ENCYCLOPEDIA OF BEST FILMS

ENCYCLOPEDIA OF
BEST FILMS

A CENTURY OF ALL THE FINEST MOVIES

Volume 4, V–Z

JAY ROBERT NASH

ROWMAN & LITTLEFIELD
Lanham • Boulder • New York • London

Published by Rowman & Littlefield
An imprint of The Rowman & Littlefield Publishing Group, Inc.
4501 Forbes Boulevard, Suite 200, Lanham, Maryland 20706
www.rowman.com

6 Tinworth Street, London SE11 5AL, United Kingdom

British Library Cataloguing in Publication Information Available

Library of Congress Cataloging-in-Publication Data

Library of Congress Control Number: 2019939590
ISBN 978-1-5381-3418-4 (cloth : alk. paper)
ISBN 978-1-5381-3419-1 (electronic)

♾™ The paper used in this publication meets the minimum requirements of
American National Standard for Information Sciences—Permanence of Paper
for Printed Library Materials, ANSI/NISO Z39.48-1992.

This work is for my wife, Judy, my son Jay and daughter-in-law Nicole, my daughter Andrea, and all other lovers of good films.

BOOKS BY JAY ROBERT NASH

FICTION

On All Fronts
A Crime Story
The Dark Fountain
The Mafia Diaries

NON-FICTION

Dillinger: Dead or Alive?
Citizen Hoover: A Critical Study of J. Edgar Hoover and His FBI
Bloodletters and Badmen: A Narrative Encyclopedia of American Criminals from the Pilgrims to the Present
Hustlers and Conmen: An Anecdotal History of the Confidence Man and His Games
Darkest Hours: A Narrative Encyclopedia of the World's Greatest Disasters
Among the Missing: An Anecdotal History of Missing Persons from 1800 to the Present
Murder, America: Homicide in the United States from the Revolution to the Present
Almanac of World Crime
Look for the Woman: A Narrative Encyclopedia of Female Criminals from Elizabethan Times to the Present
People to See: An Anecdotal History of Chicago's Makers and Breakers
The True Crime Quiz Book
The Innovators: 16 Portraits of the Famous and the Infamous
Zanies: The World's Greatest Eccentrics
The Crime Movie Quiz Book
Murder among the Mighty: Celebrity Slayings That Shocked America
Open Files: The World's Greatest Unsolved Crimes
The Toughest Movie Quiz Book Ever
The Dillinger Dossier
Jay Robert Nash's Crime Chronology
Encyclopedia of Organized Crime
Encyclopedia of 20th-Century Murder
Encyclopedia of Western Lawmen and Outlaws
Crime Dictionary
Spies: A Narrative Encyclopedia of Dirty Deeds and Double Dealing from Biblical Times to Today
Terrorism in the 20th Century: A Narrative Encyclopedia from the Anarchists through the Weathermen to the Unabomber
"I Am Innocent!": A Comprehensive Encyclopedic History of the World's Wrongly Convicted Persons

POETRY

Lost Natives & Expatriates

THEATER

The Way Back
Outside the Gates
1947 (Last Rites for the Boys)

MULTI-VOLUME REFERENCE WORKS

The Motion Picture Guide (17 volumes)
The Encyclopedia of World Crime (8 volumes)
The Great Pictorial History of World Crime (2 volumes)

INTRODUCTION

Undertaking this work was not a new chore, but an extension of lifelong research. My deep interest in motion pictures began as child in the 1940s when my mother, a singer who seemed to know everyone living in show business, introduced me to films and many of those who made and appeared in them. From childhood, I created and maintained a card system on which I made notes on every film, supplementing in my travels about the world information from movie people—directors, actors, producers, editors, writers, composers, set and art directors, and others—filling cabinets and cabinets of data, images, as well as films. I added to this a collection of books in the film field that easily occupies 20 percent of my personal library of more than 500,000 books.

Further, in my travels as a publisher and editor of various publications (*Literary Times*, *ChicagoLand Magazine*, etc.), from the early 1960s, as well as through my good friends Ben Hecht (1894-1964; the highest-paid screenwriter of his day), Stanley Ralph Ross (1935-2000; film and TV producer and my co-author of *The Motion Picture Guide*, 17 volumes), Gene Ruggiero (1910-2002; Oscar-winning film editor), along with many others, I met hundreds of Hollywood personalities (actors, actresses, producers, directors) and those related to the film industry in many capacities.

In those meetings, either formal interviews or at social events or chance encounters, I took notes on all the remarks these stellar celebrities made about their own films and the films of others, collecting over a period of more than forty years index cards upon which those remarks were recorded and filed under the title of the film those remarks best represented. Because of space, I was not able to employ these exclusive and revealing quotations in *The Motion Picture Guide*, but they have proven most applicable in this work, which concentrates on the finest films made throughout a century of moviemaking. An index shown in the back matter of this work indicates each person's remarks about specific films under an A-Z name list and where, following each name, there appears an A-Z listing of the films about which each person commented. (The acknowledgments following this introduction provide a list of those personalities.)

My first reference work on films was not published until the early 1980s, after I met and befriended Hollywood producer Stanley Ralph Ross. We met some time before he attended one of my plays then running in Hollywood and we both shared a passion for the history and quality of motion pictures. Learning that Stanley also possessed impressive personal historical archives on films, I proposed that we pool our resources and produce what later became *The Motion Picture Guide* (published from 1984 to 1999), consisting of seventeen volumes of text only and profiling in depth (complete cast, credits, synopsis, etc.) more than 65,000 theatrically released feature films, a work consisting of more than 25 million words, presently residing in every major library and is considered the definitive reference work in print on the subject (and from which, not incidentally, IMDb, the Internet Movie Database, culled the bulk of its credit information).

Of all of those films, as well as the approximately 10,000 worldwide new theatrically released feature films (dealing with no documentaries or made-for-TV or video films) to 2015, I came to realize that less than ten percent of all such films could be reasonably rated as good to masterpiece films (three, four and five-star films by my ratings). Since I had waded through all of the potboilers and programmers in the history of filmmaking, and, knowing what films were worth watching, I determined to produce the present comprehensive work of only the best films.

In the selection of the entries in this work, my criteria demands quality production as well as quality content contained in any film and, of course, a high quality of acting. Production values are based upon how well a film is constructed, from its direction to its story line and script, from its cinematography to its musical score, from its film editing to its art design and set decoration. It is the obligation of any good director to control and carefully supervise all aspects of these separate responsibilities, while visually narrating and smoothly guiding any story on film to its conclusion with consistent continuity and cohesive and effective development of characters and story line at the understandable level of the most unsophisticated viewer. Presuming knowledge or perception by that viewer is always a mistake, and such mistakes are most often made by today's directors.

"No director is a good one when he goes out of his way to make shots that visually remind the audience that he is behind the camera," director John Ford (1894-1973) told this author. Another pantheon director, Howard Hawks (1896-1977), supported that statement when telling me that "the director must be invisible and unsuspected. The story enacted on the screen by the players must make sense without the director leaving any detectable footprints." Hawks' own criteria for a good film was that it had to have at least one great scene in it, and his films invariably had more than one such scene. "Tricky shots with oddball angles are okay now and then if it helps a scene," Hawks added, "but if you overdo that, you're just posturing and strutting." Orson Welles pointed out to me that "we used a lot of unusual shots that had not been fully developed when we did *Citizen Kane*, such as deep focus, but that was to get more visual values into our scenes—and by defining those in the distance with those in the foreground at the same time, all of the characters came naturally alive."

Story and plotline are essential ingredients in any good film. The so-called Golden Age of film (1930s-1940s) was dominated by superlative writers, mostly intelligent novelists and playwrights with deep and inventive talents. These gifted writers had the ability to communicate even the most complicated story with prosaic and understandable scenes, where complex emotions and motives were translated through terse but revealing dialog. Little such "filmic literature" is present in today's films where writers chiefly rely upon the overuse of shock and sensation to produce provocative stories. Characters thusly are less believable, becoming stereotyped and, without being fully developed, preventing any talented actor from reflecting definable character traits with discernible personalities, particularly those that may be otherwise redeemable and inspiring, which is the mainstay of any good film.

Cinematography must visually translate scene for scene the story line without distracting from the actions of the players while logically unraveling all important aspects of that story line in the process. Working in tandem with cinematography, a good musical score should commensurately enhance each type of scene, whether mellifluously or discordantly, to achieve the most effective emotional impression best suited to that scene and its characters. Good editing is simply cleaning up or eliminating excessive footage or lack of continuity that either encumbers or slows down any given scene (and is not and never has been a responsibility to preempt the work of the director). Production design, art direction and set decoration, all essential elements in making a good film, must accurately reflect the period and location of the film, as well as effectively establish its ambience and atmosphere.

This is the criteria I established when producing my seventeen-volume reference work, *The Motion Picture Guide*, and is the same criteria I apply for this work. At the time I was producing that work, this author was visited by film critic Roger Ebert (1942-2013). I had known Ebert since he was a college student at the University of Illinois (he had, in the early 1960s, attended some poetry readings I was producing at Marina City in Chicago). Ebert always contended that *Citizen Kane* is the one and only best film. When he asked me what I thought was the best film ever made, I jocularly told him: "Why that's no problem at all, Roger—the greatest film ever made is *Bela Lugosi Meets a Brooklyn Gorilla* [1952]." Roger's mouth gaped and he finally said: "Are you kidding?"

I replied: "Of course, I am kidding. There is no such thing as the best film ever made." I went on to ask him if *Citizen Kane* was the best western ever produced. Was it the best comedy ever made? Was it the best musical ever made? Was it the best science fiction movie ever made? Was it the best espionage film ever made? Was it the best war film ever made? I pointed out to him that there are many great films separately addressing different themes, genres and subjects. *Citizen Kane* is a drama and, even in that instance, dramas must be subdivided by types of drama in order to determine the best films in that genre—and there are dozens of such films. *Citizen Kane* deals with one man and his corruption through wealth and power. It is senseless to make it compete against other great dramas with widely divergent themes and characters, such as *The Best Years of Our Lives* (1946), which deals with a readjusting generation of wounded persons displaced by war, or *Casablanca* (1942), a drama dealing with star-crossed lovers and the plaintive call to a noble cause. They have wholly separate and individualistic techniques, story lines, motivations, characters and literatures. It is too convenient and simplistic, as would a child filling slots with block figures, to single out only one film and place it at the top of an imaginary filmic totem pole.

I think this was somewhat lost on Ebert, fine film critic that he was, as it is by those who impulsively make up those useless pecking order lists of best films where an uninformed majority decides the jockeying position from one generation to another of such arbitrarily selected films based upon au courant popularity. This is blatantly evident in such ambiguous online sites as Wikipedia and IMDb, which present no recognized authority for any of its statements and thus no worthwhile or acceptable evaluations). This work, however, profiles approximately 7,000 best films, of which several hundred are rated by me as masterpiece (five-star) films in their respective genres. All entries offer something redeemable or worthwhile to qualify for inclusion in this work in accordance with the criteria aforementioned.

Only feature-length, theatrically released films are addressed in this work, covering films from 1913 through 2015. Such features were first produced by Hollywood and a few foreign companies in the early 1910s when shorts were expanded to tell a more complete story with some character development. The standard running time for a feature was then about forty minutes. The average feature film today runs between seventy and two hundred minutes. Between 400 and 600 feature films are made each year by Hollywood and, approximately, another 2,000 worldwide, including documentaries.

Given the enormous budgets for films today, some running into the hundreds of millions, one might believe that such funding is so plentiful as to provide unlimited funding to produce more films than what are actually made. The star system, however, has isolated most Hollywood funds, where the bulk of money goes to a few film celebrities. This system came into existence with the collapse of the studio system in the early 1960s, so that, by the 1980s, a handful of film stars dictated the overall available funds for their own productions.

I am reminded of a film production in which I was involved (where I wrote the script) at that time; the producer, a wealthy Canadian, offered Jack Nicholson's agent, Sandy Bresler, $1 million up front for Nicholson to appear in the film. Bresler had asked for an up front payment of $3 million, and when offered the lesser amount, he flatly turned down the offer. Of course, it is the job of any agent to get whatever he or she can for their clients, but the extravagant payments to such stars might preclude the availability of funds that otherwise might be allocated to smaller-budgeted films where new talent might be exposed and nurtured to maturity. Just the opposite existed under the old studio system where inexpensive programmers or "B" films were produced that showcased thousands of such newcomers.

Further and sadly, Hollywood too seldom tells a good story anymore, let alone constructs and conveys a reasonable plotline and presents admirable characters. It relies upon the most unattractive canned themes and clichéd characters—endlessly predictable rites of passage and coming-of-age tales, or mindless fright films too often peopled by stereotyped serial killers, blood-sucking vampires, soul-clutching devils, perverted parents, and anyone afflicted with drug addiction or any exotic phobia and incurable disease or malady, all of it as ambiguously presented as possible. People struggling with commonplace problems and who constitute most of the walking world, seems to hold little interest for Hollywood.

A generation of writers blossomed and grew rich writing such vacuous screenplays, and equally less talented producers and directors advanced such empty product to the forefront where even the best of actors were compelled to extraneously create their performances if they wanted to work. To be sure, there are still great creative talents such as Steven Spielberg, George Lucas, Ron Howard, Clint Eastwood, George Clooney, Tom Hanks, Meryl Streep, Mel Gibson, Cate Blanchett, Russell Crowe and others who continue to provide and appear in wonderful and entertaining films with good stories (with a beginning, a middle and an end) and have done so in the last three decades, but they are in the diminishing minority.

Most theatrically released feature films today exalt violence and mayhem, assaulting audiences with explicit sex that obliterates true affection and cheapens healthy love. It attacks viewers with visual slaughter and gore at every turn, even in digitalized animation (the chief technical god of Hollywood), eliminating human sensitivity and decency. It has largely abandoned good adult taste. Language in film has turned into that of uneducated savages or gutter rats, the more crude and offensive, the better. The reason for this social sabotage is simply that such language and explicit violence and sex is not permitted on public TV, Hollywood's original chief competitor against its theatrically released feature films.

Some films heralded as superior by others have not been included in this work as the violence employed in these films is overwhelmingly gratuitous. Thus, I do not include certain films extolling violence, vengeance and vigilantism insidiously disguised as heroism, although I do include films where violence is reasonably endemic to character development.

Then again, one must remember that Hollywood is a business that is aimed first, last and always to make money, with art as a remote afterthought. That dollar is nevertheless dwindling as are the better made and worthwhile watching new films. Hollywood stopped thinking about what the public wanted several decades ago. An executive at a major Hollywood studio told me in 1980: "We give the public the kind of films we want to make, the films that return the top dollars. If all they get is what we make then that is what they have to buy."

However, as Abraham Lincoln once said: "You can fool some of the people most of the time, and most of the people some of the time, but you can't fool all the people all the time." By the late 1990s, the attraction to Hollywood's brutal product began to wane, as did box office receipts. Theaters began closing, and ten years later, top video distributors, which had flourished in the suburbs, went out of business. The reason was clear—the suburban upscale viewer, better educated and more sophisticated, was no longer interested in paying to see bad films. Hollywood still peddles such inferior product, but thrives less handsomely from diminishing revenues that stem now from inner-city theaters and foreign distribution.

Hollywood attempted to address the concerns of parents, teachers and librarians regarding its most offensive product by establishing the Motion Picture Association of America, which created its own children's ratings (MPAA; all of which can be found in my reviews) for films released since the late 1960s. However, since this organization is industry sponsored, its ratings are not reliable and have been manipulated in the past to the advantage of production companies and studios and to the disadvantage of parents looking for guidance. I have established my own rating for children (under the age of thirteen), which appears in each and every review, including those going back to the first feature films. This work offers reviews of only theatrically released feature films from 1913 to 2015 and does not address documentaries, feature films exclusively made-for-TV, or video productions.

Hollywood, since the 1970s, has deluded itself into believing that by making certain family-oriented films those films will be acceptable for children because of their basic characters or creatures, for instance, loveable dogs, and have then proceeded to impose upon the story lines of such productions stressful adult situations. They subsequently use the unreliable MPAA rating system as a misleading smokescreen to present such films as acceptable family fare, which they are not. Today's film producers would do well to consult child behavior specialists before undertaking such productions if their films are to be truly aimed at the children's market.

In all fairness, this author wants to emphasize the superlative work of the better angels of Hollywood and the finest product it has produced over the last century and it is that product upon which this work focuses. There is much to be admired, so many thousands of films that it would take the lifetime (as it has this author) of any reader to view them, and I hope the readers of this work will attempt to do exactly that, particularly those four-and five-star films I have extensively profiled. Within the framework of these reviews, the reader will find, following my "Author's Notes," additional production information, "inside" perspectives of participants through exclusive quotes, and a wealth of other information regarding the background and genesis of these films as to their historic and biographical accuracy. All of the text for this work has been freshly written and, to my understanding, its entries far surpass in comprehensiveness any other film work to date.

Jay Robert Nash, Chicago, 2017

ACKNOWLEDGMENTS

My deep appreciation goes to Cathy Edens, page designer for this work, and her production assistant, Diane Anetsberger, as well as to Walter Oleksy for his excellent research in providing updated information on credits and video information for this work. All images employed for this work come from the Jay Robert Nash Collection and are specifically acknowledged by production company and studio in the backmatter. I am also grateful for the comments—exclusively quoted in this work—from hundreds of worldwide personalities used in this work, including, but not limited to Robert Aldrich; Don Ameche; Jean Arthur; Fred Astaire; Mary Astor; Lew Ayres; Richard Basehart; Ralph Bellamy; Jack Benny; Ingrid Bergman; Busby Berkeley; Richard Boone; Charles Boyer; Peter Boyle; Marlon Brando; Charles Bronson; Louise Brooks; Clarence Brown; Charles Bukowski; Henry Bumstead; W. R. Burnett; James Cagney; Frank Capra; Art Carney; Lon Chaney Jr.; Eduardo Ciannelli; Claudette Colbert; Marc Connelly; Elisha Cook Jr.; Gary Cooper; Joseph Cotten; James Craig; Joan Crawford; Donald Crisp; Hume Cronyn; Bing Crosby; George Cukor; Rodney Dangerfield; Bette Davis; Laraine Day; Frances Dee; Marlene Dietrich; Brian Donlevy; Irene Dunne; Douglas Fairbanks, Jr.; Peter Falk; Alice Faye; Henry Fonda; Glenn Ford; John Ford; Samuel Fuller; Greta Garbo; Greer Garson; William Taylor "Tay" Garnett; Samuel Goldwyn; Betty Grable; Cary Grant; Andy Griffith; Alec Guinness; Henry Hathaway; Howard Hawks; Susan Hayward; Rita Hayworth; Ben Hecht; Ernest Hemingway; Katharine Hepburn; Charlton Heston; Alfred Hitchcock; William Holden; Earl Holliman; Bob Hope; Dennis Hopper; Rock Hudson; Ruth Hussey; John Huston; Betty Hutton; Sam Jaffe; Nunnally Johnson; Van Johnson; Boris Karloff; Danny Kaye; Buster Keaton; William Keighley; Brian Keith; Gene Kelly; Deborah Kerr; Henry King; Don Knotts; Stanley Kramer; Stanley Kubrick; Veronica Lake; Hedy Lamarr; Burt Lancaster; Priscilla Lane; Jack Lemmon; Mervyn LeRoy; Harold Lloyd; Ida Lupino; Fred MacMurray; Rouben Mamoulian; Joseph Mankiewicz; Fredric March; George Marshall; Lee Marvin; Groucho Marx; James Mason; Raymond Massey; Walter Matthau; Victor Mature; Leo McCarey; Joel McCrea; Norman Z. McLeod; Steve McQueen; Melina Mercouri; Lewis Milestone; Ray Milland; Vincent Minnelli; Robert Mitchum; Zero Mostel; Paul Muni; Patricia Neal; Tom Neal; Jean Negulesco; Paul Newman; David Niven; Lloyd Nolan; George O'Brien; Pat O'Brien; Laurence Olivier; Dorothy Parker; John Payne; Gregory Peck; Tony Perkins; Christopher Plummer; Otto Preminger; Vincent Price; Anthony Quinn; George Raft; Claude Rains; Basil Rathbone; Nicholas Ray; Michael Rennie; Marjorie Reynolds; Jason Robards Jr.; Edward G. Robinson; Stanley Ralph Ross; Robert Rosson; Gene Ruggiero; Jane Russell; Rosalind Russell; Robert Ryan; George Sanders; William Saroyan; Roy Scheider; Budd Schulberg; George C. Scott; Randolph Scott; Sylvia Sidney; Don Siegel; Jean Simmons; Frank Sinatra; Curt Siodmak; Douglas Sirk; Red Skelton; Ann Sothern; Robert Stack; Barbara Stanwyck; Rod Steiger; John Steinbeck; George Stevens; James Stewart; Paul Stewart; John Sturges; Jessica Tandy; Elizabeth Taylor; Robert Taylor; Spencer Tracy; Claire Trevor; Dalton Trumbo; Lana Turner; King Vidor; Raoul Walsh; Harry Warren; Ruth Warrick; John Wayne; Orson Welles; William A. Wellman; Billy Wilder; Henry Wilcoxon; William Wyler; Jane Wyman; Frank Garvin Yerby; Loretta Young; Robert Young; Darryl F. Zanuck; Fred Zinnemann.

HOW TO USE INFORMATION IN THIS WORK:

The following fields of information apply to all reviews in this work:

Title (in boldface) is the most current title used in the U.S. (alternate titles appear in a separate index).

Star Ratings: ★★★ (good); ★★★★ (excellent); ★★★★★ (masterpiece).

Year of release is the year a film was released in the U.S.

The country in which the film was produced is stated.

The running time is shown in minutes (i.e., 60m; sometimes reels for silent films) at time of release.

Names of producing companies and studios are stated.

Major studios are abbreviated: AA: Allied Artists; COL: Columbia; FOX: 20th Century Fox and 21st Century Fox; MGM: Metro-Goldwyn-Mayer; PAR: Paramount; REP: Republic; RKO: RKO Radio Pictures; UA: United Artists; UNIV: Universal; WB: Warner Brothers.

Color or Black-and-White (B/W) is stated.

Genres specified: Adventure; Animated Feature; Biographical Drama; Children's and Family Film; Comedy, Crime Drama; Drama; Fantasy; Horror; Musical; Mystery; Sports Drama; Spy Drama; Science Fiction; Romance; War; Western.

Author's Children Ratings (the reasons for cautionary and unacceptable film ratings are often explained in text): Recommended; Acceptable; Cautionary; Unacceptable.

MPAA ratings (from the late 1960s; not always available) are stated.

Video Availability: BD: Blu-ray Disc; DVD: Digital Versatile System; VHS: Video Home System (video cassette); 3-D: three-dimensional movies; IV: Internet Viewing (streaming). (All of these video applications can be purchased or rented from local or national video outlets.)

In-depth review and background information (following "Author's Note") appears in each entry.

Cast and credits: p: producer; d: director; cast: cast of six to twelve leading players appearing in a film; w: screenwriter and/or adaptation (with credit for original story, book or play); c: cinematographer (often with additional technical information—i.e., Panavision; Technicolor); m: composer of musical score (for musicals, songs are listed with composers and lyricists); ed: film editor; prod d: production designer; art d: art designer; set d: set decorator or designer; spec eff: special effects or visual effects director.

Indices: Alternate Titles (3438-3449); Events (3450-3464); Fictional Persons (3465-3525); Great Last Lines (3526-3532); Historical Persons (3533-3703); Institutions and Organizations (3704-3723); Lines That Live Forever (3724-3736); Personalities Quoted (3737-3751); Photos: Name Index (3752-3762); Photos: Studio Index (3763-3765); Photos: Title Index (3766-3777); Subject Index (3778-3877).

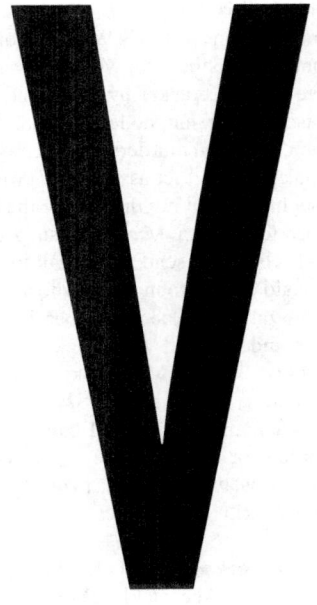

Elizabeth Taylor and Richard Burton in *The V.I.P.s, 1963.*

The V.I.P.s ★★★ 1963; U.K.; 119m; MGM; Color; Drama; Children: Unacceptable; **DVD**; **VHS**; **IV**. This slick soap opera offers outstanding performances from the love team (and real-life spouses) of Burton and Elizabeth Taylor, who were then at the height of their popularity, having just appeared in the epic **Cleopatra**, 1963. The film concentrates on several people assembled in the V.I.P. (very important persons) lounge at London's Heathrow Airport as they wait for the fog to lift so they can embark upon a plane heading for NYC. The lives of these wealthy and famous people interconnect as they contend with separate crises in their lives. Elizabeth Taylor arrives at the lounge with lover Jourdan, bent on leaving her enormously rich husband, Burton, after concluding that Burton loves his business more than her. She has left him a letter, telling him that she is going to New York to find happiness with another. Welles is another important passenger, a powerful film producer, who wants to get out of London quickly with his alluring protégé, Martinelli, in order to avoid paying a hefty tax bill. Rutherford, an elderly, titled lady, is also traveling to New York, and then to Florida, to take a job in order to make enough money to continue to own her historic estate. She is a nervous wreck as she has a deep fear of flying and is forever popping pills to calm down. Australian contractor Rod Taylor also arrives at the lounge with his secretary, Smith, who loves him from afar, knowing that, if her employer does not get to New York the next day, he will most likely lose his firm in a hostile takeover. Meanwhile, Burton, after reading Elizabeth Taylor's farewell letter, realizes that she is more important to him than all of his far-flung enterprises and he rushes to the airport to tell her that and that his life means nothing without her. Burton proves he is a caring person, after listening to Smith's plea on behalf of Rod Taylor, when he loans Rod Taylor the needed funds to prevent the loss of his company. Welles' dilemma is solved by his unctuous accountant, Miller, who tells him that, if he marries Martinelli, and transfers his wealth to her name, he will avoid the heavy taxes he owes to more than one country. When Welles learns of Rutherford's plight, he comes to her rescue by telling her that he will rent her estate for his next film production, paying her the funds she needs to keep her landmark home. At the finale, Elizabeth Taylor forgives Burton and decides to remain at his side, saving his life, as he had seriously considered committing suicide if she had flown off with the now rejected gigolo, Jourdan. Asquith does a good job balancing the tales of each of his principal characters, cleverly cutting from one to another to blend their separate lifestyle and problems. In addition to Burton and Elizabeth Taylor, the performances from Welles, Rutherford, Rod Taylor and Smith are exceptional. The film was a great box office success, earning more than $15 million against a $4 million budget. ***Author's Note***: The story of this film was based upon the real-life experience between stellar actors Laurence Olivier and his wife Vivien Leigh. When their marriage seemed to be at an end, Leigh planned to leave Olivier, going to Heathrow Airport with actor Peter Finch, but their scheduled flight to NYC was delayed by heavy fog. Olivier, learning of Leigh's plan, arrived at the airport and confronted Leigh and Finch, convincing Leigh to return home with him. They would remain together (from 1940) until Leigh sued for divorce in 1961, naming actress Joan Plowright as co-respondent. "I thought **The V.I.P.s** was a good love story," Burton told this author, "but I was concerned that it might turn too sentimental. The script and the good dialog, however, prevented that from happening." Elizabeth Taylor told this author that "I liked doing that picture because it was very easy to do since it was shot mostly on one set—the airport lounge where we were all waiting to take a plane that is grounded by fog. What would moviemakers do without fog? It's wonderful for atmosphere and all kinds of mystery and that helped a lot when we were making **The V.I.P.s.**" Welles believed that his role in this film was true to life, telling this author: "I played a filmmaker in that picture, who is dodging tax collectors all around the world, and, to tell you the truth, that had been my case in many instances when making pictures. Those people were like the hounds of hell, tracking you down to every closet and bathroom. You could not escape from them. True misery can be best learned by encountering such bloodhounds." Elizabeth Taylor got to wear some of her famous gems in this film, including the fabulous emerald brooch Burton had given her, her first gift from him, inscribed: "If it's Tuesday, I love you." She also wears a diamond tiara at the beginning of the film during an opening dinner party scene, this tiara given to her by her third husband, film producer Michael Todd (Burton was the fifth husband out of a total of eight). Elizabeth Taylor had married Todd in 1957, but he was killed in a plane crash the following year, most of his remains unrecognizable following the plane's explosion. He was buried in Chicago's Forest Lawn Cemetery where, on June 27, 1977, the body was stolen. Taylor had visited Todd's grave only a few days earlier where she had placed flowers. Police were baffled and Taylor was outraged after law enforce-

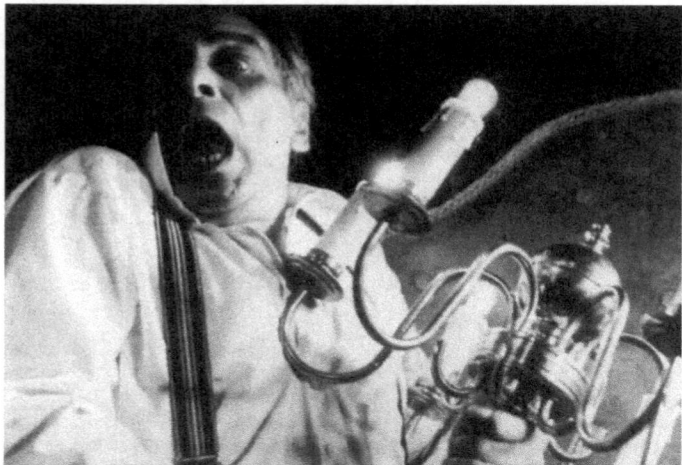

Witold Pyrkosz in *Vabank*, 1982.

ment officials could give her no explanation. She quickly hired a private detective in Chicago, Anthony J. "Tony" Pellicano, who was then this author's friend. "A gang of punks stole that body," Pellicano told this author, "because they thought that Elizabeth Taylor had placed a ten-carat diamond ring inside the casket as a memento to the man she had loved, but they quickly found out that no such ring existed after they stole the body and took it to a hideout to inspect the bag it was in. The first thing I did to track down that body was to contact some people in the Outfit [local organized crime in Chicago; Pellicano reportedly talked with none other than Mafia boss Anthony "Joe Batters" Accardo, 1906-1992, who allegedly stated to Pellicano after hearing about the ghoulish crime that "those bastards are giving us a bad name!]", and they agreed to help. They knew the gang of punks who had taken the body and a few of the 'boys' took me to their hideout where we confronted them with guns pointed at their heads. We made them take the body back to the cemetery that night, leaving it close to the spot where they had dug up the grave. I called the cops the next day and told them where they could find the body and said that I had received a tip from an informant, but that's all I told them." Following the forty-eight-hour caper solved by Pellicano, Todd's body was reinterred and remained unmolested thereafter. Pellicano's success with this case sadly inspired him to go to Hollywood where he became a high profile private eye for movie moguls, and that landed him into a lot of trouble, eventually sending him to prison for wiretapping and possession of dangerous arms (he is still serving time at this writing). Tony was, in the estimation of this author, one of the most unorthodox and inventive private detectives in that always dangerous profession. The allure of Hollywood and its seamy underbelly, however, undid what would have otherwise been a spectacular career. Nevertheless, Dashiell Hammett and Raymond Chandler would have been intrigued with this bold and passionate man, who remains behind bars, to my best understanding, for refusing to give up his sources, doggedly maintaining the code of the private eye to the bitter end. I remember meeting with Tony before he left for Tinsel Town, saying to him: "Don't go out there. It's a swamp for a guy like you. It's not only quicksilver but quicksand, and you'll get sucked down and never surface again." He replied: "I can't make enough money in Chicago. I need to follow the big fees." That he did, going right into that swamp like a wayward Cabeza de Vaca in search for those elusive Seven Cities of Gold. For more information on this fascinating character (whose sensational life begs for a motion picture), see my work *Encyclopedia of World Crime*, Volume II (CrimeBooks, Inc., 1990; Pellicano, Anthony J., pages 2437-2438). **p**, Anatole de Grunwald; **d**, Anthony Asquith; **cast**, Elizabeth Taylor, Richard Burton, Louis Jourdan, Elsa Martinelli, Margaret Rutherford, Maggie Smith, Rod Taylor, Orson Welles, Linda Christian, Dennis Price, Martin Miller, Ronald Fraser, David Frost,

Stringer Davis; **w**, Terence Rattigan; **c**, Jack Hildyard; **m**, Miklos Rozsa; **ed**, Frank Clarke; **art d**, William Kellner; **set d**, Pamela Cornell; **spec eff**, Tom Howard.

Vabank ★★★ 1982; Poland; 108m; Zespol Filmowy; Color; Crime/Comedy; Children: Unacceptable; **DVD**. Clever crime caper with a lot of comedic elements begins in 1930s Warsaw, Poland. After serving six years in prison for a bank robbery for which he was framed, Machulski seeks revenge. He is a safecracker by trade, and takes pride in his work. Upon his release from prison, he learns that a friend with whom he played in a jazz band has been murdered by Pietraszak, the man who framed him for the bank robbery. Pietraszak, now a wealthy banker, tells Machulski he will pay him for taking the fall for the bank robbery, but actually hires a hit man to kill him. Machulski suspects that Pietraszak is out to kill him, and sets out to send Pietraszak to prison instead. To that end, he enlists the aid of two young men who admire him, and they turn the tables on Pietraszak in an elaborate caper that returns the money to all bilked parties and, indeed, sends Pietraszak behind bars. (In Polish; English subtitles.) **d&w**, Juliusz Machulski; **cast**, Jan Muchulski, Leonard Pietraszak, Witold Prykosz, Ewa Szykulska, Krysztof Kiersznowski, Zdzislaw Kuzniar, Josef Para, Elzbieta Zajacowna, Jacek Chmielnik, Zofia Charewicz, Henryk Bista; **c**, Jerzy Lukaszewicz; **m**, Henryk Kuzniak; **ed**, Miroslawa Garlicka; **prod d**, Jerzy Skrzepinski; **aset d**, Andrzej Przedworski.

Vacation from Marriage ★★★ 1945; U.K.; 111m; MGM; B/W; Romance/War Drama; Children: Acceptable; **DVD**; **VHS**; **IV**. Top-notch performances are rendered by Donat and Kerr in this poignant tale. Sickly Donat and drab Kerr are a thirty-something married couple living unhappily in a London flat that has only a window facing a brick wall, a blatant symbol of their dead-end marriage. They are bored with each other and only keep the marriage going because each feels the other would be lost if they divorced. World War II (1939-1945) begins and Donat goes off to serve in the Royal Navy while Kerr joins the Wrens, which is part of the British women's civilian defense home front army. Donat becomes healthy and alive in the navy and romantically interested in Todd, a widowed nurse. Kerr becomes friends with scatterbrained Johns, who introduces her to lipstick, smoking, and encourages her to have an affair with Culver. When the war is over, Donat and Kerr both dread going back to their old humdrum marriage, but, after they see each other again, amid the destruction of German bombings, he sees a new and vibrant wife and she a much-changed husband. They fall in love again and, after they return to their old apartment, they see that bombs destroyed the brick wall so now they can look out upon the city. London may be damaged, like their marriage had been, but the city will be built again and so too will be their lives together, thanks to their vacation from marriage. This very popular and engaging film won an Academy Award for Best Original Story (Dane). A sixty-minute radio adaptation was aired by Lux Radio Theater on May 26, 1947, with Kerr reprising her role. Songs: "These Foolish Things" and "I Don't Want to Be Hurt Again" (Jack Strachey, Eric Maschwitz), "Daisy Bell" (Harry Dacre), "Home Sweet Home" (H.R. Bishop, John Howard Payne), "There Is a Tavern in the Town" (traditional), "I've Got Sixpence" (Elton Box, Desmond Cox, Lawrence Hall), "The Old Folks at Home" (Stephen Foster), "Wedding March" (Felix Mendelssohn-Bartholdy), "Auld Lang Syne" (traditional), "Little Grey Home in the West" (Hermann Lohr, D. Eardley-Wilmot). *Author's Note*: Always concerned with quality, Korda presents a film with high production values, despite the fact that the city of London, which is where this film was produced, was then under consistent attack from German V-1 and V-2 rockets. Korda had signed a deal with MGM to produce several films and, after making that deal, announced that its first production would be **War and Peace**, directed by Orson Welles and staring Welles and Merle Oberon, who was then married to Korda. That film was not produced, this one replacing it and being the only film ever produced in that package deal with MGM. Kerr told this author: "Working with Robert Donat (1905-1958) was a great pleasure. He was a gentle and considerate man who had to overcome many problems in life. He stammered as a child and overcame that by taking elocution lessons for years. He also struggled with acute asthma throughout his life and tired easily whenever he had to perform any strenuous scenes, but he never complained about that. He played courageous persons in pictures and he was a courageous man in real life." Roger Moore, a future James Bond, plays a soldier in this, his film debut. **p&d**, Alexander Korda; **cast**, Robert Donat, Deborah Kerr, Ann Todd, Glynis Johns, Roland Culver, Ivor Barnard, Muriel George, Allan Jeayes, Eliot Makeham, Elliott Mason, Roger Moore; **w**, Clemence Dane, Anthony Pelissier (based on a story by Dane); **c**, Georges Perinal; **m**, Clifton Parker; **ed**, Edward B. Jarvis; **art d**, Vincent Korda; **spec eff**, W. Percy Day.

Vagabond ★★★ 1985; France; 86m; Cine Tamaris/Grange; Color; Drama; Children: Unacceptable; **DVD**; **VHS**. Taut tale begins with a grim scene where Bonnaire, a young woman, who is an unkempt vagabond, is found frozen to death in a ditch in winter in the south of France. Through flashbacks she is seen in her final weeks as she camps alone or falls in with various men and women, some forcing their needs on her, while others try to give her life some direction and meaning. She spends some time smoking hash with a man in an old house, falls in love with a Tunisian laborer, and then works beside him pruning grape vines. Then she stays with a couple shepherding goats, meets a nature conservationist trying to save trees, gets tipsy with an old woman, and then receives an offer to appear in pornographic films. She goes nowhere but down, and winds up dead in the ditch. Though depressing and somber, the film is rescued by a powerful performance from Bonnaire. Songs: "Variations sur la Vita" (Joanna Bruzdowicz), "The Changeling" and "A Contre-Courant" (Valerie Lagrange, Ian Jelfs), "Oh Baby" and "Freedom Is Slavery" (Theo Hakola. Denis Goulag), "Marcia Baila" and "In My Tea" (Catherine Ringer, Fred Chichin), "Sur la mer toujours recommencee calmee" (Puccini, Slim Batteux). **p**, Oury Milshtein; **d&w**, Agnes Varda; **cast**, Sandrine Bonnaire, Setti Ramdane, Francis Balchere, Jean-Louis Perletti, Urbain Causse, Christophe Alacazar, Dominique Durand, Joel Fosse, Patrick Schmit, Daniel Bos; **c**, Patrick Blossier; **m**, Joanna Bruzdowicz; **ed**, Varda, Patricia Mazuy.

The Vagabond King ★★★ 1930; U.S.; 104m; PAR; Color; Musical; Romance; Children: Acceptable; **IV**. Entertaining musical packed with some great songs begins with weak and ineffectual French King Louis XI (1423-1483), played by Heggie, and who is at war with the Duke of Burgundy, an opponent bent on unseating or killing the monarch and taking over the country. Meanwhile, the handsome, roguish poet Francois Villon (1431-1463?), played broadly by King (reprising his Broadway success) and Roth, his lady love, are entertaining the people of Paris with his acerbic poems, all aimed at ridiculing Heggie. Royalists consider King to be a troublesome thief, a French Robin Hood stealing from the rich to give to the poor as leader of a gang of vagabond thieves. Commoners consider him their hero. Heggie has King sentenced to hang for his derogatory poems, but offers him a temporary reprieve if he can defeat the invading Burgundians. Heggie's beautiful niece, MacDonald, is kidnapped by an angry crowd, and King not only rescues MacDonald, but falls in love with her, which does not sit well with Roth. A lavish party is held in the palace during which Oland, an avowed enemy of Heggie, plans to kill him, but King again saves the day by preventing the assassination. Roth then saves King from being killed, at the cost of her own life, and he rallies the people to put down the Burgundian revolt and save the monarchy, ending this opus in the arms of MacDonald, and where they sing a love song duet. The film was remade in 1956, starring Kathryn Grayson. Francois Villon was the hero of the 1927 film **The Beloved Rogue**, starring John Barrymore, as well as the 1938 film **If I Were King**, starring Ronald Colman as the vagabond king and with Frances Dee as his co-star. Director Berger

Sandrine Bonnaire and Macha Meril in *Vagabond*, 1985.

presents some outstanding production numbers (including an impressive battle montage) while delivering a lively story that sees good performances from all, particularly Roth, who was a teenager when making this, her third feature film. Berger, a German director, also presents this enthralling songfest with pioneering two-strip Technicolor process, one of the first all-color films, albeit the film seems somewhat stagey as Berger literally followed the Broadway production's continuity. Songs: "Love Me Tonight," "Only a Rose," "Huguette Waltz," "Song of the Vagabonds," "Some Day," "Nocturne" (music; Rudolf Friml; lyrics: Brian Hooker); "King Louis," "Mary, Queen of Heaven," "If I Were King," "What France Needs" (Sam Coslow, Newell Chase, Leo Robin). *Author's Note*: The history of this story is long, beginning with Russell's 19th-Century novel, which was adapted for a New York play in 1901 under the title "If I Were King," and produced first for the screen as a silent in 1920 with that title and starring William Farnum. The story was converted to a musical under the title of "The Vagabond King," which opened on Broadway in 1925 as an operetta with music from Friml and lyrics by Hooker and was produced on the London stage two years later, before it was brought to the screen with this production. Composer Friml had a clause in his contract with Paramount that prohibited any inclusion of songs other than those he created. When Friml learned that Paramount thought to change the title to "If I Were King," and include songs composed by others, he sued the studio. Paramount quickly went back to the original title and then paid Friml an additional $50,000 for including additional songs by others. King, a prima donna of sorts, did not get along well with MacDonald, who appears here in her second feature film. She, in turn, disliked King immensely for his hogging of scenes. In one scene where MacDonald is singing the memorable "Only a Rose," King purposely invaded her close-up to hog the shot with his profile, and MacDonald thereafter referred to that scene and its song as "Only a Nose." Friml's heartwarming, sentimental style of music faded in popularity over the years, as was remorsefully remembered by poet Ogden Nash. In 1969, to celebrate Friml's 90th birthday, Nash sent Friml (1879-1972) a clever couplet ending with: "I trust your conclusion and mine are similar: T'would be a happier world if it were Frimler." **p**, Adolph Zukor; **d**, Ludwig Berger, (not credited) Ernst Lubitsch; **cast**, Dennis King, Jeanette MacDonald, O.P. Heggie, Lillian Roth, Warner Oland, Arthur Stone, Thomas Ricketts, Lawford Davidson, Christian J. Frank, Elda Voelkel, Iris Adrian; **w**, Herman J. Mankiewicz (based on a story by Mankiewicz, the novel by R.H. Russell, the play "If I Were King" by Justin Huntly McCarthy, and book of the 1925 operetta "The Vagabond King" by Brian Hooker, William H. Post); **c**, Henry W. Gerrard, Ray Rennahan (two-strip Technicolor); **m**, W. Franke Harling, John Leipold, Oscar Potoker, Max Terr; **ed**, Merrill G. White; **art d**, Hans Dreier.

Oreste (kneeling) with Kathryn Grayson in *The Vagabond King*, 1956.

The Vagabond King ★★★ 1956; U.S.; 85m; PAR; Color; Musical; Children: Acceptable; **DVD**; **VHS**. In this very entertaining and most lavish filming of the Friml operetta, French King Louis (1423-1483), played by Hampden, again faces being overthrown by his enemies in 1461. Many noblemen fear he is going to take their lands and castles, so they join with his main adversary, the Duke of Burgundy, Duggan, who is building an army to oppose his reign. Duggan learns about Francois Villon (1431-1463?), played by Oreste, a poet whose writings are critical of the king, and leader of a group of vagabonds that steal from the rich and give to the poor. Oreste and his girlfriend, Moreno, also sing songs on the streets of Paris that are based on his poems critical of the king. Duggan gets Oreste to join his Burgundian army in attacking Paris, but Oreste and his two cohorts are captured by Hampden's soldiers. By now, Oreste realizes that Hampden really does love his people and switches his alliance from Duggan to him. Hampden also comes to realize how popular Oreste is with the people and gets his help in defending Paris against the Burgundians. Oreste learns that there are two traitors in Hampden's palace, Nielsen and Morton, and exposes them. Moreno is killed during a battle with the Burgundians, and Oreste rescues Grayson, Hampden's beautiful niece, who is kidnapped by the Burgundians. Oreste leads the people of Paris to drive out the invaders, saving the king, preserving the monarchy, and winning the love of Grayson. This is a sumptuous remake of the 1930 musical film, and the 1938 film **If I Were King**, starring Ronald Colman as the vagabond king, Francois Villon. Songs: "Bon Jour," "Vive la You," "Some Day," "Companions," "This Same Heart," "Watch Out for the Devil," "Song of the Vagabonds" (music: Rudolf Friml; lyrics: Johnny Burke); "Huguette Waltz," "Only a Rose" (music: Friml; lyrics: Brian Hooker). **p**, Pat Duggan; **d**, Michael Curtiz; **cast**, Kathryn Grayson, Oreste Kirkop as Oreste, Rita Moreno, G. Thomas Duggan, Sir Cedric Hardwicke, Walter Hampde, Leslie Nielsen, William Prince, Jack Lord, Phyllis Newman, Vincent Price (narrator); **w**, Ken Englund, Noel Langley (based on the play "If I Were King" by Justin Huntly McCarthy and the book of the stage musical by Brian Hooker, William H. Post); **c**, Robert Burks (Vista Vision; Technicolor); **m**, Victor Young; **ed**, Arthur P. Schmidt; **art d**, Henry Bumstead, Hal Pereira; **set d**, Sam Comer, Grace Gregory; **spec eff**, John P. Fulton.

The Valachi Papers ★★★ 1972; France/Italy; 125m; De Laurentiis; COL; Color; Crime Drama; Children: Unacceptable (MPAA: R); **BD**; **DVD**; **VHS**; **IV**. A brutal and uncompromising film, this crime saga unveils the murderous machinations of the Cosa Nostra (Mafia) when it took hold in America during the 1920s in NYC as seen through one of its members, Joseph Valachi (1903-1971), who is powerfully essayed by Bronson. While serving a fifteen-year sentence in the federal prison at Atlanta for smuggling heroin, Bronson learns that his boss, Ventura, playing Mafia family chief Vito Genovese (1897-1969), who is also serving time at the penitentiary, has ordered him murdered, after Ventura becomes convinced that Bronson had brought about his own imprisonment. Learning of his death sentence when Ventura literally kisses him (the "kiss of death") and, realizing its lethal meaning, Bronson kisses Ventura back. Bronson contacts prison officials and cuts a deal with the FBI, offering to talk about his experiences with the Cosa Nostra in exchange for protection. FBI agent O'Loughlin agrees and places Bronson in another federal institution where he is heavily guarded and Bronson begins his long litany about his criminal past. In flashback to 1929, we see Bronson, at age thirty, getting a job as a truck driver and working for Mafia don Nazzari (as Gaetano Reina, 1889-1930), who is warring with rival Cosa Nostra chiefs, until he is killed by Ventura and Infanti (as Charles "Lucky" Luciano, 1897-1962). They then hire Bronson, seeing him as an effective "soldier" in their cadre who will obey and ruthlessly carry out their orders. Joining the gang is Bronson's close friend, Chiari. They participate in what is known as the Castellammarese War (1930-1931) where many gangsters are killed, including totemic Mafia boss Sperli (as Giuseppe "Joe the Boss" Masseria, 1886-1931) on orders of Wiseman, who plays Salvatore Maranzano (1886-1931). To prevent further bloodshed between the warring Mafia clans, Wiseman brings peace by organizing the Sicilian gangsters into five families, giving each family a territory to rule in the five boroughs of New York. He names himself Boss of Bosses and his word is law throughout his underworld fiefdom. The vainglorious Wiseman admits his powers have limits when stating at a funeral: "I cannot bring back the dead. I can only kill the living." Bronson then marries Ireland (Bronson's real-life spouse), who is the daughter of his murdered boss, and a lavish reception is held for them at a huge ballroom. Gang members and bosses appear to bestow expensive gifts and cash upon the newlyweds (such generous gangland gift-giving to newlyweds is shown in many other related Mafia films such as **The Godfather**, 1972, and **GoodFellas**, 1990). Bronson's narrative depicts the assassination of Wiseman and the rise of new, ruthless gangsters like Ventura, who is the most lethal of all the Cosa Nostra leaders. When Prohibition (1920-1933, a U.S. law prohibiting the production or sale of any alcoholic drinks) is repealed, Bronson and his ilk enter other rackets and Bronson grows rich enough to buy a small nightclub. Flash forward to 1963 where Infanti is sent to prison after being convicted of a felony and Ventura, to escape the same fate, flees to his native Italy where he remains in hiding. Before departing, Ventura entrusts the welfare of his mistress, Baxa, to Chiari, who is assigned as her bodyguard. When the crime boss returns, he discovers that, in his absence, Chiari and Baxa have developed a romance. Ventura takes revenge for this betrayal by having Chiari castrated. Rather than see his old friend suffer with such pain, Bronson ends Chiari's life in a mercy killing. Bronson's seemingly endless testimony then describes the Mafia summit meeting in Apalachin, New York, at the remote country estate of mob boss Joseph "Joe the Barber" Barbara (1905-1959), on November 14, 1957. Barbara's home had been bugged by the FBI and its wiretapping listeners are able to hear the plans of Ventura and others. The bosses are then informed that the place is surrounded by law enforcement officers and Ventura and others flee in all directions. Ventura and Bronson are captured and, after a series of legal battles, both wind up in the federal prison at Atlanta, where the always paranoid Ventura wrongfully concludes that Bronson was the informant that sent him behind bars. He orders Bronson killed within the walls of the prison, offering $100,000 for the murder. (When hearing of this, Valachi mistook a fellow convict for a Mafia assassin then serving time at Atlanta, and, using a pipe at a construction site, bludgeoned the man to death, which brought about his cooperation with the FBI in a plea-bargaining arrangement.) O'Loughlin then persuades Bronson to go before a U.S. subcommittee investigating the Mafia. Bronson (as did Valachi) makes historic appearance before that body to testify on a nation-wide TV airing, one that shocks the country as he discloses in gruesome detail the bloody history and operations of the Cosa Nostra or Mafia. After seeing himself testifying on a prerecorded TV show, Bronson becomes depressed at the thought that he has violated the Cosa Nostra code of "omerta" ("silence"), and rips the cord from the TV set, using it in attempt to hang himself. FBI guards, however, are able to save his life, and, as the credits roll at the finale, the viewer learns that Bronson outlived his nemesis, Ventura. (Genovese died in prison of a heart attack on February 14, 1969, at the federal correction facility in Springfield, Missouri, while Valachi died of a heart attack on April 3, 1971, at the federal correction facility at La Tuna, Texas.) Director Young does a valiant job in piecing the episodic tale together, using flash-forward and flashback scenes to show the rise of the Cosa Nostra (meaning "Our Thing") in NYC. The stoic Bronson gives a powerful performance as a remorseless killer and Ventura is equally mesmerizing as his ruthless boss, neither of them having any redeeming qualities and who live out their lives as human monsters. The film had a healthy box office response, earning more than $17 million in its initial release. *Author's Note*: Many original viewers of this film thought that it was hastily constructed in order to cash in on the enormous box office popularity of **The Godfather**, 1972. The popular Maas nonfiction book, upon which this film was made, however, was published in 1968, before Mario Puzo's classic crime novel, *The Godfather*, 1969. Producer De Laurentiis acquired the rights to the Maas book in 1969, but delays postponed its film production, which started in New York. The producer was met with hostility by Italian-American groups during the production, including an official condemnation from what was called the Italian-American Civil Rights League, a bogus organization led by Mafia family chief Joseph Colombo (1924-1978), who used that organization as a front for a lot of his illegal operations (and reaped a whirlwind of opposition from other Mafia chiefs opposed to Colombo's blatant public posture and later ordered him assassinated). Bronson told this author that "I thought Mr. De Laurentiis showed a lot of courage in making **The Valachi Papers**. He was threatened all along by the Cosa Nostra, or by the Mafia, if you want to call it that. He was told long before we went into production to give up the idea of making the picture, but he went ahead anyway. When we were in New York making the picture, a lot of so-called 'accidents' occurred, and these were created by underworld thugs, who controlled some of the unions we had to use—the usual sabotage—heavy lights falling close to the actors, cars that lost their brakes, that sort of thing. Anyone who had an Italian name who was connected with that picture became a suspected saboteur and the 'outside' thugs creating those 'accidents' banked on creating that kind of suspicion to slow down everything. I played an evil man in that picture like everyone else, but the real evil was coming from those that wanted that picture shut down. Well, Mr. De Laurentis finally had enough and stopped everything in New York, and, suddenly, overnight, we were all on our way to Rome to finish the picture. When we got there, the producer had armed guards surround his studio to make sure we completed the picture, and we did. I and a lot of the other actors were offered guns to defend ourselves. I refused to carry one because I knew that if someone really wanted to bump me off, no pistol would prevent that." Several scenes depicting events (including the castration scene) and some of the dialog (including Wiseman's comments as Boss of Bosses) were purely fictional. The film also suffers from a lack of continuity where modern cars and skyscrapers can be seen in scenes depicting 1930s settings, particularly those illustrating the NYC locale. This was undoubtedly due to the hurried filming in that city while the producers were being constantly harassed by Mafia minions. Before production, Young, other than selecting Bronson and a few other experienced actors, elected to cast those with little acting experience and having no name recognition simply because they had the kind of unglamorous (outright ugly or vicious-looking) faces that Young thought would distinguish them as underworld figures and which Young later described as "incredible." The prison scenes in this film were shot at Sing Sing Prison in Ossining, New York, and more than 100 of its actual convicts appear as extras. Producers got the cooperation of the fa-

Gerald O'Loughlin and Charles Bronson in *The Valachi Papers*, 1972.

cility after making a donation to Sing Sing's recreation fund. For more information on the Cosa Nostra/Mafia, see my books *Encyclopedia of World Crime*, Volume III (CrimeBooks, Inc., 1990; pages 2079-2086), and *The Great Pictorial History of World Crime*, Volume II (History, Inc., 2004; pages 1448-1462). For an extensive list of films depicting the Cosa Nostra/Mafia, see Index, Organizations: Organized Crime. (In Italian; dubbed in English) **p**, Dino De Laurentiis; **d**, Terence Young; **cast**, Charles Bronson, Lino Ventura, Jill Ireland, Walter Chiari, Joseph Wiseman, Gerald O'Loughlin, Amedeo Nazzari, Fausto Tozzi, Pupella Maggio, Angelo Infanti, Maria Baxa; **w**, Stephen Geller (based on the book by Peter Maas); **c**, Aldo Tonti (Technicolor); **m**, Riz Ortolani, Armando Trovajoli; **ed**, Johnny Dwyre, Monica Finzi; **prod d**, Mario Garbuglia; **set d**, Boris Juraga, Ferdinando Ruffo; **spec eff**, Paul J. Lombardi, Eros Bacciucchi.

Valdez Is Coming ★★★ 1971; U.S.; 90m; Ira Steiner Productions/Norlan Productions/UA; Color; Western; Children: Unacceptable (MPAA: PG-13); **DVD**; **VHS**; **IV**. Tough western tale sees Lancaster as a tenacious but compassionate Mexican-American lawman, Bob Valdez, seeking justice from Cypher, a ruthless cattle baron. Lancaster discovers a group of cowboys led by Jordan firing at a shack where Monson, a black man, is hiding after having been wrongly accused of killing a trader. Lancaster halts the gunfire and persuades Monson to surrender, but Monson is shot and killed by one of the vigilantes. Lancaster feels that Monson's Indian widow, who is now impoverished, should be given $200 in compensation and he raises half that amount from local residents before he visits Cypher at his ranch to ask for the balance of $100. Cypher is incensed that the elderly and wizened Lancaster would dare to ask him for such a contribution. He belittles Lancaster's authority as a law enforcement officer, and orders his men to tie Lancaster to a cross and then orders him to walk through the blistering desert to his small town. Lancaster struggles to survive the ordeal, the central pole of the cross being so long that it compels him to walk bent forward and unable to see where he is going. It appears that he will die under the weight of the cross until he encounters an oasis with two trees that he rams with the end of the crossbar of the cross to free himself. In his struggling effort to free himself, Lancaster breaks the cross, but its jagged ends are driven painfully into his back in the process. Immobilized and unable to go further, he is saved by none other than Jordan, one of Cypher's cowboys, who takes pity on Lancaster, freeing him from the cross by cutting the ropes binding him, but Jordan's knife slips in the process and he superficially slashes Lancaster's wrist. The unconscious Lancaster, however, does not know the identity of his benefactor as Jordan leaves him in the desert. Regaining consciousness, Lancaster staggers and crawls to the ranch of a friend, Silvera, who nurses him back to health.

Burt Lancaster and Frank Silvera in *Valdez Is Coming*, **1971.**

Lancaster then returns to his home and opens a trunk where he retrieves his old U.S. Cavalry uniform. He is an experienced scout and Indian fighter and vows retribution from Cypher. He arms himself with his old Sharps rifle, a long-range weapon (originally designed by Christian Sharps in 1848, a large bore single-shot rifle widely known for its pinpoint accuracy, the weapon profiled in other westerns such as **Billy Two Hats**, 1974; **Geronimo: An American Legend**, 1993; **Quigley Down Under**, 1990; **Rancho Deluxe**, 1975; **Silverado**, 1985; **True Grit**, 1969; **True Grit**, 2010; **Unforgiven**, 1992; and **Up**, 2009). He then sets out for Cypher's ranch. He encounters Elizondo, one of Cypher's outriders, and wounds him before sending him to Cypher, with a message: "Valdez is coming." To that end, Lancaster enters the compound of Cypher's ranch at night, sneaking into the main house where he finds Cypher in bed with his woman, Clark. A gunfight ensues and Lancaster escapes, taking Clark as a hostage to lure Cypher and his men after him. Cypher and his small army of men pursue Lancaster, who takes to the hills, and he captures Jordan, using him also as a hostage with Clark. He forces Jordan as a target for Cypher's men, until Jordan screams: "I cut you loose!" He proves that to Lancaster by pointing out the slash mark on Lancaster's wrist, and Lancaster then acts more leniently toward Jordan. Meanwhile, Clark, who has nothing but admiration for Lancaster's courage and resolve, admits that she had killed the trader, who had been her abusive husband, before going to live with Cypher. As Cypher and his men, led by foreman Heyman, ride after Lancaster, he picks them off one by one with his Sharps rifle. Heyman tells Cypher that their efforts are useless against Lancaster as he can stay out of range while using that rifle to kill his opponents at a range of 1200 yards. Eventually, Heyman and his men trap and capture Lancaster and Cypher then orders him killed. Jordan refuses, saying he has no gun. Heyman, who has come to admire the dogged Lancaster, orders his men not to shoot the intrepid lawman. It is now up to Cypher to perform his own orders, but he proves his cowardice when facing Lancaster, who is also armed. Lancaster warns him that he should have paid the $100 as both men face each other, the viewer left to conclude that the cowardly Cypher will take no action and that Lancaster will receive that payment. Lancaster presents a stoic but believable image of a Mexican-American lawman with a deep sense of justice while he receives strong support from Clark, Cypher, Jordan, Silvara and Heyman. *Author's Note*: Steiner, who was a producer at MGM, had obtained the rights to the Leonard story and gave the novel to Lancaster, who agreed to co-produce it, stating that he would play the role of the rancher and that Marlon Brando should play Valdez, wanting Sidney Pollak to direct the film. The production was postponed while Lancaster appeared in **Airport**, 1970. Lancaster later decided to play Valdez, and Cypher, appearing in his first theatrically released feature film (as was also the case for Jor-

dan) was cast in the role of the rancher. Lancaster told this author that "I was concerned about my character, especially his speech patterns and mannerisms, so I worked with a speech coach who knew all about the way such Latinos talked during the 1890s in the American Southwest." He also consulted with Mexican students, who gave him insights into his interpretation of his character. The film was shot on location in southern Spain, locales that resembled the American Southwest. Lancaster ran into some trouble with the American Humane Association after its members condemned some scenes showing horses colliding and receiving injuries. Violence prohibits viewing by children. **p**, Ira Steiner; **d**, Edwin Sherin; **cast**, Burt Lancaster, Susan Clark, Frank Silvera, Jon Cypher, Richard Jordan, Barton Heyman, Hector Elizondo, Phil Brown, Jose Garcia Garcia, Nick Cravat; **w**, Roland Kibbee, David Rayfiel (based on the novel by Elmore Leonard); **c**, Gabor Pogany (DeLuxe Color); **m**, Charles Gross; **ed**, James T. Heckert, George Rohrs; **art d**, Jose Maria Tapiador; **set d**, Rafael Salazar; **spec eff**, Charles Gaspar.

Valentin ★★★ 2003; Argentina/Netherlands/France/Spain/Italy; 86m; First Floor Features; Color; Drama; Children: Unacceptable (MPAA: PG-13); **DVD**; **VHS**; **IV**. Poignant tale begins with Noya, who plays eight-year-old Valentin, a boy living with Maura, his poor, widowed paternal grandmother, in 1967 Buenos Aires, Argentina. Noya has not seen his mother since he was three. His grandmother tells him that his mother was unfaithful to his father, but nonetheless he misses her. His father is a womanizing traveling salesman frequently away, and when he does come home, it is always with a new girlfriend. Valentin dreams of becoming an astronaut and builds rocket models and space suits, which diverts his mind from domestic problems. But it is unlikely he will ever become an astronaut because he is slightly cross-eyed and nearsighted. Valentin is adrift in an adult world, but we are confident he will thrive because of his indomitable spirit. A charming film offers outstanding performances from Noya and Maura. Gutter language and thematic elements prohibit viewing by children. **p**, Julio Fernandez, Thierry Forte, Laurens Geels, Massimo Vigliar, Pablo Estaban Wisznia, Rene Goossens, Annemiek van Gorp; **d&w**, Agresti; **cast**, Rodrigo Noya, Julieta Cardinali, Alejandro Agresti, Carmen Maura, Jean Pierre Noher, Mex Urtizberea, Lorenzo Quinteros, Carlos Roffe, Marina Glezer, Stefano Di Gregorio; **c**, Jose Luis Cajaraville; **m**, Luis Salinas, Paul M. van Bruggen; **ed**, Alejandro Brodersohn; **prod d**, Floris Vos; **spec eff**, Floris van der Veen.

The Valiant ★★★ 1929; U.S.; 66m; FOX; B/W; Crime Drama; Children: Unacceptable. Strange and compelling tale sees a powerful performance from Muni. He is a drifter, who murders a man. He later turns himself in, but gives a false name. Muni gives no defense, saying only that the man he killed deserved to die. He is convicted and sentenced to death, his execution scheduled in the near future. Newspapers report the story about this mystery man waiting to be killed in the electric chair, and his photo is seen in an Ohio newspaper by his mother, Yorke, and his sister, Churchill. Both go to the prison to confirm Muni's identity. When Churchill meets with Muni in the office of the prison warden, Jennings, she pleads with him to allow her to prove that he is innocent. He nevertheless denies knowing her, and she then realizes that Muni is prepared to go to his death under an assumed name so that she and Yorke will not have to live in shame under his real name. Despite Churchill's efforts to save her brother, Muni goes valiantly to the chair. The prosaic story is greatly enhanced by Muni's stellar performance, one where he is making his film debut. Muni received an Oscar nomination as Best Actor, and Barry also received an Oscar nomination for Best Writing. *Author's Note*: The film stemmed from a play on Broadway that ran for only one performance at the Nora Bayes Theater on May 4, 1926. The play took its title from William Shakespeare's "Julius Caesar" (act II, scene II), where Caesar states to wife Calpurnia: "Cowards die many times before their deaths. The valiant never taste death but once." Muni had established himself on the Broadway stage as a strong and upcoming actor and Fox responded by giving him a contract to appear in **The Valiant**. Studio chief William Fox, however, viewed the rushes for this film, then halfway in production, and decided that Muni had no "sex appeal" and ordered production chief Winfield Sheehan to close down the production. "Sheehan was in my corner," Muni told this author. "He convinced Mr. Fox to continue the picture, telling him that it would cost the studio more money to close it down than to complete and release it. Mr. Fox, however, never liked the picture and gave it no promotion or widespread distribution, so very few persons saw that picture when it was released. They kept me at Fox where I appeared in another picture that same year, **Seven Faces** [1929]. But that picture, too, saw little response after it was released. I heard that Mr. Fox told friends that he felt embarrassed after I received an Oscar nomination for my role in **The Valiant**, in the following year. By that time, however, Mr. Fox had a lot of problems that caused him to lose control of his studio." Fox (1879-1952) lost controlling interest in Fox Studios following a hostile takeover in 1930. He had been battling other movie moguls like Louis B. Mayer at MGM after Fox bought out Loew's Theater chain, which left Mayer and others without interest in that powerful distributing arm. Fox lost a fortune in the 1929 stock market crash and eventually declared bankruptcy in 1936. He worsened his own plight by attempting to bribe Judge Warren Davis at his bankruptcy hearing and where he was also found guilty of perjury, both offenses causing him to be sent to jail for six months. Fox retired thereafter, dying at age seventy-three on May 8, 1952. None of his fellow moguls attended his funeral. **p&d**, William K. Howard; **cast**, Paul Muni, Marguerite Churchill, Johnny Mack Brown, DeWitt Jennings, Henry Kolker, Edith Yorke, Richard Carlyle, Clifford Dempsey, Robert Elliott, Henry Hall, Helen Parrish; **w**, Tom Barry, John Hunter Booth (based on the play by Robert Middlemass, Holworthy Hall); **c**, Lucien Andriot, Glen MacWilliams; **ed**, Jack Dennis.

Valiant Is the Word for Carrie ★★★ 1936; U.S.; 110m; PAR; B/W; Drama; Children: Unacceptable. Stage actress George gives a powerful performance while making her film debut as Carrie Snyder, a Louisiana prostitute in the 1930s Great Depression. Social workers force her to give up her two youngsters, played as children by Moran and Wyatt. She becomes prosperous by owning some stores, but, after some years, she is arrested. Rather than face a jury trial that would reveal to her now teenage children, Howard and Judge, that she has been a lady of the night, she agrees to a short jail sentence. *Author's Note*: George, a superb actress who had made her mark on Broadway as a comedian, was equally at ease with drama, as her outstanding performance in this film proves. She was put under contract by Paramount after her successful Broadway performance in "Personal Appearance," which was later produced by Paramount as **Go West, Young Man**, 1936. Instead of giving the part George had made famous in that story, the studio gave the role to Mae West. **p&d**, Wesley Ruggles; **cast**, Gladys George, Arline Judge, John Howard, Dudley Digges, Harry Carey, Isabel Jewell, Jackie Moran, Charlene Wyatt, John Wray, William Collier Sr., Hattie McDaniel, Grady Sutton; **w**, Claude Binyon (based on the novel by Barry Benefield), **c**, Leo Tover; **m**, Frederick Hollander; **ed**, Otho Lovering; **art d**, Hans Dreier, Ernst Fegte.

Valkyrie ★★★★ 2008; U.S./Germany; 121m; MGM/UA; Biographical Drama; War Drama; Children: Unacceptable (MPAA: PG-13); **BD**; **DVD**; **IV**. This gripping and sumptuously produced tale details the failed 1944 assassination attempt against German dictator Adolf Hitler (1889-1945) by the intrepid Clause von Stauffenberg (1907-1944), wonderfully played by Cruise, along with many other high-ranking German officers. The film opens in Tunisia where Cruise is serving in the Africa Corps during WWII (1939-1945). After RAF planes bomb and strafe a German troop area, Cruise is horribly wounded, losing his right hand, left eye, and two fingers on his left hand. He is evacuated to Germany where he slowly recovers. Meanwhile, several high-ranking German officers have concluded that the only way they can successfully end the

Tom Cruise as German hero Claus von Stauffenberg and Carice van Houten as his wife Nina in *Valkyrie*, 2008.

war is to kill Hitler, who is played by Bamber. To that end, Branagh, who plays General Hermann Henning von Tresckow (1901-1944), has an unwitting German officer carry on to Hitler's plane a bomb disguised as a gift for another officer in Berlin. The bomb, however, fails to explode and Branagh flies to Berlin to successfully retrieve the bomb while accompanied by co-conspirator Nighy, who plays General Friedrich Olbricht (1888-1944). Cruise, who has recovered from his wounds and who is staunchly opposed to the Hitler regime, is then recruited into the conspiracy by Nighy. However, after he attends a meeting with others in the conspiracy to kill Hitler, he discovers that they have no plan to take control of the government once the dictator is dead. The other conspirators include General Ludwig Beck (1880-1944), played by Stamp; Field Marshal Erwin Witzleben (1881-1944), played by Schofield; and Dr. Carl Goerdeler (1884-1945), who is essayed by McNally. Cruise comes to realize that the conspirators can establish national order if they use the Reserve Army to suppress fanatical Nazi elements and key figures following Hitler's assassination. To that end, Cruise and Nighy go to Wilkinson, who plays General Friedrich Fromm (1888-1945), who heads the Reserve Army, and offer him the position of chief of the army after the fall of Hitler's Third Reich. The always cautious and circumspect Wilkinson tells them that he will not consider using the Reserve Army for their plot as long as Hitler is alive. Wilkinson, however, tacitly supports the plotters when arranging for Cruise to accompany him to Hitler's mountain retreat, the Berghof in Bavaria, where Cruise presents Hitler (Bamber) with the rewritten Operation Valkyrie that will activate the Reserve Army. Bamber, who is in conference with his top advisors, hurriedly reviews the new document and signs it. At another meeting, McNally urges Cruise to kill Bamber as well as Heinrich Himmler (1900-1945), who is played by Freihof, and who heads Hitler's personal bodyguard, the SS, as well as the Gestapo, when Cruise attends a conference at Bamber's secret military headquarters, the Wolf's Lair, in Prussia. Cruise attends the conference on July 15, 1944, but, after he sees that Freihof is not in attendance with Bamber, he takes no action. Nighy, however, thinking that Cruise has eliminated Bamber, activates the Reserve Army. When Cruise is able to contact Nighy to tell him that he has put off the assassination, Nighy orders the Reserve Army to stand down and its officers then believe that the alert was only a training test. When Cruise returns, he and Nighy are chastised by an enraged Wilkinson, who tells them that if they attempt to activate the Reserve Army again, he will have them both arrested. Cruise then bids goodbye to his wife, Nina Stauffenberg (1913-2006), played by van Houten, when he again goes to the Wolf's Lair on July 20, 1944, with his adjutant, Parker, and plants a bomb hidden in a briefcase beneath a large conference table where Bamber and others are reviewing military strategy. He leaves the building and, after a terrific explosion takes place, immediately speeds

Thomas Kretschmann as Otto Ernst Remer in *Valkyrie*, 2008.

away in a car to a nearby airport, taking a plane back to Berlin. Meanwhile, Izzard, who plays General Fritz Erich Fellgiebel (1886-1944), shuts down all communications at the Wolf's Lair, as per his instructions from Cruise. Before communications are shut down, Izzard contacts Berkel, who is Nighy's aide, to tell him that the explosion has taken place, but that he is not sure that Bamber is dead. Nighy, wanting confirmation of that death, refuses to again activate the Reserve Army, but Berkel forges Nighy's signature to again activate Operation Valkyrie. By the time Cruise returns to Berlin, he, Nighy and Berkel confront Wilkinson, who calls the Wolf's Lair to learn that Bamber has survived the explosion. Wilkinson attempts to place the conspirators under arrest, but he, instead, is arrested by the plotters. Meanwhile, Kretschmann, playing Major Otto Ernst Remer (1912-1997), one of the commanders of the Reserve Army, goes to the offices of ardent Nazi Joseph Goebbels (1897-1945), played by Friedman, who then contacts the Wolf Lair and where Bamber tells Kretschmann that he is, indeed, alive, and to arrest the conspirators. Cruise, who has actually taken control of the German government, is, along with his fellow plotters, confronted by Kretschmann and his troops and is placed under arrest. Wilkinson, to hide his own complicity in the failed plot, then orders Cruise, Nighy, Berkel, Parker and others to be immediately executed. They are taken to a courtyard and shot to death, ending this thrilling and well-presented docudrama. Director Singer does a fine job incorporating the complex elements of the actual plot to kill Hitler into many dramatic scenes that build suspense toward that startling assassination attempt. He also exceptionally defines the divergent characters who were involved in the actual plot, many of whom had separate agendas in their desire to eliminate madman Hitler. Cruise presents a riveting performance of a reserved, conscious-stricken German officer, who is dedicated to ridding his country of a maniacal dictator, a masterfully understated performance (Stauffenberg proved to be one of Germany's bravest heroes). Cruise receives marvelous support from a talented cast, particularly the conniving Wilkinson, the wavering Nighy and the dedicated Kretschmann, Berkel and Parker. The very effective visual effects employed in the early battle scenes in Africa, and the explosion taking place at the Wolf's Lair, are shockingly believable. Other than some minor quibbles (such as Cruise avidly listening to Richard Wagner's music where the real Stauffenberg detested that composer), the film is faithful to the facts of event. The film was a success at the box office, earning more than $200 million in its initial release against a budget of $75 million. Songs: "They'll Remember You" (John Ottman, Lior Rosner), "Die Walkurie: Ride of the Valkyries" (Richard Wagner), "Die Entfernte Melodie" (Lior Rosner), "Fur Eine Nacht Voller Seligkeit" (Peter Kreuder, Guenther Schwenn), "Badenweiler Marsch" (George Furst). *Author's Note*: Filmed in Germany, the German government originally

prohibited shooting at the Bendlerblock, the actual government building in Berlin where the plotters attempted to control the government. Officials relented and allowed shooting in that building (now a memorial to Stauffenberg and the other conspirators) after Cruise and producer McQuarrie made a personal appeal to them. For reliable details on the 1944 plot to kill Hitler, see my two-volume work *The Great Pictorial History of World Crime*, Volume I (History, Inc., 2004; pages 138-148). Stauffenberg has been portrayed by many other actors in many other films, including **Claus Graf Stauffenberg**, 1970 (made-for-TV; Horst Naumann); **Die Stunde der Offiziere**, 2004 (made-for-TV; Harald Schrott); **The Desert Fox**, 1951 (Eduard Franz); **Fliegen und Sturzen: Portrat der Melitta Schiller-Stauffenberg**, 1974 (made-for-TV; Wolfgang Arps); **The Great Battle**, 1973 (Alfred Struwe); **Hitler**, 1962 (William Sargent); **I Spy**, 1955-1957 (TV series; "Canaris Story": Michael Ingram); **It Happened on July 20th**, 1955 (Bernhard Wicki); **The Night of the Generals**, 1967 (Gerard Buhr); **Ohne Kampf kein Sieg**, 1966 (TV miniseries; Alfred Struwe); **Operation Valkyrie**, 2004 (made-for-TV; Sebastian Koch); **Operation Walkure**, 1971 (made-for-TV; Joachim Hansen; Jean Berger in French version); **The Plot to Assassinate Hitler**, 1955 (Wolfgang Preiss); **The Plot to Kill Hitler**, 1990 (made-for-TV; Brad Davis); **War and Remembrance**, 1988 (TV miniseries; Sky du Mont); and **The Wednesday Play**, 1964-1970 (TV series; "The July Plot," 1964 episode: John Carson). **p**, Christopher McQuarrie, Bryan Singer, Gilbert Adler, Nathan Alexander, Christoph Fisser, Henning Molfenter, Jeffrey Wetzel, Charlie Woebcken; **d**, Bryan Singer; **cast**, Tom Cruise, Kenneth Branagh, Bill Nighy, Tom Wilkinson, Thomas Kretschmann, Terence Stamp, Carice van Houten, David Schofield, Christian Berkel, Jamie Parker, Harvey Friedman, Eddie Izzard, Kevin R. McNally, Tom Hollander, David Bamber, Matthias Freihof; **w**, McQuarrie, Alexander; **c**, Newton Thomas Sigel; **m&ed**, John Ottman; **prod d**, Lilly Kilvert, Patrick Lumb; **art d**, Cornelia Ott, Keith Pain, Ralf Schreck, John Warnke; **set d**, Bernhard Henrich; **spec eff**, Alex Gunn, Mark Freund, Richard R. Hoover, Ken Nakada.

Valley Girl ★★★ 1983; U.S.; 95m; Atlantic; Color; Romance; Children: Unacceptable (MPAA: R); **DVD**; **VHS**. Crude but entertaining teen romance begins with Cage, a grungy punk rocker from Hollywood, who crashes a party of rich, young high school kids in the San Fernando Valley. It's instant love between him and Foreman, a beautiful young debutante from the Valley. They are a Romeo and Juliet pair from different cultures (her father's name is Richman), but they nevertheless spend the night together. Cage is worried that Foreman's parents, Forrest and Camp, will not like him because he is so different from Foreman. He also thinks they are probably rich snobs, but he's surprised to see they are more liberal than their daughter. Under pressure from her friends, Foreman dumps Cage and again dates her old boyfriend, Bowen, a jock with only two things on his shallow mind, sex and sports. Cage crashes the high school prom in an effort to win Foreman back, and does (shades of **The Graduate**, 1967). Songs: "Everywhere at Once" (1983; Peter Case), "A Million Miles Away" (1983; Peter Case, Joey Alkes, Chris Fradkin), "He Could Be the One" and "Johnny Are You Queer?" (1982; Bobby Paine, Larson Paine), "School Is In" (1961; Josie Cotton), "Girls Like Me" (Bonnie Hayes), "Shelley's Boyfriend" (Bonnie Hayes, S. Savage), "Eyes of a Stranger" (Paul Hyde, Rob Rock), "Love My Way" (John Ashton, Richard Butler, Tim Butler, Vince Ely), "Angst in My Pants" and "Eaten by the Monster of Love" (Ron Mael, Russell Mael), "Jukebox" (Bobby Orlando), "I Melt with You" (Modern English), "I La-La-La Love You" (Pat Travers), "She Talks in Stereo" (Gary Myrick), "Time to Win" (Gary Myrick, Jay Ferguson, Curly Smith), "Who Can It Be Now?" (Colin Hay), "Electric Avenue" (Eddy Grant). Gutter language and sexuality prohibit viewing by children. **p&w**, Wayne Crawford, Andrew Lane; **d**, Martha Coolidge; **cast**, Nicolas Cage, Deborah Foreman, Elizabeth Daily, Michael Bowen, Cameron Dye, Frederic Forrest, Colleen Camp, Joanne Baron, David Ensor, Christopher Murphy; **c**, Frederick Elmes; **m**, Marc Levinthal,

Scott Wilk; **ed**, Eva Gardos; **prod d**; Marya Delia Javier; **set d**, Barbara Benz.

The Valley of Decision ★★★ 1945; U.S. 119m; MGM; B/W; Drama; Romance; Children: Cautionary; **DVD**; **VHS**. Outstanding drama set in 1880 Pittsburgh pits the steel magnates of that day against the struggling union workers laboring in their unsafe mills where two lovers from those opposing camps try to resolve their universal problems. This dynastic family saga begins when Garson, a young Irish woman from a working family, goes to work as a maid in the mansion of steel tycoon Crisp. Her father, Barrymore, is utterly opposed to such employment as he is a disabled steel worker injured years earlier in one of Crisp's plants and blames Crisp for the unsafe conditions in his plants that brought about his disability. Garson nevertheless stays on and proves to be a dedicated worker, who is cherished by Cooper, Crisp's wife, endearing herself to Crisp's children, Peck, Hunt, Thompson and the conniving Duryea. Garson becomes a close friend of Hunt's, helping her face problems, and becomes far more than just a household servant, serving as a confidante to the entire family, including Crisp, who welcomes the idea of her becoming his daughter-in-law after she and Peck fall in love. That marriage is seriously imperiled when a widespread strike takes place that is heartily backed by the embittered Barrymore, who insists that Garson takes sides with him and the workers. Crisp resorts to hiring gangs of strikebreakers, but, before they clash with Barrymore and the workers, Garson attempts to quell the fight by arranging a meeting between Crisp and Barrymore. During that meeting, the strikebreakers appear and Barrymore, feeling betrayed, calls upon the workers to confront them. A battle ensues that sees both Barrymore and Crisp killed, and now Garson feels that these deaths have been brought about by her own willful machinations. She leaves the Crisp household and remains away from Peck, the man who loves her, for a decade. The lonely Peck then marries Tandy, a domineering woman he does not truly love. When Cooper grows ill, she asks that old friend Garson return to her mansion to look after her and Garson does. This angers Tandy, who believes that Garson will worm her way back into Peck's heart, although she has never left that spot. Though Garson lovingly cares for Cooper, the ailing woman nevertheless dies and then leaves her share of the company to Garson. Cooper, when making changes in her will before she passes, is convinced that Garson will never injure her family's interests, the other portions of the company owned by Cooper's children: Peck, Hunt, Thompson and Duryea. Peck wants to hold on to the company, but Hunt, Thompson and Duryea want to sell the mill. Garson takes sides with Peck and convinces the others to hold on to their interests as she has become the surrogate matriarch of the family, replacing Cooper. Tandy, Peck's shrewish wife, hates Garson for her strength and because she believes Peck is still in love with her. She verbally abuses Garson, and Peck comes to Garson's aid by angrily rebuking Tandy. This is where this sprawling, sumptuous domestic drama ends, leaving the viewer to think that Garson and Peck just might repair their broken romance and see future happiness together. Garnett's direction is firm as he unfolds the developing romance between Peck and Garson while subtly weaving its accompanying conflict created by their disparate social backgrounds. He does a good job in profiling the looming violence to come between the owners and workers of the mill, which presents a microcosm of the then widespread conflicts between management and labor as unions in America began to take hold. Garson is wonderful as the mediating force that holds the tycoon's family together and she is strongly supported by powerful performances from Peck, Cooper, Barrymore, Crisp and Hunt, all enhanced by superb photography from Ruttenberg and Stothart's moving and dynamic score. Tandy as the self-serving and artful wife also provides a riveting profile as a conniving villainess. Garson received an Oscar nomination for Best Actress (her fifth consecutive nomination out of total of six, which tied the record with Bette Davis, standing unmatched today. These nominations were for **Blossoms in the Dust**, 1941; **Mrs. Miniver**, 1942, where she was the winner; **Madame Curie**, 1943; and **Mrs. Parkington**, 1944; her sixth nomination was for

Greer Garson and Gregory Peck in *The Valley of Decision,* **1945.**

Sunrise at Campobello, 1960, where she played Mrs. Eleanor Roosevelt). The film also received an Oscar nomination for Best Music (Stothart). The film was an enormous box office success, earning more than $8 million in its initial release against a budget of $2.1 million. A sixty-minute radio adaptation was aired by Lux Radio Theater on January 14, 1946, with Garson and Peck reprising their roles. A thirty-minute radio adaptation was later aired by the Screen Guild Theater on May 17, 1951, with Garson again reprising her role. Songs: "Molly Baun" (traditional Irish ballad), "Pop Goes the Weasel" (traditional English song). *Author's Note*: Garson was twelve years older than co-star Peck when they appeared together in this film, although her youthful appearance offset that actual age difference. "I spent most of my time in **Valley of Decision** caring after the members of a wealthy family," Garson told this author. "In **Blossoms in the Dust**, I was caring after children. In **Mrs. Miniver**, I was caring after a family and a rose garden. In **Madame Curie**, I was mothering radiation. I could have been the poster lady for the Red Cross." Peck was impressed with Garson when he began working with her in this film, later telling this author that "she was the most dedicated actress I had met to that time, always rehearsed and ready for her scenes. She never missed a beat and her delivery was perfect for her character, which she fully understood in her heart and mind." Peck was then a freelance actor, but MGM mogul Louis B. Mayer saw his potential and did everything he could in an aggressive attempt to sign Peck to a long-term contract with his studio. "I never saw anything like it," Peck told this author. "Mayer called me into his office and begged me to sign that contract. When I resisted, he actually began to shed tears, acting like an injured father. I knew that he pulled that corny routine on others to get his way, so I merely patted him on the shoulder and gave him a polite no. He lowered his head and began sobbing all the more and that's how I left him. The man was not only a great producer but a terrific actor." Garnett knew that Mayer had handpicked this film as a Garson vehicle, telling this author: "Mayer looked upon Garson as MGM's walking saint. To him, she was the world's most trusted and loving wife and mother on the screen, representing everything good and wholesome. He had picked all her films at the studio and had an instinctive way of knowing what would be the perfect part for her. When she later made **Adventure** [1945], Mayer had a fit. He tried every which way to talk her out of playing a librarian who has an affair with a port-of-call sailor, played by Clark Gable. But, no, she insisted on playing that part. He told her that the role would cheapen her image and, in fact, took her into his office and said: 'Why do you want to look like some woman with loose morals that will jump into bed with a bozo off a tramp freighter?' She replied: 'Because the woman is in love with that bozo, Mr. Mayer.' Well, she made the film with Gable and it was a very good one, but Mayer was right. Her image got stained

James Franciscus and Gila Golan in *The Valley of Gwangi*, 1969.

and she lost a lot of fans, who wanted her to go on being the saint Mayer had created." Crisp told this author that his role in **The Valley of Decision** "was clear to everyone. The model for my character in that picture was Andrew Carnegie [1835-1919], the steel magnate who built his financial empire in Pittsburgh. He was a tough, old bird in business, but he had a lot of compassion for literature and the arts. He wanted to die as being known as America's greatest philanthropist. Like my character, he had no use for unions and considered strikes and strikers un-American. In the Homestead Strike [of 1892], Carnegie opposed the union strikers by hiring an army of strikebreakers and then brought in the Pinkerton detectives to protect those strikebreakers. Many persons were killed when those forces clashed. It was terrible, but Carnegie did not regret what he did. Unlike my character, he died peacefully in bed, rich as Croesus." Dean Stockwell, who began as a child actor, makes his film debut in this film. Other films profiling steelworkers include **Acciaio**, 1933; **All the Right Moves**, 1983; **Bootmen**, 2000; **The Deer Hunter**, 1978; **The Fighter**, 1983 (made-for-TV); **Flashdance**, 1983; **Flesh and Blood**, 1968 (made-for-TV); **The Full Monty**, 1997; **Heart of Steel**, 1983 (made-for-TV); **Her Husband's Secretary**, 1937; **Homefront**, 1991-1993 (TV series); **Hot Steel**, 1940; **Kept Husbands**, 1931; **The Light at Dusk**, 1916; **Man of Iron**, 1935; **Man of Marble**, 1981; **No Other Woman**, 1933; **Rudy**, 1993; **Stranded**, 1935; **Tomato**, 1990; **Two Seconds**, 1932; **Udaan**, 2011; and **24 City**, 2008. **p**, Edwin H. Knopf; **d**, Tay Garnett; **cast**, Greer Garson, Gregory Peck, Donald Crisp, Lionel Barrymore, Preston Foster, Marsha Hunt, Gladys Cooper, Reginald Owen, Dan Duryea, Jessica Tandy, Barbara Everest, Marshall Thompson, Arthur Shields, Dean Stockwell, Connie Gilchrist; **w**, John Meehan, Sonya Levien (based on the novel by Marcia Davenport); **c**, Joseph Ruttenberg; **m**, Herbert Stothart; **ed**, Blanche Sewell; **art d**, Cedric Gibbons, Paul Groesse; **set d**, Edwin B. Willis; **spec eff**, A. Arnold Gillespie, Warren Newcombe, Mark Davis.

The Valley of Gwangi ★★★ 1969; U.S.; 96m; Morningside/WB; Color; Science Fiction; Children: Unacceptable (MPAA: G); **DVD**; **VHS**; **IV**. Superb special effects crown this science fiction tale where Franciscus is an American cowboy, who rides into a strange valley in Mexico in 1912. He finds a gigantic Tyrannosaurus Rex living there, although the species became extinct fifty million years ago. The creature has been earlier seen battling other prehistoric creatures before it is captured by Franciscus and others, who rope and corral it like wild stallion. Franciscus calls the creature "Gwangi," and takes it to a circus in a town, but it does not like being confined and being put on display, so it escapes, killing several people, including a circus elephant (similar to the battle of the prehistoric monster from space battling an elephant in Rome in **20 Million Miles to Earth**, 1957), as well as wreaking havoc on the

town. The residents flee to a cathedral to escape the monster, but it breaks into the church to attack more inhabitants. Survivors flee the place while Franciscus traps the creature inside the cathedral, which is set on fire and where the monster dies in screeching agony. Song: "Gypsy Flamenco" (Roland Harker). ***Author's Note***: This film was inspired by special effects pioneer Willis O'Brien, who created the special effects for **King Kong**, 1933. The exciting special effects from Harryhausen seen in this film took more than a year to create where more than 300 "dynamation" cuts were employed. Harryhausen's most intensive work addressed the scene where the creature is roped by Franciscus and others who are on horseback. **p**, Charles H. Schneer; **d**, James O'Connolly; **cast**, James Franciscus, Gila Golan, Richard Carlson, Laurence Naismith, Freda Jackson, Gustavo Rojo, Dennis Kilbane, Mario de Barros, Curtis Arden, Jose Burgos; **w**, William E. Bast, Julian More (based on a story by Bast and the unproduced film project "Gwangi" by Willis H. O'Brien); **c**, Erwin Hillier; **m**, Jerome Moross; **ed**, Henry Richardson; **art d**, Gil Parrondo; **spec eff**, Ray Harryhausen, Arthur Hayward, Gerald Larn.

Valley of the Heart's Delight ★★★ 2009; U.S.; 100m; Banana Peel Entertainment/Indican Pictures; Color; Crime Drama; Children: Unacceptable (MPAA: PG-13); **DVD**; **IV**. All is peaceful in San Jose, California, in 1933 during the Great Depression until Mann, a rookie newspaper reporter, goes to his typewriter, working it as one might fire a submachine gun. He writes a story about a fatal kidnapping that has turned the town upside down, where two men are about to be lynched for the crime. Mann believes the men are innocent, so he takes on the town fathers and most of the townspeople to prove it before they can be strung up by an angry, bigoted mob. Boxell presents a moody and tension-filled tale where Mann and a good supporting cast are standouts. The true story upon which this film is based had inspired Fritz Lang's classic crime production, **Fury**, 1936. ***Author's Note***: The film is based on the 1933 kidnapping of Brooke Hart, a young department store heir abducted in San Jose, California, at gunpoint and held for ransom by Thomas Harold Thurman and John Maurice Holmes. They were caught red-handed after Thurman was captured while still negotiating the ransom on a phone. Both were taken from the San Jose Jail by more than 15,000 San Jose residents and lynched, with the tacit approval of the then governor of California, James "Sunny Jim" Rolfe Jr., who purposely delayed sending national guardsmen to rescue the kidnappers from the mob. For more details on this case, see my two-volume work *The Great Pictorial History of World Crime*, Volume I (History, Inc., 2004; pages 672-774). **p&w**, Miles Murphy; **d**, Tim Boxell; **cast**, Pete Postlethwaite, Gabriel Mann, Emily Harrison, Diana Scarwid, Bruce McGill, Tom Bower, Ron Rogge, Val Diamond, Ed Holmes, David Barth, Michael Sommers; **c**, Hiro Narita; **m**, Richard Gibbs, Nicholas O'Toole; **ed**, Jay Boekelheide; **prod d**, Douglas Freeman; **set d**, Mikey Pitchers.

The Vampire Bat ★★★ 1933; U.S.; 63m; Majestic Pictures/Capitol Film Exchange; B/W; Horror; Children: Unacceptable; **DVD**; **VHS**; **IV**. Villagers are found dead in their beds, all blood drained from their bodies. They fear that a vampire is on a murdering rampage, and that suspicion is endorsed when a large swarm of bats invade the village. The villagers come to believe that Frye is the vampire because of his affection for bats. Another villager, a woman, dies bloodless, and the village doctor, Atwill, says he is certain that a vampire killed her and drank her blood. The villagers pursue Frye to his death before they drive a stake through his heart to keep him permanently dead. Villagers then learn that Atwill has been conducting some secret experiments without even the knowledge of his assistants, Wray and Frazer. Atwill has been using blood to bring to life a being he has created. Atwill hypnotizes Frazer into strangling his servant, Adams, so as to use her blood. The hypnotized Frazer awakes without any recollection of having murdered Adams. As bloodless victims continue to add to the fatality rate, villagers fear that Frye has returned from the dead, which causes police inspector Douglas to investigate. Atwill is afraid that Douglas will discover his activities, so he again hypnotizes Frazer, ordering him to kill Douglas. Wray then discovers Atwill's murderous machinations, but, before she can warn Douglas, Atwill ties her up and tells her about his experiments to create human life. Douglas manages to bring Frazer out of his hypnotic state, and together they go after Atwill. Frazer now realizes how Atwill has used him to murder victims, and both are killed in a struggle in which Atwill's subhuman creation is also destroyed. Everyone then realizes that Atwill was the murderer wanting his victims' blood for his lunatic science, and that no vampire ever existed. Strayer offers a chilling portrait packed with suspense, and Morgan's creative lensing of deep shadows and dark streets greatly add to the creepy atmosphere gripping the village and its hapless inhabitants. Atwill's over-the-top performance is forgivable, and even adds to the gruesome luster of this tale in that he is playing a deranged scientist assiduously performing over-the-top experiments on human beings. *Author's Note*: Wray told this author that "**The Vampire Bat** was made very fast by a small production company that borrowed me and Lionel [Atwill] from Warner Brothers. We had appeared together in another horror picture, **Doctor X** [1932], and we had just made another fright picture called **Mystery of the Wax Museum** [1933]. The producers of **The Vampire Bat** wanted to cash in on both of those pictures, which were big box office hits. To make sure they rounded out a cast with an actor associated with a classic vampire picture, they hired Dwight Frye, the little guy who played the part of Renfield in **Dracula** [1931]. Dwight was really a gentle man, always kind and considerate to everyone. He died of a heart attack when he was in his forties and was a great loss as I always thought he was a terrific actor. In **The Vampire Bat**, Lionel played the same kind of character he had played in **Doctor X**, a madman creating monsters. Most actors do not like to repeat the characters they have played in different stories so when I asked Lionel if he was upset about repeating his character in the **The Vampire Bat**, he grinned and said: 'It's just another well-paid bow, my dear.'" Majestic produced this film on Universal's back lot, employing as Atwill's home and laboratory the eerie mansion and its furnishings from Universal's **The Cat and the Canary**, 1927, and **The Old Dark House**, 1932. The producers also availed themselves of the European village set at Universal that had been used for **Frankenstein**, 1931. For a comprehensive list of films profiling vampires, see Subject Index, Vampires. **p**, Phil Goldstone; **d**, Frank Strayer; **cast**, Lionel Atwill, Fay Wray, Melvyn Douglas, Maude Eburne, George E. Stone, Dwight Frye, Robert Frazer, Rita Carlisle, Lionel Belmore, William V. Mong; **w**, Edward T. Lowe; **c**, Ira Morgan; **ed**, Otis Garrett; **art d**, Charles D. Hall.

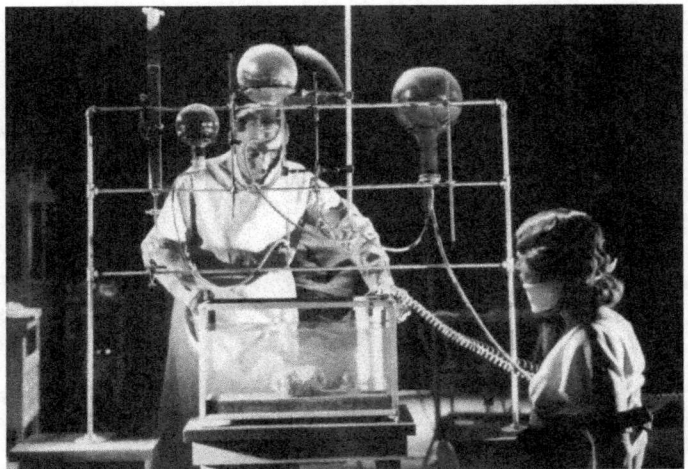

Lionel Atwill and Fay Wray in *The Vampire Bat*, 1933.

Vampyr ★★★ 1932; Germany/France; 83m; Tobis Filmkunst/General Foreign Sales Corp.; B/W; Horror; Children: Unacceptable; **BD**; **DVD**; **VHS**; **IV**. Pantheon director Dreyer made his first talkie film with this eerie production, one where the director relies upon the viewer to interpret the evils of his characters without specifically depicting their heinous acts. The film opens with West, a young man, who arrives at an inn in a strange European village. A room has already been reserved for him, and after he goes to sleep, he is awakened by Schutz, an old man, who is the lord of the manor. Schutz gives him a package and tells him that West must open it after he, Schutz, is dead. He then disappears and West comes to believe that he has imagined the visit. Nevertheless, he picks up the square package (containing a book about vampires), and Schutz has obliquely asked West to save his two daughters, Mandel, and her older sister, Schmitz, from a predatory vampire. West wanders the village streets that night, seeing and then following the disembodied shadow of a one-legged man, Boidin, who leads him to an eerie-looking castle. Inside, West finds more shadows dancing madly to weird music, which comes to a halt when Gerard, a wizened old woman, enters the room and orders silence. Gerard then meets with village physician Hieronimko, who gives her a bottle containing poison. West departs the

castle, still following Boidin's shadow, which reunites with Boidin's body, that of a gamekeeper, who then goes about building caskets. Boidin again leaves his body and West follows the shadow as it goes to Schutz's manor house. As West peers through a window, he sees Schutz, the old man who gave him the book, and Schutz is fatally shot. West is permitted to enter the manor house by some servants, who, along with Mandel, Schutz's youngest daughter, cannot save the lord of the manor. Mandel tells West that she now fears for the life of her older sister, Schmitz, who is gravely ill. (One of many chilling scenes shows Schmitz glaring hungrily at sister Mandel as if craving for her blood.) West then remembers the book Schutz had given him, one titled *Strange Tales of Vampires*, and he begins reading it. From its contents, West concludes that Schmitz is a victim of a vampire and that vampires can compel even unbitten humans to do their biddings. He and Mandel then see Schmitz wandering about the mansion grounds in her sleep and they become alarmed when she collapses. Suddenly, Gerard, the old woman, is then seen hovering above the seemingly unconscious Schmitz before Gerard utterly disappears. Hieronimko, the physician, examines Schmitz and tells West and Mandel that Schmitz's great loss of blood demands a transfusion. West provides the needed blood, but, during the operation, becomes delusional. He awakens to find Hieronimko with a vial of poison in his hand, which he drops before fleeing. West, looking for the missing Mandel, follows Hieronimko to the castle and prevents Hieronimko from killing Mandel. The doctor then flees. West, still suffering from the loss of blood, believes that he is being buried alive. He is inside a coffin with a small window that allows him to look upward where he sees Gerard peering down at him, and then sees trees and the tops of buildings as he is carted inside of that casket toward a cemetery. West is now convinced that Gerard is the vampire preying upon Schmitz and the rest of the village's inhabitants, and that local doctor Hieronimko has been acting as her familiar or surrogate. West then recovers from the operation, realizing that he imagined that he was about to be buried alive, and, after wandering in cemetery, he meets Bras, who was one of Schutz's devoted servants. Both then search for and find Gerard's grave. Bras, too, has read the book his master had given to West, and now knows how to destroy the vampire, Gerard. When they find her grave next to the village chapel, they disinter the corpse, and Bras hammers an iron bar through Gerard's body, its flesh dissolving into dust. The spirits of Gerard's many victims then rise from their graves, seeking revenge against Gerard's surrogates. They chase gamekeeper, Boidin, so that he falls down a flight of stairs to his death. They then pursue Hieronimko, who has fled to an old mill, finding himself in a chamber where flour sacks are stored. The servant Bras then activates the mill's machinery, causing Hieronimko to suffocate to death from a shower of flour that engulfs him. Bras, West and Mandel realize

The image of Death rings a bell in Dreyer's impressionistic horror film, *Vampyr*, 1932.

that the curse of the vampire has been destroyed with the deaths of Gerard, Hieronimko and Boidin after they see Schmitz fully recovered. West and Mandel then cross a fog-bound river, and, as they reach the far bank, a rising sun floods a clearing with light, presenting a tranquil landscape that symbolically promises a safe and secure future for one and all. Dreyer presents a chilling portrait of the undead, but he offers a less theatrical presentation that can be found in other films where the vampire is more acutely defined in its conduct and modus operandi (**Nosferatu**, 1922, or **Dracula**, 1931, and its many spinoffs). His is a dreamlike portrayal that suggests rather than visually pinpoints the evil workings of the vampire, embracing the folklore traditions and canards of such creatures rather than approaching the subject from any scientific perspective. Dreyer, at one point, shot a scene where Gerard summons a pack of lethal wolves to do her sinister work, but the director thought this scene too overt and cut it from the film, wanting to present an oblique, undefined portrait of the undead fiend. As such, it made less impact upon the viewing audience of the day and was widely criticized in Europe at the time of its release as having little theatrical value or social significance. It is nevertheless a powerful and compelling portrait of evil incarnate and provides a deep sense of dread and foreboding, and West, Gerard, Mandel, Schmitz and others provide impressive performances. The film was a financial failure at the box office, but it eventually earned the status of a cult classic in the genre of horror. *Author's Note*: Dreyer, following his powerful **The Passion of Joan of Arc**, 1928, was exploring several subjects for his next film. He knew that that film had to be a talkie as the advent of sound had overwhelmed the film industry. He went to England where sound technicians were most advanced in pursuing that new technical application and, while there, read dozens of books about the supernatural, including those dealing with vampires. "We can make this stuff, too," he remarked to a friend and decided to film **Vampyr**. When finding no way to fund the project, he met with West, a French-born member of Russian nobility who bore the real name of Baron Nicolas de Gunzburg and who was enormously wealthy. West financed the film in exchange for playing the leading man. (West had serious arguments with members of his titled family, which he solved by assuming the alias of Julian West; he would later migrate to the U.S. where he established himself as a fashion journalist and became an adviser to international designers like Calvin Klein.) Other than Schmitz and Schutz, all of the other actors appearing in this intriguing and experimental film are non-professionals. To have fresh faces for this production, Dreyer sent his associates to the most impoverished areas of Paris, culling potential cast members from shanties in hobo camps, those living under viaducts and in flophouses, the homeless, the alcoholics, even those from the world of crime. They were mostly undernourished, gaunt-looking people, all having a drawn appearance as if drained of blood. Hieronimko, who plays the doctor, was a Polish journalist with not an ounce of acting experience. Gerard was the mother of an actress. When he began filming, Dreyer became upset at the sharpness of his scenes as he was striving for a hazy, diffused look to the production. When reviewing a scene he had shot, he realized that it had been undeveloped and that light had seeped into its frames, but this is exactly the look Dreyer wanted, and purposely had master cinematographer Mate employ that technical "accident" thereafter by placing a thin gauze over the lens as a filter to achieve the overall foggy appearance of the film. Dreyer's use of sound in this early talkie era is deftly handled, where the viewer hears muffled conversations or undistinctive words while hearing, as if from a great distance, babies crying, parrots squawking, and dogs barking (sounds performed by professional imitators), to indicate that something is amiss down the street or around the corner. Unlike the visceral horror films of **Dracula** and **Frankenstein**, 1931, Dreyer took, as usual, a detached approach to his subject, making the pensive **Vampyr** with overwhelming elements of the sensual, the moody and the emotionally impressionistic and surrealistic. He distorts many of his images, such as showing huge faces outside of windows (which would be emulated more than fifty years later by director George Miller when making **The Witches of Eastwick**, 1987, when showing the gigantic face of Jack Nicholson, who plays a devil). Dreyer's visual approach, however, had little appeal for the audiences of that day, and, in fact, in some instances, viewers reacted violently to the film. Dreyer recalled that, in this film's Paris premiere, "some of those in the audience got so angry with the picture that they threw things at the screen and shouted. They did not understand it." Few filmmakers in the horror genre followed in Dreyer's tradition of the intangible, except for some of the early 1940s films from the gifted Jacques Tourneur (**Cat People**, 1942; **I Walked with a Zombie**, 1943; **The Leopard Man**, 1943) where the unseen and not anything graphically shown holds the most terror. This film was shot on location in Countepierre, France, and an actual castle, the manor house and the village were used in the location shots. In the original script Hieronimko was to end his life while fleeing into a swamp, but Dreyer's assistants found an old flour mill that had eerie-looking white shadows around its doors and windows, and chose this place for the evil doctor's demise. The chapel where the grave of Gerard is found was actually a barn that art director Warm converted into a chapel, as well as its adjacent graveyard. Cobwebs and filth seen in the castle were created by special effects supervisor Armand, as well as Dreyer, who broke several jars of jams and jellies and left the smashed remains standing for a month so that the area was crawling with spiders and other insects when Dreyer came to film that scene. The legend of the vampire chiefly stems from the heinous exploits of Vlad Tepes, 1431-c.1477, the Romanian ruler who impaled his enemies on pikes and reportedly drank their blood. He became the role model for Dracula in ancient legends perpetuated by the inhabitants of the Carpathian Mountains and upon which Hungarian author Armin Vambery and British author Bram Stoker based their books about Dracula. For more information on Vlad Tepes, see my two-volume work *The Great Pictorial History of World Crime*, Volume II (History, Inc., 2004; pages 937-938). Other than a few classic horror films such as **Dracula**, 1931, vampires in films attracted little audience attention until the 1950s, and were viewed, before that time, as pagan-like curiosities. By the 1980s, the vampire in film attracted, as it does today, chiefly adolescent audiences that viewed the creature as campy or "cool." By the 2000s, such films became a public mania or craze, offering less logical and more bizarre scripts that any ten-year-old might scribble. Money-hungry producers eschewed any well-written scripts when producing such films (from the ridiculous to the puerile), while preying upon a public that had become as insatiable for vampires as those mythical creatures lusting for human blood. Some of those productions centering on gratuitous gore have reaped hundreds of millions of dollars in box office revenues. The perverse vampire was no longer an isolated fantasy on film, but a gigantic, creatively undemanding (as well as boringly repetitive) Hollywood commodity, designed to drain, like its blood-sucking subjects, endless dollars from the pockets of the naïve and the mordantly morose (or any poor soul suffering from necrophilia). Interestingly, the genre has kept pace with the world's ever-increasing drug culture as the subject now basically serves as a cheaply purchased visual narcotic. The filmic vampire has incredibly achieved its universal goal by invading almost every household where it is no longer looked upon as an unwholesome, lethal creature. Instead, it is tolerated and weirdly nurtured as one might protectively harbor a distempered or deranged pet (or as the compassionate George shields the brutish Lennie in **Of Mice and Men**, 1939), despite any reluctant urgings to humanely put it to sleep (which George exactly does when mercifully killing the mindless murderer as an act of euthanasia). Other films portraying vampires include **Abbott and Costello Meet Frankenstein**, 1948; **The ABC Saturday Night Superstar Movie**, 1972-1974 (TV series; "The Mad, Mad, Mad Monsters," animated 1972 episode); **About Adam**, 2000; **Abraham Lincoln: Vampire Hunter**, 2012; **The Addiction**, 1995; **Against the Dark**, 2009; **Ahkea Khots**, 1961; **Alraune**, 1918; **Andy Warhol's Dracula**, 1974 (aka: **Blood for Dracula**); **Awake**, 2007; **Batman Dracula**, 1964; **Batman Fights Dracula**, 1967; **Billy the Kid vs. Dracula**, 1966; **Black Sabbath**, 1964; **Black Sunday**, 1960; **Black Vampire**, 1988; **Blacula**, 1972; **The Black Water Vampire**, 2014; **Blade**, 1998; **Blade: Trinity**, 2004; **Blade II**, 2002; **Blood**, 1974; **Blood and Donuts**, 1995; **Blood and Roses**, 1960; **Blood Bath**, 1966; **Blood Beast Terror** (aka: **The Vampire Beast Craves Blood**), 1969; **The Blood Drinkers** (aka: **The Vampire People**), 1966; **Blood for Dracula**, 1974; **Blood of Dracula's Castle**, 1969; **Blood of the Vampire**, 1958; **Blood: The Last Vampire**, 2000; **Blood: The Last Vampire**, 2009; **Blood Ties**, 1991 (made-for-TV); **BloodRayne**, 2006; **Bonnie & Clyde vs. Dracula**, 2008; **Bordello of Blood**, 1996; **Bram Stoker's Dracula**, 1974; **Bram Stoker's Dracula** (aka: **Dracula**), 1992; **The Breed**, 2001; **The Brides of Dracula**, 1960; **Buffy the Vampire Slayer**, 1992; **Buffy the Vampire Slayer**, 1997-2003 (TV series); **Byzantium**, 2013; **Captain Kronos—Vampire Hunter**, 1974; **The Caretaker**, 2012; **Carry On Christmas**, 1969 (made-for-TV); **Chica Vampiro**, 2013 (TV series); **Cirque du Freak: The Vampire's Assistant**, 2009; **Count Dracula**, 1973; **Count Dracula's Great Love**, 1974; **Count Yorga, Vampire**, 1970; **Countess Dracula**, 1971; **Cowboys and Vampires**, 2010; **The Creeps**, 1997; **Cronos**, 1994; **The Curse of Dracula**, 1979 (TV series); **Curse of the Undead**, 1959; **Curse of the Vampires**, 1970; **Crypt of the Vampire**, 1964; **The Dark Crystal**, 1982; **Dark Prince: The True Story of Dracula**, 2000; **Dark Shadows**, 2012; **Daughters of Darkness**, 1971; **Day Watch** (aka: **Night Watch II**), 2006; **Daybreakers**, 2009; **Desire, the Vampire**, 1982 (made-for-TV); **The Devil's Commandment** (aka: **Vampires**), 1957; **Die Hard Dracula**, 1998; **Doctor Dracula**, 1978; **Dr. Terror's Gallery of Horrors**, 1967; **Dracula**, 1931; **Dracula**, 1931 (Mexican version); **Dracula**, 1972 (made-for-TV); **Dracula**, 1973 (made-for-TV); **Dracula**, 1979; **Dracula**, 1980 (animated made-for-TV); **Dracula**, 2002 (made-for-TV;); **Dracula**, 2007 (made-for-TV); **Dracula**, 2013- (TV series); **Dracula A.D. 1972**, 1972; **Dracula and Son**, 1979; **Dracula contra Frankenstein**, 1972; **Dracula: Dead and Loving It**, 1995; **Dracula in Istanbul**, 1953; **Dracula in Pakistan**, 1967; **Dracula Has Risen from the Grave**, 1969; **Dracula: Pages from a Virgin's Diary**, 2003; **Dracula: Prince of Darkness**, 1966; **Dracula Reborn**, 2012; **Dracula Rising**, 1993; **The Dracula Saga**, 1973; **Dracula: The Dark Prince**, 2013; **Dracula (The Dirty Old Man)**, 1969; **Dracula: The Series**, 1990-1991 (TV series); **Dracula 3D**, 2013; **Dracula 3000: Infinite Darkness**, 2004 (made-for-TV); **Dracula II: Ascension**, 2003; **Dracula 2000**, 2000; **Dracula 2012**, 2013; **Dracula Untold**, 2014; **Dracula vs. Frankenstein** (aka: **Blood of Frankenstein**), 1971; **Dracula's Daughter**, 1936; **Dracula's Death**, 1921; **Dracula's Dog** (aka: **Zoltan: Hound of Dracula**), 1978; **Dracula's Family Visit**, 2006; **Dracula's Guest**, 2008; **Drakula halala**, 1921; **El Vampiro**, 1957; **Embrace of the Vampire**, 1995; **The Empire of Dracula**, 1967; **The Era of Vampires**, 2003; **Eulogy for a Vampire**,

Enormous face outside a window in Dreyer's chilling *Vampyr*, 1932.

2009; **The Fearless Vampire Killers**, 1967; **Fist of the Vampire**, 2007; **The Forsaken**, 2001; **Frankenstein and Me**, 1997; **Frankenstein's Aunt**, 1987; **Freckled Max and Spook**, 1987; **Fright Night**, 1985; **Fright Night**, 2011; **Fright Night Part II**, 1989; **Fright Night 2**, 2013; **From Dusk Till Dawn**, 1996; **Frostbite** (aka: **Frostbitten**), 2006; **Ganja & Hess**, 1973; **Genuine**, 1920; **Ghost in the Water**, 1982 (made-for-TV); **God of Vampires**, 2010; **Grave of the Vampire**, 1972; **The Great Bear Scare**, 1983 (animated feature made-for-TV); **Guess What Happened to Count Dracula?**, 1970; **Habit**, 1997; **The Hamiltons**, 2006; **Haunted**, 1993; **The Hilarious House of Frankenstein**, 1971 (TV series); **Hope**, 2001 (made-for-TV); **Horror of Dracula** (aka: **Dracula**), 1958; **Horror of the Blood Monsters** (aka: **Vampire Men of the Lost Planet**), 1970; **Hotel Transylvania**, 2012 (animated feature); **House of Dark Shadows**, 1970; **House of Dracula**, 1945; **House of Frankenstein**, 1944; **House of the Wolf Man**, 2009; **The Hunger**, 1983; **Hysterical**, 1983; **I Am Legend**, 2007; **I Kissed a Vampire**, 2012; **I Sell the Dead**, 2008; **Immortality**, 2000; **Innocent Blood**, 1992; **Interview with the Vampire: The Vampire Chronicles**, 1994; **Jonathan** (aka: **Jonathan: Vampire Sterben Nicht**), 1970; **Joe Vampire**, 2012; **Jugular Wine: A Vampire Odyssey**, 1994; **The Keep**, 1983; **The Ketchup Vampires**, 1992; **Killer Barbys vs. Dracula**, 2005; **Kiss of the Damned**, 2013; **The Kiss of the Vampire**, 1963; **La fille de Dracula** (aka: **Dracula's Daughter**), 1972; **Ladies Night**, 1983; **Lady Dracula**, 1977; **The Lair of the White Worm**, 1988; **Lake of Dracula**, 1973; **The Last Man on Earth**, 1924; **The Last Man on Earth**, 1964; **Le Viol du Vampire** (aka: **The Rape of the Vampire**), 1968; **The League of Extraordinary Gentlemen**, 2003; **The Legend of the 7 Golden Vampires**, 1979; **Lemora: A Child's Tale of the Supernatural**, 1975; **Leptirica**, 1973 (made-for-TV); **Let Me In**, 2010; **Let the Right One In**, 2008; **Let's Scare Jessica to Death**, 1971; **Lifeforce**, 1985; **Lilith and Ly**, 1919; **The Little Vampire**, 1986 (TV series); **The Little Vampire**, 2000; **Little Vampire**, 2004 (TV series); **London after Midnight** (aka: **The Hypnotist**), 1927; **The Lost Boys**, 1987; **Lost Boys: The Thirst**, 2010; **Lost Boys: The Tribe**, 2008; **Lost Empires**, 1986 (TV miniseries); **Love at First Bite**, 1979; **Love Bites**, 1993; **Lust for a Vampire**, 1971; **Lust of the Vampire**, 1963; **Mad Monster Party?**, 1967 (animated feature); **Mark of the Vampire**, 1935; **Martin**, 1978; **Matinee Theater**, 1955-1958 (TV series; "Dracula," two 1956 episodes); **Midnight Son**, 2011; **Mr. Vampire**, 1916; **Modern Vampires**, 1998 (made-for-TV); **Mona the Vampire**, 1999-2003 (TV series); **Monkeybone**, 2001; **The Monster Club**, 1981; **Monster Mash: The Movie**, 1995; **Monster Squad**, 1976 (TV series); **The Monster Squad**, 1987; **Moon Child**, 2004; **The Moth Diaries**, 2012; **My Babysitter's a Vampire**, 2010 (made-for-TV); **My Babysitter's a Vampire**, 2011-2012 (TV series); **My Best Friend Is a Vampire** (aka:

Alexandra London and Jacques Dutronc as Vincent Van Gogh in *Van Gogh*, 1991.

I Was a Teenage Vampire), 1988; My Son the Vampire (aka: Vampire over London), 1963; My Stepbrother Is a Vampire !?!, 2013; Mystery and Imagination, 1966-1970 (TV series; "Dracula," 1968 episode); Nadja, 1995; Near Dark, 1987; Never on a Sunday, 2006; New Blood Rising, 2014; A Night of Horror, 1916; Night of the Vampire Hunter, 2000; Night of the Vampires, 1966; Night People, 2006; Night Watch, 2004; Ninjas vs. Vampires, 2010; Nocturna: Granddaughter of Dracula, 1979; Nosferatu, 1922; Nosferatu the Vampyre, 1979; Not Like Others (aka: Vampyrer), 2008; Not of This Earth, 1957; Not of This Earth, 1988; Not of This Earth, 1995; The Nude Vampire, 1970; Old Dracula (aka: Old Drac; Vampira), 1975; The Omega Man, 1971; Once Bitten, 1985; One More Time, 1970; Only Lovers Left Alive, 2013; Perfect Creature, 2007; Planet of the Vampires, 1965; Priest, 2011; Queen of the Damned, 2002; Rabid, 1977; The Rape of the Vampire, 1968; Red Blooded American Girl, 1990; Renfield the Undead, 2011; Requiem for a Vampire, 1973; The Return of Dr. X, 1939; The Return of Dracula, 1958; The Return of the Vampire, 1944; A Return to Salem's Lot, 1987; Rise: Blood Hunter, 2007; Robo Vampire, 1988; Rockula, 1990; Rosario + Vampire, 2008 (TV series); Saint Dracula 3D, 2012; Samurai Vampire Bikers from Hell, 1992; The Satanic Rites of Dracula, 1978; Scars of Dracula, 1970; Shadow of the Vampire, 2000; The Shiver of the Vampires, 1978; Sifu vs. Vampire, 2014; Slayer, 2006 (made-for-TV); Sleepwalkers, 1992; Son of Darkness: To Die For II, 1991; Son of Dracula, 1943; Son of Dracula, 1974; Stake Land, 2010; Strange Things Happen at Sundown, 2003; Sun Shadows: Faithful Kiss, 2011; Sundown: The Vampire in Retreat, 1989; Tales of a Vampire, 1993; Taste the Blood of Dracula, 1970; Teenage Space Vampires, 1999; Terror of Dracula, 2012; Thirst, 1979; The Thirst, 2006; Thirst, 2009; Thirty Days of Night, 2007; Thirty Days of Night: Dark Days, 2010; To Die For, 1989; Trouble Every Day, 2001; Twilight, 2008; The Twilight Saga: Eclipse, 2010; The Twilight Saga: New Moon, 2009; The Twins Effect, 2003; Two Orphan Vampires, 1997; Ultraviolet, 2006; Underworld, 2003; Underworld: Awakening, 2012; Underworld: Evolution, 2006; Underworld: Rise of the Lycans, 2009; Valerie and Her Week of Wonders, 1971; Vamp, 1986; Vampira, 1956 (TV series); Vampira, 1971 (made-for-TV); Vampira, 1994; The Vampire (aka: El Vampiro), 1957; The Vampire, 1968; The Vampire, 2007; Vampire, 2010; Vampire, 2011; The Vampire, 2013; Vampire Academy, 2014; The Vampire and the Ballerina, 1962; The Vampire Bat, 1933; Vampire Bats, 2005; Vampire Blvd., 2004; Vampire Boys, 2011; Vampire Boys II: The New Brood, 2013; Vampire Camp, 2012; Vampire Child, 1999; Vampire Circus, 1972; Vampire City, 2009; Vampire Clan, 2002; Vampire Cop, 1990; Vampire Cop Ricky, 2006; The Vampire Diaries, 2009 (TV series); Vam-

pire Diary, 2007; Vampire Dog, 2012; Vampire Effect, 2003; Vampire High, 2001 (TV series); The Vampire Hookers (aka; Sensuous Vampires; Cemetery Girls), 1979; Vampire Hunter D, 1993; Vampire Hunter D: Bloodlust, 2001; Vampire Idol, 2011-2012 (TV series); Vampire in Brooklyn, 1995; Vampire in Vegas, 2009; Vampire in Venice (aka: Nosferatu in Venice), 1988; Vampire Killers, 2009; The Vampire Lovers, 1970; Vampire Night, 2000; Vampire Noir, 2007; Vampire over London, 1952; Vampire Prosecutor, 2011 (TV series); The Vampire Secrets, 2011 (TV series); Vampire Sunrise, 2014; Vampire Vixens from Venus, 1995; The Vampires (aka: Las Vampiras; The Vampire Girls), 1969; Vampires, 1986; Vampires (aka: John Carpenter's Vampires), 1998; Vampires, 2011; Vampires, 2012 (TV series); Vampires Anonymous, 2003; Vampire's Embrace, 1991; The Vampire's Ghost, 1945; Vampires in Venice, 2013; Vampire's Kiss, 1989; Vampires: Los Muertos, 2002; The Vampire's Night Orgy, 1974; The Vampires of Bloody Island, 2009; Vampires of Warsaw, 1925; Vampires: Rise of the Fallen, 2012; The Vampire's Seduction, 1998; Vampires Suck, 2010; A Vampire's Tale, 2009; Vampires: The Turning, 2005; The Vampire's Tomb, 2013; Vampiresas, 1996 (made-for-TV); Vampiresas 1930, 1962; Vampiro, 2009; Vamps, 2012; Vampyres, 1975; Van Helsing, 2004; Vegas Vampires, 2007; Vlad (aka: The True Life of Dracula), 1982; Vlad, 2003; Vlad Tepes, 1979; Waxwork, 1988; Way of the Vampire, 2005; We Are the Night, 2010; and The Worst Crime of Them All! (aka: Mondo Keyhole), 1966. (In French and German; dubbed in English.) **p**, Baron Nicolas de Gunzberg, Carl T. Dreyer; **d**, Dreyer; **w**, Dreyer, Christen Jul (based on stories from *In a Glass Darkly* by J. Sheridan Le Fanu); **cast**, Julian West, Henriette Gerard, Jan Hieronimko, Maurice Schutz, Rena Mandel, Sybille Schmitz, Albert Bras, N. Babanini, Jane Mora, Georges Boidin; **c**, Rudolph Mate, Louis Nee; **m**, Wolfgang Zeller; **ed**, Tonka Taldy; **art d**, Hermann Warm; **spec eff**, Henri Armand.

Van Gogh ★★★ 1991; France; 158m; Erato Films/StudioCanal/Sony Pictures Classics; Color; Biographical Drama; Children: Unacceptable (MPAA: R); **BD**; **DVD**; **VHS**. Compelling biopic sees a riveting performance from Dutronc, who plays the emotionally troubled but brilliant Dutch artist Vincent Van Gogh (1853-1890). Set in the last two months of his life, Dutronc lives at a small inn in the village of Auvers sur Oise, about fifteen miles from Paris. He is moody and mercurial as he strolls about the village and into the neighboring fields, often carrying his canvases and brushes, but we do not see the artist at work (as is shown in **Lust for Life**, 1956, where Kirk Douglas essayed Van Gogh). He chats, jokes and drinks with the local residents, often becoming pensive and withdrawn and, on other occasions, expressive and outgoing. He consorts with the local whores, but always seems unsatisfied. Le Coq, who plays his supportive brother Theo Van Gogh (1857-1891), a successful art dealer, visits him, and he acts as an emotional therapist to boost Dutronc's spirits. Dutronc nevertheless slips ever downward into depression and madness. He has long developed a deep resentment of being wholly dependent upon Le Coq for total financial aid, considering himself an utter failure as an artist. Meanwhile, he is treated by local doctor Sety for his increasing headaches, this physician being the actual reason why Dutronc has moved to the small village. (One of Van Gogh's most famous artworks is of this physician, titled *Portrait of Dr. Gachet*.) London, who is Sety's fetching daughter, falls in love with the withdrawn, cerebral Dutronc and follows him about like some devoted puppy. Dutronc's deep moods sink ever downward into dark depression and he argues and insults everyone, his brother, his brother's wife, the physician and eventually the person who loves him deeply, London. He then shoots himself and is bedridden, angrily denouncing all who arrive to console and comfort him (and these scenes are much too overdrawn), until he finally dies. Pialat directs this introspective film at an almost leisurely pace but nevertheless draws forth an outstanding and unnerving performance from Dutronc while the production values are high with appropriate period costumes and settings. Songs/Music: "Dexuième

Symphonie, Pour Cordes" (Arthur Honegger), "Où va la jeune indoue (L'air des clochettes)" (from "Lakmé" by Leo Delibes), "Je suis Monsieur Lautrec" (Bernard Le Coq, Pialat), "Le temps des cerises" (music: Antoine Renard; lyrics: Jean-Baptiste Clement). *Author's Note*: Many other actors have played Vincent Van Gogh in many other films, including **Around the World in 80 Days**, 2004 (Perry Andelin Blake); **Artists' Notebooks**, 1964 (TV series; Alan Dobie voiceover); **Besuch bei Van Gogh**, 1985 (Christian Grashof); **Dreams**, 1990 (Martin Scorsese); **Full Moon Fables**, 2004 (Dan DePaola); **Gauguin the Savage**, 1980 (made-for-TV; Barrie Houghton); **Histeria!**, 1998-2000 (TV series; "Inventors Hall of Fame: Part I," 1998 episode: Frank Welker voiceover); **Langs de kant van de weg**, 1990 (TV series; Ids van der Krieken); **Lautrec**, 1999 (Karel Vingerhoets); **Le voyage du Hollandais**, 1981 (made-for-TV; Gerard Desarthe); **Lust for Life**, 1952 (Kirk Douglas); **Medium**, 2005-2011 (TV series; "Still Life," 2005 episode: Ed Baccari); **Mon cher Theo Van Gogh**, 1980 (made-for-TV; Gregory Knop voiceover); **Moulin Rouge, a Vida de Toulouse-Lautrec**, 1963 (TV series; Rolando Boldrin); **Omnibus**, 1967-2003 (TV series; "Vincent the Dutchman," 1972 episode: Michael Gough; "Van Gogh," 1990 episode: Linus Roache); **Out of the Box**, 1998-2004 (TV series; "Mirror, Mirror" episode: Sal Viviano); **Paradise Found**, 2003 (Peter Varga); **Paul Gauguin**, 1975 (TV miniseries; Jean de Coninck); **The Philco-Goodyear Television Playhouse**, 1948-1956 (TV series; "The Life of Vincent Van Gogh," 1959 episode: Everett Sloane); **Starry Night**, 2003 (Abbott Alexander [David Abbott]); **Van Gogh**, 1969 (made-for-TV; Herbert Fleischmann); **Van Gogh; een huis voor Vincent**, 2013 (TV series; Barry Atsma); **Van Gogh: Painted with Words**, 2010 (made-for-TV; Benedict Cumberbatch); **Vincent and Theo**, 1990 (Tim Roth); **Vincent et moi**, 2001 (Tcheky Karyo); **Vincent Van Gogh**, 1988 (made-for-TV; Timo Torikka); and **The Yellow House**, 2007 (made-for-TV; John Sim). **p, d&w**, Maurice Pialat; **cast**, Jacques Dutronc, Alexandra London, Bernard Le Coq, Gerard Sety, Corinne Bourdon, Elsa Zylberstein, Leslie Azoulai, Jacques Vidal, Chantal Barbarit, Claudine Ducret; **c**, Gilles Henry, Jacques Loiseleux, Emmanuel Machuel; **m**, Andre Bernot, J.M. Bourget, Jacques Dutronc, P. Revedy; **ed**, Yann Dedet, Nathalie Hubert, Helene Viard; **prod d**, Philippe Pallut, Katia Vischkof.

Van Helsing ★★★ 2004; U.S./Czech Republic; 131m; UNIV; Color; Horror; Children: Unacceptable (MPAA: PG-13); **BD**; **DVD**; **IV**. Action-packed horror film with amazing special effects sees Jackman playing the title character, a late 19th-Century man seeking adventure by being a globe-trotting vampire hunter in the pay of a secret organization operating out of a basement in the Vatican. First, he and his bumbling assistant, Wenham, go after a computer-generated Mr. Hyde in a tower at Notre Dame Cathedral in Paris. After battling and tearing the limbs from that monster before killing him, Jackman then goes back in time to medieval Transylvania in search of Count Dracula, who is wonderfully played by Roxburgh, and who has teamed up with a rabid Wolf Man, Kemp, and the Frankenstein Monster, Hensley. In Transylvania, Jackman is assisted by sultry Beckinsale, a gypsy princess, who also is a vampire exterminator in a village near Roxburgh's castle. She wants to end a curse on her family by destroying the vampire. Together they go after Roxburgh and his undead, but at a terrible cost, including Beckinsale's brother, Kemp, who has turned into a werewolf. Violent creature action, frightening images, sensuality and gore prohibit viewing by children. Special effects artists Cremin, Jaffar and Elmendorf did more than commendable work in this thriller, providing one horrific scene after another. Typical of that action is where Jackman battles three flying vampire wives of Roxburgh's, dispatching one with an arrow soaked in holy water from a crossbow, and in his subsequent titanic struggle with the all-powerful Roxburgh. Vlad Tepes, 1431-c.1477, the Romanian ruler who impaled his enemies on pikes and reportedly drank their blood is the role model for Dracula in ancient legends perpetuated by the inhabitants of the Carpathian Mountains and

Will Kemp and Kate Beckinsale in *Van Helsing*, **2004.**

upon which Hungarian author Armin Vambery and British author Bram Stoker based their books about Dracula. For more information on Vlad Tepes, see my two-volume work *The Great Pictorial History of World Crime*, Volume II (History, Inc., 2004; pages 937-938). For a comprehensive list of actors who have played Dracula, see Index, Fictional Characters, Dracula. **p**, Bob Ducsay, Stephen Sommers; **d&w**, Sommers; **cast**, Hugh Jackman, Kate Beckinsale, Richard Roxburgh, David Wenham, Shuler Hensley, Elena Anaya, Will Kemp, Kevin J. O'Connor, Alun Armstrong, Silvia Colloca; **c**, Allen Daviau; **m**, Alan Silvestri; **ed**, Ducsay, Kelly Matsumoto, Jim May; **prod d**, Allan Cameron; **art d**, Steve Arnold, Keith P. Cunningham, Giles Masters, Tony Reading, Jaromir Svarc; **set d**, Cindy Carr, Anna Pinnock; **spec eff**, Steve Cremin, Gary Elmendorf, Kamil Jaffar.

Vanilla Sky ★★★ 2001; U.S./Spain; 136m; Cruise/Wagner/PAR; Color; Mystery; Children: Unacceptable (MPAA: R); **BD**; **DVD**; **IV**. Strange but absorbing tale focuses upon egocentric Cruise, who is in prison on a murder charge. He tells Russell, a police psychologist, how the killing happened. He held the major share of stock in a big publishing company, which he inherited from his parents when they died some years earlier. He is considered too immature and irresponsible to run the company of which he is now virtually in control. He and close friend Lee compete for the affections of Cruz. Cruise is in an auto accident that disfigures his handsome face and he kills the person who caused the accident. In telling his story, Cruise is not sure if it all happened or if it was just a dream. Remake of the 1997 film **Abre Los Ojos/Open Your Eyes**. Songs: "Vanilla Sky" (Paul McCartney), "Everything in It's Right Place" and "I Might Be Wrong" (2000; Thomas Yorker, Edward O'Brien, Colin Greenwood, Jonathan Greenwood, Philip Seaway), "From Resole with Love" (1999; Neil Claxton, Chris Baker, John Mayer), "Have You Forgotten" (1996; Mark Keeled), "All the Right Friends" (1987; Bill Berry, Peter Buck, Mike Mills, Michael Stripe), "My Robot" and "Monde '77" (2000; Stuart David, Scott Stenholm, Ronnie Black, Karn David), "My Favorite Things" (1959; music: Richard Rodgers; lyrics: Oscar Hammerstein II), "Keep on Pushing" (1964; Curtis Mayfield), "Directions" (2000; Josh Rouse), "Solsbury Hill" (1983; Peter Gabriel), "Wrecking Ball" (2001; Ian Sefchick, Sharky Laguana), "I Fall Apart" (2001; Nancy Wilson, Cameron Crowe), "Last Goodbye" (1994; Jeff Buckley), "Svefin-g-englar" and "Agaetis Bryjun" (1999; Orri P. Dyrason, Kjarta Sveinsson, Jon Tor Birigisson, Georg Holm, Agust Aevar Gunnarsson), "Earth Time Tapestry" (1999; Spacecraft), "Indra" (2000; Rob Garza, Eric Hilton), "Afrika Shox" (1999; Neil Barnes, Paul Daley, Nicholas Rapoccioli, Afrika Bambaataa), "Loops of Fury" (Thomas Rowlands, Edmund Simons), "Rez" (Rick Smith, Karl Hyde, Darren Emerson), "Too Good

Warwick Ward and the consummate vamp of the silent era, Lya De Putti, in *Variety*, 1925.

to Be Strange" (1995; Andrea Parker, David Morley), "Sweetness Follows" (1992; Bill Perry, Peter Buck, Mike Mills, Michael Stripe), "One of Us" (1995; Eric Bazilian), "Fourth Time Around" (1966; Bob Dylan), "Wild Honey" (2000; music: U2; lyrics: Bono), "Porpoise Song" (theme from "Head," 1968; Gerry Goffin, Carole King), "Jingle Bell Rock" (1957; Joseph Bell, James Boothe), "It's Slinky" (Homer Fraperman, Charles Wragley), "Western Union" (1967; John Durrill, Norman Ezell, Mike Rabon), "Heaven" (1981; Mick Jagger, Keith Richards), "Can We Still Be Friends" (1976; Todd Rundgren), "Good Vibrations" (1967; Brian Wilson, Mike Love), "Summer's End" (1962; Elmer Bernstein), "The Healing Room" (2000; Sinead O'Connor), "The Nothing Song/Njosnavelin" (2001; Orri P. Dyrason, Kjartan Sveinsson, Jon Tod Birgisson, George Holm), "Doot Doot" (1983; Rick Smith, Alfred John Thomas, Karl Hyde), "Where Do I Begin" (1997; Thomas Rowlands, Edmund Simons), "Ladies and Gentlemen, We Are Floating in Space" (1997; Jason Pierce). Sexuality and gutter language prohibit viewing by children. **p**, Cameron Crowe, Tom Cruise, Paula Wagner, Donald J. Lee, Jr.; **d&w**, Crowe (based on the film **Abre Los Ojos/Open Your Eyes** by Alejandro Amenabar, Mateo Gil); **cast**, Cruise, Penelope Cruz, Cameron Diaz, Kurt Russell, Jason Lee, Noah Taylor, Timothy Spall, Tilda Swinton, Michael Shannon, Delaina Mitchell. In cameo roles, comedian-talk show host Conan O'Brien plays himself and producer Stephen Spielberg is a party guest; **c**, John Toll; **m**, Nancy Wilson; **ed**, Joe Hutshing, Mark Livolsi; **prod d**, Catherine Hardwicke; **art d**, Beat Frutiger, John Chichester, Michael Rizzo; **set d**, Cloudia Rebar; **spec eff**, Gary D'Amico, Steven Kirshoff.

The Vanishing ★★★ 1990; Netherlands/France; 107m; Argos Films/Tara; Color; Mystery; Children: Unacceptable; **BD**; **DVD**; **VHS**; **IV**. Enthralling mystery begins with Bervoets and Steege, who are deeply in love, this young Dutch couple first seen on a cycling vacation in France when the wife, Steege, disappears while buying snacks at a busy gas station. Bervoets dedicates the next three years trying to find her before he receives some postcards from her abductor, Le Sache. The kidnapper promises to reveal what has happened to her as Bervoets pursues him to learn if his wife is alive and safe. What he learns is even more sinister than he dared imagine for a nail-biting, unhappy ending. This film was less successfully remade in 1993. Frightening scenes prohibit viewing by children. (In Dutch; English subtitles.) **p**, George Sluizer, Anne Lordon; **d&w**, Tim Krabbe (based on an adaptation by Sluizer of Krabbe's novel *The Golden Egg*); **cast**, Bernard-Pierre Donnadieu, Gene Bervoets, Johanna ter Steege, Gwen Eckhaus, Bernadette Le Sache, Tania Latarjet, Lucille Glenn, Roger Souza, Caroline Appere, Pierre Forget; **c**, Toni Kuhn; **m**, Henny Vrienten; **ed**, Lin Friedman, Sluizer; **art d**, Santiago Isidro Pin.

Vanya on 42nd Street ★★★ 1994; U.S.; 119m; Channel 4/Sony; B/W; Comedy/Drama; Children: Unacceptable (MPAA: PG); **BD**; **DVD**; **VHIS**; **IV**. Lively tale centers on a group of New York actors at a run-down theater on 42nd Street, who are performing an uninterrupted rehearsal of Chekhov's play "Uncle Vanya." The play is shown act-by-act with only brief breaks to move props or for refreshments. The lack of costumes, real props, and scenery is forgotten as the actors perform the play in street clothes and improvised props or none at all. Experimental and highly innovative, the story receives standout performances from the entire cast. Mature subject matter prohibits viewing by children. **p**, Fred Berner; **d**, Louis Malle; **cast**, Phoebe Brand, Lynn Cohen, George Gaynes, Jerry Mayer, Julianne Moore, Larry Pine, Brooke Smith, Wallace Shawn, Andre Gregory, Madhur Jaffrey, Oren Moverman; **w**, Andre Gregory (based on an adaptation by David Mamet of the play "*Uncle Vanya*" by Anton Chekhov); **c**, Declan Quinn; **m**, Joshua Redman; **ed**, Nancy Baker; **prod d**; Eugene Lee; **art d**, Daniele Perna.

Variety ★★★★ 1925 (silent); Germany; 112m/7 reels; UFA/PAR; B/W; Drama; Children: Unacceptable; **DVD**. Dynamic tale with powerful performances from Jannings and De Putti depicts in mesmerizing detail how a good man becomes corrupt under the spell of a manipulative vixen. Jannings is first seen as a convict in prison where he tells his tale to the warden. In flashback, we see Jannings operating a shabby sideshow in a small amusement center. He is married and has a small son, but he is unhappy as he longs for his former life as a celebrated trapeze artist, a profession he was forced to abandon after having been injured. One day, he is thunderstruck when a sailor arrives with De Putti, a sultry, young girl, in tow. She claims to be an orphan and quickly puts Jannings under her spell. (De Putti, as did her contemporaries Louise Brooks and Colleen Moore, wears her black, shimmering hair in a page boy hair-do, cropped and with bangs on her forehead.) Jannings becomes her love slave and both then depart the amusement park, Jannings abandoning his wife and child. They put together a trapeze act and become aerialists working with carnivals. While both are performing in Berlin, Jannings is introduced by the carnival manager to world famous aerialist Ward, who tells Jannings that his act was destroyed when his brother had an accident and he now needs a catcher. Ward is not sure he wants Jannings for that role as he is only a common carnival performer. Ward changes his mind when he spots the alluring De Putti, who not only leads him on, but convinces Jannings to join Ward against his better instincts. Ward and De Putti then begin a torrid but clandestine affair that Jannings learns about when going to a restaurant and there sees a fellow performer drawing a cartoon on a tablecloth. The caricatures show Ward and De Putti together and Jannings as a duped goat. Jannings is in a rage, and we see him purposely drop Ward while Ward is doing an in-air triple somersault, plunging to his death. That scene, however, takes place within Janning's imagination as, professional that he is, he could never bring himself to commit such an act during a performance. Jannings, however, after concluding the act and when the show ends, stoically goes to Ward's apartment where he finds the cuckolding De Putti and Ward. Jannings stabs Ward to death in front of De Putti and then washes the blood from his hands as she stares in shock. When he turns about and begins to leave her, however, De Putti, ever the opportunist, realizes that she has lost her meal ticket and clutches to Jannings like a clinging African vine. Ignoring her, Jannings plods from the place, going down some stairs, but the frantic De Putti clings to his leg like a tenacious terrier. The powerful Jannings goes down the stairs, dragging the woman, who apparently breaks her neck and dies. He is oblivious to her corpse as he goes to the street. He takes a taxi and goes to a police station where he reports his crime. We see Jannings in flash-forward talking with the prison warden, who acts like a priest in stating that he has suffered enough and, more or less, gives Jannings absolution. The finale shows the prison gates opening as if to symbolically indicate that Jannings is now free of the pain and agony he has undergone. Dupont directs this riveting film with great care, and master cinematographer

Freund provides a fluid camera and myriad innovative shots and arresting camera angles that become more distorted as the characters are slowly engulfed in betrayal and murder. The ever-increasing visual pace of the film thusly presents tremendous suspense and increasing tension. The action is often seen through reflections of glass windows or the lenses of binoculars, or through whirring blades of an electric fan, or via the POV of the characters to further isolate and emphasize these chilling scenes. Song: "Vaudeville" (used for British release; music: Vivian Ellis; lyrics: William Helmore). *Author's Note*: **Variety** was a tour de force at the box office and proved to be Dupont's most important film. He, Jannings and De Putti were all summoned to Hollywood where Jannings became a great success during the silent era. When talkies appeared, however, his studio, Paramount, felt that his thick German accent would not be acceptable to the American public and severed its relations with him. Jannings returned to Europe where he remained a great film star. Dupont was not successful at all in the U.S., and soon returned to Europe. De Putti, who radiated sensuality on the screen, went on to play vamps, but never equaled her riveting role in this absorbing film. She appeared in only a few films before returning to Europe to make another film in 1929, and she accidentally fell from a second-floor window. Although the press claimed she had attempted suicide, the actress denied it. Fully recovered, she returned to the U.S. in 1931, and, late that year, after swallowing a chicken bone at dinner, was rushed to a NYC hospital where the bone was removed. De Putti, however, developed a throat infection. She was removed to the Harbor Sanitarium in Manhattan where she became delirious and, while evading nurses, left her room and was later found lying in a corridor. She developed pleurisy and then pneumonia in both lungs. She remained unconscious for two days until dying on November 27, 1931, at age thirty-four. Other films profiling trapeze artists include **Alegria**, 1999; **Annie Get Your Gun**, 1950; **The Aristocats**, 1970; **The Big Cage**, 1933; **Big Top Pee-Wee**, 1988; **The Biggest Robbery Never Told**, 2002; **Charlie Chan at the Circus**, 1936; **The Circus**, 1928; **Circus Girl**, 1937; **Circus of Horrors**, 1960; **Circus World**, 1964; **Comrade Kim Goes Flying**, 2012; **Dante's Inferno**, 1935; **The Dark Tower**, 1943; **Das Schlangenei**, 1978; **Fire-Eater**, 1998; **4 Devils**, 1928; **Freaks**, 1932; **The Girl of Your Dreams**, 1988; **Gorilla at Large**, 1954; **The Greatest Show on Earth**, 1952; **Homicide for Three**, 1948; **I'm No Angel**, 1933; **It's Easier for a Camel...**, 2004; **Las Vegas Lady**, 1975; **Madagascar 3: Europe's Most Wanted**, 2012; **The Master Touch**, 1974; **O'Shaughnessy's Boy**, 1935; **Pandora's Box**, 1929; **Phantom of the Rue Morgue**, 1954; **Polly of the Circus**, 1932; **Seven Murders for Scotland Yard**, 1971; **The Story of Three Loves**, 1953; **Strike Me Pink**, 1936; **Thirteen Women**, 1932; **Trapeze**, 1932; **Trapeze**, 1956; **Trigger, Jr.**, 1950; **Tsirk**, 1936; **Two Tickets to Broadway**, 1951; **Undiscovered**, 2005; **Van Helsing**, 2004; **Water for Elephants**, 2011; **When Night Is Falling**, 1995; and **Wings of Desire**, 1988. p, Erich Pommer; d&w, Ewald Andre Dupont (based on the German novel *The Oath of Stephen Huller* by Felix Hollaender); cast, Emil Jannings, Maly Delschaft, Lya De Putti, Warwick Ward, Alice Hechy, Georg John, Kurt Gerron, Paul Rehkopf, Charles Lincoln, Georg Baselt, Trude Hesterberg, Werner Krauss; c, Kral Freund, Carl Hoffmann; m, Erno Rapee; art d, Alfred Junge, Oscar Friedrich Werndorff; spec eff, Ernst Kunstmann, Eugen Schüfftan.

Variety Girl ★★★ 1947; U.S.; 93m; PAR; B/W/Color; Musical; Children: Acceptable; **VHS**. Entertaining songfest opens with Hatcher and San Juan, two aspiring movie actresses, who meet in Hollywood and become starlets for a review benefiting the Variety Clubs, a charitable show business organization. A thin plot presents some humorous confusion as San Juan is mistaken for Hatcher as the "Variety Girl," but all comes right as a number of good tunes are offered. Most of the stars at Paramount Studios at the time appear in the film as well as directors Cecil B. DeMille, Mitchell Leisen, George Marshall, and Frank Butler. Some of the best numbers were Alan Ladd as a singing pilot with stew-

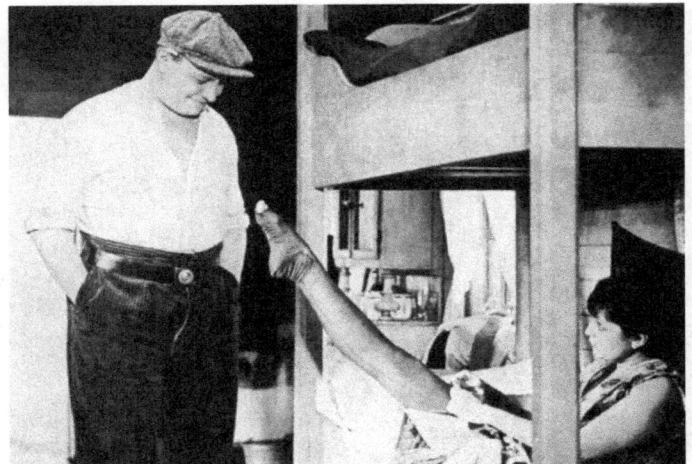

Emil Jannings and Lya De Putti in *Variety*, 1925.

ardess Dorothy Lamour aboard an airplane, and William Holden and Ray Milland dancing and singing in a quartet with Joan Caulfield and Cass Daley. Songs: "Your Heart Calling Mine," "Tallahassee, "Tired," "He Can Waltz" (Frank Loesser); "Romeo and Julicat" (Edward H. Plumb); "Tiger Rag" (Edwin B. Edwards, Nick LaRocca, Tony Sbarbaro, Henry Ragas, Larry Shields); "Harmony" (music: Jimmy Van Heusen; lyrics: Johnny Burke); "Mildred's Boogie" (Jimmy Mulcay, Mildred Mulcay); "Lohengrin, Prelude to Act III" (Richard Wagner). p, Daniel Dare; d, George Marshall; cast, Mary Hatcher, Olga San Juan, DeForest Kelly, George Reeves, Jack Norton, Howard Da Silva, William Demarest, Patric Knowles, Cecil Kellway, Richard Webb, Frank Faylen, Walter Abel, Johnny Coy, Mikhail Rasumny, and guest stars in musical numbers and skits: Pearl Bailey, William Bendix, Macdonald Carey, Joan Caulfield, Gary Cooper, Bing Crosby, Cass Daley, Billy De Wolfe, Barry Fitzgerald, Mona Freeman, Paulette Goddard, Sterling Hayden, William Holden, Bob Hope, Spike Jones, Alan Ladd, Veronica Lake, Dorothy Lamour, Burt Lancaster, John Lund, Diana Lynn, Ray Milland, Robert Preston, Gail Russell, Lizabeth Scott, Barbara Stanwyck, Sonny Tufts, and among the beautiful Variety Girls: Virginia Field, Wanda Hendrix, Paula Raymond, Arlene Whalen; w, Monte Brice, Edmund L. Hartmann, Frank Tashlin, Robert L. Welsh; c, Lionel Lindon, Stuart Thompson (Technicolor; cartoon sequence); m, Joseph J. Lilley; ed, LeRoy Stone; art d, Robert Clatworthy, Hans Dreier; set d, Sam Comer, Ross Dowd; spec eff, Farciot Edouart, Gordon Jennings.

Variety Lights ★★★ 1965; Italy; 93m; Capitolium/Pathe Contemporary Films; B/W; Drama/Romance; Children: Unacceptable; **DVD**. Absorbing tale is centered about a group of traveling entertainers in Italy, who are joined by a beautiful young woman, Del Poggio, who has run away to perform with them as a lively dancer. She is soon the main attraction and becomes famous as the vaudevillians entertain to packed houses in small towns. The troupe's aging comedian, De Filippo, falls in love with the group's ingenue, Masina. She admires him, but does not love him and is being wooed by Lulli, who is an assistant to a major impresario. To complicate matters, Del Poggio leaves the group in order to perform in high-class entertainments. Masina and Fellini were real-life husband and wife, and she starred in most of his films. This film was originally released in Italy in 1950. (In Italian; English subtitles.) p&d, Alberto Lattuada, Federico Fellini; cast, Peppino De Filippo, Carla Del Poggio, Giulietta Masina, John Kitzmiller, Dante Maggio, Checco Durante, Gina Mascetti, Giulio Cali, Silvio Bagolini, Giacomo Furia; w, Fellini, Alberto Lattuada, Tullio Pinelli (based on a story by Fellini); c, Otello Martelli; m, Felice Lattuada; ed, Mario Bonotti; art d, Aldo Buzzi; set d, Luigi Gervasi.

Leo Genn and Rosalind Russell in *The Velvet Touch*, 1948.

Vatel ★★★ 2000; France/U.K./Belgium; 103m; Legende Enterprises; Miramax Films; Color; Biographical Drama; Children: Unacceptable (MPAA: PG-13); **DVD**; **IV**. Intriguing historical biopic takes place in 1671 France, as war is about to start with Holland. Glover, a penniless prince, invites King Louis XIV (1754-1793), played by Sands, to three days of festivities in a chateau in Chantilly as a bribe because the prince wants a commission as a general. In charge of the affair is a steward, Vatel, played by Depardieu, who is a lowly born, talented man of honor. He becomes attracted to Thurman, the king's new mistress, and she finds him to be refreshingly principled in an otherwise hypocritical royal court. Their romance is doomed because of class differences. Frustrated by insults from the aristocrats and realizing that his love for Thurman is hopeless, Vatel commits suicide and Thurman is grief-stricken, but cannot show she cares. Music: "La Bourree," "Contredance from Les Indes galantes," "Temple sacre" (Jean-Philippe Rameau); "Secundo pezzo" (Ennio Morricone); "Music for the Royal Fireworks" (George Frideric Handel); "L'Air from Absalom" (Giovanni Paolo Colonna). (In French; English subtitles.) **p**, Roland Joffe, Alain Goldman, Timothy Burrill; **d**, Joffe; **cast**, Gerard Depardieu, Uma Thurman, Tim Roth, Timothy Spall, Julian Glover, Julian Sands, Murray Lachlan Young, Hywel Bennett, Richard Griffiths, Arielle Dombasle; **w**, Jeanne Labrune, Tom Stoppard; **c**, Robert Fraisse; **m**, Ennio Morricone; **ed**, Noelle Boisson; **prod d**, Cecilia Montiel, Jean Rabasse; **art d**, Louise Marzaroli; **set d**, Francoise Benoit-Fresco; **spec eff**, Eve Ramboz, Pascal Molina, Guy Monbillard, Annie Dautane.

The Velvet Touch ★★★ 1948; U.S.; 100m; Independent Artists/RKO; B/W; Crime Drama; Children: Unacceptable; **DVD**; **VHS**. Russell is a standout as she plays a Broadway stage actress starring in Henrik Ibsen's play "Hedda Gabler." Her producer, Ames, tries to stop the production and also keep her from marrying a rival, Genn. She kills Ames and, in a flashback, remembers meeting Genn. Her relations with Ames result in an argument with him during which she hits him over the head with a statuette. Police investigator Greenstreet suspects that the murder was actually committed by Trevor, Ames' jealous former girlfriend. She is arrested and charged with the murder. Trevor is convicted, but rather than go to prison for a crime she did not commit, she kills herself. Russell becomes guilt-ridden and confesses that she killed Ames in a fit of anger. The taut and clever script, along with superb performances from Russell, Trevor and Greenstreet, make for a suspenseful tale where the tension is sustained throughout. The atmosphere of the legitimate stage is everywhere in this tale to further interest lovers of the theater. A sixty-minute radio adaptation was aired by Lux Radio Theater on January 10, 1949, with Russell and Greenstreet reprising their roles. A second sixty-minute radio adaptation was aired by Screen Director's Playhouse on August 23, 1951, with Russell reprising her role. Song: "The Velvet Touch" (Mort Greeene, Leigh Harline). *Author's Note*: This was the first film produced by a company owned by Russell and her husband, Brisson. Russell told this author that "I enjoyed making **The Velvet Touch** because it was a serious drama, a crime story, really, and it got me away from comedies. I really kill poor Leon [Ames] by accident, but he is still dead as a doornail, in the picture, of course." Trevor, too, liked working in this film, telling this author that "I played the other woman again in that picture, but this time I was the fall girl, blamed for bumping off a man who jilted me for Roz [Rosalind Russell]. She goes to pieces over killing him, but it does me no good since I am dead by then. Now that's about as jilted as you can get." **p**, Frederick Brisson; **d**, Jack Gage; **cast**, Rosalind Russell, Leo Genn, Claire Trevor, Sydney Greenstreet, Leon Ames, Frank McHugh, Walter Kingsford, Lex Barker, Nydia Westman, Michael St. Angel, Martha Hyer; **w**, Leo Rosten (adapted by Walter Reilly from a story by William Mercer, Annabel Ross); **c**, Joseph Walker; **m**, Leigh Harline; **ed**, Chandler House; **prod d**, William E. Flannery; **set d**, Darrell Silvera, Maurice Yates; **spec eff**, Russell A. Cully.

Vengeance Valley ★★★ 1951; U.S.; 83m; MGM; Color; Western; Children: Unacceptable; **DVD**; **VHS**; **IV**. Action-packed western presents top-drawer performances from Lancaster, Walker and a strong supporting cast. Walker is the son of Collins, an invalided cattle baron, who depends on Lancaster, his strong-willed foreman, to keep Walker on the straight and narrow. Walker, however, is sneaky, cowardly and spoiled rotten to the core. Married to Dru, he has earlier fathered an illegitimate child with Forrest, but he has insidiously placed the blame for that transgression on Lancaster. Ireland and O'Brian, who are Forrest's brothers and pair of back-shooting rustlers stealing from Collins' herd, hear that Lancaster is the culprit and they go gunning for him. Though Forrest refuses to identify her baby's father, she accepts $500 Lancaster gives her to raise the child. Actually, Lancaster has made this payment on behalf of Walker, but Forrest's brothers believe him to be the father of their nephew. They pick a fight with Lancaster, but both are badly beaten and thrown into jail to reconsider their motives. They nevertheless swear to get even, planning their vengeance. Meanwhile, Collins learns that Walker has overdrawn $500 from the bank, but Walker tells him that he needed it to pay off some old debts and the always tolerant Collins mildly chastises him. Walker tells Collins that he will feel better if Collins officially gives him half of the ranch as Collins has promised to do. Collins agrees, saying that the other half of the ranch will go to Lancaster, whom Collins has raised as a foster son. Dru, however, is not taken in by Walker's lies. She knows that the $500 Walker took from the bank has gone to Forrest and that he has cheated on her. She locks him out of her room while Walker thinks Dru has now given her affection to the upstanding Lancaster. Walker then plans to steal the ranch's entire herd at spring round-up, while ridding himself of Lancaster by paying Ireland and O'Brian to ambush and kill Lancaster during the cattle drive. During the drive, Strange, who has purchased the herd from Walker, arrives at Lancaster's camp during a rainstorm, telling Lancaster about the transaction, which surprises Lancaster. The following day, Carpenter, one of the cowboys loyal to Lancaster, reports cattle rustling and, after Lancaster rides to investigate, Ireland and O'Brian, hiding behind rocks, shoot and wound him. Lancaster, however, manages to kill O'Brien and Ireland is killed when Carpenter and some other cowboys ride to the rescue. Lancaster now knows that Walker has been behind the ambush and finds him on the trail. Walker decides to have a showdown with the man who has been his lifelong protector, telling him that he is faster on the draw than Lancaster. That matters not when both men go for their guns. Walker is faster, but misses his mark while Lancaster's steady aim sends a bullet into the conniving Walker to end his life. Lancaster is shown at the end with Collins, who has come to realize that he has raised a treacherous son, but appreciates that he has the noble Lancaster as the inheritor of his vast ranch while Dru and Lancaster look forward to a life together. Thorpe directs this fine oater in a straightforward manner while carefully developing its characters, which are much more defined than what is found in most westerns. Walker's character is that of a conniving snake, nestling in Collins' heart while waiting to poisonously strike all who love him. Though the admirable Lancaster is impressively towering in this gritty tale, Walker steals every scene with his manipulative manner and insidious word. The film was a success at the box office, earning more than $3.1 million in its initial release against a $1 million budget. *Author's Note*: Thorpe told this author that "Burt [Lancaster] was perfect in **Vengeance Valley** as a robust ranch foreman. The guy is physical in everything he does, broad shoulders and powerful arms. He did it all, actually branding steers, racing horses, roping cattle, and no actor ever looked better in a cowboy fistfight than Burt did in the battles he has in that picture." Lancaster had nothing but admiration for his co-star Walker, who was long years dead when Lancaster told this author: "Bob [Walker] was a greater actor than most thought. He played the kind of role that made him famous, an Iago. You can see him in that kind of role when he appeared in **Strangers on a Train** [1951], where he played a millionaire's son plotting to murder his father, or in **My Son John** [1952], where he is a much-loved son, who is really a traitorous communist spy. Oh, Bob was a master of such characters. He was a very troubled man and I think he drew upon his agonies to play those parts. He died about three weeks after **Vengeance Valley** was released [on August 28, 1951, at age thirty-two], from drinking and an overdose of pills. What a waste of such a talented and gifted man." Ireland, however, was leery of Walker during this production, telling this author: "He made my flesh crawl. I played another baddie in **Vengeance Valley**, but Bob [Walker] was outright evil. I asked him how he thought about his character and he said: 'I am playing my rotten self.' Can you imagine a guy saying something like that? Very creepy—I couldn't wait for our scenes together to end so I could get away from him. Some people smell of doom and he was one of those persons." Other western films depicting the spoiled and errant sons of cattle barons include **Duel in the Sun**, 1946; **Gunman's Walk**, 1958; **Last Train from Gun Hill**, 1959; and **The Man from Laramie**, 1955. **p**, Nicholas Nayfack; **d**, Richard Thorpe; **cast**, Burt Lancaster, Robert Walker, Joanne Dru, Sally Forrest, John Ireland, Carleton Carpenter, Ray Collins, Ted De Corsia, Hugh O'Brian, Will Wright, Stanley Andrews, Grayce Mills, Glenn Strange, Jim Hayward, James Harrison; **w**, Irving Ravetch (based on the novel by Luke Short); **c**, George J. Folsey (Technicolor); **m**, Rudolph G. Kopp; **ed**, Conrad A. Nervig; **art d**, Cedric Gibbons, Malcolm Brown; **set d**, Edwin B. Willis.

Vera Cruz ★★★ 1954; U.S.; 94m; Hecht-Lancaster Productions/UA; Color; Adventure/Western; Children: Unacceptable; **BD**; **DVD**; **VHS**. Gritty tale set during the Mexican Revolution of 1867-1868 sees stalwart Cooper and freewheeling Lancaster join forces in an uneasy relationship to fight as mercenaries on the side of Maximilian I (1832-1867), the puppet emperor of Mexico, who is played by Macready. Cooper is an ex-Confederate officer looking for military employment following the collapse of the Confederacy in the American Civil War (1861-1865), and he rides to Mexico, looking for employment. He encounters Lancaster, who heads a gang of gunfighters that include Borgnine, Bronson and Elam, and they decided to join forces, planning to work for Macready. They meet Montiel, however, a sultry Mexican patriot working as a secret agent for the insurrectionists led by Benito Juarez (1806-1872), not seen. As she falls in love with Cooper, she tries to persuade him to fight for the rebels, but he and Lancaster are offered a fortune by Romero, a French aristocrat, to fight for Macready and his shaky throne, and the lure of money is too strong for them. Meeting Macready in Mexico at his palace, Cooper and Lancaster put on a display of sharpshooting, impressing the emperor with their use of Winchester repeating rifles. Macready hires them, paying them $50,000 to escort Darcel, a beautiful countess, to the seaport city of Vera Cruz. She is also accompanied on that journey by a small contin-

Paul E. Barnes, Robert Walker and Burt Lancaster in *Vengeance Valley,* **1951.**

gent of French cavalry led by Romero. When the carriage carrying Darcel is mired at a shallow river crossing, Cooper notices that the vehicle is heavier than it should be. Lancaster takes notice of the same overweight carriage and Cooper and Darcel later find Lancaster inspecting its hollow bottom to discover six crates containing gold coins. Darcel admits that the carriage is carrying more than $3 million in gold coins, which is earmarked for the payment of French troops supporting Macready's oppressive regime. Darcel, ever the opportunistic vixen, suggests that she, Cooper and Lancaster make off with the loot and split its spoils three ways. Cooper seems bound to duty while Lancaster works on his conscience. Meanwhile, Ankrum, a revolutionary general in the service of Juarez suspects that the caravan contains much-needed riches to fund the insurrection and sets ambushes for the travelers, but the attacks are beaten back. Then Lancaster's unsavory crew, including Borgnine, Elam and Bronson, learn about the hidden gold and demand that Lancaster lead them in stealing it. Romero, who is loyal to Macready, however, learns of their plot, and he and his troops make off with the carriage, taking it to the fortress at Vera Cruz. A bloody battle ensues between the Juaristas and the monarchists, ending with the revolutionaries victorious. By this time, however, Darcel has arranged to have the gold sent to a waiting ship, but Lancaster learns of her plot and seizes the gold. Cooper is no longer in agreement with Lancaster, thanks to the pleadings of rebel Montiel, and resolves that the gold should go to the rebels fighting a dictatorial regime. To decide the fate of the treasure, Cooper and Lancaster face off in a one-to-one duel, and Cooper shoots and kills his untrustworthy ally to end this rousing adventure epic. Aldrich orchestrates some fine and considerable action in this well-crafted and spritely written story, and the heroic Cooper and the enterprising Lancaster provide sterling performances as they warily wait for their final confrontation. Laszlo's lensing of the Mexican landscape is often breathtaking, and the film impressively offers sumptuous sets and rich costumes that accurately befit the period. The film had an enormous box office success, earning more than $11 million against a budget of $1.6 million. Song: "Vera Cruz" (music: Hugo Friedhofer; lyrics: Sammy Cahn). *Author's Note*: Clark Gable, who was Cooper's friend, warned him that if he appeared with Lancaster in this film, the dynamic Lancaster would "blow you off every scene." Cooper nevertheless took the chance and signed on (and later reminded Gable of his remarks when Gable appeared with Lancaster in **Run Silent, Run Deep**, 1958). Cooper told this author that "Burt [Lancaster] is a roaring boy, who talks with his whole body, arms and hands waving, but that's because he is very physical, having been a circus acrobat before he got into pictures. I really did not have any problems with him and we got along fine together in **Vera Cruz**." Cooper did not get along at all with supporting Mexican siren Sarita Montiel, telling friends that "she smelled like a

Peter Lorre and Sydney Greenstreet in *The Verdict*, 1946.

skunk. The woman apparently never bathed or washed her greasy hair. The only time I was safe from being overcome by her stench was when I was standing downwind of her." Aldrich (this film remaining his favorite) told this author that "I had made **Apache** [1954] with Burt [Lancaster] just before we did **Vera Cruz**. Burt, who financed that film, had a lot of confidence in me because **Apache** was a success, and he let me have my way with things in **Vera Cruz**. I shot that picture with more than a thousand takes, all clipped to speed up the momentum and pace. We shot it on location entirely in Mexico, and I purposely portrayed the Mexican players the way they truly looked back then, shabby, dirty and woebegone. The Mexican government, after its officials saw the picture, hated it." Actor Eli Wallach, who later appeared in **The Magnificent Seven**, 1960, which was also shot on location in Mexico, later claimed that because **Vera Cruz** had portrayed Mexicans so miserably, the Mexican government insisted that its censors approve of how its citizens were portrayed in the latter film. They did approve since all of the peons are shown wearing immaculate white attire. Lancaster told this author that "I was able to convince Coop [Gary Cooper] to play in **Vera Cruz** after I told him that he would get top billing and disapprove of any scene. Well, he did a lot of that, changing every little detail about his character where he thought that character might be shown to be anything but a shining knight. We did not complain because Coop always played such characters and he knew what his fans wanted. At one point, he took me aside and said: 'I am playing an ex-Confederate officer and he would never fight on the side of the peons, but with Emperor Maximilian.' I told him: 'Well, let's just say you lose your grip at the end to let the peons win for a change.' He pushed his lower lip into the top one and said: 'I never lose my grip.' That was Coop. By that time, he was not feeling too well because he had been injured when our special effects guys used too much dynamite to blow up a bridge in one of the action scenes and Coop got hit by some of the flying debris. He was on medication after that and pretty damned irritable. I didn't blame him for that either." Borgnine told this author that "we had a ball when we made **Vera Cruz** with the great Gary Cooper and Burt [Lancaster]. I got into some trouble when we were down there in Mexico though after we ran out of cigarettes. Me and Charlie [Bronson] were big smokers and, after one scene, while we were still in costume and wearing our guns and bandoliers of bullets, just climbed on our horses and rode for the nearest town to buy some butts. Well, some federal soldiers stopped us and gave us a hell of a time." Bronson, in a later meeting, told this author: "Because we were wearing our costumes, those federal troops thought we were real bandits, and there were still plenty of those fellows riding around in the hills, and we had to explain that we were appearing in a picture. They checked with Bob [Aldrich], who told them that we were part of his production and finally let us go. It was embarrassing as hell.

Years later, when I was down in Mexico working on a similar picture, **The Magnificent Seven** [1960], I made sure I had plenty of cigarettes. I wasn't going to be caught again by those federal soldiers, who are pretty rough customers. The first time around I almost got a rifle butt in the face when I talked back to one of them, not to say that wouldn't have improved my looks." Other films depicting the Mexican Revolution of 1867-1868 include **Adios Sabata**, 1971; **Aquellos anos**, 1974; **Blood Red Rose**, 1946; **Cinco de Mayo, La Battala**, 2013; **The Cisco Kid**, 1994 (made-for-TV); **Cuando lloran los valientes**, 1947; **El carruaje**, 1972 (TV series); **El Condor**, 1970; **El joven Juarez**, 1954; **El vuelo del aguila**, 1994 (TV series); **The Hourglass Sanatorium**, 1973; **Juarez**, 1939; **Juarez and Maximillian**, 1935; **La Tormenta**, 1967 (TV series); **The Mad Empress**, 1939; **Major Dundee**, 1965; **Maximilian von Mexiko**, 1970 (made-for-TV); **Mexicanos al grito de guerra**, 1943; **Prariejager in Mexiko: Benito Juarez**, 1988; **Treasure of the Aztecs**, 1966; **Two Mules for Sister Sara**, 1970; **The Undefeated**, 1969; **Visita al Pasado**, 1981; and **Zorro's Fighting Legion**, 1939. **p**, James Hill, (not credited) Harold Hecht, Burt Lancaster; **d**, Robert Aldrich; **cast**, Gary Cooper, Lancaster, Denise Darcel, Cesar Romero, Sarita Montiel, George Macready, Morris Ankrum, Jack Elam, Ernest Borgnine, Henry Brandon, Charles Buchinsky (Charles Bronson); **w**, Roland Kibbee, James R. Webb (based on the story by Borden Chase); **c**, Ernest Laszlo (SuperScope; Technicolor); **m**, Hugo Friedhofer; **ed**, Alan Crosland, Jr.; **prod d**, Alfred Ybarra; **spec eff**, Russell Shearman.

The Verdict ★★★ 1946; U.S.; 86m; WB; B/W; Mystery; Children: Unacceptable; **DVD**. Tension-filled whodunit sees the final film in which the dynamic Greenstreet and the laconic Lorre appear together. Greenstreet is the aging but agile superintendent of Scotland Yard in 1890 London. He makes a serious mistake in a murder case where an innocent man is convicted and executed. Admitting his error, he steps down and is replaced by posturing, gloating Courlouris. The new superintendent denigrates Greenstreet's police methods, branding them outmoded while boasting that his law enforcement procedures have always been superior to that of his predecessor. Sometime later, Greenstreet is summoned by the landlady of a boarding house across from his own residence. She fears that Lowry, one of her tenants, may have been the victim of foul play as he is now silent and inside his locked room. Greenstreet goes to the boarding house and, after Lowry does not respond, he breaks down the door. He finds Lowry prone on the floor, and the police soon arrive after having been called by the landlady. Lowry has been stabbed to death, and when Couloris arrives to take over the case, he is met with a baffling mystery as the victim has been found in a locked room with no clues to indicate his killer. Greenstreet continues to observe the new superintendent's handling of this strange case, as does his friend, Lorre, an artist who has been illustrating grim portraits for a book about crime detection Greenstreet is writing to while away his retirement hours. To prove that he is a greater detective than Greenstreet, the haughty Coulouris makes some quick deductions and promptly arrests Cavanagh, who is another friend of Greenstreet's. Cavanagh is charged with the murder of Lowry and, through Coulouris' thin circumstantial evidence, is convicted and sentenced to death. While Cavanagh's date of execution fast approaches, Greenstreet sets out to solve the crime. He learns from singer Lorring that a woman who could provide Cavanagh with an alibi has fled to the European Continent. Greenstreet pursues her, only to find that she has died. Since Greenstreet knows that Cavanagh is innocent, he admits that he is Lowry's killer and that he was simply dispatching tardy justice. He explains that Lowry was the killer who had caused the innocent man to be executed under Greenstreet's watch. He has brought about his own brand of retribution by arranging for Lowry's "perfect murder." He had drugged Lowry's drink before Lowry returned home so that, after Lowry locked himself inside of his room, he was unconscious when Greenstreet was summoned by Lowry's landlady and broke down the door to Lowry's room. While the landlady assumed that Lowry was dead and left to summon police, Greenstreet stabbed the unconscious Lowry to death and the landlady's later statements about finding Lowry dead when Greenstreet broke down the door removed all suspicion from Greenstreet. Though Greenstreet has proven to be a greater detective than Coulouris, he must now face his own hanging as a confessed murderer. Siegel, in his film debut as a director of a feature film, deftly handles this complex mystery as he carefully unravels its slim clues while drawing a riveting performance from Greenstreet. Despite some carping from contemporary critics, Siegel sustains high suspense throughout with fast-paced cross-cutting scenes and an intelligent script from Milne, all enhanced by cinematographer Haller's strong sense of moody lighting and eye-arresting scene setups. Songs: "Give Me a Little Bit" (music: M.K. Jerome; lyrics: Jack Scholl), "Sobre las olas (Over the Waves)" (1887; Juventino Rosas). *Author's Note*: Siegel told this author: "In my first assignment with a full-length picture, I was handed an old chestnut to burn, a story that had been published in 1892. Peter [Milne] and I gave it some new twists to make the story more of a mystery. When John Huston used Sydney [Greenstreet] in that actor's first picture, **The Maltese Falcon** [1941], he accented Sydney's corpulent body by filling the screen with it to give the image of an overwhelming criminal mastermind. I used the same technique when making **The Verdict**, with full shots of him taking up every frame, but where Sydney's huge body represents the authority of the law. When Sydney saw some of the rushes from those scenes, he grinned and said: 'I must go on a diet. It looks like I put on fifty pounds since yesterday.' Lorre complained to this author that "Sydney [Greenstreet] got almost all the scenes in **The Verdict**. It was really his picture, not mine. I am only around for some ghoulish laughs as I am an artist illustrating a crime book he is writing and, to tell you the truth, those drawings were simply ghastly." As usual the two stars got along famously, as they did with Siegel, and they shared more than one "inside" joke during the production. At one point, Lorre relishes the disinterring of a body from a grave by calling it "exciting," and, in another scene, Greenstreet belittles his own girth by stating that his competitor Coulouris "is getting too big for his breeches, but not big enough for mine!" Greenstreet and Lorre appeared in nine films together: **The Maltese Falcon**, 1941 (Greenstreet's film debut); **Casablanca**, 1942 (where they had no scenes together); **Background to Danger**, 1943; **Passage to Marseille**, 1944; the classic **The Mask of Dimitrios**, 1944 (their very best film together); **The Conspirators**, 1944; **Hollywood Canteen**, 1944; **Three Strangers**, 1946; and **The Verdict**, 1946. This mystery had been brought to the screen in 1928 under the title of **The Perfect Crime**, starring Clive Book and Irene Rich, which was a part-talkie that jumbled sound and title cards in a rather confusing way. It was again filmed as **The Crime Doctor**, 1934, starring Otto Kruger and Karen Morley. When Warner Brothers was fielding about for another vehicle in which to again star Greenstreet and Lorre, they purchased this story from RKO for a pittance (reportedly $13,500), and assigned Siegel to direct. Siegel, at that time, had been working at the studio for quite a number of years in many capacities, as a film librarian, montage specialist and as a highly respected second unit director, before the front office gave him the chance to direct this superior whodunit. He went on to prove his considerable directorial worth with such superior thrillers as **Invasion of the Body Snatchers**, 1956; **The Lineup**, 1958; **Hell Is for Heroes**, 1962; **Madigan**, 1968; **Coogan's Bluff**, 1968; **Dirty Harry**, 1971; and **The Shootist**, 1976. **p**, William Jacobs; **d**, Don Siegel; **cast**, Sydney Greenstreet, Peter Lorre, Joan Lorring, George Coulouris, Rosalind Ivan, Paul Cavanagh, Arthur Shields, Morton Lowry, Holmes Herbert, Art Foster; **w**, Peter Milne (based on the novel *The Big Bow Mystery* by Israel Zangwill); **c**, Ernest Haller; **m**, Frederick Hollander; **ed**, Thomas Reilly; **art d**, Ted Smith; **set d**, G.W. Bernsten, Jack McConaghy; **spec eff**, Robert Burks, William McGann, Russell Collings.

The Verdict ★★★★★ 1982; U.S.; 129m; FOX; Color; Drama; Children: Unacceptable (MPAA: R); **DVD**; **VHS**; **IV**. Newman gives one of his best performances in this fascinating courtroom drama where he

James Mason and Paul Newman in *The Verdict*, 1982.

is fighting to not only win a malpractice case for a permanently damaged woman, but salvage his ruined career and repair his long-damaged spirit. Years earlier, Newman had been a top graduate from Boston College Law School and had been one of Boston's most promising young attorneys. He worked for a distinguished law firm, but his reputation was ruined by a senior partner of that firm who framed him on a charge of jury tampering. Newman now practices alone in a dingy office, taking any ambulance case he can find. He has tried four cases in the last three years and has lost all of them. Much of that failure is due to his heavy drinking, and he appears to be nothing more than a drunk posturing as a lawyer. Warden, who has been Newman's teacher and mentor and who has been attempting to revitalize Newman's career if not his shabby social life, sends him a malpractice case that assures a sizeable defense settlement. The case involves Benenson, a young woman who is in a coma, surviving on a respirator in a hospital. She had been given an anesthetic while giving birth, but choked on her own vomit and was permanently damaged after being deprived of oxygen. Hart, the victim's sister, and her husband, Handy, are counting on a settlement that will allow them to provide continued care for Benenson, who lives bedridden and almost as a vegetable. Newman takes the case, assuring Hart and Handy that their case is a strong one and promises a quick settlement. Though he outwardly exudes confidence toward his clients, Newman is deeply unsure of his abilities to properly settle the case and, as usual, resorts to his drinking to bolster his diminishing resolve. While in his favorite bar, he meets sultry, long-haired Rampling and the two begin an affair. Rampling boosts Newman's confidence and tries to help him as he struggles to make the settlement. He visits the comatose Benenson in the hospital and is deeply moved by her plight. He then meets with Binns, who is the Archbishop of the Catholic diocese that owns the hospital where Benenson suffered her permanent disability. The Archbishop's representative then expectedly offers Newman a settlement of $210,000 to close his client's case. Newman, who by then believes that this case represents his last chance to actually prove himself as an attorney, refuses in the belief that he can achieve an outright win in court. He makes the mistake of not telling his clients about the offer and his declining of it. When brother-in-law Handy learns of this, he and his wife, Hart, angrily confront Newman. Handy shouts at him and threatens to attack him, but is restrained. Newman, however, goes forward with the case, although he sees one setback after another. He then discovers that his top medical expert, who was to testify on behalf of his client, has suddenly taken an extended trip out of town and is no longer available. Newman appeals to O'Shea, the judge presiding in the case, but O'Shea refuses to give him a continuance and is clearly in the camp of the opposing attorney, Mason, who heads a powerful legal firm. Newman angrily tells O'Shea in his chambers that he knows how corrupt he

Lindsay Crouse being questioned on the witness stand by James Mason in *The Verdict*, 1982.

is, that O'Shea has been a failed attorney and a "bagman" for the town's political machine. O'Shea becomes enraged and orders Newman to try the case immediately, and Newman tells him that he will not only try the case, but he will win it. Newman goes to trial with a substitute physician, Seneca, an elderly, black doctor on the staff of a small clinic. Seneca's testimony and expertise on anesthesia, however, is limited, and Mason quickly calls his credentials into question when cross-examining him. Further, O'Shea impedes Newman's moves at every turn and it now appears that Newman is in a hopeless position without any witnesses. He cannot find anyone connected to the hospital or those present in the operating room to testify on his behalf. He attempts to find the whereabouts of Crouse, the nurse who admitted his client on the day of the operation, but she has left the nursing profession. He locates Bovasso, a nurse at the hospital and close friend of Crouse's, but she refuses to tell Newman where he can find Crouse. When Newman persists, Bovasso, who harbors a deep resentment toward attorneys, as well as physicians, explodes, shouting at him: "You know, you guys are all the same! You don't care who you hurt! All you care about is the dollar! You're a bunch of whores! You got no loyalty, no nothing! You're a bunch of whores!" Newman, however, is able to learn that Crouse now lives in New York City and, through an exhausting number of phone calls, locates her, learning that she is now teaching young children. He flies to New York and meets with her, asking for her help, but the viewer does not know if Crouse will cooperate. While Newman is in New York, Warden, who has been helping him, along with Rampling, discovers that Rampling is being paid by Mason to spy on Newman and report back to Mason. Warden flies to NYC and tells Newman about this just before Newman is to meet with Rampling at a restaurant in that city. Enraged, Newman goes to the restaurant, walks up to Rampling and strikes her so hard that he knocks her down before departing. Newman goes ahead with the trial, but surprises the court and Mason when he calls Crouse to the stand. She states that she was the nurse who admitted Benenson, and that Benenson told her that she had eaten a full meal one hour before the operation and that she had written that down on the admitting form. Addy, the physician performing the operation, Crouse states, had had several operations that day and was tired and neglected to note that the patient had eaten only one hour before he operated. Because of that, the patient vomited and choked during the operation, which left her in a comatose state. Crouse further testifies that Addy, when discovering his negligence to note that one hour, ordered Crouse to change the number "1" representing that one hour on the admitting form, to the number "9," to falsely indicate that the patient had eaten nine hours before the operation, so that the altered admitting form could not implicate Addy in the future. Crouse, in an emotional display, then states that Addy, by forcing her to falsify the record caused her to quit her profession. She

then further startles Mason and O'Shea by providing a copy of the original admitting form to show that she had originally written down the number "1." Mason desperately insists that the copy of the form is not admissible in court as it is not the original, which is the one on record and has been altered and O'Shea agrees. Before leaving the witness stand, the deeply disturbed Crouse blurts: "He [Addy] told me to change the one to a nine...or else... or else he said he would fire me...that I would never work again...Who were these men?...Who were these men?...I wanted to be a nurse!" Crouse leaves the stand, and Mason urges O'Shea to dismiss Crouse's testimony. O'Shea does, telling the jury to ignore Crouse's testimony, but her moving and revealing remarks remain powerfully influential as to the outcome of the case and everyone knows it. It is now up to Newman to win his own case in summation (one of the finest ever written for the screen). He is hesitant and full of doubt as he approaches the jury to begin his address to its members, stating: "You know, so much of the time we're lost. We say, 'Please, God, tell us what is right, tell us what's true. There is no justice. The rich win...the poor are powerless.' We become tired of hearing people lie. After a time, we become dead, a little dead. We begin thinking of ourselves as victims...and we become victims...and we become weak...and doubt ourselves, and doubt our institutions...and doubt our beliefs. We say, for example 'the law is a sham...there is no law...I was a fool for having believed there was.' But, today, *you* are the law...and not some book and not some lawyers, or the marble statues or the trappings of the court. All that they are is symbols of our desire to be just. All that they are, in effect, is a prayer...a fervent and a frightened prayer. In my religion, we say 'Act as if you had faith and faith will be given to you.' If...if we would have faith in justice, we must only believe in ourselves...and act with justice. And I believe that there is justice in our hearts. Thank you." Newman sits down and Warden, sitting next to him, pats his hand appreciatively for his emotionally moving summation. The jury deliberates and then surprises O'Shea by asking him if they can award more money than what the plaintive has asked. Shocked, O'Shea is forced to tell them that they can. Newman lowers his head. Warden looks skyward as if to thank the Powers Above for this outcome that signals that Newman has not only won his case but that his is a landmark victory. When Newman leaves the court, he is congratulated by other attorneys who no longer view him a failed lawyer. He sees Rampling standing nearby, but ignores her. Rampling is then seen in her room, drinking heavily to the point of being inebriated as she calls Newman on the phone. Newman is at his desk in his shabby office, drinking coffee, but does not pick up the phone. He knows that Rampling is on the other end of that line. He lets it ring and ring and ring as the film ends. Everything about this masterpiece film is genuine, natural and without synthetic posturing and all of that is embodied in Newman's utterly mesmerizing performance. This marvelous actor essays a man who turns defeat into victory through his passionate will to be better than what he is for a helpless patient. His is the stuff of true heroism and sacrifice as he fends off insidious alcoholism, the betrayal of a woman he has loved, a hostile court, and a powerful adversary. He overcomes those impossible odds to emerge victorious, thanks to the courageous testimony of Crouse and his spiritual ability to inspire a compassionate response from a jury seeking true justice. There have been many superlative courtroom films, but few so closely examine the conscience of an attorney while incisively examining a frail judicial system as does this film. Lumet's deliberate direction assiduously dissects Newman's complex character while seamlessly weaving into the fabric of the story its subtle and telling nuances, and the gifted Lumet also exacts superlative performances from Rampling, Mason, Warden, O'Shea and the rest of the fine cast. He does not waste a single frame in this film, sustaining tension throughout to provide a stunning finale where victory is achieved but at a great emotional cost. Though much of writer Mamet's works are pedestrian, this outing proved his ability to excel his talents in providing a brilliant script, albeit he had a fine novel upon which to base the screenplay. The film received Oscar nominations for

Best Picture; Best Director (Lumet); Best Actor (Newman), Best Supporting Actor (Mason), and Best Screenplay Based on Material from Another Medium (Mamet). The film was a great success at the box office, earning more than $53.9 million against a budget of $11 million. The story for this film has no relation to the 1946 film by the same name. *Author's Note*: The book by Reed, published in 1980, and the subsequent Mamet script, owes much to a similar case of a woman left in a comatose state after a botched operation, and which was superbly profiled in a made-for-TV production titled **In the Matter of Karen Ann Quinlan**, 1977. Mamet first showed his script to actor Robert Redford, who then had other writers work on it, but eventually declined to play in the film as he did not want to portray an alcoholic. Director Lumet then read the script and decided to make the film and several top actors were considered for the riveting role of the boozy attorney, including Frank Sinatra, who told this author: "Hell, I loved that part and I would have played that guy for nothing, but Paul [Newman] landed that fish and he brought it into the boat big time!" Others thought suited to the part were William Holden, Dustin Hoffman, Jon Voight, Roy Scheider and even Cary Grant, until Newman, who was selected by Lumet, was signed for the role. Newman told this author: "It was a damned challenging part because the character is a total loser and a lush, and knows he is only dreaming when he thinks he can score in court against a powerful legal firm. All he has in his pockets is loose change and everything else about him is loose—his next-to-nothing law practice, his shabby love life, and, especially, his future. He's got nothing to risk when he goes for broke except his pride in his profession, and, for this guy, that is risking all he has." Mason was circumspect when talking with this author about **The Verdict**, saying: "I played the big shot corporate lawyer the way I have always seen them, very precise. Everything my character does is measured and decided upon in advance. He is a strategist, who has been to all the legal battlefields, but he overlooks the little tactics that sometimes win those battles. He has no morality at all and his only purpose in life is to win, and he tells that to all who work for him, win at all costs. To tell the truth, that man was probably the most despicable character I ever played." Mason got his role by default in that Burt Lancaster was originally cast in that role of the corporate attorney, but when Lancaster dropped out of the cast, Mason was hired. Although Lumet, a fast worker, shot this film in forty-three days, more than a week against schedule, he had his principal players rehearse the story for more than three weeks. Bruce Willis can be seen at the end of the film as an extra. Other films depicting medical malpractice include **Awake**, 2007; **The Babymaker: The Dr. Cecil Jacobson Story**, 1994 (made-for-TV); **Bedside**, 1934; **Betrayal of Trust**, 1994 (made-for-TV); **Cimarron City**, 1958-1960 (TV series; "Medicine Man," 1958 episode); **The Citadel**, 1938; **The Critical List**, 1978 (made-for-TV); **Dead Sleep**, 1992; **Detective Story**, 1951; **The Good Doctor**, 2011; **Green Light**, 1937; **The Hand That Rocks the Cradle**, 1992; **Heaven**, 1999; **The Horse Soldiers**, 1959 (John Wayne talks about the medical malpractice of doctors who brought about his wife's death); **The Hospital**, 1971; **In the Matter of Karen Ann Quinlan**, 1977 (made-for-TV); **Infection**, 2004; **Inspector Morse**, 1987-2000 (TV series; "Deadly Slumber," 1993 episode); **Isolation**, 2011; **Jeans**, 1998; **Kingdom Hospital**, 2004 (TV series; "Goodbye Kiss," 2004 episode); **Kings Row**, 1942; **A Little Help**, 2010; **M*A*S*H***, 1972-1983 (TV series; "The Novocaine Mutiny," 1976 episode; "Preventative Medicine," 1979 episode); **Malpractice**, 2001; **Miracle on 34th Street**, 1947; **Miracle on 34th Street**, 1973 (made-for-TV); **Negotiator**, 2003 (made-for-TV); **Not as a Stranger**, 1955; **Open Heart**, 2004 (made-for-TV); **The Penalty**, 1920; **Saving Hope**, 2012- (TV series; "Defense," 2013 episode); **Speaking of Sex**, 2001; **Terminal Choice**, 1985; **True Crimes: The First 72 Hours**, 2003 (TV series; "Good Doctor," 2006 episode); **Waking the Dead**, 2000- (TV series; "Double Bind," 2007 episodes); **Where Does It Hurt?**, 1972. **p**, Richard D. Zanuck, David Brown; **d**, Sidney Lumet; **cast**, Paul Newman, Charlotte Rampling, Jack Warden, James Mason, Milo O'Shea,

Paul Newman, an attorney with an impossible case, in *The Verdict*, 1982.

Lindsay Crouse, Edward Binns, Julie Bovasso, Roxanne Hart, Joe Seneca, James Handy, Wesley Addy, Bruce Willis, Susan Benenson; **w**, David Mamet (based on the novel by Barry Reed); **c**, Andrzej Bartkowiak (Panavision; DeLuxe Color); **m**, Johnny Mandel; **ed**, Peter Frank; **prod d**, Edward Pisoni; **art d**, John Kasarda; **set d**, George DeTitta.

Veronica Guerin ★★★ 2003; Ireland/U.K./U.S.; 92m; Touchstone; Buena Vista; Color; Biographical Drama; Children: Unacceptable (MPAA: R); **DVD**; **IV**. Absorbing biopic is based on true events in Ireland, where Veronica Guerin (1958-1996), played by Blanchett, is an Irish journalist for a Dublin newspaper, *the Sunday Independent*. She is distressed by gangs selling drugs to the city's children and teenagers. In 1994, some young addicts tell her about gangs using them as drug sellers in the city's housing projects. She begins efforts to expose the dealers, endangering her husband, their child, and herself. Hinds, who is a low-level crook, becomes concerned about her safety, and warns her that she is in real danger. She ignores his and her husband's warnings and goes ahead with her investigation, even recklessly walking into the home of the top Irish mafia boss and asking him why he sells drugs to children. She manages to expose the top drug dealers, but then one of their assassins shoots and kills her. This gritty and uncompromising film sees a startling and intense performance from Blanchett where she believably portrays the courageous Guerin. The film was not a success at the box office, earning less than $10 million against a budget of $17 million. Songs: "Funeral Song," "One More Day" (Harry Gregson-Williams, Hugh Marsh, Patrick Cassidy, Trevor Horn); "Aftermath" (Adrian Thaws); "Everlasting Love" (Buzz Cason, Mac Gayden); "Fields of Athenry" (Pete St. John). *Author's Note*: The film was shot on location in Dublin, as well as in Kildare and Wicklow counties. Colin Farrell appears in a cameo role as a tattooed man attending a soccer match. Violence, gutter language and drug content prohibit viewing by children. **p**, Jerry Bruckheimer; **d**, Joel Schumacher; **cast**, Cate Blanchett, Ciaran Hinds, Gerald McSorley, Brenda Fricker, Colin Farrell, Laurence Kinlan, Paul Ronan, Philip O'Sullivan, Niall Tobin, Kevin McHugh; **w**, Carol Doyle, Mary Agnes Donoghue (based on a story by Doyle); **c**, Brendan Galvin; **m**, Harry Gregson-Williams; **ed**, David Gamble; **prod d**, Nathan Crowley; **art d**, Patrick Lumb, Julie Ochipinti; **set d**, Paki Smith; **spec eff**, Kevin Byrne, Aidan Byrne, Paul Byrne.

Veronika Voss ★★★ 1982; West Germany; 104m; Bavaria Film/UA; B/W; Drama; Children: Unacceptable (MPAA: R); **DVD**; **VHS**. Unnerving but fascinating tale profiles Zech, a fading German film star, who has an affair in Munich in 1955 with Thate, a sportswriter, while being sadistically fed drugs by her female doctor, Duringer. Zech be-

James Stewart clinging from a San Francisco rooftop in *Vertigo*, 1958.

comes so dependent on morphine that she gives all of her personal property to Duringer. On Easter Sunday, Duringer locks Zech in a room and she suffers severe withdrawal from being denied morphine, but she is given enough sleeping pills to kill herself, which she does. Thate and his girlfriend try to expose Duringer to authorities, but the girlfriend is mysteriously run over by a car and the deaths of both women remain a mystery. Song: "Run, Boy, Run" (Lee Hazelwood). *Author's Note*: The film is based loosely on the life of Sybille Schmitz (1909-1955), a German film star, who committed suicide in 1955, unable to adjust to the decline of her film career. Sexuality and drug use prohibit viewing by children. (In German; English subtitles) **p**, Thomas Schuhly, Bertram Vetter, Rainer Werner Fassbinder, Horst Wendlandt; **d**, Fassbinder; **cast**, Rosel Zech, Annemarie Duringer, Hilmar Thate, Cornelia Froboess, Doris Schade, Erik Schumann, Peter Berling, Gunther Kaufmann, Sonja Neudorfer, Lilo Pempeit; **w**, Fassbinder, Pea Frohlich, Peter Marthesheimer; **c**, Xaver Schwarzenberger; **m**, Peer Raben; **ed**, Juliane Lorenz; **prod d**, Rolf Zehetbauer; **art d**, Walter Richarz.

Vertigo ★★★ 1958; U.S.; 128m; PAR; Color; Mystery; Children: Unacceptable; **BD**; **DVD**; **VHS**; **IV**. Pantheon director Hitchcock presents his most fetish-infested fears in this bizarre and often distressing whodunit. The tale deals less with crime and more with the abiding fixation of its protagonist, Stewart, a retired San Francisco police detective. Stewart obsessively goes about recreating the sex symbol of his carnal desires a la Pygmalion, but where the reincarnated lady presents no nobility or spiritual compassion, only the lurid image of a submissive, lowlife femme fatale. The film opens with an exciting rooftop chase where Stewart and a fellow detective are pursuing an elusive felon. Losing his footing while chasing after the criminal, Stewart slides downward from a roof and pitches over its side, saving his life by clutching a sagging gutter while looking bug-eyed in fear to the street many stories below. His acrophobia (fear of heights) is aggravated by his own vertigo (a dizzying sensation) as he desperately clings on that ledge. The other detective attempts to pull Stewart to safety, but loses his grip and plunges downward to his death. Stewart manages to save his own life, but the death of his fellow cop causes him to retire from the SFPD. Stewart spends considerable time with Bel Geddes, a designer and his former fiancée, who tells him that the only way he will ever conquer his fear about heights is when he experiences another traumatic shock like the rooftop disaster. Then Stewart receives a call from Helmore, a shipping magnate, and a college classmate, and, in a meeting with him, tells Stewart that he is worried about his wife, Novak. Helmore tells Stewart that Novak is suffering from a strange malady, a form of necrophilia (another fetish Hitchcock introduces with relish and mustard). Helmore tells Stewart that his wife is morbidly obsessed with an alluring dead

woman named Carlotta Valdes. "Do you believe that someone dead, someone out of the past, can take possession of a living being?" Helmore asks Stewart. He indicates that no, he does not believe that, but, after Helmore asks him to shadow Novak for her safekeeping, he nevertheless accepts the assignment. We next see Stewart following Novak, who is primly attired in conservative dress suits. He sees her go to a flower shop where she buys a floral arrangement and then trails her to a cemetery where Novak places the bouquet at the grave of Carlotta Valdes. Stewart next follows Novak to a museum where she sits staring at a portrait of Valdes as if she is in a trance. He takes note of the fact that Novak wears her hair exactly like that shown in the portrait of Valdes, her blonde hair pulled tight to the back and pinned inside of a bun. Novak then goes to a shabby, small hotel, but she disappears. When Stewart goes to her room to find it empty, the landlady, Corby, tells him that "Miss Valdes," the name Novak has used to rent a room, visits the place infrequently, appearing every few weeks. When visiting again with Helmore, Stewart learns that Novak is possessed by the spirit of Valdes, an ancestor of Novak's who once lived in that old hotel. Helmore says that his wife's obsession with Valdes is purely subconscious, and that she does not actually know that Valdes is her great-grandmother. Intrigued, Stewart has Bel Geddes take him to a bookdealer, Shayne, who is an expert on obscure San Francisco history and its strangest denizens. Shayne tells Stewart that Valdes lost her mind when her husband deserted her and she wandered the streets as a mad woman looking for a lost child, until she committed suicide at the age of twenty-six, which is Novak's very age. Stewart continues his surveillance of Novak, following her to Fort Point, where she lingers beneath the Golden Gate Bridge. He is shocked to see Novak suddenly leap into the choppy waters of San Francisco Bay in an inexplicable attempt to take her own life, as did her ancestor. Stewart dives in after her and drags her to safety. Stewart takes the dazed Novak to his apartment where they spend the night together. She awakes naked beneath the sheets of his bed to see her dry clothes and stockings hanging nearby. She dresses and then departs and Stewart (as well as the viewer) is left to think that Novak has no recollection of her death-wishing behavior. Yet, she returns to Stewart's apartment and leaves a thank you note for saving her life. Stewart meets her and they spend time at a beach where they embrace and kiss as the surf splashes about them. When Stewart returns home, he finds Bel Geddes waiting for him. She presents him with a painting she has done of herself, a portrait of herself as Carlotta Valdes, but where she is wearing Bel Geddes' traditional glasses. Stewart does not find this gesture humorous, and Bel Geddes, ashamed at her blatant faux pas, destroys the painting. Stewart is now convinced that the down-to-earth but gauche Bel Geddes is not his kind of woman. That night, the ethereal-like Novak appears at Stewart's apartment and tells him about a dream she has had. From her description of the location in her dream, Stewart recognizes it as a place called San Juan Bastista, an old mission that has been recently restored. We see Stewart and Novak kissing and they are now in a barn at San Juan Bastista, and Novak wants to impulsively go to the tower of the church. "No one possesses you," Stewart tells her, "You're safe with me." Novak replies as she breaks free: "It's too late. There's something I must do. It shouldn't have happened this way." She runs frantically toward the church, Stewart racing after her. Novak goes up the stairs and Stewart attempts to go after her, but the higher he climbs the dizzier he becomes as his acrophobia grips him. He has a distorted vision of the towering stairs, the narrowing walls and the floor seeming to come upward toward him. He then hears a scream and watches from a window in horror as a woman's body plunges downward from the top of the tower to her death. Helmore is forgiving and finds no fault in Stewart over his wife's death, which is ruled a suicide. Stewart, however, is so depressed that he is institutionalized in an almost catatonic state. He sits motionless while listening to the strains of Mozart, but, when Bel Geddes arrives to see him in this unresponsive condition, she verbally attacks his physician for not doing more to bring Stewart to his senses and leaves enraged, never to be seen again (except for a tacked-on ending shown only in Europe). When recovered, Stewart can only think of Novak and spends his time revisiting the places where he had known her, the old hotel, the museum, a restaurant. One day he sees a beautiful brunette, who is Novak's lookalike (and who is also played by Novak) and he obsessively follows her. Although she initially resists meeting with Stewart, Novak finally agrees to have dinner with him. Stewart is enthralled with this new Novak, although he sees her only as the former blonde and the two begin to develop a deep relationship. Although she claims that she is from Salina, Kansas, and has never known Stewart until now, we see in flashback that she is the same blonde Stewart earlier fell in love with, but who was only impersonating Helmore's wife in a murder scheme. Novak thinks to end her ties with Stewart by writing him a letter in which she explains how she impersonated that wife and how Helmore used Stewart's acrophobia to prevent her from ostensibly leaping from that church tower, and how Helmore actually pushed his wife from that tower. Novak, however, because she has always loved Stewart, tears up the letter and decides to continue the charade by seeing Stewart, while pretending to be a different woman. In that developing relationship, Stewart sees the present Novak only as the reincarnated woman he thinks fell from that church tower. Stewart insists that the new Novak dye her hair blonde and wear it in the fashion of the woman he formerly knew, as well as dress identically as that woman and Novak, out of slavish love, complies. When Stewart sees her wearing the necklace that he recognizes as having being worn in the portrait of Valdes, he now realizes Novak's complicity in Helmore's elaborate murder scheme and how he has been duped. He drives Novak to the mission to recreate the staged death of Helmore's real wife and then forces Novak up the stairs to the bell tower, struggling against and finally conquering his acrophobia as they reach the top of the tower. Stewart then tells Novak: "He [Helmore] made you over just like I made you over, only better. Not only the clothes and the hair, but the looks and the manners and the words. And those beautiful phony trances. And then what did he do? Did he train you? Did he rehearse you? Did he tell you exactly what to do and what to say? You were a very apt pupil, weren't you? A very apt pupil!" Novak then admits her culpability, but she declares that she nevertheless loves Stewart, and even then, Stewart, despite everything about Novak that he knows is fake and synthetic, still loves her. As they embrace, a darkly clad figure suddenly appears in response to the commotion Stewart has created, a nun who works at the mission. Her abrupt appearance so startles Novak that she steps backward through an open portal of the tower, onto its ledge, and then into space as she topples downward to her death (in one of the most ironic retribution scenes ever created). The horrified nun begins ringing the bell (another of Hitchcock's ironic touches where he sounds John Donne's "for whom the bell tolls" signature line about the universality of mankind). As the bells clang and ring, the shocked Stewart, helpless to the last, can only look down to see the body of the woman who betrayed and loved him in this strangest finale of star-crossed lovers. Hitchcock methodically presents this subtle thriller, inveigling the viewer into its labyrinth plot as much as Stewart is lured into its elaborate vortex, with one clever and enticing scene after another, more of a picture puzzle than the plotline for a film. In some scenes where Hitchcock has the camera remain focused upon a building or a portrait, the film seems to dissolve into a still picture, as to make an arcane implication about the characters and the events engulfing them, but these are visual red herrings artfully designed by the gifted and sometimes capriciously bedeviling director. (These scenes irked reviewers of the day, who claimed that the film was either "too slow" or that it "bogged down," but, as Hitchcock told this author, his pace in that regard was intentional.) Some of his scenes approach the static as he obsessively dwells upon Novak's character as seen through Stewart's POV. Stewart is outstanding as the lovesick detective struggling with his acrophobia (even when standing on a small ladder in Bel Geddes' studio where he becomes dizzy). He provides a wonderfully understated performance of a man perversely indulging his obsession to recreate out of whole cloth

James Stewart and Kim Novak in *Vertigo*, 1958.

another woman to replace the one he believes he has lost. (Therein Stewart fulfills the secret desires of many a married man, not to mention Hitchcock's sly, mea culpa exhibition of his own myriad phobias, and, as such, presents his most personally revealing film). Novak, who almost always speaks in a near whisper and was one of the most unresponsive beauties of the screen, is perfect for her role. She is a female automaton (as might be seen in **Metropolis**, 1927), who is essentially Stewart's (and Hitchcock's) exquisite and slavishly submissive mannequin, as if shaped and reshaped from the common clay of Stewart's memory and, originally, from Helmore's lethal imagination. She is nevertheless the master director's own warped model of Eliza Doolittle, a malleable and malevolent look-alike, who is also Hitchcock's most insidious sex symbol. The film received two Oscar nominations, one for Best Art Direction (Pereira, Bumstead; and set decoration: Comer, McKelvy), and one for Best Sound (George Dutton). Despite the pans of the day, the film, on the strength of the director's great reputation, did well at the box office, earning more than $14 million against a budget of more than $2.4 million. Songs/Music: "Symphony No. 34 in C K. 338, 2nd Movement, Andante di Molto (piu tosto allegretto)" (Wolfgang Amadeus Mozart), "Sardis #4" ("Forever Female," from **Skylark**, 1941; Victor Young). ***Author's Note***: Hitchcock always had Stewart in mind for the role of the acrophobic detective, and wanted to cast Vera Miles, who had appeared in his previous film, **The Wrong Man**, 1956, as the impersonating look-alike in **Vertigo**. She, however, had become pregnant and was not available. He then, with some hesitancy, cast Novak in the role, getting her on loan from Columbia where she was under exclusive contact to mogul Harry Cohn, but only under the understanding that Stewart would appear with Novak in a forthcoming Columbia production, **Bell, Book and Candle**, 1958. Hitchcock told this author that, "I believe it was a mistake to hire her [Novak] for the role. I later felt that the picture did not do as well as it might because she was too young [twenty-four-years-old] at that time, very inexperienced, and that Jimmy [Stewart] was just too old [forty-nine-years-old] to play her lover. I think the picture would have gotten better reviews and made a lot more money if I had cast a younger man in that part. Jimmy was then beyond his prime." Stewart never again worked with Hitchcock after this film, and had no regrets about it, telling this author (in 1987): "I did not really like the role I played in **Vertigo**. The character was too weak and he would not have been a police detective on the San Francisco force at all because of that. Those are tough boys. I also felt that my character was sleazy. There was something unclean about him as he tries to mold a woman into the living duplication of a dead lover, necrophilia, I think they call it. The whole thing made me feel like I had been taking a mud bath and I wanted to take a shower after every scene. I told Hitch [Hitchcock] about that and I think he took offense, as if I might be accusing

Kim Novak with director Alfred Hitchcock on the set of *Vertigo*, 1958.

him of making an unwholesome picture, which, in hindsight, I think he did. The whole thing was a disappointment for me. I really wanted to clean up my character, but Hitch would not budge on any scene. He did the same thing when Kim [Novak] asked him some questions about her death-loving character and he told her that she should 'not probe too much about things you do not understand.' Well, I saw it all coming anyway. Some years earlier, Hitch had me playing a voyeur in **Rear Window**, and then he had me playing some ghoulish guy wanting to recreate a dead woman with a naïve young lady, and he uses her love for him to do it. Hitch did not fool me. When he did **Vertigo**, he was remaking a modern version of **The Bride of Frankenstein** [1935], a woman made out of the flesh of dead persons, only he was doing the same thing metaphorically. What is the first thing Kim [Novak] does when I am shadowing her—she buys some flowers and takes them to a cemetery and that graveyard really represents everything that is going on in **Vertigo**." Stewart was even more emphatic about his contentions regarding this film when, three years later (in 1990), he told this author: "The whole thing disturbed me from the beginning. The detective I was playing was a seasoned law enforcement veteran, whom, I believe, would never let his fears and lust interfere with his surveillance assignment in that case. I told Hitch that and he only shrugged. I did it his way, as usual, but I felt somehow 'dirty' in that performance. I was playing a man in love with what he knew to be a dead woman, and then remaking her for his own sexual purposes." Stewart's affliction is really acrophobia, not vertigo, which is a misapplied term for his condition, the word "vertigo" appearing only once in the film. Though latter-day film reviewers (including my friend Roger Ebert) readdressed **Vertigo** to proclaim it a masterpiece, it is far from that, remaining an offbeat, sordid and depressing tale where the performances, other than that of Stewart, are as anemic as its characters and rather muddled plotline. It is saved by Stewart's intense performance, Hitchcock's arresting setups (he drew his own storyboards to set up each and every scene and every shot from every camera angle, as well as precisely positioning all characters in those scenes), the crisp lensing from Burks, and a befittingly haunting score from the gifted Herrmann. European censors objected to the fact that Helmore, the wife-killer, is not shown being brought to justice at the end, so Hitchcock, to appease those censors for the European release of this film, tacked on a finale where Stewart and Bel Geddes are listening to the radio to hear that Helmore, who has fled to Europe, has been arrested and charged with his wife's murder as both stare vacantly out of a window to view the waters of San Francisco Bay. The on-location shooting in San Francisco took Hitchcock only sixteen days, but the director spent several days at the California Palace of the Legion of Honor where the Carlotta Valdes painting was on display and where Novak endlessly rivets a vacant stare at that portrait. To achieve the vi-

sual appearance of the dizziness Stewart experiences, Hitchcock repeatedly used the "dolly in/zoom out" technique. Hitchcock's obsessive penchant for casting icy, sophisticated blondes in his films is epitomized by Novak in this production. The director, throughout his distinguished career, went out of his way to break down the reserved and prim and proper posture of such blonde actresses, beginning with the stunningly beautiful actress Madeleine Carroll, who starred in Hitchcock's **The 39 Steps**, 1935. "She was a bother from beginning to end in that picture," Hitchcock told this author. "She did not want to appear stupid or crude, and, in fact, I first show her reading a book on a train in **The 39 Steps** to prove her literacy. She hated the scenes where she was handcuffed to Robert Donat, and where he drags her about, because he, not her, was in control. She was, like most of the blonde ladies I directed, what I would call a 'control actress,' and where she had to be in charge of her scenes. Well, she was not in charge of any of the scenes I directed, I can tell you. She put up a terrible fuss when she had to unhook her stockings from her garters in one scene and remove them from beneath her dress when she is on the run and hiding at an inn with Mr. Donat. She did not want her thighs shown, but that was inevitable. How else was she to remove the stockings? I had to deal with that kind of thing over and over with many other actresses, their wills against mine, you know." Hitchcock had idealized blonde women at an early age, seeing them as ultra-sophisticated and utterly detached from the common events of the world, and it is obvious in most of his films that he set out to dismantle that lofty image by showing them as flesh and blood human beings, vulnerable and even treacherous. As such, he psychologically tortures cool blonde Joan Fontaine in **Rebecca**, 1940; and does the same thing to her later in **Suspicion**, 1941. He punctures the propriety posture of blonde Priscilla Lane in **Saboteur**, 1942, by having her rudely kidnapped, and reduces glamorous blonde Tallulah Bankhead to a disheveled survivor in **Lifeboat**, 1944. He depicts ultra-confident blonde psychiatrist Ingrid Berman to sexually submit herself to a mentally unbalanced imposter in **Spellbound**, 1945, and portrays the blonde Bergman again as a woman of loose morals in **Notorious**, 1946 (excusing her sexual transgressions as part of her undercover work for the FBI), and, still later, shows the blonde Bergman as an adulterous wife in **Under Capricorn**, 1949. Not even his favorite blonde actress, Grace Kelly, escapes Hitchcock's excoriating scalpel, wherein he profiles her as a cheating wife in **Dial M for Murder**, 1954; as an aloof model perversely excited about a murderer in **Rear Window**, 1954, and as a detached heiress in **To Catch a Thief**, 1955, who again is sexually aroused when having an affair with a cat burglar. Hitchcock relentlessly went on vivisecting his blondes by having self-contained blonde Doris Day become an emotional wreck over the kidnapping of her son in **The Man Who Knew Too Much**, 1954. He profiles cool blonde Eva Marie Saint as an alluring sleep-around trollop working for U.S. intelligence in **North by Northwest**, 1959. He shows more than once the voluptuous blonde Janet Leigh wearing only bra and slip in **Psycho**, 1960, viewed by berserk killer Anthony Perkins (along with the viewing audience) as the degraded subject of a Peeping Tom. Tippi Hedren, the director's last "find" as one of his leading ladies, became his penultimate cool blonde in **The Birds**, 1963, who is in total control of everything until a swarm of the fine feathered friends tear her to pieces to leave her in a comatose state, and he profiles Hedren once more in **Marnie**, 1964, as a conniving kleptomaniac. In **Topaz**, 1969, he has blonde Dany Robin as a cheating wife (and where Robin wears a decidedly ill-fitting blonde wig throughout the film), and, in his final film, **Family Plot**, 1976, Hitchcock has kidnapper Karen Black don a blonde wig as part of her lethal impersonation. "They say I took some sort of revenge on blonde women in my pictures," Hitchcock told this author, "but that's a lot of nonsense. Of course, I wanted those blonde leading ladies in my pictures because they suited the characters they were playing. Everything else is coincidence, even though most do not believe that. I controlled my pictures, but I cannot control what people want to believe and they believe all sorts of God awful things, don't they?" Hitchcock, as this author learned from personal experience with the director, suffered from a number of phobias. He was afraid of driving cars. He was afraid of nighttime intruders who might invade his homes. He was afraid to eat in restaurants, distrusting unseen chefs in kitchens and what they might be doing to his food. He was afraid of police, and this was a phobia stemming from his childhood, as mentioned in earlier remarks by this author in other entries. He was afraid of edged weapons (and this might explain why he shows in his films so many of his victims with knives buried in their backs). Hitchcock was also deeply afflicted by acrophobia, having such a deep fear of heights that he refused to fly, invariably traveling by train and ship. Nevertheless, he emphasized his acrophobia by placing his characters in precarious positions, threatening them with the possibilities of falling to their doom from great heights (they might fall, but he would not). These films include **Blackmail**, 1929, where blackmailer Donald Calthrop is pursued by police over the dome of the British Museum and where he later dangles in mid-air on a chain while attempting to flee in the museum's towering Egyptian Exhibit; **The Man Who Knew Too Much**, 1934, where child Nova Pilbeam clings to the side of a London rooftop while anarchist Frank Vosper is attempting to shoot her; **The 39 Steps**, 1935, where victimized Robert Donat clings to the girders of Scotland's Firth of Forth Bridge to escape pursuers; **Foreign Correspondent**, 1940, where Joel McCrea must escape killers by precariously walking on the high ledge of a hotel in Holland and where later is almost pushed from a cathedral tower in London by assassin Edmund Gwenn, and, still later, where journalist George Sanders escapes a ring of spies by dropping from a third floor window to have his fall broken by an awning, and, still later, where McCrea and other passengers on board a damaged plane are later shown crashing horribly into the sea; **Suspicion**, 1941, where Cary Grant appears that he might send a car carrying wife Joan Fontaine over a high cliff; **Saboteur**, 1942, where spy Norman Lloyd clings to the arm of the Statue of Liberty, his sleeve clutched by Robert Cummings, which then begins to tear away until he falls horribly downward and to his death; **Shadow of a Doubt**, 1943, where serial killer Joseph Cotten attempts to throw his niece, Teresa Wright, from a speeding train; **Spellbound**, 1945, where Gregory Peck and Ingrid Bergman are racing down a snow-coated slope on skis to almost sail over a cliff to their doom, and, later, when the mentally disturbed Peck recalls how his brother died when, as a child, he slid down a stair ramp to send the boy off its end and onto an iron fence where the boy is impaled (in what is Hitchcock's cruelest scene); **Rear Window**, 1954, where invalided James Stewart clings to a windowsill as killer Raymond Burr attempts to push him downward to his death; **To Catch a Thief**, 1955, where Cary Grant traps a cat burglar atop a building and holds her by one hand as she dangles in mid-air until she confesses her crimes to police waiting below; **North by Northwest**, 1959, where Cary Grant and Eva Marie Saint precariously cling to the side of Mount Rushmore as villains attempt to force them to fall to their deaths; **Torn Curtain**, 1966, where Paul Newman and Julie Andrews are ostensibly hiding in a trunk that hangs precariously in a cargo net high over a dockside ship that is riddled with machine gun fire; **Topaz**, 1969, where undercover agent Roscoe Lee Browne escapes Cuban communist thugs by dropping from a third-floor window to have his fall broken by an awning (which repeats the scene Hitchcock employed in **Foreign Correspondent** as mentioned above). Other films dealing with acrophobia (fear of heights, often wrongly called vertigo, which afflicts people with dizziness who perceive usually a spinning motion due to a dysfunction of the vestibular system) include **The Andromeda Strain**, 2008 (TV miniseries); **Animal**, 1977; **Antz**, 1998; **Baby's Day Out**, 1994; **The Barefoot Executive**, 1971; **The Brave Little Toaster**, 1987; **The Children of the Century**, 1999; **Cliffhanger**, 1993; **Continental Divide**, 1981; **Deewana Mastana**, 1997; **Dick Francis: Twice Shy**, 1989 (made-for-TV); **Divergent**, 2014; **Don't Look Down**, 1998 (made-for-TV); **Driving In**, 1990; **Empire Falls**, 2005 (made-for-TV); **Enduring Love**, 2004; **Evil under the Sun**, 1982; **The Face of Fear**, 1990 (made-for-TV); **Fear of Heights**, 1994; **Flame over India**, 1960; **Futureworld**, 1976; **Hero**,

Faye Emerson, Eleanor Parker, Dennis Morgan and Dane Clark in *The Very Thought of You*, 1944.

1992; **High Anxiety**, 1977; **High Lane**, 2009; **A History of Violence**, 2005; **Horatio Hornblower: Retribution**, 2001 (made-for-TV); **The In-Laws**, 2003; **Jack the Giant Slayer**, 2013; **Journey to the Center of the Earth**, 1959; **Le chanteur de Mexico**, 1956; **The Legend of Lylah Clare**, 1968; **A Likely Story**, 1947; **The Mad Miss Manton**, 1938; **Matador**, 1986; **The Meteor Man**, 1993; **The Night the World Exploded**, 1957; **Open Your Eyes**, 1997; **OSS 117: Lost in Rio**, 2009; **The Pagemaster**, 1994; **Passengers**, 2008; **Patchwork Family**, 2014; **Planes**, 2013; **Police Academy: Mission to Moscow**, 1994; **The Reluctant Astronaut**, 1967; **Samba**, 2014; **Steel**, 1979; **Stolen Hours**, 1963; **Switching Channels**, 1988; **Three Dancing Slaves**, 2004; **Thunder Birds**, 1942; **Topkapi**, 1964; **Up, Down, Fragile**, 1995; **Vanila Sky**, 2001; **White Squall**, 1996; and **The Winning Team**, 1952. **p&d**, Alfred Hitchcock; **cast**, James Stewart, Kim Novak, Barbara Bel Geddes, Tom Helmore, Henry Jones, Raymond Bailey, Ellen Corby, Konstantin Shayne, Lee Patrick, David Ahdar, Hitchcock; **w**, Alec Coppel, Samuel Taylor (based on the novel *D'entre les morts* by Pierre Boileau, Thomas Narcejac); **c**, Robert Burks; **m**, Bernard Herrmann; **ed**, George Tomasini; **art d**, Hal Pereira, Henry Bumstead; **set d**, Sam Comer, Frank McKelvy; **spec eff**, Farciot Edouart, John P. Fulton, Wallace Kelley.

The Very Thought of You ★★★ 1944; U.S.; 99m; WB; B/W; Drama; Romance; Children: Acceptable. Heartwarming tale begins with Morgan, a soldier stationed in Southern California before being shipped overseas in WWII (1939-1945). He falls in love with Parker, who is part of a dysfunctional family. Her parents, Bondi and Travers, are constantly bickering, her married sister does not respect her marriage vows, and her emotionally unstable brother may be one slice of bread short of a sandwich. Despite these obstacles, they marry and soon are parents themselves. Meanwhile, Clark, who is Morgan's army buddy, and Emerson fall in love. Not related to a 1998 film with the same title. Songs: "The Very Thought of You" (Ray Noble), "California, Here I Come" (music: Joseph Meyer; lyrics: Buddy G. DeSylva), "Cuddle Up a Little Closer" (music: Karl Hoschna; lyrics: Otto A. Harbach), "Wedding March" from "A Midsummer Night's Dream" (Felix Mendelssohn-Bartoldy), "Bridal Chorus" (from "Lohengrin" by Richard Wagner). *Author's Note*: Clark told this author that "I had a second fiddle role in **The Very Thought of You**, but I was still climbing the Hollywood ladder then, and I was grateful for any role they gave me. The song that has the same title as the picture became a big hit because it reminded every guy about the girl or wife he left behind when they went off to fight in the war, and every gal loved that song, too, because it called up the memories of their loved ones overseas. Tunes like that stayed with those in our generation through all the years of our lives." **p**, Jerry Wald; **d**, Delmer Daves; **cast**, Dennis Morgan, Eleanor Parker, Dane Clark,

Sylvia Sims and Dirk Bogarde in *Victim*, 1962.

Faye Emerson, Beulah Bondi, Henry Travers, William Prince, Andrea King, John Alvin, Richard Erdman, Angela Greene, Colleen Townsend; **w**, Daves, Alvah Bessie (based on a story by Lionel Wiggam); **c**, Bert Glennon; **m**, Franz Waxman; **ed**, Alan Crosland Jr.; **art d**, Leo Kuter; **set d**, Fred M. MacLean; **spec eff**, Warren Lynch.

Vice Versa ★★★ 1988; U.S.; 98m; COL; Color; Comedy/Fantasy; Children: Cautionary (MPAA: PG); **DVD**; **VHS**; **IV**. Entertaining fantasy begins when Reinhold returns from a buying trip abroad for a department store and finds he is in possession of a strange ornamental skull. Divorced, he is taking care of his son, Savage, for a few days. The skull has fantastic powers, similar to Aladdin's magic lamp, so when Reinhold and Savage wish that they could trade places, their personalities actually exchange bodies (shades of **Freaky Friday**, 1976, and its 1995 and 2003 remakes). Reinhold goes to school and Savage goes to work at the department store and also has to deal with his father's girlfriend. On top of that, smugglers want to get the skull away from them to obtain its magical powers and that leads into a lot of exciting mayhem. This is a lively remake of the 1948 British film that offers a well-scripted tale and some top-flight performances. Songs: "Set the Night to Music" (Diane Warren), "Crazy in the Night" (Mick Zane, Mark Behn, James Neal), "Vice Versa" (Mark Zane, Mark Behn, Paul Sabu). **p**, Dick Clement, Ian La Frenais; **d**, Brian Gilbert; **cast**, Judge Reinhold, Fred Savage, Corinne Bohrer, Swoosie Kurtz, Jane Kaczmarek, David Proval, William Prince, Gloria Gifford, Beverly Archer, Jane Lynch; **w**, Clement, La Frenais (based on the novel by F. Anstey); **c**, King Baggot; **m**, David Shire; **ed**, David Garfield; **prod d**, James L. Schoppe; **art d**, Eva Anna Bohn; **set d**, Karen O'Hara; **spec eff**, Louis Schwartzberg, Randall Rudd.

Vicky Christina Barcelona ★★★ 2008; Spain/U.S.; 96m; Weinstein Co.; Color; Drama/Romance; Children: Unacceptable (MPAA: PG-13); **BD**; **DVD**; **IV**. Good script, direction and acting make this absorbing romantic tale worth the watching. American girlfriends Cristina, played by Johansson, and Vicky, played by Hall, are on vacation in Barcelona, Spain, living at the home of Hall's relative, Clarkson. Johansson becomes attracted to Bardem, a seductive young painter, but Hall is reluctant to enter into a sexual adventure because she is about to be married. Bardem is attracted to both of them while still enamored of his mentally and emotionally unstable ex-wife, Cruz. Hall's feelings for Bardem become stronger, but change when Cruz bursts in on them with a gun and Hall is shot in the hand. That convinces Hall to exit an unstable relationship and she and Johansson return to America where Hall marries and Johansson is convinced to look elsewhere for romance as she does not want a man like Bardem in her life. Songs/Music: "Granada" and

"Asturias" (Isaac Albeniz), ""Entre Las Olas" and "Gorrion"(Juan Serrano), "Entre Dos Aguas" (Paco de Lucia, Jose Torregrosa), "El Noi de la Mare" (traditional Catalonian folk song), "La rey del retiro" (Giulia Tellarini, Maik Alemany, Alejandro Mazzoni, Jens Neumaier), "Your Shining Eyes" and "When I Was a Boy" (Biel Ballester), "Big Brother" (Stephane Wrembel). Sexuality and smoking prohibits viewing by children. **p**, Letty Aronson, Stephen Tenenbaum, Gareth Wiley, Helen Robin; **d&w**, Woody Allen; **cast**, Rebecca Hall, Scarlett Johansson, Javier Bardem, Penelope Cruz, Patricia Clarkson, Chris Messina, Kevin Dunn, Julio Perillan, Juan Quesada, Ricard Salom, Christopher Evan Welch (narrator); **c**, Javier Aguirresarobe; **ed**, Alisa Lepselter; **prod d**, Alain Bainee; **art d**, Inigo Navarro; **set d**, Sol Caramilloni, Sylvia Steinbrecht; **spec eff**, Adrienne Winterhalter, Randall Balsmeyer.

Victim ★★★ 1962; U.K.; 90m; Allied Film Makers/Astor Pictures; B/W; Crime Drama; Children: Unacceptable; **BD**; **DVD**; **VHS**; **IV**. Bogarde renders a powerful performance in this sensitive crime drama that unstintingly shows the plight of blackmailed homosexuals living in England. He plays a very successful London lawyer, seemingly happily married to Syms. McEnery, a handsome, young, working-class man, who is a homosexual, attempts to seduce Bogarde, who resists, thinking he is being set up for blackmail. It turns out that McEnery is himself a victim of blackmailers, who know of his relationship with Bogarde, and have a photograph of them together in a car where McEnery is crying. McEnery wants Bogarde to help him since he has stolen money to pay the blackmailers and now police are investigating him for homosexual activity. Homosexual acts between males were illegal in England and Wales, and those convicted were often sent to prison. In 1967, the Sexual Offences Act changed that, but police restraint did not prevent the blackmailing of victims. Police learn why McEnery is being blackmailed and he fears that Bogarde will be discovered as his partner, so he hangs himself in a police lockup. Bogarde then takes on the blackmailers and learns about a male hairdresser, who has also become a victim of the same blackmailers. The hairdresser is visited by one of the blackmailers and becomes so frightened that he has a heart attack. Before dying, he telephones Bogarde to leave a message about another victim of the blackmail ring. Bogarde contacts this man, a famous actor, played by Price, but Price, fearing for his reputation, refuses to help him, so as to keep his secret. Syms then learns about McEnery's suicide and demands Bogarde tell her the truth about his relationship with McEnery. He reminds her that, before marrying her, he had admitted to having homosexual tendencies, but promised he would no longer give in to them. However, Syms leaves him. The blackmailers then harass Bogarde, painting words such as "queer" on his garage doors. Bogarde now tells police he will help them catch the blackmailers and testify in court. Together they trap the blackmailers, who are arrested, and Bogarde repeats that he will testify against them. Syms returns to their home and agrees to stand by him at the trial and afterward, believing he is now able to overcome his homosexual tendencies. He then burns the incriminating photo and looks forward to a new future. Not related to 2010 and 2011 films with the same title. Songs: "String Quartet, Op. 18" (Ludwig van Beethoven), "Long Stringy Baby" (Trevor Peacock). *Author's Note*: Bogarde (1921-1999) was reportedly for many years a closet homosexual, living with his manager, Anthony Forwood, who was once married to British actress Glynis Johns. Bogarde, knowing well the then repressive criminal laws against homosexuals in England, never proclaimed his sexual preference, which many claimed prevented him from moving to Hollywood to pursue a film career there. Mature subject matter prohibits viewing by children. **p**, Michael Relph; **d**, Basil Dearden; **cast**, Dirk Bogarde, Sylvia Sims, Dennis Price, Anthony Nicholls, Peter McEnery, Peter Copley, Norman Bird, Donald Churchill, Derren Nesbitt, John Barrie; **w**, Janet Green, John McCormick; **c**, Otto Heller; **m**, Philip Green; **ed**, John D. Guthridge; **art d**, Alex Vetchinsky.

Victor/Victoria ★★★ 1982; U.K./ U.S.; 132m; MGM; Color; Comedy/Musical/Romance; Children: Unacceptable (MPAA: PG); **BD**; **DVD**; **VHS**; **IV**. Amusing sex farce begins with Andrews, who is a British singer who can't find a job in 1934 Paris because there is no market for female singers. She is so destitute that she has no money for food or shelter. Her prospects brighten when she meets charming and clever Preston, who is a gay cabaret singer just fired from his gig. He comes up with a scheme that can make them both comfortably in the money. He convinces her to let him be her manager in a plan where she will sing as a man, Victor, pretending to be a female impersonator, Victoria. They pull this off and all goes well until Garner, a Chicago nightclub owner, sees Andrews' act and not only loves it, but falls in love with her, thinking she is a man. She falls in love with him, too, but, if she reveals she is pretending to be a man, she will be out of work again. Further complicating matters, Preston falls for Karras, a gay man, who is Garner's macho-appearing bodyguard. Garner's blonde girlfriend, Warren, becomes jealous of Andrews, and tries to throw a monkey wrench into the Victor/Victoria scheme. The delightful farce ends with Andrews admitting the scheme to Garner and he is relieved to know he loves a woman instead of a man. Songs: "You and Me," "The Shady Dame from Seville," "Le Jazz Hot," "Gay Paree," "Chicago, Illinois," "Crazy World," "Alone in Paris," "Kings Can," "Cat and Mouse" (music: Henry Mancini; lyrics: Leslie Bricusse). Mature subject matter prohibits viewing by children. **p**, Blake Edwards, Tony Adams; **d&w**, Edwards (based on a concept by Hans Hoemburg and a 1933 script by Reinhold Schunzel for the German film **Viktor und Vicktoria**); **cast**, Julie Andrews, James Garner, Robert Preston, Lesley Ann Warren, John Rhys-Davies, Graham Stark, Peter Arne, Herb Tanney, Michael Robbins, Norman Chancer; **c**, Dick Bush (Panavision; Metrocolor); **m**, Henry Mancini; **ed**, Ralph E. Winters; **prod d**, Rodger Maus; **art d**, Tim Hutchinson, William Craig Smith; **set d**, Harry Cordwell; **spec eff**, Martin Gutteridge, Neil Courbould, Albert Whitlock.

Victoria the Great ★★★★ 1937; U.K.; 112m; Herbert Wilcox Productions/RKO; B/W/Color; Biographical Drama; Children: Acceptable; **DVD**. Beautifully made biopic is wonderfully enacted by Neagle, who plays England's Queen Victoria I (1819-1901). The film concentrates on Victoria's early years and ends with her Diamond Jubilee, celebrating a reign of sixty years. The film opens when Neagle is eighteen and inherits the throne, her three elder brothers all having died. She is gracefully courted by the elegant Walbrook, who plays Prince Albert (1819-1861), her first cousin, and they eventually marry. An assassin, Barnard, who plays Edward Oxford (1822-1900), attempts to murder Neagle, but the gallant Walbrook shields her from the attack and she remains safe. This depiction of the first of eight assassination attempts against the queen graphically and faithfully follows the actual event of June 10, 1840, when Victoria and Albert left Buckingham Palace in their carriage on their daily drive through the Constitution Hill area. Barnard, like Oxford, is seized by a crowd outside the palace and is dragged away to a police station (Oxford would later be adjudged insane and confined in Bethlehem Royal Hospital, known as Bedlam, and remained there until released in 1867 when he was ordered to migrate from England. For details and illustrations of this event and subsequent attempts on the life of Victoria, see my two-volume work *The Great Pictorial History of World Crime*, Volume I (History, Inc., 2004; pages 20-22). Episodic scenes then profile the domestic life between Neagle and Walbrook and where Walbrook is, as was Albert, a dutiful husband and prince consort, living his life at every turn in polite deference to a wife, who is foremost his queen. The couple produces nine children and Walbrook, like Albert, feels constrained over his total absence of authority, but he nevertheless uses his masterful influence to convince Neagle to discreetly use her authority when dealing with Parliament. He manages Neagle's household and estates as he involves himself in many social causes such as educational reform and the abolishment of slavery. His crusade to end slavery earns England the friendship of U.S. President Abraham Lincoln (1809-1865), who is played in cameo by

Anton Walbrook as Prince Albert and Anna Neagle as Queen Victoria I in *Victoria the Great*, 1937.

Parsons. Upon Walbrook's untimely death in 1861, Neagle is devastated and so deeply mourns his loss that she is inconsolable, her mourning continuing almost to the end of her reign. Neagle nevertheless continues to manage her affairs while dealing with the most distinguished men of her age, including the Duke of Wellington (Field Marshal Arthur Wellesley, 1769-1852), played by Dale; Prime Minister Sir Robert Peel (1788-1850), played by Carson; Prime Minister Lord Palmerston (1784-1865), impressively played by Aylmer; Prime Minister William Gladstone (1809-1898), played by Young, and Prime Minister Benjamin Disraeli (1804-1881), played by De Marney. The film ends with Neagle's Diamond Jubilee as queen of England (these sequences are shown in vivid Technicolor) and where she has lived to see her nation become one of the world's leading powers while bringing peace and prosperity to her people. Neagle's performance is nothing short of masterful as she portrays the venerated queen with all the style and elegance Victoria exuded where she became the national icon of stability as she upholds the strict standards of morality that epitomized the Victorian era. Neagle brings to her role a deep sense of humanity, but without weakening her character with sentimentality, her sensitivity and concern for her family and her people displayed in every scene in understated gestures and words. Hers is one of the most memorable essays of Victoria to ever grace the screen as she wholly captures the character of this benevolent and loving monarch. Wilcox does a superb job of directing this sumptuously produced biopic, mixing well the intimate scenes between Neagle and Walbrook with the significant historical events and personalities of that imperial age. This film was enormously successful throughout the United Kingdom, being released on the 100th anniversary when Victoria I became queen of Great Britain and Ireland, as well as Empress of India. It also saw very good box office in the U.S., but only in major cities. Songs/Music: "The Water Music" (George Frideric Handel), "Land of Hope and Glory" (from "Pomp and Circumstances No. 1" by Edward Elgar), "Soldiers of the Queen" (Leslie Stuart), "Praise God from Whom All Blessings Flow" (music: Louis Bourgeois; lyrics: Thomas Ken), "God Save the Queen" (Henry Carey). ***Author's Note***: This film was so successful that Wilcox (who would marry Neagle in 1943, a union lasting until his death in 1977) made a sequel, **Sixty Glorious Years**, 1938, an all-color production starring Neagle and Walbrook, but where Victoria's sixty-year reign concentrates upon the political events of her elegant era. Wilcox later edited the two films together, combining the first half of **Victoria the Great** with the second half of **Sixty Glorious Years**, to produce a separate film, **Queen Victoria**, 1942. Wilcox first thought to produce **Victoria the Great** after he was contacted by England's short-lived King Edward VIII, who abdicated the throne (which he assumed on January 20, 1936) on December 11, 1936, so that he could marry commoner Wallis Simpson, and

Melina Mercouri and George Peppard in *The Victors*, 1963.

then became the Duke of Windsor. As such, the Duke called Wilcox and personally requested he make a film about his illustrious ancestor. Wilcox immediately warmed to the subject, having Neagle in mind in the role of the queen. Although the film was shot in incredible speed, completed within five weeks, its attention to historic detail in its sets, costumes and vehicles are amazingly accurate and visually astonishing. Neagle's impressive costumes were copied from the original dresses held at the British Museum and palace sets were duplicated from those found at Buckingham Palace and elsewhere. Wilcox even employed the use of England's most famous historical train, "The Lion," built in 1837, that once transported passengers and freight from Liverpool to Manchester. The train was fully restored to operation for this film and presently resides in the Museum of Liverpool. Wilcox negotiated a lucrative deal with RKO for the distribution of this film in the U.S., one that included several more features he was to produce for that studio. The deal greatly aided independent producers such as Wilcox, in that it reduced England's restrictive quotas on domestic screenings of imported productions. As part of the RKO deal, Wilcox and Neagle toured the U.S. to promote **Victoria the Great** after it was released in America. Actor Paul Henreid appears in this, his first British-produced film, under his actual name. Many other actresses have portrayed Victoria I in many other films, including **The Adventure of Sherlock Holmes' Smarter Brother**, 1975 (Susan Field); **Adventures in Paradise**, 1959-1962 (TV series; "Blueprint for Paradise," 1962 episode: Pilar Seurat); **Annie Get Your Gun**, 1950 (Evelyn Beresford); **Around the World in 80 Days**, 1989 (TV miniseries; Anna Massey); **Around the World in 80 Days**, 2004 (Kathy Bates); **Balaclava**, 1930 (Marian Drada); **Barnum**, 1986 (made-for-TV; Bronwen Mantel); **The Battle of the Waltzes**, 1934 (Hanna Waag); **BBC Play of the Month**, 1965-1983 (TV series; "Gordon of Khartoum," 1966 episode: Gladys Spencer); **Bewitched**, 1964-1972 (TV series; "Aunt Clara's Victoria Victory," 1967 episode: Jane Connell); **Bismarck**, 1940 (Marga Riffa); **Buffalo Bill**, 1944 (Evelyn Beresford); **Court Waltzes**, 1933 (Madeleine Ozeray); **David Livingstone**, 1936 (Pamela Stanley); **Disraeli**, 1916 (Mrs. Henry Lytton); **Disraeli**, 1929 (Margaret Mann); **Disraeli: Portrait of a Romantic**, 1978 (TV miniseries; Rosemary Leach); **East Lynne**, 1976 (made-for-TV; Shirley Steedman); **Edward the King**, 1975 (TV series; Annette Crosbie); **The Edwardians**, 1972-1973 (TV series; 'Daisy," 1973 episode: Mollie Maureen); **Entente cordiale**, 1939 (Gaby Morlay); **Fall of Eagles**, 1974 (TV miniseries; "The English Princess," 1974 episode; Perlita Neilson; "The Last Tsar," 1974 episode: Mavis Edwards); **The Flaxton Boys**, 1969-1973 (TV series; "1854: The Dog," 1969 episode; Christine Ozanne); **Gilbert and Sullivan**, 1953 (Muriel Aked); **The Great McGonagall**, 1975 (Peter Sellers); **Hands of a Murderer**, 1990 (Honora Burke); **Hans Christian Anderson: My Life as a Fairy Tale**, 2003

(made-for-TV; Nina Lutjens); **Happy and Glorious**, 1952 (TV series; Renee Asherson); **Her Majesty; Mrs. Brown**, 1997 (Judi Dench); **Invincible Mr. Disraeli**, 1963 (Kate Reid); **Journey to Midnight**, 1971 (Fay Compton); **Journey to the Unknown**, 1968 (TV series; Fay Compton); **The Lady with a Lamp**, 1951 (Anna Neagle); **Let's Make Up**, 1956 (Anna Neagle); **Lillie**, 1978 (TV miniseries; Sheila Reed); **The Little Princess**, 1939 (Beryl Mercer); **Livingstone**, 1925 (Blanche Graham); **Marigold**, 1938 (Pamela Stanley); **Melba**, 1953 (Sybil Thorndike); **The Mudlark**, 1950 (Irene Dunne); **Mystery of the Wax Museum**, 1933 (Margaret Mann as the wax effigy of Queen Victoria); **Omnibus**, 1967-2002 (TV series; "Landseer: A Victorian Comedy," 1980 episode; Pamela Binns); **Paul Kruger**, 1956 (Gwen Ffrangcon Davies); **The Pearls of the Crown**, 1938 (Yvette Pienne); **Pervirella**, 1997 (Sexton Ming); **Preussen uber alles—Bismarcks deutsche Einigung**, 1971 (TV miniseries; Renate Pichler); **The Prime Minister**, 1942 (Fay Compton); **The Private Life of Sherlock Holmes**, 1970 (Mollie Maureen); **The Ravelled Thread**, 1979-1980 (TV series; 'The Spy," 1980 episode: Muriel Pavlow); **Rhodes**, 1996 (TV miniseries; "The Price of My Blood," 1996 episode: Margaret Heale); **Robert Montgomery Presents**, 1950-1957 (TV series; "Victoria Regina," 1951 episode: Helen Hayes; "Victoria Regina," 1957 episode: Claire Bloom); **Shadow Play**, 2004 (TV series; Doreen Mantle); **Shanghai Knights**, 2003 (Gemma Jones); **Sixty Glorious Years**, 1938 (Anna Neagle); **Sixty Years a Queen**, 1913 (Blanche Forsythe); **Station Jim**, 2001 (made-for-TV; Prunella Scales); **The Story of Alexander Graham Bell**, 1939 (Beryl Mercer); **The Story of Vickie**, 1958 (Romy Schneider); **The Symbol of Sacrifice**, 1918 (Mrs. D. Buxton); **Tall Tales and Legends**, 1985-1988 (TV series; "Annie Oakley," 1985 episode: Lu Leonard); **Those Fantastic Flying Fools**, 1967 (Joan Sterndale-Bennett); **Uncle Kruger**, 1941 (Hedwig Wangel); **Victoria & Albert**, 2001 (made-for-TV; Victoria Hamilton); **Victoria Regina**, 1964 (TV miniseries; Patricia Routledge); **Voyagers!**, 1982-1983 (TV series; "Buffalo Bill and Annie Play the Palace," 1983 episode; Lurene Tuttle); **The White Angel**, 1936 (Fay Holden); **Witness to Yesterday**, 1970-1976 (TV series; "Queen Victoria," 1973 episode: Kate Reid); **The Wrong Box**, 1966 (Avis Bunnage); **The Yankee Clipper**, 1927 (Julia Faye); **The Young Visitors**, 2003 (made-for-TV; Janine Duvitski); and **Zorro in the Court of England**, 1971 (Barbara Carroll). **p&d**, Herbert Wilcox; **cast**, Anna Neagle, Anton Walbrook, Walter Rilla, H.B. Warner, Mary Morris, James Dale, Greta Wegener, Felix Aylmer, Charles Carson, Arthur Young, Gordon McLeod, C.V. France, James Dale, Derrick De Marney, C. Aubrey Smith, Percy Parsons, Ivor Barnard; **w**, Miles Malleson, Charles de Grandcourt (based on the play "Victoria Regina" by Laurence Housman); **c**, F. A. Young, William V. Skall (Technicolor sequences); **m**, Anthony Collins; **ed**, Jill Irving; **prod d**, Tom Heslewood; **art d**, Lawrence P. Williams; **spec eff**, W. Percy Day.

The Victors ★★★ 1963; U.S./U.K.; 175m; COL; B/W; War Drama; Children: Unacceptable; **DVD**; **VHS**. Sprawling WWII (1939-1945) film grimly focuses upon a squad of U.S. soldiers fighting in Sicily, Italy, France and, finally, into Germany to see the end of the war. Each of the members of this squad are shown in vignette scenes, almost isolated from the other members as they experience personal relationships with the citizens of the war-torn landscapes they traverse, most of these relationships as vicious as the actual combat so sparingly depicted. Peppard, who receives most of the attention throughout the film, is first shown standing in the rain waiting for a bus while on leave in England. He is invited to wait inside the home of a working-class family until the bus arrives and promptly falls asleep in an armchair. When he departs, he finds that a ten shilling note has been slipped into the pocket of his uniform. Later, when at the front, Peppard has an affair with a woman, who persuades him to desert and become rich by operating with black market thieves, but, when he sees his unit leaving for the front, he joins his buddies at the last moment. Most of the other vignettes are less merciful to their characters and the viewing audience. Another member of the squad takes advantage of a lonely woman whose husband has been killed. Another squad member finds a dog and tries to take the animal along when his unit leaves for the front, but his fellow soldiers toss the dog from the truck and, as it runs after the vehicle, use it for target practice (one of the cruelest scenes ever shown on film and one that drew rage from animal cruelty groups). Wallach, the avuncular, tough sergeant guiding the young members of his squad through the war, is terribly wounded and is then sent to a hospital. When Peppard visits him with a bottle of whiskey as a present, he is sickened to discover that Wallach's face has been all but blown away, and Wallach shouts at Peppard to get away from him. The squad members are later shown being trucked through a tranquil appearing landscape during Christmastime in France, but their unit is diverted so that they and others can witness an execution. The squad members join long ranks of GIs to see Chase, a U.S. soldier convicted of desertion, being dragged shaking and quivering to a stake (while director Foreman cynically has the soundtrack playing Frank Sinatra's song "Have Yourself a Merry Little Christmas" to underscore his savage irony of this gruesome scene). When Chase is then shot and remains a sagging, bleeding hulk at that stake, we hear the even more inappropriately sardonic strains of "Hark! The Herald Angels Sing," before the stunned troops leave this stark scene. (This scene is based upon the execution of U.S. Private Eddie Slovik, 1920-1945, an unrepentant deserter, who was, out of more than 21,000 desertions by U.S. personnel, including forty-nine death sentences in WWII, the only person to be put to death, killed by a firing squad on January 31, 1945, and was excruciatingly profiled in the made-for-TV **The Execution of Private Slovik**, 1974, starring Martin Sheen as Slovik.) One by one, the members of the squad fall victim to the war. The final scene shows a drunken Hamilton, whose German girlfriend has left him for a Russian soldier, confronting Finney, a Soviet soldier in Berlin shortly after the war has ended. Both men are drunk and show their hostility toward one another by refusing to give way and while shouting at each other, but not understanding each other's language. Both pull knives and attack and kill each other, falling in such a way as to make their bodies appear to be a "V," standing for "Victory." Foreman's portrait of WWII is ferocious and often gratuitously violent to make his anti-war statements. His vignette approach to his characters, none of which are appealing or have redeemable values (other than, perhaps, Peppard), is visually jarring. To provide relief from his relentless depressing scenes, Foreman interjects home front sequences of innocuous events via newsreel clips, but the film nevertheless suffers from continuity gaps that go unexplained. Yet, this remains a memorable film in that it went against the grain of popular perspectives about WWII in a bold attempt to convince viewers that there was nothing glorious or heroic about that worldwide conflict. His is a brilliantly conceived and innovative portrait of hell at various levels of the lower depths of man, and where all humans are reduced to every miserable status of survival, including a pitiful portrait of a young French boy, who tries to sell his body to the squad, saying that even "the Germans like me." (This homosexual scene where GIs give the boy food for his carnal favors was later trimmed on orders of Hollywood censors.) Foreman ends this sad and morose tale with the words of British poet Wilfred Owen (1893-1918), who was killed in WWI (1914-1918) on the Western Front on November 4, 1918, only seven days before the Armistice: "My subject is War and the pity of War. The Poetry is the pity. All a poet can do today is warn…" The film did not do well at the box office, generating only about $2.3 million in its initial release. Hamilton later stated that the film was "way too dark, foreshadowing the great paranoid movies of the later sixties, ahead of the bad times that seemed to begin with the Kennedy assassination [the murder of President John F. Kennedy in Dallas, Texas, on November 22, 1963, this film being released one month later]. Songs: "March of the Victors," "No Other Man," "Sweet Talk" (Sol Kaplan, Freddy Douglass); "My Special Dream" (Sol Kaplan, Freddy Douglass, Howard Greenfield); "Does Goodnight Mean Goodbye" (Howard Greenfield, Gerry Goffin, Jack Keller); "Have Yourself

George Hamilton, Vincent Edwards, James Mitchum and George Peppard in *The Victors*, 1963.

a Merry Little Christmas" (Ralph Blane, Hugh Martin); "Hark! The Herald Angels Sing" (music: Felix Mendelssohn-Bartholdy; lyrics: Charles Wesley); "Vainqueurs" (Sol Kaplan, Carl Foreman, Edmond Bacri); "The Wedding March" (1843; from "A Midsummer Night's Dream, Op. 61" by Felix Mendelssohn-Bartholdy); "Montserrat" (Monia Liter), "Neutral Mood" (Cyril Watters); "Victors' (Trevor Duncan); "Fame and Glory" (Albert Matt); "Up With the Curtain" (Jack Strachey); "Symphony No. 4" (Lev Knipper); "Humoresque in G Flat Major, Op. 10, No. 7" (Anton Dvorak); "Happy Days Are Here Again" (1929; music: Milton Agar; lyrics: Jack Yellen); "Jack O'Lantern" (Roger-Roger); "Red Sails in the Sunset" (1935; Hugh Williams [Wilhelm Grosz]); "Pennies from Heaven" (1936; music: Arthur Johnston; lyrics: Johnny Burke); "Senator," "The Diplomat" (Charles Williams); "The Glory of Love" (1936; Billy Hill); "Shoo Shoo Baby" (1943; Phil Moore); "Let's Fall in Love" (1933; music: Harold Arlen; lyrics: Ted Koehler); "Bless 'Em All" (1917; Fred Godfrey); "One Night of Love" (1934; music: Victor Schertzinger; lyrics: Gus Kahn); "Remember Pearl Harbor" (1941; music: Don Reid, Sammy Kaye; lyrics: Don Reid). *Author's Note*: Foreman had served in the U.S. Signal Corps during WWII, working under pantheon film director Frank Capra, who was then making training and motivational films for the armed services. Foreman was always a left-wing political activist and wound up on Hollywood's blacklist in the early 1950s for his communist affiliations; he left the country in 1951 to live in England, not returning to Hollywood until a decade later. Other films focusing upon squads of soldiers in WWII include **Attack**, 1956; **Bataan**, 1943; **Battleground**, 1949; **Between Heaven and Hell**, 1956; **The Big Red One**, 1980; **The Dirty Dozen**, 1967; **Eight Iron Men**, 1952; **Halls of Montezuma**, 1951; **Hell Is for Heroes**, 1962; **Home of the Brave**, 1949; **Kelly's Heroes**, 1970; **The Naked and the Dead**, 1958; **Pride of the Marines**, 1945; **Sands of Iwo Jima**, 1949; **Saving Private Ryan**, 1998; **The Story of G.I. Joe**, 1945; and **To Hell and Back**, 1955; and **Too Late the Hero**, 1970. p,d&w, Carl Foreman (based on the book *The Human Kind* by Alexander Baron); cast, Vince Edwards, Albert Finney, George Hamilton, Melina Mercouri, Jeanne Moreau, George Peppard, Maurice Ronet, Romy Schneider, Rosanna Schiaffino, Elke Sommer, Eli Wallach, Michael Callan, Peter Fonda, Jim Mitchum, Senta Berger, Peter Vaughan, Alf Kjellin, James Chase; c, Christopher Challis; m, Sol Kaplan; ed, Alan Osbiston; prod d, Geoffrey Drake; art d, Maurice Fowler; spec eff, Cliff Richardson, Wally Veevers.

Vidocq ★★★ 2007; France; 98m; RF2K Productions/Lions Gate; Color; Mystery; Children: Unacceptable (MPAA: R); **DVD**; **IV**. A famous detective, Eugene Francois Vidocq (1775-1857), played energetically by Depardieu, is not seen again in 1830 Paris while pursuing an

Jean Sorel, Carol Lawrence and Raf Vallone in *A View from the Bridge*, 1962.

assassin known as the Alchemist. Depardieu's young biographer, Etienne Boisset, essayed by Canet, believes the Alchemist killed Vidocq, and begins an investigation. He learns that Depardieu had been investigating some murders involving lightning that put him on the trail of the Alchemist. Canet further learns that the Alchemist is a kind of wizard, who disguises himself or herself by wearing a mirrored mask and, like a vampire, kills virgins and drinks their blood believing he/she can remain youthful forever. The Alchemist's sex is a mystery because he/she sometimes sighs like a female. The mystery ends when Canet discovers that Depardieu is alive, living in hiding. Canet locates him and puts on a mirrored mask that reveals him to be the Alchemist. Depardieu has known Canet's identity as the killer from the start and defeats him in a final confrontation. The film ends with audiences believing that the Alchemist may have survived (to possibly present a sequel). Moody period film is convincingly staged, and the acting from the entire cast is top drawer, their outstanding performances sustaining suspense and tension throughout this good whodunit. Songs: "Hope Vol. 2" (Matthias Sayer, J. Collier, Eicca Toppinen), "Symphony No. 29 KV 201" (Wolfgang Amadeus Mozart), "Concerto for Mandolin RV 426, allegro and RV 532, adante" (Antonio Vivaldi). *Author's Note*: Vidocq was reportedly born in prison, his mother a convicted thief and, in his youth, practiced the same lowlife pursuits as a petty crook. After escaping prison, he resolved to change his ways and pursued malefactors as a detective while using his knowledge of criminal modus operandi when tracking down scores of criminals he had known in his earlier life. French author Victor Hugo used Vidocq as his two main characters, Jean Valjean, an escaped criminal, and Javert, a police inspector tracking him, in his classic 1862 novel, *Les Miserables*. Many other actors have portrayed the great French detective in many other films, including **Adventures of Criminalistics**, 1989-1993 (TV series; "Stopa," 1989 episode: Boris Rosner); **Les Miserables**, 1917 (role models for William Farnum and Hardee Kirkland); **Les Miserables**, 1927 (role models for Gabriel Gabrio and Jean Toulout); **Les Miserables**, 1935; (role models for Fredric March and Charles Laughton); **Les Miserables**, 1936 (role models for Harry Baur and Charles Vanel); **Les Miserables**, 1944 (role models for Domingo Soler and Antonio Bravo); **Les Miserables**, 1952 (role models for Gino Cervi and Hans Hinrich); **Les Miserables**, 1952 (role models for Michael Rennie and Robert Newton); **Les Miserables**, 1958 (role models for Jean Gabin and Bernard Blier); **Les Miserables**, 1972 (TV miniseries; role models for Georges Geret and Bernard Fresson); **Les Miserables**, 1978 (role models for Richard Jordan and Anthony Perkins); **Les Miserables**, 1982 (role models for Lino Ventura and Michel Bouquet); **Les Miserables**, 1995 (role models for Jean-Paul Belmondo and Philippe Khorsand); **Les Miserables**, 1998 (role models for Liam Neeson and Geoffrey Rush); **Les Miserables**, 2012 (role models

for Hugh Jackman and Russell Crowe); **Les nouvelles aventures de Vidocq**, 1971-1973 (TV series; Claude Brasseur); **A Scandal in Paris**, 1946 (George Sanders); **Vidocq**, 1923 (Rene Navarre); **Vidocq**, 1939 (Andre Brule); **Vidocq**, 1967 (TV series; Bernard Noel); **Vidocq**, 2010 (TV series; Bruno Madinier). For more details on Vidocq, see my eight-volume work *Encyclopedia of World Crime*, Volume IV (CrimeBooks, Inc., pages: 3047-3049). Violence, sexual content, nudity and drug material prohibit viewing by children. (In French; English subtitles.) **p**, Dominique Farrugia; **d**, Pitof (Jean-Christophe Comar); **cast**, Gerard Depardieu, Guillaume Canet, Ines Sastre, Andre Dussollier, Edith Scob, Moussa Maaskri, Jean-Pierre Gos, Isabelle Renauld, Jean-Pol Dubois, Andre Penvern; **w**, Pitof, Jean-Christophe Grange (based on the memoirs of Eugene Francois Vidocq); **c**, Jean-Pierre Sauvaire, Jean-Claude Thibaut; **m**, Bruno Coulais; **ed**, Thierry Hoss; **prod d**, Jean Rabasse; **art d**, Herve Gallet; **set d**, Fabien Belinguier, Francoise Benoit-Fresco, Jean Rabase; **spec eff**, Julien Poncet de la Grave.

A View from the Bridge ★★★ 1962; France/Italy; 110m; Transcontinental Films/Continental Distributing; B/W; Drama; Children: Unacceptable; **DVD**. This well-made filmed version of Miller's play about obsessive and unnatural love sees Vallone playing a Brooklyn longshoreman recently arrived from Sicily. He becomes an American citizen and is unhappily married to Stapleton while he is strongly attracted to Lawrence, the beautiful niece he and Stapleton have reared since she was a child and have brought with them to America. Two brothers, Sorel and Pellegrin, both illegal immigrants from Italy, begin lodging with them, and Lawrence falls in love with handsome Sorel. Vallone is unable to fight off his feelings for Lawrence, which are virtually incestuous, and his jealousness of Sorel creates friction. He is uncertain whether Sorel really loves Lawrence or would just feign love and use her to marry her, since she is an American citizen and this would allow him to permanently live in the United States. Vallone furthermore tries to break up the couple by telling Lawrence that Sorel is a homosexual and hopes to prove it by kissing him on the lips, which makes viewers wonder if Vallone has gay tendencies. This backfires on Vallone, and Lawrence and Sorel talk of getting married. To prevent this, Vallone reports both brothers to authorities so they will be deported back to Italy. The brothers are put in jail to await a deportation hearing, but Pellegrin is released on bail. He goes to Vallone's home and spits in his face, then forces him to his knees and compels Vallone to admit with others watching that he is a scoundrel. Pellegrin is to be deported, but a helpful attorney gets Sorel released after learning that he and Lawrence are to be married. Before he can be deported, Pellegrin stabs Vallone in the neck with a longshoreman's hook, killing the troublesome brute. Vallone gives a powerful performance of a man whose lust overtakes his reason and brings about his own death. The supporting cast members are also standouts in their roles. (In French and Italian; English subtitles.) *Author's Note*: The talented Miller later became Marilyn Monroe's husband, her third and final marriage (1956-1961), one that ended in divorce a year before her untimely death at age thirty-six. **p**, Paul Graetz; **d**, Sidney Lumet; **cast**, Raf Vallone, Jean Sorel, Maureen Stapleton, Carol Lawrence, Raymond Pellegin, Morris Carnovsky, Harvey Lembeck, Mickey Knox, Vincent Gardenia, Frank Campanella; **w**, Norman Rosten (based on the play by Arthur Miller) **c**, Michel Kelber; **m**, Maurice Le Roux; **ed**, Francoise Javet; **prod d**, Jacques Saulnier.

The Vikings ★★★ 1958; U.S.; 116m; Bavaria Film/UA; Color; Adventure; Children: Unacceptable; **DVD**; **VHS**; **IV**. Action-packed Norsemen saga begins when Borgnine, a Viking king, leads a raid against Northumbria (which is a part of present-day Scotland), and he kills the king. Thring, the king's ruthless, power-craving cousin, seizes the throne once Borgnine and his raiding Vikings depart. The widowed queen is left pregnant with Borgnine's child after the raider raped her, but she hides this from Thring, knowing he will kill the child when born. The child is sent to Italy to be raised abroad, but the ship sailing for that destination is waylaid by Vikings and the child becomes a slave, growing up to be Curtis. Donald, a nobleman in Thring's court, who is opposed to the ruler, learns that Curtis is of royal blood, but says nothing about it. After Donald defects to Borgnine, he recognizes Curtis as the heir to the Northumbria throne from an amulet Curtis wears about his neck that was placed there by his mother when he was a child. Douglas, who does not know that he is Curtis' half brother, abuses Curtis and Curtis orders his falcon to attack Douglas where the bird pecks out one of Douglas' eyes. For this offense, Curtis is sentenced to death. Way, who loves Curtis and is a powerful court prophetess, warns the court that Odin, the chief Viking god, will curse anyone who harms Curtis. Borgnine orders that Curtis be left in a tide pool to drown, but Way calls upon Odin to shift winds that turn back the waters that would otherwise drown Curtis and he is saved. Donald then claims Curtis as his slave to not only protect him but to later serve Donald's own ends. Leigh, a voluptuous Christian princess who is betrothed to Thring, is abducted in a Viking raid and held hostage by Borgnine. Both Curtis (who was then married to Leigh, this being the third of five films in which they would appear together) and Douglas fall in love with Leigh. When she shows favoritism toward Curtis, Douglas, during a court feast, persuades his drunken father, Borgnine, to give him permission to take Leigh by force. As Douglas begins to rape Leigh, Curtis intervenes, knocking Douglas senseless while he is drunk. Curtis escapes in a small boat with Leigh, Way, Connor, who is a fellow slave and friend of Curtis, and Leigh's maid, Nichols. Regaining his senses, Douglas, along with Borgnine, pursues with several Vikings in larger ships. Curtis manages to evade the pursuers when a fog enshrouds their passage and Connor gives him a crude compass, which is a magnate he had earlier found in a distant land, that guides Curtis toward Northumbria. Borgnine's ship strikes a rocky reef and sinks, but Curtis finds the drowning Viking king and saves Borgnine, taking him to Northumbria where Thring makes Borgnine a prisoner. By this time, Curtis and Leigh are deeply in love and Leigh resolves to ask Thring to release her from her marriage vows to him. Meanwhile, believing that Borgnine has gone down with his ship, Douglas abandons the pursuit and returns to his homeland. Thring is not a noble host to Borgnine, ordering Curtis to throw Borgnine into a pit prowled by starving wolves, a horrible death Curtis will not tolerate for his captive. Instead, Curtis cuts the ropes that bind Borgnine's hands and gives him a sword so that he can enter Valhalla as a fighting Viking. Bognine laughs and then leaps to his death in the pit while wielding the sword against the ravenous wolves. Thring looks upon Curtis' actions as an act of defiance and betrayal and orders that one of his hands be cut off. Thus mutilated, Curtis is put back into his boat and set adrift. Curtis returns to Douglas' fortress where he explains how Borgnine died and how Thring cut off his hand by allowing Bogrnine to die an honorable death. Both put aside their animosities toward each other and Douglas assembles all the Vikings to mount an attack on Thring's castle in Northumbria, with Curtis showing them the way through the fog-bound waters. Once they arrive before Thring's castle, the Vikings use battering rams and a ladder of axes thrown against the gate of the castle so that Douglas can climb the axes to the top of the battlement and then lower himself into the tower to release the drawbridge. The Vikings then storm into the castle and overwhelm the defenders. Douglas finds Thring and throws him into the pit, where starving wolves devour him, and Douglas then races toward the highest tower, as does Curtis, to find Leigh. Douglas locates Leigh first, grabbing her and telling her that he is going to make her his queen. Leigh tells Douglas that she despises him and loves only Curtis. Douglas then calls Curtis to a final showdown and both men furiously fight each other with swords until Curtis delivers a mortal blow. Curtis gives Douglas a sword so that he can enter Valhalla and meet Odin in death as a warrior. Douglas dies and is then given a Viking funeral at sea, his body placed in a longboat and flaming arrows fired into it until it sails onward, burning its corpse to end this tale of violent Norsemen. Fleischer does a fine job directing this adventure tale, mixing well its many well-choreographed action scenes with the tender mo-

Tony Curtis and Kirk Douglas in *The Vikings*, 1958.

ments shared between Curtis and Leigh, and where they and Douglas present convincing performances, as do the rest of the cast members essaying their historical characters. The ancient period is aptly portrayed in that Fleischer and his assistants made every effort to accurately recreate the castle sets and Viking ships, along with the costumes and customs of that day. For that reason, along with the bravura performances from Douglas and Borgnine, this film is most likely the best to profile the lusty Norsemen of historic Scandinavia. The film was successful at the box office, earning more than $6 million in its initial release against a budget of more than $2.5 million. ***Author's Note***: Fleischer spent more than two years researching Norse history before going into production with this film, replicating the long Viking ships from those held in a museum in Norway. He incorporated many of the customs employed by the Vikings, including the walking upon the oars outside of the ships for recreation. "Though he was about forty at that time," Fleischer told this author, "Kirk [Douglas] walked those oars as if he had been born a Viking. He fell into the icy water at one time, but calmly swam over to the boat where we had the cameras to ask if he had done the scene okay before he swam back to the Viking ship, as if he were swimming in his pool at home. I don't think any other actor, except for maybe Kirk's friend, Burt Lancaster, could have performed such athletic prowess." Curtis remembered this film as being uncomfortable when telling this author: "It was always cold up there since we shot **The Vikings** on location in Norway. Janet [Leigh] and I were shivering all the time and we had to swallow down some hot coffee to keep our teeth from chattering before we did our love scenes together." Borgnine told this author that "I got a big bang from working in that picture and Dick [Fleischer] let me roar about like a wild man in all of my scenes, carousing, drinking and lopping off heads for a laugh. Dick told me: 'It is impossible for you to go over the top in any of your scenes, Ernie. You are a Viking and anything goes!' Well, that's the way I played my character, but I would never, ever want to meet anyone like that in real life, and neither would you." Douglas wore an opaque scleral lens in the one eye that was supposed to be blind, but it was so painful that he could tolerate it for only a few minutes of shooting. The cast and crew were housed on two vessels moored in a Norwegian fjord while on location and a score of old PT-boats shuttled them back and forth to locations during the production that took about two months to complete. Much of that time was slowed down by rainy weather. Bresler, the producer, who hired scores of local residents to play Viking extras, stopped one of them and asked: "Does it always rain here?" The brawny youth shrugged and replied: "I don't know. I am only eighteen." To promote the film, dagger letter openers with elaborate Viking symbols embossed upon them were sent with press releases going to reviewers. As another publicity stunt, seven Norwegian seamen sailed a longboat from Oslo to New York Harbor

Robert Viharo, Yul Brynner, Charles Bronson and Robert Mitchum in *Villa Rides*, 1968.

and another longboat was hoisted above the marquee of the NYC theater where the film premiered. Other films profiling Vikings include **Erik the Conqueror**, 1963; **Erik the Viking**, 1989; **Exodus: Gods and Kings**, 2014; **The Long Ships**, 1964; **The Norseman**, 1980; **Northmen: A Viking Saga**, 2014; **Tales of the Vikings**, 1959 (TV series); **The 13th Warrior**, 1999; **The Viking**, 1928; **The Viking Sagas**, 1997; **Viking Quest**, 2014 (made-for-TV); **Vikingdom**, 2013; **Vikings!**, 1980 (TV series); and **Vikings**, 2013- (TV series). **p**, Jerry Bresler; **d**, Richard Fleischer; **cast**, Kirk Douglas, Tony Curtis, Ernest Borgnine, Janet Leigh, James Donald, Alexander Knox, Maxine Audley, Frank Thring, Eileen Way, Edric Connor, Dandy Nichols, Orson Welles (narrator); **w**, Calder Willingham (based on an adaptation by Dale Wasserman of the novel *The Viking* by Edison Marshall); **c**, Jack Cardiff (Technirama; Technicolor); **m**, Mario Nascimbene; **ed**, Elmo Williams; **prod d**, Harper Goff.

Villa Rides ★★★ 1968; U.S.; 125m; PAR; Color; War/Western; Children: Unacceptable (MPAA: R); **DVD**; **IV**. Action-loaded biopic sees Mitchum as a Texas gunrunner and pilot caught up in the Mexican Revolution of 1912. He smuggles guns from Texas to a counterrevolutionary captain, Wolff, who is fighting an insidious revolutionary general, Victoriano Huerta (1850-1916), who is played by Lom, and his underling, patriot Pancho Villa (1878-1923), played by Brynner. Mitchum's plane is damaged on one flight and he waits for its repair in a Mexican village where he witnesses Wolff lead a merciless attack on the peasants living there. Wolff and his soldiers are driven off by Bronson, one of Brynner's aids, Rodolfo Fierro (1880-1915), who lines up three of Wolff's men and shoots them all through the heart with one bullet. (This is based on actual fact as Fierro executed more enemies in such brutal fashion on more than one occasion.) Brynner learns that Mitchum has been supplying guns to the Mexican loyalists and orders him to be executed. Before Mitchum faces a firing squad, Brynner offers to let him go, if he consents to fly for the revolutionaries. Mitchum agrees and is assigned to bomb government troops with handmade grenades while Brynner and his men attack a train and a nearby town. Meanwhile, Lom, in a power struggle with Brynner, sends him on a sure-death mission; he accomplishes it with Mitchum's help, but Mitchum crashes his plane. Lom then has Brynner arrested for disobeying orders. Mitchum has had enough of the revolution and returns to Texas. Lom has Mexican president Francisco Madero (1873-1913), played by Knox, executed and sets himself up as dictator. Brynner escapes arrest and goes to Texas where he convinces Mitchum to rejoin the revolution. Inspired as a patriot, Mitchum is last seen going willingly to fight with Brynner. Mitchum, Brynner, Bronson and Lom are standouts in their historic roles, and director Kulik moves the action along at a furious pace. *Au-*

thor's Note: The film takes liberties with the historic facts about the Mexican Revolution, but many of its more colorful events, such as where Villa (Brynner) talks his way out of being executed by a firing squad, is based on that actual harrowing event. "I know my character as a pilot in **Villa Rides** is purely fictional, but some old double-wing crates were used during that Revolution as scout planes, not that they did any good," Mitchum told this author in 1990. "It is a fact that there were some Americans down there in Mexico fighting with Villa. A picture that came out last year called **Old Gringo** [1989], has Gregory Peck playing a guy based on the American writer, Ambrose Bierce [1842-c.1914], who fought with Villa." Bronson told this author that "I researched my character, Rodolfo Fierro, and he was really the kind of killer I played in **Villa Rides**. He was Villa's executioner, and had no regrets about killing anyone and he killed hundreds of men he thought might be enemies. When Villa captured a town, Fierro would ask prisoners if they wanted to go home to their families or to fight with Villa. If they said they wanted to go homes he was convinced they would later join the enemy, so he executed them. He gave a gun and some bullets to those that said they wanted to fight with Villa. The man was feared by everyone, maybe even Pancho Villa. When Fierro and his horse landed in some quicksand and he began to sink under the weight of all the weapons and gold he was carrying, he cried out for help, but even his own men ignored him, and were glad to see that killer sink under that quicksand [at the Casas Grandes Lagoon while marching with his men toward Sonora, Mexico, on October 14, 1915]. Nobody wept any tears over him." John Ireland told this author (in 1990, two years before his death) that "the only reason I have a small role in a barbershop scene in **Villa Rides** is because my pal, Bob Mitchum, wanted me in the picture. We lived in the same Santa Barbara [California] area where I owned a restaurant and Bob would often drop by to have coffee. Bob was always a generous guy and a good friend." Violence prohibits viewing by children. **p**, Ted Richmond; **d**, Buzz Kulik; **cast**, Yul Brynner, Robert Mitchum, Charles Bronson, Grazia Buccella, Herbert Lom, Alexander Knox, Frank Wolff, Fernando Rey, Jill Ireland, John Ireland, Enrique Santiago, Jose Riesgo; **w**, Robert Towne, Sam Peckinpah (adapted by William Douglas Lansford from his novel *Pancho Villa*); **c**, Jack Hildyard; **m**, Maurice Jarre; **ed**, David Bretherton; **prod d**, Ted Haworth; **art d**, Jose Alguero; **set d**, Roman Calatayud; **spec eff**, Milt Rice, Luciano Rodriguez.

Village of the Damned ★★★ 1960; U.K.; 77m; MGM; B/W; Horror/Science Fiction; Children: Unacceptable; **DVD**; **VHS**; **IV**. This very frightening film begins in an English village when everyone falls into a deep, mysterious sleep in the middle of the day. A few months later, every woman capable of child-bearing is pregnant and the children who are born seem to grow very fast and all have the same blond hair and strange, penetrating eyes that hypnotize people into doing things they would not otherwise do. The children are actually aliens from another dimension. Shelley, the wife of Sanders, a local physicist, gives birth to the leader of the alien children. After discovering this insidious alien invasion, Sanders takes action, but loses his life when destroying the aliens. *Author's Note*: Sanders reportedly took over the leading role in this thriller after Ronald Colman, scheduled for the role, unexpectedly died, and, in fact, Sanders married Colman's widow, Benita Hume, a union that lasted until her death in 1967. Sanders told this author that "Aliens were all the rage at the time we made that picture, which was, by any standards, one of the weirdest stories ever concocted—aliens invading Earth by impregnating every available woman. Can you imagine that? Well, it was no more outlandish than giant sea pods taking over whole communities by duplicating everyone inside of those pods in **Invasion of the Body Snatchers** [1956]. Those damnable aliens are an inventive lot." Violence and fright scenes prohibit viewing by children. **p**, Ronald Kinnoch; **d**, Wolf Rilla; **cast**, George Sanders, Barbara Shelley, Martin Stephens, Michael Gwynn, Laurence Naismith, Richard Warner, Jenny Laird, Sarah Long, Thomas Heathcote, Charlotte

Mitchell; **w**, Rilla, Sterling Silliphant, George Barclay (Ronald Kinnoch), based on the novel *The Midwich Cuckoos* by John Wyndham); **c**, Geoffrey Faithfull; **m**, Ron Goodwin; **ed**, Gordon Hales; **art d**, Ivan King; **spec eff**, Tom Howard.

Vincent and Theo ★★★ 1990; Netherlands/U.K./France/Italy/Germany; 138m; Belbo Films/Hemdale Films; Color; Biographical Drama; Children: Unacceptable (MPAA: PG-13); **BD**; **DVD**; **VHS**; **IV**. The tragic story of the Dutch post-Impressionist master painter Vincent van Gogh (1853-1890) receives a chronological telling in this superior biopic filmed in many of the locations where he lived and created his masterpieces in and around Paris in the late 1800s. Roth plays van Gogh, and Rhys essays his loyal art dealer younger brother Theo Van Gogh (1857-1891), who largely supported him, while Yordanoff portrays his fellow artist friend Paul Gauguin (1848-1903). Most of the dramatic scenes follow Roth's often angry encounters with those unable to understand his mercurial temper or his genius, including his lovers, creditors, art dealers, and the public. The film, however, gives the viewer a fine window into how an artist creates his work, while following Roth through a lifetime of rejection of his erratic, impoverished lifestyle, as well as his then radical artworks. We witness the artist's decline into madness and eventual suicide where he shoots himself. Altman faithfully captures the colorful landscapes and the era it represents with accurate historic sets and impressive period costumes while he draws outstanding performances from Roth, Rhys, Yordanoff and the rest of the fine cast. Produced by several countries, the film is in English. **p**, Ludi Boeken, David Conroy, Emma Hayter; **d**, Robert Altman; **cast**, Tim Roth, Paul Rhys, Jip Wijngaarden, Johanna Ter Steege, Wladimir Yordanoff, Jean-Pierre Cassel, Bernadette Giraud, Adrian Brine, Yves Dangerfield, Jean-Francois Perrier, Hans Kesting, Peter Tuinman, Marie Louise Stheins, Oda Spelbos, Anne Canovas; **w**, Julian Mitchell; **c**, Jean Lupine; **m**, Gabriel Yared; **ed**, Francoise Coispeau, Geraldine Peroni; **prod d**, Stephen Altman; **spec eff**, Matthew Altman, Olivier De Laveleye.

The Violent Men ★★★ 1955; U.S.; 96m; COL; Color Western; Children: Unacceptable; **DVD**; **VHS**; **IV**. Top-drawer western sees Robinson as a crippled Texas rancher ruthlessly taking the land of smaller ranchers and farmers with the aid of his equally ruthless wife, Stanwyck, and crooked brother, Keith, who serves as Robinson's gunman enforcer. Robinson is too obsessed with building an empire to realize that Stanwyck and Keith are lovers. Living in the area is Ford, a former Union officer in the American Civil War (1861-1865), who has become a pacifist. He plans to sell his ranch to Robinson and move East with his fiancée, Wynn, but Robinson's offer is too low. Wynn then leaves Ford because he is unwilling to fight Robinson. Ford decides to keep his ranch, because of Robinson's bullying and high-pressuring. When one of Ford's ranch hands is shot dead by Jaeckel, who is one of Robinson's gunmen, Ford finally stands up against Robinson by fatally shooting Jaeckel. Ford then causes fires and horse stampedes on Robinson's land, and, during an ambush, Stanwyck and Keith are both killed. Robinson sees his ranch and home destroyed by Ford and his dreams of being a land baron go up literally in smoke. Ford, meanwhile, has fallen in love with Robinson's daughter, Foster, and they will marry and live on his ranch. Ford, Stanwyck, Robinson and Keith render strong performances under Mate's steady direction, and the director presents some finely orchestrated action scenes, particularly where Ford's men ambush the small army Keith leads to destroy them. *Author's Note*: Stanwyck told this author that "**The Violent Men** was a pleasure to make with Rudy [Rudolph Mate], who began as a cinematographer working in Europe with Karl Freund and Alexander Korda. He was the photographer who shot **Stella Dallas** [1937], and where he captured some of the best scenes I ever had in any picture. He had an unerring eye in framing a good dramatic or action shot and that made him a double threat as a director. The best directors know what the camera can do and not do, and Rudy was one of those." Ford told this author that "I was up against a

Glenn Ford and Warner Anderson in *The Violent Men*, 1955.

master actor in my scenes with Eddie [Robinson]. I knew I could never take any scene from him as his intensity and concentration is always there in every scene. So I underplayed my scenes with him to make him appear the aggressor, which is really the character he played, a ruthless cattle baron." Robinson told this author that "I appeared in that picture as a replacement. Broderick Crawford was actually playing the cattle baron when they began shooting **The Violent Men**, but he fell from a horse and was so badly injured that he could not continue, so they asked me to take over the part. Oddly enough, I am playing an invalid, who has to move around on crutches from an injury gotten years earlier, so it looks like I was the one who fell off the horse, not Brod [Broderick Crawford]." Keith recalled this film when telling this author that "**The Violent Men** was one of three pictures I appeared in and were released in the same year, 1955, and I played the heavy in all three. I played a treacherous brother having an affair with Babs [Stanwyck] behind Eddie Robinson's back in **The Violent Men**. Then, in my next picture that year [**Tight Spot**, 1955], I played a corrupt cop who arranges the murder of Ginger Rogers, a woman he is supposed to protect. In the picture after that one [**5 against the House**, 1955], I played a psychopath who tries to rob a Las Vegas casino. I was getting a lot of work, but I was getting damned nervous about being typecast as a villain." **p**, Lewis J. Rachmil; **d**, Rudolph Mate; **cast**, Glenn Ford, Barbara Stanwyck, Edward G. Robinson, Dianne Foster, Brian Keith, May Wynn, Warner Anderson, Basil Ruysdael, Lita Milan, Richard Jaeckel, Jack Kelly, Harry Shannon, Richard Farnsworth; **w**, Harry Kleiner (based on the novel *Rough Company* by Donald Hamilton); **c**, W. Howard Greene, Burnett Guffey (CinemaScope; Technicolor); **m**, Max Steiner; **ed**, Jerome Thoms; **art d**, Carl Anderson, Ross Bellah; **set d**, Louis Diage.

Violent Saturday ★★★ 1955; 91m; FOX; Color; Crime Drama; Children: Unacceptable; **BD**; **DVD**; **VHS**; **IV**. A small mining town in Arizona is the objective of three hardened criminals, Naish, McNally and Marvin, who plays a Benzedrine-sniffing addict. After checking into a local hotel, the three men methodically plan to rob the local bank on the forthcoming Saturday. McNally, the point man, poses as a traveling salesman while Naish spends his time reading books and the sadistic Marvin looks about for some excitement. The town thrives from a successful copper mining operation run by workaholic Egan whose sexy wife, Hayes, routinely cheats on him between golf outings, her present beau being the arrogant Dexter. Although Egan loves Hayes, he takes to drink over his wife's flagrant and widely known affairs, and thinks of having his own affair with alluring nurse Leith, who is attracted to him but keeps her distance. Mature, who is an engineer working with Egan, has his own problems with his son, who thinks that Mature is a coward since he did not fight in WWII (1939-1945) as have most of the

Richard Egan and Victor Mature in *Violent Saturday*, 1955.

men in the town. Meanwhile, Sidney, who is the local librarian, is about to lose her house when she cannot make a mortgage payment. Fate provides unsavory relief when a library patron mistakenly leaves her purse behind and the desperate Sidney steals it, taking the money she finds to make a payment on her mortgage. When Sidney goes to deposit the stolen money at the local bank, Noonan, its manager, discovers her theft. Sidney, however, pressures Noonan into silence by threatening him with his own moral misconduct as Sidney has earlier discovered that Noonan is a Peeping Tom, who has been ogling Leith while she undresses in her room. On the Friday night before the thieves plan to rob the bank, the crooks go to a local bar for some relaxation. They see wealthy Egan drowning his sorrows with Leith. Egan makes a feeble attempt to seduce Leith, which she tolerates out of affection. When Egan gets drunk, Leith takes him home and puts him to bed. As Leith is leaving, Hayes arrives from one of her nightly trysts and Leith warns the cuckolding Hayes that she had better behave as a decent wife or that she will soon be losing her devoted husband. Hayes and Egan later argue about Hayes' infidelities and Egan's attraction to Leith, but Egan then realizes that he has caused his wife to seek affection elsewhere by placing his business before his marriage. They resolve their differences and decide to make a go of their union, planning on a vacation together. To obtain traveler's checks for that trip, Hayes goes to the local bank the next Saturday morning, and Sidney, too, has arrived at the bank to make her mortgage payment. Just that moment, McNally, Naish and Marvin enter the bank and hold it up, but Noonan, showing courage for the first time in his sneaky life, retrieves a weapon to prevent the robbery. A wild gunfight ensues where Noonan is wounded and Hayes is killed outright in the crossfire. In making their escape, the three robbers overwhelm Mature, taking him and his car and driving wildly into the countryside where they turn in at an Amish farm operated by Borgnine. The thieves bind Mature and Borgnine, along with Borgnine's family members, some of whom break their bounds. Mature asks farmer Borgnine to help him overcome the lethal robbers, but he tells him that his religion prohibits him from bringing about any violence. Mature is able to dispatch one of the thieves, and Borgnine goes to his assistance after one of his children is accidentally shot by one of the other two robbers. Mature eliminates one of the remaining two killers while Borgnine, grabbing a pitchfork, drives the implement into the other. Mature returns to his family where his son now sees his father as a hero while the traumatized Borgnine wrestles with his guilt over violating his pacifist scruples. Leith gives comfort to Egan while he mourns over his loss of Hayes and it appears that they will see a life together as this grim and uncompromising film ends. Fleischer does a marvelous job weaving all of the story's subplots into a complete fabric, culminated by the chaotic bank robbery and where all the cast members convincingly portray their col-

orful characters, Sidney, Borgnine and Marvin being standouts. Friedhofer's strident score perfectly emphasizes the mounting suspense so expertly created by Fleischer as he unfolds this tale of small-town inhabitants suddenly attempting to survive the life-claiming violence of ruthless intruders. The story is really a series of good character studies where all are at hazard and everyone has a hidden agenda beyond the calculating killers. The film earned more than $1.2 million in its initial release against a budget of more than $900,000. ***Author's Note***: Fleischer told this author that he thought "**Violent Saturday** was really a western story upgraded to a modern setting where three robbers appear like a tornado to tear up the lives of those living in a small town." Mature told this author: "My character in that picture did not call for me to act, only react to three thugs who shoot up a bank and take me hostage. This guy thinks he is going to be killed, so he fights for his life and is lucky enough to take out some of the bad guys. That makes him a hero to his son, but he is not a hero, only a guy trying to stay alive." Sidney did not like her character, telling this author: "There was something cynical about my character, a sweet little old lady who runs the library, but who turns thief to keep her house. A lot of women go through life living with desperation, but they do not become crooks. When I was younger, I played women of virtue, who had noble natures. Age wears everything down, even what you believe in most." Borgnine had no illusions about his character, telling this author that "I know the Amish are non-violent and my character is the same, but he is a man and a father after all. When some killer shoots one of his kids, he does what any man would do—he goes after the man who injured his child. That's where basic instinct, not religion, takes over." Marvin remembered this film as "another picture where I play a wacko druggie, who lives to hurt others, pretty much the same kind of character I played a year earlier in **The Raid** [1954]. In that one, I almost botch up a bank robbery during the Civil War [1861-1865] after I drink some of the liquid fire the raiders use to torch a small town in Vermont. My character in **Violent Saturday** is just as untrustworthy, but he is also outright stupid and I had to ask myself why any professional bank robbers would take along such a looney on a heist. Dillinger would have dropped a goofball like that into a lake before taking him on a job. I mentioned that to Dick [Fleischer] and he said: 'You're playing a mindless goon, who is needed for brute force backup, that's all.' Okay, I gave Dick the best goon I could dream up." **p**, Buddy Adler; **d**, Richard Fleischer; **cast**, Victor Mature, Richard Egan, Stephen McNally, Virginia Leith, Tommy Noonan, Lee Marvin, Margaret Hayes, J. Carrol Naish, Sylvia Sidney, Ernest Borgnine, Dorothy Patrick, Brad Dexter, Billy Chapin, Raymond Greenleaf, Donald Gamble, Robert Adler, Richey Murray, Noreen Corcoran, Ann Morrison, Kevin Corcoran, Noreen Corcoran; **w**, Sydney Boehm (based on the novel by William L. Heath); **c**, Charles G. Clarke (CinemaScope; DeLuxe Color); **m**, Hugo Friedhofer; **ed**, Louis Loeffler; **art d**, Lyle Wheeler, George W. Davis; **set d**, Walter M. Scott, Chester Bayhi; **spec eff**, Ray Kellogg.

Violette ★★★ 1978; France/Canada; 124m; Filmel/Cinevideo/New Yorker Films; Color; Crime Drama; Children: Unacceptable; **BD**; **DVD**. Absorbing tale offers a well-acted biopic based on the life of murderess Violette Nozière (1915-1966), superbly played by Huppert. She is an eighteen-year-old Frenchwoman living with her parents in a small apartment in Paris in 1933 when she attempts to kill them by lacing their drinks with a lethal dose of barbiturates. Her father dies after consuming his drink, but her mother survives after only drinking half of her glass. When arrested, Huppert tells police that her father had been raping her since she was twelve years old and that her mother knew about the incestuous transgressions, but did nothing to stop him. She gets no sympathy for the alleged sexual abuse from anyone, including the public and the press. The judge at her trial cautions jurors that Huppert was promiscuous and known to be an incorrigible liar. Jurors find her guilty of murder and she is sentenced to life imprisonment, but is released in 1945 and dies in 1966. The attractive Huppert renders a cold-blooded essay of her character, which is in keeping with the actual personality of this calculating killer. This film was remade in 2013. *Author's Note*: Violette Noziere (January 11, 1915-November 26, 1966) poisoned her father, Jean-Baptiste Noziere, with veronal, on August 21, 1933. She was convicted and sentenced to death on October 13, 1934, but her sentence was commuted to life imprisonment on December 24, 1934. She was released on August 29, 1945. See my profile of her in *Look for the Woman* (M. Evans, 1981; pages 312-313). **p**, Denis Heroux, Eugene Lepicier **d**, Claude Chabrol; **cast**, Isabelle Huppert, Stephane Audran, Jean Carmet, Jean-Francois Gerreaud, Guy Hoffmann, Jean Dalmain, Lisa Langlois, Francois Maistre, Philippe Procot, Mario David; **w**, Odile Barski, Herve Bromberger, Frederic Grendel (based on the book by Jean-Marie Fritere); **c**, Jean Rabier; **m**, Pierre Jansen; **ed**, Yves Langlois; **prod d**, Jacques Brizzio; **set d**, Robert Christides.

The Virgin Queen ★★★ 1955; U.S.; 92m; FOX; Color; Biographical Drama; Children: Unacceptable; **DVD**; **VHS**. Rousing biopic shows the tempestuous relationship between Elizabeth I of England (1533-1603), wonderfully played by Davis, and her most mercurial and ambitious courtier, Sir Walter Raleigh (1554-1618), played with gusto by Todd. This intriguing story opens in 1581 when Todd compels the patrons of a rural pub to move a carriage mired in deep mud on the nearby road. The carriage belongs to Marshall, who is playing Robert Dudley, Earl of Leicester (1532-1588), and who is Davis' most trusted adviser. When Marshall asks Todd how he can repay his service, Todd requests that Marshall introduce him to Davis. Marshall agrees. Todd greatly impresses Davis when meeting her as he speaks plainly and without any personal agendas, all of which is refreshing to a queen surrounded by conspiratorial advisers, such as Douglas, who takes an immediate dislike to Todd. When Davis and her retinue leave the throne room to venture into a courtyard, Davis is met with a large puddle. Todd (as did Raleigh in a celebrated gesture of grand chivalry), withdraws his elegant cape (borrowed from a London tailor) to place over the puddle so that Davis can walk safely to dry ground. Todd then tells Davis of his dream to sail a British fleet to the New World, so that he can glean its riches for England. Kindling this thought, Davis appoints Todd as captain of her private guards and Todd then makes O'Herlihy, an Irish nobleman, his second-in-command. This appointment not only irks Douglas, but Robinson, who is another courtier advising the Queen, especially since Robinson urged Davis not to make that appointment. Meanwhile, Collins, who plays Elizabeth Throgmorton (1565-c.1647), one of Davis' ladies-in-waiting, is attracted to the dashing Todd, and he reciprocates her subtle advances as they develop a deep love for each other. Collins is jealous of every attention Todd pays to Davis while Davis becomes more and more irritated with Todd's incessant talk about sailing to the New World. Further, Douglas informs Davis that Todd has given a post in the guards to O'Herlihy, saying that, as an Irishman, he cannot be trusted and is most likely plotting against the throne. An apprehensive Davis orders Todd to dismiss O'Herlihy, but Todd refuses, insisting that O'Herlihy is loyal to her. For his stubborn refusal, Davis strips Todd of his captaincy of the guards and banishes him from the court. While away from the court, Todd and Collins secretly marry without informing Davis. Meanwhile, Davis reconsiders her treatment of Todd and recalls him back to duty where she not only makes him a knight (as Sir Walter Raleigh), but tells him that she will not give the three ships he wants to sail to the New Land, but will allow him one vessel to make that expedition. The ecstatic Todd equips and supplies that ship while it is at harbor, but Collins then overhears Davis saying that, although she has granted Todd a ship, she will not actually allow him to sail from England. Todd then makes plans to sail to North America without notifying Davis. Then Douglas learns of Todd's intentions and informs Davis, along with telling her that her favorite has also wedded Collins in a clandestine marriage. Davis is enraged at the thought that Collins did not seek her obligatory permission to wed anyone, let alone a man Davis jealously promoted to a high position. She considers both Todd and Collins traitors and orders their arrest. Learning of this, Todd sends

Richard Todd as Sir Walter Raleigh and Joan Collins as Lady Throgmorton in *The Virgin Queen*, **1955.**

Collins with O'Herlihy, ordering his friend to take Collins to Ireland where she will be safe and beyond the wrathful reach of Davis. Troops, however, find O'Herlihy and Collins on a lonely road, and O'Herlihy is killed while defending Collins. She is arrested as is Todd and both are placed in the Tower of London to await execution. Davis, however, pays a visit to Todd's cell before his execution (as Davis did when playing Elizabeth I in **The Private Lives of Elizabeth and Essex**, 1939, where she attempted to prevent the death of her lover, Essex, played by Errol Flynn, one she had herself decreed). Davis' heart softens when she realizes that Todd has loved her as a queen but never a woman and that he married the woman he loved, Collins. She rescinds her death decree and allows Todd and Collins to sail on for the New World, but only on the promise that Todd returns with the great wealth he has promised to acquire for England. Koster directs this historical saga with considerable skill in compressing a rather complex story into a reasonable chronology, and Davis is a superb Elizabeth while Todd presents a powerful portrait of the chivalric Raleigh. The film received an Oscar nomination for Best Costume Design (Charles LeMaire, Mary Wills). It did well at the box office, recouping its considerable budget of more than $1.6 million. *Author's Note*: Davis told this author that "I had not played Elizabeth for sixteen years, ever since we made that other picture with Errol Flynn [**The Private Lives of Elizabeth and Essex**], and I think age gave me a deeper understanding of that woman. She was older than Raleigh, in middle age, when she was taken with that dashing cavalier. That is the way I played her—a lonesome woman, who is suspicious of everyone. She wants only to be loved and knows all of her courtiers are mostly liars, and that makes her sometimes mean. Elizabeth was a very vulnerable woman, but she knew she had to be foremost and always the queen. That was my posture when we made **The Virgin Queen**." Davis had the script altered so that her part was considerably enlarged, but she only worked for sixteen days during the film's production, although she seems to be everywhere throughout its scenes. She shaved two inches of hair from her forehead to show that Elizabeth was bald beneath the many wigs she wore and powdered her face so thickly that she sometimes appears to be anemic or drained of blood, which was the very complexion Elizabeth possessed. Marshall, who plays Davis' most trusted adviser, told this author: "No actress up to the time of that picture ever played Elizabeth more impressively and with such authority than Bette. Flora Robson came close when she appeared in **The Sea Hawk** [1940] with Errol Flynn, but Bette's startling performance made Elizabeth a woman who was very human, someone you could love or even hate. Evoking that kind of passion about a character is the test of great acting." Historical facts were condensed and even altered to fit the story line of this film. Elizabeth I has been profiled by many other actresses in many other films, including **Border Warfare**, 1990 (made-for-TV;

Birgitta Pettersson, center, in *The Virgin Spring*, 1960.

Juliet Cadzow); **Dorothy Vernon of Haddon Hall**, 1924 (Clare Eames); **Drake the Pirate**, 1936 (Athene Seyler); **Drake's Venture**, 1980 (made-for-TV; Charlotte Cornwell); **Elizabeth**, 1998 (Cate Blanchett); **Elizabeth R**, 1971-1972 (TV miniseries; six episodes: Glenda Jackson); **Elizabeth Rex**, 2004 (made-for-TV; Diane D'Aquila); **Elizabeth: The Golden Age**, 2007 (Cate Blanchett); **Elizabeth the Queen**, 1968 (made-for-TV; Judith Anderson); **The Eternal Strife**, 1915 (Maud Yates); **Fire over England**, 1937 (Flora Robson); **Gloriana**, 1984 (made-for-TV; Sarah Walker); **Gloriana**, 2000 (made-for-TV; Josephine Barstow); **Gunpowder, Treason & Plot**, 2004 (made-for-TV; Catherine McCormack); **The Heart of the Queen**, 1940 (Maria Koppenhofer); **Henry VIII**, 2003 (made-for-TV; Lorna Lacey); **The Hourglass Sanatorium**, 1973 (Zofia Bajuk); **I Married an Angel**, 1942 (Edwina Coolidge); **Jubilee**, 1978 (Jenny Runacre); **Loves and Adventures in the Life of Shakespeare**, 1914 (Aimee Martinek); **Mary of Scotland**, 1936 (Florence Eldridge); **Mary Stuart**, 1982 (made-for-TV; Rosalind Plowright); **O Principe E o Mendigo**, 1972 (TV series: Adriana de Goes; Suzana Goncalves); **The Other Boleyn Girl**, 2008 (Maisie Smith); **The Pearls of the Crown**, 1938 (Yvette Pienne); **The Prince and the Pauper**, 1977 (Lalla Ward); **The Prince and the Pauper**, 1996 (TV series; six episodes: Elizabeth Ann O'Brien); **The Private Lives of Elizabeth and Essex**, 1939 (Bette Davis); **Queen Elizabeth**, 1912 (Sarah Bernhardt); **The Queen's Traitor**, 1967 (TV series; Susan Engel); **Regal Cavalcade**, 1935 (Athene Seyler); **The Sea Hawk**, 1940 (Flora Robson); **Seven Seas to Calais**, 1963 (Irene Worth); **Shirley Temple's Storybook**, 1958-1960 (TV series; "The Prince and the Pauper," 1960 episode: Portland Mason); **The Story of Mankind**, 1957 (Agnes Moorehead); **Time Flies**, 1944 (Olga Lindo); **Tower of London**, 1939 (Barbara O'Neil); **The Tudors**, 2007-2010 (TV series; Laoise Murray; Claire Macaulay; Kate Dugan); **The Virgin Queen**, 1923 (Diana Manners); **The Virgin Queen**, 2005 (TV miniseries; Anne-Marie Duff); and **Young Bess**, 1953 (Jean Simmons). **p**, Charles Brackett; **d**, Henry Koster; **cast**, Bette Davis, Richard Todd, Joan Collins, Jay Robinson, Herbert Marshall, Dan O'Herlihy, Robert Douglas, Terence de Marney, Patrick O'Moore, Rod Taylor; **w**, Harry Brown, Mindret Lord (based on Brown's story "Sir Walter Raleigh"); **c**, Charles G. Clarke (CinemaScope; DeLuxe Color); **m**, Franz Waxman; **ed**, Robert Simpson; **art d**, Lyle Wheeler, Leland Fuller; **set d**, Walter M. Scott, Paul S. Fox; **spec eff**, Ray Kellogg.

The Virgin Spring ★★★ 1960; Sweden; 88m; Svensk Filmindustri; Janus Films; B/W; Drama; Children: Unacceptable; **DVD**; **VHS**; **IV**. This dire and chilling film from pantheon director Bergman presents a heavy-handed medieval saga of rape, murder and revenge. Set in 14th-Century Sweden, Christianity struggles against the ancient pagan faiths of its more uneducated inhabitants clinging to their heathen practices and superstitions. Sydow is a wealthy landowner and devout Christian, who has, along with his wife, Valberg, spoiled their virginal fifteen-year-old daughter Pettersson. She has been planning to attend a far-off church where she is to light candles before the statue of the Virgin Mary and asks permission from Sydow if she can wear a special gown reportedly sewn by fifteen virgins. Pettersson further implores Sydow if Lindblom, her half sister, can accompany her on this sacred mission. The overindulgent Sydow can deny Pettersson nothing and agrees. Lindblom, who is secretly pregnant, is permitted to accompany Pettersson, but is jealous of the attentions and favors Pettersson enjoys. Moreover, Lindblom nurtures another hidden agenda in that she secretly worships the pagan god Odin. The two girls ride horses toward the church, reaching a bridge at the edge of a forest. Slangus, an enigmatic, one-eyed bridge keeper, greets them, and after Lindblom asks his name, he cryptically replies: "None in these days." He invites the girls to stay at his hut to rest, but Pettersson declines and proceeds into the forest while Lindblom remains with Slangus. The strange bridge keeper tells her that he can see things others cannot, intriguing her. When he makes some lewd advances toward her in a clumsy attempt to seduce her, Lindblom, terrified, flees. Meanwhile, Pettersson encounters three herdsmen in the forest, two men, Duberg and Isedal, and a boy, Porath. She invites them to share her lunch. Watching them from behind some trees is Lindblom, who has followed Pettersson, but she does not join the group. Duberg and Isedal then sexually attack Pettersson, brutally raping her while Porath regretfully watches and, helpless, does nothing to aid Pettersson. Lindblom, too, watches the assault from afar, becoming excited, as if enjoying the attack on the half sister she has jealously envied all her life. Pettersson cries bitter tears, and Duberg and Isedal realize that they cannot leave her live to later testify against them so they beat her to death with a heavy stick. They then strip the elegant gown from her, departing with it to see if they can sell it. Irony, always at the core of Bergman's films, finds the herders at the very door of Sydow's home where they are given shelter and food, and where they are also allowed to sleep in a shed. In the middle of the night, Porath, who is haunted by Pettersson's death, yells out while having a nightmare and Valberg goes to investigate. She sees Porath with the gown her daughter has worn, but Porath insists that the garment belongs to his sister. Valberg goes to Sydow, telling him about her discovery and then Lindblom arrives to weep and describe how Pettersson had been violated and killed. The enraged Sydow grabs a long knife and goes to the shed where he kills all three herders, stabbing one to death and strangling the other two. He and Valberg are then led by Lindblom to the woods where they find the naked body of their daughter. Sydow begins to lose his faith in God, asking how such a thing could be permitted by the Almighty. Sydow nevertheless regains his faith, begs forgiveness for taking vengeance upon his daughter's killers, and swears that he will build a church on the spot where Pettersson has died. As he lifts her corpse to his bosom, a spring miraculously erupts on that very spot to end the film. As is the case with all of Bergman's films, the cast members render their characters with stoic performances, so detached as to seem bloodless and without genuine compassion. Sydow is riveting as a forceful, powerful patriarch, and the sweet Pettersson is wonderfully empathetic as the naïve daughter. They, however, like all the other characters, act as automatons oblivious to the normal hazards of that crude era while mindlessly inviting carnage and chaos. The illogical hole in this tale, and it is a gaping one, is that no overly protective and wise father as Sydow portrays, would allow his cherished daughters to ride alone unescorted and unprotected through a dangerous countryside he knows is rife with primitive and brutish denizens. Bergman expects, even demands, that the viewer abandon that logic in order to allow his gruesome tale to unfold. Further, he dwells upon the sexual assault to the point of making it embarrassingly gratuitous, and thus artfully compels the viewer in this much too overlong sequence to unexpectedly share in the perverse actions of the assailants. In accepting the carefully engineered art of Ingmar Bergman, one must accept the bad with the good, and some of it is bad in this obsessive, if not insidious, folktale turned nightmare. To be sure, the director's masterful techniques, his fluid camera, arresting set-ups and distorted angles are in impressive evidence throughout this film. However, that little offsets the emotionally disturbing nature of the daughter's viciously construed plight, wherein an inescapable and unsavory element of visual sadism seeps into every frame to seemingly celebrate the victimization of this young girl. To somehow remove the stain of her violation, Bergman conveniently redeems with meandering mea culpa her savage fate. He anoints her with some sort of grassroots sainthood with a revitalizing spring of pure water gushing from the earth where she was raped and murdered. One might think that Bergman was mindful of the moving scene where a young French girl claws a pure spring from the earth at the urging of a spiritual visitor in the classic film **The Song of Bernadette**, 1943. Although this production won an Oscar as Best Foreign Film, its grim and morose story was not popular at the box office, earning less than $700,000 when first released. (In Swedish; English subtitles.) **p**, Ingmar Bergman, Allan Ekelund; **d**, Bergman; **cast**, Max von Sydow, Birgitta Pettersson, Gunnel Lindblom, Birgitta Valberg, Axel Duberg, Tor Isedal, Allan Edwall, Ove Porath, Axel Slangus, Gudrun Brost; **w**, Ulla Isaksson (based on the 14th-Century ballad "Tores Dotter I Vange"); **c**, Sven Nykvist; **m**, Erik Nordgren; **ed**, Oscar Rosander; **art d**, P.A. Lundgren.

Virginia City ★★★★ 1940; U.S.; 121m; WB; B/W; Western; Children: Unacceptable; **DVD**; **VHS**. Superb western with fine performances from Flynn, Scott and Hopkins is set during the American Civil War (1861-1865) and begins in the musty, dank cells of Libby Prison in Richmond, Virginia. Flynn, a captured Union officer, is shown with two of his men, Hale and Williams, attempting to dig their way to freedom. Their efforts are met with failure, however, when they emerge from their tunneling to find Scott, a Confederate officer, waiting for them with a unit of armed guards. They are returned to their cells, but Flynn vows to escape. Flynn and his two companions later manage to escape and make their way back to Union lines where Flynn is given a new assignment. Hall, who plays Union General George Meade (1815-1872), orders Flynn to travel to Virginia City, Nevada, a booming gold mining town. Flynn is to identify and prevent a number of Rebel sympathizers from shipping more than $5 million in gold to Texas and then on to Richmond to aid the sagging economy of the Confederacy. While traveling by stagecoach toward his destination, Flynn meets and begins a romance with fellow passenger, Hopkins, an attractive and cultured lady. Unknown to Flynn is the fact that Hopkins is not only Scott's fiancée, but she is a Southern spy, sent on orders from Confederate President Jefferson Davis (1808-1889), played by Middleton, to aid the Rebels in Virginia City and learn of any Union plans to stop that gold shipment. Also traveling on the stagecoach is Bogart, who claims that he is a traveling gun salesman, but he is, in reality, the notorious bandit John Murrell. Bogart (who wears an uncustomary pencil mustache) actually intends to rob the passengers of the coach with some cohorts, but Flynn becomes suspicious of his actions and turns the tables on the bandit. Bogart, however, manages to make an escape. When Flynn arrives in Virginia City, he is surprised to see Scott, who tells him that he received a wound in battle and is no longer active in the war, a lie Flynn does not believe. Flynn is further surprised to see that the woman he loves is not what she seemed to be when Hopkins appears on stage as a singing showgirl, displaying her (rather knock kneed) legs as she dances with a bevy of chorus girls. Flynn, accompanied by his old companions Hale and Williams, then begin searching the town. They follow Scott to a blacksmith's stable where the gold is being loaded into the false bottoms of covered wagons that leave just as Flynn and his companions arrive. A shootout ensues, but Scott escapes to the home of a physician, Olsen, one of the Southern ringleaders. The bandit Bogart arrives, asking that Olsen set his broken arm, and Scott then offers Bogart $10,000 for him and his men to attack the Union garrison as a diversion that will allow

Miriam Hopkins and Errol Flynn in *Virginia City,* 1940.

the wagon train to depart Virginia City undetected. Scott then uses Hopkins to lure Flynn to Olsen's home where Flynn is captured and held prisoner. Scott takes him along as the wagon train leaves the town just as Bogart and his men make their attack, planning to return Flynn to Libby Prison once he and the Southerners reach Richmond. Flynn now feels betrayed by the woman he loves, and Hopkins is distressed at having hoodwinked the man she has come to also love. The wagon train moves southeastward toward Texas, but is stopped at a Union outpost. When some soldiers insist on searching one of the wagons, a gunfight breaks out and the Federal troops are shot down, but Flynn leaps onto a horse in the confusion and flees with Scott and others in hot pursuit. Flynn, in trying to escape, rides his horse down a steep ridge, but the animal stumbles and Flynn is thrown to land unconscious. Scott and others think him dead and ride off. Once Flynn returns to the outpost, he sends a message by wire to Union commander Dumbrille, who responds by leading his troops to the outpost. Once Dumbrille arrives, Flynn explains that Scott and the Southerners are heading for Texas with gold for the Confederacy and Dumbrille orders a pursuit. Dumbrille, however, fails to heed Flynn's advice in tracking the Rebels and loses track of the wagon train. Flynn then persuades Dumbrille to give him a small detachment so that he can follow his instincts as to the direction the wagon train has most likely taken. Dumbrille heads his main force in another direction. Meanwhile, the Southerners battle wind storms and suffer thirst for lack of water as they meet one dried-up water hole after another along their perilous trek. Worse, the Southerners are then met by Bogart and his bandits, who suspect that the wagon train is carrying riches and, when Scott refuses to turn over its treasure, the horde of outlaws attack the wagon train. Flynn, however, arrives to see the circled train under attack and rides to the side of the Southerners with his small detachment, while sending a rider to Drumbrille to bring on the main Union force. Flynn and his few Union troopers help the Rebels beat back Bogart and his men, but Scott is mortally wounded in one of the bandit assaults. Flynn is with Scott just before he dies, and Scott begs him to preserve the gold, which honestly belongs to the Southern-born miners. Scott knows that the South will lose the war, and that its crippled economy will sorely need the gold to rebuild following the war. Before Scott dies, the noble Flynn promises that he will preserve the gold for the South. As night falls, Flynn and a few others move the gold from the wagons and hide it in a remote canyon. The following day, Bogart and his men resume their attack, but, just as they are about to overwhelm the Southerners, Dumbrille arrives with his Union troopers and attack the bandits. Bogart is shot and killed from his horse as he attempts to flee and the remainder of the outlaws are also killed or driven off. Dumbrille then asks Flynn about the gold, but Flynn refuses to identify its whereabouts. The enraged Dumbrille orders Flynn to stand a court mar-

Humphrey Bogart and Randolph Scott in *Virginia City*, 1940.

tial where he again refuses to pinpoint the location of the gold, saying that it will be needed after the war to rebuild the shattered South. He is convicted of treason and sentenced to be executed on April 9, 1865. A day before Flynn is scheduled to die, Hopkins, still desperately in love with Flynn, manages to get an appointment with President Abraham Lincoln (1809-1865), who is played by Kilian (shown only from the back and part of his profile). Kilian tells Hopkins that General U.S. Grant (1822-1885) and General Robert E. Lee (1807-1870) are at that very moment ending the war at Appomattox Court House, and, as an act of conciliation toward the South, he pardons Flynn, uttering the words of this second inauguration: "With malice toward none; with charity for all…" Flynn and Hopkins are then shown together as they are making their way westward to begin a new life together. Action director Curtiz presents a fast-moving story with many exciting scenes as he carefully unfolds the plot and well develops its characters, strongly supported by another dynamic and memorable score from the gifted Steiner. Flynn, Scott and Hopkins are standouts in their roles, albeit Bogart is somewhat miscast as a slippery bandit using a suspicious Mexican accent. The film did very well at the box office, earning more than $2 million against a budget of less than $1 million. A sixty-minute radio adaptation of this story was aired by Lux Radio Theater on May 26, 1941, with Flynn reprising his role. Songs: "The Battle Hymn of the Republic" (music [1856]: William Steffe; lyrics [1862]: Julia Ward Howe), "(I Wish I Was in) Dixie's Land" (1860; Daniel Decatur Emmett), "We Will Hang Jeff Davis to a Sour Apple Tree" (sung to the melody of "The Battle Hymn of the Republic"), "The Battle Cry of Freedom" (1862; George Frederick Root), "Oh! Susanna" (1846; Stephen Foster), "Can-Can" (composer unknown), "Kingdom Coming" (aka: "The Year of Jubilo"; 1862; Henry Clay Work), "Little Brown Jug" (1869; Joseph Winner), "The Captain with His Whiskers" (1820; music: Sidney Nelson; lyrics: Thomas Haynes Bayley). *Author's Note*: There was trouble with this production right from the beginning when it went into on-location production at Flagstaff, Arizona. Screenwriter Koch told this author that "the script [his first involving a feature film] was not complete when Curtiz began shooting. We [he, Buckner and Raine] were still working out scenes and toying with different endings and all of that drove Errol [Flynn] crazy. He did not get along well with Curtiz, as they had had falling outs in previous pictures they did together, especially over the dangerous stunts Curtiz forced Flynn to perform. Both spent their time shouting at each other until Flynn sent a wire to Hal B. Wallis, who headed production at Warner Brothers, to complain about the delay. Then Curtiz sent a wire to Wallis complaining about Flynn's obstreperous conduct, accusing Flynn of acting like a Nazi storm trooper. Oh, it was a donnybrook right from the start." Wallis finally wired back to Flynn: "Will show you [completed] copy [of the script]

just as soon as [it is] ready. Thanks, old fellow. Keep up the good work." Scott told this author that "I got along all right with Errol [Flynn], but he was aggravated over production delays in that picture and then got very upset when Olivia de Havilland, who was to play the leading lady, dropped out, and was replaced by Brenda Marshall. She, too, dropped out, and Miriam Hopkins took the part, which then upset Curtiz, as he thought Miriam acted like a prima donna, although I never saw any evidence of that. Bogey [Bogart], who played a bandit in the picture, hated his role. He got that part by default when Victor Jory, who was slated to play the bandit leader, was scratched, and Bogart replaced him. To show his disgust for his character, Bogey caricatured his part with one of the worst Mexican accents I have ever heard. I think he did that on purpose to ridicule his own part and everyone else. He was sullen and unfriendly throughout the shooting out there in Flagstaff and, unfortunately, none of us got along with old Bogey." Bogart's role as John Murrell (1806-1844) is in error in that Murrell died a decade before the Civil War began and never operated in the Far West, but preyed upon travelers along the Mississippi River. The weather in Flagstaff during the six-week production presented several rainstorms, which caused Flynn to become ill, and he complained about not being able to sleep at night as he fought off colds. One of the most convivial members of the cast was stuntman Yakima Canutt, who performs some spectacular feats in this film, enacting the amazing somersault for Flynn from his horse when Flynn is being pursued down that steep ridge, and, later, in the wild wagon rush where Canutt falls between the runaway horses of one racing covered wagon when the bandits attack and where the wheels of that wagon (shot at low angle) almost crush him. He then amazingly hauls himself upward onto the wagon's tailgate, the same eye-popping stunt Canutt had performed for John Ford in the classic **Stagecoach**, 1939. Canutt was also an assistant director of note, who organized many mass cavalry vs. Indian charges in westerns and is best remembered for choreographing the spectacular chariot race in William Wyler's biblical epic, **Ben-Hur**, 1959. Burly character actor Williams plays one of Flynn's two sidekicks in this film, as does the equally brawny Hale, in **Dodge City**, 1939, and **Santa Fe Trail**, 1940. Williams became one of Flynn's closest friends and drinking buddies and served as one of the pallbearers (along with Mickey Rooney, Raoul Walsh, Otto Reichow, Mike Romanoff and Jack Oakie) at Flynn's Forest Lawn funeral in Glendale, California, on October 19, 1959. Other films showing Confederates operating in the Far West during the American Civil War include **Arizona**, 1940; **Escape from Fort Bravo**, 1953; **The Good, the Bad and the Ugly**, 1966; **Kansas Raiders**, 1950; **Last Stand at Saber River**, 1997 (made-for-TV); **The Outriders**, 1950; **Ride with the Devil**, 1999; **Rocky Mountain**, 1950 (also starring Flynn, but this time as a Rebel officer); **Siege at Red River**, 1952; **Springfield Rifle**, 1952; **A Time for Killing**, 1967; and **Two Flags West**, 1950. **p**, Robert Fellows; **d**, Michael Curtiz; **cast**, Errol Flynn, Miriam Hopkins, Randolph Scott, Humphrey Bogart, Frank McHugh, Alan Hale, Guinn "Big Boy" Williams, John Litel, Douglass Dumbrille, Moroni Olsen, Dickie Jones, George Reeves, Russell Simpson, Victor Kilian, Charles Middleton, Ward Bond; **w**, Robert Buckner, (not credited) Norman Reilly Raine, Howard Koch); **c**, Sol Polito; **m**, Max Steiner; **ed**, George Amy; **art d**, Ted Smith; **spec eff**, Byron Haskin, H.F. Koenekamp.

The Virginian ★★★★ 1929; U.S.; 92m; PAR; B/W; Western; Children: Unacceptable; **VHS**. Cooper is wonderful in this landmark western that established him as the consummate on-screen taciturn and courageous cowboy. Cooper, in his first all-talking film, plays the part of a rugged, no-nonsense foreman of the Box H Ranch near Medicine Bow, Wyoming. He is shown in a saloon where he draws the attention of bargirl Quartero, which causes Huston, a mean-minded gunman named Trampas, to jealously insult Cooper. Both go for their guns, but Cooper is faster, leveling it at the now hesitant Huston and saying: "If you want to call me that, smile." Huston warily gives him a crooked smile and the confrontation ends. Cooper then hires Arlen, a close friend, as one of his cowboys to work at the Box H Ranch, and both then proceed to court the beautiful Brian, who has recently arrived in Medicine Bow to become the local schoolteacher. She is immediately drawn to the reserved Cooper (who appears to be shy when with young women). This so crushes Arlen's spirit that he leaves the ranch and turns outlaw, becoming a rustler under the evil guidance of the sinister Huston. Cooper finds Arlen changing the brands of some cattle belonging to the Box H, but Arlen pretends that he has made a mistake and Cooper lets him go with a stern warning. After another raid against the Box H herd, Cooper leads a number of vigilantes to track down three rustlers. One of them turns out to be his close friend Arlen. The captured rustlers stoically accept the fate that awaits them: hanging. After giving the three some time to write letters and pray, Cooper reluctantly orders all three to be hanged. (This is one of the most heart-wrenching scenes in any western, especially since Cooper cannot bring himself to witness his friend's death, turning away when the horses on which the rope-tied men are lashed to speed them forward.) When Brian learns how Cooper has sent the fun-loving and affable Arlen to his death, she rejects Cooper, refusing to see him again. Cooper, plagued by guilt over Arlen's death, seethes with anger at Huston, knowing it was Huston who had Arlen and the two others rustle the cattle. Cooper confronts the deadly Huston and is wounded in a gunfight. Brian, however, shows that she still loves Cooper by taking care of him until he is mended, and, by that time, the two grow even closer together and plan to marry. Huston, however, will not let things rest, and, on the day Cooper is to be married, the villain challenges him to a final showdown in the middle of the main street of Medicine Bow. Brian sees that Cooper cannot back down from the taunting Huston and threatens not to marry him if he steps into the street. Cooper places his manly obligations first and straps on his gun belt and goes into that street where he confronts the menacing Huston. Both men go for their guns and Cooper is faster, shooting Huston dead before he returns to the waiting arms of Brian to end this outstanding western. Cooper, Arlen and Huston are standouts in their rugged roles, and Brian presents a fetching young lady attempting to bring sanity and civilization to the Old West. Pantheon director Fleming presents a well-organized, fast-moving tale while also offering many sensitive scenes that capture in natural terms the close cowboy friendships and an awkward but endearing romance. The film was a big box office success and made Cooper an overnight star. The Owen Wister novel, published first in 1902, saw a stage adaptation (by Wister and Kirk La Shelle), which opened in NYC on January 5, 1904. It was filmed as two silent movies in 1914 and 1923. This was the first talkie version of the exciting story, which would see a good remake starring Joel McCrea in 1946. A sixty-minute radio adaptation was aired by Lux Radio Theater on November 2, 1936, with Cooper reprising his role. Songs: "Pop! Goes the Weasel!" (traditional), "Three Blind Mice" (traditional children's song), "Bury Me Not On the Lone Prairie" (traditional). *Author's Note*: Cooper was hesitant when going into the production for this film, believing that this, his first talkie, would prove to be a disaster and that his voice would be inadequate. His terse dialog with "yep" and "nope" answers, however, made him boyishly empathetic to viewers. "To tell the truth," Cooper said to this author, "I thought that picture would doom my career in movies. Just the opposite took place and it became a big hit. **The Virginian** has stayed with me like an old, best friend, and I guess it is my favorite picture." Ironically, two years earlier, Richard Arlen had been the star, along with Charles "Buddy" Rogers and Clara Bow, in **Wings**, 1927, Cooper made his first important appearance in a small supporting role. The roles between Cooper and Arlen were now reversed, with Arlen in a small supporting role. While Cooper shot to superstardom and would remain one of Hollywood's icons for decades to come, Arlen's career quickly went into decline. Randolph Scott, who was then just beginning his Hollywood career and would also become a Hollywood icon, chiefly in westerns, had a small role in this film. His main job, however, as he told this author, was "to try to teach Coop [Cooper] how to speak with a Virginia drawl. Since I was from that State, I simply sat around with him and we

Gary Cooper and Mary Brian in *The Virginian*, 1929.

talked while he mostly listened to my speech patterns. He did not really have any long speeches in **The Virginian**, so his task to imitate my drawl was not too difficult." Fleming used sound periodically without dialog to give further symbolism to his scenes, the noise of cattle and horses punctuating silences. He shot the film on location at Sonora and Lone Pine, California, as well as shooting its train depot scenes at Jamestown, California. **p**, B.P. Schulberg, (uncredited) Louis D. Lighton; **d**, Victor Fleming; **cast**, Gary Cooper, Walter Huston, Richard Arlen, Mary Brian, Helen Ware, Chester Conklin, Eugene Pallette, Victor Potel, E.H. Calvert, Ernie Adams, Willie Fung, Nena Quartero, Charles Stevens, Jack Pennick, George Chandler, Randolph Scott; **w**, Howard Estabrook, Edward E. Paramore, Jr., Grover Jones, Keene Thompson (based on the play by Owen Wister, Kirk La Shelle, and the novel by Wister); **c**, J. Roy Hunt, Edward Cronjager; **m**, Karl Hajos; **ed**, William Shea.

The Virginian ★★★ 1946; U.S.; 90m; PAR; Color; Western; Children: Unacceptable; **DVD**; **VHS**. In this good remake of the 1929 classic, stalwart McCrea is from Virginia, but becomes a Wyoming rancher living a peaceful life until he has a fatal falling out with his best friend, Tufts. After Tufts has joined a gang of cattle rustlers led by Donlevy (playing the great western villain Trampas), McCrea tries to warn him that ranchers are not going to stand for their losses much longer. He's right, and on another cattle raid, Tufts is among those rustlers caught by a posse that wants to string up the outlaws. As a member of the posse, McCrea can do no more than stand by and watch as his old saddle mate Tufts is hanged from a tree. McCrea had been slowly winning the affections of Easterner Britton, the town's recently arrived schoolmarm, but she, too, had liked the charming Tufts and becomes cold to McCrea for not saving his life. McCrea cannot convince her that out West, the law is the law, and Tufts paid the ultimate price for cattle rustling. She finally sees things his way and consents to marry him. On their wedding day, McCrea and Donlevy have the ultimate showdown, and, in an exchange of gunfire, Donlevy is killed. This film was made as silent films in 1914 and 1923 and as talkies in 1929, 1962, 2000, and 2014. A television series having little to do with the original story ran from 1962 to 1971, offering 249 episodes. The 1929 version of this classic western tale, which starred Gary Cooper, remains the best. *Author's Note*: McCrea thought this film one of his best, pointing out to this author that "Gary Cooper did not really deliver the famous Owen Wister line to the villain in the 1929 picture. He said: 'If you want to call me that, smile.' I delivered the actual line for the first time when I said to Brian [Donlevy], who played that villain in the 1946 remake: 'When you call me that, smile.'" Donlevy told this author that he thought his role in **The Virginian** "was not much different than the villain I played in **Jesse James** [1929], ex-

Fernando Rey, Silvia Pinal and Margarita Lozano in *Viridiana,* **1962.**

cept I was a crooked railroad man in that picture and a killer and rustler in the other." Lawrence, who plays another heavy in this film, recalled, when talking with this author, that "**The Virginian** reminded me of another picture I was in, **The Ox-Bow Incident** [1943], which is centered about a lynching. Three rustlers get lynched in **The Virginian** and they did it about the same way, not showing the men hanging, but only the horses running off to leave them dancing in the air." **p**, Paul Jones; **d**, Stuart Gilmore; **cast**, Joel McCrea, Brian Donlevy, Sonny Tufts, Barbara Britton, Fay Bainter, Tom Tully, Henry O'Neill, Bill Edwards, William Frawley, Paul Guilfoyle, Marc Lawrence, Vince Barnett; **w**, Frances Goodrich, Albert Hackett (adapted by Howard Estabrook from the novel by Owen Wister and the play by Wister and Kirk LaShelle; **c**, Harry Hallenberger (Technicolor); **m**, Daniele Amfitheatrof; **ed**, Everett Douglas; **art d**, Hans Dreier, John Meehan; **set d**, John MacNeil; **spec eff**, Farciot Edouart, Gordon Jennings, Paul K. Lerpae.

Viridiana ★★★★ 1962; Spain/Mexico; 90m; UNINCI/Kingsley International Pictures; B/W; Drama; Children: Unacceptable; **BD**; **DVD**; **VHS**; **IV**. Technically an outstanding film from pantheon director Brunel, this production nevertheless presents the director's most obsessive polemic against social regimen, wealthy estate owners, and the Catholic Church. The film opens with Pinal as Viridiana, a novice in a convent who is about to take her final vows in becoming a nun. Before Pinal takes those vows, however, Yarza, the mother superior, tells her that she should visit her uncle, Rey, who has paid for Pinal's studies and supported her throughout her stay at the convent. Pinal states that she has no recollection of Rey. She says that, since Rey has never visited her, she sees no reason to make such a visit to see him. Yarza persists (and it is suggested that Yarza has an unsavory, unreligious hidden agenda here as if Pinal must make that visit as a repayment for Rey's financial support to this Catholic institution), and, thus pressured by Yarza, Pinal, who has a preconceived image of Rey as a person up to no good, reluctantly agrees to visit him. When she does, she vows that she will deny herself any of the many luxuries available to her at Rey's sprawling estate. She finds Rey living in a large house with a few servants, Lozano being his devoted housekeeper. Pinal soon discovers that Rey is kind and considerate, but she suspects something is amiss with him when he tells her that she bears a strong resemblance to his deceased wife, a woman he has never stopped passionately loving. Rey's wife died thirty years earlier on their wedding night, and he has forever harbored the perverse thought of possessing her through the lookalike Pinal. Before Pinal is to return to the convent, Rey asks her as a favor to don the wedding dress his wife had worn shortly before she died. Although Pinal thinks this request somewhat strange, she now feels obligated to Rey for the kindness he has shown to her, and agrees to indulge Rey's

whim. Rey, however, has Lozano drug Pinal's tea so that he can have his way with the young woman. While wearing the wedding dress and now in a drugged state, Pinal is carried by Rey to his bridal suite where he places her on a bed. He thinks to rape her, but has second thoughts and does not violate her. In the morning, however, Rey vindictively lies to Pinal, saying that he took her "virginity" the night before and, now that she is no longer chaste, she cannot therefore return to the convent. Pinal decides that she will nevertheless return to the convent and Rey then admits that he lied, that he did not violate her. Now Pinal is uncertain as to whether or not she remains a virgin. She rushes to a bus stop to travel back to the convent, but she is detained by police, who return her to the estate where she learns that Rey has hanged himself (using the jump rope of Lozano's small daughter). Rey has ended his life over remorse in attempting to ruin Pinal's hopes for a religious life at the expense of his nagging and perverse action. He has, however, left half of his estate to Pinal, the other half going to his illegitimate son, Rabal, a thoughtful and hard-working young man. Pinal decides that she will not return to the convent to take her final vows, but remain at the estate where she naively plans to do good by aiding homeless and deprived persons. To that end, Pinal invites many beggars and impoverished people to stay at the estate, offering them food and shelter in exchange for their work in improving the dilapidated estate. Rabal sees no sense in Pinal's generosity as he rightly looks upon those invited to live at the estate nothing more than loafers. He moves into the main house with his girlfriend, Zinny, who becomes jealous when she sees that Rabal, like his father, Rey, is sexually attracted to Pinal. This is confirmed when Rabal makes a pass at Pinal and Zinny promptly leaves. Rabal then takes up with Lozano, but he still has an abiding fascination with Pinal. When Rabal and Pinal leave the estate and go to the village to attend to business, the beggars break into the main house and, awed by its furnishings and plentiful food and wine, conduct a drunken feast which resembles Da Vinci's *Last Supper*, where a blind beggar (Bunuel admitted that he had a dislike for blind people) pretends to be the figure of Jesus during this drunken revel (atheist Bunuel savagely mocks the Catholic religion in this rather crude visual mimicry). Throughout, a record player emphasizes the ridicule by blaring the "Hallelujah Chorus" from Handel's "Messiah." Rabal and Pinal return unexpectedly early and confront the debauching vagrants, who, one by one, depart after making feeble excuses for making the house a shambles. One beggar, however, attacks Pinal and Rabal goes to her rescue, but is knocked out and tied up by another beggar. Rabal regains consciousness and bribes one of the beggars to kill the man attempting to rape Pinal. The police then arrive to reestablish order. Pinal later enters a room to find Rabal and Lozano playing cards, and Pinal declares that she will remain on the estate. Lozano stands up and is about to leave when Rabal asks her to stay with him and Pinal and the three then begin playing cards together, Bunuel indicating that this is now the beginning of a *ménage a trois*. Bunuel's direction is flawless and the acting from Pinal, Rey, Rabal and Lozano is outstanding, each portraying their intriguing characters with marvelous distinction. The story line, however, blatantly indicts the Catholic Church as a money-grubbing agency, Spanish gentry as licentious manipulators, and the unwashed and uneducated of the country as no more than worthless and conniving cretins as lustful as the seemingly more noble principal persons of the wobbly plot. All of this represents Bunuel's rather hortatory social and political agendas that he makes little effort to disguise, imposing his credos within the predictable rationales and behavior of his puppet-like characters. This film, which amply displays Bunuel's brilliant arrays of avant-garde surrealism in most of its scenes, won the Cannes Film Festival Golden Palm Award when released, but was banned in Spain, the country of its origin. It was not well received worldwide, thought to be little more than Bunuel's far-left political propaganda dressed as a drama, and where Bunuel shocks and insults the intellectual bourgeoisie, as he had throughout his life as a filmmaker. There is nothing visually complex about this film as Bunuel traditionally uses no camera tricks or exaggerated angles or distorted sets to emphasize its story line or attempts to impress the viewer with his directorial presence. All is shot in a straightforward manner and, as such there is a poetic simplicity to his often mesmerizing scenes. The film is also an impressive if not subliminal indictment of the fascist dictatorship of Francisco Franco (1892-1975), who was then in power in Spain. Songs/Music: "Hallelujah Chorus" (1741; from "Messiah" by George Fredric Handel), "Shimmy Doll" (composer unknown), "Requiem" (1791; Wolfgang Amadeus Mozart), "Et Incarnatus Est" (1749; from "Mass in B Minor" [BMV 232] by Johann Sebastian Bach). *Author's Note*: Bunuel was a devout communist (joining that Party in 1931 when living in Spain, and he supported the most radical left-wing elements fighting with the Republicans against Franco's nationalists during the Spanish Civil War). He was also a dedicated atheist, who had a decided hatred for the Catholic Church in Spain, which had sided with the Nationalists during the Civil War, and he took pains to insert scenes in all of his films to mock the traditions and beliefs of that Church, as he decidedly does in **Viridiana**. He had been absent from his native Spain for twenty-five years when he was invited by the Franco government to return to his country a make a film of his choice. The Franco regime extended in the mid-1950s the same invitation to many other artists it had earlier considered political enemies, such as author Ernest Hemingway, who had published *For Whom the Bell Tolls* in 1940, which depicted Franco and his nationalists as vicious oppressors of the Spanish people. Bunuel returned to Spain to make **Viridiana**, but was warned that the completed film would be subject to the national censors. Bunuel anticipated that those censors would ban the film after they viewed it, and took the precaution of secretly sending a print to Paris where he could edit the film without interference from the Spanish censors, and it was this edited version that was submitted to the Cannes Film Festival. The Spanish censors, when seeing the final print, promptly prohibited its showing in Spain. Further, the Vatican labeled the film "blasphemous," to which Bunuel replied: "I didn't set out to be blasphemous, but then Pope John XXIII [1881-1963] is a better judge of such things than I am." The director faced even further wrath in Italy when the film was shown in Milan and the local public prosecutor threatened to arrest and imprison Bunuel if he dared to enter the country, that prosecutor announcing that **Viridiana** was "sacrilegious." Brunel conceived of the story for this film while traveling by boat from Mexico, where he had lived in exile, to Spain, and later stated that he thought at that time about a minor Spanish saint named Viridiana he learned about when he was a child. "I remembered my old erotic fantasy about making love to the Queen of Spain when she was drugged and decided to combine the two [Viridiana and the Queen]." Actually, the Spanish censors had, according to Bunuel, improved this film's ending. In the original script he submitted to the censors, Pinal knocks on Rabal's door, as if she is soliciting sex with him and the censors suggested that, instead, she play cards with her intended lover at the finale. Of course, the artful Bunuel used that very scene, which he liked better than his original ending, but has Lozano remain with the lovers to indicate that they are now a romantic threesome. (In Spanish; English subtitles.) **p**, Ricardo Munoz Suay, Gustavo Alatriste, Pedro Portabella; **d**, Luis Bunuel; **cast**, Silvia Pinal, Francisco Rabal, Fernando Rey, Jose Calvo, Margarita Lozano, Rosita Yarza, Jose Manuel Martin, Victoria Zinny, Luis Heredia, Joaquin Roa, Lola Gaos, Maruja Isbert; **w**, Bunuel, Julio Alejandro (based on their story, and (uncredited) the novel *Halma* by Benito Perez Galdos); **c**, Jose F. Aguayo; **m**, Gustavo Pittaluga; **ed**, Pedro del Rey; **art d&set d**, Francisco Canet.

Virtue ★★★ 1932; U.S.; 68m; COL; B/W; Drama/Romance; Children: Unacceptable. Lombard is exceptional when playing a fallen woman, a Manhattan prostitute with a heart of gold. She is given the choice of a term in jail or to leave town. She opts for leaving and takes a train out of the big city, but has no intention of leaving, so she later gets off the train and takes a taxi back to her old street to return to her shady lady trade. She doesn't have the money to pay the taxi driver, O'Brien, but

Carole Lombard in *Virtue*, 1932.

soon charms him and he falls in love with her. They marry, but, on their wedding night, police arrive to arrest her. O'Brien, however, sweet-talks the cops out of booking his wife. Lombard then visits Methot, a girlfriend, going to Methot's hotel room to collect $200 loaned to her. O'Brien learns that Lombard has visited this hotel, noted for its unsavory occupants, and he falsely suspects that Lombard is back in the hooker business. Someone in the hotel is murdered and police suspect Lombard as the killer. With O'Brien's help, however, Lombard clears herself of the crime, and she and O'Brien live happily ever after. Song: "My Gal Sal" (1905; Paul Dresser). Buzzell directs a prosaic story and infuses a good sense of realism in his fast-moving scenes, drawing good performances from Lombard and O'Brien, who were then making their way to Hollywood superstardom, although O'Brien had already become an overnight hit with his appearance as the fast-talking newsman in Hecht and MacArthur's **The Front Page**, 1931. *Author's Note*: Lombard was on loan from Paramount when making this film and her first meeting with Columbia mogul Harry Cohn was not a pleasant one, according to O'Brien, who told this author: "Fireworks went off when those two first met. Cohn was a very blunt man who spoke his mind without really caring what he said. He took a look at Carole's [Lombard's] platinum-blonde head and said: 'Your hair is too white. It makes you look like a whore.' Well, Cohn was in for a surprise because Carole never took any guff from anyone. She immediately replied: 'That's the character I am playing in this picture, Mr. Cohn. I will admit that, if anyone would know what a whore looks like, it would be you.'" Mayo Methot, who plays another prostitute in this film, had been a Broadway musical star before appearing in films, mostly in supporting roles. She was married to Humphrey Bogart from 1938 to 1945, before Bogart met and fell in love with Lauren Bacall. The Methot-Bogart marriage was turbulent and, on one occasion, she reportedly trained a gun at Bogart while arguing with him as their dinner guests, actress Gloria Stuart and her husband, feared for their lives, but the gun was never fired. On another occasion, however, Methot, while in her cups with Bogart when they were on board their anchored boat, stabbed the actor, a serious wound that required medical attention and stitches. **d**, Edward Buzzell; **cast**, Carole Lombard, Pat O'Brien, Ward Bond, Mayo Methot, Shirley Grey, Jack La Rue, Willard Robertson, Arthur Wanzer, Jessie Arnold, Edwin Stanley, Harry Semels; **w**, Robert Riskin (based on the story by Ethel Hill); **c**, Joseph Walker; **ed**, Maurice Wright.

I Vitelloni ★★★ 1956; Italy/France; 101m; Cite Films/Janus Films; B/W; Drama; Children: Unacceptable; **DVD**; **VHS**; **IV**. Intriguing film from gifted director Fellini depicts five Italian youths refusing to grow up and accept responsibility. One of the gang, Fabrizi, seduces Ruffo, sister of his friend, Interlenghi, and he is forced to marry her. He remains

Ann-Margaret performing in *Viva Las Vegas,* 1964.

a womanizer and tries to seduce the wife of his boss, and is fired from his job as a salesman of religious objects. Ruffo gives up on Fabrizi, and leaves with their child, going to live with his father, Brochard, who gives Fabrizi a well-deserved thrashing. This earthy tale is a partially autobiographical film based on Fellini's youth. Song: "Io Cerco la Titina" (traditional). Sexuality prohibits viewing by children. (In Italian; English subtitles.) **p,** Mario De Vecchi, Jacques Bar, Lorenzo Pegoraro; **d,** Federico Fellini; **cast,** Franco Interlenghi, Franco Fabrizi, Alberto Sordi, Leopoldo Trieste, Riccardo Fellini, Leonora Ruffo, Jean Brochard, Claude Farell, Carlo Romano, Enrico Viarisio; **w,** Fellini, Ennio Flaiano (based on the story by Fellini, Flaiano, Tullio Pinelli); **c,** Otello Martelli, Luciano Trasatti, Carlo Carlini; **m,** Nino Rota; **ed,** Rolando Benedetti; **prod d,** Mario Chiari; **spec eff,** Luigi Giacost.

Vitus ★★★ 2007; Switzerland; 100m; Vitusfilm/Sony; Color; Drama; Children: Unacceptable; **DVD; IV.** Absorbing tale packed with entertaining classical music begins with Vitus, played by Borsani, who is a boy of six and whose parents, Jenkins and Jucker, make demanding and ambitious plans for him to become a concert pianist, which will also make them rich. He plays the piano very well at that age, but is distracted by having a crush on a much older girl, Lykowa, who is his babysitter. He continues to play piano beautifully, but, by the time he is twelve, as Gheorghiu, he is unwilling to follow his parents' wishes and rebels because he wants to follow his own dream. He fakes a head injury and secretly amasses a fortune on the stock market. The money allows his beloved grandfather, Ganz, to purchase an airplane. The film ends with teenage Gheorghiu trying to be reunited with his former babysitter, now played by Scarpellini, after playing Robert Schumann's Piano Concerto on stage with the Zurich Chamber Orchestra. The film stars real-life piano child protégé Gheorghiu. Songs: "Allegro barbaro" (Charles Henri Alkan), "Islamej Oriental Fantasy" (Mili Balakirew), "Rondo a-Moll KV 511" and "Requiem in d-Moll, K 626" (Wolfgang Amadeus Mozart), "Lichtstuck No. 1 and 4" (Mario Beretta), "Etude" (Carl Czerny), "Alborado del Gracioso" (Maurice Ravel), "Sonata 263" (Domenico Scarlatti), "Der wilde Reiter" (Robert Schumann), "Hungarian Rhapsody No. 6" (Franz Liszt), "La Campanella" (Niccolo Paganini), "Klavierkonzert in a-Moll Op, 5e4" (Robert Schumann), "Goldberg Variation 29, 30" (Johann Sebastian Bach), "Nutbush City Limits" (Tina Turner). Thematic elements and gutter language prohibit viewing by children. **p,** Christian Davi, Christof Neracher; **d,** Fredi M. Murer; **cast,** Fabrizio Borsani, Teo Gheorghiu, Julika Jenkins, Urs Jucker, Bruno Ganz, Daniel Rohr, Norbert Schwientek, Heidy Forster, Daniel Fueter, Livia S. Reinhard; **w,** Murer, Peter Luisi, Lukas B. Suter; **c,** Pio Corradi; **m,** Mario Beretta; **ed,** Myriam Flury; **prod d,** Susanne Jauch.

Viva Las Vegas ★★★ 1964; U.S.; 85m; MGM; Color; Musical; Children: Acceptable; **BD; DVD; VHS; IV.** Presley is a standout in this delightful musical as "Lucky Jackson," a race car driver arriving in Las Vegas with his entry in the city's first Grand Prix race. He has hopes of winning the race against a longtime rival, Danova. Presley is broke and needs money to have a new engine installed in his racer. He wins it in the casinos, but soon mislays it when Ann-Margret, the beautiful manager of a hotel swimming pool, takes his mind off car racing and races his heart instead. He also finds competition from Danova for Ann-Margret's affections. Presley proves to be lucky in both love and the race. Songs: "The Yellow Rose of Texas/The Eyes of Texas" (Don George, adapted by Randy Starr, Fred Wise, John Lang Sinclair), "The Lady Loves Me" (Sid Tepper, Roy C. Bennett), "What'd I Say" (Ray Charles), "Viva Las Vegas" (Doc Pomus, Mort Shuman), "I Need Someone to Lean On" and "Come On, Everybody" (Stanley Chianese), "Today, Tomorrow and Forever" (Bill Giant, Bernie Baum, Florence Kaye), "Santa Lucia" (traditional), "If You Think I Don't Need You" (Bob "Red" West), "Appreciation" and "My Rival" (Marvin More, Bernie Wayne), "The Climb" (Dan Anthony, John Case Schaeffer II). *Author's Note*: Presley was reportedly jealous of the attention Ann-Margret got from her vivacious appearance in the film, but it was said that nonetheless they began an affair on the set that lasted until 1967. **p,** Jack Cummings, George Sidney; **d,** Sidney; **cast,** Elvis Presley, Ann-Margret, Cesare Danova, William Demarest, Eddie Quillan, Robert Williams, Ivan Triesault, Mike Ragan, Francis Ravel, and bit parts were played by television comedian Jack Carter as a casino performer, actress Teri Garr as a show girl, and television actor Kent McCord ("Adam-12") as a casino patron; **w,** Sally Benson; **c,** Joseph Biroc; **m,** George Stoll, Robert Van Epps; **ed,** John McSweeney; **art d,** Edward Carfagno, George W. Davis; **set d,** Henry Grace, George R. Nelson.

Viva Villa! ★★★★ 1934; U.S.; 115m; MGM; B/W; Biographical Drama; Children: Unacceptable; **DVD; VHS.** Rousing biopic recounts the colorful exploits of Mexican bandit, patriot and revolutionary Pancho Villa (Jose Doroteo Arango Arambula; 1878-1923), who is expansively played by Beery. This saga opens with Cooper, who plays Pancho as a boy and witnesses his father, Puglia, being beaten to death for a minor offense by a brutal soldier serving the country's vicious dictator, Porfirio Diaz (1830-1915). Cooper later kills the soldier and flees to the mountains where he grows to be the adult Beery, an uneducated and raucous bandit. He gathers a number of dedicated followers and then rides down into the valleys to attack and pillage the estates of the wealthy, giving some of the spoils to the poor peons who come to idolize him as a latter-day Robin Hood. While on one of his raids, Beery meets American newspaper man Erwin, and they become friends. Erwin serves as Beery's biographer, writing exciting tales about this modern-day bandit, who wants to return the great estates to the penniless farmers that work on them. Also in his manic meanderings, Beery encounters landowner Cook, and his attractive sister, Wray, both believing that Beery's goals in aiding the downtrodden are worthwhile and noble, although Wray is often offended by Beery's uncouth and almost savage conduct. Through these wealthy supporters, Beery meets revolutionary leader Francisco Madero (1873-1913), who is empathetically played by Walthall. Through Walthall's patient urgings, Beery, who has come to love the older patriot, agrees to join his forces to a ragged peasant army that has risen in revolt against Diaz's regime. Then Schildkraut, whose role model is based upon Victoriano Huerta (1850-1916), an opportunistic general leading a separate force, joins with Beery and they sweep through Mexico, toppling Diaz's dictatorship to establish a free Mexico. Walthall becomes the new President of Mexico and Beery disbands his army, retiring to his ranch. He later beats a bank teller to death when arguing with him about a withdrawal, and Schildkraut, Beery's fiercest rival, orders him put to death. At the last moment when Beery is facing a firing squad, his life is spared by Walthall, who pardons him, but orders him to leave the country. Beery goes to the U.S., but then learns that his good friend Walthall has been murdered by the usurping Schildkraut, who has become dictator of Mexico. When learning of this, Beery, enraged, rides back into Mexico with his erstwhile aide Carrillo, and reorganizes his army, sweeping like a whirlwind through Mexico to defeat Schildkraut's forces. He is no longer guided by the compassionate Walthall, and slaughters anyone he thinks to be his enemy, his wanton killings alienating Cook and Wray, who refuse to support him. Incensed, he tries to assault Wray, whom he has always coveted, and she shoots him, wounding him in an arm. He orders Wray whipped, and, later, Wray is killed by a stray bullet fired by one of Beery's rampaging men. Beery then defeats Schildkraut in a final battle, and, after capturing his treacherous enemy orders Schildkraut staked out and coated with honey to be eaten alive by ants. "Put it [the honey] on his ears, his eyes, his nose," Beery shouts. "Put it everyplace on him—*everyplace!*" Schildkraut meets a tortuous, screaming death and Beery becomes president of Mexico. He has no idea how to run the country and he soon quits his position and retires once more to his ranch. He then takes a trip to Mexico City where he meets his old friend Erwin. Just then, Cook, who blames Beery for his sister's death, uses a rifle to mortally wound Beery. Erwin cradles Beery in his arms as he lies dying and Beery asks him to write a memorable epitaph for him. Erwin promises he will, saying he will write that his last words were "Goodbye, my Mexico, forgive me for my crimes. Remember, if I sinned against you, it was because I loved you too much." Beery is confused, saying to Erwin: "Forgive me? Johnny—what I done wrong?" He then dies to end this memorable film. Hawks depicts the Mexican Revolution (1910-1920) in all of its grim realities showing chaotic battles, mass executions by hanging and firing squads, pillaging and looting and everywhere flaming carnage. Beery's riveting portrait of an uncivilized Villa, half child, half brute, is one of the finest performances in his long career, wholly capturing the true nature of this tempestuous man. His supporting players, Cook, Wray, Carrillo, Walthall, Schildkraut, Erwin and others are outstanding as the equally fascinating persons they essay. The film's amazing visual vitality should be credited to its brilliant cinematographer, Howe, one of the best action photographers in Hollywood. John Waters received an Oscar as Best Assistant Director, and the film also received Oscar nominations for Best Picture, Best Adapted Screenplay (Hecht), and Best Sound Recording (Douglas Shearer). The film was an enormous box office success, earning more than $3 million against its budget of less than $1 million. A sixty-minute radio adaptation was aired by Lux Radio Theater on October 10, 1938, with Beery reprising his role. Songs: "La Cucaracha" (traditional Mexican song; new lyrics: Ned Washington), "Madre Mia" (1934; music: Herbert Stothart; lyrics: Henry H. Tobias), "The Wedding March" (1843; from "A Midsummer Night's Dream Op. 61" by Felix Mendelssohn-Bartholdy), "Artist's Life, Op. 316" (1867; Johann Strauss). ***Author's Note***: Hawks, who directed much of this film, shooting it in Mexico, told this author that the production "went haywire after we cast Lee Tracy as the reporter who follows Beery around to record his exploits. Tracy was one of the worst boozers in Hollywood, a cantankerous guy after he drank too much, which was pretty much always. Well, we were pretty far along in the picture when he went on an overnight bender and then staggered to the balcony of his hotel room and saw a parade of Mexican soldiers passing beneath. Tracy did not like soldiers and began urinating on these troops, which caused a hell of an uproar. He was seized and jailed and we suddenly had a formal complaint from the Mexican government. Tracy talked his way out of the pokey and flew right back to the States, but he was fired immediately by MGM, and they brought in Stuart Erwin to replace him. Louis B. Mayer, who ran MGM, ordered me to fly to Los Angeles and he was boiling mad. He told me that, to appease the Mexican government, he wanted Tracy to go to prison and wanted me to testify against him. I refused and was fired on the spot. They then brought in Jack Conway to finish the picture, a few weeks shooting. Tracy, who was an MGM contract player, was not only fired, but barred from the MGM lot for life. I saw him a few days later and all he said was: 'Who cares. I can get work

Fay Wray and Wallace Beery in *Viva Villa!*, 1934.

at a lot of other studios.' And he did." Wray, like Erwin, was a replacement since the leading lady was Mona Maris. Beery disliked Maris so much that he demanded another actress take her place and Wray was hired for the role. Wray, however, thought that "Wally [Beery] was almost as boorish and brutish off camera as the man he was playing in that picture, Pancho Villa. A lot of us knew that Wally was a really crude man with an explosive temperament. We also knew that he was only playing himself in that picture, maybe more of himself than he really wanted to show. He manhandled me very roughly in one scene where he is supposed to sexually assault me, and he truly frightened me, and I think he enjoyed that. There was a streak of sadism in that man. I saw that when he ordered me to be whipped for rejecting him. When I objected to that treatment, Howard [Hawks] said: 'Oh, they flog women all the time down here, Fay. Think nothing of it.' Of course, the whip never touched my flesh, but it was nevertheless a degrading scene that I hated doing." Hecht, who wrote the superb script for this film (paid $15,000), agreed with Wray that the overall portrait of Mexicans in this film showed them to be merciless savages, which, not incidentally, created severe criticism from the Mexican government when the film was released. Hecht told this author: "After I finished writing the script [for **Viva Villa!**], I pointed out to Howard [Hawks] that there was a great deal of newsreel footage that had been taken of Villa during the Revolution, and we watched those newsreels together, hours of them. The boys who shot those actual newsreels did not pull any punches. They showed the savagery of the battles down there, the headlong charges of peons into machine-gun fire where they were mowed down like bowling pins, and the mass hangings of prisoners who refused to join the victors following the battles. They were hanging from trees by the dozens. It was all very grim and gruesome, and that is exactly the way Hawks shot the film, showing no regard for human life at all. As such, he actually produced a great visual document that was almost as real as the events that took place during the Revolution. Howard [Hawks] later told me that, while he was shooting down there in Mexico, he had a tough time handling the more than seven thousand extras he used in some of the battle scenes [shot both by Hawks and Conway], and that some of the extras were real revolutionaries carrying loaded guns. He was threatened several times by some of these characters, so he took to carrying a loaded pistol himself. He was glad to get out of there after he had an argument with Louis B. Mayer over an actor [Lee Tracy], who had to be replaced when he created an international incident down there during the filming of the picture. They then brought in Bill Wellman, who did a few scenes before Jack Conway took over the direction." Many other actors have portrayed the fiery Villa in many other films, including **Ah! Silenciosa**, 1999 (Carlos Roberto Majul); **American Family**, 2002-2004 (TV series; "Mexican Revolution," 2002 episode: Edward James

Marlon Brando in *Viva Zapata!*, **1952.**

Olmos); **And Starring Pancho Villa as Himself**, 2003 (made-for-TV: Antonio Banderas); **Aqui esta Pancho Villa**, 1960 (TV series; Pedro Armendariz); **Between Pancho Villa and a Naked Woman**, 1996 (Jesus Ochoa); **Caballo prieto azabache (La tumba de Villa)**, 1968 (Raul "Chato" Padilla); **El centauro Pancho Villa**, 1967 (Jose Elias Moreno); **El encanto del aguila**, 2011 (Enoc Leano); **El 7 leguas**, 1955 (Victor Alcocer); **Ethel Barrymore Theater**, 1956 (TV series; "This Is Villa," 1956 episode: Akim Tamiroff); **La estampida**, 1959 (Jose Chavez); **La muerte de Pancho Villa**, 1974 (Antonio Aguilar); **La sangre de un valiente**, 1993 (Antonio Aguilar); **Las tres pelonas**, 1958 (Jose Chavez); **Let's Go with Pancho Villa**, 1939 (Domingo Soler); **The Life of General Villa**, 1914 (Raoul Walsh as a young Villa; Pancho Villa as himself); **Old Gringo**, 1989 (Pedro Armendariz Jr.); **Reed, Mexico Insurgente**, 1974 (Heraclio Zepeda); **Pancho Villa**, 1972 (Telly Savalas); **Pancho Villa and Valentina**, 1960 (Pedro Armendariz); **Pancho Villa Returns**, 1950 (Leo Carrillo); **Patria**, 1917 (Wallace Beery); **Red Bells Part I: Mexico on Fire**, 1982 (Jorge Reynoso); **Senda de Gloria**, 1987 (TV series; Guillermo Gil); **She Came to the Valley**, 1979 (Freddy Fender); **This Was Pancho Villa**, 1957 (Pedro Armendariz); **The Treasure of Pancho Villa**, 1936 (Juan F. Triana); **Villa!**, 1958 (Rodolfo Hoyos); **Under Strange Flags**, 1937 (Maurice Black); **Villa Rides**, 1968 (Yul Brynner); **Viva Mexico**, 1980 (made-for-TV; Jose Vilamor); **Viva Zapata!**, 1952 (Alan Reed); **Vuelve Pancho Villa**, 1950 (Pedro Armendariz); **Wanted: The Sundance Woman**, 1976 (made-for-TV; Hector Elizondo); **Why America Will Win**, 1918 (George Humbert); **With Villa's Veterans**, 1939 (Luis Alvarez); **Zapata**, 1970 (David Reynoso); and **Zapata—El sueno del hero**, 2004 (Luis Enrique Parra). **p**, David O. Selznick; **d**, Jack Conway, (not credited) Howard Hawks, William A. Wellman; **cast**, Wallace Beery, Fay Wray, Stuart Erwin, Leo Carrillo, Donald Cook, Henry B. Walthall, Joseph Schildkraut, Katherine de Mille, George E. Stone, Frank Puglia, David Durand, Henry Armetta, Noah Beery Jr., Chris-Pin Martin, Arthur Treacher, Mischa Auer, John Merkel, Phillip Cooper, Francis X. Bushman Jr., Adrian Rosley, Harry Cording, Sam Godfrey, John Davidson, Brandon Hurst, Leonard Mudie; **w**, Ben Hecht (based on the book by Edgecumb Pinchon, O.B. Stade); **c**, James Wong Howe, Charles G. Clarke; **m**, Herbert Stothart; **ed**, Robert J. Kern; **art d**, Harry Oliver; **set d**, Edwin B. Willis; **spec eff**, Slavko Vorkapich.

Viva Zapata! ★★★★★ 1952; U.S.; 113m; FOX; B/W; Biographical Drama; Children: Unacceptable; **BD**; **DVD**; **VHS**; **IV**. Brando is magnificent in playing the iconic Mexican revolutionary Emiliano Zapata (1879-1919) in this masterpiece biopic from the brilliant Kazan. This stirring and often inspiring film opens in 1909 in a sprawling room of the presidential palace in Mexico City. Roope, who plays a patronizing

Porfirio Diaz (1830-1915), meets with a group of reticent peons, who have come from the southern province of Morelos. As they nervously clutch their tattered sombreros, Gilbert, one of the peons, hesitantly tells Roope that the boundary markers on their land have been moved and that rich landowners have taken over their farms and that they are now displaced from their homesteads. Roope tells them that his officials will look into the matter, checking the boundaries with ancient land grants, and that they must be patient until their claims are verified by labyrinthine records. A tall, young man, Brando, steps from the crowd to firmly tell Roope in a quiet voice that there is no time for all that, and that the farmers must plant their crops of corn now to see an early harvest to feed their families. Roope tells him that he and his companions must check their boundaries, and Brando nods and says: "We shall do as you suggest, my president." Before Brando and the delegation depart, Roope, realizing that Brando is not just another gullible and easily manipulated peon, suspiciously asks for his name as Roope scans the list of these visitors, and, after hearing Brando utter his name, "Emiliano Zapata," draws a circle around that name as one to be closely watched. We next see Brando and his brother, Eufemio Zapata (1873-1917), played by Quinn, entering a cornfield with a group of peasants as they check its boundary markers. Suddenly, police arrive on horseback and attack the peons. Another group of armed police quickly set up a machine gun and begin shooting down fleeing peasants. Brando, atop a white stallion, races forward and lassos the machine gun, knocking down the gun crew and taking the gun in his wake as he rides away. He and Quinn then ride to the hills where they take refuge as police hunt for them. While hiding out in the mountains, Gilbert, one of Brando's closest friends, urges him to establish a relationship with Gordon, who plays Mexican patriot and revolutionary leader Francisco Madero (1873-1913), telling Brando that Gordon is leading the fight against Roope's tyrannical regime. Brando asks Gilbert that, if that is the case, why is Gordon waging that fight while in the U.S., instead of being in Mexico. Then they hear a voice below their hilltop perch calling "Zapata! Emiliano Zapata!" They see Wiseman, a dark-hatted political activist, climbing aggressively toward them, and Quinn fires a warning shot at Wiseman. "Careful you don't hit him," Gilbert cautions Quinn. "When I want to hit him, I'll hit him! When I want to miss him, I'll miss him!" Quinn replies. "A man's been known to die of a close miss," Gilbert says. Wiseman, however, rifle fire or not, will not be put off, and continues to awkwardly climb upward (his moves here amazingly duplicate the jerky movements seen in early silent films before filming was standardized at twenty-four frames per second; this was an intentional director's touch by Kazan, who admitted to this author that he wanted to visually impact the viewer with its recollection of that bygone era by shooting this little sequence at twenty fps). Wiseman finally reaches the small group where he addresses Brando, telling him that Gordon wants to see him and asks that he go to the U.S. to visit with Gordon to possibly join Gordon's movement against Roope. Brando is so evasive that he refuses to admit that he is Zapata, and prepares to leave. He nevertheless tells Gilbert to go and see Gordon, saying: "Look into Madero's eyes and tell me what you see." He then rides away as does Quinn. Margo, Gilbert's woman and a camp follower, hurriedly gathers up some meager cooking utensils and also departs. Wiseman is dumbfounded by the actions of these enigmatic outcasts, stating with disgust: "This is all very disorganized." Brando, however, is torn between aiding his oppressed people and becoming a respectable person of property in the area so that he will be an acceptable husband for Peters. She is the beautiful daughter of Ames, a wealthy merchant, who thinks Brando is nothing more than a worthless roustabout. Brando puts his best foot forward and takes a job with rich horse breeder Moss, who hires Brando to raise his thoroughbreds. When inspecting Moss' stables, however, Brando sees a little boy taking some food from a horse trough. Thomajan, a stable boss, also sees the boy and takes a whip to the boy, but Brando leaps forward and knocks Thomajan down. Before he can further beat Thomajan, Moss intervenes, restraining Brando, who angrily states: "The boy was hungry!" Moss tells Brando that he must control his impulse to right the wrongs of the world and that he has risked himself by using his influence to settle matters with the authorities over Brando's earlier transgressions. "But the boy was hungry!" Brando shouts. The patient Moss states: "You cannot be the conscience of the world." Brando accepts Moss' cool logic and, calming down, apologizes to Thomajan, who gratefully accepts that apology as he warily backs away from Brando. Later, Brando sits uncomfortably in the parlor of merchant Ames where he politely courts the sultry Peters while her mother, Dunnock, her father, Ames, and other relatives watch his every move. His exchanges between himself and Peters are forced as they discuss in abstract terms their prospect of marriage. Brando succeeds in impressing Peters' family that he is now a man of position with Moss and has a promising future. He is then interrupted when Gilbert arrives and Brando confers with him. Gilbert tells him that he is very impressed with Gordon, who is leading the fight against the despotic Roope, but Brando seems to have no more desire to topple the tyrant, repeating Moss' cautionary words: "I cannot be the conscience of the whole world." He is then seen riding with Gilbert, Wiseman and Quinn to witness an elderly peasant with a rope about his neck and his hands tied behind his back being pulled along a road by a policeman on horseback. Brando recognizes the peasant and asks him why he is in custody, but the man cannot speak as the ever tightening rope chokes off his words. Brando rides to the captain of the guard, asking him what the peasant has done, and the captain gives him an ambiguous answer: "They are always doing something." The captain yanks the rope so hard that the captive stumbles forward. Brando, resting his hand on his revolver, says to the captain: "I think you had better let him go." The policeman kicks his horse and races forward, pulling the captive downward into the dusty road so that he is horribly dragged by the neck in the wake of the policeman's galloping horse. Brando races after him and manages to cut the rope with one swipe of his machete. When Brando dismounts and examines the captive, he finds him dead. Peasants surround Brando, one saying that he will now be a hunted man and that he can hide in his house. Another offers the same kind of shelter. The peasants surrounding Brando look upon him as their heroic savior, the one man they have long been waiting for to free them from Roope's oppressive yoke. Quinn, who has chased the policemen and lost them, returns to tell Brando: "You should have cut the rope sooner." Brando then goes to a church where he tells Peters that they should be married, but she reminds him that he has broken his promise to her that he will live a non violent life and financially provide for her. When later visiting Peters and her family at her father's store, Ames tells Brando that he is unfit to be his future son-in-law. Brando grabs Ames, shaking him, saying: "What is wrong with me?" Ames angrily replies: "A fighter, a brawler, these things you are, but a man of substance, no!" Brando angrily states: "Find her a mousy, moth-eaten man like yourself!" As he leaves the store, Brando is seized by a number of policemen and a rope is placed about his neck before he, like the victim he earlier tried to save, is forced to follow on foot behind the horse of a policeman, who is surrounded by a number of other mounted guards. Brando's closest friends, Quinn, Gilbert, Margo and others begin striking rocks against each other, this signal picked up by other villagers until the village clicks and clacks with the reverberating sounds of the clashing rocks. Quinn, Gilbert and other villagers then trail the police leading Brando out of the village and along a road. As Brando is led along the road, peons appear from forests and crops, joining the procession, until hundreds of these peasants swell and clog the road before and behind the mounted policemen. Brando is yanked along by the rope around his neck, his hands tied behind his back, stumbling forward, and with a slight smile on his face, he sees the scores of farmers coming to his aid. (Kazan presents this scene with spectacular overhead shots to show hundreds of the machete-carrying peons streaming onto the road so that the procession is now a streaming river of humanity.) The procession slows as more and more peons jam the road and the nervous policeman in charge says to a peon walking beside his horse: "What are

Jean Peters and Marlon Brando in *Viva Zapata!*, 1952.

you doing?" The farmer replies: "Protecting the prisoner, because, if he escaped, you would be forced to shoot him in the back." The policeman in charge, knowing his task is hopeless, gets off his horse and walks to Brando, removing the rope from his neck and those binding his hands. Quinn, Wiseman and Gilbert arrive on horseback and bring a horse for Brando, who mounts. Wiseman points to a nearby telegraph pole, telling Brando: "Cut the wire! He'll use it!" Quinn rides to the pole, raising his machete, and the officer shouts: "Stop! Cut that wire and you'll be committing sedition!" Brando shouts to Quinn: "Cut the wire!" Quinn then savagely hacks away at the telegraph wire with his machete, severing it to start a full-scale revolution in the State of Morelos. The revolution is evidenced in the next scene where Brando inspects a derailed train his troops have blown off a track, checking the boxcars as he looks for weapons. He discovers his brother, Quinn, in a car full of harlots with a bottle in his hand, inviting him to join him. Brando has no time for that as he then learns that a cache of gun powder has been found in another car, saying that it will have to meet their needs. Those needs involve the siege of a federal fortress commanded by Biberman, who is seen looking about at his badly injured men inside that bastion and then over the rampart to see what the revolutionaries are doing. All Biberman and his men can see are some women in the bombed-out square as they carry flower baskets. "That's a good sign, don't you think, captain?" one of Biberman's men asks him. Suddenly, Margo appears to lead the women in a headlong race toward the gates of the fortress with their baskets in hand, placing them there as they contain gun powder and with a long trail of gun powder leading to those baskets. A woman then runs forward with a flaming torch to ignite the trail of gun powder. She is shot down by Bibmerman's men but, in a dying effort, manages to ignite the powder that burns rapidly toward the stacked baskets, setting off a terrific explosion that blows open the fort's gates and allows the revolutionaries to charge into the fortress, capturing it. Brando and his followers celebrate the victory, and Brando gives gifts to his adoring army of peasants. He hands out chickens and pigs as simple gifts of gratitude for their service, but when a boy, who has lost two older brothers in the battle and who has killed several federal soldiers, asks that Brando give him his magnificent white horse, the great leader hesitates, saying: "That's a good horse." A soldier standing next to the boy states: "That's why he wants him." Brando gives the boy his horse, a magnanimous gesture that further endears him to his already devoted followers. Now that Brando is a victorious general, Ames welcomes Brando into his family. Brando weds Peters, but, on their wedding night, he is restless and tells Peters that he is troubled because he cannot read, asking her to teach him. She promises to do so, but his always impulsive nature demands that she begin that very night and she gets a book where she begins instructing him word by word. Outside Brando's window, Quinn and oth-

Anthony Quinn, Marlon Brando, Lou Gilbert and Harold Gordon in *Viva Zapata!*, 1952.

ers drink and serenade their hero, all but the cold-blooded Wiseman, who does not imbibe or consort with women, as Quinn so liberally does. Quinn tells Wiseman "I love you, but I do not like you." Wiseman tells him that there will be many more battles to come. Quinn agrees, but insists that he and everyone else, except Wiseman, are human and have the need to relax and enjoy their brief moment of freedom. Then word comes that Roope has fled the country and that the Revolution is over. Brando, Quinn, Wiseman and Gilbert travel to Mexico City to meet with the new president, Gordon, who offers Brando a large ranch as a reward for his services in their victorious revolution. Brando, incensed, shouts at Gordon: "I didn't fight for a ranch!" He insists that Gordon immediately restore the stolen lands to the peasants and Gordon tells him that it will take time to do that, but the farmers will eventually regain their farmlands. He then asks Brando to have his troops lay down their arms. Brando replies that should he and his men disarm, they will have little ability to recoup and hold onto their land. He graphically demonstrates his point by aiming his rifle at Gordon and demanding that Gordon give him his watch. Gordon meekly hands over his watch and Brando then thrusts the rifle into Gordon's hands so that it is now aimed at Brando, and Brando states: "*Now* you can have your watch back!" Brando tells Gordon that he is going back to his province of Morelos and will wait, but warns that he will not wait too long to see land reforms enacted by Gordon and his new regime. After Brando leaves, Silvera, who plays the ruthless Mexican general Victoriano Huerta (aka: The Jackal; 1850-1916), urges Gordon to get rid of the pesky Brando, saying: "Shoot that Zapata now!" The well-intentioned Gordon tells Silvera that Brando has many good points as does Silvera. When Gordon leaves the room, the insidious Silvera tells his military aides that both Gordon and Brando must go, sarcastically bemoaning Gordon's noble intentions by stating: "Oh, the odor of goodness." Brando and his men do not disarm, and Gordon travels to Morelos where he persuades Brando and his followers to stack their arms. As they are so doing, however, Quinn arrives on horseback with news that Silvera's troops have invaded the province and are soon to arrive in the area. The ever trouble-making Wiseman accuses Gordon of betrayal, but Gordon is dumbfounded and confused, stating that Silvera must have misunderstood his orders and that he will stop Silvera's troops. "If you don't, I will!" Brando angrily states before he rides off to lead his troops to meet this new threat. Gordon returns to Mexico City, but he is held captive in the presidential palace until taken to a remote area at night and, after getting out of a car and thinking to meet with Silvera, is assassinated. (Madero was taken from the presidential palace in Mexico City on the night of February 22, 1913, by a unit of federal troops commanded by Captain Francisco Cardenas, an officer working in liaison with Huerta. As Cardenas and his men were transporting Madera and his Vice President, Jose Marie Pino Suarez,

1869-1913, to a nearby penitentiary for incarceration, Cardenas later claimed that a rebel force attacked the two cars transporting the captives and killed them both, a fabrication in that Cardenas ordered both men killed. Cardenas later fled to Guatemala where he committed suicide in 1920 rather than face extradition back to Mexico where he had been indicted for Madero's murder.) Brando and his men fiercely battle Silvera's troops, and in the process, Brando finds himself ordering the executions of some of his own men, who have fraternized with the enemy, including Gilbert, who had attempted to arrange a truce. Gilbert asks that Brando himself personally execute him instead of strangers, asking before Brando complies: "Can good come from a bad thing?" (Throughout the chaotic Mexican Revolution, such mass executions were routine as factions changed sides and tenuous allegiances were shattered by the shifting tides of battles, which the brilliant Steinbeck knew well when writing the great script for this film.) Silvera's savage regime, like Roope's before him, is toppled (in 1914) by Brando's forces in the South and those in the North led by Pancho Villa (1878-1923), played by Reed. Both Brando and Reed meet in Mexico City's presidential palace, and Brando insists that Reed sit in the throne chair occupied by so many other victorious conquerors as they have their picture taken together. Both later relax beneath a tree on a small island to debate the future of Mexico, and Reed insists that Brando become the country's president to finally establish the social and economic reforms they have so long fought to establish. Reed tells Brando that he is sick of war, that, after he beats one bloody tyrant, another arrives and that there is no end to the Revolution. He is tired, Reed says, and he is going to retire to his ranch. "Do I look like a president?" he states. He asks Brando if he can read and Brando smiles and nods. "It's settled then," Reed tells him. "You are the president." Brando assumes the office of president, but finds that he is facing obstacles at every turn when he tries to institute his agrarian reforms (based on Zapata's rebuilding of the State of Morelos, according to Zapata's 1911 Plan de Ayala wherein the hacienda lands of the former estate owners were to be redistributed to the peasant farmers). A delegation of farmers from Morelos arrives to beg Brando to do something about his brother, Quinn, who has seized their lands. Brando tells them that he will look into that, but he is challenged by one of the delegates, Silva (in his film debut), who defiantly tells him, as Brando told Roope years earlier, that there is no time for prolonged record-checking as crops must be planted to feed the hungry peasants. Incensed by Silva's bold assertions, Brando takes the list of the names of the delegation and draws a circle around the name "Hernandez," which is Silva's name. He then leans forward upon a table to hauntingly remember that Roope did the same thing with his name, marking him for possible extermination as a potential upstart and troublemaker. (The memorable adage of "The Past is Prologue" is thusly and powerfully exhibited with biting irony in this scene.) Brando now sees himself as he saw Roope, a dictator no longer in touch with his people, and he immediately decides to abandon his ineffective position of authority. He goes to another room with Wiseman, the ever-present, eternal Iago, following him and nervously asking: "Where are you going?" Brando tells Wiseman that he is going home to Morelos. "So you're throwing it away!" Wiseman shouts. "Leave tonight and your enemies will be here tomorrow, in this room, at that desk. They won't walk away. They'll hunt you down till you get your rest in the sun with the flies on your face! Leave now and I promise you that you won't live long." Brando replies: "I won't live long anyway." Wiseman blocks his path, saying: "In the name of all we fought for, don't go!" Brando answers: "In the name of all we fought for, I am going!" Wiseman tells Brando that he will not go with him. Brando nods, saying: "I don't expect you to… Now I know you…No woman…no friends…no love. You only destroy—that is your love. And I will tell you what you will do now. You will go to [Zapata's then enemies] Obregon [Alvaro Obregon, 1880-1928], or Carranza [Venustiano Carranza, 1859-1920], and you will never change!" With that, Brando grabs his rifle and leaves the room. When returning to Morelos, Brando enters the dilapidated rooms of a once resplendent hacienda to find Quinn drunk on a couch with a woman he has stolen from a farmer, who stands with a group of peons behind Brando. Quinn points a sword at Brando, knowing why he has come and says: "Be careful what you say to me, brother." Brando, enraged, grabs Quinn by the hair, yanking his face to his own, shouting, "You drunken pig!" Quinn breaks free to defiantly face Brando, shouting: "We beat Diaz! He's living in a palace in Spain! We beat Huerta! He's living as a rich man in the United States! Look at me! I am a general!" He reaches into his pocket, turning it inside out to show it empty. "Here's my pay—a hunk of dust!" He admits that he took the lands of the peons, and, motioning toward the woman, says: "I took their women, too. And nobody had better stop me!" With that he motions the woman to follow him as they both go down a corridor and into another room. The aggrieved farmers gather about Brando, who tells them: 'There are no strong men…they die…they desert." He motions in the direction Quinn has taken, saying, "they change…there is only a strong people." At that moment, firing breaks out as the farmer attacks Quinn, fatally shooting him as Quinn shoots back, killing the farmer at the end of a long hall. Quinn then cries out: "Emiliano!" before collapsing and Brando runs to him to cradle his body, inconsolable as he weeps for his dead brother. The farmers offer to bury Quinn with full honors as a former general, but Brando tells them no, "he did not die in battle." (Zapata's brother, Eufemio Zapata, actually died on June 18, 1917, in Cuautla, Morelos, when the womanizing Eufemio, while drunk, began beating for no reason the father of Sidronio Comacho, one of Emiliano Zapata's commanders; Comacho shot Eufemio in the abdomen before throwing him face down upon an anthill to meet an agonizing death. Comacho, who later joined Emiliano Zapata's enemies for safety, said to the dying Eufemio Zapata: "You have made many people suffer a great deal. Live a little longer so that you also will learn what it is to suffer.") Quinn's death symbolically marks Brando's decline of fortune as he and his troops are defeated by the forces of Obregon and Carranza, the very enemies who now occupy the presidential palace; the opportunistic Wiseman is their adviser and now Brando's avowed enemy. Brando lives in the mountains in a small hut with Peters, and he has only a small force of followers. Silva arrives to tell him that DeKova, a federal colonel, has agreed to defect and join Brando in his ongoing revolution, claiming that DeKova has "passed every test" in displaying his loyalty to Brando, and that DeKova will also turn over arms and heavy guns to the revolutionaries. Brando decides to accept DeKova's offer, but Peters begs him not to go to Chinemeca to meet the defecting colonel. Brando ignores her apprehensions, even after she clings to him and his horse until falling away when he rides off with his men. Brando arrives at a large hacienda where arms are stacked and waiting for him, the gates to its high walls open wide. DeKova stands at the entrance to welcome him, surprising Brando when he embraces and kisses him (as if with a Judas kiss). DeKova (in his film debut) is a strange sight to behold. Everything about him is ungainly and repulsive—a bowlegged, pigeon-toed man with crossed eyes and the stiff mannerisms of a puppet on a string. (He plays Colonel Jesus Guajardo, who commanded the 50th Cavalry Regiment, and who pretended to defect to Zapata, and when Zapata arrived at his headquarters on April 10, 1919, was immediately shot to death by Guajardo's troops.) As Brando enters the hacienda, he sees his favorite white horse standing in the square and impulsively goes to the animal, petting it, and saying: "You've changed…gotten old." As Brando fondles the horse, DeKova apprehensively draws his sword to give the signal for hundreds of soldiers to suddenly appear on the walls of the hacienda and where they unleash a thundering fusillade of bullets that rip into Brando, who falls to the ground, drawing himself into a fetal position, the bullets renting his flesh and clothes until Brando's hands and feet quiver before becoming still to indicate his death. The horse bolts and races from the hacienda and Wiseman appears, screaming for the troops to shoot the horse, but the animal swiftly escapes unharmed. Garrick, an elderly general, appears to look down upon Brando's corpse, saying: "They must have been ter-

Anthony Quinn and Nina Varela in *Viva Zapata!*, 1952.

ribly afraid of him—they shot him to pieces." Wiseman shouts: "Cut off the head of the snake and the body will die." Garrick shakes his head: "I don't know. Sometimes a dead man can be a terrible enemy." Wiseman states that they will place the riddled body of the heroic revolutionary in the town square "so that they can all see that he is dead." The body is then carried to the town square where it is dumped, and Margo and other women rush to it, covering Brando's face and covering the body with flowers. Several peons who have known their leader gather next to the body. One of them states: "He could be anybody, shot up that way." None of the farmers believe that the dead man is that of their idealized leader. "Whenever we need him, he will come," one says. "He is in the mountains." They look to the high mountains looming nearby and another says: "Yes, he is in the mountains." The camera then shows the escaped white stallion standing in those high mountains to symbolize the undying spirit of the great leader of the Mexican Revolution to end this passionately stunning and emotionally stirring masterpiece. Pantheon director Kazan robustly helms this unforgettable biopic by seamlessly unfolding its traumatic historical events in very human terms that memorialize its colorful characters. Each one of those characters is distinctively developed by the always innovative Kazan, where the lowliest peon shines with a separate personality. The acting throughout is consistently forceful and effectively believable, from Brando's bravura performance to Gordon's noble essay, from Gilbert's pensive portrait to Quinn's expansive and outgoing profile. Evil oozes through the sharply etched characters of Roope's patronizing Diaz, Silvera's ruthless Huerta, and Wiseman's classic portrait of an insidiously betraying Iago, one of the most dangerous and treacherous characters ever recorded on the screen. The script is a gem of authenticity, packed with wit and irony but couched in the simple and understandable terms of prosaic people. Quinn deservedly won an Oscar for Best Supporting Actor, and the film received Oscar nominations for Best Actor (Brando), Best Screenplay (Steinbeck), Best Music (North), and Best Art Direction (Wheeler, Fuller; set decoration: Little, Carpenter). The film did well at the box office, earning almost $2 million, but those revenues barely covered its staggering budget of more than $1.8 million. A sixty-minute radio adaptation was aired by Lux Radio Theater on November 3, 1952, with Peters reprising her role. ***Author's Note***: Kazan admitted to this author that "we took a few liberties with the Zapata story, but not many. The main thing is that we showed Zapata in a great performance from Marlon [Brando] as a genuine crusader for political and economic emancipation in Mexico. He sacrificed his life for his people." Kazan also admitted that his perspective of Zapata and the Mexican Revolution was deeply influenced by Sergei Eisenstein's **Que Viva Mexico!**, 1932, a docudrama about the Revolution as seen through the eyes of a peasant family, as well as the startling and uncensored con-

Marlon Brando and Lou Gilbert in *Viva Zapata!*, 1952.

temporary newsreels that documented the uncompromising savagery and atrocities of that conflict. Steinbeck, too, told this author that "some of the little things about Zapata needed additional dramatic elements to identify him with the illiterate peons he led. I know the real Zapata lived above the poverty level of most of his people as his family members were better off and he had some education. In showing his desire to learn how to read, I was showing the desire of his people to better their lot." Kazan told this author that he and Steinbeck wrote the script together while spending time in Steinbeck's NYC home, recalling how "we talked our way through that incredible story, and, while we talked about the Mexican Revolution and Zapata, John [Steinbeck] whittled away on a stick. I looked down to the shavings at his feet and they reminded me of corn husks, like the ones we showed in the fields the peasants are trying to reclaim in the picture." Kazan had wanted to do a film about Zapata for many years and approached several studio chiefs with the idea, getting tepid responses until Fox head Darryl Zanuck got excited about the project in 1949. Zanuck told this author: "We wanted to make the picture [**Viva Zapata!**] in Mexico, but, when we contacted officials there, they refused, saying that when another picture was made about Pancho Villa [**Viva Villa!**, 1934], the producers of that picture portrayed Villa and Mexicans as moronic savages, and they wanted no more American pictures that might show Mexicans the same way." Undaunted, Zanuck personally scouted southwest Texas and discovered between the Pecos and Rio Grande Rivers an area almost identical to the State of Morelos in Mexico, and this film was mostly shot on location near Roma, Texas. Additional on-location filming took place in Durango, Colorado, and in New Mexico. Kazan thought that the Mexican government was attempting to sabotage this film when it was in production, telling this author: "Almost every day, hundreds of Mexican men would swim the Rio Grande and appear near our set without any clothes on and wanting to be hired as extras and I had to chase them away, but they kept swimming that river day after day, until one day I got a pistol and fired several shots when I saw them all swimming toward the American side of the Rio Grande, and they turned around like obedient dolphins and swam the other way back to Mexico." The working title for this film was "Beloved Tiger," and Brando was slated to play the lead role at that time. Brando had already made himself famous with his theatrical and filmic portraits of the brutish Stanley Kowalksi in **A Streetcar Named Desire**, 1951 (directed by Kazan), but Quinn had also scored as a hit in that same role in separate theatrical productions. When Quinn was approached with a request to appear in this film, he willingly agreed, but then, as he later stated to this author: "They led me to believe that I would play Zapata. So when I learned that I was to play Zapata's brother and that Marlon [Brando] was going to play Zapata, I got damned angry. I thought about it for a while and then changed my mind and decided

that I would do the part they wanted me to play and it was a good decision because I wound up by winning an Academy Award and Marlon did not. But make no mistake, Marlon was terrific in that role and deserved an Oscar as well. What made me decide to play Marlon's brother in that picture was when I learned that Gadg [Kazan] was thinking of casting Jack Palance in that part. Well, hell, I grabbed the part before I lost that one, too! I thought Joe [Wiseman] was also outstanding in that picture. A more frightening warmonger never existed on film, I have always thought when thinking about his performance. He was such a strange guy, with lightning moves and a screaming voice that could turn your blood cold. He was absolutely perfect in his role." Quinn and Brando nevertheless quickly bonded when they went into this production, especially after they went to the Rio Grande when on location to relieve themselves and held a urinating contest as to see which one could send their emissions farther into that river. Quinn admitted to this author that he and Brando held such an unlikely competition, saying: "I guess we were as crude as the characters we were playing. In case you're wondering, Marlon won that contest." Brando was rather outlandish during this production in that he told reporters that he had eaten just about everything in his life, including grasshoppers and the eyes of gazelles. At one point, he climbed a tree outside of Jean Peters' hotel room to serenade her and later set off a string of firecrackers in the lobby of his hotel "to liven up things." The actor, however, took his role as Zapata very seriously, telling this author: "Some critics said I went out of my way to look Oriental when I played Zapata, but I had my face made up to look just the way Zapata looked in the Diego Rivera portraits and the many historical photos of him. I studied those pictures of him for some time, and I did a lot of research about that great Mexican hero before I went into the picture. He was a great patriot and deserved the best I could give him." To achieve Zapata's native Indian appearance, Brando designed his own makeup, taping his eyelids so that they had the appearance of the Mexican Indian, which was part of Zapata's heritage, and where Brando used metal rings to flare his nostrils. Though the actual Zapata was a small man with delicate features, large eyes and small hands and feet, Brando nevertheless in heart and mind embodies the spirit of that great leader in every frame of this film. Oddly, Brando was not Zanuck's first choice for the role of Zapata as he had his reigning star, Tyrone Power, in mind for that part, particularly since Power had played another Mexican hero in **The Mark of Zorro**, 1940. Kazan talked Zanuck out of casting Power in that role. "I told Darryl [Zanuck] that Ty [Tyrone Power] was good in **The Mark of Zorro** because he was playing the sophisticated son of a great landowner, but he was too polished and handsome to play the peasant leader, Zapata. That's when we started talking about Marlon Brando, one of America's greatest actors." When Fox starlet Marilyn Monroe learned about the production, she tried to be cast in the role of Brando's wife, but Zanuck thought her acting abilities "were extremely limited" and she was forgotten. So, too, was actor Richard Conte, who had lobbied for the role of Zapata. Julie Harris was originally signed to play Brando's wife, but Brando wanted an actress who appeared to be more sultry and tempestuous, and Peters was then hired for that role. For extensive details on the Mexican Revolution and comprehensive information about the many assassinations of its leaders (Madero, 1913; Zapata, 1919; Carranza, 1920; Villa, 1923; Obregon, 1928), see my two-volume work *The Great Pictorial History of World Crime*, Volume I (History, Inc., 2004; pages 84-96). Other actors playing Emiliano Zapata in other films include **El encanto del aguila**, 2011 (Tenoch Huerta); **El vuelo del aguila**, 1994 (TV series; Oscar Castaneda); **Lauro Punales**, 1969 (Jaime Fernandez); **Lucio Vazquez**, 1968 (Jaime Fernandez); **Mexikanische Revolution**, 1968 (made-for-TV; Erik Schumann); **Pafnucio Santo**, 1977 (Gina Morett); **Red Bells Part I: Mexico on Fire**, 1982 (Jorge Luke); **Santos peregrinos**, 2004 (Alberto Estrella); **Senda de Gloria**, 1987 (TV series; Manuel Ojeda); **Trini**, 1979 (Iwan Tomow); **Viva Mexico**, 1980 (made-for-TV; Claude Juan); **Zapata**, 1970 (Antonio Aguilar); **Zapata: Amor en rebeldia**, 2004 (TV miniseries; Demian Bichir); and **Zapata—El sueno** del heroe, 2004 (Alejandro Fernandez). Other films depicting the Mexican Revolution of 1910-1920 include **The Abandoned**, 1945; **Adventurous Youth**, 1928; **American Family**, 2002-2004 (TV series; "Mexican Revolution," 2002 episode); **And Starring Pancho Villa as Himself**, 2003 (made-for-TV); **Antonieta**, 1982; **Aqui esta Juan Colorado**, 1947; **Bandido**, 1956; **Bandits**, 1991; **Bad Man's River**, 1974; **Behind the Clouds**, 1963; **A Bullet for the General**, 1968; **Café Colon**, 1959; **Cannon for Cordoba**, 1970; **Capitan de rurales**, 1951; **Como agua para chocalate**, 1993; **Companeros**, 1972; **Cuando Viva Viva!...es la muerte**, 1961; **Cuartelazo**, 1977; **Django 2—Il grande ritorno**, 1987; **Don't Turn the Other Cheek**, 1974; **Duck, You Sucker**, 1972; **Duelo en las montanas**, 1950; **El caudillo**, 1968; **El diablo en persona**, 1973; **El escapulario**, 1968; **El ojo de vidrio**, 1969; **El principio**, 1973; **The Five Man Army**, 1970; **Godfather Mendoza**, 1934; **The Guns of Juana Gallo**, 1962; **Guns of the Magnificent Seven**, 1969; **The Hidden One**, 1957; **Il lungo giorno della violenza**, 1971; **Impatient Heart**, 1960; **Killer Kid**, 1967; **La Bandida**, 1963; **La Cebra**, 2011; **La chamuscada**, 1971; **La constitucion**, 1970; **La genererala**, 1971; **La guerrillera de Villa**, 1967; **La parajera**, 1945; **La tormenta**, 1967 (TV series); **La trinchera**, 1969; **La Valentina**, 1966; **Land of Darkness**, 1995; **Las fuerzas vivas**, 1975; **Las tres pelonas**, 1958; **The Light of Western Stars**, 1940; **Los cuatro Juanes**, 1966; **Los de abajo**, 1940; **Los de abajo**, 1978; **Morir de pie**, 1957; **Old Gringo**, 1989; **100 Rifles**, 1969; **Pancho Villa**, 1973; **Pancho Villa and Valentina**, 1961; **Pedro Paramo**, 1967; **Prision de mujeres**, 1977; **Prisoner 13**, 1933; **A Professional Gun**, 1970; **The Professionals**, 1966; **Pueblo en armas**, 1959; **Run, Man, Run**, 1968; **Sangre derramada**, 1975; **Senda de gloria**, 1987 (TV series); **Shadow of Pancho Villa**, 1934; **She Came to the Valley**, 1979; **Si Adelita se fuera con otro**, 1948; **The Soldiers of Pancho Villa**, 1961; **Sucedio en Jalisco**, 1972; **They Came to Cordura**, 1959; **Tepepa**, 1979; **This Was Pancho Villa**, 1959; **A Town Called Hell**, 1972; **The Treasure of Pancho Villa**, 1957; **Un treno per Durango**, 1968; **Valente Quintero**, 1973; **Valentin de la Sierra**, 1968; **Villa Rides**, 1968; **Vino el remolino y nos alevanto**, 1950; **Viva Benito Canales!**, 1966; **Viva Cangaceiro**, 1970; **Viva Maria!**, 1965; **Viva Villa!**, 1934; **Vuelve Pancho Villa**, 1950; **Wanted: The Sundance Woman**, 1976 (made-for-TV); **What Am I Doing in the Middle of the Revolution**, 1972; **The Wild Bunch**, 1969; and **Wings of the Hawk**, 1953. **p**, Darryl F. Zanuck; **d**, Elia Kazan; **cast**, Marlon Brando, Jean Peters, Anthony Quinn, Joseph Wiseman, Arnold Moss, Alan Reed, Margo, Fay Roope, Mildred Dunnock, Harold Gordon, Lou Gilbert, Frank Silvera, Nina Varela, Florenz Ames, Bernie Gozier, Frank DeKova, Joseph Granby, Pedro Regas, Guy Thomajan, Henry Silva, Philip Van Zandt, Nestor Paiva, Richard Garrick, Abner Biberman; **w**, John Steinbeck (based on the novel *Zapata the Unconquered* by Edgecumb Pinchon); **c**, Joe MacDonald; **m**, Alex North; **ed**, Barbara McLean; **art d**, Lyle Wheeler, Leland Fuller; **set d**, Thomas Little, Claude Carpenter; **spec eff**, Fred Sersen.

Vivacious Lady ★★★ 1938; U.S.; 90m; RKO; B/W; Comedy/Romance; Children: Acceptable; **DVD**; **VHS**. Pleasant romantic comedy sees Stewart as a mild-mannered University botany professor in a small town dominated by his father, Coburn, who runs the school and everyone else. He is sent to New York to retrieve fun-loving cousin Ellison, who is frequenting all the Big Apple night spots. In one of the bistros, Stewart becomes taken by the charms of Rogers, a lively and free-spirited singer. She is unlike any girl he has ever known, and soon falls head over heels in love and marries her. His troubles begin when he takes his bride home to meet his disapproving father, mother, Bondi, and former fiancée, Mercer. Stewart can't get up the gumption to introduce Rogers as his wife, so Mercer engages her in a no-holds-barred, hair-pulling hen fight. Rogers comes out on top and eventually everyone, except Mercer, accepts her as Stewart's feisty spouse. Stewart and Rogers give marvelously animated performances under the taut helming by pantheon director Stevens. This film received Oscar nominations for Best Cine-

Director George Stevens, Ginger Rogers and James Stewart on the set of *Vivacious Lady,* 1938.

matography (de Grasse), and Best Sound Recording (John Aalberg). A thirty-minute radio adaptation was aired by the Screen Guild Theater on April 7, 1940, with Rogers reprising her role and Fred MacMurray in Stewart's role. The story saw a second radio adaptation aired by Lux Radio Theater on January 6, 1941, with Don Ameche in the Stewart role and Alice Faye in the role played by Rogers. A third thirty-minute radio adaptation was aired by the Screen Guild Theater on December 3, 1945, with Stewart reprising his role. This film did well at the box office, earning more than $1.2 million in its initial release against a $700,000 budget. Songs: "You'll Be Reminded of Me" (1938; George Jessel, Jack Meskill, Ted Shapiro), "Here Comes the Bride (Bridal Chorus)" (1850; from the opera "Lohengrin" by Richard Wagner), "The Wedding March" (1843; from "A Midsummer Night's Dream" by Felix Mendelssohn-Bartholdy), "Down By the Old Mill Stream" (1910; Tell Taylor). *Author's Note*: Stevens, who had, a year earlier, directed Rogers, along with her long-time dancing co-star Fred Astaire, in **Swing Time**, 1936, told this author that "Ginger's [Roger's] legs had been insured for $500,000, so, when we filmed that wild, hair-pulling fight between her and Frances [Mercer], we had to protect Ginger's fabulous legs by having them specially wrapped with padding." Rogers recalled that event, saying to this author: "I hated that because all that padding made me look too heavy, like I had just eaten half a steer and all the new weight had gone straight to my thighs." Stewart told this author: "Although we had not appeared in any pictures together, Ginger [Rogers] asked that I be her co-star in **Vivacious Lady**. I was eager to do that picture, but I got so ill in the first week of production that they had to shut it down. By the time I was able to get back, they had replaced the actors playing my parents [Donald Crisp and Fay Bainter] with Charles Coburn and Beulah Bondi. Beulah played my mother in quite a number of pictures, and I used to call her 'Mom' off camera." Other than this film, Bondi played Stewart's mother in four other productions: **Of Human Hearts**, 1938; **Mr. Smith Goes to Washington**, 1939; **It's a Wonderful Life**, 1946; and on a 1971 TV episode of "The Jimmy Stewart Show". **p&d**, George Stevens; **cast**, Ginger Rogers, James Stewart, James Ellison, Beulah Bondi, Charles Coburn, Franklin Pangborn, Russell Wade, Grady Sutton, Jack Carson, Willie Best, Maude Eburne, Hattie McDaniel, Dennis O'Keefe, Frances Mercer; **w**, Ernest Pagano, P.J. Wolfson, Anne Morrison Chapin (based on a story by I.A.R. Wylie); **c**, Robert de Grasse; **m**, Roy Webb; **ed**, Henry Berman; **art d**, Van Nest Polglase, Carroll Clark; **set d**, Darrell Silvera.

The Voice of the Turtle ★★★ 1947; U.S.; 103m; WB; B/W; Comedy; Romance; Children: Acceptable; **DVD**; **VHS**; **IV**. Entertaining romance has Parker as a Broadway actress hoping the man of her dreams comes along soon, but the pickings are slim during World War II (1939-1945)

Ronald Reagan and Eleanor Parker in *The Voice of the Turtle*, 1947.

with most eligible men off fighting the war. Smith, her producer boyfriend, gives her up, and she is becoming desperate. Then she meets Reagan, a soldier who is in New York looking to meet up with his girlfriend, Arden, who also is an actress. Flighty and wisecracking, Arden has forgotten she has a date with Reagan and is concentrating on Morris, a navy commander. When Reagan finds them together, Arden says Morris is her husband. Reagan dejectedly departs, but needs somewhere to sleep for the night, so Parker says he can stay in her apartment, but on a strictly platonic basis (shades of the hilarious sleeping arrangements made between Joel McCrea and Jean Arthur in the WWII comedy **The More the Merrier**, 1943). Fickle Arden then decides she likes Reagan best after all and she becomes jealous of Parker as Reagan and Parker draw closer. Arden does all she can to keep them apart, but her ridiculous antics backfire and Reagan and Parker fall in love and soon head for the altar. Songs: "The First Noel" (traditional), "Silent Night, Holy Night" (music: Franz Gruber; lyrics: Joseph Mohr), "The Sailor's Hornpipe" (traditional), "A Little on the Lonely Side" (Richard Robertson, Frank Weldon, James Cavanaugh), "Londonderry Air/Danny Boy" (traditional), "How Many Hearts Have You Broken/With Those Great Big Beautiful Eyes" (Al Kaufman), "Time Waits for No One" (Cliff Friend), "Gotta Be This or That" (Sunny Skylar). **p**, Charles Hoffman; **d**, Irving Rapper; **cast**, Ronald Reagan, Eleanor Parker, Eve Arden, Wayne Morris, Kent Smith, John Emery, Erskine Sanford, Douglas Kennedy, Ross Ford, Ernest Anderson; **w**, John Van Druten (based on his play, additional dialogue by Charles Hoffman); **c**, Sol Polito; **m**, Max Steiner; **ed**, Rudi Fehr; **art d**, Robert Haas; **set d**, William Kuehl; **spec eff**, Harry Barndollar, Edwin DuPar.

Volver ★★★ 2007; Spain; 107m; Canal+Espana/Sony; Color; Drama; Children: Unacceptable (MPAA: R); **BD**; **DVD**. This offbeat, but intriguing film profiles an eccentric family of women from a region south of Madrid, Spain. The action centers on Cruz, a working-class woman forced to go to great lengths to protect her teenage daughter, Duenas, who has killed her father (de la Torre). Cruz's mother, Maura, comes back from the dead to help everyone. The name "Volver" is Spanish for "to return." Song: "Volver" (Carlos Gardel, Alfredo Le Pera). Sexual content and gutter language prohibit viewing by children. (In Spanish; English subtitles.) **p**, Esther Garcia; **d&w**, Pedro Almodovar; **cast**, Penelope Cruz, Carmen Maura, Lola Duenas, Blanca Portillo, Yohana Cobo, Chus Lampreave, Antonio de la Torre, Carlos Blanco, Maria Isabel Diaz, Neus Sanz; **c**, Jose Luis Alcaine; **m**, Alberto Iglesias; **ed**, Jose Salcedo; **prod d**, Salvador Parra; **set d**, Mara Matey; **spec eff**, Eduardo Diaz.

Von Richthofen and Brown ★★★ 1971; U.S.; 97m; Corman Co./UA; Color; War Drama; Children: Unacceptable (MPAA: PG-13); **BD**;

DVD; **VHS**; **IV**. This action-loaded film begins during the last days and flight of World War I (1914-1918) German fighter pilot Manfred von Richthofen (1892-1918). Known as the Red Baron, he was considered the top flying ace of the war, officially credited with eighty air combat victories. Played by Law, Richthofen and his comrades daily face an Allied squadron whose ace is Arthur Roy Brown (1893-1944), played by Stroud, a cynical and ruthless Canadian who does not fly by Richthofen's code of aerial chivalry. Richthofen and Brown engage each other in two aerial battles, and, in the second confrontation, Richthofen is shot down and killed at the age of twenty-five on April 21, 1918, flying his triplane over Morlancourt Ridge, near Vaux-sur-Somme, France. Controversy still exists regarding who was responsible for shooting him out of the skies. It is widely believed that the fatal shot was not fired by Brown, but by someone on the ground. A national hero to the Germans and highly respected by Allied pilots, von Richthofen was buried in Berlin with full military honors. This was Roger Corman's final film, and he does a more than credible job in presenting some very exciting aerial combat scenes. Many other actors have enacted Richthofen in many other films, including **Angry Nazi Zombies**, 2012 (Sam Smith); **Blackadder Goes Forth**, 1989 (TV series; "Private Plane," 1989 episode; Adrian Edmondson); **The Blue Max**, 1966 (Carl Schell); **Darling Lili**, 1970 (Ingo Morgendorf); **Fantasy Island**, 1977-1984 (TV series; "The Red Baron/Young at Heart," 1979 episode: Ron Ely); **The Great Waldo Pepper**, 1975 (Art Scholl); **Handle with Care**, 1977 (Harry Northup); **Man, Moment, Machine**, 2005-2007 (TV series; "The Red Baron & the Wings of Death," 2006 episode: Alexander Cukor); **The Red Baron**, 2010 (Matthias Schweighofer as the adult Manfred von Richthofen; Tomas Koutnik as the young Manfred von Richthofen); **Revenge of the Red Baron**, 1994 (John C. McDonnell voiceover); **Richthofen**, 1929 (George Burghardt); and **War of the Worlds: Goliath**, 2012 (Matt Letscher voiceover). **p**, Gene Corman; **d**, Roger Corman; **cast**, John Phillip Law, Don Stroud, Barry Primus, Corin Redgrave, Karen Huston, Hurd Hatfield, Stephen McHattie, Brian Foley, Robert La Tourneaux, Peter Masterson; **w**, John William Corrington, Joyce Hooper Corrington; **c**, Michael Reed; **m**, Hugo Friedhofer; **ed**, Alan Collins; **art d**, Jimmy T. Murakami; **set d**, Maureen Roche; **spec eff**, Peter Dawson, Noel Gallagher.

Von Ryan's Express ★★★★ 1965; U.S.; 117m; P-R Productions/FOX; Color; War Drama; Children: Unacceptable; **BD**; **DVD**; **VHS**; **IV**. This taut and suspenseful thriller sees superb performances from Sinatra and Howard, who battle each other's authority as they battle Italian and German enemies in this outstanding WWII (1939-1945) escape film. The film opens with Sinatra, a U.S. Army Air Force colonel named Joseph L. Ryan, who is shot down over Italy and taken to a POW camp guarded by Italian soldiers and occupied mostly by British troops commanded by Howard. The camp is controlled by Italian fascist officer Celi, who treats the prisoners with cruel indifference and metes out harsh punishment for the slightest infraction. Sinatra joins the POWs and, as the ranking officer, soon takes command when he objects to how Howard is managing things. Sinatra and Howard soon clash after Sinatra learns that Dexter, one of the eight U.S. servicemen held in the camp, is about to be punished for stealing medicine to aid one of his ailing fellow GIs. Howard has ordered Dexter's punishment, even though he admits that he has been hoarding that medicine for an eventual prison break. Sinatra demands to be shown where the drugs are hidden and, after seeing the cache of medicine, angers Howard by ordering that all of the drugs be dispensed to sick prisoners as they need them. Seeing that conditions at the camp are intolerable and that the hygiene is terrible, Sinatra meets with Celi and agrees to work with him if Celi improves conditions at the camp, including better food and providing basic needs, such as soap and water. Celi agrees and, in return for Celi's promise, Sinatra shows Celi and his guards the hidden tunnels that have been dug by Howard's men. This enrages Howard, who nevertheless defers to Sinatra's superior rank and continues to take Sinatra's orders. One of the orders Sinatra gives him is to have all the Allied prisoners strip naked and stand in the center of the compound where their ragged, dirty uniforms are burned. Celi orders his men to put out the fire, but their small water engine malfunctions. Celi is then forced to issue new uniforms for the POWs, which he has been holding back, but takes revenge on Sinatra by having him placed in a metal sweat box. (This scene is not dissimilar to the treatment given to commanding officer Alec Guinness in **The Bridge on the River Kwai**, 1957, after Guinness defies the Japanese commander of a POW camp and is placed in a sweat box.) Suddenly, Italy signs a truce with the Allies and the camp guards all flee. Sinatra is freed only to find that Howard is trying Celi as a war criminal in a kangaroo military court, where Fantoni, Celi's compassionate second-in-command, attempts to defend Celi. The desperate Celi denounces fascism and pleads for his life after he has been sentenced to death. Sinatra, however, commutes that death sentence and orders that Celi be placed in the sweat box where he has tortured so many Allied prisoners in the past. The prisoners then flee the camp, moving across the Italian countryside, and Fantoni, who has joined their cause, is sent to contact Allied troops. Meanwhile, German troops arrive at the deserted prison camp to find Celi, releasing him from the sweat box, and the Germans then begin hunting for the escaped POWs. The POWs take refuge in some ancient Roman ruins that night, but they find themselves surrounded by swarms of heavily armed German troops at dawn. Several POWs attempt to flee and are shot down. The rest are herded to a railroad siding where they are ordered to enter boxcars that are then sealed. Sinatra and Howard believe that Fantoni has given them away, but they find Fantoni beaten and made prisoner for siding with the POWs in the boxcar they share while they see Celi outside with the German commander and realize that it was Celi, an unrepentant fascist, who has betrayed them. Howard blames Sinatra for the botched mass escape, especially after the Germans shoot some of the sick and wounded POWs before the train moves off; Howard shouts at Sinatra: "You'll get your Iron Cross now, *Von Ryan!*" When the train reaches Rome, the POWs are allowed to eat, and Preiss, a German major, takes command of the train, occupying the last car, which has a comfortable office area and several sleeping compartments, one of which is occupied by Preiss' Italian mistress, the alluring Carra. Realizing that they are being shipped to Germany, Sinatra, Howard and others plan another escape. They tear apart some rotting floorboards from the boxcar, and, when the train stops that night to refuel at a remote area, Sinatra, Howard and Leyton slip through a hole in the floor and kill several of the guards. They then free some of the prisoners in another car, who kill the remaining guards before Sinatra, Howard and others take over the rear car and capture Preiss and Carra. When they see another train approaching, the train picks up steam with Scotti, the engineer, working the throttle after Fantoni has persuaded him to help the POWs. As several of the POWs don the uniforms of the German guards they have killed and pose as those guards while riding atop the boxcars, the captured Preiss tells Sinatra that the train following theirs is a German troop train on the same schedule so that they will never have the time to stop and make good their escape. Preiss also informs them that it is essential (in order to stay alive) that he be present when the train stops at every station the POWs are fed while the train remains in the station, and where he must personally get official clearance from the German commander in every station to continue the train's passage. Sinatra agrees, but plans to replace Preiss with British officer and chaplain Mulhare, who speaks fluent German. Although Mulhare adamantly refuses to enact such an impersonation, he is persuaded to do so and soon convinces everyone, including himself, that he is that very haughty and demanding German officer epitomized by Preiss. When the train stops at the next station, Florence, Mulhare orders the armed guards, who are escaped POWs wearing the German uniforms of the real guards they have killed, to remain at their posts, perched atop the railroad cars, so that these men will not be forced to speak German with other real German guards at that station. Mulhare further demands that the German officer giving clearance for the train to proceed imme-

Frank Sinatra and Trevor Howard in *Von Ryan's Express*, 1965.

diately button his tunic on the threat of being sent to the Russian Front to fight. Mulhare thus convinces that German officer, who clears the train to travel to its next stop, that Mulhare is another dangerous and fanatical Nazi officer. Mulhare's impersonation impresses Sinatra and Howard, but, after Mulhare reenters the command car, he faints dead away from his tense experience. While inspecting the maps Preiss has been given, Sinatra, realizes that their train, as well as the following troop train, is headed for Innsbruck, Austria, where the POWs will be imprisoned. When the POW train next stops in Bologna, Mulhare again impersonates Preiss to have the train's passage approved, and he is accompanied by Sinatra and Howard, who pose as German guards. Berger, a Gestapo agent, spots the American-made wristwatch Sinatra wears and follows Sinatra, Howard and Mulhare to the command car where Berger barters with Sinatra for the watch. He first offers Sinatra nylons, then cigarettes, until Sinatra wordlessly nods to make the exchange before Berger departs, relieving the anxiety of Mulhare and others in the car. Meanwhile, Preiss and Carra, believing that they will be killed when the POWs reach a safe destination, are held in a compartment where they are bound and gagged. Sinatra releases Carra, and, when she sees that a nylon stocking he has received from the Gestapo agent dangling from one of his pockets, she withdraws the nylons and provocatively slips the stockings onto her attractive legs in an effort to seduce Sinatra, which he resists, leaving her alone. When the train stops beneath a bridge to take on water for its engine, a crowd of Italian citizens shout insults at what they think are Germans escorting Allied POWs. (This scene, like so many made in the U.S. during and after WWII, is used as convenient and traditional propaganda to convince viewers that the Italian public as a whole barely tolerated Benito Mussolini's fascist regime and not only never sided with that regime's ally, Germany, but held contempt and hatred for the Nazis that had led them into the war.) A short time later, Preiss and Carra escape the command car, Preiss killing Leyton. They attempt to flee by hiding between the cars as Sinatra and Howard, dressed as German guards, chase them. Sinatra shoots and kills Preiss. When Carra runs to a nearby stairway leading upward to the bridge, Sinatra calls to her, asking her to stop. She continues to climb the stairs and, to prevent her from betraying him and the others as impersonators, Sinatra reluctantly shoots and kills her, An Italian boy stands nearby hatefully glaring at Sinatra, thinking him to be just another murderous German soldier. When the train reaches a siding, the POWs think to escape, but Allied bombers bombard the area, setting fire to some of the cars and injuring some of the POWs. Sinatra orders the men back onto the unscathed cars, and engineer Scotti races the train through the flaming area to safety. Fantoni then tells Sinatra and Howard that Scotti, the engineer, who has taken up the cause of the POWs, knows of a spur beyond their next stop, Milan, that will take the

Trevor Howard and Raffaella Carra in *Von Ryan's Express*, 1965.

train to Switzerland instead of Austria, and, if they can reach that neutral country, the POWs will be given sanctuary. Sinatra and Howard learn that, should they be able to destroy the control signals in a tower at the outskirts of Milan, the Germans will not be able to track their train's course, and, by manually switching some of the rails at that location, they will then be able to move the train onto the old, unused line leading to Switzerland. Sinatra and others do just that when they reach the first signal tower, smashing its electronic equipment. By this time, van Dreelen, a German officer, realizes that the POW train is escaping, once that train manages to skirt Milan and go toward Switzerland, and he orders troops onto another train to pursue the POW train. Now it becomes a frantic race toward the high mountains of Switzerland that loom in the welcoming distance. As the POW train races for the Alps, three German fighter planes appear in the skies overhead, firing at the train; the POWs, posing as German guards, fire back with their submachine guns. The train hurtles through several tunnels during the air attack, and one of the planes manages to disable a rail just before the POW train runs off the track. The POWs frantically remove a rail from behind the train to replace the disabled rail in front while disabling van Dreelen's following German troop train. While the repairs on the rail beneath a trestle are underway, a walkway on the side of the mountain is discovered, one that offers a passage into Switzerland, but when the POWs stream on to it, German planes dive at it. They manage to shoot down one of the planes, but another blows up a part of the walkway, forcing the POWs back to their train. They continue repairs, but, by this time, the German troop train has arrived a short distance away and Sinatra, Howard and others make a stand behind the POW train, fighting off the German troops. Some of the POWs, including Dexter, are killed, but the rail is finally replaced and the POW train begins to move through the last tunnel into Switzerland. Howard and others race to the departing train, managing to climb onto the platform of the command car, but Sinatra, who is the last POW running after that train, is shot and killed by pursuing German troops. He falls between the rails in the wake of the departing train while chaplain Mulhare makes the sign of the cross as he and Howard stand sorrowfully on the platform as the train disappears into the darkness of the tunnel to end this exciting war saga. Robson directs this film with gusto as he presents one great action scene after another while drawing from Sinatra, Howard and others memorable performances. This is really an all-Sinatra film, and he excels as the conscientious but firm American officer, defying British military protocol while leading his fellow POWs to freedom at the cost of his own life. The film received an Oscar nomination for Best Sound Editing (Walter Rossi) and went on to become a smash at the box office, earning more than $17.1 million in its initial release against a budget of $5.7 million. *Author's Note*: This film was envisioned as a money-making

blockbuster by Fox, which was then attempting to recoup its staggering losses from the extravagant epic **Cleopatra**, 1963. David, in his debut as a producer for Fox, rightly insisted that the film be shot on location in Northern Italy, the setting for the story, and most of the production took place near Florence; that city's railroad station was also used as a set. Many of the interiors, however, were shot at the Fox studio in Los Angeles. Although some miniatures were employed, director Robson used life-sized trains, planes and other vehicles for the film, and hundreds of extras played the POWs and German and Italian troops. The POW camp was built especially for the film. Although Sinatra was always the first choice to play the American pilot, the role of the British commander was first offered to Jack Hawkins and then Peter Finch, both of whom turned down the part, and Howard was then hired for that role. Sinatra was treated like a royal prince during the production, being flown about from one location to another in a private helicopter. Sinatra also insisted that he be shown dying at the end of this film as he did not want to make a sequel, and that, most likely, was based upon the arduous routines and physical exercises he was obligated to perform in this production. Sinatra confirmed that when telling this author: "Oh, that picture made a bundle when it got to the theaters [10th largest grossing film in 1965 and Sinatra's highest grossing film in the 1960s], but it was a backbreaker for me. Between having to sweat like a pig in a tincan prison box, I had to run around like a maniac. I was not in the kind of shape that called for such frantic action and when I went to sleep at night every bone in my body was shouting at me with a different complaint. [Sinatra was age fifty at that time.] They say that you're as young as you feel. Well, forget that. You are as young as far as you can walk. Sucking on one cigarette after another doesn't help either. I thought my co-star in that picture, Trevor Howard, was aces in **Von Ryan's Express**. He's one of those few actors who can say everything by keeping his mouth shut and staring right through you. Some of the British actors have great reserve, great presence, and he is one of those. I think that picture is one of my best." Dexter, who plays a tough sergeant in this film, had become a close Sinatra friend after he saved Sinatra's life on May 10, 1964, along with that of Ruth Koch, wife of producer-writer Howard W. Koch. Sinatra and Ruth Koch had gone swimming at Kauai, Hawaii, during the production of **None But the Brave**, 1965, a film in which Dexter was appearing as a supporting player. A former amateur boxer and always in good physical condition, Dexter saw Sinatra and Koch being swept out to sea by huge waves and dove into the surf, swimming to them. He kept them afloat for more than forty-five minutes, but Sinatra, exhausted, started to give up the struggle, saying to Dexter: "It's all over…please take care of my kids… I'm going to die." Dexter somehow held on to Sinatra, along with Koch, saying to Sinatra: "You're not going anywhere, Frank, except back to your kids." By that time, Sinatra and Koch became unconscious, but two surfers then arrived and aided Dexter in bringing both Sinatra and Koch safely back to the shore. Sinatra bonded closely with Dexter after that, until their relationship was shattered over Sinatra's new romance. During the production of this film, actress Mia Farrow, then twenty, visited the set to see her friend, Leyton, where she met Sinatra, who immediately fell in love with her, even though he was thirty years her senior. Dexter advised Sinatra not to marry Farrow, advice that turned his relationship with Sinatra sour, and Sinatra ended their friendship on the spot. Sinatra's marriage to Farrow (his third of four marriages) lasted two years. Other films depicting POW escapes during WWII include **Back to Bataan**, 1945 (escape of more than 500 American POWs held at the Japanese concentration camp in Cabanatuan, Philippines in January 1945 in a daring raid by U.S. Army Rangers); **The Bridge on the River Kwai**, 1957 (from a Japanese POW camp); **The Colditz Story**, 1955 (Allied officers escaping from a so-called escape-proof castle in Germany); **Escape**, 1940 (from a German concentration camp); **Force 10 from Navarone**, 1978 (escape from a Nazi camp in Yugoslavia); **The Great Escape**, 1963 (from a German POW camp); **The Great Raid**, 2005 (escape of more than 500

American POWs held at the Japanese concentration camp in Cabanatuan, Philippines in January 1945 in a raid by U.S. Army Rangers); **The McKenzie Break**, 1970 (from a British POW camp in Scotland); **Northern Pursuit**, 1943 (from a POW camp in Canada); **Sailor of the King**, 1953 (British sailor from German custody); **The Seventh Cross**, 1944 (from a German concentration camp); **Stalag 17**, 1953 (from a German POW camp); **Where Eagles Dare**, 1968 (from a German fortress in the Alps); and **The Wooden Horse**, 1951 (from a German POW camp). For a detailed list (300 plus) of films depicting escapes, see Index, Escapes. **p**, Saul David; **d**, Mark Robson; **cast**, Frank Sinatra, Trevor Howard, Raffaella Carra, Adolfo Celi, Brad Dexter, Sergio Fantoni, John Leyton, Edward Mulhare, Wolfgang Preiss, Vito Scotti, James Brolin, John van Dreelen, William Berger; **w**, Wendell Mayes, Joseph Landon (based on the novel by David Westheimer); **c**, William H. Daniels (DeLuxe Color); **m**, Jerry Goldsmith; **ed**, Dorothy Spencer; **art d**, Jack Martin Smith, Hilyard Brown; **set d**, Walter M. Scott, Raphael G. Bretton; **spec eff**, L.B. Abbott, Emil Kosa Jr.

Voyage to the Bottom of the Sea ★★★ 1961; U.S.; 105m; Windsor; FOX; Color; Adventure; Children: Unacceptable; **BD**; **DVD**; **VHS**. Exciting adventure tale has Pidgeon inventing a nuclear submarine that can dive far deeper than any previously constructed sub. When the world's survival is threatened by the Van Allen radiation belt going out of control, he defies the United Nations by launching missiles from his sub to blow up the belt. He is opposed by other ships and by scientist Fontaine, who tries to sabotage his efforts. A giant squid almost proves to be even more a danger to Pidgeon's mission, but, in the end, despite the squid, the distracting sexy dancing of Eden (who was then married to co-player Ansara), and the machinations of the moody Lorre, Pidgeon does, indeed, save the world. The film earned more than $2.3 million at the box office in its initial release against a then staggering budget of more than $1.5 million. Song: "Voyage to the Bottom of the Sea" (Russell Faith). *Author's Note*: Producer Allen spent more than $400,000 building the interior set for thesubmarine and recouped his investment by persuading ABC to launch a subsequent TV series about the subject. Richard Basehart took over Pidgeon's role as the commander, and the series proved to be more profitable than this film. Lorre, who died three years after this film was released, was much overweight and ailing during its production, telling this author a short time after its completion: "I sat sweating through my scenes and I felt like I was gaining weight from the hot lights they turned on when they rolled the cameras. I don't remember a single word of my lines in that film." **p&d**, Irwin Allen; **cast**, Walter Pidgeon, Joan Fontaine, Barbara Eden, Peter Lorre, Robert Sterling, Michael Ansara, Frankie Avalon, Regis Toomey, John Litel, Henry Daniell, Skip Ward, Art Baker; **w**, Allen, Charles Bennett (based on a story by Allen); **c**, Winton C. Hoch (CinemaScope; DeLuxe Color); **m**, Paul Sawtell, Bert Shefter; **ed**, George Boemler; **art d**, Herman A. Blumenthal, Jack Martin Smith; **set d**, Walter M. Scott, John Sturtevant; **spec eff**, Johnny Borgese, L.B. Abbott.

Voyager ★★★ 1992; U.S.; 117m; Action Films/Castle Hill; Color; Drama/Romance; Children: Unacceptable (MPAA: PG-13); **BD**; **DVD**; **VHS**. This intriguing romantic drama is set in the 1950s where Swiss engineer and international traveler Shepard survives a plane crash. Not wanting to take to the air again, he books passage on the next ship. On board, he meets beautiful Delpy and they have a passionate love affair as they travel to her home in Greece. But Shepard's past soon surfaces to spoil things. He had been involved with a German Jew, Sukowa, before World War II (1939-1945), but, after she became pregnant, he sent her off to have an abortion and they have not seen each other since. During his travels, Shepard learns that a friend, Zirner, who married Sukowa, has committed suicide in South America. While Shepard is having the affair with Delpy, Sukowa reenters his life, to complicate Shepard's romance. The story is highlighted by standout performances from Shepard, Delpy and Sukowa. Sexuality prohibits viewing by chil-

Walter Pidgeon and Joan Fontaine in *Voyage to the Bottom of the Sea*, 1961.

dren. **p**, Eberhard Junkersdorf; **d**, Volker Schlondorff; **cast**, Sam Shepard, Julie Delpy, Barbara Sukowa, Dieter Kirchlechner, Traci Lind, August Zirner, Deborra-Lee Furness, Thomas Heinze, Bill Dunn, Peter Berling; **w**, Rudy Wurlitzer (based on the novel by Max Frisch); **c**, Giorgos Arvanitis, Pierre Lhomme; **ed**, Dagmar Hirtz; **prod d**; Nicos Perakis; **art d**, Benedikt Herforth; **spec eff**, Kay Albrecht, Robbie Knott.

W.C. Fields and Me ★★★ 1976; U.S.; 111m; UNIV; Color; Biographical Drama; Children: Unacceptable (MPAA: PG); **DVD**; **VHS**; **IV**. Steiger does a wonderful job in playing the legendary screen comedian Fields (1880-1946). He is performing in the Ziegfeld Follies in 1924, but showman Florenz Ziegfeld (1867-1932), played by Stewart, dislikes his ribald humor. At the same time, Steiger's girlfriend runs off with another man and his investment broker loses his life savings. Steiger and friend Barty go to California where they operate a wax museum in Santa Monica. Steiger soon starts a film career and becomes an immediate star. At a party with drinking pals including John Barrymore (1882-1942), played broadly by the always grinning Cassidy, Steiger meets struggling young actress Carlotta Monte (1907-1993), played by Perrine. Cassidy and others, who are inebriated, play a joke on her, telling her that Steiger wants her to go to his home and talk about a possible role in a movie. She suspects it's a hoax but goes there anyway the next day, and Steiger surprisingly offers her a job as his live-in secretary. She accepts and Steiger arranges a screen test for her, but first assures himself that she will fail by asking producer Marley to jinx her career. Paramount Pictures producer Marley, however, thinks Perrine has some talent, but Steiger threatens to break his contract with the studio if Perrine is encouraged as an actress. Steiger, by now an alcoholic, goes on a binge in Mexico, and, upon returning to New York, has an argument with Marley that creates problems with studio relations for years to come. Perrine then learns about Steiger's ruining her film chances, but returns to him to console him upon the death of Cassidy (Fields and Barrymore were the closest of friends, along with Errol Flynn). Perrine urges Fields to marry her, but he is reluctant. She learns why while visiting Steiger on the set of **My Little Chickadee**, 1940, where she meets Parks, who tells her that he is Steiger's son from a marriage that has not yet been legally ended. Over the next few years, Steiger's health declines from his drinking and he finds it impossible to sleep, telling Perrine that he could always sleep as a child when he heard rain on the roof. To that end, Perrine sneaks out that night and sits on the lawn of Steiger's home while he tosses and turns in bed, until he hears rain on the roof and goes to blissful sleep. It is not rain, however, but Perrine, who has turned on a hose outside and sits holding that hose, aiming at the roof of the house

Betty Grable in *Wabash Avenue,* **1950.**

number that brought criticism from the Hollywood censors. Harris, the conniving casino's owner where Grable works, has cheated Mature, his former partner, out of a half interest in the business. Mature, with the help of sidekick Gardiner, schemes to ruin Harris. He also wants to get Grable away from Harris to star her in a Broadway musical and also have this sexy blonde bombshell for himself. Harris quells a melee in his saloon by pushing a colorful drunk, Barton, who strikes his head on a bar rail and is unconscious. Mature and Gardiner carry Barton to a nearby wax museum where Mature sees a wax figure that amazingly resembles Barton. He then gets the idea to blackmail Harris into giving him back half of his interest in the raucous saloon by telling Harris that he has killed Barton and holds a mock funeral for the old drunk, using the wax figure as his body while sending Barton on a long boat trip. Harris now believes that he has accidentally killed Barton and, rather than face a charge of involuntary manslaughter, lets Mature run things, particularly how the musical performers are presented. Mature starts with feisty Grable before she is to present her next number, removing several accoutrements to her gaudy, feathery gown. He compels her to stand still on the stage, instead of shaking her ample endowments, and she is confined to simply singing a sweet ballad. She is so effective that she becomes a singing star and is now grateful to the manipulative Mature, falling in love with him. When Harris sees Barton inadvertently resurface, Harris turns the tables on the artful Mature, but, in the end, he sees that Grable loves Mature, and allows her to see happiness with the charming con artist. Koster does a fine job in presenting this wild and wooly musical, presenting its lively tunes with gusto, and his lowlife saloon scenes crackle with rowdy action as befitting the rousing era. Grable is a standout in her dancing and singing numbers, and Mature and Harris are exceptional as the two men fighting for her attentions. The film received an Oscar nomination for Best Original Song ("Wilhelmina"; Myrow, Gordon). The film, which was a remake of **Coney Island**, 1943 (also starring Grable, with George Montgomery and Cesare Romero), was a big hit at the box office, earning more than $2 million in its initial release. A sixty-minute radio adaptation was aired by Lux Radio Theater on November 13, 1950, with Grable and Mature reprising their roles. Songs: "Down on Wabash Avenue," "Baby Won't You Say You Love Me?," "May I Tempt You with a Big Red Rosy Apple?," "Wilhelmina," "Clean Up Chicago" (music: Josef Myrow; lyrics: Mack Gordon); "I Wish I Could Shimmy Like My Sister Kate" (1919; Armand J. Piron, Clarence Williams); "I've Been Floating Down the Old Green River" (1915; music: Joe Cooper; lyrics: Bert Kalmar); "What Do You Want to Make Those Eyes at Me For?" (1916; Joseph McCarthy, Howard Johnson, James V. Monaco); "Honey Man/My Little Lovin' Honey Man" (1911; music: Al Piantadosi; lyrics: Joseph McCarthy); "Are You from Dixie?" (1915; music: George L. Cobb; lyrics: Jack Yellen); "I Remember You" (1908; music: Harry von Tilzer; lyrics: Vincent Bryan); "Billy/I Always Dream of Bill" (1911; music: James Kendis, Herman Paley; lyrics: Joe Goodwin); "Harrigan" (1907; from "Fifty Miles from Boston" by George M. Cohan); "Over the Waves" (1888; Juventino Rosas). *Author's Note*: Grable told this author that "I really wanted to get away from musicals for a while and make dramatic pictures, like the one I did with Vic [Victor Mature] called **I Wake Up Screaming** [1941], and when I mentioned that to Darryl Zanuck, he said, 'sure, sure, Betty, we'll put you into your next picture with Vic.' Well, he did, but guess what? It was another musical, a remake of a picture I did some years earlier, **Coney Island** [1943]. I could not escape from myself." The title for this film, Mature told this author, was originally intended to be used for a biopic about songwriter Gus Kahn (1886-1941), who, after migrating from Germany, was raised in Chicago and his songs were first sung in the bistros along Wabash Avenue. "That production was put on hold," Mature told this author, "but since exhibitors had been promised a film with that title, Fox rushed **Wabash Avenue** into production to satisfy those theater-owners. Movie-making is, after all, a business." Indeed it is; Mature was earning less than $500 a week in Hollywood when he appeared with Grable in **I Wake Up**

where Steiger sleeps. (This is one of the few scenes in the film that is actually taken from Monti's book.) Steiger is eventually hospitalized, with Perrine taking a room nearby, but he dies in 1946 on Christmas Day, a day he intensely disliked, besides children and dogs. Hiller does a fine job in presenting this complex biopic while keeping the expansive Steiger from going over the top in many of his more tempestuous scenes. Many of the famous anecdotes concerning Fields find their way into this film, not the least of which is when he is visited in the hospital by a friend who finds him reading the Bible, a book that the agnostic Fields disavowed. When asked why he had been reading the Holy Scriptures, Fields replied: "I was looking for loopholes." *Author's Note*: Steiger told this author that, in preparing for his role in this film, "I did not want to just copy or mimic the great Fields. I gave his character my own interpretation, along with that exaggerated drawl of his, and all of his quirky body movements, arms flapping like a duck and fingers pointing to the heavens. Fields was a very complicated man with a lot of internal problems beyond his being a serious drunk. God knows how he ever controlled that drinking to make such wonderful pictures. So there are scenes in the picture where I just shut up, put my head down, and thought the way Fields might be thinking after he had made a fool of himself with his friends and the woman that loved him more than he loved himself. I think he loved Carlotta [Monti], but he did not want to ever show it, because he had been deeply and emotionally damaged in his youth when risking his love with others." The Pacific Railroad car used in this film was somehow retrieved from a scrap area and refitted with a motor and rubber tires. The electric streetcars that traversed L.A. until 1950 were electronic and moved at thirteen mph. The system, also known as the Red Car Line, was the central theme in the film **Who Framed Roger Rabbit**, 1988. For more details about W.C. Fields, see my book *Zanies: The World's Greatest Eccentrics* (New Century Publishers, 1982; pages 125-134). Excessive drinking and drunken scenes prohibit viewing by children. **p**, Jay Weston; **d**, Arthur Hiller; **cast**, Rod Steiger, Valerie Perrine, John Marley, Jack Cassidy, Bernadette Peters, Dana Elcar, Paul Stewart, Billy Barty, Linda Purl, Allan Arbus; **w**, Bob Merrill (based on the book by Carlotta Monti with Cy Rice); **c**, David M. Walsh (Panavision; Technicolor); **m**, Henry Mancini; **ed**, John C. Howard; **prod d**, Robert F. Boyle; **set d**, Arthur Jeph Parker; **spec eff**, Stan Winston, Albert Whitlock.

Wabash Avenue ★★★ 1950; U.S.; 92m; FOX; Color; Musical; Children: Acceptable (MPAA: PG-13); **DVD**. Lively songfest begins with Grable as a brassy burlesque queen in a dance hall in 1892 Chicago during the Columbian Exposition. Her opening number sees a very leggy Grable in a provocative, hip-grinding, flesh-quivering routine where she gyrates to the song "I Wish I Could Shimmy Like My Sister Kate," a

Screaming, but, nine years later, when he appeared with her in this film, he was being paid more than $50,000 a film. The Kahn biopic was later produced as **I'll See You in My Dreams**, 1951, with Danny Thomas playing Kahn and Doris Day as his devoted wife, Grace. **p**, William Perlberg; **d**, Henry Koster; **cast**, Betty Grable, Victor Mature, Phil Harris, Reginald Gardiner, James Barton, Barry Kelley, Margaret Hamilton, Jacqueline Dalya, Robin Raymond, Hal K. Dawson, Red Nichols; **w**, Harry Tugend, Charles Lederer; **c**, Arthur E. Arling; **m**, Cyril J. Mockridge; **ed**, Robert Simpson; **art d**, Lyle Wheeler, Joseph C. Wright; **set d**, Thomas Little, Paul S. Fox; **spec eff**, Fred Sersen.

Wag the Dog ★★★ 1997; U.S.; 97m; Baltimore Pictures; New Line Cinema; Color; Comedy; Children: Unacceptable (MPAA: R); **DVD**; **VHS**. This offbeat black comedy begins two weeks before the presidential election when Belson, the U.S. President, is enmeshed in a sex scandal involving a Girl Scout. Heche, one of Belson's top aides, calls in a spin doctor, De Niro, who enlists the aid of Hoffman, a Hollywood producer, to produce a war in Albania in order to divert the public and the media away from the real story. Though the script from Mamet is sophomoric and even puerile in places, the superlative acting from Hoffman and De Niro (even though they are a bit long in the tooth for the characters they are playing) overcomes Mamet's otherwise shaky dialog, producing a sometimes hilarious satire that was prophetically made just before President Bill Clinton's flagrant misconduct with naïve White House aide Monica Lewinsky in 1998. This film did big box office, earning more than $64.2 million against a budget of $15 million. Songs: "Thank Heaven for Little Girls" (Alan Jay Lerner, Frederick Loewe), "I Guard the Canadian Border" (Tom Bahler, Willie Nelson), "The American Dream" (Bahler), "Good Old Shoe" (Edgar Winter), "Classical Allegro" (Marc Ferrari, Nancy Hieronymous), "Courage Mom" (Merle Haggard), "Barracuda" (Ann Wilson, Nancy Wilson, Roger Fisher, Michael DeRosier), I Like the Nightlife" (Alicia Bridges, Susan Hutcheson), "God Bless the Men of the 303" (Huey Lewis), "Wag the Dog!" (Mark Knopfler). Mature themes and gutter language prohibit viewing by children. **p**, Barry Levinson, Robert De Niro, Jane Rosenthal, Eric McLeod; **d**, Levinson; **cast**, Dustin Hoffman, De Niro, Anne Heche, Jim Belushi, Woody Harrelson, Willie Nelson, Merle Haggard, Kirsten Dunst, William H. Macy, Craig T. Nelson, Jay Leno, Michael Belson; **w**, David Mamet, Hilary Henkin (based on the book *American Hero* by Larry Beinhart); **c**, Robert Richardson; **m**, Mark Knopfler; **ed**, Stu Linder; **prod d**, Wynn Thomas; **art d**, Mark Worthington; **set d**, Robert Greenfield; **spec eff**, Dennis King, Jim Hanson, Krystyna Demkowicz.

The Wages of Fear ★★★★★ 1955; France/Italy; 140m; CICC/Vera Films/DCA; B/W; Drama; Children: Unacceptable; **BD**; **DVD**; **VHS**; **IV**. This mesmerizing, fear-gripping tale is set in a remote mountainous and jungle area in southern Mexico, chiefly the crude, unpaved village of Las Piedras. Here, the children run half naked through its muddy lanes, women toil at heavy chores and men seek work from the only source of jobs, the monopolizing Southern Oil Company (SOC). An oil well ignites and is burning out of control three hundred miles from Las Piedras, and Tubbs, the callous representative for the company, asks for volunteers to undertake a near suicidal mission. Two trucks are to be driven to the oil well by two two-man teams carrying lethal nitro to be used in blowing out the fire once those explosives are delivered. Tubbs reviews a bevy of candidates, including some who go to sneaky ends to get the jobs, including Vanel, a fierce gangster, who is a wanted man. Tubbs selects Montand, a cocky Frenchman from Corsica, who is disappointed when Tubbs chooses Dest as his co-driver instead of Vanel. The other two men Tubbs chooses are Van Eyck, an arrogant German, and the brawny Lulli. Suddenly, Dest disappears and Vanel appears, ostensibly to say goodbye to his pal, Montand. When Tubbs sees that Dest has vanished, he hires Vanel to replace him, and Vanel becomes Montand's traveling companion. Montand and the others, however, suspect

Dustin Hoffman, Anne Heche and Robert De Niro in *Wag the Dog*, 1997.

that the ruthless Vanel has done away with Dest in order to get the job. Tubbs makes no excuses for his decision in selecting two trucks for the job, saying that he is sending two trucks carefully packed with nitro since he believes that one of the trucks will most likely explode when traversing the rugged terrain (and assuring the deaths of its occupants), but he thinks that the second truck will nevertheless reach its destination. With this frightening prospect in mind, the two heavy trucks with their four occupants begin their arduous trip through the dense jungles as they slowly move their vehicles over rut-gutted roads. The two trucks are driven at a safe distance of a half hour between them with Montand and Vanel leading the way and Van Eyck and Lulli in their distant wake. Vanel is behind the wheel, but he drives at such a slow pace that the gap between the two trucks soon shortens. Montand, who has thought Vanel to possess steely nerves, now comes to believe that his co-driver is gripped by fear. Vanel passes off his overly cautious driving to a fit of malaria. By this time, Van Eyck and Lulli appear and Van Eyck decides to be the leader, gunning his huge truck in front of Montand and Vanel. Van Eyck, who is driving a lighter truck, meets the first serious obstacle when he must, to make a sharp turn, back up his truck onto a weakly supported wooden structure that spans a deep ravine. Van Eyck succeeds in making the turn and proceeds along the road. When Montand, who is now behind the wheel of the second and much heavier truck, slowly backs onto the wooden structure, some of its rotting boards creak and give way and Vanel is accidentally knocked from his seat. Montand stops, sweating and now worried that he has killed his partner. When he momentarily leaves the truck, he sees the panicking Vanel running away. Montand uses his low gear to grind the truck backward slowly onto the yielding wooden structure and then moves the truck forward and just reaches the turn and safe ground when the wooden structure completely gives way and crashes into the ravine behind him. Montand at first thinks to leave Vanel behind, but then allows him to climb back into the cab of the truck. The next serious obstacle is a huge boulder blocking the road, but Van Eyck decides to risk using a portion of the nitro he is carrying and is able to blow the rock to pieces, clearing the road and allowing both trucks to move along. When Vanel again loses his nerve and runs off, Montand chases after him and savagely beats him, forcing him back into the truck. Van Eyck by then has moved his truck far in advance of Montand, but his truck suddenly explodes in a fiery ball of fire, stunning Montand and Vanel. When they arrive at the scene, they see a large crater that is now filled with oil from a damaged pipeline. Vanel regains his courage and, while wading in the oil up to his chest, he courageously guides Montand to solid ground. They later encounter a large tree branch blocking the road, and, while Montand and Vanel use a winch to lift the branch, Vanel gets entangled in the winch's wire and Montand accidentally runs him over, crushing Vanel's legs. Mon-

Yves Montand, above, and Charles Vanel in *The Wages of Fear,* **1955.**

tand manages to free Vanel and get him back into the truck, but Vanel is by now dying. Montand then arrives at the location of the burning well-fire with the dead Vanel. He receives his payment of $2,000, and when his friends in Las Piedras learn that he is the lone survivor, they have a wild celebration. The happy Montand then drives back toward the village, believing that he will soon be able to leave Mexico and return to Paris, carrying his lucky Metro ticket on the dashboard of the truck. Suddenly, he loses control of the truck and it hideously slides over an edge and plunges downward into a deep gorge, killing him. Clouzot presents a thoroughly tension-filled tale, cautiously building its suspense in the first half of the film where he develops its fascinating characters surrounded with the grubby atmosphere of the village and its impoverished, desperate denizens. In the second half of the film, he produces excruciating anxiety while visually detailing one hazardous scene after another to powerfully chronicle the dangerous trek taken by four frantic men, all seemingly defying the doom that eventually engulfs them. From the beginning, we know these men have no future as seen in an opening shot where a child is cruelly stringing four beetles together (a scene not lost on director Sam Peckinpah, who uses the same savage metaphor when showing some sadistic children burning helpless crabs as a group of doomed outlaws who have outlived their era ride into a town to rob a bank in **The Wild Bunch**, 1969). The performances from Montand, Vanel, Van Eyck and Lulli are outstanding, each providing separate and distinctive characters that remain memorable to this day. This film was a critical and financial success upon its release and remains a masterpiece thriller to this date. It won the 1953 Best Picture Award at the Cannes Film Festival where it ran for 155 minutes. When released in the U.S., the film was savagely edited down to 106 minutes, losing much of its first half, chiefly because of what was then considered to be anti-American statements made in the film. The film was restored in 1967 to 140 minutes. In later versions, it was edited down to 131 minutes. This film saw a superlative remake in 1977 under the title of **Sorcerer**, directed by William Friedkin. Music: "The Blue Danube" (Johann Strauss). *Author's Note*: Director Clouzot thought to shoot this film in the high mountains of Spain, but Montand refused to go to Spain as it was then controlled by fascist dictator Francisco Franco (1892-1975). Instead, the film was shot on location in a mountainous area in southern France and where the village was completely constructed. Iconic French film star Jean Gabin was offered the role later taken by Vanel. Gabin turned down the part because he thought his fans would not want to see him being portrayed as a coward. Both Vanel and Montand contracted conjunctivitis after spending prolonged scenes that compelled them to all but swim through pools of oil and while also inhaling gas fumes. This was Tubbs' final film. (In French; English subtitles.) **p&d**, Henri-Georges Clouzot; **cast**, Yves Montand, Charles Vanel, Folco

Lulli, Peter Van Eyck, Vera Clouzot, William Tubbs, Dario Moreno, Jo Dest, Antonio Centa, Luis De Lima; **w**, Clouzot, Jerome Geronimi (based on the novel by Georges Arnaud); **c**, Armand Thirard; **m**, Georges Auric; **ed**, Henri Rust, Madeleine Gug, Etiennette Muse; **art d&set d**, Rene Renoux.

Wagon Master ★★★ 1950; U.S.; 86m; Argosy/RKO; B/W; Western; Children: Unacceptable; **DVD**; **VHS**; **IV**. Although this film was one of director Ford's favorites, it does not present the sweep and majesties of his masterpiece westerns such as **Stagecoach**, 1939, or **Fort Apache**, 1948. It nevertheless offers an absorbing tale with some intriguing Old West characters. It begins with Mormon settlers led by Bond journeying by wagon train to their promised land in Utah where they hope they will no longer be persecuted for their religious beliefs. Bond hires two young horse traders, Johnson and Carey Jr., to guide them. Along the way they are joined by members of a traveling medicine show, Mowbray, Dru, Clifford, and Francis Ford (the director's brother playing a mute performer), who are also driven out of towns they visit. Also joining the wagon train is Kemper and his sons, who are a murderous clan of robbers. (All of the travelers in this caravan toward the Promised Land are social outcasts of one sort or another, the pariahs of a civilization that has rejected their lifestyles.) After one of Kemper's sons, Libby, attacks Castaneda, a young Navajo woman, Kemper decides to wipe out the Mormons, but Johnson, who has fallen in love with the alluring Dru, and Carey, save them by shooting the villains. Ford offers a much slower, even leisurely pace in this film as compared to his other westerns, depicting more scenic landscapes than vital action. The script from Nugent and Patrick Ford offers less urgency and more down-home palaver than can usually be found in other Ford westerns. The director spends an inordinate amount of time developing the insidious character of Kemper, the patriarch of the outlaw family, but his recidivist criminality and predictable personality remains one dimensional. This was Kemper's first appearance in a Ford film, albeit he had performed in some other significant westerns such as **Yellow Sky**, 1948, where he played an overweight, bumbling outlaw, and reprised that kind of character in **The Doolins of Oklahoma**, 1949. Songs: "Wagons West," "Song of the Wagon Master," "Shadows in the Dust," "Chuckawalla Swing" (Stan Jones); "Come, Come, Ye Saints" (1844-1846, Jesse White, William Clayton). *Author's Note*: Ford admitted when talking with this author that "**Wagon Master** suffered at the box office since I did not use any big name stars in that picture. I believe it is a significant picture, however, because it shows in very human terms the pioneers that brought civilization to the Old West. I did not want to show larger-than-life people in that picture, only those people that had to find a way to survive the wilderness as well as the evil side of their characters. The simplest stories are sometimes the very best. I do not make psychological pictures. I leave that to armchair psychiatrists posing as directors." Johnson, who was one of the director's favorite stock company characters, has the leading role in this film and performs his own spectacular stunts as an accomplished horse rider, which is how he began with Ford in earlier films. The film was shot on location in Utah. Ford developed the idea for this film when in production for **She Wore a Yellow Ribbon**, 1949, which had Dru as its female star, and he decided to use the same actress in this film. Though he hired Nugent and his son, Patrick Ford, to write the script, the director shot very little of their story, rewriting the tale as he went through the production. He is quoted as telling the writers: "I liked your script, boys. In fact, I actually shot a few pages of it." Ford was an astute student of important films made by other directors, and was not above borrowing good concepts for his own ends. When I mentioned to Ford that Dru had played a similar role of a showgirl traveling with a western troupe of entertainers in Howard Hawks' classic western **Red River**, 1948 (which starred Ford's foremost star, John Wayne), Ford immediately countered by saying to me: "I used such entertainers in my pictures before **Red River**. I had Alan [Mobray] appearing as an eastern actor in **My Darling Clementine** [1946], so I took a page from my own book, not someone else's." Other films depicting covered wagons and wagon trains include **Across the Plains**, 1939; **Adventures of Frank and Jesse James**, 1948; **Arizona**, 1940; **Arrow in the Dust**, 1954; **Bad Men**, 1926; **Bend of the River**, 1952; **Beyond the Last Frontier**, 1943; **Beyond the Law**, 1975; **The Big Stampede**, 1932; **The Big Trail**, 1930; **The Big Trees**, 1952; **The Blocked Trail**, 1943; **Brigham Young: Frontiersman**, 1940; **Broken Lance**, 1954; **Bullwhip**, 1958; **Can't Help Singing**, 1944; **Canyon Passage**, 1946; **Cavalry**, 1936; **The Cherokee Strip**, 1937; **Chisum**, 1970; **Cimarron**, 1931; **Cimarron**, 1960; **City Slickers**, 1991; **Cole Younger, Gunfighter**, 1958; **The Command**, 1954; **Conagher**, 1991 (made-for-TV); **The Covered Wagon**, 1923; **Covered Wagon Days**, 1940; **Covered Wagon Raid**, 1950; **Covered Wagon Trails**, 1930; **Covered Wagon Trails**, 1940; **Crooked River**, 1950; **The Culpepper Cattle Company**, 1972; **Daniel Boone: Frontier Trail Rider**, 1966; **Dark Command**, 1940; **Davy Crockett: Indian Scout**, 1950; **Desperados of the West**, 1950; **The Desperate Mission**, 1969 (made-for-TV); **Dodge City**, 1939; **Drums along the Mohawk**, 1939; **El Condor**, 1970; **End of the Trail**, 1932; **Fighting Caravans**, 1931; **Fighting Pioneers**, 1935; **Finger on the Trigger**, 1965; **Flame of Barbary Coast**, 1945; **For a Few More Dollars**, 1967; **Fort Worth**, 1951; **Fort Yuma**, 1955; **4 Dollars of Revenge**, 1966; **The General**, 1926; **Ghost of Zorro**, 1949; **The Great Sioux Massacre**, 1965; **Heroes of the West**, 1930; **Home on the Range**, 1946; **Home on the Range**, 2004; **Hondo**, 1953; **How the West Was Won**, 1962; **In Old California**, 1942; **In Old Chicago**, 1938; **Into the West**, 2005 (TV miniseries); **Kit Carson**, 1940; **Land Raiders**, 1970; **The Lawless Breed**, 1953; **The Lone Ranger**, 1938; **The Lone Ranger Rides Again**, 1939; **Man in the Saddle**, 1951; **Man with the Steel Whip**, 1954; **Massacre Canyon**, 1954; **Mogambo**, 1953; **Monte Walsh**, 2003 (made-for-TV); **North to Alaska**, 1960; **The Oklahoman**, 1957; **Once upon a Time in the West**, 1969; **Open Range**, 2003; **The Oregon Trail**, 1939; **The Outriders**, 1950; **The Painted Desert**, 1931; **The Paleface**, 1948; **Pioneers of the West**, 1940; **Prairie Schooners**, 1940; **The Proud Ones**, 1956; **Puss in Boots**, 2011; **Rango**, 2011; **Red Fork Range**, 1931; **Red River**, 1948; **Ride with the Devil**, 1999; **Riders of the Deadline**, 1943; **Riding West**, 1944; **Rio Grande**, 1950; **Rolling Down the Great Divide**, 1942; **The Sacketts**, 1979 (made-for-TV); **Saddlemates**, 1941; **Sam Whiskey**, 1969; **The Scalphunters**, 1968; **Scarlet River**, 1933; **September Dawn**, 2007; **Shane**, 1953; **She Wore a Yellow Ribbon**, 1949; **Seven Men from Now**, 1956; **7th Cavalry**, 1956; **The Shakiest Gun in the West**, 1968; **Shoot, Gringo...Shoot!**, 1968; **The Silver Treasure**, 1926; **Silverado**, 1985; **The Singing Cowboy**, 1936; **Sitting Bull**, 1954; **Soldier Blue**, 1970; **Son of Oklahoma**, 1932; **Song of the Buckeroo**, 1938; **The Stranger Wore a Gun**, 1953; **Take a Hard Ride**, 1975; **Tall Man Riding**, 1955; **The Tall Men**, 1956; **The Tall Stranger**, 1957; **The Tall Texan**, 1953; **The Texan**, 1930; **Texas**, 1941; **They Died with Their Boots On**, 1941; **3 Godfathers**, 1948; **The Thundering Herd**, 1933; **Thundering Thomas**, 1929; **To the Last Man**, 1933; **The Topeka Terror**, 1945; **The Undefeated**, 1969; **Untamed**, 1955; **Valley of Vengeance**, 1944; **Vengeance**, 1977; **Vera Cruz**, 1954; **Virginia City**, 1940; **Wagon Wheels**, 1934; **Wagon Train**, 1957-1965 (TV series); **Wagons East**, 1954; **Wagons West**, 1952; **West of the Rockies**, 1931; **The Westerner**, 1940; **Westward Ho the Wagons**, 1956; **Westward the Women**, 1951; **Wheels of Destiny**, 1934; and **Wyoming**, 1947. **p**, John Ford, Merian C. Cooper; **d**, Ford; **cast**, Ben Johnson, Joanne Dru, Harry Carey Jr., Ward Bond, Charles Kemper, Alan Mowbray, Jane Darwell, Ruth Clifford, Russell Simpson, James Arness, Hank Worden, Francis Ford, Fred Libby, Movita Castaneda; **w**, Frank S. Nugent, Patrick Ford (based on a story by Ford); **c**, Bert Glennon; **m**, Richard Hageman; **ed**, Jack Murray; **art d**, James Basevi; **set d**, Joseph Kish; **spec eff**, Jack Caffee.

The Wagons Roll at Night ★★★ 1941; U.S.; 84m; WB; B/W; Drama; Children: Unacceptable; **DVD**; **VHS**; **IV**. Bogart, Sidney and Albert

Ben Johnson, Harry Carey Jr. and Joanne Dru in *Wagon Master*, **1950.**

shine in this offbeat tale about a cheap traveling carnival that provides entertaining thrills for customers as well as tragedy for its performers. Bogart is the tough, no-nonsense boss of that seedy carnival and circus on wheels (its wagons rolling at night from one tank town after another to provide brief performances before traveling on). He is also the overly protective brother of a younger sister, Leslie, who is kept safe and content at a distant farm. Bogart refuses to have her travel with the carnival, believing that its more sleazy members might easily corrupt or violate Leslie. Sidney, who is the carnival's fortune teller (billed as "Madame Florina"), is in love with Bogart and he feels the same way about her, but he tries not to show it as he has other problems to deal with, especially Rumann, the alcoholic lion tamer. When the carnival stops in a small town, Rumann becomes so drunk that he accidentally opens a cage to let loose a fierce lion. The cat enters a grocery store, shocking a female customer who is at that moment smelling some limburger cheese, and courageous clerk Albert alertly grabs a pitchfork to corner the big cat. Albert's cool nerve and easy way with the cat soon prompts Bogart to offer him Rumann's job, which the adventurous and somewhat naïve youth gladly accepts, thinking he is stepping into bigtime show business. Rumann is sent packing, but he angrily vows revenge. Sidney, who is drawn to the charismatic Albert, is unhappy with her lot and wants Bogart to sell the traveling show and settle down with her, but she knows his nomadic nature will never permit her to have that bit of happiness. (There are some very touching scenes where the sensitive Sidney marvelously displays her emotional vulnerability while trying to put up a brave front with Bogart.) Meanwhile, Albert discovers Leslie at the farm and both fall in love, but the obsessively protective Bogart becomes so enraged about this relationship that he plots to kill Albert by sending him into a cage to face Caesar, the fiercest of the lions. Sidney learns of this lethal scheme and fetches Leslie in an effort to change Bogart's mind. Albert is nevertheless sent into the lion's cage where his life is threatened by the ferocious Caesar (a well-staged sequence with plenty of fright). Bogart, who has even gone to the murderous length of making sure that there are no bullets in Albert's revolver, is nevertheless seized by his conscience when he sees that Albert is about to be killed. He rushes into the cage to help the beleaguered Albert and, in the process, is mortally wounded by the animal. Albert not only drives the big cat back into a separate cage, but dispatches a berserk, murder-bent Rumann when he returns with gun in hand to vent his hatred for earlier being sacked. Sadly, Bogart dies in Sidney's arms, but he is now looked upon as a hero and, before passing on, sardonically states: "I wonder if they can use a good promoter where I'm going?" Albert and Leslie then look to a future together without any interference from hungry lions. Enright excels himself with this exciting tale, and he presents superbly staged action scenes, injecting many montage sequences to

Humphrey Bogart, Sylvia Sidney, John Ridgely and Joan Leslie in *The Wagons Roll at Night,* 1941.

quicken the pace; the sets, costuming and score are outstanding ingredients that strengthen the tension-filled story that also offers a taut script with some very witty dialog. This film, a box office success, is a remake of **Kid Galahad**, 1937, where lion-taming replaces prizefighting, a film that starred Edward G. Robinson and with Bogart in a supporting role as the villain. Songs: "The Billboard March" (1901; John N. Klohr), "Waves of the Danube" (1880; Ion Ivanovici), "Coney Island" (1935; music: Harry Warren; lyrics: Al Dubin), "Aloha Oe" (1878; Queen Liliuokalani), "The Umbrella Man" (1939; Vincent Rose, Larry Stock, James Cavanaugh), "From Me to You" (1933; Fabian Andre, Wayne King, Nat Conney). *Author's Note*: Sidney told this author that "playing opposite Bogey [Bogart] was a special treat because he was very professional. He never missed a cue or flubbed a line. I don't think I ever met another actor so well prepared for his scenes. He was all business, just as he was when we made **Dead End** [1937], although we did not have any scenes together in that picture. **The Wagons Roll at Night** was the first picture where Bogey got top billing, but he was not too happy about the part of the story where he is crazy to keep his sister away from carnival people, including myself, I guess. 'I don't like my character,' he told me. 'It makes me feel creepy, as if I am doing what Paul Muni did in **Scarface** [1932] in protecting his sister against people like himself, a gangster.' I recognized that, too, that Muni's character had a pathological fixation on protecting his sister in a covetous way that indicated incestuous desires. I think that's why Bogey did not like his character because it was too much like Muni's nutcase gangster, who is secretly lusting after his sister. Bogey still did a great job in that picture." Other films profiling lion tamers include: **The Adventures of Huckleberry Finn**, 1960; **Big Top Pee-Wee**, 1988; **Billy Rose's Jumbo**, 1962; **Captive Wild Woman**, 1943; **Circus Girl**, 1937; **The Circus Kid**, 1928; **Congo Bill**, 1938; **Fixer Dugan**, 1939; **Frontier Circus**, 1961-1962 (TV series; "Depths of Fear," 1961 episode); **The Greatest Show on Earth**, 1953; **I'm No Angel**, 1933; **Kristina Talking Pictures**, 1976; **La tendre ennemie**, 1936; **La venenosa**, 1928; **Las doce sillas**, 1962; **The Lost Jungle**, 1934; **Man on a Tightrope**, 1953; **The Mighty Gorga**, 1969; **The Miracle**, 1991; **Only One Night**, 1939; **The Postman Always Rings Twice**, 1981; **Psycho-Circus**, 1966; **Rain or Shine**, 1930; **Red Barry**, 1938; **Red Wagon**, 1933; **Ring of Fear**, 1954; **Roselyne and the Lions**, 1989; **She Made Her Bed**, 1934; **Side Show**, 1981 (made-for-TV); and **Zirkus Palestina**, 1998. Other films depicting fortune-tellers include: **Along the Navajo Trail**, 1945; **Are You With It?**, 1948; **Batman**, 1943; **A Bay of Blood**, 1971; **Bear's Kiss**, 2002; **Before Sunrise**, 1995; **The Bicycle Thief**, 1946; **Black Magic**, 1944; **Black Magic**, 1949; **The Black Widow**, 1947; **Broadway Danny Rose**, 1984; **Broadway Rhythm**, 1944; **Brotherhood of the Wolf**, 2001; **Bunco Squad**, 1950; **Bunker Bean**, 1936; **Burnt Money**,

2001; **California Frontier**, 1938; **Carny**, 2009 (made-for-TV); **The Case of the Black Parrot**, 1941; **Celebrity**, 1998; **Chinese Odyssey 2002**, 2003; **The Circus**, 1928; **The Countess of Baton Rouge**, 1997; **Crime Doctor's Man Hunt**, 1946; **Crime Ring**, 1938; **The Crystal Ball**, 1943; **Cuban Fireball**, 1951; **The Cuckoos**, 1930; **Danger! Women at Work**, 1943; **Dangerous Davies: The Last Detective**, 1981 (made-for-TV); **Dante's Inferno**, 1935; **Dead Man's Folly**, 1986 (made-for-TV); **The Devil's Messenger**, 1961; **Dirty Gertie from Harlem, U.S.A.**, 1946; **Doctor Mabuse**, 2013; **The Doorway to Hell**, 1930; **Du Barry Was a Lady**, 1943; **Edmond**, 2005; **Eye's Bayou**, 1997; **Feast of Love**, 2007; **Fellini Satyricon**, 1969; **Feudin' Rhythm**, 1949; **Fight for Your Lady**, 1937; **First Snow**, 2006; **Five Angles on Murder**, 1952; **Flesh and Fantasy**, 1943; **For Your Consideration**, 2006; **For Whom the Bell Tolls**, 1943; **Forever, Lulu**, 1987; **The Fortune Teller**, 1920; **The Fortune Teller**, 1946; **Frankie and Johnny**, 1966; **Freshman Love**, 1936; **Games**, 2007; **The Gift**, 2000; **Golden Earrings**, 1947; **The Great Jasper**, 1933; **Greenwich Village**, 1944; **Hard Boiled Mahoney**, 1947; **Head in the Clouds**, 2004; **Heaven on Earth**, 1931; **Hell's Highway**, 1932; **Holes**, 2003; **Honeymoon in Bali**, 1939; **The Hottest State**, 2006; **I'm No Angel**, 1933; **Inside Daisy Clover**, 1965; **It Can't Last Forever**, 1937; **I've Been Waiting for You**, 1998 (made-for-TV); **I've Got Your Number**, 1934; **Journey to the Sun**, 2001; **A Kid for Two Farthings**, 1956; **La Vie en Rose**, 2007; **Labyrinth**, 1986; **The Landlord**, 1970; **The Last Days of Man on Earth**, 1974; **Le grand jeu**, 1934; **The Legend of Suram Fortress**, 1987; **The Leopard Man**, 1943; **Let Joy Reign Supreme**, 1977; **Live and Let Die**, 1973; **Long Life, Happiness & Prosperity**, 2003; **Lord of Illusions**, 1995; **Love, Honor and Goodbye**, 1945; **Love Is A Many Splendored Thing**, 1955; **Lucky Me**, 1954; **The Man from Monterey**, 1933; **Man from Music Mountain**, 1938; **The Man in Grey**, 1946; **The Medium**, 1951; **Melody Trail**, 1935; **Men in Black III**, 2012; **Mildred Pierce**, 1945; **Min and Bill**, 1930; **The Mind Reader**, 1933; **Ministry of Fear**, 1944; **Miracle in Milan**, 1951; **A Modern Hero**, 1934; **Murder-Rock: Dancing Death**, 1984; **The Murderers among Us**, 1946; **My Lucky Star**, 1938; **My Mom's a Werewolf**, 1989; **The Mysterious Mrs. Musslewhite**, 1917; **Network**, 1976; **Night of Terror**, 1933; **Nightmare Alley**, 1947; **Noi the Albino**, 2003; **Old Mother Riley's Circus**, 1941; **Once upon a Time**, 1973; **One Night in Rome**, 1924; **Onegin**, 1999; **Only You**, 1994; **Ossessione**, [1942] 1959; **The Painted Veil**, 1934; **Palmy Days**, 1931; **Panic**, 1947; **Papa, Mama, My Wife and Me**, 1955; **Pee-wee's Big Adventure**, 1985; **Pepe Le Moko**, 1937; **The Perils of Pauline**, 1914; **The Perils of Pauline**, 1947; **Playmates**, 1941; **The Puppetmaster**, 1993; **The Rainbow Thief**, 1990; **The River**, 1951; **The River**, 1997; **The Rogue's Tavern**, 1936; **Rough Riders' Round Up**, 1939; **Roustabout**, 1964; **The Royal Mounted Rides Again**, 1945; **The Saddest Music in the World**, 2004; **Santa Fe Trail**, 1940; **Saving Face**, 2004; **7 Faces of Dr. Lao**, 1964; **A Shadow You Soon Will Be**, 1994; **Sherlock Holmes: A Game of Shadows**, 2011; **Shoeshine**, 1947; **Sing As We Go**, 1934; **Sinister Hands**, 1932; **Sinners in Paradise**, 1938; **Six-Gun Trail**, 1938; **Slacker**, 1991; **Son of Dracula**, 1943; **South of Caliente**, 1951; **South of the Border**, 1939; **Starstruck**, 1982; **State Fair**, 1945; **Sudden Manhattan**, 1996; **Suez**, 1938; **Swashbuckler**, 1971; **Tales from the Crypt**, 1972; **Theatre of Death**, 1967; **The 13th Warrior**, 1999; **The 39 Steps**, 1959; **Tokyo Decadence**, 1993; **Torture Garden**, 1968; **Touch of Evil**, 1958; **Villa des Roses**, 2002; **A Walk on the Moon**, 1999; **When's Your Birthday?**, 1937; **The Wizard of Oz**, 1939; **The Wolf Man**, 1941; **Wolves of the Range**, 1943; **Yankee**, 1966; and **You Can't Escape Forever**, 1942. **p**, Harlan Thompson; **d**, Ray Enright; **cast**, Humphrey Bogart, Sylvia Sidney, Eddie Albert, Joan Leslie, Sig Rumann, Cliff Clark, Charley Foy, John Ridgely, Clara Blandick, Frank Wilcox, Aldrich Bowker, Garry Owen, Frank Mayo, Eddie Acuff; **w**, Fred Niblo Jr., Barry Trivers (based on the novel *Kid Galahad* by Francis Wallace); **c**, Sid Hickox; **m**, Heinz Roemheld; **ed**, Mark Richards; **art d**, Hugh Reticker; **spec eff**, Byron Haskin, Hans F. Koenekamp.

Waikiki Wedding ★★★ 1937; U.S.; 89m; PAR; B/W; Musical; Children: Acceptable; **DVD**, VHS. Delightful musical sees Crosby as a pineapple conglomerate's public relations man assigned to take "Miss Pineapple" beauty contest winner Ross on a tour of the Hawaiian Islands. Ross brings her friend Raye along and Crosby adds his daffy pal Burns to the tour. Ross becomes bored and books passage to return to mainland America. This gives Crosby's boss, Barbier, headaches, so Crosby thinks he will solve the problem by hiring Quinn and some local natives to "kidnap" the four of them, saying they believe the four possess a sacred jewel. The hoax is exposed, but that matters not in that Ross and Crosby fall in love and so do Raye and Burns and the foursome look forward to a double Waikiki wedding. This film did well at the box office and received an Oscar for Best Song ("Sweet Leilani"; Rainger, Robin); Songs: "Sweet Is the Word for You," "Blue Hawaii," "In a Little Hula Heaven," "Nani Ona Pua," "Okolehau" (Ralph Rainger, Leo Robin), "Sweet Leilani" (Harry Owens). *Author's Note*: Crosby told this author that he thought this film "was just another soufflé, but musicals really need very little story line to excuse a parade of songs. Audiences always put aside the story in those pictures. They were just waiting for the next song to be sung. And that's what we gave them, young man, a song and dance." Quinn told this author that his role in this film "could have been played by any guy who looked like a big goon. Those are the kind of roles I got in those days—goons, thugs and heavies. I figured if I kept doing those parts, someone would eventually give me a role with some meat on it and that eventually happened. The youngsters in today's business want that to happen overnight because they have no patience, or maybe, it's just plain stupidity." **p**, Arthur Hornblow Jr.; **d**, Frank Tuttle; **cast**, Bing Crosby, Bob Burns, Martha Raye, Shirley Ross, George Barbier, Leif Erickson, Anthony Quinn, Grady Sutton, Granville Bates, Mitchell Lewis; **w**, Frank Butler, Don Hartman, Walter DeLeon, Francis Martin (based on a story by Butler, Hartman); **c**, Karl Struss; **m**, Leo Shuken; **ed**, Paul Weatherwax; **art d**, Hans Dreier, Robert Usher; **set d**, A.E. Freudeman; **spec eff**, Farciot Edouart, Loyal Griggs.

Wait Until Dark ★★★★ 1967; U.S.; 108m; WB; Color; Horror; Children: Unacceptable; **DVD**; **VHS**; **IV**. Superbly acted and directed taut thriller sees the always endearing Hepburn in dark peril. Her hazards are darker still in that Hepburn is a blind housewife being manipulated by a gang of murderous drug peddlers. These killers have invaded her home in a desperate search for a priceless package of heroin her husband, Zimbalist, has inadvertently brought home. Zimbalist, while traveling from Montreal, Canada, does a kindness by transporting a doll for a woman. The woman, Jones, asks him to a hold the doll just before he is to board his NYC-bound flight, but she then disappears and Zimbalist simply carries the doll with him and, when reaching his home in Greenwich Village, gives it to his wife, Hepburn. At the time Jones disappears, Crenna and Weston, two petty swindlers, meet with Arkin, a crack-brained character who thinks he is a criminal mastermind. Arkin tells them he has killed Jones because she betrayed them by hiding the heroin. They by then identify Zimbalist as the person who carried the doll from the airport and they now plot to get into Zimbalist's NYC apartment to recoup the doll. To that end, Crenna pretends to be one of Zimbalist's ex-Marine buddies, arranging to meet with Zimbalist in New Jersey. When Zimbalist leaves for that destination, Crenna, Weston and Arkin use a series of ruses to gain entrance to his apartment. Knowing Hepburn is blind, the men employ a number of disguises beginning with Arkin and Weston, who arrive to tell Hepburn that they are two police detectives investigating the murder of Jones, the very woman Arkin has killed, stating that Zimbalist, the last person to have seen her, may have had something to do with Jones' death. The two men keep their story straight when talking to Hepburn by writing notes to each other and then reading them off to Hepburn, who thinks they are writing down notes relative to their ongong investigation. Unbeknownst to the imposters, as well as Hepburn, the doll the men seek is nowhere in Hepburn's apart-

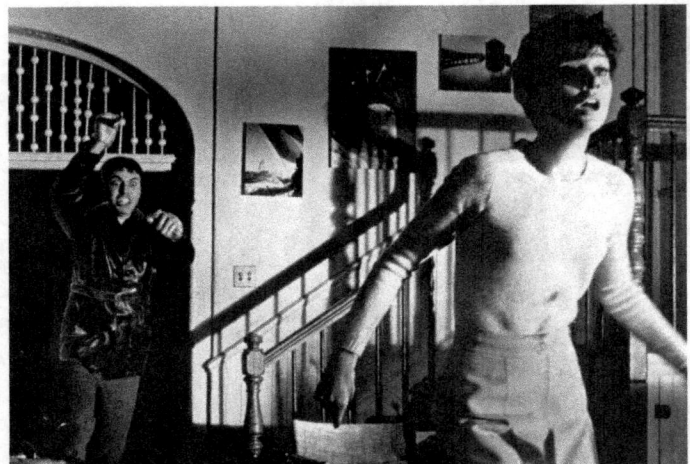

Alan Arkin and Audrey Hepburn in *Wait Until Dark*, 1967.

ment as Herrod, the little girl who lives upstairs, after learning that the doll was not a gift intended for her, has stolen it. After Arkin and Weston ask Hepburn to give them the doll, saying that it might be a clue to solving their case, she searches for it, but cannot find it. The two imposters leave to plot their next move and then Herrod appears, returning the doll. The good-natured Hepburn then thinks to call Crenna, the ex-Marine who has left a phone number, thinking he might be able to contact her husband, who can then give the doll to the detectives. When making that call, however, Hepburn learns that it is the phone number of a phone booth that is immediately across the street from her apartment. She now knows that the whole thing has been a ruse and she desperately sends Herrod to the train station to retrieve Zimbalist. She next tries to call police, but discovers that the phone line has gone dead. Crenna then appears and begins to have empathy for the near helpless Hepburn. He finally confesses that he only pretended to be Zimbalist's ex-service pal and that he and his associates are only interested in obtaining the doll. Once they have gotten that item, they will no longer bother Hepburn. Arkin then bursts into the apartment, a man who has lost his sanity by not being able to locate the doll. He blames his bumbling associates, and has just murdered Weston. He then kills Crenna and begins to terrorize Hepburn. Arkin splashes gas throughout the apartment, planning to burn Hepburn alive once he finds the doll, but the terrified Hepburn regains her senses and realizes that her only chance of survival is to even the odds with the deranged Arkin. She smashes all the light bulbs in the apartment so that the place is now pitched into the darkness she has known all her life. Her opponent is now trapped within that unseeing void so that he must grope about to find his way. When he lights matches, Hepburn douses him with some gasoline to prevent him from again using matches. The shrieking Arkin staggers about before he realizes that there is another source of light and finds the refrigerator, opening it and its light now exposes Hepburn's close presence. When Arkin reaches for her, however, she knows what he has done, and reaches behind the refrigerator to unplug it, again causing the place to be shrouded in darkness. While Arkin searches for her, Hepburn finds a butcher knife and, just as Arkin reaches her, she plunges the blade into him. She moves frantically about the dark apartment, only to find to her horror that Arkin is still alive when he clutches her leg. She breaks free, and the incensed Arkin removes the knife and uses it as a device to pull his way across the floor, intent on killing Hepburn at all costs, including his own miserable life. At that moment, Zimbalist, accompanied by police, breaks into the apartment to find Hepburn alive, and, only inches away from Arkin, who is now dead. Young does a masterful job in building suspense throughout this unique thriller, and the sweet-as-apple-pie Hepburn is magnificent in her role as the blind victim, showing empathetic vulnerability in every frame of this taut nail-biter. Crenna and We-

Barbara Britton and Macdonald Carey in *Wake Island*, 1942.

ston are standouts as the oily con artists, and the gifted Arkin is a sight to behold as one of the most evil villains to ever sully any movie screen. His facial expressions, alternating from the benign to the berserk within seconds, along with his manic moves to chillingly display a person consumed by murderous dementia, presents an unforgettable monster in human flesh. (When asked later why he was not nominated for an Oscar for his performance in this film, Arkin wryly replied: "You don't get nominated for being mean to Audrey Hepburn!") Arkin certainly goes over the top and chews every bit of the furniture in the process, but that is all acceptable since he is playing a lunatic, and where reason and rationale have no application to his grotesque character. The object of everyone's concern, the doll containing the heroin, serves as the evil catalyst in this tension-filled tale, much the same way the doll containing stolen bank money drives a desperate thief, Robert Mitchum, to chase after and possibly kill two children having that doll in another great thriller, **The Night of the Hunter**, 1955, which must certainly have inspired playwright Knott when writing this story. This film was a box office smash, earning more than $17.5 million in its initial release against a budget of $4 million. To heighten audience anxiety, theater owners shut down all of the lights in theaters during the last fifteen minutes of the film, and women routinely screamed and fainted (but, thankfully, no heart attacks were recorded). Song: "Wait Until Dark" (music: Henry Mancini; lyrics: Jay Livingston, Ray Evans). *Author's Note*: The play upon which this outstanding thriller was based was directed by Arthur Penn and opened on Broadway at the Ethel Barrymore Theatre on February 2, 1966, running for 374 performances. Ironically, Young, the director of this film, first met its star, Hepburn, when she was only sixteen years old and was serving as a nurse's aide at a hospital in Holland (she was born in Belgium) where she looked after wounded British soldiers during the 1944 Battle of Arnhem. One of those wounded soldiers was none other than Young. When Hepburn was signed for her part in this film, she began to plague Warner Brothers boss Jack Warner with constant requests that this film be shot in England, which he refused. She then demanded that the production in Hollywood close down at 4 p.m. every day so that she, Young, who was also British, and others, could have their afternoon tea. To placate Hepburn, Warner had his set builders create a tea set next to the apartment set for that purpose. A year after this film was released, Hepburn divorced her actor-producer husband, Mel Ferrer, who produced this film; he reportedly began to romance several would-be starlets auditioning for the role that eventually went to Jones. Hepburn quit Hollywood after this film, planning to permanently retire, but returned to the screen ten years later when appearing with Sean Connery in **Robin and Marion**, 1976. Many other films have profiled home invasions, including **Act of Valor**, 2012; **The Aggression Scale**, 2012; **The Air I**

Breathe, 2007; Angst, 1983; Assassins, 1995; Bad Boys, 1995; Batman, 1989; Batman Forever, 1995; Beverly Hills Cop, 1989; The Big Lebowski, 1998; Black Christmas, 1974; Black Christmas, 2006; Blind Alley, 1939; Boxcar Bertha, 1972; Boys Don't Cry, 1999; The Cable Guy, 1996; Cape Fear, 1962; Cape Fear, 1991; Cassandra's Dream, 2007; Cheery Tree Lane, 2010; A Christmas Story, 1983; The Chronicles of Reddick, 2004; A Clockwork Orange, 1971; Close Encounters of the Third Kind, 1977; Cobra, 1986; Coffy, 1973; The Collector, 2009; Contagion, 2011; Contraband, 2012; Copycat, 1995; Crime Wave, 1954; Cul-de-sac, 1966; Curfew, 1989; The Dark Hours, 2005; The Dark Knight Rises, 2012; The Dark Past, 1948; Daybreakers, 2009; Death Weekend, 1976; Death Wish, 1974; Desperado, 1995; The Desperate Hours, 1955; The Desperate Hours, 1990; Devil in a Blue Dress, 1995; The Devil's Own, 1997; Dial M for Murder, 1954; Escape in the Desert, 1945; Fast Five, 2011; Fatal Attraction, 1987; Fear, 1996; The Fear Inside, 1992; Felon, 2008; Fight for Your Life, 1977; Firewall, 2006; Flesh and Bone, 1993; Foxy Brown, 1974; Frequency, 2000; The Fugitive, 1993; Funny Games, 1997; Funny Games, 2008; A Funny Thing Happened on the Way to the Forum, 1966; Gangster Squad, 2013; The Girl Next Door, 2004; G-Men, 1935; The Great Train Robbery, 1979; Grosse Point Blank, 1997; The Hand That Rocks the Cradle, 1992; He Ran All the Way, 1951; Henry: Portrait of a Serial Killer, 1990; Hesher, 2010; Hider in the House, 1991; High Tension, 2005; Home Alone, 1990; Home Invasion, 2012; Hostage, 2005; The House on the Edge of the Park, 1985; The Hurt Locker, 2009; If I Die Before I Wake, 1998; In Cold Blood, 1967; In the Line of Fire, 1993; In Their Skin, 2012; Inside, 2007; The Ipcress File, 1965; Invaders from Mars, 1953; Invaders from Mars, 1986; The Jackal, 1997; Key Largo, 1948; Kidnapped, 1938; Kidnapped, 1960; Kidnapped, 1971; Kill the Irishman, 2011; Lady in a Cage, 1964; Lakeview Terrace, 2008; Last Action Hero, 1993; Last House on Dead End Street, 1977; The Last House on the Left, 1972; The Last House on the Left, 2009; Law Abiding Citizen, 2009; Lethal Weapon 2, 1989; Limitless, 2011; The Lincoln Lawyer, 2011; Live Free or Die Hard, 2007; The Long Kiss Goodnight, 1996; The Lost Boys, 1987; The Lovely Bones, 2009; Machete, 2010; Manhunter, 1986; Marathon Man, 1976; Martin, 1976; Martyrs, 2008; Nevada Smith, 1966; The Omega Man, 1971; The Outlaw Josey Wales, 1976; Pacific Heights, 1990; Pain & Gain, 2013; Panic Room, 2002; Patriot Games, 1993; The Penthouse, 1967; The People Under the Stairs, 1991; A Perfect Murder, 1998; The Petrified Forrest, 1936; Point Blank, 1967; Posse from Hell, 1961; A Prayer for the Dying, 1987; Prisoners, 2013; The Proposition, 2006; The Prowler, 1951; The Purge, 2013; The Ref, 1994; Rolling Thunder, 1977; Savages, 2012; Scream, 1996; The Seven Ups, 1973; Shoot Out, 1971; Silent House, 2011; Single White Female, 1992; Skyfall, 2012; Something of Value, 1957; The Sorcerer's Apprentice, 2010; Sorry, Wrong Number, 1948; The Strangers, 2008; Straw Dogs, 1971; Straw Dogs, 2011; Suddenly, 1954; Supremacy, 2014; Them, 2006; Thief, 1981; Tiger House, 2014; Trespass, 2011; Unbreakable, 2000; The Unforgiven, 1960; Underworld: Awakening, 2012; Unknown, 2011; Unlawful Entry, 1992; Unleashed, 2005; Visiting Hours, 1982; When a Stranger Calls, 1979; When a Stranger Calls, 2006; When a Stranger Calls Back, 1993; White Sands, 1992; The Whole Town's Talking, 1935; The Wild Geese, 1978; Will Penny, 1968; Year of the Dragon, 1985; and You're Next, 2011. **p**, Mel Ferrer; **d**, Terence Young; **cast**, Audrey Hepburn, Alan Arkin, Richard Crenna, Efrem Zimbalist Jr., Jack Weston, Samantha Jones, Julie Herrod, Robby Benson, Jean Del Val, Gary Morgan, Ferrer (voice only); **w**, Robert Carrington, Jane-Howard Carrington (based on the play by Frederick Knott); **c**, Charles Lang Jr. (Technicolor); **m**, Henry Mancini; **ed**, Gene Milford; **art d**, George Jenkins; **set d**, George James Hopkins.

Wake Island ★★★★ 1942; U.S.; 87m; Paramount; B/W; War Drama;

Children: Unacceptable; **DVD**; **VHS**. Stirring and patriotic, the film opens with a brief description of Wake Island, a tiny, remote American stronghold in the Pacific. It is defended by the First Battalion of the U.S. Marine Corps and a squadron of fighter planes flown by Marine pilots. (The defense forces were made up of 450 officers and men of the U.S. Marines, the island fortifications were still under construction by more than 1,200 civilian workers when the Japanese attacked the island following Japan's attack on Pearl Harbor, Hawaii, on December 7, 1941.) The story opens with Marine officers and men saying good-bye to their loved ones at Pearl Harbor, before going to their posts at Wake Island, including Donlevy, a major commanding the garrison (who represents USMC Major James P. Devereux, 1903-1988); Carey, a Marine flier; and Dekker, boss of the construction workers on the island. These men then board the Pan American Clipper, which makes regular flights to Wake, and, while on board, Donlevy and Dekker immediately clash. The by-the-book Donlevy suggests that the roughhouse Dekker shave, and the construction chief immediately fires back that he does not take such orders from the U.S. military. Meanwhile, Bendix and Preston, two career Marines, are relaxing on a beach at Wake Island, discussing Bendix's future while playing with the garrison's dog and mascot, Skipper. Bendix is about to be discharged in a few days and will be leaving the island, telling his buddy Preston that he is thinking of becoming a hog farmer. When Preston reminds him that Bendix once thought to raise turkeys, Bendix states that turkeys have too many diseases. Both then spot a glass float used by fishermen to buoy their nets and which both collect. They race to the water to retrieve it, but, when struggling over it, break it. Blaming each other for the wreckage, they get into a fight that is quickly interrupted when they hear the call summoning the garrison to chow. They run to the mess area where they get in line and where they begin to torment Van Zandt, a corporal named Goebbels. Although Van Zandt is not related to Nazi propaganda minister Joseph Goebbels, Preston and Bendix sneakily suggest that he is by shouting "Zieg Heil!" behind Van Zandt's back. This angers Van Zandt no end, as he is a patriotic American, but he can never identify those calling out the epithet behind his back. After Bendix learns that Donlevy is on his way to take command of the island, he states to his fellows: "The honeymoon is over! From now on, you're Marines!" When Donlevy arrives the following day, he makes a thorough inspection of the island, making note of its six heavy guns (which had been stripped from the decommissioned U.S. battleship USS *Texas*, and shipped to Wake Island in early 1941). After Bendix and Preston are identified as troublemakers, Donlevy orders that they be put to work digging slit trenches. Dekker, who has had his crews also building slit trenches, as well as expanding the airfield on the island, arrives to see Bendix and Preston at work. He orders them to fix a nearby truck that has broken down, and, after they refuse, he attempts to force them to the work. Preston stands up to the brutish Dekker, and Preston intends to "teach him a lesson." Instead, Dekker does the teaching by repeatedly knocking Preston down until Preston lands a powerful punch on Dekker's jaw that sends him flying into a slit trench. Donlevy arrives to ask Dekker what has happened and Dekker tells him that he fell into the trench and then goes about his business. Dekker and Donlevy later clash when Dekker arrives at Donlevy's headquarters to complain about the incessant practicing of air raids that sends his men to shelter and interrupts their work, and Dekker tells Donlevy to stop sounding those air raid warnings. Donlevy tells him that he will obey his commands or suffer the consequences. That night, Abel, who is the commanding U.S. Navy officer (representing Commander Winfield S. Cunningham, 1900-1986), hosts a dinner party for Loo, playing Japanese special envoy Saburo Kurusu (1886-1954), who is en route to Washington, D.C., to meet with U.S. Secretary of State Cordell Hull (1871-1955) in an effort to avoid war between the U.S. and Japan. (As events turned out, this visit by Kurusu was nothing more than a smokescreen and diplomatic stall while Japanese militarists planned and executed the sneak attack against Pearl Harbor, on December 7, 1941; Kurusu had been Japan's ambassador to Germany, 1939-1941, and had

Brian Donlevy, Bill Goodwin, William Bendix and Robert Preston in *Wake Island*, 1942.

signed the Tripartite Pact with Germany and Italy on September 27, 1940, unifying those three aggressor countries in a military alliance.) At the dinner, Abel, Loo, Donlevy and others toast U.S. President Franklin D. Roosevelt (1882-1945) and Japan's Emperor Hirohito (1901-1989), all expressing hope for peace. Bendix is discharged the following day, December 7, 1941, and has already donned a set of civilian clothes, a garish checkered suit and a straw boater, intending to fly from the island that day on board the Pan American Clipper. News of the bombing of Pearl Harbor is then received and Donlevy orders all military on full alert. Carey, one of the pilots flying a Wildcat fighter plane, talks with his mechanic, Rasumny, who tells Carey that he has a wife in Warsaw, which is now under German occupation. Carey apprehensively tells Rasumny that he has a wife in Pearl Harbor. When Dekker arrives once more to complain to Donlevy about the air raid siren again interrupting the ongoing construction of his work crews, he is told that Pearl Harbor has been bombed and he can leave the island on the Clipper if he so chooses. Dekker elects to stay. Bendix, still wearing civilian clothes, joins the construction workers as they scramble into air raid shelters when Japanese bombers appear over the island (thirty-six medium Mitsubishi Japanese bombers attacked Wake Island on December 8, 1941) and begin dropping bombs. Although four of the Wildcat fighter planes are in the air and on patrol at that time, eight of the twelve total fighter planes stationed at the island are destroyed in the bombing, along with most of the fuel for the remaining planes. Carey and his fellow pilots, who are then in the air, shoot down some of the attacking Japanese planes and, that night, Carey learns from Donlevy that his wife has been killed in the Pearl Harbor bombing the previous day. Donlevy gently explains that since he is a widower, both of them have suffered the loss of their spouses, so he knows the sorrow Carey is suffering. He adds that they are not alone in their grief as the thousands of others have endured the same fate as bombs all over the world are being dropped by aggressor nations such as Japan. Bendix later appears before Donlevy, who tells Bendix to "take off that dog catcher's suit," and orders him to get back into uniform and back to duty, orders the Marine-loving Bendix is happy to hear. Meanwhile, the undamaged Pan American Clipper flies off without Dekker and Bendix, who is now wearing his Marine uniform. A Japanese invasion fleet is spotted by Carey while flying a Wildcat patrolling the area off the island (that fleet consists of three cruisers, six destroyers, two PT-boats and two transports). Donlevy, by that time, has camouflaged his six five-inch coastal artillery guns to repel just such an invasion by the Japanese. (The guns were moved after the first bombing and disguised while the original emplacements were substituted by wooden logs to simulate the appearance of the guns and these decoy emplacements were later attacked by Japanese bombers instead of the actual guns.) The Japanese

Robert Preston and Brian Donlevy in *Wake Island*, 1942.

signal to the island, demanding surrender, but Donlevy does not respond. Donlevy orders his men to remain under cover and for his gun crews to hold their fire until the Japanese fleet comes within range of the coastal guns. (That order was actually issued by U.S. Navy Commander Cunningham, not his Marine counterpart and subordinate, Major Devereux, as Cunningham was the commanding officer on the island during the Battle of Wake Island, December 8-23, 1941.) Donlevy asks one of his officers, Cameron, if he remembers the words of Colonel William Prescott (1726-1795) at the Battle of Bunker Hill (June 17, 1775); Donlevy quotes Prescott's cautionary words about the approaching enemy when saying to his men: "Don't fire until you see the whites of their eyes!" When the Japanese fleet does come within range (on December 11, 1941), the coastal guns open fire, and the Japanese fleet meets with disaster, one of its light cruisers (*Yubari*) being badly damaged. Two destroyers are sent to the bottom (*Hayate* sunk at a distance of four thousand yards by one of the island's guns, the first capital ship sunk during the U.S.-Japanese war, and *Kisaragi*, which was sunk by one of the four remaining Wildcats on the island piloted by Captain Henry T. Elrod, 1905-1941, and who would later shoot down two Japanese planes before being killed and who would posthumously receive the Congressional Medal of Honor; he is the role model for Carey's character). When the Japanese fleet withdraws without landing any troops, Donlevy reviews his losses and prepares for another attack. Carey then returns from a patrol to report that he has spotted a heavy Japanese cruiser that can remain at sea beyond the range of the island's guns and bombard the island. Carey, however, tells Donlevy that, if his plane is stripped down and he carries a double load of bombs, he might be able to sink the Japanese warship. Donlevy approves of the mission, and Carey attacks the cruiser, sinking it, but is mortally wounded, and when he lands his plane, mechanic Rasumny finds him dead inside the cockpit. He is buried that night with Donlevy reading solemn words over his grave and while taps is played. A U.S. PBY arrives, and Donlevy orders Cameron to fly off with it so that he can give a full report to U.S. Navy superiors; Donlevy also sends a farewell letter to his small daughter, who is living in Pearl Harbor. While the Marines prepare for the next attack, Bendix discovers that his dog, Skipper, has given birth to several puppies. He and Preston are dumbfounded as they know of no other dog on the island, but suspect that a canine from a visiting tanker may have been that mystery animal fostering Skipper's progeny. (The story of the island's dog was perpetuated on film a year later in Howard Hawks' **Air Force**, 1943, when crew members of a B-17 bomber briefly visit the island before it falls to the Japanese and, before resuming its flight to the Philippines, taking with them a dog called "Tripoli" that belongs to the Marine defenders.) Then Marines prepare to meet the next attack, one they know will most likely overwhelm their small force. When Van Zandt inspects the ma-

chine-gun nest manned by Bendix and Preston, both shout "Heil!" to let him know that they are the ones who have been so long tormenting him, but the three end their petty squabbles in light of the battle to come. Another Japanese fleet arrives and begins to land troops. Donlevy goes to a machine-gun nest, joined by Dekker, and where both repel an attack and where Dekker grabs a grenade tossed into their position and throws it back to kill several Japanese soldiers. In a brief respite, Dekker provides two bottles of beer and gives one to Donlevy, explaining that he developed his "pitching arm" while playing football at Notre Dame, and that he is a graduate of that university in 1928. Donlevy toasts him with his bottle of beer, stating that he is a graduate of the Virginia Military Institute (VMI) in 1928. The Japanese then launch an all-out attack against all of the Marine positions that are shown overrun and its defenders killed. In a voiceover epilog, the viewer hears that "the good fight" fought by the Marines does not mark "the end," but the beginning of a war the U.S. will win. Farrow does a splendid job in developing the many diversified characters in this exciting fact-based film, and performances from Donlevy, Abel, Carey, Dekker, Preston and Bendix are outstanding. The battle scenes, including the miniature sequences at sea, and the aerial combat scenes are exceptional, as are the special effects. Buttolph's stirring score dramatically emphasizes the many action scenes so expertly choreographed. The film received Oscar nominations for Best Picture, Best Director (Farrow), Best Supporting Actor (Bendix) and Best Original Screenplay (Burnett, Butler). It was a huge box office hit, one of the biggest grossing films in the U.S. for the year 1942, earning more than $3.5 million in its initial release. A sixty-minute radio adaptation was aired by Lux Radio Theater on October 26, 1942, with Donlevy and Preston reprising their roles. Songs/Music: "Marine Hymn" (1867; Jacques Offenbach), "Taps" (1862; Daniel Butterfield), "Aloha Oe (Farewell to Thee)" (c.1877; Queen Liliuokalani). ***Author's Note***: Farrow shot this film on location at Coachella and Imperial valleys, as well as the Salton Sea. Donlevy told this author that "**Wake Island** was probably responsible for more enlistments than any other picture made that year. Young men saw the picture and when they left theaters and went into lobbies, they were greeted by recruitment officers from the Army, Navy and the Marines, and they signed up on the spot, thousands of those boys. They all wanted to avenge the defeat at Wake Island." That defeat cost the U.S. fifty-two military deaths and seventy civilians were killed. The Japanese losses were, by comparison, staggering, between 800 to 1,500 Japanese troops and sailors lost during the fifteen-day battle. Some of the facts in this film were altered. Abel, the U.S. Navy commander, dies but where Cunningham, the actual commander, surrendered the island and survived imprisonment. Devereux, who is Donlevy's role model, also survived the battle and imprisonment. The defiant message sent from Wake after the first enemy attack is recorded: "Send us more Japs!" The final message sent from that beleaguered isle was a chilling one: "Enemy on island...issue in doubt." One of the many heinous atrocities committed by the Japanese during the war occurred at Wake when its Japanese commander, Rear Admiral Shigematsu Sakaibara (1898-1947), fearing a U.S. invasion, ordered the mass murder of ninety-eight American civilian workers captured in 1941 and held on the island as slave laborers. They were blindfolded and then shot to death with machine guns on October 7, 1943. One escaped to record the atrocity on a rock before he was captured and also murdered. After the island was recaptured by U.S. Marines in September 1945, Sakaibara was found guilty of the mass killings and was executed by hanging as a war criminal. The island was continually attacked by U.S. naval forces throughout the war, but an invasion was thought to be too costly in overwhelming the island's 2,000 Japanese defenders. One of the attacks by air on the island involved U.S. Navy pilot and future U.S. President George H.W. Bush. Other films profiling WWII in the Pacific Theater include **Above and Beyond**, 1953 (atom bombing of Hiroshima, 1945); **Abroad with Two Yanks**, 1944 (Australia); **Admiral Yamamoto**, 1968 (Japanese Pearl Harbor Attack, December 7, 1941; Pacific, 1942-1943); **Aerial Gun-**

ner, 1943 (Pacific, 1942); **Air Force**, 1943 (Japanese attack against Pearl Harbor, 1941; Philippine Defense, 1942); **Ambush Bay**, 1966 (Philippines, 1944); **American Guerrilla in the Philippines**, 1950 (Philippine Defense, 1942; Leyte, 1944); **Attack Force Z**, 1982 (Pacific island); **Australia**, 2008; **Away All Boats**, 1956 (Okinawa, 1945); **Back Door to Hell**, 1964 (Philippines, Leyte, 1944); **Back to Bataan**, 1945 (Philippine Defense, 1941-1942; Leyte invasion, 1944; begins with the spectacular raid against Japanese prison camp at Cabanatuan, Luzon, Philippines, where more than 500 prisoners were rescued on April 30, 1945); **The Bamboo Blonde**, 1946 (B-29 crew in the Pacific); **Bataan**, 1943 (Philippine Defense, 1941-1942); **Battle at Bloody Beach**, 1961 (Philippine Resistance, 1943); **Battle Cry**, 1955 (Guadalcanal, 1942; Tarawa, 1943); **Battle of Blood Island**, 1960 (Pacific island); **Battle of the Coral Sea**, 1959 (Pacific, 1942); **Beach Red**, 1967 (Bougainville, 1943-1944); **Beachhead**, 1954 (Choiseul Island in Bougainville Campaign, 1943-1945); **Between Heaven and Hell**, 1956 (Philippines, 1944); **Blood Oath**, 1990 (Laha Massacre, 1942); **Bombardier**, 1943 (Pacific, 1942); **Bombs over Burma**, 1943 (Burma Road, 1942); **The Bridge on the River Kwai**, 1957 (Burma, 1942-1943); **The Burmese Harp** [1956], 1967 (Burma, 1941-1945 from the Japanese perspective; remade as a color version in 1985); **The Camp on Blood Island**, 1958 (Japanese POW camp holding British captives in Malaya); **China**, 1943 (China, 1941); **China Girl**, 1942 (Burma, China, 1941); **China Sky**, 1945 (Sino-Japanese War, 1937-1945); **Codename: Fox**, 2001 (aka: **Battle of the Pacific**; **Oba: The Last Samurai**; Japanese fighting U.S. forces on Saipan); **Corregidor**, 1943 (Philippine Defense, 1941-1942); **Cry Havoc**, 1943 (Bataan, Philippines, 1941-1942); **Cry of Battle**, 1963 (Philippine Defense, 1941-1942); **The Deep Six**, 1958 (Aleutian Islands); **Destination Gobi**, 1953 (Mongolia); **Destination Tokyo**, 1943 (Aleutian Islands; Honsho, Japan; Doolittle Raid against Japan, April 18, 1942); **Don't Go Near the Water**, 1957 (Pacific island); **Dragon Seed**, 1944 (Sino-Japanese War, 1942); **Empire of the Sun**, 1987 (Allied prisoners in Shanghai, 1939-1945); **Ensign Pulver**, 1964 (Pacific island); **Escape from Hong Kong**, 1942; **The Eve of St. Mark**, 1944 (Philippine Defense, 1941-1942); **The Extraordinary Seaman**, 1969 (fighting at sea in the Pacific); **Farewell to the King**, 1987 (Borneo); **Father Goose**, 1964 (coast watcher on a Pacific island); **The Fighting Seabees**, 1944 (Pacific, 1943); **Fire on That Flag!**, 1944 (Corregidor, Philippines); **Fires on the Plain**, 1963 (released in Japan in 1959; Japanese soldier attempting to survive on Leyte in February 1945); **Fires on the Plain**, 2014 (remake of 1959 film; Japanese soldier attempting to survive on Leyte in February 1945); **First to Fight**, 1967 (Guadalcanal, 1942); **First Yank into Tokyo**, 1945 (Honshu, Japan, 1943); **Flags of Our Fathers**, 2006 (Iwo Jima, 1945); **Flight for Freedom**, 1943 (Pacific island; fictional portrait of Amelia Earhart, 1897-1939); **Flying Leathernecks**, 1951 (Guadalcanal, 1942); **Flying Tigers**, 1942 (China, Burma, 1941); **For the Boys**, 1991; **The Frogmen**, 1951 (Southwestern Pacific); **From Here to Eternity**, 1953 (Japanese attack against Pearl Harbor, 1941); **The Gallant Hours**, 1960 (Guadalcanal, 1942); **The Girls of Pleasure Island**, 1953 (Pacific island where Marines are building an air base in 1945); **God Is My Co-Pilot**, 1945 (China, Burma, 1941-1942); **Grave of the Fireflies**, 1994 (released in Japan in 1988; animated tale of two children trying to survive the devastation of WWII in Kobe, Japan, just after the war in September 1945); **Grave of the Fireflies**, 2005 (made-for-TV live-action remake of 1988 film where two children try to survive the devastation of WWII in Kobe, Japan, just after the war in September 1945); **The Great Raid**, 2005 (details the spectacular raid against Japanese prison camp at Cabanatuan, Luzon, Philippines, where more than 500 prisoners were rescued on April 30, 1945); **Guadalcanal Diary**, 1943 (Battle of Guadalcanal, August 7, 1942-February 9, 1943); **Guerillas in Pink Lace**, 1964 (Invasion of the Philippines, 1941-1942); **Gung Ho!**, 1943 (Makin Island); **A Guy Named Joe**, 1943 (Pacific Island); **Halls of Montezuma**, 1951 (Okinawa, 1945); **Heaven Knows, Mr. Allison**, 1957 (a nun and a Marine trapped on a Japanese-held island in the Pacific); **Hell in the Pacific**,

Marines under attack in *Wake Island*, 1942.

1968 (Pacific island); **Hell to Eternity**, 1960 (Saipan, 1944); **High Barbaree**, 1947 (shot down Navy pilot and companion survive at sea in the Pacific); **The Highest Honor**, 1984 (British POWs in Singapore in 1943); **Hiroshima mon amour**, 1959 (dropping of the atom bomb on Hiroshima, 1945; remade in 2001 as **H Story**); **Home of the Brave**, 1949 (Pacific island, 1944); **Hong Kong 1941**, 1984 (Japanese occupation); **The Horizontal Lieutenant**, 1962 (Japanese-held island); **I Was an American Spy**, 1951 (Philippine Defense, 1941-1944; based on the exploits of Claire Phillips, 1908-1960); **In Harm's Way**, 1965 (Japanese attack against Pearl Harbor, 1941; Solomon Islands, 1942); **Island of Desire**, 1952 (aka: Saturday Island; marooned on a Pacific island); **Isoroku Yamamoto: The Commander-in-Chief of the Combined Fleet**, 2011 (Japanese naval operations in the Pacific); **Jungle Fighters**, 1962 (aka: **The Long and the Short and the Tall**; British forces fighting in Burmese jungles during the 1942 Malayan Campaign); **King Rat**, 1965 (Allied POWs in Malaysia); **Kokoda: 39th Battalion**, 2007 (Australian forces during the Kokoda Trail Campaign, July-November 1942); **The Last Emperor**, 1987 (Sino-Japanese War, 1937-1945); **Letters from Iwo Jima**, 2006 (Japanese defenders on Iwo Jima); **Lost Battalion**, 1962 (guerrillas fighting in Japanese-occupied Philippines); **MacArthur**, 1977 (Gregory Peck portrays U.S. five-star general Douglas MacArthur, 1880-1964, and his campaigns in the Philippine Defense, 1941-1942, and his island-hopping campaigns, 1943-1945, and his campaigns in the Korean War); **Malaya**, 1949 (rubber smuggling in Japanese-occupied Malaya); **The Man in the Gray Flannel Suit**, 1956 (Pacific island); **Manila Calling**, 1942 (Philippine Defense, 1942); **Marine Raiders**, 1944 (Guadalcanal, 1942; Solomon Islands, 1943); **Merrill's Marauders**, 1962 (Burma, 1944); **Merry Christmas, Mr. Lawrence**, 1983 (British soldiers in a Japanese POW camp); **Midway**, 1976 (Doolittle Raid against Japan, April 18, 1942; Coral Sea and Midway, 1942); **Minesweeper**, 1943 (Japanese attack against Pearl Harbor, December 7, 1941); **Mister Roberts**, 1955 (Pacific island); **Mr. Winkle Goes to War**, 1944 (Pacific island); **Monkey on My Back**, 1957 (biopic of prizefighter Barney Ross, 1909-1967, winning the Silver Star for heroism when fighting at Guadalcanal, but became addicted to drugs when treated with morphine to combat malaria); **The Mountain Road**, 1960 (China, 1944); **The Naked and the Dead**, 1958 (Pacific island); **Never So Few**, 1959 (Burma, 1943); **1941**, 1979 (California); **No Man Is an Island**, 1962 (Guam, 1941-1944); **None But the Brave**, 1965 (Pacific island); **Objective, Burma!**, 1945 (based on the 1944 raids by Merrill's Marauders in 1944); **Okinawa**, 1952; **Once Before I Die**, 1966 (Philippine Defense, 1941-1942); **Operation Bikini**, 1963 (U.S. submarine in the Pacific); **Operation Pacific**, 1951 (based on the exploits in the Pacific of USS *Darter*, SS-227, 1943-1944); **Operation Petticoat**, 1959 (submarine

Adele Mara and Gig Young in *Wake of the Red Witch,* **1949.**

operations in the Pacific); **The Outsider**, 1961 (portraying the exploits of Marine and Pima Native American Ira Hayes, 1923-1955, one of those who raised the American flag at Mount Suribachi during the battle of Iwo Jima, and who is enacted by Tony Curtis); **The Pacific**, 2010 (cable-TV miniseries; Guadalcanal, 1942; Peleliu, 1944; Iwo Jima, 1945); **Paloh**, 2003 (Japanese occupation of Malaya); **Paradise Road**, 1997 (Sumatra, 1941-1945); **Pearl Harbor**, 2001 (Japanese attack at Pearl Harbor, 1941); **Pilot No. 5**, 1943 (Java, 1942); **Pride of the Marines**, 1945 (Guadalcanal, 1942); **Prisoner of Japan**, 1942 (Pacific island); **The Proud and the Profane**, 1956 (Marines fighting in the Pacific); **PT-109**, 1963 (Tulagi in the Solomon Islands, 1943); **The Purple Heart**, 1944 (Doolittle Raid against Japan, April 18, 1942; U.S. POWs tried for the attack); **The Purple Plain**, 1954 (Burma); **The Railway Man**, 2014 (captives in a Japanese POW camp in Burma); **Remember Pearl Harbor**, 1942 (Japanese attack against Pearl Harbor, December 7, 1941); **Return from the River Kwai**, 1989 (British POWs in Burma); **Run Silent, Run Deep**, 1955 (Bungo Straits, Japan, 1944); **Salute to the Marines**, 1943 (Philippine Defense, 1941-1942); **Sands of Iwo Jima**, 1949 (Tarawa, 1943; Iwo Jima, 1945); **The Secret of Blood Island**, 1965 (British soldiers in a Japanese POW camp); **7 Women from Hell**, 1961 (women captives in a Japanese POW camp); **Shima**, 2007 (Japanese war survivors on a remote island); **So Proudly We Hail!**, 1943 (Philippine Defense, Bataan and Corregidor, 1941-1942); **Somewhere I'll Find You**, 1942 (Manila, Philippine Defense, 1941-1942); **South Sea Woman**, 1953 (Guadalcanal, 1942); **Stand By for Action**, 1942 (Pacific, 1942); **The Steel Claw**, 1961 (Philippine Defense, 1941-1942); **Storm Over the Pacific**, 1960 (Japanese attack against Pearl Harbor, December 7, 1941, Battle of Midway, 1942); **The Story of Dr. Wassell**, 1944 (Java, 1942); **Submarine Command**, 1951 (Pacific, 1945; Korean War); **Submarine Seahawk**, 1958 (operations in the Pacific); **Submarine Raider**, 1942 (Japanese attack against Pearl Harbor on December 7, 1941); **Suicide Battalion**, 1958 (U.S. forces fighting in the Philippines); **The Sullivans**, 1944 (aka: **The Fighting Sullivans**; USS *Juneau*, CL-52, sunk during action off Guadalcanal, Solomon Islands, November 13, 1942, where all five Sullivan brothers were lost); **Sunset at Chaophraya**, 1996 (Japanese and resistance fighters in Thailand; remade in 2013); **Tarawa Beachhead**, 1958 (Guadalcanal, 1942; Tarawa, 1943); **Task Force**, 1949 (USS *Franklin*, CV-13/AVT-8, Bonin and Mariana Islands, Peleliu, Leyte, 1944; Honshu, Japan, 1945); **They Met in Bombay**, 1941 (China, 1941); **They Were Expendable**, 1945 (Philippine Defense, 1942); **The Thin Red Line**, 1964 (Guadalcanal); **The Thin Red Line**, 1998 (Guadalcanal, 1942); **Thirty Seconds over Tokyo**, 1944 (Doolittle Raid against Japan, April 18, 1942); **36 Hours to Hell**, 1969 (Pacific island); **Three Came Home**, 1950 (Battle of Borneo, 1941-1942); **To End All Wars**, 2001 (British troops in a POW camp in Burma); **Tora! Tora! Tora!**, 1970 (Japanese attack against Pearl Harbor, 1941); **Too Late the Hero**, 1970 (New Hebrides); **Torpedo Alley**, 1952 (Pacific, 1945; Korean War); **Torpedo Run**, 1958 (Philippine Defense; Honshu, Japan, Aleutian Islands, 1942); **A Town Like Alice**, 1958 (Japanese invasion of Malaya, 1942); **Unbroken**, 2014 (biopic of Louis Zamperini, 1917-2014, who survived several Japanese prison camps); **Up Periscope**, 1959 (Kosrae Island, Micronesia, 1944); **The Wackiest Ship in the Army**, 1960 (operations in the Pacific); **We've Never Been Licked**, 1943 (Pacific, 1942); **Windtalkers**, 2002 (Navajo Marines use their native language to communicate and confuse Japanese listeners during the Battle of Saipan, June 15-July 9, 1944); **Wing and a Prayer**, 1944 (Coral Sea, Midway, 1942); **Women of Valor**, 1986 (made-for-TV; U.S. nurses captured on Bataan, Philippines, in 1942 and held in a Japanese POW camp); and **A Yank on the Burma Road**, 1942 (Burma, 1942). **p**, Joseph Sistrom; **d**, John Farrow; **cast**, Brian Donlevy, Macdonald Carey, Robert Preston, William Bendix, Albert Dekker, Walter Abel, Mikhail Rasumny, Rod Cameron, Bill Goodwin, Frank Albertson, Hugh Beaumont, Don Castle, Damian O'Flynn, Barbara Britton, Hillary Brooke, James Brown, Dane Clark, Alan Hale Jr., Phillip Terry, Philip Van Zandt, Keith Richards, Rudy Robles, Marvin Jones, Willard Robertson, Charles Trowbridge, Richard Loo, **w**, W.R. Burnett, Frank Butler (based on a story by Burnett); **c**, William C. Mellor, Theodor Sparkuhl; **m**, David Buttolph; **ed**, LeRoy Stone, Frank Bracht; **art d**, Hans Dreier, Earl Hedrick; **set d**, Bertram Granger; **spec eff**, Barney Wolff, Farciot Edouart, Gordon Jennings.

Wake Me When It's Over ★★★ 1960; U.S.; 126m; FOX; Color; Comedy; Children: Cautionary; **DVD**; **VHS**. Humorous film begins with a government mix-up where GI Shawn is on the record as having been killed in action during World War II (1939-1945). However, he is later found to have been a prisoner of war. He winds up back in uniform at a U.S. Air Force radar station on a small and almost forgotten island near Japan. A non-conformist pilot, Kovacs, is in charge, and he and Shawn team up to open a resort hotel, using the base men as laborers and its supplies to furnish the hotel, which is staffed by forty young women from a village on the island. These offbeat entrepreneurs flourish until a congressional committee investigates and blows the whistle on their wacky operations. Songs: "Wake Me When It's Over" (Jimmy Van Heusen, Sammy Cahn), "You Make Me Feel So Young" (Josef Myrow), "Give Me the Simple Life" (Rube Bloom). **p&d**, Mervyn LeRoy; **cast**, Ernie Kovacs, Dick Shawn, Margo Moore, Jack Warden, Robert Strauss, Noreen Nash, Parley Baer, Robert Emhardt, Marvin Kaplan, Tommy Nishimura; **w**, Richard L. Breen (based on the novel by Howard Singer); **c**, Leon Shamroy; **m**, Cyril J. Mockridge; **ed**, Aaron Stell; **art d**, Lyle R. Wheeler, John Beckman; **spec eff**, L.B. Abbott.

Wake of the Red Witch ★★★ 1949; U.S.; 106m; REP; B/W; Adventure; Children: Unacceptable; **BD**; **DVD**; **VHS**; **IV**. Exciting South Seas tale is set in the 1860s in the East Indies and, while offering two extensive flashbacks, begins with the adventure-seeking Wayne, who offends a tribe on an island and must swim out to sea for his life. He is rescued by Adler, a shipping magnate, who takes him aboard his yacht. Wayne immediately sees the wealthy Adler for the greedy person he is, a man who places riches before anyone or anything else on earth. He tells Adler about a great cache of pearls inside of a chest residing in an undersea cavern on a remote island. The problem is that the chest of pearls is guarded by a gigantic octopus that has killed many undersea divers going after the pearls. Wayne tells Adler that he will take him to that island, but only if he becomes the captain of the ship and is allowed a portion of the spoils after the pearls are retrieved. After the yacht arrives at the island, Adler has Wayne clapped in irons as he begins searching for the pearls. Wayne is later released and, with the help of native girl Mara, locates the lagoon leading to the cavern where the pearls are hidden. By this time, Wayne has met and fallen in love with attractive Russell, the daughter of Daniell, who is the French governor of the island. Daniell, who is as greedy as Adler, has made a secret pact with the tycoon where Adler will share the pearls with Daniell in exchange for Russell's hand in marriage. After Adler, who also learns of the location of the treasure cavern, sends a native diver to retrieve the chest of pearls, but he becomes trapped and Wayne dives into the waters to save him. Wayne then later finds and retrieves the chest of pearls with the help of some natives and then attacks and kills the octopus with a knife, but is almost killed himself in the fierce struggle. Russell finds him injured and tells him that she loves him, not knowing that her father has arranged for her marriage to Adler. When Wayne learns about this, he goes on a drunken bender. Russell marries Adler and, seven years later, Wayne is now commanding one of Adler's ships, the *Red Witch,* and Wayne finally takes his revenge against Adler for stealing Russell. When the ship is approaching an island, Wayne has some of his crew members, Young, his first mate, and Fix, a trusted crew member, lock Corey, the navigator, inside of his cabin, so that the ship, which is carrying more than $5 million in gold, strikes a reef and sinks. By this time, Russell, who has never stopped loving Wayne, falls ill from a mysterious disease and expresses her love for Wayne before she dies. Wayne, who has been charged with dereliction of duty, finally agrees to locate the *Red Witch,* which teeters on an underwater ledge. He dives and loads the gold onto a diving basket, which is hauled to safety, but a wild storm turns the sea into a stirring cauldron that topples the *Red Witch* from its precarious perch and takes Wayne with it to the bottom. A final scene shows Wayne and Russell sailing away together in a world much better than the one that brought them so much misery and pain. Ludwig does a good job presenting a complicated story, albeit a linear progression of the tale might have better served the continuity of its twisting and complex subplots than its prolonged and somewhat confusing flashbacks. The action scenes are stunningly and realistically choreographed, especially the battle between Wayne and the octopus. The acting from all is superior, as are the good period sets and the sleek sailing ships, and the tropical island atmosphere is seductively convincing. The film was popular at the box office, more than recouping its budget of $1.2 million. Music: "Nocturne in E Flat Major, Opus 9, No. 2" (Fredric Chopin). *Author's Note*: Wayne told this author that "**Wake of the Red Witch** has been compared to another seafaring picture I made with the great Cecil B. DeMille, **Reap the Wild Wind** [1942] and where I also have to fight a giant octopus, but the two pictures have much different stories and characters. I don't think any octopus ever grew to the size of the monsters shown in those pictures, but 'seeing is believing' when everything goes onto the screen." The huge rubber octopus employed in this film was filched by poverty row film producer Ed Wood, when he produced his overnight cheapie, **Bride of the Monster**, 1955; its star, the by then morphine-addicted Bela Lugosi, was compelled to wrap the creature's rubber tentacles around him since the always inept Wood had failed to also steal the creature's motor. This was the second film in which Wayne appeared with Russell, both having made **The Angel and the Badman**, 1947, two years earlier and where both stars reportedly had a brief, torrid affair (denied by both years later). Other films profiling underwater divers include **The Abyss**, 1989; **Act of Valor**, 2012; **The Adventures of TinTin**, 2011; **Bear Island**, 1979; **Bedknobs and Broomsticks**, 1971; **Beneath the 12-Mile Reef**, 1953; **Boy on a Dolphin**, 1957; **The Bulldog Breed**, 1960; **City in the Sea**, 1965; **Cocoon**, 1985; **Creature from the Black Lagoon**, 1954; **The Deep**, 1977; **DeepStar Six**, 1989; **The Diving Bell and the Butterfly**, 2007; **Doc Savage: The Man of Bronze**, 1975; **The Dragon Murder Case**, 1934; **The Embalmer**, 1965; **The Fabulous World of Jules Verne**, 1961; **Fanny**, 1961; **Ffolkes**, 1980; **The Flesh Eaters**, 1964; **Fool's Gold**, 2008; **The Frogmen**, 1951; **Ghost in the Shell**, 1996; **Isle of Fury**, 1936; **It Came from Beneath the Sea**, 1955; **King of California**, 2007; **Leviathan**, 1989; **Loch Ness**, 1996; **The Mechanic**, 1972;

Ben Bernie, Jack Haley, Walter Winchell and Alice Faye in *Wake Up and Live,* 1937.

Men of Honor, 2000; **Mud**, 2013; **Mysterious Island**, 1961; **Parker**, 2013; **The Perils of Pauline**, 1914; **The Perils of Pauline**, 1947; **The Phantom Submarine**, 1940; **Pineapple Express**, 2008; **Reap the Wild Wind**, 1942; **Red Barry**, 1938; **Revenge of the Creature**, 1955; **The Sea Hound**, 1947 (serial); **Sh! The Octopus**, 1937; **Sink the Bismarck!**, 1960; **Sphere**, 1998; **That Burning Feeling**, 2013; **They Were Expendable**,1945; **Tillie and Gus**, 1933; **Titanic**, 1997; **20,000 Leagues under the Sea**, 1954; **Undersea Girl**, 1957; **Underwater!**, 1955; **Voyage to the Bottom of the Sea**, 1961; and **When Eight Bells Toll**, 1971. **p**, Edmund Grainger; **d**, Edward Ludwig; **cast**, John Wayne, Gail Russell, Gig Young, Adele Mara, Luther Adler, Eduard Franz, Grant Withers, Henry Daniell, Paul Fix, Dennis Hoey, Jeff Corey, Erskine Sanford, Duke Kahanamoku, Henry Brandon; **w**, Harry Brown, Kenneth Gamet (based on the novel by Garland Roark); **c**, Reggie Lanning; **m**, Nathan Scott; **ed**, Richard L. Van Enger; **art d**, James Sullivan; **set d**, John McCarthy, Jr., George Milo; **spec eff**, Howard Lydecker, Theodore Lydecker.

Wake Up and Live ★★★ 1937; U.S.; 91m; FOX; B/W; Musical Comedy; Children: Acceptable; **DVD**; **VHS**. Lively songfest begins when, to get more publicity, radio columnist Winchell and bandleader Bernie pretend to be feuding. Haley and Bradley come to New York to seek their fortune in radio. Haley's sister, Kelly, who works for Winchell, gets them an audition, but Haley gets microphone fright and botches their chances. Singer Alice Faye comes to Haley's rescue and they become a hit song team while Winchell and Bernie end their phony feud. Winchell and Bernie resumed their fake feud in a sequel, **Love and Hisses**, 1937. This film saw a one-hour radio adaptation aired by Lux Radio Theater on February 21, 1944, with Marilyn Maxwell playing the role essayed by Faye. Songs: "There's a Lull in My Life," "Wake Up and Live," "Never in a Million Years," "I'm Bubbling Over," "It's Swell of You," "Oh, But I'm Happy," "I Love You Too Much, Muchacha," "Red Seal Malt," "Bernie's Love Song" (Harry Revel, Mack Gordon). *Author's Note*: Faye told this author that "Walter [Winchell] was the most powerful man in the media in those days. Millions of people read his syndicated gossip column and he could make or break careers by lifting one eyebrow. We all stayed on the good side of that man, believe me, and I went out of my way to treat him like a king when we made **Wake Up and Live** together. Watch out, brother, if you got onto his mean streak. Walter was not only all-powerful, but a very dangerous man to be around." **p**, Darryl F. Zanuck; **d**, Sidney Lanfield; **cast**, Walter Winchell, Ben Bernie and His Band, Alice Faye, Patsy Kelly, Ned Sparks, Jack Haley, Walter Catlett, Grace Bradley, Joan Davis, William Demarest, Elyse Knox, Eddie "Rochester" Anderson, Robert Lowery, Lynn Bari; **w**, Harry Tugend, Jack Yellen (based on a story by Curtis

Dennis O'Keefe, Louis Hayward and Louise Allbritton in *Walk a Crooked Mile,* **1948.**

Keynon and the novel by Dorothea Brande); **c**, Edward Cronjager; **m**, Cyril J. Mockridge; **ed**, Robert L. Simpson; **prod d**, William S. Darling; **art d**, Mark-Lee Kirk; **set d**, Thomas Little.

Walk a Crooked Mile ★★★ 1948; U.S.; 91m; Edward Small/COL; B/W; Spy Drama; Children: Unacceptable; **DVD**; **VHS**. Tense tale depicts a communist spy ring that has infiltrated a Southern California atomic plant to try to steal secrets from scientists working on nuclear research in a sacrosanct laboratory in Lakeview. O'Keefe is an FBI agent who teams with Hayward, a Scotland Yard British intelligence officer, to investigate. Together they uncover the ring and its leader, Stewart, in this taut documentary-style film that follows the operations of both spy organizations. O'Keefe is exceptional as the FBI agent, a role similar to the federal agent he played in the classic **T-Men**, 1947, but where, in that film, he was battling a ring of murderous counterfeiters. For other films depicting Cold War spies, see Subject Index, Espionage (Cold War). **p**, Edward Small, Grant Whytock; **d**, Gordon Douglas; **cast**, Louis Hayward, Dennis O'Keefe, Louise Allbritton, Carl Esmond, Onslow Stevens, Raymond Burr, Art Baker, Lowell Gilmore, Philip Van Zandt, Gale Storm (voice), narrated by Reed Hadley; **w**, George Bruce (based on a story by Bertram Millhauser); **c**, Edward Colman, George Robinson; **m**, Paul Sawtell; **ed**, James E. Newcom; **art d**, Rudolph Steernad; **set d**, Howard Bristol.

Walk, Don't Run ★★★ 1966; U.S.; 114m; COL; Color; Comedy; Children: Acceptable; **DVD**; **VHS**; **IV**. This entertaining outing sees Cary Grant's last film, a remake of **The More the Merrier**, 1943, which follows the earlier plot about a shortage of hotel rooms. Reset from Washington, D.C., during World War II, it is now Tokyo during the 1964 Summer Olympic Games. Grant plays a British industrialist who can't find a hotel room. He convinces Eggar, a British embassy secretary, into renting him a room in her apartment. He rents part of his room to Hutton, a young member of the U.S. Olympic walking team, and then plays matchmaker. An arranged marriage takes place between Eggar and Hutton to make things look right, but they fall in love and decide to stay married while Grant returns to jolly old England. Songs: "An Affair to Remember" (Harry Warren, Harold Adamson, Leo McCarey); "Charade" (Henry Mancini); "Stay with Me," "Happy Feet" (Quincy Jones, Peggy Lee). *Author's Note*: Grant whistles the two tunes in this film that are from two of his earlier films, **An Affair to Remember**, 1957, and **Charade**, 1963, and this reminiscent whistling somehow helped him to decide to quit the screen. "Here I was," Grant told this author, "whistling tunes that recalled my previous pictures and I knew I was looking more into the past than into the future. Besides, I was not playing the romantic lead in **Walk, Don't Run**, but reprising a role played

by Charles Coburn in **The More the Merrier**, and Coburn was about sixty-six or sixty-seven when he played that role. My fans wrote to me to say that they were disappointed that I was now playing supporting parts. I knew I was much too old to play the romantic leading man, so it was time for me to hang my hat on the wall rack. A lot of actors and actresses do not know when it is time to quit, but that picture [**Walk, Don't Run**] flashed the red light for me." This was also Walter's last production as a director of theatrically released feature films. **p**, Sol C. Siegel; **d**, Charles Walters; **cast**, Cary Grant, Samantha Eggar, Jim Hutton, John Standing, Miiko Taka, Ted Hartley, Ben Astar, George Takei, Teru Shimada, Lois Kiuchi; **w**, Sol Saks (based on a story by Robert Russell, Frank Ross); **c**, Harry Stradling, Sr.; **m**, Quincy Jones; **ed**, Walter Thompson, James Wells; **prod d**, Joe Wright; **set d**, George R. Nelson, Robert Priestley.

Walk East on Beacon! ★★★ 1952; U.S.; 98m; COL; B/W; Spy Drama; Children: Unacceptable; **DVD**; **VHS**. Based on a *Reader's Digest* tale written by FBI chief J. Edgar Hoover (1895-1972), this often riveting film profiles KGB agents working in the U.S. to steal nuclear secrets. The film opens with Graves, an American-born citizen with a Polish background, who has been coerced by his Soviet spymasters to filch top U.S. secrets. Specifically assigned to secretly obtain information on a U.S. top secret titled "Falcon," Graves botches his job and is immediately replaced by top Soviet agent Stepanek. Graves is then smuggled out of the country on a freighter heading for communist-controlled Poland, the land of Graves' ancestors. (This is a duplication of the kidnapping of a German-American spy in **Confessions of a Nazi Spy**, 1939, where a failed Nazi agent is held captive on board a ship heading to Germany to face the consequences of his inept espionage.) Pettit, who is Graves' wife and knows nothing of his spying activities, becomes alarmed when he does not return and, frantic to know his whereabouts, goes to the FBI to report him missing. Boston-based FBI supervisor Murphy immediately goes into action with his Bureau subordinates, and quickly identifies the Soviet ring. He then learns that Stepanek is coercing scientist Currie to give him what he knows about a top secret project he is supervising. To convince Currie to cooperate, Stepanek tells the elderly scientist that, unless he turns over the secrets, Currie's son, who is living in Europe, will be killed. The patriotic Currie, however, contacts Murphy and the FBI fabricates a plan to have Currie supply the Soviets with the wrong data. Stepanek, however, is too shrewd to be hoodwinked and obtains the top secrets he has been seeking. Murphy and his agents are just one step behind Stepanek and they quickly round up all the Soviet spies, but Stepanek eludes the dragnet, abducting Currie in the process. He plans to leave the country with the plans in a submarine off the coast of Massachusetts, as well as smuggling the captive Currie on board that sub. Murphy, however, alerts the U.S. Coast Guard and its cutters soon trap Stepanek and where Currie is rescued and returned to his post. Werker does a fine job sustaining high suspense throughout this taut film by presenting a very gritty portrait of its fascinating characters in a terse, docudrama approach. Standout performances are seen from Murphy, Currie and the insidious Stepanek, who work with a very good script that offers sharp and believable dialog. De Rochemont had earlier produced several top spy films, including **The House on 92nd Street**, 1945 (where the FBI battles Nazi agents), and **13 Rue Madeleine**, 1947 (where the OSS battles Nazis in occupied France during WWII), both presenting stories in a similar semi-documentary style. The film was a box office success, earning more than $1.3 million in its initial release. Songs: "Sobre las olas (Over the Waves)" (1887; Juventino Rosas), "I'm Tickled Pink" (music: Jack Shaindlin). *Author's Note*: This film, like many others produced in Hollywood, was closely supervised by J. Edgar Hoover through his FBI minions working with the producer and director. Though the story upon which this film is based originally depicted the condemned Soviet spies Julius (1918-1953) and Ethel (1915-1953) Rosenberg, who successfully stole U.S. atomic bomb secrets, the film tells a different story.

This story focuses upon scientist Currie, who proves to be a heroic patriot, instead of the traitors the Rosenberg couple represented. Much of the film promotes the good image of the FBI and, in an ancillary way, furthers the legend of the always self-promoting Hoover. For extensive details on Hoover, see my book *Citizen Hoover: A Critical Study of the Life and Times of J. Edgar Hoover and His FBI.* (Nelson-Hall, 1972), which was the first biography published about the totemic Bureau chief. Hoover, from the very beginning of his career (he made his name as a young attorney when working at the Department of Justice after preparing indictments of left-wing radicals during the "Red Menace Scare" of 1919), was obsessed with the communist threat to the U.S. and free world and often pressured Hollywood into producing films that exposed that very real threat, but more as propaganda tools advancing the image of the FBI. Such films flourished during the political witch-hunts conducted in the U.S. during the late 1940s and early 1950s and led by U.S. Senator Joseph Raymond McCarthy (1908-1957), and Hoover supplied McCarthy and others information that prompted those probes that also investigated and purged Hollywood of left-leaning radicals. These films include **I Was a Communist for the F.B.I.**, 1951 (FBI; KGB); **My Son John**, 1952 (KGB; FBI); **Pickup on South Street**, 1952 (NKVD; KGB; FBI); **The Thief**, 1952 (KGB; FBI); **Walk a Crooked Mile**, 1948 (FBI; Scotland Yard's Special Branch; KGB); and **The Woman on Pier 13**, 1949 (KGB; FBI). **p**, Louis de Rochemont; **d**, Alfred Werker; **cast**, George Murphy, Finlay Currie, Virginia Gilmore, Karel Stepanek, Louisa Horton, Peter Capell, Ernest Graves, Rosemary Pettit, Bruno Wick, Jack Manning, Karl Weber, Rev. Robert Dunn, Westbrook Van Voorhis (narrator); **w**, Leo Rosten, Virginia Shaler, Emmett Murphy, Leonard Heideman (Laurence Heath), (based on the magazine article "The Crime of the Century" by J. Edgar Hoover); **c**, Joseph Brun; **m**, Louis Applebaum; **ed**, Angelo Ross; **art d**, Herbert Andrews.

A Walk in the Clouds ★★★ 1995; U.S.; 102m; FOX; Color; Drama/Romance; Children: Unacceptable (MPAA: PG-13); **DVD**; **VHS**; **IV**. Absorbing drama begins when GI Reeves returns from WWII (1939-1945) and meets on a bus Sanchez-Gijon, a young woman who is heading home from college to help her domineering, Old World Mexican father, Quinn, with the grape harvest on a field called Las Nubes, which means "the clouds." She is pregnant, but unmarried, and is afraid her strict father will kill her over her sexual transgressions. Reeves offers to pose as her husband, and they become lovers. Reeves and Quinn get into a fight that leads to a fire on the grape field, but they finally reconcile. Songs: "Mariachi Serenade," "Crush the Grapes" (Alfonso Arau, Leo Brouwer); "Beer Barrel Polka" (Wladimir A. Timm, Jaromir Vejvoda, Lew Brown); "Cancion Mixteca" (Jose Lopez Alavez). This film proved to be very successful at the box office, earning more than $50 million in its initial release against a budget of $20 million. *Author's Note*: Quinn told this author that "I played a cranky old farmer in that picture, but who can blame anyone for that since I was a cranky old man pushing eighty when we made **A Walk in the Clouds**. Old guys like me don't get a lot of juicy parts thrown their way and when you get one, you gobble it like steak." Sensuality and war violence prohibit viewing by children. **p**, David Zucker, Jerry Zucker, Gil Netter, Bill Johnson; **d**, Alfonso Arau; **cast**, Keanu Reeves, Aitana Sanchez-Gijon, Anthony Quinn, Giancarlo Giannini, Angelica Aragon, Evangelina Elizondo, Freddy Rodriguez, Debra Messing, Febronio Covarrubias, Roberto Huerta; **w**, Robert Mark Kamen, Mark Miller, Harvey Weitzman (based on the story and screenplay "Quattro Passi fra le nuvole" by Piero Tellini, Cesare Zavattini, Vittorio de Benedetti); **c**, Emmanuel Lubezki; **m**, Maurice Jarre; **ed**, Don Zimmerman, Christine Sheaks, Melissa M. Thomas; **prod d**, David Gropman; **art d**, Daniel Maltese; **set d**, Denise Pizzini; **spec eff**, Robert Stromberg, John McLeod, Bruno Van Zeebroeck.

Walk in the Shadow ★★★ 1966; U.K.; 109m; Allied Film Makers; Continental Distributing; B/W; Drama; Children: Unacceptable. Sen-

George Murphy and Karl Weber in *Walk East on Beacon!*, 1952.

sitive tale begins when Taylor, the young daughter of Craig and Munro, is seriously injured in a boating accident and needs an urgent blood transfusion in order to live. Craig is a member of a strict religious sect that does not allow doctors to operate on its members. Munro, who opposes this, tells a doctor, McGoohan, to go ahead with the transfusion. He does this, but, unfortunately, it is too late and the child dies. At an inquest, Craig is cleared of all blame, but McGoohan tries to get police to press manslaughter charges against Craig. At a court hearing, Rogers, a Jewish lawyer, gets Craig acquitted, but afterward Craig attempts suicide. This causes McGoohan to help him face the fact that he asked God to perform a miracle and he should have let his daughter get medical help. Munro, who has left Craig after Taylor's death, realizes he needs her love and returns to him. Well-directed and superbly acted, this strong drama presents a subject seldom shown in films. **p**, Michael Relph, Basil Dearden; **d**, Dearden; **cast**, Michael Craig, Patrick McGoohan, Janet Munro, Paul Rogers, Malcolm Keen, Megs Jenkins, Michael Bryant, Leslie Sands, Norman Wooland, Lynn Taylor; **w**, Janet Green, James McCormick (based on a play by Green); **c**, Otto Heller; **m**, William Alwyn; **ed**, John D. Guthridge; **art d**, Alex Vetchinsky; **set d**, Arthur Taksen.

A Walk in the Sun ★★★★★ 1945; U.S.; 117m; FOX; B/W; War Drama; Children: Unacceptable; **DVD**; **VHS**; **IV**. Pantheon director Milestone presents one of the greatest war films dealing with WWII (1939-1945) in this riveting profile of a U.S. platoon of GIs who are part of the invasion of Italy in 1943 at Salerno (the film was later released under the title **Salerno Beachhead**). The film opens before dawn on the day of that invasion as the platoon of men ride inside of a landing craft approaching the Italian coast; Meredith narrates (as he periodically does throughout the film), introducing in voiceover some of the GIs. He states that this story "happened long ago, way back in 1943, when the lead platoon of the Texas division hit the beach at Salerno, sunny Italy." He describes some of the men riding in a barge that perilously closes upon that beach in the murky dawn, the camera closing upon their solemn faces. He talks about Andrews, a sergeant, who "never had much urge to travel. Providence, Rhode Island may not be much as cities go, but it was all he wanted...a one-town man." Meredith then mentions Conte, an "Italian-American. Likes opera and would like a wife and kids, plenty of kids." The camera shows the beefy Tyne and Meredith says that he is a "lathe operator and amateur boxing champion" from New York City. He cites Ireland, a "minister's son...Canton, Ohio. Used to take long walks alone and just think." The camera focuses upon Bridges, whom Meredith describes as a "farmer...Knows his soil, good farmer." We next see Holloway, who is described by Meredith as a "first aid man...slow, Southern, dependable." The camera

Lloyd Bridges and Dana Andrews in *A Walk in the Sun*, 1945.

eye then shows the viewer Lloyd, "platoon scout and prophet. Talks a lot, but he's all right." The camera finally stops at the jittery Rudley, who is described by Meredith as having "a lot on his mind…a lot on his mind." Meredith then presents a plaintive song (sung throughout the film by William Gillespie) describing these GIs from many parts of the United States but now all thrown together in war and how "they came across the sea to sunny Italy, and took a little walk in the sun." As the landing barge approaches the beach, Lowell, the young lieutenant in charge of the platoon, dangerously peers through binoculars as he leans above the side of the barge where enemy shells explode nearby. One of the enemy shells exploding close to the barge so seriously wounds Lowell that most of his face is blown away. He lies dying in the barge that continues toward the beach. Willis, the ranking sergeant, takes command of the platoon, telling Rudley, another sergeant, that he is to take the platoon onto the beach and inland where he and the platoon are to wait for him as he finds the captain in charge of the company and receives orders. Rudley, a veteran of the North African Campaign, is not a well man, battle weary and uncertain about everything, which is evident to Andrews, Bridges and Cardwell, three other sergeants, as well as Ireland, an observant and introspective private studying the nervous Rudley. While Holloway, the corpsman, a slow Southerner, stays with the dying Lowell, the platoon races onto the beach after the barge lands and they move over a hill and down into a ditch where they wait for Willis to rejoin them. As they wait, Milestone moves his camera from one GI to another as they pensively think of home and their loved ones, especially wives and girlfriends, and their thoughts are heard in voiceover. As the sun rises and enemy planes appear overhead, the alert Andrews suggests to Rudley that he take the men into some nearby woods to protect them against possible air attacks. Rudley, embarrassed that he has not had this thought, agrees and leads the platoon toward the woods while Andrews remains behind in the ditch, waiting for Holloway and Willis to return. While waiting, Andrews sees Holloway almost leisurely strolling over the sand dune as he approaches the ditch. Andrews, knowing enemy planes are overhead, is disturbed by Holloway's nonchalant attitude, telling him: "The way you come walking over that ridge…like you were back in Missouri looking for daisies!" Holloway tells Andrews that the lieutenant has died and that Willis, too, has been killed on the beach, but he has retrieved Willis' dispatch bag and gives this to Andrews. Holloway then tells Andrews that the action on the beach is fierce with battle. He asks Andrews to loan him the binoculars he wears so that he can climb to the top of the sand dune and report back to him what he sees on that beach. Andrews agrees and Holloway climbs to the top of the sand dune, lying down and watching the beach with the binoculars, marveling at the action as would a spectator at a sports event. Bombing at the beach drowns out Holloway's words as he shouts back

to Andrews, who waits in the ditch, and when an enemy plane descends, Holloway stands up and runs toward the ditch, but the diving plane fires at him, killing him. Andrews marks his fallen body with a rifle driven into the sand next to his body and then leaves the ditch to rejoin the platoon. Meanwhile, Rudley leads his men into a wooded area on the run as German planes swoop down from the skies, strafing them and spraying the area with bullets that slice through the trees and leaves, wounding Cardwell and Dante and killing another GI. Rudley finds Lloyd standing next to the dead soldier, stunned by his death and telling Rudley that his friend had been talking to him and had been instantly killed "right in the middle of a word." When Andrews rejoins the platoon in the woods, he tells Rudley about the deaths of Lowell, Willis and Holloway and, since Rudley is now the ranking sergeant, he is in command of the platoon. Rudley, along with Andrews and Bridges, then meet with Cardwell, a wounded sergeant, looking over the map of the area, and Cardwell tells them that the platoon's objective, a farmhouse some six miles away, commands a bridge that must be blown up. "Gerry [the Germans] will bring stuff over that bridge," Cardwell tells them. Rudley begins asking Cardwell questions about petty problems and the wounded Cardwell, holding a tourniquet on his wounded leg, angrily replies: "Look, man, you're in command. Don't ask so many dopey questions. Leave me alone." Rudley finally gets a grip on himself and orders his men to follow a road in three squads, sending out Lloyd and others as point men to scout ahead. Andrews, who commands the last squad, goes to Cardwell, who plans to remain in the woods with Dante until support units arrive. Cardwell warns Andrews to "keep your head. You're a smart apple…keep your head." He adds: "Keep your eye on Porter [Rudley]. I think he's gonna crack." Andrews asks him why he thinks that and Cardwell simply replies: "He's a good man, but I think he's gonna crack…He's got a lot on his mind." Andrews leaves some cigarettes with Cardwell and moves off with the platoon. As the GIs move along the road, the camera cuts back and forth among them to show their constant chatter that disguises their apprehensions and fears. Hall, a GI, walks with another GI, talking about Russ Colombo, a crooner of the 1930s, and how his sister "stayed in her room all the time the day he died." An enemy plane suddenly appears overhead and the GIs scatter from the road, running to a nearby gully, but several soldiers are strafed, one killed, another wounded by the diving plane. As the GIs look skyward, they see an Allied plane (P-38) attacking the German fighter, and Tyne shouts: "Shoot him! Shoot him!" After the enemy plane is driven off, the platoon goes back to the road with Lloyd leading the way. Lloyd, like Rudley, is a troubled man, angered over the loss of his friend, who was shot next to him in the woods and he kicks the dirt in front of him as he mumbles to himself, predicting that the war will go on and on, and that the GIs will eventually be fighting in Tibet. He suddenly sees two Italian soldiers in the distance, and several GIs capture them. Benedict, who speaks Italian, explains to Rudley and Andrews that the two unarmed Italian soldiers are deserters. The deserters tell them that there are German forces in the area, but they do not know exactly where, especially at the farmhouse, which they have been assigned to capture. The GIs give the Italian deserters some K-rations and then move on. Conte gives the K-rations to Benedict to hand to one of the Italian soldiers, saying: "When they eat that, they'll wish that Italy never went out of the war." (The pathetic scene of the two Italians left behind all but duplicates a sequence in **Sahara**, 1943, where Italian captive J. Carroll Naish is left to die in the desert after being given K-rations by Allied soldiers departing in an American tank operated by Humphrey Bogart.) Ireland looks back to see the Italian deserters standing without hope, and we hear his thoughts as he mentally composes another letter to his girlfriend: "Dear Frances: Just left a couple of Italian soldiers standing in the road. No, cross that out: Just left a couple of ex-Italian soldiers standing in the road. Poor suckers, they still don't know what hit them. And, in a way, it's their own fault. They let themselves be sold a bill of goods that they were going to boss the world. And now the guys who sold them are gone and they're left holding the bag. Poor suckers, right now they don't even own their own country." As the men move along the road, Rudley tells Andrews that he has a headache and is having difficulty making decisions. He asks him, if necessary, can he take command of the platoon. Turner, a scout riding a motorcycle, appears and offers to scout ahead to see if any Germans block the platoon's path. After Turner leaves, Rudley begins to worry that they will never see him again and Andrews says to Rudley: "I don't know what's eating you, but you need to snap out of it. What's eating you?" Rudley can only reply: "I don't know." The GIs then enter a woods, and Rudley orders them to take a break while he slips to the ground, holding his head. Andrews instinctively takes command, sending a squad of men, including all bazooka men along the road, telling them to stay about a mile ahead of the platoon. Rudley, who should have thought of giving that order, thanks Andrews, but finds that he is unable to continue as the platoon takes a rest in the woods. Bridges, a farmer in civilian life, examines a handful of Italian dirt, saying that "the soil's no good around here. It's no good at all. It's old and tired and worn out. Yes, the soil's no good, no good at all." The introspective Ireland adds: "Maybe too many soldiers have been walking on it. They've been walking on it for a long time. That's what always happens to a country when soldiers walk on it." Rudley then tells Bridges that he can't go on any longer as platoon leader and that Andrews will take command. Andrews tells Rudley that he can go on, but Rudley is by this time a bundle of nerves, insisting that he lie down and he buries his head in the dirt, weeping. Lloyd spots a German armored car coming along the road and shouts the alarm, and all of the GIs take cover in a ditch, unseen by the enemy, the armored car then disappearing along the road. The advance unit returns to report that they allowed the armored car to escape so that they could attack two tanks and another armored car, which they destroyed with their bazookas, but they are now out of ammunition and know that the second armored car is sure to return. Rudley is now a cringing, sobbing man, no longer able to command, and Andrews assumes authority over the platoon, positioning its men along the ditch; when the armored car returns, they are to hurl grenades along its path, hoping to destroy its tires or underbelly and disable it. Meanwhile, the pensive Ireland remains with the sobbing Rudley (musing in voiceover as if addressing Rudley): "You're crying because you're wounded. You don't have to be bleeding to be wounded. You've just had one battle too many. Yeah. You're out of it now. No more guesswork and waiting and wondering for you. You've built yourself a foxhole…up here [in your mind]. Ain't nothing in the world can make you come out of it. Go ahead…keep crying. We understand." Conte, who mans the platoon's machine gun, sets up the weapon to be aimed on the armored car when it appears, telling Tyne, his companion who is to feed the machine gun's ammunition, that when he went to Coney Island as a kid and tried to shoot down miniature airplanes at a shooting gallery that "I never could hit those airplanes. I used to miss those airplanes all the time." Tyne asks him: "How did you get to be a machine gunner?" "I bribed a guy," Conte replies. "I want a transfer," Tyne retorts. The German armored car then reappears, and, as it moves along the road, one GI after another hurls a grenade, their explosions jarring and tossing the vehicle as it races along. At the same time, Conte fires the machine gun, its tracers following the course of the armored car, bullets pinging and ricocheting from its steel plates. (Here director Milestone employs his traditional tracking shot to keep pace with the moving armored car while showing the GIs in the ditch parallel to the road attacking it, another one of his well-choreographed and very exciting battle scenes.) When one of the car's tires explodes, the car careens off the road and bullets are fired through a slit in its turret to kill the last live occupant, his hand slipping from the opening to show a ring with a large ruby on a finger. Andrews then orders the platoon to again take to the road, leaving a GI behind to look after Rudley. As Conte, Tyne and Brodie move along the road, Tyne tells Conte that he is "a traveling salesman selling democracy to the natives…you're a decadent democrat." Conte nods and says: "That's what I am all right." The platoon soon arrives at a long stone wall that runs before an open

Chris Drake and Richard Conte in *A Walk in the Sun*, 1945.

field and, in the distance is the platoon's military objective, a two-story farmhouse where no one can be seen, but Andrews and Bridges conclude is occupied by German soldiers. Andrews sends a patrol over the wall, which is led by Bridges, its members crawling through the cornfield toward the farmhouse. Its occupants suddenly appear at the building's windows with machine guns, firing at the GIs in the field. The members of the patrol then race back toward the stone wall, but two are killed in the process. Now desperate, Andrews and Bridges are baffled as to how to proceed until Ireland suggests that a squad of men circle around the farmhouse, slip into the river behind the farmhouse and blow up the bridge there with grenades while the main force waits in the field to attack the farmhouse. Andrews and Bridges accept the plan (showing that the average GI could design effective tactics), and Bridges leads a squad of men, including Ireland, toward the river. Conte is positioned behind the stone wall with the machine gun and is to open fire on the farmhouse at a certain time. When Conte begins firing, Andrews tells all, Bridges and his men will attack the bridge with grenades and Andrews will lead the rest of the platoon in an all-out attack against the farmhouse. While Bridges and Ireland take their squad to the river, Andrews and the rest of the platoon leap over the stone wall and begin slowly crawling toward the farmhouse. Andrews, worried about the pressures of command, thinks about the GIs who have already given their lives since the time they left the beach and walked inland for six miles to this farmhouse and we hear his thoughts in voiceover: "We've come a long way…long six miles…six miles closer to San Francisco, Hoskins…six miles closer to Joplin, Mack…six miles closer to St. Paul, Tinker. It's a long way. It's the shortest way home…the only way home for all the decent guys in the world." Andrews looks up to see the sky spinning, the field and the farmhouse spinning, but everything he sees suddenly halts into freeze frames when Conte opens fire on the farmhouse, raking its walls and windows with bullets. At the same time, Bridges and his squad attack the bridge, hurling grenades to blow it up. Andrews then stands up and leads his men in a headlong charge against the farmhouse where German defenders open up with machine guns. Several GIs are killed in the charge, including Lloyd, but most break into the building, killing its German defenders as they leap through windows and doors. (Again Milestone uses the same kind of tracking and dolly shots he employed in his classic WWI film, **All Quiet on the Western Front**, 1930, showing the charging line of GIs as they assault the building while the dramatic strains of "The Battle Hymn of the Republic" can be heard.) The farmhouse is taken, and the victorious GIs, including Andrews and others, emerge from it to survive for another battle. Ireland is shown approaching the farmhouse from the river and across a field, composing another letter to his sweetheart in his mind (heard in voiceover): "Dear Frances; We just blew up a bridge and took

Diane Lane and Anna Paquin in *A Walk on the Moon,* **1999.**

a farmhouse. It was so easy...so terribly easy." Milestone directs this compelling war saga from the POV of its soldiers, effectively merging their introspective scenes with startling live-action sequences that abruptly bring them to their grim senses as all risk their lives on a single day of this devastating war. Every member of the cast, from Andrews to Rudley, from Lloyd to Bridges, from Ireland to Holloway, present unforgettable portraits of widely divergent characters, who are empathetic, vulnerable and heroic beyond their palavering and wisecracking bravado. These portraits, depicted in close-ups and in group shots by the visually incisive Milestone, evoke a deep sense of loneliness for these young men, who seem to age frame by frame, their foreboding and apprehensions evidenced in every scene. Throughout there exists a stark realization of the futility of war and the ever present threat of death. None of the characters are spectacular. They are all common men from all walks of life, but uncommon in their universal dedication to defeat an evil enemy, uncommon in their desire to make free a small piece of earth for mankind, as they liberate six miles of road, a bridge, and a farmhouse in Italy. This true-to-life film presents a magnificently stated prosaic story of how that war was won by the free world, not by sweeping armies, but by small groups of men representing "all the decent guys in the world," who inched forward at the cost of their lives to gain a few miles. Songs: "The Ballads" and "It Was Just a Little Walk in the Sun" (music: Earl Robinson; lyrics: Millard Lampell), "Caissons Keep Rolling Along" (1908; Edmund L. Gruber, William Bryden, Robert Danford), "The Bonnie Blue Flag [We Are a Band of Brothers]" (1861; Harry McCarthy), "Battle Hymn of the Republic" (music [1856]: William Steffe; lyrics [1862]: Julia Ward Howe). *Author's Note*: Milestone told this author that "**A Walk in the Sun** was a pet project for Burgess Meredith, who had played the role of war correspondent Ernie Pyle [1900-1945] in **The Story of G.I. Joe** [1945]. He took the novel to his friend and producer Samuel Bronstein, who launched its production, but Bronstein got into financial trouble and another company took it over and called me in to direct. Bronstein got hopping mad and sued, but he settled out of court for a piece of the profits and we then went ahead with the picture, which we shot at the Fox ranch and some other places. Darryl Zanuck, who ran Fox and was a writer before anything else, loved the script written by Rossen because it was very down-to-earth and where we dumped all of the supermen antics shown in other war pictures during that time and concentrated on the average GIs. It proved to be one of my most satisfying productions." Andrews told this author that "I had played one of Doolittle's pilots in **The Purple Heart** [1944] a year before we made **A Walk in the Sun,** so I had some credibility as an American fighting man on the screen. I played a sergeant in that picture and had some of the best natural dialog for my character I could wish for, just another dogface taking command after his superior

goes to pieces. He doubts his ability to make everything go right, but has enough guts to go ahead anyway. I think that's how the war was really fought, with men like that." Ireland was circumspect about his character in this film when talking with this author, telling me: "My character lives more in his head than in the real world. They allowed me to voice my thoughts in that picture, a very unusual approach for those days, but I was being directed by a brilliant director, Lewis Milestone, who always took chances with new ideas. I really liked my character and that picture is one of my favorites to this day." This was the film debut for Ireland and Horton. Other films depicting the military campaign in Sicily and Italy include **Abandoned**, 1955; **And Agnes Chose to Die**, 1976; **Anni difficili**, 1950; **Anzio**, 1968; **The Art of Getting Along**, 1954; **The Assissi Underground**, 1985; **Baaria**, 2010; **Baciami piccina**, 2006; **Before Him All Rome Trembled**, 1947; **A Bell for Adano**, 1945; **The Big Red One**, 1980; **Blood of the Losers**, 2008; **Cloak and Dagger**, 1946; **Cobari**, 1970; **A Day for Lionhearts**, 1961; **Days of Glory**, 2006; **The Days of Rage**, 2001; **The Devil's Brigade**, 1968; **The English Patient**, 1996; **Escape by Night**, 1982; **Everybody Go Home!**, 1962; **The Fallen**, 2004; **The Fascist**, 1965; **Fighter Attack**, 1953; **Force of Arms**, 1951; **The Four Days of Naples**, 1963; **From the Clouds to the Resistance**, 1979; **Generale Della Rovere**, 1961; **Hidden Children**, 2004 (made-for-TV); **Honey Sweet Love**, 1996; **Hotel Meina**, 2007; **Il cielo cade**, 2000; **Il gobbo**, 1963; **It Happened in '43**, 1960; **La grande quercia**, 1997; **Last Days of Mussolini**, 1974; **Life Is Beautiful**, 1999; **Little Teachers**, 1998; **The Man in the Gray Flannel Suit**, 1956; **The Man Who Will Come**, 2010; **Men or Not Men**, 1981; **Miracle at St. Anna**, 2008; **Monte Cassino**, 1948; **Mussolini: The Untold Story**, 1985 (TV series); **The Night of the Shooting Stars**, 1982; **1900**, 1977; **Open City**, 1946; **Paisan**, 1948; **Passione**, 2011; **Patton**, 1970; **The Pigeon That Took Rome**, 1962; **Portrait: A Man Whose Name Was John**, 1973 (made-for-TV); **Private Angelo**, 1949; **Rosolino Paterno, soldato...**, 1970; **Salvo D'Acquisto**, 1974; **The Secret of Santa Vittoria**, 1969; **The Secret War of Harry Frigg**, 1968; **Seven Beauties**, 1976; **The Story of G.I. Joe**, 1945; **Tea with Mussolini**, 1999; **To Hell and Back**, 1955; **Two Anonymous Letters**, 1947; **The Two Marshals**, 1961; **Two Women**, 1960; **Up Front**, 1951; **Von Ryan's Express**, 1965; and **The White Ship**, 1941. **p&d**, Lewis Milestone; **cast**, Dana Andrews, Richard Conte, John Ireland, George Tyne, Lloyd Bridges, Sterling Holloway, Norman Lloyd, Herbert Rudley, Steve Brodie, Richard Benedict, Huntz Hall, James Cardwell, John Kellogg, Robert Horton, George Offerman Jr., Danny Desmond, Victor Cutler, Anthony Dante, Matt Willis, George Turner, Robert Lowell, Burgess Meredith (narrator); **w**, Robert Rossen (based on a story by Harry Brown); **c**, Russell Harlan; **m**, Fredric Efrem Rich; **ed**, Duncan Mansfield; **art d**, Max Bertisch.

A Walk on the Moon ★★★ 1999; U.S./Australia; 107m; Miramax; Drama/Romance; Children: Unacceptable (MPAA: R); **DVD**; **IV**. This moving and well-made romantic drama is set during the summer of the 1969 Woodstock Festival in Bethel, N.Y., four days of sex, drugs, and rock 'n' roll that defined the 1960s hippie counterculture. Lane, who married early, is unhappy with her television repairman husband Schreiber, and they live in a bungalow in a Catskills resort near the festival. While he is out of town, Lane spends the weekend with their teenage daughter, Paquin, younger son, Boriello, and Schreiber's mother-in-law Feldshuh. Along comes Mortensen, "The Blouse Man," a long-haired young man, who drives his truck from resort to resort selling blouses and accessories at discount prices. He thinks Lane is looking for more than a new blouse, so he offers her a free tie-dyed T-shirt and gives her his phone number. She calls Mortensen and it leads to them watching a television program of astronauts walking on the moon, an event that arouses her sexual desires and yearning for freedom from what she considers to be a dull life. Lane and Mortensen go nude bathing together and then she goes to the Woodstock Festival while he follows, but gets stuck in a concert-goers traffic jam. Who does Lane see at the concert but Paquin, who is there with her first-ever boyfriend.

Feldshuh, meanwhile, has seen Lane go off and figures she is going to the festival and will be with Mortensen, so she phones her son to warn him that his marriage is in deep trouble. He drives home from the city, goes after his wife, and everyone may not dance, but, in the end, they face the marital music. Sexuality, language, and drug use prohibit viewing by children. Not related to the 1987 film with the same name. Songs: "More (Ti guardero nel cuore)" (1962: Riz Ortolani, Norman Newel, Nino Oliviero, Marcello Ciorciolini), "The Name Game" (1964: Lincoln Chase, Shirley Elliston), "King Rat" (1965: John Barry), "Danke Schoen" (1962: Kurt Schwabach, Milton Gabler, Bert Kaempfert), "Wishin' and Hopin'" (1963: Burt Bacharach, Ha; David), "Ripple" and "Uncle John's Band" (1970: Jerry Garcia, Robert Hunter), "For Your Love" (1958: Earl Townsend), "Sunlight" (1969: Jesse Colin Young), "Summertime" (from "Porgy and Bess," 1935: music: George Gershwin; lyrics: Ira Gershwin, DuBose Heyward, Dorothy Heyward), "Sally Go Round the Roses" (1963: Abner Spector), "Today" (1967: Marty Balin, Paul Kantner), "Embryonic Journey" (1967: Jorma Kaukonen), "Kiss of Fire" (1952: Lester Allen, Robert Hill, Angel Gregorio Villoldo), "Cactus Tree" (1968: Joni Mitchell), "Who Knows Where the Time Goes" (1966: Sandy Denny), "Town Without Pity" (1961: music: Dimitri Tiomkin; lyrics: New Washington), "Crimson & Clover" (1968: Tommy Jones, Peter Lucia), "Freedom" (1969: Richie Havens), "The Fish Cheer" (1969: Joe McDonald), "I-Feel-Like-I'm-Fixin'-to-Die Rage" (1968: Joe McDonald), "Subterranean Homesick Blues" (1965: Bob Dylan), "White Bird" (1969: David LaFlamme, Linda LaFlamme), "Israelites" (1968: Desmond Dekker), "When You're Smiling (The Whole World Smiles with You" (1928: Mark Fisher, Joe Goodwin, Larry Shay), "Purple Haze" (1967: Jimi Hendrix), "Follow" (1967: Jerry Merrick), "Helplessly Hoping" (1969: Stephen Stills), "Crystal Blue Persuasion" (1969: Tommy James. Mike Vale, Ed Gray). **p**, Jay Cohen, Tony Goldwyn, Lee Gottsegen, Dustin Hoffman, Murray Schisgal; **d**, Goldwyn; **cast**, Diane Lane, Viggo Mortensen, Liev Schreiber, Anna Paquin, Bobby Boriello, Tovah Feldshuh, Julie Kavner, Stewart Bick, Jess Platt, Mahee Paiement; **w**, Pamela Gray; **c**, Anthony B. Richmond; **m**, Mason Daring; **ed**, Dana Congdon; **prod d**, Dan Leigh; **art d**, Gilles Aird; **spec eff**, Louis Craig, Antonio Vidosa, Lisa Bechard, Lisa Wyse, Colin Cunningham.

Walk on the Wild Side ★★★ 1962; U.S.; 114m; Famous Artists Productions/COL; B/W; Drama/Romance; Children: Unacceptable; **DVD**; **VHS**. Controversial at its time of release, this tawdry but compelling tale is set in 1931 during the Great Depression, where Harvey, a young man searching for his lost love, Capucine, rides a freight train from Texas to New Orleans, Louisiana, to find her. He meets Fonda along the way, a girl of loose virtues, who, once they arrive in the Big Easy, steals at a restaurant owned by Baxter. Harvey cannot abide such conduct and compensates Baxter for the theft, his honorable conduct so impressing Baxter that she gives him a job. He then learns that the beautiful Capucine is the star attraction at the Doll's House, an upscale brothel in the French Quarter operated by Stanwyck. A shrewd and manipulative madam, Stanwyck, it is soon seen, is very possessive of Capucine, not only as her prized prostitute, but because Stanwyck is (implied only) in love with her celebrated boarder (and here the specter of lesbianism is more than subtly suggested). Stanwyck's love for her husband, Swenson, has waned after he lost his legs in an accident and where she has transferred her now offbeat sexual preference to Capucine, who tolerates if not enjoys this relationship. Harvey tries to convince Capucine to give up her lifestyle with Stanwyck, but she is happy with her comfortable surroundings, where Stanwcyk encourages her to continue her hobby in sculpting. (Her sculptures represent the same kind of unimaginative and barren abstracts created by the sculpturing Hildegard Neff [Knef], a wealthy lesbian living on the Riviera and supporting writer Gregory Peck in **The Snows of Kilimanjaro**, 1952.) Stanwyck, meanwhile, has Fonda released on bail to her custody after Fonda has been jailed for vagrancy, and Fonda becomes one of Stan-

Jane Fonda and Laurence Harvey in *Walk on the Wild Side*, 1962.

wyck's employees and joins her pampered prostitutes. Harvey by this time resolves to rescue Capucine from her unsavory lifestyle, but she sends him away. He returns, insisting that she go back with him to Texas where they can make a life together. Seeing that Capucine is beginning to seriously think about resuming her relationship with Harvey, Stanwyck threatens Harvey with arrest, saying that she will have him sent to prison for illegally transporting the underage Fonda from Texas to Louisiana, for immoral purposes and statutory rape, unless he leaves Capucine alone and returns to Texas. When Harvey refuses, Stanwyck has her sadistic bouncer, Rust, and her vicious-minded husband, Swenson, beat Harvey senseless. Fonda, who has witnessed the savage assault, helps Harvey return to Baxter's restaurant where Baxter nurses Harvey back to health. Capucine, learning of the beating, goes to see Harvey, and, when Stanwyck learns of her absence, she follows her to the restaurant, accompanied by her goons. When Stanwyck and her thugs attempt to force Capucine back to the brothel, a fight ensures and Capucine is fatally struck by a stray bullet, dying in Harvey's arms. At the end, a newspaper report describes how Fonda's testimony has sent Stanwyck and her goons to prison. Everyone in this film is somehow crippled, Swenson physically by the absence of his legs, Stanwyck and Capucine by their unnatural sexual relationship, Fonda by her various perversions, and Harvey, an emotional invalid in not being able to recoup his love for a lost woman. Harvey, Stanwyck and Baxter render top-notch performances under Dmytryk's firm direction, and the sets of New Orleans' old French Quarter are impressively offered. The film received an Oscar nomination for Best Song ("Walk on the Wild Side"; Bernstein and David). It did fairly well at the box office, earning back its $2 million budget. Songs: "Walk on the Wild Side" and "Somewhere in the Used to Be" (music: Elmer Bernstein; lyrics: Mack David). *Author's Note*: This production was awash with dissension among the cast, the director and the producer from the beginning. Dmytryk told this author that "**Walk on the Wild Side** was a big headache for me. I inherited a group of actors who did not like each other. Some of them interfered with the script, which was always being rewritten at their insistence, and my work throughout the production was a miserable experience." The director's woes began when he was confronted by his producer, Feldman, who was then living with Capucine, and insisted that she wear the latest gowns designed by Pierre Cardin. "I told him [Feldman] that those dresses were too modern for the setting of the picture [of 1931]," Dmytryk told this author, "but, no, he wanted her in those modern designer gowns come what may, even though he knew that they did not belong." Feldman, at Capucine's urgings, kept bringing in new writers to rewrite the script, particularly Capucine's lines. Clifford Odets was hired, telling Feldman that "I can make any scene interesting, even though it may have nothing to do with the story." His scenes were never

Joseph Cotten and Alida Valli in *Walk Softly, Stranger,* **1950.**

used in the film. Pantheon screen writer Ben Hecht was also briefly hired. "I wrote several new scenes for the picture," Hecht told this author, "but Charles [Feldman] called me up one day and said that none of my scenes were 'sexy enough.' I told him to hire Henry Miller and hung up." Fonda reportedly brought another problem to the production when she first appeared with her "secretary," a Greek ex-dancer, who advised her as to how she should act in her scenes. He and Fonda quickly bonded with Capucine and Feldman and would gather at Feldman's residence each evening to rehash the day's shooting. Dmytryk called them all "conspirators." Meanwhile, Stanwyk was her usual forceful, no-nonsense self when showing up for the first day's shooting. She spied Harvey lounging in a chair wearing a gold brocaded bathrobe and sipping champagne. "He looked like some little prince expecting to be waited upon by one and all," Stanwyck told this author. "I told him: 'Okay, Larry, get off your butt and let's go to work. I don't have any time for prima donnas. His mouth dropped open and that turned into a grin and he let out a laugh. We became friends on the spot and then went to work together, which is more than I can say for others in that cast." Harvey had a great dislike for the haughty Capucine. She felt the same way toward him, and, when it came to a kissing scene between them, she explained to Dmytryk that she appeared unenthusiastic because Harvey "is not enough of a man for me." Harvey gave her back a piece of his own mind, shouting: "If you were more of a woman, I would be more of a man. Kissing you is like kissing the side of a beer bottle!" He later told her that she should have remained a model (which is what she was when producer Feldman discovered her) and that she could not act at all, a remark that caused Capucine to sulk throughout the production. Baxter, too, had problems with her scenes in the film as she was then six months pregnant and could not move about with alacrity. Dmytryk told this author that, at the end of the picture, "Capucine is shot and is dying. She ignored my advice and followed the directions of her own advisers, drawing out that death scene to the point of being ludicrous. Her death scene was something out of a ballet put on by high school kids and I told her so. She began to argue with me until Larry [Harvey] blew up and told her to stop being a prima donna and follow my directions. She finally complied but, oh, what a pain in the neck she was." Capucine, who was never an emotionally stable woman, had been briefly married in 1949, and never again married. She had several affairs after Feldman, including reported relationships with John Wayne (when appearing with Wayne and again playing a prostitute in **North to Alaska**, 1960), and with actor William Holden (while appearing with Holden in **The Lion**, 1962, and later in **The 7th Dawn**, 1964). Suffering from a prolonged ailment and consistent depression, Capucine committed suicide by leaping from the eighth floor window of her apartment in Lausanne, Switzerland, where she had lived for twenty-eight years,

on March 17, 1990. She was sixty-two years old. **p**, Charles K. Feldman; **d**, Edward Dmytryk; **cast**, Laurence Harvey, Capucine, Jane Fonda, Anne Baxter, Barbara Stanwyck, Joanna Moore, Richard Rust, Karl Swenson, Donald Barry, Juanita Moore, John Anderson; **w**, John Fante, Edmund Morris, (uncredited, Raphael Hayes, Ben Hecht), (based on the novel *A Walk on the Wild Side* by Nelson Algren); **c**, Joe MacDonald; **m**, Elmer Bernstein; **ed**, Harry Gerstad; **prod d**, Richard Sylbert; **set d**, William Kiernan.

Walk Softly, Stranger ★★★ 1950; U.S.; 81m; Vanguard-RKO/RKO; B/W; Crime Drama; Children: Unacceptable; **DVD**; **VHS**; **IV**. Cotten renders an impressive performance as a charming gambler and con man, who attempts to escape his notorious past by hiding out in the small town of Ashton, Ohio, under a new name. His sweet old landlady, Byington, thinks he's wonderful, and he gets a job in a shoe factory owned by Puglia, where he flirts with his boss's daughter, Valli. She is embittered ever since she has been paralyzed and confined to a wheelchair following a skiing accident. Cotten so impresses Valli with his easygoing ways that she talks her doting father, Puglia, into giving Cotten a higher position in the company's sales division, a promotion that Cotten declines. He finds, however, that he is truly falling in love with the beautiful young woman, which causes Cotten to rethink his shady career, and he entertains the idea of going straight after possibly marrying Valli, her hard shell attitude having melted under Cotten's affectionate attentions. His noble plans go awry with the arrival of his former crony, Stewart, who is now on the run from Petrie, a gambler he and Cotten robbed of $200,000. Petrie, who knows he cannot report the theft, intends to personally recoup the stolen cash and mete out his own justice to Stewart and Cotten. He arrives with his goons and kills Stewart and then abducts Cotten, telling him that, unless Cotten helps him bilk Valli out of her fortune, he will expose him. Cotten refuses and, while riding in Petrie's car, struggles with the driver and is wounded. The car goes out of control and all are killed, except for Cotten, who is found in a prison hospital by Valli. They both know that Cotten must be sent to prison for his past offenses, but Valli promises to be waiting for him when he is released. The somewhat clichéd story is vastly improved by Cotten's performance and that of the fetching Valli, although this better-than-average film noir entry flopped at the box office, losing more than $775,000. *Author's Note*: Cotten told this author that "**Walk Softly, Stranger** deserved a better fate at the box office than what it got. That picture suffered by comparison to another picture that was released the same year, **The Third Man** [1950], a picture I appeared in with Alida [Valli] and Orson Welles. That picture stole all the impact from **Walk Softly, Stranger**, which was actually made a year earlier, but withheld by RKO for a year, so that it could share the success of the Welles picture. The problem was that we were competing with a masterpiece." **p**, Robert Sparks; **d**, Robert Stevenson; **cast**, Joseph Cotten, Alida Valli, Spring Byington, Paul Stewart, Jack Paar, Jeff Donnell, John McIntire, Frank Puglia, Esther Dale, Marlo Dwyer; **w**, Frank Fenton (based on a story by Manny Seff, Paul Yawitz); **c**, Harry J. Wild; **m**, Frederick Hollander; **ed**, Frederic Knudtson; **art d**, Albert S. D'Agostino, Alfred Herman; **set d**, Harley Miller, Darrell Silvera; **spec eff**, Russell A. Cully.

Walk the Line ★★★ 2005; U.S./Germany; 136m; FOX; Color; Biographical Drama; Children: Unacceptable (MPAA: PG-13); **BD**; **DVD**; **IV**. Absorbing biopic profiles the life and career of country music star Johnny Cash (1932-2003), who is ably played by Phoenix. The son of a cotton share cropper in Arkansas, he becomes one of the top stars of country, rock, and gospel songs, many of which he writes, including "Folsom Prison Blues," which he wrote after serving seven short prison terms for misdemeanors, but not for drugs. His first marriage ends in divorce and, after a ten-year courtship, he marries country star June Carter (1929-2003), who is played by Witherspoon, but their marriage and his career is troubled because of his addiction to alcohol and drugs. The film ends in 1968 with Phoenix, then thirty-six, giving his landmark concert at Folsom Prison with Witherspoon at his side (as Carter would be until her death in 2003). Phoenix and Witherspoon give strong acting and singing performances in the film, which movingly dramatizes their love for each other and their music. Songs: "Cocaine Blues" (Red Arnall); "Dark Was the Night, Cold Was the Ground" (Blind Willie Johnson); "The Sea of Gallilee," "Engine 143" (A.P. Carter); "Didn't It Rain" (Marie Knight, Sister Rosetta Tharpe); "I Walk the Line," "You're My Baby," "Get Rhythm," "Rock 'N Roll Ruby," "Folsom Prison Blues," "Hey Porter" (John R. Cash); "I Was There When It Happened" (Fern Jones); "Try Me One More Time" (Ernest Tubb); "Milk Cow Blues" (Kokomo Arnold); "Time's A-Wastin'" (Boudleaux Bryant); "Ain't That Right" (Eddie Snow); "Lewis Boogie" (Jerry Lee Lewis); "Boogie Blues" (Earl Peterson); "Juke Box Blues" (Helen Carter, Maybelle Carter); "Defrost Your Heart" (Quinton Claunch, William Cantrell); "I Miss You Already" (Faron Young, Marvin Rainwater); "Bop Baby" (Dick Penner, Wade Moore); "Feelin' Good" (Herman Parker, Jr.); "Rock with Me Baby" (Billy Lee Riley, Jack Clement, R. Wallace); "She Wears Red Feathers" (Bob Merrill); "That's All Right" (Arthur Crudup); "Home of the Blues" (Cash, Lillie McAlpin, Glenn Douglas); "Fujiyama Mama" (Jack Hammer); "Candy Man Blues" (John S. Hurt); "Easy Does It" (Stephen Lang, Jamie Dunlap, Scott Nickoley); "Wildwood Flower" (A.P. Carter); "Highway '61 Revisited," "It Ain't Me Babe" (Bob Dylan); "You Get to Me" (L. Stuart); "Jackson" (Jerry Leiber, Billy Edd Wheeler); "Light of the Night" (Werner Tautz); "I Got Stripes" (Cash, Charlie Williams); "Ring of Fire" (June Carter Cash, Merle Kilgore); "Cartoon World" (Billy Sherwood); "I'm a Long Way from Home" (Hank Cochran); "Ghost Town/Poem for Eva" (Bill Frisell); "In the Sweet By and By" (Sanford F. Bennett, Joseph P. Webster); "Long Legged Guitar Pickin' Man" (Marshall Grant); "I'm Goin' to Jackson" (Johnny Cash, June Carter Cash). Sexuality, language, drugs, and alcohol prohibit viewing by children. **p**, James Keach, Cathy Konrad; **d**, James Mangold; **cast**, Joaquin Phoenix, Reese Witherspoon, Ginnifer Goodwin, Robert Patrick, Dallas Roberts, Dan John Miller, Larry Bagby, Shelby Lynne, Tyler Hilton, Waylon Malloy Payne, Shooter Jennings; **w**, Gill Dennis, James Mangold (based on the books *Man in Black* by Johnny Cash and *Cash: The Autobiography* by Cash, Patrick Carr); **c**, Phedon Papamichael; **m**, T Bone Burnett; **ed**, Michael McCusker; **prod d**, David J. Bomba; **art d**, John R. Jensen, Rob Simons; **set d**, Carla Curry; **spec eff**, Ron Bolanowski, Robert Stromberg, Paul Graff.

Walkabout ★★★ 1971; U.K.; 95m; Si Litvinoff Film/FOX; Color; Drama; Children: Unacceptable; **BD**; **DVD**; **VHS**; **IV**. Director Roeg presents a jarring, disturbing tale where two children, Agutter, and her brother, John, are left stranded in the Australian outback when their father goes insane and kills himself. After several days, they meet a young Aborigine, Gumpilil, on a "walkabout," a rite to manhood from his tribe, and he shows them how to survive in the wilderness. He also commits suicide, but they nevertheless find their way back to civilization, and we learn their adventure happened years before and is told in a flashback. Songs: "Hymen" (Karlheinz Stockhausen), "Gasoline Alley" (Rod Stewart), "Los Angeles" (Warren Marley). Sexuality, mature themes and suicide prohibit viewing by children. **p**, Si Litvinoff; **d**, Nicolas Roeg; **cast**, Jenny Agutter, Lucien John, David Gumpilil, John Meillon, Robert McDara, Pete Carver, John Illingsworth, Hillary Bamberger, Barry Donnelly, Noelene Brown, Carlo Manchini; **w**, Edward Bond (based on the novel by James Vance Marshall); **c**, Nicolas Roeg (Eastmancolor); **m**, John Barry; **ed**, Antony Gibbs, Alan Pattillo; **prod d**, Brian Eatwell; **art d**, Terry Gough.

The Walking Dead ★★★ 1936; U.S.; 66m; WB; B/W; Horror; Children: Unacceptable; **DVD**. This genuinely frightening film sees Karloff as a gentle, ex convict, who is framed by gangsters Cortez and MacLane for the murder of King, the judge who sent Karloff to prison. After Karloff is found guilty at a trial, evidence surfaces that proves his innocence, but it is too late, and he is executed by the electric chair. Realizing

Boris Karloff in *The Walking Dead*, **1936.**

that they have executed an innocent man, authorities allow a scientist, Gwenn, to try to restore Karloff to life. Gwenn succeeds in this, but Karloff now has the appearance of the Frankenstein monster, and acts like a zombie. Karloff visits those who convicted him of murdering the judge and each of them dies, although Karloff never touches them and their deaths are apparently self-inflicted. Cortez and MacLane, fearing for their lives, follow Karloff into a graveyard inhabited by the undead and kill him. They then flee in a car, but the auto strikes a power line and they are ironically killed in the same manner Karloff met his fate, electrocution. *Author's Note*: Karloff told this author that "**The Walking Dead** was much more than a routine horror film because it was directed by Curtiz, a master filmmaker. He used many creative camera angles and low-key lighting that gave the picture an eerie atmosphere and where all the production values were of the highest order. Curtiz was a perfectionist and very demanding, but that is precisely why his pictures were so good." Other than **Frankenstein**, 1931, this was the best of Karloff's many films where he played "undead" characters, the others being **Before I Hang**, 1940; **The Devil Commands**, 1941; **The Man They Could Not Hang**, 1939; **The Man Who Lived Again**, 1936; and **The Man with Nine Lives**, 1940. **p**, Louis F. Edelman; **d**, Michael Curtiz; **cast**, Boris Karloff, Ricardo Cortez, Edmund Gwenn, Marguerite Churchill, Warren Hull, Barton MacLane, Henry O'Neill, Joseph King, Addison Richards, Joe Sawyer; **w**, Ewart Adamson, Peter Milne, Robert Andrews, Lillie Hayward (based on a story by Adamson, Joseph Fields); **c**, Hal Mohr; **ed**, Thomas Pratt; **art d**, Hugh Reticker.

Walking on Air ★★★ 1936; U.S.; 70m; RKO/B/W; Musical Comedy; Children: Acceptable. Sothern shines in this charming comedy where she loves Curtis, but her father, Stephenson, and aunt, Ralph, disapprove of him because he is divorced. To make him look better in their eyes, Sothern hires Raymond to play a rude French playboy count, who courts her. In the process, she falls in love with Raymond, a singer, and dumps Curtis. Songs: "Cabin on the Hilltop" (music: Harry Ruby; lyrics: Bert Kalmar), "My Heart Wants to Dance" and "Let's Make a Wish" (music: Harry Ruby; lyrics: Bert Kalmar, Sid Silvers). **p**, Edward Kaufman; **d**, Joseph Santley; **cast**, Gene Raymond, Ann Sothern, Jessie Ralph, Henry Stephenson, Alan Curtis, George Meeker, Gordon Jones, Maxine Jennings, Anita Colby, Patricia Wilder; **w**, Kalmar, Harry Ruby, Viola Brothers Shore, Rian James (based on the story "Count Pete" by Francis M. Cockrell); **c**, J. Roy Hunt; **m**, Nathaniel Shilkret; **ed**, George Hively; **art d**, Van Nest Polglase; **spec eff**, Vernon L. Walker.

Walking Tall ★★★ 1973; U.S.; 125m; Bing Crosby Productions/Cinerama; Color; Crime Drama; Children: Unacceptable (MPAA: R); **BD**; **DVD**; **VHS**; **IV**. This hard-hitting crime tale is based on the colorful

Michael Douglas and Charlie Sheen in *Wall Street,* **1987.**

life of wrestler-sheriff Buford Pusser (1937-1974), who is strongly played by Baker. He is a wrestler whose wife, Hartman, wants him to settle down, so they move to his hometown in Tennessee where he plans to go into business with his father. He soon finds that the town is under the control of graft and corruption, so he runs for sheriff and wins. The corrupt element goes after him and murders Hartman. Baker takes matters into his own hands and, while wielding a baseball bat and other weapons, kills several of the crooks, and cleans up the town. The film was followed by **Walking Tall, Part 2,** 1975, and **Final Chapter-Walking Tall,** 1977, and also spawned a short-lived television series, and was remade in 2004. Song: "Walking Tall" (music: Walter Scharf; lyrics: Johnny Mathis). Excessive violence prohibits viewing by children. **p,** Mort Briskin; **d,** Phil Karlson; **cast,** Joe Don Baker, Elizabeth Hartman, Leif Garrett, Dawn Lyn, Noah Berry, Jr., Lurene Tuttle, Ed Call, Kenneth Tobey, Russell Thorson, Arch Johnson; **w,** Briskin, Stephen Downing, John Michael Hayes; **c,** Jack A. Marta; **m,** Walter Scharf; **ed,** Harry Gerstad; **prod d,** Stan Jolley; **spec eff,** Sass Bedig.

Wall Street ★★★★ 1987; U.S.; 126m; FOX; Color; Drama; Children: Unacceptable (MPAA: R); **BD**; **DVD**; **VHS**; **IV**. Riveting tale depicts the gnawing greed of man to not only enrich oneself, but to acquire all the vast power accompanying wealth, and, like the adage, losing one's soul in the process. Charlie Sheen is a young and ambitious junior stock broker at Jackson Steinem & Co., who wants to emulate his business idol, Douglas (Gordon Gekko), a celebrated Wall Street czar. He has attempted to contact Douglas dozens of times in an effort to go to work for Douglas' firm, but to no avail. He makes a bold move by crashing Douglas' birthday party and presenting the manipulating stock player with a box of Douglas' preferred Cuban cigars, which are highly desired contraband (Cuba then under U.S. trade sanctions). This audacious gesture impresses Douglas, who grants Sheen an interview. Sheen proposes some stock deals to Douglas that do not interest him and, desperate to get Douglas' ear, gives him inside information about Bluestar Airlines, having learned some inside data about that firm from his father (Martin Sheen), a union worker there. Douglas appears only mildly interested, telling Sheen he will think about it. Sheen goes back to his firm feeling dejected over having lost an opportunity to work with Douglas, but is then surprised when Douglas buys some Bluestar stock, thus becoming Sheen's customer. Douglas gives Sheen some investment funds, but Sheen loses the money on poor stock selections. The artful Douglas, however, plays the avuncular patron, allowing Sheen to redeem himself by spying on Stamp, a British tycoon. Sheen learns that Stamp is attempting to take over a steel firm and gives this inside information to Douglas, who, in turn, buys stock in that firm in order to prevent its purchase by Stamp, who must then buy Douglas' stock

at exorbitant prices before he manages the takeover. Sheen becomes a senior stock broker and Douglas, elated at Sheen's underhanded tactics, rewards him with a lavishly appointed penthouse apartment and the alluring company of Hannah, who had once been Douglas' mistress. Sheen now thinks he has entered Mount Olympus, but his greed has no bounds and he goes to Douglas with a new scheme. Using information he has gotten from his unwitting father (Martin Sheen), who is on the union board of Bluestar's employees, Sheen tells Douglas that he should buy the financially healthy Bluestar as a going concern and make him president, a purchase easily made through savings from union concessions Sheen thinks he can get via his father's influence, as well as the union's overfunded pension. Martin Sheen refuses to help his son in the buyout, rightly distrusting Douglas, but Charlie Sheen manages to get the support of the airline's union leaders for the buyout where the union will participate in ownership. As the deal progresses toward conclusion, Charlie Sheen is shocked to learn that the insidious Douglas plans to buy the airline only to financially gut it once he has acquired ownership. He will then dissolve the company and sell off its assets in order to obtain the cash in the firm's pension plan. Martin Sheen, when hearing of this, suffers a heart attack. Charlie Sheen is now racked with guilt over his involvement in Douglas' vicious scheme, knowing that the deal will make him wealthy beyond his expectations, but that his father and everyone else working at Bluestar will be unemployed. He confides his anger to Hannah, telling her that he plans to upset Douglas' financial plot, but she remains loyal to her former lover and they end their relationship, which has always been based on sex and not true love. Sheen devises his own scheme to drive Bluestar's stock upward before arranging it to lose its values. To that end, he meets with Bluestar's union leaders and they approach tycoon Stamp, who begins buying Bluestar stock, with the understanding that he will have controlling interest in the airline, but at a substantial discount. Meanwhile, investigators for the Securities and Exchange Commission are now probing Sheen's activities after some of his questionable trades have come to their attention. When Douglas' stock begins to plummet, Sheen advises Douglas to dump all of his stock in the company, which he does. That evening, Douglas learns that Sheen has betrayed him when he reads in a newspaper that Stamp has been buying up Bluestar stock. Feeling that he has absolved himself, Sheen goes back to his firm, but is greeted by federal officers who arrest him on charges of illegal insider trading. Sheen agrees to cooperate with authorities and meets with an irate Douglas in Central Park where Sheen wears a hidden tape recorder to preserve any incriminating comments Douglas might make. Douglas lambasts Sheen for betraying him, pointing out how he had made Sheen a rich, young man through their joint stock manipulations and that all he, Douglas, has gotten in return is ingratitude from Sheen and the likelihood of being indicted. Sheen later turns the tape over to officials and is told that he might see a lighter prison sentence for helping them prepare a case against the omnipotent Douglas. A short time later, Sheen is driven to the Supreme Court Building in downtown Manhattan by his father, Martin Sheen, who is now proud of him for saving the airline, even at the cost of his own freedom. Charlie Sheen alights from the car and mounts the steps of the courthouse, knowing that he will most likely face prison time and that his career in the stock market is over. He also knows that he has preserved something much more precious—his integrity. This film from the gifted Stone presents a powerhouse drama with great performances from Douglas and Charlie and Martin Sheen (albeit Martin Sheen's performance is all but limited to a cameo performance). All directors are not dissimilar to talented lathe operators (the French surname "Tourneur," as in French film director Jacques Tourneur, literally means "lathe operator"). Some are better than others in producing a more finite product, but all nevertheless work in the same factory, confined and limited to their intensely focused station of operation. Stone, in this instance, has honed from his lathe a memorable tale from an otherwise unimaginative subject. His characters come alive with human emotion, transcending the deadening mechanics of stock trading to the exciting level of the human spirit where conscience and intellectual courage expose the unemotional and often destructive mathematics of wealth. Douglas deservedly won an Oscar as Best Actor and the film was a box office smash, earning almost $44 million in its initial release against a budget of $15 million. A less than impactful sequel, **Wall Street: Money Never Sleeps**, 2010, is also directed by Stone, where Douglas reprises his despicable character. Songs: "Fly Me to the Moon" (1954; Bart Howard), "America Is Waiting" and "Mea Culpa" (Brian Eno, David Byrne), "Desafinado" (music: Antonio Carlos Jobim; lyrics: Newton Mendonica), "Quiet Nights of Quiet Starts" (Antonio Carlos Jobim), "Midnight Motion' (Kenny G.), "Burning Guitar" (Dave Alvin, Steve Berlin), "Rigoletto" (1851; Giuseppe Verdi), "Moonlight Magic" (Alan Moorhouse), "This Must Be the Place (Naïve Melody)" (David Byrne, Jerry Harrison, Tina Weymouth, Chris Frantz), "Happy Birthday to You" (1893; Mildred J. Hill, Patty S. Hill). *Author's Note*: Stone thought to make this film as early as 1981, inspired by his own father's background (Lou Stone, a broker during the Depression at Hayden, Stone & Co.). Stone and Weiser visited brokerage houses for several weeks in researching the script, its chief character being a high-wheeling NYC businessman Stone reportedly knew who took great risks and lost his great fortune in doing so. Douglas' celebrated line, "greed is good," stems from a remark made by stock trader Ivan Boesky, who reportedly said "greed is right." Weiser was later quoted as creating Douglas' rapid-fire speech after Stone's own speech patterns, especially when he and Stone were discussing the script over the phone. Douglas did his own research for his character by studying the careers of business tycoons T. Boone Pickens (1928-), and Carl Icahn (1936-). Charlie Sheen was allowed to select the actor who played his father and he chose his real-life father, Martin Sheen. Hannah was never comfortable in her role in that her materialistic and money-clutching character conflicted with her own ideals. She received considerable criticism for her rather lame performance. The film was shot on location in NYC and several New York movers and shakers appeared as advisers and in cameo roles, including investment bankers Jeffrey "Mad Dog" Beck and Kenneth Lipper. **p**, Edward R. Pressman, A. Kitman Ho; **d**, Oliver Stone; **cast**, Michael Douglas, Charlie Sheen, Daryl Hannah, Hal Holbrook, Terence Stamp, Martin Sheen, James Spader, Sean Young, Millie Perkins, Liliane Montevecchi, Monique van Vooren; **w**, Stone, Stanley Weiser; **c**, Robert Richardson; **m**, Stewart Copeland; **ed**, Claire Simpson; **prod d**, Stephen Hendrickson; **art d**, John Jay Moore, Hilda Stark; **set d**, Leslie Bloom, Susan Bode; **spec eff**, Andrew Francis.

Wallace & Gromit in The Curse of the Were-Rabbit ★★★ 2005; U.K./U.S.; 85m; Aaroman/DreamWorks; Color; Animated Comedy; Children: Acceptable (MPAA: G); **BD**; **DVD**. Delightful tale begins with a British inventor, Wallace (Sallis voiceover), and his dog Gromit, as they set out to learn the mystery behind sabotage in a garden that plagues their village and threatens the annual giant vegetable-growing contest. This happens while they operate a humane pest-control outfit, "Anita-Pesto," that is overrun by rabbits. They encounter and overcome many exciting obstacles before they solve the mystery. Based on a British comic strip and series of short films, the characters are made from molded plasticine modeling clay on metal armatures and filmed with stop motion clay animation. This well-made film was a hit at the box office, producing more than $192 million in its initial release against a budget of $30 million. Songs: "We Plow the Fields and Scatter" (Matthias Claudius, Johann A.P. Schultz), "The Stripper" (David Rose), "Bright Eyes" (Mike Batt). **p**, Nick Park, Peter Lord, Claire Jennings, Carla Shelley, David Sproxton; **d**, Steve Box, Park; **cast**, (voiceovers) Peter Sallis, Ralph Fiennes, Helena Bonham Carter, Peter Kay, Nicholas Smith, Liz Smith, John Thomson, Mark Gatiss, Vincent Ebrahim, Geraldine McEwan; **w**, Box, Bob Baker, Mark Burton (based on characters created by Park); **c**, Tristan Oliver, Dave Alex Riddett;

Michael Douglas in *Wall Street*, 1987.

m, Julian Nott; **ed**, David McCormick, Gregory Perler; **prod d**, Phil Lewis; **art d**, Alastair Green, Sarah Hauldren, Matt Perry; **spec eff**, Paddy Eason, Paul Driver.

WALL-E ★★★ 2008; U.S.; 98m; Pixar Animation Studios/Walt Disney; Color; Animated Comedy; Children: Recommended (MPAA: G). **BD**; **DVD**; **IV**. This delightful and visually sumptuous tale begins sometime in the future where mankind has abandoned Earth because it has become a trash can of used products. A garbage collecting robot, WALL-E (Burtt voiceover) is left to clean up the mess, alone on Earth except for a pet cockroach. One day, Eve (Knight voiceover), a beautiful robot, is sent to earth to find proof that life there is once again sustainable. Burtt falls in love with Knight and they go on an outer space adventure that changes the destiny of both his kind and humanity. The computer-animated film with some live-action sequences was a huge success with critics and audiences and won the Academy Award for Best Animated Feature. The film was an overwhelming smash at the box office, earning more than $521 million in its initial release against a staggering budget of $180 million. Songs: "Put on Your Sunday Clothes" and "It Only Takes a Moment" (Jerry Herman), "Don't Worry, Be Happy" (Bobby McFerrin), "La Vie en Rose" (Louis Guglielmi, Edith Piaf, Mack David), "Down to Earth" (Peter Gabriel, Thomas Newman), "Also Sprach Zarathustra" (Richard Strauss), "BNL Jingle" (Thomas Newman, Bill Bernstein). **p**, Jim Morris, Lindsey Collins; **d**, Andrew Stanton; **cast**, (voiceovers) Ben Burtt, Elissa Knight, Jeff Garlin, Fred Willard, MackIn Talk, John Ratzenberger, Kathy Najimy, Sigourney Weaver, Lori Alan, Bob Bergen, Laraine Newman; **w**, Stanton, Jim Reardon (based on the story by Stanton, Pete Docter); **m**, Thomas Newman; **ed**, Stephen Schaffer; **prod d**, Ralph Eggleston; **spec eff**, Ed Hirsh, Richard Hollander, Stacy Bissell.

The Walls of Jericho ★★★ 1948; U.S.; 106m; FOX; B/W; Drama; Children: Unacceptable. This intriguing tale begins with Wilde, who is an attorney in the small town of Jericho, Kansas, in 1908. His wife, Dvorak, is an alcoholic and doesn't care who knows it. Wilde falls in love with Baxter, another lawyer in town, while Darnell, the wife of his best friend, Douglas, has romantic interest in him. Wilde does not encourage Darnell, so she takes revenge by getting Douglas, publisher of the newspaper in town, to write editorials accusing Wilde of sexual transgressions, which could ruin the ambitious lawyer's chances to run for public office. Wilde becomes fed up and leaves town, so Douglas runs for office, wins an election, and goes to Washington, D.C. Wilde and Baxter meet again while Darnell still pursues him, and, incensed at again being rejected, she shoots him, wounding him. Darnell goes on trial for manslaughter, but Baxter effectively represents her, bringing about her

Cornel Wilde and Anne Baxter in *The Walls of Jericho,* **1948.**

release. Wilde finally calls his marriage to Dvorak a big mistake, and, by this time, Douglas has abandoned the tempestuous and unpredictable Darnell. A well-made soap opera, this film, despite above-average performances from its cast, did not fare well with the public. **p**, Lamar Trotti; **d**, John M. Stahl; **cast**, Cornel Wilde, Linda Darnell, Anne Baxter, Kirk Douglas, Ann Dvorak, Marjorie Rambeau, Henry Hull, Colleen Townsend, Barton MacLane, William Tracy, Griff Barnett, Art Baker, Ann Doran, Patricia Morison; **w**, Trotti (based on the novel by Paul Wellman); **c**, Arthur C. Miller; **m**, Cyril J. Mockridge, Alfred Newman; **ed**, James B. Clark; **art d**, Lyle Wheeler, Maurice Ransford; **set d**, Thomas Little, Paul S. Fox; **spec eff**, Fred Sersen.

The Walls of Malapaga ★★★ 1950; France; 89m; Italia Productions; Films International; B/W; Drama; Children: Unacceptable. Gabin gives another exceptional performance in this murky but compelling tale where he is on the run, wanted for murdering his mistress. After stowing away on a freighter, Gabin disembarks at Genoa where he suffers from a toothache that sends him in search of a dentist. While getting his tooth treated, Gabin meets Talchi, a little girl, who introduces him to her mother, Miranda. She works as a waitress and Miranda gives Gabin a meal before taking him home with her. They soon develop a romance, but Talchi becomes jealous of her mother's attentions to Gabin, which creates problems. The relationship comes to an abrupt end when Gabin is arrested and taken back to France to face charges in the death of his mistress, an eventuality Gabin has long been resigned to facing. Stark and earthy, the story is told in plain terms, and Talchi and Miranda lend fine supporting performances to Gabin's captivating character, a man without a future and knows it. Although the film is reminiscent of **Pepe Le Moko**, 1937, which also starred Gabin, it has its own distinctive story line and separately memorable characters, presented by the gifted Clement in the classic neorealism style of Italian filmmakers. (In French and Italian; English subtitles.) **p**, Alfredo Guarini; **d**, Rene Clement; **cast**, Jean Gabin, Isa Miranda, Vera Talchi, Andrea Checchi, Robert Dalban, Ave Ninchi, Carlo Tamberlani; **w**, Jean Aurenche, Pierre Bost (based on story by Suso Cecchi D'Amico, Cesare Zavattini, Guarini); **c**, Louis Page; **m**, Roman Vlad; **ed**, Mario Serandrei; **prod d**, Piero Filippone, Luigi Gervasi.

Waltz of the Toreadors ★★★ 1962; U.K.; 104m; Independent Artists/CD; Color; Comedy; Children: Unacceptable; **DVD**; **VHS**; **IV**. Subtle but entertaining comedy sees the brilliant Sellers as a retired British army general just before the start of World War I (1914-1918). He plans to write his memoirs at the Sussex manor house of his wealthy wife, Leighton, who is a shrew and hypochondriac he now loathes but she still loves him. He remembers Robin, a beautiful French mistress with whom he had an affair seventeen years earlier. She arrives at the estate insisting Sellers consummate their relationship, but that is postponed by circumstances and he puts her in the care of a young soldier and aide, Fraser. Within two days, Fraser has accomplished with Robin what Sellers had put on hold for so many years. Sellers takes revenge by having Fraser face a court-martial. At a resulting trial, Sellers learns that Fraser is his illegitimate son, so he drops the charges and allows Fraser and Robin to marry. Sellers is so depressed afterward, thinking about the rest of his life with Leighton, that he puts a gun to his head. He is about to pull the trigger when a beautiful maid enters and he finds a new interest in living. Sellers is outstanding as the grumpy but still lusty aging military man whose clumsy efforts at romance produce many mirthful scenes. The film is reminiscent of **Colonel Blimp**, 1945, but nevertheless offers a distinctive story line. **p**, Peter De Sarigny, Leslie Parkyn, Julian Wintle; **d**, John Guillermin; **cast**, Peter Sellers, Dany Robin, Margaret Leighton, John Fraser, Cyril Cusack, Prunella Scales, Denise Coffey, Jean Anderson, Raymond Huntley, Cardew Robinson; **w**, Wolf Mankowitz, Lucienne Hill (based on the play by Jean Anouilh); **c**, John Wilcox (Eastmancolor); **m**, Richard Addinsell; **ed**, Peter Taylor; **prod d**, Wilfred Shingleton; **art d**, Harry Pottle.

Wanda ★★★ 1971; U.S.; 101m; Foundation for Filmmakers/Bardene International; Color; Crime Drama; Children: Unacceptable (MPAA: GP); **DVD**. Pensive drama presents a powerful character study of a lonely housewife, Loden, who has no self-esteem. Uneducated and living in a coal county, she is easily manipulated by her husband. When he seeks a divorce and custody of their two children, Loden meekly complies, stating that "I'm just no good." She becomes a drifter, unable to find work after she leaves her hometown in Pennsylvania, and is picked up by a traveling salesman, who sleeps with her and then abandons her the next morning as he cruelly drives off, leaving her at a roadway stop. She gets to the next town and goes to a movie theater to take a nap, but her money is stolen while she sleeps. Loden then goes to a bar to use the ladies' room and makes conversation with the man behind the bar, Higgins, thinking he is the bartender. Higgins, however, is actually robbing the bar and finds that he cannot rid himself of Loden when he makes his getaway. Higgins takes her along but routinely mistreats Loden, who discovers that he is a career criminal, a neurotic thief, who tells her: "If you don't want anything, you don't have anything, and, if you don't have anything, you're as good as dead." His attitude toward her softens and Loden begins to fall in love with Higgins, since he is the only man who has ever paid any attention to her, perversely sadistic as that attention might be. She decides to be his accomplice, and, after she performs well in a robbery, Higgins buys Loden a dress and compliments her. Receiving the first encouragement of her life, Loden is now devoted to the erratic Higgins, who decides to quit crime after committing one last heist, a bank robbery. Higgins goes to the bank and is shot and killed during the robbery. Loden, who was to meet him outside the bank, is not recognized as Higgins' accomplice, and she escapes undetected. A stranger then picks her up and tries to rape her, but Loden manages to escape. She is last seen at a bar where she is offered cigarettes and drinks by several men attempting to pick her up, a grim finale to a stark story. Loden's performance is startlingly impressive as a woman without any roots or a dependable man to love. Her only family consists of drifters and social pariahs like herself, and her loneliness and sense of futility is evidence in every grueling frame of this telling, gritty portrait. Loden's sensitive performance is unforgettable as she presents the image of an attractive but utterly vulnerable woman, not unlike that of Marilyn Monroe, and she bears a striking resemblance to actress Joanne Woodward. The film saw very limited release, but it was widely acclaimed at the Venice Film Festival where it received the International Critics' Prize as Best Film. Seldom seen, it nevertheless became a cult classic. *Author's Note*: Loden (1932-1980) began her career as a magazine model and was then "discovered" by film director Elia Kazan, becoming his protégé, and she appeared in small roles in some of Kazan's films (**Wild River**, 1960; **Splendor in the Grass**, 1961). Kazan married Loden, her second marriage, in 1967, and she retired from the screen (that marriage lasted until her untimely death from breast cancer in 1980 at age forty-eight). Loden had nevertheless long nurtured the ambition of making this film. She claimed that the story was partly autobiographical and she was inspired to make the film after she read a newspaper account about a self-deprecating woman thanking a judge for sentencing her to prison. Kazan told this author: "I wrote the first draft of the screenplay for **Wanda**, but Barbara [Loden] kept rewriting it until it became her own script. She had a hidden talent I did not know she possessed, especially for creating the very strong central character, herself, in that picture." Loden worked with a shoestring budget of $115,000 to make this film, which was shot on 16mm and then blown up to 35mm for theatrical release. **Wanda** is one of the few theatrically released feature films directed by a woman during the 1970s. Kazan told this author that "Barbara studied the photographs taken during the Depression [1929-1939] by Dorothea Lange. One of those photographs, which was titled "Migrant Mother," gave her the idea of how her character and others should look in the picture she made. She wanted to capture the hopelessness of those people and I think she did. Her picture is definitely not the product of an amateur. It may even be a great one." **p**, Harry Shuster; **d&w**, Barbara Loden; **cast**, Loden, Michael Higgins, Charles Dosinan, Frank Jourdano, Dorothy Shupenes, Peter Shupenes, Jerome Their, Marian Their, Anthony Rotell, M.L. Kennedy, Gerald Grippo, Milton Gittleman; **c&ed**, Nicholas T. Proferes (Kodachrome).

The Wanderers ★★★ 1979; U.S.; 117m; Orion; Color; Teenage Drama; Children: Unacceptable (MPAA: R); **DVD**; **VHS**; **IV**. Tough tale profiles the adventures of a gang of Italian-American teenagers in the Bronx, New York, in 1963, called "The Wanderers." Their stories are told in an episodic style that mainly focuses on a football game where gangs play with and against each other. Winners and losers come together afterward to be sort-of united and defend their turf against outsiders. The film's action is set against a strong rock 'n' roll music background. Songs: "The Wanderer," "Runaround Sue" (Ernie Maresca); "The Times They Are a Changin'" (Bob Dylan); "Sherry," "Walk Like a Man," "Big Girls Don't Cry" (Bob Gaudio); "Soldier Boy" (Luther Dixon, Florence Green); "Baby, It's You" (Burt Bacharach, Hal David); "Ya Ya" (Clarence Lewis, Lee Dorsey, Bobby Robinson, Morris Levy); "Shout – Part 1" (O'Kelly Isley, Ronald Isley, Rudolph Isley); "I Love You" (Chuck Dukowski, Willie Ewing, Gordon Jenkins, Ernest Newsom, Jerry Jeff Walker); "Granada" (Augustin Lara); "Pipeline" (Bob Pickard, Brian Carman); "Tequila" (Chuck Rio); "You've Really Got a Hold on Me" (Smokey Robinson); "Stand By Me" (Ben E. King, Jerry Leiber, Mike Stoller); "Do You Love Me" (Berry Gordy); "My Boyfriend's Back" (Bob Feldman, Jerry Goldstein, Richard Gottehrer); "Wipe Out" (Robert Berryhill, Patrick Connolly, Jim Fuller, Ronald Wilson); "You Can't Go Home Again" (Don Sebesky); "Anaklasis," "Flourescences" (Krzysztof Penderecki); "La Femina" (Terri Perri); "Stranger Girl" (Jim Youngs); "Volare" (Domenico Modugno); "Stranger on the Shore" (Acker Bilk); "Adagio and Fugue in C" (Johann Sebastian Bach). Violence and gutter language prohibit viewing by children. **p**, Martin Ransohoff; **d**, Philip Kaufman; **cast**, Ken Wahl, John Friedrich, Karen Allen, Toni Kalem, Alan Rosenberg, Jim Youngs, Tony Ganios, Linda Manz, William Andrews, Val Avery, Dolph Sweet, Olympia Dukakis; **w**, Philip and Rose Kaufman (based on the novel by Richard Price); **c**, Michael Chapman; **ed**, Stuart H. Pappe, Ronald Roose; **prod d**, John Jay Moore; **set d**, Thomas Tonery.

The Wandering Jew: The Life of Theodore Herzl ★★★ 1923 (silent); U.K.; 80m; Stoll Picture Productions; B/W; Drama; Children: Unacceptable; **DVD**. Lang gives a moving performance as the cursed Jew, who lived through the Crusades (1095-1291) and then in medieval Italy, only to die during the Spanish Inquisition (1478-1834). This story was

Raymond Huntley and Margaret Leighton in *Waltz of the Toreadors*, **1962.**

filmed as silent in 1912 and 1916, and remade with various different plots and time settings in 1933, 1935, 1940 (a virulent anti-Semitic Nazi propaganda film), 1948, in 1988 (under the title of **The Seventh Sign** where a Catholic priest has lived on for centuries as the porter of Pontius Pilate, who had helped scourge Jesus), and in **Forever**, 2014, a TV series where a physician named Dr. Henry Morgan claims to have lived more than two thousand years. **p&d**, Maurice Elvey; **cast**, Matheson Lang, Hutin Britton, Malvina Longfellow, Isobel Elsom, Florence Saunders, Shayle Gardner, Hubert Carter, Jerrold Robertshaw, Winifred Izard, Fred Raynham; **w**, Alice Ramsey (based on a play by E. Temple Thurston).

The Wandering Jew ★★★ 1935; U.K.; 111m; Julius Hagen Productions/Olympic Pictures; B/W; Drama; Children: Unacceptable. Veidt gives a powerful performance as a Jew who witnesses the crucifixion of Jesus Christ at Golgotha, and, after he expresses unconcern in the gruesome fate of Christ, Jesus, before dying, tells him: "You will remain here [on Earth] until I return." For his callous attitude, Veidt is condemned by God to live forever and to wander the earth as a displaced pariah. He endures incredible hardships through the ages, including the many savage Crusades, until he is allowed to perish during the Spanish Inquisition (1478-1834). Director Elvey presents a haunting tale (which is not found either in the Bible or any Christian teachings), paying attention to historic detail in his sumptuous sets and costumes. Veidt is impressively supported by a strong cast, many of its members going on to stellar film careers. **p**, Julius Hagen; **d**, Maurice Elvey; **cast**, Conrad Veidt, Marie Ney, Basil Gill, Cicely Oates, Anne Grey, Dennis Hoey, Bertram Wallis, Hector Abbas, Jack Livesey, Kenji Takase, Joan Maude, John Stuart, Arnold Lucy, Abraham Sofaer, Felix Aylmer, Francis L. Sullivan, Peggy Ashcroft, Ivor Barnard, Conway Dixon; **w**, H. Fowler Mear (based on a play by E. Temple Thurston); **c**, Sydney Blythe; **m**, Hugo Riesenfeld; **ed**, Jack Harris; **art d**, James A. Carter.

The Wandering Jew ★★★ 1949; Italy; 100m; CDI/Globe Film Distributors; B/W; Drama; Children; Unacceptable. Gassman gives a memorable performance as the ostracized Jew, who looks upon Jesus Christ as a disruptive element in Israel's fight for freedom against Rome. He not only denounces Jesus, but prevents his wife from giving Jesus a drink of water while Jesus is dying on the cross at Golgotha. His merciless attitude toward Jesus causes him to be condemned to eternal life on earth and where he must wander through the ages without roots or a country he can call his own. We finally see Gassman as a wealthy banker in Paris in 1940 as the Nazis conquer and take over the country. Although he has the means to escape, he prefers to stay behind with his fellow Jews and help them all he can while they are being persecuted by the Nazis during the Holocaust. He is sent to a German concentration

Fay Bainter, Jean Rogers, Halliwell Hobbes and Spring Byington in *The War against Mrs. Hadley,* 1942.

camp where Jews are systematically being exterminated, but, being healthy and robust, he organizes resistance before escaping with several others. Gassman learns that, if he does not return voluntarily to the camp, 100 Jews will be killed, and he sacrifices his life to redeem these captives and thus earns his "freedom" from eternal life by dying a martyr. Alessandrini presents this age-old tale with considerable tension and provides many compelling soul-searching scenes where the introspective Gassman battles with his conscience. Cortese, who plays the woman who comes to love him, provides exceptional strong support. (In Italian; English subtitles.) **p**, Nino Angioletti; **d**, Goffredo Alessandrini; **cast**, Vittorio Gassman, Valentina Cortese, Inga Gort, Noelle Norman, Harry Feist, Pietro Sharoff, Giovanni Heinrich, Cesare Polacco, Egisto Olivieri, Renato Malavasi; **w**, Alessandrini, Flaminio Bollini, Ennio De Concini, Anton Giulio Majano, Guido De Luca, Enrico Fulchignoni, Aldo Bizzarri, Mario Monicelli, Giorgio Prosperi, Steno, Baccio Agnoletti (based on a story by Gian Battista Angioletti and the novel *Le juif errant* by Eugene Sue); **c**, Vaclav Vich; **m**, Enzo Masetti; **ed**, Otello Colangeli; **prod d**, Arrigo Equini.

The War against Mrs. Hadley ★★★ 1942; U.S.; 86m; MGM; B/W; Drama; Children: Acceptable. Good social tale profiles Bainter, a wealthy society woman in a small town during World War II (1939-1945). She refuses to take part in wartime conservation programs, which creates friction and animosity from her family members and neighbors. She gives up her resistance after realizing that by joining in the programs she is helping the servicemen overseas, one of whom is her son, Ney. Songs: "Happy Birthday" (1893; Mildred J. Hill, Patty S. Hill), "Symphony No. 5 in E Minor, Op. 64" (1888; Pyotr Ilyich Tchaikovsky), "Hark! The Herald Angels Sing" (1840; music: Felix Mendelssohn-Bartholdy; lyrics: hymn, 1730, Charles Wesley). **p**, Irving Asher; **d**, Harold S. Bucquet; **cast**, Edward Arnold, Fay Bainter, Richard Ney, Jean Rogers, Sara Allgood, Spring Byington, Van Johnson, Isobel Elsom, Frances Rafferty, Dorothy Morris, Halliwell Hobbes, Stephen McNally as Horace McNally, Rags Ragland, Mark Daniels, Carl Switzer, **w**, George Oppenheimer; **c**, Karl Freund; **m**, David Snell; **ed**, Elmo Veron; **art d**, Cedric Gibbons; **set d**, Edwin B. Willis.

War and Peace ★★★★ 1956; U.S./Italy; 208m; PAR; Color; Historical Drama; Children: Unacceptable; **BD**; **DVD**; **VHS**; **IV**. Tolstoy's sweeping tale of Russia engulfed in the Napoleonic Wars comes to vibrant life under the firm direction of pantheon director Vidoionr and fine performances are seen from Fonda, Hepburn, Ferrer, Lom, Homolka, Gassman and others. The film begins with Lom, who plays Napoleon I (1769-1821), as he covetously eyes the sprawling expanse of Russia on a European map, thinking to invade this vast land, now that he has conquered

most of Europe. Meanwhile, in tranquil Russia, mild-mannered and scholarly aristocrat Fonda visits the estate owned by the kind-hearted Jones, although Hepburn, Jones' attractive daughter, is the real reason why he has made this call. Although Fonda is deeply in love with Hepburn, he cannot bring himself to declare that love to her as he feels unworthy of her station since he is the illegitimate son of a nobleman. Fonda's father, a count, shortly dies and not only leaves a vast inheritance to Fonda, but recognizes him as his son and legitimizes him in the aristocratic world. He is now able to propose marriage to the lovely Hepburn, but Ekberg, a voluptuous vixen, enters his life and entangles him in her sensuous web, inveigling the naïve young man into marrying her. Meanwhile, Ferrer, who is Fonda's closest friend, a wealthy prince who has been waging war against Lom under the direction of Homolka, playing Russian Field Marshal Mikhail Kutuzov (1745-1813), returns to his estate to recuperate from a wound. He is further burdened with tragedy when his wife dies giving birth to their child. So depressed is Ferrer that he contemplates suicide, but the ever self-sacrificing Fonda comes to his rescue, arranging for Ferrer to meet Hepburn, the woman Fonda nobly gives up for the sake of his friend's security and health. Meanwhile, Ekberg, who has no moral values whatsoever, regularly cheats on Fonda with Russian military officers Gassman and Dantine. Fonda finally learns of her cuckolding escapades and gets rid of the Amazonian tramp. Ferrer and Hepburn (who were married in real life at the time) are now deeply in love and plan their marriage. Ferrer, however, is called back to duty when Lom invades Russia, and Ferrer goes to the front to lead his troops. Fonda, who has no military skills, also goes to the front as an observer, and is shocked by the slaughter he sees at the Battle of Borodino (September 7, 1812, the bloodiest single day of the Napoleonic Wars where more than 70,000 casualties occurred; the battle itself is brilliantly choreographed by Vidor, with considerable help from second unit director Mario Soldati). Fonda is so horrified by the widespread death and destruction he finds on the battlefield that he resolves to personally kill Lom, a man he considers a brutal mass murderer. He goes to Moscow to see it being evacuated before Lom and his French legions enter the city. Ferrer also arrives in the city, but he has been fatally wounded. Hepburn and Jones find a sanctuary outside of Moscow, an ancient abbey where they take Ferrer, who dies in Hepburn's arms. Meanwhile, Fonda searches for Lom when the French emperor enters Moscow. He fails to slay Lom and is, instead, taken prisoner. When the French realize that their capture of Moscow is a hollow victory and Lom knows that his supply lines back to France are failing, he orders his historic retreat from Moscow. Fonda is taken along with the retreating French troops, watching Lom's legions crumble under the severe Russian winter, thousands of these soldiers freezing to death. Homolka, who has again gathered a Russian army, then attacks at Berezina (November 26-29, 1812) where the Russian army devastates Lom's legions. Lom, however, manages to get most of his beaten army across the Berezina River to continue his bloody retreat. Fonda manages to escape his captors and makes a torturous trip back to Moscow where he begins to aid returning soldiers and civilians, all beginning to rebuild the city as well as the nation. Fonda and Hepburn meet once again and this time they declare their love for one another and begin to plan their future together to end this stunning opus. Vidor does a marvelous job in presenting the massive Tolstoy novel (600 pages) in a condensed but sensible format and where he retains its major characters while providing a cohesive story that mandatorily centers upon the romances of Hepburn (who is the quintessential Natasha) and the two men who love her, Ferrer and Fonda, all three giving stunning performances. Gassman and Dantine, as the adventuresome-seeking officers who act like sexual predators are also exceptional in their roles while the avuncular Jones and Homolka suitably represent the stability of the Russian aristocracy and its monarchy. Lom renders a credible performance as Napoleon, a difficult part to manage in presenting that complex and enigmatic person, showing more of his ruthlessness than his compassion. The battle scenes are superbly managed, and Cardiff's masterful lensing is apparent in every frame as this saga is seamlessly unfolded. The film received Oscar nominations for Best Director (Vidor), Best Cinematography, Color (Cardiff), and Best Costume Design, Color (Maria De Matteis). Unfortunately, this film, which was competing with several other historical epics that year (**Around the World in 80 Days** and DeMille's **The Ten Commandments**), did not do well at the box office, earning about $6.3 million in its initial release against a then staggering budget of $6 million. The story had been filmed in Russia as a silent in 1916, six years after Tolstoy died, and it would be lavishly remade in Russia in 1968 and as a TV series in 1972 and 2007. Songs/Music: "Grande Valse Brillante in E Flat Major, Op. 18" (1834; Fredric Chopin), "Die Rose von Novgorod" (music: Nino Rota; lyrics: Wolfgang Schrauth, S. Krapp), "Les roses de Novgorod" (music: Nino Rota; lyrics: Nadine Laik), "Masquerade Waltz" (1941; Aram Khachaturian). *Author's Note*: Fonda told this author that "I was not happy with my performance in **War and Peace**. My character, Pierre, was impossible to begin with as he is not a man of action in a world full of action. To make him appear intellectual, I wore small glasses, but that only made me appear more limp-wristed. In half of that picture I am walking around in a daze, wondering why old Russia has been turned into a charnel house by Napoleon. My character is an ineffectual twit and I think I detested him. He doesn't have the guts to tell the girl he loves that he loves her, but that's the way Tolstoy wrote him and that's how I had to play the character. Tolstoy was bigger than Hollywood and still is." Fonda was fifty years old when making this film and he was playing the part of a man in his twenties, and he even admitted that to this author that he had been miscast. Hepburn did not want Fonda as her co-star, and lobbied to have Gregory Peck, her co-star in **Roman Holiday**, 1953, cast in the role of Pierre, but her pleas were ignored and Fonda was cast in that part. Marlon Brando was offered the part of Pierre, but turned it down flat, saying that he did not want to appear with Hepburn. (Brando told this author that "Audrey Hepburn was forever playing giggling girls who are in the tenth grade. I never saw her as a mature woman any man would want to sleep with. She has the sex appeal of a Maypole. If that sounds cruel, well, so be it.") Vidor told this author that "**War and Peace** exhausted the hell out of me. I had to coordinate thousands of Italian extras in the battle scenes, but that was an easy chore, compared to the inside bickering of the cast members, who were always insisting that their parts be improved, especially Audrey [Hepburn] and to the point where I started calling her 'heartburn.' She is a fine actress, but I think she got an overblown head by the time we made **War and Peace**. She got more money for that part than was ever paid to an actress." Hepburn received $350,000 for playing Natasha, an amount that staggered her and where she reportedly stated to her agent: "I'm not worth it. It's impossible. Please don't tell anyone." Shot in Italy, Vidor was deeply concerned about the risks the extras and stunt people had to take in the battle scenes. "Other directors like Michael Curtiz never gave a damn what happened to extras and stuntmen in their productions," Vidor told this author. "I did not want anyone accidentally killed in **War and Peace**, and went out of my way to prevent that from happening. I hired dozens of doctors to mix in with the extras in those battle scenes and Napoleon's retreat from Moscow, so that, if any of them got hurt, they would get immediate medical attention. Thankfully only minor injuries happened when we were shooting those sequences. One of the extras got a bad cut on his arm during a sabre fight, but he was treated for the wound right away. After the shot, with his arm bandaged, the man ran up to me, and, being Italian, who are very emotional and demonstrative, embraced me as a way of thanking me for the medical attention. It was very embarrassing." For a complete list of actors who have played either Napoleon I or Mikhail Kutuzov, see Index, Historical Characters. **p**, Dino De Laurentiis; **d**, King Vidor; **cast**, Audrey Hepburn, Henry Fonda, Mel Ferrer, Vittorio Gassman, Herbert Lom, Oscar Homolka, Anita Ekberg, Helmut Dantine, Tullio Carminati, Barry Jones, Milly Vitale, Wilfred Lawson, May Britt, Jeremy Brett, John Mills; **w**, Bridget Boland, Robert Westerby, Vidor, Mario Camerini, Ennio De

Henry Fonda and Mel Ferrer in *War and Peace*, 1956.

Concini, Ivo Perilli, Gian Gaspare Napolitano, Mario Soldati, (uncredited) Irwin Shaw (based on the novel by Leo Tolstoy); **c**, Jack Cardiff (VistaVision; Technicolor); **m**, Nino Rota; **ed**, Leo Catozzo; **art d**, Mario Chiari; **set d**, Piero Gherardi; **spec eff**, Tell (Costel) Grozea.

War and Peace ★★★★ 1968; USSR/Germany/France; 427m; Mosfilm/Continental Distributing; Color; Drama; Children: Unacceptable; **DVD**; **VHS**. This is really a series of films presented in one mammoth production and financed by the Soviet government, one shown in four parts and encompasses the totality of Tolstoy's classic epic and does a superlative job in the process. Part I sees Pierre, played by Bondarchuk, who is introduced into Russian society as the intellectual and illegitimate son of a nobleman. He befriends Andrei, a rich prince, who is played by Tikhonov, who, in turn enlists in the Russian army as a high-ranking officer and serves under Field Marshal Mikhail Kutuzov (1745-1813), who is played by Zakhava. Andrei goes off to fight in the War of the Third Coalition against Napoleon I (1769-1821), who is played by Strzhelchik, while Pierre's father dies and leaves him his fortune as well as recognizes him as his legitimate son. Pierre then meets and marries the seductive Helene, played by Skobtseva, who proves to be a cheating wife, and Pierre later discards her. Andrei, meanwhile, takes part in the campaign against Napoleon in Austria, witnessing the Allied defeat at the Battle of Austerlitz (December 2, 1805), which proves to be Napoleon's greatest victory. Wounded in that battle, Andrei is taken home to recuperate, and his wife dies of childbirth. Pierre, knowing his friend's depression now borders on suicide, thinks to lighten Andrei's spirits by generously introducing Andrei to the beautiful Natasha, the daughter of a wealthy count, and who is played by Savelyeva. Natasha is a woman Pierre himself loves, but he has never been able to bring himself to declare his affection for her. Part II opens as the year 1809 is coming to a close where the radiant Natasha attends her first ball. She and Andrei fall in love and plan to wed, but Natasha's father insists that they wait some time before marrying. Andrei travels abroad and, in his absence, Natasha falls in love with another man, planning to elope with him, but she has second thoughts and abandons her lover. Andrei, hearing of this relationship, tells Natasha that he no longer wants to marry her and Natasha becomes deeply depressed. She is comforted by Pierre, who finally gets up enough nerve to tell her that he, too, loves her. Part III opens in the year 1812, and Napoleon is marching with his army toward Moscow in an effort to conquer Russia. Kutuzov asks Andrei to serve on his staff, but the prince insists that he be given a field command. Pierre travels with the Russian army and witnesses the slaughterhouse Battle of Borodino (September 7, 1812), and Pierre aids a Russian battery during the fight. He and Andrei are wounded and retreat with the beaten Russian army back toward

Audrey Hepburn and Henry Fonda in *War and Peace*, 1956.

Moscow, Napoleon and his victorious French army hot on their heels. Part IV opens with Moscow being torched by retreating Russian troops. Natasha and her family leave their mansion and go to a distant estate, taking with them many wounded Russian soldiers, including Andrei. Dying of his wounds, Andrei forgives Natasha for her transgressions and dies. Meanwhile, Pierre dresses as a peasant and attempts to assassinate Napoleon, but he is captured and forced to accompany the retreating French army as it makes its torturous way back to France in defeat, hounded all the way by attacking Russian forces. Pierre is rescued by some Russian troops and returns to Moscow where he is reunited with Natasha and they marry as Moscow is being rebuilt. Fanatically faithful to the Tolstoy epic, this film is brilliantly directed by Bondarchuk, who also produced and starred, and Saveleva is a wonderful Natasha and Tikhonov a noble Andrei. The attention to historic detail in sets and costuming is awe inspiring, and the battle scenes are stunningly portrayed with all of their gruesome gore. The film received an Oscar as Best Foreign Language Film and received an Oscar nomination for Best Art Direction (Bogdanov). The film, financed by the Soviet government, cost more than $96 million to produce, the most expensive film up to that time. *Author's Note*: Bondarchuk produced this mammoth film from 1961 to 1967, overcoming many political obstacles in the process, particularly concerned with the script, which miraculously appears to have little communist propaganda. The Soviet army provided thousands of troops that participated in the historic battles, and more than forty museums were looted of costumes, props and military ordnance that were employed in the production. More than 1,000 horses were culled from distant outposts, including the mounted police of Moscow, to make up the cavalry units depicted in the battle scenes. Mature subject matter and war violence prohibit viewing by children. (In Russian; dubbed in English.) Music: Selection from "The Coronation of Poppea" (music: Claudio Monteverdi; lyrics: Giovanni Francesco Busenello). **p&d**, Sergey Bondarchuk; **cast**, Bondarchuk, Lyudmila Saveleva, Vyacheslav Tikhonov, Boris Zakhava, Anatoli Ktorov, Anastasiya Vertinskaya, Irina Skobtseva, Antonina Shuranova, Oleg Tabakov, Viktor Stanitsyn, Vladislav Strzhelchik, Boris Smirnov; **w**, Bondarchuk, Vasiliy Solovyov (based on the novel by Leo Tolstoy); **c**, Iolanda Chen, Anatoliy Petritskiy, Aleksandr Shelenkov; **m**, Vyacheslav Ovchinnikov; **ed**, Tatayana Likhachyova; **prod d**, Mikhail Bogdanov, Aleksandr Dikhtyar, Said Menyalshchikov, Gennady Myasnikov; **set d**, Georgi Koshelev. V. Uvarov.

War Horse ★★★★ 2011; U.S.; 146m; DreamWorks SKG/Touchstone Pictures; Color; War/Drama; Children: Unacceptable (MPAA: PG-13); **BD; DVD; IV**. Inspiring film begins when Mullan, a farmer in Dartmoor, a region in south Devon, England, buys a thoroughbred horse in

1914 rather than a plough animal, to the dismay of his wife, Watson. Their teenage son, Irvine, grows to love the horse as he trains him, calling him Joey, and the two become inseparable. When his harvest fails, Mullan is forced to sell Joey to the British cavalry, which is in need of horses to serve in World War I (1914-1918). Joey is shipped to France where, after a failed offensive by British troops, he is captured by German soldiers. Joey changes owners twice more before becoming trapped in barbed wire in No Man's Land in France and finally freed by British soldiers. Irvine, now a private in the British army in France, although temporarily blinded by gas during another offensive, recognizes Joey and the horse recognizes him. As the war ends, Joey is to be auctioned off, but Irvine is able to convince authorities the horse is his and they are sent back home together. Spielberg directs this film with great affection for its subject, Joey, and his battle scenes and landscapes of war are superlative, as well as the performances he draws from Irvine and the rest of the cast. The film received Oscar nominations for Best Film; Best Original Score (Williams); Best Cinematography (Kaminski); Best Art Direction (Carter, Sandales), Best Sound Editing (Richard Hymns, Gary Rydstrom), and Best Sound Mixing (Rydstrom, Andy Nelson, Tom Johnson, Stuart Wilson). The film was a box office smash, earning more than $177.6 million against a budget of $77 million. Songs: "The Scarlet and the Blue" (John Tams, Adrian Sutton), "Roses of Picardy" (Frederick E. Weatherly, Haydn Wood), "Blue Bonnets Over the Border" (traditional). **p&d**, Steven Spielberg; **cast**, Jeremy Irvine, Peter Mallen, Emily Watson, Niels Arestrup, David Thewlis, Tom Hiddleston, Benedict Cumberbatch, Julian Wadham, Celine Buckens, Toby Kebbell, Patrick Kennedy; **w**, Lee Hall, Richard Curtis (based on the novel by Michael Morpurgo and the play by Nick Stafford); **c**, Janusz Kaminski; **m**, John Williams; **ed**, Michael Kahn; **prod d**, Rick Carter; **art d**, Andrew Ackland-Snow, Molly Hughes, Neil Lamont; **set d**, Lee Sandales; **spec eff**, Neil Corbould.

War Hunt ★★★ 1962; U.S.; 81m; T-D Enterprise/UA; B/W; War Drama; Children: Unacceptable; **DVD; VHS; IV**. Redford, in his film debut, plays a G.I. replacement sent to a front-line platoon near the close of the Korean War (1950-1953). He's an idealist and inexperienced in war. Saxon plays a psychotic private, who goes on one-man patrols slitting enemy throats under cover of night. His only companion is an eight-year-old Korean orphan boy, Matsuda. Redford follows Saxon and sees his strange behavior after killing some Koreans and concludes that Saxon has gone insane. A cease-fire is declared, ending the war, but Saxon goes on another night war hunt for North Koreans, taking Matsuda along. Redford, Aidman and Pollack go after him and find him. Saxon fires at them and Aidman kills him. Frightened, Matsuda runs off into no-man's-land. This rather rare film horrifyingly deals with homicidal psychopaths in war, and where standout performances are seen from Saxon and Redford. The subject was also treated in **Night of the Generals**, 1966. Saxon's chilling portrait of a psychopathic soldier is not unlike the savage sergeant essayed by Aldo Ray in the WWII drama **The Naked and the Dead**, 1958. This poverty-row production was made on a meager budget of $250,000 and shot in fifteen days, but nevertheless proved successful at the box office. *Author's Note*: Many connected with this little film went on to spectacular film careers. Redford, of course, eventually became a superstar. Francis Ford Coppola, who worked as a crew member and helped to drive an army truck in this film, went on to become a pantheon film director and producer. MacLeod went on to star in TV comedies, and Skerritt (also in his film debut) saw similar success on TV and in feature films. Pollack quit acting and became a director, this film so bonding him with Redford that they would make many films together as director and actor, including **Jeremiah Johnson**, 1972; **The Way We Were**, 1973; **Three Days of the Condor**, 1976; **The Electric Horseman**, 1979 and **Out of Africa**, 1985. Other films that profile the Korean War include **All the Young Men**, 1960; **The Amazing Colossal Man**, 1957; **...And the Earth Did Not Swallow Him**, 1995; **The Bamboo Prison**, 1954; **Battle Circus**, 1953; **Bat-**

tle Flame, 1959; Battle Hymn, 1957; Battle Taxi, 1955; Battle Zone, 1952; Battleground 625, 2005; Before the Deluge, 1954; The Big Chase, 1954; Big Fish, 2003; The Blue Peter, 1957; Bombers B-52, 1957; The Bridges at Toko-Ri, 1954; Canon Cheol-jin's Mission, 1977; Chattahoochee, 1990; Collision Course: Truman vs. MacArthur, 1976 (made-for-TV); Combat Squad, 1953; Cry for Happy, 1961; Day Zero, 2007; Dragonfly Squadron, 1954; Field of Honor, 1986; Fixed Bayonets!, 1951; Flat Top, 1952; For the Boys, 1991; The Front Line, 2011; Geisha Girl, 1952; Give 'Em Hell, Harry!, 1975; The Glory Brigade, 1953; The Great Imposter, 1961; Heartbreak Ridge, 1986; A Hill in Korea, 1956; Hold Back the Night, 1956; The Hook, 1963; The Hunters, 1958; I Die Alone, 2013; I Want You, 1951; Inchon, 1982; Japanese War Bride, 1952; Jet Attack, 1958; Korea Patrol, 1951; The Korean War, 2001 (TV series); Last Exit to Brooklyn, 1989; The Last Picture Show, 1971; Love Is a Many Splendored Thing, 1955; The Manchurian Candidate, 1962; Marines, Let's Go, 1961; M*A*S*H, 1970; M*A*S*H, 1972-1983 (TV series); Mask of the Dragon, 1951; MacArthur, 1977; The McConnell Story, 1955; Men in War, 1957; Men of the Fighting Lady, 1954; Mission over Korea, 1953; The Nun and the Sergeant, 1962; One Minute to Zero, 1952; The Orphan, 2008; Period of Adjustment, 1962; Pork Chop Hill, 1959; The Price of Heaven, 1997 (made-for-TV); Prisoner of War, 1954; The Rack, 1956; Retreat!, 2012; Retreat, Hell!, 1952; The Reluctant Heroes, 1971 (made-for-TV); Sabre Jet, 1953; Sayonara, 1957; Sergeant Ryker, 1968; 71: Into the Fire, 2010; Shang gan ling, 1956; Sniper's Ridge, 1961; Soldiers of Innocence, 1987; Starlift, 1951; The Steel Helmet, 1951; Submarine Command, 1951; Tae Guk Gi: The Brotherhood of War, 2004; Taebaek sanmaek, 1994; Take the High Ground!, 1953; Tank Battalion, 1958; Target Zero, 1955; Time Limit, 1957; Tokyo File 212, 1951; Toward the Unknown, 1956; War Is Hell, 1963; A Yank in Korea, 1951; and The Young and the Brave, 1963. p, Terry Sanders, Denis Sanders; d, Denis Sanders; cast, John Saxon, Robert Redford, Charles Aidman, Sydney Pollack, Tommy Matsuda, Gavin MacLeod, Tom Skerritt, Anthony Ray, William Challee, Nancy Hsueh. Francis Ford Coppola plays an army truck driver. w, Stanford Whitmore; c, Ted D. McCord; m, Bud Shank; ed, John Hoffman; art d, Edgar Lansbury; spec eff, Joe Lombardi.

War Is Hell ★★★ 1963; U.S.; 81m; Allied Artists; B/W; War Drama; Children: Unacceptable; DVD; VHS. Offbeat but absorbing war tale sees Russel as a glory-seeking G.I. sergeant, who leads his platoon on a mission against the enemy during the Korean War (1950-1953). He does not, however, tell his men that a cease-fire was just declared ending the war. He wants to win medals and be hailed a hero. To that end, he sends his men to take an enemy bunker and they take it, but most of the troops are killed. Russel claims he led the raid and that the other survivors are cowards. He expects a medal, but doesn't get it because he is found out. After an officer learns the truth, Russel kills him. The communists, however, have had enough of Russel, and kill him. p, Burt Topper, Ross Hahn; d&w, Topper; cast, Tony Russel, Baynes Barron, Michael Bell, Bobby Byles, Wally Campo, Kei Thin Chung, J.J. Dahner, Judy Dan, Robert Howard, Tony Rich, Topper, Audie Murphy (narrator); c, Jacques Marquette; m, Ronald Stein; ed, Ace Herman; spec eff, Pat Dinga.

The War Is Over HHH 1967; France/Sweden; 121m; Europa Film; Image Entertainment; B/W; Drama/War; Children: Unacceptable; DVD. Tension-filled tale is set following the end of the Spanish Civil War (1936-1939), and Montand, who has fought on the Loyalist side of the war against the fascist legions of Francisco Franco (1892-1975), is a war-weary survivor of that war living in exile in Paris. He is first shown leaving Spain and entering France, but he is stopped at the border by the Guardia Civil, who become suspicious when inspecting his passport and identification papers. He gives the Spanish guards a phone number

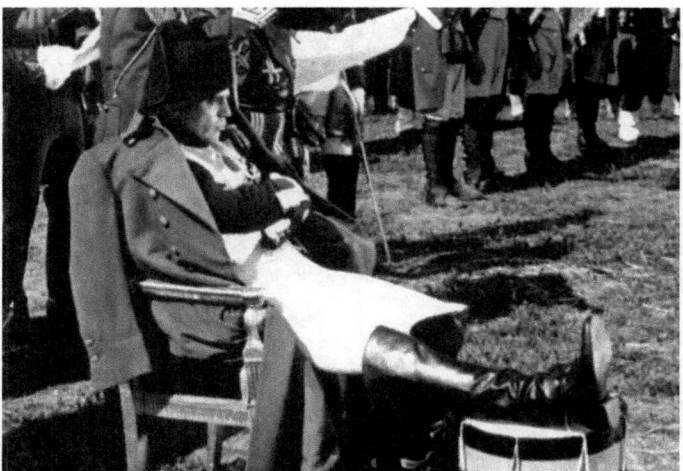

Herbert Lom as Napoleon I (sitting) before the 1812 Battle of Borodino in *War and Peace,* 1956.

in Paris to call and they ring up Bujold, a student in Paris, who is working in a revolutionary group fighting Franco's fascist regime. She corroborates Montand's identification and he is allowed to enter France. After Montand arrives in Paris, he learns to his dismay that many of his friends have been captured in Spain and that his closest associate, Remi, has gone back into Spain at the same time Montand was traveling to Paris. Montand realizes that Remi is going to his death and tries to warn him through Crauchet, who manages all missions for the revolutionaries. Crauchet tells Montand that he cannot bother with Remi as he is, at that moment, organizing a massive general strike. Montand, who has been using the passport belonging to Bujold's father, meets Bujold. They fall in love and spend a night together. He then returns to Thulin, a divorcee who is raising a son, to resume his relationship with her, but his affections for his long-standing mistress is waning in light of Montand's new love for Bujold. Montand then learns that Bujold is involved with another revolutionary faction that is planning an attack in Spain. He wants to join this group, but members in his own cell warn him that he cannot go back to Spain because he will be instantly recognized and killed. Bouise is sent to Spain instead of Montand, who tells his fellow conspirators that the general strike will be ineffective and this causes his associates to now distrust his judgment. After it is learned that Bouise has been killed, Montand is sent to Spain as his replacement. Bujold believes that Montand has been sent on a fool's errand and that the cell leaders simply want to get rid of him, so she warns Thulin. The devoted mistress is now the only one who can warn Montand before he is either captured or killed, so she takes a plane to Spain in order to intercept him and save his life, but even Montand knows that he is going to his doom, a fate he accepts as inevitable. Resnais directs this thriller with great skill, and Montand, Bujold and Thulin render fine performances in what is a bleak and melancholy tale that painfully details the reluctance of the communist fighters to give up a war that has already been irretrievably lost. This well-made film was widely acclaimed and it received an Oscar nomination for Best Screenplay (Semprun). Not related to 1989 and 2010 films with the same name. *Author's Note*: Montand was in real life a fashionable communist and so hated the Franco regime that he refused to appear in any films that were shot on location in Spain while Franco was in power. Other films profiling the Spanish Civil War include The Anarchist's Wife, 2009; Angel of Death, 2002; The Angel Wore Red, 1960; Arch of Triumph, 1948; Arise My Love, 1940; As Long as You Live, 1955; Ay, Carmela!, 1991; Behold a Pale Horse, 1964; Belle Epoque, 1992; Bethune, 1977 (made-for-TV); Black Bread, 2011; Blockade, 1938; Broken Silence, 2001; Butterfly (aka: Butterly's Tongue), 2000; Carmen among the Reds, 1939; Carol's Journey, 2003; Confidential Agent, 1945; Cousin Angelica, 1974; Dancing at Lughnasa, 1998; Death in

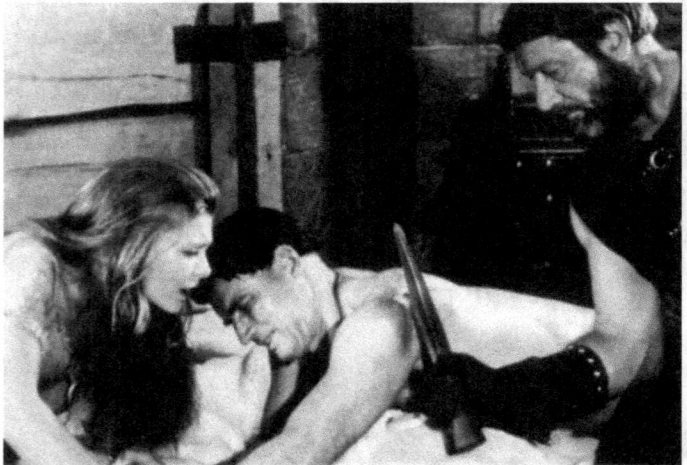

Rosemary Forsyth holds onto Charlton Heston as Richard Boone cauterizes a wound in *The War Lord,* **1965.**

Granada (aka: **The Disappearance of Garcia Lorca**), 1997; **Desire**, 2002; **The Devil's Backbone**, 2001; **Dr. Bethune** (aka: **Bethune: The Making of a Hero**), 1993; **Doomed Souls**, 1975; **Dragon Rapide**, 1986; **El Mar**, 2000; **En la ciudad sin limites**, 2002; **The End of a Mystery**, 2003; **Espionage Agent**, 1939; **The Fallen Sparrow**, 1943; **Fiesta**, 1995; **For Whom the Bell Tolls**, 1943; **A Forbidden God**, 2013; **Front of Madrid**, 1939; **Funf Patronenhulsen (Five Cartridges)**, 1960; **The Girl of Your Dreams**, 1998; **Head in the Clouds**, 2004; **The Heifer**, 1985; **Hemingway & Gellhorn**, 2012 (made-for-TV); **I Am Curious (Yellow)**, 1969; **If They Tell You I Fell**, 1992; **In Praise of Older Women**, 1997; **Ispansi!**, 2011; **The Keep**, 1983; **Land and Freedom**, 1996; **Las 13 rosas**, 2007; **The Last Circus**, 2010; **The Last Train from Madrid**, 1937; **Libertarias**, 1996; **A Life Sold**, 1976; **Little Ashes**, 2008; **The Long Holidays of 1936**, 1976; **Long Live Death**, 1971; **The Long Winter**, 1992; **Lovers of the Arctic Circle**, 1999; **The Madness**, 1976 (made-for-TV); **Madrid**, 1987; **The Man of the Legion**, 1940; **The Mirror**, 1983; **The 100-Year-Old Man Who Climbed Out of the Window and Disappeared**, 2013; **Painless**, 2012; **Pan's Labyrinth**, 2007; **Paul Robeson**, 1979 (made-for-TV); **The Prime of Miss Jean Brodie**, 1969; **Raza**, 1942; **Riders of the Dawn**, 1990 (TV series); **Roads to the South**, 1978; **Shadow of a Hero**, 2015; **Ship of Fools**, 1965; **The Siege of the Alcazar**, 1940; **Slacker**, 1991; **The Sleeping Voice**, 2012; **The Snows of Kilimanjaro**, 1952; **Soldiers of Salamis**, 2004; **Special Correspondents**, 1943; **The Spirit of the Beehive** (1973); **Spitfire**, 1943; **Talk of Angels**, 1998; **There Be Dragons**, 2011; **Thunder Rock**, 1944; **The Time of the Doves**, 1982; **The Tree of Guernica**, 1976; **Under a Blanket of Stars**, 2014; **Valentina**, 1982 (made-for-TV); **Voyage to Nowhere**, 1986; **The War We Left Behind**, 1980; **Wings of the Morning**, 1937; **Year of Enlightenment**, 1988; and **Your Name Poisons My Dreams**, 1996. War violence prohibits viewing by children. **p**, Anatole Dauman, Gisele Rebillon, Catherine Winter, **d**, Alain Resnais; **cast**, Yves Montand, Ingrid Thulin, Genevieve Bujold, Jean Daste, Dominque Rozan, Jean-Francois Remi, Paul Crauchet, Marie Mergey, Jean Bouise, Michel Piccoli, Anouk Ferjac; **w**, Jorge Semprun; **c**, Sacha Vierny; **m**, Giovanni Fusco; **ed**, Eric Pluet, Ziva Postec; **prod d**, Jacques Saulnier.

The War Is Over ★★★ 1989; France/West Germany; 105m; Camera Noire; Color; War Drama; Children: Unacceptable; **DVD**. Grim but intriguing tale begins when the fighting in World War II (1939-1945) is over, but not completely for some German and French soldiers. Bohringer, a German soldier who has gone absent without leave, is befriended by two teenage French boys, Antoine and Julien Hubert, who try unsuccessfully to save his life, and Bohlinger is put to death by the French military. The boys are the real-life sons of director-writer Hubert.

This well-made drama is not related to the 1966 and 2003 films with the same title. **p**, Gerhard Schmidt, Jean-Claude Fleury; **d&w**, Jean-Loup Hubert; **cast**, Richard Bohringer, Antoine Hubert, Julien Hubert, Martin Lamotte, Isabelle Sadoyan, Raoul Billerey, Jean-Francois Derec, Jacques Mathou, Roger Miremont, Marie Pillet, Oliver Nembi, Judith Henry; **c**, Claude Lecomte; **m**, Jurgen Knieper; **ed**, Benedicte Brunet; **prod d**, Thierry Flamand.

The War Lord ★★★★ 1965; U.S.; 123m; UNIV; Color; Historical Drama; Children: Unacceptable; **DVD**; **VHS**. Heston is compelling as a medieval Norman knight of the 11th Century whose his love for a young woman sets in motion a small war. The film opens with Heston and his minions battling invading Frisians and driving them off from a small Druid community. Heston becomes the lord of the area, maintaining order from a castle that towers over the town. When he later sees Forsyth bathing in a stream, he is attracted to her, but soon discovers that she is betrothed to Farentino, the son of the town's leader, MacGinnis. When Forsyth is married, Heston exercises an old custom, *le droit du seigneur*, which allows the local warlord the privilege of first consummating any marriage with a newly wedded bride (this crude and draconian tradition, also depicted in **Braveheart**, 1995). The brief union blossoms into genuine romance as Heston and Forsyth fall in love and Forsyth then refuses to go back to Farentino, who threatens a rebellion. To quell the natives, Heston captures and holds hostage the son of the Frisian king, but Farentino nevertheless attacks Heston's keep. Meanwhile, Stockwell, who is Heston's brother, jealous of his sibling's station and reputation, attempts to wrest control of the countryside. He and Heston do mortal battle and Stockwell is killed. To keep peace, Heston returns the captive prince to the Frisians and also sends Forsyth to them for safety. The vengeance-seeking Farentino, however, continues his attacks, and Heston is wounded in battle. Heston nevertheless escapes with the help of his supporter and friend Boone, and finds Forsyth, both of them fleeing with the hope of finding happiness together. Director Schaffner presents a stark portrait of medieval life in this captivating historical epic. His attention to detail in profiling the period is exact, from its plain, homespun costumes, huge iron swords and other crude implements of the day, as well as stark sets, particularly the dank and uninviting tower castle where Heston lives and holds court. Forceful performances are seen from Heston, Boone, Stockwell and Farentino while Forsyth offers a comforting ray of gentility and tenderness in an otherwise savage society. Produced on a budget of $3.5 million, this film did not fare well at the box office, although it remains a superior period film. *Author's Note*: Schaffner was disappointed by the studio's handling of this film in that it was heavily edited before its release. The director later complained that the injudicious edits considerably damaged the overall look of the film, stating that it had lost "those fragile but always terribly consequential subtleties that you put into a film, so important to character motivation and reaction." The film nevertheless remained one of Heston's favorites, the actor telling this author: "**The War Lord** is a genuine profile of that long-ago age. I appeared in another picture that showed life in the 11th Century called **El Cid** [1961], but that production showed a much more elegant era than what truly existed, more of a Hollywood than a historical portrait." Boone, too, liked his character, telling this author: "I am a strong-arm man in that picture. I do the dirty jobs of the local lord, who was enacted by the magnetic Charlton [Heston]. The way those people lived in those days, without indoor plumbing, no medicine, or any concept of hygiene, was incredible. It is a wonder that they even lived to be about forty years old, the average lifespan in those days. These ignorant people thought they were living full lives, even when they were hacking each other to pieces with broadswords. Of course, if they had radio, TV, cars and refrigerators, their suicide rate would most likely have increased. Everything evens out." Joe Canutt, who was the son of spectacular stuntman Yakima Canutt, doubled for Stockwell in his swordplay with Heston. Stockwell, the brother of Dean Stockwell, makes his debut in this film.

He later became a play producer in Los Angeles to supplement his acting career and, in 1979, produced this author's play, "Last Rites for the Boys." **p**, Walter Seltzer; **d**, Franklin J. Schaffner; **cast**, Charlton Heston, Richard Boone, Rosemary Forsyth, Maurice Evans, Guy Stockwell, Niall MacGinnis, James Farentino, Henry Wilcoxon, Sammy Ross, Woodrow Parfrey, John Alderson, Paul Frees (narrator); **w**, John Collier, Millard Kaufman (based on the play "The Lovers" by Leslie Stevens); **c**, Russell Metty (Panavision; Technicolor); **m**, Hans J. Salter, Jerome Moross; **ed**, Folmar Blangsted; **art d**, Alexander Golitzen, Henry Bumstead; **set d**, Oliver Emert, John McCarthy Jr.; **spec eff**, Albert Whitlock, Jim Danforth.

The War Lover ★★★ 1962; U.S./U.K.; 105m; COL; B/W; War Drama; Children: Unacceptable; **DVD**; **VHS**. Gripping tale sees McQueen as a hotshot American bomber pilot (of a B-17), who loves aerial combat. He is stationed in Britain during World War II (1939-1945), but his co-pilot, Wagner, and his crew members do not like him because of his irresponsible, daredevil ways. They nevertheless respect his flying ability as he survives one mishap after another. One of his missions is aborted because of dense cloud cover, but McQueen ignores orders and flies beneath the clouds to complete his mission, but his following squadron suffers considerable damage, including the loss of one of its B-17s as well as its entire crew. McQueen is forever seeking combat and bristles when he is ordered to drop propaganda leaflets over enemy territory instead of bombs. In defiance, he buzzes his home airfield, which causes his commander to rebuke him. His superiors know McQueen is not a team player and is out for glory, but they also know he is the best pilot in the group so his antics are tolerated. The group's physician is consulted about McQueen's conduct, and the diagnosis is that McQueen is either a courageous leader or a death-seeking psychopath. McQueen takes an interest in Wagner's English girlfriend, Field, but she thinks he's too immature for a serious relationship. Attracted to both McQueen and Wagner, Field finally selects Wagner and they begin an affair, although Field worries that Wagner will leave her forever when his tour of duty ends and he returns to the U.S. Meanwhile, McQueen's risky conduct so alarms his navigator, Cockrell, that they become contentious. McQueen arranges for Cockrell to be transferred to another bomber. Cockrell is then killed in action, which causes Wagner to lose respect for McQueen. Then the group is ordered to bomb Leipzig, and, while completing that long-range bombing run, McQueen's B-17 is badly damaged by flak. The damaged plane barely reaches the English coast with its bomb doors unable to close and a bomb still stuck in its rack. With the plane losing altitude, McQueen notifies sea rescue units to pick up his crew, and then orders all the members to parachute into the English Channel. He remains doggedly at the controls, believing out of arrogance or overconfidence that he can nevertheless bring the bomber to a safe landing. As he approaches the White Cliffs of the Kent coastline, he struggles with the lowering bomber, urging and pleading with it as if it were a reluctant horse, to remain airborne, but, at the last moment, to his horror, sees that he cannot bring the plane above the approaching cliffs as it crashes and explodes into one of the cliffs, killing McQueen in the process. (The film leaves viewers guessing whether McQueen's death was heroic or a suicidal death wish.) Wagner, who has survived, then reunites with Field, telling her that McQueen's end "is what he always wanted." The lovers are last seen walking together. The film did not fare too well at the box office as it was unfavorably compared to other war films depicting B-17 pilots, particularly the classic **Twelve O'Clock High**, 1949. It nevertheless offers an exciting, even mesmerizing portrait of a war-obsessed pilot in the riveting performance from McQueen. Songs: "Roll Me Over" (Robert Musel, Desmond O'Connor), "In Pride of May" (John Jeffreys), "Song of Liberty" (Richard Addinsell, Raymond Anzarut), "Je vous aime" (Henry Bataille, Rene Mercier, Charles Potier). **Author's Note**: McQueen told this author that "my character in **The War Lover** is a nut. The guy loves combat and just can't wait to

Danny DeVito and Kathleen Turner in *The War of the Roses,* **1989.**

get at the enemy. To tell you the truth, I don't think there were too many guys like that in the Second World War, especially those flying B-17s, or they would have been washed out early. Most of the guys I talked to who flew those planes only wanted one thing—to complete their tour of duty (twenty-five missions) and go safely home to their families." McQueen was as much a daredevil on the ground as his character is in this film in the air. When the production was almost completed, McQueen indulged his favorite pastime, race car driving, and, in one high speed run, spun out and crashed his car, luckily emerging with only a split lip. The scar was, however, evident, and he finished his final scenes wearing an oxygen mask while flying his bomber in order to cover the scar on his lip and chin. Three still serviceable B-17s were used in the making of this film, which was shot on location in England. Some actual WWII newsreel footage of B-17s were used briefly in this film, as well as the spectacular belly-landing crash shown at the beginning of **Twelve O'Clock High** (performed by expert pilot Paul Mantz). Stuntman Mike Reilly, who doubled for Wagner when parachuting out of the plane, was killed. Other films profiling bombers chiefly in WWII include **Above and Beyond**, 1953 (U.S. B-29); **Air Force**, 1943 (U.S. B-17); **Battle of Britain**, 1969 (German Dornier, Heinkel and Junker); **The Best Years of Our Lives**, 1946 (U.S. B-17); **Bombardier**, 1943 (U.S. B-17); **Command Decision**, 1948 (U.S. B-17); **Desperate Journey**, 1942 (British Wellington); **Destination Tokyo**, 1943 (U.S. B-25); **Flying Fortress**, 1942 (U.S. B-17); **International Lady**, 1941 (U.S. B-17); **Memphis Belle**, 1990 (U.S. B-17); **Missing Jane**, 2004 (U.S. B-17); **One of Our Aircraft Is Missing**, 1942 (British Wellington); **Pearl Harbor**, 2001 (U.S. B-25); **Strategic Air Command**, 1955 (U.S. B-36; U.S. B-47); **Thirty Seconds over Tokyo**, 1944 (U.S. B-25); **Tora! Tora! Tora!**, 1970 (U.S. B-17); **Twelve O'Clock High**, 1949 (U.S. B-17); and **The Way to the Stars**, 1945 (aka: **Johnny in the Clouds**; U.S. B-17). **p**, Arthur Hornblow, Jr.; **d**, Philip Leacock; **cast**, Steve McQueen, Robert Wagner, Shirley Anne Field, Michael Crawford, Bill Edwards, Gary Cockrell, Chuck Julian, Robert Easton, Al Waxman, Tom Busby; **w**, Howard Koch (based on the novel by John Hersey); **c**, Bob Huke; **m**, Richard Addinsell; **ed**, Gordon Hales; **art d**, Bill Andrews; **set d**, Andrew Low; **spec eff**, Ted Samuels, Wally Veevers.

The War of the Roses ★★★ 1989; U.S.; 116m; FOX; Color; Comedy/Romance; Children: Unacceptable (MPAA: R); **DVD, VHS; IV**. Entertaining comedy begins with DeVito, a callous divorce lawyer, who is of the opinion that marriages are never happy and end up in divorce, but one can survive the ordeal. He tells a client about one of his cases in an attempt to prove his contentions. It involves the divorce of a couple named Rose, Douglas and Turner, who meet at an auction and bid on the same cheap statuette, then go to bed together. Douglas is a wealthy

Martian space ships attacking in *The War of the Worlds,* **1953.**

lawyer and Turner becomes his housewife, spending a lot of money to furnish the house. They have two children, who grow up and leave home. Turner grows weary of just caring for a house so she sells some of her homemade liver pate to a friend and realizes it is the first money she has ever earned. Feeling a streak of independence, Turner asks Douglas for a divorce, but wants to keep the house, which by now is a museum full of unneeded things she has bought over the past seventeen years of their marriage. They go to see DeVito and things go from bad to worse and they are never happy again. This black comedy, expertly helmed by DeVito, was a box office bonanza, producing more than $160.1 million in its initial release against a budget of $50 million, and Douglas and Turner are standouts as the disenchanted couple. Songs: "Only You/And You Alone" (Buck Ram, Ande Rand), "We Wish You a Merry Christmas" (traditional), "Pretty Lady, Lovely Lady" (Nicky Addeo). Mature themes and sexuality prohibit viewing by children. **p**, James L. Brooks, Arnon Milchan, Michael Leeson; **d**, Danny DeVito; **cast**, Michael Douglas, Kathleen Turner, Danny DeVito, Marianne Sagebrecht, Sean Astin, Heather Fairfield, G.D. Spradlin, Peter Donat, Dan Castellaneta, Mary Fogarty, Peter Hansen; **w**, Michael Leeson (based on the novel by Warren Adler); **c**, Stephen H. Burum; **m**, David Newman; **ed**, Lynzee Klingman; **prod d**, Ida Random; **art d**, Mark Mansbridge; **set d**, Anne McCulley; **spec eff**, John Frazier, Lyle Carolus.

The War of the Worlds ★★★★ 1953; U.S.; 85m; PAR; Color; Science Fiction; Children: Unacceptable; **DVD**; **VHS**; **IV**. Superb science fiction thriller brings to vibrant and frightening life the classic H.G. Wells tale of Martians invading Earth. This exciting film opens with a narrative from Frees, who describes how new and sophisticated weapons in the 20th Century have revolutionized modern warfare. Hardwicke then begins to narrate (as he periodically does throughout the film) how Mars has become a dying planet and its living creatures must now find another world to occupy in order to survive. We next see a meteor streaking across the night skies over the small California town of Rosa Linda, crashing into a field. Barry, a scientist at Pacific Tech, who has been fishing nearby with colleagues, learns of the crash and he and two associates go to investigate. When he arrives, he meets fetching Robinson, and her uncle, Martin, a local minister. He and others stand near the meteor, but soon realize that it is too hot to closely examine and Barry and the others depart, planning to return later, but leaving three men on guard. They hear a grinding sound and then see the top of the meteor unscrewing to make an opening for a metallic machine with a cobra-like head and three different colored eyes, supported by an extending metallic goose-neck. The three men attempt to befriend this strange visitor, walking slowly toward it, calling out greetings and waving a small

white flag of truce. The cobra-like head of the machine then focuses upon the three men and suddenly fires a blinding heat ray that immediately vaporizes the approaching men. The ray also destroys a nearby electrical tower that causes all of the power in nearby Rosa Linda to shut down. Further, Barry notices that everyone's watch has stopped as has all of the town clocks and that the compass owned by Sande, the local sheriff, is now pointing away from magnetic north and toward the crash site of the meteor. At that site, a Martian machine floats from the meteor while two other meteors crash nearby, and two more deadly machines emerge from them to form a formation of three floating machines all with the same cobra-like head and goose necks stemming from the saucer-like crafts and all spitting out devastating heat rays that vaporize everything they touch. Nothing is left of the disintegrated humans and objects except a black smear on the ground. A heavily armed U.S. Marine unit surrounds the crash site to confront the alien machines, but, before the military takes action, Martin surprises the stunned humans by stepping forth from a barricaded position, walking calmly toward the first of the three floating machines, quoting the Bible (Psalm 23), and telling the Martians that he comes in peace. His voice is stilled by the Martian machine that vaporizes Martin with a blast of its heat ray, each blast accompanied by the eerie sound of a pulsating screech. The Marines open fire, but their attack proves utterly ineffective as the Martian craft are shielded by an impenetrable force field, and bullets, shells and missiles harmlessly bounce away from the floating targets. In response, the Martians return fire, vaporizing and disintegrating weapons and men with ease, and the remaining military units retreat. It is learned that the Martians have landed spacecraft all around the world in their global invasion of Earth. Meanwhile, the Rosa Linda area remains under attack and, to escape the area, Barry and Robinson find a small plane and take flight. To avoid swooping Air Force jets attacking the Martian ships, Barry is forced to fly at tree-top level and crashes the plane. He and Robinson find the area devastated as Martian ships float over the landscape firing heat rays at anything that moves. They discover an abandoned farmhouse where Barry comforts Robinson over the loss of her uncle and both draw closer together while Robinson makes Barry some breakfast. Then another Martian ship crashes, its meteor shell landing next to the farmhouse and plowing the earth around it into the building to half collapse the farmhouse and where Barry and Robinson survive in the wreckage. The Martian ship sends an electronic eye extending on a long metallic cable into the farmhouse, searching for any occupants. Seeing this, Barry takes an ax and chops the cable, examining its severed eye and cable. At that moment, a living Martian appears in the shadows, its pipe-like arm extending a hand consisting of three suckered fingers, resting that hand on Robinson's shoulder. When she sees this grotesque-looking limb, Robinson screams in fright and Barry throws the ax at it, striking the creature and wounding it as it screams in agony and flees through the murky ruins of the farmhouse. Barry and Robinson then barely escape the farmhouse before the hovering spacecraft blasts it to pieces with its devastating heat ray. Barry has taken with him the camera eye and part of its cable. Meanwhile, the Martian ships are shown throughout the world, destroying everything in their path, where they routinely destroy some of the world's great landmarks. (A photo shows the Eiffel Tower in Paris being snapped like a tree branch by a Martian attack and stock footage of worldwide disasters and battles is employed in montage to simulate other horrific attacks.) Barry returns to the laboratory at Pacific Tech where he and other scientists examine the electronic eye he has captured, as well as some Martian blood that has been left on Robinson's scarf after Barry wounded the creature. The scientists conclude, after testing the electronic eye and the blood sample that the Martians see Earth and its natives as magnified objects and that the creatures are anemic, a physical weakness that Earthlings might use to somehow defeat the invaders. Everything the armies of the world do, however, make no impact upon the Martians or impede the ongoing carnage created by the alien invaders. As the Martian ships advance toward Los Angeles, the White House decides to use the atomic bomb to destroy the Martians. A U.S. Air Force Flying Wing is assigned the job of dropping the bomb and it is shown flying toward the outskirts of L.A. (Footage of a Northrup YB-49 Flying Wing is used here; there were only two of these jet-and-piston-engine planes built shortly after WWII and both later crashed, but their aerial techniques were later incorporated into the U.S. B-2 Stealth Bomber produced in the 1990s.) Barry and his fellow scientists are with Tremayne, a U.S. Army general, when all observe from a fortified position the Flying Wing approach a bevy of the advancing Martian ships and where the bomb is dropped, creating a huge cloud of smoke. To the horror of the observers, the bomb is wholly ineffective in piercing the force fields shielding the Martian craft that sail undamaged through the atomic dust cloud and proceed to attack and destroy large parts of Los Angeles as its inhabitants flee to the hills. The Pacific Tech scientists conclude that the Martians will conquer the planet within six days, one day less than the Bible sets the time for God's creation of Earth. The scientists, however, still believe that they can find the Martian's vulnerability and they preserve their research and instruments, packing their equipment onto trucks. As they drive through the ruins of Los Angeles, a mob of looters attacks the caravan, stopping the trucks and taking away the scientific equipment. In the struggle, Barry is separated from Robinson. Barry later searches through the devastated streets for Robinson, finding her in a church where he, she and others pray for deliverance as the screech of the Martian heat rays are heard in the distance, sounding the doom of the human race. The screeching sounds of the Martian attack rays, however, lessn, and then come to stop as crashing noises are heard. An eerie silence envelops the city. Leaving the church, Barry, Robinson and others see a Martian ship wobbly in the air and then crash into a building, then another falls to earth and yet another. The Martians are now all dying, ironically from the Earth's bacteria and viruses (as stated by Wells in his novel), against which human beings have long earlier developed immunity. Hardwicke ends this startlingly exciting film with the narration: "It is the littlest things that God in his wisdom had put upon the Earth that saved mankind." Haskin directs this thriller with great skill, merging the shocking Martian attacks with realistic dramatic scenes that show a desperate humanity attempting to survive, along with many tender moments between Barry and Robinson, who are standouts in their roles. The film deservedly received an Oscar for its wonderful special effects and received Oscar nominations for Best Editing (Douglas) and Best Sound Recording (Loren L. Ryder). The film more than recouped its $2 million budget in its initial box office release in the U.S. alone. The story was remade in 1981 in a Polish production, again as a TV series in 1988, in an independent production in 2005 titled **H.G. Wells' War of the Worlds**, and yet again as a technically lavish feature film in 2005, starring Tom Cruise. Song: "Flop-Eared Mule (Without Calls)" (Zip Wilson). *Author's Note*: Pal, who had produced two outstanding science fiction films, **Destination Moon**, 1950, and **When Worlds Collide**, 1951, had long wanted to film the Wells novel, and was amazed to learn that Paramount had owned the film rights for the book since 1925 when that studio's then foremost director, Cecil B. DeMille, intended to make the film version. DeMille's many film projects, however, put the production on delay and it was forgotten. The story was assigned to Russian director Sergei Eisenstein in 1930 when he briefly visited the U.S., but that production never got off the ground. Pantheon director Alfred Hitchcock thought to make this film in the late 1930s, telling this author: "I was having breakfast years ago with H.G. Wells on the Blue Train going down to the South of France, and I was discussing with him about making *The War of the Worlds* into a movie. This was way back about 1936 or 1937. 'No,' he said, 'if that had to be made into a film, I'd have to rewrite it and invent all new weapons because the weapons I put into *The War of the Worlds* have all been used—poison gas and all the rest.' So, he declined to think about making a picture at that time. The picture George Pal produced [in 1953] comes up with all those new weapons that Wells did not want to think about and it is a very good movie that still keeps the Wells story intact, except

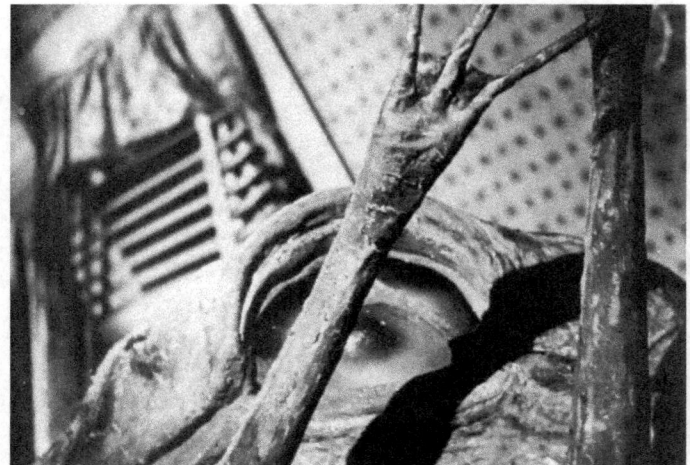

A one-eyed, three-fingered Martian in *The War of the Worlds*, 1953.

that the original story was set in London and Pal relocated the setting to California. The audience, however, has a hard time getting involved on a personal level with such stories. They must be detached, like distant spectators watching a sports event. They find it impossible to relate to these alien creatures, so these pictures become impersonal things to watch and not to be closely involved with. To be sure, there are elements of horror and mystery there, but they are not of this earth. At one point, another pantheon director-actor, Orson Welles, was approached with the idea that he helm a film based upon the Wells classic. Welles told this author: "Some producers came to me and energetically pressured me to make the Wells story into a picture, but I wanted no more to do with that tale. I had produced a very controversial radio version of that story [a dramatic one-hour presentation by Welles' Mercury Theater Productions, which was aired by CBS on October 30, 1938]. We reported the Martian invasion as if it was actually happening. We had eye-witnesses describing how the Martians were destroying everything in their path and reporters who announced news bulletins as the Martians attacked everywhere. Even though we stated several times in that broadcast that it was a dramatic presentation and not reality, a lot of folks tuning in did not hear those announcements, and thought it was a real event. Hundreds of people, maybe a lot more, panicked and did a lot of desperate things and all hell broke loose later and where I got into a lot of trouble with government people [based on complaints received by the Federal Communications Commission]. No, sir, I did not want to relive that experience and remind everyone how we scared the hell out of America, even though that was never our intent." Nevertheless, that radio broadcast forever established the media persona of the brilliant Welles, who went on to become one of the world's most illustrious filmmakers. When Pal approached Paramount, he received DeMille's endorsing consent (and Pal later paid homage to DeMille by showing the title of that director's latest film, **Samson and Delilah**, 1949, on the marquee of a theater in the film), and was given the rights to film the story, with Paramount as its releasing studio. Pal was then shocked to learn that Paramount owned only the rights to film a silent version of the story. He contacted the author's son, Frank Wells, who graciously gave Pal the rights to make a sound film version and the production went ahead. Of the $2 million budget Pal had at hand to make the film, he used $1,300,000 for the elaborate special effects, but even then, Pal was cautious in how he spent the money. Gordon Jennings, the special effects wizard for the film, originally developed the Martian ships as the tripod-walking craft originally described by Wells in his novel. Pal, however, thought such spacecraft would be too expensive and opted for a hovercraft vehicle with a snakelike head and cable protruding from it, firing yellow rays from the head and green rays from the body to represent the alien space ships. About twenty wires were used for each ship to maneuver them in mid-

Tim Robbins, Tom Cruise and Dakota Fanning in *War of the Worlds,* **2005.**

air, while other wires powered the lights and mechanisms, particularly the flashing heat rays fired by the ships. The rays consisted of burning welding wire with sparks flying from it when a blowtorch was applied to it. Albert Nozaki designed the spacecraft, combining the images of swans, cobras and manta rays to make up their overall appearance. The ships were made out of copper and no longer exist, having been donated to a Boy Scout copper drive. Jennings and his assistants created an amazing array of Martian images, suspending the hovering spaceships on wires as they move over landscapes and along city streets, creating destruction everywhere. He used for these scenes life-size models of the spacecraft, as well as exacting miniatures, glass paintings, and matte backgrounds with startling results. Sound experts Gene Garvin and Harry Lindgren produced the pulsating and piercing sound of the heat rays emanating from the craft by recording three specific notes played on three guitars that were then played backward. They also created the Martian's scream (when injured by Barry with the axe) by combining a woman's scream with dry ice scraped across a microphone, which were then played backward. They created similar unearthly sounds for the unscrewing of the meteor before the spacecraft was released, as well as the sounds of collapsing buildings and jarring explosions. To heighten the visual tension, Pal wanted to show the last portion of the film, from the dropping of the atom bomb to the crashing of the Martian ships in 3-D, but Paramount refused, concluding that that technique was nothing more than a passing fad. Jennings never saw his superlative special effects on the screen as he died on January 11, 1953, at age fifty-seven, seven months before this film was released. The small town of Corona, California, substituted for the fictitious Rosa Linda, and St. Brendan's Catholic Church (310 Van Ness Avenue, Los Angeles) was the setting for the climatic ending of this superlative film. Other location shots were taken of the rolling hills outside of El Sereno, an L.A. suburb, as well as some of its thoroughfares. Pal got permission to use the Harbor Freeway, which had just been completed, and his crew and cast members were permitted to drive on it and photograph some scenes before it was opened to the public. The planets the Martians consider invading, which are shown at the beginning of the film, were meticulously painted by Chesley Bonestell, who had provided engineering drawings for the construction of San Francisco's Golden Gate Bridge and who later became an esteemed matte artist for film productions. He was selected by Pal in his meticulous research after the producer saw Bonstell's astronomical paintings of the other planets in our solar system that appeared in a 1944 edition of *Life Magazine*. Pal invariably found a way to insert the image of cartoon character Woody Woodpecker in his films. Pal was close friends with that character's creator, Walter Lantz. Woody appears in this film in a tree at the beginning of the film just as the first Martian meteor flies over it. The Wells estate owners were so impressed with

this film that they offered Pal the selection of any other Wells novel Pal might want to be convert into a film and he chose one, which resulted in another fine science fiction film, **The Time Machine**, 1960. Other films profiling Mars and Martians include **Aelita: Queen of Mars**, 1929; **Alfred Hitchcock Presents**, 1955-1962 (TV series; "Human Interest Story," 1959 episode); **The Angry Red Planet**, 1959; **Attack from Mars**, 1988; **Batman: The Brave and the Bold**, 2008-2011 (TV series); **Ben X**, 2007; **Bill & Ted's Bogus Journey**, 1991; **Contamination**, 1980; **The Day Mars Invaded Earth**, 1963; **D-Day on Mars**, 1966 (made-for-TV); **Devil Girl from Mars**, 1954; **Doom**, 2005; **Duck Dodgers**, 2003- (TV series); **Five Million Years to Earth**, 1968; **Flash Gordon's Flight to Mars**, 1938; **Flight to Mars**, 1951; **Flying Disc Man from Mars**, 1950; **Flying Saucer Rock 'N' Roll**, 2006; **Frankenstein Meets the Space Monster**, 1965; **Ghosts of Mars**, 2011; **The Great Martian War, 1913-1917**, 2013 (made-for-TV); **The Infinite Worlds of H.G. Wells**, 2001 (TV miniseries); **Invaders from Mars**, 1953; **It! The Terror from beyond Space**, 1958; **John Carter**, 2012; **Justice League**, 2001-2006 (TV series; "Secret Origins," 2001 episode; "Secret Origins: Part II," 2001 episode; "Injustice for All," 2002 episode; "The Cat and the Canary," 2005 episode); **Looney Tunes: Back in Action**, 2003; **Los astronautas**, 1964; **Mars Attacks!**, 1996; **Mars Attacks the World**, 1938; **Mars Needs Moms**, 2011; **Mars Needs Women**, 1967 (made-for-TV); **A Martian Christmas**, 2008; **The Martian Chronicles**, 1980 (TV miniseries); **Martians Go Home**, 1989; **Mercano the Martian**, 2002; **Missile Monsters**, 1958; **Mission to Mars**, 2000; **Murdoch Mysteries**, 2008- (TV series: "The Annoying Red Planet," 2008 episode); **My Favorite Martian**, 1963-1966 (TV series); **My Favorite Martian**, 1999; **Pajama Party**, 1964; **The Purple Monster Strikes**, 1945; **Quartermass and the Pit**, 1958 (TV miniseries); **Radio-Mania**, 1922; **Rocketship X-M**, 1950; **Santa Claus Conquers the Martians**, 1964; **Santo vs. la invasion de los marcianos**, 1967; **Satan's Satellites**, 1958 (feature version of serial **Zombies of the Stratosphere**); **Tales of Tomorrow**, 1951-1953 (TV series; "Test Flight," 1951 episode; "Appointment on Mars," 1952 episode; "Plague from Space," 1952 episode); **Tracker**, 2001-2002 (TV series); **A Trip to Mars**, 1918; **Twilight Zone**, 1961-1964 (TV series; "People Are Alike All Over," 1960 episode; "Mr. Dingle, the Strong," 1961 episode); **The War of the Worlds: Next Century**, 1981; **The War of the Worlds**, 1988 (TV series); **The War of the Worlds**, 2005; **Warlords of the Deep**, 1978; **Wehan Ke Log**, 1967; **The Wizard of Mars**, 1965; and **Zombies of the Stratosphere**, 1952 (serial). **p**, George Pal; **d**, Byron Haskin; **cast**, Gene Barry, Ann Robinson, Les Tremayne, Bob Cornthwaite, Sandro Giglio, Lewis Martin, Houseley Stevenson Jr., Walter Sande, Paul Frees, William Phipps, Henry Brandon, Jack Kruschen, Sir Cedric Hardwicke (commentator); **w**, Barre Lyndon (based on the novel by H.G. Wells); **c**, George Barnes (Technicolor); **m**, Leith Stevens; **ed**, Everett Douglas; **art d**, Hal Pereira, Albert Nozaki; **set d**, Sam Comer, Emile Kuri; **spec eff**, Gordon Jennings, Wallace Kelley, Paul Lerpae, Farciot Edouart, Ivyl Burks, Jan Domela, Irmin Roberts, Walter Hoffman, Chesley Bonestell.

The War of the Worlds ★★★ 2005; U.S.; 116m; DreamWorks/PAR; Color; Science Fiction; Children: Unacceptable (MPAA: PG-13); **BD**; **DVD**; **IV**. Sumptuous and ultraviolent production retells the Wells classic science fiction tale of Martians invading Earth. Cruise gives an outstanding portrayal of a working-class father desperately attempting to save the lives of his children during the devastating nightmare of that bloody and destructive invasion. Cruise works as a crane operator and longshoreman in Bayonne, New Jersey. He is divorced from wife Otto and has been estranged from his two children, his ten-year-old daughter, Fanning, and teenage son, Chatwin. Otto drops the two children off at Cruise's home before she makes a visit to her parents in Boston, Massachusetts. Cruise attempts to bond with the two children while they notice unusual weather patterns, especially dangerous lightning strikes occurring during a clear day. Cruise then hears a commotion at a square in the town and goes to investigate with hundreds of other people. A building has been damaged and the earth begins to move in the square as the cemented roadway breaks away, and from the earth emerges a huge, towering Martian machine, walking on three mechanical legs, this strange machine called a Tripod (as they were originally described in the 1898 novel by H.G. Wells). The walking machine fires heat rays that disintegrate humans running before it, and Cruise, who races down streets along with others, narrowly escapes the purging attacks. To take refuge and shield his children, Cruise drives to Otto's suburban home with Fanning and Chatwin. The next morning, Cruise sees a 747 crash in the street outside of the house and, while investigating, learns from a news crew that the three-legged Martian machines are everywhere, destroying structures and thousands of human beings in London, Washington, D.C., New York and elsewhere and that the Martians entered the machines inside capsules sent Earthward by the lightning strikes. Cruise then has difficulty with patriotic Chatwin, who insists that he join the U.S. armed forces battling the alien invaders. While they are driving from the area, a mob stops their car and appropriates it. They make their way to the Hudson Ferry, which is packed with desperate people and which is sunk when it attempts to leave the wharf by a three-legged Tripod. Cruise then is challenged to decide whether to protect his daughter or prevent his son from joining the Marines en route to battle the Martians. He remains with Fanning as Chatwin disappears in the rush to join the military. The ensuing battle is one-sided as the Marines and their supporters are all but wiped out by the attacking Tripods, which have energy shields that make them invulnerable to attacks by any Earthly weapons. As they flee, Cruise and Fanning are offered shelter by farmer Robbins, who tells Cruise that he believes they can learn the weaknesses of the aliens by observing them since Robbins' half-ruined house is located in the camp of the Martian Tripods. They hide from the Martians that send probes into to the basement of the house, and then Robbins has a nervous breakdown after witnessing how the aliens are scooping up human beings, crushing them in a giant hopper to use their human tissue and blood to fertilize a red weed (a fictional plant on Mars that survives on blood and which has given the planet its red hue observed by astronomers for centuries). Robbins, who has gone mad, begins loudly raving and, fearing that Martians will overhear his outbursts, and, to protect himself and Fanning, Cruise kills him. An alien probe discovers the pair sleeping and Cruise uses an axe to dismantle the probe. Fanning, however, panics and runs outside where a Tripod scoops her up into a basket. Cruise then allows himself to be captured so that he can join his captured daughter and others. The Tripod selects Cruise to be crushed to pulp, and he is about to be sent into a tube for that purpose (where others are crushed as one might squeeze the juice from an orange, one of the many gory scenes in this horrific film). Cruise, however, has brought along a number of grenades that he releases into the scoop, and while he is saved by others, the grenades explode, causing the basket holding the prisoners to release them. Cruise and Fanning then make their way to Boston, a city ravaged by the Tripods, but where they see the alien red weeds dying and the Tripods collapsing. When Cruise sees birds landing atop a still moving Tripod, he alerts a nearby military unit that the Tripod has lost its protective energy shield. The troops then bombard and destroy the Tripod that tumbles in a heap to the ground. Cruise and Fanning then arrive at the home of Otto's parents to see Otto and her family members, along with Chatwin, waiting for them. They rush into each other's arms and Cruise then learns that commonplace bacteria on Earth has brought about the mass destruction of the invading Martians, bacteria to which human beings long ago have become immune. Pantheon director Spielberg presents a truly frightening film, but, as was the case with his futuristic **A.I. Artificial Intelligence**, 2001, he presents so much violence that it becomes offensively gratuitous, albeit, as usual, his production values are superb. Cruise's riveting performance of a stunned and protective father is one of his best (and this film proved to be his most financially successful film), and he receives fine support by stellar performances from Fanning, Chatwin and Rob-

Tom Cruise trapped in a beam of Martian light in *The War of the Worlds,* 2005.

bins. The special effects are outstanding, so much so that they often overshadow the live-action human story, which was not the case in Spielberg's other fine films involving space visitors, **Close Encounters of the Third Kind**, 1977, and **E.T.: The Extra-Terrestrial**, 1982. The film received Oscar nominations for Best Special Effects (Blitstein, Brink, Repecka, Mahan); Best Sound Mixing (Andy Nelson, Anna Behlmer, Ron Judkins); and Best Sound Editing. It was a huge box office smash, earning more than $591.7 million against a budget of $132 million, much of the paying audience being video game enthusiasts (and where Spielberg has been active in such productions). Songs: "Little Deuce Coupe" (Brian Wilson, Roger Christian), "Hushabye Mountain" (Richard M. Sherman, Robert B. Sherman), "Flatline" (Jeffrey Scott Harber, Jayce Alexander Basques, William Peng, Drew Dehaven Hall), "If I Ruled the World" (Leslie Bricusse, Cyril Ornadel), "Nobody Move" (Michael Ashby, Benjamin Mallon, Eric Joy, William Sherwin, Omari Edwards, Glenn Kuchenbeiser), "Enigma Vibe 2" (Nicholas Carr), "Sailor Moon BGM" (Arisawa Takanori), "Inferno" (Santino), "Fa Wat" (Christopher Shawn King). *Author's Note*: A great deal of research and preparation went into this lavishly appointed production, but the director shot it in a whirlwind seventy-two days. On-location shooting took place in New York, New Jersey, Connecticut, Virginia and California. The scene where the first Tripod erupts from the roadway was shot at Ferry and Merchant Streets and Wilson Avenue in Newark, N.J. **p**, Kathleen Kennedy, Colin Wilson; **d**, Steven Spielberg; **cast**, Tom Cruise, Dakota Fanning, Tim Robbins, Miranda Otto, Justin Chatwin, Rick Gonzalez, Yul Vazquez, Lenny Venito, Lisa Ann Walter, Ann Robinson, Gene Barry; **w**, Josh Friedman, David Koepp (based on the novel by H.G. Wells); **c**, Janusz Kaminski; **m**, John Williams; **ed**, Michael Kahn; **prod d**, Rick Carter; **art d**, Tony Fanning, Doug J. Meerdink, Andrew Menzies, Norman Newberry; **set d**, Anne Kuljian; **spec eff**, David Blitstein, Connie Brink, Gintar Repecka, Shane Mahan.

The War Wagon ★★★ 1967; U.S.; 96m; Batjac/UNIV; Color; Western; Children: Unacceptable; **BD**; **DVD**; **VHS**; **IV**. Rousing western opens when Wayne is released from prison after having been framed by Cabot, a greedy mine owner. He returns to his ranch and is intent on recouping the gold that Cabot stole from him. There he makes a deal with Douglas, who had shot him five years earlier when Douglas was in league with Cabot. Douglas agrees to partner with Wayne against Cabot and steal a $500,000 gold dust shipment being transported in a heavily guarded armored stagecoach called a "war wagon." Douglas, meanwhile, is offered a hefty bribe by Cabot to kill Wayne, but Douglas decides his share of the gold would be a lot more, so he remains loyal to Wayne. Their friendly rivalry and partnership is learned by Cabot's men, and there is a gunfight in which both Wayne and Douglas survive.

Kirk Douglas and John Wayne in *The War Wagon*, 1967.

The partners then enlist three helpers: Keel, a wise-cracking Indian; Walker, an alcoholic dynamite expert, and Wynn, a former employee of Cabot's, who wants to get even with him. Wayne also enlists the aid of local Indians eager to go on the warpath against Cabot for his efforts to relocate them off of their reservation so he can get their land which may contain more gold. Wayne has Wagner set explosives at a bridge the war wagon is to cross, and, after it explodes, some of Cabot's men guarding the wagon are killed. Cabot takes control of a rapid-firing Gatling gun on the wagon, but is killed when the wagon crashes, and Wayne and his partners recover the gold. Wynn hides the gold in flour sacks as the Indians then turn against Wayne to get the gold. Another blast kills some of the Indians and Wayne is injured by a gun shot. A horse carrying the gold dust becomes frightened and runs away, leaving a trail of gold dust and flour that is recovered by the Indians. The gold had been theirs all along because Cabot had stolen it from their land. Wayne and his partners are left with only about a fifth of the fortune for which they risked their lives, but they settle for that, instead of nothing. The film borrows from other gold-seeker productions, including elements of **The Treasure of the Sierra Madre**, 1948, but offers its own unique brand of action (especially a wild barroom brawl where Douglas swings from a chandelier), and Wayne and Douglas are very good together as friendly enemies. The film was a box office hit, earning more than $6 million in its initial release. Song: "Ballad of the War Wagon" (music: Dimitri Tiomkin; lyrics: Ned Washington). *Author's Note*: This was the third and final film in which Wayne and Douglas appear together, the previous two productions being **In Harm's Way**, 1965, and **Cast a Giant Shadow**, 1966. Wayne had nothing but praise for his co-star in this film when telling this author that "Kirk [Douglas] plays a very shifty character in **The War Wagon**, the kind of role, I think, he likes most, one where the viewer never really knows whether he is going to turn out to be good or bad. He has been keeping them wondering for a lot of years with roles like that." Wayne had a difficult time in performing some of his more energetic feats in the action scenes of this film as he had had a lung and several ribs removed in a cancer operation in 1964, as a result of his lifelong chain-smoking. He proclaimed at that time that he had "beaten the Big C [cancer]," but the same disease would claim his life fifteen years later. **p**, Marvin Schwartz; **d**, Burt Kennedy; **cast**, John Wayne, Kirk Douglas, Howard Keel, Robert Walker, Jr., Keenan Wynn, Bruce Cabot, Joanna Barnes, Bruce Dern, Gene Evans, Sheb Wooley; **w**, Clair Huffaker (based on his novel *Badman*); **c**, William H. Clothier (Panavision; Technicolor); **m**, Dimitri Tiomkin; **ed**, Harry Gerstad; **art d**, Alfred Sweeney; **set d**, Ray Moyer; **spec eff**, Albert Whitlock.

Warlock ★★★★ 1959; U.S.; 121m; FOX; Color; Western; Children: Unacceptable; **BD**; **DVD**; **VHS**; **IV**. Though this outstanding western profiles as role models the legendary Wyatt Earp (1848-1929), played by Fonda, Doc Holliday (1851-1887), essayed by Quinn, and others of the real Old West, it also presents a good psychological tale that probes the emotional motivations of these celebrated lawmen and gunslingers. The setting is a small Utah mining town called Warlock in 1881, and its law-abiding citizens are plagued by a gang of lawless cowboys led by ruthless rancher Drake. Whenever these hellions arrive in Warlock, they make it their pleasure to shoot up the place and even commit a random killing. One deputy sheriff after another standing up to them (as is shown in the opening scene when Coy is physically degraded and then packed onto a horse and driven out of town) is bullied and humiliated into leaving town. The irate citizens have had enough and they hire top gunman Fonda as their town marshal, giving him a free hand to keep law and order at any price. He is paid a meager wage, which he supplements by establishing a gambling and saloon operation that is overseen by his right-hand man and closest friend, Quinn, who is also a fast-draw artist. Fonda, when meeting with the town leaders, tells them that they will initially be grateful for the protection he provides for them. They will, he points out, eventually tire of his total authority in acting as lawman, judge and jury and meting out justice as he sees fit. They will, Fonda assures them, want him to leave after realizing that his authority is all-powerful and he will then depart, which has been his lifestyle as he and Quinn nomadically move throughout the West. Ford, a crusty old self-appointed judge, condemns Fonda, even though he admits that Fonda "is a decent man." Although she does not approve of Fonda's new authority, Michaels, a beautiful single woman, is attracted to him and he to her. Meanwhile the club-footed Quinn, who idolizes Fonda, prepares lavish rooms for him upstairs from their newly opened saloon, the French Palace. (We see them arriving in town with that sign to indicate that that operation accompanies Fonda and Quinn wherever Fonda becomes the town marshal, not dissimilar to how Wyatt Earp and his brothers operated in the Old West when moving from town to town, Ellsworth, Wichita and Dodge City in Kansas, and Tombstone, Arizona.) Drake and his undisciplined cowboys arrive in Warlock to have some rowdy fun, but they are met by Fonda, who tells them that he will shoot and kill anyone who draws a gun, unless he himself is killed, and he backs up his promise when confronting Kelley, who is Drake's fastest gun. Kelley challenges Fonda in the French Palace, mocking Fonda's gold-plated six-guns, but he soon learns that Fonda is faster on the draw and, after Fonda gets the drop on him, Kelley drops his six-gun to the floor, whistling at Fonda's amazing speed. (Kelley's character is called "Curly" and he is playing a role model of western gunslinger William "Curly Bill" Brocious, 1845-1882, who was one of Wyatt Earp's adversaries in Tombstone, and Drake's character is the role model for that town's gang leader, Ike Clanton, 1847-1887.) With Drake and his minions subdued, the cowboys depart the town, but without one of their members, Widmark, who has grown tired of the gang's wild behavior, including that of his brother, Gorshin, who is one of Drake's cowboys (and whose character is the role model for outlaw Billy Clanton, 1862-1881). Widmark decides not to return to the ranch and remains in town where the townsfolk look upon him suspiciously and where no one trusts him. Meanwhile, Quinn learns that Malone (whose character is based upon "Big Nose" Kate Fisher, 1850-1940, a notorious prostitute who was the on-and-off mistress of John Henry "Doc" Holliday) is traveling toward Warlock in a stagecoach, accompanied by gunfighter Gorss, who is the brother of another gunslinger slain earlier by Fonda at the urging of Quinn after Malone left Quinn for that dead gunman. Quinn rides into the countryside to await the arrival of the stagecoach, which, ironically, is stopped by Gorshin and another cowboy working for Drake, both intending to rob the coach. They order the passengers to alight, and, after Gorss steps from the coach, he is shot dead by Quinn, who wields a rifle while hiding behind some rocks. Gorshin and his companion are startled and order the coach to proceed while they gather up its strongbox and ride off. Gorshin and his accomplice are later identified by Malone when she arrives in Warlock and they are arrested, but, after a brief trial, released under pressure from Drake. Malone, however, believes that Quinn was behind the murder of Gorss, although all she has to go on is her intuition. Sanders, who is the sheriff for the entire county, arrives in Warlock and disapproves of Fonda, saying that he is nothing more than a killer-for-hire, and he offers the badge of deputy sheriff to anyone who has the courage to take the job. When no one responds, Widmark asks for the job and Sanders swears him into the office and where Widmark now makes his office at the town jail. He is, however, in competition with Fonda and knows it, as well as with Quinn, who deeply resents Widmark undermining Fonda's authority. Gorshin then arrives in Warlock, calling Fonda to the street as he attempts to take revenge for his arrest in the stagecoach robbery. Widmark confronts his brother, telling Gorshin to leave town. When Gorshin tells Widmark that he is siding with Fonda, Widmark replies: "I ain't backing him because you're my brother. I ain't backing you because you're wrong." Widmark then stands helplessly by as Fonda appears in the street and all but begs Gorshin and two other cowboys not to draw on him. Gorshin, however, goes for his gun and the lightning-fast Fonda shoots and kills him, along with another cowboy. Kelley and others then arrive in town and post their own proclamations, claiming that they are "regulators" entitled to enforce their brand of law the same way Fonda metes out his own type of justice. Fonda ignores these taunts as he now considers quitting his dangerous profession by marrying and settling down with Michaels, as both have fallen in love. This vexes the possessive Quinn no end, who wants to go on and on with Fonda to clean up one town after another. When Quinn learns that Drake and his cowboys are attempting to take over the town by shooting down Widmark, he prevents Fonda from going to Widmark's aid. Widmark has been earlier wounded in his gun hand by the vicious Drake, who had driven a knife through it, and he realizes that he will not be much of a match for Drake and his gunmen. Kelley, however, who has his own sense of justice, goes to Widmark and promises him "a fair fight." Widmark then steps into the street, removing the bandage from his gun hand and confronts Drake. Several of Drake's back-shooting cowboys, however, are positioned in hiding places on the street, but, when they go for their guns, all are stopped by townsmen, who have decided to support their deputy sheriff, as well as Kelley, who has knocked out one of Drake's men hiding in a wagon. Drake, who is now alone in facing Widmark, goes for his gun, but Widmark, diving to earth, shoots and kills Drake. He has now emerged a town hero and is held in higher esteem than paid killer Fonda. At this time, Fonda calls it quits with Quinn after being held in his room at gunpoint so he could not go to Widmark's aid. He has also learned that Malone's accusations about Quinn are correct, that Quinn arranged for him to shoot down Malone's former lover. Quinn takes to drinking and, before Fonda can leave town, confronts his former idol, telling Fonda that he is the faster gunslinger and that he has saved Fonda's life countless of times. He goads Fonda into a gunfight and is mortally shot by Fonda, who then carries Quinn's body into the French Palace where he forces Ford and other townspeople to sing "Rock of Ages" in honor of Quinn, who has died in Fonda's arms. The next day, Fonda confronts Widmark, drawing both gold-plated guns faster than Widmark can respond, but, on each occasion, Fonda throws the two guns into the dust of the street to signify that he has quit his role as a gunfighter. He then mounts his horse and rides slowly from Warlock. Dymtryk directs this western saga with great vigor, and its action is both believable and excitingly choreographed. Fonda, Quinn, and Widmark are standouts in their roles, each providing memorable characterizations without any stereotypes. The film saw moderate success at the box office, but failed to recoup its $2.4 million budget in its initial release. The 1989 horror film **Warlock** is unrelated to this production. Songs: "Beautiful Dreamer" (1864; Stephen Foster), "John Brown's Body" (1858; composer unknown), "Rock of Ages" (1763; music: Thomas Hastings; lyrics: Augustus Montague Toplady). *Author's Note*: Fonda told this author that "I had played Wyatt Earp by name in a John Ford picture, **My Darling Clementine**

Dolores Michaels, Henry Fonda and Anthony Quinn in *Warlock*, **1959.**

[1946], and here I was, more than a decade later, playing the same person, but with a different name. In the Ford picture, Victor Mature played my sidekick, Doc Holliday, but, in **Warlock**, that role is played by Tony [Anthony] Quinn, and he did a great job of showing Holliday's competitive nature as a gunfighter." Quinn did not like his role in this film, telling this author: "I am a screwed up gunfighter clomping around with a clubfoot, and that makes me into a vicious killer, who both loves and hates his closest friend [Fonda]. Now that's really a screwed up guy." Widmark, on the other hand, liked his part, saying to this author: "I don't do anything spectacular in **Warlock**, except to step into the street, knowing that I am probably going to be killed by other gunmen. Maybe that was spectacular enough." Dymtryk told this author that "**Warlock** is a much different type of western. It is an "adult" western and there were very few of those, except for some of Anthony Mann's pictures, like **Winchester '73** [1950] and **The Tin Star** [1957] that also starred Hank [Fonda]. We dealt with psychological problems with some of the characters in **Warlock**, especially Tony [Anthony] Quinn's role, which was very complex, but I think that went over the viewer's head and maybe caused a lack of interest at the box office. It's still one of my favorite films." The set for the town of Warlock is the same set used for a number of other Fox westerns, including **The Ox-Bow Incident**, 1943, which also starred Fonda; **The Gunfighter**, 1950; and **River of No Return**, 1954. For other films depicting Wyatt Earp and Doc Holliday, see Subject Index, Historical Persons. For more details on these legendary westerners, see my book *Encyclopedia of Western Lawmen and Outlaws* (Paragon House, 1992; Wyatt Earp: pages 110-121; Doc Holliday: pages 162-165; Clanton-McLowery Gang: pages 75-77). **p&d**, Edward Dmytryk; **cast**, Richard Widmark, Henry Fonda, Anthony Quinn, Dorothy Malone, Dolores Michaels, Wallace Ford, Tom Drake, Richard Arlen, De Forest Kelley, Regis Toomey, Vaughn Taylor, Don Beddoe, Whit Bissell, Don "Red" Barry, Ann Doran, Frank Gorshin, Hugh Sanders, Gary Lockwood, Walter Coy, Sol Gorss; **w**, Robert Alan Aurthur (based on the novel by Oakley Hall); **c**, Joe MacDonald (CinemaScope; Technicolor); **m**, Leigh Harline; **ed**, Jack W. Holmes; **art d**, Lyle R. Wheeler, Herman A. Blumenthal; **set d**, Walter M. Scott, Stuart A. Reiss; **spec eff**, L.B. Abbott, Fred Etcheverry.

Warning Shot ★★★ 1967; U.S.; 100m; Bob Banner Associates/PAR; Color; Crime Drama; Children: Unacceptable; **DVD**; **IV**. Tense crime thriller begins with Janssen, an L.A. plainclothes police sergeant, who is searching for a murderer. He is waiting in hiding outside an apartment complex when he sees a man dash across the lawn holding a gun. Janssen shouts for the man to stop, but the sprinting man ignores his warning and Janssen fires and kills the runner. The dead man turns out to be Curtis, a respected physician known for aiding impoverished Mex-

David Janssen and George Grizzard in *Warning Shot*, 1967.

icans living south of San Diego. A thorough search of the area unearths no weapon, although Janssen swears he saw the man carrying a handgun. Begley, who is a police captain and Janssen's immediate superior, has had trouble with Janssen in the past and suspects that Janssen has never mentally recovered from having been shot a year earlier while he was on duty. Begley places Janssen on suspension and he is then charged with manslaughter by overzealous prosecutor Wanamaker, who thinks all cops are trigger-happy. To clear his name and be reinstated, Janssen resolves to find that weapon and returns to the scene of the shooting. There he encounters Gish, a kind and elderly woman, who tells Janssen that Curtis was her doctor and often visited her at her efficiency apartment. She points out how kind Curtis was in that every time he visited her he brought a little toy for her dog. He then meets and befriends Grizzard, a high-living airline pilot, who offers to help Janssen if he can. In fact, Grizzard offers to fly Janssen to Mexico to find out why Curtis was making so many visits to that country. Janssen interviews Sanders, who had been Curtis' financial adviser, and also meets and talks with Parker, Curtis' boozy and cheating wife, who is now a widow and not in mourning at all as she sloppily flirts with Janssen. He later meets sultry Powers, who has been Curtis' nurse and who tells Janssen that the dead doctor was a great humanitarian, selflessly providing medical attention to destitute natives of Mexico. Throughout, Janssen is hounded by reporters, and the press profiles him as a gun-happy cop, except for acerbic TV personality Allen, who comes to his defense. When Janssen pays a call on Allen to thank him, the TV pundit cold-bloodedly tells him that he is only defending him because it increases his viewership. Now full of contempt for this manipulative media creature, Janssen tells Allen: "Be against me. I'd feel cleaner." Janssen later learns from Gish that her dog has died and that she has buried the animal in a pet cemetery, along with all the toys Curtis had provided for the animal. Janssen then finds Powers' body in Curtis' ransacked office, discovered with that body by his former detective partner, Wynn, who reluctantly puts him under arrest. By this time, Janssen has solved the mystery. He overpowers Wynn and locks him in a closet and then goes to the pet cemetery with the helpful Grizzard. Both dig up Gish's dog, and Janssen finds the pistol he saw Curtis carrying when he shot the doctor. It is not real, however, but a toy pistol. Upon closer inspection, Janssen sees that the toy is packed with heroin. Grizzard confirms Janssen's suspicions that the huge amounts of money Sanders had been sending Curtis were payoffs for drug deliveries and that Sanders and Curtis were partners in a drug smuggling ring, and the too-friendly Grizzard was the airline pilot flying the drugs from Mexico into the U.S. for distribution. Grizzard pulls a gun, but, before he can shoot Janssen, the detective fires his own weapon, killing Grizzard, who symbolically topples into the open grave to end this superbly made thriller. Kulik directs this fascinating tale at a

whirlwind pace, and Janssen is a standout as a man trying to vindicate his actions while he is supported by a bevy of top-notch players. Parker, although her part is almost that of a cameo appearance, is excellent as the boozy floozy of a wife. *Author's Note*: This film was shot at the time that Janssen was appearing in his hit TV series, **The Fugitive**, 1963-1967, and he appeared in this production between the third and fourth year's shooting of that series. This film, written by Rubin, who had written one of the episodes for **The Fugitive**, this story originally intended as a made-for-TV film, but its violence and mature themes caused producers to release the film theatrically. The arch and always detached Sanders' small role in this film prompted him to later state to this author, "I felt that I was being paid to walk into and out of my scene like a bit player." He died five years later by suicide. In 1937, he remarked to David Niven (as Niven confirmed to this author) that he intended to kill himself later in life and, on April 25, 1972, he made good his promise in a hotel room in Barcelona, Spain, from an overdose of drugs. He left an acerbic note stating: "Dear World: I am leaving because I am bored. I feel that I have lived long enough. I am leaving you with your worries in this sweet cesspool. Good luck." The venerable Gish was celebrating her 55th anniversary in films when appearing in this stellar production. **p**, Bob Banner, Buzz Kulik; **d**, Kulik; **cast**: David Janssen, Ed Begley, Keenan Wynn, Sam Wanamaker, Lillian Gish, Stefanie Powers, Eleanor Parker, George Grizzard, George Sanders, Steve Allen, Carroll O'Connor, Joan Collins, Walter Pidgeon, Vito Scotti, David Garfield, Robert Williams, Jerry Dunphy, Romo Vincent, Paul Bradley, Donald Curtis, Phil Chambers, Brian Dunne, Robert Osterloh; **w**, Mann Rubin (based on the novel *711—Officer Needs Help* by Whit Masterson); **c**, Joseph Biroc (Technicolor); **m**, Jerry Goldsmith; **ed**, Archie Marshek; **art d**, Roland Anderson, Hal Pereira; **set d**, Robert R. Benton, George R. Nelson; **spec eff**, Farciot Edouart, Paul K. Lerpae.

The Warriors ★★★ 1955; U.K.; 85m; AA; Color; Adventure; Children: Unacceptable; **BD**; **DVD**. The British have won the Hundred Years' War (1337-1453), defeating France. British King Edward III (1312-1377), played by Hordern, returns to England, but has his son, Prince Edward, played by Flynn, remain in France to look after matters in now French-controlled Aquitainia where there is an uprising to resist British rule. Finch, the leader of the resistance, a more self-serving than patriotic French count, takes Dru, a beautiful British noblewoman, as a hostage in a now British-held castle, hoping Flynn will try to rescue her. Flynn learns that Finch only has a small army, which he defeats in a climactic battle. It was Flynn's last film as a swashbuckler and he gives it his all in an exciting production packed with action. Song: "Bella Marie" (music: Cedric Thorpe Davie; lyrics: Christopher Hassall). **p**, Walter Mirisch; **d**, Henry Levin; **cast**, Errol Flynn, Joanne Dru, Peter Finch, Michael Hordern, Yvonne Furneaux, Patrick Holt, Jack Lambert, Ian Bannen, Christopher Lee, Patrick McGoohan; **w**, Daniel B. Ullman (based on his story); **c**, Guy Green (CinemaScope; Technicolor); **m**, Cedric Thorpe Davie; **ed**, Edward B. Jarvis; **art d**, Terence Verity; **set d**, Harry White.

The Warriors ★★★ 1979; U.S.; 90m; PAR; Color; Drama; Children: Unacceptable (MPAA: R). **DVD**; **VHS**; **IV**. This taut tale is set in a future New York City where turf gangs rule the streets. Hill, the leader of the most powerful gang, the Gramercy Riffs, calls for a midnight meeting for all the area gangs. Most gangs cooperate, but Kelly, leader of the Rogues, shoots Hill and frames a rival Coney Island, Brooklyn, gang, the Warriors, for the murder. The Warriors have to find their way home from the Bronx to Coney Island through hostile gang territory. Two Warriors become rivals for the gang's leadership. Beck, second in command, takes charge, while hot-headed Remar wants to be acting gang warlord. The Warriors finally make it back to their home turf only to find the Rogues waiting for them. The Riffs arrive and defeat the Rogues, allowing the Warriors to walk away. Songs: "In the City" (Joe Walsh, Barry De Vorzon), "No Where to Run" (Brian Holland, Lamont

Dozier, Eddie Holland), "In Havana" (Steve Nathanson, Artie Ripp), "Echoes in My Mind" (Carlos Wilson, Louis Wilson, Claude Cave, Richard Wilson, Wolfredo Wilson), "Love Is a Fire" (Vinnie Poncia, Johnny Vastano), "You're Movin' Too Slow" (Eric Mercury, William Smith), "Last of an Ancient Breed" (Desmond Child), "Night Run" (Philip Marshall). Violence and gutter language prohibit viewing by children. **p**, Walter Hill, Laurent Bouzereau, Freeman Davies, Jr., Lawrence Gordon; **d**, Hill; **cast**, Roger Hill, David Patrick Kelly, Michael Beck, James Remar, Dorsey Wright, Brian Tyler, David Harris, Tom McKitterick, Marcelino Sanchez, Terry Michos, Deborah Van Valkenburgh, Lynne Thigpen, Mercedes Ruehl; **w**, David Shaber, Hill (based on the novel by Sol Yurick); **c**, Andrew Laszlo; **m**, Barry De Vorzon; **ed**, Davies, Jr., David Holden, Susan E. Morse, Billy Weber; **art d**, Don Swanagan, Bob Wightman; **set d**, Fred Weiler; **spec eff**, Edward Drohan.

The Warrior's Husband ★★★ 1933; U.S.; 75m; FOX; B/W; Comedy; Children: Unacceptable. Rambeau is the queen of a group of Amazonian women in 800 B.C. ruling over mostly weakling men. She decides to take meek Truex as a husband, despite his pansy nature, and because his mother is rich. Her daughter, Landi, leads an army of women against an invading Greek army led by stalwart Manners. Landi and Manners, however, soon fall in love, and the Amazonians, not used to seeing virile men, let them take over their realm (a situation unlikely to occur in 1970s America during the Women's Liberation Movement). Song: "Amazon Blues" (music: Arthur Lange; lyrics: Val Burton, Will Jason). **p**, Jesse L. Lasky; **d**, Walter Lang; **cast**, Elissa Landi, David Manners, Ernest Truex, Marjorie Rambeau, Lionel Belmore, Claudia Coleman, Maude Eburne, Ferdinand Gottschalk, Catherine Hayes, Tiny Sanford; **w**, Lang, Sonya Levien, Ralph Spence (based on the play by Julian Thompson); **c**, Hal Mohr; **m**, Arthur Lange; **ed**, Paul Weatherwax; **art d**, Max Parker.

Warui yatsu hodo yoku nemuru ★★★ 1963; Japan; 107m; Kurosawa Production Company/Toho Company; Color; Drama; Children: Unacceptable. This intense and well-crafted tale is set in Japan after World War II (1939-1945). Mifune, in a brilliant performance, plays a young man who uses his position in a corrupt company to expose the men who were responsible for his father's death. The masterful techniques of pantheon director Kurosawa are evident in almost every frame of this intriguing film. (In Japanese; English subtitles.) **p**, Akira Kurosawa, Tomoyuki Tanaka; **d**, Kurosawa; **cast**, Toshiro Mifune, Masayuki Mori, Kyoko Kagawa, Tatsuya Mihashi, Takashi Shimura, Ko Nishimura, Takeshi Kato, Chishu Ryu, Kamatari Fujiwara, Seiji Miyaguchi; **w**, Kirosawa, Hideo Oguni, Eijiro Hisaita, Ryuzo Kikushima, Shinobu Hashimto; **c**, Yuzuru Aizawa; **ed**, Kurosawa; **prod d**, Yoshiro Muraki.

Washington Square ★★★ 1997; U.S.; 115m; Alchemy Filmworks; Buena Vista; Color; Drama/Romance; Children: Unacceptable (MPAA: PG); **DVD**; **VHS**; **IV**. This absorbing drama begins in a fashionable area of New York City shortly before the American Civil War (1861-1865). Leigh is a plain-looking young woman who finds the handsome young man of her dreams in the charming form of Chaplin. But he's poor and her wealthy doctor father, Finney, strongly disapproves of her marrying him because he thinks Chaplin is a fortune-hunter. Finney disapproves of everything Leigh does because his wife died giving Leigh birth and Finney blames her for his wife's death. Leigh is determined to marry Chaplin, even if she loses her inheritance, but, when he learns she may lose her money, Chaplin stops visiting her. In a later change of mind or heart, he plans to elope with her, but, by then, Leigh does not trust him, believing that her father, Finney, now deceased, was correct in believing that Chaplin is nothing more than a calculating fortune-hunter. Though he knocks and knocks at her front door, Leigh locks Chaplin out of her house and heart. We're never certain whether Chaplin has truly loved her. Well-made adaptation of an earlier version, **The Heiress**, 1949, that

George Coulouris, Donald Woods, Bette Davis, Lucile Watson and Paul Lukas in *Watch on the Rhine,* **1943.**

was a triumph in which Olivia de Havilland won an Academy Award as best actress for her great performance. Songs: "The Tale of the String" (Alan Bergman, Marilyn Bergman), "Tu chiami una vita" (Salvatore Quasimodo, Jan A.P. Kaczmarek), "L'Absence" (Theophile Gautier, Kaczmarek), "Please Don't Come Here Again" (unknown composer). Sensuality, a childbirth scene, and brief gutter language prohibit viewing by children. **p**, Roger Birnbaum, Julie Bergman Sender; **d**, Agnieszka Holland; **cast**, Jennifer Jason Leigh, Albert Finney, Ben Chaplin, Maggie Smith, Judith Ivey, Arthur Laupus, Jennifer Garner, Robert Stanton, Betsy Brantley, Nancy Daly, Sara Ruzicka; **w**, Carol Doyle (based on the novel by Henry James); **c**, Jerzy Zielinski; **ed**, David Siegel; **art d**, Alan E. Muraoka; **set d**, William A. Cimino; **spec eff**, Pascal Charpentier, Paul Swendsen.

Watch on the Rhine ★★★★ 1943; U.S.; 114m; WB; B/W; Drama; Children: Unacceptable; **DVD**; **VHS**. Davis and Lukas give bravura performances as refugees from Nazi persecution, entering the U.S. from Mexico. They are married and are first seen on a train, traveling toward Washington, D.C., with their children, Buka, Roberts and Wilson. They plan to visit Davis' mother, Watson, who has not seen her daughter for seventeen years, and looks forward to seeing her grandchildren for the first time. Woods, Watson's son, as well as housekeeper Bondi, who is a cherished member of Watson's household, are also eagerly looking forward to seeing Davis and her family. Already in residence at Watson's luxurious mansion is Coulouris, a manipulating Romanian aristocrat, and Fitzgerald, his American-born wife. From the beginning, Coulouris manifests the traits and furtive conduct of a spy, although viewers can only early-on suspect that that is his true persona. When Davis and family arrive, she tells Watson how she married Lukas and lived in Europe where her husband became an active anti-Nazi, working with the underground, and that they were forced to come to the U.S. when the Nazis learned of Lukas' activities. All they seek now is peace and quiet in the sanctuary of America, but they soon become threatened by the scheming Coulouris, who is secretly working with German agents in the nation's capital (this shortly before the U.S. entered WWII to fight Germany, Italy and Japan). As soon as Lukas regains his health, Davis tells Watson, they plan to return to Europe where Lukas will resume his "business." Coulouris, meanwhile, spends more and more time at the German Embassy where he plays poker with Nazi spymaster Katch and where he is barely tolerated as a Nazi sympathizer. While probing Lukas' past, Coulouris opens Lukas' briefcase to find a great deal of money and a gun. He now believes that Lukas may be an enemy of the Third Reich. Katch tells Coulouris that the Gestapo has captured an underground leader in Europe, but, despite incessant torture, were unable to force the resistance leader to reveal the name of his leader, who may be in the

Bette Davis, Donald Woods and Lucile Watson in *Watch on the Rhine*, 1943.

U.S. Coulouris concludes that that secret leader is Lukas and asks Katch if he will pay him to reveal the identity of that leader. Katch agrees and Coulouris becomes a full-fledged Nazi agent probing Lukas' past. He discovers that Lukas plans to return to Germany with the money he has collected to continue to finance the operations of the underground and he then tells Lukas that, if Lukas pays him $10,000, he will not identify him to the Nazis. To keep Coulouris quiet, Lukas kills his tormentor and then plans to return to Germany via Mexico in an effort to release the leader in Germany, if he can. He kisses Davis and his children good-bye, and Watson and Woods tell him that they will not inform authorities about Coulouris' death until Lukas is safely across the border. Nothing is heard from Lukas for some months. Then Buka states that, when he turns eighteen, he is going to Germany to aid his father in his fight against fascism, and a reluctant Davis gives him her blessing, knowing that she has sacrificed her husband and oldest son in the cause of free-dom. Although the dialog is sometimes bloated with talky propaganda, the story is nevertheless powerfully presented by Shumlin, who pro-duced and directed the stage version of this tale. In fact, this production was one of those rare films that actually improved the story presented on the stage, and crime writer Hammett more sharply honed the original dialog written by his longtime live-in lover, Hellman. Davis, Lukas, Watson, Woods and Fitzgerald give impressive performances, and Coulouris is a shuddering standout as a sinister villain. Lukas, in his finest role, received an Oscar for Best Actor, and the film also received Oscar nominations for Best Supporting Actress (Watson), and Best Adapted Screenplay (Hammett). The film did well at the box office, chiefly because of Davis' drawing power, as Warner Brothers expected. A thirty-minute radio adaptation was aired by the Screen Guild Theater on January 10, 1944, with Davis and Lukas reprising their roles. It was again aired as a thirty-minute radio adaptation by Academy Award The-ater on August 7, 1946, with Lukas reprising his role. Songs/Music: "America, My Country 'Tis of Thee" (1832; Lowell Mason, using 1744 music composed by Harry Carey for "God Save the King"), "Akademis-che Festouverture (Academic Festival Overture), Op. 80" (1880; Jo-hannes Brahms). *Author's Note*: The Hellman play premiered at the Martin Beck Theater in NYC on April 1, 1941, closing on February 21, 1942, after 378 performances, starring Lukas and Mady Christians (in the Davis role), along with supporting players Courlouris, Watson, Wil-son, Roberts, and Helen Trenholme (in the Fitzgerald role). Warner Brothers boss Jack Warner recognized the play as a perfect propaganda vehicle indicting the Nazi regime in Germany, and bought the film rights from Hellman for $150,000, and assigned her and her lover, Hammett, to write the screenplay. Hellman, however, got involved with writing the script for **The North Star**, 1943, and was unable to continue work on the script for **Watch on the Rhine**, and asked Warner to give that

writing assignment exclusively to Hammett, who was apparently then in need of money. Warmer was the leading Hollywood mogul then pro-ducing films that exposed the ruthless Third Reich for the oppressive government it truly was. He had produced the first such Nazi-damning film as early as 1939 when making **Confessions of a Nazi Spy**, although Darryl F. Zanuck, head of Fox, quickly followed suit with his anti-Nazi film, **The Man I Married**, 1940. Producer Wallis wanted Davis in the role of Lukas' wife, but she was then busy making **Now, Voyager**, 1942, so he approached Margaret Sullivan, who declined the part. Wallis toyed with the idea of casting in that role Rosemary DeCamp, Helen Hayes and Edna Best, but he kept going back to Davis. The script being written by Hammett was delayed when that writer suffered an injury, and, by the time he completed the screenplay, Davis had finished making **Now, Voyager**. Wallis then sent the script to Davis, who told this author: "I loved it at the first reading. I knew my role in that picture was a sup-porting one, and I had not taken such roles for many years when I was climbing up the Hollywood ladder. The Lillian Hellman play was so powerful and Dash [Hammett] had written such a stunning screenplay, that I felt it was my patriotic duty to appear in the picture. [Davis was a strong supporter of then U.S. President Franklin D. Roosevelt, and who shared Roosevelt's passionate desire to see fascism defeated.] The pic-ture really belonged to Paul [Lukas], who was marvelous as the anti-Nazi leader in that picture, a sensitive and dedicated performance that won him an Oscar." Although Lukas had starred in the play version, Wallis had considered casting Charles Boyer in the Lukas role. Boyer told this author: "Hal [Wallis] came to me with the idea of putting me into **Watch on the Rhine**, but I pointed out to him that I would not be suitable since my French accent did not fit the character, who is a native of Germany. I had seen Paul [Lukas] in the original play on Broadway and I urged Hal to use Paul for a role he was born to play." Wallis then cast Lukas in the part, and he and Davis got along famously as they shared the same political views. This was not the case with Watson, who was a staunch Republican and, after she voiced some criticisms about President Roosevelt, Davis responded by telling Watson to "keep your political opinions to yourself." Watson bristled at this, and, according to Davis' comments to this author: "Gave me what for by telling me: 'Bette, we are making a picture that indicts a regime in Germany that suppresses everyone's free speech. Are you suggesting that the same harsh conditions exist in America?' Well, she was right, of course, but we did not get along after that. Republicans like Lucile were all right, but just as long as they did not climb over my fence and come into my backyard to tell me how to think." Wallis announced that he was going to give Davis top billing and Davis immediately went to Wallis and told him that she was playing a supporting role and did not deserve that recognition and that Lukas should receive top billing. Wallis success-fully convinced her that her star status would make the film a success and she relented. Director Shumlin and Davis did not get along too well as Davis ignored Shumlin's directives to tone down her performance, which had come to Wallis' attention when he screened daily rushes. Davis stated to this author: "I suppose they thought I was trying to make up for my small role in that picture by over-emphasizing my lines. That was not the case as my speeches were very telling as I am the wife and mother of a family that is being torn apart by the Nazis, and that was the case with half the world then. Well, I brought my delivery down a few notches to make everybody happy. The whole thing was a little silly. I am an intense actress and that's why I was given that role and then they told me not to be so intense." This author met Shumlin years later when he was producing "Inherit the Wind" on Broadway and starring Paul Muni. He proved to be a gentle and kind man, who went out of his way to introduce this author to Muni, who had been one of my boyhood movie idols. Hammett, after completing the script for this film, enlisted in the Army and was sent to the Aleutians, where he edited an army pub-lication, *The Adakian*. Hollywood censors took objection to how Lukas kills Nazi agent Coulouris without being punished, even though he has dispatched an evil man. To appease the censors, the studio provided oblique retribution for Lukas' actions by tacking on a brief epilog to indicate that Lukas, after returning to Germany, has either been captured or killed. Shumlin had a difficult time with his cinematographer, Gerstad, who told him that he could not make too many retakes since there was a shortage of celluloid because of the war, which caused Gerstad to be replaced by the more cooperative Mohr. Films that profiled how the insidious philosophy of the Nazis crept into American households is also shown in such films as **Tomorrow the World**, 1944, and **The Stranger**, 1946. **p**, Hal B. Wallis; **d**, Herman Shumlin; **cast**, Bette Davis, Paul Lukas, Geraldine Fitzgerald, Lucile Watson, Beulah Bondi, George Coulouris, Donald Woods, Henry Daniell, Eric Roberts, Donald Buka, Anthony Caruso, Helmut Dantine, Kurt Katch, Alan Hale Jr.; **w**, Dashiell Hammett (based on the play by Lillian Hellman); **c**, Merritt Gerstad, Hal Mohr; **m**, Max Steiner; **ed**, Rudi Fehr; **art d**, Carl Jules Weyl; **set d**, Julia Heron; **spec eff**, Edwin B. DuPar, John Holden.

Water for Elephants ★★★★ 2011; U.S.; 120m; FOX; Color/B/W; Adventure/Romance; Children: Unacceptable (MPAA: PG-13); **BD**; **DVD**; **IV**. Marvelously presented and highly poignant tale begins with Holbrook, a man in his early eighties. He tells a circus owner of his years in another circus during the Great Depression of the 1930s. The film flashes back to those years when he was a young veterinary medicine student, played by Pattinson, but who has to leave college after the death of his parents. He joins a traveling circus as its vet, even though he is not licensed, and falls in love with Witherspoon, the beautiful young wife of the emotionally unstable circus owner, Waltz. Pattinson becomes especially concerned about Waltz's mistreatment of one of the circus' star performers, Rosie, an elephant. Waltz beats Witherspoon because he believes she and Pattinson have become lovers. She learns that Waltz plans to throw Pattinson from the moving train, so she and Pattinson run away together. Waltz learns they have gone to a hotel and sends men to bring her back to him and beat up Pattinson. The climax sees Pattinson and Waltz fighting soon afterward, but Rosie kills Waltz by hitting him on the back of the head with a metal spike with which Waltz had previously used to beat her. In flash-forward, Holbrook says he finished college and became a certified veterinarian, and he and Witherspoon married. Before her death, they had five children, and they kept Rosie until the elephant's death many years later. Holbrook gets hired to sell tickets at the circus owned by the man to whom he tells his story and he is happy to be home again in a circus. Lawrence vigorously directs this fascinating story, presenting the day-to-day operations of a small circus while merging into that fabric a sensitive love story. Pattinson and Witherspoon are exceptional in their roles as innocent young perople engulfed by an economically oppressive Depression (and their naïve personalities are well suited to that era), as well as the draconian antics of Waltz, who presents a mesmerizing performance of a man slowly becoming mentally unhinged. The production values are exceptional, from the crisp cinematography by Prieto, to the moving score by Howard, and the costumes, sets and vehicles are stunningly accurate to the period. The film was a hit at the box office, earning more than $117 million in its initial release against a budget of $38 million. Songs: "Chiribiribin" (George Wilson, A. Pestalozza), "Taps" (Dick Stephen Walter), "Smile Please" (Robert Viger), "I'd Like to Be Beside the Seaside" (George Wilson, John Glover Kind), "Jelly's Blues," "Creole Clarinet," "South Side Shuffle" (Keith Nichols), "Hush Little Baby" (traditional), "I'm Confessin' That I Love You" (Doc Daugherty, Ellis Reynolds, Al Neiburg), "Sheep Walk" (Marc Durst), "Button Up Your Overcoat" (Lew Brown, Buddy G. DeSylva, Ray Henderson), "Sheep's Eyes" (Lionel Weindling), "Creole Clarinet" (Keith Nichols), "Don't Tell Him What Happened to Me" (Brown, DeSylva, Henderson), "I Need a Little Sugar in My Bowl" (J. Tim Brymn, Clarence Williams, Daily Small), "Barnum & Bailey's Favorite March" (Karl King), "Stomp Time Blues" (Tiny Parham). *Author's Note*: Witherspoon and Pattinson had appeared in another film together, **Vanity Fair**, 2004, and where Pattinson played Witherspoon's estranged son, but this scene was deleted before

Robert Pattinson and Tai the Elephant in *Water for Elephants,* **2011.**

that film was released. Sean Penn, who was noted for playing neurotic characters, was cast in the role of the circus owner, but dropped out of the production and was, thankfully, replaced by Waltz. The film was shot on location in Tennessee, Georgia and California. Two antique trains were employed in this film, Number 610 of the Tennessee Valley Railroad, and, especially, Number 18 of the McCloud River Railroad, which had been built in 1914 and was in mint condition when profiled in this fine film. Other films profiling circuses, carnivals and arcade operations include **Across the Universe**, 2007; **Adam Resurrected**, 2008; **Adventureland**, 2009; **Air Bud: Golden Receiver**, 1998; **The Ape**, 1940; **Arizona Mahoney**, 1936; **Around the World in 80 Days**, 1956; **At the Circus**, 1939; **Au Hazard Balthazar**, 1970; **Barnum!**, 1986 (made-for-TV); **Bells of Rosarita**, 1945; **Bengal Tiger**, 1936; **Berserk**, 1967; **Beyond the Blue Horizon**, 1942; **The Big Cage**, 1933; **The Big Circus**, 1959; **The Big Show**, 1961; **Big Top**, 1950-1957 (TV series); **Big Top Pee-Wee**, 1988; **Bill and Coo**, 1948; **Billy Rose's Jumbo**, 1862; **Bimbo the Great**, 1961; **Black Magic**, 1949; **Blind Justice**, 1916; **The Boy Who Stole the Elephant**, 1970 (made-for-TV); **Bozo's Circus**, 1961-1980 (TV series); **Bronco Billy**, 1980; **A Bug's Life**, 1998; **Buffalo Bill**, 1944; **Bye Bye Blackbird**, 2005; **Caged Fury**, 1948; **Captive Wild Women**, 1943; **Carnival**, 1935; **Carnivale**, 2003-2005 (TV series); **Chad Hanna**, 1940; **Charlie Chan at the Circus**, 1936; **The Circus**, 1928; **The Circus**, 1951; **Circus**, 1988 (made-for-TV); **Circus**, 1989 (TV series); **Circus**, 2010 (TV series); **Circus Angel**, 1965; **Circus Boy**, 1947; **Circus Boy**, 1956-1958 (TV series); **Circus Cavalcade**, 1945; **The Circus Clown**, 1934; **Circus Girl**, 1937; **The Circus Kid**, 1926; **The Circus Kid**, 1928; **Circus of Horrors**, 1960; **Circus of the Dead**, 2014; **The Circus Queen Murder**, 1933; **Circus World**, 1964; **The City of Lost Children**, 1995; **Clowning Around**, 1992; **Dangerous Curves**, 1929; **Dante's Inferno**, 1935; **The Dark Tower**, 1943; **Darkest Africa**, 1936; **The Devil's Circus**, 1926; **Dhoom: 3**, 2013; **Dumbo**, 1941; **8½**, 1963; **Elephant**, 2011; **The Enigma of Kasper Hauser**, 1975; **Escape to Grizzly Mountain**, 2000; **Far from the Madding Crowd**, 1967; **The Fat Man**, 1951; **Finding Neverland**, 2004; **Fixer Dugan**, 1939; **Flesh and Fantasy**, 1943; **The Flying Devils**, 1985; **4 Devils**, 1928; **Freaks**, 1932; **Frontier Circus**, 1961-1962 (TV series); **Fun and Fancy Free**, 1947; **Funny Bones**, 1995; **The Girl on the Bridge**, 1999; **Gorilla at Large**, 1954; **The Great Wallendas**, 1978 (made-for-TV); **The Greatest Show on Earth**, 1952; **The Hairy Ape**, 1944; **He Who Gets Slapped**, 1924; **The Holy Mountain**, 1973; **I Am David**, 2004; **I'll Give a Million**, 1935; **I'm No Angel**, 1933; **Inland Empire**, 2006; **Inside Daisy Clover**, 1965; **Invitation to the Dance**, 1956; **It's a Small World**, 1950; **Jealousy**, 1925; **Juliet of the Spirits**, 1965; **King of the Arena**, 1933; **King of the Circus**, 1925; **King of Thieves**, 2004; **La Strada**,

Alex Etel and friend in *The Water Horse: Legend of the Deep*, 2007.

1956; **La Vie en Rose**, 2007; **Lady in the Dark**, 1944; **Larger than Life**, 1996; **The Last Circus**, 2010; **Laugh, Clown, Laugh**, 1928; **Legend of the Werewolf**, 1975; **Let's Fall in Love**, 1933; **Life Is a Circus**, 1960; **Lili**, 1953; **Little Big Top**, 2006; **The Little Unicorn**, 2002; **Lola Montes**, 1959; **Mad Max Beyond Thunderdome**, 1985; **Madeline**, 1998; **Man on a Tightrope**, 1953; **The Man Who Laughs**, 1928; **Mary**, 1931; **The Men in Her Life**, 1941; **Merry Andrew**, 1958; **The Mighty Barnum**, 1934; **The Miracle Woman**, 1931; **A Modern Hero**, 1934; **The Monkey Talks**, 1927; **Moscow on the Hudson**, 1984; **Mother Machree**, 1928; **Murder!**, 1930; **Murders in the Rue Morgue**, 1932; **Ned Kelly**, 2003; **Nightmare Alley**, 1947; **Octopussy**, 1983; **Once in a Blue Moon**, 1935; **Only One Night**, 1939; **Open Season 3**, 2011; **Our Vines Have Tender Grapes**, 1945; **Outrage**, 1993; **P.T. Barnum**, 1999; **Papa's Delicate Condition**, 1963; **Parade**, 1974 (made-for-TV); **Peck's Bad Boy**, 1921; **Peck's Bad Boy with the Circus**, 1938; **Pennies from Heaven**, 1936; **Polly of the Circus**, 1917; **Polly of the Circus**, 1932; **Rain or Shine**, 1930; **Red Stallion in the Rockies**, 1949; **Red Wagon**, 1936; **Ring Circus**, 1954; **Ring of Fear**, 1954; **Saboteur**, 1942; **Sally of the Sawdust**, 1925; **Santa Sangre**, 1990; **Sawdust and Tinsel**, 1956; **Sawdust Tales**, 1997; **7 Faces of Dr. Lao**, 1964; **The Shadow**, 1937; **She Made Her Bed**, 1934; **The Side Show**, 1931; **Sideshow**, 1928; **Sinner's Holiday**, 1930; **Something Wicked This Way Comes**, 1983; **Souls for Sale**, 1923; **Stage Door**, 1937; **The Story of Three Loves**, 1953; **Street Angel**, 1928; **The Stunt Man**, 1980; **Sunny**, 1930; **Susan Lenox: Her Fall and Rise**, 1931; **Swing High**, 1930; **Things Are Looking Up**, 1935; **Thirteen Women**, 1932; **Thousands Cheer**, 1943; **Three-Ring Marriage**, 1928; **A Tiger Walks**, 1964; **Tillie's Punctured Romance**, 1928; **The Tin Drum**, 1980; **Toby Tyler, or Ten Weeks with a Circus**, 1960; **Tough Luck**, 2003; **Trapeze**, 1931; **Trapeze**, 1956; **Tricks of Life**, 1935; **True to the Army**, 1942; **Two Brothers**, 2004; **Two Flaming Youths**, 1927; **Under the Big Top**, 1938; **Under the Top**, 1919; **The Unholy Three**, 1925; **The Unholy Three**, 1930; **The Unknown**, 1927; **The Valley of the Gwangi**, 1969; **Variétés**, 1935; **Varsity Blues**, 1999; **The Wagons Roll at Night**, 1941; **Whispering Moon**, 2006; **Wings of Desire**, 1988; **The Winning Team**, 1952; **The Woman for Joe**, 1955; **The Woman from Hell**, 1929; **You Can't Cheat an Honest Man**, 1939; **You Never Know Women**, 1926; and **Zouzou**, 1989. Moments of intense violence, animal abuse, and sexual content prohibit viewing by children. **p**, Gil Netter, Erwin Stoff, Andrew R. Tennenbaum; **d**, Francis Lawrence; **cast**, Reese Witherspoon, Robert Pattinson, Christoph Waltz, Paul Schneider, Hal Holbrook, Jim Norton, Mark Povinelli, Richard Brake, Stephen Monroe Taylor, Ken Foree; **w**, Richard LaGravenese (based on the novel by Sara Gruen) **c**, Rodrigo Prieto; **m**, James Newton Howard; **ed**, Alan Edward Bell; **prod d**, Jack

Fisk; **art d**, David Crank; **set d**, Jim Erickson; **spec eff**, Mark R. Byers, Steve Austin.

The Water Horse: Legend of the Deep ★★★ 2007; U.S.; 112m; Revolution Studios/COL; Color; Fantasy; Children: Cautionary (MPAA: PG); **BD**; **DVD**; **IV**. Delightful fantasy begins in present-day Scotland where an American couple meets an old man in a bar, who tells them a story about the Loch Ness Monster. The film flashes back to 1942 when a Scottish boy, Etel, lives in a large manor house on the shores of Loch Ness with his mother, Watson, and sister. His sailor father is believed lost at sea in World War II (1939-1945). Etel finds a large mysterious egg and cares for it until it hatches a "Water Horse," a mythical Celtic creature that Etel keeps a secret and believes is the Loch Ness Monster or its offspring. British troops arrive, commanded by Morrissey, to defend the area from possible German U-boats in the lake. The water horse is injured by a shell fired when a gunner thinks it is a U-boat, and the creature vanishes in the lake. Afterward, no one knows for certain if the water horse was the Loch Ness Monster or not, and we learn that the old man in the bar in the present day who tells the story about it is Etel as he has aged over the years. This heartwarming story is told with considerable care by director Russell, and Etel is outstanding as the believing boy. The special effects are outstanding in profiling the mythical water horse. The film did well at the box office, earning more than $103 million in its initial release against a budget of $40 million. Songs: "Back Where You Belong" (Sinead O'Connor), "Magic" (Tim Myers, David Lichens), "I'm Nobody's Baby" (Milton Ager, Benny Davis, Lester Santley), "If I Had a Talking Picture of You" (Lew Brown, Buddy G. Desylva, Ray Henderson), "I Stumbled over Love" (Chet Forrest, Bob Wright), "String Quartet in G Major" (Wolfgang Amadeus Mozart), "Goody Goody" (Matty Malneck, Johnny Mercer), "It's Only a Paper Moon" (E.Y. "Yip" Harburg, Harold Arlen, Billy Rose), "Mount Phoebus Hunt" (traditional), "Garden in the Rain" (James Dyrenforth, Carroll Gibbons). **p**, Robert Bernstein, Charlie Lyons, Barrie M. Osborne, Douglas Rae; **d**, Jay Russell; **cast**, David Morrissey, Emily Watson, Alex Etel, Ben Chaplin, Brian Cox, Carl Dixon, Craig Hall, Bruce Allpress, Geraldine Brophy, Edward Campbell, Peter Corrigan, **w**, Robert Nelson Jacobs (based on the novel *The Water Horse* by Dick King-Smith); **c**, Oliver Stapleton; **m**, James Newton Howard; **ed**, Mark Warner; **prod d**, Tony Burrough; **art d**, Dan Hennah, Simon Bright, Brad Mill; **set d**, Hennah; **spec eff**, R. Christopher White, Erik Winquist.

Waterhole No. 3 ★★★ 1967; U.S.; 95m; Blake Edwards-Geoffrey; PAR; Color; Comedy/Western; Children: Unacceptable (MPAA: PG-13); **DVD**; **VHS**; **IV**. This well-crafted spoof of westerns begins in 1888, where a renegade former Confederate cavalry sergeant, Atkins, and two other soldiers rob a fortune of gold from his army post. They bury the loot near an isolated waterhole in the desert. Coburn, a professional gambler, fights a duel with one of the robbers, kills him, and finds on his body a map to the treasure. Coburn busies himself by locking the local sheriff, O'Connor, in his own jail, before seducing the sheriff's lovely daughter, Blye, and stealing the sheriff's horse. O'Connor frees himself and rides after Coburn, arresting him and taking the gold. But Atkins and an accomplice attack O'Connor, recover the gold, free Coburn, and they ride off to Mexico to live like kings. *Author's Note:* Veteran character actor Whitmore told this author that "I don't think there were too many successful spoofs about the Old West like **Waterhole No. 3**. The Old West is looked upon by Americans with great respect, even though it was a terrible time to live in and where violence was everywhere and no one was safe. The story we show in **Waterhole No. 3** is one where everyone is trying to con everyone else. It's ridiculous, but I think appropriate because that's exactly what was going on in the Old West back then." Song: "The Ballad of Waterhole #3/Code of the West" (Dave Grusin, Robert Wells). **p**, Joseph T. Steck, (uncredited) Blake Edwards; **d**, William Graham; **cast**, James Coburn, Carroll

O'Connor, Margaret Blye, Claude Akins, Joan Blondell, Timothy Carey, Bruce Dern, James Whitmore, Harry Davis, Roy Jenson; **w**, Steck, Robert R. Young; **c**, Robert Burks; **m**, Dave Grusin; **ed**, Warren Low; **prod d**, Fernando Carrere; **set d**, Reg Allen, Jack Stevens; **spec eff**, Farciot Edouart, Paul K. Lerpae.

Waterloo ★★★ 1971; Italy/USSR; 123m; PAR; Color; Biographical Drama; Children: Unacceptable (MPAA: G); **DVD**; **VHS**. Steiger renders a fascinating portrait of Napoleon I (1769-1821) in the last days of his empire, where he meets his military debacle at the Battle of Waterloo (Sunday, June 18, 1815) in what is present-day Belgium. Steiger is shown in his throne room in 1814 where his advisers tell him that he must abdicate. He has the great powers of Europe aligned against him— England, Prussia, Austria and Russia. He is then informed that his last army has been defeated. The French emperor then reluctantly abdicates and is seen in a touching farewell to his loyal troops and marshals before he sails into exile on the bleak island of Elba. Steiger escapes from Elba and returns to France, gathering an army as he proceeds toward Paris. Michel Ney (1769-1815), who is superbly played by O'Herlihy, a former marshal under Steiger, is sent by Louis XVIII (1755-1824), played by Welles, to meet and destroy Steiger's army, which threatens to dismantle the restored French monarchy. O'Herilhy, however, cannot resist Steiger's magnetic sway and, rather than attack Steiger and his troops, joins them. (Napoleon gave Ney the command of the left wing of his army as Ney had always been one of his favorite commanders and it was Ney who commanded the rear guard that allowed Napoleon to retreat from Russia with his tattered army in 1812 and where Napoleon called Ney "the bravest of the brave.") Steiger enters Paris in triumph as Welles and his royal entourage flees. The Allied Powers declare war against the restored emperor (of 100 days), and Steiger must now face the military might of all major European countries, especially England, its troops commanded by the able Field Marshal Arthur Wellesley, 1st Duke of Wellington (1769-1852), staunchly played by Plummer. When Plummer attends a ball, he learns that Steiger has invaded Belgium and that his British troops might be cut off from Prussian forces supporting him. Steiger quickly stops the British at Quatre-Bras (on June 16, 1815) and defeats a Prussian army under the command of Field Marshal Gebhard Blucher (1742-1819), who is played by Zakariadze, at Ligny (June 16, 1815). Against the advice of his aides, Zakariadze refuses to retreat and moves to support Plummer, rightly believing that Steiger's next move will be to attack the British at Waterloo. That is exactly what happens on June 18, 1815, when Steiger orders Millot, who plays Marshal Emmanuel de Grouchy (1766-1847), to pursue the Prussians led by Zakariadze while he attacks Plummer's British forces at Waterloo. The night before that titanic battle, a wild storm rages throughout the area and Steiger grows ill with severe stomach pains. By dawn, he has improved but is angered to hear that his cannon cannot be moved because they are mired in mud from the night's rainfall and the artillery must wait until the earth dries. At 11:30 a.m., Steiger orders his artillery to open fire and sends a diversionary attack against Plummer's right flank at the Chateau Hougoumont, but Plummer does not take the bait by sending reinforcements to that area and where his troops stand firm against repeated attacks (although Wellington did send some of his artillery to Hougoumont to repel the almost suicidal attacks of the French forces there). The British resistance at Hougoumont proves important in that Steiger keeps sending more and more troops to that area without success, draining his reserves in the process. Steiger then orders his main force to attack the center of Plummer's line and these troops break through. However, Plummer sends reinforcements to plug the gap under the command of Hawkins, who plays the valiant General Sir Thomas Picton (1758-1815). The reinforcements drive back the French troops, but at the cost of Hawkins' death. As the French retreat from the British salient, a British cavalry unit called the Scots Guard, led by Wilding, who plays General William Ponsonby (1772-1815), follows the fleeing French troops. The retreating French, however, turn about to attack the

Rod Steiger as Napoleon Bonaparte in *Waterloo*, 1971.

British cavalry, which is cut to pieces by withering volley fire, and Wilding, his horse sinking in mud, is killed. As the see saw battle continues, new forces come upon the battlefield to the east, and Steiger anxiously waits to learn whether those fresh troops are commanded by his own general, Millot (Grouchy), or they are Prussian troops under the command of Zakariadze (Blucher). Steiger becomes depressed when learning that the arriving troops are Prussian, not letting his troops know about this new turn of events. He suffers severe stomach pains and leaves the field, putting O'Herlihy (Ney) in command. When O'Herlihy sees that Plummer has shifted troops in his line of defense he misinterprets this as a retreat and he masses all the French cavalry available and leads a wild charge against these forces (director Bondarchuk employs awesome overhead shots to show this massive charge). O'Herlihy then sees that the British troops have been formed into squares and his cavalry attacks these squares piecemeal, being repulsed at every quarter. (Ney and his troops at this point in the battle captured a good deal of British artillery but failed to spike the guns, even though they had the implements with them to dismantle these cannon, which were later recovered by the British and were used to bombard Napoleon's last formations, which largely contributed to the Allied victory.) While the British deflect O'Herlihy's savage attacks, Peter Davies, playing Lord Hay (1797-1815), a youthful ensign, rallies the British troops to throw back the French, but is killed in the process (Hay was actually killed at Quatre Bras two days earlier). Steiger then returns to the battlefield (as did Napoleon), learning of O'Herlihy's disastrous charge and Steiger angrily rebukes his marshals for allowing Ney to make such an impetuous attack. He then learns that British troops have been overcome at a point in Plummer's defense line and believes that the British are on the point of collapse. Steiger then orders his best reserves, his Imperial Guard, to attack the center of Plummer's line, but, when the French troops charge over the top of a hill, they see massed British formations rising from high grass where they have been hidden on orders of the shrewd Plummer, and their volley fire devastates the French troops, driving them back in retreat. Plummer then realizes that he has broken Steiger's once grand army and orders all of his British troops to advance while Zakariadze marches from the east to support Plummer's forces. Steiger now realizes that all is lost, but he insists that he remain with the Imperial Guard as it forms squares in a last stand. His marshals, however, drag him from the battlefield. The Imperial Guard is asked to surrender, but refuses, and Plummer orders his artillery (earlier captured but left intact and then abandoned by O'Herlihy's forces) to pound the stubborn French troops to pieces. The barrage annihilates the Imperial Guard and the battle is ended. Plummer then mournfully walks the battlefield to see the carnage and loss of life. Meanwhile, the defeated Steiger rides in a coach, glumly heading for

Mae Clarke and Kent Douglass in *Waterloo Bridge*, 1931.

Paris where he will again abdicate and then go into permanent exile on the isle of St. Helena to end his reign of wars and conquest. Bondarchuk does a fine job orchestrating this complicated battle, and his action scenes are well choreographed, replete with accurate costuming and weaponry. Steiger is a standout as the always aggressive Napoleon, as is Plummer as the stalwart Wellington, both receiving fine support from O'Herlihy, Hawkins, Wilding and the rest of the resplendent cast. This was one of the most expensive films made to its time, costing more than $35 million to produce, and, unfortunately it did not recoup its investment at the box office. ***Author's Note***: Steiger told this author: "Playing Napoleon Bonaparte is an impossible assignment as the man's personality was much too complex to completely capture and show on the screen. I played him as he was, moody and impulsive, but also clever and sometimes brilliant. It was the best I could do. I was flattered to later hear that they were thinking of hiring Richard Burton to play that role, but opted to hire me for the job." Plummer told this author: "It was no one's fault that **Waterloo** failed at the box office. The subject matter was just not that popular." In fact, Stanley Kubrick had been preparing a film about Napoleon, but he failed to get any backing for that project when **Waterloo** proved to be a financial failure. Welles told this author that "I played Louis XVIII in that film, but you would hardly know it as I am in and out of the throne room in a few minutes. I wasn't kidding myself about my role. I was on screen for name recognition only." Bondarchuk had been hired to helm this film on the strength of his massive production of **War and Peace**, 1968. To acquire enough funding for the film, producer De Laurentiis allied himself with Mosfilm, the Soviet-financed film company, and the film was shot mostly in Ukraine (then a part of the USSR), as well as in Italy and elsewhere on a twenty-eight-week schedule. Thousands of Russian troops were used as extras for the battle scenes, but they panicked when they were charged by the cavalry and had to be reorganized again and again for that sequence to be completed. The Soviet intelligence agency, KGB, monitored all non-Russian cast and crew members while they were working in Russia. The film was originally released at 134 minutes, but was edited when later released in the U.S. at 123 minutes. The 1815 Battle of Waterloo has been profiled in **Becky Sharp**, 1935; **Sabotage!**, 2001; and, obliquely, **Desiree**, 1954. (Dubbed in English.) **p**, Dino De Laurentiis; **d**, Sergey Bondarchuk; **cast**, Rod Steiger, Orson Welles, Virginia McKenna, Michael Wilding, Jack Hawkins, Christopher Plummer, Ian Ogilvy, Dan O'Herlihy, Rupert Davies, Peter Davies, Sergo Zakariadze, Philippe Forquet, Gianni Garko, Charles Millot, Terence Alexander; **w**, H.A.L. Craig, Bondarchuk, Vittorio Bonicelli; **c**, Armando Nannuzzi (Panavision; Technicolor); **m**, Nino Rota; **ed**, Richard C. Meyer; **prod d**, Mario Garbuglia; **art d**, Ferdinando Giovannoni, A. Menialshikov, Semyon Valiushek; **set d**, Emilio D'Andria, Kenneth Mugglestone;

spec eff, Vladimir Likhachov, Giulio Molinari.

Waterloo Bridge ★★★★ 1931; U.S.; 81m; UNIV; B/W; Drama/Romance; Children: Unacceptable; **DVD**. This excellent film version of the poignant Robert E. Sherwood play about two star-crossed lovers during WWI (1914-1918), opens with Clarke, an American chorus girl, who has fallen on hard times. To make ends meet, she has turned to prostitution, picking up her customers at Waterloo Bridge, where soldiers on leave invariably arrive. Clarke is standing on the bridge when an air raid occurs just as she meets Douglass, a Canadian soldier on leave. As everyone takes shelter, Clarke takes Douglass to her apartment where she tells him that she has lost her job as a chorus girl, and, taken with her, Douglass offers to pay her rent. She is touched by Douglass' offer but refuses to take his money, and, after he leaves, she returns to the streets. Douglass returns to her rooming house, and Griffies, the landlady, allows him to enter Clarke's apartment. There he meets Lloyd, who is Clarke's closest friend and neighbor and who tells Douglass that Clarke is a lonely girl who needs someone to love her and look after her. Clarke returns after Douglass has gone and Lloyd urges her to marry Douglass, but Clarke resents Lloyd's advice and that she has interfered with her life by urging her to wed Douglass so as to improve her lifestyle. Douglass, however, is deeply in love with Clarke, and, after he takes her to his country estate to meet his mother, Bennett, and his sister, Davis, he proposes to her. Later that night, Clarke confesses her lifestyle to a sympathetic Bennett, who, to protect her son, urges Clarke not to marry Douglass. Clarke leaves the estate alone the next morning, returning to London by train. Douglass later finds her and asks her why she vanished. When she gives no explanation, he pleads with her to marry him, and she agrees. However, while Douglass waits outside her room, Clarke flees through a window. When landlady Griffies goes to Clarke's apartment and finds her suddenly departed, she believes that Clarke has fled to avoid paying her back rent and this prompts the angry Griffies to tell Douglass the truth about how Clarke makes her living. Douglass, though shocked by this revelation, nevertheless loves Clarke and searches for her, finding her at Waterloo Bridge. He tells her that her past means nothing to him. A policeman then orders Douglass to get into a truck to join his military unit, which is being shipped to France. Douglass begs Clarke to wait for him so that, upon his return, they can be married. Clarke promises that she will wait for him, and a happy Douglass rides away. A short time later, a wailing air raid siren sends everyone running for cover. While looking for a shelter, a bomb is dropped, and Clarke is killed in the explosion to end this tragic romance. Whale directs this sensitive and haunting tale with a careful hand, bringing forth fine performances from Clarke and Douglass, as well as the rest of the cast members, particularly Lloyd's role as an empathetic friend of a doomed young woman. Whale innovatively uses many overhead shots and quick cuts in his fluid camera shots, and allows the story to naturally unfold to show small, tender moments that never sink into the bathos of a soap opera. His atmospheric profile of moody, fog-bound London prophecies the tragedy that eventually envelops the young lovers, although Whale allows some overdone Cockney accents to be employed. He further and inventively employed off-screen sounds, then a novelty, which increased the tension in the most dramatic scenes. The film was a critical and commercial success, easily recouping its initial budget of $252,000 in its initial release. This story was remade in an equally superlative production in 1940, starring Vivien Leigh and Robert Taylor and remade again as **Gaby**, 1956, with John Kerr and Leslie Caron, a disappointing third entry. Song: "God Save the King" (composer unknown; sometimes attributed to John Bull, 1619). ***Author's Note***: Playwright Sherwood based his story on his own experiences when he served in WWI, serving in a Canadian regiment. He had met an unemployed American chorus girl turned prostitute at Waterloo Bridge in London during the war and it was her story he used for this touching drama and forlorn romance, along with the German bombing raids then plaguing the city. Viewers today may realize that London was bombed during WWII (particularly during the Blitz, September 7, 1940, through May 21, 1941, and periodically thereafter, including attacks on the city by VI and V1 German rockets), but few remember that the Germans bombed London regularly in WWI, beginning in 1916 and continued such attacks until the end of the war in 1918. The attacks were made by mostly dirigibles, called airships, where fifty-four German Zeppelins bombed London, bringing about 554 deaths and 1,358 injuries. An early-day German bomber called the Gotha also conducted such raids, but proved less effective. Sherwood's play opened on Broadway at the Fulton Theater on January 6, 1930, running for sixty-four performances. Though not a critical or commercial success, Universal chief Carl Laemmle saw the play and considered it such a prestigious work that he purchased its film rights from Sherwood. He assigned Whale to direct the film because the director had scored a hit with another WWI-based production, **Journey's End**, 1930. Whale first thought to cast Rose Hobart in the role of the doomed young woman, but chanced upon budding actress Clarke, a contract player at Universal, and hired her for the part. Clarke, who would be best remembered for her brief role as a trollop receiving a grapefruit in the face from a roughhouse James Cagney in **The Public Enemy**, 1931 (released five months before this film), was in awe of Whale and considered him a "master" filmmaker, following his every direction to her to the letter, which Whale implied rather than overtly dictated when directing. "He wouldn't say *how* to do it," Clarke later stated. "He would tell you *what* was happening." Davis, who plays Douglass' sister in the film, told this author: "Mae followed Whale around like an adoring puppy when she was playing the part of a streetwalker in **Waterloo Bridge**. [Davis had little respect for Whale at that time, thinking him just another Hollywood director and not then knowing that he had deep theatrical experience.] Every actress wants to play the part of a fallen woman once in her life and Mae was magnificent in the role, underplaying her character at Whale's insistence. I played a similar role as Mildred in **Of Human Bondage** [1934] with Leslie Howard. But Mae was a saint in **Waterloo Bridge** compared to my role in **Of Human Bondage** where I was really a vicious bitch to the end of my little toes. I was just starting out in Hollywood and my small appearance in **Waterloo Bridge** was only my third picture. I must admit I envied Mae for her stunning portrayal and there was some talk that she might get an Oscar for that performance. She certainly deserved it, but nothing came of that because the Academy people probably thought that her role was just too unsavory in those days. Much later on, any woman playing a whore or lunatic had a good shot at the Oscar. One must then ask: 'Do times change for the worse?'" Sherwood was so impressed with Clarke's performance that he gave her an autographed photo reading: "For Mae Clarke, who did right by **Waterloo Bridge**." Whale shot this film within twenty-six days and came under budget by $25,000, which so edified the cost-conscious Laemmle that he told Whale that he could choose any subject he wanted in making his next film for Universal, which proved to be the colossal horror hit, **Frankenstein**, 1931. The Hollywood censorship board insisted that certain scenes be edited before this film was released, and, after that board instituted and strictly enforced its Production Code in July 1934, this film could not thereafter be released. It was thought for some time that the film was lost, its rights having been purchased by MGM, but a print of this version was found in the MGM vaults in 1977, and it was later released in limited showings and eventually on DVD. Supporting actresses Rita Carlisle [Carlyle] and Ethel Griffies appear in both this version and in its 1940 remake but as separate characters. **p**, Carl Laemmle, Jr.; **d**, James Whale; **cast**, Mae Clarke, Kent Douglass (Douglass Montgomery), Doris Lloyd, Frederick Kerr, Enid Bennett, Bette Davis, Ethel Griffies, Rita Carlisle [Carlyle], Ruth Handforth, Billy Bevan, Louise Emmons; **w**, Benn Levy, Tom Reed (based on the play by Robert E. Sherwood); **c**, Arthur Edeson; **m**, Val Burton; **ed**, Clarence Kolster, (uncredited) Whale; **art d**, Charles D. Hall; **spec eff**, John P. Fulton.

Waterloo Bridge ★★★★ 1940; U.S.; 108m; MGM; B/W;

Robert Taylor and Vivien Leigh in *Waterloo Bridge,* **1940.**

Drama/Romance; Children: Unacceptable; **DVD**; **VHS**; **IV**. In this wonderful remake of the Sherwood tale, LeRoy presents a memorably moving story of two star-crossed lovers, Leigh and Taylor, meeting on London's legendary Waterloo Bridge during WWI (1914-1918). The film begins during WWII (1939-1945) when Taylor, a middle-aged British colonel riding in his chauffeured limousine, is stopped during a blackout. He steps from the car to find himself on Waterloo Bridge and fondles a small charm, which had been given to him by the girl he loved many years earlier. He leans on the bridge's railing and, peering downward to the river, poignantly recalls the lost love of his life, Leigh. In flashback we see Taylor as a dashing, handsome young captain serving in a regiment commanded by his uncle, Smith, during WWI. He is walking on Waterloo Bridge in 1917 when a group of chatting girls pass him, including Leigh, who accidentally drops her purse, spilling its contents. An air raid ensues and, after Taylor helps Leigh gather her possessions, both take shelter together, and Taylor learns that Leigh is an apprentice ballerina. Leigh suggests that Taylor attend that night's ballet performance, and, smitten with the beautiful, Taylor Leigh, forsakes a formal dinner with his uncle, Smith, and, instead, goes to the ballet where he is impressed with Leigh's appearance. He sends a note backstage asking Leigh to join him, but Ouspenskaya, the draconian ballet director, intercepts the note and forbids Leigh to see Taylor, stating that it is her strict rule that none of her dancers begin relationships with men so as to preserve their discipline and careers in the demanding lifestyle of ballet performers. (Noted Russian actress Ouspenskaya invariably played empathetic and kindly old women, from mothers to gypsies, but here she is an intolerant tyrant running the lives of all the young women she supervises.) Leigh defies Ouspenskaya and meets Taylor, both enjoying a romantic evening at a restaurant. Taylor, now thoroughly in love with Leigh, proposes marriage when he returns from the front as he is being sent overseas immediately. He promises, however, that his wealthy family will protect and take care of Leigh. When Ouspenskaya learns that Leigh has established a relationship with Taylor, she fires Leigh from her esteemed troupe. Field, who is Leigh's close friend, then upbraids Ouspenskaya for attempting to disrupt Leigh's life, and, for her defense of her friend, Field, too, is fired by the fiery Ouspenskaya. Leigh and Field then look for work after they take a small apartment together. Watson, who is Taylor's mother, then arranges to meet Leigh in a tea room, but, while waiting, the anxious Leigh reads a newspaper and sees Taylor's name on a list of British officers who have been killed. She faints and, when coming to, drinks too much wine. When Watson appears, Leigh cannot bring herself to tell Watson that her son is dead, and her babbling, near-incoherent rambling convinces Watson that Leigh is not the right girl for her son and departs. Not finding work, Leigh becomes ill and then learns that her noble friend Field has been

Robert Taylor and Vivien Leigh in *Waterloo Bridge,* **1940.**

supporting them both with money she has earned as a streetwalker. She feels that she has distanced herself from Watson after their awkward meeting, deciding not to seek help from her. Leigh then unhappily joins Field in that sad profession. A year passes and, by then, Leigh is a professional prostitute, picking up servicemen at the train station near Waterloo Bridge. Then she is shocked to see Taylor alive and he is delighted to see her. Leigh learns that he had only been wounded and held a prisoner of war, and Taylor, still loving her, takes her to his family estate in Scotland. Once there, Leigh is warmly greeted by Watson, who now understands why Leigh acted so strangely at their first meeting when Watson had no knowledge of the grim but wrong news about her son that Leigh had learned and nobly kept from her. Leigh is also lovingly accepted into Taylor's family by the venerable Smith, who tells her how proud he is that Taylor has selected such a fine woman to be his future wife. But when he tells Leigh that he is positive that she will never bring shame upon Taylor and the family, Leigh is grimly reminded of her unsavory past and is consumed by guilt. Leigh now concludes that she will only bring unhappiness to Taylor after he inevitably discovers the truth about her. She confides her background to Watson, who is sympathetic and seems to forgive her, but Leigh cannot forgive herself and breaks off her engagement with Taylor, leaving him a brief note and returning alone to London. Taylor follows her to London where he finds Field, learning the truth about Leigh. That matters not to him. He loves Leigh and still wants to marry her, and he and Field then desperately search for her. It is too late. Leigh, now depressed and realizing she has no future, returns to the first rendezvous she had with Taylor, Waterloo Bridge. There she recalls her bittersweet memories of him before she purposely walks in front of an oncoming truck to end her life. In flashforward we see the now aged Taylor still holding the charm Leigh had given him and how he remembers her last loving words to him. He then pockets the charm, steps back into his car, and leaves. LeRoy masterfully directs this haunting film, which, thanks to the powerful performances of Leigh and Taylor, remains fresh and appealing to this day, despite its melancholy theme and tragic ending. LeRoy presents many sensitive scenes that remain poignantly memorable. Typical of such scenes is where Taylor and Leigh dance to "Auld Lang Syne" without ever exchanging a word. The film received two Oscar nominations for Best Cinematography (Ruttenberg), and Best Original Score (Stothart). The film was a success at the box office, earning more than $2.5 million in its initial release against a budget of more than $1.1 million. A thirty-minute radio adaptation was aired by the Screen Guild Theater on January 12, 1941, with Brian Aherne and Joan Fontaine playing the ill-fated lovers. It was aired again in a thirty-minute adaptation by the Screen Guild Theater on September 9, 1946, with Taylor reprising his role and where his then wife, Barbara Stanwyck, played Leigh's role. A third

thirty-minute adaptation was aired by Screen Directors Playhouse on September 28, 1951, with Norma Shearer essaying the Leigh role. Songs/Music: "Swan Lake, Op. 20" (1877; Peter Ilyich Tchaikovsky), "Smiles" (1917; music: Lee S. Roberts; lyrics: J. Will Callahan), "It's a Long, Long Way to Tipperary" (1912; Jack Judge, Henry James "Harry" Williams), "Candlelight Waltz" (1940; music: E Flat; lyrics: Artur Buel), "Auld Lang Syne" (traditional Scottish folksong; lyrics [1788]: Robert Burns), "Comin' Thro' the Rye" (traditional Scottish children's song; lyrics [1782]: Robert Burns), "The Bonnie Banks O' Loch Lomond" (1841; traditional Scottish song), "Let Me Call You Sweetheart" (1910; music: Leo Friedman; lyrics: Beth Slater Whitson), "Das Lied vom Abschied" (1940; music: Melichie; lyrics: Artur Buel), "Valcikna Rozloucenou" (Robert Burns), "The Minstrel Boy" (1798; Thomas Moore). ***Author's Note***: Because of the serious censorship problems the first version of this story faced in 1931, MGM had the original Sherwood script altered and sanitized to make Leigh a victim of circumstances, who is compelled into a tawdry profession rather than willingly becoming a streetwalker, and her death by suicide represents her repentance of sorts. This concept was advanced in the revised script and subtly foisted upon an earlier and more naïve public that still clung to Puritan ethics and its ardent credos concerning the "Scarlet Letter." Moreover, the lovers are British and not American and Canadian as originally profiled in the 1931 production. The flashback and flash-forward scenes were devised to bring the story into the current events of its day, WWII. One of the reasons for the film's great box office success is the fact that it was the film Leigh made immediately after appearing as the tempestuous heroine, Scarlett O'Hara, in **Gone with the Wind**, 1939, a blockbuster film that made Leigh an international star of unimaginable magnitude. Leigh was, at the time she went into this production, desperately in love with actor Laurence Olivier. In order to marry Olivier, Leigh was then in divorce proceedings with her husband, Herbert Leigh Holman, an English barrister she married at age nineteen in 1932 because he looked like her film idol, Leslie Howard, and she would use his middle name as her last name when launching her acting career. At the same time, Olivier, who was also then married, was divorcing his wife, Jill Esmond. Leigh expected Olivier to be cast with her in **Waterloo Bridge**, believing that their combined salary from this film would bolster the pooled funds they had assembled to produce their own theatrical version of "Romeo and Juliet." (Leigh had been paid $25,000 for her appearance in **Gone with the Wind** and $100,000 for her part in **Waterloo Bridge**.) She was devastated when learning that Taylor, not Olivier, would be her co-star in this film, writing to her convivial ex-husband-to-be Holman: "Robert Taylor is the man in the picture, and as it was written for Larry [Olivier], it's a typical piece of miscasting. I am afraid it will be a dreary job." It proved to be otherwise as Leigh soon grew to respect Taylor's adult sensibilities and she fell in love with her role and the story itself, which became her favorite film. Taylor told this author that "I heard that Vivien [Leigh] did not want me in the picture, but I resolved to play a serious man who genuinely falls in love with a sweet girl, despite the bad luck that sends her to the streets. After a few scenes together, she accepted me as her leading man, even though I knew I was competing with the love of her life, Laurence Olivier. I set very high standards for myself when we made **Waterloo Bridge**, and I believed I achieved them for the first time in my career. That picture remains my favorite to this day." LeRoy told this author that "I approached that picture with the resolve of showing a love story between two sensitive persons and we used a lot of the original dialog from Sherwood's play instead of the script used for the 1931 production. In many scenes, however, I used no dialog at all, but just let the actors play out their feelings for each other with gestures and facial expressions." **p,** Sidney Franklin; **d,** Mervyn LeRoy; **cast,** Vivien Leigh, Robert Taylor, Lucile Watson, Virginia Field, Maria Ouspenskaya, C. Aubrey Smith, Leo G. Carroll, Janet Shaw, Janet Waldo, Steffi Duna, Florence Baker, Phyllis Barry, Ethel Griffies, Rita Carlyle [Carlisle], Tom Conway (voice only); **w,** S.N. Behrman, Hans Rameau, George Froeschel (based on the play by Robert E. Sherwood); **c**, Joseph Ruttenberg; **m**, Herbert Stothart; **ed**, George Boemler; **art d**, Cedric Gibbons; **set d**, Edwin B. Willis.

Waterloo Road ★★★ 1948; U.K.; 73m; Gainsborough Pictures/Eagle-Lion Films; B/W; Drama/Romance/War; Children: Unacceptable; **DVD**. This fascinating film begins as England enters World War II (1939-1945), where a London railway worker, Mills, reports for military duty. He suspects that Shelton, the woman he has just married, has been seeing Granger, a draft dodger and a womanizer. Mills is unsuccessful at getting leave, so he goes AWOL and spends a day to visit Shelton just after Granger has seen his wife, while narrowly evading military police and nearly being killed in German air raids on the city. Along the way, Mills gets unexpected help from one of Granger's jilted girlfriends and a kindly doctor, Sim. Mills finally confronts Granger and, while bombs fall around them, they get into a no-holds-barred fist-fight, which Mills wins. He reconciles with his wife before being arrested for being AWOL and it looks like Granger will soon be wearing an army uniform. Mills and Granger are standouts in their competitive roles, and director Gilliat moves this entertaining film along at a brisk pace. Songs: "Who's Gonna Take You Home Tonight?" (Michael Carr, Irwin Dash as Lewis Ilda), "Letter from Home Sweet Home" (Harry Leon as Art Noel, Don Pelosi, John Rivers), "In My Dream Parade" (Aldred Reader, Alfred Reader), "Nobody's Sweetheart" (Ernie Erdman, Gus Kahn, Billy Meyers, Elmer Schoebel), "Tell Me the Truth" (Harry Leon, Jimmy Messini), "It Happened Just Like That" and "Spring Don't Mean a Thing to Me" (Val Guest, Manning Sherwin), "Bird of Love Divine" (music: Haydn Wood; lyrics: Kathleen Birch). *Author's Note*: Ian Fleming, who has a bit role as an officer at a police station, is not related to the author of the James Bond novels. Adult material prohibits viewing by children. Not related to a 2006 film with the same name. **p**, Edward Black; **d**, Sidney Gilliat; **cast**, John Mills, Stewart Granger, Alastair Sim, Joy Shelton, Alison Leggatt, Beatrice Varley, George Carney, Leslie Bradley, Jean Kent, Wylie Watson, Ben Williams, Anna Konstam, Ian Fleming; **w**, Gilliat (from a story by Val Valentine); **c**, Arthur Crabtree, Phil Grindrod; **ed**, Alfred Roome; **art d**, Alex Vetchinsky.

Watermelon Man ★★★ 1970; U.S.; 100m; Johanna/COL; Color; Comedy/Drama; Children: Unacceptable (MPAA: R); **DVD**; **VHS**; **IV**. A hilarious black comedy begins with hoarse-throated Cambridge, who is a white insurance agent living in an all-white suburban neighborhood with his wife, Parsons, and two young children, Garrett and Moran. Cambridge is a racist, who often taunts and harasses black people on and off the job. He wakes up one morning to find that he is now a black man. Nothing wipes off the black so he goes to Kuter, his doctor, a black man, but learns there is nothing that can be done to turn him back into a white man. He feels the stings of racism right away as his neighbors shun him and are afraid that other blacks will move into the community and lower real estate values. To get rid of Cambridge, they take up a collection to have him move away. Caine, who is Cambridge's boss, is astonished to see that Cambridge is now black, but thinks he can be useful in selling more insurance policies to black prospects. Parsons gives up under the pressure and takes the children to live with her mother in Indiana. Cambridge also gives up and accepts that he is going to stay black and moves to a black neighborhood where he opens up a black insurance agency. Cambridge is terrific and very funny in this outlandish film, which devastatingly spoofs **Black Like Me**, 1964, a film where actor James Whitmore plays a reporter posing as a black man to test racial hatred in his community. Cambridge had earlier presented another hilarious black character (Uncle Gitlow Judson) when savagely spoofing the Uncle Toms of the Old South in **Gone Are the Days!**, 1963. **p**, John B. Bennett; **d**, Melvin Van Peebles; **cast**, Godfrey Cambridge, Estelle Parsons, Howard Caine, D'Urville Martin, Mantan Moreland, Kay Kimberly, Kay E. Kuter, Scott Garrett, Erin Moran, Eddie "Rochester" Anderson, Mae Clarke; **w**, Herman Raucher; **c**, W.

Godfrey Cambridge and Estelle Parsons in *Watermelon Man,* **1970.**

Wallace Kelley; **m**, Van Peebles; **ed**, Carl Kress; **art d**, Malcolm C. Bert, Sydney Z. Litwack; **set d**, John Burton.

Watership Down ★★★ 1978; U.K.; 101m; Nepenthe Productions; AVCO Embassy; Color; Animated Drama; Children: Unacceptable (MPAA: PG); **BD**; **DVD**; **VHS**; **IV**. Rabbits try to establish a new colony free of tyranny and human intervention in this absorbing animated production. The film, however, is surprisingly violent and not recommended for young children, especially due to some frightening and bloody scenes. The story was remade in 1999. Song: "Bright Eyes" (Mike Batt). **p,d&w**, Martin Rosen (based on the novel by Richard Adams); **cast**, (voiceovers) John Hurt, Richard Briers, Michael Graham-Cox, Denholm Elliott, Zero Mostel, Ralph Richardson, Terence Rigby, Roy Kinnear, Harry Andrews, Nigel Hawthorne, Michael Hordern, Joss Ackland; **m**, Angela Morley; **ed**, Terry Rawlings; **spec eff**, Philip Campbell.

Waxworks ★★★ 1929 (silent; released in Germany in 1923); Germany; 65m; Neptune Film/Film Arts Guild; B/W; Horror; Children: Unacceptable; **DVD**. This episodic horror film offers some truly frightening scenes where several killers stalk their innocent victims. The film opens with Dieterle (who later became a distinguished film director), a poet looking for employment. He finds work at a wax museum where the owner hires him to write some tales about some of the most sinister-looking models on exhibit, these stories later to be told those attending the museum. Three of these evil-bent images represent Harun al-Rashid (763-809), a ruthless Arabian caliph, played by Jannings; blood-thirsty Russian czar Ivan the Terrible (1530-1584), played by Veidt; and Jack the Ripper (the London serial killer of 1888), played by Krauss. As Dieterle writes about these dreadful characters, he has three separate dreams, where he is accompanied by Belajeff, the fetching daughter of his employer. Each character represents three separate episodes of the film. In the first episode, Jannings, the caliph, is playing chess in his resplendent palace when his game is disrupted by smoke from a local bakery, which Dieterle operates with his wife, Belajeff. Offended by the smoke, Jannings sends his Grand Vizier to investigate. The delegate returns to tell Jannings that he has not located Dieterle, but has found something better, his beautiful wife. Curious, Jannings dresses as a commoner and goes among his people incognito to discover Belajeff's beauty on his own. Jannings goes to the bakery and attempts to seduce Belajeff while Dieterle steals the caliph's wishing ring to use in making a better life for himself and his wife. When Dieterle returns to the bakery, he finds the place locked and is forced to break into the building. Before he enters, Belajeff hides Jannings in the baking oven. Jannings' guards have been searching for him and they break into the bakery, but,

Colin Farrell and Ed Harris in *The Way Back*, 2010.

before they can arrest Dieterle, Belajeff uses the wishing ring to bring forth Jannings from the oven. The caliph then reconciles his interference with Dieterle and Belajeff by making Dieterle his official baker. The second episode profiles a mad Ivan the Terrible, dynamically played by Veidt, described in Dieterle's writings as a ruthless monarch who turns "cities into cemeteries." Veidt is shown sadistically enjoying his victims die as they are slowly poisoned to death on his orders. Veidt's poison-mixer marks the name of each victim on an hourglass and, as each victim dies, the hourglass is turned over, the victim dying just as the last gram of sand drops. When the poison-mixer takes pity on a victim, Veidt marks the poison-mixer as his next victim, but the poison-mixer writes a strange encryption on the hourglass. Veidt must make a visit to the wedding of a nobleman's son, but he fears assassination and compels the nobleman to dress as Ivan the Terrible and then Veidt drives the sled to the wedding, pretending to be a lowly chauffeur. The nobleman is killed by an arrow and the son and his bride-to-be are then shocked to see Veidt supervise their wedding. He throws the groom into a torture chamber and takes the bride for his own pleasures, only to learn that he himself has been poisoned. In an effort to reverse his grim fate, Veidt races to the torture chamber where he frantically turns the hourglass over and over and over, and where Dieterle has written that Veidt has become "mad and turned the glass over and over till the end of his days." The third episode deals with the worst of the lot, Jack the Ripper, played by Krauss. Dieterle awakes from the second dream to see that the wax figure of Krauss has come to life and it pursues him and Belajeff through the dark corridors of the museum, his knife drawn. No matter where they hide, Krauss finds them and begins stalking them, until he finally corners the two victims. Just as Krauss raises his long knife to slash his victims to death, Dieterle awakes from his third and final dream to end this shuddering film. All of the players perform well in this nightmare production, and Leni, who managed all the sets, and Birinsky, who directed all the actors, provide a memorable thriller. (In German; English subtitles.) **p**, Leo Birinsky, Alexander Kwartiroff; **d**, Birinsky, Paul Leni; **cast**, Emil Jannings, Conrad Veidt, Werner Krauss, William Dieterle, Olga Belajeff, John Gottowt, Georg John, Ernst Legal; **w**, Henrik Galeen; **c**, Helmar Lerski; **art d**, Paul Leni.

The Way Back ★★★ 2010; U.S.; 133m; Exclusive Films/Newmarket Films; B/W/Color; War Drama; Children: Unacceptable (MPAA: PG-13); **BD**; **DVD**; **IV**. Gripping war tale begins in 1941 when three men escape from a Siberian prison camp during World War II and reach India from Tibet, having walked 4,000 miles. Sturgess is the leader of the group, a Pole condemned by accusations secured when his wife was tortured. Escaping with him are Farrell, a Russian, and Harris, an American. The film tells their story and that of four others, who escaped with

them, as well as Ronan, a young Polish woman, who joins them in flight. They face freezing nights, disease, lack of food and water, mosquitoes, an endless desert, the Himalayas, and moral questions of when it is necessary to leave someone behind. Weir delivers a strong film of courage and survival. Though well made and superbly enacted, this film did not do well at the box office, earning more than $20 million in its initial release against a budget of $30 million. Violence and gutter language prohibit viewing by children. **p**, Peter Weir, Duncan Henderson, Joni Levin, Nigel Sinclair, Roee Sharon Peled; **d**, Peter Weir; **cast**, Colin Farrell, Mark Strong, Jim Sturgess, Ed Harris, Saoirse Ronan, Gustaf Skarsgard, Alexandru Potocean, Sebastian Urzendowsky, Dragos Bucur, Sally Edwards; **w**, Weir, Keith Clarke (based on the novel *The Long Walk: The True Story of a Trek to Freedom* by Slavomir Rawicz); **c**, Russell Boyd; **m**, Burkhard Dallwitz; **ed**, Lee Smith; **prod d**, John Stoddart; **art d**, Kes Bonnet; **set d**, Goro Deyanov; **spec eff**, Jason Troughton.

Way Down East ★★★★★ 1920 (silent); U.S.; 145m/13 reels; D.W. Griffith Productions/UA; B/W; Drama; Children: Unacceptable; **BD**; **DVD**; **VHS**; **IV**. Pantheon filmmaker Griffith provides another masterpiece in this stunning melodrama, and its stars, Gish and Barthelmess are mesmerizing in their prosaic roles as simple back country people. The film opens with Gish living with her mother, Landau, in a New England village. They are hard-pressed for money, and Landau pleads with Gish to go to their wealthy relatives in Boston to seek some financial aid. Gish visits Bernard, the snobbish patriarch of that family, who, along with her arrogant daughters, treat her as unwanted family baggage. She attends a social gathering, and Gish draws the attention of Sherman, a rich playboy who indulges his every whim without a care for anyone else. Sherman overwhelms her with attention and then tricks her into marrying him in a mock wedding. He convinces her to keep their union a secret, saying that if his wealthy father learns that he has married beneath his station in life, his father will cut off the handsome allowance that permits him to continue enjoying his hedonistic lifestyle. After Gish becomes pregnant, Sherman tells her the truth, that they are not legally married, and that he has no obligations toward her. He then deserts her. After Landau dies, Gish takes a room in Belden, Massachusetts, where she delivers her child in crude conditions. While alone, she baptizes her child in her miserably spare room and then discovers to her horror that the child is dead. (This scene is one of many powerful sequences where Gish displays her extraordinary acting abilities.) She stares straight ahead in shock at this most awful news, rocking back and forth in a chair before she begins to slowly move her head from left to right in denial of the horrible occurrence. Gripped by the shock of her baby's death, she remains in a catatonic state (an unforgettable evocative image frozen in the history of filmmaking, one that only Griffith in his intense artistic rapport with the gifted Gish could have achieved). Fitzroy, a cold-hearted landlady, suspects that Gish has no husband and has given birth to a child out of wedlock (an event in those days made a person an instant social pariah). She viciously evicts Gish, who must then find work and lodging somewhere. Going to a village, she finds work on a farm that is owned by a wealthy family, where Bathelmess, the hard-working son of the family patriarch, McIntosh, is immediately taken by the empathetic Gish. Even though Gish is a hired hand, McIntosh, and his kindly wife, Bruce, treat Gish as a family member and Bathelmess quickly falls in love with her. McIntosh wants Barthelmess to marry his attractive cousin, Hay, but he and Hay are only friends and Hay soon becomes emotionally involved with Hale, a visiting professor. Then Sherman resurfaces as his family owns a nearby estate. The lustful rake plies his wiles to Hay, but, when he sees Gish living with McIntosh, he urges her to return to him. Gish by this time has fallen in love with the gentle Barthelmess, but she feels that her shadowy past prevents her from seeking happiness with him. Gish's predicament worsens when Fitzroy, her former landlady, sees her on a visit to the area and tells local gossip Ogden about Gish's past indiscretions. Ogden, in turn, when attending a local barn dance, spreads this damaging tale to others, specifically informing McIntosh about Gish's past. McIntosh makes sure of this tale by going to Belden to meet with Fitzroy, who confirms the scandal about Gish. When McIntosh returns home, he angrily orders Gish from his home. She accepts her miserable lot, but, before leaving, Gish turns on the man who has brought shame and disgrace to her, Sherman, who has audaciously visited McIntosh's family. She denounces him, exposing the secret that he has been the man who has so treacherously deceived, betrayed and violated her. After Gish goes into a snow storm, the irate Barthelmess explodes and attacks Sherman, soundly thrashing him before he races after Gish. Wandering exhausted through the storm, Gish reaches the river and, consumed by grief and hysterical at her plight, staggers onto the frozen river and faints. The river is just then undergoing a spring thaw and the ice begins to break up. Meanwhile, Barthelmess searches frantically for Gish until he reaches the river and sees to his horror that the river's ice has broken up into large floating cakes and that Gish lies unconscious on one of those ice cakes, her right hand dangling into the freezing river waters, which are being swiftly sent toward a waterfall and Gish's certain death. The courageous Barthelmess leaps upon a floating ice cake and then on to another and yet another as he works his arduous way toward the fallen Gish and as the ice floe rushes toward the falls. (This sequence is one of the most harrowing action scenes ever filmed, showing Barthelmess leaping and keeping his balance on the wobbly, slippery slabs of ice that threaten to capsize him into the freezing water at any moment.) Barthelmess finally reaches the prostrate Gish and sweeps her into his arms, carrying her from the ice cake and onto another and another to reach the riverbank, but only at the last moment before both might go crashing over the waterfalls. This triumphant scene is followed by a happy epilogue where McIntosh begs forgiveness of Gish for his actions and she lovingly accepts his apology. The film ends with the triple marriage of Gish and Barthelmess, of Hay and Hale, and of town gossip Ogden and Strong, an eccentric who has been chasing Ogden for twenty years. Griffith directs this film with great care, unfolding its story of tragedy and woe in such simplistic terms that the melodrama never becomes mawkish or saccharine. This is chiefly due to his insistence that the players understate their roles and that is magnificently achieved by Gish, Barthelmess and the rest of the outstanding cast. Sherman, who later became a successful director, is wonderful as a villainous rake whose money and position he thinks puts him above the law and the standards of human decency, the kind of effective role he played throughout the silent era. Griffith's action scenes, particularly the spectacular ice floe sequence at the end, are thrilling, heart-pounding wonders to behold, especially since he achieved these perilous scenes without the benefit of special effects. There are many brief shots that cheerfully buoy the viewer's sense of gloom and doom such as a cheerful and lively barn dance, the bountiful McIntosh farmhouse, its abundance of food and a little white kitten falling asleep with family members. Griffith's deep sense of humanity floods even the smallest scenes, such as where Gish, who is still grieving over the loss of her own child, is going to a store and, seeing a child being pulled on a sled through the snow, movingly pauses to briefly caress the baby. Unlike his previous films, Griffith essentially provides a prosaic tale without subtleties that glorifies the American home and where everything seems natural, even his small comedy sketches, which, in his other films sometimes proved embarrassing, but here befitted the characters of the story's simple lifestyle. This film challenged the then viewing audience that had become much more worldly, if not jaded and hedonistic, following the ungodly destruction of WWI (1914-1918), powerfully drawing those viewers back into their old best memories, as if presenting each an urn of native soil into which they could sink their nostrils and smell the sweet scent of their native hearths. His is a great portrait of the impregnable and irresistible force of love that, despite all obstacles, invariably triumphs, as is so spectacularly manifested by the heroic Barthelmess. The film was a tremendous success at the box office, earning more than $4.5 million in its initial release against a budget of $1 million, and

Lillian Gish and Richard Barthelmess in _Way Down East,_ 1920.

proved to be Griffith's most commercially successful film to date. It became the fourth largest-grossing silent film in the history of motion pictures. Those attending its premieres in New York and Chicago paid $10 plus tax for a seat, even after the Chicago _Tribune_ inexplicably accused Griffith of being a megalomaniac for producing this film. The film had been produced as two silent shorts in 1908 and 1914, and was remade as a talkie in 1935, with Henry Fonda as its star. **_Author's Note_**: The original Parker play, written and produced in the 1890s (and revised by Joseph R. Grismer as a novel published in 1900), was very popular in its day as a William A. Brady stage production. Its thickly melodramatic tale underscored the draconian standards of the Victorian era where unwed mothers were routinely branded social outcasts. The play saw perennial road show tours and it was, by the time Griffith considered it for a film version, considered an old-fashioned story. It was therefore a little more than amazing that Griffith paid $175,000 for its film rights, something he had never done before as he invariably worked without established literary works and with his own makeshift scripts. Gish and others close to Griffith believed that he has abandoned his good judgment when he acquired this antique work, but the incisive director believed that the old-fashioned values inherent in the story still flowed in the American bloodstream and was as potent a tale as was _Little Women_ and as poignantly reminiscent of a print by Currier and Ives. Griffith would reinforce the staunch ethics of that bygone era with title cards at the beginning of the film that advocated a strict monogamy for women in the period setting, but nevertheless exposed its draconian morality for the filmgoers of a later time, banking on emotional nostalgia to serve as the film's chief motivation. In this he was shrewdly correct. Women of all ages and by the tens of thousands wept unashamedly when seeing this film, even the most hard-hearted, flippant, cigarette-smoking, cocktail-drinking flappers of that day (as depicted in Frances Marion's film, **Flapper**, 1920, released the same year). Griffith employs, chiefly in the second half of the film, his traditional intercutting and parallel action shots. One of his most effective intercutting scenes occurs when he shows in grim contrast the despondent Gish with her dead child in a lonely room and then cuts to the arrogant Sherman luxuriating at his lavishly appointed estate. The scenes of the blizzard into which Gish takes flight were shot in March 1920 at Orienta Point, near Griffith's studio at Mamaroneck, New York, and where the director, cast and crew had waited all winter for that storm to arrive. The frozen river scenes were shot at White River Junction during frozen weather. The scenes showing Barthelmess rescuing Gish just before both go over the waterfalls (stock footage of Niagara Falls was employed in brief cuts) were shot at Farmington, Connecticut, during the summer, and the actual falls were about fifteen feet high. The ice cakes used in these shots were made of blocks of floating wood painted white and to which piano wires were

Jackie Combs and Emil Jannings in *The Way of All Flesh*, 1927.

attached to allow manipulation and direction of movement. All of these various shots were then expertly patched together in editing by Griffith that resulted in the overall action sequences. When shooting the actual frozen river scenes, Griffith's crew members had to saw and even dynamite some of the river's frozen ice. Gish lies sprawled upon one of those severed pieces of ice and, while slowly floating down the river while unconscious, has her dangling right hand immersed in the frozen water. Her hair not only froze, but so did her right hand and she lost some feeling in her fingers for some time thereafter. It was Gish's idea to trail her hand in that frozen river for the sake of realism, and, even a half century later, she had problems with that right hand. She and Barthelmess did their own stunts and never complained to Griffith about the risks they were taking or the discomforts they endured. During the blizzard, icicles formed on Gish's eyelashes, and closing her eyes for some time after that caused her considerable pain. In the river scenes (Allan Law and Elmer Clifton doubled for Gish in some of the long shots), Gish spent more than three weeks on that slab of ice, and about twenty times a day, until cameraman Bitzer caught just the right action scenes that Griffith wanted. A small fire was kept burning beneath Bitzer's camera during the blizzard and river scenes in order to keep the camera's oil from freezing. Griffith did not escape the brutality of some of his realistic winter scenes as much of his face froze while he stood next to Bitzer when making those scenes. The role played by Hay, enacting McIntosh's niece, was originally assigned to Clarine Seymour, who had long been a Griffith contract player, but she became ill from a strangulated intestine during the production and underwent an emergency operation, resulting in her untimely death at age twenty-one, on April 25, 1920. Hay, who somewhat resembled Seymour, was then cast in that role and Seymour's scenes were then reshot, although Seymour can still be seen in some long shots. Another tragedy linked to this production is that of Bobby Harron (1893-1920), one of Griffith's young feature players, who ended his life at age twenty-seven, with a self-inflicted gunshot wound to the left lung (although he denied on his deathbed that he never intended to commit suicide). It was known that Harron was deeply depressed when Griffith, who had starred Harron in his masterpiece film, **Intolerance: Love's Struggle Throughout the Ages**, 1916, but who had refused to cast him in the lead role of **Way Down East**, and assigned Barthelmess that role after he had become Griffith's new protégé. Harron was to attend the New York premiere of this film, but, instead, went to his hotel room and somehow shot himself on the night of September 3, 1920, his death occurring two days later, ruled (mercifully for his family, Griffith and others) as "an accidental gunshot wound." Sherman's presence in this film continued to raise curious suspicions. He emotes, as was his style throughout his acting career, with effeminate mannerisms, accenting his fey character with

heavily mascaraed eyes, sashay walk and limp wrists. It was long felt that Sherman was a closet gay (he was a close friend of director George Cukor, who was, indeed, homosexual), but defenders point out that Sherman had married three times, albeit he wound up divorcing all three women. Some state censorship boards demanded that Griffith heavily edit this film before allowing it to be shown in theaters. The State of Pennsylvania demanded that more than sixty edits be made to eliminate any scenes where Gish is wedded in a pretended marriage, and later become pregnant. Griffith reluctantly complied, these edits damaging the film's continuity and which later produced considerable puzzlement for viewers in that state when they suddenly saw Gish with an unexplained baby in later scenes. **p&d**, D.W. Griffith; **cast**, Lillian Gish, Mrs. David Landau, Josephine Bernard, Mrs. Morgan Belmont, Lowell Sherman, Burr McIntosh, Richard Barthelmess, Kate Bruce, George Neville, Porter Strong, Mary Hay, Emily Fitzroy, Creighton Hale, Vivia Ogden, (extras) Norma Shearer, Una Merkel; **w**, Anthony Paul Kelly, Griffith (based on the play by Lottie Blair Parker, William A. Brady); **c**, G.W. Bitzer, Hendrik Sartov, Paul H. Allen, Charles Downs; **m**, Louis Silvers, William Frederick Peters; **ed**, James and Rose Smith; **art d**, Charles O. Seessel, Clifford Pember.

The Way of All Flesh ★★★★ 1927 (silent); U.S.; 94m/9 reels; PAR; B/W; Drama; Children: Unacceptable. Jannings gives a powerful performance as a good man whose life is ruined through a single folly in this fine domestic saga expertly wielded by pantheon director Fleming. Jannings is a well-to-do bank clerk living in Milwaukee with his wife Bennett and their six children. He is a devoted husband and dotes upon his children, teaching his youngest son, De Lacy, how to play the violin. Jannings is always punctual in arriving at his job and prides himself with his attention to detail. He religiously lives a structured life and is therefore upset when he is given a special assignment by the bank to deliver a packet of bonds worth $1,000 to a bank in Chicago. He is reluctant to undertake this chore, but he nevertheless agrees to deliver the bonds, and leaves home for the first time since his honeymoon. Once on the train, Jannings meets blonde flapper Haver, who is seated next to him. When the conductor asks for his ticket, Jannings withdraws it from a pocket, and Haver sees the bonds he is carrying. Haver overwhelms Jannings with her charms and talks him into buying her some champagne. The next thing he can remember is waking up in the bedroom of a seedy Chicago boarding house. His money and the bonds are gone and so is Haver. He nevertheless is successful in tracking down the vixen to a roughhouse saloon where he confronts Haver, but Kohler, her boyfriend, who is also the saloon owner, along with his thugs, beat Jannings senseless. He is then dragged to a railroad yard, but before Kohler can put an end to him, Jannings revives and struggles with his assailant. Kohler is knocked onto a track where an oncoming train strikes and kills him. At that moment, Jannings sees how he might overcome his terrible predicament by exchanging clothes with the dead man. He does so and flees. The mangled corpse is now identified as that of Jannings and he is considered a victim instead of the foolish man who lost the money entrusted to him by his bank, thus protecting his family from scandal. Jannings, assuming an alias, goes on to live in obscurity as a trash collector in a park in his hometown but he never contacts his family, although he watches his loved ones from afar over a twenty-year period, even when they go to a grave to lay a wreath to honor his eldest son, who has been killed in WWI (1914-1918). When his youngest son, who has grown to be Keith, gives his first violin performance, Jannings scrapes together enough money to see Keith perform; Keith plays one of his father's favorite compositions, shedding a tear as he plays in memory of Jannings, who, unknown to Keith, is sitting in the audience. During a Christmas snowstorm, Jannings goes to his old home to see his loved ones enjoying the Yuletide, but, before turning away, Keith encounters him and, thinking him to be nothing more than a penniless tramp, kindly gives Jannings a silver dollar before going into his home. Jannings says nothing as he walks away alone with his bittersweet memories to end this poignantly memorable film. Fleming directs this tragedy in a straightforward manner without milking its many emotional scenes to make it overly sentimental, drawing from Jannings a marvelous portrait of a man having to live with the one mistake that has destroyed his happy life. Jannings received an Oscar for his performance in this film, as well as for his appearance in **The Last Command**, 1928, the only time that the award was given for multiple performances by the same actor. The film was a box office success and its story was remade in 1940, with Akim Tamiroff essaying the Jannings role. *Author's Note*: This author saw the complete film many years ago while living in Milwaukee as a college student; it was shown on Super 8mm by a film collector long since dead. All prints of this film, other than a few segments, have since been lost. Stellar film director Henry Hathaway, who was an assistant director to Fleming during this production, told this author: "Jannings had such a thick German accent that we had a hard time communicating with him as we did not speak fluent German. Vic [Fleming] had to use an interpreter when giving him directions and his script was written in German. Once he understood his character, however, he became that person. That transition was something to behold. Emil [Jannings] was one of the world's great actors." It was claimed in 1999 by Frederica Sagor (1900-2012), an early-day Hollywood scriptwriter, who lived to the incredible age of 111, that the script for this film had been written by her husband, Ernest Maas, also a screenwriter and film producer. Maas, who was a German-American and a friend of Jannings, gave the script to the actor, but Jannings then gave the script to Paramount and Maas was never contacted again after the film went into production. Stealing ideas and even scripts in the silent era was rampant, but, as years went by, writers and film directors filched any good idea or scenes they thought would work well in their own productions. For instance, the scene where Jannings goes to see his son perform as an accomplished violinist is very much like the scene in **Showboat**, 1936, where a long-absent father, Allan Jones, arrives to see his grown daughter perform as a singer on the stage. The ironic ending of **The Way of All Flesh** where Jannings peers hauntingly and lovingly at his family members inside of his former home during Christmastime was duplicated in the finale of **Stella Dallas**, 1925, the earliest version of that wonderful soap opera also starring Belle Bennett (as well as its 1937 remake starring Barbara Stanwyck). The most flagrant filching from this film was committed by none other than the gifted writer-director Preston Sturges when making his masterpiece comedy-drama **Sullivan's Travels**, 1941. Joel McCrea, the star of that film, told this author: "Preston has one scene in that picture where a tramp hits me over the head and I am left with amnesia while the tramp runs off with my wallet that identifies me and is then killed by an oncoming train and his unrecognizable body is then identified as mine. Well, I had seen **The Way of All Flesh** and that very scene, or one very close to it, appeared in that picture. When I mentioned that to Preston, he only smiled and said: "One good scene deserves another." The Anne Sheridan appearing in this film is not to be confused with the Ann Sheridan who was the Warner Brothers superstar of the 1940s. **p**, Adolph Zukor, Jesse L. Lasky; **d**, Victor Fleming; **cast**, Emil Jannings, Belle Bennett, Phyllis Haver, Donald Keith, Fred Kohler, Philippe De Lacy, Mickey McBan, Betsy Ann Hisle, Carmencita Johnson, Gordon Thorpe, Anne Sheridan; **w**, Jules Furthman, Lajos Biro, Julian Johnson (titles), (based on the story by Perley Poore Sheehan); **c**, Victor Milner.

The Way of the Dragon ★★★ 1974; Hong Kong; 90m; Concord Productions/Bryanston Distributing; Color; Comedy/Crime; Children: Unacceptable (MPAA: R); **BD**; **DVD**. Above-average actioner sees Lee, a martial artist known as the Dragon, going to Rome, Italy, to help his cousins, who own a Chinese restaurant there. Crime syndicate tough guys are pressuring the cousins to sell their property to them, but they are unable to fight off Lee. The syndicate boss then hires the best Japanese and European martial artists to take on Lee, but he easily defeats them. The syndicate then hires Norris, a major American martial artist,

Stan Laurel and Oliver Hardy in *Way Out West*, 1937.

and he and Lee engage in a titanic martial arts showdown in the city's historic Coliseum where Lee emerges the victor. Music: "As a Judgment/Colt's Theme" (Ennio Morricone). Violence prohibits viewing by children. **p**, Raymond Chow, Bruce Lee; **d&w**, Lee; **cast**, Lee, Chuck Norris, Nora Miao, Paul Wei Ping-Ao, Wang Chung Hsin, Robert Wall, Ing-Sik Whang, Ti Chin, Tony Liu, Little Unicorn, Malisa Longo, Tommy Chen, Wu Ngan; **c**, Tadashi Nishimoto as Ho Lang Shang; **m**, Joseph Koo; **ed**, Yao Chung Chang as Chang Yao Chung; **art d**, Chen Hsin.

Way Out West ★★★★ 1937; U.S.; 65m; Hal Roach Studios/MGM; B/W; Comedy; Children: Acceptable; **DVD**; **VHS**. Master comedians Laurel and Hardy shine in this hilarious spoof of the Old West, one of their finest outings. We see the two as prospectors wandering West with their mule, Dinah, on a mission to deliver the deed of a gold mine to Lawrence, the daughter of their deceased partner, but they become hopelessly lost. To their relief, they come upon a signpost, but the fierce winds keep turning that post to show different directions, causing them more confusion. (This scene was inexplicably shown only in the version in Europe in the film's initial release.) The boys are trying to reach Brushwood Gulch and decide that it lies beyond what appears to be a shallow stream. They and their mule Dinah cross the stream, but, in the middle of the gently flowing waters, they completely disappear into a deep sinkhole. Managing to escape this underwater cavern, the boys then see a stagecoach approaching and Laurel flags it to a stop by lifting one leg of his pants to expose a bare leg. (This was only one of Laurel's little parodies in this delightful romp, a ridiculous gesture that satirized a famous scene in **It Happened One Night**, 1934, where actress Claudette Colbert lifts her skirt to show her shapely leg, stopping a car driven by Alan Hale, who gives her and Clark Gable a lift.) After they tie their mule to the coach, the boys climb aboard. Hardy attempts to be civil toward Oakland, a female passenger and the wife of Fields, the sheriff of Brushwood Gulch, by bombarding her with banal remarks such as "we've been having a lot of weather lately." Although Oakland makes every effort to tolerate Hardy's incessant chatter, it is evident that she wishes above all else that he cease his moronic babbling. When the coach arrives in Brushwood Gulch, Oakland is welcomed by her husband Fields. She tells him that her trip was made a lot more uncomfortable by Hardy's constant blather and Fields casts a suspicious eye upon the boys, telling them that they had better take the next stagecoach out of town, or else they will be "riding out of here in a hearse." (Fields demonstrates his usual nature of a brawling barroom bouncer rather than that of an upstanding sheriff, but his unlikely personality all the more emphasizes the misfit absurdity of this uproarious satire.) Since the next stage will not be leaving for some time, the boys dally outside of a sa-

Robert Redford and Barbra Streisand in *The Way We Were*, 1973.

loon where they sing impromptu while performing a soft shoe routine (the action in the distance shown on a rear projection screen). They are accompanied by the Avalon Boys in this delightful number, a member of which is future character actor Chill Wills. Though the boys are sworn to secrecy about their mission, Laurel tips their hand to Finlayson, the bartender and owner of the saloon, and who, along with his slatternly wife, Lynne, are Lawrence's guardians. Lawrence has long been mistreated by these two conniving characters, forced to slave endless hours in their emporium as a scullery maid. The shifty Finlayson (who had acted for years in the Laurel and Hardy films as their cross-eyed nemesis) directs the boys to Lynne, instead of Lawrence. Lynne, a blonde long beyond her best years, is a scheming harridan if there ever was one, shedding crocodile tears when hearing about her "father's" death. Although everyone in town except the naïve Laurel and Hardy know that Lynne is not the heir to the deed to the gold mine, the boys politely turn over that deed to Lynne. When they then meet Lawrence, the real heir, they now know that they have been hornswoggled. They return to the saloon and demand that Lynne return the deed. She defiantly refuses and a wild tug of war, replete with traditional Laurel and Hardy slapstick, ensues. Laurel manages to wrest the deed from Lynne after pursuing her to her bedroom, but she knows his weak spot and begins tickling him, reducing him to hysterical laughter (in another fine comedic scene where Laurel's high-pitched squeals of laughter became universally infectious with viewing audiences) until he is too weak to hold onto the deed and Lynne retrieves it. She and Finlayson then put the deed in their safe while the boys summon police. The police turn out to be the abrasive Fields, who orders Laurel and Hardy out of town. The boys doggedly return that night and resolve to get into Finlayson's saloon by using an elaborate pulley, which is weighted by their mule, Dinah, and where Laurel is to be raised to the second story of the building. Hardy is about to activate the pulley by spitting on his hands as would a baseball slugger approaching the plate, but, before he can go to work, Laurel crashes earthward. This alarms Finlayson, who emerges with a shotgun and begins chasing the boys, a pursuit that takes the hectic runners in and out of the building, and the boys finally take refuge inside of a grand piano that collapses and breaks to pieces under their weight. During the wild melee, Hardy's head becomes stuck in a trap door and, while attempting to free him, Laurel stretches his partner's neck at least three feet (achieved through wonderful special effects). Lawrence then arrives to aid the boys and, after they disarm Finlayson, they compel him to open the safe and turn over the deed to Lawrence. She and the boys then hastily depart Brushwood Gulch to ostensibly grow rich by working that promising gold mine. They are last seen singing their way toward a sunset, crossing the same stream, and Hardy once more drops into the sinkhole and out of sight. The film received

an Oscar nomination for Best Musical Score (Hatley) and was a great success at the box office. The film was colorized in 1985, but that version is seldom shown. Songs: "Will You Be My Lovey-Dovey?" (1936; music: Marvin Hatley; lyrics: Portia Lanning), "At the Ball, That's All" (1913; J. Leubrie Hill), "The Trail of the Lonesome Pine" (1913; music: Harry Carroll; lyrics: Ballard MacDonald), "I Want to Be in Dixie" (1912; music: Ted Snyder; lyrics: Irving Berlin), "Bohemian Girl" (1936; Nathaniel Shilkret), "Dance of the Cuckoos" (1930; Marvin Hatley), "Cheyenne" (1906; Egbert Van Alstyne), "Poet and Peasant Overture" (1846; Franz von Suppe). ***Author's Note***: Producer Roach allowed Laurel to co-produce this marvelous comedy, and the comedian doted on every scene, introducing all sorts of funny bits of business, much to Roach's delight (Laurel had also produced **Our Relations**, 1936). When Laurel and Hardy are singing the enchanting "Trail of the Lonesome Pine" (which became a hit when released on record), Laurel's voice abruptly switches from basso to high falsetto, these two passages dubbed by Chill Wills and Rosina Lawrence. Dinah, the mule, had appeared in a number of "Our Gang" comedy shorts, as well as with Laurel and Hardy in their classic comedy short, **The Music Box**, 1932, where, as delivery men, they struggle with a huge piano that must be taken up a flight of endless stairs. Hardy was thirty-four and Laurel thirty-six when they first met and they appeared together in sixty shorts and twenty-seven features, this one being one of their very best. Other films that spoof westerns include **Along Came Jones**, 1945; **The Beautiful Blonde from Bashful Bend**, 1949; **Big Money Rustlas**, 2010; **Blazing Saddles**, 1974; **Carry On Cowboy**, 1965; **Cat Ballou**, 1965; **Crazy Westerners**, 1973; **Dirty Dingus Magee**, 1970; **For a Few Dollars Less**, 1966; **Go West**, 1940; **Lemonade Joe**, 1966; **A Million Ways to Die in the West**, 2014; **The Outlaws Is Coming**, 1965; **Petticoat Planet**, 1996; **Ride 'Em Cowboy**, 1942; **Rustlers' Rhapsody**, 1985; **The Secret Life of Walter Mitty**, 1947 (western daydream sequence); **Shanghai Express**, 1986; **Texas Across the River**, 1966; **Waterhole No. 3**, 1967; and **Zachariah**, 1971. **p**, Stan Laurel, (uncredited) Hal Roach; **d**, James W. Horne; **cast**, Stan Laurel, Oliver Hardy, Sharon Lynne, James Finlayson, Rosina Lawrence, Stanley Fields, Vivien Oakland, Dinah, The Avalon Boys, Mary Gordon, Art Green, Chill Wills, Fred "Snowflake" Toones; **w**, Charles Rogers, Felix Adler, James Parrott (based on a story by Jack Jevne, Rogers); **c**, Art Lloyd, Walter Lundin; **m**, Marvin Hatley; **ed**, Bert Jordan; **art d**, Arthur I. Royce; **set d**, W.L. (William) Stevens; **spec eff**, Roy Seawright.

The Way We Were ★★★★ 1973; U.S.; 118m; Rastar Productions; COL; Color; Romance; Children: Unacceptable (MPAA: PG); **BD**; **DVD**; **VHS**; **IV**. A touching and sensitive tale that wonderfully evokes the period of WWII (1939-1945) and post-war America as two completely opposite personalities, Redford and Streisand, fall in love, marry and then grow apart over politics, but never abandon their feelings for one another. Handsome Redford is a WASP college student with ambitions to become a writer and has no more idea about politics than he does about beekeeping. He meets Streisand at a college dance just before WWII. They meet again shortly before WWII ends. Streisand finds Redford drunk and takes him home to her apartment where they attempt to make love, but Redford passes out. Years pass and both meet once more. By now, Redford has realized his dreams, having recently published a novel, which Streisand has read and admires. Streisand, a Jewish girl who is a social activist with decidedly Marxist views, intrigues the rather sedate Redford. By this time, Streisand is involved in every current campaign and appears in every available social protest where she can march, wave a flag or poster or voice her strong political opinions. She is the quintessential epitome of a person attracted to causes rather than a cause attracting a person a la Eric Hoffer's "True Believer" concept. Redford, who has served as a naval officer in the South Pacific, is trying to find his way as he studies literature and he becomes intrigued by Streisand and her outspoken and radical beliefs. She works at a radio station, and when she meets Redford's conservative college friends, she becomes the butt of their demeaning jokes. Redford, however, reserves any opinion about her. When Redford's friends show no remorse over the death of U.S. President Franklin D. Roosevelt (1882-1945), Streisand becomes incensed at their indifference, as well as Redford's noncommittal attitude about her many causes. He, in turn, can no longer abide her lack of social etiquette and he severs their relationship. (He breaks up with her even though he knows she loves him, at one time telling her: "When you love someone, from Roosevelt to me, you go deaf, dumb and blind.") Their love for one another, however, is so strong that they reunite, thinking they might make a go of it if they move from NYC to California where Redford has an opportunity to write screenplays. They live a comfortable if not luxurious life in the Golden State, but Streisand's deep senses for causes resurfaces and she tells Redford that he is selling out his fine talents for Hollywood big bucks. Moreover, the Red Menace raises its head when the U.S. House Un-American Activities Committee (HUAC) begins to probe Hollywood, especially its many left-wing writers. Streisand bristles at this and leaves for Washington, D.C., where she fights against the oppressive right-wing politicians (who were successful in having many Hollywood writers blacklisted, some even jailed for not cooperating with HUAC, ruining many careers and even causing some suicides). In her absence, Redford has an affair with Chiles, the wife of Redford's friend, Dillman. Streisand, who is pregnant, learns about the relationship and finally realizes that the man she has married is not the man she first idealized years earlier and that he has not only proved to be a cheating husband, but will use his talents for any purpose to make money. Redford, too, is worn out with Streisand's demands that he be something more than what he truly is and both decide to end their union. Some years after their divorce, they meet once more in front of NYC's Plaza Hotel. Accompanying Redford is a stylish, beautiful woman. Streisand is remarried and learns that Redford is now very successfully writing sitcoms for TV. He asks about their daughter, but shows no desire to visit the girl. They still love each other and Redford admits that he was at his artistic and altruistic best when living with Streisand. They are, however, now worlds - apart as might be strangers. After they say goodbye, Redford watches as Streisand begins handing out "Ban the Bomb" leaflets. He smiles and calls after her: "You never give up, do you?" Streisand replies: "Only when I'm forced to. I'm a very good loser." Pollack gently guides this sweet romance through its time-wearing scenes to subtly show the widening breach between two lovers unable to close the ever-widening social and political chasms between them. Redford and Streisand are marvelously true to their divergent characters, one easily accepting the ebb and flow of life, the other dynamically attempting to change its course of events and consequences, both poignantly empathetic as they drift apart as would two ships at sea sailing in opposite directions. It is a bittersweet tale of star-crossed lovers, and, thanks to the compelling performances of its magnetic stars, an unforgettable film. The film is decidedly campy, even predictable, but delightfully so, and there is enough syrup on the cement to provide some dangerous pratfalls, but no one stumbles. The innocent generation it represents through its loving characters—and there is greatness of principle and emotional heroism in them—was made of sterner stuff, much of its youthful bone and sinew sacrificed to save the world from tyrannical domination. Every scene is natural and seamlessly woven into the flexible fabric of that nostalgically remembered era. It becomes a timeless tale encompassing millions of lovers who danced to the mellifluous strains of Glenn Miller, drove an indefatigable Ford, and, without regret, left their blood on the sands of Iwo Jima and Omaha Beach. Although self-serving film reviewers demeaned this film, it is far better than what their secular and unreasonably demanding agendas reflect. The public, on the other hand, rightfully knew that love has its reasons of which reason does not know and accepted this romantic tale for what it was, loving its lovers and flocking to the box office where it earned more than $45 million in its initial release against a $15 million budget. The film received an Oscar for Best Musical Score (Hamlisch), and Best Song ("The Way We Were"; Ham-

Barbra Streisand and Robert Redford in *The Way We Were*, 1973.

lisch), and it received Oscar nominations for Best Actress (Streisand); Best Cinematography (Stradling); Best Art Direction (Grimes; set decoration: Kiernan); and Best Costume Design (Dorothy Jeakins, Moss Mabry). Songs: "The Way We Were" (1973; music: Marvin Hamlisch; lyrics: Marilyn [Bergman], Alan Bergman), "Red Sails in the Sunset" (1935; Will Grosz), "The Glory of Love" (1936; Billy Hill), "On the Sunny Side of the Street" (1930; music: Jimmy McHugh; lyrics: Dorothy Fields), "Wrap Your Troubles in Dreams (And Dream Your Troubles Away)" (1930; Harry Barris), "In the Mood" (1939; Joe Garland, Andy Razaf), "Paper Doll" (1915; Johnny Black). *Author's Note*: Laurents, who wrote the novel and screenplay with some considerable help from a bevy of talented writers, based his tale upon a life experience. As a student at Cornell in 1937, he met a Jewish student, who was a member of the Young Communist League, a girl passionately involved with the movement against Francisco Franco (1892-1975), the fascist leader then attempting to usurp the Republic in Spain during the Spanish Civil War (1936-1939). She was a tempestuous radical, who organized rallies against Franco and she so impressed Laurents that, though he later lost touch with this fiery young woman, he never forgot her and used her as the role model for his novel's heroine, the character Streisand so perfectly enacts in this film. Streisand was always the first choice for that role, Laurents stating that he had her in mind when writing the script. Laurents recommended Pollack direct, and Pollack, in turn, wanted Warren Beatty for the leading man. When Beatty refused, he turned to Redford, but Redford took his time in accepting that role, showing reluctance to enact another "pretty boy." When Ryan O'Neill was then considered for the part, Redford finally accepted, but there was friction on the set when the film went into production. Streisand demanded extensive talks about each scene and seemingly endless rehearsals which frustrated Redford no end as he believed in a more impulsive and impromptu approach with scenes. Pollack later complained that he spent most of his time trying to please both stars and the contentious atmosphere on the set was later described as "doing overtime at Dachau [the German concentration camp in WWII]." Much of the friction was attributed to Streisand, who meddled incessantly with production matters endemic to producer Stark or director Pollack, and it was felt that she really wanted to helm this film, a desire she later fulfilled when becoming an independent director. The college scenes were shot at Union College in Schenectady, New York. The Medberry Hotel in Ballston Spa, New York, was used for the restaurant meeting between Redford and Streisand and other scenes were shot in NYC and in California. The scenes that depicted the HUAC hearings were later drastically edited, which caused Streisand to later state: "There weren't many movies made about this period of time in the blacklist, and that's why it killed me to have those two scenes taken out. I was really heartbroken."

Stefan Arngrim and Kirk Douglas in *The Way West*, 1967.

She and Redford were very much like the characters they played with decidedly different personalities and perspectives, but, according to all reports, they respected each other and remained cordial after the completion of this film. Other films profiling HUAC include: **Big Jim McLain**, 1952; **Citizen Cohn**, 1992 (Roy Cohn) **Guilty by Suspicion**, 1991; **J. Edgar**, 2011 (J. Edgar Hoover); **J. Edgar Hoover**, 1987 (made-for-TV); **Hoover**, 2000 (J. Edgar Hoover); **The Majestic**, 2001; **Marathon Man**, 1976; **One of the Hollywood Ten**, 2000; **Paul Robeson**, 1979 (made-for-TV); **The Private Files of J. Edgar Hoover**, 1977; **Tail Gunner Joe**, 1977 (made-for-TV; Joseph McCarthy); and **Three Brave Men**, 1956. **p**, Ray Stark; **d**, Sydney Pollack; **cast**, Barbra Streisand, Robert Redford, Bradford Dillman, Lois Chiles, Patrick O'Neal, Viveca Lindfors, Allyn Ann McLerie, Murray Hamilton, Herb Edelman, Sally Kirkland, Marcia Mae Jones, Don Keefer, James Woods, Susan Blakely; **w**, Arthur Laurents, (uncredited) Alvin Sargent, David Rayfiel, Francis Ford Coppola, Dalton Trumbo (based on the novel by Laurents); **c**, Harry Stradling Jr. (Panavision; Eastmancolor); **m**, Marvin Hamlisch; **ed**, John F. Burnett; **prod d**, Stephen Grimes; **set d**, William Kiernan.

The Way West ★★★ 1967; U.S.; 122m; Harold Hecht/UA; Color; Western; Children: Unacceptable (MPAA: PG-13); **DVD**; **VHS**; **IV**. Gritty western with a sterling cast begins with Douglas, a widowed U.S. senator, who leads a wagon train of pioneers from Missouri to Oregon to start a new settlement in the West in the mid-1800s. A truculent trail scout, Mitchum, is second in command and is often at odds with Douglas on which best routes to take, and it doesn't help much that Mitchum's eyesight is failing. Douglas and one of the newcomers to the journey, Widmark, clash over Douglas' iron will and forceful leadership. While on the trek, newlyweds Witney and Justice have a falling out, and Witney seduces and impregnates the young and naive Field. The settler families face many hardships besides weather and Sioux Indians, especially after Witney accidentally kills a young Indian boy, who is disguised in a wolf skin. To make peace with the Sioux, Douglas has Witney hanged. Douglas pays dearly for his draconian edict as if Providence has turned against him. His son, Arngrim, is killed in a stampede, and Douglas, feeling that God has punished him for taking Witney's life, orders his slave, Glenn, to whip him. Meanwhile, the distraught Field, realizing that she is facing unwed motherhood, is touched when McGreevey, who is Widmark's teenage son, asks her to marry him. The caravan is about to be joined by a protective unit of U.S. cavalry, but Douglas, who fears losing his authority, sends the troops away with a false claim that the homesteaders are infected by smallpox. Learning this, Widmark decides to take command of the wagon train and Douglas becomes a traveling, lonesome pariah. When the train encounters its last obstacle where it

must lower horses and wagons over a perilous cliff, Douglas plunges to his death, the rope holding him cut by Justice in revenge for his having had her husband hanged to appease the blood-seeking Sioux. The wagon train finally reaches Oregon and the pioneers start their settlement. The film is beautifully lensed in radiant color by master cinematographer Clothier and it did well at the box office, but hardly recouped its whopping budget of more than $5 million. Song: "The West" (Bronislau Kaper, Mack David). ***Author's Note***: Mitchum told this author that "**The Way West** was the second picture I appeared in with Kirk [Douglas]. We had worked together in **Out of the Past** [1947], but that was twenty years earlier where I was the star of that picture and Kirk was in a supporting role. I guess we were vying for the leading role when we did that western together, but, mind you, Kirk let everyone know that he was the big shot in that picture, as well as a big pain in the butt." Widmark echoed these sentiments when telling this author: "The way [Kirk] Douglas acted when we were shooting **The Way West**, you would think that he was running United Artists [the studio releasing this film]. He was playing the part of a bossy wagon master in that picture and I think he took his role to heart because he was bossing everybody off camera, too. I am the first to admit that he is a terrific actor, but John Ford he is not!" This film saw some harrowing accidents during its production. A helicopter crashed on the set, but little damage was done. Worse, a wagon turned over during a river crossing that trapped Albright inside of it. She was pinned underwater by some of the props inside the wagon and was rescued just in time when crew members pulled her out in an unconscious state. She was hospitalized for the day, but returned the next morning where a double took her place when the river crossing scene was reshot. Albright stated that she remained traumatized by the accident long after the film was completed. This was the film debut for Justice and Field, the latter leaving her mousey roles to become a dynamic leading lady a decade later. **p**, Harold Hecht; **d**, Andrew V. McLaglen; **cast**, Kirk Douglas, Robert Mitchum, Richard Widmark, Lola Albright, Patric Knowles, Katherine Justice, Sally Field, William Lundigan, Harry Carey Jr., Elisabeth Fraser, John Mitchum, Jack Elam, Michael Witney, Michael McGreevey, Stefan Arngrim, Stubby Kaye, Peggy Stewart, Nick Cravat, Roy Glenn; **w**, Ben Maddow, Mitchell Lindemann (based on the novel by A.B. Guthrie, Jr.); **c**, William H. Clothier (Panavision; DeLuxe Color); **m**, Bronislau Kaper; **ed**, Otho Lovering; **art d**, Ted Haworth; **set d**, Robert Priestley; **spec eff**, Daniel Hays, Albert Whitlock.

Ways of Love ★★★ 1950; Italy/France; 119m; Joseph Burstyn; B/W; Drama; Children: Unacceptable; **DVD**; **VHS**. Three well-crafted episodes about love and lovers make up this absorbing film. In the first episode, "A Day in the Country," a working-class woman and her daughter become involved with two oarsmen. In the second story, "The Miracle," a woman, Magnani, sleeps with Fellini, a bum, and becomes pregnant, believing she is carrying the child of Saint Joseph. (Fellini made his only screen appearance in this film.) The final episode, "Jofroi," is about a peasant who sells his land and then will not let the owner cut down the olive trees on it. (In French and Italian; English subtitles.) "A Day in the Country": **p**, Pierre Braunberger; **d&w**, Jean Renoir (based on a story by Guy de Maupassant); **c**, Claude Renoir, Jean Bourgoin; **m**, Joseph Kosma; **ed**, Marguerite Renoi; **prod d**, Christian Berard; "The Miracle": **p&d**, Roberto Rossellini; **cast**, Anna Magnani, Federico Fellini; **w**, Rossellini, Tullio Pinelli (based on a story by Fellini); **c**, Aldo Tonti; **ed**, Eraldo Da Roma; **m**, Renzo Rossellini; "Jofroi": **d**, Marcel Pagnol; based on the story "Jofroi De La Maussan" by Jean Giono).

We Are Not Alone ★★★ 1939; U.S.; 112m; WB; B/W; Drama; Children: Unacceptable. Muni presents another powerful performance in this forceful drama of a middle-aged physician tied to a shrewish wife while falling in love with a beautiful, young dancer. Muni is a country doctor with a practice in a small community in England in 1914. He is married to Robson, a woman with a heart of stone, and he spends most of his leisure hours doting on their young son, Severn, and playing the violin. Bryan, an Austrian dancer, is treated by Muni, who sets her broken wrist. He sees that she is so depressed in not being able to find work that she contemplates suicide. Muni comforts her and, while she looks for employment, provides a place for her to stay. So that Severn will not come under the domination of harsh Robson, Muni hires Bryan to be the boy's governess, and the young woman and boy quickly develop a deep bond while Severn stays with Bryan during the daytime, until Muni finishes his medical chores and returns home in the evening. Robson resents being usurped as the boy's mother by Bryan, and, after learning that Bryan had been, of all things, a dancer, and, worse, tried to kill herself, she demands that Muni fire her. When he refuses, Robson sends Severn to live with Napier, who is Robson's stiff-lipped brother and an archdeacon residing in a remote village. Muni then helps Bryan to enter a music school and continues to aid and see her. Meanwhile, Severn rebels against his severe environment and sneaks back into his home and, while searching for a pocket knife Robson earlier took from him, he knocks over some bottles in Muni's office, breaking some and spilling others. He desperately stuffs the pills into other bottles, not knowing that taking some of these pills may prove fatal to any user. After WWI (1914-1918) begins, irate citizens run amuck and begin attacking and destroying any shop or residence operated or occupied by anyone with a German-sounding name. Muni realizes that Bryan's Austrian background puts her in jeopardy and he spirits her to another town where she prepares to return to her native country. Robson, at this time, is suffering from a severe headache and takes some pills from the cabinet in Muni's office, not realizing that Severn has inadvertently mixed some dangerous pills with simple aspirin. She soon grows ill and dies. Her death is ruled a homicide and Muni and Bryan are arrested and charged with murder. They are tried, convicted and sentenced to death, mostly because of the prejudice jurors have against Bryan's Austrian heritage. Muni realizes that Severn innocently caused his mother's death, but he keeps this a secret so as to protect the boy from any future guilt. He and Bryan are allowed to see each other shortly before they are executed and they declare their love for one another, believing that they will find happiness together in the next world. Despite the rather depressing ending, this film is presented by director Goulding with great sensitivity, and Muni's superlative performance as a gentle and loving person sustains deep interest throughout. Robson and Bryan also provide sterling performances as the two women who bring about the destruction of Muni's otherwise tranquil life. The period is well captured in sets and costumes, and the peaceful English countryside is sumptuously lensed by master cinematographer Gaudio. Though this film was not popular at the box office, it remained one of Muni's best outings on film. Songs/Music: "Rondo in A Minor, K.511" (1787; Wolfgang Amadeus Mozart), "Die Krahe (The Raven) Op. 89, No. 15" (Franz Schubert), "Romance in Eb, Op. 44, No. 1" (Anton Rubenstein), "God Save the King" (1744; Henry Carey), "It's a Long, Long Way to Tipperary" (1912; Jack Judge, Harry Williams), "Symphony No. 4 ('Surprise'): Andante" (1791; Joseph Haydn). *Author's Note*: Muni told this author that he felt his appearance in this film, his tenth and final screen production for Warner Brothers, was "one of my best performances as I had a fine script to work with and my character was intelligent and compassionate. I was even allowed to do my own violin playing, although I do not claim to be a concert performer. To be sure, **We Are Not Alone** is a tragedy, but it also shows the mass hysteria during World War One when hatred and prejudice controlled the public's temper." Dolly Haas was originally cast as the younger woman, but reportedly suffered a nervous collapse due to the stressful nature of her role and was replaced by Bryan. In truth, Haas left the production after she and Muni had one too many arguments about "creative differences" in their scenes together. There is no mistaking that author Hilton, when writing *We Are Not Alone*, employed the sensational murder case involving mild-mannered Dr. Hawley Harvey Crippen (1862-1910), who murdered his domineering wife, Cora, on January 31, 1910, so that he could run away with a younger

A tiger friend and Matt Damon in *We Bought a Zoo*, 2011.

woman, Ethel Le Neve (1883-1967), and was apprehended, tried, convicted and executed by hanging on November 23, 1910. For comprehensive information on this case, see my work *World Encyclopedia of 20th Century Murder* (Paragon House, 1992; pages: 145-152). Other actors depicting Crippen include **Dr. Crippen**, 1942 (Rudolf Fernau); **Dr. Crippen**, 1964 (Donald Pleasence); and **The Suspect**, 1944 (Charles Laughton). **p**, Henry Blanke; **d**, Edmund Goulding; **cast**, Paul Muni, Jane Bryan, Flora Robson, Una O'Connor, Raymond Severn, Henry Daniell, Montagu Love, James Stephenson, Cecil Kellaway, Alan Napier, Douglas Scott, Phyllis Barry, Lucile Fairbanks, Doris Lloyd; **w**, James Hilton, Milton Krims (based on a novel by Hilton); **c**, Tony Gaudio; **m**, Max Steiner; **ed**, Warren Low; **art d**, Carl Jules Weyl; **spec eff**, Byron Haskin, H.F. Koenekamp.

We Bought a Zoo ★★★ 2011; U.S.; 124m; FOX; Color; Comedy; Drama; Children: Unacceptable (MPAA: PG0; **BD**; **DVD**; **IV**. This entertaining tale is based on the autobiographical memoirs of Mee, a journalist, played by Damon, a young widower who really buys a zoo. In reality, it was the Dartmoor Zoological Park in Devon, England, closed in 1968; the Mee family bought it in 2006. However, the film sets the family and zoo in Southern California. The film opens with Damon rearing his mid-teenage son, Ford, and daughter, Jones, who is seven. Ford is arrested for shoplifting and Damon decides it's best to bring up the children in the country, so they leave the big city and he finds a house that is equipped with some animals since it was once a private zoo, but has been closed for lack of money and zoning problems. Johansson takes care of the animals with help from her teenage niece, Fanning, and a Scotsman, Macfadyen. Damon buys the place, including the zoo, despite the advice of his accountant brother Church. Damon and Johansson disagree on whether to put down Spar, an old Bengal tiger that is depressed. Meanwhile, an animal control officer, Higgins, imposes strict standards for the care and housing of the animals on the property. All is finally resolved and Damon and Johansson and the kids and animals become one happy family. Songs: "Don't Come around Here No More" (Tom Petty, Dave Stewart); "Do It Clean" (Ian Stephen McCulloch, William Sergeant, Leslie Thomas Pattinson, Pete De Freitas); "Airline to Heaven" (Woody Guthrie, Jay Bennett, Jeffrey Tweedy); "Don't Be Shy" (Cat Stevens as Yusuf Islam); "Do Go," "Sinking Friendships," "Aevin Endar," "Boy Lilikoi" (Jon Thor Birgisson); "Living with the Law" (Chris Whitely); "Last Medicine Dance," "Ashley Collective," "Throwing Arrows" (Mike McCready); "Buckets of Rain" (Bob Dylan); "No Soy Del Valle" (William Holland, Nidia Gongora); "Like I Told You" (Acetone: Mark Lightcap, Richie Lee, Steve Hadley); "For a Few Dollars More" (Lee Perry); "Hunger Strike" (Chris Cornell); "Mariachi el Bronx" (Vincent Hidalgo, Joby J.

Eric Portman and John Mills in *We Dive at Dawn*, 1943.

Ford, Jorma Vik, Ray L. Suen, Brad Magers, Ken Horne, Matt Caughthran); "Haleakala Sunset" (Carlton Kaller, Christopher Kaller); "Cinnamon Girl" (Neil Young); "Holocene" (Justin Vernon); "All Your Love/I Miss Your Loving" (Otis Rush); "I Think It's Going to Rain Today" (Randy Newman); "Hoppipolla" (Jon Thor Birgisson, Orri Pall Dyrason, Georg Holm, Kjartan Sveinsson); "Gathering Stories" (music: Jon Thor Birgisson; lyrics: Birgisson, Cameron Crowe). Gutter language and thematic elements prohibit viewing by children. **p**, Cameron Crowe, Julie Yorn, Rick Yorn, Paul Deason, Marc R. Gordon, Aldric La'auli Porter; **d**, Crowe; **cast**, Matt Damon, Scarlett Johansson, Thomas Haden Church, Colin Ford, Maggie Elizabeth Jones, Angus Macfadyen, Elle Fanning, Patrick Fugit, John Michael Higgins, Carla Gallo, J.B. Smoove, Michael Panes, Kym Whitley; **w**, Crowe, Aline Brosh McKenna (based on the book by Benjamin Mee); **c**, Rodrigo Prieto; **m**, Jon Thor Birgisson as Jonsi; **ed**, Mark Livolsi; **prod d**, Clay Griffith; **art d**, Peter Borck, Domenic Silvestri; **set d**, Wayne Shepherd; **spec eff**, Burt Dalton, Dale Ettema.

We Dive at Dawn ★★★★ 1943; U.K.; 98m; Gainsborough/GFD; B/W; War Drama; Children: Unacceptable; **DVD**; **VHS**. Top-notch submarine tale sees fine performances from Portman, Mills and others in this exciting drama set in WWII (1939-1945). Mills, the youthful commander of a British submarine, returns with his crew from an unsuccessful mission at sea. He and his crew members are given shore leave and we see several of these seamen going home. Portman, who has a strained relationship with his wife, finds that she and his son have left him. MacGinnis goes home to be married, but his wedding is postponed when he and the rest of the crew are abruptly recalled to duty. Initially relieved at not having tied the knot, MacGinnss has second thoughts and feels guilty in not marrying the woman he loves. Mills and his crew are informed that the new German pocket battleship *Brandenburg* has suddenly left its home port at Bremerhaven and is making for the Baltic Sea to undergo sea trials and Mill's submarine, *Sea Tiger*, is assigned to sink it before it reaches the Kiel Canal to cross the Danish Peninsula. (Actually, at the time of WWII, the *Brandenburg*, which was launched in 1890, no longer existed, as it was scrapped in 1920; the battleship referenced in this film is most likely the much-sought-after *Tirpitz*.) While sailing toward its objective, the *Sea Tiger* spots a rescue buoy to which three Luftwaffe airmen are clinging after having been shot down. Mills and his crew members mercifully rescue these enemy airmen before continuing their perilous journey. Their compassionate conduct, however, upsets their timetable and delays their arrival at the Canal. As the *Sea Tiger* enters a minefield, one of the German airmen panics and states that the German battleship is far ahead of the pursuing submarine. Realizing that the *Brandenburg* has already entered the Canal, Mills thinks to sail

around the Danish Peninsula and confront the German battleship when it emerges from the Canal. His decision puts his command at even greater risk as he must now navigate through the Baltic Sea, which is totally controlled by German ships and airplanes. Mills' gamble pays off as the *Brandenburg* is seen making for the open sea when the *Sea Tiger* reaches the other side of the Canal. Mills orders all of his submarine's torpedoes fired at once, hoping that one or more of its spread of underwater missiles will strike the target. Since the battleship is accompanied by several German destroyers, Mills orders a crash dive, hoping to avoid the many depth charges to come from those searching destroyers. The *Sea Tiger* takes a terrible pounding from incessant depth charges exploding all around it. To hoodwink the German destroyers, Mills orders that oil be released, along with debris, to convince the enemy ships that the submarine has been sunk. (This ploy was used in many similar films dealing with submarines; in **Run Silent, Run Deep**, 1958, submarine commander Clark Gable orders the same flotsam and jetsam released, along with two bodies of U.S. sailors who have been crushed in a depth charge attack to assure a Japanese destroyer that it has destroyed its undersea target.) After the German destroyers leave the area, the *Sea Tiger* escapes, but Mills and his crew do not know if they have sunk the *Brandenburg*. The submarine, however, is so short of fuel that it may not be able to return to England. To solve that problem, Portman, a former merchant seaman who speaks fluent German, dons the German uniform of one of the captive Luftwaffe airmen and is put ashore on a Danish island. Portman finds an oil tanker docked at the island's port and signals the submarine to sail into its harbor where it refuels from that tanker's contents. Meanwhile, the German garrison occupying the island attacks the *Sea Tiger*, but, with the help of Danish resistance fighters, the submarine manages to escape back to sea and eventually reaches the safety of English waters. When the *Sea Tiger* reaches port, Mills and its crew learn to their delight that they have sunk the *Brandenburg*. Waiting for Portman is his wife and son, and MacGinnis finds to his heart's delight that his fiancée is there to welcome him into her arms. Asquith directs this film with great attention to the detail of submarine operations while sustaining tension and suspense throughout, and Mills, Portman and MacGinnis provide riveting performances. The film was a success at the box office in England as well as in the U.S. Songs: "Thora" (Stephen Adams, Frederick Edward Weatherly), "The Last Rose of Summer" (traditional), "Here Comes the Bride" ["Bridal Chorus"] (1850; from "Lohengrin" by Richard Wagner), "The Shag" (Milton Ager, Al Neiburg, Jerry Livingston). ***Author's Note***: To prepare for his role, Mills became a passenger on a British submarine that sailed down the Clyde River on a training exercise, and Mills was astounded to learn that its captain was no older than twenty-one years old. When the submarine crash-dived, the actor later related his experience, stating: "The ship then seemed to stand on her nose and I felt her speeding like an arrow toward the sea bed; charts and crockery went flying in all directions; I hung on to the rail near the periscope trying to look heroic and totally unconcerned; the only thing that concerned me was the fact that I was sure that my face had turned a pale shade of pea-green." Interior shots were made at Gaumont-British Studios in London and with the full cooperation of the British Admiralty. Exterior shots profiled two British submarines, the P614 and the P615, two of four submarines constructed in 1939 by the Vickers Company that were to be delivered to Turkey. With the onset of WWII, however, these submarines, which were similar but smaller than the S Class British submarines, were requisitioned by the British Admiralty and designated the P611 Class while serving in the British Fleet. Other films profiling submarines include **Above Us the Waves**, 1956 (Atlantic; WWII); **The Abyss**, 1989; **Action in the North Atlantic**, 1943 (WWII); **Arise, My Love**, 1940 (Atlantic; WWII); **Around the World under the Sea**, 1966; **Atlantis: The Lost Empire**, 2001; **The Atomic Submarine**, 1959 (Cold War); **Back to Bataan**, 1945 (Pacific; Leyte, Philippines Invasion of 1944); **Battle of the Coral Sea**, 1959 (Pacific; WWII); **The Bedford Incident**, 1965 (Arctic; Cold War); **Below**, 2002 (Atlantic; WWII);

Captain America: The First Avenger, 2011; Corvette K-225 (Atlantic; WWII); Crash Dive, 1943; Crimson Tide, 1995; The Cruel Sea, 1953 (Atlantic; WWII); Dangerously They Live, 1941; Dark Journey, 1937 (Atlantic; WWI); Darling Lili, 1970; Das Boot, 1981 (Atlantic, Mediterranean, WWII); The Desert Fox: The Story of Rommel, 1951 (Mediterranean; WWII); Destination Tokyo, 1943 (Pacific; WWII); Destroyer, 1943 (Atlantic; WWII); Devil and the Deep, 1932; Diamonds Are Forever, 1971; Down Periscope, 1996; The Enemy Below, 1957 (Atlantic; WWII); Eye of the Needle, 1981 (Irish Sea; WWII); Fantastic Voyage, 1966; Firefox, 1982; For Your Eyes Only, 1981; 49th Parallel, 1941 (Hudson's Bay; WWII); Full Fathom Five, 1990; Generale Della Rovere, 1961; Gray Lady Down, 1978; The Great Race, 1965; Gung Ho!, 1943 (Pacific; Makin Island Raid; WWII); Hell and High Water, 1964 (Pacific; Cold War); Hell Below, 1933; Hellcats of the Navy, 1957 (Pacific; WWII); The Hunt for Red October, 1990; I Was an American Spy, 1951 (Pacific; WWII); Ice Station Zebra, 1968 (Arctic; Cold War); In Enemy Hands, 2004 (Atlantic; WWII); In Which We Serve, 1943 (Atlantic; Mediterranean; WWII); The Incredible Mr. Limpet, 1964 (Pacific; WWII); It Came from Beneath the Sea, 1955; K-19: The Widowmaker, 2002; The Land That Time Forgot, 1975 (South Atlantic; WWI); Lifeboat, 1944 (Atlantic; WWII); License to Kill, 1989; The Man Who Never Was, 1956 (Atlantic; WWII); The McKenzie Break, 1970 (Atlantic; WWII); Men of Honor, 2000; Morituri, 1965 (Atlantic; WWII); Murphy's War, 1971 (South Atlantic; WWII); Mysterious Island, 1961 (Pacific); Mystery Submarine, 1950 (South Atlantic; WWII); Nazi Agent, 1942 (Atlantic; WWII); Never Say Never Again, 1983; 1941, 1979 (Pacific; WWII); Northern Pursuit, 1943; Okinawa, 1952 (Pacific; WWII); On the Beach, 1959; Operation Disaster, 1950; Operation Pacific, 1951 (WWII); Operation Petticoat, 1959 (Pacific; WWII); Our Man Flint, 1966; Pearl Harbor, 2001 (Pacific; WWII); Phantom, 2013; Prisoner of Japan, 1942 (Pacific; WWII); Raiders of the Lost Ark, 1981; Run Silent, Run Deep, 1958 (Pacific; WWII); The Russians Are Coming, The Russians Are Coming, 1966; Sea Wife, 1957 (Pacific; WWII); Sealed Cargo, 1951; The Silver Fleet, 1945; The Spy in Black, 1939 (Atlantic; WWI); Spy Kids, 2001; The Spy Who Loved Me, 1977; Submarine, 1928; Submarine Command, 1951 (Pacific; WWII; Korean War); Submarine Seahawk, 1958 (Pacific; WWII); Submarine Patrol, 1938; Submarine X-1, 1969 (Atlantic; WWII); Task Force, 1949 (Pacific; WWII); They Came to Blow Up America, 1943 (Atlantic; WWII); They Were Expendable, 1945 (Pacific; WWII); Titanic, 1997 (Atlantic; finding and exploring the ship's wreck); Tora! Tora! Tora!, 1970 (Pacific; attack on Pearl Harbor; WWII); Torpedo Alley, 1953 (Pacific; Korean War); Torpedo Run, 1958 (Pacific; WWII); 20,000 Leagues Under the Sea, 1954 (Pacific); U-571, 2000 (Atlantic; WWII); U-47, 1958 (Atlantic; WWII); Up Periscope, 1959 (Pacific; WWII); Voyage to the Bottom of the Sea, 1961; Yellow Submarine, 1958; and You Only Live Twice, 1967. p, Edward Black; d, Anthony Asquith; cast, Eric Portman, John Mills, Reginald Purdell, Niall MacGinnis, Joan Hopkins, Josephine Wilson, Louis Bradfield, Ronald Millar, Jack Watling, Leslie Weston, Ian Fleming, Philip Friend; w, J.B. Williams, Val Valentine, (uncredited) Frank Launder; c, Jack Cox; m, Hubert Bath; ed, R.E. Dearing; art d, Walter Murton.

We Live Again ★★★ 1934; U.S.; 85m; Samuel Goldwyn Company; UA; B/W; Drama; Children: Unacceptable; DVD; VHS. Tolstoy's novel *Resurrection* comes to vivid life under the careful direction of pantheon director Mamoulian, and March and Sten give wonderful performances as star-crossed lovers in oppressive czarist Russia. The story begins with March, who is a prince living on a countryside estate; he befriends peasant girl Sten, who works as a servant for March's aunts Griffies and Logan. Although their stations in life are worlds apart, the two treat each other as equals and Sten soon falls deeply in love with March. After serving two years in the military, March returns to his estate to find Sten waiting for him, and her love for him has not dimin-

Fredric March and Anna Sten in *We Live Again*, 1934.

ished. March strolls through his estate with Sten and then seduces her in a greenhouse. He departs the next morning without saying good-bye or leaving a note, only some money, which disappoints and angers Sten. March completely ignores Sten, and has no knowledge that she has become pregnant. Sten still clings to the hope that March will return to her, and, at one point, she runs after a train during a storm in an effort to contact him, but March is oblivious to the girl while he plays cards with his fellow aristocrats. Now abandoned, Sten is fired when her employers learn of her unwed condition and she goes to Moscow where, failing to find any work, she becomes a prostitute, living a degraded and miserable life. Meanwhile, March becomes engaged to Baxter, the daughter of powerful judge Smith. When he is asked to become a juror reviewing a murder case, March is shocked to see Sten as one of the defendants charged with killing a merchant. He then learns how Sten, to survive, became a prostitute, and March blames himself for the downfall of this innocent, young woman. Sten is found guilty through a misreading of the jury's verdict, the jury really intending to free her. Smith, a draconian jurist, however, sentences her to hard labor in Siberia for five years. The guilt-ridden March realizes that he has never stopped loving Sten and attempts to get her released from prison. Failing that, he offers to marry her, but, when he returns to the prison, he finds that she has been sent by train to Siberia. March then gives up all his worldly possessions, dividing his estate among the peasants who have worked for him. He then follows and finds Sten at the Siberian border, where he declares his love for her, vowing to stay with her forever when saying: "All I ask is to live again with your forgiveness and your help and your love." Mamoulian carefully unfolds this stunning atmospheric tale of a man who seeks and gains redemption for his callous behavior, as well as the love of a woman he has scorned and almost destroyed. Everywhere throughout this film is producer Goldwyn's lavish taste for period films as it offers marvelous sets and elaborately rich costumes, all wonderfully photographed by master cinematographer Toland. Though March and Sten provide sensitive and memorable performances as the tragic lovers, this film, like two others producer Goldwyn expensively showcased with his protégé, Sten (Nana, 1934; The Wedding Night, 1935), proved to be a financial disappointment at the box office. The story had been made as three silent versions, in 1909 by D.W. Griffith; in 1918, starring Pauline Frederick; and in 1927, starring Rod LaRocque and Dolores Del Rio. It saw a talkie version in 1931, starring Lupe Velez and John Boles that was offered in English and Spanish. The story was filmed many times thereafter, including film versions in 1938, 1943, 1958, 1960, and in 2001 as a made-for-TV production. *Author's Note*: When the obstinate Goldwyn was informed that this story had been filmed many times, the producer responded with his typical aplomb: "It hasn't been made until I make

Chris Klein and Mel Gibson in *We Were Soldiers*, 2002.

it!" He saw the story as an ideal vehicle for Sten, the actress he had found and was grooming as "the Russian Garbo," and felt that, since the Tolstoy tale emanated from Sten's native country, she would be able to bring a Slavic persona to her role that others could not. Though Sten received admirable kudos from critics for her performance in this film, she never enamored the public and for reasons that remain inexplicable. The producer doted on this film, working closely with Mamoulian, who told this author: "Sam [Goldwyn] was always invading the set and it made me nervous to have him leaning over my shoulder, but I knew that he was an incorrigible meddler, so I put up with his never-ending suggestions about fixing this scene or that." March told this author that "Goldwyn would concentrate on a single scene in his pictures and then demand that it be presented to perfection. In **We Live Again**, he focused on a Russian Orthodox Easter Mass to make sure that that sequence (lasting more than ten minutes) displayed all the pageantry of its age. Those scenes were absolutely amazing as you heard the Gregorian chants and we were all awed by the procession of Russian priests with their long beards, carrying golden ikons that shimmered and glowed under the hot lights of the set. Goldwyn fell so much in love with that sequence that no one had the courage to tell him that, after that very expensive shooting was completed, the music for the mass had been mistakenly recorded onto the soundtrack backward." Goldwyn told this author: "Poor Anna Sten. She was the most misunderstood actress of her aura [sic]. Nobody could ever figure out why the public did not like her. Maybe because she was just too beautiful and all the lovely ladies who came to see her pictures got so green with envy that they never showed up at the theaters to watch her pictures." Following one more expensive try to put Sten across to the public, **The Wedding Night**, 1935, which also failed at the box office, Goldwyn gave up and released Sten from her contract with him. Goldwyn was in his word-mangling métier when he saw an ad for this film written by his publicity people that read: "The directorial genius of Mamoulian, the beauty of Sten, and the producing genius of Goldwyn have combined to make the world's greatest entertainment." Said Goldwyn: "That's the kind of ad I like. Facts. No exaggeration." **p**, Samuel Goldwyn; **d**, Rouben Mamoulian; **cast**, Anna Sten, Fredric March, Jane Baxter, C. Aubrey Smith, Sam Jaffe, Ethel Griffies, Gwendolyn Logan, Jessie Ralph, Leonid Kinskey, Cecil Cunningham, Mary Forbes, Nina Koshetz; **w**, Maxwell Anderson, Leonard Praskins, Preston Sturges, (uncredited) Thornton Wilder (based on the novel *Resurrection* by Leo Tolstoy); **c**, Gregg Toland; **m**, Alfred Newman; **ed**, Otho Lovering; **prod d**, Sergei Soudeikin; **art d**, Richard Day.

We of the Never Never ★★★ 1983; Australia; 134m; Adam Packer Film Productions/Triumph Releasing Corp.; Color; Biographical Drama; Children: Acceptable (MPAA: G); **BD**; **DVD**. This moving tale begins in 1901 Australia, where McGregor, a genteel woman from the city of Victoria, marries Digman and moves with him to the desolate wilds of the Northern Territory Outback (in Australia the Outback is also called the Never Never) to manage a station, which is a large ranch. They are the only Caucasians living among Aborigines' and she gradually learns to give up her city ways and becomes a member of a new class of women sometimes called "Australian Outback Women." She also learns to appreciate the difficult lives of the natives. The film is based on the diaries of Jeannie Gunn (1870-1961), the woman McGregor so perfectly profiles in this absorbing film. **p**, Greg Tepper, John B. Murray, Phillip Adams; **d**, Igor Auzins; **cast**, Angela Punch McGregor, Arthur Dignam, Martin Vaughan, Lewis Fitz-Gerald, John Jarratt, Tony Barry, Tommy Lewis, Donald Blitner, Mawuyul Yanthalawuy, Cecil Parkee, Sibina Willy, Tex Morton, Kim Chiu Kok; **w**, Peter Schreck (based on the book by Mrs. Aeneas Gunn); **c**, Gary Hansen; **m**, Peter Best; **ed**, Clifford Hayes; **prod d**, Josephine Ford; **art d**, Ro Bruen-Cook, Graeme Dunesbury, Greg Nelson; **spec eff**, Reece Robinson, Glenn Ruehland, Peter Sloss.

We Were Soldiers ★★★ 2002; U.S./Germany; 138m; Icon Entertainment/PAR; Color; War Drama; Children: Unacceptable (MPAA: R); **BD**; **DVD**; **VHS**; **IV**. Action-packed tale takes place during the Vietnam War in 1965, where U.S. Army Col. Howard G. Moore, who is ably played by Gibson, and 400 young troopers from the newly formed elite American 7th "Air" Cavalry are surrounded by 2,000 North Vietnamese soldiers. The ensuing battle was one of the most savage in U.S. history, taking place on a football-sized clearing later called "The Valley of Death." It is shown here as the signal encounter between the American and North Vietnamese armies, and its realistic choreographing is truly harrowing. Based on a book by Moore, this expertly directed film pays tribute to the courage and loyalty of these valiant soldiers, and Gibson and a stellar cast shine in their heroic roles. Sequences segues between the battle scenes in Vietnam and the wives and girlfriends of the soldiers waiting at home for them, and how most of these women painfully receive telegrams telling them that their loved ones have been killed in action; some of the wives actually deliver those messages in order to ease the trauma endured by the recipients. Songs: "Hold On I'm Coming" (Isaac Hayes, Jr., David Porter), "Hold Me, Thrill Me, Kiss Me" (Harry Noble), "Sgt. MacKenzie" (Joseph Rizza Kilna), "Mansions of the Lord" (Nick Glennie-Smith, Randall Wallace). War violence prohibits viewing by children. **p**, Randall Wallace, Bruce Davey, Stephen McEveety, Danielle Lemmon, Stephen Zapotoczny; **d&w**, Wallace (based on the book *We Were Soldiers Once... and Young* by Lt. Gen. Howard G. Moore, Joseph L. Galloway); **cast**, Mel Gibson, Madeleine Stowe, Greg Kinnear, Sam Elliott, Chris Klein, Keri Russell, Barry Pepper, Duong Don, Ryan Hurst, Robert Bagnell, Jon Hamm; **c**, Dean Semler; **m**, Nick Glennie-Smith; **ed**, William Hoy; **prod d**, Tom Sanders; **art d**, Daniel T. Dorrance, Kevin Kavanaugh; **set d**, Gary Fettis; **spec eff**, Richard S. Wood, Paul Lombardi, David Goldberg, Kevin Lingenfelser, Paul Abatemarco.

We Were Strangers ★★★ 1949; U.S.; 106m; Horizon/COL; B/W; Adventure; Children: Unacceptable; **DVD**; **VHS**. The dynamic Garfield presents another intense portrayal in this intriguing tale of revolutionaries and two tempestuous rebels who become lovers. Garfield is an American, who returns to his native Cuba in 1933 to help the people in their revolution. Sensual Jones joins the Cuban underground movement after her brother is killed by Armendariz, the ruthless chief of the secret police. She meets and falls in love with Garfield. He plans to assassinate some Cuban government officials at a state funeral by detonating explosives in a tunnel under the cemetery where the officials will be gathered for a burial ceremony. Garfield enlists the aid of three comrades, but one of them, Roland, balks because he is afraid some innocent people might also be killed in the explosion. The plan is discovered and the funeral is moved to another location. Police then track down Garfield and his group and he and the loyal Jones are killed in a gun battle, but in dying, Garfield hears people in the streets starting their revolution. Though director Huston sustains suspense and dread throughout this tension-filled tale, the film did poorly at the box office. Song: "We Dig All Day We Dig All Night" (unknown composer). *Author's Note*: Though it is unstated, Garfield and other rebels are attempting to end the oppressive regime of Gerardo Machado, 1871-1939, and where an assassination attempt was made on Machado's life when he was scheduled to attend the funeral services of a fellow politician. The ceremony, however, was moved elsewhere and the attempt was aborted. Huston told this author that he and Viertel, his co-writer for this film, went to Cuba to research this story and "we wound up sailing about the Cuban waters with Ernest Hemingway, who was then living in Cuba and was a friend of Peter's [Viertel's]. Hemingway suggested that we have everyone trying to assassinate a Cuban dictator killed at the end of our picture, which, he said, was the real case about the story we were writing. Hemingway was a dangerous guy. On one hand, he was full of ideas about how to make movies, and, on the other hand, he spent most of his time with us telling us how stupid and rotten everyone was in Hollywood." **p**, Sam Spiegel as S.P. Eagle; **d**, John Huston; **cast**, Jennifer Jones, John Garfield, Pedro Armendariz, Gilbert Roland, Ramon Navarro, Wally Cassell, David Bond, Jose Perez, Morris Ankrum, Abdullah Abbas, J. Huston; **w**, Huston, Peter Viertel (based on the novel *Rough Sketch* by Robert Sylvester); **c**, Russell Metty; **m**, George Antheil; **ed**, Al Clark; **art d**, Cary Odell; **set d**, Louis Diage; **spec eff**, Lawrence W. Butler.

Weary River ★★★ 1929; U.S.; 86m; First National Pictures; B/W; Crime Drama/Romance; Children: Unacceptable; **DVD**. Well-made tale sees Barthelmess, a youthful gangster, framed for a crime he did not commit by rival hoodlum Natheaux. He is sent to prison where he feels his life has ended. Holden, the compassionate warden, befriends the new inmate at his prison, believing that Barthelmess has redeeming qualities and that he can be rehabilitated. When Holden learns that Bathelmess has a good singing voice, he encourages him to form a prison band. The band, with Barthelmess doing its vocals, is aired on the radio and Barthelmess' singing voice captivates thousands of listeners. So popular does he become that the governor is moved to give him a pardon. Upon his release, Barthelmess becomes a hit in the vaudeville circuit where he is known as the Master of Melody. Some in the audiences, however, have learned of his past and Barthlemess hears the word "convict" repeated more than once, which begins to disturb his concentration when performing and undermines his confidence as an entertainer. Unable to perform well, Barthelmess quits his profession and returns to his old gang where he resumes his romance with Compson. Natheaux, his old nemesis, again becomes a threat and Barthelmess resolves to kill his underworld antagonist. Compson begs Barthelmess to quit his vendetta against Natheaux, and, failing this, she contacts the avuncular warden, Holden. Before Barthelmess takes bloody revenge against Natheaux, Holden persuades him to put aside his thirst for revenge and remain on the good side of the law. Barthelmess leaves the rackets to make a new life with Compson and then becomes a singing star on the radio. Though thick with melodrama, the tale is told so well by director Lloyd, that its characters become appealing and empathetic, and Barthelmess is a standout in his role of an indecisive but good-hearted youth finding salvation through the spirit of song. The film received an Oscar nomination for Best Director (Lloyd) and did well at the box office. Songs: "Weary River" and "It's Up to You" (1929; music: Louis Silvers; lyrics: Grant Clarke), "Frankie and Johnny" (traditional), "The Prisoner's Song" (1924; music: Guy Massey), "Hail! Hail! The Gang's All Here" (1917: music: Arthur Sullivan; lyrics: Theodore Morse). *Author's Note*: This film was part silent and part talkie, and Barthelmess, who had been a silent screen star, made his successful transition to talkies with this absorbing drama. Singer Johnny Murray dubbed all the singing vocals for Barthelmess and was so effective that he was put under exclusive con-

John Garfield and Jennifer Jones in *We Were Strangers,* 1949.

tract in the event that Barthelmess appeared in any upcoming films where he would be required to sing. Future western film star Randolph Scott made an appearance in this, his second feature film, telling this author: "I had a bit part in **Weary River** where I am sitting in a theater audience. I was doing a lot of that when I started out. In my first film [**Sharp Shooters**, 1928], I was sitting in a café. I figured that this was pretty easy work and decided to stay in Hollywood in case the parts got bigger and they certainly did." Sally Eilers was also just then starting out in films and she appears here in a bit part as a hatcheck girl. The William Holden (1862-1932), who plays the warden, is not to be confused with the latter-day matinee idol, William Holden (1918-1981). **p&d**, Frank Lloyd; **cast**, Richard Barthelmess, Betty Compson, Raymond Turner, Gladden James, Louis Natheaux, George E. Stone, Ernie Adams, Brooks Benedict, William Holden, Ruth Cherrington, Robert Emmett O'Connor, Sally Eilers, Randolph Scott, Louis Mercier, Johnny Murray (singing voice for Barthelmess); **w**, Bradley King, Paul Perez, Thomas J. Geraghty (based on a story by Courtney Riley Cooper); **c**, Ernest Haller; **m**, Louis Silvers; **ed**, James Gibbon, Edward Schroeder; **art d**, John J. Hughes; **set d**, Ray Moyer.

The Weather Man ★★★ 2005; U.S.; 116m; PAR; Color; Drama; Children: Unacceptable (MPAA: R): **DVD**; **IV**. Compelling tale begins with Cage, who is a Chicago television weatherman. He is doing well professionally, but his personal life is a shambles. His relationships with his perfectionist writer father, Caine, and neurotic ex-wife, Davis, and their children, are in a crash mode. He is tentatively offered an attractive new job as weatherman on a television talk show in New York City and is conflicted about whether to take it and escape his personal problems or to remain and face them. He goes to New York and performs so well on the talk show he is offered the job. He asks Davis to reconcile with him, but she decides to marry someone else; amid this, Caine dies. Cage moves to New York to begin a new and less stormy weather life (he hopes). This film, though well-made and offering superior performances, was a disappointment at the box office, earning $19 million in its initial release against a budget of $22 million. Songs: "The Passenger" (Iggy Pop, Ricky Gardiner), "Windy Day" (Robin L. Klein, Scott P. Schreer), "I Can See Clearly Now" (Johnny Nash), "Like a Rock" (Bob Seger), "Transitions" (Michael Louis Diamond, Adam Nathaniel Yauch), "Sweet Lorraine" (Clifford Burwell, Mitchell Parish). Gutter language and sexual content prohibit viewing by children. **p**, Steve Tisch, Todd Black, Jason Blumenthal, Steven Conrad; **d**, Gore Verbinski; **cast**, Nicolas Gage, Michael Caine, Hope Davis, Nicholas Hoult, Michael Rispoli, Gemmenne De La Pena, Gil Bellows, Judith McConnell, Chris Marrs, Dina Facklis; **w**, Conrad; **c**, Phedon Papamichael; **m**, Hans Zimmer, James Levine; **ed**, Craig Wood; **prod d**, Tom Duffield;

Gemmenne De La Pena and Nicolas Cage in *The Weather Man*, 2005.

art d, Patrick Sullivan; **set d**, Rosemary Brandenburg; **spec eff**, Charles Gibson, David Sosalla, John D. Milinac, Rodman Kiser.

The Web ★★★ 1947; U.S.; 87m; UNIV; B/W; Crime Drama; Children: Unacceptable; **DVD**. Taut crime yarn begins when Leiber is released after five years in prison for embezzling from the firm of his employer, Price. After Price suspects that Leiber is threatening him, he hires O'Brien as his secret bodyguard. Leiber breaks into Price's room at home with a gun and O'Brien kills Leiber. O'Brien is attracted to Price's secretary, so he remains in the shadows, learning that Price has used him to get rid of Leiber, who had not embezzled from Price in the first place. With the help of a friend, Bendix, a tough police lieutenant, O'Brien tricks Price into confessing it all. *Author's Note*: Price delighted in his villainous role in this above-average film noir outing, telling this author: "Oh, yes, I was up to my double-dealing self in **The Web**. My character was a very clever fellow, setting himself up to be a victim, so that he can rid himself of someone who has the goods on him. He is really not that clever at the end because he gets tangled up in his own involved set of lies to once again prove that crime does not pay." Violence prohibits viewing by children. **p**, Jerry Bresler; **d**, Michael Gordon; **cast**, Ella Raines, Edmond O'Brien, William Bendix, Vincent Price, Maria Palmer, Fritz Leiber, John Abbott, Howland Chamberlin, Gino Corrado, Tito Vuolo, Wilton Graff; **w**, William Bowers, Bertram Millhauser (based on the story by Harry Kurnitz); **c**, Irving Glassberg; **m**, Hans J. Salter; **ed**, Russell Schoengarth; **art d**, Bernard Herzbrun, James W. Sullivan; **set d**, Russell A. Gausman, William Stevens.

A Wedding ★★★ 1978; U.S.; 125m; Lion's Gate/FOX; Color; Comedy; Children: Unacceptable; **DVD**; **VHS**. This offbeat film offers little more than social calamity, but it is nevertheless fascinating, thanks to its impossible characters. The story focuses upon a lavish wedding that merges a middle-class Southern family with a wealthy Chicago clan that has connections to organized crime. Stryker, the daughter of a Louisville truck driver, is to marry Arnaz, the scion of a very wealthy Chicago family headed by his father, Gassman, but the reception at the family estate is closely watched by police. Stryker's sister, Farrow, has earlier had an affair with Arnaz and is now pregnant. Their mother, Burnett, is bored with her husband, Dooley, and is involved in an affair with Arnaz's uncle, McCormick. Chaplin, who is the wedding's coordinator, is a lesbian, and the priest, Cromwell, is so senile that he winds up talking to a corpse and doesn't know it. Duff is a drunken doctor getting personal with all the women except Gish, who is Arnaz's grandmother and who dies early on the wedding day. The day ends with the bridal couple being killed in an automobile accident. Altman, who was probably the laziest director of them all, allowed the actors to ad-lib anything they wanted in this scattergun film. The chaos thus created inadvertently presents a nutcase, utterly confusing comedy that produces hilarity in spite of itself and the sloppy Altman. The improvised chatter is often wholly unrelated to the story and verges on the idiotic as the actors make up everything as they collect their bloated salaries. This outrageous production may be the most blatant visual rip-off in film history. Songs: "Bird on a Wire" (1968; Leonard Cohen), "Hungarian Dance No. 5" (1969; Johannes Brahms), "Bridal Chorus" from "Lohengrin" (1850; Richard Wagner), "Funiculi Funicula" (1880; Luigi Denza), "Beautiful Dreamer" (1862; Stephen Foster), "Love Is a Many-Splendored Thing" (1955; music: Sammy Fain; lyrics: Paul Francis Webster), "You Make Me Feel So Young" (1946; music: Josef Myrow; lyrics: Mack Gordon), "Fools Rush In/Where Angels Fear to Tread" (1940; Rube Bloom), "The More I See You" (1945; music: Harry Warren; lyrics: Mack Gordon), "The Second Time Around" (1960; music: Jimmy Van Heusen; lyrics: Sammy Cahn), "Give Me the Simple Life" (1946; music: Rube Bloom; lyrics: Harry Ruby); "Heavenly Sunlight" (1899; music: George Harrison Cook; lyrics: Henry J. Zelley), "Again" (1948; music: Lionel Newman; lyrics: Dorcas Cochran). Adult material prohibits viewing by children. **p&d**, Robert Altman; **cast**, Carol Burnett, Mia Farrow, Desi Arnaz Jr., Lillian Gish, Viveca Lindfors, Vittorio Gassman, Amy Stryker, Nina van Pallandt, Howard Duff, Dina Merrill, Pat McCormick, Ruth Nelson, Geraldine Chaplin, Lauren Hutton, John Cromwell, Paul Dooley, Dennis Franz, John Malkovich, Gary Sinise, Peggy Ann Garner, Gerald Busby; **w**, Altman, John Considine, Patricia Resnick, Allan Nichols (based on a story by Altman, Considine); **c**, Charles Rosher (Panavision; DeLuxe Color); **m**, John Hotchkis; **ed**, Tony Lombardo; **art d**, Dennis J. Parrish.

The Wedding March ★★★★ 1928 (silent); U.S.; 113m/11 reels; PAR; B/W; Drama; Children: Unacceptable; **VHS**. Lavishly appointed melodrama once again sees the inimitable and mesmerizing Stroheim as a Germanic nobleman. This time, however, he becomes the victim of his love for commoner Wray, instead of the savagely abusive Hun he so often essayed in the silent era. The setting is Vienna in 1914, and Stroheim is first shown getting out of his princely bed and preparing to ride in the grand procession honoring the Feast of Corpus Christi. Stroheim is to act as the commander of the cavalry guard for Emperor Franz Joseph (1830-1916), who is played by Vaverka. Stroheim, a prince, and his haughty parents, are rich with titles, but have no wealth and are in an impoverished state. Before going to the ceremony, Stroheim asks his parents for money, but they sneeringly decline, more or less suggesting that he should marry into a wealthy family or kill himself. (As usual, Stroheim, who dominated the script for this opus, injects his thick brand of cruelty into almost all of his characters, exposing their self-serving and heartless motivations.) While organizing his troops in front of St. Stephen's Cathedral, Stroheim spots the beautiful Wray in the crowd with her parents and Betz, a butcher and her crude fiancé. The family is eating at this time, and the uncouth Betz spits, embarrassing Wray and her family members. (As usual, Stroheim goes out of his way to display any crude or ungainly gesture to further emphasize the demeanor of his earthy characters; in this case, Betz is profiled as a grotesque cretin of a man, unworthy of any good woman's attentions.) In an amazingly startling sequence of at least 200 quick cuts, Stroheim (as the director) shows how Stroheim (as the prince) and Wray are magnetically drawn to each other without showing them both in the same frame. This stunning montage culminates as Wray places a bouquet of flowers at Stroheim's bootstrap. At that moment, Stroheim's horse is spooked by a gun salute and rears upward before landing a crushing hoof onto Wray's foot. Stroheim immediately dismounts and attends to the injured Wray, arranging for her to be sent to a hospital for treatment. Betz recognizes what is happening and lunges at Stroheim, but he is quickly arrested and taken to jail. The procession is then shown in all of its resplendent pomp and splendor (this sequence was filmed in the old three-strip Technicolor process). Without revealing his princely identity, Stroheim visits Wray in the hospital and, after she has recuperated, goes to the wine garden and pub, owned by her parents, where she works as a harpist. They befriend each other and then go to the Danube, where Wray tells Stroheim about the legend of the Iron Man and the Danube maidens, symbolizing evil and good. Stroheim and Wray are then shown beneath an apple bower where tender white blossoms slowly flutter in the soft wind and float downward upon them (in what is one of Stroheim's most tender moments put on celluloid). Stroheim strays by patronizing an upscale bordello, but he leaves early, drawn back toward the innocent Wray. The director then brilliantly shows a series of cross-cutting scenes to profile Fawcett, Stroheim's father, drunk and disorderly at the bordello. Fawcett arranges for his son to marry Pitts, the invalided daughter of a wealthy nobility-climbing corn-plasterer, in exchange for wealth, and that family acquiring Stroheim's aristocratic name and title. Fawcett indulges in an orgy (the typical Bacchanalian bash that Stroheim's so ardently offered in his silent films), where the director cuts to Wray, awakening from a dream where she has seen the Iron Man of evil as a warning image of doom. A dog also sees this grim specter and begins to bark, awakening Betz, who has recently been released from jail. Betz, realizing that Stroheim is now the love object of sweetheart Wray, attacks Stroheim, but is thrown into a pigsty. Wray then goes to the cathedral where she confesses her sin of seducing Stroheim, and Stroheim shows her absolution in many stunning, ethereal images in that symbolic church environment, where the statues of saints seem to nod approval of this young woman as if to bestow their blessings upon her. Meanwhile, to prevent his family's financial ruin, and, in spite of the fact that he does not love Pitts, Stroheim agrees to marry the crippled woman. Stroheim marries Pitts and Betz shows a newspaper article about the nuptials to Wray, demanding that she marry him. Wray tells Betz that she loathes him and that she still loves Stroheim. Betz then threatens to murder Stroheim unless Wray agrees to marry him and Wray relents. During that wedding ceremony, Wray faints before the union between her and Betz is finalized and now Betz vows to kill his nemesis by going to Stroheim's honeymoon lodge. He confronts his romantic adversary with a gun, while Wray arrives but fails to stop Betz. Pitts, however, steps in front of Stroheim and is struck by the bullet. Betz escapes and goes into hiding, now a wanted criminal. Pitts is told that she can recover from her wound, but only if she remains perfectly still. Realizing that Stroheim loves only Wray, Pitts purposely ends her life by leaving her bed to crawl to a massive crucifix and dies in her heroic, self-sacrificing effort. Stroheim, depressed, returns to Vienna and finds the wine garden and pub once owned by Wray's parents closed and Wray gone. He then revisits the bordello, only to be recalled to duty when war is declared (WWI; 1914-1918). He is placed in command of troops assigned to suppress a ruthless band of renegades terrorizing Austrian communities along the Serbian border. One of those communities houses the convent of the Sisters of the Bleeding Heart, where Wray has taken shelter. The community and the convent is attacked by the renegades, among whom is the savage Betz (proving that he may be one of the most indefatigable and enduring villains in filmic history). Just as the interlopers break into the convent and Betz is about to rape Wray, Stroheim suddenly appears with his troops and dispatches Betz and his murderous companions. Stroheim and Wray are then married at the convent's altar before Stroheim leads his troops off to the front. He turns about to wave at Wray, shouting (on a title card): "Nobody can say—we didn't have a lot of music—such as it was." Stroheim is his old magnetic self in the role of the love-smitten prince, and Wray gives a powerful performance as the woman who loves him above all else, Pitts is equally impressive as the sweet and retiring invalid victimized by circumstances and the insanity of a jealous lover. The film, though inventively directed and masterfully photographed, presented a rather thick melodrama that had worked for Stroheim years earlier. Its lavish sets and costumes constituted a costly proposition for producer Powers and Paramount, the studio producing this film with a budget of more than $1.2 million, then a

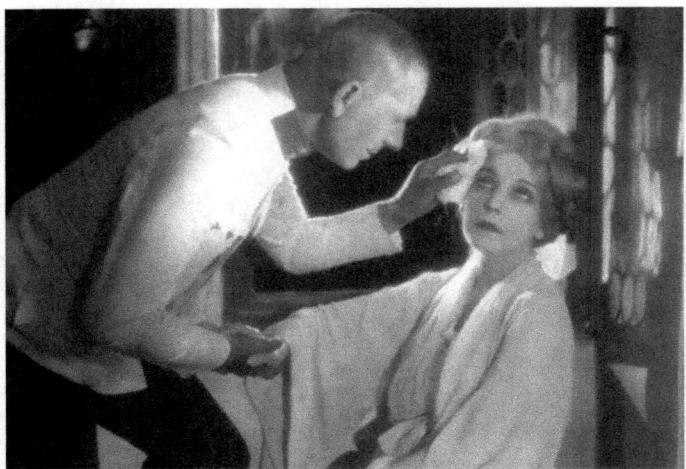

Erich von Stroheim and ZaSu Pitts in *The Wedding March*, 1928.

staggering sum. It was a box office failure and did not recoup its original investment, but, over the years, this film became a cult classic. Song (played in theaters when originally released): "Paradise (The Love Theme)" (1928; music: J.S. Zamecnik; lyrics: Harry D. Kerr). ***Author's Note***: By the time Stroheim undertook this film, he had worn out his welcome with most Hollywood studios and producers through his expensive excesses and total unconcern for restrictive budgets, not to mention his autocratic attitudes that alienated movie moguls of his day (including Louis B. Mayer, head of MGM, who became so incensed with Stroheim's insulting conduct that he physically thrashed him and sent him to the hospital). Wealthy producer Pat Powers, however, still had trust in Stroheim, wanting the temperamental director to helm a film starring Peggy Hopkins Joyce, who was Powers' love interest at that time. Stroheim, however, persuaded Powers to finance this project. Stroheim wrote a 154-page script that really called for two films based on the same characters, **The Wedding March** and **The Honeymoon**. He also planned to add a third story to the overall saga. Stroheim worked with a co-author, Harry Carr, a laborious exercise on Carr's part, as he later related. They had initially created a motherless heroine (essayed by Wray), but, as Carr later related, Stroheim insisted that he "could not write about a motherless girl unless he knew what her mother was like. So we had to sit down and spend days manufacturing the life story of a woman who was never intended to appear in the story." Such was Stroheim's penchant for irrelevant and harassing detail, which was demonstrated when he was making the exorbitant **The Merry Widow**, 1925. In that very expensive production, Stroheim insisted that all of his principal male actors have and wear costly monogrammed underwear, even though these undergarments would never be seen by any viewer; Stroheim said that "the actors will know it and give them confidence in their roles as aristocrats." He took the same approach with **The Wedding March**. "He insisted on retaking even the smallest scene over and over until he was satisfied with it," Wray told this author. "When someone complained about that, he exploded and shouted that he would make twenty thousand takes of a single scene until the actors 'got it right.' We believed him. He almost did make that many takes. That production went on and on and on, until we all thought that it would be our life's work. I think the only person who agreed with Stroheim was Mr. Betz, who was also a German and used a "von" with his name in real life. He changed his mind about the director when Stroheim ordered Mr. Betz to eat maggot-infested meat that caused Mr. Betz to throw up. Stroheim walked away at that time and we heard him say: 'Isn't that very funny?' It was one of the most sadistic acts I have ever seen in Hollywood. I got so frustrated at times with Stroheim's shouting directions that I confided in Zasu [Pitts], who had been the director's star in **Greed** [1924], asking her if Stroheim was mentally stable. She

Erich von Stroheim on the set with Fay Wray in *The Wedding March*, 1928.

smiled, patted my hand, and said: 'Of course, dear, he's as mad as a hatter, but he is also a genius, and, in our business, that is one and the same thing.' I kept my mouth shut and did as I was told until the producer and the people at Paramount ordered Stroheim to close down the production. Then we all ran like chickens escaping the coop." To maintain his rigid regimen for reality, the director hired several dozen Hollywood prostitutes to play the harlots in the bordello scenes, and he had them and professional actors guzzling real imported champagne (these scenes shot on a closed and guard set). Stroheim, who had begun with a budget of $300,000 and had exceeded that by $950,000, bristled when ordered to cut down the length of this film, but agreed to edit what film he had produced and it was enormous, more than 200,000 feet of film shot over a six-month period. Stroheim and Hull spent the next seven months editing this footage until he finally presented a single feature combining both **The Wedding March** and **The Honeymoon** elements. The film retained the wonderful cathedral and street sets of old Vienna and its hundreds of ornately costumed extras, and many of its finely honed scenes remained intact, even after Paramount had the gifted director, Josef von Sternberg, further edit the film. Stroheim, however, always felt that this film, like so many of other films he had directed, had been ruined by front office meddling. **p**, P.A. (Pat) Powers; **d**, Erich von Stroheim; **cast**, Stroheim, Fay Wray, Zasu Pitts, Matthew Betz, George Fawcett, Maude George, George Nichols, Dale Fuller, Hughie Mack, Cesare Gravina, Anton Vaverka; **w**, von Stroheim, Harry Carr; **c**, Hal Mohr, Ben F. Reynolds, William C. McGann, Harris Thorpe; **m**, J.S. Zamecnik, Louis De Francesco; **ed**, Frank E. Hull, von Stroheim, Julian Johnston; **art d**, Richard Day, Stroheim.

The Wedding Night ★★★ 1935; U.S.; 82m; Howard Productions/UA; B/W; Drama/Romance; Children: Unacceptable; **DVD**; **VHS**. Polished tale begins with Cooper, a novelist, who suffers a flop with his newest book. His publisher suggests that he go to a Connecticut farmhouse with his devoted wife, Vinson, to relax and see if he can write a better book. There he meets Sten, a daughter of a local Polish immigrant tobacco farmer, and is impressed with her simple way of looking at life. The wealthy Ruman then enriches Cooper and Vinson by $5,000 when buying a field they own to add to his own property. Vinson, meanwhile, becomes disenchanted with country life and, at Cooper's urging, returns to New York City to enjoy a vacation with their newfound money. In Vinson's absence, Cooper decides to write his new novel about Sten and her uncomplicated lifestyle. He then learns that her father, Ruman, has betrothed her to Bellamy, a dull-witted fellow residing in a stuffed shirt. Cooper hires Sten to be his cook and housekeeper, and she soon prefers Cooper to Bellamy. During a heavy storm, she and Cooper spend the night together in the farmhouse, but the honorable Cooper refrains from

taking advantage of the willing young woman and secludes himself in his bedroom and away from temptation. Ruman suspects Sten is forcing herself on Cooper, so he insists she marry Bellamy immediately. Vinson returns to the farmhouse and, reading the first chapters of Cooper's new novel, concludes that Sten is the heroine of his story and tries to convince Sten that she will not win Cooper away from her. Sten gives up on Cooper and marries Bellamy, but, on their wedding night, Bellamy is rejected by Sten. Bellamy convinces himself that his newly acquired wife has lost her virginity to Cooper. Becoming enraged at this thought, Bellamy storms into Cooper's farmhouse and he and Cooper have a battle royal. Sten rushes into the fray and then falls to her death down a flight of stairs, but not before Cooper declares his love for her. This improbable romance and abrupt tragedy is nevertheless so well presented by Vidor that its stylized story line and sterling performances from Cooper, Sten, Bellamy and Vinson make it thoroughly appealing. Character actor Brennan provides some good comic relief as a rustic cabdriver. The film was disappointing at the box office, as was the case with two previous and lavishly produced films (**Nana**, 1934, and **We Live Again**, 1934) where Goldwyn mightily attempted to make Sten a star (paying her $2,500 a week in this production). Songs: "Shall We Gather at the River" (1964; Robert Lowry), "Trail to Mexico/Bury Me Not on the Lone Prairie" (traditional), "Wabash Blues" (1921; music: Fred Meinken; lyrics: David Ringle). *Author's Note*: Sten's thick Russian accent was a big stumbling block with the American public and most likely contributed to her unpopularity, even though she was incessantly trained by voice coaches. "I put that beautiful young lady into three quality pictures," Goldwyn told this author, "but none made any money, so it was three strikes and I was out standing on her base." Vidor told this author that "Anna [Sten] was a good actress, but when she opened her mouth, all of Moscow came out, instead of Cleveland or Springfield. No matter how hard she tried to deliver believable lines, she sounded wooden and stilted. I broke my back trying to put her across to the American public, but I knew from the start that it was a battle I would lose." When this author talked with Cooper shortly before he died, he recalled this picture with only memories of the colorful Goldwyn, who had pried him away from Paramount for this production. "He was very worried that the picture would not go over, like a few others he had produced for his protégé, Anna [Sten]. He came onto the set one day to interrupt a love scene between Anna and me and took over the direction from King [Vidor]. After he gave us some ideas about how to clinch, Goldwyn said 'If this scene isn't the greatest love scene ever put into a picture then the whole goddamn picture will go right up out of the sewer.' Well, I don't think it went out of any sewer, but I don't think it ever got into any American cup of tea." Bellamy told this author that "Anna [Sten] was as beautiful as a porcelain doll, but there was something wooden about her personality. She never clicked with the public. She appeared in three beautifully made pictures and then drifted into productions that got cheaper and cheaper, and that was her tragedy." **p**, Samuel Goldwyn; **d**, King Vidor; **cast**, Gary Cooper, Anna Sten, Ralph Bellamy, Helen Vinson, Sig Ruman, Esther Dale, Leonid Snegoff, Milla Davenport, Walter Brennan, Dennis O'Keefe; **w**, Edith Fitzgerald (based on a story by Edwin Knopf); **c**, Gregg Toland; **m**, Alfred Newman; **ed**, Stuart Heisler; **art d**, Richard Day.

Weddings and Babies ★★★ 1960; U.S.; 81m; FOX; B/W; Drama; Children: Unacceptable; **DVD**; **VHS**; **IV**. Absorbing domestic tale sees Lindfors impatient for her fiancé, Myhers, to set the date to marry her because she is anxious to start a family. He is a wedding and baby photographer, who wants to wait until he becomes a film director and financially secure before wedding Lindfors, who works as his assistant. Moreover, he devotes most of his time caring for his senile mother, Barile. At one point, Barile escapes a home for the elderly and must be tracked down to a cemetery where she is searching for the grave of her deceased husband and the plot awaiting her next to his interred corpse. Myhers uses his savings to buy a movie camera to increase his business, but it is damaged and he must now overcome another setback. There is nothing stylized or eloquent about this film, which is often banal and even crude in its lensing, but its docudrama approach, intentional or not, thus enhances its realistic story line. This good character study presents mature themes that prohibit viewing by children. *Author's Note*: Engel was the first to use a handheld 35mm camera in making a feature film. He had discovered Barile while she was sitting on a stoop in front of a NYC rooming building. She died before this film was released and never saw her performance on the big screen. **p&d**, Morris Engel; **cast**, Viveca Lindfors, John Myhers, Chiarina Barile, Leonard Elliott, Joanna Merlin, Mary Faranda, Gabriel Kohn, Kristoffer Tabori; **w**, Engel, Mary-Madeleine Lanphier, Blanche Hanalis, Irving Sunasky (based on a story by Engel); **c**, Engel; **m**, Eddy Lawrence Manson; **ed**, Michael Alexander, Stan Russell.

Wee Geordie ★★★ 1956; U.K.; 93m; Individual Films/Times Film Corp.; Color; Comedy; Children: Acceptable; **DVD**. Delightful comedy begins with Young, a Scottish boy who is small in stature, but who aspires to compete in the Olympics one day, so he sends for a mail order body-building course. By the time he is twenty-one, he's a strong, big highland lad grown to become Travers, who has a special talent for hammer-throwing. He is selected to represent Britain in the 1956 Olympic Games in Melbourne, Australia, but insists upon wearing a Scottish kilt. Officials object to that at first, but relent. Sim plays a cooperating Laird who advances Travers' ambitions. The muscular lad becomes involved with Danish amazon Goddard, but departs her domineering company in favor of the gentle and fetching Gorsen, who is the Scottish girl of his heart. In the happy ending, Travers wins and sets a new world's record in hammer-throwing. Well made and acted with gusto, the film provides enjoyable entertainment throughout. Songs: "Highland Laddie," "The British Grenadiers," Yankee Doodle" (all traditional);"Gilbert and Sullivan Medley" (William S. Gilbert, Arthur Sullivan); "Radetzky March" (1848; Johann Strauss Sr.); "The Stars and Stripes Forever" (1896; John Philip Sousa). **p**, Frank Launder, Sidney Gilliat; **d**, Launder; **cast**, Alastair Sim, Bill Travers, Norah Gorsen, Molly Urquhart, Francis De Wolff, Jack Radcliffe, Brian Reece, Raymond Huntley, Miles Malleson, Jameson Clark; **w**, Launder, Gilliat (based on a novel by David Walker); **c**, Wilkie Cooper (Technicolor); **m**, William Alwyn; **ed**, Thelma Connell; **art d**, Norman Arnold.

Wee Willie Winkie ★★★★ 1937; U.S.; 100m; FOX; B/W; Adventure; Children: Acceptable; **DVD**; **VHS**; **IV**. The adorable Temple is at her precocious best in this exciting Kipling tale about colonial India from pantheon director Ford. Temple and her penniless and widowed mother, Lang, are escorted to a remote British outpost by McLaglen, a gruff but kindhearted British army sergeant. Temple and Lang are coldly received by Smith, who is Lang's stern father-in-law and who is the colonel commanding the garrison. Temple works her childish wiles on the stiff-upper-lip Smith, her endearing ways soon softening his heart and where he grows delighted at the sight of the child. Meanwhile, Lang is befriended by handsome officer Whalen and the two develop a romantic relationship. The visitors then witness the capturing of Romero, a rebel leader, who is held captive at the post, and Temple befriends him. Meanwhile, McLaglen acts as Temple's guide and protector, and she dons the Scottish uniform of the regiment, replete with tunic and kilt and is dubbed "Wee Willie Winkie" as she accompanies McLaglen on his rounds. She routinely upsets the rigid military structure of the post, but hers is a healthy and happy chaos. Then Romeo's band raids the post and rescues him. McLaglen is sent on a patrol to retrieve the captive but is carried back to the post, mortally wounded. Temple visits her dear friend as McLaglen dies in the post hospital while Temple (in a truly heart-wrenching scene) sings "Auld Lang Syne" to him. Temple resolves to end the fighting between the Indian rebels and the British troops by visiting Romero with the help of Fung, who is really Romero's spy. Romero is delighted to see his old friend Temple and

Bill Travers, center, getting sick in *Wee Geordie,* **1956.**

treats her with kindness and respect, but insidiously thinks to hold her captive in order to lure Smith and his soldiers to their doom. Smith, of course, resolves to rescue his granddaughter at any cost and marches his troops toward Romero's bastion. Keeping his men out of the rifle range of Romero's followers, Smith heroically walks toward the stronghold alone to demand the return of his granddaughter. A few of Romero's rebels fire at him, narrowly missing their target. Seeing this, the alarmed Temple runs to Smith and stands defiantly with him as they face Romero together. Romero, filled with admiration for their courage, orders a truce and then agrees to terms that peacefully end the revolt. Ford directs this endearing film with his usual gusto, presenting all the pomp and resolve of the British military and drawing excellent performances from Temple and the rest of the cast, particularly his favored actor, McLaglen (who had earned an Oscar as Best Actor two years earlier for his portrayal in Ford's classic, **The Informer**, 1935). Ford also suppresses his directorial impulses to address in detail the British imperialism and the Indian rebellion of that era by placing emphasis on the restoration and preservation of a family. Temple's family, where McLaglen becomes an added and vital member, is a much more important entity than England's vast and powerful empire, as earlier and more broadly depicted in Ford's **The Black Watch**, 1929. Ford wisely allows Temple, through her wholesome naiveté and the simplicity of her childish heart, to triumphantly resolve such complex matters of state. The film received an Oscar nomination for Best Art Direction (Darling, Hall; set decoration: Little), and proved an enormous box office success, earning three times its then staggering budget of about $1 million, that success undoubtedly attributable to Temple's universal popularity. Songs: "Auld Lang Syne" (1788; traditional), "Wha Wanda Fecht for Charlie" (traditional), "Comin' Thro' the Rye" (traditional), "God Save the King!" (1744; Henry Carey). *Author's Note*: Ford knew full well that, by undertaking this production, he was playing second fiddle to child star Temple and that his usual themes and messages would not be present in the story line. He was nevertheless, as he admitted to this author, attracted to the project because of the enormous budget Fox provided for the film. Ford never worked well with child actors as he had no patience with their naturally unpredictable or impulsive behavior, and he was cold toward Temple when she first showed up on the set with her mother, Gertrude Temple, her constant chaperone. But when Mrs. Temple became ill with a severe stomach ailment and Shirley became distraught, Ford became her avuncular protector. "She [Shirley Temple] had been in pictures for five years before we made **Wee Willie Winkie** together," Ford told this author. "I had seen a few of her pictures and knew she was an adorable little tyke and very sincere and nothing phony about her ways. I did not think of her as someone who could really act, other than being what she was, a little girl. Well, I was in for

Cesar Romero and Shirley Temple in *Wee Willie Winkie,* 1937.

the surprise of my life when she did the deathbed scene with Vic [Victor McLaglen], the rough-and-tumble sergeant who became her friend in that picture. Her tears and facial expressions and trembling little hands in that very touching scene proved to me and the rest of the world that Shirley Temple was no poster girl, but one of the world's greatest actresses. She was wonderful. She stunned me and held me so captive by what she was doing that I let the scene go overlong, something I never did. She took me away from what I was, from what I had to do. She was that powerful in that scene. After that, I guess I treated her like royalty, but she took no notice of that because there was not an artful or egotistical bone in her little body. That sweet, pure little girl was everything in real life that you saw on the screen. She was innocent and completely without artifice. You know, in the silent days, they called Mary Pickford 'America's Sweetheart,' but Shirley became "America's Sweetheart' from the first moment she showed up on the screen in the talking days of the Thirties. And I think she stayed there forever." Temple, who was the top box office star in the U.S. from 1935 to 1938, was also subjected by Ford to her first and only spanking on film in this production. She makes an infraction that upsets some military protocol and Lang, playing her mother, is compelled to spank her. "June [Lang] did not want to do that," Ford recalled for this author. "In fact, she was trembling when she told me in a voice I could hardly hear that she refused to spank Shirley. I asked her why and she replied: 'Mr. Ford, it will be the end of my career in movies and I will be hounded and harassed on every street in America, that's why.' I managed to calm her down and then got her to do it and Shirley took all that very well, but June dreaded the release of the picture with that scene in it." So did Darryl Zanuck, head of Fox, who told this author: "Hell, I took one look at that scene and told Jack [John Ford]: "You are not going to destroy us with a scene where our greatest star is spanked like an unruly child. She's not part of the 'Our Gang' crowd. That scene goes where it belongs, on the cutting room floor." That's where the scene went before this film was released. Years later, Temple stated that **Wee Willie Winkie** remained her favorite film, saying in her autobiography: "Of all my films, I rate **Wee Willie Winkie** the best, but for all the wrong reasons. It was best because of its manual of arms, the noisy marching around in military garb with brass buttons, my kilts bouncing. It was best because of daredevil stunts with snipers and stampeding horses. It was also best because I finally seemed to earn the professional respect of someone so blood and thunder macho as [John] Ford. Best of all, the watery-blue color of my portable dressing room had been painted in regimental red." Even the tough McLaglen, a former world-class prizefighter, was putty in Temple's hands. Ford quoted McLaglen's words to this author, when McLaglen told the director during the production: "Aww, she can make me do anything. Jump over a fence, roll down a hill, spin like a top, anything to please

that little darling." Ford remained a friend of Temple's for years thereafter and even became the godfather for one of Temple's children. The original Kipling story profiled a boy, Percival Williams, as its protagonist, but the gender was changed for Temple, who becomes Priscilla Williams in this wonderful film. The film was shot mainly at Chatsworth, California, where the military post was constructed, along with Romero's stronghold. This was due to the then ongoing labor problems plaguing Hollywood studios in Los Angeles, including Fox. "Gangsters were then using a lot of strong-arm tactics with us through the theatrical unions they controlled in order to get payoffs," Zanuck told this author. "At one point, I sent an assistant up to Chatsworth with a message for Jack [Ford], and, while he was there, he saw a union crew member doing a sloppy job and bawled him out. A short time later, a heavy light was dropped on his head, knocking him senseless, although the crew members claimed that was an accident, which it was not. Someone even blamed poor little Shirley for all the problems we were having and I think one of the underworld goons allied with one of the unions was the one who took a shot at her when she and her mother were entering their home a short time later. They were not hurt and I think it was done to warn our studio." At that time, Hollywood was undergoing great pressure from organized crime figures that were extorting studios out of sizeable kickbacks on the promise that they would suppress exorbitant demands being made by unions they controlled and where these gangsters were actually dictating those demands. The leading gangster at that time involved in such Hollywood labor racketeering was William Morris "Willie" Bioff (1900-1955), who had been sent to the Coast in the mid-1930s by Chicago crime boss Frank "The Enforcer" Nitti (1886-1943) to take control of unions in the film industry. Bioff formed a liaison with George E. Browne, who later became the president of The International Alliance of Theatrical Stage Employees. Bioff and Browne successfully extorted millions from the studios, until their racket was exposed, and Browne went to prison in 1943 after being convicted of extortion. Bioff was killed, literally blown to pieces, after getting into his truck on November 4, 1955, and dynamite wired to its starter exploded after Bioff turned on the ignition. Other films depicting British control of India (during the British Raj) include: **Around the World in 80 Days**, 1956; **The Bandit of Zhobe**, 1959; **Before the Rains**, 2008; **Bengal Brigade**, 1954; **The Bengali Night**, 1988; **Bhowani Junction**, 1956; **Black Narcissus**, 1947; **The Black Watch**, 1929; **Bonnie Scotland**, 1935; **The Brigand of Kandahar**, 1965; **Carry On...Up the Khyber**, 1968; **The Charge of the Light Brigade**, 1936; **The Chess Players**, 1978; **Clive of India**, 1935; **The Crucifer of Blood**, 1991 (made-for-TV); **The Drum**, 1938; **Flame over India**, 1960; **Frontier**, 1968 (TV series); **Ganadevata**, 1979; **Gandhi**, 1982; **The Green Goddess**, 1923; **Gunga Din**, 1939; **Indiana Jones and the Temple of Doom**, 1984; **The Jewel in the Crown**, 1984 (TV miniseries); **Jinnah**, 1998; **Jungle Book**, 1942; **Junoon**, 1979; **Kim**, 1950; **Kim**, 1984 (made-for-TV); **King of the Khyber Rifles**, 1953; **Khyber Patrol**, 1954; **The Legend of Bhagat Singh**, 2002; **The Lives of a Bengal Lancer**, 1935; **The Long Duel**, 1967; **The Man Who Would Be King**, 1975; **Mard**, 1985; **Miss Beatty's Children**, 1992; **The Moonstone**, 1997 (made-for-TV); **Neel Akasher Neechey**, 1959; **1942: A Love Story**, 1994; **Palay Khan**, 1986; **Passage to India**, 1984; **The Rains Came**, 1939; **The Rains of Ranchipur**, 1955; **Rang De Basanti**, 2006; **The Rising: The Ballad of Mangal Pandey**, 2005; **The River**, 1951; **Rudyard Kipling's The Jungle Book**, 1994; **Shadows of Time**, 2005; **Sharpe's Challenge**, 2006 (made-for-TV); **Sharpe's Peril**, 2010 (made-for-TV); **Soldiers Three**, 1951; **Staying On**, 1980 (made-for-TV); **Storm over Bengal**, 1938; **The Stranglers of Bombay**, 1960; **Those Daring Young Men in Their Jaunty Jalopies**, 1969; **Thunder in the East**, 1953; **22 June 1897**, 1979; **Veta**, 2014; and **Water**, 2006. **p**, Gene Markey; **d**, John Ford; **cast**, Shirley Temple, Victor McLaglen, C. Aubrey Smith, June Lang, Michael Whalen, Cesar Romero, Constance Collier, Douglas Scott, Gavin Muir, Willie Fung, Mary Forbes, Lynn Bari; **w**, Ernest Pascal, Julien Josephson (based on a story by Rudyard Kipling); **c**, Arthur Miller; **m**, Alfred Newman; **ed**, Walter Thompson; **art d**, William S. Darling, David S. Hall; **set d**, Thomas Little.

Weekend ★★★ 1968; France/Italy; 105m; Comacico Films/Grove Press; Color; Comedy/Drama; Children: Unacceptable; **BD**; **DVD**; **VHS**; **IV**. Offbeat but fascinating story begins with what is to be an idyllic weekend trip to the countryside for an upper-class Paris couple, Yanne and Darc. That ostensibly pleasant trip turns into a never-ending nightmare of traffic jams, revolution, murder and cannibalism as French bourgeois society starts to collapse under the oppressive weight of its own preoccupations with consumerism. When the two arrive at their destination, the home of Darc's mother, they are cruelly refused a loan they are seeking, and they brutally murder the elderly lady. When returning to Paris, they meet a group of radical outcasts, who attack and murder Yanne. Darc then becomes a member of these moronic killers, only to learn that they are cannibals when she is served a stew that contains some of her husband's remains. A stunning and shockingly paranoid Godard film laced with analogies and allegories that will rivet viewers, although it and they are never quite sure where it and they are going or have been. Song: "Allo, tu m'entends" (Guy Beart). Violence and mature themes prohibit viewing by children. (In French; English subtitles.) **d&w**, Jean-Luc Godard (based on the short story "La Autopista del Sur" by Julio Cortazar); **cast**, Mireille Darc, Jean Yanne, Jean-Pierre Kalfon, Yves Afonso, Yves Beneyton, Juliet Berto, Michele Breton, Michel Cournot, Omar Diop, Jean Eustache; **c**, Raoul Coutard (Eastmancolor); **m**, Antoine Duhamel, Wolfgang Amadeus Mozart; **ed**, Agnes Guillemot.

Week-End at the Waldorf ★★★ 1945; U.S.; 130m; MGM; B/W; Drama; Children: Acceptable; **DVD**; **VHS**. This superbly made episodic tale vaults the elegance of Park Avenue's Waldorf-Astoria and follows in the exciting tradition of **Grand Hotel**, 1932, which its story line emulates. We first see Rogers, a successful film actress (essaying the Garbo role in the earlier version), who is tired of her luxurious lot in life, no longer enjoying her fame and worn out with being a celebrity. Rogers has DeCamp as a maid and is so protective of her that, after she hears that DeCamp's boyfriend is involved in some crooked dealings, she resolves to set the man straight by talking him into changing his ways. She mistakes the charming Pidgeon for this person, calling him "Duke," and Pidgeon, enamored of Rogers and her attentions toward him, plays along with her, pretending to be that errant lover (his role being a loose version of John Barrymore's part in the 1932 film). Pidgeon and Rogers not only have a heart-to-heart, but fall in love with each other in the process. Rogers pays homage to the earlier film by saying in response to one of Pidgeon's remarks: "That's right out of **Grand Hotel**." Thaxter then becomes involved with Rogers when she refuses to marry Anderson, a physician, thinking that Anderson is romantically involved with superstar Rogers. To convince Thaxter otherwise, Rogers fibs and says that she is secretly married to Pidgeon, and, before Rogers can suppress her fabrication, the tale is rumored down every hall in the hotel. Meanwhile, hotel stenographer Turner hopes to marry a Park Avenue suitor that will take her away from her lowly domicile on Tenth Avenue. (She plays the role enacted by Joan Crawford in the original film, but is nowhere near the amoral lady Crawford essayed.) Turner meets personable Johnson, an Army Air Force officer, who is about to undergo a life-and-death operation where shrapnel received in battle (during WWII, 1939-1945) is lodged close to his heart and must be removed. Turner is offered all the comforts of the world if she will become the mistress to tycoon Arnold (enacting the role Wallace Beery played in the original film). The clean-living Turner cannot lend herself to such an unsavory relationship and loses her heart to Johnson when they later meet in the hotel's nightclub. While all of these romantic relationships are being resolved, investigative reporter Wynn manages to upset the evil applecart wheeled by Arnold, who is attempting to swindle Arab businessman Zucco, and the suave Pidgeon aids Wynn in exposing the underhanded

Ginger Rogers and Walter Pidgeon in *Week-End at the Waldorf,* **1945.**

Arnold. All ends well for the several lovers as Rogers and Pidgeon make arrangements to meet in England where they will wed as Thaxter and Anderson tie the knot, as do Turner and Johnson, and where it is shown that he will survive his hazardous operation. Providing comic relief throughout this romantic saga is the very witty Benchley, a notorious hotel gossip who agonizes over his pregnant Scotch terrier while downing endless glasses of booze until the canine delivers triplets. Leonard directs this multi-storied tale with great skill, seamlessly merging its separate tales and bringing outstanding performances from its stellar cast. Rogers and Pidgeon and Turner and Johnson especially shine in their roles as unlikely but inevitable lovers. The script crackles with wit and humor throughout while Green provides a lively and lyrical score. The film was a huge box office success, earning more than $6.1 million in its initial release against a budget of $2.5 million, becoming the fourth largest grossing film for the year 1945. Songs: "And There You Are" (1940; music: Sammy Fain; lyrics: Ted Koehler), "Guadalajara" (1937; Pepe Guizar), "Once Upon a Dream" (1890; from "Sleeping Beauty" by Peter Ilyich Tchaikovsky), "I've Got You Under My Skin" (1936; Cole Porter), "Here Comes the Bride" ["Bridal Chorus"] (1850; from "Lohengrin" by Richard Wagner). *Author's Note*: Rogers told this author that "**Week-End at the Waldorf** was a picture America needed. Everyone was worn out with the war [WWII, 1939-1945], which ended only a few months before the picture was released, and the public wanted to laugh and be happy again. When audiences left the theater after seeing that picture, they felt good about everything, especially themselves. I know that may sound silly, but people live inside their best memories and we gave them good, warm ones in that picture." Johnson recalled for this author one of those good, warm memories when talking about his role in this film, saying: "Some of the interior and exterior shots of the actual Waldorf were shot on location in New York for that picture, and I can tell you that that wonderful hotel was one of my favorites. It offered the kind of old world elegance you didn't see except for some of the great European hotels, with enormous imported rugs in that grand foyer and tapestries and marbled pillars. It was like checking into the Taj Mahal." Though some shots of the Waldorf were shot for this film, most of the interiors, the Starlight Roof, lobby and guest rooms were reconstructed and used at the MGM studio in Culver City, California. These sets were later used in another MGM production made that same year, **Her Highness and the Bellboy**, 1945. Turner told this author: "They spent a lot of money to produce **Week-End at the Waldorf**. Everything about it was lavish, but when they saw they were spending so much money on that picture, they did a little cost-cutting when it came to my role. In one scene I am wearing an evening gown. It was a beautiful dress with a beaded laurel-leaf pattern, but when I looked at it in the mirror, it reminded me of another picture, and, sure

John Payne and Alice Faye in *Week-End in Havana*, 1941.

enough, Joan Crawford had worn that same dress in **Reunion in France** [1942; originally created by renown costumer designer Irene], and the costume department had simply refitted it for me. I did not feel I was wearing a hand-me-down. Not a bit. I felt I was in very good company." Waldorf management did not demand a cent for the use of its name and location shooting, rightly believing that this film would serve as a wonderful publicity and promotion vehicle for its operation. Mrs. Lucius Boomer, who was the wife of the president of the Waldorf Corporation, served as an adviser on this production, but when she and others suggested that MGM shoot the film in color to show the hotel at its best, MGM executives balked. They were told that, if the Waldorf made that a condition, the studio would set the location at another, mythical hotel located in San Francisco and title the film **Palace in the Sky**. Waldorf management dropped the idea. The acerbic and always entertaining Benchley, who provided some mirthful scenes for this film, had already appeared in four more unreleased films. He never saw any of them on the big screen, including this one, as that grand and witty man was too ill when this film was released, dying a month later on November 21, 1945. There was too much story for this film that required one sequence, which depicts Constance Collier as a one-time opera prima donna destined for a retirement home, to be cut from the film. **p**, Arthur Hornblow, Jr.; **d**, Robert Z. Leonard; **cast**, Ginger Rogers, Lana Turner, Walter Pidgeon, Van Johnson, Edward Arnold, Keenan Wynn, Robert Benchley, Phyllis Thaxter, Warner Anderson, Leon Ames, Lina Romay, Samuel S. Hinds, Porter Hall, George Zucco, Rosemary DeCamp, Constance Collier, Xavier Cugat and His Orchestra; **w**, Sam and Bella Spewack (based on an adaptation by Guy Bolton of the play "Grand Hotel" by Vicki Baum); **c**, Robert Planck; **m**, Johnny Green; **ed**, Robert J. Kern; **art d**, Cedric Gibbons, Daniel B. Cathcart; **set d**, Edwin B. Willis; **spec eff**, Warren Newcombe, A. Arnold Gillespie, Mark Davis.

Week-End in Havana ★★★ 1941; U.S.; 81m; FOX; Color; Musical Comedy/Romance; Children: Acceptable; **DVD, VHS**. Delightful songfest sees Faye as a New York City department store salesgirl who saves her money for a Caribbean vacation cruise, but the ship runs aground off the Florida coast. The ship company compensates her by giving her an all-expenses-paid week-end tour of pre-revolutionary Havana, Cuba. Payne, a company official, is assigned as her escort. Payne, who would rather remain in New York to marry his fiancée, Wright Jr., agrees reluctantly to accompany Faye to restaurants and gambling casinos. In one of the casinos, they meet Romero, a penniless gambler, and his singing Hispanic firecracker girlfriend, Miranda. The fiery Miranda becomes jealous when Romero makes a play for Faye, thinking she is wealthy. This goes nowhere because by then Faye and Payne have fallen in love. Faye is outstanding and radiant and sees good singing compe-

tition from the colorful Miranda. Songs: "A Week-End in Havana," "When I Love, I Love," "Tropical Magic," "The Man with the Lollypop Song," "The Nango" (music: Harry Warren; lyrics: Mack Gordon); "Rebola a Bola/Embolada" (music: Aloysio De Oliveira, Nestor Amaral; lyrics: Francisco Eugenio Brant Amaral); "Romance and Rhumba" (music: James V. Monaco; lyrics: Mack Gordon). *Author's Note*: Faye told this author that "they were thinking of starring Betty Grable in **Week-End in Havana**, but I was happy to get the role. They were always pitting Betty and me against each other, as if they thought we were fierce competitors, but that was never the case. We really liked each other and pretended we were serious rivals just to keep the front office at Fox jumping." Faye had recently married bandleader and actor Phil Harris and was pregnant at the time she made this film. Darryl Zanuck, head of Fox, told this author that "**Week-End in Havana** was the perfect kind of picture for Alice [Faye]. She played a Macy's department store clerk in that musical and is very down to earth, which was her real personality and that is how we always wanted her to be portrayed. She was the kind of star that appealed to both men and women and that always meant box office for our studio." Payne told this author that "the real scene-stealer in **Week-End in Havana** was Carmen [Miranda]. She was so wonderful in mangling the English language that we had a hard time stifling our laughter in scenes with her. Her flashing large eyes and rubbery facial expressions belonged only to her and she had more energy than a Marine Corps band." Miranda was aware of all of that, and her agents worked out a tough agreement with Fox where none of Miranda's musical numbers could be interrupted by cutaways to other actors speaking dialog while she was performing a number. She was reportedly paid $5,000 a week for her role in **Week-End in Havana**. "Oh, we paid through the nose to get Carmen [Miranda]," Zanuck told this author. "She was worth every dime." It was this film and the outlandish hats bedecked with imitation fruit that Miranda wore that inspired an army of cartoonists to begin drawing caricatures of her, much to the delight of Fox, as well as Miranda's millions of fans. **p**, William Le Baron; **d**, Walter Lang; **cast**, Alice Faye, John Payne, Carmen Miranda, Cesar Romero, Cobina Wright Jr., George Barbier, Sheldon Leonard, Leonid Kinskey, Chris-Pin Martin, Billy Gilbert, Bob Crosby, **w**, Karl Tunberg, Darrell Ware; **c**, Ernest Palmer (Technicolor); **m**, Alfred Newman; **ed**, Allen McNeil; **art d**, Richard Day, Joseph C. Wright; **set d**, Thomas Little.

Weekend of Shadows ★★★ 1978; Australia; 105m; Australian Film Commission; Color; Crime Drama; Children: Unacceptable; **VHS**. The well-made, tension-filled tale presents a murder tale that depicts the mounting bloodlust of a posse that turns into a lynch mob. Waters becomes a member of a posse out to catch a Polish immigrant farmhand, who is suspected of killing a rancher's wife. Roberts, a police sergeant, leads the chase and is determined to hunt down the fugitive so as to regain lost stature after having brought about the deaths of two young people. Waters, however, comes to believe that the fugitive may be innocent and increasingly defends him, which pits him against Roberts. Meanwhile, the disorganized posse bogs down with disinterest, and some of its members drink themselves into boozy oblivion. Tautly directed by Jeffrey, the well-written script and top-flight performances keep this tale and its dogged hunt very much alive until its grim conclusion. Violence and alcoholism prohibit viewing by children. **p**, Tom Jeffrey, Matt Carroll; **d**, Jeffrey; **cast**, John Waters, Melissa Jaffer, Wyn Roberts, Barbara West, Graham Rouse, Keith Lee, Bill Hunter, Kit Taylor, Les Foxcroft, Graeme Blundell, Kevin Miles; **w**, Peter Yeldham (based on the novel *The Reckoning* by Hugh Atkinson); **c**, Richard Wallace (Eastmancolor); **m**, Charles Marawood; **ed**, Rod Adamson; **prod d&art d**, Christopher Webster.

Week-End with Father ★★★ 1951; U.S.; 83m; UNIV; B/W; Comedy/Romance; Children: Acceptable. Entertaining domestic tale has Heflin and Neal as single parents, as both are widowed. They meet at a train station where he is sending his two young daughters and she is packing off her two young sons to summer camp. Heflin and Neal fall in love, but Heflin's former girlfriend, the attractive Field, a television star, thinks Heflin plans to marry her. Then the boundlessly energetic Denning, the camp's athletic counselor (and a fanatic health nut if there ever was one) becomes interested in Neal. It turns into a wild weekend. At first, the children try to keep their parents apart, and do a devilishly good job of alienating them from one another. However, the ever observant Perreau, one of Heflin's daughters, sees that Heflin and Neal really love each other and persuades the other children to help her get their parents back together. This works so well that the adults are soon heading for the altar and their two broods will soon be one. *Author's Note*: Heflin told this author that "I and Patricia [Neal] may have gotten top billing in **Week-End with Father**, but we are not the stars. Doug [Douglas Sirk] made the kids playing our children the stars of that picture. I actually enjoyed that comedy, which was a relief from the kind of intense roles I had played, like the man on the run in **Act of Violence** [1948], or the indecisive lover of Barbara Stanwyck in **B.F.'s Daughter** [1948]." Neal echoed these sentiments when telling this author: "Van [Heflin] and I are strictly second fiddles to a passel of kids in **Week-End with Father**, but I am not complaining because those little tykes really stole the show with performances that would put some adult actors and actresses to shame." Sirk admitted to this author that "I made that picture strictly for the children. I had used the same theme where children really substitute for fate by determining what happens to adults in **All That Heaven Allows** [1955]. In that picture, selfish children try to sabotage a marriage between Rock Hudson and Jane Wyman. I never tried to show children as basically mean or evil. They know the world is controlled by adults, but they also know that they have a lot to say in the little worlds they live in and they naturally try to protect what emotional comfort they have in those isolated worlds." Sirk became a vegetarian while making this film and admitted to this author that Denning's outlandish health-obsessed character was "a bit of a self-satire." **p**, Ted Richmond; **d**, Douglas Sirk; **cast**, Van Heflin, Patricia Neal, Gigi Perreau, Virginia Field, Richard Denning, Jimmy Hunt, Janine Perreau, Tommy Rettig, Gary Pagett, Forrest Lewis; **w**, Joseph Hoffman (based on a story by George W. George, George F. Slavin); **c**, Clifford Stine; **m**, Frank Skinner; **ed**, Russell Shoengarth; **art d**, Bernard Herzbrun, Robert Boyle; **set d**, Russell A. Gausman, Ruby R. Levitt.

Welcome Stranger ★★★ 1947; U.S.; 107m; PAR; B/W; Comedy; Drama; Children: Acceptable; **DVD, VHS**. Entertaining tale reunites Crosby and Fitzgerald, who had scored a hit with **Going My Way**, 1944, but this time they are physicians instead of priests. Fitzgerald is a small-town Maine doctor at a clinic with a poor bedside manner, who hires Crosby, sight unseen, to help him. They don't get along, mainly because Fitzgerald has little trust in a doctor who sings and the happy-go-lucky Crosby is forever warbling. Crosby agrees to stay after seeing beautiful school teacher Caulfield. She shows little interest in him because she is to marry the local druggist. The inhabitants are also so cool and suspicious of Crosby that he feels that he might as well depart, but Patterson, Fitzgerald's maid, convinces Crosby to have a heart-to-heart talk with curmudgeon Fitzgerald. He does and Fitzgerald's attitude toward Crosby softens and, gradually, the two medics get to like each other. Fitzgerald gains respect for Crosby's medical skills, especially after Fitzgerald needs emergency surgery for an appendectomy, and the singing doctor performs the operation well. Both are stunned when Young, a posturing doctor, is given the post of director of the new hospital where he is confronted with a sudden medical crisis. Four boys are stricken with what Young determines to be equine encephalitis, a viral brain fever contracted from diseased horses. His diagnosis is challenged by Crosby and Fitzgerald after Crosby finds four half-smoked cigars hidden in a locker room and the boys admit to puffing on the stogies. The discredited Young departs and Fitzgerald and Crosby become the directors of the new clinic. Better still, Caulfield has decided that Crosby is the man for

Joan Caulfield and Bing Crosby in *Welcome Stranger,* 1947.

her. Well handled by director Nugent (who also offers a cameo as a physician), this film belongs to Crosby and Fitzgerald, who shine through their heartwarming shenanigans. Patterson, Kilbride and Faylen provide lively portrayals as flinty New Englanders, and Hendrix, who soon became a leading lady, is a little gem of a lovesick teenager swooning over Crosby's crooning. The songs from Van Heusen and Burke are exceptional and one, "Country Style," leads to a toe-tapping square dance production number. This delightful film proved to be a great success at the box office, earning more than $6.1 million in its initial release. It saw a thirty-minute radio adaptation aired by the Screen Guild Theater on October 14, 1948, with Crosby and Fitzgerald reprising their roles, and a sixty-minute radio adaptation aired by Lux Radio Theater on April 5, 1954, with Fitzgerald reprising his role. Songs: "Smile Right Back at the Sun," "Country Style," "My Heart Is a Hobo," "As Long As I'm Dreaming," "Smack in the Middle of Maine" (music: Jimmy Van Heusen; lyrics: Johnny Burke). *Author's Note*: Crosby told this author: "I think the reason why the script for **Welcome Stranger** had so many clever and funny lines is because one of the writers, Art Sheekman, wrote for the Marx Brothers pictures. He had a knack in seeing the average Joe as a comical character. He was a terrific wordsmith and always knew where laughter could be found." Not related to the 1924 and 2006 films of the same title. **p**, Sol C. Siegel; **d**, Elliott Nugent; **cast**, Bing Crosby, Joan Caulfield, Barry Fitzgerald, Wanda Hendrix, Frank Faylen, Elizabeth Patterson, Robert Shayne, Larry Young, Percy Kilbride, Charles Dingle, Don Beddoe, Thurston Hall, Lillian Bronson; **w**, Arthur Sheekman, N. Richard Nash (based on a story by Frank Butler); **c**, Lionel Lindon; **m**, Robert Emmett Dolan; **ed**, Everett Douglas; **art d**, Franz Bachelin, Hans Dreier; **set d**, Sam Comer, John MacNeil; **spec eff**, Farciot Edouart.

Welcome to Hard Times ★★★ 1967; U.S.; 103m; MGM; Color; Drama/Western; Children: Unacceptable; **DVD**; **VHS**; **IV**. Gritty, almost savage western sees Fonda as the spineless mayor of a dying small town called Hard Times (ostensibly located in Nevada), who is the brunt of frequent abuse by Ray, who is called the Man from Bodie. Fonda refuses to use a gun to corral this roaring bully and does nothing as the drunken Ray begins to threaten everyone in the small town. He is a wandering gunman who kills at his pleasure. When two of the town's leading citizens, Birch, the founder of Hard Times, and Cook, the local undertaker, stand up to him, Ray shoots and kills them both. (Cook's cruel demise is not unlike the scene where he is shot to death in a muddy street by villainous gunslinger Jack Palance in the classic western **Shane**, 1953.) Ray then rapes McCrea, who is Birch's woman, before he burns down the town. Ray, who even shoots his own horse before stealing another, departs in a laughing frenzy, reveling in his bloodletting and wan-

Maura Tierney and Ray Romano in *Welcome to Mooseport*, 2004.

ton destruction. Fonda, who adopts Birch's son, Shea, promises to rebuild the town after Ray moves on, but the townspeople give up and leave. Rule, who is now terrified that Ray might return, stays in town, and Shea becomes her protector, believing that her lover Fonda is nothing but a weakling. A wagon load of prostitutes employed by Wynn then arrives, and Wynn plans to open a new saloon, using these loose ladies as shills for the miners who sometimes come down from the hills. Wynn and Fonda undertake to rebuild the town. Rule wants revenge on Ray, and Fonda promises that, if Ray returns, things will be different. This proves true when Ray does come back to town and Fonda straps on a gun. He and Ray blast it out together and Ray falls under a hail of bullets fired by Fonda. Carrying the body of the outlaw to Rule to prove to her that this awful menace is dead, Ray suddenly comes back to terrifying life, grabbing Rule's hand. She screams and Shea comes on the run with his shotgun, wildly firing the weapon, which strikes Ray in the face and finally kills this human monster, but the blast also strikes Rule, fatally wounding her. Fonda cradles her in his arms as she dies, ironically and inadvertently slain by the boy who has vowed to protect her from the devastating Ray. Fonda and Shea then stand at Rule's gravesite, looking back upon the town, which has been rebuilt. Kennedy does a good job in offering this violent and often gruesome tale as an unforgettable grim portrait of the Old West as a living nightmare. Fonda is captivating as a hesitating hero, and Rule rivets as a woman wholly consumed by dread and fear. The burly, hoarse-throated Ray gives a fantastic performance as a berserk sociopath, one of the most frightening performances of his career. Ray had shown a strong proclivity for such roles when earlier portraying a psychopathic soldier in **The Naked and the Dead**, 1958. The film saw a modest success at the box office. Songs: "Little Brown Jug" (1869; Joseph Winner), "Buffalo Gals" (1844; John Hodges), "Silent Night" (1859; music: Franz Gruber; lyrics: Joseph Mohr), "O, Come, O Ye Faithful/Adeste Fideles" (Frederick Oakeley), "The Bridal Chorus" (1850; Richard Wagner). *Author's Note*: Fonda told this author that "**Welcome to Hard Times** was made in 1966 and was originally planned as a TV production, but it was so violent that the networks would not air it, so it was released in theaters instead. None of its characters are likeable, even those who are victims. It's really a horror story or a study in terror. Aldo Ray scared the hell out of all of us when we were making that picture as well as anyone who saw it. If there had been ten real lunatics like him back then, the Old West would have been nothing but ghost towns." This film was shot on location at the Conejo Ranch in Thousand Oaks, California. Another western offers almost the same story where ineffective James Stewart attempts to defend a miserable western town in **Firecreek**, 1968, which also stars Fonda as one of several bad men threatening the terrified inhabitants. **p**, David Karr, Max E. Youngstein; **d**, Burt Kennedy; **cast**, Henry Fonda, Janice Rule,

Keenan Wynn, Janis Paige, John Anderson, Warren Oates, Fay Spain, Edgar Buchanan, Aldo Ray, Denver Pyle, Lon Chaney Jr., Royal Dano, Alan Baxter, Paul Fix, Elisha Cook Jr.; **w**, Kennedy (based on the novel by E.L. Doctorow); **c**, Harry Stradling Jr. (Metrocolor); **m**, Harry Sukman; **ed**, Aaron Stell; **art d**, Carl Anderson, George W. Davis; **set d**, Henry Grace, Joseph J. Stone.

Welcome to Mooseport ★★★ 2004; U.S./Germany; 110m; FOX; Color; Comedy; Children: Unacceptable (MPAA: PG-13); **BD**; **DVD**; **IV**. Entertaining comedy begins with Hackman, a former U.S. President, who retires to his vacation home-town of Mooseport in Maine. He will take endorsement deals and speaking engagements while developing his own presidential library. He is offered the local position of mayor, but finds an unlikely opponent in a hardware store owner, Romano. A simple competition escalates into all-out war between the two mayoral candidates. They decide neither will vote for himself or the other candidate, but Hackman deceptively votes for himself and wins by one vote. Hackman's conscience gets the better of him and he reveals that he voted for himself, and concedes the election to Romano. But Romano admits he voted for himself and declines the office, so Hackman becomes mayor. Both men also have girlfriend problems which are resolved. Hackman and Romano offer very good performances as two conniving politicians, who turn out to be friendly enemies rather than ruthless competitors. Hackman retired from acting after this film, which did not do well at the box office, earning about $14.5 million in its initial release against a budget of $30 million. Songs: "Small Town" (John Mellencamp), "Hail to the Chief" (James Sanderson), "The Thunderer" and "Semper Fidelis" (John Philip Sousa), "Mandy" (Scott David English, Richard Buchanan Kerr), "For He's a Jolly Good Fellow," "Horse Race Bugle Call" (both traditional), "Woods Plot" (John Frizzell), "Why Can't We Be Friends" (Sylvester Allen, Harold R. Brown, Morris D. Dickerson), "Mayor of Simpleton" (Andy Partridge). Sexual content and nudity prohibit viewing by children. **p**, Tom Schulman, Marc Frydman, Basil Iwanyk; **d**, Donald Petrie; **cast**, Gene Hackman, Ray Romano, Marcia Gay Harden, Maura Tierney, Christine Baranski, Fred Savage, Rip Torn, June Squibb, Wayne Robson, John Rothman; **w**, Schulman (based on the story by Doug Richardson); **c**, Victor Hammer; **m**, John Debney; **ed**, Debra Neil-Fisher; **prod d**, David Chapman; **art d**, Michael Shocrylas; **set d**, Gordon Sim; **spec eff**, John T. Van Vliet, Martin Malivoire, Dennis Petersen.

The Well ★★★ 1951; U.S.; 86m; UA; B/W; Drama; Children: Unacceptable; **DVD**; **VHS**; **IV**. Taut tale takes on the sensitive racial issue between whites and blacks in a small town. Laster, a five-year-old black girl, falls into a forgotten well on her way to school, but nobody notices. Sheriff Rober checks on a report that the girl was earlier seen with a white stranger, and rumors start to fly. An investigation leads to Morgan, who is innocent, but the racially divided town believes he killed the girl. Morgan is jailed on suspicion of having kidnapped Laster, who remains missing. Morgan is soon released for lack of evidence. A search of the area near the school leads to the discovery that Laster is down in the well. Rober asks Morgan, who has experience in engineering, to try to dig Laster out. Morgan, however, is bitter about having been accused and jailed for something he did not do, and refuses. He then thinks it over, and his conscience acts for him as he agrees to go down into the well. By this time, the blacks and whites of the community have gathered at the shaft site and tension mounts as they wait for Morgan to reemerge from the well. When he does, he is holding a barely alive Laster, and he, who had been earlier labeled a killer, is now hailed as the girl's rescuer. All of the principal players, especially Morgan and Rober, are standouts in their roles. The film also offers a good study of the kind of racial tension profiled in other small American towns in such films as **Intruder in the Dust**, 1949, and **To Kill a Mockingbird**, 1962. This engrossing rescue film was released the same year as was another, somewhat similar but more cynical film, **The Big Carnival** (aka: **Ace**

in the Hole), 1951, which deals with a man trapped inside of a mountainous cavern. **p**, Harry M. Popkin, Clarence Greene; **d**, Leo C. Popkin, Russell Rouse; **cast**, Gwendolyn Laster, Richard Rober, Henry (Harry) Morgan, Maidie Norman, George Hamilton, Ernest Anderson, Dick Simmons, Lane Chandler, Pat Mitchell, Margaret Wells, Michael Ross; **w**, Greene, Rouse; **c**, Ernest Laszlo; **m**, Dimitri Tiomkin; **ed**, Chester Schaeffer; **prod d**, Rudolph Sternad; **set d**, Murray Waite.

Wells Fargo ★★★ 1937; U.S.; 97m; PAR; B/W; Adventure; Children: Unacceptable; **DVD**; **VHS**. A lot of action is packed into this fictionalized tale about the Wells Fargo express company. Beginning in the early 1840s, McCrea, an employee, comes upon a broken carriage in the countryside and gives a young lady, Dee, and her mother, Nash, a lift into Buffalo, New York, although he is in a hurry to deliver some fresh oysters for his firm, Wells Fargo. He gets them there in time to enable his boss, Henry Wells, played by O'Neill, to impress some bankers with the speed of his delivery service. O'Neill assigns McCrea to set up a branch office in St. Louis, where Dee and her mother live, and they begin seeing each other. McCrea is then sent in 1846 to open trails to California and takes along a frontiersman, Burns, and Burns' Pawnee Indian friend, Siegel. One of McCrea's duties is to transport gold from a mining camp to San Francisco, and one of his customers is a prospector, Cummings, who is shot by robbers and left for dead. Cummings recovers, but other miners think he intended to rob the gold. Cummings produces a draft from Wells Fargo that will cover their losses. McCrea and Cummings, who has recovered from his wound, meet a ship in San Francisco in 1851 and see that Dee is a passenger, with her father, Morgan. McCrea and Dee marry and have two children together. Their union is strained when McCrea is away often after the start of the American Civil War (1861-1865), protecting gold shipments from the west that are intended for the Union, but that are intercepted by Confederates. Wells Fargo is assigned to transport $2 million in gold, and McCrea is assigned to lead the wagon train. McCrea meets President Abraham Lincoln (1809-1865), played by McGlynn, who emphasizes how crucial the gold is to the Union. Complicating matters for McCrea is Dee and Nash, who are strong Southern supporters, Dee's brother having been killed while fighting for the Confederacy. Dee tries to talk McCrea out of his job of protecting the gold shipment, but he remains steadfast in his duty to the Union. Dee learns the secret route McCrea will take and writes it down. At the last minute, she crumples up the note, but Nash passes it along to Confederate officials. A Confederate force attacks McCrea and his wagon train, and McCrea survives, but not Burns or Siegel. McCrea finds the note about the route he is taking and recognizes his wife's handwriting. When he returns to San Francisco, he finds that his wife and children have gone to live with Nash. Years later, McCrea goes east for a dinner in his honor and is visited by his daughter, Stewart, now a teenager. She invites him to her seventeenth birthday party and, when he arrives, he sees Dee and discovers she did not betray him after all, and they become reconciled. Episodic and where the story freely mixes fact with fiction, the tale is nevertheless portrayed with wonderful action scenes under the firm hand of director Lloyd. McCrea and Dee (they were married at that time, a union that lasted from 1933 to his death in 1990) are compelling as the at-odds lovers, who are divided over loyalties that also tear apart the fabric of America. Paramount spent lavishly on this film and its fine production values show it, from its appropriately appointed period sets to its authentic stagecoaches, drawn by six speedy horses. The film received an Oscar nomination for Best Sound (Loren L. Ryder), and it proved very popular with the public, returning twice its investment budget of more than $1.5 million at the box office in its initial release. Songs: "Where I Ain't Been Before" (1937; music: Burton Lane; lyrics: Ralph Freed), "Symphony No. 9, 4th Movement" (1893; Antoin Dvorak). *Author's Note*: McCrea admitted to this author that "**Wells Fargo** was really a picture made up of a lot of stories about several competing express companies in the 19th Century, not just Wells Fargo, but it made for an exciting picture. There was so much to say

Joel McCrea in *Wells Fargo*, 1937.

about those stagecoach days that maybe we showed more than what was needed, but that always happens when you are filming an epic. I took some personal pride in appearing in **Wells Fargo** because my grandfather had been a stagecoach driver and had fought off outlaws and Apaches while driving stagecoaches to the safety of small towns." Dee told this author that "Joel [McCrea] was in his element when we appeared together in **Wells Fargo**. He always felt more comfortable when he was playing in a western as he was a free-and-easy cowboy by nature." **p&d**, Frank Lloyd; **cast**, Joel McCrea, Bob Burns, Frances Dee, Lloyd Nolan, Henry O'Neill, Mary Nash, Ralph Morgan, John Mack Brown, Porter Hall, Robert Cummings, Peggy Stewart, Harry Davenport, Scotty Beckett, Richard Denning, Willie Fung; **w**, Paul Schofield, Gerald Geraghty, Frederick Jackson (based on a story by Stuart N. Lake); **c**, Theodor Sparkuhl; **m**, Victor Young; **ed**, Hugh Bennett; **art d**, Hans Dreier, John Goodman; **spec eff**, Gordon Jennings.

We're No Angels ★★★★ 1955; U.S.; 106m; PAR; Color; Comedy; Children: Cautionary; **DVD**; **VHS**; **IV**. Very funny story proved that tough Bogart was as brilliant with comedy as he was with any film noir tale. We see Bogart, Ustinov and Ray escaping the dreaded penal colony of Devil's Island (in French Guiana). All have been serving life terms, Bogart for forgery and Ustinov and Ray for murder. They make good their escape just before Christmas and arrive at a small French colonial town. They go to a store owned by Carroll and Bennett, who have a young daughter, Talbott, and discover that this is the only store that allows purchases on credit. Penniless, however, they cannot buy the clothes and supplies they need to continue their flight to freedom, so the escaped convicts offer to fix the store's leaking roof in exchange for a night's lodging. This arrangement has been made under Carroll's misunderstanding that he thinks the three are paroled convicts and have been sent to make those repairs. The trio really plans to wait until nightfall until they can steal what they need and then board a ship waiting in the harbor without ever making those repairs. However, as they wait, they learn that their kind benefactors are in distress and hard-pressed for money. The naive and trusting nature of their hosts causes the escapees to have a change of heart, and they prepare a succulent Christmas dinner for the family, which is made up of mostly foodstuffs they have stolen. The conniving trio concludes that hiding out as workers for Carroll is the safest way to wait out the intense and widespread hunt for him, until searchers quit their pursuit. Further, they decide to improve the family's finances. Bogart uses his criminal expertise to juggle the store's books so that it appears that the operation is flourishing, while Ray and Ustinov find ways of making the store operate more efficiently to cut costs. The enterprising trio soon charms Carroll's customers into paying their long overdue accounts, and the convicts convince patrons

Peter Ustinov, Aldo Ray, Humphrey Bogart and Leo G. Carroll in *We're No Angels,* **1955.**

to buy things from the store that they would otherwise never think to purchase. Carroll is amazed at this profitable turnaround, which provides Bennett and daughter Talbott with the reassurance of a secure future. Bogart and friends then discover that Carroll is not the actual owner of the store, but only manages it for his distant relative, Rathbone, a mean-minded, penny-pinching businessman, who arrives from Paris with all of his pompous airs and demanding demeanors, along with Baer, his nephew. Talbott is immediately attracted to the handsome Baer, although he is a bit of a rake in that he encourages the naïve Talbott even though he is engaged to another woman. Rathbone believes that Carroll has been running an unprofitable operation and intends to take over the store. He audits the books and sees Bogart's manipulations therein, convincing himself that Carroll has been illegally siphoning off money for his own ends and he threatens to bring criminal charges against him. This grim outcome will not be permitted by the now avuncular Bogart, Ustinov and Ray. Ustinov prevents Rathbone from destroying Carroll and his family by placing Adolphe, his pet and a very poisonous snake, into a basket conveniently positioned in Rathbone's path when Rathbone is searching through the store for what he thinks is money hidden by Carroll. When reaching into that basket, Rathbone is immediately bitten by Adolphe and dies an unceremonious off-screen death. Baer, who is just as greedy and self-serving as his vicious uncle, ignores Rathbone's demise and begins his own search for money. When rummaging through Rathbone's pockets, Baer encounters Adolphe, who bites him, too, quickly sending Baer along the dark path Rathbone has taken. With these two villains out of the way, the store reverts to the ownership of Carroll, Bennett and Talbott, who also inherit Rathbone's vast holdings. The convicts are left with only one problem to solve, and that is finding a suitable suitor for the now pining Talbott. They solve this by arranging for Smith, a young and dashing medical officer, to meet Talbott. Both are immediately drawn to each other and a healthy romance ensues. Having done their good deed, the convicts depart for the ship in the harbor, but they have more than second thoughts about continuing their flight to freedom, which, they believe, will not be freedom at all. They conclude that the world is peopled with many more criminals with whom they would have to compete than those inside the prison that has been their predictable home for so many years. They decide to go back inside of the prison walls and regain the security they offer. As they make their way toward their old warders, a halo appears, one after another, over the heads of Bogart, Ustinov and Ray, and, finally, over the basket Ustinov carries containing Adolphe, although his halo is decidedly off-kilter. Macabre, if not bizarre, as this clever film is, it is nevertheless presented by the gifted Curtiz as a wonderful dark comedy packed with witty lines and mirthful scenes. Bogart, Ustinov and Ray are at their mischievous best, and they get strong support from a talented

cast in the form of that arch villain, Rathbone, as well as Carroll, Bennett, and Talbott. This film was a great box office hit, earning more than $3 million in its initial release against a budget of more than $1.6 million. The story was remade with disappointing results in 1989 with Robert De Niro and Sean Penn in the leading roles. Songs: "Sentimental Moments" (music: Friedrich Hollaender; lyrics: Ralph Freed); "Ma France Bien-Aimee" (music: G. Martini; lyrics: Roger Wagner), "Three Angels" (music: Edward J. Hopkins; lyrics: Troy Sanders). *Author's Note*: Rathbone told this author that "I have but a few scenes in **We're No Angels** and where I played, as usual, a villain. I thought it a very entertaining picture, and my only regret is that I wished I had had more scenes with that amazing actor, Humphrey Bogart, who only needed to walk into a scene in order to dominate it. He was in stature a rather small man with thin, bony shoulders, but he radiated a magnetic force that captivated every living thing in that production, including that unreliable little snake." Other films depicting convicts at or escaping from the penal colony at French Guiana, which incorporates Devil's Island, include **The Devil Doll**, 1936; **Devil's Island**, 1926; **Devil's Island**, 1939; **Escape from Devil's Island**, 1935; **Hell on Devil's Island**, 1957; **I Escaped from Devil's Island**, 1973; **L'affaire Seznec**, 1993 (made-for-TV); **The Life of Emile Zola**, 1937 (which depicts Alfred Dreyfus' incarceration at Devil's Island); **Pappillon**, 1973; **Passage to Marseille**, 1944 (where Bogart is also a convict and escapes); **Strange Cargo**, 1940; **Terror of the Bloodhunters**, 1962; and **Women of Devil's Island**, 1962. **p**, Pat Duggan; **d**, Michael Curtiz; **cast**, Humphrey Bogart, Aldo Ray, Peter Ustinov, Joan Bennett, Basil Rathbone, Leo G. Carroll, John Baer, John Smith, Gloria Talbot, Lea Penman, George Dee; **w**, Ranald MacDougall (based on the play "La cuisine des anges" by Albert Husson); **c**, Loyal Griggs (VistaVision; Technicolor); **m**, Frederick Hollander; **ed**, Arthur Schmidt; **art d**, Hal Pereira, Roland Anderson; **set d**, Sam Comer, Grace Gregory; **spec eff**, John P. Fulton.

We're Not Dressing ★★★ 1934; U.S.; 74m; PAR; B/W; Musical Comedy; Children: Acceptable; **DVD**; **VHS**. In this superior musical adaptation of the play "The Admirable Chrichton," Lombard is a wealthy heiress, who invites some society friends on a cruise to the South Seas aboard her yacht. Crosby, a deckhand, is given the chore of walking Lombard's pet bear about the ship while wealthy guests like Milland and Henry luxuriate and brag about their lofty aristocratic stations in life. Errol, a pompous clown, believes he is a born navigator and takes control of the ship, promptly driving it onto a reef, and it sinks. None of the crew survives except Crosby, a singing sailor, and, with his help, the passengers make their way ashore to an island. They all prove to be useless as survivors, so Crosby takes over and assigns everyone chores as the servant becomes the master. Crosby and friends find that Burns and Allen, a married couple, are living on the other side of the island. They are botanists who have set elaborate traps to capture exotic animals on the island, and this later presents a series of hilarious mishaps. Crosby and Lombard fall in love, and a ship comes along to rescue everyone. Burns and Allen, although they appear briefly, steal the show with their funny lines that show how mentally dense Gracie Allen was (which she was not). At one point, Burns talks about the "flora and fauna" to be found on the island, and Allen thinks he is talking about a vaudeville act. The film's title refers to not dressing formally for dinner. The story was originally filmed as a silent in 1918 as **The Admirable Chrichton**, and a year later as another silent titled **Male and Female**, 1919, directed by Cecil B. DeMille and starring Gloria Swanson and Thomas Meighan. It later was remade in 1957 as **Paradise Lagoon**, starring Kenneth More, and in 1967 and 1968 as **The Admirable Chrichton**, both made-for-TV. It made again in 1974 and 2002 under the title of **Swept Away**. Songs: "Sailor's Chanty/It's a Lie," "May I?," "Goodnight Lovely Little Lady," "She Reminds Me of You," "Love Thy Neighbor," "Let's Play House" "It's Just a New Spanish Custom," "It's the Animal in Me," "I Positively Refuse to Sing" (1934; music: Harry Revel; lyrics: Mack Gordon); "Did You Ever See a Dream Walking?,"

"Once In a Blue Moon" (1933; Harry Revel); "Billy Boy" (traditional); "Stormy Weather" (1933; music: Harold Arlen; lyrics: Ted Koehler); "Who's Afraid of the Big Bad Wolf" (1933; music: Frank Churchill; lyrics: Churchill, Ann Ronell); "The Last Round-Up/Get Along, Little Doggie, Git Along" (1933; Billy Hill); "El Capitan" (1896; John Philip Sousa); "Aloha Oe" (1908; Queen Liliuokalani). *Author's Note*: "I got to sing a lot of songs in that picture," Crosby told this author, "and I think they were better songs than the rather silly ones you hear these days. To tell the truth, I was a lot more interested, even excited, about singing when we made **We're Not Dressing**. I've lost a lot of enthusiasm for songs since those good old days, but, again, I think it's because the caliber of the songs they are writing today do not have the catchy melodies composed by those earlier songsmiths. Guess I sound more like a crotchety old man looking over his shoulder than straight ahead." **p**, Benjamin Glazer; **d**, Norman Taurog; **cast**, Bing Crosby, Carole Lombard, George Burns, Gracie Allen, Ethel Merman, Leon Errol, Ray Milland as Raymond Milland, Jay Henry, Ernie Adams, Sam Ash; **w**, Horace Jackson, Francis Martin, George Marion, Jr. (based on stories by Glazer, Walton Hall Smith, and the play "The Admirable Chrichton" by James M. Barrie); **c**, Charles Lang; **m**, Howard Jackson; **ed**, Stuart Heisler; **art d**, Hans Dreier, Ernst Fegte; **spec eff**, Barney Wolff.

We're Not Married! ★★★ 1952; U.S.; 85m; FOX; B/W; Comedy; Children: Unacceptable; **DVD**; **VHS**; **IV**. Genuinely funny tale begins when Moore, a bumbling justice of the peace, starts marrying couples on Christmas Eve, but his appointment is not valid until January 1, so the couples are not legally married. The blooper is not discovered until two years later when one of the couples files for divorce. Moore has to track down the other couples and inform them of his error. Rogers and Allen are a husband-and-wife radio team, who are lovey-dovey on the air, but off the wire would love to cut each other's throat. Wayne is a stay-at-home father whose beautiful wife, Monroe, has just won the "Mrs. Mississippi" pageant and he fears her success will spoil their marriage. Douglas and Arden rarely speak to each other, and he has a roving eye for someone to replace her. Bracken is a G.I. about to be shipped overseas while his wife, Gaynor, is pregnant. Calhern is a kind millionaire whose gold-digging wife, Gabor, intends to divorce him and make off with his millions. All the couples eventually remarry except Calhern and Gabor, and Calhern is grateful for an official mistake that saves his fortune and preserves his happiness. Songs: "Cuddles" (Edmund Goulding), "The Wedding March" from "A Midsummer Night's Dream" (Felix Mendelssohn-Bartholdy), "The First Noel" (traditional), "Silent Night" (music: Franz Gruber; lyrics: Joseph Mohr), "Coppelia Waltz" (Leo Delibes), "Home Sweet Home" (H.R. Bishop), "Sweet and Lovely" (Gus Arnheim, Harry Tobias, Neil Moret as Jules LeMare), "Baby Face" (Harry Akst), "Perfidia" (Alberto Dominguez). *Author's Note*: Rogers told this author that "I really liked doing **We're Not Married**, mostly because I got to work with Fred Allen, who was one of the funniest guys on radio and with a wit so sharp that it could cut through barbed wire. I think we got most of the best lines that produced the laughs, but there was plenty to go around in that picture. Marilyn [Monroe] played another one of her 'dumb blonde' characters in that picture, but I can tell you that she was only acting because she was really one sharp cookie." **p**, Nunnally Johnson; **d**, Edmund Goulding; **cast**, Ginger Rogers, Fred Allen, Victor Moore, Marilyn Monroe, David Wayne, Eve Arden, Paul Douglas, Eddie Bracken, Mitzi Gaynor, Louis Calhern, ZsaZsa Gabor, James Gleason, Paul Stewart, Jane Darwell, Lee Marvin, Marjorie Weaver, Noreen Nash; **w**, Johnson, Dwight Taylor (based on a story by Gina Kaus, Jay Dratler); **c**, Leo Tover; **m**, Cyril Mockridge; **ed**, Louis Loeffler; **art d**, Leland Fuller; Lyle Wheeler; **set d**, Claude Carpenter, Thomas Little; **spec eff**, Ray Kellogg.

Werewolf of London ★★★ 1935; U.S.; 75m; UNIV; B/W; Horror; Children: Unacceptable; **DVD**; **VHS**; **IV**. Character actor Hull is mesmerizing in this lycanthropic tale about a man who is bitten by a were-

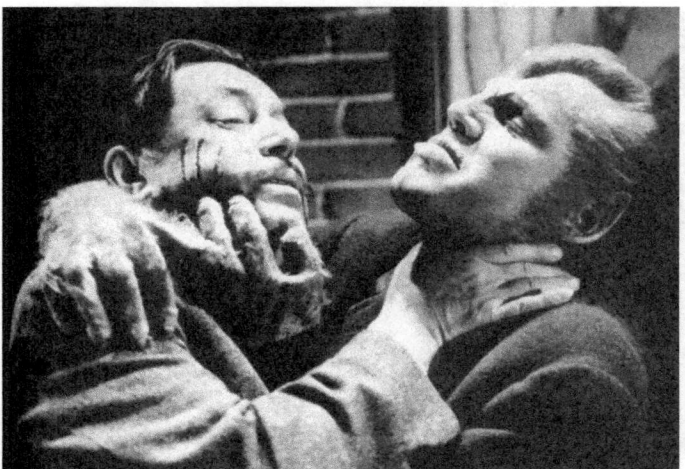

Warner Oland and Henry Hull in *Werewolf of London*, 1935.

wolf and then becomes one to ravage the streets of London. Hull is first seen scrambling through the high passes of the Himalayas in Tibet. He is a botanist and is in obsessive search for the Mariphasia Lupina Lumina, a very rare photo-luminescent orchid only found in these mountainous climes. Hull acquires the rare plant, but just then he is attacked and bitten by a hairy creature later determined to be a werewolf. Hull returns to London with his treasured plant, keeping it alive and growing in his nursery. Knowing that the plant will only bloom when flooded with the light of a full moon, Hull rigs a lamp to shine on the flowering plant, one that simulates the light of the full moon. He is then visited by Oland, a learned Oriental botanist. Oland tells Hull that, when the plant is in full bloom, it will produce a juice that, when taken as an antidote by a human being bitten by a werewolf, he will be temporarily cured of becoming a werewolf himself (such are the mystical vagaries attached to the imperfect science of lycanthropy, the psychiatric term applied to those suffering from the delusion that, at certain times, they uncontrollably turn into werewolves). Hull believes none of this, dismissing Oland's cautionary remarks as nothing but old wives' tales. He changes his mind when he sees fur rapidly grow on his hands when he places them beneath his moon lamp. Hull is shocked to see the same thing when he stands that night beneath the glowing light of a full moon. At that moment, Hull is on his way to attend a party being given by an aunt of his wife, Hobson, who is already attending that festive event with a former suitor, Matthews. Realizing that he is now undergoing the transformation to a werewolf, Hull races back to his laboratory to take the antidote. He discovers that Oland has already taken the two blossoms from the rare plant. One blossom remains with the plant, but it has yet to bloom and Hull is now unable to prevent his transformation into a bloodthirsty werewolf. (That transformation is impressively shown in a series of zoomorphic dissolves where Hull's human features alter into that of an upright, hairy-faced, hairy-armed beast bearing the black nose of an animal and with long fangs protruding from its mouth.) Now completely transformed into a werewolf, Hull dons his hat and cloak and goes into the street, looking for victims. He finds a lonely, young woman and attacks and kills her. Returning home, and with the coming of dawn, Hull transforms back to his human form. He is now terrified of having any relationship with Hobson, keeping his distance from her and causing her alarm and endless concern. To keep himself from harming Hobson lest he again transform into a werewolf, Hull rents a cheap room far from his luxurious home, remaining there at night, especially on nights offering full moons. He once again becomes a werewolf, and this transformation is heard by two elderly landladies at the boarding house, Tilbury and Griffies, who are in their cups and become terrified when hearing the commotion coming from Hull's room. Hull escapes the room through a window and begins another hunt for victims. Days later, Hull

Lois Moran and John Gilbert in *West of Broadway,* **1931.**

reads about these gruesome murders, realizing that one or more lunatics have been killing people in addition to the lives that he himself has claimed. When suffering a third attack, Hull races to his laboratory to use the remaining blooming flower as an antidote. While his back is turned, Oland takes the flower, but Hull catches him and they struggle. Hull kills Oland, realizing that Oland had been the very werewolf that had attacked and bitten him in Tibet. The third bloom is too damaged to be of use, and Hull agonizingly transforms again into a werewolf. This time, he begins to hunt for Hobson, intent of making her his next victim. As he confronts her, however, police arrive with Matthews, and Hull is fatally shot before he can attack Hobson. As he lies upon the floor, he transforms back into human form, horrifying Hobson, Matthews and officers and, before dying, expresses his gratitude for being mercifully killed, saying: "Thanks for the bullet." Walker helms this genuinely terrifying film with great skill, unfolding its horrific tale with considerable speed (shot within five weeks and on a budget of $195,000), and the chilling makeup created for Hull's transformations by Jack Pierce, along with the special effects from Fulton and Horsley, are outstanding, setting the bar for those to later depict the werewolf on the screen. Hull is superb as the helpless victim as is the insidious Oland. Their struggle, however, is shown not to revel in their ability to transform and murder at will, but to prevent themselves from once more taking a human life and therefore they evoke pity if not empathy for the tragic characters they essay. Songs/Music: Music from **The Invisible Man** (1933; Heinz Roemheld), Music from **The Black Cat** (1934; Heinz Roemheld), "Scenes That Are Brightest" (1845; from the grand opera "Maritana," by William Vincent Wallace), "Tales from the Vienna Woods, Op. 325" (1868; Johann Strauss). *Author's Note*: The startling transformation of Hull was achieved in a series of tracking shots where he walks along a street, his features altering as he passes behind a series of pillars, but the edited shots are shown as one long and uninterrupted tracking shot to make Hull appear that he is undergoing that transformation before the eyes of the viewers. The camera was stopped when each pillar obscured its lens, and Pierce then added more and more makeup to Hull, until he was that werewolf. Boris Karloff was originally slated for the leading role in this film, but Hull was then selected, although Hull never liked the part and hated the makeup he was compelled to wear, refusing to sit for prolonged periods as Pierce applied that makeup. This film became somewhat forgotten through the years, preempted by the more popular **The Wolf Man**, 1941, starring Lon Chaney Jr., which is not a sequel to this film and offers a much different story. For a comprehensive list of films depicting werewolves, see Subject Index, Werewolves. **p**, Stanley Bergerman; **d**, Stuart Walker; **cast**, Henry Hull, Valerie Hobson, Warner Oland, Lester Matthews, Lawrence Grant, Spring Byington, Clark Williams, J.M. Kerrigan,

Charlotte Granville, Ethel Griffies, Zeffie Tilbury, Wong Chung; **w**, John Colton, Harvey Gates, Robert Harris (based on a story by Harris); **c**, Charles Stumar; **m**, Karl Hajos; **ed**, Russell Schoengarth, Milton Carruth; **art d**, Albert S. D'Agostino; **spec eff**, John P. Fulton, David S. Horsley.

West of Broadway ★★★ 1931; U.S.; 68m; MGM; B/W; Drama; Children: Unacceptable; **DVD**; **IV**. Absorbing tale sees Gilbert, a millionaire, returning home to New York after serving in the army in World War II (1914-1918). His health is so poor that his doctor says he only has six months to live. He decides to hurry his grim fate along by drinking himself to death. That causes Evans, his fiancée, to leave him. He wakes up from one of his binges to find himself married to Moran, assuming she is a gold digger after his money. He leaves her and goes to a ranch in Arizona to dry out and start divorce proceedings. Gilbert eventually learns that Moran really loves him and he loves her and they plan a life together, especially after the Arizona weather has improved Gilbert's health. Gilbert does a good job essaying the role of a doomed man, and Moran gives him strong support as the woman who refuses to desert him. The film did not do well at the box office as MGM did not strongly support its promotion. Songs: "Smiles" (1918; music: Lee S. Roberts; lyrics: J. Will Callahan), "Mademoiselle from Armentieres," "Over There" (George M. Cohan), "The Wedding March" (1843; from "A Midsummer Night's Dream" by Felix Mendelssohn-Bartholdy), "The Strawberry Roan" (traditional). *Author's Note*: Gilbert, a former matinee idol in the silent screen era, had been feuding with MGM boss Louis B. Mayer for many years, their contentious encounters beginning in 1926 when Gilbert fell in love with the studio's top star, Greta Garbo, and they became the top on-screen romance team of that era. Garbo, however, left Gilbert standing alone at the altar in 1927 after Garbo got cold feet and refused at the last minute to marry him. Mayer had attempted to stop the Gilbert-Garbo romance, and Gilbert always believed that Mayer had persuaded Garbo to jilt him. Gilbert had an iron-clad contract with MGM and was receiving a then whopping $250,000 per picture, including this one, which served as a constant irritation for Mayer. The studio boss went out of his way to rid himself of Gilbert by making sure he was given scripts for his early talkies that were poorly written and loaded with corny dialog. He believed that Gilbert's many fans would eventually desert him, which they did by the early 1930s. The gifted Gilbert, however, made much more out of his empathetic character in this film, and even Mayer grudgingly admitted that his performance in **West of Broadway** was exceptional. Gilbert was reunited with Garbo in **Queen Christina**, 1933 (at Garbo's generous insistence, or through a sense of mea culpa), but his star had by then long faded with the public. He made one more film after that, **The Captain Hates the Sea**, 1934, and died of a heart attack on January 9, 1936, at age thirty-nine. This film is not related to the 1926 silent film with the same title. **d**, Harry Beaumont; **cast**, John Gilbert, Lois Moran, El Brendel, Madge Evans, Ralph Bellamy, Frank Conroy, Hedda Hopper, Gwen Lee, Willie Fung, Kermit Maynard, Dennis O'Keefe, Kane Richmond; **w**, Ralph Graves, Bess Meredyth, J.K. McGuiness, Gene Markey (based on a story by Graves, Meredyth); **c**, Merritt B. Gerstad; **ed**, George Hively; **art d**, Cedric Gibbons.

West of the Pecos ★★★ 1945; U.S.; 66m; RKO; B/W; Western; Children: Acceptable; **DVD**; **VHS**. Lively western begins when Hale, a young society woman from the East, takes a stagecoach going west to get to the family ranch in Texas. She travels disguised as a boy for safety reasons. After the stage is robbed, Mitchum, a cowboy who lives in his saddle and travels with his pal, Martin, finds her lost in the desert. Hale and Mitchum do not get along and he, thinking she is a boy and after she gives him some trouble, tosses her into the Pecos River. She emerges soaking wet, which gives away her sex masquerade. Mitchum and Martin fight off outlaws and then take her to the family ranch where they are offered work. By then Mitchum and Hale have fallen in love and there will soon be a wedding at the ranch. Mitchum and Hale are stand-outs in this exciting Zane Grey tale, which had been filmed as a silent in 1922, and in 1934, starring Richard Dix. Song: "Cielito Lindo" (Quirino Mendoza). *Author's Note*: Mitchum told this author that "I don't remember much about that oater except that I enjoyed working with Barbara Hale, a real down-to-earth gal. It was one of the first films where I got top billing. Only a few years before that, I was playing so many bit parts that I could not remember one picture from another." In 1943, Mitchum appeared in twenty films. This was one of Mitchum's early feature films, made before he served in the U.S. Army during World War II (1939-1945). After his return, he soon became a rising star and then a superstar. Hale and Williams met during this production and married a year later, both becoming television stars. **p**, Herman Schlom; **d**, Edward Killy; **cast**, Robert Mitchum, Barbara Hale, Richard Martin, Thurston Hall, Rita Corday, Bill Williams, Russell Hopton, Bruce Edwards, Harry Woods, Perc Launders, Bryant Washburn, Jason Robards Sr.; **w**, Norman Houston (based on the novel by Zane Grey); **c**, Harry J. Wild; **m**, Paul Sawtell; **ed**, Roland Gross; **art d**, Albert S. D'Agostino, Lucius Croxton; **set d**, Darrell Silvera, William Stevens.

West Point ★★★ 1927 (silent); U.S.; 95m/9 reels; 95m; MGM; B/W; Drama/Romance; Children: Acceptable; **DVD**. Haines is outstanding as a wisecracking plebe after enrolling in the U.S. Army at West Point to become a cadet and subsequently an officer upon graduation. He tries out for the football team and proves to be a great running back, but he soon rubs angry elbows with competitor Neely, an upperclassman. Haines then meets attractive Crawford, who is the daughter of a local hotel owner, and who attends all the football practices. She is enthralled by Haines' gridiron feats and becomes his ardent fan, cheering him on as he becomes the team's leading player. Haines, however, sees that he has sharp competition from Neely for Crawford's attentions. Neely is always the gentleman with Crawford, but roughhouse Haines takes the liberty of forcing a kiss on her and she resents his aggressive manner, rejecting him. Haines continues to force himself upon Crawford, but that only deepens her dislike for him, until he completely alienates himself from the girl who once adored him. He also angers football coach Moses after Haines accuses Moses of showing favoritism with other team members like Neely. Haines and Moses get into a shouting match in the locker room, and Haines explodes, yelling: "To hell with the Corps!" Full of anger, Haines quits the team, and gossip about Haines' scandalous conduct spreads through West Point. Haines' doubtful allegiance to this esteemed military academy causes Haines' close friend, Bakewell, to take him aside, and he attempts to talk reason with the now seething Haines. In response, Haines knocks Bakewell down and Bakewell suffers a head injury. Haines is now full of remorse for his impetuous actions and tries to make amends, but to no avail, and he thinks to resign from West Point. He speaks with the superintendent, but reconsiders his decision to resign, believing that he will be deserting the school's football team in its time of need. However, when it comes time to play in the crucial Army-Navy game, Moses keeps Haines on the bench. With the game almost over and with Army losing, Moses relents and sends Haines onto the field. He scores a touchdown at the last minute, winning the game. In a very moving scene, Haines then apologizes to his teammates for his former obnoxious behavior, winning back their friendship and recouping the love that Crawford has always had for him. Sedgwick does an exceptional job in moving this exciting romantic tale along and provides plenty of gridiron action; Haines, Crawford, Neely, Bakewell and Moses are exceptional in their roles, and the superlative lensing from Morgan fully captures the atmosphere of the hallowed West Point. *Author's Note*: For all of his outwardly manly appearances, Haines was gay, something he never hid from anyone. In fact, Haines' sexual relationship with Jimmy Shields (they would remain together throughout their lives, Shields committing suicide out of remorse over Haines' death in 1973) so incensed MGM chief Louis B. Mayer that the mogul released Haines from his MGM contract. Though

Barbara Hale and Robert Mitchum in *West of the Pecos,* **1945.**

Haines' film career thereafter petered out, he flourished as an interior decorator for Bloomingdale's Department Store and decorating the homes of many of Hollywood's foremost denizens. Crawford, who also remained friends with Haines through his lifetime, told this author: "Billy [Haines] was a terrific actor and one of the most charming persons I ever met. We all knew he was gay, but that did not matter with most of us [including actress Marion Davies, who was the mistress of the all-powerful media magnate William Randolph Hearst]. Mr. Mayer, who ran MGM, decided that Billy's private life would spill into the newspapers and on radio back then and feared that his homosexuality would damage MGM its prestige. Mr. Mayer had Billy brought to his office and ordered him to break off his relationship with Jimmy [Shields] and, can you imagine, told him to marry a woman, any woman, and right away! When Billy refused, Mr. Mayer told him that he was through in pictures. Billy did not care. He always wanted to be an interior decorator and he was soon doing that and becoming rich and famous in that new profession. In 1930, Billy and I were listed as the two top movie stars in Hollywood, but that meant nothing to Mr. Mayer. All he was concerned about was his studio's reputation. Billy did the decorations for many of the homes of Hollywood stars, including Fredric March, William Powell, Claudette Colbert, Jack Warner, Constance and Joan Bennett and Carole Lombard. Producers asked him to return to the screen years later, but Billy told them no, he was happy doing what he was doing. Carole [Lombard] thought the world of Billy and it was she who got all of her Hollywood friends to hire Billy as an interior decorator. She once told me that she asked Mr. Mayer if he would like to have Billy design some rooms in his home and Mr. Mayer replied: 'If you dare bring that creature into my house, I will have you and him arrested.' As I have said, Mr. Mayer did not like Billy at all. I don't think Mr. Mayer hated Billy because he was homosexual. It was because Billy had dared to stand up to him and no one, but no one, ever defied Mr. Louis B. Mayer." This film was shot on location at West Point. Its identical story was used in another film released the same year, **Dress Parade**, 1927, directed by Cecil B. DeMille and starring William Boyd and Bessie Love. Other films depicting West Point include **Arizona**, 1931; **Army Girl**, 1938; **Assault at West Point: The Court Martial of Johnson Whittaker**, 1994 (made-for-TV); **Benedict Arnold: A Question of Honor**, 2003 (made-for-TV); **Branded**, 1965-1966 (TV series; "That the Brave Endure," 1965 episode); **Cadet Girl**, 1941; **Class of '61**, 1993 (made-for-TV); **Come On, Leathernecks!**, 1938; **A Distant Trumpet**, 1964; **Dress Parade**, 1927; **Flirtation Walk**, 1934; **God Is My Co-Pilot**, 1945; **Hold 'Em Navy**, 1937; **Ike**, 1986 (made-for-TV); **King of Diamonds**, 1961-1962 (TV series; "Guided Tour de Force," 1962 episode); **Knute Rockne—All American**, 1940; **The Last Castle**, 2001; **The Long Gray Line**, 1955; **MacArthur**, 1977; **Rosalie**,

Doris Day in *The West Point Story*, 1950.

1937; **Santa Fe Trail**, 1940; **The Scarlet Coat**, 1955 (Benedict Arnold); **The Silence**, 1975 (made-for-TV); **The Spirit of West Point**, 1947; **Ten Gentlemen from West Point**, 1942; **They Died with Their Boots On**, 1941; **War of 1812**, 1999 (TV miniseries); **West Point**, 1956-1957 (TV series); **The West Point Story**, 1950; **Wild Stallion**, 1952; **Women at West Point**, 1979 (made-for-TV). **p&d**, Edward Sedgwick; **cast**, William Haines, Joan Crawford, William Bakewell, Neil Neely, Ralph Emerson, Leon Kellar, Raymond G. Moses, Edward Brophy, E.H. Calvert; **w**, Raymond L. Schrock, Joseph Farnham; **c**, Ira Morgan; **m**, David Davidson (2002 version); **ed**, Frank Sullivan.

The West Point Story ★★★ 1950; U.S.; 107m; WB; B/W; Musical Comedy; Children: Acceptable; **DVD**; **VHS**; **IV**. Lively songfest begins with Cagney, an unemployed musical director, who is approached by producer Winters, who asks him to direct a musical at West Point. Cagney, though he doesn't like the manipulative Winters, agrees to go to West Point and organize its annual 100th Night Show. There is a hitch to the job in that the scheming Winters, after the show becomes a hit, wants to move the show to Broadway with MacRae, who has written the show and is a cadet at West Point. It is Cagney's additional job to persuade the talented MacRae to resign from West Point and join the production when it moves to Broadway. Cagney undertakes the job, but he is frustrated by all the rules and regulations at West Point that constantly interrupt his production schedules and rehearsals. Further, he gets nowhere in attempting to persuade MacRae to leave the Academy and becomes so irritable that he alienates his girlfriend, Mayo, who has accompanied him to the Academy and where she is to play one of the female leads in the show. Worse, Cagney loses his control during a rehearsal and strikes a cadet. He is ordered to either leave the Academy, or stay and continue to produce the show, but only if he becomes a cadet at the Academy and follows all of its rules. A contrite Cagney agrees, and this middle-aged man is soon wearing the Academy's gray uniform and undergoing hazing as would any plebe. Cagney shows he is made of sterner stuff and puts up with all the harassing while he follows the rules and still manages to put the show in order. Then Day, one of the female stars Cagney has hired for the show, arrives and wows the cadets, especially MacRae, who falls head-over-heels in love with the bubbly blonde singer. When Day returns to Hollywood, MacRae, who is lovesick without her, goes AWOL and chases after Day. Cagney, realizing that MacRae has jeopardized his military career, follows and persuades MacRae to return to the Academy. When he arrives, he is arrested and the show is summarily canceled. Cagney solves his and MacRae's dilemma by discovering that there is an old Academy proviso that allows any visitor of recognized authority to request that punishments for cadets be dismissed. He uses the French medal he has earlier won when serving

in France to convince the French Attaché to make that request and MacRae is not only pardoned, but Day arrives to be reunited with him. The show goes on and it's a great success, with Cagney replacing Nelson, an injured cadet, and dancing with the curvaceous Mayo to "It Could Only Happen in Brooklyn." MacRae is so grateful for Cagney's help that he assigns the rights to the show to him, and Cagney prepares to take the show to Broadway with the loyal Mayo at his side. Though there are a few stagnant scenes, this film otherwise offers an energetic Cagney, who dominates every scene with his frenetic dancing and charismatic character. The film received an Oscar nomination for Best Music (Heindorf) and it did well at the box office, earning more than $1.8 million in its initial release. Songs: "Alma Mater" (music: Friedrich Wilhelm Kucken [Kuecken]; lyrics [1911]: Paul S. Reinecke, USMA); "It's Raining Sundrops," "By the Kissing Rock," "Long Before I Knew You," "This Is the Finale," "Ten Thousand Two Hundred and Thirty-Two Sheep," "The Military Polka," "You Love Me," "It Could Only Happen in Brooklyn" (music: Jule Styne; lyrics: Sammy Cahn); "One Hundred Days Till June" (Francis E. Resta); "The Corps" (W. Franke Harling); "The Toy Trumpet" (1937; Raymond Scott); "Semper Fidelis" (1888; John Philip Sousa). ***Author's Note***: Cagney told this author that he had trouble with dance director LeRoy Prinz when making this film, saying: "He knew that I knew that he did not know one foot from the other. I think he quickly grew to hate me because he knew I saw through him, so our relationship was strained throughout the production. I really enjoyed the other actors in that picture—Gordon [MacRae], who has a wonderfully throaty singing voice, and Doris [Day], who sings like no other female singer, and, of course, my old pal, Ginny [Virginia Mayo], who co-starred with me a year before we made **The West Point Story** in a wild gangster picture called **White Heat** [1949]." Cagney rehearsed his dancing for his number in this film with a partner who was much lighter than Mayo, so that when it came to dance and lift Mayo in the final number, the aging Cagney found it stressful. Mayo told this author: "Jimmy told me that after we did our number in **The West Point Story** that he was getting just too old for the kind of acrobatic dancing we had to perform. He told me: 'From now on, Ginny, I do all my pictures sitting down.'" **p**, Louis F. Edelman; **d**, Roy Del Ruth; **cast**, James Cagney, Virginia Mayo, Doris Day, Gordon MacRae, Gene Nelson, Alan Hale, Jr., Raymond Roe, Roland Winters, Jerome Cowan, John Baer, Jack Kelly, Tommy Kelly; **w**, John Monks, Jr., Charles Hoffman, Irving Wallace (based on the story "Classmates" by Wallace); **c**, Sid Hickox; **m**, Ray Heindorf; **ed**, Owen Marks; **art d**, Charles H. Clarke; **set d**, Armor E. Marlowe; **spec eff**, Edwin DuPar.

West Side Story ★★★★★ 1961; U.S.; 152m; Mirisch/Seven Arts/UA; Color; Drama/Musical/Romance; Children: Unacceptable; **BD**; **DVD**; **VHS**; **IV**. This stunning and emotionally moving production deservedly won more Oscars (ten) than any other musical while presenting a dynamic drama and a tragic romance that is set on the West Side of Manhattan. This modern-day version of "Romeo and Juliet" begins with an overhead helicopter shot of Manhattan, showing its neighborhoods in geometric patterns until the camera zooms downward to select the Lincoln Square area in "Hell's Kitchen." Members of two rival gangs, the Jets, a white gang led by Tamblyn (Riff), and the Sharks, a Puerto Rican gang led by Chakiris (Bernardo), get into a brawl that is stopped by police officers Oakland (Lt. Schrank) and Bramley (Officer Krupke). This only angers Tamblyn, who, along with Jet gang members, decide to confront the Sharks in an all-out rumble at an upcoming dance. Tamblyn goes to his best friend Beymer (Tony), who co-founded the Jets, but has since left it, and asks him to reenlist and fight with the gang ("Jet Song"). Tamblyn tells Beymer to be available for an important upcoming gang event ("Something's Coming"), but Beymer is no longer interested in gang activities. Wood (Maria), who is the younger sister of Sharks leader Chakiris, tells Moreno (Anita), who is Chakiris' girlfriend, how excited she is in looking forward to attending the dance. Once the two gangs arrive at the event ("Dance at the Gym") the gang members and their girlfriends refuse to mingle with each other. This is not the case when Beymer and Wood meet and dance together. They quickly fall in love. When Chakiris sees the two together, he explodes and orders Beymer to stay away from his sister before Chakiris orders Wood to go home. Tamblyn then suggests that he and Chakiris meet later at a drugstore. Meanwhile, Moreno upbraids Chakiris for being overly protective of Wood and attempting to destroy her chances of romance. Both then compare lifestyles in the United States and Puerto Rico ("America"). Beymer, however, has no intention of never again seeing Wood and secretly visits her on a fire escape, and they again declare their love for one another ("Tonight"). Bramley believes that the Jets are planning something and visits some of its members, cautioning them not to create any problems. The Sharks then arrive and agree with the Jets to have a one-on-one fistfight under a bridge the next evening. Officer Oakland arrives and tries to learn what the gangs are planning, but the rival gang members tell him nothing as they pretend to be friendly toward each other. The next day, Moreno tells Wood about the upcoming rumble, and Wood later meets with Beymer and asks him to prevent the fight in order to protect her brother, Chakiris. Beymer promises to do what he can to stop the fight, and they fantasize about being married ("One Hand, One Heart"). That night, the Jets and Sharks meet beneath a highway ("Quintet"), and Beymer tries to stop the rumble. Chakiris sneeringly ridicules Beymer's peacemaking efforts, and, angered at Beymer's humiliation, Tamblyn attacks Chakiris with a knife. When Beymer attempts to separate the two, Tamblyn is killed by Chakiris, and Beymer picks up Tamblyn's knife and uses it to kill Chakiris. Police sirens are heard and the gang members suddenly take flight, leaving the bodies of Tamblyn and Chakiris. Beymer goes to Wood, meeting her on a rooftop, and he tells her what has happened and how sorry he is for what he has done. He begs her forgiveness, saying that he is going to turn himself into the police. Wood tells him that she still loves him, asking him to stay with her ("Somewhere"). Smith, who has become the new leader of the Jets, orders his gang members to say nothing to the police about the rumble ("Cool"). He then warns Beymer that DeVaga, who has become the Sharks leader, is looking to seek vengeance upon him for killing Chakiris. Beymer can only think about Wood, visiting her at her apartment, and he tells her that he is going to get some money so they can elope and live elsewhere in peace. When Moreno sees Beymer leave, she criticizes Wood for carrying on with Beymer, the boy who has killed her lover, Chakiris ("A Boy Like That"). Wood, however, begs Moreno to help her elope with Beymer ("I Have a Love"). Beymer and Wood get separated, but later meet in a playground where they run toward each other. De Vega, however, arrives and fatally shoots Beymer, who dies in Wood's arms ("Somewhere"). Wood then confronts both the Jets and Sharks by taking the gun from De Vega and telling both gangs that their own hate had brought about the deaths of Tamblyn, Chakiris and Beymer, and they end their war. Police arrive and then arrest De Vega and lead him away into custody ("Finale") to end this utterly riveting tale. The brilliant Wise directs this tragedy with great skill, seamlessly balancing its dramatic scenes with its captivating musical numbers, and the choreography by Robbins is outstanding. The overall image of this mesmerizing film offers a marvelous blend of reality and fantasy. Beymer and Wood are superlative as the star-crossed lovers, and wonderful support is provided by Tamblyn, Chakiris and Moreno. The film received ten Oscars for Best Film; Best Director (Wise, Robbins); Best Supporting Actor (Chakiris); Best Supporting Actress (Moreno); Best Cinematography, Color (Fapp); Best Original Score; Best Film Editing (Stanford); Best Art Direction (Leven; set decoration: Gangelin); Best Costume Design (Irene Sharaff); and Best Sound (Gordon Sawyer, Fred Hynes). It was an enormous hit at the box office, earning more than $43.7 million in its initial release against a budget of $6 million, becoming the second highest grossing film in the U.S. for the year. Songs/Music: "Overture," "Prologue," "Dance at the Gym," "Intermission," "The Rumble," "End Credits" (Elmer Bernstein) "Jet Song,' "Something's Coming," "Maria,' "America," "Tonight," "Gee,

George Chakiris, Richard Beymer and Russ Tamblyn in *West Side Story,* **1961.**

Officer Krupke!," "I Feel Pretty," "One Hand, One Heart," "Quintet," "Somewhere," "Cool," "A Boy Like That/I Have a Love" (music: Elmer Bernstein; lyrics: Stephen Sondheim); "America, My Country 'Tis of Thee" (1832; based on "God Save the King!," 1744 by Henry Carey); "La Cucaracha" (traditional). *Author's Note*: This highly stylized iconic version of "Romeo and Juliet" proved to be one of the most enduringly popular musicals in film history, ranking with **Grease**, 1978; **Mary Poppins**, 1964; **My Fair Lady**, 1964; and **The Sound of Music**, 1965. The film ran in Paris for 249 weeks, a record in theatrical showings. Wise was selected to direct this story because he had helmed several successful urban dramas such as **Odds against Tomorrow**, 1959 (he wanted but failed to cast Elvis Presley in the role played by Beymer), but he had limited experience with musicals. Robbins, who had never directed a film but had directed the stage version (opening at the Winter Garden on September 26, 1957, and running for 732 performances), was hired to direct the singing and dancing segments of this film. Robbins tirelessly rehearsed the cast for three months before the film went into production and remained until toward the end of the six-month shooting when he was fired when his segments ran overlong (and after suffering a near-nervous breakdown). Wise, however, who recognized Robbins' great contribution, insisted that Robbins share a co-director credit with him, although Wise directed the bulk of this film. As is the case with the stage version, the empathy, such as it is, was placed with the Puerto Rican gang, which appears to be the underdog, while the Anglo gang consists mostly of brutal and insensitive louts, a "politically correct" stance that grew to outlandish proportions in Hollywood's later years to prove that minorities could do no wrong. Wood, a fine actress, had to struggle at times with her Puerto Rican accent, and Beymer seems almost miscast as a youth too clean-cut to be the leader of a street gang. Beymer later complained that he wanted to play his role of Tony as a much tougher character in bringing a more real portrait of a gang leader, but director Wise refused to allow him to be anything other than the nicest guy on the block. Some of the scenes struck too close to home, such as when Moreno is viciously attacked by the Jets and where she begins to cry uncontrollably. She recalled at those moments how she had been raped as a child, and this scene brought back that vicious memory so acutely that it dismantled her concentration. She was consoled by members of the cast playing those Jets, who told her that they, not she, would be universally hated by audiences for what they were doing to her, but this was little emotional compensation for the traumatic scars she bore. Wood's singing voice was provided by Marni Nixon, who had provided the vocals for Audrey Hepburn in **My Fair Lady**. Larry Kert was thirty when playing the part of Tony in the stage version, and Carol Lawrence was twenty-nine when playing the role of Maria in the stage production. Both were thought by Hollywood pro-

Rita Moreno, right, dancing in *West Side Story,* 1961.

ducers as being too old to appear in the film version. Many of Hollywood's top stars were considered for the role of Tony, some even auditioning for that part, including Tony Perkins, Warren Beatty, Bobby Darin, Tab Hunter, Troy Donahue, Burt Reynolds, Richard Chamberlain, Gary Lockwood and Dennis Hopper. Tamblyn auditioned for the role, but, after Beymer was given the part, Tamblyn was called back and given the role of Riff. Other films profiling street gangs around the world include **Aberdeen**, 2000; **Adventures in Babysitting**, 1987; **American Graffiti**, 1973; **American Me**, 1992; **An American Tail**, 1986; **Angel**, 1999-2004 (TV series); **Angel Town**, 1990; **The Angels Wash Their Faces**, 1939; **Angels with Dirty Faces**, 1938; **Assault on Precinct 13**, 1976; **Attack the Block**, 2011; **Attack the Gas Station!**, 1999; **Band of the Hand**, 1986; **Batman Forever**, 1995; **Batman: The Dark Knight Returns, Part 1**, 2012; **Batman; The Movie**, 1999 (made-for-TV); ***batteries not included**, 1987; **The Baytown Outlaws**, 2013; **Being There**, 1979; **A Better Life**, 2011; **The Big Boss**, 1981; **Big Trouble in Little China**, 1986; **Billy Jack Goes to Washington**, 1971; **Blackboard Jungle**, 1955; **Boyz 'n the Hood**, 1991; **A Brighter Summer Day**, 2011; **Brighton Rock**, 1947; **Brighton Rock**, 2011; **Bruce Almighty**, 2003; **Bulletproof Monk**, 2003; **City of God**, 2000; **City of Joy**, 1992; **City of Men**, 2002-2005 (TV series); **Clockers**, 1995; **A Clockwork Orange**, 1971; **Colors**, 1988; **The Cool World**, 1963; **The Corruptor**, 1999; **Crank**, 2006; **Crash**, 2005; **Crime in the Streets**, 1956; **Crime Spree**, 2003; **Dead End**, 1937; **Death Wish**, 1974; **Death Wish 3**, 1985; **Death Wish II**, 1982; **The Departed**, 2006; **Deuces Wilde**, 2002; **Downtown**, 1990; **8 Mile**, 2002; **End of Watch**, 2012; **The Enforcer**, 1976; **Escape from New York**, 1981; **A Family Thing**, 1996; **Gangs of New York**, 2002; **Germany Year Zero**, 1949; **Gran Torino**, 2008; **Grease**, 1978; **Harsh Times**, 2006; **Hazard**, 2005; **Heartless**, 2009; **Hey Good Lookin'!**, 1982; **The Hoodlum Priest**, 1961; **Hue and Cry**, 1951; **In the Heat of the Night**, 1967; **Josh**, 2000; **Kids Return**, 1996; **Kill the Irishman**, 2011; **King Creole**, 1958; **King of New York**, 1990; **Knights of the City**, 1986; **Knock on Any Door**, 1949; **Kung Fu Hustle**, 2005; **Life Is Hot in Crackdown**, 2009; **Lionheart**, 1991; **Los Olvidados**, 1950; **Mean Streets**, 1973; **Medium Cool**, 1969; **The New Centurions**, 1972; **The New Kids**, 1985; **1990: The Bronx Warriors**, 1982; **No Way Out**, 1950; **On the Waterfront**, 1954; **The Onion Field**, 1979; **Only the Strong**, 1993; **The Outsiders**, 1983; **Painted Fire**, 2002; **The Perfect Weapon**, 1991; **Police Academy 2: Their First Assignment**, 1985; **The Public Enemy**, 1931; **The Purple Gang**, 1960; **The Quest**, 1996; **Ratcatcher**, 1999; **Red Heat**, 1988; **Ring of Fire**, 1991; **River Gang**, 1945; **Romeo + Juliet**, 1996; **Rumble Fish**, 1983; **Rumble in the Bronx**, 1996; **Salaam Bombay!**, 1988; **The Sandpit Generals**, 1972; **Seven Hours to Judgment**, 1988; **Sinners and Saints**, 2010; **Six Bridges to Cross**, 1965; **Somebody Up**

There Likes Me, 1956; **Sons of Anarchy**, 2004-2008 (TV series); **Straw Dogs**, 1971; **Teenage Mutant Ninja Turtles**, 1990; **Teenage Mutant Ninja Turtles II: The Secret of the Ooze**, 1991; **Tell No One**, 2006; **They Call Me Mr. Tibbs!**, 1970; **3:15**, 1986; **The Tin Drum**, 1980; **To Live and Die in L.A.**, 1985; **Tokyo Tribe**, 2014; **Touch and Go**, 1986; **Trading Places**, 1983; **Training Day**, 2001; **The Warriors**, 1979; **Wild at Heart**, 1990; **Wild Boys of the Road**, 1933; **Who's That Knocking at My Door**, 1967; and **The Young Savages**, 1961. **p**, Robert Wise; **d**, Wise, Jerome Robbins; **cast**, Natalie Wood, Richard Beymer, Russ Tamblyn, Rita Moreno, George Chakiris, Simon Oakland, Ned Glass, William Bramley, Tucker Smith, Jose De Vega, Marni Nixon (singing voice of Wood and for some songs for Moreno), Betty Wand (singing voice for Moreno for "A Boy Like That"), Jimmy Bryant (singing voice for Beymer); **w**, Ernest Lehman (based on the stage play by Arthur Laurents, inspired by the play "Romeo and Juliet" by William Shakespeare); **c**, Daniel L. Fapp (Panavision; Technicolor); **m**, Leonard Bernstein; **ed**, Thomas Stanford; **prod d**, Boris Leven; **set d**, Victor Gangelin; **spec eff**, Saul Bass, Linwood Dunn.

Westbound ★★★ 1959; U.S.; 72m; WB; Color; Western; Children: Acceptable; **DVD**; **VHS**. Solid western offers exciting action and good performances from a talented cast. Scott is a Union officer during the American Civil War (1861-1865) assigned to take over a stagecoach line in Colorado in 1864, and deliver gold shipments from Colorado to California for the North. He is hindered by Duggan, who wants to intercept the gold for the Confederates. Duggan is killed in a skirmish while honorably defending Scott. Duggan's dying wish is that Scott will look after his wife, Mayo, which Scott agrees to do. His heart is in that since he had earlier lost Mayo to Duggan. *Author's Note*: Scott told this author that "I thought it was ironic that I played a Union officer to preserve gold for the Union during the Civil War in **Westbound**. Two decades earlier I played a Confederate officer during the Civil War in **Virginia City** [1940]. In that picture I was trying to get gold from the West to the South and where Errol Flynn was playing a Union officer searching for that gold. Times change, but Hollywood scripts don't age too much. Switch uniforms and you have a new story." Mayo told this author that "Randy [Scott] is one of the finest gentlemen I ever met and it was a real treat to work with him on **Westbound**. He is a Southerner, you know, a Virginian, and he has those genteel manners going back to the old Plantation South. I always had the image of him sitting on a huge veranda in front of an old Southern mansion with huge white pillars and sipping a mint julip. Funny, how you think about people." **p**, Henry Blanke; **d**, Budd Boetticher; **cast**, Randolph Scott, Virginia Mayo, Karen Steele, Michael Dante, Andrew Duggan, Michael Pate, Wally Brown, John Daheim as John Day, Walter Barnes, Peter Brown (voice); **w**, Berne Giler (based on the story "The Great Divide No. 2" by Giler, Albert Shelby LeVino); **c**, J. Peverell Marley; **m**, David Buttolph; **ed**, Philip W. Anderson; **art d**, Howard Campbell; **set d**, Gene Redd.

Western Union ★★★★★ 1941; U.S.; 93m; FOX; Color; Western; Children: Unacceptable; **DVD**; **VHS**; **IV**. Rousing tale from pantheon director Lang chronicles the building of Western Union's telegraph operation from Omaha, Nebraska, to Salt Lake City, Utah, during the American Civil War (1861-1865). Scott (Vance Shaw) and others are seen fleeing from a posse after committing a robbery, riding pell-mell across the plains while lawmen are in hot pursuit. The outlaws separate, riding in different directions, and Scott's horse breaks a leg and he sadly shoots it and then proceeds on foot. He comes across Jagger (Edward Creighton), who is riding a horse and pulling along some burros laden with equipment and goods. Scott pulls a gun and aims it at Jagger, telling him that he needs his horse, but, when Jagger, who has been injured, falls from his mount, Scott discovers that Jagger has broken ribs. Instead of fleeing, Scott binds Jagger and then places him back on his horse and leads the horse and burros to a nearby cabin. He fires a shot to alert its occupants and leaves, riding Jagger's horse, which Jagger allows him to take with his blessing for saving his life. When Jagger returns to Omaha, he puts in motion his plan to link Omaha to Salt Lake City by wire so that the Union will be able to maintain instant communication with the West during this crucial period of the Civil War (an operation that had been personally encouraged by President Abraham Lincoln, 1809-1865). Through Watson, who is Jagger's foreman, workers are then hired, including pioneers Wills and Kilian, along with Summerville, a cook, who is an expert chef, but hates any kind of violence. (Before being hired Summerville flaunts his expertise with cuisine by proudly declaring: "There are nine different ways to cook mutton and I know them all!") The men are examined by Carradine, a doctor who works exclusively for Western Union, and who passes each man as healthy and ready for duty after a cursory inspection of their tongues, and by tapping on their chests. Striding into Jagger's office is brash Young (Richard Blake), who is an expert at Morse code and who is immediately taken by Gilmore, Jagger's attractive sister, who works in the office as a telegrapher. Young, who is a green tenderfoot and a Harvard-educated engineer, tells Jagger that he has been sent by the front office to serve in any capacity, adding that he is proficient in all uses of Morse code. Actually, Jagger has hired the overconfident Young at the request of Young's wealthy father, who wants to make a man of his braggadocio offspring. Jagger later goes to a nearby corral to inspect the horses that have recently been purchased for Western Union and he is surprised to see that Watson has hired Scott as a horse wrangler. Scott, who has decided to abandon his outlaw pursuits and work as an honest man, is shocked to see Jagger, but Jagger pretends that he has never before met him. Meanwhile, Young reappears after having purchased a garish western outfit, replete with a buckskin jacket ornately decorated with braided designs. He brags that he has ridden all sorts of horses, and Jagger, Gilmore and others then have him ride a mount in a corral, one that has never been broken and is a bucking bronco from head to hoof. Young surprises Jagger, Scott, Gilmore and others by staying on that snorting, kicking and leaping wild horse until it settles down to calmly saunter about the corral with Young triumphantly in the saddle. (This superbly choreographed action scene equals any bucking bronco sequence to come, including where tenderfoot Jack Lemmon is ordered to break a bronco in **Cowboy**, 1958, or the wildly spectacular bronco-busting ride Lee Marvin takes in **Monte Walsh**, 1970, where his horse all but destroys a Cowtown street and nearly kills him.) That night Jagger finds Scott packing his belongings and telling him that he is moving on. Jagger, however, asks him to stay on with Western Union as a troubleshooter and horse buyer. Scott states: "I like being alone." Jagger knowingly replies: "The best place to be alone sometimes is in a crowd." Scott nods and says: "That's the way I figured it...until I ran into you." Jagger tells him that he has never met him before as a way of thanking him for earlier saving his life as well as forgiving Scott's shady past, which he is obviously attempting to reform. Scott decides to remain with Western Union, mostly because he is attracted to Gilmore, but he finds that, whenever he visits the beautiful young woman, Young also appears to compete for Gilmore's attentions. Then, on July 4, 1861, Jagger orders his wagons and crews to roll westward and they begin constructing a line of telegraph poles rigged with wiring to stretch Western Union's communication system across the wild plains. While Jagger and his crews are camped for a night, they are suddenly attacked by a band of rampaging Indians, killing a worker and running off most of Jagger's cattle. Scott then investigates, tracking down the Indians to their camp and finding that they are not Indians at all, but a band of outlaws wearing war paint and Indian garb. They are led by MacLane, who is Scott's brutal brother, the very band of brigands to which Scott had once belonged. (MacLane is named Jack Slade, the actual name of one of the West's deadliest gunmen, Joseph Alfred "Jack" Slade, 1831-1864, who had once been a Pony Express and stagecoach superintendent, and who is profiled as such by Mark Stevens in **Jack Slade**, 1953, and where, ironically, MacLane plays a rival gunman slain by Stevens in that film.) MacLane welcomes Scott when seeing him, believing that Scott is re-

Randolph Scott and Robert Young in *Western Union*, 1941.

joining him. Scott tells him otherwise, saying that he has found a decent life while working for Western Union. He demands that MacLane and his cohorts return the stolen steers. MacLane, however, says that he and his henchmen are now guerrillas fighting for the Confederacy and refuses to return the cattle. Scott rides back to Jagger's camp to report that Indians, indeed, stole the cattle, but that he could not locate their whereabouts, thus shielding his brother, MacLane, and his former outlaw friends. Scott suggests that Jagger simply buy another herd of cattle and leave the Indians alone to prevent further bloodshed. Jagger, though suspicious, takes Scott's advice. A short time later, Scott and Young are working at a forward area when a number of drunken Indians appear, demanding whiskey. When one of the Indians takes some equipment, Young, despite's Scott's warning not to take any action, impulsively shoots the Indian, driving off the others. They then learn that the main camp is under attack by a larger band of Indians, and Scott, Young and others rush back to defend that camp. The attackers, however, prove to be MacLane and his outlaws, again dressed as Indians, this proven when one of them is shot and found so disguised. The raiders have stolen all the horses in the camp, and Jagger is compelled to buy more mounts at a nearby town where he must deal with seller MacLane, who claims he purchased the horses from Indians. Jagger sees through this lie, but has no choice but to buy back his own stolen herd of horses from the very man who has taken them. During that meeting with MacLane, Jagger realizes that Scott and MacLane recognize each other, and Scott later admits to Jagger that he knows MacLane and some of his gang members. Richards, the commanding officer of a local U.S. Cavalry unit in the area, then informs Jagger that Indians led by Chief Big Tree (Chief Spotted Horse), has refused to allow Jagger to construct any more telegraph poles and wires through his territory because Young had impulsively shot and wounded his drunken son. Jagger is not to be halted in his dedicated task and meets with Chief Big Tree and his braves, who are ready for war and arrayed before him on the prairie at the point where the last telegraph pole stands and where the wire has been cut by the Indians. Scott interprets the chief's words for Jagger, telling him that the chief warns that "there won't be any peace if you try to take the singing wire through the Oglala nation." Jagger replies: "Tell him that the Great White Father, who speaks with lightning over the singing wire, is sorry for the wounding of his Indian son, but the lightning talk is strong medicine and it must go through." When the chief remains adamant, Jagger tells him that he will prove how the Great White Father is all-powerful and must be obeyed. He has the chief's strongest braves hold a wire that is extended to a telegraph shack, and, unseen by the chief and his followers, Young sends a bolt of electricity through the wire, causing the braves to traumatically leap and quiver and scream in shock until Jagger orders Young to stop. This amazing demonstration

Randolph Scott, Dean Jagger and Robert Young in *Western Union*, **1941.**

convinces the chief that he is dealing with mystical powers he cannot control, and he allows Jagger to build his telegraph line through the territory. Jagger and his men leave as the chief and his followers chant prayers of obedience to the telegraph line towering above them. MacLane and his outlaws, however, remain a constant threat to Jagger's operations, and Scott knows it when he is summoned to a meeting with his errant brother. MacLane tells Scott that he belongs to the outlaw way of life and insists that Scott rejoin the gang. Scott refuses as he is now a reformed man and grateful for the decent and honest way of life Jagger has allowed him to live. MacLane announces that he and his men are going to destroy Western Union operations that night by attacking Jagger's camp. He orders his men to bind Scott, so that he cannot interfere with the raid and then leaves Scott helplessly hogtied next to a burning campfire. While MacLane and his men ride away, Scott struggles with the ropes that bind him, edging close enough to the campfire to work his hands over some burning embers. He manages to burn away the rope but at the cost of seriously damaging his hands. Meanwhile, MacLane and his cohorts enter Jagger's camp, spreading coal oil everywhere and then setting fire to wagons and equipment before riding away. Chaos erupts as the wagons and tents burst into shooting flames, and the Western Union workers desperately try to save what they can, racing wagons from the site toward a nearby river. Scott, who has freed himself, arrives to help save some of the equipment, and his horribly burned hands are attributed to the fire set by MacLane and his outlaws. Afterward, Jagger confronts Scott, and, getting no explanation from Scott, fires him. Scott now resolves to have a final showdown with MacLane, but, before leaving the camp, he confides to Young that MacLane is his brother and he intends to stop MacLane and his men from further damaging Western Union. "I'd like to go with you," Young says. Scott replies: "Sorry, this is one job I don't trust to a tenderfoot, no matter how good he is." Scott rides to a nearby town where MacLane and his henchmen are in a barber shop where MacLane is being shaved by barber Bacon. When MacLane gets word that Scott is looking for him, he has his men take cover, and they draw their guns, MacLane concealing his six-gun beneath the barber's sheet. Scott then resolutely goes along the wooden walkway leading to the barber shop, slowly removing the bandages from his burned hands that edge toward his guns. He enters the shop and tells MacLane that he is there to stop him and his men once and for all from further damaging Western Union. MacLane, a cruel smile on his face, shoots Scott through the barber's sheet, and Scott fires back, shooting and killing some of MacLane's men, until MacLane sneaks to a window and shoots and kills Scott, who falls dead outside the shop. MacLane steps outside to see his fallen brother, only to then see Young, a gun strapped to his side, advancing toward him. Seeing his friend Scott dead, Young fires at MacLane, who fires several shots in return, but Young's aim is

better and his bullets strike and kill MacLane, who falls dead into a puddle of the muddy street, ending this savage outlaw's reign of terror. We next see crowds celebrating the successful linking of Western Union's operations between Omaha and Salt Lake City. Young, Jagger and Gilmore stand together as Young listens to the messages being sent out over the wires of Western Union. "Makes a nice sound, doesn't it," says Young, "coming across a continent." Jagger states: "It's music." Gilmore, who has loved Scott as much as she loves Young, sadly laments Scott's passing, saying: "I wish Shaw [Scott] could hear it." The sympathetic Jagger replies: "It's a long way from Salt Lake City to Boot Hill in Elkville, but I think he can hear it." At that moment, we see Scott's final resting place, a lonely grave with a crude marker next to a string of telegraph poles stretching into hills flooded by the fading light of a crimson sunset. We also hear the plaintive, haunting strains of "Bury Me Not on the Lone Prairie," serving as Scott's poignant epitaph while this memorably evocative scene dissolves. Lang directs his second western with this superlative film (following **The Return of Frank James**, 1940, which, like this film, depicts an outlaw attempting to abandon his criminal lifestyle). Lang's diligent attention to historic detail is apparent in every frame, and this would remain his favorite film. The Zane Grey tale, upon which this exciting tale is based, offers a highly fictionalized version of events of those early days of Western Union, but it is told with such conviction and panache that its scenes compellingly linger as a fond image of the Old West to this day. The photography from Cronjager and Davey, in brilliant Technicolor (the older process that presented much deeper and richer hues), breathtakingly presents a stunning portrait of the Old West and its rolling plains. Its many heart-pounding action scenes are well choreographed, and the performances from Scott, Jagger, Young, Gilmore and a bevy of talented character actors are outstanding. MacLane, as the savage outlaw, gives a truly frightening performance of a man so evil that he does not have a smidgeon of remorse in shooting and killing his own brother. (Stephen McNally, another fine character actor, would play a similar evil brother in another classic western, **Winchester '73**, 1950, where he is forever attempting to kill his brother, James Stewart, who is attempting to do the same thing to him because McNally has fatally shot their father in the back.) Summerville is exceptional in providing many subtle laughs as a timid cook frightened of any noise. The befuddled and often terrified Summerville presents a hilarious scene when the Western Union camp is raided while he is busy preparing dinner inside the cook wagon. He has already cut and bandaged every finger on his hands at the slightest provocation, and when chaos ensues during the raid, Summerville bounces and tosses about inside that wagon until he lands into a tub of peeled potatoes. The score from Buttolph is memorable as he weaves "Bury Me Not on the Lone Prairie" throughout its scenes, foreshadowing the fate of Scott's doomed character. The film was a box office success and greatly furthered the careers of Scott, Jagger and Young. Songs: "Gwine to Run All Night (De Camptown Races)" (1850; Stephen Foster), "The Little Brown Jug" (1869; Joseph Winner), "Bury Me Not on the Lone Prairie" (Cowboy folk song). *Author's Note*: Jagger's role is based on the real-life Edward Creighton, 1820-1874, who built a transcontinental telegraph line from Omaha, Nebraska, to Sacramento, California, financed by Western Union. The line was begun on July 2, 1861, and completed on October 24, 1861. In reality, Western Union had little difficulty in building its telegraph line in 1861, except for the fact that the company ran out of telegraph poles after roaming buffalo began knocking them down. These beasts scratched themselves on the rough-hewn exteriors of the poles, their hunters later finding their hides studded by wooden splinters. Creighton made friends with the many Indian tribes along that route and championed their cause, defending Indian rights to the point where he was in conflict with many politicians and military leaders, as well as his own brother, John A. Creighton, 1831-1907, who became a packing plant tycoon in Omaha. Both brothers were abolitionists and pro-Union during the American Civil War. Young recalled this film with warm memories, telling this author: "Lang was a tough director, who had very little patience with actors showing up unprepared for a scene, and I knew that, so I was always ready and as sharp as I could be when doing my scenes under his supervision. I appreciated all that because it made us all better actors. I was in very good company in that picture with Dean [Jagger], Randy [Randolph Scott], and Ginny [Virginia Gilmore]. Ginny was one of the great Hollywood beauties of that day, although she did not have too many scenes in that picture. It was a man's picture to the bone and it mostly belonged to Randy, who was terrific. I think that picture, more than most, made him decide that he belonged more in westerns than in any other kind of picture." Scott told this author: "I don't think I ever played a more sympathetic character than the one I played in **Western Union**. He is a man running from his past until he realizes that he cannot escape it. He is killed when trying to defeat that past and meets a hero's death. There were many kinds of martyrs in the Old West. My character was one of them, a martyr to his brutal past." Fox chief Zanuck particularly liked this film, but thought that MacLane had gone "over the top" when essaying the outlaw leader, as Zanuck told this author. "MacLane had leather lungs," Zanuck said to this author. "He was a man who never spoke his words normally. He shouted them. I once asked him if he spoke that way in a restaurant when ordering a meal and he replied: 'What are you talking about?' He was shouting when he said that." The vital necessity and dependence upon communication via telegraph lines in the Old West was forever being depicted in westerns. When telegraphers discovered those lines had gone dead, it invariably signaled a disastrous event, most likely the result of raiding Indians, as is shown in John Ford's classic westerns, **Stagecoach**, 1939, and **Fort Apache**, 1948. Such imperative use of the telegraph, however, was not confined to the American West. At the beginning of another classic film, **Gunga Din**, 1939, a telegraph signal from a remote outpost in India abruptly stops that leads to the discovery of a widespread revolt led by a killer cult known as Thuggee. The eerie atmosphere created by a telegraph line going dead was an essential dramatic ploy accepted by pantheon director Lang, who would go on to make one more western, **Rancho Notorious**, 1952, starring his fellow native German, Marlene Dietrich. Lang truly loved the American West and spent much time researching its past, particularly its Indian culture when taking extensive vacations in its wilds. He took great pains to present the Indians in accurate dress and mannerisms while directing this epic film. Scriptwriter Carson pretty much used the Grey story in name only, replacing its tale with a plot that accented a human drama. Lang did not like the script and began making changes, but Fox boss Zanuck stepped in and ordered Lang to follow the Carson story line. He complied and later thanked Zanuck for preserving a tale that Lang came to believe was his best effort on film. Exteriors were shot on location at House Rock Canyon, Arizona, and extensively at Kanab, Utah, and at the Zion National Park near Springdale, Utah. Interiors were shot at the Fox Studio at Century City, Los Angeles, California. **p**, Darryl F. Zanuck; **d**, Fritz Lang; **cast**, Robert Young, Randolph Scott, Dean Jagger, Virginia Gilmore, John Carradine, Slim Summerville, Chill Wills, Barton MacLane, Russell Hicks, Victor Kilian, Minor Watson, Chief Big Tree, Chief Thundercloud, Addison Richards, Irving Bacon, George Chandler, James Flavin, Dick Rich, Iron Eyes Cody, Francis Ford, Charles Middleton, Harry Strang, Jay Silverheels; **w**, Robert Carson (based on the novel by Zane Grey); **c**, Edward Cronjager, Allen M. Davey (Technicolor); **m**, David Buttolph; **ed**, Robert Bischoff, (uncredited) Gene Fowler, Jr.; **art d**, Richard Day, Wiard B. Ihnen, Albert Hogsett; **set d**, Thomas Little; **spec eff**, William F. Mittlestedt, Ben Southland.

The Westerner ★★★★★ 1940; U.S.; 100m; UA; B/W; Western; Children: Unacceptable; **DVD**; **VHS**. Pantheon director Wyler presents a masterpiece film that captures and presents a gritty and unforgettable image of the Old West while memorably portraying its earthy, compelling characters as realistic denizens roaming that ferocious landscape. The film opens as the camera inspects the ramshackle town of Vinega-

Gary Cooper, Doris Davenport and Walter Brennan in *The Westerner*, 1940.

roon, Texas (which later became the town of Langtry, in Val Verde County, Texas), the center of which is a crude saloon. This broken-down bar is operated by Brennan, who plays the outlandish Judge Roy Bean (1825-1903), an uncouth, uneducated ruffian. Brennan has made himself the supreme law of this town of thieves and killers. Possessing a single law book that he seldom consults, Brennan has appointed himself as the local judge and brags that he is "the only law west of the Pecos." We see Brennan conducting trials at his saloon where he illegally collects fines and seizes property for the smallest infraction, or none at all. Those so foolish to defy his draconian edicts are summarily hanged at his orders, executions he calls his "suspended sentences." Cooper, an amiable drifter, arrives at this hellhole and is in immediate trouble with Brennan, after Cooper is brought to the saloon and charged with stealing a horse belonging to one of Brennan's slavish henchmen, Hurst. Cooper claims innocence, insisting that he bought the horse from another man, but when he cannot produce that man, Brennan, in a whirlwind mock trial, sentences Cooper to death by hanging. Cooper, however, knows that Brennan is obsessed with the beautiful British actress Lily Langtry (1853-1929, played by Bond), who is then touring the eastern cities of the U.S. Cooper tells Brennan that he has not only met the wonderful actress, but that she allowed him to cut a lock of her hair, which Cooper has secreted elsewhere. Coveting that priceless keepsake, Brennan postpones Cooper's execution as he subtly negotiates with the conniving cowboy to obtain that desired lock of hair. Cooper, who claims that he will send for the lock of hair, which is being kept for him in El Paso, is given a momentary respite while Brennan thinks about obtaining that lock of hair. That night, Cooper escapes and finds refuge at the home of farmer Stone, and his beautiful daughter, Davenport. They invite him to dinner in the hopes that Cooper will stay on as a much needed farmhand. Tucker is already working for them and he resents Cooper's intrusive arrival, believing that he might win the attentions of Davenport, the girl Tucker loves. Stone and other farmers in the area are under constant pressure from cattle ranchers, who want the farmers off the range; Brennan works in league with the ranchers to drive off the farmers. Meanwhile Tyler, the real horse thief, is unearthed and killed in a shootout. Now that he is vindicated and his sentence of death removed by the utterly corrupt Brennan, Cooper remains in the area as he is now smitten by the fetching Davenport. In one of their more tender moments together, Cooper is able to clip a lock of her hair (even though she petulantly refuses), which he preserves in a small leather pouch. Brennan then befriends Cooper, thinking the younger man to be very much like himself in his youthful days (Brennan, in reality, was only seven years older than Cooper when making this film). Brennan looks upon Cooper as a man possessing his own daring and bonds with him after Cooper gives him the lock of hair he has taken from Davenport, pretending that

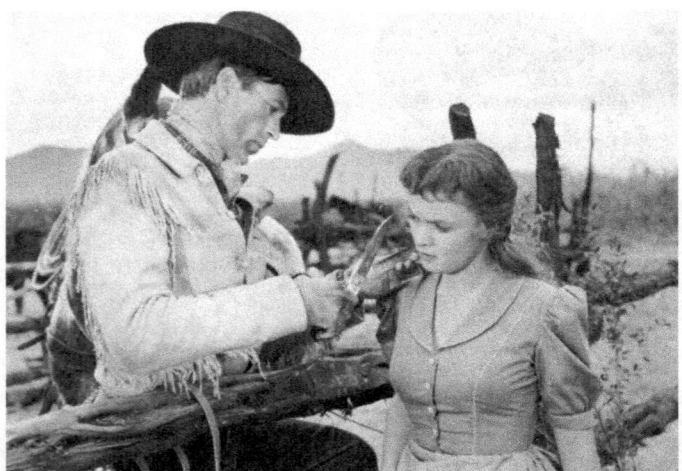

Gary Cooper cutting a lock of Doris Davenport's hair in *The Westerner,* 1940.

it is from the illustrious head of Langtry, and it becomes Brennan's most prized possession. Cooper's friendship with Brennan alienates him from the homesteaders he has befriended and this leads to a savage fight between Cooper and Tucker, one where Cooper barely manages to hold his own. Brennan continues to harass the homesteaders by deputizing his thug friends, who then terrorize the farmers to the point where the homesteaders decide to take the law into their own hands. They ride in a wagon, all heavily armed, going to town, which Brennan has renamed "Langtry" after the woman he loves from afar. The farmers, led by Tucker, barge into Brennan's saloon and aim their guns at him, planning to lynch him. Cooper, however, manages to disarm them, saving Brennan's life and ordering the farmers back to their wagon where they ride humiliated from the town. Brennan's gratitude toward Cooper is mixed with his hatred for the upstart homesteaders and he resolves to destroy them for daring to threaten his life. He unleashes his minions in an all-out war against the farmers, burning their crops and homes, and Stone is killed defending his homestead. The mourning Davenport is left alone, but refuses to leave her burned-out homestead, defiantly saying she will rebuild. She wants no more part of Cooper, believing he has somehow been part of the raids that claimed her father's life and ruined her farm. Cooper, too, refuses to accept defeat and resolves to put an end to Brennan's terrorist activities once and for all. He visits the county sheriff in a neighboring town where he is deputized and given warrants for Brennan's arrest, along with his criminal associates. When riding to the town of Langtry, however, Cooper finds that Brennan and his closest cohorts have departed, all riding to the town of Fort Davis to see the one and only Lily Langtry, who is appearing in the local theater. Brennan has donned his old Confederate uniform and saber that he once wore in the Civil War to appear at his regal best when meeting Langtry. To have the performance of the beautiful actress exclusive to himself, Brennan has henchman Wills buy out all the tickets for that performance. Ordering his men to remain outside, Brennan enters the theater to become the only spectator, taking a seat upfront and in the center of the middle aisle to face the stage. He watches as members of the orchestra take their places and anxiously peers to the stage with great anticipation in seeing for the first time the woman he adores. Finally, the orchestra begins to play introductory music and the curtain slowly rises, but, instead of seeing Langtry, Brennan is amazed to see Cooper standing at center stage, his hands next to his guns, looking down upon him and telling him that he is putting him under arrest. Brennan goes for his gun and both begin firing at each other as they take cover. Cooper then fatally shoots Brennan, but the dying man has only one last request and that is that he has one look at Lily Langtry. Cooper carries Brennan backstage and into the dressing room of the actress, played by Bond, and Brennan stands briefly alone, kissing Bond's hand before her image, as seen from Bren-

nan's POV, begins to blur, fade and then dissolve as Brennan dies. Cooper and Davenport are then seen together as man and wife, watching from their farm window as new settlers arrive, now that Cooper has made that once hazardous area safe for decent folks to live. Cooper begins to wax optimism for the future, but his ramblings are cut off when Davenport embraces and kisses him for a passionate and loving finale. Wyler brilliantly presents a somber and very dangerous West where no one is safe and where its inhabitants have to struggle to stay alive each and every day. Through Toland's crisp lensing, Wyler offers an uninviting landscape through which dirt-covered cowboys drive mean-looking herds of cattle and where raw-boned farmers fight to grow water-starved crops of corn. Dust rises from the parched earth with the slightest movement of a horse or a walking man in almost every scene. Winds howl and whip the desert sands down the lonely, barren street of Vinegaroon, and across the bleak Texas prairies. Cooper is at his most reliable stalwart best as a nomadic saddle tramp finding his way and sinking his roots into the same earth so energetically cultivated by Davenport, Stone and their hardworking fellow farmers. In so doing, he betrays his own wild cowboy class, opposing its ruthless and reckless pillaging and bloodletting. He does not go easy to that decision as he befriends the utterly corrupt but colorful Brennan, who Cooper knows to be protectively avuncular, but, at the same time, is as unpredictable as a treacherous rattlesnake. Brennan really steals this film by rendering a memorable portrait of one of the West's most irascible, contemptible and outlandish characters. Brennan deservedly received an Oscar as Best Supporting Actor (his third and final such award), and the film also received Oscar nominations for Best Story (Lake) and Best Art Direction (Basevi; set decoration: Heron). The film was a success at the box office, earning back more than double its budget of more than $1 million in its initial release. The story received a sixty-minute radio adaptation that was aired by Lux Radio Theater on September 23, 1940, with Cooper, Brennan and Davenport reprising their roles. The 1919 and 1934 films with the same title have no relationship to this story. *Author's Note*: The story line for this film plays fast and loose with the legend of Roy Bean. He was, indeed, a self-styled justice of the peace, who idolized actress Lily Langtry and changed the name of Vinegaroon, Texas, to Langtry, Texas. Bean actually saw Langtry in 1888 in San Antonio when she was then on tour in the U.S. The cantankerous Bean, however, did not die in a gunfight as shown herein, but peacefully in his bed in 1903. A few months later, Langtry, out of curiosity, visited the town named after her, but by then her most ardent admirer in that dust-clogged community was already residing underground at Boot Hill. Goldwyn had some difficulty with Cooper before making this film, as Cooper, who was under exclusive contract to Goldwyn, believed that his role was a minor one and that Brennan, as the eccentric Roy Bean, was at the dramatic center of the story. Goldwyn told this author: "I told Coop [Gary Cooper] that his role was the leading part in **The Westerner** and that he would be seen more on screen than any other player and we kept that promise." Nevertheless, Cooper wrote to Goldwyn, telling the producer that he would live up to his contractual obligations, and give his role his best efforts, but that he wanted to sever relationships with Goldwyn following the completion of this film. No such thing happened as Cooper and Goldwyn went on to work together on **The Pride of the Yankees,** 1942 (where Cooper won an Oscar as Best Actor, and where Brennan played a supporting actor). "I got the girl in **The Westerner,**" Cooper told this author, "but Walter [Brennan] walked away with all the good scenes by playing that crazy old coot, Roy Bean." Brennan told this author: "I knew that Coop [Gary Cooper] was worried about all the good scenes I had in **The Westerner,** so I underplayed my part and let him have most of the close-ups with no complaint. Hell, he was the star, not me. It was my character that fascinated everyone and landed me another Oscar. I spent a lot of time researching that man [Roy Bean] and when I learned that Bean had survived a hanging, I used that in the film. I regularly got a crick in my neck and I cocked my chin at a twisted angle so that Coop had to straighten out my neck by punching my jaw. Coop was a regular and fair-minded fellow and I always believed in the characters he played in the pictures we made together. We went back a long ways, all the way back to 1925, when we were both going to the casting offices in Hollywood to get bit parts. I did well over the years, but Coop became one of Hollywood's greatest stars. I always knew he would get to the big time because he had that boyish charm that made every man and woman like him." Wyler told this author that "No other actor looked better on a horse than Coop [Gary Cooper]. He had injured his back when he was much younger and trained himself how to ride a horse so that he never jostled or bounced in the saddle. He always looked like he and the horse were one, even when the horse was at a full gallop, and he photographed beautifully when he was mounted in action scenes." Andrews, who made his debut in this film, told this author: "I had a bit part in **The Westerner**, but Willy [William Wyler] must have seen something in me that he liked, because, five years later, he gave me one of my greatest roles when he cast me in a leading part in his picture, **The Best Years of Our Lives** [1946]. Willy is a perfectionist, the kind of director who will make dozens of takes until he thinks he has gotten a scene right. Any actor willing to work under that kind of tough schedule always made the grade with him." Davenport, who had been a Goldwyn Girl, had been one of the finalists auditioning for the leading part of Scarlett O'Hara in **Gone with the Wind**, 1939, and this so impressed Goldwyn that he cast her as the heroine in **The Westerner**, much to the chagrin of Wyler, who felt her acting skills were limited. Sadly, just after this film was completed, Davenport was involved in a car accident where her legs were crushed and she was compelled thereafter to walk with the support of a cane. She made only one film after this one, **Behind the News**, 1940, a programmer produced by Republic. Davenport died at age sixty-three in 1980. This was also Tucker's debut. Exteriors were shot at the Bull Farm outside of the arid town of Continental, Arizona. Roy Bean has been portrayed by many other actors in many other films, including **Colt 45**, 1957-1960 (TV series; "Law West of the Pecos," 1959 episode: Frank Ferguson); **Death Valley Days**, 1952-1970 (TV series; "A Sense of Justice," 1966 episode: Tom Skerritt); **The Gambler Returns: The Luck of the Draw**, 1991 (made-for-TV; Brad Sullivan); **Hell Town**, 1985 (made-for-TV; Warren Vanders); **Judge Roy Bean**, 1956-1957 (TV series; Edgar Buchanan); **Judge Roy Bean**, 1971 (Pierre Perret); **The Life and Times of Judge Roy Bean**, 1972 (Paul Newman); **Lillie**, 1978 (TV miniseries: Tommy Dugan); **Lives and Deaths of the Poets**, 2011 (Jim Epstein); **Streets of Laredo**, 1995 (TV miniseries; Ned Beatty); and **A Time for Dying**, 1982 (Victor Jory). Lily Langtry has been essayed by many actresses in many other films, including **Edward the King**, 1975 (TV series; two episodes: Francesca Annis); **Gambler V: Playing for Keeps**, 1994 (made-for-TV; Dixie Carter); **Incident at Victoria Falls**, 1992 (made-for-TV; Jenny Seagrove); **The Life and Times of Judge Roy Bean**, 1972 (Ava Gardner); **Lillie**, 1978 (TV miniseries; Francesca Annis); **Oscar**, 1985 (TV series; Catherine Strauss); and **The Trials of Oscar Wilde**, 1960 (Naomi Chance). **p**, Samuel Goldwyn; **d**, William Wyler; **cast**, Gary Cooper, Walter Brennan, Doris Davenport, Fred Stone, Forest Tucker, Paul Hurst, Chill Wills, Lilian Bond, Dana Andrews, Charles Halton, Tom Tyler; **w**, Jo Swerling, Niven Busch (based on a story by Stuart N. Lake); **c**, Gregg Toland; **m**, Dimitri Tiomkin, (uncredited) Alfred Newman; **ed**, Daniel Mandell; **art d**, James Basevi; **set d**, Julie Heron; **spec eff**, Archie Stout, Paul Eagler.

Westfront 1918 ★★★ 1931; Germany; 75m; Bavaria Film/Embassy; B/W; War Drama; Children: Unacceptable; **DVD**. Pantheon German director Pabst presents a stunning if not oppressive portrait of the last year of WWI (1914-1918). The POV through most of the film is that of four German soldiers desperately attempting to survive constant threats of death in the trenches of the Western Front. The four are Kampers, Diessl, Moebis (called "the student"), who are enlisted men, and Clausen, who is a young lieutenant commanding their trench area.

Walter Brennan, Gary Cooper and Lilian Bond (as Lillie Langtry) in *The Westerner*, 1940.

Diessl and Clausen are given a brief furlough, but they quickly see how the war has devastated their hometown and their families. So desperate for food is Heller, Diessl's mother, that, when seeing him on the street, she does not go to him in fear of losing her place in the queue of people waiting for rations to be distributed. So much hunger and hopelessness greet these two soldiers that they quickly return to the front to be with those having more compassion for each other. When part of a dugout collapses upon Diessl and Clausen, Moebis comes to their rescue, digging them out. Moebis serves as a runner, moving between the trenches and the rear area where artillery is located, bringing information that pinpoints the distant targets for these big guns. Diessl, Kampers and Clausen then come under a murderous artillery barrage that is mistakenly fired by their own artillery, and Moebis once more risks his life to save his comrades by racing through the barrage to have the German artillery cease its bombardment. Diessl is given another brief leave and, when he returns home, he finds his cheating wife, Hoessrich, in bed with Balhaus, the local butcher. So disgusted with this, he again leaves for the front. He finds that, in his absence, Moebis has been mortally stabbed. Just then the French attack with tanks that quickly penetrate the thin German defenses, followed by massive lines of French infantry. As the Germans retreat, Diessl and Kampers are part of the rear guard, fighting furiously to ward off advancing French troops. Both are wounded, and they are taken to a hospital where they see Clausen, who has lost his sanity as he salutes and addresses a row of dead German soldiers. Diessl is slowly dying from his wounds, overworked physicians finding no way to save him. Feverish and hallucinating, Diessl sees his wife Hoessrich once more, reconciling with her just before he dies. His final words are "we are all to blame." His body is covered by a sheet, his hand protruding from that shroud, and a wounded French soldier takes his hand, saying: "Comrades…not enemies." The final word on the screen, "End" has an added question mark. Pabst directs this grim story with well-orchestrated war action scenes, and his players are believably realistic in their roles, each of them portrayed as pitiful, doomed men with no hope of surviving an all-destroying war. *Author's Note*: The tone of this powerful film is decidedly anti-war, and its logical pacifism was condemned when the Nazis came to power a few years later in 1933, who banned this film in Germany. Joseph Goebbels, Nazi minister of propaganda and who controlled the German film industry, branded this film as "a very one-sided and therefore false representation of war." Goebbels went on to state that **Westfront 1918** jeopardized "the vital interest of the state to preserve the military will of the people." The film is not dissimilar to Lewis Milestone's classic **All Quiet on the Western Front**, 1930, andPabst honors that film by emulating its action and carnage when depicting trench warfare in all its horrors. **p**, Seymour Nebenzal; **d**, Georg Wilhelm (G.W.) Pabst; **cast**,

Robert Taylor and women in *Westward the Women*, 1951.

Fritz Kampers, Gustav Diessl, H. J. Moebis, Claus Clausen, Jackie Monnier, Hanna Hoessrich, Elsa Heller, Carl Balhaus, Aribert Mog, Gustav Puttjer, Vladimir Sokoloff; **w**, Ladislaus Vajda, Peter Martin Lampel (based on the novel *Vier von der Infanterie* by Ernst Johannsen); **c**, Charles Metain, Fritz Arno Wagner; **m**, Alexander Laszlo; **ed**, W.L. Bagier, Jean Oser, Marc Sorkin; **art d**, Erno Metzner.

Westward Ho, the Wagons! ★★★ 1956; U.S.; 86m; Walt Disney; Buena Vista; Color; Western; Children: Acceptable; **DVD**; **VHS**; **IV**. Parker is a standout as a scout for a wagon train heading west to Oregon. Along the way, the pioneers are attacked by hostile Indians, but Parker saves them by staging a cattle stampede. Later, they encounter friendly Indians, and Parker, who claims to be a doctor, saves the chief's injured son, but he is careful not to upstage the tribe's medicine man by enlisting his help in the boy's recovery. Director Beaudine provides a fascinating portrait of pioneers surviving the wilderness as they make their way through undiscovered landscapes, and the action scenes are well choreographed. Songs: "Westward Ho the Wagons" and "The Ballad of John Colter" (George Bruns, Tom Blackburn), "Wringle Wrangle" (Stan Jones), "I'm Lonely My Darlin' (Bruns, Fess Parker, based on "Green Grow the Lilacs" [traditional]), "Pioneer's Prayer" (Paul J. Smith, Hazel George). *Author's Note*: George Reeves had a small supporting role in this film, made during his years playing "Superman" on television (1952-1958). Reeves died at home, a suspected suicide, a year after the series ended, and after he had difficulty finding other roles. **p**, Bill Walsh; **d**, William Beaudine; **cast**, Fess Parker, Kathleen Crowley, Jeff York, David Stollery, George Reeves, Sebastian Cabot, Doreen Tracey, Barbara Woodell, John War Eagle, Iron Eyes Cody; **w**, Thomas W. Blackburn as Tom Blackburn (based on the novel *Children of the Covered Wagon* by Mary Jane Carr); **c**, Charles P. Boyle; **m**, George Bruns; **ed**, Cotton Warburton; **art d**, Marvin Aubrey Davis; **set d**, Emile Kuri, Bertram Granger; **spec eff**, Peter Ellenshaw, Ub Iwerks, Albert Whitlock.

Westward the Women ★★★ 1951; U.S.; 116m; MGM; B/W; Western; Children: Unacceptable; **DVD**; **VHS**. Offbeat but compelling tale from pantheon director Wellman sees a wagon train of pioneering women traveling from Chicago, Illinois, to California, to meet and marry men they have never before seen. The film opens in 1851 where McIntire has recruited 138 sturdy women to travel at his expense from the Windy City to a community he has established in California and there to meet and marry the men who are working in that valley. McIntire warns these volunteer women that at least one third of them will most likely not survive the perils and hazards of the trek. He shows the marital candidates daguerreotype photos of the bachelors waiting for them in California,

which are posted on a large board and where women are asked to select the man they want to marry. McIntire is very selective in choosing the right women for the trip. He accepts Emerson, a towering, robust woman from New England, who lost her sailing husband and sons in a storm at sea and now wants to start life anew. He also chooses Dennis, a young unmarried woman who is pregnant and wants to leave her shame behind. When McIntire rejects some women who are garishly dressed as showgirls, Darcel and Bishop leave the hall and change from their flashy attire to more sedate dresses. McIntire has noted this, but accepts the two anyway, believing that Darcel and Bishop are honestly attempting to improve their lifestyles. Meanwhile, Taylor, a seasoned wagon master and pioneering scout, has been hired by McIntire to lead the women to their waiting husbands-to-be, a chore the tough, no-nonsense Taylor does not relish. McIntire and Taylor then take the women to St. Joseph, Missouri, where wagon teams and the men Taylor has hired to protect the caravan are waiting for them. Taylor immediately warns the men that he will shoot any of them taking liberties with the women. He, along with the men he has hired, have the women experienced in driving wagons help the others to learn how to harness teams and drive those wagons. Nakamura, a personable Japanese worker, who has been hired as the wagon train's cook, serves as Taylor's amiable assistant and quickly befriends the women. As Taylor expected, some of the men begin to make unwanted advances toward the women, and Taylor shoots one of them for sexually attacking Bishop. All of the hired men, except Nakamura and Conway, who has fallen in love with Dennis, desert the wagon train, taking eight of the women with them. Taylor wants to turn back now that the men have deserted, believing that the women alone, with only four men to guide them, do not stand a chance of surviving the wilderness. The women rebel against this idea. Emerson and other outspoken leaders of the women refuse, saying that, since they have gone halfway to their destination, they must continue. McIntire sides with them, believing that they can do what men can accomplish, if they only know how to manage their wagons. Taylor grudgingly trains the women how to drive their teams, but Martufi, the young son of Italian mother Vanni, is killed during this training period. Vanni, who speaks only Italian, a language unfamiliar to all the others, refuses to leave the boy's gravesite after he is buried on the prairie. To save her life, Taylor has no choice but to knock her out, tie her up, and place her into the wagon driven by Emerson and Darcel. The caravan proceeds into storms, where a stampede routes and destroys some of the wagons. When descending into a gorge, some of the wagons break apart and one woman is killed. Then Indians attack and the heroic women fight off the assailants, Conway and McIntire being killed, along with several women. The wagon train, though badly damaged, reaches a riverbank, but when a violent storm causes the riverbank to give way, the wagon carrying Bishop collapses, and she is drowned. Throughout these many hardships, Darcel proves to the taciturn and tough Taylor that she has the bravery of a lioness, as do the indefatigable women surviving the terrible trek, and Taylor comes to respect and admire them, as well as falling in love with Darcel. To overcome their last obstacle, a scorching desert, Taylor orders all the wagons lightened by having the women discard their prized furniture and most of their belongings, including their fancy gowns. Dennis then goes into labor and delivers a baby boy. Crossing the desert, the wagon train arrives at a lake where the thirsty passengers slake their thirst. They are now outside McIntire's valley, but the women refuse to go further until Taylor obtains for them some decent clothing that will make them presentable to their prospective husbands. They also tell Taylor that he is to inform those potential spouses that anyone of them daring to approach the wagon train before the women obtain their new clothes will be shot on sight. Taylor complies and the anxious men in the valley assemble every kind of feminine attire they can provide for the women. Once again dressed in their feminine garb, the women drive their wagons into the settlement, all carrying the pictures of the men they have carried throughout their torturing trip. Emerson, the towering spokeswoman of the group, tells the men that it will be the women choosing their mates, not the other way around. Each woman finds the man they want, all of these patient men showing gratitude to their future brides for the heroic sacrifices they have made in making the hazardous journey to their valley. Even Vanni finds a man who speaks Italian, an orange grower from Genoa, and Dennis pairs off with a considerate farmer eager to welcome her and her infant son to his homestead. Nakamura plays Cupid by urging Darcel to go to Taylor before he rides away, knowing that they love each other. Darcel does just that and soon she and Taylor are joining the line of couples heading toward a preacher, who is marrying one couple after another, this joyful procession serving as this fine film's finale. Wellman, as usual, pays close attention to historic detail, which is evident in every one of his carefully organized scenes, and his action is exciting and well choreographed. Mellor's gritty lensing dynamically captures the changing landscape of plains, mountains, rivers and deserts, and the intelligent script from Schnee is commendable, replete with some witty dialog. At one point, McIntire describes the caravan of women he is taking westward to Taylor by saying: "One man's eye for beauty is another man's eyesore!" The assertive Emerson has many very funny lines, not the least of which is her delivery to the waiting men at the end of the trail where she states: "You can look us over, but don't think you're going to do the choosing. All the way from Independence [Missouri], I have been staring at two things: One is this picture [of the man she had originally selected before making the trip], and the other was a rump of a mule...and don't ask me which was prettier!" Taylor is outstanding as the resolute wagon master, as is the visionary McIntire and the precocious Nakamura. Darcel is at her feisty best, and Bishop, Dennis and Emerson are exceptional as some of the courageous women. The film was a box office success, earning almost $4 million in its initial release against a budget of $2.2 million. The story saw a sixty-minute radio adaptation aired by Lux Radio Theater on December 29, 1952, with Robert Taylor reprising his role. Song: "To the West! To the West!" (Henry Russell). *Author's Note*: Director Frank Capra wrote the unusual story for this film and thought to direct it himself, telling this author: "I was fascinated as a youth when I learned how mail order brides were ordered in the Old West, women and men agreeing to marry each other sight unseen. That's what gave me the idea for **Westward the Women**. The trouble was that I got involved with some other projects and did not have the time to make the picture, so I contacted my good friend and neighbor, Bill Wellman, who immediately warmed to the idea." Wellman bought the film rights to the story, telling this author: "It was a roaring good story, all these women willing to risk their pretty necks to find a good husband thousands of miles away that they had never laid eyes on. I must admit that I risked their necks all right, and some of the action scenes came close to sending some of those brave ladies to the hospital. The actresses were just as courageous as the characters they were playing and none of them gave me any trouble and put up with every damned snake and sand fly. What a great bunch of gals. I was bowled over by Hope [Emerson], an amazon of a woman. She stood more than six-feet-two and weighed more than 220 pounds. Nobody, including me, bossed that woman around. When I was preparing what I thought was going to be a very difficult action scene, she said to me: 'You just dish it out, Bill. We'll do it and dish it right back to you!'" Taylor, too, told this author that Emerson was always calming the actresses when it came to undertaking hazardous scenes. "I heard her telling the other ladies before one of those scenes," Taylor told this author, "that they could not afford to be 'delicate' and that they could do any scene any man could do, but she had the edge on them as she was almost twice the size of all of them. Well, they all followed Hope's [Emerson's] lead and the scene worked perfectly." Taylor was not the first choice for the role of the wagon master. Capra thought to have Gary Cooper play that role, but, after Wellman took over, he cast Taylor, who was then one of MGM's leading stars. This was the film debut of Conway. Other films depicting wagon trains include **Across the Plains**, 1939; **Adventures of Frank and Jesse James**, 1948; **Arizona**, 1940; **Arrow in the Dust**, 1954; **Bad Men**, 1926; **Bend of the River**, 1952;

Robert Taylor and Denise Darcel in *Westward the Women*, 1951.

Beyond the Last Frontier, 1943; **Beyond the Law**, 1975; **The Big Stampede**, 1932; **The Big Trail**, 1930; **The Big Trees**, 1952; **The Blocked Trail**, 1943; **Brigham Young: Frontiersman**, 1940; **Broken Lance**, 1954; **Bullwhip**, 1958; **Can't Help Singing**, 1944; **Canyon Passage**, 1946; **Cavalry**, 1936; **The Cherokee Strip**, 1937; **Chisum**, 1970; **Cimarron**, 1931; **Cimarron**, 1960; **City Slickers**, 1991; **Cole Younger, Gunfighter**, 1958; **The Command**, 1954; **Conagher**, 1991 (made-for-TV); **The Covered Wagon**, 1923; **Covered Wagon Days**, 1940; **Covered Wagon Raid**, 1950; **Covered Wagon Trails**, 1930; **Covered Wagon Trails**, 1940; **Crooked River**, 1950; **The Culpepper Cattle Company**, 1972; **Daniel Boone: Frontier Trail Rider**, 1966; **Dark Command**, 1940; **Davy Crockett: Indian Scout**, 1950; **Desperados of the West**, 1950; **The Desperate Mission**, 1969 (made-for-TV); **Dodge City**, 1939; **Drums along the Mohawk**, 1939; **El Condor**, 1970; **End of the Trail**, 1932; **Fighting Caravans**, 1931; **Fighting Pioneers**, 1935; **Finger on the Trigger**, 1965; **Flame of Barbary Coast**, 1945; **For a Few More Dollars**, 1967; **Fort Worth**, 1951; **Fort Yuma**, 1955; **4 Dollars of Revenge**, 1966; **The General**, 1926; **Ghost of Zorro**, 1949; **The Great Sioux Massacre**, 1965; **Heroes of the West**, 1930; **Home on the Range**, 1946; **Home on the Range**, 2004; **Hondo**, 1953; **How the West Was Won**, 1962; **In Old California**, 1942; **In Old Chicago**, 1938; **Into the West**, 2005 (TV miniseries); **Kit Carson**, 1940; **Land Raiders**, 1970; **The Lawless Breed**, 1953; **The Lone Ranger**, 1938; **The Lone Ranger Rides Again**, 1939; **Man in the Saddle**, 1951; **Man with the Steel Whip**, 1954; **Massacre Canyon**, 1954; **Mogambo**, 1953; **Monte Walsh**, 2003 (made-for-TV); **North to Alaska**, 1960; **The Oklahoman**, 1957; **Once upon a Time in the West**, 1969; **Open Range**, 2003; **The Oregon Trail**, 1939; **The Outriders**, 1950; **The Painted Desert**, 1931; **The Paleface**, 1948; **Pioneers of the West**, 1940; **Prairie Schooners**, 1940; **The Proud Ones**, 1956; **Puss in Boots**, 2011; **Rango**, 2011; **Red Fork Range**, 1931; **Red River**, 1948; **Ride with the Devil**, 1999; **Riders of the Deadline**, 1943; **Riding West**, 1944; **Rio Grande**, 1950; **Rolling Down the Great Divide**, 1942; **The Sacketts**, 1979 (made-for-TV); **Saddlemates**, 1941; **Sam Whiskey**, 1969; **The Scalphunters**, 1968; **Scarlet River**, 1933; **September Dawn**, 2007; **Shane**, 1953; **She Wore a Yellow Ribbon**, 1949; **Seven Men from Now**, 1956; **7th Cavalry**, 1956; **The Shakiest Gun in the West**, 1968; **Shoot, Gringo...Shoot!**, 1968; **The Silver Treasure**, 1926; **Silverado**, 1985; **The Singing Cowboy**, 1936; **Sitting Bull**, 1954; **Soldier Blue**, 1970; **Son of Oklahoma**, 1932; **Song of the Buckeroo**, 1938; **The Stranger Wore a Gun**, 1953; **Take a Hard Ride**, 1975; **Tall Man Riding**, 1955; **The Tall Men**, 1956; **The Tall Stranger**, 1957; **The Tall Texan**, 1953; **The Texan**, 1930; **Texas**, 1941; **They Died with Their Boots On**, 1941; **3 Godfathers**, 1948; **The Thundering Herd**, 1933; **Thundering Thomas**, 1929; **To the Last Man**, 1933;

Neil Hamilton and Myrna Loy in *The Wet Parade*, 1932.

The Topeka Terror, 1945; **The Undefeated**, 1969; **Untamed**, 1955; **Valley of Vengeance**, 1944; **Vengeance**, 1977; **Vera Cruz**, 1954; **Virginia City**, 1940; **Wagon Master**, 1950; **Wagon Wheels**, 1934; **Wagon Train**, 1957-1965 (TV series); **Wagons East**, 1954; **Wagons West**, 1952; **West of the Rockies**, 1931; **The Westerner**, 1940; **Westward Ho the Wagons**, 1956; **Wheels of Destiny**, 1934; and **Wyoming**, 1947. **p**, Dore Schary; **d**, William A. Wellman; **cast**, Robert Taylor, Denise Darcel, Hope Emerson, John McIntire, Julie Bishop, Lenore Lonergan, Henry Nakamura, Frankie Darro, Marilyn Erskine, Beverly Dennis, Pat Conway, Renata Vanni, Guido Martufi; **w**, Charles Schnee (based on the story by Frank Capra); **c**, William Mellor; **m**, Jeff Alexander; **ed**, James E. Newcom; **art d**, Cedric Gibbons, Daniel B. Cathcart; **set d**, Edwin B. Willis, Ralph S. Hurst.

Westworld ★★★ 1973; U.S.; 88m; MGM; Color; Science Fiction; Children: Unacceptable (MPAA: PG); **BD**; **DVD**; **VHS**; **IV**. Weirdly fascinating tale begins when robots give rich vacationers a chance to live out their fantasies at a futuristic adult-themed amusement park. Benjamin and Brolin are two visitors, who chose a Wild West adventure, but, in a computer breakdown, they find they are being stalked by Brynner, a rogue robot gunslinger. After a series of harrowing action scenes, Brolin is killed, but Benjamin manages to subdue Brynner before the robot can kill more humans. The film is eerily presented, and Brynner presents a chilling mechanical killer, who makes the real outlaws of the Old West look like pansies. The film scored well at the box office, earning more than $10 million in its initial release against a budget of $1.2 million. *Author's Note*: This was Crichton's first feature film as a director and it pioneered the use of digital image processing, simulating the android's POV with pixelated photography. **p**, Paul N. Lazarus III; **d&w**, Michael Crichton; **cast**, Yul Brynner, Richard Benjamin, James Brolin, Norman Bartold, Alan Oppenheimer, Victoria Shaw, Dick Van Patten, Linda Scott, Steve Franken, Michael Mikler; **c**, Gene Polito (Panavision; Metrocolor); **m**, Fred Karlin; **ed**, David Bretherton; **art d**, Herman Blumenthal; **set d**, John Austin; **spec eff**, Charles Schulthies, Brent Sellstrom.

The Wet Parade ★★★ 1932; U.S.; 120m; MGM; B/W; Drama; Children: Unacceptable. Fascinating tale profiles two families affected by alcohol during the Prohibition Era (1920-1933). One family is in the North, where Huston is a frequent bar drinker in New York City, and the other in the South, where Stone, also a heavy drinker, runs a bootlegging operation. Huston becomes drunk on some bad booze, killing his wife, Blandick, in anger when she breaks a bottle of bourbon intentionally in front of him and he is sent to prison for life. Stone is married to Dunn and the father of beautiful Jordan, a nice girl, and

Hamilton, who migrates to New York to become a writer. Stone drinks some bad liquor, falls into a deep depression, and slits his throat. Meanwhile, Huston's son, Young, joins the Prohibition agents and, together with Durante, tracks down some bootleggers. Jordan and Young meet, fall in love, and marry. Hamilton becomes a successful Broadway playwright and also marries, but he, too, becomes a victim to some bad liquor. He goes blind and his wife, Loy, leaves him. Meanwhile, Durante pursues the bootleggers and is killed in a gunfight while trying to save Young. Fleming directs this gangster film with great energy and inserts a running historic travelogue throughout the dramatic scenes, beginning with the Temperance Movement (starting in 1916). Fleming uses footage to show the presidential race between Woodrow Wilson (1856-1924) and Charles Evans Hughes (1862-1948), and WWI (1914-1918), as well as the wild Prohibition era, detailing the making of illicit liquor, from its mash to bottling, labeling and distribution. He seamlessly weaves the story's dramatic elements throughout to offer a devastating chronicle of that reckless age. Comedian Durante plays an uncommon serious character and does a fine job of playing a Prohibition agent who hates the gangsters peddling the rotgut booze, but also decries the law that spawned the gangster era leading to organized crime. (Like most of those in the U.S. at that time, Durante considers Prohibition a "bad law," but keeps his vows to uphold it, even at the cost of his life.) Songs: "Columbia, the Gem of the Ocean" (1843; David T. Shaw), "Arise, My Country, 'Tis of Thee" (1831; traditional), "Swanee River/Old Folks at Home" (1851; Stephen Foster), "My Old Kentucky Home" (1853; Foster), "Alexander's Ragtime Band" (1911; Irving Berlin), "A Hot Time in the Old Town" (1896; Theo. A. Metz), "Over There" (1917; George Cohan), "The Star-Spangled Banner" (1814; John Stafford Smith), "Hail! Hail! The Gang's All Here!" (1917; Arthur Sullivan, Theodore Morse), "Merrily We Roll Along" (traditional), "Viva la Company" (traditional), "Auld Lang Syne" (1600s; traditional), "Chicago That Toddlin' Town" (1922; Fred Fisher), "For He's a Jolly Good Fellow" (traditional). **p**, Hunt Stromberg; **d**, Victor Fleming; **cast**, Walter Huston, Lewis Stone, Dorothy Jordan, Jimmy Durante, Neil Hamilton, Myrna Loy, Emma Dunn, Robert Young, Wallace Ford, Joan Marsh, John Miljan, Clarence Muse, Clara Blandick; **w**, John L. Mahin (based on the novel by Upton Sinclair); **c**, George Barnes; **m**, William Axt; **ed**, Anne Bauchens; **art d**, Cedric Gibbons.

We've Never Been Licked ★★★ 1943; U.S.; 103m; UNIV; B/W; War Drama; Children: Unacceptable; **VHS**. Exceptional wartime propaganda film is set in the United States shortly before World War II (1939-1945). Quine is a student at Texas A&M University with sympathies for the Japanese, which make him unpopular with other students. He is expelled for allegedly stealing a secret formula for a poison gas antidote from a professor and giving it to Frawley, a spy working for the Japanese. Quine goes to Japan where he broadcasts Japanese propaganda. However, he is really a double agent and not disloyal to the U.S., and is using his work to learn Japanese war plans. He tips off U.S. military about Japan's plan to invade the Solomon Islands. Later, he boards a Japanese bomber planning to strike an American aircraft carrier where his college buddies are aviators. He manages to take control of the plane and sacrifices his life by crashing the plane onto a Japanese carrier, sinking that flagship. Songs: "The Aggie War Hymn" (J.V. "Pinky" Wilson), "The Marine's Hymn" (traditional), "Me for You, Forever" (music: Harry Revel; lyrics: Paul Francis Webster), "Silent Night" (music: Franz Gruber; lyrics: Joseph Mohr), "Spirit of Aggieland" (music: Richard J. Dunn; music: Marvin H. Mimms), "I'd Rather Be a Texas Aggie" (Jack H. Littlejohn). *Author's Note*: Quine had been a child actor, but always wanted to be behind the camera instead of in front of it. He appears here in his film debut, but later became an accomplished director, helming such hits as **Pushover**, 1954; **My Sister Eileen**, 1955; **The Solid Gold Cadillac**, 1956, and **Bell Book and Candle**, 1958. Robert Mitchum appears in a bit part as one of the Aggies, one of almost two dozen such roles he played in 1943, long before Mitchum became a Hollywood superstar. **p**, Walter Wanger; **d**, John Rawlins; **cast**, Richard Quine, Anne Gwynne, Noah Berry Jr., Martha O'Driscoll, William Frawley, Edgar Barrier, Robert Mitchum, Bill Stern, Mantan Moreland, Harry Davenport, Moroni Olsen, John James, Paul Langton, Cliff Robertson; **w**, Nick Grinde (based on the story "The Fighting Sons of Texas A&M" by Norman Reilly Raine); **c**, Milton R. Krasner; **m**, Frank Skinner; **ed**, Philip Cahn; **art d**, Alexander Golitzen, John B. Goodman; **spec eff**, John P. Fulton.

Whale Rider ★★★ 2003; New Zealand/Germany; 101m; South Pacific Pictures/Newmarket Films; Color; Drama; Children: Unacceptable (MPAA: PG-13); **DVD**. Exciting tale begins with a tribe of people on the east coast of New Zealand, who believe that their origins date back thousands of years to a single ancestor, Paikea, and who escaped death when his canoe capsized by riding to shore on the back of a whale. Thereafter, tribal chiefs considered the first-born males to be Paikea's direct descendants. Pay (Castle-Hughes), a twelve-year-old Maori girl, believes she is destined to be the new chief, but her grandfather, Paratene, is bound by tradition to pick a male leader. Though she loves him, she must oppose Paratene and a thousand years of tradition to fulfill her destiny. She rides the back of the largest whale seen in the area and almost drowns, but Paratene declares her the tribe's leader. Well made and with lively performances from the entire cast, this film was a great success at the box office, earning more than $41.5 million in its initial release against a budget of $3.5 million. Songs: "Kaikoura Dub" (Michael Hodgson, Paddy Free), "U Want Beef" (John Chong-Nee, Mark Sagapolutele, Demetrius Savelio, Daniel Maoate, David Puniani), "Voice/Percussion Loop" (Hirini Melbourne, Richard Nunns), "Just Passing Through" (Nick Theobald). *Author's Note*: Castle-Hughes was the youngest ever nominee for a Best Actress Academy Award as she was twelve years old in 2002 when she was nominated. Violence prohibits viewing by children. **p**, John Barnett, Frank Hubner, Tim Sanders, Richard Brundig; **d&w**, Niki Caro (based on the novel by Witi Ihimaera); **cast**, Keisha Castle-Hughes, Rawiri Paratene, Vicky Haughton, Cliff Curtis, Grant Roa, Mana Taumaunu, Rachel House, Taungaroa Emile, Tammy Davis, Mabel Wharekawa-Burt; **c**, Leon Narbey; **m**, Lisa Gerrard; **ed**, David Coulson; **prod d**, Grant Major; **art d**, Grace Mok; **spec eff**, Phil Addenbrook, Dean Clarke, Christel Brunn, Manfred Buttner.

The Whales of August ★★★ 1987; U.S.; 90m; Nelson Entertainment; Color; Drama; Children: Unacceptable; **DVD**; **VHS**; **IV**. Touching tale has Davis and Gish as two elderly widowed sisters, who spend a summer in a cottage on an island in Maine, recalling their troubled relationship as young women and the summers they enjoyed there over the years. Davis, blind and near death, has become bitter and cold-hearted. Gish is softer and more tolerant, nursing Davis and trying to get her to reconcile with her past. Price, an aristocratic Russian fisherman, is a sort-of suitor for Gish, who helps her remember better days, as does Sothern, a lifelong friend of the sisters. But times have changed as whales no longer pass close to the shore as they did during the two sisters' youth, and it's unlikely that true reconciliation will happen between them before it's too late. Gish thinks it may be time to sell the cottage and find a nursing home for Davis, but still clings to the hope that this will not be her sister's fate. Both Davis and Gish are wonderful in their roles as elderly women nurturing bittersweet memories in their waning years. The sensitive script is intelligent and does not pander to its poignant subject. The film did moderate box office, earning more than $1.4 million in its initial release. Song: "Roses of Picardy" (Haydn Wood, Frederick Edward Weatherly). *Author's Note*: Gish appeared in this film at the age of ninety-three, making her the oldest actress to ever play in a leading role in any feature film, which was her last, ending a seventy-five-year career in films. Gish would die six years later at the age of ninety-nine. The always competitive Davis got along well with Gish,

Lillian Gish and Bette Davis in *The Whales of August*, 1987.

but when director Anderson complimented Gish by saying: "Miss Gish, you have given me a perfect close-up," Davis responded by saying: "She should. She invented them." Davis died two years after making this film at the age of eighty-one. This was also the last film for Sothern, who died in 2001 at the age of ninety-two. Sothern told this author that "just walking onto the set to act with Lillian Gish was one of the great professional treats of my life. She was the sweetest thing wearing shoes, not an egotistical bone in her little body, and she was sharp as a tack and could recall any scene she ever played in, but what she liked to talk about most was the great director, D.W. Griffith. He was her idol when she was a teenager and he was her idol when she went to her grave." Price told this author that "I was overwhelmed by talent in that picture—up against Lillian Gish, Bette Davis and Ann Sothern—I didn't stand a chance of stealing one second in any scene." **p**, Mike Kaplan, Carolyn Pfeiffer; **d**, Lindsay Anderson; **cast**, Bette Davis, Lillian Gish, Vincent Price, Ann Sothern, Harry Carey, Jr., Frank Grimes, Margaret Ladd, Tisha Sterling, Mary Steenburgen, Frank Pitkin, Mike Bush; **w**, David Berry (based on his play); **c**, Mike Fash; **m**, Alan Price; **ed**, Nicolas Gaster; **prod d**, Jocelyn Herbert; **art d**, Bob and K.C. Fox; **set d**, Sosie Hublitz.

What About Bob? ★★★ 1991; U.S.; 99m; Touchstone/Buena Vista; Color; Comedy; Children: Unacceptable (MPAA: PG); **DVD**; **VHS**; **IV**. Entertaining comedy begins with Dreyfuss, a self-centered psychiatrist, who is eager to appear on a "Good Morning America" telecast so he can plug his new book, *Baby Steps*. That book presents his theory of how to treat emotional disorders and phobias. Murray plays "Bob," a man afraid to leave his own apartment, who becomes Dreyfuss' new patient. Murray becomes attached to Dreyfuss like a fly to flypaper, which becomes very annoying to Dreyfuss. Dreyfuss hopes to escape Murray by going away for a month's vacation at a peaceful New Hampshire lakeside cottage with his wife, Hagerty; son, Korsmo; and daughter, Erbe. Murray has other plans and forces himself to go there. Murray's needs drive Dreyfuss to the breaking point, and Dreyfuss kidnaps Murray in the woods at gunpoint and straps explosives to him, calling it "death therapy." This backfires on Dreyfuss and the cottage is blown up. Dreyfuss later regains his composure at a friend's wedding, but he is still in a psychological quandary about what he should do about Murray. Dreyfuss is exceptional as a vainglorious shrink, and Murray is a scream as his incurable patient in this very dark comedy. This film was a box office smash, earning almost $64 million in its initial release against a budget of $35 million. Songs: "Jolt" (Gerry Hurtado, Chris Abbott), "The Brady Bunch Theme" (Frank De Vol, Sherwood Schwartz), "Singin' in the Rain" (Arthur Freed, Nacio Herb Brown), "Good Morning America Theme" (Marvin Hamlisch, Richard Hazard). **p**, Laura Ziskin, Bernard

Robin Williams and Annabella Sciorra in *What Dreams May Come,* **1998.**

Williams; **d**, Frank Oz; **cast**, Bill Murray, Richard Dreyfuss, Julie Hagerty, Charlie Korsmo, Kathryn Erbe, Tom Aldredge, Susan Willis, Roger Bowen, Fran Brill, Brian Reddy, Joan Lunden; **w**, Tom Schulman (based on a story by Alvin Sargent, Ziskin); **c**, Michael Ballhaus; **m**, Miles Goodman; **ed**, Anne V. Coates; **prod d**, Leslie Dilley; **art d**, Jack Blackman; **set d**, Anne Kuljian; **spec eff**, Richard O. Helmer.

What Doesn't Kill You ★★★ 2008; U.S.; 100m; Battleplan Productions/Yari Film Group; Color; Crime Drama; Children: Unacceptable (MPAA: R); **BD**; **DVD**; **IV**. Taut heist tale opens as an armored car is robbed by three men. A policeman exchanges gunfire with one of the robbers. In a flashback, we meet two friends, Hawke and Ruffalo, who are petty thieves on the mean streets of South Boston. They join a gang of other young crooks and Hawke becomes their leader. Ruffalo drinks and is on drugs and ignores his wife, Peet, and two young sons while he hangs out with Hawke, but finds it increasingly hard to maintain his criminal lifestyle. Ruffalo decides to change and goes to Alcoholics Anonymous meetings, but Hawke doesn't want him to go straight, so he tells Ruffalo about his plan to rob an armored car. In flash-forward, we again see the armored car robbery and shooting, but we don't know who is shot and probably killed, but strongly suspect it is Ruffalo. Songs: "Funktastic Galactical Rock" and "Buzzard Luck" (Swamp Dogg as Jerry Williams), "Put a Little Nasty on It" (James Edward Alexander, Larry Charles Dodson, Jazze Pha as Anton Phalon Alexander, Anthony Michael Dortch), "Bounce, Rock, Skate, Roll" (Vaughan Mason Jr., Gregory Bufford, Jerome Bell), "Of Foreign Lands and Peoples" (Robert Schumann), "On the Road" and "Help Me Baby" (Richard Wagner), "Yeah Yeah Yeah" (Gary Cherone, Leo J. Mellace, Stephen M. Catizone). Gutter language, drug and alcohol use, violence, and brief sexuality prohibit viewing by children. *Author's Note*: This story is based upon the director's own background with the South Boston Irish Gang. **p**, Bob Yari, Rod Lurie, Marc Frydman; **d**, Brian Goodman; **cast**, Mark Ruffalo, Ethan Hawke, Amanda Peet, Will Lyman, Goodman, Donnie Wahlberg, Edward Lynch, Angela Featherstone, Mike Yebba, Brian Connolly; **w**, Goodman, Wahlberg, Paul T. Murray; **c**, Chris Norr; **m**, Alex Wurman; **ed**, Robert Hoffman; **prod d**, Henry Dunn; **set d**, Jennifer Engel; **spec eff**, Tim Jacobsen, Mitch Gates.

What Dreams May Come ★★★ 1998; U.S.; 115m; UNIV; Color; Fantasy; Children: Unacceptable (MPAA: PG-13); **BD**; **DVD**; **VHS**; **IV**. Offbeat fantasy encompasses the hereafter, heaven, hell and a strange redemption. While vacationing in Switzerland, Williams, an American physician, meets artist Sciorra. They fall in love, marry, and have two children. A few years later, the children die in a car crash, and Sciorra suffers a nervous breakdown. The couple considers divorce, but they remain together. However, on the anniversary of the day they decide not to divorce, Williams is killed in another car crash. Williams remains on Earth and tries to communicate with Sciorra to console her, but some presence says this will only cause her more pain. He gives up on that and awakens in heaven. There he meets Gooding, whom he remembers as a friend and mentor from his medical residency and who now will guide him in his new afterlife. Gooding teaches Williams how to travel to Earthlings' "dreams." Williams now sees his daughter and they share a tearful reunion. Meanwhile, Sciorra is so depressed that she commits suicide and is sent to hell. Williams is determined to rescue her and bring her to heaven with him. Gooding finds Williams a "tracker" to help him search for Sciorra's soul. Williams now realizes that Gooding is his son as the two make their journey together. They find Sciorra at her house in hell, but are warned that, if Williams stays with her for more than a few minutes, he may be permanently trapped in Hades. All he can hope for or expect is a brief visit to say farewell to her. Sciorra, suffering from amnesia, cannot remember her suicide. Despite that, Williams decides to stay with her. Hearing this intention, Sciorra regains her memory and ascends to heaven, bringing Williams with her. They are reunited with their children in heaven, and Williams then suggests reincarnation, so he and Sciorra can experience life together again. The film ends with them meeting again as young children. The film earned $74.5 million at the box office in its initial release, but did not earn back its entire budget of $85 million. Songs: "Chris & Annie's Theme" (Michael Kamen, Mark Snow as Martin Fulterman), "Hymn II from Three Sacred Songs" (Alfred Schnittke). Mature themes and suicide prohibit viewing by children. **p**, Barnet Bain, Stephen Deutsch as Stephen Simon; **d**, Vincent Ward; **cast**, Robin Williams, Cuba Gooding Jr., Annabella Sciorra, Max von Sydow, Jessica Brooks Grant, Josh Paddock, Rosalind Chao, Lucinda Jenney, Maggie McCarthy, Matt Salinger, Werner Herzog; **w**, Ron Bass (based on the novel by Richard Matheson); **c**, Eduardo Serra; **m**, Michael Kamen; **ed**, David Brenner, Maysie Hoy; **prod d**, Eugenio Zanetti; **art d**, Jim Dultz, Tomas Voth, Christian Wintter; **set d**, Cindy Carr, Josh Fifarek; **spec eff**, Roy Arbogast, Tom Sindicich, James Reedy.

What Lies Beneath ★★★ 2000; U.S.; 130m; DreamWorks; Horror; Mystery; Children: Unacceptable (MPAA: PG-13); **DVD**; **VHS**; **IV**. Strange but compelling horror tale sees Ford, a Vermont university research scientist, becoming increasingly concerned about the mental health of his wife, Pfeiffer, a retired concert cellist, who, a year earlier, was involved in a serious car accident. After sending their daughter off to college, Pfeiffer tells Ford that she hears voices and has seen some strange things going on in and around his old family house that he is having renovated. Doors and windows open and close by themselves, framed pictures fall off the walls, and the bathtub fills itself with water. The house is on the shores of a lake where she believes she sees the face of a young woman reflected in the water. She thinks the house is being haunted by the ghost of a woman her next-door neighbor murdered (not proven, but believed because the woman disappeared mysteriously). Ford urges Pfeiffer to see Baker, a psychiatrist, and she tells him she believes the house is being haunted by a ghost. Baker suggests that Pfeiffer make contact with the ghost, so she gets help from her best friend, Scarwid, and they try to figure it out with, of all things, a Ouija Board. This provides little insight into Pfeiffer's problems, and she eventually discovers that Ford is the culprit, who has created the spooky images while attempting to murder her, as he has the woman in the lake. He attempts to drown Pfeiffer, but the rotten corpse of the woman Ford killed breaks free of its moorings and allows Pfeiffer to swim to the surface while holding Ford beneath the water to drown. Eerie and haunting throughout, this stylized thriller offers standout performances from Pfeiffer and Ford. The film was a box office hit, earning more than $291.4 million in its initial release against a budget of $100 million. Songs/Music: "Too Late" (Justine Brandy, Katie Harris, Lissa Beltri, Claudia Rossi, Doug DeAngelis), "Domination" (Adam Hamilton), "Gymnopedie No. 1" (Erik Satie), "The Four Seasons: Autumn" (Antonio Vivaldi). Terror, violence, sensuality and gutter language prohibit viewing by children. **p**, Jack Rapke, Steve Starkey, Robert Zemeckis; **d**, Zemeckis; **cast**, Harrison Ford, Michelle Pfeiffer, Katharine Towne, Miranda Otto, James Remar, Victoria Bidewell, Diana Scarwid, Ray Baker, Dennison Samaroo, Jennifer Tung, Eliott Goretsky, Rachel Singer; **w**, Clark Gregg (based on a story by Gregg, Sarah Kernochan); **c**, Don Burgess; **m**, Alan Silvestri; **ed**, Arthur Schmidt; **prod d**, Rick Carter, William James Teegarden; **art d**, Stefan Dechant, Tony Fanning, Elizabeth Lapp; **set d**, Karen O'Hara; **spec eff**, Charles Belardinelli, Ron Bolanowsi, Keith Marbory.

What Price Glory ★★★★ 1926 (silent); U.S.; 116m/12 reels; FOX; B/W; War Drama; Children: Unacceptable. Pantheon director Walsh presents a rousing tale of two army buddies battling Germans and themselves in WWI (1914-1918). The film begins with McLaglen (Flagg) and Lowe (Quirt) as two Marine sergeants serving in Peking, China, and then in Shanghai, where both compete for the attentions of Haver (Shanghai Mabel). They are next battling insurgents in the Philippines as well as each other over the affections of Filipino girl Jurado, these two bruisers never hesitating to use their fists to settle matters between them. The two are finally shown in France in 1917 (as part of the 1st Marine Division). McLaglen has, by this time been promoted to the rank of captain. He arrives in a small French village to take command of a Marine company and addresses his men with tough caution, saying that he will not tolerate any of his men "running wild with these French dames, getting drunk, and fighting among yourselves." McLaglen, as well as Lowe, have routinely violated these cardinal rules. McLaglen's life soon becomes more complicated and frustrating when Lowe is assigned to his company as its top sergeant. The two immediately clash, particularly over the beautiful del Rio (the celebrated Charmaine), who is the daughter of Mong, the keeper of the inn where they are staying. Mong later comes to McLaglen to complain that Lowe has been dallying with his daughter, del Rio. Mong wants Lowe to marry his daughter, but McLaglen, who is also attracted to the French beauty, gives Mong empty promises. McLaglen and Lowe settle their battle over del Rio by playing a winner-take-all card game. McLaglen wins del Rio, but he decides not to collect his "winnings" after he sees that del Rio truly loves Lowe. The two then join their men as they go to the front and are assigned to capture a German officer, which costs the lives of several of their best men (the battle scenes, shown at night, are exceptionally choreographed and are truly frightening). McLaglen and Lowe accomplish their mission and their company is relieved, McLaglen taking a furlough while Lowe recovers from a wound. When McLaglen returns to the village, he finds Lowe waiting for him, slapping a helmet on to McLaglen's head as they have been ordered back to the front lines and they gladly go arm in arm toward that uncertain destiny. Walsh directs this fast-paced story with great energy, and his outstanding action scenes are shown with quick cross-cutting, employing overhead and tracking shots to heighten the tension of the battle sequences. McLaglen and Lowe are marvelous to behold as tenacious competitors, but their loyalty and deep friendship for each other is never in doubt. Del Rio, one of the most beautiful actresses to ever grace the screen, is captivating as the adorable Charmaine, and the supporting players are standouts in their roles, particularly Fenton, who plays a young, wounded officer and asks that pacifist question of McLaglen—what price glory? This film, like its original play, was an enormous box office success, earning more than $2 million in its initial release against a budget of $370,000, becoming one of the top box office hits for the year. The New York *Times* listed this film as one of the ten best films for 1926. Sequels: **The Cock-Eyed World**, 1929; **Women of All Nations**, 1931; and **Hot Pepper**, 1933. McLaglen and Lowe played similar characters in **Call Out the Marines**, 1942. The film saw an equally superior remake by John Ford in 1952, starring James Cagney and Dan Dailey in the Flagg-Quirt roles. McLaglen and Lowe reprised their roles in several radio adaptations that were aired by the Blue Network (September

Victor McLaglen, Dolores del Rio and Edmund Lowe in *What Price Glory*, 1926.

28, 1941, and January 25, 1942), and NBC (February 13, 1942, and April 3, 1942). Song (played in theaters when film was released): "Charmaine" (1926; music: Erno Rapee; lyrics: Lew Pollack). *Author's Note*: The Stallings-Anderson play, produced in 1924, saw Louis Wolheim as Flagg and William 'Stage' Boyd as Quirt (both would reprise their characters under different names in **Two Arabian Knights**, 1928). Where the play specifically delivered its anti-war sentiments in dialog, Walsh effectively manages to exhibit that sentiment through visuals in the film version, where he employs a minimum of title cards. Walsh also used for the first time some special effects to heighten the tension of his battle scenes, but he allowed actors McLaglen and Lowe to verbally assault each other with endless profanities, not realizing that thousands of lip readers would later easily determine the curses they were delivering, and which resulted in hundreds of written protests to Fox. Walsh spent more than two weeks shooting the nighttime battle scenes, and the blasts from explosions used for those scenes blew out windows of nearby Beverly Hills homes and did other damage. Police so routinely responded to these explosions that Walsh used up a half dozen assistants to deal with complaints. Walsh told this author: "I hired these young men to be fall guys when the cops showed up at the back lot. The cops would ask: 'Who is in charge here?' One of my assistants would say, 'I am,' and he would be immediately arrested on charges of disturbing the peace and taken to the pokey and we would bail him out the next day. That went on almost every night for about two weeks until I got what I needed for those nighttime trench warfare scenes." Fox later paid out an estimated $70,000 to cover damages to homes in the area. The director admitted that "my demolition people warned the actors not to go into certain areas on the battlefield set, but some of them ran into those areas during the night battles we staged and were injured by some of the explosions." Actor Jack Fay had been seriously injured by just such an explosion, eventually dying from the injury on November 25, 1928, at age twenty-five. Fox re-released this film in January 1927 with added synchronized sound effects and music while employing the newly developed Movietone system. The song "Charmaine," which was composed for this film, was recorded later by Guy Lombardo and his Orchestra and it became a huge hit, remaining at the top of the chart for seven weeks in 1927. It was integrated into the score for the 1952 remake and it also appears in the film **Two Girls and a Sailor**, 1944, where Harry James played the song, his record of that tune that year also topping the charts. Several other versions were recorded and the song became a perennial. **d**, Raoul Walsh; **cast**, Victor McLaglen, Edmund Lowe, Dolores del Rio, Victor V. Mong, Phyllis Haver, Elena Jurado, Leslie Fenton, Barry Norton, Sammy Cohen, J. Carrol Naish, Patrick Rooney, Jack Pennick; **w**, James T. O'Donohoe, Malcolm Stuart Boylan (titles), (based on the play by Laurence

James Cagney, Corinne Calvet and Dan Dailey in *What Price Glory,* **1952.**

Stallings, Maxwell Anderson); **c**, Barney McGill, Jack A. Marta, John Smith; **m**, Erno Rapee; **spec eff**, L.B. Abbott.

What Price Glory ★★★★ 1952; U.S.; 111m; FOX; Color; Comedy; War Drama; Children: Unacceptable; **DVD**; **VHS**. Master filmmaker Ford presents a wonderful remake of the 1926 classic, and Cagney is brilliant as the strutting Captain Flagg and Dailey a delightfully conniving Sergeant Quirt. The film opens with Cagney commanding a Marine unit stationed in a small French village, along with his two lieutenants, Hill and Adams. Cagney at this time is romancing Calvet (Charmaine), the daughter of an innkeeper, who wants to accompany Cagney on his furlough to Paris. Cagney tells her that he cannot take her along because he is married, which is a lie. Before he departs, a large number of untried new replacements arrive to be trained for upcoming battle in the front lines. Cagney also awaits the arrival of a top sergeant, who is to train these recruits, and he is infuriated when that seasoned non-commissioned officer turns out to be his old rival, Dailey. These two men have been conducting their own private war with each other over their many years in the service, from their days in China and the Philippines. They now find themselves serving together once more in 1918, the last year of WWI (1914-1918). Cagney orders Dailey to whip the recruits into disciplined soldiers before he departs for Paris in a motorcycle and sidecar driven by his long-time aide and corporal, Demarest. He also warns Dailey to stay away from Calvet, which is a red flag to Dailey, who has been forever competing with Cagney over women. Of course, in Cagney's absence, Dailey finds time to begin his own romance with the attractive Calvet as he rigorously trains the recruits. One of those recruits is youthful Wagner, who meets French school girl Pavan and the two quickly fall in love. When Cagney returns, he finds that Dailey has trained his Marines well, but is alarmed when French innkeeper Letondal comes to him with a serious complaint about Dailey, saying that Dailey must marry his daughter, Calvet, now that he has become her fiancé. Dailey denies such an engagement, but Cagney now sees a way of getting even with Dailey, who has been stealing his girlfriends over the years. He orders Dailey to marry Calvet and, in that way, preventing Dailey from poaching upon his romantic partners in the future. Though Dailey angrily protests such a shotgun marriage, Cagney orders that the wedding be scheduled as soon as possible. Meanwhile, Wagner asks Cagney for permission to marry Pavan, the lovesick private admitting to Cagney that he has only known the girl for eight days. The avuncular Cagney tells him to wait and think about taking such a serious step. Just then, Gleason, the commanding general, arrives and orders Cagney to immediately take his unit into the front lines, and he asks that Cagney, at all costs, capture a German prisoner so that information can be learned about enemy operations from that captive. Gleason promises that, if Cagney captures and sends back that prisoner, he will relieve his unit, withdrawing them from the front lines, and give Cagney a week's furlough. Dailey, too, gives Cagney an ultimatum when he refuses to marry Calvet, telling Cagney that he has only two choices as to how he treats him. He can either take him to the front with the rest of the troops or he can send him to a court-martial. Cagney elects to take Dailey with him to the front lines, where both renew their feud as they try to capture a German officer. Adams is killed and Hill, the remaining lieutenant, is wounded, becoming bitter over the useless casualties of war; he asks Cagney "what price glory now, Captain Flagg?" Hill challenges Cagney to capture his own prisoner and he sets out to do exactly that. He and Dailey manage to find and bring back to their trench line a German colonel, but the German officer is killed in a sudden enemy barrage. Dailey, who has been slightly wounded in the leg, crows to Cagney that his injury will now send him right back to the village where he can continue his romance with Calvet, but without the frills of a wedding. Thinking he has bested Cagney, Dailey leaves for the base hospital and then Wagner arrives with a German lieutenant, a prisoner that he alone has captured. Cagney congratulates Wagner, but the youthful Marine is quickly killed when another German barrage bombards the dugout. Cagney is beside himself at the wasteful killing of such youthful soldiers as Wagner, crying out: "Little boys!...Little boys!" He becomes further disillusioned after calling Gleason to tell him that his unit has captured that German prisoner, who is being sent back for interrogation. Gleason then tells Cagney that he cannot keep his word as Cagney and his men are needed at the front until replacements can be sent to relieve them. Cagney then leads an all-out attack against German positions while Dailey is seen arriving at the inn in the village to resume his wooing of Calvet. Cagney's unit is then given a brief respite and pulled from the lines. When Cagney returns to the village, he tells Calvet that he loves her and that he lied when telling her that he was married. He proposes, but Calvet is now confused, saying that she loves both Cagney and Dailey. Both men then get into a fight over her, but they decide to settle the matter with a game of cards. Cagney wins after bluffing Dailey, who flees for his life as they agreed that the winner would shoot the other. Cagney crows with triumph, but Demarest appears, telling him that he and his unit have been ordered back to the trenches. Cagney states that he has had enough of war and will not take his men back into that awful carnage, but reason gets the better of him and he reluctantly orders his men to assemble. He then tells Demarest that he has been discharged and that he has been holding his discharge papers for about a year since he so much relies upon the faithful Demarest. It matters not as Demarest refuses to be left behind and joins Cagney as the Marines begin to slowly trudge back to the front. Dailey, too, cannot shirk his duties or his deep loyalty to Cagney. Though wounded, he kisses Calvet goodbye and then joins the column of Marines, slinging a rifle onto his shoulder as he marches into the darkness with Cagney and the rest of the Marines. Ford directs this film with a firm hand, providing exciting action scenes on the well-staged battle sets while offering many comedic scenes between Cagney and Dailey, as well as strong support from the other cast members. Cagney and Dailey are entertainingly impressive as the warring pals, and supporting players Demarest, Morgan, Vernon and Gleason are also standouts in their colorful roles. Calvet is sensually attractive, and Pavan (the twin sister of actress Pier Angeli) convincingly plays a sensitive young girl falling in love for the first time with charming Wagner. The film was a box office hit, earning more than $2 million in its initial release. Songs: "Oui, Oui, Marie" (music: Fred Fisher; lyrics: Al Bryan, Joseph McCarthy), "My Love, My Life" (Jay Livingston, Ray Evans), "It's a Long Way to Tipperary" (1912; music: Jack Judge; lyrics: Henry James "Harry" Williams), "Charmaine" (1926; music: Erno Rapee; lyrics: Lew Pollack); "The Marines' Hymn" (music [1859]: Jacques Offenbach (based on his opera "Genevieve de Brabant"; lyrics [1917]: W.E. Christian, in his book, *Rhymes of the Rookies*), "The Battle Hymn of the Republic" (music [1856]: William Steffe; lyrics [1862]: Julia Ward Howe),

"Semper Fidelis" (1888; John Philip Sousa), "Over There" (1917; George M. Cohan), "Here Comes the Bride" ["Bridal Chorus"] (1850; from "Lohengrin" by Richard Wagner), "Columbia, Gem of the Ocean" ["The Red White and Blue"] (1843: Thomas a Becket Sr.), "Smiles" (1917; music: Lee S. Roberts; lyrics: J. Will Callahan), "There's a Long, Long Trail" (1913; music: Alonzo "Zo" Elliott; lyrics: Stoddard King). *Author's Note*: Though this film did not fare well with reviewers at the time of its release, it deserved a much better fate than the rough treatment it received, where Ford experimented with artificial colors to present an eerie, ethereal visual effect in some of the battle scenes. Fox producers originally thought to remake the Walsh classic (Ford had worked as an assistant to Walsh on the 1926 silent version of this story) as a musical, which so intrigued Cagney that the actor readily agreed to appear in the film. Ford, however, did not like the idea of trying to make a musical out of a rather grim war story and thought that that approach, as he told this author "would mock the many brave men who fought and died in that war. I told the front office at Fox that if they wanted to make a musical to get someone else and that I would not dance on the graves of those great Marines." Conversely, when the film went into production, Cagney was reluctant when hearing that Ford was going to shoot the film as a straight comedy-drama. "Well, I had committed myself," Cagney told this author. "So, I gave it my best. Dan [Dailey] and I had a tough time trying to outdo Vic [Victor McLaglen] and Edmund [Lowe], who had appeared in the original silent version, a real classic. Some of the cast members were old friends of mine, including Wally [Vernon], who, in his earlier days, was a terrific dancer." Cagney recalled for this author that, in one scene with veteran character actor Demarest, he almost joined Demarest in the hospital. "Bill [Demarest] had been a motorcyclist during the Great War [WWI], so when I had to do a scene with him where he drives that cycle and I am sitting it its sidecar, I did not have any concerns about his driving abilities. Pappy [Ford] warned me not to do that scene, saying that I should just walk up the road as he did not trust motorcycles. When I insisted on doing that scene, Pappy said: 'All right, go ahead, but *I* wouldn't do it.' Well, we roared away up the street and they got the scene, but then the damned cycle wouldn't stop—they later found out that the breaking pads were worn out—and Bill crashed the cycle. He broke both legs and a nearby electrician got injured, too. Both went to the hospital. I was lucky. I got only a few scratches. So when I limped back to see Pappy, there he was standing with his hands on his hips and chewing on his pipe. 'I told you so,' he said." Ford had directed a stage version of this story in 1949 with John Wayne, and he wanted Wayne as the leading player in his film version, but Wayne was not then available. Most of the dialog in the original play by Stallings and Anderson was discarded when scriptwriters Henry and Phoebe Ephron (parents of comedian and author Nora Ephron) wrote the screenplay. The Ephron couple overheard Ford telling some jokes to some friends off the set that they interpreted as being Anti-Semitic (which Ford always denied) and they refused to return to the production thereafter. This is Pavan's film debut. Other films depicting U.S. Marines include **Air Devils**, 1938; **Air Force**, 1943 (Marines at Wake Island); **All the Young Men**, 1960 (Korean War); **Ambush Bay**, 1966 (WWII; Philippines); **American Beauty**, 1999; **American Sniper**, 2014 (Iraq); **American Son**, 2008; **Annapolis**, 2006; **Atlanta Convoy**, 1942; **Battle Cry**, 1955 (WWII; Guadalcanal; Tarawa); **Battle of Los Angeles**, 2011; **Beach Red**, 1967; **Beachhead**, 1954 (WWII; Bougainville); **Black Hawk Down**, 2001 (Somalia, 1993); **Born on the Fourth of July**, 1989; **The Boys in Company C**, 1978; **The Brig**, 1964; **Busses Roar**, 1942; **Call Out the Marines**, 1942; **Charo and the Sergeant**, 1976 (made-for-TV); **The Cock-Eyed World**, 1929; **Come On, Leathernecks!**, 1938; **Come On, Marines!**, 1934; **Company K**, 2004; **Coronado**, 1935; **Corregidor**, 1943 (WWII; Philippine Defense, 1941-1942); **Cover-Up**, 1991; **Crazylegs**, 1953 (Elroy Hirsch); **Cuban Love Song**, 1931; **The D.I.**, 1957; **Death before Dishonor**, 1987; **Devil Dogs of the Air**, 1935; **Dog Tags**, 2008; **Down in San Diego**, 1941; **A Few Good Men**, 1992; **55 Days at Peking**, 1963 (China; Boxer Rebel-

James Cagney, Corinne Calvet and Dan Dailey in *What Price Glory*, 1952.

lion, 1900); **Fighting Coastguard**, 1951; **The Fighting Devil Dogs**, 1938; **The Fighting Devil Dogs**, 1943; **The Fighting Marines**, 1935; **First to Fight**, 1967 (WWII; Guadalcanal); **Flags of Our Fathers**, 2006 (WWII; Iwo Jima); **Flight**, 1929; **Flying Leathernecks**, 1951 (WWII; Guadalcanal); **The Flying Marine**, 1929; **Full Metal Jacket**, 1987 (Vietnam); **Fury to Freedom**, 1985 (Vietnam; Raul; Ries); **The Girls of Pleasure Island**, 1953 (Pacific island where Marines are building an air base in 1945); **Good Morning, Vietnam**, 1987; **Green Dragon**, 2001; **Guadalcanal Diary**, 1943; **Gung Ho!**, 1943 (Carlson's Makin Island Raid); **A Guy, a Gal and a Pal**, 1945; **Hail the Conquering Hero**, 1944; **Halls of Montezuma**, 1950 (WWII; Okinawa); **Heartbreak Ridge**, 1986; **Heaven Knows, Mr. Allison**, 1957 (WWII; Pacific island); **Hell to Eternity**, 1960 (WWII; Saipan; Guy Gabaldon); **Here Come the Marines**, 1952; **Highway Dragnet**, 1954; **Hot Pepper**, 1933; **Ice Station Zebra**, 1968; **If I Had a Million**, 1932; **In Harm's Way**, 1965; **Instant Justice**, 1986; **The Iron Major**, 1943; **Island of Desire**, 1952; **Isle of Destiny**, 1940; **Jarhead**, 2005; **Johnny Doesn't Live Here Anymore**, 1944; **Lady Be Careful**, 1936; **The Last Castle**, 2001; **A Line in the Sand**, 2009; **Loot**, 1919; **Lost Battalion**, 1962 (WWII; Philippines); **Maisie Goes to Reno**, 1944; **Major Payne**, 1995; **The Marine**, 2006; **Marine Raiders**, 1944 (WWII; Guadalcanal, 1942; Solomon Islands, 1943); **A Marine Story**, 2010; **The Marines Are Coming**, 1934; **The Marines Are Here**, 1938; **The Marines Fly High**, 1940; **Marines, Let's Go**, 1961; **Max**, 2015 (Afghanistan); **Memorial Day**, 1983 (made-for-TV); **Miss Sadie Thompson**, 1953; **Most Wanted**, 1997; **1941**, 1979; **None But the Brave**, 1965; **Operation C.I.A.**, 1965; **The Outsider**, 1961 (WWII; Iwo Jima; Ira Hamilton Hays); **The Pacific**, 2010 (TV cable series; John Basilone at Guadalcanal and Iwo Jima); **Pacific Rendezvous**, 1942; **Parachute Jumper**, 1933; **Pride of the Marines**, 1945 (WWII; Al Schmid at Guadalcanal); **The Profiteer**, 1919; **Rain**, 1932; **Red Dawn**, 2012; **Retreat, Hell!**, 1952 (Korean War); **Rosie the Riveter**, 1944; **Rules of Engagement**, 2000; **Sadie Thompson**, 1928; **Safe Passage**, 1994; **Salute to the Marines**, 1943 (WWII; Philippine Defense, 1941-1942); **Sands of Iwo Jima**, 1949 (WWII; Tarawa and Iwo Jima); **Sarge Goes to College**, 1947; **Semper Fi**, 2001 (made-for-TV); **Seven Days in May**, 1964; **The Siege of Firebase Gloria**, 1989 (Vietnam); **The Singing Marine**, 1937; **Slave Girl**, 1947; **Snafu**, 1945; **Sniper**, 1993; **Sniper: Reloaded**, 2011; **The Soldier**, 1982; **Soldiers and Women**, 1930; **South Sea Woman**, 1953 (WWII; Guadalcanal); **Stateside**, 2004; **The Steel Claw**, 1961 (WWII; Philippines); **Step by Step**, 1946; **The Story without a Name**, 1924; **Strangers in the Night**, 1944; **Sweethearts on Parade**, 1930; **Taking Chance**, 2009 (made-for-TV; Michael Strobl); **Tell It to the Marines**, 1918; **Tell It to the Marines**, 1926; **The Thin Red Line**, 1964 (WWII; Guadalcanal); **The Thin Red Line**, 1998 (WWII; Guadal-

William Demarest and James Cagney in *What Price Glory,* 1952.

canal); **Thunderbolt's Tracks**, 1927; **To the Shores of Tripoli**, 1942; **Tribes**, 1970 (made-for-TV); **Tripoli**, 1950; **True to the Navy**, 1930; **United States Smith**, 1928; **The Walking Dead**, 1995 (Vietnam); **Wake Island**, 1942 (WWII); **War Dogs**, 1942; **The War of the Worlds**, 1953; **A Warm Wind**, 2011; **Warrior**, 2011; **A Wave, a WAC and a Marine**, 1944; **We've Never Been Licked**, 1943; **What Price Glory**, 1926 (WWI; France); **When the Lights Go On Again**, 1944; **The Wind and the Lion**, 1975 (1904 Morocco; Perdicaris Affair); **Windtalkers**, 2002 (WWII; Saipan); **Women of All Nations**, 1931; and **Yellow Jack**, 1938. **p**, Sol C. Siegel; **d**, John Ford; **cast**, James Cagney, Corinne Calvet, Dan Dailey, William Demarest, Craig Hill, Robert Wagner, Marisa Pavan, Casey Adams (Max Showalter), James Gleason, Wally Vernon, Harry Morgan, Luis Alberni, Henri Letondal, Paul Fix, Tom Tyler, William Henry, Sean McClory; **w**, Henry and Phoebe Ephron (based on the play by Maxwell Anderson, Laurence Stallings); **c**, Joe MacDonald; **m**, Alfred Newman; **ed**, Dorothy Spencer; **art d**, Lyle Wheeler, George W. Davis; **set d**, Thomas Little, Stuart Reiss; **spec eff**, Ray Kellogg.

What Price Hollywood? ★★★★★ 1932; U.S.; 88m; RKO; B/W; Drama; Children: Unacceptable; **DVD**; **VHS**; **IV**. Pantheon director Cukor made his first superlative film with this critical profile of Hollywood in its halcyon heydays of the early 1930s. Up to the time of this film, Tinsel Town had mostly been profiled as a pristine palace housing illustrious Mount Olympus type personalities. Cukor strips away all of its gossamer illusions, laying bare that community's corrupting and debilitating influences, ending the career of one stellar denizen via alcoholism and suicide while his protégé goes on to become a luminous superstar. The film opens at Hollywood's famous eatery, the Brown Derby, peopled by movie moguls, arrogant directors and posturing stars. Working the tables of this celebrated restaurant is waitress Bennett, a fetching, savvy blonde, who has ambitions to join the illustrious clientele she serves. She spots Sherman, a famous director, entering the restaurant and taking a table. Bennett persuades the waitress serving that table to switch positions with her so that Bennett can wait on Sherman and she quickly dazzles him with her insouciant patter and palaver. Sherman is in his cups, but he nevertheless takes a liking to the personable Bennett and invites her to accompany him to a movie premiere at Grauman's Chinese Theater. Thrilled at this opportunity, Bennett goes home and dresses to the nines, but is surprised when the capricious and still inebriated Sherman arrives to pick her up in a broken-down heap of a car instead of the traditional limousine. When they arrive at the premiere, Sherman tips the parking valet by telling him to keep the jalopy. This extravagant gesture is typical of Sherman's lifestyle, which he has earlier summed up for Bennett when telling her: "Remember our

motto—'It's all in fun.' Always keep your sense of humor and you can't miss!" The eccentric director introduces Bennett to Ratoff, one of Hollywood's foremost producers. Sherman then takes Bennett to his lavish mansion that night (he sleeps in his bedroom alone, she on a couch), and he remembers nothing when he awakes. Bennett, however, reminds him that he promised to give her a screen test. Bennett likes her new friend, but she expresses her concern about Sherman's heavy drinking, sarcastic perspectives, and, despite the servants and slavish aides who surround him, a lifestyle that is decidedly solitary. Sherman ignores her stated concerns and then arranges for her to have a screen test where she comes down a long flight of stairs to talk to a suitor. Bennett's bubbly and blurted line only convinces Sherman that Bennett, beautiful though she might be, has little or no talent for the screen. Before Sherman walks off the set, Bennett pleads with him for another chance and he reschedules the test for the next day. That night, Bennett practices her brief scene, taking her time in delivering her line and speaking it slowly so that she is not only clearly heard, but that there is hidden implications in her words. She makes the test with Sherman the next day and then goes to a screening room to wait and see the response from Ratoff. After seeing the test, the producer thinks Bennett has great potential and signs her to a long-term contract, telling her that, in a few years, she will be a rich and famous Hollywood star. All of this palaver is no news to Sherman, who, though suffering a hangover while slouching in his chair in the screening room, has recognized Bennett's hidden talents in her second test. We see in montages how Bennett appears in one film after another, becoming an enormous success and a foremost Hollywood actress. Sherman, who directs her films, however, refuses to develop a romance with Bennett, who is in love with him. Sherman is convinced that his long career in movies is on the decline and he does not want to have a relationship with Bennett in order not to sully her meteoric career with his failing image. When attending a polo match, Bennett catches the eye of handsome playboy and polo player Hamilton, who quickly falls in love with her. To protect her career, Sherman and Ratoff warn Bennett against establishing a relationship with the wealthy Hamilton, but the playboy amuses her and she encourages him. Hamilton then invites Bennett to a formal dinner he has arranged at his mansion, replete with full orchestra, but she fails to appear. (Director Billy Wilder would copy this very scene when making his classic film **Sunset Boulevard**, 1950, where he profiled an aging Hollywood star of the silent period, who persuades a young scriptwriter into becoming her gigolo.) Incensed at being rebuffed, Hamilton angrily goes to Bennett's residence and yanks her from her bed, bundling her up and taking her to his home where servants then present her with a lavish dinner. She eventually agrees to marry Hamilton, but, as Sherman and Ratoff have earlier predicted, the union is in trouble from the start after Hamilton is compelled to wait endless hours for Bennett to finish her work at the film studio. Worse, Hamilton becomes angered about the racy articles published about his wife in Hollywood fan magazines. When a magazine writer contacts him and tells Hamilton that he wants to write an article about him and wife Bennett titled "Great Lovers of Today," the irate husband explodes at what he considers to be a blatant invasion of his private life. Feeling used for Bennett's publicity purposes, Hamilton leaves Bennett, a separation that causes her anguish. Sherman offers little comfort, more or less telling his protégé that he warned her from the beginning how dangerous a movie career would be, cynically stating: "I made you what you are today. I hope you're satisfied." Hamilton and Bennett divorce and then Bennett discovers that she is pregnant. Her disillusionment with Hollywood life and the shambles of her own life are then lifted when she wins an Oscar as Best Actress in a screen performance. She is now at the top of the Hollywood heap, but Sherman has, by this time, become an incurable alcoholic. His degradation and disgrace is accented when Bennett must bail him out from jail after he has been arrested for drunk driving. She takes Sherman to her lavish home where she encourages him to rehabilitate himself. The once celebrated director, however, is resigned to his self-ruination, saying: "I'm washed up. It's all gone." He looks into a mirror to see a dissolute drunk standing before him and then compares that repulsive image with a photograph of himself in his happier, sober days, a grim visual comparison that convinces Sherman that his life is at an end. He finds a gun inside of a drawer and decides without remorse or concern for anyone that he should finish himself and perfunctorily fires a bullet into his chest, killing himself. Sherman's suicide in Bennett's home causes a widespread scandal, and reporters, hungry for any sensational tale, descend like hawks upon Bennett. After one reporter asks Bennett if she is going to be able to keep custody of her young son because of the scandal now surrounding her, the actress panics and flees to France with the boy. Hamilton learns where Bennett and the boy are living and visits them. He begs forgiveness from Bennett for deserting her and asks that she give him another chance to restore their marriage and make a better life for them and their child. The compassionate Bennett embraces him and accepts his offer and promise that happiness awaits them in the future. Cukor directs this tale in whirlwind fashion, moving its characters and events along at a racetrack pace, and Bennett is superb in her role, convincingly transitioning from ingénue to superstar. She would later state that she thought her role in this film was the best performance of her long Hollywood career. Hamilton is impressively empathetic as the loving husband, but Sherman steals the film with his riveting portrayal of a jaded film director almost routinely accepting his spiraling downward fate, as if eager to leap into an all-destructive whirlpool. Cukor employs many innovative visual techniques to emphasize the story line's most dramatic elements, particularly toward the end when the dimming fates of its characters are seen by Cukor through a glass darkly. Sherman's suicide, for instance, is viewed through many strange camera angles, all shown in a montage of alarmingly distorted, quick cuts to visually compare Sherman's tranquil handsome past to his traumatic ugly present (a portrait of Dorian Gray in reverse), and the unthinking savagery of a gunshot abruptly overwhelms peaceful reasoning or any love of life. The film received an Oscar nomination for Best Story (St. Johns), but it was, however, not a box office success, earning almost $600,000 in its initial release against a budget of more than $400,000. The film was successfully remade by Selznick as **A Star Is Born**, 1937, starring Janet Gaynor and Fredric March and directed by William Wellman. It was again remade in 1954, also as **A Star Is Born**, starring Judy Garland and James Mason, and Cukor again directed the story. The tale was yet remade once more in 1976, but with disappointing results. Songs: "Three Little Words" (1930; music: Harry Ruby; lyrics: Bert Kalmar), "The Wedding of the Painted Dolls" (1929; Nacio Herb Brown), "Louise" (1929; music: Richard A. Whiting; lyrics: Leo Robin), "Happy Days Are Here Again" (1929; music: Milton Ager; lyrics: Jack Yellen), "The Wedding March" (1843; from "A Midsummer Night's Dream," Op. 61 by Felix Mendelssohn-Bartholdy), "Parlez-moi d'amour" (1930; Jean Lenoir), "All of Me" (1931; Gerald Marks, Seymour Simons). *Author's Note*: Producer Selznick had long been interested in making a film that candidly portrayed the filmmaking industry and, to that end, he contacted top scriptwriter Adela Rogers St. Johns, telling her: "It's time we made a really good picture about Hollywood, so why don't you go ahead and find us a story?" St. Johns put together a story that was based upon actress Colleen Moore and her husband, John McCormick, who was an alcoholic producer. She enriched her tempestuous tale by including Sherman's character, based upon the tragic, brief life of film actor and director Tom Forman (1893-1926), who directed some significant films before being reduced to directing potboilers for poverty-row production companies and, in despair over his failing career and while suffering a nervous breakdown, committed suicide by shooting himself in the heart on November 7, 1926. Sherman admitted that he "borrowed" a lot of his mannerisms and eccentricities for his character from his then brother-in-law and famous actor John Barrymore. Selznick originally wanted silent screen siren Clara Bow to play the heroine in this film, but Bow was by then overweight, as well as an alcoholic, and was in no shape to undertake the acting assignment. The role then went to Bennett.

Constance Bennett tested for stardom by Lowell Sherman in *What Price Hollywood?*, 1932.

The startling montage of Sherman, which grimly ends when Sherman falls dead in slow motion to the floor, was actually constructed by Hollywood montage and special effects expert Slavko Vorkapich, who had arrived in Hollywood in 1922 from Austria. He produced with experimental director Robert Florey an amazing eleven-minute short in 1928 titled **The Life and Death of 9413, a Hollywood Extra**, which excoriated Hollywood for dehumanizing those appearing before its cameras. The hero of that short film arrives in Tinsel Town with the hopes of becoming a star, just like Bennett in this film, and finds only work as an extra where he is identified only as a number, 9413, which is written on his forehead, and which he must wear until he dies and goes to heaven where that stigmatizing number is finally removed. Screenwriter Ben Hecht (who was this author's mentor of sorts) told this author that "Slavko [Vorkapich] is an amazing guy I met back in the late 1920s when I first arrived in Hollywood. He produced montages for several pictures that captioned the most eye-popping images, especially visuals that most disturbed the human psyche. After I saw what he did for George [Cukor] in **What Price Hollywood?**, I later asked him to put together a montage for a picture I produced and directed called **Crime without Passion** [1934] and he put together almost overnight a series of wraiths sailing through the corridors of skyscrapers in New York, which I labeled 'the Furies' to indicate how these vengeance-seeking spirits haunted Manhattan's canyons to bring about death and destruction of the high and mighty". Cukor told this author that "David [Selznick] approached me a few years after we made **What Price Hollywood?**, and asked me to direct a picture almost identical to that story, and I refused, telling him that RKO would most likely sue him if he lifted that story for another production. Well, he went out and got Bill Wellman to direct that picture and, sure enough, RKO called him to tell him that they were going to sue him for plagiarism after he released **A Star Is Born** [1937]. RKO, however, backed down, and never went on with a legal case. Irony overtook us all when, many years later, I wound up directing the great Judy Garland in the remake of **A Star Is Born** [1954]. In Hollywood what goes around comes around again and again, as long as the audiences keep filling up the theaters." Other films about filmmakers and filmmaking include **Adaptation**, 2002; **After the Fox**, 1966; **All That Jazz**, 1979; **Analyze That**, 2002; **Anchors Aweigh**, 1945; **Annie Hall**, 1977; **The Anniversary Party**, 2001; **Ararat**, 2002; **The Aviator**, 2004; **The Bad and the Beautiful**, 1952; **The Bank Dick**, 1940; **The Barefoot Contessa**, 1954; **Barton Fink**, 1991; **Beloved Infidel**, 1959; **Beyond the Sea**, 2004; **The Big Knife**, 1955; **The Black Camel**, 1931; **Blazing Saddles**, 1974; **Bolt**, 2008; **Bombshell**, 1933; **Boy Meets Girl**, 1938; **Bugsy**, 1991; **The Buster Keaton Story**, 1957; **Callaway Went Thataway**, 1951; **The Cameraman**, 1928; **The Carpetbaggers**, 1964; **Caught in the Draft**, 1941;

Helen Hunt and Mel Gibson in *What Women Want*, 2000.

Celebrity, 1998; **Chaplin**, 1992; **Cinema Paradiso**, 1988; **The Cotton Club**, 1984; **The Country Girl**, 1954; **Crimes and Misdemeanors**, 1989; **Dancing in the Dark**, 1949; **Day for Night**, 1973; **The Day of the Locust**, 1975; **De-Lovely**, 2004; **Ed Wood**, 1994; **8½**, 1963; **The Extra Girl**, 1923; **Follow the Boys**, 1944; **Footlight Parade**, 1933; **Frances**, 1982; **Free and Easy**, 1930; **The French Lieutenant's Woman**, 1981; **Gable and Lombard**, 1976; **Get Shorty**, 1995; **The Godfather**, 1972; **Going Hollywood**, 1933; **Good Morning, Babylon**, 1987; **The Great Waldo Pepper**, 1975; **Harlow**, 1965 (with Carroll Baker); **Harlow**, 1965 (with Carole Lynley); **Hearts of the West**, 1975; **The Helen Morgan Story**, 1957; **Henry Aldrich Gets Glamour**, 1942; **Hitchcock**, 2012; **Hold Back the Dawn**, 1941; **Holiday Inn**, 1942; **Hollywood Boulevard**, 1976; **Hollywood Canteen**, 1944; **Hollywood Cavalcade**, 1939; **Hollywood Hotel**, 1937; **Hollywood Shuffle**, 1987; **Hollywood Story**, 1951; **Hollywoodland**, 2006; **Hugo**, 2011; **I Wake Up Screaming**, 1941; **In a Lonely Place**, 1950; **Incendiary Blonde**, 1945; **It's a Great Feeling**, 1949; **Jeanne Eagels**, 1957; **Jolson Sings Again**, 1949; **The Jolson Story**, 1946; **King Kong**, 1933; **L.A. Confidential**, 1997; **La Dolce Vita**, 1961; **Lady Killer**, 1933; **The Last Command**, 1928; **The Last Movie**, 1971; **The Last Tycoon**, 1976; **Leaving Las Vegas**, 1995; **The Legend of Lylah Clare**, 1968; **Lost in Translation**, 2003; **The Lost Squadron**, 1932; **Love Me or Leave Me**, 1955; **The Loved One**, 1965; **Mad about Music**, 1938; **The Magic Box**, 1952; **Man of a Thousand Faces**, 1957; **Man on the Moon**, 1999; **Merton of the Movies**, 1947; **Midnight in Paris**, 2011; **The Miracle of the Bells**, 1948; **Miss Tatlock's Millions**, 1948; **Mrs. Parker and the Vicious Circle**, 1994; **Mommie Dearest**, 1981; **Moon over Parador**, 1988; **Movie Crazy**, 1932; **My Favorite Year**, 1982; **Mulholland Dr.**, 2011; **My Week with Marilyn**, 2011; **Nickelodeon**, 1976; **Nine**, 2009; **One of the Hollywood Ten**, 2000; **The Oscar**, 1966; **Paramount on Parade**, 1930; **The Perils of Pauline**, 1947; **The Player**, 1992; **Postcards from the Edge**, 1990; **The Purple Rose of Cairo**, 1985; **Ragtime**, 1981; **Second Fiddle**, 1939; **Shadow of the Vampire**, 2000; **Show People**, 1928; **Silent Movie**, 1976; **Singin' in the Rain**, 1952; **Sitting Pretty**, 1933; **Something to Sing About**, 1937; **Souls for Sale**, 1923; **Stand-In**, 1937; **A Star Is Born**, 1937; **A Star Is Born**, 1954; **Star Spangled Rhythm**, 1942; **Stardust Memories**, 1980; **Starlift**, 1951; **The Stuntman**, 1980; **Sullivan's Travels**, 1941; **Sunset**, 1988; **Sunset Boulevard**, 1950; **Thank Your Lucky Stars**, 1943; **Two Weeks in Another Town**, 1962; **Valentino**, 1951; **Valentino**, 1977; **W.C. Fields and Me**, 1976; **Wag the Dog**, 1997; **The Way We Were**, 1973; **Whatever Happened to Baby Jane?**, 1962; **White Hunter, Black Heart**, 1990; **Who Framed Roger Rabbit**, 1988; **Won Ton Ton: The Dog Who Saved Hollywood**, 1976; and **The World's Greatest Lover**, 1977. **p**, David O. Selznick; **d**, George Cukor; **cast**, Constance

Bennett, Lowell Sherman, Neil Hamilton, Gregory Ratoff, Brooks Benedict, Louise Beavers, Eddie "Rochester" Anderson, King Baggot, Sam Armstrong, Zeena Baer; **w**, Jane Murfin, Ben Markson, Allen Rivkin, Gene Fowler, Rowland Brown, Robert Presnell, Sr. (based on a story by Adela Rogers St. Johns, Louis Stevens); **c**, Charles Rosher; **m**, Max Steiner; **ed**, Del Andrews, Jack Kitchin; **art d**, Carroll Clark; **spec eff**, Lloyd Knechtel, Sklavo Vorkapich.

What Women Want ★★★ 2000; U.S.; 127m; PAR; Color; Comedy; Romance; Children: Unacceptable (MPAA: PG-13); **BD**; **DVD**; **IV**. Entertaining comedy with a touch of fantasy makes this tale come alive after Gibson, a hot shot advertising executive, is in an accident that enables him to hear what women think. He wants to rid himself of what he considers to be a curse, but a psychologist tells him he can work it to his advantage. Gibson eavesdrops on women's thoughts at the office and uses their ideas as his own. Then he tries his new thing on Hunt, the woman who got the promotion he wanted. He takes her ideas for a new advertising campaign as his own, but then regrets it because she is then fired. Then, as love's arrow strikes them both during a storm, Gibson loses his power to know what women want. He explains everything to Hunt and she forgives him. She gets her job back, but Gibson is fired. No matter, he'll get another job, and they will get married. He knew she wanted him all along. Songs: "Something's Gotta Give" (Johnny Mercer), "Bitch" (Meredith Brooks, Shelly Peiken), "The Best Is Yet to Come" (Cy Coleman, Carolyn Leigh), "I See You Baby" (Andrew Cato, Tom Findlay, Tod Wooten), "Mack the Knife" (Kurt Weill, Bertolt Brecht, Marc Blitzstein), "Nobody But Me" (Billy Myles), "Until We Meet Again" (Joe Lervold), "We Think It's Love" (Leah Haywood, Jorgen Eloffson), "Work Me to the Bone" (Stephen Edwards), "Yay Boy" (Pape Serigne Seck), "I Won't Dance" (Oscar Hammerstein II, Otto A. Harbach, Dorothy Fields, Jimmy McHugh, Jerome Kern), "My Pander Bear" (Mark Isham), "Night and Day" and "I've Got You Under my Skin" (Cole Porter), 'Steel Drum Cruise" (D. Overberger), "C'est la vie" (Tracy Ackerman, Raymond Hedges, Martin Brannigan, Sinead O'Carroll, Edele Lynch, Keavy Lynch, Lindsay Armaou), "It's All Your Fault" (Robbie Nevil, Joey Schwartz), "What a Girl Wants" (Guy Roche, Shelly Peiken), "Cake" (Matty Selman), "I've Got the World on a String" (Harold Arlen, Ted Koehler), "If I Had You" (Jimmy Campbell, Reg Connelly, Ted Shapiro), "Too Marvelous for Words" (Johnny Mercer, Richard A. Whiting). Sexual content and gutter language prohibit viewing by children. **p**, Nancy Meyers, Susan Cartsonis, Bruce Davey, Gina Matthews, Matt Williams, Bruce A. Block; **d**, Meyers; **cast**, Mel Gibson, Helen Hunt, Marisa Tomei, Alan Alda, Ashley Johnson, Mark Feuerstein, Lauren Holly, Delta Burke, Valerie Perrine, Judy Greer, Sarah Paulson; **w**, Josh Goldsmith, Cathy Yuspa (based on a story by Goldsmith, Yuspa, Diane Drake); **c**, Dean Cundey; **m**, Alan Silvestri; **ed**, Thomas J. Nordberg, Stephen A. Rotter; **prod d**, Jon Hutman; **art d**, Gae Buckley, Tony Fanning; **set d**, Rosemary Brandenburg; **spec eff**, Kenneth Van Order, Tim Cunningham, Kenneth Jones.

What Ever Happened to Aunt Alice? ★★★ 1969; U.S.; 101m; Palomar/Cinerama; Color; Comedy/Horror; Children: Unacceptable (MPAA: M); **DVD**; **VHS**. Offbeat comedic horror story begins with Page, a widow, who learns that her late husband, supposedly wealthy, left her penniless, bequeathing her only a stamp collection. She concocts a deadly scheme to live comfortably by moving to the Arizona desert near Tucson where she hires elderly housekeepers with no known relatives but substantial life savings, then kills them one by one. She takes what money they have and their remains become mulch for her garden. Elderly Gordon, as Aunt Alice, becomes her latest housekeeper in order to learn what happened to her missing widowed friend, Dunnock, who had been Page's last housekeeper. Gordon's nephew helps her sleuth and falls in love with Forsyth, a young widow living next door to Page. Page eventually murders Gordon, and then Fuller reveals that she is a serial killer. It is later learned that Page need not have turned to murder for a living, since the stamp collection her husband left her is valued at more than $100,000. A clever ending to a fine dark comedy sees stand-out performances from veteran actresses Page and Gordon, with strong support from a fine cast. **p**, Robert Aldrich; **d**, Lee H. Katzin, Bernard Girard; **cast**, Geraldine Page, Ruth Gordon, Rosemary Forsyth, Robert Fuller, Mildred Dunnock, Joan Huntington, Peter Brandon, Michael Barbera, Peter Bonerz, Richard Angarola; **w**, Theodore Apstein (based on the novel *The Forbidden Garden* by Ursula Curtis); **c**, Joseph F. Biroc (Metrocolor); **m**, Gerald Fried; **ed**, Frank J. Urioste; **art d**, William Glasgow; **set d**, John Brown.

What Ever Happened to Baby Jane? ★★★★ 1962; U.S.; 132m; Seven Arts/WB; B/W; Horror; Children: Unacceptable; **BD**; **DVD**; **VHS**; **IV**. Davis and Crawford are superb in this contest of mentally disturbed wills that produced a gothic horror tale involving sibling sav-age revenge, remorseful retribution and sanity-testing survival. Both are elderly sisters and former actresses, their stage and Hollywood heydays long gone; they reside in a decrepit mansion in Los Angeles' Hancock Park. In flashback to 1917 we see Davis as a childhood star in vaudeville known as Baby Jane, who moves on to silent films and is the rage. Her career, however, slowly wanes and she takes to drink while Crawford becomes a superstar on the screen. By 1935, Davis is only working in small roles that Crawford arranges for her, which causes Davis to harbor deep and abiding resentment. Both are leaving a party when they are in-volved in a terrible accident, and Crawford is permanently crippled, un-able to walk and later confined in a wheelchair. She is later unable to move from her bed and is now, in the present time (1962), wholly de-pendent upon her sister, Davis. Crawford receives more attention and empathy from Norman, her cleaning lady, than she does from her sister and befriends Norman, who realizes the hostility Davis increasingly shows to Crawford. When Norman suggests as a warning that Davis is becoming mentally unstable, Crawford instinctively and protectively defends Davis, but she knows that Norman is right. When Crawford be-comes convinced that Davis demonstrates manifestations of delusions and mental illness, she decides that she will sell the mansion and place Davis in a sanitarium. Learning of this, Davis disconnects the phone in Crawford's room, cutting her off from the outside world, and then vi-ciously kills Crawford's pet parakeet. As Davis sinks into a deranged mental state, she serves that parakeet and even a dead rat on an elegant covered silver serving dish to Davis as meals, which convinces Craw-ford that she is now dealing with an uncontrollable psychopath. Craw-ford, now desperate, writes a note to her neighbor, Lee, pleading for help and throwing the note from her bedroom window. Davis, however, finds the note when returning home and confronts and taunts the helpless Crawford with all of her old grudges against her over Crawford's imag-ined treatment of her as a second-hand sister. Davis sends cleaning woman Norman away and then decides that she will return to the stage as a singer and places an ad in a theatrical publication for a piano ac-companist. Buono, an overweight mother-dominated bachelor, replies to the ad. Davis hires him, and the two prepare Davis' comeback act where she grotesquely costumes herself with her old childhood attire to replay her child act that had been popular decades earlier. She patheti-cally croaks out "I've Written a Letter to Daddy" as Buono dutifully ac-companies that song on the piano. After Davis drives Buono home, Crawford manages to leave her room and searches for food, discovering a number of checks that Davis has forged in her name to accumulate cash. Using the downstairs phone, Crawford calls the family doctor, begging him to immediately come to her home, but Davis finds Craw-ford having this conversation and hangs up the phone before beating Crawford into unconsciousness. She then calls the doctor back and, im-itating Crawford's voice (which was actually Crawford's voiceover), tells the physician not to pay any visits to her house. Davis then drags Crawford back to her bedroom where she ties her up and sadistically taunts the now terrorized, starving woman. The next day, Norman ar-rives and finds Crawford. As she is attempting to free the captive, Davis

Bette Davis and Joan Crawford on the set and laughing over the outlandish script for *What Ever Happened to Baby Jane?*, 1962.

appears and kills Norman. Buono then arrives, and when he hears Craw-ford screaming for help, he goes upstairs to see, to his horror, Crawford struggling to free herself. Terrified, the weak-willed and easily cowed Buono runs from the house. When Davis sees Buono fleeing, she be-lieves he is going to notify the police, so she bundles the helpless Craw-ford into the family car and drives to Malibu Beach, thinking to bury Crawford beneath its sands. Meanwhile, police investigate the mansion to find Norman's body and then begin a search for Davis and Crawford. While on the beach, Crawford admits to Davis that she had arranged that accident in 1935 in an attempt to run over Davis, but crashed the car and brought about her own paralysis and that Davis was then totally unaware of Crawford's insidious plot as she was then too drunk to know anything. Crawford's confession sparks a commiserating response from Davis, who meditatively states: "All this time we could have been friends." Police then find the sisters on the beach, and the viewer is left to wonder if Crawford is by then still alive. When officers approach, Davis, now totally unhinged, begins a hideous performance of her little girl act, as she mentally regresses to that forgotten age to end this eerie and truly frightening tale. Aldrich directs this horror story at a relentless pace, he holds back nothing repulsive or disgusting in order to reveal-ingly peel back the layers of lies, deceits and hidden secrets shared by the sisters. Davis and Crawford are at their very inventive bests in pre-senting chilling performances. These two consummate scene stealers are wonderful to watch as they vie with each other for every on-screen second as they sink ever lower into monstrous depravity. The film re-ceived an Oscar for Best Costume Design, Black and White (Norma Koch), and received Oscar nominations for Best Actress (Davis); Best Supporting Actor (Buono); Best Cinematography, Black and White (Haller); and Best Sound (Joseph D. Kelly). The film was a box office success, earning more than $9 million in its initial release against a budget of more than $1 million. Songs: "I've Written a Letter to Daddy" (music: Frank De Vol; lyrics: Bob Merrill), "Old Folks at Home" ["Swa-nee River"] (1851; Stephen Foster). ***Author's Note***: The celebrated feud between Davis and Crawford, which had lasted for more than three decades as these two great actresses competed for roles and star status, continued unabated during the production of this film. Although Craw-ford played her role as an understated character, Davis exploited her in-sane character, eventually engulfing Crawford's character by broadly playing that demented sister. Aldrich employs many arresting visual shots to increase the suspense and viewer anxiety, including a startling overhead shot looking down upon Crawford as she momentarily loses control of her senses and moves her wheelchair erratically and violently about her room as would a starving caged tigress. The trapped character Crawford enacts is reminiscent of the riveting performance of Barbara Stanwyck, who plays a paralyzed woman awaiting her own murder in

Leonardo DiCaprio and Johnny Depp in *What's Eating Gilbert Grape,* **1993.**

Sorry, Wrong Number, 1948. Similarly, Davis' wretched attempt to return to the stage recalls the image of Gloria Swanson's delusionary conduct as a faded movie siren at the end of **Sunset Boulevard**, 1950, where she thinks she is enacting a scene in "Salome" before cameras that are actually recording her arrest for murder. Aldrich told this author that "I had a hell of a time keeping those two lionesses [Davis and Crawford] from devouring each other. They looked for every opportunity to upstage each other, but since both had such obsessive and self-centered characters, they were tilting at windmills. I knew that they despised each other and I must admit that I encouraged that mutual dislike to aggravate each of their scenes together, by complimenting one and then the other all the time. To tell the truth, it emotionally drained me, because these two powerful and intense actresses are what I call 'psychic sappers.' They draw energy from others to channel their performances. I suppose that terribly suggests the bloodsucking of vampires." Davis told this author that, following the release of the film and while she was being interviewed by reporters: "I quoted Jack Warner, who, after someone suggested Joan [Crawford] and I star in **What Ever Happened to Baby Jane?**, said: 'I wouldn't give a plug nickel for either one of those two old broads.' That was repeated in a published story and then I got a wire from Joan that read: 'In future, do not refer to me as an old broad!' Well, I followed her advice and referred to her thereafter as 'a broken-down old broad." Crawford told this author that "when Bette [Davis] and I were rehearsing the script for that picture, we realized how ridiculous its plot and characters were—really outlandish, something out of a lunatic asylum, and we suddenly burst into uncontrollable laughter. The director [Aldrich] said: 'Ladies—this is a serious story.' Bette replied: 'That's what you and the writers think.' We did not have to believe the story, only act out its characters, both of whom are crazy as loons. Our roles reminded me of the batty sisters in **Mr. Deeds Goes to Town** [1936], but they were tame compared to the lunatics we played in **What Ever Happened to Baby Jane?**" Crawford was upset when she was not nominated for an Oscar for her role in this film and even more disturbed when Davis received an Oscar nomination. To upstage her lifelong rival, Crawford lobbied the other Best Actress nominees, asking them if she could accept their Oscar in the event that any of them won. Anne Bancroft, who had been nominated for the Oscar for her startling performance in **The Miracle Worker**, 1962, responded by asking Crawford to accept that Oscar for her if she won as she would be unable to attend the Academy Award ceremonies. When Bancroft was announced as the winner, Crawford triumphantly went to the podium, reportedly passing Davis, a loser waiting in the wings, and saying: "Excuse me— I have an Oscar to accept." Davis admitted that, when insisting on doing her own makeup for her role in this film, "I think I went a bit too far, pasting more and more white makeup onto my kisser until I looked like

a ghost drained of all blood. I wanted to have my character look unearthly, but, when seeing the finished picture, I realized I had made that character ungodly. It really did not matter. I was playing a total nut and total nuts can get away with anything." **p&d**, Robert Aldrich; **cast**, Bette Davis, Joan Crawford, Victor Buono, Wesley Addy, Julie Allred, Ann Barton, Marjorie Bennett, Bert Freed, Anna Lee, Maidie Norman, Dave Willock, Bobs Watson, Andrew Duggan (narrator); **w**, Lukas Heller (based on the novel by Henry Farrell); **c**, Ernest Haller; **m**, Frank De Vol; **ed**, Michael Luciano; **art d**, William Glasgow; **set d**, George Sawley; **spec eff**, Donald Steward.

What's Eating Gilbert Grape ★★★★ 1993; U.S.; 118m; PAR; Color; Drama; Children: Unacceptable (MPAA: PG-13); **BD**; **DVD**; **IV**. Intriguing tale with a clever script begins with Depp (Gilbert Grape), a twenty one year old man living in a small Iowa town. He did not have an easy time growing up. Depp's father hanged himself when Depp was four-years-old. He lives in an old house with his obese mother, Cates; two sisters, Schellhardt and Harrington; and seventeen-year-old brother, DiCaprio, who is mentally impaired. Cates, a widow, weighs about 500 pounds and can hardly walk, so she spends most of her time in a chair at home while watching television. Neighborhood boys hear about his enormous mother and want to see this huge woman as curious spectators might want to see a sideshow freak. Depp allows them this strange vision and lifts them up to see her through a window. Depp and his two younger sisters often bring the kitchen table with dinner on it to Cates so she doesn't have to move from her chair. (This scene is acutely reminiscent of those sequences showing Ayllene Gibbons, the obese and gluttonous mother coddled with mounds of endless food by son Rod Steiger in the black comedy **The Loved One**, 1965.) Depp works at a small grocery store whose owner worries because a supermarket has just opened in town to give him competition. While delivering groceries, Depp meets and then develops an awkward affair with gawky Steenburgen, a lonely widow whose husband drowned in a wading pool after suffering a heart attack. (There is no end to these weird people or the oddball fates that befall their loved ones.) Depp takes on the job of caring for the family and doing repairs on their old house. His main responsibility is looking after DiCaprio, who has the habit of climbing the water tower in town, but never reaches the top and needs help climbing back down. Lewis, a lovely teenager, arrives in town with her grandmother, Branning, after their car breaks down. The auto needs repair which will take about a week, so they are stranded in this backwater community. Lewis and Depp become attracted to each other and an awkward romance begins. Depp pays so much attention to Lewis that he ignores DiCaprio. He leaves DiCaprio alone to spend some time with Lewis while DiCaprio is bathing at home. Depp returns home late, but does not look for DiCaprio. The next morning he finds DiCaprio is still in the bathtub and shivering because the water has turned icy cold. Depp feels guilty for having left his brother alone and also feels the criticism of his mother and sisters. Meanwhile, willy-nilly Steenburgen leaves town to find a new life for herself. While Lewis talks to Depp about her ambitions, they lose sight of DiCaprio, who climbs the water tower again, but this time is arrested for trespassing. Cates, who has not left her house in seven years, goes to the police station and manages to get DiCaprio released. When he is back home, DiCaprio resists taking another bath and tries to run away, which causes Depp, who has always tried to be patient and loving toward him, to hit him. Frustrated and feeling guilty for his violent act, Depp gets into his car and drives off. DiCaprio leaves the house and goes to Lewis, who looks after him until his sisters come for him. Lewis manages to talk Depp into returning home for DiCaprio's eighteenth birthday party. He does, and everyone forgives him and he introduces his mother to Lewis, which he had not done earlier because he was ashamed of Cate's weight. After the party, Cates walks up the stairs to her bedroom, which she has not been able to do since her husband's suicide. When DiCaprio goes to look in on her, he finds that she has died in bed. Townspeople had laughed at Cates for being so fat when she went to the police station, so Depp, DiCaprio, and their sisters decide not to have her body taken out of the house for burial, and, instead, cremate the corpse. A year passes and Depp, DiCaprio, and their sisters wait by a roadside for Lewis to take them to a better life in her trailer and where they plan to tell Lewis what became of them after their mother's death. This is a moving film with little action, but where gentleness and good humor radiate from its characters, who elicit more compassion than pity as most appear to be dysfunctional people. What is most touching is Depp's demonstration of love for his mentally disabled brother and his determination to always be there for him. DiCaprio steals this film with his mesmerizing performance, one that offsets the somewhat annoying and distracting usual blank stare and deadpan face presented offhandedly by Depp (and where he sometimes appears to have taken a massive overdose of Pepto-Bismol), as well as Steenburgen's equally harassing little girl voice, which is invariably delivered in a bland squeak. The production values are nevertheless superior with outstanding lensing from Nykvist and a strong score from Isfalt and Parker. The offbeat story and bizarre characters most likely turned off the public as this film was a failure at the box office, earning only about $10 million against a budget of $11 million. Songs: "This Magic Moment" (Doc Pomus, Mort Shuman), Music from "Sorry, Wrong Number" (Franz Waxman), Music from "Harmony Lane" (Arthur Kay), "Foodland Muzak" and "Waterfalls" (Joseph S. DeBeasi). Mature subject matter prohibits viewing by children. **p**, David Matalon, Bertil Ohlsson, Meir Teper; **d**, Lasse Hallstrom; **cast**, Johnny Depp, Leonardo DiCaprio, Juliette Lewis, Mary Steenburgen, Darlene Cates, Laura Harrington, Mary Kate Schellhardt, Kevin Tighe, John C. Reilly, Crispin Glover, Penelope Branning; **w**, Peter Hedges (based on his novel); **c**, Sven Nykvist; **m**, Bjorn Isfalt, Alan Parker; **ed**, Andrew Mondshein; **prod d**, Bernt Capra; **art d**, John Myhre; **set d**, Gretchen Rau, Jarrell Jay Knowles; **spec eff**, Howard Jensen, Scott Prescott, Paul Stewart.

What's Love Got to Do with It ★★★ 1993; U.S.; 118m; Touchstone; Buena Vista; Color; Biographical Drama; Children: Unacceptable (MPAA: R); **BD**; **DVD**; **VHS**; **IV**. Well-made biopic sees Anna Mae Bullock (Kelly), born and reared in the small town of Nutbush, Tennessee, abandoned by her parents when she is a little girl, her parents taking her sister with them. She lives with her grandmother until she is a teenager. After that woman's death, she moves to St. Louis where she reunites with her mother and sister. She becomes a beautiful young woman with an equally beautiful singing voice and becomes attracted to Ike Turner (Fishburne), leader of a rock band. She becomes the band's singer, then she and Fishburne marry and she becomes known as Tina Turner (Bassett). She also becomes the mother of their children and those of his from previous liaisons. They soon gain musical success together as Ike and Tina Turner. She becomes well known as a singer while Fishburne, jealous of attention paid to her and not him, turns to drugs and begins to beat her. She endures his physical abuse for the sake of the children, and a friend introduces her to Nichiren Buddhism in the hope that it will emotionally help her. Becoming more self-confident, she finally musters the courage to leave Fishburne. She becomes a rock singing superstar and Fishburne tries to win her back, but she resists and becomes a rhythm and blues solo star without him. This film is not related to the 2002 and 2013 documentaries or a television series of the same title. Songs: "What's Love Got to Do with It" (Terry Britten, Graham Lyle), "Why Must We Wait Until Tonight" (Bryan Adams, Robert John Lange), "Proud Mary" (John Fogerty), "I Don't Wanna Fight" Lulu [Marie Lawrie], Billy Laurie, Steve DuBerry), "Rock Me Baby" (Riley King, Joe Josea), "Disco Inferno" (Leroy Green, Ron Kersey), "Nutbush City Limits" (Tina Turner), "Darlin', You Know I Love You" (B.B. King, Jules Taub), "A Fool in Love" (Ike Turner), "It's Gonna Work Out Fine" (Rose McCoy, Sylvia McKinney), "Shake a Tail Feather" (Verlie Rice, Otis Hayes, Andre Williams), "Tina's Wish" (Ike Turner, Tina Turner), "I Might Have Been Queen" (Jeanette Obstoj, Rupert Hine,

Angela Bassett in *What's Love Got to Do with It*, 1993.

Jamie West-Oram), "River Deep, Mountain High" (Phil Spector). **p**, Doug Chapin, Barry Krost, Pat Kehoe; **d**, Brian Gibson; **cast**, Angela Bassett, Laurence Fishburne, Rae'Ven Kelly, Cora Lee Day, Jennifer Lewis, Phyllis Yvonne Stickney, Sherman Augustus, Chi McBride, Terrence Riggins, Gene "Groove" Allen; **w**, Kate Lanier (based on the book *I, Tina*, by Tina Turner with Kurt Loder), **c**, Jamie Anderson; **m**, Stanley Clarke; **ed**, Stuart Pappe; **prod d**, Stephen Altman; **art d**, Richard L. Johnson; **set d**, Rick Simpson; **spec eff**, James K. Fredburg.

What's New Pussycat? ★★★ 1965; U.S./France; 108m; Famous Artists/UA; Color; Comedy; Children: Unacceptable; **BD**; **DVD**; **VHS**; **IV**. Amusing tale begins with O'Toole, a notorious womanizer who wants to be faithful to his fiancée, Schneider, but has problems in that because every woman he meets falls in love with him. Among these female suitors is Prentiss, a neurotic American; a stripper at a night club owned by Allen; and Andress, a parachutist, who accidentally lands in O'Toole's car. His married psychoanalyst, Sellers, is totally occupied with courting one of his patients, Capucine (who also loves O'Toole), and is therefore too busy to help O'Toole resolve his romantic dilemmas. Everyone checks into a French countryside hotel for the weekend, unaware of each other's presence. It all ends with O'Toole marrying Schneider, the only girl he ever loved. This is a fast and funny romantic comedy that was Allen's film debut as an actor (his first produced script). Richard Burton appears in a cameo appearance at the strip club bar. The film was a success at the box office, producing more than $18.8 million in its initial release. Songs: "What's New Pussycat?," "Here I Am," "My Little Red Book," "Dance Mamma, Dance Pappa, Dance" (Burt Bacharach, Hal David); "Boston City" (traditional). Sexual subject matter prohibits viewing by children. **p**, Charles K. Feldman; **d**, Clive Donner; **cast**, Peter Sellers, Peter O'Toole, Romy Schneider, Capucine Paula Prentiss, Woody Allen, Ursula Andress, Edra Gale, Katrin Schaake, Eleanor Hirt, Richard Burton, Louise Lasser; **w**, Allen; **c**, Jean Badal (Technicolor); **m**, Burt Bacharach; **ed**, Fergus McDonell; **art d**, Jacques Saulnier; **spec eff**, Robert MacDonald.

What's Up, Doc? ★★★ 1972; U.S.; 94m; Saticoy/WB; Color; Comedy; Children: Acceptable (MPAA: G); **BD**; **DVD**; **VHS**; **IV**. Bogdanovich pays homage to the 1930s screwball comedies in this often hilarious outing where the accidental mix-up of four identical plaid overnight bags creates a series of funny situations. Streisand, O'Neal, Kahn, and Mars are all researchers, who go to San Francisco to compete for a research grant in music. They all wind up in court and it ends with Streisand and O'Neal kissing on an airplane while their in-flight movie shows Bugs Bunny in one of his cartoons saying the famous line that gave the film its title. The director takes a story line leaf from many

Ryan O'Neal and Barbra Streisand in *What's Up, Doc?*, 1972.

films, especially **Bringing Up Baby**, 1938, but offers a distinctive brand of humor in his own right; the cast members give top-flight performances. The film saw considerable success at the box office, earning more than $66 million in its initial release against a budget of $4 million. Songs: "You're the Top" (Cole Porter), "As Time Goes By" (Herman Hupfeld), "Santa Lucia" (Teodoro Cottrau). **p&d**, Peter Bogdanovich; **cast**, Barbra Streisand, Ryan O'Neal, Madeline Kahn, Kenneth Mars, Austin Pendleton, Michael Murphy, Philip Roth, Sorrell Booke, John Hillerman, Stefan Gierasch, Mabel Albertson, Randy Quaid, Patricia O'Neal; **w**, Buck Henry, David Newman, Robert Benton (based on a story by Bogdanovich); **c**, Laszlo Kovacs (Technicolor); **m**, Artie Butler; **ed**, Verna Fields; **prod d**, Polly Platt; **art d**, Herman A. Blumenthal; **set d**, John Austin; **spec eff**, Robert MacDonald.

What's Up, Tiger Lily? ★★★ 1966; U.S./Japan; 80m; Benedict Pictures/American International/Focus Features; Color; Comedy; Children: Unacceptable (MPAA: PG); **DVD**; **VHS**. This wacky tale was created when Allen adapted the 1965 Japanese action film **International Secret Police: Key of Keys** and dubbed it in English, changing the plot to make it center around a secret egg salad recipe. The film is mainly a farce, an excuse for sight gags, puns, and poking fun at Asian stereotypes. It follows the misadventures of a secret agent (Allen voiceover), who is hired by the Grand Exalted High Majah of Raspur of a mythical country, to find a secret egg salad recipe that someone stole from him. In searching for the thief, Allen is vamped by beautiful Wakabayashi (voiceover), who join him in his spying, and we learn that the thief is Nakamaru (voiceover), the leader of a gang of thugs. Meanwhile, Kurobe (voiceover), another gangster, appears to be helping Allen, but is only trying to steal the recipe. Mature subject matter prohibits viewing by children. *Author's Note*: This was Allen's directorial debut of a theatrically released feature film, and he made this film on the shoestring budget of less than $400,000. **p**, Reuben Bercovitch, (Japanese version) Tomoyuki Tanaka; **d**, Woody Allen, (Japanese version) Senkichi Taniguichi; **cast**, Allen, and the voices of Julie Bennett, Frank Buxton, Louise Lasser, Mickey Rose, Bryna Wilson; **w**, Allen, Julie Bennett, Buxton, Lasser, Len Maxwell, Rose, Ben Shapiro, Wilson, **c**, Kazuo Yamada (Tohoscope; Eastmancolor); **m**, The Lovin' Spoonful (Steve Boone, Joe Butler, John Sebastian, Zal Yanovsky); **ed**, Richard Krown.

When Did You Last See Your Father? ★★★ 2007; UK/Ireland; 92m; Film4/Sony; Color; Drama; Children: Unacceptable (MPAA: PG-13); **BD**; **DVD**; **IV**. Fascinating family story begins with Firth, who is a British writer with unresolved relationship problems with his father, Broadbent, who has been diagnosed with terminal intestinal cancer. Firth leaves his wife and children to drive to a Yorkshire village where he

spent his childhood and adolescence to help his mother and sister care for Broadbent in his final days. Broadbent has been a doctor in practice with his wife, Stevenson, also a doctor. Firth suspects that Broadbent has been having an affair with one of Firth's aunts, Lancashire. This is typical of Broadbent, a man of considerable charm, and Firth has been out-charming him for women they have both pursued. Firth also resents his father for mistreating Firth's mother. Broadbent is under sedation so communication with him is difficult. Firth confides most in his first love, the family maid, Cassidy, their romance beginning when he was a boy (played by Johnson). Firth also recalls happier days as a boy and teenager when he and his father went camping and when Broadbent taught him how to drive a car. Another resentment Firth has against his father is that Broadbent was strict with him about having relations with girls, and considered him to be the "sex police" while Broadbent violated his own principles by being unfaithful to his own wife. Also, Firth resents it that Broadbent disdains his occupation as a writer, and that Broadbent only read one book all the way through his life. Firth and Broadbent never get to talk father-and-son, and Firth only forgives him after his father dies. This is a rather grim tale (reminiscent of the more gentle **I Never Sang for My Father**, 1970), but realistically enacted with top performances from all, greatly aided by a strong, intelligent script. Songs/Music: "Cold Cold Feeling" (J.M. Robinson), "Put a Little Love in Your Heart" (Jimmy Holiday, Randall Meyers, Jackie De Shannon), "Mayor of Simpleton" (Andy Partridge), "I'm Gonna Tell Santa on You" (Thelma Blackmon), "Winter Weather" (Ted Shapiro), "I, Yi, Yi, Yi, Yi/I Like You Very Much" (Harry Warren, Mack Gordon), "One Fine Day" (Carole King, Gerry Goffin), "I Can't Let Go" and "Don't Ever Change" (Chip Taylor, Al Gorgoni), "Casta Diva" (from the opera "Norma" by Vincenzo Bellini), "Andante" (from "Keyboard Concerto in G Minor" by Johann Sebastian Bach), "Adagio" (from "Piano Trio in E Flat Major" by Franz Schubert). Sexual content, thematic material and gutter language prohibit viewing by children. **p**, Elizabeth Karlsen, Stephen Woolley, Laurie Borg; **d**, Anand Tucker; **cast**, Colin Firth, Jim Broadbent, Claire Skinner, Juliet Stevenson, Gina McKee, Elliot Avery, Rhiannon Howden, Elaine Cassidy, Tom Butcher, Sarah Lancashire, Naomi Allisstone; **w**, David Nicholls (based on the book by Blake Morrison); **c**, Howard Atherton; **m**, Barrington Pheloung; **ed**, Trevor Waite; **prod d**, Alice Normington; **art d**, Lynne Huitson; **set d**, Barbara Herman-Skelding; **spec eff**, Ian Rowley.

When Father Was Away on Business ★★★ 1985; Yugoslavia; 136m; Centaur Film/Cannon; Color; Drama; Children: Unacceptable (MPAA: R); **DVD**; **VHS**. When Marshal Tito broke up with Stalin in 1948, dangerous years loomed for many hard-core Yugoslav communists. A careless remark about a newspaper cartoon gets Manojlovic arrested. His wife, Karanovic, and young son, Bartolli, are forced to wait for his return from prison. She tells him his father is merely "away on business," but he gradually comes to understand the politics of the country that straddles East and West. This good character study also incisively profiles the changing politics in multi national Yugoslavia at the beginning of the Cold War. (In Serbian; English subtitles.) **p**, Mirza Pasic; **d**, Emir Kusturica; **cast**, Moreno D'E Bartolli, Miki Manojlovic, Mirjana Karanovic, Mustafa Nadarevic, Mira Furlan, Predrag Lakovic, Pavle Vujisic, Slobodan Aligrudic, Eva Ras, Aleksandar Dorcev; **w**, Abdulah Sidran; **c**, Vilko Filac; **m**, Zoran Simjanovic; **ed**, Andrija Zafranovic; **prod d**, Predrag Lukovac.

When Harry Met Sally ★★★ 1989; U.S.; 116m; Castle Rock-Nelson Entertainment/COL; Color; Comedy/Romance; Children: Unacceptable (MPAA: R); **BD**; **DVD**; **VHS**; **IV**. Lighthearted story entertainingly profiles Crystal and Ryan, first showing their graduation from the University of Chicago. They drive to New York City together, she to start journalism school while he begins a business career. The film then chronicles their next twelve years and raises the question of whether men and women can merely be friends while maintaining a romance.

Ryan believes they can be friends without sex, but he wants that, too. They do have sex one night and eventually get married. The always empathetic Crystal and the alluring Ryan are exceptional in their roles, providing provocative character studies while a robust script examines what works in maintaining a loving relationship. This film saw a great box office success, earning more than $92.8 million in its initial release against a budget of $16 million. Songs: "It Had to Be You" (Isham Jones, Gus Kahn); "Our Love Is Here to Stay" and "Let's Call the Whole Thing Off," (George Gershwin, Ira Gershwin); "Don't Pull Your Love" (Brian Potter, Dennis Lambert); "Ramblin' Man " (Forrest Richard Betts); "Rag Time Of the Night" (Peter McCann); "Where Or When," "But Not for Me," "I Could Write a Book" "Isn't It Romantic" (music: Richard Rodgers; lyrics: Lorenz Hart); "Lady's Lunch" (Marc Shaiman); "The Tables Have Turned" (Laura Kenyon, Shaiman, Scott Wittman); "Plane Cue" (Max Steiner); "Autumn in New York" (Vernon Duke); "Winter Wonderland" (Felix Bernard, Richard B. Smith); "The Surrey with the Fringe on Top" (Richard Rodgers, Oscar Hammerstein II); "Say It Isn't So" (Irving Berlin); "Mozart String Quintet in E Flat Major" (Wolfgang Amadeus Mozart); "Stompin' at the Savoy" (Benny Goodman, Chick Webb, Edgar Sampson, Andy Razaf); "Don't Be That Way" (Goodman, Sampson, Mitchell Parish); "Have Yourself a Merry Little Christmas" (Ralph Blane, Hugh Martin); "Call Me" (Tony Hatch); "Don't Get Around Much Anymore" (Duke Ellington, Bob Russell);, "Auld Lang Syne" (Robert Burns). Sexuality prohibits viewing by children. **p,** Rob Reiner, Andrew Scheinman, Steve Nicolaides, Jeffrey Stott; **d,** Reiner; **cast,** Billy Crystal, Meg Ryan, Carrie Fisher, Bruno Kirby, Steven Ford, Lisa Jane Persky, Michelle Nicastro, Gretchen Palmer, Robert Alan Beuth, David Burdick, Joe Viviani, Harley Jane Kozak, Joseph Hunt; **w,** Nora Ephron; **c,** Barry Sonnenfeld; **ed,** Robert Leighton; **prod d,** Jane Musky; **set d,** George R. Nelson, Sabrina Wright-Basile.

When Knighthood Was in Flower ★★★ 1922 (silent); U.S.; 120m/12 reels; Cosmopolitan Productions/PAR; B/W; Adventure; Children: Unacceptable. Sumptuous epic sees fetching Davies as Mary Tudor (1496-1533), who falls in love with nobleman Sir Charles Brandon (1484-1545), played by Stanley. Davies wants to marry Stanley, but her brother and king, Henry VIII (1491-1547), played by Harding, angrily opposes that union, insisting that Davies solidifies a political alliance with France by wedding that country's elderly Louis XII (1462-1515), who is played by Norris. Davies cannot abide such a marriage, and when she resists, Stanley is framed for murder and is imprisoned. Davies disguises herself as Stanley's younger brother and manages to help him escape. The two lovers flee, only to have Harding order his troops to pursue her. They are captured at a Bristol inn, but not without a fight (where Davies battles six men with a huge broadsword in one of many spectacular scenes). Once subdued, Davies pleads for Stanley's life, promising Harding that she will marry the doddering Norris, but on the condition that Stanley's life is spared. (Mary also asked Henry that, upon the death of Louis XII, who was thirty-four years older than Mary, she would be allowed to marry Brandon.) Harding relents and Stanley is banished, sent into exile. Davies obediently prepares to marry Norris, and another touching scene shows her nonchalantly selecting fabric for her wedding dress, a very amusing scene that wonderfully demonstrated Davies' great talent for comedy. Norris believes that he is still young and virile enough to satisfy the needs of such a young and vibrant woman as Davies, but drops dead when attempting to prove his manhood. Powell, who plays Francis I (1494-1547), who is heir to the French throne, then asks Harding if he can wed Davies. Stanley, who has been living in exile, returns to rescue Davies from another terrible marriage and both are married. Harding accepts their union, saying: "I should have consented in the first place, and saved us all this trouble." (The union between Mary Tudor and Louis XII was short-lived. They married on October 9, 1514, and, three months later, on January 1, 1515, Louis died, apparently from over-exertions in their bedchamber.) This

Meg Ryan and Billy Crystal in _When Harry Met Sally,_ 1989.

epic was lavishly produced, offering majestic sets, rich costumes and more than 3,000 extras, offering a rich pageant of the Tudor era. Davies, Harding and Powell are exceptional in their roles, but director Vignola presents rather stagey scenes and his camera cries out for mobility, although the lensing from Morgan and Wenstrom is nevertheless exceptional. **_Author's Note_**: The production company behind this opus was Cosmopolitan Pictures, which was owned by media magnate William Randolph Hearst, and which was devoted to productions starring Davies, Hearst's mistress. Hearst personally selected this story for Davies after being impressed by such costume epics as **Madame Du Barry**, 1919, and **Anna Boleyn**, 1920, both German productions directed by the gifted Ernest Lubitsch, as well as Fred Niblo's **The Three Musketeers**, 1921, starring swashbuckler Douglas Fairbanks Sr. Hearst spent lavishly on this production, $1.5 million, but it was money well spent in that the film earned back more than twice that investment in its initial release, becoming not only the most expensive film made to that time, but the sixth biggest financial hit of the year. A short time after the release of this film, a friend of Hearst's told the media mogul that "there is a lot of money in pictures." Hearst nodded and replied: "Yes, I know—mine." This was Powell's second feature film and he was given the role of Francis I after the actor originally cast in that part grew ill. Powell told this author: "I played a villain in that picture, black mustache and goatee and heavy black wig, and where I had to be menacing toward Marion [Davies]. Threatening that radiant woman was extremely difficult because she was such a wonderful person, perhaps the nicest actress I ever met. She was always so friendly and outgoing on the set that she made working in pictures in those days a happy experience for everybody, actors and crew members alike. Her productions were financially backed by one of the most powerful men in the world [Hearst], but you would never know it from Marion. Everybody called her their friend, and she was. I can't tell you the number of down-and-out actors and actresses she later helped out when times were tough in the Depression [of the 1930s], getting them jobs, places to live, food to eat and even paying their medical bills. There was no one like her." The sets for this film were so enormous that Paramount had to rent additional sound stages from two other studios before the production was completed. When the film was released, the publicity department working for Hearst made sure that the lobbies of all the first-run theaters showing this film were filled with flowers. Director Orson Welles recalled for this author how, when he was only about six or seven, he was taken to see this film "and I never forgot how the theater, from its entrance and foyer, right up to where the doors opened to the theater aisles were filled with flowers. This was a grand gesture Hearst personally made to honor Marion Davies, and I later learned that he spent more than $50,000 filling up theaters with flowers for the picture's opening. I never forgot

William Powell menacing Marion Davies (as Mary Tudor) in *When Knighthood Was in Flower*, 1922.

that, so when we made **Citizen Kane** [1941], I had the opera singer coming back onto the stage to be inundated with flowers." Mary I of England has been enacted by many other actresses in many other films, including **Anne of the Thousand Days**, 1969 (Nicola Pagett); **Die Liebe und die Konigin**, 1977 (made-for-TV; Inge Keller); **Elizabeth**, 1998 (Kathy Burke); **Elizabeth R**, 1971-1972 (TV miniseries; "The Lion's Club," 1971 episode: Daphne Slater); **Henry VIII**, 2003 (made-for-TV; Lara Belmont); **Lady Jane**, 1986 (Jane Lapotaire); **Lady Jane Grey**, 1936 (Gwen Ffrangcon-Davies); **Mary Tudor**, 1917 (Jeanne Delvair), **Mary Tudor**, 1920 (Ellen Richter); **Mary Tudor**, 1966 (made-for-TV; Francoise Christophe); **The Other Boleyn Girl**, 2008 (Constance Stride); **The Pearls of the Crown**, 1938 (Yvette Pienne); **Piece of the Sky**, 1958 (Lia Ferrel); **The Six Wives of Henry VIII**, 1970 (TV miniseries; Alison Frazer, Verina Greenlaw); **The Sword and the Rose**, 1953 (Glynis Johns); **The Tudors**, 2007-2010 (TV series; Sarah Bolger) as older Mary; Blathnaid McKeown as oung Mary; and **The Twisted Tale of Bloody Mary**, 2008 (made-for-TV; Miranda French as older Mary; Lizzie Rees as young Mary) **d**, Robert G. Vignola; **cast**, Marion Davies, Forrest Stanley, Lyn Harding, Theresa Maxwell Conover, Pedro de Cordoba, Ruth Shepley, Ernest Glendinning, Arthur Forrest, Johnny Dooley, William Norris, William Powell (as "William H. Powell"); **w**, William LeBaron, Luther Reed (based on the novel by Charles Major); **c**, Ira H. Morgan, Harold Wenstrom; **m**, William Frederick Peters; **art d**, Joseph Urban; **spec eff**, Harry Redmond, Sr.

When Ladies Meet ★★★ 1933; U.S.; 73m; MGM; B/W; Comedy/Romance; Children: Unacceptable. Exceptional performances are seen from a bevy of fine actors in this rakish comedy. Morgan is a book publisher married to Harding but attracted to Loy, one of his authors, a novelist who has become his mistress. Montgomery, who also is attracted to Loy, arranges for her and Harding to meet, neither knowing the other's true identity. The two women become friends while discovering they are rivals for Morgan; they decide he is a womanizer and Loy gives him up to Harding and falls into the arms of Montgomery. Brady provides humor as a hostess, who pretends to be addle-brained, but is as shrewd as a racetrack tout. The film received an Oscar nomination for Best Art Direction (Gibbons).The story was remade in 1941. Songs: "Love, You Funny Thing" (1932; Fred E. Ahlert), "I Love But Thee/Jeg elsker Dig!" (1864: music, Edvard Grieg; lyrics: Hans Christian Andersen), "Try a Little Tenderness" (1932: Harry M. Woods). *Author's Note*: The play upon which this film was based opened on Broadway at the Royale Theater on October 6, 1932, and ran for 173 performances. Loy told this author that "I was blessed to have Bob [Montgomery] as my co-star in that picture, a sophisticated actor, who was also as witty off

the set as he was before the cameras." Montgomery recalled for this author that "Frank Morgan played an utter cad in **When Ladies Meet**. He uses women in that picture as one might discard paper napkins, so it is odd to think of him now as the wonderful and jovial character actor he later became, everybody's kind and benevolent uncle, the kind of role I believe he always preferred to play." **p**, Lawrence Weingarten; **d**, Harry Beaumont; **cast**, Ann Harding, Robert Montgomery, Myrna Loy, Alice Brady, Frank Morgan, Martin Burton, Luis Alberni, Sterling Holloway, David Newell; **w**, John Meehan, Leon Gordon (based on the play by Rachel Crothers); **c**, Ray June; **m**, William Axt; **ed**, Hugh Wynn; **art d**, Cedric Gibbons.

When Ladies Meet ★★★ 1941; U.S.; 105m; MGM; B/W; Comedy; Drama; Romance; Children: Unacceptable; **DVD, VHS**. In this fine remake of the 1933 original version, Crawford is a novelist with advanced ideas about love and marriage. She is in love with her publisher, Marshall, but he is married to Garson. Crawford decides to lure Marshall away from his wife and marry him, but her friend, Taylor, who is in love with her and pursues her, has ideas of his own on how to deal with the two-timing Marshall. He decides to bring Crawford and Garson together at the house of a friend, Byington, in order to have them become friends so Crawford will not take Garson's husband away from her. Crawford and Garson, who do not know each other, meet at Byington's house and come to like each other. Crawford appreciates and respects Garson's maturity and wisdom, and the two ladies become friends. While learning from Garson that Marshall is a philandering womanizer of long standing, Crawford realizes she cannot love him or be as tolerant of him as is Garson, so she decides she will make a life with Taylor after all. The performances from Crawford, Garson, Marshall and Taylor are top notch in this sophisticated comedy. The film received an Oscar nomination for Best Art Direction (Gibbons; set decoration: Willis; Gibbons having received the same Oscar nomination for the original 1933 version). The subject matter, while tastefully handled, is too mature for children. Songs: "I Love But Thee/Jeg elsker Dig!" (1864; music: Edvard Grieg; lyrics: Hans Christian Andersen), "Yo Ho Ho and a Bottle of Rum" (traditional), "Jeanie with the Light Brown Hair" (1854; Stephen Foster). Remake of 1933 film. *Author's Note*: Crawford told this author that "I knew I had considerable competition when acting opposite Greer [Garson] in **When Ladies Meet**. She was being groomed for stardom at MGM by studio boss Louis B. Mayer. I think we spent most of our time in our scenes together underplaying each other." Garson told this author that "Joan Crawford was one of the reigning queens at MGM when we appeared together in **When Ladies Meet**, a mantle she had been slowly taking away from Norma Shearer. I felt that she felt I was challenging her status at the studio, so we had more than a few tense moments while we were making that picture." Taylor liked his role in this film, telling this author that "the toughest kind of role to play is always in comedies like **When Ladies Meet**, although that was really a sophisticated drama with elements of comedy thrown into its plot. You have to convince an audience that you have a sense of humor when doing comedies and that's always the toughest nut to crack." The always circumspect Marshall recalled this film for this author by saying: "My character in that picture is a habitual cheating husband, who is always being forgiven by a very tolerating wife. That was Greer Garson in that picture. I have never really believed that any sensible wife ever forgives a cheating husband, unless she is doing the same thing, and those tit-for-tat marriages never last." **p**, Robert Z. Leonard, Orville O. Dull; **d**, Leonard; **cast**, Joan Crawford, Robert Taylor, Greer Garson, Herbert Marshall, Spring Byington, Mona Barrie, Rafael Storm, Max Willenz, Florence Shirley, Leslie Francis; **w**, S.K. Lauren, Anita Loos (based on the play by Rachel Crothers); **c**, Robert Planck; **m**, Bronislau Kaper; **ed**, Robert J. Kern; **art d**, Cedric Gibbons; **set d**, Edwin B. Willis.

When My Baby Smiles at Me ★★★ 1948; U.S.; 98m; FOX; Color; Musical; Children: Unacceptable; **DVD**. Lively and very entertaining songfest has Grable and Dailey as a married vaudeville team in the late 1920s and where she sings and he plays a clown. Dailey becomes a Broadway star, but it goes to his head and he takes to the bottle, winding up in Bellevue Hospital. Grable divorces him and is romanced by Arlen, a wealthy rancher. Dailey's best friends, Oakie and Havoc, help him to overcome his alcoholism and he makes a triumphant return to the stage. Teaming again with Grable, they become a hit together on Broadway and Grable returns to his arms. Based on the stage play "Burlesque," the story was filmed twice earlier, as **The Dance of Life**, 1929, and **Swing High, Swing Low**, 1937. Songs: "When My Baby Smiles at Me" (Bill Munro, Ted Lewis, Andrew Sterling II), "By the Way" and "What Did I Do?" (Josef Myrow, Mack Gordon), "Oh! French" (Con Conrad, Sam Ehrlich), "Bye Bye Blackbird" and "Bam Bam Bamy Shore" (Ray Henderson, Mort Dixon), "Oui, Oui, Marie" (Fred Fisher, Al Bryan, Joseph McCarthy), "Don't Bring Lulu" (Ray Henderson, Billy Rose, Lew Brown), "Ain't We Got Fun" (Richard A. Whiting, Ray Egan, Gus Kahn), "The Birth of the Blues" (Ray Henderson, Buddy G. DeSylva, Lew Brown), "Sweet Georgia Brown" (Maceo Pinkard, Kenneth Casey), "The Daughter of Rosie O'Grady" (Walter Donaldson, Monty C. Brice), "Say 'Si Si'" (Ernesto Lecuona, Francia Luban, Albert Stillman), "And He'd Say 'Oo-La-La Wee-Wee'" (Harry Ruby, George Jessel), "Oh, My Love" (James V. Monaco, Joseph McCarthy), "How 'Ya Gonna Keep 'em Down on the Farm/After They've Seen Paree?" (Walter Donaldson, Sam Lewis, Joe Young), "Bridal Chorus" (from "Lohengrin" by Richard Wagner). *Author's Note*: Grable told this author that "I thought that Dan [Dailey] proved to everyone that he was not just a song-and-dance man when we did **When My Baby Smiles at Me**. He played a man who drowns in alcohol and his scenes as a drunk shocked and amazed us all. It was truly great acting." **p**, George Jessel; **d**, Walter Lang; **cast**, Betty Grable, Dan Dailey, Jack Oakie, June Havoc, Richard Arlen, James Gleason, J. Farrell MacDonald, Noel Neill, Louise Allen, Maxine Ardell, Jean Wallace; **w**, Lamar Trotti (based on an adaptation by Elizabeth Reinhardt of the play "Burlesque" by Arthur Hopkins, George Manker Watters); **c**, Harry Jackson; **ed**, Barbara McLean; **art d**, Lyle Wheeler, Leland Fuller; **set d**, Thomas Little, Ernest Lansing; **spec eff**, Fred Sersen.

When Strangers Marry ★★★ 1944; U.S.; 67m; King Brothers/MON; B/W; Mystery; Children: Unacceptable; **DVD**. Superlative film noir entry has Hunter, a small-town girl, going to New York City to be with her new husband, Jagger, whom she married without really knowing him. Jagger doesn't show up for their meeting, and she asks a friend, Mitchum, to help her find Jagger. He urges her to call the police. Jagger finally phones Hunter and arranges a meeting, but she is to keep the location secret. Meanwhile, Hamilton is a cop investigating the murder of a drunken conventioneer, Elliott. Jagger tells her he knew Elliott, but did not kill him, and she then suspects that Mitchum might have killed Elliott. With Hamilton's help, Hunter traps Mitchum and he admits being the killer. Mitchum is arrested and Hunter and Jagger finally go off on their belated honeymoon. This "sleeper" film was shot on a ten-day schedule and with a shoestring budget by poverty-row studio Monogram, but it proved to be a big hit. Castle maintains tension and suspense throughout the film, drawing fine performances from Hunter, Jagger and Mitchum. The film also has an outstanding score from the gifted Tiomkin. Hunter, Mitchum, and Fleming were then at the start of their film careers. Song: "Boogie Woogie" (Lorenzo Flennoy). *Author's Note*: Mitchum told this author that "I think they paid me about $100 a day for about eight or nine days to make **When Strangers Marry**. It was a cheaply made whodunit, but it had a good script and Bill [Castle] knew what he was doing when he made that picture. I was in a lot of clinkers in those days, but that picture gave me a good shot with a leading role and I wasn't complaining. Kim Hunter and Dean Jagger were in that picture and they were very good in their parts." **p**, Frank King, Maurice King; **d**, William Castle; **cast**, Dean Jagger, Kim Hunter, Robert Mitchum, Neil Hamilton, Rhonda Fleming, Byron Foulger,

Kim Hunter and Robert Mitchum in *When Strangers Marry*, 1944.

Marta Mitrovich, Fred Aldrich, Marie Bryant, Minerva Urecal; **w**, Philip Yordan, Dennis J. Cooper (based on a story by George Moskov); **c**, Ira Morgan; **m**, Dimitri Tiomkin; **ed**, Martin G. Cohn; **art d**, F. Paul Sylos.

When the Clouds Roll By ★★★★ 1919 (silent); U.S.; 68m/6 reels; Douglas Fairbanks Pictures/UA; B/W; Comedy/Fantasy; Children: Cautionary; **DVD**. This extraordinary satire sees Fairbanks in an outlandish but fascinating tale that begins with the intriguing title card: "Guinea pigs and rabbits are often sacrificed for scientific purposes. But here is a new one." We then see Grimwood, a psychiatrist, lecturing at a strange convention, and he states: "The power of suggestion can destroy both mind and body. But first I weaken the power of resistance in my subject by implanting psychic germs of fear, worry, superstition, and kindred annoyances." Grimwood's "subject" is Fairbanks (named Daniel Boone Brown), who is America's most superstitious person and lives in Greenwich Village. Gimwood and his insidious henchmen do their psychological utmost to drive this young man to a state of insanity where he contemplates suicide. Fairbanks advertises for a servant, and Campeau, one of Grimwood's aides, applies and gets the job. He immediately prepares and serves Fairbanks an exotic dinner of lobster, Welsh rarebit, onions and mince pie. As expected, when Fairbanks goes to sleep, his digestive tract rebels against what he has consumed, and we are treated to a shot of the inside of his stomach where the rancorous food creates turmoil and Fairbanks has one nightmare after another. He awakens to discover an elongated figure sleeping next to him, and, after he pushes it from his bed, it transforms into a weird cutout figure that bounces menacingly upright. As giant white hands reach for him, the terrified Fairbanks leaps away, crashing through a wall to wind up in the middle of a meeting of ladies. When he notices that his pajama bottoms are beginning to fall, he dives into a painting of a seascape, landing into a pool. After he climbs from the pool, he sees the items of food that he ate are now enormous figures and they begin to chase him. Although Fairbanks is running at full speed, he seems to get nowhere and is shown moving in slow motion. In his desperation to escape his bizarre pursuers, Fairbanks leaps fences, rolls precariously in front of an oncoming truck, jumps onto the back of a running horse, and then crashes through another wall. He finds himself inside a large house and begins to investigate it by walking up a wall, across a ceiling and down another wall (Fred Astaire would do the same thing in an amazing dance number thirty years later when performing in **Royal Wedding**, 1951.) A door opens, and the aggravating food pours into the room, again chasing him. He manages to escape the house and is again furiously running, this time directly toward the camera, again in slow motion. Fairbanks reaches a chimney and dives down its shaft to land upon a giant drum where all sorts of people are beating upon it. Suddenly, Fairbanks awakes from

Kay Francis and Broderick Crawford (as outlaw Bob Dalton) in *When the Daltons Rode,* **1940.**

this sequence of nightmares to answer the door of his house. The visitor is another one of Grimwood's assistants, who is there to apply more torture, this time to awaken all of Fairbanks' many superstitions. Umbrellas open everywhere in his residence while endless mirrors shatter to pieces. To avoid a black cat crossing his path, Fairbanks bounds through windows and over buildings. Grimwood then frames Fairbanks on charges of stealing oil properties from the father of the woman he loves, so that his sweetheart, Clifford, and her father, turn their backs on him in shame and disgust. The police arrive and begin chasing Fairbanks everywhere inside his house, but these are fake officers working for Grimwood. Fairbanks slips into a closet to hide and there sees the inside of his own head, with a female figure called "Reason" sitting on her throne, and another figure called "Sense of Humor" sits at her feet. Then other figures, called "Worry" and "Discord," seize "Reason" and take her away. Groggy and stunned by what he has seen, Fairbanks leaves the closet, but does not realize that Grimwood has slipped a revolver into his pocket. Just when Fairbanks is about to use that revolver to end his agonies, he sees attendants from a lunatic asylum seizing Grimwood, who turns out to be an escaped madman. Fairbanks then finds Clifford to make amends to her, offering a fantastic proposal of marriage as he hangs by his feet on a swinging door, and gleefully increasing the speed of that door when she accepts. Just then they are engulfed by a fierce hurricane that sends everything and everyone flying about, subsiding into a wild flood, and Fairbanks and Clifford find themselves sitting atop the roof of a floating house. Another house comes floating by carrying a minister and they have the preacher marry them to end this wild fantasy of a film. Although Fairbanks would go on to appear in many spectacular swashbuckling films, from **Robin Hood**, 1922, to **The Black Pirate**, 1926, he would never again make such a capricious or delightful satire as this most imaginative production represents. Bizarre and eccentric in every sense, this film nevertheless presents a visual treat of early-day special effects while lampooning psychiatrists as the energetic and acrobatic Fairbanks performs some of his greatest physical feats. Much of the visual achievements for this exceptional film are attributable to the inventiveness of pantheon helmsman Fleming, who makes his directorial debut here. *Author's Note*: Although much of the nightmare sequences showing spectacular images were presented as miniatures, many action shots were accomplished with life-sized scenes. To create the flood, Fairbanks had a small dam destroyed (and repaired later) and he used actual transportation vehicles, like speeding trains over which he scampers and the Lackawanna Ferry, on top of which he performs some greased lightning stunts. Fairbanks' attitude toward psychiatrists in this film did not endear him to these professionals as he basically tells viewers in this amazing film to stop fretting about *why* things happen, and take life as it comes with a smile on your face and without

taking anything too seriously. This was the second film Fairbanks released through United Artists, the studio he had established that year with actress Mary Pickford (who would marry Fairbanks in 1920), comedian Charles Chaplin and master filmmaker D.W. Griffith. He would make two other such (but less spectacular) films, **The Mollycoddle**, 1920, and **The Nut**, 1921, before devoting himself entirely to the production of swashbuckling films. After U.S. President Woodrow Wilson (1856-1924) suffered a paralyzing stroke on October 2, 1919, Fairbanks, who had supported Wilson's administration, provided the White House with a film projector and copies of his films to entertain the suffering Chief Executive. When watching this film (Wilson had the use of only one eye at that time), the President became so enamored of its fantastic images that he asked that it be shown again. Wilson spent almost every afternoon watching films at the White House, until leaving office more than a year later when President Warren G. Harding (1865-1923) became the new President. By then, William Gibbs McAdoo Jr., who was Wilson's son-in-law and an attorney, had become the chief legal counsel for United Artists. **p**, Douglas Fairbanks; **d**, Victor Fleming; **cast**, Fairbanks, Herbert Grimwood, Kathleen Clifford, Frank Campeau, Albert MacQuarrie, Ralph Lewis, Daisy Jefferson, Bull Montana, Fleming, Harris Thorpe; **w**, Fairbanks, Tom Geraghty; **c**, William C. McGann, Thorpe; **art d**, Edward M. Langley.

When the Daltons Rode ★★★ 1940; U.S.; 81m; UNIV; B/W; Western; Children: Unacceptable; **DVD**. An entertaining western that is a sanitized fictionalization of the Dalton Gang, mostly brothers and outlaws in the American West from 1890 to 1892 that specialized in bank and train robberies. In this film, Scott is a young lawyer, who arrives in Kansas to visit the Dalton brothers, who are law-abiding rancher friends. The Dalton brothers are Crawford (Bob Dalton, 1869-1892), Donlevy (Gratton "Grat" Dalton, 1861-1892), Albertson (Emmett Dalton, 1871-1937), and Erwin (Ben Dalton, 1852-1936), their mother played by Gordon. They are in danger of losing their homestead to a corrupt land development company. Albertson accidentally kills one of the land grabbers, and Scott defends him at a court trial. A scuffle breaks out at the trial and Erwin is shot in the back, and the three brothers shoot their way out of the courtroom. This turns the Daltons into outlaws, but they are portrayed more as victims than villains. Meanwhile, Scott falls in love with Francis, Crawford's former fiancée. The brothers turn to robbing banks and railroads. Scott urges them to give themselves up, and they agree, but decide to pull one more bank job in Coffeyville, Kansas, a decision that costs them their lives in a wild shootout with lawmen on October 5, 1892, when the gang boldly attempts to rob two banks at one time in broad daylight. *Author's Note*: Marshall admitted to this author that "when we made that picture about the Dalton boys, we used a lot of fictional elements to build up the dramatic scenes, but we stuck mostly to the facts when it came to the daring robberies they committed." Donlevy told this author that "I played one of the Dalton brothers in that picture [Gratton Dalton], a hardhead, and that is just the way my real-life character was, shoot first and ask questions later. We played those boys as amiable fellows, but, in truth, they were very dangerous persons and you would not want to get into a poker game with any of them." Scott, when recalling his role in this film, told this author: "My character in **When the Daltons Rode** is pretty much like the role I had in **Jesse James** [1939] where I am a friend of the outlaws and try to get them to go straight. A lot of the real facts about the Daltons were ignored by the scriptwriters, especially where they show Emmett Dalton [played by Albertson] being killed in the final scenes of the Coffeyville raid. Emmett was the only brother that survived. He went to prison, and, when he got out, he wrote the book upon which the film was based. Could you call that ghost-writing?" For more details on the Dalton Gang see my book *Encyclopedia of Western Lawmen and Outlaws* (Paragon House, 1992; pages 94-101). **d**, George Marshall; **cast**, Randolph Scott, Kay Francis, Brian Donlevy, George Bancroft, Broderick Crawford, Stuart Erwin, Andy Devine,

Frank Albertson, Mary Gordon, Fay McKenzie, Edgar Buchanan (narrator); **w**, Harold Shumate (based on the book by Emmett Dalton, Jack Jungmeyer Sr.); **c**, Hal Mohr; **m**, Frank Skinner; **ed**, Ed Curtiss; **art d**, Jack Otterson; **set d**, Russell A. Gausman.

When the Legends Die ★★★ 1972; U.S.; 107m; Sagaponack/FOX; Color; Western; Children: Unacceptable (MPAA: PG); **DVD**; **VHS**. Action-packed western sees Forrest, a young and rebellious Ute Indian, joining the rodeo circuit and meeting Widmark, a former rodeo rider, who has fallen on hard times and is a heavy drinker, but who becomes his mentor. With Widmark's tutoring, Forrest becomes a rodeo star. Widmark, however, fixes some events and gambles away the winnings on liquor without Forrest knowing about it. Forrest is injured in a rodeo event and is hospitalized. Afterward, he finds Widmark dying and, despite their past differences, takes Widmark's body to the Ute reservation for burial. Forrest then gives up rodeos and remains on the reservation to become a teacher of Indian culture. Well acted and firmly directed, this film shows some very good rodeo footage. For a comprehensive list of similar films, see Subject Index, Rodeos and Rodeo Performers. *Author's Note*: Widmark told this author that "a lot of the plot and characters in **When the Legends Die** are very similar to another rodeo picture, **The Lusty Men** [1952], except that we have a lot of new twists to the characters. When making movies it is almost impossible for story lines not to bump into each other." **p**, Stuart Millar, Gene Lasko; **d**, Millar; **cast**, Richard Widmark, Frederic Forrest, Luana Anders, Jack Mullaney, Vito Scotti, Herbert Nelson, John War Eagle, John Gruber, Garry Walberg, Malcolm Curley, Roy Engel; **w**, Robert Dozier (based on the novel by Hal Borland); **c**, Richard H. Kline (DeLuxe Color); **m**, Glenn Paxton; **ed**, Louis San Andres; **art d**, Angelo Graham; **set d**, Jerry Wunderlich.

When the Sky Falls ★★★ 2000; UK/Ireland/U.S.; 107m; Icon Entertainment International; Color; Crime Drama; Children: Unacceptable (MPAA: R); **BD**; **DVD**. This suspenseful thriller is a fact-based film about Irish crime investigating reporter Sinead Hamilton, played by Allen. She invades the Irish underworld and tries to expose the illegitimate activities she finds. Hampered by the system, a police consort is unable to aid her. Her husband, McNally, hates her activities and the dangers in which she places herself, but grudgingly admires her persistence and ultimately encourages her investigation. The story is based on the activities of Veronica Guerin (1958-1996), a crime reporter writing about drugs for the Irish newspaper the *Sunday Independent*, that led to investigating drugs and murder, but the heroic Guerin was murdered while conducting her investigations. Her story was also depicted in **Veronica Guerin**, 2003. Songs: "Full Circle" (Loreena McKennitt), "Sleep with the Ancients" (Jimmy Smyth, Pearse Dunne, Jenny Newman), "Don't It Make My Brown Eyes Blue" (Richard Leigh), "Open Asylum," "Blockhead." Excessive violence, gutter language, drug content and some sexuality prohibit viewing by children. **p**, Nigel Warren Green, Michael Wearing, David McLoughlin; **d**, John Mackenzie; **cast**, Joan Allen, Kevin McNally, Patrick Bergin, Pete Postlethwaite, Liam Cunningham, Jimmy Smallhorne, Gerard Flynn, Jason Barry, Des McAleer, Owen Roe; **w**, Ronan Gallagher, Colum McCann, Michael Sheridan, Guy Andrews; **c**, Seamus Deasy; **m**, Pol Brennan; **ed**, Graham Walker; **prod d**, Mark Geraghty; **art d**, Conor Devlin; **set d**, Johnny Byrne; **spec eff**, Graham Bushe.

When Willie Comes Marching Home ★★★ 1950; U.S.; 82m; FOX; B/W; Comedy/War Drama; Children: Acceptable; **DVD**. Entertaining comedy has Dailey playing Willie Kluggs, who is the first in his hometown of Punxatawney, West Virginia, to enlist in the U.S. Army Air Forces after the attack on Pearl Harbor on December 7, 1941, that brings the United States into WWII (1939-1945). His father, Demarest; mother, Varden; and girlfriend, Townsend are proud of him, and they and the rest of the town give him a big send-off. He wants to become a war hero

Richard Widmark and Frederic Forrest in *When the Legends Die*, 1972.

and tries to become a pilot, but washes out. He is, however, an excellent aerial gunner so he is made a gunnery instructor assigned to a base near his hometown. After two years of stateside duty near home, the townspeople brand him a coward, even though he keeps requesting a transfer that will take him into combat. Finally, he gets his transfer when a gunner on a B-17 Flying Fortress bomber falls sick and Dailey is allowed to take his place. The plane takes off for England, but a heavy fog settles in and it is unable to land while the plane runs low on fuel. The crew is ordered to bail out, but Dailey is asleep and does not parachute out of the plane until it is over German-occupied France. He is captured by a French resistance unit led by beautiful Calvet and with them sees a secret German rocket launch of the lethal V-2 that has been used to bombard London, which is filmed by the French. He and the film are picked up by a British torpedo boat and taken to England where he passes the vital film on to generals, first in London, and then in Washington, D.C. He has trouble sleeping so is given liquor, which makes him ill and he is hospitalized. He is mistakenly put in a psychopath ward, but escapes and heads home on a freight train. Back home again, Dailey recounts his fantastic exploits (all occurring only four days since he left), but his parents and girlfriend don't believe his story. They finally believe him after officers arrive from the Pentagon to return him to Washington to be personally decorated by the President. Dailey is superb as the belated, zany hero, and pantheon director Ford provides a lot of exciting action and many mirthful scenes. He nevertheless balances the comedic elements with more somber scenes when Dailey and the French underground witness the launching of the V-2 rocket. The film received an Oscar nomination for Best Story (Gomberg). Songs: "When Johnny Comes Marching Home" (Patrick Gilmore as Louis Lambert), "Shall We Gather at the River" (Robert Lowry), "Somebody Stole My Gal" (Leo Wood), "Hail! Hail! The Gang's All Here" (Arthur Sullivan, Theodore Morse), "You're in the Army Now" (music: Isham Jones; lyrics: Tell Taylor, Ole Olsen), "Deep in the Heart of Texas" (1941; Don Swander), "You've Got Me This Way/Whatta-Ya Gonna Do About It" (music: Jimmy McHugh; lyrics: Johnny Mercer), "The Army Air Corps Song" (Robert Crawford), "Frere Jacques" (French traditional), "The Yankee Doodle Boy" (1905; George M. Cohan), "The Whiffenpoof Song" (Tod B. Galloway), "Don't Sit Under the Apple Tree with Anyone Else But Me" (Sam H. Stept). *Author's Note*: This film was one of Ford's favorites, but he nevertheless admitted to this author that "although the story is based on the real experiences of a gunner in WWII, we took a few pages out of Preston Sturges' **Hail the Conquering Hero** [1944] when we made **When Willie Comes Marching Home**. We even used Bill Demarest, who was in the Sturges picture, but he plays a different character in our production. The film was not made for just laughs, but has some very serious moments about how the Nazis were

Colleen Townsend and Dan Dailey in *When Willie Comes Marching Home,* **1950.**

using rockets to kill innocent citizens in London." Ford then recalled his own experiences in WWII when he made documentaries for the U.S. Army and U.S. Navy, stating: "That was my racket for some time during the war, and there wasn't anything funny about that war. I even lost some of my crew members, who were killed making those pictures. I suppose some S.O.B. will make a comedy out of Vietnam someday." The story upon which this film is based recounted the exploits of Sy Gomberg, who was shipped out of the country in WWII on a Friday afternoon, and he shot down a Japanese plane while his own plane was being staffed and how he was returned home the following Monday, a four-day harrowing exploit even Gomberg found hard to believe. Silent screen star Mae Marsh appears in a bit part as do Vera Miles and Alan Hale Jr., who were then beginning their careers in Hollywood. **p**, Fred Kohlmar; **d**, John Ford; **cast**, Dan Dailey, Corinne Calvet, Colleen Townsend, William Demarest, James Lydon, Lloyd Corrigan, Evelyn Varden, Alan Hale Jr., Charles Halton, Vera Miles, Mae Marsh, Kenneth Tobey, Hank Worden; **w**, Mary Loos, Richard Sale (based on the story "When Leo Comes Marching Home" by Sy Gomberg); **c**, Leo Tover; **m**, Alfred Newman; **ed**, James B. Clark; **art d**, Lyle Wheeler, Chester Gore; **set d**, Bruce Macdonald, Thomas Little.

When Worlds Collide ★★★ 1951; U.S.; 83m; UNIV; Color; Science Fiction; Children: Unacceptable; **DVD**; **VHS**; **IV**. Exciting and well-made doomsday tale begins when Derr, a skilled pilot, is paid to deliver some mysterious photographs from one eminent astronomer to another. The recipient, space scientist Keating, confirms that the star Bellus will collide with Earth and wipe out all of humanity. Despite widespread disbelief, two philanthropists give Keating some money to build an enormous rocket ship that will, at least they hope, take selected humans to Zyra, a planet orbiting Bellus, which may or may not be able to sustain human life. The rest of the money needed comes from Hoyt, a wheelchair-bound tycoon, who insists he be taken along, despite limitations on space for passengers and cargo. Meanwhile, as doomsday approaches, Derr finds himself in a love triangle with Keating's beautiful daughter, Rush, and her fiancé, Hansen. It becomes a rush against time as the rocket ship is being built before the world ends. The special effects include New York City being flooded and the rocket ship's takeoff and landing on the new planet, which, fortunate for the migrating humans, is livable. This above-average science fiction film did well at the box office, earning more than $1.6 million in its initial release. *Author's Note*: Pal, who would go on to produce the outstanding **War of the Worlds**, 1953, meticulously researched this futuristic tale, hiring gifted artist Chesley Bonestell to draw the colliding worlds as well as the space ark that takes Earthlings to their new home in space. Pal thought to make a sequel to this film, but was unable to secure financial backing. Alyn,

who has a small role in this film, had had his share of futuristic films when he starred as Clark Kent and Superman in the 1948 film serial **Superman**. **p**, George Pal; **d**, Rudolph Mate; **cast**, Richard Derr, Barbara Rush, Peter Hansen, John Hoyt, Larry Keating, Hayden Rorke, Kirk Alyn, Mary Murphy, John Ridgely, Stuart Whitman; **w**, Sydney Boehm (based on the novel by Edwin Balmer, Philip Wylie); **c**, W. Howard Greene, John F. Seitz (Technicolor); **m**, Leith Stevens; **ed**, Arthur Schmidt; **art d**, Hal Pereira, Albert Nozaki; **set d**, Sam Comer, Ross Dowd; **spec eff**, Gordon Jennings, Farciot Edouart, Paul K. Lerpae.

When You're in Love ★★★ 1937; U.S.; 110m; COL; B/W; Musical/Romance; Children: Acceptable; **DVD**; **VHS**. Poignantly memorable musical begins with Moore, an opera singer, who is stranded in a town in Mexico and is unable to return to the United States because of visa problems. Grant, an artist, is also stranded there, unable to pay his hotel bill. They agree to an arrangement whereby Grant agrees to marry Moore if she pays him $2,000, which will enable her to return to New York to resume her career and where Grant can pay off his debts. It doesn't take long before the marriage-for-convenience couple fall in love with each other. Moore's career obligations take their toll on Grant and they file divorce papers. True love, however, wins out and they reconcile. A highlight of the film is when Moore joins a small band to sing "Minnie the Moocher." Songs: "Minnie the Moocher" (Cab Calloway, Irving Mills, Clarence Gaskill), "Our Song" and "The Whistling Boy" (Jerome Kern, Dorothy Fields), "Serenade" (Franz Schubert), "Siboney" (Ernesto Lecuona), "The Waltz Song" (from "Romeo and Juliet" by Charles Gounod, Jules Barbier, Michel Carre), "In the Gloaming" (Annie Fortescue Harrison, Meta Orred), "Vissi D'Arte" (from "Tosca" by Giacomo Puccini). *Author's Note*: Moore died in a plane crash ten years after this film was made and the world was deprived of a great talent. Silent film star Louise Brooks returned to the movies after an absence of seven years to appear in a small role as a ballet dancer. The sultry actress had been a top star in the silent era, but fell out with movie moguls when she refused to appear in talking pictures during the early 1930s. She appeared in several important European films, including **Diary of a Lost Girl**, 1929, and **Pandora's Box**, 1929, but, when she returned to the U.S., almost all the Hollywood studios turned their backs on her. Grant told this author that "Louise [Brooks] was absolutely radiant in her small part in **When You're in Love**, which the studio promoted as her comeback, but they did it in such a way as to make sure she would be going nowhere. She was terribly treated." Columbia's publicity department purposely demeaned Brooks as a temperamental, unreliable actress (on orders from Columbia boss Harry Cohn), its humiliating release stating: "Louise Brooks, former star who deserted Hollywood at the height of her career, has come back to resume her work in pictures. But seven years is too long for the public to remember and Louise courageously begins again at the bottom." Brooks, many years later, told this author (in her Rochester, N.Y. residence): "Those people in the publicity department at Columbia told me that Harry Cohn had really written that release that made me look like some orphan. I then marched right into Cohn's office and confronted him with that and he snarled at me and said: 'You told us [Hollywood moguls] all to go to hell when you went to Europe, and tramped around with all those goddamned communists and anarchists, who call themselves moviemakers. Then you come back here and expect us to treat you like you have never been gone. We don't owe you a damned thing, lady. You're lucky I let you on our [Columbia's] lot.' I made only two pictures after that, one at my old studio, Paramount, where they dumped my scenes [from **King of Gamblers**, 1937], and my last picture, at Republic, a western [**Overland Stage Riders**, 1938] with that wonderful John Wayne, who was instrumental in getting me the role of his leading lady in that film. After that, I opened a dance studio, but had some problems and finally left Hollywood in 1940 and I haven't missed one day of its sunshine since." Brooks had married only twice and later had affairs with millionaires, including William S. Paley (1901-1990), head of CBS, who provided her with a small lifetime annuity, which, Brooks later claimed, prevented her from contemplating suicide. Wayne told this author that: "It was a crying shame how Louise Brooks was treated in the late 1930s when she tried to make a comeback in pictures. I talked executives at Republic into casting her in one of my westerns [**Overland Stage Riders**], and one of them said at that time: 'She's got a terrible reputation.' 'As what,' I said, 'a great actress?' Well, they put her into the picture, but that was her last go-round before the cameras. What a loss." **p**, Everett Riskin; **d**, Robert Riskin; **cast**, Grace Moore, Cary Grant, Aline MacMahon, Henry Stephenson, Thomas Mitchell, Catherine Doucet, Luis Alberni, Emma Dunn, Scotty Beckett, Louise Brooks, Ann Doran, Billy Gilbert, Dave O'Brien; **w**, Robert Riskin (based on an idea by Ethel Hill, Cedric Worth); **c**, Joseph Walker; **m**, Alfred Newman; **ed**, Gene Milford; **art d**, Stephen Goosson.

Where Danger Lives ★★★ 1950; U.S.; 84m; RKO; B/W; Crime Drama; Children: Unacceptable; **DVD**. Mitchum gives a fascinating performance of a compassionate physician who sinks ever downward into a whirlpool of infidelity, deceit and murder in this riveting film noir tale. He is involved with O'Sullivan, a nurse, who works with him, and they are planning a life together. Mitchum's peaceful life all changes when he begins treating sultry Domergue, a patient at the San Francisco Hospital where she has been admitted for attempting suicide. She recovers and departs, but leaves a note for Mitchum, saying that if he wants to know her story, he should contact her. Worried that Domergue might try again to take her life, Mitchum breaks a date with O'Sullivan and finds Domergue living at a huge mansion and surrounded by great wealth. Mitchum falls deeply in love with Domergue, and when she later tells him that she will be flying to Nassau with her father, a trip she does not want to make, Mitchum tries to stop her. He tells Rains that he is in love with his daughter, asking permission to marry her. Rains smugly informs Mitchum that Domergue is not his daughter, but his wife, and that she is a scheming woman who married him only to obtain his money. Domergue protests, but Mitchum is disgusted with the both of them and begins to leave. He hears Domergue scream and returns to find her holding a bloody ear where her earring has been ripped from the lobe. Incensed at Rains' brutal treatment of Domergue, Mitchum gets into a struggle with Rains. Grabbing a fireplace poker, Rains repeatedly hits Mitchum with it. Mitchum fends Rains off by pushing him hard to the floor where the elderly husband strikes his head and becomes unconscious. Going to a bathroom to attend to his bloody head, Mitchum returns to find Rains dead. Dazed, he is convinced by the desperate Domergue to flee after she says that police will accuse them of murdering Rains. They first think to use the airline tickets Domergue has for Nassau, but, when they see police officers gathered at the airline counter, they decide to escape to Mexico in Domergue's expensive convertible. While driving toward the Mexican border, they realize that police will be looking for Domergue's car, so they trade it in for a beat-up truck, driving to Roseville, Arizona, where they plan to sneak across the border to Mexico. Mitchum is still suffering from the concussion he received from the beating administered by Rains, and he diagnoses his condition with dire predictions. He tells Domergue that the mental fog he is suffering stems from a concussion that could lead to paralysis of his limbs or one side of his body and, should that happen, he could slip into a coma within twenty-four to forty-eight hours. When arriving at Roseville, they are suddenly picked up by local police, but Mitchum finds that it is a local custom to waylay any man who is not wearing a false beard since the town is celebrating "Wild West Whiskers Week." Domergue explains that they are planning to get married in Mexico, and police chief Kemper says that his town specializes in marrying eloping lovers, insisting that the couple wed in Roseville. They are cowed into accepting a honeymoon room. When Mitchum leaves that room, Domergue hears a police report on the radio that reports Rains' death and she throws a wild temper tantrum when the broadcast relates how she has been undergoing psychiatric treatment and is described as mentally un-

Robert Mitchum, Claude Rains and Faith Domergue in *Where Danger Lives,* **1950.**

stable. After she and Mitchum then slip away, heading for the border, Kemper identifies a photo of Domergue as being wanted for a murder, and he notifies the border patrol. It is then reported that Rains died from asphyxiation after being smothered by a pillow. Reaching a border town, the couple pawns Domergue's $9,000 bracelet for $1,000; the pawnbroker sends them to Van Zandt, a theater owner, who offers to smuggle them into Mexico for $1,000. As they are fleeing, Mitchum is seized by paralysis, and realizes, finally, that Domergue is mentally deranged. He tells her that he will not accompany her to Mexico. She explodes, knocking him down and smothering him. Mitchum, however, recovers, and manages to stumble after her. When she sees him approaching, Domergue withdraws a pistol and begins firing at Mitchum, but border patrol agents arrive and, when Domergue refuses to surrender, she is fatally shot. Before dying, however, Domergue absolves Mitchum of any blame in the death of her husband, Rains. Mitchum is shown recovering back at his hospital in San Francisco. When a doctor leaves his room, he asks a nurse to attend to Mitchum and that nurse is O'Sullivan, who reunites with the man she loves. Farrow does a fine job in developing the complex characters of Domergue and Mitchum, and both excel in presenting those complicated people. The tale is well told from a clever script by Bennett (who had written the adaptation for **The 39 Steps**, 1935, and the screenplay for **Foreign Correspondent**, 1940, both classic film noir entries from Alfred Hitchcock), and Musuraca's gritty lensing adds great film noir atmosphere. Webb's discordant score lends an eerie sense to the increasing hallucinations suffered by Mitchum and those harbored by Domergue. Songs: "There's Nothing Else To Do in Ma-La-Ka-Mo-Ka-Lu" (Cliff Friend, Sidney D. Mitchell), "I'm Living in a Great Big Way" (music: Jimmy McHugh; lyrics: Dorothy Fields), "You May Not Remember" (music: Ben Oakland; lyrics: George Jessel), "I Haven't a Thing to Wear" (Mort Greene, Harry Revel), "Pau Loke" (Gene Rose, Roy Webb). *Author's Note*: Mitchum told this author that "Faith [Domergue] was Howard Hughes' hand-picked protégé. He paired me with her in **Where Danger Lives**, believing that that picture would establish her as a screen siren, and that she would become as famous as Jane Russell, another gal Howard promoted into superstar status. That just didn't happen. Faith never caught on with the public like Jane did. Howard thought that his money could make anyone a star, but it cost him a pretty dollar to find out otherwise." **p**, Irving Cummings, Jr.; **d**, John Farrow; **cast**, Robert Mitchum, Faith Domergue, Claude Rains, Maureen O'Sullivan, Charles Kemper, Ralph Dumke, Billy House, Harry Shannon, Philip Van Zandt, Jack Kelly, Philip Ahlm, Jack Kruschen, Angela Stevens; **w**, Charles Bennett (based on a story by Leo Rosten); **c**, Nicholas Musuraca; **m**, Roy Webb; **ed**, Eda Warren; **art d**, Albert S. D'Agostino, Ralph Berger; **set d**, Darrell Silvera, John Sturtevant.

Richard Burton and Clint Eastwood in *Where Eagles Dare,* 1969.

Where Does It Hurt? ★★★ 1972; U.S.; 72m; Josef Shafter Productions/Cinerama Releasing Corp.; Color; Comedy; Children: Unacceptable (MPAA: R); **DVD**. This offbeat film satirizes medical scammers, who are epitomized by the hilarious Sellers, a blatantly unscrupulous hospital administrator. He gets rich by duping insurance companies, having unnecessary surgery performed on patients, padding their bills, and falsifying records. Lenz, an out-of-work construction worker, arrives at his hospital for a chest X-ray and Sellers learns that he owns a house, so he and Morita, a greedy laboratory technician, conspire to get it away from him. An admitting nurse, Pflug, tells Lenz that he needs to have his appendix removed, and, after the surgery, he learns that the operation was not necessary and he might now sue the hospital. Sellers retaliates by having Pflug, his girlfriend, seduce Lenz while he films the encounter. She gets even with Sellers by having a Mexican festival held at the hospital just as a hospital administrator, McKinley, arrives to inspect conditions and finds the place a disorganized disaster. He fires Sellers and sends him to jail for a short time. After serving his time in jail, Sellers returns to the hospital seeking revenge. He pretends to be a patient and has himself operated on, then plans to sue the hospital for malpractice. Gould, an inept doctor, performs the surgery while closing his eyes. Try as he may, however, Sellers' plot backfires on him and he finds that he just can't win. Songs: "Where Does It Hurt?" (Keith Allison), "When I'm Calling You" (from the operetta "Rose Marie"; music: Rudolf Friml; lyrics: Oscar Hammerstein II). Mature material and gutter language prohibit viewing by children. **p**, Rod Amateau, William Schwartz; **d**, Amateau; **cast**, Peter Sellers, Jo Ann Pflug, Rick Lenz, Harold Gould, Eve Bruce, Hope Summers, Pat Morita, Paul Lambert, Brett Halsey, Norman Alden, Keith Allison, Albert Reed, Jean Byron, Ed Begley Jr., Kathleen Freeman; **w**, Amateau, Budd Robinson (based on their novel *The Operator*); **c**, Brick Marquard (Eastmancolor); **m**, Keith Allison; **ed**, Mario Mora, Stanley Rabjohn; **prod d**, Antonio Sarzi-Braga; **art d**, Michael D. Haller.

Where Eagles Dare ★★★★ 1969; U.K./U.S.; 155m; MGM; Color; Spy Drama; Children: Unacceptable (MPAA: M); **BD**; **DVD**; **VHS**; **IV**. Outstanding espionage tale sees Burton leading a small group of British commandos and one American officer, Eastwood, on a daring raid behind enemy lines to rescue a captured U.S. general in WWII (1939-1945). This intriguing, complex tale begins when Beatty, a U.S. general who knows the plans for the Allied invasion of Europe (Normandy), is made captive after his plane crashes off Crete and is taken by the Germans to an Alpine fortress in Bavaria where he is held for interrogation. In England, a group of commandos are ordered to rescue Beatty, the group including Burton, a major, along with Eastwood, a U.S. lieutenant in the Rangers, and British commandos Houston, Barkworth,

Squire, Williams and McCarthy. Assigning this group to this near-impossible mission is Hordern, a British admiral, and Wymark, a British colonel, both spymasters for MI6. The group is told at a briefing that they must parachute close to the mountain fortress, infiltrate its defenses, locate Beatty, and somehow rescue and take him to freedom before he can reveal the details of the Allied invasion to the Germans. The group is then shown flying toward their destination in a German bomber (a Junker JU 52 to disguise its occupants); Ure, another MI6 agent, is secreted on board that plane and is to accompany the group, but her presence is known only to Burton. The attractive Ure and Burton are more than co-spies on this mission as they have been long-standing lovers. After the group successfully parachutes into deep mountain snows in Bavaria, Burton finds Williams, one of the NCOs and the radio operator, dead. He discovers that Williams has been struck on the back of his head, his neck broken, realizing that he has been murdered by one of the other parachutists, but he reports the death as an accident to Hordern via a short-wave radio (where his memorable call signal is "Broadsword calling Danny Boy"). When McCarthy, another NCO, is also found mysteriously murdered by Burton, he inexplicably reports that he, too, died from an unexplained mishap. Burton uses the short-wave radio carried by Williams to contact Horndern and Wymark, reporting the two deaths but giving his superiors no explanations for those fatalities. Burton and the other surviving four members of his team then meet at a prearranged rendezvous, a mountain cabin, and, while the others rest, Burton goes to a nearby shack to secretly meet with Ure, who has parachuted last from the plane and remains unknown to others in Burton's team. She separately makes her way from the snow-swept mountain to the village in the valley below, going to an inn where she is met by Pitt, who pretends to welcome her as a visiting relative. Burton and the other four agents then go to the same inn, and they are dressed as German soldiers, Burton and Eastwood as officers and Houston, Barkworth and Squire dressed as German enlisted men. Burton sits down with a group of other German officers and makes outlandish passes at waitress Pitt. When another German officer criticizes his behavior as being conduct unbecoming an officer, Burton lashes out at him, saying that he is related to SS and Gestapo leader Heinrich Himmler (1900-1945), and that if the critical German officer knows what is good for him and wants to avoid being sent to the Russian Front (known to be a deathtrap by all German troops), he had better keep his remarks to himself. Eastwood is more than puzzled by Burton's eccentric behavior, but does nothing. German troops then enter the inn, led by an officer who states that enemy parachutists have been detected in the area disguised as German soldiers, and everyone in the inn is ordered to stand up for inspection. Burton further amazes Eastwood by nonchalantly approaching the German officer to tell him that he and Eastwood, along with Houston, Barkworth and Squire, are the men he is seeking, and all meekly submit to arrest. Burton and Eastwood are separated from the other three agents as they are wearing German officer uniforms and are to be separately interrogated. As both are being driven to an interrogation area, Burton and Eastwood overwhelm their guards, killing them. They then place the bodies of the Germans into the command car and push it over a cliff so that it crashes downward into a ravine, landing in a river and where it explodes. They then make their way back to the village where they sneak into an ammunition warehouse, stealing explosives and, before leaving, set a time bomb. When investigating Germans enter the warehouse, a searching German officer trips a wire and sets off an explosion that blows up the place. In the confusion, Burton and Eastwood kill two Germans riding on a motorcycle with a sidecar, and then use that vehicle to ride through the village as Germans are rushing to put out the fire at the destroyed warehouse. They then use the cycle to drive along a roadway to prepare their future escape route, affixing explosives to telephone poles and trees that they wire to roadway markers. Meanwhile, Pitt arranges for Ure to work as a maid at the castle fortress that looms above the village, and they take a cable car—the only access to the castle—riding upward to the castle with

Gestapo officer Nesbitt, an arrogant and fanatical Nazi major who makes advances toward Ure. A short time later, Burton and Eastwood secretly climb onto the top of the next cable car going upward to the castle, and reach a roof where, unseen, they climb to the foot of the castle and where Ure lowers a rope from the window of a safe room. Burton climbs upward and enters the room, followed by Eastwood, who seems to struggle in reaching that room. Ure asks Burton why he does not help Eastwood climb to the room, and Burton casually tells her that since he climbed up to the room on his own, it is Eastwood's obligation to do the same. (His is an ironic remark in that when Burton made that climb he was then overweight and out of condition and had to be lifted by a crane with unseen wires to that room.) Once Eastwood arrives, he is introduced to Ure, and he and Burton then plan their next move. Meanwhile, Mayne, a German general, arrives by helicopter at the castle where he is warmly greeted by Diffring, a German colonel and where Mayne and Diffring later conduct an interrogation of Beatty, the captive American general, probing his knowledge about the anticipated Allied invasion of France. The three British agents, Houston, Barkworth and Squire, are then brought to that interrogation area and it is revealed that they are actually German double agents, who have penetrated British intelligence. As planned, Burton and Eastwood then enter the room, training guns on the German interrogators, and Burton announces, after surprisingly disarming Eastwood, that he is not a British agent, but a German intelligence officer working for the SD, the espionage arm of the German SS. To convince Mayne, Diffring and the traitorous three German agents that he is what he says he is, Burton states that Beatty is not an American general at all, but an American actor, who is actually a corporal in the U.S. Army, and whose impersonation is designed to mislead the Germans about where the Allies will next invade France. Burton further proves his true identity as a German agent by having Mayne talk to a German spymaster on the phone, who confirms Burton's role as a German double spy. Burton states that he believes that Houston, Barkworth and Squire are actually British agents pretending to be German spies and tells them that the only way he will accept them as German agents is for them to write down their German contacts in England. The three dutifully write down lists of those contacts and give the lists to Burton. Once Burton has pocketed this information, he summarily shoots and kills Mayne and Diffring, while Eastwood, who has been allowed to rearm himself, shoots and kills a German female stenographer attempting to flee the room, along with Gestapo major Nesbitt, who has earlier come upon the enclave. Burton, it is now clear, has been playing a triple game to obtain information from the three German double agents. He and Eastwood then order Houston, Squire and Barkworth, as well as Beatty, to accompany them back to their escape room and where Ure waits for them. While Eastwood plants explosives in various areas of the castles to create diversions—these time-bomb explosions creating chaos among the garrison—Burton contacts Hordern and Wymark by radio to tell them that he has obtained the information they were seeking and are about to escape, asking that the escape plane be sent to a nearby airport. The group then gets into several firefights with garrison troops, until Burton uses Squire as a decoy by ordering him to descend down a rope from the escape room and where German troops find and kill him. Burton and the others then go to the cable car control room, killing its operators, but Houston and Barkworth take over one of the cable cars and begin to descend toward the valley. Burton leaps onto the top of the cable car and a fight between him and the two German agents ensues, ending after Burton kills both men, and then leaps from that descending cable car to one ascending toward the castle. (The fantastic stunts performed in this amazing sequence, where Burton leaps through the air from one cable car to another duplicates a scene shown in an equally superb espionage film, **Night Train to Munich**, 1940, where actor Rex Harrison enacts almost the same stunts.) When reaching the cable car control room with the ascending cable car, Burton has Ure, Eastwood and Beatty get into it and they ride it downward. As planned, when the cable car descends and passes over a river, all four

Derren Nesbitt, Ingrid Pitt and Mary Ure in *Where Eagles Dare*, 1969.

occupants drop into the freezing waters, swimming to and climbing onto the riverbank and then going to a garage to find, as prearranged, a bus affixed with a snowplow, boarding this vehicle. Meanwhile, German troops assemble at the platform to await the descending cable car, having been informed that it contains the fleeing saboteurs. However, the cable car explodes in the faces of these waiting German troops from a time bomb Burton has earlier left in the car. Burton then drives the bus through the village, with Eastwood and Ure firing at German guards attempting to stop it, racing it along the escape route Burton and Eastwood explored and where they had planted explosives. When German troops give chase in armored vehicles, Burton strikes the road markers to break the wires attached to those explosives affixed to poles and trees. The explosions then topple the poles and trees to prevent the Germans from following the bus, which Burton then crashes through a fence, racing it onto an airfield, and he drives the bus to make glancing blows against German parked planes, damaging them and setting them afire. Only moments earlier, the escape plane Burton has called for, has arrived, disguised again as a German bomber, and is waiting for the agents. Burton and the others fire and dismantle several pursuing German vehicles and their troops before climbing into the plane, which then takes off. On board that plane is Wymark, who congratulates Burton for accomplishing his challenging mission. Part of that accomplishment, Burton announces, involves exposing the top German agent in England, one of the real purposes for the mission, and Burton then tells Wymark that he, Wymark, is that Nazi mole, information Burton has confirmed during the mission. Wymark, stunned, sits glaring at Burton as the plane climbs higher and higher over the Alps and heading for England. Wymark points a Sten gun at Burton, but Burton tells him that the gun has no firing pin, which, he says, has been removed by Hordern before Hordern gave Wymark that gun. Burton tells Wymark that this has been done on the suspicion that Hordern shared with Burton, that Wymark was that German spymaster in England. Wymark squeezes the trigger of the gun, but nothing happens. He then asks Burton if he has any options and Burton gentlemanly allows him only one, other than returning to England to be executed as a spy. Wymark thanks him and, opening the door of the plane, leaps without a parachute to his certain death. Ure then comforts Burton by bandaging one of his injured hands while Eastwood, amazed at all the double-crossing he has witnessed during this incredible mission, tells Burton that, if and when Burton plans another such mission, he make it an "all-British" operation and without including him. The plane then flies onward toward freedom to end this very exciting film. Director Hutton provides an adventure tale packed with almost nonstop action, and where the script has so many clever turns and twists that even the actors cannot keep up with them. The pace is frenetic, and the acting from Burton, Eastwood and the rest of the cast members per-

Richard Burton and Clint Eastwood in *Where Eagles Dare*, 1969.

fectly matches the cartoon-strip characters they so convincingly enact. The viewer will easily accept this fantastic tale when watching this incessantly barraging film as its mesmerizing action allows little or no time for its scenes to be analyzed, let alone any belief put to the test. This film saw a great box office success, earning more than $21 million in its initial release against a budget of $7 million. *Author's Note*: The genesis for this film began when some of Burton's family members urged him to make an adventure film, an idea he warmed to in that he wanted relief from the heavy dramas he had been essaying. He approached producer Kastner, who, in turn, asked author MacLean to write a new espionage story for this film, and MacLean produced the book and script within six weeks. The lightning speed by which he achieved this feat might be due to his culling several real-life spy stories dealing with WWII, as well as looking keenly back upon a little remembered gem of a spy film titled **Night Train to Munich**, 1940. That film was helmed by pantheon director Carol Reed and starred Rex Harrison as a valiant MI6 agent who penetrates the German High Command in order to rescue an important scientist and his attractive daughter. That film's most spectacular sequences occur in the Alps, where Harrison leaps through mid-air from one cable car to another passing cable car in a battle with pursuing Gestapo agent Paul Henreid. When Burton is shown doing the same thing, he had a talented stuntman double, Alf Joint, performing those stunning feats, and who lost three teeth when performing that amazing stunt. When Eastwood was watching this stunt and others performed, he quipped that the film should be titled "Where Doubles Dare." Burton enjoyed great riches from this film through a whopping salary ($1,200,000) and a percentage of the profits. He told this author that "**Where Eagles Dare** almost broke my back—all that slogging through snowdrifts and mountain climbing. You had to be part goat to go anywhere. I don't know how they do it on the Matterhorn or Mount Everest—they must be made of iron and steel instead of flesh and blood. The air up there [at Hohenwerfen Castle south of Salzburg, Austria, where the film was shot on location] was pretty thin so it was no place for smokers. I think it might have been the most strenuous picture I ever made, other than another war picture called **The Desert Rats** [1953], but, thank God, in that picture, we were running around in the warm desert. I think we wiped out half the German army in that picture [**Where Eagles Dare**], but you must realize that MacLean [author of the script and novel] used the old serial techniques for his action characters, and they do all the impossible things that no humans can possibly do. That picture is a damned good cartoon strip put on film." Eastwood, who received $800,000 for his role, did not like the script when first reading it and asked that some of his lines be given to others, and some were later incorporated into Burton's speeches. Meanwhile, Eastwood, always an actor relying more on action than words, became the center of the

more spectacular energy-filled scenes. The Polish-born Pitt, who played the barmaid, had a difficult time with this film as the sight of the Nazi uniforms brought back nightmare images of her own real-life persecutions under the Nazis during WWII. The Hohenwerfen Castle used for the on-location shooting, located south of Salzburg, Austria, was then being used as a training center for police. There are no cable cars running to that bastion, so the cable car sequences were filmed at Ebensee, Austria. The airport scenes were shot at Aigen im Ennstal, Austria. The title for this film stems from William Shakespeare's "Richard III," Act I, Scene III: "The world has grown so bad that wrens make prey where eagles dare not perch." Other films profiling espionage and their intelligence agencies during WWII include **Above Suspicion**, 1943 (MI6; Abwehr); **Across the Pacific**, 1942 (Kempeitai; MI); **Action in Arabia**, 1944 (MI6; O.S.S.); **Adventures of Tartu**, 1943 (Gestapo; MI6); **Against the Wind**, 1949 (SOE; Abwehr); **All through the Night**, 1942 (Abwehr); **An American Guerrilla in the Philippines**, 1950 (U.S. naval intelligence; Filipino underground); **The Angels of Death Island**, 2003 (O.S.S.); **The Assassination of Trotsky**, 1972 (KGB); **Back-Room Boy**, 1942 (Abwehr); **Back to Bataan**, 1945 (Filipino Underground); **Background to Danger**, 1943 (O.S.S.; Abwehr); **Beachhead**, 1954 (U.S. military intelligence); **Behind the Rising Sun**, 1943 (Japanese Intelligence; Kempeitai); **Betrayal from the East**, 1945 (Japanese intelligence; Kempeitai); **Betrayed**, 1954 (Dutch intelligence); **Blood on the Sun**, 1945 (Kempeitai); **Bombay Clipper**, 1942 (Kempeitai); **Carve Her Name with Pride**, 1958 (SOE); **Circle of Deception**, 1961 (MI6; Abwehr); **Cloak and Dagger**, 1946 (O.S.S.; Abwehr); **Company Business**, 1991 (CIA: KGB); **Confessions of a Nazi Spy**, 1939 (Abwehr; FBI); **Count Five and Die**, 1958 (O.S.S.; MI6; Abwehr); **Counter-Espionage**, 1942 (MI5; Abwehr); **Decision Before Dawn**, 1951 (MIG; O.S.S.; Gestapo; Abwehr); **The Eagle Has Landed**, 1977 (Abwehr); **Enemy Agent**, 1940 (Abwehr; FBI; German agents after plans for the B-17 bomber and its bomb-sight); **Eye of the Needle**, 1981 (Abwehr); **Eyes in the Night**, 1942 (Abwehr); **The Falcon's Brother**, 1942 (Abwehr); **First Yank into Tokyo**, 1945 (O.S.S.; Kempeitai); **Foreign Correspondent**, 1940 (Abwehr); **The Good Shepherd**, 2007 (O.S.S.); Hidden Enemy, 1940 (Abwehr); **The House on 92nd Street**, 1945 (Abwehr; FBI); **I See a Dark Stranger**, 1947 (Abwehr; MI5); **I Was an American Spy**, 1951 (Filipino Underground); **Joan of Paris**, 1942 (French Underground; Gestapo); **The Lone Wolf Spy Hunt**, 1939; **The Man Who Never Was**, 1956 (NID; Abwehr); **Manila Calling**, 1942 (Filipino Underground); **Meet Boston Blackie**, 1941; **Ministry of Fear**, 1944 (Abwehr; Scotland Yard); **My Favorite Spy**, 1942 (MIG); **Nazi Agent**, 1942 (Abwehr); **Never So Few**, 1959 (MIG; O.S.S.); **Northern Pursuit**, 1943 (Canadian intelligence); **Notorious**, 1946 (FBI); **Odette**, 1951 (SOE); **Operation Crossbow**, 1965 (O.S.S.; MI6; Abwehr); **Operation Secret**, 1952 (O.S.S.; Abwehr); **O.S.S.**, 1946; **Paris Calling**, 1942 (French underground; Gestapo); **Rogue's Regiment**, 1948 (O.S.S.); **Saboteur**, 1942 (FBI; Abwehr); **Sherlock Holmes in Washington**, 1943 (Abwehr; FBI); **Seven Miles from Alcatraz**, 1942; **13 Rue Madeleine**, 1947 (O.S.S.; Abwehr; Gestapo); **36 Hours**, 1965 (Abwehr); **This Gun for Hire**, 1942 (fifth columnists working for Japan); **To Be or Not to Be**, 1942 (MI6; Abwehr); **Triple Cross**, 1966 (MI5; MI6; Abwehr); **The Two-Headed Spy**, 1959 (MI6; Abwehr); **Waterfront**, 1944 (Abwehr); **The Whip Hand**, 1951 (Abwehr); and **Yellow Canary**, 1944 (Abwehr; MI5). For comprehensive details on espionage agents, agencies and operations during WWII, see my book *Spies: A Narrative Encyclopedia of Dirty Deeds & Double Dealing from Biblical Times to the Present* (M. Evans, 1997). **p**, Elliott Kastner; **d**, Brian G. Hutton; **cast**, Richard Burton, Clint Eastwood, Mary Ure, Patrick Wymark, Michael Hordern, Donald Houston, Anton Diffring, Peter Barkworth, William Squire, Robert Beatty, Ingrid Pitt, Derren Nesbitt, Ferdy Mayne, Brook Williams, Neil McCarthy; **w**, Alistair MacLean (based on his novel); **c**, Arthur Ibbetson (Panavision; Metrocolor); **m**, Ron Goodwin; **ed**, John Jympson; **art d**, Peter Mullins; **spec eff**, Richard Parker, Fred Hellenburgh, Tom Howard.

Where East Is East ★★★ 1929 (silent); U.S.; 65m/7 reels; MGM; B/W; Drama/Romance; Children: Unacceptable; **DVD, IV**. Chaney again performs a stunning characterization, this time as a respected trapper of jungle animals for zoos and circuses in the Orient. He is a loving father to his beautiful daughter, Velez, as well as being overly protective of her well-being. He becomes suspicious of the intentions of Hughes, the son of a wealthy circus owner to whom he provides animals. Hughes' sincerity eventually wins Chaney over, and they take a river boat to Saigon to see the lad's father. Aboard ship, Chaney's wife, Taylor, a notorious seducer of men who has earlier run away from Chaney, returns to vamp Hughes. Chaney prevents her from breaking up their daughter's engagement to Hughes by releasing a gorilla that kills Taylor and badly mauls Chaney. Shortly after seeing Velez and Hughes marry, Chaney dies happy, knowing his daughter is in good hands. **p**, Hunt Stromberg, (not credited) Irving Thalberg; **d**, Tod Browning; **cast**, Lon Chaney, Lupe Velez, Estelle Taylor, Lloyd Hughes, Louis Stern, Mrs. Wong Wing, Willie Fung, Duke Kahanamoku, Chris-Pin Martin, Richard Neill (as the gorilla); **w**, Joseph Farnham (adapted by Waldemar Young from a story by Browning, Harry Sinclair Drago); **c**, Henry Sharp; **m**, William Axt; **ed**, Harry Reynolds; **art d**, Cedric Gibbons.

Where the Sidewalk Ends ★★★★ 1950; U.S.; 95m; FOX; B/W; Crime Drama; Children: Unacceptable; **DVD**. Hard-hitting film noir tale from top screenwriter Ben Hecht sees Andrews as a NYPD detective who hates criminals, tracking them down and beating them senseless before dragging them to the local precinct for booking. His seething rage against the underworld is rooted to a deep-seated hatred for his own father, who had been a corrupt cop, and Andrews will do anything to rid himself of that "sins-of-the-father" stigma. Andrews is already in trouble for his roughhouse treatment of hoodlums when he investigates the murder of wealthy von Zell, who has been killed after being bilked in a rigged gambling game. Stevens has acted as a shill to inveigle von Zell to that gambling operation, which is controlled by gangster Merrill. Andrews confronts Stevens but, when he resists interrogation, the two get into a brawl and Andrews knocks Stevens down. He hits his head, which contains a steel plate from a war wound, and is killed. Panicking, Andrews hides the body by dumping it into a nearby river. He is then assigned to investigate Stevens' disappearance while he attempts to plant evidence that will implicate Merrill in Stevens' death. Andrews has nothing but hatred for Merrill as the gangster, who had corrupted Andrews' father with payoffs. Malden, a police lieutenant supervising the case, believes that Tully, a hardworking and honest cabdriver, is responsible for Stevens' disappearance. Malden knows that Tully has had a long-standing grudge against Stevens, who was the estranged husband of Tully's daughter, Tierney. Andrews learns that Tierney had tolerated an abusive relationship with Stevens, and, after meeting her, he and Tierney become romantically involved. In an effort to clear Tully from suspicion, Andrews creates his own tangled web that brings him face to face with Merrill and his thugs. He leaves a letter exonerating Tully, who has been jailed and faces murder charges, and confesses in that letter that he alone killed Stevens, explaining that Stevens' death was an accident. Andrews then locates Merrill in a massage parlor and boldly threatens him, punching Merrill in the face and purposely provoking Merrill's goon Brand and others to beat him up. Merrill says that Andrews is really trying to get his goons to kill him so that he, Merrill, and his thugs will then be found guilty of Andrews' murder. In this the shrewd Merrill has read Andrews' disturbed mind. Merrill and his thugs then tie up Andrews and flee after they are alerted that police are about to raid their lair. Andrews breaks free, obtains a gun and attempts to stop Merrill and his men and is wounded in the resulting shoot-out. Police arrive to arrest Merrill and his thugs. Tully is then cleared and released and Tierney expresses her love to Andrews. He and she meet with Andrews' superior, Simon, a police inspector, who congratulates him on capturing Merrill and his gang. Andrews, however, relieves his burden of guilt by handing Simon the self-incriminating letter he has earlier written. Simon reads it and tells

Craig Stevens, Gene Tierney and Gary Merrill in *Where the Sidewalk Ends,* 1950.

Andrews that he must face the consequences of his actions, but Andrews accepts whatever fate awaits him, comforted by knowing that Tierney will be at his side. Preminger directs this gritty and violent tale with expertise, seamlessly unfolding the story's complicated twists and turns without red herrings or distracting subplots. Andrews gives a marvelous performance of a dedicated detective haunted by the gnawing memory that he has crossed the thin line between law enforcement and the criminal underworld, destroying his own code of strict ethics, until regaining self-respect by doing the right thing. Tierney is her beautiful self, a woman who finally finds an honorable man, but he is a man struggling to maintain his honor without losing her love. Merrill, too, is outstanding as the conniving and insidious crime boss, and Tully is very appealing as the empathetic father. This film proved successful at the box office and greatly advanced the careers of Andrews and Tierney. This story saw a sixty-minute radio adaptation aired by Lux Radio Theater on April 2, 1951, with Andrews reprising his role. Song: "Street Scene" (Alfred Newman). ***Author's Note***: The original story for this film began as a 1949 episode titled "Night Cry" in the serialized radio series called "Suspense." This was the last film Preminger directed for Fox. He told this author: "I had directed Dana [Andrews] and Gene [Tierney] in another crime picture called **Laura** [1944], which I believed made them both big Hollywood stars, and I wanted them both back together when we made **Where the Sidewalk Ends** as I always thought they had some special magnetism in their scenes together." Preminger also directed Andrews in another outstanding film noir tale from Fox, **Fallen Angel**, 1945, and he had directed yet another excellent film noir production with Tierney in **Whirlpool**, 1949, which, like this film, had been written by master screenwriter Ben Hecht. That writer told this author that "Preminger had the look of a Prussian officer, but he was really a very cooperative and amiable director. I never really had any problem with him. He looked over my script for **Where the Sidewalk Ends** and simply nodded. He rolled up the manuscript and then used it as a makeshift riding crop to slap his flanks with it as he walked away." Andrews told this author that "I always thought that **Where the Sidewalk Ends** was one of my best pictures, along with **The Best Years of Our Lives** [1946] and a number of very hard-hitting crime pictures like **Laura** [1944], **Fallen Angel** [1945] and **Boomerang!** [1947]. All of them gave me down-to-earth characters with a lot of substance." Tierney told this author that "I think too many people underestimated Dana's [Andrews'] acting of ability. He is the kind of actor who always underplays his characters and you can almost always see what he is thinking through his very small but telltale gestures. That is great acting." Malden recalled his role in this film for this author by stating: "I played a mean-minded police detective in **Where the Sidewalk Ends**, a part almost as the small one I had in another picture I did with Dana [Andrews] called

Dana Andrews, Sally Forrest, Thomas Mitchell and Ida Lupino in *While the City Sleeps,* **1956.**

Boomerang! And I played a cop in that one, too. In those days, directors thought I had the kind of face that belongs to a flatfoot." He was not alone, as character actor Simon also learned. This was Simon's film debut when playing the NYPD police official; ten years later he would again play a similar role in **Pay or Die**, 1960, when essaying the role of the commissioner of the NYPD. This film was shot entirely on location in NYC's Washington Heights and Manhattan. **p&d**, Otto Preminger; **cast**, Dana Andrews, Gene Tierney, Gary Merrill, Bert Freed, Tom Tully, Karl Malden, Ruth Donnelly, Craig Stevens, Robert F. Simon, Fred Aldrich, Don Appell, Neville Brand, Harry von Zell, Oleg Cassini; **w**, Ben Hecht, Frank P. Rosenberg, Victor Trivas, Robert E. Kent (based on the novel *Night Cry* by William L. Stuart); **c**, Joseph LaShelle; **m**, Cyril Mockridge; **ed**, Louis Loeffler; **art d**, Lyle Wheeler, J. Russell Spencer; **set d**, Walter M. Scott, Thomas Little; **spec eff**, Fred Sersen.

Where's Charley? ★★★ 1952; U.K.; 97m; WB; Color; Musical Comedy; Children: Acceptable; **DVD**. Based on the Broadway stage musical comedy, this entertaining songfest begins with Bolger and Shackleton, who are Oxford roommates during the reign of Queen Victoria (1819-1901). They are both in love with McLerie, while Germaine would like to date them but strict social conduct requires she have a chaperone. Bolger's aunt is enlisted to come from Brazil and be the chaperone for both young women, but is delayed. Bolger solves the problem by dressing up as his aunt. Cooper, who is Germaine's guardian, takes a romantic interest in Bolger (while he impersonates his aunt), and so does Shackleton's father, who thinks "aunt" Bolger is rich. The real aunt, Scott, finally arrives, and all the apple carts are toppled before everything is straightened out and the boys and girls get together. The film is a tour de force for singing-dancing Bolger, who recreates his stage success. It saw success at the box office, earning more than $1.5 million in its initial release. This is a remake of **Charley's Big-Hearted Aunt**, 1940, and **Charley's Aunt**, 1941. Songs: "The New Ashmolean Marching Society and Students' Conservatory Band," "My Darling, My Darling," "Once in Love with Amy", "At the Rose Cotillion," "Better Get Out of Here" (Frank Loesser). *Author's Note:* Bolger was forty-eight years old when performing his marvelous and acrobatic dances in this delightful film, attesting to his eye-popping durability and physical abilities. He was the only American in a lead role, the film being shot entirely at the Warner Brothers Studio in England. **p**, Ernest H. Martin, Cy Feuer; **d**, David Butler; **cast**, Ray Bolger, Allyn McLerie, Robert Shackleton, Horace Cooper, Margaretta Scott, Howard Marion-Crawford, Mary Germaine, Henry Hewitt, H.G. Stoker, Martin Miller; **w**, John Monks Jr. (based on the musical play by Frank Loesser, George Abbott from the play "Charley's Aunt" by Brandon Thomas); **c**, Erwin Hillier (Technicolor); **m**, Ray Heindorf, Howard Jackson; **ed**, Reginald Mills; **art d**, David

Ffolkes, Albert Witherick, **set d**, David Ffolkes.

Where's Poppa? ★★★ 1970; U.S.; 83m; UA; Color/B/W; Comedy; Children: Unacceptable (MPAA: R); **BD**; **DVD**; **VHS**. Hilarious and outlandish black comedy has New York City attorney Segal living with Gordon, his eccentric and slightly batty eighty-seven-year-old widowed mother. Segal promised his late father on his deathbed that he would always take care of his mother and never put her in a rest home. But Segal doesn't like having to take care of her and deal with her strange ways. He hires a series of caretakers to look after her, but they all quit because they cannot deal with Gordon's bizarre and unpredictable behavior. Segal then hires Van Devere, a private nurse, not knowing that patients in her care have a habit of dying. They fall in love at first sight and Segal is eager to marry Van Devere and start a new life free of caring for his mother, so he considers murdering her, or maybe even worse, putting her in a home for senile seniors. He tries to scare her to death by dressing in a gorilla costume and attacking her in bed, but she fends off the beast with her cane. She then pulls down Segal's pants and gives him a love bite on his bare butt. Segal tries to get his brother, Leibman, to take Gordon off his hands, but Leibman can barely take care of himself, being one of the world's eternal victims, and where he is repeatedly mugged in Central Park. After Van Devere tells him that she can't stand another second with Gordon and threatens to leave him, Segal finally gives up and takes Gordon to a rest home and drops her off at the entrance, telling her that Poppa (her deceased husband) is there. Then he drives away to be with Van Devere. Gordon is magnificent as the impossible mother (she had played many an eccentric characters), and Segal is a standout as the frustrated son. Director Reiner, an outstanding comedian in his own right, does a fine job moving this wacky film along at a fast pace. Mature subject matter prohibits viewing by children. Songs: "Where's Poppa?," "Move It!," "Freedom," "Pleasure Palace," "The Goodbye Song" (music: Jack Elliott; lyrics: Norman Gimbel); "Louise" (1929; music: Richard A. Whiting; lyrics: Leo Robin); "If You Were the Only Girl in the World" (1916: Nat Ayer). **p**, Jerry Tokofsky, Marvin Worth; **d**, Rob Reiner; **cast**, George Segal, Ruth Gordon, Ron Leibman, Trish Van Devere, Barnard Hughes, Vincent Gardenia, Rae Allen, Paul Sorvino, Michael McGuire, Rob Reiner, Penny Marshall; **w**, Robert Klane (based on his novel); **c**, Jack Priestley; **m**, Jack Elliott; **ed**, Chic Ciccolini, Bud Molin; **art d**, Warren Clymer; **set d**, Herbert F. Mulligan.

While the City Sleeps ★★★★ 1956; U.S.; 100m; RKO; B/W; Crime Drama; Children: Unacceptable; **DVD**; **VHS**; **IV**. Pantheon director Lang presents a fast-moving, taut tale of NYC mayhem and murder as reported through several news-gathering personalities, who are overseen by media mogul Price (called "Kyne," easily substituting for "Kane" as in **Citizen Kane**, 1941). Price is a dilettante when it comes to understanding how his vast news organization operates. He has inherited the media empire from his father, Warwick, who has recently died. He does not plan to direct that organization first-hand, wanting someone else to successfully guide it to more success. To that end, he establishes a dog-eat-dog competition for the title of editor-in-chief of the organization's flagship, a daily tabloid called the New York *Sentinel*. The three competitors are Mitchell, the managing editor of the newspaper; Sanders, who controls the wire service; and Craig, head of the company's photo division. Price tells these three power-hungry newshounds that whichever one of them is responsible for identifying a stalking murderer, who has been plaguing the city, before police capture that slayer, will get the top job. Barrymore is that demented serial killer, who has been dubbed "The Lipstick Killer." He is called by this name because, after sexually attacking and slaying his female victims, he leaves messages for the police written with the lipsticks of his victims. He is a mama's boy, dominated by mother Marsh, living alone with her and hating her. Meanwhile, Mitchell, a hard-drinking Irishman, wants the job simply to have the salary raise accompanying the promotion. The suave Sanders, on the other hand, wants the lofty position because it will enhance his social position. Photo chief Craig, on the other hand, exerts little effort in the competition, believing he can get the job through his adulterous relationship with Price's wife, the sultry Fleming, who has been cuckolding Price for years. Mitchell enlists the aid of his friend Andrews, who is the firm's TV news commentator, and Sanders gets Lupino, who is the paper's foremost columnist, to be his eyes and ears when tracking the story about the killer. Mitchell believes that Andrews can be of special assistance as he has recently fallen in love with and is engaged to Forrest, who is Sanders' executive secretary. While these self-serving individuals go about their dirty business, they easily discard their professional ethics as well as abandoning their morals. Andrews, for a sum of money promised by Mitchell, if he gets the promotion, plans to use the attractive Forrest as bait in luring the killer to her apartment, which Andrews will monitor. Sanders has no scruples in asking Lupino to seduce Andrews to find out what he knows, and Lupino, for a promised raise, agrees to attempt just such an assignation. Using information from his friend, Duff, who is a police lieutenant, Andrews appears on TV and directly challenges the killer, daring him to make another attack and he uses Forrest as the bait for that possible assault. Barrymore, watching the TV broadcast, accepts Andrew's challenge and goes to the apartment building where Forrest lives. When failing to gain entrance to her apartment, he sees alluring Fleming enter another apartment, ironically where Fleming meets to have her secret trysts with Craig. Barrymore forces his way into that apartment and attacks Fleming, who struggles wildly, screaming as Barrymore strips away her clothes and mauls her. She manages to escape, running into the hallway; Forrest, who has heard the commotion, quickly takes her into her apartment, slamming and locking the door just as Barrymore arrives in the hallway. Andrews, who has been watching the building and has seen Barrymore enter it, arrives and pursues Barrymore, as do police officers. A wild chase leads Andrews into the subway system where he runs after Barrymore down the tracks. Catching the killer, Andrews battles Barrymore, but, just as two on-coming trains arrive, both men separate. Andrews is almost struck by one train going one way, and Barrymore escapes the on-rushing train going in the other direction. Andrews sees Barrymore climbing some stairs and gives chase, but Barrymore is then cornered and captured by police, dragged away into custody while screaming like a wounded animal. Lang superbly balances the several coinciding stories that make up this thriller, increasing the suspense by intercutting from the newspaper coterie and their calculated hunt for the killer to the lethal Barrymore. His performance is one of his best as he manifests in every frame the habits and manners of a terrifying psychopath. Andrews, Mitchell, Sanders and Price are exceptional in their roles, and Fleming, Lupino and Forrest are standouts as the feminine leads. This film was a box office success and it has no relation to the 1928 silent film of the same title. *Author's Note*: Andrews told this author that "I really didn't like my character too much in **While the City Sleeps**, as he is an opportunist using his own girlfriend to attract a killer in order to get a story. I had to console myself with the thought that all the other characters in that picture were doing about the same thing." Sanders delighted in his role, telling this author: "I played an underhanded newspaper boss in that picture and where I will do anything, sell out anyone, to get more prestige for myself. Come to think of it, isn't that what all actors do in Hollywood?" Price stated to this author that "I had experience in playing a wealthy tycoon who connives to get everybody else to do his dirty work in **While the City Sleeps**. A few years earlier, I had played a similar character in **Champagne for Caesar** [1950], only in that picture I was a conniving tycoon running a soap company. If you have seen one tycoon, you have seen them all." The character played by Barrymore is based upon Chicago serial killer William George Heirens (1928-2012) who was sent to prison for life after being convicted of murdering three people, albeit he may have killed many more in a crime spree during the late 1940s. He was a burglar who strangled most of his female victims (abducting one six-year-old child and murdering her when he failed to obtain ransom money).

Myrna Loy and Spencer Tracy in *Whipsaw*, 1935.

He was called, like Barrymore in this film, the "Lipstick Killer," because he wrote messages to the police after committing his crimes with the lipstick of his victims. One of those messages, written on the mirror of one of the residences he burglarized, read: "Stop me before I kill more. I can't help myself." For details on Heirens, see my book *The Great Pictorial History of World Crime*, Volume II (History, Inc., 2004; pages 269-274). Though the setting for this riveting film is NYC, it was shot entirely in Los Angeles and the old Pacific Electronic Belmont tunnel doubled for the NYC subway system. Though they have no scenes together, Lupino and Duff were married at the time of this production. **p**, Bert Friedlob; **d**, Fritz Lang; **cast**, Dana Andrews, Rhonda Fleming, George Sanders, Howard Duff, Thomas Mitchell, Vincent Price, Sally Forrest, John Drew Barrymore, James Craig, Ida Lupino, Robert Warwick, Mae Marsh, Celia Lovsky, Vladimir Sokoloff; **w**, Casey Robinson (based on the novel *The Bloody Spur* by Charles Einstein); **c**, Ernest Laszlo; **m**, Herschel Burke Gilbert; **ed**, Gene Fowler, Jr.; **art d**, Carroll Clark; **set d**, Jack Mills.

Whipsaw ★★★ 1935; U.S.; 78m; MGM; B/W; Crime Drama/Romance; Children: Unacceptable; **DVD**. Nifty crime caper film begins with Loy, Stephens, and Clement stealing some jewels in Paris and heading for New York. While traveling across the country with the loot, the jewels are stolen by two other thieves, Harrigan and Gleckler. Loy recovers the jewels and goes off with Tracy, thinking he is another crook\ who has pitched in to help her out of her dilemma. However, Tracy is a government agent. On their travels they stop at the country home of Qualen, where a romance develops between Loy and Tracy. They become even more domesticized when they help Qualen's pregnant wife deliver a set of twins. Then Stephens and Clement, who have been pursuing Loy, find Loy and Tracy and hold them hostage in order to recover the gems. Loy tells them the jewels are back in New York, and the foursome travel back to the Big Apple to retrieve the gems. Tracy then reveals that he is a G-Man and, following a battle with the two crooks, aids police in their arrest (at that time federal agents did not have the power of arrest and had to employ local police to make such arrests). Loy is brought to trial, but Tracy confesses that he loves her and, no matter what happens, he will help with her defense to keep her out of prison and in his arms. Tracy and Loy show a lot of exciting chemistry together in this fast-paced yarn from Wood, who makes much more out of the pedestrian script by showing its action and story line through inventive lensing from master cinematographer Howe. The film was a success at the box office, earning more than $1 million in its initial release. *Author's Note*: MGM had originally thought to star William Powell and Myrna Loy together in this film as they were grooming them as a romantic team. They had clicked well a year earlier when appearing

Richard Conte and Gene Tierney in *Whirlpool,* **1949.**

with Clark Gable in the gangster hit **Manhattan Melodrama**, 1934, **Evelyn Prentice**, 1934, and, especially, **The Thin Man**, 1934; they first took their bows as married sleuths Nick and Nora Charles, these memorable characters created by master detective fiction writer Dashiell Hammett. This production, however, was delayed when Loy put her pretty foot down and demanded not only better pay but better scripts with more substance as befitting the superstar status MGM boss Louis B. Mayer was creating for her. Loy went on a strike, more or less stalling the studio, in order to get what she wanted. Such tactics did not work well in Hollywood with the then all-powerful movie moguls running the studios, and any actor or actress using such strong-arm measures were invariably put on suspension and were mostly not heard from thereafter. However, Bette Davis had effectively employed these tactics to better herself at Warner Brothers and Loy knew that, so she daringly made her demands, and, after a while, Mayer came around to her way of thinking and agreed to the salary hike. His decision was most likely influenced by a romantic crush he had for Loy, one the actress knew about but did not encourage. "I can't say at that time that I had Mr. Mayer around my little finger," Loy told this author. "Let's say that we both knew that he had been spending quite a bit of money in making me one of the studio's leading actresses and he did not want to lose his investment by giving me the old heave-ho, so he gave in and I got my raise." All of this took so much time that Powell had by then been cast in another film. Irving Thalberg, head of MGM production, then brought Tracy in to co-star with Loy in **Whipsaw**, but where Loy received top billing. Workhorse Wood was assigned the directorial job, but he and Tracy immediately got into squabbles over Wood's penchant for making endless takes of the smallest scenes. "Aww, he [Sam Wood] drove us all nuts when we made **Whipsaw**," Tracy told this author. "He sat on every line like some mother hen waiting to hatch a golden egg with every scene." Thalberg ended the on-set arguments by going to Wood to ask him to make less takes. At that moment, he asked Wood what he thought of Tracy, and the director surprised Thalberg by replying: "I think the red-headed bastard is the best actor on the lot!" Tracy was not enamored of his role in this film, believing his character to be too insensitive. This was manifested by the lines he was given, such as when he tells Loy, who is worried about her former criminal friends tracking them down and Tracy's ability to protect her: "Will you quit worrying about those guys! You'd think you were traveling with a cripple or an interior decorator!" The reference to an "interior decorator" in those days suggested a homosexual. Tracy also rendered mild criticisms to Loy about her performance until she realized that these harassments disguised a genuine off-set romantic interest, and the pair, who had never before appeared together in a film, began a very secret and very torrid affair that ended with the production, but resumed when they again ap-

peared together in **Libeled Lady**, 1936. Tracy was then married to Louise Treadwell, a marriage that began in 1923 and lasted until his death in 1967. He was unhappy in that marriage by the early 1930s, but, being a Catholic, refused to ever consider a divorce, doggedly clinging to that marriage also for the sake of the two children its union produced. MGM got wind of the affair and counseled both Tracy and Loy to maintain a very low romantic profile and no publicity about this on-and-off-again affair was ever leaked, until Loy herself many years later admitted to those brief romances. Tracy would also have a lingering affair with actress Loretta Young in the 1930s, and, in 1942, met the true love of his life, Katharine Hepburn, the two becoming lovers for the remainder of Tracy's life. MGM's careful nurturing of Loy's career led to her being named in a national poll as Queen of the Movies in 1936, a year after this film was released. So protective of Loy was MGM that its executives examined each and every scene in which she appeared to make sure she was filmed as a beautiful woman. In one scene in this film, she awakes at Qualen's farm with her hair so tousled that it appeared to be a rat's nest. Howe, who was one of Loy's favorite cinematographers, was called on the carpet for shooting Loy in that condition. The scene was cut from the film. **p**, Harry Rapf; **d**, Sam Wood; **cast**, Myrna Loy, Spencer Tracy, Harvey Stephens, William Harrigan, Clay Clement, Robert Gleckler, Robert Warwick, Paul Stanton, John Qualen, Wade Boteler, Robert Livingston; **w**, Howard Emmett Rogers (based on a story by James Edward Grant); **c**, James Wong Howe; **m**, William Axt, Edward Ward; **ed**, Basil Wrangell; **art d**, Cedric Gibbons.

Whirlpool ★★★ 1949; U.S.; 97m; FOX; B/W; Crime Drama; Children: Unacceptable; **DVD**. Intriguing and suspense-filled tale has Tierney as a beautiful young kleptomaniac, who is married to a psychoanalyst Conte. She enjoys an upscale lifestyle in Los Angeles and has a happy marriage with Conte, but, try as she might, Tierney cannot suppress her gnawing compulsion to steal. She has been suffering from kleptomania since adolescence, but, so far, has been able to hide this dark practice from husband Conte. After she filches an expensive brooch at a department store, she is caught red-handed by store detective MacDonald. To prevent Tierney from being arrested and booked for shoplifting, Ferrer, a self-styled healer who practices hypnosis, comes to her rescue. He persuades store officials not to press charges and becomes Tierney's avuncular savior, but Ferrer has sinister motives in his feigned magnanimous act of kindness. The suspicious Tierney does not immediately accept Ferrer as a gallant knight, thinking he will later want to blackmail her to keep the theft of the brooch from her husband, Conte. She offers Ferrer a bribe, but he refuses. The glib Ferrer easily convinces Tierney that his motives are honorable. She hires him to treat her so that she can sleep at night, and Ferrer further assures her that he can cure her of her habitual stealing through his hypnotherapy, and she readily becomes his patient. Ferrer has by then bilked his mistress, O'Neil, a former patient, out of a fortune, and she is about to expose the subtle, scheming quack. He plans to murder her to keep her silent and his thieving ways a secret while framing the gullible Tierney as the killer. He hypnotizes Tierney and then sends her to the mansion of socialite O'Neil where she is able to break inside and wander about when O'Neil is absent, leaving clues as to her presence everywhere. After undergoing a painful operation on his gall bladder, Ferrer hypnotizes himself while recovering in a hospital so that he has the stamina to stealthily leave the clinic, go to O'Neil's residence, kill her, and then return to his hospital room undetected. When O'Neil is found dead, police, led by lieutenant Bickford, conclude that Tierney was the killer since it is determined that she was at the scene of the crime. Charged with murder, Tierney tells police and her understanding and loyal husband Conte that she has no recollection of being at O'Neil's home or any memories of committing any crime. Bickford, a tough and cynical cop, thinks she is feigning amnesia. Tierney insists that she is innocent and Conte believes her. Bickford, through Conte's analysis of what happened, softens his attitude toward Tierney and comes to believe, like Conte, that the insidious Ferrer somehow manipulated Tierney's memory and has a psychological hold on her mind. They set a clever trap to find out how Ferrer was able to commit the murder while recently undergoing a debilitating medical operation. Ferrer then inadvertently exposes his murderous machinations and is impaled on his own psychological petard as he identifies himself as the culprit while returning to the scene of the crime, and he is killed in a shoot-out with police. Tierney, who has escaped a calculated nightmare created by Ferrer, is now happily reunited with Conte. The always meticulous Preminger presents an engrossing and harrowing portrait of a woman being sucked into a mental whirlpool that threatens to destroy her mental and physical well-being as he works with a well-thought-out script by Hecht and Solt. Tierney, one of the most beautiful actresses of her day, gives a stunning performance as a woman looking for the blank spaces in a clouded mind, and Ferrer presents a shuddering performance as an artful, intellectual villain, a Machiavellian character so darkly complex that the viewer is riveted to his every cunning move. Song: "Again" (Lionel Newman). *Author's Note*: Preminger told this author: "I was directing Gene [Tierney] again in **Whirlpool**. We had a very good relationship when we did **Laura** [1944] together some years earlier and, like **Laura**, she again played a victim, but in a much more subtle way. Instead of becoming a potential murder victim as in **Laura**, she was mentally framed for a murder in **Whirlpool** through a mind-controlling killer. The ability to manipulate someone's mind has long been shown on the screen and I think we did that better in **Whirlpool** than what you might see in other pictures." Preminger would go on to direct Tierney in another outstanding film noir production, **Where the Sidewalk Ends**, 1950, and in **Advise and Consent**, 1962. Tierney told this author that "**Whirlpool** was a very demanding picture. My character was accused of murdering someone and had no memory of it. Trying to convince moviegoers that my character's mind was blank was not an easy chore. I was working with nothingness and had to express it, so I had to express the fear of not knowing anything through frustration and some very traumatic scenes. I did not sleep well when we were doing that picture." Hecht, who wrote most of the screenplay, admitted to this author: "Some of the story line elements we used for **Whirlpool** can be seen in a picture I wrote for Alfred Hitchcock, and was called **Spellbound** [1945]. In the Hitchcock picture, a man [Gregory Peck] thought to be a murderer, suffers from amnesia. Because of a childhood trauma, he blocks out a memory that would otherwise vindicate him. The new twist we added to that in **Whirlpool** is that the woman [Tierney] accused of murder who can remember nothing about the killing, is being manipulated by a hypnotist, who is the actual killer and who is using his patient as the scapegoat." At the time he wrote the screenplay for this film, Hecht was suffering from Hollywood pressures relating to his considerable aid to Israel in its struggle for independence from British rule (the U.K. then controlling Palestine as a province of its realm before it granted that independence). He had made some anti-British statements in public about how England was reluctant to grant Israel its independence and the British distributors of this film took vengeance upon him by arbitrarily changing his name credit in **Whirlpool** to Lester Barstow. For some years, Hecht had collected funds from Hollywood moguls (most of whom were Jewish) and used these monies to arm Israeli military organizations that were fending off incessant Arab attacks attempting to prevent the establishment of the State of Israel. One of the donors to that cause was Harry Cohn, head of Columbia, who later, according to what Hecht told this author, summoned Hecht to his office and upbraided him after Cohn saw a small gunboat the Israelis were using and upon which had been painted the name "S.S. *Ben Hecht*." Cohn angrily asked Hecht why his name, Cohn, instead of Hecht's name, was not on that gunboat. 'Because you told me not to mention to anyone that you were helping to fund the Israelis,' Hecht replied. 'I did,' Cohn said, 'but I never told you not to put my name on a boat!' This was Collier's final film. Other films depicting hypnotists and hypnotism include **Abbott and Costello Meet Frankenstein**, 1948; **Abbott and Costello Meet the Killer: Boris Karloff**, 1949; **The Adventures of Rocky and Bull-**

Jose Ferrer and Gene Tierney in *Whirlpool*, 1949.

winkle, 2000; **The Affairs of Anatol**, 1921; **Alice**, 1990; **Amy George**, 2011; **Archangel**, 1991; **Atlantis, the Lost Continent**, 1961; **Audrey Rose**, 1977; **Battle Beneath the Earth**, 1968; **The Bells**, 1918; **Beautiful People**, 1999; **Bewitched**, 1945; **The Black Cat**, 1984; **The Black Doll**, 1938; **Black Magic**, 1949; **Black Shadows**, 1920; **Blithe Spirit**, 1945; **Blind Alley**, 1939; **The Blood Beast Terror**, 1969; **Blood of Dracula**, 1957; **The Bride and the Beast**, 1958; **Bride of the Monster**, 1956; **The Brides of Fu Manchu**, 1966; **Broadway Danny Rose**, 1984; **The Cabinet of Dr. Caligari**, 1921; **Calling Dr. Death**, 1943; **Captain America**, 1944; **Captain Kronos—Vampire Hunter**, 1974; **Carefree**, 1938; **Carnival Magic**, 1981; **Carry On Spying**, 1964; **The Case of Becky**, 1921; **Chandu the Magician**, 1932; **Charlie Chan at Treasure Island**, 1939; **Close Your Eyes**, 2002; **Communion**, 1989; **Conan the Barbarian**, 1982; **Contamination**, 1982; **Count Yorga, Vampire**, 1970; **The Court Jester**, 1956; **Cowboy from Brooklyn**, 1938; **The Crawling Eye**, 1958; **Cure**, 2001; **The Curse of the Alpha Stone**, 1985; **Curse of the Demon**, 1958; **The Curse of the Jade Scorpion**, 2001; **The Dark Past**, 1948; **The Dark Tower**, 1943; **Dead Again**, 1991; **Dead on Sight**, 1994; **The Dead Pit**, 1989; **Devil Doll**, 1964; **The Devil Rides Out**, 1968; **The Devil's Mask**, 1946; **The Devonsville Terror**, 1983; **Disturbing Behavior**, 1998; **Divorce American Style**, 1967; **Doctor Dracula**, 1978; **Dr. Morelle: The Case of the Missing Heiress**, 1949; **Cat-Women of the Moon**, 1953; **Dracula**, 1931; **Dracula**, 1979; **Dracula**, 1992; **Dracula: Dead and Loving It**, 1995; **Dracula Has Risen from His Grave**, 1969; **Dracula—Prince of Darkness**, 1966; **Dracula's Daughter**, 1936; **Elvira's Haunted Hills**, 2002; **Evil Deeds**, 2012; **The Evil of Frankenstein**, 1964; **Exorcist II: The Heretic**, 1977; **Faces in the Crowd**, 2011; **Fear in the Night**, 1947; **The Fighting Gringo**, 1917; **Flash Gordon**, 1936; **Four Rooms**, 1995; **The Frozen Ghost**, 1945; **Future Shock**, 1994; **Girl Crazy**, 1932; **Ghost Chasers**, 1951; **Glitch!**, 1988; **The Great Buck Howard**, 2009; **Happiness Runs**, 2010; **Her Jungle Love**, 1938; **Hold That Hypnotist**, 1957; **Horrors of the Black Museum**, 1959; **The Hot Rock**, 1972; **House of Dracula**, 1945; **How to Be Very, Very Popular**, 1955; **How to Make a Monster**, 1958; **Hypnosis**, 1963; **The Hypnotist**, 2001; **Hypnotized**, 1932; **I Was a Teenage Werewolf**, 1957; **The Illusionist**, 2006; **I'm from the City**, 1938; **Invasion of the Star Creatures**, 1962; **The Invisible Avenger**, 1958; **Island Empire**, 2006; **J. D.'s Revenge**, 1976; **Judgment**, 1992; **The Jungle Book**, 1942; **The Jungle Book**, 1967; **The Keeper**, 1976; **Kim**, 1950; **King of the Zombies**, 1941; **The Killer Eye**, 1999; **Kiss the Girls**, 1997; **Kisses for Breakfast**, 1941; **Konga**, 1961; **Let's Kill Uncle Before Uncle Kills Us**, 1966; **Lizzie**, 1957; **London After Midnight**, 1927; **Lord Love a Duck**, 1966; **Lost in a Harem**, 1944; **Love at First Bite**, 1979; **The Love Captive**, 1934; **The Magician**, 1926; **The Man in the Moonlight**, 1919; **The Man**

Alan Ladd, John Eldredge and Robert Preston in *Whispering Smith*, 1948.

Who Knew Too Much, 1934; The Man Who Saw Tomorrow, 1922; The Man with Two Faces, 1934; The Manchurian Candidate, 1962; Mark of the Vampire, 1935; The Mask of Diijon, 1946; The Matrimonial Bed, 1930; Mausoleum, 1983; Mesmerized, 1986; Messengers, 2004; Mirage, 1965; Mr. Hex, 1946; Mountain Rhythm, 1939; Mountains of the Moon, 1990; Nicholas and Alexandra, 1971; No Dessert, Dad, Till You Mow the Lawn, 1994; Nothing But the Night, 1975; On a Clear Day You Can See Forever, 1970; On Her Majesty's Secret Service, 1969; One Hour Before Dawn, 1920; Operation Kid Brother, 1967; Palmy Days, 1931; Paranormal Xperience 3D, 2011; The Pirate, 1948; The Pit and the Pendulum, 2009; The Plague of the Zombies, 1966; Possession, 2008; Psycho Beach Party, 2000; Raising Cain, 1992; Rasputin, 1985; Rasputin and the Empress, 1932; Rasputin the Mad Monk, 1966; Rawhead Rex, 1987; The Razor's Edge, 1946; Reckless, 1995; Revenge of the Ninja, 1983; Road to Rio, 1947; Running Wild, 1927; The Search for Bridey Murphy, 1956; The Secret Life of Walter Mitty, 1947; The Seven-Per-Cent Solution, 1976; The Seventh Veil, 1946; The Shadow, 1994; Shadow of Chinatown, 1936; The She Creature, 1956; She's Got Everything, 1937; Sin You Sinners, 1963; Sing Your Worries Away, 1942; Sisters, 1973; Stir of Echoes, 1999; Sum of Existence, 2005; Svengali, 1931; Tales of Terror, 1962; A Taste of Blood, 1967; The Terror, 1963; Terror, 1979; Theater of Death, 1967; The Thief of Bagdad, 1940; Thirteen Women, 1932; The Three Faces of Eve, 1957; The Tomb of Ligeia, 1965; Tomie, 1999; Trilby, 1923; Twilight of the Ice Nymphs, 1997; The Two-Soul Woman, 1918; The Undead, 1957; Under the Top, 1919; Undersea Kingdom, 1936; The Unholy Night, 1929; Unmasked, 1929; The Untameable, 1923; Vampire at Midnight, 1988; Violent Love, 1967; Voodoo Man, 1944; What Happened Then?, 1934; White Goddess, 1953; Wild Wild West, 1999; The Witch, 1916; The Woman in Green, 1945; The Year My Voice Broke, 1987; and Zelig, 1983. Violence prohibits viewing by children. p&d, Otto Preminger; cast, Gene Tierney, Richard Conte, Jose Ferrer, Charles Bickford, Barbara O'Neil, Eduard Franz, Constance Collier, Fortunio Bonanova, Sally Forrest, Joyce Mackenzie, Larry Keating, Helen Westcott, Ian MacDonald; w, Ben Hecht (as Lester Barstow in England), Andrew Solt (based on the novel by Guy Endore); c, Arthur Miller; m, David Raksin; ed, Louis Loeffler; art d, Lyle Wheeler, Leland Fuller; set d, Thomas Little, Walter M. Scott; spec eff, Fred Sersen.

The Whisperers ★★★ 1967; U.K.; 105m; Seven Pines/UA/Lopert; B/W; Drama; Children: Unacceptable; DVD; VHS. Evans delivers a tour de force performance as a woman confronting her old age after her husband, Portman, has left her years ago. She lives alone in an impoverished apartment in Manchester, England, and hears voices through the walls and pipes. Her grown son, Fraser, is a rascal and a thief who stashes some money in her closet. She thinks it is a windfall from her father, and Fraser and a neighbor, Bunnage, drug her and leave her in an alley. Evans is found by sympathetic neighbor Newman (who was then married to director Forbes), who takes her to a nearby clinic and where Evans is suffering from the first stages of pneumonia. She recovers in the hospital and officials then dig up the long-gone Portman in an attempt to have him reconcile with Evans. Portman, however, is still a self-serving rake and steals the money Fraser had stolen, and again leaves Evans alone in her damp, cold flat. She is alone again, continuing to hear those haunting whispers, pathetically calling out at the grim finale: "Are you there?" Forbes directs this rather bleak film with great care, drawing from Evans one of the greatest performances of her long career; she deservedly received an Oscar nomination as Best Actress. p, Michael Laughlin, Ronald Shedlo; d&w, Bryan Forbes (based on the novel *Mrs. Ross* by Robert Nicolson); cast, Edith Evans, Eric Portman, Nanette Newman, Gerald Sim, Avis Bunnage, Ronald Fraser, Kenneth Griffith, Margaret Tyzack, Lionel Gamlin, Leonard Rossiter; c, Gerry Turpin; m, John Barry; ed, Anthony Harvey; art d, Ray Simm; set d, Peter James.

Whispering Smith ★★★★ 1948; U.S.; 88m; PAR; Color; Western; Children: Unacceptable; DVD. The taciturn and tough Ladd is outstanding as a no-nonsense railroad detective in this superlative western, a role he would only surpass when essaying a magnificent gunfighter in Shane, 1953. Ladd plays Luke "Whispering Smith," thus called because of his soft, low voice and his quiet demeanor. He is called into action after three outlaw brothers, Vye, Wood, and Kortman, rob a train and shoot a guard. After the brothers rob several more trains, Ladd secrets himself aboard another train and, when the outlaws next strike, he shoots and kills Wood and Kortman, but Vye escapes. In his battle with the outlaws, Ladd is knocked from the train and lands unconscious along the railway. He is later found by attractive Marshall, who had been Ladd's great love in the past, but who is now married to Ladd's friend, Preston. Ladd is taken to Preston's ranch where he is nursed back to health, but he and Marshall keep their long-ago romance a secret from Preston. The amiable Preston is getting rich by salvaging railroad wrecks and keeping whatever spoils he finds. When Ladd sees that Preston is keeping company with wealthy rancher Crisp, he warns Preston that Crisp has a bad reputation of consorting with outlaws. Crisp has been harboring Vye and, after Ladd tracks down and kills the outlaw, Crisp hires deadly gunslinger Faylen with the hopes that his new hired hand will soon kill the pesky Ladd. When Ladd later finds Preston looting the salvage from another train wreck, he reports the theft and Preston is fired. Preston now not only becomes Ladd's enemy but eagerly joins Crisp's growing gang of outlaws. Crisp then leads the gang in another series of robberies, but Ladd forms a super posse to track down the outlaws. In an ensuing battle, Faylen, who has ruthlessly killed a helpless postal worker, kills Crisp when he thinks he is going to double-cross him. Ladd then confronts Faylen and outguns him, shooting the gunslinger dead (a precursor to the way Ladd would later dynamically dispatch gunslinger Jack Palance in Shane). Preston, who has been wounded in the shoot-out, rides to his ranch to find Marshall packing. She has decided to leave Preston, no longer able to tolerate his criminal pursuits. Preston believes Marshall is leaving him to be with Ladd, now that he has discovered his wife's former relationship with the railway detective. He strikes her just as Ladd arrives to subdue Preston. Then Preston, as devious as his dead associates, oozes an apology to his former friend Ladd for all of his criminal activities. But, when Ladd turns his back on Preston, the outlaw pulls a gun and is about to shoot Ladd. However, he is unable to pull the trigger as the wound he has earlier received is fatal and Preston crashes to the floor dead. Ladd's assignment to quell the crime spree is now over and he prepares to move on to face more challenges, the viewer left to wonder if he and Marshall will see happiness together in the future. Fenton directs a taut, action-packed film that presents wonderful color visuals from Rennahan that show snow-capped mountains, verdant meadows, and golden rolling plains. Through this rich and splendorous landscape Ladd convincingly rides in his first western as an indefatigable hero of the Old West. Crisp and Preston are standouts as ruthless villains, and Faylen, who otherwise usually played amiable supporting players, steals every scene as a vicious and unconscionable killer. The darkly alluring Marshall is empathetic in her role of a woman trapped into a marriage with a man dedicated to going bad. The film was a box office success and it was later offered in a thirty-minute radio adaptation aired by Screen Director's Playhouse on September 16, 1949, with Ladd reprising his role. This story had been filmed as silent films in 1916, 1917, 1926 (with H.B. Warner playing the intrepid railway detective), 1927, and, as talkies, in 1930, 1935, 1948 (this production), and 1952. It was the basis of a TV series beginning in 1961, starring Audie Murphy as Whispering Smith. Songs: "Laramie" (Jay Livingston, Ray Evans), "Auld Lang Syne" (traditional Scottish folksong; lyrics [1788]: Robert Burns), "Billy Boy" (1930; traditional folk and children's song). *Author's Note*: Crisp told this author that "my character in **Whispering Smith** was despicable. I spent most of my scenes smiling and pretending that I loved everybody while I was planning their murders. The two pictures I made before and after that western had me playing a kindly old man loving a dog called Lassie, the kind of role I always liked and preferred. Casting directors can take you a long way away from the real person you are." The character "Whispering Smith," created by author Spearman, is based upon several actual railway detectives of the Old West, including James L. "Whispering" Smith, Timothy Keliher, and Joe Lefors (1865-1940). Faylen's character, Whitey Du Sang, is based upon Wild Bunch outlaw Harvey Logan (aka: Kid Curry; 1865-1904). For more information on these Old West lawmen and outlaws, see my book *Encyclopedia of Western Lawmen and Outlaws* (Paragon House, 1992). **p**, Mel Epstein; **d**, Leslie Fenton; **cast**, Alan Ladd, Robert Preston, Brenda Marshall, Donald Crisp, William Demarest, Fay Holden, Murvyn Vye, Frank Faylen, John Eldredge, J. Farrell MacDonald, Will Wright, Robert Wood [Ward Wood], Bob Kortman, Don Barclay, Terry Frost, Hank Worden; **w**, Frank Butler, Karl Kamb (based on the novel by Frank H. Spearman); **c**, Ray Rennahan (Technicolor); **m**, Adolph Deutsch; **ed**, Archie Marshek; **art d**, Hans Dreier, Walter Tyler; **set d**, Sam Comer, Bertram Granger; **spec eff**, Gordon Jennings, Farciot Edouart.

The Whistle at Eaton Falls ★★★ 1951; U.S.; 96m; COL; B/W; Drama; Children: Unacceptable. This riveting drama, expertly crafted in docudrama style by the gifted Siodmak, offers the grassroots problems of a small plant in New England that is on the verge of a financial collapse that will destroy the community that depends upon it. McKee, the president of a plastics plant in Eaton Falls, New Hampshire, is killed in a plane crash, and Bridges, a bright and ambitious worker at the plant, is suddenly appointed to fill that vacancy by Gish, the wealthy widow who now owns most of the interest in the company. Bridges is greeted with more trouble than anticipated when realizing that the plant, which is the main source of income for the community, is on the verge of bankruptcy and shutting down. It has lost many contracts and new orders and its income is dwindling. Bridges, an inventive self-starter, thinks to cut costs by using a new automatic cutter that will produce plastic parts at a faster and cleaner rate. What challenges Bridges most is the fact that he must cut costs to save the plant, but he also knows that that draconian measure will also see widespread layoffs. He is immediately challenged by aggressive and insulting union leader Hamilton, who seems to be more self-serving than advancing the interests of the workers he represents. Hamilton threatens Bridges with the ultimatum that if any jobs are lost, a full-scale strike will close down the plant. The close-down, Bridges knows, will guarantee the death of the plant, and turn Eaton Falls into an impoverished ghost town. He is now faced with a ninety-day deadline to not only modernize the plant and obtain new orders, but

Frank Faylen, Donald Crisp and Alan Ladd in *Whispering Smith*, 1948.

amicably settle all management-labor problems. Hamilton stirs up so much antagonism against Gish and Bridges that he and union workers finally compel the plant's closing. Bridges' innovative production techniques, however, allow him to offer better deals for the plant's products to buyers and orders begin to flow into the office, allowing Bridges to reopen the plant and keep everyone at their jobs. It appears at the end that the plant will not only survive but thrive in the future. Bridges, in one of his first leading roles, is superb as a business wunderkind, who saves the only company he has ever worked for, as well as assuring a good financial future for those he has known and loved in his hometown. The supporting cast, especially Gish and Hamilton, are standouts in their roles, and the gritty lensing from Brun adds stark reality to the absorbing story. There are strong similarities between this film and **Executive Suite**, 1954, where the president of a furniture plant unexpectedly dies and the future of the company is at risk. This film, however, closely examines the strained relations between management and labor where the latter film profiles the struggle of a company's hierarchy to determine its corporate leadership and the quality of products it will produce. This film was well received and remains a minor classic of its genre. Song: "Ev'ry Other Day" (Carleton Carpenter). *Author's Note*: This was the second feature film in which Ernest Borgnine appeared, that actor telling this author: "I had a small part in that picture, which was all about union workers trying to hold onto their jobs and that was dear to all of our hearts because that's what we actors were trying to do, too. I remember how impressed I was with the intensity of Lloyd's [Bridges'] acting. He acted as if lightning had struck him. He generated so much energy it was like seeing lightning bolts in his scenes." The film offers no political agendas as producer De Rochemont and director Siodmak confined the story to the struggle of management and labor to survive together and, as such, produced a sterling and memorable film. **p**, Louis De Rochemont; **d**, Robert Siodmak; **cast**, Lloyd Bridges, Dorothy Gish, Carleton Carpenter, Murray Hamilton, James Westerfield, Lenore Lonergan, Russell Hardie, Diana Douglas, Anne Francis, Anne Seymour, Ernest Borgnine, Arthur O'Connell, Donald McKee; **w**, Lemist Esler, Virginia Shaler, Laurence Heath (based on the research of J. Sterling Livingston); **c**, Joseph Brun; **m**, Louis Applebaum; **ed**, Angelo Ross; **art d**, Herbert Andrews.

The Whistle Blower ★★★ 1987; U.K.; 100m; Portreeve/Hemdale Film; Color; Spy Drama; Children: Unacceptable (MPAA: PG); **BD**; **DVD**; **VHS**; **IV**. Taut espionage tale begins with Havers, who is a Russian translator for the British intelligence agency (GCHQ) during the Cold War. A Soviet mole is discovered at the agency, and Havers becomes suspicious that strange things are going on within the agency; security is pressuring everyone to inform on one another. Tensions have

John Gielgud and Michael Caine in *The Whistle Blower*, 1987.

mounted to the point where some supposed suicides have occurred. Moreover, directors of the agency fear that, if they do not clean house, the CIA will stop working closely with them. Havers confides his suspicions with his father, Caine, a retired British naval officer and a veteran of the Korean War (1950-1953). Caine is concerned that Havers not make waves at the agency if he wants to keep his job. Havers is thinking of leaving the agency and marrying Dean, an older woman with a young daughter, but Caine is not in favor of that union. He advises his son to remain with the agency, a decision he lives to regret when Havers is found dead. Havers reportedly committed suicide by leaping to his death. Caine does not believe this official report and asks a friend, Foster, who is with MI6, to look further into his son's death. He then meets with Colley, a journalist and a radical socialist, who tells Caine that he was to meet with his son before Havers' death as Colley was aware of problems within British intelligence and hoped to get some insight about those problems from Havers. Caine then begins a deep investigation, only to discover that several rogue directors of the agency have faked the suicides at the agency to cover their own traitorous operations. Fox, Jackson and Gielgud are implicated, and, when Caine finally confronts Gielgud, he forces him to write out a confession. Gielgud then attempts to destroy that confession by killing Caine, but is killed himself in a struggle. Caine then leaves Gielgud's corpse and the signed confession to be found later to end this thriller. Langton presents a very complex tale with many subplots and legions of red herrings, but Caine's intense and riveting performance sustains interest throughout. The film saw a modest success at the box office, earning more than $1.5 million in its initial release. Not related to the 2013 film with the same title. *Author's Note*: Much of the story is reminiscent of the traitorous British double agents, who were recruited as Soviet spies in the 1930s at Cambridge University. These traitors included Anthony Blunt (1907-1983), Kim Philby (1912-1988), Guy Burgess (1911-1963), Donald Maclean (1913-1983), and John Cairncross (1913-1995), as well as wealthy American publisher Michael Whitney Straight (1916-2004). For more details on these secret Soviet agents see my book *Spies: A Narrative Encyclopedia of Dirty Tricks & Double Dealing from Biblical Times to the Present* (M. Evans, 1997). Other films depicting intelligence agencies and their operations during the Cold War include **Assignment: Paris**, 1952; **Arctic Flight**, 1952; **Avalanche Express**, 1979; **Berlin Express**, 1948 (neo-Nazism); **Billion Dollar Brain**, 1967; **Cornered**, 1945 (neo-Nazism); **Counterspy Meets Scotland Yard**, 1950; **The Deadly Affair**, 1967 (MI5; KGB); **Die Another Day**, 2002; **Diplomatic Courier**, 1952; **Dr. Strangelove**, 1964; **The Double**, 2011; **The Double Man**, 1968 (CIA; KGB); **The Falcon and the Snowman**, 1985 (KGB; FBI); **Family of Spies**, 1990 (made-for-TV; the Walker family); **Foreign Intrigue**, 1956; **The Fourth Protocol**, 1987 (KGB);

From Russia with Love, 1964; **Funeral in Berlin**, 1966 (KGB); **Hell and High Water**, 1954; **High Treason**, 1952 (Scotland Yard's Special Branch; KGB); **The Holcroft Covenant**, 1985 (neo-Nazism); **The Hunter**, 1952 (TV series); **I Was a Communist for the F.B.I.**, 1951 (FBI; KGB); **The Ipcress File**, 1965; **The Iron Curtain**, 1948 (KGB); **Jet Attack**, 1958 (KGB); **The Jigsaw Man**, 1984 (KGB; MI6); **The Kremlin Letter**, 1970 (KGB); **License to Kill**, 1989; **The Looking Glass War**, 1970 (MI6); **The Mackintosh Man**, 1973 (MI6); **The Manchurian Candidate**, 1962; **The Manchurian Candidate**, 2004; **Marathon Man**, 1976; **My Son John**, 1952 (KGB; FBI); **Night People**, 1954 (KGB; G-2); **North by Northwest**, 1959 (CIA; KGB); **Notorious**, 1946 (neo-Nazism); **Notorious**, 1992 (made-for-TV); **The Odessa File**, 1974 (neo-Nazism); **Our Man in Havana**, 1959 (MI6); **Pickup on South Street**, 1952 (NKVD; KGB; FBI); **The Quiller Memorandum**, 1966 (neo-Nazism); **Salt**, 2010; **Security Risk**, 1954; **Spies Like Us**, 1985; **The Spy Who Came in from the Cold**, 1965 (KGB; MI5); **The Spy Who Loved Me**, 1977; **The Russia House**, 1990 (MI6; KGB); **The Stranger**, 1946 (neo-Nazism); **The Thief**, 1952 (KGB; FBI); **The Third Man**, 1950 (MI6; KGB); **Three Days of the Condor**, 1975 (CIA); **Topaz**, 1969 (CIA; KGB); **Torn Curtain**, 1966 (CIA; KGB); **Walk a Crooked Mile**, 1948 (FBI; Scotland Yard's Special Branch; KGB); **Walk East on Beacon!**, 1952 (FBI; KGB); and **The Woman on Pier 13**, 1949 (KGB; FBI). **p**, Geoffrey Reeve; **d**, Simon Langton; **cast**, Michael Caine, James Fox, Nigel Havers, John Gielgud, Felicity Dean, Barry Foster, Gordon Jackson, Kenneth Colley, David Langton, Peter Miles; **w**, Julian Bond (based on the novel by John Hale); **c**, Fred Tammes; **m**, John Scott; **ed**, Robert Morgan; **prod d**, Morley Smith; **art d**, Chris Burke; **spec eff**, Tony Willis.

Whistle Down the Wind ★★★ 1961; U.K.; 98m; Beaver-Allied Film Makers/Pathe-America; B/W; Drama; Children: Unacceptable; **DVD**; **VHS**. Absorbing tale begins in Lancashire, England, where three farm children discover Bates, a fugitive bearded man hiding in their barn. Influenced by stories they recently heard at Sunday school, they mistake him for being Jesus. He makes no effort to correct them, especially when he sees that Mills, the eldest child, is determined to protect him from being discovered by local police. We learn from a poster that Bates is wanted for murder. Lee, who is Mills' father, eventually learns that Bates is hiding in the barn and notifies police. Mills feels she has let Jesus down and apologizes to Bates. Before surrendering to police, Bates forgives her, and tells her that they will meet again one day. Two very young children, who have heard about the stranger, ask to see Jesus, and Mills tells them they missed him this time, but that he will be back. This charming, allegorical film sees outstanding performance from Mills and the other children, as well as Bates, who makes his debut here in his first starring role. The screenplay was adapted from the novel by Mills' mother, Mary Hayley Bell. The story was further adapted into a stage musical by Andrew Lloyd Webber and Jim Steinman in 1998. Songs: "We Three Kings" (Rev. John Henry Hopkins Jr.), "What a Friend We Have in Jesus" (Charles Converse, Joseph Scriven). **p**, Richard Attenborough; **d**, Bryan Forbes; **cast**, Hayley Mills, Bernard Lee, Alan Bates, Diane Holgate, Alan Barnes, Norman Bird, Diane Clare, Patricia Heneghan, John Arnatt, Elsie Wagstaff, Hamilton Dyce; **w**, Keith Waterhouse, Willis Hall (based on the novel by Mary Hayley Bell); **c**, Arthur Ibbetson; **m**, Malcolm Arnold; **ed**, Max Benedict; **art d**, Ray Simm.

Whistle Stop ★★★ 1946; U.S.; 85m; Nero Films/UA; B/W; Crime Drama; Children: Unacceptable; **DVD**; **VHS**; **IV**. Slick and moody tale begins when beautiful Gardner returns to her small whistle stop hometown of Ashbury (state not mentioned) after many years of living in Chicago. She left this town with nothing but has returned with considerable cash and is wearing a mink coat. She is looking for handsome Raft, her former beau, hoping that he has reformed. Raft is glad to renew his romance with the alluring Gardner, but she soon realizes that he is still the same old time-wasting gambler and has no intention of reforming. Gardner decides to look for greener pastures and finds Conway, a suave nightclub owner, who lavishes money and attention on her. McLaglen, a former bartender at Conway's upscale saloon, learns that Raft now despises Conway for stealing Gardner away from him. McLaglen uses this to have Raft focus upon a scheme where Raft can take revenge against the nightclub owner, and where McLaglen, too, can take revenge against Conway for firing him. The two plot to rob and kill Conway, but Gardner hears of this lethal plan and goes to Raft, begging him not to go through with it. Raft truly loves her and decides that her way of thinking is best. He quits the scheme and Gardner dumps Conway to remain at Raft's side, especially since he has now promised to reform and get a legitimate job. Now it is time for Conway to seek revenge for being discarded by Gardner, blaming Raft and McLaglen as the catalysts who caused Gardner to desert him. Conway plans a robbery of his own nightclub, kills his bouncer, and then frames Raft and McLaglen for the murder. Police arrive at the saloon and there is some gunplay in which Raft is wounded. He and McLaglen go to St. Louis to hide out, but McLaglen lusts for Conway's blood and soon returns to the nightclub. In a wild shoot-out, both he and Conway are killed. Raft is cleared of the bouncer's murder and Gardner joins him in St. Louis to start a new life. This was the last of three American films (including **Paris After Dark**, 1943, and **Action in Arabia**, 1944) directed by Moguy, a French filmmaker, and he provides a provoking and atmospheric tale thick with film noir touches. Raft is at his tough guy best, and the chemistry between him and the sultry Gardner crackles and pops in every scene they have together. Conway is convincing as the debonair club owner, and McLaglen provides just the right amount of hulking menace to round out a cast of characters living on the wrong side of the law. Not related to a 1965 film of the same title. Songs: "Once Again" and "Turkey in the Straw" (traditional), "Little Brown Jug" (Joseph Winner), "She'll Be Coming 'Round the Mountain" (traditional), "I've Been Working on the Railroad" (traditional). *Author's Note*: Gardner had already appeared in small roles in many films, and had already married and divorced actor Mickey Rooney, and was then married to bandleader Artie Shaw by the time she made this film. It was this film where she caught the attention of the public, as the actress admitted to this author: "**Whistle Stop** gave me my first leading role and that led to my next picture, **The Killers** [1946], where I played opposite the powerful Burt Lancaster, and I was a terrible vixen in that picture, ruining everybody's life, including my own. I was a much nicer gal when sparking with Georgie [Raft] in **Whistle Stop**, just another gal looking for a decent guy to settle down with, which may be the story of my life." Raft told this author that "my character in **Whistle Stop** was pretty much like my own lifestyle, I guess. I played a guy who spent most of his time gambling and going to nightclubs. The best thing about that picture was that I had the beautiful Ava Gardner as my co-star and I don't think any guy could ask for more than that." Raft was once quoted as saying: "I must have gone through $10 million in my career. Part of the loot went for gambling, part for horses, and part for women. The rest I spent foolishly." **p**, Seymour Nebenzal; **d**, Leonide Moguy; **cast**, George Raft, Ava Gardner, Victor McLaglen, Tom Conway, Jorja Curtright, Jane Nigh, Florence Bates, Charles Drake, Charles Judels, Carmel Myers; **w**, Philip Yordan (based on the novel by Maritta M. Wolff); **c**, Russell Metty; **m**, Dimitri Tiomkin; **ed**, Gregg Tallas; **art d**, Rudi Feld; **spec eff**, R.O. Binger.

The Whistler ★★★ 1944; U.S.; 59m; Larry Darmour Productions; COL; B/W; Crime Drama; Children: Unacceptable; **DVD**. Engrossing crime tale begins with Dix, a wealthy industrialist who becomes despondent when learning that his wife drowned at sea in the Pacific. He hires Naish, a hit man, to kill him, because he lacks the courage commit suicide. He then learns that his wife is alive and is being held as a prisoner by the Japanese on an island in the Pacific during World War II (1939-1945). He tries to call off the hit by finding an intermediary, Costello, with whom he had made the contract with Naish. Unfortunately,

Ava Gardner and George Raft in *Whistle Stop*, 1946.

Costello has been shot dead by police and his widow thinks Dix set him up. Dix then becomes the victim of a car crash and spends the night in a flop house, then tries to stow away on a Red Cross ship. Meanwhile, Naish plans to kill Dix by frightening him to death. Stuart, Dix's private secretary, who secretly loves him, struggles to save him. Each time Naish is about to kill him, Dix hears mysterious whistling from an unseen presence that warns him that he is in danger. Dix is eventually saved by Stuart. In each of the six films in this series, the victim is a different person saved by The Whistler's warning. Dix is superb as a man trying to cancel a murder he has arranged for himself, and Castle, who came into his own as a director with this film, presents a thoroughly and frightening film through many innovative camera techniques and an eerie score. Song: "The Whistler" theme (Wilbur Hatch). *Author's Note*: Castle, who made this film on the feeble budget of $75,000, was able to get an exceptional performance of intense anxiety from Dix, who was already an outstanding actor when going into this film, by making him a nervous wreck when insisting that Dix quit smoking and undertake a severe diet. Castle further put Dix on edge by calling him very early in the morning and then, when he arrived on the set, made the actor wait hours before calling him before the camera. He would then demand that Dix do endless retakes "until he was ready to explode," according Castle statements. "He [Dix] was constantly off-center, restless, fidgety, and nervous as a cat." Further, to give the film an eerie feeling, Castle used low-key lighting and wide-angle lenses while also using hand-held cameras (a novelty for that day) "to give a sense of reality to the horror." **p**, Rudolph C. Flothow; **d**, William Castle; **cast**, Richard Dix, Gloria Stuart, J. Carrol Naish, Alan Dinehart, Trevor Bardette, Kermit Maynard, Joan Woodbury, Pat O'Malley, Walter Soderling, Charles Wagenheim, Otto Forrest (not seen, The Whistler); **w**, Eric Taylor (based on a story by J. Donald Wilson); **c**, James S. Brown; **m**, Rene Garriguenc, Lucien Moraweck; **ed**, Jerome Thoms; **art d**, George Van Marter; **set d**, Sidney Clifford.

Whistling in Brooklyn ★★★ 1943; U.S.; 87m; MGM; B/W; Mystery; Children: Acceptable; **DVD**; **VHS**. A lot of mirthful buffoonery is presented by the talented comedian Skelton, who plays a master detective on radio called "The Fox." He is about to take fiancée Rutherford to Niagara Falls to get married. Meanwhile, Ragland, his valet, pulls a prank on him by telling a newspaper reporter that Skelton is a "constant reader," who has sent information to newspapers about people who have been murdered and where to find the bodies, so as to make the police look ineffectual. The police believe that the "constant reader" is the killer himself, since no one else could know all the details about each crime. They begin a chase for Skelton that leads to abandoned warehouses and mansions with orders to kill him on sight. Skelton also is

Kay Francis as Florence Nightingale in *The White Angel*, 1936.

now being pursued by the killer. Skelton goes to the Brooklyn Dodgers baseball park and disguises himself as a bearded ballplayer, and he saves police inspector O'Neill from the murderer before police arrest the real "constant reader" serial killer. Song: "Auld Lang Syne" (1788; music: traditional; lyrics: Robert Burns). *Author's Note*: This was the third in the series starring Skelton, which also co-stars the fetching Rutherford. That actress told this author that "I don't think there were other comedians back then in the movies who could match the antics of Red [Skelton]. He was a master at doing pratfalls and was very physical in all of his scenes when we did those comedies together. It is a wonder to me how such a human being could constantly run into walls, fall from buildings, and be chased everywhere all the time without winding up in a sanitarium." The other two films of the series are **Whistling in the Dark**, 1941, and **Whistling in Dixie**, 1942. **p**, George Haight; **d**, S. Sylvan Simon; **cast**, Red Skelton, Ann Rutherford, Jean Rogers, Rags Ragland, Ray Collins, Henry O'Neill, William Frawley, Sam Levene, Steven Geray, Howard Freeman; William Bishop, Leo Durocher; **w**, Nat Perrin, Wilkie Mahoney, Stanley Roberts; **c**, Lester White; **m**, George Bassman; **ed**, Ben Lewis; **art d**, Cedric Gibbons; **set d**, Edwin B. Willis; **spec eff**, Warren Newcombe.

Whistling in Dixie ★★★ 1942; U.S.; 74m; MGM; B/W; Mystery; Children: Acceptable; **DVD**; **VHS**. This second in a good comedy series begins when Skelton, a radio detective called "The Fox," and his fiancée, Rutherford, delay their marriage to go to Georgia and try to help Rutherford's old college friend, Lewis. They are soon investigating a murder and hunting for Civil War gold hidden in an old mansion. Local crooks menace Skelton by mistaking him for a treasure hunter. Ragland plays two roles, that of a reformed convict, and also his twin brother, a lunatic murderer on the loose. Providing a lot of good slapstick, the film is highlighted by Ragland's hilarious dual roles, and the viewer has a hard time knowing which one of him is the homicidal nutcase out to croak the radio detective and which is Skelton's devoted friend. Songs: "Dixie" (1860; Daniel Decatur Emmett), "Here Comes the Bride" ["Bridal Chorus"] (1850; from "Lohengrin" by Richard Wagner), "Yankee Doodle" (1755, traditional), "Morning" (1876; from "Peer Gynt Suite No. 1" by Edvard Grieg), "Anvil Chorus" (1853; from "Il Trovatore" by Giuseppe Verdi). *Author's Note*: Rutherford told this author that "Rags [Ragland] stole that picture from Red [Skelton] and me when he played twins. It was amazing how the special effects people were able to show him in the same frame wrestling, punching and rolling all over the place with himself." The other two films in the series include **Whistling in the Dark**, 1941, and **Whistling in Brooklyn**, 1943. **p**, George Haight; **d**, S. Sylvan Simon; **cast**, Red Skelton, Ann Rutherford, George Bancroft, Guy Kibbee, Diana Lewis, Rags Ragland, Peter Whitney, Mark Daniels,

Celia Travers, Lucien Littlefield, Hobart Cavanaugh, Billie "Buckwheat" Thomas; **w**, Nat Perrin, Wilkie C. Mahoney; **c**, Clyde DeVinna; **m**, Lennie Hayton; **ed**, Frank Sullivan; **art d**, Cedric Gibbons; **set d**, Edwin B. Willis.

Whistling in the Dark ★★★ 1941; U.S.; 78m; MGM; B/W; Comedy/Mystery; Children: Acceptable; **DVD**; **VHS**. First of three in a very funny series, this outing sees Skelton, a radio detective known as "The Fox," and his fiancée, Rutherford, being kidnapped by Veidt, head of a phony religious cult. Veidt demands that Skelton, because of his vaunted expertise in criminology (which he has none) help him plan a perfect murder. Skelton is forced to concoct a non-detectable poison to be put into millionaire Corrigan's toothpaste. Skelton, however, warns the victim by radio while he is on an airplane flight not to brush his teeth. Corrigan obeys the warning, Skelton and Rutherford are rescued by police, and the demented Veidt and his followers are arrested and sent either to prison (or a lunatic asylum). Two sequels of this delightful series are **Whistling in Dixie**, 1942, and **Whistling in Brooklyn**, 1943. *Author's Note*: This is a remake of a 1933 film with the same title, which was based upon an original play that opened on Broadway on January 19, 1932, and ran for 265 performances, starring Edward Arnold, Claire Trevor and Ernest Truex. Rutherford told this author that she was "very impressed with the acting ability of Conrad Veidt, a European actor who had been appearing in films since the early silent days. He was very intense when appearing with Red [Skelton] and me in **Whistling in the Dark**, so much so that he genuinely frightened me with all his menacing moves and facial expressions, and, when you can scare your fellow actors, that, to me, is the sign of great acting." **p**, George Haight; **d**, S. Sylvan Simon; **cast**, Red Skelton, Conrad Veidt, Ann Rutherford, Virginia Grey, Rags Ragland, Henry O'Neill, Eve Arden, Lloyd Corrigan, Don Douglas, William Tannen, Reed Hadley, Mark Daniels, Dorothy Morris; **w**, Robert MacGunigle, Harry Clork, Albert Mannheimer, (uncredited, Elliott Nugent, Eddie Moran), (based on the play by Laurence Gross, Edward Childs Carpenter); **c**, Sidney Wagner; **m**, Bronislau Kaper; **ed**, Frank E. Hull; **art d**, Cedric Gibbons; **set d**, Edwin B. Willis.

The White Angel ★★★ 1936; U.S.; 92m; First National/WB; B/W; Biography/Drama; Children: Unacceptable. Inspiring fictionalized biopic of Florence Nightingale (1820-1910) is exceptionally played by Francis. She is a British woman determined to bring sterile medical conditions to the wounded on battlefields during the Crimean War (1853-1856), which Russia lost against an alliance of Britain, France, the Ottoman Empire, and Sardinia. Francis overcomes many obstacles from the military, medical, and political establishment in her quest to save lives through good sanitary conditions. The film opens when Francis puzzles her upscale family in England by expressing her desire to become a nurse. She travels to Germany to attend the only school then offering such education for female students and endures hardship and extraordinary demands before graduating. When she returns to England, she finds that no one will employ her. She sees her opportunity to put her medical knowledge to practice after the Crimean War takes place and the London *Times* decries the horrible medical conditions endured by Allied troops during that conflict. Francis befriends Hunter, the author of the *Times* articles, and through him and other influential male persons, she is permitted to organize a small group of female nurses; she and her nurses are sent to Scutari, Turkey, where these women tend to soldiers wounded in that war. Francis encounters stern resistance from Crisp, the chief physician in charge of the hospital, who has no regard for females in medicine. She nevertheless endures Crisp's insults and criticism, and she and her nurses soon become beloved by the patients they treat. Francis, ever concerned about the condition of her patients, enters the hospital wards each night, going from bed to bed with a burning lamp, to inspect the well-being of patients (and where she earned the sobriquet "Lady with the Lamp"). That lamp and its glimmering rays that pierced a darkness where all was anxiety, discomfort and pain, becomes for the suffering a reassuring symbol of the careful and compassionate care Nightingale so diligently applied, and that these patients were not alone or forgotten. The mortality rate is then reduced through Francis' indefatigable efforts, her fame is spread by newspapers while poet Henry Wadsworth Longfellow (1807-1882) immortalizes her in a famous poem. Francis decides that she can be more effective by treating the wounded at the front to prevent disease from spreading early on. Leaving her most trusted assistant Malyon in charge at Scutari, Francis goes close to the battle lines, but again meets resistance from physician Crisp. Her cause, however, is championed by Hobbes, who plays Lord Raglan (1788-1855); she is then allowed to treat the wounded as they immediately return from the front, and her nursing regimen begins to save even more lives at her field hospital. Francis is then struck down by cholera, and, ironically, she is nursed back to health by Mauch, a drummer boy Francis herself nursed back to health when he was close to death. While she is still recuperating, Francis is alarmed to see Malyon arrive to tell her that Crisp has replaced her at the Scutari hospital with Gerald, an irresponsible socialite that Francis had earlier dismissed from her service as being incompetent. Malyon reports that the patients at Scutari are now suffering much worse under the lax supervision of Gerald. Francis returns to Scutari where she confronts Crisp and again sends Gerald away to quickly improve conditions at the hospital. Returning to England when the war ends, Francis has the satisfaction of knowing that Crisp has finally accepted her nursing standards as life-saving methods now essential to the practicing of good medicine. When back in her native England, however, she is again met with stubborn resistance to her practices by a chauvinistic Love, the undersecretary of war, and who goes out of his way to poison the mind of Queen Victoria (1819-1901) against Francis. Victoria, who is played by Holden, knows well, however, the great sacrifices and very good work that Francis has done, and, instead, recognizes her achievement by bestowing a commemorative brooch upon her to end this fine film. Dieterle presents this biopic with great care, concentrating upon the development of Francis' character and her unswerving dedication to improving the awful medical conditions of her era, as was the case with Nightingale. Although the script takes liberties with the actual facts, the spirit of this great and foremost nurse is fully captured, and Francis, Hunter, Malyon and Crisp render exceptional performances. The film was a great box office success, earning more than $1.5 million in its initial release against a budget of $500,000. Not related to the 1994 film of the same title. Song: "Auld Lang Syne" (traditional Scottish folksong; lyrics [1788]: Robert Burns). *Author's Note*: Dieterle told this author: "For the sake of dramatic purposes, we had to take some liberties with the actual story about Florence Nightingale, but we did not distort her position in history. That was all a matter of time lapses in her lifetime and the continuity we needed for the picture." Crisp told this author that "Florence Nightingale was facing the impossible when she embarked upon her crusade to improve sanitary conditions in medicine simply because she was a woman. Women in her day could not even vote and had no real rights in society, so when she stormed into the hallowed halls of medicine where men controlled everything, she was thought to be a witch stirring up a poisonous brew. I have to hand it to her. She had more courage than most men of her day and the wonder is that she was able to achieve her goals when everyone and everything was against her." Florence Nightingale has been profiled by many other actresses in many other films, including **Alfresco**, 1983-1984 (TV series; 1983 episode: Emma Thompson); **BBC Learning: True Stories**, 2012 (TV series; 2012 episode: Emily Speed; Lucinka Eisler); **Big Train**, 1998-2002 (TV series; 2002 episode: Amelia Bullmore); **The Charles Dickens Show**, 2012 (TV series; "Health," 2012 episode: Amanda Lawrence); **Emergency Ward 10**, 1957-1967 (TV series; "Ben Gunn's Christmas Journey," 1964 episode: Iris Russell); **Florence Nightingale**, 1915 (Elizabeth Risdon); **Florence Nightingale**, 1952 (made-for-TV; Sarah Churchill); **Florence Nightingale**, 1985 (Jacklyn Smith); **Florence Nightingale**, 2008

Charles Bronson as Wild Bill Hickok in *The White Buffalo*, 1977.

(made-for-TV; Laura Fraser); **Histeria!**, 1998-2000 (TV series; "Better Living through Science," 1999 episode: Tress MacNeille); **The Holy Terror**, 1965 (made-for-TV; Julie Harris); **The Lady with a Lamp**, 1951 (Anna Neagle); **Looking About**, 1961-1962 (TV series; "Florence Nightingale," 1961 episode: Clare Austin); **Magic Grandad**, 1993- (TV series; "Famous People: Florence Nightingale," 1994 episode: Kate Isitt); **Mary Seacole: The Real Angel of the Crimea**, 2005 (made-for-TV; Michelle Bunyan); **Miss Nightingale**, 1974 (made-for-TV; Janet Suzman); **NDP Philo Café**, 2006 (Jade Taylor); **Palabra por palabra**, 2008 (Simone Yenkinson); **The Passionate Pilgrim**, 1949 (made-for-TV; Betty Cooper); **Sixty Glorious Years**, 1938 (Joyce Bland); **A Skirt through History**, 1994 (TV series; "The Experiment," 1994 episode: Rosalie Crutchley); **A Word in Your Eye**, 1992 (TV series; 1992 episode: Helen Lederer); and **Wrath of Jealousy**, 1936 (Fay Compton). **p**, Henry Blanke; **d**, William Dieterle; **cast**, Kay Francis, Ian Hunter, Donald Woods, Nigel Bruce, Donald Crisp, Henry O'Neill, Billy Mauch, Halliwell Hobbes, Eily Malyon, Ara Gerald, Montague Love, Fay Holden, E.E. Clive, Mary Forbes, Mary Gordon, Fay Holden, Zeffie Tilbury; **w**, Michael Jacoby, Mordaunt Shairp (based on the biography of Florence Nightingale by Lytton Strachey and the poem "The Lady with the Lamp" by Henry Wadsworth Longfellow); **c**, Tony Gaudio; **m**, Heinz Roemheld; **ed**, Warren Low; **art d**, Anton Grot; **spec eff**, Fred Jackman.

The White Buffalo ★★★ 1977; U.S.; 97m; Dino De Laurentiis/UA; Color; Horror/Western; Children: Unacceptable (MPAA: PG); **BD**; **DVD**; **VHS**. Offbeat and allegorical, this strange but compelling biopic of western gunslinger James Butler "Wild Bill" Hickok (1837-1876), is ably played by the taciturn Bronson. The famed lawman and gunfighter is suffering from bad vision and nightmares about a gigantic white buffalo that menaces him in his troubled sleep. Bronson goes to a doctor, who tells him that his vision is failing and that he has glaucoma and is suffering from ophthalmitis (inflammation of the eyes), and basically, there is no cure. This grimly assures Bronson that he will soon be unable to face down any of the countless gunmen that want to take his life for the sake of simply killing the legendary gunfighter. (Hickok was actually diagnosed with this affliction by a physician in Kansas City, Missouri, only months before he was murdered by Jack McCall in Deadwood, Dakota Territory [South Dakota] on August 2, 1876.) He wanders westward wearing dark glasses to protect his sensitive eyesight, and meets an old flame, Novak, an aging madam. She runs a whorehouse and Bronson briefly resumes a romance with her before moving on. He meets and backs down gunmen such as Walker, and then renews his friendship with old buffalo hunter Warden. He and Warden then undertake to hunt down a legendary white buffalo, one that has also been

Richard Carlson, Hedy Lamarr and Walter Pidgeon in *White Cargo*, 1942.

haunting Bronson's dreams. While on such a hunt, they encounter a band of Indians led by Thompson, a weird Indian chief called Frozen Dog Pimp. The eccentric Thompson, bedecked in white war paint, spares the lives of Bronson and Warden during a blinding blizzard because of Bronson's display of courage, but tells him that the next time he sees Bronson, he will kill him. When later attacked by Crow Indians, Bronson and Warden are aided by a lone Sioux (Oglala Lakota) Indian chief, Sampson, who plays Chief Crazy Horse (1840-1877). With Sampson's help, they beat off the Crow warriors, and Bronson later invites Sampson to his campfire where they talk about hunting the white buffalo, which has killed Sampson's child and which he must kill in order to complete his rites as a brave. Bronson, however, tells Sampson that he must kill the enormous beast to rid himself of its nightmare images. The two then compete separately in hunting the beast. The hunt culminates when the beast is trapped in a canyon during a blinding snowstorm and where Bronson, aided by Warden, is about to kill the buffalo as it charges wildly at him. His frozen rifle malfunctions and Bronson is almost killed, but he is saved when Sampson appears and attacks the beast, killing it with his knife. Though poorly received, this film deserved a better fate as it is a tautly made story and Bronson, Warden, Sampson and others render above-average performances. Its production values are high, with Lohmann's lensing presenting crisp visuals and the special effects dealing with the buffalo are exceptional. Producer De Laurentiis provided a then sizeable budget of $5 million to produce this tale. *Author's Note*: Director Thompson admitted that the film is loosely based upon Melville's classic tale *Moby Dick*, and that Sampson plays the role of the obsessed Ahab, who fanatically pursues a gigantic white whale that is substituted for the buffalo in this opus and where Bronson's character substitutes for the harpooner Queequeg. Bronson told this author that "from my own research before we made **The White Buffalo**, I learned that Hickok really wanted to quit his wild life in the Old West. He tried that by going east to appear in some Wild West shows, but that did not work out for him. He went back to the West, but his heart was not in it anymore and, by the time he was killed, he just didn't give a damn whether he lived or died. That was clear when he sat down in Saloon Number 10 and did what he never did, sat with his back exposed and that is when Jack McCall shot him—in the back." The film's exterior shots were made on location in New Mexico and Colorado and interiors shot in Los Angeles. Carlo Rambaldi, who had created the moving parts of the animated beast in **King Kong**, 1976, for De Laurentiis, was hired by the producer to create an animatronic out-sized bison for this film, one that moved on tracks. For more details about James Butler "Wild Bill" Hickok, see my book *Encyclopedia of Western Lawmen and Outlaws* (Paragon House, 1992; pages 155-160). Many other actors have essayed Wild Bill in many other films, including **Aces** **and Eights**, 1936 (Karl Hackett); **Across the Sierras**, 1941 (Bill Elliott); **Adventures of Wild Bill Hickok**, 1951-1958 (TV series; Guy Madison); **Badlands of Dakota**, 1941 (Richard Dix); **Beyond the Sacramento**, 1940 (Bill Elliott); **Bronco**, 1958-1962 (TV series: "Montana Passage," 1960 episode: Charles Cooper; "One Evening in Abilene, 1962 episode: Jack Cassidy); **Buffalo Girls**, 1995 (made-for-TV; Sam Elliott); **Bullets for Bandits**, 1942 (Bill Elliott); **Calamity Jane**, 1953 (Howard Keel); **Calamity Jane**, 1963 (made-for-TV; Art Lund); **Calamity Jane**, 1984 (made-for-TV; Frederic Forrest); **Custer's Last Stand**, 1936 (serial; Allen Greer): **Dallas**, 1950 (Reed Hadley); **Deadwood**, 2004-2006 (TV series; Keith Carradine); **Deadwood Dick**, 1940 (serial; Lane Chandler); **Deadwood '76**, 1965 (Robert Dix); **Death Valley Days**, 1952-1970 (TV series: "A Calamity Called Jane," 1966 episode: Rhodes Reason); **The Devil's Trail**, 1942 (Bill Elliott); **Frontier Scout**, 1938 (George Houston); **The Great Adventure**, 1963-1964 (TV series: "Wild Bill Hickok: The Legend and the Man," 1964 episode: Lloyd Bridges); **The Great Adventures of Wild Bill Hickok**, 1938 (Bill Elliott); **Hands across the Rockies**, 1941 (Bill Elliott); **I Killed Wild Bill Hickok**, 1956 (Tom Brown); **The Iron Horse**, 1924 (Jack Padjan); **Jack McCall, Desperado**, 1953 (Douglas Kennedy); **King of Dodge City**, 1941 (Bill Elliott); **The Last Frontier**, 1926 (J. Farrell MacDonald); **The Lawless Breed**, 1953 (Robert Anderson); **Legend**, 1995 (TV series; William Russ); **The Legend of Calamity Jane**, 1997-1998 (TV series; Clancy Brown); **The Legend of the Lone Ranger**, 1981 (Richard Farnsworth); **Little Big Man**, 1970 (Jeff Corey); **The Lone Star Vigilantes**, 1942 (Bill Elliott); **The Meant to Be's**, 2008 (made-for-TV; Jon Eric Price); **North from the Lone Star**, 1941 (Bill Elliott); **The Outlaws Is Coming!**, 1965 (Paul Shannon); **Overland Trail**, 1960 (TV series: "Westbound Stage" episode: Adam West); **Party Wagon**, 2004 (animated; made-for-TV; Dan Castellaneta voiceover); **The Plainsman**, 1936 (Gary Cooper); **The Plainsman**, 1966 (Don Murray); **Pony Express**, 1953 (Forrest Tucker); **Prairie Gunsmoke**, 1942 (Bill Elliott); **Prairie Schooners**, 1940 (Bill Elliott); **Purgatory**, 1999 (made-for-TV; Sam Shepard); **The Raiders**, 1963 (Robert Culp); **Roaring Frontiers**, 1941 (Bill Elliott); **Seven Hours of Gunfire**, 1965 (Adrian Hoven); **Son of the Renegade**, 1953 (Ewing Miles Brown); **This Is the West That Was**, 1974 (made-for-TV; Ben Murphy); **Wild Bill**, 1995 (Jeff Bridges); **Wild Bill Hickok**, 1923 (William S. Hart); **Wild Bill Hickok Rides**, 1942 (Bruce Cabot); **Wild Times**, 1980 (TV series; L. Q. Jones); **The Wildcat of Tucson**, 1940 (Bill Elliott); **The World Changes**, 1933 (Charles Middleton); **Young Bill Hickok**, 1940 (Roy Rogers); and **The Young Riders**, 1989-1992 (TV series; 1992 episodes; Josh Brolin). p, Dino De Laurentiis, Pancho Kohner; d, J. Lee Thompson; **cast**, Charles Bronson, Jack Warden, Kim Novak, Clint Walker, Stuart Whitman, Slim Pickens, Will Sampson, John Carradine, Ron Thompson, Cara Williams, Douglas Fowley, Ed Lauter; w, Richard Sale (based on his novel); c, Paul Lohmann; m, John Barry; ed, Michael F. Anderson; **prod d**, Tambi Larsen; **art d**, James Berkey; **set d**, Dennis Fill; **spec eff**, Roy Downey.

White Cargo ★★★ 1942; U.S.; 88m; MGM; B/W; Adventure/Drama; Children: Unacceptable; **VHS**. The sultry Hedy Lamarr sizzles in this tropical tale of desire, deceit and murder. Set in the African Congo of 1910, the film begins with Pdigeon, who is the bored and burned-out station superintendent at a remote British rubber plantation. Carlson arrives as a new assistant to replace Fletcher, who is leaving after suffering a mental and physical breakdown. Carlson is determined not to let the work or the Congo heat get to him on his four-year assignment there. Problems arise with the arrival of Lamarr, a dark-skinned beauty wearing a revealing sarong. She is a Caucasian mix and daughter of an Egyptian who enjoys vamping men everywhere. She turns her charms on Carlson, who falls fast for her, but Pidgeon tries to caution him that Lamarr is nothing but an insincere gold digger. Carlson is too much in love with her to follow Pidgeon's warning, and marries her. Lamarr soon grows bored with Carlson and starts lacing his drinks with poison. Pidgeon catches her at this and, instead, gives her a drink she has poisoned. He then sends Lamarr into the jungle where she dies. This causes Carlson to fall apart and he leaves the station as another new assistant replaces him, to suggest that nothing changes in this ever ongoing debilitating and destructive tropical climate. This film had one of the most memorable opening lines for any actress when gorgeous Lamarr, skimpily draped with a sarong, slinks into a sweltering plantation room filled with males to announce: "I am Tondelayo," as if the room wasn't already hot enough. The film is well directed by Thorpe, and the performances from Pidgeon, Carlson and Lamarr are outstanding. Not related to 1973 or 1996 films of the same title. Songs: "The Wedding March" (1843; from "A Midsummer Night's Dream" by Felix Mendelssohn-Bartholdy), "There's No Place Like Home" (1823; music: H.R. Bishop; lyrics: John Howard Payne), "The Oceana Roll" (1911; music: Lucien Denni; lyrics: Roger Lewis), "Rooty-Toot, She Plays the Flute" (composer unknown), "Under the Bamboo Tree" (1902; Bob Cole, James Weldon Johnson, Rosamond Johnson), "Ma Blushin' Rosie" (1900; music: John Stromberg; lyrics: Edgar Smith). *Author's Note*: The play upon which this film is based opened on Broadway on November 5, 1923, and ran for 257 performances. In that original stage production the part played by Lamarr was portrayed by a black woman, and this was the case when a British film used the same story for its 1930 production. Hollywood censors refused to give its sanctions for that version because of the miscegenation attached to the story line. To meet Hollywood censor standards, MGM had scriptwriter Gordon change the female lead to being half Arab and half Egyptian for this version, so that her marriage to a white man would be acceptable. Thorpe told this author that "the race problem with the story was very serious back then. The KKK still controlled the South and the picture would never be exhibited there unless the female lead was shown to be mostly a white woman." Lamarr told this author that "I thought my part in **White Cargo** was ridiculous—that all I had to do was wiggle my hips and arch my eyebrows to lure men to their doom. Then again, that's how a lot of men are lured into movie theaters." **p**, Victor Saville; **d**, Richard Thorpe; **cast**, Hedy Lamarr, Walter Pidgeon, Frank Morgan, Richard Carlson, Reginald Owen, Henry O'Neill, Bramwell Fletcher, Clyde Cook, Oscar Polk, Jim Davis; **w**, Leon Gordon (from his stage play based on the novel *Hell's Playground* by Ida Vera Simonton); **c**, Harry Stradling; **m**, Bronislau Kaper; **ed**, Fredrick Y. Smith; **art d**, Cedric Gibbons; **set d**, Edwin B. Willis.

White Christmas ★★★★ 1954; U.S.; 120; PAR; Color; Musical/Romance; Children: Acceptable; **BD**; **DVD**; **VHS**; **IV**. Delightful Yuletide tale offers blockbuster songs from the great Irving Berlin while showcasing the marvelous talents of Crosby, Kaye, Clooney and Vera-Ellen. The film begins in Europe in 1944 during WWII (1939-1945) where two GIs, Crosby, who is a successful Broadway entertainer in civilian life, and Kaye, a wannabe Crosby, team up to present a show for their unit, the 151st Infantry Division. While entertaining the troops, they learn that their commanding officer, Jagger, a general they call the "Old Man," has been relieved of duty, and, at the finale, Jagger delivers a compassionate farewell to his men. Following the war, Crosby and Kaye team together, presenting a successful act in nightclubs, then on radio and finally on Broadway. They become so successful that they begin producing their own shows. They receive a letter from one of their old army buddies, asking them to watch a sister act, and both go to a nightclub to see Clooney and Vera-Ellen perform ("Sisters"). Crosby becomes smitten with Clooney and Kaye pairs off with Vera-Ellen. The foursome go to Pine Tree, Vermont, where the sisters are booked to perform at a lodge, but when they arrive they find the lodge almost deserted since this skiing area is absent of snow. The lodge, ironically, is owned and operated by Jagger, who had once been Crosby's and Kaye's commander. Jagger has invested every dime he has in the lodge and, because of the uncooperative weather, faces financial failure. To bring guests to the lodge, Crosby and Kaye arrange for the entire cast of their current

Rosemary Clooney and Bing Crosby in *White Christmas*, 1954.

Broadway show, "Playing Around," to come to Vermont to reprise their hit at the lodge and they add to their ensemble Clooney and Vera-Ellen. While Crosby and Clooney cement their romance ("Count Your Blessings"), it is learned that Jagger's request to rejoin the U.S. Army has been denied. To boost Jagger's morale as well as to swell the audience for the special show at the lodge, Crosby has an old friend, Grant, who hosts a TV variety show, to publicly invite all of the soldiers who had served under Jagger to attend the upcoming show. When talking to Grant on the phone about this, Grant suggests that Crosby allow him to air the show on national TV to provide Crosby and Kaye free advertising for their ongoing Broadway show. Crosby rejects this idea, but Wickes, his devoted housekeeper, overhears only the first part of this conversation and later repeats what she knows to Clooney. Thinking that Crosby is now just a limelight-seeking promoter, Clooney grows cold toward Crosby, which baffles him. Further, Vera-Ellen is convinced that Clooney will never establish a serious relationship until she, Vera-Ellen, first becomes engaged, so she convinces Kaye to make a phony announcement that he and Vera-Ellen have become engaged. Clooney, however, has already left for NYC to appear at a nightclub. Crosby follows her to see her new act ("Love, You Didn't Do Right By Me"), but when he tries to find what is behind Clooney's coldness toward him, he gets nowhere. Meanwhile, Kaye distracts Jagger from seeing Grant's broadcast and to maintain the surprise visit to the lodge to be made by Jagger's former troops by faking an accident. Crosby appears on Grant's broadcast and invites all of the survivors of the 151st Division to attend the show at Pine Tree, Vermont, at Christmas time ("What Can You Do with a General?"). Clooney sees the broadcast and now realizes that she was all wrong about Crosby. Returning to the lodge, Clooney is reunited with Crosby, and when Jagger enters the packed lodge, he sees that it is packed by members of his old division, who warmly greet him ("The Old Man"), and they recall fond memories of serving together ("Gee, I Wish I Was Back in the Army"). Just then, Jagger is overjoyed, as is everyone else, to see snow finally falling outside, and the film ends with Crosby and others singing "White Christmas." Though the plot is a bit thin, the film is loaded with many laugh-filled scenes, due to the eccentric antics of Kaye, and the singing and dancing is exceptional from Crosby, Clooney, Vera-Ellen and others. Curtiz directs this very entertaining frolic with skill, presenting some wonderfully choreographed dance numbers with the talented Vera-Ellen. The film received an Oscar nomination for Best Song (Berlin: "Count Your Blessings Instead of Sheep") and it was a great success at the box office, earning more than $12 million in its initial release (premiering at NYC's Radio City Musical Hall on October 14, 1954). Subsequent releases soared earnings to more than $30 million. It was the top grossing film for 1954, followed by **The Caine Mutiny**, 1954, which earned $8.7 million in its initial re-

Danny Kaye, Vera-Ellen and Bing Crosby in *White Christmas*, 1954.

lease (oddly enough, one of the leading players in that film, Jose Ferrer, was Rosemary Clooney's husband). A stage adaptation of this story was produced in 2004, premiering in San Francisco, and saw a limited engagement on Broadway at the Marquis Theater from November 14, 2008, to January 4, 2009, running for fifty-three performances. Songs: "White Christmas," "The Old Man," "Hi Hup," "Heat Wave," "Blue Skies," "Sisters," "The Best Things Happen When You're Dancing," "Snow," "Minstrel Show," "Mandy," "Count Your Blessings Instead of Sheep," "Choreography," "Abraham," "Love, You Didn't Do Right By Me," "What Can You Do with a General?" "Gee! I Wish I Was Back in the Army," "Let Me Sing and I'm Happy" (Irving Berlin). *Author's Note*: This film was originally designed to reunite Crosby and Fred Astaire, who had appeared together in two Irving Berlin musicals, the memorable **Holiday Inn**, 1942, which introduced the great standard "White Christmas," and **Blue Skies**, 1946. "Fred had to bow out," Crosby told this author, "as he had prior commitments, so Donald O'Connor replaced him, but then that fine dancer got hurt and then Danny [Kaye] and I were teamed to make **White Christmas**. It was a brilliant stroke of luck, because Danny provided a lot of wonderful moments of comedy in that picture. He was so funny in creating a lot of his antic routines that he broke us all up when we did our scenes with him. That drove Mike [director Michael Curtiz] nuts, because he had to redo those scenes." Kaye did not come cheap; he demanded and got $200,000 and 10 percent of the gross for his role. Berlin and Crosby split 50 percent of the profits, the balance going to Paramount. Since O'Connor, a dancer, was out of the film and had been replaced by Kaye, who was no dancer, another dancer, Brascia, was hired to perform the dances that had already been choreographed for O'Connor. (Brascia would later team with wife Jordan Michaels to perform together in a successful dancing act in nightclubs, an act known as Brascia and Tybee.) A very youthful George Chakiris, who would go on to star in **West Side Story**, 1961, appears as a specialty dancer, and Barrie Chase, another exceptional dancer, also appears here. Some of the scenes in this delightful film were created during production. Kaye told this author: "Bing [Crosby] and I were clowning around on the set and doing impromptu impersonations of Rosemary [Clooney] and Vera-Ellen and Mike [Curtiz] thought that all of that nonsense was so funny that he had the scriptwriters do a special scene for us called "The Sisters," and that went right into **White Christmas**." The wonderful clarity of this film achieved by cinematographer Griggs was greatly enhanced when Paramount combined Technicolor and VistaVision, which was used for the first time here. That innovative technical process involved running the film past the lens in a horizontal position in order that each frame occupied the space of two 35mm frames. Enriching the sound and its entertaining Berlin music was another newly introduced technical achievement, Perspecta, a directorial sound system

employing three inaudible tones that panned the monaural sound to left, center and right. Crosby had introduced the song "White Christmas" in **Holiday Inn**, 1942 (singing it with the beautiful Marjorie Reynolds), and he sang it again in **Blue Skies**, 1946, and yet again in this outstanding production, furthering its enormous popularity and where it again went to the top of the charts. The perennial song remains a standard at Christmas time. The set for the Vermont inn used for this film is actually the remodeled set used for **Holiday Inn**, which was then a lodge supposedly in Connecticut. Character actor Percy Helton makes an appearance here as a music conductor, having appeared earlier in another classic Christmas film, **Miracle on 34th Street**, 1947, as a drunken Santa Claus in Macy's Thanksgiving Day Parade, and who draws the ire of and is replaced by Edmund Gwenn (the real Santa Claus). Other films that focus upon or take place at the time of Christmas include **An Affair to Remember**, 1957; **All I Want for Christmas**, 1991; **An American Girl Holiday**, 2004 (made-for-TV); **Arthur Christmas**, 2011; **Babes in Toyland**, 1934; **Babes in Toyland**, 1986 (made-for-TV); **Bad Santa**, 2003; **The Bells of St. Mary's**, 1945; **The Best Man Holiday**, 2013; **The Bishop's Wife**, 1947; **A Boyfriend for Christmas**, 2004 (made-for-TV); **A Bride for Christmas**, 2012 (made-for-TV); **Bright Eyes**, 1934; **Catch a Christmas Star**, 2013 (made-for-TV); **A Charlie Brown Christmas**, 1965 (made-for-TV); **The Cheaters**, 1945; **Christmas**, 2009; **Christmas Angel**, 2012 (made-for-TV); **Christmas Belle**, 2013 (made-for-TV); **The Christmas Candle**, 2013; **The Christmas Card**, 2006 (made-for-TV); **A Christmas Carol**, 1938; **A Christmas Carol**, 1951; **A Christmas Carol**, 1984 (made-for-TV); **A Christmas Carol**, 1999 (made-for-TV); **A Christmas Carol**, 2009; **Christmas Carol: The Movie**, 2001; **Christmas Cupid**, 2010 (made-for-TV); **Christmas Eve**, 1947; **Christmas Eve**, 2015; **Christmas Holiday**, 1944; **A Christmas Kiss**, 2011 (made-for-TV); **A Christmas Kiss II**, 2014 (made-for-TV); **Christmas in Connecticut**, 1945; **Christmas in Connecticut**, 1992 (made-for-TV); **Christmas in Conway**, 2013 (made-for-TV); **Christmas Lodge**, 2011 (made-for-TV); **A Christmas Memory**, 1997 (made-for-TV); **Christmas on the Bayou**, 2013 (made-for-TV); **The Christmas Parade**, 2014 (made-for-TV); **The Christmas Secret**, 2014 (made-for-TV); **The Christmas Shoes**, 2002 (made-for-TV); **A Christmas Story**, 1983; **Christmas under Wraps**, 2014 (made-for-TV); **Christmas Vacation**, 1989; **Christmas Vacation 2: Cousin Eddie's Island Adventure**, 2003 (made-for-TV); **A Christmas Wedding Date**, 2012 (made-for-TV); **A Christmas Wish**, 2011 (made-for-TV); **Christmas with Holly**, 2012 (made-for-TV); **Christmas with the Kranks**, 2004; **Come to the Stable**, 1949; **A Cookie Cutter Christmas**, 2014 (made-for-TV); **Dear Santa**, 2011 (made-for-TV); **Deck the Halls**, 2006; **Elf**, 2003; **Ernest Saves Christmas**, 1998; **An Evergreen Christmas**, 2014; **A Fairly Odd Christmas**, 2012 (made-for-TV); **Finding Christmas**, 2013 (made-for-TV); **The Fitzgerald Family Christmas**, 2012; **Four Christmases**, 2008; **Fred Claus**, 2007; **Good Luck Charlie, It's Christmas!**, 2011 (made-for-TV); **Grumpy Cat's Worst Christmas Ever**, 2014 (made-for-TV); **Happy Christmas**, 2014; **A Heartland Christmas**, 2010 (made-for-TV); **Help for the Holidays**, 2012 (made-for-TV); **Holiday**, 1938; **The Holiday**, 2006; **Holiday Engagement**, 2011 (made-for-TV); **Holiday in Handcuffs**, 2007 (made-for-TV); **Holiday Inn**, 1942; **The Holly and the Ivy**, 1954; **Home Alone**, 1990; **Home Alone 2: Lost in New York**, 1992; **Home Alone 4**, 2002 (made-for-TV); **Home Alone: The Holiday Heist**, 2011 (made-for-TV); **How About You...**, 2007; **How the Grinch Stole Christmas**, 2000; **I'll Be Home for Christmas**, 1998; **I'll Be Seeing You**, 1944; **It's a Wonderful Life**, 1946; **Jingle All the Way**, 1996; **Joyeux Noel**, 2005; **The Lemon Drop Kid**, 1951; **The Lion in Winter**, 1968; **The Lion in Winter**, 2003 (made-for-TV); **Love Affair**, 1939; **Love at the Christmas Table**, 2012 (made-for-TV); **Love Finds Andy Hardy**, 1938; **The Man Who Came to Dinner**, 1942; **Meet John Doe**, 1941; **Meet Me in St. Louis**, 1944; **Merry Christmas, Drake & Josh**, 2008 (made-for-TV); **Merry Christmas, Mr. Lawrence**, 1983; **A Midnight Clear**, 1992; **Miracle at Sage Creek**, 2005; **Miracle on 34th Street**,

1947; **Miracle on 34th Street**, 1994; **The Mistle-Tones**, 2012 (made-for-TV); **The Most Wonderful Time of the Year**, 2008 (made-for-TV); **The Muppet Christmas Carol**, 1992; **The Nativity Story**, 2006; **The Nightmare before Christmas**, 1993; **The Nine Lives of Christmas**, 2014 (made-for-TV); **Noel**, 2004; **Northpole**, 2014 (made-for-TV); **Nothing Like the Holidays**, 2008; **The Nutcracker**, 1993; **O. Henry's Full House**, 1952 ("The Gift of the Magi" sequence); **One Magic Christmas**, 1985; **One Starry Christmas**, 2014 (made-for-TV); **Pete's Christmas**, 2013 (made-for-TV); **Pocketful of Miracles**, 1961; **The Polar Express**, 2004; **Prancer**, 1989; **A Princess for Christmas**, 2011 (made-for-TV); **Remember the Night**, 1940; **A Royal Christmas**, 2014 (made-for-TV); **Rudolph, the Red-Nosed Reindeer**, 1964 (made-for-TV); **Santa Claus**, 1959; **Santa Claus**, 1985; **The Santa Clause**, 1994; **Santa Claus Conquers the Martians**, 1964; **Santa Claus Is Comin' to Town**, 1970 (made-for-TV); **The Santa Clause 3: The Escape Clause**, 2006; **The Santa Clause 2**, 2002; **Saving Christmas**, 2014; **Scrooge**, 1970; **Scrooged**, 1988; **The Shop around the Corner**, 1940; **Stella Dallas**, 1925; **Stella Dallas**, 1937; **Surviving Christmas**, 2004; **This Christmas**, 2007; **The Three Godfathers**, 1916; **Three Godfathers**, 1936; **3 Godfathers**, 1948; **To Grandmother's House We Go**, 1992 (made-for-TV); **The Tree That Saved Christmas**, 2014 (made-for-TV); **The Trouble with Angels**, 1966; **A Very Brady Christmas**, 1988 (made-for-TV); **The Way of All Flesh**, 1927; and **The Year without a Santa Claus**, 1974 (made-for-TV). **p**, Robert Emmett Dolan; **d**, Michael Curtiz; **cast**, Bing Crosby, Danny Kaye, Rosemary Clooney, Vera-Ellen, Dean Jagger, Johnny Grant, Mary Wickes, John Brascia, Anne Whitfield, Percy Helton, George Chakiris, Barrie Chase, Grady Sutton; **w**, Norman Krasna, Norman Panama, Melvin Frank; **c**, Loyal Griggs (VistaVision; Technicolor); **m**, Joseph J. Lilley; **ed**, Frank Bracht; **art d**, Hal Pereira, Roland Anderson; **set d**, Sam Comer, Grace Gregory; **spec eff**, Farciot Edouart, John P. Fulton.

The White Cliffs of Dover ★★★★ 1944; U.S.; 126m; MGM; B/W; Drama; Children: Cautionary; **DVD**; **VHS**. Dunne gives one of her finest performances as a long-suffering wife and mother, sacrificing her husband and son to the cause of freedom in two separate wars, WWI (1914-1918), and WWII (1939-1945). Dunne is first seen as a Red Cross supervisor, who, along with her nurses, is awaiting wounded servicemen in England during WWII. As she sits at her desk, she recalls how she left America and migrated to her adopted country many years earlier. In flashback, we see Dunne and her father, Morgan, a publisher of a small-town newspaper, arriving in England for a brief vacation. They meet affable Smith, a colonel in the British army, who introduces them to handsome Marshal, a knighted aristocrat who owns a large estate and luxurious mansion. Marshal and Dunne are immediately attracted to one another and fall in love. Although there is some resistance from her father, Morgan, and some of Marshal's family members, to their marriage because Dunne is an American, the couple weds. A short time later WWI breaks out and Marshal is called to duty as an officer in his regiment. He is sent to France and Dunne agonizes over his safety and well-being, especially after Cooper, her mother-in-law, informs her that her younger son, Warburton, has been killed in action. Marshal, however, returns to Dunne's side and they have a brief, romantic reunion in Dieppe. While there, they learn that the U.S. has entered the war and will soon be sending its troops to aid England and its allies. Marshal then rejoins his regiment at the front, and Dunne returns to England where she bears a son. She, along with her child, and the protective Smith anxiously read daily casualty reports from France, dreading what might happen to Marshal. Their spirits are lifted when they see American troops arrive and march along London streets. The war rages on until the world is relieved to see that an Armistice has been signed on November 11, 1918, ending the war. Then the horrible news arrives to inform Dunne that Marshal has been killed in the closing days of the war and that he will never again see Dunne or the child he has never seen. The child, McDowall, is raised as the young heir to Marshal's estate where Dunne resides as a titled

Irene Dunne and Alan Marshal in *The White Cliffs of Dover,* 1944.

lady, along with Cooper. McDowall befriends and develops a crush on Taylor, a pretty girl who is the daughter of one of his estate's tenant farmers, a friendship that will last until adulthood. After McDowall invites two German boys, the sons of a wealthy German, to his estate, the boys alarm Cooper, Dunne and Morgan, who is visiting the estate, with their pro-Nazi statements. One of the boys even suggests that the estate would be ideal for landing gliders loaded with German troops. All of this talk is too ominous for Cooper, Dunne and Morgan, who remember the sacrifice made in the last war and know well about the impending war between Germany and the free world that looms for the future. Dunne harbors the persistent fear that McDowall will have to fight in that future war, which will invariably involve England. After Cooper dies, and to save her son from the fate that befell his father, Dunne makes plans to sell the estate and take McDowall to America to live with Morgan and where he will be safe and not have to fight in the next war. When she tells McDowall this, he tells her no, that he will not leave and that his place is in England and his responsibility and allegiance is to the country where he was born. She sadly agrees and remains at the estate. When WWII breaks out, her son has grown to be Lawford, and he, like his father, dutifully joins his regiment as an officer, while the little girl he has always loved (and grown up to be Lockhart) joins the Wrens. Lawford goes off to war and Dunne joins the Red Cross to serve at a London hospital. In flash-forward, we see her back at her desk being informed that wounded soldiers are entering the hospital and, among the injured, she is shocked to see her son. Lawford has been mortally wounded and there is nothing Dunne can do to save his life. She is with him when she hears a band playing American marital music to herald the arrival of American troops and, while peering from a window, describes for Lawford how wonderfully the arriving Americans march, until Lawford dies to conclude this tragedy. Sentimental and a grand melodramatic tearjerker, this film nevertheless presents a wonderful and stirring pageant of several generations of loving people facing the challenge of their own survival as well as that of their country. Brown, always skilled at developing his characters, does a great job in presenting in-depth profiles superbly enacted by Dunne, Marshal, Cooper, Morgan and Lawford. The evocative tale is poignantly memorable and received an Oscar nomination for Best Cinematography, Black and White (Folsey). The film was a great hit at the box office, earning more than $6.2 million in its initial release. The story saw a thirty-minute radio adaptation aired by Academy Award Theater on September 18, 1946, with Dunne reprising her role. Songs: "Auld Lang Syne" (traditional Scottish folksong; lyrics [1788]: Robert Burns), "Land of Hope and Glory" (1901; based on "Pomp and Circumstance, March No. 1 in D"; music: Edgar Elgar; lyrics: Arthur C. Benson), "Kunstlerleben (Artist's Life), Op. 316" (1867; Johann Strauss), "Rosen aud dem Suden (Roses

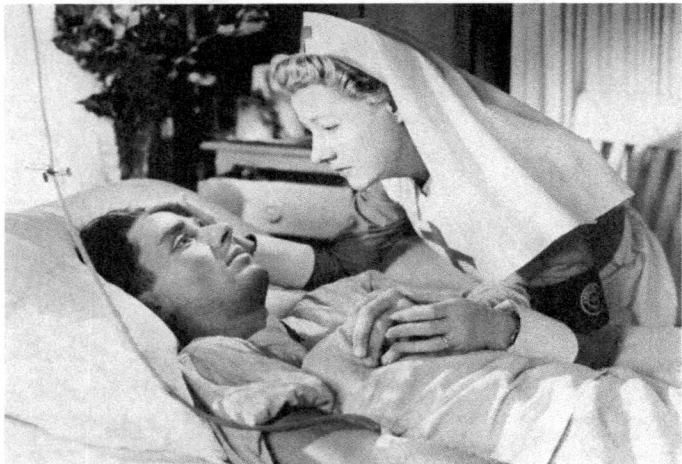

Peter Lawford and Irene Dunne in *The White Cliffs of Dover*, 1944.

from the South), Op. 388" (1880; Johann Strauss), "God Save the King!" (1744; music: Henry Carey), "Flow Gently Sweet Afton" (1786; music: Alexander Hume; lyrics: Robert Burns), "The Wedding March" (1843; from "A Midsummer Night's Dream, Op. 61" by Felix Mendelssohn-Bartholdy), "There's a Long, Long Trail" (1913; music: Alonzo "Zo" Elliott; lyrics: Stoddard King), "Pack Up Your Troubles in Your Old Kit Bag and Smile, Smile, Smile" (1915; music: Felix Powell; lyrics: George Asaf), "The Star Spangled Banner" (1814; music: John Stafford Smith; lyrics: Francis Scott Key), "Liebestraum nach dem Balle, Intermezzo, Op. 356" (1890; Alphons Czibulka), "The Stars and Stripes Forever" (1896; John Philip Sousa), "Over There" (1917; George M. Cohan), "When Johnny Comes Marching Home" (1863; Louis Lambert), "Taps" (1862; Daniel Butterfield). *Author's Note*; Brown told this author that "I had purchased the rights to the Miller poem from actor Ronald Colman, and knew that MGM was looking for another pro-British picture to make like **Mrs. Miniver** [1942], and the poem was a perfect vehicle, showing the great sacrifice England was making against German aggression. MGM bought the idea and then hired me to direct the picture." Dunne was MGM's first choice to play the pivotal character, but she was already cast in the production of another WWII film, **A Guy Named Joe**, 1943. She was nevertheless able to star in this film after a tragic accident occurred in the early stages of **A Guy Named Joe**. Dunne told this author: "Van Johnson, a very talented, young actor, was involved in a terrible car accident that closed down the production for **A Guy Named Joe**. Poor Van was almost killed, a terrible gash made in his forehead and he had to have a metal plate inserted to save his life. They thought about replacing him, but Spence [Spencer Tracy], who was the star of that picture, went to MGM's front office and said he would not appear in the picture unless Van remained in the cast. They agreed, and so we waited for Van to heal. Well, that waiting time allowed me to go into the production for **The White Cliffs of Dover**. Van got well enough to go back into the production for **A Guy Named Joe**, and here I was, running back and forth to appear in scenes for both of those pictures almost at the same time. It was hectic, but very exhilarating. Both of those pictures were inspirational, patriotic stories, told with great sensitivity, and I was proud to appear in both of them." **p**, Sidney Franklin; **d**, Clarence Brown; **cast**, Irene Dunne, Alan Marshal, Frank Morgan, Roddy McDowall, Van Johnson, C. Aubrey Smith, Dame May Whitty, Gladys Cooper, Peter Lawford, John Warburton, Jill Esmond, Tom Drake, Isobel Elsom, Doris Lloyd, June Lockhart, Arthur Shields, Elizabeth Taylor; **w**, Claudine West, Jan Lustig, George Froeschel (based on the poem "The White Cliffs" by Alice Duer Miller, with additional poetry by Robert Nathan); **c**, George Folsey; **m**, Herbert Stothart; **ed**, Robert J. Kern; **art d**, Cedric Gibbons; **set d**, Edwin B. Willis; **spec eff**, Arnold Gillespie, Warren Newcombe.

The White Countess ★★★ 2005; U.K./U.S./Germany/China; 135m; Merchant Ivory/Sony; Color; Drama; Children: Unacceptable (MPAA: PG-13); **DVD**; **IV**. Absorbing atmospheric tale has a group of displaced persons attempting to survive in Shanghai in the late 1930s. Richardson, a beautiful young countess who has escaped the Bolshevik Revolution, works as a taxi dancer in a seedy bar to support her daughter, her mother-in-law, Lynn Redgrave, and an aunt, Vanessa Redgrave, who hypocritically scorn her for her work although her meager salary keeps them alive. Richardson meets Fiennes, a former official of the U.S. State Department whose wife and children were killed in terrorist bombings in Shanghai, which has left him blind. He uses winnings from a horse race to open an elegant nightclub catering to the upper class and hires Richardson to be the club's main hostess, naming the place after her by calling it "The White Countess." They gradually fall in love, but must leave the club and Shanghai when it is besieged in the Second Sino-Japanese War. Ivory does a fine job in presenting the ambience of a grubby and frenetic Shanghai in those turbulent days and draws top performances from Richardson and Fiennes as tempest-tossed lovers in a world of uncaring expatriates. The film earned more than $4 million in its initial release and was the last film by Ivory and producer Merchant. Songs/Music: "The Tolstoy Waltz" (Leo Tolstoy); "Pink Sea," "Yellow Angel" (Alexandr Vertinsky); "Polite Conversation" (Graham Preskett); "The Old Teahouse," "Butterfly Dance," "Shanghai Blues" (John Huie); "Two Guitars" (David Bahanovich); "Avalon" (Vincent Rose, Al Jolson, Buddy G. DeSylva); "The Song You're Hearing" (Ming Yao, Lian Sun Chen); "Magic Love" (Ching Kwang Lee, Wei Zhang); "Camptown Races" (Stephen Foster); "When Will He Come Back" (Lin Bei, Xue An Liu); "Rose Rose I Love You" (Chen Ng, Ge Xi Chen); "That Rhythm Man" (Harry Brooks, Fats Waller, Andy Razaf); "Mood Indigo" (Duke Ellington, Barney Bigard, Irving Mills); "The Cocktail Wine" (Di Yi Chen, Ming Yao); "Look at Me" (Che His Yen); "Joe Ramsbottom Buys a Piano" (Norman Evans); "Nocturne #9 in E Minor" (John Field), "Carnivale Op. 9" (Robert Schumann); "I Should Say So" (Robb Wilton); "Sweet Lorraine" Clifford Burwell); "Chinese Laundry Blues" (Jack Cottrell); "Shanghai Lil" (Harry Warren, Al Dubin); "Russian Lullaby" (traditional); "It's Not Too Late" (Ching Kwang Lee, Xiao Zhong Yang); "After You've Gone" (Turner Layton, Henry Creamer); "HMS Pinafore Overture" (William S. Gilbert, Arthur Sullivan). **p**, Ismail Merchant, Andreas Grosch, Zhong-lun Ren, Paul Bradley, Richard Hawley; **d**, James Ivory; **cast**, Ralph Fiennes, Natasha Richardson, Vanessa Redgrave, Lynn Redgrave, Madeleine Potter, Madeleine Daly, John Wood, Allan Corduner, Timur Engalychev, Lucy Sutton, Lin Dong Fu, Ying Da, Jeff Harding; **w**, Kazuo Ishiguro; **c**, Christopher Doyle; **m**, Richard Robbins; **ed**, John David Allen; **prod d**, Andrew Sanders; **art d**, Chen Shaomian, Steve Simmonds, Yu Baiyang; **set d**, Lan Bin, Bian Qi, Shanqing Wang; **spec eff**, David Fletcher, Zhu Weiyuan, Tom Kittle, Rick Sun.

White Dog ★★★ 1982; U.S.; 90m; PAR; Color; Horror; Children: Unacceptable (MPAA: PG); **BD**; **DVD**; **VHS**; **IV**. Frightening tale begins when McNichol, a young movie actress, accidentally drives over a stray white German shepherd dog at night. She has it cared for by a veterinarian and adopts it, against the wishes of her boyfriend, Parker. They don't know that the dog was earlier trained by a white racist to attack black people on sight. It sneaks out of the house one night and kills a black trash man. When McNichol takes the dog to work, it attacks a black actress. Ives, a dog trainer, tells her to have the dog put down, but she allows another dog trainer, Winfield, a black man, to try to re-educate the dog. During the course of training, the dog escapes and kills an elderly black man in a church. Winfield manages to keep the dog from being euthanized, hoping to de-program it so as to discourage other white racists not to train dogs to kill blacks. Winfield finally succeeds in changing the dog's behavior so it is friendly to blacks. Carruthers, the dog's white owner, comes to claim it, and McNichol lambasts Carruthers for his racist attitude, telling him that the dog has been retrained and is now friendly. The dog attacks Carruthers and Winfield now believes that somehow the re-training has programmed the dog to attack white people. To protect McNichol and other whites, Winfield shoots the dog. Although this is a good study in racism, it was not well received as being "politically incorrect" and was not therefore released in U.S. movie theaters, but was shown on cable television and in Europe before being released on DVD in 2008. *Author's Note*: The genesis of this terrifying tale began when Sean Seberg, who was the actress-wife of writer Romain Gary found a white German shepherd when the couple was living in Hollywood and kept it as her own. The dog attacked their black gardener and then another black person and yet a third black person until they came to believe that it had been trained to attack blacks. Gary wrote a story about their experience with this dog that later blossomed into a novel that became the subject for this film. Paramount was nervous about the production from the start. Fuller told this author: "The studio's front office let every kind of political activist to roam my set when we were in production for **White Dog**. The NAACP was there in force and they immediately began making demands about how to change this scene or that. They even asked me to have Paul's [Winfield's] character have a college degree so that he would appear more educated and be less inclined to be a black racist. The whole thing turned ridiculous. Paramount got so frightened by threats made by the NAACP and other social groups that they would boycott the picture when it was released that they decided to release it only abroad. That was like locking up my own new-born child in a jail cell!" Fuller was so disgusted and angered that he went to live in Paris where this film was widely acclaimed as an anti-racist masterpiece. **p**, John Davison; **d**, Samuel Fuller; **cast**, Kristy McNichol, Paul Winfield, Burl Ives, Jameson Parker, Marshall Thompson, Vernon Weddle, Karl Lewis Miller, Karrie Emerson, Fuller, Paul Bartel; **w**, Fuller, Curtis Hanson (based on the story by Romain Gary); **c**, Bruce Surtees (Metrocolor); **m**, Ennio Morricone; **ed**, Bernard Gribble; **prod d**, Brian Eatwell; **set d**, Barbara Krieger.

White Fang ★★★★ 1991; U.S.; 107m; Walt Disney Pictures/Buena Vista; Color; Adventure; Children: Unacceptable (MPAA: PG); **DVD**; **VHS**; **IV**. The vibrant Jack London adventure tale comes to exciting life in this superb production of the Alaskan Gold Rush of the 1890s, where a youthful gold seeker befriends and bonds with a once savage wolfdog called White Fang. Hawke arrives in Alaska from San Francisco, seeking to work his dead father's claim. The naïve young man is befriended by Remar, a vicious trapper, who promptly steals his money. Bereft of funds, the penniless Hawke meets Cassel, who drives dogsleds and is called a musher. Cassel, who had been a friend of Hawke's father, introduces Hawke to Brandauer, an enigmatic, no-nonsense guide, who compassionately takes Hawke under his avuncular wing and agrees to take him to his father's claim. (In his climb to reach the base camp where Cassel and Brandauer are staying, Hawke joins a seemingly endless line of gold seekers trudging upward over a snowswept mountain, a stunning scene that duplicates an equally impressive sequence in Charles Chaplin's classic silent comedy **The Gold Rush**, 1925.) Brandauer, Cassel and Hawke trek into the hinterlands to cross wide vistas of deep snow and frozen rivers until they make camp. That night, they are threatened by a pack of howling wolves. A female wolf lures one of the sled dogs away from the camp, another wolf driving the dog into some woods. Cassel goes in search of the dog and uses up his ammunition in shooting one wolf, but is then attacked and devoured by the pack of wolves. The pack then attacks Brandauer and Hawke, but they manage to drive off the hungry beasts with burning branches from their campfire. (This scene is reminiscent of the wolf pack attack shown in another fine Jack London tale, **Call of the Wild**, 1935, starring Clark Gable and Loretta Young.) By morning Brandauer and Hawke had used up their supply of burning wood to fend off the wolves and the beasts move in for the kill. Both are saved, however, when another sled of gold seekers arrive and one of them shoots a female wolf, driving off the others, and the pup of that dead wolf must now fend for himself to survive. As Hawke

Ethan Hawke in *White Fang*, 1991.

and Brandauer reach a small town and plan to stay there for the winter, the pup is found and raised by a band of Indians and the chief names him White Fang. When spring arrives, Hawke and Brandauer resume their trek to find the gold claim, stopping off at the Indian camp where they see White Fang. Hawke tries to befriend the dog, but he is warned by the chief that White Fang is not a friendly dog and has been trained only to obey. The dog, however, seems to have an attraction to Hawke, and when he strays from the settlement and is attacked by a grizzly bear, White Fang goes to his rescue, driving off the bear. After Hawke and Brandauer leave the Indian camp, White Fang is taken by some Indians to a nearby white settlement where Remar threatens the Indians to trade White Fang to him by insisting that it is illegal to have a wild dog. Believing that they will be arrested, the Indians trade White Fang, and Remar, along with his brutal cohorts, then train White Fang to be a vicious attack dog so that they can match him against other dogs in illegal dogfights. Meanwhile, Brandauer and Hawke find the gold site and begin rebuilding an old cabin which has long been in disrepair and then begin working the claim. When going to a nearby white settlement, Hawke comes upon a dogfight where White Fang has been matched against a ferocious bulldog and he is in jeopardy of losing his life. Hawke saves White Fang's life at the last moment and brings him back to his claim site where he nurtures the dog back to health and tries to rid the dog of his combative training. Hawke and Brandauer, with the help of White Fang, then strike it rich when discovering gold. Accumulating their wealth, they take it to town where they register their claim. Remar sees White Fang and decides to seek vengeance against Hawke. He and his henchmen follow Hawke and Brandauer back to their cabin and attack both of them, but Brandauer and Hawke, anticipating this, outwit and capture them with the help of White Fang. They take the thugs back to town where they are arrested. Later, as Brandauer and his wife are leaving, they ask Hawke to accompany them back to San Francisco. Brandauer, however, tells Hawke that he cannot take White Fang to that city as the dog needs to live in the wilds where he was born. Hawke agrees and uses a stick to drive White Fang away, although the dog does not understand why he is being separated from the one human being he has come to love. Just as he is about to board a ship bound for San Francisco, Hawke changes his mind and feels that his place is living at his father's claim site and returns to the cabin in the wilds. In a short time, Hawke finds that he is not alone, as White Fang has chosen not to live in the wilds and has found his way to that cabin where both are happily reunited. Kleiser does a wonderful job directing this classic outdoor tale, the snow-bound wilderness landscapes beautifully lensed by cinematographer Pierce-Roberts. Hawke, Brandauer, Cassel and Remar are standouts in their rugged roles, presenting understated performances to genuinely create authentic-looking pioneer characters, and the action is

Virginia Mayo and James Cagney in *White Heat*, 1949.

breathtakingly choreographed. Jed the Dog impressively presents the legendary White Fang, both fierce and endearing as he transcends from wild animal to loving companion. The story was shown in many versions, including a 1936 release under the same title, and this film saw a sequel, **White Fang 2: Myth of the White Wolf**, 1994. This film was a hit at the box office, earning almost $35 million in its initial release against a budget of $14 million. *Author's Note*: Jed the Dog appeared in **The Thing**, 1982, and **The Journey of Natty Gann**, 1985. Other films depicting the Alaskan or Klondike Gold Rush of the 1890s include **Belle of the Yukon**, 1944; **Call of the Wild**, 1935; **The Call of the Wild**, 1972; **The Call of the Wild: Dog of the Yukon**, 1997; **Call of the Wild 3D**, 2009; **Carmen of the Klondike**, 1918; **The Chechacos**, 1923; **The Far Country**; 1954; **The Flame of the Yukon**, 1926; **Gold**, 2013; **The Gold Rush**, 1925; **Gold Rush: A Real Life Alaskan Adventure**, 1998 (made-for-TV); **The Grub Stake**, 1923; **Jack London**, 1943; **Klondike Annie**, 1936; **Klondike Fever**, 1980; **The Legend of White Fang**, 1992-1994 (TV series); **Lure of the Yukon**, 1924; **Nikki, Wild Dog of the North**, 1961; **The North Star**, 1996; **North to Alaska**, 1960; **Road to Utopia**, 1946; **The Spoilers**, 1914; **The Spoilers**, 1923; **The Spoilers**, 1930; **The Spoilers**, 1942; **The Spoilers**, 1955; **Those Redheads from Seattle**, 1953; **The Trail of '98**, 1928; and **White Fang**, 1936. p, Marykay Powell; d, Randal Kleiser; cast, Klaus Maria Brandauer, Ethan Hawke, Seymour Cassel, Susan Hogan, James Remar, Bill Moseley, Clint B. Youngreen, Pius Savage, Aaron Hotch, Charles Jimmie, Sr., Bart the Bear, Jed the dog as White Fang; w, Jeanne Rosenberg, Nick Thiel, David Fallon (based on the novel by Jack London); c, Tony Pierce-Roberts; m, Basil Poledouris; ed, Lisa Day; prod d, Michael Bolton; art d, Sandy Cochrane; set d, Brian Kasch; spec eff, John Thomas, Mike Vezina, Lyn Caudle.

White Feather ★★★ 1955; U.S.; 102m; Panoramic Productions/FOX; Color; Western; Children: Unacceptable; **DVD**. Exciting and action-packed western begins when the Cheyenne Indians are persuaded to peacefully leave their Wyoming hunting grounds in 1877 to make way for white settlers. Cavalry Colonel Lund is in charge of resettling the Native Americans, and gets help from surveyor Wagner, who befriends two young Cheyenne leaders, Hunter and O'Brian. Complications arise when Hunter's Indian girlfriend, Paget, falls in love with Wagner. This leads to the Cheyenne launching an arrow with a white feather signaling they intend to attack the cavalry. Wagner suggests that the matter be solved by single combat, but, after O'Brian turns to treachery, a Cheyenne chief, Franz, shoots him. Hunter then alone charges the cavalrymen and they are compelled to shoot and kill him. Wagner arranges his friend Hunter's body for traditional Cheyenne burial and the tribe agrees to go peacefully to the reservation. Webb presents a sympathetic

view toward Native Americans, and Wagner, Hunter, Lund, and O'Brian give exceptional performances. Paget is fetching and empathetic as the beautiful Indian girl, a role she essentially reprises from her performance in **Broken Arrow**, 1950. Violence prohibits viewing by children. p, Robert L. Jacks; d, Robert D. Webb; cast, Robert Wagner, John Lund, Debra Paget, Jeffrey Hunter, Eduard Franz, Noah Beery Jr., Virginia Leith, Hugh O'Brian, Milburn Stone, Emile Meyer, Iron Eyes Cody; w, Delmer Daves, Leo Townsend (based on a story by John Prebble); c, Lucien Ballard (CinemaScope; Technicolor); m, Hugo Friedhofer; ed, George A. Gittens; art d, Jack Martin Smith; set d, Richard Siegel.

White Gold ★★★ 1927 (silent); U.S.; 73m/7 reels; DeMille Pictures Corp./Producers Distributing Corp.; B/W; Western; Children: Unacceptable. Exciting and introspective western begins with Thomson, who is an Arizona sheep rancher. He falls in love and marries Goudal, a beautiful young Mexican girl. They go to the ranch where they live with his elderly father, Nichols, who does not take to sharing him with anyone and immediately dislikes his son's bride. Nichols devotes himself to making life as miserable as possible for Goudal and tries to turn her against Thomson, while also making his son doubt her marital fidelity. Nichols purposely creates this suspicion when he hires Bancroft, a sheep herder, when he arrives at the ranch looking for work and Nichols sees that he is attracted to Goudal. Thomson and Goudal argue and he leaves her to go sleep in the ranch bunkhouse. Bancroft sees his chance to make love to Goudal, visiting her that night. The next morning, Bancroft is found dead of a gunshot wound. Nichols tells Thomson that he shot Bancroft because he caught Goudal having an affair with him. Thomson now believes his father, instead of his wife. Goudal, distraught because her husband thinks she has been unfaithful to him, does not defend herself. Instead she leaves, and, along her way to freedom from an impossible relationship, discards the gun with which she shot and killed Bancroft. This film is not related to the 2003, 2009, 2014 films with the same title. p, Cecil B. DeMille; d, William K. Howard; cast, Jetta Goudal, Kenneth Thomson, George Bancroft, George Nichols, Robert Perry, Clyde Cook; w, Garrett Fort, Tay Garnett, Marion Orth (based on the play by J. Palmer Parsons), John Krafft, John Farrow; c, Lucien Andriot; ed, John Dennis; art d, Anton Grot.

White Heat ★★★★★ 1949; U.S. 114m; WB; B/W; Crime Drama; Children: Unacceptable; **BD**; **DVD**; **VHS**; **IV**. Cagney gives a volcanic and unforgettable portrayal of a psychopathic criminal in this quintessential gangster film, presented with terrifying gusto by pantheon director Walsh. Set in the contemporary time of the then present era of the late 1940s, the film opens with the robbing of a train in northern California by Cagney and his gang. After the train is stopped, Rainey (in his film debut) takes over the engine, but makes the mistake of mentioning Cagney's name ("Arthur Cody Jarrett"), and an angry Cagney snorts: "Why didn't you give him [the engineer] my address, too?" Cagney shoots and kills both the engineer and fireman so that they cannot later identify him. After the gang loots the mail car of a fortune, Rainey is badly scalded when searing steam from the engine is accidentally released. He is taken to the gang's hideout where his badly burned face is bandaged. The gang remains at this remote cabin, even though gang member Cochran, who is called Big Ed, thinks that they should immediately leave the area. Cagney cancels that idea, ordering everyone to remain. He slowly cleans his revolver, eyeing the defiant Cochran, saying slowly: "Big Ed...Great Big Ed. You know why they call him Big Ed? Because he's got big ideas...and someday he's gonna get a really big one...about me...It'll be his last!" Cochran shrugs off the notion while Mayo, Cagney's slatternly wife, sleeps away the day until she is awakened to make some food. It is shown that Mayo and Cochran are drawn to one another, but they cautiously keep their distance whenever Cagney and his protective mother, Whycherly, are present. Suddenly, Cagney is seized by one of his head-splitting migraine headaches and falls to the floor, accidentally firing a shot from his revolver. He staggers to his feet, and Whycherly guides him into a bedroom where she rubs the back of his head to ease his pain, telling him: "It's these mountains, Cody, cold all the time. Can't breathe the air…Let's get out, son." When the seizure passes, Cagney gets to his feet, saying: "It's like having a red-hot buzz saw inside my head." Wycherly tells him not to let the others see him in such a shaken condition. "Always thinking about your Cody," Cagney says to her. With that he sits in her lap as if he were a little boy while she continues to comfort him, reassuring him that he can achieve anything to reach "the top of the world." When Cagney regains his composure, Wycherly tells him: "Now, go on out [into the outer room]. Show them you're all right!" When Cagney returns to his apprehensive gang members, he once again takes command, saying: "What are you all gaping at?" (While Cagney has been secluded with mother Wycherly, Cochran and Mayo are shown together, and Cochran tells Mayo, as well as viewers, that Cagney is insane, stating "He's nuts, like his old man" and that he, Cochran, is just biding his time to wait for the best opportunity to take over control of the gang.) Knox, one of the gang members, runs into the house to tell Cagney that he has just heard on a car radio that a big storm is coming, and Cagney says: "That is what I have been waiting for." He orders everyone to pack and get into the cars waiting outside as they will now drive to Los Angeles under the cover of that storm. The unpredictable Cagney then punches and knocks Knox down, snarling: "I told you to stay away from that radio! If that battery is dead, it'll have company!" As they are packing, the conniving Mayo sees the piles of money stolen from the train and suggests that Cagney does not split with the other gang members, saying: "Why don't you keep it all?" Cagney replies: "You're cute." Mayo persists, adding: "Why don't you? We could travel, buy things. That's what money is for. I would look good in a mink coat, honey." Cagney ignores her by saying: "You'd look good in a shower curtain." Everyone leaves the house except the badly burned Rainey who lies on a couch, and Cassell. Rainey begs Cassell, his friend, to look after him, saying: "You'll see that I get away all right, see that I get to a doc." Cassell tells him not to worry. When Wycherly sees Cassell leave the house, she reminds Cagney that Rainey, who is being left behind, has a way of talking. Cagney orders Cassell to go back into the house and kill Rainey, so that no live witnesses remain for police to find. Cassell returns to Rainey, gives him a pack of cigarettes and then fires shots into the air to pretend that he has murdered his friend before running outside and getting into one of the two cars packed with the fleeing gangsters just as they drive off. Before driving away, the cold-blooded Cagney says to Wycherly: "Rest easy. We're miles from the tunnel [the location of the train robbery]. What have they got? A corpse [Rainey] without a record. Nothing to tie him in with the tunnel job or us." Meanwhile, Archer, a U.S. Treasury agent is assembling information about the train robbery. He learns that Rainey's corpse (he has died from his injuries) provides no information except that he has suffered scalding wounds, and Archer surmises that those wounds are from the engine of the train. Moreover, an examination of the pack of cigarettes in Rainey's possession yields a separate set of fingerprints that identifies "Giovanni 'Cotton' Valletti," who is Cassell, and he is then identified as a known member of the Cody Jarrett gang. Archer tells his assistant, Montgomery, that Wycherly is the key to finding Cagney and his gang, saying: "Wherever Ma goes, Cody goes." One of Archer's men then spots Wycherly shopping at a Los Angeles supermarket, buying strawberries, which is Cagney's favorite fruit. He ties a white rag to the fender of Wycherly's car so that she can be followed by other agents. Wycherly gets into her car and the ever-alert old woman, suspecting that she is being followed, drives a circuitous route back to the auto court where she, Cagney and Mayo are staying in a cabin. Before her arrival, Cagney waits in that court as Mayo stands on a chair to admire in a mirror the new mink coat she is wearing. Cagney has learned that Rainey's corpse has been found and that he has been linked to the train robbery. "We're all hot as pistols," Cagney tells Mayo. "I don't know how they did it. Somebody must have tipped

James Cagney in *White Heat*, 1949.

them." Mayo sneers at his anxiety as he paces back and forth, replying: "It's always 'somebody must have tipped them,' never 'the cops are smart.'" When Mayo tells Cagney that Wycherly has gone shopping, he replies: "We had enough food for the week. Why did she go out?" Mayo sarcastically replies: "You like strawberries, don't you? Well, she just had to get some for her boy!" Cagney, incensed at any critical remark about Wycherly, angrily kicks the stool from beneath Mayo, toppling her disheveled onto a bed. Archer, by this time, has followed reports about where Wycherly has driven and drives to the auto court. He sees Cagney as he is leaving his cabin and orders him to surrender. Cagney produces a gun and shoots and wounds Archer and then hustles Wycherly and Mayo into a car, driving off at top speed. Montgomery, Archer's aide, then drives up to see Archer wounded, and Archer tells him to follow Cagney and Montgomery gives pursuit. Cagney wheels his car along L.A. streets, hearing Montgomery's siren wailing behind him. He sees an outdoor drive-in movie theater and slowly drives into the area, parking his car, and he, Wycherly and Mayo pretend to watch the outdoor movie. Montgomery's car and other police squad cars drive past the theater and Cagney plots his next move. He calms Wycherly by telling her that he is going to go to Illinois and confess to a hotel robbery in that state, saying that he will get only a few years in prison for that offense to avoid being prosecuted for the train robbery and its attendant murders, which could mean the death sentence. Wycherly wickedly beams with pride over Cagney's inventive alibi scheme, saying: "You're the smartest there is!" Mayo kisses Cagney, saying: "I'll be waiting for you, honey!" Archer, who is recovering from his wound but works in his office, later has Wycherly and Mayo brought to his office, but both women claim that they have not seen Cagney for some time and that they know nothing about Archer being shot, saying that they were watching a movie at the time of the shooting. Archer asks them what film they were watching and Wycherly says: "**Task Force** [1949], exciting, Verna [Mayo] liked it a lot." Archer tells her that she knows Cagney has shot him, but the crafty Wycherly states: "Of course, being an old woman, I wouldn't know much about the law, but I hear you have to have witnesses to make anything stand up in court." Archer tells her that he knows that Cagney engineered the murderous train robbery six weeks earlier, and Wycherly becomes indignant, saying: "I'm not going to sit here and hear you accuse my boy without proof. Besides, I know my rights. You can't keep us here. You've got nothing on us." Mayo pretends to cry and Wycherly states: "Come on, Verna, stop crying. Nobody's going to hurt you." The two women leave, and Archer then summons special Treasury agent O'Brien, briefing him about Cagney's clever ruse. O'Brien remarks: "Who checks confessions in Springfield [Illinois]?" Archer then assigns O'Brien to go undercover as a convict, to be sentenced at the same day that Cagney

James Cagney, Edmond O'Brien and Wally Cassell in *White Heat,* **1949.**

appears in court to receive his sentence for the hotel robbery. O'Brien, who has been acting as an undercover agent for years in prisons as a pretended convict to obtain needed information, states: "I joined the Department [U.S. Treasury Department] to put criminals behind bars and here I am, stir crazy!" He undergoes intensive briefing about those he might see in the Illinois penitentiary, identifying MacDonald, who will spot him as a federal agent. Archer tells O'Brien not to worry as MacDonald will be paroled before he, O'Brien, joins Cagney behind bars. Archer warns O'Brien that there is a streak of insanity that runs through Cagney's family. He tells him that Cagney's father died in an insane asylum. Archer adds: "[Cagney] used to fake headaches when he was a kid to get his mother's attention away from the rest of the family. It worked. As he grew up, the fancied headaches became real…until now they tear him to pieces. Any moment, he's apt to crack open at the seams [and] there goes our case. So, you'll be working against time. [Cagney's] not easy to get close to in a hurry…The only person he's ever trusted or cared about is his mother. No one else has ever made a dent, not even his wife." O'Brien replies: "You mean I'm supposed to take mama's place." He is specifically tasked with finding out from Cagney the identity of the man who plans Cagney's spectacular robberies and then fences the stolen money. To that end, O'Brien goes to Illinois and, after Cagney is sentenced to three years in prison at the Illinois state penitentiary, O'Brien is then sent to the same prison, becoming one of Cagney's cellmates, as is prearranged by Archer with the prison warden. O'Brien attempts to befriend Cagney, sharing the cell with him and two other hardened convicts, Osterloh, and Collins, who is called "Reader" because he has the ability to read lips. Cagney, however, keeps a tight lip and reveals nothing to O'Brien, keeping O'Brien at arm's length. Meanwhile, Wycherly keeps a close watch on Mayo, who finds furtive ways to secretly rendezvous with Cochran, cheating on Cagney in his absence with Cochran while Cochran tells her that he has a friend serving time in the Illinois penitentiary that will "take care of" Cagney, so that he will become the boss of the gang and have Mayo in the process. Cochran's contact inside the penitentiary is Guilfoyle, a convict who operates an overhead crane that moves heavy equipment in the vast machine shop where Cagney, O'Brien and scores of other convicts work. Just as Cagney is wheeling a barrel of waste metals down an aisle of the shop, Guilfoyle positions a huge piece of machinery above Cagney's head and then "accidentally" releases it. The alert O'Brien sees this and dives at Cagney, driving him to safety just as the machinery falls, and Cagney nevertheless strikes his head against some equipment. O'Brien tells Cagney that it was lucky "that I saw that [the machinery about to fall] just in time." Cagney replies: "What do you want—a medal?" Guilfoyle nervously apologizes to Cagney, who tells him: "Accidents will happen." Later that day, Cagney learns that Guilfoyle's actions were

not accidental when he meets in the visiting room with Wycherly, who warns him that Cochran is plotting against him and that Cochran has a friend in the prison who might do Cagney harm. Cagney rubs his bruised forehead, realizing what she means. Wycherly says that Cochran and Mayo have run off together and she feels that she has let Cagney down. She vows to take care of Cochran and leaves with Cagney pleading with her not to take any action and that he will take care of Cochran and Mayo when he gets out. Wycherly nevertheless leaves to seek vengeance against the betraying Cochran and Mayo and with Cagney vainly calling out after her not to take any action against Cochran. When Cagney returns to the machine shop, he glares at Guilfoyle, saying he is not going to do anything about the "accident," but that he will "let you stay awake nights…sweat it out, and when I get ready, good and ready, I'll pay you back." Cagney then suffers another one of his splitting headaches and collapses to the floor, asking O'Brien to "cover for me," so that guards will not send him to any doctors for examination. O'Brien not only shields Cagney from patrolling guards, but massages his head and tells him that he has always admired him and, from his youth, has had only one ambition and that is to join his gang. O'Brien thus becomes a surrogate mother, instead of Wycherly, who can no longer care for her imprisoned son. Now Cagney fully trusts O'Brien, looking upon him as his closest friend. Cagney no longer thinks to wait out his sentence inside the walls, but has only one ambition and that is to break out of prison and eliminate Cochran before his mother is endangered by that lethal gangster. Cagney enlists the aid of his cellmates O'Brien, Osterloh and Collins, but his plans for a breakout come unglued when Cagney receives news that his mother is dead while he is eating in the prison mess hall with hundreds of other inmates. Shocked by the news that Wycherly is dead, Cagney goes berserk, screaming incoherently as he slams down a cup on the table and then erupts from his seat, climbing atop the mess hall table and stumbling almost blindly along its length, stunning hundreds of convicts into silence. He roars: "I gotta get out of here!" As he slips to the floor, a guard rushes up to him and Cagney knocks him unconscious. Another guard runs to him, slamming his club onto Cagney's head without stopping him, and Cagney punches the guard into unconsciousness. A third guard strikes Cagney as he stumbles along an aisle between the eating tables and, he too, strikes Cagney but he is also knocked down by the raging Cagney. Several guards then close in and subdue him, dragging him away as his piercing screams echo throughout the mess hall with "Get me out! Get me out!" (This utterly traumatic scene is one of the most explosive sequences ever put on film, where Cagney transcends from a docile inmate to a wild animal attempting to break from its cage, becoming a roaring, raging maniacal creature savagely using what appears to be superhuman strength to ward off guards in his frantic but futile attempt to gain immediate freedom.) Cagney is taken to the prison infirmary where he is held in a guarded cell and lies on a bed while wearing a straitjacket. Osterloh, one of Cagney's cellmates, later arrives with food and attempts to feed the restrained Cagney, who spits out the soup, but whispers to Osterloh that the next time he comes he is to bring the gun Osterloh has been hiding. Meanwhile, Archer and his federal agents, who have been preparing to follow Cagney, O'Brien and others after a prearranged prison escape has occurred, are informed that Cagney has become a raving lunatic and is in confinement. Archer then abandons his plans, telling his fellow agents: "Sorry boys, they [plans] can't all work out." Osterloh then returns with another plate of food just when two psychiatrists have arrived at the penitentiary to take Cagney to an asylum. The prison doctor calls the warden to state that Cagney is incurably insane and will be driven from the penitentiary that night by the visiting psychiatrists, and taken to a mental institution. While a guard and the doctors are distracted, Osterloh enters Cagney's cell and unties Cagney from the straitjacket he wears before slipping a gun to him. Cagney throws off the straitjacket, pointing the gun at the two doctors while Osterloh takes the guard's club and slugs him unconscious. Cagney then forces the doctor to call a cell block, ordering a guard to bring Cagney's cellmates O'Brien and Collins to the infirmary, as well as telling the guard to bring along Guilfoyle. When the guard arrives with O'Brien, Collins and Guilfoyle, he is disarmed and locked up with the other guard and the prison doctor. The two psychiatrists are then forced at gunpoint by Cagney to leave the infirmary with the other escaping inmates, and they go to a waiting car in the prison yard. Guilfoyle knows why he has been included in the prison break, saying to Cagney: "You've got me wrong. I've got nothing against you. It was Big Ed [Cochran] who told me to do it [the earlier attempt to drop the machinery on Cagney to kill him]. You wouldn't kill me in cold blood, would you?" Cagney sneers at him, saying: "I'll let you warm up a little." After Cagney orders Guilfoyle to get into the car's trunk, he and others hide on the floor of the car while the psychiatrists drive the car from the prison yard toward the prison's main gate. Cagney warns them that "If we don't make it, I've got six slugs in this gun, one for each of us!" The tower guard recognizes the psychiatrist driving the car and opens the gate and the car drives from the penitentiary. Archer then learns that Cagney has escaped and he waits to hear from O'Brien, who is now traveling with the fleeing convicts. Cagney and others are then seen in a remote farmhouse they have taken over. The two psychiatrists are bound to chairs, stripped of their clothes; Cagney, wearing one of their suits, says sarcastically to them: "I like your tailor. How do you like mine?" The hall phone begins to ring and Cagney calls out for O'Brien, who is trying to find a way to contact Archer. Cagney meets O'Brien in the hallway and rips the phone from its wall moorings before they step outside to a car as Cagney chews on a chicken leg. Before he gets into another car, Cagney hears Guilfoyle calling out from the trunk of the car they are abandoning (the one driven by the psychiatrists as it can be identified). Cagney stands next to the trunk of the car, calling out: "How are you doing, Parker [Guilfoyle]?" Guilfoyle replies from within the trunk: "It's stuffy in here. I need some air!" Cagney withdraws a gun and points it at the trunk, saying: "Stuffy, huh? I'll give it a little air!" With that, he fires several shots into the trunk, the bullets piercing the metal hood, and ostensibly and brutally killing Guilfoyle in revenge for his earlier attempt to kill Cagney in the prison machine shop. (This casual, seemingly off-hand murder is all the more shocking to the viewer in that it horrifically shows the utter callousness possessed by the brutal Cagney, who has no regard for human life and that murdering anyone is merely a perfunctory act in a bestial lifestyle where endless killings are routine. Moreover, Guilfoyle is shown being killed without actually being seen shot to death, which conforms to the old Hollywood censorship code that insisted that a killer could not be seen in the same frame with a victim while taking the life of that victim. When Cagney earlier shoots and kills the engineer and fireman in the train robbery, he is shown firing the shots, but the victims are shown collapsing to death in separate frames.) While Cagney and the escaped prisoners are driving toward California, Cochran and Mayo are hiding out at a remote farmhouse and where Cochran, now that he knows Cagney has escaped, will be gunning for him. He is shown rigging up a bell at the front door and making other preparations to warn himself when Cagney enters the building and where he intends to kill his former boss. Mayo is beside herself with anxiety as she awaits the return of her lethal husband, begging Cochran to flee with her. "Take it easy, baby," soothes Cochran. "We're ready for him [Cagney] when he comes." Mayo cannot be calmed, saying: "I can't stand another night, Ed, listening, going crazy. It ain't like waiting for some human being who wants to kill you. Cody [Cagney] ain't human! Fill him full of lead and he'll still come at you!" Cochran sneers at this, replying: "Plug him and he drops, same as anybody else." She tells Cochran that she wants to live and plans to leave. Cochran warns her that no place is really safe for her: "The world ain't big enough, sugar, not when he [Cagney] finds out what you did to his ma." Cochran tells her that if Mayo runs out on him and he survives Cagney's expected attack, he will tell Cagney how Mayo killed Wycherly, adding that Cagney "ain't gonna like to hear that she got it in the back!" Thoroughly intimidated, Mayo agrees to stay with Cochran

James Cagney and Margaret Wycherly in *White Heat*, 1949.

and face Cagney. When Cochran is absent, however, Mayo dons her overcoat and slips from a window and runs to the garage, entering it, only to be suddenly grabbed by Cagney, who has been waiting there in the dark. She is terrified as Cagney braces her neck with both arms, snarling: "Now tell me you're glad to see me, but say it low so that nobody can hear." Mayo, eyes wide with fear, gives Cagney what he wants to hear, stating: "I'm so glad to see you. I've been praying that you'd come back." She tells him that Cochran has been beating her and keeping her a prisoner and that he threatened to kill Cagney unless she remained with him, so she has therefore sacrificed herself to preserve his life (or so she claims). Mayo further lies to Cagney when telling him that it was Cochran who murdered his mother, blurting: "He got her in the back!" She then warns Cagney about entering the farmhouse, telling him: "You've got to be careful…he's got the house rigged up like a trap. You can't get in unless I tell you how." Now in league with Cagney, Mayo returns to the house, and Cochran hears her downstairs. She goes upstairs to admit to him that she thought of running away, but that she changed her mind and has decided to stay with him. Cochran grabs her and says: "You're my honey!" He passionately kisses her, but she nervously breaks away, knowing that Cagney is now in the next room. Cagney emerges from that room, gun in hand. Cochran turns with a drink in his hand to see him and then throws the drink at Cagney, running from the room, closing the door behind him. Cagney fires several shots through the door and we then see Cochran in the hall, staggering toward the stairs, having been shot in the back in the manner Wycherly has been earlier killed. He collapses dead at the top of the stairs. Cagney steps into the hall with Mayo and looks down at Cochran's crumpled body. At that moment, O'Brien, Osterloh and Collins burst through the front door and stand at the bottom of the stairs. Cagney smirks down at them, saying: "Catch!" He then kicks Cochran's body, which tumbles down the stairs to crash at the bottom. Cagney later meets with members of his old gang, Cassell, Coby, and Knox, with the added members of escaped convicts Osterloh and Collins, as well as undercover man O'Brien. The old gang members tell Cagney how they had been planning a big robbery with Cochran and where they planned to use a gas truck in that robbery. They then surprise Cagney by telling him that they actually purchased a large gas truck for $12,000 and have it hidden next to the barn. Cagney and the others then inspect the truck, and Cagney gets a better idea on how to use that vehicle in a spectacular robbery, using the truck as an analogy for the legendary giant wooden horse that hid Greek warriors who then conquered the otherwise impregnable city of Troy. Meanwhile, O'Brien is attempting to find a way to contact Archer, but is surprised to see a fisherman, Clark, appear at the remote farmhouse, asking if he can use the phone. Cagney tells him yes, and escorts him into the house. O'Brien joins them and asks Clark what he

Edmond O'Brien, James Cagney and Virginia Mayo in *White Heat*, 1949.

is fishing for and, when Clark says "bass," O'Brien pulls a gun and trains it on Clark, telling Cagney that Clark is a phony, that there is no bass in any of the local waters, and that "this is trout country." Cagney laughs and waves off O'Brien, telling Clark that "he got you." He then introduces Clark to O'Brien as the planner of his robberies and middle-man who fences all the stolen loot, the very man O'Brien has been assigned to identify. Cagney then goes on to tell Clark that O'Brien is now his partner, saying "I split even with Ma, didn't I?" (In this statement, Cagney tacitly admits that O'Brien, who has soothed his splitting headaches and has bolstered his confidence at every turn, has, indeed, replaced Wycherly in Cagney's warped affections.) That night, now that O'Brien has learned that Cagney and his gang will be robbing the pay-roll of a large chemical plant, O'Brien tries to leave the farm, but is stopped on the grounds outside the farmhouse by gang member Knox. When Knox tries to prevent him from leaving, O'Brien tosses him over his shoulder in a quick judo move, but is further stopped when Cagney appears from the shadows. O'Brien tells Cagney that he was going to L.A. to see his wife since he has not seen her since they broke out of prison, but Cagney tells him that no one is allowed to leave the place, forgiving O'Brien for breaking his rules. The two walk through some woods and Cagney again confides in O'Brien, telling him that "you're just lonesome...lonesome like me...All I ever had was Ma...I was just talking [to her] out there." Knowing that O'Brien knows that Wycherly is dead, Cagney asks: "That sound funny to you?...Some might think so...My old lady never had anything...always on the run, always on the move, some life. First, it was my old man, died kicking and screaming in a nut house. Then my brother...and, after that, it was taking care of me. Always trying to put me on top—'Top of the world,' she used to say. And then, times when I'd be losing my grip, there she'd be, right behind me...pushing me back up again. That was a good feeling out there...talking to her...just me and Ma. A good feeling—I liked it." He stares at O'Brien and then says: "Maybe I am nuts." The next day, the gang prepares to rob the chemical plant, and O'Brien, who has shown his ability to fix equipment by ostensibly fixing Mayo's radio, slides beneath the gas truck to affix an oscillator made from that radio, one that will send out signals to indicate the location of the truck. When Cagney orders everyone to move, he asks O'Brien what he is doing beneath the truck and O'Brien glibly tells him that it is customary for any gas truck with a full load of gas to drag a chain to get rid of any electricity. Most of the gang members then hide inside the truck's empty gas tank via a hole that one of the gang members has cut with an acetylene torch. When the truck stops at a gas station, O'Brien makes his move, going to the station washroom where he uses a bar of soap to write a message on the mirror above the sink, the message telling the station attendant to contact Archer. O'Brien then goes outside to complain to the station attendant

that his washroom is filthy, hoping that will cause the attendant to inspect the washroom, see his message and contact Archer. Meanwhile, the gang has a rendezvous with Clark, and Cagney and O'Brien join the other gang members hiding inside the tank of the truck while a new driver takes over the wheel of the truck. The new driver of the truck is one that knows the route to the plant and has been assigned by Clark. However, that driver turns out to be MacDonald, who does not see O'Brien, a man he knows to be a federal agent, get into the gas tank with Cagney. The truck begins traveling along its route to the chemical plant. By this time Archer has been contacted by the gas station attendant, and he and his agents are able to track its route via the signals emitted from the oscillator planted beneath the truck by O'Brien. The agents plot the truck's course on a map at headquarters as direction-finding cars pick up the signals at various intersections the truck passes. The truck stops at a huge chemical plant and Archer and his agents now know where the robbery is taking place, 198th and Figueroa streets. Agents and police then begin to converge on that location. Meanwhile, MacDonald enters an office area of the chemical plant, and disarms an armed guard before Cagney and the other gang members enter to loot its safe. Just then MacDonald spots O'Brien and tells Cagney that O'Brien is a Treasury agent. Cagney is incensed, shouting: "A copper... and I went for it. Treated him like a kid brother...and I was going to split with a copper! Maybe they're waiting to pin a medal on him!" O'Brien trains a gun on Cagney and the rest of the gang members, replying: "Solid gold! Come on...get your hands up!" Cassell, however, moves into the office behind O'Brien and knocks him to the floor. At that moment, police arrive and Archer calls out through a bullhorn for Cagney to surrender. Cagney replies by firing a B.A.R. that strikes nearby pipes and sends police to cover, and police begin shooting tear gas through the office windows, clouding the interior with smoke. Cagney turns to shoot and kill O'Brien, who is then staggering to his feet, but Cagney misses his target and shoots Cassell instead. O'Brien makes a break from the building and races to the police lines while Cagney and the rest of his gang members take flight into the interior of the plant's grounds, which contains many huge chemical tank towers. The police and agents pursue the thieves through this area, careful not to fire at the tanks lest they set the entire field afire. While on the run, Cagney shoots several officers, but his men are picked off, one after another, until only he and Osterloh remain hiding beneath a huge chemical tower as night falls and searchlights now play over the area, searching for the thieves. Police then bring Mayo to the area and she offers to coax Cagney to surrender, but only if she is let free. Archer looks upon the deceitful gun moll in disgust, ordering her to be locked up. Cagney, hiding with Osterloh, states: "They think they've got Cody Jarrett. They haven't got Cody Jarrett!" Cagney orders Osterloh to accompany him as he climbs the tower to its top platform, but Osterloh has had enough and runs toward a police line, shouting that he is surrendering. Cagney, feeling that he is once more being betrayed, shoots and kills Osterloh, giving away his position, and searchlights flood searing light upon the platform where Cagney defiantly stands. Using a long-range sniper's rifle with a telescope, O'Brien picks out Cagney as a target and fires, hitting him and knocking him down. Cagney gets up, laughing, wildly firing his pistol to pierce a pipe and ignite its chemical contents that burst into shooting flames. O'Brien fires again and again, knocking down Cagney, who, incredibly rises again and again to his feet, firing his pistol at random. "What's holding him up?" O'Brien says, astonished that Cagney continues to live. Cagney fires another wild shot that sets off a terrific explosion behind him, and the fierce gangster raises his arms akimbo, looking skyward to shout: "Made it, Ma! Top of the world!" With that, the entire chemical tower blows up, killing him, and setting off a chain reaction where one chemical tower after another explodes in blasting white heat fireballs. We then hear Archer's grim epitaph for the dead gangster: "Cody Jarrett. He finally got to the top of the world and it blew right up in his face!" One terrible, blinding explosion after another fills the screen as this utterly gripping and emotionally draining film ends. The gifted Walsh robustly directs this classic gangster film to show in shuddering detail the modus operandi of criminals of that era. In his fascinating process, Walsh also incisively reveals through his demonstrative scenes the innermost thoughts of a criminal mastermind who is both insidiously creative and decidedly demented, a man whose mind has been crippled through the evil domination of a venal and vicious mother, so excruciatingly portrayed by Wycherly in what must be her most impressive performance (albeit she played just the opposite as a benign and loving mother in **Sergeant York**, 1941). Cagney, of course, is the centerpiece of this madhouse melodrama and he unleashes tremendous energy to electrify, startle and amaze in one dynamic scene after another. His is a uniquely bravura performance that will most likely never be equaled, and, as such, sets the bar for even the most gifted actor thinking to follow in his inimitable footsteps. Mayo, too, is a wonder to watch as she marvelously presents a totally worthless human being, all crass, all greed, all deceiving. She is the consummate gun moll, a beautiful, alluring tramp to end all tramps. The darkly featured Cochran also astounds as the artful, oily gangster eager to replace his boss so as to have the unnerving power to command and kill at will. O'Brien is the only saving grace, albeit obliquely, as the intrepid undercover agent, who ruthlessly gains the twisted affection of a mentally crippled man. In so doing, however, he becomes as devious and conniving as the criminal mentor he so assiduously and perversely nurtures for whatever personal redemption law enforcement might later bestow upon him. The supporting players are also convincing with their every gesture and word to round out this horrendous portrait of a modern-day hell on earth (and in imagery worthy of the most nightmare creations from Hieronymous Bosch). The film received an Oscar nomination for Best Story (Kellogg). The film was a box office smash and remains one of Cagney's hallmark films to this day. Song: "Five O'Clock Whistle" (1940; music: Josef Myrow, Kim Gannon, Gene Irwin). *Author's Note*: Cagney appears here in his first gangster film since making **The Roaring Twenties**, 1939, and it was a film that he was reluctant to make. "I did not want to go back to the hoodlums again," he told this author. "My studio, Warner Brothers, or, chiefly, Jack Warner, talked me into doing **White Heat**. Well, since I was going to do it, I decided I would go all out with the berserk character I had to play. I had had some experience in understanding how such demented persons acted when, as a young fellow, I went to Ward's Island with a pal of mine, who wanted to see his uncle. The uncle was a patient in the asylum there and I got a good look at how those suffering people act. My God, all the screaming and shouting and struggling of those patients—it was unforgettable—and you must realize that they were under restraint, some in straitjackets, others even chained to their beds. So when it came to acting like that, I leaned on my old, dark memories to create my character. When we did that mess hall scene and where I throw a fit, I almost broke my neck when falling off a table. And then, when struggling with an actor playing a guard, I missed pulling my punch and really hit him square, and he retaliated by striking me very hard on the side of my head with his guard's club. I didn't blame him. I had it coming. The pain I felt from that blow—well, I used that pain when I was struggling and shouting and pleading to get out of that prison. Believe me, what I really wanted was to get out of that scene." The mess hall scene was one of the most expensive sequences in the film, one where hundreds of extras played prison inmates in a vast mess hall patrolled by dozens of guards. Studio boss Jack Warner asked director Walsh to save some money and shoot the scene instead in a chapel where less extras would be required. "I anticipated that," Walsh told this author, "so I beat Jack [Warner] to the punch by shooting that scene before he made a beef about it. When I told him it was already in the can, he got very mad, but kept his mouth shut and just marched away." Mayo told this author that "I played a deceitful, money-grubbing wife in **The Best Years of My Life** [1946], and I never thought I would get another part as good as that. Then we made **White Heat**, and I was able to play one of the worst females to ever put on a dress, a back-shooting killer, really, that no good man would ever

James Cagney goes out in a blaze in *White Heat,* 1949.

bother to spit on. What a wonderful role, but it would have meant nothing if I had not been playing opposite James Cagney, one of the world's greatest actors. He made me and everybody else always look good. I think it was his energy—like streams of light bursting from the sun—that caused you to try to be as good as he was, which, of course, was impossible. Jimmy always believed that he was the character he was playing. In that picture, he was playing a man who should have been in a lunatic asylum, instead of running a big-time robbery gang. But when you look at that picture, you realize that his role is perfect because everyone in that picture, except for those playing the cops, are about the worst lot of people that ever walked the earth—all of them thieves and killers, and none of them having a good heart." Actor George C. Scott was a lifetime admirer of Cagney and told this author that this film represented "the quintessential Cagney in all of his explosive temperament. From beginning to end in **White Heat** he is a time bomb waiting to explode. No other actor could use his body to express and define his character as could Cagney. He demonstrated that to the world in that unforgettable prison scene where he goes berserk when hearing that his mother has died. His body is something out of a fireworks display, leaping, jumping, writhing, staggering, crouching, punching, every kind of distortional position the human body can perform—all of it is there in that incredible and electrifying scene, one that I daresay will never be equaled." Actor-director Orson Welles also admired this film, telling this author that "**White Heat** is a very cleverly designed crime film that shows you its horrifying plot, all of its ugly actions, without hiding anything, and, at the same time, the director [Walsh] brilliantly uses his scalpel to cut open the mind of the gang leader, Cagney, to show everyone that he is insane but still a criminal mastermind, who can outwit police, almost at every turn. He is not caught through the logic of old-fashioned police procedures, but through newly developed electronic devices [direction finders in the cars tracking the gas truck to its destination]. It is the modern age that catches up with the outdated gangster and destroys him in the end and that is the true moral of **White Heat**." The character Cagney plays, Arthur Cody Jarrett, is unmistakably based upon 1930s bank robber and kidnapper Arthur "Doc" Barker (1899-1939). He was one of the four Barker brothers, all raised by the criminally bent Arizona Donnie Clarke "Ma" Barker (1873-1935), who was shot to death in a shoot out in Florida with one of her other sons, Fred Barker (1901-1935). Arthur, indeed, suffered from severe headaches throughout his life, which only his mother seemed to quell. Walsh confirmed this when saying to this author: "Doc Barker was the role model for Jimmy's [Cagney's] character in **White Heat**. He and his brothers were all psychopathic killers and kidnappers. Barker was killed while trying to escape Alcatraz. He got as far as the water's edge and when the guards told him to surrender, he laughed at them like a lunatic and they shot him. He kept going to-

George Dzundza and Clint Eastwood in *White Hunter Black Heart*, 1990.

ward the water and they shot him again and again until he finally dropped dead. We used that at the end of **White Heat** where Eddy [Edmond O'Brien] shoots Jimmy [Cagney] several times when trying to kill him." Cagney reaffirmed this when saying to this author: "Doc Barker was a mama's boy and, whenever he got into trouble, even as a grown man, he ran home to Ma Barker, who would cradle him like a little baby. I knew that, so I used it for one of the scenes I had with Margaret [Wycherly]. After I got a headache, which is sort of an attack of epilepsy, I told her that I would sit on her lap and she should pet me like I was a little boy to ease my pain, and that is what we did. I didn't tell Uncle [Walsh] that we were going to do it. We just did the scene, and Uncle congratulated us after we did that. You have to realize that Ma Barker was as loose-brained and fierce as her sons, a lioness protecting her cubs, so that they could grow up and become predators. There were a lot of beasts like that roaming America back in the Thirties." For more information on Doc and Ma Barker, see my eight-volume work *Encyclopedia of World Crime*, Volume I (CrimeBooks, Inc., 1990; Barker brothers: pages 235-243). Other actors playing Arthur "Doc" Barker in other films include **Bloody Mama**, 1970 (Clint Kimbrough); **The F.B.I. Story: The FBI Versus Alvin Karpis, Public Enemy Number One**, 1974 (made-for-TV; Charles Cyphers); **Guns Don't Argue**, 1957 (Lash La Rue); **The Kansas City Massacre**, 1975 (made-for-TV; Gary Sandy); **Ma Barker's Killer Brood**, 1960 (Gary Ammann as a boy; Ronald Foster as a man); **Murder in the First**, 1995 (Michael Melvin); **Public Enemies**; 2009 (Steve Key); and **The Untouchables**, 1959-1963 (TV series; Peter Baldwin). Other actresses playing Ma Barker in other films include **Bloody Mama**, 1970 (Lisa Linsky as girl; Shelley Winters as woman); **The FBI Story**, 1959 (Jane Crowley); **The F.B.I. Story: The FBI Versus Alvin Karpis, Public Enemy Number One**, 1974 (made-for-TV; Eileen Heckart); **Gang Busters**, 1952- (TV series, two 1952 episodes: Jean Harvey); **Guns Don't Argue**, 1957 (Jean Harvey); **Ma Barker's Killer Brood**, 1960 (Lurene Tuttle); **Queen of the Mob**, 1940 (role model for Blanche Yurka); **Spirits of St. Paul: The Gangster Era**, 2012 (Carol Vnuk); **The Untouchable Family**, 1988 (Caridad Sanchez); **The Untouchables**, 1959-1963 (TV series; "Ma Barker and Her Boys," 1959 episode: Claire Trevor); and **The Witness**, 1960-1961 (TV series; "Ma Barker," 1961 episode: Joan Blondell). This film was shot on location at the Southern Pacific Railroad Tunnel in the Santa Susana Mountains near Chatsworth, California (the train robbery), at the San Val Drive-In Theater in Burbank, California, and at the Shell Oil Plant at 198th and Figueroa streets in Los Angeles, California (the chemical plant robbery). The train robbery depicted in this film reenacts the sensational and bloody robbery of the Southern Pacific Railroad, Train No. 13, committed by the three D'Autremont brothers on October 11, 1923, at Siskiyou, Oregon, just north of the California

border, where they robbed its mail car and killed four railroad workers in the process. For details on this robbery gang and that event, see my work*Encyclopedia of World Crime*, Volume II (CrimeBooks, 1990; D'Autremont brothers: pages 878-880). **p**, Louis F. Edelman; **d**, Raoul Walsh; **cast**, James Cagney, Virginia Mayo, Edmund O'Brien, Margaret Wycherly, Steve Cochran, John Archer, Wally Cassell, Fred Clark, Paul Guilfoyle, Ian MacDonald, Robert Osterloh, Joel Allen, Fred Coby, Mickey Knox, G. Pat Collins, Eddie Foster, Ray Montgomery, Sid Melton, Ray Bennett; **w**, Ivan Goff, Ben Roberts (based on a story by Virginia Kellogg); **c**, Sid Hickox; **m**, Max Steiner; **ed**, Owen Marks; **art d**, Edward Carrere; **set d**, Fred M. MacLean; **spec eff**, Roy Davidson, H.F. Koenekamp.

White Hunter Black Heart ★★★ 1990; U.S.; 112m; Malpaso Productions/WB; Color; Biographical Drama; Children: Unacceptable (MPAA: PG); **DVD**; **VHS**; **IV**. Offbeat but fascinating drama sees Eastwood playing against type as an autocratic film director (based on pantheon helmsman John Huston, 1906-1987), who spends his time shooting animals and a film at the same time in the wilds of Africa. The story begins in England where Eastwood convinces writer Fahey (playing scriptwriter Peter Viertel, 1920-2007) to write a screenplay about a WWI (1914-1918) adventure set in Africa (based on **The African Queen**, 1951, which starred Humphrey Bogart and Katharine Hepburn). Eastwood, a grumpy, truculent person, then persuades producer Dzundza (who portrays movie producer Sam Spiegel, 1901-1985) to finance the production. He further signs on actress Berenson (playing Hepburn, 1907-2003) and actor Vanstone (who plays Bogart, 1899-1957) to star in the film. The group then travels to Africa where Eastwood delays the production and thus increases its costs by making outlandish demands for script rewrites and impossible location shoots. He then becomes obsessed with shooting a rogue elephant and spends so much of his time hunting the mammoth beast that the film is woefully delayed. In the process, Eastwood manages to alienate almost everyone involved in the film production and even brings tragedy to the gun bearers and aides helping him hunt down that evasive elephant, not to mention picking numerous fistfights and creating, out of sheer orneriness, many other nasty confrontations. The film gets made, but leaving everyone with a bad experience. Moreover, Eastwood dwells upon the long-standing condemnation of shooting African beasts for sport, and his character admits that such sport is "a sin." It takes the life of Boy Mathias Chuma, who plays Eastwood's devoted guide, to ultimately convince him not to shoot the elephant. Eastwood directs as well as stars in this strange outing, and he is fascinating to behold as he indulges himself as much as did the real Huston favor his own image and authority. It is a well-made drama that closely examines the complex persona of a gifted director, but it nevertheless presents a one-sided perspective that does not do justice to the genius that was John Huston. This film was not popular with the public and earned about $2 million in its initial release against a budget of $24 million. Songs: "Satin Doll" (Duke Ellington, Johnny Mercer, Billy Strayhorn), "Rowan Tree" (traditional), "Massa's in De Cold Ground" (1852; Stephen Foster). *Author's Note*: This author has never met Eastwood, but I did meet Huston several times and he never impressed me as the totally self-serving person that Eastwood depicts. This author believes that Eastwood, when making this film, unfairly, if not enviously, competed against the then dead Huston by savagely and too simplistically caricaturizing Huston's complex persona (including Eastwood's exaggerated and unconvincing speaking habits by drawing out vowels to poorly imitate if not to mock Huston's manner of deliberate speech), instead of profiling that director as the truly gifted and compassionate man he was. This author admits that Huston sometimes physically manifested his rugged individualism that sometimes led him astray from his own creative purposes and personal integrity, but he was never the self-destructive weirdo as shown herein. Further, Eastwood employs the considerable venom spewed forth from the vengeance-seeking Viertel, who had long harbored resentments against Huston over their earlier confrontations when working together on **The African Queen**. Eastwood himself is an admirable, multitalented man, but, in this instance, he diminished his own lofty stature and did a great disservice to John Huston with this nevertheless superior production. **p**, Clint Eastwood, Stanley Rubin; **d**, Eastwood; **cast**, Eastwood, Jeff Fahey, Charlotte Cornwell, Norman Lumsden, George Dzundza, Edward Tudor Pole, Roddy Maude-Roxby, Boy Mathias Chuma, Richard Warwick, John Rapley, Marisa Berenson, Richard Vanstone, Mel Martin, Timothy Spall; **w**, Peter Viertel, James Bridges, Burt Kennedy (based on the novel by Viertel); **c**, Jack N. Green; **m**, Lennie Niehaus; **ed**, Joel Cox; **prod d**, John Graysmark; **art d**, Tony Reading; **set d**, Peter Howitt; **spec eff**, John Evans, Roy Field, Peter Field.

White Lightning ★★★ 1973; U.S.; 101m; UA; Color; Crime Drama; Children: Unacceptable (MPAA: PG-13); **BD**; **DVD**; **VHS**; **IV**. Exciting, action-packed tale begins with Reynolds, who is arrested for selling illegally-made liquor and is given a choice of jail or informing on his moonshine suppliers and helping catch them. He chooses the latter, but believes that Beatty, the sheriff who offered the deal, has murdered his younger brother, a civil rights activist. With the help of Clark, a fellow informant, Reynolds infiltrates the moonshine organization and discovers that its leader is Beatty. Reynolds exposes Beatty as the gang leader and killer while stealing Billingsley, the girlfriend of hot car driver Hopkins. Reynolds gives a riveting performance in this tension-filled tale, which proved to be a hit at the box office, earning more than $6.5 million in its initial release. A less successful sequel, **Gator**, followed in 1976. Song: "Way Down Under" (Charles Bernstein). Excessive drinking and violence prohibit viewing by children. *Author's Note*: Other films depicting moonshiners include **Amigo**, 2011; **Bad Georgia Road**, 1977; **The Belles of St. Trinian's**, 1954; **Big Bad Mama**, 1974; **Bootleggers**, 1974; **The Burning Hills**, 1956; **Carbine Williams**, 1952; **The Cat's Meow**, 2001; **Cherokee Uprising**, 1953; **Coal Miner's Daughter**, 1980; **Dixie Dynamite**, 1976; **The Egg and I**, 1947; **The Flim-Flam Man**, 1967; **Foxfire Light**, 1982; **Frozen Heart**, 1993; **Harlan County War**, 2000 (made-for-TV); **Hooch**, 1977; **Hot Lead and Cold Feet**, 1978; **The Howling Miller**, 1982; **It's Up to Us**, 1973; **The Jerk**, 1979; **Judith of the Cumberlands**, 1916; **Juha**, 2003; **Kentucky Moonshine**, 1938; **King of the Pack**, 1926; **Kissin' Cousins**, 1964; **The Last American Hero**, 1973; **The Last of the High Kings**, 1988; **Lawless**, 2012; **Lucky Lady**, 1975; **Make Mine Music**, 1946; **A Man without a Wife**, 1983; **Mongoland**, 2000; **Monsieur Gangster**, 1963; **Moonrunners**, 1975; **Moonshine**, 2006; **Moonshine County Express**, 1977; **Moonshine Highway**, 1996 (made-for-TV); **Moonshine Mountain**, 1964; **The Moonshine War**, 1970; **My Dog Skip**, 2000; **The Nest of the Cuckoo Bird**, 1965; **The Night Watch**, 1926; **Nightmare Alley**, 1947; **Our Mr. Sun**, 1956 (made-for-TV); **Paper Moon**, 1973; **The Quiet Village**, 1997; **The Road Hustlers**, 1968; **Rocco and His Brothers**, 1962; **Ruby Gentry**, 1953; **The Rutherford County Line**, 1987; **The Scarlet Drop**, 1918; **Sheffey**, 1977; **The Shepherd of the Hills**, 1919; **The Shepherd of the Hills**, 1941; **The Silent Avenger**, 1926; **Soggy Bottom U.S.A.**, 1981; **Song of Warsaw**, 1953; **Swamp County**, 1966; **The Tender Warrior**, 1971; **They Live by Night**, 1949; **Thunder Road**, 1958; **Walking Tall**, 1973; **A Wicked Woman**, 1934; and **The Wind Journeys**, 2010. **p**, Arthur Gardner, Jules V. Levy, (not credited) Arnold Laven; **d**, Joseph Sargent; **cast**, Burt Reynolds, Jennifer Billingsley, Ned Beatty, Bo Hopkins, Matt Clark, Louise Latham, Diane Ladd, R.G. Armstrong, Dabbs Greer, Conlan Carter, Laura Dern; **w**, William W. Norton; **c**, Edward Rosson (DeLuxe Color); **m**, Charles Bernstein; **ed**, George Nicholson; **spec eff**, Cliff Wenger.

White Mischief ★★★ 1988; U.K./U.S.; 107m; COL; Color; Crime Drama; Children: Unacceptable (MPAA: R); **DVD**; **VHS**. Well-directed and extremely well-acted crime tale profiles the sensational murder case involving the shooting death of Josslyn Hay, 22nd Earl of Erroll, 1901-1941, who is played by Dance. The man accused of killing Josslyn was

Geraldine Chaplin and Greta Scacchi in *White Mischief*, 1988.

wealthy Sir Henry Jock Delves Boughton, 1883-1942, played by Ackland. Both men who were vying for the affections of Boughton's alluring wife, Diana Caldwell Boughton, who is played by Scacchi. The film faithfully follows the melodramatic story when Dance's body is found in his car, shot to death. He is a resident of Happy Valley in colonialized Kenya, an exclusive area where British landed gentry reside and spend most of their time pursuing decadent lifestyles, excessively drinking, taking drugs, and, chiefly, having adulterous affairs. The marriage between Scacchi and Ackland, who is thirty years older than his wife, is one of hedonistic convenience. In their prenuptial agreement, both consented to the fact that, if either of them entered into an extramarital romance, the other would not interfere with that ongoing affair. To that precarious end, Scacchi enters into a torrid romance with Dance while also involving herself with the drug-taking lifestyle of the loose-living American heiress Miles, and Scacchi, like Miles and others, is often out of touch with reality. Dance truly loves Scacchi and wants her to divorce Ackland and marry him. Scacchi does not want to leave the security that Ackland's wealth affords her, knowing that Dance is low on funds and has little prospects of improving his financial future. She does not know, however, that her husband's fortune has dwindled and he, too, is in financial trouble. Ackland is keenly aware of his wife's infidelity with Dance and gets drunk at his exclusive club, mockingly toasting Scacchi's romance with her lover and politely requesting that Dance get his wife home to him at a decent hour after the two complete their assignation. Ackland's intoxication, however, is a pretense as he is sober that night. After Dance dallies with Scacchi and takes her home, he is later found shot to death in his car, which is located close to Ackland's estate. Ackland is then charged with Dance's murder. Emotionally devastated over Dance's death, Scacchi is consoled by rich plantation owner Hurt, who then astounds her when he proposes marriage to her. Ackland stands trial, but since there are no witnesses against him and the circumstantial evidence in the case is too flimsy to convict him, he is acquitted and set free. Scacchi later discovers evidence that would have convicted her husband, but, before she brings this to the attention of officials, Ackland, in a fit of rage, threatens to kill her with a shotgun. Instead, he takes his own life, the blast coating Scacchi with his blood. In shock, and coated with Ackland's gore, Scacchi leaves her home, going to find comfort from her friends. She finds them all at a drunken revel being held at the grave of Miles, who has earlier died from an overdose of drugs, completing this grim portrait of debauchery and degenerate social behavior. Though the film is a blatant indictment of the British idle rich that too often obsessively dwells upon the perversions of its subjects (even the austere Howard is shown to be a morally corrupted Peeping Tom), the acting is exceptional. The film is further enhanced by its richly presented period sets, costumes and

Renee Zellweger and Michelle Pfeiffer in *White Oleander*, 2002.

vehicles, as well as inventive lensing from Deakins and a haunting score from Fenton. The film did not do well at the box office, earning about $3 million in its initial release against a budget of more than $5.3 million. Songs: "The Alphabet Song" (George Fenton), "Begin the Beguine" (1934; Cole Porter), "The Dance of the Sugar Plum Fairy" (1892; from "The Nutcracker" by Peter Illyich Tchaikovsky). *Author's Note*: Miles' character, Alice de Janze (nee Silverthorne; 1899-1941), did not die of a drug overdose as depicted herein, but committed suicide by shooting herself on September 30, 1941, after being diagnosed with uterine cancer and becoming depressed at her fading looks. Her once attractive appearance had been considerably altered to a careworn, haggard image by years of drug and alcohol abuse. She was a multi-millionaire and whose father had been a leader in the textile industry. She was one of the leading New York and Chicago socialites of the 1920s, leading an extravagant lifestyle. She later became an expatriate in Paris, where, on March 25, 1927, she shot her lover Raymond De Trafford, as well as herself, after De Trafford refused to divorce his wife and marry her. She was married at that time and had been carrying on an affair with De Trafford. Both survived. Alice had always lived a troubled life, having been raped at an early age by her own father, William Edward Silverthorne. Her mother, Julia Belle Chapin, was related to the Armour family of Chicago, which owned one of the world's largest meatpacking firms. She, like Diana Boughton, had had a torrid affair with Josslyn Hay, and many believed that it was Alice de Janze who killed Hay, not the often cuckolded Jock Delves Boughton, who did not, as depicted in this film, kill himself in Kenya. He took an overdose of morphine and died on September 5, 1942, in a hotel in Liverpool, after he had been rejected by the Happy Valley community following his acquittal and his return to England. For more facts about the Boughton-Hay case, see my two-volume work *The Great Pictorial History of World Crime*, Volume II (History, Inc., 2004; pages 873-875). **p**, Simon Perry; **d**, Michael Radford; **cast**, Greta Scacchi, Charles Dance, Joss Ackland, Hugh Grant, John Hurt, Trevor Howard, Sarah Miles, Geraldine Chaplin, Ray McAnally, Susan Fleetwood, Susannah Harker; **w**, Radford, Jonathan Gems (based on the novel by James Fox); **c**, Roger Deakins; **m**, George Fenton; **ed**, Tom Priestley; **prod d**, Roger Hall; **art d**, Len Huntingford, Keith Pain.

White Oleander ★★★ 2002; U.S.; 109m; WB; Color; Drama; Children: Unacceptable (MPAA: PG-13); **DVD**; **VHS**; **IV**. Strange but compelling tale begins when Lohman is a fifteen-year-old living in California with her mother, Pfeiffer, who is a beautiful, free-spirited poet. Pfeiffer falls in love with Connolly, who breaks her heart. She murders him by putting poison in her favorite flower, a white oleander, and is sent to prison for life. Lohman is sent to one foster home after another

where, over the course of about ten years, she experiences forbidden love, starvation, drug use, religion, near-death, and also how it feels to be loved by someone. During these years she writes letters to her mother in prison sharing encouragement; Lohman teaches her mother about love and Pfeiffer teaches Lohman how to survive. Often morose and depressing, the film is saved and sustained by the exceptional performances of Lohman and Pfeiffer. Songs: "Melissa's Dream" (Earl Rose), "One Perfect Thing" (Girls Against Boys: Eli Janney, Scott McCloud, Johnny Temple, Alexis Fleisig), "Black Hearted Ways" (Tim Easton), "What's Inside Me" (Raile), "The Good Life" (Leslie Mills, Chris Pelcer), "When They Make Me Bang" (R. Patterson, J. Martinez), "S.S.T." (Thomas Barnett, Eric Kane, Garth Petrie, Matt C. Sherwood, Matt Smith), "Happy Hour" (The Promise Ring: Davey von Bohlen, Dan Didier, Jason Gnewikow, Scott Schoenbeck, Scott Beschta), "Menina D'Agua/Girl of the Sea" (Marcelo C. Madeira, Gabi V. Rossi), "Bang Bang" (Steve Clark, Tom McKay), "Plank of Fire" (Dimitri Coats), "Safe and Sound" (Sheryl Crow). Drug content, gutter language, violence, sexuality, and mature themes about dysfunctional relationships prohibit viewing by children. **p**, Hunt Lowry, John Wells; **d**, Peter Kosminsky; **cast**, Alison Lohman, Michelle Pfeiffer, Billy Connolly, Robin Wright as Robin Wright Penn, Noah Wyle, Renee Zellweger, James Lashly, Amy Aquino, John Billingsley, Melissa Marsala, Kali Rocha, Mark Soper; **w**, Mary Agnes Donoghue (based on the novel by Janet Fitch); **c**, Elliot Davis; **m**, Thomas Newman; **ed**, Chris Ridsdale; **prod d**, Donald Graham Burt; **art d**, Anthony Rivero Stabley; **set d**, Bryony Foster; **spec eff**, Jeff Denes, Thad Beier, Jay Mark Johnson.

White Palms ★★★ 2007; Hungary; 97m; Filmpartners/Strand Releasing; Color; Sport Drama; Children: Unacceptable; **DVD**; **IV**. Action-filled drama begins with Hajdu, who is a boy in Hungary; outstandingly performs as a gymnast, but suffers under a brutal Communist-era coach. He becomes a champion gymnast nonetheless and then moves to Canada. After he becomes a coach, he finds himself in a similar abusive situation from his pupils. His situation improves and he gains a new understanding of the coach-pupil connection when he coaches a troubled young Canadian teenager, Shewfelt, who has the potential of becoming a world champion. They are first teacher and student rivals, but eventually become friends. Hajdu and Shewfelt are real-life gymnasts. The film's title refers to the white rosin gymnasts put on their hands while performing. (In Hungarian and German; English subtitles.) **p**, Ivan Angelusz, Mathieu Kassovitz, Gabor Kovacs, Agi Pataki, Peter Reich, Andras Poos; **d&w**, Szabolcs Hajdu; **cast**, Zoltan Miklos Hajdu, Kyle Shewfelt, Gheorghe Dinica, Andor Lukats, Oana Pellea, Orion Radies, David Horvath, David Vecsernyes, Peter Deeri, Krisztian Oltyan; **c**, Andras Nagy; **m**, Ferenc Darvas; **ed**, Peter Politzer; **prod d**, Monika Esztan; **art d**, Szilvia Ritter; **set d**, Attila Feherhegyi; **spec eff**, Gyula Krasnyanszky, Laszlo Pinter, Ritter.

The White Ribbon ★★★ 2009; Germany/Austria/France/Italy; 144m; X-Films Creative Pool/Sony; Color; Mystery; Children: Unacceptable (MPAA: R); **BD**; **DVD**; **IV**. Eerie mystery begins when strange things begin to happen in a German village, these inexplicable events lasting from July 1913 to the start of World War I (1914-1918). A horse trips on a wire and the rider is thrown off, a woman falls to her death walking on rotted planks, the son of the town's baron, Tukur, is hung upside-down in a mill, parents bully and slap their children for no reason, a man sexually abuses his daughter, and people vanish without explanation. Friedel, a callous teacher who courts a nanny in the baron's household, narrates this weird story while investigating possible connections of those involved in the crimes and disappearances. Songs/Music: "O Sacred Head Now Wounded" (music: Hans Leo Hassler), "A Mighty Fortress Is Our God" (Martin Luther). Violence and sexuality prohibit viewing by children. **p**, Stefan Arndt, Veit Heiduschka, Margaret Menegoz, Andrea Occhipinti; **d&w**, Michael Haneke (based on his story); **cast**, Christian Friedel, Ernst Jacobi (voice only), Leonie Benesch, Ulrich Tukur, Ursina Lardi, Fion Mutert, Michael Kranz, Burghart Klaussner, Steffi Kuhnert, Maria-Victoria Dragus, Leonard Proxauf; **c**, Christian Berger; **ed**, Monika Willi; **prod d**, Christoph Kanter; **art d**, Anja Muller; **set d**, Heike Wolf; **spec eff**, Gerd Feuchter, Rolf Hanke.

The White Rose ★★★★ 1923 (silent); U.S.; 100m/12 reels; D.W. Griffith Productions/UA; Drama; Children: Unacceptable; **DVD**. Master filmmaker Griffith relies on a traditional morality story in depicting this tale of a fall from grace and redemption by a young preacher, who starts out to save the souls of the world and jeopardizes his own. The film begins with Novello, the son of a wealthy Southern family who is about to take his vows as a minister. Having led a protected life, he decides to travel about to see the levels of society he will encounter when becoming a preacher. To that end, he arrives at a town outside of New Orleans where he meets beautiful Marsh, an alluring flapper. She is really anything but that. Marsh is a naive orphan, who is innocent of the wiles and ways of the world. She works at the hotel and has been taught how to dress and act like a modern siren, donning short skirts, heavy makeup and employing the come hither actions of a vamp, all of this play-acting earning her the nickname "Teazie." Such conduct is truly foreign to Marsh, her exaggerated profile apparent to any sophisticated man. Yet the local unworldly bumpkins are taken in by her awkward disguise and are awed and overwhelmed by her struggling but endearing efforts to present herself as a vixen. So too is the unsophisticated Novello when he meets her, mesmerized by her antic actions. He makes a clumsy attempt to reform Marsh by suggesting she read the Bible, particularly passages referencing the harlot, Jezebel. All of this is lost on Marsh, who does not know what he is talking about and is really as innocent as a babe in the manger. She is nevertheless enamored of the handsome Novello and they spend the night together. At dawn, Novello, now ridden with guilt over trysting with Marsh (his histrionics in a nearby woods at losing his virginity is somewhat embarrassing, but nevertheless in keeping with the moral code and acting style of the day), quickly departs to return home where he resumes his coddled relationship with fetching Dempster. Hamilton, the poor boy next door, who works as a grocery clerk, adores Dempster from afar, although he believes his station in life will never allow him to marry her as she, like Novello, is a member of high society. For her part, Dempster toys with the slavish-like Hamilton, thinking him to be amusing, but never taking him seriously as a suitable husband. While Novello goes on to take his vows and enter the ministry, Marsh, who has become pregnant, is now looked upon by her peers as a fallen woman. She delivers a baby and loses her job and she is now branded a social pariah. Penniless and without shelter, she is taken in by a compassionate black woman, La Verne (who, also in the custom of the day, plays the role of Auntie Esther in blackface as do all other white actors essaying blacks in this film, such minstrel performances traditional throughout Griffith's films). Some time passes and Novello becomes the pastor of an upscale church where he delivers impassioned sermons against the sinful ways of mankind, using the inflated memories of his one-night stand with Marsh to remind himself of such evildoing. His spiritual visions collide with the realities of life when Marsh appears at the church with their child. Novello, realizing that he has always loved Marsh and not Dempster, practices what he preaches by marrying Marsh, redeeming himself and removing the stain that has sullied Marsh's social image at the same time. Dempster, by this time, is now courted by a wholly different Hamilton, who has left town and returned a successful businessman, and when he proposes to her, Dempster, who has fallen in love with this "new man," readily accepts. Griffith presents a straightforward domestic tale, depicting this story in such a prosaic fashion—unencumbered by any cultured airs or designs—that it remains a pristine sentimental portrait of artless young lovers overcoming social barricades and draconian religious beliefs to find happiness. Marsh, who was twenty-eight when making this film, gives the finest performance of her life, never again to equal her sterling essay. She is just as convincing and empathetic when playing an out-

Actual members of The White Rose group: Hans Scholl, Sophie Scholl and Christoph Probst, all profiled in *The White Rose*, 1983.

landish fifteen-year-old in this film as she is when she comes to maturity and motherhood, where her acting becomes marvelously restrained. Though Novello, a British matinee star and popular song composer at the time he made this film, is exceptional as the soul-searching young minister, it is Marsh and her stunning performance that perpetuates the most lingering memories of this superlative production. Griffith spent more than $650,000 to produce this film, but, sadly, it barely earned back its investment at the box office. *Author's Note*: Griffith shot this film on location at Bayou Teche in Louisiana and along areas of the New River near Fort Lauderdale, Florida. The resplendent mansion that serves as the residence for Novello's wealthy family is actually the Weeks House, which was built in 1830, and is located at New Iberia, Louisiana. This visually beautiful film was photographed by the legendary cinematographer Billy Bitzer, who recorded all of Griffith's greatest films; he originally employed tinted and toned nitrate film that is sadly lacking in the rather washed-out, dull-appearing prints of this film that are stored at the Museum of Modern Art. D.W. Griffith (writing as Irene Sinclair); **cast**, Mae Marsh, Carol Dempster, Ivor Novello, Neil Hamilton, Lucille La Verne, Porter Strong, Jane Thomas, Kate Bruce, Erville Alderson, Herbert Sutch; **c**, G.W. Bitzer, Hendrik Sartov, Harold S. Sintzenich; **m**, Joseph Carl Breil; **art d**, Charles M. Kirk; **spec eff**, Edward Scholl.

The White Rose ★★★★ 1983; West Germany; 108m; Central Cinema/TeleCulture; Color; Drama; Children: Unacceptable; **DVD**. This well-acted, well-directed film presents a searing profile of the resistance to Nazi authorities led by a nonviolent intellectual group of Munich University students. That actual and courageous group operated with the help of a philosophy professor from June 1942 until February 1943, and was known as "The White Rose." The name came from a banned 1929 book and was given to a graffiti campaign and an anonymous leaflet the secret group circulated to the student body in its attempt to gain support to resist Nazi control of Germany and to oppose the regime of Adolf Hitler (1889-1945). The student movement's origins begin in the summer of 1942 when several of its members are forced to serve for three months on the Russian front alongside male medical students from the University of Munich. There they observe the horrors of war, witness beatings and other mistreatment of Jews by the Nazis, and hear about the persecution of Jews from other sources. Massive support begins for the movement until the Gestapo learns of it and begins a crackdown. The movement's six leading members are caught, tried for treason, and beheaded in February 1943, shortly after the German defeat at Stalingrad, Russia, in World War II (1939-1945). The film predates **Sophie Scholl: The Final Days**, 2005, which also told the story of the heroic resistance movement. Verhoeven also directed another film, **The Nasty**

Monte Blue and Raquel Torres in *White Shadows in the South Seas*, 1928.

Girl, 1990, about Sophie Scholl, one of the White Rose participants. Not related to the 1923 or 1992 films with the same name. *Author's Note*: The group's sixth leaflet was smuggled out of Germany through Scandinavia to the United Kingdom and, in July 1943, millions of copies were dropped over Germany by Allied planes, retitled "The Manifesto of the Students of Munich." Another member of the group, Hans Conrad Leipelt, who distributed the sixth leaflet in Hamburg, was executed in 1945 for his participation. Originally released in Germany in 1982, the film was not released in the United States until 2013. Violence and gutter language prohibit viewing by children. (In German; English subtitles.) **p**, Senta Berger, Artur Brauner, Hans Prescher, Dietmar Schings, Michael Verhoeven, **d**, Verhoeven; **cast**, Lena Stolze, Wulf Kessler, Oliver Siebert, Ulrich Tukur, Werner Stocker, Martin Benrath, Anja Kruse, Ulf-Jurgen Wagner; **w**, Mario Krebs, Verhoeven; **c**, Axel de Roche; **m**, Konstantin Wecker; **ed**, Barbara Hennings; **prod d**, Les Oelvedy.

White Shadows in the South Seas ★★★ 1928 (silent); U.S.; 88m; MGM; B/W; Drama/Romance; Children: Unacceptable; **DVD**; **IV**. Blue is exceptional in his role as a successful physician in America, who becomes disillusioned with civilization. He decides to give up his career and live a more simple and carefree life in the South Seas. He takes to drink and becomes a boozy sot (a role he would effectively reprise as Mary Astor's drunken father in **Across the Pacific**, 1942). He then befriends Anderson, a vicious opportunist, who leads a gang of cutthroats. Anderson, a pearl trader, and his associates are endangering the lives of natives working for them as pearl divers. It becomes a war of wills between Blue and Anderson as Blue condemns the pearl trader's greed and tries to stop Anderson's abuse. But Anderson will do anything to protect his way of life by exploiting the natives. Blue so angers Anderson that he has his thugs lash Blue to the wheel of a schooner reportedly filled with the bodies of plague victims and sent adrift. The small vessel is caught in a wild storm and tossed wildly about, but Blue manages to free himself and dives overboard before the schooner sinks. He winds up on the sandy shore of a beautiful island where the natives are in awe of him as he is the first white man they have ever seen. Blue's dissolute life comes to an end when he falls in love with Torres, a native beauty, but his tranquil life is threatened when he goes pearl diving and finds a huge cache of pearls. He becomes, like Anderson, the man he loathes, greedy for pearls and the riches they might bring him. Now that he is rich, Blue thinks to leave his tropical paradise with his newly found riches and sends a smoke signal, hoping to be rescued. Ironically, it is Anderson and his henchmen who see the signal and sail to the unchartered island. There they enslave the natives, compelling them, as before, to risk their lives diving for pearls. Enraged,

Blue attacks Anderson, but he is shot to death by one of Anderson's men, ending this sultry tale of greed and murder in the South Seas. Van Dyke and Flaherty share the director's credit here, the former helming the dramatic sequences while Flaherty, a maker of tropical documentaries, filmed the exotic exterior shots, all of which give a lush and sultry look to this fascinating tale; Blue, Anderson and Torres are standouts in their roles. The film did well at the box office and earned an Oscar for Best Cinematography (De Vinna, Nogle, Roberts, awarded in 1930). The story, based on a travel book, vastly influenced many films to come that were set in the South Seas, particularly the pearl-diving scenes appearing in **Wake of the Red Witch**, 1948. *Author's Note*: Flaherty shot this film in Tahiti and MGM released it as its first sound feature after its top sound technician, Douglas Shearer (the brother of MGM superstar Norma Shearer), added a musical score, sound effects and one word, "hello." It was then presented with a synchronized score when it was premiered at Grauman's Chinese Theater in Hollywood on August 3, 1928. The film also offered, for the first time, the studio's famous Leo the Lion, roaring for the first time on the screen. Flaherty would go on to make another exceptional South Seas film with gifted director F.W. Murnau entitled **Tabu: A Story of the South Seas**, 1931. Van Dyke was brought in to support Flaherty, but Flaherty left before the production was completed, having helmed the lagoon and island scenes. As would be the case with **Tabu**, when Flaherty found it too difficult to deal with Murnau, he encountered the same difficulties with Van Dyke. Other films depicting pearl-divers and pearl-diving include **Adventure's End**, 1937; **Amphibian Man**, 2006; **Anokha Moti**, 2000; **Badjao: The Sea Gypsies**, 1962; **Beyond the Reef**, 1981; **The Blue Lagoon**, 1980; **Brides of Sulu**, 1937; **Cruel Sea**, 1972; **The Flaming Signal**, 1933; **Hitokui ama**, 1958; **In a Savage Land**, 1999; **Isle of Fury**, 1936; **My Mother the Mermaid**, 2004; **The Millionaire Pirate**, 1919; **Paradise Island**, 1930; **Port of Hate**, 1939; **Return to the Blue Lagoon**, 1991; **Soldiers of Fortune**, 1955-1957 (TV series; "Pearls Off Dondra Head," 1955 episode); **Tabu: A Story of the South Seas**, 1931; **Tarzan and the Mermaids**, 1948; **A Thief in Paradise**, 1925; **Vengeance of the Deep**, 1938; **Wake of the Red Witch**, 1948; **Wallaby Jim of the Islands**, 1937; **A Woman There Was**, 1919; and **Zetsurin ama: Shimari-gai**, 1985. **p**, Hunt Stromberg, (not credited) Irving Thalberg; **d**, W.S. Van Dyke, Robert J. Flaherty; **cast**, Monte Blue, Raquel Torres, Robert Anderson, Renee Bush, Dorothy King, Napua; **w**, Ray Doyle, Jack Cunningham (based on the novel by Frederick O'Brien), John Colton; **c**, Clyde De Vinna, George Nogle, Bob Roberts; **m**, William Axt, David Mendoza; **ed**, Ben Lewis.

The White Sister ★★★★ 1923 (silent); U.S.; 143m; Inspiration Pictures/Metro Pictures; B/W; Drama/Romance; Children: Unacceptable; **DVD**. Gish gives a marvelous performance in this powerful tale about an Italian princess cruelly deprived of her inheritance. Gish is in love with Colman, a dashing army officer; they plan to marry, but her father, Lane, who knows nothing of this romance, arbitrarily arranges for Gish to marry Martinelli, the dissolute son of Ibanez, a wealthy count. That marriage never takes place as Lane is accidentally killed while riding to hounds. Gish's vindictive sister, Kane, who hates Gish for having been first in Lane's heart, destroys their father's will. She further burns all other family papers that show Gish's rightful place in the family so that Gish now appears to have been born out of wedlock in a second marriage and thus has no right to the family's aristocratic name. When the vengeance-seeking Kane informs Ibanez about Gish's affair with Colman, the count then destroys the marriage contract between Gish and Martinelli. Ordered from her palatial home, Gish is taken in by La Violette, her compassionate chaperone, and she is further comforted by Colman, who, unfortunately, gives her the bad news that he has been ordered to a remote African outpost. Colman nevertheless promises that they will be wed the moment he returns. A short time later, Italian newspapers report that the African outpost has been attacked by Arabs and all members of the garrison, including Colman, have been killed. Upon learning this, Gish goes into shock, remaining catatonic. She is removed to a hospital supervised by nuns, and, through their loving care, her mental well-being is restored. Gish then decides that she will, to honor Colman's memory, become a nun. The day she takes her vows, Gish returns to work at the hospital and there sees Colman very much alive. He had languished in an Arab jail for two years until managing to escape. When they first meet, Colman takes Gish into his arms and passionately kisses her and she responds in kind, until she realizes that she is now a nun and runs to her room. Sherry, the hospital's monsignor, prevents Colman from following Gish, telling him that Gish is now married to the Catholic Church. Colman refuses to accept this covenant and tries to get Gish to ask the Pope for a dispensation that will release her from her vows. Gish, however, refuses. Meanwhile, Vesuvius, the always active volcano, begins to erupt and citizens flee to safety. Among those seeking shelter is Kane, who is being driven in her carriage when lightning causes its horses to bolt, wrecking the carriage and fatally injuring Kane. She crawls to a nearby church where, ironically, Gish is praying. Kane confesses that she had destroyed their father's will that made Gish a placeless person and begs Gish's forgiveness. Gish hesitates, but, in a sensitive scene of soul-searching, finds enough compassion in her heart to forgive Kane before she dies. Vesuvius erupts in all of its explosive fury, spewing forth fireballs, ash and lava, destroying a dam that takes countless victims. Colman dies in this calamity after saving the lives of several people. When Gish learns of his death, she prays that God will keep him safe until she and Colman can be united in the hereafter. Though fraught with thick sentimentality, this heavy melodrama is saved from sinking into mawkish bathos by the expert direction of King and masterful essays from Gish and Colman, who give marvelously restrained performances. The action scenes during the volcanic eruptions are stunningly choreographed and excitingly recorded by cinematographer Overbaugh. The story was filmed as an earlier silent in 1915, and as a superior talkie in 1933. *Author's Note*: King told this author that "I had some problems when it came to shooting the scene where Lillian [Gish] must take her vows as a nun [the Assumption of the Veil], and I mentioned that to a member of a Vatican delegation that was traveling on the same ship I was taking to Europe to make the picture. [The film was shot entirely on location in Italy for $300,000.] Well, when we came to shoot that scene, the Vatican sent its ceremonial director with a complete script for that scene. We shot it from eight in the morning until seven that night and that little fat priest really did all the direction for that sequence. It proved to be one of the best scenes in the picture and I told him he was a born director." That scene, like so many in this film, is, indeed, memorably moving as Gish, surrounded by radiant light, takes her vows. King later became a convert to Catholicism. Colman, who had been "discovered" by Gish and King in a Broadway play, had appeared in a few films before making his appearance in **The White Sister**. It was his empathetic performance in this film, however, that made him a superstar, even without the benefit of audiences being able to hear his mellifluous voice in that silent era. Although Hollywood studios thought that religious films such as this one were acceptable fare, distributors considered these productions box office poison. Inspiration Films had no national distributor for this film until it received rave reviews when it was premiered in New York, and it was immediately picked up by Metro Pictures, becoming a widespread success, this only nine months before Metro merged with Mayer and Goldwyn studios to become Metro-Goldwyn-Mayer (MGM). Other films depicting volcanic eruptions include **Aloma of the South Seas**, 1941; **Alvin and the Chipmunks: Chipwrecked**, 2011; **Apocalypse Pompeii**, 2014; **Atlantis, The Lost Continent**, 1961; **Atlantis: The Lost Empire**, 2001; **Behemoth**, 2011 (made-for-TV); **Black Paradise**, 1926; **The Black Scorpion**, 1957 (Mexico); **Colossus and the Headhunters**, 1963; **Congo**, 1995; **The Croods**, 2013; **Dante's Peak**, 1997 (Pacific Northwest); **The Deep**, 2012; **Deep Core**, 2000; **The Devil at Four O'-Clock**, 1961; **Devil Goddess**, 1955; **Doomsday Prophecy**, 2011 (made-for-TV); **Fantasia**, 1940; **Her Jungle Love**, 1938; **Hercules the**

Clark Gable and Alan Edwards in *The White Sister*, 1933.

Avenger, 1965; **In Search of the Castaways**, 1962; **Journey to the Center of the Earth**, 1959; **Journey to the Center of the Earth**, 2008; **Journey 2: The Mysterious Island**, 2012; **King of the Rocket Men**, 1949; **King Solomon's Mines**, 1937; **King Solomon's Mines**, 1985; **Krakatoa: East of Java**, 1969 (May-August 1883); **Krakatoa**, 2008 (made-for-TV; May-August 1883); **The Land That Time Forgot**, 1975; **The Last Days of Pompeii**, 1913 (Vesuvius, 79 A.D.); **The Last Days of Pompeii**, 1935 (Vesuvius, 79 A.D.); **Last Days of the Dinosaurs**, 2010 (made-for-TV); **Leopardi**, 2014; **The Lord of the Rings: The Return of the King**, 2003; **Lost Continent**, 1951; **Magma: Volcanic Disaster**, 2006 (made-for-TV); **Melody in Love**, 1978; **Mysterious Island**, 1961; **Mysterious Island**, 2005 (made-for-TV); **The Naked Kiss**, 1964; **Night at the Museum: Secret of the Tomb**, 2014; **The Night the World Exploded**, 1957; **100 Degrees below Zero**, 2013; **Our Man Flint**, 1966; **Phantom of the Jungle**, 1955; **Pompeii**, 2014 (Vesuvius, 79 A.D.); **Raptor Island**, 2004 (made-for-TV); **Robinson Crusoe of Clipper Island**, 1936; **Robot Monster**, 1953; **Rodan**, 1956; **St. Helens**, 1981; **Scorcher**, 2002; **The Secret Life of Walter Mitty**, 2013; **The Secret of Treasure Island**, 1938; **79 A.D.**, 1962 (Vesuvius); **She Demons**, 1958; **Son of Kong**, 1933; **Star Trek: Into Darkness**, 2013; **Stromboli**, 1950; **Supergirl**, 1984; **Superman IV: The Quest for Peace**, 1987; **Switching Channels**, 1988; **The Time Machine**, 1960; **2012**, 2009; **Two Lost Worlds**, 1951; **Untamed Women**, 1952; **Volcano**, 1997 (Los Angeles, California); **When Time Ran Out**, 1980; **The Wild**, 2006; **Wrath of the Titans**, 2012; and **Yog: Monster from Space**, 1970. **p&d**, Henry King; **cast**, Lillian Gish, Ronald Colman, Gail Kane, J. Barney Sherry, Juliette La Violette, Gustavo Serena, Alfredo Bertone, Roman Ibanez, Alfredo Martinelli, Carloni Talli; **w**, George V. Hobart, Charles Whittaker, titles by Will M. Ritchey, Don Bartlett (based on the novel by Francis Marion Crawford); **c**, Roy Overbaugh; **m**, Joseph Carl Breil; **ed**, Duncan Mansfield; **art d**, Robert Haas.

The White Sister ★★★ 1933; U.S.; 110m; MGM; B/W; Drama/Romance; Children: Unacceptable; **DVD**. Good remake of the outstanding 1923 version has Hayes as a young woman whose father, Stone, has forced her into an arranged marriage, but she does not love the man he has chosen. Before she weds, Hayes meets Gable at a religious event. They fall in love and run away together. World War I (1914-1918) breaks out and Gable becomes a pilot. He is later reported dead and Hayes joins a convent. Gable is not dead, however, but in an Austrian POW camp, unable to contact her. After two years of confinement in the camp, Gable escapes, stealing an Austrian plane and flying to friendly lines. He searches for Hayes and finds her at the convent where she has already taken her final vows as a nun. Gable begs her to get a dispensation from

Jeff Bridges, center, and youthful crew members in *White Squall*, 1996.

the Pope so they can marry, but she refuses. Gable leaves, only to later return to the convent, but is killed just outside the gate when an Austrian plane drops a bomb. He dies in Hayes' arms, letting her know he accepts her decision to remain faithful to her vows. Hayes and Gable provide outstanding performances in this well-made tearjerker expertly crafted by pantheon director Fleming. Of exceptional note are the will-staged aerial scenes showing Italian and German WWI fighter bi-planes in exciting action. This film proved to be a box office success, earning more than $1.7 million in its initial release. This story, in addition to the 1923 silent version that starred Lillian Gish and Ronald Colman, had been produced as an earlier silent in 1915, with Viola Allen and Richard Travers. It was remade as an Italian production in 1973, starring Sophia Loren as the star-crossed nun, a wholly disappointing version in which the earthy Loren was wholly miscast. Songs: "O Sole Mio" (1898; music: Eduardo Di Capua, Alfredo Mazzucchi; lyrics: Giovanni Capurro), "Finiculi, Finicula" (1880; Luigi Denza), "Patriotic Song" (traditional). *Author's Note*: Hayes felt that her young co-star, Gable, was self-conscious in playing the honorable lover, stating that he was forever attempting to "hide his hands, which bore many scars," despite the considerable efforts of the makeup department to disguise them. Gable, before becoming an actor, had done extensive manual labor, scarring his hands when working as a rigger in the Oklahoma oil fields with his father. The senior Gable never approved of his son's chosen profession as an actor, considering that livelihood "unmanly." Gable, always a "man's man," downplayed his great success as an actor, sharing his father's perspective that acting was "too easy a way to make a living." Although director Fleming shot all the interiors for this film at the MGM studio in Culver City, California, the aerial combat scenes were shot outside of Reno, Nevada, where pilot Paul Mantz staged some spectacular dogfights. p, Hunt Stromberg; d, Victor Fleming; cast, Helen Hayes, Clark Gable, Lewis Stone, Louise Closser Hale, May Robson, Edward Arnold, Richard Bennett, Gino Corrado, Nat Pendleton; w, Donald Ogden Stewart (based on the play by Walter Hackett and the novel by Francis Marion Crawford); c, William Daniels; m, Herbert Stothart; ed, Margaret Booth; art d, Cedric Gibbons.

White Squall ★★★ 1996; U.S.; 129m; Hollywood Pictures/Buena Vista; Color; Adventure/Drama; Children: Unacceptable (MPAA: PG-13); **BD; DVD; VHS; IV**. This exciting film is based on the sinking of a sea training ship, the brigantine *Albatross*, on May 21, 1961, allegedly because of a white squall storm. A crew of teenage boys, whose parents think they need some toughening up, learn lessons of seamanship and life from each other and the ship's captain, Bridges, who the boys call "Skipper." He is a tough and seasoned young man of the sea, who teaches them discipline, often at the expense of their pride and sensibil-

ities. Bridges bonds with Wolf, who is a clean-cut All-American boy, a troubled rich kid, Sisto, shy Phillippe, and bad-boy Cole. When a white squall threatens the ship, the boys try to use what Bridges has taught them so they can survive, but the ship goes down, taking with it Bridges' wife, Goodall, while the others survive. Despite the unhappy and tragic ending, the tale presents some fine character development from gifted director Scott, and top performances from the entire cast. The film earned more than $10 million at the box office in its initial release, but did not recoup its budget of $38 million. Songs: "Valpariso" (Sting: Gordon Sumner), "Be My Guest" (Fats Domino as Antoine Domino, John Marascalco, Tommy Boyce), "I Wanna Walk You Home" (Antoine Domino), "Somethin' Else" (Sharon Sheeley, Bob Cochran), "The Twist" (Hank Ballard), "Yellow Basket" (Duke Reid, Tommy McCook), "In the Mood" (Joe Garland), "Teenage SKA" (Duke Reid), "Amazing Grace" (1779; John Newton), "South Australia/Bound for South Australia" (1800s British sea shanty). *Author's Note*: The actual vessel used for this film is called *The Eye of the Wind*, which was originally constructed as a top-sail schooner in 1911. It was refitted as a brigantine in 1975 and is presently rigged as a brig. The ship was used in other films, including **The Blue Lagoon**, 1980, **Savage Island**, 1985, and **Tai-Pan**, 1986. Director Scott reportedly stated that he would direct this film after reading its script within ninety minutes. Other films depicting storms at sea include **Abandon Ship!**, 1957; **The Adventures of Baron Munchausen**, 1989; **The Adventures of Robinson Crusoe**, 1954; **The Adventures of Swiss Family Robinson**, 1998 (TV series); **All the Brothers Were Valiant**, 1953; **Aloma of the South Seas**, 1926; **Alone on the Pacific**, 1964; **An American Tail**, 1986; **The Bermuda Depths**, 1978 (made-for-TV); **Beyond the Poseidon Adventure**, 1979; **Bitter Moon**, 1994; **The Black Stallion**, 1979; **The Bounty**, 1984; **The Caine Mutiny**, 1954; **Cast Away**, 2000; **China Seas**, 1935; **The Chronicles of Narnia: The Voyage of the Dawn Treader**, 2010; **Cloud Atlas**, 2012; **Crusoe**, 1988; **Dead Calm**, 1989; **Deep Waters**, 1948; **Doctor Dolittle**, 1967; **Down to the Sea in Ships**, 1949; **Eight Bells**, 1935; **Far From Home: The Adventures of Yellow Dog**, 1995; **Ffolkes**, 1980; **The Finest Hours**, 2015; **Flood**, 2007; **Foreign Correspondent**, 1940; **Frozen**, 2013; **The Giants of Thessaly**, 1963; **Golden Door**, 2006; **Golden Rendezvous**, 1978; **The Golden Voyage of Sinbad**, 1974; **Goliath Against the Giants**, 1963; **Gorgo**, 1961; **The Guardian**, 2006; **The Guns of Navarone**, 1961; **Hawaii**, 1966; **Hawks of the Wilderness**, 1938; **Hercules in the Haunted World**, 1964; **Hornblower: Duty**, 2003 (made-for-TV); **Hornblower: Mutiny**, 2001 (made-for-TV); **The Hurricane**, 1937; **Ice Age: Continental Drift**, 2012; **The Immortal Voyage of Captain Drake**, 2009 (made-for-TV); **Indiana Jones and the Last Crusade**, 1989; **Jamaica Inn**, 1939; **Journey to the Center of the Earth**, 1959; **Journey to the Center of the Earth**, 2008; **Journey 2: The Mysterious Island**, 2012; **Kidnapped**, 1948; **King Kong**, 2005; **Kon-Tiki**, 2013; **The Last Voyage**, 1960; **Life of Pi**, 2012; **Lifeboat**, 1944; **Mantango**, 1963; **Mara Maru**, 1952; **Master and Commander: The Far Side of the World**, 2003; **Mysterious Island**, 1961; **Napoleon**, 1927; **New Moon**, 1940; **Nim's Island**, 2008; **No Way Out**, 1987; **North of Nome**, 1936; **Ordinary People**, 1980; **Pacific Rim**, 2013; **The Perfect Storm**, 2000; **Pirates of the Caribbean: The Curse of the Black Pearl**, 2003; **Plymouth Adventure**, 1952; **Port Sinister**, 1953; **The Poseidon Adventure**, 1972; **Reap the Wild Wind**, 1942; **Robinson Crusoe**, 1997; **Safe Harbor**, 2009 (made-for-TV); **The Sea Beast**, 2008 (made-for-TV); **Sea Wife**, 1957; **The Sea Wolf**, 2008 (made-for-TV); **Ship of Fools**, 1965; **Sinbad: Legend of the Seven Seas**, 2003; **Six Days Seven Nights**, 1998; **Souls at Sea**, 1937; **Swiss Family Robinson**, 1940; **Swiss Family Robinson**, 1960; **Tarzan**, 1999; **Tarzan and the Green Goddess**, 1938; **300: Rise of the Empire**, 2014; **The Thief of Bagdad**, 1940; **Thunder Bay**, 1953; **Thunder Rock**, 1944; **The Truman Show**, 1998; **Two Years Before the Mast**, 1946; **Una noche**, 2012; **Virus**, 1999; **Wake of the Red Witch**, 1948; **The Wolf of Wall Street**, 2013; **The Wreck**

of the Mary Deare, 1959; and **Yankee Buccaneer**, 1952. Sexuality and scenes of the traumatic shipwreck prohibit viewing by children. **p**, Mimi Polk Gitlin, Rocky Lang, Todd Robinson, Nigel Wooll; **d**, Ridley Scott; **cast**, Jeff Bridges, Caroline Goodall, Balthazar Getty, John Savage, Scott Wolf, Jeremy Sisto, Ryan Philippe, David Lascher, Eric Michael Cole, Jason Marsden, David Selby, Zeljko Ivanek, Ethan Embry, Jordan Clarke; **w**, Todd Robinson (based on the book *The Last Voyage of the Albatross* by Charles Gieg Jr., Felix Sutton); **c**, Hugh Johnson; **m**, Jeff Rona; **ed**, Gerry Hambling; **prod d**, Peter J. Hampton, Leslie Tomkins; **art d**, Joseph P. Lucky; **set d**, Rand Sagers; **spec eff**, Kent Houston, Mario Cassar, Kenneth Cassar.

The White Tower ★★★★ 1950; U.S.; 98m; RKO; Color; Adventure; Children: Unacceptable; **DVD**; **VHS**. Superb mountain-climbing thriller sees a strange lot of adventurers attempting to conquer a challenging snow-capped peak in the Swiss Alps (ostensibly the redoubtable Matterhorn, a mountain that had taken the lives of many, albeit its peak had, indeed, been reached). Beginning shortly after the end of WWII (1939-1945), Ford, an American, arrives at a Swiss lodge and meets alluring Valli, a native who belongs to a legendary mountain-climbing family. Looming above the lodge is a mountain called The White Tower, a peak that has never been climbed. Valli both loves and hates this mountain in that her father, an experienced climber, was killed while scaling its craggy cliffs. Ford soon falls in love with Valli, but, before they can make any plans together, Valli insists that he join her and others in making one last climb to conquer the mountain. Ford, who has only limited experience as a mountaineer, is slow to accept her offer. He is an ex-GI, wearied from the recent war, and all he wants to do is enjoy life, not risk his life again, especially in what he thinks is a foolish exercise to prove that man can best anything on earth. Valli is disappointed in him, but nevertheless assembles a team of climbers to accompany her in an attempt to conquer the mountain. These include Rains, an alcoholic French writer; Hardwicke, a British naturalist; and Homolka, a brawny Alpine guide, who has climbed higher on this mountain than any other. When Bridges, a former German officer in the war, insists on joining the team, Ford decides to go along, at least in the first stages of the climb. This group now constitutes climbers from major countries, an international team inspired by the lofty ambitions of the eager Valli. The climbers slowly make their way up the mountain, with Homolka leading the way, ropes extended from one climber to the next, so that, in the event that one might fall, the others might save that climber. By the time they reach their first campsite, the elderly Hardwicke calls it quits as he is too exhausted to continue and where he can only gaze longingly toward the highest peak looming above. The others continue their climb at dawn, leaving Hardwicke behind. Struggling to the next campsite is Rains, who admits that he can no longer go on. Rains then crawls into a small tent while a snowstorm swirls about him, feeling that he is as much a failure as a climber as he has been as a writer. Ford, by this time, has become protective of Valli and resolves to keep climbing with her. He, Valli, Bridges and Homolka laboriously scale ever upward, inching from one rocky ledge to another. At the next campsite, Valli now questions her motives for making the climb, realizing how life-threatening the challenge has become. She nevertheless follows Homolka ever upward. When Holmolka reaches one ledge, he finds that he cannot reach upward to the next, admitting failure by saying "it won't go." Bridges refuses to admit defeat, slipping past Holmolka, saying "it must go!" He is a man more possessed of achieving victory than the others. Throughout the climb, Bridges has sarcastically remarked about the weaknesses and inabilities of his fellow climbers and has displayed contempt for them, if not outright hatred. His once friendly character has now been abandoned to reveal his true ruthless nature. He is, as Ford realizes, a Nazi to the core, a man believing that he is far superior to others, one believing himself to be an Aryan superman. Ford then focuses upon the small insignia centered on the cap Bridges wears, one showing the symbol of the German army of Hitler's Nazi Third Reich.

Mountain-climbers Oscar Homolka, Cedric Hardwicke, Glenn Ford and Lloyd Bridges in *The White Tower*, 1950.

Ford realizes that Bridges has never really left that army and is still fighting the war, one that his country lost, but here, on this mountain, Bridges will achieve victory to prove himself to be the superior member of the group. Ford, who had foolishly neglected to bring along his snow goggles, is going temporarily blind in the incessant snow storms, but he decides to compete with Bridges to prove that Bridges is not the superman the Nazi regime so fanatically advanced during the late war. With Homolka gone to safeguard Hardwicke, Ford is left alone with Valli and Bridges. When they reach a narrow ledge that may lead them to the top of the mountain, Bridges refuses Ford's help in crossing a chasm on that ledge, determined to lift himself alone to the next ledge. He makes a superhuman effort to cross that wide gap and, in so doing, falls to his death. Valli, now realizing that Ford is dearer to her than her ambition to conquer the mountain, leads the snow-blind Ford down the mountain and to safety where they plan a life together. Tetzlaff does a fine job combining the exciting mountain-climbing scenes with the dramatic elements, and Ford, Valli, Rains, Hardwicke and Homolka are standouts in their divergent roles. The film, however, really belongs to the subtle and utterly riveting performance by Bridges, who is wholly captivating as a cunning and artful mountaineer. He carefully nurtures, from the beginning, a sinister purpose as he is not climbing for sport, but to vindicate to the world his Nazi superiority over all other fellow human beings. By achieving his ends, Bridges attempts to reaffirm the ruthless credos of the Nazi regime. We see him affable and charming at the beginning, but, as the climb proceeds, his true vicious nature slowly emerges, and Bridges makes a shuddering transformation from a friendly companion to a savage competitor, that performance guaranteed to send cold shivers up and down any viewer's spine. He is, in the end, more lethal than the mountain as he will jeopardize the lives of others, as well as himself, to win his own private war. At one point, when everyone decides to take a rest, Bridges reveals his brutal character, stating: "To rest is not to conquer!" He, like his fellow Nazis, loses that war, as well as his life through his own fanaticism. His is one of the finest character studies of the Nazi persona ever put on film. *Author's Note*: This film was expensively produced, shot on location in the French Alps near Haute-Savoie, France, and the Technicolor process provides myriad breathtaking panoramas of that mountain range via Rennahan's outstanding lensing. Ford told this author: "All of the cast members in that picture had to learn how to actually climb a mountain, using the correct moves, from footwork to hand-grasping onto ledges. We used mountaineer hammers and steel studs to pound into rocky crevices and all of our clothing and gear was accurate. I think I lost more than ten pounds when scaling that damned mountain." Rains told this author: "I was just too old for my role in **The White Tower**. In one scene, I must stop because I cannot catch my wind. Well, I was not act-

Robert Mitchum and Susan Hayward in *White Witch Doctor*, 1953.

ing, believe me. After that one, I started looking about for roles where I could deliver my lines from an easy chair." Other films depicting mountain climbing, mountain climbers and mountaineers include **The Abominable Snowman**, 1957 (Yeti); **The Ascent**, 1994; **Aguirre: The Wrath of God**, 1972; **Auntie Mame**, 1958 (Matterhorn); **Alive**, 1993; **Beyond the Rocks**, 1922; **Blind Husbands**, 1919; **Bridal Suite**, 1939; **The Bulldog Breed**, 1960; **Canoa**, 1976; **Cast Away**, 2000; **The Challenge**, 1939 (1865 climb on Matterhorn); **Cliffhanger**, 1993; **The Climb**, 1986; **Courage Mountain**, 1990; **Death Hunt**, 1981; **The Devil's Brigade**, 1968; **Devil's Pass**, 2013; **Drums in the Deep South**, 1951; **The Eiger Sanction**, 1975; **The Endless Knot**, 2007; **Everest**, 2007 (TV miniseries); **A Farewell to Arms**, 1932; **A Farewell to Arms**, 1957; **Final Ascent**, 2000 (made-for-TV); **The Girl from the Chartreuse**, 2005; **The Gold Rush**, 1925 (Alaska); **Goodbye, Mr. Chips**, 1939; **Goodbye, Mr. Chips**, 2002; **Gran Paradiso**, 2000; **The Guns of Navarone**, 1961; **High Ice**, 1980 (made-for-TV); **The Holy Mountain**, 1973; **Into Thin Air: Death on Everest**, 1997 (made-for-TV); **K2**, 1991; **Letter from an Unknown Woman**, 1948; **The Longest Day**, 1962 (climbing Pointe du Hoc, a 100-foot cliff, during the 1944 Normandy invasion); **Lost Continent**, 1951; **Lost Horizon**, 1937 (Himalayas); **Love and Bullets**, 1979 (Matterhorn); **Magic Boy**, 1961; **Man Beast**, 1956 (Yeti); **The Mountain**, 1956; **Never Again as Before**, 2005; **Nim's Island**, 2008; **North Face**, 2008; **Pathfinder**, 1988; **The Place of the Dead**, 1997; **Premier de Cordee**, 1999 (made-for-TV); **Private Lives**, 1931; **Road to Utopia**, 1946; **Scream of Stone**, 1991; **Secret Agent**, 1936; **Seven Years in Tibet**, 1997; **She**, 1935; **The Silent Barrier**, 1920; **The Squaw Man**, 1914; **Storm and Sorrow**, 1990 (made-for-TV); **Storm Over Mont Blanc**, 1932; **Survival Quest**, 1988; **Third Man on the Mountain**, 1959; **The Treasure of the Sierra Madre**, 1948; **Vertical Limit**, 2000; **What Lies Above**, 2004; **Where Eagles Dare**, 1969; **White Fang**, 1991 (Alaskan Gold Rush); **Wide Country**, 1962-1963 (TV series; "A Cry from the Mountain," 1963 episode); **A Wife Confesses**, 1961; and **With a Friend Like Harry**, 2001 (Matterhorn). **p**, Sid Rogell; **d**, Ted Tetzlaff; **cast**, Glenn Ford, (Alida) Valli, Claude Rains, Oscar Homolka, Sir Cedric Hardwicke, Lloyd Bridges, June Clayworth, Lotte Stein, Edit Angold, Fred Essler; **w**, Paul Jarrico (based on the novel by James Ramsey Ullman); **c**, Ray Rennahan (Technicolor); **m**, Roy Webb; **ed**, Samuel E. Beetley; **art d**, Albert S. D'Agostino, Ralph Berger; **set d**, Darrell Silvera, Harley Miller; **spec eff**, Norman Breedlove, Harold Wellman.

White Witch Doctor ★★★ 1953; U.S.; 96m; FOX; Color; Adventure/Romance; Children: Unacceptable; **DVD**; **VHS**. Superior adventure tale begins when Hayward, a missionary nurse, is assigned to the Belgian Congo in 1907 to bring modern medicine to the native peoples. She hires Mitchum, an animal wrangler and fortune hunter, and Slezak, a guide, to take her into the interior to reach the mission. They reluctantly agree to be her guides and begin a hazardous journey in which they battle gorillas, hostile natives, and get bitten and scratched by lions. Slezak is then seized with gold fever after seeing a necklace of gold around the neck of a sick boy being nursed by Hayward. He is convinced that there is gold to be found, which eventually creates conflict between him and Mitchum. They engage in a struggle and Mitchum's gun goes off accidentally and kills Slezak. Upon their arrival at the mission, Hayward and Mitchum must cope with hostile native witch doctors, who want no part of modern medicine. On their way, despite their differences, Hayward and Mitchum fall in love. They manage to overcome the objections of the superstitious natives and begin to save lives by administering modern medicine. Both decide to remain together at the mission to help the natives, as well as make a life together. Ironically, Hayward must contend with meddling witch doctors to save the life of the chief's son in this film, just as much as she had to tolerate a witch doctor trying to save her ailing husband, played by Gregory Peck, in **The Snows of Kilimanjaro**, 1952. This film earned more than $2.5 million at the box office in its initial release against a budget of $2 million. *Author's Note*: Trouble reared itself from the beginning when this film went into production. Hayward told this author that "I was very unhappy with the script and so was Bob [Mitchum], so I marched into Darryl's office [Darryl F. Zanuck, head of Fox Studio] and told him that, unless the script was rewritten with better dramatic scenes, Bob and I would walk. He told me that the studio could not afford to do that, so I got up and headed for the door. He stopped me, and told me that he would do something about that. What he did was to have Henry [Hathaway] rewrite the script, which really was an improvement, so we went ahead with the production." Mitchum echoed this feeling when telling this author: "The script was strictly from hunger when we got it—the story centering on too much missionary history—so it got rewritten. I later pulled a little joke on Henry [Hathaway] when I came on to the set and told him that I could not remember my lines. He blew his top and I asked for a copy of the six or so pages covering that scene. I took only a few minutes to glance at the pages and then did the scene without a hitch and Henry almost fell out of his chair. I never told him that I had been up all night memorizing those lines." Hathaway later told this author that "Bob [Mitchum] came on to the set one day to tell me his mind had gone blank and he could not recall any of his lines. I threw a script at him and he flipped through the pages for that scene in about twenty seconds. He then did the scene perfectly, delivering every one of his lines without error. I was amazed. I told Darryl [Zanuck] later: 'Bob Mitchum is one of the greatest actors on planet earth!'" Additional stress permeated the production in that the intense and forceful Hayward did not like working with the demanding Hathaway, who was chiefly an action director, and also resented the laidback attitude Mitchum invariably displayed. She had had difficulties with Hathaway when working with him on **Rawhide**, 1951, a rough-and-tumble western where she co-starred with Tyrone Power. She had, as she told this author, "a tough time with Bob [Mitchum] when we did **The Lusty Men** [1952], and where the director of that film [Nicholas Ray] allowed Bob to ride roughshod all over my lines and scenes. I wasn't having any more of that when we did **White Witch Doctor** together, and I told Henry [Hathaway] and Bob that in no uncertain terms." All the scenes involving the principal actors were shot at the Fox studio, but, with Zanuck's approval, Hathaway sent a second unit to Africa to shoot location scenes at an additional cost of $600,000, and artifacts from the Dark Continent were retrieved and used in the production. Other films depicting witch doctors include **Altered States**, 1980; **Arizona Dream**, 1992; **Art of the Devil**, 2004; **Australia**, 2008; **Belizaire the Cajun**, 1986; **Booloo**, 1938; **Cabeza de Vaca**, 1991; **Captive Girl**, 1950; **Carry On Up the Jungle**, 1970; **Child's Play**, 1988; **The Comedians**, 1967; **Congo Bill**, 1948; **Dance with the Devil**, 1997; **Danger Island**, 1931; **Darkest Africa**, 1936; **Daughter of the Jungle**, 1949; **The Dead**, 2010; **Demon**

Hunter, 1983; **The Diving Bell and the Butterfly**, 2007; **Down among the Sheltering Palms**, 1953; **East of Sudan**, 1964; **Exorcist II: The Heretic**, 1977; **Father and Sons**, 2003; **The Four Skulls of Jonathan Drake**, 1959; **Hawk of the Wilderness**, 1948; **How to Stuff a Wild Bikini**, 1965; **Jungle Drums of Africa**, 1953; **Jungle Gents**, 1954; **Jungle Girl**, 1941; **Jungle Gold**, 1966 (made-for-TV); **Jungle Jim**, 1948; **Jungle Mystery**, 1932; **Jungle Raiders**, 1945; **Killers of Kilimanjaro**, 1959; **King Kong**, 1933; **King of the Islands**, 1936; **King Solomon's Mines**, 1937; **King Solomon's Mines**, 1950; **King Solomon's Mines**, 1976; **The Kingdom**, 1994 (TV miniseries); **Land of Fury**, 1954; **The Last King of Scotland**, 2006; **Law of the Jungle**, 1942; **The League of Extraordinary Gentlemen**, 2003; **Madagascar: Escape 2 Africa**, 2008; **Manhunt in the Jungle**, 1958; **Manhunters of the Caribbean**, 1936; **The Men's Club**, 1986; **The Mighty Gorga**, 1969; **Mirrors**, 1978; **The New World**, 2005; **The Oblong Box**, 1969; **Operation Petticoat**, 1959; **Outbreak**, 1995; **The Perfect Snob**, 1941; **The Princess and the Frog**, 2009; **The Punisher**, 2004; **Robinson Crusoe of Clipper Island**, 1936; **The Rum Diary**, 2011; **Sacrifice!**, 1972; **The Snows of Kilimanjaro**, 1952; **Son of Kong**, 1933; **Souls**, 2010; **The Stick**, 1988; **Tarzan and the She-Devil**, 1953; **Tarzan's Fight for Life**, 1958; **Tarzan's Savage Fury**, 1952; **Too Hot to Handle**, 1938; **Uncivilized**, 1937; **U-238 and the Witch Doctor**, 1966 (made-for-TV); **Vengeance**, 1930; **Voodoo Woman**, 1957; **Walk into Hell**, 1956; **White Goddess**, 1953; **White Zombie**, 1932; and **Yesterday**, 2004. Mature themes and violence prohibit viewing by children. **p**, Otto Lang; **d**, Henry Hathaway; **cast**, Susan Hayward, Robert Mitchum, Walter Slezak, Timothy Carey, Mashood Ajala, Joseph C. Narcisse, Elzie Emanuel, Otis Greene, Michael Ansara, Myrtle Anderson; **w**, Ivan Goff, Ben Roberts (based on the novel by Louise A. Stinetorf); **c**, Leon Shamroy (Technicolor); **m**, Bernard Herrmann; **ed**, James B. Clark; **art d**, Lyle R. Wheeler, Mark-Lee Kirk; **set d**, Stuart A. Reiss; **spec eff**, Ray Kellogg, Matthew Yuricich.

White Zombie ★★★ 1932; U.S.; 69m; UA; B/W; Horror; Children: Unacceptable; **BD**; **DVD**; **VHS**; **IV**. Strange horror film begins with beautiful Bellamy and handsome Harron, a young couple in love who are coaxed by an acquaintance, Frazer, to hold their wedding on his plantation in Haiti. They agree, not realizing Frazer intends to use zombie tactics to convince Bellamy to run away with him. Frazer does this by enlisting the help of Lugosi, who runs a mill where his employees work as slaves as they have been turned into zombies. Lugosi gives Frazer a potion that puts Bellamy under his control, but Frazer becomes dissatisfied because she is emotionless. Frazer wants her changed back, but Lugosi, instead, drugs Frazer and turns him into a zombie. A local priest tells Harron that Bellamy may still be alive, and in the end, Lugosi and Frazer fight and fall off a cliff to their deaths. Bellamy recovers and ends up in the arms of her true love, Harron. Thickly melodramatic and stagey, the film nevertheless offers considerable fright, and the eerie atmospheric sets and weird angle lensing add to the suspense. Lugosi, who had recently scored with **Dracula**, 1931, goes over the top in almost all of his scenes, entertainingly adding to the inadvertent campiness of this oddball production. Though the film did well at the box office, it received savage condemnation from reviewers, mostly over its cornball script, somewhat slipshod production designs, and erratic continuity. Lugosi's broad and fulsome performance, however, preserves this film as a horror keeper. Almost everything awful happens off-screen, which was intentional by director Halperin, who opted to present a horror tale by suggesting its actions rather than depicting them, much the same way Carl Dreyer created his haunting **Vampyr**, 1932; Songs: "Here Comes the Bride" ("Bridal Chorus") (1850; from the opera "Lohengrin" by Richard Wagner); "Liebestraum" (1850; Franz Liszt); "Chant" (Guy Bevier); "Listen to the Lambs" (Nathaniel Dett); "Incidental Symphonies," "Agitato," "Agitato Pathetique," "Appassionata" (Gaston Borch); "Death of a Great Chief" (Hugo Riesenfeld); "Spanish Jota" (Xavier Cugat); "Ill at Ease" (H. Maurice Jacquet); "Incidental Sym-

Bud Abbott and Lou Costello in *Who Done It?*, 1942.

phony" (Leo Kempinski); "S.O.S.," "In the Depths" (Nem Herkan); "Cavatina" (Carl Bohm). *Author's Note*: This film was made on a shoestring budget of $75,000, and the actors were paid next to nothing for their performances, Lugosi receiving $5,000. The producers rented some space at Universal's smallest sound stage and shot the film in ten days. Somewhat crude wired camera setups were employed to give the film a distorted visual appearance, and the discordant music (some even provided by bandleader Xavier Cugat) was designed to jar the senses of viewers. This was the first feature-length film to profile zombies, spawning dozens more to come, the best of which was Jacques Tourneur's **I Walked with a Zombie**, 1943. A hilarious comedy titled **The Ghost Breakers**, 1940, has Bob Hope, Paulette Goddard and Willie Best being chased about by a zombie played by Noble Johnson, the black actor who impressively portrayed the tribal chief in **King Kong**, 1933. Scenes from this production were used by the Halperin brothers when they made another poverty-row film titled **The Revolt of the Zombies**, 1936. **p**, Edward Halperin, (uncredited) Phil Goldstone; **d**, Victor Halperin; **cast**, Bela Lugosi, Madge Bellamy, John Harron, Robert Frazer, Joseph Cawthorn, Brandon Hurst, George Burr MacAnnan, Frederick Peters, Annette Stone, Clarence Muse; **w**, Garnett Weston (based on a story by Weston and the novel *The Magic Island* by William Seabrook); **c**, Arthur Martinelli; **ed**, Harold McLernon; **art d**, Ralph Berger; **spec eff**, Howard A. Anderson as Harold Anderson.

Who Done It? ★★★ 1942; U.S.; 77m; UNIV; B/W; Comedy; Children: Acceptable; **DVD**; **VHS**. A lot of good comedy is served up by Abbott and Costello, who are soda jerks dreaming of writing radio mysteries. They work in the same building as a major radio studio and, after a network president is murdered, they masquerade as detectives to solve the crime. They are believed as detectives but bungle things as badly as Bendix, a real detective investigating the crime. There are lots of laughs before the would-be detectives solve the mystery, including Costello hanging high above the ground from the station's aerial antenna. The dynamic duo presents several of their classic burlesque routines, including their memorable "Alexander 2222" and "Who's on first?" Universal put all the best technical people behind this film to create great film noir atmospheres, from crackling lightning, eerie sounds and some very good special effects (such as where a terrified Lou runs through a pane of glass, leaving his outlined image in his pudgy wake). Packed with whirlwind slapstick, this is one of the better outings from these two fine comedians, who dominated Hollywood's laughter charts in the early 1940s. Other films profiling soda jerks include **Assassin of Youth**, 1937; **The Bank Dick**, 1940 (Shemp Howard); **The Best Years of Our Lives**, 1946 (Dana Andrews); **Blast from the Past**, 1999; **Blue Denim**, 1959; **Calling All Marines**, 1939; **College**, 1927 (Buster Keaton); **The Con-**

Baby Herman (Lou Hirsch voiceover) and Bob Hoskins in *Who Framed Roger Rabbit,* **1988.**

stant Woman, 1933; **Dames**, 1934; **The Gangster**, 1947 (Harry Morgan); **Good News**, 1947 (Peter Lawford); **The Great Rupert**, 1950; **Happiness C.O.D.**, 1935; **Has Anybody Seen My Gal?**, 1952; **The Headleys at Home**, 1938; **It's a Wonderful Life**, 1946; **Larceny, Inc.**, 1942; **My Sister Eileen**, 1942; **My Sister Eileen**, 1955; **99 River Street**, 1953; **One Hour Late**, 1934; **Playing Around**, 1930; **Pleasantville**, 1998 (Jeff Daniels); **Reefer Madness**, 1936; **Slightly Dangerous**, 1943; **The Sniper**, 1952; **Speedy**, 1928 (Harold Lloyd); **Start Cheering**, 1938; **Stranger on the Third Floor**, 1940; **Tension**, 1949; **They Won't Forget**, 1937 (Elisha Cook Jr.); **Thousands Cheer**, 1944; **20,000 Men a Year**, 1939; **Wide Open Faces**, 1938 (Joe E. Brown); and **Zis Boom Bah**, 1941. **p**, Alex Gottlieb; **d**, Erle C. Kenton; **cast**, Bud Abbott, Lou Costello, Patric Knowles, William Gargan, Louise Allbritton, William Bendix, Thomas Gomez, Don Porter, Jerome Cowan, Mary Wickes, Ludwig Stossel, Gladys Blake; **w**, Stanley Roberts, Edmund Joseph, John Grant (based on a story by Roberts); **c**, Charles Van Enger; **m**, Frank Skinner; **ed**, Arthur Hilton; **art d**, Robert F. Boyle, Jack Otterson; **set d**, Russell A. Gausman, A.J. Gilmore.

Who Framed Roger Rabbit ★★★★★ 1988; U.S.; 104m; Amblin/Silver Screen/Walt Disney/Touchstone; Color; Fantasy; Children: Unacceptable (MPAA: PG); **BD**; **DVD**; **VHS**; **IV**. Wonderfully created animation and live action provides an exciting film noir fantasy of Hollywood's toon underbelly of 1947. Cartoon characters called "Toons" live in an animated district of Hollywood called "Toon Town," and serve as paid actors in films produced by Hollywood studios. One of the reigning toon stars is Roger Rabbit (Fleischer voiceover), who works with another toon named Baby Herman (Hirsch voiceover) in animated shorts, but Roger has of late given poor performances. Tilvern (R.K. Maroon), who heads Maroon Studios that produces Roger's films, believes that his star is about to have a nervous breakdown because of rumors that his sexy wife, Jessica Rabbit (Turner voiceover), is having an extramarital affair. Tilvern hires Hoskins (Eddie Valiant), an alcoholic private detective, to investigate the matter. Hoskins begins snooping at the Ink & Paint nightclub where Jessica sings, and, while watching her sultry act, meets several old toon friends, including Betty Boop (Questel voiceover), a one-time toon star of the early 1930s, who has been reduced to selling cigarettes to customers at the club. Meanwhile, toons Donald Duck and Daffy Duck duel at separate pianos in a wild rendition of "Hungarian Rhapsody No. 2." Hoskins sees Hollywood agent Kaye (Marvin Acme) ogling Jessica while she performs and later takes photos of Kaye with Jessica in her dressing room where they are playing patty-cake. Hoskins takes this incriminating evidence to Tilvern's studio offices and, after Tilvern and Roger see them, Roger goes berserk, literally blowing his top. He angrily vows that he and Jes-

sica will have a happy marriage or else, his red eyes popping and long ears flopping and twisting into knots while he spins wildly about the office before crashing through a window and wildly fleeing the studio. The next morning LeParmentier (LAPD Lieutenant Santino) meets with Hoskins in Hoskins' seedy office (which is patterned after the rundown office occupied by Dick Powell while playing private eye Philip Marlowe in **Murder, My Sweet**, 1944), and which is also his living quarters, to tell Hoskins that Roger is suspected of killing Kaye by dropping a safe on him, the same manner in which Hoskins' brother had been murdered years earlier. Hoskins accompanies LeParmentier to the scene of the crime where they also meet Lloyd (Judge Doom), who presides with draconian authority over Toon Town and all of its residents. Lloyd explains that he intends to have his henchmen, a pack of vicious toon weasels, find Roger and eliminate him with what he calls "The Dip," a toxic liquid of his own invention (a combination of turpentine, benzene and acetone). When returning to his office, Hoskins meets Baby Herman, who tells Hoskins that Kaye's will is missing and, if it is not found by midnight, Toon Town will be taken over by a corrupt company called Cloverleaf Industries, which is also buying up the interest in the Pacific Electric trolley cars. Once Hoskins enters his office, he pours himself a drink and moodily recalls his dead brother, only to discover that Roger is hiding there. He angrily accuses Roger of killing Kaye, but Roger pleads with him to believe that he is innocent and that he has been framed. The toon weasels and Lloyd then arrive to search Hoskins' office, but Hoskins hides Roger in a sink full of water. Hoskins then goes to a nearby bar operated by his girlfriend Cassidy (Dolores), smuggling Roger into the place, which is also raided by the searching toon weasels. Hoskins manages to once again hide Roger in a hidden room while attempting to puzzle out who killed Kaye. Hoskins manages to hide Roger into the trunk of Benny the Cab (another toon; Fleischer voiceover), and is driven to Tilvern's office where Hoskins gets the movie mogul to admit that he blackmailed Kaye into compromising Jessica in order to get to the bottom of who is trying to take over the trolley car system as well as his own studio. Tilvern is then mysteriously killed by an unknown assailant. When Hoskins sees Jessica fleeing the studio lot, he pursues her to Toon Town where he encounters a hideously ugly female toon he mistakes for Jessica and who pursues him everywhere as the goofy toon is smitten with him. He finally eludes this wild toon to find Jessica, who tells him that Lloyd is behind all the killings in that he is the secret owner of Cloverleaf, the firm that is taking over the trolley car system in order to build a freeway and where he needs to eliminate Toon Town and its major studio, once owned by Tilvern, as its stands in the way of that freeway. They then go in search of Kaye's will, which leaves Toon Town to its residents, thus shielding them from ruthless businessmen like Lloyd. They go to Kaye's gag factory in search of the will, but are trapped in the factory by Lloyd and his toon weasels. Lloyd then has henchmen roll in a huge machine, which contains Lloyd's deadly "Dip." Roger arrives and attempts to save Jessica, but he and she are tied up and suspended in the air. The toon weasels and Lloyd aim the Dip machine's spout at them, its lethal stream of Dip narrowly missing them many times as Hoskins misdirects the machine. He manages to have the toon weasels die of laughter one by one by causing them to laugh uncontrollably through his wild antics. (Hoskins is absolutely marvelous in performing a makeshift vaudeville act as he frantically dances and recites nonsensical forced rhymes, which is nothing more than miserable but hilarious kitsch.) Lloyd screams with rage as his toon weasels are all destroyed through Hoskins' zany routines, and the viewer sees these creatures leave their bodies as floating spirits, ascending with halos about their heads as they drift upward to toon Heaven. Hoskins then manages to direct the Dip machine into a huge brick wall, crashing through so that it enters Toon Town, and its happy characters sing and dance, oblivious to this death-dealing apparatus, which is promptly run over by a speeding toon train. Roger and Jessica are saved, and Lloyd gets his just deserts when he is flattened by a steamroller. To everyone's amazement, he springs back to life in his natural state, that of an evil toon, but he is dispatched when trapped by his own Dip and melts to death (much the same way the Wicked Witch of the West melts when doused with water in **The Wizard of Oz**, 1939). Hoskins then floods the factory floor with fresh water as LAPD officers arrive to learn that Lloyd has not only been the killer they have been seeking, but Hoskins learns that it was Lloyd who had killed his brother years earlier. The toon characters then stream into the factory after Roger finds Kaye's will, which is stated on the back of a love poem Roger has earlier written to Jessica. He has inadvertently saved Toon Town and all of its happy inhabitants celebrate at the victory, singing and dancing. Roger, believing that Hoskins still dislikes him and all toons, is surprised to see that Hoskins' good nature has returned when Hoskins gives Roger a sloppy kiss. Cassidy and Hoskins then join Roger and Jessica and all the rest of the toon characters (including Mickey Mouse, Donald Duck, Bugs Bunny, Tweety Bird, Sylvester, Daffy Duck and many others) as they dance their way into Toon Town, and Porky Pig (Blanc voiceover) ends the film with his catchphrase "Tha-tha-tha-tha-that's all folks!" Tinker Bell then waves her wand to sprinkle her magic. Zemeckis directs this wild story with great zest, where he seamlessly weaves his animated characters into the visual fabric of the live action sequences. Hoskins is wonderful as the beefy, down-and-out private eye, and Lloyd is a very frightening villain, about as evil as they come. All of the supporting players are standouts in their outlandish roles, and the action is almost nonstop, a breathless visual treat far surpassing anything in its unusual and captivating genre. The script from Price and Seaman is brilliantly sardonic and is packed with wit. In one exchange, Jessica, who is shown as a tall, voluptuous toon woman with a peek-a-boo red hairstyle the same hairstyle worn by blonde Veronica Lake, a film star of the 1940s), says to Hoskins: "You don't know how hard it is being a woman looking the way I do." Hoskins replies: "You don't know how hard it is being a man looking at a woman looking the way you do." Jessica then gives him her classic retort: "I'm not bad. I'm just drawn that way." The film won Oscars for Best Film Editing (Schmidt); Best Special Effects (Lantieri, Lince, Biggs), and Best Sound Editing (Charles L. Campbell, Louis Edemann). It won a Special Achievement Award from the Academy for "animation, creation and direction of the cartoon characters" (Richard Williams). It received Oscar nominations for Best Cinematography (Cundey); Best Art Direction (Cain, Scott); and Best Sound (Robert Knudson, Tony Dawe, John Boyd and Don Digirolamo). The film was an enormous box office success, earning more than $329 million in its initial release against a whopping budget of $70 million, the most expensive feature-length film using animation to that date. Songs: "Why Don't You Do Right?" (1936; Joseph "Kansas Joe" McCoy), "The Merry-Go-Round Broke Down" (1937; Cliff Friend, Dave Franklin), "Smile, Darn Ya, Smile" (1931; Jack Meskill, Charles O'Flynn, Max Rich), "Witchcraft" (1957; music: Cy Coleman; lyrics: Carolyn Leigh), "Hungarian Rhapsody No. 2" (1847; Franz Liszt), "The Stars and Stripes Forever" (1896; John Philip Sousa), "Giant Killers" (Len Stevens). *Author's Note*: The Disney Company purchased the film rights to the Wolf novel shortly after its 1981 publication and soon partnered with Steven Spielberg's Amblin Company, and several others. When Zemeckis was hired to direct, he and Spielberg essentially controlled the production, which was approved at a $30 million budget that soon spiraled upward, more than doubling that cost before the film was completed. Spielberg convinced many studios with notable cartoon characters to cooperate in loaning those characters for the production, and these very temperamental stars were given equal attention in their scenes together (Paramount and MGM did not participate). Writers Price and Seaman did good research in steeping themselves in the productions of Warner Brothers cartoon characters, as well as those made by Tex Avery and others. They used some of the plot themes of **Chinatown**, 1974, for their Cloverleaf plot, and added to that the actual corruption of the old Red Car service in L.A. in the 1940s by those with investments in the new freeway system

Roger Rabbit (Charles Fleischer voiceover) and Bob Hoskins in *Who Framed Roger Rabbit,* **1988.**

(the freeways now run along the routes once taken by that colorful trolley car system). Hoskins later stated that, after he and his two young sons watched this film, his sons refused to talk to him for several weeks. He then learned that they were peeved at the fact that their father appeared with their favorite cartoon characters and never introduced those sterling players to them. Animation director Williams employed many new techniques for this visual masterpiece, including special lighting that would accent both live action and animation in the same scenes. He also has the animated characters interact with not only live action humans but with myriad live action objects to make the animated characters all the more realistic. Williams also had the camera in constant motion to prevent the animated characters from appearing to be simply pasted on flat backdrops. Although Turner (who did not receive credit) did the voiceover for the alluring Jessica Rabbit, the character's singing vocals were rendered by Amy Irving. Several life-sized rubber Roger Rabbits were constructed so that live actors could have an idea of the imaginary co-star with whom they were interacting. Roger is an out-sized character, one not unlike the huge invisible rabbit seen in a portrait in the comedy **Harvey**, 1950. More than 82,000 frames of animation were drawn by 326 animators for this amazing film. Other films offering scenes combining animation and live action include **Absolutely Anything**, 2015; **The Adventures of Rocky and Bullwinkle**, 2000; **Alice**, 1988; **Alice in Wonderland**, 1949 (French version); **Anchors Aweigh**, 1945; **Annie Hall**, 1977; **Arthur and the Invisibles**, 2007; **Arthur 3: The War of the Two Worlds**, 2010; **Arthur 2: The Revenge of the Maltazards**, 2009; **Babes in Toyland**, 1961; **Bedknobs and Broomsticks**, 1971; **Belle's Tales of Friendship**, 1999; **Best Player**, 2011 (made-for-TV); **Brasil Animado**, 2011; **Captain EQ**, 1986; **Casper: A Spirited Beginning**, 1997; **Charlotte's Web**, 2006; **A Christmas Carol**, 2009; **Christmas Carol: The Movie**, 2001; **The Congress**, 2014; **Conspirators of Pleasure**, 1997; **Cool World**, 1992; **Coonskin**, 1975; **Creepshow**, 1982; **Creepshow 2**, 1987; **Dangerous When Wet**, 1953; **The Daydreamer**, 1966; **Dibu 3**, 2002; **Dinosaur**, 2000; **Dot and the Kangaroo**, 1977; **Elf**, 2003; **Enchanted**, 2007; **Evil Toons**, 1992; **The Extraordinary Adventures of Adele Blanc-Sec**, 2010; **A Fairly Odd Christmas**, 2012 (made-for-TV); **A Fairly Odd Movie: Grow Up, Timmy Turner!**, 2011 (made-for-TV); **A Fairly Odd Summer**, 2014 (made-for-TV); **Fantasia 2000**, 1999; **Fat Albert**, 2004; **Faust**, 1995; **(500) Days of Summer**, 2009; **The Flying Machine**, 2011; **Fun and Fancy Free**, 1947; **Garm Wars: The Last Druid**, 2014; **The Great Rock 'n' Roll Swindle**, 1990; **Greedy Guts**, 2001; **Gulliver's Travels**, 1981; **The Hairy Tooth Fairy**, 2007; **Happy Feet**, 2006; **Happy Feet 2**, 2011; **Hollywood Party**, 1934; **Honey, I Blew Up the Kid**, 1992; **Honey, I Shrunk the Kids**, 1989; **Hop**, 2011; **How to Eat Fried Worms**, 2006; **Howl**, 2010; **Immortal**

Bob Hoskins and Jessica Rabbit (Kathleen Turner voiceover) in *Who Framed Roger Rabbit,* **1988.**

(Ad Vitam), 2004; **The Incredible Mr. Limpet**, 1964; **The Invincible Piglet**, 2015; **James and the Giant Peach**, 1996; **Journey Back to Oz**, 1974; **Judy Moody and the Not Bummer Summer**, 2011; **King of Jazz**, 1930; **The Lego Movie**, 2014; **The Lizzie McGuire Movie**, 2003; **Lunacy**, 2006; **Main Krishna Hoon**, 2013; **The Many Adventures of Winnie the Pooh**, 1977; **Maria, Mirabella**, 1981; **Mary Poppins**, 1964; **McDull, the Alumni**, 2006; **Melody Time**, 1948; **Metamorphoses**, 1978; **Monkeybone**, 2001; **Monty Python and the Holy Grail**, 1975; **Monty Python's Life of Brian**, 1979; **Moonwalker**, 1988; **Movie 43**, 2013; **Mrs. Doubtfire**, 1993; **My Dream Is Yours**, 1949; **My Friend Ganesha**, 2007; **My Friend Ganesha 3**, 2010; **My Friend Ganesha 2**, 2009; **Natural Born Killers**, 1994; **Neon Genesis Evangelion: The End of Evangelion**, 2002; **The New Gulliver**, 1935; **9 to 5**, 1980; **O'Faby**, 1993; **Osmosis Jones**, 2001; **Out of an Old Man's Head**, 1969; **The Outrageous Baron Munchausen**, 1964; **The Pagemaster**, 1994; **Pete's Dragon**, 1977; **The Phantom Tollbooth**, 1970; **Pink Floyd The Wall**, 1982; **The Pink Panther**, 1964; **The Pink Panther**, 2006; **The Pink Panther 2**, 2009; **The Pink Panther Strikes Again**, 1976; **Pooh's Heffalump Halloween Movie**, 2005; **Problem Child 2**, 1991; **Ra One**, 2011; **Raggedy Ann and Andy**, 1977; **Raja Chinna Roja**, 1989; **Re-Animated**, 2006 (made-for-TV); **The Reluctant Dragon**, 1941; **The Return of the Pink Panther**, 1975; **Revenge of the Pink Panther**, 1978; **Robosapien: Rebooted**, 2013; **Rock-A-Doodle**, 1992; **Run Lola Run**, 1999; **The Secret of the Magic Gourd**, 2007; **A Shot in the Dark**, 1964; **The Smurfs**, 2011; **The Smurfs 2**, 2013; **Son of the Pink Panther**, 1993; **Song of the South**, 1946; **Space Jam**, 1996; **The SpongeBob Movie: Sponge Out of Water**, 2015; **The SpongeBob SquarePants Movie**, 2004; **Stay Tuned**, 1992; **The Stolen Airship**, 1967; **Super**, 2011; **Surviving Life**, 2010; **Tank Girl**, 1995; **Taxandria**, 1994; **Thomas and the Magic Railroad**, 2000; **The Three Caballeros**, 1944; **Trail of the Pink Panther**, 1982; **The Trigger Movie**, 2000; **Tron**, 1982; **Troop Beverly Hills**, 1989; **Twice Upon a Time**, 1983; **A Very Harold & Kumar 3D Christmas**, 2011; **Volere Volare**, 1993; **Walking with Dinosaurs 3D**, 2013; **Wall-E**, 2008; **The Water Babies**, 1978; **Winnie the Pooh**, 2011; **Winnie the Pooh: A Valentine for You**, 1999; **Winnie the Pooh: A Very Merry Pooh Year**, 2002; **Xanadu**, 1980; and **Yogi Bear**, 2010. **p**, Frank Marshall, Robert Watts; **d**, Robert Zemeckis; **cast**, Bob Hoskins, Christopher Lloyd, Joanna Cassidy, Stubby Kaye, Alan Tilvern, Richard Le Parmentier, Betsy Brantley, Joel Silver, and (voiceovers) Charles Fleischer, Kathleen Turner, Lou Hirsch, Mae Questel, Amy Irving, Mel Blanc, April Winchell, Tony Anselmo, Joe Alaskey, Russi Taylor, Les Perkins, June Foray, Fred Newman, Mary T. Radford; **w**, Jeffrey Price, Peter S. Sea-

man (based on the novel *Who Censored Roger Rabbit?* by Gary K. Wolf; **c**, Dean Cundey; **m**, Alan Silvestri; **ed**, Arthur Schmidt; **prod d**, Roger Cain, Elliot Scott; **spec eff**, Michael Lantieri, Brian Lince, Peter Biggs.

Who's Afraid of Virginia Woolf? ★★★★ 1966; U.S.; 131m; WB; B/W; Drama; Children: Unacceptable; **DVD**; **VHS**; **IV**. Cathartic and emotionally draining, this taut drama, expertly directed by Nichols, sees bravura performances from married couple Taylor and Burton, who play a married couple loving and hating each other at the same time. Burton is a burned-out college professor of history while Taylor is his shrewish wife, who is forever comparing her husband to the sterling image of her father, who is the college president (and who is never seen). Taylor, a heavy drinker, constantly taunts Burton, who is somewhat docile, but invariably replies with acid-filled comments about her overweight and the frazzled appearance of a middle-aged woman, chipping away at her already badly damaged self-confidence. After the two attend a cocktail party, Taylor invites a naïve young couple, Segal and Dennis, to have nightcaps with them. Segal is a young biology professor with ambitions to rise within the academic hierarchy, thinking that his new relationship with Burton and Taylor may lead to promotion. He and Dennis, however, are soon shocked to see Taylor and Burton heaping abuse upon one another. After Taylor and Dennis go off together for a heart-to-heart talk, Dennis returns to tell Segal while Burton listens in, that Taylor told her that she and Burton are preparing to celebrate their son's sixteenth birthday. Burton becomes enraged that Taylor would reveal this information, but, when Taylor appears, he can only vent his anger by making sly, derogatory remarks about her. Taylor then brags about having humiliated Burton in front of her esteemed father. Dennis, who has had too much to drink, then races to the washroom to vomit. While Taylor goes to the kitchen to make coffee, Burton and Segal step outside where Segal admits that he married Dennis out convenience, not love, since Dennis comes from a well-to-do family. Further, Segal confesses, he wedded Dennis only after she told him that she was pregnant with their child, which, either by accident or on purpose, turned out to be untrue. Burton, too, admits that his marriage is one of continuing aggravation where he must accommodate a wife with a prestigious family name. Burton then recalls in a rambling narrative his memories of a boy who accidentally killed his mother and father and lived out his life in a mental institution, all of this lost on the self-centered Segal. Segal tells Burton that he intends to sleep with the right women at the college to advance his career and then crudely jokes that he should start with Burton's wife, Taylor. When Segal and Dennis state that they are leaving, Burton and Taylor suggest they drive them home, but, while driving, Dennis spots a roadhouse and insists that they stop and dance at this low dive. Dennis, who is still drunk, dances seductively alone until Segal stops her and has her sit down. Then Taylor has Segal dance with her, ande her suggestive moves so anger Burton that he unplugs the jukebox and announces that "the game is over." Incensed at his behavior, Taylor angrily tells Segal and Dennis how Burton is a failure in not being able to finish a novel about a young man who may have murdered his parents. She bluntly adds that that very young man is no one other than the now aging Burton. In explosive response, Burton begins to strangle Taylor, but Segal stops him. They then persuade the owner to give them a final round of drinks, and Segal suggests that they play a humiliation game where Burton should be humiliated while Taylor is sexually seduced. In retaliation, Burton says he is thinking of writing a second novel based upon an ambitious young professor who has recently married a naïve young woman for her money and out of her claimed pregnancy. Dennis now realizes that Segal has disclosed their innermost family secret to Burton and runs off. Segal promises to take revenge on Burton before he runs after his emotionally distraught wife. Burton then finds Taylor in the parking lot and he tells her that he will no longer tolerate her constant humiliation of him, but Taylor lashes back, stating that that is exactly what he wants her to perversely do, more than implying that

Burton is a masochist has also perversely forced her to become a savage sadist. She then drives off to catch up with the fleeing Segal and Dennis, leaving Burton to make his way home alone on foot. By the time Burton arrives at home, he finds the car crashed in the driveway and Dennis semi-conscious in its backseat. Looking upward to his bedroom window, Burton sees the silhouettes of what appears to be Segal and Taylor having sex. He then learns from the half coherent Dennis that her pregnancy was real and that she apparently aborted the fetus. Burton then plots revenge against Taylor. Inside the house, Taylor accuses a sexually inadequate Segal of being impotent, but he claims that his poor sexual performance was based upon consuming too much liquor. Burton then arrives to throw snapdragons at both of them and announces that he received a telegram stating that their son was killed while driving on a road, his car crashing when he attempted to avoid a porcupine. Taylor becomes emotionally unhinged, begging Burton not to "kill" their son. Segal then realizes that this deeply dysfunctional couple has never had a son and that that cherished offspring has been created out of their strange imaginations (ostensibly in miserable compensation over the suggested fact that Taylor is barren and could never have children as Burton earlier mentioned that she never had any pregnancies). For Taylor, this is the last straw, accusing Burton of destroying the myth of their child, but Burton states that she herself ruined that lifelong emotional game by revealing its secret to Dennis. Segal and Dennis then leave the house wordlessly. Taylor and Burton sit grimly together as dawn breaks and Burton asks Taylor: "Who's Afraid of Virginia Woolf?" Taylor phlegmatically replies: "I am, George, I am." Though depressing and disturbing throughout, this emotionally debilitating (for the actors as well as the viewers) drama rivets attention in every scene as its wholly indulgent and self-destructive characters create an incisive and socially suicidal Gotterdammerung. This grimly introspective portrait is magnificently achieved through the gifted direction of Nichols and the stunning performance of the principal actors. The human psyche is mercilessly examined here, as would a brain surgeon meticulously use a scalpel to expose a cancerous tumor (not to mention the film's overall scathing portrait of a pampered academia without moral purpose). In this regard, watching this film is as psychologically challenging as is Eugene O'Neill's soul-searching **Long Day's Journey into Night**, 1962. None of the characters in this story are worthwhile, all of them cruelly trapped by their corrupted visions of life, selfishly willing to destroy what tattered vestiges of civilized behavior that remain in their vain efforts to seal open and unhealable self-inflicted wounds. The film received an astounding Oscar nomination for every Academy Award in every available category (the only other to do so being **Cimarron**, 1931). It won for Best Actress (Taylor); Best Supporting Actress (Dennis); Best Cinematography, Black and White (Wexler); Best Art Direction (Sylbert; set decoration: Hopkins); and Best Costume Design, Black and White (Irene Sharaff). It received Oscar nominations for Best Film; Best Director (Nichols); Best Actor (Burton); Best Supporting Actor (Segal); Best Adapted Screenplay (Lehman); Best Original Score (North); Best Sound Mixing (George Groves); and Best Film Editing (O'Steen). It was also, much due to the star status of Taylor and Burton, a great box office success, earning more than $40 million against a budget of more than $7.5 million. (Taylor received $1.1 million; Burton $750,000; playwright Albee $500,000 plus percentages.) *Author's Note*: The Albee play opened on Broadway at the Billy Rose Theater on October 13, 1962, and closed on May 16, 1964, after 664 performances. The three-act play was overlong (particularly the third act, which could have sacrificed twenty minutes without any impact, as was the case with the film), running more than three hours with two ten-minute intermissions. Albee got the idea for the play's title when visiting a men's room in a NYC saloon and where some wag had written "Who's Afraid of Virginia Woolf?" on its wall to mimic the children's song "Who's Afraid of the Big Bad Wolf?" Albee originally envisioned Bette Davis and James Mason for the roles taken by Taylor and Burton, where Davis would have actually parodied herself in delivering a classic Davis line

Elizabeth Taylor and Richard Burton in *Who's Afraid of Virginia Woolf?*, 1966.

Albee lifted from an old Davis film when Taylor's character says "what a dump!" Taylor told this author that "I thought my role as Martha in that picture was probably my best performance. It got me my second Oscar [after **Butterfield 8**, 1960]. I won my first Oscar by playing a tramp and, in the Albee story, I was a bitch. Did anyone notice the difference?" Taylor was thirty-three at the time she essayed that unforgettable role, one where she was playing a woman of fifty-two. She put on thirty or more pounds to play the part and wore her hair unkempt and frazzled. "Liz deglamorized herself for that role," Burton told this author, "and I thought that was one of her more heroic moments." Burton appears with Taylor in their fourth outing out of eleven films they made together. Oddly, Jack Lemmon was the first actor to be offered the role played by Burton. Lemmon accepted the part, but, on the following day, stated that he would not play the part and no explanation was given. It was later claimed in an unsubstantiated report that Lemmon dropped out because Jack Warner would not meet his asking price. Lemmon's inexplicable behavior was matched by movie queen Marlene Dietrich, who, when visiting the set, completely ignored Taylor and restricted her conversations to director Nichols and Burton. "I thought it was strange when Marlene [Dietrich] did that," Taylor told this author, "but I think she did it because she was an actress of the older generation and may have resented the status my generation had gained in pictures. She had been in the movies since the 1920s and they said she was ageless, but I could see the telltale crow's feet at her eyes. Vanity makes people do some strange things, and I always thought that Marlene was pretty strange to begin with, so I was not that put out by her eccentric behavior." This was one of the first films to challenge the Hollywood censors as its dialog is liberally peppered with profanities and crude gutter language (to further unseat the lofty image of educated people, an Albee trait if not crusade). Studio head Jack Warner personally championed this film, convincing the censors to allow the film after Warner stated that only adults would be allowed into theaters to view the film, thus creating the necessity for the MPAA rating for children to be established a short time later. Gutter language and sexuality prohibit viewing by children. **p**, Ernest Lehman; **d**, Mike Nichols; **cast**, Elizabeth Taylor, Richard Burton, George Segal, Sandy Dennis, Agnes and Frank Flanagan; **w**, Lehman (based on the play by Edward Albee); **c**, Haskell Wexler; **m**, Alex North; **ed**, Sam O'Steen; **prod d**, Richard Sylbert; **set d**, George James Hopkins.

Who Is Killing the Great Chefs of Europe? ★★★ 1978; U.S./Italy; France; West Germany; 112m; Aldrich Co./WB; Color; Comedy; Children: Unacceptable (MPAA: PG); **DVD**; **VHS**. Macabre, mirth-filled tale sees Morley needing to lose 140 pounds for his health. The problem is that he loves and cannot resist the gourmet foods of the top chefs in

Janet Leigh in *Who Was That Lady?*, 1960.

Europe. Each of these master food artists dies mysteriously in ways similar to their culinary specialties. One is baked in his own oven, another's head is crushed in a duck press. Is Morley the killer? He's the logical villain (and the red herring throughout this hilarious romp through upscale Europe). The murderer, however, is his faithful assistant, Ryan, who does in the chefs in a vain attempt to keep Morley on his diet. The frosting on the cake is a captivating romantic subplot involving Segal, an entrepreneurial fast-food operator, and Bisset, a chef noted for her succulent desserts, and where she, too, is on Ryan's elimination list. **p**, William Aldrich; **d**, Ted Kotcheff; **cast**, George Segal, Jacqueline Bisset, Robert Morley, Jean-Pierre Cassel, Philippe Noiret, Jean Rochefort, Nigel Havers, Madge Ryan, Joss Ackland; John Carlisle; **w**, Peter Stone (based on the novel *Someone Is Killing the Great Chefs of Europe* by Ivan and Nan Lyons); **c**, John Alcott (Metrocolor); **m**, Henry Mancini; **ed**, Thom Noble; **prod d**, Rolf Zehetbauer; **art d**, Werner Achmann.

Who's Minding the Mint? ★★★ 1967; U.S.; 97m; COL; Color; Comedy; Children: Acceptable; **DVD**; **VHS**; **IV**. This slaphappy comedy begins when Hutton, a money checker for the U.S. mint in Philadelphia, accidentally tosses some awful-tasting fudge made by Provine, his girlfriend, into a bag that is dumped into the garbage disposal, along with some money that sticks to the fudge. He decides to cover the loss by breaking into the mint and printing some replacement money. He soon discovers that others want in on the job, including Brennan, a retired money printer, Gilford, a deaf safecracker, and Berle, a pawnshop owner. The scheme is pulled off and Hutton gets the money he needs, but the rest of it is accidentally tossed out to sea, so the others leap frantically into the water to try to find it. This very funny comedy of errors sees top-notch performances from Hutton, Provine and the rest of the cast. *Author's Note*: More than $1 million in actual U.S. currency was used in making this film, and armed guards were close by the sets to protect that money during the production. When shown in close-ups, the currency was enlarged beyond its usual proportions to distort the face of the bills so that counterfeiters could not have genuine copies to use in producing their own bills. **p**, Norman Maurer; **d**, Howard Morris; **cast**, Jim Hutton, Dorothy Provine, Milton Berle, Joey Bishop, Bob Denver, Walter Brennan, Victor Buono, Jack Gilford, Jamie Farr, Paul Winfield; **w**, R.S. Allen, Harvey Bullock; **c**, Joseph F. Biroc (Technicolor); **m**, Lalo Schifrin; **ed**, Adrienne Fazan; **art d**, John Beckman; **set d**, Budd Friend, Morris Hoffman; **spec eff**, Richard Albain.

Who's That Knocking at My Door ★★★ 1967; U.S.; 90m; Trimrod Films/Joseph Brenner; B/W; Drama; Children: Unacceptable (MPAA: R); **DVD**; **VHS**; **IV**. Exceptional drama sees Keitel playing J.R., an Italian-American living in New York's Little Italy neighborhood, and who hangs out with his buddies and gets into minor scrapes. His carefree life changes radically when he falls in love with Bethune, an art student who has far more education and sophistication than does Keitel. He nevertheless decides to marry her and settle down. After he learns that she was once raped, however, he backs away from their relationship. He is in conflict with his strict Catholic upbringing and his conscience that tells him to accept Bethune as the good person she truly is. He finally forgives her and wants to marry her, but she does not forgive him and refuses him because she rightly feels that she has nothing over which to be forgiven. He returns to his buddies and their street life, and when he goes to church for answers, he finds none, leaving viewers with a somewhat dismal ending. This was director Scorsese's first feature film, where he displays his exceptional abilities to develop fascinating characters. This was also the first film in which Keitel received screen credit and where he proves to be captivating in his earthy role. Songs: "The End" (Jim Morrison), "Don't Ask Me to Be Lonely" (Richard Blandon), "Who's That Knocking?" (Claude Johnson, Fred Jones), "Jenny Take a Ride" (Bob Crewe, Enotris Johnson, Little Richard (Richard Wayne Penniman), "I've Had It" (Carl Bonura, Ray Ceroni), "El Watusi" (Ray Barretto), "Shotgun" (Junior Walker), "Ain't That Just Like Me?" (Earl Carroll, Billy Guy), "The Plea" (Arlene Smith). *Author's Note*: This film began as a project undertaken by Scorsese when he was a film student at New York University where he was mentored by Professor Haig Manoogian, who became one of the producers for this film. The original production was widely condemned when first seen at New York University, prompting Scorsese and Manoogian to rewrite the script and then reshoot the film, all of this achieved on a miserable budget of $35,000. The story was actually part of an envisioned film trilogy, this being the second in that series, the third resulting in Scorsese's outstanding **Mean Streets**, 1973. The first film of that trilogy, titled "Jerusalem, Jerusalem," was never produced, although Scorsese used elements from that original script for this film. Strong subject matter prohibits viewing by children. **p**, Betzi Manoggian, Haig Manoogian, Joseph Weill; **d**, Martin Scorsese; **cast**, Zina Bethune, Harvey Keitel, Ann Collette, Lennard Kuras, Michael Scala, Harry Northrup, Bill Minkin, Tsuai Yu-Lan, Catherine Scorsese, Martin Scorsese; **w**, Scorsese, Betzi Manoogian; **c**, Richard H. Coll, Michael Wadleigh (as Michael Wadley) ; **ed**, Thelma Schoonmaker.

Who Was That Lady? ★★★ 1960; U.S.; 115m; Ansark-Sidney/COL; B/W; Comedy; Children: Unacceptable; **DVD**. Entertaining tale begins with Curtis, a college chemistry professor whose wife, Leigh, catches him in his laboratory kissing another woman. She immediately files for divorce, but he wants to prevent that, so he asks his best friend, Martin, a television writer, to help him. Martin comes up with a scheme in which Curtis lies to Leigh, claiming that he is not really a professor, but an undercover agent for the FBI. Martin even gets Curtis a fake gun and authentic-looking FBI identification card. Leigh believes Curtis and becomes so impressed with him as a heroic FBI agent that she tells her friends and urges Curtis to do more secret mission work. Martin helps Curtis in this ruse by setting up a date with two beautiful blondes and promising to spend a weekend together with them. This leads to misadventures with some real FBI agents, the CIA, and some Soviet secret agents, which culminates in a room in the sub-basements of the Empire State Building. There Curtis and Martin think they are Soviet prisoners on an enemy submarine and patriotically sing "The Star-Spangled Banner" as they try to sink the vessel, but only succeed in rocking the building. Some real FBI agents arrive to save them and Leigh forgives Curtis since he has made such a fantastic effort to save their marriage (they were married in real life). Songs: "Who Was That Lady?" (Sammy Cahn, James Van Heusen), "Your Smile" (music and lyrics: Andre Previn, Dory Previn), "The Star-Spangled Banner" (1814; music: John Stafford Smith; lyrics: Frances Scott Key). *Author's Note*: Curtis told this author that this film "was a breeze to do, but anyone watching it would think that I would have to have a screw loose to cheat on a hot-looking wife like Janet [Leigh]. But those were the days when the public easily suspended disbelief and accepted whatever nonsense they saw on the big screen, thankfully for us actors." **p&w**, Norman Krasna (based on his play "Who Was That Lady I Saw You With?"); **d**, George Sidney; **cast**, Tony Curtis, Dean Martin, Janet Leigh, James Whitmore, John McIntire, Barbara Nichols, Larry Keating, Larry Storch, Joi Lansing, Wally Brown, Alan Carney, "Snub" Pollard, and Jack Benny in a bit guest appearance; **c**, Harry Stradling; **m**, Andre Previn; **ed**, Viola Lawrence; **art d**, Edward Hayworth; **set d**, James M. Crowe.

The Whole Town's Talking ★★★★★ 1935; U.S.; 95m; COL; B/W; Crime/Comedy; Children: Unacceptable; **DVD**; **VHS**; **IV**. Terrific Ford film sees marvelous performances from Arthur as a bored secretary, who falls in love with meek-mannered clerk Robinson. He loves Arthur from afar, but does not have the nerve to make any advances and it appears that his uneventful life will remain in limbo. Robinson (called Arthur Ferguson Jones) prides himself in having a spotless work record. He has worked at his firm for eight years and is always punctual. However, he oversleeps one morning and arrives late and is summarily fired. He then goes to lunch with Arthur and is spotted in the restaurant by searching detectives, who amaze Robinson when they put him under arrest and drag him away, thinking him to be a notorious gangster. To his further amazement, Robinson sees that he is almost the identical twin of the gangster police have been frantically attempting to capture. That gangster, known as "Killer Mannion," has recently escaped from prison to gather his old gang together to commit spectacular robberies. Robinson is put under endless interrogation, and, despite his protests, police refuse to believe that he is an innocent office worker. Arthur fuels the police fervor by making up a lot of ridiculous remarks about the recent robberies committed by Robinson's lookalike. (Her raucous behavior includes her pretending to be a gun moll, sneering and talking out of the side of her mouth as she rattles off gibberish confessions, providing one of the many hilarious sequences in this outstanding film. Arthur's outlandish behavior would be emulated by Katharine Hepburn when she and Cary Grant are inadvertently jailed in **Bringing Up Baby**, 1938, where Hepburn pretends to be part of a mob, making wisecracks and outlandish claims of having committed spectacular crimes.) Girardot, a manager from Robinson's office, arrives at police headquarters and identifies Robinson as one of his clerks. Byron, the district attorney, then realizes that Robinson is so much a lookalike for the wanted gangster that he will be arrested again and again whenever he makes a public appearance. Byron solves that problem by giving Robinson a written pass that Robinson can show to police whenever he is again mistaken for Public Enemy Number One. (Ironically, Byron played the warden in the earlier prison drama **20,000 Years in Sing Sing**, 1932, where he jeopardizes his career by giving convict Spencer Tracy a 24-hour pass to see his injured girlfriend on Tracy's promise that he will return to prison of his own volition.) The newspapers hear about the strange story of mistaken identity and Robinson suddenly becomes a local hero. He is not only rehired by Harvey, the head of the firm, but Harvey thinks all the publicity about Robinson is good for his business. When Ford, a newspaper editor and friend of Harvey's, suggests that Robinson write a series of articles about his lookalike gangster, Harvey is all for it. Harvey tells Robinson that his new job is writing a column for Ford's newspaper and where he will essentially present the biography of his gangster doppelganger while obliquely promoting Harvey's business. Harvey gives Robinson a raise and promotes him, but Robinson finds it difficult to write anything about the gangster who had caused him so much trouble. Arthur, however, uses her vivid imagination to supply Robinson with grist for the column as well as shrewdly negotiates his increased salary. When Robinson the gangster reads about how Robinson the clerk has a pass that will allow him to go unmolested throughout the city, the gangster visits the clerk at his rooming house. (The scene between the two is an amazing sequence of special effects where Robinson interacts with himself as he and the gangster move about that room.) The gangster

Edward G. Robinson in dual roles (a gangster and a mild-mannered clerk) in *The Whole Town's Talking,* 1935.

threatens the clerk into allowing him to sleep in his room during the day and use his police pass at night to conduct his illegal activities while the clerk goes to work at his office during daytime. Using this ruse, the gangster and his henchmen commit several more robberies, using the clerk's pass to escape. Police realize that the only way they can capture the gangster is to put the clerk behind bars and he is imprisoned for his own protection and so that he can be identified as the innocent twin in this vexing scenario. The gangster cannily uses this situation to enter the prison so that he can murder an inmate that earlier informed on him, and, during the process, also sets up the clerk to be framed in a subsequent robbery where the clerk and not the gangster will be killed by unwitting but obliging police. Thus, the gangster will be able to make a permanent escape and live out his life as the innocent clerk. Meanwhile, to make sure that the clerk does as he is ordered, the gangster has Arthur and others kidnapped and held at the gang's hideout. Meanwhile, the clerk, as usual, fumbles his assignment before he goes to the bank where police lay in waiting to waylay the gangster. The absent-minded clerk returns to the hideout to retrieve a check he has forgotten to deposit in the bank that is to be robbed, and, in the process, unwittingly leads police to that hideout. When he appears, the gang members are dumbfounded by the appearances of the clerk and the gangster, not knowing which one is their true leader. The clerk, who has gained the confidence of his evil twin, seizes this confusion to assume command of the gang, and, using the perfect persona of the gangster, ruthlessly orders the gang members to shoot and kill the gangster. The police then arrive to arrest the henchman and the clerk establishes his real identity. Robinson the clerk has not only rescued Arthur and others, but becomes a great hero, receiving a huge reward for eliminating the lethal gangster. He and Arthur then happily make a life together by sailing to Shanghai on their honeymoon, which had been the clerk's fondest ambition. Ford achieves a fine blend of comedy and drama in this gangster spoof and avoids gimmicks and tricks to convincingly present the nuances and subtleties of his well-developed characters. His rapid delivery eliminates any pensive scenes as the story moves along like a speeding train. Robinson's dual essay of a cowering milquetoast and a savage gangster is nothing short of masterful. He persuasively defines these divergent characters with decidedly separate personalities, giving each individual mannerisms and quirks as well as providing distinctive body motions for each character and different manners of speech. Arthur, too, is a radiant standout in her role of a rebellious office worker, who is savvy to the wiles of mankind. The film was successful at the box office and boosted the careers of Ford, Robinson and Arthur while adding a new twist to the film noir genre. ***Author's Note***: Ford told this author that "I never warmed up to crime stories, but the story for **The Whole Town's Talking** was so unusual—where the same actor would play two completely different per-

Jean Arthur and Edward G. Robinson in *The Whole Town's Talking*, 1935.

sons—that it appealed to me. We were able to put that one in the can [complete production] in about ten weeks because I had some real pros, Eddie [Robinson] and Jean [Arthur], working with me. They both came through like champions in that picture, even though I had to put up with a lot of interfering nonsense from Harry Cohn [the head of Columbia]. Harry always thought he knew how to better shoot a scene than any of the directors working for him. He was a pain in the neck. He never bothered me as much as he did poor Frank Capra, who turned out one great picture after another for Harry. I think Harry was just plain jealous of Frank." Capra told this author that, after seeing this Ford gem, "I was so impressed with Jean's worldly and very funny gun moll mimicking in that picture that it stayed with me and where I always wanted her in some of the pictures we went on to make together. She was my tough-skinned reporter hiding a generous heart in **Mr. Deeds Goes to Town** [1936], and played the same kind of part as an in-the-know secretary in **Mr. Smith Goes to Washington** [1939]. There was no one like that brilliant and lovely lady." Robinson was startled when he learned that he had been cast in this film without being told by his home studio, Warner Brothers. "I learned about that when I was reading a gossip column written by Louella Parsons," he told this author. "Here Louella was announcing to the world that Warner Brothers had loaned me out to Columbia to play a gangster in **The Whole Town's Talking**, and nobody had said a thing about that to me. It unnerved me, but, after I read the script, I thought Jack Warner had done me a great service as the dual roles I would be playing were very challenging and all actors want to test their abilities. I was also glad to see that that story had been written by a very talented Chicago crime writer, W.R. Burnett, who had written the story for **Little Caesar** [1931] and that was the picture that sent my career into orbit, so I knew I was in very good hands, especially when I learned that Pappy [John Ford], a master filmmaker, would be behind the camera." Arthur thought her role in this film was one of her best to date, saying to this author: "Oh, I got to clown around a lot in **The Whole Town's Talking** as a brassy secretary, who is too smart for her own good. I went out of my way not to overplay the part as the great John Ford was directing, and I knew that he watched every flicking finger before the camera like a hawk. I think every actor always gave Mr. Ford their very best because they were always impressed with him and wanted to please him. I was no exception." Francis Ford, the director's older brother, appears as a reporter, Ford always careful to have his sibling cast in some sort of role, although the brothers were not friendly toward each other throughout life. Lucille Ball has a bit part as a bank employee. Many films have portrayed actors in dual roles to enact twins or lookalikes, including **The Ace of Scotland Yard**, 1929; **Adam and Evil**, 1927; **Adaptation**, 2002; **Adolf Armstarke**, 1937; **Adventures of Texas Jack**, 1934; **Ali Baba Goes to Town**, 1937; **Alice in Wonder-**

land, 1933; **Alice in Wonderland**, 1951; **Alice in Wonderland**, 2010; **Alien 3**, 1992; **Among the Living**, 1941; **Angels and Insects**, 1996; **Anna the Adventuress**, 1920; **The Arizona Cyclone**, 1928; **Around the World in 80 Days**, 2004; **Atom Man vs. Superman**, 1950; **Back to the Future Part III**, 1990; **Bad Company**, 2002; **Bad Man from Red Butte**, 1940; **Bad Man of Deadwood**, 1941; **The Baron's African War**, 1966 (made-for-TV; repackaging of Republic's 1943 serial "Secret Service in Darkest Africa"); **Barry McKenzie Holds His Own**, 1974; **The Beast of the City**, 1932; **Before Night Falls**, 2000; **Berkeley Square**, 1933; **Bicentennial Man**, 1999; **Big Calibre**, 1935; **The Big Show**, 1936; **Bikini Beach**, 1964; **Billy the Kid Returns**, 1938; **Black Bandit**, 1938; **Black Is White**, 1920; **Black Magic**, 1949; **The Black Room**, 1935; **Black Waters**, 1929; **Blake of Scotland Yard**, 1937; **Blazing Aacross the Pecos**, 1948; **Blazing the Western Trail**, 1945; **A Blind Bargain**, 1922; **Blueprint**, 2003; **Bonanza Town**, 1951; **Born to Gamble**, 1935; **Both Barrels Blazing**, 1945; **Brazil**, 1944; **Breed of the Sea**, 1926; **Brenda Starr, Reporter**, 1945; **Brothers**, 1930; **Bruce Gentry**, 1949; **Buried Treasure**, 1921; **Callaway Went Thataway**, 1951; **Canadian Mounties vs. Atomic Invaders**, 1953; **Captain America**, 1944; **Captain America**, 1979 (made-for-TV); **Captain America**, 1990; **Carolina Blues**, 1944; **Casualties of War**, 1989; **Cat Ballou**, 1965; **Chaplin**, 1992; **Chatterbox**, 1943; **The Cheerful Fraud**, 1926; **The Chinese Cat**, 1944; **A Chump at Oxford**, 1940; **The Circus Clown**, 1934; **City Slickers II: The Legend of Curly's Gold**, 1994; **A Close Call for Boston Blackie**, 1946; **Cobra Woman**, 1944; **The Cobra Strikes**, 1948; **Coffee and Cigarettes**, 2004; **Conceiving Ada**, 1997; **Confessions of a Vice Baron**, 1943; **The Conquerors**, 1932; **Constantine**, 2005; **Copacabana**, 1947; **Corpus Christi Bandits**, 1945; **The Corsican Brothers**, 1941; **Cover Girl**, 1944; **Covered Wagon Days**, 1940; **Crime Doctor's Man Hunt**, 1946; **Crime Over London**, 1936; **Crimes at the Dark House**, 1940; **Cuban Fireball**, 1951; **Custer's Last Stand**, 1936; **Daredevils of the Red Circle**, 1939; **The Daring Young Man**, 1942; **The Dark Half**, 1993; **The Dark Mirror**, 1920; **The Dark Mirror**, 1946; **Dark Streets**, 1929; **A Date with the Falcon**, 1942; **Dave**, 1993; **Dead Again**, 1991; **Dead Men Walk**, 1943; **Dead Ringer**, 1964; **Dead Ringers**, 1988; **Deadwood Dick**, 1940; **Deceptions**, 1985 (made-for-TV); **The Desert Hawk**, 1944; **The Desert Horseman**, 1946; **Django Unchained**, 2012; **Don Q: Son of Zorro**, 1925; **Don Ricardo Returns**, 1946; **Don't Get Personal**, 1942; **Double, Double, Toil and Trouble**, 1993 (made-for-TV); **Double Impact**, 1991; **Dracula**, 1992; **The Drifter**, 1944; **The Driftin' Kid**, 1941; **Duplicate**, 1998; **Eadie Was a Lady**, 1945; **Echo**, 1997 (made-for-TV); **England Made Me**, 1973; **Equinox**, 1992; **The Errand Boy**, 1961; **Fahrenheit 451**, 1966; **False Face**, 1977; **The Far Side of the Moon**, 2005; **The Fighting Frontiersman**, 1946; **The Fighting Renegade**, 1939; **Folies Bergere**, 1935; **The Forbidden City**, 1918; **The Forbidden Street**, 1949; **Four Mothers**, 1941; **Freddie Steps Out**, 1946; **Frontier Gunlaw**, 1946; **Fugitive at Large**, 1939; **Fugitive from Sonora**, 1943; **Galloping Thunder**, 1946; **The Gay Deceiver**, 1926; **The Gay Vagabond**, 1941; **Genealogies of a Crime**, 1998; **Get That Man**, 1935; **Ghost of Zorro**, 1949; **The Ghosts of Yesterday**, 1918; **The Girl Without a Soul**, 1917; **G-Men Never Forget**, 1948; **God's Gun**, 1976; **Gold Dust Gertie**, 1931; **The Great Dictator**, 1940; **The Great Race**, 1965; **The Green Archer**, 1940; **Gunfire**, 1950; **Gunning for Vengeance**, 1946; **The Hawk of Wild River**, 1952; **Heading West**, 1946; **The Hell of Frankenstein**, 1960; **Her Splendid Folly**, 1933; **Here Come the Waves**, 1944; **His Brother's Ghost**, 1945; **History of the World: Part I**, 1981; **Hit and Run**, 1957; **House of Numbers**, 1957; **House of Terror**, 1973; **I'll Never Forget You**, 1951; **In His Brother's Place**, 1919; **The Indians Are Coming**, 1930; **Irish Luck**, 1925; **It Came from Outer Space**, 1953; **Jesse James at Bay**, 1941; **Joe Palooka Meets Humphrey**, 1950; **Joy of Living**, 1938; **Junction City**, 1952; **Just Suppose**, 1926; **Kaminey: The Scoundrels**, 2009; **The Kid from Amarillo**, 1951; **King of the Bullwhip**, 1950; **A Kiss Before Dying**, 1993; **Kissin' Cousins**, 1964; **The Krays**, 1990; **La**

Conga Nights, 1940; Lady of the Night, 1925; Landrush, 1946; The Last Days of Boot Hill, 1947; The Last Starfighter, 1984; Law and Order, 1942; Lawless Breed, 1946; The Lawless Breed, 1953; Lawless Empire, 1945; The Lawless Rider, 1954; Leaves of Grass, 2009; Les Misérables, 1935; Les Misérables, 1952; Les Misérables, 1995; Les Misérables, 1998; Les Misérables, 2000 (TV miniseries); Lightning Guns, 1950; Lights of Old Broadway, 1925; Liquid Sky, 1982; Little Lord Fauntleroy, 1921; Little Miss Broadway, 1938; The Lizzie McGuire Movie, 2003; The Lone Hand Texan, 1947; The Lone Ranger Rides Again, 1939; Lonely Wives, 1931; The Long Shadow, 1992; Lord of the Flies, 1963; The Love Bug, 1968; Make Mine a Double, 1961; The Man in the Iron Mask, 1939; The Man in the Iron Mask, 1998; The Man Who Loved Redheads, 1955; Manhattan Moon, 1935; Man's Country, 1938; Marked for Death, 1990; Marriage in Transit, 1925; Mary Poppins, 1964; Mary Reilly, 1996; Mask of Death, 1996; The Masked Pirate, 1949; Maximum Risk, 1996; Mexican Spitfire's Elephant, 1942; The Million Dollar Dollies, 1918; Miss V from Moscow, 1942; Mistaken, 2013; Mr. Lemon of Orange, 1931; Mr. Murder, 1998 (made-for-TV); Model Behavior, 2000 (made-for-TV); Modesty Blaise, 1966; The Mosquito Coast, 1986; Mother Night, 1996; Murder by Television, 1935; Murder He Says, 1945; Nazi Agent, 1942; Now or Never, 1935; Obsession, 1976; Om Shanti Om, 2007; On the Riviera, 1951; The One, 2001; One Touch of Venus, 1948; The Other Me, 2000 (made-for-TV); Outlaw Treasure, 1955; Outlaws of Santa Fe, 1944; Outlaws of the Rockies, 1945; The Parent Trap, 1961; The Parent Trap, 1998; Partners in Crime, 1928; The Persuader, 1957; Peter Pan, 1953; The Phantom, 1943; The Phantom Cowboy, 1935; Phantom Patrol, 1936; The Phantom Rider, 1946; Phantom Valley, 1948; Pioneers of the West, 1940; Pocahontas, 1995; Port Said, 1948; Prairie Raiders, 1947; Prairie Rustlers, 1945; The Prince and the Pauper, 1937; The Prince of Tides, 1991; The Prisoner of Zenda, 1922; The Prisoner of Zenda, 1937; The Prisoner of Zenda, 1952; The Purple Rose of Cairo, 1985; Redline, 1997; Renegades of the Sage, 1948; Replicant, 2001; The Return of Daniel Boone, 1941; The Return of the Durango Kid, 1945; Riders of the Lone Star, 1947; Rim of the Canyon, 1949; The River Pirates, 1988; Riverboat Rhythm, 1946; River's End, 1940; Road to Paradise, 1930; Romance of the Rio Grande, 1941; The Saint's Double Trouble, 1940; Schizopolis, 1997; Scouts to the Rescue, 1939; A Scream in the Night, 1935; Sealed Lips, 1942; Secret Agent X-9, 1937; The Secret Code, 1942; The Secret of Treasure Island, 1938; Secret Service in Darkest Africa, 1943 (serial); Secrets of Scotland Yard, 1944; Separated by Murder, 1994 (made-for-TV); The Shadow Returns, 1946; She Gets Her Man, 1945; Shooting High, 1940; The Sickle or the Cross, 1949; The 6th Day, 2000; Sky Raiders, 1941; Slap Shot, 1977; Slightly Scandalous, 1946; Smart Politics, 1948; So I Married an Axe Murderer, 1993; So You Won't Talk, 1940; The Social Network, 2010; Son of a Badman, 1949; The Son of Dr. Jekyll, 1951; The Son of the Sheik, 1926; Son of Zorro, 1947; Special Effects, 1984; Speed to Spare, 1937; The Sphinx, 1933; The Spider Returns, 1941; The Spider's Web, 1938; The Spiderwick Chronicles, 2008; Spy Smasher, 1942; Stars Over Texas, 1946; Start the Revolution Without Me, 1970; Stella Maris, 1918; A Stolen Life, 1946; The Strange Death of Adolf Hitler, 1943; Sunset in El Dorado, 1945; The Sunset Legion, 1928; Superman, 1948; Swing It, Soldier, 1941; Swing Out, Sister, 1945; The Tabasco Kid, 1932; A Tale of Two Cities, 1935; A Tale of Two Cities, 1958; A Tale of Two Cities, 1980 (made-for-TV); Tango & Cash, 1989; Tanu Weds Manu Returns, 2015; Teenage Mutant Ninja Turtles, 1990; Texas Dynamo, 1950; Thank Your Lucky Stars, 1943; A Thousand Elephants, 2008; The Time Machine, 1960; The Tioga Kid, 1948; Tom and Thomas, 2002; The Tomb of Ligeia, 1964; Tombstone Terror, 1935; Trail of Terror, 1943; Trail to Laredo, 1948; Trapped in Tia Juana, 1932; The Truman Show, 1998; Tumbledown Ranch in Arizona, 1941; Twice Blessed, 1945; Twin Dragons, 1992; Two-Faced Woman, 1941; Two-

Nick Nolte and Tuesday Weld in *Who'll Stop the Rain,* 1978.

Fisted Stranger, 1946; Two Gun Sheriff, 1941; Two Sisters, 1929; Under California Stars, 1948; Vertigo, 1958; The Vigilante: Fighting Hero of the West, 1947; Watch the Birdie, 1950; West of Sonora, 1948; Westwind, 2011; Wheel of Chance, 1928; While the Patient Slept, 1935; Whirlwind Raiders, 1948; Whistling in Dixie, 1942; White Comanche, 1968; The White Shadow, 1924; The Wife of General Ling, 1938; Wild Horse Rustlers, 1943; Windwalker, 1980; The Woman in White, 1948; Wonder Man, 1945; The Wonderful Adventure, 1915; Wyoming, 1947; and Zorro Rides Again, 1937. p, Lester Cowan; d, John Ford; cast, Edward G. Robinson, Jean Arthur, Arthur Byron, Arthur Hohl, James Donlan, Wallace Ford, Donald Meek, Etienne Girardot, Edward Brophy, Paul Harvey, Lucille Ball, Francis Ford; w, Jo Swerling, Robert Riskin (based on the story "Jail Breaker" by W.R. Burnett); c, Joseph August; ed, Viola Lawrence.

Who'll Stop the Rain ★★★ 1978; U.S.; 126m; Katzka-Jaffe/UA; Color; Crime Drama; Children: Unacceptable (MPAA: R); DVD; VHS. Taut crime yarn begins in Philadelphia in the late 1960s where Nolte is a veteran of the attritional Vietnam War (1961-1975) and is now in the Merchant Marine and has done some marijuana drug smuggling. He allows his buddy, Moriarty, who had been traumatized by the war and is now a newspaper reporter, talk him into helping smuggle some heroin into the United States. Nolte's job is to bring in the heroin and deliver it to Moriarty's wife, Weld, who is a drug addict, and wait for Moriarty to sell the goods. After Nolte sees that he is being followed by two gunmen, Masur and Sharkey, he flees with Weld and the heroin. Before Nolte can find a buyer for the drugs, Masur and Sharkey, who are working for corrupt narcotics agent Zerbe, find them hiding in a hippie commune. Zerbe wants Nolte and his friends eliminated as they are cutting into his own drug trafficking. There is a shootout and Nolte is shot and dies miserably on some railroad tracks, ending this morose and jolting tale. A lot of symbolism is employed to demonstrate the decline of ethics and loss of idealism in the 1960s, as well as the destroyed belief of youth in its leaders. Songs: "Philadelphia Fillies," "Put a Little Love in Your Heart" (Jackie DeShannon, Jimmy Holiday, Randall Meyers); "American Pie" (Don McLean); "I'll Step Down" (Slim Whitman); "Hey Tonight," "Who'll Stop the Rain," "Proud Mary" (John Fogerty); "Gimme Some Lovin'" (Steve Winwood, Muff Winwood, Spencer Davis); "Golden Rocket" (Hank Snow). *Author's Note*: Nolte's character is based upon Beat Generation writer Neal Cassady (1926-1968), who died in San Miguel, Mexico, after attending a wedding party, walking through a rainstorm while in a debilitated state from the overuse of drugs. He was found comatose alongside some railroad tracks and died a short time later at the age of forty-one. Drugs and violence prohibit viewing by children. p, Herb Jaffe, Gabriel Katzska; d, Karel Reisz;

Ethel Shutta and Eddie Cantor in *Whoopee!*, 1930.

cast, Nick Nolte, Tuesday Weld, Michael Moriarty, Anthony Zerbe, Richard Masur, Ray Sharkey, Gail Strickland, Charles Haid, David Opatoshu, Joaquin Martinez, Wings Hauser; **w**, Robert Stone, Judith Rascoe (based on the novel *Dog Soldiers* by Stone); **c**, Richard H. Kline; **m**, Laurence Rosenthal; **ed**, John Bloom; **prod d**, Dale Hennesy; **set d**, Robert De Vestel; **spec eff**, Paul Stewart, Charles E. Dolan.

Whoopee! ★★★★ 1930; U.S.; 93m; Goldwyn/UA; Color; Musical Comedy; Children: Acceptable; **DVD**; **VHS**. Superb early-day musical comedy sees Cantor shine in one of his most memorable roles. Cantor resides in an eastern city and is the world's leading hypochondriac, having a special nurse, Shutta (in her one and only film), to be on hand to deal with every disease and malady he believes is invading his vulnerable immune system. To improve what he thinks is his failing health, Cantor moves west to Arizona with the ever faithful Shutta and settles at an upscale dude ranch. He meets fetching Hunt, who is pursued by fiancé Rutherford, the local sheriff, but Hunt does not love the brusque lawman. Her heart belongs to Indian brave Gregory and the ever-meddling Cantor decides to play Cupid and arranges for Hunt to end up with Gregory. It turns out that the handsome Gregory is not an Indian, but a white man who, as a child, had been abandoned and raised by the local tribe (this twist to appease the then deep concerns about miscegenation matching). Freeland provides a delightfully frothy musical with a number of outstanding Busby Berkeley production numbers peopled by many leggy Goldwyn Girls (who make their debut here), not the least of whom is a very young (age fourteen) Betty Grable. Cantor is the centerpiece of this entertaining frolic and has several side-splitting scenes, including one where he explains that he could die of any number of deadly diseases attacking him. The film received an Oscar nomination for Best Art Direction (Day), and was a solid box office hit, earning more than $2.6 million in its initial release against a budget of $1.3 million. The film was remade with another exceptional production by Goldwyn as **Up in Arms**, 1944, starring Danny Kaye, another latter-day Goldwyn protégé. Songs: "Makin' Whoopee" (1928; music: Walter Donaldson; lyrics: Gus Kahn); "Cowboys," "Today's the Day," "A Girlfriend of a Boyfriend of Mine," "My Baby Just Cares for Me," "Stetson," "The Song of the Setting Sun" (all 1930; music: Walter Donaldson; lyrics: Gus Kahn); "I'll Still Belong to You" (1930; music: Nacio Herb Brown; lyrics: Edward Eliscu); "The Wedding March" (1843; from "A Midsummer Night's Dream" by Felix Mendelssohn-Bartholdy); "Here Comes the Bride" ("Bridal Chorus") (1850; from "Lohengrin" by Richard Wagner); "Ol' Man River" (1927; music: Jerome Kern; lyrics: Oscar Hammerstein II). *Author's Note*: Goldwyn purchased the film rights to the smash Broadway hit produced by Flo Ziegfeld and worked with Ziegfeld as his partner (the first and only time

since Goldwyn had become an independent film producer in 1923) to make this film. The original production opened at the Amsterdam Theater on December 4, 1928, and ran for 407 performances. In 1929, Ziegfeld lost everything in the Stock Market Crash and, to recoup his terrible losses, closed the show and sold the film rights to Goldwyn, even though the show could have run for another year on Broadway. Cantor, who had appeared in the Broadway production, was ideal for the character he reprises with his ebullient and energetic comedic talents. This film made him an overnight Hollywood superstar. This film marked the high water of Cantor's career. He not only sings the memorable "Whoopee," but also "My Baby Just Cares for Me," where he does his trademarked blackface routine (and he would present that routine in every one of his subsequent movies). He would go on to make a total of six films with Goldwyn, being paid in these Depression days an astronomical salary of $150,000 per picture plus 10 percent of the profits, or an average of $250,000 per film. Omitted from the film version is singer Ruth Etting, who appeared in the Broadway production, along with her signature song, "Love Me or Leave Me," which would be showcased by Doris Day when essaying Etting in the outstanding biopic, **Love Me or Leave Me**, 1955. Buddy Ebsen also appeared in the Ziegfeld stage production, but not in this film version. Goldwyn took an expensive plunge in opting to make this story as one of the first color musical comedy films, where the old two-color Technicolor process was employed. The genesis of this tale began as a serial titled "The Wreck," beginning in December 1921 in *Argosy/All Story Magazine*. Owen Davis adapted the serial as a play in 1923, titled "The Nervous Wreck," starring Otto Kruger, Albert Hackett and June Walker. It was adapted for the screen as a silent in 1926 by Al Christie that starred Harrison Ford, Chester Conklin and Phyllis Haver. Goldwyn told this author that "I always wanted to make that Cantor musical as a talkie, even way back in the silent days. I admired that little guy [Cantor] even after his blackface routine went out of fashion." Grable was barely a teenager when she appeared in this film, telling this author: "I was in the chorus for the 'Cowboy' number and some others in that picture. Busby [Berkeley] ran the production numbers and he ran us all ragged when we did them, I can tell you. What a slave driver! The numbers were spectacular. When we all looked back at what he did on the screen, well, you had to admire Busby's brilliant choreography, which he always planned in detail in advance like some general before going to war." Sothern, too, was beginning her career when appearing in this film, stating to this author: "I was just starting out in pictures then when I was selected to be one of the Goldwyn Girls. We all went into that Eddie Cantor production. There was a leggy gal hoofing right next to me named Betty Grable and, after she told me that she was underage, I promised not to snitch on her. I told her to go back to school and forget about the movies. Well, what did I know? Betty became one of the Hollywood greats and that all started with **Whoopee!**" Others in the choruses of the Goldwyn girls in this film include Paulette Goddard and Virginia Bruce, both going on to become leading ladies in the 1930s and 1940s. The film premiered in New York on September 30, 1930, at $5 per seat and was sold out for weeks. Many other films depict hypochondriacs, including **All Mine to Give**, 1957; **Amelie**, 2001; **The Aviator**, 2004; **The Band Wagon**, 1953; **Bandits**, 2001; **Born Romantic**, 2000; **Burn Notice**, 2007-2013 (TV series); **Carry On Matron**, 1972; **Checking Out**, 1989; **The Citadel**, 1938; **Crimes at the Dark House**, 1943; **A Day at the Races**, 1937; **Day of the Wacko**, 2002; **Dr. Bull**, 1933; **Dr. Socrates**, 1935; **Dogville**, 2004; **Down to Earth**, 1917; **The Egg and I**, 1947; **Emma**, 1972 (TV miniseries); **Emma**, 1996 (made-for-TV); **Ethan Frome**, 1993; **Ferris Bueller's Day Off**, 1986; **The Gangster**, 1947; **Gold Diggers of 1937**, 1936; **The Great Madcap**, 1977; **A Guy and a Gal**, 1975; **Hannah and Her Sisters**, 1986; **Hav Plenty**, 1997; **Home**, 2009; **How I Was Systematically Destroyed by an Idiot**, 1983; **Hypochondriac**, 1979; **I Take This Woman**, 1940; **In the Land of Women**, 2007; **An Indecent Obsession**, 1985; **Innerspace**, 1987; **Le Corbeau: The Raven**, 1948; **The Little Shop of Horrors**, 1960; **Lovely Loneliness**,

2009; **Madagascar**, 2005; **Meet the Girls**, 1938; **A Night of Terror**, 1937; **Not as a Stranger**, 1955; **The Odd Couple**, 1968; **Piku**, 2015; **Pinching Penny**, 2011; **Play It Again, Sam**, 1972; **Poison Ivy**, 1992; **Pollyanna**, 1960; **Red Desert**, 1965; **The Saddest Music in the World**, 2003; **Saddle Pals**, 1947; **Send Me No Flowers**, 1964; **Sorry, Wrong Number**, 1948; **Sorry, Wrong Number**, 1989 (made-for-TV); **The Street with No Name**, 1948; **The Strawberry Blonde**, 1941; **Swing High, Swing Low**, 1937; **Uptown Girls**, 2003; **Ship Ahoy**, 1942; **Supercondriaque**, 2014; **The Switch**, 2010; **Trilogy: Two**, 2002; **2 Days in Paris**, 2007; **Up in Arms**, 1944; **Wake Up Love**, 1997; **Why Worry?**, 1923; **Wild and Wonderful**, 1964; **Wonderful Summer**, 2010; and **You Really Got Me**, 2001. **p**, Samuel Goldwyn, Florenz Ziegfeld; **d**, Thornton Freeland; **cast**, Eddie Cantor, Ethel Shutta, Paul Gregory, Eleanor Hunt, Jack Rutherford, Walter Law, Dean Jagger, Virginia Bruce, Claire Dodd, Paulette Goddard, Betty Grable, Ann Sothern; **w**, William M. Conselman (based on the Ziegfeld stage musical by William Anthony McGuire, Walter Donaldson, Gus Kahn, the stage comedy "The Nervous Wreck" by Owen Davis, and the story "The Wreck" by E.J. Rath); **c**, Lee Garmes, Ray Rennahan, Gregg Toland; **m**, Alfred Newman, Donaldson, Kahn, Nacio Herb Brown, Edward Wliscu; **ed**, Stuart Heisler; **art d**, Richard Day.

Whose Life Is It Anyway? ★★★ 1981; U.S.; 119m; MGM/UA; Color; Drama; Children: Unacceptable (MPAA: R); **DVD**; **VHS**; **IV**. Absorbing offbeat tale sees Dreyfuss as a happily married artist who creates sculptures. He is in a car accident and his life is dramatically altered when he finds himself paralyzed from a neck injury. All he can do is talk, and wants to die. In hospital, he is befriended by some of the staff and his doctor, Lahti, and hospital administrator Cassavetes, who try to talk him out of taking his own life. Dreyfuss hires lawyer Balaban and takes his case to court requesting he be allowed to die. Dreyfuss and Balaban win, and a judge, McMillan, rules that Dreyfuss can leave the court and live or die as he chooses. The morbid and somewhat depressing tale is saved by Dreyfuss' outstanding performance. Songs: "Hospital Ladies" (Arthur B. Rubinstein), "Punkette Nights" (Michael Starobin). **p**, Lawrence P. Bachmann; **d**, John Badham; **cast**, Richard Dreyfuss, John Cassavetes, Christine Lahti, Bob Balaban, Kenneth McMillan, Kaki Hunter, Thomas Oms, Janet Eilber, Kathryn Grody, George Wyner; **w**, Brian Clark, Reginald Rose (based on the play by Clark); **c**, Mario Tosi; **m**, Arthur B. Rubinstein; **ed**, Frank Morriss; **prod d**, Gene Callahan; **art d**, Sydney Z. Litwack; **set d**, Jerry Adams; **spec eff**, Terry W. King, Charles Schulthies.

Why Be Good? ★★★ 1929 (silent); U.S.; 84m; First National/WB; B/W; Romance; Children: Unacceptable; **DVD**. This entertaining tale of a frivolous flapper centers on Moore, who works as a sales clerk at a department store and gets a notorious reputation through no fault of her own. Moore is really a stay-at-home young lady who lives with her doting mother, Rosing, and father, Sainpolis. Moore is like any other girl of her generation, one who lives for jazz and dancing. She meets handsome, young Hamilton and goes on the town with him. They dance through the night so that when she gets home she falls asleep exhausted and is late when reporting for work the next morning. She is called into the manager's office to explain her tardiness and is surprised to see that Hamilton is not only her boss, but the son of the department store owner, Martindel. The owner sees the fetching Moore and thinks that, because of her skimpy dress and modern bobbed hair (which Moore wears in her patented bangs), she is not the right girl for his son and has her fired. Moore thinks that Hamilton has caused her dismissal and will have nothing more to do with him. Hamilton, however, is smitten with Moore and tells Martindel that he loves the girl. Martindel, in an effort to protect his son, suggests that Hamilton test her by taking her to a hotel to see if she can be easily seduced. Hamilton grudgingly agrees and, through a ruse, inveigles Moore into that very compromising rendezvous. Moore,

Colleen Moore and Neil Hamilton in *Why Be Good?*, 1929.

however, resists any suggested assignation and leaves Hamilton, thus proving that she is the very good young lady Hamilton has always believed her to be. After Hamilton proves to his father that Moore has passed the test with flying colors, she is accepted into the upscale family, although Hamilton has a difficult time convincing Moore that his intentions were strictly honorable from the beginning to the happy ending where Moore and Hamilton plan a life together. Moore and Hamilton are standouts as naïve, young lovers and the supporting cast members are exceptional in their roles. Songs: "I'm Thirsty for Kisses—Hungry for Love," "Here Comes My Ball and Chain," "A Love-Tale of Alsace Lorraine" (music: J. Fred Coots; lyrics: Lou Davis); "Blazin'" (Joe Sanders); "Freshman Hop" (Al Goering, Jack Pettis); "Who Wouldn't Be Jealous of You?" (George Frommel, Haven Gillespie, Larry Shay); "Sweet Georgia Brown" (Maceo Pinkard); "That's Her Now" (Milton Ager); "If You Want the Rainbow, You Must Have the Rain" (Oscar Levant); "He's Tall and Dark and Handsome" (Al Sherman); "Give Your Baby Lots of Lovin'" (Joseph A. Burke); "My Angeline" (Mabel Wayne); "My Suppressed Desire" (Chester Cohn); "Rag Time" (Edwin B. Edwards, Nick LaRocca, Henry Ragas, Tony Sbarbaro, Larry Shields); "Doin' the Raccoon" (music: J. Fred Coots; lyrics: Raymond Klages); "Changes" (Walter Donaldson); "I Faw Down an' Go Boom" (James Brockman, Leonard Stevens); "Honey" (Richard A. Whiting); "Hello Montreal" (Harry Warren); "It Goes Like This/That Funny Melody" (Cliff Friend); "Sweet Adeline" (music: Harry Armstrong; lyrics: Richard H. Gerard); "Bon Vivant," "Le Chant des Boulevards," "Violence" (J.S. Zamecnik); "Moto Perpetuo" (Max Bergunker); "Suite Domestica" (Hugo Risenfeld); "Narcissus" (Ethelbert Nevin); "In the Hall of the Mountain King" from "Peer Gynt Suite No. 1" (Edvard Grieg); "Baby Face" (Harry Akst); "Flapperette" (Jesse Greer); "Moon Madness" (T. Henry Lodge); "Intermezzo Perpetual" (W.W. Lowitz); "Happy Moods" (Paul Marquardt); "Crazy Rhythm" (Joseph Meyer, Roger Wolfe Kahn); "Oh! You Have no Idea" (Dan Dougherty); "High Up on a Hill-top" (Abel Baer, Ian Campbell, George Whiting); "When Erastus Plays His Old Kazoo" (Sammy Fain, Sam Coslow, Larry Spier); "Don't Be Like That" (Archie Gottler, Charles Tobias, Maceo Pinkard); "Disperazione" (Giuseppe Beece); "Appassionato No. 2" (William Axt). *Author's Note*: Seiter told this author that "directing Colleen [Moore] was a pleasure as she was a natural actress and one of the prettiest young ladies in Hollywood in the late 1920s. She wore her jet black hair in bangs, the same kind of hairstyle Louise Brooks had, but Colleen always played wholesome, young ladies where Louise was always playing vamps and sirens. Colleen had an enormous following, probably more fans in those days than most other actresses. The title of that picture— **Why Be Good?**—is really ironic because Colleen was always a good girl." This film was released as a silent without dialogue, but it was ac-

Joel McCrea and Vera Miles in *Wichita*, 1955.

companied by a lively Vitaphone soundtrack loaded with sound effects, music and songs with singers. The film was considered lost for decades, but a 35mm print was located and was restored in 2014. Also appearing in this film early in their careers is Jean Harlow, who plays a blonde on a rooftop bench at a party; Phil Harris, who is a band drummer; and Andy Devine, who is a man at a nightclub. Norton plays a hilarious drunk, the kind of specialty role he essayed for decades, although Norton was a teetotaler. **p**, John McCormick; **d**, William A. Seiter; **cast**, Colleen Moore, Neil Hamilton, Bodil Rosing, John Sainpolis (St. Polis), Dixie Gay, Mischa Auer, Jack Norton, Andy Devine, Jean Harlow, Phil Harris, Grady Sutton, Virginia Sale; **w**, Carey Wilson, Paul Perez (based on a story by Wilson); **c**, Sidney Hickox; **ed**, Terry Morse.

Why Does Herr R. Run Amok? ★★★ 1977; Germany; 88m; Antiteater Produktion/New Yorker Films; B/W; Crime Drama; Children: Unacceptable (MPAA: PG-13); **DVD**; **VHS**. This strange but absorbing film focuses upon Raab, a technical draftsman, who gets along with others at work and is content with his life, his wife, Ungerer, and his son. His problems begin when his social-climbing wife pushes him to seek a promotion. His is further aggravated when his parents visit and his mother criticizes Ungerer. Old school friends and neighbors visit, some commenting on his wife's expensive tastes. His chances of promotion are jeopardized when he gives a dull toast while having too much to drink at an office party. Watching television at home with his wife and son, Raab becomes disturbed at his wife, who is talking with a friend. He picks up a heavy candelabra, and beats his family to death. The next day, he hangs himself. Viewers are left to wonder what drove Raab to such violence, but the clues of boredom and dissatisfaction with life are present to bring viewers to their own conclusions. Raab is exceptional in this pensive character study from Fassbinder, whose directorial career is studded with such unnerving and brutal tales. Song: "Stand by Me" (Ben E. King, Jerry Leiber, Mike Stoller). Mature themes and violence prohibit viewing by children. (In German; English subtitles.) **d&w**, Rainer Werner Fassbinder, Michael Fengler; **cast**, Kurt Raab, Lilith Ungerer, Lilo Pempeit, Franz Maron, Harry Baer, Peter Moland, Hanna Schygulla, Ingrid Caven, Irm Hermann; **c**, Dietrich Lohmann; **prod d**, Kurt Raab.

Why Rock the Boat? ★★★ 1974; Canada; 113m; National Film Board of Canada/COL; Color; Comedy; Children: Unacceptable (MPAA: PG); **VHS**. Set in 1940s Montreal, Canada, the film begins with Gillard, a naïve young reporter who gets a job on the worst newspaper in the city. While struggling with assignments and a tyrannical boss, and being seduced by the city editor's wife, he meets and falls in love with Leek, a reporter for a competing paper. Leek forms a local union for journalists

that strains Gillard's relationship with her. He nevertheless wants to impress her, so he finally helps her in unionizing the city's newspaper editors and writers, an effort that unites them for a happy ending. Howe directs an easygoing, charming comedy where Gillard, Leek and the rest of the cast give impressive performances. Sexual matter prohibits viewing by children. **p&w**, William Weintraub (based on his novel); **d**, John Howe; **cast**, Stuart Gillard, Tiiu Leek, Ken James, Budd Knapp, Henry Beckman, Sean Sullivan, Patricia Gage, Ruben Moreno, Cec Linder, Henry Ramer; **c**, Savas Kalogeras; **m**, Howe; **ed**, Marie-Helene Guillemin; **art d**, Denis Boucher; **set d**, Boucher, Ronald Fauteux, Earl G. Preston.

Why Worry? ★★★★ 1923 (silent); U.S.; 63m/6 reels; Hal Roach Studios/Pathé Exchange; B/W; Comedy; Children: Acceptable; **DVD**. Lloyd uses all his inventive and most effective slapstick techniques in presenting this laugh riot of a film. Lloyd is a multimillionaire hypochondriac, who, with his constant nurse, Ralston, thinks to improve his health by moving to an island off the coast of South America. Once Lloyd arrives, he is greeted by a widespread revolution, although he thinks this mayhem is being especially staged to provide him with amusement. He learns to his great discomfort that this social upheaval is for real after he is imprisoned in a cell with a giant named Colosso (Aasen), who is suffering from a head-pounding toothache. Lloyd is initially terrified by this raging behemoth of a man, until he befriends him by pulling that aggravating molar (not unlike removing the painful burr from the lion's paw to befriend the wild beast in the children's fairy tale), and Aasen is now Lloyd's private guardian and Goliath-like warrior. The duo, in a series of fantastic sight gags (not the least of which is an uncooperative cannon that consistently flops its muzzle in the direction of the heroes), are able to rescue the imperiled Ralston and subdue the wild rebels. They further track down the American renegade responsible for the upheaval, delivering to him his just deserts. Lloyd is overjoyed at realizing that all of his hazardous actions on the island have so busily preoccupied him that he is now cured of his imaginary maladies. He returns to California where he spends his time doing good deeds, including pulling strings so that a friend can become a traffic cop in downtown L.A. He then marries Ralston and begins living a life without ailments and allergies. This film, like so many others starring Lloyd and produced by Roach (**A Sailor-Made Man**, 1921; **Grandma's Boy**, 1922; **Dr. Jack**, 1922; and **Safety Last!**, 1923), was a huge hit, and it was the last film Lloyd made with Roach. *Author's Note*: Lloyd had accrued so much money through his association with Roach that he decided to produce his own films and amicably severed his relationship with Roach, who wished the comedian well. By the time Lloyd made this last film with Roach he was already making most of the major decisions. For instance, Lloyd personally contacted Ringling Brothers and hired that circus' resident giant, William George Auger (1881-1922), who was billed as the Cardiff Giant (and who stood 7'5"). Auger, however, died during the production of this film on November 30, 1922, and Lloyd desperately searched about for another giant, luckily finding the Norwegian-born John Aasen (1890-1938), a native of Minnesota (who stood more than 7'2"). Lloyd cast Aasen in the role of the giant in this film; Lloyd reshot all the scenes in which Auger had appeared, and Aasen proved to be a natural actor. This was Ralston's first feature film where she was a leading lady and she would go on to make five more films with Lloyd. His previous leading lady, Mildred Davis, had retired from the screen to become Lloyd's wife, a union that would produce three children and last until her death in 1969. The comedy **Whoopee!**, 1930, starring Eddie Cantor, takes a large leaf from this film in that its leading character, Cantor, like Lloyd, is a hypochondriac, who moves to a different climate to cure his imagined illnesses. **p**, Hal Roach; **d**, Fred Newmeyer; **cast**: Harold Lloyd, Jobyna Ralston, John Aasen, Leo White, James Mason, Wallace Howe, Gaylord Lloyd, Mark Jones, William Gillespie, Lee Phelps, Charles Stevenson, Sam Lufkin; **w**, Sam Taylor (story), H.M. Walker (titles); **c**, Walter Lundin; **ed**, Thomas J. Crizer.

Wichita ★★★ 1955; U.S.; 81m; AA; Color; Biographical Drama/Western; Children: Unacceptable; **DVD**. Superior biopic is set in 1874 when former buffalo hunter Wyatt Earp (1848-1929), played by McCrea, arrives in the lawless cattle town of Wichita, Kansas. His skills as a gunfighter make him a perfect candidate when town elders ask him to be the new town marshal, but he refuses the job. When things get really out of control with lawlessness, he decides he has to bring law and order to the town. He immediately prohibits guns from being carried in town and jails the rowdy trail crew of Sande's ranch for tearing up the town after they return from a Texas cattle drive. The town banker, Coy, the mayor, Reid, and others think McCrea has gone too far, but he won't rescind his strict rules of law enforcement. Coy then turns against him until his wife, Clarke, is shot dead. A saloon owner, Buchanan, plots to have McCrea killed, but McCrea gets help from his brothers Jim Earp (1841-1929) played by Smith, and Morgan Earp (1851-1882), played by Graves, and a local reporter, William "Bat" Masterson (1853-1921), played by Larsen. McCrea is also supported by Coy's beautiful daughter, Miles. Buchanan enlists Sande's gunmen, Bridges and Barnes, but McCrea and his fellow lawmen overwhelm Buchanan and his men to finally bring law and order to Wichita. The gifted Tourneur takes an average western saga and turns it into a compelling and suspenseful tale, using his strong visual style and hurrying the pace of the film throughout to increase tension. McCrea gives a strong performance of the legendary lawman and is well supported by a talented cast, where Bridges is exceptional as a ruthless gunslinger. *Author's Note*: McCrea told this author that "the writers for **Wichita** took some liberties when writing the screenplay, even though Stuart Lake, who wrote the definitive biography about Wyatt Earp, was a technical adviser for the picture. Earp really began his career as a law enforcement officer in Wichita, but some of the events of that time that we show in that picture were a bit exaggerated for dramatic purposes. I believe I kept Earp's character intact. He was a stoic man of deliberate purpose and took his job seriously. He had to, if he wanted to stay alive." This was Allied Artist's first CinemaScope production. Future director Sam Peckinpah has a bit part as a bank teller in this film. Many other actors have essayed Wyatt Earp in many other films, including **The Adventures of Young Indiana Jones: Hollywood Follies**, 1994 (made-for-TV; Leo Gordon); **Alias Jesse James**, 1959 (Hugh O'Brien); **Alias Smith and Jones**, 1971-1973 (TV series; "Which Way to the O.K. Corral?," 1972 episode: Cameron Mitchell); **Alien Nation**, 1989-1990 (TV series; "Spirit of '95," 1990 episode: Mark Thomas Miller); **Appointment with Destiny**, 1971-1973 (TV series; "Showdown at O.K. Corral," 1972 episode: David H. Vowell); **Any Last Words?**, 2012 (Scott Jefferies); **The Arizonian**, 1935 (role model for Richard Dix); **Badman's Country**, 1958 (Buster Crabbe); **Bat Masterson**, 1958-1961 (TV series; Ron Hayes); **Buffalo Bill, Jr.**, 1955-1956 (TV series; "First Posse," 1955 episode: Walter Reed); **Cheyenne Autumn**, 1964 (James Stewart); **Dawn at Socorro**, 1954 (role model for James Millican); **Deadwood**, 2004-2006 (TV cable series; Gale Morgan Harold); **Death Valley Days**, 1952-1970 (TV series; "After the O.K. Corral," 1964 episode; Jim Davis); **Doc**, 1971 (Harris Yulin); **Doctor Who**, 1963-1989 (TV series; John Alderson); **Dodge City**, 1939 (role model for Errol Flynn); **Four Eyes and Six-Guns**, 1992 (made-for-TV; Fred Ward); **Frontier Marshal**, 1934 (George O'Brien as "Michael Wyatt"); **Frontier Marshal**, 1939 (Randolph Scott); **The Gambler Returns: The Luck of the Draw**, 1991 (made-for-TV; Hugh O'Brien); **Goldrush: A Real Life Alaskan Adventure**, 1998 (made-for-TV; David Longworth); **Gun Belt**, 1953 (James Millican); **Gunfight at the O. K. Corral**, 1957 (Burt Lancaster); **Gunmen of Rio Grande**, 1965 (Guy Madison); **Guns of Paradise**, 1988-1990 (TV series; Hugh O'Brien); **Hannah's Law**, 2012 (made-for-TV; Greyston Holt); **Horse Opera**, 1993 (made-for-TV; Rik Mayall); **Hour of the Gun**, 1967 (James Garner); **I Married Wyatt Earp**, 1983 (made-for-TV; Bruce Boxleitner); **Law and Order**, 1932 (role model for Walter Huston); **The Life and Legend of Wyatt Earp**, 1955-1961 (TV series; Hugh O'Brien); **Masterson of Kansas**, 1954 (Bruce Cowling); **Maverick**,

Herbert Marshall, Faith Brook, Arlene Dahl and Philip Carey in *Wicked as They Come*, **1957**.

1957-1962 (TV series; "Marshal Maverick," 1962 episode: Med Flory); **My Darling Clementine**, 1946 (Henry Fonda); **The Outlaws Is Coming**, 1965 (Bill Camfield); **Pistols 'n' Petticoats**, 1966-1967 (TV series; "Shootout at O.K. Corral," 1966 episode: Roy Engel); **The Secret World of Eddie Hodges**, 1960 (made-for-TV; Hugh O'Brien); **Sunset**, 1988 (James Garner); **Stories of the Century**, 1954 (TV series; "Doc Holliday," 1954 episode: James Craven); **Tombstone**, 1993 (Kurt Russell); **Tombstone: The Town Too Tough to Die**, 1942 (Richard Dix); **Wagon Train**, 1957-1965 (TV series; "The Silver Lady," 1965 episode: Don Collier); **Wild Bill Hickok**, 1923 (Bert Lindley); **The Wild West**, 2006-2007 (TV miniseries; "The Gunfight at the O.K. Corral," 2007 episode: Liam Cunningham); **Winchester '73** (Will Geer); **Wyatt Earp**, 1994 (Kevin Costner); **Wyatt Earp: Return to Tombstone**, 1994 (made-for-TV; Hugh O'Brien); **Wyatt Earp's Revenge**, 2012 (Val Kilmer as old Earp; Shawn Roberts as Earp in 1878); and **You Are There**, 1953-1957 (TV series; "The Gunfight at the O.K. Corral," 1955 episode; Robert Bray). **p**, Walter Mirisch, Richard V. Heermance; **d**, Jacques Tourneur; **cast**, Joel McCrea, Vera Miles, Lloyd Bridges, Wallace Ford, Edgar Buchanan, Peter Graves, Keith Larsen, Carl Benton Reid, John Smith, Robert Wilke, Jack Elam, Mae Clarke, Walter Sande, Rayford Barnes; **w**, Daniel B. Ullman (based on his story); **c**, Harold Lipstein (CinemaScope, Technicolor); **m**, Hans Salter; **ed**, William Austin; **art d**, David Milton; **set d**, Joseph Kish.

Wicked as They Come ★★★ 1957; U.K.; 94m; Frankovich Productions/COL; B/W; Drama; Children: Unacceptable. The beautiful Dahl gives a top-notch performance as one of the most artful vixens on film in this fascinating tale of a young woman with ruthless ambitions. She begins her climb to riches by entering a beauty contest, using her wiles to have Kossoff, the elderly manager of the show, to fix the results so that she wins the grand prize, a paid trip to Europe. Afterward, Dahl promptly drops Kossoff and flies to London. (Her scheming vengeance against the opposite sex is early on displayed when she states: "You tried to buy me...with the contest. You men just don't like it, do you, when your dirty game is played back!") During the flight to London, she meets handsome Carey, and, though she is attracted to him, she sets her sights on Goodliffe, a well-healed photographer, who falls head over heels for her. After she accepts his proposal, she uses his credit card to buy a wedding dress and many other expensive items. She then pawns all of these goods for cash and jilts Goodliffe. She then goes back to Carey and gets a job at the advertising firm where Carey works. Dahl then sets covetous eyes on the firm's manager, Marshall, who is a happily married man. Marshall then falls hopelessly in love with Dahl, who demands that he divorce his wife, Brook, whose father, Truman, owns the agency. Brook, desperate to save her marriage, tries to pay off Dahl

Jean Parker, Charles Bickford and Mady Christians in *A Wicked Woman*, 1934.

to leave her husband alone. Dahl, instead, transfers to the agency's Paris office where she promptly seduces Truman, who marries her. Dahl now believes she has achieved her goal in life, living in the lap of luxury, but she becomes frightened when a stalker begins threatening her through the mails and over the phone (not unlike the kind of torturous harassment Doris Day undergoes in **Midnight Lace**, 1960, as she is stalked by a unknown killer). When Dahl believes that the stalker has entered her home, she uses a gun to shoot and kill the intruder, but it turns out to be Truman, her husband. She is charged with murder and, after no one believes the story of the stalker, she is convicted and sentenced to death. Carey, however, who has always loved Dahl, looks into her past. He explains to authorities how Dahl had been assaulted as a young girl and had been cruelly treated by men thereafter, causing her to develop a loathing for men and where she took emotional revenge upon them. The emotionally injured Goodliffe, who had been earlier jilted by Dahl, then softens his heart toward the traumatized Dahl and admits that he had been stalking her to the point where she was frightened for her life and rashly killed Truman by mistake. This confession causes Dahl's death sentence to be commuted to a lighter sentence. Dahl is not only grateful to Carey for saving her life, but expresses true love for him, hoping that when she is released they might make a life together. Hughes does a fine job helming this intriguing tale, and Dahl surprises by giving one of her best performances. Dahl had been a star at MGM but had been cast in roles where she was little more than attractive window-dressing. Here she has a role that allows her to show her wide range of acting abilities and where she essays an unforgettable femme fatale. *Author's Note*: Marshall recalled this film when stating to this author: "My role in **Wicked as They Come** was not unlike the part I played in **The Letter** [1940] where I was the cuckolded husband of Bette Davis, a man so hopelessly in love with his wife that he cannot envision her possibly betraying him for another man. She murders that man and he still goes on believing in her innocence. That was the kind of emotionally blind person I played in **Wicked as They Come**. I must admit that Arlene [Dahl is so stunningly beautiful that any man, let alone my character, would turn to putty in her hands, and, of course, I do, wrecking my own marriage and getting nothing in return but the old heave-ho." This film is also known as **Portrait in Smoke**. The film was shot on location in London. **p**, M.J. Frankovich, Maxwell Setton; **d**, Ken Hughes; **cast**, Arlene Dahl, Philip Carey, Herbert Marshall, Michael Goodliffe, Ralph Truman, David Kossoff, Faith Brook, Sidney James, Frederick Valk, Patrick Allen, Marvin Kane, Jacques B. Brunius, Larry Cross; **w**, Hughes, Sigmund Miller (story by Robert Westerby, based on a novel *Portrait in Smoke* by Bill S. Ballinger); **c**, Basil Emmott; **m**, Malcolm Arnold; **ed**, Max Benedict; **art d**, Donald M. Ashton; **set d**, Terence Morgan II.

The Wicked Lady ★★★ 1946; U.K.; 104m; Gainsborough/UNIV; B/W; Adventure/Crime Drama; Children: Unacceptable; **DVD**; **VHS**. Exciting tale sees Lockwood as a 17th-century British beauty, who is bored with her aristocratic life. To enliven her dull life, she becomes a highway robber and has an affair with Mason, a fellow highwayman. After they become partners in crime, Aylmer, an aging Lockwood family servant, discovers Lockwood's double life and she kills him before he can disclose her covert lifestyle. She then kills a farmer in her attempt to steal a gold shipment. Although Lockwood loves Rennie, he abandons her to marry Roc. Lockwood steals Rennie from Roc, but, when satiated with her emotional victory, Lockwood then marries Mason. After Mason is arrested for being a highwayman, he is sentenced to death, but, before he can be hanged, rioters save him. Lockwood kills again and is bound to meet a bad end, which she does. The jilted Rennie shoots her, but she escapes on horseback to continue her wicked ways. Arliss provides a lot of stimulating action in this saga, and Lockwood and Mason are exceptional in their daring roles. This film was enormously popular in England, proving to be a top box office success in its initial release. This story was remade in 1983, but with disappointing results. Songs: "Love Steals Your Heart" (Hans May, Alan Stranks); "Highwayman's Song" (Hubert Bath); "Courante," "Wedding Music," "Gigue," "Minuet," "Rondeau," "Christening Hymn" (Henry Purcell); "The Barley Mow" (traditional); "Down Among the Dead Men" (traditional). *Author's Note*: Mason told this author that "The reason why **The Wicked Lady** was so successful is because the legends of highwaymen are as popular in England as your gunfighters of the Old West are in America. Our highwaymen have always been presented as romantic figures defying authority, but, in truth, they were nothing much more than a lot of murderous thugs. For them to be attractive in pictures they must be shown to have some nobility and saving graces and that's where actors like me come in." The role played by Lockwood is based upon Lady Katherine Ferrers (1634-1660), who was known as the "Wicked Lady," and who terrorized the countryside of Hertfordshire when committing many daring robberies. She undertook these daring raids to replenish the funds of her dwindling estate and legend has it that she fell in love with an accomplice named Ralph Chaplin, who was caught and executed on the night Ferrers was killed in a running gunfight. For more details about this extraordinary woman, see my eight-volume work *Encyclopedia of World Crime*, Vol. II (CrimeBooks, Inc., 1990; page 1152). This film was thought to be risqué at the time it was released in the U.S., and Hollywood censors insisted that some of the scenes showing plunging cleavages for Lockwood and Roc be reshot, which they were. Violence prohibits viewing by children. **p**, R.J. Minney; **d**, Leslie Arliss; **cast**, Margaret Lockwood, James Mason, Michael Rennie, Patricia Roc, Griffith Jones, Felix Aylmer, Enid Stamp-Taylor, Jean Kent, Francis Lister, Martita Hunt; **w**, Arliss, Aimee Stuart, Gordon Glennon (based on the novel *The Life and Death of the Wicked Lady Skelton* by Magdalen King-Hall); **c**, Jack E. Cox; **m**, Hans May; **ed**, Terence Fisher; **art d**, John Bryan.

A Wicked Woman ★★★ 1934; U.S.; 72m; MGM; B/W; Drama/Romance; Children: Unacceptable. This well-made melodramatic tearjerker begins with Christians, who is close to delivering her fourth child when Harvey, her abusive and alcoholic husband, leaves her in Louisiana, taking their money with him. She goes after Harvey and, while Christians is protecting her children, he is killed in a struggle with him. She tries to cover his death by dumping his body in a swamp and keeps his death a secret. Christians goes back to town and finds work, but Jennings, the local sheriff, comes looking for Harvey, so Christians moves to another town and changes her last name. She starts a sewing business at home and eventually opens a dress shop. She rears her children to be tough but honest and intends one day to confess that she killed her husband and stand trial. Ten years pass, however, and the children grow up and all find good jobs, and romance reenters Christians' life when she falls in love with newspaper reporter Bickford. She eventually gives herself up and stands trial, but her now-grown children, Parker, Henry, and Furness, testify that she was trying to protect them when she killed Harvey and their moving testimony brings about Christians' acquittal, the jury deciding that she killed her husband in self-defense. The syrupy story is redeemed through the strong performance of Christians, a talented Viennese actress, who stunningly underplays her much victimized character. Songs: "Oh Susanna" (1846; Stephen Foster), Old Folks at Home/Swanee River" (1851; Stephen Foster), "My Old Kentucky Home" (1853; Stephen Foster), "In Louisiana " and "In the Hash" (1935; Burton Lane), "Swing Low, Sweet Chariot" (Wallis Willis), "The Wedding March" from "A Midsummer Night's Dream" (1843; Felix Mendelssohn-Bartholdy). *Author's Note*: This was one of Robert Taylor's first roles in a feature film where he plays a young cad wooing Parker. Taylor told this author: "I was just starting out then, in 1934, the year I broke into pictures, and my part in **A Wicked Woman** called for me to be a bit of a rake trying to take advantage of a naïve young lady [Parker]. I got a bigger break the following year when I played opposite the wonderful Irene Dunne in **Magnificent Obsession** [1936], but I was still getting hammered by critics who called me a flash-in-the-pan. Not until I appeared with the great Greta Garbo in **Camille** [1936] did the critics think me worthy of their attention. We were always at the mercy of the critics, some of whom dipped their pens in poison and others used them as daggers aimed at our throats." **p**, Harry Rapf; **d**, Charles Brabin; **cast**, Mady Christians, Jean Parker, Charles Bickford, Betty Furness, William Henry, Jackie Searle, Betty Jane Graham, Paul Harvey, DeWitt Jennings, Samuel S. Hinds, Charles Lane, Sterling Holloway, Georgie Billings; **w**, Florence Ryerson, Zelda Sears, Maurine Dallas Watkins (based on the book by Anne Austin). **c**, Lester White; **m**, William Axt, **ed**, Ben Lewis; **art d**, Cedric Gibbons.

The Wicker Man ★★★ 1975; U.K.; 102m; British Lion/WB; Color; Horror/Mystery; Children: Unacceptable (MPAA: R); **BD**; **DVD**; **VHS**; **IV**. Bizarre and savage, this terror tale is set in Scotland, where Woodward is an unmarried, aging police sergeant and lay Christian minister. He receives a photograph of a girl, Cowper, in his mail, along with a note that reports that she is missing. Woodward travels to the remote island community from which Cowper is reported missing to search for her, but no one there ever heard of her. He discovers that the islanders practice a form of Celtic paganism and, to his horror, that he is their next intended victim at a May Day festival. The inhabitants plan to sacrifice him to appease the sun god that has caused their crops to fail. Woodward is attacked at the festival, stripped, and dressed in ceremonial robes, then led to a cliff where he is locked inside a giant, hollow statue of a wicker man, an effigy used in human sacrifice by the ancient Gauls. The islanders fear that the true God has deprived them of their harvest because of their paganism. As the wicker man is set afire, Woodward prays to God for ascension to heaven and screams the name of Jesus Christ as he mercilessly perishes. A grim and uncompromising horror story, there is little or no redemption, but the story is so well enacted and written that it captivates throughout. This film was remade in 2006, with a sequel, **The Wicker Tree**, in 2011. Songs: "Corn Rigs," "Gently Johnny," "Willows Song," "Maypole Song," "Tinker Of Rye," "The Landlord's Daughter," "Chop Chop," "Fire Leap" (Paul Giovanni);"Summer Is Icumen In" (traditional). Violence prohibits viewing by children. **p**, Peter Snell; **d**, Robin Hardy; **cast**, Edward Woodward, Christopher Lee, Diane Cilento, Britt Ekland, Geraldine Cowper, Lindsay Kemp, Russell Waters, Aubrey Morris, Irene Sunters, Walter Carr; **w**, Anthony Shaffer; **c**, Harry Waxman (Eastmancolor); **m**, Paul Giovanni; **ed**, Eric Boyd-Perkins; **art d**, Seamus Flannery.

Widow's Peak ★★★ 1994; U.K./Ireland; 102m; British Screen Productions; Color; Comedy/Mystery; Children: Unacceptable (MPAA: PG); **DVD**; **VHS**; **IV**. This well-made comedy is set in 1920s Dublin, Ireland, where Richardson moves into a neighborhood called "Widows' Peak." The area is thus called because most of the husbands of the fe-

Jim Broadbent, Joan Plowright and Mia Farrow in *Widow's Peak*, 1994.

male inhabitants are deceased. The residents are curious about the new arrival, but, try as they may, find it next to impossible to learn anything about her. Not even the leader of the group, the busybody Plowright, can get any details about Richardson's past, even though her son, Dunbar, is dating Richardson. It doesn't help that Farrow and Richardson form an immediate dislike for each other as they vie for Dunbar's attentions. Richardson soon begins to feel as if Farrow is trying to ruin her and spoil her relations with Dunbar. The mystery becomes the area's chief and abiding obsession, until it is finally resolved when a family secret is revealed. Well directed and acted, this tale sustains interest throughout. Songs: "I'll Be Your Sweetheart" (Henry Dacre), "The Sweetheart of Sigma Chi" (F. Dudleigh Vernor, Byron D. Stokes), "Mother Machree" (Ernest Ball, Chauncey Olcott, Rida Johnson Young). Mature themes and gutter language prohibit viewing by children. **p**, Jo Manuel, Prudence Farrow, Tracey Seaward; **d**, John Irvin; **cast**, Mia Farrow, Joan Plowright, Natasha Richardson, Adrian Dunbar, Jim Broadbent, Anne Kent, John Kavanagh, Rynagh O'Grady, Gerard McSorley, Michael James Ford; **w**, Hugh Leonard (based on his story); **c**, Ashley Rowe; **m**, Carl Davis; **ed**, Peter Tanner; **prod d**, Leo Austin; **art d**, Richard Elton, David Wilson; **spec eff**, Gerry Johnston, Craig Chandler.

Wife, Husband and Friend ★★★ 1939; U.S.; 80m; FOX; B/W; Comedy/Romance; Children: Acceptable; **DVD**. This delightful comedy begins with attractive Young, a New York socialite, who has aspirations of becoming an opera singer. She is being trained by lecherous voice teacher Romero, who knows Young has limited talent, but nevertheless encourages her training in order to receive lucrative fees as well as the opportunity of bedding this curvaceous wife. Her husband, Baxter, a down-to-earth building contractor, rightly thinks that Young has only mediocre singing talent, but he grudgingly encourages her. Barnes, an opera star, who is attracted to Baxter, on the other hand, convinces him that *he* has an outstanding singing voice and should become an opera star. He secretly takes singing lessons and then appears in some showcase concerts where all politely praise his throaty performances, so much so that Barnes insists that Baxter appear with her in a grand opera. Now it is Baxter's head that is ballooned to vainglorious proportions and he egotistically thinks he is ready for the big time. He appears in that opera, but his clumsiness and ineptitude make him a laughing stock, not to mention embarrassing the posturing Barnes to the point of hysteria (these scenes are absolutely hilarious). Booed off the stage in his professional debut, Baxter and Young come to their senses, realizing that they will never become opera stars. They are relieved and happier than ever in seeing that their best dream is their happiness together. Young and Baxter are outstanding as a married couple out of

Myrna Loy, Clark Gable and Jean Harlow in *Wife vs. Secretary,* **1936.**

their professional depth and Barnes is also exceptional as the opera diva who thinks she knows where all talent resides. Their standout performances can be largely credited to the firm helming of director Ratoff, who specialized in pleasant comedies like this one, which was a hit at the box office. The story was adapted for the radio by Lux Radio Theater, aired on April 28, 1941, with George Brent, Priscilla Lane and Gail Patrick essaying the roles of Baxter, Young and Barnes. The film was remade as **Everybody Does It**, 1949. Songs: "Drink from the Cup of Tomorrow" and "Arlesiana" (Samuel Pokrass, Walter Bullock), "Songs My Mother Taught Me" (Antonin Dvorak, Natalie MacFarren), "On the Road to Mandalay" (Oley Speaks, Rudyard Kipling), "Beyond the Blue Horizon" (Richard A. Whiting, W. Franke Harling, Leo Robin). *Author's Note*: The unlikely author for this good comedy was James M. Cain, who was known for his hard-hitting crime novels and short stories, and who was paid $8,000 for the film rights for this story. Cain later admitted that he was the actual role model for the Baxter character in this story as Cain had a good baritone voice and had trained as an opera singer, and he often inserted characters in his tales with operatic backgrounds. Myna Loy was first cast in the role that later went to Young, who resented getting hand-off roles, telling this author: "Although I enjoyed making **Wife, Husband and Friend**, I was tired of being at the mercy of Fox or any other studio that could use you as a replacement for some Hollywood star and where you had to pick up their discarded roles. I decided about that time that I would become an independent actress and I did a short time later. Darryl Zanuck, who ran Fox, told me that I was ruining my career and that I would go nowhere unless I was under contract to some studio. Well, his predictions were wrong. I did fine on my own." And that also meant that Young won an Oscar as an independent actress when she appeared in **The Farmer's Daughter**, 1947. When remaking this film in 1949, director-writer Nunnally Johnson told this author: "The original script for **Wife, Husband and Friend** was so tautly written that I hardly changed a word when I wrote the screenplay for the remake under the title of **Everybody Does It**. The remake starred Paul Douglas, Linda Darnell and Celeste Holm. Douglas was very good in playing the part Baxter had done, although I always had fond memories for Baxter, who did a great job playing Dr. Samuel Mudd [1833-1883] in John Ford's **The Prisoner of Shark Island** [1936], and I wrote the script for that one, too." p, Darryl F. Zanuck, Nunnally Johnson; d, Gregory Ratoff; cast, Loretta Young, Warner Baxter, Binnie Barnes, Cesar Romero, Robert Kellard, George Barbier, J. Edward Bromberg, Eugene Pallette, Helen Westley, Ruth Terry, Renie Riano; w, Johnson (based on the novel *Two Can Sing* by James M. Cain); c, Ernest Palmer; m, Charles Maxwell; ed, Walter Thompson; art d, Richard Day, Mark-Lee Kirk; set d, Thomas Little.

Wife vs. Secretary ★★★★ 1936; U.S.; 88m; MGM; B/W; Drama; Children: Acceptable; **DVD**; **VHS**; **IV**. This thoroughly absorbing, sophisticated drama from pantheon director Brown sees sterling performances from Gable, Harlow and Loy. Gable is a hard-driving magazine publisher who is deeply in love with his wife, Loy. His high-pressure job demands that he have a capable and reliable secretary available to him at all times, and that devoted employee is the alluring Harlow. Gable and Loy are celebrating their third anniversary of wedded bliss, and he gives her a stunning diamond bracelet (which he has hidden in a brook trout that Loy is about to eat). Robson, who is Gable's protective and meddling mother, thinks that Harlow is too much of a temptation for her son and warns Loy that the efficient secretary poses a threat to her marriage. Loy has heard this before from Robson and others, but her rock-steady devotion to Gable remains undisturbed as she believes that Gable will never stray from her side. Stewart, who is crazy about Harlow and wants to marry her, suspects, like Robson, that Harlow's relationship with Gable is much too cozy and objects to Harlow's close association with her boss, especially when Gable calls her one evening and asks her to work with him on the very evening that he and Loy are celebrating their anniversary. Stewart asks Harlow to marry him, but she refuses as she is much too consumed in her work, and this convinces Stewart that Harlow secretly loves her boss. Following an argument, they break up. Meanwhile, Gable tries to buy Barbier's publication and is very secretive about his business dealings so that his competitors will not know about the transaction. He even keeps Loy in the dark about these dealings, allowing only Harlow to know about and attend his meetings with Barbier. When he returns from his meeting with Barbier, Gable tells Loy that he has been at his club, but Loy discovers that that is not the case. When Loy gets sick and cannot attend a skating party, Gable and Harlow innocently go skating together. When this is reported to Loy, she begins to suspect that the rumors she hears from friends that her husband is having an affair with Harlow might be a reality. When they get into a car, Loy tells Gable that he should arrange for Harlow to work at another firm, but Gable angrily refuses, insisting that Harlow is one of his best employees. Loy and Gable argue and Loy then coldly treats Gable for the rest of the evening, until she has second thoughts and becomes once more the loving if not completely trusting wife. Gable, realizing that he has been ignoring Loy, makes up with her when he proposes that they take another honeymoon trip alone together. Loy is ecstatic that her husband thinks only of her, but she is jarred when hearing from Gable that he must postpone that vacation since he must now make a hurried business trip to Havana, Cuba. Gable has learned that Barbier is about to sell his publication there and Gable flies off alone to make the acquisition. He then summons Harlow to follow him so that she can help him close the deal. They are successful and, after Gable buys Barbier's publication, he and Harlow celebrate, but have too much to drink and flirt dangerously together. Gable, however, nobly keeps his distance. Loy, at this time, calls Gable, and Harlow answers the phone. Loy is stunned to realize that Harlow is in Cuba with her husband and is now utterly convinced that the blonde secretary is trysting with her husband. When Gable returns to New York City, he finds Loy demanding a divorce. She tells him that she is leaving and books passage on a ship sailing for Europe. Before the liner leaves the dock, however, Harlow arrives to tell Loy that she is foolish and that her husband has never really strayed from her side, but that, if she does not take action, she will, indeed, lose Gable forever. When Harlow returns to her office, she finds Gable, who, depressed and angry, tells her that he is going to Bermuda and, if she wants to go with him, she had better quickly pack her bags. That is not necessary as Loy suddenly appears and rushes into Gable's welcoming arms and where the couple are now reunited in an even stronger bond of caring trust. Harlow departs, only to find the ever patient Stewart waiting for her and she leaves with him, ostensibly to make a new life with this persistent suitor. The viewer is left to wonder if Harlow is truly in love with Gable, but that matters not, as he remains a husband jarred back into a happy marriage with the inimitable Loy. Brown does a marvelous job in keeping this domestic tale from sinking into a vast sea of sudsy melodrama, presenting terse scenes at a fast pace while still maintaining well-defined character development. Gable and Harlow (in their fifth out of six films together) work well together, but their chemistry is that of brother and sister rather than the kind of torrid romances they exhibited in earlier films such as **Red Dust**, 1932, **Hold Your Man**, 1933, and **China Seas**, 1935. Gable and Loy, on the other hand (in their fourth out of seven films together) are exceptional as a loving couple who will not give up on each other. The film was a great box office hit, earning more than $2 million in its initial release against a budget of more than $500,000. Songs: "Thank You for a Lovely Evening" (1934; Jimmy McHugh), "Happy Birthday to You" (1893; Mildred J. Hill, Patty S. Hill), "She Was Poor But She Was Honest" (1930; music: R.P. Weston; lyrics: Bert Lee), "At Dawning" (1906; Charles Wakefield Cadman), "Pack Up Your Troubles in Your Old Kit Bag and Smile, Smile, Smile!" (1915; music: Felix Powell; lyrics: George Asaf), "Skater's Waltz" (1882; Emile Waldteufel), "Crack the Whip" (Carl Maria von Weber), "Peanut Vendor" (1927; Moises Simons), "Mama Inez" (1931; music: Eliseo Grenet; lyrics: L. Wolfe Gilbert), "Ay-Ay-Ay" (1913; Osman Perez Freire), "Cuban Love Song" (1931; Dorothy Fields, Jimmy McHugh, Herbert Stothart). *Author's Note*: Harlow was delighted to act in this film as she had been badgering MGM to put her into films where she was not playing oversexed platinum blondes. Here she gets to act as a normal lady wanting to do a good job as an efficient secretary, and the studio allowed her to tone down her hair color. She is not out to vamp anyone in this pleasing tale and proves it in one scene by good-heartedly putting an inebriated Gable to bed without a touch of sensuality, all due to the good taste direction of Brown. Loy told this author that "**Wife vs. Secretary** was one of the best sexy pictures I ever made, especially because all of its sex is subtly suggested and where good taste abounded. I 'abounded' a lot with Clark in that picture, but, even though we are playing a married couple, the closest thing we came to 'abounding' was talking through a door about what we might have done together the night before. Today, everything is on the table and there is no mystery to romance, only flesh about to be chopped up and served without dressing to the viewers." Brown stated to this author that "I had a great script to work with when we made that picture. The writers loaded it with wit and humor and all of the players were likeable adults who are fond of one another, even though there is a suggested affair running through the entire story. I could not have had better people than Clark [Gable], Jean [Harlow] and Minnie [Loy] when we made that picture." Stewart told this author that "I was playing the third wheel in **Wife vs. Secretary**, the kind of part they routinely gave me at MGM for years. Four years after we made that picture I was still playing the third wheel in **The Philadelphia Story** [1940, and Stewart won an Oscar as Best Actor for playing that third wheel], only that time I was not trying to marry Jean Harlow but Katharine Hepburn and where I lose out to Cary [Grant] instead of Clark [Gable]. Who could ever compete with those handsome fellows? Anyway, I got to kiss Jean Harlow in **Wife vs. Secretary**, and, in fact, I purposely botched that smooching scene several times so that Clarence [Brown] demanded that we reshoot it. I was dizzy for days after that." **p**, Hunt Stromberg; **d**, Clarence Brown; **cast**, Clark Gable, Jean Harlow, Myrna Loy, May Robson, George Barbier, James Stewart, Hobart Cavanaugh, Tom Dugan, Gilbert Emery, Marjorie Gateson, Gloria Holden, John Qualen; **w**, Norman Krasna, Alice Duer Miller, John Lee Mahin (based on the novel by Faith Baldwin); **c**, Ray June; **m**, Herbert Stothart, Edward Ward; **ed**, Frank E. Hull; **art d**, Cedric Gibbons.

Wild at Heart ★★★ 1990; U.S.; 125m; PolyGram Filmed Entertainment/Samuel Goldwyn; Color; Crime Drama; Children: Unacceptable (MPAA: N-17); **BD**; **DVD**; **VHS**. Weird romantic drama sees Dern and Cage as lovers in North Carolina who are separated when he is jailed for killing Dandridge, a man who attacked him with a knife. Ladd, Dern's mother, who hates Cage, had hired Dandridge to kill him. After

Nicolas Cage and Willem Dafoe in *Wild at Heart*, 1990.

Cage serves a term in prison, Dern meets him and they go to a hotel and make love. They then go to a nightclub and Cage gets into a fight with a man who flirts with Dern. It seems that wherever they go in their area, violence follows. They decide to run away to California, which breaks Cage's parole. Ladd hires Stanton, her boyfriend, who is a private detective, to find them and bring them back. She also hires Freeman, a gangster, to track them and kill Cage. Freeman's minions capture and kill Stanton, sending Ladd into a psychosis fueled by guilt. Meanwhile, Dern and Cage witness an automobile accident in which a young woman, Fenn, dies in front of them and they consider it a bad omen. They are broke, so they head for Big Tuna, Texas, where Cage contacts an old friend, Rossellini, who might help them, although Dern believes that Rossellini is under contract by her mother to kill Cage. Needing money, Cage joins gangster Dafoe in robbing a feed store. Dern waits for him in a hotel room, trying to hide the fact that she is pregnant with Cage's child. The robbery goes wrong when Dafoe shoots two clerks in the store. Sheriff's deputies arrive and open fire on Dafoe who accidentally blows his own head off with his shotgun. Cage is arrested and sentenced to five years in prison. While Cage is in prison, Dern gives birth to their son. When Cage is released from prison, Dern reunites once more with him, again against Ladd's strong objections. But Cage now thinks he is no good for Dern or their child and says he will leave them both, for their own good. He then encounters a gang of men who surround him. He insults them and they knock him out. While unconscious, he sees a vision of Glinda, the good witch from *The Wizard of Oz*, who tells him not to turn away from love. When he awakens, he apologizes to the men who beat him, then runs after Dern. While driving his car back to them, there is a traffic jam and Cage runs over the roofs and hoods of the stalled cars to get back to Dern and their son. This strange but compelling tale of lowlifes is well enacted and directed (albeit it appears that Cage, Stanton and others compete to present the most oddball characterizations). The film earned more than $14.5 million in its initial release against a budget of $10 million. Not related to a 2006 film with the same title. Songs: "Slaughter House" (Joel DuBay, Jeffrey Litke, Adrian Liberty); "In the Mood" (Joe Garland); "Love Me" (Jerry Leiber, Mike Stoller); "First Movement" (Duke Ellington, Ray Brown); "Chrysanthemum" (Shony Alex Braun); "Streamline" (John Ewing, Charles Tomas, Charles Lane, Jesse Sailes, Russell Weathers); "Smoke Rings" (Ned Washington, H.E. Gifford); "Up in Flames" (David Lynch, Angelo Badalamenti); "Buried Alive" (Billy Swan); "Avant du mourir" (Shony Alex Braun); "Far Away Chant" (A. Maxwell, M. William); "Love Me Tender" (Elvis Presley, Vera Matson); "In Abendrot" (from "Four Last Songs"; music: Richard Strauss; lyrics: Joseph Freiherr von Eichendorff); "Baby Please Don't Go" (Joe Williams); "Boomada" (Les Baxter); "Be-Bop-a-Lu-La" (Gene Vincent, Tex Davis); "Kosmogonia"

Jeff Bridges as Wild Bill Hickok and Ellen Barkin as Calamity Jane in *Wild Bill*, 1995.

(Krzysztof Penderecki); "Wicked Game," "Blue Spanish Sky," "In the Heat of the Jungle" (Chris Isaak); "Wrinkles" (Lafayette Leake). Violence and gutter language prohibit viewing by children. **p**, Steve Golin, Monty Montgomery, Sigurjon Sighvatsson; **d**, David Lynch; **cast**, Nicolas Cage, Laura Dern, Diane Ladd, Harry Dean Stanton, J.E. Freeman, Willem Dafoe, Isabella Rossellini, Sherilyn Fenn, Crispin Glover, W. Morgan Sheppard, Grace Zabriskie, Calvin Lockhart, Gregg Dandridge; **w**, Lynch (based on the novel *Wild at Heart: The Story of Sailor and Lula* by Barry Gifford); **c**, Frederick Elmes; **m**, Angelo Badalamenti; **ed**, Duwayne Dunham; **prod d**, Patricia Norris; **spec eff**, David Domeyer.

Wild Bill ★★★ 1995; U.S.; 98m; Zanuck Company/UA; Color; Biographical Drama/Western; Children: Unacceptable (MPAA: R); **DVD**. Though this film did not do well at the box office and many reviewers gave it a bad time when it was released, it nevertheless presents one of the best character studies ever presented about the legendary James Butler "Wild Bill" Hickok (1837-1876), who is wonderfully (and accurately) essayed by the talented Bridges. His past packed with gunfights, lost ambitions, fleeting women and failing eyesight, Bridges arrives in Deadwood, Dakota Territory, in 1876. He renews his friendship with roughhouse stagecoach driver Calamity Jane (1852-1903), who is aggressively played by Barkin, as well as Gammon, who plays his old friend, California Joe. Bridges' debut in this wild town is announced by Hurt, who plays "Charley Prince" (in real life his name was Charlie Utter, known as Colorado Charlie), and who narrates this tale throughout. Bridges, as usual, wears his two Colt revolvers high on his hips and everyone fears his ire, although he is affable and easygoing, as he is looking to improve his financial lot in gambling and, perhaps, the gold fields. He is immediately challenged by Jack McCall (1952-1877), played by Arquette, a youth who bears a long-standing grudge against Bridges and announces in front of a saloon crowd that he is going to kill him. Bridges slaps Arquette's face and Gammon then runs the boy out of the bar, dismissing him as nothing more than an ignorant, bragging teenager. As Bridges settles into a routine of poker playing, Hurt recalls many of his legendary feats. We see in black-and-white flashback Bridges' gunfight with Dern and Dern's brother, where Bridges kills the brother and cripples Dern for life. Dern is later shown in a wheelchair and he calls Bridges to a gunfight. Bridges responds by strapping himself to a chair (to fairly compensate Dern for his physical handicap) in the middle of the street; both pull their six-guns, and Dern is promptly shot to death (this encounter and Dern's character is pure fiction if not western hokum). In another flashback, we see Bridges attempting to reform his notorious western past by traveling East to appear in a vaudeville show run by his old friend, William F. "Buffalo Bill" Cody

(1846-1917), played by Carradine. The scene where Bridges first appears fumbling, hesitant and unsure in that show as his famous self and fails to respond from a cue from Carradine, who must repeat it before Bridges acclimates himself to a live audience, is a priceless bit of groping showmanship. (Hickok moved in 1867 to Niagara Falls, N.Y., where he attempted to make a living on the stage in a play titled "The Daring Buffalo Chasers of the Plains," but he proved to be such a miserable actor—booed from the stage several times—that he soon abandoned that profession.) Meanwhile, in flash-forward, we see Bridges entering a saloon to have a peaceful drink, but he is waylaid by a group of drunken soldiers, who attack him and where he dispatches the lot of them in a wild brawl and shootout. (This event was based on Hickok's actual encounter with troopers from the U.S. 7th Cavalry in Hays City, Kansas, on July 17, 1870; Hickok wounded trooper Jeremiah Lonergan in the knee and fatally shot trooper John Kyle.) Bridges later seeks relief by visiting a Chinese opium den where he dreams his most haunting dreams. At the same time, Arquette takes up with trollop Applegate and plots to kill Bridges at the best opportunity. A gang of killers seek to do the same thing, and compel Arquette to accompany them in that goal, but their plot goes awry and Bridges find them all in a livery stable, shooting and killing these would-be assassins, but oddly sparing the life of Arquette, who still vows to send Bridges to Boot Hill. Barkin comes to think that Arquette is not bluffing and tries to convince Bridges that Arquette's threats are real, but Bridges strangely waves off such warnings, almost inviting his self-destruction. The reason for Arquette's seething hatred for Bridges is that Bridges deserted Arquette's mother, Lane, and that Arquette is actually Bridges' illegitimate son (this contention a complete myth created by playwright Babe). Arquette eventually achieves his lethal goal by shooting Bridges in the back while he is playing poker, his last "dead man's hand" showing aces and eights. Here we see a close-up of Bridges' distorted face of flickering eyes and scowling mouth that seems to grimly express his resolve to accept his murderous fate. Hill introspectively directs this superior western as a psychiatrist might reveal layer by layer the many psychological problems of a troubled patient, carefully merging Bridges' past and present through flashbacks (in black-and-white) and flash-forward scenes. Bridges gives an outstanding performance of a man always uncomfortable with his lethal fame. He appears throughout to be annoyed by the constant reminders of that fame through the loud, laudatory comments of his friends Barkin, Gammon and narrator Hurt, all convincing heralds who chronicle Bridges' stoic journey to doom, step-by-barroom-step. The film, after savaged by reviewers, including Roger Ebert, did poor box office, earning about $2 million in its initial release against a budget of $30 million, but it deserved a much better fate. This film is not related to the 2002 and 2011 films with the same name. Songs: "The Yellow Rose of Texas" (traditional), "The Battle Hymn of the Republic" (music [1856]: William Steffe; lyrics [1862]: Julia Ward Howe). *Author's Note*: This author confronted old friend Roger Ebert after Ebert slammed this film, asking him if he had explored Hickok's past and he admitted that he had not. "I reviewed the movie, not Wild Bill Hickok," he said to me. "How can you review a biographical movie," I asked, "if you know nothing about the real-life person the actor [Bridges] represents?" He replied: "I know nothing about the Old West. I leave that to historians like you." Roger thought his point was well taken, but his point was that he just did not give a damn about Hickok's true character or whether or not Bridges had fully captured the actual complex persona of that character. In truth, Roger was always an innocent, popcorn-munching child watching and responding to biopic movies for what they flatly told him on the screen, intellectually oblivious to any true-to-life genuineness those characters might represent on that screen. He saw them all as fictional characters and believed that it was his job to interpret the worth of their theatrical credibility. Beyond that, he would not or could not go. As such, he successfully mirrored and championed millions of viewers seeking only entertainment while happily content with their own cocoon-like ignorance. This is the case with almost all living film reviewers, who, sadly, lack Ebert's superb writing abilities. The relationship between Hickok and the tempestuous, hard-drinking Calamity Jane is well captured in this film in that Hickok met and befriended Calamity Jane (Martha Jane Canary) a short time before he arrived in Deadwood, telling a friend that he had "absolutely no use" for her. Bridges repeatedly expresses his disdain for this wild woman throughout the film by fending off Barkin's passionate advances as one might shoo away a pesky fly. Calamity Jane, years after Hickok's death, claimed that she and Hickok had been secretly married, but there is no record to prove this claim. Hickok, in fact, had married Agnes Thatcher Lake, a fifty-year-old woman who owned a small circus in Cheyenne, Wyoming Territory, a short time before he moved to Deadwood in 1876, writing his last letter to her with affectionate terms shortly before he was murdered by Jack McCall. Many other actors have profiled James Butler "Wild Bill" Hickok in many other films, including **Aces and Eights**, 1936 (Karl Hackett); **Across the Sierras**, 1941 (Bill Elliott); **Adventures of Wild Bill Hickok**, 1951-1958 (TV series; Guy Madison); **Badlands of Dakota**, 1941 (Richard Dix); **Beyond the Sacramento**, 1940 (Bill Elliott); **Bronco**, 1958-1962 (TV series: "Montana Passage," 1960 episode, Charles Cooper; "One Evening in Abilene, 1962 episode: Jack Cassidy); **Buffalo Girls**, 1995 (made-for-TV; Sam Elliott); **Bullets for Bandits**, 1942 (Bill Elliott); **Calamity Jane**, 1953 (Howard Keel); **Calamity Jane**, 1963 (made-for-TV; Art Lund); **Calamity Jane**, 1984 (made-for-TV; Frederic Forrest); **Custer's Last Stand**, 1936 (serial; Allen Greer): **Dallas**, 1950 (Reed Hadley); **Deadwood**, 2004-2006 (TV series; Keith Carradine); **Deadwood Dick**, 1940 (serial; Lane Chandler); **Deadwood '76**, 1965 (Robert Dix); **Death Valley Days**, 1952-1970 (TV series; "A Calamity Called Jane," 1966 episode: Rhodes Reason); **The Devil's Trail**, 1942 (Bill Elliott); **Frontier Scout**, 1938 (George Houston); **The Great Adventure**, 1963-1964 (TV series; "Wild Bill Hickok: The Legend and the Man," 1964, Lloyd Bridges); **The Great Adventures of Wild Bill Hickok**, 1938 (Bill Elliott); **Hands across the Rockies**, 1941 (Bill Elliott); **I Killed Wild Bill Hickok**, 1956 (Tom Brown); **The Iron Horse**, 1924 (Jack Padjan); **Jack McCall, Desperado**, 1953 (Douglas Kennedy); **King of Dodge City**, 1941 (Bill Elliott); **The Last Frontier**, 1926 (J. Farrell MacDonald); **The Lawless Breed**, 1953 (Robert Anderson); **Legend**, 1995 (TV series; William Russ); **The Legend of Calamity Jane**, 1997-1998 (TV series; Clancy Brown); **The Legend of the Lone Ranger**, 1981 (Richard Farnsworth); **Little Big Man**, 1970 (Jeff Corey); **The Lone Star Vigilantes**, 1942 (Bill Elliott); **The Meant to Be's**, 2008 (made-for-TV; Jon Eric Price); **North from the Lone Star**, 1941 (Bill Elliott); **The Outlaws Is Coming!**, 1965 (Paul Shannon); **Overland Trail**, 1960 (TV series: "Westbound Stage" episode: Adam West); **Party Wagon**, 2004 (animated; made-for-TV; Dan Castellaneta voiceover); **The Plainsman**, 1936 (Gary Cooper); **The Plainsman**, 1966 (Don Murray); **Pony Express**, 1953 (Forrest Tucker); **Prairie Gunsmoke**, 1942 (Bill Elliott); **Prairie Schooners**, 1940 (Bill Elliott); **Purgatory**, 1999 (made-for-TV; Sam Shepard); **The Raiders**, 1963 (Robert Culp); **Roaring Frontiers**, 1941 (Bill Elliott); **Seven Hours of Gunfire**, 1965 (Adrian Hoven); **Son of the Renegade**, 1953 (Ewing Miles Brown); **This Is the West That Was**, 1974 (made-for-TV; Ben Murphy); **The White Buffalo**, 1977 (Charles Bronson); **Wild Bill Hickok**, 1923 (William S. Hart); **Wild Bill Hickok Rides**, 1942 (Bruce Cabot); **Wild Times**, 1980 (TV series; L. Q. Jones); **The Wildcat of Tucson**, 1940 (Bill Elliott); **The World Changes**, 1933 (Charles Middleton); **Young Bill Hickok**, 1940 (Roy Rogers); and **The Young Riders**, 1989-1992 (TV series;1992 episodes, Josh Brolin). For more details about James Butler "Wild Bill" Hickok, see my book *Encyclopedia of Western Lawmen and Outlaws* (Paragon House, 1992; pages 155-160). Sexual scenes and violence prohibit viewing by children. **p**, Lili Fini Zanuck, Richard D. Zanuck; **d**, Walter Hill; **cast**, Jeff Bridges, Ellen Barkin, John Hurt, Diane Lane, Keith Carradine, David Arquette, Christina Applegate, Bruce Dern, James Gammon, Marjoe Gortner, Luana Anders; **w**, Hill (based on the book *Deadwood* by Pete Dexter and the play "Fathers and Sons" by

Jeff Bridges as Wild Bill Hickok in *Wild Bill*, 1995.

Thomas Babe); **c**, Lloyd Ahern; **m**, Van Dyke Parks; **ed**, Freeman Davies; **prod d**, Joseph Nemec III; **art d**, Daniel Olexiewicz; **set d**, Gary Fettis; **spec eff**, Casey Cavanaugh, Lawrence J. Cavanaugh, Sean Cavanaugh, Joseph P. Mercurio.

Wild Bill Hickok ★★★ 1923 (silent); U.S.; 70m; Famous Players/PAR; B/W; Biographical Drama/Western; Children: Unacceptable. Veteran silent cowboy star Hart gives a good performance of the famous James Butler "Wild Bill" Hickok (1837-1876) in this action-packed saga. He is first shown in Washington, D.C., toward the close of the Civil War (1861-1865) and where he meets President Abraham Lincoln (1809-1865). After establishing his fame as a gunfighter, Hart decides, because of his failing eyesight, to hang up his guns and become a gambler when he moves to Dodge City. He befriends fellow lawmen William Barclay "Bat" Masterson (1853-1921), who is played by Gardner, and Wyatt Earp (1848-1929), played by Lindley. Hart also befriends the town hellion, Calamity Jane (1852-1903), played by Terry. Gang leader Farley, realizing that Hart's vision is failing, brazenly tells the deadly gunman that he has lost his nerve and challenges him, but Hart refuses to face his opponent. He meanwhile falls in love with O'Connor, but she is a married woman and Hart respectfully keeps his distance. Farley and his gang then rob a stagecoach, and Gardner and Lindley ask Hart to help them track down these desperadoes. Hart cannot refuse his old friends and joins their pursuit of Farley and his henchmen. They track down the thieves, killing and capturing them, but Farley escapes. The indefatigable Hart nevertheless tracks down the outlaw and, following a wild gun battle, shoots and kills him. Hart returns to Dodge City, but, realizing that he can never have the woman of his heart, leaves town, heading for Deadwood and a rendezvous with death. Though the script abandons historical facts—Hickok never served as a lawman in Dodge City—Hart nevertheless gives a powerful and convincing performance of the great gunfighter, full of stoic resolve to uphold the law at all costs. The film did not do well at the box office, this being the third to the last western film Hart would make. **p**, Adolph Zukor, William S. Hart; **d**, Clifford S. Smith; **cast**, Hart, Ethel Grey Terry, Kathleen O'Connor, James Farley, Jack Gardner, Carl Gerard, William Dyer, Bert Sprotte, Leo Willis, Bert Lindley; **w**, Hart, J.G. Hawks; **c**, Arthur Reeves, Dwight Warren.

The Wild Blue Yonder ★★★ 1951; U.S.; 98m; REP; B/W; War; Drama; Children: Unacceptable. Good action tale shows Corey and Tucker as Army Air Corps officers flying a B-29 Superfortress bomber during World War II (1939-1945). They are assigned to bomb a target in the South Pacific. Before they go on that hazardous mission, both compete for the affections of Ralston, a nurse. Corey begins flying as part of the program designed to test the new bomber, which can fly

Flight crew preparing to board a B-29 in *The Wild Blue Yonder*, 1951.

faster, higher and farther than any other bomber. In that test, however, Corey pushes the plane to its maximum and, while at a high altitude, it loses its air compression, bringing about a near disaster. One crewman is sucked from the plane but is saved when he parachutes safely to the ground. Upon landing, Corey is upbraided by Tucker, his superior, for exceeding test instructions and endangering the lives of his men. Brennan, the general in charge, then determines that the pilots have completed their training with the B-29s and he flies with them and their new bombers to China and then to attack Japanese targets. After flying several missions, the air group is transferred to Guam where Corey and Tucker are reunited with Ralston, who has been transferred to that base. At Guam, the aggressive General Curtis LeMay (1906-1990), who is played by Witney, decides that the bombers will be more effective at lower levels and orders carpet firebombing of major cities in Japan. In a raid on Tokyo that includes almost all available B-29s, Corey is wounded by anti-aircraft fire, but Tucker manages to fly the crippled, burning plane back to base. Corey is helped from the plane, but when Tucker goes back into the burning wreckage to save another crew member, the plane explodes, killing him. Corey and Ralston grieve over Tucker's death as they begin to make a life together. A short time later, a lone B-29 takes off from the island of Tinian to drop the atomic bomb on Hiroshima, and, a few days later, another B-29 drops another A-bomb on Nagasaki, which ends the war. In addition to a good script and top-flight acting by all, the film offers some great aerial combat footage. The film saw considerable success at the box office, earning more than $1 million in its initial release. The story was adapted for radio and aired by Lux Radio Theater on September 24, 1951, with Corey, Tucker and Ralston reprising their roles. This film is not related to the 2005, 2007 films with the same title. Songs: "The U.S. Air Force" (Robert Crawford), "The Heavy Bomber Song" (music: Victor Young; lyrics: Ned Washington), "The Man Behind the Armor-Plated Desk" (music: traditional; lyrics: Allan Dwan), "The Thing" (music: based on the traditional melody "Taylor's Boy"; lyrics: Charles R. Green). *Author's Note*: The role played by David Sharpe (as Sgt. "Red" Irwin) is based upon the real-life U.S. airman, Henry E. Erwin (1921-2002), who was flying in a B-29 over Tokyo on April 12, 1945, when a phosphorous bomb failed to release. Though terribly wounded, Erwin carried that bomb through the length of the plane to throw it from the window of the cockpit, saving the plane and its crew and for which he received the U.S. Congressional Medal of Honor. His heroic act is faithfully depicted in this film. So badly wounded was Erwin that it was believed that he would soon die after the plane landed; he was rushed to a hospital, and General LeMay and other high-ranking officers immediately approved of awarding the Medal of Honor so that Erwin would be alive to receive it. He nevertheless survived. Flown back to the U.S., he underwent forty-one surgi-

cal operations over thirty months that restored his eyesight and the use of one arm. He worked for thirty-seven years as a benefits counselor at the Veteran's Hospital in Birmingham, Alabama, until retiring. His son, Hank Erwin, became an Alabama state senator. Republic got considerable assistance from the USAF and Marine Corps when making this film. It was shot on location at March Field Air Base and the Mojave Airport Marine Base in California, and at Davis-Monthan Field in Tucson, Arizona, and Walker Air Force Base in Roswell, New Mexico. Other films depicting bomber planes include **Above and Beyond**, 1953 (U.S. B-29); **Air Force**, 1943 (U.S. B-17); **Battle of Britain**, 1969 (German Dornier, Heinkel and Junker); **The Best Years of Our Lives**, 1946 (U.S. B-17); **Black Book**, 2006 (U.S. B-17); **Bombardier**, 1943 (U.S. B-17); **Command Decision**, 1948 (U.S. B-17); **Desperate Journey**, 1942 (British Wellington); **Destination Tokyo**, 1943 (U.S. B-25); **Flying Fortress**, 1942 (U.S. B-17); **Forever Young**, 1992 (U.S. B-24); **Hiroshima**, 1995 (made-for-TV; U.S. B-29); **International Lady**, 1941 (U.S. B-17); **Johnny in the Clouds** (aka: **The Way to the Stars**), 1945 (U.S. B-17); **Memphis Belle**, 1990 (U.S. B-17); **Missing Jane**, 2004 (U.S. B-17); **One of Our Aircraft Is Missing**, 1942 (British Wellington); **Pearl Harbor**, 2001 (U.S. B-25); **Strategic Air Command**, 1955 (U.S. B-36; U.S. B-47); **Thirty Seconds Over Tokyo**, 1944 (U.S. B-25); **Tora! Tora! Tora!**, 1970 (U.S. B-17); **Twelve O'Clock High**, 1949 (U.S. B-17); **The War Lover**, 1962 (U.S. B-17); and **We'll Meet Again**, 1982 (TV miniseries; U.S. B-17). **p**, Herbert J. Yates, John H. Auer; **d**, Allan Dwan; **cast**, Wendell Corey, Vera Ralston, Forrest Tucker, Phil Harris, Walter Brennan, William Ching, Ruth Donnelly, Harry Carey Jr., Penny Edwards, Wally Cassell, James Brown, Richard Erdman, Reed Hadley, David Sharpe, Jack Kelly, Peter Coe, Jay Silverheels, William W itney, Robert Kent; **w**, Richard Tregaskis (based on a story by Andrew Geer, Charles Grayson); **c**, Reggie Lanning; **m**, Victor Young; **ed**, Richard L. Van Enger; **art d**, James W. Sullivan; **set d**, John McCarthy Jr., Charles S. Thompson; **spec eff**, Ellis F. Thackery, Howard Lydecker, Theodore Lydecker.

Wild Boys of the Road ★★★★★ 1933; U.S.; 77m; First National/WB; B/W; Drama; Children: Unacceptable; **DVD**. Pantheon director Wellman presents a shockingly realistic slice of Americana during the Great Depression (1929-1939), and Darro and Phillips give marvelous performances of youths uprooted from disintegrating families, who must now struggle for survival in a hostile and desperate world. The two boys are attending high school and live in comfortable homes. Darro and Phillips attend a school dance where girls wear evening gowns, dancing with eager boys to "The Skater's Waltz." Signs of financial discontent, however, appear almost immediately when a boy is denied admission to the dance because he lacks the needed 75¢ entry price. Further, a sense of desperation is evidenced when one of the boys finds that the gas from his jalopy has been siphoned off. Security for all of these teenagers begins to erode when Phillips later tells Darro that he is dropping out of school and will try to get a job in order to help provide his financially strapped family. Darro tells Phillips that he will ask his father, Mitchell, to give him a job, but Darro then learns that Mitchell has lost his own job and is struggling to pay pressing bills. Darro sells his jalopy for a paltry $22 to help out Mitchell, who is a loving and caring father, but this will hardly keep the family in food for a week. With their families now facing eviction, Darro and Phillips decide to leave home so that they will no longer be financial burdens to their loved ones and they hop a freight heading for Chicago, Illinois, hoping that they can find work in the Windy City. They are soon amazed to see dozens of other teenagers doing the same thing, leaping into boxcars. Along with these "wild boys of the road," they meet Coonan, a teenage girl who is dressed as a boy and has had to leave home. Coonan tells Darro and Phillips that she hopes that Gombell, her aunt in Chicago, will give her a temporary home until she can get a job. Cold, hungry and dispirited, the teenagers finally reach the vast train yards in Chicago, only to be detained by railway police. Coonan, however, shows officers a letter she has received from Gombell inviting her to live with her. The police allow her to go free, along with Darro and Phillips, after Coonan lies in saying that the two boys are her cousins. Gombell welcomes Coonan and the two boys into her home, but their stay is a brief one as Gombell has been up to no good and the teenagers flee after police raid the place. They soon return to the road, hopping another freight train going toward Cleveland, Ohio. Again, the train is packed with runaway teenagers, premature hobos trying to survive, and they are invariably met by small armies of railway workers or police wielding clubs, and the teenagers shower their oppressors with pelting rocks. At one point, firemen arrive to hose down the teenagers with powerful sprays of water that bowl over the kids. This is the kind of unsavory work the firemen do not enjoy, one of them saying: "This is a rotten trick!" Another fireman agrees, replying: "How do you think I feel with two kids of my own?" Everywhere Darro, Phillips and Coonan go, they are met with the homeless and must scrounge for morsels of food. Some of their adult persecutors are ruthless, such as Bond, a brutal train brakeman, who catches Hudson, another girl dressed as a boy, and rapes her. When the other kids learn what Bond has done, they pursue him along the top of a moving train, attacking him so that he falls to his death as the train nears Cleveland. As the train approaches the city, all of the destitute riders leap off, but Phillips strikes his head on a switch and, while half-conscious, begins crawling across some tracks, only to see an oncoming train rushing toward him. He manages to get off the rail, except for one foot, which is mangled when the train strikes him. His leg must then be amputated and he and Coonan support him as they go to live in "Sewer Pipe City." Penniless, Darro steals a prosthetic leg for Phillips, the theft and other disturbances causing city officials to drive the kids from the area. They move on, riding the rails to New York, and here they have little semblance of the decent teenagers they once were. All have lost their spirit to improve their lot, and their hope in the American dream has vanished. They are simply animals trying to find shelter and food to survive. Then Darro becomes elated when he is offered a job, but he needs $3 to buy a coat for that position. The kids begin panhandling for the needed cash. Two men then offer Darro $5 if he will deliver a note to the cashier of a nearby theater. When Darro delivers the note, the cashier and theater manager call the police and have Darro arrested as the note was a threatening demand for money. Darro, as well as Phillips and Coonan, are taken into custody and brought before a judge, Barrat. Darro lashes out at the court and officialdom in general for the way he and his friends have been treated. He shouts that all they ever wanted to do was to find decent work to regain their self-respect and dignity, and, instead, were shuttled from city to city like unwanted flotsam and jetsam. Barrat listens patiently and, after reviewing the history of these three teenagers, realizes the terrible injustices they have had to endure. He promises that Darro will get that job and that they will get help to improve their otherwise miserable lifestyle. He then dismisses all charges against them, and when the three leave the court, Darro is now overjoyed that they will now have a chance at life. So exuberant is he that he dances and cartwheels along the street and then, for a stunning climax to this outstanding film, turns himself upside down and spins wildly on his head like a top (in one of the most astounding acrobatic movements ever put on film). Wellman delivers this great film with a simple message and that is that the Depression is tearing the social fabric of America to pieces, brilliantly delineating his prosaic statement by graphically depicting the woes of a generation of displaced youths. It is a grim, unstinting and unappealing portrait, but so powerfully presented that it rivets attention in every fast-moving frame. Darro gives the performance of his life and he is wonderfully supported by Phillips, Coonan, Hudson and a bevy of other teenagers, along with a strong adult cast. Many reviewers criticized Wellman for taking a rather naïve and simplistic view of the economic strife then plaguing the country, as well as the benevolent image of Barrat (who is the visual surrogate for then President Franklin D. Roosevelt and his "New Deal" philosophy). The film was only marginally successful at the box office, but its stature over the years has rightly grown to that

Dorothy Coonan, Frankie Darro and Rochelle Hudson in *Wild Boys of the Road,* **1933.**

of a masterpiece. Songs: "The Gold Diggers' Song (We're in the Money)" (1933; Harry Warren), "In a Shanty in Old Shanty Town" (1932; music: Ira Schuster, Jack Little; lyrics: Joe Young), "Shadow Waltz" (1933; Harry Warren), "Pettin' in the Park" (1933; Harry Warren), "High Life" (1933; Harry Warren), "Forty-Second Street" (1933; Harry Warren). *Author's Note*: Wellman told this author: "I got attacked for giving **Wild Boys of the Road** a happy ending, but the odd thing is that I really wanted the judge to throw the book at the boy [Darro], sending him to a reform school and putting the other kids into a juvenile institution. The front office insisted that I give the picture an upbeat finish and I did. They were right. It saved the picture from being a completely depressing story. People need to have hope, and that includes kids, or life is not worth living anymore. That is what the public wanted more than anything back then when grown men could not afford to buy a loaf of bread and some lunch meat to feed to their families. Half the country was out of work and tens of thousands were starving to death. FDR [Franklin D. Roosevelt, 1882-1945] changed a lot of that. He put thousands of young men who had no homes to work in clean camps and where they worked in the CCC [Civilian Conservation Corps, 1933-1942]. They restored the American national parks and forest preserves. It was a wonderful program." The CCC planted more than three billion trees and restored and improved more than 800 national parks, as well as building a nation-wide network of service areas and public roadways, along with updating forest fire fighting methods. John Ford was originally asked to direct this film at the same time Wellman was approached. "Bill [Wellman] and I both talked about it," Ford told this author, "and we decided that it was better suited to Bill. He went on to make an uncompromising picture that remains in the memories of just about everyone who have ever seen it." A year after this film was released Wellman married Coonan, a union that lasted for more than forty years until his death in 1975. Many other films have profiled hobos, including **A nous la liberte**, 1931; **The Abandonment**, 1916; **Across the Bridge**, 1957; **Adventures of a Young Man**, 1962; **The Adventures of Rex and Rinty**, 1935 (serial); **Almost a Gentleman**, 1939; **Always a Bridesmaid**, 1943; **American Psycho**, 2000; **The Arkansas Traveler**, 1938; **The Assistant**, 1997; **The Ballad of Cable Hogue**, 1970; **Bank Alarm**, 1937; **Barefoot in the Park**, 1967; **The Beachcomber**, 1938; **Beggars of Life**, 1928; **Beloved Infidel**, 1959; **The Big Show-Off**, 1945; **Bindlestiffs**, 2012; **A Bird in the Bush**, 2008; **The Black Dahlia**, 2006; **Black Eagle**, 1948; **Boom Town**, 1940; **Border Incident**, 1949; **Born to Fight**, 1936; **Boulder Dam**, 1936; **Bound for Glory**, 1976; **Bowery at Midnight**, 1942; **Boxcar Bertha**, 1972; **Breakfast with Scot**, 2008; **Bruce Almighty**, 2003; **Bud Abbott and Lou Costello in Hollywood**, 1945; **Calling All Husbands**, 1940; **Central Park**, 1932; **Chronically Unfeasible**, 2000;

Ernest Borgnine, Warren Oates, William Holden and Ben Johnson in *The Wild Bunch*, 1969.

C.H.U.D., 1984; **Cinderella Man**, 2005; **City Lights**, 1931; **Come Live with Me**, 1941; **Come the Morning**, 1993; **Conflict**, 1945; **The Cosmic Monster**, 1958; **Cosmopolis**, 2012; **Crimson Gold**, 2003; **The Crossing Guard**, 1995; **Danger Lights**, 1930; **Date with Death**, 1959; **Drillbit Taylor**, 2008; **Easy Living**, 1937; **Elmer Gantry**, 1960; **Emperor of the North Pole**, 1973; **End of Days**, 1999; **Escape in the Desert**, 1945; **A Face in the Crowd**, 1957; **The Falcon Strikes Back**, 1943; **The Fighting Peacemaker**, 1926; **Flying Fists**, 1937; **The Footloose Heiress**, 1937; **Gangway for Tomorrow**, 1943; **The Gay Falcon**, 1941; **Girls on the Road**, 1940; **The Gold Rush**, 1925; **The Grapes of Wrath**, 1940; **The Great Debaters**, 2007; **Grind**, 2003; **Happenstance**, 2001; **Heaven with a Barbed Wire Fence**, 1939; **Henry and Dizzy**, 1942; **Heroes for Sale**, 1933; **Hidden Places**, 2006 (made-for-TV); **Hobo with a Shotgun**, 2011; **A Hobo's Christmas**, 1987 (made-for-TV); **I Am a Fugitive from a Chain Gang**, 1932; **The Illustrated Man**, 1969; **I'll Give a Million**, 1937; **I'm Not There**, 2007; **Into the Wild**, 2007; **Iron Sky**, 2012; **It Happened on Fifth Avenue**, 1947; **It Happened One Night**, 1934; **Joe Gould's Secret**, 2000; **Joe the King**, 1999; **The Journey of Natty Gann**, 1985; **Junior Army**, 1942; **The Kid**, 1921; **Killer: A Journal of Murder**, 1995; **King of the Underworld**, 1939; **Kisses for Breakfast**, 1941; **Kit Kittredge: An American Girl**, 2008; **La Chienne**, 1931; **Lady Killer**, 1933; **The Landloper**, 1918; **Little Caesar**, 1931; **The Little Red Schoolhouse**, 1936; **The Littlest Hobo**, 1979-1985 (TV series); **The Live Wire**, 1925; **Long Live the Hobos**, 1995; **The Lost Squadron**, 1932; **Love on a Bet**, 1936; **The Lovers on the Bridge**, 1991; **Maisie**, 1939; **The Man Who Found Himself**, 1937; **The Man Without a Past**, 2002; **The Manipulator**, 1971; **Masked and Anonymous**, 2003; **Meet John Doe**, 1941; **Melvin and Howard**, 1980; **Merrily We Live**, 1938; **Midnight Court**, 1937; **Miracle in Milan**, 1951; **Miss Nobody**, 1926; **Mr. Nobody**, 2011; **Mokey**, 1942; **The Moonlighter**, 1953; **Mountain Rhythm**, 1939; **My Man**, 1997; **My Man Godfrey**, 1936; **My Summer Vacation**, 1996; **New York, I Love You**, 2009; **Nightmare Alley**, 1947; **Oliver & Company**, 1988; **On the Road**, 2012; **On Our Merry Way**, 1948; **Our Hospitality**, 1923; **The Outfit**, 1993; **The Penalty**, 1941; **The Petrified Forest**, 1936; **Pippi**, 2006; **The Plot Thickens**, 1936; **The Polar Express**, 2004; **Prince of Darkness**, 1987; **The Rainmakers**, 1935; **Resurrecting the Champ**, 2007; **Riffraff**, 1936; **Samuel Fuller's Street of No Return**, 1991; **Scarecrow**, 1973; **Seabiscuit**, 2003; **Starlight Hotel**, 1988; **The Stratton Story**, 1949; **Sullivan's Travels**, 1941; **Superman and the Mole-Men**, 1951; **Syncopation**, 1942; **Thank You for Smoking**, 2006; **That I May Live**, 1937; **Them!**, 1954; **There Goes My Girl**, 1937; **They Wanted to Marry**, 1937; **Things That Hang from Trees**, 2006; **The Time of Your Life**, 1948; **Tombstone Terror**, 1935; **The Treasure of the Sierra Madre**, 1948;

The Trouble with Harry, 1955; **12 Monkeys**, 1995; **24 Hour Party People**, 2002; **The Ultimate Life**, 2013; **Union Depot**, 1932; **Vagabond**, 1985; **Wanda**, 1971; **The Way of All Flesh**, 1927; **The Way of All Flesh**, 1941; **Wendy and Lucy**, 2008; **Wyatt Earp**, 1994; and **Young Fugitives**, 1938. **p**, Robert Presnell, Sr.; **d**, William A. Wellman; **cast**, Frankie Darro, Edwin Phillips, Rochelle Hudson, Dorothy Coonan, Sterling Holloway, Minna Gombell, Grant Mitchell, Robert Barrat, Ward Bond, Charley Grapewin, Alan Hale, Jr., George Offerman, Jr.; **w**, Earl Baldwin (based on the story "Desperate Youth" by Daniel Ahearn); **c**, Arthur L. Todd; **ed**, Thomas Pratt; **art d**, Esdras Hartley.

The Wild Bunch ★★★★★ 1969; U.S.; 143m; WB; Color; Western; Children: Unacceptable (MPAA: R); **BD**; **DVD**; **VHS**; **IV**. Until the appearance of this brilliant landmark film there had never been a western that so accurately and excruciatingly depicted the death throes of the Old West, and in such a spectacular display of that passing period's ultra-violence. The film is set in Texas in 1913, just before the outbreak of WWI (1914-1918), where civilization has made great progress in taming the wild west of yesteryear. Holden leads a gang of aging outlaws into a small town in Texas, all disguised in the uniforms of troopers from the U.S. Cavalry. The vicious disdain for any kind of life is early on demonstrated when the gang rides past a group of children at play, grimly noticing that their childish merriment is focused upon the brutal torture of some scorpions they have trapped and are now being attacked by swarms of red ants. (This shocking scene quickly establishes the tone and temperament of the times and is emphasized by the gleeful laughter of the children, their presumed innocence utterly shattered as they sadistically enjoy the agonizing deaths of the squirming scorpions; this is a graphic analogy ignorantly lost by the adult riders as these outlaws represent those very scorpions and the red ants the ever advancing civilization that is soon to devour them.) The smiling, sweet-faced children are later shown dropping handfuls of burning straw onto the scorpions to set them on fire, horribly killing these hapless creatures, frantically quivering and quavering as their limbs crackle under the flames. It is but a gruesome game to these ignorant children, a mindless, savage exercise to edify their newly discovered power of life and death. The outlaws ride leisurely into the town, passing a group of Temperance activists led by Taylor, who loudly sermonizes against the evils of Demon Rum. Dismounting near a railroad office, the object of their mission, the outlaws withdraw their rifles and empty saddle bags. Holden accidentally bumps into a woman, knocking a package from her arms. He apologizes and Borgnine, another member of the gang, cavalierly picks up the package and returns it to her as they both escort the woman across the street to the railroad office. Watching the outlaws entering the railroad office is a number of roughneck bounty hunters led by Ryan, all lining the rooftop of a building across the street from the railroad office. Dekker, a ruthless railroad official who has hired the bounty hunters to destroy Holden and his gang in what has been a well-designed trap, orders Ryan and his men to hold their fire and "wait till they come out [of the railroad office]. Catch them in the act." He turns to Ryan and says: "Then you kill him [Holden] or go back to Yuma." Ryan grimly nods, realizing that he has little choice. Ryan had once ridden with Holden and the gang, but had been captured and sent to the prison in Yuma, Arizona. He has been released on his promise that he will track down and kill Holden and the gang, which has been plaguing Dekker and his railroad for years with countless robberies. Meanwhile, Holden, Borgnine, Sanchez, Hopkins and Oates enter the railroad office to loot it of a shipment of silver while Johnson, who is Oates' brother, and others wait outside with the horses and stand guard. A clerk asks Holden what he wants and Holden grabs him, pushing him across the room toward the office's vault, stating to his outlaw companions regarding the other workers and customers in the office: "It they move, kill 'em!" Holden, Borgnine, Oates and Sanchez quickly loot the office of its huge cache of silver, putting the heavy sacks into their saddlebags, and then leave the office, telling Hopkins to keep the workers and customers there until he is called to the street to escape from the office. Hopkins, a psychopathic killer, tells Holden that he will keep the hostages in place "until hell freezes over or you say different." Just as the Temperance group begins a parade down the main street, the gang prepares to leave and Ryan's men open fire from their perches on the rooftop, creating a mass slaughter. The citizens and Temperance activists flee in all directions, mingling with the outlaws and many of these innocent people are wantonly shot down as Holden and his companions make their escape, although some of the gang members are shot from their saddles. (This scene is reminiscent of the disastrous bank raid in Northfield, Minnesota, on September 7, 1876, by the James-Younger gang, where most of the robbers were either killed or captured, as shown in **Jesse James**, 1939, and many other films.) The outlaws ride wildly out of town, only six of them surviving their raid, including Holden, Borgnine, Oates, Johnson, Sanchez and Barnes. Blinded by gunfire, Barnes falls from his horse, calling out to Holden to keep his promise to shoot him should this very condition exist and to keep him from being captured alive. Holden hesitates, but then draws his gun and shoots and kills Barnes before he and the others ride off. (This scene duplicates the mercy killing shown in **For Whom the Bell Tolls**, 1943, when Loyalist saboteur Gary Cooper shoots a wounded companion, Feodor Chaliapin Jr., rather than see his cohort fall into the hands of the brutal enemy when they flee from Federal troops after blowing up a train during the Spanish Civil War, 1936-1939.) Johnson tells Holden that Barnes "was a good man. We should bury him." Oates agrees. Borgnine, realizing that they must make their escape, says sarcastically: "I'd like to say a few words for the dear, dear departed. Maybe a few hymns would be in order! Followed by a church supper and a choir!" The gang then rides away. Meanwhile, Hopkins, berserk with power, is seen marching his captives about in the railroad office, but, when they flee, he fires at them with a shotgun, ostensibly killing them (the captives not then seen) and saying with a maniacal grin: "They shouldn't have run!" Dekker and his bounty hunters then close in on the office and Hopkins shoots and kills a number of them before he himself is mortally wounded. Dekker stands over him and Hopkins looks up at him, full of contempt, saying: "How'd you like to kiss my sister's black cat's ass?" Dekker then shoots Hopkins to death—there is no mercy from either those upholding the law or those breaking it. In the street, bounty hunters Martin and Jones fight like vultures over the possessions they strip from the dead robbers while Dekker upbraids Ryan for botching the well-planned trap to finally destroy Holden and his gang. Ryan complains that the men Dekker has given him are nothing but inept, low-life predators, but Dekker tells him that he must do with what he has and Dekker further tells some of the bounty hunters that, if Ryan does not remain loyal to his task, they are to shoot him. By this time, Holden and the other survivors of his gang reach a Mexican farm in the desert where O'Brien, a grizzled, old henchman, has been waiting for them with fresh horses. Brothers Oates and Johnson bitterly blame Holden for not foreseeing the trap sprung by Ryan. When Holden tells old friend O'Brien that he saw Ryan with the bounty hunters, O'Brien becomes dismayed, remembering back to the old days when Ryan rode stirrup to stirrup with Holden and him. The gang members then unload their stolen sacks, opening them to find to their shock that they all contain metal washers and not the silver they thought they were robbing. Oates angrily shouts: "We shot our way out of that town for a dollar's worth of steel holes!" Holden disgustedly states: "They set it up." Oates says: "Who the hell is they?" O'Brien sees the grim folly of it all, ridiculing Oates' naïve question with: "They? They is just the plain and fancy 'they'! That's who 'they' is! Caught you, didn't they. Tied a can to your tail! Led you in and waltzed you out again! Oh my, what a bunch! Big tough ones! Here you are with a handful of holes, a thumb up your ass, and a big grin to pass the time of day with! 'They!' Who the hell is 'they'!" The gang talks about their future, which seems grim. Holden proposes that they hide across the border to Mexico and where they might plan to rob a payroll or a bank, saying: "We've got to think

William Holden and Jaime Sanchez in *The Wild Bunch,* **1969.**

beyond our guns. Those days are closing fast." The scene ends as all realize how absurd the venture has been and begin laughing uproariously. When O'Brien later makes a clumsy mistake, Johnson tells Holden that O'Brien is a liability and he intends to kill the old man. Holden explodes and tells him that he won't permit that, shouting: "When you side with a man, you stay with him! If you can't do that, you're like some animal! You're finished! We're finished! All of us!" To his surprise, Holden learns from O'Brien that Hopkins, the crazy killer left behind in the raid, had been O'Brien's grandson. O'Brien tells Holden that he never mentioned that since Holden had "enough on his mind" when leading that raid. O'Brien is content to know that Hopkins did his duty during the raid, his death acceptable under the circumstances of their dangerous profession. The gang then arrives in a Mexican village, which is Sanchez's home and where the outlaws are given food and shelter, whiling away leisurely hours as they make their plans, and where Holden nurtures an old leg wound that has worsened to the point where he finds it difficult to mount his horse. Urueta, the village elder, tells Holden and others that he and his people are much oppressed by a Mexican rogue general, Fernandez, who recently raided the village, killing all the young men and running away with Amelio, who was Sanchez's girlfriend. Urueta tells Sanchez that the girl went willingly with Fernandez and Sanchez vows to retrieve her, as well as arm his village as soon as he can obtain weapons, so that the villagers can take revenge on Fernandez. Sanchez is really a patriot by nature and inclination and not an outlaw like the gang members he accompanies. In fact, he has warned his companions not to mention what they do for a living as the villagers do not know that he has turned outlaw. It is implied that the gang will somehow aid the villagers, and when the outlaws ride from the town, the villagers now look upon them as heroic redeemers. The gang rides to Fernandez's stronghold, which is garrisoned by hundreds of heavily-armed irregular troops. The outlaws are startled to see for the first time a bright, red auto being driven into the area with Fernandez sitting smugly in the back seat, the general clutching Sanchez's former girlfriend, Amelio, who later presents a horse to the strutting general. So incensed is Sanchez at seeing his old flame in the arms of the aging Fernandez that he draws his six-gun and fires at her, killing her. Everyone is shocked into silence. Holden and his other gang members raise their hands to indicate that they have had no part in this violent act as Sanchez is seized, beaten and dragged away. Fernandez, who is being controlled by Wagner, a German officer, asks Holden and his men to have a drink with him. Fernandez, at Wagner's insistence, asks Holden if he and his men can obtain some heavy weapons for Fernandez, especially machine guns, which Fernandez says he needs to subdue an ongoing rebellion. Holden is asked to raid a U.S. Army supply train north of the border, a robbery that Fernandez cannot perform without creating an international

William Holden in *The Wild Bunch*, 1969.

incident. Holden tells Fernandez that they can do just that, but only if they are well paid. Fernandez offers Holden and his men $10,000 in gold in exchange for the weapons. Holden agrees to steal the weapons for Fernandez, but only under the condition that Sanchez is released to him and his gang members as Sanchez is needed in getting those much-wanted weapons. Fernandez agrees and the badly beaten Sanchez rejoins the gang as they ride away. Meanwhile, Ryan and his bounty hunters are searching into Mexico for Holden and his men, but Ryan realizes that his irresponsible, sleazy followers are all but useless in finding their prey. Sanchez later tells Holden that he wants his share of the payment in the form of some of the guns they are about to steal so that he can arm his villagers against Fernandez. Holden tries to talk Sanchez out of such noble notions, but Sanchez replies: "Would you give guns to someone to kill your father, or your mother, or your brother?" The cynical Holden responds: "Ten thousand [dollars] cuts an awful lot of family ties." Nevertheless, Holden agrees to give Sanchez a crate of rifles instead of his share of the gold as he and the rest of his men know full well that they cannot trust Fernandez. By this time, Ryan gets wind of the impending raid to be conducted by Holden, an attack on a train carrying U.S. Army weapons. He and his bounty hunters board that train, as do a company of regular U.S. soldiers, but Ryan knows these troopers are nothing more than "green recruits" and will be of little help in capturing the elusive Holden and his men. As the U.S. Army train moves along an overpass where Holden and his men are waiting, the outlaws secretly work their way onto the train, taking over the engine and uncoupling the flatcar containing the arms shipment so that the passenger coaches carrying Ryan and his bounty hunters and another coach packed with army recruits are left stranded on the track. Seeing that he has been again outwitted, Ryan orders his men to unload their horses from a boxcar and they give pursuit while the soldiers clumsily retrieve their mounts and follow. Meanwhile, the engine and flatcar arrive at a rendezvous where O'Brien awaits with a wagon and the arms are removed from the flatcar and loaded into a wagon, the outlaws then moving over a trestle spanning the Rio Grande to re-enter Mexico. As they cross that trestle, Sanchez lights some dynamite that has been planted on the trestle and, when Ryan and his men appear, the trestle explodes, sending the bounty hunters, horses and all, plunging downward into the river. (Clint Eastwood would take a leaf from this spectacular scene when making **The Outlaw Josey Wales**, 1976; he shoots the ropes pulling a ferry packed with horses and posse members pursuing him so that the ferry goes out of control and plunges the pursuers helplessly into a river and where Eastwood makes good his escape.) Holden and his men then hide the cache of weapons, including a machine gun, a weapon they did not expect to find. Realizing that they cannot trust the treacherous Fernandez, the outlaws devise a clever plan to obtain their payment. They

begin to deliver the arms in separate caches, obtaining incremental payments and then leaving. The final delivery is made by Borgnine and Sanchez. After the machine gun is delivered, Borgnine is paid the share of gold, but Sanchez is seized on Fernandez's orders, and the general tells Borgnine that he has learned from the mother of the girl Sanchez has killed, that Sanchez has held out a crate of weapons. For that, Fernandez plans to punish Sanchez. Borgnine, surrounded by dozens of Fernandez's men, is helpless to aid Sanchez and rides away to rejoin Holden, Oates and Johnson. Meanwhile, O'Brien, who has rounded up fresh horses for the gang, is trapped by Ryan and his bounty hunter, who wound O'Brien in the leg during a running gunfight, but the crafty O'Brien nevertheless manages to escape. Enriched with Fernandez's gold, Holden, Borgnine, Oates and Johnson go to a nearby town and revel with booze and women, but all of this now seems empty and without meaning. Holden has had enough and tells the others that he intends to get Sanchez. Oates stares at him for a moment, knowing that his intent is lethally dangerous, but he, like the others, are now resigned to meet their eventual fate and where Oates tersely states: "Why not?" The four finally accept the grim fact that their days at outlaws are at an end and vow that they will all uphold Holden's credo of "all for one and one for all" by going into Fernandez's stronghold to retrieve the captive Sanchez, although all know this most decidedly means certain death for all of them. The four—Holden, Borginine, Oates and Johnson—all heavily armed, begin to march four-abreast toward Fernandez's lair, past scores of staring soldiers, women and children. (Here Peckinpah uses an ironic image, one shown in many previous westerns—**My Darling Clementine**, 1946; **Gunfight at the O.K. Corral**, 1957; **Hour of the Gun**, 1967—and that is where the three Earp brothers, accompanied by John H. "Doc" Holliday, 1851-1887, stoically march four-abreast to the O.K. Corral in Tombstone, Arizona, on October 26, 1881, to shoot it out with the Clanton-McLowery outlaw clan, except that in this director's stoic-heroic image, Peckinpah conversely, if not perversely, substitutes outlaws for lawmen.) The four outlaws enter Fernandez's heavily guarded compound only to see Sanchez being dragged behind the moving car as Fernandez sits inside of it, drinking and reveling with a number of whores. When the car stops, Holden demands that Fernandez turn over the badly wounded Sanchez to him and his companions. Fernandez gives Holden a crooked grin and agrees. He then holds the semi-conscious Sanchez upright, but, instead of handing Sanchez over to his friends, produces a sharp knife and cuts Sanchez's throat, murdering him on the spot. Holden, enraged, draws his gun, as do his companions, and shoots and kills Fernandez on the spot. All hell breaks loose as the outlaws then begin shooting at every one of Fernandez's scampering men, who return blistering fire from all directions. The four outlaws have taken on hundreds of troops in this battle and each of the outlaws are wounded again and again as they shoot down scores of their enemies, including Wagner, the German officer (who obliquely represents a threat to the U.S., the native country of the outlaws, as Wagner's country is plotting a world war against democracies). Then each of the four outlaws take turns firing the machine gun, which has been earlier mounted and where Fernandez has used it in wild target shooting. The outlaws mow down rank upon rank of charging troops as they attempt to reach a patio where the outlaws have taken refuge. Each of them, Oates, Johnson, Borgnine, and finally, Holden, are shot and killed while manning that machine gun, Holden dying as he crumples to the ground while still clutching the handle of the weapon. The slaughter is widespread and devastating, a Gotterdammerung massacre (and undoubtedly the most violent sequence ever put on film as the agonizing death throes of the outlaws symbolize the death of the Old West they have so colorfully represented). Ryan and his bounty hunters then come upon the gruesome scene, a grisly charnel house littered with myriad, bullet-shredded bodies; the savage Martin and Jones become ecstatic when discovering the bodies of the notorious outlaws, stripping them of their belongings. Ryan is disgusted with this ravaging sight and remains behind as Martin, Jones and others pack up the bodies of the dead outlaws to return them to collect their rewards. Ryan, wise to the ways of O'Brien, however, knows what awaits the bounty hunters, who are waylaid and killed by O'Brien and the villagers from Sanchez's town who have armed themselves with the weapons provided by Sanchez. O'Brien then rides back to see Ryan sitting outside of Fernandez's destroyed hacienda. They are old friends who have long ago followed the outlaw trail together. O'Brien motions toward the villagers who have accompanied him and says: "Well, me and the boys here, we got some work to do. Want to come along? Ain't like it used to be, but it will do." Ryan is happy to agree, joining O'Brien and the others as they carry their revolution to an oppressive enemy to end this bloody saga. Peckinpah directs this startling film with great energy, using many visual techniques (and more than 2,700 edits) to convey the storyline while effectively defining its crude characters in this epic western. In addition to his many-angled shots, quick cuts and brilliant cross-cutting, he adds, at the ending, slow-motion scenes that accent the gory demises of his anti-heroes. Holden is superb as the gang leader and he is superbly supported by wonderful character actors Borgnine, Johnson, Oates and O'Brien. Sanchez is perfect as the idealized young Mexican wanting a better life for his people while Fernandez is equally impressive as a villain oozing evil at every turn. The film received Oscar nominations for Best Screenplay (Green, Peckinpah, Sickner), and Best Musical Score (Fielding). It was a huge success at the box office, earning almost $12 million in its initial release against a budget of $6 million. Songs: "Polly Wolly Doodle" (traditional), "Shall We Gather at the River?" (1864; Robert Lowry), "La Golondrina" (1862; Narciso Serradell Sevilla). *Author's Note*: Although Holden was always one of the first actors Peckipah considered for the role of the outlaw leader, he also considered James Stewart, Burt Lancaster, Gregory Peck, Richard Boone, Robert Mitchum, Sterling Hayden, and Charlton Heston. "I think my role as the gang leader in **The Wild Bunch**," Holden told this author, "was one of my most significant performances. You know, another picture was made the same year we made **The Wild Bunch**, one with Paul Newman and Robert Redford, called **Butch Cassidy and the Sundance Kid** [1969], and that picture carries the same message, that the outlaws have outlived their time. At one point in that picture, someone [Jeff Corey] tells both of those outlaws that their days are over and all they can do is die bloody, and that is what happens to the outlaws in **The Wild Bunch**. In fact, the real Butch Cassidy led an outlaw gang that was then called the Wild Bunch." Borgnine recalled his experience in this film as very painful, telling this author: "I had broken my foot in a picture [**The Split**, 1968] I made just before we made **The Wild Bunch**, and I had to wear a cast on that foot with a specially made boot to cover it. But all that riding and running around in that picture caused me a lot of agony. If I moved the wrong way, I got slivers of pain up my leg. I was really relieved when Bill [Holden] and I and the rest of us got shot to pieces and that movie ended, so I could finally sit down and stay off my injured foot." Ryan was not happy with his performance in this film, telling this author that "I played a traitor who works for a ruthless railroad tycoon and with the only purpose of tracking down and killing the only friends I ever had. What kind of a character is that?" The film was shot on location in Mexico near Torreon, Saltillo, Coahuila, and on the Rio Nazas, which duplicates for the Rio Grande. The blowing up the trestle over that river was an expensive proposition where five stuntmen were paid $2,000 each to fall into that river when the trestle explodes. Six cameras were used to record that action, one camera lost in the river during the explosion. Veteran western star John Wayne saw this film and did not like what he saw. He later told this author: "That picture goes out of its way to destroy the good myths of the Old West, the kind of decency and honor the westerners really had back then. Only Peckinpah is the kind of snotty, upstart director who would make a picture like that." Western star Joel McCrea echoed these sentiments when telling this author that "**The Wild Bunch** is not a western, only a picture dressed up to look like one. It aims to show how the days of the Old West were closing and violent men of those waning days are living their last hours.

Ernest Borgnine and William Holden in *The Wild Bunch*, 1969.

It is really a gangster picture made in a western setting and the machine gun used to kill an army of people in that picture relates to the underworld of the 1920s and early 1930s. In **The Public Enemy** [1931], a heavy machine gun is used to try to kill Jimmy [James] Cagney and a friend, both playing gangsters. Peckinpah used the same device for the finish of **The Wild Bunch**. I made a picture with Sam [Peckinpah] called **Ride the High Country** [1962] some years before **The Wild Bunch** was made, and I think that picture gives a better, more reasonable portrait of fading gunmen in the Old West and without all those damned blood pellets exploding in the viewer's face." This was the last film for character actor Albert Dekker, who, a short time after this film was completed (in eighty-one days; Dekker had been paid $30,000 for his role), was found dead in his Hollywood apartment, strangled to death with a noose about his neck that was looped about a curtain rod in his bathtub and where lewd words had been written on his body. His death was ruled an "accident" as Dekker was known to practice strange masochistic rituals. Dekker's grim ending mirrored the very kind of obsessive violence so forcefully exhibited in this film. Director Martin Scorsese, a close friend of Peckinpah's, sat in the screening room with Peckinpah to watch this film, which Scorsese, for technical reasons, proclaimed a "masterpiece," and which vastly influenced that director when making his future films. Unfortunately, this film also set the bar for the many gratuitous bloodbath westerns to come. **p**, Phil Feldman; **d**, Sam Peckinpah; **cast**, William Holden, Ernest Borgnine, Robert Ryan, Edmond O'Brien, Warren Oates, Jaime Sanchez, Ben Johnson, Emilio Fernandez, Strother Martin, L.Q. Jones, Albert Dekker, Bo Hopkins, Dub Taylor, Jorge Russek, Alfonso Arau, Chano Urueta, Sonia Amelio, Rayford Barnes, Aurora Clavel, Elsa Cardenas, Fernando Wagner, Paul Harper, Constance White, Lilia Castillo, Matthew Peckinpah; **w**, Walon Green, Peckinpah (based on a story by Green, Roy N. Sickner); **c**, Lucien Ballard (Panavision; Technicolor); **m**, Jerry Fielding; **ed**, Louis Lombardo; **art d**, Edward Carrere; **spec eff**, Bud Hulburd, Ralph Ayres, James Rugg.

The Wild Child ★★★ 1970; France; 83m; Les Artistes Associes/UA; Color; Drama; Children: Unacceptable (MPAA: PG); **DVD**; **VHS**. This offbeat but riveting tale is based on true events, beginning on a summer day in 1798 when a naked boy about twelve years old, Cargol, wanders through a forest in southern France. A woman sees him, then runs off screaming, and tells some hunters she saw a wild boy. They hunt him down with a pack of dogs. Cargol has lived for years like a wild animal, unable to speak or understand any language. He is brought to Paris and placed in a school for deaf mutes where Truffaut takes custody of him at his home outside the city. Truffaut is convinced that Cargol is not an idiot, but a victim of his environment as a child. Gradually, Cargol be-

Alan Ladd and Dorothy Lamour in *Wild Harvest*, 1947.

comes educated and civilized. Truffaut presents a sensitive portrait of early-day education and enlightenment, and he and Cargol offer outstanding performances. **p**, Nestor Almendros; **d**, Francois Truffaut; **cast**, Jean-Pierre Cargol, Truffaut, Francoise Seigner, Jean Daste, Annie Miller, Claude Miller, Paul Ville, Nathan Miller, Mathieu Schiffman, Jean Gruault, Laura Truffaut, Eva Truffaut; **w**, Truffaut, Gruault (based on the journals published by Jean-Marc Gaspard Itard, "Memoire et raport sur Victor de l'Aveyron"); **c**, Almendros; **ed**, Agnes Guillemot; **art d**, Jean Mandaroux.

The Wild Geese ★★★ 1978; U.K./Switzerland; 134m; Richmond Film Productions/Allied Artists; Color; Adventure; Children: Unacceptable (MPAA: R); **BD**; **DVD**; **VHS**; **IV**. Exciting adventure begins when Burton, a middle-aged British mercenary and former army colonel, arrives in London from Switzerland to meet the rich and ruthless merchant banker Granger, who has financial interest in Africa. Granger hires Burton to rescue Ntshona, an imprisoned president of a central African country, who is to be executed after a *coup d'etat* by Baptiste, a usurping colonel. Burton enlists his friends, Moore, a British pilot; Kruger, a German Afrikaner; and Harris, a skilled military tactician. Fifty mercenaries are trained for the dangerous mission. Harris gets Burton to promise to watch over his son if he fails to return from Africa. They rescue Ntshona, who is very ill and wounded by rifle fire, and await a plane to take them back to England, when Granger cancels the flight after making a private deal with Ntshona's captors. Burton, his friends, and the mercenaries flee into the bush country, pursued by hostile troops. They head for Ntshona's home village, hoping to get support for him there, but, en route, are fired upon by pursuers and Harris is gravely wounded. Burton is forced to shoot him, to save him from their pursuers. During an ambush, Kruger also is killed, while shielding Ntshona. At the village, Finlay, an Irish missionary priest, tells Burton that there is an old transport plane nearby that might be used to make an escape. They board the plane and Flynn attempts to get the stalled engine started, and the mercenaries flee to it under a hail of gunfire. Moore pilots the plane into nearby Rhodesia, but, by then, Ntshona has died from his injuries. Back in England, Burton breaks into Granger's home, taking all the cash from a wall safe to compensate for the payment he was promised for Ntshona's rescue, then kills Granger and leaves. He then fulfills his promise to Harris by visiting his son's boarding school to tell the boy, Spurrier, about his father's bravery and that he will look after him. Burton and the rest of the cast give exceptional performances in this fast-paced action tale. This film is not related to a 1927 film of the same name. Songs: "Flight of the Wild Geese" (Joan Armatrading), "Sammy's Theme/Dance of Death" (Jerry Donahue, Marc Donahue), "Rafer's Theme" (Aleksandr Borodin). *Author's Note*:

Burton told this author that "I originally turned down the role I played in **The Wild Geese** as I have no use for mercenaries, but, in hindsight, I realized these mercenaries were conducting a mercy mission, so I agreed to make the picture. It was hell shooting that picture in Africa and we were plagued every moment by the heat and the insects, not to mention the bad food and miserable sleeping accommodations. I couldn't wait for that picture to end so I could get the hell out of there." Violence prohibits viewing by children. **p**, Euan Lloyd, Douglas Netter; **d**, Andrew V. McLaglen; **cast**, Richard Burton, Stewart Granger, Roger Moore, Richard Harris, Hardy Kruger, Winston Ntshona, Jack Watson, Frank Finlay, Kenneth Griffith, Barry Foster, Ronald Fraser, Thomas Baptiste, Paul Spurrier; **w**, Reginald Rose (based on the novel by Daniel Carney); **c**, Jack Hildyard; **m**, Roy Budd; **ed**, John Glen; **prod d**, Syd Cain; **art d**, Bob Bell; **spec eff**, Kit West.

Wild Geese Calling ★★★ 1941; U.S.; 77m; FOX; B/W; Adventure; Drama; Children: Unacceptable. Fonda is superb in his role as a lumberjack with a yen for wandering, especially after he hears wild geese calling as they fly overhead each year. He finally decides to seek adventure in the 1890s when he quits his job and goes to Seattle to look for William, an old friend who is a con artist. He meets Bennett, a dance hall girl, and they fall in love, but she doesn't tell him that she once was William's girlfriend, but nonetheless they marry. William is being sought by gambler MacLane, who was fleeced earlier with some loaded dice used by William. To escape MacLane's wrath, William flees to Alaska and Fonda and Bennett go along. Fonda and Bennett move into a cabin in the wilderness, and, in a nearby town Bennett meets Munson, a prostitute. William tries to kiss Bennett just as Fonda walks in to see them. He thinks of leaving Bennett, but changes his mind when he learns that Bennett is going to have his child. When Fonda goes to town for a doctor to deliver his child, MacLane shoots and wounds him. William arrives and confronts MacLane, killing him. He and Munson then sail a small boat back to the cabin during a heavy rainstorm. Munson delivers Bennet's child, and William confesses to Fonda that he forced himself on Bennett when trying to steal a kiss. Fonda forgives his old friend and the wife he loves above all else. Fonda then settles down as a contented husband and father. He no longer hears the wild geese calling that urged him to go wandering each year. *Author's Note*: Fonda told this author that "I made that picture just after doing **The Lady Eve** [1941], a sophisticated comedy with Babs [Barbara] Stanwyck. I did that picture on a loan-out to Paramount, and when I returned to my home studio [Fox], I was told by Darryl [Zanuck], the boss of the studio, that he was putting me into a lumberjack picture called **Wild Geese Calling**. I felt like I was going back to the third grade, but the studio gave me some very fine supporting players and I enjoyed making that picture and where I got to dig deeply into my character. More than thirty years later I appeared in a picture with Paul Newman called **Sometimes a Great Notion** [1970] and here I was again playing the part of a lumberjack, only this time I have my own logging company and my sons are working for me. How's that for irony?" **p**, Harry Joe Brown; **d**, John Brahm; **cast**, Henry Fonda, Joan Bennett, Warren William, Ona Munson, Barton MacLane, Russell Simpson, Iris Adrian, Mary Field, Stanley Andrews, Charles Middleton; **w**, Horace McCoy (based on the novel by Stewart Edward White); **c**, Lucien Ballard; **m**, Alfred Newman; **ed**, Walter Thompson; **art d**, Richard Day, Albert Hogsett; **set d**, Thomas Little.

Wild Harvest ★★★ 1947; U.S.; 92m; PAR; B/W; Drama; Children: Unacceptable; **DVD**; **VHS**. Ladd gives a strong performance as the head of an itinerant farming combine crew, working wheat harvests against a rival crew bossed by Wright. This involves moving the wheat harvested from the panhandle of Texas through Oklahoma, Kansas, Nebraska, Colorado, and into the Dakotas each season. Ladd's pal, Preston, joins his crew, and, at a farm stop, they meet Lamour, a farmer's daughter. Lamour falls for Ladd, but he isn't interested, so, out of spite, she marries Preston. Lamour then gets Preston to double-cross Ladd by skimming off some of the money from the harvest, which Ladd badly needs to pay for farm machinery. After Ladd finds out that Preston is stealing from him, Preston flees with Lamour. She then tells Preston that she only married him so she could be close to Ladd. When Ladd catches up with Preston, he and Ladd have a ferocious fight. Their battle ends when they decide that the scheming Lamour isn't worth fighting over. They renew their friendship and go off together, leaving the scheming Lamour stranded in Nebraska. Garnett presents an absorbing, well-written drama, and Ladd, Preston and Lamour are standouts in their roles. Not related to a 1962 film of the same name. *Author's Note*: This film reunites Ladd and Preston, who had appeared together in the hard-hitting film noir **This Gun for Hire**, 1942. They would appear together again in this picture and, a year later, in an outstanding western, **Whispering Smith**, 1948. Lamour told this author that "acting opposite Alan Ladd in **Wild Harvest** was a real challenge. He is a very intense actor and you had to be on your toes when mixing with him before the camera. He always came prepared for his scenes, very sharp, like a cat ready to pounce on any miscued line. He is a very captivating man, so you risked flubbing your scenes with him if you concentrated on his good looks. I never stared into his eyes, only at his eyebrows, so I could concentrate on my own lines. When my gaze wandered downward, I saw that he was staring straight into my eyes, and never missed a line. What concentration!" Garnett told this author that Paramount was having a difficult time when, during the production of this film, the Studio Painters and Carpenters Union went on strike. "We got around that by having crew members stay at the sound stages late into the night until the strikers left and the crew members could go home without crossing the picket lines. It was a tiring time, but we made the most of it by having a little party at the end of each day's shooting. Well, at one of those parties, some big bozo crashed the party and I told Alan [Ladd] about him. Alan stood only about five feet five inches or so, but he was a tough bird. We always made Alan appear taller in scenes by having him stand on specially built planks. Well, he spotted this loud-mouth gatecrasher and marched up to him. The big bozo called Alan 'shorty' and Alan thundered at him: 'You're leaving this party right now!' When the guy clenched his fists, Alan turned around and said with a straight face: "Get my planks!" Everybody broke up with that, some of them laughing so hard that they went to the floor. I had two crew members grab the gatecrasher and throw him out." **p**, Robert Fellows; **d**, Tay Garnett; **cast**, Alan Ladd, Dorothy Lamour, Robert Preston, Lloyd Nolan, Dick Erdman, Allen Jenkins, Will Wright, Griff Barnett, Anthony Caruso, Walter Sande, Frank Sully, Vernon Dent; **w**, John Monks Jr. (based on a story by Houston Branch); **c**, John Seitz; **m**, Hugo Friedhofer; **ed**, Billy Shea, George Tomasini; **art d**, Hans Dreier, Haldane Douglas; **set d**, Sam Comer, Frank McKelvy; **spec eff**, Farciot Edouart.

Wild Hearts Can't Be Broken ★★★ 1991; U.S.; 88m; Walt Disney; Buena Vista; Color; Biographical Drama; Children: Cautionary (MPAA: PG); **DVD**; **VHS**; **IV**. Riveting biopic is based on the memoirs of Sonora Webster Carver (1904-2003), who is ably played by Anwar, and her adventures in horse diving. As a teenage runaway from a farm during the 1930s Depression, Anwar becomes a stable hand for Robertson, who has a girl-and-horse high diving act at carnivals and circuses. Her goal is to learn to star in such an act. Robertson's son, Schoeffling, helps her tame a wild horse, and, as Schoeffling trains her, he falls in love with her. York, the show's star diver, is injured and the act is booked in Atlantic City. Robertson dies and Schoeffling takes over, asking Anwar to marry him before her first dive. She accepts him, but has an accident in the dive that leaves her permanently blind. She mounts her horse and makes a perfect dive to prove to everyone and herself that she can accomplish the difficult feat, and without the audience knowing she is blind. In a voiceover at the end of the film we learn that she continued horse diving for eleven years and that she and Schoeffling married and lived happily ever after. This well-made, inspirational film offers two charismatic performances by the talented Anwar and Schoeffling.

Michael Schoeffling and Gabrielle Anwar in *Wild Hearts Can't Be Broken*, 1991.

Songs: "Happy Days Are Here Again" (Jack Yellen, Milton Ager), "On the Boardwalk in Atlantic City" (Mack Gordon, Josef Myrow), "Weren't So Bad What Used to Be" (Mason Daring). **p**, Matt Williams, Robin S. Clark; **d**, Steve Miner; **cast**, Gabrielle Anwar, Michael Schoeffling, Cliff Robertson, Dylan Kussman, Kathleen York, Frank Renzulli, Nancy Moore Atchison, Lisa Norman, Lorainne Collins; **w**, Williams, Oley Sassone; **c**, Daryn Okada; **m**, Mason Daring; **ed**, Jon Poll; **prod d**, Randy Ser; **art d**, Thomas Fichter; **set d**, Jean Alan; **spec eff**, David K. Phillips, Peter Montgomery.

Wild Is the Wind ★★★ 1957; U.S.; 114m; PAR; B/W; Drama; Children: Unacceptable; **VHS**. The earthy Magnani and Quinn are outstanding in this intense tale from pantheon director Cukor. Quinn is an uncomplicated sheepherder with a small ranch in Nevada. After his wife dies, Quinn travels to his native Italy and meets and marries the sister of his deceased spouse, taking her back to his ranch. Quinn, however, is still so much in love with his dead wife that he repeatedly utters her name when addressing Magnani. When he misspeaks that name at a birthday party, Magnani becomes offended. Sexually ignored by Quinn, she turns elsewhere for attention and quickly finds it in the form of ranch hand Franciosa, who has been raised from boyhood by Quinn. Magnani slowly falls in love with Franciosa, who patiently teaches her English. After Quinn insults her by again calling her by her dead sister's name, Magnani locks Quinn from her bedroom, telling him to go to the grave of his dead wife and sleep there. She then begins an affair with Franciosa, but, when Quinn learns about this, he does not get angry, realizing that he has created the situation. Franciosa admits that he has trifled with Magnani, but tells Quinn that he has broken off the affair and, in respect for his friendship with Quinn, leaves. Magnani by then has resolved to return alone to Italy, but Quinn pleads with her to remain at his side, promising that he will be a true husband to her. At the last minute, Magnani relents and decides to give her marriage with Quinn one more chance. The simple story is sensitively presented by Cukor, who focuses much upon the gifted Magnani as what might be expected as Cukor was known as "a woman's director." The film received Oscar nominations for Best Actor (Quinn), Best Actress (Magnani) and Best Original Song ("Wild Is the Wind"; Tiomkin/Washington). Ironically, Franciosa received an Oscar nomination as Best Actor the same year, but for his appearance in **A Hatful of Rain**, 1957. This film had been previously made as an Italian production titled **Furia**, 1948. Songs: "Wild Is the Wind" (music: Dimitri Tiomkin; lyrics: Ned Washington), "Canzone Napoletana" (1838-1840; from "Venezia e Napoli" by Franz Liszt), "Scapricciatiello" (music: Fernando Albano; lyrics: Pacifico Vento). *Author's Note*: Cukor told this author that "I thought that the chemistry between Tony [Quinn] and Anna [Magnani] was wonderful when we

Stewart Granger being attacked by a wolf in *The Wild North,* 1952.

made **Wild Is the Wind** and I enjoyed directing both of these very dedicated actors. That almost did not happen as John Sturges was hired to direct that picture. He was an action director to the bone so when he realized that the picture was really a love story, he backed out of the production and I was brought in to direct." Quinn told this author that "I really loved making that picture as it gave me a character I could develop from the inside out. I played a man struggling with the loss of a wife he loved and who replaces her as a substitute wife instead of seeing that second wife as a woman who has her own different personality. There was a lot to chew on in that story." During the production, Franciosa and Magnani developed their own passionate affair, and when Franciosa's then wife, Shelley Winters, heard about that, she flew from California to Nevada, where the film was being shot on location, putting a halt to that affair and preserving her marriage to Franciosa for another three years. **p**, Hal B. Wallis; **d**, George Cukor; **cast**, Anna Magnani, Anthony Quinn, Anthony Franciosa, Joseph Calleia, Dolores Hart, Lily Valenty, James Flavin, Dick Ryan, Joseph Vitale, Ruth Lee; **w**, Arnold Schulman (based on the novel *Furia* by Vittorio Nino Novarese); **c**, Charles Lang; **m**, Dimitri Tiomkin; **ed**, Warren Low; **art d**, Hal Pereira, Tambi Larsen; **set d**, Sam Comer, Arthur Krams; **spec eff**, John P. Fulton, Farciot Edouart.

The Wild North ★★★ 1952; U.S.; 97m; MGM; Color; Adventure; Western; Children: Unacceptable; **DVD**. Good action-packed tale begins with Granger, an easygoing French Canadian fur trapper in the wild Northwest. He befriends Charisse, a beautiful Native American girl, but, at the same time, Granger makes an enemy of a bully, Petrie. Nonetheless he agrees to travel with him. Petrie then tries to kill them both, but Granger kills Petrie in self-defense. Corey, a Royal Canadian Police Mountie, pursues Granger doggedly, following the time-honored tradition of the service that "we always get our man." The pursuit takes them all through rugged country, white water rapids, wolf packs, snowstorms, and desperadoes. Finally capturing Granger, Corey becomes lost and relies on Granger to find the right route back to civilization. At first, Granger purposely misleads Corey, but, after Corey grows ill, Granger nurtures Corey back to health. By then Corey believes Granger when told that the shooting of Petrie was in self-defense. Corey then magnanimously gives Ganger his freedom. Marton directs this action-packed saga at a quick pace, drawing exceptional performances from Granger, Corey and the sultry Charisse. The film was a box office hit, earning more than $4 million in its initial release against a budget of more than $1.2 million. Song: "Northern Lights" (Charles Wolcott). *Author's Note*: Granger told this author that "**The Wild North** took a lot out of all of us as that picture was shot on location in the deep snows of Idaho. It was so cold half the time that the cameras had to be warmed up before

they would work and some of the cast and crew members got frozen faces and hands. The steam viewers saw coming out of our mouths and nostrils was for real. To tell the truth, I would have rather been sweating in India or Africa." The film went beyond its schedule, causing it to be halted and then resumed when Granger had to make a commitment to another production, **The Light Touch**, 1952. Corey's character was based upon an intrepid Mountie named Albert Pedley, who, in 1904, tracked and captured a wanted criminal, bringing him hundreds of miles through rough country to justice. The Mounties have been profiled in many other films, including **Ace High**, 1918; **Agent of Influence**, 2002 (made-for-TV); **April One**, 1994; **Border Saddlemates**, 1952; **Cameron of the Royal Mounted**, 1921; **Canadian Mounties vs. Atomic Invaders**, 1953; **The Canadians**, 1961; **Clancy of the Mounted**, 1933; **Code of the Mounted**, 1935; **The Code of the Scarlet**, 1928; **Courage of the North**, 1935; **Crashing Through**, 1939; **Danger Ahead**, 1940; **Dangerous Nan McGrew**, 1930; **Dangers of the Canadian Mounted**, 1948; **Daredevils of the Clouds**, 1948; **The Dawson Patrol**, 1978 (made-for-TV); **Death Goes North**, 1939; **Death Hunt**, 1981; **Fangs of the Arctic**, 1953; **Fighting Mad**, 1939; **The Fighting Trooper**, 1934; **God's Country and the Man**, 1937; **His Fighting Blood**, 1935; **In the Line of Duty**, 1931; **Jaws of Justice**, 1933; **King of the Mounties**, 1942; **King of the Royal Mounted**, 1940; **The Man from Montreal**, 1939; **Menace**, 2008 (made-for-TV); **The Missouri Breaks**, 1976; **Murder on the Yukon**, 1940; **The Mysterious Pilot**, 1937 (serial); **North of the Rockies**, 1942; **Northern Pursuit**, 1943; **Northwest Mounted Police**, 1940; **Northwest Trail**, 1945; **On the Great White Trail**, 1938; **Outpost of the Mounties**, 1939; **Perils of the Royal Mounted**, 1942; **Perils of the Wilderness**, 1956; **Phantom Patrol**, 1936; **Pony Soldier**, 1952; **R.C.M.P.**, 1959-1960 (TV series); **Renfrew of the Royal Mounted**, 1937; **Riders of the North**, 1931; **Rose Marie**, 1936; **Rose Marie**, 1954; **The Royal Mounted Patrol**, 1941; **The Royal Mounted Rides Again**, 1945; **Saskatchewan**, 1954; **Secret Patrol**, 1936; **Sky Bandits**, 1940; **The Silent Code**, 1935; **Sky Bandits**, 1940; **South of Northern Lights**, 1922; **Susannah of the Mounties**, 1939; **Tangled Trails**, 1921; **Timber Terrors**, 1935; **The Trail Beyond**, 1934; **Trail of the Mounties**, 1947; **Trail of the Yukon**, 1949; **Trails of the Wild**, 1935; **Trial by Fire**, 2000 (made-for-TV); **Trooper O'Neill**, 1922; **Undercover Men**, 1934; **The Untouchables**, 1987; **What Price Vengeance**, 1937; **Where the North Holds Sway**, 1927; **Wildcat Trooper**, 1936; **Yukon Fight**, 1940; **Yukon Gold**, 1952; and **Yukon Manhunt**, 1951. **p**, Stephen Ames; **d**, Andrew Marton; **cast**, Stewart Granger, Wendell Corey, Cyd Charisse, Morgan Farley, J.M. Kerrigan, Howard Petrie, Houseley Stevenson, John War Eagle, Lewis Martin, Rex Lease; **w**, Frank Fenton (based on his story); **c**, Robert Surtees (Ansco Color); **m**, Bronislau Kaper; **ed**, John D. Dunning; **art d**, Cedric Gibbons, E. Preston Ames; **set d**, Edwin B. Willis, Alfred E. Spencer; **spec eff**, A. Arnold Gillespie, Warren Newcombe, Max Fabian.

The Wild One ★★★ 1953; U.S.; 79m; COL; B/W; Drama; Children: Unacceptable; **BD**; **DVD**; **VHS**; **IV**. Brando gives another mesmerizing performance in this offbeat biker tale where he plays an angry man-child leading a gang of cretin-like motorcycle thugs who briefly terrorize the small California town of Wrightsville. The film opens with Brando leading the Black Rebels Motorcycle Club into Carbonville, California, where a motorcycle race is being held. Stratton, a member of the gang and lickspittle to Brando, steals the second-place trophy to be awarded in the race and gives it to Brando, apologizing because the first-place trophy was too large to hide in the theft. Brando mounts the trophy on the handlebars of his cycle and the gang is ordered by police to leave. They roar off, going to Wrightsville, California, where they harass Wright, an old man, who is driving too slowly for them along a street. The bikers distract him to the point where he crashes his car into a pole. Keith, the elderly town constable and only law enforcement officer in the town, appears and realizes he cannot alone handle these rowdies. He manages to make peace with them and Wright, pacifying all parties. As the bikers go through the town and pour into the local bar, Brando spots pretty girl Murphy and follows her into a small restaurant where she is the lone counter waitress. Murphy works for her uncle, Teal, who is Keith's brother, the owner of the restaurant and adjoining bar. Teal looks upon the bikers as lucrative visitors who might bring him more business than usual. Meanwhile, Brando learns to his surprise that Murphy is Keith's daughter and also that she is less than impressed with him. To gain her favor, Brando makes Murphy a gift of the stolen trophy, pretending that he rightfully won the award. Murphy is strangely attracted to the brooding Brando, but she politely refuses to accept the trophy. Marvin and his own gang of bikers, the Beetles, then arrive in town, and Marvin, a raging brute who had been a one-time member of Brando's pack, takes pleasure in challenging Brando. He attempts to take the trophy from Brando's bike and he and Brando get into a savage fight. The two viciously maul each other until Brando gets the better of Marvin, leaving him beaten and bloody. Some of the townsfolk become angry with Keith for not maintaining order and driving the bikers from the town. One incensed citizen, Sanders, purposely drives his car into a stand of motorcycles, knocking them down. Since these bikes belong to the Beetles, Marvin drags Sanders from his car, intending to punish him for damaging the bikes. He and his gang members damage Sanders' car. Keith arrives and realizes that the bikers have now gone too far and he is compelled to act. He arrests Marvin, who is drunk, putting him into a jail cell. That night, the two gangs work in unison to further create mayhem in the town, Marvin's gang members intimidating the lone switchboard operator into fleeing so that they can then disrupt the local phone operations. Brando's gang members then abduct Sanders and drag him to the jail, putting him into the same cell occupied by Marvin, who is sleeping off a bender. The bikers then go on a violence binge, smashing store windows and vandalizing the town. Murphy is chased by a group of bikers led by Clarke, but Brando interferes, and, after rescuing her, takes her on a long motorcycle ride into the country where Murphy comes to like Brando. When she shows her affection toward him, however, he rejects her after returning her to the town. When Wright sees Murphy running away toward home and crying, he believes that Brando has assaulted her and this later leads town vigilantes, led by Sanders, who has been released from the jail, to track down and attack Brando. Keith arrives and tries to stop the vigilantes, but they seize Brando and mercilessly beat him. He then escapes on his bike, but someone in the crowd throws a tire iron at him, knocking him unconscious, and his cycle goes out of control, striking and killing Vedder. County Sheriff Flippen arrives with his deputies, restoring order as they quickly round up the bikers. When Flippen charges Brando with Vedder's death, Murphy goes to Brando's aid, pleading on his behalf. This moves Teal and Wright, who head the vigilantes, to admit that Vedder's death was an accident and that Brando was not to blame. Although these offended citizens have come to defend the very man who is mostly responsible for the chaos in their town, they receive no thanks from Brando, who cannot bring himself to show any gratitude to them or anyone else. After the bikers are compelled to pay for the damage they have created, they are ordered to leave the county. Brando goes with the gang, but then turns around and returns to Wrightsville, going to the restaurant where Murphy works. He has a cup of coffee with her and then leaves, but returns to place the stolen trophy on the counter, leaving it as a gift for her before he smiles and goes to his bike and rides away. Benedek directs this film with a firm hand, building subtle tension as violence increases and while he expertly balances the tender moments between Brando and Murphy and the wild antics of the bikers. Brando gives a powerful performance as a rebellious youth who wants no home to call his own and finds very good support from the entire cast. Marvin as the sleazy, unwholesome biker also gives a stunning essay as a dirty, uncouth and savage-natured gang leader, the kind of terrifying role for which this hoarse-voiced actor was best known. This was the first film to depict the outlaw motorcycle gang violence that was to plague the U.S. for years to come, as well as spawning a spate of biker films that also in-

Marlon Brando, right, and motorcycle friends in *The Wild One*, 1953.

cluded many parodies of these moronic and often bestial predators in a series of bikini beach films. The film did well at the box office, thanks to Brando's by then established fame. Songs: "Chino," "Blues for Brando," "The Wild One," "Windswept" (Leith Stevens). *Author's Note*: The story upon which this film is based was inspired by the 1947 biker riot occurring in Hollister, California, on a Fourth of July weekend where a rally of more than 4,000 members of the American Motorcycle Association was in progress and the bikers literally wrecked the town. Brando told this author that "I played my character in **The Wild One** the way he and all of his fellows truly are, as a child. He is petulant, impetuous, impulsive, selfish and arrogant without any true wisdom. He knows all of these things about himself, which is why he breaks down and weeps like a child at one point. That is what he is, a child that never grew up. You must realize that these bikers are very stupid people, mostly men who think to prove their manhood through the speed and noise of their bikes as they roar about without really having any place to go that wants them. They are nomads, gypsies, garbage people, really, who have thrown away their lives. Anyone who reads any significance into these people is as idiotic as the bikers themselves. Personally, I detest the whole, stinking lot of them and, if they were to all suddenly disappear from the roads of California, the hard-working citizens of this state would be very grateful, including yours truly." Kramer admitted to this author that Brando was not enthusiastic about appearing in this film, telling me: "I think Marlon [Brando] agreed to play that rebel only because he had started out with me in his first important feature film, **The Men** [1950]. He did not like most of the players in that picture, especially the actual bikers I hired who played dozens of extras. In fact, I asked one of those anti-social bikers: 'What are you rebelling against?' He replied: 'Whaddya got?' We used that exchange in the dialog and Marlon gives that universal answer. The truth is I wanted to make that picture to show the reasons why these nomadic young men and women were rebelling against society, but I am afraid that all I achieved was to show how senseless and brutal these people really are." Brando's iconic image—long sideburns, leather jacket and biker cap—was later adopted by myriad bikers. He and this film became an anthem for the disaffected youth of the era. Marvin, who did not know how to drive a motorcycle when cast in this film, trained himself to drive a Harley-Davidson (Brando and his gang ride British Triumphs). "I knew Marlon had his own cycle and was always scooting around the Hollywood hills," Marvin told this author, "but I was determined to become as good as he was on a cycle and worked so hard that he refused to race with me. I bugged him a lot when we were making that picture to the point where we had a fight and he took his revenge by actually bopping me on the head with that trophy he rides around with. I told him at the time: 'I know that was an accident, so let's forget it.' He floored me when he replied: 'That was

Marlon Brando in *The Wild One*, 1953.

no accident.'" British officials banned this film in England where it was not shown until fourteen years later in 1968 and then only for a limited engagement. Officials felt that the film would incite young people in England to defy authority and the kind of widespread violence so routinely practiced by bikers in the U.S. **p**, Stanley Kramer; **d**, Laslo Benedek; **cast**, Marlon Brando, Mary Murphy, Robert Keith, Lee Marvin, Jay C. Flippen, Peggy Maley, Hugh Sanders, Ray Teal, John Brown, Will Wright, Robert Osterloh, John Doucette, Timothy Carey, Angela Stevens, Gil Stratton, Jerry Paris, Keith Clarke, William Vedder, Yvonne Doughty, Pat O'Malley, Robert Bice, Alvy Moore, Harry Landers; **w**, John Paxton, Ben Maddow (based on a story by Frank Rooney); **c**, Hal Mohr; **m**, Leith Stevens; **ed**, Al Clark; **prod d**, Rudolph Sternad; **art d**, Walter Holscher; **set d**, Louis Diage.

Wild Orchids ★★★ 1929 (part silent); U.S.; 100m; MGM; B/W; Drama/Romance; Children: Unacceptable; **DVD**. Garbo is stunning in this taut domestic drama that begins when she marries kind and considerate Stone, a man almost twice her age. The couple sails for Java and while on board their luxury liner, Garbo sees a handsome, well-attired man strike one of his servants. Garbo is both repelled and fascinated by the looks and actions of this man. She quickly retreats to her cabin where she is frustrated by her new husband, as Stone is always too occupied with business to pay her any romantic attention. Stone is planning to operate a tea plantation on Java and is aided by Asther, a Javanese prince, who has deep knowledge about the operations of such plantations. Stone introduces Garbo to Asther and she is startled to see that he is the very same man she saw aboard the ship physically rebuking a servant. Asther is attracted to Garbo and uses every opportunity to be with her alone, but she manages to evade his advances until one night he forcibly grabs and kisses her. Garbo can no longer resist the passionate Asther and embraces him. Stone see this passionate scene, but only as two silhouettes through a screen and is uncertain as to whether or not Garbo is cheating on him with Asther. His suspicions are later confirmed after he finds a misplaced necklace and he resolves to kill Asther on a tiger hunt. Garbo, sensing the danger, tries to convince Stone to take her away, but he keeps his distance from her while he makes his murderous plans. Asther is wounded in that hunt where Stone cannot bring himself to murder the man who has seduced his wife. Stone then tells Garbo that he is returning to the U.S., and prepares to leave without her. She, however, truly loves Stone and, after convincing him that her heart belongs only to him, the couple departs, wiser for their torrid experience on exotic Java. Franklin does a good job in presenting consistent tension throughout this tale of deceit and reaffirmed love while Garbo and Asther present steamy encounters in their every scene together. Of special note is the lush photography cinematographer Daniels lavishes upon Garbo, surrounding her with halos of light and bathing her with light whenever Asther appears. The scene where Asther's bedroom door opens is visually astounding as Garbo is engulfed with shimmering light while Asther's shadow slowly crawls over her body. Garbo's character in this film is far from the vixen or sophisticated vamp her myriad fans always expected. She plays a good-hearted woman, who, despite her brief dallying with Asther, remains true to her husband. The film was a hit at the box office, earning more than $1.1 million in its initial release against a budget of $320,000. Garbo would appear in **The Painted Veil**, 1934, a talkie that offered much the same story line. This film was not entirely silent, offering sound effects and a musical score. Song: "You Are Like Wild Orchids" (music: Georg Enders; lyrics: Nils-Georg). *Author's Note*: Garbo told this author that just when she went into production for this film she learned that her mentor, film director Mauritz Stiller, had died in Sweden. "That wonderful man's death so devastated me that I did not think I would ever give another good performance," she said to this author. In fact, at the time of that production and after hearing that news, Garbo dramatically told Stone and Asther: "You will have something dead on the screen. It will have no life." However, always the consummate actress, Garbo gave a marvelous performance in **Wild Orchids**. The day Garbo received that dreadful news about Stiller she walked off the set and went to her dressing room where Asther heard her laughing hysterically. He entered to find her holding a small bottle of brandy that had been sent to her by MGM chief Louis B. Mayer, along with a note reading: "My sympathies for your sorrow. But the show must go on. Louis B. Mayer." Asther, like so many others who played opposite of her, fell in love with his co-star and they had a brief affair. When the film ended, Asther proposed marriage to Garbo, but she rejected his offer, just as she had with many other handsome costars, including the inimitable John Gilbert. When the film was completed, Garbo left immediately for Sweden to visit Stiller's grave, ignoring Mayer's request that she remain for retakes, and Mayer briefly suspended her contract with MGM for her defiance. After arriving in Sweden, Garbo visited a storeroom where all of Stiller's belongings were kept and Stiller's attorney recalled how she lovingly touched those possessions, much the same way she would passionately fondle the furniture in the love chamber she shared with Gilbert when making **Queen Christina**, 1933. She then visited Stiller's grave, which was located in a Jewish cemetery, where she spent many hours mourning over the loss of this man, who died at age forty-five and who many have been Garbo's lover as well as her professional inspiration. It was no secret that Garbo then and throughout her life was fiercely pro-Jewish (and pro-Israel when that nation came into existence in 1948). At one point in the early 1930s, knowing how Adolf Hitler and his regime intended to exterminate the Jews, Garbo confided to a friend that she had the urge to visit Hitler with a gun hidden in her purse and assassinate him. Other films dealing with or set in Java include **Breed of the Sea**, 1926; **Celine and Julie Go Boating**, 1974; **Dead Time: Kala**, 2008; **Dr. Renault's Secret**, 1942; **Java Heat**, 2013; **Krakatoa**, 2008 (made-for-TV); **Krakatoa, East of Java**, 1969; **Lord Jim**, 1965; **Merry Christmas, Mr. Lawrence**, 1983; **Nemesis**, 1993; **November 1828**, 1979; **The Rebellious Woman**, 1982; **Requiem from Java**, 2007; **The Story of Dr. Wassell**, 1944; **Thundering Dawn**, 1923; and **We Go Fast**, 1941. **p, d**, Sidney Franklin; **cast**, Greta Garbo, Nils Asther, Lewis Stone, Dick Sutherland; **w**, Marian Ainslee, Ruth Cummings, Hans Kraly, Richard Schayer (based on Willis Goldbeck's adaptation of a story by John Colton); **c**, William H. Daniels; **ed**, Conrad A. Nervig; **art d**, Cedric Gibbons.

The Wild Party ★★★ 1929; U.S.; 77m; PAR; B/W; Comedy/Romance; Children: Unacceptable. In her first talking picture, Bow plays a beautifu loose-living young woman who goes to college just to have fun. She and her girlfriends take a class presided over by March, not that they're interested in the subject he expertly teaches, but because they think he's cute. He is a strict professor and they try to loosen him up by playing pranks on him. Bow attends a wild party, but is kicked out because her dress is cut too low at the bodice. She goes to a roadhouse where Hendricks tries to seduce her. Who wanders into the roadhouse but March, who spots his student and promptly rescues her from the lecherous clutches of cad Hendricks. Compton, one of Bow's classmates, sees her leaving in March's car and thinks they are having an affair. Her gossip about them spreads across the campus, and March lectures Bow sternly in class to prove he does not have any passion for her. She then goes to another wild party with O'Hara, who falls in love with Luden. Hendricks, angry that March interfered with his lovemaking, shoots him. March is wounded and Bow then tells March that she loves him. A spicy letter O'Hara writes to Luden then spreads across the college and causes a scandal, but Bow claims responsibility for the letter and, in disgrace, leaves college. She boards a train in despair, but March follows her aboard and declares his love for her and his plan to leave the college and marry her. The beautiful Bow with her bee-stung lips is thoroughly entertaining in this college romp, and March is the perfect stick-in-the-mud-turned-lover. This film is not related to the 1923, 1956, 1975, and 1998 films with the same name. Song: "My Wild Party Girl" (1929; music: Richard A. Whiting; lyrics: Leo Robin). *Author's Note*: March told this author that "**The Wild Party** was my second feature film where I was the leading man. I played a straight-laced professor at a college where I get involved with red-headed Clara Bow, who played a pretty coed. Clara was very nervous when we made that picture as it was the first time audiences would hear her voice and we all took turns calming her down before she did her scenes." The crude sound techniques of that era caused Bow's voice to be extremely loud in some scenes and somewhat garbled in others. Bow had become an overnight sensation in **It**, 1927, and had been known thereafter as "The It Girl." To take advantage of that reputation, Paramount promoted Bow's first talkie with such slogans as "You had an eyeful of IT...now get an earful." Bow's star would fade within a few years, but March would go on to become one of the most respected and accomplished actors in Hollywood. This film was released in England as a silent. Future stars Holmes and Oakie have bit parts in the film. Excessive drinking prohibits viewing by children. **p**, E. Lloyd Sheldon **d**, Dorothy Arzner; **cast**, Clara Bow, Fredric March, Phillips Holmes, Jack Oakie, Marceline Day, Shirley O'Hara, Adrienne Dore, Joyce Compton, Jack Luden, Alice Adair, Kay Bryant, Marguerite Cramer, Ben Hendricks Jr.; **w**, Sheldon (based on a story by Samuel Hopkins Adams as Warner Fabian); **c**, Victor Milner; **m**, John Leipold; **ed**, Ohto Lovering.

Wild River ★★★ 1960; U.S.; 110m; FOX; Color; Drama; Children: Unacceptable; MPAA: PG; **BD**; **DVD**; **VHS**; **IV**. Clift gives a compelling performance as a young field administrator for the Tennessee Valley Authority. He arrives at rural Tennessee to oversee the building of a dam on the Tennessee River in the early 1930s. He meets with strong opposition when many homeowners resist government attempts to buy their homes and demolish them because they are in the path of the dam building. The most resistant of these homeowners is Van Fleet, an elderly woman who refuses to give up her home on an island in the river. Meanwhile, Clift falls in love with Remick, who is Van Fleet's widowed granddaughter. In the end, the government wins the battle and Clift wins Remick. In addition to Clift's exceptional performance, Van Fleet is a standout as the strong-willed homeowner, playing a woman of eighty (when the actress was then forty-one and where makeup artist Ben Nye did wonders to convincingly age the actress). Songs: "He Walks with Me" (traditional), "In the Garden" (C. Austin Miles). *Author's Note*: Kazan admitted to this author that "I had visited Tennessee when that dam-building was going on back then in the 1930s, and I always wanted to make a picture about that era and the tough people who lived there. It took me three decades to get back to that project." Barbara Loden, who was Kazan's wife and later directed the exceptional film **Wanda**, 1971, has a bit part in this film. This is the film debut of actor

Greta Garbo, embracing flowers as if they were her lover in *Wild Orchids*, **1929.**

Bruce Dern. **p&d**, Elia Kazan; **cast**, Montgomery Clift, Lee Remick, Jo Van Fleet, Albert Salmi, Jay C. Flippen, James Westerfield, Barbara Loden, Frank Overton, Malcolm Atterbury, Bruce Dern, Pat Hingle; **w**, Paul Osborn (based on the novels *Mud on the Stars* by William Bradford Huie, *Dunbar's Cove* by Borden Deal); **c**, Ellsworth Fredericks (CinemaScope; DeLuxe Color); **m**, Kenyon Hopkins; **ed**, William Reynolds; **art d**, Lyle R. Wheeler, Herman A. Blumenthal; **set d**, Walter M. Scott, Joseph Kish.

Wild Rovers ★★★ 1971; U.S.; 136m; MGM; Color; Western; Children: Unacceptable (MPAA: PG-13); **DVD**; **IV**. Holden plays an aging cowboy and O'Neal his younger pal, both working on a ranch owned by Malden. Holden wonders what will become of him when he's too old to do his ranch work, and O'Neal wants a better and more exciting life. One of the other cow hands on the ranch is killed in a corral accident, and O'Neal suggests to Holden that they improve their status in life by robbing a bank. Holden reluctantly agrees and they rob a local bank, making good their escape, but are then followed by Malden and his two grown sons, Skerritt and Baker. They find the culprits and a shootout occurs which leaves both Holden and O'Neal full of holes. The story is as prosaic as the uneducated cowboys it so revealingly profiles, and Holden and O'Neal are standouts as the simplistic cowhands. Songs: "Ballad of the Wild Rovers" (Jerry Goldsmith), "Wild Rover" (music: Goldsmith; lyrics: Ernie Sheldon). *Author's Note*: Holden admitted to this author that "**Wild Rovers** certainly follows a lot of the elements seen in another fine western, such as **Monte Walsh** [1970], where cowboys attempt to improve their miserable lot by becoming thieves. There is no patent on such ideas as most of the outlaws of the Old West started as cowboys. The tragedy is that most of them wound up the same way Ryan [O'Neal] and I do in that picture, shot down like dogs by a posse. Life was hard in the Old West, and only a few in those days ever went easy to Death." **p**, Blake Edwards, Ken Wales; **d&w**, Edwards; **cast**, William Holden, Ryan O'Neal, Karl Malden, Lynn Carlin, Tom Skerritt, Joe Don Baker, James Olson, Leora Dana, Moses Gunn, Victor French, Rachel Roberts, Alan Carney; **c**, Philip Lathrop; **m**, Jerry Goldsmith; **ed**, John F. Burnett; **art d**, George W. Davis, Addison Hehr; **set d**, Reg Allen, Robert R. Benton; **spec eff**, Earl McCoy, Charles Schulthies.

Wild Strawberries ★★★★★ 1959; Sweden; 90m; Svensk Filmindustri/Janus Films; B/W; Drama; Children: Unacceptable; **BD**; **DVD**; **VHS**; **IV**. This masterpiece film from pantheon director Bergman introspectively examines the past of a brilliant professor as he reviews his long life while traveling to receive an honorary degree. Sjostrom [Seastrom] is a respected medical professor specializing in bacteriology and he is

Victor Sjostrom and Bibi Andersson in *Wild Strawberries*, 1959.

on his way by car from Stockholm to Lund to receive recognition for his fifty years of educational service, the very university where he graduated fifty years earlier. Traveling with Sjostrom is Thulin, his pregnant daughter-in-law, who has left her husband, Bjornstrand, because he does not want a child to complicate his life. That strained relationship is mirrored in Thulin's feelings for Sjostrom as she thinks he has the same strong and unyielding personality exhibited by her truculent spouse, who is Sjostrom's only son. During the journey, Sjostrom is plagued by haunting memories, daydreams and nightmares that compel him to reevaluate a lifetime while he grows anxious over his advancing age (he is seventy-eight) and the threat of nearing death. The catalysts for Sjostrom's reveries are a number of hitchhiking travelers who briefly join Sjostrom and Thulin. The first of these is a young couple who recall for Sjostrom his earliest love, Andersson, when he visits his ancestral home. While walking about the place, Sjostrom sees in flashback Andersson, the first woman he ever loved, as she picks wild strawberries before joining the family for dinner (although Sjostrom is not seen in these scenes nor does he interact with these spectral visions). Andersson gives the strawberries to her deaf grandfather while having a conversation with Sjostrom's brother. After watching the family have dinner, Sjostrom is awakened (in flash-forward) by a teenaged Andersson (playing dual roles), who asks for a ride. She, along with two young male friends, her admirers, then join Sjostrom and Thulin on their journey. After their car collides with and damages another car, its occupants, a loud and angry middle-aged couple, Brostrom and Sjoberg, are given a lift by Sjostrom. The couple's vociferous and sadistic comments so anger everyone else that Thulin stops the car and orders them from the auto. The others continue their journey until they stop to have lunch and the two young males playfully fight with one another. Sjostrom then dreams that he is being examined by a demanding Sjoberg, who orders Sjostrom to read foreign words written on a blackboard and, when Sjostrom fails to do so, Sjoberg reads for him, the translation stating: "A doctor's first duty is to ask forgiveness." Sjoberg then pronounces that Sjostrom is "guilty of guilt." While looking at the seaside, Sjostrom wistfully recalls how the Andersson of this youth married his brother. The group then travels on, stopping to visit Sjostrom's elderly and embittered mother, who is ninety-five and constantly complains that she has lived throughout her life while feeling cold. They then visit Sjostrom's middle-aged son, and Sjostrom makes peace with his troubled memories, accepting his past and present life and now willing to accept the death he knows is fast approaching. They stop at an old house and Sjostrom's medical expertise is put to the test when he must examine an old woman, but he fails to diagnose that she is dead. After the travelers reach Lund, Sjostrom receives his honorary degree, but the award seems empty to the old man. He then returns to the home of his son,

Bjornstrand, and, when going to sleep, enjoys for the first time in many years a blissful sleep where all the issues he has had with Thulin, Bjornstrand and others are amicably resolved and Sjostrom is finally at peace with himself. This evocative journey into the past is marvelously presented by Bergman, who seamlessly balances the reality and dream sequences with great care to give unforgettable definition to the failing mind and rising spirit of the old doctor. Sjostrom, Thulin, Bjornstrand, Andersson and the rest of the cast are outstanding in their distinctive roles, and some of the dream sequences are bone chilling, particularly the opening expressionist scenes where Sjostrom confronts his own death. In that sequence, he walks through an abandoned town, seeing a man without a face and a clock without hands (to signify his own unidentified self and the unknown amount of time left in his own life). A funeral wagon moves with clacking echoes over the empty streets and, when it turns a corner, its wheel becomes snagged with a post that causes the wheel to fall off, but the wagon continues its bleak journey. A coffin slides from the wagon to land on the street, and when Sjostrom reaches into the coffin his hand is grabbed by the hand of the dead person inside of that casket, the body being himself. He struggles with the dead creature, which tries to take him into that coffin, momentarily freeing himself in what is otherwise a futile effort to escape death. (This scene was hilariously parodied by Mel Brooks when making **Young Frankenstein**, 1974, where Gene Wilder, the creator of the monster, pretends to hold his own hand, which is that of the monster's and which has slipped from a coffin dislodged from a wagon, after an investigating constable arrives upon the ludicrous scene.) As usual, the always professorial and hortatory Bergman overdramatizes his scenes by encouraging extraordinary theatrics from his cast members, heavily lacing his scenes with symbolism while intellectualizing what he presents through heavy analysis. In this film, however, which is an utterly captivating, intensive and inhibiting analyzation of a human life, all of these lifelong filmic traits are not bugbears but essentially needed ingredients that make up the whole of this magnificent spiritual portrait. This was Sjostrom's final film and his swansong performance is undoubtedly his greatest. The film received an Oscar nomination for Best Original Screenplay (Bergman). Songs: "Kungliga Soedermanlands Regementes" (Carl Axel Lundvall), "Marcia Carolus Rex" (Wilhelm Harteveld), "Parademarsch der 18: Er Husaren" (Alwin Mueller), "Under Roenn Och Syren/Blommande Skoena Dalar" (music: Herman Palm; lyrics: Sakari Topelius), "Ja Maa Han Leva!" (traditional), "Fugue No. 8 in E-Flat Major" (Johann Sebastian Bach). ***Author's Note***: Bergman admitted that he got the idea for this film when visiting his grandmother's house and, before entering its door, had the idea that when he opened that door all of the visions he remembered from his childhood would greet him. "So it struck me," he said, "what if you could make a film about this—that you could just walk up in a realistic way and open a door, and then you walk into your childhood. And then when you open another door…come back to reality." In 1957, Bergman was treated for two months with gastric problems and stress in Stockholm's Karolinska Hospital, which is where he got the idea for this film. He used this hospital as the workplace for Sjostrom's character, spending his two months there writing the script for the film while recovering from his ailments. The director's life was then in great disarray, his third marriage crumbling and his long-standing affair with actress Bibi Andersson ending. Although he had recently reconciled with his mother, his relationships with his family members were strained and all of this Bergman incorporated into the film's story line. Sjostrom was ailing and in his advanced years when Bergman called him and asked him to play the leading role in this film. The old actor had been retired, but he told Bergman that he would think about it. He called back to say he would play the part as long as Bergman returned him to his home by 5 p.m. each day so he could have his grog of whiskey. This was done punctually, although the crew feared that Sjostrom might die any day during the production as his health weakened throughout the production. The actor died a year after this film was released at the age of eighty. (In

Swedish; English subtitles) **p**, Allan Ekelund; **d&w**, Ingmar Bergman; **cast**, Victor Sjostrom, Bibi Anderson, Ingrid Thulin, Gunnar Bjornstrand, Jullan Kindahl, Folke Sundquist, Naima Wifstrand, Gunnar Sjoberg, Gunnel Brostrom, Gertrud Fridh, Max von Sydow; **c**, Gunnar Fischer; **m**, Erik Nordgren, Gote Loven; **ed**, Oscar Rosander; **prod d**, Gittan Gustafsson.

The Wild Thornberrys Movie ★★★ 2002; U.S.; 85m; PAR/Nickelodeon Movies; Color; Animated Adventure; Children: Cautionary (MPAA: PG); **DVD**; **IV**. This delightful feature-length animated film entertainingly profiles an eccentric family on safari in Africa, which is based on the television series (1998-2001). Curry and Carlisle (voiceovers for Mr. and Mrs. Thornberry) and their children travel in a mobile home while Carlisle films their adventure with a camera and the youngest daughter (Chabert voiceover) talks to a pet monkey (Kane voiceover) and other animals. After they encounter poachers, the family rescues three panther cubs in a helicopter, and finally save a herd of elephants from extinction. Songs: "The Wild Thornberrys Theme" (Drew Neumann), "Iwoya" (Angelique Kidjo, Jean Hebrail, David J. Matthews), "Accident" (Sean Caruth), "Father and Daughter" (Paul Simon), "I Am the Very Model of a Modern Major-General" (William S. Gilbert, Arthur Sullivan), "She's a Lady" (Paul Anka), "Monkey Man" (Frederick Hibbert), "The Dream" (Youssou N'Dour, Jonathan Sharp), "Get Out of London" (Simon Fellowes, Simon Gillham), "Animal Nation" (Peter Gabriel), "Don't Walk Away" (Youssou N'Dour, Jonathan Sharp, Cameron McVey, Michael Power), "Shaking the Tree" (Gabriel, N'Dour, O. Burrell), "End of Forever" (Nick Carter, Guy Chambers), "Oombe" (Ayub Ogada, Ishmael Pamphille), "Motla Le Pula/The Rainmaker" (Hugh Masekela), "Africa/Ila Re Waisco" (Consuelo Apo Batupa, Josefina Loribo Apo), "Awa Awa" (Wes Madiko, Michel Sanchez), "Dance with Us" (Nisan Stewart, Mechalle Jamison, Dante Nolan, Sean Combs, Varick Smith, Rahman Griffin), "Bridge to the Stars" (Randy Kerber, J. Peter Robinson), "Happy" (Tobias Gad, Jacqueline Nemorin). Violence makes this cautionary viewing by children. **p**, Gabor Csupo, Arlene Klasky, Tracy Kramer, Sean Lurie, Terry Thoren, Norton Virgien; **d**, Cathy Malkasian, Jeff McGrath; **cast**, (voiceovers) Tim Curry, Marisa Tomei, Lynn Redgrave, Rupert Everett, Brock Peters, Alfre Woodard, Brenda Blethyn, Lacey Chabert, Laraine Newman, Tom Kane; **w**, Kate Boutilier (based on characters created by Arlene Klasky, Csupo, Steve Pepoon, David Silverman, Stephen Sustarsic); **m**, Paul Simon, Randy Kerber, Drew Neumann; **ed**, John Bryant; **prod d**, Dima Malanitchev; **spec eff**, Dee Farnsworth, Nadja Bonacina, Brice Mallier, Jerry Mills.

Wildrose ★★★ 1985; U.S.; 95m; Ely Lake Films/New Front Films; Color; Drama; Children: Unacceptable (MPAA: PG-13); **VHS**. Captivating tale sees Eichhorn and Bower as co-workers on the Iron Range in northern Minnesota in the 1980s. They fall in love and then must face the difficulties of combining love and work, even though they do not marry. They are both laid of and Bower moves back to his hometown of Bayfield, Wisconsin, to return to commercial fishing on Lake Superior, while Eichhorn remains in Minnesota, hoping to be rehired. She is finally rehired, but Bower stays in Wisconsin. The film does a good job exploring the difficulties in live-in unions as the female actively seeks a career. **p**, Sandra Schulberg; **d**, John Hanson; **cast**, Lisa Eichhorn, Tom Bower, James Cada, Cinda Jackson, Dan Nemanick, Lydia Olsen, Bill Schoppert, James Stowell, Steve Yokam, Vienna Maki, Joel Thingvall; **w**, Hanson, Eugene Corr (based on a story by Hanson, Schulberg); **c**, Peter Stein; **m**, Bernard Krause, Gary Malkin as Gary Remal; **ed**, Arthur Coburn; **art d**, Shirley Morton, Cate Whittemore.

Will Penny ★★★★ 1968; U.S.; 109m; WB; Color; Western; Children: Unacceptable; **DVD**; **VHS**; **IV**. Heston and Hackett are outstanding in this prosaic western where an aging cowboy takes pity on a homeless woman and her child, becoming their reluctant protector. Set in Montana

Tom Bower and Lisa Eichhorn in *Wildrose*, 1985.

in the 1880s, Heston and fellow cowboys Zerbe and Majors are nomadically looking for work after helping to drive a cattle herd to the state. The three encounter Pleasence, a berserk preacher, and his three savage sons, who attack them, as they fight over a dead elk. Zerbe is wounded and Heston shoots and kills one of the sons before driving off Pleasence and his other two deadly offspring, with Pleasence shouting that he will later take bloody vengeance upon Heston. Taking Zerbe to a nearby roadhouse where he can be mended, Heston meets pioneer woman Hackett, and her small son, Francis, who are traveling to California to reunite with Hackett's husband. They have an unreliable guide, who is to take them over the mountain. Hackett urges Heston and Majors to take Zerbe to a town to see a doctor instead of allowing him to die at the roadhouse. Heston and Majors continue on to a small town where Schallert, the local barber and physician, undertakes to save Zerbe's life. Heston meanwhile finds it difficult to find work, although he is a reliable and seasoned cowhand. He bathes about nine or ten times a year, mends his own clothing and minds his own business. He and Majors part and Heston later comes upon a dead cowboy who has been bucked from his horse. Heston takes the body to the Flatiron Ranch where he lands a job when Johnson hires him at $30 a month to replace the dead line rider, and where Heston must look out for wandering steers in the high country. When he arrives at the line cabin, he is surprised to see Hackett and Francis living there. Hackett explains that their guide deserted them and they have no place to live. Heston takes pity on them and allows them to stay for a brief while, but tells them that they must soon move on, as he does not own the cabin or land and is merely a line rider. While riding the high territory, Heston is ambushed by Pleasence and his two sons, who beat him so mercilessly that they leave him for dead. He nevertheless manages to get to the cabin occupied by Hackett and Francis and Hackett patiently nurses him back to health over a long period of time; they get to know each other and develop genuine affection for one another. Further, Heston becomes genuinely paternalistic toward Francis, who looks upon him as a father figure. Heston comes to think that he might give up his nomadic way of life as he slowly falls in love with Hackett, considering that he might actually settle down and farm the land as Hackett urges. He has little time to think about altering his life after the maniacal Pleasence and his two sons reappear, invading the cabin and making Heston, Hackett and Francis prisoners. They turn Heston into a slave and Pleasence conducts a marriage between Hackett and one of his lustful sons. Heston, however, escapes after Majors comes to his rescue, and the two then battle Pleasence and his two sons, who are all killed. Heston then realizes that he cannot change his lifestyle and rides away from Hackett and Francis to continue his restless roaming through the West. Heston gives one of his finest performances in this down-to-earth and very realistic western, his character and those

Gene Rutherford, Donald Pleasence, Bruce Dern and Quentin Dean in *Will Penny,* **1968.**

surrounding him all carefully developed by director Tom Gries (whose son, Jon, plays Hackett's son). Hackett and Jon Gries are standouts in their roles Francis and Francis Pleasence chews up the rugged landscape as a hissing villain, a truly frightening portrait, which is equaled by Dern, one of his unbalanced sons. The script is superbly written and the dialog accurately reflects the argot as expressed by the uneducated westerners of its era, where all is genuinely gritty and hardscrabble. This sincere western, unfortunately, did not do well at the box office, earning more than $1.8 million in its initial release against a budget of $1.4 million. Song: "The Lonely Rider" (David Raksin, Robert Wells). *Author's Note*: Heston told this author that "**Will Penny** has always been my favorite picture. I think it offers one of the best performances of my career, but it suffered at the box office because of the downbeat ending where I leave the woman [Hackett] and child [Francis] at the end. Audiences love a happy ending, like the one in the war epic, **55 Days in Peking** [1963] where I played a U.S. Army captain. At the end of that picture, I was leading my troops from the city, but I turned in my saddle and reached down to take a Chinese girl [Lynne Sue Moon], the daughter of a fellow officer, who has been killed, along with me. That happy ending rang up the dollars. Also, I think that Paramount did not really get behind **Will Penny** and lacked the enthusiasm to give that picture the promotion it deserved." Hundreds of films have profiled in detail the lifestyle of the cowboy in the Old West, some of the best of these, in addition to this fine film, include **Appaloosa**, 2008; **The Big Country**, 1958 (which also stars Heston); **Cattle Drive**, 1951; **The Cheyenne Social Club**, 1970; **Chisum**, 1970; **Cowboy**, 1958; **The Cowboys**, 1972; **The Culpepper Cattle Company**, 1972; **The Far Country**, 1955; **Lonely Are the Brave**, 1962; **Monte Walsh**, 1970; **Oklahoma!**, 1955; **Open Range**, 2003; **The Ox-Bow Incident**, 1943; **Quigley Down Under**, 1990; **Red River**, 1948; **Silverado**, 1985; **Vengeance Valley**, 1951; **The Virginian**, 1929; **The Virginian**, 1946; **The Virginian**, 2000 (made-for-TV); **The Westerner**, 1940; **Wild Rovers**, 1971; and **The Winning of Barbara Worth**, 1926. For a more extensive list, see Subject Index, Cowboys. **p**, Fred Engel, Walter Seltzer; **d&w**, Tom Gries; **cast**, Charlton Heston, Joan Hackett, Jon Gries [Francis], Donald Pleasence, Lee Majors, Bruce Dern, Ben Johnson, Slim Pickens, William Schallert, Clifton James, Anthony Zerbe, Roy Jenson, G.D. Spradlin; **c**, Lucien Ballard (Technicolor); **m**, David Raksin; **ed**, Warren Low; **art d**, Hal Pereira, Roland Anderson; **set d**, Ray Moyer, Robert Benton; **spec eff**, Paul K. Lerpae.

Will Success Spoil Rock Hunter? ★★★★ 1957; U.S.; 94m; FOX; Color; Comedy; Children: Acceptable; **BD**; **DVD**; **VHS**; **IV**. Randall is uproariously hilarious as an ambitious young man bumbling his way to

the top in this wild spoof about advertising agencies and where the voluptuous Mansfield makes her most pulchritudinous mark. Randall works as a copy writer for an upscale ad agency in NYC while he takes care of his niece, Gentle, a teenage celebrity activist (her name is April, but Randall, who is the inimitable Rockwell P. Hunter, affectionately calls her "Ape"). We first see Randall entering his offices to greet the august Williams, owner of the agency, as he passes Randall in the hallway. Williams takes no notice of Randall as he goes his aloof way, but lowly Randall is accustomed to such snubs. He is so far down on the totem pole that he does not have a key to the executive men's room, possession of that key representing the success Randall so ardently craves. He learns that day from Jones, his conniving superior (who slyly utters all the advertising buzz words that encapsulate his authority) that the agency is about to lose its chief client, Stay-Put Lipstick. This means that Jones may be ousted and that Randall is certainly facing dismissal. While pondering this fate at home one morning (his secretary and fiancée, Drake, lives one floor above Randall's apartment), Randall sees that his niece Gentle has skipped school to go to the airport with other screaming teenage girls who make up the Rita Marlowe fan club. That movie star, played by the Amazonian Mansfield, arrives from California and TV cameras close upon her as she walks down the stairs leading from a plane, opening her coat to display a buxom body wearing only a scanty swimsuit, and she is described as the movie star with the "oh-so-kissable-lips." Mansfield has arrived in NYC to further advance her career, but, in reality, she is running away from he-man Hollywood movie star Hargitay (who would become Mansfield's second husband the next year). Gentle breaks through a police line to get Mansfield's autograph and, when Randall sees her on TV, he gets an idea that might save the Stay-Put Lipstick account as well as his job. By this time, Randall has resolved to get Mansfield's endorsement for Stay-Put Lipstick and learns from Gentle where the movie star is staying (Randall tracks down Gentle to a movie theater where Randall triples her allowance for such inside information). Mansfield and her loyal aide, Blondell, have checked into an upscale hotel and Blondell is massaging Mansfield on a table (where she is adorned in only a long towel) when Randall arrives. At that time, Mansfield is in an argument with Hargitay in a long distance phone call conversation. When she learns that Randall is there representing an advertising agency, she makes up a big story about him as her new lover to spite Hargitay. She tells Hargitay over the phone that Randall is the president of a powerful ad agency and that she calls him "Lover Doll," claiming that Randall is one of the world's most romantic Casanovas, although he is far from that. To get Mansfield's endorsement, Randall goes along with her tall tale, talking pompously over the phone to Hargitay. He so impresses the impressionable Mansfield that she becomes passionately involved with him on the spot, grabbing him and giving him the most passionate kiss of his lifetime. He is shown leaving the hotel a short time later in a daze, and he is almost run over by passing cars to which he is oblivious. He later prepares promotional material about Mansfield's endorsement and tells Drake, his secretary and intended, that he is going to put his idea across with Williams. He rushes into Williams' elegantly appointed office to show his promotions, but the standoffish Williams treats Randall indifferently, believing that the agency has lost the Stay-Put Lipstick account. Williams summarily fires Randall, who, in turn, gives Williams a piece of his mind, but his fulminations make no impact. Storming from Williams' office, Randall bumps into a man entering the agency in the lobby, the collision causing Randall to drop and leave all his promotions showing Mansfield's endorsement of Stay-Put Lipstick. He returns to his office to angrily tell Drake that he has been sacked. Randall begins packing up his personal belongings, including a bevy of pipes. He tells Drake that he always wanted to smoke a pipe to have the right executive look, but was always unable to keep any pipe lit and thereby be able to smoke it. Randall leaves to get drunk at a nearby bar. Meanwhile, Mansfield sees her estranged lover, Hargitay, being interviewed on TV and where he takes a break from one of his jungle TV series by climbing down from a tree while attired in a loin cloth and baring a chest as hairy as a lion. Hargitay tells an interviewer that the wayward Mansfield has run away from him but will never find another great lover such as himself and brags that she will be soon come running back to him. Hargitay then demeans Mansfield's new heartthrob, Rockwell P. Hunter, mocking the name "Lover Doll" that Mansfield has given him. Everyone who is anyone in America watches this coast-to-coast network show, and Randall is now known as one of the world's great lovers. When ad executive Jones is summoned to the agency, he learns that the owner of Stay-Put Lipstick is the man Randall bumped into and that he has become overjoyed at Randall's promotions about getting Mansfield's endorsement. Williams, the agency owner, is now desperate to have Randall back in the fold. Jones and Drake find Randall under a table at a local bar; he has drunk so much that he is unconscious (and they find several unlit pipes protruding from his mouth). He is taken home to sober up and is later told by Jones that Williams has not only rehired him, but given him a promotion. Meanwhile, Mansfield has become so angry that she tells Blondell that she will never return to the arrogant Hargitay and fixes her passion on Randall to further make Hargitay jealous. Then Mansfield arrives at Randall's apartment building with great fanfare, reporters and TV personnel interviewing her as she arrives while her fans scream in joy to see her. Randall peers from his apartment window with Jones, telling Jones that Mansfield "is a nut," but that he intends to seal the deal with her whatever it takes so he can become the success he has always envisioned and then marry Drake. His fiancée, however, sees Mansfield arriving and drops a plant of flowers from her window to the one below, striking Randall, to show just how jealous *she* has become for his lavishing attentions on the film siren. Randall is nevertheless promoted to vice president and is awed when he is finally given the much desired key to the executive men's room. He and Mansfield then have a number of engagements, attending nightclubs and dancing until dawn, all of this infuriating Drake. When Randall returns to his office one day, he is inundated with thousands of letters from fans, who are enthralled with his image as "Lover Doll." Drake has been exhaustively performing rigorous exercises to enlarge her breasts so that she can compete with the bosomy Mansfield. When this does not improve her appearance, she wears enormous falsies in Randall's office, moving sensually about and squealing as she talks to mock and mimic Mansfield. She breaks off her engagement with Randall, who has become miserable. He has acquired Mansfield's endorsement for Stay-Put Lipstick and, after arranging for a TV spectacular starring Mansfield, he becomes the president of the ad agency. Williams then happily retires to raise his cultured roses. Williams admits he inherited the company from his draconian father and never liked advertising and that he assumed a haughty attitude because he was insecure, apologizing to Randall for his earlier mistreatment of him. The TV spectacular ensues and Mansfield is a big hit, but is stunned to see a "surprise guest" appear, her first love, Groucho Marx, who takes her into his arms and passionately kisses her. Randall, now that he is at the top of his game, realizes that the success he so desired is empty without Drake and he, like Williams, turns the ad agency over to Jones. Drake takes Randall back and both are married and move to the country where they are shown to be deliriously happy as chicken farmers to end this wacky and utterly humorous story. Randall is superb as the would-be advertising tycoon, and Mansfield, who parodies the stereotypical dumb blondes of the movies, such as Marilyn Monroe as well as Mansfield herself, is perfect in what became her signature film. Drake, Blondell, Gentle, Williams and Jones give outstanding support as the tale is moved along at a whirlwind pace by writer-director Tashlin. In writing the script, Tashlin lampooned television as a poor substitute for Hollywood films, and this is repeatedly enforced by Randall, who addresses the viewer directly more than once to interrupt the story with many absurd, annoying and interruptive advertisements. The film was a box office smash, earning $5 million in its initial release against a budget of $1 million. Song: "You Got It Made" (Bobby Troup). *Author's Note*: The film was based upon the hit Broad-

Tony Randall and Betsy Drake in *Will Success Spoil Rock Hunter?*, **1957.**

way play that opened at the Belasco Theater on October 13, 1955, and ran for 444 performances. The play starred Mansfield, Walter Matthau, Orson Bean, Tom Posten and Tina Louise. Tashlin rewrote the Axelrod play and Fox bought the story chiefly to acquire its title and basic story line, along with wanting to get Mansfield in the bargain as her image as a screen siren was then soaring. Although Mansfield plays an addle-brained blonde bombshell, she was in real life a very savvy woman (with an IQ of 163), fluently speaking five languages and having a college education. She was more than capable at playing the violin and had given concerts in her youth. She always knew what she and her image were about and promoted her sex symbol image with great expertise, until she was horribly killed in a terrible car accident outside of Slidell, Louisiana, on June 29, 1967, dying at age thirty-four. She was not decapitated in that accident as it was later and erroneously reported. Other films profiling advertising agencies include **According to Spencer**, 2001; **Agency**, 1981; **Artists and Models**, 1937; **Beauty for the Asking**, 1939; **Being Nice**, 2014; **Bewitched**, 1964-1972 (TV series); **Bosom Buddies**, 1980-1982 (TV series); **Bounce**, 2000; **Branded**, 2012; **The Circle**, 1970; **Confessions of a Sociopathic Social Climber**, 2005 (made-for-TV); **Crazy People**, 1990; **The Days**, 2004- (TV series); **Definitely, Maybe**, 2008; **Derailed**, 2005; **Distracted**, 1970; **Doin' the Town**, 1941; **Elvis Has Left the Building**, 2004; **The Ex**, 2006; **A Face in the Crowd**, 1957; **Fancy Dancing**, 2002; **Good Neighbor Sam**, 1964; **Good Night, and Good Luck**, 2005; **H.M. Pulham, Esq.**, 1941; **Happiness Never Comes Along**, 2012; **How to Get Ahead in Advertising**, 1989; **Howl**, 2010; **The Hucksters**, 1947; **The Human Contact**, 2008; **I Want to Get Married**, 2011; **A Job to Kill For**, 2006 (made-for-TV); **Kate & Leopold**, 2001; **The Last Kiss**, 2006; **Laura**, 1944; **Live!**, 2007; **The Long Weekend**, 2006; **Lost in America**, 1985; **Loulou**, 1980; **Mad Men**, 2007-2015 (made-for-TV); **Madison Avenue**, 1961; **Marjorie Morningstar**, 1958; **Me and My Girl**, 1984-1988 (TV series); **Melancholia**, 2011; **Melody Lane**, 1941; **A Merry War**, 1998; **Million Dollar Murder**, 2005 (made-for-TV); **Mr. Blandings Builds His Dream House**, 1948; **Ned and Stacey**, 1995-1997 (TV series); **99 Francs**, 2007; **No**, 2012; **North by Northwest**, 1959; **Oh Happy Day**, 2007; **Old Dogs**, 2009; **One Way**, 2006; **Passkey to Danger**, 1946; **Perfect Stranger**, 2007; **Private Road**, 1973; **Putney Swope**, 1969; **Sweetheart of the Fleet**, 1942; **Syrup**, 2013; **A Taste of Success**, 1983; **They Want to Marry**, 1947; **Three Cases of Murder**, 1955; **388 Arletta Avenue**, 2012; **Viktor Vogel—Commercial Man**, 2001; **What to Do in Case of Fire**, 2002; **Weekend for Three**, 1941; **Wicked as They Come**, 1956; and **The Woman in Red**, 1984. **p,d&w**, Frank Tashlin (based on the play by George Axelrod); **cast**, Jayne Mansfield, Tony Randall, Betsy Drake, Joan Blondell, John Williams, Henry Jones, Lili Gentle, Mickey Hargitay, Georgia Carr, Barbara Eden, Grou-

Jean Marsh as Queen Bavmorda in *Willow*, 1988.

cho Marx; **c**, Joe MacDonald (CinemaScope; DeLuxe Color); **m**, Cyril
J. Mockridge; **ed**, Hugh S. Fowler; **art d**, Lyle B. Wheeler, Leland
Fuller; **set d**, Walter M. Scott, Bertram Granger; **spec eff**, L.B. Abbott.

Willow ★★★ 1988; U.S.; 126m; Imagine Films/Lucasfilm/MGM/;
Color; Fantasy; Children: Unacceptable (MPAA: PG); **BD**; **DVD**; **VHS**;
IV. Fascinating fantasy begins when a baby girl is found in a river by
Vande Brake and Downing, children of Willow Ufgood, played by
Davis, a dwarf farmer and magician. The child is taken in by Davis and
his family. When a doglike creature attacks their village seeking the
baby, Davis goes to the High Aldwin, played by Barty, for advice. Barty
gives Davis a task to leave the village and give the baby to a responsible
person. Davis learns that the baby is Elora Danan (Ruth and Kate Greenfield), who is destined to bring down the evil sorceress, Queen Bavmorda, played by Marsh. Davis gets help from a swordsman, Kilmer, a
good sorceress, Hayes, and two brownies, Overton and Pollak, in protecting Greenfield from Marsh. Meanwhile, Davis and the others are
being pursued by Marsh's daughter, Whalley, and army general Roach.
Davis and his friends emerge victorious after Davis and his comrades
defeat Marsh and her minions, and Greenfield assumes her rightful place
as ruler in place of Marsh. Violence prohibits viewing by children. **p**,
Nigel Wooll; **d**, Ron Howard; **cast**, Val Kilmer, Joanne Whalley, Warwick Davis, Jean Marsh, Patricia Hayes, Billy Barty, Pat Roach, Kevin
Pollak, Rick Overton, Ruth Greenfield, Kate Greenfield; **w**, Bob Dol-
man (based on a story by George Lucas); **c**, Adrian Biddle; **m**, James
Horner; **ed**, Daniel Hanley, Michael Hill, Richard Hiscott; **prod d**, Allan
Cameron; **art d**, Tim Hutchinson, Jim Pohl, Tony Reading, Kim Sin-
clair, Malcolm Stone; **spec eff**, John Richardson.

Willy Wonka & the Chocolate Factory ★★★ 1971; U.S.; 98m;
Wolper/PAR; Color; Comedy/Fantasy/Musical; Children: Cautionary
(MPAA: G); **BD**; **DVD**; **VHS**; **IV**. Wilder is very weird in his strange
and magnetic role of Willie Wonka, the enigmatic owner of a chocolate
factory in an unspecified European city. Ostrum, an innocent young boy,
regularly visits the local candy store, but where other parents and children buy the wonderful candies available, he is too poor to buy anything
and simply stares through the store window at the succulent goods displayed as the shop owner sings "The Candy Man." Ostrum receives his
meager pay for selling newspapers and uses it to buy a loaf of bread,
taking this home to his starving family. While going home, Ostrum
passes the Wonka chocolate factory and meets Capell, a mysterious tinker, who tells him that "no one ever goes in and no one ever goes out"
of that factory. When reaching his home, Ostrum is greeted by his family, its members living in a cold hut where they are forever freezing and
covered with heavy blankets. They are his widowed mother and his four

ailing grandparents. When Ostrum tells his grandfather, Albertson, about
meeting the tinker, the kindhearted old man tells him that Wilder closed
his factory after he learned that Meisner, his sneaky competitor, and
other unethical candy makers, had sent spies into the factory in an effort
to steal Wilder's candy recipes. Wilder then disappeared for three years,
but has reopened his factory and is producing more candy than ever, although no one knows anything about the workers laboring inside the
factory. Then the pop-eyed Wilder announces to the world that he has
hidden five "Golden Tickets" inside his Wonka Chocolate Bars, and
those finding those tickets will get a free tour of the factory and a lifetime supply of his wonderful candy. We see, as does Ostrum, four lucky
children finding those tickets. They are Bollner, an overweight German
boy with a tendency toward gluttony; Cole, a pampered British girl;
Nickerson, an American girl who is forever chewing gum; and American
boy Themmen, who is a television fanatic. As each is shown with a
covetous ticket, a sinister-looking man is seen whispering in each child's
ear. A fifth ticket is found in South America and this news shatters Ostrum, but it is then announced that the ticket is a forgery. Fortune then
smiles on Ostrum when he finds money in a gutter and uses it to buy
not one but two of the chocolate bars, one of which Ostrum intends to
give to his family. After he finds the last of the five Golden Tickets, he
is approached by the same sinister-looking man, who turns out to be
Wilder's underhanded competitor, Meisner, and who offers money to
the boy for a sample of the new chocolate bar, which Ostrum refuses to
provide. When Ostrum announces the news to his family that he has
found one of the tickets, Albertson becomes so overjoyed that his ability
to walk is restored. Ostrum then picks him to be his chaperone in his
tour of the factory as each of the five children must be accompanied by
an adult. When entering the factory, the children and their chaperones
are greeted by a scowling Wilder. He trusts no one and tells everyone
that, if any of them touches anything, their agreement with him will be
over. He is so suspicious that he insists that all sign a strict contract with
him before the tour begins. The visitors then see the wonders of the factory as they sail along a river of running chocolate and see wallpaper
that can be licked and mushrooms that are edible. Working to manufac-
ture Wilder's wonderful confectionaries is a small army of green-haired,
orange-skinned dwarfs called Oompa-Loompas. As the tour proceeds,
each of the spoiled children routinely violate the terms of their agreement with Wilder and meet frightening fates. The first of these is the fat
German boy, Bollner, who tries to drink from the chocolate river and
falls into it, being sucked up a pipe to the Chocolate Smelting Room.
Nickerson inflates to a giant blueberry, billowing upward and out of
sight after she prohibitively chews a three-course meal gum. When Albertson and Ostrum reach the Fizzy Lifting Drinks Room, they drink
some of the beverages, and this causes them to float to the factory ceiling, but they manage to hide their violation. The spoiled Cole then demands in a temper tantrum a priceless goose laying golden chocolate
eggs, and her unruly behavior is rewarded when she is sent down a
garbage chute that leads to a furnace. Themmen then becomes so obsessed with "Wonkavision" that he is teleported to a reduced size of only
six inches tall. With all the visitors eliminated, Ostrum and Albertson
reach the "Inventing Room" where Ostrum is given an "Everlasting
Gobstopper." This is not an all-day sucker, but a lifelong sucker that
never wears out. Wilder, however, demands the return of the lifelong
sucker, stating that Ostrum and his grandfather broke their agreement
when they wrongfully drank Fizzy Lifting Drinks, ordering them to
leave the factory. Albertson becomes enraged, verbally insulting Wilder
as a treacherous person. He then tells Ostrum to give the "Everlasting
Gobstopper" to Wilder's competitor, Meisner. Ostrum, however, does
not have a mean bone in his body and is honest to the core. He turns the
lifelong sucker over to Wilder. A broad smile floods Wilder's face as he
tells Ostrum that the entire tour was a test to see which of the children
would be honest and only Ostrum has passed that test. Meisner then appears and is introduced as Wilder's agent, not Wilder's competitor, and
that Meisner's job being to test the honesty of the children. In addition

to keeping the lifelong sucker, Ostrum and Albertson are then treated by Wilder to a ride in Wilder's "Wonkavator," an elevator that soars upward, breaks through the roof and then sails over the city. Wilder then tells Ostrum that the real prize is that Ostrum is now the owner of the chocolate factory and he and his impoverished family can now move into the place while he, Wilder, retires. Wilder gives one of his most bizarre performances in this well-made, often exciting, but somewhat disturbing film, one where he plays the avuncular benefactor, who is nevertheless unlikable and even abnormally frightening. This eerie fantasy is Teutonic in nature and with many abusive scenes couched as artful humor that teach its moral lessons with draconian results. Severe punishment is meted out to those children so foolish as to violate the rules of conduct set down by the dictatorial Wilder. He acts like a punitive chocolate Kaiser, rather than a benevolent and kindly candy-maker. The outlandishly grim fates of the violating children therefore present a frightening black comedy that may disturb any young child viewing this offbeat film, not to mention sensitive parents eschewing corporal punishment. It must then be asked what kind of audience the producers had in mind when making this fascinating but ominous-looking production for there is strong evidence of brutality and even sadism appearing in many of its more spectacular scenes. Ironically, Albertson appeared (in his third feature film) as the capricious postal worker who urges that all the undeliverable mail sent to Santa Claus during Christmastime be rerouted to a courthouse. That action saves Edmund Gwenn at a sanity hearing, officially verifying Gwenn as the one and only true Santa Claus, in the warmhearted **Miracle on 34th Street**, 1947, a film in temperament and theme just the opposite of this mean-spirited film. But that 1947 film, of course, was made in a kinder, gentler era, and this film was made almost three decades later when innocence was viewed by a jaundiced Hollywood eye and where smart-set adult cynicism had replaced the uncomplicated trust of any believing child. A fearful and always wielding rod is not spared in this film. The film was a success at the box office, earning more than $10 million, and earning twice that amount in rereleases over the next twenty years, against a budget of more than $4 million. This film was remade as **Charlie and the Chocolate Factory**, 2005, starring Johnny Depp, a disappointing production where the posturing Depp is wholly miscast. Songs: "The Candy Man," "Cheer Up, Charlie," "(I've Got a) Golden Ticket," "Pure Imagination," "Oompa-Loompa-Doompa-De-Do," "I Want It Now!," "Wondrous Boat Ride" (Leslie Bricusse, Anthony Newley). **p**, David L. Wolper, Stan Margulies; **d**, Mel Stuart; **cast**, Gene Wilder, Jack Albertson, Peter Ostrum, Roy Kinnear, Julie Dawn Cole, Leonard Stone, Denise Nickerson, Dodo (Nora) Denney, Gunter Meisner, Peter Capell, Michael Bollner, Paris Themmen, Ursula Reit, Stephen Dunne; **w**, Roald Dahl, (uncredited) David Seltzer (based on the novel *Charlie and the Chocolate Factory* by Dahl); **c**, Arthur Ibbetson; **m**, Walter Scharf; **ed**, David Saxon; **art d**, Harper Goff; **spec eff**, Logan R. Frazee, Jim Danforth.

Wilson ★★★ 1944; U.S.; 154m; FOX; Color; Biographical Drama; Children: Acceptable; **DVD**; **VHS**; **IV**. In his finest role, Knox is movingly convincing as the idealistic U.S. President Woodrow Wilson (Thomas Woodrow Wilson, 1856-1924) in a sumptuous production that chronicles his life from his presidency at Princeton to his becoming the Chief Executive in the White House. The film opens in 1909 where Knox is the highly respected president of Princeton University (1902-1910) in New Jersey. He is approached by Democratic Party officials to run as a candidate for governor of the state and he accepts. Winning, Knox becomes so successful that his party leaders think he can be elected to the presidency and he runs as a Progressive Democrat in the 1912 election, winning after the Republican Party splits, giving him a forty percent plurality. During Knox's first term of office, WWI (1914-1918) breaks out, but he maintains a rigid policy of neutrality, and institutes many reforms, despite the strong opposition of his Republican leaders, such as Hardwicke, who plays a severe and aggressive Henry Cabot Lodge (1850-1924), the unwavering U.S. senator from Massa-

Thomas Mitchell, Alexander Knox (as Woodrow Wilson) and Geraldine Fitzgerald in *Wilson*, 1944.

chusetts. Knox further deals with the deep loss of his wife, Nelson, who plays Ellen Wilson (1860-1914). When Knox runs for reelection he promises to keep America out of that war, but this proves to be all but impossible as German submarines begin sinking U.S. merchant vessels. He then discovers that Germany is attempting to persuade Mexico to wage war on the U.S. as a German ally, this information unearthed through the interception of British intelligence of the notorious Zimmermann Telegram (sent by German Foreign Secretary Arthur Zimmermann, 1864-1940, to the German ambassador to Mexico on January 11, 1917). Knox becomes furious over this blatant subterfuge and calls Selwart, who plays Count Johann Heinrich von Bernstorff (1862-1939), the German ambassador to the U.S., to the White House. In an explosive scene, Knox loudly upbraids Selwart for his country's underhanded and warmongering tactics and then orders him to leave the country, closing all relations with Germany. Despite warnings from his top adviser, Price, who plays Knox's son-in-law and U.S Secretary of the Treasury William G. McAdoo (1863-1941), Knox asks Congress to declare war on Germany. Knox agonizes over his decision, but he receives the strong support of his wife, Fitzgerald, who plays Edith Wilson (who was married to Wilson in 1915). The couple startles U.S. Army troops before they are to leave for Europe and the front when they both appear at a train station to serve coffee and doughnuts to the "Doughboys." Knox at that time reassures the eager young men that they are fighting in a just war that must be won for the freedom-loving people of the world. When the war is won, Knox goes to Europe to make peace with the other Allied leaders, convincing them to establish a League of Nations that will hopefully keep the world from ever again entering such a devastating war. Knox returns to the U.S., but is told by his old nemesis Hardwicke that America is still an isolationist country and wants no part of the League of Nations. Knox takes to the stump, traveling across the country by train and making speeches to all who will listen as he urges the U.S. to join the League. The campaign is too much for him, ruining his health and he returns to the White House only to see Congress reject the League. He then suffers a stroke and Fitzgerald becomes not only his nurse and protector, but guardedly acts as a surrogate President, until Knox leaves office and the great man dies. Though somewhat overlong and some of the scenes drag, the film nevertheless offers a fascinating portrait of one of America's most distinguished and courageous Presidents. Knox, in a marvelously understated performance, well captures this thoughtful and compassionate leader, receiving great support from a talented cast. The film received Oscars for Best Writing, Original Story (Trotti); Best Cinematography (Shamroy, Palmer); Best Film Editing (McLean), Best Art Direction (Ihnen, Basevi; and set decoration: Little); and Best Sound Recording (E. H. Hansen). It also received Oscar nominations for Best Film; Best Director (King); Best Actor (Knox); Best

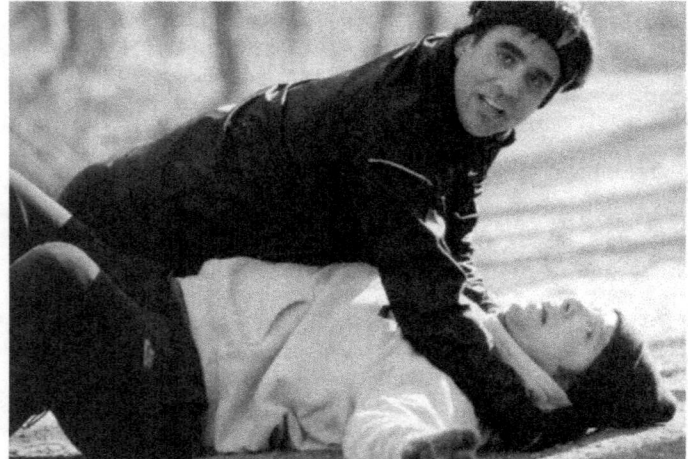

Bobby Cannavale and Paul Giamatti in *Win Win*, 2011.

Music (Newman), and Best Special Effects (Sersen). Although this film received an amazing ten Oscar nominations (winning five), it did poorly at the box office, stunning Fox and its chief, Darryl Zanuck. It earned about $2 million in its initial release against a whopping budget of more than $3 million (which was more than the cost to make the lavish **Gone with the Wind**, 1939, and, in fact, the most expensive film made by Hollywood up to that time). *Author's Note*: Zanuck told this author that this film "was a story I wanted to make for years as I always had a deep admiration for President Wilson. We threw everything we had into that production, so I was shocked when the public simply did not respond. I was so upset about the picture's no-show that I did not want its title mentioned to me for years after that." Zanuck premiered this film in his tiny hometown of Wahoo, Nebraska, and was very disappointed when it made little impact there and where the theater was only half-filled when it was first shown. "I think," Zanuck said to this author, "that because the Second World War was still going on, the public did not want to be reminded of the Great War that had taken place only twenty years earlier. The country was just worn out by war by that time with too many gold stars hanging in the windows of American homes." Those gold stars represented sons, fathers, and brothers who had been killed in WWII (1939-1945). Then President Franklin D. Roosevelt (1882-1945) admired this film and specifically ordered that **Wilson** be screened when he attended the Second Quebec Conference in 1944, but even his closest ally at that time, Winston Churchill (1864-1965), walked out on the film, stating that he was too exhausted to continue watching and went to bed. Price told this author that "**Wilson** was a terrific picture and Alex [Knox] was outstanding when playing President Wilson. He not only looked like him, but he acted like him in a very measured and tightly controlled performance. No actor speaks the English language more precisely than that accomplished actor, absolutely no one, not even me." King told this author that "Darryl [Zanuck] wanted everything accurate when we did that picture so he hired Eleanor Wilson McAdoo [1889-1967] to be our technical adviser. Well, lovely lady that she was, she drove us nuts with 'oh, no, my father did not use his fork that way when eating,' or 'oh, no, my father never wore his hats tilted to one side or the other.' You would think that she was at her father's side every second of his life." Woodrow Wilson has been profiled by man other actors in many other films, including **Backstairs at the White House**, 1979 (TV miniseries; episode 1.1.: Robert Vaughn); **The Conquerors**, 1932 (himself in archive footage); **The Great Victory, Wilson or the Kaiser? The Fall of the Hohenzollerns**, 1919 (Fred C. Truesdell); **First Ladies Diaries: Edith Wilson**, 1976 (made-for-TV; Michael Kane); **Freedom to Speak**, 1982 (TV miniseries; Mason Adams); **Frontiers of Faith**, 1951-1970 (TV series; "A Dream of Earth," 1955 episode; Reynolds Evans); **The Great War and the Shaping of the 20th Century**, 1996 (TV minis-

eries; several episodes; Martin Landau); **Iron Jawed Angels**, 2004 (made-for-TV; Bob Gunton); **The Kaiser, The Beast of Berlin**, 1918 (Orlo Eastman); **Nzabyvaemyy 1919 god**, 1951 (L. Korsakov); **Oh! What a Lovely War**, 1969 (Frank Forsyth); **Omnibus**, 1952-1961 (TV series; "He Shall Have Power," 1960 episode; Harry Townes); **On the Jump**, 1918 (Ralph Faulkner); **Polonia restituta**, 1981 (Jerzy Kaliszewski); **Profiles in Courage**, 1964-1965 (TV series; "Woodrow Wilson," 1965 episode; Whit Bissell); **The Prussian Cur**, 1918 (Ralph Faulkner); **The Story of Will Rogers**, 1952 (Earl Lee); **Time Squad**, 2001- (TV series; "White House Weirdness" episode: Rob Paulsen); **The Wet Parade**, 1932 (himself in archive footage); **Why America Will Win**, 1918 (Ralph Faulkner); **You Are There**, 1953-1971 (TV series; "The Secret Message That Plunged America into World War I, March 1, 1917," 1955 episode: Edward Earle); **You Can't Buy Everything**, 1934 (Fred Lee); **The Young Indiana Jones Chronicles**, 1992-1993 (TV series; "Paris, May 1919," 1993 episode; Josef Sommer). **p**, Darryl F. Zanuck; **d**, Henry King; **cast**, Alexander Knox, Charles Coburn, Geraldine Fitzgerald, Thomas Mitchell, Ruth Nelson, Sir Cedric Hardwicke, Vincent Price, William Eythe, Mary Anderson, Ruth Ford, Sidney Blackmer, Stanley Ridges, Eddie Foy, Jr., Francis X. Bushman, Tonio Selwart; **w**, Lamar Trotti; **c**, Leon Shamroy, Ernest Palmer (Technicolor); **m**, Alfred Newman; **ed**, Barbara McLean; **art d**, Wiard Ihnen, James Basevi; **set d**, Thomas Little; **spec eff**, Fred Sersen.

Win Win ★★★ 2011; U.S.; 106m; FOX Searchlight; Color; Sport Drama; Children: Unacceptable (MPAA: R); **BD**; **DVD**. Exciting and action-packed film begins with a discouraged Providence, New Jersey attorney, Giamatti, who spends nights as a high school wrestling coach and comes upon Shaffer, a boy with potential of becoming a star athlete. Lynskey, Shaffer's mother, comes out of drug rehabilitation and threatens to upset Shaffer's chances of being a winning wrestler. Giamatti and his wife, Ryan, take Shaffer into their home in exchange for Lynskey leaving her son alone. It's a "win win" situation for everyone that leads to Shaffer's success as a championship wrestler. This film is not to be confused with a 2013 Switzerland-Belgium film of the same title but with a different plot. Songs: "Runaway" (Bryan Crouch, Joe Barlow, Drew Dockrill, Chad Richardson, Darryl Romphf, Alex Aligizakis); "Nearer My God to Thee" (1841; Sarah Flower Adams); "Sexy Muzaak Esm," "Convenience Store Muzaak Esm," "Mellow Muzaak Esm" (Michael Tavera); "Mary Had a Little Lamb" (traditional); "Reconnect" (Dystrophy: Aristotle Mihalopoulos as Ari, Phil Tschechaniuk, Joe Fox, Erik Tisinger); "Blonde Bad and Beautiful" (Joel Francis O'Keeffe, Ryan O'Keeffe); "Until the Day," "I Am You" (Ryan Young, Justin Francis); "Cornucopia" (Tom Keane); "Revolution" (Damien Starkey, Kevin Renwick, Bobby Amaru); "Out of Control" (James Lum); "Thrust" (Marvin Gordy III, Thomas Brissette); "Fight! Fight! Fight! A" (Will Schaefer); "Scratch Anthem" (Rob Swift); "Have a Nice Day" (Jon Bon Jovi, Richie Sambora, John Shanks); "Gladiator March" (traditional); "Terrified" (Hubert Clifford); "Think You Can Wait" (Matt Berninger, Aaron Dessner). Gutter language prohibits viewing by children. **p**, Thomas McCarthy as Tom McCarthy, Lisa Maria Falcone, Michael London, Mary Jane Skalski, Jacqueline Brogan; **d**, McCarthy; **cast**, Paul Giamatti, Amy Ryan, Alex Shaffer, Bobby Cannavale, Jeffrey Tambor, Burt Young, Melanie Lynskey, Margo Martindale, David Thompson, Mike Diliello; **w**, McCarthy (based on a story by McCarthy, Joe Tiboni); **c**, Oliver Bokelberg; **m**, Lyle Workman; **ed**, Tom McArdle; **prod d**, John Paino; **art d**, Scott Anderson; **set d**, Amanda Carroll; **spec eff**, Mark Skversky, Phillip Beck, Jake Braver, Chris Gelles, David Isyomin.

Winchester '73 ★★★★★ 1950; U.S.; 92m; UINV; B/W; Western; Children: Unacceptable; **DVD**; **VHS**; **IV**. Gritty and realistic in every frame, this masterpiece western from Mann sees one of James Stewart's finest performances as a man obsessed with seeking vengeance upon the killer who murdered his father. The person for whom he desperately searches is McNally, who also renders one of his best performances as a ruthless outlaw and who is none other than Stewart's brother. The film opens during the pivotal year of 1876 when the command of George Armstrong Custer (1839-1876) has been wiped out by the Sioux at the Little Big Horn, celebrated gunman James Butler "Wild Bill" Hickok (1837-1976) has been killed in Deadwood, Dakota Territory, and the James-Younger Gang has been all but destroyed in an abortive bank robbery raid at Northfield, Minnesota. It is the same year in which a prized Winchester rifle exchanges hands in one ironic twist of fate after another and where most of its owners meet violent ends. Stewart and his close friend Mitchell arrive in Dodge City, believing McNally (calling himself "Dutch Henry Brown") has arrived in that town. As Stewart rides into the town, he sees Winters, a pretty blonde woman, being roughly escorted to a stagecoach that is about to depart. Stewart tries to intervene with Geer, the man escorting Winters. Geer prevents Stewart from taking any action when he affably exhibits his authority by pinning his marshal's badge onto his vest and introduces himself as Wyatt Earp (1848-1929). Winters is being sent out of town because her notorious dance hall reputation has caused the ire of the town's decent and upstanding women, many of whom stand by to see that she leaves, and Geer admits to Stewart that his chore is an unpleasant one. Winters thanks Stewart for his efforts on her behalf and takes her place in the stage, telling Stewart that she hopes to see him again before the stagecoach is driven away. Geer then tells Stewart and Mitchell that they are welcome to stay in Dodge as long as they check their guns, which they do. Geer explains that they have arrived at a propitious moment in that the town is celebrating the Fourth of July. A shooting match is to be held that day and many sharpshooters have arrived to participate in the contest, not the least of whom is McNally, the very man Stewart so passionately seeks. After checking their guns at Geer's office, stored by Wilkerson (who plays Virgil Earp, 1843-1905), Geer then accompanies Stewart and Mitchell to a saloon. When they enter, Stewart sees McNally and both impulsively reach for their guns before they realize that their holsters are empty and that Geer has already taken those six-guns. Stewart and Mitchell go to the end of the bar while McNally and his two gunmen companions, Millican and Brodie, go to the opposite end of that bar. The sneering McNally then orders milk to be served to Stewart and, when that drink is placed before him, Stewart thinks to go after McNally, but the peace-keeping Geer holds him in his place, not knowing the reason why these two men hate each other. A short time later, Geer stands in the town square, holding aloft a beautiful new rifle, the Winchester '73, which he states is "one in a thousand" made, that it is a perfect weapon and that the rifle will be the prize awarded to the best marksman shooting that day. Stewart, McNally and many others enter the contest and begin shooting at targets. Stewart and McNally are the only ones to hit consistent bull's eyes and the targets are removed to farther distances, but the same results are seen. To settle the match, Geer throws coins into the air, but both men hit the coins with single shots. Stewart then purchases a hollow Indian ornament from Chief Yowlachie for $1 and both he and McNally shoot at it after Geer tosses it into the air. Both seem to miss, but Stewart claims that he shot through the hollow of the ornament. He then borrows a postage stamp from one of Geer's deputies, pasting the stamp over the ornament's hollow area, saying that if he hits the ornament he wins, if he misses, he loses to McNally. "I'll take that bet," McNally tells him. Mitchell objects, saying that "if you have to shoot, he has to shoot." Stewart nevertheless insists that they go ahead with the hit-or-miss trial and Geer tosses the ornament skyward. After Geer picks up the ornament, he proclaims Stewart the winner, showing that Stewart has shot through the postage stamp covering the hollow of the ornament. Stewart is awarded the Winchester rifle, but, when he later enters his hotel room, McNally and his two henchmen are waiting there and attack him. McNally knocks Stewart out and takes the rifle, but Geer and Mitchell realize what is going on and fire at the outlaws, who flee the hotel and escape the town on horseback, but with only the Winchester and without their own guns. Geer arrives to see Stewart coming to his senses,

James Stewart and Stephen McNally in *Winchester '73*, 1950.

and Geer tells him that whatever has caused the feud between him and McNally, Stewart can now add the stolen Winchester to their longstanding grudge. Stewart and Mitchell then collect their six-guns and leave Dodge to continue their pursuit of McNally. Meanwhile, McNally and his two companions reach a roadhouse operated by Alexander, where gunrunner McIntire is playing solitaire as he waits word from a local Indian chief to meet with him so that McIntire can sell him his used guns. Alexander warns McIntire that he is playing a dangerous game in selling weapons to Indians, especially after they have learned that the Sioux have wiped out Custer and his command at the Little Big Horn, and that the Indian tribe McIntire is dealing with may be on the same warpath. McNally, Millican and Brodie then try to purchase six-guns and rifles from McIntire, but they do not have enough money to buy any. When McIntire sees the Winchester carried by McNally, however, he offers to give McNally $300 in gold coins, as well as guns to him and his friends. McNally, however, pools the money he and his friends have and plays poker with McIntire, winning enough money to purchase other weapons from the gun dealer. McNally then plays poker once more with McIntire and, when believing he has a winning hand, bets the Winchester. When McIntire wins that pot and the Winchester, McNally threatens McIntire and Alexander, holding a shotgun on McNally and his two friends, and orders them to leave his place. The three, now having used six-guns and rifles, depart. McIntire is then summoned to the camp of Indian chief Hudson, who inspects the guns offered by the gunrunner. Hudson tells McIntire that all of the weapons he is offering for sale are worn out and next to useless and says that all white men lie all the time to Indians. He then sees the Winchester that McIntire has in the scabbard strapped to his horse and withdraws it. McIntire tells Hudson that he will never have enough money to buy that rifle and that it is not for sale. Hudson snarls: "This is the gun I want!" McNally and his cohorts later come upon McIntire, who is sitting in the distance at a smoking campfire. McNally uses one of the rifles he has earlier gotten from McIntire to shoot the gunrunner, and, after McIntire topples to the ground, McNally rides to the campfire site to recoup the Winchester. He and his companions, however, find that McIntire is dead, killed much earlier by Hudson, as clearly indicated when Brodie states: "Why do they always have to scalp [their victims]?" We next see Hudson, the very man who has killed McIntire, with his warriors, all mounted and wearing war paint, planning to war on the whites as has their neighbors, the Sioux (Hudson's tribe is not specified but one might assume that he and his followers are Cheyenne, which allied itself with the Sioux in the Indian wars of 1876). Now it is Hudson, not McIntire, who possesses the much-coveted Winchester. Hudson at that moment sees in the far distance a couple traveling in a buckboard, and we then see Winters with Drake, the man who has long

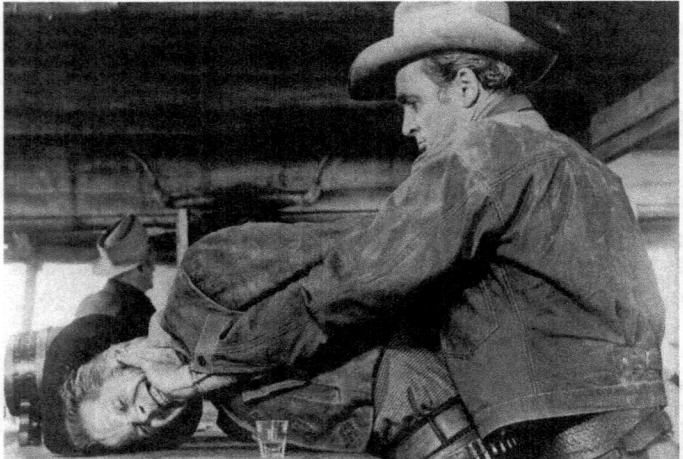

Dan Duryea and James Stewart in *Winchester '73*, 1950.

promised to marry her and save her from the barroom shames that drove her from Dodge City. Suddenly, they see Hudson and his braves riding along a ridge and heading their way, and Drake whips the horses into a furious pace. When Drake sees that the Indians are gaining on him and Winters, he panics, stopping the buckboard and mounting his horse which has been tied to the buckboard and races off, shouting back to Winters that he is going for help. Drake is, however, as Winters and he both know well, racing off to save his own life at the sacrifice of hers and that he is an utter coward. When Drake reaches a knoll and looks downward, however, he sees a campsite where U.S. Cavalry troops are gathered. He then turns about and races back to Winters, rejoining her and urging her to lash the horses of the buckboard forward as the Indians race and whoop after them. Riding furiously down a slope and outdistancing Hudson and his warriors, Drake and Winters reach the cavalry camp where they are welcomed by seasoned sergeant Flippen. Winters is so relieved to see this grizzled old army veteran that she gives him a kiss. Flippen, however, offers dire news in that he and his men, a small contingent of raw recruits en route to a nearby fort, have been pinned down for some time by the Indians led by Hudson. As Winters takes refuge next to a wagon, she grows cold toward Drake, who becomes guilt-ridden and sheepish for having momentarily deserted her. That night, Stewart and Mitchell have reached Alexander's roadhouse where they are having supper and hearing the news that McNally and his men were there only a short time earlier and are on their way to a nearby town, perhaps to rob a bank. Although Mitchell wants to remain at the roadhouse and rest, he obediently follows his friend Stewart, who insists that they ride on in order to find McNally. While riding through the twilight of the countryside, they hear the birdcalls and other sounds of Indians in the area and Stewart now has second thoughts about continuing his pursuit of McNally. Just as the Indians close in, Stewart and Mitchell gallop over a ridge and, like Winters and Drake before them, see the U.S. Cavalry camp and ride pell-mell to it. Flippen, the sergeant in command, tells Stewart that his raw recruits have never fought Indians before and Stewart tells him that, since night is falling, Flippen and his troopers can rest easy until dawn, which is when the Indians will attack. Stewart then resumes his acquaintanceship with Winters, who has a warm feeling toward him as he was the only one in Dodge who showed her respect and kindness. Stewart gives his six-gun to Winters to use in defending herself, but it is understood between them that the last bullet in that gun is reserved for herself and to be used to take her own life to prevent her live capture at hands of the savages. Stewart and Mitchell, who are veteran Indian fighters, then tell Flippen that when the Indians attack, they will come in waves and that, while the troopers fire their single-shot U.S. Army rifles, he, Mitchell and Drake, who all have repeating rifles, will hold their fire until the second wave attacks and drive

back the Indians. This alternating firing power, Stewart says, might repel and even defeat the Indians being led by Hudson. As predicted, when dawn arrives, Hudson sends his warriors in mounted attacking waves against the camp. The troopers shoot down most of those in the first wave and Stewart, Mitchell and Drake drive back the second wave. In a final attack, Stewart is able to shoot and kill Hudson, the chief, which causes the remaining Indians to call off their attack. Now safe to resume their journey, Flippen thanks Stewart and Mitchell for their help and Winters fondly keeps a single bullet she had saved from the six-gun Stewart gave her for self-protection during the attack. Stewart tells her that he hopes he will see her again and rides off with Mitchell. Curtis, one of the troopers, then finds the new Winchester next to the body of the fallen Hudson, and Flippen gives the rifle to Drake as his way of thanking him for helping to fight off the Indians. Drake and Winters then resume their journey on their buckboard until, that night, they reach a small farm where Winters is to stay while Drake meets with gang leader Duryea. Nothing remains peaceful there for too long as a hard-riding outlaw band led by Duryea arrives at the farm, taking refuge inside the farmhouse as a posse in hot pursuit of the outlaws surround the place and besiege the outlaws. Trapped inside the home is Mullen, a farm woman, and her two children, Eddy and Jackson, along with Drake and Winters. During the siege, Duryea not only covets Winters, but wants the Winchester Drake possesses. Drake refuses to sell it to Duryea so the gang leader demeans and belittles him by forcing him to make coffee and serve it to him. He finally goads Drake into a gunfight that Drake knows he cannot win, killing Drake and taking the Winchester. As the posse begins to fire upon the farmhouse, Winters convinces Duryea to let Mullen and her children go outside before they are injured, but Duryea insists that Winters remain with him. After his men are being shot down by the posse members, Duryea escapes through a window, taking Winters with him and fleeing the place. He later arrives at the mountain hideout of McNally and his henchmen. When McNally sees Duryea with the Winchester, he demands that Duryea give it to him, saying that it is his rifle. Rather than shooting it out with McNally, Duryea gives up the prized weapon. Winters later finds a picture of McNally and Stewart together with their father and now knows that the two are blood related. After McNally outlines his plan to rob the bank in nearby Tascosa, Texas, he rides off with his men. Winters then tells Duryea that he is a strange man in that Duryea shot and killed one man, Drake, to get the Winchester, but then meekly surrendered the gun to McNally. "Aww, I'll get it back from old Dutch," Duryea grins, indicating that he will recoup the rifle the same way he got it from Drake, by killing fellow outlaw McNally after they rob the bank together. Stewart and Mitchell then ride into Tascosa, going to the saloon, and there meet Winters once more. She is playing the piano and tells Stewart that Duryea knows where Stewart can find McNally, pointing out Duryea, who stands at the bar. It is Duryea's job and that of two other henchmen to cover McNally and others after they rob the bank across the street. Before Stewart goes to Duryea, Winters warns Stewart, saying "watch his left hand," as she remembers how Duryea earlier killed Drake. Stewart goes to the bar and tells Duryea that he is looking for McNally and wants to know McNally's whereabouts. Duryea stalls Stewart, slowly pouring a drink and purposely spilling it on his left hand, and, as if to wipe that hand, reaches for his six-gun. Stewart, thus alerted by Winters, grabs Duryea's left arm and twists it behind Duryea's back, forcing Duryea's head to the bar and shouting to know where he can find McNally. Duryea tells him that he will lead him to McNally. As Duryea walks slowly from the saloon, he pulls a gun from the holster of a man outside, but Stewart shoots him before Duryea can aim and fire at Stewart. Duryea fires several wild shots before collapsing dead in the middle of the street. Two of Duryea's henchmen try to kill Stewart, but Mitchell shoots one while Stewart struggles with the other. At that moment, McNally and others emerge from the bank after just having robbed it. Pandemonium ensues in the street with horses and citizens running wildly about. Winters sees a child and runs to it, saving the child, but is shot and wounded in the melee. Stewart, having subdued his assailant, races to her. Seeing that Winters is wounded, he tells Mitchell to look after her as he watches McNally riding away alone. As Stewart rides in fast pursuit after the outlaw, Winters tells Mitchell to stop him, but Mitchell explains that Stewart must right an old terrible wrong, explaining that Stewart and McNally are brothers, one of them good, the other, McNally, bad to the bone. McNally robbed a bank, Mitchell tells Winters, and then went home to hide from pursuing lawmen. When his father refused to give him sanctuary, McNally murdered his father, shooting him in the back. Stewart by this time is following McNally through the desert in a wild chase that leads to the mountain hideout. McNally dismounts and begins climbing through the high rocky terrain, firing at Stewart, who climbs after him. Both men duel with rifles, narrowly missing each other while they exchange threats, and they remind each other how their father taught them to shoot more effectively than the deadly marksmanship they are demonstrating. Finally, Stewart traps McNally at the top of a high cliff and, after McNally exposes himself to fire rapidly at his opponent, Stewart takes careful aim and shoots and kills McNally. The outlaw topples dead from his high perch while Stewart hangs his head in sorrow at having taken the life of his murderous brother. Winters then sees Stewart arrive in the town, and she and Mitchell are reunited with Stewart, the camera then closing on the prized Winchester, which has returned to its rightful owner and now rests in the scabbard tied to Stewart's horse. Mann helms this superb frontier saga with a sharp eye to detail while seamlessly weaving the episodic segments to show how the Winchester exchanges several hands, all with evil purposes, except for those exhibited by the upstanding Stewart. This was a new kind of western in that it presents no glorified myths of the Old West and where everyone is careworn in a hardscrabble and menacing landscape. Mann also does not shirk from showing the routine brutalities of that age from bloodletting Indians to bestial bandits having no compunction in taking human life. Even when cornered and knowing they are most likely facing death, the outlaws following the insidious Duryea laugh and make crude jokes as they exchange shots with posse members. This was heralded as one of the first "psychological" westerns in that it examines through its well-defined characters the obsessive passions that motivate their violent actions. It would influence countless westerns to adapt a more introspective attitude than the many previous sanctified and sanitized screen portraits of the Old West. Stewart is outstanding and surprisingly convincing as a man as savage as the man he seeks to kill, a man obsessed by unrelenting revenge. The scene where Stewart brutally manhandles Duryea shocked Stewart's millions of fans when seeing this otherwise gentle and retiring man become as explosively ferocious as the most mindless barbarians he routinely encounters, but a scene that convincingly shows that he is one and the same as those who inhabit his primitive and always clawing society. McNally and Duryea, too, are riveting as ruthless, cunning outlaws, and Mitchell is reassuring as Stewart's friend, as loyal a sidekick as ever rode stirrup-to-stirrup with any companion. (Mitchell would play a similar role as an avuncular lawman and long-time friend of Gregory Peck, an outlaw on the dodge in another gritty western made the same year, **The Gunfighter**, 1950.) Winters is a gem as she once more plays her traditional role as a shady lady (as she would in many other films, from the waitress-mistress in a **Double Life**, 1947, to the cheating, cheap wife in **The Great Gatsby**, 1949, from the never-to-be-married mistress in **Executive Suite**, 1954, to bordello madam Polly Adler, 1900-1962, in **A House Is Not a Home**, 1964). Geer is believable in his role of famed Wyatt Earp, albeit this veteran character actor later claimed that he was woefully miscast as being much too old to play that energetic marshal at the peak of his law-enforcing prime. The film was a huge success, earning more than $2.2 million, this being the first of many westerns made by Stewart and the gifted Mann. The film was remade as a made-for-TV production in 1967 that starred Duryea. A sixty-minute radio adaptation of this story was aired by Lux Radio Theater on November 5, 1951, with Stewart reprising his role. *Author's Note*: Fritz Lang was originally hired to direct

James Stewart, Millard Mitchell and Will Geer in *Winchester '73*, 1950.

this film, but he backed out and Stewart immediately suggested that Mann helm the production. Stewart told this author that he had met Mann many years earlier when they had worked together in theater productions and he was the actor's first choice to direct this superlative western. "We wanted everything to look authentic," Stewart said to this author, "and that meant that I had to learn how to actually shoot that Winchester. I practiced with that rifle so hard and long that I made my knuckles raw. I learned how to not only hold, aim, fire and cock that rifle, but how to properly cradle it in my arms when carrying it. That rifle is really the star of that picture." Mann used sharpshooter Herb Parsons to shoot through the postage stamp after the holed ornament was tossed into the air during the shooting contest. Stewart wisely forwent his usual $200,000 fee per picture when making this film and settled for a percentage of the profits, which reportedly netted him more than $600,000 (in a deal that also included Stewart's appearance in the delightful fantasy film **Harvey**, 1950, made the same year by Universal). Winters told this author that "Jimmy [Stewart] was the best of gentlemen when we did that picture together and he even had the director shoot my best profile instead of his when we were in scenes together. He is a very gracious and considerate man and a pleasure to work with, even though I was competing with a rifle in the movie." The character McNally plays, Dutch Henry Brown, is based upon real-life lawman-turned-outlaw Henry Newton Brown (1857-1884). He was, at one time, the town marshal of Tascosa, Texas, and he was given a Winchester rifle with his name emblazoned on its stock in thanks for his service. He later turned outlaw and was captured along with three others in a botched bank robbery in Medicine Lodge, Kansas, in April 1884 where the bank president and a clerk were killed. Brown and the others were told that they could write letters to their loved ones before they were hanged, and Brown wrote a touching missive to his wife, asking her to visit his grave after he was executed. He stated: "I will send you all my things and you can sell them. But keep the Winchester." Brown considered this rife the most prized possession of his life. He made an attempt to escape, but was shot to death. His companions were then promptly hanged. For more details about Brown, see my book *Encyclopedia of Western Lawmen and Outlaws* (Paragon House, 1992; pages 54-55). Future superstars Rock Hudson and Tony Curtis have small roles in the film, which was shot on location at Six Points, Texas; Mescal and Tucson, Arizona; and at the Universal backlot in Los Angeles. **p**, Aaron Rosenberg; **d**, Anthony Mann; **cast**, James Stewart, Shelley Winters, Dan Duryea, Stephen McNally, Millard Mitchell, Charles Drake, John McIntire, Will Geer, Jay C. Flippen, Rock Hudson, Steve Brodie, Abner Biberman, James Millican, John Alexander. Ray Teal, Virginia Mullens, Guy Wilkerson, Chief Yowlachie, John Doucette, Tony Curtis, James Best, Bonnie Kay Eddy, Gary Jackson;

Lillian Gish in _The Wind,_ 1928.

w, Robert L. Richards, Borden Chase (based on the story by Stuart N. Lake); c, William Daniels; m, Joseph Gershenson, Jesse Hibbs; ed, Edward Curtiss; art d, Bernard Herzbrun, Nathan Juran; set d, Russell A. Gausman, A. Roland Fields.

The Wind ★★★★ 1928; U.S.; 74m (95m in later releases); MGM; B/W; Drama; Children: Unacceptable; **DVD.** Gish gives another bravura performance in this taut pioneering drama set in the desolate deserts of the southwest. Gish travels by train from Virginia to live with her cousin, Earle, in Texas. She is constantly vexed by the howling desert wind as that train makes its agonizingly slow way through an endless Texas. Love, a cattle buyer traveling on that train, covets the fetching Gish, but makes no advances, other than to cruelly tell Gish that the fierce desert winds have driven many a woman insane. When arriving at Sweet Water, Texas, Gish is met by Hanson, a roughneck cowboy, and balding wrangler Orlamond, who are there to escort her to Earle's remote ranch. Before leaving for that ranch, the unctuous Love tells Gish that he will pay her a visit now and then to see how she is getting along. Gish is not enthusiastic about such prospective visits as she has little or no use for Love, or for Hanson either, as the cowboy makes crude advances to her, which Gish routinely rebuffs. Gish and her escorts, after what seems like an endless journey, finally arrive at Earle's ranch, and her cousin warmly greets her. Cumming, who is Earle's possessive wife, however, shows immediate resentment for Gish because of the affection existing between her and her husband. Cumming further becomes angry and frustrated when her children come to love Gish, giving her more devoted attention than they show to Cumming. Later, a party is held at Earle's ranch, and Hanson, Orlamond and Love attend. A fierce windstorm sends everyone to shelter in the basement and there cowboys Hanson and Orlamond toss a coin to see which of them will be the first to ask Gish for her hand in marriage. Gish thinks this is a game, but the commonplace cowboys are serious. So, too, is the conniving Love, who also asks Gish to marry him. Cumming then confronts Gish and tells her that she wants her to leave the ranch as she can no longer tolerate her dominating the affections of her husband and children. Gish explains that she is without money and has no other place to go. Cumming tells her that she must select one of her suitors and she reluctantly chooses Love. Gish is shocked to then learn from Love that he cannot marry her as he is already married and only wants her to become his mistress. Gish angrily rejects this proposition and Cumming then tells Gish that she must now choose either Hanson or Orlamond as her future husband. Gish selects Hanson and they are married. Hanson takes her home to his small house and attempts to kiss her, but Gish, feeling that she is nothing more than chattel, is unresponsive. When Hanson becomes more forceful in his advances, Gish openly resists him

and tells him that his brutal lovemaking only creates a feeling of loathing for him. Hurt and stunned, Hanson tells her that he will never again touch her and promises to make enough money so that he can send her back to Virginia. Gish meanwhile does all the chores at the house, but is constantly annoyed and haunted by the ceaselessly howling wind. Meanwhile, Hanson tells Gish that he must attend a cattlemen's meeting to deal with the widespread drought that is causing their cattle to die. Gish is now terrified of being left alone in the house with the vexing wind as her only companion and begs to be taken on that trip. Hanson agrees and has her mount a horse, but she cannot manage to ride the animal. Hanson then attempts to take her along with her riding behind him on his horse, but she constantly falls off and the frustrated Hanson then tells Orlamond to take her home. When Hanson returns from his trip, he brings along Love, who has been injured, and Gish nurses Love back to health. Hanson then asks Love to join him and others in a cattle roundup that will provide cash for everyone and Love agrees. Love, however, deserts the cowboys and sneakily returns to the small ranch to make advances toward Gish. By this time, a fierce windstorm is raging and between the menacing Love and the howling wind, Gish is overcome by fear and faints. Love carries Gish to her bed before the scene closes (and it is suggested that Love has sexually attacked her). The following morning, Love demands that Gish go away with him, but she refuses. Love states that when Hanson finds her and him together, he will kill them both. The lust-driven Love then makes another move toward Gish, but she arms herself with a revolver and points it at Love, ordering him to keep his distance. Love does not believe Gish will actually shoot him and grabs the gun, which accidentally goes off, killing him. Filled with panic, the hysterical Gish drags Love's body outside and attempts to bury it, but the gusting winds consistently blow away the sand covering the corpse. Gish thinks that the wind represents the unseen hand of God and is further terrified that she cannot hide the body of the man who has brought so much shame to her. Returning to her house, Gish awaits the inevitable and when Hanson returns she is so relieved to see him that she passionately kisses him and then confesses that she killed Love after he attempted to seduce her. Hanson and Gish then look for the corpse, but it is nowhere to be seen. The compassionate and forgiving cowboy then tells Gish that the wind can obliterate any evidence when a killing is done in self-defense. He tells her that he has gotten enough money to send her back to Virginia, but Gish no longer wants to leave, telling Hanson that she wants to remain at his side as his loving wife and that she no longer fears the wind to close this stunning melodramatic saga. Seastrom directs this domestic tale with a firm hand, introducing many startling scenes that combine the menacing, blowing winds with Gish's hallucinatory responses. He carefully builds these scenes to the tremendous visual crescendo of Love's death and an unseen hand of nature that symbolically refuses to allow Gish to hide the shame forced upon her. The ever-present wind is presented as initially insidious, as it blinds vision and physically alters the barren landscape to fateful designs, until, at the finish, it acts as Gish's benefactor and protector. Gish gives a magnificent performance of a woman beset with imaginary and very real fears, and Hanson is the alter ego of that wind, at first uncontrollable and unpredictable, and then as a comforting shield. Love is exceptional as the scheming cad, the kind of reprehensible character he so often played during the silent era, until he became more avuncular and benign in his roles during the subsequent talkie period. Seastrom, who would be hailed as the father of Swedish film, would go on to inspire Ingmar Bergman and countless others with his use of natural symbolism as he so masterfully displays in this film, as well as exhibiting through one telling scene after another a deep sense of guilt, which is invariably relieved through demonstrative redemption. As was his lifelong tradition, he advances through Gish's always jeopardized character, the evolvement of women as individuals in a society then hazardous and prejudicial toward them. The wind that drives sand into every corner of every house, into clothing and into food, is a metaphor for all the emotional plagues besetting

Gish and bedeviling her psyche. Seastrom makes the wind the catalyst and symbol of everything evil and eventually, everything benevolent. The film did not do well at the box office, but remains a classic of its kind. *Author's Note*: The idea for this film emanated from Gish, who went to MGM production chief Irving Thalberg, asking that he produce the story and where she would star. Gish had had a satisfying experience with Seastrom when they made **The Scarlet Letter**, 1926, together, also at MGM. She asked and got Seastrom as her director and then asked for Hanson to play her leading man after Gish had seen Hanson playing opposite the alluring and enigmatic Greta Garbo in the Swedish film **Gosta Berlings saga**, made in 1924 and released in the U.S. in 1928. The original ending for this film had Gish being driven insane by the wind and, after having killed Love, she wanders into the desert until she is entirely shrouded by swirling dust driven by the wind. MGM executives saw that depressing ending and put their foot down, insisting that a happy finale replace that rather dismal finish. Seastrom and Gish obliged. Although this was shot as a silent, MGM added a soundtrack before the film was released, and the wind can be heard whispering and howling throughout. The film presented considerable hardships for the cast and crew as it was entirely shot in the Mojave Desert where everyone suffered under the sweltering heat of between 100 to 115 degrees. The area was so hot that when Gish placed her hand on a metal door handle, it scalded her. The propellers of eight aircraft were employed to create the powerful gusts of wind that sent crusted earth flying in all directions. Cast (whenever not before the cameras) and crew members were compelled to use goggles, long-sleeved clothing, bandanas around their necks and greasepaint covering their hands and faces to protect themselves from the blinding and stinging sand blown throughout the sets. **d**, Victor Seastrom (Sjostrom); **cast**, Lillian Gish, Lars Hanson, Montagu Love, Dorothy Cumming, Edward Earle, William Orlamond, Carmencita Johnson, Laon Ramon (Leon Janney), Billy Kent Schaefer; **w**, Frances Marion (based on the novel by Dorothy Scarborough); **c**, John Arnold; **m**, William Axt; **ed**, Conrad A. Nervig; **set d**, Cedric Gibbons, Edward Withers.

Wind Across the Everglades ★★★ 1958; U.S.; 93m; Budd Schulberg/WB; Color; Drama/Romance; Children: Unacceptable; **DVD**. Plummer gives an exceptional performance as an alcoholic conservationist with the Audubon Society in the Florida Everglades in the early 1900s where he tries to protect the swamps from real estate developers and poachers who are killing some of the wildlife. Some plume birds are especially sought for their colorful tail fathers that are used to decorate fashionable hats for women. Ives is head of the poachers and he and Plummer eventually clash. Before Plummer can capture him, Ives is killed. Songs: "Empty Pockets Blues" (Budd Schulberg), "Kissin' 'n' Killin'" (Schulberg, Totch Brown, Burl Ives), "Lonely Boy Blues" (Schulberg, Rufus Beecham, Nicholas Ray), "Lostman's River," (Shear 'Em Sheep, Shear 'Em" (Totch Brown). *Author's Note*: Ray, who was one of the best innovative directors of the 1950s, told this author that "I did not have a good time when making that picture. I clashed a lot with Budd [Schulberg] as this was his pet project, a crusade to point out how the wildlife in the Everglades has been slaughtered and were still being decimated when we made **Wind across the Everglades**. We argued about almost every scene until he arranged for me to leave the production and I was glad to go." Schulberg stated to this author that "Nick [Ray] saw that story one way and I saw it another and we just couldn't get together on how that story had to be told, so we parted ways and I reshot most of the film, but Nick had to get credit under the terms of our agreement. I still think that picture told a powerful story." Plummer offhandedly told this author that "I played a boozy character trying to preserve wildlife in a swamp that nobody entered or cared about. It was a very strange story." Falk recalled for this author how "that picture was the first feature I appeared in and my role was so small and I had so few lines that I forget who I was or what I said, except that I know I was there. How's that for a spectacular debut?" Falk played the part of a

George Voskovec, Christopher Plummer and Gypsy Rose Lee in *Wind across the Everglades,* 1958.

writer, and also in bit parts were the famous clown Emmett Kelly and the author MacKinlay Kantor. **p**, Stuart Schulberg; **d**, Nicholas Ray; **cast**, Burl Ives, Christopher Plummer, Gypsy Rose Lee, Chana Eden, Tony Galento, Sammy Renick, Pat Henning, Peter Falk, Cory Osceola, George Voskovec, Totch Brown, Emmett Kelly, MacKinlay Kantor, Dick Wesson (narrator); **w**, Budd Schulberg; **c**, Joseph Brun (Technicolor); **m**, Paul Sawtell, Bert Shefter; **ed**, Georges Klotz, Joseph Zigman; **art d**, Richard Sylbert.

The Wind and the Lion ★★★★ 1975; U.S.; 119m; MGM; Color; Adventure; Children: Unacceptable (MPAA: PG); **DVD**; **VHS**; **IV**. Connery is compelling as the fierce Moroccan tribal chief Raisuli (Mulai Ahmed er Rausuni (1871-1925). He kidnaps American woman Bergen (as Mrs. Eden Pedecaris) and her two children, Harrison and Gottesman, holding them for ransom, and creates the considerable ire of a feisty President Theodore Roosevelt (1858-1919), played by Keith in a marvelously expansive performance. Set in 1904 when the great European powers of England, Germany and France are trying to influence the destiny of Morocco, Connery kidnaps Bergen and her children in a raid on her home, taking them to his remote stronghold. Connery has done this to embarrass Zuber, the Sultan of Morocco, as well as Sheybal, the Pasha of Tangier, in order to set off a civil war, and where Connery, a Berber leader, intends to lead that insurrection. Seeking reelection to the White House, Keith sends a "Big Stick" message to the Sultan of Morocco: "We want Pedecaris alive or Raisuli dead!" This alarms Keith's Secretary of State John Hay (1838-1905), who is played by Huston. (Actually, it was Hay, who, during the crisis where Greek-American playboy Ion Pedecaris, 1840-1925, was kidnapped and held for ransom by Raisuli, sent that fire-and-brimstone message to Samuel Rene Gummere, 1849-1920, who was the U.S. Consul-General in Tangier.) When Gummere, played by Lewis, is unable to negotiate the release of Bergen and her children, Keith angrily sends the U.S. South Atlantic fleet to Tangier Harbor to intimidate the Sultan and Pasha into taking action against the rogue Connery. Keith privately admits to Baxter, who plays Alice Roosevelt (1884-1980), his daughter, oldest child and devoted admirer, that he has great respect for Connery, believing that, even if Connery is his enemy, he is nevertheless an honorable and courageous man. At one point, Keith demands to know what kind of rifle Connery uses so that he can also have the same kind of weapon as Keith is (as was outdoorsman Roosevelt) an avid hunter and marksman. Keith is shown at a firing range where he shoots at a target upon which is emblazoned the image of Germany's Kaiser Wilhelm II (1859-1941) and where he tells Baxter that he has gone blind in one eye, but she is not to tell anyone about it, stating that he hopes that his vision in that eye might surprisingly return. Meanwhile, Bergen attempts to persuade Connery to

Candice Bergen and Sean Connery in *The Wind and the Lion*, 1975.

release her and her children, but the Berber chief is adamant that he must keep her in custody until he achieves his political ends in Morocco. She calls him a "brigand" and a "lout," and warns him that American President Roosevelt (Keith) will not tolerate his actions and that he will soon be facing the might of the U.S. Connery remains unperturbed, but proclaims his admiration for Keith and his manly ways. Desperate to return to her home, Bergen bribes one of Connery's men to help her and her children escape. She and her children and the defecting Berber ride from Connery's bastion to a seaside hideout where the guide shows his true colors and offers to sell Bergen and her children to a group of Arab cutthroats. They gather about Bergen, Harrison and Gottesman, but the little family manages to ward them off with a long spear Harrison seizes. Then the bandits see a lone rider atop a distant dune. It is Connery, who uses his long-range rifle to shoot and kill one of the leaders of the band. Several others mount their horses and charge Connery, who races toward them, his large scimitar swinging wildly; he kills his opponents, the last of whom he decapitates before rescuing Bergen and the children. Vexed by Bergen's actions, Connery tells her: "You are a lot of trouble!" When Connery later tells Bergen his story, especially how he was imprisoned in a dungeon for years by his brother, Sheybal, Bergen's attitude toward the Berber chief softens and he and she become enamored of each other. Jenson, the admiral commanding the U.S. fleet that has anchored in Tangier Harbor, confers with Consul-General Lewis and brash Kanaly, a U.S. Marine captain, urges military intervention to force Sheybal into conceding to Connery's demands in order to retrieve Bergen and her children. To that end, Kanaly lands two reinforced companies of Marines in Tangier and marches to Sheybal's palace where they make a wild charge, killing all of the palace guards and taking Sheybal hostage. Sheybal watches all of this carnage with disdain as he lies upon a lounge chair, and when Kanaly tells him that he is his prisoner, Sheybal archly replies: "Your president is insane and you are a dangerous man." Kanaly smiles, salutes and happily says: "Yes, sir!" (Although the unwelcomed U.S. fleet was, indeed, anchored at Tangier Harbor, the patriotic military action herein so excitingly shown, never occurred as the actual hostage, Pedecaris, was released through negotiations.) Sheybal meets Connery's demands and a hostage exchange takes place at a seaside town where Kanaly and a small Marine detachment arrive to retrieve Bergen and her children. Moroccan troops, however, under the command of German officer Saint-John, traps Connery and makes him prisoner. Connery's lieutenant, Sawalha, however, leads his men in a wild attack on the town and Connery is set free after Saint-John and his forces are defeated. Bergen and her children are then safely returned to their home and, in the U.S., Keith is cheered for heroically saving these American lives. Keith then receives a letter from Connery, stating: "I [Raisuli], like the lion, must stay in my place, while you, like the wind, will never know

yours." Milius, a superb action director, lets no viewer down when presenting this exciting and often mesmerizing film, although it is evident that the director was deeply influenced by **Lawrence of Arabia**, 1962, and **The Wild Bunch**, 1969 (particularly when the Sultan test fires his new Maxim gun, making a shambles of his elegant palace, not unlike the Mexican general wildly firing his newly acquired heavy machine gun in **The Wild Bunch**). The scene where Kanaly leads his Marines with rifles held high and affixed with bayonets at a running, thundering pace through the streets of Tangier is breathtakingly choreographed, with natives and animals scattering before them, until they reach the resplendent palace and form for their attack. Connery rivets as the unwavering Berber chief who knows no fear and accepts all challenges. Keith gives a wonderful rendition of a bold Teddy Roosevelt, one where he also makes fun of his own public posturing. In one scene, Keith climbs atop a desk to pose in what he thinks his bear—which he has earlier killed in a western hunt and is being stuffed—should look like when placed on exhibit. Bergen is fetching and the rest of the cast convincingly perform their historic roles. The film received an Oscar nomination for Best Original Score (Goldsmith) and Best Sound Mixing (Harry W. Tetrick, Roy Charman, Aaron Rochin and William L. McCaughey). The film was a success at the box office, earning more than $5 million in its initial release against a budget of $4 million. Song: "For He's a Jolly Good Fellow" (traditional). *Author's Note*: Although the writers played fast and loose with the actual story of Ion Pedecaris, as well as manufacturing events that never took place, such as the attack on the Tangier palace, the film nevertheless captures the fiery spirit of the two-fisted Roosevelt era where a U.S. President considered going to go to war over the abuse of a lone American. Roosevelt was not unmindful of the heroic actions of the U.S. fleet that sailed to Tripoli in 1804 to punish the Libyan pirates that had been plaguing U.S. commerce and where the bold Commodore Stephen Decatur (1779-1820) distinguished himself in defeating a fleet of these Tripolitan brigands. Keith told this author: "It was impossible to play the great Teddy Roosevelt except as a caricature because that man was larger than life and larger than anyone living at his time. He was a true adventurer who would rather go on a big game hunt than sit in the Oval Office. He was the roaring boy of his era and everybody loved him, even his enemies, like the character Sean [Connery] played in **The Wind and the Lion**. And I loved playing that wonderful man." The film was shot entirely in Spain. Many other actors have portrayed Theodore Roosevelt in many other films, including **Bordertown**, 1989-1991 (TV series; "Four Eyes," 1990 episode: Wayne York); **Bret Maverick**, 1981-1982 (TV series; "Horse of Yet Another Color," 1982 episode: William Hootkins); **Brighty of the Grand Canyon**, 1967 (Karl Swenson); **Bronco**, 1958-1962 (TV series; "Yankee Tornado," 1961 episode: Peter Breck); **Buffalo Bill**, 1944 (Sidney Blackmer); **Bully: An Adventure with Teddy Roosevelt**, 1978 (One-man show; James Whitmore); **Captains and Kings**, 1976 (TV miniseries; Lee de Broux); **Cavalcade of America**, 1952-1957 (TV series; "The Tenderfoot," 1953 episode: Tom Brown); **Circus Boy**, 1956-1958 (TV series; "General Pete," 1957 episode: Ed Cassidy); **Citizen Kane**, 1941 (Thomas A. Curran); **Cook and Peary: The Race to the Pole**, 1983 (made-for-TV; Walter Massey); **The Conquerors**, 1932 (himself in archive footage); **The Copperhead**, 1920 (Jack Ridgway [Jack Ridgeway]); **The Curious Case of Benjamin Button**, 2008 (Ed Metzger); **Cowboys from Texas**, 1939 (himself in archive footage); **Deadliest Warrior**, 2009-2011 (TV series; "Teddy Roosevelt vs. Lawrence of Arabia," 2011 episode: Matt Allman); **Eleanor and Franklin**, 1976 (made-for-TV; William Phipps); **Eleanor and Franklin: The White House Years**, 1977 (made-for-TV; David Healy); **End of the Trail**, 1936 (Erle C. Kenton); **Fancy Pants**, 1950 (John Alexander); **The Fighting Roosevelts**, 1919 (Roosevelt as a boy: Francis J. Noonan; Roosevelt as a young man: Herbert Bradshaw; Roosevelt as president: E.J. Ratcliffe); **The First Traveling Saleslady**, 1956 (Ed Cassidy); **The Ford Television Theatre**, 1952-1957 (TV series; "With No Regrets," 1957 episode: Larry Thor); **Freedom to Speak**, 1982 (TV miniseries; Sam Waterston); **The Gambler Returns: The Luck of the Draw**, 1991 (made-for-TV; Claude Akins); **Geronimo**, 1993 (made-for-TV; Ray Geer); **Gilded Lilys**, 2013 (made-for-TV; Lou Carbonneau); **I Loved a Woman**, 1933 (E. J. Ratcliffe); **I Wonder Who's Kissing Her Now**, 1947 (John Merton); **In Old Oklahoma**, 1943 (Sidney Blackmer); **Incident at Victoria Falls**, 1992 (made-for-TV; Claude Akins); **The Indomitable Teddy Roosevelt**, 1983 (Bob Boyd); **Jack London**, 1943 (Wallis Clark); **Law of the Plainsman**, 1959-1960 (TV series; "The Dude," 1959 episode: Robert Vaughan); **The Legend of Tarzan**, 2001-2003 (TV series; "Tarzan and the Rough Rider," 2001 episode: Stephen Root); **The Life and Times of Grizzly Adams**, 1977-1978 (TV series; "The Tenderfoot," 1977 episode: Charles Martin Smith); **Lights of Old Broadway**, 1925 (Buck Black); **The Magnificent Yankee**, 1965 (made-for-TV; William Griffis); **Meeting of the Minds**, 1977-1981 (TV series; two 1977 episodes: Joe Early); **My Friend Flicka**, 1955-1960 (TV series; "Rough and Ready," 1956 episode: Frank Albertson); **My Girl Tisa**, 1948 (Sidney Blackmer); **Never Kick a Man Upstairs**, 1953 (made-for-TV; Sidney Blackmer); **Newsies**, 1992 (David James Alexander); **Night at the Museum**, 2006 (Robin Williams); **Night at the Museum: Battle of the Smithsonian**, 2009 (Robin Williams); **Night at the Museum: Secret of the Tomb**, 2014 (Robin Williams); **Omnibus**, 1952-1961 (TV series; "He Shall Have Power," 1960 episode: Larry Blyden); **Ordeal by White House**, 1952 (made-for-TV; Howard Wierum); **Ragtime**, 1981 (Robert Boyd); **The Right Man**, 1960 (made-for-TV; Edward G. Robinson); **The Road to Galveston**, 1996 (made-for-TV; Alex Morris); **The Rough Riders**, 1927 (Frank Hopper); **Rough Riders**, 1997 (made-for-TV; Tom Berenger); **Silk Hat Kid**, 1935 (Frankie Genardi); **Sugarfoot**, 1957-1961 (TV series; "Man from Medora," 1960 episode: Peter Breck); **Sun Valley Cyclone**, 1946 (Ed Cassidy); **Sundown**, 1924 (E. J. Ratcliffe); **Take Me Out to the Ball Game**, 1949 (Ed Cassidy); **This Is America, Charlie Brown**, 1988-1989 (TV miniseries; "The Smithsonian and the Presidency," 1989 episode: Frank Welker); **This Is My Affair**, 1937 (Sidney Blackmer); **The Virginian**, 1962-1971; "Riff-Raff," 1962 episode: Karl Swenson); **Voyagers!**, 1982-1983 (TV series; "Bully and Billy," 1982 episode: Gregg Henry); **War of the Worlds: Goliath**, 2012 (Jim Byrnes voiceover); **Wild and Wooly**, 1978 (made-for-TV; David Doyle); **The Wright Stuff**, 2005-2006 (TV series: Ethan Phillips); **Why America Will Win**, 1918 (W. E. Whittle); **Yankee Doodle Dandy**, 1942 (Wallis Clark); **You Are There**, 1953-1971 (TV series; "Dewey's Victory at Manila, May 1, 1898," 1955 episode: Grandon Rhodes; "Attempt to Assassinate Theodore Roosevelt, October 14, 1912," 1957 episode: Roland Winters); and **The Young Indiana Jones Chronicles**, 1992-1993 (TV series; "British East Africa, September 1909," 1992 episode: James Gammon). **p**, Herb Jaffe; **d&w**, John Milius; **cast**, Sean Connery, Candice Bergen, Brian Keith, John Huston, Geoffrey Lewis, Steve Kanaly, Vladek Sheybal, Nadim Sawalha, Simon Harrison, Polly Gottesman, Antoine Saint-John, Roy Jenson, Deborah Baxter, Marc Zuber, Shirley Rothman, Rusty Cox, Larry Cross; **c**, Billy Williams (Panavision; Metrocolor); **m**, Jerry Goldsmith; **ed**, Robert L. Wolfe; **prod d**, Gil Parrando; **art d**, R. Antonio Paton; **spec eff**, Alex Weldon, Matthew Yuricich.

The Wind in the Willows ★★★ 1997; U.K.; 88m; Allied Filmmakers; Buena Vista; Color; Fantasy; Children: Acceptable (MPAA: PG); **DVD**; **VHS**. Well-made fantasy remake of the classic 1949 animated Disney film **The Adventures of Ichabod and Mr. Toad** begins when spring arrives with good weather. Good-natured Mole (Coogan) loses interest in spring cleaning in his underground home, so he emerges to take in the sights and goes down to the nearby river, which he has never seen before. There he meets Ratty (Idle), a water rat, who takes Coogan for a ride in his row boat. Over the next few days, Idle teaches Coogan the ways of the river. One summer day, the friends disembark near the grand Toad Hall and pay a visit to Toad (Jones), a rich, friendly, and kind-hearted but aimless and conceited toad. He is a willy-nilly sort, who

Terry Jones as Toad in *The Wind in the Willows*, 1997.

adopts one fad after another and soon abandons them. His current passion is his horse-drawn caravan and he takes Coogan and Idle for a drive in it. A speeding motorcar scares the horse and the caravan overturns into a ditch. While Coogan calms the horse, Jones decides that driving a motorcar is for him. On a snowy day, while Idle naps, Coogan goes off to explore the Wild Wood. He hopes to meet Badger (Williamson) there, but gets lost and sees some scary faces. He becomes frightened and hides in the roots of a tree. Idle goes in search of Coogan, armed with two pistols, and after finding him, they stumble upon Williamson's underground home and he invites them in to have a meal and dry their wet clothes. Williamson learns from Coogan and Idle that Jones has crashed seven cars and been hospitalized three times. The three of them decide to save Jones from himself because they are all friends who want to help each other. With the arrival of summer again, they go to Toad Hall and try to talk Jones out of his penchant for his new obsessions like motoring. Jones rejects their suggestion, so they put him under house arrest with themselves as guards, until Jones changes his mind. Jones eludes them, steals a car, and drives it recklessly until he is stopped by police. He is sent to prison on a twenty-year sentence. While Jones is in prison, Coogan and Idle live in Toad Hall hoping that Jones will return there. Jones escapes from prison with the help of the jailor's daughter and appropriates a car, again driving recklessly until he has an accident. Police pursue him again until he reaches a river that takes him to Idle's house. There he learns that weasels and ferrets from the Wild Wood have driven out Coogan and Williamson. Jones wants to rescue his friends, realizing their caution about his adventures consisted of good-natured help from friends. Williamson leads the friends through a tunnel and they chase out the weasels and ferrets. Jones celebrates by hosting a banquet and thanks his friends, after which they all live together in comfort at Toad Hall. Songs: "Messing About on the River" (music: Tony Hatch; lyrics: Terry Jones); "Secret of Survival," "Mr. Toad," "AS Friends Is What We Is" (music: John Du Prez; lyrics: Terry Jones); "Miracle of Friends" (music: Dave Howman, Andre Jacquemin; lyrics: Terry Jones). **p**, Jake Eberts, John Goldstone; **d**, Terry Jones; **cast**, Steve Coogan, Eric Idle, Terry Jones, Antony Sher, Nicol Williamson, John Cleese, Stephen Fry, Michael Palin, Bernard Hill, Nigel Planer; **w**, Jones (based on the novel by Kenneth Grahame); **c**, David Tattersall; **m**, John Du Prez, Andre Jacquemin; **ed**, Julian Doyle; **prod d**, James Acheson; **art d**, Keith Pain; **set d**, Anna Pinnock; **spec eff**, Peter Chiang, Dave Crownshaw, Peter Hutchinson.

The Wind Journeys ★★★ 2010; Colombia/Germany/Argentina; 117m; Cuidad Lunar/Razor Film/Film Movement; Color; Drama; Children: Unacceptable; **DVD**; **IV**. Intriguing tale begins with Martinez, who is a wandering musician traveling the villages of northern Colombia

Liam Cunningham in *The Wind That Shakes the Barley*, 2007.

playing folk songs on his accordion, a legendary instrument that is said to have once belonged to the devil. After some traveling, he marries and settles in a small town. When his wife dies traumatically, he vows never again to play the accordion, which he believes is cursed. He then goes on a journey to return the instrument to its owner. Along the way, he is followed by Nunez, a teenager who wants to become his apprentice. Not wanting to be alone, Martinez takes Nunez under his wing as his pupil and they travel the country, discovering the musical diversity of Colombian cultures. Martinez tries to discourage Nunez from following his lonely life of wandering, but destiny has its own exciting plans for them. (In Spanish; English subtitles.) **p**, Diana Bustamante, Cristina Gallego, Gerhard Meixner, Roman Paul, Ana Maria Velasco; **d&w**, Ciro Guerra; **cast**, Marciano Martinez, Yull Nunez, Agustin Nieves, Jose Louis Torres, Carmen Molina, Erminia Martinez, Justo Valdez, Juan Batista Martinez, Hector Brito, Guillermo Merlo, Clemente Herrera, **c**, Paula Andres Perez; **m**, Ivan Ocampo; **ed**, Ivan Wild; **prod d**, Angelica Perea; **spec eff**, Leonardo Quartieri, Roberto Zambrino.

The Wind That Shakes the Barley ★★★★ 2007; Ireland/U.K.; 127m; Sixteen Films/Matador Pictures/Pathé International; Color; War Drama; Children: Unacceptable; **DVD**; **IV**. Taut tale with many harrowing scenes depicts the struggle for Ireland's independence, beginning in 1920. Murphy is a young physician whose brother, Delaney, commands a unit of the IRA (Irish Republican Army, est. 1913), which is fighting British forces to gain that independence. Delaney attempts to persuade his brother to join the IRA, but Murphy has resolved to leave his village and practice medicine in a hospital in London, telling Delaney that the war against the British cannot be won. Even after Barry, who is Murphy's close friend, is executed by the British paramilitary force, the Black and Tans, he cannot bring himself to join the Irish cause. Just before leaving his village, Murphy sees Cunningham, the Irish engineer, as well as a guard, of a train, adamantly refusing to allow British troops to take over their train. Murphy is so impressed with their defiant resistance that their actions convince him to remain at home and he joins Delaney's IRA unit. Murphy trains in the hills before he and others conduct a raid against the barracks of the Royal Irish Constabulary and there obtain weapons, using these guns to execute four pro-British members of the Auxiliaries that are associated with the Constabulary. In response to these assassinations, Allam, a wealthy pro-British landowner, pressures Crean, one of his servants and an IRA member, into giving information about the local IRA unit, which leads to the mass arrest of all of its members. While imprisoned, Murphy meets and befriends Cunningham, the defiant train engineer, and Murphy soon realizes that both share the same socialist beliefs. Delaney, by this time, has been tortured, his fingernails torn from his hands after he refuses

to name the members of the IRA unit. Ruane, a British soldier who has Irish ties, arranges for all of the IRA members, except three, to escape. As Delaney is still recovering from the injuries to his hands, Murphy assumes command of the IRA unit. When he learns how Allam and Crean betrayed the IRA, both are seized and held hostage. After news is received that the three IRA members still held in prison have been summarily executed, Murphy receives orders from higher-ups to execute hostages Allam and Crean. Although Crean has been a lifelong friend, Murphy, now wholly dedicated to the IRA cause, shoots and kills him, along with Allam. Murphy and others then ambush a large Auxiliaries unit, and, in retaliation, British forces begin burning the farms throughout the area and subjecting civilians to harsh punishments for harboring IRA members. This includes Murphy's sweetheart, Fitzgerald, who is humiliated when her hair is shaved so closely that razor-sharp cuts remain on her bald skull, injuries that Murphy later treats. News then arrives that the British and Irish opponents have agreed to a cease-fire. The Anglo-Irish Treaty is signed (between England's Prime Minister, David Lloyd George, 1863-1945, and Ireland's Michael Collins, 1890-1922, and Arthur Griffith, 1872-1922, on December 6, 1921), which brings momentary peace to Ireland. The terms of this agreement, however, soon create widespread division in Ireland. Many IRA leaders and members oppose the agreement, which calls for Ireland to remain in the British Empire with dominion status, but where the Irish will now have representation. Delaney supports the agreement, stating that, in time, Ireland will gain its full independence, but others vehemently oppose the treaty as it continues to subjugate the country to British rule. While Delaney and others join the Irish Army led by Collins, Murphy and Cunningham become their enemies, violently opposing the Treaty, even though Ireland becomes the Irish Free State and is no longer under direct rule by Great Britain. The anti-Treaty forces, however, wage a civil war against the pro-Treaty forces and, during a raid made by the IRA forces led by Murphy and Cunningham at a Free State barracks commanded by Delaney, Cunningham is killed and Murphy taken prisoner. Delaney begs his brother to tell him where a cache of rifles have been hidden by the IRA, promising him amnesty and freedom so that Murphy can finally marry Fitzgerald and live in peace. Murphy refuses to betray his cause and is sentenced to death. Before he is executed, Murphy writes a moving letter to Fitzgerald, and he is then shot and killed by a firing squad as the heartbroken Delaney witnesses his brother's death. Delaney then sorrowfully delivers that letter to Fitzgerald, who is devastated at Murphy's death. She then tells Delaney that she never again wants to see him to end this exciting but anguishing tale where families are torn apart, along with a nation struggling to gain independence. Loach energetically directs this film, expertly merging its historic events with dramatic sequences and where the action is well-choreographed. Murphy, Delaney, Cunningham and Fitzgerald are standouts in their roles and they are ably supported by a talented supporting cast. The film was a great success at the box office, earning more than $22 million in its initial release against a budget of $7 million, and it did surprisingly well in the U.K., that public seldom receptive to any film empathetic with the IRA cause. It became the most popular independently produced film in Ireland. Where the superb **Michael Collins**, 1996, profiles the early-day IRA struggles at the hierarchy of that organization, this film magnificently details its rank and file to show a savage and uncompromising microcosm of that struggle. Songs: "The Wind That Shakes the Barley," "Amhrain Na bhFiann," "Oro! Se Do Bheatha 'Bhaile," "The Doon Reel" (traditional). ***Author's Note***: The title for this outstanding film is taken from a song composed by Robert Dwyer Joyce (1830-1883), which tells the story of a young Irish revolutionary who joins the 1798 rebellion in Ireland after the violent death of his true love. The film was shot entirely in Ireland, chiefly in the County of Cork. Hundreds of extras were culled from the ranks of Scout troops, and the British soldiers were enacted by members of the local units of the Irish Army Reserve. Although the cast members are Irish, Loach, the director, is British. Many other films profile the

IRA (Irish Republican Army), including **Angela's Ashes**, 2000; **Anton**, 2008; **Beloved Enemy**, 1936; **Bloody Sunday**, 2002; **Blown Away**, 1994; **The Bombmaker**, 2001 (made-for-TV); **Borstal Boy**, 2001; **The Boxer**, 1997; **The Break**, 1998; **Breakfast on Pluto**, 2005; **Cal**, 1984; **Circle of Deceit**, 1993 (made-for-TV); **The Craic**, 1999; **The Crying Game**, 1992; **The Dawning**, 1988; **The Devil's Own**, 1997; **Disappearing in America**, 2009; **Divorcing Jack**, 1998; **The Eagle Has Landed**, 1976; **The Enigma of Frank Ryan**, 2012; **An Everlasting Piece**, 2000; **Exiled**, 1999; **Fifty Dead Men Walking**, 2009; **Five Minutes of Heaven**, 2009; **48 Angels**, 2007; **The General**, 1998; **Giro City**, 1984; **The Glory Boys**, 1984 (TV series); **Guests of the Nation**, 1981 (made-for-TV); **Harry's Game**, 1982 (TV series); **Hennessy**, 1975; **Hidden Agenda**, 1991; **Hunger**, 2008; **In the Name of the Father**, 1993; **I.R.A.: King of Nothing**, 2007; **I See a Dark Stranger**, 1947; **In This Corner**, 1985 (made-for-TV); **The Informer**, 1935; **The Informant**, 1998; **The Jackal**, 1997; **Johnny Was**, 2006; **Liam**, 2001; **The Long Good Friday**, 1982; **The Man Who Never Was**, 1956; **Michael Collins**, 1996; **Midnight Man**, 1997 (made-for-TV); **The Night Fighters**, 1960; **Odd Man Out**, 1947; **Omagh**, 2004 (made-for-TV); **Ordinary Decent Criminal**, 2000; **The Outsider**, 1980; **Patriot Games**, 1992; **Peacefire**, 2009; **The Plough and the Stars**, 1936; **A Prayer for the Dying**, 1987; **The Quiet Man**, 1952; **The Rising of the Moon**, 1957; **Riot**, 1996; **Ronin**, 1998; **Ryan's Daughter**, 1970; **The Secret Invasion**, 1964; **Shake Hands with the Devil**, 1959; **Shergar**, 1999; **Some Mother's Son**, 1996; **Sword in the Desert**, 1949; **Ticker**, 2001; **Titanic Town**, 1999; **Veronica Guerin**, 2003; **When the Sky Falls**, 2000; and **The Year London Blew Up: 1974**, 2005 (made-for-TV). **p**, Rebecca O'Brien, Redmond Morris; **d**, Ken Loach; **cast**, Cillian Murphy, Padraic Delaney, Liam Cunningham, Orla Fitzgerald, Mary Riordan, Mary Murphy, Laurence Barry, Damien Kearney, Roger Allam, John Crean, William Ruane, Frank Bourke, Myles Horgan; **w**, Paul Laverty; **c**, Barry Ackroyd; **m**, George Fenton; **ed**, Jonathan Morris; **prod d**, Fergus Clegg; **art d**, Michael Higgins, Mark Lowry; **spec eff**, Pat Redmond, Aidan, Brendan, and Kevin Byrne.

The Window ★★★★ 1949; U.S.; 73m; RKO; B/W; Crime Drama; Children: Unacceptable; **DVD**; **VHS**; **IV**. Chilling thriller set in the tenements of NYC sees a marvelous performance from child actor Driscoll, along with riveting portrayals from his overworked parents Hale and Kennedy, and the scheming killers Driscoll discovers, Stewart and Roman. Driscoll is a precocious boy with an imagination too vivid for his own good, and he is forever making up scary stories to tell his parents in this modern-day version of the tale about the boy who cried wolf. On one sweltering night, Driscoll leaves his stuffy bedroom and climbs onto the fire escape, taking his pillow and blanket to sleep at the level one floor above his own apartment. Before dozing off, he sees through a window his neighbors Stewart and his wife Roman with Benedict, a drunken seaman, sitting at a table. He then sees Stewart stab and murder Benedict with scissors and, terrified, Driscoll scrambles down the fire escape to retreat back into his room. Driscoll, knowing that his parents have routinely dismissed the wild tales he has told them, is hesitant to tell Kennedy and Hale what he has seen. He nevertheless works up his courage to describe the murder, and, as he expected, Kennedy and Hale tell him that he must curb his imagination and stop inventing such terrible stories. So unnerved is Driscoll for being disbelieved that he goes to the local police station where he tells his story to detective Ross, who places little credence in the tale, but is obligated to investigate. Ross accompanies Driscoll to his tenement building, and, while the boy remains in a hallway, Ross pretends to be a housing appraiser for the owner of the building. He tells Stewart and Roman that he must inspect their premises to see if painting and other improvements are necessary and is thus allowed to look into all of the rooms in their apartment. He finds nothing incriminating and then takes Driscoll back to his own apartment where Driscoll is upbraided by his father and mother for spreading such horrible tales about their neighbors. By this time, Stewart and Roman

Killers Paul Stewart and Ruth Roman in *The Window,* **1949.**

know that Driscoll is on to them, especially after Hale takes Driscoll to their apartment and demands that Driscoll apologizes to them for spreading a wild tale about his neighbors. After Driscoll refuses to apologize, Kennedy punishes him by locking him into his room before Kennedy leaves for work and while Hale is away visiting a sick relative. Stewart and a reluctant Roman then decide that they must eliminate the only person who can implicate them in Benedict's murder by killing Driscoll. Stewart gets into Driscoll's apartment and sees that the boy is trying to escape his room by pushing the key out of its lock. Stewart aids Driscoll in getting that key by nudging it close enough to the bottom crack of the door so that Driscoll can retrieve it, unlock the door, and escape his room. When Driscoll steps beyond that room, however, he is greeted by Stewart and Roman, who tell him that they are upset that Driscoll thinks so much ill of them. Under the pretext of taking him to the police station, however, they take him to a dark alley. He escapes, but they recapture him and then take a cab back to their apartment. When the taxi stops at a corner where a beat cop is on patrol, Driscoll calls out for help, but Stewart and Roman convince the policeman that Driscoll is their own child and is merely giving them a hard time. The officer remembers Driscoll as the boy who earlier visited the precinct office and where his tale was considered a false report. Before walking away, the cop tells Driscoll: "A good licking never hurt anybody, boy. My old man used to give me enough of them when I was a kid. Hey, still in all, I never thought of calling the cops when he did." As the cab drives away, Driscoll becomes violent, and Roman shields him from the cabdriver's view, so that Stewart can slug the boy unconscious. Stewart tells the driver that he has fallen asleep and the driver casually replies that that's always the case with children. After Stewart and Roman take Driscoll back to their apartment, Kennedy, who has been worried about his son, returns unexpectedly to his apartment to check on Driscoll. When he finds him absent, he begins looking for him and then goes to the police and officers aid him in searching the nearby streets for Driscoll. The boy, by that time, tells Stewart that he will not retract his story about how he saw Stewart kill Benedict, and Stewart resolves to kill Driscoll, who abruptly escapes by going through a window to the fire escape and climbing upward to the roof. Roman, who no longer has the stomach to murder the child, tries to stop Stewart from going after Driscoll, but is knocked aside as Stewart desperately climbs upward after the boy. Scampering across the rooftop, Driscoll manages to enter another building, one that has long been vacant and is in so much disrepair that its floorboards and walls are about to collapse. Driscoll hides from one empty dark room to another until he climbs outward onto a huge rafter that is so poorly moored to a wall that it appears that it will give way and fall to the three floors below where all is rubble. Stewart finds this cavern and slowly climbs onto another wobbling rafter in an

Paul Stewart pursuing Bobby Driscoll in *The Window,* 1949.

effort to reach the cringing Driscoll. The boy screams for Stewart to stay away from him, but Stewart, now possessed with the one idea of eliminating Driscoll, continues inching toward him in an attempt to get onto the other rafter. Just as he is about to reach his goal, however, the rafter on which Stewart crawls breaks loose from its moorings and crashes downward, killing Stewart. The rafter to which Driscoll clings then begins to give way and, as it precariously wobbles in mid-air, Driscoll begins screaming for help. Neighbors hear the screams and police soon arrive, along with Kennedy, as well as Hale, who has returned to her apartment. They see Driscoll high above on the rafter, and firemen arrive with a net, urging Driscoll to jump before the rafter gives way. Though terrified, the boy finally leaps downward to be caught safely by the net and Kennedy and Hale rush to Driscoll to embrace him. By this time, police have found Benedict's body and have arrested Roman to prove that Driscoll has been telling the truth all along. A policeman congratulates Driscoll for bravely making the jump and the boy states to Kennedy: "I'm never going to be a fireman. I don't like jumping in[to] those nets." Kennedy tells him that he is proud of him and Driscoll promises that he will always tell him and Hale the truth and that he will never make up another imaginary story in the future. Kennedy holds Driscoll close as he says: "I'll bet when we get down to the station all the guys are going to point to me and say: 'There goes Tommy Woodry's father!'" To this, Driscoll responds with a beaming smile. Tetzlaff, who began as an accomplished cinematographer of mostly film noir productions, including Hitchcock's masterful **Notorious**, 1946, maintains suspense throughout this harrowing tale while increasing tension in every frame. Driscoll gives a wonderful and utterly believable performance as the jeopardized child, who becomes the target of killers he has so courageously identified, in spite of his warnings being totally ignored by an indifferent adult world. Driscoll received a special Oscar as an outstanding juvenile actor for his appearance in this film as well as Disney's **So Dear to My Heart**, 1948, an award that was periodically bestowed. Knudtson also received an Oscar for Best Editing. The film, which was produced for less than $220,000, was a hit at the box office and was remade with altering story lines as **The Boy Cried Murder**, 1966; **Eyewitness**, 1970; and **Cloak and Dagger**, 1984. *Author's Note*: This film was actually produced in 1947, but was shelved by then RKO chief Howard Hughes and not released until 1949. Driscoll, who excelled as a child actor, found little film work by the time he reached adulthood and became addicted to drugs, dying miserably in NYC on March 30, 1968, from a heart attack brought on by drugs at the age of thirty-one. Stewart told this author: "It was a grim irony that Bobby [Driscoll] died in the same kind of run-down tenement building in New York that was shown in the picture we made together [**The Window**]. In fact, when they found his body, they could not identify him right away

and it was some time before they knew who he was. He was a terrific child actor, one of the very best, and for him to end his young life the way he did was a terrible tragedy." Other films that depict witnesses seeing crimes through windows include **The Bedroom Window**, 1987; **The Boy Cried Murder**, 1966; **Cloak and Dagger**, 1984; **Eyewitness**, 1970; **The House on Carroll Street**, 1988; **Lady on a Train**, 1945; **My Cousin Vinny**, 1992; **Rear Window**, 1954; **12 Angry Men**, 1957; **Who Framed Roger Rabbit**, 1988; **Witness**, 1985; and **Witness to Murder**, 1954. For a more extensive listing see Subject Index, Witnesses to Crimes. **p**, Frederic Ullman, Jr.; **d**, Ted Tetzlaff; **cast**, Barbara Hale, Bobby Driscoll, Arthur Kennedy, Paul Stewart, Ruth Roman, Anthony Ross, Tom Ahearne, Richard Benedict, Tom Coleman, Lloyd Dawson, Carl Faulkner; **w**, Mel Dinelli (based on the novelette *The Boy Who Cried Murder* by Cornell Woolrich); **c**, William Steiner, Robert De Grasse; **m**, Roy Webb; **ed**, Frederic Knudtson; **art d**, Albert D'Agostino, Sam Corso, Walter E. Keller; **set d**, Darrell Silvera, Harley Miller; **spec eff**, Russell A. Cully.

Windtalkers ★★★ 2002; U.S.; 134m; Lion Rock Productions/MGM; Color; War/Drama; Children: Unacceptable (MPAA: R); **BD**; **DVD**; **IV**. Based on real events and characters, this offbeat but engrossing tale involves the heroic roles played by members of the Navajo Indian tribe during World War II (1939-1945). The film opens with Cage, an army corporal, who survives a battle against the Japanese in the Solomon Islands in the Pacific and where his entire squad has been killed. When he returns to active duty, he is assigned to protect Beach, a Navajo code talker. Slater also receives a similar assignment to protect Navajo code talker Willie. The Navajo code is one based on two parts: the difficult Navajo language and a code embedded in it that would even confuse native speakers and was considered virtually unbreakable by monitoring Japanese. The "windtalker" code talkers are trained to send and receive coded messages that direct battleship bombardments of Japanese positions. Cage and Slater are told that, since captured Navajos are always tortured to death, the code cannot fall into Japanese hands, and they are to execute these important code talkers to prevent them from ever being captured should their capture appear to be a certainty. They all engage in the invasion and battle of Saipan (Mariana Islands, June 15, 1944-July 9, 1944). Because Beach's radio is destroyed, the U.S. Navy convoy is unable to call off the bombardment, resulting in friendly fire raining down upon the Marines. Beach disguises himself as a Japanese soldier and goes behind enemy lines, pretending to take Cage as his supposed prisoner of war, as he searches for a radio. Cage and Beach kill several Japanese soldiers including a Japanese radioman. Beach then uses the Japanese radio to contact U.S. artillery, redirecting its fire on the Japanese positions, which wins the fight for that day. The next morning, Japanese soldiers raid the U.S. position in a village and Slater is decapitated while his code talker, Willie, is about to be captured. Cage sees Willie beaten, and then being dragged off by the Japanese, but Cage has run out of ammunition. Willie urges Cage to throw a grenade at him in order to protect the code, and Cage does that, the explosion killing both Willie and his captors. Beach returns to the front line and, outraged at learning that Cage killed Willie, aims his weapon at him, but cannot pull the trigger. The Marines camp in a village they think is secured, but they are ambushed. Still enraged over the death of Willie, Beach charges the enemy fearlessly, but loses the radio needed to call in bombardments. In trying to recover the radio, both Beach and Cage are shot. Cage, although wounded in the chest, carries Beach to safety. Dying, Cage admits to Beach that he hated having to kill Willie, but that his mission was to protect the Navajo code above everything else. Back in the U.S., Beach and his wife and son sit atop Point Mesa in Monument Valley, Arizona, and perform the Navajo ritual of paying respects to Cage, the man who saved his life. In an epilogue, the film explains that the Navajo code, critical to America's victory against Japan in the war, was never broken. Well directed with exceptional battle scenes, this film sees outstanding performances from Cage, Beach, Slater, Willie and the rest of the cast. Though this film produced more than $77 million at the box office in its initial release, it did not recoup its investment of more than $115 million. Songs: "Little Jug" and "Everything Goes" (Ib Glindemann), "Voice of the Mountain" (Kaaren Whitewind, Tom Bee), "What Shall We Do with the Drunken Sailor?/Early in the Morning" (traditional), "The Marine's Hymn" (music: Jacques Offenbach), "Ia 'Oe e Ka La" (traditional). *Author's Note*: Film critic Roger Ebert unfairly slammed this film, saying that it was overburdened with "battle clichés," a remark that could have been made about any war film. I knew Ebert well throughout his adult life, beginning when he was a student at the University of Illinois. One night when drinking with him at the old O'Rourke's Pub in Chicago's Old Town, a group of young Marines entered that bar, and I bought them a round of drinks. "Don't encourage them," Ebert told me. "They are just a bunch of freeloaders." My response to that was: "That's rich, coming from a guy like you, who never put on his country's uniform. Sometimes it is very difficult to be your friend." Ebert was oblivious to those who thus served their country, as he was to their history of battles and wars (he repeatedly and blatantly told this author, as if proud of his ignorance, that he knew little or nothing about history). He was what I call a hothouse human being, protected and pampered from childhood by a domineering mother (whom this author knew), nurtured by Academia until he got a job with his one and only employer, the Chicago *Sun-Times* where he became its film reviewer and lofty superstar. He later acquired yearly multi-million dollar contracts from ABC and Disney for his TV appearances and lived out a life of luxury with mansions and fat bank accounts. He never had to worry about paying a bill or buying a pair of shoes, let alone experience the loneliness of being a member of the armed services, accepting its risks and sacrifices. He never wanted to know anything about all of those "freeloaders," who safeguarded his comfortable and sacrosanct lifestyle. He was a paradoxical person in that he was an avowed Socialist and yet a social elitist. He was therefore incapable of understanding the true character and dedication of the kind of heroic people depicted in this film. This film was shot on location in Hawaii, many of its battle scenes made at Kualoa Ranch. Extras were culled from the ranks of the U.S. Army stationed at Schofield Barracks at Pearl Harbor, Oahu, Hawaii, as well as Hickam Air Force Base and the U.S. Navy Base at Pearl Harbor. Other films depicting the Battle of Saipan in WWII include **Battle Cry**, 1955; **Codename: Fox**, 2001; **Golden Partners**, 1979; **Hell to Eternity**, 1960; and **Not Forgotten**, 2000. Violence and gutter language prohibit viewing by children. **p**, John Woo, Terence Chang, Tracie Graham-Rice, Alison R. Roszenzweig, Arthur Anderson, Caroline Macaulay; **d**, John Woo; **cast**, Nicolas Cage, Adam Beach, Mark Ruffalo, Christian Slater, Brian Van Holt, Martin Henderson, Roger Willie, Frances O'Connor, Peter Stormare, Noah Emmerich, **w**, John Rice, Joe Batteer; **c**, Jeffrey L. Kimball; **m**, James Horner; **ed**, Jeff Gullo, Steven Kemper, Tom Rolf; **prod d**, Holger Gross; **art d**, Kevin Ishioka; **set d**, Richard Goddard; **spec eff**, Jan H. Aaris, Fred Cervantes, John Frazier.

Windwalker ★★★ 1980; U.S.; 108m; Santa Fe International/Pacific International Enterprises; Color; Western; Children: Unacceptable (MPAA: PG); **DVD**; **IV**. Offbeat but fascinating tale depicts a Cheyenne tribe struggling to survive the harsh living conditions in what later became Utah while battling their lifelong foes, the Crow tribe. Howard is a resolute Cheyenne warrior (played by Remar as a young man), who has seen countless hardships and was forced to witness the murder of his beloved wife, Hedin, at the hands of invading Crow warriors, as well as the kidnapping of one of his twin sons. Howard spends years searching for that abducted child, but to no avail and, grown old and weary, he dies in the winter of 1797. Howard receives a ceremonial funeral supervised by his son, Ramus, who then leads his family south to rejoin the Cheyenne tribe. While migrating southward, Remus and his family are attacked by Crow Indians. They beat them off, but Ramus is badly wounded and his family members hide him from the pursuing enemy.

Nicolas Cage and Adam Beach in *Windtalkers*, 2002.

At this time, the Great Spirit awakens Howard from his death sleep and he then goes to the aid of his family members, using an old Indian remedy to nurture Ramus back to health while guiding him and others to a cave held sacred by the Cheyenne. Howard helps Ramus and his two sons set ingenious traps for the searching Crow warriors that destroy them, so that only its chief and another warrior remain. Howard and Ramus then discover that the remaining Crow warrior is none other than Howard's long-missing son, who is Ramus' brother. When Howard offers peace to the Crow chief, he refuses and attacks, but the restored son turns on the chief and kills him. Now that his family is safe, Howard returns to the spirit land of the dead and we see him reunited with his wife, Hedin, as his family members make their way southward to join what remains of the Cheyenne nation. Merrill does a fine job in sympathetically portraying the lifestyle of this Indian family, presenting authentic customs and habits endemic to the Cheyenne. His characters are depicted as decent and noble human beings, emulating John Ford's classic **Cheyenne Autumn**, 1964, instead of the cardboard savages so routinely and carelessly displayed in most Hollywood westerns, and predates by a decade that kind of realistic and fair-minded portrayal as seen in **Dances with Wolves**, 1990, which humanized the Sioux tribe. Howard, Ramus, Remar and the rest of the cast members are standouts in their roles. The film did well at the box office, earning more than $18 million in its initial release. *Author's Note*: To make the film credible from the Indian POV, director Merrill insisted that the dialog be spoken in the native languages of the Cheyenne and Crow tribes, and he employs English subtitles. He further wanted an all-Indian cast, selecting Chief Dan George (1899-1981) to play the aging Indian family leader. Dan George, however, grew ill and could not enact the role, which then went to Howard (at the insistence of producers who wanted to have some appealing star status to promote the film), and who does an amazingly convincing job of playing that Indian patriarch. Other films depicting the Cheyenne tribe or its members include **Battling with Buffalo Bill**, 1931; **Before the White Man Came**, 1920; **The Big Sky**, 1952; **Brave Eagle**, 1955-1956 (TV series); **Buffalo Bill**, 1944; **Cavalry Scout**, 1951; **Cheyenne**, 1947; **Cheyenne Autumn**, 1964 (Southern Cheyenne); **The Cheyenne Cyclone**, 1932; **The Cheyenne Kid**, 1930; **The Cheyenne Kid**, 1933; **The Cheyenne Kid**, 1940; **Cheyenne Rides Again**, 1937; **Cheyenne Roundup**, 1943; **Cheyenne Takes Over**, 1947; **Cheyenne Tornado**, 1935; **Cheyenne Trails**, 1928; **Cheyenne Wildcat**, 1944; **Custer of the West**, 1967; **Goodnight for Justice**, 2011 (made-for-TV); **Grayeagle**, 1977; **Hell on Wheels**, 2011- (TV series); **The Plainsman**, 1936; **Prudence and the Chief**, 1970 (made-for-TV); **She Wore a Yellow Ribbon**, 1949 (Southern Cheyenne); **Stagecoach West**, 1960-1961 (TV series; "The Bold Whip," 1961 episode); **Tales of Wells Fargo**, 1957-1962 (TV se-

Don Ameche and Charles Bickford in *Wing and a Prayer*, 1944.

ries; "Renegade Raiders," 1957 episode); **Treachery Rides the Range**, 1936; **Wagons West**, 1952; and **White Feather**, 1955. For detailed compilations of films depicting other American Indian tribes, see Organizations Index. (In Cheyenne and Crow; English subtitles.) **p**, Thomas E. Ballard, Arthur R. Dubs; **d**, Kieth Merrill; **cast**: Trevor Howard, Nick Ramus, James Remar, Serene Hedin, Dusty "Iron Wing" McCrea, Silvana Gallardo, Emerson John, Jason Stevens, Roberta Deherrera, Ivan Naranjo, Chief Tug Smith, Fredelia Smith; **w**, Ray Goldrup (based on the novel by Blaine Yorgason); **c**, Reed Smoot; **m**, Merrill Jenson; **ed**, Janice Hampton, Steven L. Johnson, Peter L. McCrea; **prod d**, Thomas Pratt; **set d**, Rick Barker, Richard Jamison; **spec eff**, Rick Josephsen, Lynn Maughan, Kieth Richins.

Wing and a Prayer ★★★★ 1944; U.S.; 97m; FOX; B/W; War Drama; Children: Unacceptable; **DVD**; **VHS**. Taut tale tells the story of one of the U.S. carriers that survived the annihilating attack on the American fleet at Pearl Harbor on December 7, 1941, and how it was used to decoy the Japanese fleet into a decisive U.S. naval victory at Midway six months later. Ameche, who is the ship's flight commander, welcomes a new detachment of bomber pilots led by Lieutenant Andrews, just as the carrier heads for an unspecified destination. One of the members of that new squadron is Eythe, a former Hollywood star and Academy Award winner, who bears the nickname "Oscar." Eythe displays a cavalier if not indifferent attitude toward his duties, which alarms by-the-book Ameche. Andrews is told by Ameche that he will not tolerate any careless behavior by his pilots as that can jeopardize the ship as well as its secret mission. Exactly that happens during a training exercise where Morgan, one of Andrews' pilots, accidentally drops a bomb close to the carrier. Ameche immediately grounds Morgan, which raises the ire of his fellow pilots. Then O'Shea, who is one of the most experienced pilots and who has earned the Navy Cross for his heroic actions during the Battle of the Coral Sea (May 4-8, 1942), botches a takeoff from the deck of the carrier and is compelled to ditch his plane in the sea. O'Shea, like Morgan, is then grounded. Meanwhile, Hardwicke, the commanding admiral, and Bickford, the ship's captain, receive top secret orders to sail the carrier to the Solomon Islands in a deceptive course that is intended to convince the Japanese that the ship represents more than one U.S. carrier. The ship sails several divergent courses, always managing to avoid contact with Japanese warships searching for it. This evasive action appears to Andrews and his pilots that the carrier and its commanders are intentionally avoiding battle, these seemingly cowardly tactics so infuriating the pilots that they come close to open rebellion. Finally, however, the carrier has accomplished its mission, convincing the Japanese that the U.S. carriers are so scattered about the Pacific that the U.S. Navy will not be able to meet a concentrated attack by a huge

Japanese fleet against the U.S. island of Midway, a strategic military base. The carrier, however, joins the U.S. fleet at Midway as planned and it ambushes the Japanese warships converging on that island. During the Battle of Midway (June 3-7, 1942), Andrews and his pilots perform heroically. Morgan and O'Shea, because of the need for pilots, are allowed to return to duty, and O'Shea again performs heroically, this time sacrificing his life by crashing his plane into a diving Kamikaze plane before that enemy warplane can crash into the carrier. Bickford and Ameche listen over the radio to hear their pilots in combat as they attack the Japanese fleet, and learn how they sink one Japanese carrier after another (the Japanese lost four class "A" carriers during the Battle of Midway, a defeat that crippled the Japanese navy for the remainder of the war). They also agonize as they hear many of their pilots being shot down, some resigning themselves to their grim fate as they crash into the sea (one stating to his fellow crewman: "We'll take this ride together"). The effort results in a great U.S. victory, but not without great losses. When Andrews and others return to the carrier by making safe landings, it is learned that Eythe, who has performed bravely during the battle, is returning to the carrier with a damaged plane. Night has fallen and Andrews pleads with Ameche to have him turn on the carrier's landing lights so that Eythe can find the ship and safely land. Ameche adamantly refuses, saying that he cannot jeopardize the carrier as Japanese submarines may be lurking nearby. When Andrews challenges Ameche's genuine concern for the pilots, Ameche explodes, telling Andrews and other pilots that it is his job to protect the ship at all costs, but for anyone to think that he does not care about the lives of the men he commands is wrong. He does care and deeply so, but his obligation to duty will not permit him to do other than what he does, despite his personal inclination to do otherwise. He admits that some must be sacrificed in order to preserve the others and the ship's ability to continue taking the fight to the enemy. It is then believed that Eythe, who has run out of fuel, has crashed his plane in the sea and is now lost. News is then received that tells everyone that Eythe is very much alive, as he has been rescued by a destroyer. We then see Ameche going about his duties, walking through the corridors of the carrier to its deck which is rain-swept and, after being drenched, goes to his command room and begins giving orders for the next day's operations to end this fine film. Pantheon director Hathaway presents this story with great economy and offers a realistic portrayal of the carrier and its day-to-day operations while drawing from its fine cast outstanding performances. The film was a hit at the box office and received an Oscar nomination for Best Original Screenplay (Cady). Songs: "Anchors Aweigh" (1906; music: Charles A. Zimmerman; lyrics: Alfred Hart Miles), "A Weekend in Havana" (1941; music: Harry Warren; lyrics: Mack Gordon), "My Bonnie Lies over the Ocean" (1881; H.J. Fuller, J.T. Wood [pseudonyms]), "Till We Meet Again" (1918; music: Richard A. Whiting; lyrics: Raymond B. Egan), "Deep in the Heart of Texas" (1941; music: Don Swander; lyrics: June Hershey), "I Know Why (And So Do You)" (1941; music: Harry Warren; lyrics: Mack Gordon), "You Say the Sweetest Things (Baby)" (1940; music: Harry Warren; lyrics: Mack Gordon), "The Sheik of Araby" (1921; music: Ted Snyder; lyrics: Harry B. Smith, Francis Wheeler), "Taps" (1862; Daniel Butterfield). ***Author's Note***: Hathaway told this author that "we got a lot of help from the U.S. Navy when we made **Wing and a Prayer**. It allowed us to go on board the new carrier, the *Yorktown* (CV-10), named after the old *Yorktown* [CV-5], which was lost at the Battle of Midway, when that new flattop was going through its shakedown cruise in 1943. We were able to shoot all of its interior and its deck and got some great action shots. We merged those shots with aerial combat shots we got from the Navy." Ameche told this author that he thought his role in this film "was one of the best I ever got, the part of a flight commander who must send pilots to their death and suppress his feelings about them in order to maintain discipline and keep them flying. It was men like that that helped us win that terrible war. I knew that there would be very little empathy for that character as he juggles schedules and orders men into the air. That was the most challenging part in enacting that role." Andrews recalled this film for the author by stating: "The film I made just before **Wing and a Prayer** was **The Purple Heart** [1944], another war story and where I played one of the pilots in the Doolittle Raid on Japan [April 18, 1942]. Oddly enough, I and seven other airmen are captured and must protect the name of a carrier from which their plane was launched in that attack [USS *Hornet*, CV-8]. And here I was playing another pilot flying from another aircraft carrier in **Wing and a Prayer**." O'Shea, who appears in this film as a heroic pilot, also played one of the airmen captured with Andrews in **The Purple Heart**. The title of this film was taken from a 1943 hit song titled "Coming In on a Wing and a Prayer." Other films depicting aircraft carriers include **Act of Valor**, 2012; **Air Force**, 1943 (WWII); **Apollo 13**, 1995; **The Avengers**, 2012; **Battle of the Coral Sea**, 1959 (WWII; USS *Lexington*, CV-2; USS *Yorktown*, CV-5); **Battleship**, 2012; **Behind Enemy Lines**, 2001(Kosovo Campaign of 1999); **Between Heaven and Hell**, 1956 (WWII); **Bombardier**, 1943 (WWII; USS *Hornet*, CV-8); **The Bridges at Toko-Ri**, 1954 (Korean War; USS *Oriskany*, CV-34); **The Caine Mutiny**, 1954 (WWII; USS *Kearsarge*, CV-33); **Captain Phillips**, 2013; **Crimson Tide**, 1995; **The Deer Hunter**, 1978 (Vietnam War); **Destination Tokyo**, 1943 (WWII; USS *Hornet*, CV-8); **Dive Bomber**, 1941 (pre-WWII; USS *Enterprise*, CV-6); **The Final Countdown**, 1980 (WWII; USS *Nimitz*, CVN-68); **Flat Top**, 1952 (Korean War; USS *Princeton*, CV-37); **Flight Command**, 1940 (pre-WWII; USS *Enterprise*, CV-6); **The Flight of the Intruder**, 1991 (Vietnam War; USS *Independence*, CV-61); **The Flyboys**, 2008; **Freedom Strike**, 1998; **The Gallant Hours**, 1960 (WWII); **Godzilla**, 2014; **A Guy Named Joe**, 1943 (WWII; mythical German aircraft carrier); **Hell Divers**, 1931 (1930s; USS *Saratoga*, CV-3); **Here Come the Waves**, 1944; **Hot Shots!**, 1991; **I Am Legend**, 2007; **Men of the Fighting Lady**, 1954 (Korean War; USS *Oriskany*, CV-34); **Midway** (WWII; USS *Enterprise*, CV-6; USS *Hornet*, CV-8; USS *Yorktown*, CV-5); **A Mighty Heart**, 2007; **Olympus Has Fallen**, 2013; **Operation Pacific**, 1951 (WWII); **Our Man Flint**, 1966; **Pacific Rim**, 2013; **Pearl Harbor**, 2001 (WWII; USS *Hornet*, CV-8); **The Purple Heart**, 1944 (WWII; USS *Hornet*, CV-8); **Rescue Dawn**, 2007; **The Right Stuff**, 1983; **Rules of Engagement**, 2000; **Sink the Bismarck!**, 1960 (WWII; HMS *Ark Royal*, 91); **Supercarrier**, 1988 (TV series); **Task Force**, 1949 (pre-WWII and WWII; USS *Enterprise*, CV-6; USS *Franklin*, CV-13; USS *Hornet*, CV-8; USS *Langley*, CV-1; USS *Saratoga*, CV-3; USS *Yorktown*, CV-5); **Tears of the Sun**, 2003; **Thirty Seconds Over Tokyo**, 1944 (WWII; USS *Hornet*; CV-8); **Top Gun**, 1986 (Vietnam War); **Torpedo Run**, 1958 (WWII); **Tora! Tora! Tora!**, 1970 (WWII; Japanese carriers; USS *Hornet*, CV-8); **Transformers**, 2007; **The Wind Rises**, 2014; **World War Z**, 2013; and **Zero Dark Thirty**, 2012. **p**, William A. Bacher, Walter Morosco; **d**, Henry Hathaway; **cast**, Don Ameche, Dana Andrews, William Eythe, Charles Bickford, Sire Cedric Hardwicke, Kevin O'Shea, Richard Jaeckel, Henry (Harry) Morgan, Richard Crane, Charles Lang, Glenn Langan, Robert Bailey, Reed Hadley, Dave Willock, Jimmie Dodd, Blake Edwards, Raymond Roe, Murray Alper; **w**, Jerome Cady, (uncredited) Mortimer Braus (based on a story by Cady); **c**, Glen MacWilliams; **m**, Hugo W. Friedhofer; **ed**, J. Watson Webb; **art d**, Lyle Wheeler, Lewis Creber; **set d**, Thomas Little; **spec eff**, Fred Sersen.

Winged Victory ★★★ 1944; U.S.; 130m; FOX; B/W; War Drama; Children: Acceptable. Superior WWII (1939-1945) propaganda film profiles a group of young recruits who are trained to become B-24 bomber pilots. The story focuses upon one cadet, McCallister, who, along with companions O'Brien, Taylor, Daniels and others, undergoes rigorous training. Sharing their anxieties are the females in their lives, Crain, Holliday and Ball. The cadets struggle to maintain the demanding regimen, and one of the wives becomes pregnant. She does not want to worry her husband about the responsibilities of fatherhood and keeps that a secret. He crashes in a solo flight and never knows that he has a child. Others get washed out when they fail to meet flying standards,

Don Ameche and William Eythe in *Wing and a Prayer*, 1944.

but most of the cadets finally get their wings. In a moving finale scene, their women are shown in a San Francisco hotel, watching from the windows as their planes fly overhead and into the skies over the Pacific to carry the war to the enemy. Many scenes show the comradeship and esprit de corps of the cadets, and pantheon director Cukor mixes the sometimes hum-drum training exercises with considerable mirth. One of the more humorous scenes depicts three of the cadets performing their imitation of the then popular singing group, the Andrews Sisters, all wearing wigs and in drag, including budding comedian Red Buttons. The film was a huge hit at the box office as was the Moss Hart play upon which it was based. Songs: "You're So Sweet to Remember" (1944; music: Billy Rose; lyrics: Leo Robin), "The Army Air Corps Song" (1939; Robert Crawford), "Gee, Mom, I Want to Go Home (I Don't Want No More of Army Life)" (1944; Charlotte Kackley), "Mademoiselle from Armentiers" (composer unknown), "Spirit of the Corps" (William J. Clinch), "I've Been Working on the Railroad" (traditional), "I've Got Sixpence (As I Go Rolling Home)" (Elton Box, Desmond Cox), "Wait for Me Mary" (1943; Charles Tobias, Nat Simon, Harry Tobias), "For Me and My Gal" (1917; George W. Meyer, Edgar Leslie, E. Ray Goetz), "I Can't Give You Anything but Love, Baby" (1928; music: Jimmy McHugh; lyrics: Dorothy Fields), "The Whiffenpoof Song" (music [1898]: Guy H. Scull; lyrics [1910]: Mead Minnigerode), "Chica Chica Boom Chic" (1941; music: Harry Warren; lyrics: Mack Gordon), "Silent Night, Holy Night" (music [1818]: Franz Xaver Gruber; lyrics [1816] Joseph Mohr), "Pennsylvania Polka" (1942; Lester Lee, Zeke Manners). ***Author's Note***: Cukor told this author that "Bill [William] Wellman was originally hired to direct **Winged Victory** because of his aviation experience [Wellman had been a pilot in WWI, 1914-1918], but, after he dropped out, I was signed for the job. The original play on Broadway by Moss Hart was a big morale booster during the war [WWII] and when it closed, Fox rushed it into production for the screen. It was mostly a lighthearted story about patriotic young men eager to serve their country and the women who loved them. It was a poignant tale that years later reminded everyone about the sacrifice those fine young men made to help us win that terrible war." Crain recalled for this author how "My first leading roles in pictures began with Lon [McCallister], and that was in 1944 when I appeared with him in **Home in Indiana** and **Winged Victory**. I remember those pictures with fondness. They were full of sweet and caring people, much different from today's pictures." Future film stars appearing in this film include Judy Holliday, Edmond O'Brien, Jeanne Crain, Barry Nelson, Don Taylor, Karl Malden, Peter Lind Hayes, George "Superman" Reeves, Red Buttons, Lee J. Cobb, Kevin McCarthy, and Gary Merrill. The film marked the screen debut of Brad Dexter, who appears in a bit part. This was one of the few films that profiled in detail the four-engine B-24 Liberator

Charles "Buddy" Rogers, Richard Arlen and Gary Cooper in *Wings*, **1927.**

bomber plane. **p**, Darryl F. Zanuck; **d**, George Cukor; **cast**, Pvt. Lon McCallister, Jeanne Crain, Sgt. Edmond O'Brien, Jane Ball, Sgt. Mark Daniels, Jo-Carroll Dennison, Cpl. Don Taylor, Judy Holliday, Cpl. Lee J. Cobb, T/Sgt. Peter Lind Hayes, Cpl. Red Buttons, Cpl. Barry Nelson, Cpl. Garry Merrill, Sgt. George Reeves, Cpl. Karl Malden, Pfc. Martin Ritt, Dick Hogan, Brad Dexter, Keith Andes, Mario Lanza, Kevin Mc-Carthy, Ray McDonald, Richard Travis; **w**, Moss Hart (based on his play); **c**, Glen MacWilliams; **m**, Sgt. David Rose; **ed**, Barbara McLean; **art d**, Lyle Wheeler, Lewis Creber; **set d**, Thomas Little; **spec eff**, Fred Sersen.

Wings ★★★★★ 1927 (silent); U.S.; 111m (144m restoration); PAR; B/W; War Drama; Children: Unacceptable; **BD**; **DVD**; **IV**. Pantheon director Wellman presents a startling WWI (1914-1918) epic that brilliantly weaves into its war-torn fabric the lives of three people—Rogers, Arlen and the effervescent Bow. The film opens in a small town in America where Rogers and Arlen compete for the affections of the most desired young lady, Ralston. Bow is the girl living next door to Rogers and who has always loved him, but Rogers looks upon her as simply a good friend. When he tinkers with his racing car, Bow helps him make repairs, including the painting of the car's name, "The Shooting Star." Once repaired, however, Rogers disappoints Bow (as he constantly does) by driving off without her so that he can take Ralston for a spin. When America enters the war, both Rogers and Arlen enlist in the Army Air Corps, and Rogers thinks that Ralston has selected him as her beau. She has, however, fallen in love with Arlen, who is more withdrawn, although Ralston cannot bring herself to let Rogers know about her true affections for his close friend. Rogers and Arlen are sent together to a training camp and are billeted in the same tent where they meet Cooper, an experienced pilot they instantly admire for his quiet resolve and pluck. Arlen offers him a bite from his candy bar and Cooper chews a piece. He then displays his lucky charm before he is called to duty to test a new fighter plane, which, all know, presents lethal hazards. Cooper shows his nerve, however, by telling his new young friends (on a title card): "When your time comes, you're going to get it." Rogers and Arlen soon learn how serious is their new service life when they see the plane that Cooper is flying crash and he is killed. Rogers and Arlen are further troubled when talking about Ralston and both become enemies over their feelings for her. By the time they complete their training and are ordered to France to go into combat, they have become friends once more. In France, we now see Bow, who has joined the Ambulance Service, and is driving a lorry in a long line of similar trucks. She learns that a new American ace called "The Shooting Star" is none other than the man she loves, Rogers. When arriving in Paris, Bow finds Rogers tipsy at a bistro, and he is being wooed by two streetwalkers.

Realizing that Rogers jeopardizes his career by going AWOL with these two girls, Bow rescues him by pretending to be an alluring French girl, taking him back to his hotel room to sleep it off. While changing back into her uniform, however, MPs rush in to find her in this compromising position and she is later compelled to resign from the service and return to the U.S. in disgrace. Meanwhile, Rogers and Arlen undertake several hazardous missions, not the least of which is shooting down enemy observation balloons during the raging battle of Saint-Mihiel (September 12-15, 1918). Arlen is later shot down and Rogers believes he has been killed. He becomes obsessed with taking revenge on the enemy for his friend's death and becomes a one-man air force, taking to the air and shooting down every German plane he can find, as well as attacking German ground troops. Arlen, however, has survived. He finds and steals a German fighter plane and escapes with it, flying toward the Allied lines. Just then he sees Roger's plane with its insignia, "The Shooting Star," and frantically signals to his friend. Rogers, however, does not recognize Arlen and believes he is just another German fighter pilot, and attacks the German plane, shooting it down. Rogers then lands his plane to cut away the identification number of the plane he shot down, but finds, to his horror, that he has shot down his dearest friend, Arlen. Rogers weeps as he cradles the dying Arlen in his arms, begging his forgiveness. Arlen dies and Rogers kisses him goodbye and then flies off. The war then ends and Rogers returns home to a hero's welcome. He cuts the ceremonies short to go to Arlen's parents and where he begs their forgiveness for having killed their son. Arlen's mother does forgive him, saying that it was not Rogers, but the war that killed her son. Rogers then sees Bow, who has been anxiously waiting for him, and he realizes how much he loves her, and they joyously reunite, planning a life together. Wellman presents this story in deeply moving scenes that exhibit the innocence of the youthful pilots and their eventual introduction to the horrors of warfare while integrating tender scenes between Bow and Rogers. The aerial scenes are astonishing for their day, unparalleled action sequences that depict breathtaking dogfights, spinouts, explosions and flaming deaths. Wellman equals these amazing scenes with his battle sequences on the ground where thousands of Doughboys attack entrenched German positions with charging bayonets and tanks during a restaging of the Battle of Saint-Mihiel. The acting from Rogers, Arlen, Bow and Ralston is exceptional, and the usual histrionic theatrics of the day are kept to a minimum. Bow, who sacrifices her reputation for the young man she loves above all else, gives one of her finest and more subdued performances as a good-hearted and memorably endearing young woman, a role for which she would always be fondly remembered. The film received the first Oscar for Best Picture (in 1929), as well as an Oscar for Engineering Effects (Roy Pomeroy), a category later abandoned by the Academy. **Wings** proved to be a box office smash, earning more than $4 million in its initial release against a budget of $2 million. Songs (played in theaters in the 1927 release): "A Midsummer Night's Dream, Op. 61" (1843; excerpts; Felix Mendolssohn-Bartholdy), "Wings" (1927; J.S. Zamecnik). ***Author's Note***: Largely contributing to the success of this film was the public's heightened awareness of aviation as Charles Lindbergh made the first solo flight from New York to Paris on May 20-21, 1927. That historic flight was made one day after this film was shown as a sneak preview in a theater in San Antonio, Texas, on May 19, 1927. The film officially premiered on August 12, 1927, at the Criterion Theater in New York and ran for sixty-three weeks, and, after it was similarly shown in first-run theaters, it then moved on to second-run theaters. When Paramount decided to produce this very expensive film, it first got the complete cooperation from the U.S. War Department, agreeing to provide a $10,000 insurance policy on every person in the U.S. armed services participating in the film. The studio also agreed that the film would also serve as a training vehicle for U.S. Army Air Force pilots and that it would not release the film without government approval. Among the fliers piloting the many WWI biplanes in that film were youthful aviators Frank Maxwell Andrews (1884-1943) and Hoyt Vandenberg (1899-1954), both of whom later became generals in the U.S. Air Force. The film was shot chiefly at Kelly Field near San Antonio, Texas, and locations near the 2nd Infantry Division and its Corps of Engineers stationed at Corpus Christi, Texas. Thousands of troops stationed there were used to recreate the Battle of Saint-Mihiel (this same division would make up the extras used in the made-for-TV production of **Rough Riders**, 1997). Arlen was a natural selection for the film as he had been a WWI pilot in France (a member of the Royal Canadian Air Force, but he did not see combat). Rogers had no flying experience, but that was solved when Vandenberg hid in the back seat of a plane operating the controls while Rogers acted before the camera in the front seat. Like all the other planes, Rogers' craft had a camera strapped to its cowling, and the pilot actors had to also operate those cameras while, at the same time, enacting their roles. Paramount selected Wellman to helm this epic, but the front office was very uneasy about allowing this twenty-eight-year-old director to head the production as he had directed only a bevy of "B" productions. He was, however, the only director in Hollywood who had first-hand experience with aerial combat, Wellman having been a fighter pilot in the illustrious flying group known as the Lafayette Escadrille during WWI. Wellman shot down three enemy planes and possibly downed another five before his own plane, "Celia" (named after his mother), was shot down while he served as a fighter pilot in France. That crash injured one of his legs, causing Wellman to walk thereafter with a decided limp. Wellman had to pass a severe test before he was fully accepted as the director, however, when appearing before the top Army brass at a dinner in San Antonio, Texas. He was greeted curtly at that time by the commanding general, but, when he addressed the dinner guests, he won the hearts of the officers' wives by treating his role cavalierly, saying that the Paramount executives were "idiots" as they had entrusted this expensive film to him, a man of limited experience, but one who had seen aerial combat, had been married twice, and had been lucky enough to have met Clara Bow, the reigning film star of the day. So candid and refreshing was his approach that the wives burst into applause, followed by the officers, who then accepted Wellman into their fold. The production sapped Wellman's strength as he worked night and day to complete the picture, which began on September 6, 1926, and did not end until seven months later, on April 7, 1927. Wellman had begun with a budget of more than $1 million. He added more and more aerial combat scenes so that, by the time he was ready to film the more than five-minute sequence that showed the Battle of Saint-Mihiel, he was far beyond his budget. Those battle scenes, he knew, would cost several hundred thousand more dollars. He spent ten days preparing those sequences, all meticulously shot with more than sixty aircraft, culled from every available field, and he used more than 3,500 extras on the ground. He directed one scene involving several thousand extras attacking German positions over many acres of landscape that had been turned into a vast no-man's-land from a huge tower. He alone set off the charges that had been planted on the battleground from that tower, and, while he was so doing, someone shouted a question at him. "Get the hell out of here, you idiot!" Wellman shouted down to whoever had asked that question, as he continued to set off those dangerous detonations, worried that any more interruptions might cause him to set off explosives that could injure some of the extras charging over the battlefield. Fortunately, Wellman kept his concentration and all went well. "I was lucky," Wellman told this author. "I got it all and nothing went wrong. It was as perfect as it would ever be. I knew, however, that I had gone way over the budget, especially after I waited day after day to see some clouds in the sky. Without the clouds, the planes looked like a swarm of flies. The clouds were essential, as Howard Hughes learned the hard way when making **Hell's Angels** [1930], because they give the viewer the proper perspective of a plane's speed and direction of movement. I felt that the money people, three of the biggest bankers in the country, who had bankrolled Paramount to make the picture, had run out of patience with me. I believed they were down there in San Antonio to fire me. I figured that **Wings** would mark

Charles "Buddy" Rogers, Clara Bow and Richard Arlen in *Wings*, 1927.

the end of my career in pictures. After getting that battle scene done, I went back to my room [at the Saint Anthony Hotel in San Antonio] and started guzzling from a bottle of whiskey. I got sick and went into the shower to try to sober up and, while I was soaking, I heard a knock on the door. I threw on a robe and, dripping wet, opened the door to see those three bankers standing in the hall and glaring at me. They weren't smiling. 'Okay,' I told myself. 'Here it comes. This is where I get the sack.' I invited them into the room and offered them a drink. Two of them took little sips from their glasses, but the most important banker, Otto Kahn [1867-1934], refused. Kahn paced up and down the room and I felt like I was going to throw up, so I ran into the bathroom and closed the door. When I opened it, I saw that all three were gone. Then there was more knocking and I found Mr. Kahn standing in the hall. 'We really like you, young man,' he said. 'We saw the battle scene and a lot of the others you have put into the picture and we think it is all wonderful. You can have anything you want or need to finish the picture. By the way, I was the 'idiot' who interrupted you today when you were on the tower. I apologize.' With that, he walked down the hall. I closed the door and sank to the floor in such relief that I found myself crying like a baby. It was one of the most emotional moments of my life." Cooper remembered this classic film with the same kind of terse words he would emulate when essaying his many memorable stoic characters in films to come. "I had about two minutes on the screen in **Wings**," he told this author. "I chew some candy, say a few words, then take off in a plane that crashes. That was the end of me in that picture. Did it make me a star overnight? I don't think so, but it sure helped." Paramount was then grooming Cooper for stardom and purposely had his role inserted into the story line to showcase this upcoming leading player, who, within a few years, was one of Hollywood's leading male stars. Bow, who carried on a brief and torrid affair with Cooper during and after this film, was constantly battling with the costume department about the uniform she wore as an ambulance driver, insisting that it be refitted so that it was tight enough to display her voluptuous body. There were only two serious injuries in this epic production, one involving veteran stunt pilot Dick Grace, who failed to jump clear of his plane when it crashed and struck the fuselage, breaking his neck. He recovered in a hospital and returned six weeks later to resume his duties. There was one fatality when a U.S. Army pilot was killed, the Army officials held the pilot responsible and not Wellman. The film was edited by Wellman (over a six-week period) down to 111 minutes when it was first released, but, when edited footage was restored years later, the film ran in its original 144 minutes. The original release featured color-tinted scenes in prints shown in first-run theaters, as well as an early-day wide screen process. In a rerelease in 1981, Carmine Coppola conducted a full-scale orchestra with additional sound effects to accompany that

Panoramic air and ground battle action in William Wellman's classic WWI film, *Wings*, 1927.

showing at NYC's Radio City Music Hall. This film also marked another "first" for U.S. feature films in that it has some brief nude scenes of Bow, but showing her only from the back in those fleeting sequences. Wellman himself appears briefly in a cameo role in this film as a U.S. infantryman advancing over the difficult terrain of no-man's-land during a battle and where he is wounded. Other films depicting WWI pilots and/or aerial combat include **Ace of Aces**, 1933; **Aces High**, 1977; **The Blue Max**, 1966; **Body and Soul**, 1931; **Captain Eddie**, 1945; **The Court Martial of Billy Mitchell**, 1955; **Crimson Romance**, 1934; **Darling Lili**, 1970; **The Dawn Patrol**, 1930; **The Dawn Patrol**, 1938; **The Eagle and the Hawk**, 1933; **Flyboys**, 2006; **The Great Dictator**, 1940; **The Great Waldo Pepper**, 1975; **Hell in the Heavens**, 1934; **Hell's Angels**, 1930; **Lafayette Escadrille**, 1958; **The Last Flight**, 1931; **The Legion of the Condemned**, 1928; **L'equipage**, 1938 (aka: **Flight into Darkness**; remade as **The Woman I Love**, 1937); **Lilac Time**, 1928; **The Lost Squadron**, 1932; **Mata Hari**, 1931; **Men Must Fight**, 1933; **The Red Baron**, 2010; **Revenge of the Red Baron**, 1994; **Richthofen**, 1929; **A Romance of the Air**, 1918; **The Sky Hawk**, 1929; **The Story of Vernon and Irene Castle**, 1939; **Suzy**, 1936; **The Tarnished Angels**, 1958; **To Each His Own**, 1946; **Today We Live**, 1933; **Von Richthofen and Brown**, 1971; **War Nurse**, 1930; **War of the Worlds: Goliath**, 2012; **The Woman I Love**, 1937; **Young Eagles**, 1930; and **Zeppelin**, 1971. **p**, Lucien Hubbard; **d**, William A. Wellman; **cast**, Clara Bow, Charles "Buddy" Rogers, Richard Arlen, Jobyna Ralston, El Brendel, Richard Tucker, Gary Cooper, Henry B. Walthall, Roscoe Karns, Hedda Hopper; **w**, Hope Loring, Louis D. Lighton, Julian Johnson (titles), (based on a story by John Monk Saunders); **c**, Harry Perry, E. Burton Steen, Cliff Blackston, Russell Harland, Bert Baldridge, Frank Cotner, Foxon M. Dean, Ray Olsen, Herman Schoop, L. Guy Wilky, Al Williams; **m**, J.S. Zamecnik; **ed**, Lucien Hubbard, E. Lloyd Sheldon; **art d**, Hans Dreier; **spec eff**, Roy Pomeroy, Barney Wolff.

Wings in the Dark ★★★ 1935; U.S.; 75m; PAR; B/W; Adventure/Romance; Children: Acceptable; **DVD**. Exciting tale begins with Grant, an American aeronautical engineer, who, with his mechanic and best friend, Cavanaugh, is developing technology to enable pilots to safely fly blind in bad weather and fog. Loy is an aviatrix who writes messages in the sky and performs death-defying aerial acrobatics at the instigation of Karns, a crafty entrepreneurial showman. Karns has a newspaper story prematurely published that reports how Grant plans to fly a long distance mission to test his technology. Before he can undertake that alleged flight, Grant is nearly blinded in a gasoline explosion in his workshop. Loy, who has fallen in love with him, takes on even more dangerous flying stunts to earn money to keep his research going. Her checks are sent to Grant, but he does not know they are from her. Meanwhile,

Grant, with the help of his faithful dog and Cavanaugh, writes magazine articles to earn some money, but they are all rejected. Loy then pilots a plane on a dangerous non stop flight from Moscow to New York City, and, upon her return, her plane becomes in danger of crashing in heavy fog over Newfoundland. She radios for help and a sportscaster, Mc-Namee, broadcasts her plight to the world. Grant learns of it and, after using his old plane and with Cavanagh to aid him, flies to Loy's rescue. As he flies to her in-flight location, he radios help to her, based on his technology that enables her to safely land at Roosevelt Field in New York where they are reunited for a happy ending. Though far-fetched, the tale is presented with some exciting aerial action, provided by stunt pilot Paul Mantz (flying a Lockheed Vega), and Grant and Loy are standouts in their offbeat roles. ***Author's Note***: Loy told this author that "it was no secret that the aviatrix I was playing in **Wings in the Dark** was based upon the famous female pilot Amelia Earhart [1897-1937], although I was a sky-writer in that picture and Amelia was never that. Roz [Rosalind] Russell later appeared in a wonderful picture called **Flight for Freedom** [1943] and her character is definitely based on that great heroine." Earhart actually visited the set for this film and acted as an adviser on some of its aerial techniques. Loy was on loan-out from MGM to Paramount to make this film and she was still feuding with her home studio about the kind of pay she was receiving as a leading lady. It was at this time that she demanded and got a better contract from MGM boss Louis B. Mayer. Grant, a rising Paramount star, told this author that "my role in **Wings in the Dark** was a strange one. Here I had beautiful Minnie [Myrna Loy] running after me and I keep putting her off because I am too busy inventing something that will allow pilots to fly blind in dense fog. Now that is about the densest character I ever played." **p**, Arthur Hornblow Jr.; **d**, James Flood; **cast**, Myrna Loy, Cary Grant, Roscoe Karns, Hobart Cavanaugh, Dean Jagger, Russell Hopton, Matt McHugh, Graham McNamee, Hanley Andrews, Samuel S. Hinds, Stanley Andrews; **w**, Jack Kirkland, Frank Partos, Dale VanEvery, Earl H. Robinson, Paul Girard Smith (based on the story "Eyes of the Eagle" by Nell Shipman, Philip D. Hurn); **c**, William C. Mellor; **m**, Heinz Roemheld; **ed**, William Shea; **art d**, Hans Dreier, A. Earl Hedrick; **spec eff**, Dewey Wrigley.

Wings of Desire ★★★ 1988; West Germany/France; 128m; Road Movies Filmproduktion/Orion Classics; Color/Sepia; Fantasy; Children: Unacceptable (MPAA: PG-13); **DVD**; **VHS**; **IV**. This absorbing allegorical drama uniquely presents guardian angels who have been watching events on Earth since its beginning. Invisible to humans, these other world beings watch and listen above the divided city of Berlin after World War II, but they are not permitted to change events. Two of the angels, Ganz and Sander, listen to the thoughts of an old Holocaust victim and others including a circus aerialist, who is afraid she will fall. Ganz falls in love with her and wishes he was human so as to experience the joys of love and everyday human sensory pleasures. The enjoyable film makes us think about the unanswerable questions such as why are we here, where did we come from, and where do we go after death. This film was remade as the U.S. film **City of Angels**, 1998. Songs: "Zirkusmusik," "Les Filles du Calvaire" (Laurent Petigand); "Six Bells Chime," "The Carny," "From Here to Eternity" (Nick Cave); "Pas Attendre" (Sprung aus den Wolken); "Some Guys" (Tuxedomoon); "Angel Fragments" (Laurie Anderson); "Der Karibische Western" (Die Haut). Mature subject matter prohibits viewing by children. (In German; English subtitles.) **p**, Wim Wenders, Anatole Dauman; **d**, Wenders; **cast**, Bruno Ganz, Solveig Dommartin, Otto Sander, Curt Bois, Peter Falk, Hans Martin Stier, Elmar Wilms, Sigurd Rachman, Beatrice Manowski, Lajos Kovacs, Bruno Rosaz; **w**, Wenders, Peter Handke, Richard Reitinger; **c**, Henri Alekan; **m**, Jurgen Knieper; **ed**, Peter Przygodda; **prod d**, Heidi Ludi; **set d**, Esther Walz.

The Wings of Eagles ★★★ 1957; U.S.; 110m; MGM; Color; Adventure/Biographical Drama; Children: Cautionary; **DVD**; **VHS**; **IV**. The iconic Wayne gives a powerful performance as writer and U.S. Navy aviation pioneer Frank W. "Spig" Wead (1895-1947) in this exciting and colorful biopic, expertly directed by pantheon director Ford. Opening just after WWI (1914-1918), Wayne and his fellow aviator friends in the U.S. Navy, including close pal Curtis, try to convince the top brass that seaplanes and carrier-based planes will be essential in future wars. To prove their point, Wayne and company establish several air races, robustly competing with U.S. Army pilots led by Tobey, his role based upon aviation pioneer James H. "Jimmy" Doolittle (1896-1993). So obsessed with this campaign is Wayne that he ignores his devoted wife, O'Hara, and their children, which places a terrible strain on their relationship. Complicating that relationship is Wayne's carefree, heavy-drinking lifestyle, especially with roustabout U.S. sailor and lifetime friend, Dailey. When O'Hara gives birth, Wayne finds that the baby has died and he can find no way to console O'Hara. He becomes a stranger to her and their two daughters while his aviation antics become more and more outrageous, such as where he lands an airplane in the swimming pool of an admiral opposed to the expansion of naval aviation. O'Hara, instead of being alarmed at such outlandish conduct, hopes that Wayne will continue in his errant ways so that he will be cashiered from the Navy and he can then spend time with her and their children. Just the opposite happens. Wayne is promoted and appointed to head a new U.S. Navy fighter squadron. On the night he receives that encouraging news, Wayne falls down the stairs in his home and becomes paralyzed. He is rushed to a hospital, but doctors report that Wayne has severed his spinal cord and that there is little or no hope that he will ever recover or be able to regain the use of his legs. He is so depressed that he rejects O'Hara's comfort and support and will only see his old Navy pals Curtis and Dailey. While wallowing in self-pity and believing his life is over and that he is of no more use to O'Hara, Wayne tells her to leave him and make a new life with their children. Curtis and Dailey visit Wayne in his hospital room daily, encouraging him to get over his depression and make an effort to rehabilitate his legs. Dailey in particular routinely arrives each day to urge Wayne to make use of any part of his legs. Wayne at this time is prone with face down and Dailey rigs up a mirror where Wayne can look at his naked feet. Dailey then begins a regimen where he pressures Wayne to move only one toe on one foot, chanting endlessly "I'm gonna move that toe!" Through constant exercise and sheer will power, Wayne begins to see movement in that toe and finally his feet and, partially, his legs. He not only sees considerable recovery, although he must walk on crutches, that he also begins a new career as a writer, which is also incessantly encouraged by the loyal and tireless Dailey. Wayne's exciting stories about his Navy experiences, couched as fictional tales, take hold and he begins to be published. Moreover, he meets Bond, a famous film director, who admires him (based on Ford himself, who was a lifelong U.S. Navy advocate and reserve officer and a close friend of Wead), and is hired to write scripts that become successful films. (The scene where Bond is shown in his office is replete with Oscars won by Ford, as well as Ford's pipes and hollow cane.) Meanwhile, O'Hara, who has become a successful businesswoman, reunites with Wayne and they begin planning another life together. Their plans are interrupted when the Japanese attack Pearl Harbor and America becomes involved in WWII (1939-1945). Wayne's expertise in the Navy is then needed and he returns to service where he struggles to create much-needed new aircraft carriers and where, at Wayne's insistence, he has Dailey once more at his side. Wayne (like Wead) then creates a new type of small aircraft carriers he calls "jeep" carriers, which are designed to ferry new fighter and bomber planes to replace those lost in battle from the larger carriers. This not only meets the crucial demand for these warplanes, but helps to shorten the war against the Japanese in the Pacific. During the Battle of Kwajalein (January 31, 1944-February 3, 1944) Dailey is crucially wounded after saving Wayne's life from strafing by an attacking Japanese plane. The strain of battle causes Wayne to suffer a heart attack, which sends him into retirement and where he tries to rekindle his much damaged relationship with O'Hara

John Wayne, Maureen O'Hara and Dan Dailey in *The Wings of Eagles,* **1957.**

to end this fine biopic. Ford presents a compassionate profile filled with good action and some memorably tender moments between Wayne and O'Hara, who give exceptional performances. Dailey, too, provides a wonderful essay as Wayne's doggedly faithful friend, one of the best sidekick roles ever presented. The aerial sequences are fascinating to watch, and the script bristles with irony and wit. The film earned more than $3.6 million in its initial release against a budget of more than $2.6 million. Songs: "Anchors Aweigh" (1906; music: Charles A. Zimmerman; lyrics: Alfred Hart Miles), "Mama Inez" (1931; music: Eliseo Grenet; lyrics: L. Wolfe Gilbert), "Song of the Islands" (1940; Charles E. King), "You're In the Army Now" (1917; music: Isham Jones; lyrics: Tell Taylor, Ole Olsen), "Toot Toot Tootsie (Goodbye)" (1922; Al Jolson), "The Wearing of the Green" (traditional), "Aloha Oe" (c.1877; Queen Liliuokalani). *Author's Note*: Ford told this author that "everything we showed in **The Wings of Eagles** is based on real facts, even the cake-throwing scene between the Navy and Army pilots. I know that happened because I was right there in the middle of that doughy battle. Spig actually crash-landed a plane in an admiral's pool and we showed that, too. He was not only one of the most colorful characters in my life, but he was also a brilliant Navy officer and a terrific writer. He knew what people wanted to see up there on the big screen and, thankfully, I helped him put some of those stories there." Wayne told this author that "Pappy [John Ford] loved the guy I was playing in **The Wings of Eagles**, an old Navy pal of his, who, according to Pappy, walked on water. So I walked on eggs when playing that Navy hero as Pappy watched my every move. I mean he got so picky that he once said: 'No, Spig did not squint like that. He squinted like this.' And then he showed me how the man squinted by wrinkling his nose. How picky could Pappy get? Down to every hair on your head, that's how." This would be the third of five films in which O'Hara appeared with Wayne, the other four being **Rio Grande**, 1950 (also directed by Ford); **The Quiet Man**, 1952 (also directed by Ford); **McLintock!**, 1963; and **Big Jake**, 1971. My good friend, Gene Ruggiero, edited this film, telling me that: "I had to tow Ford's mark when working on that picture. Ford watched all film editors working on his pictures like a hawk. It was the editor's job to point out to him imperfections or technical errors in scenes, but you didn't dare edit out or clip any of his scenes, unless you wanted to go to the hospital. He was a tough bird. I knew that he once found an editor clipping out a scene from one of his pictures and he knocked him out cold. That wasn't going to happen to me, no sir, so on **The Wings of Eagles** I had very little work to do. Most of the time, Ford was standing next to me, looking over my shoulder as I worked the moviola. He made me nervous as hell and I think he enjoyed doing that to everyone. Nobody ever talked back to John Ford, and I mean nobody! When we finished he thanked me and told me I had done a good job. I went home, lit a cigar, had a

Henry Fonda and Annabella in *Wings of the Morning*, 1937.

stiff drink, and then asked myself, 'What the hell did he thank me for?' All I did was preview the picture for him. You must realize, however, that Ford was such a good director that he edited his films as he shot them, so all of his continuity was always in place and his timing and everything was right on the money. Working with him was another matter, like being in the same room with Attila the Hun." The film was shot in Hollywood and also on location in Pensacola, Florida, where Ford employed as extras many U.S. Navy flight cadets as well as their instructors and where, in defiance of the Navy restrictions, he gave these extras bonus payments for their appearances. Film stories and screenplays written by Wead include **Air Mail**, 1932; **The Beginning or the End**, 1947; **Blaze of Noon**, 1947; **Bombardier**, 1943; **Ceiling Zero**, 1936; **China Clipper**, 1936; **The Citadel**, 1938; **Dirigible**, 1931; **Destroyer**, 1943; **Dive Bomber**, 1941; **Hell Divers**, 1931; **International Squadron**, 1941; **Test Pilot**, 1938; and **They Were Expendable**, 1945. **p**, Charles Schnee; **d**, John Ford; **cast**, John Wayne, Dan Dailey, Maureen O'Hara, Ward Bond, Ken Curtis, Edmund Lowe, Kenneth Tobey, James Todd, Barry Kelley, Sig Ruman, Henry O'Neill, Dorothy Jordan, Veda Ann Borg, Olive Carey, William Henry, Mae Marsh, May McAvoy, William Tracy; **w**, Frank Fenton, William Wister Haines (based on the life and writings of Comdr. Frank W. "Spig" Wead, U.S.N., and the biography *Wings of Men*); **c**, Paul C. Vogel (Metrocolor); **m**, Jeff Alexander; **ed**, Gene Ruggiero; **art d**, William A. Horning, Malcolm Brown; **set d**, Edwin B. Willis, Keogh Gleason; **spec eff**, A. Arnold Gillespie, Warren Newcombe.

The Wings of the Dove ★★★ 1997; U.K./U.S.; 102m; Miramax; Color; Drama/Romance; Children: Unacceptable (MPAA: PG-13); **DVD; IV**. Engrossing tale begins with Carter and Roache, who are young London lovers wanting to marry, but have very little money. Carter lives with Rampling, a domineering aunt, while Roache writes sensational stories for newspapers and magazines. Elliott, a young American heiress with a possibly fatal illness, visits London and meets Carter and Roache at a party. Elliott falls in love with Roache while Carter becomes her companion; believing Elliott may soon die, Carter talks Roache into pretending he loves Elliott so he can marry her and, after Elliott dies, she and Roache can live happily ever after on Elliott's fortune. Roache agrees, but his conscience gets the better of his underhanded ambitions. Elliott learns about Carter's plot to get her money and falls gravely ill. She dies and Roache learns that she left him most of her fortune, but he follows his heart, deciding that he will not touch the money. He also now rejects Carter, and she, too, has a guilty conscience and won't take any of Elliott's money left to her. The former lovers now separate, knowing that their ruthless plotting will never allow them to be as they were. Softley helms this offbeat romantic drama with

commendable restraint, and Carter, Roache and Elliott deliver fine performances. The film received Oscar nominations for Best Actress (Carter); Best Adapted Screenplay (Amini); Best Cinematography (Serra); and Best Costume Design (Sandy Powell). The film earned more than $13.6 million in its initial release. Sexuality prohibits viewing by children. **p**, Stephen Evans, David Parfitt; **d**, Iain Softley; **cast**, Helena Bonham Carter, Linus Roache, Alison Elliott, Michael Gambon, Elizabeth McGovern, Alex Jennings, Charlotte Rampling, Alexander John, Diana Kent, Shirley Chantrell; **w**, Hossein Amini (based on the novel by Henry James); **c**, Eduardo Serra; **m**, Edward Shearmur; **ed**, Tariq Anwar; **prod d**, John Beard; **art d**, Martyn John, Andrew Sanders; **set d**, Joanne Woollard; **spec eff**, Dominic Tuohy, Steve Warner, Tez Palmer.

Wings of the Morning ★★★ 1937; U.K.; 89m; New World/FOX; Color; Drama/Romance; Children: Acceptable; **DVD; VHS**. This fine film is set in 1889 Ireland where Banks, an Irish lord, marries Annabella, a beautiful gypsy girl. Soon after, Banks is thrown by his horse and dies. His family, who hates Annabella, forces her out of her home and she takes refuge in Spain. Nearly half a century later in 1937, the gypsy girl (played now by Vanbrugh) flees the Spanish Civil War (1936-1939) and returns to Ireland with her granddaughter (also played by Annabella), and where Vanbrugh intends to enter a horse in the Epsom Downs Derby. Annabella wants to ride the horse in the race, so she disguises herself as a boy. Fonda, a Canadian horse trainer, learns her secret when he sees her dressed as a woman at a party. He falls in love with her and she with him, despite the fact that she is engaged to Underdown, who lives in Spain. The horse wins the derby and Underdown arrives from Spain, but, after he sees that Annabella loves Fonda, he nobly breaks off their engagement so that the lovers can marry. Shuster presents a tender love story that is enhanced through the rich but subdued hues of the new Technicolor process (this film being the first color film made in England). Annabella and Fonda shine in their roles as the hesitant lovers. This film is not related to a 1919 silent film of the same name. Songs: "Believe Me If All Those Endearing Young Charms" (music: traditional; lyrics: Thomas Moore), "Killarney" (music: Michael William Balfe; lyrics: Edmund Falconer), "Come Back to Erin" (Charlotte Barnard), "At the Dawning of the Day" (traditional), "Wiener Blut/Vienna Blood" (Johann Strauss Jr.), "Marche Militaire" (Bronislau Caper, Walter Jurmann). Songs sung by Irish tenor John McCormack. *Author's Note*: Fonda told this author that "I looked forward to appearing in **Wings of the Morning** because it gave me my first chance to visit the Continent where it was shot on location. It was beautifully filmed in the old Technicolor process, which was used for the first time in America as an all-outdoor color picture a year before and I appeared in that film, too." That picture was **Trail of the Lonesome Pine**, 1936, and, like this one, was shot in three-strip Technicolor, which offered more muted, softer colors than the latter-day process that more sharply (if not garishly) defined color. Fonda, to his surprise, suddenly came to the attention of the amorous Annabella, the French star quickly developing a romantic crush for Fonda. When he discovered this, he made a hasty retreat, leaving the set every time after finishing his scenes with her. She nevertheless pursued him and he did everything possible to avoid her when off the set. Annabella's husband received a note from the actress that told him that she was in love with Fonda and that the actor was in love with her. The husband, Jean Murat, flew to London where the film was nearing completion and confronted Fonda. The actor patiently explained that no romance whatsoever existed between him and his wife, and Murat accepted his explanation. Thereafter, Annabella kept her distance from Fonda. She would later set her sights on handsome American matinee idol Tyrone Power Jr., and would eventually marry him (her third and final husband). Though Fonda was able to ward off the affections of Annabella, he met a beautiful, young American socialite, Frances Seymour Brokaw, who, along with a group of other Americans, was visiting the set. Fonda and Brokaw were immediately attracted to each other and soon married, a union that would last until her death in 1950. **p**, Robert Kane; **d**, Harold D. Schuster; **cast**, Annabella, Henry Fonda, Leslie Banks, Stewart Rome, Irene Vanbrugh, Edward Underdown as Teddy Underdown, Mark Daly, Sam Livesey; Harry Tate, Helen Haye; **w**, Thomas J. Geraghty, John Meehan, Gilbert Wakefield (based on stories by Donn Bryne); **c**, Ray Rennahan (Technicolor); **m**, Arthur Benjamin; **ed**, James B. Clark; **prod d&art d**, Ralph W. Brinton.

Winner Take All ★★★ 1932; U.S.; 68m; WB; B/W; Sports Drama; Children: Unacceptable; **DVD**. Cagney gives another dynamic performance in this action-loaded prizefighting drama. He is a New York City boxer recovering in a New Mexico health resort from injuries and fast living with women and alcohol. He falls in love with Nixon, a former nightclub singer. She needs $600 to keep her sickly young son, Moore. To help her, Cagney risks his health with a tough boxing match in Tijuana, Mexico. He wins the fight and settles Nixon's financial problems, but he suffers a broken nose in the south-of-the-border brawl. Cagney returns to New York, intending to become a champion. There he meets Bruce, a beautiful society woman, and falls for her. To improve his looks so that the elitist Bruce will accept him, Cagney undergoes plastic surgery that fixes his smashed nose and cauliflower ear. Further, he takes etiquette lessons from Mowbray and now he feels that Bruce will accept him. Moreover, he thinks to become a champ in the ring after Kibbee, his manager, arranges a lightweight championship bout. Kibbee, however, thinks Cagney is aiming too high by pursuing the snooty Bruce and sends for Nixon. When Nixon arrives, Cagney sheepishly admits that he plans to tie the knot with Bruce. With his fixed face and inflated ego, Cagney tells Bruce that he intends to win the championship bout and win enough money so that they can be married. However, when Cagney gets into the ring to compete in that match, he is so protective of his nose, that Cagney is booed by fight fans. He sees that Bruce is not at the ringside seat he has reserved for her and then learns that she is about to sail to Europe on an ocean liner. Cagney panics and forgets about his nose, which is promptly broken once more, but he savagely attacks his opponent, knocking him out. He rushes from the stadium to the dockside liner and boards it, finding Bruce in her cabin. She invents the excuse that she must travel to Europe to aid her sister, but her lie is quickly exposed when Roche, Bruce's current lover, enters the cabin. Cagney immediately recognizes that Bruce has merely been toying with him and never had any affection for him. He punches Roche unconscious and, after Bruce leans over to check on Roche, he kicks her soundly in the backside and departs. He then meets Nixon, the woman who truly loves him, and Cagney realizes that she is the woman for him. Del Ruth offers a fine drama with exceptional character development, especially the transformation of Cagney from careless pug to considerate human being. The boxing sequences are also well choreographed, and Cagney appears genuine as a professional prizefighter (he would go on to play another prizefighter in an outstanding sports drama, **City for Conquest**, 1940). The film was a box office hit and greatly enhanced Cagney's climb to superstardom. This film is not related to a 1939 film with the same title. Songs: "The Sidewalks of New York" (1894; Charles Lawlor), "Beyond the Blue Horizon" (1930; Richard A. Whiting, W. Franke Harling), "Was That the Human Thing to Do?" (1932; music: Sammy Fain; lyrics: Joe Young), "St. Louis Blues" (1914; W. C. Handy). *Author's Note*: Cagney took his role in this film seriously, telling this author: "I trained as a prizefighter with Harvey Perry, who was a one-time welterweight fighter, and who taught me all the right moves to make in the ring, along with how to throw my punches and protect myself in the clinches." Perry also has a small role in the film. Further aiding Cagney was his dazzling footwork in the boxing scenes, and where he incorporated his dancing expertise. So effective was he that rumors in Hollywood had it that Cagney had, before turning to acting, been an amateur boxer. Briefly seen in the film is a clip from **Queen of the Night Clubs**, 1929, with nightclub owner-entertainer Texas Guinan and

Charles Coleman, James Cagney and Virginia Bruce in *Winner Take All*, **1932.**

George Raft. For a comprehensive list of prizefighting films, see Subject Index, Boxers and Boxing. **p&d**, Roy Del Ruth; **cast**, James Cagney, Marian Nixon, Virginia Bruce, Dickie Moore, Guy Kibbee, Alan Mowbray, John Roche, Esther Howard, Clarence Muse, Clarence Wilson, Ralf Harolde, Sheila Bromley, George "Gabby" Hayes, Allan Lane, Chris-Pin Martin, Texas Guinan, George Raft; **w**, Robert Lord, Wilson Mizner (based on the story "133 at 3" by George Beaumont); **c**, Robert Kurrle; **m**, W. Franke Harling; **ed**, Thomas Pratt; **art d**, Robert Haas.

Winnie the Pooh ★★★ 2011; U.S.; 116m; Walt Disney/Buena Vista; Color; Animated Comedy; Children: Recommended (MPAA: G); **BD**; **DVD**; **IV**. During an ordinary day in the Hundred Acre Wood, Winnie the Pooh (Cummings voiceover) sets out to find some honey. Misinterpreting a note from Christopher Robin (Boulter voiceover), Owl (Ferguson voiceover), Tigger (Cummings voiceover), Rabbit (Kenny voiceover), Piglet (Oates voiceover), Kanga (Anderson-Lopez voiceover), Roo (Hall voiceover) and Eeyore (Luckey voiceover), they all think Pooh has been captured by a creature named "Backson" and set out to save him in what turns out to be a number of precocious and entertaining adventures. This charming entry in the Disney animated series of films about Pooh and friends is thoroughly entertaining and provides meticulously created and highly innovative animation. Songs: "The Tummy Song," "A Very Important Thing to Do," "Everything Is Honey," "The Winner Song," "The Backson Song," "It's Gonna Be Great" (Robert Lopez, Kristen Anderson-Lopez); "Winnie the Pooh," "The Wonderful Thing Abut Tiggers" (Richard M. Sherman, Robert B. Sherman); "So Long" (Zooey Deschanel). **p**, Peter Del Vecho, Clark Spencer; **d**, Stephen J. Anderson, Don Hall; **cast**, Jim Cummings, Bud Luckey, Craig Ferguson, Jack Boulter, Travis Oates, Kristen Anderson-Lopez, Wyatt Dean Hall, Tom Kenny, Huell Howser, John Cleese (narrator); **w**, Hall, Anderson, Clio Chiang, Don Dougherty, Kendelle Hoyer, Brian Kesinger, Nicole Mitchell, Jeremy Spears, Paul Briggs, Chris Ure (based on the "Winnie the Pooh" stories of A.A. Milne, Ernest Shepard); **c**, Julio Macat; **m**, Henry Jackman; **ed**, Lisa Linder; **art d**, Paul Felix, Patrick M. Sullivan Jr.; **spec eff**, Tim Gospodnetich, George C. Stevens.

Winning ★★★ 1969; U.S.; 123m; Jennings Lang; Newman-Foreman/UNIV; Color; Sports Drama; Children: Unacceptable; **DVD**; **VHS**. Newman gives a riveting performance as a professional race car driver with dreams of winning the Indianapolis 500, but his wife, Woodward, resents the fact that he spends more time in the garage tinkering with his car than with her. The frustrated Woodward seeks comfort in the arms of Wagner, who is Newman's main rival on the track. Woodward's son, Thomas, a child from a previous marriage and whom Newman adopted, comes to their rescue to save their marriage. That union is sev-

Vilma Banky and Gary Cooper in *The Winning of Barbara Worth*, 1926.

ered, however, after Newman finds Wagner in bed with Woodward, who has sought his rival's affections out of Newman's neglect of her. Wagner's car suffers engine trouble in the Indy 500 race, but he is driven out of anger and desperation from the event of his personal life to drive the race of his life, which Newman nevertheless wins. Following the win, Newman attends a victory party where he is surrounded by fawning beautiful women, none of whom having any appeal for him. Wagner then seeks him out and apologizes for his tryst with Woodward, and Newman responds by punching the marital interloper unconscious. Newman then finds Woodward and tells her that he wants to start over again with her, but she remains unsure, the last scene being a freeze frame of them together to emphasize their uncertain future together. An exciting auto race film, Goldstone offers many harrowing racetrack scenes, along with developing the trouble-haunted characters with care. The film was a great box office success, earning more than $14.5 million in its initial release. ***Author's Note***: Newman told this author that "I guess I indulged myself a lot in **Winning** as I love race car driving, a real passion. I don't know whether it's the speed or the control of the car that intrigues me, maybe both." Newman and Woodward were married in real life, and Newman did his own driving in the film (the studio insured him for $3 million). For a comprehensive list of films depicting race car drivers, see Subject Index, Race Cars and Race Car Drivers. **p**, John Foreman; **d**, James Goldstone; **cast**, Paul Newman, Joanne Woodward, Robert Wagner, Richard Thomas, Clu Gulager, David Sheiner, Barry Ford, Robert Shayne, Bobby Unser, Tony Hulman, Bobby Grim, Dan Gurney, Roger McCluskey; **w**, Howard Rodman; **c**, Richard Moore (Panavision; Technicolor); **m**, Dave Grusin; **ed**, Edward A. Biery, Richard C. Meyer; **art d**, Alexander Golitzen, John J. Lloyd, Joe Alves; **set d**, John McCarthy, George Milo; **spec eff**, Frank Brendel.

The Winning of Barbara Worth ★★★★ 1926 (silent); U.S.; 89m/9 reels; Samuel Goldwyn Company/UA; B/W; Western; Children: Unacceptable; **DVD**. Outstanding western from Goldwyn sees exceptional performances from Colman and Banky, along with newcomer Cooper, playing a shy cowboy who almost steals Banky's heart, along with the film (his debut as a leading player). The film opens with a pioneering family crossing a desert; the husband dies and his wife, who has just given birth and is also played by Banky, buries him, using the slats of her child's cradle to make a crude cross that marks his grave. The mother also dies in a fierce sandstorm, but the child is rescued when Lane (as Jefferson Worth), a land developer, finds the baby. He raises the child as his own and she grows to adulthood as Banky (Barbara Worth). Banky idolizes her foster father Lane and energetically supports his dream of reclaiming the desert by using the Colorado River to irrigate thousands of desert acres. Needing money for this expensive project,

Lane heavily borrows money from corrupt New York banker Ratcliffe, who arrives with his stepson Colman, an engineer. As they review the project, Colman and Banky are drawn together. The project sees the rise of a town that Lane calls "Barbara Worth," after his adopted daughter. While Colman is wooing Banky, he sees competition from another young engineer, Cooper. The two become enemies in their joint affection for the beautiful Banky, who cannot decide which of them she wants for her husband. Meanwhile, Ratcliffe's greed gets the best of him, and, after he sees that irrigated land will produce a fortune in crops and nurture livestock, he decides to take the project from Lane. When realizing Ratcliffe's land-grabbing scheme, Lane orders Ratcliffe from his property. Lane also and wrongly concludes that Colman is in league with Ratcliffe and orders that he, too, leave the area. Lane plans to finish the project on his own, which includes the final construction of a huge dam. He fires all the engineers working for him, including Cooper. Lane soon runs out of cash and is further hampered when Ratcliffe incites Lane's workers to riot when demanding their unpaid wages. Former enemies Colman and Cooper then join forces to aid Lane when both ride all day to a distant location to obtain needed cash that will satisfy the workers. Knowing this, Ratcliffe sends his minions after the pair, and, as they are returning with the needed cash, they are ambushed and Cooper is seriously wounded. The noble Cooper, realizing that Banky truly loves Colman, tells Colman to leave him behind and ride on to meet the crisis facing Lane. The grateful Colman does exactly that, arriving just in time to quell the rioting workers, paying them off before they are about to lynch Lane. Tragedy then strikes when the gerrymandered dam constructed with faulty materials used by Ratcliffe, gives way and wipes out the town. (This is the most spectacular scene in the film, an awesome disaster expertly displayed in miniature.) The hardy pioneers are undaunted, however, as Lane and his followers decide to rebuild the dam and reclaim the desert while Colman and Banky make happy plans to go to the altar. King directs this action-filled film with gusto and draws fine performances from Banky and Colman, as well as the reserved Cooper. The film was a hit at the box office as Banky and Colman were then matinee idols. ***Author's Note***: Goldwyn had long thought to produce this story as a significant western and had eyed the novel published by Wright in 1911 for some years. He learned in 1925 that film producers Sol Lesser and Mike Rosenberg, who headed Principal Pictures, wanted the story and they were attempting to acquire the film rights of Wright's western. Goldwyn immediately acquired those rights by paying Wright a staggering $125,000, an unprecedented amount in those days. "My star in that day was Vilma Banky," Goldwyn told this author, "and I put her into that story as her wedding gift." Banky was planning to marry film star Rod La Roque, the couple marrying in 1927, that union lasting until his death in 1969. Colman was a natural choice as Banky's leading man, this film being their second of five films they made together. The third leading role of the cowboy engineer was assigned to Harold Goodwin, but when Goodwin was held up with another production, King, who was then ready to go into production, desperately fielded about for another leading player. "I knew a bit player, a lanky young cowboy, who I had hired at $50 a week after I saw a screen test he had made by himself," King told this author. "That extra was Coop [Gary Cooper]. I convinced Sam [Goldwyn] that Coop was perfect for the part. Sam was nervous about it, but he let me cast him anyway and Coop proved to be perfect for the role of the other man in Vilma's [Banky's] life. To tell you the truth, I had to do a lot of coaching to get Coop to make the right moves and got away with all that because Sam was too busy with another production to see how much of a rookie actor Coop really was." Cooper got a $15 raise for his role in this film, taking home $65 a week. "The pay wasn't much," Cooper told this author, "but just being in that picture gave me the big break that established my career in the movies. I always remembered Henry [King] with gratitude for giving me that break." The public responded well to this film and Cooper did not go unnoticed as thousands of fans wrote letters to him, flooding Goldwyn's office and where Goldwyn rightly believed he had another great star. Goldwyn, however, thought that King had hired Cooper to a long-term agreement under the Goldwyn banner. King thought Goldwyn had done the same thing. Neither had gotten Cooper's signature on a contract, a mistake they soon came to deeply regret. Paramount, after seeing this film, immediately signed Cooper to a long-term contract and he would stay with that studio for many years to come. **p**, Samuel Goldwyn; **d**, Henry King; **cast**, Ronald Colman, Vilma Banky, Gary Cooper, Charles Lane, Paul McAllister, E.J. Ratcliffe, Clyde Cook, Erwin Connelly, Ed Brady, Sammy Blum, Fred Esmelton; **w**, Frances Marion (based on the novel by Harold Bell Wright); **c**, Gregg Toland, George Barnes; **m**, Ted Henkel; **ed**, Viola Lawrence; **art d**, Karl Oscar Borg.

The Winning Team ★★★ 1952; U.S.; 98m; WB; B/W; Biographical Drama; Sports Drama; Children: Cautionary; **DVD**; **VHS**; **IV**. Reagan gives a superlative performance as one of baseball's greatest hurlers, Grover Cleveland Alexander (1887-1950), with wonderful support by the talented Day, who plays his loyal wife. The film opens with Reagan working as a telephone lineman in Nebraska and where he is engaged to local belle Day. He is forever spending all of his leisure time pitching for the local amateur team until he is discovered by talent agent Jones. Reagan marries Day, and they settle down to a happy life on a farm. He is finally signed by the Philadelphia Phillies and goes on to perform astonishing pitching records, but he is hit in the head by a ball and begins to have occasional dizzy spells. That condition is further aggravated when he serves in the U.S. Artillery during WWI (1914-1918), where the constant explosions create consistent headaches and dizzy spells. Reagan consults physicians that tell him that he should quit baseball as the rigors on the field only add to his condition, but he continues playing while keeping his medical problems to himself and from Day. While pitching, he begins to have double vision accompanied by painful headaches. To dull the pain, he begins drinking heavily. His alcoholism debilitates his ability to perform on the mound, and he is traded from one major league team to another until he is reduced to pitching in the minor leagues. When he suffers a dizzy spell on the mound and collapses, his medical malady is mistaken by critics as inebriation and Reagan finally leaves the game he loves more than anything else. By this time, Day has left him, believing that he is an incurable and irresponsible alcoholic. She then learns from Patterson, the doctor who originally diagnosed Reagan, that Reagan is suffering from a medical malady and she now realizes that her husband has a physical malady as well as dealing with a drinking problem. Day finds him appearing at a seedy side show where he gives speeches about his career, and she then goes to Lovejoy, who plays Rogers Hornsby (1896-1963), the manager-player for the St. Louis Cardinals, begging him to hire Reagan. Millican, who plays Bill Killefer (1887-1960, who was Alexander's favorite catcher), also urges Lovejoy to hire Reagan and Lovejoy does exactly that. Reagan quickly regains his status as one of the country's top hurlers by leading the Cardinals to one victory after another through his incredible pitching until they face the powerful New York Yankees in the 1926 World Series. Reagan pitches and wins two complete games in that series (games two and six), using up all of his energy. In game seven, however, the pitcher for the Cardinals develops a blister and Lovejoy calls upon Reagan to save that seventh game. He goes to the mound with the Yankees having loaded the bases and with Yankee slugger Tony Lazzeri (1903-1946) at the plate at the bottom of the seventh inning. Reagan is unsure as to whether or not he can strike out this powerful hitter and fears that he might again suffer double vision or a dizzy spell. He looks to the stands, however, to see Day sitting there and encouraging him (he has told her earlier that he has been "taking my strength from you" throughout his comeback). Reagan bears down on Lazzeri and strikes him out. He goes on to keep the Yankees scoreless and wins that seventh crucial game and the series, a fantastic feat that causes the great pitcher to be memorialized in the Baseball Hall of Fame. Seiler does an outstanding job merging the dramatic scenes with some very exciting base-

Ronald Reagan and Doris Day in *The Winning Team*, **1952.**

ball sequences, many of these culled from actual newsreel clips of the period. Reagan gives an exceptional performance of the great Alexander and the ailments that plagued him while he struggles to achieve his impossible feats on the mound. Day is her effervescent self and gives a warmhearted performance of a doggedly loyal spouse, and Lovejoy is convincing and reassuring as the great Rogers Hornsby. The film was a hit with the public, earning more than $1.7 million in its initial release. Songs: "Take Me Out to the Ball Game" (1908; music: Albert Von Tilzer; lyrics: Jack Norworth), "For He's a Jolly Good Fellow" (c.1709; traditional complimentary song), "I'll String Along with You" (1934; music: Harry Warren; lyrics: Al Dubin), "Ol' Saint Nicholas" (Inez James, Buddy Pepper), "Pack Up Your Troubles in Your Old Kit Bag and Smile, Smile, Smile!" (1915; music: Felix Powell; lyrics: George Asaf), "Ain't We Got Fun" (1921; music: Richard A. Whiting; lyrics: Raymond B. Egan, Gus Kahn), "Carolina in the Morning" (1922; music: Walter Donaldson; lyrics: Gus Kahn), "Lucky Day" (Ray Henderson). *Author's Note*: Reagan had lobbied to star in **The Stratton Story**, 1949, the story of another baseball great, Monty Stratton (1912-1982), but the role went to James Stewart. When that film proved to be a hit at the box office, Warner Brothers went ahead with this film and with Reagan as its leading man, a role that Reagan fondly remembered as one of his favorites. Alexander played professional baseball from 1911-1930 and amassed a record of (373-208) with an earned run average (E.R.A.) of 2.56 and 2,198 strikeouts. Other films profiling baseball players include **The Adventures of Frank Merriwell**, 1936 (serial); **Alibi Ike**, 1935 (Chicago Cubs); **Amos**, 1985 (made-for-TV); **Angels in the Outfield**, 1951 (Pittsburgh Pirates); **Angels in the Outfield**, 1994 (California Angels); **The Babe**, 1992 (George Herman "Babe" Ruth; New York Yankees); **Babe Ruth**, 1991 (made-for-TV; New York Yankees); **The Babe Ruth Story**, 1948 (New York Yankees); **Back in the Game**, 2013- (TV series); **The Bad News Bears**, 1976; **Bang the Drum Slowly**, 1973; **The Battery**, 2012; **Battlefield Baseball**, 2003; **The Benchwarmers**, 2006; **The Big Picture**, 1989 (George Herman "Babe" Ruth); **The Bingo Long Traveling All Stars & Motor Kings**, 1976; **The Blonde**, 2001 (TV miniseries; based on Marilyn Monroe and her relationship with New York Yankees player Joe DiMaggio); **Boys**, 1996; **Brewster's Millions**, 1985; **The Bronx Is Burning**, 2007 (TV series; New York Yankees); **Bull Durham**, 1988; **Casey at the Bat**, 1916; **Casey at the Bat**, 1927; **Cobb**, 1994 (Ty Cobb; Detroit Tigers); **Damn Yankees**, 1958 (New York Yankees); **Deadball**, 2011; **Deadline at Dawn**, 1946; **Dempsey**, 1983 (made-for-TV; George Herman "Babe" Ruth; New York Yankees); **Don't Look Back: The Story of Leroy "Satchel" Paige**, 1981 (made-for-TV; Negro Leagues); **Eastbound & Down**, 2009-2013 (TV series); **Eight Men Out**, 1988 (1919 Chicago White Sox); **Elmer the Great**, 1933 (Chicago Cubs); **Everybody Loves Ray-**

Francis L. Sullivan and Robert Donat battling in an English court in _The Winslow Boy_, 1950.

mond, 1996-2005 (TV series); **The Fan**, 1996 (San Francisco Giants); **Fear Strikes Out**, 1957 (Jimmy Piersall; Boston Red Sox); **Field of Dreams**, 1989 (1919 Chicago White Sox); **For Love of the Game**, 1999 (Detroit Tigers); **42**, 2013 (Jackie Robinson; Brooklyn Dodgers); **The Goddess**, 1958 (based on Marilyn Monroe and her relationship with New York Yankees player Joe DiMaggio); **Henry & Me**, 2014 (George Herman "Babe" Ruth; Lefty Gomez; Thurman Munson; Reggie Jackson; Michael Kay; Joe Girardi; Mickey Mantle; New York Yankees); **Hit and Run**, 1924; **Holes**, 2003; **Hot Curves**, 1930; **House on Haunted Hill**, 1999; **How Do You Know**, 2010; **I'm with Lucy**, 2002; **Insignificance**, 1985 (based on Marilyn Monroe and her relationship with New York Yankees player Joe DiMaggio); **Ironweed**, 1987; **It Happened in Flatbush**, 1942; **It Happens Every Spring**, 1949 (fictitious St. Louis team); **The Jackie Robinson Story**, 1950 (Brooklyn Dodgers); **Jim Thorpe—All American**, 1951 (New York Giants); **The Kid from Cleveland**, 1949 (Cleveland Indians); **The Kid from Left Field**, 1979 (made-for-TV); **Kill the Umpire**, 1950 (Texas League); **Ladies' Day**, 1943; **A League of Their Own**, 1992; **Little Big League**, 1994 (Minnesota Twins); **Love Affair: The Eleanor and Lou Gehrig Story**, 1978 (made-for-TV; Lou Gehrig; George Herman "Babe" Ruth; New York Yankees); **Love Finds You in Sugarcreek**, 2014 (made-for-TV); **Major League**, 1989 (Cleveland Indians); **Make Mine Music**, 1946 (animated sequence of Casey at the Bat); **Manhattan Merry-Go-Round**, 1942; **Marilyn: The Untold Story**, 1980 (made-for-TV; based on Marilyn Monroe and her relationship with New York Yankees player Joe DiMaggio); **Meet John Doe**, 1941; **The Men's Club**, 1986; **A Mile in His Shoes**, 2011 (made-for-TV); **Mr. Baseball**, 1992; **Mr. Dynamite**, 1941; **Moneyball**, 2011 (Oakland Athletics); **Moonlight in Havana**, 1942; **The Natural**, 1984 (based on Edward Stephen Waitkus, who played for the Chicago Cubs, Philadelphia Phillies and Baltimore Orioles and who was shot and critically wounded on June 14, 1949, at Chicago's Edgewater Beach Hotel by deranged fan and stalker Ruth Ann Steinhagen, 1929-2012); **Never Been Kissed**, 1999; **Norma Jean & Marilyn**, 1996 (made-for-TV; based on Marilyn Monroe and her relationship with New York Yankees player Joe DiMaggio); **The Odd Couple**, 1968; **One Hit from Home**, 2012; **Outrage**, 2003; **Outside Ozona**, 1998; **The Pride of St. Louis**, 1952 (Jerome "Dizzy" Dean; St. Louis Cardinals; Chicago Cubs); **The Pride of the Yankees**, 1942 (Lou Gehrig; New York Yankees); **Rocket Gibraltar**, 1988; **The Rookie**, 2002 (Jim Morris; Tampa Bay Devil Rays); **Rookie of the Year**, 1993 (Chicago Cubs); **Safe at Home!**, 1962 (Roger Maris; Mickey Mantle; New York Yankees); **The Sandlot**, 1993; **The Scout**, 1994 (New York Yankees); **Seven Minutes in Heaven**, 1985; **Ship of Fools**, 1965; **Shuffleton's Barbershop**, 2013 (made-for-TV); **Signs**, 2002; **Simple Men**, 1992; **61***, 2001 (made-for-TV; Roger Maris; Mickey Mantle; New

York Yankees); **Soul of the Game**, 1996 (made-for-cable-TV; Negro Leagues; Leroy "Satchel" Paige; Josh Gibson; Jackie Robinson); **Space Jam**, 1996 (Michael Jordan; Birmingham Barons, minor league team of Chicago White Sox); **Strategic Air Command**, 1955 (St. Louis Cardinals); **The Stratton Story**, 1949 (Monty Stratton; Chicago White Sox); **Summer Catch**, 2001; **Summer Wars**, 2009; **Swellhead**, 1935; **Take Me Out to the Ball Game**, 1949; **Tall Tales & Legends**, 1985-1987 (TV series; "Casey at the Bat," 1986 episode); **That Touch of Mink**, 1962 (Roger Maris; Mickey Mantle; Yogi Berra; New York Yankees); **Trouble with the Curve**, 2012; **20,000 Men a Year**, 1939; **Two's Company**, 1973 (made-for-TV); **The Upside of Anger**, 2005; **Woman of the Year**, 1942; and **Wrecking Crew**, 1942. **p**, Bryan Foy; **d**, Lewis Seiler; **cast**, Doris Day, Ronald Reagan, Frank Lovejoy, Eve Miller, James Millican, Russ Tamblyn, Gordon Jones, Hugh Sanders, Bonnie Kay Eddiy, Frank Ferguson, Walter Baldwin, Dorothy Adams, Bob Lemon, Peanuts Lowery, Hank Sauer, George Metkovich, Kenneth Patterson, Frank McFarland; **w**, Ted Sherdeman, Seeleg Lester, Merwin Gerard (based on the story by Lester, Gerard); **c**, Sid Hickox; **m**, David Buttolph; **ed**, Alan Crosland, Jr.; **art d**, Douglas Bacon; **set d**, William Kuehl; **spec eff**, H.F. Koenekamp.

The Winslow Boy ★★★★ 1950; U.K.; 97m (U.S. release; 112m in U.K.); De Grunwald Productions/Eagle-Lion Films; B/W; Drama; Children: Acceptable; **DVD**; **VHS**; **IV**. Taut tale begins in 1912 when North, a cadet at the Royal Naval College, is expelled after being accused of stealing a five-shilling postal order. Hardwicke believes his son innocent and that he has been falsely accused and his future ruined. Hardwicke resolves to defend his son and redeem his honor, but wherever he turns he is faced by indifferent bureaucrats and draconian British law that prevents him from taking any action. Supporting Hardwicke is his single-minded daughter, Leighton, who is an energetic activist for women's suffrage. Radford, their family solicitor, is asked to make inquiries which seem to go nowhere. Their last resort is to hire Donat, the most brilliant barrister in England to bring the case to a trial, where Hardwicke stakes his own reputation and risks all of his assets in defending his son. Donat finds that he has untaken one of the most difficult cases in his long and distinguished career in that he must battle the government, which, at first, refuses to allow the case to proceed in court. He finally compels authorities to grant a court proceeding and, battling bureaucratic obfuscations, manages to discredit the flimsy evidence against North. He finally puts North on the stand and patiently works from the fourteen-year-old boy an admission that he was not guilty of taking the postal order, but that he was covering up the fact that he was sneaking a smoke in his locker at the time he was accused of the theft, which caused suspicion on the part of superiors and peers. Thus penetrating the boy's code of honor, Donat exposes the truth of the events and North is exonerated. The victory, however, is a hollow one in that the exhaustive trial has taken a severe toll on the family. Hardwicke's health has been ruined, Leighton's engagement to her fiancé, Lawton, is broken off, and Watling, Hardwicke's oldest son, is forced to leave Oxford. The story is a weighty one that would, without the intense and fascinating performances from Hardwicke, Leighton and Donat, otherwise present a boggy tale. The courtroom scenes are also presented in such intensity that they provide high tension throughout, and this achievement should be credited to director Asquith and his brilliant camera work along with his fluid edits and cuts. The film was enormously popular in the U.K., and did well at the box office in the U.S. in its initial release. Songs: "Snookey Pookey Twaddle" and "You Can't Help Winning" (Howard Carr), "Bugle March" (Hubert Clifford), "Who Were You With Last Night?" (Fred Godfrey, Mark Sheridan), "In the Shadows" (Herman Finck), "Little Dolly Daydream" (Leslie Stuart), "Knocked 'Em in the Old Kent Road" (Albert Chevalier, Charles Ingle), "Wait and See" (Stanley Holloway), "All Things Bright and Beautiful" (1848; music: William Henry Monk; lyrics: Cecil Frances Alexander), "For He's A Jolly Good Fellow" (c.1709; traditional complimentary song). *Author's*

Note: The play upon which this film is based opened on Broadway at the Empire Theater on October 29, 1947, and ran for 214 performances. Unlike the play, which references the trial events involved in the story but do not appear on stage, the film offers these added scenes in captivating detail, which also allowed for additional characters such as the thunderous Sullivan. The Rattigan play was based on real events stemming from the celebrated case of George Archer-Shee (1895-1914), a fourteen-year-old cadet attending the Royal Naval College at Osbourne, who, in 1908, was accused of stealing a five-shilling postal order. His case was brought to court by one of England's foremost attorneys, Sir Edward Carson (1854-1935), and the boy was exonerated in 1910. Archer-Shee was later commissioned and served as an officer in WWI (1914-1918), killed in action at the First Battle of Ypres at age nineteen on October 31, 1914. The film was remade in 1999 where North again appears, but in an adult role. **p**, Anatole de Grunwald; **d**, Anthony Asquith; **cast**, Robert Donat, Margaret Leighton, Cedric Hardwicke, Neil North, Basil Radford, Francis L. Sullivan, Walter Fitzgerald, Frank Lawton, Hugh Dempster, Mona Washbourne, Stanley Holloway, Cyril Ritchard, Jack Watling, Wilfrid Hyde-White; **w**, Terence Rattigan, de Grunwald (based on the play by Rattigan); **c**, Freddie Young; **m**, William Alwyn; **ed**, Gerald Turney-Smith; **art d**, Andrej Andrejew; **spec eff**, W. Percy Day.

The Winslow Boy ★★★ 1999; U.K./US; 104m; Winslow Partners Ltd./Sony; Color; Drama; Children: Acceptable (MPAA: G); **DVD**; **VHS**; **IV**. This good remake of the 1950 film begins at Christmas in 1911, where Hawthorne, a London banker, is preparing for a dinner to announce the engagement of his daughter, Rebecca Pidgeon, a strong supporter of women's suffrage, to Gillett, a British army captain. Hawthorne is surprised that Edwards, his youngest son, a thirteen-year-old cadet at the Royal Naval College, has arrived at home unexpectedly. Hawthorne learns that the boy has been accused of stealing a postal order at the school. A school investigation has found him summarily guilty, and Hawthorne is requested to withdraw him from the college. Edwards insists he is innocent and Hawthorne believes him, demanding an apology from the college. College authorities refuse to reinstate Edwards, so Hawthorne decides to take the matter to court. He hires Northam, a leading barrister (attorney) to defend the boy. The government refuses to allow the case to go forward since the Naval College is part of the Admiralty and the Crown and British law presumes they are infallible and above question. The government eventually gives in and the case comes to court. Northam questions Edwards and becomes convinced that he is telling the truth and is innocent of the alleged crime. The case becomes a cause célèbre in the media. Hawthorne's fortune is fast being depleted because of legal expenses, and his health deteriorates under the strain. Hawthorne's wife, Jones, begins to wonder if the real issue is justice or her husband's stubborn pride. The eldest son, Matthew Pidgeon, is forced to leave the Naval College due to the family's lack of money, so he goes to work in Hawthorne's bank. Gillett breaks off his engagement to Rebecca Pidgeon at the insistence of his father. Edwards, meanwhile, is transferred to a different school. At the trial, Northam is able to discredit much of the supposed evidence against Edwards, and the Admiralty, no longer confident of the boy's guilt, withdraws all charges against him, proclaiming him to being entirely innocent. Only the maid, Flind, is present at the conclusion of the trial where justice has won, despite the affair taking a great emotional and financial toll. Playwright Mamet does a credible job in recreating this engrossing drama, drawing forth superior performances from the entire cast. *Author's Note*: Mamet, instead of following the script for the 1950 film, uses the story line originally appearing in the Rattigan play, where all of the courtroom events depicted in the original film are not employed. North, who played the boy in the original film, again appears here as the First Lord of the Admiralty, ironically passing judgment on the boy he played five decades earlier. **p**, Sarah Green; **d**, David Mamet; **cast**, Nigel Hawthorne, Jeremy Northam, Gemma Jones, Matthew Pid-

Phyllida Law and Emma Thompson in *The Winter Guest*, 1997.

geon, Rebecca Pidgeon, Lana Bilzerian, Sarah Flind, Aden Gillett, Guy Edwards, Colin Stinton, Neil North; **w**, Mamet (based on the play by Terence Rattigan); **c**, Benoit Delhomme; **m**, Alaric Jans; **ed**, Barbara Tulliver; **prod d**, Gemma Jackson; **art d**, Andrew Munro; **set d**, Trisha Edwards; **spec eff**, Richard Van Den Bergh.

The Winter Guest ★★★ 1997; U.S.; 108m; Capitol Films/Fine Line Features; Color; Drama; Children: Unacceptable (MPAA: R); **DVD**; **VHS**. Absorbing tale begins with Thompson, a recent widow who wants to leave Scotland and resettle in Australia with her teenage son, Hollywood, when she gets an unexpected visit from her aging mother, Law, who needs elder care. The story is told on one wintry day and mainly is a character study of the two women, well played by Law and her real-life daughter, Thompson. Song: "Take Me with You." Crude language and brief sensuality prohibit viewing by children. **p**, Steve Clark-Hall, Ken Lipper, Edward R. Pressman; **d**, Alan Rickman; **cast**, Phyllida Law, Emma Thompson, Sheila Reid, Sandra Voe, Arlene Cockburn, Gary Hollywood, Sean Biggerstaff, Douglas Murphy, Tom Watson, Jan Shand, Rickman; **w**, Sharman Macdonald, Rickman (based on the play by Macdonald), **c**, Seamus McGarvey; **m**, Michael Kamen; **ed**, Scott Thomas; **prod d**, Robin Cameron Don; **art d**, Ben Scott; **spec eff**, Dave Crownshaw, John Cox, Peter Haran, Tim Howell.

Winter Kills ★★★ 1979; U.S.; 97m; Winter Gold Productions/AVCO Embassy Pictures; Color; Drama; Children: Unacceptable (MPAA: R); **DVD**; **VHS**. Taut tale begins when the U.S. President is assassinated and, nine years later, his brother, Bridges, discovers a dying man claiming to have been the gunman. This leads Bridges to believe there may have been a plot to kill the President. As he conducts his own investigation, everyone Bridges meets come to violent ends at the hands of mysterious killers. The ending leaves us guessing whether the chief executive had been killed by Bridges' domineering father, Huston, or Huston's assistant, Perkins. The story is about control of a giant company imperiled by a meddling chief executive, where Huston ostensibly orders his son, Bridges, murdered by henchman Boone when Bridges probes too deeply into his brother's death. Boone is killed in a savage gunfight with Bridges, and Bridges then finds Huston, who has slipped over a high-rise railing, clinging in mid-air to an American flag and, businessman to the last, shouting to Bridges: "Put my money in South America!" The flag, symbolic of retribution, then rips apart and sends Huston plummeting to his doom. Though well directed (Richert's debut as a theatrical film director) and superior performances by a talented cast maintain tension and interest throughout, this film did not do well at the box office. It earned more than $1 million in its initial release against a budget of $6 million. *Author's Note*: The role of the family

Burgess Meredith, Margo, Maurice Moskovitch, Edward Ellis, Alec Craig and Eduardo Ciannelli in *Winterset*, 1936.

patriarch was originally offered to Frank Sinatra, who turned down the part, telling this author that "I did not want to appear as a crotchety character trying to control America like a corporation." Huston told this author: "I had no qualms about playing a power-mad millionaire, which is the nature of most successful businessmen." Perkins told this author that he thought "**Winter Kills** is one of those murder puzzles where all the pieces just don't quite fit, and I think that is the case with most homicides. They never get all the right pieces to finish the overall picture." Boone, when talking with this author, stated: "I played another mindless goon in that picture, the kind of role I had been enacting for too many years. No one has any empathy for a pathological killer." Meeker recalled for this author that "they kept closing down the production for **Winter Kills** because they kept running out of money. So we went off to get other gigs and returned to the production when the producers came up with more funds. It was touch-and-go to see if that picture would ever get finished." Taylor told this author that "I had a very small role, a cameo appearance, in that picture. It was done as a gesture because my husband at that time [John Warner] also appeared in that picture." She was paid $100,000 for her brief appearance in this film. The production was replete with underworld associations in that it was initially funded by two millionaire marijuana smugglers, Leonard J. Goldberg and Robert Sterling. Goldberg (1946-1979) was found murdered in his NYC apartment, handcuffed and his head blown off with a shotgun, for his unpaid debts to the Mafia. Sterling was later sentenced to forty years in prison for drug smuggling. **p**, Fred Caruso, (not credited) Daniel H. Blatt; **d&w**, William Richert (based on the novel by Richard Condon); **cast**, Jeff Bridges, John Huston, Anthony Perkins, Eli Wallach, Sterling Hayden, Dorothy Malone, Tomas Milian, Ralph Meeker, Toshiro Mifune, Richard Boone, Brad Dexter, Elizabeth Taylor in a cameo role; **c**, Vilmos Zsigmond; **m**, Maurice Jarre; **ed**, David Bretherton; **prod d**, Robert Boyle; **art d**, Norman Newberry; **set d**, Arthur Jeph Parker; **spec eff**, Larry L. Fuentes, Jim Danforth.

Winter Light ★★★ 1963; U.S.; 109m; MGM/; Color; Drama; Children: Unacceptable (MPAA: PG-13); **DVD**; **VHS**. Bergman presents a taut drama that begins with Bjornstrand, pastor of a small rural church in Sweden, who performs a service for the congregation, despite having a bad cold and a severe crisis of faith. After the service, he tries to comfort Sydow, a fisherman who is fearful about the Chinese having an atomic bomb. Bjornstrand is too self-absorbed and talks only about his troubled relationship with God, and the depressed Sydow finally commits suicide. Thulin, a schoolteacher who loves him, offers herself to Bjornstrand to console him for his loss of faith, but he resists her. When Bjornstrand goes to the church for evening vespers, he finds only Thulin there, while he still has doubts of faith. The film was the second in a

trilogy by Ingmar Bergman (1918-2007), son of a Lutheran minister, dealing with man's relationship with God, the others being **Through a Glass Darkly**, 1961, and **The Silence**, 1963. *Author's Note*: Bergman admitted that this film and the two others that ostensibly make up his spiritual trilogy were never envisioned as such and simply evolved as such because of their similar themes. **p**, Allan Ekelund; **d&w**, Ingmar Bergman; **cast**, Ingrid Thulin, Gunnar Bjornstrand, Max von Sydow, Gunnel Lindblom, Allan Edwall, Kolbjorn Knudsen, Olof Thunberg, Elsa Ebbesen, Lars-Olof Andersson, Eddie Axberg; **c**, Sven Nykvist; **ed**, Ulla Ryghe; **prod d**, P.A. Lundgren.

The Winter War ★★★ 1989; Finland; 195m; National Film Oy; Color; War Drama; Children: Unacceptable; **BD**; **DVD**; **IV**. Impactful war drama begins when army reservists in Finland leave their homes and go to war after Nazi Germany invades Poland in September 1939 to start World War II (1939-1945). The film centers on two young brothers, Taneli and Konsta Makela, who are Finnish farmers from the city of Kauhava in the province of Pohjanmaa/Ostrobothnia. They serve together in a Finnish platoon during the harsh winter of 1939-1940. The film follows the brothers and a small group of comrades as they find themselves in the front lines facing a Soviet invasion. Their main objective becomes merely to stay alive, protect each other, and follow orders as soldiers must. Well directed and acted, the film presents a realistic and gritty view of the war, depicting some unnerving battle scenes. *Author's Note*: Though extremely popular in Finland, the film did poorly in its worldwide distribution and, being then the most expensive film made in this country to date, did not recoup its huge investment, causing the production company to go bankrupt. The Makelas are real-life brothers. Violence prohibits viewing by children. (In Finnish; English subtitles.) **p**, Marko Rohr, Jukka Makela; **d**, Pekka Parikka; **cast**, Taneli Makela, Konsta Makela, Vesa Vierikko, Timo Torikka, Heikki Paavilainen, Antti Raivio, Esko Kovero, Martti Suosalo, Markku Huhtamo, Matti Onnismaa, Samuli Edelmann; **w**, Antti Tuuri, Parikka (based on the novel by Tuuri); **c**, Kari Sohlberg; **m**, Jukka Haavisto, Juha Tikka; **ed**, Keijo Virtanen; **prod d**, Pertti Hikamo; **spec eff**, Mauri Laaksonen, Esa Parkatti, Jan-Eric Nystrom.

Winterset ★★★ 1936; U.S.; 78m; RKO; B/W; Drama; Children: Unacceptable; **DVD**; **VHS**. Loosely based on the celebrated murder-robbery case involving Nicola Sacco (1891-1927) and Bartolomeo Vanzetti (1888-1927), this riveting drama begins with a prologue that depicts that crime, set in the early 1920s. Ciannelli, along with accomplices Ridges and Guilfoyle, commit a payroll robbery, murdering the paymaster, and then abandon their getaway car. Police find in that car left-wing writings by Carradine, who is then arrested and railroaded into a hasty trial and conviction that results in his execution. It is now fifteen years later, and Meredith, who is Carradine's son, sets out to vindicate his father. He tracks down Guilfoyle, who is widely rumored to have been the driver of the getaway car, and, while trying to worm the truth from Guilfoyle, Carradine meets and falls in love with Guilfoyle's sister, Margo. Realizing that Guilfoyle might reveal his identity, Ciannelli, a ruthless gangster, decides to kill Meredith. The indefatigable Meredith, however, manages to get enough information that exonerates Carradine, but his life, as well as that of Margo's is now in peril from the vengeance-seeking Ciannelli. The gangster and his goons trap Meredith and Margo and are about to shoot them to death. Meredith, however, begins playing an abandoned hurdy-gurdy to create a commotion that brings the police on the run and who then attack Ciannelli and his henchmen. Before they are captured, Ciannelli is shot and killed by accident at the hands of one of his own enforcers. Meredith and Margo are now free to live out their life together. Santell directs this rather grim tale with firm restraint and draws from Meredith, Margo and the rest of the cast outstanding performances while revealingly depicting the misery and suffering of the then on-going Depression. The film received Oscar nominations for Best Original Score (Shilkret) and Best Art Direction (Polglase). The film was a box office disappointment, earning less than $700,000 in its initial release against a budget of more than $400,000. Song: "Siboney" (1929; Ernesto Lecuona). *Author's Note*: The ending of this film sees a happy conclusion where the Anderson play ended on a sad note, with the leading characters being shot and killed by the gangsters. This was Meredith's film debut as a leading player, albeit he had appeared in a bit part as a hobo in **The Scoundrel**, 1935. Though based upon the Sacco-Vanzetti case, the details differ in this film from the actual events that led both of these anarchists to their conviction of a 1920 robbery and murder and their executions in 1927. For more details on the Sacco and Vanzetti case, see my eight-volume work *Encyclopedia of World Crime*, Volume IV (CrimeBooks, Inc., 1990; pages 2649-2652). **p**, Pandro S. Berman; **d**, Alfred Santell; **cast**, Burgess Meredith, Margo, Eduardo Ciannelli, Maurice Moscovitch, Paul Guilfoyle, Edward Ellis, Stanley Ridges, Mischa Auer, Alec Craig, John Carradine, Myron McCormick, Helen Jerome Eddy, Barbara Pepper, Paul Fix, Lucille Ball, Alan Curtis; **w**, Anthony Veiller (based on the play by Maxwell Anderson); **c**, Peverell Marley; **m**, Nathaniel Shilkret; **ed**, William Hamilton; **art d**, Van Nest Polglase; **spec eff**, Vernon Walker.

The Witches ★★★ 1990; U.S.; 109m; MGM/; Color; Fantasy; Children: Unacceptable; (MPAA: PG); **DVD**; **VHS**; **IV**. Shuddering fantasy tale begins when Fisher's parents remain in Norway while he goes with his grandmother, Zetterling, to England. They stop at a hotel where a convention of witches, with Huston as the Grand High Witch, has gathered to form a plot to rid England of all children. They turn Fisher into a mouse, and, after he escapes them, they chase after him with Huston's pet cat. After a lot of strange and spooky goings-on, Huston's mistreated assistant, Horrocks, turns Fisher back into a human. It's a fun fantasy for teenagers, but too scary for children. It seems likely that J.K. Rowling, author of the *Harry Potter* books, got her inspiration for those works from this film, which has a boy involved with witches. His best boyfriend is played by an actor named Charlie Potter. Dahl's book, *The Witches*, was published in 1983, fourteen years before Rowling's first *Harry Potter* book, *Harry Potter and the Sorcerer's Stone*, which was published in 1997, and Rowling also might have seen the movie **The Witches** in 1990, seven years before her first *Harry Potter* book was published. In interviews, Rowling acknowledged that she drew inspiration and plot ideas from many books including *the Bible*, along with histories and children's books, but never says she was influenced by Dahl's **The Witches**. Not to disparage Rowling's imagination and writing ability, but this possible inspiration for her phenomenally successful books seems likely. **p**, Mark Shivas; **d**, Nicolas Roeg; **cast**, Anjelica Huston, Mai Zetterling, Jasen Fisher, Rowan Atkinson, Bill Paterson, Brenda Blethyn, Jane Horrocks, Charlie Potter, Anne Lambton, Sukie Smith, Rose English; **w**, Allan Scott (based on the novel by Roald Dahl); **c**, Harvey Harrison; **m**, Stanley Myers; **ed**, Tony Lawson; **prod d**, Andrew Sanders; **art d**, John King, Norman Dorme; **set d**, Robin Tarsnane; **spec eff**, William Plant, David Barrington-Holt, Chris Barton.

The Witches of Eastwick ★★★ 1987; U.S.; 118m; WB; Color; Horror; Children: Unacceptable (MPAA: R); **BD**; **DVD**; **VHS**; **IV**. Wicked, weird and wondrous is this bizarre tale where the fascinating Nicholson not only goes over the top in his role as a Devil from the Netherworld, but chews up every frame in which he appears. The film opens with three women, Cher, Pfeiffer and Sarandon, all living in remote Eastwick, Rhode Island, and where they lead dissatisfied lives. Cher is a sculptor and single mother raising a daughter. Pfeiffer, another single mother with six children, writes a column for the local newspaper. Sarandon, yet another single woman, is unable to have children and teaches music. All three have bonded, not realizing that they are witches but nevertheless establishing a coven where they fanatisize about their ideal man. Suddenly, as if summoned through the fantasies of the three women, Nicholson, a mysterious stranger, arrives in town to shock the community by purchasing the most desirable real estate in the area, the

Cher, Susan Sarandon and Michelle Pfeiffer in *The Witches of Eastwick*, 1987.

Lennox Mansion and its sprawling grounds, which is a local landmark. Cartwright, the wife of Jenkins, the editor of the newspaper that employs Pfeiffer, is not a witch, but her instincts quickly tell her that Nicholson is up to no good and says so to everyone who will listen to her. When Sarandon sponsors a music recital, Nicholson appears but disrupts the proceedings by creating a scene with his outlandish conduct. When Cartwright criticizes him, Pfeiffer's necklace inexplicably breaks and spills its beads everywhere, causing Cartwright to take a fall and break her leg. Nicholson then invites Cher, Sarandon and Pfeiffer to his mansion where he makes romantic moves on all three women. When the four play tennis on Nicholson's court, they see that they can do magical things with the tennis ball, sending it skyward by thousands of feet or freezing it in mid-air. They now all realize that they possess the powers of witchcraft and they begin indulging in drugs and sex with Nicholson. Meanwhile, Cartwright continues her verbal campaign against Nicholson, publicly (and rightly) branding him the Devil. Cartwright also publicly castigates Cher, Pfeiffer and Sarandon that they become social pariahs. Then Nicholson causes the women, unbeknownst to them, to cast an evil spell on Cartwright where she becomes a screeching harridan and is continuously vomiting cherry stones. Jenkins believes his wife is becoming deranged, and, bedeviled by her harassing conduct and unable to watch her decline into insanity, grabs a poker and beats her to death. Cher, Pfeiffer and Sarandon are shaken by this murderous scandal so that they isolate themselves from each other and Nicholson. Feeling that the three witches have deserted him, Nicholson takes revenge by using his own evil powers to plague them. He causes snakes to invade Cher's bed. He turns Sarandon into a withered old hag and then causes Pfeiffer to feel constant pain. The three women realize what Nicholson is doing and, after overcoming his plagues, they meet to uniformly conspire against Nicholson. They make a wax voodoo doll in his likeness and then begin to torture it and Nicholson is then beset with excruciating pain. He returns to the mansion to wreak havoc on his tormentors, appearing as an enormous creature, but the women destroy him when throwing the wax doll into a fire. Eighteen months later, all three women are living in the mansion like princesses, along with their children, plus three new baby boys, all the offspring of their relationships with Nicholson. While the boys are watching TV, Nicholson appears on the huge screen, asking the boys to "give Daddy a kiss." The women end Nicholson's eerie contact with them and the children as they summarily turn off the TV to end this shocker. Miller robustly directs this film, creatively building its suspense while developing its central characters, the three modern-day witches, and Nicholson is a captivating and very bedeviling devil. Cher, Pfeiffer and Sarandon are convincing and intriguing while playing their roles as seductive ladies dabbling in dangerous witchcraft. Of special note are the

Jack Nicholson and Cher in *The Witches of Eastwick*, 1987.

cleverly introduced special effects that present other world images that create wonder and fright at the same time, but become so spectacular at the finish that these awesome images overwhelm the story's conclusion, settling for mayhem instead of human reasoning. The film received Oscar nominations for Best Original Score (Williams) and Best Sound (Wayne Artman, Tom E. Dahl, Tom Beckert, Art Rochester). The film proved to be a box office smash, earning more than $63 million in its initial release. Songs/Music: "Nessun Dorma" (1926; from the opera "Turandot" by Giacomo Puccini), "Feodora" (Carel Struycken), "Someone to Watch Over Me" (1926; music: George Gershwin; lyrics: Ira Gershwin), "Cello Concerto in B minor (Allegro)" (1895; Antonin Dvorak), "Devil's Dance" (John Williams). *Author's Note*: The film was shot on location in Cohasset, Massachusetts, which duplicated for the town of Eastwick, as well as Scituate, Massachusetts. Bill Murray was considered for the role subsequently essayed by Nicholson. Actresses Pam Grier and Angelica Huston were considered for roles as witches. This was the first U.S. full-length feature film helmed by Australian director Miller. For a comprehensive list of similar films, see Witchcraft in Subject Index. **p**, Peter Geuber, Jon Peters, Neil Canton; **d**, George Miller; **cast**, Jack Nicholson, Cher, Susan Sarandon, Michelle Pfeiffer, Veronica Cartwright, Richard Jenkins, Keith Jochim, Carel Struycken, Helen Lloyd Breed, Caroline Struzik; **w**, Michael Cristofer (based on the novel by John Updike); **c**, Vilmos Zsigmond; **m**, John Williams; **ed**, Hubert C. De La Bouillerie, Richard Francis-Bruce; **prod d**, Polly Platt; **art d**, Mark Mansbridge; **set d**, Joe D. Mitchell; **spec eff**, Mike Lanteri, Louis Lanteri, Don Elliot.

With a Song in My Heart ★★★★ 1952; U.S.; 116m; FOX; Color; Biographical Drama/Musical; Children: Cautionary; **DVD**. Hayward gives an exceptional performance as singer Jane Froman (1907-1980) in a sumptuously produced biopic replete with a bevy of great songs. The film opens with Hayward as an already established singing star, where she is receiving an award at a special meeting of the Newspapermen of New York. As the proceedings of that honoring meeting take place, Calhoun and Ritter, two people deeply involved in Hayward's life, reminisce about her past. In flashback to 1936, we see a young Hayward beginning her career by entering a Cincinnati radio station where she expects to have an audition for an on-airway job. She meets Wayne, mistaking him for the director she is scheduled to meet and sings for him. Wayne tells her to tone down her delivery and be very reserved about her presentation. Then Talbot, who is the actual director, arrives and, after listening to Hayward sing, tells her that she should be more dramatic and charming. She appears on the show and is a success, quickly developing a relationship with Wayne. Hayward then appears at New York's top theaters, including the Paramount and Radio City,

where she becomes an overnight sensation. Wayne is at her side, encouraging her every step of the way while asking her to marry him. Hayward is indecisive but eventually listens to her heart and marries him. The marriage becomes troubled when Wayne's own business opportunities dry up and he is strapped for money. Moreover, he becomes jealous of Hayward. After WWII (1939-1945) breaks out, she volunteers to entertain U.S. troops close to the fighting fronts. On a flight toward Portugal she meets attractive pilot Calhoun, who asks her to help him show passengers how to use life vests in the event the plane is forced down into the sea. That is exactly what happens when the plane develops engine problems and crashes. Hayward is injured but Calhoun saves her from a watery death. Hayward begins a long recovery in a Lisbon hospital where Ritter, a no-nonsense nurse, nurtures her back to health while Calhoun regularly visits her. He tells her that he is in love with her, but Hayward, as a married woman, keeps her affection for him a secret. Her injuries are serious, her left knee crushed and her right leg almost severed in the crash. Doctors believe that they will have to amputate the right leg, but believe that physicians in the U.S. might save the limb. Wayne then arrives and arranges for Hayward to fly back to the U.S. She undergoes a number of painful surgeries to save her leg, and, while she recuperates, Wayne thoughtfully provides a piano so Hayward can practice her singing. Ritter then arrives in the U.S. to continue as Hayward's stalwart and constant nurse. Although she is not fully recovered, Hayward makes a comeback on the stage in "Artists and Models," where she must wear a restrictive cast up to her right hip. She nevertheless captivates audiences that give her ovations as they welcome her back. Hayward has a relapse and, after undergoing more operations, makes another comeback by performing at a nightclub. Calhoun arrives to see her perform and is immediately confronted by Wayne, who now knows that the pilot is in love with his wife. Hayward, torn between the two men who love her, leaves again to perform for the troops overseas, appearing in these performances on crutches. She becomes unsure of herself, but her spirits are bolstered by Ritter, who accompanies her everywhere, and the indomitable spirit of the servicemen, who applaud her every song. By this time, Wayne realizes that he has lost Hayward to another man and sends her a message informing her that when she returns to the U.S., he will not be waiting for her and that their marriage is over. When Hayward does return to America, Calhoun is waiting for her, welcoming her into his arms and where they plan to make a future together. Hayward is exceptional as the heroic Froman, and the raft of tunes she sings are wonderfully presented as Froman sings those songs while Hayward lip-syncs the songs. Ritter gives a strong performance as an indefatigable nurse while Wayne and Calhoun give top-notch essays as the two men who love the same woman. Of special note is Wagner, who was then starting out in films and appears briefly in a touching scene as a wounded serviceman who asks Hayward to sing a song at a benefit. The film won an Oscar for Best Musical Score (Newman), and received Oscar nominations for Best Actress (Hayward), Best Supporting Actress (Ritter), Best Sound Recording (Thomas T. Moulton), and Best Costume Design, Color (Charles Le Maire). The film was a great success at the box office, earning more than $3.2 million in its initial release. A sixty-minute radio adaptation was aired by Lux Radio Theater on February 9, 1953, with Hayward, Ritter and Wayne reprising their roles. Songs: "With a Song in My Heart" (1929; music: Richard Rodgers; lyrics: Lorenz Hart), "Hoe That Corn" (Max Showalter, Jack Woodford), "That Old Feeling" (1937; music: Sammy Fain; lyrics: Lew Brown), "Jim's Toasty Peanuts" (Ken Darby), "I'm Thru with Love" (1931; music: Joseph Anthony "Fud" Livingston; lyrics: Matty Malneck, Gus Kahn), "Get Happy" (1930; music: Harold Arlen; lyrics: Ted Koehler), "Blue Moon" (1930; music: Richard Rodgers; lyrics: Lorenz Hart), "On the Gay White Way" (1942; music: Ralph Rainger; lyrics: Leo Robin), "The Right Kind" (1948; music: Alfred Newman; lyrics: Don George, Charles Henderson), "Home on the Range" (music [1904]: Daniel E. Kelley; lyrics [1873]: Brewster "Bruce" Higley), "Montparnasse" (music: Alfred Newman; lyrics: Eliot Daniel), "Embraceable

You" (1930; music: George Gershwin; lyrics: Ira Gershwin), "Tea for Two" (1925; music: Vincent Youmans; lyrics: Irving Caesar), "It's a Good Day" (1947; Peggy Lee, Dave Barbour), "They're Either Too Young or Too Old" (1943; music: Arthur Schwartz; lyrics: Frank Loesser), "I'll Walk Alone" (1944; music: Jule Styne; lyrics: Sammy Cahn), "America the Beautiful" (music [1882]: Samuel A. Ward; lyrics [1910]: Katharine Lee Bates), "Wonderful Home Sweet Home" (Ken Darby), "Give My Regards to Broadway" (1904; George M. Cohan), "Chicago" (1922; Fred Fisher), "California Here I Come" (1921; music: Joseph Meyer, Al Jolson; lyrics: Buddy G. De Sylva), "Carry Me Back to Old Virginny" (1878; James Allen Bland), "Stein Song" (for the University of Maine; music [1901]: E.A. Fenstad; lyrics [1910]: Lincoln Colcord), "Indiana" (1917; music: James F. Hanley; lyrics: Ballard MacDonald), "Alabamy Bound" (1924; music: Ray Henderson; lyrics: Buddy DeSylva, Budd Green), "Deep in the Heart of Texas" (1941; music: Don Swander; lyrics: June Hershey), "(I Wish I Was in) Dixie's Land" (1860; Daniel Decatur Emmett). *Author's Note*: Froman was permanently crippled after a flying boat carrying her and others to Portugal, crash-landed in the Tagus River near Lisbon, on February 22, 1943. She recovered enough to go on to entertain troops during WWII, although she performed on crutches at that time and thereafter. Hayward told this author that "I did my own singing in that picture, even though Jane's [Froman's] singing voice was used. I actually sang all those songs instead of lip-syncing so that my throat muscles would indicate that I was really delivering those tunes. Jane was a true heroine and I was proud to enact her life story. God, that woman went through hell and almost lost one of her legs, but she would not give up and I think it was her great spirit that pulled her through. Spirit always does, if you call on it, and the help of God." Hayward was not the original choice to play the celebrated singer as Fox was seriously considering Jeanne Crain, an actress the studio was then promoting for stardom, for the role, and Crain strongly lobbied for the part. Froman, however, who had the right to pick the actress who would portray her, selected the dynamic Hayward, which was the best decision anyone could make. The costume department was constantly busy during the production in providing dozens of dazzling gowns for Hayward as Froman was known as one of the world's leading clotheshorses and had appeared on many Best Dressed lists for years. Costumer designer Charles LeMaire created more than forty such stunning gowns that were worn by Hayward. "I was the best dressed actress in Hollywood when we made that picture," Hayward told this author. "I wore more designer dresses in **With a Song in My Heart** than I ever had in my closets at home." Other films depicting famous female singers include **Adriana**, 2004 (Maria Callas, portrayed by Antonio Moco); **After the Ball**, 1957 (Vesta Tilley; portrayed by Margaret Sawyer as a child; Pat Kirkwood as an adult Tilley); **Bessie**, 2015 (made-for-cable TV; Bessie Smith, portrayed by Queen Latifah); **Bowery to Broadway**, 1944 (Lillian Russell, portrayed by Louise Allbritton); **Callas e Onassis**, 2005 (made-for-TV; Maria Callas, portrayed by Luisa Ranieri); **Callas Forever**, 2002 (Maria Callas, portrayed by Fanny Ardant); **The Cotton Club**, 1984 (Fanny Brice, portrayed by Rosalind Harris); **Daphne**, 2007 (Gertrude Lawrence, portrayed by Janet McTeer); **David Harum**, 1934 (Lillian Russell, portrayed by Ruth Gillette); **Diamond Jim**, 1936 (Lillian Russell, portrayed by Binnie Barnes); **Downton Abbey**, 2010- (TV series; Nellie Melba, portrayed by Kiri Te Kanawa); **Edith and Marcel**, 1984 (Edith Piaf, portrayed by Evelyne Bouix); **Edith es Marlene**, 1992 (made-for-TV; Edith Piaf, portrayed by Erzsebet Kutvolgyi); **Edith Piaf: Une breve rencontre**, 1993 (made-for-TV; Sophie Artur); **Funny Girl**, 1968 (Fanny Brice, portrayed by Barbra Streisand); **Funny Lady**, 1975 (Fanny Brice, portrayed by Barbra Streisand); **The Gentleman from Louisiana**, 1936 (Lillian Russell, portrayed by Ruth Gillette); **Grace of Monaco**, 2014 (Maria Callas, portrayed by Paz Vega); **The Great Ziegfeld**, 1936 (Lillian Russell, portrayed by Ruth Gillette; Marilyn Miller, portrayed by Rosina Lawrence); **The Helen Morgan Story**, 1957 (portrayed by Ann Blyth); **Ike: The War Years**, 1979 (TV series; Gertrude Lawrence, por-

Susan Hayward as Jane Froman singing to U.S. servicemen in *With a Song in My Heart*, 1952.

trayed by Patricia Michael); **I'll Cry Tomorrow**, 1955 (Lillian Roth, portrayed by Susan Hayward); **Interrupted Melody**, 1955 (Marjorie Lawrence, portrayed by Eleanor Parker; singing vocals by Eileen Farrell); **ITV Sunday Night Drama**, 1959-1980 (TV series; "Remember Jack Buchanan," 1980 episode: Gertrude Lawrence, portrayed by Cheryl Kennedy); **Jackie Bouvier Kennedy Onassis**, 2000 (made-for-TV; Maria Callas, portrayed by Leslie Cottle); **La Vie en Rose**, 2007 (Edith Piaf, portrayed by Marion Cotillard); **Lady Sings the Blues**, 1972 (Billie Holiday, portrayed by Diana Ross); **Lillie**, 1978 (TV miniseries; Lillian Russell, portrayed by Christina Greateaux); **Lillian Russell**, 1940 (portrayed by Alice Faye); **Look for the Silver Lining**, 1949 (Marilyn Miller, portrayed by June Haver); **Lost Empires**, 1986 (TV miniseries; Vesta Tilley, portrayed by Julia Parrott); **Love Me or Leave Me**, 1955 (Ruth Etting, portrayed by Doris Day); **The Man Who Lived at the Ritz**, 1989 (made-for-TV; Edith Piaf, portrayed by Nathalie Cerda); **Melba**, 1953 (Nellie Melba, portrayed by Patrice Munsel); **Melba**, 1988 (TV series; Nellie Melba, portrayed by Linda Cropper, singing vocals by Yvonne Kenny); **Mitzi...Roaring the 1920s**, 1976 (TV special; Bessie Smith, portrayed by Linda Hopkins); **My Wild Irish Rose**, 1947 (Lillian Russell, portrayed by Andrea King); **Onassis: The Richest Man in the World**, 1988 (made-for-TV; Maria Callas, portrayed by Jane Seymour); **Parade of Stars**, 1983 (made-for-TV; Fanny Brice, portrayed by Dorothy Loudon; Helen Morgan, portrayed by Dinah Shore); **Playhouse 90**, 1956-1961 (TV series; "The Helen Morgan Story," 1957 episode: portrayed by Polly Bergen); **Sinatra**, 1992 (made-for-TV; Jo Stafford, portrayed by Maggie Egan; Billie Holiday, portrayed by Leata Galloway); **So This Is Love**, 1953 (Grace Moore, portrayed by Kathryn Grayson); **Somebody Loves Me**, 1952 (Blossom Seeley, portrayed by Betty Hutton); **Stage Door Canteen**, 1943 (Gertrude Lawrence, portrayed by herself); **Star!**, 1968 (Gertrude Lawrence, portrayed by Julie Andrews); **Stars in Their Eyes**, 1990- (TV series; Billie Holiday, portrayed by Deborah Christopher; Maria Callas, portrayed by Nicola Kirsch; Edith Piaf, portrayed in two separate episodes by Marie Lloyd and Esther Rantzen); **Till the Clouds Roll By**, 1946 (Marilyn Miller, portrayed by Judy Garland); **Touched by an Angel**, 1995-2003 (TV series; "God Bless the Child," 2000 episode: Billie Holiday, portrayed by Paula Jai Parker); **What's Love Got to Do with It**, 1993 (Tina Turner, portrayed by herself); **Yankee Doodle Dandy**, 1942 (Fay Templeton, portrayed by Irene Manning); and **Ziegfeld: The Man and His Women**, 1978 (made-for-TV; Fanny Brice, portrayed by Catherine Jacoby; Marilyn Miller, portrayed by Pamela Peadon); **p&w**, Lamar Trotti; **d**, Walter Lang; **cast**, Susan Hayward, Rory Calhoun, David Wayne, Thelma Ritter, Robert Wagner, Helen Westcott, Una Merkel, Max Showalter, Bill Baldwin, Leif Erickson, Lyle Talbot, Jane Froman (singing vocals for Hayward), singing groups: The Modernaires, The Skylarks, The King's

Spencer Tracy and Katharine Hepburn in *Without Love*, 1945.

Men, The Melody Men, The Four Girlfriends, The Starlighters; **c**, Leon Shamroy (Technicolor); **m**, Alfred Newman; **ed**, J. Watson Webb, Jr.; **art d**, Lyle Wheeler, Joseph Wright; **set d**, Walter M. Scott, Thomas Little; **spec eff**, Fred Sersen, Ray Kellogg.

Within Our Gates ★★★ 1920 (silent); U.S.; 79m; Micheaux Book & Film Co./Quality Entertainment Corp.; B/W; Drama/Romance; Children: Unacceptable: **DVD**. This early film about racial problems in the United States begins with Preer, who is a black woman from the South visiting her cousin, Clements, in the North where there is less racial prejudice than in her hometown of Piney Woods. She is anxiously awaiting the arrival of her fiancé, Ruffin, but Clements also has an attraction for him. Clements tricks Preer into a compromising situation when Ruffin arrives and he turns his back on her. Preer is heartbroken and returns to Piney Woods to help a minister run a school for young blacks. The ministry needs money and will have to turn away students unless it raises $5,000 to add to the $1.49 the state allocates for each student per year. To help raise the money, Preer returns to the North and helps Lucas, a kindly black doctor, regain his wallet after it is stolen. Preer then saves a child from being hit by a racing automobile, but is slightly injured. The car's owner, Mrs. Evelyn, is wealthy and, to compensate Preer, provides the needed $5,000, so the school in Piney Woods can be saved. Though the story is far fetched in places, Micheauxs' direction presents a fast-clipped tale with superior acting by the entire cast. **p,d&w**, Oscar Micheaux; **cast**, Evelyn Preer, Flo Clements, James D. Ruffin, Jack Chenault, William Smith, Charles D. Lucas, Bernice Ladd, Mrs. Evelyn, William Stark, Micheaux (presenter); **m**, Philip Carli.

Without a Clue ★★★ 1988; U.S.; 107m; Incorporated Television Co./Orion Pictures/MGM; Color; Comedy/Mystery; Children: Unacceptable (MPAA: PG); **BD**; **DVD**; **VHS**. In this comedic Sherlock Holmes film, the great detective is a fictional character created by Kingsley, who plays Dr. John Watson, to enable him to solve crimes incognito. After the public demands to see the great detective in person, Kingsley hires Caine, an unemployed actor, to play the role of the super detective. Caine has to follow Kingsley's instructions on new cases, but oversteps on a major case at a museum, so Kingsley fires him. Kingsley, however, takes him back after the British government seeks Holmes' aid in a mystery involving Bank of England £5 bank plates that have been stolen and where the printing supervisor, Warner, has gone missing on the night of the theft. Unless the plates are recovered before counterfeit currency can be printed, the British Empire's economy may collapse. Jones, who plays Inspector Lestrade of Scotland Yard, is jealous of Caine/Holmes, and spies on him and Kingsley, in order to steal their sleuthing ideas. Clues lead to Anthony, Warner's daughter, and Savage,

a twelve-year-old boy. Caine and Kingsley discover that Freeman, who plays Professor Moriarty, is the brains behind the counterfeiting scheme. Kingsley is "apparently" killed, forcing Caine to solve the case on his own. He tracks Freeman to an abandoned theater, and then discovers that Kingsley is alive and they work together to capture Freeman. Kingsley now has a new appreciation for Caine, and the public is relieved to know that Caine and Kingsley will continue their sleuthing as a team. Eberhardt directs this entertaining whodunit with a lot of delightful tongue-in-cheek scenes while Caine and Kingsley shine in their legendary roles. Songs: "Where Did You Get that Hat?" (Joseph J. Sullivan), "Rock of Ages" (music: Thomas Hastings; lyrics: Augustus Montague Toplady). **p**, Marc Stirdivant; **d**, Thom Eberhardt; **cast**, Michael Caine, Ben Kingsley, Jeffrey Jones, Lysette Anthony, Paul Freeman, Nigel Davenport, Pat Keen, Peter Cook, Tim Killick, John Warner, Matthew Savage; **w**, Gary Murphy, Larry Strawther; **c**, Alan Hume; **m**, Henry Mancini; **ed**, Peter Tanner; **prod d**, Brian Ackland-Snow, Martyn Hebert; **art d**, Terry Ackland-Snow, Robin Tarsnane; **set d**, Peter James, Ian Whittaker; **spec eff**, Ian Wingrove.

Without Apparent Motive ★★★ 1972; France/Italy; 100m; Cinetel; FOX; Color; Mystery; Children: Unacceptable (MPAA: PG); **DVD**. This taut film noir thriller begins after a series of strange murders occur and Trintignant, a wily police detective, is assigned to solve the mysterious deaths, although he is confronted with no clues. The deaths, all taking place in the sun-drenched streets of Nice, include Bardinet, a wealthy Frenchman; Segal, an astrologer; and a confidence man, Sellan. While investigating, Trintignant meets Sanda, who is Bardinet's stepdaughter and who gives him her stepfather's diary, those lurid memoirs containing a list of the dead man's lovers. Trintignant tracks down several people listed in that diary, finally locating Antonelli, who was driven insane after having been gang-raped and has been institutionalized. He then finds the culprit, Marielle, her husband, who has taken revenge by killing those who assaulted his wife. Labro helms this suspense-packed tale at a brisk pace, and Trintignant is riveting in his role of the dogged detective, strongly supported by a talented cast. (In French; English subtitles; also dubbed in English.) **p**, Jacques-Eric Strauss; **d**, Philippe Labro; **cast**, Jean-Louis Trintignant, Dominique Sanda, Sacha Distel, Carla Gravina, Paul Crauchet, Laura Antonelli, Jean-Pierre Marielle, Stephane Audran, Erich Segal, Alexis Sellan, Michel Bardinet; **w**, Labro, Vincenzo Labella, Jacques Lanzmann (based on the novel *Ten Plus One* by Evan Hunter as Ed McBain); **c**, Jean Penzer (Eastmancolor); **m**, Ennio Morricone; **ed**, Claude Barrois; **prod d**, Andre Hoss; **set d**, Louis Le Barbenchon.

Without Love ★★★ 1945; U.S.; 111m; MGM; B/W; Comedy/Romance; Children: Acceptable; **BD**; **DVD**; **VHS**; **IV**. This delightful romantic comedy begins with Tracy, who is a scientist during World War II (1939-1945). He works for the government in Washington, D.C., on a high-altitude oxygen helmet for fighter pilots that might replace the traditional oxygen mask. Housing in the nation's capital at wartime is as scarce as snow in July, and Tracy desperately needs a place to conduct his experiments in secret. Fortune smiles on him when he meets Hepburn, a young widow who owns a sprawling house with a basement that would make a good laboratory. To prevent any scandal from gossiping neighbors should the two occupy the same residence without the sanctions of marriage, Tracy and Hepburn agree to a marriage of convenience, neither of them ever having any notion that they will wed anyone out of pure love. Further, the patriotic Hepburn is persuaded to undertake this unusual arrangement because she so much wants to help the war effort. Moreover, she has fallen in love with Tracy's dog and wants that affectionate canine at her side. Instead of a honeymoon, they work together on the oxygen project as she becomes his assistant. Tracy is inclined to walk in his sleep and his dog faithfully escorts him back to bed. While they grow to feel more affectionate toward each other, Ball, a real estate agent, develops a yearning for Tracy, while Hepburn is courted by Esmond, and Tracy's former flame, Morison, comes back into his life to complicate matters. In such close quarters as a basement laboratory, Tracy and Hepburn fall in love, now glad that they are already married to each other. Tracy and Hepburn are again charming together, and the scenes where Tracy sleepwalks with his loyal dog accompanying him (and trained to keep him out of trouble) provide more than one hilarious moment. Added attractions include Wynn's ongoing drunk act and Ball's appearance as a very sexy, wisecracking business woman, where her only business is trying to steal Tracy away from Hepburn. The film was a hit at the box office, earning more than $3.7 million in its initial release against a budget of $1.8 million. Songs: "Easy to Love" (Cole Porter), "Clair de Lune" (Claude Debussy), "O! Susanna" (Stephen Foster). *Author's Note*: Hepburn had appeared in the original Barry play upon which this film is based, one that opened on Broadway at the St. James Theater on November 10, 1942, and ran for 113 performances. "Don Stewart [Donald Ogden Stewart] adapted that play for the screen," Hepburn told this author, and did a very good job of it. He was an old pro and had adapted another Barry play for me called **The Philadelphia Story** [1940], which I did with Cary [Grant] and Jimmy [James] Stewart. I knew I was in very good hands." Tracy told this author that "even though I peeked when I am supposed to be sleepwalking in that picture, I still bumped into furniture and, once, slipped and took a pratfall that made my backside sore for a week. We had to reshoot those scenes more than once. I don't know how people who are real sleepwalkers can move around before they get back to the sack without breaking their necks. It is one of the wonders of the world." Many other films depict sleepwalkers and sleepwalking (somnambulism), including: **Abbott and Costello Meet Frankenstein**, 1948; **The Affairs of Cellini**, 1934; **The Cabinet of Dr. Caligari**, 1921; **The Chinese Room**, 1968; **City of Pirates**, 1985; **Class Trip**, 1998; **The Conjuring**, 2013; **Count Dracula**, 1977 (made-for-TV); **Dark Corners**, 2006; **Dark Water**, 2002; **Dead Awake**, 2001; **The Doll**, 1919; **Donnie Darko**, 2001; **Don't Look Down**, 2008; **Don't Look Now...We're Being Shot At!**, 1969; **Dracula**, 1931; **Dracula**, 1979; **Dracula**, 1992; **Dracula: Dead and Loving It**, 1995; **Dracula Has Risen from His Grave**, 1969; **Dracula in Istanbul**, 1953; **Dracula—Prince of Darkness**, 1966; **Dracula's Daughter**, 1936; **Experience Preferred...But Not Essential**, 1983; **Eye of the Devil**, 1966; **The Eyes of Annie Jones**, 1964; **Fort Bliss**, 2014; **Gone Fishin'**, 1997; **Half Angel**, 1951; **Haxan: Witchcraft through the Ages**, 1922; **He Married His Wife**, 1940; **He Said, She Said**, 1991; **The Horn Blows at Midnight**, 1945; **Hot Water**, 1924; **Jericho Mansions**, 2003; **Killer Joe**, 2011; **La sonnambula**, 1954; **The Legend of Hell House**, 1973; **Leif**, 1987; **The Lieutenant Wore Skirts**, 1956; **Loch Ness**, 1996; **Macbeth**, 1948; **Macbeth**, 1971; **Macbeth**, 2015; **Mark of the Vampire**, 1935; **Neel Kamal**, 1968; **The New Daughter**, 2009; **A Nightmare on Elm Street 2: Freddy's Revenge**, 1985; **Nosferatu**, 1922; **Nosferatu: The Vampire**, 1979; **Paranormal Activity**, 2009; **The Parasomniac**, 2010; **The Private Lives of Pippa Lee**, 2009; **Reign over Me**, 2007; **Run & Jump**, 2013; **The Science of Sleep**, 2006; **Secondhand Lions**, 2003; **Side Effects**, 2013; **Silent Hill**, 2006; **Sinister**, 2012; **The Skull**, 1965; **Sleep Murder**, 2004 (made-for-TV); **Sleepwalk with Me**, 2012; **The Sleepwalker Killing**, 1997 (made-for-TV); **Sleepwalkers**, 1992; **Stepbrothers**, 2008; **The Towrope**, 2012; **Turtles Can Fly**, 2004; **Vampire over London**, 1952; **Viridiana**, 1962; **When Father Was Away on Business**, 1985; **The Woman in Green**, 1945; and **Wreckers**, 2011. **p**, Lawrence A. Weingarten; **d**, Harold S. Bucquet; **cast**, Spencer Tracy, Katharine Hepburn, Lucille Ball, Keenan Wynn, Carl Esmond, Patricia Morison, Felix Bressart, Gloria Grahame, Eddie Acuff, Hazel Brooks, Donald Curtis; **w**, Donald Ogden Stewart (based on the play by Philip Barry); **c**, Karl Freund; **m**, Bronislau Kaper; **ed**, Frank Sullivan; **art d**, Cedric Gibbons, Harry McAfee; **set d**, Edwin B. Willis; **spec eff**, A. Arnold Gillespie, Danny Hall.

Without Reservations ★★★ 1946; U.S.; 107m; RKO; B/W; Com-

Don DeFore, Claudette Colbert and John Wayne in *Without Reservations*, **1946.**

edy/Romance; Children: Acceptable; **DVD**; **VHS**. Though this film takes a large leaf from **It Happened One Night**, 1934, it nevertheless delivers a heartwarming and delightful story about a furtive famous writer, Colbert, and two Marines, Wayne and DeFore, accompanying her across the U.S. to Tinsel Town. Colbert has just published a bestselling novel and is traveling to California where she expects to work on the script that will take that bestseller to the screen. She does not want to be distracted by anyone so she journeys incognito. She learns from her producer just before she departs that Cary Grant was scheduled to star in the film, but has dropped out and the producer thinks that an unknown person should play the part of the hero. On board the train going west, Colbert meets Wayne and DeFore, two Marine pilots. Colbert is so taken with the heroic-appearing Wayne that she is convinced that he is the very person to play the protagonist in the movie version of her story and wires her producer about him. She does this, despite the fact that Wayne and DeFore do not like Colbert's novel, although they like her without knowing that she is the book's author. When the three arrive in Chicago, Colbert learns that Wayne and DeFore are taking another train and she hastily joins them, leaving her baggage behind. The happy threesome has a little too much to drink in the club car, and Wayne and DeFore attempt to recreate their flying exploits by assembling an airplane from furniture. Colbert joins in the antics and is blamed for the mayhem by train officials, who order her to leave the train at the next stop. Wayne and DeFore believe Colbert has been wrongly punished and get off the train with her. They buy a used car and the trio drives westward. The car breaks down, and, while DeFore works on the engine, Wayne and Colbert stroll through a farmland in the evening moonlight, resting on a haystack (this scene almost duplicates Colbert's scene with Clark Gable twelve years earlier when they sleep next to a haystack in **It Happened One Night**). When the trio arrives in New Mexico and needs cash, Colbert comes to the rescue by cashing a check, but she is compelled to use her real name and she is identified as a famous writer. A false report is then published that Colbert is already in California and Colbert is arrested in New Mexico for impersonating herself and passing a forged check! In order to raise cash to bail Colbert out of the clink, Wayne and DeFore sell their car but are amazed when Colbert's producer arrives to spring her from jail. Now that they know who Colbert is, Wayne angrily feels that Colbert has been using him and leaves for his base in San Diego. Colbert finally arrives in Hollywood and begins writing her script, but gossip columnist Louella Parsons broadcasts a report that Colbert is romantically involved with her leading man, Wayne. This so angers Wayne that he resolves to never again see Colbert. DeFore, however, plays cupid, and convinces Wayne that he has Colbert all wrong and that she truly loves him. Wayne and Colbert then reunite to make a life together. In that final scene, as Wayne

Don DeFore and John Wayne in *Without Reservations,* **1946.**

walks to Colbert's open arms, she repeats an iconic line used by fliers: "Thanks, God, I'll take it from here." The script is frothy but provides enough happy situations to sustain interest as pantheon director LeRoy energetically moves this delightful tale along at a brisk pace. Colbert is her usual effervescent self, deftly playing her invented character while Wayne is the perfect straight-laced specimen of her dreams while affable DeFore is the ideal sidekick. This film was a big success at the box office, earning more than $3 million in its initial release against a budget of more than $1.6 million. It saw a sixty-minute radio adaptation that was aired by Lux Radio Theater on August 26, 1946, with Colbert reprising her role. *Author's Note*: LeRoy told this author that "**Without Reservations** is one of those screwball comedies that was so popular back in the 1940s, and it is also a lively romance between Claudette [Colbert], a refined woman, and Wayne, a brawny but sincere down-to-earth guy. That was a winning combination then and, if you had that kind of talent available today, it would be just as popular with contemporary audiences." Colbert liked acting opposite Wayne, telling this author: "He was, when we made that picture together, bigger than life. He had won the war [WWII, 1939-1945] almost singlehanded on the screen, so when he appeared as a Marine pilot in that picture, everyone, including me, accepted him as a real-life hero." Wayne was not so sure that his role was ideal for him, saying to this author that "I felt a little uneasy about appearing with Claudette, one of the world's most beautiful actresses, a very polished lady. She has so much style that I thought I appeared clumsy and awkward in some of our scenes together. You know what it was? I was up against real class, and I knew it." Cameo appearances are made by columnist Parsons and Cary Grant, who briefly dances with Colbert. Comedian Jack Benny appears early on in the film, asking Colbert to autograph a copy of her book. Many other films depicting individuals abandoning their true identities to operate incognito, include: **The Adorable Deceiver**, 1926 (Balkan king and princess daughter disguise themselves when fleeing to America from revolutionaries with the crown jewels); **Bachelor in Paradise**, 1961 (famous author goes undercover); **Back Trail**, 1948 (former outlaw serves as respectable town banker); **The Beasts of Marseilles**, 1959; **Betty**, 1997 (famous actress disguises her identity); **The Big Mouth**, 1967; **Big Town Girl**, 1937 (department store clerk hides her identity as a famous radio singing star); **Business under Distress**, 1938 (efficiency expert goes undercover to solve financial problems at a nightclub); **Death Duel**, 1977; **The Desert Song**, 1943 (sheik poses as a lowly positioned Arab); **The Desert Song**, 1953 (sheik poses as a lowly positioned Arab); **The Devil and Miss Jones**, 1941 (tycoon takes a job as a clerk in his own department store); Elvis Meets Nixon, 1997 (made-for-TV); **Emperor Chien Lung**, 1976; **Expensive Husbands**, 1937 (prince disguises himself as a waiter at an upscale European hotel); **Go-Get-'Em Haines**,

1936 (reporter goes undercover to nab criminals); **The Goose Girl**, 1915 (German nobleman disguises his identity); **The Green Man**, 1957; **Gun Smoke**, 1945; **The Gunfighter**, 1950 (former outlaw serves as town's marshal); **Headline Crasher**, 1937 (senator's son goes undercover to aid his father's reelection); **Hey Hey It's Esther Blueburger**, 2008; **Highways by Night**, 1942; **Hollow Triumph**, 1948 (fatal irony takes place after a man disguises himself with plastic surgery); **Hollywood Road Trip**, 2015; **Holy Matrimony**, 1943 (famous painter works under a pseudonym to ruin greedy art dealers); **Honeymoon**, 2014; **I Married a Witch**, 1942 (infamous Salem witch pretends to be a victim in a modern-day fire); **Incognito**, 1998 (art expert disguises herself to expose creator of faked famous paintings); **Incognito**, 1999 (bodyguard disguises himself to protect rape victim); **Incognito**, 2005 (TV series); **Incognito**, 2009 (ambitious singer disguises himself to advance his career); **Incognito**, 2012- (TV series); **Intent to Kill**, 1959 (South American president disguises himself to evade assassins); **It Happened One Night**, 1934 (heiress disguises herself on flight from tycoon father); **Jesse James Rides Again**, 1947 (infamous outlaw goes undercover to aid ranchers); **Knight without Armor**, 1937 (countess disguises herself as a peasant to escape Bolshevik killers during the Russian Revolution); **The Lady Hermit**, 1971 (Kung Fu master goes undercover); **Lafayette**, 1963; **The Man with 100 Faces**, 1938 (society lion goes undercover as a modern-day Robin Hood); **Man with the Steel Whip**, 1954; **Mary Jane's Pa**, 1935 (long-absent father returns to aid daughter by pretending to be her housekeeper); **Melvin and Howard**, 1980 (billionaire Howard Hughes disguises himself as a hobo); **Mississippi Gambler**, 1942 (criminal disguises himself with plastic surgery); **Orlando**, 1993 (British nobleman remains young forever under many aliases); **The Panther's Claw**, 1942 (famous person becomes a secret blackmailer); **Park Avenue Logger**, 1937 (rich man's son disguises his identity); **The Rogue's Tavern**, 1936; **Set Free**, 1927 (stuntman works as clerk to rescue female storeowner); **Sitting Pretty**, 1948 (famous author goes undercover as a babysitter to write a scandalous book about neighbors); **Sudan**, 1945 (Egyptian queen pretends to be a commoner); **Sullivan's Travels**, 1941 (famous film director pretends to be a hobo); **A Taste for Women**, 1964 (cannibals pretend to operate a gourmet restaurant while looking for the ideal woman to serve at their next full-moon sacrifice, and this may be the most outlandish film ever to make it to the screen); **They All Kissed the Bride**, 1942; **The Thief of Bagdad**, 1924 (sultan pretends to be a commoner); **The Thief of Bagdad**, 1940 (sultan pretends to be a commoner); **Time Out for Romance**, 1937 (society lady hides her identity when escaping an unhappy marriage); **The Tourist**, 2010; **Twilight on the Prairie**, 1944 (musicians pretend to be cowboys to aid rancher); **Two Gun Lady**, 1955 (woman becomes a sharpshooter and goes undercover to hunt down her parents' killers); **Undercover**, 2015- (TV series); **The Vagabond King**, 1930; **The Vagabond King**, 1956; **Western Justice**, 1934 (three men use aliases in an effort to bring water to a drought-ridden town); **With Pleasure, Madame**, 1937 (British diplomat disguises himself for reasons of State); and **Woman in Distress**, 1937 (reporter goes undercover to expose art fraud). **p**, Jesse L. Lasky; **d**, Mervyn LeRoy; **cast**, Claudette Colbert, John Wayne, Don DeFore, Anne Triola, Phil Brown, Frank Puglia, Thurston Hall, Dona Drake, Fernando Alvarado, Louella Parsons, Jack Benny, Raymond Burr, Cary Grant, Bruce Lester, Dolores Moran, Ruth Roman; **w**, Andrew Solt (based on the novel *Thanks, God, I'll Take It from Here* by Jane Allen, Mae Livingston); **c**, Milton Krasner; **m**, Roy Webb; **ed**, Jack Ruggiero; **art d**, Albert S. D'Agostino, Ralph Berger; **set d**, Darrell Silvera, James Altwies; **spec eff**, Vernon L. Walker, Russell A. Cully, Harold Stine.

Without Warning ★★★ 1952; U.S.; 75m; UA; B/W; Crime Drama; Children: Unacceptable; **BD**; **DVD**; **VHS**. Taut thriller centers on Williams, a withdrawn Los Angeles gardener who becomes deranged because of the infidelity of his blonde wife. He takes out his revenge by stalking and killing blonde women. Police track him down through the use of laboratory techniques, following a key clue, a spring from a pair of garden shears. Policemen Binns and Warde nab him as he is about to kill Randall, the blonde daughter of the owner of a greenhouse. This low-budget film noir entry is firmly directed by Laven, and the cast render superior performances. Violence prohibits viewing by children. **p**, Arthur Gardner, Jules Levy; **d**, Arnold Laven; **cast**, Adam Williams, Meg Ramdall, Edward Binns, Harlan Warde, John Maxwell, Angela Stevens, Byron Kane, Charles Tannen, Robert Shayne, Robert Foulk; **w**, Bill Raynor (based on his story); **c**, Joseph F. Biroc; **m**, Herschel Burke Gilbert; **ed**, Arthur H. Nadel; **prod d**, Ted Haworth as Edward S. Haworth.

Witness ★★★★ 1985; U.S.; 112m; PAR; Color; Crime Drama; Children: Unacceptable (MPAA: R); **BD**; **DVD**; **VHS**; **IV**. Spine-tingling thriller begins when McGillis, a young Amish widow, and Haas, her eight-year-old son, are traveling to Philadelphia by train to visit McGillis' sister. As the train stops at the 30th Street Station, Haas sees a man killed by two men. Ford and Jennings, detectives, are assigned to investigate, but Haas can give them no information after he reviews mug shots and police lineups. Haas then spots a newspaper clipping with a photo of Glover and identifies him as one of the murderers. Glover is a narcotics officer with a suspicious background. Ford recalls how Glover was involved in a drug raid where most of the evidence inexplicably disappeared. Ford confides his suspicions to Sommer, his superior, who tells Ford to keep his suspicions about Glover to himself as they cautiously investigate Glover. A short time later, Glover ambushes Ford in a parking garage, shooting and wounding him before he escapes. Ford realizes that Sommer warned Glover and is somehow involved in the murder. Realizing that his witness is now in danger, Ford calls Jennings and tells him to remove the records about McGillis and Haas from police files. He then uses his sister's car to drive McGillis and Haas back to their home in Lancaster County, Pennsylvania, an Amish community, where he believes they will be safe. Just as they arrive at McGillis' farm, Harrison passes out from his wound. He is reluctantly taken in by Rubes, who is McGillis' father-in-law, and is slowly nursed back to health. Ford and McGillis develop a relationship that alarms Godunov, a neighboring Amish farmer who has been courting McGillis. Moreover, Rubes does not like the budding romance between McGillis and Ford and warns his daughter-in-law that, unless she severs her relationship with the Philadelphia detective, the Amish community might reject her and make her a social pariah. Ford, however, uses his expertise as a carpenter to help raise a barn for a newly married couple and earns the respect of Godunov and other Amish leaders. He is nevertheless treated as an outsider, and McGillis further alienates community members when she serves Ford first at a dinner. McGillis is obviously in love with Ford and, when he finds her bathing, she stands naked before him. Ford, however, leaves, later explaining that if he remained and made love to her, he or she would have to depart the community. When he later goes to town to call his partner, Jennings, he finds that Jennings has been murdered. Ford concludes that Jennings has been killed by Glover and Sommer, along with another corrupt detective, MacInnes, the second killer Haas saw with Glover at the train station. While in town, Ford sees several Amish members being harassed by local thugs. Following their strict adherence to non-violence, the Amish do not retaliate, but Ford interferes on their behalf and the brief scuffle is later reported to local police, which leads to Sommer learning of Ford's whereabouts. The three corrupt policemen arrive the next day and Ford sends Haas to a neighbor's farm for safety, but MacInnes pursues him into a silo. Haas tricks MacInnes so that he is able to suffocate him with tons of corn. Meanwhile, Ford retrieves MacInnes's shotgun and uses it to kill Glover. Sommer, however, captures McGillis and Rubes in the farmhouse, forcing them outside at gunpoint where he intends to kill them, along with Ford. Haas, seeing this, rings the warning bell, which summons the Amish to the scene. Realizing he is being seen by dozens of witnesses, Sommer has no choice but to surrender to Ford. Local police then arrive

Kelly McGillis, Lukas Haas and Harrison Ford in *Witness,* **1985.**

to place Sommer under arrest to conclude this tense tale. Weir does a good job unraveling this sinister tale among the atmosphere of the good-intentioned Amish, and, in so deftly defining that religious group doubly presents a fine profile of cultures in collision. Ford, McGillis, Haas, Rubes and Godunov render standout performances, while heavies Glover, Sommer and MacInnes provide genuinely believable villains. The film received Oscars for Best Original Screenplay (Kelley, Wallace), and Best Film Editing (Noble), while receiving Oscar nominations for Best Picture; Best Director (Weir); Best Actor (Ford); Best Cinematography (Seale); Best Art Direction (Jolley, Anderson); and Best Original Score (Jarre). It was a great success at the box office, earning more than $68.7 million against a budget of more than $12 million. Songs: "(What a) Wonderful World" (1959; Sam Cooke, Herb Alpert, Lou Adler), "Shocking Behavior" (1984; Paul Chiten, Sue Sheridan), "Party Down" (Alan Brackett, Scott Shelly). *Author's Note*: The Amish were not pleased with this film (or any other film depicting their religious practices, which includes all Anabaptists and Mennonites). This reclusive if not furtive and very peaceful religious sect is easily victimized by Hollywood with its many intrusive productions where it and its members are too often profiled as religious crackpots, or deluded misanthropes. Weir and the producers of this film are not one of those ridiculing groups, but appear to sincerely show these God-fearing people as decent and respectable human beings. However, the film inadvertently created a problem with this group where McGillis herself telegraphs that problem by telling Ford while he is recuperating at her father-in-law's farm that tourists often look upon the Amish as freaks to be stared at and that they routinely violate their privacy by trespassing on their properties to obtain souvenirs. This is exactly what happened following this film, and the Amish called for a boycott of this film, fearing that tourists would overrun their community to trespass on their farmlands and filch private items for souvenirs. Pennsylvania Governor Dick Thornburgh (1932-) was moved to publicly announce that the State would not encourage any future film producers to use Amish sites for their productions. To prepare for her role as an Amish widow, McGillis took up residence with an Amish widow with seven children to learn the practices, customs and lifestyle of the religious group. Ford, too, did his research, by working with the Philadelphia police department and even accompanying some of its detectives on police raids. Ford was not the original selection for the leading role in this film as Sylvester Stallone was first asked to play that part. He rejected the role, and it was later reported that he felt that it was one of his worst career decisions. Stallone approached this author through an agent of the William Morris Agency in 2015, asking to secure the film and/or dramatic rights to this author's work, *Bloodletters and Badmen: A Narrative Encyclopedia of American Criminals from the Pilgrims to the Present,*

Tyrone Power, Una O'Connor and Norma Varden in *Witness for the Prosecution,* **1957.**

which, to date, has sold more than four million copies. After prolonged delays, the agent informed this author that Mr. Stallone did not want to pay a cent for those rights and that I should grant those rights free to him and be paid from Mr. Stallone's sale of those rights to a TV network. I declined Mr. Stallone's less than generous offer, telling the agent to inform Mr. Stallone that "in this savvy old world of ours, you get nothing when you offer nothing." I think Mr. Stallone has a habit of making injudicious career decisions. The Amish (as well as Anabaptists and Mennonites) have been profiled in many other films, including **Aaron's Way**, 1988 (TV series); **Amish Grace**, 2010 (made-for-TV); **An Amish Murder**, 2013 (made-for-TV); **At Close Range**, 1986; **Banshee**, 2013- (TV series); **Birch Interval**, 1976; **David in Wunderland**, 1998; **Deadly Devotion**, 2013- (TV series); **Deadly Reactor**, 1989; **Diary of the Dead**, 2007; **ECW One Night Stand**, 2005 (made-for-TV); **For Richer or Poorer**, 1997; **Gypsy 83**, 2001; **Harvest of Fire**, 1996 (made-for-TV); **Hitting the Nuts**, 2010; **Holy Matrimony**, 1994; **Holyman Undercover**, 2010; **Jesus' Son**, 1999; **Kaw**, 2007; **Kingpin**, 1996; **Love Finds You in Sugarcreek**, 2014 (made-for-TV); **Lucky Numbers**, 2000; **The Night They Raided Minsky's**, 1968; **North**, 1994; **The Outsider**, 2002 (made-for-TV); **Plain Truth**, 2004 (made-for-TV); **Road Movie**, 1974; **Route 30**, 2007; **Saving Sarah Cain**, 2007; **Sex Drive**, 2008; **The Shunning**, 2011 (made-for-TV); **The Stoning in Fulham County**, 1988 (made-for-TV); **They Call Me Renegade**, 1987; **Violent Saturday**, 1955; and **Warlock**, 1989. **p**, Edward S. Feldman, David Bombyk; **d**, Peter Weir; **cast**, Harrison Ford, Kelly McGillis, Lukas Haas, Danny Glover, Patti LuPone, Josef Sommer, Jan Rubes, Alexander Godunov, Brent Jennings, Angus MacInnes; **w**, William Kelley, Earl W. Wallace (based on a story by Kelley, Earl W. and Pamela Wallace); **c**, John Seale (Technicolor); **m**, Maurice Jarre; **ed**, Thom Noble; **prod d**, Stan Jolley; **set d**, John Anderson; **spec eff**, John R. Elliott, Charles E. Dolan.

Witness for the Prosecution ★★★★ 1957; U.S.; 114m; Edward Small Productions/UA; B/W; Crime Drama; Children: Unacceptable; **BD**; **DVD**; **VHS**; **IV.** Pantheon director Wilder offers a powerful and mesmerizing courtroom drama that is based upon the story and hit play by master mystery writer Agatha Christie. Power, in his last appearance in a film, is at his very best as a charming married man and womanizer living by his wits in London. He is suddenly accused of murder and turns to the city's leading barrister, Laughton, to save him from the gallows. Laughton, however, is an ailing man who has been told by his physicians that he must retire and that conducting any more trials will put his life at risk. To that end, he is guarded night and day by watchdog nurse Lanchester (who is Laughton's real-life wife), who is aided by equally fussy butler Wolfe. To ease the strain of climbing stairs to his bedroom, a seat operated on a rail automatically going up those stairs

has been recently installed, and Laughton is enjoying its movement when Daniell, a solicitor, arrives with Power in tow. Although Laughton tells Daniell that he is no longer practicing law, he spots some cigars protruding from one of Daniell's suitcoat pockets and takes Daniell and Power into his private office, locking out a lecturing Lanchester. Laughton takes one of Daniell's cigars and Power lights it. The shrewd attorney then inspects Power with his monocle, positioning it so that sunlight from a nearby window reflects into Power's eyes to distract him as Laughton questions him. (Laughton used as his role model an attorney that represented him and Dietrich in real life and twirled a monocle when addressing juries.) Power, however, is smilingly cooperative as he tells how he met the murder victim, Varden. His narrative is shown in flashbacks as he describes his encounters with Varden, first when passing a woman's hat store to see her trying on a new bonnet. He explains that he did not approve of that hat, but nodded approval of another Varden modeled, earning the woman's gratitude. Power then goes on to explain that he met Varden again when going to a movie and they watched a film together, Varden later inviting Power to have tea at her home. He is shown in another flashback attempting to interest Varden in investing into his new invention. He demonstrates that invention, an eggbeater, in Varden's kitchen while Varden and her disapproving, partially deaf housekeeper, O'Connor, stand by and watch him operate the elaborate apparatus. He makes a perfect mess of the kitchen but nevertheless points out that his marvelous eggbeater uniquely separates yokes from whites. Varden, a wealthy widow, is enamored of the handsome Power and his bubbling personality so endears him to her that the love-starved woman makes him the chief beneficiary in her will. When she is later found dead in her lavishly appointed home, Power becomes the chief suspect in her death, especially since he has been left £80,000 by Varden in her will. Laughton at first heeds the cautions of doctors and Lanchester, turning over the case to his associate, Williams, but when Williams thinks he will lose in court, Laughton reconsiders. The persuasive Power convinces Laughton that he is innocent, and, despite objections from his doctors and household protectors, Laughton finally agrees to defend Power at a murder trial held at London's Old Bailey. Power's only alibi is that his wife, Dietrich, saw him at their home on the night of Varden's death, but since a wife's testimony is suspect in court, Laughton knows that he has very little defensive ammunition by which to save Power. He nevertheless interviews Dietrich, who gives him a lot of sarcastic answers before she finally provides that alibi by stating that Power was with her at the time Varden was killed. Dietrich tells Laughton that her testimony at Power's upcoming trial will be accepted since she is not really Power's wife and that they had wedded illegally in Germany as she was already married to a German national. Power has, by this time, been arrested by Scotland Yard on charges of murdering Varden and is held in prison to await his trial. Laughton interviews Power in his prison cell, learning from him (as seen in another flashback) that he met Dietrich when she was singing in a seedy German cabaret and enduring a miserable life. Power, then a serviceman in the British army, rescued her from her lowlife lot by marrying her and taking her to England. Laughton takes the case and begins a battle of wits with his opponent and prosecutor, Thatcher, as both maneuver their legal positions. During Power's trial, Laughton thinks to use Dietrich in his defense of Power, but he is shocked when seeing her suddenly appear as the star witness for the prosecution. Thatcher announces to the court that since Dietrich is not legally married to Power, she can testify against him and Dietrich does exactly that. She states that, although she had originally agreed to testify on his behalf and provide Power with an alibi, her conscience has given her no peace of mind and that she now wants to tell the truth. She states that Power admitted to her that he killed Varden, and Power, who stands in the box of the accused, erupts, passionately calling her a liar. The startled Laughton then labels Dietrich a flagrant bigamist whose statements cannot be reliable and, he, too, calls Dietrich a liar. He and Thatcher make their closing arguments, and the case rests to await the jury's decision. While waiting that night,

Laughton is contacted by a strange, uncouth cockney woman, who offers to sell him evidence that will save his client. Laughton and Daniell then clandestinely meet this vulgar female, who sells them a number of love letters Dietrich has written to a secret lover named "Max." The next day, Laughton convinces the court to reopen the case because of his newly acquired evidence. He calls Dietrich back to the witness box and confronts her with her incriminating love letters to the enigmatic "Max." Laughton then eloquently states to the court that the letters he offers in evidence prove that Dietrich's motive in lying about Power was to send him to his death so that she could be with her secret lover. Laughton's argument wins a favorable verdict for Power, who is then set free. Laughton celebrates his triumph by taking a stiff drink instead of his medicine, but his great victory is soon proved to be hollow. The perceptive Laughton has suspected this all along, stating immediately after winning the case that it has all been "too neat, too tidy, and, altogether, too symmetrical…" He then meets Dietrich in the empty courtroom, ostensibly by accident, and she sarcastically mimics Laughton's earlier words to her that "no jury would believe an alibi given by a loving wife." The clever and manipulative Dietrich gloats over her own inventiveness, and takes credit for saving Power, discrediting Laughton as having been duped as her ploy in achieving that acquittal. She then shocks Laughton by telling him that she forged the love letters to a mythical "Max," and disguised herself as the cockney woman (where she speaks briefly in cockney slang to prove it). She goes on to state that the only way she could save Power, the man she loves above all else, was to give false testimony against him and then be discredited by Laughton, who was armed with the very evidence Dietrich supplied that would impugn her testimony. Dietrich smugly rubs salt into her wounding words, by arrogantly telling Laughton that she has known all along that Power killed Varden, but that she nevertheless saved him from execution because she loves him. Power has heard all of this, but when Dietrich goes to him, he pushes her away, telling her that he has as cleverly used her as she has shrewdly manipulated Laughton in that he, irrespective of his innocence or guilt, cannot again be tried for the same crime under the law of double jeopardy. He not only admits his guilt but tells Laughton that he will pay for Dietrich's defense when she is brought to trial for perjury, now that Varden's fortune has been legally bestowed upon him. Power then shocks Dietrich by telling her that he is abandoning her and that he is going off with his secret lover, Lee, a much younger and more attractive woman, who suddenly appears at Power's side. The enraged Dietrich then picks up a knife, which has been used as an exhibit in Power's case and ironically used to kill Varden, and plunges the blade into Power's back, killing him. As Dietrich is seized by officers and led away, the seemingly unperturbed Laughton (nothing can shock him at this point of recurrent shocks), and at the urging of Lanchester, who has arrived with his medicine, tells his associates that he will defend Dietrich (saying that she has "executed" Power) at her upcoming trial to end this spine-tingling tale. Wilder stunningly presents this complex story and its colorful characters with many a deftly crafted scene. He meticulously builds suspense with many convincing red herrings before finally unraveling and exposing Dietrich and Power and their sinister machinations. To relieve the static boredom of courtroom procedures, Wilder uses his fluid camera techniques, flashbacks, cross-cutting, and amusing asides (Lanchester constantly nagging Laughton to take his medicine) to maintain an ever increasing pace as he mounts tension in every frame. The inimitable Laughton is the centerpiece of this tale, but his clients, Power, and, subsequently, Dietrich, dominate every scene in which they appear separately, and mesmerize when they finally appear together in the fatal finale. Both are at their exceptional best—Power as the outgoing, glad-handing entrepreneur with only murder on his mind, and Dietrich as the aging, victimized woman, who discards her morality for love—in this utterly fascinating whodunit where the supporting cast members are also outstanding in their roles. The film received Oscar nominations for Best Picture; Best Director (Wilder); Best Actor (Laughton); Best Supporting Actress (Lanchester); Best

Tyrone Power and Marlene Dietrich in *Witness for the Prosecution*, 1957.

Film Editing (Mandell); and Best Sound (Gordon E. Sawyer). It was a great success at the box office, earning more than $9 million in its initial release against a budget of $3 million. Prior to this film, the story was presented as a live telecast by Lux Video Theater on September 17, 1953, starring Edward G. Robinson, Tom Drake and Andrea King. This film was remade for TV in 1982. Song: "I May Never Go Home Anymore" (music: Ralph Arthur Roberts; lyrics: Jack Brooks). *Author's Note*: Dietrich told this author that "Billy [Wilder] wanted to show off my legs, or, at least one of them, which he thought would be an added attraction to the picture, so he wrote in a scene [a flashback to the German café where Dietrich performs] where I could sing a song ["I May Never Go Home Anymore"] and even play an accordion." Dietrich wore one of her famous slack suits in that scene, which ended in a brawl where her trousers were torn to expose one leg. That scene increased the budget by almost $100,000 as Wilder used several dozen stuntmen and about 150 extras in shooting it. Wilder told this author that "Marlene [Dietrich] spent more time on doing that little scene where she impersonates a cockney woman than the rest of her part. She even went to Charles' [Laughton's] home and pestered him and Elsa [Lanchester] on how to dress and talk like that shabby street person. When she gets something into her head, it becomes an obsession." Of particular note is the recreation of the courtroom at the Old Bailey. This was authentically recreated by art director Trauner, who had designed spectacular sets for such films as **Children of Paradise**, 1944. Trauner visited the Old Bailey, and, after being told he could not photograph any of its interior courtrooms, made meticulous sketches of one of them and then recreated that courtroom, right down to its sixty Austrian oaken wall panels, all of which could be removed when needed. He further created a moveable sectioned floor. The entire courtroom set cost $75,000. This author once asked Alfred Hitchcock if he would rank this film as one of those that approached Hitchcock's own suspense films and he replied: "Yes, well, that was an isolated film, even for him [Wilder]. That was a play written by Agatha Christie, and Billy was confined to many restrictive scenes, but he is a clever fellow who knows how to get around all that. He knows how to use the camera to make things move smoothly. He has a very good eye for that. However, it is common knowledge that Agatha Christie took a good look at my picture, **The Paradine Case** [1947], before she wrote her play, and I think Billy looked at that picture more than once before he made Christie's play into a picture. Their story has the same kind of character as you see in **The Paradine Case**, a person everyone thinks is innocent, but is really guilty. You might recall that I used a very fine actress, Norma Varden, as a potential murder victim in **Strangers on a Train** [1951], where killer Robert Walker loses self-control and almost strangles her to death at a social gathering while demonstrating how mur-

Tyrone Power in the defendant's box in *Witness for the Prosecution*, 1957.

derers throttle their victims. [Varden often played victims in films, such as in **Casablanca**, 1942, where she sits with her husband at an outdoor café while Curt Bois, a clever thief, adeptly picks her husband's wallet.] That scene must have impressed Billy, too, because he cast Norma in the role of the murder victim in **Witness for the Prosecution**. I generously call all of that filching of my work as nothing more than 'Secondhand Flattery.'" United Artists went to great length to protect the surprise ending of this film, asking those attending theaters to see it to sign pledges that they would not reveal its final scenes. They went so far as to ask Queen Elizabeth II (1926-), and her entourage to do the same when the film was privately screened at a Royal Command Performance. This was Power's last film as he suffered a massive heart attack the following year while enacting a sword-fighting scene when making **Solomon and Sheba**, 1959. Actually, Power had turned down the role as the affable killer in this film and, after William Holden, Glenn Ford, Jack Lemmon and Gene Kelly also turned it down, agreed to play the part, but on the condition that he was paid $300,000 in a two-film package, the second being **Solomon and Sheba**, which claimed his life. Yul Brynner replaced him in that production. Only diminutive O'Connor had appeared in the original Broadway production of the Christie play, one that opened at Henry Miller's Theater on December 16, 1953, and ran for 645 performances. Many other films involve courtroom and trial scenes, including **Abused Confidence**, 1938; **Accused**, 1936; **The Accused**, 1949; **The Accused**, 1988; **Accused—Stand Up**, 1930; **The Adventures of Huckleberry Finn**, 1960; **Affare Dreyfus**, 1968 (TV miniseries; Alfred Dreyfus); **An Act of Murder**, 1948 (euthanasia case); **Adam's Rib**, 1949 (attempted murder of husband); **Along the Great Divide**, 1951; **The Amazing Dr. Clitterhouse**, 1938; **An American Tragedy**, 1931 (based on the 1908 Chester Gillette murder case); **Amistad**, 1999 (based upon the 1839 mutiny case by slaves on board the ship *La Amistad*); **Anatomy of a Murder**, 1959 (murder defense based upon "irresistible impulse" and loosely based on the 1932 Massie murder trial in Hawaii where Clarence Darrow acted as defense attorney); **Anatomy of a Psycho**, 1961; **...And Justice for All**, 1979; **And the Sea Will Tell**, 1991 (made-for-TV); **Angel Face**, 1952; **The Bachelor and the Bobby-Soxer**, 1947; **The Ballad of Josie**, 1967; **Before I Hang**, 1940; **Before the Deluge**, 1954; **Bernie**, 2011 (based on the murder of millionaire Marjorie Nugent in Carthage, Texas); **Best Wishes for Tomorrow**, 2007 (military tribunal; trial of WWII Japanese war criminals); **Bewitched**, 1945; **Beyond a Reasonable Doubt**, 1956; **Black and White**, 2002; **Black Legion**, 1937 (based on the Detroit, Michigan, terrorist organization, 1933-1936, led by Harvey Davis); **Blind Faith**, 1990 (made-for-TV); **Blondes at Work**, 1938; **Blood & Orchids**, 1986 (TV miniseries; loosely based on the 1932 Massie murder trial in Hawaii where Clarence Darrow acted as defense attorney); **Bluebeard**, 1963

(based on French serial killer Henri Landru, who was found guilty of murdering at least eleven women and was beheaded by the guillotine in 1922); **Body of Evidence**, 1993; **Body of My Enemy**, 1976; **Boomerang**, 1947 (based on the 1924 murder of Father Hubert Dahme in Bridgeport, Connecticut, and the resultant trial of Harold Israel, who was saved from conviction by prosecutor Homer Cummings, and who later became the U.S. Attorney General); **Breaker Morant**, 1980 (based upon the 1902 court-martial of British officers Harry "Breaker" Morant, Peter Handcock and four others on charges of murder during the Boer War and for which the two principals were executed); **The Brief**, 2004-2005 (TV series); **Buchanan Rides Alone**, 1958; **Buried Alive**, 1939; **The Caine Mutiny**, 1954 (U.S. military tribunal); **Canyon Passage**, 1946; **The Case of the Black Cat**, 1936; **The Case of the Stuttering Bishop**, 1937; **Charlie Chan at the Wax Museum**, 1940; **The Charmer**, 1987 (TV miniseries); **The Chatterley Affair**, 2006 (made-for-TV); **The Cheat**, 1931; **Chicago**, 2002 (based on the 1924 murder committed by married Beulah Annan, who shot her lover in the back and was nevertheless acquitted by a Chicago jury); **A Civil Action**, 1998; **The Clairvoyant**, 1935; **Class Action**, 1991; **The Client**, 1994; **Compulsion**, 1959 (based on the 1924 Loeb and Leopold murder case and criminal defense attorney Clarence Darrow who is played by Orson Welles); **Counselor at Law**, 1933 (based on the courtroom exploits of criminal defense attorney William Fallon); **Counter Investigation**, 2007; **The Count of Monte Cristo**, 1934; **The Count of Monte Cristo** 2002; **Court Martial**, 1954 (military tribunal); **The Court Martial of Billy Mitchell**, 1955 (U.S. military tribunal); **Crazy in Alabama**, 1999; **The Crucible**, 1996 (Salem witch trials in 1692-1693); **Damini – Lightning**, 1993; **Darrow**, 1991 (made-for-TV; life of attorney Clarence Darrow); **Deadlocked**, 2000 (made-for-TV); **Destry Rides Again**, 1932; **Destry Rides Again**, 1939; **The Devil and Daniel Webster**, 1941 (aka: **All That Money Can Buy**; Webster defends a mortal who has made a pact with the Devil); **Dishonored Lady**, 1947; **Dorothea Angermann**, 1959; **Double Jeopardy**, 1999; **The Drake Case**, 1929; **Dress Gray**, 1986 (made-for-TV); **The Dreyfus Case**, 1930 (Alfred Dreyfus); **The Dreyfus Case**, 1931 (Alfred Dreyfus); **88 Minutes**, 2007; **Emma**, 1932; **Erin Brockovich**, 2000; **Evelyn Prentice**, 1934; **The Exorcism of Emily Rose**, 2005; **A Few Good Men**, 1992 (U.S. military trial); **Find Me Guilty**, 2006 (based upon the 1985 case against members of organized crime in New Jersey, reputedly aligned with the New York Thomas Lucchese crime family headquartered in NYC); **The Firm**, 1993; **For the Defense**, 1954 (made-for-TV); **Fracture**, 2007; **Fury**, 1936 (based upon the 1933 kidnapping-murder of department store heir Brooke Hart and the lynching of his killers, Thomas Harold Thurmond and Maurice Holmes by a mob in San Jose, California); **Gandhi**, 1982; **The Girl Who Kicked the Hornets' Nest**, 2009; **The Glass Shield**, 1994; **Good Day for a Hanging**, 1959; **The Great Sioux Massacre**, 1965 (U.S. military tribunal following the Custer massacre of 1876); **Gupt: The Hidden Truth**, 1997; **Hang 'Em High**, 1968; **High Crimes**, 2002; **Hour of the Gun**, 1967 (trials in Tombstone, Arizona, in 1881 involving the Earp-Clanton factions); **The Hour of Thirteen**, 1952; **The Hourglass Sanatorium**, 1973 (Alfred Dreyfus); **Huckleberry Finn**, 1939; **I Accuse!**, 1958 (Alfred Dreyfus); **I Want to Live!**, 1958 (based on the 1955 murder trial of Barbara Graham); **Illegal**, 1955 (based on the courtroom exploits of criminal defense attorney William Fallon); **Impact**, 1949; **The Incident**, 1990 (made-for-TV); **Incident in a Small Town**, 1994 (made-for-TV); **In Cold Blood**, 1967 (based on mass murderers Perry Smith and Richard Hickock); **Inherit the Wind**, 1960 (based on the 1925 John T. Scopes "Monkey Trial"); **Inherit the Wind**, 1988 (made-for-TV; 1925 Scopes trial); **The Iron Sheriff**, 1957; **J. Edgar**, 2011 (trials resulting from the investigations of the FBI as led by J. Edgar Hoover); **Jagged Edge**, 1985; **Jasper, Texas**, 2003 (made-for-TV; based upon the 1998 murder of black man James Byrd Jr., by three white racists); **JFK**, 1991 (trials resulting from the investigations launched by New Orleans district attorney Jim Garrison into the assassination of President John F. Kennedy);

Jimmy the Gent, 1934; Joan of Arc, 1948; Joan the Woman, 1916 (Joan of Arc); Johnny Belinda, 1948; The Judge, 2014; Judgment at Nuremberg, 1961(post-WWII Nazi trial); Judicial Consent, 1994; Kavanagh QC, 1995-2001 (TV series); King & Country, 1964 (British military tribunal); L.A. Law, 1986-1994 (TV series); La Chienne, 1931; La Chienne, 1975; The Lady from Shanghai, 1948; L'affaire Dreyfus, 1995 (made-for-TV; Alfred Dreyfus); L'affare Dreyfus, 1968 (made-for-TV; Alfred Dreyfus); The Laramie Project, 2002 (made-for-TV; based on the 1988 murder of Matthew Shepard); The Last Innocent Man, 1987 (made-for-TV); The Lawyer, 1970; Leave Her to Heaven, 1945; The Learning Tree, 1969; The Legend of Lizzie Borden, 1975 (made-for-TV; based on the 1892 ax murders of Borden's father and stepmother in Fall River, Massachusetts; she was acquitted); Let Us Live, 1939; The Letter, 1940 (trial of wife who has killed her lover); Libel, 1959; Libeled Lady, 1936; The Life of Emile Zola, 1937 (Alfred Dreyfus); The Lincoln Lawyer, 2011; A Lion Is in the Streets, 1953 (based on Louisiana demagogue Huey Long); Lizzie Borden Took an Ax, 2014 (made-for-TV; based on the 1892 ax murders of Borden's father and stepmother in Fall River, Massachusetts; she was acquitted); M, 1933 (trial held by criminals judging a child molester and killer); M, 1951 (trial held by criminals judging a child molester and killer); Madeleine, 1950 (based on the 1857 murder case of Madeleine Smith, accused of killing her lover in Glasgow, Scotland); A Man for All Seasons, 1966 (based on the 1535 trial for treason by Sir Thomas More); Man Made Monster, 1941; The Man They Could Not Hang, 1939; The Man Who Sued God, 2001; Manhattan Melodrama, 1934 (loosely based on the 1928 NYC murder of gambler and crime boss Arnold Rothstein); Marshal of Gunsmoke, 1944; Mary, 1931; Melvilisom, 2011 (Indian military trial); The Messenger: The Story of Joan of Arc, 1999; Midnight in the Garden of Good and Evil, 1997; The Missing Juror, 1944; Miracle on 34th Street, 1947 (sanity hearing); Mississippi Burning, 1988 (based on the 1964 murders of three civil Rights activists and the resultant trial of KKK members); The Missouri Breaks, 1976; Mr. Deeds Goes to Town, 1936 (sanity hearing); Mister 880, 1950 (trial of an elderly counterfeiter); The Monster and the Girl, 1941; The Mouthpiece, 1932 (based on the courtroom exploits of criminal defense attorney William Fallon); Murder!, 1930; The Murder of Mary Phagan, 1988 (TV miniseries; based upon the 1913 wrongful conviction of Leo Frank for the murder of Mary Phagan, a young girl in Atlanta, Georgia, and Frank's lynching by the KKK in 1915); Mutiny on the Bounty, 1935 (military tribunal); Mutiny on the Bounty, 1962 (British military tribunal); My Cousin Vinny, 1992; The Naked Edge, 1961; The Night of January 16th, 1941; Night without Justice, 2004 (based upon the 1933 kidnapping-murder of department store heir Brooke Hart and the lynching of his killers, Thomas Harold Thurmond and Maurice Holmes by a mob in San Jose, California); No One Killed Jessica, 2011; Oscar Wilde, 1960; Oscar Wilde, 1972 (made-for-TV); The Outrage, 1964; The Ox-Bow Incident, 1943 (trial by lynch mob); Pandora's Box, 1929; The Paradine Case, 1947; Party Girl, 1958 (trials of a criminal attorney in 1920s Chicago); The Passion of Joan of Arc, 1928; The Passion of the Christ, 2004; Paths of Glory, 1957 (French military tribunal in WWI); Penguin Pool Murder, 1932; The People Against O'Hara, 1951; The People v. Leo Frank, 2009 (based upon the 1913 wrongful conviction of Leo Frank for the murder of Mary Phagan, a young girl in Atlanta, Georgia, and Frank's lynching by the KKK in 1915); The People vs. Jean Harris, 1981 (made-for-TV); The People vs. Larry Flynt, 1996; Perfect Stranger, 2007; Peyton Place, 1957; Philadelphia, 1993; Physical Evidence, 1989; Piccadilly, 1929; A Place in the Sun, 1951 (based on the 1908 Chester Gillette murder case); Primal Fear, 1996; Prisoner of Honor, 1991 (made-for-TV; Alfred Dreyfus); Providence, 1977; Question of Love, 1978; The Rack, 1956 (U.S. court-martial of a U.S. officer accused of treason in Korean War); The Return of Frank James, 1940; Reversal of Fortune, 1990 (based upon the 1982 Claus von Bulow murder trial); Roses Are for

Tyrone Power and Charles Laughton in *Witness for the Prosecution,* 1957.

the Rich, 1987 (made-for-TV); Roxie Hart, 1942 (based on the 1924 murder committed by married Beulah Annan, who shot her lover in the back and was nevertheless acquitted by a Chicago jury); Rules of Engagement, 2000 (U.S. military trial); Runaway Jury, 2003; Salome's Last Dance, 1988 (Oscar Wilde); Scarlet Street, 1945; The Secret Six, 1931; Separated by Murder, 1994 (made-for-TV); Sergeant Rutledge, 1960 (U.S. military tribunal); Shark, 2006-2008 (TV series); Shaurya, 2008 (Indian military trial); The Shawshank Redemption, 1994; Side Effects, 2013; Silkwood, 1983; Sleep Murder, 2004 (made-for-TV); Sleepers, 1996; A Soldier's Story, 1984 (U.S. military tribunal); Solomon and Sheba, 1959; Somebody Up There Likes Me, 1956 (U.S. court-martial of prizefighter Rocky Graziano); Sorry Ain't Enough, 2006; The Sound of Fury, 1950 (based upon the 1933 kidnapping-murder of department store heir Brooke Hart and the lynching of his killers, Thomas Harold Thurmond and Maurice Holmes by a mob in San Jose, California); Stairway to Heaven, 1947 (trial held in Heaven); The Star Chamber, 1983; State's Attorney, 1932 (loosely based on the career of criminal defense attorney William Fallon); Storeyville, 1992; The Story on Page One, 1959; The Strange Case of Dr. Rx, 1942; Stranger on the Third Floor, 1940; Suing the Devil, 2011; Summer Storm, 1944; Suspect, 1987; Sway, 2007; Taxi!, 1932; They Won't Believe Me, 1947; They Won't Forget, 1937 (based upon the 1913 wrongful conviction of Leo Frank for the murder of Mary Phagan, a young girl in Atlanta, Georgia, and Frank's lynching by the KKK in 1915); This Land Is Mine, 1943; Three Strangers, 1946; Time Limit, 1957 (U.S. court-martial of a U.S. officer accused of treason in Korean War); A Time to Kill, 1996; To Kill a Mockingbird, 1962; Tom und Hacke, 2012; Tombstone, 1993 (trials in Tombstone, Arizona in 1881 involving the Earp-Clanton factions); Town without Pity, 1961; Trial, 1955; The Trial, 1963; The Trial, 2010; Trial and Error, 1962; Trial and Error, 1997; The Trial of Joan of Arc, 1965; The Trial of Madeleine Smith, 1949 (made-for-TV; based on the 1857 murder case of Madeleine Smith, accused of murdering her lover in Glasgow, Scotland); The Trial of Joan of Arc, 1965; The Trial of Mary Dugan, 1929; The Trials of Oscar Wilde, 1960; True Grit, 1969; True Grit, 2010; The Truth, 1960; 12 Angry Men, 1957 (chiefly takes place inside a jury room); Twilight of Honor, 1963; Two Men in Town, 1976; Two Seconds, 1932; The Undercover Man, 1949 (based on the 1931 tax evasion case of Chicago crime boss Al Capone); The Unholy Three, 1925; The Unholy Three, 1930; The Untouchables, 1987 (based on the 1931 tax evasion case of Chicago crime boss Al Capone); The Valiant, 1929; Valiant Is the Word for Carrie, 1936; Valley of the Heart's Delight, 2009 (based upon the 1933 kidnapping-murder of department store heir Brooke Hart and the lynching of his killers, Thomas

Judy Garland and the Singer Midgets (as the Munchkins) in *The Wizard of Oz,* **1939.**

Harold Thurmond and Maurice Holmes by a mob in San Jose, California); **The Verdict**, 1982 (medical malpractice case); **Virginia City**, 1940 (U.S. military tribunal); **The Weight of Water**, 2000; **West of Memphis**, 2012; **White Mischief**, 1988 (based on the 1941 murder trial in Kenya of Sir Henry "Jock" Delves Broughton, accused of killing Josslyn Hay, Earl of Erroll, over the affections of Broughton's much younger wife); **Whose Life Is It Anyway?**, 1981 (euthanasia case); **A Wife Confesses**, 1961; **Wilde**, 1997 (Oscar Wilde); **Witness**, 1985; **A Woman's Face**, 1941; **The Wreck of the Mary Deare**, 1959; **Wyatt Earp**, 1994 (trials in Tombstone, Arizona, in 1881 involving the Earp-Clanton factions); **You Are There**, 1953-1957 (TV series; "The Dreyfus Case," 1953 episode); **Young Adam**, 2003; **The Young Land**, 1959; **Young Mr. Lincoln**, 1939; and **The Young Savages**, 1961. **p**, Arthur Hornblow, Jr.; **d**, Billy Wilder; **cast**, Tyrone Power, Marlene Dietrich, Charles Laughton, Elsa Lanchester, John Williams, Henry Daniell, Ian Wolfe, Torin Thatcher, Una O'Connor, Norma Varden, Ruta Lee, Francis Compton, Philip Tonge, Molly Roden; **w**, Wilder, Harry Kurnitz, Larry Marcus (based on the novel and play by Agatha Christie); **c**, Russell Harlan; **m**, Matty Malneck; **ed**, Daniel Mandell; **art d**, Alexandre Trauner; **set d**, Howard Bristol; **spec eff**, Lee Zavitz.

Witness to Murder ★★★ 1954; U.S.; 81m; UA; B/W; Crime Drama; Children: Unacceptable; **BD**; **DVD**; **VHS**. Taut crime yard beings when Stanwyck witnesses a woman being murdered as she looks out of the bedroom window of her apartment on a hot night in Los Angeles. The killer, Sanders, a writer of historical novels, hides the body in the room next to Stanwyck's. His victim was his mistress whom he killed because she stood in the way of his marrying a rich woman. Stanwyck calls the police about what she has seen, but Merrill, a detective, tells her she must be mistaken. Stanwyck is taken to a mental asylum, but she is later released and sees Sanders reading a newspaper article about the murder. When she confronts him about the murder she has witnessed, he boldly admits it. She later flees to a rooftop where Sanders pursues her. They struggle high on a scaffold and he falls to his death just as police arrive. Rowland keeps a firm hand on this thriller, deftly unraveling many harrowing scenes, and Stanwyck is a standout as the witness who then becomes another potential murder victim. Song: "Nowhere Blues" (Herschel Burke Gilbert, Sylvia Fine). *Author's Note*: Stanwyck told this author that "**Witness to Murder** was a very good crime picture, but it suffered at the box office because another picture was released about the same time and had a similar story. That picture was called **Rear Window** [1954] and starred Jimmy Stewart. It was directed by Alfred Hitchcock and it took all the thunder from our picture." Sanders told this author: "Oh, what a meaty role I had in that picture, an utter cad and killer. I not only defy Babs [Stanwyck] when she tells me that she has

seen me kill my mistress, but I admit murdering the woman as casually as one might remark about the weather and then dare her to do something about it. Villainous roles like that are very rare." Violence prohibits viewing by children. **p**, Chester Erskine; **d**, Roy Rowland; **cast**, Barbara Stanwyck, George Sanders, Gary Merrill, Jesse White, Harry Shannon, Claire Carleton, Lewis Martin, Dick Elliott, Juanita Moore, Harry Tyler; **w**, Chester Erskine; **c**, John Alton; **m**, Herschel Burke; Gilbert; **ed**, Robert Swink; **art d**, William Ferrari; **set d**, Alfred E. Spencer.

The Wizard of Oz ★★★★★ 1939; U.S.; 101m; MGM; B/W/Color; Fantasy/Musical; Children: Recommended; **BD**; **DVD**; **VHS**; **IV**. Perceived at the time of its release as one of the great fantasy films, this enchanting and most beloved of films opens on a Kansas farm where Garland is a fourteen-year-old girl living with Blandick, her aunt, and Grapewin, her uncle. She is surrounded by farm animals that are tended to by hired hands Bolger, Haley and Lahr. Her closest companion is a little, precocious dog, Toto. This cute canine has, unfortunately, bitten Hamilton, a mean-minded spinster traveling around on a bicycle to annoy and vex every neighbor in the county. Lonely and longing for a more exciting life, one especially away from vicious people like Hamilton, Garland wistfully sings the plaintive "Over the Rainbow." Then Hamilton appears with a court order that allows her to take Toto away to a place where the little dog will be put to sleep as a vicious animal, even though he is anything but that. Garland pleads with Blandick and Grapewin to prevent Hamilton from taking her dog, but they are helpless and tell Garland that they must comply with the law. Blandick tells Hamilton that she is nothing more than a terrible, hate-filled reprobate, but Hamilton ignores her as she places Toto in a basket and peddles off on her bicycle with the canine. Toto, however, manages to squiggle free of the basket and escapes, running back to the farm and into the arms of the crying Garland. She resolves to save her pet by running away with him. As she travels along the prairie road, she spots an old horse-drawn wagon that has broken down. There she meets Morgan, an old-time carnival performer, who calls himself Professor Marvel, a self-styled magician. The glib-talking Morgan impresses the naïve Garland no end about his abilities to bring wonders to the world, but he demonstrates no such feats of magic, even though he claims that he has performed before the crowned heads of Europe. Garland asks that she accompany him on his travels, but, when peering into his crystal ball and, rightfully suspecting that Garland has run away from home, says he sees a kindly old woman weeping over her absence. Garland thinks Morgan is seeing in that crystal ball her generous-hearted aunt, Blandick, and becomes remorseful for running away. She thanks Morgan for his invitation to see the crowned heads of Europe, but she has decided to return home. When arriving close to her farm, Garland becomes terrified to see a towering black tornado off in the distance, churning and tearing up the earth as it makes its grinding way toward her farm. While holding on to Toto, she struggles against a fierce wind to make her way to the farm. Meanwhile, Blandick, Grapewin and their three farmhands all frantically search for Garland as the the sky turns dark and winds tear through the farmyard, sending chickens flying. They battle the winds as they make their way to an underground storm cellar, going inside and closing its heavy doors behind them. Garland arrives at the farm to see everyone gone. She tries to enter the storm cellar, but she cannot open the doors as the howling winds harass her into the house. She runs to her bedroom and a storm screen is blown from its anchors, its sash striking her and knocking her unconscious so that she falls upon her bed. There she sees in her troubled dreams the tornado consuming the farmyard and swallowing the house, sending the building upward through its hollow eye. She stands up from the bed and looks from the open window to see farm animals flying about inside the twister's vortex, as well as two men rowing a boat, and an old woman in a rocking chair, who continues to knit before she is carried away. To her horror, Garland then sees Hamilton furiously peddling her cycle, as if in pursuit of her and Toto. Hamilton further shocks Garland when she transcends into a haggard-looking old witch, now wearing flowing black robes and a peaked hat as she maniacally cackles. She is no longer peddling her cycle but riding on a broomstick. The house swirls upward and then begins to plummet, falling down and down, until it crashes, coming to rest on terra firma. The jarred Garland then apprehensively leaves her bedroom and goes to the front door of the house, opening it with anxiety, only to see a world of blinding color (the film changes at this point from sepia-black-and-white to rich Technicolor) and steps outside to find herself in the strange world of Munchkin Land. She walks with Toto into this quaint little village of thatched huts, tranquil ponds and verdant bushes and trees to eventually see its inhabitants, little people who are called Munchkins. These docile little people are delighted to see her as Garland's house has landed squarely on top of and killed the Wicked Witch of the East, the vicious old harridan who has forever been making their lives miserable. The Munchkins show their deep appreciation by singing her praises and thanking her. Suddenly, a bright light descends from the skies in the form of a shimmering white bubble that transforms into Glinda, the Good Witch of the North, who is wonderfully played by Burke. She tells Garland that she is a national hero. Then a cloud of red smoke erupts nearby from which Hamilton, the Wicked Witch of the West, emerges. She is enraged that Garland's house has killed her sister, and when she threatens Garland, Burke tells her that she has no power in Munchkin Land. Hamilton then sees the feet of her sister protruding from beneath the house that has ended her vile existence. She especially covets the powerful ruby slippers that adorn the feet of that dead witch. Before Hamilton can retrieve these magical slippers, however, Burke waves her magical wand and encases Garland's feet inside those slippers, telling her that, if she stays tight inside of those ruby slippers, no harm can befall her and her little dog. Hamilton insists that the slippers now belong to her, but, as she reaches for them, the slippers send electrical shock waves that drive her back. Hamilton then leans close to Garland, her face green with livid anger (her face is truly green) and shrieks vengeance: "I'll get you, my pretty, and your little dog, too!" With that, she clutches her broomstick and disappears in a fiery cloud of red smoke. Garland is thunderstruck by her new surroundings and tells Burke that her only wish is to return to her farm in Kansas where she can be with her family. Though Burke is lovingly protective of her, she tells Garland that her powers are limited and that the only person who can send her back to her Kansas farm is the great Wizard of Oz, who resides in far-off Emerald City. To return to Kansas, Garland must travel to that city and see the Wizard. To go to Emerald City, Burke says, Garland must follow the Yellow Brick Road. The Munchkins then encourage her to take that course by singing "Follow the Yellow Brick Road," and Garland steps onto that road and leaves Munchkin Land with Toto. As she travels to her far-off destination, she comes to a crossroads where she sees a scarecrow, played by Bolger, which surprisingly comes alive. Garland helps Bolger slip from the stake to which he is nailed and he wobbles about, spilling his innards of straw. He stuffs the straw back into his shirt, and, after Garland tells him that she is going to see the Wizard, Bolger asks her if she thinks the Wizard can give him a brain, so that he can think for himself. Garland assures him that the Wizard is all powerful and is sure that he can provide that brain and Bolger sets out with her for Emerald City. While traveling along, Garland becomes hungry and sees some apple trees, but when she tries to pick an apple from a branch, the tree comes alive and slaps her with one of its branches. She recoils in shock, but Bolger tells her that he will get her some apples and, for a scarecrow who claims he has no brain, uses his considerable wits to tell the apple tree that its apples are most likely sour and not worth eating. The tree then angrily beings throwing apples at them, and Bolger gathers these for Garland to eat. The two continue their journey and then encounter a tin man, played by Haley, who stands immobile with an ax next to the road. When they approach him, Haley manages to squeak out a plea that they retrieve a nearby oil can and oil his body parts, which have been rusted and caused him to remain rigid. Once they apply the oil to the joints of his face, neck, arms and legs, he is able to move about, expressing his gratitude

Jack Haley, Ray Bolger, Judy Garland and Bert Lahr in *The Wizard of Oz,* 1939.

for his new agility. Haley tells them that he was chopping wood in the forest when a rainstorm rusted him into a fixed position. When he learns about their journey to Emerald City to see the Wizard, he asks Garland if the Wizard will give him a heart, and he bangs on his chest so that she and Bolger can hear its hollow sound. He wants a heart so that he can show his love to the animals and all other living things, and Garland promises him that the Wizard will grant his wish. Haley then happily joins Garland and Bolger on their journey to Emerald City. As the trio proceeds into a dark forest, Garland asks her companions if it might be occupied by wild animals, and Haley informs her that the forest holds some "lions and bears." Lahr, who plays a fierce-looking lion, leaps from the forest just at that time. He threatens them with roaring and pawing, but when he attempts to capture a running Toto, Garland slaps Lahr in the face. Lahr breaks down, shaking with fear and sobbing, admitting as he trembles that he is a cowardly lion and is afraid of everybody and everything. When he learns that the trio are on their way to have the Wizard of Oz help them, he begs to go along, asking if the Wizard will grant him what he needs most in life—courage. Garland assures him that the all-powerful Wizard can do that for him and he joins her, Bolger and Haley, the foursome then happily dancing along the Yellow Brick Road as they sing "We're Off to See the Wizard." Overseeing the journey the foursome take is Hamilton, who peers through her crystal ball to watch their progress. To halt them in their tracks she guides them into a field of poppies where they can see the glimmering towers of Emerald City in the far distance. As they run toward their objective, however, the poppies (representing the drug they contain) cause them to fall asleep and collapse. Burke, however, the Good Witch of the North, comes to their rescue when seeing this and waves her wand over the prone bodies of the travelers, creating a gentle falling of snow that awakes and refreshes the four so that they regain consciousness and resume their journey, leaving the poppy field and following the Yellow Brick Road right to the closed doors of Emerald City. They bang on the doors and a guard (also played by Morgan), opens it, allowing them inside where they are transported about in a carriage driven by a coachman (also played by Morgan) and which is pulled by the "Horse of a Different Color," this horse changing from one brilliant hue to another from one cut to another. The four are then separately cleaned and coiffured in beauty parlors before their meeting with the all-powerful Wizard. However, when they appear before the closed door of the Wizard's residence, a guard (also played by Morgan) refuses to let them see the man they have traveled to meet. When Garland begins to weep, now believing that she will never be able to get back to her dear old aunt, the guard begins to cry, tears streaming down his face in pouring rivulets, saying that he will somehow arrange for them to see the Wizard and allows them to enter the Wizard's inner

Margaret Hamilton, right, as the Wicked Witch in *The Wizard of Oz,* 1939.

sanctum. While waiting to see the Wizard, Lahr longingly proclaims in a delightful song how the Wizard will give him enough courage to become "King of the Forest." However, when the four enter a large chamber, they see a towering image of the fierce-looking face of the Wizard. The face booms loudly to them as they quake and tremble before that frightening image that he, the Wizard, will grant all of their wishes. However, before granting those wishes, they must first destroy the Wicked Witch of the West (Hamilton) and prove it by bringing him her broomstick. That prospect terrifies all of them and causes the utterly cowardly Lahr to race in fear from the chamber and crash through a glass wall. The four nevertheless undertake their impossible mission, but, as they travel through a dark forest, Hamilton views their progress through her crystal ball and then orders her armies of winged monkeys to attack the foursome and bring Garland and Toto to her. The winged monkeys fly as ordered, hordes of them swooping down upon Garland, Bolger, Haley, Lahr and Toto, disabling them. They then fly off, carrying Garland and Toto, taking them to Hamilton's remote mountaintop castle. The terrified Garland is threatened by Hamilton with terrible punishments, but she is restricted from injuring her as long as Garland wears the protective ruby slippers. Hamilton places a large hourglass before her, saying that when its sand runs out, Garland will face her doom. Hamilton then attempts to injure Toto, but the little dog manages to escape the castle room, race down the stone stairs to the drawbridge and leap from it before it is lifted over a moat. Toto races off to freedom among the craggy rocks, all of this seen from a window by Garland, who triumphantly cries out, "He got away! He got away!" Toto's escape further enrages Hamilton, but she bides her time and continues to plot Garland's demise. Meanwhile, Bolger, Haley and Lahr have resolved to rescue their friend Garland and, after finding Toto, are led by the dog to Hamilton's castle where they battle three of the witch's guards (all of whom have long noses and green faces similar to that of Hamilton). They disguise themselves in the heavy uniforms of the guards and join other guards marching into the castle. They then race up the castle stairs to find Garland, but Hamilton and her army of guards pursue them through the castle's battlements, trapping them in a tower room. Cornered, Hamilton slowly approaches the four, setting fire to her broomstick and thrusting this at Bolger, saying "how about a little fire, Scarecrow?" She sets Bolger's straw to flames, and Garland desperately grabs a bucket of water and douses the fire. The water, however, drenches Hamilton, and, following the tradition that water is the enemy of all witches and will destroy them, Hamilton shrieks out that she is melting. Hamilton begins to diminish in size, crying out as her hideous form collapses and melts to nothing but a soggy rag flattened to the stone floor. The guards then kneel in gratitude that Garland has destroyed the witch that has so long dominated them and they are glad to give Garland what remains of

Hamilton's singed broomstick as she and her three friends depart for Emerald City. When they again reappear before the Wizard, they are cruelly refused their requests, despite the fact that Garland and her brave friends have destroyed Hamilton and brought her broomstick as the Wizard demanded. The Wizard nevertheless orders them to depart, but Toto goes to a nearby curtain, pulling it aside to disclose a man frantically operating the controls of an elaborate machine. He is Morgan, a human being, who, after confronted by Garland and her friends, admits that he is a humbug and the actual Wizard of Oz. He states that he is "a very good man but a very bad wizard." He nevertheless is able to grant all of their wishes. He gives Bolger a diploma and the title of Professor of Thinkology to prove that he now has a brain. He bestows upon Haley a large, red, metallic heart that is a clicking clock that beats like a heart, reminding him that it is not only important to be loved by others, but to love those very people. He then gives Lahr, the cowardly lion, a medal to prove that he has displayed incredible courage, and Lahr is now filled with bravery. He also promises to grant Garland her wish by taking her personally back to Kansas in his balloon, which is momentarily about to sail from Emerald City and the Land of Oz. After Garland makes fond farewells to Haley, Lahr and Bolger, she climbs into the basket of the balloon with Morgan. Toto, however, sees a cat and leaps from the basket to chase it and Garland goes after him. The balloon begins to ascend without her, and Garland calls out for Morgan not to leave her. Morgan shouts back that he cannot help her as he does not know how the balloon works, again proving his ineptitude, despite his good intentions. As the balloon sails skyward, leaving Garland behind, she cries uncontrollably, realizing that she may never again be able to return home. Her friends Bolger, Haley and Lahr console her, telling her that they all love her and that they are happy that she can remain with them. Going home, however, is the only consolation she seeks. At that moment, Burke, the Good Witch of the North, reappears to tell Garland that she always had the ability to return home by simply clicking her ruby slippers three times and repeating the words "There's no place like home." Garland then turns to her loving friends, kissing each one of them and bidding them farewell before she clicks the heels of her slippers three times; her fondest wish comes true as she is transported back to her home (where the scene in her bedroom is now in sepia-black-and-white). She regains consciousness to see Blandick and Grapewin sitting next to her, and the farmhands, Bolger, Haley and Lahr, standing nearby, all smiling to see that she is now all right. Morgan then appears at the window, to see that Garland has survived the attack of the tornado, and all are happy to see Garland in good health. With Toto at her side, Garland is elated to be back with her family, saying that "there's no place like home." Her joyous reunion with her family and her happy return from the wonderful Land of Oz, ends this utterly enchanting and forever memorable film. Although several other notable directors, including King Vidor, George Cukor, Norman Taurog and Richard Thorpe worked on some of the scenes in the masterpiece film, most of its unforgettable scenes were helmed by pantheon director Fleming, who, not incidentally, directed the classic **Gone with the Wind** at the same time he supervised this classic in 1939. As such, he presents a film so vibrant, so exciting and so enthralling that, in its initial release, viewers saw it over and over again, and this is exactly what has happened from one generation to the next to this day the world over. It has become, perhaps beyond any other film, the most viewed feature film in history, and deservedly so. The performances from all the players are as astounding as its amazing visual effects, lavish sets and richly appointed costumes. To that time, no one had seen such special effects, from the savage tornado destroying everything in its path (the tornado was created by a thirty-five-foot piece of muslin that was constantly twisted) to the twirling house, objects and people swirling inside of it, from disappearing and reappearing witches to flying monkeys, from intemperate trees with arms that hurled its own apples to a horse that changed brilliant color before the viewer's startled eyes. Its sets were equally eye-popping, from the miniature dwellings nestling in Munchkin Land to the elegant chambers of Emerald City, from the deep forests to the witch's foreboding castle. The costuming, too, is awesomely impressive, from the elaborate clothes and uniforms of the Munchkins, to the startling costumes worn by Bolger, who wears a rubber-like Scarecrow face stretching away from his rolling eyes and the clanking metallic body encasing Haley's Tin Man that emits puffs of whistling steam from the top of his hat, an inverted metal funnel. The costume worn by Lahr as the Cowardly Lion is, perhaps, the most astonishing of all, one where his face projects an animal's snout and where his large tail wags of its own strange accord. The acting from Garland is perfect for her role, an innocent, naïve and trusting young girl who accepts the wonders that engulf her as she bravely sets out to endure one harrowing adventure after another in order to return to the front door of her home. Her shining, starry-eyed face reflects the insecurities of childhood at every hazardous turn while her indefatigable confidence, grounded on the common sense of her rock-ribbed family roots, continues to provide reassurance that all will come right at the end, which, of course, it does. Bolger is wonderful as the optimistic and often brilliant thinking Scarecrow as he wobbles about on unstable, rubbery legs, repeatedly yanked to an upright position by a steadying Garland. Haley, who sings in a fine tenor voice, is the ever stalwart Tin Man as he bangs metallically along the roads with his friends. Lahr is an unforgettable Cowardly Lion, tremoring in fear of his own shadow, perhaps the most ridiculous and hilarious of the lot of these strange but loveable characters. Garland received an Oscar as a Special Juvenile Academy Award, which also applied to her appearance the same year in **Babes in Arms**, 1939. The film received an Oscar for Best Original Score (Stothart), and an Oscar for Best Song ("Over the Rainbow," Arlen, Harburg). It also received Oscar nominations for Best Picture; Best Cinematography, Color (Rosson); Best Art Direction (Gibbons, Horning), and Best Special Effects (Gillespie, Bloomfield). It was a box office smash, earning more than $3 million in its initial release against a budget of more than $2.7 million, and, in subsequent rereleases earned more than $22 million (or almost $250 million at today's rate). MGM gleaned millions over the years beyond its theatrical releases of this film by allowing CBS, beginning in 1976, to run the film once a year at a payment of $800,000 per airing. Almost every child the world over had seen this wonderful film by the end of WWII (1939-1945), its characters and songs embedded in the public's memory. During WWII, the song "We're Off to See the Wizard" became the official marching song of the Australian army. A sixty-minute radio adaptation was aired by Lux Radio Theater on December 25, 1950, with Garland reprising her role. The story was originally filmed as a silent, **The Wizard of Oz**, 1925, and it was remade as a Broadway play in 1975 that saw a 1978 film version starring Diana Ross. An animated spin-off, **Journey Back to Oz**, 1974, saw Hamilton reprise her role as the Wicked Witch in voiceover. Disney produced **Return to Oz**, 1985, a disappointing entry, and another stage version, "Wicked," was produced on Broadway in 1995, a musical presenting the doings of the witches prior to Dorothy's unexpected arrival in Oz. In 2005, ABC-TV offered **The Muppets' Wizard of Oz**, 2005. Related films include **After the Wizard**, 2010; **Oz the Great and Powerful**, 2014 and **Legends of Oz: Dorothy's Return**, 2014. Songs: "Over the Rainbow," "Come Out, Come Out, Wherever You Are," "The House Began to Pitch," "As Mayor of the Munchkin City," "As Coroner I Must Aver," "Ding Dong, the Witch Is Dead," "Lullaby League," "Lollipop Guild," "Follow the Yellow Brick Road," "If I Only Had a Brain," "We're Off to See the Wizard," "If I Only Had a Heart," "If I Only Had the Nerve," "The Merry Old Land of Oz," "If I Were King of the Forest" (1939; music: Harold Arlen; lyrics: E.Y. Harburg); "The Happy Farmer, Op. 68, No. 10" (1848; Robert Schumann), "In the Shade of the Old Apple Tree" (1905; Egbert Van Alstyne), "Night on Bald Mountain," (1867; Modest Mussorgsky), "Home Sweet Home" (1823; H.R. Bishop), "Scherzo in EMinor, Op. 16, No. 2" (1829; Felix Mendelssohn-Bartholdy). *Author's Note*: The success of Disney's **Snow White and the Seven Dwarfs**, 1937, proved to the world that feature-length cartoons could be immensely popular with audiences and very lucrative at

Judy Garland as Dorothy and Ray Bolger as the Scarecrow in *The Wizard of Oz*, 1939.

the box office. MGM mogul Louis B. Mayer thought that the Oz story would be perfect as just such a feature, but the rights to the Baum story were then owned by producer Samuel Goldwyn. "I had been sitting like a rooster on an egg with that story," Goldwyn told this author, "and I thought for many years to make a feature length talkie film about it with Eddie Cantor as the Scarecrow, that part being the leading character. I got busy with some other projects, so I sold the rights [in January 1938] to MGM, and that was one of the biggest mistakes I ever made." LeRoy, a talented director in his own rights was named to produce the film and he quickly went about assigning a small army of writers to do treatments as well as full-length shooting scripts. "I even leaned on my fellow directors George [Cukor] and King [Vidor] to see if they could do anything with the treatments and scripts the writers were churning out," LeRoy told this author. "God Almighty, Mervyn had everyone in Hollywood working on that script," Cukor told this author. "He had his assistant Billy Cannon [William H. Cannon] do a draft that was based on the 1925 silent version of the story that got rid of all of the magic aspects to the story, which I thought was crazy, because the magic made the story magical. In that version, the scarecrow is the leading player, a man so stupid and useless that the only job he can get is to play a scarecrow in a cornfield and he even fails at that. That was the role Goldwyn wanted Eddie Cantor to play in a picture Goldwyn never made. I told Mervyn to dump Cannon's version and use Baum's original story." Vidor told this author that he urged LeRoy to do the same thing, adding: "I got a script written by Herman Mankiewicz. Though Herman was a hopeless drunk, he had a brilliant mind that worked along the lines of the original story writer [Baum], very creative and inventive, and his script packed a lot of magical elements into the story, which is what the original writer had created. I told Mervyn that he should go with that version, although Mervyn kept adding more and more writers to the script until the manuscripts filled up a large bookcase in his office." (Vidor later took credit for directing the sepia-toned segments of this film showing Garland at the beginning and end of the production after the busy Fleming was compelled to leave the production to work on **Gone with the Wind**.) Poet Ogden Nash was added to that army of writers, along with Samuel Hoffenstein, Irving Brecher, Noel Langley, Herbert Fields, Florence Ryerson, John Lee Mahin and Edgar Allan Woolf. When the final script was ready, LeRoy began casting the film. "There had been some talk that Shirley Temple or Deanna Durbin would be very good in the role of Dorothy," LeRoy told this author, "but I wanted Judy [Garland] right from the start. She was sixteen at the time we went into production, but she had that cherubic face of the fourteen-year-girl she was supposed to play. She sang like a bird and was just right for the part." Wallace Beery, who was then a leading heavy at MGM, wanted to play the part of the Wizard, but when LeRoy told MGM boss Louis

Ray Bolger (Scarecrow), Judy Garland (Dorothy) and Jack Haley (Tin Man) in *The Wizard of Oz,* 1939.

B. Mayer about that, Mayer exploded. LeRoy quoted Mayer when telling this author: "Mayer went nuts, shouting at me: 'Beery is the biggest headache on the lot! He's half-drunk most of the time, insulting and bullying everyone and picking fights even with our child stars. Absolutely not! Keep that bozo out of that production!' I went to W.C. Fields and offered him the role of the Wizard, but that shrewd old guy wheedled about until he demanded $100,000 to play the part and that was way too much for a role that is really a minor one, compared to the other parts played. When I next offered it to Ed Wynn, he told me that he was turning down the role for that very reason, that it was just too small a part. Well, we had a very good character actor at MGM named Frank Morgan and he had been badgering me and everyone else at the studio to get that part. I thought he might pull it off, but I insisted that he test for the part. He did not argue or pull any of that 'I am an established player' stuff and he made a great test, so I signed him up as the Wizard." Buddy Ebsen was then cast as the Scarecrow, even though Bolger had lobbied for that part, and Bolger was cast as the Tin Man. Ebsen, however grew ill just before production began, and Bolger became the Scarecrow, gaining immortality by happenstance. Haley was then cast as the Tin Man, a role for which he, too, would be forever remembered, but his was the most arduous and demanding of all of the characters. He suffered greatly inside his tin-made costume, overheating to the point of utter exhaustion and dizziness. "That costume was agony," he later stated. "I couldn't bend in that Tin Man thing. The only chance I had all day to get out of that costume was when Judy [Garland] was in school. Lahr was the only one of the three of Dorothy's companions who had been originally selected for his role as the Cowardly Lion and he relished his part. He, along with Haley, added bits of dialog to their roles, along with small pieces of theatrical businesses they had both used in burlesque. "Both of them were great at that," LeRoy told this author, "as they were old pro performers who knew how to squeeze every ounce of energy from their characters." Lahr told everyone on the set that his part would establish him as a foremost character player in the future. Frank Morgan, however, somewhat dampened Lahr's ebullience when he took him aside and said to Lahr: "You're going to be a great hit in this picture, but it's not going to do you a damned bit of good because you're playing an ***animal!***" Lahr later told Morgan that he was right. After weeks of playing inside of his ninety-pound costume, he complained that he dripped sweat throughout each scene, saying to Morgan: "I am not only playing an animal, I now smell like one." The role of the Wicked Witch was originally intended for either Edna May Oliver or Gale Sondergaard, but it was awarded to Hamilton, who, according to LeRoy's comments to this author "had the perfect hatchet face to play the Witch." Her role, she learned to her dismay, was laced with actual hazards. She was, for instance, badly burned more than once when act-

ing in the scenes where she appears and disappears in clouds of red smoke. These explosive scenes caused Hamilton so many burns that she had to be medically treated. She became so wary of the stunts she was compelled to perform that, for one scene, she refused to mount her broomstick, which was to take her heavenward where she writes in the skies over Emerald City the words "Surrender Dorothy." LeRoy told this author: "Vic [Victor Fleming, the director] did everything he could to get her to do that stunt, but Margaret [Hamilton] put her foot down and refused to do it. Okay, Vic said, he would embarrass her by having a stand-in do the stunt. Well, the special effects people got this gal, Betty Danko, who was Margaret's stand-in, to take that ride on the broomstick and everything went wrong with the mechanism. She was almost blown right through the roof of the sound stage and had to be rushed to a hospital where it took her two weeks to recover from her injuries. Margaret marched up to Vic and said: 'I hate to say "I told you so," but I told you so!'" A few weeks later, technicians found the witch's hat and broomstick Danko had used in that stunt still embedded in the roof of the sound stage. The part of the Good Witch Glinda was originally assigned to Helen Gilbert, but that actress suddenly disappeared (reportedly on a romantic holiday) and the delicate Burke was given the role, and she was the perfect, gentle lady descending from the skies to protectively guide Dorothy to her destination. (Burke's singing vocals were rendered by singer Lorraine Bridges.) Of all the players in this spectacular film, the 124 midgets playing the Munchkins (AT $125 per week per midget) presented LeRoy and Fleming with the most difficult problems. Some were members of the famous Singer Midgets, a vaudeville group from Vienna, Austria, managed by Leo Singer, who additionally recruited many American-born midgets for this film. After they were assembled in Hollywood for this production, they wreaked havoc everywhere. When first ensconced in a Hollywood hotel, the midgets rebelled after seeing that they had not been given small-sized (or children's) furniture in their rooms as requested. Many of them wrecked the furniture and even set fire to some of the drapes in the rooms as a form of protest. Further, many of them spoke little English and were angry when hotel employees could not speak to them in their native tongue. "Oh, they made a hell on earth for me and others," LeRoy told this author. 'The male midgets were impossible to deal with, especially the American midgets, half of them drunk most of the time, even on the set, and you can see that in the way they are staggering around in some of the scenes. I think they were angry most of the time because they knew we had altered their voices on the sound track to make them sound like squeaking Munchkins, or with deep, quavering voices that no adult would ever have. I was forever taking booze bottles away from the little guys as they sat around the set of Munchkin Land telling dirty stories and throwing knives at each other and, especially, at crew members who were very tall. They hated tall people, I guess. Some of the adult male midgets would also run under the dresses of some of the normal sized ladies and shout obscenities. I caught one of those little guys doing that and shook him like an unruly child and ordered him to behave. He shouted back at me: 'Get your hands off of me, you big jerk, or the next time I see you doze off in your producer's chair I will sneak up on you with a baseball bat and use it to put out your lights!' Can you imagine that? Here was this vicious little midget threatening to bump me off! I went to sleep that night thinking that one of those little guys might end my career before we ever finished that picture. I can't tell you what a relief it was to wrap up the scenes with those Munchkins and send them back to wherever they came from." Fleming had very little patience with anyone interrupting the scenes he directed and, at one point, had to take Garland to task. In the scene where Lahr suddenly attacks her and the others, Garland responded to Lahr's gruff antics by laughing when she was supposed to be frightened. Fleming stopped the scene, took her aside and slapped her face, telling her that this was a serious scene. She returned to obediently do the scene as directed. "He felt terribly guilty about that," LeRoy told this author. "He said: 'For God's sake, now I am down to hitting a little girl! What kind of terrible business is this? I'm worse than that damned Wicked Witch!' I mentioned that to Judy [Garland] and she immediately went to Vic [Fleming] and kissed him on the nose to show that all was forgiven. She was the sweetest little thing in Hollywood. Vic got drunk that night." The brilliantly inventive author of this great tale, L. Frank Baum (1856-1919) was a sickly boy who was forever daydreaming and, at one time, was expelled from a military school for such endless musings. He began as a writer but never had much success publishing magazines about poultry and advertising, until he began writing tales of fantasy, but, at the beginning of his creative career as a fiction writer, he seemed to go nowhere. His wife Maud thought of him as a hopeless time waster and was forever lecturing him to abandon his fairy tale writing and get a substantial job. He moved with her and their four sons to Humboldt Park, Illinois, a suburb of Chicago, in 1891. Baum so vexed his wife with his writing and his failure to make any money from that endeavor (while meagerly supporting his family as a salesman) that she insisted he quit scribbling altogether and become a "serious" man. Baum promised to do so, but kept his dreams alive by putting his desk and writing materials in a shed in the backyard of their home where he told his wife he had to work at times to repair household tools. Maud never entered that shed as Baum warned her that it had been invaded by rodents, this fabrication assuring his peace of mind. It was in that shed in the middle of the night where the frail, sickly and much henpecked writer labored to convert his daydreams into vivid literary realities. In 1897, he wrote *Mother Goose in Prose* (illustrated by Maxwell Parrish), and its publication earned him enough money so that he could quit his door-to-door salesman's job. Two years later, he published the very successful *Father Goose, His Book*, illustrated by W.W. Denslow, which presented delightful nonsense poetry. It became the top seller in the field of children's books for 1899. The following year, 1900, Baum, again using Denslow's illustrations (they shared copyrights together), published *The Wonderful Wizard of Oz*, which became an overnight publishing sensation. The riches from its publication brought the comfort and security that Maud Baum had wanted throughout all the long suffering years of her marriage with a man she had written off as "hopeless." When she finally inspected the miserable and meager workplace she had compelled her husband to furtively occupy in that shed in creating his masterpieces, she wept and said to him: "*You* are the wizard." Yes, indeed, L. Frank Baum was that very man hiding behind the curtain, or out there in the middle of the night in that little shed, forging his daydreams into fantasies that the world would joyously and forever clutch to its universal heart. Many other films depict wizards, including **After the Wizard**, 2010; **Adventure Time**, 2010- (TV series); **Arabela**, 1979 (TV series); **Arabian Knights**, 1968 (TV series); **Arthur's Quest**, 1999 (made-for-TV; Merlin)); **Bedknobs and Broomsticks**, 1971; **The Black Cauldron**, 1985; **Blackstar**, 1981-1982 (TV series); **Captain Sinbad**, 1962; **The Care Bears Adventure in Wonderland**, 1987; **Chac**, 1975; **The Church**, 1990; **The Color of Magic**, 2008- (TV miniseries); **Conan the Adventurer**, 1992-1993 (TV series); **Conan the Barbarian**, 1982; **Conan the Destroyer**, 1984; **A Connecticut Yankee**, 1931 (Merlin); **A Connecticut Yankee in King Arthur's Court**, 1949 (Merlin); **A Connecticut Yankee in King Arthur's Court**, 1989 (made-for-TV: Merlin); **Deathstalkers**, 1983; **The Desert Hawk**, 1944; **Dr. Strange**, 1978 (made-for-TV); **Dragons: Fire and Ice**, 2004 (made-for-TV); **Dragonworld: The Legend Continues**, 1999; **The Dresden Files**, 2007- (TV series); **Dragonslayer**, 1981; **Fairy Tail**, 2009- (TV series); **Fantasia**, 1940; **Fellini Satyricon**, 1969; **Fire and Ice**, 1983; **The Flight of Dragons**, 1982; **Guinevere Jones**, 2002 (TV series; Merlin); **Harry Potter and the Chamber of Secrets**, 2002; **Harry Potter and the Deathly Hallows Part 1**, 2010; **Harry Potter and the Deathly Hollows Part 2**, 2011; **Harry Potter and the Goblet of Fire**, 2005; **Harry Potter and the Half-Blood Prince**, 2009; **Harry Potter and the Order of the Phoenix**, 2007; **Harry Potter and the Prisoner of Azkaban**, 2004; **Harry Potter and the Sorcerer's Stone**, 2001; **The Hobbit**, 1977 (made-for-TV); **The Hobbit: An Unexpected Journey**, 2012; **The**

Judy Garland, lower left, back home in Kansas with her family in *The Wizard of Oz*, 1939.

Hobbit: The Battle of the Five Armies, 2014; **The Hobbit: The Desolation of Smaug**, 2013; **Hugo**, 2011; **Ice from the Sun**, 1999; **Into the Labyrinth**, 1981-1982 (TV series); **Jack the Giant Killer**, 1962; **Journey Back to Oz**, 1974; **King Arthur and the Knights of Justice**, 1992-1993 (TV series; Merlin); **Knightriders**, 1981; **Legend of the Seeker**, 2008-2010 (TV series); **Legends of Oz: Dorothy's Return**, 2014; **The Lego Movie**, 2014; **The Lord of the Rings**, 1978; **The Lord of the Rings: The Fellowship of the Ring**, 2001; **The Lord of the Rings: The Return of the King**, 2003; **The Lord of the Rings: The Two Towers**, 2002; **The Lord Protector**, 1996; **Lucinda's Spell**, 2000; **Magic Boy**, 1961; **The Magic Sword**, 1962 (Merlin); **Magos y gigantes**, 2004; **Merlin**, 1993; **Merlin**, 1998 (TV miniseries); **Merlin and the Sword**, 1985 (made-for-TV); **Merlin: The Return**, 2000; **Merlin's Apprentice**, 2006 (TV miniseries); **Mr. Merlin**, 1981-1982 (TV series); **Monty Python and the Holy Grail**, 1975; **The Muppets' Wizard of Oz**, 2005 (made-for-TV); **The New Wizard of Oz**, 1914; **Oz the Great and Powerful**, 2014; **Paganini**, 1923; **The Prestige**, 2006; **The Prince and the Evening Star**, 1979; **The Princess Bride**, 1987; **The Princess and the Pauper**, 1997 (made-for-TV); **The Return of the King**, 1980 (made-for-TV); **Return to Oz**, 1964 (made-for-TV); **Return to Oz**, 1985; **Roar**, 1997- (TV series); **The Ruby Princess Runs Away**, 2001; **Ruslan and Ludmila**, 2006; **Santa Claus**, 1959; **The Secret of NIMH**, 1982; **Shrek**, 2001; **Shrek Forever After**, 2010; **Shrek the Third**, 2007; **Shrek 2**, 2004; **The Sign of Death**, 1939; **Sinbad of the Seven Seas**, 1989; **Sinbad: The Battle of the Dark Knights**, 1998; **The Singing Princess**, 1967; **The Slayers**, 1995 (TV series); **Sleeping Beauty**, 2014; **The Sorcerer's Apprentice**, 2010; **Star Fairies**, 1985 (made-for-TV); **Stunt Rock**, 1980; **The Sword in the Stone**, 1963 (Merlin); **Troll**, 1986; **Willow**, 1988; **The Wiz**, 1978; **The Wizard**, 1989; **The Wizard**, 2015; **The Wizard of Mars**, 1965; **The Wizard of Oz**, 1925; **The Wizard of Oz**, 1982; **The Wizard of Oz**, 1990-1991 (TV series); **The Wizard of Oz on Ice**, 1996 (made-for-TV); **The Wizard of Stone Mountain**, 2011; **Wizards**, 1977; **Wizards of the Demon Sword**, 1991; **The Wizards of the Lost Kingdom**, 1985; **Wizards of the Lost Kingdom II**, 1989; **Wizards of Waverly Place**, 2007-2012 (TV series); **The Woman in Black**, 2012; **The Worst Witch**, 1986 (made-for-TV); and **Your Highness**, 2011. Also see Merlin, in Fictional Characters Index and Witchcraft in Subject Index. **p**, Mervyn LeRoy; **d**, Victor Fleming, (not credited) King Vidor; **cast**, Judy Garland, Frank Morgan, Ray Bolger, Bert Lahr, Jack Haley, Billie Burke, Margaret Hamilton, Charley Grapewin, Clara Blandick, Pat Walshe; Terry the dog as Toto, The Singer Midgets; **w**, Noel Langley, Florence Ryerson, Edgar Allan Woolf (based on the novel by L. Frank Baum); **c**, Harold Rosson; **m**, Herbert Stothart; **ed**, Blanche Sewell; **prod d**, William A. Horning, Malcolm Brown, Jack Martin Smith; **art d**, Cedric Gibbons; **set d**,

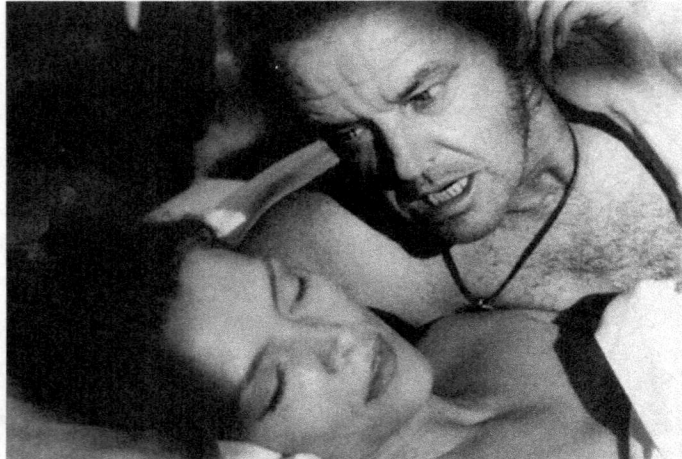

Michelle Pfeiffer and Jack Nicholson in *Wolf,* 1994.

Edwin B. Willis; **spec eff**, A. Arnold Gillespie, Edwin Bloomfield, (1998 restoration, Mark Freund).

Wolf ★★★ 1994; U.S.; 125m; COL; Color; Horror; Children: Unacceptable (MPAA: R); **BD**; **DVD**; **VHS**; **IV**. Top-notch thriller has Nicholson as an editor with a book publishing company, who, while driving home through Vermont, is bitten by a wolf that hits his car. Soon after, he is demoted from editor in chief during a takeover by Plummer, a ruthless tycoon who replaces him with Nicholson's younger and ambitious protégé, Spader. After the wolf bite, Nicholson experiences physiological changes, from increased appetites and libido, to hair regrowth and sharper sensory perceptions. Nicholson suspects his wife, Nelligan, is having an affair with Spader and, after finding them together, bites Spader. Nicholson leaves his wife and goes to a Manhattan hotel. As the moon waxes, he takes on wolf-like aggressive characteristics. With the help of Plummer's beautiful daughter, Pfeiffer, Nicholson tries to adapt to his wolf-like instincts. One night, at the guest house on the Plummer estate while visiting Pfeiffer, Nicholson partially transforms into a wolf and hunts down a deer. In the morning he finds himself by a stream with blood covering his face and hands. He seeks the advice of Puri, an Indian paranormal scholar, who gives him a silver amulet to wear around his neck to protect him from werewolf tendencies. Puri, who has been diagnosed with a terminal illness, asks Nicholson to bite him, preferring eternal damnation as a werewolf to death, but Nicholson refuses and returns to his hotel. That night, as a wolf man, he breaks into the zoo and escapes two police officers, taking their handcuffs. When muggers try to steal his money, he attacks them savagely, then returns to his hotel and sleeps, but, the next morning he remembers nothing of the previous night. Nicholson threatens Plummer by saying that most of the top writers with the publishing house will leave unless he gets the top job back. Plummer agrees, then fires Spader and Nicholson urinates on the young man's suede shoes, as a wolf might mark his territory. Nicholson finds two severed fingers in his suit coat pocket and realizes he has bitten them off as the wolf and fears the wolf is gaining control over him. Nelligan asks Nicholson to forgive her, but he refuses and immediately begins a sexual relationship with Pfeiffer in his hotel room. The next day, Jenkins, a detective, informs him that Nelligan has been savagely murdered, but it is later learned that Spader is trying to frame Nicholson in an attempt to get his job back. Jenkins learns that Nelligan's blood was contaminated by canine DNA, and Pfeiffer starts to fear that Nicholson is a murdering monster. Nicholson agrees when she suggests she lock him in the horse barn on her father's estate while she goes for police. Spader is at the police station when she arrives there and she senses he has wolf-like characteristics. She hurries back to the estate, convinced that Nicholson is innocent of his wife's murder and that Spader is the

villain and monster. She now wants to leave the country with him. Spader goes to the estate and kills two security guards. He tries to rape Pfeiffer, but Nicholson intervenes, tears off his amulet, and both men, now both werewolves, fight and are seriously injured. Spader tries to stab Nicholson with some hedge clippers, and Pfeiffer takes up the revolver that had belonged to one of the two security guards and shoots Spader dead. Nicholson, now mostly werewolf, escapes into the nearby forest. The film ends with Nicholson howling at the moon as he has transformed fully into a werewolf and then focuses on Pfeiffer whose eyes have turned amber and her gaze is no longer human as she starts to change into a wolf. Nicholson is convincing as the wolf-plagued victim turned monster and he gets good support from Nelligan, Spader, Pfeiffer and Plummer to make this a convincing and suspenseful tale of horror. The film was a hit at the box office, earning more than $131 million in its initial release against a budget of $70 million. Violence prohibits viewing by children. **p**, Douglas Wick; **d**, Mike Nichols; **cast**, Jack Nicholson, Michelle Pfeiffer, James Spader, Kate Nelligan, Richard Jenkins, Christopher Plummer, Eileen Atkins, David Hyde Pierce, Om Puri, Prunella Scales; **w**, Jim Harrison, Wesley Strick; **c**, Giuseppe Rotunno; **m**, Ennio Morricone; **ed**, Sam O'Steen; **prod d**, Jim Dultz, Bo Welch; **art d**, Tom Duffield; **set d**, Linda DeScenna; **spec eff**, Stan Parks, Alia Agha, Ryan Berg.

The Wolf Man ★★★★ 1941; U.S. 71m; UNIV; B/W; Horror; Children: Unacceptable; **BD**; **DVD**; **VHS**; **IV**. This superlative and very frightening horror tale set the bar for all of the werewolf films to come and sees exceptional performances from Chaney, Jr., Rains, and a strong supporting cast that takes a serious look at lycanthropy and those afflicted by that very real malady. Chaney is first seen as the heir to a large estate in Wales, returning to his home after completing his college education in the U.S., and where Rains, his considerate and understanding father, tolerates his inability to manage family affairs as he adjusts to his family responsibilities. While strolling in the nearby village, Chaney enters an antique store and meets attractive Ankers, the daughter of storeowner Kerrigan. After flirting with her, Chaney purchases an unusual-looking walking stick with a silver handle in the shape of a wolf's head upon which is engraved a pentagram (a five-pointed star). Ankers tells Chaney that the handle of the wolf represents an old legend about a werewolf, explaining that such a creature is a man who can somehow change into a wolf at certain times of the year. Ankers treats the subject as nothing more than an old wives' tale, playfully reciting an old cautionary poem accompanying that legend: "Even a man who is pure in heart and says his prayers by night may become a wolf when the wolfbane blooms and the autumn moon is bright." Chaney dismisses the legend as the nonsense of children and asks Ankers to accompany him that evening to visit a carnival that has just arrived in town. She agrees, but insists that they take her girlfriend, Helm, along with them. When attending the carnival that night, the trio encounters Ouspenskaya, a gypsy, and her son, Lugosi. While Helm has her fortune read by soothsayer Lugosi, Chaney and Ankers take a stroll in the moonlight. While peering into Helm's palm, Lugosi becomes alarmed at seeing the sign of the pentagram, believing this means that she is marked for death at the hands of a werewolf. Lugosi abruptly ends his palm reading and orders Helm to go away. The young woman, now frightened, runs from Lugosi's tent. Moments later, Chaney and Ankers hear Helm's screams and Chaney runs to the area. He is then attacked by a savage wolf that bites him in his chest before Chaney uses the silver-headed end of his cane to beat the savage beast to death. Chaney then collapses from his wound. Police and Ankers arrive to find him regaining consciousness while finding the bodies of Helm and Lugosi nearby. Chaney explains that a wolf attacked Helm and he ran to her rescue and was himself attacked. The police can find no dead wolf and they attribute the deaths of Helm and Lugosi to the missing beast. Bellamy, the police captain in charge of the case, however, has suspicions he keeps to himself after he sees that Helm has been murdered by having her throat savagely ripped away as if by a wild beast and Lugosi, who is barefooted, has been killed by having his head crushed. Bellamy is further confused when he finds no wound on Chaney's chest. Seeking answers, Chaney seeks out and finds Ouspenskaya, who admits that Lugosi was her son and then tells him that Lugosi was a werewolf and, now that Chaney has been bitten by him, he, too, is a werewolf. Chaney finds all of this too fantastic to believe. When the old gypsy woman looks at his chest, however, her fears are reaffirmed as she sees the image of the pentagram on Chaney's chest, the telltale sign of the werewolf. Chaney refuses to believe the gypsy's claims, even after she tells him that he will change into a wolf at the rising of the next moon, adding that a werewolf can only be killed with a silver instrument, either a knife or bullet or the kind of silver-headed cane Chaney used to kill Lugosi. Chaney returns to his family estate where he meets with his father, Rains; Bellamy; family friend Knowles, who is also interested in Ankers; and local physician William. Chaney asks William if there is any credence in the tales about were-wolves. William says that lycanthropy is a very real mental illness where deluded individuals believe that they can turn into werewolves. William refuses to believe, however, that any person can physically transform into such a savage beast. That night, Chaney locks himself inside of his bedroom, but, when the moon rises, he begins to transform into a were-wolf, his hands and feet turning into paws with long, jagged claws, his body covered with dense fur and his face distorting into that of a wolf, with a dark, wet nose and snout and a mouth snarling deadly fangs. He departs from a window and begins to search for prey. He finds a grave digger working at night and attacks him before running back to his es-tate. In the morning, Chaney awakens on his bed. He is barefooted and when he looks at the carpet and floor of his room, he sees animal tracks that lead to an open window. Bellamy and his police have by then dis-covered the body of the slain grave digger and have followed wolf tracks to Chaney's estate and manor house. Bellamy believes that a blood-thirsty wolf has killed the grave digger and has his men set traps for the animal throughout the area. That night, Chaney again transforms into a werewolf and, while stalking prey in the forest, steps into one of the traps and is caught. As the moon wanes and dawn approaches, he re-sumes his human form. Ouspenskaya, the gypsy woman, is then passing nearby in her wagon, intent on leaving the area. She helps Chaney to free himself, although she knows she cannot do a thing to lift the terrible physical curse he bears. Chaney by this time accepts the fact that he is a transforming savage beast and tells Ankers that he is a werewolf. She dismisses his statements as those of a mentally disturbed person. Chaney is convinced of his words when he sees the sign of the pentagram in the palm of her hand, now convinced that Ankers will be his next victim. He returns to his manor house where he tells Rains that he has turned into a werewolf. Rains will not accept such outlandish remarks and dis-misses such claims as nonsense. He tells Chaney that he is suffering delusions and that there is no such thing as a werewolf. Chaney insists that when the moon rises that night, he will again transform into the beast and kill once again. To prove that his son is suffering from hallu-cinations, Rains has Chaney sit in a chair and securely ties him to it so that he will not be able to leave his room, which Rains then locks. That night, Rains takes Chaney's silver-headed walking stick with him when he joins the hunting parties searching for the wolf in the forest. Mean-while, the moon rises and Chaney again transforms into the beast, easily breaking free of his bounds and escaping the mansion before entering the fog-bound forest. While Rains joins Bellamy, Knowles, William and others, Ankers enters the forest, believing that Chaney might be wan-dering about and injured if not killed when mistaken for the beast. Chaney, lurking behind a tree, sees her, and, as that very beast Ankers does not believe exists, viciously attacks her. Rains, however, comes upon the struggling couple and battles the beast while Ankers flees. Rains then ironically uses Chaney's silver-headed cane to savagely at-tack the werewolf, repeatedly striking it on the head, until killing it. To his horror, Rains looks down upon the beast to see it transform into the human form of his own son. Bellamy and others then come upon the

Lon Chaney Jr. and Maria Ouspenskaya in *The Wolf Man*, 1941.

scene where the stunned Rains remains silent and in shock. Bellamy concludes that Chaney was killed by the beast when coming to Ankers' rescue, and Rains allows him and the others to believe this false scenario for the sake of preserving his son's good name. Ouspenskaya then ap-pears to once more recite the strange prayer of the werewolf to end this superb tale of horror. Waggner directs this thriller with a firm hand and moves its well-written story along at a fast clip while Chaney, Rains, Bellamy and Ankers render standout performances. William, who had been a matinee idol in the 1930s, has a brief part in this film as the local doctor. He is marvelous when explaining in his mellifluous voice the delusionary aspects of lycanthropy, adding another chilling dimension to the concept of werewolves and their origin. Further, Ouspenskaya, a gifted European actress of great stature, lends credence to this incredible story in her restrained performance of the prophetic gypsy. The film was a tremendous hit at the box office, gleaning more than $1 million in its initial release against a budget of $180,000, this, in spite of the fact that it appeared in theaters only five days after the Japanese attacked Pearl Harbor, and even that cataclysmic event did not deter audiences from attending. ***Author's Note***: Universal had long wanted to revive its suc-cessful horror film, **Werewolf of London**, 1935, but, when doing so with this production, it decided to take an entirely different approach to the story. To that end, horror tale expert Siodmak was assigned to write a new story line for the monster. "I created that new werewolf out of whole cloth," Siodmak told this author: "Though most people thought that the poem about the moon was an old legend, I wrote that from scratch. It was so effective that it was used in a lot of the Universal films in the 1940s thereafter that dealt with the accursed creature. All that clever claptrap about how the creature could only be killed with a silver bullet or a silver weapon was exclusively mine and that went on to be-come part of the werewolf legend, too. I must admit that I consulted Bram Stoker's novel, **Dracula**, when I wrote the script for **The Wolf Man**, especially his passages about how the vampire can transform into a wolf, as well as the legends Stoker used to write that terrific tale. But the werewolf I created for that picture was all forged here [he tapped his forehead]." For many years prior to this film, Lon Chaney Jr. refused to play any monsters in films lest he invade the acting territory his cel-ebrated father, Lon Chaney Sr., had long-ago established in such silent horror classics as **The Hunchback of Notre Dame**, 1923, and **The Phantom of the Opera**, 1925. When looking at the literate and lively script the brilliant Siodmak created, however, Chaney wholeheartedly embraced the role of the werewolf. "It was my baby," he told this author. "The character of Larry Talbot became my persona and I went on to play that agonized character again and again." Chaney appeared as the lycanthropic-afflicted Talbot in such sequels as **Frankenstein Meets the Wolf Man**, 1943; **House of Frankenstein**, 1944; **House of Drac-**

Lon Chaney Jr. and Evelyn Ankers in *The Wolf Man*, 1941.

ula, 1945; and **Abbott and Costello Meet Frankenstein**, 1948. What caused Chaney the most difficulty in playing his role was the laborious makeup he had to endure as his character transforms into that werewolf. Unlike the 1935 **Werewolf of London** where Henry Hull played the beast and refused to wear the restrictive, rubbery makeup created by Jack Pierce in that production, Chaney underwent many intensive and uncomfortable hours as the same Jack Pierce applied detailed makeup to convert Chaney into that werewolf. "Jack [Pierce] was a master at makeup," Chaney told this author, "but he put me through a lot of agony to make me up into that monster. I had to sit four or five hours at a time for him to gradually apply the yak hair to my feet, arms, and hands which he singed into place with a curling iron along with spirit gum. He then slowly added the same hair and a wolf's snout to my face, along with prosthetic fangs in my mouth. During the whole procedure, the camera recorded those little changes in lap-dissolves to make it appear that I was actually transforming into that wolf. It was all achieved through his makeup working with the camera and the special effects people. When I first saw it in rushes, I was amazed and I told everyone that I would scare the hell out of anyone who went to see that picture—and I did! You know, it is a little boy's dream to be able to scare other kids and when kids can scare adults, well, that's a special treat. So, I guess it was the little boy in me that delighted in frightening people as the werewolf. After the picture came out, a woman came up to me on the street and said: 'I saw that wolf picture, Mr. Chaney, and, all I can tell you is that I would not want to be with you in a dark park at night under the moon!' I told her it was all pretend, but she looked at me as if I could actually change into that wolf. You know, when I played the same character in an Abbott and Costello picture, I tell fat, little Costello—one of the funniest men on the face of the earth—that I change into a wolf at night under a full moon. He replies: 'Yeah, you and twenty million other guys!' Well, that line so cracked me up that I had to turn away from him to keep from laughing. Are werewolves ridiculous? Of course, but people want to believe in them because they like to be scared out of their wits and that was my business." Ankers later recalled that she had a somewhat strained relationship with Chaney when first meeting him at the beginning of the film's production. Chaney had been reprimanded for trashing his dressing room when he and actor Broderick Crawford, another heavy drinker, went on a drinking spree in that dressing room. He was assigned a smaller dressing room, with the original one being assigned to Ankers. "So you're the gal who stole my dressing room?" Chaney said to her when they first met, but they soon became friends. Ankers, whose appearance in this film made her an overnight hit as a classic "screamer" in horror films, recalled how one scene in this film involved a carnival bear that Chaney wrestles and defeats. The scene, along with the bear's keeper, Kurt

Katch, was later eliminated from the film before it was released. Ankers, at that time, had become fascinated with the trained bear, which, in turn, apparently became fascinated with her. The 600-pound bear broke loose from its keeper's chain at one point and ran toward Ankers. Terrified, she climbed up a ladder toward a gaffer's platform with the bear loping after her. An electrician pulled her to safety and drove the bear away by shining a blinding klieg light in the bear's face. Adding greatly to the wonderful atmospheric scenes of this film are the well-appointed sets (by Otterson and Gausman) showing the village, the carnival grounds and the sprawling manor house where Chaney resides. The murk-filled grounds surrounding the mansion appear to be sodden with bogs and foreboding forests, where small, gnarled trees jut upward from an ugly earth that is shrouded in knee-deep fog. That fog that so doggedly clings to the earth was created with a mixture of rather dangerous chemicals and where the actors were told not to fall into them or breathe any of its fumes. Ankers, however, when rehearsing the scene where she is attacked by Chaney at the finale, went into that fog-bound area and tripped, falling and striking her head so that she was in a semi-conscious state and began inhaling the dangerous fumes in that ersatz fog. Fortunately, a crew member, when checking the area, stumbled over her prone body and quickly lifted Ankers from the fog, carrying her to her dressing room where she slowly recovered. Rains told this author that "I thought **The Wolf Man** had a very well-written script that seemed to make sense out of the nonsensical. This kind of horror story was familiar to me as I had appeared in **The Invisible Man** [1933] many years earlier and that film presented a character that was as horrific as the fang-faced creature depicted in **The Wolf Man**. Audiences love such pictures because, after they get their dose of the frights, they can leave the theater in good health while the monsters remain back there on the screen." On a personal note: This film got me into deep trouble with my mother when I first took my kid brother, Neil, to see it at the Packer Theater in Green Bay, Wisconsin (in one of its many rereleases). As soon as Chaney began to transform into the hideous-looking werewolf, Neil started to scream bloody murder (as did a lot of other younger kids in the theater). He wildly kicked the seat in front of him and pounded the arm rests and me as he continued shouting as if someone had applied a cow-prodder to him. He was the loudest screaming kid in the theater and would not stop until he fled up the aisle, running into the lobby where he continued to cry and crazily stomp around, telling the compassionate theater manager: "He's always taking me to see those boogiemen! I hate him! I hate him! Someone kick him!" He carried on so much that the manager called my mother, who roared up before the theater in her car and raced inside in what must have been a record run from our home to that theater. Neil ran into her arms, tears still streaming down his face and telling her that "Jay made me look at the boogiemen again!" My mother gave me a stern look and said: "I thought I told you to take him to see a cowboy movie!" I waved my arms in hopeless response, finally saying: "I lost my head. Sorry." My mother took Neil home, but I remained to see this film, not once, but twice more in the same day, that's how good I thought it was. Further, I did not feel a smidgeon of guilt about eating all the popcorn my brother had so foolishly abandoned while fleeing from the genuine terror of this film. Other films depicting werewolves include **Abbott and Costello Meet Frankenstein**, 1948; **An American Werewolf in London**, 1981; **An American Werewolf in Paris**, 1997; **The Beast Must Die**, 1974; **Being Human**, 2008-2014 (TV series); **Big Fish**, 2003; **Big Wolf on Campus**, 1999-2002 (TV series); **Bitten**, 2014- (TV series); **Blood of Dracula's Castle**, 1969; **The Boy Who Cried Werewolf**, 1973; **The Boy Who Cried Werewolf**, 2010 (made-for-TV); **Brotherhood of the Wolf**, 2001; **The Brothers Grimm**, 2005; **Buffy the Vampire Slayer**, 1997-2003; **The Cabin in the Woods**, 2012; **The Company of Wolves**, 1984; **Cry of the Banshee**, 1970; **Cry of the Werewolf**, 1944; **The Curse of the Werewolf**, 1961; **Dark Shadows**, 2012; **Death Valley**, 2011- (TV series); **Despicable Me**, 2010; **Dr. Terror's House of Horrors**, 1965; **Dog Soldiers**, 2002; **Dracula**, 1931; **Dracula**, 1979; **Dracula**, 1992; **Dracula Has Risen** from His Grave, 1969; Dracula—Prince of Darkness, 1966; Dracula 2000, 2000; Frankenstein Meets the Wolf Man, 1943; Fright Night, 1985; The Gates, 2010- (TV series); Ginger Snaps, 2000; Grimm, 2011- (TV series); Grindhouse, 2007; Harry Potter and the Deathly Hallows Part 1, 2010; Harry Potter and the Deathly Hollows Part 2, 2011; Harry Potter and the Half-Blood Prince, 2009; Harry Potter and the Prisoner of Azkaban, 2004; Hemlock Grove, 2013 (made-for-TV); Holloweentown, 1998 (made-for-TV); Hotel Transylvania, 2012; The House of Dracula, 1945; The House of Frankenstein, 1944; Howl, 2015; The Howling, 1981; I Was a Teenage Werewolf, 1957; Kaos, 1984; Legend of the Werewolf, 1975; The Machinest, 2004; Mad at the Moon, 1992; The Mad Monster, 1942; Mad Monster Party, 1967; The Midnight Hour, 1985 (made-for-TV); The Monster Club, 1981; The Monster Squad, 1987; The Munsters, 1964-1966 (TV series); My Mom's a Werewolf, 1989; Never Cry Werewolf, 2008 (made-for-TV); The Neverending Story, 1984; Night of the Werewolf, 1981; The Nightmare before Christmas, 1993; Nosferatu, 1922; Nosferatu: The Vampire, 1979; Penny Dreadful, 2014- (TV series); Providence, 1977; Red: Werewolf Hunter, 2010; The Return of the Vampire, 1944; Sanctuary, 2008- (TV series); Scream of the Wolf, 1974 (made-for-TV); She-Wolf of London, 1990-1991 (TV series); Silver Bullet, 1985; Spring, 2014; Supernatural, 2005- (TV series); Tales of Halloween, 2015; Teen Wolf, 1985; Teen Wolf, 2011- (TV series); The 10th Kingdom, 2000 (TV miniseries); Transylvania 6-5000, 1985; True Blood, 2008-2014 (TV series); Underworld, 2003; Underworld: Evolution, 2006; Underworld: Rise of the Lycans, 2009; The Undying Monster, 1942; The Vampire Diaries, 2009- (TV series); Van Helsing, 2004; Waxwork, 1988; What We Do in the Shadows, 2014; The Werewolf, 1956; Werewolf, 1987-1988 (TV series); Werewolf, 2012; Werewolf of London, 1935; The Werewolf of Washington, 1973; Werewolf Women, 1977; When Animals Dream, 2014; Wolf, 1994; Wolf Children, 2012; Wolf Girl, 2001 (made-for-TV); Wolfblood, 2012- (TV series); Wolfen, 1981; Wolfman, 1979; The Wolfman, 2010; Wolves, 2014; and Wolf's Rain, 2003- (TV series). p&d, George Waggner; cast, Claude Rains, Lon Chaney, Jr., Ralph Bellamy, Warren William, Patric Knowles, Bela Lugosi, Maria Ouspenskaya, Evelyn Ankers, Fay Helm, J.M. Kerrigan, Doris Lloyd; w, Curt Siodmak; c, Joseph Valentine; m, Charles Previn; ed, Ted Kent; art d, Jack Otterson; set d, Russell A. Gausman; spec eff, John P. Fulton, Ellis Burman.

The Wolf Song ★★★★ 1929 (part sound); U.S.; 93m; PAR; B/W; Romance/Western; Children: Unacceptable. Cooper and Velez sizzle in this torrid romantic film set in 1840s California and Canada. Cooper is a rugged trapper from Kentucky who has gone to the Far West to glean pelts and where he enjoys his outdoor life with pals Romanoff and Wolheim. His wild ways are tamed after he meets fiery Velez, the daughter of Mexican don Vavitch. Her father, however, does not think that ruffian Cooper is a suitable husband for Velez and refuses to sanction their union. Cooper cannot tolerate this and takes action by carrying Velez with him to his mountain retreat, and she is more than willing to elope with the rough-hewn pioneer. They are married and settle down. Cooper's wanderlust, and his yearning to be with his friends Romanoff and Wolheim, however, gets the better of him, and he goes off in search of more adventure, leaving Velez behind. He then has second thoughts about deserting the woman he loves and decides to return, but he is ambushed by a band of Indians led by Regas. Though he is wounded, and manages to eventually dispatch his old enemy Regas, Cooper finds his way back to his cabin and Velez. She seethes with resentment over his abandoning her, but she also loves her errant husband and nurtures him back to health and eventually welcomes him back into her arms. Action director Fleming (who was known as a "man's director") helms this film at a fast pace and packs considerable action into its vivid scenes where Cooper and Velez passionately spark together. The film was a hit at the box office and caused more than a little attention due to one controver-

Gary Cooper and Lupe Velez in *The Wolf Song,* 1929..

sial scene where Velez goes swimming in a mountain pool in the altogether. Fleming shot this scene, however, at such a long distance, that Velez's nude body is hardly discernible, although such a scene would never be allowed a few years later when strict censorship codes were established. Though the film is a silent, it offered sound effects and three songs that were sung by Velez and appeared with a synchronized score when the film was released. Songs: "Love Take My Heart" (Arthur J. Lamb, A. Teres), "Mi Amado" (music: Harry Warren; lyrics: Sam Lewis, Joe Young), "Yo Te Amo Mean I Love You" (music: Richard A. Whiting; lyrics: Al Bryan). *Author's Note*: Cooper told this author that **Wolf Song** "was one of my early westerns, the kind of picture where I was most comfortable. We shot that one up in the mountains, the great outdoors. I always felt uneasy when I had to play in drawing room stories. The open sky offers a greater roof than any sound stage. You know, before I went to Hollywood, I worked as a guide at Yellowstone Park and that was one of the best jobs I ever had, and maybe the healthiest." Henry Hathaway served as an assistant director on this production and later went on to direct Cooper in many of his best films, including **The Lives of a Bengal Lancer**, 1935; **Souls at Sea**, 1937; and **The Real Glory**, 1939. Hathaway told this author: "When Coop met that 'Mexican Spitfire' [Velez's nickname] on the set of **Wolf Song**, he was immediately head over heels in love with her. I mean, the man was daffy over that little lady. He mooned around when she was off the set and when they were together, well, those embraces and passionate kisses you see in that picture were for real. The studio [Paramount] did not want any part of that romance as they wanted Cooper to remain unmarried, believing that every woman who saw him on the screen wanted him for themselves. They even took Coop and Lupe aside and ordered them to not only stay apart but to even forget about getting married, especially after the gossip columnists got hold of their affair and began writing about it. That gossip helped the picture a lot at the box office, but Paramount wanted that romance to stop. It didn't. Coop and Lupe stayed together for the next couple of years before they went their separate ways." Hathaway remained one of Cooper's closest friends until the end of the actor's life, the director being one of the pallbearers at Cooper's funeral. p, Lucien Hubbard; d, Victor Fleming; cast, Gary Cooper, Lupe Velez, Louis Wolheim, Constantine Romanoff, Michael Vavitch, Ann Brody, Russ Columbo, Augustina Lopez, George Regas, Leone Lane; w, John Farrow, Keene Thompson, Julian Johnson (titles), (based on the novel by Harvey Fergusson); c, Allen Siegler; m, Gerard Carbonara, Max Bergunker; ed, Eda Warren.

Wolfen ★★★ 1981; U.S.; 115m; Orion/WB; Color; Horror; Children: Unacceptable (MPAA: R); DVD; VHS; IV. Riveting tale has Finney, a New York police captain, assigned to investigate a bizarre string of vi-

Benicio Del Toro as a werewolf in *The Wolfman*, 2010.

olent murders after wealthy Brown, his wife, Pohtamo, and bodyguard, McCurry, are slain in Battery Park. Brown's client blames the murders on terrorists, but McCurry was a 300-pound Haitian with ties to voodoo. Finney and Venora, a criminal psychologist, team to investigate. After a street person is torn to pieces at an abandoned church and, while checking it out, Finney hears a wolf's howl. Next, a bridge worker is similarly murdered. The sleuthing leads to learning that the killer is Wolfen, a wolf spirit that kills to protect its Battery Park hunting grounds. A wolfen pack nearly kills Finney and Venora, but, after Finney destroys a model of a construction project that threatened the wolfen's hunting grounds, the pack suddenly disappears. Finney is outstanding as the dogged police sleuth and gets good support from a talented cast in what is truly a frightening film from beginning to end. The film, however, did not do as well as expected at the box office, earning more than $10 million in its initial release against a budget of $17 million. Song: "Jitterbug Boy" (Tom Waits). Violence prohibits viewing by children. **p**, Rupert Hitzig; **d**, Michael Wadleigh; **cast**, Albert Finney, Diane Venora, Edward James Olmos, Gregory Hines, Tom Noonan, Dick O'Neill, Dehl Berti, Max M. Brown, Anne Marie Pohtamo, Sam Gray, John McCurry; **w**, Wadleigh, David Eyre, Eric Roth (based on a story by Wadleigh, Eyre and the novel by Whitley Strieber); **c**, Gerry Fisher (Panavision; Technicolor); **m**, James Horner; **ed**, Marshall M. Borden, Martin Bram, Dennis Dolan, Chris Lebenzon; **prod d**, Paul Sybert; **art d**, David Chapman; **set d**, Alan Hicks; **spec eff**, Conrad Brink, Roy Ottesen, Bill Traynor.

The Wolfman ★★★ 2010; U.S.; 103m; Relativity Media/UNIV; Color; Horror; Children: Unacceptable (MPAA: R); **BD**; **DVD**; **IV**. Lavishly appointed horror tale updates the 1941 classic with many new twists and no little gore. The story begins in 1891 England, where Merrells is attacked and killed by a creature in the woods on the family estate at Blackmoor. Blunt, his fiancée, contacts his brother, Del Toro, a famous Shakespearean actor, telling him that Merrells disappeared a month ago. Del Toro leaves his theatrical tour to return to Blackmoor where he is reunited with his estranged father, Hopkins. Merrells' mauled body is found and around his neck is a medallion police suspect he received from gypsies, who are camped outside the nearby town. At the town pub, Del Toro hears locals blame the gypsies and one tells of a similar killing several decades earlier when a werewolf was suspected of having killed someone. Del Toro then recalls his boyhood at Blackmoor when his mother committed suicide. He remembers seeing Hopkins standing over her dead body, and then Hopkins committing him to an insane asylum in London for suffering delusions. Del Toro visits the gypsy camp during a full moon. Townspeople raid the camp to confiscate a dancing bear they believe is the killer. (The dancing bear scene shown here takes

a large leaf from the 1941 film **The Wolf Man**, which featured a dancing bear, but that scene was cut out of that film to resurface here in its own unique sequence.) The creature attacks, slaughtering some of the people. A boy, Adams, becomes frightened and runs into the woods and Del Toro runs after him and is savagely mauled by the creature. The townspeople chase the creature away with gunfire. Chaplin, a gypsy woman, sews up Del Toro's neck wounds and her daughter insists that he be killed because he is now a werewolf and will kill again, but Chaplin refuses, saying he is still a man and that only a loved one can change him from being a werewolf. Blunt cares for Del Toro at Talbot Hall on the Blackmoor estate where he suffers some bad dreams, but, after a few weeks, he appears to have completely recovered. Malik, a family servant, shows Del Toro some silver bullets and cautions him that something monstrous is loose on the grounds of the estate. Weaving, a Scotland Yard detective, arrives to investigate the mysterious murder of Merrells and the attack on Del Toro. Because of Del Toro's mental history and his portrayals of mentally ill protagonists such as Hamlet and Macbeth, Weaving suspects he is the demented killer. Del Toro goes to his mother's crypt and she tells him he has been "dead" for years, so he locks himself in the room alone. He undergoes a transformation into the Wolfman, then runs into the woods and kills wolf hunters there. Del Toro is captured and taken to the same asylum he had been committed to as a boy. Hopkins visits him and explains that years ago, when he was hunting in India, he had been bitten by a feral boy and infected with lycanthropy. Now Del Toro realizes that when he saw Hopkins standing over the body of his mother, his father was at that moment, a werewolf who had killed her. Hopkins, again as a werewolf, had killed Merrells after a drunken argument with him. During a full moon, while in the asylum, Del Toro again transforms into his werewolf self and kills his doctor. He then goes on a murderous rampage in the streets of London as a werewolf before escaping back to Blackmoor. He confronts his father and the two accept the inevitable as they both transform into werewolves and fight to the death in a wild battle through the halls of the family mansion until Del Toro kills Hopkins. Weaving arrives just as Del Toro sees and attempts to attack Blunt, the detective firing at him. Del Toro then bites Weaving and pursues Blunt. She is trapped at a gorge and pleads with him to recognize her as the woman he loves. When Del Toro hesitates, Blunt aims and fires a revolver that sends a silver bullet into Del Toro, mortally wounding him. Del Toro, before dying in her arms, thanks her for ending his agony-filled life and killing the monster that has dwelled within him. (Again, this film takes another leaf from yet another such film, **Werewolf of London**, 1935, the film that began the werewolf craze on the screen, where Henry Hull, playing that werewolf, is shot to death by police at the finale, saying: "Thanks for the bullet!") Del Toro then changes back to his human form and dies just as Weaving arrives with a number of hunters. Weaving looks upward to see the full moon, realizing his grim fate. He had been bitten by Del Toro, and will soon join that predatory and unnatural federation of the night. At the grim finale, we hear a wolf howling in the distance. Though this film is well made and sees top-flight acting from Del Toro, Hopkins, Blunt, Weaving and the rest of the cast, it did not do as well as expected at the box office. The film earned more than $139 million in its initial release, but that did not offset its staggering budget of more than $150 million. Of special note are the amazing special effects used to transform the humans into werewolves, along with the spectacular action scenes, particularly where Del Toro rampages through London, slaying at will, and scampering and leaping from one rooftop to another. Violence and gore prohibit viewing by children. For a list of similar films see Subject Index, Werewolves. **p**, Sean Daniel, Benicio Del Toro, Scott Stuber, Rick Yorn, Stratton Leopold; **d**, Joe Johnston; **cast**, Del Toro, Anthony Hopkins, Emily Blunt, Art Malik, Hugo Weaving, Geraldine Chaplin, Simon Merrells, Gemma Whelan, Mario Marin-Borquez, Asa Butterfield, Cristina Contes, Max von Sydow; **w**, David Self, Andrew Kevin Walker (based on a 1941 screenplay by Curt Siodmak); **c**, Shelly Johnson; **m**, Danny Elfman; **ed**, Walter Murch, Dennis Virkler; **prod d**, Rick

Heinrichs; **art d**, John Dexter, Philip Harvey, Andy Nicholson; **set d**, John Bush; **spec eff**, Paul Corbould.

The Woman I Love ★★★ 1937; U.S.; 85m; RKO; Drama/Romance; Children: Unacceptable. Muni again provides a riveting performance, this time as a French pilot fighting in WWI (1914-1918). He is an indefatigable warrior of the skies, but his wife, Hopkins, who is a nurse, constantly worries about his safety, until their relationship becomes strained. Further, Muni develops the reputation of being a jinx as almost every observer and rear-seat gunner flying with him is either seriously wounded or killed. He becomes so much of a Jonah that Clive, his squadron commander, cannot persuade anyone to fly with him. This changes when Hayward reports to the squadron and readily agrees to fly with Muni. Hayward then falls in love with Hopkins, not realizing that she is Muni's wife when they first meet and begin their affair. Clive then orders his squadron into the air to accomplish an extra hazardous mission. After a wild battle in the air with the enemy, Muni manages to return to his base and land his crippled plane, but Hayward is found dead in his seat and Muni is critically wounded. He is rushed to a hospital where Hopkins nurses him back to health. In the process, Muni routinely looks over Hayward's personal effects, and is shocked to see a photo of Hopkins and an affectionate letter Hopkins had sent to the now dead Hayward. Hopkins then admits having an affair with Hayward and begs Muni to forgive her. This he finds almost impossible to do, but his love for Hopkins still abides and he finally relents as they plan a better marriage together while Muni slowly regains his health. Though the script is a bit turgid and melodramatic, the acting by all is superior and the aerial sequences choreographed by pilot Paul Mantz are impressive. The film, however, did not do well at the box office, earning less than $800,000 in its initial release against a budget of $725,000. *Author's Note*: This film was a remake of **L'equipage** (aka: **Flight Into Darkness**), which Litvak had filmed in France in 1935 and was released in the U.S. in 1938, a year after this film. When RKO decided to produce this film, Charles Boyer was offered the role of the jinxed pilot. "Charles [Boyer] did not want to play the part," Muni told this author, "and when it was offered to me, I agreed because I thought the part I would be playing had some considerable depth of character that I might explore in a wartime setting. I was never deeply interested in playing in war dramas and I only did a few of those type of pictures later on [**Commandos Strike at Dawn**, 1942; **Counter-Attack**, 1945]. War themes always dominate any story line, but in **The Woman I Love**, I was able to present an exceptional type of character, a man who becomes a pariah and is disliked by his own comrades almost as much as he is hated by the enemy. It is the irony and circumstances of war that disenfranchises him. He must battle in the air with the enemy and on the ground to regain his status within his own society. *That* I found very interesting." The film, nevertheless, remains an anomaly in that it was sandwiched between two of Muni's classic films, **The Good Earth**, 1937, and **The Life of Emile Zola**, 1937. This film marked the tragic end for former matinee idol Colin Clive, who had electrified audiences six years earlier as the creator of the monster in **Frankenstein**, 1931. He had reprised that role in the equally terrifying **The Bride of Frankenstein**, 1935, both films directed by his good friend and sometimes homosexual lover James Whale. Clive had never wanted to be an actor but had ambitions to become a distinguished officer in the British army, following in the tradition of his ancestor, Clive of India (Robert Clive, 1725-1774), who established the British Empire in India. Ironically, he appeared as just such an officer in the film about his famous antecedent, **Clive of India**, 1935, starring Ronald Colman as Clive. Early in his adult life, Clive was seriously injured when horse riding and falling from his mount, breaking a leg and causing him to walk with a slight limp thereafter. That injury prevented him from entering active service in the British army and he then pursued a career in acting. He was even then a heavy drinker when he replaced Laurence Olivier in the London stage production of "Journey's End," in 1928, which was then being directed by an

Miriam Hopkins and Paul Muni in *The Woman I Love,* 1937.

up-and-coming stage and film director, James Whale. The success of that play sent Whale to Hollywood to make its film version, **Journey's End**, 1930, with Clive playing the lead role of the alcoholic captain agonizing over the deaths of the men he sends to fight in the trenches of WWI (1914-1918). Whale perversely admitted some years later that he wanted Clive to play that role because he wanted an actual alcoholic to enact the role, and also admitted that Clive was often half inebriated when playing some of the scenes in that film. Clive attempted to rehabilitate himself many times, but to no avail. He spent his time mostly in New York, living at the Algonquin Hotel (but never participating in the meetings with the many celebrities attending its Round Table sessions), and he worked in stage productions. He got the reputation of being an unreliable drunk and few directors wanted to cast him in any role. When Otto Preminger was casting for a new production, "Libel," a courtroom drama, Clive asked that director for a role. "I knew he was a heavy drinker," Preminger told this author, "but he promised me that he was on the wagon and could manage his role, so I took a chance with him and gave him the part." Clive was sober through the play's out-of-town performances, but when Preminger held a champagne party in Philadelphia to celebrate the production's 100th performance, Clive fell off that wagon. "He had one drink after another and could not stop, until he had to be carried to his hotel room," Preminger told this author. "It was a shame, such a fine actor. Well, he went back out to Hollywood and appeared in a couple of more pictures. One of them was being directed by my good friend, Anatole Litvak, who asked me if he could rely on Clive if he cast him in that picture [**The Man I Love**], and I said, 'yes, as long as you watch him like a hawk.'" Litvak did exactly that, but was dumbfounded when he could not determine how Clive was sneaking liquor into his dressing room. Although Clive gives a top-notch performance in this film, he was drinking so heavily during its productions that all of his scenes had to be shot before noon. By that time, he was hopelessly drunk and unable to go before the camera. Preminger further recalled for this author: "Anatole [Litvak] later told me that, to complete some of Clive's final scenes, he had to be held upright while the camera shot over his shoulders." Two months after this film was released, Clive died of pneumonia, complicated by acute alcoholism, dying on June 25, 1937, at the age of thirty-seven. His good friend, James Whale, did not attend his funeral and neither did Clive's wife, actress and writer Jeanne De Casalis. She sent only a spray of flowers to his bier, her relationship with Clive having then so miserably deteriorated. When she later published her memoirs, she made no mention of her former spouse. Clive, ironically and while making this film, obliquely prophesized his own premature death when taking young Louis Hayward aside and saying to him: "My dear sir, get out of this business! It will kill you! It will kill you!" **p**, Albert Lewis; **d**, Anatole Litvak; **cast**, Paul Muni, Miriam Hop-

Sally Shepherd, Henry Daniell, Basil Rathbone (sitting), Olaf Hytten and Hillary Brooke in *The Woman in Green*, 1945.

kins, Louis Hayward, Colin Clive, Minor Watson, Elisabeth Risdon, Paul Guilfoyle, Mady Christians, Alec Craig, Sterling Holloway, Don "Red" Barry, Alan Curtis; **w**, Mary Borden (based on the novel *L'equipage* by Joseph Kessell; **c**, Charles Rosher; **m**, Arthur Honegger, Maurice Thiriet; **ed**, Henri Rust; **art d**, Van Nest Polglase; **spec eff**, Vernon L. Walker, Russell A. Cully.

The Woman in Green ★★★ 1945; U.S.; 68m; UNIV; B/W; Mystery; Children: Unacceptable; **DVD**; **VHS**; **IV**. Rathbone again plays the indefatigable Sherlock Holmes in this good mystery. He and his associate, Bruce, playing the endearing Dr. Watson, investigate after several women are murdered and their forefingers were severed. Cavanagh, a widower of British nobility, visits beautiful Brooke at her apartment where she hypnotizes him. He awakens the next morning with no memory of the night before, but he finds a forefinger in his suit coat pocket, so he believes he is the serial killer. Amber, his daughter, goes to Rathbone and Bruce, without realizing she is being followed by henchmen in the employ of Holmes' nemesis, Professor Moriarity, who is played by Daniell. Amber tells the sleuths that she saw Cavanagh bury a forefinger under some earth, and that she later dug it up, showing this grisly human artifact to them. When the two accompany Amber home, they find Cavanagh dead, and Rathbone suspects that he was murdered by someone who had been blackmailing him. Bruce then gets a phone call to help a woman who has taken a fall when feeding her pet bird. After he leaves Rathbone at their apartment, Daniell arrives and admits to the great detective that he faked the phone call, so he could talk to Rathbone alone. A sniper in a house across the street then fires at Rathbone, but the shot strikes a bust of Julius Caesar that Rathbone had placed near a window as a substitute target. Daniell escapes after his ruse misfires, and Rathbone later befriends Brooke. He rightly concludes that she is in league with Daniell. She takes Rathbone to her apartment where she believes she has hypnotized him. One of Daniell's henchmen then cuts Rathbone with a knife to verify that he is hypnotized. Rathbone is then ordered to write a suicide note, which he does. Rathbone, under supposed hypnosis, is instructed by Daniell to walk along an outdoor high ledge in Brooke's building where he will fall to his death. Rathbone walks precariously along that ledge, but, just before he plummets to his death, Bruce and Boulton, a police inspector, arrive. Rathbone calmly steps down from the ledge to prove that he was conscious all along and aware of his nemesiss' lethal intentions. He states that he had earlier taken a drug that prevented him from feeling any pain when he had been cut to test his hypnotic state. Daniell is arrested but escapes and, while leaping to another building, clings to a pipe, but it gives way and he falls to his death. Rathbone had suspected that Daniell was behind the murders in a plan to make rich, single men like Cavanagh believe they committed the crimes in order to blackmail them. Daniell had counted on the men being too terrified to expose the scheme. Neill again provides another absorbing, suspense-filled mystery, and the master sleuth is superbly represented by his most accomplished and polished interpreter, Rathbone. Bruce also provides, as usual, many humorous moments, particularly when he subjects himself to hypnotism at the Mesmer Club to unwittingly remove his shoes. Visual bonuses are presented by the beautiful Brooke and the insidious Daniell, who both convincingly provide a strong dose of villainy. **Author's Note**: Rathbone told this author that "when making that picture, Hillary [Brooke] and I attempted to entertain the cast and crew members by putting on a Drunk Act at the bar on the set of the Mesmer Club where everyone is trying to out-hypnotize each other in the story. Everyone enjoyed our impromptu performance during that break, except Mr. Daniell, who stood silently before us while the others laughed at our antics. 'What's the matter, Henry,' I asked him, 'didn't you like our little performance?' He replied with his usual dour delivery: 'I am here to perform as an actor, not to be amused by other actors.' Well, he was true to his form—sour-faced to the end." **p&d**, Roy William Neill; **cast**, Basil Rathbone, Nigel Bruce, Hillary Brooke, Henry Daniell, Paul Cavanagh, Matthew Boulton, Eve Amber, Frederick Worlock, Mary Gordon, Sally Shepherd, Fred Aldrich; **w**, Bertram Millhauser (based on characters created by Sir Arthur Conan Doyle); **c**, Virgil Miller; **m**, Paul Dessau; **ed**, Edward Curtiss; **art d**, John B. Goodman, Martin Obzina; **set d**, Russell A. Gausman, Ted Von Hemert; **spec eff**, Chris Guthrie, John P. Fulton.

Woman in Hiding ★★★ 1950; U.S.; 92m; UNIV; B/W; Crime Drama; Children: Unacceptable; **DVD**; **VHS**. This intense thriller opens with a great action shot showing Lupino driving along a road at breakneck speeds. Her car crashes and falls into a river. We next see her in flashback when she is living in a small Tennessee town and where she is the daughter of Litel, a wealthy mill owner. McNally, general manager of the mill, was once a wealthy man, but he is now in need of money, so he plans to kill Litel and marry Lupino, thereby gaining ownership of the mill and Lupino's considerable estate. Litel falls to his death at the mill, or is pushed, his grim demise unclear. The suave and conniving McNally then romances Lupino, and they are married, a union that soon begins to sour when he plots to kill her. Dow, a woman jealous of Lupino over McNally's affections, tells her that McNally only married her to gain control of the mill. Believing Dow, Lupino demands the marriage be annulled. McNally then tampers with the brakes on her car, which causes the crash into the river. We see in flash-forward to the present time as Lupino leaps from the car just before it crashes into the river, and where she moves to Knoxville under an assumed name. The handsome and rugged Duff, recently discharged from army service in World War II (1939-1945), recognizes her from notices that she is a rich man's missing wife. Duff pretends to be interested in Lupino romantically, but he is more interested in the $5,000 reward McNally has offered for her return. McNally learns of Lupino's whereabouts and, at a convention in a hotel, he almost succeeds in killing her. By this time, Duff has come to love Lupino and becomes her protector, taking her back to her small town to resolve matters with the treacherous McNally, who is now running the mill. McNally sees his chance to rid himself of Lupino once and for all when she appears at the mill, but, while searching for her in the dark, he mistakes Dow for her and kills his mistress. Duff, who has also been searching for Lupino, comes upon McNally and the two men fiercely fight and McNally is killed. Lupino is now free of being hunted like an animal and looks forward to a happy union with Duff. The acting from Lupino, McNally, Duff and Dow is superior, and the script that drives this compelling story line provides intelligent dialog and evocative scenes, all well managed under the helm of Gordon. A sixty-minute radio adaptation was aired by the Screen Guild Theater of November 30, 1950, with Lupino and Duff reprising their roles. **Author's Note**: Lupino told this author that "**Woman in Hiding** was a picture that offered a lot of depth to its characters, and it impressed me so

Is this the correct caption and photo?

much that, after I became a director about the same time we made that picture, I concentrated on film noir productions like that one. It's not enough to present frightening scenes to audiences—you have to convince viewers that those in peril are genuine people, so the scripts, like the one we had for **Woman in Hiding**, must have characters with a lot of substance." Lupino purposely set out to become a director after working at Warner Brothers as a contract actress. She visited the sets of many "A" productions, meeting and learning from top-flight directors the ins and outs of filmmaking. She began by making small-budgeted but riveting film noir films, including **Outrage**, 1949; **The Hitchhiker**, 1953; and **The Bigamist**, 1953. She became known as the only woman in Hollywood then directing films who earned widespread respect from her male peers. Lupino met Duff for the first time when making this film and they fell in love, marrying the next year, a union that lasted for thirty-three years until ending in divorce in 1984. Everyone connected to this film seemed to get into the act. Its producer, Kraike, makes a cameo appearance as a man reading a newspaper and director Gordon appears in another cameo as a man opening a locker. Dow, an attractive blonde, who started out as a model and debuted in her first feature film a year earlier, **Undertow**, 1949, would go on to appear in the classic comedy **Harvey**, 1950, starring James Stewart and released the same year as this film. She met and married Walter Helmerich, an oil man, and quit Hollywood flat (after appearing in nine feature films, from 1949 to 1951), moving to Tulsa, Oklahoma where she and her husband raised five sons. **p**, Michel Kraike; **d**, Michael Gordon; **cast**, Ida Lupino, Howard Duff, Stephen McNally, Peggy Dow, John Litel, Taylor Holmes, Irving Bacon, Don Beddoe, Joe Besser, Tony Curtis (voice only); **w**, Oscar Saul, Roy Huggins (based on the novel *Fugitive from Terror* by James Webb); **c**, William Daniels; **m**, Frank Skinner; **ed**, Milton Carruth; **art d**, Robert Clatworthy, Bernard Herzbrun; **set d**, Russell A. Gausman, Ruby R. Levitt; **spec eff**, David S. Horsley.

The Woman in Red ★★★ 1935; U.S.; 68m; First National/WB; B/W; Drama/Romance; Children: Unacceptable; **DVD**. Edgy high society drama centers on the dynamic Stanwyck, who works as a stable hand and rides show horses for Tobin, a rich widow. She meets Raymond, scion of a once-wealthy Long Island, New York, family, who now rides polo ponies for Tobin. Raymond and wealthy Eldredge, who rides his own show horses in competitions, compete for Stanwyck's affections, but she chooses Raymond. This so irritates Tobin, who also loves Raymond, that she fires Raymond, but this does not deter the two lovers from eloping. Raymond introduces Stanwyck to his family of snobs, who treat her as a person socially unfit for their elitist circles. They are further annoyed when the newlyweds begin handling horses for wealthy neighbors. Stanwyck hopes that her grandfather in Kentucky will make them a loan, but when she fails to receive those funds she borrows from Eldredge to finance her operation, but without telling Raymond. When Eldredge asks Stanwyck to help him entertain a wealthy client aboard his yacht, she agrees. The client shows up at the yacht drunk with Tree, a showgirl, in the same condition. Tree falls overboard and drowns, and one of the ship's officers blames Eldredge, who is arrested and charged with the girl's death. At the trial, it is revealed that a mysterious "woman in red" had been seen leaving the yacht that night. The evidence against Eldredge mounts and it appears that he will be convicted, until Stanwyck testifies that she was that mystery woman, testifying that she saw Tree accidentally fall overboard while drunk. Her testimony saves Eldredge, and Stanwyck now worries that her admission will ruin her marriage. Raymond, however, is an understanding and compassionate spouse, and he welcomes her back into his arms, believing that she is a courageous woman and has nothing to feel guilty about. The melodramatic story does not detract from very strong performances from Stanwyck, Raymond and Eldredge, their well-acted characters sustaining interest throughout. The film was a success at the box office. Not related to a 1984 comedy of the same name. Songs: "I Only Have Eyes for You" (1934; music: Harry Warren; lyrics: Al Dubin), "So Close to the Forest"

Joan Bennett and Edward G. Robinson in *The Woman in the Window,* 1944.

(Larry Spier). *Author's Note*: Stanwyck told this author that "Bette Davis was scheduled to play the leading lady in **The Woman in Red**, but when their feisty gal said no to the part, they gave me that hand-me-down role. Well, I couldn't afford to be as temperamental as Bette, and played the role and I played it to the hilt. I guess I wrung out every ounce of water from that part, but audiences liked it because those were the days of the great tearjerkers. Everybody had a lot to cry about. We were in a Great Depression where people could afford only to see movies as their entertainment. So we gave them everything we had, even Bette, when she deigned to appear in a picture." **p**, Harry Joe Brown; **d**, Robert Florey; **cast**, Barbara Stanwyck, Gene Raymond, Genevieve Tobin, John Eldredge, Phillip Reed, Dorothy Tree, Nella Walker, Claude Gillingwater, Doris Lloyd, Jack Mulhall, Ann Shoemaker, Arthur Treacher; **w**, Mary C. McCall Jr., Peter Milne (based on the novel *North Shore* by Wallace Irwin); **c**, Sol Polito; **m**, Bernhard Kaun; **ed**, Terry Morse; **art d**, Esdras Hartley.

Woman in the Dunes ★★★ 1964; Japan; 123m; Toho/Pathe; B/W; Drama; Children: Unacceptable; **DVD**; **VHS**; **IV**. This well-crafted tale presents a moving parable of the search for the meanings of life and love. Okada is an entomologist and educator residing in Tokyo, who visits a poor seaside village to collect and study sand insects as part of his research. He misses the last bus back to the city and spends the night in the home of Kishida, a young woman living at the bottom of a sand pit reached only by a ladder. Her husband and child had died in a sandstorm and their undiscovered bodies lie near the house. In the morning Okada finds that the ladder is gone and he is trapped with the woman. He then realizes that she has planned to trap him so that he can help her dig out the sand before it destroys her house and bury them alive. Okada tries to find a way to escape dying with the woman, but he nevertheless succeeds in saving her as well as her home. Mature themes prohibit viewing by children. **p**, Kiichi Ichikawa, Tadashi Ono; **d**, Hiroshi Teshigahara; **cast**, Eiji Okada, Kyoto Kishida, Koji Mitsui, Hiroko Ito, Sen Yano, Ginzo Sekiguchi, Kiyohiko Ichiha, Hideo Kanze, Hiroyuki Nishimoto, Tamotsu Tamura; **w**, Kobo Abe, Eiko Yoshida (based on Abe's novel *Suna no Onna*); **c**, Hiroshi Segawa; **m**, Toru Takemitsu; **ed**, Fusako Shuzui; **pro d**, Totetsu Hirakawa, Masao Yamazaki.

The Woman in the Window ★★★★ 1944; U.S.; 99m; Christie Corporation/RKO; B/W; Crime Drama; Children: Unacceptable; **DVD**; **VHS**. Robinson, Bennett, Massey and Duryea are mesmerizing in this terrific psychological crime drama from pantheon director Lang. Robinson, a reserved criminology professor, sends his wife and two children off to a vacation before he meets with his peers at their club. There they discuss the looming dangers that threaten them should they undertake

Dan Duryea and Joan Bennett in *The Woman in the Window,* 1944.

new adventures. Ironically, that very same threat becomes a reality after Robinson, while strolling along a street, stops to admire the portrait of a beautiful brunette woman depicted in a painting displayed in a store window. Oddly, Bennett, the very woman who has modeled for that painting is standing beside Robinson, as she has been watching anyone who views her portrait. She asks Robinson if he would like to have drinks with her, and Robinson, suddenly enthralled with this ravishingly beautiful woman, agrees. They go to a club and chat and then Bennett invites him to her apartment. The two are at that apartment for only a short time before wealthy financier Loft, who is Bennett's close friend, if not sugar daddy, arrives. Loft immediately and wrongly concludes that Bennett is cheating on him with Robinson and slaps her several times. He then angrily turns on Robinson, but as he attacks the astonished professor, Robinson grabs a pair of scissors and, in defending himself, fatally stabs Loft in the back. Robinson and Bennett are now terrified that they will be charged with Loft's murder and decide to dispose of the body. They suffer a number of obstacles in their gruesome task, until they manage to drive the corpse in a car to the open country as the corpse sits upright, its eyes open and seemingly glaring at them. They finally find a remote spot and dispose of the body before returning to the city. Robinson, however, can find no relief as he is continuously reminded about the killing by Massey, his friend and the district attorney supervising the investigation into the case. Robinson further agonizes over his actions when Massey invites him to visit the scene of the crime to provide any suggestions based on his deep knowledge of criminology. Through Massey, Robinson sees how the police are using all the clues he has left behind as they relentlessly pursue the culprit, himself. He is further beleaguered when Duryea, who had been Loft's bodyguard, learns the truth of his boss's demise and begins to blackmail Bennett. She, in turn, agrees to pay off the insidious blackmailer, but she uses a lethal prescription drug to lace Duryea's drink when he arrives to collect the payoff. Duryea, however, is suspicious of Bennett, and, though he takes the payoff money, refuses to down the dosed drink. Robinson then arrives to learn what has happened from Bennett, and, feeling that all is lost, drinks from the poisoned glass, ending his own life. By this time, Bennett searches for Duryea, who is confronted by police and is killed in a wild shootout. Massey and officers quickly conclude that Duryea was the man who killed Loft. When Bennett races to her apartment to tell Robinson the news that they are no longer under suspicion, she sees Robinson slumped dead in his chair. The epilogue provides ironic relief in that Robinson is then shown awakening from a long nap while sitting in a chair at his club and where he realizes that all of what has transpired has been nothing more than a gruesome nightmare. That nightmare had been created by his own previous discussion with his fellow club members and his vivid criminologist's imagination. He then takes a stroll

down a street and he then sees the same painting in the store window. When a young woman asks him for a light to ignite her cigarette, Robinson, recalling the horror of his nightmare, cowers before her and then begins to retreat down the street, until he is running from her and any prophetic fate that woman represents to end this bone-chilling thriller. Lang presents a fast-paced story that tersely unfolds its frantic characters and unnerving story line, greatly aided by Krasner's deft camerawork that provides stark lighting and deep atmospheric shadows from frame to frightening frame. Robinson is superb as the victim of his own mistaken meanderings while the alluring Bennett sizzles seductively in all of her scenes. Massey is a wonderful district attorney, full of resolve for justice at any ethical cost and Duryea is just the opposite as a lowlife hustler bartering a cover-up to murder for cold cash. The film was a great success at the box office, so much so that Lang went into another film noir production shortly thereafter with about the same cast and crew members. A sixty-minute radio adaptation of this film was aired by Lux Radio Theater on June 25, 1945, with Robinson, Bennett and Duryea reprising their roles. The story was shown on TV in the Robert Montgomery Presents series in a 1955 episode. *Author's Note*: Johnson, the producer and writer of this film, told this author that "one of the most impressive transitions of any scene in any picture was accomplished in **The Woman in the Window**. Instead of attempting to show that transition through tricky dissolves, Fritz [Lang] had an assistant creep beneath the camera which was showing Eddie's [Robinson's] head in a close-up after he has supposedly died from drinking poison. While the camera was running, the assistant snapped off the breakaway clothes Eddie was wearing while the crew changed the setting from Joan's [Bennett's] apartment to Eddie's club. The camera, still rolling, then pulled back to show Eddie peacefully asleep in his chair at that club, wearing the clothes he wore at the beginning of the picture, and very much alive. When audiences saw that scene they thought Fritz was some sort of a magician. So did most everyone who worked in Hollywood." Robinson thought his role in this film "was one of my better efforts because I was not playing another gangster, but a learned professor who had studied and understood crime, perhaps too much as his knowledge of crime creates for him the perfect criminal nightmare. Actually, a few years earlier, I played a physician studying criminal mentalities in **The Amazing Dr. Clitterhouse** [1938], and where I join an underworld gang led by Humphrey Bogart, so I can study those very types of criminals. So when Fritz [Lang] asked me to appear in **The Woman in the Window** and I read the script, I knew I was on familiar ground, although that picture has a much different plot and cast of characters." Bennett told this author that she "enjoyed playing another femme fatale, the kind of woman who purposely or accidentally lures men to their doom. I was so good at luring Eddie [Robinson] to his doom in **The Woman in the Window**, that Fritz [Lang] put us all into another picture called **Scarlet Street** [1945] and where I could lure Eddie once more to a terrible destiny. Dan [Duryea] was in that one too, helping me to destroy poor Eddie once again." Massey told this author that "the ending where Eddie [Robinson] comes out of his nightmare was dictated by the front office at Universal. The production code of that day would not allow a killer to get off scott-free, so Fritz [Lang] came up with that ending where Eddie wakes up to find out it was all a nightmare. The writer [Nunnally Johnson], who also produced the picture, did not want that ending at all, but he had to accept it or look for another job in another business." p&w, Nunnally Johnson (based on the novel *Once Off Guard* by J.H. Wallis); d, Fritz Lang; **cast**, Edward G. Robinson, Joan Bennett, Raymond Massey, Edmund Breon, Dan Duryea, Thomas E. Jackson, Dorothy Peterson, Arthur Loft, Iris Adrian, Robert Blake, George "Spanky" McFarland; c, Milton Krasner; m, Arthur Lange; ed, Marjorie Johnson, Gene Fowler, Jr., Thomas Pratt; art d, Duncan Cramer; set d, Julia Heron; spec eff, Vernon Walker, Paul K. Lerpae, Harry Redmond, Jr.

The Woman in White ★★★ 1948; U.S.; 109m; W/B; B/W; Horror; Mystery; Children: Unacceptable. Eerie thriller begins when Young, a handsome British art teacher, meets Parker (Ann), a mysterious and distressed woman dressed in white. He learns she has escaped from an insane asylum. He travels to Cumberland, hired as a drawing teacher for a wealthy family. The household includes an invalid, Abbott, his nurse, Dunn, and his niece, also played by Parker (Laura) in a dual role, and her cousin, Smith. Young immediately sees a remarkable resemblance between Ann and Laura. The woman in white (Ann) is known to the household as being mentally disabled and had lived nearby as a child and was devoted to the niece's mother, who first dressed her in white. Young and Parker (Laura) fall in love, but she has promised Abbott that she will marry nobleman Emery. Her betrothal has been cleverly arranged by the scheming Greenstreet, who plots to acquire Parker's (Laura's) vast estate through the arranged marriage while working in collusion with Emery. Smith, knowing that Parker (Laura) loves Young, advises him to forget her and leave. The other Parker (Ann) then sends a letter to Laura that warns her against marrying Emery. She then meets Young, who is convinced that Emery has been the lover of the institutionalized Parker (Ann), or was responsible for having her put into the asylum. Despite the warning, Parker (Laura) and Emery marry and travel to Italy for a few months. After their honeymoon, the newlyweds return to Emery's house in Hampshire, accompanied by Greenstreet, who is married to Moorehead, Parker's mentally unbalanced aunt. Greenstreet and Emery now scheme to find a way to murder Parker (Laura) in order to have her estate. Parker (Ann) then escapes from the asylum, and, still dressed in white (to differentiate her from the other Parker), warns her sibling that Greenstreet and Emery plan to take her life. Young then appears to help save Parker (Laura). The plot against her collapses when Moorehead goes berserk and kills Greenstreet. The long-persecuted Parker (Ann) also dies while Emery is exposed, which eventually allows Young and Parker (Laura) to make a life together. They eventually marry, have a son, and move onto their estate to live out a happy life. Godfrey does a good job sorting out the twists and turns of Collins' convoluted plot, and Parker is effective in her dual roles. Young, Greenstreet, Emery, Smith and Moorehead are exceptional as supporting characters. This film is a remake of the 1912, 1917 and 1929 silent films of the same title, as well as the talkie **Crimes at the Dark House**, 1940. The story was presented in two TV series in 1966 and 1997 and was made into a musical in 2004. **p**, Henry Blanke; **d**, Peter Godfrey; **cast**, Eleanor Parker, Alexis Smith, Sydney Greenstreet, Gig Young, Agnes Moorehead, John Abbott, John Emery, Curt Bois, Emma Dunn, Matthew Boulton; **w**, Stephen Morehouse Avery (based on the novel by Wilkie Collins); **c**, Carl Guthrie; **m**, Max Steiner; **ed**, Clarence Kolster; **art d**, Stanley Fleischer; **set d**, George Southam; **spec eff**, Robert Burks, William McGann.

The Woman Next Door ★★★ 1981; France; 106m; Le Films du Carrosse/UA; Color; Drama/Romance; Children: Unacceptable (MPAA: R); **DVD**; **VHS**. This well-made romantic drama begins with Depardieu, who is happily married to Baumgartner and has a good relationship with their son Becquaert. All that changes when a young married couple, Ardant and Garcin, become their next-door neighbors. It is an accidental reunion for Depardieu and Ardant, who had a passionate love affair some years earlier. Their strong feelings for each other resurface into an uncontrollable obsession. It ends with gruesome tragedy when Garcin plans to leave with Ardant. She cannot, however, go on living without her lover, and, while visiting Depardieu for a final embrace, shoots and kills him and then herself. Depardieu and Ardant are mesmerizing as the obsessive and star-crossed lovers as the gifted Truffaut meticulously chronicles with stunning visuals and many moving scenes their path to self-destruction. The grim finale may be too much for sensitive viewers to bear. Sexual matter and suicidal violence prohibit viewing by children. (In French; English subtitles.) **p&d**, Francois Truffaut; **cast**, Gerard Depardieu, Fanny Ardant, Henri Garcin, Michele Baumgartner, Roger Van Hool, Veronique Silver, Olivier Becquaert, Philippe Morier-Genoud, Muriel Combe, Nicole Vauthier; **w**, Truffaut,

Sydney Greenstreet and Alexis Smith in *The Woman in White,* 1948.

Suzanne Schiffman, Jean Aurel; **c**, William Lubtchansky (Fujicolor); **m**, Georges Delerue; **ed**, Martine Barraque; **prod d**, Jean-Pierre Kohut-Svelko.

A Woman of Affairs ★★★★ 1928 (silent); U.S.; 98m; MGM; B/W; Drama/Romance; Children: Unacceptable; **VHS**. Garbo is magnificent while enacting Michael Arlen's doomed flapper of the 1920s, a woman who loses the man she loves to another while her own life collapses into illicit affairs, alcoholism and suicide. The film opens with three youngsters representing Garbo, Gilbert and Brown, the two boys affectionately agog over the girl they adore. Garbo, however, prefers Gilbert, and, as they sit beneath a tree, their favorite rendezvous, they vow that, when they become adults, they will marry and have a blissful life together. Garbo becomes a radiant young woman and a lively creature of the Roaring Twenties, assuming with relish the flashy image of that era's flapper, replete with smearing lipstick, short skirts and cloche hats, and she drives a Hispano-Suiza roadster at breakneck speeds. She and Gilbert are as deeply in love as they were when adolescents. When they plan to marry, however, Bosworth, who is Gilbert's father, adamantly objects to the union. Though Garbo comes from an aristocratic British family, Bosworth does not approve of its family members. He thinks Garbo is a loose woman and that her brother, Fairbanks, is nothing more than a drunken wastrel. To make sure his son does not marry Garbo, Bosworth sends Gilbert to Egypt to manage the family business and where Gilbert is expected to increase his family's fortunes. Garbo nevertheless patiently and longingly waits two years for Gilbert to return to her. When Gilbert does not return, Garbo finally accepts Brown's proposal and they honeymoon in Paris. Their wedded bliss, however, abruptly turns to violent tragedy when Brown inexplicably commits suicide just before police arrive. The shocked Garbo then learns that Brown had stolen money to fund their marriage and took his own life when his crime was exposed. To repay the money stolen by Brown, Garbo earns money by becoming the lover of one wealthy man after another, until she is a hand-me-down woman of affairs. Throughout her descent into degradation, Fairbanks, her brother, becomes an emotionally unstable alcoholic, as he blames Garbo for the death of his close friend, Brown. Stone, a physician and family friend, is summoned to treat Fairbanks and he has the young man hospitalized. Gilbert, by this time, has returned from Egypt, and, while seeing Garbo and Stone drive past him on a street, seeks out Garbo and takes her to his apartment where they renew their passions for one another, spending the night together. That night Fairbanks dies, and the following morning Stone arrives at Gilbert's apartment to give him that news, shocked to learn that Garbo has spent the night with Gilbert. A few days later, Gilbert marries Sebastian, a wedding that has been arranged by Bosworth, although

Lewis Stone and Greta Garbo in *A Woman of Affairs,* **1928.**

Gilbert still loves Garbo. Nine months later, Garbo is hospitalized for an unspecified illness (in the original script, she suffers a miscarriage), and Gilbert and Sebastian visit her at her hospital room. Garbo, not realizing that Sebastian is in the room, tells Gilbert that she still loves him. When she realizes Sebastian's presence, she urges Gilbert to remain at his wife's side, telling him that Sebastian needs him since she is now pregnant with his child. The heartbroken Gilbert leaves Garbo once and for all, telling Sebastian that Garbo did not even recognize him, as he resolves to remain with Sebastian. Garbo, once recovered, sees no happiness in her future and drives her roadster at high speeds until she purposely crashes it into the very tree where she and Gilbert once professed their love for one another and there, beneath the bows of that tree, she dies, ending this "lost generation" tale. Brown does a fine job presenting this tragic love tale, carefully developing its fascinating characters while Garbo dominates every scene with a much more vibrant personality than the somewhat tired or waned females she had portrayed in recent films. She is as much a crazed and Jazz-loving flapper as was essayed by Louise Brooks, Clara Bow and Colleen Moore in many other films, but more so in that she uniquely creates empathy for her character as she makes her melancholy way toward her self-destruction. She conveys her excitement-seeking character through her own visual shorthand: Garbo streaks lipstick onto her lips and exhales long streams of smoke from her cigarette before ripping away her cloche hat so that the wind can whip her hair about as she races her open-car roadster. This and more exemplifies her love for life and her utter joy at living for the moment. This film also offers one of Garbo's most memorable moments on film when Gilbert leaves her hospital room and she finds the bouquet he has left behind. She substitutes the flowers for Gilbert, clutching them as she might her lover, thrusting her face into these flowers to deeply inhale their fragrance, as if to reinvigorate her wasted being with their living strength. She fondly carries the flowers back to her room, pressing them close to her cheek as a mother might caress a newborn child. This stunning scene alone is worth the whole of this film and only in **Queen Christina**, 1933, did Garbo exceed this scene when she moves about a bedroom to lovingly caress its furniture as the cherished artifacts of her lovemaking (also with Gilbert) the night before. The film received an Oscar nomination for Best Writing (Meredyth, Ainslee, Cummings) and it was a great hit at the box office, earning more than $1.3 million in its initial release against a budget of more than $320,000. The story was adapted for a Broadway play in 1925. This film was remade as **Outcast Lady**, 1934, starring Constance Bennett and Herbert Marshall. Songs (offered on a synchronized sound track at the time of release): "Love's First Kiss" (1928: music: William Axt, David Mendoza; lyrics: Raymond Klages), "Garbo Valsen" (music: Henry Southerland; lyrics: Arne Riesinger). *Author's Note*: Brown told this author that "the Michael

Arlen book, *The Green Hat*, with its notorious heroine, Iris March, and the indecent men in her life, was strictly taboo in Hollywood. That book was so infamous that we had to change the names of all of its characters. We had to change Johnny Mack Brown's character to a thief who kills himself after the police get on to him, but, in the novel, that character commits suicide because he has syphilis and has infected his new bride with that deadly disease. We also had to get rid of the heroin that the characters in the novel use, but we got away with showing Doug [Douglas Fairbanks Jr.] constantly drinking, even though Prohibition was then still in force in America because the setting was in England where drinking alcohol was legal. We danced around the Hays Office [the Hollywood censoring office at that time] like madmen to make that picture! The best part was working with Garbo, who was always very cooperative, but very shy and I learned early on to treat her gently by whispering my directions to her so that she would not be embarrassed by others listening to those directions. She was possessed of what I call an 'Inner Eye' for her scenes and where she could do things that no other actress could do with simple movements and gestures to create a wholly captivating scene. I don't think there will ever be anyone like her on the screen." Garbo told this author that she was "very pleased with **A Woman of Affairs**. I had known such tragic women, who had been deprived of love, deprived of children, deprived of all happiness in life, and even infected with that terrible sexual disease, so I knew what my character had to be. That picture was directed by one of my favorite persons, Clarence Brown, and my favorite cameraman, Billy [William] Daniels, was there for me, so I was in very good hands." **p&d,** Clarence Brown; **cast,** John Gilbert, Greta Garbo, Lewis Stone, John (Johnny) Mack Brown, Douglas Fairbanks Jr., Hobart Bosworth, Dorothy Sebastian, Gertrude Astor, Agostino Borgato, Anita Louise; **w,** Bess Meredyth, Marian Ainslee, Ruth Cummings (from the novel *The Green Hat* by Michael Arlen); **c,** William H. Daniels; **m,** William Axt, Carl Davis; **ed,** Hugh Wynn; **art d,** Cedric Gibbons.

A Woman of Paris: A Drama of Fate ★★★ 1923 (silent); U.S.; 93m/9 reels; Charles Chaplin Productions/UA; Drama; Children: Unacceptable; **DVD; VHS**. Chaplin exercises all of his creative inventiveness when directing this well-crafted melodrama that opens with Purviance, a girl living in a small French village who is in love with Miller. The two plan to elope to Paris and get married, but circumstances soon prevent them from following their dream together. Purviance climbs from her second-floor bedroom in her home to rendezvous with Miller, but, when her stern stepfather, Geldart, sees her strolling with Miller along a nearby lane, he angrily locks Purviance out of the house. Geldart does not think Miller is a suitable husband for Purviance and thinks even less of his stepdaughter, believing that she is a trollop by nature. When she returns to find the door bolted, Purviance begs to be allowed inside, but Geldart tells her to find a bed in Miller's home. Miller has his mother, Knott, prepare a bed for Purviance, but she soon realizes that Knott and Miller's father, French, also do not approve of her. The next morning, Purviance goes to the train station and Miller promises he will soon join her there. While waiting at the station, she receives a phone call from Miller, telling her he cannot go with her to Paris. Purviance, heartbroken but full of resolve to break free of the restraints in her village, boards the train bound for Paris. In Paris, Purviance attracts the lecherous eye of Menjou, a wealthy rake, who makes her his mistress. Purviance lives a life of luxury, attending one fete and party after another. She is invited to attend one such raucous revel, but, when taking a taxi to the place, she enters the wrong building and is shocked to see Miller, who has traveled with his mother to Paris to study art and is then an apprentice painter. Purviance, who is still in love with Miller, gives him her card and asks him to call on her so that he can paint her portrait. When Miller later arrives at Purviance's sumptuous apartment, she notices that he is wearing a black armband and asks for whom he mourns. Miller tells her he mourns for his father and when she asks when French died, Miller tells her "when you left [for Paris]." The two are again drawn together out of their deep love for one another and Purviance breaks her relationship with Menjou. The bounder is not perturbed as he has already become engaged to a socialite. The news that Menjou has routinely betrayed her is given to Purviance when a friend appears to show her an article in a society magazine that announces Menjou's engagement. Purviance glances at the article before tossing it aside and lighting a cigarette. When her friend leaves, however, she grabs the magazine and reads the article intently, realizing that she has become nothing more than a plaything for rich men. When Miller then proposes marriage to Purviance, she thinks he is only being kind and wants to salvage her ruined reputation as he knows about her long-standing affair with Menjou. Although Miller has made this offer out of sincere love for her, Purviance interprets his offer as a noble gesture of pity and she rejects him. Miller is crushed and later commits suicide. Now, Knott, Miller's mother, is convinced that Purviance has all along set out to destroy her innocent son and vows to take vengeance against her. When Knott meets with Purviance, however, she sees that she is overwrought with grief at Miller's death and realizes that Purviance truly loved her son. She forgives Purviance, and the two become good friends in sharing their mutual mourning over the young man they both loved. They both return to their village, vowing to perform works of charity in the name of the dead Miller. To that end, they establish a home for orphans in a cottage. The film ends on a poignantly ironic note as we see Purviance fetching some milk and being given a lift in a wagon loaded with hay, and she is accompanied by other villagers enjoying the balmy day. A chauffeur-driven automobile then approaches, one in which Menjou sits with one of his gentlemen friends. His companion asks him whatever became of his former mistress, Purviance, and Menjou only shrugs to indicate that he has no idea. An overhead shot then shows the automobile and the wagon going in opposite directions. Purviance, Miller and Menjou are superb in their roles while Chaplin directs with vitality, cleverly inserting one ironically touching scene after another to produce a grand tearjerker. This film was not well received by the public as Chaplin's millions of fans expected another comedy with him as the leading character, most likely his iconic character of the Little Tramp. Chaplin anticipated this response by issuing flyers to all those attending the picture to state that this production was a "deviation" from his usual films and that, although he had directed the film, he did not appear in it as a leading man (albeit he appears in a bit part). His fans felt betrayed and the film did poorly at the box office, earning less than $640,000 in its initial release against a budget of $350,000. *Author's Note*: Chaplin based this story on his own 1922 romance with globe-trotting Peggy Hopkins Joyce (1893-1957), American model, dancer and actress, who consorted and cavorted with American and British expatriates in Paris. "I saw Peggy and Charlie a lot together in Paris in that year," Ernest Hemingway told this author. "She wrapped that daffy little comedian around her little finger until he ran out of pratfalls to amuse her, and she dumped him, just like she dumped six rich husbands and a dozen wealthy gigolos. That dame collected more diamonds, furs and money from those suckers, including Chaplin, than a Romanov princess." Joyce was the role model mentioned by name for the gold-digging characters profiled in Anita Loos' 1925 novel, *Gentlemen Prefer Blondes*. Joyce acquired through her marital exploits the Portuguese Diamond, one of the most expensive gems in the world. She later sold it to jewelry tycoon Harry Winston, that diamond now reposing at the Smithsonian Institute. Chaplin later stated that he wanted to make Purviance, who had loyally remained with him over the years in his Little Tramp films, into a recognized dramatic actress by starring her in this film. Her career, however, never really soared beyond her celebrated partnership on screen with Chaplin as that Little Tramp. Chaplin further annoyed and disappointed his partners Mary Pickford, Douglas Fairbanks Sr. and master director D.W. Griffith, the four of them having established United Artists Studio. This film was the first that Chaplin directed under that studio's banner and its failure at the box office brought him criticism from those very close

Claire Trevor, Albert Dekker and Marion Martin in *The Woman of the Town*, 1943.

friends. Purviance's career nose-dived thereafter, and Chaplin felt so responsible for that that he demonstrated his lifelong friendship to her by paying her a full yearly salary as called for in her lifetime contract with him, right up to her death on January 11, 1958. **p,d&w**, Charles Chaplin; **cast**, Edna Purviance, Adolphe Menjou, Carl Miller, Lydia Knott, Charles K. French, Clarence Geldart, Betty Morrissey, Malvina Polo, Henry Bergman, Chaplin, Charles Farrell; **c**, Roland Totheroh, Jack Wilson; **ed**, Monta Bell; **art d**, Arthur Stibolt.

The Woman of the Town ★★★ 1943; U.S.; 90m; Harry Sherman/UA; B/W; Western; Children: Unacceptable; **DVD**; **VHS**. This gritty and action-packed western is loosely based on the life of William Barclay "Bat" Masterson (1853-1921), who is ably played by Dekker, when he was marshal of Dodge City, Kansas. Dekker is shown while working for a New York newspaper in 1919 and where he reminisces about his days in the Old West. In flashback, we see Dekker putting on a badge after he is unable to find work on the local newspaper in Dodge City. He is almost immediately confronted by Sullivan, who heads a rowdy cowboy faction. Dekker then meets Trevor, who plays Dora Hand (Fannie Keenan, 1844-1878), a social worker and dance hall singer. He soon falls in love with her after hearing Trevor sing with the choir at the local church, but when the church's pastor then learns that Trevor sings at the local saloon, he criticizes her presence among the churchgoers. Dekker then writes an article for the local newspaper in which he condemns the kind of prejudice exhibited by the pastor. Trevor realizes that Dekker has written this article as a way of protecting her good name among the city's social and religious leaders. Both soon fall in love, but Trevor fears for Dekker's life and urges him to leave Dodge City and go to work for her uncle in Kansas City, who operates a local newspaper there and where Trevor has arranged for her uncle to hire Dekker. (She does not inform Dekker that she has done this at her own sacrifice in that her uncle, after learning what she does for a living, promises to hire Dekker only on Trevor's promise that she will never appear in Kansas City again to disgrace her family with her now notorious reputation.) Dekker proposes marriage, but Trevor, knowing she cannot accompany him to Kansas City, rejects his offer and then begins seeing cattle baron Sullivan. Before Dekker leaves town, however, Sullivan kills the local mayor, Hall, and a stray bullet in the wild gunfight also claims the life of Trevor. A mournful Dekker attends her funeral and then buries his gun with her before leaving to begin his new career as a newspaperman. Trevor and Dekker render top-flight performances as star-crossed lovers in the Old West, and Sullivan is exceptional as the ruthless cattleman. Songs: "I'm a Heavy Tipper," "Poor Polly" (Lester Lee, Jerry Seelen). *Author's Note*: Trevor told this author that "I played a saloon singer who sings in a church choir in **The Woman of the Town**, but, I guaran-

Spencer Tracy and Katharine Hepburn in *Woman of the Year,* 1942.

tee you, I did not sing anything in that picture as my voice can't carry a song. They had a singer do my vocals for those songs. You may recall that the same kind of character is played by Jeanette MacDonald in **San Francisco** [1936]. She sings in a saloon operated by Clark Gable and also sings in the choir of a church where Spencer Tracy is the priest. The difference between those two pictures is that Jeanette has a great singing voice. When I was asked by director John Huston to actually sing a song in a gangster picture, **Key Largo** [1948], I sang that song["Moanin' Low"], but I sounded like a croaking frog—just terrible, and what do you know, that song helped me win an Oscar." Dora Hand was also profiled by Margaret Hayes in "The Double Life of Dora Hand," a 1956 episode in the TV series **The Life and Legend of Wyatt Earp** (1955-1961). Venerable character actor Worden told this author: "I thought that picture was an above-average western, really well written. I played a barber in that picture, but I can't recall my lines or anything. All I can remember is that Claire Trevor gave a wonderful performance as a wronged dance hall lady." Bat Masterson has been profiled by many other actors in many other films, including **Any Last Words?**, 2012 (Tom Lagleder); **Appointment with Destiny**, 1971-1973 (TV series; "Showdown at O.K. Corral," 1972 episode; Dan Ferrone); **Badman's Country**, 1958 (Gregory Walcott); **Bat Masterson**, 1958-1961 (TV series; Gene Barry); **Bordertown**, 1989-1991 (TV series; two 1990 episodes: Steve Makaj); **Doctor Who**, 1963-1989 (TV series; many episodes: Richard Beale); **The Gambler Returns: The Luck of the Draw**, 1991 (made-for-TV; Gene Barry); **The Gunfight at Dodge City**, 1959 (Joel McCrea); **Gunfight at the O.K. Corral**, 1957 (Kenneth Tobey); **Guns of Paradise**, 1988-1990 (TV series, "A Gathering of Guns," 1989 episode: Gene Barry); **The Life and Legend of Wyatt Earp**, 1955-1961 (TV series; Mason Alan Dinehart); **Masterson of Kansas**, 1954 (George Montgomery); **The Outlaws Is Coming!**, 1965 (Ed T. McDonnell); **Prince of the Plains**, 1949 (Monte Hale); **Santa Fe**, 1951 (Frank Ferguson); **Trail Street**, 1947 (Randolph Scott); **Wild Bill Hickok**, 1923 (Jack Gardner); **Winchester '73**, 1950 (Steve Darrell); **Witchita**, 1955 (Keith Larsen); **Wyatt Earp**, 1994 (Tom Sizemore); and **Wyatt Earp's Revenge**, 2012 (Matt Dallas). **p**, Harry Sherman; **d**, George Archainbaud; **cast**, Claire Trevor, Albert Dekker, Barry Sullivan, Marion Martin, Henry Hull, Porter Hall, Percy Kilbride, Beryl Wallace, Arthur Hohl, Clem Bevans, Hank Worden, George Cleveland, Russell Hicks; **w**, Aeneas MacKenzie (based on a story by Norman Houston); **c**, Russell Harlan; **m**, Miklos Rozsa; **ed**, Carrol Lewis; **art d**, Ralph Berger; **set d**, Emile Kuri.

Woman of the Year ★★★★ 1942; U.S.; 112m; MGM; B/W; Comedy/Romance; Children: Acceptable; **BD**; **DVD**; **VHS**; **IV**. Tracy and Hepburn are delightfully entertaining in this romantic romp, the first of

nine films they would make together. Both are columnists for a New York newspaper, but their similarities stop there as they are as divergent as an apple and an orange. Hepburn is sophisticated, well educated and fluently speaks several languages, and she writes a widely read foreign affairs column. Her father, Watson, is a U.S. senator and an important diplomat. Tracy, on the other hand, is a down-to-earth but knowledgeable sports writer who writes an equally popular column. The two enter a literary battle after Tracy hears Hepburn state on her radio show that baseball should be suspended until WWII (1939-1945) ends, as she believes that watching such a sport is unpatriotic. Tracy bristles at that contention, insisting that "the national pastime" is a healthy ingredient in building American morale on the home front. When they begin potshooting at each other in their columns, Owen, their editor, tells them that he will not tolerate internecine warfare among his employees and orders both to make peace with one another. Tracy arrives at Owen's office to make that peace with Hepburn, and, when he enters and sees her for the first time, she is smoothing out a nylon stocking on one of her shapely legs. Both are immediately attracted to each other (proving the old saying that "opposites attract"), and Tracy tries to show Hepburn how enjoyable it is to watch baseball by taking her to a game. His fellow sports writers are amused at how Tracy must struggle to explain the game to Hepburn, who gets everything mixed up, from plays to players. He later takes Hepburn to his hangout, a bar operated by Bendix, an ex-prizefighter fond of describing in detail his best-remembered bouts by reenacting them to customers. Hepburn is fascinated by Tracy's prosaic character and uncomplicated lifestyle where all seems colorful and entertaining. Tracy, in turn, is mesmerized by this brainy and ultra-sophisticated woman, who lives in a world of international diplomacy and high politics. They fall in love and then marry. The wedding takes place in a small community, and Tracy is hustled through the ceremony with Hepburn so that her busy father, Watson, can quickly depart to attend an important diplomatic meeting and Hepburn can report on that as well as other earth-shaking matters. The marriage is immediately on shaky ground as Hepburn is forever going off to important interviews with world leaders, and when she is at home with Tracy, which is seldom, she displays no commonplace skills as a wife. Hepburn excites Tracy by announcing that they are going to have a child. Hepburn then brings home a child, Kezas, a Greek refugee, telling Tracy that she wants to adopt him. This shocks Tracy as he has had no prior warning of Hepburn's intentions, along with the fact that the couple have hardly had any time to produce a child of their own from their tenuous union. Although Tracy initially tells Hepburn he does not want a six-year-old orphan foisted upon him, he warms to the child and welcomes him into their home. Tracy is unable to speak with him as Kezas does not speak English, although the accomplished Hepburn can converse with him in his native language. Tracy nevertheless patiently introduces Kezas to American sports. Then Hepburn is named "Woman of the Year," and wants Tracy to attend the ceremonies with her when she receives her award. Tracy, however, says that they cannot leave Kezas alone, but Hepburn insists, as that honorary award comes first with her. Tracy does attend, making a fool of himself before he returns home to find an unhappy Kezas. He then decides that Hepburn is not a fit mother and that Kezas would be better off at the orphanage and he returns the boy to that home. Tracy then packs his bags and leaves Hepburn. When she returns home, Hepburn finds both husband and child gone and she realizes the terrible mistake she has made. She goes to the orphanage in an attempt to take Kezas back home with her, but the boy refuses, insisting that he stay with the other orphans he has befriended. Hepburn then attends a wedding where her father, Watson, finally marries a woman he has waited much too long to wed. When Hepburn hears the wedding vows, she resolves to save her own marriage. She goes to Tracy's old Riverside home and, while Tracy is asleep, she begins to make him a breakfast, but everything she does proves to be a disaster. Tracy is awakened by the noises created in the kitchen by Hepburn and investigates. Hepburn tells him that she is no longer interested in being a celebrated columnist and intends to be a full-time wife and do all the daily domestic chores required of such a devoted spouse. Tracy is at first suspicious of her motives but then realizes that she is sincere. As they reconcile, Tobin, who is Hepburn's punctilious and overly efficient secretary, arrives unannounced to tell Hepburn that she has a number of important meetings to attend, not the least of which is the launching of a capital ship. Tobin has throughout the film constantly interrupted the lives of Tracy and Hepburn with such official agendas. At this moment, Tobin carries a bottle of champagne that Hepburn is to use in launching the ship. With Hepburn's blessing, Tracy leads Tobin outside and we hear the crash of a bottle. Tracy then returns alone to tell Hepburn that he has just "launched" Tobin. The couple then clinch for the happy ending. Tracy and Hepburn give sterling performances as a couple struggling to find enough common ground in their marriage upon which to build enough happiness that will sustain that union. They receive fine support from Bendix, Kezas, Tobin, Owen, Watson and others. All enjoy a brilliant and intelligent script that defines their fascinating characters while pantheon director Stevens incisively develops those characters into immensely appealing people from frame to frame. The wonderful script from Kanin and Lardner won an Oscar as Best Screenplay, and Hepburn received an Oscar nomination as Best Actress. The film was an enormous hit at the box office, earning more than $2.7 million against a budget of $1 million. A Broadway musical version of this story opened at the Palace Theater on May 29, 1981, starring Lauren Bacall and Harry Guardino, that play running for 770 performances. Songs: "Here Comes the Bride" ["Bridal Chorus"] (1850; from "Lohengrin" by Richard Wagner), "Anchors Aweigh" (1906; music: Charles A. Zimmerman; lyrics: Alfred Hart Miles). *Author's Note*: Screenwriter Garson Kanin conceived of this story, basing Hepburn's character on Dorothy Thompson, a celebrated columnist who wrote about international affairs, and he had only one actress in mind to play that "woman of the year"—Hepburn. Kanin was too busy to write a treatment for the film and gave it to his brother, Michael Kanin, and Ring Lardner Jr., both then apprentice Hollywood scriptwriters. They wrote a 30,000-word treatment and gave it to Hepburn, asking that, if she liked it, she take it to MGM mogul Louis B. Mayer for production approval. Hepburn loved the story and, being the strong-willed person that she was, walked into Mayer's office to pitch the story. She took the precaution of wearing four-inch high heels to increase her height from 5'7" to 5'11" so that she towered over the small-sized Mayer. Hepburn forcefully described the story, demanding that writers Kanin and Lardner receive $50,000 each for their treatment and subsequent screenplay. She also demanded that she be paid $100,000 for starring in the film, plus $11,000 commission for representing the script. She further demanded that she designate her own director as well as her male co-star. Mayer patiently listened to Hepburn and said nothing. She left his office believing that she had utterly failed to convince the studio head. "Well, I was in for the surprise of my life," Hepburn told this author. "Mr. Mayer called me and told me to go ahead with everything for **Woman of the Year** and that he approved of everything I wanted and without any reservations. I almost fell on the floor!" She then called George Stevens, saying that she wanted him to direct the film. Stevens told this author: "I couldn't believe that she had bullied Mayer into that production. 'Let me get this straight,' I said to her on the phone, '*you* told *him* that I was to direct this picture?' She confirmed that as a fact and I then said, 'okay, Kate, I'm your man.'" Tracy was nonchalant when he echoed Stevens' statements to this author, saying: "Kate called me and said I was going to appear with her in a picture called **Woman of the Year**." He then recounted his legendary meeting with the actress: "We first met in the MGM commissary and she was wearing very high heels and, when she stood up, she said, 'maybe I'm too tall for you.' I answered: 'Don't worry. I'll cut you down to my size.' Well, I'm not so certain who did all the cutting after that." It was during the production of this film that Tracy and Hepburn fell in love, a union that would last until his death twenty-five-years later. Tracy, a devout Catholic who was then married and with children, refused to divorce his wife, and the self-

Spencer Tracy and Katharine Hepburn in *Woman of the Year*, 1942.

sacrificing Hepburn accepted that as long as she could be with the man she loved. Even though Hepburn was totally in charge of this film, she allowed Tracy to take top billing. Garson Kanin, a close friend of Tracy's, upbraided the actor for that, saying that he should have given Hepburn top billing, telling Tracy: "She's a lady. You're the man. Ladies first?" Tracy replied: "This is a movie, Chowderhead, not a lifeboat!" Many other films have profiled newspaper columnists, including **Advice to the Lovelorn**, 1933; **Agatha**, 1979; **All about Eve**, 1950; **The Appointment**, 1991; **Attraction**, 2001; **Beau James**, 1957 (Walter Winchell narrating); **The Bellboy**, 1960 (Walter Winchell narrating); **Beloved Infidel**, 1959 (Sheilah Graham); **The Big Game**, 1936; **The Big Story**, 1949-1958 (TV series; Walter Winchell); **Big Trouble**, 2002; **The Birds, the Bees and the Italians**, 1967; **Black Angel**, 1946; **Blonde for a Day**, 1946; **A Bloody Canvas**, 2008 (made-for-TV; Paul Gallico); **The Blue Gardenia**, 1953; **Bogie**, 1980 (made-for-TV; Louella Parsons); **Breakfast in Hollywood**, 1946 (Hedda Hopper); **The Bride Came C.O.D.**, 1941; **The Bride Vanishes**, 1939; **The Bride Wore Crutches**, 1940; **Bright Young Things**, 2003; **Broadway Thru a Key-Hole**, 1933 (Walter Winchell and other columnists); **Café Society**, 1995; **The Cat's Meow**, 2001 (Louella Parsons); **Chicago**, 2002; **Christmas in Connecticut**, 1945; **Citizen Cohn**, 1992 (made-for-TV; Walter Winchell); **Climax!**, 1954-1958 (TV series; "The Louella Parsons Story," 1956 episode); **College Confidential**, 1960 (Walter Winchell, Sheilah Graham); **Confessions of a Shopaholic**, 2009; **Continental Divide**, 1981; **The Corpse Came C.O.D.**, 1947 (Louella Parsons, Hedda Hopper); **Crime of Passion**, 1957; **Daisy Kenyon**, 1947 (Walter Winchell, Damon Runyon); **Damon Runyon's Pueblo**, 1981 (made-for-TV); **Dan in Real Life**, 2007; **Dash and Lilly**, 1999 (made-for-TV; Walter Winchell); **Dempsey**, 1983 (made-for-TV; Damon Runyon); **Divorcing Jack**, 1998; **Dondi**, 1961 (Walter Winchell); **The Drag-Net**, 1936; **F. Scott Fitzgerald in Hollywood**, 1976 (made-for-TV; Sheilah Graham); **A Face in the Crowd**, 1957 (Walter Winchell); **Finnegan Begin Again**, 1985 (made-for-TV); **Fitzgerald**, 2002 (made-for-TV; Sheilah Graham); **Five Star Final**, 1931; **The Fountainhead**, 1949; **The Front Page**, 1931; **The Front Page**, 1974; **The Girl Hunters**, 1963; **The Gossip Columnist**, 1980 (made-for-TV); **The Great Jewel Robber**, 1950 (Sheilah Graham); **The Hearst and Davies Affair**, 1985 (made-for-TV; Louella Parsons); **Heartburn**, 1986; **Her Highness and the Bellboy**, 1945; **Hi, Nellie!**, 1934; **High Tide**, 1947; **Hollywood Hotel**, 1937 (Louella Parsons); **The Honor of the Press**, 1932; **Hot News**, 1953; **The House across the Street**, 1949; **House of Horrors**, 1946; **How to Handle Women**, 1928; **How to Lose a Guy in 10 Days**, 2003; **Human Cargo**, 1936; **I Wake Up Screaming**, 1942; **Impact**, 1949 (Sheilah Graham); **Impact Point**, 2008; **Incendiary Blonde**, 1945 (Louella Parsons); **International Crime**, 1938; **Is It Just**

Spencer Tracy and Katharine Hepburn in *Woman of the Year*, 1942.

Me?, 2010; **The Josephine Baker Story**, 1991 (made-for-TV; Walter Winchell); **The Jury's Secret**, 1938; **Kraft Music Hall**, 1967-1971 (TV series; "Stagedoor Johnny," 1967 episode: Walter Winchell); **Laughter on the 23rd Floor**, 2003 (made-for-TV; Walter Winchell); **Laura**, 1944; **Lepke**, 1975 (Walter Winchell); **Lonelyhearts**, 1958; **Love and Hisses**, 1937 (Walter Winchell); **Love Is News**, 1937; **The Lucy Show**, 1962-1968 (TV series; "Lucy the Gun Moll," 1966 episode: Walter Winchell); **Lux Video Theater**, 1950-1959 (TV series; Sheilah Graham in two episodes); **Ma! He's Making Eyes at Me**, 1940; **Madison Sq. Garden**, 1932 (Damon Runyon playing himself, Paul Gallico playing himself); **Malice in Wonderland**, 1985 (made-for-TV; Louella Parsons, Hedda Hopper); **The Man Who Dared**, 1946; **Marilyn and Me**, 1991 (made-for-TV; Walter Winchell, Louella Parsons); **Marilyn: The Untold Story**, 1980 (made-for-TV; Louella Parsons); **Marlene**, 2000 (Louella Parsons); **Meet John Doe**, 1941; **Mr. Deeds Goes to Town**, 1936; **Mr. Soft Touch**, 1949; **The Murder Man**, 1935; **A New Kind of Love**, 1963; **The Odd Couple**, 1968; **One Mile from Heaven**, 1937; **Over 21**, 1945; **The Paper**, 1994; **The Patsy**, 1964 (Hedda Hopper); **The Payoff**, 1935; **Pepe**, 1960 (Hedda Hopper); **The Phantom of 42nd Street**, 1945; **The Private Files of J. Edgar Hoover**, 1977 (Walter Winchell, Damon Runyon); **Red, Hot and Blue**, 1949; **The Rat Pack**, 1998 (made-for-TV; Walter Winchell); **The Reluctant Dragon**, 1941 (Walter Winchell); **The Right Approach**, 1961 (Hedda Hopper); **Ring of Passion**, 1978 (made-for-TV; Damon Runyon, Paul Gallico); **RKO 281**, 1999 (made-for-TV; Louella Parsons, Hedda Hopper); **Roxie Hart**, 1942; **Runaway Bride**, 1999; **Saving Sarah Caine**, 2007; **Scandal Sheet**, 1931; **Scandal Sheet**, 1952; **The Scarlett O'Hara War**, 1980 (made-for-TV; Walter Winchell, Louella Parsons); **Sex and the City**, 1998-2004 (TV series); **Shinbone Alley**, 1970; **Shirley Temple Story**, 1976 (Louella Parsons); **Single Room Furnished**, 1966 (Walter Winchell); **Smart Woman**, 1948; **Social Register**, 1934; **The Soloist**, 2009; **Something to Sing About**, 1937; **Sorrowful Jones**, 1949 (Walter Winchell narrating); **Spy Ship**, 1942; **Starlift**, 1951 (Louella Parsons); **State of the Union**, 1948; **The Stork Club**, 1945 (Louella Parsons); **Sunset Boulevard**, 1950 (Hedda Hopper); **Sweet Smell of Success**, 1957 (role model for Walter Winchell); **Taking a Chance on Love**, 2009 (made-for-TV); **Teacher's Pet**, 1958; **Telephone Time**, 1956-1958 (TV series; "I Get Along Without You Very Well," 1957 episode: Walter Winchell); **That's Right—You're Wrong**, 1939 (Sheilah Graham); **There's No Business Like Show Business**, 1954 (Walter Winchell narrating); **They Asked for It**, 1939; **-30-**, 1959; **To Please a Lady**, 1950; **Trocadero**, 1944; **The Untouchables**, 1959-1963 (TV series; Walter Winchell narrates); **Vicki**, 1953 (remake of I Wake Up Screaming); **Wake Up and Live**, 1937 (Walter Winchell); **The Walls**

Came Tumbling Down, 1946; **The Walter Winchell File**, 1957-1958 (TV series); **The Walter Winchell Show**, 1956 (TV series); **Where Are You, Sophia?**, 2009; **While the City Sleeps**, 1956; **Wild Harvest**, 1962 (Walter Winchell narrating); **Wild in the Streets**, 1968 (Walter Winchell); **Winchell**, 1998 (made-for-TV; Walter Winchell); **Woman of the Town**, 1943 (Bat Masterson, Louella Parsons); **Woman of the Year**, 1942; **Woman-Wise**, 1937; **The Women**, 1939; **X Marks the Spot**, 1931; **You Can't Escape Forever**, 1942; and **Young Man of Manhattan**, 1930. **p**, Joseph L. Mankiewicz; **d**, George Stevens; **cast**, Spencer Tracy, Katharine Hepburn, Fay Bainter, Reginald Owen, Minor Watson, William Bendix, Gladys Blake, Roscoe Karns, Sara Haden, George Kezas, William Tannen, Ludwig Stossel, Joe Yule; **w**, Ring Lardner, Jr., Michael Kanin; **c**, Joseph Ruttenberg; **m**, Franz Waxman; **ed**, Frank Sullivan; **art d**, Cedric Gibbons; **set d**, Edwin B. Willis.

The Woman on Pier 13 ★★★ 1949; U.S.; 73m; RKO; B/W; Crime Drama; Children: Unacceptable; **DVD**; **VHS**. Ryan gives an impressive, intense performance in this well-crafted propaganda film that seeks to indict the evils of communism. He is the vice-president of a San Francisco shipping company, who is approached by Gomez, a commissar spreading chaos in the U.S., and asked to work with communists in sabotaging waterfront operations and union workers. When Ryan refuses to cooperate, Gomez attempts to blackmail Ryan by bringing up his past when Ryan had belonged to the Communist Party many years earlier. At that time, he had accidentally killed a man, but Gomez has arranged for that death to now appear to be a murder that can be laid at Ryan's door to destroy him and his wife Day, if he does not cooperate. Ryan still stubbornly refuses to be a communist stooge, and Gomez then uses sexy Carter, a communist femme fatale to seduce Ryan's brother-in-law, Agar. Ryan's new wife, Day, senses that he and Agar are under some kind of pressure, but she is unable to learn the causes of their frustrations. After Agar is killed, Day investigates and learns that Gomez and his communists are attempting to take over the San Francisco waterfront from a guilt-ridden Carter. She tells Day that Talman, one of Gomez's henchmen, killed Agar. When Day leaves, Carter writes out a confession, indicting Gomez and her fellow communists, but Gomez appears and confiscates her note. Carter then dies after either falling out or being pushed from the window of her high-rise apartment. Meanwhile, Day tracks down Talman, finding him at an amusement center where he works. Before she can summon police, Talman kidnaps Day and takes her to a warehouse operated by Burns, which serves as a communist headquarters. By this time, Ryan is on his wife's trail, going to the warehouse where he aims a gun at Burns, who allows him into the warehouse. Ryan confronts Gomez and Talman, and a shootout takes place where Ryan kills both Gomez and Talman. Mortally wounded, Ryan is cradled by Day, who tells him that she still loves him before he dies. Though its plot is outlandish in places, Stevenson directs with a firm hand and provides a fast-paced story packed with a lot of well-choreographed action. Ryan is superb as the victimized company boss struggling with his past while testing his own allegiance to his country. The beautiful Day is suitably heroic, and Carter is captivating as the sex tool used by the communists while Gomez gives an outstandingly convincing performance as the insidious manipulator of that tool. The film did only moderate box office as the public found this tale more political than dramatic. Songs: "I Haven't a Thing to Wear" (Harry Revel), "One for My Baby/And One More for the Road" (Harold Arlen). ***Author's Note***: Ryan told this author that "**The Woman on Pier 13** was really a test that Howard Hughes made when he was running RKO. He was very patriotic and we all knew that the communists posed a threat to America, so he used this picture and a few others to root out those at RKO that might have communist sympathies. He contacted more than a dozen directors and asked them to direct **The Woman on Pier 13**, and they all refused, so he put them on his list as secret communists, or communist sympathizers or fellow travelers. He finally hired Stevenson, a British director, to supervise the production. All the moguls that ran the Hollywood studios were doing the same thing as they were scared witless that the FBI would be handcuffing them at any moment. Those were the days of the Red Scare and, believe me, they were very real. I looked upon the story for that picture as just another well-written crime yarn with the communists thrown in for good measure." Gomez told this author that "I had no regrets in playing a murderous communist in that picture. I knew all about the commies and I knew they would stop at nothing to undermine our way of life. They constituted a real threat to America and anyone who thought otherwise in those days was not in touch with reality." Other anti-communist films include **Assignment: Paris**, 1952; **Arctic Flight**, 1952; **Avalanche Express**, 1979; **Big Jim McLain**, 1952; **Billion Dollar Brain**, 1967; **A Bullet for Joey**, 1955; **Captain Scarface**, 1953; **Counterspy Meets Scotland Yard**, 1950; **The Deadly Affair**, 1967; **Die another Day**, 2002; **Diplomatic Courier**, 1952; **Dr. Strangelove**, 1964; **The Double**, 2011; **The Double Man**, 1968; **The Fearmakers**, 1958; **The Falcon and the Snowman**, 1985; **Family of Spies**, 1990 (made-for-TV); **5 Steps to Danger**, 1957; **Foreign Intrigue**, 1956; **The Fourth Protocol**, 1987; **From Russia with Love**, 1964; **Funeral in Berlin**, 1966; **Hell and High Water**, 1954; **High Treason**, 1952; **The Hunter**, 1952 (TV series); **I Was a Communist for the F.B.I.**, 1951; **Invasion U.S.A.**, 1952; **Invasion U.S.A.**, 1985; **The Ipcress File**, 1965; **The Iron Curtain**, 1948; **Jet Attack**, 1958; **The Jigsaw Man**, 1984; **The Journey**, 1959; **The Kremlin Letter**, 1970; **License to Kill**, 1989; **The Looking Glass War**, 1970; **The Mackintosh Man**, 1973; **Man on a Tightrope**, 1953; **The Manchurian Candidate**, 1962; **The Manchurian Candidate**, 2004; **My Son John**, 1952; **Night People**, 1954; **Pickup on South Street**, 1952; **Rambo: First Blood Part II**, 1985; **Rambo III**, 1988; **Red Dawn**, 1984; **Red Dawn**, 2012; **The Red Menace**, 1949; **Red Scorpion**, 1989; **Salt**, 2010; **Satan Never Sleeps**, 1962; **Security Risk**, 1954; **Shack Out on 101**, 1955; **Spies Like Us**, 1985; **The Spy Who Came in from the Cold**, 1965; **The Spy Who Loved Me**, 1977; **The Russia House**, 1990; **The Thief**, 1952; **Topaz**, 1969; **Torn Curtain**, 1966; **Trial**, 1955; **Walk a Crooked Mile**, 1948; **Walk East on Beacon!**, 1952; **The Whip Hand**, 1951; and **The Whistle Blower**, 1987. **p**, Jack J. Gross; **d**, Robert Stevenson; **cast**, Laraine Day, Robert Ryan, John Agar, Janis Carter, Thomas Gomez, Richard Rober, William Talman, Paul Guilfoyle, Paul E. Burns, Iris Adrian; **w**, Robert Hardy Andrews, Charles Grayson (based on a story by George W. George, George F. Slavin); **c**, Nicholas Musuraca; **m**, Leigh Harline; **ed**, Roland Gross; **art d**, Albert S. D'Agostino, Walter E. Keller; **set d**, Darrell Silvera, James Altwies.

The Woman on the Beach ★★★ 1947; U.S.; 71m; RKO; B/W; Drama/Film Noir/Romance; Children: Unacceptable; **DVD**; **VHS**. Pantheon French director Renoir presents an engrossing, moody film noir tale that begins with Ryan, a one-time Coast Guard officer during World War II (1939-1945). Ryan is beset with emotional problems after surviving a mine explosion that had sunk his ship. Ryan sees nothing but skeletal remains resting beneath all the nearby waters and he also sees a strange blonde woman in the distance, one he cannot ever reach. Ryan comes to believe that he is becoming insane. He then meets Leslie, a blonde woman who works at a nearby shipyard and seems to resemble the ghostly woman of Ryan's nightmares. Ryan soon proposes marriage to Leslie, and she accepts. As Ryan rides his horse along the seaside, he spots Bennett, a ravishingly beautiful brunette, who stands near the wreckage of a torpedoed boat. Ryan learns that she is unhappily married to Bickford, a famous painter whom she accidentally blinded during an argument. They live together in a small cottage crammed with Bickford's paintings, which Bickford claims are now priceless since he can no longer paint. Ryan falls under Bennett's romantic spell, and the two find each other sharing the same feeling of being trapped in life. Bickford unsettles Ryan by attempting to befriend him, sensing that Bennett is drawn to the younger man, although he is convinced that Bennett will never leave him for Ryan. For his part, Ryan resents Bickford's

Robert Ryan and Laraine Day in *The Woman on Pier 13*, 1949.

superior, avuncular attitude. Ryan begins to think that Bickford suspects he loves Bennett and also that he is not really blind, so he takes Bickford to a cliff, hoping he will fall off and die. Bickford falls but survives. Ryan then thinks to drown the blind Bickford by taking him on a fishing outing where Ryan scuttles the boat, believing that the helpless Bickford will drown. The two are nevertheless saved when a Coast Guard vessel arrives to pluck them from the sea. The boat was summoned by Bennett, who was aware of Ryan's plot and, at the last minute, refused to go along with the murder plan. While being saved, Ryan sees Leslie as part of the rescue team and now relates her image to that of the blonde woman who had earlier beckoned to him. Ryan is in a romantic dilemma and gets a phone call from Bennett urging him to come to her cottage immediately. He arrives to find it on fire, and Bickford is throwing his paintings onto the mounting flames. Bennett, who only married Bickford so that she might become rich from the sale of his paintings, reluctantly helps Bickford to safety. Bickford then tells Bennett that he destroyed his paintings because they were his obsession and caused his continuing mental anxieties. He proposes that he and Bennett return to New York where they originally found happiness together. When Bennett accepts, Ryan realizes he has no future with Bennett and departs. Renoir provides an unnerving, edgy psychological melodrama where Ryan, Bennett and Bickford are outstanding in their roles as deeply troubled people. The lensing from Tover and Wild presents a bleak landscape befitting the emotional makeup of the characters, and Eisler's powerful and haunting score enhances the fitful story line. The film did not do well at the box office as viewers found it difficult to comprehend the subtleties and nuances Renoir implanted within his characters. This film is not related to a 2006 film with the same name. *Author's Note*: No sharp and convenient definitions for the motives and goals of the characters in this film are presented by Renoir to ameliorate the public's anxieties, and the ambiguous finale seems to leave the romantic trio and their deep problems unresolved. This also troubled RKO's front office, which grossly tampered with this film, editing it to the point where gaps of continuity of the story line are obvious and some of the dialog seems inapplicable. Bennett was behind this film from the start, wanting to work with Renoir, and she had the backing of her husband, producer Walter Wanger, although Jack Gross became its producer. "The producer [Gross] suddenly got involved with other projects before the picture was completed," Bennett told this author, "and that left Jean [Renoir] to handle everything, and I think it became too much for him. That is why the picture seems to be somewhat disjointed, although it has Jean's mark of genius throughout." Ryan told this author: "I never really understood my character in that picture. Renoir never fully explained it to me, other than to tell me that my character was going mentally downhill because of his war experi-

Charles Bickford, Robert Ryan and Joan Bennett in *The Woman on the Beach,* 1947.

ences. At one point, I say about myself in that picture: 'Let's face it—I'm not well!' That only scratched the surface of my character, who can't quite decide to kill the husband of the woman he wants, but keeps trying to murder him just the same." **p**, Jack J. Gross; **d**, Jean Renoir; **cast**, Joan Bennett, Robert Ryan, Charles Bickford, Nan Leslie, Walter Sande, Irene Ryan, Glenn Vernon, Frank Darien, Jay Norris, Martha Hyer; **w**, Renoir, Frank Davis, Michael Hogan (based on the novel *Not So Blind* by Mitchell Wilson); **c**, Leo Tover, Harry Wild; **m**, Hanns Eisler; **art d**, Albert S. D'Agostino, Walter E. Keller; **set d**, Darrell Silvera, John Sturtevant; **spec eff**, Russell A. Cully.

Woman on the Run ★★★ 1950; U.S.; 77m; Fidelity/UNIV; B/W; Crime Drama; Children: Unacceptable; **DVD**; **VHS**; **IV**. Superior crime yarn has Elliott as an artist, who is walking his dog along a San Francisco beach at night when he witnesses a killing and fears for his life, so he goes into hiding. Keith, a police inspector, and Jenks, a detective, interrogate Sheridan, who is Elliott's wife, but she does not provide information that discloses his whereabouts. She is uncooperative, not happy in her marriage, and the officers have her watched, thinking that Sheridan has something to hide. O'Keefe, a tabloid reporter, helps her find her husband and offers her $3,000 for an exclusive interview. Little does she know that O'Keefe is the actual killer, who is using her to find Elliott so he can kill him and thus eliminate the only eyewitness to the murder. O'Keefe committed the murder to silence a man who was blackmailing him. The mystery ends at an amusement park where Keith kills O'Keefe just before O'Keefe can kill Sheridan and Elliott, who then reconcile for a happy ending. Foster directs this tense film noir tale at a fast clip and draws top-flight performances from Sheridan, Keith and, especially O'Keefe. **p**, Howard Welsch; **d**, Norman Foster; **cast**, Ann Sheridan, Dennis O'Keefe, Robert Keith, John Qualen, Frank Jenks, Ross Elliott, Jane Liddell, J. Farrell MacDonald, Steven Geray, Victor Sen Yung; **w**, Alan Campbell, Foster (based on a story by Sylvia Tate); **c**, Hal Mohr; **m**, Emil Newman, Arthur Lange; **ed**, Otto Ludwig; **art d**, Boris Leven; **set d**, Jacques Mapes; **spec eff**, Loyal Griggs, Robert Hansard.

Woman They Almost Lynched ★★★ 1953; U.S.; 90m; REP; B/W; Western; Children: Unacceptable; **BD**; **DVD**; **VHS**. This offbeat but intriguing western takes place during the American Civil War (1861-1865) and is set in a small town on the Kansas-Missouri border where the community has refused to take sides in the conflict. Leslie is about to be hanged as a Confederate spy, although she is innocent. She is an Easterner who wandered into town to run a saloon, and she packs a gun. The real spy is her boyfriend, Lund, who is not suspected. Meanwhile, the notorious Confederate guerrilla leader, William Quantrill (1837-

1865), played by Donlevy, rides into town with outlaws Jesse James (1847-1882), played by Cooper; his brother Frank James (1843-1915), played by Brown; and fellow outlaw Cole Younger (1844-1916), played by Davis. Donlevy and his guerrillas have arrived to loot the riches of a local mine and they come into conflict with Lund, who secretly represents the regular Confederate army. Lund is shot and wounded in a gunfight with the guerrillas, but Leslie saves his life and tells him that she loves him. Meanwhile, Leslie is seized and held as a spy by locals who are intent on lynching her. Totter, who rides with Donlevy, however, does the noble thing and tells the residents that she is the spy before Totter rides off with the guerrillas. Saved from the rope, Leslie plans a life with Lund to end this unusual oater. Songs: "All My Life" (music: Sam H. Sept; lyrics: Sidney D. Mitchell), "How Strange" (Victor Young). *Author's Note*: Donlevy told this author that "I knew my character very well when we made **Woman They Almost Lynched** as I had played Quantrill in an earlier picture called **Kansas Raiders** [1950]. Quantrill was probably the most disreputable border guerrilla during the Civil War, a bloodthirsty killer who only gave lip service to the South he pretended to fight for while he went about looting towns. The man was an outlaw, plain and simple." **p&d**, Allan Dwan; **cast**, John Lund, Brian Donlevy, Audrey Totter, Joan Leslie, Ben Cooper, James Brown, Jim Davis, Reed Hadley, Ann Savage, Virginia Christine, Richard Crane, Dick Simmons, Gordon Jones, Ellen Corby, Minerva Urecal; **w**, Steve Fisher (based on a story by Michael Fessier); **c**, Reggie Lanning; **m**, Stanley Wilson; **ed**, Fred Allen; **art d**, James Sullivan; **set d**, John McCarthy Jr., George Milo; **spec eff**, Howard Lydecker, Theodore Lydecker.

A Woman Under the Influence ★★★ 1974; U.S.; 155m; Faces International; Color; Drama; Children: Unacceptable (MPAA: R); **BD**; **DVD**; **VHS**; **IV**. Perfectionist outsider Cassavetes presents through his talented real-life wife Rowlands a mesmerizing portrait of an un-average housewife slowly losing her mind. Rowlands is married to Falk, an amiable blue-collar construction worker, and they have three well-balanced, loveable children, Cassel, Labyorteaux, and Grisanti. Rowlands is not sophisticated, coming from a lower-class family, but she is good-hearted and well intentioned, but there is a frustrating hesitancy in her manner that suggests that she is unfulfilled and searching for something better in her life. She and her family live in Los Angeles, and Rowlands maintains the household, devoting herself to her loving husband Falk and her children, so much so that there seems to be nothing left for herself. Her conduct becomes increasingly erratic while she blurts out ideas that make sense to her but alarm others, such as calmly urging her children to dance naked. She is not, to her mind, suggesting anything indecent, only her interpretation of how she loves life and how the freedom of the human body might be unashamedly shown. At one point, Rowlands tells her children: "I hope that you will never grow up." In this she obliquely identifies her own inner recognition that perceives herself to be a little girl living inside of the body of an adult (but nevertheless wholly uninhibited) woman. Her children, at another point, reply to Rowlands when she asks what they think of her that she is "funny, smart, and nervous." Of course, to the minds of her adult family members, rooted to conventional beliefs, Rowland's unconventional behavior indicates only that she is becoming mentally unbalanced. Falk, on the other hand, is an inarticulate and uneducated laborer. He loves his wife and children and shows it, but he has no patience for Rowlands' sometimes outlandish statements and her borderline manic behavior. He erupts into brief physical violence as he does equally inexplicable things such as verbally and physically abusing Rowlands, and, at one point, getting his children a bit tipsy. Such brute-like behavior is excused by others simply because he is a "man's man." Meanwhile, Rowlands loses what little is left of her own personality, as if using it up by lavishing that persona onto her loved ones in a fanatical need to please, until she is emotionally bankrupt. Falk dominates her every move and Rowlands is forever pleading with him for guidance by repeatedly stating: "Just tell me how you want me to act?" His patented response is always: "Just be yourself!" This, of course, is not what he really wants, if Falk knows at all what he really wants. When Rowlands becomes more and more erratic, Falk's family members urge him to have her institutionalized so that she can "get help" and where her mind can be restored to some self-control. To that end, Falk, who has resisted doing that very thing, finally takes Rowlands to an asylum. She is treated for six months and is then released. Before she is to arrive at her home, Falk invites a host of family and friends to welcome Rowlands back to the fold, but he thinks twice about this and sends most of the guests away. Only the immediate family is there to receive Rowlands and, when she arrives, there is a happy re-union that soon diminishes to small talk; Rowlands is shown to be just as unsure and questioning her existence as she was before she was sum-marily packed off to that institution. She manifests the same unstable tendencies as before she was institutionalized by nervously cutting her-self on the night she returns. Falk realizes that nothing has changed after Rowlands puts the children to bed. Falk and Rowlands retire for another night together where their relationship remains uncertain and all the strain and turmoil of the past hauntingly lingers to remain bitterly unre-solved. This unnerving but fascinating tale is well crafted and helmed by Cassavetes. It nevertheless serves as an obsequious visual slave to the then Women's Liberation Movement of the 1970s in its savage por-trayal of Rowlands being under the servile influence of her dominating husband, Falk, a man undeserving (as were all men according to the credo of that movement) of being a spouse. Cassavetes supported that movement and here he indicts men in general on that movement's behalf through his rather insidious portrayal of Falk as an unthinking but good-natured brute. He thus universally represents all married men of that era as depriving their wives of their own individualities, the sacred personas so assiduously and fiercely advanced by Women's Libbers. There is, however, blinding moments of brilliance shown in the direction of this offbeat tale that saves it from being an utterly hectoring moral lecture. Cassavetes inventively uses his camera for Rowlands' confused POV as it searches in hand-held jitteriness one uninviting room after another in her confining house, an unfulfilled quest for visual comfort, and where as much as Rowlands seeks the same emotional assurance. Un-fortunately, many of the scenes are way too long, as if Cassavetes him-self was unsure as to where to end a scene, even after he had exhausted all meaning and significance to a sequence. It is safe to assume that Cas-savetes would think that the viewer would excuse such technical mean-derings as being integral to the unstable mentality of Rowlands and thus provide a rationale for such irrational filmmaking. This film is far from being a masterpiece and is sometimes amateurish and awkward to the point of being sloppy, but Rowlands makes it all worthwhile seeing through her powerfully penetrating performance, which approaches the magnificent in many scenes, especially where she teeters between life-loving ebullience and stark depression over her dead-end lifestyle. Row-lands deservedly received an Oscar nomination for Best Actress, and the film received another Oscar nomination for Best Director (Cas-savetes). The film did surprisingly well at the box office, earning more than $6 million in its initial release against a poverty-row budget of about $1 million and the fact that it saw extremely limited distribution. The film eventually grossed more than $12 million. Songs/Music: "La Boheme" (1896; Giacomo Puccini), "I Get a Kick Out of You" (1934; Cole Porter), "Torna a Surriento" (1902; music: Ernesto De Curtis; lyrics: Giambattista De Curtis), "Aida" (1871; Giuseppe Verdi), "Swan Lake" (1875; Peter Ilyich Tchaikovsky), "Song of My Mother" (Angelo Grisanti). *Author's Note*: The idea for this film originated with Row-lands, who asked her husband, Cassavetes, to write a play about a woman facing contemporary problems and she would star in that stage production. The script Cassavetes wrote provided such an intense char-acter that Rowlands felt she could never stand up to playing such a men-tally disabled person night after night. Cassavetes then opted to employ the script for a film. He found little or no interest from any of the Hol-lywood studios and then decided to produce the film himself. He used

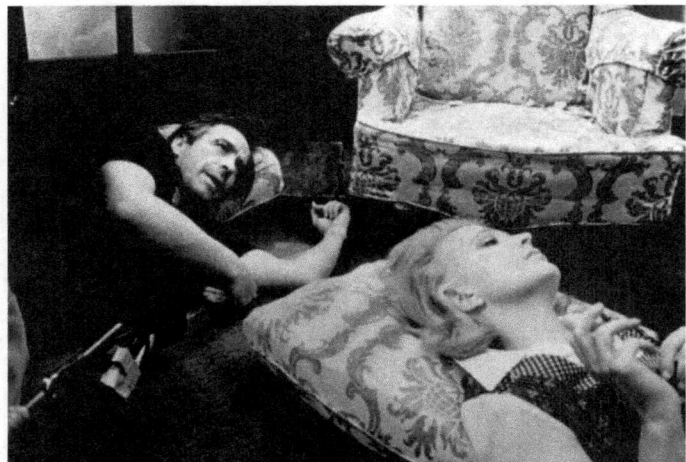

John Cassavetes directing his wife, Gena Rowlands, in *A Woman Under the Influence*, 1974.

his own money and those of friends, such as Falk (who reportedly in-vested $500,000) to eventually produce this film. When completed, Cas-savetes could not find a distributer to handle the film so he personally booked it into as many art house theaters that would show it. "I guess that picture was just about the most nerve-wracking thing I ever expe-rienced," Falk told this author. "I don't know which one of us was the nut, me or Gena [Rowlands] when we were playing man and wife in **A Woman Under the Influence**. I can only explain it with one word—relentless!" **p**, Sam Shaw; **d&w**, John Cassavetes; **cast**, Peter Falk, Gena Rowlands, Matthew Cassel, Matthew Labyorteaux, Fred Draper, Lady Rowlands, Katherine Cassavetes, Christina Grisanti, O.G. Dunn, Mario Gallo, Xan Cassavetes; **c**, Mitch Breit, Al Ruban (MGM Color); **m**, Bo Harwood; **ed**, David Armstrong, Elizabeth Bergeron, Sheila Viseltear, Tom Cornwell; **art d**, Phedon Papamichael.

Woman Who Came Back ★★★ 1945; U.S.; 68m; REP; B/W; Hor-ror; Children: Unacceptable; **DVD**; **VHS**; **IV**. Eerie tale begins when Dudgeon, an old woman, flags down a bus on a road along woods near Eden Rock, Massachusetts. She takes a seat next to Kelly, who is re-turning home to the town after being away for two years. Dudgeon surprises Kelly by calling her by name and talks about events in the town 300 years ago when women were burned at the stake as witches after trials that had been convened by Dudgeon's ancestor. The bus suddenly veers off the road and goes into a lake. Kelly survives, but Dudgeon is missing. In town, people think Kelly is descended from witches and probably is one herself. The only person glad to see Kelly is physician Loder, her former fiancé. Strange things start happening in and around town, and everyone suspects Kelly is possessed. She is so distraught that she tries suicide but survives, and then an old prophecy may be about to be fulfilled. Kelly searches her past, discov-ering that she is a descendant of a judge at the Salem Witchcraft Trials who sent fifteen women to their deaths as witches. She learns that a pact was made at that time between one of the witches and the Devil, where the evil soul of the witch is passed on to the young woman near-est to the witch following her death. Kelly now believes that the de-ceased Dungeon has passed on her evil being to her. Loder conducts his own research into the old Witchcraft trials and discovers a journal written by Kelly's ancestor where that judge admitted forging docu-ments and confessions that wrongly sent women convicted as witches to their fiery deaths. He takes this journal to Kelly but is alarmed to see her house being set on fire by residents, who are convinced that Kelly is a witch. Loder sees Kelly race from the house and flee to a nearby lake, plunging wildly into the waters. Loder runs after her, pulling her to safety. He then finds Dudgeon's body, proving that she was merely an old, demented woman, and, like the residents, was con-

Conrad Veidt bending Joan Crawford to his will in *A Woman's Face*, **1941.**

sumed by superstition. Now convinced that she is under no evil spell, Kelly plans a future with Loder. Kelly, an accomplished stage performer, does a good job as a woman haunted by her past, and Loder is a standout as the resolute doctor who brings sanity and safety to her life. For other films dealing with witches, see Witchcraft in Subject Index. **p&d**, Walter Colmes; **cast**, Nancy Kelly, John Loder, Otto Kruger, Ruth Ford, Harry Tyler, Jeanne Gail, Almira Sessions, J. Farrell McDonald, Emmett Vogan, Sam Ash, Elspeth Dudgeon; **w**, Dennis Cooper, Lee Willis (based on a story by John H. Kafka and an idea by Philip Yordan); **c**, Henry Sharp; **m**, Edward Plumb; **ed**, John Link; **set d**, Jacques Mapes; **spec eff**, Mario Castegnaro, Ray Mercer.

A Woman's Face ★★★★ 1941; U.S.; 105m; MGM; B/W; Crime Drama; Children: Unacceptable; **DVD**; **VHS**; **IV**. In this superlative remake of a 1939 Swedish film starring Ingrid Bergman, Crawford gives a memorable and powerful performance as a woman struggling between her evil past and a future that promises redemption and happiness. We see her living as a reclusive lady in Stockholm (retaining the setting of the 1939 version) where she hides her hideously disfigured face by a veil. She has had to bear that terrible face since being injured in childhood. In flashback, we then see a courtroom where Crawford stands trial for murder. Witnesses take the stand to unravel this mysterious woman's past. In further flashback, we see Crawford operating a small café outside the city. She seeks retribution for the physical and psychological injuries she has endured by involving herself with a ring of blackmailers preying upon the rich and powerful. She meets charming Veidt, a calculating member of high society whose family fortune is depleted, and he seeks to restore its assets by any means. Veidt rightly believes that Crawford is strong as iron but knows that she seeks affection like most any other person; he gives her the attentions she so desperately wants. He soon becomes Crawford's Svengali, inveigling her into a murderous plot. Veidt covets a great inheritance from his father, Bassermann, but Veidt's young nephew, Nichols, stands to receive that fortune, which will only fall to Veidt should Nichols somehow perish. It is that death that Veidt busies himself in preparing, using Crawford as his accomplice. She nevertheless continues to pursue her lucrative blackmailing operations after she obtains some scandalous letters penned by Massen, who is the wife of Douglas, a successful plastic surgeon. Crawford thinks to blackmail Massen after she realizes that Massen has been cheating on Douglas with a secret lover. She takes the letters and goes to the home of her victim. Just as Crawford confronts Massen, however, Douglas returns, going into his surgery room (his medical practice is at his residence) where Crawford has hidden herself and where she has injured her foot when attempting to flee. Massen tells the startled Douglas that Crawford is a burglar, but, when Douglas thinks to call the police,

Massen thinks twice, realizing that Crawford might reveal her secret affair and urges Douglas not to contact authorities. Douglas sees Crawford's horribly scarred face and tells her that he can use his skills as a plastic surgeon to restore her beauty. Crawford is at first reluctant to undergo such an operation, but she finally agrees. Douglas performs the surgery, and the results are stunning as Crawford is now a beautiful woman. Although both know that Douglas has beneficially altered Crawford's appearance, her psyche remains scarred with terrible memories of her past. All Crawford can think about is how her new appearance will please Veidt and she rushes to him to show her new face. Veidt states that he is pleased with this new woman, but reminds Crawford that they must proceed to the business at hand and that is dispatching Nichols. Veidt persuades the near senile Bassermann to hire Crawford as Nichols' nanny and she is soon living inside that family mansion where she soon realizes that Nichols is a likeable and innocent boy. Her heart softens toward him and they quickly bond so that Crawford now becomes as protective of the boy as if she were his own mother. All the while, Crawford struggles with her orders from Veidt where she will arrange for Nichols' "accidental" death by uncoupling a link to the system that operates a cable car going upward toward a mountain pass while Nichols is riding in that cable car. All of this takes place when there is a festive event taking place at Bassermann's mansion where, ironically, Douglas is watching the cable car slowly make its way upward toward the mountain pass (as tension inherently mounts in this anxious scene), but nothing happens. Veidt is livid, as he realizes that Crawford has betrayed him. Crawford, at the last minute, cannot bring herself to commit such a heinous act as bringing about the death of an innocent boy. Even though she loosens the bolt that will cause Nichols' death, she pulls him back to safety and hugs him with love at the last moment. When seeing how Nichols survives his murderous plot, Veidt becomes incensed by the fact that he has lost control over Crawford. He realizes with rage that she has regained her conscience and is adhering to the good heart she has always possessed while breaking free of the Svengali ties Veidt has so effectively used to control her. During festivities that celebrate Bassermann's birthday, everyone participates in sleigh rides. When Crawford sees Veidt abruptly place Nichols in a sleigh and frantically whip its horses to wildly drive off with him, she realizes that Veidt has resolved to personally end the boy's life. While she and Douglas are in another sleigh, she urges him to catch up with Veidt, confessing to the plot to murder Nichols. A frantic pursuit ensues, and Douglas manages to catch up with Veidt just as he is about to throw Nichols over the edge of a cliff and into a falls. Crawford, however, produces a gun and shoots Veidt while Douglas plucks Nichols into his own sleigh. Dying from the wound inflicted by Crawford, Veidt loses control of his sleigh and plunges to his death. In a flash-forward to Crawford's trial, Douglas testifies on Crawford's behalf, saying that she saved Nichols' life. He also admits in open court that he loves Crawford and thus tacitly intends to end his marriage with the cheating Massen. The judges weigh all the evidence and conclude that Crawford did not murder Veidt and she is exonerated, set free to begin a new life with Douglas. Cukor, the consummate "woman's director," does a fine job managing the complex plot as he carefully develops Crawford's complicated character, increasing tension as he also unfolds Veidt's insidious murder scheme, and while merging the budding romance between Crawford and Douglas. Crawford gives one of her finest performances as a woman struggling to regain her ability to love and be loved as she also makes a heroic effort to resist Veidt's evil machinations that feed her lifelong hatreds for those who have wronged her. She startlingly shows a marvelous transformation from evil to good after the loving Douglas restores her beauty with his scalpel as much as the prince awakened the sleeping beauty with his kiss. Cukor expertly exposes Crawford's true sensitivity toward beauty and goodness early on when she sits down at a piano to play an inspiring piece by Chopin for Veidt, and, more expansively, when she emerges from Douglas' operation as a woman no longer hideously scarred. At that moment, she realizes that she need no longer hide a gargoyle's image, which has been transplanted into a beautiful countenance. She joyfully removes her hat to show her new face to the world, allowing the wind to blow freely through her hair as she walks down a street full of happy confidence, as if escaping a hellish underworld to reenter the world of the living. Douglas is his pleasing and reassuring self while Veidt oozes evil as the scheming Svengali, the kind of role for which he was best known. This film did not initially do well at the box office, until MGM's publicity department boosted its image by releasing a campaign that advertised the glamorous Crawford as "a female monster" and thus causing her fans to flock into the theaters. The film subsequently realized more than $1.9 million at the box office against a budget of more than $1.3 million. It saw a thirty-minute radio adaptation that was aired by the Screen Guild Theater on April 19, 1942, with Veidt reprising his role. It saw a second radio adaptation of sixty minutes that was aired by Lux Radio Theater on November 2, 1942, with Veidt also reprising his role. *Author's Note*: Cukor told this author that "directing Joan Crawford was a delight. We worked well together when I directed her in **The Women** [1939] and in **Susan and God** [1940], and, by the time we did **A Woman's Face**, we were very comfortable with each other. By that time, she had the utmost confidence that I would bring out her best performance. She is a vibrant person with great tonal qualities to her voice, evident when she delivers her lines. But in **A Woman's Face** she is portraying a person who has no self-respect or sense of self-worth and I wanted her to reflect that by delivering a lot of her lines in a monotone. To achieve that I had Joan repeat over and over the multiplication table so that when she finally delivered her lines, she spoke in a worn-out monotone. She thought that brilliant, but I was only going back to my own childhood where I was forced to repeat those multiplication tables over and over again until I was so weary that my voice had no vitality and my words were uttered without inflection or emphasis. Good direction is sometimes based on simply recalling your own human experiences that might translate into an effective dramatic scene enacted by those that will listen to what you have to say. Joan was always a good listener." Crawford did not initially warm to her character in this film when offered the part. Crawford stated to this author: "'You want me to look like what?' I said to the Vic [Victor Saville, producer of this film] when he first told me about my role in **A Woman's Face**. He told me that I would be playing a woman so scarred and ugly that she fears showing her face to anyone. I said to him: 'My face is my career, Vic, and you want me to dump that into an ash can?' He hemmed and hawed and then said: 'You start out looking like hell, yes, but your face is restored by a plastic surgeon and your regain your beautiful looks.' Well, that intrigued me so much that, after I read the script, I could not wait to play the role, especially after I knew that George [Cukor] would be my director. I knew George would never let me stay ugly on the screen for too long. Saying that reminds me of a line the little boy [Nichols] says to me in that picture. He says: 'You could never be mean. You're too pretty.' Well, that's the way the world thinks—that beauty is good and those who are ugly are not. That part always bothered me, because there are millions of women who are not pretty, but they are wonderful and good and beneath their faces they are more beautiful than a lot of the Venus de Milos I have seen strutting around Hollywood, believe me." This was the second film that the German-born Veidt made in the U.S., following **Escape**, 1940, where he continues to play an intelligent but utterly insidious character, the kind of role that the articulate and talented Veidt wholeheartedly embraced. Unlike Veidt, Bassermann, who was also a native of Germany, never mastered the English language. In fact, he could not speak the language unless learning his lines phonetically from his patient wife, Elsa, but he nevertheless and quite amazingly delivered those lines in English with the perfect inflection to every word. Many other films depicting plastic surgeons and plastic surgery include **The Air I Breathe**, 2007; **All About My Mother**, 1999; **American Mary**, 2012; **Anna Nicole**, 2007; **Another Face**, 1935; **Another Pretty Face**, 2002 (made-for-TV); **Anthony Zimmer**, 2006; **Arsenic and Old Lace**, 1944; **Arsenic and Old**

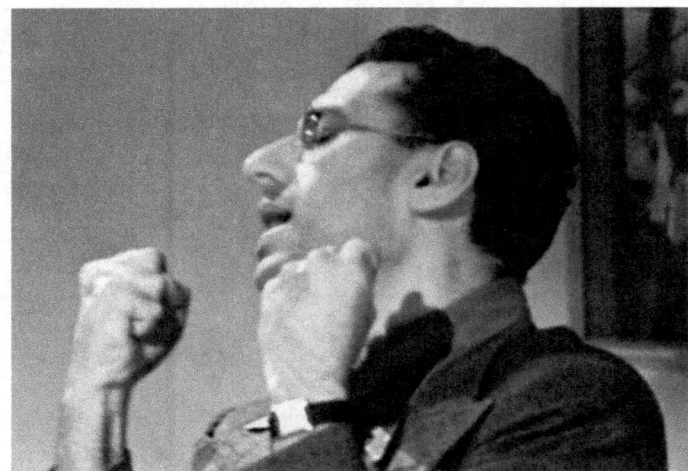

George Cukor directing a scene during the production of *A Woman's Face*, **1941.**

Lace, 1969 (made-for-TV); **Arthur 3: The War of the Two Worlds**, 2010; **Ash Wednesday**, 1973; **Bad Teacher**, 2011; **Behind the Candelabra**, 2013 (made-for-TV); **Below the Deadline**, 1936; **Bernard and Doris**, 2007; **Beyond Recognition**, 2003; **Black Dragons**, 1942; **Blackout**, 1985 (made-for-TV); **Borderline Murder**, 2011 (made-for-TV); **The Brain That Wouldn't Die**, 1962; **Brazil**, 1985; **Brief Crossing**, 2002; **Burn after Reading**, 2008; **Calendar Girl**, 1993; **Campus Confidential**, 2005 (made-for-TV); **Cape of Good Hope**, 2004; **Captain America**, 1990; **Carnage**, 2002; **Cassandra's Dream**, 2007; **Celebrity**, 1998; **Charlie Chan at the Wax Museum**, 1940; **A Chorus Line**, 1985; **Chrysalis**, 2008; **Circus of Horrors**, 1960; **City Girl**, 1938; **Confetti**, 2006; **Corruption**, 1968; **Cronos**, 1994; **Dan in Real Life**, 2007; **The Dancer Upstairs**, 2002; **Dark Passage**, 1947; **Dead End**, 1937; **Death Becomes Her**, 1992; **The Devil's Double**, 2011; **The Diabolical Dr. Z**, 1967; **Diamonds Are Forever**, 1971; **Doc Hollywood**, 1991; **Dr. Renault's Secret**, 1942; **Doctors Don't Tell**, 1941; **The Dolly Sisters**, 1945; **Escape from L.A.**, 1996; **Eyes Without a Face**, 1962; **Face/Off**, 1997; **The Face Behind the Mask**, 1941; **A Face to Die For**, 1996 (made-for-TV); **Faceless**, 1987; **False Face**, 1977; **False Faces**, 1932; **Fedora**, 1978; **First Yank into Tokyo**, 1945; **For Your Consideration**, 2006; **Foxy Brown**, 1974; **Get Smart**, 2008; **The Ghost Walks**, 1934; **The Girl in the Kremlin**, 1957; **The Girl Most Likely to…**, 1973; **G-Men Never Forget**, 1948; **Good Luck Chuck**, 2007; **Goodbye, Columbus**, 1969; **Goodnight Mommy**, 2014; **The Great Beauty**, 2013; **The Guest**, 2014; **He Who Dares: Downing Street Siege**, 2014; **Head Over Heels**, 2001; **Hello Again**, 1987; **Hired Killer**, 1966; **His Kind of Woman**, 1951; **Hollow Triumph**, 1948; **I Could Never Be Your Woman**, 2007; **The Illegal Immigrant**, 1985; **Ira & Abby**, 2006; **It's Complicated**, 2009; **Jail Bait**, 1954; **The Jigsaw Man**, 1984; **Johnny Handsome**, 1989; **Just Before Dawn**, 1946; **Just Go With It**, 2011; **Kid Monk Baroni**, 1952; **Killer Babes**, 2007; **A King in New York**, 1957; **L.A. Confidential**, 1997; **Logan's Run**, 1976; **Looker**, 1981; **Lovely & Amazing**, 2001; **Made in Italy**, 2008; **Man in the Mirror: The Michael Jackson Story**, 2004 (made-for-TV); **The Man Who Lived Twice**, 1936; **Mask of Death**, 1996; **Me, Myself & Irene**, 2000; **Melvin Goes to Dinner**, 2003; **The Menace**, 1932; **The Merry Widow**, 2007; **Mirror, Mirror**, 1979 (made-for-TV); **Mississippi Gambler**, 1942; **Mouth to Mouth**, 1997; **Movie 43**, 2013; **Murder in Texas**, 1981 (made-for-TV); **My Only Love**, 1982; **Mystery of the 13th Guest**, 1943; **The Naked Kiss**, 1964; **Nighthawks**, 1981; **Nights in Rodanthe**, 2008; **Nip/Tuck**, 2003-2010 (TV series); **Norma Jean & Marilyn**, 1996 (made-for-TV); **Once upon a Time in Mexico**, 2003; **Open Windows**, 2014; **Open Your Eyes**, 1999; **Operation Kid Brother**, 1967; **The Osterman Weekend**, 1983; **Partners in Crime**, 2012; **Passenger 57**, 1992; **Peep World**,

Cornel Wilde, June Allyson, Clifton Webb and Arlene Dahl in *Woman's World,* **1954.**

2010; **Perfect People**, 1988 (made-for-TV); **Petunia**, 2012; **Plastic Man**, 1999 (made-for-TV); **The Point Men**, 2001; **Predestination**, 2014; **Priceless**, 2008; **The Promise**, 1979; **Providence**, 1999-2002 (TV series); **Public Enemies**, 2009; **Public Hero No. 1**, 1935; **Quicksilver Highway**, 1997 (made-for-TV); **The Raven**, 1935; **Remo Williams: The Adventure Begins**, 1985; **Repo! The Genetic Opera**, 2008; **Revenge**, 2000; **Richard**, 1972; **The Right to Romance**, 1933; **Romy and Michele's High School Reunion**, 1997; **Roxanne**, 1987; **The Second Face**, 1950; **Second Nature**, 2003 (made-for-TV); **Seconds**, 1966; **Seducing Doctor Lewis**, 2003; **Sgt. Pepper's Lonely Hearts Club Band**, 1978; **A Serious Man**, 2009; **The Shape of Things**, 2003; **Shattered**, 1991; **Sherlock Holmes; A Game of Shadows**, 2011; **Sherman Oaks**, 1995-1997 (TV series); **Shiri**, 2002; **Short Night of Glass Dolls**, 1971; **Sin City: A Dame to Kill For**, 2014; **Singles**, 1992; **The Skin I Live In**, 2011; **Smile**, 2005; **Smokin' Aces**, 2006; **Southland Tales**, 2006; **Speed Racer**, 2008; **Spin the Bottle**, 2000; **Stolen Face**, 1952; **Thirteen**, 2003; **The Three Trials**, 2006; **Thunderball**, 1965; **Time**, 2006; **The Tourist**, 2010; **Traffic**, 2000; **12 and Holding**, 2006; **2012**, 2009; **Vanilla Sky**, 2001; **White Fire**, 1985; **Winner Take All**, 1932; **A Woman's Face**, 1939; **Why Me?**, 1984 (made-for-TV); and **You Are a Widow, Sir**, 2012. **p**, Victor Saville; **d**, George Cukor; **cast**, Joan Crawford, Melvyn Douglas, Conrad Veidt, Osa Massen, Richard Nichols, Reginald Owen, Albert Bassermann, Marjorie Main, Donald Meek, Connie Gilchrist, Charles Quigley, George Zucco, Henry Daniell; **w**, Donald Ogden Stewart, Elliot Paul (based on the play "Il etait une fois" by Francis de Croisset); **c**, Robert Planck; **m**, Bronislau Kaper; **ed**, Frank Sullivan; **art d**, Cedric Gibbons; **set d**, Edwin B. Willis.

Woman's World ★★★ 1954; U.S.; 94m; FOX; Color; Drama; Children: Acceptable; **DVD**; **VHS**. Absorbing domestic tale sees Webb as an automobile manufacturing tycoon whose general manager leaves the company, so he invites three of his company's regional executives of about equal ability to New York to vie for the job. He decides that the job will go to the man whose wife best fits his idea of a corporate spouse. Heflin's wife, Dahl, is ambitious and wants him to get the job at any cost. MacMurray's wife, Bacall, fears that he is such a workaholic that overwork will cause his premature death and she'll never see him again. Wilde's wife, Allyson, is a small-town girl, who wants him to get the job if he wants it, but knows she'd be happier back home in Kansas City. The sophisticated and poised Bacall proves herself to be a generous-hearted competitor by coming to the aid of the plain-looking Allyson by helping her buy a new and impressive wardrobe that will suit the demanding Webb when all the competing couples attend a weekend stay at the estate of Webb's wealthy, socialite sister, Gillmore. Although she

is sweet and appealing to everyone, Allyson is hopelessly clumsy, displaying her awkward behavior by accidentally locking herself inside of a ladies' room at one social gathering and, to add to everyone's embarrassment, spills martinis onto some of the guests. Dahl, on the other hand, is a conniving wife who schemes to make sure her husband Heflin gets the job. To that end she uses her wiles with some of the corporate executives who might influence Webb to select Heflin. Webb learns about this and removes Heflin from his list of candidates. Heflin, however, also discovers his wife's underhanded machinations and, being the deliberate and forthright man he is, goes to Webb and exposes his wife's actions, apologizing for them. He tells Webb that he wants the job, but not through any devious methods his conniving wife might have put into action. Such honesty is not lost on Webb, who then reconsiders Heflin for the job and finally decides that he is the right man to run things. Heflin then breaks with the scheming Dahl, her ruthless ploys bringing her nothing but a dissolved marriage. Wilde and Allyson return to Kansas City where they will be happier, and Bacall and MacMurray go about rebuilding their strained relationship. The acting from the entire cast is superb, especially by Bacall, Heflin, MacMurray and Allyson, and Negulesco manages to balance with sense and comprehensive continuity the various subplots that undercurrent the story line. Of special note is the rich color photography that lavishly depicts the Big Apple of the 1950s, replete with Park Avenue, Macy's, Fifth Avenue, and the elite Stork Club, which was operated by Sherman Billingsley (1900-1966) and catered to the likes of powerful gossip columnist Walter Winchell (1897-1972) and FBI chief J. Edgar Hoover (1895-1972). The film did well at the box office, earning more than $3 million in its initial release against a budget of more than $2 million. Songs: "It's a Woman's World" (Cyril J. Mockridge, Sammy Cahn), "Blue Moon" (1934; Richard Rodgers, Lorenz Hart). *Author's Note*: Negulesco told this author that "the whole point of **Woman's World** was to show the public that corporate America was not only held together by determined and intelligent men, but the women who stood behind them and who represented the solid foundations of principles and values that held their careers together." Heflin's ethical character in this film would, as he told this author, be again tested years later when "I appeared in another picture based upon the inner workings of corporate America called **Patterns**, 1956. In that picture I had to deal with a ruthless tyrant played by Everett Sloane, but, in **Woman's World**, I had to deal with a benign business patriarch played by Clifton Webb. You know, there was an interesting inside joke in **Woman's World** that was mounted on the wall of Clifton's office, where a number of portraits of women he has loved in the past are shown. One of the portraits is of actress Gene Tierney and it is the very portrait of her that was used in a very good crime picture made by the same studio, Fox, called **Laura** [1944]. Clifton played a sophisticated columnist and killer in that very picture." MacMurray told this author that he enjoyed his role in this film, stating: "Working with Betty [Lauren Bacall] was a great pleasure as she is one of the most considerate actresses in Hollywood—no phony airs, very down to earth and always well prepared for her scenes. I have had my share of the other kind, actresses who demand a lot of hand-kissing and special considerations, but Betty always gets right down to the business at hand." The story line for this film is similar to that of **Executive Suite**, 1954, which was released the same year as this film, where Allyson again plays the loyally supportive wife of an executive (William Holden), who is vying for the position of company president. The concept of pitting several executives against each other in competition for a higher corporate position was also employed in **While the City Sleeps**, 1956, which sees media mogul Vincent Price putting his top people through their paces for that top job, which goes to the one who first identifies a serial killer on the loose. **p**, Charles Brackett; **d**, Jean Negulesco; **cast**, Clifton Webb, June Allyson, Van Heflin, Lauren Bacall, Fred MacMurray, Arlene Dahl, Cornel Wilde, Elliott Reid, Margalo Gillmore, Alan Reed; **w**, Claude Binyon, Russel Crouse, Howard Lindsay, Mary Loos, Richard Sale (based on a story by Mona Williams); **c**, Joseph MacDonald (CinemaScope; Technicolor); **m**, Cyril J. Mockridge; **ed**, Louis R. Loeffler; **art d**, Lyle R. Wheeler; **spec eff**, Ray Kellogg.

The Women ★★★★★ 1939; U.S.; 132m; MGM; B/W/Color (one color sequence); Drama; Children: Acceptable; **BD**; **DVD**; **VHS**; **IV**. Superlative all-women's tale sees a wonderful performance from Shearer, who is a happily married woman with Weidler as her darling daughter. Shearer's ideal marriage is threatened after her cousin, Russell, a notorious gossip, goes to a salon to get her fingernails colored to a jungle red. Russell hears Moore, a manicurist, tell her that Shearer's husband is having an affair with Crawford, a counter girl, who sells perfumes and makes it her mission in life to steal other women's husbands. Knowing that Shearer implicitly trusts her husband and that she will discount any claims made by her, Russell arranges for Shearer to visit the same manicurist where Shearer hears the same thing about her husband. Troubled by this claim, along with her husband's insistence that he must work long hours at his office, Shearer comes to believe that there might be some truth to the gossip. Her mother, Watson, urges her not to confront her husband and consider the claims against him as purely gossip. Although Shearer is suspicious, she takes a break and goes to Bermuda with Watson. When she returns, she attends a fashion show where Crawford is in attendance, and Russell then urges Shearer to confront Crawford as she is in a dressing room trying on gowns. Crawford does not only admit that the rumors about her and Shearer's husband are true, but brazenly tells Shearer that, unless she allows her husband to go on seeing her, she will most likely wind up being divorced. Thoroughly humiliated, Shearer departs and further endures abuse by constantly hearing more gossip spread by her chatterbox cousin Russell and her friend Povah, two first-class rumor mongers, until the story reaches and is spread by a gossip columnist. It's all too much for Shearer, who takes a train to Reno to seek a divorce. While on that sad trip, Shearer meets several other women going to the same destination and with the same objective, including Boland, a countess and former show girl, who has been married so many times that she has a hard time remembering her discarded spouses. She also meets shy Fontaine and tough-talking chorus girl Goddard. Once they all take residence at a ranch run by gruff-speaking Main, who liberally gives unwanted advice to everyone all the time, Shearer learns from Goddard that she is, ironically, having an affair with Russell's husband, and plans to not only steal him away from Russell but marry the cheating spouse. Shearer learns from Fontaine that she is pregnant and still loves her husband, so she convinces Fontaine to try to patch things up and hold onto her marriage. This Fontaine does. Then Russell arrives to learn that it is Goddard who has wrecked her marriage, and the two women get into a tumbledown fight that causes Shearer and the others to laugh uncontrollably until Shearer breaks up the brawl. Goddard then tells Shearer that she should call her husband before her divorce goes through within a few hours, and Shearer takes this good advice, only to learn when making that call that her husband has just married the scheming Crawford. It is now two years later, and Shearer has moved back to New York where she lives alone, sharing visitations with Weidler. Meanwhile, Weidler is a very unhappy little girl who lives with her father and her new stepmother, Crawford. She overhears Crawford talking to her new boyfriend while Crawford takes a bubble bath. When Weidler interrupts her, Crawford tells her to go away, which is Crawford's usual treatment of the little girl. Shearer hosts a party to celebrate Boland's two-year anniversary with her new husband, who is a radio star, but when all the ladies go to a nightclub, Shearer remains at home. Weidler, who is visiting her, then tells Shearer that Crawford is cheating on her father with none other than Boland's new husband. Shearer then decides to get her husband back by using the same tactics Crawford and others have used to destroy her marriage. She dresses to the nines and then tells Watson: "I have had two years to grow claws, Mother—jungle red!" Shearer arrives at the nightclub and alerts gossip monger Russell, as well as gossip columnist Hopper, that Crawford is now cheating on her ex-husband with Boland's spouse, and

Rosalind Russell, Joan Fontaine and Norma Shearer in *The Women*, 1939.

that scandal spreads like wildfire. When Shearer confronts Crawford to tell her that her secret affair is now shared by everyone, Crawford arrogantly states that she intends to leave Shearer's ex-husband anyway so she can marry Boland's spouse. Crawford states that since Boland's husband is making a fortune as a singing cowboy on a radio program, his riches will support her in comfort for the rest of her life. Boland then steps forward to tell Crawford that her husband has no money and that she intends to withdraw her sponsorship of his radio show and he will soon be in the poorhouse where Crawford can join him. Completely undone, Crawford states that she is heading back to that perfume counter to support herself (and possibly gold-dig for another errant husband), angrily stating before she departs: "There's a name for you ladies, but it is seldom used in high society—outside of a kennel!" The triumphant Shearer then leaves to rejoin her ex-husband, who is eagerly waiting to reinstate their marriage. Shearer is wonderful as a woman victimized by her own species, and many of that species, Crawford, Russell, Goddard, Fontaine, Boland and others, are equally stunning as they play convincing and even devastatingly divergent characters, no less impressive than a bevy of fierce lionesses protecting their prides. Cukor's direction firmly unfolds this fascinating story as effective as a private eye trailing an errant spouse, albeit not a single man appears in this all-women social epic. It is a tale full of female fury and feminine tenderness, all eagerly presented with great taste by art director Gibbons; these feline creatures hunt through the hallways of high society, through upper-class penthouses, western retreats and chic nightclubs for unsuspecting male trophies while battling each other in the process. The film was a great success (mostly with females), earning more than $2.2 million in its initial release against a budget of more than $1.6 million. This film was remade in 2008 but with disappointing results. Songs: "Forevermore" (1939; music: Edward Ward; lyrics: Chet Forrest, Bob Wright), "I Cried for You" (1923; music: Arthur Freed, Abe Lyman; lyrics: Gus Arnheim), "She'll Be Comin' 'Round the Mountain When She Comes" (traditional), "Please Don't Talk About Me When I'm Gone" (1930; music: Sam H. Stept; lyrics: Sidney Clare), "On Top of Old Smokey" (traditional), "Old Chisholm Trail (Come a Ti Yi Yippee Yippee Yah)" (traditional). ***Author's Note***: Cukor, who was known as a "woman's director," was in his element with this production, telling this author: "I have never, before or after, had such a great number of talented actresses—and there were more than 140 of them cast in **The Women**. All of them had their own unique personalities and dealing with them on a one-to-one basis turned out to be the greatest challenge of my life as a director. Each one wanted special attention and I gave that to them, or, at least, I believe they came to think I did. At that time, Norma [Shearer] and Joan [Crawford] were competing for the throne of the reigning queen of MGM, and trying to get them to work together

Rosalind Russell and Joan Crawford in *The Women*, 1939.

in the same scene was often difficult. At one time, they were called to the studio to have some promotion photos taken of them together. Well, they showed up in separate limousines and neither would get out of their cars first, so I was called in and had to go out and greet them as they both got out of those limousines at the same time and they pretended that they were close friends as they had their photos taken. The studio also forced a Technicolor scene on me by insisting that I include a show the women attend to see a lot of designer dresses created by Adrian [more than 200 gowns were created for this film], the front office thinking that every woman in the world would attend theaters just to see these gowns, which was a ridiculous idea. I tried to throw out that scene, but I was stuck with it, and it was shown with the completed picture when it was first released." Crawford told this author: "That picture [**The Women**] did not belong to Norma Shearer and it did not belong to me, or any other actress. There were too many women in **The Women** for that picture for it to belong to any one actress. It really belonged to George Cukor, the director, the only man who ran that herd of females across the plains and finally into the corral." Russell told this author that "I don't think I ever played a more loose-brained person than that goofy magpie in **The Women**. What a dingbat she is—she can't keep her mouth shut for a minute. She's like a radio tower broadcasting rumor and gossip around the clock, as if her dirty little scandals are earth-shaking news stories. I hate to admit it, but how many such women did I hear from girlhood onward who leaned over the backyard fences to do the same stupid thing! The characters in **The Women** do the very same thing, except they live in a more sophisticated and chic world, but it's still the old backyard fence routine. Women make friends for life, but they are very clannish, and they compete with other clans, and all of that is like cannons booming through the neighborhood, exchanging one barrage for another. That war never ends. Men make friends for life, too, but they keep their mouths shut most of the time, I think, so that their wives don't really know what they're thinking. Neither do their buddies. Women conduct open warfare, but for men, it's espionage." **p**, Hunt Stromberg; **d**, George Cuckor; **cast**, Norma Shearer, Joan Crawford, Rosalind Russell, Mary Boland, Paulette Goddard, Phyllis Povah, Joan Fontaine, Virginia Weidler, Lucile Watson, Marjorie Main, Virginia Grey, Ruth Hussey, Hedda Hopper, Mary Beth Hughes, Margaret Dumont, Barbara Jo Allen, Betty Blythe, Muriel Hutchison, Dennie Moore; **w**, Anita Loos, Jane Murfin, (uncredited) F. Scott Fitzgerald, Donald Ogden Stewart (based on the play by Clare Boothe (Clare Boothe Luce); **c**, Oliver T. Marsh, Joseph Ruttenberg (Technicolor for one sequence); **m**, Edward Ward, David Snell; **ed**, Robert J. Kern; **art d**, Cedric Gibbons; **set d**, Edwin B. Willis, Jack D. Moore.

Wonder Bar ★★★ 1934; U.S.; 84m; WB; B/W; Musical Comedy;

Children: Unacceptable; **DVD**; **VHS**. Jolson gives a dynamic performance as the owner of a bistro in Paris called Wonder Bar (Jolson's character is named Al Wonder) where employees and customers sing, dance and romance each other, some finding happiness, others only tragedy. Jolson and Powell, his lead singer, are both in love with ravishingly beautiful Del Rio, the café's top star, but she has only eyes for dashing Cortez, her dancing partner. However, wealthy socialite Francis, even though she is married to Kolker, is agog over Cortez, and is trying to woo him away from Del Rio. Meanwhile, two rich customers, Kibbee, who is married to Donnelly, and Herbert, who is wedded to Fazenda, pursue (respectively) two of the club's hostesses, D'Orsay and Kennedy. Another customer is the dour-faced Barrat, a German officer who has lost everything in the stock market and visits the Wonder Bar to have one last fling before he commits suicide the next day. Oddly, Jolson knows of Barrat's dire intention and tries to give Barrat a good time before he takes his own life. Throughout all of these dramatic and romantic subplots, Jolson and others present a number of Harry Warren songs that are peppered with some elaborate Busby Berkeley dance numbers, not the least of which is a stunning ensemble of scores of chic-looking, well-adorned male and female dancers doing a spectacular routine with innumerable mirrors and titled "Don't Say Goodnight." The dramatic element of the many sequenced tales dealing with the trio of Cortez, Francis and Del Rio ends when Del Rio discovers that Cortez is about to run off with Francis, Kolker's unfaithful wife, and Del Rio shoots and kills Cortez for a Frankie and Johnny finish. This offbeat film sees some strange risqué doings, but its musical numbers and Jolson's performance so captivate with no little eyebrow-raising that interest is sustained throughout. The film was enormously popular at the box office, earning more than $2 million in its initial release against a budget of more than $675,000. Songs: "All Washed Up," "Tango del Rio," "You're So Devine," "Love Me Again," "Fairer on the Riviera" (Harry Warren); "Don't Say Goodnight," "Goin' to Heaven on a Mule," "Vive La France," "Why Do I Dream Those Dreams?," "Wonder Bar" (music: Harry Warren; lyrics: Al Dubin); "Elizabeth (My Queen)" (Robert Katscher); "Ochi Tchornya (Dark Eyes)" (traditional Russian song). *Author's Note*: Jolson was a top entertainer at the time this film was produced, having first appeared in this story as a musical revue staged at New York's 44th Street Theater (it never got to Broadway) and, when he agreed to appear in the film version, he demanded and got a percentage of the gross receipts, which considerably increased his personal fortune. There are two numbers that alerted the Hays Office, the then censoring Hollywood organization. One involved a young man asking to cut in on a man and woman dancing and, when the woman agrees and opens her arms to her new partner, she is shocked to see the young man dance off with her male partner. At this, Jolson slaps his own wrist in a decidedly fey gesture and says: "Boys will be boys! Woo!" The censors objected to this scene, branding it offensive as it blatantly showed homosexuals, then a major Hollywood taboo. The other scene was simply one of terrible bad taste and that is where Jolson, who had for years performed his numbers, as did the old minstrels, in blackface, sang a number titled "I'm Goin' to Heaven on a Mule" in blackface and, while en route to the pearly gates, he encounters hundreds of black children and black angels who all appear to be fawning Uncle Toms. These racial stereotypes nevertheless raised fewer objections from the censors than the brief gay scene and Jolson's limp-wristed slap, which were broadly accepted by snickering lowbrow audiences of that day as chic. Both scenes, however, remained in the film when originally released. **p&d**, Lloyd Bacon; **cast**, Al Jolson, Dolores Del Rio, Ricardo Cortez, Kay Francis, Dick Powell, Robert Barrat, Guy Kibbee, Ruth Donnelly, Hugh Herbert, Louise Fazenda, Hal Le Roy, Fifi D'Orsay, Jane Darwell, Merna Kennedy, Henry Kolker, Dave O'Brien, Dennis O'Keefe; **w**, Earl Baldwin (based on the play "Die Wunderbar" by Geza Herczeg, Karl Farkas, Robert Katscher); **c**, Sol Polito; **m**, Leo F. Forbstein; **ed**, George Amy; **art d**, Jack Okey, Willy Pogany.

Wonder Man ★★★★ 1945; U.S.; 98m; Goldwyn/RKO; Color; Fantasy; Children: Unacceptable; **DVD**; **VHS**. Kaye is hilarious as twins who have not seen each other for years and reunite only after one of them is bumped off by mobsters. One of the twins (whom we call Danny to identify his character) works as a standup comedian at a bistro called the Pelican Club while his identical sibling (whom we call Kaye to identify his separate character) busies himself by writing a history book. While the outgoing Danny outlandishly performs at that swanky watering hole, the reclusive Kaye lovingly spends most of his time doing research at the public library and where he states: "I love the smell of leather bindings." Danny presents a zany act while entertaining customers, his act so antic that one might easily think that he is constantly beset by a nagging St. Vitus Dance. Danny is engaged to be married to fetching Vera-Ellen, a dancer, and who is part of his act. The two, unfortunately, will never go to the altar because Danny has had the bad luck of witnessing a murder committed by mob boss Cochran. Knowing Danny can have him sent to prison and perhaps to the electric chair, Cochran sends his goons, Jenkins and Brophy, to eliminate that dangerous witness before Danny can spill the beans to Kruger, the district attorney. After shooting the comedian, the two goons dump the body into a lake in Brooklyn's Prospect Park. His brother, Kaye, at that time, is having a snack with his girlfriend, Mayo, in their favorite delicatessen, which is operated by roly-poly Sakall. Before Kaye takes another bite, he suddenly feels the need to leave the place and hurry to that lake in the park and where he meets once more his long-absent brother Danny. Kaye, a withdrawn type who jumps with alarm at any unexpected noise, becomes alarmed when Danny tells him that he is not only dead, but that he has been murdered by Cochran's killers. He insists that Kaye obtain evidence that will prove that slaying, as well as the murder Danny witnessed, and take the proof to Kruger, the crime-fighting district attorney. Kaye admits that he is too timid and frightened to undertake such a hazardous chore, but Danny tells Kaye that he will supply enough courage for him by periodically entering his body and taking over to get the job done whenever Kaye loses his nerve. Kaye, though apprehensive, agrees, and undertakes the assignment. Kaye then takes over Danny's role and finds Vera-Ellen always at his side and pushing hard for nuptials while Kaye loves only Mayo, who now sees that she has competition from Vera-Ellen. When mobster Cochran sees that Kaye is very much alive, he believes that his minions, Jenkins and Brophy, have botched their job and tells them to get rid of Kaye once and for all. This creates a number of hazardous moments for Kaye, who, whenever he is threatened, summons Danny to get inside of him to brazen his way out of one predicament after another. Cochran corners Kaye in a nightclub, and, as they glare at each other while sitting at the same table, Kaye, with Danny inside of him and sneeringly defiant to Cochran, gets roaring drunk. Kaye manages to slip away and later goes to Kruger's office, but Danny is no longer inside of him (and the viewer must assume that the ghost of Danny is somewhere else sleeping off a terrible hangover). Meanwhile, Brophy and Jenkins are hunting Kaye everywhere and, after they get onto his trail, Kaye flees, racing to the Metropolitan Opera where he knows Kruger is in attendance. Kaye slips backstage and, while Danny reappears to slip once more inside of him, dons a ridiculous costume, and steps onto the stage as a celebrated opera singer to warble out a wacky message about the murders to Kruger. The district attorney listens with avid interest, and then Kruger alerts the cops. Jenkins and Brophy are then apprehended just before they are about to send Kaye to the other world where Danny resides. Cochran, too, is rounded up, and now that Danny has been able to use Kaye as his private detective to solve the murders, including his own, he is content and forever leaves to take up residency in eternity. Meanwhile, Kaye is happily reunited with Mayo and they head toward the altar while Vera-Ellen happily embraces a relationship with Woods, who owns the Pelican Club and has always been in love with her. Kaye is exceptionally funny in this comedic romp where his millions of fans get a double dose of him, albeit his twin is not really seen but heard throughout, but where Kaye appears

Otto Kruger, Danny Kaye and Richard Lane in *Wonder Man*, 1945.

in just about every fast-moving scene, all in rich color. He does a good job presenting two decidedly different personalities, from the brash cabaret performer to the reticent bookworm, while working his comedic routines and patter songs (composed by his wife Fine) into the overall story line. One of those routines that he perfected in his nightclub acts involved his singing as a Russian baritone the song "Otchi Tchorniya" while he is seized by an uncontrollable sneezing fit. The other is his impossible operatic parody where, in the climax, he winds up in a wrestling match with diva Alice Mock. He receives great support from the beautiful Mayo and Vera-Ellen (her film debut), and is surrounded by colorful character actors Sakall, Jenkins, Brophy and a sinister Cochran, who went on to play sneering villains in many films to come, this being Cochran's second feature film. This film won an Oscar for Special Effects (Redman and Fulton), and received Oscar nominations for Best Song ("So in Love"; Rose and Robin), Best Sound Recording (Gordon Sawyer), and Best Musical Score (Heindorf). Songs: "Bali Boogie," "Opera Number," "Otchi Tchorniya Number," "Palpably Inadequate," "The Patter" (all 1945; Sylvia Fine); "So In Love" (1945; David Rose, Leo Robin). *Author's Note*: Producer Goldwyn told this author that "Danny [Kaye] did such a great job in the first picture we made with him [**Up in Arms**, 1944], not to mention the bonanza that picture produced, even though I am mentioning it, that I decided to put him right into another big picture and that was **Wonder Man**. He was very funny in that picture, because audiences got to see two of him playing twin brothers, so customers got two Danny Kayes for the price of one." Mayo told this author that "**Wonder Man** was the first of four pictures I made with Danny and he had everyone in stitches in that picture, just like he did in the other ones. I always wondered where he got the energy because he could do those crazy routines over and over in retakes and never lose a beat." Kaye felt that playing dual roles, according to his statements to this author, "gave me a two-man show, and where I could cut up more than usual because I have another person inside of me and making me do all the crazy things that I do. If that makes sense to you, you need to see the same psychiatrist those two guys needed to see." Kaye would go on to play twins again in another fine comedy, **On the Riviera**, 1951. Twins or lookalikes have been depicted in many other films, including **The Ace of Scotland Yard**, 1929; **Adam and Evil**, 1927; **Adaptation**, 2002; **Adolf Armstarke**, 1937; **Adventures of Texas Jack**, 1934; **Ali Baba Goes to Town**, 1937; **Alice in Wonderland**, 1933; **Alice in Wonderland**, 1951; **Alice in Wonderland**, 2010; **Alien 3**, 1992; **Among the Living**, 1941; **Angels and Insects**, 1996; **Anna the Adventuress**, 1920; **The Arizona Cyclone**, 1928; **Around the World in 80 Days**, 2004; **Atom Man vs. Superman**, 1950; **Back to the Future Part III**, 1990; **Bad Company**, 2002; **Bad Man from Red Butte**, 1940; **Bad Man of Deadwood**, 1941; **The Baron's African**

Virginia Mayo and Danny Kaye in *Wonder Man,* **1945.**

War, 1966 (made-for-TV; repackaging of Republic's 1943 serial "Secret Service in Darkest Africa"); Barry McKenzie Holds His Own, 1974; The Beast of the City, 1932; Before Night Falls, 2000; Berkeley Square, 1933; Bicentennial Man, 1999; Big Calibre, 1935; The Big Show, 1936; Bikini Beach, 1964; Billy the Kid Returns, 1938; Black Bandit, 1938; Black Is White, 1920; Black Magic, 1949; The Black Room, 1935; Black Waters, 1929; Blake of Scotland Yard, 1937; Blazing Across the Pecos, 1948; Blazing the Western Trail, 1945; A Blind Bargain, 1922; Blueprint, 2003; Bonanza Town, 1951; Born to Gamble, 1935; Both Barrels Blazing, 1945; Brazil, 1944; Breed of the Sea, 1926; Brenda Starr, Reporter, 1945; Brothers, 1930; Bruce Gentry, 1949; Buried Treasure, 1921; Callaway Went Thataway, 1951; Canadian Mounties vs. Atomic Invaders, 1953; Captain America, 1944; Captain America, 1979 (made-for-TV); Captain America, 1990; Carolina Blues, 1944; Casualties of War, 1989; Cat Ballou, 1965; Chaplin, 1992; Chatterbox, 1943; The Cheerful Fraud, 1926; The Chinese Cat, 1944; A Chump at Oxford, 1940; The Circus Clown, 1934; City Slickers II: The Legend of Curly's Gold, 1994; A Close Call for Boston Blackie, 1946; Cobra Woman, 1944; The Cobra Strikes, 1948; Coffee and Cigarettes, 2004; Conceiving Ada, 1997; Confessions of a Vice Baron, 1943; The Conquerors, 1932; Constantine, 2005; Copacabana, 1947; Corpus Christi Bandits, 1945; The Corsican Brothers, 1941; Cover Girl, 1944; Covered Wagon Days, 1940; Crime Doctor's Man Hunt, 1946; Crime Over London, 1936; Crimes at the Dark House, 1940; Cuban Fireball, 1951; Custer's Last Stand, 1936; Daredevils of the Red Circle, 1939; The Daring Young Man, 1942; The Dark Half, 1993; The Dark Mirror, 1920; The Dark Mirror, 1946; Dark Streets, 1929; A Date with the Falcon, 1942; Dave, 1993; Dead Again, 1991; Dead Men Walk, 1943; Dead Ringer, 1964; Dead Ringers, 1988; Deadwood Dick, 1940; Deceptions, 1985 (made-for-TV); The Desert Hawk, 1944; The Desert Horseman, 1946; Django Unchained, 2012; Don Q: Son of Zorro, 1925; Don Ricardo Returns, 1946; Don't Get Personal, 1942; Double, Double, Toil and Trouble, 1993 (made-for-TV); Double Impact, 1991; Dracula, 1992; The Drifter, 1944; The Driftin' Kid, 1941; Duplicate, 1998; Eadie Was a Lady, 1945; Echo, 1997 (made-for-TV); England Made Me, 1973; Equinox, 1992; The Errand Boy, 1961; Fahrenheit 451, 1966; False Face, 1977; The Far Side of the Moon, 2005; The Fighting Frontiersman, 1946; The Fighting Renegade, 1939; Folies Bergère, 1935; The Forbidden City, 1918; The Forbidden Street, 1949; Four Mothers, 1941; Freddie Steps Out, 1946; Frontier Gunlaw, 1946; Fugitive at Large, 1939; Fugitive from Sonora, 1943; Galloping Thunder, 1946; The Gay Deceiver, 1926; The Gay Vagabond, 1941; Genealogies of a Crime, 1998; Get That Man, 1935; Ghost of Zorro, 1949; The Ghosts of Yesterday, 1918;

The Girl Without a Soul, 1917; G-Men Never Forget, 1948; God's Gun, 1976; Gold Dust Gertie, 1931; The Great Dictator, 1940; The Great Race, 1965; The Green Archer, 1940; Gunfire, 1950; Gunning for Vengeance, 1946; The Hawk of Wild River, 1952; Heading West, 1946; The Hell of Frankenstein, 1960; Her Splendid Folly, 1933; Here Come the Waves, 1944; His Brother's Ghost, 1945; History of the World: Part I, 1981; Hit and Run, 1957; House of Numbers, 1957; House of Terror, 1973; I'll Never Forget You, 1951; In His Brother's Place, 1919; The Indians Are Coming, 1930; Irish Luck, 1925; It Came from Outer Space, 1953; Jesse James at Bay, 1941; Joe Palooka Meets Humphrey, 1950; Joy of Living, 1938; Junction City, 1952; Just Suppose, 1926; Kaminey: The Scoundrels, 2009; The Kid from Amarillo, 1951; King of the Bullwhip, 1950; A Kiss Before Dying, 1993; Kissin' Cousins, 1964; The Krays, 1990; La Conga Nights, 1940; Lady of the Night, 1925; Landrush, 1946; The Last Days of Boot Hill, 1947; The Last Starfighter, 1984; Law and Order, 1942; Lawless Breed, 1946; The Lawless Breed, 1953; Lawless Empire, 1945; The Lawless Rider, 1954; Leaves of Grass, 2009; Les Misérables, 1935; Les Misérables, 1952; Les Misérables, 1995; Les Misérables, 1998; Les Misérables, 2000 (TV miniseries); Lightning Guns, 1950; Lights of Old Broadway, 1925; Liquid Sky, 1982; Little Lord Fauntleroy, 1921; Little Miss Broadway, 1938; The Lizzie McGuire Movie, 2003; The Lone Hand Texan, 1947; The Lone Ranger Rides Again, 1939; Lonely Wives, 1931; The Long Shadow, 1992; Lord of the Flies, 1963; The Love Bug, 1968; Make Mine a Double, 1961; The Man in the Iron Mask, 1939; The Man in the Iron Mask, 1998; The Man Who Loved Redheads, 1955; Manhattan Moon, 1935; Man's Country, 1938; Marked for Death, 1990; Marriage in Transit, 1925; Mary Poppins, 1964; Mary Reilly, 1996; Mask of Death, 1996; The Masked Pirate, 1949; Maximum Risk, 1996; Mexican Spitfire's Elephant, 1942; The Million Dollar Dollies, 1918; Miss V from Moscow, 1942; Mistaken, 2013; Mr. Lemon of Orange, 1931; Mr. Murder, 1998 (made-for-TV); Model Behavior, 2000 (made-for-TV); Modesty Blaise, 1966; The Mosquito Coast, 1986; Mother Night, 1996; Murder by Television, 1935; Murder He Says, 1945; Nazi Agent, 1942; Now or Never, 1935; Obsession, 1976; Om Shanti Om, 2007; On the Riviera, 1951; The One, 2001; One Touch of Venus, 1948; The Other Me, 2000 (made-for-TV); Outlaw Treasure, 1955; Outlaws of Santa Fe, 1944; Outlaws of the Rockies, 1945; The Parent Trap, 1961; The Parent Trap, 1998; Partners in Crime, 1928; The Persuader, 1957; Peter Pan, 1953; The Phantom, 1943; The Phantom Cowboy, 1935; Phantom Patrol, 1936; The Phantom Rider, 1946; Phantom Valley, 1948; Pioneers of the West, 1940; Pocahontas, 1995; Port Said, 1948; Prairie Raiders, 1947; Prairie Rustlers, 1945; The Prince and the Pauper, 1937; The Prince of Tides, 1991; The Prisoner of Zenda, 1922; The Prisoner of Zenda, 1937; The Prisoner of Zenda, 1952; The Purple Rose of Cairo, 1985; Redline, 1997; Renegades of the Sage, 1948; Replicant, 2001; The Return of Daniel Boone, 1941; The Return of the Durango Kid, 1945; Riders of the Lone Star, 1947; Rim of the Canyon, 1949; The River Pirates, 1988; Riverboat Rhythm, 1946; River's End, 1940; Road to Paradise, 1930; Romance of the Rio Grande, 1941; The Saint's Double Trouble, 1940; Schizopolis, 1997; Scouts to the Rescue, 1939; A Scream in the Night, 1935; Sealed Lips, 1942; Secret Agent X-9, 1937; The Secret Code, 1942; The Secret of Treasure Island, 1938; Secret Service in Darkest Africa, 1943 (serial); Secrets of Scotland Yard, 1944; Separated by Murder, 1994 (made-for-TV); The Shadow Returns, 1946; She Gets Her Man, 1945; Shooting High, 1940; The Sickle or the Cross, 1949; The 6th Day, 2000; Sky Raiders, 1941; Slap Shot, 1977; Slightly Scandalous, 1946; Smart Politics, 1948; So I Married an Axe Murderer, 1993; So You Won't Talk, 1940; The Social Network, 2010; Son of a Badman, 1949; The Son of Dr. Jekyll, 1951; The Son of the Sheik, 1926; Son of Zorro, 1947; Special Effects, 1984; Speed to Spare, 1937; The Sphinx, 1933; The Spider Returns, 1941; The Spider's Web, 1938; The Spiderwick

Chronicles, 2008; **Spy Smasher**, 1942; **Stars Over Texas**, 1946; **Start the Revolution Without Me**, 1970; **Stella Maris**, 1918; **A Stolen Life**, 1946; **The Strange Death of Adolf Hitler**, 1943; **Sunset in El Dorado**, 1945; **The Sunset Legion**, 1928; **Superman**, 1948; **Swing Out, Sister**, 1945; **Swing It, Soldier**, 1941; **The Tabasco Kid**, 1932; **A Tale of Two Cities**, 1935; **A Tale of Two Cities**, 1958; **A Tale of Two Cities**, 1980 (made-for-TV); **Tango & Cash**, 1989; **Tanu Weds Manu Returns**, 2015; **Teenage Mutant Ninja Turtles**, 1990; **Texas Dynamo**, 1950; **Thank Your Lucky Stars**, 1943; **A Thousand Elephants**, 2008; **The Time Machine**, 1960; **The Tioga Kid**, 1948; **Tom and Thomas**, 2002; **The Tomb of Ligeia**, 1964; **Tombstone Terror**, 1935; **Trail of Terror**, 1943; **Trail to Laredo**, 1948; **Trapped in Tia Juana**, 1932; **The Truman Show**, 1998; **Tumbledown Ranch in Arizona**, 1941; **Twice Blessed**, 1945; **Twin Dragons**, 1992; **Two-Faced Woman**, 1941; **Two-Fisted Stranger**, 1946; **Two Gun Sheriff**, 1941; **Two Sisters**, 1929; **Under California Stars**, 1948; **Vertigo**, 1958; **The Vigilante: Fighting Hero of the West**, 1947; **Watch the Birdie**, 1950; **West of Sonora**, 1948; **Westwind**, 2011; **Wheel of Chance**, 1928; **While the Patient Slept**, 1935; **Whirlwind Raiders**, 1948; **Whistling in Dixie**, 1942; **White Comanche**, 1968; **The White Shadow**, 1924; **The Whole Town's Talking**, 1935; **The Wife of General Ling**, 1938; **Wild Horse Rustlers**, 1943; **Windwalker**, 1980; **The Woman in White**, 1948; **The Wonderful Adventure**, 1915; **Wyoming**, 1947; and **Zorro Rides Again**, 1937. **p**, Samuel Goldwyn; **d**, Bruce Humberstone; **cast**, Danny Kaye, Virginia Mayo, Vera-Ellen, Steve Cochran, Donald Woods, S.Z. Sakall, Allen Jenkins, Edward Brophy, Otto Kruger, Richard Lane, Natalie Schafer, Huntz Hall, Virginia Gilmore, Edward Gargan, Grant Mitchell, Alice Mock, James Flavin, Frank Orth, Karin Booth, Carol Haney, Chili Williams, The Goldwyn Girls; **w**, Don Hartman, Melville Shavelson, Philip Rapp, Jack Jevne, Eddie Moran (based on a story by Arthur Sheekman); **c**, Victor Milner, William Snyder, Karl Struss (Technicolor); **m**, Ray Heindorf, Heinz Roemheld; **ed**, Daniel Mandell; **art d**, Ernst Fegte, Perry Ferguson; **set d**, Howard Bristol; **spec eff**, Harry Redmond Jr., John P. Fulton.

The Wonderful Country ★★★ 1959; U.S.; 98m; DRM/UA; Color; Western; Children: Unacceptable; **DVD**; **VHS**. Exciting and well-acted tale begins with Mitchum, who has fled to Mexico some years ago for killing his father's murderer. He crosses back into Texas when he is hired by local "war lord" Armendariz and his brother, Mendoza, to be a gunrunner. Along the way, Mitchum breaks a leg and is cared for by London, who is unhappily married to Merrill. Through London, Mitchum discovers that Merrill is working for Armendariz, who is trying to clear the area of Apaches, who threaten the railroad from being built there. Mitchum and London fall in love, but their romance is short-lived after Mitchum becomes unhappy at working for Armendariz, who sends a gunman to kill him. Mitchum, however, kills the gunman, and he and London settle down together in Texas. This offbeat oater is thick with atmosphere and good action that is well orchestrated by Parrish and the gritty lensing from Crosby and Phillips is exceptional as well as offering breathtaking landscapes. The film did not do well at the box office, earning a little more than $1 million in its initial release. Songs: "Where Did You Get That Hat?" (Joseph J. Sullivan), "El Desterrado (The Banished)" (Jorge Negrete). *Author's Note*: Mitchum's own company produced this film, and he took great pride in the film's production values, telling this author: "I think the reason why that picture did not do as well as we hoped it would do was because we did not include the usual western formula, except for a happy ending, I guess. You know what they say—you can't please 'em all." The film was shot on location in Durango, Mexico. Legendary black baseball hurler Leroy "Satchel" Paige plays a U.S. cavalry sergeant, and Lea, the author of the novel upon which this film is based, plays a barber. Gregory Peck and Henry Fonda were both offered the role of the leading player for this film, but, after both turned down the role, Mitchum stepped up to take the part and financed its production. **p**, Chester Erskine; **d**, Robert Parrish; **cast**,

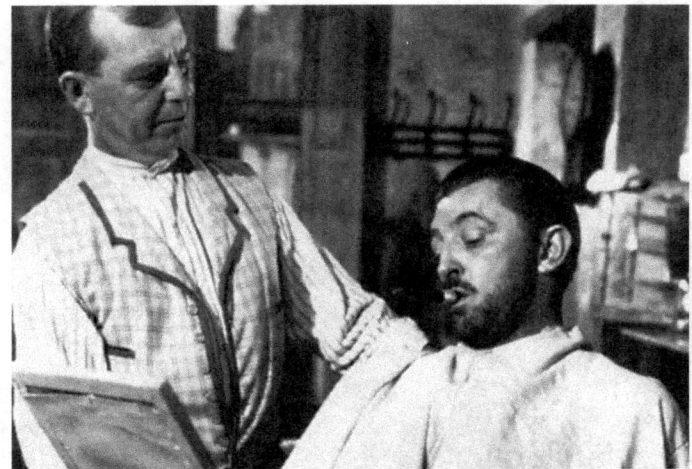

Tom Lea and Robert Mitchum in *The Wonderful Country*, 1959.

Robert Mitchum, Julie London, Pedro Armendariz, Gary Merrill, Albert Dekker, Jack Oakie, Charles McGraw, Leroy "Satchel" Paige, Anthony Caruso, Mike Kellin, Victor Mendoza, Jay Novello; **w**, Robert Ardrey, Walter Bernstein (based on the novel by Tom Lea); **c**, Floyd Crosby, Alex Phillips; **m**, Alex North; **ed**, Michael Luciano; **prod d**, Harry Horner; **spec eff**, Lester Swartz.

Wooden Crosses ★★★★ 1932; France; 110m; Pathe-Natan/Criterion; B/W; Drama/War; Children: Unacceptable; **BD**. Superb semi-documentary drama offers a dynamic anti-war film set in France during WWI (1914-1918). The film opens with a stark shot of a hillside covered with white wooden crosses to indicate the resting places of many of the French soldiers portrayed herein. We then see Blanchar joining a group of young, patriotic Frenchmen in 1914, all draftees, marching off to the Western Front in Champagne. Blanchar is a young idealist whose patriotism begins to evaporate as he and his friends come under incessant bombardments and they are shown seeking safe shelter everywhere, in dugouts, shell craters and foxholes. These hapless soldiers are further terrified when realizing that German sappers are tunneling beneath French fortifications to set enormous caches of explosives that they intend to later blow up, killing as many of their French foes as possible. Blanchar and his companions are grateful when they are ordered to withdraw from their trenches and are given a brief furlough to see their family members. That respite is too terribly brief as all are quickly called back to duty to perform in an elaborate parade only to edify their luxury living superior officers, chiefly generals who exhibit nothing but disdain for the safety of these battle-scarred troops. Blanchar and his friends are then ordered back into the trenches and, one by one, they are killed, until only Blanchar remains alive of his original contingent. He, however, meets the same awful fate and then joins his friends when he is buried next to them and a white wooden cross marks his grave. Solemn and uncompromising, this film depicts in grim reality the horrors of trench warfare and the futility and horrible attrition of that war, and where Blanchar renders a memorable performance. Bernard directs this film with great skill, and his battle scenes are breathtaking in their scope and horrifying detail. *Author's Note*: This film ranks with such classics as Lewis Milestone's **All Quiet on the Western Front**, 1930, Pabst's **Westfront 1918**, 1931, and Stanley Kubrick's **Paths of Glory**, 1957. Some of the battle scenes in this film were later used in John Ford's **The World Moves On**, 1934, and Howard Hawks' **The Road to Glory**, 1936. (In French; English subtitles,) **d**, Raymond Bernard; **cast**, Pierre Blanchar, Gabriel Gabrio, Charles Vanel, Raymond Aimos, Antonin Artaud, Paul Azais; Rene Bergeron, Raymond Cordy, Marcel Delaitre, Jean Galland; **w**, Bernard, Andre Lang (based on the novel by Roland Dorgeles); **c**, Jules Kruger, Rene Ribault; **ed**, Lucienne Grumberg; **art d**, Jean Perrier.

Mickey Rooney and Judy Garland in *Words and Music*, 1948.

The Wooden Horse ★★★★ 1951; U.K.; 101m; London Films/Snader Productions; B/W; War Drama; Children: Unacceptable; **DVD**; **VHS**. This cleverly crafted film, which is based upon actual events, depicts one of the most ingenious escapes from a German POW camp during WWII (1939-1945). The escape is conceived by British POWs penned up in Stalag Luft III in 1943. The escapees, Genn, Tomlinson and Steel, realize that the distance from their barracks to the barbed wired fence of the compound is too great for them to dig a tunnel that will take them beyond that barrier. To diminish that distance they conceive of a plot by which they will dig that tunnel in the open compound, right in front of the noses of the German guards. To that end, they construct a vaulting horse of chiefly plywood from Red Cross parcels, so that it is hollow enough for one or two prisoners to hide beneath it and be carried each day to the exact same spot where the tunnel is being dug. While many other POWs exercise for a few hours each day by vaulting over the horse, those inside of it dig out the tunnel. They cover that tunnel after a few hours of digging with wooden boards supported by sandbags over which dry sand is then placed to make the surface seem normal before they and the wooden horse are carried back to the barracks. The men dig in relays over several months, and their covert operations are almost detected on several anxious occasions by German guards. Further, they devise a way by which they can dispose of the dirt dug from the tunnel by carrying that dirt in bags affixed to the inside of the wooden horse, and that excess dirt is later disposed of when they are carried back to their barracks. The escapees finally reach a point where the tunnel is beyond the fence and in an area where, when they emerge, they will not be easily detected by guards. With the tunnel completed, one of the diggers hides inside the tunnel while the horse is taken back to the barracks where three more men hide inside the horse and are carried to the spot where the tunnel is located. Two more get into the tunnel while a third covers it up and the wooden horse is then taken back to the barracks. Inside the tunnel, Genn, Steel and Tomlison break through the surface, which is well beyond the fence, and they make their way to freedom. Genn and Steel, while traveling together, make contact with underground workers and they are spirited into Denmark and are subsequently smuggled to neutral Sweden. Tomlinson is waiting there to greet them, having traveled by train while posing as a salesman and reaching Danzig and from there arriving in Sweden. Lee directs this nail-biting tale with robust action, and Genn, Steel, Tomlinson render standout performances. The film was a box office smash in England and did very well in the U.S. in its initial release. Songs/Music: "Deutschlandlied" (Joseph Haydn), "Symphony No. 6 in F Major Pastoral Op. 68" (Ludwig van Beethoven), "Nymphs and Shepherds" (Henry Purcell). *Author's Note*: Actor John Mills attempted to buy the rights to this story, envisioning it to be a vehicle for his own talents, but he lost to another firm. The film

was shot almost entirely in Germany. Williams, who wrote the novel on which this story is based, as well as the screenplay, was an actual participant in the escape as a POW in WWII. Actor Goodliffe was also a POW during the war. Other films depicting escapes from prison camps during WWII include **Albert, R.N.** (aka: **Break to Freedom**), 1955; **As Far as My Feet Will Carry Me**, 2001; **Back to Bataan**, 1945; **Battle of the Coral Sea**, 1959; **The Beasts of Marseilles** (aka: **Seven Thunders**), 1959; **The Bridge on the River Kwai**, 1957; **The Captive Heart**, 1948; **The Colditz Story**, 1955; **The Cow and I**, 1961; **The Cross of Lorraine**, 1943; **Danger Within** (aka: **Breakout**), 1960; **Escape**, 1940; **Escape in the Desert**, 1945; **Escape to Athena**, 1979; **Escape to Victory** (aka: **Victory**), 1981; **Force 10 from Navarone**, 1978; **The Great Escape**, 1963; **The Great Escape II: The Untold Story**, 1988 (made-for-TV); **The Great Raid**, 2005; **Hannibal Brooks**, 1969; **Hart's War**, 2002; **The McKenzie Break**, 1970; **Northern Pursuit**, 1943; **The One That Got Away**, 1958; **Passage to Marseille**, 1944; **The Password Is Courage**, 1962; **Reach for the Sky**, 1957; **Sailor of the King**, 1953; **The Secret of Blood Island**, 1965; **The Secret War of Harry Frigg**, 1968; **The Seventh Cross**, 1944; **Stalag 17**, 1953; **Uncertain Glory**, 1944; **Von Ryan's Express**, 1965; and **Where Eagles Dare**, 1968. **p**, Ian Dalrymple; **d**, Jack Lee; **cast**, Leo Genn, David Tomlinson, Anthony Steel, David Greene, Peter Burton, Patrick Waddington, Michael Goodliffe, Bryan Forbes, Peter Finch, Bill Travers; **w**, Eric Williams (based on his novel); **c**, C. Pennington-Richards; **m**, Clifton Parker; **ed**, John Seabourne, Sr., Peter Seabourne; **art d**, William Kellner.

Words and Music ★★★ 1948; U.S.; 120m; MGM; Color; Biographical Drama/Musical; Children: Acceptable; **DVD**; **VHS**. This entertaining and highly fictionalized biopic is really an excuse to lavishly showcase some of the great Rodgers and Hart songs. It only incidentally depicts the lives of gifted American composer Richard Rodgers (1902-1979), who is played by Drake, and his brilliant lyricist, Lorenz Hart (1895-1943), who is extremely well played by Rooney, as Drake narrates the story. Both come from well-to-do families in NYC, Drake meeting Rooney, an undersized, brash know-it-all and mama's boy, in the early 1920s. Whatever lilting tune Rodgers can compose, Rooney has just the befitting and clever lyrics to go with it, such as the captivating "Manhattan," one of their early and most popular creations. Their collaboration is mostly sought by Rooney, and Drake is shown to be somewhat reluctant to team up with this cigar-smoking runt, but Rooney's alert mind is so quick to produce inventive lyrics that Drake soon agrees to team up with him. (Other than the outpourings from genius Cole Porter, Hart was undoubtedly one of the top lyricists of American music in the 20th Century, the master of polysyllabic internal rhymes that were full of sophisticated wit.) They are soon successful and they become writers of some of the most popular songs of the next three decades on Broadway and in films. In the film, Drake meets Leigh and they fall in love and marry while Rooney falls for Garrett. When Garrett states that she is taller than he is, Rooney rushes out to buy specially made shoes with lifts inside of them that give him a few more inches in height. This makes him tilt forward when walking (a hilarious scene, but a tragic one when considering how Hart hated his small size). Rooney repeatedly proposes to Garrett, but she rejects him. He nevertheless continues to pursue her, and, between her rejection and his other and unknown inner demons, he turns to alcohol and dies at an early age at the height of his fame. Many of the best songs written by this fabulous team are featured in the film by MGM stars including Judy Garland singing a 1937 showstopper, "Johnny One Note." Other guest performers include June Allyson, Perry Como, Lena Horne, Gene Kelly, Ann Sothern, Mel Torme and Vera-Ellen. There is not much to the story line, but the songs are well presented, especially the sumptuously mounted ensembles that recreate the numbers that appeared in the many Rodgers and Hart musicals produced on Broadway. The film was a hit at the box office, earning more than $4.5 million in its initial release against a budget of more than $3 million. Not related to the 1929 film by the same name. Other songs: "Where's That Rainbow?," "Mountain Greenery," "Blue Moon," "Thou Swell," Way Out West," "Manhattan," "Lover," "On Your Toes," "Slaughter on Tenth Avenue," "There's a Small Hotel," "Where or When," "The Lady Is a Tramp," 'I Wish I Were in Love Again," "Spring Is Here," "This Can't Be Love," "With a Song in My Heart," "A Tree in the Park," "You Took Advantage of Me," "Someone Should Tell Them," "I Didn't Know What Time It Was," "Spring Is Here," "My Romance," "We'll Be the Same," "Here in My Arms," "Yours Sincerely," "The Girl Friend," "Ship Without a Sail," "March of the Knights," "Nothing But You," "Hollywood Party," "Dancing on the Ceiling" (music: Richard Rodgers; lyrics: Lorenz Hart). *Author's Note*: Garland's brief and wonderful appearance here almost did not take place as MGM boss Louis B. Mayer had recently put her on suspension due to her many illnesses that delayed productions, as well as her drug addiction. Mayer offered Garland $50,000 to perform one song in this film and she delivered "Johnny One Note" with such panache and verve that Mayer offered her another $50,000 to sing one more song, an encore duet she sings with Rooney (the two having appeared in many earlier films together). Garland, who was underweight at that time, quickly added another twenty pounds and did the number "I Wish I Were in Love Again," so pleasing Mayer that he took her off suspension. Lorenz Hart's true secret life is not shown here as he was not only an alcoholic early on, as is indicated in the film, but was tormented by the fact that he was dwarf-sized, never standing taller than five feet (Rooney, who plays him, is two inches taller than that). What gnawed at Hart was the fact that he was a closet homosexual and his furtive escapades with abusive sailors and working men of his sexual ilk left him devastated and full of self-recrimination. He lived his entire life with his widowed mother, and, after she died, he went on a Homeric binge that so debilitated him that Rodgers found it impossible to work with him and severed their relationship in 1943, which had begun in 1919. Hart continued his drinking and indulging in his sexual proclivities, contracting pneumonia and dying on November 22, 1943, at the age of forty-eight. **p**, Arthur Freed; **d**, Norman Taurog; **cast**, Mickey Rooney, Tom Drake, Janet Leigh, Betty Garrett, Cyd Charisse, Marshall Thompson, Richard Quine, Jeanette Nolan, Clinton Sundberg, The Blackburn Twins (Ramon and Royce Blackburn), Gower Champion, Allyn Ann McLerie; **w**, Fred F. Finklehoffe (adapted by Ben Feiner Jr. from a story by Guy Bolton, Jean Holloway); **c**, Charles Rosher, Harry Stradling Sr.; **m**, Lennie Hayton, Conrad Salinger; **ed**, Albert Akst, Ferris Webster; **art d**, Cedric Gibbons, Jack Martin Smith; **set d**, Edwin B. Willis, Richard A. Pefferle; **spec eff**, Warren Newcombe.

Working Girl ★★★ 1988; U.S.; 113m; FOX; Color; Comedy/Romance; Children: Unacceptable (MPAA: R); **BD**; **DVD**; **VHS**; **IV**. This delightful romantic romp begins with Griffith, who is a secretary working in the mergers and acquisitions department of a Wall Street investment bank. Her boss, Weaver, suggests they share ideas for a possible merger with another firm, only to find that Weaver has taken credit for her idea. On top of this, Griffith finds her boyfriend, Baldwin, in bed with another woman. Griffith goes into action at a dinner meeting with bank executive Ford where she wears one of Weaver's dresses. Griffith wakes up the next morning in Ford's bed. Ford tells Griffith he had been romantically involved with Weaver, but that is finished. At a big meeting about the possible merger, Weaver accuses Griffith of stealing her idea, but Griffith proves it was hers all along and Weaver is fired. Griffith gets a more important job with the bank and keeps Ford as her lover in the bargain. Nichols directs this film with a firm hand, delivering a slick and seamless tale filled with many amusing scenes, and the script bristles with wit. Griffith, Ford, Weaver and Baldwin are standouts in their roles. The film won an Oscar for Best Song ("Let the River Run" by Carly Simon), and received Oscar nominations for Best Picture; Best Director (Nichols); Best Actress (Griffith), and Best Supporting Actress (Weaver, Cusack). The film was an enormous hit at the box office, earn-

Melanie Griffith, Harrison Ford and Sigourney Weaver in *Working Girl,* **1988.**

ing more than $102 million in its initial release against a budget of more than $28 million. Songs: "Let the River Run" (Carly Simon), "I'm So Excited" (Anita Pointer, Ruth Pointer, June Pointer, Trevor Lawrence), "The Lady in Red" (Chris DeBurgh), "Straight from the Heart" (Greg C. Jackson), "St. Thomas" (Sonny Rollins), "Isn't It Romantic" (Richard Rodgers, Lorenz Hart), "The Man That Got Away" (Harold Arlen, Ira Gershwin), "Poor Butterfly" (John Golden, Raymond Hubbell). Mature themes prohibit viewing by children. **p**, Douglas Wick; **d**, Mike Nichols; **cast**, Harrison Ford, Sigourney Weaver, Melanie Griffith, Alec Baldwin, Joan Cusack, Philip Bosco, James Lally, Kevin Spacey, Olympia Dukakis, Jeffrey Nordling; **w**, Kevin Wade; **c**, Michael Ballhaus; **ed**, Sam O'Steen; **prod d**, Patrizia von Brandenstein; **art d**, Doug Kraner; **set d**, George DeTitta; **spec eff**, John Algana, Dick Rauh.

The World According to Garp ★★★ 1982; U.S.; 136m; WB; Color; Comedy; Children: Unacceptable (MPAA: R). **DVD**; **VHS**; **IV**. Absorbing but strange tale sees Williams enacting the life of a man called Garp, and, for inexplicable reasons, all kinds of troubled women are attracted to him. He is an illegitimate son, born in 1944 to a dying World War II soldier and a nurse, Close, who wanted to be a mother but not a wife. Williams matures to become interested in wrestling, writing fiction, and women. Close is also a writer, who pens a book about human sexuality that becomes a bestseller. Her weird friends populate Williams' life as he has a passionate relationship with Hurt, the daughter of his wrestling coach. They marry, have children, and she proves to be unfaithful. Williams has a car accident and crashes into the car of his wife's lover, which is parked in their driveway. One child in the car is killed and the other suffers an eye injury. With Close's help, Williams forgives his cheating wife and himself for own mistakes in a film with myriad plots and offbeat antics. The weird story line and even more bizarre acting produced only a modest success at the box office where this film earned more than $29 million in its initial release against a budget of more than $17 million. Songs: "When I'm Sixty-Four" (John Lennon, Paul McCartney), "There Will Never Be another You" (Harry Warren, Mack Gordon), "Long Way to Go" (Michael Bruce). **p**, George Roy Hill, Robert L. Crawford; **d**, Hill; **cast**, Robin Williams, Mary Beth Hurt, Glenn Close, John Lithgow, Hume Cronyn, Jessica Tandy, Swoosie Kurtz, James McCall, Peter Michael Goetz, Amanda Plummer; **w**, Steve Tesich (based on the novel by John Irving); **c**, Miroslav Ondricek; **ed**, Stephen A. Rotter; **prod d**, Henry Bumstead; **art d**, Woods Mackintosh; **set d**, Robert Drumheller, Justin Scoppa, Jr.; **spec eff**, Albert Griswold.

The World Changes ★★★ 1933; U.S.; 91m; First National/WB; B/W; Drama; Children: Unacceptable. Muni gives a powerful performance in this episodic odyssey of a Midwestern family. It begins when Muni

Gregory Peck and Ann Blyth in *The World in His Arms*, 1952.

is a young man living on the farm of his parents, O'Neill and MacMahon, in the Dakotas in 1852. After he leaves home to take some cattle to Texas, he meets Kibbee, owner of a meat packing house in Chicago's Union Stock Yards, and they become partners. Muni marries Astor, who is Kibbee's lovely daughter, and they move into a big and luxurious house in Chicago. Muni becomes rich by learning how to ship beef in refrigerated railroad cars. Over the years, Muni and Astor have two sons and Kibbee dies. Astor has high society ambitions, but thinks Muni's reputation as merely a butcher hinders that, so she tries to persuade him to give up his business and invest in a stock brokerage firm to benefit Cook, one of their now grown sons, who is married to Lindsay, a daughter of a New York society family. Muni refuses to agree to Astor's wishes, and she becomes mentally ill and dies. Time marches on and, by 1929, Muni is a grandfather. He has sold his meat packing business and invested in Cook's brokerage firm. The stock market crashes and Muni loses his fortune so he embezzles money, is found out, and is given a prison sentence. Cook, learning that Lindsay is having an affair with one of his business associates, commits suicide. The world has changed greatly for Muni over the years, and the tragedies of losing his fortune, his son's suicide, and facing years in prison take their toll on him and he dies of a stroke when he is seventy-seven years old. Songs: "Oh, Susanna" (Stephen Foster), "Bridal Chorus" from "Lohengrin" (Richard Wagner), "On the Beautiful Blue Danube" and "Roses from the South" (Johann Strauss Jr.), "I Love You Truly" (Carrie Jacobs Bond). *Author's Note*: LeRoy told this author that "I had directed Paul [Muni] in **I Am a Fugitive from a Chain Gang** a year before we made **The World Changes** together, and he became a wholly different person for that role. He was a very rare actor, one who could successfully play just about any character and play that character better than any other actor I ever met." Muni told this author that "I aged a lot in that picture [**The World Changes**], from a young fellow to an old man, like the one you see before you. I understand how old people acted early in my life and was able to play such persons with some convincing performances. When I was twelve years old, I played a sixty-year-old man on the stage, but I had the benefit of wearing a long gray beard that disguised my boyish face." Astor had nothing but praise for her co-star of this film, telling this author: "Paul Muni is one of the world's greatest actors, bar none. I know. I appeared with him in **The World Changes** and personally witnessed his acting wizardry." **p**, Robert Lord; **d**, Mervyn LeRoy; **cast**, Paul Muni, Aline MacMahon, Mary Astor, Donald Cook, Jean Muir, Guy Kibbee, Patricia Ellis, Margaret Lindsay, Alan Dinehart, Henry O'Neill, Douglas Dumbrille, Alan Mowbray, Mickey Rooney, Dave O'Brien, Sidney Toler, Charles Middleton, Jackie Searle, Richard Quine; **w**, Edward Chodorov (based on the story "America Kneels" by Sheridan Gibney); **c**, Tony Gaudio; **m**, Bernhard Kaun; **ed**, William

Holmes; **art d**, Robert M. Haas, Jack Okey.

World for Ransom ★★★ 1954; U.S.; 82m; Plaza/AA; B/W; Crime/Drama; Children: Unacceptable; **DVD**; **VHS**; **IV**. Gritty and gripping tale has Duryea as a veteran of World War II (1939-1945) who becomes a private eye based in Singapore. Carr, a former girlfriend, hires him to get her husband, Knowles, out of an association with Lockhart, a major black marketer. Lockhart plans to kidnap Shields, a nuclear scientist, who is one of only three men in the world who knows how to detonate an H-bomb and who carries most of that knowledge inside of his head. In his scheme, Lockhart would then hold the scientist for ransom and sell him to the highest bidder from any country. To accomplish Lockhart's sinister mission, Knowles dresses as a U.S. Army officer and meets Shields at an airport, and where Shields thinks that Knowles is his protector. Knowles, however, promptly kidnaps Shields. One of Duryea's helpmates sees this meeting and takes a picture of the kidnapping. The photographer is found dead the next morning and Duryea is suspected of killing him. Detective Dumbrille questions Duryea, but Duryea knocks him out and flees, hiding out in Carr's apartment. Duryea learns that Shields is being held on a deserted jungle island, so he travels to that isle. Denny, who is a British intelligence agent, follows, and he and Duryea join forces to find Lockhart, Knowles, and Shields in a hideout. Duryea and Denny break in and rescue Shields, taking him to safety. A fight ensues in which Denny is wounded and Duryea finds himself to be in a room with Lockhart and Knowles. Duryea throws two grenades that explode and kill both Lockhart and Knowles. He then takes Shields and Denny from the island. After returning to Singapore, Duryea tells Carr that he's sorry that he was unable to save Knowles and she angrily slaps his face. He leaves, walking off alone down a street. This highly stylized film noir entry is thick with exciting atmosphere, and Aldrich draws superior performances from Duryea and the rest of the cast. Biroc's lensing is also outstanding as Aldrich guides that camera to show one claustrophobic scene after another, suggesting that all of his characters are trapped. The film was shot on a shoestring budget, but it nevertheless produced more than $700,000 in its initial release. Song: "Too Soon" (Walter Samuels). *Author's Note*: Aldrich told this author that "I shot **World for Ransom** with a few dollars I could scrape up and all the change in my pockets. I put that picture in the can within ten days, but I had to stop shooting a few times because I ran out of money and went off to direct a few TV commercials to get enough funds to complete the picture. The cast and crew members were wonderful, working for scale. I think the whole production cost about $90,000. That picture did so well that it allowed me to go on and make another crime film, **Kiss Me Deadly** [1955], and that one helped establish my career in the genre they so generously call film noir." **p**, Robert Aldrich, Bernard Tabakin; **d**, Aldrich; **cast**, Dan Duryea, Gene Lockhart, Patric Knowles, Reginald Denny, Nigel Bruce, Marian Carr, Arthur Shields, Douglass Dumbrille, Carmen D'Antonio, Keye Luke, Lou Nova, Strother Martin; **w**, Hugo Butler, Lindsay Hardy; **c**, Joseph Biroc; **m**, Frank De Vol; **ed**, Michael Luciano; **art d**, William Glascow; **set d**, Ted Offenbacker; **spec eff**, David Commons, Jack Rabin.

The World in His Arms ★★★ 1952; U.S.; 104m; UNIV; Color; Adventure; Children: Cautionary; **DVD**; **VHS**. Peck is exceptional in this rousing sea tale where he competes with Quinn in illegally poaching seals. A New Englander, Peck is forever challenging Quinn, a Portuguese with a fiery temper. They both find themselves in San Francisco (c.1850) where Peck has just completed a successful voyage and has returned with a hold full of seals. Peck takes a room at an upscale hotel in the Barbary Coast. Blyth, a Russian countess who has run away from Esmond, a man to whom she is betrothed, but a man she detests, has also arrived in town. She thinks to sail away to Sitka, Alaska, which is governed by her uncle, Ruman, believing that he will give her sanctuary and protect her from Esmond. To that end, she finds Quinn and offers him a large payment if he will use his sailing ship to take her to Alaska.

When Quinn is unable to put together a crew, Blyth then turns to Peck, who is suddenly taken with the beautiful Blyth, but not knowing that she is of rRoyal Russian blood. He refuses to sail to Alaskan waters as he has nothing but contempt for Russians, but he soon changes his mind when he takes Blyth on the town and falls in love with her. Peck proposes and Blyth accepts. They are to be wed the next day, but the nuptials are interrupted when Esmond appears in a Russian vessel and abducts Blyth and her entourage before setting sail for Alaska. When learning of this, Peck gets drunk, loses all his money, and gets into a wild fight with Quinn. When he sobers up, Peck resolves to go after Blyth and he proposes to Quinn that they race both of their ships to Sitka, the first arriving there becoming the winner of both of their boats and the catches of seals they take along the way. Quinn agrees and the two ships race northward. Peck's vessel arrives in Sitka shortly ahead of Quinn's, but both captains are soon out of the money in that Esmond orders both of their ships and their catches impounded and has Peck and Quinn and their crew members thrown into prison. Meanwhile, Esmond threatens to kill Ruman unless his niece marries him. Coupled with that threat are the lives of Peck, Quinn and their crews that now hang in the balance. Blyth, who loves Peck, then promises to marry Esmond if he orders Peck's release and that of the others. The captains are returned to their ships, but, instead of sailing away, they and their crews stealthily go to Ruman's estate where Blyth is about to be married to Esmond. They interrupt the ceremony and Peck rescues Blyth, taking her back to his ship and then sailing for San Francisco. Esmond is foiled when his gunboat is then dismantled by a revenge-seeking Quinn. Peck and Blyth are then seen at the wheel of his ship as the winds waft over them and the stars above look down upon them as they sail toward freedom and happiness. Walsh robustly directs this action-filled film, and Peck, Quinn, Blyth and Esmond are standouts in their roles. Metty's lensing is superb, as he depicts a rowdy and raucous Barbary Coast in all of its garishness while excitingly capturing many breathtaking seascapes. Of special note are the excellent special effects that offer a wild storm at sea. The film was popular at the box office, earning more than $3 million in its initial release. *Author's Note*: Walsh told this author that "Greg [Gregory Peck] came to me with only one complaint when we made **The World in His Arms** and that is where he had to be flogged. He reminded me that that flogging scene did not occur in the original Beach novel, but I told him that 'we need to have that scene so that you will appear to have some humility as you are much too arrogant.' He looked at me as if puzzled and then shrugged and walked away. He did the scene without any further complaint. He later approached me and asked me what the hell I meant when I told him about teaching him humility. I stated: 'I have no idea. I needed to say something to get you to do the scene.'" Peck told this author that "the one thing that really bothered me was how those sailors are slaughtering seals in **The World in His Arms**, but Uncle [Raoul Walsh] promised me that he did not intend to show the hunting of the seals in any detail and he kept his promise. There is a lot of talk about seal catches in the picture, but I can't remember a single scene where that kind of cruel slaughter is shown." Quinn had nothing but respect for his co-star, telling this author: "Greg [Gregory Peck] is one of most resolute actors in the business. His whole personality is like looking at the Rock of Gibraltar. The man, through his actions and that great baritone voice of his, radiates confidence. I suppose that's why he was always the hero and guys like me are lucky enough to get punched in the face by him." This was the first of three films Peck and Quinn would make together, the other two being **The Guns of Navarone**, 1961, and **Behold a Pale Horse**, 1964. **p**, Aaron Rosenberg; **d**, Raoul Walsh; **cast**, Gregory Peck, Ann Blyth, Anthony Quinn, John McIntire, Carl Esmond, Andrea King, Eugenie Leontovich, Hans Conried, Rhys Williams, Sig Ruman, Bryan Forbes, Suzan Ball; **w**, Borden Chase, Horace McCoy (based on the novel by Rex Beach); **c**, Russell Metty (Technicolor); **m**, Frank Skinner; **ed**, Frank Gross; **art d**, Alexander Golitzen, Bernard Herzbrun; **set d**, Russell A. Gausman, Julia Heron; **spec eff**, David S. Horsley.

Carl Esmond and Ann Blyth in *The World in His Arms*, 1952.

World in My Corner ★★★ 1956; U.S.; 82m; UNIV; B/W; Sports Drama; Children: Unacceptable. Absorbing tale sees Murphy as a poor boy from the New Jersey ghetto becoming a professional boxer and attracting the interest of Morrow, a wealthy businessman who lets him train in the gym at his Long Island estate. Murphy falls in love with Rush, who is Morrow's daughter, but needs money so he can marry her, although her father tries to discourage the romance. To make money faster, Murphy decides to drop his honest fight manager, McIntire, and let himself be handled by St. John, a crooked fight promoter. St. John arranges a match for Murphy against the welterweight champion but tells him he can make more money by taking a fall. Murphy refuses to throw the fight and gets badly beaten but, surprisingly, wins the title by throwing a surprise left-handed punch that knocks out the champ. Fighting honest and winning, he gains respect from Morrow, who then permits Rush to marry Murphy. Now that he has achieved his goals, Murphy decides to quit the ring. The script is intelligent and the acting from Murphy, Rush, Morrow and St. John is superior, all making this film a worthwhile viewing. **p**, Aaron Rosenberg; **d**, Jesse Hibbs; **cast**, Audie Murphy, Barbara Rush, Jeff Morrow, Tommy Rall, John McIntire, Howard St. John, Chico Vejar, Steve Ellis, Art Aragon, Dani Crayne, James F. Lennon, Sheila Bromley; **w**, Jack Sher (based on a story by Sher, Joseph Stone); **c**, Maury Gertsman; **m**, Henry Mancini, Heinz Roemheld; **ed**, Milton Carruth; **art d**, Alexander Golitzen, Bill Newberry; **set d**, Russell A. Gausman, Julia Heron.

The World Is Not Enough ★★★ 1999; U.K./U.S.; 128m; Danjao; Eon; MGM; Color; Spy Drama; Children: Unacceptable (MPAA: PG-13); BD; DVD; IV. This exciting entry into the James Bond franchise (nineteenth in the series) is played for laughs while nevertheless providing nonstop action. Brosnan plays the secret agent investigating the murder of an oil tycoon and is assigned to protect his beautiful daughter, Marceau. The chief villain of the story is Carlyle, who was shot in the head by another agent and the bullet is still lodged in his head. For revenge, Carlyle plans to blow up a pipeline. Brosnan is helped by Richards, a beautiful research scientist, but becomes suspicious of Merceau, especially when Bond's boss M (Dench) goes missing. Brosnan has to work fast to keep Carlyle from destroying Europe, as villains in the series rarely do anything small. The thrills come from car chases, a powerboat chase on the Thames River, a hot air balloon adventure, a ski race down a mountainside, hang-gliding, bungee-jumping from a tall building, bomb throwers riding snowmobiles, and a spectacular climax involving a submarine. The film was a blockbuster at the box office, earning more than $362 million in its initial release against a budget of more than $135 million. Songs: "The World Is Not Enough" (David Arnold, Don Black), "James Bond Theme" (Monty Norman). *Author's*

Maria Grazia Cucinotta in *The World Is Not Enough*, **1999.**

Note: Action locations include London, Scotland, Azerbaijan, and Spain. Intense action violence and some sexuality prohibit viewing by children. **p**, Barbara Broccoli, Michael G. Wilson; **d**, Michael Apted; **cast**, Pierce Brosnan, Sophie Marceau, Robert Carlyle, Michael Kitchen, Denise Richards, Robbie Coltrane, Judi Dench, John Cleese, Desmond Llewelyn, Maria Grazia Cucinotta, Samantha Bond, Patrick Malahide; **w**, Neal Purvis, Robert Wade, Bruce Feirstein (based on a story by Purvis, Wade and characters created by Ian Fleming); **c**, Adrian Biddle; **m**, David Arnold; **ed**, Jim Clark; **prod d**, Peter Lamont; **art d**, Neil Lamont, Simon Lamont; **set d**, Simon Wakefield; **spec eff**, Nick Finlayson, Steve Hamilton, Paul Knowles, Andy Williams.

The World Moves On ★★★ 1934; U.S.; 104m; FOX; B/W; Drama/Romance; Children: Unacceptable; **DVD**. Pantheon director Ford does a good job in presenting this episodic chronicle of a wealthy family surviving chaos and calamities for more than a century. Beginning at the time of the closing of the Napoleonic Wars, two families in the U.S. and England, with branches in Prussia and France, own huge cotton businesses (not unlike the banking family of Rothschild). The family thrives under the guidance of Tone and the beautiful Carroll (appearing in her first U.S. film production), who marry in 1825. Over the years, their sons and grandsons robustly expand the family's fortune until its operation becomes a giant in the world of commerce. Tone and Carroll reappear as those descendants throughout the decades, until Tone is shown fighting in France during WWI (1914-1918) as a member of the French Foreign Legion. Carroll, another member of the family, is, unlike Tone, utterly opposed to war and defies the government when she refuses to produce munitions to be used in that war. Tone survives the war, marries Carroll, and becomes an aggressive player in speculative investments, so much so that he loses the family fortune in the 1929 stock market crash. Carroll, playing his modern-day wife, forgives his disastrous business errors while they retreat to their ancestral home to begin again. Tone, Carroll and Denny are exceptional in their repetitive roles, and Ford excels in presenting this episodic pageant in a semi-documentary fashion. He uses impactful imagery to make his historical points, including Jesus on his Cross and where he warns in a strong anti-war statement the rising nationalism of Germany, Italy and Japan by inserting newsreel footage of Hitler, Mussolini and Japanese military leaders, becoming a filmic soothsayer to predict the eventuality of WWII (1939-1945). The film, for all of its sweep and majesty of sets and costumes, did not do as well as expected at the box office. Songs/Music: "Should She Desire Me Not" (Louis De Francesco), "The Wedding March" (Felix Mendelssohn-Bartholdy), "Ave Maria" (Charles Gounod), "Rhapsody in Blue" (1924; George Gershwin). *Author's Note*: Ford told this author that "I was not eager to make **The World**

Moves On. Fox more or less compelled me to make that picture under contract. The studio had had a great success with another episodic film, **Cavalcade** [1933, winning Oscars for Best Picture and Best Director, Frank Lloyd], which was based upon a well-to-do British family over the years. Also, I had made another picture, **Four Sons** [1928] for Fox. That story had the sons of a German family fighting on opposite sides of the war [WWI], and the same thing happens in **The World Moves On**. I argued that we were going over ground that was just too familiar, but the front office stubbornly ordered me to make the picture and I complied. The studio dumped so much money into that production that, by the time it came to photograph the episode dealing with the war [WWI], the budget was strapped. I got around that by using footage from a great French picture about that war, **Wooden Crosses** [1932], but since that picture portrayed French troops fighting in the trenches, we had to make the hero [Tone] a member of the French army. There was another episodic story that had also seen great success called **Smilin' Through**. It was made as a silent [1922] by Sidney Franklin and featured Norma Talmadge. Franklin remade that picture at MGM as a talkie [1932] with Norma Shearer, Leslie Howard and Freddie March and it was also a big hit. Then that studio remade it even one more time [in 1941], but as a musical with Jeanette MacDonald and Brian Aherne. Studios never give up on a good thing and will repeat it until they wring out every dime from its story. You know, Aherne, who is a fine actor, appeared in a terrific episodic picture called **Forever and a Day** [1943], a story where an old British house is the star of the story that shows many persons living in it over the decades and what becomes of them. That story worked very well, but others do not. I think that **The World Moves On** was a better-than-average episodic picture, but it suffered because it was made too soon after **Cavalcade**." **p**, Winfield Sheehan; **d**, John Ford; **cast**, Madeleine Carroll, Franchot Tone, Reginald Denny, Louise Dresser, Sig Ruman, Stepin Fetchit, Lumsden Hare, Dudley Digges, Russell Simpson, Francis Ford, Mary Gordon, Jack Pennick; **w**, Reginald Berkeley (based on his story); **c**, George Schneiderman; **m**, Max Steiner, R.H. Bassett, David Buttolph, Louis De Francesco, Hugo Friedhofer, Cyril J. Mockridge; **ed**, Paul Weatherwax; **art d**, William Darling; **set d**, Darling, Thomas Little.

The World of Apu ★★★ 1960; India; 105m; Satyajit Ray/ Edward Harrison; B/W; Drama; Children: Unacceptable; **DVD**; **VHS**. Another fine Indian domestic drama is seen in this third and final installment of the Apu trilogy. Apu, played by Chatterjee, is a jobless ex-student in Calcutta dreaming of becoming a famous writer. Mukherjee, an old college friend, invites him to a village wedding, which changes his life when the bridegroom turns out to be mad and Apu is asked to become the husband. Though reluctant, he agrees and takes his beautiful bride, Tagore, back to Calcutta. After she dies in childbirth, Chatterjee leaves Calcutta and abandons his son, Chakravarty, leaving him with his wife's parents. After five years of depression and grieving, with the help of Mukherjee, Chatterjee is finally able of return to his son and the world. Earlier films in the series were **Pather Panchali**, 1955, and **Aparajito**, 1956. Mature themes prohibit viewing by children. (In Bengali; English subtitles.) **p,d&w**, Satyajit Ray (based on the novel *Aparajito* by Bibhutibhushan Bandyopadhyay); **cast**, Soumitra Chatterjee, Sharmila Tagore, Alok Chakravarty, Swapan Mukherjee, Dhiresh Majumdar, Sefalika Devi, Dhiren Ghosh, Shanti Bhattacherjee, Abhijit Chatterjee, Belarani Devi; **c**, Subrata Mitra; **m**, Ravi Shankar; **ed**, Dulal Dutta; **prod d**, Bansi Chandragupta.

The World of Hans Christian Andersen ★★★ 1971; Japan/U.S.; 70m; Hal Roach/UA; Color; Animated Fantasy; Children: Recommended (MPAA: G); **DVD**; **VHS**. Well-made animated feature film combines two of the best-known tales of Danish author and poet Hans Christian Andersen (1805-1875), "The Red Shoes" and "The Poor Little Match Girl." Hans (Galen voiceover) is the son of a poor shoemaker (MacGeorge voiceover) and is unhappy because he cannot go to the opera. His Uncle Oley (McCann voiceover) comes to the shoe shop to have his shoes repaired and pays with a piece of magic red leather. There is a contest to make red shoes for the princess to wear to the opera and the red leather is very welcome by the shoemaker. McCann tells Galen that his work involves polishing the stars in the sky each week and acting as the sand man, some of the tales Hans learns and later writes about. A poor girl (Orr voiceover) selling flowers, who lives next door to the shoe shop where Galen also lives, needs the money she gets for her flowers in order to buy medicine for her ailing grandmother (Bailew voiceover), so she turns to selling matches outside the opera house. Galen works odd jobs to get money to go to the opera, and buys all of Orr's matches, instead of going to the opera. Another girl, Elisa (Orr voiceover), is selling flowers outside the opera during the performance, and Galen stays with her, spinning stories that entertain listening crowds. The governor (MacGeorge voiceover) listens to Galen's stories and is so enthralled that he makes Galen his ward. Hans' father (MacGeorge voiceover) wins the contest with the red shoes he has made for the princess to wear to the opera. This delightful film for the whole family provides stunning animation that presents the enchanting story with inventive action. *Author's Note*: In the play "Pygmalion," by George Bernard Shaw (1856-1950), which was made into a film in 1938, and was then made into the musical **My Fair Lady**, 1964, the heroine selling flowers outside the London Opera House is named Eliza, or Liza for short, while the girl doing the same thing in this entertaining film is named Elisa. Other films from tales by Andersen include **The Red Shoes**, 1948; **The Little Mermaid**, 1989; and **Thumbelina**, 1994. The author's life was profiled by Danny Kaye in **Hans Christian Andersen**, 1952. **p**, Hiroshi Okawa; **d&w**, Al Kilgore, Chuck McCann; **cast** (voices of) Hetty Galen (Hans), McCann (Uncle Oley), Corinne Orr (Elisa, Kitty Kat, Little Boy, Match Girl/Mouse), Ruth Bailew (Grandmother), Ron Dante (lullaby singer), Sidney Filson (Karen), Earl Hammond (Ducks, Theater Manager), MacGeorge (Kaspar Kat, Governor), Linda November (Lullaby singer), Lionel G. Wilson (Hannibal Mouse, Mayor, Watchdog); **m**, Ronald Frangipane, Seiichiro Uno; **ed**, Eli Haviv, Emil Haviv; **art d**, Tadashi Koyama.

The World of Henry Orient ★★★ 1964; U.S.; 106m; UA; Color; Comedy; Children: Unacceptable; **DVD**; **VHS**. A screamingly funny performance is rendered by the gifted Sellers as an egocentric, amorous concert pianist in this comedic romp. He is pursued throughout New York City by two fourteen-year-old girls, Walker and Spaeth, who are his most ardent fans. They chase the harassed Sellers all over the city, spoiling his afternoon liaisons with sultry and towering married woman Prentiss. (Prentiss stands almost 5'10" while Sellers is barely more than 5'8" and Prentiss looms over him like the shadow of the Empire State Building). Lansbury, who is Walker's mother, finds a scrapbook her daughter and Spaeth have put together that chronicles the life and times of their beau ideal, Sellers. Lansbury wrongly assumes that Sellers has taken liberties with Walker and confronts the pianist. Sellers, however, turns on his amorous charm, soon seducing Lansbury, a conquest made with her happy consent since she is bored to death with her ho-hum husband Bosley. To destroy the adoring infatuations Walker and Spaeth have for Sellers, Lansbury orders Walker to sever her relationship with Spaeth. By this time, Walker is utterly depressed and shocked that her mother has stolen Sellers from her and Spaeth. Bosley takes firmer action, ending his marriage to Lansbury and taking Walker on a trip abroad. When Walker returns, she reunites with close friend Spaeth, but the two are no longer interested in an aging pianist like Sellers as they have now discovered boys of their own age. Though Sellers is superb as a piano playing Don Juan, the film is stolen by Walker and Spaeth, who provide one delightful scene after another of two curious girls coming of age as they share their romantic fantasies. Hill's direction is sure as he unravels this entertaining tale with one good scene after another, all supported by an intelligent and very witty script that not only strips away the trappings of glamorous affairs but incisively exposes plodding

Peter Sellers at the piano in *The World of Henry Orient*, 1964.

adults that somehow cannot relate to the innocent exuberance of the younger generation. The film also benefits from a sturdy score by Bernstein and above-average lensing from Kaufman and Ornitz. The film did well at the box office, yielding more than $2.1 million in its initial release. Music: "Henry Orient Concerto" (Kenneth Lauber). **p**, Jerome Hellman; **d**, George Roy Hill; **cast**, Peter Sellers, Paula Prentiss, Tippy Walker, Merrie Spaeth, Angela Lansbury, Tom Bosley, Phyllis Thaxter, Bibi Osterwald, Al Lewis, Fred Stewart, Hermione Gingold; **w**, Nunnally and Nora Johnson (based on the novel by Nora Johnson); **c**, Boris Kaufman, Arthur J. Ornitz (Panavision; DeLuxe Color); **m**, Elmer Bernstein; **ed**, Stuart Gilmore; **prod d**, James Sullivan; **art d**, Jan Scott; **set d**, Ken Krausgill.

The World's Fastest Indian ★★★ 2005; New Zealand/U.S./Switzerland/Japan; 127m; Rights Entertainment/Magnolia Pictures; Color; Sports Drama; Children: Unacceptable (MPAA: PG-13); **BD**; **DVD**; **IV**. Hopkins is marvelous as a middle-aged man with a lifetime love affair with motorcycles. He plays Herbert James "Burt" Munro (1899-1978), who lives in Invercargill, New Zealand, where he is not well liked by his neighbors. They object to his carless lifestyle where he seldom if ever mows his lawn, routinely urinates on his lemon tree, and is noisily revving his motorbike early in the morning. Most forgive the eccentric lifestyle of Hopkins since they know he possesses the fastest motorbike in the country, a 1920 Indian motorcycle he has been remodeling and modifying for years. It has been his lifelong ambition to take that motorbike to the U.S. where he might test its endurance and speed on the Salt Flats of the Bonneville Speedway near Wendover, Utah. He fulfills his dream by using his savings to book passage on a cargo ship sailing to Los Angeles that will carry him and his motorbike to the U.S. Once he arrives, however, Hopkins is met by innumerable obstacles that threaten to stop him from reaching his destination, particularly seemingly endless bureaucratic paperwork that will allow him as a foreign national to travel about the U.S. The gregarious Hopkins overcomes these difficulties through his brusque personality and blunt manner of speaking, which somehow endears him as a colorful rustic to the many people he encounters. He checks into a motel where he befriends transvestite woman Williams, who comes to his aid so that he can clear customs. Williams further helps Hopkins buy a car from used car salesman Rodriguez. When making the deal, Rodriguez gives Hopkins permission to use his junkyard and shop to build a trailer by which Hopkins can tow his motorbike to Utah. After Hopkins fine-tunes a number of cars on Rodriguez's lot, the salesman offers him a job, but Hopkins declines as he can only focus on getting as quickly as possible to the Bonneville Speedway. Along his way, Hopkins meets several outgoing Americans who help him, including Ladd, who briefly becomes his lover. When

Aaron Murphy and Anthony Hopkins (as bike racer Burt Munro) in *The World's Fastest Indian*, 2005.

Hopkins finally arrives at the Bonneville Salt Flats, officials refuse to allow him to participate in any of the races because he has not registered his bike in advance. Further, his motorcycle lacks brakes and a parachute to safely halt the cycle when needed and its tires are worn out. When hearing about this, other contestants and spectators go to officials and persuade them to allow the aging Hopkins to race his bike. He enters a timed run where he races his bike at terrific speeds (the camera mounted on the bike shows that dizzying and breathtaking pace in all of its exciting detail). Hopkins surprises the world, as well as himself, by achieving the impossible. He sets a new land speed record at the eighth mile, reaching 201.851 mph. The incredible challenge takes its toll on Hopkins, where one of his legs is badly burned from his bike's exhaust that eventually causes him to fall with his bike, which skids to a stop and where he luckily survives. Hopkins has not only lived out his dream of glorious victory, but, after he returns to his home in New Zealand, he is universally hailed as a conquering hero. Hopkins, one of the world's great actors, gives an utterly captivating and bravura performance as a dogged man who refuses to allow old age or an indifferent world to stand in his way to a goal he set when he was a youth. He proves, through the many moving scenes in this film, that spirit, courage, know-how, and the friendship of others can lead to victory if not to a special kind of immortality. This film became one of the top grossing films in New Zealand and earned more than $25 million in its initial worldwide release. Songs: "You Are My Sunshine" (1939; Jimmie David, Charles Mitchell), "Kiss Twist" (Craig Hubber). *Author's Note*: Munro raced his Indian Scout motorcycle to set that record at the Bonneville Salt Flats on August 26, 1967, a record that stands to this day. The machine he drove and he had remodified, was forty-seven years old when Munro set that record and he was sixty-eight years old at the time of that race. He had set several speed records in New Zealand while racing his Indian cycle, one as early as 1938. Director Donaldson claimed that he had researched this film for more than twenty years, producing a short documentary for TV on Munro titled **Offerings to the God of Speed**, 1971. Hopkins later stated that he thought his role in this film was the easiest he ever played in that he shared Munro's perspectives about life. **p**, Roger Donaldson, Gary Hannam, Barrie M. Osborne; **d&w**, Donaldson; **cast**, Anthony Hopkins, Diane Ladd, Jessica Cauffiel, Christopher Lawford, Iain Rea, Tessa Mitchell, Chris Williams, Saginaw Grant, Aaron Murphy, Chris Bruno, Paul Rodriguez, Joe Howard, Tim Shadbolt, Annie Whittle, Greg Johnson, Antony Starr, Kate Sullivan, Craig Hall; **c**, David Gribble; **m**, J. Peter Robinson; **ed**, John Gilbert, Michael R. Fox, Steve Haugen; **prod d**, Robert Gillies, J. Dennis Washington; **art d**, Roger Guise, Mark Hofeling; **set d**, Jackie Gilmore, Ken Kirchner; **spec eff**, Kent Houston, Philip Cory.

World's Greatest Dad ★★★ 2009; U.S.; 99m; Magnolia Pictures; Color; Comedy/Drama; Children: Unacceptable (MPAA: R); **BD**; **DVD**; **IV**. Offbeat, unnerving tale begins with Williams, who has dreams of becoming a rich and famous writer, but who only manages to become a high school poetry teacher. He nevertheless holds on to his dream. A single parent, his only son, Sabara, is fifteen-year-old and an underachieving, sex-obsessed teenager, is viciously hostile to Williams. Williams is dating Gilmore, the school's art teacher, but she is more interested in Simmons, another teacher. One night, Sabara accidentally strangles himself in his bedroom while looking at a photograph of Gilmore's underwear. To avoid this embarrassing death from being known, Williams writes a suicide note on Sabara's computer and hangs the body of his son in a closet, perversely faking his offspring's death as a tragic suicide. The other students at school do not miss Sabara because he was widely disliked, even detested because of his anti-social behavior. One student, however, obtains the suicide note from police records and publishes it in the school newspaper. Everyone is impressed with the sensitive writing in the note, so Williams capitalizes on this by writing a journal that he claims was written by Sabara. News spreads about the journal, and Williams appears on a national telecast talk show. The school's principal decides to rename the school library in Sabara's honor. Williams now becomes rich and famous for his writing, but he cannot escape the fact that his fame and riches have resulted from his false positioning of his own writing, based on his sleazy manipulation of his son's death. Feeling guilty at the library dedication, Williams confesses his deception. The incensed Gilmore slaps him and turns to Simmons, while everyone, feeling betrayed and used by Williams, turns their back on him. In everyone's eyes, Williams has made his reprehensible son a hero to enrich himself, but, in the cruelly deceptive process, he himself has become just as reprehensible. This black comedy, couched as satire, inexplicably did extremely well at the box office, producing more than $295 million in its initial release against a budget of more than $10 million. Sexual content, gratuitous gutter language and drug use prohibit viewing by children. Songs: "The Creeper (High)," (Tom Kenny, Darius Holbert, Gerald Brunskill, Ryan Rees, Andy Paley); "Invisible," "Sneaking Up on Boo Radley," "Shadow Hand," "Song C" (Bruce Hornsby); "Is You Is, or Is You Ain't My Baby" (Billy Austin, Louis Jordan); "It's a Good Day" (Dave Barbour, Peggy Lee); "Don't Be Afraid, You're Already Dead" (Miles Seaton, Seth Olinsky, Dana Janssen, Ryan Vanderhoff); "I Hope I Become a Ghost" (William Etling, Jesse Hoy, Michael Hughes, Christopher Richard); "Genius" (Inara George); "Mandolin Rain" (Bruce Hornsby, John Hornsby); "Under Pressure" (David Bowie, Freddie Mercury, Brian May, John Deacon, Roger Taylor); "Tiny Spark" (Brendan Benson, Jason Falkner). *Author's Note*: This film and an earlier film in which Williams appeared, **What Dreams May Come**, 1998, treat with suicide, and in this film it is employed as a device to enhance one's posthumous reputation. In grim irony, Williams himself committed suicide on August 11, 2014, hanging himself with a belt in about the same manner he fakes his own son's death in this film, and one must ask if this was done for the same purpose, to somehow enhance his posthumous reputation. This author met Robin Williams three times while doing book tours in the1980s and, on each occasion, I sensed that he was completely insincere and desperate to be the center of attention by doing anything antic, like a child throwing a tantrum in order to be noticed. Everything about him was furtive, fugitive and frantic, from his seemingly endless batting of eyelids, his retentive lips (sucked inward as if to hold back a torrent of words desperate to burst forth), his wrenching of hands (as if to keep from uncontrollably flailing), his awkward, severe posturing where he appeared to disjoint his limbs to slow his body motions. He was always "on," like a shark that must keep moving to survive, and my inclination in all instances was to get as far away from this weirdo as possible, lest I contract his contagious nervous tick. On one occasion while we were both waiting to appear on a talk show, Williams displayed such jitteriness that I asked him: "What's the matter with you? Do you have to visit the men's room?" He glared at me before rapidly spitting out his words: "What the hell are you talking about?" We had no conversation thereafter. I thought that Williams was unbalanced then, and I am guessing that he most probably thought so, too, but he cleverly hid his innermost fears about that by always frenetically expressing himself, setting off endless and meaningless firecrackers to drown out the sound of the challenging voice of sanity. His true talent was that he was artfully able to control his lunacy by transitioning it into the kind of mindless comedy that wows pubescent children, not unlike hand puppets whacking each other on the head with large wooden mallets. Such insidious self-manipulation, I felt, was motivated by something perverse, even sinister, wherein he was using up what drams of sanity he did possess to preserve what he mistakenly (or knowingly) believed to be his strength, the evils of lunacy that created illusionary and deceptive mirth to greedily garner more and more attention, but that also, I believe, bedeviled his mind. His foremost comedic idol was the truly funny Jonathan Winters, who told me (and I also met the gifted Winters several times) that "Robin isn't fooling anyone. We all know he is certifiable." Winters said this with a straight face. Williams was at the top of the Hollywood heap he always wanted to conquer when he took his life. He had a huge estate worth $35 million and another $50 million in the bank. He was idolized by millions of fans. He had three healthy children and a wife who loved him. But, by then, he was broke. He had used up all the real cash he had, his last vestiges of reason, spending it on worthless self-illusions. They say "you can't take it with you," but, I believe that Williams thought otherwise. In the end, he took his most prized possession with him—himself. I do not want to be unkind or, as they say, speak ill of the dead, but Robin Williams was a long way to committing suicide before he could actually bring himself to do that unsavory deed. He thus set a perverse example for millions of his young followers, knowing full well that he had widely influenced these impressionable people, and is therefore, beyond some of his exceptional performances, best forgotten than remembered. Sad to say, every one of those often marvelous performances now bears the permanent dark stigma of this talented but tormented actor's final self-betrayal. **p**, Howard Gertler, Richard Kelly, Sean McKittrick, Tim Perell, Sarah de Sa Rego; **d&w**, Bobcat Goldthwait; **cast**, Robin Williams, Daryl Sabara, Alexie Gilmore, Henry Simmons, Geoff Pierson, Zach Sanchez, Morgan Murphy, Naomi Glick, Dan Spencer, Evan Martin, Ellie Jameson, Michael Thomas Moore, Jermaine Williams; **c**, Horacio Marquinez; **m**, Gerald Brunskill; **ed**, Jason Stewart; **prod d**, John Paino; **set d**, Rachel M. Thompson; **spec eff**, Ian T. Barbella.

The Wreck of the Mary Deare ★★★ 1959; U.K./U.S.; 105m; MGM; Color; Adventure; Children: Unacceptable; **DVD**; **VHS**; **IV**. This exciting tale begins when Heston, captain of a small rescue tugboat in the English Channel, finds the freighter *Mary Deare* drifting after a small fire takes place on its decks. The ship appears to be abandoned, but, after Heston boards the vessel, he finds Cooper, who tells him to leave because the ship is not abandoned. While attempting to return to his tugboat, Heston falls into the sea and Cooper pulls him to safety with a rope. Cooper then allows Heston to join him aboard the *Mary Deare* and then confides to Heston that he plans to ground the ship on some reefs along the channel so its owner will decide it is missing or sunk. Then Cooper will refloat the ship as its new owner. The ship's owner sends Knox to investigate, but Cooper persuades Heston not to reveal where the ship is located. A French salvage ship owner finds the ship, which eliminates any chances by Heston to claim salvage, and the secrecy of the ship's whereabouts so rigidly maintained by Cooper is shattered. While Cooper and Heston go ashore, Cooper tells Heston that the crew of the French salvage ship is working in collusion with the owner, planning to move it from its rocky moorings and sink it while it is at sea. Heston then agrees to help Cooper prove his contention when both use scuba diving gear to swim back to the stranded freighter. Harris, who heads the salvaging crew, attempts to kill them both, but, in a wild

Gary Cooper in *The Wreck of the Mary Deare*, 1959.

struggle with Cooper, is killed. A court of inquiry is later held, and Cooper now reveals the mystery behind the *Mary Deare*. Cooper testifies that the ship dropped off its cargo in Rangoon and then sailed away. While at sea, it was purposely set on fire by its owner to collect payments from an insurance company for the loss of the cargo (which had already been sold off) as well as the ship. At that time, the crew abandoned the ship, but Cooper, its captain, who had been knocked unconscious and left for dead, revived and remained on board, sailing the ship onto a rocky reef in an attempt to save the vessel. Cooper is cleared of any wrongdoing and splits reward money from the insurance company with Heston. Anderson directs this action-packed thriller with a firm hand, and Cooper gives a strong performance as the duty-bound captain, one that is matched by the dynamic Heston. Harris, then beginning his career in films, is a standout as the brutal salvage seeker. The film earned almost $3 million in its initial release against a budget of more than $2.5 million. *Author's Note*: Alfred Hitchcock was originally signed to direct this film, but, after he and writer Ernest Lehman worked on the script for some weeks, they quit the project. Hitchcock told this author: "I agreed to direct that picture because I wanted to work with Gary Cooper, but the story we developed turned into a rather tedious courtroom drama, so I decided to abandon that project, and we then concentrated on making **North by Northwest** [1959]." Cooper told this author that "I looked forward to working with Hitch [Alfred Hitchcock]. Unfortunately, he went in another direction and we wound up with another director for **The Wreck of the Mary Deare**." That director was Anderson, who worked with an entirely new script that minimized the courtroom scenes originally conceived of by Hitchcock and Lehman. Heston told this author: "The new script for that picture gave the story a lot more drama and some very good action scenes at sea. To tell you the truth, I broke my back crawling all over that wrecked freighter. It was some of the hardest scenes I ever had to perform." **p**, Julian Blaustein; **d**, Michael Anderson; **cast**, Gary Cooper, Charlton Heston, Michael Redgrave, Emlyn Williams, Cecil Parker, Virginia McKenna, Alexander Knox, Richard Harris, Ben Wright, Terence de Marney; **w**, Eric Ambler (based on the novel by Hammond Innes); **c**, Joseph Ruttenberg (CinemaScope; Metrocolor); **m**, George Duning; **ed**, Eda Warren; **art d**, Paul Groesse, Hans Peters; **set d**, Henry Grace, Hugh Hunt; **spec eff**, A. Arnold Gillespie, Lee LeBlanc, Doug Hubbard.

The Wrestler ★★★ 2008; U.S.; 109m; Wild Bunch/Fox Searchlight; Color; Sports Drama; Children: Unacceptable (MPAA: R); **BD**; **DVD**; **IV**. Absorbing tale begins with Rourke, an aging professional wrestler long past his prime and who barely survives by wrestling at small shows and working in a grocery store. At the same time he tries to reconcile with Wood, a daughter he abandoned when she was a child while he at-

Marisa Tomei and Mickey Rourke in *The Wrestler*, 2008.

tempts to form a closer relationship with Tomei, a stripper. To solve his financial woes and redeem his self-respect, Rourke makes a Herculean effort to make a wrestling comeback in a rematch with Miller, his archrival of twenty years earlier and, in that extremely violent struggle, wins the match. The quirky Rourke gives a powerful performance while strongly supported by Tomei, Wood and the rest of the cast. The film earned more than $44 million in its initial release against a budget of $6 million. Songs: "The Wrestler" (Bruce Springsteen), "Bang Your Head/Mental Health" (Frankie Banali, Carlos Cavazo, Tony Cavazo, Kevin DuBrow), "Don't Know What You've Got Till It's Gone" (Thomas Carl Keifer), "Round and Round" (Robbin Crosby, Warren Demartini, Stephen Pearcy), "Balls to the Wall" (Peter Baltes, Udo Dirkschneider, Gabrielle Hauke, Wolf Hoffman, Stefan Kaufman), "Sweet Child O' Mine" (Steven Adler, Saul Hudson, Duff McKagan, Axl Rose, Izzy Stradlin), "Animal Magnetism" (Klaus Meine, Herman Rarebell, Rudolf Schenker), "Jump" (Madonna, Stuart Price, Joe Henry), "N2 Sumthin" (Takbir Bashir), "Don't Walk Away" (Bill Snare, Bill Leverty), "Soundtrack to a War" (Georg Dolivo, Robert Downes, Bryan Forsythe, Stefan Sigerson, Jackie Enx), "Nice Guys Finish First" (Joey Johnson), "8-bit Wrestler" (Joel Feinberg), "Just Let Your Freak Out" (Eben Jones, Deesha Sarai), "Mirror" (Danny Weise, Ari Zablozki, Chrin Chin, Santo Liveo, Danny Lawrence), "No Bitterz" (Tannis Kristjanson, Ari Katz), "Strutin' Like My Daddy" (Dwayne Carter, Tristen Jones, Bryan Williams), "Dodge It" (Samsaya, Eve Nelson), "Her Name Is Alice" (Michael Draper, James MacMillan, Nathan Abner), "Hit Da Flo" (Joseph Aschalew, Bradley P. Brandon), "Dangerous" (Jeff Blando, Blas Elias, Mark Slaughter, Dana Strum), "Black Light" (Kevin Huffman), "I'm Insane" (Robin Crosby), "The Muscle" (W. Hardnett, J. Anderson, J. Lightfoot), "Jerk It" (Omalola Isis Salami, Graham Bertie), "Aloha Oa/Queen Lilluokalani" (Robert Neary), "Blowin' Up" (Solomon), "30 Stars" (Peter Walker), "Ayatollah's Theme" (Raz Mesinai), "Farewell to Thee" (Queen Lilliuokalani). *Author's Note*: Nicolas Cage was originally slated for the role of the aging wrestler, but, after he dropped out, Rourke replaced him. The film was shot on location throughout New Jersey, and the wrestling scenes were filmed in the arena in Philadelphia. Other films depicting wrestlers and wrestling include **Abbott and Costello in the Foreign Legion**, 1950; **Abe Lincoln in Illinois**, 1940; **Across the Pacific**, 1942; **Alias Betty**, 2001; **Alias the Champ**, 1949; **American Graffiti**, 1973; **Baby It's You**, 1983; **Behind the Rising Sun**, 1943; **The Big Show-Off**, 1945; **Billy Madison**, 1995; **The Blue Umbrella**, 2005; **Blue Valentine**, 2010; **Blood on the Sun**, 1945; **The Body Snatcher**, 1957; **Bodyhold**, 1949; **The Breakfast Club**, 1985; **The Calamari Wrestler**, 2005; **The Chinese Connection**, 1972; **The Crammer**, 1958; **Diary of a Wimpy Kid**, 2010; **Ed Wood**, 1994; **Fancypants**, 2011; **Fellini Satyricon**, 1969;

Fighting Coast Guard, 1951; **The Fighting Kentuckian**, 1949; **Fighting Through**, 1934; **Force 10 from Navarone**, 1978; **Foxcatcher**, 2014; **A Girl, a Guy, and a Gob**, 1941; **The Girl from Mexico**, 1939; **Goliath and the Rebel Slave**, 1963; **Goliath and the Sins of Babylon**, 1963; **Hadley's Rebellion**, 1987; **Hercules Unchained**, 1959; **Highlander**, 1986; **Hollywoodland**, 2006; **Idiocracy**, 2006; **Kid Courageous**, 1935; **Kid Nightingale**, 1939; **The Killing**, 1956; **Legendary**, 2010; **The Magic of Lassie**, 1978; **Magnificent Brute**, 1936; **Man on the Flying Trapeze**, 1935; **Man on the Moon**, 1999; **The Manchurian Candidate**, 1962; **Micki & Maude**, 1984; **Mighty Joe Young**, 1949; **Mr. Moto in Danger Island**, 1939; **Morgan!**, 1966; **The Mummy Returns**, 2001; **Munich**, 2005; **The Naked City**, 1948; **Night and the City**, 1950; **No Place to Go**, 1939; **Paper Moon**, 1973; **Park Avenue Logger**, 1937; **The Payoff**, 1935; **People Will Talk**, 1935; **Pulp Fiction**, 1994; **Quo Vadis**, 1951; **Requiem for a Heavyweight**, 1962; **Risky Business**, 1983; **Rocky III**, 1982; **Samson and Delilah**, 1949; **Santa Sangre**, 1990; **Secret Venture**, 1955; **The Sign of the Cross**, 1932; **Spartacus and the Ten Gladiators**, 1964; **Spider-Man**, 2002; **Sudan**, 1945; **Swing Fever**, 1943; **Swing Your Lady**, 1938; **The Sword and the Rose**, 1953; **Take Down**, 1979; **Tarzan and the Leopard Woman**, 1946; **True Legend**, 2011; **Uptown New York**, 1932; **The Vampires**, 1969; **Vision Quest**, 1985; **Walking Tall**, 1973; **Walking Tall Part II**, 1975; **The Waterboy**, 1998; **We're in the Money**, 1935; **The World According to Garp**, 1982; **The Wrestler**, 1974; and **The Wrestler and the Clown**, 1958. Excessive violence, sexuality, nudity, gutter language and drug use prohibit viewing by children. **p**, Darren Aronofsky, Scott Franklin, Mark Heyman; **d**, Aronofsky; **cast**, Mickey Rourke, Marisa Tomei, Evan Rachel Wood, Mark Margolis, Todd Barry, Wass Stevens, Judah Friedlander, Ernest Miller, Dylan Summers, Tommy Farra, Mike Miller; **w**, Robert Siegel; **c**, Maryse Alberti; **m**, Clint Mansell; **ed**, Andrew Weisblum; **prod d**, Tim Grimes; **art d**, Matthew Munn; **set d**, Theo Sena; **spec eff**, Drew Jiritano, Andrew Mortelliti, Dan Schrecker.

Written on the Wind ★★★★ 1956; U.S.; 99m; UNIV; Color; Drama; Children: Unacceptable; **DVD**; **VHS**. This superb, tautly drawn melodrama thinly disguises the short and troubled life of tobacco tycoon Zachary Smith Reynolds and his mysterious and violent death that may have been brought about by his straying wife, Libby Holman, a celebrated torch singer. The film concentrates on a morally bankrupt Texas family named Hadley that owns everything in sight as its members are oil barons, and the town in which they live also bears that family name. Keith is the draconian patriarch whose greed for power and money knows no end. Stack is his errant son, an alcoholic drowning in his own wealth as well as booze, and his sister, Malone, is equally disreputable as a widely known promiscuous young woman. Keith has no regard for the two children he has spoiled and looks upon down-to-earth Hudson, who works as a geologist for Keith's oil company, as a son. Hudson has known Stack and Malone from childhood and has always been a steadying force in Stack's life. While on a trip to New York, Hudson meets and is attracted to alluring Bacall, an executive secretary, who is nobody's fool. He thinks to wed this self-confident woman, but undoes his own romantic plans by introducing Bacall to Stack. Turning on his considerable charm, Stack soon woos Bacall from Hudson's side, demeaning his friend by calling Hudson his "eccentric sidekick," pointing out that Hudson is "poor." To prove that he is just the opposite, Stack offers to buy the advertising firm for which Bacall works to offer it to her. She avoids a romance with the wealthy playboy, but Stack eventually wins her over. Stack suggests they go on a vacation, and Bacall agrees to a trip to Florida with him while Hudson dutifully tags along, more as a watchdog to Stack than an unwanted third party. Bacall is stunned to witness Stack's staggering wealth when seeing that he has not only reserved a luxurious suite for her at a top Florida hotel, but has filled it with designer dresses and rare perfumes. When Stack admits that he has ordered all of these expensive gifts for Bacall by simply making a phone call, she becomes nervous, believing that Stack is attempting to buy her affections. She leaves the hotel without Stack knowing it and goes to the airport, planning to immediately return to New York. Stack, however, finds her there and persuades her not only to stay, but convinces her that marrying him will be the best thing to happen in her life. They marry and go on an around-the-world honeymoon for three weeks; Keith learns that his son has wed a mystery woman only through reports appearing in newspapers. When Stack finally surfaces in Hadley with Bacall, Keith is delighted to know that his new daughter-in-law is a wise and sophisticated woman. After welcoming her to the family, Keith has a private chat with Bacall and is further edified to learn from her that his son has stopped drinking and that he no longer keeps a loaded gun under his pillow at night. Keith has always wanted Hudson to marry his daughter, Malone, but Hudson has no thought to ever wedding the wild-living Malone, having always thought of her as a sister. Stack and Bacall have a happy marriage, but Malone's sexual adventures begin to increase tension among the family members. After she tries to seduce Larch, who is a bartender at a local saloon, Stack and Hudson arrive at the bar, and Stack and Larch get into a fight. When Stack starts to get the worst of it, Hudson steps in and knocks out Larch. Hudson then departs with Malone in her sports car where she declares that he is the only man for her. Hudson still wants no part of Malone as he is still in love with Bacall, and Bacall feels the same way about him, but both do nothing in order to maintain Bacall's marriage. Rejected by Hudson, Malone goes on the prowl later that night, and, still later, she is brought home under escort by police, along with Williams, a young gas station attendant Malone has picked up, both having been found together at a motel. Williams claims that Malone inveigled him into the assignation and Keith becomes so enraged that he grabs a gun, thinking to shoot Williams, but Hudson stops him. Malone is indifferent to it all, going upstairs to her room where she dons a red nightgown and turns on a loud, trumpet bleating cha-cha record to which she wildly dances, kicking her legs and heels in wild abandon as she cavorts about the room. With everyone gone, Keith is enraged and embarrassed by his daughter's flagrant behavior and he decides to have it out with her once and for all. As Keith resolutely marches up the long staircase to chastise Malone, he suddenly suffers a heart attack, stumbling and then falling down the stairs to his death. Malone, oblivious to her father's death, continues her self-indulgent dance while her deafening music fills the mansion. (This sequence is only one of the many stunning segments of this obsessive film, one where Sirk cuts back and forth with distorted angle shots to show both Keith and Malone as painful death embraces one and sensual ecstasy the other.) Stack is unhinged by Keith's death, coupled with the fact that he has learned that he may be sterile and incapable of fostering children, these images so haunting him that he goes back to the bottle and begins drinking incessantly. Malone, who has little or no respect for anyone, viciously tells Stack that Bacall and Hudson are having an affair. Stack explodes, shouting at her: "You're a filthy liar!" Malone nods, replying in a way where she admits that she also has no self-respect when stating: "I'm filthy, period." Malone nevertheless continues to tell Stack that his wife is unfaithful until he comes to believe that Bacall and Hudson are secretly seeing each other. Meanwhile, Bacall gets a lift from Hudson into town where she has a meeting with a physician. Hudson drops her off at the doctor's office and then visits his father, Shannon, a self-survivor like his son, who is content to reside in a small house where he spends most of his time with his gun collection, repairing and cleaning the weapons religiously. Hudson then picks up Bacall and tells her that he has decided to work in Iran for an oil conglomerate and confesses that he loves her. Bacall stuns Hudson by stating that her doctor has informed her that she is now pregnant with Stack's child. She goes on to state that the previous medical diagnosis that Stack was sterile was simply "a medical opinion, not a fact." When arriving at the Hadley mansion, Bacall thinks to brighten Stack's gloomy perspective by telling him about her pregnancy. Half drunk, Stack responds with rage, coming to the wrongful conclusion that Hudson is the father of Bacall's impend-

Rock Hudson and Dorothy Malone in *Written on the Wind,* 1956.

ing child, Stack convinced that he cannot have children. He lashes out at Bacall, shouting: "You shouldn't have done that to me!" He attacks her, knocking her down. Seeing this, Hudson intervenes and knocks Stack half-senseless before Stack manages to leave the mansion on wobbly legs with Hudson calling after Stack that, if he ever assaults Bacall again, he will kill him, this traumatic scene witnessed by several household servants. Stack then searches for his own gun, which Keith has earlier confiscated and hidden. He attempts to buy one but is unsuccessful. He returns to the mansion and tears apart his father's study, finally locating the weapon. Stack then confronts Hudson, shouting: "You lousy trash! You no-account two-faced dog! I'm going to watch you cringe and then I'm going to put a bullet in your belly." Hudson insists that he and Bacall are innocent and that nothing happened between them, but Stack is consumed by rage, further stating: "You made me small in my father's eyes. You made my sister spit on me. Then, you stole my wife!" Hudson tells him that, as a result of his attack on Bacall, she has suffered a miscarriage, and that the unborn child would have been Stack's. Malone then enters the room and, seeing Stack with the weapon, attempts to wrestle it away from him. In the struggle, Stack stumbles and the gun goes off, a fatal bullet striking Stack. Staggering out the front door of the mansion, Stack dies, and Malone is quick to take revenge on Hudson for his constant rejection of her affections by blaming him for Stack's death, especially after he again refuses to marry her after Stack's demise. The scandalous death of the oil heir makes international news and, at a resulting trial, Hudson is charged with murder. Several witnesses from the Hadley household testify that they heard Hudson threaten to kill Stack and the chief witness against him, Malone, takes the stand to say that Hudson was, indeed, responsible for Stack's death. She then has a change of heart and admits that Hudson is innocent and that Stack's death was accidental. The finale sees Hudson and Bacall driving away from the Hadley mansion to seek happiness together. Malone sits at the desk in her father's study while a portrait behind her shows Keith sitting behind that very desk and where Malone holds a miniature oil well in her hands to symbolize her ignominious inheritance. Sirk inventively provides a magnificent potboiler as sexually provocative as **The Carpetbaggers**, 1964, and as scandalous as **Peyton Place**, 1957, surpassing these productions by providing the consummate melodrama. He uses luridly garish colors to accent the lovemaking scenes, such as when Bacall and Stack arrive at the Florida hotel and later at the Hadley mansion, while a florid score gushes forth to emphasize the most torrid sequences. The performances from Stack, Hudson, Malone, Bacall and Keith are exceptional as they fully capture their separate and tempestuous personalities, and Sirk works from an inventive script with enough twists and turns to maintain tension throughout, like the venerable pot threatening to boil over at any moment, until it finally does. Sirk was a master of

Rock Hudson and Dorothy Malone in *Written on the Wind*, 1956.

exaggerated soap operas and here he overwhelms with stylish absurdity to grimly parody his tragic characters. He entirely escapes any condemnation because his well-developed characters exist far beyond reason and realistic lifestyles. In one incisive scene after another he shows how their wealth allows them to commit all forms of outlandish behavior before they occasionally retreat back into the coldhearted sanity of their money and their false aura of prestige as naively seen by have-nots viewing and accepting their seemingly all-encompassing power. Sirk nevertheless reveals how these characters are as frail and vulnerable as any sharecropper or impoverished dirt farmer and that their envied fortune is the sinister catalyst that brings about their tragic downfalls. The characters make up anything but a model American family, as they are little more than a collection of dysfunctional individuals who are all but strangers to one another in emotion and spirit. Their distinction bears an evil stigma (in the public view) in that they are the possessors of oil, the greedy energy that drives the world's economy. Only a few of the many films ever based on oil have ever shown its characters to be sympathetic; most are portrayed as avaricious proprietors. In **Boom Town**, 1940, oil is presented as a geological adventure, but here it is treated as a corruptive, murderous force of the spirit if not the body, as it is, to name only a few, in **Giant**, 1956 (released two months before this film and also starring Hudson); **Oklahoma Crude**, 1973; and **There Will Be Blood**, 2007. Malone, who gives the performance of her life as a rich trollop reveling in hedonism, deservedly won an Oscar as Best Supporting Actress. Oscar nominations were also received for Best Supporting Actor (Stack) and Best Song ("Written on the Wind"; Young, Cahn). The film did very well at the box office, earning more than $4.4 million in its initial release. Songs: "Written on the Wind" (music: Victor Young; lyrics: Sammy Cahn), "Temptation" (1933; music: Nacio Herb Brown; lyrics: Arthur Freed). *Author's Note*: Sirk admitted to this author that "I threw everything into **Written on the Wind**, from incest to alcoholism, from sterility to infidelity, from adultery to brutality, from blackmail to murder—dragging every damned skeleton from what you might find in a family closet. I wanted to add homosexuality by showing a stronger emotional bond between Bob [Stack] and Rock [Hudson], but the censors drew the line and I knew I could not get away with that. [Hudson was a closet gay all of his adult life, even though he had a three-year marriage to the secretary of his manager, a union most believed was for cosmetic purposes, designed to shield his secret sexual proclivities.] I wanted to show the most corrupt family in America and I think I came close to doing that in that picture." Hudson told this author that "I got top billing in **Written on the Wind**, but Bob [Stack] got most of the play and he did a wonderful job with a very complex character. I was rooting for him to win an Oscar and it was a shame that he did not win [Stack lost out to Anthony Quinn for his portrayal in

Lust for Life, 1956], and I was up for an Oscar that year, too [for Hudson's performance in **Giant**]." Stack told this author that "I worked very hard to develop my character in **Written on the Wind**. He is a man with very low esteem who lives in the shadow of his dominating father and he takes to drink to compensate for that and also when he learns that he is impotent, which has to jar any man. To get a feel for the scenes where I have to go on a binge, I studied alcoholics in some hospital wards and even studied some of the poor drunken devils living in L.A.'s skid row. Almost all of them had a creepy, vacant look to their eyes and I used that in my scene with Betty [Bacall] where I have to knock her over a bed that causes her to have a miscarriage. Before we did that scene, I got myself into a boiling state of emotion by recalling some of my worst memories and while pretending to be drunk, go at her. Just before we did that scene, Betty became very concerned and said: 'I think you are crazy.' I told her that that is what my character was supposed to be in that scene. She was shaking a little and replied: 'I don't mean *acting* crazy. I mean you really are crazy!' I was purposely crossing my eyes a little when we were preparing that scene and I guess that is what set her off. I told her that I was only acting crazy, but, before we did the scene, I don't think she completely believed me. It was that scene that later upset her husband, Humphrey Bogart, and I understand that he told Betty to never appear in another film like **Written on the Wind** to avoid nuts like me. I guess all of that translated into some sort of half-hearted compliment about my performance, or so I told myself." The year following this production, Sirk would direct another outstanding film, **The Tarnished Angels**, 1957, based on another dysfunctional family, a group of aviation gypsies in the early 1930s and also starring Stack, Hudson and Malone. **Written on the Wind** was based upon the fatal shooting of Zachary Smith Reynolds (1911-1932), American aviator, yachtsman, and younger son of tobacco tycoon R. J. Reynolds (Richard Joshua Reynolds, 1850-1918), founder of R.J. Reynolds Tobacco Co. Following a drunken party at the Reynolds estate in Winston-Salem, North Carolina, the twenty-year-old Reynolds was fatally shot on the night of July 5-6, 1932. The shooting occurred under mysterious circumstances, taking place in the bedroom of his wife, Broadway torch singer and actress Libby Holman (Elizabeth Lloyd Holman, 1904-1971). He died a few hours later in a hospital without regaining consciousness. Holman claimed that Reynolds had committed suicide, but gave no reasons why this young multi-millionaire would take his own life. A coroner's inquest rendered a verdict of "death from a bullet wound inflicted by a person or persons unknown to the jury," but Holman was later charged with his murder, a charge that was later dropped. At the time of the shooting, Holman was alleged to be having an affair with one of Reynolds' friends, Ab Walker, and that the shooting resulted from a confrontation between the two while Holman was present. Years later, Holman stated: "I was so drunk that night that I don't know whether I shot him [Reynolds] or not." Holman married Ralph Holmes, an aviator, seven years later. The story was also loosely profiled in **Reckless**, 1935. For more details on the Smith killing, see my two-volume work *The Great Pictorial History of World Crime*, Volume II (History, Inc., 2004; pages 1238-1246). **p**, Albert Zugsmith; **d**, Douglas Sirk; **cast**, Rock Hudson, Lauren Bacall, Robert Stack, Dorothy Malone, Robert Keith, Grant Williams, Robert J. Wilke, Harry Shannon, John Larch, Edward C. Platt, Joseph Granby, Roy Glenn, Maidie Norman, Kevin Corcoran, The Four Aces (singing the title song); **w**, George Zuckerman (based on the novel by Robert Wilder); **c**, Russell Metty (Technicolor); **m**, Frank Skinner; **ed**, Russell F. Schoengarth; **art d**, Alexander Golitzen, Robert Clatworthy; **set d**, Russell A. Gausman, Julia Heron.

The Wrong Arm of the Law ★★★ 1963; U.K.; 94m; Romulus/Continental Distributing; B/W; Comedy; Children: Acceptable (MPAA: PG-13); **DVD**; **VHS**; **IV**. Very funny cops-and-robbers film is set in London where crooks do not carry guns and no one resists the police. City-wide burglaries are committed with clockwork precision under the supervision of Sellers, who professionally leads a bunch of smoothly coordinated cohorts while managing a designer dress shop on upscale Bond Street as a front. He has so well-organized the various burglary gangs that all have maintained a code that Sellers has established, one where all keep their promise not to invade the territories of each other. Moreover, Sellers treats his minions like the benevolent president of a corporation, providing them with paid lunches, vacations in Spain and regular sessions that tutor the crooks in the latest modus operandi of other burglars by screening caper films such as **Rififi**, 1956. This underworld tranquility is shattered when a new gang appears that consists of three interloping Australians and whose members dress as cops and steal from the crooks. It takes some time for Sellers to realize that he has been outsmarted by his underworld peers, and does not know that his lover, Newman, has been working with these foreign crooks by tipping them off to Sellers' operations. This turns upside-down the relationship between police and criminals, but Sellers calls a truce with law enforcement officials, persuading them to join forces in order to catch the impersonators (not unlike the underworld of Berlin working with police to catch a child killer in the more sinister **M**, 1931). To trap the Aussies, Sellers works with Scotland Yard to set up a gold robbery where the outsiders will be caught when going after the gold. The bumbling Jeffries, however, botches up the trap and the crooks escape. Sellers then proposes another trap where the foreigners can gain access to the money held in an armored car at an airport where Sellers thinks to hoodwink not only the police but the invading crooks by stealing the money and escaping on a plane at the airport. Again Jeffries fouls up the plan by getting himself chained to the moneybox held in the armored car, but Sellers and others still manage to fly off with the loot. When they arrive at a remote tropical island, however, they find that Scotland Yard has outwitted them as the stolen money is bogus. Undaunted, Sellers and his gang members quickly adapt to their new environment by becoming businessmen and where they make grass skirts to be sold to the natives and tourists. This is the kind of wacky comedy, filled with unpredictable turns and twists for which Sellers was so well remembered and at which he was so expertly adept. Nothing is taken seriously and the story's lack of violence makes it acceptable for children. The film was enormously popular in England and did good box office in the U.S. Song: "Oh Charley, Take It Away" (Arthur Le Clerq, Frederick Malcolm, Elvin Hedges). **p**, Aubrey Baring; **d**, Cliff Owen; **cast**, Peter Sellers, Lionel Jeffries, Bernard Cribbins, Nanette Newman, Bill Kerr, Davy Kaye, Ed Devereaux, Reg Lye, Graham Stark, Dennis Price in a cameo role, and Michael Caine in a small role in a police station at the start of his film career; **w**, John Warren, Len Heath, Ray Galton, Alan Simpson, John Antrobus (based on a story by Ivor Jay, William Whistance Smith); **c**, Ernest Steward; **m**, Richard Rodney Bennett; **ed**, Tristam Cones; **art d**, Harry White; **spec eff**, Charles Staffell.

The Wrong Box ★★★★ 1966; U.K.; 107m; Salamander Film Productions/COL; Color; Comedy; Children: Unacceptable; **DVD**; **VHS**. Subtle comedy, set in Victorian England, sees some outstanding performances from Mills, Caine, Richardson, Sellers, Moore, Cook and a bevy of other talented British thespians who all conspire to obtain a cache of money that has accumulated over many years in a family tontine. This ancient money investment plan involves family members contributing cash each year to eventually benefit the last surviving member of that family. Such an investment plan now obsesses the mind of two aging brothers, Mills and Richardson, each wanting that money and each hoping that the other brother dies first. Mills is ill and angry at the thought that his brother, Richardson, might acquire the loot after he passes. To prevent that from happening, he plots Richardson's murder, hoping that, once Richardson has gone underground, the riches will go to Mills' daydreaming grandson, Caine, a medical student, who looks after Mills. Meanwhile, Cook and Moore, who are Mills' cousins, stand to benefit from Richardson's survival and they do their utmost to keep that cantankerous old man alive. Mills pretends that he is on his

Peter Cook and Dudley Moore sitting on *The Wrong Box*, 1966.

deathbed and asks his brother, Richardson, to meet with him for one last time to reconcile their long-standing differences. Mills' real reason for summoning Richardson is to have him killed. The protective Moore and Cook bundle Richardson onto a London-bound train to meet with Mills, but everything goes awry when Richardson enters a compartment occupied by a dreaded serial killer known as the Bournemouth Strangler. The addlebrained Richardson rattles off his theories of numbers, boring his fellow passenger until he takes off his coat and then steps into the corridor to smoke a cigarette. The killer dons Richardson's coat only a short time before the train is demolished in a head-on collision with another train. After the mangled and unidentifiable corpse of the serial killer is discovered wearing Richardson's coat, Moore and Cook assume that their uncle has been killed and they are now out of the family tontine fortune. To keep other family members from knowing about Richardson's fate, they place the corpse into a coffin and ship it back home. The box, however, is inadvertently sent to Mills' home. Caine finds that he suddenly has a strange corpse on his hands and, thinking he will be blamed for its death, frantically seeks to hide it and ship it elsewhere. Meanwhile, as Cook and Moore discover their error, they pay corrupt Sellers, a physician, to sign a fake death certificate that states that the body is that of their deceased uncle, Richardson. In all the confusion, Caine meets Newman, Richardson's ward, and falls in love with her. Police now know that the body found at the train wreck is that of the killer and they conduct a frantic search for that missing corpse. As the police and the family relatives chase that elusive corpse, with the body constantly being moved about, it is then discovered that Mills and Richardson are very much alive. Richardson has made his way to Mills' home; they are found bickering once more together. For all of their sinister efforts, Moore and Cook succeed in only sending themselves to prison, and Caine is named the beneficiary of the tontine cache since he and Newman are now to be wed. Forbes does a fine job guiding viewers through the chaos and confusion of this macabre and thoroughly amusing tale and where the talented cast offers an entertaining romp, which owes much to the old Mack Sennett silent comedies and where it does not stint on slapstick and even employs subtitles to clarify the calamities dumbfounding most viewers. This film is reminiscent of Alfred Hitchcock's **The Trouble with Harry**, 1955, another dark comedy about a body that will not stay buried and keeps resurfacing to vex a cast of oddball characters who decidedly want that corpse under the ground. **p&d**, Bryan Forbes; **cast**, John Mills, Ralph Richardson, Michael Caine, Peter Cook, Dudley Moore, Peter Sellers, Nanette Newman, Tony Hancock, Wilfrid Lawson, Peter Graves, Jeremy Lloyd, James Villiers, **w**, Larry Gelbart, Burt Shevelove (based on the novel by Robert Louis Stevenson and the novel by Lloyd Osbourne); **c**, Gerry Turpin (Eastmancolor); **m**, John Barry; **ed**, Alan Os-

Henry Fonda in *The Wrong Man*, 1956.

biston; **art d**, Ray Sim; **set d**, Peter James.

The Wrong Man ★★★★ 1956; U.S.; 105m; WB; B/W; Crime Drama; Children: Unacceptable; **DVD**; **VHS**; **IV**. Fonda gives a powerful performance as musician Christopher Emmanuel "Manny" Balestrero (1909-1998), who was wrongfully charged with a string of robberies in this tense tale from pantheon director Hitchcock. Fonda plays a bass in a band at the swanky Stork Club in NYC. He is a dedicated family man, who returns dutifully home after work to join his loving and devoted wife, Miles, and their two sons. The family is financially stressed, and Fonda, to make ends meet, is constantly borrowing money. Fonda plays a little game at home when reading the racetrack news in the paper as he picks winners in upcoming races, but he admits that he has never dared place a bet since he and his family are simply too poor for such extravagant gambles. When Miles desperately needs dental work to relieve the pain she is enduring, Fonda goes to his insurance company to borrow money on his wife's life insurance plan. Office employees then identify Fonda as the very man who has recently robbed them. That night, police enter the Stork Club and arrest Fonda, booking him on charges of robbery. Stone, one of the interrogating police officers, politely asks Fonda to write out a note, using the same words written by the holdup man. Fonda dutifully writes that note and is asked to write it out once more, which Fonda does. Stone then points out to Fonda that he has twice written the word "drawer" as "draw," which is the same kind of misspelling made by the holdup man. He is then placed in a police lineup and is identified by the women from the insurance firm, as well as some small shop owners, who have been robbed at gunpoint by the same man. He is then officially charged with the robberies, fingerprinted, photographed and imprisoned while he awaits his trial. Fonda insists that he is innocent, and when his wife, Miles, visits him, she is so distraught and anxious that it is Fonda comforting her instead of the other way around. After Fonda is released on bail, he retains Quayle as his attorney, but, despite his desperate efforts, he cannot find witnesses to provide an alibi for him during the time of the robberies, and it now appears that he will be facing a certain conviction and long imprisonment. When realizing this, Miles begins to go to pieces, the emotional strain giving her such anxieties and apprehension that she withdraws to her room and then into her herself, shutting herself off from Fonda and their two boys. So mentally damaged by the trauma created by her husband's trial is Miles that she becomes nonresponsive and must be placed in an institution. Fonda then goes to trial with Quayle as his defense attorney, but the proceedings are soon disrupted when it is learned that one juror asks why so many questions must be asked as he all but states that he has predetermined Fonda's guilt. A mistrial is declared and Fonda then goes into a new trial. While lan-

guishing in his prison cell, Fonda prays for his deliverance and he is inexplicably given that freedom after another man is identified and arrested for robbing a small grocery store (this is achieved when the face of that man, Robbins, is superimposed upon Fonda's face to show them to be lookalikes). Robbins is now arrested and charged with the robberies, and the same witnesses who had earlier testified against Fonda now identify Robbins as the real culprit. A grateful Fonda is released and he rushes to the asylum to give Miles the good news. She, however, remains in her near catatonic state. After she listens unemotionally to Fonda, she merely states: "That's good for you." The film closes on this depressing note, but an epilogue states that, two years later, she was fully recovered and left the institution. (In reality, Balestrero's wife not only recovered, but she, her husband and their two sons moved to Florida to live out a happy life.) Unlike almost all of his previous films, Hitchcock shot this film in a semi-documentary style as if recording a news event and shot the film on the locations of the story, including the posh Stork Club where Balestrero worked, his actual home on Seventy-Fourth Street in Queens, the Long Island Prudential Insurance office in Long Island where he was first wrongly identified, and even the very asylum where his wife was institutionalized. The performances from Fonda, Miles and Quayle are astoundingly reserved, and they realistically essay commonplace people trapped in an uncommon and threatening situation. The low-key, gritty lensing by Burks reflects the grimness of the story, Hitchcock had Burks linger his camera in many scenes to capture the tedium of police interrogations and the exhausting procedures of the court systems to most effectively show how the patience and endurance of Fonda, Miles and even attorney Quayle is tested to the point of utter exhaustion. As such, this film becomes a devastating profile of a man trapped into a system from which circumstances and happenstance may never allow him to escape. The film, like all Hitchcock films, did well at the box office, earning more than $2 million in its initial release against a budget of more than $1.2 million. *Author's Note*: Hitchcock told this author: "We did considerable research when we made **The Wrong Man**. We had long talks with the Balestrero family and with Frank O'Connor, who represented Balestrero in court. [O'Connor, 1909-1992, was a New York State senator at the time he defended Balestrero and, following that trial, became the district attorney for Queens County and later an appellate court judge.] We shot the film on location in New York and used all the actual locations that involved the case. It was not a glamorous story, like, say, **North by Northwest** [1950] with a sophisticated actor like Cary Grant wooing a beautiful blonde. No, it was just the opposite. Plain people wearing inexpensive clothes and where their talk is simple and to the point and without a bit of wit, that is what I wanted to show. Here you have a man who is wrongfully accused of a crime and, even though he is innocent, he really has no chance of proving his innocence because he has no money, no powerful friends. Only through an accident of fate, or through the intervention of the Almighty, if you like, do his chances improve and only then does he have any hope that he will see freedom and his family again." Fonda told this author that "my character in **The Wrong Man** is not anyone special in society. In fact, he is a nobody, who soon learns that being a nobody is very dangerous when you are wrongly accused for a crime you did not commit. He is lucky enough to find a good lawyer to defend him, but no one comes to his rescue, and it seems to him that no one even cares whether he is innocent or not. He is inside of a system that routinely sends people to prison, even some who are innocent, period. To me, every human being is somebody, someone special, and so was the man I played, which is why I was excited about that role right from the beginning. I was additionally eager to make that picture because I always wanted to work with the great Alfred Hitchcock." As Hitchcock told this author (as stated in my *Author's Note* in my entry for Hitchcock's **Murder!**, 1930): "Hank [Fonda] did a picture with me, **The Wrong Man** [1956] and he told me at that time how much of an admirer he was of my pictures and how he had studied them. Well, the next picture he makes is **12 Angry Men**, and what do you think? It's a takeoff on my picture, **Murder!** At least, the premise of that picture uses the beginning of my picture and takes it from there. In **12 Angry Men**, Hank is the lone juror in a room full of jurors, who are pressuring him to agree with them in convicting the defendant when he thinks the defendant might be innocent. Like Herbert [Marshall] in my picture [**Murder!**], Hank then recreates the murder right there in the jury room to finally turn everybody around so that they find the defendant innocent. I found that picture very appealing and have always thought it was Hank's left-handed way of flattering me." When this author later repeated these remarks to Fonda (who was the chief producer of **12 Angry Men**) in one of my many meetings with the actor, he replied: "That man had a memory like an elephant. He forgot nothing. I think Hitch spent a lot more time watching other people's films than he did his own, not to get ideas, but to see if his own ideas were being used. You might say he was an unusual film detective, the way he could track down how his own ideas were being used by everybody else. Sure, I watched **Murder!** and more than once before we did **12 Angry Men**. You learn all you can from master directors like Hitchcock if you want to make good films." Miles, who appeared in Hitchcock's **Psycho**, 1960, and who had also appeared in a segment of the director's TV show, "Alfred Hitchcock Presents," told this author that "Hitch was not that demanding, except that he expected you to come prepared and anyone who did not would hear from him very quickly." Hitchcock told this author that he was very disappointed when he could not have Miles as his leading lady in **Vertigo**, 1958, the next feature film he made after **The Wrong Man**. "I thought that Vera would be outstanding in that picture, but, no she had to go and get pregnant and then I was forced to use Kim Novak." The director later stated: "She [Miles] was going to be real star with this film, **Vertigo**, but she couldn't resist her Tarzan of a husband, Gordon Scott. She should have taken a jungle pill!" **p&d**, Alfred Hitchcock; **cast**, Henry Fonda, Vera Miles, Anthony Quayle, Harold J. Stone, Charles Cooper, John Heldabrand, Nehemiah Persoff, Werner Klemperer, Harry Dean Stanton, Tuesday Weld, Richard Robbins, Hitchcock; **w**, Maxwell Anderson, Angus MacPhail (based on the story "The True Story of Christopher Emmanuel Balestrero" by Anderson); **c**, Robert Burks; **m**, Bernard Herrmann; **ed**, George Tomasini; **art d**, Paul Sylbert; **set d**, William L. Kuehl.

Wuthering Heights ★★★★ 1939; U.S.; 103m; Goldwyn/UA; B/W; Drama/Fantasy/Romance; Children: Unacceptable; **DVD**; **VHS**; **IV**. This wonderful film offers a haunting romance story that remains a timeless classic with marvelous performances from Olivier, Oberon and a talented cast directed by pantheon director Wyler. Its eerie 1841 opening sees Mander stranded in a frozen English countryside during a fierce snowstorm and he desperately seeks shelter. He sees in the distance an old manor house named Wuthering Heights and finds his way to it, asking that he be given a room for the night. The occupants— Olivier, the landlord, his wife, Fitzgerald, and Carroll, the caretaker, display hostile attitudes toward Mander, but housekeeper Robson is friendly. Mander is shown to an upstairs room, which has once been a bridal chamber, and he makes himself comfortable. He is then startled to feel a rush of cold air blowing into the room and goes to the window to close a shutter being banged by the wind. As he reaches to close the shutter, an ice-cold hand clutches his, and he then hears from outside the window a woman's voice calling out: "Heathcliff!" Mander sees in the distance what seems to be the form of a woman, crying out: "Let me in! I'm out on the moors! It's Cathy!" The disturbed Mander informs Olivier about what he has heard and seen, and Olivier orders him to leave the room he has occupied and then runs from the manor house and into the snowstorm. Mander is bewildered until Robson tells him that he has seen the ghost of Oberon (Cathy), who was once Olivier's lover, but has been dead many years. Mander resolutely tells Robson that he has no belief in ghosts, but Robson tells him that he might believe in spirits after he hears Cathy's story and she begins to unfold that tragic tale as depicted in a long flashback. It is forty years earlier and

Harold J. Stone, Henry Fonda and Charles Cooper in *The Wrong Man,* 1956.

we see Heathcliff as a child, played by Downing, who is found in the streets of Liverpool by Kellaway. Downing is a homeless gypsy, and Kellaway adopts the precocious boy, bringing him home to his countryside manor house so that he might have a better life as enjoyed by his two children. Downing is not happily greeted by those two children, Cathy, played by Wooten, and her brother, Scott. Though Wooten eventually befriends Downing and they become very close, Scott resents Downing, thinking him to be an intruder into a close-knit family. Downing and Wooten play an imaginary game where they are living in a castle. They grow to adults as Olivier and Oberon, and, by this time they are in love, secretly meeting atop a rocky hilltop called Peniston Crag, the site of their imaginary castle, where they embrace and kiss (although it is implied that their affair at this time is platonic). Scott has grown to be an adult as Williams, who has continued to hate Olivier and, after Kellaway dies, Williams becomes the owner of the manor house. He turns to drink and becomes a tyrannical landlord, turning Olivier out and forcing him to work as a stable boy. Olivier, and Oberon, however, continue to secretly meet, and, while strolling one night, see a party being held by their well-to-do neighbors. They attempt to enter the grounds, but, as they climb over a garden wall, the family dogs attack them and Oberon is injured. Olivier has no choice but to leave Oberon in the care of this family. He soon resents the fact that Oberon is enamored of this family's wealth, which drew them to that party, and he exhibits his hatred for these neighbors by cursing them and their riches. Meanwhile, Niven, the son of that rich family, falls in love with Oberon and proposes marriage. After several months of recuperation, Oberon returns to her home to tell housekeeper Robson about Niven. Robson reminds Oberon that she has pledged her love to Olivier. Oberon, however, is utterly captivated by the wealth of Niven's family and tells Robson that she would feel humiliated if she married Olivier because of his lowly station in life. Olivier has overheard these terrible remarks and leaves, deeply hurt. When Oberon realizes that Olivier has overheard her hurtful remarks, she immediately feels guilty and runs after him but is caught in a storm. She is found by Niven, who returns her home and where she again falls ill. Niven takes care of her and, when she regains her health, she agrees to marry him. Olivier is thought to have disappeared forever, but he returns within a few years as a wholly different man. He has acquired great wealth and is much more refined and sophisticated. He also harbors a deep resentment over the way he has been treated in the past and seeks revenge. He discovers that Williams has fallen deeply into debt and he pays off those debts while acquiring Wuthering Heights, allowing Williams to continue living in the old manor house. Olivier nevertheless takes his revenge against Williams by treating him just as cruelly as Williams meanly treated him in the past, encouraging Williams' alcoholism in order to hasten his demise.

Laurence Olivier and Merle Oberon in *Wuthering Heights*, 1939.

Williams thinks to kill Olivier, but is too drunk to complete his grim task. Olivier viciously points out that even in this Williams has proven to be a miserable failure. Olivier further inflicts anguish on Oberon by marrying Niven's gullible sister, Fitzgerald. Olivier knows that Oberon still loves him and his loveless union to Fitzgerald has been made out of spite. Fitzgerald, who is devoted to the cold-hearted Olivier, knows that her husband still pines for Oberon and becomes so resentful of that lingering love that she hopes that Oberon will die so that Olivier will finally forget her and make a happier life with her. Oberon, for all the comfort that Niven's riches afford her, is so unhappy that she had never consummated a marriage to the only man she loves that she longs to see her life end. She grows ill and, when she is on her deathbed, Olivier, realizing all the wrong he has done to her, makes his way to Oberon's room, despite objections from the embittered Fitzgerald. When at that deathbed, Olivier tells Oberon that he has never stopped loving her and she declares her love for him, both stating that even death cannot sever their love for one another. Olivier carries Oberon to a window to show her where they once played together as children, their imaginary childhood castle at Peniston Crag. Oberon promises that, after her death, she will wait for Olivier there. Olivier asks that Oberon haunt him through the rest of his living days, even though such ghostly visitations might drive him insane. Oberon then dies in Olivier's arms. In flash-forward, we see Robson ending this strange tale, which Mander cannot believe. At that moment, Crisp, the family physician, bursts through the front door. He is highly animated, stating that he has just seen Olivier walking in the snow with his arm around a woman. "It was Cathy!" Fitzgerald shouts with fright, but Crisp shakes his head, saying: "No, I don't know who it was." Crisp continues, saying that he was thrown from his horse and then found Olivier lying in the snow alone and that only Olivier's footprints were in the snow and to all of this Crisp now says he thinks he has doubted his own sanity at what he has seen. "Is he dead?" Mander asks, referring to Oliver. Crisp sadly nods, but Fitzgerald knows otherwise, solemnly stating: "No, not dead…and not alone. He's with her. They've just begun to live." We see at this startling finale the towering Peniston Crag, the imaginary childhood castle, and, superimposed upon this rocky hillock, the spirits of Olivier and Oberon walking hand in hand through eternity together. The indefatigable Wyler exhausted his cast and crew in making this classic film, but his careful diligence to detail and penchant for perfection produced one of the most lyrical tragic romances ever put on the screen. Olivier and Oberon are magical as the star-crossed lovers, perfectly matched to produce one tender or tempestuous scene after another. The nuances of their subtle interplay—from the modulated tonal qualities of their voices to their physical movements—present a powerful emotional bonding so intense as to be mesmerizing and unforgettable. The supporting cast members, Williams,

Robson, Fitzgerald, Carroll, Kellaway, Niven, Mander and Crisp, are startlingly believable in their distinctive roles, bringing each character to life with the same kind of robust vitality as exhibited by Olivier and Oberon. Much of this is due to the patience and perseverance of the gifted Wyler, who worked all of them very hard while ordering innumerable takes until he got each scene, according to his own words, "the right way." The brilliant script from Hecht and MacArthur is, other than the sentimental ghostly ending, utterly faithful to the Bronte novel. Newman presents a melodic and dynamic score enhancing each and every scene, and the Georgian period is wonderfully recreated through Basevi's accurate and tasteful art direction, along with stunning sets from Heron. Greatly adding to the moody atmosphere throughout is the crisp lensing from master cinematographer Toland, who, two years later, went on to photograph **Citizen Kane**, 1941, for Orson Welles. He had been selected by the Mitchell Camera Corporation to be the first cinematographer to use their new BNC camera in shooting this film, that camera becoming the standard thereafter. Toland's inventive mastery of that camera here was evident to the members of the Academy Awards, who bestowed upon Toland an Oscar for Best Cinematography. The film also received Oscar nominations for Best Picture (Goldwyn); Best Director (Wyler); Best Actor (Olivier); Best Supporting Actress (Fitzgerald); Best Screenplay (Hecht, MacArthur); Best Original Score (Newman); and Best Art Direction (Basevi). The film was, unfortunately, not popular at the box office, earning less than $700,000 in its initial release, although Goldwyn recouped his investment of more than $1 million through rereleases and, by 1950, saw considerable profits from the production. The film saw a radio adaptation aired by Philip Morris Playhouse on October 17, 1941, starring Raymond Massey and Sylvia Sidney. A thirty-minute radio adaptation was aired by the Screen Guild Theater on February 25, 1946, with Oberon reprising her role. It received a sixty-minute radio adaptation aired by Lux Radio Theater on September 14, 1954, with Fitzgerald reprising her role. Several remakes include Luis Bunuel's **Wuthering Heights** (aka: **Abismos de Pasion**; made in 1953, but released in the U.S. in 1983), a 1954 Egyptian production, as well as versions in 1970, 1985, 1992, 2011, made-for-TV productions in 1998 and 2003, a TV series in 1967, and two TV miniseries in 1978 and 2009. None match the 1939 original production. Songs/Music: "Piano Sonata in A Major, K.331: Rondo alla Turca" (1778; Wolfgang Amadeus Mozart), "The Wedding March" (1843; from "A Midsummer Night's Dream, Op. 61" by Felix Mendelssohn-Bartholdy). *Author's Note*: The genesis of this film began with Wyler, who told this author that "I had wanted to make **Wuthering Heights** for many years, and I wanted Charles Boyer and Sylvia Sidney to star in that picture. I had a very good experience with Sylvia some years before that when we made **Dead End** [1936] together. I went to Sam [Goldwyn] with the idea and he got very excited and told me to assign Ben [Hecht] and Charlie [Charles MacArthur] to write the script." Hecht and MacArthur at that time were the top, highest-paid screenwriters in Hollywood. According to Hecht's remarks to this author, both were "more than enthusiastic to tackle that Bronte brute of a novel. We knew it was far too unwieldy to pack that whole story into even an overlong picture, so we settled for the first sixteen chapters [out of the total thirty-four chapters, also eliminating Cathy's daughter and Heathcliff's son, who appear in the latter half of the book, and keeping Isabella alive until the end of the film where, in the novel, she escapes Heathcliff and dies]. Sam [Goldwyn] wanted the setting changed from the Regency to the Georgian era so that he could dress up his actresses in the more elegant gowns of that period and we complied, but we labored long to keep the story line and characters intact and we followed the dialog, such as it was, with not too many frills. At the time, Charlie [Charles MacArthur] and I had residences in New York, and we did not want to write that script in Hollywood where Sam [Goldwyn] could get at us, and that would be night and day, believe me. We thought Sam might even fly to New York, so we both hid out on a little island owned by our friend Alec [Alexander] Woollcott [Neshobe Island in Lake Bomoseen, Vermont, Woollcott then being the powerful New York *Times* drama critic and the major domo of the Algonquin Round Table]. He had built a mansion on that island where he lived like a fat prince, but the only way you could get to it was by a boat run by some old geezer in Alec's employ and Alec told this Charon who he could ferry back and forth from that island. Well, when we told Alec what we were writing, he became more than curious. In fact, he thought we were nothing but a couple of pranksters taking advantage of naïve Hollywood producers. He loved the Bronte novel and was fiercely protective of it, at one time spying on us and accusing us of writing a fake script. Of course, we went out of our way to make him believe that. We wrote a phony scene in the script and left it in plain sight for Alec to find, which he did. The fake scene has Heathcliff traveling to America after Cathy marries someone else and he spends a year among the Indians to make his fortune. We wrote impossible scenes for that sequence that involve Heathcliff and a character we called Chief Crooked Head and where the dialog consisted of such lines as 'Ugh, ugh, heap big pow-wow!' After Alec found that part of the phony script, he confronted us at dinner, glaring at us through glasses that made him look like a disapproving owl. 'I think you two gentlemen are in need of a psychiatrist,' he told us. 'Emily Bronte never wrote the line 'ugh, ugh, heap big pow-wow' or any facsimile thereof! You both disgust me so much I cannot finish my dinner.' With that he threw his napkin onto his plate and departed for his inner sanctum and he refused to talk to us for several days after that, until we told him that we had been ribbing him, and that made him all the more angry. We were lucky to get off that island without suffering any serious physical damage." When Hecht delivered the script to Goldwyn and Wyler, Goldwyn, always the meddler, as he told this author, "decided that the script needed something else. It was just too grim and dim, so I gave the script to a young writer named John Huston to look it over." Huston told this author: "I was so impressed with what Ben [Hecht] and Charlie [Charles MacArthur] had done with that script that I gave it back to Goldwyn and told him that I could not find a word that I would change. It was perfect. But Goldwyn being Goldwyn just had to shove his thumbprint onto that sublime romance." Goldwyn told this author: "I did not like the ending and I had a scene added at the finish where Heathcliff and Cathy are seen as spirits walking arm and arm." When Wyler saw this scene, he refused to make it part of the production. "I told Sam that he was ruining the ending of a great story," Wyler told this author. "Sam then said to me: 'The ending is too depressing. We are *not* going to send audiences out of the theater feeling miserable! That's out! The ghosts are in for the finish and that's that.' As usual, he got his way and the spirits remained in the picture, and every time I saw it after that, *I* was the one who was miserable." There was considerable misery to go around during the production of this great film, especially among the leading players. Olivier was not the first choice to play Heathcliff as Wyler wanted Charles Boyer for that part, but he was unavailable at the time of production. Wyler then considered Ronald Colman, Douglas Fairbanks Jr., and even British character actor Robert Newton before he settled on Olivier. After Olivier signed, he began to lobby to have his fiancé, Vivien Leigh, play the role of Cathy, but Wyler had already chosen Oberon. The role of Heathcliff's wife, Isabella, was offered to Leigh, but she considered that role demeaning as she was then a leading lady and the part was a supporting role, which Leigh declined (she was signed a few months later to play the unforgettable Scarlett O'Hara in **Gone with the Wind**, 1939). Olivier told this author: "Making **Wuthering Heights** was not a pleasant time for me. I had personal problems then and I did not get along well with the leading lady [Oberon], who was a haughty prima donna, to say the least." The truth was that both Olivier and Oberon detested each other, both miserable at being separated from their loved ones, Olivier from Leigh and Oberon from film producer Alexander Korda. In one of their romantic scenes together, Oberon accused Olivier of spitting on her, shouting to Wyler: "Tell him to stop spitting on me!" Olivier shouted at Wyler: "What's a little spit between actors!" He then turned to Oberon and shouted at her: "You bloody little idiot! How dare you

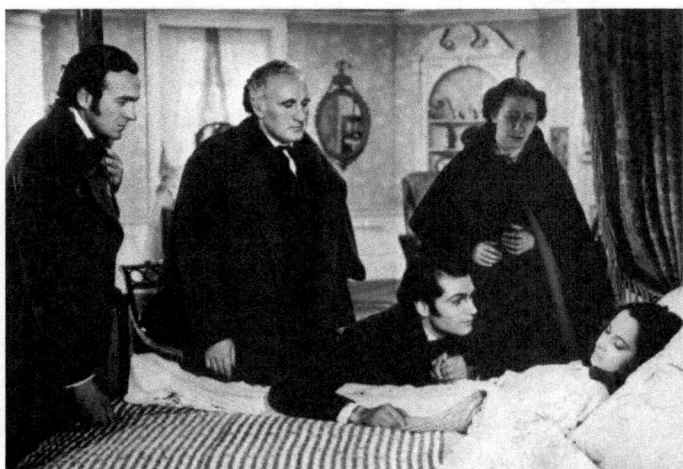

David Niven, Donald Crisp, Laurence Olivier, Flora Robson and Merle Oberon in *Wuthering Heights,* **1939.**

speak to me that way?" Oberon raced off the set in tears, taking shelter in her dressing room, and it took some time before Wyler was able to finally coax her back before the camera, but only after Wyler ordered Olivier to apologize to the actress. Wyler stated to me: "I was trying to have these two thoroughbreds run in tandem in **Wuthering Heights**, but all they could think about was breaking away from each other—the two most unlikely on-screen lovers in my entire history of filmmaking." Further, Olivier grew exasperated with Wyler's penchant for retaking a scene over and over and over, until he achieved what he thought was the best scene. "I had to wear him [Olivier] down," Wyler told this author. "He was much too theatrical, always playing to the second balcony as would a stage actor, and he did not realize that, in films, you had to be much more reserved and subtle and not 'ham it up.'" Olivier did one take after another until he asked Wyler: "How do you want me to do it?" Wyler merely replied: "I want it better." Olivier later admitted, as he did to this author, that Wyler, more than any other director, trained him how to act at his best before the camera. "I learned much from Willie [Wyler]," Olivier told this author, "but I hated him at the time I was his enslaved pupil." Years later, Olivier went on to state that Wyler had given him "the simple thought that, if you do it right, you can do anything. And if he hadn't said that, I think I wouldn't have done **Henry V** [1944; 1946 as a U.S. release] five years later." Still, the battles between Oberon and Olivier continued until veteran actor Crisp scolded them for their unprofessional behavior. Crisp told this author: "I took Merle [Oberon] aside one day and told her that her conduct with Larry [Olivier] was unbecoming of a great actress and she said: 'To hell with that—he's an arrogant lout and nothing more!' I also took Larry aside and told him about the same thing and he said: 'She can go back to the eternal hellfire where she came from!' I went to Willie [Wyler] and told him: 'I cannot help you make peace with these two—there is too much hatred to overcome.' In a way, they were emotionally ideal for their roles. Off camera, their passion was intense hatred, but, before the camera, they found a way to turn that passion around to make it appear that they loved each other without reservation, without hesitation, without a single doubt to challenge the bond between them. And that is the strangest thing of all about **Wuthering Heights**." Niven, too, had great difficulty with the production. He had had a bad time when appearing in **Dodsworth**, 1936, which was directed by Wyler and where Wyler's incessant retakes so upset Niven that he refused to appear in this production. Niven was threatened with suspension by the studio and only then did he reluctantly agree to play the second leading man in this film. Moreover, Niven had had an affair only a few years earlier with Oberon and, as he blithely told this author, "and here I was playing opposite her as her husband in **Wuthering Heights**. It was terribly uncomfortable for both of us in our scenes together. In one scene where she is dying, I

Merle Oberon and Laurence Olivier in *Wuthering Heights*, 1939.

could not, try as I might, bring myself to shed any tears. So the makeup people sprayed some menthol mist all over me, so that I could dutifully sob at Merle's passing, and Willie [Wyler] put that take into the can after about a dozen retakes. That is why I really did not want to do the picture, because Willie was never satisfied. Well, just after he got what he wanted in that final retake of that scene, the damned menthol had caused so much mucus to form in my nose that suddenly long globs of green slime poured from my nostrils in long repulsively looking strands. Merle's eyes opened wide, her mouth dropped in disgust and she bolted for her dressing room where she promptly threw up. I laughed about that sometime later, but, at that time, I felt like the most disgusting second leading man in pictures and the snottiest actor in Hollywood." Goldwyn, who always claimed that this was his favorite film, spared no expense in mounting this production. He had a resplendent manor house constructed and then converted more than 450 acres near Thousand Oaks, California, close to California Lutheran University, so that this area appeared identical to the English moors. To present even more authenticity, Goldwyn had more than 1,000 heather plants imported from England and implanted in this uninviting landscape. By the time Wyler went into production, he had to order the growth of these plants be cut back because they had so quickly flourished beneath the California sun. When Wyler was later given all the credit for this magnificent film, Goldwyn replied: "*I* made **Wuthering Heights**. Wyler only directed it!" Many other films have depicted spirits or ghosts, including **The Adding Machine**, 1969; **Adventures of Ichabod and Mr. Toad**, 1949; **The Adventures of Prince Achmed**, 1926; **The Adventures of Sir Galahad**, 1949; **After Life**, 1998; **An American Carol**, 2008; **The Amityville Horror**, 1979; **The Amityville Horror**, 2005; **Amityville 3-D**, 1983; **An American Werewolf in London**, 1981; **An American Werewolf in Paris**, 1997; **Andrea: The Revenge of the Spirit**, 2005; **Angel on My Shoulder**, 1946; **Apartment 1303**, 2007; **Apartment 1303 3D**, 2012; **Art of the Devil**, 2005; **The Asphyx**, 1973; **Banshee!!!**, 2008; **Bedazzled**, 2000; **Beetlejuice**, 1988; **Begotten**, 1991; **Behind the Wall**, 2008; **Belladonna of Sadness**, 1973; **Beloved**, 1998; **Beyond the Door**, 1975; **Beyond the Door III**, 1989; **Beyond the Door II**, 1977; **Beyond Tomorrow**, 1940; **Bhooter Bhabishyat**, 2012; **Bhoothnath**, 2008; **The Bible: In the Beginning**, 1966; **Big Trouble in Little China**, 1986; **Black Butler**, 2014; **Black Robe**, 1991; **Blackbeard's Ghost**, 1968; **The Blair Witch Project**, 1999; **Blithe Spirit**, 1945; **Blondie Has Servant Trouble**, 1940; **Body of Water**, 2011; **Book of Blood**, 2009; **The Book of Life**, 2014; **The Boy Who Wanted to Be a Bear**, 2003; **Brave**, 2012; **Brother Bear**, 2003; **Bunshinsaba**, 2012; **Burned at the Stake**, 1981; **The Canterville Ghost**, 1944; **The Canterville Ghost**, 1975 (made-for-TV); **The Canterville Ghost**, 1985 (made-for-TV); **The Canterville Ghost**, 1986 (made-for-TV); **The Canterville Ghost**, 1996

(made-for-TV); **The Canterville Ghost**, 1997 (made-for-TV); **The Canterville Ghost**, 2001 (made-for-TV); **The Canterville Ghost**, 2005 (made-for-TV); **Casper**, 1995; **Carnival of Souls**, 1962; **Carousel**, 1956; **The Cat and the Canary**, 1927; **The Cat and the Canary**, 1939; **The Cat and the Canary**, 1978; **Cello**, 2005; **Chamatkar**, 1992; **The Changeling**, 1980; **A Chinese Ghost Story**, 1988; **A Chinese Ghost Story**, 1997; **Christ Stopped at Eboli**, 1979; **A Christmas Carol**, 1938; **A Christmas Carol**, 1951; **Christmas Carol**, 1978 (made-for-TV); **Christmas Carol**, 1984 (made-for-TV); **Christmas Carol**, 1986 (made-for-TV); **A Christmas Carol**, 1999 (made-for-TV); **A Christmas Carol**, 2000 (made-for-TV); **Christmas Carol: The Movie**, 2012; **Christmas Ride**, 2013; **Cinco**, 2010; **City That Never Sleeps**, 1953; **Clash of the Titans**, 2010; **Concentration Camp**, 1938; **Conjurer**, 2008; **The Conjuring**, 2013; **Coraline**, 2009; **Corpse Bride**, 2005; **The Curse of the Crying Woman**, 1969; **The Dangerous Lives of Altar Boys**, 2002; **Darby O'Gill and the Little People**, 1959; **The Dark**, 2006; **Dark Circles**, 2013; **Dark Water**, 2002; **Dark Water**, 2005; **Daughter of the Mind**, 1969 (made-for-TV); **Dead Friend**, 2004; **Dead of Night**, 1945; **Dead Silence**, 2007; **Dead Weekend**, 2014; **Deadly Visitor**, 1973 (made-for-TV); **Death at Love House**, 1976 (made-for-TV); **Death of a Ghost Hunter**, 2007; **Dementia**, 2014; **The Demoniacs**, 1977; **Demonic Beauty**, 2002; **The Devil and Daniel Webster**, 1941; **The Devil's Backbone**, 2011; **Distant Lights**, 1987; **Don't Be Afraid of the Dark**, 1973 (made-for-TV); **Don't Be Afraid of the Dark**, 2011; **Don't Click**, 2012; **Don't Go to Sleep**, 1982 (made-for-TV); **Don't Panic**, 1978; **Dorm**, 2006; **Drag Me to Hell**, 2009; **Dragonheart**, 1996; **The Dreaming**, 1988; **Dreamkeeper**, 2003 (made-for-TV); **The Echo**, 2008; **Eliza's Horoscope**, 1975; **The Enemy**, 1974; **Enter the Void**, 2010; **The Entity**, 1983; **Esprit d'amour**, 1983; **Evil Angel**, 2009; **The Exorcism of Emily Rose**, 2005; **Extended Play**, 2006; **The Eye**, 2002; **The Eye**, 2008; **The Eye 10**, 2005; **The Eye 2**, 2004; **The Fall of the House of Usher**, 1928; **Feardotcom**, 2002; **Fear No Evil**, 1969 (made-for-TV); **Feng Sui**, 2004; **Feng Sui**, 2014; **Field of Dreams**, 1989; **Final Fantasy: The Spirits Within**, 2001; **The Fog**, 1980; **The Fog**, 2005; **1408**, 2007; **Fragile**, 2005; **Fridge**, 2012; **The Frighteners**, 1996; **Ghastly**, 2011; **The Ghost**, 1963; **Ghost**, 1990; **The Ghost**, 2001; **Ghost**, 2010; **Ghost**, 2012; **The Ghost and Mrs. Muir**, 1947; **The Ghost and Mr. Chicken**, 1966; **Ghost Banana Tree**, 2005; **The Ghost Breakers**, 1940; **The Ghost Catchers**, 1944; **Ghost Dad**, 1990; **The Ghost Goes West**, 1936; **Ghost in the Machine**, 1993; **The Ghost of Rashmon Hall**, 1953; **Ghost Rider**, 2007; **Ghost Ship**, 2002; **Ghost Story**, 1981; **The Ghost Talks**, 1929; **Ghost Town**, 2008; **The Ghost Walks**, 1934; **The Ghost That Walks Alone**, 1944; **Ghostbusters**, 1984; **Ghostbusters II**, 1989; **The Ghostmaker**, 2012; **Ghostwatch**, 1992; **The Ghosts of Berkeley Square**, 1947; **The Ghosts of Edendale**, 2003; **Ghosts of Girlfriends Past**, 2009; **The Ghosts of Hanley House**, 1968; **Ghosts of Mars**, 2001; **Ghosts That Still Walk**, 1977; **The Gift**, 2000; **Golden Door**, 2006; **Golden Earrings**, 2010; **Golpo Holeo Shotti**, 2014; **Gothika**, 2003; **Grave Encounters**, 2011; **Grave Secrets: The Legacy of Hilltop Drive**, 1992 (made-for-TV); **The Gravedancers**, 2006; **The Grudge**, 2004; **The Grudge 3**, 2009; **The Grudge 2**, 2006; **Gugure! Kokkuri-san**, 2014 (TV series); **A Guy Named Joe**, 1943; **The Halloween Tree**, 1993 (made-for-TV); **Hamlet**, 1948; **Hamlet**, 1964; **Hamlet**, 1969; **Hamlet**, 1990; **Hamlet**, 1996; **Hamlet**, 2000; **Hamlet**, 2010 (made-for-TV); **Hamlet**, 2014; **Harry Potter and the Chamber of Secrets**, 2002; **Harry Potter and the Deathly Hallows Part 1**, 2010; **Harry Potter and the Deathly Hallows Part 2**, 2011; **Harry Potter and the Goblet of Fire**, 2005; **Harry Potter and the Half-Blood Prince**, 2009; **Harry Potter and the Order of the Phoenix**, 2007; **Harry Potter and the Prisoner of Azkaban**, 2004; **Harry Potter and the Sorcerer's Stone**, 2001; **The Haunted**, 1991 (made-for-TV); **Haunted**, 1995; **The Haunted Mansion**, 2003; **The Haunting**, 1963; **The Haunting**, 1999; **The Haunting in Connecticut**, 2009; **The Haunting in Connecticut 2: The Ghosts of Georgia**, 2013; **The**

Haunting of Helena, 2013; The Haunting of Julia, 1981; The Healing, 2012; Heart and Souls, 1993; Heaven Can Wait, 1943; Heaven Can Wait, 1978; Here Comes Mr. Jordan, 1941; Hidalgo, 2004; High Plains Drifter, 1973; High Spirits, 1988; Hold That Ghost, 1941; The Horn Blows at Midnight, 1945; Horror, 2003; House, 1977; House, 1986; House of Evil, 1978; House on Haunted Hill, 1959; House on Haunted Hill, 1999; The House That Never Dies, 2014; House II: The Second Story, 1987; The House Where Evil Dwells, 1982; How Awful about Allan, 1970 (made-for-TV); How to Drown Dr. Mracek, the Lawyer, 1975; Hum Kaun Hai?, 2004; I Am ZoZo, 2012; I Married a Witch, 1942; Idle Hands, 1999; The Innocents, 1961; Insidious, 2011; The Invasion of Carol Enders, 1973 (made-for-TV); Invisible Adversaries, 1977; Invisible Ghost, 1941; The Invited, 2010; Isabel, 1968; Jack Frost, 1998; Jekhane Bhooter Bhoy, 2012; Jessabelle, 2014; Jessica; A Ghost Story, 1992; The Journals of Knud Rasmussen, 2006; Jungle Boy, 1998; Ju-on: The Grudge, 2003; Just Like Heaven, 2005; Kairo, 2001; The Keeper of the Bees, 1935; Kilometer 31, 2006; The Kingdom, 1994 (TV miniseries); Krasue Valentine, 2006; Kwaidan, 1965; La Liorona, 1960; Lady in White, 1988; Lake Mungo, 2008; The Last Airbender, 2010; The Legend of Hell House, 1973; Liliom, 1935; The Living and the Dead, 2006; Long Time Dead, 2002; The Lord of the Rings: The Return of the King, 2003; The Lovely Bones, 2009; The Magic Snowman, 1987; The Magical Legend of the Leprechauns, 1999; The Maid, 2006; Man with the Steel Whip, 1954; Marchlands, 2011 (TV miniseries); The Marsh, 2006; The Matrimony, 2007; Maxie, 1985; Maytime, 1937; The Messenger: The Story of Joan of Arc, 1999; The Messengers, 2007; A Midsummer Night's Sex Comedy, 1982; Miracle in the Rain, 1956; Mostly Ghostly, 2008; Mother of Tears, 2008; My Neighbor Totoro, 1993; My Own Love Song, 2010; Night Angel, 1990; The Night Child, 1976; Nightmare, 2007 (made-for-TV); The Nightmare before Christmas, 1993; A Nightmare on Elm Street, 1984; Nightwing, 1979; Nomads, 1986; Now and Forever, 2002; Nutcracker, 2001; Oculus, 2014; On Borrowed Time, 1939; 100 Feet, 2008; One Missed Call, 2005; One Missed Call 2, 2006; The Oracle, 1985; The Orphanage, 2008; The Other, 1972; The Other Side of the Tracks, 2008; The Others, 2001; Ouija, 2014; Over Her Dead Body, 2008; Painted Fire, 2002; The Painted Stallion, 1937; Pan's Labyrinth, 2007; Papillon, 1973; Paranormal Activity, 2007; Paranormal Activity 3, 2013; Paranormal Activity 2, 2010; ParaNorman, 2012; Phantasmagoria, 2014; Phantom Brother, 1988; The Phantom Rider, 1946; Photographing Fairies, 1997; The Piano Lesson, 1996 (made-for-TV); Pizza, 2012; Pizza 2: Villa, 2013; Playing Beatie Bow, 1986; Poltergeist, 1982; Poltergeist III, 1988; Poltergeist II, 1986; Portrait of Jennie, 1949; Practical Magic, 1988; Presence of Mind, 1999; Princess Mononoke, 1999; Pulse, 1988; Pulse, 2001; Pulse, 2006; Purgatory, 1999 (made-for-TV); R.I.P.D., 2013; Ravenous, 1999; The Red Shoes, 2005; The Remarkable Andrew, 1942; The Return of Peter Grimm, 1935; Resurrection Mary, 2008; Riding the Bullet, 2004; Ring, 1998; The Ring, 2002; Ring 2, 1999; Rinne, 2006; The Rising Light, 2013; The Rite, 2011; Road to Morocco, 1942; Route 666, 2001; The Ruins, 2008; Saint Ange, 2005; Sandcastles, 1972 (made-for-TV); Satan's Blade, 1984; Saving Hope, 2012- (TV series); Scary Movie 2, 2001; Schalken the Painter, 1979 (made-for-TV); Scooby-Doo, 2002; Scooby-Doo 2: Monsters Unleashed, 2004; The Screaming Skull, 1958; Scrooge, 1970; Scrooged, 1988; Segundo Mano, 2011; The She-Creature, 1956; Shadows of a Stranger, 2014; The Shining, 1980; Shock, 2004; Short Peace, 2014; Shutter, 2004; Shutter, 2008; Shutterbug, 2009; Silent Tongue, 1993; Silk, 2007; Simeon, 1992; The Sixth Man, 1997; The Sixth Sense, 1999; Sleepy Hollow, 1999; Sleepy Hollow, 2013 (TV series); Spectres, 2012; Spirit Warriors: The Shortcut, 2003; Spirited Away, 2003; Star Wars: Episode IV—A New Hope, 1977; Stay Alive, 2006; Stir of Echoes, 1999; Stir of Echoes 2: The Homecoming, 2007; Stormhouse, 2012; The Sullivans, 1944; Supernatural, 2005- (TV

Laurence Olivier in *Wuthering Heights,* 1939.

series); Susie Q, 1996 (made-for-TV); The Sweet House of Horrors, 1989; Tales of Terror, 1962; Tears of Kali, 2004; The Tempest, 1960 (made-for-TV); The Tempest, 1979; The Tempest, 2010; The Terror, 1963; That's My Boy, 1932; 13 Ghosts, 1960; This England, 1941; This House Possessed, 1981 (made-for-TV); Throne of Blood, 1961; Till Death, 1978; The Time of Their Lives, 1946; Topper, 1937; Topper Returns, 1941; Topper Takes a Trip, 1939; Tormented, 1960; Tormented, 2009; Torture Garden, 1967; Tower of Terror, 1997; The Triangle, 2001 (made-for-TV); Trick or Treat, 1986; Truly Madly Deeply, 1991; The Turn of the Screw, 1959 (made-for-TV); The Turn of the Screw, 1974 (made-for-TV); The Turn of the Screw, 1982 (made-for-TV); The Turn of the Screw, 1992; The Turn of the Screw, 1994 (made-for-TV); The Turn of the Screw, 2000 (made-for-TV); The Turn of the Screw, 2003; The Turn of the Screw, 2009 (made-for-TV); Two Thousand Maniacs, 1964; 2001 Maniacs, 2005; Ugetsu, 1954; Universal Grove, 2007; Universal Signs, 2008; The Uninvited, 1944; The Uninvited, 1996 (made-for-TV); The Uninvited, 2001; The Unseeable, 2006; Venus in Furs, 1970; The Victim, 2006; Visitor, 2004; Voices, 2007; The Watcher in the Woods, 1980; Wendigo, 2001; What Lies Beneath, 2000; When a Man Sees Red, 1934; When the Lights Went Out, 2012; Where Got Ghost?, 2009; White Lady, 2006; White Noise, 2005; White Noise 2, 2007; Wild Flowers, 2000; Windstruck, 2004; Witchboard, 1986; Witchboard III: The Possession, 1995; Witchboard 2, 1993; The Woman in Black, 1989 (made-for-TV); The Woman in Black, 2012; The Woods, 2006; The Wraith, 1986; You'll Find Out, 1940; and Zorro Rides Again, 1937. p, Samuel Goldwyn; d, William Wyler; cast, Merle Oberon, Laurence Olivier, David Niven, Flora Robson, Donald Crisp, Geraldine Fitzgerald, Hugh Williams, Leo G. Carroll, Miles Mander, Cecil Kellaway, Cecil Humphreys, Douglas Scott, Sarita Wooten, Rex Downing; w, Ben Hecht, Charles MacArthur, (uncredited) John Huston (based on the novel by Emily Bronte); c, Gregg Toland; m, Alfred Newman; ed, Daniel Mandell; art d, James Basevi, Alexander Toluboff; set d, Julia Heron; spec eff, W. Percy Day.

Wyatt Earp ★★★ 1994; U.S.; 191m (212m expanded edition); WB; Color; Western; Children: Unacceptable (MPAA: PG-13; BD; DVD; VHS; IV. Costner gives a fine performance as a resolute Wyatt Earp (1848-1929) in this action-packed frontier saga, one that presents the most complete portrait of that legendary lawman of the Old West under the sure direction of Kasdan. The film opens with Wyatt as a teenage boy, played by Bohen, running away from his farm in Pella, Iowa, in an effort to enlist in the Union army, so he can be with his older brothers who are then serving at the front during the American Civil War (1861-1865). He runs through a field of tall corn, trying to evade his pursuing

Kevin Costner in *Wyatt Earp*, 1994.

father, Hackman, who plays a stern but judicious Nicholas Porter Earp (1813-1907), and who is riding on horseback through that cornfield. Hackman finally finds and confronts Bohen, who mounts the horse as Hackman rides back toward their farmhouse, telling him that he is too young to fight in the war and that he is needed at home with his younger brothers to tend to the Earp farm. Bohen sadly promises to not run away again as Hackman quietly informs him that he must then punish him for his errant ways. Sometime later Bohen is outside his farmhouse to see a wagon approach that carries his older brothers James Earp (1841-1926), played by Andrews, and Virgil Earp (1843-1905), who is played by Madsen. Andrews is seriously wounded, both having returned from the war, and Bohen warmly welcomes them, as does Hackman, who waits for them with open arms at the threshold of the farmhouse. Later, at a family breakfast, Hackman tells his family members that he has decided to pull up roots and move to California, a state that he thinks offers more opportunities. The family is next seen moving westward in a caravan of prairie schooners and, while they make camp, Bohen is sent to town to purchase some supplies. While there, he witnesses two men burst from a saloon, cursing and shooting at each other as they collapse into the street, mortally wounded and dying in agony. Bohen, after viewing this senseless carnage, gets sick to his stomach and vomits. When returning to his family, Bohen is counseled by Hackman about what Bohen has just seen. Hackman tells Bohen that there are some men he will meet in life who, beyond rhyme or reason, are consumed by viciousness. He tells them that when and if he is ever confronted by such vicious men, he is to strike first and he should strike to kill in order to preserve his own life. He tells Bohen that he will know exactly when to do such a thing as "the Earps always know." We next see Wyatt Earp as an adult and played by Costner, who is shown wildly driving a freight wagon along a frontier roadway while his co-worker fires at a gang of outlaws pursuing them in order to rob them of the goods they are carrying. The outlaw gang seems to be gaining on the freight wagon as Costner furiously whips his team of horses onward. At this point, Costner shouts back to the guard to shoot the lead horse in the pursuing gang and once he does this, the outlaws give up the chase. Costner arrives in town with his freight intact and is next seen refereeing an open-air bare-knuckle boxing match where his friend, McGrady, is getting the worst of it. Rather than see McGrady beaten senseless, Costner calls off the fight and for which the badly beaten McGrady tells him: "God bless you, boy!" Minutes later, while walking away with the crowd, Costner is stopped by Kove, a powerfully built gunman, who is angry at Costner for stopping the fight and ruining his bets. Kove takes his revenge by hitting Costner squarely on the jaw and knocking him down and senseless. Later that night, Costner goes to a saloon where he is warned by a friend and a barroom girl that Kove is looking for him as Kove has heard

that Costner has threatened to settle the score with him. Costner denies this, saying that someone has made up that story, but Kove nevertheless arrives and calls Costner out. Costner tries to talk his way out of another confrontation with Kove, telling him that he is not armed. Kove tosses a six-gun onto a billiard table and tells Costner to reach for it as Kove readies himself to draw his own gun. Realizing that he is no match for Kove, Costner picks up a billiard ball and hurls it with all his might at Kove, striking the gunman in the throat so that he collapses, choking and apparently dying. Costner walks to the downed Kove and takes his gun and gunbelt, saying that "this man wanted to take my life...over nothing! He lost! I am taking his gun!" He straps the gun belt around his waist and steps outside to witness a Fourth of July fireworks display and, enthralled by the pyrotechnic explosions, draws his newly acquired six-gun and fires at the skyward fireworks to end this chapter of his young life. We next see Costner in Missouri where he is courting his childhood sweetheart, Gish, informing her parents at dinner that he has taken a job as a police officer. He and Gish marry and they move into a small house. They are happy for only a few months until Gish is stricken by typhoid and dies. So depressed is Costner that he burns down his house and takes to drink. He becomes a drifter, moving from town to town, until, broke and emaciated he robs a man in Pine Bluff, Arkansas, and steals his victim's horse. He is later found in a bordello by lawmen and arrested and thrown into jail. He awakens in his cell to see his father, Hackman, standing outside the bars, and condemning his dissolute ways. A short time later, Hackman stands outside the jail in a rainstorm with Costner, telling him that he has gotten his bail until he goes to trial. He also tells him that he will be found guilty at that trial and then hanged for stealing a horse. He tells him to get onto a horse he has provided and keep riding until he is out of the state of Arkansas and never come back. Costner then rides away. We next see Costner working as a successful buffalo hunter, shooting scores of these shaggy beasts on the plains and skinning them in order to sell their hides. He drives to a local town and goes to a bar where he orders coffee as he no longer drinks alcohol. While at the bar, Costner is approached by two brothers, Sizemore and Pullman, who play, respectively, William Barclay "Bat" Masterson (1853-1921), and Edward John "Ed" Masterson (1852-1878), who ask Costner for jobs and he hires them as buffalo skinners. At that moment, a rowdy gunman steps up to the bar next to Costner and tells him to have a drink on him. Costner tells him that he does not drink, but that he will accept the man's payment for his coffee. The gunman slams a bottle down onto the bar next to Costner and orders him to take a drink. Within seconds, Costner has his six-gun pressed against the stomach of the gunman, ordering him to drop his gun belt and get out of town. The man drops his belt and flees for his life. Sizemore and Pullman are now deeply impressed with their no-nonsense employer. Costner is later shown with his two employees as he shoots buffalo, and Sizemore and Pullman have the distasteful and foul-smelling job of skinning these beasts, a chore that causes Pullman to stagger off on the plains to vomit. In the process, Costner takes time to show these apprentices how to aim and shoot buffalo. Costner later tells Sizemore and Pullman that he no longer wants to continue killing buffalo and he is later shown in Wichita, Kansas. While shaving in his room one morning, a bullet smashes through the window, narrowly missing him. He slips outside in his bare feet where another bullet whizzes past him before he takes cover in an alleyway where the local mayor and sheriff, along with others, are cowering from the gunfire from a crazed gunman in a saloon across the street. When Costner asks the sheriff why he does not go to the saloon and arrest the gunman, the lawman tells him that he is not being paid enough to risk his life by committing suicide by confronting a berserk gunman. Costner then borrows the sheriff's six-gun and races across the street, entering the saloon and where we hear several shots being fired and then a crashing sound. Costner then reappears, dragging the unconscious gunman by the feet from the saloon and depositing him in the middle of the street. The mayor immediately offers Costner the job of deputy sheriff at the then astronomical salary of $100 per month, and

Costner takes the job. He is now a lawman and is shown aiding the local sheriff in corralling drunks and jailing them. So effective is Costner in dealing with lawbreakers that he soon earns a reputation of a sterling lawman and is recruited as a deputy to work in the wild cowboy town of Dodge City (at a lower salary but earns $2.50 for each rowdy cowhand he jails and thus makes much more money). He then influences the town officials to also hire the Masterson brothers, Sizemore and Pullman. By this time, Costner has taken up with prostitute Mattie Blaylock (Celia Ann "Mattie" Blaylock; 1850-1888), who is played by Winningham, and who becomes Costner's common-law wife (that union in reality lasted for eight years). While patrolling the streets one night, Costner is attacked by cowboys, who are hurrahing the town by shooting wildly into a saloon. One fires a shot at him and he returns fire, shooting the cowboy from his horse and killing him. This shooting is seen by Josie Marcus (Josephine Sarah Marcus Earp;1860-1944), who is played by Going, one of the dancers performing on the stage of the saloon. During another encounter on the street with two armed cowboys, Sizemore and Pullman, now deputies, attempt to disarm these men, informing them that no firearms are allowed within the city limits. When the easygoing Pullman attempts to talk the two cowboys into surrendering their weapons, Costner abruptly steps in and "buffalos" the two men by knocking them out with the butt of his six-gun (which was a favorite technique employed by Earp during his days as a lawman). Costner then criticizes both men for not acting sooner, showing them a hidden Derringer in the hands of one of the men. After locking these two lawbreakers inside of a jail cell, Costner tells Pullman that he should look for another line of work as he is "too affable," and that his easygoing ways will eventually cost him his life and perhaps the lives of other innocent men. "I am not a fool, Wyatt," Pullman says to Costner. "No," Costner replies, "you are not, but you are not a deliberate man." He adds that Pullman lacks the needed resolve to enforce the law with lethal action, if needed. Costner's no-nonsense enforcement of the law soon brings criticism that he manhandles too many rowdy citizens and he is asked to resign. Costner goes to work for the railroad, tracking down lawbreakers, and he is next seen tracking a train robber to Fort Griffin, Texas. There he meets his old friend McGrady, the former boxer he had saved from a beating and who is running a saloon in that town. When Costner asks if McGrady has seen the outlaw he is searching for, McGrady tells him that notorious gunman John H. "Doc" Holliday (1851-1887), who is played by Quaid, might know the outlaw's whereabouts. McGrady takes Costner to a tent saloon to meet Quaid, an emaciated man sitting alone at a table and playing solitaire. A former dentist, Quaid is known as one of the deadliest gunslingers in the West. Costner and Quaid, though leery of each other, become friends. Meanwhile, Pullman is seen one night in Dodge City where he politely disarms a man in a saloon, but, after stepping from the saloon, the cowboy reappears with a gun and fatally shoots Pullman as Pullman shoots and kills the cowboy and one of his friends. Pullman, shot in the side, staggers into the street calling his brother's name. Sizemore rushes to Pullman just as he collapses, and Pullman dies in his arms. (This traumatic scene, like all of the action sequences in this film, is well orchestrated and shockingly and accurately depicts how Ed Masterson actually died, the bullet entering his body at close range igniting his clothes and causing smoke to emit from him as he dies.) Costner then receives a wire from Dodge City officials asking him to return as they believe that only he can restore law and order in the town. Costner does return to Dodge City, this time backed up by Sizemore and other deputies. Costner is shown restoring a shot-up sign prohibiting the wearing of firearms in the city limits before he enters a raucous saloon to fire off a shotgun in bringing the calamitous noise to silence, and he shouts: "It all ends now!" A short time later, Quaid arrives in Dodge City with his common-law wife, Big Nose Kate (Mary Katherine Horony; 1850-1940), who is played by Rossellini, a notorious prostitute, and they take up residence there; Quaid promises to obey the law and check his guns with the lawmen. A short time later, Costner is called to their residence where Rossellini is firing a six-gun

Kevin Costner in *Wyatt Earp*, 1994.

in the room occupied by her and Quaid, who is drunk and has beaten her. Costner cautiously enters the room and is able to disarm Rossellini, who bears a bleeding nose from blows received from the drunken Quaid. Costner further strikes and knocks out Quaid when he attempts to knife Rossellini, later dragging him outside where he sobers up Quaid by ducking his head into the water of a horse trough. As he sits next to Costner, Quaid admits that he is dying from tuberculosis (consumption) and that he does not care whether he lives or dies because "everyone hates me." Costner replies: "Not everyone hates you," signifying his deep friendship for the gunman. Costner then decides that he and his brothers and their women should move to the booming mining town of Tombstone, Arizona, where the Earp family believes better opportunities await them. Costner, however, meets resistance from the wives of his brothers but ignores their insistence that they remain in Dodge City. The family, along with Quaid, moves to Tombstone where they soon enrich themselves with part gambling interests in some of the local saloons, and Madsen, playing Virgil Earp, becomes the town marshal, deputizing his brothers, Costner, and Ashby, who plays Morgan Earp (1851-1882). By this time, Winningham has taken to drugs (laudanum) and is mostly in a state of semi-consciousness. The unhappy Costner, however, is soon drawn to Going, the actress he saw in Dodge City, after she arrives in Tombstone as the fiancé of local sheriff Johnny Behan (1844-1912), who is played by Harmon. Costner later develops an emotional relationship with Going, who rejects Harmon after he shows nude pictures of her in a local saloon. Costner and his brothers are not only met with continued resistance to their activities in Tombstone by their wives, but are openly threatened by a rowdy band of cowboys led by Ike Clanton (Joseph Isaac "Ike" Clanton; 1847-1887), who is played by Fahey. That band of ruthless gunslingers includes Ike's brother, Billy Clanton (William Harrison "Billy" Clanton; 1862-1881), who is played by Folse; Frank McLaury (1849-1881), who is played by Linn; and Tom McLaury (1853-1881), who is played by Baldwin. Additional foes of Costner, his brothers and Quaid consist of such gunslingers as William "Curly Bill" Brocius (c.1845-1882), who is played by Smith; Billy Claiborne (William Floyd Claiborne; 1860-1882), who is played by Kamm; Johnny Ringo (John Peters Ringo; 1850-1882), who is played by Howell; Pete Spence (Elliott Larkin Ferguson; aka: Peter M. Spencer; 1850-1914), who is played by Fox; and Frank Stilwell (Frank C. Stilwell; 1856-1882), who is played by Johnston. Fahey and others in his band are shown planning the assassination of Tombstone sheriff Fred White (Frederick G. "Fred" White; c.1849-1880), who is played by Southerland, in that they pretend to be drunk while firing their six-guns. When Southerland hears the gunfire, he leaves his wife on a Tombstone street and runs to the backyard area where the cowboys are gathered. When he attempts to disarm Smith (Brocius), the gunman of-

Kevin Costner as Wyatt Earp and Dennis Quaid as Doc Holliday in *Wyatt Earp*, 1994.

fers him his six-gun, but then twirls the weapon about so that he shoots and kills Southerland. He and others are then arrested by Madsen and Costner. Smith claims in court that the shooting was "accidental" and is eventually set free, but the cowboys begin challenging the authority of Madsen, Costner and Ashby at every opportunity; Fahey consistently insults Quaid, knowing he is a close friend of the Earp brothers. After several of the cowboys are knocked down and jailed for drunkenness, Fahey and others openly challenge the lawmen. Fahey, Folse, Linn, Baldwin and Kamm then assemble at the O.K. Corral, defying the city ordinance by wearing their six-guns (about 3 p.m., Wednesday, October 26, 1881), challenging the lawmen to disarm them. Costner, Madsen and Ashby intend to do that, but, before they go to the O.K. Corral, they are met by Quaid, who tells Madsen that the cowboys might not want to turn over their weapons if they see the shotgun Madsen is carrying. Madsen gives the shotgun to Quaid and tells him to hide the weapon beneath his long coat. The four then begin to walk to the corral. Harmon, the corrupt county sheriff who has long been in league with the outlaws and part of their illegal operations, attempts to stop them, lying when saying that the cowboys are not armed. Costner brushes Harmon aside as the four continue their solemn walk to the corral. Arriving at the corral (which is nothing more than an open, narrow lot between two buildings on Fremont Street and six doors west of the actual corral and is accurate as to the real location of the historic gunfight), Madsen tells the cowboys that he has come to disarm them. Kamm (Claiborne) flees the scene (as the real Claiborne did in that confrontation), and Fahey, losing his braggadocio and nerve, races to Costner to tell him that he is unarmed. Costner flings him aside and Fahey flees, running into a nearby shop (this is what actually happened between Wyatt Earp and Ike Clanton, Earp reportedly shouting at Clanton: "The fight has commenced! Go to your guns or get out!"). Fahey takes shelter by running into C.S. Fly's Photographic Studio, the building next to the open lot just as Folse, Linn and Baldwin go for their guns, as do the lawmen and Quaid. The gun battle is brief (in reality about thirty shots were exchanged by the two factions within thirty seconds) with Folse, Linn and Baldwin killed and Madsen, Ashby and Quaid wounded, and only Costner left still standing and unharmed (this, too, is factual in that bullets went through Wyatt Earp's coat and hat but, like all other confrontations in his spectacular career, he miraculously remained unscathed). Following the shoot-out, Harmon attempts to arrest Costner and his associates, but Costner defies him. Costner later agrees to be tried, along with his brothers and Quaid, for the shooting, but all are acquitted. The remaining outlaw faction then takes revenge by shooting and killing Ashby through a window while he plays pool in a billiard parlor and where other shots narrowly miss their mark, Costner. Madsen is then later shot and seriously wounded while making his rounds one night in Tombstone, also shot from am-

bush. Costner, along with some supporters, puts Madsen on a train bound for California (where Virginal Earp took up residence with his father and other family members), but, while the train is stopped in Tucson, Arizona, Fahey seeks to take revenge by killing the remaining Earp brothers with the aid of gunmen Johnston (Stilwell) and Fox (Spence). Costner and Quaid, however, foil the plot and Costner finds and kills Johnston. Believing that Johnston was the one who shot and killed his brother Ashby (Morgan Earp), Costner takes special revenge by emptying his gun into the pleading, dying Johnston. Later, Costner, Quaid and some of their supporters conduct a vendetta against the remaining cowboys, hunting down and killing Smith (Brocius) and Howell (Ringo). During this relentless manhunt, Costner and Quaid sit one night at a campfire where Quaid tells Costner that "you can't get what you want," that "you can't kill them all." He urges Costner to leave Arizona and come back later and then "get them one by one." Quaid begins to cough and Costner knows that Quaid is dying, telling him that he should go to a sanitarium in Colorado where he might recover. "I'll go, if you take me," Quaid says. Costner then tells Quaid that he is the best friend he has ever had. Quaid replies: "Shut up!" In flash-forward we see an aging Costner on board a ship sailing to Alaska during the Gold Rush and standing at his side is his wife, Going (Josie Marcus Earp) and where they seek new opportunities. Astin, a young man traveling on that boat, recognizes Costner as the famous lawman, asking if it is true that he saved the life of his errant uncle, Michael "Mike" O'Rourke (1862- ?), a gambler known as "Johnny-Behind-the-Deuce," from a lynch mob. In flashback, we see Costner standing before the Tombstone jail to confront a lynch mob seeking to hang that uncle, played by Doe, who cowers inside a cell in that jail. Costner stands alone with his hand resting on his six-gun to tell the irate vigilantes that the only way they are going to get to his prisoner is over his dead body and that he intends to take a number of the vigilantes with him if they try to storm the jail. The vigilantes think twice and then back down, Costner having saved Doe's life at the risk of his own. (This incident is also based on fact; O'Rourke was truly threatened by a lynch mob in 1881, and Earp and others prevented the vigilantes from carrying out that lynching, another heroic feat added to the Earp legend.) Costner and Going then peer toward the Alaskan shoreline and Costner says: "Some say that it didn't happen that way." Going replies: "Never mind, Wyatt. It happened that way." This fine film ends with a written epilogue appearing on the screen to tell viewers that Quaid (Holliday) died six years after the Gunfight at the O.K. Corral in a hospital at Glenwood Springs, Colorado (on November 8, 1887), and that Josie and Wyatt Earp's marriage lasted for forty-seven years until Wyatt Earp's death in Los Angeles (on January 13, 1929) at the age of eighty. Though somewhat overlong, Kasdan presents an absorbing western epic that is as close to the actual facts as can be accurately relied upon, expertly balancing its well-choreographed action scenes with the many dramatic moments between Costner and his wives (O'Hara, Winningham and Going), his strange but strong friendship with gunfighter Quaid, and his interaction with his brothers and their wives. Costner is particularly remarkable for his stoic performance in that he captures the persona of Wyatt Earp more accurately than the many actors who have essayed this legendary lawman. He plays a very deliberate and even phlegmatic Earp, which was that man's actual personality (as opposed to the more animated interpretation of that character by Kurt Russell, who nevertheless rendered a fine essay of Earp in the more popular **Tombstone**, 1993). Earp was a serious man confronted with death-defying problems in the Old West. He was pragmatic, down-to-earth, and always quicker to take action against his adversaries, which preserved his life and perpetuated his admirable legend as one of the greatest lawmen of his era. Costner was unfairly criticized for his portrayal, but such criticism undoubtedly stemmed from those who knew little or nothing about the man Costner so accurately portrays. Quaid, too, is exceptional in his role as a reprehensible Doc Holliday, a man fearing no one since he knows his own death from consumption is close at hand; Quaid's emaciated and hollow-eyed appearance (the actor lost thirty pounds for his role), his raspy voice, and erratic behavior shockingly reinforces the true image of that dying but deadly gunman. All of the supporting players are standouts in their colorful roles, and the Old West is superbly represented in finely-drawn period settings where freight wagons, prairie schooners, tent saloons, and clapboard rooming houses accurately present that bygone era of the Old West. The film is beautifully photographed by Roizman, who received an Oscar nomination for Best Cinematography. Since this film was released six months after **Tombstone**, 1993, and covered much of the same historic ground, it did not fare well at the box office, earning a little more than $25 million in its initial release against a budget of $63 million. *Author's Note*: Costner was originally involved in the Tombstone production, but he differed with its scriptwriters, insisting that more emphasis be placed on the character of Wyatt Earp. He left that production to mount his own biopic of Earp, which resulted in this fine and accurate portrait. That production was first thought to be positioned as a TV miniseries, but Costner convinced producers to offer it as a theatrically released feature film. Most critics gave thumbs down to this film, but this was undoubtedly in light of their praising the previously released **Tombstone**. One such critic was Gene Siskel (1946-1999), who was well known to this author. When I asked Siskel what he disliked about **Wyatt Earp**, he replied: "I personally dislike Costner. I think he has a swell head. I just don't like the guy. **Tombstone** is a better picture." I replied: "So you panned **Wyatt Earp** because you do not personally like its leading player?" "That's right," Siskel said. "So what?" Siskel was not really a film critic or a film reviewer. He was a former sports writer who angled his way into film reviewing by teaming with Roger Ebert (1942-2013) to appear together on a TV show where they reviewed contemporary films. Siskel's knowledge about films and filmmakers was limited to the level of any high school sophomore so I easily dismissed his criticism about this film. Ebert, on the other hand, who should have known better, also panned this film, saying it was "an unfocused biography of Wyatt Earp." I confronted Ebert with this and he admitted to this author: "I am not an expert on Wyatt Earp. I leave that to historians like you. I just liked the **Tombstone** picture, which came out first. I did not care to know about this man's entire life. **Wyatt Earp** should have focused on the Gunfight at the O.K. Corral." I replied: "Like most every other film production about that subject." Ebert nodded. "All right, Roger," I said. "Since **Wyatt Earp** did not deliver your expected formula, you fobbed off the film [he had given it two stars]." To that, he shrugged and walked away. Such was the typical hackneyed approach Ebert and Siskel so often and woefully demonstrated toward films that deserved better in their heyday. For more details on Wyatt Earp, see my book *Encyclopedia of Western Lawmen and Outlaws* (Paragon House, 1992; pages: 110-121). Many other actors have essayed Wyatt Earp in many other films, including: **The Adventures of Young Indiana Jones: Hollywood Follies**, 1994 (made-for-TV; Leo Gordon); **Alias Jesse James**, 1959 (Hugh O'Brien); **Alias Smith and Jones**, 1971-1973 (TV series; "Which Way to the O.K. Corral?," 1972 episode: Cameron Mitchell); **Alien Nation**, 1989-1990 (TV series; "Spirit of '95," 1990 episode: Mark Thomas Miller); **Appointment with Destiny**, 1971-1973 (TV series; "Showdown at O.K. Corral," 1972 episode: David H. Vowell); **Any Last Words?**, 2012 (Scott Jefferies); **The Arizonian**, 1935 (role model for Richard Dix); **Badman's Country**, 1958 (Buster Crabbe); **Bat Masterson**, 1958-1961 (TV series; Ron Hayes); **Buffalo Bill, Jr.**, 1955-1956 (TV series; "First Posse," 1955 episode: Walter Reed); **Cheyenne Autumn**, 1964 (James Stewart); **Dawn at Socorro**, 1954 (role model for James Millican); **Deadwood**, 2004-2006 (TV cable series; Gale Morgan Harold); **Death Valley Days**, 1952-1970 (TV series; "After the O.K. Corral," 1964 episode: Jim Davis); **Doc**, 1971 (Harris Yulin); **Doctor Who**, 1963-1989 (TV series; John Alderson); **Dodge City**, 1939 (role model for Errol Flynn); **Four Eyes and Six-Guns**, 1992 (made-for-TV; Fred Ward); **Frontier Marshal**, 1934 (George O'Brien as "Michael Wyatt"); **Frontier Marshal**, 1939 (Randolph Scott); **The Gambler Returns: The Luck of the Draw**, 1991 (made-for-TV; Hugh O'Brien);

Wallace Beery and Leo Carrillo in *Wyoming*, 1940.

Goldrush: A Real Life Alaskan Adventure, 1998 (made-for-TV; David Longworth); **Gun Belt**, 1953 (James Millican); **Gunfight at the O.K. Corral**, 1957 (Burt Lancaster); **Gunmen of Rio Grande**, 1965 (Guy Madison); **Guns of Paradise**, 1988-1990 (TV series; Hugh O'Brien); **Hannah's Law**, 2012 (made-for-TV; Greyston Holt); **Horse Opera**, 1993 (made-for-TV; Rik Mayall); **Hour of the Gun**, 1967 (James Garner); **I Married Wyatt Earp**, 1983 (made-for-TV; Bruce Boxleitner); **Law and Order**, 1932 (role model for Walter Huston); **The Life and Legend of Wyatt Earp**, 1955-1961 (TV series; Hugh O'Brien); **Masterson of Kansas**, 1954 (Bruce Cowling); **Maverick**, 1957-1962 (TV series; "Marshal Maverick," 1962 episode: Med Flory); **My Darling Clementine**, 1946 (Henry Fonda); **The Outlaws Is Coming**, 1965 (Bill Camfield); **Pistols 'n' Petticoats**, 1966-1967 (TV series; "Shootout at O.K. Corral," 1966 episode: Roy Engel); **The Secret World of Eddie Hodges**, 1960 (made-for-TV; Hugh O'Brien); **Sunset**, 1988 (James Garner); **Stories of the Century**, 1954 (TV series; "Doc Holliday," 1954 episode: James Craven); **Tombstone**, 1993 (Kurt Russell); **Tombstone: The Town Too Tough to Die**, 1942 (Richard Dix); **Wagon Train**, 1957-1965 (TV series; "The Silver Lady," 1965 episode: Don Collier); **Wichita**, 1955 (Joel McCrea); **Wild Bill Hickok**, 1923 (Bert Lindley); **The Wild West**, 2006-2007 (TV miniseries; "The Gunfight at the O.K. Corral," 2007 episode: Liam Cunningham); **Winchester '73** (Will Geer); **Wyatt Earp: Return to Tombstone**, 1994 (made-for-TV; Hugh O'Brien); **Wyatt Earp's Revenge**, 2012 (Val Kilmer as old Earp; Shawn Roberts as Earp in 1878); and **You Are There**, 1953-1957 (TV series; "The Gunfight at the O.K. Corral," 1955 episode: Robert Bray). **p**, Kevin Costner, Lawrence Kasdan, Jim Wilson; **d**, Kasdan; **cast**, Costner, Dennis Quaid, Gene Hackman, Joanna Going, Bill Pullman, Tom Sizemore, Isabella Rossellini, David Andrews, Linden Ashby, Michael Madsen, Mare Winningham, JoBeth Williams, Tea Leoni, Adam Baldwin, Annabeth Gish, Catherine O'Hara, Brett Cullen, Mark Harmon, Jeff Fahey, Lewis Smith, Michael McGrady, Norman Howell, Boots Southerland, Kirk Fox, Mackenzie Astin, John Doe, John Dennis Johnston, Kris Kamm, Martin Kove, Gabriel Folse, Rex Linn, Ian Bohen, Jim Caviezel; **w**, Kasdan, Dan Gordon; **c**, Owen Roizman; **m**, James Newton Howard; **ed**, Carol Littleton; **prod d**, Ida Random; **art d**, Gary Wissner; **set d**, Cheryl Carasik; **spec eff**, Burt Dalton, Robert Stadd.

Wyoming ★★★ 1940; U.S.; 89m; MGM; B/W; Western; Children: Unacceptable. Beery gives an exceptional performance as a roughhouse deserter from the army, who flees to Wyoming where a cattle rancher is killed by outlaws led by Calleia. He befriends Rutherford, the rancher's daughter, and son Watson, and helps them and the other cattle ranchers to fight Calleia, who has been trying to drive all the landowners from

Halle Berry in *X-Men,* **2000.**

the territory so that he can take over their ranches and cattle. Beery and his friends get the help of General George Armstrong Custer (1839-1876), who is played by Kelly, and his troopers. After winning this battle, Beery sets off to find a former outlaw partner, Carrillo, to teach him his new respect for going straight. Not related to the 1928 and 1947 films with the same title. Songs: "Oh, Susanna" (1948; Stephen Foster), "A Bird in a Gilded Cage" (1900; music: Harry von Tilzer; lyrics: Arthur J. Lamb), "Turkey in the Straw" (traditional), "There's a Home in Wyomin'" (1933; Billy Hill, Peter De Rose). *Author's Note*: "Beery was up to his old shenanigans when we made **Wyoming**," Thorpe told this author, "boozing during the production and acting like some wild bear out of its cage. I spent half my time scolding him for his abusive behavior, but I must admit that once he was before the camera, he turned on that old craggy-faced charm of his and won everybody over." Rutherford surprisingly escaped Beery's insults and gruff behavior, telling this author: "He was an old darling, very kind and courteous to me. I heard terrible stories about his rowdy conduct, but I did not see any of that when we made **Wyoming** together. It was a case of his reputation preceding him, I guess." This was the first film pairing of Beery and Main, who became a popular duo with movie fans and who would appear in nine films together. **p**, Milton Bren; **d**, Richard Thorpe; **cast**, Wallace Beery, Leo Carrillo, Ann Rutherford, Lee Bowman, Joseph Calleia, Bobs Watson, Paul Kelly, Henry Travers, Marjorie Main, Clem Bevans; **w**, Jack Jevne, Hugo Butler; **c**, Clyde DeVinna; **m**, David Snell; **ed**, Robert J. Kern; **art d**, Cedric Gibbons; **set d**, Edwin B. Willis.

Wyoming ★★★ 1947; U.S.; 84m; REP; B/W; Western; Children: Unacceptable. Above-average oater sees Elliott and his wife settle in the Wyoming Territory where they become friends with Hayes. Elliott's wife dies in childbirth and he sends his infant daughter to Europe to be educated. Years pass while she is away, and Elliott becomes a wealthy cattle baron. The daughter grows to be Ralston as an adult, returning to Wyoming soon after it is admitted to statehood. She discovers that much of her father's former range is now open to homesteaders and a war is being waged between the sodbusters and ranchers. Carroll, who is Elliott's foreman and a former lawyer, with whom Ralston has fallen in love, cautions Elliott against using violence in dealing with the homesteaders. Dekker, a devious gang leader of cattle rustlers, becomes the spokesman for the homesteaders and uses their fight with Elliott to gain power and wealth. Dekker murders Hayes, and Elliott hires a gang of gunmen to war with Dekker and his henchmen. All ends well with Elliott avenging Hayes' murder and settling matters with Dekker and his gang. Songs: "I Ride an Old Paint," "Woopee Ti-Yi-Yo," "Git Along Little Dogies" (all traditional). **p&d**, Joseph Kane; **cast**, William Elliott, Vera Ralston, John Carroll, George "Gabby" Hayes, Albert Dekker, Virginia

Grey, Maria Ouspenskaya, Grant Withers, Minna Gombell, Ben Johnson, Roy Barcroft, Trevor Bardette, Paul Harvey, Rex Lease; **w**, Lawrence Hazard, Gerald Geraghty; **c**, John Alton; **m**, Ernest Gold, Nathan Scott; **ed**, Arthur Roberts; **art d**, Frank Hotaling; **set d**, John McCarthy Jr., George Suhr; **spec eff**, Howard Lydecker, Theodore Lydecker.

The X Files ★★★ 1998; U.S.; 121m; FOX; Color; Science Fiction; Children: Unacceptable (MPAA: PG-13); **BD**; **DVD**; **IV**. Adapted from "The X-Files" television series, the film begins with two FBI special agents, Duchovny and Anderson, who investigate the bombing of a federal building in Dallas, Texas. They learn that the terrorism has stemmed from aliens and goes back to 15,000 BC (which we see in flashback) when a prehistoric hunter wanders into a cave that later became part of north Texas and where that hunter kills a strange creature after it attacks him. The film then flashes forward to the present when a boy at the same place in Texas falls into a hole that contains a mysterious black substance. Back in the present, Duchovny and Anderson investigate the Dallas bombing and meet Landau, a doctor, who says aliens are behind the bombing and Earth is going to be destroyed by a plague from the aliens. After a lot of action and intrigue between the two agents and alien enemies, Earth is saved. The action, heavily laced by extraordinary special effects, sustains interest throughout. Songs: "Teotihuacán" (Noel Gallagher), "Walking After You" (Dave Groh), "Invisible Sun" (Sting: Gordon Matthew Sumner), "Hunter" (Bjork: Bjork Guomundsdottir), "Crystal Ship" (Jim Morrison, Ray Manzarek, John Densmore, Robby Krieger), "One" and "Red Right Hand" (Nick Cave), "Flower Man" (Emerson Hart, Jeff Russo, Dan Lavery, Kevin Shepard), "The X-Files Theme" (Mark Snow) "Beacon Light," "Deuce," "One More Murder," "More Than This," "16 Horses," "Black." Intense violence and gore prohibit viewing by children. **p**, Chris Carter, Daniel Sackheim; **d**, Rob Bowman; **cast**, David Duchovny, Gillian Anderson, John Neville, Martin Landau, William B. Davis, Blythe Danner, Mitch Pileggi, Jeffrey De Munn, Terry O'Quinn, Armin Mueller-Stahl; **w**, Chris Carter (based on a story by Carter, Frank Spotnitz); **c**, Ward Russell; **m**, Mark Snow; **ed**, Stephen Mark; **prod d**, Christopher Nowak; **art d**, Gregory Bolton, Hugo Santiago, Marc Fisichella; **set d**, Jackie Carr; **spec eff**, Stan Blackwell, Yuri Everson, Chuck E. Stewart.

X-Men ★★★ 2000; U.S.; 104m; FOX; Color; Science Fiction; Children: Unacceptable (MPAA: PG-13); **BD**; **DVD**; **IV**. This is the first of the X-Men series of films, the others being **X-2: X-Men United**, 2003, and **X-Men: First Class**, 2011. Based on Marvel Comics characters, sometime in the future both humans and mutants coexist on Earth but fear each other. Paquin, a young female mutant, runs away from home and hitches a ride with another mutant, Jackman, who is known as Wolverine. Stewart, a professor who owns a school for young X-Men mutants, sends two mutants, Berry and Marsden, to bring them back. McKellen, the leader of the Brotherhood of Mutants, intends to turn world leaders into mutants at a United Nations summit with a machine he has built to bring about acceptance of mutants, but Stewart knows that the forced mutation will result in their deaths. Wolverine and his claws prove what a hero a mutant can be in resolving this international threat. Like the rest of the series, special effects dominate almost every scene and they are spectacular. The film was an enormous box office success, earning more than $296 million in its initial release against a budget of $75 million. Songs: "Still I Long for Your Kiss" (Lucinda Williams, Duane Jarvis), "Fox News Update" (Robert Israel), "Atom Bomb" (Michael Tournier, Jonathan Fugler, Michael Bryant), "Garb of Old Gaul" (traditional), "Governor's Guard" (A.S. Leeming). Intense violence prohibits viewing by children. **p**, Lauren Shuler Donner, Ralph Winter, Joel Simon, William S. Todman, Jr.; **d**, Bryan Singer; **cast**, Hugh Jackman, Patrick Stewart, Ian McKellen, Halle Berry, James Marsden, Anna Paquin, Bruce Davison, Famke Janssen, Tyler Mane, Ray Park;

w, David Hayter (based on the story by Singer, Tom DeSanto); c, Newton Thomas Sigel; m, Michael Kamen; ed, Steven Rosenblum, Kevin Stitt, John Wright; prod d, John Myhre; art d, Paul Denham Austerberry, Tamara Deverell; set d, James Edward Ferrell; spec eff, Tony Kenny, Kaz Kobielski.

X-Men: First Class ★★★ 2011; U.S.; 132m; FOX; Color; Science Fiction; Children: Unacceptable (MPAA: PG-13); **BD**; **DVD**; **IV**. In this exciting prequel to **X-Men**, 2000, the Unites States government in 1962 enlists the help of mutants with superhuman capabilities to stop a mad dictator, who is determined to start World War III. Before mutants Charles Xavier, played by McAvoy, and Erik Lensherr, played by Fassbender, took the names Professor X and Magneto, they were young men just discovering their supernatural powers for the first time. Before becoming archenemies, they were also close friends, working together with other mutants to stop the greatest threat the world has ever known. They have a falling-out which begins an internecine war between Fassbender's Magneto Brotherhood and McAvoy's X-Men. Special effects control the story line and dominate the characters, which, though utterly synthetic, have a deep visual attraction, not unlike the mesmerizing display of dazzling fireworks. The film was a smash at the box office, earning more than $353 million in its initial release against a budget of $160 million. Songs: "Love Love" (Gary Barlow, Howard Donald, Jason Orange, Mark Owen, Robbie Williams), "Concentration Camp" (Michael Kamen), "La vie en rose" (1945; Louis Guglielmi as Louiguy, Edith Piaf), "Palisades Park" (Chuck Barris as Charles Barris), "Run/I'm a Natural Disaster" (CeeLo Thomas as Thomas Callaway, Danger Mouse as Brian Burton, Keith Mansfield), "A Little Bit of Soap" (Bert Russell), "Green Onions" (Al Jackson Jr., Booker T. Jones, Lewie Steinberg, Steve Cooper), "Hippy Hippy Shake" (Chan Romero as Robert Lee Romero), "Soviet National Anthem" (Anatoli Alexandrov). Intense violence, some sexual content, brief partial nudity and gutter language prohibit viewing by children. p, Gregory Goodman, Simon Kinberg, Lauren Shuler Donner, Bryan Singer, Jason Taylor; d, Matthew Vaughn; cast, James McAvoy, Michael Fassbender, Kevin Bacon, Laurence Belcher, Bill Milner, Rose Byrne, Jennifer Lawrence, Beth Goddard, Morgan Lily, Oliver Platt, Alex Gonzalez, Hugh Jackman in a cameo performance. w, Vaughn, Ashley Miller, Zack Stentz, Jane Goldman (based on a story by Sheldon Turner, Singer; c, John Mathieson; m, Henry Jackman; ed, Eddie Hamilton, Lee Smith; prod d, Chris Seagers; art d, Grant Armstrong, Paul Booth, Alex Cameron, Steve Cooper, Marc Fisichella, John King, Dawn Swiderski; set d, Erin Boyd, Sonja Klaus; spec eff, Shailendra Swarnkar.

X-Men Origins: Wolverine ★★★ 2009; U.S.; 107m; Fox; Color; Science Fiction; Children: Unacceptable (MPAA: PG-13); **BD**; **DVD**; **IV**. Action-packed story begins with the early life of the mutant Wolverine and his years with the U.S. government squad Team X and the impact it will have on his later years. In 1845 Canada, a boy, James Howlett, played by Sivan, sees his father killed by Jackman, a groundskeeper. The trauma activates Sivan's mutation so that bone claws protrude from his hands and he kills Jackman, who reveals before dying that he is Sivan's real father. Sivan flees along with Jackman's son, Schreiber, who is Sivan's half brother. They spend the next century as soldiers, fighting in the American Civil War (1861-1865), World War I (1914-1918), World War II (1939-1945), and the Vietnam War (1961-1975). In 1975, Schreiber kills a senior officer and Jackman defends him, so they are both sentenced to be executed by a firing squad but, instead, are held in military custody. Huston, a major, offers them a pardon if they join his Team X, a group of mutants. Sivan and Jackman remain in the team for a few years, but Jackman decides to leave because of the group's disregard for human life. Six years later, now using the alias of Logan, Jackman works as a lumberjack in Canada where he lives with his schoolteacher girlfriend, Collins. Schreiber approaches Jackman at his work and reports that two of the team members have been killed and

Michael Fassbender and James McAvoy in *X-Men: First Class,* **2011.**

that someone is believed to be targeting the remaining mutants. Jackman is urged to rejoin Huston but refuses. He changes his mind after Collins' bloodied body is found in a forest. Jackman finds Schreiber at a local bar and they fight. Huston then explains that Schreiber has gone rogue, having killed one of the team members, and offers Jackman a way to become strong enough to avenge Collins' murder. Jackman undergoes an operation to reinforce his body with a virtually indestructible metal. Then Huston attempts to betray Jackman by planning to have his memory erased, but Jackman escapes. Nothing is resolved, leaving the way for sequels in this very violent science fiction series, which nevertheless offers astounding special effects. This film did well at the box office, earning more than $373 million in its initial release against a budget of $150 million. Songs: "Havamal" (traditional), "Tie a Yellow Ribbon 'Round the Ole Oak Tree" (L. Russell Brown, Irwin Levine), "Carousel Rides" (Herman Beeftink), "Zoot Shoot" (Weevil & Riddick), "New Orleans Boogie" (Daniel May, Marc Ferrari), "Gimme One More Shot" (Jamie Dunlap, Scott Nickoley), "Shinjuku Shadows" (G.E. Stinson). Excessive violence and some partial nudity prohibit viewing by children. p, Hugh Jackman, John Palermo, Lauren Shuler Donner, Louis G. Friedman, Peter MacDonald, Marsha Swinton, Ralph Winter, Bryan Singer; d, Gavin Hood; cast, Hugh Jackman, Liev Schreiber, Danny Huston, Lynn Collins, Kevin Durand, Dominic Monaghan, Taylor Kitsch, Daniel Henney, Ryan Reynolds, Troye Sivan; w, David Benioff, Skip Woods; c, Donald M. McAlpine; m, Harry Gregson-Williams; ed, Nicolas De Toth, Megan Gill; prod d, Barry Robison; art d, Ian Gracie; set d, Rebecca Cohen, Sandy Walker; spec eff, Dan Oliver, Cam Waldbauer, Brendon Durey.

X-Men: The Last Stand ★★★ 2006; Canada/U.S./U.K.; 14m; FOX; Color; Science Fiction; Children: Unacceptable (MPAA: PG-13); **BD**; **DVD**; **IV**. This good sequel to the series begins a few months after the action in **The X-Men Files**, 1998, and where conflict returns among Earthlings and X-Men mutant aliens. Humans discover what causes them to mutate and have found a cure. The X-Men aliens, Jackman and Berry, are violently opposed to a cure, so X-Men leader Magneto, played by McKellen, assembles a mutant army and starts an all-out war with the humans. Janssen, who was killed in the previous film, mutates into The Phoenix, also played by Janssen, with mutant powers so strong she cannot control her own body. She kills Professor X, played by Stewart, and now the Earthlings must stop McKellen again to end the alien war, and also stop Janssen from causing more violence. Like the rest of the series, this entry is dominated by astounding special effects that do not stint on violence and gore. The film was a smash at the box office, earning almost $460 million in its initial release against a budget of $210 million. Song: "The Last Stand" (John Powell). Excessive violence, sex-

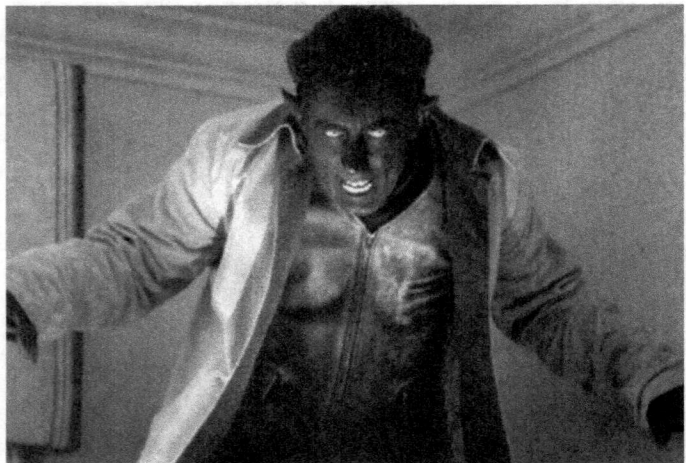

Alan Cumming in *X2: X-Men United*, 2003.

ellen's partner, Romijn, plans to break him out of prison. Stewart's X-Men school is attacked by Cox's forces, but Jackman and his companions are lucky enough to escape. The remaining X-Men meet in Boston where they form a tenuous alliance with McKellen to stop Cox and rescue Stewart. As is the case with the other entries in the series, the spectacular special effects supplant realism and even logic, but nevertheless provide fascinating interest throughout. A prequel, **X-Men: First Class**, was released in 2011, and two TV series dealing with X-Men were produced in 2009 and 2011. This film was a great box office hit, earning more than $407.7 million in its initial release against a budget of more than $110 million. Songs: "Dies Irae" from "Requiem in D Minor," "Romanze" from Eine Kleine Nachtmusik," "Sonata K545" (Wolfang Amadeus Mozart); "Evolution Exhibit," "News Theme," "Sports Jam" (Christopher Tin); "Center of the Sun" (Annie Danielewski, Rhys Fulber); "Game Show Network Original Program End Cue," "Pastoral Lands" (William Loose); "Bye Bye Bye" (Andreas Carlsson, Kristian Lundin, Jacob Schulze). Excessive violence, some sexuality and gutter language prohibit viewing by children. **p**, Ralph Winter, Lauren Shuler Donner, Ross Fanger, Kevin Feige; **d**, Bryan Singer; **cast**, Patrick Stewart, Hugh Jackman, Ian McKellen, Alan Cumming, James Marsden, Halle Berry, Famke Janssen, Anna Paquin, Brian Cox, Rebecca Romijn, Bruce Davison, Cotter Smith; **w**, Michael Dougherty, Dan Harris, David Hayter (based on a story by Singer, Hayter, Zak Penn; **c**, Newton Thomas Sigel; **m**, John Ottman; **ed**, John Ottman, Elliot Graham; **prod d**, Guy Hendrix Dyas; **art d**, Geoff Hubbard, Helen Jarvis; **set d**, Elizabeth Wilcox; **spec eff**, Gord Davis, Michael L. Fink, Stephen Rosenbaum.

ual content and gutter language prohibit viewing by children. **p**, Avi Arad, Lauren Shuler Donner, Ralph Winter, Kurt Williams, Lee Cleary, Ross Fanger, James M. Freitag; **d**, Brett Ratner; **cast**, Hugh Jackman, Halle Berry, Ian McKellen, Patrick Stewart, Anna Paquin, James Marsden, Kelsey Grammer, Famke Janssen, Rebecca Romijn, Shawn Ashmore, Aaron Stanford, Vinnie Jones; **w**, Simon Kinberg, Zak Penn; **c**, Dante Spinotti; **m**, John Powell; **ed**, Mark Goldblatt, Mark Helfrich, Julia Wong; **prod d**, Edward Verreaux; **art d**, Geoff Hubbard; **set d**, Elizabeth Wilcox; **spec eff**, W.A. Andrew Sculthorp, Mike Vezina, Cam Waldbauer.

X: The Unknown ★★★ 1957; U.K.; 81m; Hammer/WB; B/W; Science Fiction; Children: Unacceptable; **DVD**; **VHS**. Eerie and exciting sci-fi tale begins when a British army radiation unit drills at a remote 1950s Scottish base and attracts a subterranean radioactive entity that looks like a living glob of mud. Experts learn that this pulsating mass oozes out of the ground every fifty years or more and then vanishes. This time it leaves two severely radiation-burned soldiers in its wake as well as a seemingly bottomless crack in the earth. Others meet the same fate that night as the mass reappears and grows bigger. It's up to brilliant scientist Jagger to deal with it, but his problem is how to destroy something enigmatic that apparently feeds on human energy. He finally overcomes the menace by killing the mass with electronic waves, but, at the exciting finale, the viewer is uncertain as to whether or not this inexplicable and seemingly other world threat will reappear in the future. Norman sustains suspense throughout while offering many harrowing moments, and Jagger and the supporting cast are exceptional in their roles. **p**, Anthony Hinds; **d**, Leslie Norman; **cast**, Dean Jagger, Edward Chapman, Leo McKern, Anthony Newley, Jameson Clark, William Lucas, Peter Hammond, Marianne Brauns, Ian McNaughton, Michael Ripper, John Harvey; **w**, Jimmy Sangster; **c**, Gerald Gibbs; **m**, James Bernard; **ed**, James Needs; **art d**, Ted Marshall; **spec eff**, Jack Curtis.

X2: X-Men United ★★★ 2003; Canada/U.S.; 133m; FOX; Color; Science Fiction; Children: Unacceptable (MPAA: PG-13); **BD**; **DVD**; **IV**. In this fine sequel to **X-Men**, 2000, a few months have passed since the mutant X-Men, led by Stewart, defeated the evil Magneto, played by McKellen, and imprisoned him in a plastic chamber (not unlike the three traitors on Krypton who are sent into space while encapsulated in floating prisms in **Superman II**, 1980). One day, a mutant called Nightcrawler, played by Cumming, infiltrates the White House and tries to assassinate the President, portrayed by Smith. This sets off a series of anti-mutant efforts by the government. Meanwhile, the mutant Logan/Wolverine, played by Jackman, is trying to learn about his past. Cox, a scientist, discovers Stewart's secret school for mutants, and McK-

The Yakuza ★★★ 1975; U.S./Japan; 123m; WB/Toei; Color; Crime Drama; Children: Unacceptable (MPAA: R); **DVD**; **VHS**; **IV**. This tension-filled crime tale begins when Keith, a powerful American shipping tycoon, learns that his daughter, Chirillo, has been kidnapped by Okada, a leader of a Yakuza clan (Yakuza is a 400-year-old secret Japanese criminal society similar to the American-Italian Mafia). Keith has been in Okada's pay to buy and ship arms to the Yakuza. Okada kidnaps the girl to apply pressure in his dealings with Keith, who, in turn, hires Mitchum, an old army buddy from World War II (1939-1945), to rescue Chirillo. Mitchum is in the United States, a retired detective, and he accepts this assignment, despite misgivings about returning to Japan where he had been a U.S. army military policeman after the war. At that time, Mitchum had fallen in love with Keiko, a Japanese woman involved in the black market, but their relationship was brought to an end by her brother, Takakura, who disapproved of her being with an American, and Takakura joined the Yakuza. After much mayhem, Mitchum learns that Takakura is not Keiko's brother, but her husband. It all ends with Yakuza and American thieves falling out, and where Mitchum kills Keith, apologizing to Takakura for interfering in his life. Both men bow to each other at the Tokyo airport as Mitchum is about to take a flight back to the United States. The story has less to do with the sinister operations of the Yakuza than it does with complicated internecine family wars in Japan. Song: "Only the Wind" (Dave Grusin, Aku Yu). *Author's Note*: Mitchum told this author that "I thought the script for **The Yakuza** was more than a little murky and it had too many confusing characters. I don't think the writer [Schrader] knew too much about the Yakuza, a very tough criminal gang that has been around in Japan for longer than the U.S. has been the U.S. It's really a story about a detective trying to find a kidnap victim. I have played other detectives [a private detective in **Out of the Past**, 1947; a police detective in **The Racket**, 1951], but the one I played in this picture can't find a clue in a closed society. You see, in Japan, they don't really talk about their crimes and criminals because they lose face by admitting that such lawbreakers exist. The government doesn't even announce when they execute a murderer until maybe months or even years later. That's the way it is in Japan." For details on the Yakuza, see my two-volume work *The Great Pictorial*

History of World Crime, Volume II (History, Inc., under Secret Criminal Societies, Yakuza; pages: 1471-1474). Many other films have depicted the Yakuza, including **Across the Pacific**, 1942; **Adrenaline Drive**, 2000; **American Yakuza**, 1993; **Armed Response**, 1986; **Battles without Honor and Humanity**, 2004; **Beyond Outrage**, 2012; **The Bird People in China**, 1998; **Black Rain**, 1989; **The Blind Swordsman: Zatoichi**, 2004; **Blue Tiger**, 1994; **Boiling Point**, 1990; **Branded to Kill**, 1967; **Brother**, 2000; **The Challenge**, 1982; **Chocolate**, 2009; **Cold Fish**, 2011; **Contract Killer**, 1998; **Crying Freeman**, 1995; **Dead or Alive**, 2001; **Drunken Angel**, 1959; **Everything's Gone Green**, 2007; **The Fast and the Furious: Tokyo Drift**, 2006; **Fighter in the Wind**, 2004; **Fireworks**, 1998; **The Five**, 1998; **Fudoh: The New Generation**, 1996; **Ghost in the Shell**, 1995; **Ghost in the Shell: Innocence**, 2004; **Gozu**, 2003; **Graveyard of Honor**, 2003; **The Hoodlum Soldier**, 1974; **Ichi the Killer**, 2003; **Into the Sun**, 2005; **Kids Return**, 1996; **Last Life in the Universe**, 2004; **Like a Dragon**, 2010; **My Wife Is a Gangster**, 2001; **Naked Weapon**, 2002; **Nameless Gangster: Rules of the Time**, 2012; **Ninja**, 2009; **Ninja Assassin**, 2009; **No Way Back**, 1995; **Outrage**, 2010; **Pairan**, 2001; **Pale Flower**, 2005; **Pigs and Battleships**, 1963; **Predators**, 2010; **The Punisher**, 1989; **Rain Fall**, 2009; **Rainy Dog**, 1997; **Red Sun Rising**, 1994; **Rising Sun**, 1993; **RoboCop 3**, 1993; **Samurai Cop**, 1991; **Shinjuku Incident**, 2010; **Showdown in Little Tokyo**, 1991; **The Slammin' Salmon**, 2009; **Sonatine**, 1998; A **Stranger of Mine**, 2005; **The Taste of Tea**, 2004; A **Taxing Woman**, 1987; **Tokyo Decadence**, 1993; **Tokyo Drifter**, 1966; **Tokyo Godfathers**, 2003; **Versus**, 2002; **War**, 2007; **Wasabi**, 2002; **Why Don't You Play in Hell?**, 2013; **The Wolverine**, 2013; **Yakuza Apocalypse**, 2015; **Yakuza Weapon**, 2011; **Younger and Younger**, 1993; **Youth of the Beast**, 1963; and **Zatoichi**, 1989. Excessive violence prohibits viewing by children. **p&d**, Sydney Pollack; **cast**, Robert Mitchum, Brian Keith, Ken Takakura, Richard Jordan, Herb Edelman, Kishi Keiko, James Shigeta, Eiji Okada, Kyosuke Machida, Christina Kokubo, Lee Chirillo, William Ross; **w**, Paul Schrader, Robert Towne (based on a story by Leonard Schrader); **c**, Okazaki Kozo (Panavision; Technicolor); **m**, Dave Grusin; **ed**, Don Guidice, Thomas Stanford; **prod d**, Stephen Grimes; **art d**, Ishida Yoshiyuki; **spec eff**, Kasai Tomoo, Richard Parker.

A Yank at Oxford ★★★ 1938; U.S.; 82m; MGM; B/W; Comedy; Children: Acceptable. Delightful, lighthearted comedy begins with Taylor, a cocky American who has been a track athlete at a small-town college and who receives a scholarship to attend Cardinal College, Oxford University, in London. He is reluctant to accept because his father, Barrymore, has a limited income, but he nevertheless decides to study at the prestigious English school. On the train to the college, he brags about his athletic abilities to Oxford students Jones, Coote, and Croft. They think he's a brash American and pull a prank on him by convincing Taylor to get off at the wrong stop. Taylor manages to get to Oxford where students play more pranks on him, including pulling down his pants in public. He becomes attracted to O'Sullivan, who is the sister of Jones. Taylor, however, has trouble with Jones, who dislikes him. The animosity between them changes after Jones gets into trouble and Taylor takes the blame for him, risking expulsion. Barrymore takes a boat to England and arrives in time to save Taylor from disgrace. Taylor, who has earlier earned universal disapproval from the students for his unsportsmanlike conduct on the track in the quarter-mile dash, then wins everyone's approval when he wins the school rowing team's big match against Cambridge. He also wins the hand of the fetching O'Sullivan to end this campus romp. The film was a success at the box office, earning more than $2.7 million in its initial release against a budget of more than $1.3 million. The film was parodied in the Laurel and Hardy film **A Chump at Oxford**, 1940, a sequel of sorts, as well as **A Yank at Eaton**, 1942, with Mickey Rooney, and remade as **Oxford Blues**, 1984, with Rob Lowe in the Taylor role. Songs: "Academic Festival Overture in C, Opus 80" (1880; Johannes Brahms), "Yankee Doodle" (1755; traditional),

Griffith Jones and Robert Taylor in *A Yank at Oxford*, **1938.**

"Rule Brittania" (1740; music: Thomas Augustine Arne; lyrics: James Thomson), "Over There" (1917; George M. Cohan), "Battle Hymn of the Republic" (1856; music: William Steffe; lyrics: 1862; Julia Ward Howe), "There Is a Tavern in the Town" (1891; F.J. Adams), "For He's a Jolly Good Fellow" (traditional). *Author's Note*: "I had a lot to prove when we made **A Yank at Oxford**," Taylor told this author. "Up to the time we made that picture, I had been bum-rapped by some very vicious Hollywood reporters who inferred that, because of all of the romantic roles I had played, I was not very manly, and suggested that I was effeminate. That boiled my blood, so I set out to change that image when we did **A Yank at Oxford**. Fortunately, there were several scenes where I have to run in track meets and later I am in a boat race and, because I knew that the waters were freezing cold in those sculling matches, I prepared myself by soaking in tubs filled with ice water. I had done a lot of track work when I was in school and I had kept in shape so I was authentic looking when I ran in the track events in that picture. The sports togs I wore in the athletic events showed my chest and the press made a big deal out of the fact that I had a hairy chest, so that put aside any doubts about my manhood. Appearances are everything, aren't they?" The film was shot in England but was wholly financed by MGM's London office, which hired British producer Balcon to supervise the production, although MGM boss Louis B. Mayer made this film as one of his pet projects. Mayer particularly wanted this film to be a vehicle for Taylor and was so edified at the response from the press about Taylor's hairy chest and athletic prowess that, after the film became an overnight success, Mayer called Taylor to state: "Bob—you are now a man!" Mayer doted on everyone cast in this film and objected to the presence of Leigh, who plays a small but important part as a lowlife British young woman who tries to vamp Taylor. Balcon convinced Mayer that Leigh was a bargain in that since she lived in England where the film was being shot, MGM would not have to incur any traveling expenses for her. Balcon shrewdly used this ploy to win over Mayer, knowing that the studio boss was a penny-pinching mogul. Leigh, however, proved difficult during the production, not getting along well with the outgoing O'Sullivan, with whom Leigh had befriended in childhood. Leigh was apparently upset with her small role and kept complaining about the cheap clothes she had to wear in the film. She argued with director Conway and when she got nowhere, she went to Balcon, who told her: "You are playing a tart, my dear lady. Tarts wear cheap clothing and that is what you must wear." Actually, Leigh was having a lot of emotional problems at that time as she was waiting for her own divorce and that of her lover's, actor Laurence Olivier, to conclude before she could be with Olivier. She caused so much unrest that British producer Alexander Korda, to whom she was under contract, heard about her prima donna actions and contacted her, telling her that if she did not stop her tem-

Tyrone Power and Betty Grable in *A Yank in the R.A.F.*, 1941.

peramental outbursts during the production of **A Yank at Oxford**, he would cancel her agreement with him. Thereafter, Leigh was on her best behavior. Mayer's behavior, however, was even more annoying to Balcon and Conway as the mogul, who was then in England, visited the set almost every day to make sure that everything went the way he wanted it to go. This was the first MGM film shot in England, and Mayer wanted everyone to know that he was in charge. He walked about the set making critical comments about the costuming, the sets and even the props being used. At one point, he lambasted Balcon, an accomplished producer, in front of O'Sullivan, Leigh and others to the point where the producer refused to tolerate any more of Mayer's bullying. Balcon quit the production, telling Mayer that he could personally produce the film, which sent the mogul scurrying back to his hotel suite. Mayer had originally asked top screenwriter Ben Hecht to write the script for this film, but Hecht declined. "I wanted no part of that story," Hecht told this author. "I knew little about campus life and told Mayer that. I also knew that Mayer was going to be on hand during the whole production and I did not want that meddling bird pecking over my shoulder at the script. You could sell Mayer on almost any kind of story for the screen if you jazzed up the tale with a lot of action and sentimentality. Charlie [Charles MacArthur] and I once sold him a script idea while we were in an elevator with him, but you did not want to have that man around when you were writing the script because he would drive you nuts with his wacky ideas. A lot of writers worked on **A Yank at Oxford**, including F. Scott Fitzgerald, who was then a contract writer at MGM. Scott worked for several weeks on that script and added a lot of intelligent dialog and set up some of its best romantic scenes, but the guy never got a credit for all of his work. Hollywood treated Scott very badly because he had gotten the reputation of being a heavy drinker and that was a big taboo in Hollywood. They kept this great author around for window-dressing, I guess. Poor Scott, he did not have long to live by that time. He died about two years after **A Yank at Oxford** came out [on December 21, 1940] and, by that time, he was a forgotten man. That changed years later when his fine novels became popular with college teachers, who brought his works back to the public, thank God." Although Leigh's appearance in this film is a small one, she was noticed in Hollywood, especially after Taylor raved about her to David O. Selznick, who, shortly after this film was released, cast Leigh as his Scarlett O'Hara in the epic **Gone with the Wind**, 1939. **p**, Michael Balcon; **d**, Jack Conway; **cast**, Robert Taylor, Lionel Barrymore, Maureen O'Sullivan, Vivien Leigh, Edmund Gwenn, Griffith Jones, C.V. France, Claude Gillingwater, Tully Marshall, Walter Kingsford, Robert Coote, Dennis O'Keefe, Richard Todd, Doodles Weaver; **w**, Malcolm Stuart Boylan, Walter Ferris, George Oppenheimer, Leon Gordon, Sidney Gilliat, Michael Hogan (uncredited) John Paddy Carstairs, F. Scott Fitzgerald,

Angus MacPhail, Roland Pertwee, Frank Wead, based on a story by Gordon, Gilliat, Hogan, and an idea by John Monk Saunders); **c**, Harold Rosson; **m**, Hubert Bath, Edward Ward; **ed**, Charles Frend; **art d**, Lawrence P. Williams.

A Yank in the R.A.F. ★★★★ 1941; U.S.; 98m; FOX; B/W; Romance; War Drama; Children: Unacceptable; **DVD**; **VHS**. Power charms and endears in one of his biggest hits while playing a cocky American pilot who joins the R.A.F. during WWII (1939-1945). He is first seen flying from the U.S. border to Trenton, Ontario, Canada, and, when landing, states that he thought that he was flying to Trenton, New Jersey (taking a leaf from Douglas "Wrong Way" Corrigan, 1907-1995, who flew from New York to Ireland in 1938, pretending that he had a navigation error and intended to fly to California). Once in Canada, Power offers to ferry training planes from Canada to England for $1,000. This he knows is part of the plan by the then neutral U.S. to aid England, which is then at war with Germany. After Power ferries the plane to England, he runs into Grable, his old flame, who is not eager to see him since he abandoned her when she was a chorus girl in Texas. Grable has nothing but contempt for the conniving Power, calling him a "worm" and saying that he is a coward for not fighting for England. She, at this time, is performing at a London nightclub during the evenings and, during the day, serves in the Women's Auxiliary Air Force. Power, simply to impress Grable, whom he has always loved, cavalierly joins the R.A.F. (British Royal Air Force). When Sutton, who is Power's superior, learns about the fetching Grable, he becomes emotionally involved with her, although Grable tells Sutton that there is another man in her life, tacitly admitting that she is deeply in love with Power, even though he is an unreliable cad. Gardiner, one of Power's co-pilots, is also interested in Grable, but he cannot get either Power or Sutton to introduce him to the attractive blonde. Power, an experienced pilot, must nevertheless undergo training, which he routinely performs although it is all boringly repetitive for him. Upon graduation, he is assigned to Sutton's bomber squadron, which displeases Power as he wants to fly fighter planes, preferably a Spitfire. His first assignment is to go on a bombing run to Berlin, Germany, but Power is amazed and disgusted to see that, once his plane is over the target, all he is ordered to drop is propaganda leaflets instead of bombs. (This occurs during what was known as the "Phony War," an eighth-month quiet period from September 1939 until May 1940 when little or no military actions were taken between England and its allies and Germany). German ground searchlights pick them up and anti-aircraft guns begin firing at the plane. The frustrated Power feels helpless, so, instead of sending the individual propaganda leaflets downward one by one, he throws them in tied bundles at the enemy, one of those bundles managing to smash one of the searchlights. This inspires others of the crew to not only throw the bundles at the enemy, but frantically search about the plane to throw any other heavy object at the Germans, including fire extinguishers and other metal objects. This leaflet mission only further convinces Power that the war is a silly exercise and that his superiors are incompetent. Power breaks a date to see Grable after the mission when he meets an old buddy from America. Sutton then arrives to ask Grable to spend a weekend at his family estate and there he proposes marriage. Grable returns to London where she tells Power about the proposal (which she has not accepted), but is careful not to identify the suitor as Sutton. Power then offers to marry Grable, but his proposal is made in such an offhand and frivolous manner that Grable becomes incensed and tells him that their relationship is ended. By this time, Germany invades Belgium and the Netherlands, and Power is assigned to go on a mission to Dortmund, Germany. This time, the R.A.F. will be dropping bombs and not leaflets. During the mission, the plane that Sutton and Power is flying is hit by anti-aircraft fire and one of its engines is disabled, causing the plane to descend. Gardiner, flying another bomber, descends in an effort to aid his friends, but his plane is also hit by enemy fire and he crashes and is killed. Sutton orders his crew to parachute from the plane, but Power refuses and takes control of the bomber, landing it on a beach. He, Sutton and another crew member survive, but are taken prisoner by Kreuger, a German officer. The crew member sacrifices his life so that Power and Sutton can kill Kreuger. They then make their escape in a motorboat. Power awakes in a hospital, having suffered from overexposure. To glorify himself, Power shows up at Gable's flat with his arm in a sling, pretending that he has been wounded in his recent mission. Although Grable is always on the alert for Power's shenanigans, she is taken in by this ruse and is suddenly caring and concerned for him, making him comfortable. As Power attempts to embrace and kiss her, however, Grable quickly sees that there is not a thing wrong with his arm and she angrily accuses Power of being nothing more than a deceiving fraud. Before Grable throws him out, Power struggles with her to finally embrace and kiss her (and this is typical of the wrestling matches that make up their delightful and amusing love scenes). He then forces an engagement ring upon her finger. Grable then receives a call from Sutton, telling her that he must break their appointment and that all leaves are canceled. Power must then report back to his base. The evacuation of the British and French troops from Dunkirk (on May 27–June 4, 1940) is presently ongoing and all the pilots with experience flying fighter planes are pressed into service to protect the naval rescue of those British troops. Power is one of those aviators, and where he no longer looks upon the war with a detached perspective, but one that has taken the lives of his friends and he now accepts it as the somber and serious threat it truly presents to democracies and freedom. He is assigned a Spitfire fighter plane and sees action over the Channel, shooting down two German fighter planes. Power's transformation from a lighthearted and unconcerned bystander to a passionate activist is shown when he states when downing one of the enemy planes: "That's for Roger!" (That is the name of Gardiner's character, earlier shot down by the Germans.) Power is then shot down and Grable anxiously awaits his return in London. Sutton takes her to the docks to see a ship with survivors from Dunkirk arriving, and Grable is ecstatic to see a wounded Power come down the gangplank. Grable races into Power's arms, showing him that she is still wearing his engagement ring. Just then an attractive British nurse passes Power to tell him to call her up when he can. Grable begins to see that Power is up to his old tricks, but he appears contrite, saying: "I know—I'm a worm!" But the two lovers nevertheless walk off arm and arm together to end this exciting and entertaining tale. King presents a rousing adventure tale while merging an equally tempestuous romance into the fabric of this well-mounted film, bringing forth exceptional performances from Power, Grable, Sutton, Gardiner and a strong supporting cast. The aerial action scenes are also splendidly presented, combining live action combat footage with authentic-looking miniature scenes filled with impressive special effects. The lively script is packed with many amusing scenes and its dialog sparkles with wit and irony. The film received an Oscar nomination for Best Special Effects (Sersen). The film was enormously popular at the box office, becoming one of the top theatrically released feature films of the year, earning more than $2 million in its initial release against a budget of more than $200,000. A thirty-minute radio adaptation was aired by the Screen Guild Theater on October 26, 1942, with Power, Grable and Sutton reprising their roles. Songs: "These Foolish Things (Remind Me of You)" (1936; music: Jack Strachey; lyrics: Eric Maschwitz, Harry Link), "Hi-Yah, Love" (music: Ralph Rainger; lyrics: Leo Robin), "Another Little Dream Won't Do Us Any Harm" (music: Ralph Rainger; lyrics: Leo Robin), "She'll Be Comin' Round the Mountain 'When She Comes" (traditional), "I've Been Working on the Railroad" (traditional), "Bless 'Em All" (1917; Fred Godfrey), "R,A,F. March Past" (H. Walford Davies). *Author's Note*: The idea for this film began with Fox boss Zanuck, who was pro-British at the time the U.S. was attempting to maintain neutrality at the beginning of WWII, and who wanted to aid England in its war against Germany. Zanuck, who always thought of himself as a writer and as a film producer only through circumstance, wrote the screenplay under his long-standing pseudonym of Melville Crossman. In order to get support from

Betty Grable and Tyrone Power in *A Yank in the R.A.F.,* 1941.

the British, as well as combat aerial footage from the R.A.F., Zanuck sent his finished screenplay to British officials, one where Power is killed at the end while fighting in the skies over Dunkirk. "They liked the script," Zanuck told this author, "but they objected to Ty [Tyrone Power] getting killed at the end. They thought that, because he was so popular with audiences in England, his death on the screen would crush morale. Even though they did not openly state it, they thought that by showing this hero dying their efforts to recruit American pilots into the R.A.F. during those early days of the war would be diminished. All of that made sense, so I changed the script to show where Ty survived and returned to Betty [Grable] for a happy ending." At the time, Zanuck was in contact with Lord Beaverbrook (William Maxwell Aitkin, 1879-1964), who was the British Air Minister. He had been a film actor in the 1920s and was an old friend of Zanuck's. After he read the script, Beaverbrook told Zanuck that "we have enough drama these days," and asked the movie mogul to insert more comedy into the script, which Zanuck promptly did. Director King told this author that "Darryl [Zanuck] obtained from the British a great deal of combat footage that was taken over France during the early part of the war and I worked those aerial dogfights into the film. The British also gave us footage of the evacuation of their troops from Dunkirk and we used that, too, but we enlarged upon that by restaging that great rescue at sea on a beach in California." These scenes were shot at Point Mugu, California, and more than 1,000 extras were used to recreate the evacuation of British and French troops from the beaches of Dunkirk. King's masterful use of this footage, which he seamlessly wove into the fabric of the dramatic scenes of this film, impressed Zanuck, who, more than two decades later, used the same techniques when producing his epic **The Longest Day**, 1962, which depicts the Normandy invasion of June 6, 1944, but where he replaced actual footage with recreated live-action for its combat scenes. In this film, all of the aerial sequences recreating combat were staged by Hollywood aviation expert Paul Mantz, a legendary stunt pilot. During the production, two aerial photographers, Jack Parry and Otto Kanturek, were killed when filming some action scenes over Norfolk, England, on June 26, 1941. Their deaths occurred when their plane collided with a British fighter plane, or, as another report had it, were shot down by a German fighter plane. Zanuck saw this film as not only a clever propaganda tool, but as a vehicle to promote two of his leading stars of that day, Power and Grable, and he personally coached Grable for her more dramatic scenes. "He told me that he wanted me to become serious in some of the scenes in **A Yank in the R.A.F.**," Grable told this author, "because he wanted me to play an even more serious role in my next picture, a whodunit [**I Wake Up Screaming**, 1941], although there was an opportunity for me to sing and dance a little in that war picture with Ty [Tyrone Power]." Zanuck told this au-

James Cagney and Joan Leslie in *Yankee Doodle Dandy,* **1942.**

thor that "when I talked with Ty [Power] about this picture, he was a little surprised that he would be playing opposite Betty [Grable] for the first time. When I told him that, although Betty would be singing and dancing in the picture, she could handle the dramatic scenes with him. He was all for that, telling me: 'Her [singing and dancing] numbers should lighten up the story—God knows they need some of that over there in England. They are having a tough time of it.'" Other films depicting pilots and warplanes in the European and North African theaters of WWII include **The Adventures of Tartu** (aka: **Sabotage Agent**; 1943; R.A.F.; German Luftwaffe); **Angels One Five**, 1954 (R.A.F.); **Battle of Britain**, 1969 (R.A.F.; German Luftwaffe); **Battle Squadron Lutzow**, 1941 (German Luftwaffe); **Battleground**, 1949 (U.S. Air Force); **The Best Years of Our Lives**, 1946 (U.S. Air Force); **A Bridge Too Far**, 1977 (U.S. Air Force; R.A.F.); **Captains of the Clouds**, 1942 (R.A.F.; German Luftwaffe); **Command Decision**, 1948 (U.S. Air Force); **The Crew of the Dora**, 1943 (German Luftwaffe; Soviet Air Force); **Dark Blue World**, 2001 (Czech pilots in the R.A.F.); **The Desert Fox: The Story of Rommel**, 1951; **Desperate Journey**, 1942 (R.A.F.; German Luftwaffe); **The Devil's General**, 1957 (German Luftwaffe); **Eagle Squadron**, 1942 (R.A.F.); **Eagles over London**, 1973 (R.A.F.); **The English Patient**, 1996; **Fighter Squadron**, 1948 (U.S. Air Force); **Flying Fortress**, 1942 (U.S. Air Force); **Force 10 from Navarone**, 1978; **Forever Young**, 1992; **The Great Escape**, 1963 (U.S. Air Force; R.A.F.; German Luftwaffe); **The Guns of Navarone**, 1961; **The Heroes of Telemark**, 1965 (R.A.F.); **Hope and Glory**, 1987 (German Luftwaffe; R.A.F.); **International Lady**, 1941; **Into the White**, 2012 (R.A.F.; German Luftwaffe); **Johnny in the Clouds** (aka: **The Way to the Stars**; R.A.F.), 1945; **The Longest Day**, 1962 (R.A.F.; German Luftwaffe); **The McKenzie Break**, 1970 (German Luftwaffe; R.A.F.); **Memphis Belle**, 1990 (U.S. Air Force; German Luftwaffe); **Missing Jane**, 2004; **One of Our Aircraft Is Missing**, 1942 (R.A.F.); **The One That Got Away**, 1958 (German Luftwaffe); **Only Old Men Are Going to Battle**, 1974 (Soviet Air Force; German Luftwaffe); **Patton**, 1970; **Red Tails**, 2012 (Tuskegee pilots in Italy; U.S. Air Force); **Sahara**, 1943 (German Luftwaffe); **Saving Private Ryan**, 1998; **Secret Flight**, 1952 (German Luftwaffe; R.A.F.); **633 Squadron**, 1964 (R.A.F.); **Spitfire**, 1943 (R.A.F.); **Stairway to Heaven** (aka: **A Matter of Life and Death**), 1947; **The Star of Africa**, 1957 (German Luftwaffe; R.A.F.); **Stukas**, 1941 (German Luftwaffe); **13 Rue Madeleine**, 1947 (U.S. Air Force); **To Be or Not to Be**, 1942 (Polish pilots in the R.A.F.); **Torpedo Bombers**, 1983 (Soviet Air Force); **The Tuskegee Airmen**, 1995 (made-for-TV; U.S. Air Force); **Twelve O'Clock High**, 1949 (U.S. Air Force); **Valkyrie**, 2008; **Von Ryan's Express**, 1965 (German Luftwaffe); **A Walk in the Sun** (aka: **Salerno Beachhead**; German Luftwaffe; U.S. Air Force), 1945; **The War Lover**, 1962 (U.S.

Air Force); **We'll Meet Again**, 1982 (TV miniseries); and **The Winds of War**, 1983 (TV miniseries). **p**, Darryl F. Zanuck; **d**, Henry King; **cast**, Tyrone Power, Betty Grable, John Sutton, Reginald Gardiner, Donald Stuart, Ralph Byrd, Richard Fraser, John Wilde, Morton Lowry, Denis Green, Bruce Lester, Gladys Cooper, Kurt Kreuger; **w**, Darrel Ware, Karl Tunberg (based on a story by Melville Crossman [Zanuck]); **c**, Leon Shamroy; **m**, Alfred Newman; **ed**, Barbara McLean; **art d**, Richard Day, James Basevi; **set d**, Thomas Little; **spec eff**, Fred Sersen.

Yankee Doodle Dandy ★★★★ 1942; U.S.; 126m; WB; B/W; Biographical Drama/Musical; Children: Acceptable; **BD**; **DVD**; **VHS**; **IV**. The inimitable and dynamic Cagney was never more appealing than in this marvelous musical biopic of the great composer and entertainer, George M. Cohan (1878-1942), an unforgettable performance that brought Cagney an Oscar and also delightfully brought back to life scores of great songs from Cohan's era. The film opens with Cagney, who, as Cohan, has come out of retirement to appear in a Broadway musical ("I'd Rather Be Right," 1937, by George S. Kaufman and Moss Hart, music and lyrics by Richard Rodgers and Lorenz Hart) that portrays the then occupant of the White House, Franklin D. Roosevelt (1882-1945). Just as Cagney finishes the show for the night, he is summoned to the White House. After he arrives, he is shown into Roosevelt's office where he meets the President, who is played by Young. Thinking to be rebuked by the President for his satirical performance of the Chief Executive, Cagney is amazed to see that Young has asked him to visit him so that he can give him the Congressional Medal of Honor for composing his patriotic songs "Over There" and "You're a Grand Old Flag." While Cagney chats with Young, he recalls his past, beginning with his birth on the Fourth of July (albeit some records state that Cohan was born on July 3, 1878) and where his father, Huston, anxiously awaits his birth from wife DeCamp while Civil War veterans march in a parade past the theater where Huston is performing. In further flashback, we see him performing as a boy, played by Croft, with his parents, Huston and DeCamp, and his little sister, Parsons, on the vaudeville circuit, where he is always upstaging his parents and is forever creating problems for them. He is a bit of a braggart and showoff, but he loves show business as much as he does his family. He so revels in playing "Peck's Bad Boy" that, in one performance, he convinces a group of boys witnessing that show that he is that very brat, and these youthful theatergoers pretend to be his fans and wait for him following that performance. When he appears at the stage door they pummel and abuse him before he escapes back into the theater with nothing but bruises and an injured pride as his reward for proving that he is an exceptional thespian. Croft's conceit further creates problems for his parents when his arrogant attitudes antagonize theater managers. (Cohan was known to be headstrong as a child and his antics often presented temper tantrums that continually vexed his parents on and off the stage, although they and their fellow adult performers invariably forgave his transgressions as they knew Cohan was undeniably talented with amazing versatility to act, sing, dance and later compose his own unique and extremely popular songs and musical plays.) At one family performance, theater impresario Edward Franklin Albee II (1857-1930, the adoptive grandfather of future playwright Edward Franklin Albee, 1928-), played by Watson, attends one of the Cohan performances. He is so impressed that he visits the family in their dressing room, thinking to book them into some of his first-class theaters. The brash Croft, however, haughtily demands so much for his family that Watson tells Huston and DeCamp that he is withdrawing his offer and departs. This time, at the insistence of mother DeCamp, the lenient Huston is compelled to reach for a strap to tan Croft's bottom. We next see Cohan as an adult Cagney where he is appearing in a play in Buffalo, New York, as a crotchety old man with a long white beard. After the play, Leslie, a beautiful young girl, visits Cagney in his dressing room, telling him how much she admires his acting and that she has ambitions to become a theater performer. Cagney continues his role of the old man, delivering his avuncular advice to

Leslie in a croaking voice, but he then removes his false gray beard to reveal his youthful face, which so alarms Leslie that she screams. Cagney then throws the beard on the floor and stomps on it, as if eliminating a threat to the girl who has so infatuated him. He later persuades the theater manager, Catlett, to hire Leslie as a chorus girl, but then makes a secret arrangement with the leader of the pit orchestra to play an unscheduled, separate song that Leslie performs. When Catlett sees Leslie performing the song, he explodes, ordering the curtain brought down; Cagney gets into an argument with him to the point where Catlett fires not only Leslie, but cancels the act performed by Cagney and his family members. The family goes off to perform in other engagements, and Cagney routinely closes their act (in what became a classic sign-off) by thanking the audience, saying: "My father thanks you, my mother thanks you, my sister thanks you, and I thank you!" Cagney nevertheless has by this time so alienated theater managers that few will book the family's act. In order that his father, mother and sister (played by Jeanne Cagney, who is Cagney's real-life sister) can get work, Cagney leaves the act and strikes out on his own, peddling his songs in New York's Tin Pan Alley. He and Leslie give a delightful audition of one of Cohan's songs, "Harrigan," before Tobias and Clute, musical producers and song publishers. Like so many other financial backers, however, they decline to back Cagney's show, and, as he leaves, Cagney sees Whorf, who plays Cohan's future partner and producer, Sam Harris (1872-1941). Cagney sees Whorf again at a cafe where Whorf, who has failed to interest Tobias and Clute in his play, is attempting to persuade wealthy Sakall to back his own production, but he is getting nowhere. Cagney then pretends that he and Whorf are partners and implies that they already have a deal with Tobias and Clute to back Cagney's musical production, which they do not. Cagney so intrigues Sakall with his new musical and the fact that Sakall might be denied the right to back it, that Sakall finally insists that Cagney and Whorf take his check to bind the deal. The new show, "Little Johnny Jones" (1904), becomes a big hit, and Cagney's career soars upward. Sometime later, Whorf insists that Cagney meet with the then top female star on Broadway, Fay Templeton (1865-1939), played by Manning. He and Whorf arrive at the theater where Manning is performing and are warmly welcomed by her producer, Barbier, who plays A.L. Erlanger (1859-1930). Manning, however, wants nothing to do with Cagney, considering him nothing more than a flag-waving Broadway upstart and a creator of novelty tunes. Barbier tells Manning that Cagney is the brightest and newest thing along Broadway and that she should hitch her wagon to his mercurially rising star, saying: "He's the whole country squeezed into one pair of pants!" (Not so incidentally, the affable, congenial and supportive Erlanger that Barbier so warmly essays is a filmic myth in that that producer was one of the most stingy, severe, unfair and cold-hearted producers on Broadway.) Whorf manages to get a reluctant Cagney to meet with Manning in her dressing room while she changes for her next act. Manning tells both of them that she is not interested in the pedestrian musical shows they create and that she is grateful to get away from the noise and hoopla of Broadway by going to her home in New Rochelle, New York, every night after she performs, even though, she admits, her home is only forty-five minutes from Broadway. The aloof Manning then leaves Cagney and Whorf in the dressing room as she goes on to the stage to perform in her next act. While Manning is performing, Cagney, sitting at an upright piano in the dressing room, works intensively to produce a new song, which Whorf presents to Manning when she returns to her dressing room. Whorf begs Manning to look at the song that Cagney has worked so hard to produce, one titled "Forty-Five Minutes from Broadway," the title of which Cagney has satirically filched from Manning's own caustic remarks. Manning looks over the sheet music and is very much impressed with this song. To further impress her, Whorf seizes from Cagney's music case another song Cagney has composed, "Mary's a Grand Old Name," showing this to Manning. Cagney protests, as he has written that song for his now wife, Leslie, and expects that Leslie will sing that song in his next musical produc-

James Cagney and S. Z. Sakall *in Yankee Doodle Dandy,* **1942.**

tion. Manning, however, is captivated by the song, which clinches her deal with Whorf and Cagney. A short time later, Cagney arrives home with a huge bouquet of flowers and a large box of candy, presenting these gifts to Leslie. She thanks him and he then works up his courage to tell her that "I gave your song to Fay Templeton." Instead of the sadness or anger he expects from his wife, Leslie fondly kisses him, telling him that she knew he would do that and it is fine with her. They then both attend the theater where Manning performs that song and others in Cagney's new musical. At the end of the show, Leslie tells Cagney that Manning has his song, but that she has the man who created it. The show is a smash hit as were many others created by this show business dynamo (Cohan penned forty plays and composed more than 1,000 songs.) At one point, Cagney steps from a theater showing one of his hit musicals and encounters his great contemporary, Eddie Foy Sr. (1856-1928), who is played by Eddie Foy Jr., and the two get into a competitive conversation over each other's accomplishments (one of the many very funny scenes in this film). Foy finally tells Cagney that he, Foy, has accomplished something that Cagney has not surpassed, that being his siring seven children, known as the Seven Little Foys. We then see in montage many sequences showing Cagney appearing with his family members and Leslie in other shows, until Huston and DeCamp retire and his sister Jeanne Cagney marries, leaving Cagney to go on performing alone. He writes a bad serious play, "Popularity," and then sends a wire to the press apologizing for it, asking that the public not see it and announces its closing. In 1917, the U.S. becomes involved in WWI (1914-1918) and Cagney goes to a recruiting office and attempts to enlist, but he is told that he is too old. He tries to convince recruiting officers otherwise by demonstrating his energetic and acrobatic skills as a dancer, but he is told that he is too important to go "over there" to fight and must do what he can with his talent to help his country in this crisis. Cagney is later seen sitting alone on the stage of a theater slowly composing his new great song, "Over There," and he next appears on an outdoor stage with Langford, who plays Nora Bayes (1880-1928), the famous singer of that day who made that song popular. Before Cagney and Langford sit dozens of U.S. Army soldiers, and to whom Cagney and Langford sing this inspiring song, encouraging the soldiers to join in at the last chorus, which ends with a rousing cheer. That stirringly patriotic song is then heard as a montage of American troops are shown embarking for France, marching to and fighting at the front, and then returning home. By this time, Cagney's mother and sister die, and Cagney is finally called to Huston's bedside where he says a sad farewell to his dying father. Huston becomes somewhat delirious toward the end, talking to his grown son as if it were years earlier and where he warns his son, as if he were still playing "Peck's Bad Boy," not to upstage his mother and sister and reminds him to thank the audience for the finish.

Jeanne Cagney, James Cagney, Joan Leslie, Walter Huston and Rosemary DeCamp in *Yankee Doodle Dandy,* **1942.**

As Huston dies, Cagney (in one of his most touching scenes in any of his many fine films), holds his father's hands to his own face and, weeping, says: "I said my father thanks you, my mother thanks you, my sister thanks you and I thank you." (This emotionally wrenching scene where Cagney weeps at the passing of Huston so moved the hardboiled Curtiz that that draconian director found himself shedding tears, something he later denied, albeit his camera crew members all stated that they saw those stingy tears dripping from Curtiz's cheeks.) Cagney is later shown severing his partnership with Whorf as he takes an around-the-world tour with wife Leslie and they then retire to a farm. One night, Leslie tells Cagney that Whorf has been calling and needs his help to appear in a new Kaufman and Hart play based on President Roosevelt. Cagney appears reluctant to even discuss it, but Leslie urges him to go back on the stage. He finally agrees, admitting that he had earlier called Whorf and agreed to play the part of the President. In flash-forward, we now see Cagney concluding the chronicle of his life for Young (President Roosevelt, who is shown from the back only in slight profile) as they sit in an office at the White House. Cagney thanks Young for bestowing the Medal of Honor upon him and assures him that America will win the present WWII (1939-1942). After he leaves Young's office, Cagney begins to walk down the long staircase at the White House leading to its front entrance and, halfway, begins to tap his way downward while performing delightful "wings" (reminding us all of the precocious boy who still lives within him) until reaching the bottom floor where smiling servants hand him his hat and coat. He steps onto Pennsylvania Avenue where a crowd lines the street to see U.S. Army troops marching past, all singing "Over There" as they are ostensibly en route to a theater of war. Many in the crowd march alongside the soldiers, and Cagney joins them, striding alongside Faylen, a corporal, who asks him: "What's the matter, old-timer? Don't you remember this song?" Cagney replies: "It seems that I do." He then joins in singing that moving song with tears welling in his eyes for the finale. Cagney's performance is nothing short of spectacular, one where he rivets the viewer in every frame in both his dramatic and musical scenes. His singing and dancing is packed with robust energy, and his unique choreography is a sight to behold, as he appears to be a lighter-than-air puppet dancing via invisible strings. Some of his incredible dancing movements include one split second action where he literally balances on his toes as he taps and buck-and-wings his way across a stage and up its supporting wall. There was never a dancer like this, his style all his own. His memorable performance deservedly won for him his one and only Oscar as Best Actor, he being the first actor to win such an award for a musical performance. Cagney is wonderfully supported by a talented cast, and Huston, DeCamp, Jeanne Cagney, Leslie, Whorf and many others superbly enact their roles. Curtiz, one of the great action directors and the workhorse at

Warner Brothers, presents a fast-moving story and where he packs action, humor, and some great musical ensembles into its memorable scenes. The film, in addition to Cagney's award, won Oscars for Best Music (Cohan) and Best Sound (Nathan Levinson). The film received Oscar nominations for Best Picture; Best Director (Curtiz); Best Supporting Actor (Huston); Best Film Editing (Amy); and Best Original Screenplay (Buckner, Joseph). the film was a box office smash, earning almost $6 million in its original release against a budget of about $600,000. After its many rereleases, the film earned more than $12 million, becoming the studio's largest grossing film to that date. A thirty minute radio adaptation was aired by The Screen Guild Theater on October 19, 1942, with Cagney reprising his role. Songs: "The Yankee Doodle Boy" (1904; George M. Cohan), "Give My Regards to Broadway," (1904; George M. Cohan), "Over There" (1917; George M. Cohan), "You're a Grand Old Flag" (1906; George M. Cohan), "Mary's a Grand Old Name" (1906; George M. Cohan), "Forty-Five Minutes from Broadway" (1906; George M. Cohan), "So Long, Mary" (1906; George M. Cohan), "Harrigan" (1908; George M. Cohan), "I Was Born in Virginia" (1906; George M. Cohan), "The Warmest Baby in the Bunch" (1896; George M. Cohan), "Oh, You Wonderful Girl" (1911; George M. Cohan), "Blue Skies, Gray Skies" (1927; George M. Cohan), "The Belle of the Barbers' Ball" (1908; George M. Cohan), "Like the Wandering Minstrel" (1927; George M. Cohan), "Nellie, I Love You" (1922; George M. Cohan), "The Man Who Owns Broadway" (1909; George M. Cohan), "Molly Malone" (1927; George M. Cohan), "Billie" (1928; George M. Cohan), "In a Kingdom of Our Own" (1929; George M. Cohan), "You Remind Me of My Mother" (1922; George M. Cohan), "Off the Record" (1937; music: Richard Rodgers; lyrics: Lorenz Hart; additional lyrics [1942]: Jack Scholl), "At a Georgia Camp Meeting" (1897; Kerry Mills), "While Strolling through the Park One Day" (1884; Ed Haley), "Columbia, the Gem of the Ocean" [aka: "The Red, White and Blue"] (1843: David T. Shaw; arranged by Thomas A. Becket Sr.), "Keep Your Eyes on Me (Dancing Master)" (Jerry Cohan), "Good Luck, Johnny" (1942; music: M.K. Jerome; lyrics: Jack Scholl), "Little Johnny Jones" (1942; music: M.K. Jerome; lyrics: Jack Scholl), "All Aboard for All Broadway" (1942; music: M.K. Jerome; lyrics: Jack Scholl), "(I Wish I Was in) Dixie's Land" (1860; Daniel Decatur Emmett), "The Battle Hymn of the Republic" (music [1856]: William Steffe; lyrics [1862]: Julia Ward Howe), "Auld Lang Syne" (traditional Scottish folksong; lyrics [1788]: Robert Burns), "When Johnny Comes Marching Home" (1863; Louis Lambert [Patrick Sarsfield Gilmore]), "America, My Country Tis of Thee" (1832; Lowell Mason, using 1744 music composed by Harry Carey for "God Save the King"; lyrics: Samuel Francis Smith), "The Love Nest" (1920; music: Louis A. Hirsch; lyrics: Otto A. Harbach), "Jeepers Creepers" (1938; music: Harry Warren; lyrics: Johnny Mercer). ***Author's Note***: This was Cagney's favorite film and proved to be one of his biggest moneymakers, earning him more than $500,000 in profit sharing, in addition to his $150,000 salary per picture under his then contract with Warner Brothers. The story for this film was shopped through some of the Hollywood studios by Cohan himself, until Jack Warner bought the rights to the performer's life, and Cohan personally asked that Cagney portray him. "I felt that Mr. Cohan was giving me a great honor by selecting me to play him in **Yankee Doodle Dandy**," Cagney told this author. "He was a living institution on Broadway and throughout America. We all wanted to do justice to his great achievements and we tried very hard to do that when we made that picture." A lot of nonsense was gossiped years later that Cagney wanted to do this film to prove his patriotism because he had been accused of being a communist at one time. This was not the case as Cagney, though a liberal who had supported President Franklin D. Roosevelt throughout the 1930s, never had any ties to the Communist Party. Such false claims were made through equally unreliable Internet sites decades after this film was produced. Cagney's dancing style, as stunningly shown here, was unique in the history of film musicals. "Nobody I knew could ever dance like Cagney," dancer Gene Kelly told this author. "Though he appears to be stiff-legged, he moves about with such ease and combines leaps and running steps with his taps that only a master ballet dancer might achieve. He did all of that in **Yankee Doodle Dandy** and I could never figure out how it did it without breaking his ankles." Dancer Fred Astaire was equally amazed at Cagney's dancing performance in this film, telling this author: "No one, but no one, equaled that unique dancing style of his in **Footlight Parade** [1933], and, especially, in **Yankee Doodle Dandy**. He started out as a hoofer in musical revues off Broadway, but he made up his own steps as he went along. I once asked Jimmy [Cagney] about where he picked all of that up and he told me that he used to watch a street dancer on the Lower East Side of Manhattan when he was a kid and copied that guy's movements. Well, that street performer must have been one hell of a dancer!" In one of my visits with Cagney, this author spent a little time with the actor while he was working out in his exercising area (at his residence in Martha's Vineyard), which consisted of a small room with mirrors and a ballet bar, and Cagney, even at an advanced age, performed some very strenuous ballet movements. Cagney stated to this author: "I was left to my own devices in **Yankee Doodle Dandy**, especially when it came to the musical numbers. Curtiz [director Michael Curtiz] let me alone when it came to the dancing as he had very little knowledge about that and let others handle the ensembles and choreography. I added little bits of business [improvised dance movements] in my numbers as we went along, this move and that. When I walked down the stairs in the White House, I added those small wings [dance steps] to liven up that scene because I knew that Cohan used to do that, even when he was walking down a street, a little jig or a jog here and there. That man was always full of music. I think he could hear a song coming out of a taxi's horn or a whistle shrieking from a factory. America loved his songs because they had wonderful melodies that went straight into your heart, the kind of songs that took you by the hand and walked you to the front door of your mother's home. I think I understood Mr. Cohan very well as we were both Irish and everything is family with the Irish, and we show all of that in **Yankee Doodle Dandy**: The hard-working father [Huston] who loves his son enough to spank him when he gets out of line, the mother [DeCamp] who forgives every boyish brag, the sister [Jeanne Cagney], who smiles even when she gets upstaged by a swaggering brother, and the sweet girl [Leslie], who becomes the loving wife. Mr. Cohan's music naturally worked into that family story because, in a way, it is the story of this country." Cagney spent six months researching the subject, spending a great deal of time with Cohan to learn the showman's mannerisms and traits, his style of speech and even how he walked and gestured with his hands. Cagney, when performing his musical numbers, adopted the same kind of song delivery for which Cohan was known, a recitative style for lyrics that was half talking and half singing. When the film was complete, Cagney agreed to attend its premiere (something he had refused to do for any of his previous films). Cohan, by that time, was too ill to attend as he had been battling intestinal cancer for months. He was shown the film at a private screening, and, after it concluded, Cohan smiled and said: "My God! What an act to follow!" He died five months later on November 5, 1942. Cagney would play Cohan once more in a cameo appearance in **The Seven Little Foys**, 1955, where Bob Hope played the senior Foy and where both Cagney and Hope do an energetic table top dance together. Leslie was only seventeen when appearing in this film and credibly ages four decades before the film ends, thanks to some marvelous makeup creations. She was still attending school during this production, and her classroom attendance caused some shooting delays. DeCamp, who plays Cagney's mother, was actually eleven years younger than Cagney when making this film. Though Cagney liked the original Buckner and Joseph script, he asked the Epstein twins (Julius J. and Philip G. Epstein, who co-scripted **Casablanca**, 1942, with Howard Koch the same year) to see what they might add. "The screenplay was very tight," Julius J. Epstein told this author, "so we added only a few lines of dialog. We kept looking for holes, but we couldn't find any and told Jimmy [Cagney]

Joan Leslie and James Cagney in *Yankee Doodle Dandy,* **1942.**

that. 'You mean it's perfect?' he asked when we handed the script back to him with our changes. 'It is now,' I said." Of special note are the sumptuously mounted musical ensembles that recreate Cohan's many Broadway productions, all authentic to costumes and sets. Among the many exceptional talents appearing here is the outstanding singer Frances Langford, who not only appears on-screen as Nora Bayes, singing "Over There" with Cagney, but who also sings a medley of Cohan songs through a nostalgic montage sequence depicting Cohan's greatest Broadway musical hits. Although Cagney portrays President Franklin D. Roosevelt in a few dancing scenes from the Kaufman and Hart musical, it was then not widely known (when that 1937 production appeared on Broadway and at the time of this 1942 film) that Roosevelt could not walk, let alone dance, as he had been stricken with polio many years earlier and had been confined to a wheelchair (actor Jack Young, playing Roosevelt in scenes with Cagney, never leaves his chair), although Roosevelt could stand and slowly move upright when wearing two ten-pound iron braces, one affixed to each leg. This great man endured the strain and pain of such movements throughout the four terms of his presidency. "I backed Roosevelt from the first time he ran as President," Cagney told this author, "and a more courageous human being did not exist." Many other actors, as well as Cagney, have portrayed George M. Cohan in other films, including **After the Ball**, 1957 (Mark Baker); **Bob Hope Presents the Chrysler Theater**, 1963-1967 (TV series; "The Seven Little Foys," 1964 episode: Mickey Rooney); **The Ed Sullivan Show**, 1948-1971 (TV series; "Toast of the Town," 1968 episode; Joel Gray); **George M!**, 1970 (made-for-TV; Joel Gray); **The Kraft Music Hall**, 1967-1971 (TV series; "Give My Regards to Broadway," 1967 episode: Bobby Darin); **Parade of Stars**, 1983 (made-for-TV; David Cassidy); **Producer's Showcase**, 1954-1957 (TV series; "Mr. Broadway," 1957 episode: Mickey Rooney); and **The Seven Little Foys**, 1955 (James Cagney). Franklin D. Roosevelt has also been portrayed by many other actors in other films, including **Action in the North Atlantic**, 1943 (Art Gilmore); **Albert Einstein**, 1990 (TV series; Ernst Heise); **Annie**, 1982 (Edward Herrmann); **Annie**, 1999 (made-for-TV; Dennis Howard); **Back Stairs at the White House**, 1979 (TV miniseries; John Anderson); **Beau James**, 1957 (Dick Nelson); **The Beginning or the End**, 1947 (Godfrey Tearle); **Bertie and Elizabeth**, 2002 (made-for-TV; Robert Hardy); **Bonanno: A Godfather's Story**, 1999 (made-for-TV; Vlasta Vrana); **Churchill and the Generals**, 1981 (made-for-TV; Arthur Hill); **Churchill: The Hollywood Years**, 2004 (Henry Goodman); **Cradle Will Rock**, 1999 (himself in archive footage); **Crossings**, 1986 (TV miniseries; Jack Denton); **Day One**, 1989 (made-for-TV; Donald Ogden Stiers); **De Gaulle**, 2006 (TV series; Robert Hardy); **Edge of Darkness**, 1943 (voiceover of Jack Young); **Einstein**, 1984-1985 (TV miniseries; Gerard Buhr); **Eleanor and**

Loene Carmen and Ben Mendelsohn in *The Year My Voice Broke*, 1987.

Franklin, 1976 (made-for-TV; Edward Herrmann); **Eleanor and Franklin: The White House Years**, 1977 (made-for-TV; Edward Herrmann); **Enola Gay: The Men, The Mission, The Atomic Bomb**, 1980 (made-for-TV; Stephen Roberts); **The Fall of Berlin**, 1952 (Oleg Frelikh); **F.D.R.**, 1965 (TV miniseries; Charleton Heston voiceover); **F.D.R.: A One-Man Show**, 1987 (Chris Elliott); **F.D.R.: The Last Year**, 1980 (made-for-TV; Jason Robards Jr.); **F.D.R.: The Man in the White House**, 1982 (made-for-TV; Robert Vaughn); **The First Front**, 1949 (Nikolai Cherkasov); **First to Fight**, 1967 (Stephen Roberts); **For All: Springboard to Victory**, 1998 (Guaracy Picado); **Freedom to Speak**, 1982 (TV miniseries; Laurence Luckinbill); **The Great Battle**, 1973 (Stanislaw Jaskiewicz); **Hyde Park on Hudson**, 2012 (Bill Murray); **Ike: The War Years**, 1979 (TV miniseries; Stephen Roberts); **Into the Storm**, 2009 (made-for-TV; Len Cariou); **J. Edgar**, 2011 (David A. Cooper); **J. Edgar Hoover**, 1987 (made-for-TV; David Ogden Stiers); **Katastrofa w Gibraltarze**, 1984 (Andrzej Krasicki); **The Kennedys of Massachusetts**, 1990 (TV miniseries; Josef Sommer); **Kingfish: The Story of Huey P. Long**, 1995 (made-for-TV; Bob Gunton); **The Last Bastion**, 1984 (TV miniseries; Warren Mitchell); **The Long Days of Summer**, 1980 (made-for-TV; Stephen Roberts); **MacArthur**, 1977 (Dan O'Herlihy); **Mission to Moscow**, 1943 (Jack Young); **Murrow**, 1986 (made-for-TV; Robert Vaughn); **Pearl Harbor**, 2001 (Jon Voight); **The Pigeon That Took Rome**, 1962 (Dick Nelson; scenes deleted); **The Private Files of J. Edgar Hoover**, 1977 (Howard Da Silva); **The Revenge of Al Capone**, 1989 (made-for-TV; Donald Craig); **The Right Man**, 1960 (made-for-TV; Art Carney); **Roosevelt and Truman**, 1977 (made-for-TV; Art Evans); **Spies**, 1992 (made-for-TV; Chris Nubel); **Sunrise at Campobello**, 1960 (Ralph Bellamy); **This Is the Army**, 1943 (Jack Young); **Truman**, 1995 (made-for-TV; Lee Richardson, and himself, archive footage, funeral procession); **The Untouchables**, 1959-1963 (TV series; "The Unhired Assassin, Part II," 1960 episode: Paul Frees); **The Untouchables**, 1993-1994 (TV series; "Radical Solution," 1993 episode: Richard Henzel); **The Victors and the Vanquished**, 1949 (Nikolai Cherkasov); **Victory**, 1984 (Algimantas Masiulis); **Voyagers!**, 1982-1983 (TV series; Nicholas Pryor); **War and Remembrance**, 1988 (TV miniseries; Ralph Bellamy); **Warm Springs**, 2005 (made-for-TV; Kenneth Branagh); **Winchell**, 1998 (made-for-TV; Christopher Plummer); **The Winds of War**, 1983 (TV miniseries; Ralph Bellamy); **World War Two: Behind Closed Doors**, 2008 (TV series; Bob Gunton); **World War II: When Lions Roared**, 1994 (made-for-TV; John Lithgow); and **Yalta**, 1984 (made-for-TV; Robert Rimbaud); **p**, Hal B. Wallis; **d**, Michael Curtiz; **cast**, James Cagney, Joan Leslie, Walter Huston, Richard Whorf, Irene Manning, George Tobias, Rosemary DeCamp, Jeanne Cagney, Frances Langford, S.Z. Sakall, Eddie Foy Jr., George Barbier, Walter Catlett, Minor Watson, Chester Clute,

Douglas Croft (George at age thirteen), Odette Myrtil, Patsy Lee Parsons, Leslie Brooks, Charles Drake, Bill Edwards, Joyce Reynolds, Audrey Long, Jo Ann Marlowe, Henry Blair (George at age seven), Capt. Jack Young (Franklin D. Roosevelt), Pat Flaherty, William B. Davidson, Frank Faylen, Tom Dugan, Wallis Clark (Theodore Roosevelt in musical montage for "You're a Grand Old Flag"), James Flavin, Murray Alper, Lon McCallister, Dolores Moran, Art Gilmore (voiceover for Franklin D. Roosevelt), Sally Sweetland (singing voiceover for some of Leslie's songs); **w**, Robert Buckner, Edmund Joseph, (not credited) Julius J. Epstein, Philip G. Epstein (based on a story by Buckner); **c**, James Wong Howe; **m**, George M. Cohan, Leo F. Forbstein; **ed**, George Amy; **art d**, Carl Jules Weyl.

The Year My Voice Broke ★★★★ 1987; Australia; 103m; Kennedy Miller/Adventure Pictures; Color; Drama/Romance; Children: Unacceptable: (MPAA: PG-13); **DVD**. Superbly acted, sensitive coming-of-age film begins in a dilapidated small town in New South Wales, Australia, during the summer of 1962. Taylor, a fifteen-year-old boy, becomes heartsick when Carmen, his best friend and first love, who is a year older, develops a crush on Mendelsohn, an older soccer player at their high school. Mendelsohn is the town's troublemaker, and Taylor tries to send Carmen telepathic messages that would make him irresistible to her. Carmen, however, has grown to be more sexually aware of her feelings, which she doesn't understand very well. The film follows Taylor's fantasies of being a hero, especially Carmen's hero, and Carmen's struggle with losing her girlhood innocence as she begins to become a young woman. Though petty thief Mendelsohn is disliked by Taylor, the unruly boy redeems himself in Taylor's eyes by coming to his aid in fending off school bullies. The fun days end and become more serious when Carmen tells Taylor she has become pregnant (after she has slept with Mendelsohn at an abandoned house). Taylor nobly offers to marry her, but Carmen tells him that she does not want to wed anyone. Meanwhile, Mendelsohn steals a car and is sent to a detention center. Taylor then finds a locket that leads him to investigate Carmen's mysterious background, discovering that her mother was a local prostitute. He finds the woman's grave and also learns that she ironically died while trying to give birth alone to Carmen in the same deserted house where Carmen and Mendelsohn had their assignation. Mendelsohn then escapes the detention center, stealing a car and committing an armed robbery where he wounds a store clerk. Police pursue him, but he manages to return to his hometown where he reunites with Carmen at the abandoned house, learning that she is pregnant with his child. Their poignant reunion is cut short when police arrive and Mendelsohn flees, crashing his car and dying the next day. Carmen vanishes, but Taylor finds her at the abandoned house where she has miscarried and is suffering from hypothermia. He takes her to a hospital and there reluctantly tells her about her biological mother. Carmen, once she has regained her health, decides to leave town as the shame of her past there will, she believes, haunt her forever. She decides to move to a big city to remake her life, and Taylor accompanies her to the train station, giving her all the money he has saved, and they promise to keep in touch. After she departs, Taylor goes to the place where he, Carmen and Mendelsohn had met together and Taylor carves onto the face of a rock the names of Carmen, Mendelsohn and his own. In an epilogue, Taylor, by now an adult, states that he never again saw Carmen. Duigan directs this moving tale with great skill, drawing startling performances from Taylor, Carmen, Mendelsohn and the rest of the cast members. Though this bittersweet film is reminiscent of **Summer of '42**, 1971, it offers a separate and fascinating story line. Songs/Music: "The Lark Ascending" (Ralph Vaughan Williams), "The Man Who Shot Liberty Valance" (music: Burt Bacharach; lyrics: Hal David), "Corinna Corinna" (Bo Carter, Mitchell Parish, J. Mayo Williams), "That's the Way Boys Are" (Mark Barkan, Ben Raleigh), "I Remember You" (music: Victor Schertzinger; lyrics: Johnny Mercer), "Apache" (Jerry Lorden), "Temptation" (music: Nacio Herb Brown; lyrics: Arthur Freed), "Tower of Strength" (music: Burt

Bacharach; lyrics: Bob Hillard), "One Hundred Pounds of Clay" (Kay Rogers, Luther Dixon, Bob Elgin), "Diana" (Joe Sherman, Paul Anka), "Get a Little Dirt on Your Hands" (Bill Anderson), "Pastorale" (Theme for "Blue Hills" radio serial, by Ronald Hamner), "Daisy Bell" ("Bicycle Built for Two," Harry Dacre). *Author's Note*: This film was originally planned as part of a TV series but was shot on 35mm and theatrically released to earn about $500,000, albeit it saw limited distribution. The film was shot on location at Braidwood, New South Wales, Australia. **p**, Terry Hayes, George Miller, Doug Mitchell; **d&w**, John Duigan; **cast**, Noah Taylor, Loene Carmen, Ben Mendelsohn, Graeme Blundell, Lynette Curran, Malcolm Robertson, Judi Farr, Tim Robertson, Bruce Spence, Harold Hopkins, Nick Tate, Vincent Ball; **c**, Geoff Burton; **m**, Christine Woodruff; **ed**, Neil Thumpston; **prod d**, Roger Ford; **spec eff**, Roger Cowland.

The Year of Living Dangerously ★★★★ 1982; U.S.; 115m; MGM; Color; Adventure/Romance/War Drama; Children: Unacceptable (MPAA: PG); **DVD**; **VHS**; **IV**. Though this superlative adventure tale offers many divergent subplots that encompass politics, romance and even mysticism, it nevertheless offers a gripping tale with impactful performances from Gibson, Weaver, Hunt, Murphy and others. The story opens in 1965, when Gibson, an eager, young wire service reporter for an Australian network, arrives in Jakarta, Indonesia, to cover the ongoing crisis between the government of Sukarno (1901-1970), the Communist Party of Indonesia (PKI) and the right-wing Muslim military. He quickly proves unsuccessful in getting any important news in that his predecessor departs without introducing Gibson to any of his important news contacts. The members of the close-knit foreign correspondent community he meets are reluctant to share any of their contacts with the present diplomatic corps, all of them greedily competing for news items. Hunt, however, an intelligent Australian-Chinese dwarf, who is also a news photographer, takes a liking to Gibson and teams up with him, introducing Gibson to important government officials. While Gibson writes his stories, Hunt provides the photos to accompany them. Hunt, a female impersonating a male, is a master of shadow puppetry known in the Javanese theater as *wayang kulit*, showing Gibson the technique (and thereby providing the metaphor for this story). Hunt further introduces Gibson to Weaver, an attaché in the British embassy, who provides Gibson with important inside stories. In the process, Gibson and Weaver fall in love. Weaver then learns of an attempted communist coup and where the Chinese Communists are about to arm the PKI. Fearing for Gibson's life, she tells him about the impending coup and urges him to leave the city. Gibson, however, gone greedy for news, betrays Weaver's confidence and writes a major story about the imminent coup. This alienates Weaver and Hunt from him, and the only friends remaining loyal to him are Murphy, an American journalist, and his assistant and driver, Roco, who is a secret member of the PKI. When Hunt sees that Sukarno allows many of his Indonesian subjects to go hungry in the crisis, she protests by hanging a sign from the window of her hotel room that reads: "Sukarno: Feed Your People!" Security police raid the hotel and throw Hunt from the window. She is found by Gibson and dies in his arms; Hunt's death is also witnessed by Weaver. Gibson is nevertheless still obsessed with getting the big story and travels northward into the wilds against the protests of Roco. When he insists on getting information from a group of soldiers, one of them slams a rifle butt into his face, knocking Gibson senseless; he suffers a damaged retina. Gibson finds shelter in Hunt's residence where Roco later visits him and tells him that the coup has failed. Gibson, however, can only think about the fact that he is about to lose the sight of his eye unless he gets medical attention and begs Roco to drive him to the airport so that he can flee Jakarta, which is still in chaos. Roco complies and Gibson boards the last plane leaving from the city, and he is reunited with Weaver, both departing for an uncertain future. Weir employs a good deal of mysticism by repeatedly showing Hunt's shadow puppets, and Hunt narrates arcane lines about Indonesia's exotic and unpredictable history, all of

Mel Gibson and Sigourney Weaver in *The Year of Living Dangerously,* **1982.**

this adding, instead of detracting, to the overall suspense of this exciting thriller. Gibson gives a fine performance of a man too selfish for his own professional and personal good while Weaver is empathetically attractive and Hunt is often riveting as the wisest member of a foolish lot of journalists. Hunt won an Oscar as Best Supporting Actress for her cross-dressing performance. The film did very well at the box office, earning more than $12 million in its initial release against a budget of $6 million. **The Killing Fields**, 1984, which deals with a news photographer in Cambodia during Pol Pot's bloody reign of terror, explores the same subject as this absorbing film. Songs: "Beim Schlafengehen" (1948; from "Four Last Songs" by Richard Strauss), "Excerpts from L'enfant" (1979; from "Opera Sauvage" by Vangelis), "(There'll Be Bluebirds Over) The White Cliffs of Dover" (1941; music: Walter Kent; lyrics: Nat Burton), "Whole Lotta Shakin' Goin' On" (1955; Dave "Curlee" Williams, James Faye "Roy" Hall), "Long Tall Sally" (1956; Little Richard), "Beautiful Ohio Waltz" (1919; music: Robert A. King; lyrics: Ballard MacDonald), "Be-Bop-A-Lula" (1955; Gene Vincent, Bill "Tex" Davis), "Ain't That Lovin' You Baby" (1956; Jimmy Reed), "Tutti-Frutti" (1955; Little Richard [Richard Wayne Penniman], Dorothy LaBostrie). *Author's Note*: This was the first Australian film to receive full financing from a Hollywood studio (MGM). Some of its scenes were shot in the Philippines to assimilate the setting for Indonesia, but, after death threats (in written notes) were made to Weir and Gibson, ostensibly from Islamic sources that thought the film was anti-Islamic, the production moved to Australia where it was completed. The film was banned in Indonesia, but was eventually shown there in 2000 after dictator Suharto (1921-2008) resigned two years earlier. Excessive violence prohibits viewing by children. **p**, James McElroy; **d**, Peter Weir; **cast**, Mel Gibson, Sigourney Weaver, Linda Hunt, Michael Murphy, Bill Kerr, Noel Ferrier, Bembol Roco, Paul Sonkkila, Ali Nur, Dominador Robridillo; **w**, David Williamson, Weir, C.J. Koch (based on the novel by Koch); **c**, Russell Boyd (Panavision; Metrocolor); **m**, Maurice Jarre; **ed**, William Anderson; **art d**, Herbert Pinter; **spec eff**, Danny Dominguez.

Year of the Dragon ★★★ 1985; U.S.; 134m; Dino De Laurentiis; MGM; Color; Crime Drama; Children: Unacceptable (MPAA: R); **DVD**; **VHS**; **IV**. Taut thriller sees Rourke as a racist veteran of the Vietnam War (1961-1975), who becomes a New York police captain and cracks down on organized crime in Chinatown. He hates Asian people since his war service, and after he is assigned to Chinatown, he breaks the rules to go after Lone, who is head of the Chinese Triad (mafia) in the city and where both men use extreme violence to achieve their goals. As Lone wages war with competing Triad leaders, he also attempts to establish a truce with his underworld enemies. Meanwhile, Rourke es-

Mickey Rourke and John Lone in *Year of the Dragon*, 1985.

tablishes a relationship with Ariane, a Chinese TV reporter crusading against the Triads. To punish her, Lone rapes Ariane and then murders Rourke's wife, Kava, offenses over which Rourke vows revenge. Rourke selects rookie Chinese NYPD officer Dun to infiltrate Lone's operations by having him become a worker in one of Lone's restaurants. Dun learns about a huge drug shipment Lone is about to receive, but he is betrayed by Kehler, a crooked cop who informs Lone about Dun's true identity. Dun is killed, but Rourke has by then learned about the drug shipment and intercepts Lone and his bodyguard as they arrive at the waterfront to receive that shipment. Kehler sees Rourke and tries to ambush him, but Rourke shoots and kills the corrupt cop and then gets into a shootout with Lone and his bodyguard. In the melee, Lone accidentally kills his bodyguard before fleeing across a train bridge with Rourke in hot pursuit. Realizing that he is trapped, Lone turns and advances toward Rourke, both men firing wildly at each other. Lone is hit and collapses, and Rourke compassionately hands him his gun so that Lone can use it to commit suicide rather than go to prison. Grim and uncompromising, this crime yarn is well directed by Cimino, who draws exceptional performances from Rourke, Lone, Ariane and the rest of the cast members. The almost nonstop action obfuscates any viewer's desire for a literate script, as its dialog and story line basically appeals to thrill-seeking adolescents, the kind of mindless mayhem writer-director Stone would later employ to otherwise brilliantly depict the futility of war in making **Platoon**, 1986. The film did not do as well as expected at the box office, earning more than $18.7 million in its initial release and without fully recouping its budget of more than $24 million. Songs: "Dream Dance" (Lucia Hwong), "Symphony No. 2, Resurrection, 5th Movement" (Gustav Mahler), "Uphill/Peace of Mind" (Frederick Knight), "Infatuation" (Rod Stewart, Duane Hitchings, Roland Robinson). *Author's Note*: Cimino thought to write the script for this film, but his many projects prompted him to ask Stone to write the script. Stone reportedly agreed on the condition that producers additionally finance Stone's forthcoming film, **Platoon**, 1986, a deal which producer De Laurentiis allegedly later reneged upon. Cimino originally also thought to cast either Jeff Bridges or Nick Nolte as the hard-driving police captain, but he hired Rourke for that role after seeing Rourke's performance in **The Pope of Greenwich Village**, 1984. Rourke later claimed that his role had been written for Paul Newman or Clint Eastwood, who, according to Rourke, turned down the part. The realistic sets that represent NYC's Little China and the Orient were shot in sound stages in Wilmington, N.C. The title of this film, **Year of the Dragon**, stems from one of the twelve-year cycles of animals that appear in the Chinese zodiac, related to the Chinese calendar. Extreme violence prohibits viewing by children. Chinese Triads had been depicted in many other films, including **A Better Tomorrow**, 1986; **A Bittersweet Life**,

2005; **The Chinese Connection**, 1972; **The Corruptor**, 1999; **The Last Dragon**, 1985; **Shanghai**, 2010; and **Wake of Death**, 2004. **p**, Dino De Laurentiis; **d**, Michael Cimino; **cast**, Mickey Rourke, John Lone, Ariane, Leonard Termo, Dennis Dun, Ray Barry, Caroline Kava, Jack Kehler, Eddie Jones, Joey Chin, Victor Wong, Pao Han Lin, K. Dock Yip, Daniel Davin; **w**, Cimino, Oliver Stone (based on the novel by Robert Daley); **c**, Alex Thomson; **m**, David Mansfield; **ed**, Francoise Bonnot, Noelle Boisson; **prod d**, Wolf Kroeger; **art d**, Vicki Paul; **set d**, Robert Drumheller; **spec eff**, Jeff Jarvis.

The Yearling ★★★★ 1946; U.S.; 134m; MGM; Color; Drama; Children: Acceptable; **DVD**; **VHS**; **IV**. This wonderfully sensitive family drama begins in 1878 as pioneers Peck, Wyman and their preteen son, Jarman, struggle to make their small farm productive in the wilds beyond Lake George, Florida. Although Jarman has a strong and warm father-son relationship with Peck, he feels somewhat unloved by Wyman. Somber and even dour, Wyman holds her emotions tightly in reserve. She has lost three children, and their deaths have made her fearful that Jarman, too, might perish, if she gives him any motherly love. Peck, an uncomplicated and hardworking man, has but one dream and that is to produce a crop so bountiful that he will have enough money to sink a well close to their log-cabin farmhouse so that Wyman will not have to carry water from the nearby stream. Lonely and seeking affection, Jarman asks his parents if he can keep a pet. Peck agrees, but Wyman objects. Meanwhile, a rattlesnake bites Peck and Peck kills a doe, using its heart and liver to draw out the snake's poison. The doe's fawn is now orphaned, and Jarman asks if he can adopt the yearling as his pet. Overriding his wife's objections, Peck allows Jarman to keep the fawn, but warns him that he must be responsible for it and that the fawn must be set free to return to the wilds once it matures. Jarman ponders about a name to give to his pet and goes to see his only friend, Gift, but finds to his sadness that Gift has died. Gift's mother, Wycherly, however, tells Jarman that if Gift were still alive, the name he would have suggested would have been "Flag," to indicate the deer's waving white tail. Jarman and the yearling deeply bond so that they are soon inseparable, the fawn going everywhere with the boy. A year later, however, the animal has grown to the point where it presents a constant nuisance to the family. It tramples the small tobacco crop, destroys fences and eats much of the newly grown corn, thus depriving the family of much-needed food. Peck tells Jarman that, to keep the animal, he must not only replant the corn crop but must build a higher fence to protect it from his pet. Jarman struggles to build the fence, and when Wyman sees him laboring to achieve his task, she joins with him in reconstructing that higher fence. The grown deer, however, manages to get over the fence and again destroys the corn crop. Peck this time tells Jarman that he must take his pet into the woods and shoot the animal in order that the family can survive. The traumatized Jarman obeys, but, when he gets Flag into the woods, he cannot bring himself to kill his beloved pet and chases him away, hoping that the deer will now fend for itself. Flag, however, knows no home except the farm and the love of the boy that has nurtured him and returns to the farm where it again invades the corn crop. Wyman resolves to end the dilemma by shooting the deer herself, but her poor aim only wounds the animal. At Peck's insistence, Jarman is now faced with ending his pet's suffering by killing it, which, with tears streaming down his eyes and sobs choking his throat, he does. Bitter and angry, Jarman runs away and remains in the wilds for three days while his parents agonize over his disappearance. Travers, a kindhearted boat captain, finds the famished and dehydrated Jarman and returns him to his home. He and Peck embrace, resolving the anger that Jarman has harbored for his father and then learns that Wyman, frantic over his absence, is not present and is still searching for him. Jarman, exhausted, goes to sleep in his bed for the first time in days, and when Wyman returns and finds him home, she rushes to the boy, embracing him and showing him all the love she has withheld from him in the past, now believing that she will not lose her only child. Jarman, too, has learned the hard facts of life, for, like the yearling he has loved, he has grown up, realizing that his fine parents have not been cruel, only pragmatic in their universal affection for him and where they have compelled him to face his responsibilities. Brown unfolds this sensitive tale in the most prosaic terms, and its plain-speaking characters are poignantly portrayed by Peck, Wyman, Jarman and the rest of the cast members. There are no frills to this hardscrabble story where it is painfully evident in every frame that the family members must work very hard to survive from day to day in a challenging wilderness. Brown presents some very fine action scenes, particularly when Peck and Jarman are shown hunting and their dogs encounter a savage bear that injures one of their best hounds, the camera excitingly following on the heels of these two highly animated hunters as they splash through swamplands to track down that ferocious bear. The richly warming color of the film stunningly recreates the brilliant hues of the backwaters of Florida through the old Technicolor process. The film won Oscars for Best Cinematography (Rosher, Smith, Arling), and Best Art Direction (Gibbons, Groesse; set decoration: Willis). Jarman received a special Academy Juvenile Award that honored his sensitive and moving portrayal. It also received Oscar nominations for Best Picture; Best Director (Brown); Best Actor (Peck); Best Actress (Wyman); and Best Film Editing (Kress). The film was a box office smash, earning more than $7.5 million in its initial release against a budget of more than $3.8 million and became MGM's top grossing film for the year. The story had a thirty-minute radio adaptation that was aired by the Screen Guild Theater on January 6, 1947, with Peck, Wyman and Jarman reprising their roles. A sixty-minute radio adaptation was aired by Lux Radio Theater on January 19, 1948, with Peck, Wyman and Jarman reprising their roles. The story was again aired in a thirty-minute adaptation by Stars in the Air on February 7, 1952, with Peck reprising his role, supported by Jean Hagen. The story was remade as **The Yearling**, 1994 (made-for-TV), starring Peter Strauss and Jean Smart. Songs/Music: "Florida Suite" (1887; Frederick Delius), "Koanga" (1895; Frederick Delius), "Appalachia: Variations on an Old Slave Song" (1902; Frederick Delius), "A Midsummer Night's Dream: Scherzo" (1843; Felix Mendelssohn-Bartholdy). *Author's Note*: MGM bought the film rights to the 1938 best-selling novel by Rawlings and began production of the story in 1941 with Spencer Tracy in the role of the father and Anne Revere as the mother (she would play matriarchs in such films as **The Song of Bernadette**, 1943; **National Velvet**, 1944; **Body and Soul**, 1947; **Gentleman's Agreement**, 1947; **The Great Missouri Raid**, 1951, as the mother of Frank and Jesse James, and **A Place in the Sun**, 1951). Newcomer Gene Eckman was cast in the role of the boy and Roddy McDowall as his best friend while Victor Fleming directed. The production, however, encountered endless problems, including an uncontrollable plague of mosquitoes while the film was being shot on location in Florida, along with the fact that, over many months, Eckman grew too big. Fleming did not think the boy's thick southern accent worked well with that of Tracy and Revere and hated the script from John Lee Mahin. Further, the fawn used in this version grew even faster than Eckman and was constantly replaced by another animal, creating vexing problems for trainers. Moreover, producer Franklin and Fleming were constantly at odds as to how to shoot the film until Fleming bowed out. Pantheon director King Vidor was then hired, but he met with the same problems that had confronted Fleming. "Everyone was miserable down there [in Florida]," Vidor told this author. "The first thing Spence [Spencer Tracy] said to me is 'I want to get the hell out of here—the insects are eating us alive and the weather is so damp that when I get up in the morning I think that I have been sleeping in a tub of warm water!' The script had so many holes in it that, after I insisted that it be rewritten and got no approval, I had to quit. Too bad, the novel is such a great story, but then Clarence [Brown] went at it some years later and turned it into a masterpiece, but he had a much better script to work with." After an expenditure of more than $500,000, the production closed down (and Eckman never again appeared in any film). The onset of WWII (1939-1945) caused MGM to put the project on hold as the

Claude Jarman Jr. and pet fawn in *The Yearling*, 1946.

studio began to devote its fare to war films and musicals, although producer Franklin refused to give up on the story, thinking to cast Roddy McDowall as the boy. The story was dusted off after the war ended, and, in 1945, Osborn was assigned to rewrite the script. Brown was assigned to direct the film with Peck, Wyman and Jarman in the leading roles. Peck was very busy at this time, as he appeared in this production at the same time he began preparation for his role in **Duel in the Sun**, 1946. Peck told this author: "While I was working in Florida on **The Yearling**, I was traveling to Texas to appear in **Duel in the Sun**, and I had to keep adjusting to my two separate characters, one being a hardworking farmer and loving father, the other being a rotten-to-the-heart cowboy who guns down anybody he dislikes. Audiences applauded one character and hissed at the other. It was quite a year." Wyman had reservations about playing the part of the mother who withholds her love from her son and appears to be unsympathetic to him and his pet. "It was the meanest role I ever played," Wyman told this author. "My own daughter saw the picture and was so angry with my performance that she hardly said a word to me for weeks after that." Brown told this author that he had selected Jarman to play the role of the boy after testing thousands of children in a nationwide hunt that was highly promoted by the studio. Brown stated to this author: "He had long hair when I tested him because he had been too busy at school to get a haircut, but that, and his lean and lanky frame, gave him the look I thought best suited the farm boy portrayed in the story." The film was shot on location in the Prairie Wilderness Park of Florida's Ocala National Forest. In acknowledgment of the film a hiking path in the park was called The Yearling Trail. Dozens of trained animals were employed in the making of this film, including five fawns that had to be replaced during the production to conform to the animal's aging described in the story. The first fawn found by Jarman was only three days old, the animal having been rescued from a local forest fire. "The animal menagerie we had to keep when we were making that picture," Brown told this author, "would have made a dozen zookeepers busy night and day." That animal collection also included 126 deer, eighty-three chickens, fifty-three wild birds, thirty-seven dogs, thirty-six pigs, eighteen squirrels, seventeen buzzards, seventeen raccoons, nine black bears, eight rattlesnakes, four horses and one owl. Other historical or period films set in Florida include **Cabeza de Vaca**, 1991; **Cross Creek**, 1983; **Davy Crockett: King of the Wild Frontier**, 1955; **Distant Drums**, 1951; **Drums of Destiny**, 1937; **Hurricane Island**, 1951; **Juke Girl**, 1942; **Reap the Wild Wind**, 1942; **Rosewood**, 1997; **Seminole**, 1953; **Shark River**, 1953; **Warm Springs**, 2005 (made-for-TV); **Wind across the Everglades**, 1958; and **Yellowneck**, 1955. **p**, Sidney Franklin; **d**, Clarence Brown; **cast**, Gregory Peck, Jane Wyman, Claude Jarman Jr., Chill Wills, Clem Bevans, Margaret Wycherly, Henry Travers, Forrest Tucker, Donn Gift, June Lockhart, Matt Willis, Dan White,

Sandra Dorne and William Sylvester in *The Yellow Balloon*, 1953.

George Mann, Arthur Hohl, Joan Wells, Jeff York, Victor Kilian, Housely Stevenson, Chick York; **w**, Paul Osborn (based on the novel by Marjorie Kinnan Rawlings); **c**, Charles Rosher, Leonard Smith, Arthur Arling (Technicolor); **m**, Herbert Stothart; **ed**, Harold F. Kress; **art d**, Cedric Gibbons, Paul Groesse; **set d**, Edwin B. Willis; **spec eff**, Warren Newcombe.

The Yellow Balloon ★★★★ 1953; U.K.; 76m; Marble Arch Productions/Allied Artists; B/W; Drama; Children: Unacceptable; **DVD**. This fascinating film noir entry is set in London that still shows the ravages of WWII (1939-1945), many of its districts still in rubble from German bombings and the destruction of Nazi V-1 and V-2 rockets. Ray, a twelve-year-old boy, lives in one of these ravaged districts in London's East End and he has his heart set on purchasing a yellow balloon from a street peddler. His father, More, gives Ray a shilling to buy that balloon, but, when Ray sees that his close friend, Fenemore, has bought the balloon from the vender, he impulsively snatches it away from his friend and flees with the yellow balloon. Fenemore runs after Ray, and the chase leads the two boys into a large house that has been left in ruins from a bombing during the war. Ray races to an upper floor and Fenemore follows, only to slip and fall to his death. Terrified at what has happened, Ray scrambles down to try to help Fenemore, but then realizes that the boy is dead. Witnessing all of this is Sylvester, a petty thief, who has been hiding in the bombed-out house. Sylvester quickly convinces the naïve Ray that, even though Fenemore's death was the result of an accident, the police will not see his demise in that light and will think that Ray killed his friend by pushing him to his death and will charge him with murder. Sylvester, however, promises Ray that they can escape together and that Sylvester will keep what he knows about Fenemore's death a secret, but only if Ray does his criminal bidding. Thus blackmailed, Ray reluctantly steals from his parents, giving the loot to Sylvester, his conduct discovered by More and Ryan, which perplexes his compassionate father and mother. Sylvester then uses Ray as a decoy as he commits a robbery, but the holdup goes wrong and Sylvester kills the pub owner. Realizing that Ray has witnessed the murder and can implicate him, Sylvester decides to eliminate the child. Ray, however, realizes this peril and begins running for his life. As Sylvester chases him, Ray runs into de Banzie, this kindhearted woman taking him to her flat where Ray blurts out his association with Sylvester and tells her about the robbery-murder. De Banzie then takes Ray home in a taxi, dropping him off in front of his residence before she goes to the nearest police station to report the crime to officers. Meanwhile, as Ray enters his apartment building, Sylvester, hiding in the shadows of the entranceway, seizes him and takes Ray to an abandoned underground railway where he plans to kill him. Ray, however, breaks free, and a wild chase

through the underground system ensues. By this time, police have been informed by de Banzie about Sylvester and Ray, and when officers do not find the boy at home, they begin a desperate search for him, putting them onto the trail of Sylvester and his intended victim. When it appears that Sylvester is about to catch the fleeing Ray and while officers close in on him, the culprit frantically looks to escape. In his wild flight, however, Sylvester falls into a shaft and to his doom. Ray is then reunited with More and Ryan for a harrowing finish. Director Thompson presents a taut thriller, carefully building its narrowing story line while increasing suspense and tension to the very end of its nail-biting climax. Ray is exceptional as the boy harassed by his own sense of guilt into becoming the tool of a calculating criminal. That cold-hearted character is superbly enacted by Sylvester, while More, Ryan, de Banzie, and the rest of the cast members provide standout performances under the gritty, stark lensing from the gifted Taylor. *Author's Note*: The British Board of Censors thought this film much too frightening for viewing by children and prohibited anyone under the age of sixteen from seeing this film when it was released in England in 1952. Ironically, its star, Ray, who was thirteen when enacting in the film and fourteen when it was released, was thus prevented from seeing his own performance. Exhibitors protested to the censorship, stating that the film was not as shocking as the censors claimed it to be, adding that the board's decree was ruining their business as the exhibitors mostly relied upon family patronage. The board relented the following year in 1953 and lifted its ban, allowing children under the age of sixteen to see this film if they were accompanied by their parents, a modus operandi later adopted by the MPAA. Similar films where boys are manipulated by their imagination, wrong sense of guilt, or by others to act irrationally include **Decision before Dawn**, 1951; **The Fallen Idol**, 1949; **The Hunted** (aka: **The Stranger in Between**), 1952; **The Night of the Hunter**, 1955; **The Rocking Horse Winner**, 1950; and **The Window**, 1949. **p**, Victor Skutezky; **d**, J. Lee Thompson; **cast**, Andrew Ray, Kathleen Ryan, Kenneth More, Bernard Lee, Stephen Fenemore, William Sylvester, Marjorie Rhodes, Peter Jones, Brenda de Banzie; **w**, Thompson, Anne Burnaby (based on a story by Burnaby); **c**, Gilbert Taylor; **m**, Philip Green; **ed**, Richard Best; **art d**, Robert Jones; **spec eff**, George Blackwell.

Yellow Canary ★★★ 1944; U.K.; 84m; Herbert Wilcox Productions; RKO; B/W; Spy Drama; Children: Unacceptable; **DVD**. High production values and superior acting from a talented cast provides an above-average and exciting espionage tale, replete with competing British and Nazi agents operating during WWII (1939-1945). Neagle, a wealthy, attractive British socialite, publicly announces her support for Adolf Hitler (1889-1945) and his Nazi regime, a political stance that alienates her among most of her peers since it is 1940 and England and Germany are at war. (The film opens with Neagle appearing to signal German planes on where to drop their bombs on London and where she ostensibly acts as a Nazi collaborator, the title referring to Neagle's supposed cowardice in betraying her own country.) To escape the constant social harassment and condemnation she receives, Neagle books passage on a ship sailing from England to Halifax, Nova Scotia, Canada. She quickly attracts the attentions of two male passengers, Greene, who is traveling incognito but who is secretly a British naval intelligence (NID) officer, and Lieven, a Polish aristocrat. When Neagle learns that Greene may be a British agent, she rejects his advances and concentrates on Lieven. While the ship is midway to its destination, it is stopped by *Prinz Eugen*, a German heavy cruiser. Officers from this warship board the passenger vessel and arrest a man they think to be Greene, taking him on board the cruiser and sailing away. The man seized, however, proves to have been an imposter as Greene then emerges from hiding. After arriving in Halifax, Lieven introduces Neagle to his mother, Mannheim, but the two women get into an argument over Neagle's strong support of the Nazi regime and her pronounced admiration for Hitler. Neagle then attempts to sever her relationship with Lieven, but he then tells her that he is a secret agent working for German intelligence (Abwehr), and Neagle again renews her association with him. Lieven easily enlists Neagle into his spy ring, and she soon learns that Mannheim is not Lieven's mother, but the spymaster who heads that cabal of Nazi agents. She then learns that Mannheim and her cohorts have planned a devastating coup that will destroy the military and civilian port of Halifax, then a center supplying much-needed war materials to England. Neagle discovers that the agents have arranged for a cargo ship to be replaced by another vessel packed with explosives, and when that ship sails into the port of Halifax with a convoy of other vessels, it will be detonated and destroy the port. Mannheim, knowing that Greene is a British agent and that Neagle is still in touch with him, orders Neagle to call Greene and lie to him by telling him that the Nazi agents plan to blow up the British ocean liner *Queen Mary*. That ruse, Mannheim believes, will divert the British by sending its agents to protect the great British passenger ship, instead of scrutinizing the ship loaded with explosives about to arrive in the port. Neagle, however, has been playing a double game with the Nazi agents because her true loyalties are to England and she has been a British agent all along. She calls Greene and exposes the actual plot and Canadian bombers swoop down and blow up the munitions ship before it can enter Halifax Harbor. Learning that Neagle has betrayed him and his cohorts, Lieven shoots Neagle just before Greene arrives to rescue her. Neagle, however, survives since the bullet struck the cigarette case Greene has earlier given her as a gift. With the Nazi spy ring smashed, Neagle and Greene are now free to marry and begin a life together. Wilcox directs this spy thriller with a firm hand, presenting its clever twists and turns with considerable skill while Neagle gives an outstanding performance as a double agent, receiving standout support from Greene, Lieven, Mannheim and others. Of special note is the wonderful character actor Rutherford, who steals every scene in which she appears and delivers a classic line when dryly stating: "Wouldn't it be nice to do something violent?" This film is not related to a 1963 production of the same name. *Author's Note*: Much of this film is based on real people and events that made headlines before and during the war. To emphasize the dangerous activities of spies and saboteurs operating in England early in WWII, the film opens with a newspaper headline announcing a bomb attack at Buckingham Palace. Actually, seven separate such attacks occurred, the most serious taking place on the morning of September 13, 1940, when a powerful bomb damaged the memorial of Queen Victoria and the palace chapel and when George V and Queen Elizabeth were in residence. The character so expertly essayed by Neagle is based upon British socialite Unity Mitford (1914-1948), who was notorious for her pro-Nazi leanings and who had personally met with Hitler more than once. She was living in Munich, Germany, when England and Germany declared war, and, upon hearing this news, Mitford attempted suicide, but survived. She was invalided back to England but never recovered. Her sister, Diana Mitford (1910-2003), was married to Sir Oswald Mosley (1896-1980), who was the leader of the fascist movement in England (BUF, 1932-1940), and who was imprisoned in England in 1940 when his Nazi organization was dissolved (he was released in 1943). Diana Mitford married Mosley in the home of Nazi propaganda chief, Joseph Goebbels (1897-1945), and Nazi leader Adolf Hitler (1889-1945) was present at the wedding ceremonies. Like her husband, Diana Mitford was imprisoned in England for her Nazi activities for three years. The plan to destroy the port of Halifax outlined in this film is based upon the horrific explosion that all but destroyed that port during WWI (1914-1918) on December 6, 1917. At that time, the SS *Mont-Blanc*, a French freighter packed with munitions, collided with the SS *Imo*, a Norwegian freighter, causing a cataclysmic explosion (the equivalent of 2.9 kilotons of TNT), killing more than 2,000 people and injuring 9,000 others while destroying a goodly portion of the city. Greene was, at the time of this production, serving in the British army and was given a furlough to make this film. Neagle became romantically involved with the director, Wilcox, during this production, and, upon its completion, the couple married, a union that lasted until Wilcox's death in 1977. Other films depicting German agents of the Abwehr include

Anna Neagle and Richard Greene in *Yellow Canary*, 1944.

Above Suspicion, 1943; **All through the Night**, 1942; **Arch of Triumph**, 1948; **Back-Room Boy**, 1942; **Background to Danger**, 1943; **Berlin Correspondent**, 1942; **Betrayed**, 1954; **Bulldog Sees It Through**, 1940; **Carve Her Name with Pride**, 1958; **Circle of Deception**, 1961; **Cloak and Dagger**, 1946; **Clouds over Europe** (aka: **Foreign Sabotage**; **Q Planes**), 1939; **Commandos Strike at Dawn**, 1942; **Confessions of a Nazi Spy**, 1939; **Contraband** (aka: **Blackout**), 1940; **Cottage to Let** (aka: **Bombsight Stolen**), 1943; **Count Five and Die**, 1958; **Counter-Espionage**, 1942; **Decision Before Dawn**, 1951; **The Desert Fox: The Story of Rommel**, 1951; **Desperate Journey**, 1942; **The Eagle Has Landed**, 1977; **Enemy Agent**, 1940; **Enemy of Women**, 1944; **Eye of the Needle**, 1981; **Eyes in the Night**, 1942; **The Falcon's Brother**, 1942; **5 Fingers**, 1952; **Foreign Correspondent**, 1940; **The 49th Parallel** (aka: **The Invaders**), 1942; **Hidden Enemy**, 1940; **The Hitler Gang**, 1944; **Hotel Reserve**, 1946; **The House on 92nd Street**, 1945; **I See a Dark Stranger**, 1947; **Journey into Fear**, 1943; **The Lady Vanishes**, 1938; **The Lady Vanishes**, 1979; **Law and Disorder**, 1940; **Let George Do It!** (aka: **To Hell with Hitler**), 1940; **Lightning Conductor**, 1938; **The Man from Morocco**, 1946; **Man Hunt**, 1941; **The Man Who Knew Too Much**, 1935; **The Man Who Never Was**, 1956; **Ministry of Fear**, 1944; **Nazi Agent**, 1942; **Night Boat to Dublin**, 1946; **Night of the Fox**, 1990 (made-for-TV); **The Night of the Generals**, 1967; **Night Train to Munich**, 1940; **Odette**, 1951; **Operation Crossbow**, 1965; **Operation Secret**, 1952; **O.S.S.**, 1946; **Pimpernel Smith**, 1942; **Remember Pearl Harbor**, 1942; **Rogue Male**, 1977; **Sabotage**, 1937; **Saboteur**, 1942; **Sealed Cargo**, 1951; **The Seventh Survivor**, 1942; **Sherlock Holmes and the Secret Weapon**, 1942; **Sherlock Holmes in Washington**, 1943; **Shining Through**, 1992; **Snowbound**, 1949; **Sons of the Sea**, 1939; **Spies of the Air**, 1940; **Spy for a Day**, 1940; **Spy Ship**, 1942; **Squadron Leader X**, 1943; **Stalag 17**, 1953; **They Came to Blow Up America**, 1943; **They Met in the Dark**, 1945; **13 Rue Madeleine**, 1947; **36 Hours**, 1965; **This Was Paris**, 1942; **To Be or Not to Be**, 1942; **The Torso Murder Mystery** (aka: **Traitor Spy**), 1940; **Tower of Terror**, 1942; **Triple Cross**, 1966; **The Two-Headed Spy**, 1959; **Unseen Enemy**, 1942; **Waterfront**, 1944; **Where Eagles Dare**, 1968; and **The Whip Hand**, 1951. **p&d**, Herbert Wilcox; **cast**, Anna Neagle, Richard Greene, Nova Pilbeam, Albert Lieven, Lucie Mannheim, George Thorpe, Marjorie Fielding, Margaret Rutherford, Franklin Dyall, Claude Bailey, Ian Fleming; **w**, Miles Malleson, De Witt Bodeen, P.M. Bower; **c**, Max Greene; **m**, Clifton Parker; **ed**, Vera Campbell; **art d**, William C. Andrews.

Yellow Earth ★★★ 1988; China; 89m; Guangxi Films/International Film Circuit; Color; Drama; Children: Unacceptable; **VHS**. Well-made

Virginia Bruce and Robert Montgomery in *Yellow Jack,* **1938.**

tale sees Wang as a communist soldier, who is sent to the remote countryside to collect folk songs for the Communist Revolution. He stays with a peasant family and learns that the happy songs he was sent to collect do not exist, and those he does find are filled with hardships and suffering. Before he returns to the army, he promises to come back for Xue, a girl who has become spellbound by Wang's talk of the freedom women have under communist rule and where she longs to join the Communist Army. Though blatant propaganda is evident, fine acting overcomes the manipulative political message. Mature themes prohibit viewing by children. (In Mandarin; English subtitles.) **d,** Kaige Chen; **cast,** Xueyin Wang, Bai Xue, Quiang Liu, Tuo Tan; **w,** Ziliang Zhang, Chen (based on the novel by Lan Ke); **c,** Yimou Zhang; **m,** Jiping Zhao.

Yellow Jack ★★★ 1938; U.S.; 83m; MGM; B/W; Drama; Children: Unacceptable. This taut drama, based on historical events, begins in Cuba just after the end of the Spanish-American War (1898). Stone, who plays Major Walter Reed (1851-1902), a brilliant U.S. Army physician who believes that, rather than direct contact between human beings, Yellow Fever (called "Yellow Jack") plaguing U.S. army troops and civilians on the island comes from mosquitoes. After consulting with Coburn, who plays Dr. Carlos Finlay (1833-1915), and studying Coburn's research, Stone becomes convinced that mosquitoes are the source of the dreaded disease. Stone's convictions, however, bring nothing but ridicule from his medical peers, although he is encouraged to follow his beliefs by fellow physicians O'Neill, who plays Dr. William Crawford Gorgas (1854-1920), and Hale, who plays Major General Leonard Wood (1860-1927), then governor general of Cuba. However, Stone needs to prove his theory through a dangerous procedure where human guinea pigs volunteer to be quarantined within screened-in barracks swarming with these insects. When word goes round in the ranks of the U.S. soldiers stationed in Cuba, Montgomery thinks twice about being one of those volunteers as he is involved with army nurse Bruce. When seeing some gravediggers about to intern some of the victims of Yellow Fever, Montgomery states to himself: "O'Hara…suppose you do give your life [in volunteering to be a guinea pig]? It will be a noble thing, but will you be able to say so?" Montgomery hesitates until he witnesses the death of the sacrificing Hull, another tireless physician battling the disease. With Bruce's urging, Montgomery volunteers and, more or less, shames four others in his company, Levene, Ebsen, Henry and Curtis, to join him in Stone's perilous medical experiment. Three volunteers, Ebsen, Levene and Henry, are confined in "a dirty" cabin, while Montgomery and Curtis are confined to a supposedly "antiseptic" cabin where Curtis is bitten by a mosquito carrying the disease and Montgomery is not. Curtis grows ill, but Montgomery, although in close contact with Curtis, remains healthy, so Stone concludes that he may be

immune or that his belief that the disease is not contracted from one human to another is a medical certainty. To be sure, Montgomery further agrees to have himself bitten by a mosquito carrying Yellow Jack, and he, too, then grows ill, to confirm Stone's conviction. Montgomery teeters between life and death, but Bruce remains steadfastly at his side to see him recover, and they can now make plans for a life together. The film details the exact procedures conducted by Reed and his medical staff in Cuba, thanks to the meticulous care from director Seitz. The performances from Montgomery and his fine supporting cast members are superlative, and the script is both witty and inspiring, etching its characters in realistic, down-to-earth terms. A radio adaptation was aired by Philip Morris Playhouse on September 5, 1941. The play and screenplay were adapted for TV episodes aired under the title of "Yellow Jack" by Celanese Theater in 1952 and Producers' Showcase in 1955. Songs: "Battle Hymn of the Republic" (music [1856]: William Steffe; lyrics [1862]: Julia Ward Howe), "Goodbye Cuba" (unknown composer), "On the Banks of the Wabash, Far Away" (1897; Paul Dresser), "You're in the Army Now" (1917; music: Isham Jones; lyrics: Tell Taylor, Ole Olsen). *Author's Note*: The play upon which this film is a based opened on Broadway on March 6, 1934, and ran for seventy-nine performances with James Stewart in the role of the Irish sergeant, a part that brought him to the attention of MGM. "The studio signed me to a contract at that time," Stewart told this author, "and it was a lucky thing for me because I was not sure, until that happened that I wanted to spend the rest of my life as an actor. I was not surprised that I did not get the role of the sergeant in the film version of that story because I knew MGM wanted to have one of their leading men star in it. I was then at the bottom of the MGM totem pole and had to work my way up to star status. I thought that Bob [Montgomery] did a splendid job in enacting that role, although he used an Irish accent that I did not even attempt in the stage version." Montgomery told this author that "I used that accent because I knew that the character I was playing was an Irish immigrant with a thick brogue and I wanted to be as authentic as possible. I used a Welsh accent a year before when I appeared in a picture called **Night Must Fall** [1937], but that character was far from the good-hearted sergeant I played in **Yellow Jack**, as he was a deranged woman killer." Sam Levene was the only member of the film cast who had appeared in the stage version. Other films depicting Yellow Fever include **Blood and Honor**, 2000; **Captain Horatio Hornblower**, 1951; **The Courage to Love**, 2000 (made-for-TV; New Orleans); **Jezebel**, 1938 (New Orleans); **The Liberator**, 2014; **Magnificent Doll**, 1946; **A Man Alone**, 1955; **The Navy Lark**, 1959; **The Ordeal of Dr. Mudd**, 1980 (made-for-TV; Dr. Samuel Alexander Mudd; Dry Tortugas); **The Planter**, 1917; **The Prisoner of Shark Island**, 1936 (Dr. Samuel Alexander Mudd; Dry Tortugas); **The Rifleman**, 1958-1963 (TV series; "Panic," 1959 episode); **Telephone Time**, 1956-1958 (TV series; "The Quality of Mercy," 1958 episode: Dr. Samuel Alexander Mudd; Dry Tortugas); **Washington Square**, 1997; **Westinghouse Desilu Playhouse**, 1958-1960 (TV series; "The Case for Dr. Mudd," 1958 episode: Dr. Samuel Alexander Mudd; Dry Tortugas); **White Legion**, 1936 (Panama Canal); and **Women of Valor**, 1977 (made-for-TV). Other films profiling human guinea pigs in medical experiments include **After the Truth**, 1999 (Joseph Mengele); **And the Violins Stopped Playing**, 1981 (Joseph Mengele); **The Andromeda Strain**, 1971; **The Andromeda Strain**, 2008 (TV miniseries); **The Boys from Brazil**, 1978 (Joseph Mengele); **Brain Twisters**, 1991; **Bug**, 2006; **The Caller**, 1987; **The Chairman**, 1969; **Commando Mengele**, 1987 (Joseph Mengele); **Control**, 2004; **Cube Zero**, 2005; **Danger 5**, 2011- (TV series; "Lizard Soldiers of the Third Reich," 2012 episode; "Revenge of the Lizardmen," 2015 episode: Joseph Mengele in both episodes); **Devil's Plot**, 1948; **Dr. Ehrlich's Magic Bullet**, 1940; **Dr. Jekyll and Mr. Hyde**, 1920; **Dr. Jekyll and Mr. Hyde**, 1931; **Dr. Jekyll and Mr. Hyde**, 1941; **The Experiment**, 2002; **Fantastic Voyage**, 1966; **Flesh for Frankenstein**, 1974; **Frozen Scream**, 1975; **The German Doctor**, 2014 (Joseph Mengele); **Green Light**, 1937; **The Grey Zone**, 2002 (Joseph Mengele);

Heroes of the North, 2010-2011 (TV series; Joseph Mengele); Human Experiments, 1979; The Hydric Zone, 2015- (TV series; "Rise of the Mutant Wetlands," 2015 episode: Joseph Mengele); I.Q., 1994; Ilsa: She Wolf of the SS, 1975; The Invisible Man, 1933; The Invisible Man Returns, 1940; Kessler, 1981 (TV miniseries; Joseph Mengele); The Mad Doctor of Market Street, 1942; The Mad Monster, 1942; The Man with Nine Lives, 1940; The Manster, 1959; Marathon Man, 1976 (role model for Joseph Mengele); Maruta 2: Laboratory of the Devil, 1992 (Japanese eugenics on captives in Manchuria during WWII); Men behind the Sun, 1989 (Japanese eugenics on captives in Manchuria during WWII); Out of the Ashes, 2003 (made-for-TV; Joseph Mengele); The Passing, 1985; Playing for Time, 1980 (made-for-TV; Joseph Mengele); Push, 2009; Saru, 2003; Schindler's List, 1993 (Joseph Mengele); The Story of Louis Pasteur, 1936; Subject Two, 2006; Surf Nazis Must Die, 1987 (Joseph Mengele); Terminal Choice, 1985; Tobor the Great, 1954; The Unborn, 2009 (Joseph Mengele); Walking the Dead, 2000- (TV series; "Yahrzeit: Part 1," "Yahrzeit: Part 2," 2007 episodes: Joseph Mengele); Whiffs, 1975; Wit, 2001 (made-for-TV); Women's Camp 119, 1977; and Wyrmwood: Road of the Dead, 2014. p, Jack Cummings; d, George B. Seitz; cast, Robert Montgomery, Virginia Bruce, Lewis Stone, Andy Devine, Henry Hull, Charles Coburn, Buddy Ebsen, Henry O'Neill, Janet Beecher, William Henry, Alan Curtis, Sam Levene, Jonathan Hale, Stanley Ridges, Phillip Terry, C. Henry Gordon; w, Edward Chodorov (based on the play by Sidney Howard, Paul de Kruif and the book *Microbe Hunters* by de Kruif); c, Lester White; m, William Axt; ed, Blanche Sewell; art d, Cedric Gibbons.

Yellow Sands ★★★ 1938; U.K.; 68m; Associated British Pictures Corp.; B/W; Comedy/Drama; Children: Unacceptable; Unavailable. Offbeat but fascinating film begins with Tempest, who is an aging spinster residing in a British fishing village. Of all of her many relatives, she decides that, after she dies, her fortune of $20,000 will go to her idealistic left-wing nephew, Newton. A Communist, Newton has always been in contention with Tempest's financial dealings, labeling her a capitalist. He intends to use the money for a communal shelter to aid the poor. However, when he realizes he will only get a small amount for himself, he begins to wonder if he ought to go through with his munificent plan. He is further beset with constant harassment from a bevy of other relatives who have been cut out of Tempest's will. Brenon presents a clever story that is enlivened with superior performances, particularly by the dynamic Newton, and whose obsessive unpredictability provides sustaining interest. *Author's Note*: The film is based on a play that opened in London in 1925 that ran for 610 performances before moving to Broadway where it opened at the Fulton Theater on September 10, 1927, running for only twenty-five performances. The theater production was noted for the London debut of the distinguished British actor Ralph Richardson. The film version saw the debut of a youthful Roddy McDowall. p, John W. Gossage, Walter C. Mycroft; d, Herbert Brenon; cast, Marie Tempest, Belle Chrystall, Wilfrid Lawson, Robert Newton, Patrick Barr, Amy Veness, Coral Browne, Drusilla Wills, Muriel Johnston, Roddy McDowall; w, Rodney Ackland, Michael Barringer (based on the play by Adelaide Phillpotts, Eden Phillpotts; c, Walter J. Harvey; m, Hubert Bath; ed, Flora Newton.

Yellow Sky ★★★★ 1948; U.S.; 98m; FOX; B/W; Western; Children: Unacceptable; DVD; VHS. Gritty, realistic western is set in 1867 and begins when Peck leads a band of men in robbing a bank. The outlaws flee with a posse of U.S. Cavalry troopers in pursuit. When the outlaws ride into the vast salt flats (of Death Valley, California), the pursuers give up their chase, believing that no one can survive in that scalding furnace of a desert. (This predicament is earlier shown in John Ford's classic **3 Godfathers**, 1948, and its two predecessors, where three bank robbers are chased into a desert without water by their pursuers, who allow them to go their way, convinced that they will not long survive.)

Gregory Peck and Charles Kemper in *Yellow Sky,* 1948.

The outlaws, however, have no choice and continue traveling across the blistering, parched desert, husbanding their precious water. They dismount and walk their exhausted horses, Peck spilling some water from his canteen onto his kerchief to wipe away the saline rime from the mouth of his horse. (He thus indicates that he among these hard cases is the only one with common sense and compassion, the others too selfish, indifferent or stupid to understand the misery of their mounts or the necessity to preserve their horses to later enable them to survive.) Peck, Widmark, Russell, Morgan, Arthur and Kemper manage to survive the scorching heat and waterless salt flats, coming upon a ghost town called "Yellow Sky." They quench their thirst at a nearby water hole and then find Baxter, a young woman, living with her grandfather, Barton, at an old house at the outskirts of the town. While the outlaws recuperate, Widmark investigates the area and then tells Peck that he believes Barton and Baxter are working on a gold mine somewhere in the area, but Peck seems uninterested as he has become attracted to Baxter. Peck goes to the old house, and Baxter confronts him with a rifle, warning him to keep his distance. He makes the mistake of moving closer to her, and she shoots off his hat, the bullet grazing his scalp. Peck manages to disarm Baxter and then attempts to embrace and kiss Baxter, but she fights wildly in fending him off, saying: "Did anyone tell you that you stink?" Russell, the meanest of the gang, later sees Baxter arriving at the water hole where the gang is camped to fetch a bucket of water. When she does so, Russell assaults her, but Arthur, the youngest of the outlaws, who looks upon Baxter with protective idealism, interrupts, knocking Russell down. The more powerful Russell knocks Arthur into the shallow water hole, holding his head beneath the water. Peck comes upon the scene and orders Russell to let Arthur go. Russell refuses and Peck knocks Russell down and then holds *his* head beneath the water, letting him up at the last minute so that Russell can finally breathe. Widmark later convinces the outlaws that Peck can no longer think straight because of his emotional commitment to Baxter and attempts to take over the gang. Peck, however, confronts them all and tells them that he is still their leader and is willing to back up his authority with his sixguns. At that moment, a shot rings out, one fired by Baxter, which narrowly misses Widmark, and the outlaws dive for cover. Realizing that the gang intends to rob them of the gold they have labored so hard to mine, Baxter and Barton have taken to the hills and are hiding in some high rocks, both armed and ready to battle the outlaws. In an exchange of gunfire, Barton is wounded in the leg and Peck then arrives under a white flag of truce, telling Baxter that he has not only taken a bath in the water hole, but he has combed his hair "right around that part you gave me [when grazing his scalp with a bullet]." He tells her and Barton that they can come to an agreement about fairly splitting up the gold and Baxter and Barton surrender, returning to their house. Barton, in

Gregory Peck in *Yellow Sky*, 1948.

bed, attempts to negotiate a deal, and Peck finally agrees that he and his followers will take only half of the gold Barton and Baxter have mined. Barton agrees and then reveals the location of the sealed-up mine, to which the outlaws go and begin reopening its shaft. Meanwhile, a horde of Apaches ride into the ghost town, and its chief meets with Barton, an old friend. Peck sneaks back to the house to see Barton talking with the chief before sending him away. The Apaches then depart, and Peck learns that Barton has convinced the Indians to return to their reservation instead of taking to the warpath. Peck realizes that Barton could have easily asked his Apache friends to attack and wipe out the outlaws, but that he has done nothing of the kind. In gratitude for such protection, Peck guarantees Barton and Baxter that he will keep his promise to give them both fifty percent of their gold, even though Widmark and Russell have no intention of upholding that agreement. In fact, Widmark has crept onto the porch outside the room where Peck and Barton are talking and, after hearing that Peck intends to give a portion of gold to its original owners, fires a shot at Peck, which narrowly misses him. Peck then sets out after Widmark, who has also taken shots at Russell and the others in order to keep all the gold for himself. Arthur is fatally shot in the exchange of gunfire, and Peck orders Kemper to carry the youthful outlaw into the house where they, along with Barton and Baxter, are pinned down by Morgan, who has been ordered to his post by Widmark. Peck has Kemper call out to Morgan, telling him to join them in the house and he does. Now Peck only must deal with Widmark and Russell. By this time, Widmark has fled, with Russell pursuing him after Widmark has fired and missed Russell. The two end up in a dark, deserted saloon in the ghost town, and Peck enters the place where all three exchange shots at each other. Baxter, who is now attracted to Peck, goes to the saloon and finds Widmark and Russell dead and Peck wounded, the scene ending as she frantically calls out for help. We next see three reformed outlaws, Peck, Morgan and Kemper, riding back into the very town where they had robbed the bank and they enter that bank once again, holding the employees at gunpoint. Peck then delivers to the bank president the exact amount of money they had earlier stolen. Before leaving, Peck asks Guy, a woman in the bank, if he can purchase the hat she is wearing and she happily agrees. Peck, Morgan and Kemper then ride into the countryside where Baxter and Barton are waiting for them. Peck arrives to tell Baxter that, though it hurt them to do it, they returned every cent they had stolen from the bank. He then gives Baxter the hat he has purchased; Baxter, who has worn men's clothing throughout the film and has appeared to be a tomboy, is touched by this small gift that sparks her femininity and she dons the hat with Peck's grinning approval. They then all mount their horses and ride off together, ostensibly to continue law-abiding lives. Wellman offers an offbeat but very compelling western with realistic, down-to-earth characters, all with diver-

gent personalities. Peck is rewarding as the resolute outlaw with a sense of honor and decency, which is shared by the youthful Arthur, and, reluctantly, by the rather dim-witted Morgan and Kemper. Widmark and Russell are superb as the two sinister, greed-obsessed villains, ready to betray and kill anyone standing in their avaricious ways. Baxter, too, is exceptional as a callous woman forced to deny her womanhood to survive in the wilderness, but whose femininity surfaces with the arrival of the amorous Peck. Old pro Barton provides an intriguing portrait of a foxy grandpa whose only real concern in life is the welfare of his granddaughter. The script from Trotti, who also produced this film, is superlative, providing earthy humor and wit while faithfully representing the terse nomenclature and prosaic lifestyles of the Old West and who was also the screenwriter for another classic western, **The Ox-Bow Incident**, 1943. Of additional special note is MacDonald's stark, high-contrast black-and-white lensing, lending visual credibility to every frame. Newman's dynamic musical score is limited to the opening and closing scenes in this film, a score that was originally used for **Brigham Young: Frontiersman**, 1940, which was also scripted by Trotti. This exciting story was aired as a thirty-minute radio adaptation by Screen Director's Playhouse on July 15, 1949, hosted by Wellman and where Peck reprised his role. The film was remade as **The Jackals**, 1967, a South African production starring Robert Gunner and Diana Iverson and where Vincent Price played Barton's old prospector character. *Author's Note*: Fox boss Zanuck, who always thought of himself as a writer first and filmmaker second, had great admiration for the original author of this story, W.R. Burnett, who had penned the unforgettable crime novel *Little Caesar* (1929), which saw a classic screen version two years later with Edward G. Robinson in the role of the ambitious gangster. "Burnett had written a western novel that was not yet published," Zanuck told this author. "I read it in one reading and decided to make a picture out of it right away. Like all of his works, it drew a sharp and memorable portrait of the Old West and a group of outlaws and it was written in very graphic terms. It was a terrific story." The Burnett story would not be published until two years after the film was released under the title of *Stretch Dawson* (1950), although Zanuck bought its film rights for $35,000 in late 1947 from the author, almost three years before its publication. Burnett admitted to this author that "I based that western yarn on Shakespeare's 'The Tempest,' but no one realized that and when I mentioned it to Bill [William Wellman], he laughed and said: 'Maybe we ought to call this picture "The Bard Goes West."' I don't think Bill was steeped in the classics, but he could always visualize a good story for the screen." Peck thought the same way about Wellman, telling this author: "Bill is one of the great pioneers in the movie business and he knows how to effectively show a story without a lot of dialog. He lets his visuals carry the story line. He started in this business with silent classics like **Wings** [1927] when visuals were everything. That's what he did in **Yellow Sky**. When he has us [the outlaw gang] escape across the salt flats in that picture, he was actually recreating some parched earth scenes shot by Erich von Stroheim in **Greed** [1925]. Bill admitted that to me when I pointed it out to him and he said: 'I guess we watch the same pictures, Greg, at least all the good ones.'" Wellman told this author that Peck "resisted playing the outlaw leader in that picture and, at one point, he told Darryl [Zanuck] that he had been miscast. I think that was because he did not have a lot of dialog. I pointed out to him that none of the other characters did either, but that I knew he would be convincing to audiences through his special acting abilities. Well, what does that mean? It means that some actors can make a wonderful transition from fearful meanness to likeable affability in seconds on the screen through a few gestures and facial expressions, and make their characters completely understood in seconds. Greg [Peck] is one of those actors." Wellman went on to state to this author: "I made sure that everyone in **Yellow Sky** looked like they were suffering from the heat and dust and the unwelcoming landscape trapping their lives. All of them had to wear threadbare, shabby-looking clothes. Their boots were scuffed, their western hats were frayed, and when the outlaws come out of the desert to find the ghost town, they all look like a pack of scruffy hyenas, and where you can almost smell the stinking sweat dripping from their filthy bodies. In fact, I had Anne tell Greg in one scene that he stinks and should take a bath. It would not occur to any westerner in that era that his body odor offended a young and sensitive woman unless someone reminded him of that and she does." Peck added to that: "After that picture came out, people came up to me and sniffed to see if I had taken a shower that day. Movies are a powerful medium, even though they haven't figured out a way to give audiences the actual scents of the characters they see on the screen. I suppose that will be next." Widmark, who is the only one of the outlaws wearing any kind of upscale clothing (and where his character is called "Dude"), plays a gambler who has thrown in his lot with the gang, even though he is more sophisticated and seemingly more intelligent than his peers. "I had just appeared in **Kiss of Death** [1947] a year before we made **Yellow Sky**," Widmark told this author. "I played a psychopathic gangster in that first picture [his film debut] and then appeared in two more pictures where I played pretty much the same kind of wacko character [**The Street with No Name**, 1948; **Road House**, 1948]. In **Yellow Sky**, I got to show a little more humanity in my character, but he's still the same kind of conniving crumb-bum. When we were making **Yellow Sky**, Darryl [Zanuck] passed me on the lot [of the Fox studio] and asked me: 'Are we going to hear that famous laugh again, Dick?' I nodded, but I was not happy about that. I had laughed like a cackling lunatic in that first picture when I killed an old, invalided lady by shoving her in her wheelchair down a flight of stairs—and that is about as nutty as you can get. Well, that damned laugh took hold so hard that Darryl wanted me to use it again and again in one picture after another like a trademark, I guess. I always thought it sounded terrible, like I was choking on a chicken bone, but I gave out a little cackle once more in **Yellow Sky** so that the front office would be satisfied that I was earning my money." Baxter, who is wonderful in her tomboy-turned-loving-woman role, was not the first choice for her part. Zanuck first offered the role to Jean Peters, but she declined, telling Zanuck that she thought the role was "too sexy" for her, albeit Peters had been playing very sexy women in Fox films in those days, and, in fact, appeared five years later opposite Widmark as a tramp selling her favors in a superlative Cold War spy thriller, **Pickup on South Street**, 1953. Paulette Goddard was also considered for the role until Baxter was finally selected, and a better choice could not have been made. Zanuck had wanted the esteemed Walter Huston, who had transitioned from leading man in the 1920s and 1930s to a superlative character actor, to play the role of the gold-mining grandfather in **Yellow Sky**, but Huston was then busy making a film with his director son, John Huston, titled **The Treasure of the Sierra Madre**, 1948. "We then decided that Jim [James Barton] would be very good in the part of the old prospector," Wellman told this author. "He was a great versatile performer and he could do anything. He started as a dancer in vaudeville and burlesque before turning to dramatic parts. He played the kind of gruff but loveable old geezer always outfoxing younger men who think they are smarter than he is and who are not. Jim always reminded me of a British actor, Wilfrid Lawson, who was also one of those great character actors with a gravel voice like Jim's, and who could steal any scene from the best of them. I mentioned that to Jim and he gave me that famous squint of his and then said: 'Wilfrid doesn't dance.'" Exteriors for this film were shot at the Death Valley National Park in the Sierra Nevada range in California as well as Lone Pine, California. Several hundred studio craftsmen built a ghost town at Lone Pine by using the remains of a decrepit set once used by western star Tom Mix when making his film, **The Last Outpost**, 1923. Many other films depict gold miners and gold mines, including **Aces Wild**, 1936; **Across the Pacific**, 1914; **The Adventures of Bullwhip Griffin**, 1967; **Adventures of Frank and Jesse James**, 1948; **The Adventures of Mark Twain**, 1944; **The Adventures of the Masked Phantom**, 1939; **Angelique**, 2013; **Apache Rifles**, 1964; **The Apple Dumpling Gang**, 1975; **At Play in the Fields of the Lord**, 1991; **Back to God's Country**, 1953; **Bad Men**

Gregory Peck and Anne Baxter in *Yellow Sky,* **1948.**

of Tombstone, 1949; **The Badlanders**, 1958; **Badlands of Dakota**, 1941; **Bait**, 1954; **Bandits of Dark Canyon**, 1947; **Barbary Coast**, 1935; **Barbary Coast Gent**, 1944; **Battling with Buffalo Bill**, 1931 (serial); **Beaten**, 1924; **The Beautiful Blonde from Bashful Bend**, 1949; **Behind Southern Lines**, 1952; **Beings**, 1998; **Belle of the Yukon**, 1944; **Bend of the River**, 1952; **Beyond the Sierras**, 1928; **Black Arrow**, 1944; **Black Bart**, 1948; **Blind Warrior**, 1987; **The Blocked Trail**, 1943; **Border Feud**, 1987; **Border Roundup**, 1942; **Border Vengeance**, 1925; **Born to Gamble**, 1935; **Born to the West**, 1926; **The Bride Came C.O.D.**, 1941; **The Broken Law**, 1924; **The Bronze Buckeroo**, 1939; **Bulldog Courage**, 1935; **Burning Daylight**, 1928; **Bury Me Not on the Lone Prairie**, 1941; **California**, 1947; **California Firebrand**, 1948; **Call of the Coyote: A Legend of the Golden West**, 1934; **Call of the Desert**, 1930; **The Call of the Wild**, 1935; **The Call of the Wild**, 1972; **Carmen of the Klondike**, 1918; **Carson City**, 1952; **Carson City Raiders**, 1948; **The Chechahcos**, 1924; **The Cheyenne Kid**, 1933; **Choco**, 2012; **The Cisco Kid and the Lady**, 1939; **The Claim**, 2000; **Clancy of the Mounted**, 1933; **The Comeback**, 1917; **Country Gentlemen**, 1936; **The Courageous Avenger**, 1935; **Cowboy and the Senorita**, 1944; **The Cowboys**, 1972; **Crimes at the Dark House**, 1940; **The Crooked Trail**, 1936; **Cross Fire**, 1933; **Curse of the Forty-Niner**, 2002; **Danger Valley**, 1937; **Dark Mountain**, 2013; **Dead Man's Gold**, 1948; **Deadwood**, 2004-2006 (TV series); **Death Valley Rangers**, 1943; **Desert Gold**, 1936; **Desert Phantom**, 1936; **Desire under the Elms**, 1958; **Doughnuts and Society**, 1936; **Draegerman Courage**, 1937; **The Dude Goes West**, 1948; **Edge of Eternity**, 1959; **Eight Legged Freaks**, 2002; **El Cortez**, 2006; **Eureka**, 1984; **Fandango**, 1970; **The Far Country**, 1955; **Fighting Caravans**, 1931; **Fighting Frontier**, 1943; **The Firebrand**, 1962; **The Flame of the Yukon**, 1926; **Flaming Frontiers**, 1938; **For a Few More Dollars**, 1966; **Framed**, 1947; **The Frozen Limits**, 1939; **Garden of Evil**, 1954; **The Gay Defender**, 1927; **Gay Purr-ee**, 1962; **Ghost Valley**, 1932; **The Girl from Outside**, 1919; **Girl Rush**, 1944; **Goin' South**, 1978; **Gold**, 2013; **Gold Fever**, 1952; **Gold Fever in Lapland**, 1999; **Gold Is Where You Find It**, 1938; **The Gold Rush**, 1925; **The Golden Eye**, 1948; **The Golden Stallion**, 1927; **The Golden Trail**, 1940; **Goldrush: A Real Alaskan Adventure**, 1998 (made-for-TV); **Goldtown Ghost Riders**, 1953; **Gordon of Ghost City**, 1933; **Grand Larceny**, 1991 (made-for-TV); **The Great Divide**, 1929; **The Great Jesse James Raid**, 1953; **Greed**, 1924; **Gun Fever**, 1958; **Gun Gospel**, 1927; **Gunmen of Abilene**, 1950; **Guns of Hate**, 1948; **Hands Up!**, 1926; **The Hanging Tree**, 1959; **Haunted Gold**, 1932; **The Haunted Mine**, 1946; **Heading West**, 1946; **Heathens and Thieves**, 2012; **Heir to Trouble**, 1935; **Hell on Devil's Island**, 1957; **Hellhounds of the West**, 1922; **Hidden Gold**, 1940; **Holes**, 2003; **Home on the Range**,

Sophia Loren and Marcello Mastroianni in *Yesterday, Today and Tomorrow,* 1964.

1935; **How the West Was Won**, 1962; **If One Is Born a Swine**, 1967; **In Old Sacramento**, 1946; **The Indians Are Coming**, 1930; **Jack London**, 1943; **Jack McCall, Desperado**, 1953; **Junction City**, 1952; **Jungle Drums of Africa**, 1953; **Kid Courageous**, 1935; **King of the Wild**, 1931 (serial); **Klondike Fever**, 1980; **Klondike Kate**, 1943; **Lady in a Jam**, 1942; **The Law Rides**, 1936; **The Lawless Frontier**, 1934; **Le ruffian**, 1983; **The Legend of White Fang**, 1992-1994 (TV series); **Lightning Raiders**, 1945; **Lightning Range**, 1934; **The Lightning Warrior**, 1931 (serial); **The Lone Defender**, 1934; **The Lone Rider and the Bandit**, 1942; **The Lone Rider Fights Back**, 1941; **Lonesome Trail**, 1945; **The Lost Special**, 1932 (serial); **The Luck of the Roaring Camp**, 1937; **Lure of the Yukon**, 1924; **Lust for Gold**, 1949; **Mad Dog Morgan**, 1976; **The Man from Colorado**, 1949; **Man from Music Mountain**, 1938; **A Man from Nowhere**, 1920; **Man from the Black Hills**, 1952; **The Man Who Played Square**, 1924; **Mandie and the Cherokee Treasure**, 2010; **The Mask of Zorro**, 1998; **Men in the Raw**, 1923; **The Mints of Hell**, 1919; **Montana Territory**, 1952; **Mourning Becomes Electra**, 1947; **The Mysterious Rider**, 1942; **The New Land**, 1973; **Nikki, Wild Dog of the North**, 1961; **No Man's Gold**, 1926; **North of Arizona**, 1935; **The North Star**, 1996; **North to Alaska**, 1960; **North to the Klondike**, 1942; **Oblomov**, 1980; **On Our Merry Way**, 1948; **One More Train to Rob**, 1971; **Orphans of the North**, 1940; **The Overland Express**, 1938; **Overland Trails**, 1948; **Paint Your Wagon**, 1969; **The Pal from Texas**, 1939; **Pale Rider**, 1985; **Pals in Paradise**, 1926; **Panther Girl of the Kongo**, 1955; **The Pecos Kid**, 1935; **A Perilous Journey**, 1953; **Perils of the Royal Mounted**, 1942; **Phantom Gold**, 1938; **The Phantom Rider**, 1936 (serial); **Pirates on Horseback**, 1941; **The Plunderer**, 1915; **The Prime Gig**, 2001; **Quick Millions**, 1939; **The Raiders**, 1952; **Range Riders**, 1934; **Relentless**, 1948; **Renegade**, 2004; **Revenue Agent**, 1950; **Ride the High Country**, 1962; **Rider from Tucson**, 1950; **The Rider of Death Valley**, 1932; **A River of Skulls**, 2011; **Road to Utopia**, 1946; **Robin Hood of El Dorado**, 1936; **Rockin' in the Rockies**, 1945; **A Romance of the Redwoods**, 1917; **Rough Riders' Round-up**, 1939; **The Royal Mounted Rides Again**, 1945 (serial); **Rugged Gold**, 1994 (made-for-TV); **The Ruthless Four**, 1960; **Sagebrush Troubadour**, 1935; **Salt of the Earth**, 1917; **The San Francisco Story**, 1952; **Santa Fe Stampede**, 1938; **Scared Stiff**, 1953; **The Secret Menace**, 1931; **Secrets of the Wasteland**, 1941; **Senorita from the West**, 1934; **Senorita from the West**, 1945; **Set Free**, 1927; **Sheriff of Tombstone**, 1941; **Seven Guns for Timothy**, 1966; **The Silent Code**, 1935; **The Silent Hero**, 1927; **Silly Billies**, 1936; **The Singing Cowboy**, 1936; **A Sky Full of Stars for a Roof**, 1968; **The Sombrero Kid**, 1942; **Something New**, 1920; **Son of a Gun**, 2014; **Son of the Morning Star**, 1991 (made-for-TV); **Son of Zorro**, 1947; **South of Death Valley**, 1949; **Spe-**

cial Investigator, 1936; **The Spoilers**, 1914; **The Spoilers**, 1923; **The Spoilers**, 1930; **The Spoilers**, 1942; **The Spoilers**, 1955; **Spook Ranch**, 1925; **Stage to Chino**, 1940; **Stagecoach Express**, 1942; **The Strangeness**, 1987; **A Stone's Throw**, 2006; **Sudden Bill Dorn**, 1937; **Support Your Local Sheriff**, 1991; **Sutter's Gold**, 1936; **Sweet Georgia**, 1972; **The Texas Rambler**, 1935; **Texas Terrors**, 1940; **Thanks for Listening**, 1937; **There Goes the Groom**, 1937; **The 33 of San Jose**, 2010; **Those Redheads from Seattle**, 1953; **Thunder Mountain**, 1935; **Thunder over Arizona**, 1956; **Timber Wolf**, 1925; **A Tornado in the Saddle**, 1942; **Trail of Kit Carson**, 1945; **Trails of Adventure**, 1933; **Trapped**, 2010; **The Treasure of the Sierra Madre**, 1948; **Two Brothers in Trinity**, 1972; **Tyrant of Red Gulch**, 1928; **Unconquered Bandit**, 1935; **Under the Fiesta Stars**, 1941; **The Valiant Hombre**, 1948; **The Valley of Bravery**, 1926; **Valley of the Lawless**, 1936; **Valley of Vanishing Men**, 1924; **The Valley of Vanishing Men**, 1942 (serial); **Wanda Nevada**, 1979; **Way Out West**, 1937; **Welcome to Hard Times**, 1967; **Wells Fargo**, 1937; **We're Going to Be Rich**, 1938; **West of Carson City**, 1940; **Westbound Mail**, 1937; **Western Vengeance**, 1924; **Whispering Smith Rides**, 1927; **White Fang**, 1991; **White Fang 2: Myth of the White Wolf**, 1994; **Wild Geese Calling**, 1941; **Wings of the Hawk**, 1953; **Women and Gold**, 1925; **The Yellow Bullet**, 1917; **Yellow Dust**, 1936; and **Young Buffalo Bill**, 1940. p&w, Lamar Trotti (based on the novel by W.R. Burnett); d, William A. Wellman; cast, Gregory Peck, Anne Baxter, Richard Widmark, Robert Arthur, John Russell, Henry (Harry) Morgan, James Barton, Charles Kemper, Robert Adler, Victor Kilian, Paul Hurst, William Gould, Eula Guy, Norman Leavitt, Harry Carter, William Wellman, Jr., Jay Silverheels, Hank Worden, Chief Yowlachie; c, Joe MacDonald; m, Alfred Newman; ed, Harmon Jones; art d, Lyle Wheeler, Albert Hogsett; set d, Thomas Little, Ernest Lansing; spec eff, Fred Sersen.

Yellow Submarine ★★★ 1968; U.K./U.S.; 85m; Apple Corps/UA; Color; Animated Musical Fantasy; Children: Acceptable (MPAA: G); **BD**; **DVD**; **VHS**. At the height of their popularity, the singing group the Beatles composed and performed the songs in this film, but only appeared in the closing scene, while their cartoon counterparts were voiced over by other actors. A make-believe world is inhabited by the Blue Meanies, who suck the color out of people and throw big green apples at them. The Beatles ride to the rescue in a yellow submarine and encounter many adventures before finally overpowering the Meanies with love and song. This film proved to be a big hit for Beatles and cartoon movie fans. Songs: "Yellow Submarine," "Hey Bulldog," "Eleanor Rigby," "All Together Now," "Lucy in the Sky with Diamonds," "Sgt. Pepper's Lonely Hearts Club Band," "With a Little Help From My Friends," "Babe You're a Rich Man," "All You Need Is Love," "When I'm Sixty-Four," "Nowhere Man," "A Day in the Life" (John Lennon, Paul McCartney), "Love You To," "Think for Yourself," "It's All Too Much," "Only a Northern Song" (George Harrison). p, Al Brodax; d, George Dunning; cast, The Beatles (John Lennon, Paul McCartney, George Harrison, Ringo Starr, and (voiceovers), Paul Angelis, Dick Emery, Geoff Hughes, Lance Percival, Peter Batten; w, Lee Minoff, Brodax, Erich Segal, Jack Mendelsohn, Roger McGough (based on a story by Minoff from the song by Lennon, McCartney); c, John Williams (DeLuxe Color); m, The Beatles, George Martin; ed, Brian J. Bishop; art d, Heinz Edelmann; spec eff, Charles Jenkins.

Yesterday, Today, and Tomorrow ★★★ 1964; Italy/France; 119m; Compagnia Cinematographica Champion/Embassy; Color; Comedy; Drama/Romance; Children: Unacceptable (MPAA: PG-13); **BD**; **DVD**; **VHS**; **IV**. Three stories of Italian social mores are cleverly profiled in this absorbing production where the artful and endearing Mastroianni and the voluptuous Loren appear in all three episodes. In "Adelina," Mastroianni is out of work, so he and his wife, Loren, sell black market cigarettes on the streets of Naples. To avoid going to prison, Loren gets pregnant, since women cannot be jailed until six months after their child is born. When that time expires, she gets pregnant again and gets another six-month reprieve. This continues until Mastroianni is exhausted. The case then gets such media attention that the President pardons them both. In "Anna," Loren is the wife of industrialist Mastroianni in Milan. He wrecks her sports car while trying to avoid hitting a child, and she goes off with another man, proving that she is nothing more than a gold-digging sexpot. In "Mars," Loren is a prostitute, who works out of her apartment. Ridolfi, a young seminarian, becomes attracted to her while her lover and best client, Mastroianni, is away on business. Ridolfi considers either giving up his vocation to become a priest or joining the French Foreign Legion, but Loren convinces him that he should take his final vows and become a priest. She then takes a one-week vow of chastity in gratitude for Ridolfi's resolve. This vow, however, vexes Mastrioanni no end when he returns to her, especially after Loren, wearing nylons and garters, does a sensual striptease for him and then, remembering her vow, stops short and refuses him sex. This well-crafted sex farce earned an Oscar as Best Foreign Language Film and was a hit at the box office, earning more than $4 million in its initial release. Songs: "Abat-jour/Salome" (music: Robert Stolz, Bruno Cherubinias; lyrics: Ennio Neri), "Core 'ngrato/Catari, Catari" (music: Salvatore Cardillo; lyrics: Riccardo Cordiferro), "La partita di pallone" (Carlo Alberto Rossi, Edoardo Vianello), "E Cerase" (music: Nicola Valente; lyrics: Salvatore Di Giacomo). (In Italian; English subtitles.) **p**, Carlo Ponti; **d**, Vittorio De Sica; **cast**, "Adelina," Sophia Loren, Marcello Mastroianni, Aldo Giuffre, Agostino Salvietti, Tonino Cianci; "Anna," Loren, Mastroianni, Armando Trovajoli; "Mara," Loren, Mastroianni, Giovanni Ridolfi, Tina Pica; **w**, "Adelina," Eduardo De Filippo, Isabella Quarantotti; "Anna," Cesare Zavattini, Bella Billa (based on the novella "Troppo Ricca" by Alberto Moravia); "Mara," Zavattini; **c**, Giuseppe Rotunno (Techniscope; Technicolor); **m**, Armando Trovajoli; **ed**, Adriana Novelli; **prod d**, Ezio Frigerio.

Yesterday's Enemy ★★★ 1959; U.K.; 95m; Hammer/COL; B/W; War Drama; Children: Unacceptable; **DVD**. This tension-filled tale is set in Burma during WWII (1939-1945) where Baker leads a battle-scarred British army unit through the jungle. He and his men are attempting to rejoin other British troops when they come upon an enemy-held village. After overcoming the small Japanese garrison, the British find on the body of the dead Japanese colonel commanding that village a coded map that apparently anticipates the future strategies of the British in that jungle campaign. While interrogating a prisoner, Baker demands that he decipher that coded map, but the man refuses. Baker states that if he does not do as he is ordered, two innocent villagers will be summarily executed. McKern, a journalist, and Rolfe, a priest, vehemently object to Baker's brutal tactics, but Baker tells them that he has no other choice and to remain silent. When the prisoner refuses to cooperate, Baker has the two villagers shot by Jackson, his top sergeant. The prisoner then breaks down and provides the information Baker is seeking. Baker then learns that a strong Japanese force is approaching the village and he sends several soldiers to contact British HQ with the information he has gleaned, but the British soldiers are ambushed and killed. Just before the Japanese overwhelm the village, Baker has his radio operator send a message to HQ, but it is uncertain whether that message is received or not. Ahn, who is the Japanese colonel in charge of the victorious Japanese troops, tells Baker that, unless he tells him what he has learned, he will have all of the surviving British troops executed. Baker refuses and makes a futile effort to reach the radio and is killed, Ahn stating that he would have done the same thing. The surviving British soldiers are then executed while a final shot shows the British war memorial in Burma. Grim and even depressing, this film nevertheless provides a powerful indictment of war and the futility of its hapless participants. Baker and the rest of the cast give standout performances under Guest's firm direction, and Guest does not spare the brutality invariably accompanying battle action, which is also well choreographed. Song: "Burma March" (Franz Reizenstein). *Author's Note*: Baker

Timothy Bateson, Stanley Baker and Bryan Forbes in *Yesterday's Enemy,* **1959.**

thought this film to be one of his best but complained that its limited budget starved some of its production values. Based upon a war crime committed by a British captain in Burma in 1942, the tale was first shown in a 1958 BBC TV production. This film was shot entirely inside a studio within five weeks, but its sets are so realistic that the viewer might be easily convinced that the production was made on location in Burma. Other films set in Burma during WWII include **Bombs over Burma**, 1943; **The Bridge on the River Kwai**, 1957; **The Burmese Harp** [1956], 1967; **China Girl**, 1942; **Flying Tigers**, 1942; **God Is My Co-Pilot**, 1945; **Merrill's Marauders**, 1962; **Never So Few**, 1959; **Objective, Burma!**, 1945; **The Purple Plain**, 1954; **The Railway Man**, 2014; **Return from the River Kwai**, 1989; **To End All Wars**, 2001; and **A Yank on the Burma Road**, 1942. **p**, Michael Carreras; **d**, Val Guest; **cast**, Stanley Baker, Guy Rolfe, Leo McKern, Gordon Jackson, David Oxley, Richard Pasco, Philip Ahn, Bryan Forbes, Wolfe Morris, David Lodge, Percy Herbert; **w**, Peter R. Newman (based on his television play); **c**, Arthur Grant; **ed**, James Needs, Alfred Cox; **prod d**, Bernard Robinson; **art d**, Don Mingaye.

Yojimbo ★★★★★ 1961; Japan; 110m; Kurosawa Productions/Toho Company/Seneca Productions; B/W; Drama; Children: Unacceptable; **BD**; **DVD**; **VHS**; **IV**. As was his directorial wont throughout his career, pantheon director Kurosawa infuses the ancient code of ethics embodied in another Samurai warrior, who is played by Mifune. He is a ronin, a Samurai warrior who has no master during Japan's feudal period of more than seven hundred years (1185-1868). Mifune arrives in a town in 1860 that is controlled by two warring factions and he is immediately sought by both gang leaders, Kawazu and Sazanka, both asking him to fight for them. Tono, who owns the inn where Mifune is staying, urges the warrior to leave town before he is killed, but Mifune resolves to stay, saying that the leaders of the two gangs and their followers are corrupt and should all be destroyed. He agrees to fight for Kawazu and slays three of Sazanka's men. He then eavesdrops on Yamada, who is Kawazu's wife, hearing her tell her son to murder Mifune by stabbing him in the back when Mifune next goes into battle. Mifune, however, stirs up both factions and then refuses to participate in the upcoming fight. A government official then arrives to prevent that battle from happening. When the official departs, Mifune begins to stir up the factions once more. Tono then tells Mifune that Sazanka has kidnapped the wife of a farmer and given the woman to Shimura, a sake merchant. The noble Mifune then kills the guards keeping the woman hostage and releases her. For this offense, Mifune is beaten and imprisoned, but he manages to escape. By this time Sazanka has decided to wipe out his opposition altogether and sends his men in an all-out attack against Kawazu's forces. The bloody battle results in the destruction of Kawazu

Atsushi Watanabe and Toshiro Mifune in *Yojimbo*, 1961.

and his gang. Mifune, who is hiding in a cemetery where Tono brings him food, then learns that Tono has been captured. Mifune takes his revenge by attacking Sazanka and his men, killing all of them in a titanic battle. Now that he has finally brought peace to the town, Mifune decides to continue his nomadic wanderings and leaves. Kurosawa directs this startling film with his usual firm hand, unfolding the story through the measured movements of his Samurai warrior and subtly telegraphing its changing climate and events with clever images. He subtly employs wind and rain to set his scenes for impending violence and its somber results, and, on other occasions, uses more savage graphics. Just as Mifune is about to enter the town at the beginning, a dog runs from the troubled community with a human hand clenched in its jaws to indicate that the warrior is entering an evil area of carnage and where human gore is commonplace. Mifune presents a forceful and indefatigable warrior, using everything in his ample arsenal to defeat the destructive forces in the town, including considerable psychology in pitting those forces against each other. His stunning performance is strongly supported by a talented cast that Kurosawa had routinely employed in other films while the erratic but arresting score from Sato works well with the choreographed action and contrasting contemplative scenes (Sato's melodic strains were inspired by his idol, Henry Mancini, but he nevertheless slathers that score with many discordant passages to emphasize the rampant bloodletting Kurosawa unstintingly depicts). Kurosawa followed this superb film with a sequel, an equally masterful film, **Sanjuro**, 1963. *Author's Note*: The director, who was an admirer of the detective stories written by Dashiell Hammett, later claimed that he was inspired to make this film after the Hammett-based film noir classic **The Glass Key**, 1942, starring Alan Ladd, Veronica Lake and Brian Donlevy, and that he employed some of that film's plot-lines into **Yojimbo**. His star in this film, Mifune, asked Kurosawa before production began how to interpret his character, and the director told him that that a Samurai warrior was like a wolf or a wild dog. Mifune then added to his performance what would later become a trademark for that character, a routine twitching of his shoulder to simulate a dog's gesture in attempting to shake off fleas. The imaginary fleas then become a telescopic metaphor for the pesky gangsters that terrorize the inhabitants of the town and constantly antagonize the visiting warrior. To emphasize the fact that Mifune's character is somewhat of a social pariah and that he has long ago lost the sponsorship of a master, Kurosawa adorns his protagonist in a worn-out, drab-looking kimono. He is not in fashion or a part of anything contemporary, but a misanthropic character representing an ancient age and an almost forgotten order of Japanese knights and thus inherently mythical. This film is magnificently photographed by Miyagawa, who presents a stark landscape enveloping its characters with sharply defined, contrasting im-

ages, providing an uncompromising, often visually disturbing pattern of images in recording the story's savagery. This master cinematographer shows, for instance, in one scene, how Mifune demonstrates his amazing knife-throwing skills. The camera follows the course of a knife thrown by Mifune to pin a blowing leaf to a wooden floor. Miyagawa accomplished this brief but dazzling action by running the shot backward. Miyagawa had by this time already lensed such classics as **Rashomon**, 1951, and **Ugetsu**, 1954. Kurosawa, forever the perfectionist, doted on every aspect of this film as he did on all of his other productions, including its sound effects. He became obsessed with capturing just the right sound for a sword slicing into a human body and killing someone (such was this director's dispassionate insistence on achieving even the most seemingly insignificant sounds while capturing the gory reality of his bloodletting characters). He spent hours experimenting with his sound expert, Ichiro Minawa, to produce what he thought would be the correct sound. They recorded the sound of a sword slicing and hacking into slabs of raw beef and pork. The director, however, remained unsatisfied, until Minawa came up with a horrific crunching sound effect after he placed two wooden chopsticks into the innards of a raw chicken and hacked it with a sword. The more realistically presented physical elements Kurosawa could insert into his films, the more symbolic metaphors he could thus summarily add into its story lines, counterbalancing his naked, unthinking violence with his ethereal intellectual evaluations of such inhuman behavior. He therefore reflected the true history of his country, a Japan that had for centuries been ruled by ruthless warlords and rigid feudal systems, savaging the human spirit and where the welfare of mankind was in constant peril. The legacy of his nation is much in need of a Deus Machina, that redeemer becoming Kurosawa's constant valiant warrior, a rescuer, a savior, a militant messiah. Just as Kurosawa's **Seven Samurai**, 1956, would transcend into **The Magnificent Seven**, 1960, **Yojimbo** (which means "bodyguard") would become a classic spaghetti western, **A Fistful of Dollars**, 1964. Sergio Leone, the director of that latter film, however, ignored copyrights by simply lifting Kurosawa's story, causing Kurosawa to file suit against the Italian director. He stated that **A Fistful of Dollars** "was a fine movie, but it was *my* movie." Leone ignored the lawsuit, stating that his film drew elements from the story lines of many films, including such American classic westerns as John Ford's **My Darling Clementine**, 1946, and George Stevens' **Shane**, 1953, and that Kurosawa himself had, when making **Yojimbo**, used film noir story lines from Hammett's novel, *Red Harvest* (1929), as well as that author's writings that served as the story lines for the two film versions of **The Glass Key** in 1935 and 1942. Leone, however, finally relented and settled out of court with Kurosawa, allegedly paying the Japanese director fifteen percent of the worldwide receipts for **A Fistful of Dollars**, as well as $100,000 in court costs. **Yojimbo** nevertheless inspired a spate of other spaghetti westerns with the same kind of nomadic hero, as well as a number of U.S. films, including **Last Man Standing**, 1996, and Mifune's character also inspired U.S. comedian John Belushi to routinely caricaturize that Samurai warrior as moronically violent in the TV series **Saturday Night Live**. Other films depicting Samurai warriors include **Assassins**, 2011; **Battle with Top-Class Samuri**, 1980; **Brazil**, 1985; **Duel to Death**, 1983; **Forgotten Warrior**, 1986; **47 Ronin**, 2013; **47 Samurai**, 1963; **Ghost Dog: The Way of the Samurai**, 2000; **The Hidden Fortress**, 1959; **Highlander: The Final Dimension**, 1995; **Kanketsu Sasaki Kojiro: Ganryo-jima ketto**, 1951; **The Last Samurai**, 2003; **Lone Wolf and Cub: Baby Cart at the River Styx**, 1997; **Lone Wolf and Cub: Baby Cart in Peril**, 1997; **Lone Wolf and Cub: Baby Cart in the Land of Demons**, 1997; **Lone Wolf and Cub: Baby Cart to Hades**, 1973; **Lone Wolf and Cub: Sword of Vengeance**, 1973; **Lone Wolf and Cub: White Heaven in Hell**, 1997; **Rashomon**, 1951; **Rurouni Kenshin: Wandering Samurai**, 1996-1998 (TV series); **Samurai**, 2009 (made-for-TV); **Samurai Avenger: The Blind Wolf**, 2009; **Samurai Commando Mission 1549**, 2005; **Samurai Jack**, 2001-2004 (TV series); **Samurai I: Musashi**

Miyamoto, 1955; **Samurai Reincarnation**, 1981; **Samurai III: Duel at Ganryu Island**, 1967; **Samurai Two: Duel at Ichijoji Temple**, 1967; **Samurai X: Reflection**, 2001- (TV series); **Sanjuro**, 1963; **Sengoku jieitai**, 1981; **Seven Samurai**, 1956; **Shadow Hunters 2: Echo of Destiny**, 1972; **Shinsengumi: Assassins of Honor**, 1970; **The Shogun's Samurai**, 1984; **Sleepy Eyes of Death: Sword of Fire**, 1965; **The Sword of Doom**, 1966; **Ugetsu**, 1954; **Village of Eight Gravestones**, 1978; and **Yoroiden Samurai Troopers**, 1988-1995 (TV series). **p&d**, Akira Kurosawa; **cast**, Toshiro Mifune, Tatsuya Nakadai, Yoko Tsukasa, Isuzu Yamada, Daisuke Kato, Seizaburo Kawazu, Kyu Sazanka, Eijiro Tono, Takashi Shimura, Kamatari Fujiwara, Hiroshi Tachikawa, Yosuke Natsuki; **w**, Kurosawa, Ryuzo Kikushima (based on the story by Kurosawa); **c**, Kazuo Miyagawa; **m**, Masaru Sato; **ed**, Kurosawa; **art d**, Yoshiro Muraki.

Yolanda and the Thief ★★★ 1945; U.S.; 108m; MGM; Color; Musical/Fantasy/Romance; Children: Acceptable; **DVD**; **VHS**. Offbeat but delightful musical sees Astaire as a con man on the lam in a Latin-American country named Patria. He learns that Bremer is a beautiful heiress to a fabulous fortune and invades her home to steal whatever he can. During his invasive process, he overhears Bremer, who was educated in a convent, praying to her guardian angel for guidance in her business affairs. Astaire decides to materialize as her angel, gaining her confidence in order to help himself to her millions. While Astaire worms his way into Bremer's affections, he seems to have a change of heart, which is pointed out to him by his equally conniving partner, Morgan, who even believes that Astaire might have fallen in love with his intended victim. Meanwhile, Ames, an enigmatic stranger, appears and disappears with regularity until it is revealed that he is Bremer's true guardian angel. By this time, Astaire realizes that he not only loves Bremer, but has no intention of bilking her and plans to reform. With the resolve at hand, Ames gives his blessing for the two to be wed and live happily ever after. Minnelli provides a highly stylized musical fantasy with some snappy songs and good dance ensembles headed by the lively Astaire. The film, however, did not fare well at the box office, earning about $1.8 million against a budget of more than $2.4 million. Songs: "Angel," "Coffee Time," "This Is a Day for Love," "Will You Marry Me?," "Yolanda" (Harry Warren, Arthur Freed). *Author's Note*: Producer Freed envisioned this film as a vehicle that would make Bremer, his discovery and lover, a superstar. Though she proved to be a wonderful dance partner for Astaire, she never caught on with the public and her acting abilities were limited. Astaire told this author that "I worked very hard with Eugene Loring [an accomplished choreographer] to make some distinctive ensembles for **Yolanda and the Thief**." He provided Loring with more than five hours of film clips from his previous films, telling Loring that he did not want to repeat any of the numbers he had already performed. He and Loring then went to work on a prolonged ballet segment, a fantasy sequence where Astaire must decide to continue his thieving ways or accept Bremer's love and reform. This sixteen-minute dream sequence is beautifully presented and proved to be the film's highlight, but, as Astaire told this author, "it went over the heads of the critics and the public as it was the first time such a ballet was ever presented in a musical. Gene Kelly was much more successful with a similar sequence when he appeared in a marvelous Parisian ballet in **An American in Paris** [1951], but, by that time, the public had been conditioned to such ballet performances, thanks to **The Red Shoes** [1948], and many other such pictures. **Yolanda and the Thief** was simply too much ahead of its time." **p**, Arthur Freed; **d**, Vincente Minnelli; **cast**, Fred Astaire, Lucille Bremer, Frank Morgan, Mildred Natwick, Mary Nash, Leon Ames, Ludwig Stossel, Jane Green, Gigi Perreau, Leon Belasco; **w**, Irving Brecher (based on a story by Jacques Thery, Ludwig Bemelmans); **c**, Charles Rosher (Technicolor); **m**, Lennie Hayton; **ed**, George White; **art d**, Cedric Gibbons, Jack Martin Smith; **set d**, Edwin B. Willis; **spec eff**, A. Arnold Gillespie, Warren Newcombe, Mark Davis.

George Raft and Sylvia Sidney in *You and Me*, 1938.

You and Me ★★★★ 1938; U.S.; 90m; PAR; B/W; Drama/Romance; Children: Unacceptable; **DVD**. Pantheon director Lang presents an offbeat but fascinating crime-does-not-pay tale involving lovers Raft and Sidney. The film opens with Carey, a benevolent department store owner, who decides to hire a number of ex-convicts as a humanitarian effort to more easily rehabilitate them. Ex-con Raft is hired and goes to work at the store where he meets clerk Sidney. They soon fall in love and Raft proposes. Sidney is reluctant to accept since she, too, is an ex-convict, but she keeps this from Raft when she finally accepts his proposal. After they are married, Raft is stunned to learn that not only is Sidney an ex-convict like himself but that their marriage is illegal as Sidney has violated the conditions of her parole. Raft becomes so upset that he returns to his underworld pursuits, putting together a gang and planning to rob the store. Sidney learns of this plot and goes to Carey, convincing her avuncular employer that she can talk Raft and his cohorts out of their robbery. She waits for Raft and his criminal partners at the store and confronts them when they break inside. She then lectures them, pointing out in detail that the robbery will only net them each a little more than $100 but nevertheless brand them as wanted criminals. They realize that the risk of possibly going to jail is not worth their effort and Raft et al. give up the plan. Raft, however, is so humiliated by his wife's bold actions, and irrespective of her good intentions, that he vanishes. When Raft returns many months later, he learns, to his delight, that Sidney has delivered their child and he happily reunites with her, going once more to the altar to be legally married and with the baby in tow. Lang does a good job with this somewhat outlandish tale that is nevertheless made all the more believable through solid performances from Raft and Sidney. The film, however, was not successful at the box office. Songs: "Song of the Cash Register," "The Right Guy for Me," "Knocking Song" (music: Kurt Weill; lyrics: Sam Coslow). *Author's Note*: Krasna, who wrote the original story at the request of Paramount producer William Le Baron as a vehicle for Raft, did so with the ambition of directing the film. The studio approved and Raft, and Carole Lombard were slated to play the lovers. Raft refused to accept Krasna as the director and was immediately suspended. By the time he returned to the fold, Lombard had taken other assignments and Sidney was cast as his co-star, with Richard Wallace as the director. Sidney, however, successfully lobbied for Lang to replace Wallace. "I had appeared in two pictures [**Fury**, 1936; **You Only Live Once**, 1937] that had been earlier directed by Mr. Lang," Sidney told this author, "and I felt very comfortable with him, although he was very demanding." Raft, on the other hand, bristled at Lang's draconian direction, telling this author: "That guy was a petty dictator. He took so many retakes that I thought that we would never finish the picture. If you beefed about that, he would blow up. Well, I had already raised a stink about not working under one di-

Mark Ruffalo and Rory Culkin in *You Can Count on Me,* 2000.

rector [Krasna], so I had used up my complaints with the studio and just swallowed my pride and let Lang kick me around, but never again." Raft does appear in what Lang thought would be a very funny scene (and it is cleverly presented). He is shown talking like his gangster characters of old, saying: "I'm telling you that this is a good racket and there isn't a racket that I haven't tried." The camera pulls back to show that Raft is talking to a department store customer, while he is attempting to sell that customer a tennis racket. When Lang finished this film and previewed it for the Paramount front office, its executives were dumbfounded, not knowing how to promote this hybrid film, which was a half serious drama and a half tender romance. They did their best, showing Sidney and Raft in a poster that proclaimed: "Two great dramatic stars bring you the searing story of love on parole." **p&d**, Fritz Lang; **cast**, Sylvia Sidney, George Raft, Robert Cummings, Barton MacLane, Roscoe Karns, Harry Carey, George E. Stone, Warren Hymer, Guinn "Big Boy" Williams, Carol Paige, Vera Gordon, Joyce Compton, Richard Denning, Ellen Drew, John Hubbard, Cheryl Walker; **w**, Virginia Van Upp (based on a story by Norman Krasna); **c**, Charles Lang, Jr.; **m**, Kurt Weill; **ed**, Paul Weatherwax; **art d**, Hans Dreier, Ernst Fegte; **set d**, A.E. Freudeman.

You Belong to Me ★★★ 1941; U.S.; 94m; COL; B/W; Comedy/Romance; Children: Acceptable; **DVD**; **VHS**. Delightful romantic comedy begins with Fonda, a wealthy but bored playboy who meets doctor Stanwyck at a ski resort. He takes a fall in front of her while skiing, and she treats his minor injuries. Fonda, who is smitten with Stanwyck, comments: "The time I've wasted being well." They fall in love and marry, but problems arise even on their wedding night because she is busy attending to patients, Jones and Clark, two young swains who are obsessed with his wife. Stanwyck's busy work routine continues, and Fonda finds himself alone most of the time in the mansion they share. He also becomes jealous when he learns that most of her patients are handsome young men. To keep him busy, Stanwyck has Buchanan, who is Fonda's gardener, try to interest him in gardening, but Fonda proves that he has no green thumb. Next, Stanwyck urges Fonda to get a job, so he becomes a clerk in a department store. After other employees learn that he is rich, they demand he be fired because he has no need of a job and others do. He is fired, but comes up with the solution to his marital dilemma and lack of an occupation. He buys a bankrupt hospital and installs Stanwyck as its chief of the medical staff while he manages its finances. Now he and his wife can see each other more often while they work together in a good cause. Ruggles presents a spritely romp with enough amusing predicaments to make the tale pleasantly entertaining, especially via two top performances from Fonda and Stanwyck, who had recently scored in the comedy hit **The Lady Eve**, 1941, the same year. The story is cleverly scripted by Binyon, who worked from a tale by the gifted Trumbo and where the snappy dialog shows considerable wit and humor. Not related to 1954 and 2007 films with the same title. *Author's Note*: "**You Belong to Me** was the last picture I did with Henry [Fonda]," Stanwyck told this author, "which was a shame because I always thought we worked very well together and understood our personalities. We did three lighthearted pictures together [**The Lady Eve**; **The Mad Miss Manton**, 1938; and **You Belong to Me**]—they called them 'screwball comedies' in those days—and each one of them was a happy experience for me." Fonda recalled this film and the two others he did with Stanwyck as "a lot of fun. I played a filthy rich guy in two of those pictures [**The Lady Eve** and **You Belong to Me**] and Babs [Stanwyck] played a rich young lady in the other picture [**The Mad Miss Manton**]. Those pictures were made when the country was just working its way out of the Depression [The Great Depression, 1929-1939] and audiences wanted to see how the other half lived, people who lived in mansions, were members of clubs and spent most of their time at resorts. What viewers saw on the screen at that time were the kind of stories that would allow them to escape their financial woes for a few hours. I always felt a little guilty and embarrassed by playing those young millionaires with nothing to do while the rest of the world was scrambling to make a buck. Men and women had a hard time feeding their kids while Hollywood gave them a lot of fanciful illusions. When audiences left the theaters in those days, they could say that at least some people in America were eating good food. They were—if you lived in Beverly Hills." **p&d**, Wesley Ruggles; **cast**, Barbara Stanwyck, Henry Fonda, Edgar Buchanan, Roger Clark, Gordon Jones, Ruth Donnelly, Melville Cooper, Maude Eburne, Renie Riano, Mary Treen, Fritz Feld, Lloyd Bridges, Barbara Brown, Jeff Corey, Jack Norton, Larry Parks, Grady Sutton; **w**, Claude Binyon (based on a story by Dalton Trumbo); **c**, Joseph Walker; **m**, Frederick Hollander; **ed**, Viola Lawrence; **art d**, Lionel Banks.

You Can Count on Me ★★★ 2000; U.S.; 111m; Hart-Sharp Entertainment/PAR; Color; Drama; Children: Unacceptable (MPAA: R); **DVD**; **VHS**; **IV**. Well-presented slice-of-life tale begins with Linney and her brother, Ruffalo, who became very close after their parents were killed in a car accident. A few years later when Linney is a lending officer at a bank and a single mother to an eight-year-old son, Culkin, she and Culkin are excited to learn that Ruffalo is going to visit them in a small town in New York State. Ruffalo, an irresponsible drifter, arrives to dishearten Linney after she learns that he has only come to borrow money because he is broke, his traditional financial condition. Nonetheless, Linney welcomes him as being a male companion to Culkin. Linney gives Ruffalo some money, but he sends it to his girlfriend. After the girlfriend commits suicide, Ruffalo stays on with Linney and Culkin, and Linney welcomes his decision to stay. A boyfriend proposes to Linney, but she holds him off, as she already has too many responsibilities. Linney feels more comfortable in having an affair with Broderick, her new bank manager, even though he is married and his wife is pregnant. Linney decides to devote her life to Culkin and, to that end, she turns down the marriage proposal and then breaks off her relationship with Broderick. Linney also decides that Ruffalo should leave and he departs for Alaska. Linney and Ruffalo end up reconciling before he leaves, finding a degree of compatibility with their different lifestyles. Songs: "Aus Liebe will mein Heiland Sterben" (from "St. Matthew Passion"), "G Major Suite for Solo Cello" (Johann Sebastian Bach); "I'm Still in Love with You," "Harlan Man," "Pilgrim," "The Mountain," "Texas Earle" (Steve Earle); "Somebody Somewhere/Don't Know What He's Missin'" (Lola Jean Fawbush); "Long Way to Go" (Sue Foley); "Impacto Tendremos" (Jimmy Bosch); "If You're Not Gone Too Long" (Wanda Ballman); "Mendocino" (Doug Sahm); "Straight Highway," "Strange" (The V-roys: Scott Miller, Jeff Bills, Paxton Sellers, Mike Harrison); "Vampire" (Bap Kennedy); "Faraway You" (Marah); "Amy 88" (Mike Harrison); "The Other Woman" (Bety Sue Perry); "85 On 85" (Kenny Roby); "White Lies" (Cheri Knight); "La Misma Cancion"

(Ozomatli). Gutter language, drug use and sexuality prohibit viewing by children. **p**, Barbara De Fina, John N. Hart, Larry Meistrich, Jeffrey Sharp, Keith Abell, Julian Iragorri; **d&w**, Kenneth Lonergan; **cast**, Laura Linney, Mark Ruffalo, Matthew Broderick, Rory Culkin, Jon Tenney, J. Smith-Cameron, Gaby Hoffmann, Amy Ryan, Michael Countryman, Adam LeFevre, Halley Feiffer, Whitney Vance; **c**, Stephen Kazmierski; **m**, Lesley Barber; **ed**, Anne McCabe; **prod d**, Michael Shaw; **art d**, Shawn Carroll; **set d**, Lydia Marks.

You Can't Cheat an Honest Man ★★★★ 1939; U.S. 76m; UNIV; B/W; Comedy; Children: Acceptable; **DVD**; **VHS**. Fields is at his conniving best in this hilarious comedy that begins when Fields is hustling his flea-bitten circus across a state line. Hot in pursuit are police who want to nab Fields and company for confidence games artfully exercised in their town and from which the carney people have promptly fled. Fields and his rollicking caravan just manage to cross that state line, which prohibits local police from continuing their pursuit. Once they arrive at the next town, Fields and his followers pitch their tents and begin enticing local customers to their sideshows and attractions, all rigged to bilk gullible customers. Fields, who is aptly called Larson E. Whipsnade, pronounces to his naïve patrons that his operation is strictly above board (which it is certainly not), quoting his grandfather's final words ("just before they sprung the trap"): "You can't cheat an honest man…never give a sucker an even break…or smarten up a chump." Fields is in his element, but his days are darkened by one of his attractions, Bergen, and his wisecracking dummy, Charlie McCarthy, who is forever humiliating him. He would love to fire the ventriloquist and his wooden sidekick, but they have an ironclad contract with him. Fields is overjoyed to hear that Bergen is about to quit, but he quickly changes his mind when Moore, who is Fields' attractive daughter, arrives to pay her father a visit. Charlie McCarthy is so upset with Bergen's decision to remain with the dilapidated circus that he throws a temper tantrum, such is the dummy's deep desire to rid himself once and for all of the obstreperous Fields. Charlie McCarthy, too, changes his mind after Bergen informs his sidekick that Moore has a younger sister (which she does not). Meanwhile, Fields is beset with innumerable problems that make his life miserable, a pesky dog that is forever gnawing on him, the topmost flap of his wagon from which he sells tickets that collapses upon his much-abused head, and incompetent assistants who constantly raid his lunch, which consists of a whiskey bottle. When Moore finds her father, she sees that he is butt-sprung and woebegone, always dodging creditors. At one point, Fields disguises himself as a German visitor by affixing shreds of rope under his nose to create a crude fake mustache while palavering with a bill collector. Moore tells Fields that Bush, a young man from a wealthy family, is in love with her and has proposed marriage. The self-serving Fields sees this budding romance as a way of bolstering the finances of his near-destitute circus, thinking to fleece Bush and his family. The goodhearted Moore decides that she will accept Bush's proposal, even though she does not love him, so that Bush and his family can come to Fields' financial rescue. Arledge, who is Fields' son and longs for a better lifestyle than his father's, also urges Moore to marry Bush. By this time, however, Moore has fallen in love with Bergen, the couple meeting clandestinely at a balloon moored nearby. When Moore's wedding day arrives, she tells Fields that she does not have the heart to break the news of her nuptials to Bergen and asks Fields to deliver that sad news. Fields is delighted to bring his old antagonist such heartbreaking information and finds Bergen and Charlie McCarthy waiting for Moore while standing in the basket of the balloon. Pretending to whittle while he breaks the news to Bergen, Fields cuts the ropes mooring the basket and sends the ventriloquist and his dummy skyward. The balloon sails over the countryside, while, ironically, Moore is shown in a downward view as she drives to her wedding. The hapless Bergen and Charlie McCarthy are not encouraged to find another passenger sleeping beneath some rags, Mortimer Snerd, a slow-witted country bumpkin and another dummy who immediately competes

W.C. Fields in *You Can't Cheat an Honest Man*, **1939.**

with Charlie for Bergen's verbal attentions. Fields then attires himself in his best top hat and tails and has lamebrain assistant Sutton drive him to Bush's mansion in a chariot. Bergen and his two sidekicks escape the balloon at this time by parachuting to earth and they land inside the open car driven by Moore. Their parachute covers the auto so that Moore cannot see where she is driving and she promptly crashes into a gas station. All of them are arrested for reckless driving and jailed. Moore is released after it is learned that she is Bush's intended, the groom's prestigious family having sway over local officials, and she is soon escorted to the Bush mansion. Meanwhile, Fields strolls through the cavernous manor house insulting the upscale guests while Arledge dutifully trails behind him, begging him to curtail his verbal abuses. Fields ignores such advice, launching into a tale about slithering snakes, which causes Forbes, who is Bush's stuffy mother, to promptly faint since she has a deep aversion to reptiles. Forbes revives, but faints again and again as Fields repeats the word "snake"; she is finally brought around after she is given shots of whiskey. Fields then proclaims that she has had too much to drink. He next wanders into a game room where he gets involved in a fantastic ping-pong match that drives him out of the room, through several other rooms and eventually onto a patio; his final smash of the ball drives that ball into the open mouth of a startled dowager attending the wedding. (As with all of Fields' inventive comedy skits, this one is exaggerated to the point of ridiculousness, a parody within a parody.) When Moore arrives and hears everyone condemning the outlandish exploits of her father, she comes to her father's defense, breaking her promise to marry Bush, and joins Arledge in telling off Bush's parents and their snooty friends before she, Fields and Arledge climb into the chariot and race off. By this time, Bergen and his dummy friends have mounted a bicycle and they peddle frantically after Fields and his equally adventurous children. The plot for this wild tale is little more than a series of comedy sketches designed as an episodic vehicle for Fields, but its zany scenes and its offbeat action so captivate that the viewer remains mesmerized by its mirth-filled chaos. The film, the first Fields made for Universal, was a box office hit, its success prompting the studio to immediately schedule Fields in a number of future comedy films (**My Little Chickadee**, 1940; **The Bank Dick**, 1940; **Never Give a Sucker an Even Break**, 1941). Songs: "Camptown Races" (1850; Stephen Foster), "Sobre Los Olas (Over the Waves)" (1887; Juventino Rosas), "Chicken Reel" (traditional), "The Irish Washerwoman" (traditional). *Author's Note*: Universal had long wanted to add Fields to their star roster and wooed him away from his home studio, Paramount, with a very lucrative contract, paying him $100,000 for his appearance in this film (Bergen, then a huge radio star, was also paid $100,000 for his appearance in this film). The studio also paid Fields an additional $25,000 for writing the script. The script for this film was written by

Harvey Stephens, Humphrey Bogart and Billy Halop in *You Can't Get Away with Murder*, 1939.

Fields under the pseudonym of Charles Bogle and consisted to two old scripts he and others had worked on in the late 1920s and early 1930s. Fields was not happy with the end product as several of his important scenes designed to explain his character were eliminated early on, especially the opening where his wife, a trapeze artist, is killed in a fall and dies in his arms. This causes him to become an irresponsible, heavy-drinking and very caustic man. In another scene, also not shot, Fields bares his soul to his children before Moore's wedding, which causes them to empathetically rise to his defense and depart with him to make a better life together. Without these scenes, Fields believed that his image in this film was nothing more than a mean-minded, conniving curmudgeon who has no compassion for anyone, and he refused to go on a promotion tour when this film was released. Worse, Fields did not get along at all with veteran director Marshall, who told this author: "He fought me tooth and nail over every scene in that picture. Right from the beginning, Fields let me know that, even though I was directing the picture, he was in charge of everything. Well, I thought I would teach him a lesson. In one scene, he has to take a shower with Rochester [Eddie "Rochester" Anderson], and must stand beneath the trunk of an elephant who sprays the both of them. It was a funny bit, but I made them both do the scene about eight or nine times. Fields called a halt to my next retake and took Rochester into the wagon, which was his office in the picture, and locked it. They both sat inside that wagon drinking whiskey. I banged on that wagon and even had the trainer have his elephant rock it back and forth, but those two would not come out. By the time they emerged they were so tipsy I could do nothing with them. That kind of Fields hijinks went on all the time during that production." To settle things, studio bosses brought Edward Cline, who was a Fields buddy, to direct only Fields' scenes while Marshall helmed the rest of the production. Cline would direct the next three films Fields made for Universal. The studio also capitalized on a running "feud" that had been ongoing between Fields and Bergen on Bergen's immensely popular radio show, and it pits the two comedians again together in this film. That "feud," however, was mythical as both were very close friends who greatly respected one another. In fact, Fields also complained that his good friend Bergen was also being coated with too much slapstick in this film, stating: "Edgar Bergen doesn't have to be whisked around in a basket to be funny." As usual, he went too far in also demanding that Bergen's lively dummy be addressed as "Mr. McCarthy." Despite the internecine warfare involved in the production, as well as its lack of continuity, the film nevertheless is an extremely funny film, one that only the inimitable Fields could have produced. Other films depicting ventriloquists and their dummies include **Alfred Hitchcock Presents**, 1955-1965 (TV series; "And So Died Riabouchinska," 1956 episode; "Final Performance," 1965 episode); **All's Faire in Love**, 2009; **Annie**,

1982; **Arizona Stage Coach**, 1942; **Avargal**, 1977; **Best in Show**, 2000; **Big Fish**, 2003; **The Big Show**, 1936; **Bright Lights**, 1935; **Broadway Danny Rose**, 1984; **The Bronze Buckeroo**, 1939; **Bugsy Malone**, 1976; **Bullets and Saddles**, 1943; **Call the Mesquiteers**, 1938; **Charlie McCarthy, Detective**, 1939 (Edgar Bergen and Charlie McCarthy); **Charlie's Haunt**, 1950 (Edgar Bergen and Charlie McCarthy); **Chicago**, 2002; **Coming Home**, 1978; **Cowboy Canteen**, 1944; **Cradle Will Rock**, 1999; **Crash Canyon**, 2011- (TV series); **Crime Ring**, 1938; **The Danny Kaye Show**, 1963-1967 (TV series; several episodes); **Dead of Night**, 1945; **Dead Silence**, 2007; **Death Defying Acts**, 2008; **Der Mann mitt dem Glasauge**, 1969; **Devil Doll**, 1964; **Dinner for Schmucks**, 2010; **Don't Make Waves**, 1967; **Dummy**, 2002; **El as negro**, 1943; **Ellery Queen's Penthouse Mystery**, 1941; **Fight for Your Lady**, 1937; **Find the Blackmailer**, 1943; **For Your Consideration**, 2006; **Fugitive Valley**, 1941; **Fun and Fancy Free**, 1947 (Edgar Bergen and Charlie McCarthy); **Getting Any?**, 1994; **Getting Home**, 2007; **Go Chase Yourself**, 1938; **Go for It**, 1983; **Gold Diggers in Paris**, 1938; **The Goldwyn Follies**, 1938 (Edgar Bergen and Charlie McCarthy); **The Great Gabbo**, 1929; **Gunsmoke Ranch**, 1937; **Harmony Trail**, 1944; **Here We Go Again**, 1942 (Edgar Bergen and Charlie McCarthy); **Hidden Danger**, 1948; **Hit the Saddle**, 1937; **I Love Hitler**, 1984; **The Illusionist**, 2010; **The Immortals**, 1995; **The In-Laws**, 1979; **The Jack Benny Program**, 1950-1965 (TV series; "Christmas Show," 1960 episode); **Jeff Dunham: Birth of a Dummy**, 2011; **Knock on Wood**, 1954; **Knots**, 1975; **La 7eme cible**, 1984; **Land of Hunted Men**, 1943; **The Last of Sheila**, 1973; **The Last Request**, 2006; **Letter of Introduction**, 1938 (Edgar Bergen and Charlie McCarthy); **Look Who's Laughing**, 1941 (Edgar Bergen and Charlie McCarthy); **Magic**, 1978; **Magic Mansion**, 1965-1967 (TV series); **Manhattan Merry-Go-Round**, 1937; **The Men's Club**, 1986; **The Miracle Woman**, 1931; **Mr. Moto's Last Warning**, 1939; **The Muppet Movie**, 1979; **The Night Is Young**, 1987; **1941**, 1979; **Overland Stage Raiders**, 1938; **The Paper Man**, 1963; **Pecker**, 1998; **Pin**, 1989; **Poppy**, 1936; **The Purple Vigilantes**, 1938; **Range Defenders**, 1937; **Reap the Wild Wind**, 1942; **Red River Range**, 1938; **The Riders of the Whistling Skull**, 1937; **Roaring Fire**, 1982; **Rock River Renegades**, 1942; **Rosalie**, 1937; **Santa Fe Stampede**, 1938; **Seed of Chucky**, 2004; **The Shadow of the Eagle**, 1932; **The Sheriff of Medicine Bow**, 1948; **Sheriff of Sundown**, 1944; **Soap**, 1977-1981 (TV series); **Song of the Open Road**, 1944 (Edgar Bergen and Charlie McCarthy); **Stage Door Canteen**, 1943 (Edgar Bergen and Charlie McCarthy); **Stop! Look! And Laugh!**, 1960; **Swing, Cowboy, Swing**, 1946; **Swing Out the Blues**, 1943; **The Ten**, 2007; **Terror Firmer**, 1999; **The 39 Steps**, 2008 (made-for-TV); **The Three Mesquiteers**, 1936; **Tonto Basin Outlaws**, 1941; **Trigger Trail**, 1944; **Tumbledown Ranch in Arizona**, 1941; **20 Years After**, 2008; **Twilight Zone**, 1959-1964 (TV series; "Caesar and Me," 1964 episode); **Two Fisted Justice**, 1943; **Unashamed**, 1938; **Underground Rustlers**, 1941; **The Unholy Three**, 1925; **The Unholy Three**, 1930; **Variety Lights**, 1965; **A Very Long Engagement**, 2004; **West of Pinto Basin**, 1940; **What's Up, Tiger Lily?**, 1966; **When a Stranger Calls Back**, 1993 (made-for-TV); and **Zapatlela**, 1993. **p**, Lester Cowan; **d**, George Marshall, (not credited) Edward F. Cline); **cast**, W.C. Fields, Edgar Bergen, Charlie McCarthy, Eddie "Rochester" Anderson, Constance Moore, Russell Wade, Grady Sutton, James Bush, Thurston Hall, Arthur Hohl, John Arledge, Charles Coleman, Princess Baba, Irving Bacon, Mary Forbes, Edward Brophy, Ivan Lebedeff, Ferris Taylor, Jan Duggan, Mortimer Snerd; **w**, George Marion, Jr., Richard Mack, Everett Freeman (based on a story by Charles Bogle (Fields); **c**, Milton Krasner; **m**, Frank Skinner; **ed**, Otto Ludwig; **art d**, Jack Otterson; **set d**, R.A. Gausman.

You Can't Get Away with Murder ★★★ 1939; U.S.; 78m; WB/First National; B/W; Crime Drama; Children: Unacceptable; **DVD**; **IV**. Absorbing crime tale is set in NYC's Hell's Kitchen where hardworking Page tries to keep her younger brother, Halop, out of trouble. (The plot is close to that of sister Silvia Sidney protecting younger brother Halop against street evils in **Dead End**, 1937, and where Bogart represents the glorified temptation of such criminal pursuits in that earlier film.) Bogart is a ruthless petty criminal, who takes teenage Halop under his wing and makes him his apprentice in stealing. Halop admires Bogart's every move and willingly aids Bogart in robbing a gas station manned by Ridgely. Thrilled by the risk involved in the robbery and overjoyed at receiving a portion of its loot, Halop has little hesitation when Bogart orders him to steal a gun for their next caper. He filches a gun owned by Stephens, who is Page's fiancé, planning to return the weapon after it is used in an upcoming robbery. The two invade a pawnshop, but nothing goes as planned. The owner not only resists, but sets off an alarm that causes Bogart to viciously explode; he uses the gun to shoot and kill the owner, and, in his panic, leaves the weapon behind. The gun is traced to Stephens and he is quickly charged, tried and convicted for the crime and sentenced to death. Halop wants to tell the police that Stephens is innocent, but Bogart threatens him and both are then arrested and charged with robbing the gas station after their fingerprints, left at the scene of that crime, are identified. They are convicted and sentenced to Sing Sing prison, which is where the innocent Stephens awaits execution in the Death House. Halop, who is far from being a hardened criminal like Bogart, is haunted by the thought that Stephens faces death for a crime he has not committed and wants to tell the prison warden, Crehan, that Stephens is innocent. Bogart, however, orders Halop to uphold the criminal code of the underworld by keeping silent, threatening the youth with his own death by stating that, if Halop confesses, he and Bogart will be going to the electric chair in Stephens' place for murdering the pawnshop owner. Crehan and his guards think that Bogart is too much of an influence for Halop, and Halop is transferred from the prison shoe factory where he works with Bogart, to the prison library where he comes under the influence of Travers, a kindly old convict, who has retained moral values. Meanwhile, Halop is convinced that Stephens will be exonerated on his appeal, but is shocked to hear that Stephens' conviction has been upheld. Page by this time suspects that Halop knows the truth and begs him to confess, as does Travers, but Halop, who is constantly threatened by Bogart, remains silent right up to the day of Stephens' scheduled execution. On that very day, Bogart and con friends Downing and Huber plan to escape, and Bogart, to keep Halop silent, plans to kill Halop before they break out. Halop leaves a note for Travers in which he confesses all before the break, but Bogart finds the note and takes it with him when the convicts make their break. Downing and Huber are shot and killed in the prison break, but Bogart and Halop escape and hide out in a boxcar. Bogart shoots Halop, mortally wounding him. When police arrive, Bogart says their bullets killed Halop. He is shocked to see that Halop is still alive, and, before dying, Halop makes a full confession to the police. Stephens is cleared, while Bogart is sent to the electric chair in his place. Seiler directs this thick melodrama at a whirlwind pace and draws exceptional performances from Bogart, Halop and the rest of the cast. *Author's Note*: Though Bogart presents his usual electrifying performance as a cold-blooded criminal and killer in this film, he resented being once again typecast in such a role, one he did not escape for another two years until becoming an empathetic and aging robber in **High Sierra**, 1941, eventually graduating to the anti-hero detective Sam Spade in **The Maltese Falcon**, 1941, and finally achieving leading man status in **Casablanca**, 1942. Halop, who had had his film debut two years earlier in **Dead End**, in which Bogart again played a ruthless gangster, never saw his film career develop beyond his juvenile roles and who spent most of his adult career in Hollywood playing bit parts. Other films that depict Sing Sing prison include **Alias Jimmy Valentine**, 1915; **Analyze That**, 2002; **And One Was Beautiful**, 1940; **Baby Take a Bow**, 1940; **Behind the Mask**, 1932; **Castle on the Hudson**, 1940; **Citizen Saint**, 1947; **A Fugitive from Matrimony**, 1919; **The Helen Morgan Story**, 1957; **Her Story**, 1920; **Invisible Stripes**, 1939; **It's a Wonderful World**, 1939; **King of New York**, 1990; **Kiss of Death**, 1947; **Little Miss Broadway**,

Alice Faye, Don Ameche and Tony Martin in *You Can't Have Everything*, 1937.

1947; **The Lonely Woman**, 1918; **Man against Women**, 1932; **Man on a Ledge**, 2012; **The Man Who Found Himself**, 1915; **Manhattan Melodrama**, 1934; **Maniac Cop**, 1988; **Murder Man**, 1935; **Naked City**, 1958-1963 (TV series; "Prime of Life," 1963 episode); **The Naked Street**, 1955; **Phantom of the Paradise**, 1974; **Picture Snatcher**, 1933; **The Producers**, 1968; **The Producers**, 2005; **Scandal Sheet**, 1932; **Secrets of a Nurse**, 1938; **Sergeant Madden**, 1939; **Sing Sing Nights**, 1934; **Strange Justice**, 1932; **The Supreme Sacrifice**, 1916; **Sworn Enemy**, 1936; **Three Who Loved**, 1931; **20,000 Years in Sing Sing**, 1932; **Two Smart People**, 1936; and **The Valachi Papers**, 1972. Excessive violence prohibits viewing by children. **p**, Samuel Bischoff; **d**, Lewis Seiler; **cast**, Humphrey Bogart, Gale Page, Billy Halop, Henry Travers, John Litel, Harvey Stephens, Joseph Crehan, Herbert Rawlinson, Harold Huber, Joe Sawyer, Joe Downing, Robert E. Homans, Robert Emmett O'Connor, George E. Stone, John Ridgely, William Cagney, Eddie "Rochester" Anderson, Emory Parnell, Tom Dugan, Frank Faylen; **w**, Robert Buckner, Don Ryan, Kenneth Gamet (based on the play "Chalked Out" by Warden Lewis E. Lawes, Jonathan Finn); **c**, Sol Polito; **m**, Heinz Roemheld; **ed**, James Gibbon; **art d**, Hugh Reticker.

You Can't Have Everything ★★★ 1937; U.S.; 99m; FOX; B/W; Musical; Children: Acceptable; **DVD**. Delightful songfest begins with Faye, who is an aspiring playwright without money. She's hungry so she orders a spaghetti dinner in a restaurant, knowing she can't pay for it. To pay for her food, she is compelled to walk back and forth in front of the establishment wearing a sandwich board promoting the restaurant. Ameche, a successful musical writer with influence along Broadway, sees her predicament and offers to pay for her meal, but proud Faye refuses. Faye nevertheless confides in the tipsy Ameche that she has written a play and hopes that producer Winninger will buy its rights and produce it. Ameche returns home to find Lee, his girlfriend, angrily waiting for him, reminding him that he has broken their date for the night. Ameche, who is now smitten by Faye, goes to his friend Winninger and gives him Faye's play, which is called "North Wind." Even though both realize that the work is a terrible melodrama, Ameche convinces Winninger to pay the economically strapped Faye $250 for its rights. Ameche then talks Lee into taking a vacation while he begins to produce the play, even giving Faye a part in the cast. Lee returns from her vacation to find that Ameche and Faye are now involved in a romance and she warns Faye to stay away from her boyfriend. The play by then is an utter failure and Faye assumes all the responsibility, and also believes that she has stolen Lee's man from her. She leaves, and Ameche, who breaks up with Lee, is frantic to find Faye. In her absence, Ameche turns Faye's play into a musical that becomes an overnight hit on Broadway.

James Stewart and Jean Arthur in *You Can't Take It with You,* **1938.**

Faye, who has returned to her old job selling sheet music in a department store, learns about her play's success when she sees some of its songs in the sheet music she is selling. Faye returns to New York and is over-awed at the hit Ameche has brought about, and she and Ameche begin a life together, proving that sometimes you can have everything. Faye is superb as the ambitious writer, and her full-throated vocals make for wonderful listening. Ameche is his amiable and personable self in this completely entertaining musical, which is packed with a passel of fine songs. The film was a box office hit, its success aided by the appearance of the zany Ritz Brothers, these three wackos providing manic mirth in all of their frenetic scenes. Songs: "You Can't Have Everything," "Danger, Love at Work," "Afraid to Dream," "North Pole Sketch," "Please Pardon Us, We're in Love," "The Loveliness of You" (1937; Harry Revel, Mack Gordon); "Santa Lucia" (1849; traditional); "Chopsticks" (traditional); "Jingle Bells" (1857; Kames Pierpont); "Spring Song" (1842; Felix Mendelssohn-Bartholdy); "Dance Rubinoff" (David Rubinoff); "Long Underwear" (1937; Samuel Kokrass, Sid Kuller, Ray Golden); "String Quintet in E" (Luigi Boccherini); "Yankee Doodle" (1755; traditional); "It's a Southern Holiday" (1937; Louis Prima, Jack Loman, Dave Franklin); "Rhythm of the Radio" (1937; Louis Prima). *Author's Note*: This was the first of six films Faye and Ameche would make together, and one of the three films in which the Ritz Brothers appeared with Faye. "Those three boys [Ritz Brothers] were the same off camera as they were before it," Faye told this author. "They were such live wires that we all thought that they were connected to some electrical socket. Their wild gyrations and eye-popping facial expressions were so outlandish that we all had a hard time keeping straight faces in our scenes with them. They had a lot of imitators over the years, but there was never anything like that act." Ameche told this author: "The studio [Fox] was worried about casting Gypsy Rose Lee in **You Can't Have Everything** because she had the reputation of being one of America's foremost striptease artists. They decided to disguise her by having her use her given name [Louise Hovick] instead of her burlesque name, which was already famous. Well, they didn't fool anyone and they knew a lot of men would flock to see that picture anyway just to gander at her, even though she keeps all of her clothes on in that picture. I think that was Zanuck's [Darryl F. Zanuck, head of Fox] idea. He is a very clever fellow and knew how to promote his films." **p**, Darryl F. Zanuck; **d**, Norman Taurog; **cast**, Alice Faye, Ritz Brothers (Harry, Al, Jimmy Ritz), Don Ameche, Charles Winninger, Louise Hovick (Gypsy Rose Lee), Arthur Treacher, Tony Martin, Phyllis Brooks, Wally Vernon, Jed Prouty, Louis Prima, Lynn Bari, Clara Blandick, Joan Davis, Robert Lowery; **w**, Tugend, Jack Yellen, Karl Tunberg (based on a story by Gregory Ratoff); **c**, Lucien Andriot; **m**, Cyril J. Mockridge, Walter Scharf; **ed**, Hanson Fritch; **art d**, Duncan Cramer.

You Can't Take It with You ★★★★ 1938; U.S.; 126m; COL; B/W; Comedy/Romance; Children: Acceptable; **BD**; **DVD**; **VHS**; **IV**. Pantheon director Capra provides a thoroughly enjoyable romantic comedy set squarely within an eccentric family, headed by Barrymore, where his equally independent-minded granddaughter, Arthur, shares her love with Stewart, the heir to great wealth. Arthur is a stenographer, who has fallen in love with Stewart, the vice president of a huge company headed by his father, Arnold. She has a problem, however, believing that Stewart and his wealthy family will not be acceptable to her own family, which has forsaken the business of moneymaking many years earlier. Barrymore, at that time, accumulated a small fortune and decided to pursue the arts and sciences, encouraging his family, relatives and friends to join him in their many creative pursuits. Further complicating the budding romance between Arthur and Stewart is the fact that Arnold has just returned from Washington, D.C. where he engineered what amounts to a monopoly on the production of munitions. He has decided to buy up all the property in a twelve-block area of New York to build a huge plant for that purpose and has acquired all the real estate, except for one large house, occupied and owned by Barrymore. The free-thinking Barrymore has refused to sell the property, and Arnold has instructed Wilson, his real estate broker, to acquire the house at all costs. If Barrymore continues to refuse to sell, Wilson is to make life miserable for Barrymore and his artistic clan. Arthur is the only one among the unconventional family members who can be considered normal as her relatives live happily in their separate dream worlds as they pursue their different goals in life. Her mother, Byington, thinks of herself as a writer after finding a typewriter left on the doorstep of their home, and she has been writing a novel ever since. Her father, Hinds, is an inventor, who has been laboring in the basement, tinkering with dangerous explosives as he attempts to create the world's highest soaring rocket and the perfect Roman candle. Miller, their daughter, works tirelessly to become a great ballet dancer and she is hounded everywhere by the cynical Auer, her Russian mentor and ballet master, who views the world with a jaundiced eye. Taylor plays the xylophone while Meek makes toys and party masks. Meek, who, like his name, is a milquetoast, delights in sneaking up on household members to frighten them with his latest scary mask. The house is full of activity, and the calamitous sound of outlandish creativity reverberates through every room. For Barrymore and his ilk, it is a space filled with joy and peace, but to Arnold and his snooty wife, Forbes, when first entering this loosely organized mayhem, they think they have entered an asylum occupied by lunatics. This is exactly what happens after Stewart proposes to Arthur, and she bravely agrees to take him and his parents, Arnold and Forbes, to her home to meet her family. Arthur forewarns Barrymore, who, in turn, asks that his family members keep their usual antics to less than a college roar, saying that, for Arthur's sake, they make a good impression on Stewart and his parents. Unfortunately, there is a mix-up in the actual evening at which the two families are to have dinner together. Stewart, Arnold and Forbes arrive one night too early and they are exposed to the wild behavior of the family members, who are caught off guard, and Arthur and Byington frantically try to put a meal together. Arnold is dumbfounded by the strange conduct and bizarre behavior exhibited by Barrymore's clan, and Forbes is outright insulted. The chaotic evening is capped by a terrific explosion when Hinds accidentally sets off some of his incendiary materials. This causes the police to raid the house, and everyone is arrested and charged with making illegal fireworks. Both families are placed in a large drunk tank cell where they are surrounded by inebriates, tramps and the social dregs of the Great Depression (1929-1939), as they await trial in night court. Barrymore amuses himself with philosophizing about society and playing the harmonica. He tells the ruthless Arnold that, though he may accumulate much more wealth and power, he will die without any friends, all of this further antagonizing Arnold and Forbes. Everyone is then dragged before Davenport, the presiding judge. When asked what the disturbance is really about, Barrymore lamely tells Davenport that it involved Arnold's possible purchase of his house. Arthur takes exception to her grandfather's statements, believing that Barrymore is attempting to save her from embarrassment. She then declares that the disturbance was really created by the wealthy Arnold and Forbes, who did not approve of their son's marriage to her, and she cites class prejudices. Newspaper reporters in the court rush to report this scandal about the powerful Arnold just before Davenport benignly releases everyone from custody. Arthur then vanishes, and the mild-mannered Stewart finally unleashes his own accusations, all aimed at his father, pointing to his shady business deals and his social bias against Barrymore's decent family and, in particular, against the woman he loves, Arthur. Stewart then goes off in search of Arthur. Meanwhile, Warner, who is Arnold's foremost business competitor, denounces him to his face as a mean-minded predator of commerce and that he has failed as a human being. Warner dies a short time later, and Arnold, ruminating upon the comments to him from his son and from Warner, now comes to his senses. He goes to Barrymore's house to find the old man sitting outside, and Barrymore has decided to sell his beloved home. Arnold tells him that that is no longer necessary and that he and his family should remain in that old house. Both of them cement their friendship by playing a harmonica duet as Barrymore's family members happily reenter the house, and Stewart and Arthur return to plan a life together. The film ends with both families having dinner together. Capra presents the quintessential screwball comedy, offering nonstop humor where all of his manic characters are perfect in their roles, a film of well-organized chaos that keeps the viewer glued to its rollicking story line. The film received Oscars for Best Picture and Best Director (Capra) and it received Oscar nominations for Best Supporting Actress (Byington); Best Screenplay (Riskin); Best Cinematography (Walker); Best Film Editing (Havlick); and Best Sound Recording (John P. Livadary). It was a smash hit at the box office, earning more than $5.2 million in its initial release against a budget of more than $1.6 million. The film saw a radio adaptation aired by Lux Radio Theater on October 2, 1939, with Arnold reprising his role and Robert Cummings and Fay Wray playing the young lovers. Songs: "Valse Brilliante Op. 34 No. 2" (1838; Frederic Chopin), "Whistle While You Work" (1937; Frank Churchill), "Just Once Again" (1927; Walter Donaldson), "Rockin' the Town" (1938; Johnny Green), "Gypsy Dance No. 8" (Mischa Bakaleinikoff, Ben Oakland), "Hungarian Dance" (1869; Johannes Brahms), "Polly Wolly Doodle" (traditional), "Lock Lomand" (traditional Scottish folk song). *Author's Note*: The original Kaufman and Hart play, upon which this film is based, opened at New York's Booth Theater on December 14, 1936, won the 1937 Pulitzer Prize, and ran for 838 performances. The stage production was still running when this film was released. Capra had seen the play when attending the New York premiere of his classic **Lost Horizon**, 1937, and was overawed by the play's infectious hilarity and outlandish cast of characters. "I immediately went to Harry Cohn [Columbia's dictatorial chief], and asked him to purchase the rights for 'You Can't Take It with You,'" Capra told this author. "When I told him that it would cost the studio $200,000, he exploded, saying: 'Are you crazy? The rights to the Bible wouldn't cost that much!' I pointed out that the play was the biggest thing on Broadway and that if only the audiences that had seen the play came to see the picture, we would still be making a lot of money. He had someone in his office call New York every day to see the office receipts of the previous evening for that play and, only after he learned that the theater was playing to packed houses and had sold thousands of tickets far in advance, was he convinced that we had a captive audience for the picture version. Harry was the original Hollywood skinflint. He kept himself alive by nickel and diming everyone in his life. I went to sleep at night praying that he would get a visit from the three ghosts in *A Christmas Carol* to see the light, but those spirits, I guess, wanted no part of Harry Cohn, so it was up to me to battle with him for one good story after another in making the pictures I made at Columbia." Capra personally picked the cast members for this film, selecting Stewart after he saw the actor perform in **Navy Blue and Gold**,

Edward Arnold, James Stewart and Lionel Barrymore in *You Can't Take It with You*, **1938.**

1937, and liked the personable young man. "Jimmy had that look of innocent youth, something that never left his personality," Capra told this author, "and we got along great together." This film was the first collaboration between Capra and Stewart and two more would also prove to be classics, **Mr. Smith Goes to Washington**, 1939 (which also costarred Arthur) and **It's a Wonderful Life**, 1946. Stewart told this author that "working with that genius, Frank Capra, taught me more about pictures than I had learned up to that time. He was a perfectionist and liked to have as many retakes as he could until he was satisfied that he got the best from all of us. It was tiring, but very rewarding because we all became better for it." Capra shot more than 330,000 feet of film during the production, compared to the average 8,000-10,000 feet of film employed when making a feature film in that era. Much of the footage was due to Capra's constant retakes. During the production, Stewart noticed that Miller, who was debuting in this film at the age of fifteen, would do her ballet scenes and, when off the set, inexplicably begin crying. "I thought she was just nervous as this was her first picture," Stewart told this author, "and, to cheer her up, I brought her a few boxes of candy. She never told me the real reason why she was crying. Well, I learned years later that it was because her strenuous dancing [especially some extremely difficult ballet movements such as the toe pointe] had caused her considerable pain. She never complained about it. She was a great trouper right from the start." Arthur, who had become a superstar when appearing in Capra's **Mr. Deeds Goes to Town**, 1936, had nothing but admiration for the director, telling this author: "He [Capra] is one of the most considerate and gentle directors I ever met. He treated everyone with kindness and was patient with everyone. When he saw that Lionel Barrymore could no longer walk because of his painful arthritis, he simply had a false cast made for one of his legs and put him a wheelchair, explaining to the audience that his character had fallen when sliding down a bannister. He knew that Edward Arnold was notorious for flubbing his lines, but he and all of us put up with that without complaining because he was such a powerful actor. Frank [Capra] had no hesitation in using Mr. Arnold again when we all made **Mr. Smith Goes to Washington** the next year." Capra had a way of hiring everyone he could when making his films. There were only nineteen characters in the original stage production of this story, but he employed more than 150 actors and actresses in this film, particularly hiring performers who had fallen on hard times. "Harry [Cohn] confronted me one time," Capra told this author, "and accused me of 'padding' my casts. 'This studio [Columbia] is not a charity ward,' he said to me. I had to remind him all the time that extras were necessary in making any picture. 'Yeah, sure,' he griped, 'but you always add extras to the extras!'" Capra always went out of his way to aid any actor, and that was the case with Dub Taylor, who debuted in this film. Taylor, who would go on to become a veteran char-

James Stewart in *You Gotta Stay Happy*, 1948.

acter actor in scores of films (and would appear as a rascally reporter in Capra's **Mr. Smith Goes to Washington**), was out of work and his wife was expecting a baby when he answered an ad in the Hollywood trade papers that called for a character who could play the xylophone. Taylor knew how to play that instrument and enthusiastically applied for the role. Capra not only hired him, but, after learning that the starving actor was facing medical bills for the impending delivery of his child, kept Taylor on salary for the length of the eight-week production. The director used the excuse that Taylor needed to have "special musical training" in keeping him on salary, those additional payments allowing Taylor to cover his wife's hospital bill. Capra believed that this film would be the great success it became, but, on the eve of that success, Capra found no joy. While attending the premiere of this film, Capra was called away to a hospital where his three-year-old son, Johnny, had undergone a simple tonsillectomy, but a blood clot developed in the boy's brain and killed him. **p&d**, Frank Capra; **cast**, Jean Arthur, Lionel Barrymore, James Stewart, Edward Arnold, Mischa Auer, Ann Miller, Spring Byington, Samuel S. Hinds, Donald Meek, H.B. Warner, Halliwell Hobbes, Dub Taylor, Mary Forbes, Eddie "Rochester" Anderson, Clarence Wilson, Ann Doran, Christian Rub, Charles Lane, Harry Davenport, Ward Bond, Robert Greig; **w**, Robert Riskin (based on the play by George S. Kaufman, Moss Hart); **c**, Joseph Walker; **m**, Dimitri Tiomkin; **ed**, Gene Havlick; **art d**, Stephen Goosson.

You Gotta Stay Happy ★★★ 1948; U.S.; 100m; Rampart/William Dozier/UNIV; B/W; Comedy/Romance; Children: Acceptable; **DVD**; **VHS**. Delightful romantic romp begins with Fontaine, who is an heiress undecided about marrying her sixth fiancé, Parker, but is pushed into it. On the night of her wedding, she flees their honeymoon suite at a Manhattan hotel and takes refuge in the next room, which is occupied by Stewart, a commercial pilot, who craves sleep. Stewart, a WWII (1939-1945) veteran, has started a financially shaky cargo plane service, but its expenses have brought him to the brink of bankruptcy. Stewart really does not know what to do with Fontaine, believing that she is a poor young woman who has been forced to consorting with married men. He urges her to return home to her parents and lead a better life, but Fontaine pleads with him to take her from the evil ways of Manhattan and Stewart reluctantly agrees to take her along on his flight to California. That flight turns out to be a circus-like event where carefree if not careless co-pilot Albert creates considerable problems as he tells Stewart to relax and worry about nothing while Stewart is worrying about paying his bills. Fellow passengers consist of an escaped embezzler, a newly wedded smooching couple, a chimpanzee that smokes cigars, a corpse, and a perishable shipment of oysters. Everything that can go wrong does go wrong, and the plane is eventually forced to crash-land in a farmer's

field. By this time, however, Stewart and Fontaine have fallen in love and Fontaine decides to obtain a quick annulment from Parker. She and Stewart then plan to marry, and Stewart is overjoyed to realize that he will be marrying a wealthy woman who will save his embryonic air service. The lightweight script is overcome by top flight performances from Stewart and Fontaine, as well as receiving great support from the rest of the cast members. The story saw a sixty-minute radio adaptation aired by Lux Radio Theater on January 17, 1949, with Stewart and Fontaine reprising their roles. Though this is not a remake, the plot is similar to **Princess O'Rourke**, 1943. *Author's Note*: Stewart, who had been an accomplished pilot during WWII (as is his character in this film), told this author: "I had a flying jacket that I wore during the war that I felt was lucky for me and I wore that leather jacket in **You Gotta Stay Happy**. A lot of us actors did the same thing, I guess. I know that John Wayne had a lucky hat that he wore until that lid fell from his head in tatters." Actually, that leather jacket is often worn by Fontaine in the film, at the instructions of director Potter, who wanted to disguise Fontaine's appearance as she was pregnant at that time and was beginning to show her condition. **p**, Karl Tunberg; **d**, H.C. Potter; **cast**, Joan Fontaine, James Stewart, Eddie Albert, Roland Young, Willard Parker, Percy Kilbride, Porter Hall, Marcy McGuire, William Bakewell, Paul Cavanagh, Fritz Feld, Jock Mahoney; **w**, Tunberg (based on the *Saturday Evening Post* serial by Robert Carson); **c**, Russell Metty; **m**, Daniele Amfitheatrof; **ed**, Paul Weatherwax; **prod d**, Alexander Golitzen; **set d**, Russell A. Gausman, Ruby R. Levitt; **spec eff**, David S. Horsley.

You Never Can Tell ★★★ 1951; U.S.; 78m; UNIV; B/W; Comedy; Crime Drama/Fantasy; Children: Acceptable; **DVD**; **VHS**. Outlandish but cleverly presented fantasy begins with Rex, a former police and army dog. This German shepherd inherits a fortune from an eccentric millionaire, but someone poisons him to gain the fortune. Rex pleads with superiors in the Hereafter to be allowed to go back to earth so that he can track down and capture the culprits that ended his canine life. He is granted his wish and returns to Earth as Powell, a human being who is a private detective. He meets Holden, who tells him that she has joined him on earth as a female associate in his investigation, explaining that she was formerly a horse that has also been sent from Animal Heaven to assist him. (There are a lot of very funny sight gags that affix themselves to these transformed creature characters, such as Powell's inclination to pause before fire hydrants and Holden's obsession for biscuits as well as an uncontrollable snorting nigh from her now and then.) Powell's aim is really to protect Dow, the daughter of wealthy Sharpe, a young woman he had protected in his dog's life. Powell sniffs his way through scant clues, suspecting the household butler and housekeeper, but he finally focuses upon the real villain, Drake, a personable young man who is wooing Dow. Powell traps the villain and winds up remaining on earth to be with Dow while Holden, who has been advising troubled horses at a nearby racetrack, finally transforms back into her original image as a horse and gallops back to Heaven. Charming and entertaining, the film is consistently highlighted by Powell's entertaining performance. The incisive script decidedly and humorously takes the sides of animals. At one point, Holden urges Powell to be less devious and more forthcoming with people in his investigation. He replies: "These are humans we're dealing with. You can't tell them the truth and expect them to believe it." This is a fun-filled fantasy that will amuse the entire family. **p**, Leonard Goldstein; **d**, Lou Breslow; **cast**, Dick Powell, Peggy Dow, Joyce Holden, Charles Drake, Albert Sharpe, Lou Polan, Frank Nelson, Will Vedder, Frank Gerstle, Anthony George; **w**, Breslow, David Chandler (based on a story by Breslow); **c**, Maury Gertsman; **m**, Hans J. Salter; **ed**, Frank Gross; **art d**, Alexander Golitzen, Bernard Herzbrun; **set d**, Russell A. Gausman, Ruby R. Levitt; **spec eff**, David S. Horsley.

You Only Live Once ★★★★ 1937; U.S.; 86m; Walter Wanger Productions/UA; B/W; Crime Drama; Children: Unacceptable; **BD**; **DVD**;

VHS; IV. Pantheon director Lang presents a moody but powerful drama that ensnares two lovers, Fonda and Sidney, into a life of crime. These star-crossed lovers must deal with Fonda's sullied past. He has committed a number of robberies and has many convictions and is now a four-time loser. One more offense and conviction and Fonda will be imprisoned for life. Fonda, however, is determined to quit any criminal pursuits and vows to go straight. He gets a job and then marries Sidney, who has patiently waited for Fonda to have change of heart and alter his life. Fonda's past, however, haunts him and Sidney at every turn. After their landlord learns of Fonda's criminal background, he evicts the couple. Fonda, who works for a trucking company, is then fired after his employer discovers that he is an ex-convict. Then a hat belonging to Fonda is found at the scene of a bloody bank robbery where a guard has been killed. Police arrest Fonda and charge him with the crime, and he is quickly convicted and sentenced to death. Fonda now resolves to fight back at a system that has allowed him no opportunity to live a law-abiding life and decides to escape. He feigns illness and is sent to the prison hospital where he knows he can obtain a hidden gun. Once he has the gun, he uses it to hold prison doctor Cowan a hostage, using him as a shield as he makes his way into the prison yard. Gargan, the prison chaplain who has urged Fonda to keep faith, races toward him to tell him that he has been pardoned. Gargan explains that the body of the real bank robber, his getaway car and the stolen money, has been recovered from a lake and that Fonda can now become a free man. Fonda, however, has become too callous to believe anyone anymore. Fonda is convinced that Gargan is attempting to distract him so that he can be recaptured and returned to his cell on Death Row. When Gargan advances, Fonda impulsively fires the gun and kills the chaplain. Fonda then makes good his escape and reunites with Sidney. They are now wanted everywhere by police and are thought to be such dangerous criminals that they are labeled public enemies. Sidney delivers a baby, and the child is left with MacLane, who had been Fonda's devoted public defender and, at one time, Sidney's employer. Stealing a car, Fonda and Sidney begin driving toward the Canadian border in an effort to leave a country that has seemingly hounded them into crime. The couple manages to avoid dragnets and reach the Canadian border, but they lose control of the car and they set out on foot to enter Canada. New York State police, however, are waiting there for them and a police sharpshooter picks them up as they trudge forward in his telescopic sight. He fires and Sidney is mortally hit. Fonda takes her into his arms and carries her into Canada, but he, too, is fatally shot. Sidney dies in Fonda's cradling arms and he, too, then succumbs, both reaching freedom, but only in death. Lang presents a grim portrait where little or no hope is offered while he carefully crafts each uncompromising scene to make up what became a film noir classic. He brilliantly fills the screen with overcast skies and murky landscapes, where all is foreboding (as was his tradition when working in the German cinema). Fonda's portrayal as a social pariah is flawless, where irony compounds his fate into doom, while Sidney presents heart-aching empathy for a woman seeking nothing more than a safe place for her and her loved ones. She had played such roles of downtrodden characters in previous films, from **An American Tragedy**, 1931, to **Dead End**, 1937, justly earning the sobriquet 'The Face of the Great Depression.' In this film, she devastatingly represents the universal miseries and woes that beset the generation of that oppressive and impoverished decade. The film was successful at the box office and it saw a radio adaptation aired by Philip Morris Playhouse on November 28, 1941, with Burgess Meredith playing Fonda's role. A thirty-minute radio adaptation was aired by the Screen Guild Theater on October 29, 1945, with Fonda and Sidney reprising their roles. Song: "A Thousand Dreams of You" (Louis Alter). *Author's Note*: Sidney had nothing but praise for the hard-driving Lang, telling this author: "Even though you thought you had given your all in a scene, he [Lang] would have you do that scene over and over again until *he* thought you had gotten it right. We all knew he was a very demanding director, but we respected him because he wanted to

Guinn "Big Boy" Williams and Henry Fonda in *You Only Live Once,* 1937.

make the best possible picture and that meant he was working very hard to make us all be our very best." Fonda told this author: "Fritz Lang was a slave driver, one of those perfectionists that would have you do a scene over and over until you were ready to walk away or kick him. But we all knew that before we went to work in any picture with him, and we also knew that his pictures were a lot better than most of what was being made in Hollywood back then, so we went through his paces. In **You Only Live Once**, Lang exhausted us to the point where we all looked like we had been put through ringers, but that is exactly the look he wanted for characters being harassed at every turn until they have nowhere to go. I guess no one would put up with Fritz Lang today, but we sure did in the 1930s, and I think we were grateful for the experience." This film marked the debut of Jack Carson. The characters that Fonda and Sidney play are loosely based on the notorious bandits of the early 1930s, Clyde Barrow (1909-1934), and Bonnie Parker (1910-1934), both of whom were shot to death by a posse of Texas Rangers. Fonda and Sidney, however, play empathetic characters in this film, very much unlike the real Bonnie and Clyde, who were ruthless killers that took more than a dozen lives before they met their own bloody end. For more details on Bonnie and Clyde, see my two-volume work *The Great Pictorial History of World Crime*, Volume II (History, Inc., 2004; pages 1321-1326). Lang was aware of the excessive violence routinely exhibited by Bonnie and Clyde, who had been killed three years before this film was made. The director incorporated that kind of violence in a series of quick cuts to show the bank robbery for which Fonda is wrongly blamed. He showed in that startling sequence cops being shot down, along with women and children, and bullets strew the street and bombs are hurled to create bodies littering the sidewalks. The Breen Office, the then Hollywood censor, so strenuously objected to these violent shots that Lang was compelled to remove them before the film was released. **p**, Walter Wanger; **d**, Fritz Lang; **cast**, Sylvia Sidney, Henry Fonda, Barton MacLane, Jean Dixon, William Gargan, Jerome Cowan, Charles "Chick" Sale, Margaret Hamilton, Warren Hymer, Guinn "Big Boy" Williams, Ward Bond, Jack Carson; **w**, Gene Towne, Graham Baker (based on a story by Towne); **c**, Leon Shamroy; **m**, Alfred Newman; **ed**, Daniel Mandell; **art d**, Alexander Toluboff.

You Only Live Twice ★★★ 1967; U.K.; 117m; UNIV; Color; Spy Drama; Children: Unacceptable; **BD**; **DVD**; **VHS**; **IV**. This action-packed espionage tale, the fifth entry in the James Bond series, begins when an American spacecraft is hijacked from orbit by another unidentified spacecraft. The United States government believes the Soviets are responsible, but British authorities suspect Japanese involvement since the spacecraft landed in the Sea of Japan. Connery (James Bond), a British MI6 agent with the code name of 007, is assigned to investigate

Rita Hayworth and Fred Astaire in *You Were Never Lovelier*, **1942.**

and is sent to Tokyo after faking his own death and being buried at sea. In Tokyo, he is contacted by Wakabayashi, assistant to Japanese secret service chief Tamba. Wakabayashi introduces Connery to Gray, a local MI6 operative who claims to have evidence about the spacecraft that shot down the U.S. spacecraft. Gray is killed before he can tell Connery what he knows or suspects. Connery chases and kills the man who murdered Gray and then his investigation takes him to Osato Chemicals where he breaks into the office safe of the president of the company, Shimada. Leaving the building, assassins try to kill Connery, but Wakabayashi rescues him, while the assassins are killed by a magnetic device fired from a helicopter. Connery and Wakabayashi then drive to Kobe where a ship, the *Ning Po*, is docked, this vessel having delivered elements for rocket fuel. There Connery is captured by minions of Shimada, who orders Dor, his female secretary, to have him killed aboard the ship. Connery bribes Dor, and she helps him escape in a plane to Tokyo. Deceptive Dor sets off a flare in the plane while it is en route and bails out, but Connery manages to land the crashing plane and makes good his escape. Connery's investigation leads him to an island with a volcano that houses an elaborate secret rocket base inside of it. This leads Bond into more harrowing adventures including those with Japanese Secret Service ninjas until he finally discovers that the mastermind behind it all is Pleasence, the head of Connery's nemesis, SPECTRE. Pleasence activates the rocket base's self-destruct system and escapes, while Connery, Wakabayashi, and the ninjas escape the volcano before the base explodes and they are rescued by submarine. Connery has saved the world from World War III and lives to spy again. The incredible action in this film, much of it achieved through wonderfully creative gadgets and innovative special effects, provides exciting entertainment from the first scene to the last, where the indomitable Connery survives one crisis after another by using the coolest head in the realm of spies. The film was a huge box office success, earning almost $112 million in its initial release against a budget of more than $10 million. *Author's Note*: After Connery (and his wife, Diane Cilento) arrived in Tokyo to make this film, the press hounded the actor night and day, even photographing Connery in a toilet stall. He became enraged, especially after reporters insisted on calling him James Bond and not by his real name. Connery then announced that he would never again play the character, although he did return as 007 in **Never Say Never Again**, 1983. **p**, Albert R. Broccoli, Harry Saltzman; **d**, Lewis Gilbert; **cast**, Sean Connery, Akiko Wakabayashi, Tetsuro Tamba, Mie Hama, Teru Shimada, Donald Pleasence, Karin Dor, Bernard Lee, Lois Maxwell, Charles Gray, Desmond Llewelyn; **w**, Roald Dahl, Harold Jack Bloom (based on the novel by Ian Fleming); **c**, Freddie Young; **m**, John Barry; **ed**, Peter Hunt; **prod d**, Ken Adam; **art d**, Harry Pottle; **set d**, David Ffolkes; **spec eff**, John Stears.

You Were Never Lovelier ★★★★ 1942; U.S.; 97m; COL; B/W; Musical; Children: Acceptable; **DVD**; **VHS**; **IV**. Delightful songfest begins when Astaire, an American dancer, is stranded in Buenos Aires, Argentina, after losing his money betting on the horses. He hangs out at a hotel owned by Menjou, hoping to get work dancing in the hotel's stage show. Menjou has daughter problems. He has four of them and he has decided that they can marry only in order of their birth, the eldest first. Sister No. 1 marries and the two youngest want to go to the altar, but the second eldest sister, Hayworth, wants to wait for her dream man to appear. To keep peace in the family, Menjou sends flowers to Hayworth as a mystery man for her to fall in love with. Hayworth, however, falls in love with Astaire, thinking he is the mystery man after he inadvertently delivers flowers to her. Although Menjou does not approve of him, Menjou hires Astaire to go on playing that mystery man, in hopes that his mooning daughter will accept him as her groom. Astaire is, at first, reluctant to play cupid, but he slowly falls in love with Hayworth and they eventually tie the knot, which makes everyone happy. Astaire and Hayworth are terrific in this thoroughly entertaining musical, and their dance numbers are often spectacular. The film received Oscar nominations for Best Musical Score (Harline); Best Song ("Dearly Beloved"; Jerome Kern and Johnny Mercer); and Best Sound Recording (John Livadary). The film was a box office hit. Songs: "You Were Never Lovelier," "Dearly Beloved," "Wedding in the Spring," "These Orchids," "I'm Old Fashioned," "The Shorty George" (music: Jerome Kern; lyrics: Johnny Mercer); "Chiu, Chiu" (Nicanor Molinare); "Los Hijos de Buda" (Rafael Hernandez, Noro Morales); "Bim Bam Bum" (Johnnie Camacho, Noro Morales); "Echo" (Gilbert Valdes). *Author's Note*: "Of all of my pictures," Hayworth told this author, "I think that **You Were Never Lovelier** remains my very favorite. I loved dancing with Fred [Astaire], one of the greatest dancers of them all. He made you look like you were floating on air, but, believe me, we worked very hard in our rehearsals to make them look like it was all so easy." Astaire told this author that "Rita was one of my best dancing partners. She was an experienced hoofer and started out in pictures as a dancer. She was always very graceful and never seemed to tire. She was also a much better actress than a lot of people gave her credit for." Director Seiter told this author that "Fred [Astaire] wanted to have a Latin motif to all of the ensembles and dance numbers choreographed for **You Were Never Lovelier**, and I think the reason why he and Rita [Hayworth] hit it off so well was because Rita was Mexican-born and understood the tempo and pace of Latin music. They made it easy for me, because they did all the work and Fred really directed himself and Rita in those great dancing sequences." This was the second and final film together for Astaire and Hayworth who previously scored in **You'll Never Get Rich**, 1941. **p**, Louis F. Edelman; **d**, William A. Seiter; **cast**, Fred Astaire, Rita Hayworth, Adolphe Menjou, Isobel Elsom, Leslie Brooks, Adele Mara, Barbara Brown, Larry Parks, Kirk Alyn, Xavier Cugat and His Orchestra, Nan Wynn (voiceover vocals for Hayworth); **w**, Michael Fessier, Ernest Pagano, Delmer Daves (based on the story and screenplay "The Gay Senorita" by Carlos Olivari, Sixto Pondal Rios); **c**, Ted Tetzlaff; **m**, Leigh Harline; **ed**, William Lyon; **art d**, Lionel Banks.

You'll Find Out ★★★ 1940; U.S.; 97m; RKO; B/W; Comedy/Musical; Children: Cautionary; **DVD**; **VHS**. Hilarious spoof on horror films sees radio bandleader Kay Kyser and his team, known as "Kay Kyser's Kollege of Musical Knowledge," going to a mansion to perform at the twenty-first birthday celebration for Parrish, the girlfriend of their radio show's program manager, O'Keefe. They arrive at a scary-looking mansion during a heavy rainstorm in which lightning destroys a drawbridge over a moat that leaves them all stranded in the building. The ramshackle manor is full of odd objects collected over the years by Parrish's deceased father, who had been a global explorer. Parrish lives in the mansion with Kruger, her addlebrained aunt, and whose guest is Lugosi, a medium whom she hopes can contact Kruger's dead brother. Visiting in the mansion are Karloff, a retired judge, who is the family's attorney, and Lorre, a supposed psychologist and spiritualist, who Karloff has hired to expose Lugosi. Parrish's life becomes endangered when someone fires off a poisoned dart that strikes Simms, the band's female vocalist, who wears one of Parrish's dresses since her own got soaked in a rainstorm. It becomes grimly evident that someone does not want Parrish to reach her twenty-first birthday when she will inherit a large estate. Lugosi holds a séance the night just before Parrish is to become twenty-one, and she is nearly killed when a chandelier crashes nearby. Kyser and his band explore the mansion and discover mechanisms that Lugosi uses in his séances. They also realize that Lugosi, Karloff, and Lorre are all working together to kill Parrish and share the estate. The villainous trio has concocted a dynamite device intending to blow up Kyser and the others, but the elaborate explosive mechanism goes wrong and, instead, blows them up. Parrish and friends survive to celebrate her birthday and are more than grateful to eventually leave this house of manufactured horrors. This broad satire on spooks and lurking killers is packed with gags and pratfalls that keep the action moving along at a brisk pace, where fright-masters Lugosi, Karloff and Lorre are at their menacing best. Moreover, Kyser and company provide a lot of lilting tunes to bring fanciful light to all the looming shadows. This was a solid hit at the box office, earning more than $1 million in its initial release against a budget of $370,000. Songs: "(I've Grown So Lonely) Thinking of You" (1926; Kay Kyser's theme song; music: Walter Donaldson; lyrics: Paul Ash); "You've Got Me This Way," "I'd Know You Anywhere," "Like the Fella Once Said," "The Bad Humor Man," "I've Got a One Track Mind" (1940; music: Jimmy McHugh; lyrics: Johnny Mercer); "Heigh Ho" (1937; music: Frank Churchill; lyrics: Larry Morey); "My Bonnie Lies Over the Ocean" (1881; H.J. Fuller); "London Bridge Is Falling Down," "Pop! Goes the Weasel," "Three Blind Mice," "Old MacDonald Had a Farm" (traditional). *Author's Note*: Karloff told this author that "**You'll Find Out**" was a nice mixture of comedy and horror, but the frightening scenes were all played for laughs. The villain I played in that picture is not much different than the calculating cutthroat that tries to do away with timid Danny Kaye in **The Secret Life of Walter Mitty** [1946], and I had just as much fun threatening that zany, wonderful comedian as I did when I was trying to blow up Kay Kyser and his band." Lorre felt that his appearance with Lugosi, the only time the two appeared on the screen together, was personally disturbing, telling this author: "Bela was not a well man when we made that picture with Kay Kyser. He was already taking drugs and, after doing a scene, he would go off somewhere and shoot up [take an injection] of heroin or something, poor soul. I knew about his problem very well because I got addicted to morphine years earlier and it was hell kicking that habit. Bela took everything seriously, even though the picture we were making was lampooning horror pictures. I asked him once during the production: 'You don't believe in any of this murder plot nonsense, do you?' He leaned very close to me, his grim, long face only inches from my own, and said through a scowl: 'Of course I do—don't you?' Without batting an eye, he added: 'It is within us all to contemplate murder at one time or another...A little fellow like you, for instance, would make for a perfect victim.' I went out of my way to have no further conversations with him." Lorre attended Lugosi's funeral services in 1956, and remarked to a friend at that time when peering at Lugosi's casket: "Do you think we should drive a stake through his heart just to be sure?" Jeff Corey saw his film debut in this production. **p&d**, David Butler; **cast**, Kay Kyser, Peter Lorre, Boris Karloff, Bela Lugosi, Helen Parrish, Dennis O'Keefe, Alma Kruger, Joseph Eggenton, Ginny Simms, Harry Babbitt, M.A. Bogue (as Ish Kabibble), Sully Mason, Jeff Corey; **w**, James V. Kern (based on a story by Kern, Butler, Monte Brice, Andrew Bennison, R.T.M. Scott); **c**, Frank Redman; **m**, Roy Webb; **ed**, Irene Morra; **art d**, Van Nest Polglase; **set d**, Darrell Silvera; **spec eff**, Vernon L. Walker.

You'll Like My Mother ★★★ 1972; U.S.; 92m; BCP/UNIV; Color; Horror; Children: Unacceptable (MPAA: PG); **VHS**. Top-notch thriller

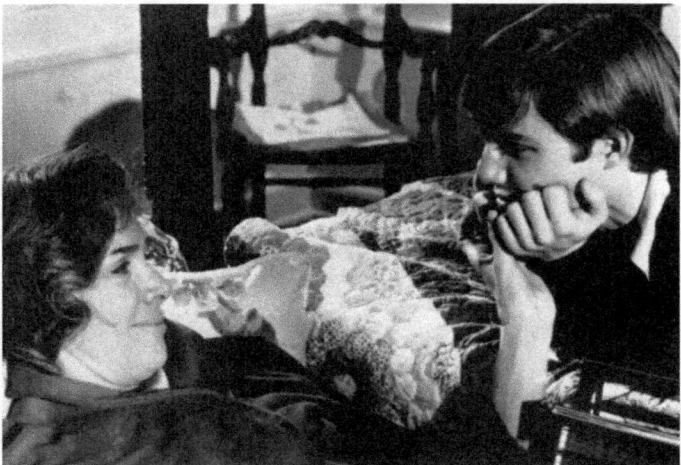

Rosemary Murphy and Richard Thomas in *You'll Like My Mother*, 1972.

begins with Duke, who is a widow made pregnant by her husband before he left for the Vietnam War (1961-1975) and was killed. She leaves Los Angeles and, while driving in a blizzard to his mansion in a Minnesota town, she arrives to find that her mother-in-law, Murphy, says her son never told her he got married. It turns out that Murphy is not Duke's mother-in-law, but an aunt masquerading as Duke's late husband's mother in an attempt to inherit the mansion. Murphy wants the house because her own son, Thomas, a homicidal maniac wanted for murder and serial rape, is hiding in the basement. Duke meets Allen, a young woman who seems mentally unbalanced and mute and who Murphy claims is Duke's sister-in-law, but she is really Murphy's own daughter. Duke shortly goes into labor and delivers a baby, but, after she revives, Murphy informs her that the child is dead and hands the baby to Allen for burial. Duke is later awakened by Allen, who leads her to the attic where she shows the newborn child to her, the baby very much alive. Duke goes unseen to the basement where she sees Thomas and Murphy in conversation and she soon realizes that Murphy and her son intend to kill her and her child so that they can inherit the fabulous mansion. When the storm abates, Murphy tells Duke that it is time for her to leave and take a bus back to L.A. Thomas is waiting to drive her to the bus station, but Duke realizes that this psychopath is present to end her life. She gives the excuse that she has forgotten her gloves and reenters the mansion, retrieving her child. Duke then attempts to escape by running from the house, but Murphy orders Thomas to track her down. Thomas chases her to a carriage house, knocking her unconscious. He then holds the baby and covers its crying mouth, sadistically grinning as he is about to murder the child. At that moment, Allen races to Thomas and stabs him in the back with a pair of scissors, killing him. Murphy is devastated and is shown cradling the dead Thomas as Duke holds her baby, and she and Allen look upon the grim scene as help arrives. Duke, Murphy, Allen and Thomas are all standouts in their roles. Director Johnson carefully unfolds this harrowing tale, using the howling storm to provide a chilling and claustrophobic atmosphere, which assured its box office success. *Author's Note*: The film was shot on location at the Glensheen Historic Estate outside of Duluth, Minnesota, where this dire story repeated itself in reality on June 27, 1977, when its millionaire owner, Elizabeth Mannering Congdon (1894-1977), and her nurse, Velma Pietila (1911-1977) were found murdered. The murders were later attributed to Marjorie Congdon, a sociopath and one of the two daughters of Elizabeth Congdon, and her boyfriend, Roger Caldwell. Both reportedly committed the murders in order to inherit the Congdon estate. Violence prohibits viewing by children. **p**, Mort Briskin; **d**, Lamont Johnson; **cast**, Patty Duke, Rosemary Murphy, Richard Thomas, Sian Barbara Allen, Dennis Rucker, Harold Congdon, James Glazman, James Neumann, Joel Thingvall; **w**, Jo Heims (based

Anthony Hopkins in *You Will Meet a Tall Dark Stranger,* 2010.

on the novel by Naomi A. Hintze); **c**, Jack A. Marta, Vincent Saizis (Technicolor); **m**, Gil Melle; **ed**, Edward M. Abroms; **art d**, William D. DeCinces; **spec eff**, Joe Goss.

You Will Meet a Tall Dark Stranger ★★★ 2010; U.S./Spain; 98m; Mediapro/Sony; Color; Comedy/Romance; Children: Unacceptable; (MPAA: R); **BD**; **DVD**; **IV**. This entertaining and hectic episodic tale records the misadventures of two married couples, Hopkins and Jones, and their daughter, Watts, and her husband, Brolin, as their sex drives, ambitions, and anxieties lead them into chaos. Hopkins has enough of Jones to see if he can reclaim his lost youth. Meanwhile, Watts loses interest in Brolin and develops a crush on her boss, Banderas, the handsome owner of an art gallery. Several other romantic misanthropes enter their lives, including a call girl and a novelist, who becomes enamored of a woman of mystery that watches him through a window. Love's own unpredictable reasoning finally brings sensibility and relief to all in this offbeat comedy. Songs/Music: "Laser Luxe" (Rupert Pope, Reece Gilmore), "When My Baby Smiles at Me" (Ted Lewis, Bill Munro, Andrew B. Sterling, Harry von Tilzer), "When You Wish Upon a Star" (Ned Washington, Leigh Harline), "If I Had You" (Reginald Connelly, James Campbell, Ted Shapiro), "Grave Assir" (from "Guitar Quintet in D Major 'Fandango'" by Luigi Boccherini), "I'll See You in My Dreams" (Gus Kahn, Isham Jones), "Let Your Body Move" (Marc Ferrari, Michael McGregor), "Serenade No. 6 in D Major, Rondo Allegretto" (Wolfgang Amadeus Mozart), "Only You/And You Alone" (Buck Ram, Andre Rand), "Tu Che a Dio Spiegasti L'ali" (from the opera "Lucia di Lammermoor, Act 3" by Gaetano Donizetti), "Mais si l'amour" (Giulia Tellarini, Maik Alemany Uson, Alejandro Mazzoni, Jens Neumaier), "I Never Loved You" (Scott Nickoley, Jamie Dunlap), "My Sin" (Lew Brown, B.G. DeSylva, Ray Henderson). Gutter language prohibits viewing by children. **p**, Letty Aronson, Jaume Roures, Stephen Tenenbaum, Helen Robin, Nicky Kentish Barnes; **d&w**, Woody Allen; **cast**, Anthony Hopkins, Naomi Watts, Josh Brolin, Antonio Banderas, Gemma Jones, Rupert Frazer, Freida Pinto, Kelly Harrison, Fenella Woolgar, Ewen Bremner, Neil Jackson, Lynda Baron; **c**, Vilmos Zsigmond; **ed**, Alisa Lepselter; **prod d**, Jim Clay; **art d**, Dominic Masters; **set d**, John Bush; **spec eff**, Stuart Brisdon.

You'll Never Get Rich ★★★ 1941; U.S.; 88m; COL; B/W; Musical; Romance; Children: Acceptable; **DVD**; **VHS**; **IV**. Entertaining tune-filled tale begins with Benchley, a Broadway theater owner and womanizer, who gets his manager, Astaire, to help him romance dancer Hayworth. However, Benchley's wife, Inescort, is aware of his latest dalliance. Hubbard, an army captain interested in Hayworth, invites her and her aunt, Gateson, to visit him and his mother, Shoemaker, at his army base. Astaire, who has just been drafted into the army at the start of World War II (1939-1945), has been posted there. MacBride is his top sergeant, and his buddies are fellow draftees Nazarro and Williams. Astaire begins to pursue Hayworth by purloining a captain's uniform to impress her. Benchley goes to the base to produce a show for the troops and assigns Astaire as his assistant. Benchley begins to pursue Massen, another dancer who he has promised to be the show's star. Hubbard learns he is to be sent to Panama and asks Hayworth to marry him and go there with him, but she is undecided. A farcical business then enters involving a diamond bracelet that will derail romances between all those involved, so Astaire goes AWOL to retrieve it from his apartment. This results in Hayworth accepting Hubbard's proposal. Inescort then arrives at the base and forces Massen to leave the show. Astaire and Hayworth are to dance and then marry in the show. Astaire, however, arranges for a genuine Justice of the Peace to officiate in the stage marriage. Astaire then confesses the wedding charade to Hayworth and she forgives him, visiting him in the guardhouse where he has been jailed for impersonating an officer. Hayworth has loved Astaire all along, so his hoodwinking fulfilled her romantic ambitions to end this romp. He is further spared a court-martial when Hubbard, who accepts the fact that Hayworth loves Astaire and not him, orders Astaire released from the guardhouse. Implausible as are most musicals, this one nevertheless presents a lively tale and some very good music and dancing ensembles where hoofers Astaire and Hayworth trip the light fantastic. Songs: "Boogie Barcarolle," "Dream Dancing," "Shootin' the Works for Uncle Sam," "Since I Kissed My Baby Goodbye," "March Milastaire," "So Near and Yet So Far," "The Wedding Cake Walk" (Cole Porter), "Fruhlingdslied/Spring Song" (Felix Mendelssohn-Bartholdy), "Taps" (Daniel Butterfield). **Author's Note**: Astaire told this author: "Fortune smiled on me when giving me Rita [Hayworth] as a new dancing partner [after he had severed dancing ties with Ginger Rogers, who wanted to concentrate on dramatic roles]. She is one of the most graceful female dancers I ever met. She instinctively follows tempo to make up what I call perfect rhythm." Hayworth, in her first starring role in a big-budgeted film at her home studio of Columbia, was an overnight sensation with this very successful film. At about the same time this film was released, she appeared in a photo spread published by *Life Magazine*, one image showing her kneeling on a bed and wearing a revealing negligee, that image immortalizing her as a foremost Hollywood sex siren. "No one like the great Fred Astaire," Hayworth told this author. "He made me look so good in our dancing numbers together, but that was not achieved overnight. Fred rehearses his numbers until every kink is gone, like all perfectionists. I am remembered for some pictures like **Gilda** [1946], but the pictures I made with Fred are the ones that made me a star and those are the ones *I* remember best." This film was Astaire's and Hayworth's first of two pairings; **You Were Never Lovelier** filmed the following year. The great composer Cole Porter unusually undertook the writing of the score for this film, composing several military-type songs that were out of the mainstream romantic ballads he invariably produced. Further, he was hampered by a meddling Harry Cohn, head of Columbia, who, even though he had a tin ear, was uncertain as to whether anyone would like Porter's new tunes. He tested them on his secretaries at Columbia to get their approval before Cohn green-lighted Porter's compositions. The song titled "You'll Never Get Rich," stems from the traditional army song that offers the lyrics: "You'll never get rich / by digging a ditch / You're in the Army now!" A lot of humor is offered by the clever Benchley, who is always a bit too clever for his own good, and Cliff Nazarro, a master of the double talk, rattling off what seemed to be logical phrases, but his words consisted of nothing more than artfully enunciated gibberish. **p**, Samuel Bischoff; **d**, Sidney Lanfield; **cast**, Fred Astaire, Rita Hayworth, Robert Benchley, John Hubbard, Osa Massen, Frieda Inescort, Guinn Williams, Donald MacBride, Cliff Nazarro, Marjorie Gateson, Ann Shoemaker, Tim Ryan, Martha Tilton; **w**, Michael Fessier, Ernest Pagano; **c**, Philip Tannura; **m**, Cole Porter, (musical director) Morris Stoloff; **ed**, Otto Meyer; **art d**, Lionel Banks.

Young and Innocent ★★★★ 1938; U.K.; 84m; Gaumont Picture Corporation; B/W; Mystery; Children: Unacceptable; **DVD**; **VHS**; **IV**. This cleverly created whodunit from pantheon director Hitchcock begins with rich actress Carme, who is arguing with Curzon, her ex-husband. Curzon, passionately jealous over Carme, mentions the name of de Marney, a young man living nearby, and Carme slaps his face. Curzon says nothing and wordlessly leaves. A short time later, de Marney is walking along the seashore when he sees to his horror the body of Carme wash ashore. He races off to notify the police, but two swimmers arrive at that time, seeing de Marney running from the corpse. After police arrive, they find a belt from de Marney's missing raincoat lying next to the body, the instrument apparently used to strangle Carme to death. De Marney immediately becomes the prime suspect in the case after it is learned that he was not only friendly with the wealthy victim but had been included in her will. Arrested, de Marney is grilled throughout the night until he faints. He is revived through the aid of Pilbeam, who has some training as a nurse and is the daughter of Marmont, the local chief constable. She is instantly attracted to de Marney and feels sorry for his plight. De Marney is then put on trial, but he realizes that his barrister is inept and that mounting circumstantial evidence will undoubtedly bring about his conviction. He disguises himself with some glasses and, in the confusion of a crowded courtroom, makes his escape. While fleeing through the countryside, de Marney meets Pilbeam, convincing her to drive him to a deserted farmhouse where he attempts to persuade the young woman that he is innocent, although Pilbeam is fearful that her association with the wanted man will bring serious repercussions from her father, Marmont. By this time, however, Pilbeam has fallen in love with the charming de Marney and she considers helping him. While de Marney hides in the farmhouse, Pilbeam joins her father and brothers for dinner, but when they all discuss de Marney's case and Pilbeam learns that de Marney is without funds, she excuses herself and returns to the farmhouse, bringing de Marney food and money. She agrees to drive him to the tavern where he left his raincoat, the very item that might prove him innocent. While driving to the tavern, de Marney carelessly attracts the attention of two inept constables, who pursue them, but the young and innocent couple escapes. When they arrive at the pub, there is a scuffle, both learning that Rigby, a tramp, now has de Marney's raincoat. They go in search of Rigby, but are sidetracked when Pilbeam must attend a birthday party where she and de Marney come under the scrutiny of relatives, especially by snoopy Clare, who is Philbeam's aunt, while a game of blind-man's-bluff is played. They manage to leave and eventually find Rigby at a homeless shelter. He gives them the raincoat, but it is missing its belt. Rigby, however, is able to provide the pair with a clue and that is that the man who gave him the raincoat has a nervous eye twitch. Police pursue the pair, chasing them to an abandoned coal mine. They ride in a coal car through the dark shaft, only to have the ceiling collapse upon them; Pilbeam is rescued at the last moment by de Marney's outstretched hand (in reality, the outstretched hand shown by Hitchcock in close-up is that of Pen Tennyson, the great-grandson of poet Alfred Lord Tennyson, who was then Hitchcock's assistant director and who would later marry Pilbeam). The couple becomes separated, and Marmont, realizing that his daughter had involved herself with a wanted man, decides to resign his post. Pilbeam and Rigby, however, are led to a hotel, going to its ballroom where dancers jam the floor and a band is playing, all of its members in blackface (as was the habit of jazz bands in that era). As Pilbeam stands nearby, Rigby, the only person knowing the identity of the man who gave him the raincoat, scans the crowd, looking for that man. His vision becomes that of the camera, which slowly pans through and over the crowd of dancers until it comes to a stop at one of the band members, the drummer. The camera then closes up on the drummer's face, narrowing to his eyes, which, when he spots Rigby, begin to twitch uncontrollably. The drummer is Curzon, the real killer. He faints, collapsing

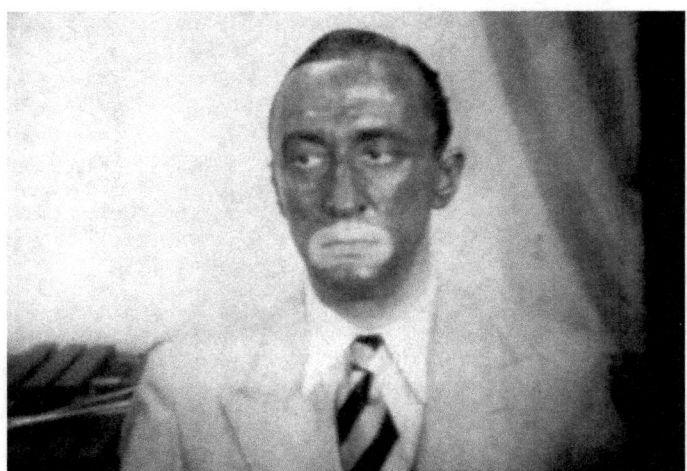

Portrait of a killer in black face: George Curzon in *Young and Innocent,* **1938.**

to the floor. When revived, he confesses to killing Carme, thus exonerating de Marney. Hitchcock deftly helms this thriller by carefully and cleverly building its scenes to the eventual crescendo of the band blaring and the drummer frenetically playing. The man-on-the-run theme is a traditional plotline for Hitchcock (as shown in such classic films as **The 39 Steps**, 1935; **Saboteur**, 1942; and **North by Northwest**, 1959) and is in harrowing evidence here. He also employs the offbeat romance of a reluctant lover, Pilbeam, who attempts to prove the innocence of the man she loves to vindicate her love for him, as can be seen in other Hitchcock films (**Rebecca**, 1940; **Stage Fright**, 1950; and **Strangers on a Train**, 1951). Pilbeam, who first appeared as a child in peril in Hitchcock's first version of **The Man Who Knew Too Much**, 1934, gives a fine performance as a young woman torn between her love for a father who upholds the law and her love for a man accused of breaking it. The personable de Marney is a standout as the wrongly accused victim, who has been framed by a calculating killer. The film was a hit at the box office in its initial release, impacting U.S. audiences to the point where Hitchcock became much in demand by Hollywood producers and studios. Songs: "No One Can Like the Drummer Man" (Samuel Lerner, Al Goodhart, Al Hoffman), "May I Have the Next Romance With You" (Mack Gordon, Harry Revel), "I've Got Something In My Eye" (James V. Monaco, Charles Newman). *Author's Note*: Hitchcock appears in his traditional cameo role about fourteen minutes into this film as a clumsy photographer outside the courtroom from which de Marney escapes. Hitchcock admitted to this author that "we took considerable liberties with the original novel on which the picture is based. The writers had to eliminate most of the novel's characters, and even changed the identity of the real killer. This was necessary in order to maintain a sense to the story line, or, as they call it, continuity. I was upset when the United States distributors for **Young and Innocent** cut the picture from eighty-four minutes to seventy minutes when it was released in America. They cut out the scenes involving the birthday party, but those scenes were important in building suspense, especially where the 'blind-man's bluff' sequence mirrors the chase involving Derek [de Marney]. Such essential subtle techniques were often lost on the less sophisticated audiences in America in those days." Hitchcock was proud of the coal shaft scene, which he had personally designed, one where a hydraulic platform eighteen feet above the floor of a sound stage was built and the coal shaft built on top of that platform. When the shaft seems to collapse, it is the platform that is actually descending as coal is showered atop the actors, the camera riding with the coal car as it descends. The marvelous dolly shot Hitchcock achieved in the ballroom of the hotel covered an area of 145 feet. In that expertly captured fluid shot, the camera swoops down upon the dancers and then slowly floats over them as they swirl beneath its lens, and the camera finally releases its visual tension by stopping

Frank Sinatra and Doris Day in *Young at Heart*, 1954.

only four inches from the face of the culprit. **p**, Edward Black; **d**, Alfred Hitchcock; **cast**, Nova Pilbeam, Derrick de Marney, Percy Marmont, Edward Rigby, Mary Clare, John Longden, George Curzon, Basil Radford, Pamela Carme, George Merritt, Jerry Verno, Torin Thatcher, Hitchcock; **w**, Charles Bennett, Edwin Greenwood, Anthoy Armstrong, Alma Reville, Gerald Savory (based on the novel *A Shilling for Candles* by Josephine Tey); **c**, Bernard Knowles; **m**, Jack Beaver; **ed**, Charles Frend; **art d**, Alfred Junge; **spec eff**, Jack Whitehead.

Young and Willing ★★★ 1943; U.S.; 83m; Cinema Guild/UA; B/W; Comedy; Children: Acceptable; **DVD**; **VHS**; **IV**. Entertaining tale begins with a group of starving actors, young and willing, who share finances and an apartment in Greenwich Village, New York. To keep the peace, Holden gets them all to agree to a policy of no romances, until they get roles on Broadway. Two of the group, Britton and Brown, are already secretly married, and Bracken, one of the other young actors, is in love with Hayward, one of the actresses. Friends of O'Driscoll visit and are shocked to see young men and women sharing the same space and they insist that O'Driscoll inform her rich father, Fassett, about such unorthodox living arrangements. Since they may lose O'Driscoll's rent (she is the only one with any money), the actors leave the apartment until Fassett visits and then departs. Fassett sees no women in the apartment until two of the girls, Britton and Hayward, arrive and accuse Fassett of being a dirty old man and he leaves befuddled. Paige, the landlady, keeps asking for rent and one day gives her boarders a manuscript for a play she has found in a hallway. The group rehearses the play and its author, Benchley, who lives downstairs, watches their rehearsal and says he will produce it, and with all of the boarders performing the play on Broadway. This solves everyone's rental problems as well as their furtive romantic situation. This wacky comedy is firmly directed by Griffith, and Holden, Hayward, and Bracken are standouts. The 1954 and 1962 films of the same name are not related to this story. *Author's Note*: This film was made in 1941, but Paramount did not release it until two years later, which explains why many of the actors appear so young (Holden, Bracken, Hayward) as they were then beginning their careers. "**Young and Willing** was one of my 'Smiling Jim' pictures," Holden told this author. "It was the kind of picture where I grin my way through the story, another lighthearted if not lightheaded character, but that picture was still a lot of fun to make." This was the last film Holden would make before he entered the U.S. Army Air Force to fight in WWII (1939-1945). Hayward told this author that "**Young and Willing** was a combination of **Stage Door** [1937] and **My Sister Eileen** [1942], but was presented as a screwball comedy. I was lucky enough to have the meatiest female part and even got to wear a slinky gown and vamp the great Robert Benchley. We weren't making a lot of money in

those days, but we had a lot fun making pictures." **p&d**, Edward H. Griffith; **cast**, William Holden, Eddie Bracken, Robert Benchley, Susan Hayward, Martha O'Driscoll, Barbara Britton, Mabel Paige, James Brown, Florence MacMichael, James Brown, Jay Fassett, Cheryl Walker; **w**, Virginia Van Upp (based on the play "Out of the Frying Pan" by Francis Swann); **c**, Leo Tover; **m**, Victor Young; **ed**, Eda Warren; **art d**, Hans Dreier, Ernst Fegte.

Young at Heart ★★★ 1954; U.S.; 117m; Arwin/WB; Color; Drama; Musical/Romance; Children: Unacceptable; **BD**; **DVD**; **VHS**. Intriguing tale begins with Young, a handsome songwriter who arrives in a small Connecticut town where three sisters, Day, Malone, and Fraser, all fall in love with him. Day and Young become engaged, but Day has second thoughts when Young's friend, Sinatra, arrives to help him with some song arrangements. Day is upbeat and full of sunshine, while Sinatra sees his glass as half empty and lives under a constant dark cloud. Despite their differing personalities, they fall in love. Meanwhile, Malone and Fraser both marry. Then Day and Sinatra marry, but he continues to feel doubts of self-worth. Sinatra becomes so depressed that one night he decides to kill himself, thinking Day would be happier with Young. Sinatra drives into oncoming traffic during a snowstorm with his windshield wipers off, and the car crashes. He survives with a new desire to live and make his marriage work. He writes a song he had been working on and finds his self-esteem with Day and their new baby. Though the entire cast renders top-notch performances, Sinatra steals the show with a bravura performance of a disillusioned but talented man who somehow cannot find his way in a world he thinks is out to crush his spirit. Day is also very good as the staunchly supportive and loving spouse, a role she had played in such films as **I'll See You in My Dreams**, 1951 (as the loyal wife of composer Gus Kahn), and **The Winning Team**, 1952 (as the devoted wife of baseball pitcher Grover Cleveland Alexander). This good remake of **Four Daughters**, 1938, proved to be a box office hit, earning more than $2.5 million at the box office in its initial release; the title song, sung by Sinatra, also went to the top of the charts. Songs: "Just One of Those Things" (Cole Porter), "Someone to Watch Over Me" (music: George Gershwin; lyrics: Ira Gershwin), "One for My Baby/and One More for the Road" (music: Harold Arlen; lyrics: Johnny Mercer), "Hold Me in Your Arms" (Ray Heindorf, Charles Henderson, Don Pippin), "Ready, Willing and Able" (Floyd Huddleston, Al Rinker, Dick Gleason), "Till My Love Comes Back to Me" (based on "On Wings of Song"; music: Felix Mendelssohn-Bartholdy, Ray Heindorf; lyrics: Paul Francis Webster), "There's a Rising Moon for Every Falling Star" (music: Sammy Fain; lyrics: Paul Francis Webster), "You, My Love" (music: Jimmy Van Heusen; lyrics: Mack Gordon), "Young at Heart" (music: Johnny Richards; lyrics: Carolyn Leigh). *Author's Note*: Sinatra told this author that "I knew what it was to be kicked around like the character I played in **Young at Heart**, so, when playing that composer, I was really playing myself in a way. I never had any illusions about life. It's a dog-eat-dog world, but you try to find some happiness wherever or whenever you can, and that's what my character does when he comes to his senses." Sinatra liked Barrymore, who was so frail (at age seventy-six) when making this film that she confined herself to a wheelchair to preserve what energy she could muster for her scenes. Sinatra thoughtfully gave her a surprise birthday party during the production that moved the celebrated actress to tears. He was less enthusiastic about Doris Day's manipulative husband, Martin Melcher, telling Day that her husband was ruining her career by his constant meddling and managing and that he was simply using her to advance his own Hollywood career as a self-styled producer. Day wanted no part of such criticism and refused to listen to Sinatra. For his part, however, Sinatra went to the front office and told studio boss Jack Warner that if he did not bar Melcher from the set of **Young at Heart**, he, Sinatra, would quit the film. Sinatra, by that time, had become a powerhouse in Hollywood, and Warner bowed to his wishes, promptly banning Melcher from the Warner Brothers lot. So powerful was Sinatra that he had cinematographer Charles Lang replaced by Ted McCord, because Lang caused too many rehearsal takes and Sinatra preferred to skip rehearsals and make only one take. **p,** Henry Blanke; **d,** Gordon Douglas; **cast,** Doris Day, Frank Sinatra, Gig Young, Ethel Barrymore, Dorothy Malone, Robert Keith, Elisabeth Fraser, Alan Hale Jr., Barbara Pepper, Tony Taylor; **w,** Liam O'Brien (based on the screenplay for the film **Four Daughters** by Julius J. Epstein, Lenore Coffee from the story "Sister Act" by Fannie Hurst); **c,** Ted McCord (Warner Color); **m,** Ray Heindorf; **ed,** William Ziegler; **art d,** John Beckman; **set d,** William Wallace; **spec eff,** H.F. Koenekamp.

Young Bess ★★★ 1953; U.S.; 112m; MGM; Color; Biographical Drama; Children: Unacceptable; **DVD; VHS.** Simmons is exceptional in essaying the early life of England's Elizabeth I (1533-1603) in this sumptuous production that shows her turbulent childhood to the eve of her accession to the throne. After the execution of her mother, Anne Boleyn (1501-1536), played by Elaine Stewart, who is accused of infidelity by her husband Henry VIII (1491-1547), outstandingly played by Laughton (who won an Oscar for playing the same role in **The Private Life of Henry VIII**, 1933), young Bess (Simmons) is declared illegitimate. Not entitled to inherit the throne, she is exiled to Hatfield House near London. Accompanying Simmons are her loyal servant Kellaway and governess Walsh. Laughton marries Lady Catherine Parr (1512-1548), played by Kerr, and, when Simmons is a teenager, she rebels against Laughton, but he so much likes her defiant behavior that he declares her legitimate and an heir to his throne. Laughton dies and Thompson, his nine-year-old son, becomes Edward VI (1537-1553). Simmons falls in love with Admiral Thomas Seymour (1509-1549), played by Granger, whose brother Ned (Rolfe) has become Thompson's guardian and Lord Protector. Simmons sees Granger in the arms of Kerr, but Kerr soon after falls ill and dies. Rolfe, jealous of Granger's ambitions, has him arrested and charged with treason, while also accusing Simmons of plotting with Granger to overthrow Thompson. Simmons gets Thompson to write a pardon for Granger, but is too late to save him from execution. Thompson soon afterward dies, leaving Simmons next in line for the throne. Although the scriptwriters took liberties with the facts concerning this tempestuous royal family, Franklin nevertheless offers a thoroughly absorbing historical epic with superb production values and outstanding performances from Simmons, Granger, Kerr and Laughton. The film was a hit at the box office, earning more than $4 million in its initial release against a budget of more than $2.4 million. *Author's Note*: MGM bought the rights to the Irwin novel in 1945. "At that time," Kerr told this author, "they were thinking of putting Elizabeth Taylor in the role of young Bess, but they realized she was too young for the part. They had the scriptwriters rewrite the role for an older Bess and signed me to play the part. The project was sidetracked for some time and Jean Simmons was later given the role, and I was signed to do the role of one of Henry's wives [Catherine Parr]. In Hollywood, everyone ages a lot faster than in real life, and promised roles disappear even faster." Granger told this author that "I got to do my derring-do again in **Young Bess**, one of my favorite costume epics, but I did not get involved with the spectacular swordplay I had a few years earlier in **Scaramouche** [1952]. That was all well and good since I almost broke my neck in fencing with Mel Ferrer in **Scaramouche**." Granger was married to Simmons when they appeared in this film together. Many other actresses have essayed Elizabeth I of England in many other films, including **Border Warfare**, 1990 (made-for-TV; Juliet Cadzow); **Dorothy Vernon of Haddon Hall**, 1924 (Clare Eames); **Drake the Pirate**, 1936 (Athene Seyler); **Drake's Venture**, 1980 (made-for-TV; Charlotte Cornwell); **Elizabeth**, 1998 (Cate Blanchett); **Elizabeth R**, 1971-1972 (TV miniseries; six episodes: Glenda Jackson); **Elizabeth Rex**, 2004 (made-for-TV; Diane D'Aquila); **Elizabeth: The Golden Age**, 2007 (Cate Blanchett); **Elizabeth the Queen**, 1968 (made-for-TV; Judith Anderson); **The Eternal Strife**, 1915 (Maud Yates); **Fire over England**, 1937 (Flora Robson); **Gloriana**, 1984 (made-for-TV; Sarah Walker); **Glori-**

Jean Simmons and Stewart Granger in *Young Bess,* 1953.

ana, 2000 (made-for-TV; Josephine Barstow); **Gunpowder, Treason & Plot**, 2004 (made-for-TV; Catherine McCormack); **The Heart of the Queen**, 1940 (Maria Koppenhofer); **Henry VIII**, 2003 (made-for-TV; Lorna Lacey); **The Hourglass Sanatorium**, 1973 (Zofia Bajuk); **I Married an Angel**, 1942 (Edwina Coolidge); **Jubilee**, 1978 (Jenny Runacre); **Loves and Adventures in the Life of Shakespeare**, 1914 (Aimee Martinek); **Mary of Scotland**, 1936 (Florence Eldridge); **Mary Stuart**, 1982 (made-for-TV; Rosalind Plowright); **O Principe E o Mendigo**, 1972 (TV series: Adriana de Goes; Suzana Goncalves); **The Other Boleyn Girl**, 2008 (Maisie Smith); **The Pearls of the Crown**, 1938 (Yvette Pienne); **The Prince and the Pauper**, 1977 (Lalla Ward); **The Prince and the Pauper**, 1996 (TV series; six episodes: Elizabeth Ann O'Brien); **The Private Lives of Elizabeth and Essex**, 1939 (Bette Davis); **Queen Elizabeth**, 1912 (Sarah Bernhardt); **The Queen's Traitor**, 1967 (TV series; Susan Engel); **Regal Cavalcade**, 1935 (Athene Seyler); **The Sea Hawk**, 1940 (Flora Robson); **Seven Seas to Calais**, 1963 (Irene Worth); **Shirley Temple's Storybook**, 1958-1960 (TV series; "The Prince and the Pauper," 1960 episode: Portland Mason); **The Story of Mankind**, 1957 (Agnes Moorehead); **Time Flies**, 1944 (Olga Lindo); **Tower of London**, 1939 (Barbara O'Neil); **The Tudors**, 2007-2010 (TV series; Laoise Murray; Claire Macaulay; Kate Dugan); **The Virgin Queen**, 1923 (Diana Manners); **The Virgin Queen**, 1955 (Bette Davis); and **The Virgin Queen**, 2005 (TV miniseries; Anne-Marie Duff). **p,** Sidney Franklin; **d,** George Sidney; **cast,** Jean Simmons, Stewart Granger, Deborah Kerr, Charles Laughton, Kay Walsh, Guy Rolfe, Kathleen Byron, Cecil Kellaway, Rex Thompson, Robert Arthur, Leo G. Carroll, Alan Napier, Noreen Corcoran, Elaine Stewart, Doris Lloyd; **w,** Jan Lustig, Arthur Wimperis (based on the novel by Margaret Irwin); **c,** Charles Rosher (Technicolor); **m,** Miklos Rozsa; **ed,** Ralph E. Winters; **art d,** Cedric Gibbons, Urie McCleary; **set d,** Edwin B. Willis, Jack D. Moore; **spec eff,** A. Arnold Gillespie, Warren Newcombe.

Young Cassidy ★★★ 1965; U.K.; 108m; MGM; Color; Biographical Drama; Children: Unacceptable; **DVD; VHS.** Taylor gives a dynamic performance when essaying Irish playwright Sean O'Casey (1880-1964) in this well-produced biopic. The film is set in Dublin in 1911 where Taylor lives with his ailing mother, Robson, in a miserable hovel in northern Dublin. The self-taught Taylor works as a laborer and is an ardent member of the Irish movement against the oppressive methods employed by British rulers. Taylor reads books at night and, after several clashes with the British establishment, turns to writing pamphlets against the British instead of actually battling England's minions in the streets of Dublin. He meets Christie, an attractive streetwalker, and they have a torrid but brief affair. Taylor then turns his romantic attention to Smith, who operates the bookstore which he routinely visits and where he buys

Maggie Smith and Rod Taylor in *Young Cassidy,* **1965.**

his books. Smith urges Taylor to write more freely, and he begins to write plays that depict the struggles of the Irish movement, which later develops into the IRA (Irish Republican Army) that would make open revolution against England in 1916. The play, "The Plough and the Stars," is accepted by the Abbey Theatre, championed by its leader, William Butler Yeats (1865-1939), who is wonderfully played by Redgrave, but when it premieres, the audience riots, even though the play is later proclaimed to be a masterpiece. Taylor sees little joy in his literary triumph as his sick mother, Robson, dies in poverty, and Taylor's discovery of her death is one of the many touching scenes in this moving film. The final scene sees Taylor leaving for England where he would be acclaimed as one of the world's greatest playwrights. The direction from Cardiff (and with some scenes helmed by the great John Ford) is outstanding, capturing the period with all of its class turmoil, and Taylor, Robson, Christie, Smith and Redgrave are superb in essaying their distinctive characters. This film did not do well at the box office, initially struggling to regain its original budget of more than $1 million. *Author's Note*: Producers Graff and Ginna were excited when director John Ford was hired to helm this picture, agreeing to direct it for only $50,000, much less than his standard fee. When Ford first arrived at the Dublin airport, however, the producers were shocked to see an ailing and inebriated Ford. He was unshaven and disheveled and told the producers that he had only a week to work on the film before he had to return to the U.S. for the premiere of his latest U.S. film, **Cheyenne Autumn**, 1964, but that he would return following that premiere. He did return, but, as Ford told this author: "I got very sick over there [in Ireland] while we were making **Young Cassidy**, and, unfortunately, I had to quit the picture. Things like that did not usually happen to me and I felt that I was disappointing everyone, including myself." Actually, Ford left the production high and dry, and when the producers complained, he reportedly stated: "What do you expect for a lousy fifty grand?" The producers replaced him with the gifted cinematographer-turned-director Jack Cadiff. The most startling scenes in the film unmistakably bear the Ford imprimatur, those between Taylor and Robson and those between Taylor and Christie. Before leaving, Ford wanted the producers to add a poignant final scene between Christie and Taylor, one where Christie, by then a woebegone prostitute, greets Taylor after seeing his play and tells him how wonderful it is before she walks away down a dark street and out of his life. That scene was never shot. Sean Connery and Richard Harris were at one time or another given the role of O'Casey/Cassidy, until Taylor was hired for the part. O'Casey personally approved of the script and Taylor. Other films profiling the IRA (Irish Republican Army) include **Angela's Ashes**, 2000; **Anton**, 2008; **Beloved Enemy**, 1936; **The Black Windmill**, 1974; **Bloody Sunday**, 2002; **Blown Away**, 1994; **The Bombmaker**, 2001 (made-for-TV);

Borstal Boy, 2001; **The Boxer**, 1997; **The Break**, 1998; **Breakfast on Pluto**, 2005; **Cal**, 1984; **Circle of Deceit**, 1993 (made-for-TV); **The Craic**, 1999; **The Crying Game**, 1992; **The Dawning**, 1988; **The Devil's Own**, 1997; **Disappearing in America**, 2009; **Divorcing Jack**, 1998; **The Eagle Has Landed**, 1976; **The Enigma of Frank Ryan**, 2012; **An Everlasting Piece**, 2000; **Exiled**, 1999; **Fifty Dead Men Walking**, 2009; **Five Minutes of Heaven**, 2009; **48 Angels**, 2007; **The General**, 1998; **Giro City**, 1984; **The Glory Boys**, 1984 (TV series); **Guests of the Nation**, 1981 (made-for-TV); **Harry's Game**, 1982 (TV series); **Hennessy**, 1975; **Hidden Agenda**, 1991; **Hunger**, 2008; **In the Name of the Father**, 1993; **I.R.A.: King of Nothing**, 2007; **I See a Dark Stranger**, 1947; **In This Corner**, 1985 (made-for-TV); **The Informer**, 1935; **The Informant**, 1998; **The Jackal**, 1997; **Johnny Was**, 2006; **Liam**, 2001; **The Long Good Friday**, 1982; **The Man Who Never Was**, 1956; **Michael Collins**, 1996; **Midnight Man**, 1997 (made-for-TV); **The Night Fighters**, 1960; **Odd Man Out**, 1947; **Omagh**, 2004 (made-for-TV); **Ordinary Decent Criminal**, 2000; **The Outsider**, 1980; **Patriot Games**, 1992; **Peacefire**, 2009; **The Plough and the Stars**, 1936; **A Prayer for the Dying**, 1987; **The Quiet Man**, 1952; **The Rising of the Moon**, 1957; **Riot**, 1996; **Ronin**, 1998; **Ryan's Daughter**, 1970; **The Secret Invasion**, 1964; **Shadow Dancer**, 2012; **Shake Hands with the Devil**, 1959; **Shergar**, 1999; **Some Mother's Son**, 1996; **Sword in the Desert**, 1949; **Ticker**, 2001; **Titanic Town**, 1999; **Veronica Guerin**, 2003; **When the Sky Falls**, 2000; **The Wind That Shakes the Barley**, 2007; and **The Year London Blew Up: 1974**, 2005 (made-for-TV). **p**, Robert D. Graff, Robert Emmett Ginna; **d**, Jack Cardiff, John Ford; **cast**, Rod Taylor, Julie Christie, Maggie Smith, Michael Redgrave, Edith Evans, Flora Robson, Jack MacGowran, Sian Phillips, T.P. McKenna, Julie Ross, Robin Sumner; **w**, John Whiting (based on the autobiography *Mirror in My House* by Sean O'Casey); **c**, Ted Scaife (Metrocolor); **m**, Sean O'Riada; **ed**, Anne V. Coates; **art d**, Michael Stringer.

Young Chopin ★★★ 1952; Poland; 98m; UFF/Artkino Pictures; B/W; Biographical Drama; Children: Acceptable. Fine biopic chronicles the early formative years in the life of Polish composer-pianist Frederic Chopin (1810-1849) from 1825 to 1831. It was a time of social unrest throughout Europe, of rising nationalism, and cries for political and social reform. Chopin, played by Wollejko, is an outstanding musical student, caught up in the revolutionary spirit in Poland and who gives piano recitals that are praised by the aristocracy. He goes on tour throughout Europe and, while performing in Vienna, learns of the November 1831 revolutionary uprising in Warsaw. He attempts to return and join the fight, but his carriage breaks down and he becomes ill. His doctor warns him to stop traveling because of poor health, so he settles down to a quieter life in Paris where he continues composing. Ford does a fine job fusing the dramatic and musical elements of this compelling tale, and Wollejko gives a powerful performance of the great composer. Music: "Polonaise in D Minor," "Sonata in C Major, Opus 4," "Mazurka in A Minor, Opus 17, No. 4," "Mazurka in C Sharp Minor, Opus 6, No. 4)," "Hulanka," "Concerto in E Minor, Opus 11," "Etude in E Major, Opus 10, No. 3," "Etude in A Minor, Opus 25, No. 11)," "Etude in C Minor, Opus 10, No. 12" (Frederic Chopin). *Author's Note*: Chopin's life before and beyond the years in this film was fictionalized in the 1945 film **A Song to Remember**, 1945, to great success; Cornel Wilde essayed the composer. Other actors profiling Chopin in many other films include: **Bohemian Rapture**, 1948 (Vaclav Voska); **Chopin: Desire for Love**, 2004 (Piotr Adamczyk); **Coup de Grace**, 1978 (Bruno Thost); **Die lachende Grille**, 1926 (Alfred Abel); **Ein Winter auf Mallorca**, 1982 (made-for-TV; Krystian Martinek); **Farewell**, 1935 (Jean Servais); **Farewell Waltz**, 1934 (Wolfgang Liebeneiner); **George and Fanchette**, 2010 (made-for-TV; Fabrice Pruvost); **George Sand**, 1958 (TV series; Egidio Eccio); **George Who?**, 1973 (Pierre Kalinovski); **Impromptu**, 1991 (Hugh Grant); **International**, 1969 (Christopher Sandford); **La note bleue**, 1991 (Janusz Olejniczak); **La rebellion de los fantasmas**, 1949 (Francisco Valera); **La Valse de l'adieu**, 1928 (Pierre Blanchar); **Liszt Ferenc**, 1982 (TV miniseries; Laszlo Galffi); **Lisztomania**, 1975 (Ken [Kenneth] Colley); **Nocturne in Scotland**, 1951 (made-for-TV; Hugh Burden); **Nocturno der Liebe**, 1919 (Conrad Veidt); **Notorious Woman**, 1974 (TV miniseries; George Chakiris); **Pontcarral, colonel d'empire**, 1942 (Jean Chaduc); **Preludio, A Vida de Chopin**, 1962 (TV series; Claudio Marzo); **Song without End**, 1960 (Alex [Alexander] Davion); **Szerelmes szivek**, 1944 (Gyula Benko); and **Toute la ville en parle**, 2000 (made-for-TV; Maurice Mons). (In Polish/English subtitles.) **d**, Aleksander Ford; **cast**, Czeslaw Wollejko, Zbigniew Lobodzinski, Jozef Nieweglowski, Jerzy Duszynski, Jerzy Pietraszkiewicz, Leon Pietraszkiewicz, Aleksandra Slaska, Jan Kurnakowicz, Gustaw Buszynski, Tadeusz Bialosczynski; **w**, Ford, Leon Kruczkowski (based on the novella *Niezatarte slady* by Gustaw Bachner, Jerzy Broszkiewicz, Stanislaw Hadyna, Jan Korngold); **c**, Jaroslav Tuzar; **m**, Kazimierz Serocki; **ed**, Krystyna Tunis; **prod d**, Roman Mann.

Young Dr. Kildare ★★★ 1938; U.S.; 81m; MGM; B/W; Drama; Children: Acceptable; **DVD**; **VHS**. One of the better entries in the series, this tale sees Ayres as Dr. James Kildare just graduated from medical school. He chooses not to join his father's country medical practice, disappointing his father, Hinds, and mother, Dunn, as well as his childhood sweetheart, Carver. Instead, he takes an internship at large Blair General Hospital in New York City. There he meets grumpy Dr. Leonard Gillespie, superbly played by Barrymore, who soon becomes his mentor. Barrymore is the hospital's resident diagnostician and he challenges all of the new hospital interns to diagnose him. All are reluctant to do that, except Ayres, who immediately finds favor with the demanding Barrymore. Ayres is assigned to ambulance duty, working with attendant Pendleton, and his first case is that of a man passed out in a bar. Pendleton believes the man is drunk, but Ayres thinks that he is suffering from another and more serious problem and tells Pendleton to give the patient oxygen all the way to the hospital while Ayres answers another urgent call. Pendleton fails to apply the oxygen and the man dies, but Ayres nobly takes responsibility and saves Pendleton's job. Ayres finds himself in deep trouble when he saves a suicidal woman, Sayers, who is an heiress from a powerful family. While attending Sayers, no signs of life are found, but Ayres refuses to declare her dead and manages to revive her. Woolley, the hospital's psychiatrist, thinks that Sayers is certifiable, but Ayres, after talking with Sayers, is convinced that she is sane, and that she was driven to end her life. When he refuses to disclose what Sayers has told him in confidence, Ayres is suspended by hospital director Kingsford. Ayres does his own investigation and learns that Sayers had gone alone to a nightclub after arguing with her fiancé, Bradley, and had too much to drink. She was taken to a private room upstairs and remembered nothing thereafter until finding herself walking along a dark street. Found by a policeman and taken home, Sayers, fearful of what might have happened, attempted to take her life. After avuncular Barrymore urges Ayres to probe on his own, the young doctor visits Sayers and assures her that nothing happened to disgrace her on the night she blacked out at the nightclub. He tells her that the man at the nightclub who found her simply dropped her off on a street after she revived, knowing she was from a wealthy and powerful family and was fearful of what might happen to him if he had taken advantage of her. Ayres further coaches her on how to respond to further tests conducted by Woolley so that he is not compelled to send her to an insane asylum. Ayres is fired for insubordination, although hospital administrators know nothing of Ayres' private investigation into Sayer's problems. Hinds, Dunn and Carver arrive to be told by Ayres that he has decided to return home and become his father's medical partner, but Barrymore changes all that when he summons Ayres to his office and tells him that he is hiring him as his assistant as he is the only intern who has correctly diagnosed his condition as cancer-based melanoma and that he wants the courageous and brilliant Ayres to eventually become his successor. *Au-*

Lionel Barrymore and Lew Ayres in *Young Dr. Kildare*, 1938.

thor's Note: Of the ten films based on Dr. James Kildare, the first film to depict this character starred Joel McCrea in **Interns Can't Take Money**, 1937. This film was the first of a nine-picture series starring Ayres as Dr. Kildare that later spun off into the Dr. Gillespie series with Barrymore. The other Kildare films starring Ayres are **Calling Doctor Kildare**, 1939; **Dr. Kildare Goes Home**, 1940; **Dr. Kildare's Crisis**, 1940; **Dr. Kildare's Strange Case**, 1940; **Dr. Kildare's Victory**, 1941; **Dr. Kildare's Wedding Day**, 1941; **The People vs. Dr. Kildare**, 1941; and **The Secret of Dr. Kildare**, 1939. The films of the Dr. Gillespie series are **Between Two Women**, 1944; **Calling Dr. Gillespie**, 1942; **Dark Delusion**, 1947; **Dr. Gillespie's Criminal Case**, 1943; **Dr. Gillespie's New Assistant**, 1942; and **Three Men in White**, 1944. Ayres told this author that "I was not happy with the role of Dr. Kildare, but the character took such a strong hold on the public's imagination that I was trapped into that role for a number of years. I know that Basil Rathbone played Sherlock Holmes so many times that he wanted to escape the character, but he found himself playing that character again and again, just as I kept playing Dr. Kildare. I asked Basil about that and he said: 'Sherlock wears me out, but I must admit that he is as comfortable as old, worn-out slippers.' What do they say—if the shoe fits, wear it?" Nevertheless, the role of Dr. Kildare fit Ayres like a surgeon's plastic glove while Dr. Kildare became the personification of America's idea of the ideal doctor, a character for which Ayres is forever remembered, just as Basil Rathbone and Sherlock Holmes are umbilical within the public's memory. **p**, Lou L. Ostrow; **d**, Harold S. Bucquet; **cast**, Lionel Barrymore, Lew Ayres, Lynne Carver, Nat Pendleton, Jo Ann Sayers, Samuel S. Hinds, Emma Dunn, Walter Kingsford, Monty Woolley, Truman Bradley, Nella Walker, Don "Red" Barry, Don Castle, Phillip Terry, Bobs Watson; **w**, Harry Ruskin, Willis Goldbeck (based on characters created by Max Brand); **c**, John Seitz; **m**, David Snell; **ed**, Elmo Veron; **art d**, Cedric Gibbons; **set d**, Edwin B. Willis.

Young Frankenstein ★★★★ 1974; U.S.; 108m; Crossbow Productions/FOX; B/W; Comedy/Horror; Children: Unacceptable (MPAA: PG); **BD**; **DVD**; **VHS**. By far and away one of Brooks' and Wilder's funniest films (ranking with such classics as **The Producers**, 1967, and **Blazing Saddles**, 1974) this outlandish and outrageous spoof of horror films, particularly the eerie Frankenstein legend, was never better parodied. This comedic work of genius from Brooks sees utterly captivating performances from Wilder, Boyle, Feldman, Garr, Kahn, Leachman, and a bevy of other gifted supporting players as they pratfall and satirize their antic ways through Mary Shelley's most horrific nightmares. This ogling opus begins with Wilder as a respected physician at an esteemed American medical school where he is demonstrating nervous reaction from a human guinea pig who has received an injection and who goes

Teri Garr, Gene Wilder and Madeline Kahn in *Young Franken-stein*, 1974.

limp after Wilder finishes his medical monolog. One of his students asks Wilder about his infamous grandfather, the berserk medical scientist who created the Frankenstein monster long ago. Wilder bristles at the wrong pronunciation of his name, insisting that his name be pronounced "*Fronkensteen*" so as to distance himself from that deranged ancestor, angrily stating that his forefather's sinister experiments with the undead were nothing but "doo-doo." Distracted and unnerved, he makes his point by driving a sharp scalpel into his own leg, and then nervously rolls his eyes while shielding the faux pas of the protruding instrument from public view. Wilder is engaged to Kahn, a fussy prima donna, and looks forward to their wedding, but his plans drastically alter when he is informed that he is the heir to a vast estate in Transylvania, and he decides to travel to that distant country to claim his inheritance. Kahn sees him off at a train station, but where she will not allow Wilder to kiss her so as to keep her cosmetically made-up face intact and so they simply gesture affectionate farewells. Wilder is then shown arriving by train in Transylvania (and where a newspaper boy mimics the Glenn Miller song title "Pennsylvania 6-5000"). Wilder is greeted by family servant Feldman, a bug-eyed dwarf with a humpback (and where the hump on his back invariably moves from one side to another in different shots, baffling Wilder). Feldman introduces himself as "Igor," but, as Wilder has given a different emphasis to the pronunciation of his own name, Feldman insists upon being called "Eye-Gore." Also greeting Wilder is fetching blonde Garr, who becomes Wilder's sexy assistant. They arrive at the Frankenstein castle in a horse-drawn carriage and stand before its huge doors that are adorned with ornate door knockers. "What knockers!" Wilder exclaims. Garr, who wears a revealing blouse showing considerable cleavage, blushes and states: "Thank you!" The door of the castle opens to show Leachman, the housekeeper, a beak-nosed woman so ugly that when she states her name of "Frau Blucher" that she frightens the horses drawing the carriage, prompting them to rear upward and loudly whinny and bray in fearful repulsion (when her name is mentioned thereafter the viewer hears those horses whinnying). When Wilder is shown to his quarters, the master bedroom where his crackpot ancestor slept, he sees a portrait of that forefather and where Leachman, thinking she is unobserved, kisses the picture before saying goodnight. When attempting to sleep that night, Wilder hears strange music and leaves the chamber to investigate. He meets with Garr, who has also heard the eerie music, and they go to the mansion's library. While Wilder is leaning on one of the bookcases, Garr inadvertently removes a burning candle from its place that causes the bookcase to quickly swivel about, wedging Wilder between the library and an inner passageway. He manages to work himself free after Garr returns the candle to its place and they both then explore the secret passageway, going down stone stairs to find the hidden large laboratory where Wilder's

grandfather created the Frankenstein Monster. Investigating further, Wilder and Garr find Feldman hiding behind a case of wax heads and they later discover the office of Wilder's grandfather, finding a book titled *How I Did It*. The book fascinates Wilder as he reads how his ancestor pieced together human body parts and brought to life the Monster. Wilder becomes obsessed with continuing his ancestor's work, which he had formerly branded as lunacy but now accepts as the work of a genius. He is enthusiastically aided by his mindless assistants, Feldman and Garr, as well as the deranged Leachman, who admits that Wilder's deceased and wacky grandfather was her "boyfriend." Wilder and Feldman visit a graveyard where the corpse of a deceased criminal is being buried. They patiently wait for the body to be interred and, after the gravediggers depart, they unearth the body, taking it back to Wilder's castle and placing it in the old laboratory. Wilder then tells Feldman to go to a nearby medical center with orders to steal the healthy brain of a famous and recently deceased historian, Hans Delbruck. While performing this gruesome chore, a lightning storm rattles Feldman so much that he drops and breaks the glass container holding the historian's brain, ruining the specimen. He then takes another glass containing a second brain, ignoring its label, which reads: "Abnormal Brain! Do Not Use!" Wilder then transplants that brain into the lifeless corpse, not knowing that he has inserted the brain of a vicious criminal. Using the elaborate equipment employed by his grandfather (including similar gadgets and dynamos emitting crackling electronic pulses and waves used by director James Whale in the original **Frankenstein**, 1931), Wilder rides with the body on a platform as it is elevated to a tower where it is infused with the lightning of a fierce storm and then descends back into the laboratory. At first, it seems that the dramatic experiment is a failure, but the creature, Boyle, comes to life as a crazed giant, breaking the massive straps that bind it to the operating table and attacking Wilder. He, with the help of Garr and Feldman, however, manages to inject a sedative into Boyle so that he is rendered unconscious. The experiment, with all of its attendant noise and racket, alerts the local authorities and townspeople in a nearby village, causing police inspector Mars to make a visit to Wilder. Mars (in a brilliant parody of Lionel Atwill who plays the police inspector in **Son of Frankenstein**, 1939) warily converses with Wilder as they play a wild dart game and where Wilder evades questions from Mars about whether or not Wilder has resumed his grandfather's dangerous experiments. Mars adopts a German accent that is so thick that no one can understand what he says, compelling him to repeat his lines in clearly pronounced words in order to communicate. After Mars departs, Wilder returns to the laboratory where Feldman accidentally sets up some of the machines, their noise and bolts of electricity causing Boyle to regain consciousness and flee the castle to roam free through the countryside and nearby village. He meets a young girl and plays with her in her backyard on a teeter-totter, but, when she makes the wrong move, he slams down the seesaw, sending her flying upward and through the upstairs window of her bedroom so that she lands in her bed just as her worried parents rush into that room to find her safe and sound. (In this scene, Wilder and Brooks have sanitized for laughs a more sinister sequence from the original **Frankenstein** where the monster meets and plays with a little girl, and winds up throwing her into a lake and drowning her.) Boyle next visits Hackman, a blind hermit living in an isolated cottage; the lonely Hackman, eager for human contact, welcomes the monster into his humble home (this sequence spoofing the monster's encounter with a blind hermit in the classic James Whale film **The Bride of Frankenstein**, 1935). He gives Boyle wine, but, when toasting, smashes Boyle's cup. He then ladles out some hot soup for Boyle, but, being blind, misses his mark and, instead of dumping the scalding soup into Boyle's bowl, splashes the searing hot soup onto Boyle's lap, causing him to scream in pain. Hackman then offers Boyle a cigar, but, when lighting the stogie, he mistakenly lights Boyle's finger, causing the flesh to ignite into flames; the antagonized Boyle races howling with pain from the cottage. A disappointed Hackman stands at the doorway to say: "I was going to make espresso!"

Wilder, by this time, recaptures Boyle and locks him into a secure cell in the basement of the castle. Wilder then braves Boyle's locked room, telling Garr, Feldman and Leachman that, whatever he says when he is within that locked room with the monster he has created, they are not to let him out. Once inside, Boyle makes some menacing moves toward Wilder and Wilder panics, pleading and begging for his associates to open the door. He then adopts a patronizing attitude where he tells Boyle that he is merely an unloved and misunderstood creature and praises Boyle's monstrous appearance, telling him that he is much loved. Thus bolstering Boyle's low self-esteem, the monster embraces Wilder as his only friend, the single person who compassionately understands him. This triumph of the will inspires Wilder to finally acknowledge his own strange heritage when he proudly shouts: "My name is *Frankenstein!*" Wilder is next seen at a theater packed with noted medical authorities and their wives. He stands on the stage dressed in tie and tails, introducing his new creation, a spotlight then showing Boyle, the creature also formally attired in tie and tails. Wilder then orders Boyle to demonstrate his physical coordination by stepping forward and back before Wilder tells the conductor of the pit orchestra to begin playing Irving Berlin's "Puttin' on the Ritz." Wilder and Boyle then go into a top hat and tails dance while Garr, watching from the wings, is thrilled to see the pair performing their buck-and-wing routine. The audience responds with applause, but all goes wrong when one of the stage lights malfunctions and explodes, the flames causing Boyle to revert to his bestial nature of roars and flailing of arms. This prompts the audience to pelt Boyle with bits of garbage so that he becomes even further enraged and charges into the audience where spectators flee in panic. Police rush down the aisle and subdue Boyle, taking him to a jail where he is held in a dungeon-like cell and chained to a chair. Wilder, now conscious-wracked over Boyle's imprisonment, is consoled by Garr. He is then visited by his fiancée, Kahn, who takes up residence in the castle. By this time, a sadistic guard taunts the chained Boyle so that he explodes in rage, breaking his chains and escaping the prison cell to once again roam the countryside. He returns to the castle like a homing pigeon and sees the voluptuous Kahn combing her luxuriant hair before going to bed. Boyle invades her room, taking her to his lair. She at first resists him, but his sexual stamina and prowess soon sees her as a willing partner as she sings "Ah, Sweet Mystery of Life." Meanwhile, Wilder entices Boyle to his side by playing the violin and attempts to once more stabilize the monster's troubled brain and correct its irrational behavior. Townspeople, however, led by Mars, march by torchlight to the castle to make an end to Boyle once and for all. By the time the mob arrives, they find that Wilder has transferred much of his intellect to the creature and Boyle is able to rationally reason with the invaders, sending them shamefacedly back to their homes. Boyle then marries Kahn and they settle down (Kahn's outlandish cone-like hair-do duplicates the very same coiffure as worn by Elsa Lanchester when playing the intended wife of the monster in **The Bride of Frankenstein**). Garr, who has paired off with Wilder, is then delighted to learn that Wilder has acquired the sexual extremity of his creation in his last experiment to end this magnificent farce. Brooks directs this, his most accomplished film, with amazing style that emulates the best of the classic Frankenstein films. He brilliantly balances the traditional grim tale by cleverly inserting in just the right sequences the quirky brand of humor that hilariously alters each sinister event to memorable clownish scenes. Wilder and Brooks include in their script innumerable crudities throughout their script to add to its nonstop zaniness, packing it with sight gags and endless moronic non sequiturs, their idiotic characters drawn as tightly as outstretched rubber bands to snap mirthfully back into the face of the viewer. Wilder and Brooks not only milk every laugh from their script, but squeeze each comedic line and scene limp, out-burlesquing burlesque, fusing sophisticated satire and pubescent humor with reckless abandon. One does not tire of this flagrant technique since it so cleverly includes the viewer as a participant in the impossible charade, where the fourth wall (addressing the viewer directly with words or looks) is

Marty Feldman in *Young Frankenstein*, 1974.

often invaded by the endearing actors. What seems to be throw-away lines and gestures are nothing of the kind, all being imaginatively conceived bits of business that compete on many levels for the anxious attention of the viewer. Wilder is superb as the out-of-kilter medical scientist and Boyle a wonderful lumbering monster-turned-sophisticated gentleman (who ends up reading the *Wall Street Journal* in his final scene with Kahn). Feldman and Garr, to be sure, are also standouts in their rollicking roles, holding their own with the manic Wilder and the phlegmatic Boyle; Kahn, Hackman, Leachman and Mars add fine performances, all making up one of the most entertaining menageries of any classic comedy. The film received Oscar nominations for Best Adapted Screenplay (Wilder, Brooks), and Best Sound Recording (Richard Portman, Gene Cantamessa). The film was a box office smash, earning more than $86 million in its initial release against a budget of more than $2.7 million. A musical version was adapted by Brooks and was produced at Seattle's Paramount Theater, opening on August 7, 2007, and closing on September 1 that same year. It saw a Broadway production that opened at NYC's Hilton Theater on November 8, 2007, and closing on January 4, 2009, after twenty-nine previews and 485 performances, starring Roger Bart in the Wilder role and Shuler Hensley as the creature. Songs: "Ah, Sweet Mystery of Life" (1910; from "Naughty Marietta"; music: Victor Herbert; lyrics: Rida Johnson Young), "Puttin' on the Ritz" (1927; published in 1929; Irving Berlin), "The Battle Hymn of the Republic" (music [1856]: William Steffe; lyrics [1862]: Julia Ward Howe), "Ave Maria" (1825; Franz Schubert), "I Ain't Got Nobody (And Nobody Cares for Me)" (1915; music: Spencer Williams; lyrics: Roger A. Graham), "Here Comes the Bride" ["Bridal Chorus"] (1850; from "Lohengrin" by Richard Wagner). *Author's Note*: This film remained Wilder's favorite and Brooks felt that it was his most professionally produced film, but not, however, his funniest. The idea for the film was conceived by Wilder, who approached Brooks more than once, asking that he direct it, but that he not appear in it (although Brooks does provide the howling of the werewolf, the screeching of the cat who is struck by a wayward dart during the contest between Wilder and Mars, and the voiceover of Wilder's ancestor). Brooks turned down the idea until Wilder mentioned that the character he would play wanted nothing to do with his ancestors and was utterly ashamed of them. "That's funny," Brooks replied and decided to do the film with Wilder. The two wrote the script together, but they battled throughout that struggling writing period. At one point, Wilder reportedly yelled at Brooks: "I don't want this to be a 'Blazing Frankenstein!'" Brooks yelled back: "I don't want an art film that only fourteen people see!" They somehow managed to work all of their separate ideas into the film, including puns, slapstick, double entendre and sight gags that later so seamlessly worked with the story line. When the film went into

Gene Wilder and (prone as the monster) Peter Boyle in *Young Frankenstein*, 1974.

production, Brooks insisted that it be shot in black and white to conform to the B/W images of its straightforward predecessors, and used the same techniques employed in the making of **Frankenstein**, 1931; **The Bride of Frankenstein**, 1935; **The Son of Frankenstein**, 1939 (from which Wilder draws his characterization, originally essayed by Basil Rathbone); and **The Ghost of Frankenstein**, 1942 (culling from the latter two films the characterization of the evil Ygor, who was originally essayed by Bela Lugosi, but who in this film is enacted by the zany Feldman). So faithful was Brooks to the previous horror classics, that he shot **Young Frankenstein** at a 1:85 ration, as had been done in those previous films, and while also using the same visual techniques of iris up, wipes, and fadeouts. He even went to the length of securing the original laboratory equipment used in the first film that had been created by Kenneth Strickfaden, who had stored that very equipment in his garage and who loaned it to Brooks for this production, as well as adding new gadgets for this film. The spectacular sets were also dictated by Brooks, who recreated the looming castle, and the nearby village with its odd-angled buildings and slippery wet cobblestone streets. The lighting also imitates the original productions to present stark rays of searing light and looming shadows. Many of the classic lines and inside jokes appearing in this film were provided by the actors, notably Feldman (who purposely moved his hump back and forth until it was noticed by production assistants and was incorporated as a joke), and Hackman, who plays the gay hermit and who added the line: "I was going to make espresso." The brain destroyed by Feldman in the film is labeled: "Hans Delbruck, scientist and saint." Just such a man truly existed, Hans Delbruck, 1848-1929, who was a noted German historian. Brooks initially offered the film to Columbia Studio, but when its producers only offered a budget of $1.7 million, he took the idea to Fox, which gave Brooks an initial budget of $2.3 million and judiciously signed Brooks and Wilder to long-term contracts. Though both would later go on to produce and star in many more films, neither ever equaled the masterpiece level of this wonderful comedy. This was the final film for Richard Haydn and Oscar Beregi Jr., and was the film debut of Jeff Maxwell. The Frankenstein Monster has been enacted by many actors in many other films, including **Abbott and Costello Meet Frankenstein**, 1948 (Glenn Strange); **The ABC Saturday Night Superstar Movie**, 1972-1974 (TV series; "The Mad, Mad, Mad Monsters," animated 1972 episode: Allen Swift voiceover); **Andy Warhol's Frankenstein**, 1973 (Srdjan Zelenovic; Miomir Aleksic); **Big Monster on Campus**, 2000 (Matthew Lawrence); **Billy Frankenstein**, 1998 (Brian Carrillo); **Blood: The Last Vampire**, 2009 (Joey Anaya; Khary Payton); **The Bride**, 1985 (Clancy Brown); **The Bride of Frankenstein**, 1935 (Boris Karloff); **Carry On Christmas**, 1969 (made-for-TV; Bernard Bresslaw); **Casanova Frankenstein**, 1975 (Aldo Maccione); **Casino Royale**, 1967 (David

Prowse); **The Creeps**, 1997 (Thomas Wellington); **The Curse of Frankenstein**, 1957 (Christopher Lee); **Dracula vs. Frankenstein**, 1971 (aka: **Blood of Frankenstein**; John Bloom); **The Erotic Rites of Frankenstein**, 1973 (Fernando Bilbao); **The Evil of Frankenstein**, 1964 (Kiwi Kingston); **Flesh for Frankenstein**, 1974 (Srdjan Zelenovic); **Frankenstein**, 1931 (Boris Karloff); **Frankenstein**, 1984 (made-for-TV; David Warner); **Frankenstein**, 1987 (made-for-TV; Chris Sarandon); **Frankenstein**, 1992 (made-for-TV; Randy Quaid); **Frankenstein**, 2004 (made-for-TV; Vincent Perez); **Frankenstein**, 2004 (TV miniseries; Luke Goss); **Frankenstein**, 2007 (made-for-TV; Julian Bleach); **Frankenstein**, 2011 (Dean Gangle); **Frankenstein and the Monster from Hell**, 1974 (David Prowse); **Frankenstein and the Werewolf Reborn!**, 2005 (Ethan Wilde); **Frankenstein: Birth of a Monster**, 2003 (made-for-TV; David Schofield); **Frankenstein Conquers the World**, 1966 (Koji Furuhata; young Frankenstein: Sumio Nakao); **Frankenstein Created Woman**, 1967 (Robert Morse); **Frankenstein: Day of the Beast**, 2011 (Tim Krueger); **Frankenstein General Hospital**, 1988 (Irwin Keyes); **Frankenstein Meets the Space Monster**, 1965 (Bruce Glover); **Frankenstein Meets the Wolf Man**, 1943 (Bela Lugosi); **Frankenstein Must Be Destroyed**, 1970 (brain: George Pravda; body: Freddie Jones); **Frankenstein—1970**, 1958 (Mike Lane); **Frankenstein 90**, 1984 (Eddy Mitchell); **Frankenstein Reborn!**, 1998 (Ethan Wilde); **Frankenstein Reborn!**, 2005 (Joel Hebner); **Frankenstein Rising**, 2010 (Randal Malone); **Frankenstein: The True Story**, 1973 (made-for-TV; Michael Sarrazin); **Frankenstein Unbound**, 1990 (Nick Brimble); **Frankenstein vs. the Creature from Blood Cove**, 2005 (Lawrence Furbish); **Frankenstein's Aunt**, 1987 (TV series; Gerhard Karzel); **Frankenstein's Daughter**, 1958 (Harry Wilson); **Frankenstein's Great Aunt Tillie**, 1984 (Miguel Angel Fuentes); **Frankenstein's Monster**, 2013 (Matt Risoldi); **Frankenstein's Planet of Monsters!**, 1995 (Mike Brunelle); **Frankenstein's Wedding**, 2011 (made-for-TV; David Harewood); **Frankenweenie**, 1984 (Sparky); **The Ghost Busters**, 1975 (TV series; "Dr. Whatsisname," 1975 episode: Bill [William] Engesser); **The Ghost of Frankenstein**, 1942 (Lon Chaney, Jr.); **Gothic**, 1987 (Kiran Shah); **Haunted**, 1993 (David Sanders); **Hellzapoppin'**, 1941 (Dale Van Sickel); **The Horror of Frankenstein**, 1971 (Dave [David] Prowse); **House of Dracula**, 1945 (Glenn Strange); **The House of Frankenstein**, 1944 (Glenn Strange); **House of Frankenstein**, 1997 (made-for-TV; Peter Crombie); **House of the Wolf Man**, 2009 (Craig Dabbs); **I, Frankenstein**, 2014 (Aaron Eckhart); **I Was a Teenage Frankenstein**, 1957 (Gary Conway); **Jesse James Meets Frankenstein's Daughter**, 1966 (Cal Bolder); **Lady Frankenstein**, 1973 (Peter Whiteman); **Life without Soul**, 1915 (Percy Darrell Standing); **Mary Shelley's Frankenstein**, 1994 (Robert De Niro); **Mr. Stitch**, 1995 (made-for-TV; Wil Wheaton); **Monster Brawl**, 2011 (Robert Maillet); **Monster Mash: The Movie**, 1995 (Deron McBee); **Monster Squad**, 1976 (TV series; Mike Lane); **Monstrosity**, 1988 (Haal Borske); **Munster, Go Home!**, 1966 (Fred Gwynne); **Necropolis**, 1970 (Bruno Corazzari); **The Prey**, 1984 (Carel Struycken); **The Revenge of Frankenstein**, 1958 (Michael Gwynn); **The Rocky Horror Picture Show**, 1975 (Peter Hinwood); **Son of Dracula**, 1974 (Morris Bush); **Son of Frankenstein**, 1939 (Boris Karloff); **Tales of Tomorrow**, 1951-1953 (TV series; "Frankenstein," 1952 episode: Lon Chaney Jr.); **Terror of Frankenstein**, 1977 (Per Oscarsson); **Van Helsing**, 2004 (Shuler Hensley); **Waxworks II: Lost in Time**, 1992 (Stefanos Miltsakakis); and **The Wide World of Mystery**, 1973-1978 (TV series; two 1973 episodes: Bo Svenson). **p**, Michael Gruskoff; **d**, Mel Brooks; **cast**, Gene Wilder, Peter Boyle, Marty Feldman, Cloris Leachman, Teri Garr, Madeline Kahn, Kenneth Mars, Richard Haydn, Liam Dunn, Danny Goldman, Oscar Beregi Jr., Arthur Malet, Jeff Maxwell; **w**, Wilder, Brooks (based on characters from the novel *Frankenstein* by Mary Wollstonecraft Shelley); **c**, Gerald Hirschfeld; **m**, John Morris; **ed**, John C. Howard; **prod d**, Dale Hennesy; **set d**, Bob de Vestel; **spec eff**, Henry Millar, Jr., Hal Millar, Matthew Yuricich.

The Young Girls of Rochefort ★★★ 1967; France; 125m; Madeleine Films/Miramax; Color; Musical Comedy; Children: Acceptable; **BD**; **DVD**. Lively songfest begins with Deneuve and Dorleac, who are beautiful twin sisters owning a dance studio in Rochefort-sur-Mer, a town along the northwest coast of France. Chakiris and Dale, two young boat salesmen, arrive to sell their wares at a carnival and become attracted to the sisters. Their beautiful mother, Darrieux, runs a café and dreams of being reunited with Piccoli, her long-lost love who owns a nearby music shop. The sisters dream of romance which comes in the form of Kelly and Perrin. Perrin is an artist, who paints his dream girl and discovers that Dorleac is that lucky girl. Kelly is an American concert pianist, who is in Rochefort and finds a romantic musical score written by Deneuve. Chakiris and Dale leave town, thereby leaving Deneuve to Kelly and Dorleac to Perrin. Love also finally comes to Darrieux as Piccoli finally reunites with her. Deneuve and Dorleac were real-life sisters, but not twins. Songs/Music: "Le Pont Transbordeur," "Arrive des Camioneurs," "Chanson des jumelles," "De Delphine a Lancien," "Nous voyageons de ville en ville," "Chanson de Delphine," "Chanson de Simon," "Marins, amis, amants ou maris," "Andy amoureux/Chanson d'Andy," "Chanson de Maxence," "De Hambourg a Rochefort," "La femme coupee en corceaux, "Les rencontres," "Kermesse," "Chanson d'un jour d'ete," "Tourjour, Jamais," "Concerto," "Depart des Forains" (Michel Legrand); "Chanson d'Yvonne" (Legrand, Demy). **p**, Gilbert De Goldschmidt; **d&w**, Jacques Demy; **cast**, Catherine Deneuve, Francoise Dorleac, Gene Kelly, Danielle Darrieux, George Chakiris, Jacques Perrin, Michel Piccoli, Jacques Riberolles, Grover Dale, Genevieve Thenier, Henri Cremieux, Pamela Hart, Leslie North; **c**, Ghislain Cloquet (Franscope; Technicolor); **m**, Michel Legrand; **ed**, Jean Hamon; **prod d**, Bernard Evein; **set d**, Louis Seuret.

Young Guns ★★★ 1988; U.S.; 107m; Morgan Creek Productions; FOX; Color; Western; Children: Unacceptable (MPAA: R); **BD**; **DVD**; **VHS**. Exciting, action-filled western chronicles the violent Lincoln County War of 1878 and thereafter in New Mexico Territory. The film opens with Stamp, who plays John Turstall (1853-1878), a well-educated English immigrant who has established a large ranch in Lincoln County. Stamp sees tough competition from Palance, who plays Lawrence Murphy (1831-1878), and who also owns a large cattle ranch; the ruthless Palance aligns himself with local corrupt officials. Stamp routinely hires young drifters notoriously known for using their guns to settle arguments, but Stamp tries to curb them of such violence, believing that all matters can be settled peacefully. He takes under his avuncular wing William H. Bonney, better known as Billy the Kid (1851-1881), played by Estevez, along with Josiah Gordon "Doc" Scurlock (1849-1929), played by Sutherland; Jose Chavez (1851-1924), played by Phillips; Richard M. "Dick" Brewer (1850-1878), played by Sheen (who is Estevez's real-life brother); Charles "Charlie" Bowdre (1848-1880), played by Siemaszko; and "Dirty" Steve Stephens, played by Mulroney. Where Palance has allied himself with leading citizens in the town of Lincoln, Stamp establishes a partnership with lawyer and storeowner Alexander McSween (1843-1878), who is played by O'Quinn. Stamp, a religious man, holds Bible sessions with his cowboys, and particularly advises the most dangerous of his wards, Estevez "He who sows the wind will reap the whirlwind." Tension between rivals Stamp and Palance escalate to the point where Stamp is murdered on orders of Palance and at the hands of Palance's henchmen while Stamp is riding alone on the range. O'Quinn manages to get warrants for those responsible for Stamp's death and is able to deputize Estevez and the rest of the cowboys at Stamp's ranch to issue those warrants and arrest the culprits. The cowboys call themselves "Regulators" and quickly seek out the guilty parties. While tracking some of these suspects, the hotheaded Estevez ignores the directions of nominal leader Sheen and guns down some of these Palance gunmen. He also shoots and kills Blake, who has recently joined the Regulators, but who Estevez believes is still in league with Palance. For these transgressions, the Reg-

Lou Diamond Phillips in *Young Guns,* 1988.

ulators are stripped of their badges and branded outlaws. They decide to continue pursuing Stamp's killers instead of leaving the area. They then encounter deadly gunman Andrew L. "Buckshot" Roberts (d.1878), played by Keith, an aged gunslinger who is seeking to kill the Regulators. The cowboys trap Keith in an outhouse and a wild gunfight ensues where Sheen is killed, along with Keith. Estevez then assumes the leadership of the gang, vowing to track down and kill Palance and his cohorts. Pursued by the U.S. Cavalry, the gang goes to Mexico where Siemaszko is married and where Estevez meets for the first time and befriends Pat Garrett (1850-1908), played by Wayne, and before Garrett had become a lawman, the very man who tracked down and killed his old friend, Billy the Kid. Wayne tells Estevez and his friends that Palance and his men plan to kill their one-time supporter, O'Quinn, the following day. Estevez and the others immediately leave for Lincoln to save O'Quinn. They arrive to take shelter in O'Quinn's home, but the house comes under siege by Palance and his men and an ongoing firefight ensues. The U.S. Cavalry arrives to aid Palance and his men, and they set the house on fire. Estevez and others, though wounded, manage to escape, except for Siemaszko, who is killed. O'Quinn then attempts to surrender and he is murdered. During the melee, Sutherland manages to rescue Carter, who is Palance's Chinese sex slave, riding off with the girl (he had earlier been attracted to her and asked her to leave the area with him). Palance shouts curses as the boys ride away, but Estevez turns his horse about and rides back toward Palance, shouting: "Reap the whirlwind, Murphy!" He fires and his lethal aim is true, the bullet striking Palance square in the forehead and killing him. Estevez then rides away with the fleeing gang. The final scene offers a voiceover from Sutherland, who explains how he moved East and married Carter, that Phillips went to work in California, and O'Quinn's widow, Thomas, demanded and got a congressional investigation into her husband's murder and the real culprits that caused the Lincoln County War. The film, helmed by several people, presents a good retelling of this Old West saga, and outstanding performances are seen from Estevez, Sutherland, Palance, Stamp, Phillips, Keith (who appears briefly but is electrifying as a death-defying killer) and others. The facts concerning the real events are mostly correctly shown here, but some embellishments are included to accommodate the action scenes (such as where Estevez escapes the burning O'Quinn house while hiding in a large trunk that is thrown from a second-floor window). This film was a huge box office hit, earning more than $45.6 million in its initial release against a budget of $11 million. ***Author's Note***: Of all the many portrayals of Billy the Kid, Estevez's portrait is one of the most impressive and accurate, albeit the Kid was also effectively portrayed by Paul Newman in **The Left-Handed Gun**, 1958. For further information about Billy the Kid, see my book *Encyclopedia of Western Lawmen and Outlaws* (Paragon

Christian Slater in *Young Guns II,* **1990.**

House, 1992; pages 38-45). Many other actors have essayed Billy the Kid in other films, including **Another Man, Another Chance**, 1977 (Tony Crupi); **Bill & Ted's Excellent Adventure**, 1989 (Dan Shor); **Billy the Kid**, 1925 (Franklyn Farnum); **Billy the Kid**, 1930 (Johnny Mack Brown); **Billy the Kid**, 1941 (Robert Taylor); **Billy the Kid**, 1964 (Jack Taylor); **Billy the Kid**, 1989 (made-for-TV; Val Kilmer); **Billy the Kid**, 2013 (Christopher Bowman); **Billy the Kid in Santa Fe**, 1941 (Bob Steele); **Billy the Kid in Texas**, 1940 (Bob Steele); **Billy the Kid Outlawed**, 1940 (Bob Steele); **Billy the Kid Returns**, 1938 (Roy Rogers); **Billy the Kid: Showdown in Lincoln County**, 2015 (Christopher Bowman); **Billy the Kid Trapped**, 1942 (Buster Crabbe); **Billy the Kid vs. Dracula**, 1966 (Chuck Courtney); **Billy the Kid Wanted**, 1941 (Buster Crabbe); **Billy the Kid's Fighting Pals**, 1941 (Bob Steele); **Billy the Kid's Gun Justice**, 1940 (Bob Steele); **Billy the Kid's Range War**, 1941 (Bob Steele); **Billy the Kid's Round-Up**, 1941 (Buster Crabbe); **Billy the Kid's Smoking Guns**, 1942 (Buster Crabbe); **Birth of a Legend: Billy the Kid & the Lincoln County War**, 2011 (Robert Shrimplin); **Blazing Frontier**, 1943 (Buster Crabbe); **The Boy from Oklahoma**, 1954 (Tyler MacDuff); **Cattle Stampede**, 1943 (Buster Crabbe); **Chisum**, 1970 (Geoffrey Deuel); **Copperhead**, 2008 (made-for-TV; Keith Stone); **Dirty Little Billy**, 1972 (Michael J. Pollard); **The Fourth Horseman**, 1932 (Paul Shawhan); **Fugitive of the Plains**, 1943 (Buster Crabbe); **A Girl Is a Gun**, 1971 (Jean-Pierre Leaud); **Horse Opera**, 1993 (made-for-TV; Jonathan Moore); **I Shot Billy the Kid**, 1950 (Don "Red" Barry); **I'll Kill Him and Return Alone**, 1967 (Peter Lee Lawrence); **The Kid from Texas**, 1950 (Audie Murphy); **The Kid Rides Again**, 1943 (Buster Crabbe); **Law and Order** (aka: **Billy the Kid's Law and Order**), 1942 (Buster Crabbe); **The Law vs. Billy the Kid**, 1954 (Scott Brady); **The Left Handed Gun**, 1958 (Paul Newman); **The Life and Times of Judge Roy Bean**, 1972 (Mark Headley); **Lucky Luke**, 2009 (Michael Youn); **The Mysterious Rider**, 1942 (Buster Crabbe); **The Outlaw**, 1943 (Jack Buetel); **The Outlaws Is Coming!**, 1965 (Johnny Ginger); **The Parson and the Outlaw**, 1957 (Anthony Dexter); **Pat Garrett and Billy the Kid**, 1973 (Kris Kristofferson); **Purgatory**, 1999 (made-for-TV; Donnie Wahlberg); **Redemption**, 2009 (Owen Conway); **The Renegade**, 1943 (Buster Crabbe); **Return of the Bad Men**, 1948 (Dean White); **Sheriff of Sage Valley**, 1942 (Buster Crabbe); **Son of Billy the Kid**, 1949 (William Perrot); **Strange Lady in Town**, 1955 (Nick Adams); **The Tall Man**, 1960-1962 (TV series; Clu Gulager); **Timemaster**, 1995 (George Pilgrim); **Western Cyclone**, 1943 (Buster Crabbe); and **Young Guns II**, 1990 (Emilio Estevez). p, Christopher Cain, d, Joe Roth, Paul Schiff, Irby Smith; Cain; **cast**, Emilio Estevez, Kiefer Sutherland, Lou Diamond Phillips, Charlie Sheen, Dermot Mulroney, Casey Siemaszko, Terence Stamp, Jack Palance, Alice Carter, Terry O'Quinn, Sharon

Thomas, Brian Keith, Patrick Wayne, Geoffrey Blake; **w**, John Fusco; **c**, Dean Semler; **m**, Brian Banks, Anthony Marinelli; **ed**, Jack Hofstra; **prod d**, Jane Musky; **art d**, Harold Thrasher; **set d**, Robert Kracik; **spec eff**, Johnny Hale, Greg Hull, Dale L. Martin, William Purcell, Joe Quinlivan.

Young Guns II ★★★ 1990; U.S.; 104m; Morgan Creek Productions; FOX; Color; Western; Children: Unacceptable (MPAA: PG-13); **DVD**; **VHS**; IV. Good sequel to the 1988 film opens with Estevez, who plays Billy the Kid (1851-1881), as well as Brushy Bill Roberts (1859-1950), who claimed to be the Kid in the 1940s (a claim rejected by most, including some of his relatives), and who narrates this story. Estevez, as Brushy Bill Roberts, has contacted Whitford, a New Mexico attorney in 1950, telling Whitford that he is really Billy the Kid. He states that he wants the pardon once offered to him decades earlier by Lew Wallace (1827-1905), then governor of New Mexico Territory, and who is played by Wilson. Estevez then begins narrating this tale, saying that, after the Lincoln County War ended, he and his "Regulators" had gone their separate ways. Estevez is shown joining a new gang of outlaws that includes Pat Garrett (1850-1908), played by Petersen, and gunman David "Dave" Rudabaugh (1854-1886), who is played by Slater. Wilson, the new governor of New Mexico Territory, has by then ordered that the Regulators led by Estevez be tracked down and Josiah Gordon "Doc" Scurlock (1849-1929), played by Sutherland, and Jose Chavez (1851-1924), played by Phillips, are captured and placed in an underground cell in Lincoln and are soon to be hanged for their former crimes. Estevez then meets with Wilson, who offers him a pardon if he agrees to testify against members of the faction he fought against in the old Lincoln County War, and Estevez agrees. With the help of Petersen and Slater, Estevez and his friends pose as vigilantes wearing hoods to free Sutherland and Phillips. The gang decides to escape to Mexico along a secret trail called the Mexican Blackbird, known to only Estevez and a few others, but Petersen decides to quit the outlaw life and leaves to open a boarding house. Estevez, Slater, Sutherland and Chavez, who are joined by Getty, playing Tom O'Folliard (1858-1880), and Ruck, who plays Hendry William French, before the gang rides toward Mexico. Meanwhile, Wilson, in league with rancher John Chisum (1824-1884), who is played by Coburn, summons Petersen and offers him the job of sheriff of Lincoln County and $1,000 if he will track down and kill Estevez and his gang members. Petersen accepts and forms a posse that goes in pursuit of the outlaws. The gang by then has arrived in the small town of White Oaks and taken refuge in a brothel run by Wright. A local lynch mob led by a local deputy, Knepper, tries to negotiate with Estevez, saying that if he turns over Phillips, he will allow the rest of the outlaws to flee. Estevez refuses and uses Knepper as a shield to escape. Petersen then arrives at White Oaks with his posse, but too late to capture the outlaws. He later tracks them down and, in a shootout, kills Getty, who is only fourteen years old and idolizes Estevez (although O'Folliard was twenty-two when killed). Estevez then confesses that the secret broken trail to Mexico is a myth he made up to keep the gang together, and the disgusted Sutherland decides to quit and leave for the East. He is waylaid by one of Petersen's deputies, however, and sacrifices himself so that Estevez and the others can escape. Estevez, however, is captured and brought back to Lincoln where he is jailed, knowing he faces a kangaroo court that will convict him and sentence him to hang. He is visited by his old bordello friend Wright, and she smuggles a gun to Estevez with which he makes his escape. By that time, Slater has ridden to Mexico, but he is ostensibly killed by villagers. Estevez rides to Old Fort Sumner to find that Phillips is dying from a gunshot wound. Estevez hides out with a protective Mexican family, but Petersen tracks him down. Estevez asks his old friend to let him ride away to Mexico, and tell the authorities that he has shot him. Petersen tells Estevez that he does not trust him and that he will only return and that will not only brand him, Petersen, a liar, but bring about his own death. The unarmed Estevez then turns his back on Petersen, daring him to shoot him in the back. Petersen cannot bring himself to do such a cowardly act. The next day, a fake burial is conducted and Petersen's horse is stolen by an unidentified person (Estevez), who rides out of the country. In flash-forward, we see Estevez telling attorney Whitford that he stole that horse and Whitford agrees to aid him. An epilogue states that Petersen wrote a book about this saga that was not popular and was later shot and killed and that Brushy Bill later met with the governor of New Mexico, but that his claims were discredited and he died a month later. The final shot shows Estevez pointing his six-gun at an unknown target and where he states (a laughing line often repeated in this film and its predecessor) before firing a shot: "I'll make you famous!" This film sees a lot of startling action and good performances from Estevez, Slater, Petersen, Sutherland and Phillips. Even though the actual facts in the case are altered to suit the story line, the film enhances the myth of Billy the Kid and sustains interest throughout. The film was a great box office success, earning more than $44.1 million in its initial release against a budget of $10 million. Songs: "Blaze of Glory," "Billy Get Your Guns," "Miracle," "Blood Money," "Santa Fe," "Justice in the Barrel," "Never Say Die," "You Really Got Me Now," "Bang a Drum," "Dying Ain't Much of a Livin'" (Jon Bon Jovi), "Guano City" (Alan Silvestri). *Author's Note*; Phillips was injured during the production when Estevez fired a shot that spooked a horse and dragged Phillips some distance and where he broke his kneecap and an arm. To compensate for the broken arm, a scene was added where Slater and Phillips get into a fight and Slater drives a knife into Phillips' arm, causing him to wear splints thereafter to cover a real arm cast. Ironically, Coburn, who plays cattle baron John Chisum in this film and who convinces Petersen, playing Pat Garrett, to go after Billy the Kid, played that very lawman in **Pat Garrett and Billy the Kid**, 1973. Although this film depicts Garrett and the Kid riding together as outlaws, that was never the case, although they were passing acquaintances when they first met at Beaver Smith's Saloon in Old Fort Sumner and where they often played Casino (the Kid called Garrett "Big Casino" and Garrett called the Kid "Little Casino"). Throughout this film, as well as its predecessor, Estevez emits a unique and memorable laugh, which is more of a stuttering cackle, although not as high pitched as the hyena-like laugh rendered by Tom Hulce in **Amadeus**, 1984, or the snorting, phlegm-filled laugh delivered by Richard Widmark in **Kiss of Death**, 1947, and many other films. **p**, Paul Schiff, Irby Smith, **d**, Geoff Murphy; **cast**, Emilio Estevez, Kiefer Sutherland, Lou Diamond Phillips, Christian Slater, Viggo Mortensen, William Petersen, James Coburn, Balthazar Getty, Bradley Whitford, Scott Wilson, Alan Ruck, Jenny Wright, Robert Knepper, Jon Bon Jovi; **w**, John Fusco (based on characters created by Fusco); **c**, Dean Semler; **m**, Alan Silvestri; **ed**, Bruce Green; **prod d**, Gene Rudolf; **art d**, Christa Munro; **set d**, Andrew Bernard, Pasco Di Carlo, Flint Esquerra, Steve Joyner; **spec eff**, Robin L. D'Arcy, Peter Chesney.

The Young in Heart ★★★★ 1938; U.S.; 90m; Selznick International Pictures/UA; B/W; Comedy; Children: Cautionary; **DVD**; **VHS**. Delightful story presents a family of con artists who are first seen duping wealthy visitors to the French Riviera. Young is the patriarch of this swindling clan, a one-time Canadian actor who impersonates a former British officer of the Bengal Lancers of India, and his wife, Burke, aids him in his confidence games. Their two children, Gaynor and Fairbanks, are equally adept at enacting scams and concentrate on fortune-hunting. Gaynor sets her sights on Carlson, but she dumps him after learning that he has no money. Meanwhile, Fairbanks chases Early, a wealthy heiress, but his plans to ensnare Early are preempted by Young, who promptly cheats her father, Cobb, out of a large sum of money while playing cards. French officials realize that the family is nothing more than a pack of charming flimflammers and order them to leave the country, providing them with complimentary train tickets. While on the train, they meet dowager Dupree, thinking she will be their next victim after Gaynor befriends the lonely, aging spinster. Dupree confides to Gaynor

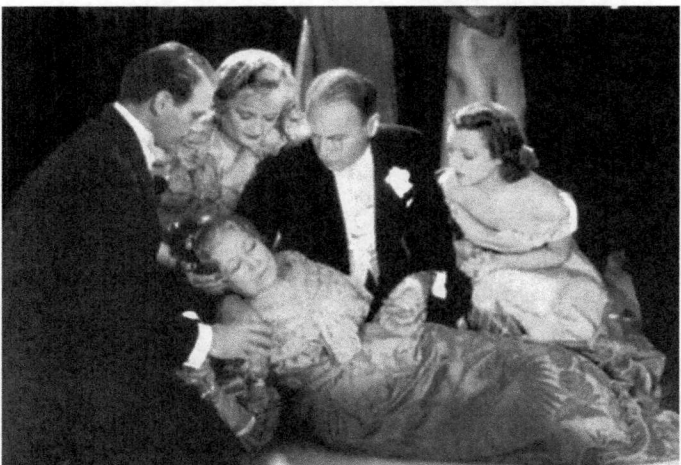

Douglas Fairbanks Jr., Billie Burke, Roland Young, Janet Gaynor and (prone) Minnie Dupree in *The Young in Heart*, 1938.

that she has been left a great fortune by a former fiancé she rejected many years earlier. She invites Gaynor and her family members to dinner, and they all become friends. When the train is later derailed in an accident, the family saves Dupree's life, and she is so grateful that she invites them all to stay at her luxurious mansion in London. The family accepts with alacrity, believing that they can so ingratiate themselves to Dupree that she will, when passing, leave them her money (she is aptly named Ellen Fortune). While the con artists spend enjoyable evenings with Dupree, Young and Fairbanks, to offset the deep suspicions harbored about them by Dupree's attorney, Stephenson, proclaim that they are going to apply for jobs, even though neither has worked a day in their conniving lives. Carlson then appears, looking for Gaynor, even though he knows she has used him in the past and that he has nothing much to offer her and that her family members are much less than reputable. Carlson endears himself to Gaynor by helping Young get a job as a salesman for Flying Wombat cars, a position Young quickly comes to appreciate when he takes pride in making his first sale. Young becomes so successful that he is named the London manager and is given a substantial raise. Fairbanks then halfheartedly applies for a job as a clerk at an engineering firm, and he is hired through the efforts of attractive Goddard, who works there and to whom Fairbanks is deeply attracted. Goddard knows that Fairbanks is not on the up-and-up, but through her guidance, he comes to appreciate the value of honest work and makes plans to attend night courses so that he can become an engineer. He and his father Young by now have deep regrets about possibly fleecing the generous and kindhearted Dupree, as do Burke and Gaynor, who look after the sweet old lady. None of the family members, however, believe that any of the others have had a change of heart and that each of them still plots to inherit Dupree's fortune. Dupree then learns the true background of the family she is hosting, but she only regrets that these people, who have become her dear friends, have chosen such an unsavory way of life. She nevertheless instructs Stephenson to draw up a new will in which she leaves everything to Young and his family. She then presides at a white tie dinner party where her guests are told about the inheritance, but she collapses and Stephenson tells the stunned guests that Dupree's fortune has evaporated to the point where she owns nothing, not even the resplendent mansion where they all live. That matters nothing to Young, Burke, Gaynor and Fairbanks. Their only concern is for the welfare of their wonderful host and they tell Stephenson that *they* will now take care of Dupree. The happy ending sees Dupree living in a comfortable cottage with Young and Burke, along with Fairbanks and Goddard, and Gaynor and Carlson, these two couples having happily gone to the altar. This warmhearted tale is told with great sensitivity by Wallace, and all of the actors are superb in their roles, particularly where Young, Burke, Gaynor and Fairbanks subtly transition from

Marlon Brando and Maximilian Schell in *The Young Lions*, 1958.

crooks to kindhearted, rehabilitated people through the affection they have for and receive from the marvelous Dupree. This is not one of the screwball comedies so popular in the 1930s, although it is reminiscent of **The Lady Eve**, 1941, where a father and daughter are con artists out to bilk a young millionaire. The film is also not dissimilar in modus operandi with **I Was an Adventuress**, 1940, where a phony countess falls in love with her victim, which brings about her reformation, or **They Met in Bombay**, 1941, where man-and-woman jewel thieves re-form after they fall in love. The film received Oscar nominations for Best Cinematography (Shamroy), and Best Musical Score (Waxman). The film did not do as well as expected at the box office, but later became a minor classic. Songs/Music: "Funeral March" (Charles Valentin Alkan), "Gary Owen" (traditional Irish song), "Loch Lomond" (Scottish traditional song), "Anvil Chorus" ["Gypsy Chorus"] (1853; from "Il Trovatore" by Giuseppe Verdi), "Flight of the Valkyries" ["Ride of the Valkyries"] (1851; from "Die Wakkure" by Richard Wagner). *Author's Note*: Fairbanks told this author that "the Flying Wombat car Roland [Young] sells in **The Young in Heart** was a hybrid auto specifically built for the picture [at a cost of $12,000], and it was designed by, of all people, Rust Heinz, whose family sold the ketchup and mustard [57 varieties]. It was a six-passenger coupe that he and others thought to sell as a customized car [1938 Phantom Corsair] back then, but that car never got to the marketplace." Gaynor retired after this film, but she returned to appear in one more production, **Bernadine**, 1957. Dupree was not the first choice to play the dowager, as icons Laurette Taylor and Maude Adams were first tested for the part. This was Richard Carlson's feature film debut. This film has no relation to the film **Young at Heart**, 1954, starring Frank Sinatra and Doris Day. **p**, David O. Selznick; **d**, Richard Wallace; **cast**, Janet Gaynor, Douglas Fairbanks, Jr., Paulette Goddard, Roland Young, Billie Burke, Minnie Dupree, Henry Stephenson, Richard Carlson, Irvin S. Cobb, Lucile Watson, Margaret Early, Lya Lys, Billy Bevan; **w**, Paul Osborn, Charles Bennett (based on the novel *The Gay Banditti* by I.A.R. Wylie); **c**, Leon Shamroy; **m**, Franz Waxman; **ed**, Hal C. Kern; **prod d**, William Cameron Menzies; **art d**, Lyle R. Wheeler; **spec eff**, Jack Cosgrove.

Young Jesse James ★★★ 1960; U.S.; 73m; AP/FOX; B/W; Biographical Drama/Western; Children: Unacceptable. Solid biopic details the early life of the infamous outlaw, which begins when the father of brothers Jesse James (1847-1882) and Frank James (1843-1915) is unjustly hanged by Union troops during the American Civil War (1861-1865). Their mother's arm is amputated after their home is bombed by Union zealots, so the boys join Quantrill's Raiders and meet outlaws Cole Younger (1844-1916) and Belle Starr (Myra Maybelle Starr, 1848-1889). In this telling of the legend of the James Brothers, Jesse, played

by Stricklyn, wants only to settle down and become a farmer, but destiny sends him in the direction of crime. Frank James is played by Robert Dix, Cole Younger by Willard Parker, Belle Starr by Merry Anders, and William Quantrill (1837-1865) by Emile Meyer, all of whom, along with Stricklyn, are impressive in their historic roles. Song: "Young Jesse James" (Irving Gertz, Hal Levy). *Author's Note*: Though the writers of this film play fast and loose with the actual facts about these legendary outlaws, the film nevertheless captures the true personalities of the errant brothers. For more details about Jesse James, see this author's works, *Encyclopedia of Western Lawmen and Outlaws* (Paragon House, 1992; pages 172-189), and the two-volume *The Great Pictorial History of World Crime*, Volume II (History, Inc., 2004; pages 1342-1359). Outstanding films about the James Brothers include **Jesse James**, 1939; **The Return of Frank James**, 1940; **The True Story of Jesse James**, 1957; **The Last Days of Frank and Jesse James**, 1986; **Frank and Jesse**, 1995; and **The Assassination of Jesse James by the Coward Robert Ford**, 2007, while Gene Tierney profiled Belle Starr in the 1941 movie of that name. **p**, Jack Leewood; **d**, William F. Claxton; **cast**, Ray Stricklyn, Willard Parker, Merry Anders, Robert Dix, Emile Meyer, Jacklyn O'Donnell, Rayford Barnes, Rex Holman, Boyd Holister, Sheila Bromley; **w**, Jerry Sackheim, Orville H. Hampton; **c**, Carl Berger; **m**, Irving Gertz; **ed**, Richard C. Meyer; **art d**, Lyle Wheeler, John B. Mansbridge; **set d**, Mac Mulcahy; **spec eff**, Stuart Moody.

The Young Lions ★★★★ 1958; U.S.; 167m; FOX; B/W; War Drama; Children: Unacceptable; **DVD**; **VHS**. Brando, Clift and Martin give stunning performances as vastly different men caught up in WWII (1939-1945), the former fighting for the Germans, the latter two as GIs, fate bringing them grimly together on a European battlefield. The film opens in 1938 in Bavaria, where American tourist Rush is taking skiing lessons from Brando, a German ski instructor. They are attracted to each other, but that changes when Brando invites Rush to a New Year's Eve party at the inn where she is staying. The festivities are interrupted by military songs and praise for the present leader of Germany, Adolf Hitler (1889-1945), and this spoils the party for Rush, who has no respect for the German dictator. While she and Brando stand outside the inn, Brando tells her that he believes that Hitler may improve his country's economy and restore Germany's prestige among nations. For this reason, Rush breaks off her brief romance with the handsome, blond-haired Brando and returns to the U.S. to resume her long-standing relationship with Martin, a self-centered Broadway playboy. Meanwhile, Clift, a young Jewish man, visits his estranged and impoverished father only to see him die in a seedy hotel room. When WWII (1939-1945) begins, Brando joins the German army with the rank of lieutenant and, while serving under the command of Schell, participates in the Battle for France in 1940. While the Germans close on Paris, Brando leads a unit of German troops against undermanned French soldiers, overwhelming their position and where he is congratulated for his military skills. He and Schell are later seen in Paris where they pose for photographs at the landmark of Sacré-Coeur, and Brando's friend, Baer, a sergeant who later becomes a German officer, is also present. Stationed in Paris, Brando is given police duty, working with the SS, and he finds the torturing of prisoners so distasteful that he asks that he be transferred to the front in North Africa. Meanwhile, Rush urges Martin to join the fight against the Nazis, but he has no desire to give up his luxurious lifestyle. After the U.S. enters the war, Martin is summoned to a draft board where, despite his protests, he is drafted, along with others, including Clift, a clerk in a department store. Martin befriends Clift, inviting him to a party where he meets Rush and her friend, Lange, a young woman from a small town. Clift and Lange fall in love, but Lange's father, Taylor, a merchant, is not sure that he wants a Jew for a son-in-law. Lange brings Clift home and Taylor is impressed with the sincere young man (and where he meets a Jew for the first time in his life) and he approves the marriage between Clift and Lange. We now see Brando serving in the German Africa Corps, and he is under the command of

Schell, who sets an ambush for a unit of British troops at camp. The Germans attack the camp with mortar shells and machine guns and other automatic fire, slaughtering the mostly unarmed British soldiers. Brando orders his men to cease fire after seeing no resistance from the British, but Schell ruthlessly countermands that order by having his men continue to bombard and rake the camp with shells and gunfire. When the Germans enter the camp, Shell sees a blinded British trooper staggering forward and orders Brando to shoot him. Brando refuses to commit what he believes to be an outright murder, and Schell angrily executes the wounded soldiers, upbraiding Brando for not having the will to destroy the enemy and obey his orders. Brando is sickened by such slaughter and is now completely disillusioned with the war and, especially, the dishonorable conduct of his fellow German soldiers. By this time, Clift and Martin have been sent to a GI training camp where they are commanded by Rudley, an anti-Semitic captain who singles out Clift for company punishment for having dirt at his bed station and where Rudley punishes the entire platoon at the same time. This causes some of the other GIs to abuse Clift. After some of his personal belongings are destroyed, and while ignoring warnings from Martin not to seek revenge, Clift challenges his antagonists, the four biggest GIs in his platoon, to separate fistfights. One by one, these brutes savagely beat Clift, but he insists on fighting each man. He finally beats the last man, but tends to that man's bloody wounds, befriending him. All of the men he has fought, however, eventually show their respect for Clift. At the same time, Martin protests the beatings Clift has been taking to Rudley, who tells him that, unless he keeps quiet, he will not be transferred to the cushy job he seeks and will remain in an infantry company and be sent to the front where he might be easily killed. Martin ignores that warning and goes over Rudley's head, reporting him to his superior. Rudley is later called before his commander and is relieved of his command and ordered to face a court-martial. In Africa, the tide of war has turned against the Germans and Brando is shown driving a motorcycle with Schell clinging to him on that cycle as they flee a battlefield with British planes pursuing them and other retreating German forces. They strike a land mine and the two are blown from the cycle, and where Brando is wounded and Schell is terribly disfigured. Brando, recovered, later visits Schell in a hospital, where Schell's head is completely bandaged, with only a small opening for his mouth. Schell asks Brando to secretly bring him a bayonet, but Brando hesitates until Schell explains that the weapon is for his suffering roommate, not for himself, and where that wounded soldier has asked Schell to end his suffering by ending his life. Brando reluctantly agrees to bring Schell the bayonet. Brando is reassigned to Paris where he resumes his friendship with Baer, who has acquired a French girlfriend, and who introduces Brando to her friend, Doll. The young French woman, however, has nothing but resentment for Germans and insults Brando. He simply accepts the degradation, which causes Doll to regret her remarks, and the two have a brief affair. Meanwhile, Martin has managed to get himself a safe assignment in London where Rush is serving as an assistant to an American general. Rush believes that Martin is shirking his duty and shames him into requesting a front line assignment. At that time, Clift and his company are serving at the front in France and are commanded by Franz, a compassionate lieutenant. The company is trapped at an advanced position when Germans attack the area, and Franz orders everyone to retreat back to the American lines and they flee in twos and threes. Clift and two others reach a river, but one of the men refuses to cross as he cannot swim. Clift helps the other soldier to cross, and they reach the safety of the American lines. Clift then swims back across the river to retreat the other soldier and helps him swim the river to safety. At that time, Martin arrives to resume his friendship with Clift. Brando, by this time, returns to Germany on a brief furlough. As he walks through the ruins of a bombed-out German city, he sees a small one-legged boy trying to maneuver through the rubble, an image that convinces Brando that the war is lost to his country. He visits Britt, who is Schell's widow, to pay his respects. He has earlier visited this blonde vixen, knowing she has rou-

Montgomery Clift and Dean Martin in *The Young Lions*, 1958.

tinely cheated on Schell with high-ranking German officers. She is no longer living in luxury, her once well-appointed apartment now a shabby, clapboard affair. When Britt sees Brando, she is also no longer the ravishing beauty Brando had earlier seen, but is now careworn and haggard. Britt shocks Brando when telling him that her husband committed suicide with a bayonet, the very weapon that Brando had smuggled to Schell. Britt, desperate for any creature comforts, looks upon Brando as someone who can improve her miserable lifestyle. She attempts to seduce him, stating that she will make herself more appealing to him, but when she tries to embrace him, Brando violently throws her against a wall as he finds her as repulsive as the evil regime for which he has fought, and he hastily departs. Brando is later seen alone, uniform in tatters and carrying a submachine gun, as he makes his way to a German concentration camp; he meets its commander, Katch, who gives Brando some meager food to eat as Brando has been wandering hungry for days. Katch then receives a call from Berlin and angrily hangs up on his superior, complaining to Brando that his superior has asked that he do the impossible and that is murder all of the thousands of Jews at that camp immediately. Katch tells Brando that he does not have the men or equipment to commit such a mass extermination, particularly since American troops are nearby and advancing on the camp. Stunned by what is a grim revelation to him, Brando now realizes the true evils brought about by the Nazi regime and he leaves in revulsion and shame. American troops then come upon the camp and the GIs entering it are led by Franz, his forces including Clift and Martin. A local German official then appears before Franz to tell him that the German community nearby will not tolerate a demonstration by the Jewish inmates, who want to hold a religious service for the first time in years to honor their many dead. Franz then tells the official that he intends to place armed guards in the towers and around the camp with orders to shoot anyone who attempts to interfere with those Jewish services and that if the official ever dares to enter the camp again, he, Franz, will personally throw him out on his ear. Franz, realizing that Clift is Jewish and has been traumatized by what he has seen at this awful place, tells him to leave the camp and sends Martin to go with him. The two roam down a road, and Clift is wracked with agony at seeing the horror camp where his fellow Jews have been systematically exterminated under Hitler's genocidal practices. He tells Martin that he hopes that men with conscience and a sense of justice like Franz will be running the world when the war ends. Meanwhile, Brando has made his own personal peace with the world, quitting the German army by destroying his submachine gun before he stumbles through some woods. Clift and Martin hear Brando approaching and Martin sees Brando moving through some woods, shouting for Clift to take cover while Martin fires at Brando. Fatally shot, Brando falls forward into a shallow stream, his head beneath the

Marlon Brando and May Britt in *The Young Lions*, 1958.

waters where his last gurgling gasps are shown as bubbles bursting at the surface. Martin and Clift silently watch Brando die before slowly walking back toward the camp. A final scene shows Clift emerging from the subway station that he left when joining the army; Lange sees him from the upstairs window of their apartment and joyfully holds up the little daughter Clift has never seen. He eagerly goes up the stairs to enter the brownstone to end this stirring and memorable film. Dmytryk helms this episodic tale with great skill as he seamlessly merges one tale into the other while chronicling the unfolding events of the war, and he effectively uses newsreel footage to link those events. The acting from Brando, Clift, Martin and Lange is superb as they fully capture the personas of their widely divergent characters. Of particular note is the ruthless Schell, a dedicated Nazi, and Britt, his slutty, self-serving wife. They both represent all that is corrupt about the Hitler regime they so fanatically support, and their miserable fates incisively example the overall justice the world meted out to that vile dictatorship. The film received Oscar nominations for Best Cinematography (MacDonald), Best Dramatic or Comedy Score (Friedhofer), and Best Sound Recording (Carlton W. Faulkner). The film did very well at the box office, earning more than $4.4 million in its initial release against a budget of $3.5 million. Songs: "The Blue Danube" (1866; Johann Strauss), "Horst Wessel Song" ["The Flag on High"] (1930; lyrics: Horst Wessel), "Deutschland Uber Alles" (music [1797]: Joseph Haydn; lyrics [1841]: August Heinrich Hoffman von Fallersleben), "There'll Always Be an England" (1939; Ross Parker, Hughie Charles), "Bless 'Em All" (1917; music: Robert Kewley; lyrics: Fred Godfrey), "How About You?" (1941; music: Burton Lane; lyrics: Ralph Freed), "Blue Moon" (1934; music: Richard Rodgers; lyrics: Lorenz Hart). *Author's Note*: Although Anhalt's script is faithful to the powerful Shaw novel, the film ends in a much different way, a change made at Brando's insistence. In the novel, the character played by Brando is an unrepentant Nazi to the very end; he kills the Jewish GI and is then killed by the character played by Martin. Brando told this author: "My view was that Shaw had written his novel just after the war when tempers were still hot and he could not have any forgiveness for the Germans. We were showing a vicious German officer already in the role played by Schell, so it was pointless to have two characters have the same attitudes." Brando, of course, a powerhouse in Hollywood at that time, had his way, although Shaw later told Brando that he would have written his characters the same way even if he had written his novel a decade after the war was over. Shaw, who had fought in WWII in Europe as a warrant officer, published his novel, his first, in 1948, three years after the war ended. "The truth of the matter was that Marlon could not tolerate playing a character that had no sense of decency or honor," Dmytryk told this author. "The real problems we had existed between Marlon and Monty, both prima donnas." Brando

reportedly spied on Clift's scenes while standing behind the camera crew, but Clift refused to watch any of Brando's scenes. When Brando suggested that his character die with a Christ-like image, one where his arms would be shown outstretched on barbed wire, Clift exploded. Dmytryk told this author: "Monty came to me and said: 'If you let him get away with that crucifixion death, I will quit this picture.' It took me a half hour to calm him down and assure him that Marlon's death would not be like that. A friend of mine later said: 'What do you expect? When Monty's around, there can only be one Jesus Christ.'" Clift had found a picture of Jewish writer Franz Kafka in a magazine and tore it out, keeping it at his dressing room table where he made himself up, altering his face by using putty to enlarge his ears so that they would stick out and also enlarging his nose so that it had an even more hooked appearance. All of this was to make himself resemble Kafka. "He thought he looked more Jewish by doing all that," Dmytryk told this author, "but all he succeeded in doing was making himself less attractive and appealing. To be liked by an audience, an actor should do everything to appear empathetic, including how they look. Monty, to tell you the truth, looked like hell in that picture, although he bragged to people later that he thought it was one of his best performances." Brando, too, thought his portrayal was one of the best he had rendered on film and even named his son "Christian," after his character's name of "Christian Diestl." Martin was not the first choice to play Clift's friend, that role first assigned to Tony Randall, but Randall had to drop out and Martin got the role. This departure from his teaming with comic Jerry Lewis proved to be so impressive that Martin went on to become a serious film actor, rendering many memorable performances, such as John Wayne's alcoholic deputy in **Rio Bravo**, 1959. Martin later stated that he was indebted to Clift, who gave him many acting tips during the production. They later became friends, and Martin remained a friend to Clift long after that actor alienated most of his associates through his use of alcohol and drugs. Where Clift and Martin became friends, so too did Brando and Schell. The gifted German actor, however, could not speak English at the time he made this film, and Brando patiently worked with him, teaching Schell how to pronounce his words phonetically. **p**, Al Lichtman; **d**, Edward Dmytryk; **cast**, Marlon Brando, Montgomery Clift, Dean Martin, Hope Lange, Barbara Rush, May Britt, Maximilian Schell, Lee Van Cleef, Arthur Franz, Parley Baer, Dora Doll, Liliane Montevecchi, Vaughn Taylor, Herbert Rudley, Kurt Katch; **w**, Edward Anhalt (based on the novel by Irwin Shaw); **c**, Joe MacDonald (CinemaScope); **m**, Hugo Friedhofer; **ed**, Dorothy Spencer; **art d**, Lyle R. Wheeler, Addison Hehr; **set d**, Walter M. Scott, Stuart A. Reiss; **spec eff**, L.B. Abbott.

The Young Lord ★★★ 1970; West Germany; 137m; UNITEL/International Television Trading; Color; Musical Drama/Opera; Children: Unacceptable. This superior adaptation of the German opera "Der Junge Lord" by Hans Werner Henze and Ingeborg Bachmann is set in 1830 when Graf, an elderly nobleman, arrives in a town with servants and pets. Townspeople are in awe of him, but he shows only contempt for the inhabitants. He expresses his feelings by creating Grobe, a mythical "young lord," trying to convince everyone that the fellow exists. (In German English subtitles.) **d**, Ernst Wild; **cast**, Donald Grobe, Edith Mathis, Loren Driscoll, Barry McDaniel, Otto Graf, Vera Little, Lisa Otto, Margrette Ast, Gita Mikes, Bella Jaspers, Manfred Rohrl, Ivan Sardi; **w**, Ingreberg Bachmann (based on the German fable "Der Scheik von Alexandria und seine Sklaven" by Wilhelm Hauff); **c**, Wild (Eastmancolor); **m**, Hans Werner Henze.

Young Man with a Horn ★★★★ 1950; U.S.; 112m; WB; B/W; Drama; Children; Unacceptable; **DVD**; **VHS**; **IV**. Douglas gives another intense and compelling performance as an ambitious trumpet player, his riveting role inspired by legendary jazz cornetist Leon "Bix" Beiderbecke, 1903-1931. He attempts to achieve great musical heights are almost at the cost of his life in his obsessive quest for the perfect note.

The film begins with narration from pianist-composer Carmichael (1899-1981), who was a friend of Beiderbecke's, describing how Douglas, as a child, played by Lindgren, came to the world of music. In flashback, we see Lindgren staring into a pawnshop window at an old trumpet. In order to buy the instrument, he works at a bowling alley setting pins. Once he buys the trumpet, however, he has no knowledge of how to play it. To that end, he roams the streets at night, listening to the black jazz bands playing their distinctive music. He climbs onto the ledge of a window above a door of one club to watch Hernandez and his band play the music he has come to love. When the band ends for the night, Hernandez sees Lindgren and invites him to have sandwiches with him and his band members. When Hernandez learns that Lindgren wants to learn how to play the trumpet he has purchased, as well as to play jazz, the avuncular Hernandez takes the boy under his wing. He becomes his teacher and closest friend, as well as a kindhearted father figure. (Lindgren, a white boy, is not shown with any family members and it is assumed that he is homeless, but one without prejudice in that he fully accepts the friendship and guidance of a man and his talented band members who are all black, this in an era when America was racially segregated.) Hernandez, an accomplished jazz musician, patiently tutors the boy with his unique brand of music until he grows to manhood as Douglas, cautioning him now not to develop a "roll" on his tongue that might destroy his ability to play the trumpet. Douglas gets a job with a band led by Reed where he meets and befriends piano player Carmichael and is attracted to the band's beautiful blonde singer, Day, who thinks he is a brilliantly gifted musician. Douglas then gets into trouble with bandleader Reed when, one night, tiring of the same musical routines the band is compelled to play, he improvises on his solo of a song, instead of playing it according to the way it was composed. Though Reed warns him never again to do that, Douglas encourages Carmichael to help him create a new arrangement with a few of the other band members and they play a hot jazz number. Enraged at Douglas' impromptu jam session, Reed fires Douglas, along with Carmichael, and both leave to go on the road together. They play at inexpensive road-houses where they make little money, but they are playing the kind of music both love. Day, however, has never forgotten Douglas, and, in fact, loves him. When Carmichael tires of the poor pay and nomadic life with Douglas, he quits and goes back home to Indiana. Douglas then goes to New York to see if he can find work as a musician. He finds Day singing with a dance band at an upscale nightclub. He and Day then go to a small café where Douglas is shocked to see his mentor, Hernandez, playing there, but Hernandez is now old and ailing and can no longer perform well. Douglas helps him by playing with him, and his performance so impresses Cowan, who is Day's bandleader employer, that Cowan hires Douglas for his band. Douglas soon becomes the lead trumpet player in the band and rises to superstardom, now recognized as a wizard with his horn and where he thrills audiences with his startling solo performances. One night, Day brings her friend Bacall to the club to listen to Douglas, and Bacall is more than impressed by this talented young man. When they meet, Douglas, much to Day's regret, is taken with the haughty Bacall. She comes from great wealth and is studying to become a psychiatrist, but this is but a fad to while away her time as Bacall is a dilettante who has dabbled with many pursuits, mastering none. She harbors doubts and fears ever since her own mother committed suicide, and she admits that she is an emotionally unstable woman. Nevertheless, Douglas and Bacall have a torrid affair, but Bacall blatantly tells Douglas that she is incapable of receiving or giving love. Despite that dire warning, Douglas continues to pursue Bacall and the two eventually marry, but it is a union doomed from the start. Bacall looks upon Douglas not as a husband, but as another possession, a trophy to be displayed to her elitist friends. She insists that he attend parties she gives where he is surrounded by self-serving snobs like Bacall, who have no regard for his talent or the passion he has for creative music. Actually, Bacall is jealous of Douglas and his unique brand of music. After Hernandez is killed by a hit-and-run driver, Douglas misses a large

Orley Lindgren (boy at left) and Juano Hernandez in *Young Man with a Horn*, 1950.

party Bacall gives in order to attend his mentor's funeral. When he returns, he is greeted by a livid Bacall, who accuses him of insulting her and her friends. She perversely resents Douglas' affection for the dead black musician where she can give no affection or accept any from Douglas. Bacall demonstrates her hatred for his creativity and love of music by smashing Douglas' prized and rare record collection of great jazz artists. This ends the marriage, and Douglas, who has taken to drink, increases his binges to the point where he is unreliable and is fired from the band by Cowan. He drifts through a series of low dives, playing his kind of jazz, but his drinking debilitates his ability to play. Day finds him and secures a job for him where Douglas is to accompany her during a recording session. When it comes to his solo, however, Douglas breaks up and is unable to play the high notes he easily achieved in the past. He becomes so angry and frustrated with himself that he smashes his trumpet, his most beloved possession. Douglas then goes on a Homeric bender that eventually sends him to the alcoholic ward where, in his delusional state, he hears the wailing of a distant police siren and thinks that piercing sound is the very note he has sought to find and play throughout his life before he collapses unconscious. Day and Carmichael then find Douglas in the hospital. It appears through Carmichael's narration that Douglas will not only recover, but that he will rehabilitate his life with Day and eventually find peace, accepting the limits of his talent and his continued ability to play the horn. In addition to Douglas' bravura performance, Bacall renders a mesmerizing essay of a beautiful but vicious person who uses her wealth and position to demean and destroy those with talent in order to advance her warped sense of superiority. This was one of Bacall's most stunning performances, one that proved her deep talent as a first-class actress. Hernandez, too, is outstanding as the generous mentor, and Carmichael shines as the piano-playing sidekick, a role the composer-turned-actor patented over the years. Day is her sunny self, and Curtiz does a fine job unfolding this bittersweet rags-to-riches-to-rags tale with great directorial skills, seamlessly merging some great musical numbers with well-constructed melodramatic scenes. The real musical star of the film is the brilliant Harry James, who performed Douglas' trumpet playing (Jimmy Zito dubbed the trumpet playing for Hernandez; Buddy Cole did some of Carmichael's piano playing). Day's vocals are outstanding, and here she is playing a role from real life as she began her career as a singer in a band. The film was a success at the box office and received a one-hour radio adaptation aired by Lux Radio Theater on March 3, 1952, with Douglas reprising his role and with singer Jo Stafford and actress Patrice Wymore in support. Songs: "In the Sweet By and By" (1868; music: Joseph P. Webster; lyrics: S. Fillmore Bennett), "Moanin' Low" (1929; music: Ralph Rainger; lyrics: Howard Dietz), "Chinatown, My Chinatown" (1910; music: Jean Schwartz; lyrics: William Jerome), "Shadow Waltz" (1933; Harry Warren), "The Very

Hoagy Carmichael and Kirk Douglas in *Young Man with a Horn*, 1950.

Thought of You" (1934; Ray Noble), "Baby Face" (1926; music: Harry Akst; lyrics: Benny Davis), "Sweet Georgia Brown" (1925; music: Ben Bernie, Maceo Pinkard; lyrics: Kenneth Casey), "Get Happy" (1930; music: Harold Arlen; lyrics: Ted Koehler), "Lovin' Sam (The Sheik of Alabam)" (1922; music: Milton Ager; lyrics: Jack Yellen), "Silent Night, Holy Night" (music [1818]: Franz Gruber; lyrics [1816] Joseph Mohr), "Too Marvelous for Words" (1937; music: Richard A. Whiting; lyrics: Johnny Mercer), "Ain't She Sweet" (1927; music: Milton Ager; lyrics: Jack Yellen), "Blue Room" (1926; music: Richard Rodgers; lyrics: Lorenz Hart), "Can't We Be Friends?" (1929; Katharine Faulkner "Kay" Swift), "I Only Have Eyes for You" (1934; music: Harry Warren; lyrics: Al Dubin), "Tea for Two" (1925; music: Vincent Youmans; lyrics: Irving Caesar), "The Man I Love" (1924; music: George Gershwin; lyrics: Ira Gershwin), "I May Be Wrong (but I Think You're Wonderful)" (1929; music: Henry Sullivan; lyrics: Harry Ruskin), "What Is This Thing Called Love?" (1929; Cole Porter), "'S Wonderful" (1927; music: George Gershwin; lyrics: Ira Gershwin), "Limehouse Blues" (1922; music: Philip Braham; lyrics: Douglas Furber), "Swing Low, Sweet Chariot" (c.1862; Wallis Willis), "Nobody Knows the Trouble I've Seen" (c.1867; traditional Negro spiritual), "Someone to Watch Over Me" (1926; music: George Gershwin; lyrics: Ira Gershwin); "Carolina in the Morning" (1922; music: Walter Donaldson; lyrics: Gus Kahn), "With a Song in My Heart" (1929; music: Richard Rodgers; lyrics: Lorenz Hart), "Pretty Baby" (1916; music: Egbert Van Alstyne; lyrics: Tony Jackson, Gus Kahn); "The Japanese Sandman" (1920; music: Richard A. Whiting; lyrics: Raymond B. Egan), "Love for Sale" (1930; Cole Porter), "If I Could Be with You (One Hour Tonight)" (1926; music: James P. Johnson; lyrics: Henry Creamer), "Nocturne, Op. 9, No. 2 in E Flat Major" (1830-1832; Frederic Chopin). *Author's Note*: Bacall was eager to play her role as a cold-hearted wealthy woman, even though there is not a bit of empathy in her character, to prove her superb acting abilities. She serves as a psychic sapper, draining all of the emotion and strength from Douglas' jazzman. Further, it is evident in one scene where Douglas finds Bacall with a female friend, a somewhat cross-eyed sculptor, that Bacall is a closet lesbian, but this is subtly suggested as the censors of that day banned such sexual references from the screen. Douglas went after this role as he did with all others with zealous dedication, working for three months with Larry Sullivan, who was the lead trumpet player for the studio orchestra, learning the valve movements of the trumpet and where he could reasonably play the instrument, although he lip syncs his numbers in the film. He nevertheless continued to loudly practice on the instrument throughout the production, creating so much racket in his dressing room that he disturbed the rest of the cast and director Curtiz had to ask him to cease. Day did not find the film personally rewarding, later complaining that her costars,

Douglas and Bacall, cold-shouldered her. Bacall and Douglas had once dated when they were struggling at the beginning of their careers in New York, and Bacall was later instrumental in bringing Douglas to Hollywood's attention. Day stated many years later that she was undergoing a lot of stress in this film because it reminded her of the emotionally draining experiences she had had when she began her own career as a singer in a band. (Day had begun her singing career at age eighteen in 1939 as a singer with band leader Les Brown and she would go on to record more than 650 songs and become one of America's leading singers as well as one of the most popular film actresses in the 20th Century.) Day was friendly with the director of this film, Curtiz, who had auditioned her for her first film role in **Romance on the High Seas**, 1948. She never befriended Douglas, stating later that the actor was too self-centered to make friends with anyone (other than old acquaintance Bacall). Though Douglas loosely plays the life of Bix Beiderbecke, he plays a trumpet throughout the film where Beiderbecke played a cornet, the preferred instrument of any jazz player and one that produces richer tonal qualities than the more shrilly trumpet. Douglas is shown surviving his severe alcoholism in this film, but Beiderbecke did not, dying at the early age of twenty-eight, in a seedy Queens, New York, boarding room of a heart attack after a bender that brought on pneumonia. Fellow tenant George Kaslow heard Beiderbecke screaming on the night of August 6, 1931, and ran into the jazzman's room to find him trembling. "He was screaming that there were two Mexicans hiding under his bed with long daggers," Kraslow later stated. Kraslow humored Beiderbecke by looking under the bed to assure him that there were no intruders in his room and, when he stood up, Beiderbecke fell forward, a dead weight, into Kraslow's arms. A doctor shortly pronounced the great jazzman dead. Oddly, none of Beiderbecke's outstanding jazz recordings, mostly from the 1920s, including "Big Boy," "Oh Baby!," "Riverboat Shuffle," "Tiger Rag," "Singin' the Blues," "I'm Coming Virginia," "Sorry," and "Jazz Me Blues" appear in this film. James, superb musician that he was, could never have duplicated these classics and where more mainstream popular tunes were selected for mass audience identification. This author's mother, a singer in the late 1920s to the early 1940s, met the great Beiderbecke about a year before his death and where he was playing with a small jazz group in a NYC speakeasy. In 1974, she recalled for me her meeting with the legendary jazzman: "He sat down with us, this clean-cut looking fellow from Davenport, Iowa, and began drinking so quickly that his head was soon down on the table. Someone told me that this was the great Bix Beiderbecke, but I could hardly believe it. Yet, when someone shook him to tell him that his session was beginning, he revived like a rose opening with sunlight and jumped to his feet. He raced to the small bandstand where he grabbed his cornet and began playing. We were all stunned. Only a few minutes earlier, this young man seemed to be in a drunken stupor. And here he was blasting out some of the purest jazz notes the world has ever heard! It was thrilling. I had heard [Louis] Armstrong and many other great horn players, but none compared to Bix. His attack was so aggressive and the force of his delivery was unlike anything else in the world of jazz in those days. His music was different, sort of a combination of New Orleans jazz and Midwestern ragtime and where his tempo was tremendous, like a train gathering steam to speed down a track. We all knew that night that this was a man who lived only for his music, and, sadly, he died for it only about a year later. When someone told me that he was dead, I burst into tears, and I said to a friend: 'That poor, sad, young man, all alone in the world with only his horn.' About a year later, I sat with Hoagy [Carmichael], a close friend of Bix's, who told me that Bix used to listen to records of King Oliver and other New Orleans jazzmen when he was a kid. And he bought an old cornet and taught himself how to play it as he played along with those records, which is how, I guess, he developed his unique playing style. Hoagy said: 'I don't think I ever saw that sweet kid when he wasn't carrying that beat-up old horn of his.' That horn gave Bix his only joy, but it could not save his life." My mother had collected all of Beiderbecke's early records and, as Bix had listened to Oliver as a child, I had listened to Bix's music as a child, poignant and powerful jazz music that has remained rewardingly vivid and lasting in my memory. Other films profiling jazz players, jazz bands and jazz music include **All Dogs Go to Heaven**, 1989; **All Night Long**, 1963; **American Blue Note**, 1989; **An American in Rome**, 1954; **American Pop**, 1981; **Anatomy of a Murder**, 1959; **And All That Jazz**, 1983; **At the Circus**, 1939; **The Benny Goodman Story**, 1956; **Belle of the Nineties**, 1934; **The Big Bang**, 2010; **Bird**, 1988; **Birth of the Blues**, 1941; **The Black Glove**, 1954; **The Blues Brothers**, 1980; **Blues in the Night**, 1941; **Bombay Velvet**, 2015; **Bullet to the Head**, 2012; **The Cabin in the Cotton**, 1932; **Chico & Rita**, 2010; **Compulsion**, 1959; **The Cotton Club**, 1984; **The Crimson Canary**, 1945; **Dancing on the Edge**, 2013 (TV miniseries); **Dementia**, 1955; Dr. Rhythm, 1937; **The Drag-Net**, 1936; **Drillinge an Bord**, 1959; **Every Other Weekend**, 1991; **The Fabulous Dorseys**, 1947; **False Face**, 1977; **The Five Pennies**, 1959; **Follow the Boys**, 1944; **Follow the Fleet**, 1936; **The Gene Krupa Story**, 1959; **Glory Alley**, 1952; **Groundhog Day**, 1993; **Hard Boiled**, 1993; **Havoc**, 1972; **High Society**, 1956; **Houseboat**, 1958; **The Hustler**, 1961; **Imaginary Heroes**, 2004; **Innocent Sorcerers** [1960], 2014; **Jam Session**, 1944; **The Jazz Singer**, 1927; **The Jazzband Five**, 1932; **Just Friends**, 1993; **Just Wright**, 2010; **Kansas City**, 1996; **Kettle of Fish**, 2006; **King of California**, 2007; King of Jazz, 1930; **The Kovak Box**, 2006; **Kung Fu Hustle**, 2004; **The Lady Says No**, 1951; **Lady Sings the Blues**, 1972; **Make Believe Ballroom**, 1949; **A Man Called Adam**, 1966; **Miles Ahead**, 2015; **Mo' Better Blues**, 1990; **My Man Godfrey**, 1936; **New Orleans**, 1947; **New York, New York**, 1977; **Night Owl**, 1993 (made-for-TV); **Nightmare**, 1956; **Paris Blues**, 1961; **The Party's Over**, 1966; **Pete Kelly's Blues**, 1955; **Play Misty for Me**, 1971; **Rachel Getting Married**, 2008; **Rififi**, 1956; **Roberta**, 1935; **'Round Midnight**, 1986; **St. Louis Blues**, 1939; **St. Louis Blues**, 1958; **Second Chorus**, 1940; **Shadows**, 1959; **The Snows of Kilimanjaro**, 1952; **A Song Is Born**, 1948; **Space Is the Place**, 1974; **Stormy Monday**, 1988; **Stormy Weather**, 1943; **The Strip**, 1951; **The Sun Also Rises**, 1957; **Sweet and Low-Down**, 1944; **Sweet and Lowdown**, 1999; **Sweet Smell of Success**, 1957; **Swing**, 1999; **Swing Kids**, 1993; **The Ten**, 2007; **Thank You Satan**, 1989; **Three on a Match**, 1932; **Thrill of a Romance**, 1945; **The Tic Code**, 2000; **Tightrope**, 1984; **Tony Takitani**, 2005; **Too Late Blues**, 1962; **Treme**, 2010-2013 (TV series); **28 Days**, 2000; **Up at the Villa**, 2000; **Vabank**, 1982; **Where the Boys Are**, 1960; **Whiplash**, 2014; **You, the Living**, 2007; and **Young and Innocent**, 1938. p, Jerry Wald; d, Michael Curtiz; cast, Kirk Douglas, Lauren Bacall, Doris Day, Hoagy Carmichael, Juano Hernandez, Jerome Cowan, Mary Beth Hughes, Nestor Paiva, Walter Reed, Keye Luke; w, Carl Foreman, Edmund H. North (based on the novel by Dorothy Baker); c, Ted McCord; m, Ray Heindorf; ed, Alan Crosland, Jr.; art d, Edward Carrere; set d, William Wallace.

Young Man with Ideas ★★★ 1952; U.S.; 85m; MGM; B/W; Comedy/Romance; Children: Acceptable; **DVD**. Ford and Roman are standouts as a newly married couple who move with their children to California to make a better life. Ford works as a legal researcher while he is studying to pass the California bar; he meets seductive Foch, a fellow student, who makes moves on him. He also encounters French chanteuse Darcel, who is so smitten with the handsome Ford that she considers giving up her movie career to be with him. Ford, however, fends off advances from her as well as Foch. He is a well-married man and loves wife Roman, intending to make his marriage as much a success as his legal profession. Things get even more complicated when Ford's phone keeps ringing with calls from people wanting to make bets. The phone number assigned to Ford in his new home, unfortunately, had earlier been used by a notorious bookie. Roman, who thinks someone is playing a practical joke by constantly calling to make bets, finally takes one of those bets, thinking she is going along with the joke. Roman, however, has taken a winning bet, and when hoodlums led by

Henry Fonda as Abraham Lincoln in *Young Mr. Lincoln,* **1939.**

Leonard go to Ford's home to collect, they are told that Ford is not a bookie and it is all a mistake. Leonard threatens Ford and Roman, but police arrive to arrest the lot of them. Ford, however, shows his legal expertise by presenting himself and Roman and cleverly winning his own case. Roman is consumed with guilt for having created all the confusion, but she is comforted at the finale when she sees that Ford's career as a lawyer is successfully launched after an established attorney offers Ford a job with his firm. In addition to a clever script, director Leisen does a fine job handling the comedic story line, and Leonard, who routinely played gangsters and thugs, presents a hilarious menace. The film did not do well at the box office, however, earning less than $900,000 in its initial release without earning back its budget of more than $1.2 million. *Author's Note*: Ford told this author that "**Young Man with Ideas** was one of my first pictures where I had a shot at comedy, which is much more difficult for an actor, because you are trying to make audiences laugh rather than frightening or saddening them in a dramatic role. Sheldon [Leonard] gave me a good tip when he said to me: 'The more you nervously smile at me when I snarl at you the more laughs you will get.' I think he was right. Sheldon was one of the great heavies in pictures back then before he became a producer and got rich." Director Leisen, who had worked for Paramount, made his first film for MGM with this film. p, Gottfried Reinhardt, William H. Wright; d, Mitchell Leisen; cast, Glenn Ford, Ruth Roman, Denise Darcel, Nina Foch, Donna Corcoran, Ray Collins, Mary Wickes, Bobby Diamond, Sheldon Leonard, Dick Wessel, Fay Roope, Carl Milletaire, Curtis Cooksey; w, Arthur Sheekman; c, Joseph Ruttenberg; m, David Rose; ed, Fredrick Y. Smith; art d, Cedric Gibbons, Arthur Lonergan; set d, Edwin B. Willis, Hugh Hunt; spec eff, A. Arnold Gillespie.

Young Mr. Lincoln ★★★★ 1939; U.S.; 100m; FOX; B/W; Biographical Drama; Children: Cautionary; **DVD**; **VHS**. Fonda renders a memorable performance as a young Abraham Lincoln (1809-1865) under the firm helming of pantheon director Ford. The film opens with Fonda delivering a speech in 1832 to members of the Whig Party, the party to which he then belonged before becoming a Republican and where the slow drawling Fonda opens with: "You all know me..." A short time later, Fonda is shown in New Salem, Illinois (where Lincoln lived from 1831 to 1837), with Moore, who plays Ann Rutledge (1813-1835) and where the two fall in love (this romance is contended by many Lincoln historians). Fonda is uncertain about his future, but Moore reassures him that whatever profession he chooses will be the correct one. Fonda by this time has become a rail-splitter, boatman and later operates a general store in this frontier town. The years pass quickly, and Fonda is shown in flash-forward standing at the very spot where he once talked with Moore along a riverbank. He is alone, now, as Moore is dead and he

Pauline Moore and Henry Fonda in *Young Mr. Lincoln*, 1939.

stands next to her grave (Ann Rutledge died from a typhoid epidemic that swept New Salem in 1835). By this time, an immigrant family, headed by matriarch Brady, arrives in town and goes to Fonda's store, seeking foodstuffs. They have no money but offer to trade a barrel of old books, including one law book, *Blackstone's Commentaries*. Fonda makes the exchange and begins reading the law book. While standing at Moore's grave, he jams a stick into the earth, stating that if the stick falls upon her grave, he will become a lawyer. The stick collapses on the grave, and Fonda later sets himself up as an attorney, going to Springfield (on a mule as he is too poor to afford a horse) where he practices law with partner Maxwell. Fonda's practice is meager where he settles disputes with clients with prosaic country-style persuasion. Two of his clients are so contentious that they adamantly refuse the compromise Fonda proposes. A man who tells stories to illustrate his points, Fonda then states: "Do you two fellows ever hear about the time when I butted two heads together?" Both quickly get Fonda's point and promptly settle their dispute, and Fonda collects his fee for arbitrating their case. Fonda is then seen on the Fourth of July as a judge at a pie-eating contest. During the festivities we see two roughnecks, Bond and Kohler, drinking heavily and carousing through the crowds; they attempt to seduce one of the two young wives of Cromwell and Quillan, who are brothers, and a quarrel ensues. Later that night, Bond and Kohler get into a vicious argument and Kohler is killed, but it is Cromwell and Quillan who are accused of murdering him. They are jailed, and their mother, Brady, the very woman who had traded the law book to Fonda for foodstuffs years earlier in New Salem, goes to Fonda, asking that he defend her sons. He agrees and, that night, after he sees a lynch mob assembling at the jail, stands before the angry vigilantes, asking them not to hang his clients, saying that they will be depriving him of his first real law case. Fonda's humor quells and humors the mob to the point where they depart and where Fonda has saved the lives of his clients, Cromwell and Quillan. Seeing Fonda overcome this crisis is Weaver, who plays Mary Todd (1818-1882), and Stone, who plays Stephen A. Douglas (1813-1861), and they are impressed with the young attorney. (Todd would go on to marry Lincoln, and Douglas and Lincoln would later become political opponents, conducting legendary debates in their runs for office.) Weaver invites Fonda to a party given by her sister where he meets members of Springfield's high society, but he appears awkward and even clumsy when attempting to converse with these wealthy and powerful people. Weaver nevertheless sees in Fonda something unique and appealing in this earnest young lawyer. Before Fonda goes to trial, Charters, the presiding judge, urges Fonda to turn over the murder case involving Cromwell and Quillan to a much more experienced attorney. He suggests that Stone, a seasoned trial lawyer, who is now Fonda's rival for Weaver's hand, take over the case. Fonda refuses

and prepares for the trial by first going to Brady, who apparently witnessed the death of Kohler. She, however, cannot or will not tell Fonda which one of her sons may have been the actual killer. He tells her that by keeping silent, she may be sending both of her sons to the gallows, but Brady's motherly love prevents her from singling out one of her sons for what appears to be certain death. When the case goes to trial, Bond, the chief witness against the boys, admits that he quarreled with Kohler. He states that he left Kohler in a clearing and Kohler was attacked by one of the brothers, saying that "it was the bigger of the two," meaning the taller Cromwell. Fonda asks how, at such a long distance, Bond could identify the killer, and Bond replies that he could clearly see since the evening was "moon bright." Such certain eyewitness testimony appears to damn Cromwell, but Fonda then recalls Bond to the witness stand, accusing him of lying. Bond insists that he has stated the truth, but Fonda provides startling new evidence that utterly refutes Bond's claim. He produces an almanac that states that, on the night of the killing, the moon was in almost a total eclipse and that it could not have provided enough light for Bond to have witnessed the murder. Jarred by this evidence and flustered by Fonda's incessant accusations, Bond loses control and blurts out an admission of guilt, saying that Kohler was his friend and he did not mean to kill him. Cromwell and Quillan are set free, and Bond is arrested and jailed as the actual killer. Following the trial, Weaver and Stone congratulate Fonda, and Stone tells Fonda that he will never again underestimate him. Fonda later walks through the countryside with old friend Collins, and he meets Brady, her sons and their wives as they are about to leave. Brady gives him a small payment and her gratitude for saving the lives of her sons before they ride off in their covered wagon. Collins then watches as Fonda strolls slowly up the road to the top of hill and Ford ends this memorable frontier saga. Ford builds this tale at a slower pace than what is seen in his other action-packed films, his camera lingering long on scenes and ending them with slow dissolves to better capture the nuances and emotions of his characters. He carefully constructs the scenes until he reaches the climactic courtroom sequence while inserting poignant images that illustrate the heartiness and resolve of the pioneers of early-day America. Fonda is magnificent as a young Lincoln trying to find his way in life, uneasy with the authority of his legal profession, but full of rock-ribbed confidence that he will find a way to bring justice to his clients. He receives superlative support from a talented cast, and Bond, a Ford favorite, gives one of his best performances as a boisterous, conniving killer. Trotti's powerful and meaningful script received an Oscar nomination as Best Story. The film did well at the box office in its initial release, earning almost twice its original budget of $1.5 million. A thirty-minute radio adaptation was aired by Academy Award Theater on July 10, 1946, with Fonda reprising his role. Songs: "Yankee Doodle" (c.1755; traditional), "Turkey in the Straw" (traditional), "The Dew Is On the Blossom" (traditional), "Battle Cry of Freedom" (1862; George Frederick Root), "Battle Hymn of the Republic" (music [1856]: William Steffe; lyrics [1862]: Julia Ward Howe). *Author's Note*: Neither Ford nor Fonda wanted to make this sterling film. Ford had recently completed his western masterpiece **Stagecoach**, 1939, when Darryl Zanuck, head of Fox, approached him with this project. "Ford told me that films about Lincoln had been 'done to death,' and that all the good material about that great man had been exhausted," Zanuck told this author. "He changed his mind after I gave him a copy of the script [by Trotti], and that so impressed him that he agreed to direct the picture. What changed Ford's mind was that the story was a little known part of Lincoln's history, chiefly his winning a case where his poor client was accused of murder." That case involved William "Duff" Armstrong (1833-1899), who was accused of murder; Lincoln defended Armstrong in Beardstown, Illinois, in 1858. The defendant was the son of Jack Armstrong, a friend of Lincoln's when Lincoln was studying law in New Salem, Illinois, and Lincoln offered to defend him pro bono. The prosecution's case rested on the testimony of Charles Allen, who stated on the witness stand that he saw, from a distance of 150 feet, Armstrong use a slingshot to kill James Preston Metzker on the night of August 29, 1857, in Mason County, Illinois. Allen insisted that he could clearly see the killing since the moon was full and provided enough light. Lincoln produced a reliable almanac that utterly refuted that claim, one that showed that the moon on that night was in partial eclipse and that it could not have produced enough light for anyone to witness the crime. The jury acquitted Armstrong on its first ballot. After Ford learned that Fonda had refused to play Lincoln, saying that the character of the iconic President was too much for his abilities, the director summoned the actor to his office. Ford told this author: "I said to Hank [Henry Fonda] that he was not playing the Great Emancipator—that image had been very well captured by Walter Huston in Griffith's **Abraham Lincoln** [1930]. I told him: 'Look, you are playing a young, inexperienced lawyer with no courtroom knowledge. He is a country bumpkin, but he is smart enough to see through the perjury of the real killer.' I had reduced the story to a whodunit, but with great history and Lincoln thrown into the lot and that convinced Hank to play the role. He understood his character very well and gave me a first-class performance. As years went on and we continued to work together, his performances got even better, but Hank's head got so big that he thought he knew more about making pictures than people like me and that is what finished us." This was the first of many films involving Ford and Fonda, one that resulted in six subsequent and superlative films, including **Drums along the Mohawk**, 1939; **The Grapes of Wrath**, 1940; **My Darling Clementine**, 1946; **The Fugitive**, 1947; **Fort Apache**, 1948; and **Mister Roberts**, 1955. This author met Fonda three years after he had completed **Mister Roberts** with Ford, and where Fonda called Ford a "S.O.B." and then added that Ford was "a cantankerous, mean-minded man. I admit that he was a genius who made some of the world's greatest pictures, but that did not excuse the fact that he was also one of the world's most miserable human beings!" Fonda was still stinging from his brief brawl with Ford when making **Mister Roberts**, where Ford hit Fonda with his fist and knocked him down, forever ending their relationship (as detailed in my **Author's Note** about this incident in my entry for **Mister Roberts** in this work). Regarding this film, Fonda stated to this author: "The scriptwriter [Trotti] for **Young Mr. Lincoln** told me that he had included the part, which was entirely fictional, where the mother refuses to identify either one of her sons, even though she knows that both might be executed. He [Trotti] told me that he had been a reporter in the South and covered a case where a mother did exactly that and the brothers were convicted and hanged. That made my blood run cold and stayed with me when I played my scene with Alice Brady, who played the mother in that picture, especially where I beg her to name one of her sons, but she refuses, so it is up to me to save them both." Ford actually had Fonda do a screen test for his role as Lincoln, where makeup people altered Fonda's nose and gave him bushier eyebrows and thicker hair. He also wore specially made boots that made him appear taller. After Fonda looked at the test, as he later exclaimed: "I felt as if I were portraying Christ himself!" He then agreed to do the part. This was the final film by veteran actress Brady. Many other actors have essayed Abraham Lincoln in many other films, including **Abe Lincoln: Freedom Fighter**, 1978 (Allen Williams); **Abe Lincoln in Illinois**, 1940 (Raymond Massey); **Abe Lincoln in Illinois**, 1945 (made-for-TV: Stephen Courtleigh); **Abe Lincoln in Illinois**, 1964 (made-for-TV; Jason Robards Jr.); **Abraham Lincoln**, 1930 (Walter Huston); **Abraham Lincoln: Vampire Hunter**, 2012 (Benjamin Walker as adult Lincoln; Lux Haney-Jardine as young Lincoln); **Action Family**, 1986 (made-for-TV; Drummond Erskine); **The Adams Chronicles**, 1976 (TV miniseries; Stephen D. Newman); **Alcoa Presents: One Step Beyond**, 1959-1961 (TV series; "The Day the World Wept: The Lincoln Story," 1960 episode: Barry Atwater); **America: A Call to Greatness**, 1995 (made-for-TV; Raymond Baker); **American Inventory**, 1951-1952 (TV series; "Abe Lincoln's Story," 1952 episode: Crahan Denton); **Apache Ambush**, 1955 (James Griffith); **Appointment with Destiny**, 1971-1973 (TV series; "Surrender at Appomattox, 1972 episode: Joseph

Lynch mob led by Jack Pennick (center) in *Young Mr. Lincoln,* **1939.**

Leisch Jr.); **Are We Civilized?**, 1934 (Frank McGlynn Sr.); **The Battle Cry of Peace**, 1915 (William J. Ferguson); **The Big Picture**, 1989 (Richard Blake); **Bill and Ted's Excellent Adventure**, 1989 (Robert Barron); **The Birth of a Nation**, 1915 (Joseph Henabery); **The Blue and the Gray**, 1982 (TV miniseries; Gregory Peck); **Captains and Kings**, 1976 (TV series; Ford Rainey); **Carl Schurz**, 1968 (Christian Rode); **Cavalcade of America**, 1952-1957 (TV series; "Moonlight Witness," 1954 episode: Bruce Bennett; "New Salem Story," 1953 episode: James Griffith; "The Palmetto Conspiracy," 1955 episode: Richard Hale); **The Civil War**, 1990 (TV miniseries; Sam Waterston voiceover); **The Conspirator**, 2011 (Gerald Bestrom); **Courage of the West**, 1937 (Albert Russell); **The Crisis**, 1916 (Sam D. Drane); **Cybill**, 1995-1998 (TV series; "It's for You, Mr. Lincoln," 1996 episode: Charles L. Brame); **The Day Lincoln Was Shot**, 1998 (made-for-TV; Lance Henriksen); **Days That Shook the World**, 2003-2013 (TV series; "Terror Made in America: Assassination of Abraham Lincoln…," 2004 episode: Jim Babel); **The Dramatic Life of Abraham Lincoln**, 1924 (George A. Billings as adult Lincoln; Danny Hoy as a young Lincoln); **Dream West**, 1986 (TV miniseries; F. Murray Abraham); **The DuPont Show of the Month**, 1957-1961 (TV series; "The Lincoln Murder Case," 1961 episode: Drummond Erskine); **The Faking of the President**, 1976 (William J. Daprato); **FDR: A One Man Show**, 1987 (made-for-TV; Drummond Erskine); **Ford Star Jubilee**, 1955-1956 (TV series; "The Day Lincoln Was Shot," 1956 episode: Raymond Massey); **The Fortune Cookie**, 1966 (John Anderson); G. E. True Theater, 1953-1962 (TV series: "Prologue to Glory," 1956 episode: John Ireland); **The Great Battles of the Civil War**, 1994 (TV miniseries; Charlton Heston); **The Great John Ericsson**, 1938 (John Ericsson); **The Great Man's Whiskers**, 1973 (made-for-TV; Dennis Weaver); **Guardian of the Wilderness**, 1976 (Ford Rainey); **Hands Up!**, 1926 (George A. Billings); **Happy Gilmore**, 1996 (Charles L. Brame); **The Heart of Lincoln**, 1915 (Francis Ford); **The Heart of Maryland**, 1927 (Charles Edward Bull); **Hearts in Bondage**, 1936 (Frank McGlynn Sr.); **Her Country's Call**, 1917 (Benjamin Chapin); **Histeria!**, 1998-2000 (TV series; four 1998 segments: Maurice LaMarche); **How the West Was Won**, 1962 (Raymond Massey); **In the Days of Buffalo Bill**, 1922 (Joel Day); **The Iron Horse**, 1924 (Charles Edward Bull); **Ironclads**, 1991 (made-for-TV; James Getty); **Lincoln**, 1974-1975 (TV series; Hal Holbrook); **Lincoln**, 1988 (TV miniseries; Sam Waterston); **Lincoln**, 1992 (made-for-TV; Jason Robards Jr.); **Lincoln**, 2012 (Daniel Day-Lewis); **Lincoln: American Mastermind**, 2009 (made-for-TV; Fritz Klein); **Lincoln and the War Within**, 1992 (made-for-TV; Jason Robards Jr.); **The Lincoln Conspiracy**, 1977 (John Anderson); **The Lincoln Cycle**, 1917 (Benjamin Chapin); **The Lincoln-Douglas Debates**, 1976 (made-for-TV; Scott Mandrell); **Lincoln-Douglas Galesburg Debate**, 1994

Henry Fonda staring down a lynch mob in *Young Mr. Lincoln,*
1939.

(made-for-TV; Michael Krebs); **The Lone Ranger**, 1938 (Frank McG-
lynn Sr.); **The Littlest Rebel**, 1935 (Frank McGlynn Sr.); **Lost River:
Lincoln's Secret Weapon**, 2009 (Fritz Klein); **Lux Video Theater**,
1950-1959 (TV series; "Abe Lincoln in Illinois," 1951 episode: Ray-
mond Massey); **The Mad Empress**, 1939 (Mexican version of **Juarez**,
1939; Frank McGlynn Sr.); **Madame Who**, 1918 (Clarence Barr);
Medic, 1954-1956 (TV series; "Black Friday," 1955 episode: Austin
Green); **Mister Lincoln**, 1981 (made-for-TV; Roy Dotrice); **My Own
United States**, 1918 (Gerald Day); **New Mexico**, 1951 (Hans Conried);
North and South, Book II, 1986 (TV miniseries; Hal Holbrook); **Of
Human Hearts**, 1938 (John Carradine); **Omnibus**, 1952-1961 (TV se-
ries; "Mr. Lincoln," five parts, 1952-1953: Royal Dano); **Out of This
World**, 1987-1991 (TV series; "Honest Evie," 1989 episode: Robert
Barron); **The Perfect Tribute**, 1991 (made-for-TV; Jason Robards Jr.);
Philco-Goodyear Television Playhouse, 1948-1956 (TV series; "Ann
Rutledge," 1950 episode: Stephen Courtleigh); **The Plainsman**, 1936
(Frank McGlynn Sr.); **Police Squad!**, 1982 (TV series; many segments:
Rex Hamilton); **Prince of Players**, 1955 (Stanley Hall); **The Prisoner
of Shark Island**, 1936 (Frank McGlynn Sr.); **Pulitzer Prize Playhouse**,
1950-1952 (TV series; "Abe Lincoln in Illinois," 1950 episode: Ray-
mond Massey); **Red Dwarf**, 1988- (TV series; "Meltdown," 1991
episode: Jack Klaff); **The Right Man**, 1960 (made-for-TV; Richard
Boone); **The Rivalry**, 1975 (made-for-TV; Arthur Hill); **Riverboat**,
1959-1961 (TV series; "No Bridge on the River," 1960 episode: Sandy
Kenyon); **Rock Island Trail**, 1950 (Jeff Corey); **San Antoine**, 1953
(Richard Hale); **Saving Lincoln**, 2013 (Tom Amandes); **Schlitz Playhouse**, 1951-1959 (TV series; "Washington Incident," 1956 episode:
Mark Stevens); **Screen Director's Playhouse**, 1955-1956 (TV series;
"Lincoln's Doctor's Dog," 1955 episode: Robert Ryan); **The Secret
Diary of Desmond Pfeiffer**, 1998 (TV series; four segments: Dann Florek); **The Slacker's Heart**, 1917 (Benjamin Chapin); **Stage to Tucson**,
1950 (James Griffith); **The Story of Mankind**, 1957 (Austin Green);
Studio One in Hollywood, 1948-1958 (TV series; "Abraham Lincoln,"
1952 episode: Robert Pastene); **Sunday Showcase**, 1959-1961 (TV se-
ries; "An American Heritage: Shadow of a Soldier," 1960 episode: Ford
Rainey); **Tad**, 1995 (made-for TV; Kris Kristofferson); **The Tall Target**,
1951 (Leslie Kimmell); **Telephone Time**, 1956-1958 (TV series; "The
Stepmother,' 1956 episode: Ronnie Lee); **They've Killed President
Lincoln!**, 1971 (made-for-TV; Joseph Leisch Jr.); **This Is America,
Charlie Brown**, 1988 (TV miniseries; "The Smithsonian and the Pres-
idency," 1989 episode: Frank Welker); **The Time Tunnel**, 1966-1967
(TV series; "The Death Trap," 1966 episode: Ford Rainey); **Trailin'
West**, 1936 (Robert Barrat); **Treasure of the Aztecs**, 1965 (Jeff Corey);
TV Reader's Digest, 1955-1956 (TV series; "How Chance Made Lin-
coln President," 1955 episode: Richard Gaines); **Twilight Zone**, 1959-

1964 (TV series; "The Passerby," 1961 episode: Austin Green); **Two
Fisted Justice**, 1931 (Joseph Mills); **Virginia City**, 1940 (Victor Kilian); **Voyagers!**, 1982-1983 (TV series; "The Day the Rebs Took Lincoln," 1982 episode: John Anderson); **Weird Science**, 1994-1996 (TV
series; "Community Property," 1996 episode: Gary Bullock); **Wells
Fargo**, 1937 (Frank McGlynn Sr.); **Western Gold**, 1937 (Frank McG-
lynn Sr.); **Woman with a Sword**, 1952 (made-for-TV; Henry Sharp);
Wrongfully Accused, 1998 (Mark Francis); and **You Are There**, 1953-
1957 (TV series; "The Emancipation Proclamation," 1955 episode: Jeff
Morrow; "The Gettysburg Address," 1953 episode: Paul Tripp; "The
Nomination of Abraham Lincoln," 1954 episode: Jeff Morrow). **p**, Dar-
ryl F. Zanuck, Kenneth Macgowan; **d**, John Ford; **cast**, Henry Fonda,
Alice Brady, Marjorie Weaver, Arleen Whalen, Eddie Collins, Pauline
Moore, Richard Cromwell, Donald Meek, Eddie Quillan, Ward Bond,
Fred Kohler Jr., Edwin Maxwell, Spencer Charters, Charles Halton,
Francis Ford, Dickie Jones, Robert Lowery, Russell Simpson, Milburn
Stone; **w**, Lamar Trotti; **c**, Bert Glennon, Arthur C. Miller; **m**, Alfred
Newman; **ed**, Walter Thompson; **art d**, Richard Day, Mark-Lee Kirk;
set d, Thomas Little.

The Young Mr. Pitt ★★★★ 1943; U.K., 118m; FOX; B/W; Biographical Drama; Children: Acceptable; **DVD**. Donat gives an exceptional
performance of William Pitt the Younger (1759-1806), who was one of
England's greatest prime ministers. The film opens with Donat, playing
his own father, William Pitt the Elder, the Earl of Chatham (1708-1778),
and who was also prime minister of England. He makes a passionate
speech in the House of Lords in 1770, decrying England's assault on
"its brethren," the colonists of America, stating that, if a foreign power
were to do to England what England is doing to America, its people
would, like the colonists in America, never lay down their arms. He is
known as the "Great Commoner," and he tries to convey his beliefs to
his son, Atkins, who plays William Pitt the Younger as a boy, telling him
that he should never seek success through war, the great sin of mankind.
Meanwhile, another child is born into Atkins' generation, that of
Napoleon Bonaparte (Napoleon I, 1769-1821), who is later shown as
an adult by Lom. Meanwhile, the British government is controlled by a
corrupt political coalition led by Morley, who plays Whig leader Charles
James Fox (1749-1806) and Aylmer, who plays Lord North (1732-
1792). By this time, William Pitt the Younger has grown to an adult,
also played by Donat, and George III (1738-1820), played by Lovell,
asks Donat to become England's prime minister. Patriotic and totally
devoted to England, Donat wins election as England's prime minister
on his promise of peace and prosperity, an astounding victory in that he
is only twenty-four when achieving that lofty position. Morley becomes
Donat's constant nemesis, attempting to block every move Donat makes
as prime minister. And here Morley all but steals every scene in this film
with his droll delivery and dry humor. In one scene where Morley is
being entertained by his elitist friends, a brick comes crashing through
the window. When someone asks what has happened, Morley dryly
replies with sarcasm: "The voice of public opinion." After Donat's position is in question in 1793 when France threatens England, he makes
a passionate speech for the support of England against the mounting
threat of the enemy; he is greeted by stuffy indifference, and his opponents, led by Morley, idly chat with each other while ignoring him.
Donat convinces Lovell to dissolve Parliament and compel a general
election to replace its representatives. At the same time, Lom (as
Napoleon) is shown rising higher in the ranks of the French military.
When Lom plans to invade Holland, he has his French envoy, Charles
Talleyrand (1754-1838), played by Lieven, propose to Donat that England join with France to conquer and control the whole of Europe, a proposal Donat rejects out of hand. Donat urges his country to prepare for
a war with Lom, knowing well that the French emperor will eventually
attack his country. His struggles drain his energies as he seeks comfort
from Calvert, who plays Eleanor Eden (d. 1851), the woman he loves,
but never marries. Exhausted after England suffers a number of battle-

field defeats, mainly brought about through debilitating appeasements offered by the insidious Morley, Donat resigns his post in 1801. When Lom suffers military reversals in 1804, Donat is summoned back to office to continue his struggle to support England's war against the French dictator. He lives to see the significant British naval victory against the French fleet at Trafalgar in 1805, achieved by England's great admiral, Lord Horatio Nelson (1758-1805), who is played by Haggard. Donat does not live to see Lom eventually defeated, dying in 1806, and Donat is nationally revered as one of England's most stalwart defenders and leaders. Pantheon director Reed helms this episodic biopic with great care, diligently presenting history as it actually occurred, and Donat is mesmerizing at the indomitable Pitt. Morley also gives a superb performance as an oozing, oily opponent, his marvelous essay being the essence of artful connivance. Mills, who plays Pitt's most loyal supporter and friend, William Wilberforce (1759-1833), is also excellent in his role (and it was Wilberforce who led the crusade against slavery, but that just movement is mentioned in this film only briefly). The sets for this period film are marvelous to behold, exact to the era from the reliable Vetchinsky, and the richly decorated costumes, also religiously faithful to that period, were designed by the gifted Cecil Beaton and Elizabeth Haffenden. What also markedly stands out is the brilliant script that so wittily and incisively encompasses the years of Pitt's spectacular public life. Songs/Music: "Piano Sonata No. 4 in E-Flat Major" (1774; Wolfgang Amadeus Mozart), "Symphony No. 41 (Jupiter)" (1788; Wolfgang Amadeus Mozart), "God Rest You Merry Gentlemen" ["God Rest Ye Merry Gentlemen"] (c.1790; English traditional Christmas carol; composer unknown), "Tom Tough" (traditional), "Jolly Waterman" (traditional), "A Life on the Ocean Wave" (traditional). *Author's Note*: Donat appears wane and careworn in many scenes to effectively depict his character's declining health, but such scenes actually reflected Donat's own frail health in that he suffered from acute asthma. Mills, who would go on to appear with Lom in **War and Peace**, 1956, and where Lom again essayed Napoleon I, was called in to play his part in this film in a matter of hours as the actor hired to play Wilberforce died while in rehearsal. William Pitt the Younger has been played by other actors in other films, including **Admiral Ushakov**, 1954 (Nikolay Volkov); **Amazing Grace**, 2007 (Benedict Cumberbatch); **America**, 1924 (Charles Bennett); **Austerlitz, la victoire en marchant**, 2006 (Jonathan Sawdon); **The Battle of Austerlitz**, 1960 (Anthony Stuart); **Battle of the Brave**, 2004 (Tim Roth); **Beau Brummell**, 1954 (Paul Rogers); **The Fight against Slavery**, 1975 (TV miniseries; Ronald Pickup); **The First Black Britons**, 2005 (made-for-TV; Alister Barton); **The Madness of King George**, 1994 (Julian Wadham); **Mrs. Fitzherbert**, 1950 (Henry Oscar); **Nelson**, 1918 (Ernest Thesiger); **Number 10**, 1983 (TV miniseries; Jeremy Brett as adult Pitt; Daniel Matthews as Pitt as a boy); **Prince Regent**, 1979 (TV miniseries; David Collings); **The Scarlet Pimpernel**, 1934 (Bruce Belfrage); and **You Are There**, 1953-1971 (TV series; "William Pitt's Last Address to Parliament," 1954 episode: Lorne Greene). **p**, Edward Black, Maurice Ostrer; **d**, Carol Reed; **cast**, Robert Donat, Robert Morley, Phyllis Calvert, John Mills, Geoffrey Atkins, Jean Cadell, Felix Aylmer, Raymond Lovell, Max Adrian, Herbert Lom, Albert Lieven, Kathleen Byron, Stephen Haggard, Philip Friend, Leo Genn; **w**, Frank Launder, Sidney Gilliat, Viscount Castlerosse; **c**, Freddie Young; **m**, Charles Williams; **ed**, R.E. Dearing; **art d**, Alex Vetchinsky.

The Young One ★★★ 1961; Mexico/U.S.; 96m; Producciones Olmeca/Valiant Films; Color; Drama; Children: Unacceptable; **DVD**. A lesser known film from pantheon director Bunuel begins on the Carolina coast where black jazz clarinetist Hamilton is wrongly accused of raping a white woman. He flees in a small boat to an island that is a hunting area for rich southerners. He meets young girl Meersman, who is the granddaughter of the island's handyman who has recently died. She lives in a small cabin alone, and, after Hamilton gives the girl some money for foodstuffs and supplies, they become friends. Scott, who owns a bee

Jack Oakie, Shirley Temple and Charlotte Greenwood in *Young People,* 1940.

farm on the island, and who is attracted to Meersman, finds Hamilton's boat, and, thinking that an intruder has stolen some of his money, he shoots holes in the boat. When he later finds Hamilton attempting to repair the boat, he pursues Hamilton with his rifle, but Hamilton is also armed, having taken a shotgun from Meersman's cabin. When Scott and Hamilton finally confront each other, they learn that they were both veterans in WWII (1939-1945), and Scott allows Hamilton to remain on the island as the new handyman. Scott, by this time, has returned from the mainland with gifts for Meersman, a dress and a pair of high heels (continuing Bunuel's traditional foot fetish). He has the girl sit in his lap and tells her: "Don't let anyone hold you like this." When he tries to kiss her, however, Meersman avoids his lips and caresses. Scott has Hamilton occupy Meersman's cabin while he has Meersman move into his own cabin. Meersman, a naïve adolescent (her age is never specified) does not understand why Scott and Hamilton are constantly on guard against each other. Hamilton finally tells her: "It's easy for him to kill me. It's hard for me to kill him." Meersman then persuades Hamilton to play his clarinet for her before she returns that night to the cabin occupied by Scott. That night Scott grabs and roughly kisses the girl before a fadeout that implies that he has raped her. The following day, Brook, a local preacher from the mainland, arrives with boatman Denton. He has arrived to baptize Meersman and then take her to a welfare home, but Brook soon becomes suspicious that Scott has illegally seduced the girl. Meanwhile, the visitors learn of Hamilton's presence, and they search for him. Scott helps Hamilton to escape back to the mainland and then returns to Brook and Denton and tells them that Meersman will remain on the island as he intends to marry her and that is where this offbeat, but strangely compelling film ends. Scott, Hamilton and Meersman are all standouts in this gritty drama, one with many unsettling issues that remain unresolved by Bunuel. It is another slice of life from the director, well constructed and with high tension mounting to its finale, but not as satisfying as Bunuel's previous sterling films. Song: "Sinner Man" (Leon Bibb). *Author's Note*: Shot on location in Mexico, this was Bunuel's second and final film made for Hollywood. **p**, George P. Werker; **d**, Luis Bunuel; **cast**, Zachary Scott, Bernie Hamilton, Key Meersman, Crahan Denton, Claudio Brook; **w**, Bunuel, Hugo Butler (based on the story "Travellin' man" by Peter Matthiessen); **c**, Gabriel Figueroa; **ed**, Carlos Savage; **art d**, Jesus Bracho.

Young People ★★★ 1940; U.S.; 78m; FOX; B/W; Drama/Musical; Children: Acceptable; **DVD**; **VHS**; **IV**. Temple is exceptional in this delightful musical drama. She plays a twelve-year-old orphan who is adopted by Oakie and Greenwood, a vaudeville song-and-dance team. They retire to a small town, but are not accepted by local residents, who look down on show business performers. Their attitude changes after a

Paul Newman in *The Young Philadelphians*, 1959.

big storm strikes the area and Oakie proves himself to be a hero. He and Greenwood put on a show, with help from Temple, to entertain and lift the spirits of the devastated inhabitants. Whelan and Montgomery are young lovers who befriend the show biz folk, and who also make them acceptable to the community. Songs: "Fifth Avenue," "I Wouldn't Take a Million," "The Mason-Dixon Line," "Tra-La-La-La," "Young People" (all 1940; music: Harry Warren; lyrics: Mack Gordon); "On the Beach at Waikiki" (1915; music: Henry Kailimai; lyrics: G.H. Stover); "Baby Take a Bow" (1934; music: Lew Brown, Jay Gorney; lyrics: Les Brown); "Flow Gently, Sweet Afton," Auld Lang Syne," "The Farmer in the Dell," "Turkey in the Straw" (traditional); "The Japanese Sandman" (1920; music: Richard A. Whiting; lyrics: Raymond B. Egan). This film is not related to 1952 and 1961 films of the same name. *Author's Note*: Dwan cleverly makes use of clips from Temple's earlier films to demonstrate her past with her adoptive parents while providing a poignant chronicle of the tyke's fame and where, in previous years, she was the number one Hollywood star. **p**, Harry Joe Brown; **d**, Allan Dwan; **cast**, Shirley Temple, Jack Oakie, Charlotte Greenwood, Arleen Whelan, George Montgomery, Kathleen Howard, Minor Watson, Frank Sully, Mae Marsh, Darryl Hickman; **w**, Edwin Blum, Don Ettlinger (based on their story); **c**, Edward Cronjager, Arthur C. Miller; **m**, Cyril J. Mockridge; **ed**, James B. Clark; **art d**, Richard Day, Rudolph Sternad; **set d**, Thomas Little.

The Young Philadelphians ★★★ 1959; U.S.; 136m; WB; B/W; Drama; Children: Unacceptable; **DVD**; **VHS**; **IV**. This well-enacted soap opera sees Newman as a lawyer climbing the social and corporate ladder in Philadelphia society. The episodic tale opens in 1924 where poor girl Brewster jilts lover Keith in order to gain entrance to society by marrying wealthy West. After they are wed, however, West proves to be impotent on his wedding night and, devoured by shame, commits suicide by crashing his car. Realizing that she might not have a toe-hold in West's prominent family, Brewster races back to Keith where she inveigles him into an assignation and later delivers his child, claiming the baby to be West's offspring. Elsom, who is Brewster's mother-in-law and the dominating patriarch of West's family, suspects that Brewster is lying and disinherits her and her baby. Brewster nevertheless raises the child, who grows to an adult as Newman, as if he were a member of that elitist family, even though both live their lives on the wrong side of the tracks Brewster has not escaped. Newman puts himself through Princeton law school by working in construction and meets beautiful Rush one day when she has a minor accident. They fall in love and develop an affair, even though Rush is engaged to be married to wealthy Eisley, who is a member of the society set. Rush is torn between her love for Newman and her obligation to Eisley, but Vaughn, who is a friend to Newman and Rush, cautions Rush not to ruin her life, as he has done, by allowing social pressures to come between her and the person she loves. Newman persuades Rush to elope with him, but Williams, her wealthy father, asks Newman to postpone the wedding between his daughter and Newman, offering him a job as an attorney in his law firm. Newman, as ambitious as his mother Brewster to better himself, accepts the lucrative position' and this so shocks Rush that she breaks up with Newman and sails to Europe. Eisley goes after her and she marries him. Meanwhile, Newman has become adept in the way of advancing himself through the power structures of the world in which he wants to live. He ingratiates himself to wealthy attorney Kruger through the influence of Kruger's wife, Smith, whom Newman seduces. Newman then rids himself of Smith when she arrives one night for another assignation and where he tells her that she must divorce her husband and start all over with him, something Newman knows Smith is unwilling to do. When the Korean War (1950-1953) breaks out, Eisley is drafted and is killed, leaving Rush a widow. Newman also serves in that war but remains safe as a legal officer in the Judge Advocate General's Corps (JAG). His friend Vaughn also serves and loses an arm in battle. Upon his return, Newman meets wealthy woman Burke by chance, and she asks his legal advice about amending her will. He shows her how to position her riches so that she will not have to pay excessive taxes, and Burke is so impressed that she fires Williams, Newman's old foe and Rush's father, and designates Newman as her estate attorney and where he manages all of her finances. This legal coup allows Newman access to Philadelphia's elite, and he soon becomes the legal darling of the social set, finally gaining the status he has always longed to achieve. He then goes about mending his old fences with Rush, who still loves him. That love is tested when Newman is suddenly confronted with a murder case involving his old friend Vaughn, who has become a disheveled drunk and is charged with killing his rich uncle, Douglas, who had served as the mean-minded guardian of Vaughn's inheritance, and who had been miserly doling out small funds to him for years. Vaughn pleads with Newman to defend him at his trial, convinced that Conroy, the family patriarch, is not interested in seeing Vaughn proven innocent and wants to avoid a scandal at all costs. Newman knows very little about criminal law but agrees to take the case. He is then confronted by Conroy, who tells him that, if he proceeds with the case and brings scandal to his family, Conroy will reveal that Keith is really Newman's father and that Newman was born illegitimate. Moreover, Rush offers to provide an experienced criminal attorney to defend Vaughn, and Newman realizes that she still distrusts him and fears that he has again sold his integrity to Conroy. Newman proves her wrong by maintaining his integrity and trying the case where he thoroughly discredits Deacon, who was Douglas' butler, regarding the details involving Douglas' death. He then places Conroy on the stand and compels him to admit that Douglas had a brain tumor and was in a state of deep depression before he died, strongly implying that Douglas most likely committed suicide. His argument wins over the jury, and a verdict of "not guilty" is rendered for Vaughn. Having shown himself to be self-sacrificing and bravely honest, Newman regains the love and confidence of Rush, and the two then plan their future together. Newman's outstanding performance preserves this film as a superior drama, his intense character sustaining interest throughout while strongly hinting at his fine work to come. Songs: "When Irish Eyes Are Smiling" (1912; music: Ernest Ball; lyrics: Chauncey Olcott, George Graff), "The Kiss Waltz" (1930; music: Joseph Burke; lyrics: Al Dubin), "Too Marvelous for Words" (1937; music: Richard A. Whiting; lyrics: Johnny Mercer). *Author's Note*: Newman told this author that "my role in **The Young Philadelphians** was not unlike the character I played the next year in **From the Terrace** [1960] where I played another young man so ambitious that he is eager to sell his integrity, but for Wall Street instead of the legal world." **d**, Vincent Sherman; **cast**, Paul Newman, Barbara Rush, Alexis Smith, Brian Keith, Diane Brewster, Billie Burke, John Williams, Robert Vaughn, Otto Kruger, Adam West, Fred (Anthony) Eisley, Peter Brown, Frank Conroy,

Robert Douglas, Isobel Elsom, Richard Deacon; **w**, James Gunn (based on the novel *The Philadelphian* by Richard Powell); **c**, Harry Stradling, Sr.; **m**, Ernest Gold; **ed**, William Ziegler; **art d**, Malcolm Bert; **set d**, John P. Austin.

The Young Savages ★★★ 1961; U.S.; 103m; Contemporary Productions/UA; B/W; Crime Drama; Children: Unacceptable; **BD**; **DVD**; **VHS**; **IV**. In an area of New York City known as Spanish Harlem controlled by a Puerto Rican-American gang of teenage boys, three teenagers—Kristien, Chandler, and Nephew—who are members of a street gang called the Thunderbirds, fatally stab Perez, a blind Puerto Rican teenage boy. Perez is the leader of a Puerto Rican gang called the Horsemen. District Attorney Lancaster is assigned to prosecute the racially charged case. He wants convictions of first degree murder for all three boys even though one of them, Kristien, is the son Lancaster's former girlfriend, Winters. Lancaster gets help from police lieutenant Savalas in investigating the case. They learn that the victim was one of the leaders of the Puerto Rican gang and may have pulled a knife on the three boys accused of his murder. Lancaster comes to realize that it was not a case of murder, but of self-defense. One of the boys gets twenty years in prison, another is sent to a mental hospital, and Kristien is acquitted. Frankenheimer presents a riveting film about racial strife in the big city, and Lancaster is a standout as a prosecuting attorney torn between his allegiance to his job and his emotional ties to Winters as he struggles with his conscience. *Author's Note*: Frankenheimer told this author that "working with Burt [Lancaster] was always satisfying as he never missed a beat, knew his lines as well as everyone else's and brought many great ideas to the production." For his part, Lancaster stated to this author that he was "surprised when I first walked onto the set for **The Young Savages**. The first thing I saw was a camera on the floor and aimed upward, the kind of angle shot very few directors used, so I knew that John [Frankenheimer] was a very innovative guy, although such shots were not new. Gregg Toland used those kinds of shots when he and Orson [Welles] made **Citizen Kane**." Frankenheimer, however, was so blunt in his dealing with actress Dina Merrill that, after the first day's shooting, she was reduced to tears. He had told her that she was the worst actress he had ever met. Lancaster later came to her defense and complimented Frankenheimer for not criticizing Merrill in her next shot with him. Excessive violence prohibits viewing by children. **p**, Pat Duggan; **d**, John Frankenheimer; **cast**, Burt Lancaster, Dina Merrill, Shelley Winters, Telly Savalas, Stanley Kristien, John Davis Chandler, Edward Andrews, Larry Gates, Vivian Nathan, Jody Fair, Jose Perez, Neil Nephew, Pilar Seurat, Roberta Shore; **w**, Edward Anhalt, J.P. Miller (based on the novel *A Matter of Conviction* by Evan Hunter); **c**, Lionel Lindon; **m**, David Amram; **ed**, Eda Warren; **art d**, Burr Smidt; **set d**, James Crowe.

Young Sherlock Holmes ★★★ 1985; U.S.; 109m; UNIV; Color; Adventure/Family; Children: Unacceptable (MPAA: PG-13); **DVD**; **VHS**; **IV**. Intriguing Sherlockian tale begins with teenagers Rowe, who plays Sherlock Holmes, and Cox, who plays John Watson, meeting and becoming good friends while they are students at London's less-than-prestigious Brompton Academy. Rowe introduces Cox to his mentor, Stock, a retired schoolmaster and inventor. Stock's niece, Ward, is also Rowe's close friend and love interest. At school, Rowe is considered to be brilliant, but an undisciplined troublemaker. He is closely advised by Higgins, a professor, and Higgins, his fencing instructor. Higgins cautions Rowe that he is too emotional and impulsive. A hooded figure uses a blowpipe to shoot two teachers, one of them a minister, with hallucinogenic thorns, causing them to have nightmares resulting in their deaths. Rowe suspects their deaths are connected, but Scotland Yard policeman Lestrade, played by Ashton-Griffiths, rebuffs him. Rhodes, a rival student, gets Rowe unjustly expelled from the academy. As Rowe prepares to leave, Higgins is shot with a hallucinogenic thorn and accidentally kills himself when trying to fight off imaginary gremlins. Before dying,

Sophie Ward and Alan Cox in *Young Sherlock Holmes,* 1985.

Higgins whispers to Rowe, "Eh-tar." Rowe, Cox, and Ward investigate and try to figure out clues, including a jingling bell sound made by the killer, a piece of cloth, and the blowpipe which was dropped at Higgins' murder scene. This leads them to uncover the existence of Rame Tep, an ancient Egyptian cult of Osiris worshippers. Their main weapons are blowpipes through which they shoot thorns dipped into a solution made of a plant extract that causes nightmarish hallucinations. The trio tracks the cult to a London warehouse where cult members are performing human sacrifices in a secret underground area shaped as a wooden pyramid. The young sleuths interrupt one of the cult's ceremonies and are chased and shot at with thorns, barely escaping. The next night, at Higgins' loft, Rowe and Cox find a picture of the three murder victims and a fourth man, Jones. The boys are found there and are to be expelled in the morning. That night, Ward joins them and they locate the fourth man, Jones, who explains that, in his youth, he and the other two men had discovered the underground pyramid of Rame Tep while planning to build a hotel in Egypt. Their discovery led them to an uprising that was put down by the British army. A local boy named Eh-tar and his sister vowed revenge after their parents were killed in the uprising. Jones is then shot by a poisoned thorn and tries to kill Rowe, but he is knocked unconscious by Ashton-Griffiths, who has changed his mind and has come to suspect as Rowe has all along, that the deaths were related because he, too, was poisoned by the hallucinogen. Rowe now realizes that Higgins is Eh-Tar, but he and Cox arrive too late to stop him and his sister, Fleetwood, from abducting Ward, and where they intend to sacrifice her and then set the cult's pyramid on fire. Higgins escapes with Ward while Fleetwood swallows one of her own hallucinogenic thorns during a fight with Rowe. Higgins tries to escape, but Cox damages his carriage. Higgins then tries to shoot Rowe with a poisoned dart, but Ward takes it instead. Rowe then duels with Higgins along the frozen River Thames, and the villain falls through the ice to his doom. Rowe holds Ward in his arms as she dies. Rowe explains later to Cox that he figured out who the killer was when he realized that "Eh-Tar" is "Rathe" spelled backwards. When they part, Cox says he hopes he and Rowe will become sleuths in future adventures, and, in a post-credits scene, Higgins is revealed to be alive, checking himself into an Alpine inn under a new name, "Moriarity." Songs: "Young Sherlock Holmes Main Theme," "Young Sherlock Holmes—Waxing Elizabeth" (Bruce Broughton). Levinson directs this action-packed tale with gusto, and where Rowe, Cox, Ward and the rest of the cast are standouts in their legendary roles. The period sets and costuming are superior as is the crisp lensing from Goldblatt. **p**, Mark Johnson, Henry Winkler; **d**, Barry Levinson; **cast**, Nicholas Rowe, Alan Cox, Sophie Ward, Anthony Higgins, Susan Fleetwood, Freddie Jones, Nigel Stock, Roger Ashton-Griffiths, Earl Rhodes, Brian Oulton; **w**, Chris Columbus (based on

Rupert Friend as Prince Albert and Emily Blunt as Victoria I in
The Young Victoria, **2009.**

characters created by Sir Arthur Conan Doyle); **c**, Stephen Goldblatt; **m**, Bruce Broughton; **ed**, Stu Linder; **prod d**, Norman Reynolds; **art d**, Charles Bishop, Fred Hole; **set d**, Michael Ford; **spec eff**, Kit West, Trevor Wood.

Young Tom Edison ★★★ 1940; U.S.; 86m; MGM; B/W; Biographical Drama; Children: Acceptable; **DVD**; **VHS**. Rooney is terrific as an adolescent Thomas Alva Edison (1847-1931), his curiosity and inventions often creating more trouble than his parents can bear. He is a bright but unruly teenager so obsessed with his ideas for inventions that he ignores his school and home obligations. His teachers and neighbors think he's crackbrained, but Bainter, his patient mother; Bancroft, his loving father, and Weidler, his supportive younger sister, tolerate his outlandish behavior because they think he is destined for great things. His mother is his biggest supporter, believing in Rooney after each time he fails and gets into mischief. He helps to save her life when she becomes ill. Corrigan, the doctor attending Bainter at her home, must perform an immediate operation, but he does not have enough light by which to perform that surgery. Rooney desperately rigs up a wall mirror and reflects from it intensive light from several lamps so that the physician can see to perform that delicate operation, one which Bainter survives. Then, to earn enough money that will finance his inventions, Rooney sells fruit and reading materials on trains while he learns Morse code from a telegrapher. Some of his ideas so infuriate his employer that Rooney is fired. He then learns that his family members are riding on a train that is speeding toward a railway bridge spanning a deep gorge and has collapsed. Rooney convinces an engineer to race his engine toward that train, and Rooney uses the engine's whistle to send out a shrill message in Morse code that warns of the collapsed bridge, the message understood by Weidler, who then informs the engineer driving the imperiled train and who stops the train just in time to save all of its passengers. Rooney is not only hailed a hero, but now earns the respect of the adults of his community who had earlier written him off as a hopeless fool. This film was a huge box office success and greatly advanced Rooney's career. His acting is much more reserved than in his previous film, and he suppresses his normal boyish exuberance and youthful ebullience (albeit the undersized Rooney was twenty when he made this film). Taurog, who specialized in directing juveniles, does a fine job in helming this very exciting and entertaining film, which is studded with fine performances from its supporting players. The film saw a sixty-minute radio adaptation aired by Lux Radio Theater on December 23, 1940, with Rooney and Weidler reprising their roles. Songs: "Sweet Genevieve" (George Cooper, Henry Tucker), "Jingle Bells" (1858; James Pierpont). *Author's Note*: This production was made at the same time MGM produced **Edison, the Man**, starring Spencer Tracy as the

great inventor. Many other actors have essayed Thomas Edison in many other films, including **The Adventures of Young Tom Edison**, 2008 (made-for-TV; Randy Rossilli); **Bill and Ted's Bogus Journey**, 1991 (Hal Landon Sr.); **General Electric Theater**, 1953-1962 (TV series, "Edison the Man," 1954 episode: Burgess Meredith); **The Hourglass Sanatorium**, 1973 (Stanislaw Tylczynski); **Let There Be Light: Nicola Tesla**, 2005 (made-for-TV; Robert Goss); **Lights of Old Broadway**, 1925 (Frank Glendon); **Nikola Tesla**, 1977 (TV series; three episodes: Buzancic); **Tall Tales and Legends**, 1985-1988 (TV series; "Annie Oakley," 1985 episode: John Achorn); **Tom Edison: The Boy Who Lit Up the World**, 1979; (made-for-TV; David Huffman); and **The Young Indiana Jones Chronicles**, 1992-1993 (TV series; "Princeton, February 1916," 1993 episode: Richard K. Olsen). **p**, John W. Considine Jr.; **d**, Norman Taurog; **cast**, Mickey Rooney, Fay Bainter, George Bancroft, Virginia Weidler, Eugene Pallette, Victor Kilian, Bobby Jordan as Bobbie Jordan, J.M. Kerrigan, Lloyd Corrigan, John Kellogg, Clem Bevans, Harry Shannon, and Spencer Tracy in a cameo role as man looking at a portrait of Edison; **w**, Bradbury Foote, Dore Schary, Hugo Butler (based on material gathered by H. Alan Dunn); **c**, Sidney Wagner; **m**, Edward Ward; **ed**, Elmo Veron; **art d**, Cedric Gibbons; **set d**, Edwin B. Willis.

Young Torless ★★★ 1968; West Germany/France; 90m; Franz Seitz Filmproduktion/Nouvelles Editions de Films/ Kanawha; B/W; Drama; Children: Unacceptable; **DVD**; **VHS**. Well-told, taut story profiles three students at a boarding school in the Austro-Hungarian Empire prior to World War II (1939-1945). Carrriere, Dietz, and Tischer catch a classmate, Seidowsky, stealing money from one of them. Rather than report him to school authorities, the boys decide to punish him themselves. Two of the boys, Dietz and Tischer, torture, degrade, and humiliate Seidowsky with sadistic delight, but the third boy, called Torless, who is played by Carriere, watches and refuses to take part in the torture while he analyzes his friends' abnormal behavior. School officials learn of the incident and Carriere admits he was part of the brutal procedure. Carriere is asked to leave the school, while the other two boys are turned over to police. The well-acted film serves as an allegory of what happened to many German people during the war, particularly those who may not have taken part in atrocities and the Holocaust but morally shared the responsibility. A fascinating film but too violent for children. (In German; English subtitles.) **p**, Franz Seitz, Louis Malle; **d**, Volker Schlondorff (based on an adaptation by Herbert Asmodi of the novel *Die Verwirrungen des Zoglings Torless* by Robert Musil); **cast**, Matthieu Carriere, Marian Seidowsky, Bernd Tischer, Fred Dietz, Lotte Ledl, Jean Launay, Barbara Steele, Herbert Asmodi, Hanna Axmann-Rezzori, Fritz Gehlen; **c**, Franz Rath; **m**, Hans Werner Henze; **ed**, Claus von Boro; **set d**, Maleen Pacha.

The Young Victoria ★★★ 2009; U.K./U.S.; 105m; GK Films/Apparition; Color; Biography; Children: Unacceptable (MPAA: PG); **BD**; **DVD**; **IV**. Blunt is superb in presenting a convincingly authentic young queen of England in her riveting role of Victoria I (1819-1901). There is much British court intrigue about who Blunt should marry, and finally the young queen not only settles on her German cousin Prince Albert (1819-1861), who is played by Friend, but falls in love with him, and he with her. Friend becomes her primary adviser, and they have nine children together who become the royal families of most of Europe. Friend saves her life from a would-be assassin and later dies of typhoid fever at the age of forty-two, leaving Blunt devastated. Not entirely historically accurate, this film nonetheless is a fine biopic, and the direction, for the most part, accurately chronicles this fascinating royal saga. All of the cast members are standouts in their historic roles, and the production values—lavish sets and rich costumes—are accurate to that ornate and decorous period. The film won an Oscar for Best Costume Design (Sandy Powell), and received Oscar nominations for Best Art Direction (Walker, Lowe, Inglis; and set decoration: Gray), and Best Makeup (Jon Henry Gordon, Jenny Shircore). The film did not do as well as expected at the box office, earning more than $27.4 million in its initial release against a budget of $35 million. Songs: "Ado the Priest" (George Frederic Handel), "Vine, far quested brachia" from "I Puritan" (Incense Belling), "The Cold Song" (Henry Purcell), "Pa Pace Domino" (Argo Part), "Only You" (Ian Sheri, Scott Shields, Nikki Anders, Pam Shayne), "Walker a la Again" (Johann Strauss, Jr.), "Tausendapperment Walzer" and "Contredances op. 44" (Johann Strauss, Sr.), "Swan Song" (Franz Schubert), "Serenade for Strings in E Major" (Antonin Dvorak), "L'elisir d'amour" (Gaetano Donizetti), "What Power Art Thou?" (Henry Purcell). *Author's Note*: The most egregious inaccuracy in the film is where Friend, while shielding Blunt against an assassin (several attempts were made against Victoria's life in her long reign), is grazed by a bullet. Albert was never wounded in any of those assassination attempts, although he did shield the queen with his body in one attempt. Many other actresses have essayed Victoria I in many other films, including **The Adventure of Sherlock Holmes' Smarter Brother**, 1975 (Susan Field); **Adventures in Paradise**, 1959-1962 (TV series; "Blueprint for Paradise," 1962 episode; Pilar Seurat); **Annie Get Your Gun**, 1950 (Evelyn Beresford); **Around the World in 80 Days**, 1989 (TV miniseries; Anna Massey); **Around the World in 80 Days**, 2004 (Kathy Bates); **Balaclava**, 1930 (Marian Drada); **Barnum**, 1986 (made-for-TV; Bronwen Mantel); **The Battle of the Waltzes**, 1934 (Hanna Waag); **BBC Play of the Month**, 1965-1983 (TV series; "Gordon of Khartoum," 1966 episode: Gladys Spencer); **Bewitched**, 1964-1972 (TV series; "Aunt Clara's Victoria Victory," 1967 episode: Jane Connell); **Bismarck**, 1940 (Marga Riffa); **Buffalo Bill**, 1944 (Evelyn Beresford); **Court Waltzes**, 1933 (Madeleine Ozeray); **David Livingstone**, 1936 (Pamela Stanley); **Disraeli**, 1916 (Mrs. Henry Lytton); **Disraeli**, 1929 (Margaret Mann); **Disraeli: Portrait of a Romantic**, 1978 (TV miniseries; Rosemary Leach); **East Lynne**, 1976 (made-for-TV; Shirley Steedman); **Edward the King**, 1975 (TV series; Annette Crosbie); **The Edwardians**, 1972-1973 (TV series; "Daisy," 1973 episode; Mollie Maureen); **Entente cordiale**, 1939 (Gaby Morlay); **Fall of Eagles**, 1974 (TV miniseries; "The English Princess," 1974 episode; Perlita Neilson; "The Last Tsar," 1974 episode: Mavis Edwards); **The Flaxton Boys**, 1969-1973 (TV series; "1854: The Dog," 1969 episode: Christine Ozanne); **Gilbert and Sullivan**, 1953 (Muriel Aked); **The Great McGonagall**, 1975 (Peter Sellers); **Hands of a Murderer**, 1990 (Honora Burke); **Hans Christian Andersen: My Life as a Fairy Tale**, 2003 (made-for-TV; Nina Lutjens); **Happy and Glorious**, 1952 (TV series; Renee Asherson); **Her Majesty; Mrs. Brown**, 1997 (Judi Dench); **Invincible Mr. Disraeli**, 1963 (Kate Reid); **Journey to Midnight**, 1971 (Fay Compton); **Journey to the Unknown**, 1968 (TV series; Fay Compton); **The Lady with a Lamp**, 1951 (Anna Neagle); **Let's Make Up**, 1956 (Anna Neagle); **Lillie**, 1978 (TV miniseries; Sheila Reed); **The Little Princess**, 1939 (Beryl Mercer); **Livingstone**, 1925 (Blanche Graham); **Marigold**, 1938 (Pamela Stanley); **Melba**, 1953 (Sybil Thorndike); **The Mudlark**, 1950 (Irene Dunne); **Mystery of the Wax Museum**, 1933 (Margaret Mann as the wax effigy of Queen Victoria); **Omnibus**, 1967-2002 (TV series; "Landseer: A Victorian Comedy," 1980 episode: Pamela Binns); **Paul Kruger**, 1956 (Gwen Ffrangcon-Davies); **The Pearls of the Crown**, 1938 (Yvette Pienne); **Pervirella**, 1997 (Sexton Ming); **The Pirates! Band of Misfits**, 2012 (Imelda Staunton voiceover); **Preussen uber alles—Bismarcks deutsche Einigung**, 1971 (TV miniseries; Renate Pichler); **The Prime Minister**, 1942 (Fay Compton); **The Private Life of Sherlock Holmes**, 1970 (Mollie Maureen); **The Ravelled Thread**, 1979-1980 (TV series; "The Spy," 1980 episode: Muriel Pavlow); **Rhodes**, 1996 (TV miniseries; "The Price of My Blood," 1996 episode: Margaret Heale); **Robert Montgomery Presents**, 1950-1957 (TV series; "Victoria Regina," 1951 episode: Helen Hayes; "Victoria Regina," 1957 episode: Claire Bloom); **Shadow Play**, 2004 (TV series; Doreen Mantle); **Shanghai Knights**, 2003 (Gemma Jones); **Sixty Glorious Years**, 1938 (Anna Neagle); **Sixty Years a Queen**, 1913 (Blanche Forsythe); **Station Jim**, 2001 (made-for-TV; Prunella Scales); **The Story of Alexander Graham Bell**,

Emily Blunt as Victoria I of Great Britain in *The Young Victoria*, 2009.

1939 (Beryl Mercer); **The Story of Vickie**, 1958 (Romy Schneider); **The Symbol of Sacrifice**, 1918 (Mrs. D. Buxton); **Tall Tales and Legends**, 1985-1988 (TV series; "Annie Oakley," 1985 episode: Lu Leonard); **Those Fantastic Flying Fools**, 1967 (Joan Sterndale-Bennett); **Uncle Kruger**, 1941 (Hedwig Wangel); **Victoria & Albert**, 2001 (made-for-TV; Victoria Hamilton); **Victoria in Dover**, 1936 (Jenny Jugo); **Victoria in Dover**, 1958 (Romy Schneider); **Victoria Regina**, 1964 (TV miniseries; Patricia Routledge); **Victoria the Great**, 1937 (Anna Neagle); **Voyagers!**, 1982-1983 (TV series; "Buffalo Bill and Annie Play the Palace," 1983 episode: Lurene Tuttle); **The White Angel**, 1936 (Fay Holden); **Witness to Yesterday**, 1970-1976 (TV series; "Queen Victoria," 1973 episode: Kate Reid); **The Wrong Box**, 1966 (Avis Bunnage); **The Yankee Clipper**, 1927 (Julia Faye); **The Young Visitors**, 2003 (made-for-TV; Janine Duvitski); and **Zorro in the Court of England**, 1971 (Barbara Carroll). **p**, Martin Scorsese, Sarah Ferguson, Tim Headington, Denis O'Sullivan, Anita Overland, **d**, Jean-Marc Vallee; **cast**, Emily Blunt, Rupert Friend, Paul Bettany, Miranda Richardson, Jim Broadbent, Thomas Kretschmann, Mark Strong, Jesper Christensen, Harriet Walter, Julian Glover, Jeanette Hain, Michael Maloney; **w**, Julian Fellowes; **c**, Hagen Bogdanski; **m**, Ilan Eshkeri; **ed**, Jill Bilcock, Matt Garner; **prod d**, Patrice Vermette; **art d**, Alexandra Walker, Christopher Lowe, Paul Inglis; **set d**, Maggie Gray; **spec eff**, Stuart Brisdon, Marc Cote.

Young Winston ★★★ 1972; U.K./U.S.; 157m (initial U.S. release; 146m in later release; Open Roads/COL; Color; Biographical Drama; Children: Unacceptable (MPAA: PG); **DVD**; **VHS**; **IV**. The aggressive and talented Foreman was personally selected by Winston Churchill (1874-1965) to produce this dynamic and compelling biopic of his book, *My Early Life: A Roving Commission*. This episodic film spans the years 1881 to 1901, and opens with Lewis, who plays Churchill at age seven; he is a lonely boy, mostly ignored by his demanding father, Lord Randolph Churchill (1849-1895), who is played by Shaw, and who is forever busy with British politics. His mother, Lady Randolph Churchill (Jennie Jerome; 1854-1921), who is played by Bancroft, is a former American socialite. She, too, is also so busy with her social affairs that she finds little time to pay much attention to her son, although she loves and encourages him to strive for great things. Moreover, as Audreson at age thirteen, the young Winston Churchill finds no joy at his school where he does not relate to his classmates and is often in trouble. He grows to manhood as Ward and is in India and where, as an ambitious junior officer in the army, thinks to make his reputation. A fellow officer suggests that, if Ward wants to makes his mark, he should become a correspondent for one of the English newspapers and this he does. After he helps to suppress an uprising, he begins to send dis-

Simon Ward and John Mills in *Young Winston*, 1972.

patches to a newspaper. He then writes a popular book about the crisis, one that angers his superiors because of his critical opinions on how the uprising was managed by those superiors. By this time, Shaw, who is the Chancellor of the Exchequer, has so many stressful arguments over new arms expenses with his political foes that he resigns his post out of frustration. Shaw contracts syphilis and that eroding disease soon causes his political star to descend. This is painfully evident when, to their shock and horror, Bancroft and Ward, while in the gallery of the House of Commons, watch Shaw attempt to make a speech and where his address is reduced to incoherent babbling. Upon Shaw's death, Ward realizes that Shaw dies believing that his son will never amount to much, and Ward resolves to prove him wrong by continuing to risk himself in one spectacular adventure after another. He goes to the Sudan as a cavalry officer, serving under the command of Field Marshal Horatio Herbert Kitchener (1850-1916), who is ably played by Mills. The British reconquer the Sudan during the battle of Omdurman (September 2, 1898), where Ward distinguishes himself in a cavalry charge. The Dervishes and their Arab allies, even though they vastly outnumber the British forces, are defeated in this decisive battle due to the modern machine guns and artillery employed by the British army. Ward's impeccable war record convinces him to return to England where he runs for Parliament, but his bid for office is rejected when he loses the election. Undaunted, Ward then serves in South Africa as an officer and a war correspondent during the Second Boer War (1899-1902). When a British armored train is ambushed by Boers, Ward supervises a counterattack that saves the train, but he is then captured and confined in a POW concentration camp. He and fellow prisoner Woodward, however, manage a sensational escape, which, along with the dispatches that Ward has been sending to British newspapers, makes him a figure of national attention. With the reputation of a hero, Ward returns to England and again runs for Parliament, but this time he is elected at the age of twenty-six and his political career is firmly established, promising all the great things to come. Ward has become the important person he has sought to be, vindicating Bancroft's belief in him while posthumously proving his father wrong. After winning the election, he makes a moving speech in the House of Commons, echoing the impassioned words of his father for a vigilant England, and Bancroft beams proudly as she watches her son from the gallery. Ward, a newcomer, is exceptional as the dedicated Churchill (and he would go on to play a much older Churchill in the 1994 TV miniseries **Kurtulus**), and he is strongly supported by Shaw and Bancroft, who render memorable performances as his celebrated parents. The supporting cast is also notable, particularly Mills, Hawkins, Hopkins and Woodward, the latter going on to appear in the exceptional **Breaker Morant**, 1980, which brought Woodward into the first acting ranks of filmdom. Attenborough, an established actor, had already dis-

tinguished himself as a superb director when helming the musical **Oh! What a Lovely War**, 1969, and his good sense of history is evident throughout this impressively mounted production, including his depiction of the Battle of Omdurman, which was earlier captured on a mammoth scale in Alexander Korda's classic adventure film **The Four Feathers**, 1939. Attenborough presents a life full of riveting action, but allows little time for an introspective view of Churchill. He cannot be faulted for profiling a vigorous young man who has yet to become the political savant the world would know years later. A final scene showing Ward as an aging Churchill sleeping before one of his landscape paintings while dreaming of his father coming to him to state that he still does not understand his actions was cut from the film, but later restored in some releases. The film received Oscar nominations for Best Screenplay (Foreman); Best Art Direction (Ashton, Drake, Graysmark, Hutchinson; set decoration: James); and Best Costume Design (Anthony Mendleson). The film did well at the box office, earning more than $2.1 million in its initial release. Songs: "Forty Years On" (traditional), "The Lincolnshire Poacher" (traditional), "Sunny Bank" (traditional), "Sarie Marais" (traditional), "The British Grenadiers" (traditional), "Bonnie Dundee" (traditional), "Jenny's Bawbee" (traditional), "March of the Victors" (1963; from **The Victors**; Sol Kaplan, Freddy Douglass), "For Thy Mercy and Thy Grace" (1841; Henry Downton), "The Man on the Flying Trapeze" (1867; music: Gaston Lyle, Alfred Lee; lyrics: George Leybourne), "Iolanthe" (1882; music: Arthur Sullivan; lyrics: W.S. Gilbert), "Enigma Variations" ["Variations, Op. 36"] (1898-1899; Edward Elgar), "Scipio" (1726; from "Scipione"; music: George Frederic Handel; lyrics: Paolo Antonio Rolli), "Soldiers of the Queen" (1898; Leslie Stuart), "Wiener Blut" (1873; Johann Strauss II), "Pomp and Circumstance" (1901; Edward Elgar), "Toreador Song" (1875; from "Carmen" by Georges Bizet), "Triumphal March" (1897-1898; from "Caractacus" by Edward Elgar). *Author's Note*: Churchill was impressed with Foreman's production, **The Guns of Navarone**, 1961, and met with the director at that time, discussing the possibility of his making a film based upon Churchill's memoirs of his early life. Foreman made plans to produce the film, but other projects delayed the film, and, by the time Foremen went into production, Churchill had died six years earlier. Bancroft told this author that "I played Winston Churchill's mother in that picture, but the actor [Simon Ward] playing my son was only about ten years younger than me. An actress always feels that she is as young as she looks, but when you start playing mother roles, you must settle for looking like an older woman. That does not go over too well with some actresses, but I always thought such roles challenged my ability as an actress." Foreman asked Attenborough to not only direct this film, but to play the role of Randolph Churchill. When Attenborough accepted the job as director, he declined the role that eventually and wisely went to Shaw, who provided a forceful and intense characterization befitting the character. The film was shot on location in the U.K. and in Morocco. Many other actors have essayed Winston Churchill in many other films, including **Above and Beyond**, 2006 (TV miniseries; Joss Ackland); **Above Us the Waves**, 1956 (Peter Cavanagh); **Allegiance**, 2005 (Mel Smith); **An American in Paris**, 1951 (Dudley Field Malone); **Annie: A Royal Adventure**, 1995 (made-for-TV; David King); **The Battle of Sutjeska**, 1973 (Orson Welles); **Bertie and Elizabeth**, 2002 (made-for-TV; David Ryall); **Bomber Harris**, 1989 (made-for-TV; Robert Hardy); **Bullet for Heydrich**, 2013 (Richard Syms); **Callas e Onassis**, 2005 (made-for-TV; Gerry George); **Captains of the Clouds**, 1942 (Miles Mander); **Casablanca Express**, 1989 (John Evans); **Castles in the Sky**, 2014 (Tim McInnerny); **Churchill and the Generals**, 1981 (made-for-TV; Timothy West); **Churchill: 100 Days That Saved Britain**, 2015 (made-for-TV; Robert Hardy); **Churchill: The Hollywood Years**, 2004 (Christian Slater); **Churchill: When Britain Said No**, 2015 (made-for-TV; Christian Rodska); **Churchill's First World War**, 2013 (made-for-TV; Adam James); **Days of Betrayal**, 1973 (Jan Vitek); **De Gaulle**, 2006- (TV series; David Ryall); **Deadline Gallipoli**, 2015 (TV miniseries; Simon Maiden); **The Desert Fox**, 1955 (voiceover of Jack Moyles);

Dieppe, 1993 (made-for-TV; W.B. Brydon); **Dunkirk**, 2004 (made-for-TV; Simon Russell Beale); **The Eagle Has Landed**, 1977 (Leigh Dilley); **Edward & Mrs. Simpson**, 1978 (TV miniseries; Wensley Pithey); **Edward the King**, 1975 (TV series; Christopher Strauli); **F.D.R.: The Last Year**, 1980 (made-for-TV; Wensley Pithey); **The Fall of Berlin**, 1952 (Viktor Stanitsyn); **The Gathering Storm**, 1974 (made-for-TV; Richard Burton); **The Gathering Storm**, 2002 (made-for-TV; Albert Finney); **The Great Battle**, 1973 (Yuri Durov); **The Great Escape II: The Untold Story**, 1988 (made-for-TV; Ronald Lacey); **Heyday!**, 2006 (made-for-TV; Frank Holden); **Hiroshima**, 1995 (made-for-TV; Timothy West); **Hiroshima**, 2005 (made-for-TV; Robert Austin); **Honey Sweet Love...**, 1994 (John Evans); **Ike: Countdown to D-Day**, 2004 (made-for-TV; Ian Mune); **Ike: The War Years**, 1979 (TV miniseries; Wensley Pithey); **Inglourious Basterds**, 2009 (Rod Taylor); **Into the Storm**, 2009 (made-for-TV; Brendan Gleeson); **Jennie: Lady Randolph Churchill**, 1974 (TV miniseries; Warren Clarke); **The King's Speech**, 2010 (Timothy Spall); **Kurtulus**, 1994 (TV miniseries; Simon Ward); **The Last Bastion**, 1984 (TV miniseries; Timothy West); **The Life and Times of David Lloyd George**, 1981 (TV series; William Hootkins); **A Man Called Intrepid**, 1979 (TV miniseries; Nigil Stock); **The Man Who Never Was**, 1956 (Peter Sellers voiceover); **Masterpiece Theatre: Lord Mountbatten—The Last Viceroy**, 1986 (TV miniseries; Malcolm Terris); **Matinee Theatre**, 1955-1958 (TV series; "Savrola," 1956 episode; David Frankham); **Menzies and Churchill at War**, 2008 (made-for-TV; Charles "Bud" Tingwell); **Mission to Moscow**, 1943 (Dudley Field Malone); **Number 10**, 1983 (TV miniseries; Terence Harvey); **Onassis: The Richest Man in the World**, 1988 (made-for-TV; Thorley Walters); **Operation Crossbow**, 1965 (Patrick Wymark); **Peenemunde**, 1970 (made-for-TV; Alfred Schieske); **Queen of the Desert**, 2015 (Christopher Fulford); **Regal Cavalcade**, 1935 (C.M. Hallard); **The Siege 1922** (2013; Mario Rosenstock); **The Siege of Sidney Street**, 1961 (Jimmy Sangster); **Sinking of the Lusitania: Terror at Sea**, 2007 (made-for-TV; Martin Le Maitre); **Stalingrad**, 1990 (Ronald Lacey); **Suez 1956**, 1979 (made-for-TV; Wensley Pithey); **The Treaty**, 1991 (made-for-TV; Julian Fellowes); **Truman at Potsdam**, 1976 (made-for-TV; John Houseman); **Two Men Went to War**, 2004 (David Ryall); **The Unforgettable Year: 1919**, 1952 (Viktor Stanitsyn); **Wallis & Edward**, 2005 (made-for-TV; David Calder); **War and Remembrance**, 1988 (TV miniseries; Robert Hardy); **The Winds of War**, 1983 (TV miniseries; Howard Lang); **Winston Churchill: The Valiant Years**, 1960-1963 (TV series; Richard Burton); **Winston Churchill: The Wilderness Years**, 1981 (TV series; Robert Hardy); **The Woman He Loved**, 1988 (made-for-TV; Robert Hardy); **The Woman I Love**, 1972 (made-for-TV; Henry Oliver); **World War Two: Behind Closed Doors**, 2008-2009 (TV series; Paul Humpoletz); **World War II: When Lions Roared**, 1994 (made-for-TV; Bob Hoskins); and **Yalta**, 1984 (made-for-TV; Bernard Fresson). **p**, Carl Foreman, (uncredited) Richard Attenborough; **d**, Attenborough; **cast**, Simon Ward, Robert Shaw, Anne Bancroft, Jack Hawkins, Ian Holm, Anthony Hopkins, Michael Audreson, Russell Lewis, Patrick Magee, Edward Woodward, John Mills, Laurence Naismith, Robert Hardy, Jane Seymour, Pat Heywood, Nigel Hawthorne; **w**, Foreman (based on *My Early Life: A Roving Commission* by Sir Winston Churchill); **c**, Gerry Turpin (Panavision; Eastmancolor); **m**, Alfred Ralston, Sir Edward Elgar; **ed**, Kevin Connor; **prod d**, Don Ashton, Geoffrey Drake; **art d**, John Graysmark, William Hutchinson; **set d**, Peter James; **spec eff**, Cliff Richardson, Tom Howard, Charles Staffel.

Young Wives Tale ★★★ 1952; U.K.; 79m; Associated British Pictures; B/W; Comedy/Romance; Children: Acceptable; **DVD**. Because of a post-WWII (1939-1945) housing shortage, Greenwood, a shy British woman, and Patrick, her playwright husband, share their house with another married couple, Cherry and Farr, and a single woman, Hepburn. The couples feud while Hepburn becomes infatuated with Patrick. The household is in constant mayhem, with service people and a dog that

George Hamilton as country singer Hank Williams and Susan Oliver in *Your Cheatin' Heart*, 1964.

keeps stealing everyone's dinner, adding to the constant calamities. Broadly played for laughs, this bickering farce includes some amusing slapstick, and it is a delight to watch a young Audrey Hepburn in an early role. **p**, Victor Skutezky; **d**, Henry Cass; **cast**, Joan Greenwood, Nigel Patrick, Derek Farr, Guy Middleton, Audrey Hepburn, Athene Seyler, Helen Cherry, Fabia Drake, Selma Vaz Dias, Irene Handl; **w**, Anne Burnaby (based on the play by Ronald Jeans); **c**, Erwin Hillier; **m**, Philip Green; **ed**, Edward B. Jarvis; **art d**, Terence Verity.

Your Cheatin' Heart ★★★ 1964; U.S.; 100m; Four Leaf/MGM; B/W; Biographical Drama; Children: Unacceptable; **DVD**; **VHS**; **IV**. This lively biopic provides a convincing portrait of the life and career of country singer and song writer Hank Williams (1923-1953), who is ably played by Hamilton, and who rose to fame in the 1940s and 1950s. His career begins by singing in a traveling medicine show where he meets and falls in love with Oliver, who likes the film's title song and sends it to a music publisher on Hamilton's behalf. The song becomes a success and furthers Hamilton's career. He and Oliver marry, and he becomes a regular on radio and with the Grand Ole Opry. With fame comes a drinking problem that lasts through the rest of Hamilton's short life, alcoholism causing him to die of heart failure at the age of twenty-nine. In addition to Hamilton's fine performance, Ingram is exceptional in his scenes with Losby, who plays Williams at age fourteen, where Ingram teaches Losby how to play the guitar. Williams left behind many classic country songs, many of which are included in this film: "Your Cheatin' Heart," "Long Gone Lonesome Blues," "I Saw the Light," "I Can't Help It," "Jambalaya," "Cold, Cold Heart," "I'm So Lonesome I Could Cry," "Hey Good Lookin'," "Ramblin' Man," "Kaw-Liga,"and "You Win Again." The songs are sung by his son, Hank Williams, Jr. Excessive drinking prohibits viewing by children. **p**, Sam Katzman; **d**, Gene Nelson; **cast**, George Hamilton, Susan Oliver, Red Buttons, Arthur O'Connell, Shary Marshall, Rex Ingram, Donald Losby, Chris Crosby, Rex Holman, Hortense Petra, Roy Engel; **w**, Stanford Whitmore; **c**, Ellis W. Carter; **m**, Fred Karger; **ed**, Ben Lewis; **art d**, George W. Davis, Merrill Pye; **set d**, Henry Grace, Don Greenwood, Jr.

Your Past Is Showing ★★★ 1958; U.K.; 87m; RANK-Anglofilm; RANK; B/W; Comedy; Children: Unacceptable; **DVD**; **VHS**; **IV**. Delightful black comedy begins with artful Price, who is the publisher of a British scandal magazine, but who is clever enough to show some caution before printing his outlandish tales. Before publishing each story, he approaches the subject whose scandalous behavior is to be implied, not described, in order to avoid libel. He promises to suppress the story in return for money, which amounts to a clever bribe. His victims are Terry-Thomas, a racketeering peer; Mount, a female writer; Eaton, a

Eddie Albert, Millard Mitchell and Gary Cooper in *You're in the Navy Now,* **1951.**

beautiful model; and Sellers, a popular television personality. Each of them tries to kill the conniving Price, but fail, so they join forces and succeed in getting rid of him, to prevent him from revealing their scandalous lives in his magazine or at any trial. The most laugh-filled scenes in this good comedy involve the wild antics the victims enact while attempting to rid themselves of the scandal-peddling, blackmailing Price. **p&d**, Mario Zampi; **cast**, Terry-Thomas, Peter Sellers, Peggy Mount, Shirley Eaton, Dennis Price, Georgiana Cookson, Joan Sims, Miles Malleson, Kenneth Griffith, Moultrie Kelsall, Wally Patch; **w**, Michael Pertwee; **c**, Stanley Pavey; **m**, Stanley Black; **ed**, Bill Lewthwaite; **art d**, Ivan King.

Your Three Minutes Are Up ★★★ 1973; U.S.; 93m; Minutes/Cinerama; Color; Comedy/Drama; Children: Unacceptable (MPAA: PG); **DVD**; **VHS**. Enjoyable "buddy" tale begins with Bridges, who works at a dull office job and is engaged to Margolin, a neurotic woman. He and his pal, Leibman, who takes life less seriously, take a road trip together to California and reexamine their lives. They get involved with a few minor confidence games while meeting some fetching women and further bond by getting to know each other and themselves. Songs: "It's Only Me," "Get Hold of Yourself" (Dennis Lambert, Brian Potter, Perry Botkin Jr.). Mature themes prohibit viewing by children. **p**, Jerry Gershwin, Mark C. Levy; **d**, Douglas N. Schwartz; **cast**, Beau Bridges, Ron Leibman, Janet Margolin, Kathleen Freeman, David Ketchum, Stu Nisbet, Read Morgan, Jennifer Ashley, Sherry Bain, Paul Barselou; **w**, James Dixon; **c**, Stephen M. Katz (DeLuxe Color); **m**, Perry Botkin, Jr.; **ed**, Aaron Stell; **art d**, Joseph Crowingham.

You're a Big Boy Now ★★★ 1966; U.S.; 96m; Seven Arts; Color; Drama/Romance; Children: Unacceptable; **DVD**; **VHS**. Absorbing coming-of-age tale sees Torn taking his son, Kastner, and telling him two strict words: "Grow up!" He urges him to untie the apron strings his doting mother, Page, has tied around him. Kastner takes Torn's advice and moves from his security blanket home on Long Island. He rents a room in a boarding house in New York City run by Harris. Kastner gets a job at the New York City Public Library and falls under the sex and drugs influence of his swinging coworker, Bill. Kastner rejects a romance with Black, a nice girl who really likes him, and he becomes obsessed with Hartman, a disco dancer, who secretly hates men. Hartman's problem is that she has been emotionally damaged by her conniving high school counselor, a lecherous hypnotherapist. Kastner finally sees the light and focuses on Black, with whom he finds a warm and welcoming relationship. Coppola presents a sensitive and goodhearted story with inviting characters, and Kastner, Torn, Page, Black, Harris and Bill are standouts in their roles. Mature themes prohibit

viewing by children. **p**, Phil Feldman; **d&w**; Francis Ford Coppola; **cast**, Elizabeth Hartman, Geraldine Page, Julie Harris, Peter Kastner, Rip Torn, Michael Dunn, Tony Bill, Karen Black, Dolph Sweet, Michael O'Sullivan; **c**, Andrew Laszlo (Pathe Color); **m**, Robert Prince; **ed**, Aram Avakian; **art d**, Vassele Fotopoulos; **set d**, Marvin March.

You're in the Navy Now ★★★ 1951; U.S.; 93m; FOX; B/W; Comedy; Children: Acceptable; **DVD**; **VHS**. Offbeat but entertaining tale for superstar Cooper begins in the first months of 1942, during America's entrance into World War II (1939-1945). Cooper is an inexperienced U.S. Navy lieutenant, a "90-day wonder," who is assigned as the new skipper of a submarine chaser equipped with an experimental steam engine. He bids goodbye to his wife, Greer, and hopes that the crew of his ship, the U.S.S. *Teakettle*, can help him do his job. It turns out that most of the crew is just as inexperienced as he is, only having worked in ships with diesel engines. The only one aboard with any naval experience is Mitchell, the ship's chief machinist's mate, but Mitchell cannot handle all the problems that arise as the ship goes through a series of tests at sea. Not the least of Cooper's problems is Webb, his engineering officer, who has no training or knowledge about engineering, and Erdman, the mess officer, who suffers from constant seasickness and who creates nothing but chaos in the kitchen galley. Nothing goes right during the sea trials, and, while being distracted, Cooper sees his ship ram an aircraft carrier, not once, but twice. He and his crew nevertheless manage to complete their mission, successfully testing the steam engine, and everyone receives commendations for their hard work. Hathaway keeps the action moving at a brisk pace, and Cooper, along with a strong supporting cast, provide top-notch performances. The film did not do well at the box office when first released under the title of **U.S.S. Teakettle**, but it was renamed under the above title and did much better when shortly rereleased, earning more than $1.6 million. This film is not related to the 1926 film of the same name. Song: "Yours/Quiereme Mucho" (Augustin Rodriguez, Gonzalo Roig, Jack Sherr). *Author's Note*: Cooper told this author that "I had played a number of U.S. Navy officers in other pictures. In one I played an officer on a submarine [**The Devil and the Deep**, 1932]. In another I played a U.S. Navy doctor [**The Story of Dr. Wassell**, 1944], and in another picture I skippered aircraft carriers [**Task Force**, 1949]. In **You're in the Navy Now**, I played the most fouled-up officer the Navy ever saw, and I had a crew that was just as ignorant. The whole lot of us should have been thrown into the brig." Greer told this author that "I did not have much to do in that picture with Gary [Cooper], except to smile sweetly and send him off to sea with a hug and a kiss, and I guess that is what millions of other women were doing during the war [WWII]." Hathaway, who would make six films with Cooper, told this author: "We got complete cooperation from the Navy to make **You're in the Navy Now**, and shot a lot of it on location at the Norfolk Naval Yard at Hampton Roads, Virginia. When the Navy brass previewed the picture later, they were not so cooperative after they saw how a bunch of inexperienced clowns were running one of their ships. I got a lot of heat for that, but they forgave us because they liked Coop [Gary Cooper], especially after he had played a heroic Navy doctor and a skipper of an aircraft carrier in WWII in **The Story of Dr. Wassell** and **Task Force**, which were big favorites with the Navy." This film was also exceptional in that it saw the screen debuts of some very talented actors: Lee Marvin, Jack Warden, Charles Bronson and Harvey Lembeck. **p**, Fred Kohlmar; **d**, Henry Hathaway; **cast**, Gary Cooper, Jane Greer, Millard Mitchell, Eddie Albert, John McIntire, Ray Collins, Harry Von Zell, Jack Webb, Richard Erdman, Harvey Lembeck, Ed Begley, Charles Bronson, Lee Marvin, Biff McGuire, George Nader, Damian O'Flynn, Jack Warden; **w**, Richard Murphy (based on a *New Yorker* magazine article by John W. Hazard); **c**, Joe MacDonald; **m**, Cyril Mockridge; **ed**, James B. Clark; **art d**, Lyle Wheeler, J. Russell Spencer; **set d**, Thomas Little, Fred J. Rode; **spec eff**, Ray Kellogg, Fred Sersen.

You're Telling Me! ★★★★★ 1934; U.S.; 66m; PAR; B/W; Comedy; Children: Acceptable; **DVD**; **VHS**. This hilarious outing sees the inimitable Fields as an inventor, who is always on the verge of triumph but success treacherously eludes him. While struggling to find enough money to support his family, he becomes so frustrated that he takes to drink and returns home so tipsy with blurred vision that he finds it next to impossible to insert his key into the lock of his front door. Fortunately, Fields has invented a device to meet such unwieldy challenges, a keyhole finder that is an odd-looking funnel he uses to guide the key into the lock. Once he gains entrance, he is confronted by wife Carter, who is very much awake and waiting. To his great relief, Fields discovers that Carter has not been pacing the floor and waiting for him, but their daughter, Marsh, who is out too late once again with playboy Crabbe, and who is the scion of a millionaire family. When Marsh finally returns home, she exuberantly announces that she is now engaged to Crabbe. This news brings no joy to either Fields or Carter as they know their financial problems do not put them into the same class as Crabbe's upper-class family. Howard, who is Crabbe's mother, wants nothing to do with Fields, thinking him to be a worthless loafer, a negative opinion shared by Carter, who believes her husband wastes his time in creating gadgets and devices that never work and that he is not smart enough to put on the kind of social airs that might accept them into high society. Nevertheless, the undaunted Fields desperately attempts to create an invention that will make him and his family as rich as those of his intended son-in-law. He invents a puncture-proof tire that will revolutionize the auto industry (something today's drivers take for granted). A leading tire company invites Fields to its headquarters to demonstrate his new tires. He arrives in his car, one that has four of those new supposedly indestructible tires, parking it in front of the company headquarters building, but makes the mistake of parking in a no-parking zone. He enters the office of the National Tire Company to discuss his invention with corporate executives, headed by Irving, who is president of the firm. Fields then invites Irving and his associates outside to see a demonstration where he plans to shoot at his tires and catch the ricocheting bullets with a baseball glove. Fields fires a shot into one tire and he is shocked to see it deflate. He fires another shot into a second tire and that, too, deflates. Fields is nonplussed, not realizing that he is not shooting at the tires of his own car. While he was conversing inside the office building, a police car moved his car out of its parking place and, in the process, left the police car, which is identical to Fields' auto, in its place. Police officers returning to their car see Fields' destruction of their tires and immediately pursue him (in what is a duplication of the Keystone Kops routine of the silent film era). Taking the train home, Fields is so despondent that he thinks to drink a bottle of iodine to commit suicide, so as not to further embarrass his daughter Marsh. He pours some of the iodine onto a spoon, but it spills before he can swallow the lethal fluid, not realizing that he has used his own invention, a collapsible spoon. He looks upon this as a providential warning. A short time later, he sees pretty young Ames in a different compartment on board the train; she is about to also use some iodine for what he thinks is the same fatal purpose, but she intends to use it for a small cut. He rushes into her compartment and smashes the bottle and then tells her his own woes and that no matter how many problems in life one might encounter, preserving your life is more important at all costs. "When you wake up in the morning and find yourself dead," he intones, "you'll regret it." Ames is deeply touched by Fields' sincere concern over her and she decides to help him out of his troubles. Unknown to Fields is the fact that Ames is a real-life princess from a foreign land who is making a state visit to the U.S. Ames then arrives in Fields' hometown with great pomp and circumstance as the celebrated princess. The first thing she publicly states is that she must see Fields, a great man, who has saved her life. The local bigwigs, including Crabbe and his snooty family, are aghast that such an international celebrity is indebted to and has such deep affection for Fields, who has otherwise been looked upon as a shiftless no-account. When Ames goes to the Fields residence, she tells his wife,

Adrienne Ames and W.C. Fields in *You're Telling Me!*, 1934.

Carter: "you're the luckiest woman in the world." Carter replies with a sour face: "Is my husband dead?" Fields is suddenly the center of everybody's attention, gaining enormous respect. He believes that Ames is merely returning a favor by pretending to be a princess and he congratulates her on her disguise and convincing everyone with her sham. Town officials now consider Fields one of their most prominent citizens and invite him to host the opening of the town's new golf course. Meanwhile, Irving, the president of the tire firm, has seen Fields' car and tested its tires to see that they are, indeed, puncture proof. Irving is now desperately searching for Fields to make a deal with him for his marvelous invention. By this time, Fields is pompously officiating at the opening of the new golf course and is the first person to tee off. He goes into his patented golf routine (incorporating and reprising his antics that had appeared in Fields' silent feature, **So's Your Old Man**, 1926, and the sound short, **The Golf Specialist**, 1930) while Crabbe, Marsh and Ames stand by. He has Young as his inept and moronic caddy, who keeps supplying Fields with unwieldy or gerrymandered golf clubs, and the overconfident Fields booms to his friends and foes: "Stand clear and keep your eye on the ball!" At that moment, Irving arrives to tell Fields that his own experts at his tire company have tested the tires on Fields' car and that he wants to purchase the invention. He offers Fields $20,000, but the helpful Ames steps forth and states that she wants to buy the patent for Fields' invention, and Irving then gets into a bidding war with Ames. The frustrated Irving offers Fields $1 million and a royalty payment for the sale of each and every one of his impregnable tires, and the astounded Fields finally accepts. (This scene somewhat repeats Fields' other comedy classic of the same year, **It's a Gift**, 1934, where he buys unseen a dilapidated orange grove in California, but is tipped off by a helpful neighbor that a consortium must buy the property for a new sports arena and where Fields negotiates a fabulous offer before selling the property.) Now wealthy and with Marsh happily married to Crabbe, and his own future comfortably secure and his reputation from loafer to stellar citizen is established, Fields bids a fond farewell to Ames, still not knowing that she is truly a princess and believing that she has been putting on an act all along. He praises her for "putting one over" on the entire community. Before she drives off and Fields happily strolls away, Ames smiles and says: "You're telling me!" Brilliantly written by Fields, McAvoy and others, the story is more complex and linear than what most of Fields' other films offer, allowing him many opportunities to demonstrate his unique comedic routines as well as provide some dramatic scenes where Fields is both sensitive and effectively serious. The scene where Fields considers suicide is a startling mixture of drama and comedy, pathos and humor, and the viewer is torn between weeping and laughing. The gifted Fields demonstrates a moving depth of feeling, espe-

Meg Ryan and Tom Hanks in *You've Got Mail,* **1998.**

cially when pleading with Ames not to take her life, showing the kind of compassion not seen in his other films. Like some of Fields' other opuses, especially **It's a Gift,** he is again a much-harassed and henpecked husband. At one point, he tells daughter Marsh as she contemplates marriage with Crabbe: "Pick and choose, dear. Liberty is sweet. Once you're married, it's just like being in jail." The film was a great success at the box office and furthered Fields' career. Song: "Sympathizin' with Me" (music: Arthur Johnston; lyrics: Sam Coslow). *Author's Note*: Fields was a man who husbanded all of his ideas and found ways to work them into all of his films. In this film he talks about the possibility of catching burglars in the basement of his house and befriending them through social drinking, the very scene Fields would employ the next year in his film **Man on the Flying Trapeze,** 1935. The ever-alert Fields noticed that one of the characters in this film was named Charlie Bogle, and he appropriated that name when later using it many times as a pseudonym when writing scripts for his future films. Part of this film was shot on location in Sierra Madre, a town located in Los Angeles County, where local residents attempted to blackmail producers. They demanded that they be paid in order to keep the peace and intimidated the producers by playing loud music and creating other outlandish rackets. Residents organized gangs of children that ran screaming through areas that were being filmed and send packs of dogs barking and howling as they raced through the streets with tin cans tied to their tails. Sierra Madre was thereafter blacklisted as a possible location for any film. Song: "Sympathizin' with Me" (Arthur Johnston, Sam Coslow). **p,** William LeBaron; **d,** Erle C. Kenton; **cast,** W.C. Fields, Joan Marsh, Larry "Buster" Crabbe, Adrienne Ames, Louise Carter, Kathleen Howard, Tammany Young, Dell Henderson, James B. "Pop" Kenton, Robert McKenzie, George Irving, Nora Cecil; **w,** Walter DeLeon, Paul M. Jones, J.P. McEvoy (based on the story "Mr. Bisbee's Princess" by Julian Street); **c,** Alfred Gilks; **m,** John Leipold, Tom Satterfield; **ed,** Otho Lovering; **art d,** Hans Dreier, Robert Odell.

Yours, Mine and Ours ★★★ 1968; U.S.; 116m; Walt Disney/Buena Vista; Color; Comedy; Children: Unacceptable (MPAA: PG); **DVD**; **VHS**; **IV**. Delightful comedy has Fonda as a widower with ten children, who marries Ball, a widow with eight children and they all live together as one big happy family, or that is the plan. Fonda, a U.S. Navy officer, and Ball, a nurse, spend most of their time refereeing internecine family battles. Even in a big house there never seems to be enough bedrooms or bathrooms and it's a chore to make eighteen school lunches. Family resentments and squabbles subside when Ball's son, Shea, comes to idolize Matthieson, Fonda's eldest son, especially when Matthieson goes off to war and a new blessed event is coming. It's an often hilarious family-friendly comedy with the two stars giving entertaining perform-

ances. The film proved to be a great box office success, earning more than $25.9 million against a budget of $2.5 million. So successful was this film that it led to the creation of the TV series **The Brady Bunch**, 1969-1974. *Author's Note*: The story was inspired by the real-life family of Frank and Helen Beardsley, both widowed and having eighteen children between them, and two more children were added through their marriage. Fonda told this author that "I had appeared with Lucy [Lucille Ball] almost twenty-five years earlier in another picture called **The Big Street** [1942, which was Ball's favorite film]. She was terrific then and she was the same great personality when we made **Yours, Mine and Ours**. By that time she was known as a comedy star, but she was also a very good dramatic actress. To play good comedy, you must understand and be more than able to undertake dramatic roles. She has always understood that and her fine performances in both areas prove it." Fred MacMurray was originally slated to play Ball's husband in this film, but he had to drop out and was replaced by Fonda, who eagerly embraced the role. Produced by Ball's Desilu Productions (with one-time husband Desi Arnaz, a Cuban singer and actor), this film made more money than the comedienne ever anticipated in that she had not provided for any personal tax shelters when undertaking the project. The millions of profit the film produced mostly went to taxes other than into her personal account, which caused Ball to express anger, mostly against herself. **p,** Robert F. Blumofe; **d,** Melville Shavelson; **cast,** Lucille Ball, Henry Fonda, Van Johnson, Louise Troy, Sidney Miller, Tom Bosley, Nancy Howard, Walter Brooke, Tim Matthieson (Matheson), Gil Rogers, Jennifer Leak; **w,** Shavelson, Mort Lachman (based on the story by Madelyn Davis, Bob Carroll, Jr., from the book *Who Gets the Drumsticks?* by Helen Eileen Beardsley); **c,** Charles F. Wheeler (DeLuxe Color); **m,** Fred Karlin; **ed,** Stuart Gilmore; **art d,** Arthur Lonergan; **set d,** James Payne.

You've Got Mail ★★★ 1998; U.S.; 107m; UNIV; Color; Comedy/Romance; Children: Unacceptable (MPAA: PG-13); **BD**; **DVD**; **VHS**; **IV**. Entertaining tale opens with Ryan, who is the owner of a small New York City bookstore called "The Shop around the Corner" that is close to going out of business. Her boyfriend, Kinnear, is a leftist newspaper writer always rooting for the underdog. While he is busy at his typewriter, Ryan spends a lot of time on her laptop computer looking at her e-mail. Using the screen name "Shopgirl," she reads an e-mail from "NY152," the screen name of Hanks. His family operates Fox Books, a chain of mega bookstores. They frequent the same neighborhoods and pass each other on their ways to work, and finally meet when he takes his divorced brother's two children to her bookstore for a story time. Ryan tells Hanks she has fears about a new big bookstore opening soon just around the corner from her own small operation. That threatening firm, of course, is the very bookstore chain owned by Hanks' family. Hanks and Ryan meet again at a publishing party where Ryan discovers Hank's family connection. She then begins a media war, boycotting Fox Books. While this is going on, both are corresponding via e-mail and getting interested in each other. Hanks knows who Ryan really is, but she doesn't know he is Mr. Fox Books. He arranges to meet her at a café as she is "Shopgirl" and neither is happy with the meeting. Ryan breaks up with Kinnear, and Hanks and Ryan begin dating. It all ends well with both falling in love with each other, despite the e-mail dating and misunderstandings. The loveable catalyst that brings them permanently together at Riverside Park is Hanks' dog, and Ryan finally admits that she hoped all along that "NY152" would turn out to be Hanks. The acting is top notch, and the gifted Ephron moves this delightful story along at a fast clip, presenting enough obstacles for the hoped for lover to overcome. Some of the scenes become a little too precious, but the fine acting overrides these annoyances. The film was a great success at the box office, earning more than $250 million in its initial release against a budget of $65 million. The film is an updated version of **The Shop around the Corner**, 1941, and the 1949 musical remake **In the Good Old Summertime**. Songs: "The Puppy Song," "Remember," "I Guess the Lord Must Be in New York City" (Harry Nilsson); "Dreams" (Noel Hogan, Dolores O'Riordan); "Rockin' Robin" (Leon Rene as Jimmie Thomas); "Never Smile at a Crocodile" (Frank Churchill, Jack Lawrence); "Splish Splash" (Bobby Darin, Jean Murray); "Dummy Song" (Lew Brown, Billy Rose, Ray Henderson); "Tomorrow" (Charles Strouse, Martin Charnin); "River," "Both Sides Now" (Joni Mitchell); "Dream" (Johnny Mercer); "Lonely at the Top" (Randy Newman); "Signed Sealed Delivered I'm Yours" (Steve Wonder, Syreeta Wright, Lee Garrett, Lula Mae Hardaway); "Over the Rainbow" (E.Y. Harburg, Harold Arlen); "Anyone at All" (Carole King, Carole Bayer Sager); "I'm Gonna Sit Right Down and Write Myself a Letter" (Joe Young, Fred E. Albert); "The Instrument Song" (traditional); "Let's All Go to the Lobby," "Westminster Quarters" (traditional). *Author's Note*: The film was shot on location through NYC's Upper West Side. The bookstore operated by Ryan was actually the Cheese and Antique Shop owned by Maya Sharper, which was rented by the producers. The owner took a vacation while the shop was remodeled as a bookstore and then restored to its original state when the production was over. The shop was selected for its "homey and quaint" look that best suited the children's bookstore operated by Ryan. **p**, Nora Ephron, Lauren Shuler Donner, Donald J. Lee Jr.; **d**, Nora Ephron; **cast**, Tom Hanks, Meg Ryan, Greg Kinnear, Parker Posey, Jean Stapleton, Steve Zahn, Heather Burns, Dave Chappelle, Dabney Coleman, John Randolph, Hallee Hirsh; **w**, Nora Ephron, Delia Ephron (based on the play "Parfumerie" by Nikolaus Laszlo); **c**, John Lindley; **m**, George Fenton; **ed**, Richard Marks; **prod d**, Dan Davis; **art d**, Ray Kluga, Beth Kuhn; **set d**, Susan Bode, Ellen Christiansen; **spec eff**, J.C. Brotherhood, Steve Kirshoff.

Z ★★★★ 1969; France/Algeria; 127m; Raggane-Valoria Films/Cinema 5 Distributing; Color; Drama; Children: Unacceptable (MPAA: M); **BD**; **DVD**; **VHS**; **IV**. Masterful political thriller from Costa-Garvas begins at a lecture hall where a speaker drones on and on about a country's (ostensibly Greece) agricultural policy, which is accompanied by an equally dull slide show. The lecture in the large meeting hall is suddenly interrupted by the leader of the military police that enforces the dictates of right-wing government leader Dux. He states in bombastic and impassioned terms how the government is presently combating the evils of leftism. This interruption causes Montand, a government deputy and leader of the left-wing element of the government, to hold his meeting in a smaller hall. Montand obtains permission to hold this meeting only after appealing to Dux, who allows him to hold his meeting in a small lecture room having only 200 seats. Realizing that more than 4,000 of his followers are expected for this meeting, Montand requests that a loudspeaker system be installed so that his address can be heard by those standing outside the hall. At the same time Montand finally conducts his speech, he realizes that he is now competing with the premiere performance of the Bolshoi Ballet to which all of the city's high society and political bigwigs are attending. Meanwhile, outside the hall, Montand's peace-abiding supporters are harassed and insulted by members of a right-wing faction while the police, who are present to maintain order, do nothing to stop the violent right wingers. Montand begins delivering his speech, but an opponent sneaks up behind him and clubs him on the head. The opponent is seized and hustled away and Montand recovers enough to continue speaking, but the loudspeakers are then cut off and Montand goes into the street to find out why he has been prevented from concluding his address. As he crosses a street from the hall, a speeding truck narrowly misses him, and one of its occupants leans forward, clubbing Montand on the head; Montand falls unconscious. He is taken to a hospital and where Papas, his wife, soon arrives to be with her husband. While physicians attend to Montand, Dux pretends to be concerned about the incident, appointing Trintignant as a special investigator to look into the matter. Trintignant, who is thought to be nothing more than a slavish pawn of the right-wing government, begins to ques-

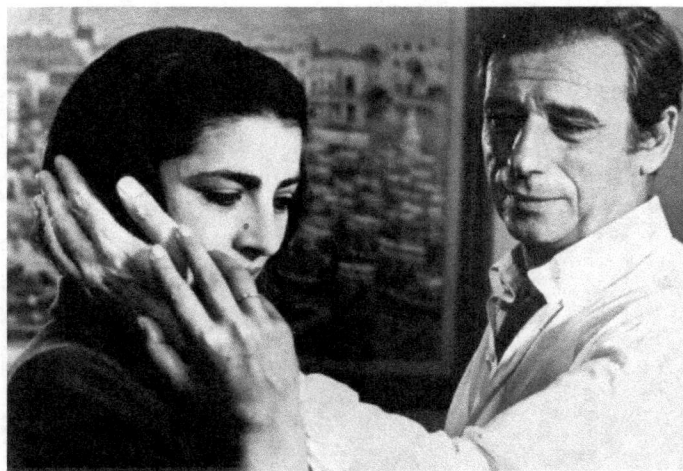

Irene Papas and Yves Montand in *Z*, 1969.

tion the report that states that Montand was "accidentally" struck in a hit-and-run incident. Witnesses come forward to insist that Montand was struck by a drunk driver and that Montand injured himself when his head struck the pavement, but Trintignant concludes that all of these eyewitness accounts have been manufactured by stooges of the government. By this time, doctors report that, despite their considerable efforts to save Montand, he has died from his head injury. Trintignant then obtains the autopsy performed on the dead Montand, and it proves that he died by being struck on the head. Further, Trintignant gets help from Perrin, a photojournalist, and Geret, a courageous informant, that allows him to learn that Montand was assassinated in a carefully planned execution by a secret rightwing-group called C.R.O.C., which stands for "Royalist Forces of the Christian West" and has strong ties to Dux and his hierarchy. Dux and his henchman pressure Trintignant to abandon his investigation, but he shocks his superiors when he defies Dux's corrupt fascist regime. He publicly announces that Montand's death was part of a conspiracy led by members of the government and he indicts several officials, including the very general who appointed him to his investigative post. Papas is told that her husband has not died in vain and that his wrongful death is being exposed. The film ends, however, where evil, not good, triumphs. A TV report states that, following the indictments, a military force has engineered a coup that takes over the government and that a fascist regime now controls the country with an iron fist. Witnesses that have worked with Trintignant have mysteriously vanished or have been killed. Trintignant is removed from his office and Perrin is jailed for disclosing official documents. All of those officials who have been earlier indicted have received full pardons from the military junta in power. Further, strict bans have been enforced against any peace movements, such as that led by Montand, along with the wearing of long hair, listening to the Beatles, and, especially, the letter "Z," which represents the slain Montand and symbolically means "He is Alive." Costa-Gravas directs this riveting and powerful film with a firm hand, building tension by increasing the speed of his scenes through accelerated cross-cutting and where the action accordingly keeps pace with that technique. The lensing from Coutard aids this technique with its fluid and sweeping coverage of events, and where the score from Theodorakis provides just the right discordant passages to emphasize and sometimes telescope the sinister events that unfold. Montand, Papas, Trintignant, Perrin, Geret, Dux and others are outstanding in their captivating roles. The film received an Oscar for Best Foreign Language Film and Best Film Editing (Bonnot), and it received Oscar nominations for Best Film; Best Director (Costa-Gravas); and Best Adapted Screenplay (Semprun, Costa-Garvas). The film was a huge success at the box office, earning more than $14.3 million in its initial release, becoming the fourth largest grossing film in France for 1969, and the twelfth

Jonah Bobo in *Zathura: A Space Adventure*, 2005.

largest grossing film in the U.S. in the same year. Song: "Messe pour le temps Present—psyche rock" (Pierre Henry). ***Author's Note***: The film is rooted to the assassination of leftist Greek politician Gregoris Lambrakis (1912-1963), who opposed the military regime in Greece and, after delivering an anti-war speech in Thessaloniki, was struck on the head by two men driving a truck, on May 22, 1963; he died from those head injuries five days later. Lambrakis is certainly the role model for the character so superbly played by Montand. Costa-Garvas, the son of a liberal activist in Greece, had long wanted to make a film about this political martyr and, after the Vassilikos novel appeared, immediately acquired its rights and went into production with this outstanding film. (In French; English subtitles in some U.S. releases.) **p**, Jacques Perrin, Ahmed Rachedi; **d**, Costa-Gavras; **cast**, Yves Montand, Irene Papas, Jean-Louis Trintignant, Perrin, Charles Denner, Francois Perier, Pierre Dux, Georges Geret, Bernard Fresson, Renato Salvatori; **w**, Costa-Gavras, Jorge Semprun (based on the novel by Vassili Vassilikos); **c**, Raoul Coutard (Technicolor); **m**, Mikis Theodorakis; **ed**, Francoise Bonnot; **prod d** & **set d**, Jacques D'Ovidio.

Zathura: A Space Adventure ★★★ 2005; U.S.; 113m; COL; Comedy/Fantasy; Children: Unacceptable (MPAA: PG); **DVD**; **IV**. Bobo and Hutcherson are brothers who are always at odds with each other while driving their parents crazy as their older sister, Stewart, tries to ignore them. The boys try to settle their differences by playing an old mechanical board game called Zathura. After their very first move, the game transports them and Stewart and the house into outer space. They believe the only way they can get back home is to finish the game, but, with every new move, more dangers challenge them. They are harassed by Oz, a defective robot, and a bevy of reptilian aliens. A stranded robot, Shepard, attempts to help them, explaining that he and his brother had played the game and, after Shepard wished his brother away, he was left alone with the entrapping game. While evading the aliens throughout the house, the boys learn that the game they are playing is really a black hole in space that has sucked them and their house into its void, and, at the end, returns them to earth just as their parents arrive. Playing the game teaches the brothers to cooperate and they learn they are important to each other. The appeal of this innovate film is its stunning special effects, albeit the film did not do as well as expected at the box office, earning about $64 million in its initial release against a budget of $65 million. Songs: "Hey Man" (The Vacancies), "SportsCenter Theme" (John Colby), "Slippin" (Tom Hammer), "Tidal" (Jay Skinner), "Numb" (Bonnie Borst, Andy Zulla, Tiff Eaves, Sam Schlesinger), "Can't Be Bothered" (Kate Turley, Graham Turley), "Loves Me Like a Rock" (Paul Simon). A good adventure film but rated PG for fantasy action and peril, language. **p**, Michael De Luca, Scott Kroopf, William Teitler,

Peter Billingsley; **d**, Jon Favreau; **cast**, Jonah Bobo, Josh Hutcherson, Dax Shepard, Kristen Stewart, Tim Robbins, Frank Oz, John Alexander, Derek Mears, Douglas Tait, Joe Bucaro, Jeff Wolfe; **w**, David Koepp, John Kamps (based on the book by Chris Van Allsburg); **c**, Guillermo Navarro; **m**, John Debney; **ed**, Dan Lebental; **prod d**, J. Michael Riva; **art d**, David Klassen, Richard F. Mays; **set d**, Lauri Gaffin; **spec eff**, Joe Bauer, Greg Baxter.

Zazie dans le metro ★★★ 1961; France/Italy; 89m; Nouvelles Editions de Films; Astor Pictures; Color; Comedy; Children: Acceptable; **BD**; **DVD**; **VHS**. Cute and enjoyable family tale begins when her mother goes off with a new boyfriend and eleven-year-old Zazie, played by Demongeot, is compelled to stay two days with her uncle, Noiret, in Paris. Demongeot goes off to explore the city on her own, but is kept from riding the subway because of a strike by the Paris Metro. She nonetheless takes Noiret on a merry chase throughout the city, and, at one point when in pursuit of her, he is compelled to parachute from the Eiffel Tower with a balloon. The strike ends and Demongeot finally gets to ride the subway, but she is so worn out by her own exploits that she falls asleep in her seat on the way back home and misses most of the ride. This is an early and very entertaining outing from the gifted Malle, who would go on to produce **Atlantic City**, 1980. (In French; English subtitles.) **p&d**, Louis Malle; **cast**, Catherine Demongeot, Philippe Noiret, Hubert Deschamps, Carla Marlier, Annie Fratellini, Vittorio Caprioli, Jacques Dufilho, Yvonne Clech, Odette Piquet, Nicolas Bataille; **w**, Malle, Jean-Paul Rappeneau (based on the novel *Zazie dans le metro* by Raymond Queneau); **c**, Henri Raichi; **m**, Fiorenzo Carpi, Andre Pontin; **ed**, Kenout Peltier; **prod d**, Bernard Evein.

Zelary ★★★ 2003; Czech Republic/Slovakia/Austria; 150m; ALEF Film & Media Group/Sony; Color; Drama; Children: Unacceptable (MPAA: R); **DVD**; **VHS**. Geislerova, a medical student in Prague in the early 1940s, has her training interrupted by the Nazi occupation of Czechoslovakia during World War II (1939-1945). She is discovered as a resistance worker and is sent to Zelary, a remote mountain village in the country, to marry an uneducated sawmill worker, Cserhalmi. She is more cultured than the simple man she marries but comes to love him as Russian troops, not the Germans, march into the village. The film is actually an episodic portrayal of many of the villagers living in the small community and how they relate to each other. This well-made and exceptionally enacted film was deservedly nominated for an Oscar as Best Foreign Language Film. Violence and sexual themes prevent viewing by children. Songs: "The Moon" (Petr Ostrouchov), "Zakazane ovoce" (George Voskovec, Jan Werich). **p**, Ondrej Trojan, Helena Uldrichova, Pavel Borovan, Danny Krausz, Jaroslav Kucera, Kurt Stocker, Marian Urban; **d**, Trojan; **cast**, Anna Geislerova, Gyorgy Cserhalmi, Jaroslava Adamova, Miroslav Donutil, Jaroslav Dusek, Iva Bittova, Ivan Trojan, Jan Hrusinsky, Tomas Zatecka, Anna Vertelarova; **w**, Petr Jarchovsky (based on the novel *Jozova Hanule* by Kveta Legatova); **c**, Asen Sopov; **m**, Petdr Ostrouchov; **ed**, Vladimir Barak; **prod d**, Milan Bycek; **spec eff**, Vit Komrzy, Jan Vseticek.

Zelig ★★★1983; U.S.; 80m; Orion/WB; B/W/Color; Comedy; Children: Cautionary (MPAA: PG); **DVD**; **VHS**. Offbeat and weird, Allen offers a zany docudrama (or mockumentary) that purports to chronicle the life of a chameleon-like personality, Zelig, played by his inimitable self, who is all persons to all people and who seems to know everyone of note on the planet. Set in the Great Depression of the 1930s, a narrator tells the story of Leonard Zelig (Allen) and how he has the amazing ability to adapt and be accepted at all levels of society. He is shown being accepted at a party by a bevy of affluent Republicans, but, when he slips into the kitchen to mingle with the household help, he becomes unsophisticated and speaks the argot of the uneducated and all believe him to be a Democrat. In what are assimilated newsreel clips, Allen is shown standing in the deck circle of a baseball field as he waits for New

York Yankee slugger Babe Ruth (1895-1948) to go to the plate before a new cut shows him transforming into an Oriental, a black man, and then a long-bearded Hassidic rabbi. Farrow, a psychiatrist, watches some of these newsreels and becomes fascinated with the multiple personalities Allen so rapidly represents. She interviews him and then hypnotizes him to discover that Allen's myriad transformations are the result of his craving to be loved by anyone and everyone. Allen becomes a one-man national craze as songs are based upon him and sung everywhere. Warner Brothers produces a biopic about him, and he inspires a new dance that is named after him. Meanwhile, Allen is shown with scores of real-life celebrities from the political, sports and movie worlds that emulate the newsreels of the 1930s (and copies the same technique as can be seen in Orson Welles' **Citizen Kane**, 1941, where Welles' character appears with international figures such as Benito Mussolini, 1883-1945, and Adolf Hitler, 1889-1945). Color montages are then interspersed between these newsreel clips to show Dr. Bruno Bettelheim, Susan Sontag, Irving Howe, Saul Bellow and other celebrities attempting to make cogent comments about this amazing man, who, according to Bettelheim, is not amazing at all, but who considers him "the ultimate conformist." Even though Farrow falls in love with Allen, the fickle man goes off with another woman. Allen vanishes, but Farrow learns that he is in Germany and has reportedly become a fanatical Nazi and a close adviser to Adolf Hitler (this prior to the outbreak of WWII, 1939-1945). Farrow goes to Germany and finds Allen there, discovering that he wants to escape the fascist country and they both flee. Reaching safety, they marry, and resume residence in the U.S., where both have been hailed as heroes. The film is entertaining, and Allen's throwaway gags are in full force, but the use of the old newsreel clips is done to such excess that this technique somewhat tires the viewer through repetition. Allen is at his nerdy best and the fetching Farrow the most believable as she rattles off her psychiatric discourses while carnally coveting the myopic twerp who obsesses her. The rest of the cast, professional actors and famous pe0ple, appear serious and straight-faced with strictly tongue-in-cheek cameos. The film received Oscar nominations for Best Cinematography (Willis) and Best Costume Design (Santo Loquasto). It fared moderately at the box office, earning more than $11.7 million. Songs: "Leonard the Lizard," "Doin' the Chameleon," "Chameleon Days," "You May Be Six People, But I Love You," "Reptile Eyes," "The Changing Man Concerto" (all 1983; Dick Hyman); "I've Got a Feeling I'm Falling" (1929; music: Thomas "Fats" Waller, Harry Link; lyrics: Billy Rose); "I'm Sitting on Top of the World" (1925; music: Ray Henderson; lyrics: Samuel M. Lewis, Joe Young); "Ain't We Got Fun" (1921; music: Richard A. Whiting; lyrics: Raymond B. Egan, Gus Kahn); "Sunny Side Up" (1929; music: Ray Henderson; lyrics: Lew Brown, Buddy De Sylva); "I'll Get By" (1928; music: Fred E. Ahlert; lyrics: Roy Turk); "I Love My Baby, My Baby Loves Me" (1925; music: Harry Warren; lyrics: Bud Green); "Runnin' Wild" (1922; music: A.H. Gibbs; lyrics: Joe Grey, Leo Wood); "A Sailboat in the Moonlight" (1937; Carmen Lombardo, John Jacob Loeb); "Charleston" (1923; music: James P. Johnson; lyrics: Cecil Mack); "Chicago (That Toddling Town)" (1922; Fred Fisher); "Five Feet Two, Eyes of Blue" (1925; music: Ray Henderson; lyrics: Samuel M. Lewis, Joe Young); "Anchors Aweigh" (1906; music: Charles A. Zimmerman; lyrics: Alfred Hart Miles; music modified [1950]: Dominico Savino; additional lyrics [1950]: George D. Lottman); "Take Me Out to the Ballgame" (1906; Albert von Tilzer); "The Internationale" (1888; Pierre Degeyter). *Author's Note*: The most appealing aspects of this strange film are the visual marvels achieved by Willis while merging live-action shots of Allen with historic personalities appearing in the newsreels of the 1920s and 1930s, this being accomplished through the then extant bluescreen technology. The same technology was applied to another film of that era, **Dead Men Don't Wear Plaid**, 1982, but where the leading actor was merged as new footage into black-and-white archival footage from feature film noir productions of the 1940s. The same approach was taken in the making of **Forrest Gump**, 1994, but where that character, essayed by Tom Hanks, was incorporated into

Woody Allen and Herbert Hoover in *Zelig*, 1983.

color archival footage through the more modern process of digital technology. The brief clip showing novelist F. Scott Fitzgerald in this film is most likely the only clip extant of this great author. Other films profiling those with multiple personalities include **All around the Town**, 2002 (made-for-TV); **Angel's Dance**, 1999; **The Befallen**, 2003 (TV miniseries); **Bewitched**, 1945; **Color of Night**, 1994; **Dark Corners**, 2006; **Dear Diary**, 1989; **Dr. Jekyll and Mr. Hyde**, 1920; **Dr. Jekyll and Mr. Hyde**, 1931; **Dr. Jekyll and Mr. Hyde**, 1941; **Dorothy Mills**, 2008; **Eden Log**, 2007; **Femme Fatale**, 1991; **The Five of Me**, 1981 (made-for-TV); **Flirting with Danger**, 2006 (made-for-TV); **Frankie & Alice**, 2010; **H**, 2002; **Hangover Square**, 1945; **Hangover Square**, 2009; **Her Deadly Rival**, 1995 (made-for-TV); **Heroes**, 2006-2010 (TV series); **A History of Violence**, 2005; **House of Dust**, 2013; **I'm Not There**, 2007; **Identity**, 2003; **Keep My Grave Open**, 1976; **Keiho**, 1999; **Lizzie**, 1957; **Loose Cannons**, 1990; **Mad Detective**, 2008; **Madonna of the Seven Moons**, 1945; **Me Myself and I**, 1992; **Me, Myself & Irene**, 2000; **Mirage**, 1965; **Mirage**, 1995; **Never Talk to Strangers**, 1995; **9**, 2009; **The Nines**, 2007; **Norma Jean & Marilyn**, 1996 (made-for-TV); **On the Count of Zero**, 2007; **One Life to Live**, 1968-2013 (TV series); **Passion of the Mind**, 2000; **Primal Fear**, 1996; **Psycho**, 1960; **Psycho**, 1998; **Psycho Beach Party**, 2000; **Raising Cain**, 1992; **Rampage: The Hillside Strangler Murders**, 2006; **A Reflection of Fear**, 1992; **The Scribbler**, 2014; **Secret Window**, 2004; **Session 9**, 2001; **Shattered Image**, 1998; **6 Souls**, 2010; **Ski Patrol**, 1990; **Sybil**, 1976 (TV miniseries); **The Terror Inside**, 1996 (made-for-TV); **Thr3e**, 2007; **The Three Faces of Eve**, 1957; **Three Lives and Only One Death**, 1997; **Twin Peaks**, 1990-1991 (TV series); **Twin Peaks: Fire Walk with Me**, 1992; **United States of Tara**, 2009-2011 (TV series); **Voice**, 2005; **Voices Within: The Lives of Truddi Chase**, 1990 (made-for-TV); and **Wicked Wicked Games**, 2006- (TV series). **p**, Robert Greenhut; **d&w**, Woody Allen; **cast**, Allen, Mia Farrow, John Buckwalter, Mavtin Chatinover, Stanley Swerdlow, Paul Nevens, Howard Erskine, George Hamlin, Ralph Bell, Richard Whiting, Patrick Horgan (narrator); **c**, Gordon Willis; **m**, Dick Hyman; **ed**, Susan E. Morse; **prod d**, Mel Bourne; **art d**, Speed Hopkins; **set d**, Les Bloom, Janet Rosenbloom; **spec eff**, Stuart Robertson.

Zeppelin ★★★ 1971; U.K.; 100m; Getty+Fromkess Corp./WB; Color; War Drama; Children: Unacceptable (MPAA: PG); **DVD**. This exciting tale takes place during World War I (1914-1918), where York, a Scottish officer of German descent, is a lieutenant in the British army. He meets Stewart, a beautiful German spy, and falls in love with her. She suggests that he escape to Germany to reunite with his family and friends. He reports this to his commanding officer, Davies, who also wants York to go to Germany on a secret mission to steal information on a new type

Gene Kelly and Fred Astaire in *Ziegfeld Follies*, 1945.

of zeppelin under development there. York goes to Germany under the pretense of being a deserter, convincing Germans of his loyalty. He arrives at the airport where the zeppelin is being kept and meets a long-time friend, Goring, a professor, who has a beautiful, much younger wife, Sommer. Diffring, a German intelligence colonel, insists that York be on board the zeppelin when it takes part in a military operation. This involves stealing many British historical documents, including the *Magna Carta* from its secret storage at Balcoven Castle in Scotland by a team of German soldiers using the zeppelin. After refueling in Norway, the zeppelin, with York aboard, takes on some German soldiers, and the airship proceeds to Balcoven Castle. York enters the castle with the German raiding party, but slips away in the dark and finds the castle's communications room. A radio operator thinks he's a spy and shoots him in an arm. The British admiralty dispatches several squadrons of aircraft and ground troops to the castle. The Germans retreat rather than risk losing the zeppelin, but some pursuing British planes damage it. The zeppelin's pilot manages to crash it near the coast of neutral Holland. York, Sommer, and the surviving crew members land in shallow water and make their way to the shore as the zeppelin explodes behind them. York is exceptional as the bogus British deserter, receiving strong support from Sommer, Goring and the rest of the cast. Of particular note is the use of the zeppelin, a giant airship that is a wonder to behold. The film did well at the box office and was remade again in 1981. *Author's Note*: Exterior shots of the zeppelin were made of models constructed at 37'x17', which duplicates the *R33* British airship and the captured German *LZ76* zeppelin of WWI. Close-ups and interiors were shot of a control car and cabins copied from the original *R33*, its blueprints furnished by the British Air Museum for this production. During the aerial filming, a flown replica of a WWI fighter plane collided with a helicopter that was filming the action, and four of the camera crew members were killed. Other films that profile dirigibles include **The Airship**, 1994; **Around the World in 80 Days**, 1989 (TV miniseries); **The Assassination Bureau**, 1969; **Batman: The Animated Series**, 1992-1995 (TV series); **British Intelligence**, 1940; **Buck Rogers**, 1939 (serial); **Buck Rogers**, 1977 (edited version of 1939 serial); **Charlie Chan at the Olympics**, 1937; **The Court Martial of Billy Mitchell**, 1955; **Darling Lili**, 1970; **The Desert Fox: The Story of Rommel**, 1951; **Devil Dogs of the Air**, 1935; **Dirigible**, 1931; **Equilibrium**, 2002; **The Fabulous World of Jules Verne**, 1961; **The Fighting Devil Dogs**, 1938 (serial); **Fly Away Baby**, 1937; **Flyboys**, 2008; **The Go Getter**, 1937; **The Golden Compass**, 2007; **The Great Love**, 1918; **Hell Divers**, 1931; **Hell's Angels**, 1930; **Here Comes the Navy**, 1934; **The Hindenburg**, 1975; **Hindenburg**, 2007 (made-for-TV); **Hindenburg: The Last Flight**, 2011 (made-for-TV); **Hope and Glory**, 1987; **Indiana Jones and the Last Crusade**, 1989; **The Island at the**

Top of the World, 1974; **Joe and Max**, 2002 (made-for-TV); **Kiki's Delivery Service**, 1989; **King of the Texas Rangers**, 1941 (serial); **The League of Extraordinary Gentlemen**, 2003; **The Lost Jungle**, 1934; **The Lost Zeppelin**, 1929; **The Lottery Bride**, 1930; **Madam Satan**, 1930; **Master of the World**, 1961; **Murder in the Air**, 1940; **The Red Tent**, 1971; **Riverworld**, 2010 (made-for-TV); **Robinson Crusoe of Clipper Island**, 1936 (serial); **Shanghai Knights**, 2003; **Sky Bandits**, 1986; **Sky Captain and the World of Tomorrow**, 2004; **The Sky Hawk**, 1929; **Snow White**, 2012; **Southland Tales**, 2006; **Steamboy**, 2004; **The Sum of All Fears**, 2002; **Synecdoche, New York**, 2008; **Tailspin Tommy in the Great Air Mystery**, 1935 (serial); **Thunder in the City**, 1937; **Two Years' Vacation**, 1967; **Up**, 2009; **A Very Long Engagement**, 2005; **A View to a Kill**, 1985; **Waterloo Bridge**, 1931; **Wings**, 1927; and **Zeppelin**, 1981. **p**, Owen Crump; **d**, Etienne Perier; **cast**, Michael York, Elke Sommer, Peter Carsten, Marius Goring, Anton Diffring, Andrew Keir, Rupert Davies, Alexandra Stewart, William Marlowe, Richard Hurndall; **w**, Arthur Rowe, Donald Churchill (based on a story by Owen Crump); **c**, Alan Hume (Panavision; Technicolor); **m**, Roy Budd; **ed**, John Shirley; **prod d**, Fernando Carrere; **art d**, Bert Davey; **set d**, Arthur Taksen; **spec eff**, Cliff Richardson.

Ziegfeld Follies ★★★ 1945; U.S.; 110m (original running time: 273m); MGM; Color; Musical Comedy; Children: Acceptable; **DVD**; **VHS**; **IV**. Delightful songfest begins with Powell, who plays deceased showman Florenz Ziegfeld Jr. (1867-1932), and who looks down from heaven to recall his first Broadway show, the Ziegfeld Follies of 1907. It leads him to think about producing one more show, and he ponders about who might appear in that new extravaganza. What he imagines becomes a star-filled follies to end all follies, with talent including (alphabetically) Fred Astaire, Lucille Ball, Lucille Bremer, Fanny Brice, Cyd Charisse, Judy Garland, Kathryn Grayson, Lena Horne, Gene Kelly, James Melton, Victor Moore, Virginia O'Brien, Red Skelton, and Esther Williams. The concept for the thin story line is really a good excuse to present one lavish musical ensemble after another. The film was a smash hit at the box office, earning more than $5.3 million in its initial release against a budget of $3.5 million. Songs: "Here's to the Girls" (music: Roger Edens; lyrics: Arthur Freed), "Bring on the Wonderful Men" (music: Roger Edens; lyrics: Earl K. Brent), "Libiamo ne'lieti calici" from *La Traviata* (Giuseppe Verdi), "This Heart of Mine" (music: Harry Warren; lyrics: Arthur Freed), "Love" (music: Hugh Martin; lyrics: Ralph Blane), "Limehouse Blues" (music: Philip Braham; lyrics: Douglas Furber), "A Great Lady Has an Interview" (music: Roger Edens; lyrics: Kay Thompson), "The Babbitt and the Bromide" (music: George Gershwin; lyrics: Ira Gershwin), "There's Beauty Ev'rywhere" (music: Harry Warren; lyrics: Arthur Freed), "Wot Cher! Knock'd 'em in the Old Kent Road" (music: Charles Ingle; lyrics: Albert Chevalier). *Author's Note*: Among its many highlights, this film marked the first film in which sterling dancers Astaire and Kelly appeared together (in a sequence of three scenes titled "The Babbitt and the Bromide," they challenge each other in several period dance scenes, but where one cannot top the other. They would not appear again together on the screen until the making of **That's Entertainment, Part II**, 1976. This extravaganza was created to celebrate the twentieth anniversary of MGM as a studio, which purchased the rights to Ziegfeld's story from his widow and actress Billie Burke, as well as theatrical impresario Lee Shubert, paying them $100,000. Powell told this author: "I guess I was the logical candidate to play Flo Ziegfeld in **Ziegfeld Follies** since I had played that great showman in another picture almost ten years earlier [**The Great Ziegfeld**, 1936]. I don't do a lot in that picture as I am long gone and taking it easy in a luxurious apartment in Heaven where I spend my time dreaming up my next super production. It was a terrific memory lane picture where all of Ziegfeld's stars are recalled. I remember fondly a great touch of showmanship Vincent Minnelli added and that was where he had a lot of the older lovely ladies, who had been the real

Ziegfeld Girls, parade in one spectacular number ["Bring on the Beautiful Girls"]. Ziggie would have loved that picture, or should I say, he probably looked down upon it and applauded. You know, I had a lot of reservations when I first played him. He was a complex man, not just a showman, but a man who wanted most of all to glorify women. They were all beautiful to him and he put them on pedestals as high as the one holding the Statue of Liberty. Everyone who left his theaters felt like they had been in a special place. That was part of his legend. How do you do justice to a man who can put that kind of feelings into human beings?" Freed was given more than $3 million to produce this musical epic and he spent every dime of it well with the help of MGM's best director of musicals, Minnelli, who had, early in his career, worked on some of Ziegfeld's musical revues. Minnelli tapped just about every big star on the MGM roster for this film, calling them away for their brief scenes from ongoing productions. Astaire appeared in one other sequence, but his scene was cut from the film before it was released. Astaire told this author: "I had just gotten about a half dozen vaccinations because I was about to leave on a USO tour to entertain the troops [in WWII]. When it came to do that scene with Judy Garland, I had a temperature of 102 and the huge set, which was a pile of rocks with beautiful women standing on them, went spinning around, that's how dizzy I got. They had created a lot of synthetic bubbles for that scene and the chemicals they used got all the girls sick and the cameraman fainted. The number wound up on the cutting room floor." The wonderful sequence where Astaire and Kelly dance together was taken from a 1927 routine Astaire had performed with his sister Adele in the Broadway show "Funny Face." Kelly recalled doing that number for the author, stating: "Fred [Astaire] and I got along great when we did that routine, but the producer [Freed], who doted on every scene in that picture, stopped us at one point and said: 'Look, fellas, you are so nice to each other and are willing to follow each other's style that you're missing the point. You're playing old friends, sure, but you are competing with each other throughout your lives and that competition has got to be when you dance together.' Well, we went to town with that and I guess we made our steps as competitive as we could without appearing to try to top each other. I know one thing—we both had a lot of fun doing it." Minnelli told this author: "Oh, we had so many wonderful scenes and numbers in that picture that we outdid Ziegfeld. The film ran 273 minutes when we finally put it into the can and we knew that that was way too long and we had to cut a lot of very good scenes. A lot of the comedy bits went onto the floor, along with a great scene with Fanny Brice, and we also had to cut a terrific Gershwin tune, "Liza," a scene [with singers Avon Long and Lena Horne] I liked so much that I named my daughter after it [Liza Minnelli]. But what we saved was the crème de la crème." Ziegfeld has been portrayed by many other actors in other films, including **Deep in My Heart**, 1954 (Paul Henreid); **The Eddie Cantor Story**, 1953 (William Forrest); **Ellis Island**, 1984 (TV miniseries; Julian Holloway); **Funny Girl**, 1968 (Walter Pidgeon); **The Great Ziegfeld**, 1936 (William Powell); **The Helen Morgan Story**, 1957 (Walter Woolf King); **I'll See You in My Dreams**, 1951 (William Forrest); **The Jolson Story**, 1946 (Eddie Kane); **Look for the Silver Lining**, 1949 (William Forrest); **Polly of the Follies**, 1922 (Bernard Randall); **The Story of Will Rogers**, 1952 (William Forrest); **W.C. Fields and Me**, 1976 (Paul Stewart); **Ziegfeld: The Man and His Women**, 1978 (made-for-TV; Paul Shenar). **p**, Arthur Freed; **d**, Vincente Minnelli, (not credited) Lemuel Ayers, Roy Del Ruth, Robert Lewis, George Sidney, Merrill Pye, Charles Walters; **cast**, William Powell, Edward Arnold, Marion Bell, Hume Cronyn, William Frawley, Keenan Wynn, Karin Booth, Hazel Brooks, Peter Lawford, Tommy Rall, Audrey Totter; **w**, David Freedman, Hugh Martin, Ralph Blane, John Murray Anderson, Peter Barr, Guy Bolton, Allen Boretz, Irving Brecher, Eddie Cantor, Erik Charell, Harry Crane, Roger Edens, Devery Freeman, Everett Freeman, E.Y. Harburg, Cal Howard, Al Lewis, Robert Lewis, Max Liebman, Eugene Loring, Wilkie C. Mahoney, William Noble, James O'Hanlon, Samuel Raphaelson, Philip Rapp, William Schorr, Joseph Schrank, Red

Fanny Brice and Hume Cronyn in *Ziegfeld Follies*, 1945.

Skelton, Frank Sullivan, Kay Thompson, Harry Tugend, Charles Walters, William K. Wells, George White, Edgar Allan Woolf, Joseph Erens, Edna Skelton; **c**, George Folsey, Charles Rosher, Ray June (Technicolor); **m**, Roger Edens, Lennie Hayton, Conrad Salinger; **ed**, Albert Akst; **art d**, Cedric Gibbons, Merrill Pye, Jack Martin Smith, Lemuel Ayres, Edward C. Carfagno, Harry McAfee; **set d**, Edwin B. Willis; **spec eff**, A. Arnold Gillespie, Warren Newcombe, Mark Davis.

Ziegfeld Girl ★★★ 1941; U.S.; 132m; MGM; B/W; Musical/Romance; Children: Unacceptable; **DVD**; **VHS**; **IV**. Three beautiful young women find that their lives change when they are chosen by impresario Florenz Ziegfeld Jr. (1867-1932) to become "Ziegfeld Girls" in his Broadway musicals. Garland is a singer who reluctantly leaves a father-and-daughter song-and-dance team with Winninger. Turner is a working girl who has to choose between Stewart, the poor man she loves, and millionaire Hunter. Lamarr is married to Dorn, a struggling concert violinist, who detests that she is exposing her beauty in skimpy costumes. The lives of these three fetching ladies are chronicled between musical numbers featuring a bevy of beauties. After Garland leaves her father, she meets and falls in love with Turner's brother, Cooper. Turner, who is discovered by a Ziegfeld talent scout while she works as an elevator operator, gives up her job and avidly pursues the bright lights, abandoning truck driver Stewart, a down-to-earth young fellow who only wants to marry Turner and raise a family. When Turner meets wealthy playboy Hunter, she is agog with his presents and the high life he can offer her. To compete with Hunter, Stewart awkwardly attempts to make a lot of money as a bootlegger, but that only brings misery to him as he is arrested and jailed. Lamarr, who is married to the penniless Dorn, also heads for the bright lights, leaving the man she loves behind. She soon learns that Dorn means much more to her than all the glittering life of a Ziegfeld Girl and she quits the Follies and returns to her husband, who goes on to perform as a brilliant violinist and who becomes an international sensation. Garland, too, finds happiness with Cooper, but Turner is doomed. She takes to drink and becomes an alcoholic and is dropped from the Follies. She deludes herself that she is still performing in a Ziegfeld show and, while descending the staircase of a theater lobby, falls to her death (which is left uncertain as the finale offers an upbeat Garland scene). Intriguing as the three separate stories are, the film is highlighted by the sumptuous musical ensembles offered, where scores of beautiful women parade while wearing some of the most stunning costumes ever designed. Garland and Lamarr are outstanding, and Turner renders an unexpectedly strong performance, proving she was more than just beautiful. Stewart, although he has but a few scenes, is also a standout as the stranded, sincere lover. The film proved to be a big box office hit, earning more than $3.1 million in its initial release against a budget of $1.4

Brian Cox as famed U.S. attorney Melvin Belli in *Zodiac*, 2007.

million. Songs: "You Never Looked So Beautiful" (1936; music: Walter Donaldson; lyrics: Harold Adamson), "Minnie from Trinidad" (1941; Roger Edens), "I'm Always Chasing Rainbows" (1918; music: Harry Carroll; lyrics: Joseph McCarthy), "Laugh? I Thought I'd Split My Sides" (Roger Edens), "You Stepped Out of a Dream" (music: Nacio Herb Brown; lyrics: Gus Kahn), "Whispering" (1920; music: John Schonberger; lyrics: Marvin Soberer), "Bridal Chorus" from "*Lohengrin*" (Richard Wagner), "The Wedding March" from "A Midsummer Night's Dream: (1843: Felix Mendelssohn-Bartholdy), "Caribbean Love Song" (music: Roger Edens; lyrics: Ralph Freed), "Mr. Gallagher and Mr. Shean" (1922; Edward Gallagher, Al Shean), "Ziegfeld Girls" (1941; Roger Edens), "You Gotta Pull Strings" (1936; music: Walter Donaldson; lyrics: Harold Adamson). *Author's Note*: Stewart told this author that "I have a very fond memory for **Ziegfeld Girl** because it was the last picture I made before I went into the service. I did not return to Hollywood until five years later when I was fortunate enough to be in Frank Capra's **It's a Wonderful Life** [1946]. **Ziegfeld Girl** had three of the most wonderful actresses of that golden era—Judy Garland, Lana Turner and Hedy Lamarr. MGM knew that with those three ladies in that picture it could not miss and it didn't." This film was originally planned in 1938 as a sequel by MGM to its great biopic hit **The Great Ziegfeld**, 1936, and it hired the same writer, McGuire, who had written the 1936 production, to do the story for this film. McGuire wrote the story, but died before the film went into production. Other delays caused it to be postponed for several more years until producer Berman, who had been the production workhorse at RKO, moved to MGM. He liked the story and put everything he had into the production, bringing in the gifted Busby Berkeley to create its lavish musical numbers. "Busby studied the revues that Ziegfeld had produced," Lamarr told this author, "and he outdid them with even more elaborate arrangements than Ziegfeld could ever get onto a stage." Turner told this author that "when we walked and strolled and sauntered through those Busby Berkeley numbers we were all wearing the most elaborate costumes I had ever seen—all designed by Adrian, a genius at such creations. Talk about glorifying the American girl, well, that picture sure did all of that." Other films profiling Ziegfeld Girls and the Ziegfeld Follies include **Beau James**, 1957; **Deep in My Heart**, 1954; **The Eddie Cantor Story**, 1953; **Funny Girl**, 1968; **Glorifying the American Girl**, 1929; **The Great Ziegfeld**, 1936; **I'll See You in My Dreams**, 1951; **The Jolson Story**, 1946; **Look for the Silver Lining**, 1949; **Polly of the Follies**, 1922; **Singin' in the Rain**, 1952; **The Story of Will Rogers**, 1952; **W.C. Fields and Me**, 1976; **Ziegfeld Follies**, 1945; and **Ziegfeld: The Man and His Women**, 1978 (made-for-TV). **p**, Pandro S. Berman; **d**, Robert Z. Leonard; Busby Berkeley (musical numbers); **cast**, James Stewart, Judy Garland, Hedy Lamarr, Lana Turner, Tony

Martin, Jackie Cooper, Ian Hunter, Charles Winninger, Edward Everett Horton, Philip Dorn, Paul Kelly, Eve Arden, Dan Dailey, Al Shean, Fay Holden, Felix Bressart, Rose Hobart, Mae Busch, Reed Hadley, Joyce Compton, and as Ziegfeld Girls: Leslie Brooks, Patricia Dane, Myrna Dell, Louise La Planche, Jean Wallace; **w**, Sonya Levien, Marguerite Roberts (based on a story by William Anthony McGuire), **c**, Ray June; **m**, Herbert Stothart; **ed**, Blanche Sewell; **art d**, Cedric Gibbons; **set d**, Edwin B. Willis.

Zig Zag ★★★ 1970; U.S.; 105m; Freeman-Ender/MGM; Color; Mystery; Children: Unacceptable (MPAA; PG); **DVD**; **VHS**; **IV**. Tension-filled thriller begins with Kennedy, an insurance investigator dying from a brain tumor. He confesses to murdering an industrialist so that his family will be provided for with the reward money. But he later learns by way of new laser surgery that he is cured. With the help of Wallach, his attorney, he learns that Murphy, daughter of the murdered man's associate, was the mistress of the victim. Her father, Brooke, who was the real killer, shoots Kennedy and is then gunned down by police. Colla provides a taut whodunit with a clever script, and Kennedy is exceptional in the role of a seemingly helpless victim. No relation to the 2002 film of the same title. Songs: "Zig Zag" (Mike Curb, Robert Enders, Guy Hemric), "On Green Dolphin Street" (Bronislau Kaper, Ned Washington). Violence prohibits viewing by children. **p**, Robert Enders, Everett Freeman; **d**, Richard A. Colla; **cast**, George Kennedy, Anne Jackson, Eli Wallach, Steve Ihnat, William Marshall, Joe Maross, Dana Elcar, Walter Brooke, Anita O'Day, Joan Tompkins; **w**, Enders, John T. Kelley; **c**, James A. Crabe (Panavision; Metrocolor); **m**, Oliver Nelson; **ed**, Ferris Webster, Hal G. Davis; **art d**, George W. Davis, Marvin Summerfield; **set d**, Robert R. Benton, Don Greenwood Jr.; **spec eff**, Robert R. Hoag.

Zodiac ★★★ 2007; U.S.; 157m; Phoenix Pictures/PAR/WB; Color; Crime/Drama/Mystery/Serial Killer; Children: Unacceptable (MPAA: R); **BD**; **DVD**; **VHS**; **IV**. Based on a real serial killer, this riveting film begins when Gyllenhaal, a San Francisco political cartoonist, becomes an amateur detective trying to track down a murderer the press calls Zodiac. The psychopathic killer sends cryptic letters taunting the police, and Downey, a crime reporter, becomes impressed when Gyllenhaal is able to translate one of the letters. The two team up in an attempt to identify this clever and sadistic murderer, but he eludes them at every turn as he (or she) continues to evade the widespread dragnet conducted by the police. Their investigations span several years and more murders occur that are attributed to the maniac, but the killer is never found. Firm direction delivers a suspense-filled tale, with Gyllenhaal and Downey delivering top-flight performances. The film earned more than $84.8 million in its initial release against a budget of $65 million. Songs: "Hurdy Gurdy Man" (Donovan Leitch), "Solar" (Miles Davis), "Inner City Blues/Make Me Wanna Holler" (Marvin Gaye, James Nyx), "Bang Bang/My Baby Shot Me Down" (Sonny Bono), "Sky Pilot" (Vic Briggs, Eric Burdon, Barry Jenkins, Danny McCulloch, John Weider), "Brother Louie" (Errol Brown, Anthony Wilson), "Young Girl" (Jerry Fuller), "Baker Street" (Gerry Rafferty), "Easy To Be Hard" (Galt MacDermot, James Rado, Gerome Ragni), "Soul Sacrifice" (David Brown, Marcus Malone, Gregg Rolie, Carlos Santana), "It's Not for Me to Say" (Robert Allen, Albert Stillman), "Jean" (Rod McKuen), "Don't Let the Sun/Catch You Crying" (Les Chadwick, Leslie Maguire, Fred Marsden, Gerry Marsden), "Tar Sequence" (Lalo Schifrin), "Bernadette" (Lamont Dozier, Brian Holland, Eddie Holland Jr.), "Crystal Blue Persuasion" (Tommy James, Ed Gray, Mike Vale), "There Is No Christmas Like a Home Christmas" (Mickey J. Addy, Carl Sigman), "I Never Promised You a Rose Garden" (Joe South), "I Want to Take You Higher" (Sylvester Stewart), "Arrivederci, Roma" (Renato Ranucci, Allessandro Giovanninoi, Pietro Garinei), "Snowbird" (Gene MacLellan), "Mary's Blues" (Pepper Adams), "Spooky Nights" (Thomas Chase Jones), "The New Scooby Doo Movies" (William Hanna, Joseph Barbera, Hoyt

Curtin), "Deacon Blues" (Walter Becker, Donald Fagen), "Lowdown" (Boz Scaggs as William Scaggs, David Paich). *Author's Note*: The serial killer who plagued the San Francisco Bay Area during the late 1960s and early 1970s, preying on victims in lovers' lanes, was never tracked down, his murders remaining one of the city's most infamous unsolved series of crimes. For more information on this enigmatic killer, see my books *Open Files: A Narrative Encyclopedia of the World's Greatest Unsolved Crimes* (McGraw-Hill, 1983; pages 276-279), and *The Great Pictorial History of World Crime*, Volume II (History, Inc., 2004; pages 1264-1267). This film was shot on location in San Francisco and is noteworthy for its special effects, achieved through digital enhancements when showing action shots as well as the development of forensic evidence mounted against the killer. Violence, drug material, and brief sexual images prohibit viewing by children. **p**, Cean Chaffin, Bradley J. Fischer, Mike Medavoy, Arnold W. Messer, James Vanderbilt; **d**, David Fincher; **cast**, Jake Gyllenhaal, Robert Downey Jr., Mark Ruffalo, Anthony Edwards, Brian Cox, John Carroll Lynch, Richmond Arquette, Bob Stephenson, John Lacy, Chloe Sevigny, Candy Clark; **w**, James Vanderbilt (based on the book by Robert Graysmith); **c**, Harris Savides; **m**, David Shire; **ed**, Angus Wall; **prod d**, Donald Graham Burt; **art d**, Keith Cunningham; **set d**, Victor Zolfo; **spec eff**, Rodney Byrd, Douglas Calli, Burt Dalton.

Zoo in Budapest ★★★ 1933; U.S.; 85m; FOX; Drama/Romance; Children: Unacceptable; **DVD**. Lee provides a fascinating tale where Young, a Hungarian orphan, is about to become an indentured worker until reaching an adult age. To avoid such an enslaving fate, she slips away from her classmates while they are attending the zoo. Meanwhile, Raymond, who has always worked at the zoo as a keeper, is criticized by supervisor Heggie, an otherwise kindly person, for being too gentle with the animals, coddling them to the point where they seem to refuse the commands of other keepers. Further, Raymond detests any of the fashionable women visiting the zoo who wear animal furs, and he has the habit of stealing these luxurious garments. When a wealthy woman states that she wants to buy one of the animals so she can have it killed and its hide converted to a fur coat, Raymond grabs the fur she is wearing and runs off with it, hiding in the zoo. To Raymond, such women represent predators that cruelly kill the very beasts he loves. (His actions in this film to protect animals would later become a widespread movement in the U.S. in the 1970s and 1980s, where women wearing expensive furs were actually attacked and acid thrown onto their fur neckpieces and coats.) Raymond is then sought by other zookeepers and police, a search party Heggie reluctantly organizes as he is fond of the idealistic Raymond. After meeting fellow fugitive Young, Raymond falls in love with the beautiful girl and becomes her protector, hiding her in his secret places in the zoo. While hiding in a bear cave, and while Raymond is gone, Young is trapped by Fix, a sadistic zookeeper, who attacks her. Raymond appears at that moment and beats Fix senseless, saving Young. A short time later, a small boy becomes trapped in a tiger's cage, and panic ensues throughout the zoo. Some of the wild beasts get loose and roam throughout the zoo while spectators run from them. In the chaos, Raymond keeps his head and uses an elephant to save the little boy from a tiger attempting to devour him. The boy's wealthy father is so grateful to Raymond that he hires him as his gamekeeper for his huge estate, and also, at Raymond's urging, agrees to adopt Young. Raymond and Young then plan to wed when Young comes of age. The story is a simple one, but told in such gentle terms that the sensitive tale becomes an ethereal plea for the humane treatment of animals as well as human beings. A dream-like image is captured by director Lee, who keeps his cameras fluid as he pans and dollies through the zoo among mists and fogs, wading through spectators and singling out the animals in their confining environments. Raymond and Young are exceptional in their roles as naïve victims of an unthinking society. The film was a success at the box office and advanced the careers of its stars as well as director Lee. Music: "Rhapsodie Hongroise" (music: Marcel Delannoy; lyrics:

Anthony Quinn and Alan Bates in *Zorba the Greek*, 1964.

Jacques Brillouin, Serge Plaute). *Author's Note*: Young told this author that "I played a teenaged orphan in **Zoo in Budapest**, but I was nineteen when I was hired for that role a year [1932] before we went into production. It was a strange story, but very exciting. The animals in the zoo were really the stars of the picture." Other films profiling zoos include **An American Werewolf in London**, 1981; **Anchorman: The Legend of Ron Burgundy**, 2004; **Creature Comforts**, 1996; **Elephant Fury**, 1956; **Fierce Creatures**, 1997; **Harry Potter and the Sorcerer's Stone**, 2001; **Hero**, 1992; **Rise of the Planet of the Apes**, 2011; **We Bought a Zoo**, 2011; **Withnail & I**, 1987; and **Zookeeper**, 2011. **p**, Jesse L. Lasky; **d**, Rowland V. Lee; **cast**, Loretta Young, Gene Raymond, O.P. Heggie, Wally Albright, Paul Fix, Murray Kinnell, Ruth Warren, Roy Stewart, Frances Rich, Jane Withers; **w**, Dan Totheroh, Louise Long, Lee (based on a story by Melville Baker, Jack Kirkland); **c**, Lee Garmes; **ed**, Harold Schuster; **art d**, William Darling.

Zorba the Greek ★★★★★ 1964; Greece/U.S.; 142m; FOX; B/W; Drama; Children: Unacceptable; **BD**; **DVD**; **VHS**; **IV**. The gifted Quinn makes his career performance in this marvelous profile of a free-spirited, nomadic man whose love of life is unbounding, a bravura performance that endeared the actor to audiences and critics the world over. The film opens at the Athens port of Piraeus where Bates, a writer who is half British and half Greek, is waiting to take a boat to the island of Crete. Quinn, an animated Greek peasant with an exuberant nature and who is called Zorba, meets and befriends Bates. Bates explains that he is planning to reopen a lignite mine left to him by his father. Bates also states that he hopes his experience in Greece will rid him of his writer's block. Quinn convinces Bates that he would be a good assistant in helping him develop the mine, and Bates hires him. When the two arrive in Crete, they drive to the village where Bates owns land and stay at a small hotel operated by Kedrova, an aging courtesan who has been widowed in WWII (1939-1945). Kedrova openly admits that she has been a French prostitute and the mistress of four admirals and that she was once a celebrated cabaret dancer. The lusty Quinn encourages Bates to have an assignation with the elderly madam, and, when Bates politely declines, Quinn promptly seduces the flattered woman. Bates and Quinn then attempt to work the mine, but they find the decrepit shaft in such bad shape that they realize that it is unsafe and they think to give up mining the lignite. Quinn, however, has noticed that neighboring land has a thick forest and he suggests to Bates that they use the lumber to restore the mine. Even though a nearby monastery owns the forest, the audacious Quinn goes to the monastery and convinces the monks to cooperate by getting them all drunk. He returns triumphant to Bates where he dances in joy, which both fascinates and disturbs the reserved Bates. Quinn then urges Bates to make advances to attractive Papas, a widow

Anthony Quinn and Alan Bates dancing on the beach in *Zorba the Greek*, 1964.

who is coveted by many of the young men in the village, but who has spurned all of her admirers. During a rainstorm, Bates meets Papas and offers his umbrella to her, which she reluctantly accepts. Quinn tells Bates that Papas is attracted to him and that he should pursue her. Bates thinks Quinn believes that all women are attracted to all men and refuses to visit the widow. Meanwhile, Quinn thinks that enough lumber can be used to shore up the dilapidated mine and he convinces Bates to give him money so that he can go to the big city and buy equipment that will allow him and Bates to move the lumber over difficult terrain to the mine. While in the city of Chania, Quinn indulges himself in drinking and entertainment and has a brief affair with a young dancer, writing to Bates about his latest romantic exploits and, in his usual extravagant manner, declaring that he has finally found love in his life. Bates gets angry, believing that Quinn is simply squandering his money and spitefully lies to the love-craving Kedrova that Quinn is in love with her and that he intends to marry Kedrova when he returns to the village. Then Moustakas, the village idiot, returns Bates' umbrella to Bates on behalf of Papas. That night, urged by Kedrova, the shy Bates works up enough courage to visit Papas. Bates is seen leaving Papas' home, and a scandal soon erupts throughout the village. Voyadjis, the young man who slavishly loves Papas, is ridiculed by villagers pointing out that Papas has scorned him by giving her love to the visiting stranger, Bates. So humiliated is Voyadjis that he wades into the sea and commits suicide by drowning himself. Quinn then returns and asks Bates what he was doing the night earlier and learns that he has gone to see Papas. By this time, the body of Voyadjis is found washed up on a beach and a funeral is later held. Papas goes to the church to attend the ceremonies, but she is blocked by villagers from entering, all of whom blame her for Voyadjis' death. Bates sees that Papas is trapped in a courtyard where villagers beat her and threaten to stone her to death. Unable to take action, the mild-mannered Bates sends Moustakas to find Quinn. Just before one of the villagers can knife Papas, Quinn appears and disarms the man. Thinking Papas is safe, Quinn tells her to follow him, but, when he turns his back, the dead youth's father takes terrible revenge by slitting Papas' throat, killing her. Horrified, Bates and Quinn stand by helplessly to see her die. A short time later, Kedrova confronts Quinn, asking why he has not made arrangements for their marriage. Quinn stalls, saying that he is waiting for the delivery of an elaborate wedding dress he has ordered for her. She then presents two gold rings she has made and states that they should announce their engagement. Quinn again stalls, but suddenly comes alive with enthusiasm for their union and excitedly agrees, astounding Bates. Kedrova contracts pneumonia while Quinn and Bates work the mine, and when she takes a turn for the worse, Quinn arrives with Bates and where Quinn tenderly holds her in his arms as she dies. Women of the town then strip Kedrova's room of all of her belongings

as she is a foreigner with no heirs and her possessions, under the law, belong to the state. Bates is horrified by this, but Quinn tells him that that is the way of life in Greece. Nothing is left in the room except a bird in a cage, and Quinn takes this with him when he and Bates leave. Bates and Quinn return to their labors, and, after Quinn announces that the contraption that is to transport the lumber is now in place, the villagers turn out to celebrate its launching. Quinn fires a shot into the air to unleash the first log, but it rushes downward with such speed that it damages the transporting equipment. A second and third log so further damages the contraption that the whole system lies in ruins, the villagers by then having fled, believing that Quinn has created a dangerous apparatus. All of their plans now in ruins, Bates bemoans the fact that he is now broke and with no opportunities left. Quinn consoles him when Bates says that he plans to return to England to start anew and Quinn tells him that he will be missing all the fine madness of life if he leaves Greece. Bates looks upon the ruins of what he and Quinn have tried to create and then erupts with hysterical laughter. Bates asks Quinn to teach him how to perform the Greek dance, Sirtaki, and Quinn happily complies. Both men then begin to dance (choreographed by Giorgos Provias) on the beach, laughing at the misfortunes of life, but reveling in life itself to end this marvelous film. Quinn's great performance is utterly mesmerizing as a carefree lover of life, where he radiates an indomitable spirit that cannot be crushed by any adversity. Bates presents the perfect counterbalance to the abandoned spirit of Quinn as a man who finally emerges from his protective emotional shell to become another liberated human being. Wonderful supporting performances are rendered by Papas and Kedrova as well as the rest of the cast under the superlative direction of Cacoyannis. The film received Oscars for Best Supporting Actress (Kedrova); Best Cinematography, Black and White (Lassally); and Best Art Direction, Black and White (Photopoulos). The film received Oscar nominations for Best Picture; Best Director (Cacoyannis); Best Actor (Quinn); and Best Screenplay Based on Material from another Medium (Cacoyannis). The film was an enormous success at the box office, earning more than $23.5 million in its initial release against a budget of more than $783,000, becoming the nineteenth highest grossing film for 1964. The story was adapted for a musical that opened at New York's imperial theater on November 16, 1968, and ran for 305 performances, starring Herschel Bernardi. The musical was revived in 1983, with Quinn and Kedrova in the starring roles, and that revival ran for 362 performances. Song: "Riri Ririka" (Stathis Mastoras). *Author's Note*: Every Hollywood studio turned down this production until Darryl Zanuck, head of Fox, agreed to fund the film. Quinn was not the first choice to play the amiable Zorba, that role first offered to Burt Lancaster and then to Burl Ives, both turning down the part. Quinn was then hired for the magnetic role of Zorba. Quinn told this author that "I injured my foot when we were making **Zorba the Greek** so I could not leap about at the end of the picture in some wild dance they wanted me to perform. Instead, I made up my own slow dance where I sort of shuffled around. When they asked me what dance that was, I told them it was a traditional Greek dance and they accepted that. I did that a lot in my career. When I played an Indian in **The Plainsman** [1936], I chanted out a lot of gibberish and the director [Cecil B. DeMille, who later became Quinn's father-in-law] thought I was speaking the actual language of a Cheyenne Indian. That was the only way I got that job in that picture. My philosophy has always been—what they don't know can't hurt them, as long as they think they are getting what they want. Sometimes you have to walk in the footsteps of an idiot to please everyone. As long as you give them a lot of good entertainment, no harm is ever done. Besides, that's what acting is all about, isn't it?" The role of the former madam who operates the hotel originally went to French actress Simone Signoret, but, after a few days shooting, Cacoyannis realized she was not right for the part and went to Zanuck, asking permission to replace her. Zanuck agreed, suggesting Bette Davis, Barbara Stanwyck or even the temperamental Tallulah Bankhead for the part. Cacoyannis, however, wanted Kedrova for the role. "I had never even seen this actress in any film," Zanuck told this author, "but I trusted the director, so I told him to hire her, and what happens? She wins an Oscar. We did not allow a big budget for that picture, so we felt there was little risk. We did not really think mainstream audiences would respond well, so we booked that picture through the art houses we controlled. Then it won a bunch of Oscars and everybody had to see it, so we put it into general distribution and it went through the roof. Zorba was a sleeper and its snoring woke up everybody." The film was shot on location in Crete, and the dance at the end of the film was shot on the beach outside the village of Stavros. **p,d&w**, Michael Cacoyannis [Kakogiannis] (based on the novel by Nikos Kazantzakis); **cast**, Anthony Quinn, Alan Bates, Irene Papas, Lila Kedrova, Sotiris Moustakas, Anna Kyriakou, Eleni Anousaki, George Voyadjis, Takis Emmanuel, George Foundas, George P. Cosmatos; **c**, Walter Lassally; **m**, Mikis Theodorakis; **ed**, Mihalis Kakogiannis; **art d**, Vassilis Photopoulos.

Zou-Zou ★★★ [1934] 1989; France; 92m; Les Film H. Roussillon; Kino; B/W; Drama/Romance; Children: Unacceptable; **DVD**. Intriguing tale sees Baker and Gabin working in a traveling circus in France, although she is dark skinned and he is light. She grows up to love him, but Gabin looks upon Baker as a sister. He becomes an electrician in a Paris music hall and she is a laundress, who delivers clean underwear to the performers. Baker makes the mistake of introducing Gabin to her friend at work and they fall in love. Gabin thinks that Baker has such great talent that she could star in the show at the music hall. To that end, he conspires to get the show's star out of town so he can audition Baker off to the theater manager. The manager is impressed with Baker's lively and sexy performance and makes her the fill-in star of his show. She is a smash hit and not only has a new career, but earns enough money to pay for Gabin's defense when he is wrongfully accused of a murder. During Gabin's trial, Baker becomes a star and her fame and money save him from the gallows, and she hopes that she will eventually win his heart. Songs: "Viens Vivine/Come Vivian," "Haiti," "For Me There's Only One Man in Paris" (Alain Romans, Vincent Scotto, Georges Vab Parys). *Author's Note*: This film was originally released in France in 1934, but not shown in the United States until 1989. **p**, Arys Nissotti; **d**, Marc Allegret; **cast**, Josephine Baker, Jean Gabin, Pierre Larquey, Yvette Lebon, Illa Meery, Palau, Madeleine Guitty, Claire Girard, Marcel Vallee, Roger Blin, Geo Forster, Viviane Romance; **w**, Carlo Rim (based on the novel *Zouzou*); **c**, Boris Kaufman, Michel Kelber, Jacques Mercanton, Louis Nee; **m**, A. Romans, Scotto, Van Parys; **ed**, Denise Batcheff; **set d**, Lazare Meerson, Alexandre Trauner.

Zulu ★★★★★ 1964; U.K.; 135m; Diamond Films/Embassy Pictures; Color; Adventure; Children: Unacceptable; **BD**; **DVD**; **VHS**. One of the great adventure films, this riveting tale takes place during the Anglo-Zulu War of 1879 in South Africa, and opens with narration (by Richard Burton) that explains how the British have just suffered a crushing defeat at the Battle of Isandlwana on January 22, 1879. The Zulus are shown rummaging through the ruins of the battlefield, collecting rifles to supplement their armament of spears and rawhide shields and then begin converging on the tiny British garrison at Rorke's Drift, Natal Province, South Africa (occupied by 140 regular British troops and fifteen other combatants of the 24th Regiment of Foot). Hawkins, a Swedish missionary, and his daughter, Jacobsson, are at a large Zulu village to witness a multiple wedding ceremony. News is brought to the Zulu King Cetewayo (1826-1884, played by Chief Mangosuthu Buthelezi) of the victory over the British and he orders his warriors to prepare for an attack at Rorke's Drift. Hawkins, a heavy drinker, panics and flees in a horse-drawn carriage with Jacobsson, the Zulu chief allowing them to leave unharmed. All is quiet at Rorke's drift where officer Caine (playing Lt. Gonville Bromhead, 1845-1891) is shown hunting wild game and returning to the base with a dead leopard to see Baker (playing John Rouse Merriott Chard, 1847-1897), an engineering officer attempting to repair a small bridge. Hawkins arrives to give the British troops warn-

Stanley Baker and troops in *Zulu*, 1964.

ing that as many as 4,000 Zulus are approaching Rorke's Drift to wipe out the company of British soldiers stationed there. Van Den Bergh, who is the commander of the Native Natal Contingent, also warns the base that this overwhelming force of warriors is about to attack. The command of the post goes to Baker, who is senior in rank to Caine, although Caine, who comes from landed gentry, is somewhat miffed that he is relegated to being second in command, stating that he is expected to live up to the exploits of his illustrious military ancestors. Baker, a practical man, immediately begins to organize a defense of the small post, having his troops make gun ports in the closely grouped buildings at the post so that they can catch any advancing enemy in murderous crossfires. He builds barricades with wagons and mealie bags, including a last redoubt of mealie bags that will allow three ranks of soldiers to release consecutive volleys of fire. When Baker and Caine ignore Hawkins' warnings to abandon the post, he tells them that they and all of their soldiers are going to be killed. Frustrated at being unable to convince these officers to leave the area, Hawkins takes to drink and, while inebriated, tries to convince the unsophisticated soldiers to desert the post. He is interrupted by Green, a by-the-book color sergeant, who, under orders from Baker, locks Hawkins up in a small room where he continues his rants. Baker has finally had enough of Hawkins, and he and Jacobsson are placed into their carriage and ordered to drive off to safety. A contingent of Boer cavalry arrives, its commander telling Baker that he and his men stand no chance of survival if they make a stand against the Zulus. The Boers then ride off, despite Baker's pleas for them to stay and help defend the post. A short time later, a deep and prolonged chant of thousands of Zulus is heard as they appear on the ridges surrounding the post, their war chant not dissimilar to the sound of an approaching train. Hawkins and Jacobsson are seen by the Zulus as they race in their carriage from the post and a chief signals to his warriors to allow the missionaries to leave the area unmolested. The Zulus then begin attacking in waves, first at one point and then at another. Van Den Bergh, who has survived the disastrous battle at Isandlwana and knows the battle tactics of the Zulus, tells Baker and Caine that the chief is testing the strength of the garrison to find its weakest point at the sacrifice of his warriors. At each point, the soldiers unleash withering volley fire that mows down the spear-carrying Zulus, their bodies heaped before the defensive barricades. The attacks cease and then the soldiers come under fire from the hills by Zulus who are using the rifles they have obtained from the slain British at Isandlwana. Baker orders his men to climb onto the roofs of some of the buildings to fire back at these marksmen. As the battle continues into the evening, the Zulus realize that the weak point in the British defense is the building housing the hospital where about thirty sick men have been firing their muskets from windows. The Zulus set fire to the thatched roof of the building, climbing

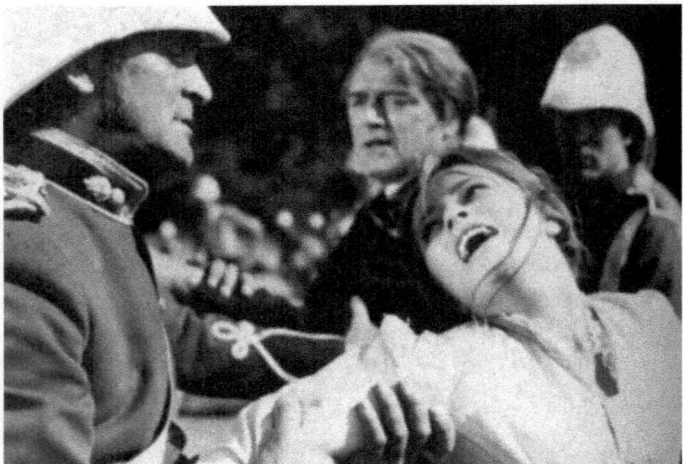

Stanley Baker, Jack Hawkins and Ulla Jacobsson in *Zulu*, 1964.

on top of it and dropping into one of its rooms where a fierce fight ensues and where Booth, who plays Private Henry Hook (1850-1905), a notorious drinker and shirker, takes charge and organizes a defense. Booth kills several Zulus and, after he and another soldier break through several partitions of the building, leads the survivors from the burning structure. The Zulus attempt to break through another area, but a herd of cattle is accidentally let loose and stampedes through the charging ranks of the attackers, killing them by the dozens. The next morning, the Zulus begin chanting their war song and they are answered by Emmanuel and several other soldiers who are part of the regimental singers, and who loudly and defiantly sing the stirring "Men of Harlech," ending with the line: "Welshmen will not yield!" The Zulus then make a final assault, hundreds of their warriors charging forward and breaking through the now thinly defended perimeter. Baker orders all of his surviving men into the final redoubt, where they form three ranks. He and Caine take turns ordering one rank after another to fire separate and continuous volleys as the Zulus make an all-out charge, but the attackers are slain by the scores under these incessant firing ranks. The Zulus retreat after they realize that they cannot break the British formation. Disappearing over a ridge, thousands of the Zulus reappear, holding their spears high and chanting. Baker and Caine are aghast, believing that the Zulus are again preparing to attack once more. Van Den Bergh gives out a nervous laugh, telling both Baker and Caine that the Zulus are not going to again make an assault but that they are sending the British troops a cheer that recognizes the bravery of the defenders. The Zulus then leave the area and the survivors count the living and dead. As Baker and Caine reorganize their men and the area, Burton narrates the epilog to state how eleven of the defenders received England's highest medal, the Victoria Cross, more than ever awarded to a single regiment to that time. Endfield directs this breathtaking film with great expertise, seamlessly merging its dramatic scenes with some of the most astoundingly realistic battle sequences ever filmed. The desperation of close in-fighting is graphically detailed as the ferocious Zulus charge wildly into the ranks of the British defenders and are greeted with volley fire and then the cold steel of British bayonets; the viewer is not spared the resulting carnage and chaos. Few films have ever so effectively captured on film the hand-to-hand struggles of these 19th-Century infantrymen. The resolute Baker and the inventive Caine (in his first leading role in a major film) are superlative as the heroic officers resolved to fight to the last as are all of the defenders, and the heroism of the Zulus is also shown with equal fervor. Hawkins gives a memorable performance as the tortured and alcoholic missionary, and Booth, as the shirker turned hero, is magnificent; Green wonderfully epitomizes the stalwart British soldier as a stern sergeant oblivious to fear. The film was a great success at the box office, earning more than $8 million in its initial release against a budget

of more than $3.5 million. An outstanding prequel, **Zulu Dawn**, was released in 1979. Songs: "Men of Harlech" (traditional), "Stamp and Shake" (Michael Z. Gordon). *Author's Note*: The malingering soldier portrayed by Booth, Private Hook, was not in real life a slovenly and unreliable soldier, but a model soldier, who was a Methodist preacher, a teetotaler, and, who, before the battle at Rorke's Drift, had received the good conduct medal. Further, the Zulus did not depart peacefully on the second day of the battle, but fled the area with the approach of a British relief column led by General Frederic Chelmsford (1827-1905). The battle of Rorke's Drift, occurring on January 22-23, 1879, was recreated near the Tugela River in South Africa, where more than 700 Zulu extras were hired to play the attacking warriors, many of them being descendants of the original warriors involved in the actual battle. Chief Mangosuthu Buthelezi was the great-grandson to the very man he plays in the film, Chief Cetewayo. Since most of the Zulus had never seen a film before, Baker showed a Gene Autry film for these extras. Baker's production company produced this film, one which Baker likened to a Hollywood western where the British troops represented the U.S. Cavalry and the Zulus represented American Indians. The film was banned from viewing by blacks in South Africa, its then officials believing that the film might "incite them to revolt." **p**, Stanley Baker, Cy Endfield; **d**, Endfield; **cast**, Baker, Jack Hawkins, Ulla Jacobsson, James Booth, Michael Caine, Nigel Green, Ivor Emmanuel, Paul Daneman, Glynn Edwards, Gert Van Den Bergh, Neil McCarthy, Patrick Magee, Chief Mangosuthu Buthelezi, Richard Burton (narrator); **w**, Endfield, John Prebble (based on an article by Prebble); **c**, Stephen Dade (Technirama 70; Technicolor); **m**, John Barry; **ed**, John Jympson; **art d**, Ernest Archer.

Zulu Dawn ★★★ 1979; U.S./South Africa/U.K./Netherlands; Zulu Dawn NV/American Cinema Releasing; Color; Adventure; Children: Unacceptable (MPAA: PG); **BD**; **DVD**; **VHS**. This fascinating slice of British war history sees the captivating Lancaster as one-armed British colonel Anthony William Durnford (1830-1879) leading his ill-fated troops into the Battle of Isandlwana at about 11 a.m. on January 22, 1879, during the Anglo-Zulu War. The film opens at a conference of high-ranking British officials in Cape Colony, South Africa, where O'Toole, playing the arrogant British general Lord Frederic Chelmsford (1827-1905) and Mills, playing the conniving Sir Henry Bartle Frere (1815-1884), conspire to dismantle neighboring Zululand. They issue an ultimatum to Zulu King Cetewayo (1826-1884), who is played by Sabela, demanding that the Zulu leader dissolve his kingdom. Sabela responds by assembling an army of Zulus made up of thousands of fierce warriors. The Zulu chief is ready to repel any British troops that might invade his empire. O'Toole then leads his British army, made up of regular British troops and Boer volunteers, into Zululand, going toward Ulundi, its capital. Accompanying the troops is a long line of supply wagons that becomes overstretched and distant from the main body of troops. En route, British scouts capture and torture some Zulus, attempting to learn Sabela's battle plans, but they learn nothing. The pompous O'Toole halts his stretched-out army at the base of Mount Isandlwana, ignoring warnings that he is exposing his troops to attack. O'Toole then accepts a false report as reality and leads half his army on a chase after a phantom Zulu army, taking with him his best infantry, artillery and cavalry. The troops remaining are mostly inexperienced volunteers commanded by Lancaster and they are summarily attacked by thousands of Zulus. Lancaster's troops are stretched out over open terrain and when his advanced units run out of ammunition, they find it next to impossible to get back to the main camp to resupply that needed ammunition. The relentless Zulus attack in sweeping waves that engulf small units of British soldiers, and the disorganized defenders never assemble a formidable British square to repel the attackers. The British nevertheless resolutely stand their ground in small groups, fighting with the butts of their rifles and bayonets, but they are overwhelmed. Hoskins is one of those dedicated soldiers, a sergeant who fiercely fights the enemy, killing several Zulus while attempting to protect a young recruit, Bradley, but he, too, is speared to death, along with Bradley. The surviving British troops fight a rearguard delaying action as they make a hurried retreat back toward their main camp, but the Zulus swarm over them, killing most of them before they can reach that camp. Massive formations of Zulus then encircle the camp and charge from all sides, massacring the remaining troops, including Lancaster, who has made a last stand at an ammunition wagon. Elliott, who plays Colonel Henry Pulleine (1838-1879), seeing that the command is being wiped out, entrusts the regimental colors to lieutenants Ward, Faulkner and Cazenove, ordering them to take the flag to safety. They ride through the devastated area only to be attacked as they attempt to cross the Buffalo River, all fatally wounded and falling from their horses while a Zulu grabs the flag. In a dying effort, Ward fires his pistol at the Zulu, killing him so that the British flag falls into the river and its current carries the banner away from the clutches of the enemy. O'Toole, after abandoning his wild goose chase of a mythical Zulu army, returns in shock to see half of his army slaughtered in what has been one of England's most ignominious and humiliating defeats at the hands of a primitive enemy. Hickox does a good job handling the unwieldy action and faithfully follows the actual events of the battle, drawing standout performances from Lancaster, O'Toole, Hoskins and the rest of the cast. Endfield, who had directed and written the script for **Zulu**, 1964, wrote the intelligent screenplay for this production. The battle scenes are both breathtaking and horrific as they detail the brutal hand-to-hand death struggles of the combatants. The producers of this film expected to see the same success as Stanley Baker's **Zulu**, but this film fared poorly at the box office, although it deserved a better fate. Song: "Men of Harlech" (traditional). *Author's Note*: Stanley Baker, producer of the classic **Zulu**, wanted to make a film about this battle, but he died a few years before this film went into production; Lancaster played the role Baker had thought to enact. Lancaster told this author that "I think the reason why **Zulu Dawn** did not go over with the public is that it showed the massacre of a British army at a time when Western audiences did not want to see such setbacks. Strange, many successful films show the massacre of George Armstrong Custer [1839-1876] at the Little Big Horn. I guess there has always been more empathy for the Indians who wiped out Custer than for the Zulus that destroyed that British army because they lived in a distant land that no one knew much about. Nevertheless, the Zulus were just as noble and brave as the American Indians. After all, the Zulus were protecting their homeland against a powerful invader. If that happened to you, you'd fight like hell, too!" More than 1,300 British soldiers were killed at the Battle of Isandlwana at the hands of more than 20,000 Zulus, their own fatalities exceeding more than 1,000. Shot on location in South Africa, more than 11,000 Zulus were used as extras in this epic film. **p**, Nate Kohn, James Faulkner; **d**, Douglas Hickox; **cast**, Burt Lancaster, Peter O'Toole, Simon Ward, John Mills, Denholm Elliott, Peter Vaughan, James Faulkner, Christopher Cazenove, Bob Hoskins, Nicholas Clay, Simon Sabela, Nigel Davenport, Michael Jayston, David Bradley, Ronald Pickup; **w**, Cy Endfield, Anthony Storey (based on a story by Endfield); **c**, Ousama Rawi (Panavision; Technicolor); **m**, Elmer Bernstein; **ed**, Malcolm Cooke; **prod d**, John Rosewarne; **art d**, Peter Williams; **spec eff**, Richard Richtsfeld.

Rorke Denver in *Act of Valor,* **2012.**

2012-2015 FILMS

Act of Valor ★★★ 2012; U.S.; 110m; Relativity Media; Color; Thriller/War; Children: Unacceptable (MPAA: R); **BD**; **DVD**. Riveting tale begins with Sanchez, a CIA agent, who is kidnapped in Costa Rica and taken hostage. Then Cottle, an Islamic terrorist in the Philippines, kills the U.S. ambassador and his son and dozens of other school children before he escapes to a training camp in Indonesia. Cottle's aim is to bring holy war to the United States. An elite team of Navy SEALs embark on a covert mission to recover Sanchez and learn who killed those in the Philippines. Their mission leads them to Costa Rica, then Somalia, and another in the South Pacific as they leave a trail of bodies behind them. They discover that Cottle and some other terrorists are located on an island off Baja, California, and attack and kill almost all of them. Veadov, a drug dealer, admits that he has been aiding Cottle whom they learn is planning to set off explosive vests at strategic places throughout the U.S. in order to kill important people. With the help of Mexican Special Forces, the SEALs neutralize the targets. U.S. Marines then relieve the SEALs, who go on to Mexico to help Mexican Special Forces attack a drug cartel factory where one of the SEALs, Denver, sacrifices his life by throwing his body onto grenade that explodes and kills him, his heroism giving the film its title. The remaining SEALs team members then kill Cottle. Partly based on true events, this exciting film presents almost nonstop action, and all of the cast members are standouts in their roles. The film was a success at the box office, earning more than $81.2 million in its initial release against a budget of $12 million. Songs: "Te Vi" (Jesus A. Perez-Alvarez), "For You" (Keith Urban). Excessive violence prohibits viewing by children. **p**, Mike McCoy, Scott Waugh, Duncan Smith; **d**, McCoy, Waugh; **cast**, Rorke Denver, Jason Cottle, Nestor Serrano, Roselyn Sanchez, Alex Veadov; **w**, Kurt Johnstad; **c**, Shane Hurlbut; **m**, Nathan Furst; **ed**, Siobhan Prior, Michael Tronick, Scott Waugh; **prod d**, John Zachary; **art d**, Randy Ser; **set d**, Julie Kaye Fanton; **spec eff**, Charlie Bonilla, Danny Cangemi, Watcharachai Panichsuk.

Admission ★★★ 2013; U.S.; 107m; UNIV; Color; Drama/Romance; Children: Unacceptable (MPAA: PG-13); **BD**; **DVD**. Heart-warming romantic tale begins with by-the-book admissions officer Fey at Princeton University. She visits a high school and finds that she and the principal, Rudd, had been college classmates some years earlier. They are attracted to each other, although they are total opposites in personality, she being more conventional and he being more easygoing. Wolff, who is one of Rudd's students, is very bright and Fey would like him to enroll at Princeton, even though she has reservations about Wolff, as he

is unconventional and not what she considers to be typical Princeton material. While she begins to bend the rules so Wolff can be admitted to Princeton, Rudd suspects that Wolff may be the son Fey gave up for adoption when he was an infant. Straight-laced Fey begins to relax her strict admission rules to accommodate Wolff's personality while she and Rudd fall in love. She ends up not only admitting Wolff to Princeton, but Rudd into her heart. Fey, Rudd, Wolff and the rest of the cast render top-notch performances in this intelligently written story, which sees firm and rewarding direction from Weitz. The film earned more than $18 million in its initial release against a budget of $13 million. Songs: "We Are Young" and "Naturally" (Christopher Cosgrove, Dan Marcellus), "Careful" (Claire Marie Grater), "Cool Samba" (Andrew Prosser, Mark Allaway, Melissa Heathcote), "George Was Here" (Michael A. Levine), "Lucky" (Kat Edmonson, Kevin Lovejoy), "Peaceful Carillon" (Christy Carew), "Bless the Most" (Hampton Hawes), "Shine Right Through" (Angela Correa), "Make Your Heart" (Orenda Fink, Maria Taylor), "Tigertown Blues" (Dick Armstrong), "Hasta Quemarnos" (Carlos Chairez, Ulises Lozano, Omar Gongora, Gilberto Cerezo, Cesar Pliego), "It's Amazing" (Jem Griffiths, Lester Mendez), "Shapiro, the Kid" (David Torn), "What I Wouldn't Do" (Alison Sudol). Gutter language and some sexual material prohibit viewing by children. **p**, Paul Weitz, Kerry Kohansky-Roberts, Andrew Miano, Dan Balgoyen; **d**, Weitz; **cast**, Tina Fey, Paul Rudd, Nat Wolff, Ann Harada, Ben Levin, Daniel Joseph Levy, Maggie Keenan-Bolger, Gloria Reuben, Wallace Shawn, Elaine Kussack, Christopher Evan Welch; **w**, Karen Croner (based on the novel by Jean Haniff Korelitz; **c**, Declan Quinn; **m**, Stephen Trask; **ed**, Joan Sobel; **prod d**, Sarah Knowles; **set d**, Susan Perlman; **spec eff**, Drew Jiritano, Vico Sharabani, Jim Rider.

The Age of Adaline ★★★ 2015; U.S./Canada; 112m; Lakeshore Entertainment/Lionsgate; Color; Romance/Fantasy; Children: Unacceptable (MPAA: PG-13); **BD**; **DVD**, **IV**. This enchanting romantic fantasy wonderfully captures the genre of romantic time-skipping. In this well-constructed paranormal film, Adaline, played by Lively, somehow remains young, twenty-nine years old for more than a century. She has lived a somewhat remote life by herself, seldom getting close to anyone who might discover her ageless secret. We first meet her when she has acquired a fake driver's license that identifies her as Jennifer Larson, age twenty-nine, and is driving in present-day San Francisco. Who taught her to drive is anyone's guess. We learn more about her life in flashbacks to the early 20th Century photographs and an antique typewriter, as well as an early newsreel. She was born in 1908 and as a beautiful, young woman married to a handsome young engineer, and she gave birth to a daughter, Flemming. Her husband dies young and she is grief-stricken. While driving on a snowy night in northern California, her car crashes into a freezing cold river, but she is miraculously rescued by a bolt of lightning that restarts her heart and also stops her aging process. A voice (Ross, voiceover) tells her she is to be spared "the ravages of time." This sounds good, but it condemns her to a lonely, mostly solitary life. Lively only tells her aging daughter, played as an adult by Burstyn, about the miracle of her agelessness. Her desire for love and romance resurfaces when she meets Huisman, a charismatic philanthropist, at a New Year's Eve party. The truth behind her agelessness is threatened when she spends a weekend with him and his parents, Ford and Baker, and she has to make a decision that will change her life forever. Ford seems to immediately recognize Lively, calling her Adaline, and Lively vaguely recalls him until she realizes that Ford had been a young man who had proposed to her decades earlier and she had rejected him. Lively covers her past by saying that Adaline was her mother, who died many years ago, but Ford remains puzzled if not suspicious about her true identity. His recognition causes Lively to panic and she decides to abandon her love for Huisman, not wanting to outlive him and all those she loves. She departs, but, while driving away, Lively changes her mind and stops to call Burstyn, telling her that she has stopped running away from her fate. She turns the car around but a towtruck accidentally strikes her car and she is left alone to freeze and die. An ambulance arrives and medics apply an electric defibrillator that revives her. Huisman visits her in the hospital and they declare their love for one another. A year later, she and Huisman, now married, are about to attend a New Year's Eve party, and, just before leaving, Lively peers into a mirror to see her first gray hair, gratefully realizing that she is now aging normally with the man she loves. Lively gives a captivating performance as an ageless woman and is supported by a fine cast, with strong performances from Burstyn and Ford, all thriving through Krieger's fine direction. The film did well at the box office, earning more than $57.7 million in its initial release against a budget of $25 million. Songs: "Since I Don't Have You" (James Beaumont, Walter Lester, John Taylor, Joseph Verscharen, Janet Vogel), "I'm Just a Jitterbug" (Mack David, Jerry Livingston), "Tear for You My Dear" and "Walking Empire" (Jeromy Allinger, Martin Gibson), "Auld Lang Syne" (lyrics: Robert Burns; music: traditional), "Goodnight" (Stephen Lu), "Let's Trip the Light Fantastic" (Chris Walden), "The Rainbow People" (Dexter Gordon), "Success" (Raney Schockne), "Don't Watch me Dancing" (Fabrizio Moretti, Binki Shapiro, Rodrigo Amarante), "Drift Dive" (Peter Silberman, Darby Cicci, Michael Lerner), "Comin' Back to Me" (Marty Balin), "Gimme Some Lovin'" (Spencer Davis, Muff Winwood, Steve Winwood), "Brighter in the Night" (Nancy McCallion), "Simple Twist of Fate" (Bob Dylan), "Start Again" (Bob Simonsen, Nathan Johnson, Katie Chastian). Rated PG-13 for suggestive content. **p**, Sidney Kimmel, Gary Lucchesi, Tom Rosenberg, Brad Van Arragon; **d**, Lee Toland Krieger; **cast**, Blake Lively, Michiel Huisman, Harrison Ford, Ellen Burstyn, Kathy Baker, Amanda Crew, Lynda Boyd, Hugh Ross, Richard Harmon, Fulvio Cecere, Anjali Jay; **w**, J. Mills Goodloe, Salvador Paskowitz (based on their story); **c**, David Lanzenberg; **m**, Rob Simonsen; **ed**, Melissa Kent; **prod d**, Claude Pare; **art d**, Martina Javorova; **set d**, Shannon Gottlieb; **spec eff**, Paul Benjamin, Kyle T. Moore.

Age of Uprising: The Legend of Michael Kohlhaas ★★★ 2013; France/Germany; 122m; Les Films d'Ici/Music Box Films; Color; Drama; Children: Unacceptable (MPAA: PG-13); **BD**; **DVD**. Based on a true story, a horse dealer named Michael Kohlhaas, essayed by Mikkelsen, lives a peaceful life with his family in Colln, Germany (now incorporated into the city of Berlin), and sets out to sell a few of his horses at the Leipzig Trade Fair in 1532. En route to the fair in the neighboring electorate of Saxony, Mikkelsen passes the estate of a Saxon baron, who seizes two of his horses in lieu of a fee for passage through his land, although toll fees have been abolished in the area for some time. Mikkelsen then takes the matter to a Saxon court, but some of the baron's relatives are jurors and he loses his case. Failing to achieve compensation legally, he sets fire to the baron's castle, but the baron escapes and hides in a monastery disguised as a nun. Mikkelsen's wife, Chuillot, is later attacked by some of the baron's men and dies from her injuries. Mikkelsen then raises a small army and sets fire to more houses over the next six years. Finally arrested in 1540, he is brought to trial and tortured on the wheel, later dying in Colln. The gritty, sometimes grim tale is well directed and acted with a good sense of the history it represents. The film saw limited distribution, earning a little more than $800,000 in its initial release. Song: "Drive the Cold Winter Away/The Beggar Boy" (Martin Wheeler). *Author's Note*: Earlier films based on the life of Michael Kohlhaas (1500-1540) are **Michael Kohlhaas** and **Michael Kohlhaas, The Rebel**, both released in 1969. Violence prohibits viewing by children. (In French; English subtitles.) **p**, Serge Lalou, Remi Burah, Gunnar Dedio, Martina Haubrich; **d**, Arnaud des Pallieres; **cast**, Mads Mikkelsen, Melusine Mayance, Delphine Chuillot, David Kross, Brujno Ganz, Denis Lavant, Roxane Duran, Paul Bartel, David Bennett, Swann Arlaud, Amira Casar; **w**, des Pallieres, Chriselle Berthevas (based on the novella by Heinrich von Kleist); **c**, Jeanne Lapoirie; **m**, Martin Wheeler, The Witches (Claire Michon, Freddy Eichelberger, Odile Edouard, Pascale Boquet, Sylvie Moquet); **ed**,

Rorke Denver in *Act of Valor*, 2012.

Sandie Bompar, des Pallieres; **prod d&set d**, Yan Arlaud; **spec eff**, Bernard Chevreul, Mikael Tanguy.

Agneepath ★★★ 2012; India; 174m; Dharma Productions; Color; Crime Drama; Children: Unacceptable; **BD**; **DVD**. The title of this riveting tale is Hindi for "The Path of Fire," and it begins on the island village of Mandwa, India. A highly respected schoolteacher, Pandit, tells villagers not to give away their lands on lease to Dutt, the son of the village leader who plans to start a drug mafia. Dutt decides to get rid of Pandit by framing him for murder. Dutt ambushes and murders a young girl inside the school, blaming Pandit for her death. With the support of villagers, Dutt kills Pandit by hanging him from a tree. The hanging is witnessed by Pandit's young son, Bhiwandiwala, who, together with his mother, Wahab, then leave the village. Destitute, they find shelter in the city of Mumbai. Bhiwandiwala grows up with one aim in life and that is to avenge his father's death by returning to Mandwa and killing Dutt. While in Mumbai, Wahab delivers a baby girl named Shiksha. Her son, now grown into a young man, played by Roshan, becomes associated with Kapoor, a local girl-trafficker, who is an enemy of Dutt. Roshan joins Kapoor's gang and becomes his trusted right-hand man. Meanwhile, Puri, a new drug commissioner, acts as a silent guardian for Roshan and tries to end crime in Mumbai. To retaliate, Dutt sends his aid, Jhankal, to Mumbai to fight against Puri. Together, Roshan and Puri disrupt Dutt's plans, while Roshan takes a bullet intended for Dutt's son, Tandon. Roshan then murders Tandon, bringing his corpse to Kapoor, who falls sick and is admitted to a hospital. Roshan takes over Kapoor's empire and stops all crimes committed by Kapoor's gang. Roshan then tries to strike a deal with Dutt to hand over the drug business in Mumbai to him and, in return, take over the drug business in Mandwa. Dutt agrees to the arrangement on the condition that Puri be killed. Kapoor regains health and learns the truth behind Tandon's death, but Roshan kills him. Dutt then sends a man to kill Kapoor, and soon after, Dutt sends a hit man to assassinate Puri. The hit man identifies Roshan as the son of the teacher killed by Dutt and reports this to Dutt. In trying to assassinate Puri, the hit man is killed by Roshan. Roshan then marries Chopra, but she is killed during a shooting with Dutt's men. Roshan then leaves for Mandwa to avenge the death of his father and his wife, and kills Dutt by hanging him from the same tree from which his father was hanged. However, Roshan succumbs to injuries in the gunfight with Dutt's men and dies in the arms of his mother. The film's title refers to a difficult path, one that is very difficult to walk on, and, in the poem by Harivansh Rai Bachman, it means a tough life, with all the problems working as fire on the path of life. The action is well choreographed in this thriller and where the acting is exceptional, albeit the violence is almost nonstop and prohibits

Action scene in *Act of Valor*, 2012.

viewing by children. The film was successful at the box office, earning more than $29 million in its initial release against a budget of more than $9 million. This film is a superior remake of a 1990 film with the same title. (In Hindi and English). **p**, Hiroo Johar, Karan Johar; **d**, Karan Malhotra; **cast**, Hrithik Roshan, Priyanka Chopra, Sanjay Dutt, Rishi Kapoor, Madhurjeet Sarghi, Chetan Pandit, Rajesh Tandon, Kanika Tiwari, Om Puri; **w**, Malhotra, Ila Bedi Dutta, Piyush Mishra; **c**, Kiran Deohans; **m**, Ajay Gogavale, Atul Gogavale; **ed**, Akiv Ali; **art d**, Santosh Kotkar, Suresh Selvarajan; **spec eff**, Agnelo D'Souza.

Ain't Them Bodies Saints ★★★ 2013; U.S.; 96m; Sailor Bear/IFC Films; Color; Crime Drama; Children: Unacceptable (MPAA: R); **BD**; **DVD**. Gritty thriller presents a fascinating latter-day Bonnie and Clyde tale where Affleck and his pregnant girlfriend, Mara, go on a Midwestern crime spree in the 1970s. They are pursued by police and hide out in a farmhouse, but are found there and gunfire is exchanged. Mara shoots one of the sheriff's deputies and Affleck is wounded. Fearing for Mara's life, Affleck surrenders and says he shot the policeman, not Mara. He is sent to prison while Mara is acquitted. While Affleck is in prison, Mara gives birth to a daughter and, over the next four years, tries to go straight, becoming attracted to Foster, the policeman she had earlier shot. Affleck breaks out of prison and looks for Mara, along the way hijacking a woman and hopping a train to where he believes Mara is now living. While Mara and Foster fall in love, Affleck seeks shelter with his adoptive father, Carradine, as police get closer to finding him. Bounty hunters then hunt Affleck as he arrives in the Texas area where Mara is living and he is seriously wounded in a firefight. He manages to find Mara, and the child he has never seen. Foster allows the dying Affleck to be cradled in Mara's arms while he takes the daughter away. Grim and uncompromising, there is a melancholy quality to this film that presents some standout performances from Affleck, Mara, Foster and the rest of the cast. The film, beautifully photographed and shot on location in Louisiana and Texas, saw limited distribution and realized about $1 million at the box office in its initial release. Songs: "The Lights" (Jonathon Price); "Where Had You Gone?," "Appalachian Abduction," "Bluegrass Vamp," "Bluejay Lullaby," (Curtis Heath); "Ain't Long Enough," "I Will Go A'wandering No More," "Here We Are" (Andrew Tinker). Rated R for violence. **p**, Cassian Elwes, Toby Halbrooks, James M. Johnston, Amy Kaufman, Lars Knudsen, Jay Van Hoy, Michael Sledd; **d&w**, David Lowery; **cast**, Casey Affleck, Rooney Mara, Ben Foster, Keith Carradine, Kennadie Smith, Jacklynn Smith, Nate Parker, Robert Longstreet, Charles Baker, Augustine Frizzell; **c**, Bradford Young; **m**, Daniel Hart; **ed**, Craig McKay, Jane Rizzo; **prod d**, Jade Healy; **art d**, Jonathan Rudak; **set d**, Adam Willis; **spec eff**, Katie Riggs.

All Is Bright ★★★ 2013; U.S.; 107m; GreeneStreet Films/Anchor Bay Films; Color; Comedy/Drama; Children: Unacceptable (MPAA: R); **BD**; **DVD**. Offbeat but entertaining tale sees Giamatti as an ex-convict whose former wife, Landecker, tells their teenage daughter that he died of cancer. He rejoins his associate in petty crime, Rudd, who is now dating Landecker, and the two French Canadian friends travel to New York City as Christmas approaches. The petty thieves plan to sell Christmas trees that Rudd steals. They sleep in a wooden trailer along the way, while Hawkins, the eccentric wife of a dentist, complicates their lives. Despite these and other obstacles that upset their venal operations, the friends look forward to a merry Christmas. Giamatti and Rudd are exceptional as the clumsy thieves, and director Morrison hurries this often very funny story along at a brisk pace. Songs: "Joy" (Tracey Thorn), "Kiss Me Baby" (Ernest Chapman), "Big Big Heart" (Bob Lawton), "The First Noel" (traditional), "Slavanye." Gutter language and brief nudity prohibit viewing by children. **p**, Daniel Carey, Elizabeth Giamatti, Sidney Kimmel, John Penotti, Luca Borghese, Louise Lovegrove; **d**, Phil Morrison; **cast**, Paul Rudd, Paul Giamatti, Sally Hawkins, Amy Landecker, Peter Hermann, Colman Domingo, Halley Feiffer, Liza Colon-Zayas, Morgan Spector, Barbara Vincent, Curtiss Cook; **w**, Melissa James Gibson; **c**, W. Mott Hupfel III; **m**, Graham Reynolds; **ed**, Jeff Buchanan; **prod d**, Mary Frederickson; **art d**, Morgan Sabia; **set d**, Kelley Burney; **spec eff**, Drew Jiritano, Luke DiTommaso.

All Is Lost ★★★ 2013; U.S.; 105m; Before the Door Pictures/Lionsgate/Roadside Attractions; Color; Adventure; Children: Unacceptable (MPAA: PG-13); **BD**; **DVD**. Absorbing film opens with Redford adrift in a small yacht in the Indian Ocean, saying to himself: "I'm sorry, I tried. To be true, to be strong, to be kind, to love, to be right, but I wasn't. All is lost." In a flashback to eight days earlier, Redford finds that water is flooding his boat after it has collided with a floating shipping container that has ripped a hole in the hull. He uses a hand bilge pump to remove the water in the cabin, only to discover that the boat's navigational and radio systems have been damaged in the collision. As he climbs the mast to repair the radio antenna, Redford sees an oncoming storm and tries to prepare for it. The storm strikes and he is washed overboard, but, after nearly drowning, he gets back on deck. The boat then loses its mast and capsizes with the equipment on board, but Redford climbs into an inflatable life raft. He has managed to salvage a sextant from the boat and finds that he is near a major shipping lane. Ocean currents begin to pull his raft toward the shipping lanes when another storm approaches. He survives that storm, but, by then, he is very low on food and his drinking water is contaminated with salty sea water. His raft reaches the shipping lane so he sends up signaling flares, but he is passed unnoticed by two ships. His raft drifts out of the shipping lane and Redford is now out of both food and water. On the eighth day, lost at sea, he writes a letter and puts it in a jar, tossing it into the water as a message in a bottle for anyone to find. That night he sees a light in the dark and thinks it is from a ship, but he has run out of signaling flares, so he tears pages from his charts and a journal he has been keeping and sets them aflame as a fire signal. The fire gets out of control, consumes his life raft, and he is pitched into the ocean. He struggles to stay afloat, but then becomes too tired and allows himself to sink. When all truly looks lost, he sees the hull of a boat with a search light approaching. He swims toward the light and grasps an outstretched hand as he is rescued. Although his essay cannot compare with the bravura performance of Spencer Tracy in Hemingway's allegorical classic, **The Old Man and the Sea**, 1958, Redford (at age seventy-seven) nevertheless gives a very strong performance of a person struggling to survive alone with only his determined will and indomitable spirit to guide him toward that possible survival. The film had a modest box office showing, earning more than $13.6 million in its initial release against a budget of $8.5 million. Song: "Amen" (Alex Ebert). **Author's Note**: Redford claimed that he injured an ear during this production, which was largely shot for about two months in the tank at Baja Studios, Rosarito Beach, Mexico, where

Titanic, 1997, was filmed. Veteran sailors criticized this film for the utter lack of seamanship demonstrated by Redford's character. It is not determined, however, that Redford's character is a seasoned seaman or an inexperienced landlubber, so the obvious mistakes he makes in the film that eventually renders him helpless in the water may be accepted as unforeseeable events and routine accidents occur. Other films dealing with survivors at sea include **Abandon Ship!**, 1957 (lifeboat); **Action in the North Atlantic**, 1943 (raft); **The Adventures of Robinson Crusoe**, 1954; **The Adventures of Tintin**, 2011; **The African Queen**, 1951; **Arise My Love**, 1940 (lifeboats); **Atlantic Adventure**, 1935 (lifeboat); **Atlantis**, 1914; **Beat the Devil**, 1953; **Ben-Hur**, 1959 (raft); **Black Island**, 1979; **The Blue Lagoon**, 1949; **The Blue Lagoon**, 1980; **The Bounty**, 1984 (lifeboat); **Britannic**, 2000 (made-for-TV); **By the Bluest of Seas**, 1936 (fishing boat); **Captain Eddie**, 1945 (lifeboat); **Captain Phillips**, 2013; **The Chambermaid on the Titanic**, 1998 (lifeboats); **Crash Dive**, 1943; **Crusoe**, 1988; **Crusoe**, 2008-2009 (TV series); **Cyclone**, 1979 (tour boat); **Dead Calm**, 1989 (yacht); **Death Ship**, 1980 (floating wreckage); **The Devil Pays Off**, 1941 (lifeboat); **The Disappeared**, 2013 (lifeboat); **Eight Bells**, 1935 (lifeboat); **Go-Get-'Em Haines**, 1936; **The Heroes of Telemark**, 1965; **The Hurricane**, 1937 (lifeboats; sailboat); **I Love You Again**, 1940 (lifeboat); **In Which We Serve**, 1942 (lifeboat); **The Intruder**, 1933 (lifeboat); **Island Captives**, 1937 (lifeboat); **The Island of Dr. Moreau**, 1977; **Island of Lost Souls**, 1932; **Jaws**, 1975 (fishing boat); **Jaws 2**, 1978 (sailboats); **Juggernaut**, 1974 (lifeboat); **Jungle Bride**, 1933; **King Kong**, 1976; **The Land That Time Forgot**, 1988; **The Last Survivors**, 1975 (made-for-TV); **The Last Voyage**, 1960; **The Legend of the Titanic**, 1999; **Life of Pi**, 2012 (lifeboat); **Lifeboat**, 1944 (lifeboat); **Lt. Robin Crusoe, U.S.N.**, 1966; **Little Robinson Crusoe**, 1924; **Lord Jim**, 1965 (lifeboats); **The Lost Continent**, 1968; **Madame Spy**, 1942 (lifeboat); **Miss Robin Crusoe**, 1954; **The Most Dangerous Game**, 1932; **Mutiny on the Bounty**, 1935 (lifeboat); **Mutiny on the Bounty**, 1962 (lifeboat); **A Night to Remember**, 1958 (*Titanic*; lifeboats); **Nim's Island**, 2008; **No Greater Love**, 1995 (made-for-TV; *Titanic*; lifeboats); **Once upon a Honeymoon**, 1942 (lifeboat); **Open Water**, 2004; **Out to Sea**, 1997; **The Poseidon Adventure**, 1972; **The Poseidon Adventure**, 2005; **Prometheus**, 2012; **Regeneration**, 1923 (lifeboat); **Road to Rio**, 1947 (raft); **Robinson Crusoe**, 1927; **Robinson Crusoe**, 1997; **S.O.S. Titanic**, 1979 (made-for-TV; lifeboats); **Scarlet Seas**, 1928; **Sea Wife**, 1957 (life raft); **The Sea Wolf**, 1920 (always at sea); **The Sea Wolf**, 1941 (always at sea); **The Sea Wolf**, 1971 (TV miniseries; always at sea); **The Sea Wolf**, 2008 (made-for-TV; always at sea); **Seas Beneath**, 1931 (lifeboat); **Seven Were Saved**, 1947 (life raft); **Shout at the Devil**, 1976; **Souls at Sea**, 1937 (lifeboat); **The Spy in Black**, 1939 (lifeboats); **Stand By for Action**, 1942; **Stranded**, 2002 (made-for-TV); **Strange Holiday**, 1970 (made-for-TV); **Swiss Family Robinson**, 1940; **Swiss Family Robinson**, 1960; **A Talking Picture**, 2003; **Titanic**, 1943 (lifeboats); **Titanic**, 1953 (lifeboats); **Titanic**, 1997 (lifeboats); **Titanic**, 2012 (TV miniseries); **Titanic: The Legend Goes On**, 2000; **Topper Returns**, 1941; **Two Came Back**, 1997 (made-for-TV; life raft); **U-571**, 2000; **Unbroken**, 2014 (life rafts); **Under False Colors**, 1917 (lifeboat); **The Unsinkable Molly Brown**, 1964 (*Titanic*; lifeboats); **Waterworld**, 1995; **When a Man Loves**, 1927; and **Whom the Gods Destroy**, 1934 (lifeboat). Gutter language prohibits viewing by children. **p**, Neal Dodson, Anna Gerb, Justin Nappi, Teddy Schwarzman, Sean Akers; **d&w**, J.C. Chandor; **cast**, Robert Redford; **c**, Frank G. DeMarco, Peter Zuccarini (underwater photography director), **m**, Alex Ebert; **ed**, Pete Beaudreau; **prod d**, John P. Goldsmith; **art d**, Marco Niro; **set d**, Gabriela Ramirez; **spec eff**, Frank Iudica, Brendon O'Dell.

The Amazing Spider-Man 2 ★★★ 2014; U.S.; 142m; Marvel Enterprises/COL; Color; Adventure/Fantasy; Children: Unacceptable (MPAA: PG-13); **BD**; **DVD**; **3D**. In this good sequel to **Spider-Man 2**, 2004, scientist Peter Parker, played by Garfield, again masquerades as crime fighter Spider-Man. DeHaan, Garfield's friend when they were

Action scene in *Act of Valor,* 2012.

boys, goes to New York City to be with his father, Cooper, who is the head of Oscorp and is terminally ill. Cooper tells his son that the illness he has is hereditary and will now inflict him, then gives him a small device containing his life's work. Cooper dies the following day, and DeHaan becomes the new CEO of Oscorp. He then accuses its board of directors of trying to take control of the company and says he knows they know about Cooper's secret biogenic methods he had been working on for foreign militarists. Foxx, who idolizes Garfield, is electrocuted by genetically modified electric eels while doing some work in an Oscorp laboratory. The eels mutate him into becoming a living electronic generator. Garfield, meanwhile, is having relationship problems with his girlfriend, Stone, who wants him to stop being Spider-Man. She threatens to move to England to take a college scholarship if he refuses. Foxx now accidentally causes a blackout in Manhattan and police fire at him. He is wounded and hospitalized. DeHaan's mysterious illness begins working in him and he believes that only an infusion of Spider-Man's blood will save him, so he asks Garfield to find the crime fighter. Garfield is reluctant to give DeHaan any of his blood, not sure of how it might affect his friend. When Garfield refuses to give him some of his blood, DeHaan starts to hate Spider-Man. Now Oscorp board members frame DeHaan for not revealing Foxx's accident and remove him as CEO. DeHaan gets Foxx's help in getting back inside the Oscorp building and finds a suit of armor made with genetically altered spiders. The spider venom advances DeHaan's illness and turns him into a goblin-like creature, but the suit miraculously restores him to good health. Garfield finds a videotape in an Oscorp laboratory saying he had to leave the company because he refused to work on its biogenic warfare projects. Garfield then learns from Stone that she is going to go to London to accept a scholarship at Oxford University. Before she leaves, Garfield tells her he loves her. Foxx now causes another blackout in Manhattan and falls ill, so Garfield and Stone try to comfort him, but in restoring power, Foxx's body is overloaded with electricity and he dies. DeHaan now knows Spider-Man's true identity and kidnaps Stone. He and Spider-Man fight each other at the top of a high clock tower and Spider-Man subdues him, but Stone falls to her death. Garfield now gives up being Spider-Man, but changes his mind when hearing Stone's high school graduation speech being read at the ceremony and decides he will continue to be the crime crusader. His work will be cut out for him since his old nemesis, Giamatti, who has been in prison, escapes and begins a new crime spree. The hallmark of this film, like its predecessors, is its astounding special effects, which provide mesmerizing action. The film had an enormous success at the box office, earning more than $709 million in its initial release against a budget of $255 million. Songs: "A Night That Never Comes" (Chester Bennington, Mike Shinoda), "Here" (Pharrell Williams). Excessive violence, mayhem, gutter

Bradley Cooper in *American Hustle*, 2013.

language and some sexuality prohibit viewing by children. **p**, Avi Arad, Matthew Tolmach; **d**, Marc Webb; **cast**, Andrew Garfield, Emma Stone, Jamie Foxx, Dane DeHaan, Campbell Scott, Embeth Davidtz, Colm Feore, Paul Giamatti, Sally Field, Martin Sheen; **w**, Alex Kurtzman, Roberto Orci (based on a story by James Vanderbilt and characters by Stan Lee, Steve Ditko),; Jeff Pinkner; **c**, Dan Mindel; **m**, Pharrell Williams, Hans Zimmer; **ed**, Elliot Graham, Pietro Scalia; **prod d**, Mark Friedberg; **art d**, Kim Jennings, Richard L. Johnson; **spec eff**, John Frazier, Eric Frazier, Bruce D. Hayes.

American Hustle ★★★ 2013; U.S.; 138m; Atlas Entertainment/COL; Color; Crime Drama; Children: Unacceptable (MPAA: R); **BD**; **DVD**. This tension-filled tale is a fictional version of the true story of Abscam, the FBI's 1980 undercover sting operation to uncover suspected corruption in Congress. Bale and Adams, the latter posing as a British aristocrat, are con artists working together while also in a relationship together. Bale's life is further complicated as he must consistently deal with problems created by Lawrence, his unstable wife. He fears that if he leaves Lawrence, he will lose contact with her adopted son. Lawrence also threatens to expose him to police if he leaves her. Cooper, an AFI agent, catches Bale and Adams in a loan scam but says he will not turn them in if Bale will help him in four more arrests. Bale has a friend, Pena, who pretends to be a rich Arab sheikh looking to make American investments. An associate of Bale's suggests that the sheikh do business with Renner, the corrupt mayor of Camden, New Jersey, who wants to revitalize gambling in Atlantic City but is having trouble getting money for that plan. Bale plans to make Renner the victim of a sting operation. Adams helps him manipulate a FBI secretary into making a $2 million wire transfer. Bale arranges for Renner to meet the sheikh, but has Whigham, another FBI agent, pose as the sheikh. Renner takes the sheik to a casino party where mobsters are gambling. Bale becomes concerned after Adams drops her English accent and admits to being American. Bale tries to protect her and stop their deal with Cooper, but Cooper says if they back out, De Niro will learn of the scam and murder them all, including Lawrence and her son. Lawrence then begins an affair with Huston, a mobster she has met at the party. She tells him she believes that Bale is working with the IRS, and this causes Huston to threaten Bale. In response, Bale promises to prove that the sheikh's investment is real. Bale then confronts Lawrence, who admits she confided in Huston and promises to keep quiet but insists on having a divorce. With Renner's help, Bale and Cooper videotape members of Congress receiving bribes. Feds inform Bale that their $2 million is missing and they have gotten an anonymous offer to return the money in exchange for immunity and a reduced prison sentence for Renner. Cooper then accuses Bale of theft, but Bale tells Cooper that Cooper ei-

ther has the money or is incompetent for having lost it. In fact, Bale says, they never met with De Niro's lawyer. Instead, Bale had a friend pose to con Cooper. Bale is then taken out of the case, which sends him back into obscurity. Bale and Adams begin living together and open an art gallery, while Lawrence lives with Huston and shares custody of her son with Bale. Complex, overlong and sometimes confusing, the film nevertheless offers a thoroughly entertaining black crime comedy with good performances by all. The elderly De Niro contributes little (other than his patented grimaces), his star status used as window dressing. The film did very well at the box office, earning more than $251 million in its initial release against a budget of $40 million. Songs: "Jeep's Blues" (Duke Ellington, Johnny Hodges); "A Horse with No Name" (Dewey Bunnell); "Dirty Work" (Walter Becker, Donald Fagen); "Does Anybody Know What Time It Is" (Robert Lamm); "Blue Moon" (music: Richard Rodgers; lyrics: Lorenz Hart); "I've Got Your Number" (Cy Coleman, Carolyn Leigh); "Live to Live" (Chris Stills); "La chatte a la Satie" (Gian Piero Piccioni); "The Coffee Song/They've Got an Awful Lot of Coffee in Brazil" (Bob Hilliard, Richard Miles); "Straight, No Chaser" (Theolonious Monk); "Stream of Stars," "Long Black Road," "10538 Overture" (Jeff Lynne); "It's De-Lovely" (Cole Porter); "I Saw the Light" (Todd Rundgren); "I Feel Love" (Peter Bellotte, Giorgio Moroder, Donna Summer); "Don't Leave Me This Way" (Kenneth Gamble, Cary Gilbert, Leon Huff); "Delilah" (Barry Mason, Les Reed); "I Was Born to Love You" (Booker T. Jones, Jr., David Porter, Shirley Walton); "Goodbye Yellow Brick Road" (Elton John, Bernard Taupin); "Papa Was a Rollin' Stone" (Barrett Strong, Norman Whitfield); "Evil Ways" (Clarence Arthur Henry); "The Evening News" (John Ross); "White Rabbit" (Grace Wing Slick); "How Can You Mend a Broken Heart" (Barry Gibb, Robin Gibb); "To the Station" (Evan Lurie); "Live and Let Die" (Paul McCartney, Linda McCartney); "The Jean Genie" (David Bowie); "Clair de lune" (Claude Debussy). Gutter language, sexual content and violence prohibit viewing by children. **p**, Charles Roven, Richard Suckle, Andy Horwitz, Megan Ellison, Mark Kamine; **d**, David O. Russell; **cast**, Christian Bale, Bradley Cooper, Robert De Niro, Jeremy Renner, Amy Adams, Shea Whigham, Louis C.K., Jennifer Lawrence, Michael Pena, Jack Huston, Elisabeth Rohm, Erica McDermott; **w**, Eric Warren Singer; **c**, Linus Sandgren; **art d**, Jesse Rosenthal; **prod d**, Judy Becker; **set d**, Heather Loeffler; **spec eff**, John Ruggieri, Lindsay Boffoli.

American Sniper ★★★★★ 2014; U.S.; 132m; Village Roadshow Pictures/WB; Color; Biographical Drama/War Drama; Children: Unacceptable (MPAA: R); **BD**; **DVD**; **IV**. Gritty, grim and unforgettable, this electrifying film is based on the true story of Chris Kyle (1974-2013), who is marvelously played by Cooper. He is a Texas rancher who survives four tours of duty as a U.S. Navy SEAL in the Iraq War (2003-2011). With 160 confirmed sniper kills out of a possible 255, he earns the title of the deadliest shooter in American history. Cooper is first seen when he is assigned as an "overhead" sniper on rooftops to protect squads of Marines going door-to-door in Fallujah. His first kills in Iraq are a mother and her little boy, who are holding explosives and attempt to run toward an American unit of soldiers in an obvious suicidal effort to kill them. Before shooting both to death, Cooper pauses and we are unsure as to whether he can bring himself to fire upon a woman and a child, but, at the last moment, he does exactly that. Following this horrific chore, guilt and shame become Cooper's constant companions, but he reminds himself that he is a soldier and his job is to try to protect his comrades. He shoots with pinpoint accuracy, saving countless lives of his comrades on the battlefield, and as reports of his courageous marksmanship spread, he earns the nickname "Legend," although when he hears it, he looks away in self-recrimination. At the same time, his reputation grows behind the enemy lines and a price is put on Cooper's head so that he becomes a prime target of Arab terrorists. The film shows Cooper accepting his military service every day of his four tours of duty while his wife Taya, who is played by Miller, and their two children wait anxiously for him to return home. Sometimes he is able to telephone his wife at home to let her know he is alive and all right. While Cooper is on leave between tours, he is under great stress from his war experiences and finds it difficult to adjust to civilian life and the world around him. When he is home and looking at his wife and children, he is unable to connect to them or to share his war experiences with his wife when she asks about his lengthy tours of duty. On his fourth tour, and after nine months of duty, the trauma of Cooper's war experiences begins to emotionally overwhelm him and he breaks down while phoning his wife, weeping as he tells her exhaustively: "I'm coming home." He heads home to the family ranch, but is unable to complete the trip, calling his wife while at a bar in the United States and telling her that he's not yet ready to face her, the children, or other family or friends. Cooper finally goes home and hugs his wife and plays with his young children, tossing them into the air. He is a hero to the public, but his ghastly life-taking war experiences as a military marksman have taken their toll on him as he struggles to live with what he has done to others as well as to himself. He admits to his wife that all he really wanted to be was a cowboy. He later goes for some counseling sessions for posttraumatic war stress, visits wounded warriors at their homes and in hospitals. His peacetime life starts to move forward again, until he is briefly seen by his wife and the viewer with a disturbed veteran, the man who inexplicably murders him. The film ends with an on-screen epilogue that reads: "Chris Kyle was killed that day by a veteran he was trying to help." The viewer then sees from the POV of Kyle's funeral procession, mourners lining the roads and, later, crowds attending his burial services. Not for the squeamish, this candid and unrelenting film presents a patriotic and heroic portrait of a self-sacrificing young American, a microcosm of tens of thousands such Americans caught up in the Middle Eastern wars. It is also a devastatingly cathartic indictment of war itself and all of the barbaric inhumanities attending its carnage and death. In one scene we see Cooper talking on the phone to Miller while he is in actual combat and under fire. When Miller realizes this and Cooper must quit the conversation to go into battle but where the phone connection remains live, his wife panics and is emotionally torn as much a part as her husband, who is, at that moment, facing front-line fire. Eastwood, who has become a pantheon director in the last two decades, presents a straightforward story with no frills and without any glorification of battle in this stunning and shocking war chronicle. It is a magnificent portrait of a stalwart soldier, representing innumerable other soldiers, one that lingers long in memory and will stir the conscience of any viewer that holds all life dear. Cooper is superb as that soldier and he receives wonderful support from a talented cast. The battle scenes, especially the lonely and murderous chore of Cooper's sniping and the Arab sniper who attempts to take his life, are particularly astonishing in their stark realities. The film received an Oscar for Best Sound Editing (Alan Robert Murray, Bub Asman), and it received Oscar nominations for Best Picture; Best Actor (Cooper); Best Adapted Screenplay (Hall); Best Film Editing (Cox, Roach); and Best Sound Mixing (John T. Reitz, Gregg Rudloff, Walt Martin). The film was an enormous success at the box office, earning more than $547.3 million in its initial release against a budget of more than $58.8 million, becoming the highest grossing film in the U.S. in 2014. Songs: "Taya's Theme" (Clint Eastwood), "Someone Like You" (Van Morrison), "The Funeral" (Enio Morricone). *Author's Note*: The concept for the Arab sniper recruited to specifically find and kill Cooper was originally advanced by Steven Spielberg, who thought to direct this film (and where that personal sniper duel had been introduced and extensively portrayed in **Enemy at the Gates**, 2001). When Spielberg dropped out, Eastwood almost immediately took the job of helming this film. Other films depicting military snipers include **Aerial Gunner**, 1943; **Air Force**, 1943; **All Quiet on the Western Front**, 1930; **Back to Bataan**, 1945; **Bataan**, 1943; **Beach Red**, 1967; **Beachhead**, 1954; **Behind Enemy Lines**, 2001; **Between Heaven and Hell**, 1956; **The Big Red One**, 1980; **Black Hawk Down**, 2001; **The Bourne Identity**, 2002; **The Bourne Supremacy**, 2004; **The Bridge at Remagen**, 1969;

Bradley Cooper (right foreground) in *American Sniper*, 2014.

The Bridges at Toko-Ri, 1954; **A Bridge Too Far**, 1977; **Casualties of War**, 1989; **Clear and Present Danger**, 1994; **Cold Mountain**, 2003; **Courage under Fire**, 1996; **Cross of Iron**, 1977; **Cry Havoc**, 1943; **Days of Glory**, 1944; **Enemy at the Gates**, 2001; **Executive Action**, 1973; **The Fighting Seabees**, 1944; **Flags of Our Fathers**, 2006; **For Your Eyes Only**, 1981; **For Whom the Bell Tolls**, 1943; **The Four Feathers**, 2009; **From Russia with Love**, 1963; **Full Metal Jacket**, 1987; **Gettysburg**, 1993; **Goldfinger**, 1964; **The Great Raid**, 2005; **The Green Berets**, 1968; **Green Zone**, 2011; **Guadalcanal Diary**, 1943; **Gunga Din**, 1939; **The Guns of Navarone**, 1961; **The Hurt Locker**, 2009; **I Was an American Spy**, 1951; **Joyeux Noel**, 2005; **Kelly's Heroes**, 1970; **Letters from Iwo Jima**, 2006; **The Lives of a Bengal Lancer**, 1935; **The Living Daylights**, 1987; **The Lost Patrol**, 1934; **The Mark of Cain**, 2008; **Men in War**, 1957; **Miracle at St. Anna**, 2008; **Platoon**, 1986; **Rambo**, 2008; **Sands of Iwo Jima**, 1949; **Saving Private Ryan**, 1998; **Shock**, 1934; **Ski Patrol**, 1940; **Sniper**, 1993; **Soldiers**, 2010; **The Steel Helmet**, 1951; **Tears of the Sun**, 2003; **The Thin Red Line**, 1964; **The Thin Red Line**, 1998; **Three Kings**, 1999; **Thunderbirds**, 1952; **Twilight's Last Gleaming**, 1977; **The Wild Geese**, 1978; **X-Men Origins: Wolverine**, 2009; and **Zulu**, 1964. Excessive war violence, gutter language and sexual references prohibit viewing by children. **p**, Clint Eastwood, Bradley Cooper, Andrew Lazar, Robert Lorenz, Peter Morgan; **d**, Eastwood; **cast**, Bradley Cooper, Sienna Miller, Kyle Gallner, Cole Konis, Ben Reed, Elise Robertson, Luke Sunshine, Troy Vincent, Brandon Salgado Telis, Keir O'Donnell, Marnette Patterson; **w**, Jason Hall (based on the book *American Sniper: The Autobiography of the Most Lethal Sniper in U.S. Military History* by Chris Kyle, Scott McEwen, Jim DeFelice); **c**, Tom Stern; **ed**, Joel Cox, Gary Roach; **prod d**, Charisse Cardenas, James J. Murakami; **art d**, Harry E. Otto, Dean Wolcott; **set d**, Gary Fettis; **spec eff**, Steve Riley, Brendon O'Dell.

Amour (Love) ★★★ 2012; France/Germany/Austria; 127m; Les Films du Losange/Sony; Color; Drama/Romance; Children: Unacceptable (MPAA: PG-13); **BD**; **DVD**. Trintignant and Riva are retired music teachers in their eighties who make up a couple. Riva has a stroke at breakfast, which instigates her physical and mental decline as Trintignant tries to care for her at home. Huppert, a grown daughter living abroad, comes to visit, but Riva suffers a second stroke that leaves her unable to speak and her right side is paralyzed. Huppert wants her mother to be put into a nursing home, but Trintignant continues home care for his wife. One day, desperate and unable to help Riva, Trintignant tells her a story about his childhood and as he finishes, picks up a pillow and smothers her. Then, as spirits, they both walk out the door together. A beautifully made film, but a sad character study that often depresses

Jean-Louis Trintignant and Emmanuelle Riva in *Amour (Love)*, **2012.**

instead of inspires, its morose message overcome through the touching expressions of love exampled by the superb performances by Trintignant and Riva. The film won an Oscar as Best Foreign Language Film and it received Oscar nominations for Best Picture; Best Actress in a Leading Role (Riva); Best Direction (Haneke); and Best Original Screenplay (Haneke). Songs: "Impromptu Opus 90, Nos. 1 and 3," "Bagatelle Opus 126, No. 2" (Ludwig van Beethoven), "Prelude Choral, Ich ruf zu dir, Herr Jesu Christ" (Johann Sebastian Bach; Ferruccio Busoni). Mature thematic material and brief gutter language prohibit viewing by children. **p**, Stefan Arndt, Michael Katz, Margaret Menegoz, Michael Andre, Alice Girard, Hans-Wolfgang Jurgan, Heinrich Mis, Bettina Reitz, Bettina Ricklefs; **d&w**, Michael Haneke; **cast**, Jean-Louis Trintignant, Emmanuelle Riva, Isabelle Huppert, Alexandre Tharaud, William Shimell, Ramon Agirre, Rita Blanco, Carole Franck, Dinara Drukarova, Suzanne Schmidt; **c**, Darius Khondji; **ed**, Nadine Muse, Monika Willi; **prod d**, Jean-Vincent Puzos; **set d**, Susanne Haneke, Sophie Reynaud; **spec eff**, Arnaud Fouquet, Geoffrey Kleindorfer, Julien Meesters.

And So It Goes ★★★ 2014; U.S.; 94m; Castle Rock/Clarius; Color; Comedy/Romance; Children: Unacceptable (MPAA: PG-13); **BD**; **DVD**. Entertaining comedy begins with Douglas, a realtor who is not people friendly. He wants to sell one more house, then retire and live peacefully. That all changes when his estranged son leaves him with Jerins, a granddaughter he never knew existed, and she turns his life upside down. He hasn't any idea about how to care for the sweet abandoned nine-year-old, so he gives her to his friendly neighbor, Keaton, and tries to get on with his life. Jerins, however, gradually opens Douglas' heart to her, as well as blossoming a romance with Keaton, and life itself becomes enjoyable. This engaging film fared well at the box office, earning more than $25.3 million in its initial release against a budget of $18 million. Song: "Get It Rite" (Steve Hoplins, William Levell Hansbrough). Sexual references and drug elements prohibit viewing by children. **p**, Rob Reiner, Mark Damon, Alan Greisman; **d**, Reiner; **cast**, Michael Douglas, Diane Keaton, Frankie Valli, Yaya Alafia, Sterling Jerins, Frances Sternhagen, Paloma Guzman, Andy Karl, Austin Lysy, Theo Stockman; **w**, Mark Andrus; **c**, Reed Morano; **m**, Marc Shaiman; **ed**, Dorian Harris; **prod d**, Ethan Tobman; **art d**, Matteo De Cosmo, Jan Jericho; **set d**, Carrie Stewart.

The Angel's Share ★★★ 2012; U.K./France/Belgium/Italy; 101m; Entertainment One/Sundance Selects; Color; Comedy/Drama; Children: Unacceptable; **BD**; **DVD**. Offbeat but engrossing comedy begins in Glasgow, Scotland, where Brannigan avoids a jail term for beating up a college boy by doing community service. He is broke and visits Reilly, his girlfriend, in a hospital where she has just given birth to their son.

That blessed event compels Brannigan to make a vow to himself that he will change his rowdy and disorganized life. Henshaw, a kindhearted social worker managing Brannigan's community service sentence, gets him lodging, and he visits a malt whiskey distillery. Brannigan learns there is a rare cask of whiskey about to be offered for auction for hundreds of thousands of pounds, so he enlists the aid of his community service pals, Ruane, Maitland, and Riggins, to obtain a bottle. Brannigan hides in the warehouse overnight and overhears two men planning to buy two bottles of the rare brew before they go on auction in the morning. When they leave, Brannigan siphons most of the expensive whiskey into an empty bottle and pours a little of the brew into a bottle of cheaper whiskey. In the course of some wheeling and dealing, Brannigan gets away with one of the bottles. The bottle Brannigan gets away with pays for a new car in which he and his girlfriend and their baby leave for a new life. A frothy production, even with its mismanaged morality, offers good performances from Brannigan and the cast. The film's title refers to the angels' share of whiskey lost to evaporation each year. Songs: "Some Clouds" (Joel Zimmerman), "I'm Gonna Be/500 Miles" (Charles Stobo, Craig Morris Reid). Too mature for children. **p**, Rebecca O'Brian; **d**, Ken Loach; **cast**, Paul Brannigan, John Henshaw, Gary Maitland, Jasmine Riggins, William Ruane, Roger Allam, Siobhan Reilly, James Casey, Roderick Cowie, Paul Donnelly, Scott Dymond; **w**, Paul Laverty; **c**, Robbie Ryan; **m**, George Fenton; **ed**, Jonathan Morris; **prod d**, Fergus Clegg; **art d**, Zoe Wight; **spec eff**, Sav Akyuz, Simon Kilroe.

Anna Karenina ★★★ 2012; U.K.; 129m; UNIV/Focus Features/Working Title; Color; Drama/Romance; Children: Unacceptable (MPAA: R); **BD**; **DVD**. Good retelling of the classic tale opens in Imperial Russia in 1874, where beautiful aristocratic Anna, played by Knightley, travels from St. Petersburg to Moscow to try and save the marriage of her brother, Prince Oblonsky, played by Macfadyen, and who has had an affair with his housemaid. Knightley is unhappily married to older Count Alexei Karenin, played by Law, and they have a young son. Knightley meets a handsome young Count Vronsky, played by Taylor-Johnson, and they fall in love. Knightley manages to quell a scandal about Macfadyen's infidelities, but then creates a scandal by beginning an open romance with Taylor-Johnson. Law gives Knightley an ultimatum: either she gives up her lover or he will make her a social pariah, ostracizing her from his family while he keeps their son. She is too much in love with Taylor-Johnson and by now despises Law, so she chooses to say goodbye to her son and leaves. Knowing that Law will not give her a divorce and carrying on the romance with Taylor-Johnson will never be acceptable to her peers, Knightley throws herself under the wheels of an on-coming train to end her agony and life. This version of Tolstoy's classic story is lavishly produced and well acted, but it cannot equal the Greta Garbo film in 1935 and the Vivien Leigh essay of Anna Karenina in 1948. The film nevertheless did exceptionally well at the box office, earning more than $68.9 million in its initial release. Other film productions of the novel were released in 1967, 1976, 1979, and television versions were produced in 1985, 1996, 2000, and 2009. Song: "Masha's Song." *Author's Note*: Knightley had played Elizabeth Bennett in **Pride and Prejudice**, 2005, with Macfadyen as Mr. D'Arcy, but they play brother and sister in this film. **p**, Tim Bevan, Paul Webster, Alexander Dostal, Alexandra Ferguson; **d**, Joe Wright; **cast**, Keira Knightley, Jude Law, Matthew Macfadyen, Emily Watson, Michelle Dockery, Olivia Williams, Luke Newberry, Kelly Macdonald, Bryan Hands, Aruhan Galieva; **c**, Seamus McGarvey; **m**, Dario Marianelli; **ed**, Melanie Oliver; **prod d**, Sarah Greenwood; **art d**, Thomas Brown, Nick Gottschalk, Tom Still, Niall Moroney; **set d**, Katie Spencer; **spec eff**, Mark Holt, James Davis III, David Holt.

Ant-Man ★★★ 2015; U.S.; 117m; Marvel Studios/Walt Disney; Color; Adventure/Science-Fiction; Children: Unacceptable (MPAA: PG-13); **3D**; **BD**; **DVD**. Outlandishly fascinating, this rowdy tale sees Rudd in tights as Scott Lang, a superhero who can make himself tiny, talk to ants, and save the world from a crazed scientist. A well-meaning burglar, Rudd is transformed into Ant-Man, created by aging scientist Douglas, who invented Rudd's costume and formerly wore it. The film starts in 1989 as Douglas resigns from S.H.I.E.L.D. when he learns that the agency is going to make an identical copy of his ant-man shrink technology that he believes is dangerous and wants to hide it as long as he lives. Stoll, a former Douglas protégé, forced him out of his own company, and Stoll is working on a shrinking costume of his own called the Yellowjacket, which alarms Douglas because of its evil and destructive possibilities. Rudd can't find work because of his criminal record so he burglarizes a house owned by Douglas and cracks its safe. Rudd finds what he thinks is an old motorcycle suit and takes it to his apartment. There he dons the suit and is shrunk to the size of an ant. Frightened, he takes the suit back to Douglas' house, but is arrested. Douglas owns the house and the ant suit and visits Rudd in his prison cell, bringing the ant suit along to help him break out of prison. Douglas tells Rudd that he will help him escape, but only if Rudd becomes a new Ant-Man and steals the Yellowjacket suit from Stoll. Rudd agrees, escapes prison, and then leads a swarm of flying ants to thwart Stoll when stealing the Yellowjacket. Rudd and Douglas, however, are captured by Stoll, who plans to sell both costumes to the demonic agency Hydra. Rudd manages to pursue Stoll, but Stoll puts on the Yellowjacket suit and attacks Rudd. Then Rudd is arrested by Cannavale. Stoll then takes Greer hostage to lure Rudd into another fight, but Rudd kills him. Rudd then abandons his role as Ant-Man, and Cannavale kindly covers for him to keep Rudd from going back to prison. Rudd, Douglas and cast render top-flight performances in this exciting story, which is highlighted by some astounding special effects. The film reaped enormous profits at the box office, earning more than $518.2 million in its initial release against a budget of $130 million. Songs: "Borombon" (Javier Vazquez), "Shingalin en Panama" (Luis Jacinto Argumedes Mateus), "Antmusic" (Adam Ant, Marco Pirroni), "Live It Up" (Dwayne Alo, Jaron Lamot, Colton Fisher, Jason Rabinowitz), "La Cucaracha" (traditional), "Hot Poppin Popcorn" (Murray Cook, Jeff Fatt, Anthony Field, John Field, Sam Moran, Paul Paddick), "Escape" (Roy Ayers), "I'm Ready" (Milan Williams), "Our Time Now" (Kelli Wakili, Michael Meyeda, Colton Fisher, Jason Rabinowitz, Jaron Lamot), "Pink Gorilla" (Roberto Callero Ross, Colton Fisher, Jason Rabinowitz), "It's a Small World" (Robert B. Sherman, Richard M. Sherman), "Plainsong" (Robert Smith, Simon Gallup, Porl Thompson, Boris Williams, Roger O'Donnell, Laurence Tolhurst), "50 Year Old Ghost Story" (Henry Jackman). Excessive violence prohibits viewing by children. **p**, Kevin Feige, Brad Winderbaum; **d**, Peyton Reed; **cast**, Paul Rudd, Michael Douglas, Evangeline Lilly, Corey Stoll, Bobby Cannavale, Anthony Mackie, Judy Greer, Abby Ryder Fortson, Michael Pena, David Dastmalchian, Hayley Atwell; **w**, Joe Cornish, Adam McKay, Paul Rudd, Edgar Wright (based on a story by Cornish, Wright, and the Marvel comic books by Jack Kirby, Stan Lee, Larry Lieber); **c**, Russell Carpenter; **m**, Christophe Beck; **ed**, Dan Lebental, Colby Parker Jr.; **prod d**, Shepherd Frankel, Marcus Rowland; **art d**, Cameron Beasley, Nigel Churcher, David Lazan; **set d**, Leslie A. Pope; **spec eff**, Daniel Sudick; Joel Mitchell, Wayne Newland, Darin O'Neill.

Anything Is Possible ★★★ 2013; U.S.; 93m; D Street Films/Color; Drama; Children: Unacceptable (MPAA: R); **BD**; **DVD**. Intriguing tale begins with Bortnick, a ten-year-old boy who is separated from his mother, Chabert. She is a U.S. Army lieutenant who goes missing during a rescue mission to Japan after it is struck by a 2011 tsunami. Living in Detroit, Bortnick discovers that his father, Bennett, is not his biological father. Fearing that Child Care Services might take him, he runs away. Bennett searches for Bortnick while the boy takes to the streets where he meets Miles, a homeless Iraqi war veteran. Miles takes him to the home of Atkins, a wealthy philanthropist whose ten-year-old daughter, Ptacek, hides them in the basement. Atkins learns by accident that Bort-

Jude Law and Keira Knightley in *Anna Karenina*, 2012.

nick is a gifted pianist. Atkins reunites Bortnick with Bennett, but, until social workers can straighten things out, Bortnick will remain in the custody of the state in an orphanage. The orphanage is to be closed for lack of operating funds, so Bortnick, Ptacek, and the other children organize a fundraiser, a concert starring Bortnick at the piano. The concert raises enough money to keep the orphanage open. There's just one thing missing now for Bortnick and that is his missing mother. Good script and acting sustains interest throughout in what becomes a heartwarming story. In real life, Ethan Bortnick (2000-) is a child protégé pianist, composer, singer, and actor. Songs: "All About Music," "Anything Is Possible," "Looking Up to You," "Showtime," "That's Not Me," "We're All Family," "Blow a Kiss," "Everything's Gonna Be Alright," "They Shine" (all by Ethan Bortnick, Harry Baker); "It's a Miracle" (Bortnick). **p&d**, Demetrius Navarro; **cast**, Ethan Bortnick, Jonathan Bennett, Lacey Chabert, Elizabeth Atkins, Fatima Ptacek, David Haines, Erlinda Navarro, Kym Whitley, Stephane Nicoli, Mila McConaughey, Enrico Natale, Daniel Lujan; **w**, Navarro, Carlos R. Bermudez; **c**, Keith L. Smith; **m**, Ethan Bortnick; **ed**, Andrew Brzozowski, Jon Vasquez.

Argo ★★★★★ 2012; U.S.; 120m; WB; Color; Drama; Children: Unacceptable (MPAA: R); **BD**; **DVD**. Taut thriller begins when Iranian militarists take more than fifty members of the U.S. embassy staff in Iran as hostage on November 4, 1979, in retaliation for U.S. President Jimmy Carter (1924-) giving asylum to the Shah of Iran (Mohammad Reza Pahlavi, 1919-1980) in the U.S. during the Iranian Revolution. Six staff members escape capture by hiding in the home of Canadian ambassador Kenneth Taylor (1934-2015), who is played by Garber. Tony Mendez (Antonio Joseph "Tony" Mendez, 1940-), played by Affleck, a U.S. CIA infiltration specialist, is brought into the crisis, but he is doubtful about U.S. State Department strategies in freeing the hostages, although he has no better plan of his own. He then decides to go to Iran, using the cover of a film crew to scout locations for making a movie. Affleck joins with Goodman, a Hollywood makeup artist, who creates disguises for the CIA, and Arkin, a film producer, and they set up a bogus movie production company for a science fiction film called "Argo." Affleck poses as a producer for the film, enters Iran, and meets with the six escapees in the Canadian ambassador's home. He gives them all Canadian passports and fake identities to enable them to get by airport security guards. Meanwhile, revolutionaries rummaging through documents shredded by Americans before they were captured in the embassy piece some of the shredded photos to learn that some of the embassy personnel are missing and not in their custody. Tension rises when the escape plan is officially canceled so that it will not conflict with a U.S. military plan to rescue the hostages held by the revolutionaries (this being the abortive attempt the Carter administration put into place to

John Goodman and Alan Arkin in *Argo*, 2012.

bring about that rescue). However, Affleck proceeds with his plan to liberate those six embassy employees hiding in the Canadian ambassador's home. The fugitives are concerned about Affleck's ability to rescue them, but they agree to follow his instructions since they realize that he is risking his own life to save theirs. To enforce their posture of making a movie, Affleck and his so-called film crew go to a bazaar in Tehran under the pretense of getting some on-location shots, but when it is learned that they are Americans, several natives show hostility and threats. The Iranian cultural affairs representative, however, manages to hustle the fake film crew from the area and to safety. When it appears that the revolutionaries might identify and locate the missing six embassy employees, Affleck pressures his superiors to obtain flight tickets on a Swissair airliner. The embassy personnel and the fake film crew then arrive at the Tehran Airport but they are detained by suspicious revolutionaries who are closely scrutinizing all passengers. The potential escapees nervously wait to board the plane while a revolutionary guard puts a phone call through to Hollywood to confirm the existence of the film crew, and Arkin and Goodman almost miss that call. They, however, answer it and lie to the revolutionaries that the film crew has been, indeed, in Iran to make a film. Also, at the last minute, the flight reservations and boarding passes are approved and the escapees board the plane. As the plane taxies to a runway for takeoff, a revolutionary guard who has identified the escapees and now believes that they are on that Swissair plane, races through the airport to stop the plane. By the time he reaches his superiors, however, the plane has taken off and is in the air and heading westward to safety (the actual flight landed in Zurich, Switzerland). Affleck does a wonderful job in presenting this harrowing tale, carefully mounting suspense in every taut scene. He expertly intercuts from bureaucratic negotiators to those nerve-wracked escapees in hiding to the revolutionaries discovering and then desperately searching for the fugitives that have escaped their clutches. The acting throughout is realistically exceptional and the crisp lensing superbly adds to the tension through fluid shots that capture in the action of each jittery scene. There is a deep sense of visual intimacy to almost every scene in this cliff-hanging film that emphasizes the anxiety of the fugitives. Their eventual rescue provides a great emotional relief and satisfaction for the viewer (as it most assuredly did for the actual escapees), a true-to-life triumph over the evil actions of life-taking terrorists, which is masterfully recreated in this great escape film. The film deservedly won Oscars for Best Picture; Best Adapted Screenplay (Terrio); and Best Film Editing (Goldenberg). It received Oscar nominations for Best Supporting Actor (Arkin); Best Original Score (Desplat); Best Sound Editing (Erik Aadahl, Ethan Van der Ryn); and Best Sound Mixing (John Reitz, Gregg Rudloff, Jose Antonio Garcia). The film enjoyed a great box office success, earning more than $232.3 million in its initial

release against a budget of $44.5 million. The story of the rescue was told earlier in the 1981 television movie **Escape from Iran: The Canadian Caper**. Songs: "Al Adhan" (traditional), "Dance the Night Away" (Edward Van Halen, Alex Van Halen, Michael Anthony, David Lee Roth), "Hip Hug-Her" (Steve Cropper, Donald Dunn, Al Jackson Jr., Booker T. Jones), "Little Y&A" (Mick Jagger, Keith Richards), "Sultans of Swing" (Mark Knopfler), "When the Levee Breaks" (Jimmy Page, Robert Plant, John Paul Jones, John Bonham), "Upside Down" (Mark Isham), "Charlie's Tune" (Joseph Liebman), "March to the Dead City" (Leonard Rosenman), "Stalking Stars" (Andrew Lockington), "Do You Miss London" (Harry Gregson-Williams), "Hace Tuto Guagua" (traditional), "Concrete Jungle" (Rod Byers), "Adham, Call to Prayer" (traditional), "Abwoon Call to Prayer" (Jahanara Laura Mangus), "Eftekhar" (Gaynor O'Flynn, Qoqnus), "Taedol" (Gaynor O'Flynn). *Author's Note*: In the actual takeover of the U.S. embassy in Tehran, all the hostages taken were freed on January 20, 1981. The escape of the six embassy employees was not made public until sometime later in order to protect the Canadian government and the identities of the escaped Americans, as well as the heroic Mendez. The film was criticized for some historical inaccuracies including minimizing the role that the Canadian embassy played in the rescue and for falsely claiming that the six Americans had been turned away by the British and New Zealand embassies. The movie's plot was adapted from the book *The Master of Disguise* by CIA operative Tony Mendez and the 2007 article "The Great Escape" by Joshuah Bearman in *Wired* magazine. Mendez stated that long after the CIA had closed the fake Hollywood office for the equally phony film production company, Studio Six, dozens of film scripts arrived for that company's consideration. **p**, Ben Affleck, George Clooney, Grant Heslov, Amy Herman; **d**, Affleck; **cast**, Affleck, Bryan Cranston, Alan Arkin, John Goodman, Victor Garber, Tate Donovan, Clea DuVall, Zeljko Ivanek, Scoot McNairy, Rory Cochrane, Christopher Denham; **w**, Chris Terrio (based on a selection from *The Master of Disguise* by Tony Mendez as Antonio J. Mendez, and the article "The Great Escape" by Joshuah Bearman); **c**, Rodrigo Prieto; **m**, Alexandre Desplat; **ed**, William Goldenberg; **prod d**, Sharon Seymour; **art d**, Peter Borck; **set d**, Jan Pascale; **spec eff**, R. Bruce Steinheimer, Barry McQueary.

Arthur Newman ★★★ 2013; U.S.; 101m; Vertebra Films/Cinedigm Entertainment Group; Color; Drama; Children: Unacceptable (MPAA: R); **BD**; **DVD**. Offbeat but intriguing tale sees Firth as a former professional golfer who has become bored with his life as he works as a FedEx floor manager in Florida. His marriage has failed and he is not happy with his current girlfriend, Heche. His life is further troubled by Hedges, his teenage son, who dislikes him. Firth decides to make an entirely new life by faking his own death in a drowning accident on a lonely Florida beach. After acquiring a forged passport, he travels under a new name, "Arthur Newman," and resumes his former profession as a professional golfer, playing at a club in Terre Haute, Indiana. Along the way there he meets Blunt, a beautiful but troubled young thief. He finds her at his motel swimming pool, unconscious from having taken drugged cough syrup. He takes her to a hospital and learns she also has been living under a false identity, that of her twin sister who is a schizophrenic, and that she has fled her home in North Carolina. Firth and Blunt then fall in love while traveling together to Indiana. Blunt comes up with a way to make money and find living accommodations by breaking into the homes of wealthy people while dressed in their clothes, and pretending to be these victims. Hedges, meanwhile, becomes friends with Firth's former girlfriend and they try to understand why he deserted both of them. Firth and Blunt eventually tire of their con game and take a fresh look at their lives. Firth drives Blunt back to her hometown so she can look after her schizophrenic sister, and he then drives back to Florida to reconcile with his son. This prosaic story about two sad people, who find a little happiness together, provides good performances from Firth and Blunt. Sexual content, gutter language and brief drug use prohibit viewing by children. **p**, Becky Johnston, Mac Cappuccino, Brian Oliver, Alisa Tager, Stefan Sonnenfeld; **d**, Dante Ariola; **cast**, Colin Firth, Emily Blunt, Anne Heche, Kristin Lehman, Sterling Beaumon, David Andrews, Nicole LaLiberte, Autumn Dial, Peter Jurasik, Steve Coulter, Dean Chekvala, Lucas Hedges; **w**, Johnston; **c**, Eduard Grau; **m**, Nick Urata; **ed**, Olivier Bugge Coutte; **prod d**, Christopher Glass; **art d**, Quito Cooksey; **spec eff**, William Purcell.

The Artist ★★★★ 2012 (almost all silent); France/Belgium/U.S.; 100m; Studio 37/Weinstein Co.; B/W; Comedy/Drama/Romance; Children: Unacceptable (MPAA: PG-13); **BD**; **DVD**. Entertaining and moving almost all-silent film provides outstanding performances from Dujardin and Bejo, who depict two movie stars of the silent era and nostalgically mirror a more genteel and glamorous Hollywood. The story takes place between 1927 and 1932 and focuses on the relationship of an older silent film star, Dujardin, and a rising young actress, Bejo, at the time when silent films are being replaced by sound films called "talkies." Dujardin is posing for pictures outside the premiere of his latest hit film when Bejo, a young woman, stumbles into him accidentally. He is amused and has his picture taken with her. The next day, Bejo sees herself on the cover of *Variety* with the heading "Who's That Girl?" Dujardin next sees her when she auditions as a dancer, and he insists to his bosses at Kinograph Studios that she be given a part in his next movie. Big shot producer Goodman protests with his usual blimpy fulminations, but Dujardin, who is a reigning star, gets his way. While dancing together in a scene for the new film, Dujardin and Bejo show great chemistry. He grooms her for stardom by putting a beauty spot on her face (a la Clara Bow), which becomes her trademark, and she slowly rises from an extra to starring roles. Two years pass and Goodman announces that the studio won't make any more silent films, but Dujardin thinks "talkies" are going to be a short-lived novelty. He then decides to produce and direct his own silent film, financing it himself. His movie opens on the same day as Bejo's new sound film is released, the very day of the 1929 stock market crash. Dujardin's hopes for survival rest with his new film becoming a hit, but audiences ignore it and, instead, flock to see Bejo's talkie. Dujardin is ruined financially, and his wife evicts him from their lavish mansion. He moves into an apartment with Cromwell, his devoted chauffeur-valet, and his dog. Bejo then becomes a major Hollywood star. Dujardin is bankrupt and auctions off his personal belongings and ends Cromwell's services by giving him his car because he has been unable to pay him for a year. Dujardin becomes drunk and depressed, setting fire to his private collection of his earlier films. As the films blaze into a huge fire, he falls unconscious from inhaling the smoke, still clutching one film canister. His dog howls for help and a policeman rescues him. Bejo visits him in a hospital where he is recovering from injuries in the fire, and he later wakes up in a bed in her house, happily discovering that the loyal Cromwell is working for her. Bejo insists that her studio allow Dujardin to be her co-star in her next film or she will quit. Dujardin then learns that Bejo bought all of his possessions that he had auctioned off and, in despair, he returns to his burned-out apartment. Bejo goes there are finds that he is about to attempt suicide. They reconcile, and, remembering how well they danced together, she persuades Goodman to star them in a musical together. The viewing audience now hears sound as the film starts rolling (in some color sequences) for a dance scene, and their tap dancing is heard as well as their sighs as they now become lovers both off-screen and on. The on-screen director shouts "Cut!" He then requests one more take, and Dujardin utters his only audible line in this film: "With pleasure!" In addition to the sterling essays rendered by Dujardin and Bejo, the rest of the cast, especially Cromwell, Miller and Pyle, deliver standout performances under the firm direction of Hazanavicius. The innovative technique of filming this story as a silent, except for its very satisfying ending, startled audiences and critics alike, but the absence of sound did not reduce the powerful impact of the performances, which was thankfully recognized by the Academy. The film won Oscars for

Ben Affleck moving in a Tehran crowd in *Argo*, 2012.

Best Picture; Best Actor (Dujardin); Best Cinematography (Schiffman); Best Original Score (Bource); and Best Costume Design (Mark Bridges). It was a smash hit at the box office, earning more than $133.4 million in its initial release against a budget of more than $15 million. Not related to a 2008 film with the same name. Songs: "Estancia Op. 8" (Alberto Ginastera), "Jubilee Stomp" (Duke Ellington), "Imagination" (Livingston), "Pennies from Heaven" (music: Arthur Johnston; lyrics: Johnny Burke), "Love Scene" (Bernard Herrmann), "Dirty Tap Dancing" (Ludovic Bource). *Author's Note*: The story line for this superlative film evokes many other productions that deal with Hollywood's transition from silent films to the talkies, where the silent stars of yesteryear failed to become successes in the new sound era, such as **Singin' in the Rain**, 1952. It most closely recalls the tragic film career of John Gilbert, co-star and lover of the great Greta Garbo, who saw his star fade with the coming of sound films. The film employs the concepts of the several versions of **A Star Is Born** (1937, 1954, 1976), where a fading film star grooms a novice for stardom at the sacrifice of his own career, and also **What Price Hollywood?**, 1932, where an alcoholic director makes a star out of an unknown and inexperienced actress at the cost of his life. Launching a major theatrically released silent film in 2012 was undoubtedly risky business. Such approaches had not worked well in the past. Mel Brooks tried that approach with his **Silent Movie**, 1976 (which has only one word spoken), and, even though that film was very funny, it did not see the box office success anticipated. The characters so wonderfully depicted in this film, however, become so endearing and empathetic that one yearns for their success and happiness. Lensing, lighting and camera techniques—iris up and down, wipes and fadeouts—are employed throughout to simulate the movie making techniques of the silent era and all to exceptional effect. Shot in Hollywood, the film was made on a whirlwind schedule of thirty-five days. Retired film actress Kim Novak accused producers of misappropriating the musical score composed by Bernard Herrmann for Alfred Hitchcock's **Vertigo**, 1958, but this proved not to be the case as they had gotten permission to use some of Herrmann's passages for Bource's score. Hazanavicius publicly answered Novak with: "**The Artist** was made as a love letter to cinema, and grew out of my (and all of my cast and crew's) admiration and respect for movies throughout history. It was inspired by the work of Hitchcock, Lang, Ford, Lubitsch, Murnau and Wilder. I love Bernard Herrmann and his music has been used in many different films and I'm pleased to have it in mine. I respect Kim Novak greatly and I am sorry that she disagrees." **p**, Thomas Langmann, Jean Dujardin, Jeremy Burdek, Nadia Khamlichi, Adrian Politowski, Gilles Waterkeyn; **d&w**, Michel Hazanavicius; **cast**, Jean Dujardin, Brnice Bejo, John Goodman, James Crowell, Penelope Ann Miller, Missi Pyle, Beth Grant, Ed Lauter, Joel Murray, Malcolm McDowell; **c**, Guillaume Schiffman;

Jean Dujardin in *The Artist*, 2012.

m, Ludovic Bource; **ed**, Anne-Sophie Bion; **prod d**, Laurence Bennett; **art d**, Gregory Hooper; **set d**, Robert Gould; **spec eff**, David Waine.

At Any Price ★★★ 2012; U.S.; 105m; Black Bear Pictures/Sony; Color; Drama; Children: Unacceptable (MPAA: R); **BD**; **DVD**. Quaid is outstanding as a ruthless Midwest farmer, who owns more than 3,500 acres he inherited from his father and which he intends to pass along to his youngest son, Efron. Quaid is a shark in the competitive world of modern agriculture whose slogan is "Expand or die." He heartlessly buys up farms on the cheap when their owners die. A family crisis arises when an investigation exposes Quaid's shady business practices. Quaid also represents the Liberty Seed Co. which sells genetically modified seeds. A rather devious opportunist, he finds himself at odds with the seed company and also at home where his eldest son, Stevens, has left the family to climb mountains in South America. Efron, meanwhile, prefers to be a NASCAR driver rather than be a farmer or salesman. Quaid's wife, Dickens, meanwhile, is loyal and patient with him. Both Quaid and Efron gradually learn there are limits they can go to in order to achieve what they want. In addition to Quaid's riveting essay, Efron, Dickens and Stevens render standout performances under the tight direction of Bahrani. Songs: "I Remember You" (Jorge Harada, Danielle Ruby Phillips, Elizabeth Ann Smith, Peter Evan Smith, Francis Warren Lewis), "Badly Bent" and "Two for the Road" (Joshua Pless Harris), "Lions of Least" (Jennings Carney, Lain Carney, Van Carney), "Hash" (RTX), "The Party's at Lightning Rock, Bro, B.Y.O.L.B." (Jake Palladino, Shane Medanich, Dave Fallis), "Still Got My Summer" (Louis Yoelin), "Dearest Lady" (John Burton Kerry), "The Man I Am" (John Eddie, Adam Schoenfeld), "Butcher" (Matt Cherry, Dave Eidson, James Halcrow, Dan Nadolny, Sean Sawyer). Sexual content, graphic sexual images and gutter language prohibit viewing by children. **p**, Ramin Bahrani, Justin Nappi, Teddy Schwarzman, Kevin Turen, Christine Vachon, Declan Baldwin, Pamela Koffler, Andrew Levitas; **d**, Bahrani; **cast**, Dennis Quaid, Zac Efron, Kim Dickens, Aaron B. Oduber, Jacob R. Oduber, Patrick W. Stevens, Guy Massey, John Hoogenakker. Laura Atwood; **w**, Bahrani, Hallie Elizabeth Netwon, **c**, Michael Simmonds; **m**, Dickon Hinchliffe; **ed**, Alfonso Goncalves; **prod d**, Chad Keith; **art d**, Jonathan Guggenheim; **set d**, Adam Willis; **spec eff**, John D. Milinac, Blake E. Matthys, Andre Basso, Rob Richert.

At Middleton ★★★ 2014; U.S.; 99m; CineSon Enterprises/Anchor Bay; Color; Comedy/Romance; Children: Unacceptable (MPAA: R); **BD**; **DVD**. Bittersweet romantic tale begins with Vera Farmiga, a businesswoman, who is taking her eighteen-year-old daughter, Taissa Farmiga, on a tour of potential colleges. Garcia is a heart surgeon accompanying his son, Lofranco, on the same tour, although the young man has no strong desire to attend any college. The foursome's paths cross at Middleton College in the Pacific Northwest. Their offspring would rather be on their own, so the adults find themselves with a free day as they tour the campus together. They appear to have nothing in common beyond both being single parents with a university-bound child, but, after meeting during a group campus tour, they form a relationship as they reflect on their own college days and talk about their lives. Meanwhile, their offspring enter a relationship. Garcia and Taissa Farmiga shine in their roles, receiving good support from the rest of the cast. The film is reserved and full of dry humor as its restrained characters examine their rather vacuous lives but just hoping that they might fulfill those lives by having some happiness together. Songs: "The Great Divide" (David Applebaum, Colin Dieden, Matthew Dipanni, Kathryn Earl, Spencer Gongwer, Christian Hand, Joshua Hogan, Peter Mallinger, Michael Vincze), "Beacon" (Matt Duncan), "Give Me the Go" and "Dance If You Like" (Max Brodie), "Piano Sonata, Opus 57, No. 23, Appassionata" (Ludwig van Beethoven), "Bad Name" (McGowan Southworth), "Two Fingered Salute" (Aleksander Dimitirijevic), "Tijuana" (Tobias Jesso, Buck Spencer), "Musical Chairs" (Joey Stephens, Ricardo Robles, Andrew Parker), "Otto Wood" (Michael Rank), "What's Next" (Jean Burden, Christian Devivo, Mark Pistel, Mark Weiner), "The Quiet Crowd" (Patrick Watson, Mikhail Stein, Robbie Kuster, Simon Angell), "Fanfare for the Common Man" (Aaron Copland), "Chop Sticks" (Euphemia Allen). Drugs and brief sexuality prohibit viewing by children. **p**, Andy Garcia, Glenn German, Sig Libowitz, Joe Drago; **d**, Adam Rodgers; **cast**, Garcia, Vera Farmiga, Taissa Farmiga, Spencer Lofranco, Nicholas Braun, Tom Skerritt, Peter Riegert, Mirjana Jokovic, Stephen Borrello, Daniella Garcia-Lorido; **w**, Glenn German, Rodgers; **c**, Emmanuel Kadosh; **m**, Arturo Sandoval; **ed**, Suzy Elmiger; **prod d**, Vincent DeFelice; **set d**, Debbie Dahlstrom; **spec eff**, Travis Berry, Jason Mckee.

August: Osage County ★★★ 2013; U.S.; 121m; Weinstein Co.; Color; Drama; Children: Unacceptable (MPAA: R); **BD**; **DVD**. This offbeat but intriguing tale begins with a dysfunctional rural Oklahoma family, estranged for years, but who reunite at the funeral for Streep's husband, Shepard, who had once been a famous poet before turning into an alcoholic and who is believed to have committed suicide by drowning. Streep has three daughters. One of them, Roberts, who never got along with Streep, has married and moved to Colorado. Lewis also left but she has forever desperately sought Streep's approval. The third sibling, Nicholson, has remained to take care of her parents. Streep had become addicted to medication for various illnesses, including nagging oral cancer, as well as having deep emotional problems, much of this caused when Shepard turned to drink. The film follows these people and their husbands or boyfriends as everyone's inner secrets and sexual desires are brought to the surface. The film ends with Streep blaming Roberts for Shepard's suicide, but Streep also reveals that his suicide might have been preventable. But Streep by now has slipped beyond Roberts' help and leaves the house. Streep breaks down and the film ends with a quote from a poem by T.S. Eliot: "This is how the world ends" (not with a bang, but with a whisper). Streep and Roberts, who have the same deep-seated mean-minded personalities, are superb when confronting each other and blaming each other for their emotional and family problems, almost as a cathartic exercise to purge their mutual guilt for having mismanaged their lives. Streep received an Oscar nomination for Best Actress and Roberts for Best Supporting Actress. On the strength of these two sterling actresses, this film saw good success at the box office, earning more than $74.1 million at the box office in its initial release against a budget of more than $25 million. Songs: "Hinnom, TX" (Justin Vernon); "Don't Let Go," "The Decision," "Forward" (Adam Taylor); "I'll See You Again," "Little White Lies," "Violet's Song" (James Dolan, Marc Copely, Adam Levy); "Lay Down Sally" (Eric Clapton, George Terry, Marcella Detroit as Marcy Levy); "Hetch" (John Morgan Askew, Bruce David Winter, Erik Todd Herzog); "Last Mile Home" (Caleb, Nathan, Jared, and Matthew Followill), "The Kiss" (Adam Taylor),

"2nite We Gonna Live It Up" (John Costello, David Hilker, Aaron Paul Nelson); "Push It" (Herby Azor); "The Stroke" (Billy Squier); "Livin' la Vida Loca" (Desmond Child, Draco Rosa as Robi Rosa); "Silent Film" (Mateo Messina); "Gawd Above" (John Fullbright, Dustin Welch); "Sanford and Son Theme" (Quincy Jones); "The Big One" (Alan Tew); "Can't Keep It Inside" (Brett Dennen). Gutter language, sexual references and drug material prohibit viewing by children. **p**, George Clooney, Harvey Weinstein, Jean Doumanian, Grant Heslov, Steve Traxler; **d**, John Wells; **cast**, Meryl Streep, Julia Roberts, Ewan McGregor, Julianne Nicholson, Chris Cooper, Benedict Cumberbatch, Sam Shepard, Dermot Mulroney, Margo Martindale, Abigail Breslin, Juliette Lewis; **w**, Tracy Letts (based on his play); **c**, Adriano Goldman; **m**, Gustavo Santaolalla; **ed**, Stephen Mirrione; **prod d**, David Gropman; **set d**, Nancy Haigh; **spec eff**, Jo Martin, Wilson Tang.

The Avengers ★★★ 2012; U.S.; 143m; Marvel Studios/PAR/Walt Disney; Color; Science Fiction; **BD**; **DVD**. Exciting sci-fi tale begins with Jackson, who is the director of S.H.I.E.L.D., an international peace-keeping agency whose superheroes include Iron Man (Downey), Captain America (Evans), the Incredible Hulk (Ruffalo), Thor (Hemsworth), Hawkeye (Renner), and Black Widow (Johansson). They all go into action when villain Loki, played by Hiddleston, threatens to destroy the world with the Tesseract, a cube of pulsating energy that opens a gateway to the cosmos. He plans to attack Earth with machines that look like metal monster reptiles. The superheroes start out competing with each other but soon learn that teamwork is what is needed to best the villain. Most of the action takes place in midtown Manhattan, which the monsters try to take over. They soon learn that they do not have a chance against the combined heroics of the Avengers. The film opens with Asgardian Hiddleston encountering the Other (Denisof), leader of an extraterrestrial race known as the Chitauri. In exchange for retrieving the Tesseract, a powerful energy source, Denisof promises Hiddleston an army with which he can subjugate Earth. Nick Fury (Jackson), director of the espionage agency S.H.I.E.L.D., and his lieutenant agent, Hill (smulders), arrive at a remote research faculty where physicist Selvig (Skarsgard) is leading a team experimenting on the Tesseract. Agent Coulson (Gregg) explains that the Tesseract has been radiating an unusual kind of energy. It suddenly activates and opens a wormhole that allows Hiddleston to reach Earth. He takes the object and uses his scepter to enslave Skarsgard and some other agents including Clint Barton/Hawkeye (Renner) to help him in a getaway. Jackson responds to the attack by reactivating the "Avengers Initiative." Agent Johansson is sent to Calcutta to recruit Bruce Banner/Hulk (Ruffalo) to trace the Tesseract through its gamma radiation emissions. Gregg then visits Tony Stack-Iron Man (Downey), to have him review Skarsgard's research, and Jackson assigns Steve Rogers/Captain America (Evans) to retrieve the Tesseract. In Stuttgart, Germany, Renner steals iridium needed to stabilize Tesseract's power, while Hiddleston causes a distraction that leads to a confrontation with Evans, Renner, and Ruffalo that ends when Hiddleston surrenders. While Hiddleston is escorted to S.H.I.E.L.D., Thor (Hemsworth), who is his adoptive brother, arrives and frees him, hoping to convince him to abandon his plan and return to Skarsgard. Hemsworth agrees to take Hiddleston to S.H.I.E.L.D.'s flying aircraft carrier, the Helicarrier. There, Hiddleston is imprisoned while Ruffalo and Downey try to locate the Tesseract. The Avengers become divided over how to approach Hiddleston and the revelation that S.H.I.E.L.D. plans to harness the Tesseract to develop weapons against hostile extraterrestrials. As the Avengers argue, Renner and Hiddleston's other possessed agents attack the Helicarrier, disabling its engines in flight and causing Ruffalo to transform into the Hulk. Downey and Evans try restarting the damaged engine, and Hemsworth tries to stop Ruffalo's rampage. Ruffalo fights Renner and knocks him unconscious, which breaks Hiddleston's mind control. Hiddleston then kills Gregg and escapes, ejecting Hemsworth from the airship, while the Hulk (Ruffalo) falls to the ground after attacking a S.H.I.E.L.D. fighter jet. Jackson uses

Uggie and Berenice Bejo in *The Artist*, 2012.

Gregg's death to motivate the Avengers into working as a team. Downey and Evans realize that Hiddleston's defeat of them will not be sufficient. He needs to overpower them publicly so as to validate himself as ruler of Earth. Hiddleston uses the Tesseract, together with a device Skarsgard made, to open a wormhole above Stark Tower to the Chitauri fleet in space, launching his invasion. The united avengers meet in defense of New York City, where the wormhole is located, but realize they will be overwhelmed as waves of Chitauri descend upon Earth. Ruffalo arrives and transforms into the Hulk, and together he, Downey, Evans, Hemsworth, Renner, and Johansson battle the Chitauri while evacuating civilians. Ruffalo finds Hiddleston and beats him into submission. Johansson makes her way to the wormhole generator where Skarsgard, freed of Hiddleston's control, reveals that Hiddleston's scepter can be used to shut down the generator. Meanwhile, Jackson's superiors attempt to end the invasion by launching a nuclear missile at Manhattan. Downey's space suit runs out of power, and he falls back through the wormhole just as Johansson closes it. Downey goes into freefall, but Evans saves him. Hemsworth returns Hiddleston and the Tesseract to Skarsgard and the crisis is over. Jackson is confident that the Avengers will return if and when they are needed. The overwhelming attraction of this film is its nonstop action and phenomenal special effects achieved through digital enhancements, the dominating commercial factor in today's films (where character development and story line have become marginal if not unnecessary). It is an eye-popping visual light show that is both mesmerizing and, because of its incessant, edgy action, unnerving and somewhat disturbing. Its audience is chiefly those adolescents addicted to video game shows, the more violent the better, and that is what this film delivers, one rapid wallop after another to the head and eyes without end. The indefatigable heroes, who have been saving the world in our comics for almost a century, are inhuman towers of strength as are the villains, and their much battered punching bag is the viewer (or those who might cry out in perverse pain: "Beat me some more—I love it!"). Admirers of Shakespeare, Eugene O'Neill, or even Mickey Spillane, should look elsewhere, but those craving mindless, dehumanizing action and visual destruction of any kind of physical matter will find this film rewarding. This film was a mega-blockbuster at the box office, earning more than $1.520 billion against a budget of more than $220 million, becoming the fourth largest grossing film to date (after **Avatar**, 2009, at $2.787 billion; **Titanic**, 1997, at $2.186 billion; and **Jurassic World**, 2015, at $1.668 billion). Not related to the 1961-1969 TV series and 1998 film. Songs: "Black Dirt" (Emile Millar, Michael Baiardi, Mick Flowers), "Shoot to Thrill" (Angus Young, Malcolm Young, Brian Johnson), "Live to Rise" (Chris Cornell), "String Quartet No. 13" (Franz Schubert). ***Author's Note***: The film was shot on location in Albuquerque, New Mexico; Cleveland, Ohio; Pittsburgh, Pennsylva-

Jean Dujardin and Berenice Bejo in *The Artist,* **2012.**

nia; and New York City where mammoth sets to show widespread destruction were created. Excessive violence and drug references prohibit viewing by children. **p,** Kevin Feige, Alexander Ward; **d,** Joss Whedon; **cast,** Robert Downey Jr., Chris Evans, Mark Ruffalo, Chris Hemsworth, Scarlett Johansson, Jeremy Renner, Tom Hiddleston, Samuel L. Jackson, Gwyneth Paltrow, Clark Gregg, Stellan Skarsgard, Powers Boothe, Jenny Agutter, Harry Dean Stanton; **w,** Joss Whedon (based on a story by Whedon and Zak Penn); **c,** Seamus McGarvey; **m,** Alan Silvestri; **ed,** Jeffrey Ford, Lisa Lassek; **prod d,** James Chinlund; **art d,** Benjamin Edelberg, Jann K. Engel, Gregory S. Hooper, William O. Hunter, Randy Moore, Richard L. Johnson; **set d,** Victor J. Zolfo; **spec eff,** Chris Brenczewski, Daniel Sudick.

Avengers: Age of Ultron ★★★ 2015; U.S.; 141m; Marvel Studios/Walt Disney; Color; Science Fiction; Children: Unacceptable (MPAA: PG-13); **3D; BD; DVD; IV.** This exciting sequel to the 2012 film **The Avengers** sees the further adventures of characters in the Marvel comic books in which Downey and Avenger vigilante superheroes attempt to restart a dormant peacekeeping program called Ultron, but things go wrong and they have to try to stop it from destroying the universe (that's right, the universe, not merely Earth). The other Avengers include Evans as Captain America, Hemsworth as Thor, Ruffalo as Hulk, Remmer as Hawkeye, and Johansson as Black Widow. The story takes place in the mythical East European country of Sokovia where the Avengers raid an evil Hydra outpost led by Kretschmann, who is experimenting on humans by using twins (Taylor-Johnson), who have superhuman speed, and Olsen, a mind-controller. Downey and Ruffalo discover an artificial intelligence in a scepter and use it to complete Ultron's defense system. Ultron believes it has to kill off all humans in order to save Earth, so it minions build an army of robot drones. The Avengers then go to Africa to obtain a mineral that might save humans from annihilation. Back in Sokovia, the Avengers fight Ultron's robots, win the battle, and more Avengers are then trained to protect against a similar threat in future and the human race is again saved. Like its predecessor, this film presents dazzling digitally enhanced special effects, which is at the core of its attraction. This film had a colossal success at the box office, earning more than $1.405 billion in its initial release against a budget of $279.9 million, becoming the sixth-largest grossing film to this date. Songs/Music: "Concerto for Piano and Orchestra in C Major: Larghetto" (Antonio Salieri), "Themes from Marvels from "Marvel's The Avengers" (Alan Silvestri), "Casta Diva" from the opera "Norma" (Vincenzio Bellini), "Great Intentions" (Jason French Muniz, Colton Fisher, James Katabalas, Jason Rabinowitz), "Liquid Spirit" (Gregory Porter), "I Can't Get Started" (Ira Gershwin, Vernon Duke), "Evening of Elegance" (Bill Keis), "Drum Duel" (Brian Tyler), "I've Got No Strings" (Leigh Har-

line, Ned Washington), "Cinderella" from the ballet by Sergei Prokofiev), "Berliner Messe, Kyrie" (Arvo Part), "Full Dress Hop" (Gene Krupa, David Roy Eldridge), "Hikari" (Hikaru Utada). Excessive violence prohibits viewing by children. **p,** Kevin Feige, Mitchell Bell; **d,** Joss Whedon; **cast,** Robert Downey Jr., Chris Evans, Chris Hemsworth, Mark Ruffalo, Scarlett Johansson, Paul Bettany, Jeremy Renner, James Spader, Thomas Kretschmann, Samuel L. Jackson, Don Cheadle, Aaron Taylor-Johnson, Elizabeth Olsen; **w,** Whedon (based on Marvel comic books by Jack Kirby, Stan Lee); **c,** Ben Davis; **m,** Danny Elfman, Brian Tyler; **ed,** Jeffrey Ford, Lisa Lassek; **prod d,** Charles Wood; **art d,** Ray Chan; **set d,** Chris Howes, Sheona Mitchley, Richard Roberts; **spec eff,** Paul Corbould, Ian Corbould.

Bahubali: The Beginning ★★★★ 2015; India; 159m; Arka Mediaworks; Color; Adventure; Children: Unacceptable; **DVD.** This exciting two-part epic from India begins with two brothers competing for the rule of a kingdom. The film opens with Krishnan, a young queen of an ancient kingdom in India, coming out of a cave near a waterfall with an infant in her arms. Under threat of pursuing soldiers, she decides to save the baby boy by drowning herself, but keeping the baby's head above the water on top of her head. Rohini, a villager, saves the boy, and names him Sivudu. She and her husband rear the child as their own son, hiding themselves in the cave, which is sealed by a removable large rock. The boy Sivudu, played by Prabhas, wants to climb the waterfall, but repeatedly falls in every attempt. Rohini asks Bharani, a holy man, for help, and is told to pour water on the boy's head 116 times in order for her prayers to be answered. From atop the falls, a mask descends onto Prabhas and creates an imprint of the person to whom the mask belongs, a beautiful girl. Prabhas holds her image in his mind and eventually manages to climb the waterfall. There he discovers that the mask belongs to Bhatia, a rebellious female warrior who is waging guerrilla warfare against Daggubati, the king of the realm. Prabhas learns that the former queen has been chained in the palace by the king for the past twenty-five years. Bhatia falls in love with Prabhas when she learns that her image inspired him to climb the waterfall. It is then learned that Prabhas is the son of a former king of the land. In a flashback, we learn of a conflict between cousins Prabhas and Daggubati, whose father, Nassar, was denied the throne because of the imperfection of a disfigured hand. His brother became the new king, but died young. Krishnan becomes steward until a new king can be crowned. Prabhas and Daggubati are brought up together as brothers, but Daggubati is obsessed with gaining the throne. They are now both trained in the martial arts and warfare, but both have differing ideas about how to be a king. Prabhas is generous and giving to everyone but Daggubati is violent and self-serving. When another kingdom wages war against theirs, the brothers learn that whichever of them brings the head of the enemy ruler will become the new king of their land. Daggubati slaughters innocent people as well as the enemy in order to win the war. But Krishnan proclaims Prabhas as the new king because of his fair play and nobility and leadership in the war. Daggubati becomes the general of the kingdom's army, a position that allows him to accrue power and eventually oppose Prabhas, which sets the stage for the second part of this fine epic, which is scheduled for release in 2016. Though the story line is reminiscent of the biblical tale of Moses and Rameses in ancient Egypt, it nevertheless provides a provocative tale that is enacted by the entire cast. The film saw success at the box office, earning more than $91 million in its initial release. Songs: "Pacha Bottasi," (Anant Sriram), "Neeva Nadhi (Inaganti Sundar); "Dheerava" (Ramajogayya Sastry); "Mamatala Talli" (K. Shiva Shaki Datta), "Nippulaa Swasa Ga" (Inaganti Sundar), "Manohari" (Chaitanya Prasad); "Sivuni Aana" (Sundar); "Dheerava" (Aditya, Neol Sean); "Pachai Thee," "Deeva Nadhi,:" "Dheerane Tamil," "Irulkonda," "Moochile," "Manohari," "Siva Sivaya" (Madhan Karky); "Mamta Se Bhari," "Jal Rahin Hain," "Swapri Sunehere," "Khoya Hain," "Jaun Hai

Who," "Panchhi Bole," "Manohari" (Manoj Muntashir); "Siva Sivaya," "Irul Thingum Vaanil," Manohari," "Njan Chendana," "Pancha Theeyanu Nee," "Punnara Kanavine," "Theekanal Jwalayayi" (Mankombu Gopalakrishnan). **p**, Prasad Devineni, Shobu Yarlagadda; **d**, S.S. Rajamouli; **cast**, Prabhas, Rana Daggubati, Anushka Shetty, Tamannaah Bhatia, Ramya Krishnan, Nasser, Sudeep, Satyaraj, Tanikella Bharani, Gabriella Bertante, Nora Fatehi, Prabhakar; **w**, Rajamouli (based on a story by Vijayendra Prasad); **c**, Senthil Kumar; **m**, M.M. Keeravani; **ed**, Venkateswara Rao Kotagiri; **prod d**, Sabu Cyril; **art d**, Manu Jagadh; **spec eff**, Walt Jones.

The Bag Man ★★★ 2014; U.S.; 108m; Cinedigm; Color; Crime Drama; Children: Unacceptable (MPAA: R); **BD**; **DVD**. Taut thriller sees Cusack as a hit man on the run from a dark past that involves an ex-wife, who was murdered after they had an argument about his murder-for-hire job. Crime boss De Niro hires him to get a mysterious black leather bag from a New Orleans bayou motel, but not to open it. He is to wait with the bag in his room for more instructions. When one of De Niro's henchmen delivers the bag to Cusack, he shoots at him, wounding Cusack in the hand and Cusack, in turn, shoots and kills the goon, hiding his body in the trunk of his car. Cusack phones De Niro about the attack, but is told only to follow his orders. The motel is run by wheelchair-bound Glover, and is occupied by a bunch of violent misfits, including two psychotic pimps, Fingaz and Klebba. When Cusack learns that two men in the hotel are making inquiries about him, he breaks into their room and kills them both in a firefight, only to learn that they were FBI agents. He disposes of the bodies, but, when returning to his room, he finds another guest, Da Costa, a beautiful prostitute, hiding in his room. She has fled from her pimps, who menace her. Cusack decides to help Da Costa, but, while driving her to a bus station, Fingaz and Klebba arrive to attack them both, and Cusack kills these berserk flesh peddlers. Cusack takes Da Costa back to his room, but Glover calls the local sheriff, Purcell, after Cusack refuses to pay him more money for double occupancy since Da Costa is now staying with him. Purcell arrives to briefly question Cusack. After he leaves, Cusack gets into a fight with Glover, killing him. Purcell returns, asking what has happened to Glover, but before Purcell begins to torture Cusack, Da Costa arrives to aid him and where Cusack kills Purcell. When De Niro finally arrives, he tells Cusack that his mission was simply a test to see if he was still following orders. Everyone Cusack was compelled to dispatch, De Niro sadistically states, were on his payroll, including the police officers, but who we unwitting participants in De Niro's bloodletting test to challenge Cusack's loyalties to him. Da Costa then makes the mistake of telling Cusack that she had looked into that bag, and Cusack now believes that for her violation of De Niro's orders, both will be killed by the crime boss. Nevertheless, Cusack informs De Niro about this and De Niro tells him to kill Da Costa. Instead, Cusack, by this time, has looked into the mysterious bag to see the head of his wife, who had been ordered killed by De Niro to prevent him from quitting him. Cusack then gets into a battle with De Niro and De Niro explodes the motel with previously set charges in an attempt to kill Cusack, but Da Costa, who has been wounded in the battle, kills De Niro. She later receives a huge reward for ridding the world of De Niro and she and Cusack then drive away to begin a new life together. All of the murder and mayhem in the crazy quilt story line of this film is well orchestrated, a chaotic madness where Cusack and Da Costa give riveting performances. The viewer's sense of improbability that any crime boss would go to the detailed lengths enacted herein to assure the dedication of a prized employee is overwhelmed by the almost nonstop perils and action, which are cleverly presented by director Grovic. The cat-and-mouse game over what might be contained in that bag is ancillary to the life-and-death exercise De Niro decrees and serves as a catalyst to the grim events that follow. This concept undoubtedly inspired several other film noir entries, most notably **Night Must Fall**, 1937, where charming serial killer Robert Montgomery, who travels about with a leather case containing the head of

Quvenzhane Wallis in *Beasts of the Southern Wild*, 2012.

one of his female victims, and the more grisly underworld tale, **Bring Me the Head of Alfredo Garcia**, 1974. Such gory artifacts have surfaced in other films, even the classic adventure tale **Northwest Passage**, 1940, where one of the colonists who has attacked an Indian village carries a sack with the head of one of those dead Indians as a source of food! This film is not related to a 2005 film with the same name. Songs: "Numb" (Gary Clark Jr.), "Beacon" (David Frost), "Stand My Ground" (John O'Regan), "Lezz Bounce" (Dorian Childs), "I Can Handle It" (Darryl Warren, Stacey Justice), "Wolf Teeth" (Jonathan McPherson, James Sutton), "Day Is Done" (Nick Drake), "I Got Loaded" (Camille Bob), "Chopin Waltz" (Frederic Chopin). Excessive violence, sexual content, and gutter language prohibit viewing by children. **p**, Peter D. Graves, Warren Ostergard; **d**, David Grovic; **cast**, John Cusack, Rebecca Da Costa, Robert De Niro, Crispin Glover, Dominic Purcell, Sticky Fingaz, Martin Klebba, David Shumbris, Chazz Mendez, Ian Mclaughlin; **w**, Grovic, Paul Conway, based on the screenplay **Motel** by James Russo and inspired by the story "The Cat" by Marie-Louise von Franz. **c**, Steve Mason; **m**, Tony Morales, Edward Rogers; **ed**, Devin Maurer, Michael R. Miller; **prod d**, J. Dennis Washington; **art d**, Kelly Curley; **set d**, Cynthia Anne Slagter; **spec eff**, Peter Chesney.

Bajrangi Bhaijaan ★★★ 2015; India; 107m; Eros International; Color; Comedy/Drama; Children: Unacceptable. **DVD**. Sensitive and rewarding film begins with Malhotra, a speech-impaired Muslim girl who is taken to Delhi, India, by her mother in hopes of praying for her speech to return. Nothing helps her, and, on their return to their village, the train stops and Malhotra gets out to help a lamb stuck in a ditch on the India-Pakistan border. Lost in India, she boards a freight train and arrives in a town where Salman Khan, a devout Brahmin, feeds her and tells her to call him uncle. Khan eventually takes her to his home in Delhi. He later learns what village she is from, and, after many misadventures, she not only returns home, but has regained her ability to speak as thousands of Indians and Pakistanis cheer her. This film saw success at the box office where it earned more than $95 million in its initial release against a budget of $14 million. Songs: "Selfie Le le Re" and "Chicken Song" (Mayur Puri), "Pushkarna" (Tu Chahiye), "Bhar Do Jholi Meri" and "Tu Jo Mila" (Kausar Munir), "Aaj Ki Party" (Shabbir Ahmed), "Zindagi" (Neelesh Misra). **p**, Kabir Khan, Salman Khan, Sunil Lulla, Rockline Venkatesh, Amar Butala; **d**, Kabir Khan; **cast**, Salman Khan, Kareena Kapoor, Harshaali Malhotra, Nawazuddin Siddiqui, Om Puri, Sharat Saxena, Meher Vij, Najeem Khan, Kamlesh Gill; **w**, Vijayendra Prasad, Kabir Khan, Parveez Sheikh, Asad Hussain (based on a story by Prasad); **c**, Aseem Mishra; **m**, Julius Packiam; **ed**, Rameshwar S. Bhagat; **prod d**, Snigdha Basu, Sumit Basu; **spec eff**, Keith Devlin.

Quvenzhane Wallis in *Beasts of the Southern Wild*, 2012.

Beasts of the Southern Wild ★★★ 2012; U.S.; 93m; Cinereach/FOX Searchlight; Color; Fantasy; Children: Unacceptable (MPAA: PG-13); **BD**; **DVD**. Entertaining tale has Hushpuppy, a six-year-old girl played by Wallis, living with her father, Henry, in the Bathtub, a remote southern bayou region. She doesn't know where her mother is, but we presume she has died. Henry gives Wallis tough love to prepare her for when he's no longer alive to protect her. He falls ill of a mysterious malady, and nature goes wild as temperatures rise and ice caps melt, this abrupt and radical climate change releasing an army of prehistoric creatures called aurochs. With Henry's health fading and these monstrous creatures arriving, Wallis nevertheless goes in search of her mother. This takes her on adventures in which she defies the aurochs. Further, she learns to have courage and where she finds love, albeit she does not locate her mother, even though she meets a cook who may be that long-sought person. Wallis is wonderful, and the whole story is superbly presented by director Zeitlin. This film received Oscar nominations for Best Picture; Best Director (Zeitlin); Best Actress (Wallis, who at age nine, became the youngest such nominee in film history); and Best Adapted Screenplay (Alibar, Zeitlin). The film did well at the box office, earning more than $21.9 million in its initial release against a budget of $1.8 million. Songs: "Valse de Balfa" (Will Balfa), "Henry" (Louis Michot), "Les veuves de la coulee" (Leroy LeBlanc, Oran Guidry), "La danse de Mardi Gras" (Dewey Balfa), "Jole Blon" (Buddy Dee), "It Will Have to Do/Until the Real Thing Comes Along" (Sammy Cahn, Saul Chaplin, L.E. Freeman, Mann Holiner, Alberta Nichols). Thematic material, including child imperilment, disturbing images, gutter language and brief sexuality prohibit viewing by children. **p**, Michael Gottwald, Dan Janvey, Josh Penn, Chris Carroll, Matthew Parker; **d**, Benh Zeitlin; **cast**, Quvenzhane Wallis, Dwight Henry, Levy Easterly, Lowell Landes, Pamela Harper, Gina Montana, Jonshel Alexander, Nicholas Clark, Joseph Brown, Philip Lawrence; **w**, Zeitlin, Lucy Alibar (based on the play "Juicy and Delicious" by Alibar); **c**, Ben Richardson; **m**, Dan Romer, Zeitlin; **ed**, Crockett Doob, Affonso Goncalves; **prod d**, Alex DiGerlando; **art d**, Dawn Masi; **set d**, Erin Staub; **spec eff**, Neil Stockstill, Ian M. Stockstill.

Beautiful Creatures ★★★ 2013; U.S.; 124m; Alcon Entertainment; WB; Color; Fantasy/Romance; Children: Unacceptable (MPAA: PG-13); **BD**; **DVD**. This fascinatingly eerie tale begins in a small town in South Carolina, where Ehrenreich, a young man, awakens from a recurring dream about a girl he has never met. In voice-over narration, he talks about his obsession of reading banned books, his despair of living in a small town, and how he goes to college. In his junior year at that college he sees beautiful young Englert, who looks like the girl in his haunting dreams. Englert is not popular at school, and rumors circulate about her reclusive uncle, Irons, and that her family members are devil worshippers. When classroom windows shatter, classmates and others in town believe Englert has caused these disturbances, all believing that she is a witch. Ehrenreich almost runs down Englert with his car and gives her a ride home. They quickly find that they have some things in common, such as a love of poetry and that their mothers have both died. Ehrenreich finds a locket Englert has left in his car and returns it to her in the mansion where she lives. Touching the locket, Englert is transformed back to the era of the American Civil War (1861-1865) and Ehrenreich awakens back at his home, as if this experience is another one of his strange dreams. Irons senses the young people are in love and attempts to keep them apart. Ehrenreich nevertheless continues to pursue Englert and she tells him that she and her family are "casters," beings capable of performing magical spells such as changing the weather and casting illusions. Englert believes that on her 16th birthday, she will lean toward her light or dark side, the latter causing her to become consumed by evil and where she will hurt those she loves. Ehrenreich tries to assure her that she is responsible for her own choices and that she is a good person. Two casters then appear and attempt to persuade Englert to enter her dark side. They are Rossum, Englert's cousin and childhood friend, and Thompson, who is Englert's mother, who takes possession of the mind and body of Mary Todd Lincoln (1818-1882). Thompson foresees Englert becoming a very powerful caster who can rid the Earth of humans, leaving casters to rule in their place. The weird adventures then continue until Englert finds herself to be a half-dark, half-light caster, but she rids herself of her dark side through the love expressed by Ehrenreich, who, while driving away from the college, shouts her name. Though well acted and directed with gusto by LaGravenese, this strange, compelling film did not do well at the box office, earning more than $60 million in its initial release against a budget of $60 million. Songs: "Never Too Late" and "Run to Me" (Dhani Harrison), "Subterranean Homesick Blues" (Bob Dylan), "Theme from 'A Summer Place'" (Max Steiner), "Make It Home" (Dhani Harrison, Jonathan Sadoff), "Needle and Thread" (Alice Englert). ***Author's Note***: One of the banned books Ehrenreich and Englert share is written by underground poet Charles Bukowski (Henry Charles Bukowski, 1920-1994), who was a friend of this author, and this author published one of Bukowski's books, *Cold Dogs in the Courtyard*, 1965, through my newspaper, *Literary Times*, which I was then publishing in Chicago. Bukowski, a brilliant loner who wore a pock-marked face from a childhood disease and worked as a mail sorter in the Los Angeles Post Office, churned out poetic polemics against all manner of Establishment forces for years when not boozing himself into prolonged benders. In one of our many conversations together (when I made one of my infrequent visits to Bukowski in L.A.), I asked Charlie if he believed in the Hereafter and he replied: "No, I don't believe in ghosts either or any of that other spiritual crap that people use to make themselves believe that their mortality is somehow immortal. I do believe in some human beings, but only a few." I asked him to name some of those human beings and he said: "You, for one, because you're buying the drinks tonight." Violence, frightening images and some sexual material prohibit viewing by children. **p**, Broderick Johnson, Andrew A. Kosove, Molly Mickler Smith, Erwin Stoff, Steven P. Wegner; **d&w**, Richard LaGravenese (based on the novel by Kami Garcia and Margaret Stohl); **cast**, Alden Ehrenreich, Alice Englert, Jeremy Irons, Emmy Thompson, Eileen Atkins, Viola Davis, Emma Rossum, Thomas Mann, Margo Martindale, Zoey Deutch, Tiffany Boone; **c**, Philippe Rousselot; **m**, Thenewno2; **ed**, David Moritz; **prod d**, Richard Sherman; **art d**, Lorin Flemming; **set d**, Matthew Flood Ferguson; **spec eff**, Matt Kutcher, Donnie Dean, Jonathan Dunn.

Before I Go to Sleep ★★★ 2014; UK/U.S./France/Sweden; 92m; Film i Vasi/Filmgate Films/Clarius Entertainment; Color; Mystery/Thriller; Children: Unacceptable (MPAA: R); **BD**; **DVD**. Intriguing psychological drama sees Kidman waking up every morning in bed with Firth, a man who says repeatedly that he is her husband. However, she does not know who he is, and he tells her that she has amnesia from a car accident ten years earlier, to keep Kidman from knowing the truth so as to save her trauma. Strong, a hospital neurologist, tells Kidman that she lost her memory after having been sexually attacked. She then learns that she had been married, but, in an affair with another man who sexually assaulted her, she developed amnesia to stave off any traumatic memories. Strong says that her attacker was later arrested, and all ends well as she finally recognizes Firth as her real husband. Kidman, Firth and Strong give impressive performances in this carefully made tale from Joffe. This film did not fare well at the box office, earning a little more than $15 million in its initial release against a budget of more than $22 million. Songs: "You Keep Me Hangin' On" (James Holland Jr.), "Girls on Top" (Nina Ossoff, Dana Calitri, Martin Briley). Brutal violence and gutter language prohibit viewing by children. **p**, Ridley Scott, Tony Scott, Mark Gill, Avi Lerner, Liza Marshall, Matthew O'Toole, Jack Arbuthnott, Peter Heslop; **d&w**, Rowan Joffe (based on the novel by S.J. Watson); **cast**, Nicole Kidman, Colin Firth, Mark Strong, Anne-Marie Duff, Dean-Charles Chapman, Jing Lusi, Adam Levy, Llewella Gideon, Rosie MacPherson, Charlie Gardner; **c**, Ben Davis; **m**, Ed Schearmur; **ed**, Melanie Oliver; **prod d**, Kave Quinn; **art d**, Mark Raggett, Tim Blake, John West; **set d**, Niamh Coulter; **spec eff**, Mark White, Alan Banis.

Before Midnight ★★★ 2013; U.S.; 109m; Castle Rock/Sony; Color; Drama/Romance; Children: Unacceptable (MPAA: R); **BD**; **DVD**. In a sequel to **Before Sunset** (1995) and **Before Sunrise** (2004), this pleasant romantic drama opens with the aging lovers Hawke and Delpy living in Paris, he as a novelist and she is thinking of becoming a government worker. They have become parents to twin girls, and Hawke is not having an easy time with his teenage son, Davey-Fitzpatrick, who lives in Chicago with Hawke's ex-wife. Davey-Fitzpatrick has been spending the summer with Hawke's ex-wife on a Greek island. The couple has long conversations about sex, their children, their careers, and whatever happened to them over the years, all enlivened by beautiful Greek location filming. At one point, they argue when Hawke tells Delpy that he wants to relocate to Chicago to be closer to son Davey-Fitzpatrick, which would spoil Delpy's career plans. The confrontation becomes so bitter that she tells him that she no longer loves him. He meets with her later and brings her a letter, telling her that he is a time traveler and gives her a letter written when she was eighty-two and where she describes their last night together as the most wonderful moment of her life. He tells her that he loves her. Delpy laughs, joining with Hawke in the amusing joke, and it appears that they will reconcile and continue their lives together. The story is a simple one, but so well-acted by Hawke, Delpy and Davey-Fitzpatrick as sincere and appealing characters that it sustains interest throughout. The intelligent script received an Oscar nomination as Best Adapted Screenplay (Linklater, Hawke, Delpy). The film did well at the box office, earning more than $23.3 million in its initial release against a budget of $3 million. Songs: "Gia Ena Tango" (Charis Alexiou), "Stou Mema Ta Traina" and "O Antonis O Kekes" (Nikos Kalogeropoulos). Sexual content, nudity and gutter language prohibit viewing by children. **p**, Richard Linklater, Sara Woodhatch, Christos V. Konstantakopoulos, Vincent Palmo Jr., Athina Rachel Tsangari; **d**, Linklater; **cast**, Ethan Hawke, Julie Delpy, Seamus Davey-Fitzpatrick, Jennifer Prior, Charlotte Prior, Xenia Kalogeropoulou, Walter Lassally, Ariane Labed, Yiannis Papadopoulos, Panos Koronis; **w**, Linklater, Hawke, Delpy (based on characters created by Linklater, Kim Krizan); **c**, Christos Voudouris; **m**, Graham Reynolds; **ed**, Sandra Adair; Anna Georgiadou.

Belle ★★★ 2014; U.K.; 105m; DJ Films/Fox Searchlight; Color; Drama/Biography/History; Children: Unacceptable (MPAA: PG-13); **BD**; **DVD**. This good period drama was inspired by the true story of Dido Elizabeth Belle (1761-1804), played by Mbatha-Raw, who is the illegitimate mixed-race daughter of a British Royal Navy admiral.

Quvenzhane Wallis and beast in *Beasts of the Southern Wild,* 2012.

Reared by her aristocratic great-uncle Lord Mansfield, played by Wilkinson, and his wife, Watson, Belle's lineage allows her certain privileges. However, her dark skin color prevents her from fully participating in the traditions of her social standing. Left to wonder if she will ever find love, she begins a romance with Goode, an idealistic young vicar's son who is bent on social change. With her help, he gets Wilkinson, as Lord Chief Justice, to end slavery in England. The film ends with Mbatha-Raw and Goode being married and having children. The acting is top notch from Wilkinson, Mbatha-Raw and Goode, along with the rest of the cast, all firmly directed by Asante, who shows an accurate eye for historical accuracy. The film saw modest success at the box office, earning more than $16.5 million in its initial release against a budget of $10.9 million. Music: "Piano Suite in G Minor, Allemande" (George Frideric Handel), "Fugue No. 8 in E Flat Minor" and "Violin Partita No. 2 in D Minor, Corrente & Sarabande" (Johann Sebastian Bach), "The Island of Beauty" (John Pepusch), "Concerto Grosso Op. 6, No. 5 in F Major, Andante Larghertto," "Concerto Grosso Grosso Op. 6, No. 11 in A Major, Andante Larghetto" (Handel). *Author's Note*: Little is known about the real Dido Elizabeth Belle, who is shown in the 1792 painting with her cousin, Lady Elizabeth Murray (1760-1825), so the writers of this film had the luxury of creating their own portrait of this enigmatic woman. Of special note are the startlingly impressive sets, particularly the recreation of the 18th-Century docks in Bristol, England, which were meticulously constructed on the Isle of Man by outstanding production designer Bowles. Equally astounding is the recreation of Kenwood House, also by Bowles, who recreated this lavish mansion along the lines of the most stately houses to be found in London. The film was shot on location at Oxford, London and the Isle of Man. Thematic elements, gutter language and smoking prohibit viewing by children. **p**, Damian Jones, Robert Norris, Jane Robertson; **d**, Amma Asante; **cast**, Gugu Mbatha-Raw, Tom Wilkinson, Emily Watson, Miranda Richardson, Matthew Goode, Penelope Wilton, Timothy Walker, Andrew Woodall, James Northcote, James Norton; **w**, Misan Saga; **c**, Ben Smithard; **m**, Rachel Portman; **ed**, Victoria Boydell; Pia Di Cataula; **prod d**, Simon Bowles; **art d**, Claudio Campena, Ben Smith; **set d**, Tina Jones; **spec eff**, Chris Reynolds, Angela Barson.

The Best Exotic Marigold Hotel ★★★★ 2012; U.K./U.S./United Arab Emirates; 124m; Participant Media/Fox Searchlight; Color; Comedy/Drama; Children: Unacceptable (MPAA: PG-13); **BD**; **DVD**. Delightful tale sees seven British senior citizens deciding that they can live more cheaply at a retirement hotel in India than in England, so they answer an online advertisement that promotes a luxurious hotel with very inexpensive rates. Dench wants to go to India to live more comfortably after her husband has died and left her with staggering debts.

Dev Patel in *The Best Exotic Marigold Hotel*, 2012.

Wilkinson, a retired high court judge, wants to return to India where he spent eighteen years in residence when he was much younger. Wilton and Nighy, an aging married couple, are also seeking a cheap but nice place to live after having lost most of their life savings on their daughter's failed Internet business. Aging playboy Pickup wants to go to India in an effort to renew his youth by developing new romances. Imrie is an aging divorcee seeking to find a new spouse and retired housekeeper, Smith, even though she is prejudiced against Indians, wants to go to India to get an inexpensive operation for a hip replacement. They all travel to Jaipur where, to their collective disappointment, they find the hotel to be far less than luxurious and run by an overly energetic and optimistic young manager, Patel. While struggling to find funds to renovate the hotel, Patel also works hard to keep a relationship with girlfriend Desae, which Patel's mother opposes. Meanwhile, the new British guests each affect each other in different ways. Wilton becomes interested in Wilkinson until he confides that he is gay and looking for his male lover from years ago. He finds that aging man, but learns that he is about to enter an arranged marriage. Wilkinson gives up the ghost by dying from exhaustion. Meanwhile, the other Britons become so disenchanted with the hotel they talk of leaving, until Smith convinces them it can be renovated. Smith's xenophobic prejudices have evaporated after she has developed a good relationship with her helpful Indian physician, and through the good service she receives from an Indian maid working at the hotel. The British guests agree to stay while the assertive Smith takes charge of the hotel's renovations and front desk operations. Dench by this time has gotten a job with a call center dealing with relocated Britons and then introduces her supervisor, Hardcastle, to lothario Pickup, both quickly developing a relationship. For most, the stay has proven a happy adjustment, and the hotel's new success inspires Patel to defy his mother's edicts by telling her that he is going to marry Desae, the girl he loves. All of the acting is exceptional in this inspiring story that proves that the elderly share the same emotional desires as their younger counterparts and that world still welcomes lovers no matter how old they might be. Patel is remembered for starring as the young quiz show contestant in **Slum Dog Millionaire**, 2008. The way was left open for a sequel that was released in 2015 under the title **The Second Best Exotic Marigold Hotel**, especially after the surprise enormous success this film enjoyed at the box office where it earned more than $136.8 million in its initial release against a budget of $10 million. Songs: "Strangers in the Night" (Bert Kaempfert, Charles Singleton, Eddie Snyder), "Arroz Con Pollo" (Ali Dee as Ali Theodore, Julian Davis, Jordan Yaeger), "Piano Sonata No. 15" (Ludwig van Beethoven), "Circus Hour Goat Curry Sauce Tumbi Tumbi" (Tony Lewis, Mike Reed), "Clara" (Leo Nissim), "Raga Khamaj" (Karl Lundeberg), "A Touch of Elegance" (Peter Falkner), "Le Freak" (Nile Rodgers, Bernard

Edwards), "Cham Cham Chamke Chuari" (traditional). ***Author's Note***: This surprise international hit originally had trouble finding a producing company after several studios rejected the story, thinking it unmarketable. The producers, however, managed to convince some investors to back the film and the rest is history. On-location shooting took place in Jaipur and Udaipur, India, and the hotel used was the Ravla Khempur, located outside Udaipur, an equestrian hotel that had once been the palace of a tribal chieftain. Sexual content and gutter language prohibit viewing by children. **p**, Graham Broadbent, Peter Czernin, Sarah Harvey, Caroline Hewitt; **d**, John Madden; **cast**, Maggie Smith, Judi Dench, Tom Wilkinson, Bill Nighy, Penelope Wilton, Ronald Pickup, Diana Hardcastle, Lucy Robinson, Celia Imrie, Dev Patel, Tena Desae, Sara Stewart, Patrick Pearson; **w**, Ol Parker (based on the novel *These Foolish Things* by Deborah Moggach); **c**, Ben Davis; **m**, Thomas Newman; **ed**, Chris Gill; **prod d**, Alan MacDonald; **art d**, Dilip More, Peter Francis; **set d**, Tina Jones; **spec eff**, Shiva Nanda.

The Best Offer ★★★ 2014; Italy; 131m; Paco Cinematografica; WB/ICF Films; Color; Crime Drama; Children: Unacceptable (MPAA: R); **BD**; **DVD**. Intriguing and cleverly written crime tale begins with Rush, an aging art expert, who is hired by Hoeks, a reclusive young heiress, to auction off the large art and antiques collection left to her by her parents. For some reason, she refuses to be seen in person. Sturgess helps Rush to restore some odd mechanical parts he finds among Hoeks' belongings. At the same time, Sturgess gives Rush advice on how to become Hoeks' friend and deal with his feelings toward her. Rush learns that Hoeks suffers from agoraphobia (fear of traveling far from home and thinking that unknown places present dangerous environments) and, for the most part, remains in her living quarters. Slowly, Rush falls in love with the younger Hoeks. In what is a deceptive and manipulative transaction, Sutherland, another friend of Rush's, helps Rush acquire a secret private collection of very valuable paintings by masters. Rush slowly instills confidence in him by Hoeks, who overcomes her fear of leaving her premises and moves in with the art dealer, where he shows her his priceless art collection. He returns home one day to find all of his prized art works are missing and gone with them is Hoeks. Rush then realizes that Hoeks and all connected with her were part of an elaborate plan to steal his art collection. After months of recovering from the shock of Hoeks' betrayal, Rush travels to Prague and goes to a restaurant that Hoeks had once mentioned as one of her favorite places. He waits alone, and that is where this film ends. The acting by Rush, Hoeks, Sturgess and Sutherland is exceptional in a well-plotted tale that somewhat blindsides the viewer with its surprising ending, but one so well developed by director Tornatore that the viewer does not feel cheated. The film saw a modest success at the box office, earning more than $20.8 million in its initial release against a budget of $18 million. The film was shot within five weeks on location in northern Italy, Vienna and Prague. Sexuality and graphic nudity prohibit viewing by children. **p**, Isabella Cocuzza, Arturo Paglia; **d&w**, Giuseppe Tornatore; **cast**, Geoffrey Rush, Jim Sturgess, Sylvia Hoeks, Donald Sutherland, Philip Jackson, Dermot Crowley, Kiruna Stamell, Liya Kebede, Caterina Capodilista, Gen Seto; **c**, Fabio Zamarion; **m**, Ennio Morricone; **ed**, Massimo Quaglia; **prod d**, Maurizio Sabatini; **art d**, Maurizio di Clemente; **set d**, Raffaella Giovannetti; **spec eff**, Stefano Corridori, Francesca Baiardi.

Bethlehem ★★★ 2014; Israel/Germany/Belgium; 99m; Entre Chien et Loup/Adopt Films; Color; Drama; Children: Unacceptable; **BD**; **DVD**. Suspenseful film presents the police procedures in the West Bank of Bethlehem that concerns the world of the Israeli intelligence and police and their extensive use of Palestinian informants to prevent Islamic terrorist attacks. The Israelis need these informants to watch neighborhoods where radical Islamic terrorists are given safe haven, and the Palestinians, despite divided loyalties, are forced to cooperate, often to save their own lives. The film opens with, Mar'i, a teenager, who lives and works as a busboy in Bethlehem. His older brother, Kopty, is a terrorist and a prominent member of the al-Aqsa Martyrs' Brigades, but who may be deceiving his fellow terrorists by also working with the militant group Hamas, another terrorist organization. Kopty goes into hiding in Bethlehem after claiming responsibility for a bombing in Jerusalem that kills thirty Israelis. Halevi, an Israeli agent who recruited Mar'i when he was fifteen years old with the purpose of getting information on Kopty, acts as the boy's protector. Halevi spends more time with Mar'i than he does with his own children and has a fatherly feeling toward him, advising him not to consort with bad people. Kopty is on the run but gives statements that air on the nightly news. Mar'i has to keep Kopty's activities a secret from the family and from his brother's dangerous associates, who are led by Omari. Mar'i relies more and more on Halevi for protection while, at the same time attempting to take Kopty's place, playing Hamas and al-Aqsa members off each other. Mar'i is consumed by a life of secrecy. Halevi senses this but has conflicted loyalties, to help Mar'i or be a good law enforcement agent. When Mar'i is finally ordered to kill his brother, Halevi, despite protests from his wife and his Israeli commander, rushes to the boy and prevents him from participating in the murder plot, his rationale either being that he should preserve the boy as an informant or because he has genuine affection for Mar'i, and wants to save his life. Soon everything falls apart for everyone as events reach a deadly climax. In addition to the superb acting by the entire cast, director Adler equally depicts the brutal violence shown by the Palestinian terrorists and the Israelis, leaving the viewer to make a personal assessment in this taut apolitical tale. This film was shot on location in Jerusalem, Bethlehem, Jaffa and Ramla. Violence prohibits viewing by children. (In Hebrew; Arabic/English subtitles.) **p**, Sebastian Delloye, Diana Elbaum, Sonja Ewers, Osnat Handelsman-Keren, Steve Hudson, Talia Kleinhendler; **d**, Yuval Adler; **cast**, Tsahi Halevi, Shadi Mar'i, Hitham Omari, Michal Shtamler, Tarik Kopty, George Iskandar, Yossi Eini, Penina Mezei, Dudu Niv, Irad Rubenstein, Ibrahim Saqallah; **w**, Adler, Ali Wakad; **c**, Yaron Scharf; **m**, Ishai Adar; **ed**, Ron Omer; **art d**, Yoav Sinai; **spec eff**, Mirko Burchartz, Nicolai Cronau.

Beyond the Hills ★★★ 2012; Romania/France/Belgium; 150m; Mobra Films/Sundance Selects; Color; Drama; Children: Unacceptable; **BD**; **DVD**. Unnerving but intriguing tale profiles Flutur and Stratan, two young women who have been close friends since their years in a boarding school, and who later become lesbian lovers, who vow never to part. But materialistic Flutur migrates to Germany and becomes a barmaid, leaving Stratan, who is more serene and enters an Orthodox convent in rural Moldavia, becoming a devout Christian of the Romanian Orthodox Church and plans to become a nun. Flutur goes to the convent and tries to persuade Stratan to go to Germany with her. Stratan has a difficult choice to make. She now considers her intimacy with Flutur to be sinful and tries to persuade Stratan to join the convent and also become a nun. Andriuta, a priest, regards Flutur as Satan trying to steal the faithful from God and he resorts to an exorcism of Stratan, one wherein she dies. Stratan, Flutur and Andriuta render standout performances in this offbeat film. *Author's Note*: This film is based upon an actual case involving twenty-three-year-old Maricica Irina Cornici, a mentally ill nun in a monastery of the Romanian Orthodox Church in Tanacu, Romania; a priest and four nuns performed an exorcism on Cornici in January 2005. Her hands and feet were bound and a towel was stuffed into her mouth to keep her from screaming. She was found dead from dehydration, exhaustion and a lack of oxygen. The priest and nuns were arrested, charged with murder and sent to prison, the nuns serving short prison terms and the priest released four years later. Sexual themes and exorcism prohibit viewing by children. **p**, Cristian Mungiu, Pascal Caucheteux, Jean-Pierre Dardenne, Luc Dardenne, Vincent Maraval, Bobby Paunescu, Gregoire Sorlat; **d&w**, Cristian Mungiu (inspired by nonfiction novels of Tatiana Niculescu-Bran); **cast**, Cosmina Stratan, Christina Flutur, Valeriu Andriuta, Valeriu Andriuta, Dana Tapalaga, Catalina Harabagiu, Gina Tandura, Vica Agache, Nora Covali, Dionisie

Tom Wilkinson in *The Best Exotic Marigold Hotel,* 2012.

Vitcu, Liliana Mocanu; **c**, Oleg Mutu; **ed**, Mircea Olteanu; **prod d**, Calin Papura, Mihaela Poenaur.

Beyond the Lights ★★★ 2014; U.S.; 116m; Relativity Media; Color; Drama/Romance; Children: Unacceptable (MPAA: PG-13); **BD**; **DVD**. Entertaining romantic tale begins with Mbatha-Raw, who is a young musician and who has just won a Grammy award and is on the brink of super-stardom. Pressures of her success are so great that she nearly ends her life, but she is saved by Parker, a young black police officer. They fall in love despite protests of their parents, who want each to focus on their own career ambitions. Parker's love for the young woman provides the missing piece that unlocks Mbatha-Raw's true artistic potential. A good cast and an intelligent script serves up a thoroughly satisfying story. The film received an Oscar nomination for Best Song ("Grateful"; Diane Warren). Songs: "Grateful" (Diane Warren), "2 AM" (Christopher Chrishan Dotson, Kyle Coleman, Anthony Franks, Dominic Woods), "Blackbird," "Masterpiece," "Extraordinary Love," "Lights and Camera," "C'mon Boy," "Fly Before You Fall," "Drunk in Love," "Just Girly Things," "Private Property," "Shelter," "Worthy, "Don't Let Me Down." Gutter language and thematic elements prohibit viewing by children. **p**, Stephanie Allain, Reggie Rock Blythewood, Ryan Kavanaugh, Marc Ambrose; **d&w**, Gina Prince-Bythewood; **cast**, Minnie Driver, Gugu Mbatha-Raw, Danny Glover, Nate Parker, Aisha Hinds, Hayley Marie Norman, Aml Ameen, Jordan Belfi, Joseph Aviel, Tyler Christopher; **c**, Tami Reiker; **ed**, Terilyn A. Shropshire; **prod d**, Cecilia Montiel, Hannah Purdy Foggin; **art d**, Nick Ralbovsky; **set d**, Lori Mazuer; **spec eff**, Tim Carras.

Big Eyes ★★★ 2014; U.S.; 105m; Silverwood Films/Weinstein Co.; Color; Biographical Drama; Children: Unacceptable (MPAA: PG-13); **BD**; **DVD**. The fascinating biopic follows the phenomenal success of painter Margaret Keane (Peggy Doris Hawkins, 1927-), portrayed by Adams, who became famous in the 1950s for her paintings of people with enormous eyes. The film chronicles her subsequent legal problems with her husband, Walter Keane (1915-2000), played by Waltz, who, in the 1960s, claimed credit for her works. Waltz, claiming to be the artist of the work of Adams, becomes a national celebrity on television talk shows after he pioneers mass production of prints of the big-eyed children painted by Adams, and selling them cheaply in hardware stores and at gas stations across the country, signing his name to the paintings. This ends in a court battle when Adams claims that Waltz is insane. The judge puts up two easels, side by side, and challenges each of them to start painting. Waltz begs off, claiming a shoulder injury, while Adams dashes off one of her familiar big-eyed creations and wins the court case. Adams and Waltz are outstanding as the contesting couple, and the

Judi Dench and Celia Imrie in *The Best Exotic Marigold Hotel*, 2012.

viewer is treated to myriad images of Keane's haunting, vacant-eyed children. Songs: "Big Eyes," "I Can Fly" (Lana Del Ray). *Author's Note*: In the court challenge, where Walter Keane begged off from painting one of the big-eyed children, Margaret Keane completed her portrait within fifty-three minutes and a jury awarded her $4 million in damages, which an appeals court later reversed. Thematic elements and gutter language prohibit viewing by children. **p**, Tim Burton, Scott Alexander, Lynette Howell, Larry Karaszewski, Bob Weinstein, Harvey Weinstein; **d**, Tim Burton; **cast**, Amy Adams, Christoph Waltz, Krysten Ritter, Jason Schwartzman, Danny Huston, Terence Stamp, Stephanie Bennett, Jon Polito, Andrew Airlie, Heather Doerksen, Elisabetta Fantone; **w**, Alexander, Karaszewski; **c**, Bruno Delbonnel; **m**, Danny Elfman; **ed**, J.C. Bond; **prod d**, Rick Heinrichs; **art d**, Chris August; **set d**, Shane Vieau; **spec eff**, Sean House.

Big Hero 6 ★★★ 2014; U.S.; 108m; Walt Disney Studios; Color; Animated Comedy; Children: Unacceptable (MPAA: PG); **BD**; **DVD**. This visually sumptuous story begins when a special bond develops between a large inflatable robot named Baymax (Adsit voiceover) and his prodigy, Hiro Hamada (Potter voiceover). When a devastating event happens in the city of San Fransokyo that catapults Potter into danger, he turns to Adsit and his other close friends, Chung, Wayans Jr., and Rodriguez. To uncover the mystery, Porter transforms his friends into a band of high-tech heroes called "Big Hero 6." The film received an Oscar for Best Animated Feature and it was a megahit at the box office, earning more than $657.8 million in its initial release against a budget of more than $165 million. Songs: "Immortals" (Andy Hurley, Joe Trohman, Patrick Stump, Pete Wentz), "Boca Dulce Boca" (F. Estefano Salgado, Flavio Enrique Santander), "Eye of the Tiger" (James Michael Peterik, Frank Sullivan), "Edge of the Earth," "My Songs Know What You Did in the Dark," "Top of the World." Crude humor and thematic elements prohibit viewing by children. **p**, Roy Conli, Kristina Reed; **d**, Don Hall, Chris Williams; **cast**, (voiceovers) Scott Adsit, James Cromwell, Ryan Potter, Daniel Henney, T.J. Miller, Jamie Chung, Damon Wayans Jr., Genesis Rodriguez, Alan Tudyk, Maya Rudolph; **w**, Jordan Roberts, Daniel Gerson, Robert L. Baird (from a story by Hall, Roberts, Paul Briggs, Joseph Mateo, and concept and characters created by Duncan Rouleau, Steven T. Seagle); **m**, Henry Jackman; **ed**, Tim Mertens; **prod d**, Paul A. Felix; **art d**, Scott Watanabe; **spec eff**, Nathan Curtis, Tony Chai, Chris Carignan.

Big Stone Gap ★★★ 2015; U.S.; 103m; Altar Identify Studios/Picture House; Color; Comedy/Romance; Children: Unacceptable (MPAA: PG-13); **BD**; **DVD**. This delightful film is based on the first of four novels by Adriana Trigiani and set in 1978 in a small town in the Blue Ridge

Appalachian Mountains of Virginia. Judd, a thirty-five-year-old pharmacist, accepts the unwelcome fact that she is a spinster. She has good friends and keeps busy as co-captain of the town's Rescue Squad and director of its popular outdoor play. One day, she discovers a skeleton in her family's closet that sends her life into orbit. She finds herself deciding between marriage proposals from Wilson and Sarandon, conducts a family feud, plans a journey to Europe, and helps her best friend, Elfman, the high school band director, put on a football halftime show. That musical extravaganza is designed to entertain if not overwhelm visiting movie star Elizabeth Taylor, who is coming to town with her husband John Warner, and who is on a U.S. senatorial campaign tour. A great deal of fine comedy is presented through a bevy of eccentric characters while the viewer appreciates that Judd's best days are far from over and that her most rewarding times are yet to come. Judd, Sarandon, Wilson, Elfman and the rest of the cast shine in their roles as director Trigiani delivers a thoroughly entertaining story. Suggestive material prohibits viewing by children. **p**, Joseph E. Craig, Donna Gigliotti, James Spies, Matthew T. Weiner; **d&w**, Adriana Trigiani (based on the novel by Trigiani); **cast**, Ashley Judd, Patrick Wilson, Jenna Elfman, Jane Krakowski, Chris Sarandon, Whoopi Goldberg, Dagmara Dominczyk, Anthony LaPaglia, Jasmine Guy, James Hampton, Carlo Trigiani; **c**, Reynaldo Villalobos; **m**, John Leventhal; **ed**, Christopher Passig; **prod d**, Eloise Crane Stammerjohn; **set d**, Deana Goodwin Stoddard, Emily Weston; **spec eff**, Gary Pilkinton.

Birdman or (The Unexpected Virtue of Ignorance) ★★★★ 2014; U.S.; 119m; Fox; Color; Comedy/Drama; Children: Unacceptable (MPAA: R); **BD**; **DVD**. Manic comedy sees Keaton as a has-been actor, who became famous for playing a superhero called Birdman in the movies, and he decides to stage a comeback in a Broadway play. Pressures mount leading up to the play's opening night as the quirky Keaton battles his ego and tries to win back his family while, at the same time, reestablishing his career and finding himself in the process. The rest of those in the film are all struggling with one personal crisis after another. Stone is a drug addict, Norton has sexual problems, and Watts is preoccupied with self-realization. While rehearsing the play, Keaton sees his drug-afflicted daughter Stone being kissed by lothario Norton and worries about this new tenuous relationship, especially after Stone has told him that his play is nothing more than an expensive exercise to bolster his vanity. So upset with this is Keaton that he accidentally locks himself out of the theater while he is about to change clothes for the play's next scene. To reenter the theater, he must walk through Times Square in his underwear. This embarrassing trek is caught by amateur photographers, and his underwear walk goes viral on the Internet. Keaton then runs into Duncan, who is one of NYC's leading theater critics. She tells him that she hates Hollywood film stars like him, stating that Keaton is nothing more than an untalented, phony actor, and she guarantees to destroy his play's success with a damning review on opening night. (This situation is just the hilarious reverse in **The Producers**, 1967, as well as its 2005 remake, where, in the original film, theater producer Zero Mostel hands cash on the opening night of his terrible play as a blatant bribe to the New York *Times* theater critic, in attempt to assure a deprecating review.) Duncan's spine-chilling threat so discombobulates Keaton that he drinks himself into a stupor, collapsing on a street. The next day, his hallucinations grip his sense of reality, and he imagines as reality a meeting with his other superhero self from Hollywood, the indomitable Birdman, that fictional character demanding that Keaton abandon his Broadway airs and make another film starring, of course, Birdman. At one point, Keaton's hallucinations joyfully embrace this suggestion, and he visualizes himself soaring through the streets of Manhattan as that unstoppable superhero. He comes down to earth in time to return to theater where Stone shows him a video of him walking through Times Square in his underwear, and both see the mirthful ridiculousness of it all. Stone now sees her father as a down-to-earth human being, and both begin to develop the deep bond they have always wanted. Keaton, nevertheless, is deeply haunted by Duncan's threat to destroy his stage opus. Utterly despondent on opening night, Keaton replaces his prop pistol with a real gun, intending to actually commit suicide at the play's finale. At the end of the play, Keaton shoots himself and the audience erupts, giving him and his play a standing ovation as drama critic Duncan flees the theater. Keaton, however, is revealed the next day to be very much alive. He bungled his suicide, succeeding in only blowing off his nose, and we see him at the hospital where that nose has already been surgically replaced. Galifianakis, who is Keaton's close friend and attorney, visits the bedridden actor to inform him that Duncan has written a rave review of the play and his place on Broadway is now successfully planted. Stone then visits him to tell him how proud she is of his acting ability and his success. As she momentarily leaves, Keaton goes to the private bathroom in his room where he dismisses Birdman. When he sees some birds outside, he gingerly climbs onto the window ledge. Stone then reappears and, not finding Keaton in his room, goes to the bathroom to see the open window. She looks downward to the street far below and then slowly looks upward to the sky and a smile floods her face. Keaton is wonderful in this hilarious comedy, offering in his doubt-filled character myriad eccentricities that fascinate from frame to frame. He is supported with equal excellence by Stone, Norton, Galifianakis, Duncan, Ryan, Watts and the rest of the cast. Director Inarritu does a great job hurrying this hectic tale along, slathering its well-written story line with rich theatrical ambience and flavor. The film hit the top charts at the Academy Awards, receiving nine Oscar nominations and winning in four categories: Best Picture; Best Director (Inarritu); Best Original Screenplay (Inarritu, Giacobone, Dinelaris, Bo); and Best Cinematography (Lubezki). It received Oscar nominations for Best Actor (Keaton); Best Supporting Actress (Stone); Best Supporting Actor (Norton); Best Sound Editing (Martin Hernandez, Aaron Glascock); and Best Sound Mixing (Jon Taylor, Frank A. Montano, Thomas Varga). The film was a huge box office success, earning more than $103.2 million in its initial release against a budget of $18 million. Songs: "Birdman Blind Melody" (Joan Valent), "Harpad" and "Jazz Bar Music" (Victor Stumpfhauser), "BB Drum Beats" (Brian Blade), "Pavane for a Dead Princess" and "Passacallie" (Maurice Ravel), "Symphony No. 9 in D" and "Ich bin der Welt" (Gustav Mahler), "Symphony No. 5, Andante Cantabile" and Symphony No. 4, Andantino" (Pyotr Ilyich Tchaikovsky), "Dream Team" (Jeff Bernat, Joel Cowell), "Chorus of Exiled Palestinians" (from "The Death of Klinghoffer"; music: John Adams; lyrics: Alice Goodman), "Harmonium III, Wild Nights" (John Adams), "Symphony No. 2, Movements 1 and 2, Largo, Allegro Moderato" (Sergei Rachmaninoff). *Author's Note*: Keaton, who carries the whole story, was the first choice to play the aging actor in this mirthful romp. He has had an up-and-down career, providing some failed throwaway essays such as **Johnny Dangerously**, 1984, and more superb performances in many films, from **Beetlejuice**, 1988, to his several Batman characterizations, that superhero serving as the heroic character this film incisively and brilliantly parodies. At one point, Keaton is shown being interviewed by the press in his dressing room, where he says he has not played Birdman since 1992, and that is the last year that Keaton played his last role in the Batman series. In real life, Keaton later stated that the character he plays in this film was the most difficult he ever undertook as that character is completely opposite his own persona. Before going into production, director Inarritu showed a picture to the entire cast and crew, one that showed tightrope walker Philippe Petit dangerously working his way along a rope stretched between the Twin Towers; the director then pointed out the fine line the film was walking (between cornball burlesque and great comedy), saying: "Guys, this is the movie we are doing—if we fall, we fail." The director's approach to this film involved his ambition to shoot it as one long take, but when meeting with pantheon director Mike Nichols before going into production, Nichols told him that he was inviting disaster as such a technique would not allow him to use cuts in editing and thereby inhibit the flow of the comedic story. This same ambition was embraced by master filmmaker

Maggie Smith in *The Best Exotic Marigold Hotel*, 2012.

Alfred Hitchcock when he made **Rope**, 1948, attempting to capture its story and characters in one long take, this technique proving to be a failed experiment. Inarritu attempts the same thing here, but allowed about a dozen visible cuts. The film was shot on a whirlwind schedule and completed in about two months, including rehearsal, and since the film was shot in sequence it was easily edited within two weeks. Inarritu demanded and got from his cast intensive acting periods to keep his tight schedule, and those actors performed as many as fifteen pages of the script each day. This caused many of them to flub their lines, but they quickly corrected their mistakes to keep pace with their high speed director. The film was shot on location in New York City, the theater profiled being the St. James Theatre at 246 W. 44th Street. Other films dealing with Broadway productions and shows include **All About Eve**, 1950; **All That Jazz**, 1979; **At the Stage Door**, 1921; **Author! Author!**, 1982; **Babes on Broadway**, 1941; **The Band Wagon**, 1953; **The Barkleys of Broadway**, 1949; **Bedtime Story**, 1941; **The Big Street**, 1942; **Black Widow**, 1954; **Bloodhounds of Broadway**, 1952; **Blossoms on Broadway**, 1937; **Bowery to Broadway**, 1944; **Bring Your Smile Along**, 1955; **Broadway**, 1929; **Broadway**, 1942; **The Broadway Boob**, 1926; **Broadway Broke**, 1923; **Broadway Daddies**, 1928; **The Broadway Melody**, 1929; **Broadway Melody of 1936**, 1935; **Broadway Melody of 1938**, 1937; **Broadway Melody of 1940**, 1940; **Broadway Scandals**, 1929; **Chasing Rainbows**, 1930; **Chicken a La King**, 1928; **Chip Off the Old Block**, 1944; **Cinderella Swings It**, 1943; **City for Conquest**, 1940; **Cowboy in Manhattan**, 1943; **David Harum**, 1934; **Deep in My Heart**, 1954; **Delightfully Dangerous**, 1945; **De-Lovely**, 2004; **Diamond Jim**, 1936; **A Double Life**, 1947; **Down to Earth**, 1947; **The Eddie Cantor Story**, 1953; **Ellis Island**, 1984 (TV miniseries); **Follow the Band**, 1943; **Footlight Parade**, 1933; **Footlight Serenade**, 1942; **Forty Naughty Girls**, 1937; **42nd Street**, 1933; **Funny Girl**, 1968; **Funny Lady**, 1975; **The Gentleman from Louisiana**, 1936; **George White's Scandals**, 1934; **Gildersleeve on Broadway**, 1943; **The Girl He Didn't Buy**, 1928; **Gold Diggers of 1933**, 1933; **Gold Diggers of 1935**, 1935; **Gold Diggers of 1937**, 1936; **Good Morning, Judge**, 1943; **The Great Flirtation**, 1934; **The Great Victor Herbert**, 1939; **The Great Ziegfeld**, 1936; **Grief Street**, 1931; **Haywire**, 1980 (made-for-TV); **The Helen Morgan Story**, 1957; **I'll See You in My Dreams**, 1951; **It Could Be Worse**, 2013 (TV miniseries); **The Jazz Singer**, 1927; **The Jazz Singer**, 1952; **The Jazz Singer**, 1980; **Jeanne Eagels**, 1957; **Jolson Sings Again**, 1949; **The Jolson Story**, 1946; **Lillian Russell**, 1940; **Lillie**, 1978 (TV miniseries); **Lily in Love**, 1985; **Look for the Silver Lining**, 1949; **Love Happy**, 1949; **Love Me or Leave Me**, 1955; **Lovestruck: The Musical**, 2013 (made-for-TV); **Lucky Me**, 1954; **Lullaby of Broadway**, 1951; **Make a Wish**, 1937; **The Matinee Idol**, 1928; **Meet Me after**

Tena Desae and Dev Patel in *The Best Exotic Marigold Hotel*, **2012.**

the Show, 1951; **Mr. Big**, 1943; **My Best Gal**, 1944; **My Gal Sal**, 1942; **My Wild Irish Rose**, 1947; **New York, New York**, 1977; **Night and Day**, 1946; **On Broadway**, 2007; **Polly of the Follies**, 1922; **Prince of Players**, 1955; **The Producers**, 1967; **The Producers**, 2005; **Rainbow over Broadway**, 1933; **Regal Cavalcade**, 1935; **Repeat Performance**, 1947; **Scattergood Meets Broadway**, 1941; **The Seven Little Foys**, 1955; **Smash**, 2012-2013 (TV series); **Somebody Loves Me**, 1952; **Stage Door**, 1937; **Stage Door**, 1948 (made-for-TV); **Star!**, 1968; **Staying Alive**, 1983; **The Story of Vernon and Irene Castle**, 1939; **The Story of Will Rogers**, 1952; **Submissions Only**, 2010- (TV series); **Tea for Two**, 1950; **This Is the Army**, 1943; **Three for the Show**, 1955; **Thrill of a Lifetime**, 1937; **Till the Clouds Roll By**, 1946; **Tonight We Sing**, 1953; **Two Blondes and a Redhead**, 1947; **The Velvet Touch**, 1948; **W.C. Fields and Me**, 1976; **Walking Down Broadway**, 1938; **Wives and Lovers**, 1963; **Words and Music**, 1948; **Yankee Doodle Dandy**, 1942; **You're the One**, 1941; **Ziegfeld Follies**, 1945; **Ziegfeld Girl**, 1941; and **Ziegfeld: The Man and His Women**, 1978 (made-for-TV). Gutter language, sexual content and brief violence prohibit viewing by children. **p**, Alejandro G. Inarritu, John Lesher, Arnon Milchan, James W. Skotchdopole; **d**, Inarritu; **cast**, Michael Keaton, Edward Norton, Zach Galifianakis, Amy Ryan, Emma Stone, Naomi Watts, Lindsay Duncan, Andrea Riseborough, Merritt Wever, Damian Young, Natalie Gold; **w**, Inarritu, Nicolas Giacobone, Alexander Dinelaris, Armando Bo; **c**, Emmanuel Lubezki; **m**, Antonio Sanchez; **ed**, Douglas Crise, Stephen Mirrione; **prod d**, Kevin Thompson; **set d**, Geore DeTitta Jr.; **spec eff**, Conrad V. Brink, Jr., Denis Lavigne.

A Birder's Guide to Everything ★★★ 2014; U.S.; 86m; Dreamfly Productions/Screen Media/Focus World; Color; Drama; Children: Unacceptable (MPAA: PG-13); **BD**; **DVD**. Absorbing coming-of-age tale opens with Smit-McPhee, a fifteen-year-old boy, who is grieving for the death of his mother when his father, Le Gros, decides to remarry. His mother-to-be is Lavender, the nurse who took care of his mom in her final months. A shy, emotional boy, Smit-McPhee throws himself into amateur bird-watching, which had been his mother's passion. He becomes part of a birding club at school, which consists of only two other members, Chen and Wolff, and all are serious birders. While riding home from school one day, Smit-McPhee sees an unusual-looking duck waddling across the road. He takes a picture of the bird and shows it to Kingsley, a famous local ornithologist who says it has been thought to be extinct. Kingsley has devoted his life to birding, even lost a leg because of it, and wrote a memoir called "Look to the Skies," which Smit-McPhee has read five times. Kingsley tells Smit-McPhee and his two birder club friends that the bird's migration pattern means it may be in an anticipated place the next weekend, if they want to track it.

That is the same weekend Smit-McPhee's father is to remarry, and Smit-McPhee is not happy about that because he fears that Lavender will take his mother's place in his father's heart, so he decides to risk not being at the wedding and, instead, follow the duck. He and his pals borrow a car from a friend and take a road trip to find the bird. They need a better camera so when they meet Chang, a new girl in town, and tell her about their plans to look for the rare bird, she agrees to come along. Although she is not a birder, she brings her camera with telephoto lens. The birders go into the wooded area where Kingsley says the duck may be, and Smit-McPhee tells Chang about bird-watching as she grows more interested. The trek enables Smit-McPhee to have his first real interaction with a girl, which gradually enables him to accept his dad's remarriage. Gutter language, sex and drug references, as well as brief partial nudity prohibit viewing by children. **p**, Kirsten Duncan Fuller, Lisa K. Jenkins, Dan Lindau, R. Paul Miller, Linda Moran; **d**, Rob Meyer; **cast**, Ben Kingsley, Kodi Smit-McPhee, James Le Gros, Alex Wolff, Katie Chang, Briana Marin, Stephen Kunken, Daniela Lavender, Ethan Cohn, Ira Hawkins; **w**, Meyer, Luke Matheny; **c**, Tom Richmond; **m**, Jeremy Turner; **ed**, Vito DeSario; **prod d**, Elizabeth J. Jones; **art d**, Brian Goodwin; **set d**, Armann Ortega; **spec eff**, Dean Winkler, Ralph Scaglione.

Black Nativity ★★★ 2013; U.S.; 93m; Fox Searchlight; Color; Drama/Musical; Children: Unacceptable (MPAA: PG); **BD**; **DVD**. Good coming-of-age tale sees Latimore as a streetwise teenager from Baltimore (one of the most violence-plagued cities for blacks in America), who has been reared by single mother Hudson. He journeys to New York City to spend the Christmas holiday with his estranged relatives, Whitaker, a minister, and his wife, Bassett. Latimore is unwilling to live by Whitaker's strict rules and wants to return home to his mother, so he goes off on a journey that is both surprising and inspirational, meeting new friends. With some divine intervention, he discovers the true meaning of faith, healing, and family. This film did not fare well at the box office, earning less than $7.5 million in its initial release against a budget of $17.5 million. Songs: "Coldest Town" (Raphael Saadig, Taura Stinson, Kasi Lemmons), "Motherless Child" (traditional), "Hush Child/Get You Through This Silent Night" (Kasi Lemmons, Taura Stinson, Taylor Gordon), "He Loves Me" (Raphael Saadig, Taura Stinson, Darien Dorsey), "Sweet Little Jesus Boy" (Robert MacGimsey), "Fix Me Jesus" (traditional), "Be Grateful" (Walter Hawkins), "Can't Stop Praising His Name" (Ricky Grundy, Herman Netter), "Test of Faith" (Raphael Saaquid, Taura Stinson), "Silent Night" (music: Franz Gruber; lyrics: Joseph Mohr); "The First Noel," "Jesus Is on the Mainline," "Rise Up Shepherd and Follow" (traditional), "As" (Stevie Wonder). Thematic material, gutter language and menacing situations prohibit viewing by children. **p**, William Horberg, Galt Niederhoffer, Celine Rattray, Trudie Styler, Bergen Swanson; **d**, Kasi Lemmons; **cast**, Angela Bassett, Jennifer Hudson, Forest Whitaker, Mary J. Blige, Jacob Latimore, Tyrese Gibson, Vondie Curtis-Hall, Samantha Gelnaw, Nas, Rotimi, Chris Nunez; **w**, Lemmons, Langston Hughes (libretto); **c**, Anastas N. Michos; **m**, Laura Karpman, Raphael Saadig; **ed**, Terilyn A. Shropshire; **prod d**, Kristi Zea; **art d**, Doug Huszti; **set d**, Diane Lederman; **spec eff**, Edward Drohan IV, Eric J. Robertson.

Bless Me, Ultima ★★★ 2013; U.S.; 106m; Sony; Drama; Children: Unacceptable (MPAA: PG-13); **BD**; **DVD**. Absorbing drama where orthodox religion is challenged by ancient mysticism. The film opens in a New Mexico village during World War II (1939-1945), where Ganalon, a boy, lives with his parents and aunts and uncles. When Ultima (Colon), an elderly medicine woman, comes to live with them Ganalon's boyish notions about his religion become shaken. Colon has a strong influence on Ganalon, teaching him the power of the spiritual world. He begins to question the strict Catholic doctrines taught him by his parents, Heredia and Martinez. Through a series of mysterious and, at times, terrifying events, Ganalon grapples with questions about his own destiny, the relationship between good and evil, and, ultimately, how to reconcile Colon's powers with those of the God of his church. This well-made film saw limited distribution and earned only about $1.5 million in its initial release. Songs: "Muy Sabroso Blues" (Lalo Guerrero), "La Feria de Las Flores" (Jesus Monge). *Author's Note*: Christy Walton, heiress to the Walton fortune, provided upfront funds for this production, which was shot on location in New Mexico. Violence and some sexual references prohibit viewing by children. **p**, Jesse Beaton, Sarah DiLeo, Mark Johnson, Tom Williams; **d&w**, Carl Franklin (based on the novel by Rudolfo Anaya); **cast**, Luke Ganalon, Miriam Colon, Benito Martinez, Dolores Heredia, Castulo Guerra, Joaquin Cosio, Manuel Garcia-Rulfo, Reko Moreno, Luis Bordonada, Joseph A. Garcia; **c**, Paula Huidobro; **m**, Mark Kilian; **ed**, Alan Heim; **prod d**, David J. Bomba; **art d**, John R. Jensen; **set d**, Carla Curry; **spec eff**, Daniel Holt, Marco Recuay.

Blind ★★★ 2014; Norway; 96m; Lemming Film/Cineart; Color; Drama; Children: Unacceptable; **BD**; **DVD**. Compelling story sees Petersen, a blind author, retreating to the security of her home where she can feel in control and be alone with her husband, Rafaelsen, as well as her innermost thoughts. However, her deep-seated fears and harassing fantasies plague her until she realizes that her real problems lie within herself, not beyond the walls of her apartment or in a world she cannot see. Mature subject matter prohibits viewing by children. Not related to 2007 and 2011 films with the same title. (In Norwegian; English subtitles.) **p**, Sigve Endresen, Hans-Jorgen Osnes, Joost de Vries, Leontine Petit, Derk-Jan Warrink; **d&w**, Eskil Vogt; **cast**, Ellen Dorrit Petersen, Henrik Rafaelsen, Vera Vitali, Marius Kolbenstvedt, Stella Kvam Young, Isak Nikolai Moller, Jacob Young, Nikki Butenschon, Erle Kyllingmark, Fredrik Sandahl; **c**, Thimios Bakatakis; **m**, Henk Hofstede; **ed**, Jens Christian Fodstad; **prod d**, Jorgen Stangebye Larsen; **art d&set d**, Solfrid Kjetsa; **spec eff**, Sander Jansen.

Blood Ties ★★★ 2014; U.S./France; 127m; Les Productions du Tresor/Roadside Attractions; Color; Crime Drama; Children: Unacceptable (MPAA: R); **BD**; **DVD**. In 1974 Manhattan, Owen is released from prison on good behavior after serving several years involved in a gangland murder (where Owen killed a rapist in the brutal act). His younger brother, Crudup, a cop with a bright future, reluctantly meets him outside the gates. They are not alike in nature and their father, Caan, has always favored Owen. Caan and his daughter, Taylor, want only for Owen and Crudup to get along together. Crudup, who hopes Owen will straighten out his life, shares his home with the ex-con, finds him a job, and helps him get back with his children and ex-wife, Cotillard. After seeing that Cotillard is a drug-addicted prostitute, Owen begins a new relationship with Kunis and tries to start a legitimate business. His new business is sabotaged by underworld goons, and Owen goes back to a life of crime. Crudup, who has his own personal troubles, banishes Owen from his life. Their destinies, as misfortune decrees, are nevertheless bound together. Violence, gutter language, sexual content and brief drug use prohibit viewing by children. This taut tale is well-enacted and is expertly directed by Canet, but it failed miserably at the box office, earning only about $2.4 million in its initial release against a budget of $26 million. This film is not related to a 2006 film of the same name. **p**, Guillaume Canet, Alain Attal, John Lesher, Hugo Selignac, Christopher Woodrow; **d**, Canet; **cast**, Clive Owen, Billy Crudup, Marion Cotillard, James Caan, Lili Taylor, Zoe Saldana, Mila Kunis, Noah Emmerich, Griffin Dunne, Eve Hewson, **w**, Canet, James Gray (based on the novel *Deux frerer, un flic, et truand* by Bruno Papet, Michel Papet, and the film **Les liens du sang** screenplay by Jacques Maillot, Pierre Chosson, Eric Veniard); **c**, Christophe Offenstein; **ed**, Herve de Luze; **prod d**, Ford Wheeler; **art d**, Henry Dunn; **set d**, Heather Loeffler, Cherish Magennis; **spec eff**, Jeff Brink, Kevin Hannigan.

Blue Jasmine ★★★★ 2013; U.S.; 98m; Perdido Productions/Sony;

Penelope Wilton in *The Best Exotic Marigold Hotel*, 2012.

Color; Drama; Children: Unacceptable (MPAA: PG-13); **BD**; **DVD**. A superb performance is seen from Blanchett, who marvelously plays a one-time top New York wealthy socialite, who is now reduced to poverty and must return to her estranged sister, Hawkins, in San Francisco. In flashbacks, Blanchett recalls her past life in New York with her husband, Baldwin, a wealthy businessman. Some years earlier, Hawkins and Clay, her working-class husband, visited New York and Blanchett provided a car and driver so they could tour the city and paid for a stay in a hotel so as to avoid spending any time with them. Hawkins and Clay win $200,000 in the lottery and Clay plans to use it to start a construction business, but Blanchett offers him Baldwin's help in investing the money instead, and they accept. Then Hawkins sees Baldwin kissing another woman, who later appears at Blanchett's birthday party. Hawkins decides not to tell Blanchett about her, hoping not to trouble her marriage. Baldwin now is revealed to be a fraud, losing money for many investors, including the investment money Hawkins and Clay had given him. Hawkins defends Blanchett, but Clay blames her for ruining his life. Baldwin is sentenced to a term in prison for fraud, but kills himself. Hawkins divorces Clay and begins dating Cannavale, a mechanic. Blanchett suffers a nervous breakdown and is briefly hospitalized before going to San Francisco to see Hawkins. When she relocates to that Bagdad on the Bay, Blanchett decides to become an interior designer and takes an Internet course, but discovering that she has no computer skills, looks elsewhere for a job. She gets work as a telephone receptionist to a dentist, Stuhlbarg, who makes sexual advances, which causes Blanchett to quit. Blanchett then meets Sarsgaard, a wealthy widower, at a party, discovering that he is a diplomat with aspirations of becoming a U.S. congressman. Meanwhile, Hawkins meets a man at the same party and breaks up with Cannavale. Hawkins then learns that the man is married and returns to Cannavale. Blanchett lies to Sarsgaard about her past life, telling him that her husband was a surgeon who died of a heart attack. Sarsgaard is about to buy her an engagement ring when they bump into Clay outside the jewelry store. He yells at Blanchett about how Baldwin ruined his life and also reveals that Blanchett's estranged stepson, Ehrenreich, is living nearby in Oakland. Shocked, Sarsgaard calls off the engagement. Blanchett goes to Oakland and finds Ehrenreich, who tells her he never wants to see her again. In a flashback, we see how Blanchett finally learned about Baldwin's many affairs and then confronted him. Hearing that Baldwin wants to leave her for a teenage girl, the enraged Blanchett exposes his fraudulent business dealings to the FBI and he is arrested. Blanchett returns to Hawkins' apartment and finds her back with Cannavale, who blames Blanchett again for ruining his life. Blanchett lies to Hawkins that she is going to marry Sarsgaard and moves out. The film's downbeat finale sees Blanchett sitting alone on a park bench, talking to herself about her troubles. Allen

Edward Norton in *The Bourne Legacy,* 2012.

presents an unlikely classic profile here of a woman who carelessly destroys her own life and, through misfortune, vainly struggles to reconstruct that life into a semblance of comfort and love. Blanchett deservedly won the Best Actress Academy Award for her bravura performance, and she is strongly supported by the entire cast, especially the gifted Hawkins, and where the invariably abusive Clay renders a particularly impressive essay. The film received Oscar nominations for Best Supporting Actress (Hawkins); and Best Original Screenplay (Allen). The film enjoyed a great success at the box office, earning more than $97.5 million in its initial release against a budget of $18 million. Songs: "Back O'Town Blues" (Louis Armstrong, Luis Carl Russell), "Speakeasy Blues" (Clarence Williams, Joseph Oliver), "Blues My Naughty Sweetie Gives to Me" (Carey Morgan, Arthur M. Swanstrom, Charles R. McCarron), "A Good Man Is Hard to Find" (Eddie Green), "Blue Moon" (music: Richard Rodgers; lyrics: Lorenz Hart), "Aunt Hagar's Blues" (W.C. Handy), "House Party" (Mezz Mezzrow, Sidney Bechet), "Great White Way" and "Yacht Club" (Julius Block), "The Vision" (J.J. Aljaro), "Ipanema Breeze" (Paul Abler), "Out on the Town" (Kelly Bhamra, Gussy G, Taren Bilkhu), "Human Static" (Bob Bradley, Matt Sanchez, Gavin McGrath), "Average Joe" (Stephen Emil Dudas), "Miami Sunset Bar" (Mireya Medina, Raul Medina), "Welcome to the Night" (Andrew Bojanic, Wendy Page, James Fenton Marr), "Love Theme" (David Chesky), "My Baby Sends Me/My Daddy Rocks Me" (J. Berni Barbour), "West End Blues" (Clarence Williams, Joseph Oliver), "Black Snake Swing" (Victoria Spivey). Mature themes, gutter language and sexual content prohibit viewing by children. **p**, Letty Aronson, Helen Robin, Stephen Tenenbaum, Edward Walson; **d&w**, Woody Allen; **cast**, Cate Blanchett, Sally Hawkins, Alec Baldwin, Andrew Dice Clay, Bobby Cannavale, Alden Ehrenreich, Peter Sarsgaard, Martin Cantu, Daniel Jenks, Max Rutherford, Kathy Tong, Ted Neustadt; **c**, Javier Aguirresarobe; **ed**, Alisa Lepselter; **prod d**, Santo Loquasto; **art d**, Michael Goldman; **set d**, Kris Boxell; **spec eff**, Jake Braver.

The Book of Life ★★★ 2014; U.S.; 95m; Reel FX Creative Studios/FOX; Color; Animated Adventure; Children: Unacceptable (MPAA: PG); **BD**; **DVD**. Entertaining and well-animated tale begins with some children who behave badly on a trip to a museum, so their tour guide (Applegate voiceover) shows them a display and tells them an old tale that takes place in Mexico. In the story, Luna is a poetic musician who wants to be a guitar player, but his father wants him to become a bullfighter. Luna's gentle nature makes him think it is wrong to kill a bull in an arena for sport. Another young man (Tatum voiceover), a soldier, wants to save his village from bandits and become a hero. Both of them compete for the love of lovely Saldana. Which of them wins her hand and heart largely depends on the influence of two others who

are supernatural beings: del Castillo, the queen of the beautiful Land of the Remembered, and Perlman, who rules the grim Land of the Forgotten. They bet on who will win Saldana, with del Castillo choosing Luna, while Perlman prefers Tatum. The rival suitors try their best until a tragedy occurs and it's up to one of them to use his sincere heart to find his way back into the arms of Saldana. This 3-D computer-animated story offers breathtaking images as well as a good story and fanciful characters enlivened with a fine script. The film was a success at the box office, earning more than $99.8 million against a budget of $50 million. This production is not related to a 1998 film with the same title. Songs: "Peer Gynt Suite No. 1, Op. 46, Morning Mood" (Edvard Grieg); "Deceptacon" (Johanna Bateman, Kathleen Hanna, Sadie Benning); "La Cucaracha" (traditional); "Ave Maria" (traditional); "Jarabe Tapatio" (traditional); "I Will Wait" (Edward Dwane, Benjamin Lovett, Winston Marshall, Marcus Mumfod); "Mas"" (Augustin Cerezo Garza, Carlos Chairez Garcia, Joaquim Lozano Aguire, Juan Gongora Rangel); "Symphony No. 9 in D Minor, Ode to Joy" (Ludwig van Beethoven); "Ecstasy of Gold" (Ennio Morricone); "Creep" (Albert Hammond, Michael Hazlewood, Colin Greenwood, Jonathan Greenwood, Edward O'Brien, Philip Selway, Thomas Yorke); "Piano Concerto No. 22" (Wolfgang Amadeus Mozart); "Just a Friend" (Marcel Theo Hall); "Do Ya Think I'm Sexy" (Rod Stewart, Carmine Jr. Appice, Duane Hitchings); "I Love You Too Much" (music: Gustavo Santaolalla; lyrics: Paul Williams); "The Apology Song" (Santaolalla, Williams); "Can't Help Falling in Love" (Luigi Creatore, George David Weiss, Hugo Peretti); "El Aparato" (Ruben Isaac Albarran Oretga, Emmanuel del Real Diaz, Enrique Rangel Arroyo, Jose Alfredo Rangel Arroyo); "Carmen Overture" (Georges Bizet); "La Negra" (Silvestre Vargas Vazques, Ruben Fuentes Gasson); " Chon" (traditional); "La Donna e Mobile" from "Carmen" (Giuseppe Verdi); "Cielito Lindo" (traditional); "Home" (Alex Ebert, Jade Castrinos); "No Matter Where You Are" (Michael Alvardao, Carissa Alvarado); "Live Life" (Nate Company, Allan Grigg, Tirzah Joy Huerta Uecke, Jesse Eduardo Huerta Uecke); "Take It All Away, "Do or Die," "Te Amo y Mas" (Santaolalla); "Si Puedes Perdonar" (Santaolalla). Rude humor, some thematic elements and brief frightening images prohibit viewing by children. **p**, Aaron Berger, Brad Booker, Guillermo del Toro, Carina Schulze, Geoffrey Stott, Matthew Teevan; **d**, Jorge R. Gutierrez; **cast**, (voices only) Diego Luna, Zoe Saldana, Channing Tatum, Ron Perlman, Ice Cube, Christina Applegate, Kate del Castillo, Hector Elizondo, Danny Trejo, Moosie Drier; **w**, Gutierrez, Doug Langdale; **m**, Gustavo Santaolalla; **ed**, Ahren Shaw, Steven Liu; **prod d**, Paul Sullivan, Simon Valdimir Varela; **art d**, Paul Sullivan; **spec eff**, Erich Turner, Andrew Anderson.

The Book Thief ★★★ 2013; U.S./Germany; 131m; FOX; Color; Drama; Children: Unacceptable (MPAA: R); **BD**; **DVD**. This grim but intriguing tale is based upon an Australian young adult novel set in Germany during World War II (1939-1945), and which is narrated by Death (Allam voiceover). It begins with Nelisse, a nine-year-old girl, who goes to live with a foster family headed by Rush and Watson in a German working-class neighborhood. Her parents have given Nelisse up to distance her from their past communist sympathies. She arrives after having stolen her first book, *The Gravedigger's Handbook*, which begins her love affair with books. Rush teaches her how to read and write, and she helps Watson washing and delivering laundry to neighbors. Rush's son is a staunch member of the Nazi Party, but Rush is opposed to the Third Reich and all of its oppressive policies. Nelisse becomes friends with Liersch, a neighbor boy, but resists his kissing advances. During a public book burning by Nazis, Nelisse steals a second book and keeps on stealing more. Meanwhile, Nelisse witnesses the horrors of Nazi Germany and anti-Semitism as Rush and Watson hide Schnetzer, a Jewish refugee, under the stairs in their house. As the family continues to shield and hide other Jews, Nelisse shares the books she has stolen with them. Many years later, Death comes for Nelisse when she is ninety-years-old and living in Sydney, Australia. Death reveals to her that he has carried one of her books, *The Book Thief*, with him for years, implying that she had become a writer. She asks if he could understand it, and he tells her that she was one of the few human beings that made him long to understand "what it is to live," adding, "I am haunted by humans." Nelisse, Watson and Rush give outstanding performances in this incisive view of Nazi Germany. The direction from Percival is robust, and Williams presents a powerful and moving score that received an Oscar nomination. The film did well at the box office, earning more than $76.6 million in its initial release against a budget of more than $19 million. Songs: "Wiegenleid: Guten Abend, Gut Nacht" (Johannes Brahms), "Deutschlandlied" (music: Joseph Haydn; lyrics: August Heinrich Hoffman von Fallersleben), "Die Fledermaus" and "The Blue Danube" (Johann Strauss, Jr.), "Kampflied der National Sozialisten" (Albert Methfessel), "Herbstweisen" (Emil Waldteufel), "Silent Night" (music: Franz Gruber; lyrics: Joseph Mohr); "Die Gedanken Sind Frei" (traditional). *Author's Note*: In addition to the widespread book burnings conducted by the Nazis, the film also depicts the Nazi destruction of Jewish stores and synagogues during Kristallnacht (November 9-10, 1938), so called for the extensive broken glass from the smashed windows of those buildings. This tale evocatively recalls other films that have surgically shown the underbelly of Hitler's vile regime before WWII, including **Above Suspicion**, 1943 (honeymooners act as British spies in Nazi Germany prior to WWII); **Address Unknown**, 1944 (art dealer returns to his native Germany to embrace Nazi beliefs); **Bonhoeffer: Agent of Grace**, 2000 (life of German clergyman Dietrich Bonhoeffer, who opposed Hitler's regime); **Confessions of a Nazi Spy**, 1939 (espionage agents in Germany and the U.S. prior to WWII); **The Damned**, 1969 (the rise of Hitler's SA Storm Troopers and SS); **Enemy of Women**, 1944 (rise of Nazi propaganda minister Paul Joseph Goebbels); **Escape**, 1940 (American attempts to get his mother released from a Nazi concentration camp in 1938); **Good**, 2008 (the rise of National Socialism); **The Hindenburg**, 1975 (the sabotaging of the Nazi dirigible LZ 129 in 1937); **Hitler: Beast of Berlin**, 1939 (anti-Nazi activists in Germany prior to WWII); **The Hitler Gang**, 1944 (the rise of Adolf Hitler in Germany); **Hitler's SS: Portrait in Evil**, 1985 (made-for-TV); **Joe and Max**, 2002 (made-for-TV; story of German prizefighter Max Schmeling, who fought U.S. boxer Joe Louis); **Julia**, 1977 (American playwright Lillian Hellman smuggles money into Nazi Germany to aid her closest friend and other members of the underground); **The Man I Married**, 1940 (American woman marries a German, who becomes a Nazi); **The Mortal Storm**, 1940 (rise of Hitler's SA Storm Troopers); **None Shall Escape**, 1944 (the rise to power of a Nazi officer); **Pastor Hall**, 1940 (profile of German clergyman Martin Neimuller, who opposed the Nazis); **Seven Journeys**, 1951 (profiles seven owners of a car during the years of Nazi Germany); **Spitfire**, 1943 (scenes showing how Germany is building a massive air force before WWII); **Taking Sides**, 2003 (the life of Berlin orchestra leader Wilhelm Furtzwanger); **13 Minutes**, 2015 (profiling Georg Elser, who attempted the assassination of Adolf Hitler in 1939); and **The Tin Drum**, 1980 (the Nazi takeover of Danzig). Violence and intense images prohibit viewing by children. **p**, Ken Blancato, Karen Rosenfelt, Christoph Fisser, Henning Molfenter, Charlie Woebcken; **d**, Brian Percival; **cast**, Geoffrey Rush, Emily Watson, Sophie Nelisse, Ben Schnetzer, Nico Liersch, Joachim Paul Assbock, Kirsten Block, Roger Allam, Sandra Nedeleff, Ludger Bokelmann, Rafaek Gareisen; **w**, Michael Petroni (adapted from the novel by Markus Zusak); **c**, Florian Ballhaus; **ed**, John Wilson; **prod d**, Simon Elliott; **art d**, Jens Lockmann, Anja Muller, Bill Crutcher; **set d**, Mark Rosinski; **spec eff**, Wolfgang Higler, Jens Schmiedel.

The Bourne Legacy ★★★ 2012; U.S.; m; UNIV; Color; Spy Drama; Children: Unacceptable; MPAA: PG-13; **BD**; **DVD**. In this exciting fourth entry in the Bourne series, the CIA has lost track of the Moscow whereabouts of Jason Bourne (who was played by Matt Damon in the first three entries). Meanwhile, Aaron Cross, played by Renner, is a government agent assigned to Operation Outcome, a Department of Defense

Jeremy Renner and Rachel Weisz in *The Bourne Legacy*, 2012.

program that uses experimental pills known as "chems" to enhance the physical and mental abilities of their users. Renner is assigned to Alaska for a training exercise under weather extremes. In New York, when an illegal adaptation of the program is exposed, CIA Director Glenn and his deputy Allen are ordered to investigate. Help is gotten from Keach, a retired Navy admiral, who has Norton, a retired Air Force colonel, to also investigate. Norton, who is responsible for overseeing research and development of various clandestine enhancement programs used by the CIA and Defense, discovers a scandalous video on the Internet showing Finney, the Treadstone medical director, in a romantic situation with male doctor Cunningham, who is Outcome's medical director. To prevent the members of the U.S. Congress from learning about Outcome, and to protect the next generation supersoldier program, LARX, Norton deploys drones to eliminate two Outcome agents in Alaska. One of those agents, Renner, hears the drone approach and leaves moments before a missile destroys the cabin he occupies. He then removes the radio-frequency identification device implanted in his thigh and force feeds this into the mouth of a wolf, that animal destroyed by a missile. Thus, Renner has tricked Norton into believing he is dead. Before he can reveal anything in his scheduled appearance before the U.S. Senate, Finney conveniently dies of a heart attack. Then Ivanek, a research doctor at a bio-genetics lab, uses a pistol to shoot and kill all but one of his top-level colleagues employed by Outcome, and, just as security guards rush into his laboratory, he turns the weapon on himself, committing suicide. The only survivor of this group is Weisz. Renner saves Weisz's life, and she tells Renner that he has been genetically modified to retain his mental and physical abilities without the green chemicals anymore. He still requires regular doses of blue chemicals to maintain his intelligence, but his supply of blue chemicals is limited. Renner and Weisz go to the Philippines where the chemicals are manufactured, to try to infect him with a virus so he will not need the blue chemicals. They go to Manila where Weisz injects Renner with live virus stems, and where they narrowly escape capture. Norton orders a chemically brainwashed supersoldier to track down and kill them. They take shelter in a flophouse while Renner recovers from flu-like symptoms while suffering from wild hallucinations about his Outcome training. Philippine police surround the flophouse, but Renner escapes with Weisz by motorcycle. Now they are pursued both by police and LARX agent Changchien. A manic motorcycle chase ensues through the marketplaces of Manila where Renner and Weisz lose the police, but Changchien doggedly races after them. Both Renner and Changchien exchange gunfire, wounding each other, but Weisz saves herself and Renner when causing Changchien's cycle to crash and where he is killed. Weisz then persuades a Filipino boatman to help her and the wounded Renner to escape in a boat and they sail to safety at sea. The film ends with official

Rachel Weisz and Jeremy Renner in *The Bourne Legacy,* 2012.

Straitharn lying to the U.S. Senate in false testimony that covers up the entire CIA debacle. Though complicated and complex to the point of some confusion, this espionage tale provides great eye-popping action and enough subterfuge to intrigue even the most jaded viewer; Renner, Norton, Weisz and the rest of the cast are standouts in their conniving roles. Lavishly produced, this thriller was a great box office success, earning more than $276.1 million in its initial release against a budget of $125 million. Songs: "Kongkkakji" (Bi Ryong Choi, Jun Ho Choi), "Cleaning This Gun/Come on in Boy" (Casey Beathard, Marla Cannon-Goodman), "Patcha" (Arlen P. Mandangan, Cieleto A. Diola), "Extreme Ways/Bourne's Legacy" (Moby: Richard Melville Hall). *Author's Note*: Matt Damon, who had starred in the previous Bourne films, does not appear in this entry as he wanted to bow out of the role, as much as Sean Connery eventually tired of his 007 persona in the James Bond spy series. Renner, however, is a superb replacement as he provides an intense portrayal of a secret agent struggling to do his job while freeing himself of the biochemicals that control his life. This film was shot in a more conventional style than its predecessors in that the camera work is less visually intrusive by its lack of the hand-held shots that so densely inhibited the previous films of the series. Having served in U.S. intelligence, this author can state with some certainty that the Bourne stories are far-fetched to the point of absurdity, and this one challenges logic and reason to their very breaking points. To be fair, however, so did the James Bond series, although Bourne and his ilk are all government pawns fiercely chained to sinister ambitions while Bond inhabits a world of adventurous, tongue-and-cheek playboys dabbling in the deadly world of espionage. The CIA (U.S. Central Intelligence) invariably takes the brunt for all of the evil machinations that take place in the Bourne series, that agency having been so consistently profiled that it has never bothered to respond to this series or any other such film production, out of professional indifference to Hollywood and by following its own protective protocol. One of its high ranking members once said to this author: "What they show about the agency in movies doesn't mean a damned thing to us. The world knows that those Hollywood writers are amateurs and know nothing about what we really do. They can make up whatever myths they want, but that doesn't mean they are presenting facts. None of those writers, or any of the actors playing our agents would survive one hour in our world." The CIA has been profiled in many other films, including **Agent Cody Banks**, 2003; **Aldrich Ames: Traitor Within**, 1998 (made-for-TV); **Apocalypse Now**, 1979; **The A-Team**, 2010; **Act of Valor**, 2012; **Argo**, 2012; **Bad Company**, 2002; **The Barbarian Invasions**, 2003; **Black Dynamite**, 2009; **Body of Lies**, 2008; **The Bourne Identity**, 2002; **The Bourne Supremacy**, 2004; **The Bourne Ultimatum**, 2007; **Burn After Reading**, 2008; **The Chairman**, 1969; **Charade**, 1963; **Charlie Wilson's War**, 2007; **The**

Case of the Red Monkey (aka: **Little Red Monkey**), 1955; **Casino Royale**, 1967; **Casino Royale**, 2006; **Columbiana**, 2011; **Company Business**, 1991; **Company Man**, 2001; **Confessions of a Dangerous Mind**, 2002; **Criminal**, 2016; **Danger Route**, 1967; **The Dark Knight Rises**, 2012; **Die another Day**, 2002; **Dr. No**, 1962; **The Double Man**, 1968; **Erased**, 2012; **Escape Plan**, 2013; **Executive Action**, 1973; **Fair Game**, 2010; **5 Steps to Danger**, 1957; **From Paris with Love**, 2010; **Goldfinger**, 1964; **A Good Day to Die Hard**, 2013; **The Good Shepherd**, 2006; **Green Zone**, 2010; **Hanna**, 2011; **The Innocent**, 1995 (Berlin Tunnel); **Innocent Bystanders**, 1973; **The In-Laws**, 1979; **The Ipcress File**, 1965; **Keeping Track**, 1986; **The Killer Elite**, 1975; **Knight and Day**, 2010; **Laser Mission**, 1989; **License to Kill**, 1989; **Live and Let Die**, 1973; **The Living Daylights**, 1987; **Lockout**, 2012; **Madame Sin**, 1972; **Man on a String**, 1960; **Man on Fire**, 2004; **The Man with One Red Shoe**, 1985; **The Means War**, 2012; **Meet the Parents**, 2000; **Moonraker**, 1979; **Night People**, 1954; **North by Northwest**, 1959; **The November Man**, 2014; **The Numbers Station**, 2013; **Once upon a Time in Mexico**, 2003; **The Operative**, 2000; **The Osterman Weekend**, 1983; **Outrageous Fortune**, 1987; **Pineapple Express**, 2008; **Red**, 2010; **Red 2**, 2013; **Rendition**, 2007; **Ronin**, 1998; **The Russia House**, 1990; **Safe House**, 2012; **Salt**, 2010; **Salting the Battlefield**, 2014 (made-for-TV); **Scavengers**, 1987; **The Sell-Out**, 1977; **Spies Like Us**, 1985; **Spy Game**, 2001; **The Sum of All Fears**, 2002; **Three Days of the Condor**, 1975; **3 Days to Kill**, 2014; **Thunderball**, 1965; **Topaz**, 1969; **Torn Curtain**, 1966; **Turks and Caicos**, 2014 (made-for-TV); **2 Guns**, 2013; **World War Z**, 2013; **X-Men: First Class**, 2011; **Yuri Nosenko: Double Agent**, 1986 (made-for-TV); and **Zero Dark Thirty**, 2012. Violence prohibits viewing by children. **p**, Patrick Crowley, Frank Marshall, Ben Smith, Jeffrey M. Weiner, Andrew R. Tennenbaum; **d**, Tony Gilroy; **cast**, Jeremy Renner, Rachel Weisz, Edward Norton, Joan Allen, Albert Finney, David Straithairn, Scott Glenn, Stacy Keach, Zeljko Ivanek, Louis Ozawa Changchien, Sam Ibram; **w**, Tony Gilroy, Dan Gilroy (based on a story by Tony Gilroy); **c**, Robert Elswit; **m**, James Newton Howard; **ed**, John Gilroy; **prod d**, Kevin Thompson; **art d**, Molly Hughes; **set d**, Leslie Rollins; **spec eff**, Gary Elmendorf.

Boyhood ★★★ 2014; U.S.; 165m; IFC Films; Color; Drama; Children: Unacceptable (MPAA: R); **BD**; **DVD**. Unique coming-of-age film shot intermittently over an eleven-year period from May 2002 to October 2013 shows the growth of a young boy from age five to eighteen and his older sister to adulthood. In 2002, six-year-old Mason Evans Jr. (Coltrane) and his sister Samantha (Lorelei Linklater) live with their single mother Olivia (Arquette) in Texas. Coltrane overhears Arquette arguing with her boyfriend, saying she cannot enjoy life because she no longer has any free time. Arquette moves the family so she can complete her degree by attending the University of Houston and where she might get professional work. In Houston, Coltrane's father (Hawke) takes the children bowling, and assures them that he will spend more time with them before he takes them home. He then gets into an argument with Arquette as the children overhear. Two years later, Arquette takes Coltrane to one of her college classes, introducing him to Perella, her professor, and Coltrane sees his mother flirting with that teacher. Arquette and Perella marry and merge their two families, including Perella's two children from a previous marriage. Arquette continues her studies and is initially supportive of Perella's strict style of parenting and where he imposes heavy chores on all the children and then orders Coltrane to cut his long hair. The no-nonsense Perella alters for the worse as alcoholism changes his strict regimen to abusiveness. After Perella assaults Arquette and threatens the children with physical violence, Arquette finally takes action, moving the family into a friend's house and filing for a divorce. In 2008, Hawke learns that Linklater has a boyfriend and talks to her and Coltrane about contraception, cautioning them about the hazards of sex. Hawke and Coltrane then bond as father and son when they go camping at a state park and share their affections for the Star Wars movies as well as music, and Coltrane expresses his interest in girls. The children develop new lifestyles in San Marcos, a town close to Austin, Texas, where Arquette teaches psychology at a college. Coltrane is ridiculed by bullies at school and is razed during a camping trip, but he now enjoys attention from girls, who take an interest in the sensitive youth. Arquette then falls in love with Hawkins, one of her students, and develops a relationship with him as they live together. Hawkins is a veteran of the Afghanistan/Iraq War, who demonstrates the same rigid personality exhibited by Perella. Coltrane then experiments with marijuana and alcohol as he begins dating girls. On Coltrane's fifteenth birthday, Hawke remarries and, with a baby from that union, takes Coltrane and Linklater to visit his new wife's parents. Coltrane meets Graham at a party and she becomes his girlfriend. After Coltrane arrives home late one night from a party, Hawkins, who has been drinking heavily, confronts Coltrane about his late hours. Arquette, seeing she is reliving the life she had with Perella, breaks up with Hawkins. In 2012, Coltrane and Graham visit Linklater at the University of Texas at Austin. In Coltrane's senior year, he has a painful breakup with Graham. He has become interested in photography and wins a silver medal in a state contest and is awarded college scholarship money. The family holds a party to celebrate Contrane's high school graduation, and all toast his future success. Hawke then gives Coltrane advice about the boy's breakup with Graham. Arquette plans to sell her house and asks Coltrane and Linklater to sort through their possessions. As Coltrane prepares to leave for college, Arquette breaks down, saying she is disappointed with life. At college, Coltrane moves into his dorm room, goes hiking in Big Bend National Park with his roommate's girlfriend, and her roommate, who gives him drugs. Coltrane and the girl who gives him drugs then talk about "seizing the moment," and Coltrane agrees that they are always "in the moment." The film ends on the same kind of ambiguous note that has highlighted the lifestyles of these emotional nomads, but where one poignant and telling scene after another reminds identifying viewers of their own passage through life. Linklater presents an evocative episodic family tale where the entire cast renders top-notch performances. Nothing startling disrupts this prosaic story, but it is told in such a direct and impactful way that interest is sustained throughout. Arquette received an Oscar for Best Supporting Actress, and the film received Oscar nominations for Best Picture; Best Director (Linklater); Best Supporting Actor (Hawke); Best Original Screenplay (Linklater); and Best Film Editing (Adair). The film did well at the box office, earning more than $46.4 million in its initial release against its budget of $4 million. Songs: "Yellow" (Guy Berryman, Jonny Buckland, Will Champion, Chris Martin), "Hate to Say I Told You So" (Randy Fitzsimmons), "Anthem Part Two" (Thomas DeLonge), "Try Again" (Stephen Garrett, Tim Mosley), "Soak Up the Sun" (Sheryl Crow, Jeff Trott), "Island in the Sun" (Rivers Cuomo), "What Is Life" (George Harrison), "Get Lucky" (Thomas Bangalter, Guy-Manuel de Homen-Christo, Pharrell Williams, Nile Rodgers), "Hero" (Joseph Keefe), "Let It Die" (Dave Grohl), "Oops! I Did It Again" (Max Martin, Rami Yacoub), "Crank That, Soulja Boy" (DeAndre Way), "Band on the Run" (Paul McCartney, Linda McCartney), "Do You Realize" (Wayne Coyne, Steven Drozd, Michael Ivins, Dave Fridmann), "Whomping Willow and the Snowball Fight" (from **Harry Potter and the Prisoner of Azkaban** by John Williams), "Could We" (Chan Marshall), "My Good Gal" (Ketch Secor), "Rock and Roll, Part 2" (Mike Leander, Gary Glitter), "Split the Difference" (Ethan Hawke), "Freaks! Freaks!" (John Dust, Nazereth Nirza), "I Held Onto My Pride and Let Her Go" (Dale Watson), "Crazy" (Danger Mouse, Thomas Callaway, Gian Piero Reverberi, Gianfranco Reverberi), "We're All in This Together" (Matthew Gerrard, Robbie Nevil), "Hate It Here" (Nels Cline, John Chadwick Stirratt, Glenn Kotche, Mikael Jorgensen, Pat Sansone, Jeff Tweedy), "One/ Blake's Got a New Face" (Ezra Koenig, Rostam Batmangli, Christopher Tomson), "LA Freeway" (Guy Clark), "1901" (Frederic Moulin, Thomas Croquet, Christian Mazzalai), "Lovegame" (Lady Gaga as Stefani Germanotta, Nadir Khayat), "Desencabulada"

Merida (center) at an archery contest in *Brave*, 2012.

(Luis Felipe Gama, Rodrigo Campos), "Good Girls Go Bad" (Kara Elizabeth DioGuardi, Jacob Kasher Hindlin, Kevin Rudolf, Gabe Saporta), "Lero Lero" (Luisa Maita), "Sous la soileil" (Aurelia Ikor, P. Brunko, C. Bovet, Mimmo Pisino, T. Borgas, Jaba Seiler), "Radioactive" (Caleb Followill, Oivan Followill, Jared Followill, Matthew Followill), "Wish You Were Here" (David Gilmour, Roger Waters), "Beyond the Horizon" (Bob Dylan, Hugh Williams, James Kennedy), "Sunshine Day" (Solomon Amarfio, Francis Teddy Osei, Michael Tontoh), "Telephone" (Lady Gaga), "Ryan's Song" (Ethan Hawke), "Happy Birthday to You" (1893; Mildred J. Hill, Patty S. Hill), "She's Long Gone" (Dan Auerbach, Patrick Carney), "Notre Dame Victory March" (John F. Shea, Michael J. Shea), "Pout" (David Clark, Sam Dillon), "Helena Beat" (Mark Foster), "Suburban War" and "Deep Blue" (Win Butler, William Butler, Regine Chassagne, Jeremy Gara, Tim Kingsbury, Richard Reed), "Somebody That I Used to Know" (Walter Andre De Backer, Luiz Bonfa), "Gobbelins" (Sean Tracey), "I'll Be Around" (Georgia Hubley, Ira Kaplan, James McNew), "Trojans" (Keith Jeffrey, Michael Jeffrey, Steven Jeffrey, Darren Sell), "Nao acorde o nenem" and "Coisa Boa" (Moreno Veloso, Domenico Lancellotti), "Em Todo Lugar Voz Boa" (Moreno Veloso), "Que Mala" (Freddy Fender as Eddie Medina), "The Dog Song" (Marlon Sexton), "Summer Noon" (Jeff Tweedy). Lorelei Linklater is director Richard Linklater's daughter in real life. Drug use and mature material prohibit viewing by children. **p**, Richard Linklater, Jonathan Sehring, John Sloss, Cathleen Sutherland, Sandra Adair, Kirsten McMurray, Vincent Palmo Jr.; **d&w**, Linklater; **cast**, Ellar Coltrane, Patricia Arquette, Ethan Hawke, Elijah Smith, Lorelei Linklater, Steven Prince, Bonnie Cross, Marco Perella, Jamie Howard, Andrew Villarreal; **c**, Lee Daniel, Shane F. Kelly; **ed**, Sandra Adair; **prod d**, Rodney Becker, Gay Studebaker; **set d**, Melanie Ferguson; **spec eff**, Parke Gregg, Nick Smith.

Brave ★★★★ 2012; U.S.; 93m; Walt Disney/Pixar; Color; Animated Adventure/Fantasy; Children: Unacceptable (MPAA: PG); **BD**; **DVD**. This thoroughly engrossing mythological Scottish tale begins with young Princess Merida (Macdonald voiceover). She has a strong independent streak and is a skilled archer. Macdonald's father, King Fergus (Connolly voiceover) gives her a bow for her birthday, much to the dismay of her mother, Queen Elinor (Thompson voiceover). When Macdonald turns sixteen, Thompson tells her she is to marry a man from one of her father's allied clans, but, if she refuses the clan tradition, it could harm the kingdom. The first-born sons of three clans try to win her hand in an archery match, but she defeats them all because she does not want to marry any of them. Macdonald then follows a ghost-like light called a will-o'-the-wisp that leads her to a witch (Walters voiceover). Walters gives her a magical cake that is supposed to change

Merida and an enchanted bear in *Brave*, 2012.

Thompson's mind about her marrying one of the clansmen. Instead, the cake transforms Thompson into a large bear. Macdonald learns that the spell that has transformed Thompson will remain forever unless undone before the second sunrise. To undo the curse, Macdonald must repair an ornate tapestry she had earlier damaged when arguing with Thompson as well as defeat an ogre prince, who has similarly been transformed into a beast. In achieving her goals, Macdonald exacts a promise from the clans that, once she has lifted the curse and has chosen a husband, her offspring will be able to choose their spouses as they see fit in the future, thus breaking the old tradition of the clans. After confronting the ogre and defeating him, the monster transforms back into his human form as a prince, expressing his gratitude to Macdonald for lifting the curse that has made his life miserable. Macdonald has also restored her mother, Thompson, to human form to end this visually stunning film. Wonderfully crafted by Pixar, this exciting film deservedly won an Oscar as Best Animated Feature Film and was a great success at the box office, earning more than $539 million in its initial release against a budget of $185 million. Songs: "Touch the Sky" (Alex Mandel, Mark Andrews), "Into the Open Air" (Mandel), "Learn Me Right" (Mumford & Sons), "Song of Mor Du" (Patrick Doyle, Steve Purcell), "Noble Maiden Fair" (Doyle). Frightening action and crude humor prohibit viewing by children. **p**, Katherine Sarafian; **d**, Mark Andrews, Brenda Chapman, Steve Purcell; **cast** (voiceovers), Emma Thompson, Kelly Macdonald, Kevin McKidd, Robbie Coltrane, Steve Purcell, Patrick Doyle, Craig Ferguson, Sally Kinghorn, Eilidh Fraser, Peigi Barker, Steven Cree; **w**, Andrews, Purcell, Brenda Chapman, Irene Mecchi, Michael Arndt (based on a story by Brenda Chapman); **m**, Patrick Doyle; **ed**, Nicholas C. Smith; **prod d**, Steve Pilcher; **spec eff**, David MacCarthy.

Bridge of Spies ★★★★★ 2015; U.S.; 135m; Amblin Entertainment; DreamWorks/Fox 2000/Walt Disney; Color; Spy Drama; Children: Unacceptable (MPAA: PG-13); **BD**; **DVD**. This compelling Cold War thriller's title refers to a real "bridge of spies" that linked West Berlin to Potsdam in East Germany and where the intelligence agencies of the U.S. and Soviet Union traded prisoners along the bridge. The 3D film tells the true story of James B. Donavan (1916-1970), portrayed by Hanks, a New York insurance attorney whose boss, Alda, has him assigned to negotiate the release of Francis Gary Powers (1929-1977), played by Stowell, a U.S. Air Force captain whose U-2 spy plane was shot down over the Soviet Union on May 1, 1960, and he is being held as a spy. The U.S. claims that Powers was on a weather reconnaissance mission whose plane strayed into Soviet air space. But, after the plane has been shot down and the Soviets recover its equipment, it shows that the craft was not a weather recon plane, but a highly sophisticated air-

craft with advanced photographic technology aimed at capturing surveillance information. The film opens three years earlier in 1957 when Soviet KGB spymaster Rudolf Abel (1903-1971), portrayed by Rylance, goes to a park in Brooklyn, New York, and retrieves a message from one of his agents that is hidden beneath a bench. He returns to his photographic studio, which Rylance uses as a cover, but FBI agents burst inside. Rylance manages to destroy the message, but other paraphernalia and evidence found in that studio brings about his arrest as an enemy espionage agent. Hanks is recruited by his firm to represent Rylance in court, and, after meeting with Rylance in prison, the Soviet agent agrees to accept Hanks' legal representation. Hanks makes such a vigorous defense for the spymaster that he shocks his legal peers, his family and the court. Rylance, like the real Abel, refuses to aid his own case by giving U.S. intelligence any information about his activities or connections during his stay in the U.S. (1948-1957; he had illegally crossed from Canada into the U.S. where he established his espionage network). While demonstrating his energetic defense of his client, Hanks further shocks everyone by demanding that Rylance be acquitted. This brings down upon Hanks' head a storm of angry protests from his own family and friends, as well as the American public. He receives a torrent of hate mail and even threats on his life, but he continues his legal battle undaunted. Rylance is nevertheless convicted of all the charges leveled against him, although Hanks persuades the judge to give Rylance only a thirty-year prison sentence, successfully and prophetically arguing that Rylance might be later used as an exchange pawn to retrieve any U.S. spy captured by the Soviets. Even though Rylance goes behind bars, Hanks continues to fight for his freedom, making an appeal to the U.S. Supreme Court where he argues that Rylance should be acquitted on the grounds that the prosecution provided tainted evidence and that Rylance had been arrested through an invalid search warrant. Hanks, however, loses his case in a 5-4 decision. Three years pass and Stowell, playing U-2 pilot Francis Gary Powers, goes on his mission, is shot down and captured by the Soviets in Russia. At about the same time, Frederic Pryor (1933-), an American college student who is played by Rogers, visits his German girlfriend in East Berlin at the same time the Berlin Wall is being constructed by the Soviet-controlled regime of East Germany. When Rogers tries to smuggle that girlfriend into West Berlin, he is arrested and jailed as a U.S. spy. Rylance then receives a letter from his family (Abel was married with two sons), which is really an indirect message for Hanks that tells Hanks that the USSR will exchange U-2 pilot Stowell for Rylance and Hanks contacts U.S. authorities. He tells the CIA (Central Intelligence Agency, for which Stowell has worked as a U-2 pilot) that he thinks he can not only negotiate the release of Stowell, but also that of the imprisoned student, Rogers. The CIA approves of the two-for-one exchange, but only under the condition that Hanks does not jeopardize the release of Stowell. Hanks works hard as he separately negotiates with his East German and USSR counterparts, but the East Germans suddenly break off negotiations after they learn that Hanks has been also negotiating with the Soviets in Moscow. The CIA, believing that Hanks might fail to free Stowell, tells him to forget about the hapless Rogers, but Hanks will not forsake the American student. He tells the East Germans that, if they do not release Rogers, they will be risking the continued imprisonment of Rylance, who will be further interrogated and might reveal Soviet secrets, all because of the truculence of the East Germans, who will then be blamed by the Soviets for not retrieving their spymaster. The East Germans relent and release Rogers. Meanwhile, Hanks supervises the dramatic exchange of Rylance and Stowell on the night of February 10, 1962. Hanks stands on the Glienicke Bridge (the legendary bridge of spies where secret agents have been exchanged) that spans the Havel River and which links West Belin to Potsdam. He watches as U.S. officials release Rylance from one end of that bridge while the Soviets release Stowell from the other side of the bridge. The two slowly walk toward each other and then wordlessly pass each other until both reach freedom. Hanks is then recognized for bringing about the freedom of not only Stowell but American student

Rogers to end this thoroughly gripping thriller. Pantheon director Spielberg brilliantly builds suspense from the first frame to the last while he fully develops the divergent and shifty characters, all having their own manipulative agendas except for the patriotic and fair-minded Hanks. Again, Hanks renders another great performance in his quietly managed heroic role, where he utterly mesmerizes as a brilliant attorney and master negotiator, sensitive in every harrowing second to the protection of the lives placed in his hands. The film was successful at the box office, earning more than $88 million in its initial release (and to the time of this writing) against a budget of $40 million. *Author's Note*: The idea for this film had been discussed for decades in Hollywood. In 1964, Donovan published his memoirs about this event, *Strangers on a Bridge: The Case of Colonel Abel and Francis Gary Powers*. In 1965, Gregory Peck, in response to the Donovan book, pitched the idea to MGM, stating that he would play attorney Donovan and Alec Guinness would play Rudolf Abel and where the gifted screenwriter Sterling Silliphant would script the story. MGM, however, in light of the tension then existing between the U.S. and the USSR, declined to produce a politically oriented espionage film. Spielberg and his DreamWorks studio bought the story in 2014 and shortly launched the production, which was shot in New York; Berlin and Potsdam, Germany; Poland; and California. The same story is loosely profiled in **The Serpent**, 1973, where a Soviet spymaster is exchanged for a downed U.S. pilot. This author (who served in a branch of U.S. Intelligence other than the CIA) met Powers in Chicago a few years before he was killed in 1977 when a helicopter in which he was flying for a Los Angeles TV station crashed. Powers told this author that "when Abel and I were exchanged, we each started from the end of a bridge and walked toward each other. In the middle of the bridge I looked at this bird, but he kept his head straight forward and refused to look at me when we passed each other. I think the reason why it took them so long to catch Abel is because he looked like Uncle Fudd, the kind of man you would never think to be a spymaster. Well, what did I look like? They caught me red-handed after I parachuted out of my plane. So I must have looked like the chump of the world!" For more details on this case, see my book *Spies: A Narrative Encyclopedia of Dirty Deeds and Double Dealing from Biblical Times to Today* (M. Evans, 1997; Abel: pages 13-17; Powers: pages 394-397). Other films portraying spies and intelligence agencies during the Cold War and afterward include **Agent 8¾** (aka: **Hot Enough for June**, 1965 (MI6; KGB); **Alex Rider: Operation Stormbreaker**, 2006 (MI6); **Assignment K**, 1968 (MI6; East German Stasi); **Assignment: Paris**, 1952; **Arctic Flight**, 1952; **Avalanche Express**, 1979; **Bang! Bang! You're Dead!** (aka: **Our Man in Marrakesh**), 1966; **Battle beneath the Earth**, 1968 (Chinese Intelligence); **Berlin Express**, 1948 (neo-Nazism); **Billion Dollar Brain**, 1967 (MI5); **The Black Windmill**, 1974 (MI6; IRA); **Blue Ice**, 1992 (MI6); **Bullet to Beijing**, 1997 (made-for-TV; MI5; KGB); **Callan**, 1974 (SIS; KGB); **Caravan to Vaccares**, 1974 (KGB); **Carry On Spying**, 1965; **The Case of the Red Monkey** (aka: **Little Red Monkey**), 1955 (Scotland Yard's Special Branch; CIA; KGB); **The Chairman**, 1969 (CIA); **Charlie Muffin**, 1983 (made-for-TV; MI6; KGB); **Che!**, 1969 (KGB); **Company Business**, 1991 (CIA; KGB); **Company Man**, 2001 (CIA); **Confessions of a Dangerous Mind**, 2002 (CIA); **Conspirator**, 1949 (MI5; KGB); **Cornered**, 1945 (neo-Nazism); **Counterspy Meets Scotland Yard**, 1950; **Criminal**, 2016 (CIA); **A Dandy in Aspic**, 1968 (MI6; KGB); **Danger Route**, 1968 (MI6); **The Deadly Affair**, 1967 (MI5; KGB); **Death Has a Bad Reputation**, 1990 (made-for-TV; MI6; Carlos the Jackal); **Death Train**, 1993 (made-for-TV; MI6); **The Devil's Agent**, 1962 (KGB; Stasi); **Dick Barton at Bay**, 1950 (MI5); **Dick Barton Strikes Back**, 1949 (MI5); **Dick Barton, Special Agent**, 1948 (MI6); **Die another Day**, 2002; **Diplomatic Courier**, 1952 (KGB; U.S. Army Intelligence); **Dr. Strangelove**, 1964; **The Double**, 2011; **The Double Man**, 1968 (CIA; KGB); **The Executioner**, 1970 (MI5; KGB); **The Executioner** (aka: **Permission to Kill**), 1975; **The Falcon and the Snowman**, 1985 (KGB; FBI); **Family of Spies**, 1990 (made-for-TV; the Walker family);

Merida and friends in *Brave*, 2012.

Fathom, 1967 (NATO); **Foreign Exchange**, 1970 (made-for-TV; KGB; MI6); **Foreign Intrigue**, 1956; **The Fourth Protocol**, 1987 (KGB); **From Russia with Love**, 1964; **Funeral in Berlin**, 1966 (MI5; KGB); **Hammerhead**, 1968 (MI6; NATO); **Hell and High Water**, 1954; **High Treason**, 1952 (Scotland Yard's Special Branch; KGB); **Highly Dangerous**, 1951 (MI6; KGB); **The Holcroft Covenant**, 1985 (Neo Nazism); **The Human Factor**, 1979 (MI6; KGB); **The Hunter**, 1952 (TV series); **I Was a Communist for the F.B.I.**, 1951 (FBI; KGB); **The Innocent**, 1995 (MI6; CIA; KGB; Berlin Tunnel); **Innocent Bystanders**, 1973 (MI6; KGB; CIA); **The Intelligence Men**, 1965 (MI5; KGB); **The Internecine Project**, 1974 (MI6); **The Ipcress File**, 1965 (MI5); **The Iron Curtain**, 1948 (MGB/MVD; RCMP); **Jet Attack**, 1958 (KGB); **The Jigsaw Man**, 1984 (KGB; MI6; Kim Philby); **Johnny English**, 2003 (MI6; KGB); **Johnny English Reborn** (aka: **Johnny English Returns**), 2011 (MI6; KGB); **Keep Your Fingers Crossed** (aka: **Catch Me a Spy**), 1971 (KGB; MI6); **Kingsman: The Secret Service**, 2014; **The Kremlin Letter**, 1970 (KGB); License to Kill, 1989; **The Liquidator**, 1966 (MI6); **The Looking Glass War**, 1970 (MI6; KGB); **The Mackintosh Man**, 1973 (MI6); **Madame Sin**, 1972 (CIA); **The Man Between**, 1953 (MI6; KGB); **The Man in the Glass Booth**, 1975 (role model for Adolf Eichmann; Mossad); **Man on a String**, 1960 (CIA; KGB); **The Man Who Knew Too Much**, 1956 (MI5; KGB); **The Manchurian Candidate**, 1962; **The Manchurian Candidate**, 2004; **Marathon Man**, 1976; **Master Spy**, 1964 (MI5; KGB); **Midnight in Saint Petersburg**, 1996 (MI6; KGB); **MI-5** (aka: **Spooks: The Greater Good**), 2015 (MI5); **My Son John**, 1952 (MGB/MVD; FBI); **The Naked Runner**, 1967 (MI6; KGB); **Night People**, 1954 (KGB; U.S. G-2); **Night Train to Paris**, 1964 (French intelligence; KGB); **Nightwatch**, 1995 (made-for-TV; UN agents); **No. 1 of the Secret Service**, 1970 (MI6); **North by Northwest**, 1959 (CIA; KGB); **Notorious**, 1946 (neo-Nazism; FBI); **Notorious**, 1992 (made-for-TV); **The Numbers Station**, 2013 (CIA); **The Odessa File**, 1974 (neo-Nazism); **Otley**, 1969; **Operation Eichmann**, 1961 (neo-Nazism; Mossad); **Operation Manhunt**, 1954 (KGB; Canadian intelligence; RCMP); **Our Man in Havana**, 1959 (MI6); **Page Eight**, 2011 (MI5); **Pickup on South Street**, 1952 (NKVD; KGB; FBI); **The Quiller Memorandum**, 1966 (neo-Nazism); **Ring of Treason** (aka: **Ring of Spies**), 1964 (MI5; KGB; Portland Spy Ring); **Salt**, 2010; **Salting the Battlefield**, 2014 (made-for-TV; MI5; CIA); **The 2nd Best Secret Agent in the Whole Wide World** (aka: **Licensed to Kill**), 1965 (MI6); **Security Risk**, 1954; **The Sell-Out**, 1977 (CIA; KGB; Mossad); **Shadow Dancer**, 2012 (MI5; IRA); **Shoot First** (aka: **Rough Shoot**), 1953 (MI5; KGB); **Some Girls Do**, 1971; **Some May Live**, 1967 (U.S. Army Intelligence); **Spies Like Us**, 1985; **Spooks**, 2002-2011 (TV series; MI5); **The Spy Killer**, 1969 (made-for-TV; MI6; KGB); **Spy**

Bear cubs in *Brave*, 2012.

Story, 1976 (MI6; KGB); **The Spy Who Came in from the Cold**, 1965 (KGB; MI6; MI5); **The Spy Who Loved Me**, 1977; **The Russia House**, 1990 (MI6; KGB); **The Stranger**, 1946 (neo-Nazism); **Subterfuge**, 1969 (MI6); **Survivor**, 2015 (MI6); **They Can't Hang Me**, 1955 (Scotland Yard's Special Branch; KGB); **The Thief**, 1952 (KGB; FBI); **The Third Man**, 1950 (MI6; KGB); **Three Days of the Condor**, 1975 (CIA); **Tinker Tailor Soldier Spy**, 1979 (TV miniseries); **Tinker Tailor Soldier Spy**, 2011 (MI5; KGB); **Topaz**, 1969 (CIA; KGB); **Torn Curtain**, 1966 (CIA; KGB); **Turks and Caicos**, 2014 (made-for-TV; MI5; CIA); **Walk a Crooked Mile**, 1948 (FBI; Scotland Yard's Special Branch; KGB); **Walk East on Beacon!**, 1952 (FBI; KGB); **Where the Bullets Fly**, 1967; **Where the Spies Are**, 1966; **The Whistle Blower**, 1987 (MI6); **The Woman on Pier 13**, 1949 (KGB; FBI). Violence and gutter language prohibit viewing by children. **p**, Steven Spielberg, Kristie Macosko Krieger, Marc Platt, Christopher Fisser, Charlie Woebcken, Henning Molfenter; **d**, Spielberg; **cast**, Tom Hanks, Eve Hewson, Amy Ryan, Alan Alda, Mark Rylance, Peter McRobbie, Billy Magnussen, Austin Stowell, Will Rogers, Domenick Lombardozzi, Michael Gaston, Sebastian Koch; **w**, Matt Charman, Ethan Coen, Joel Coen; **c**, Janusz Kaminski; **m**, Thomas Newman; **ed**, Michael Kahn; **prod d**, Adam Stockhausen; **art d**, Marco Bittner Rosser, Kim Jennings; **set d**, Rena DeAngelo, Bernhard Henrich; **spec eff**, Gerd Nefzer, Bernd Rautenberg, Steven Kirshoff.

Caesar Must Die ★★★ 2012; Italy; 77m; Kaos Cinematografica/Adopt Films/Sacher Distribution; B&W/Color; Drama; Children: Unacceptable (MPAA: R); **BD**; **DVD**. Fascinating tale begins with inmates in a theatre program in Rebibbia Prison in a suburb of Rome, Italy. They stage a production of William Shakespeare's "Julius Caesar" that is well received. The film is told in flashback several months before when its co-ordinators announce that the play will be the group's production of the year. A cast is auditioned and the inmates, many of them serving long sentences or life for serious crimes, find, as they rehearse, that the play has special meaning to them in contrast to their confining prison lives. This very unusual film was a surprise winner of the Golden Bear award at the 62nd Berlin International Film Festival. (In Italian; English subtitles) **p**, Grazia Volpi, Agnese Fontana, Donatella Palermo, Laura Andreini Salerno, Cecilia Valmarana; **d&w**, Paolo Taviani, Vittorio Taviani (based on the play "Julius Caesar" by William Shakespeare); **cast**, Giovanni Arcuri, Cosimo Rega, Salvatore Striano, Antonio Frasca, Juan Dario Bonetti, Vincenzo Gallo, Rosario Majorana, Francesco De Masi, Gennaro Solito, Vittorio Parrella; **c**, Simone Zampagni; **m**, Giulian Taviani, Carmelo Travia; **ed**, Roberto Perpignani.

Cake ★★★ 2014; U.S.; 102m; Cinelou Films; Color; Drama; Children: Unacceptable (MPAA: R); **BD**; **DVD**. Aniston renders a stunning performance as a successful and wealthy Los Angeles divorcee who is nonetheless an emotional and physical wreck. She is a chronic pain sufferer who belongs to a group of similarly afflicted people. With scars on her face and limbs, she is bitter and argumentative, relying on substances she even steals to obtain and swallow with wine. She is miserable while sleeping with her gardener and no one can stand her, even those she employs, such as her swim therapy instructor. The only person who will tolerate her is her sympathetic and supportive Mexican housekeeper, Barraza. The film opens with Aniston being banished from her support group by its leader, Huffman, after Aniston expresses sympathy for Kendrick, a member of the group who was so desperate she killed herself by leaping from a freeway overpass. Aniston is out of pills, so she asks Barraza to drive her across the border to Tijuana to get refills of the illegal tranquilizing substances at a drug store there. The store clerk sells Aniston what she wants but stores it in a holy statuette. This distresses Anniston because she is not religious, but she tolerates the ruse. Barraza is more emotionally stronger than her employer and is able to illicit some hidden sense of kindness within Anniston. This is offset by Aniston's nightmares in which she is visited by Kendrick and they engage in discussions about suicide, which may be a dire self-therapy exercised by Aniston to help her relieve her misery. She also finds solace in a relationship with Kendrick's widower, Worthington, and young son. Despite her failings, we have a sense of sympathy for Aniston, a woman who badly needs someone to love and want her and, metaphorically speaking, bake a cake for her. Aniston stuns in a dynamic performance where the viewer seems to feel her pain and agony and Barraza also gives a sterling essay as the only person in the world who can tolerate this intolerable, nerve-wracked woman. Barnz directs with a careful hand as he fully develops these characters that are strangely repulsive and appealing at the same time, particularly drawing grudging empathy from viewers otherwise unsympathetic to Aniston's antisocial persona. The film did poorly at the box office, earning less than $2.4 million in its initial release against a budget of more than $7 million. Songs: "Goodbye" (Gary Romero), "Bludan" (Eddie Cano), "Desaparecido" (Manu Chao), "El Cucuy' and "Moreno Mexicana" (Geoff Levin, Bruce Chianese), "John and James" (Herbert Frederick, Arthur Stanley Reid), "Let's Get Started" (Dylan Gardner), "Honestly" (Billy Joel), "Simple Simon" (Elizabeth Goose, Andrew Green), "Magical Embrace Trumpet" (Randy Goodman, Timothy Hosman), "Ole por Nos" (Vinicius Gageiro Marques), "Dig It" (Hal Borne, Johnny Mercer), "Halo" (Evan Bogart, Beyonce Knowles, Ryan Tedder). Gutter language, substance abuse and brief sexuality prohibit viewing by children. **p**, Jennifer Aniston, Ben Barnz, Mark Canton, Kristin Hahn, Courtney Solomon, Stephanie Caleb, Elizabeth Destro, Scott Karol, Wayne Marc Godfrey; **d**, Daniel Barnz; **cast**, Aniston, Adriana Barraza, Anna Kendrick, Sam Worthington, William H. Macy, Mamie Gummer, Felicity Huffman, Chris Messina, Lucy Punch, Britt Robertson, Paula Cale, Ashley Crow; **w**, Patrick Tobin; **c**, Rachel Morrison; **m**, Christophe Beck; **ed**, Kristina Boden, Michelle Harrison; **prod d**, Joseph T. Garrity; **art d**, Brittany Bradford; **set d**, Lisa Son; **spec eff**, Gary Monak.

The Calling ★★★ 2014; U.S.; 103m; Stage 6 Films/Vertical Entertainment; Color; Crime Drama/Horror; Children: Unacceptable (MPAA: PG-13); **BD**; **DVD**. Grim and eerie tale sees Sarandon as the sheriff in a small Canadian town that has very little crime for her to investigate, so her middle age and alcoholism doesn't interfere with her work. She gets it done with the help of deputy Bellows and a new cop on the force, Grace. Sarandon then finds the body of a local friend from church sitting in a living room chair without a head completely attached. The female victim's throat has been nearly severed, and her mouth has been twisted into an artificial scream. While investigating that murder, another person is killed, the victim's stomach removed and fed to some dogs. Sarandon and her police associates now believe a very violent serial killer is at loose. They suspect Heyderdahl, a spooky man who comes to town in a long black coat carrying a mysterious bag. Sarandon and her police associates follow Heyderdahl and learn he is the serial killer, as well as his motives which turn out to be religious. After dispatching several other people, Heyderdahl traps Sarandon, explaining that he is taking revenge for his brother's suicide, as both he and his brother had been orphans living in an asylum supervised by Sutherland, a priest. Heyderdahl has also killed Sutherland, as the priest was terminally ill, as were the rest of the serial killer's victims, who is performing his own brand of euthanasia or mercy killing. He believes Sarandon is also terminally ill and offers her a cup of his own brewed tea, which contains poison. Sarandon, weary of life, is about to swallow this vile bile, but then refuses. Astonishingly, the mentally deranged Heyderdahl does the next best thing and joins his brother in death by committing suicide. Sarandon gives a stellar performance as a tortured woman, her will lingering between life and death. Burstyn plays Sarandon's mother in the film and Donald Sutherland appears in two scenes to explain the plot. The film was first released to video but saw limited theatrical distribution, earning about $3 million in its initial release. Not related to a 2000 film with the same title. Violence, disturbing images and gutter language prohibit viewing by children. Song: "Jesus Loves Me, This I Know" (William Batchelder Bradbury). **p**, Scott Abramovitch, Lonny Dubrofsky, Randy Manis, Nicholas Tabarrok, Ricky Tollman; **d**, Jason Stone; **cast**, Susan Sarandon, Ellen Burstyn, Topher Grace, Gil Bellows, Donald Sutherland, Chrisopher Heyderdahl, Ella Ballentine, Kristin Booth, Katy Breier, Amanda Brugel, Shane Daly; **w**, Abramovitch (based on the novel by Inger Ash Wolfe); **c**, David Robert Jones; **m**, Grayson Matthews; **ed**, Aaron Marshall; **prod d**, Oleg M. Savytski; **set d**, Christina Kuhnigk; **spec eff**, Dennis Temprile.

Captain America: The Winter Soldier ★★★ 2014; U.S.; 128m; Marvel Entertainment/Disney; Color; Adventure/Science Fiction; Children: Unacceptable (MPAA: PG-13); **BD**; **DVD**. In this eye-popping sequel to **Captain America: The First Avenger** (2011), Steve Rogers, played by Evans, who has the superman powers of Captain America, struggles with his new role in the modern world and battles a new threat from his old adversary, the Soviet agent Bucky Barnes, played by Stan, who is also known as the Winter Soldier. Two years after the Battle of New York, Evans attempts to adjust to contemporary society as he works in Washington for the espionage agency S.H.I.E.L.D., and under supervisor Jackson. Evans and agent Johansson are sent with the agency's counterterrorism team led by agent Grillo to free hostages aboard an agency vessel from St-Pierre and his mercenaries. Evans discovers that Johansson has another agenda, to get data from the ship's computers to give to Jackson. Evans returns to the Triskelion, the agency's headquarters, to confront Jackson and is briefed about Project Insight involving three helicarriers linked to spy satellites that are designed to eliminate threats. After he is unable to decrypt the data recovered by Johansson, Jackson becomes suspicious and asks Redford, the agency senior official, to put the project on hold. Jackson is then ambushed by assailants led by a mysterious assassin, Stan, called (the Winter Soldier) when attempting a rendezvous with Smulders. Jackson escapes, going to Evans' apartment where he warns him that the agency has been compromised, giving Evans a flash drive that contains data from the ship, before he is fatally shot by Stan. After Jackson dies in surgery, Hill recovers his body and, the next day, Redford orders Evans to report to the Triskelion. Evans withholds the information given to him by Jackson and Redford orders Evans arrested. While being sought by S.T.R.I.K.E., Evans meets with Johansson. When using data in the flash drive, they learn about a secret S.H.I.E.L.D. bunker in New Jersey where they activate a supercomputer containing Jones' preserved consciousness. Jones relates how Hydra has secretly operated within S.H.I.E.L.D. after World War II (1939-1945), and, as that agitating mole, has created worldwide unrest, its aim to have the world seek security in exchange for freedom. When a S.H.I.E.L.D.

Tom Hanks and Halle Berry in *Cloud Atlas,* 2012.

missile strikes and destroys the bunker, Evans and Johansson narrowly escape death, and they now know that Redford is the secret leader of Hydra. They enlist the aid of Mackie, a former U.S. Air Force rescue expert whom Evans had earlier befriended, and obtain his powered "Falcon" wing pack. They pinpoint S.H.I.E.L.D. agent Hernandez as a Hydra mole, and compel him to divulge information that explains how Jones developed a data-mining algorithm that identifies enemies of Hydra. To destroy those enemies, Hydra plans to use satellite-guided guns manned in Insight Helicarriers. Evans, Johansson, and Mackie are then ambushed, and Stan kills Hernandez. During this fierce firefight, Evans recognizes his friend Stan, remembering how Stan was captured and underwent experiments during WWII. (Stan's programming is not unlike that which takes over the mind and personality of Laurence Harvey in **The Manchurian Candidate**, 1962, where he does the murderous bidding of his controllers, automatically responding to lethal orders without question as does the somnambulist played by Conrad Veidt in **The Cabinet of Dr. Caligari**, 1921, or the mindless zombies controlled by Voodoo masters in the Caribbean islands.) Smulders is able to rescue Evans, Johansson, and Mackie, taking them to a safe house where they are surprised to see Jackson very much alive. He has not only faked his death, but has plans to sabotage the Helicarriers by sabotaging their controller chips. When World Security Council members arrive for the launch of the Helicarriers, Evans tells everyone at the Triskelion about Hydra's insidious and widespread conspiracy. Redford is disarmed by Johansson, who has disguised herself as a council member. Jackson then compels Redford to unlock S.H.I.E.L.D.'s database, so that Johansson can obtain classified information to be disseminated to the public and where Hydra can be exposed as an evil organization. A wild struggle takes place where Redford is shot dead by Jackson. Meanwhile, Evans and Mackie get into two Helicarriers and replace the controller chips, but Stan destroys Mackie's suit and battles Evans. Fending off Stan, Evans manages to replace the final chip that allows Smulders to take control to have the vessels destroy each other. As a ship collides with the Triskelion, Evans is blown into the Potomac River. Stan rescues the unconscious Evans before vanishing. S.H.I.E.L.D. is now a shambles as Johansson appears before a senate subcommittee to reveal its corrupt elements. Jackson, meanwhile, maintains his cover (of having been killed), and travels to Eastern Europe to track down the remaining elements of Hydra. Evans and Mackie then resolve to find and battle Stan, while, following Triskelion's destruction, Grillo, who was a double agent for Hydra, is hospitalized. As the film's closing credits roll, Baron Wolfgang von Sturker, played by Kretschmann, is seen at a Hydra laboratory where he proclaims that the "age of miracles" has begun. Scientists are then shown examining an energy-filled scepter and two prisoners. One prisoner possesses superhuman speed, the other prisoner

Halle Berry and Keith David in *Cloud Atlas,* **2012.**

possesses extraordinary telekinetic powers. Evans, Stan, and Johansson are standouts in their roles and receive strong support from a talented cast, but the centerpiece of this riveting action-packed thriller is its amazing special effects, which received an Oscar nomination. The film was an enormous box office success, gleaning more than $714.4 million in its initial release against a budget of $170 million. Songs: "It's Been a Long, Long Time" (Jule Styne, Sammy Cahn), "Trouble Man" (Marvin Gaye), "Score from Captain Avenger: The First Avenger" (Alan Silvestri). **p**, Kevin Feige, Nate Moore; **d**, Anthony Russo, Joe Russo; **cast**, Chris Evans, Scarlett Johansson, Samuel L. Jackson, Robert Redford, Dominic Rains, Jenny Agutter, Anthony Mackie, Cobie Smulders, Maximiliano Hernandez, Hayley Atwell, Emily VanCamp, Sebastian Stan, Thomas Kretschmann, Toby Jones, Georges St-Pierre, Frank Grillo; **w**, Christopher Markus, Stephen McFeely (based on a concept and story by Ed Brubaker and the comic book by Joe Simon, Jack Kirby); **c**, Trent Opaloch; **m**, Henry Jackman; **ed**, Jeffrey Ford; **prod d**, Peter Wenham; **art d**, Thomas Valentine; **set d**, Leslie A. Pope; **spec eff**, Daniel Sudick, Garry Elmendorf, Katrissa Peterson, Jen Underdahl, Geoffrey E. Baumann.

Captain Phillips ★★★★ 2013; U.S.; 134m; Scott Rudin/COL; Color; Adventure/Biographical Drama; Children: Unacceptable (MPAA: PG-13); **BD**; **DVD**. This tense thriller is based upon the hijacking of the unarmed U.S. container ship *Maersk Alabama* by a crew of Somali pirates, who seized the ship 145 miles off the Somali coast, the crisis ending on April 12, 2009. The ship's captain, Richard Phillips (1955-), played by Hanks, takes command in the port of Salalah in Oman. He receives orders to sail the vessel through the Gulf of Aden to Mombassa in the African Great Lakes region. Hanks, as well as his first officer, Chernus, are acutely aware of the fact that there is pirate activity off the coast of the Horn of Africa. Ordering strict security measure, Hanks and Chernus conduct rigorous emergency drills to avoid being captured by pirates. During a drill, Somali pirates chase the ship in two skiffs, prompting Hanks to radio for help. Knowing that the pirates are monitoring his SOS messages, Hanks pretends to answer his own call, promising immediate air support that will summarily destroy the pirates. His ruse works as one pirate skiff turns about while the other goes dead in the water when it loses engine power. The pirates, however, persist, and, the next day, one of the skiffs, fitted with outboard engines, returns with four heavily armed pirates, who are led by Abdi. They secure a ladder to the ship and begin to climb on board. While the crew hides in the engine room on Hanks' orders, the pirates take over the ship and Hanks allows himself to be taken prisoner. Hanks immediately tries to barter for the ship's freedom, offering Abdi $30,000 from the ship's safe. The pirate leader, however, is under orders to ransom the ship and crew in

exchange for millions of dollars of insurance money, and he refuses Hanks' proposal. Meanwhile, the alert Chernus monitors the movements of the pirates as they search for the ship's crew. He sees that Abdirahman, the youngest of the pirates, wears no sandals and is moving about on bare feet. He orders the crew members to line the engine room corridor with broken glass, while Warshofsky, the chief engineer, turns off the power inside the ship, plunging the lower decks into darkness. As anticipated by crew members, Abdirahman cuts his feet on the glass and Abdi is compelled to continue the search alone. The crew members overwhelm Abdi but they agree to release him into a lifeboat if the pirates abandon the ship. However, the pirates refuse to release Hanks and they launch a lifeboat, leaving the ship with Hanks. As the lifeboat heads for shore, the pirates lose contact with their mother ship. Ahmed, one of the pirates, argues with others as he tries to persuade them to kill Hanks. The U.S. Navy destroyer USS *Bainbridge* then intercepts the lifeboat. Vasquez, the destroyer's captain, has been ordered to prevent the pirates from reaching the shore. Abdi, however, despite the arrival of more rescue ships, refuses to surrender. The lifeboat is eventually taken over by a Navy SEAL team that has parachuted into the area. Abdi now agrees to board the *Bainbridge*, when he is told that his clan elders have arrived to negotiate Hanks' ransom. Ahmed, who is still in control of the lifeboat, orders his fellow pirates to blindfold Hanks. Seeing that Hanks is about to be executed, a SEAL marksman takes careful aim and shoots and kills all of the pirates. Abdi is then seized while he is aboard the destroyer and charged with piracy. Hanks, who is disoriented and in shock, is then taken from the lifeboat and he expresses his gratitude to the sharpshooter for saving his life at the last moment. Harrowing and horrific from one frame to another, this film rivets as Greengrass carefully builds the tension naturally unfolding in the actual events. Hanks is mesmerizing in the role of the heroic captain, who is both negotiator and victim, a seemingly nerveless man dealing with lethal kidnappers who have no hesitation in taking his life at any moment. The screenplay chronicles the grim events in terse and uncompromising terms while the lensing and production values are superb. The film received Oscar nominations for Best Picture; Best Supporting Actor (Abdi); Best Screenplay (Ray); Best Film Editing (Rouse); and Best Sound Mixing (Mark Taylor, Chris Burdon, Mike Prestwood Smith, Chris Munrod). It was a great box office hit, earning more than $218.8 million in its initial release against a budget of $55 million. Songs: "Up in Here" (Kovasciar Myvette), "Hilm B Hilm" (Musa Hanhan), "Wonderful Tonight" (Eric Clapton), "The End" (John Powell). *Author's Note*: The film was shot on location off the coast of Malta in the Mediterranean Sea on a nine-week shooting schedule. Abduwali Muse (c.1990-), the only pirate to survive the abortive seizure of the *Maersk Alabama*, was convicted of piracy and ship hijacking, and is presently serving a thirty-three-year prison sentence in a U.S. federal prison. Other films that profile the attempted seizure or seizure of ships include **All the Brothers Were Valiant**, 1953; **Amistad**, 1997; **The Bounty**, 1984; **The Caine Mutiny**, 1954; **Captain Blood**, 1935; **Captain Horatio Hornblower**, 1951; **China Seas**, 1935; **City Hunter**, 1993; **Final Voyage**, 1999; **The French Atlantic Affair**, 1979 (TV miniseries); **The Ghost Ship**, 1943; **Golden Rendezvous**, 1978; **A Hijacking**, 2013; **King of Alcatraz**, 1938; **The Land That Time Forgot**, 1975; **The Lightship**, 1986; **Morituri**, 1965; **Mutiny on the Bounty**, 1935; **Mutiny on the Bounty**, 1962; **Passage to Marseilles**, 1944; **The Sea Hawk**, 1940; **The Sea Wolf**, 1941; **Speed 2: Cruise Control**, 1997; **Two Years before the Mast**, 1946; **Under Siege**, 1992; and **Voyage of Terror: The Achille Lauro Affair**, 1990 (made-for-TV). Sustained intense sequences of menace, violence with bloody images and substance use prohibit viewing by children. **p**, Dana Brunetti, Michael De Luca, Scott Rudin, Michael Bronner, Christopher Rouse; **d**, Paul Greengrass; **cast**, Tom Hanks, Catherine Keener, Barkhad Abdi, Barkhad Abdirahman, Faysal Ahmed, Mahat M. Ali, Michael Chernus, David Warshofsky, Corey Johnson, Chris Mulkey, Yul Vazquez; **w**, Billy Ray (based on the book *A Captain's Duty: Somali Pirates, Navy SEALS, and Dangerous Days* *at Sea* by Richard Phillips, Stephen Talty); **c**, Barry Ackroyd; **m**, Henry Jackman; **ed**, Christopher Rouse; **prod d**, Paul Kirby; **art d**, Su Whitaker; **set d**, Dominic Capon; **spec eff**, Caius Man, Brian Ricci, Dominic Tuohy.

Cesar Chavez ★★★★ 2014; U.S./Mexico; 101m; Canana Films/Lionsgate; Color; Biographical Drama; Children: Unacceptable (MPAA: PG-13); **BD**; **DVD**. This fine dramatization of the birth of a modern American social movement follows the life and work of Mexican American civil rights and labor organizer Cesar Chavez (1927-1999), who is superbly played by Pena. He is torn between his duties as a husband and father and his commitment to securing a living wage for 50,000 farm workers in California, who were temporary workers from Mexico. Pena sees how the Mexican migrants suffer drastically from poor working conditions, and, at the same time, are victims of racism and brutal treatment by their employers, as well as local Californians. To improve living and working conditions, Pena organizes a labor union called the United Farm Workers (UFW), but his efforts are met with staunch opposition by the owners of large industrial farms, including Malkovich, owner of a large industrial grape farm. Some of his adversaries resort to force, causing widespread violence to erupt. The patient Pena, however, persists, and his organization takes root and its workers begin to see the benefits of their membership in better living and working conditions, as well as a more friendly relationship between the workers and their employers. Pena's success inspires millions of Americans from all walks of life who never worked on a farm to fight for social justice. The film touches on several major nonviolent campaigns by the UFW, the Delano grape strike, the Salad Bowl strike, and the 1975 Modesto march. This film, unfortunately, did not do well at the box office, earning less than $6.7 million in its initial release against a budget of more than $10 million. Songs: "Good Love" (L. Stuart), "Estoy perdido" (Victor Manuel Mato Argumedo), "If That Old Jukebox Could Talk" (Jody Reynolds), "Darktown Strutters Ball" (Shelton Brooks), "De manana en adelante" (Copyright Control), "No nos moveran" (traditional), "Lazy Daisy Blues" (Samuel Stuart Kaplan), "De colores" (traditional), "Amor sin medida" (Jose Alfredo Jimenez), "Beale Street Blues" (W.C. Handy), "Solo le pido a Dios" (Ulises Lozano). Mature subject matter prohibits viewing by children. **p**, Pablo Cruz, Lianne Halfon, Diego Luna, Larry Meli, Keir Pearson, Russell Smith, Georgina Teran; **d**, Diego Luna; **cast**, Michael Pena, America Ferrera, John Malkovich, Michael Cudlitz, Rosario Dawson, Gabriel Mann, Kevin Dunn, Mark Moses, Jacob Vargas, Lisa Brenner; **w**, Keir Pearson, Timothy J. Sexton; **c**, Enrique Chediak; **m**, Michael Brook; **ed**, Douglas Crise, Miguel Schverdfinger; **prod d**, Ivonne Fuentes, Krystyna Loboda; **set d**, Robert Wischhusen-Hayes; **spec eff**, Raul Prado.

Chef ★★★ 2014; U.S.; 115m; Aldamisa Entertainment/Open Road Films; Color; Comedy; Children: Unacceptable (MPAA: R); **BD**; **DVD**. Favreau (who not only stars in this entertaining film but produced, wrote and directed it) is a Miami-born chef who tries to open a restaurant in Los Angeles, but it fails. He returns to Miami to fix up a food truck in an attempt to reclaim his culinary creative promise, while trying to get back with Vergara, his wealthy ex-wife. Undaunted, Favreau plans to drive across the country to reclaim his reputation as a preeminent chef. Along the way, he serves his own creations of po' boys and barbequed brisket-of-beef, and becomes a great success. The film did well at the box office, earning more than $46 million against a budget of $11 million. Songs: "Brother John Is Gone/Herc-Jolly-John" (The Wild Magnolias: Theodore Dollis, June Yamagishi, Norwood Johnson, Gerard Dollis, Queen Rita, Monk Boudreaux), "Tired of Being Alone" (Al Green), "Rudy, a Message to You" (Robert Livingstone Thompson), "I Like It Like That" (Tony Pabon, Manny Rodriguez), "Lucky Man" (Courtney Morrison, Nicole Sharpe, John Holt, Tyrone Evans, Howard Barrett), "C.R.E.A.M." (Dennis Coles, Robert F. Diggs, Gary E. Grice, Lamont Hawkins, Isaac Hayes, Jason Hunter, Russell T. Jones, David

Hugh Grant in *Cloud Atlas,* 2012.

Porter, Clifford Smith, Corey Woods), "Cavern" (Scott Hartley, Richard McGuire, Salvatore Principato, Dennis Young), "Hung Over" (Charles Axton, Leroy Hodges, Mabon Hodges, Johnny Keys, Archie Mitchell), "Bang Bang" (Joe Cuba, Jimmy Sabater), "La Quimbumba" (Jose Caridad Hernandez), "The Champ" (Harry Palmer), "The Hustler" (Willie Colon), "Tabaco y Ron" (Manuel Roche Dominguez), "Que Se Sepa" (Titti Sotto), "Acid" (Ray Barretto), "Ali Baba" (Louie Ramirez), "Homenaje al Benny (Castellano Que Bueno Balia Usted" (Alexander Delgado, Yosdany Jacob, Fernando Otero), "My Swing es Tropical" (Nicolas Desimone, Hector Alomar, Will Holland), "Bustin' Loose" (Charles L. Brown), "Sexual Healing" (Odell Brown, David Ritz, Marvin Gaye), "Travis County" (Gary Clark, Jr.), "When My Train Pulls In" (Clark, Jr.), "Oh, Didn't He Ramble" (traditional), "West Coast Poplock" (Roger Troutman, Larry Troutman, Mikel Hooks, Ronnie Hudson), "Oye Como Va" (Tito Puente). Gutter language and suggestive material prohibit viewing by children. ***Author's Note***: This film was shot on location in Los Angeles; Miami, Florida (using the Fontainebleau Hotel and its famed Versailles Restaurant); Austin, Texas; and New Orleans, Louisiana. Other films profiling chefs and cooks include: **The Adventures of Robin Hood**, 1938; **All Quiet on the Western Front**, 1930; **Angels Fall**, 2007 (made-for-TV); **Anything Can Happen**, 1952; **Back to Bataan**, 1945; **Bataan**, 1943; **Battleground**, 1949; **A Better Life**, 2012; **Big Night**, 1996; **The Blues Brothers**, 1980; **Buck Privates**, 1941; **Burning Man**, 2011; **Burnt**, 2015; **Carnival of Sinners**, 1947; **The Case of the Curious Bride**, 1935; **Chef!**, 1993-1996 (TV series); **The Chef**, 2005; **Chef's Special**, 2009; **Chowder**, 2007-2010 (TV series); **Cover Girl**, 1944; **Cowboy**, 1958; **The Culpepper Cattle Company**, 1972; **The Dark Knight Rises**, 2012; **Destination Tokyo**, 1943; **The Devil Wears Prada**, 2006; **Dinner Rush**, 2000; **Dishdogz**, 2006; **The Duchess of Duke Street**, 1976-1977 (TV series); **East Side Story**, 2006; **Eat Drink Man Woman**, 1994; **Everybody Sing**, 1938; **Felicia's Journey**, 1999; **The Fighting Chefs**, 2013; **Follow the Leader**, 1930; **Fools for Scandal**, 1938; **Freddie**, 2005-2006 (TV series); **The Freshman**, 1990; **The Glass Slipper**, 1955; **The Godfather**, 1972; **The Golden Palace**, 1992-1993 (TV series); **The Great Race**, 1965; **Guadalcanal Diary**, 1943; **Haute Cuisine**, 2013; **He Stayed for Breakfast**, 1940; **Here Comes Cookie**, 1935; **History Is Made at Night**, 1937; **Hit Parade of 1947**, 1947; **The Hundred-Foot Journey**, 2014; **I Am Love**, 2010; **If You Could Only Cook**, 1936; **Julie & Julia**, 2009; **Kitchen Confidential**, 2005- (TV series); **The Killers**, 1946; **Lady Bodyguard**, 1943; **Le Chef**, 2012; **Le Grand Chef**, 2007; **Le Grand Chef 2: Kimchi Battle**, 2010; **Let's Dance**, 1950; **The Longest Day**, 1962; **Love's Kitchen**, 2011; **Majestic Hotel Cellars**, 1945; **A Matter of Minutes**, 1959; **Mr. Nice Guy**, 1998; **Monte Walsh**, 1970; **Monte Walsh**, 2003 (made-for-TV); **Mostly**

Jim Sturgess and Hugo Weaving in *Cloud Atlas*, 2012.

Martha, 2001; **Murder by Death**, 1976; **My Big Love**, 2008; **My Darling Clementine**, 1946; **A Night at the Ritz**, 1935; **A Night in Casablanca**, 1946; **No Reservations**, 2007; **Obliging Young Lady**, 1942; **Pack Up Your Troubles**, 1932; **Panman**, 2011; **Patton**, 1970; **Perfect Sense**, 2011; **PT 109**, 1963; **Queen for a Day**, 1951; **The Ramen Girl**, 2008; **The Ranger, the Cook and a Hole in the Sky**, 1995 (made-for-TV); **Ratatouille**, 2007; **Red River**, 1948; **Recipe for Disaster**, 2003 (made-for-TV); **Simply Irresistible**, 1999; **The Slammin' Salmon**, 2009; **Soul Kitchen**, 2010; **Spanglish**, 2004; **The Swan**, 1956; **They Were Expendable**, 1945; **Three's Company**, 1977-1984 (TV series); **Till We Meet Again**, 1936; **To Catch a Thief**, 1955; **Toast**, 2011; **Today's Special**, 2009; **Tortilla Soup**, 2001; **Vatel**, 2000; **Wake Island**, 1942; **Who Is Killing the Great Chefs of Europe?**, 1978; and **You Really Got Me**, 2001. **p**, Jon Favreau, Sergei Bespalov, Karen Gilchrist, Olga Lesnova; **d&w**, Favreau; **cast**, Scarlett Johansson, Robert Downey Jr., Dustin Hoffman, Sofia Vergara, Jon Favreau, John Leguizamo, Russell Peters, Bobby Cannavale, Amy Sedaris, Oliver Platt; **c**, Kramer Morgenthau; **ed**, Robert Leighton; **prod d**, Denise Pizzini; **art d**, Alicia Maccarone; **set d**, Bryan Venegas; **spec eff**, Mark R. Byers.

Cinderella ★★★★ 2015; U.S./UK; 105m; Allison Shearmur Productions/Walt Disney; Color; Drama/Family/Fantasy; Children: Acceptable (MPAA: PG); **BD**; **DVD**; **IV**. Superb version of this eponymous tale sees Ella, played by Webb as a ten-year-old, living on a beautiful estate in a kingdom with her wealthy father, Chaplin, and mother, Atwell, who teaches her to believe in magic. Webb befriends animals on the estate, particularly mice. All is peaceful and bliss until Atwell dies. Her deathbed words to Webb are to always be courageous and show kindness to others. Webb's father remarries a few years later to the widow of an old friend, Blanchett. Blanchett, who is now Ella's stepmother, has two selfish daughters, McShera and Grainger, who are instantly hostile toward Ella, and their cat, Lucifer, viciously stalks Ella's pet mice. Now a few years older, Ella, played by James, has to protect her mice from Blanchett's cat. When Chaplin is called away on business, Blanchett becomes downright mean to James and sends her to live in the attic, while her daughters share her room. Word soon arrives that Chaplin has fallen ill and died. In need of money, Blanchett dismisses the servants and assigns James to do all the work in the house. James also is denied meals with the others and sleeps by the fireplace for warmth. In the morning, her face is covered with cinders so her stepsisters mockingly call her "Cinderella." One day while in the woods she sees a hunting party pursuing a stag and meets an apprentice named Kit, played by Madden, who lives in the palace, not knowing the handsome fellow is the son of the kingdom's dying king, Jacobi. Madden is enchanted by James' kind-

liness and charm, becoming infatuated with her. Jacobi believes his life is waning and insists that Madden find a bride at an upcoming ball at the palace, but she must be a princess. Madden, who cannot forget the enchanting James, persuades Jacobi to agree to invite every single maiden in the land to attend the ball. Blanchett is excited about the ball, hoping Madden will choose one of her daughters as his bride. Blanchett plans not to have James attend the ball, but, on that night, with the help of her mice friends, James fixes up an old pink dress of her birth mother's. Before leaving for the ball, Blanchett has her daughters tear up James's dress. After they leave for the palace, James goes into her garden and sobs, telling her mother that she doesn't know how she can keep her promise to be courageous and kind. An old beggar woman, played by Carter, then appears to state that she is her fairy godmother. Carter uses magic to transform James's dress into a beautiful blue gown. She then waves her magic wand to change a pumpkin into a stunning carriage, four mice into horses, two lizards into footmen, and puts a beautiful pair of glass slippers on James' dainty feet. Carter sends James off to the ball, but cautions her that the magic spell she has performed will end at the final stroke of midnight. James becomes the belle of the ball, especially enrapturing Madden, while she learns he is the prince and heir to the throne of the kingdom. They dance together, but, as the clock starts to strike midnight, James flees, accidentally leaving one of her glass slippers behind on the palace stairs. She returns home and hides the other shoe in her room as a reminder of having fallen in love with the prince, and he with her. Before Jacobi dies, he grants Madden's request that he can marry any girl he wishes. Madden soon becomes king and decrees that every maiden in the land try on the glass slipper he has found at the ball to see if it fits. Blanchett now believes that James was the mystery girl at the ball, and demands that she be the head of the royal household if James marries Madden, and that her stepsisters are to be paired with suitable husbands. James refuses the requests, which are more like demands, and Blanchett locks her in the attic, after breaking the glass slipper to pieces. She takes the shards to the Grand Duke, played by Skarsgard, and says she will tell him the identity of the mystery girl if he agrees to make her a countess and finds suitable husbands for her birth daughters. Meanwhile, Madden travels the land to find the maiden whose foot fits the glass slipper he has kept. Blanchett's daughters try on the slipper, but it does not fit either of them. Before leaving their house, Madden hears James singing "Lavender Blue" through a window that the mice have opened so he can hear her. Madden has James try on the slipper, it fits, and she and Madden embrace and she leaves with him, after forgiving Blanchett and her stepsisters. Blanchett winds up with Skarsgard, and they and her daughters leave the kingdom. Carter, as the fairy godmother, narrates an epilogue that states that Madden and James become the most cherished monarchs of the kingdom and where they not only rule with courage and kindness, but enjoy a happy life together. The attractive James and Madden provide stirring romantic essays, while Blanchett rivets as a cunning and insidious stepmother. The production values are stunning, and the special effects are wonders to behold. This film saw great success at the box office, earning more than $542.7 million in its initial release against a budget of more than $95 million. Songs: "Lavender Blue" (traditional); "Oh, Sing Sweet Nightingale," "A Dream Is a Wish Your Heart Makes," "Bibbidi-Bobbidi-Boo" (Al Hoffman, Jerry Livingston, Mack David); "It Was a Lover and His Lass" from "As You Like It" (music: Patrick Doyle; lyrics: William Shakespeare); "Strong" (Patrick Doyle, Kenneth Branagh, Tommy Danvers); "Making Today a Perfect Day" (Kristen Anderson-Lopez, Robert Lopez); "Happy Birthday to You" (Mildred J. Hill, Patty S. Hill). Thematic materials prohibit viewing by children. **p**, David Barron, Simon Kinberg, Allison Shearmur; **d**, Kenneth Branagh; **cast**, Cate Blanchett, Lily James, Richard Madden, Helena Bonham Carter, Nonso Anozie, Stellan Skarsgard, Sophie McShera, Derek Jacobi, Ben Chaplin, Holliday Grainger, Hayley Atwell, Eloise Webb; **w**, Chris Weitz (based on the 1697 fairy tale by Charles Perrault); **c**, Haris Zambarloukos; **m**, Patrick Doyle; **ed**, Martin Walsh; **prod d**, Dante Ferretti; **art d**, Gary

Freeman, Leslie Tomkins; **set d**, Casey Banwell, Francesca Lo Schiavo; **spec eff**, David Watkins, Kevin Gilmartin.

Cloud Atlas ★★★ 2012; U.S.; Germany/Hong Kong/Singapore; 172m; Color; WB; Drama/Science Fiction; Children: Unacceptable (MPAA: PG-13); **BD**; **DVD**. This fascinating tale presents six stories about people whose lives are interrelated and span different time periods from the South Pacific Ocean in 1849 to the post-apocalyptic future. The first story involves slavery and an abolitionist movement. Next the story moves to England and Scotland in 1936 in which Whishaw, a bisexual English musician, composes his masterpiece, "The Cloud Atlas Sextet" and after a plagiarism attempt, commits suicide. Next, we see San Francisco in 1973 where several people are involved with assassinations regarding those in charge of a new nuclear reactor that benefits major oil companies. The saga continues to London in 2012 when a book publisher, Broadbent, is sent to prison for murdering a critic of a book authored by a gangster, Hanks. We are next in Seoul, Korea, in 2144, where Bae, a female genetically engineered clone, is interviewed before her execution and tells of her life and how fabricants like her are killed and recycled into food for future fabricants. After exposing the slavery and cloning, she is executed. The film ends with an epilogue in which Hanks tells the stories to his grandchildren in a safe colony of Earth on another planet. Episodic and experimental, this tale attempts to integrate the evil of slavery imposed upon mankind from one era to the next, first in the form of actual slaves and then to the enslavement of mankind through dependence upon oil and finally upon fabricants, destroying human values in the process. Visually electrifying and with strong performances from a talented cast who play multiple roles, the script nevertheless grasps at Orwellian straws that challenge viewer belief. It is reminiscent of the editorial aims and time-spanning organization of another intriguing offbeat sci-fi entry, **The Illustrated Man**, 1969, that attempted to chronicle such dire events in episodic format. This film barely earned back its investment, gleaning more than $130 million in its initial box office release against a budget of $128 million. Songs: "Looking for Freedom" (Jack White, Gary Cowtan), "Chimhyang Moo" (Byungki Hwang). Excessive violence, gutter language, sexuality, nudity and drug use prohibit viewing by children. **p**, Tom Tyker, Andy Wachowski, Lana Wachowski, Stefan Arndt, Grant Hill, Alex Boden, Roberto Malerba, Alexander Rodnyansky, Alexander van Duelman; **d&w**, Tom Tykwer, Andy Wachowski, Lana Wachowski (based on the novel by David Mitchell); **cast**, Tom Hanks, Halle Berry, Jim Broadbent, James D'Arcy, Hugo Weaving, Jim Sturgess, Doona Bae, Ben Whishaw, Keith David, Susan Sarandon, Hugh Grant, David Gyasi; **c**, Frank Griebe, Jon Toll; **m**, Reinhold Heil, Johnny Klimek, Tom Tykwer; **ed**, Alexander Berner, Claus Wehlisch; **prod d**, Hugh Bateup, Uli Hanisch; **art d**, Daniel Chour, Sabine Engelberg, Stephan O. Gessler, Thorsten Sabel, David Scheunemann, Steve Summersgill, Kai Koch, Nicki Mc-Callum, Charlie Revai, **set d**, Rebecca Alleway, Peter Walpole; **spec eff**, Uli Nefzer, Andy Williams.

Cloudy with a Chance of Meatballs 2 ★★★ 2013; U.S.; 95m; Sony/COL; Color; Animated Comedy; Children: Unacceptable (MPAA: PG); **3-D**; **BD**; **DVD**. This visually satisfying sequel to the 2009 film is a computer-animated movie that begins after a disastrous food storm in the first film, as Flint (Hader voiceover) and his friends are forced to leave the town. He accepts an invitation from his idol, Chester V (Forte voiceover) to join the Live Corp Company which has the task of cleaning the island. The best investors in the world have gathered there to create technologies for the betterment of mankind. When Hader discovers that his machine still operates and now creates mutant food beasts, including living pickles, hungry tacodiles, shrimpanzees, and apple pie-thons, he and his friends must return to save the world. The film was a hit at the box office, earning more than $274.3 million in its initial release against a budget of $78 million. Songs: "Caramelldansen," "We Run the Night," "Scream and Shout" (Will i Am ft., Britney Spears);

Jim Broadbent and Ben Whishaw in *Cloud Atlas*, 2012.

"New" (Paul McCartney); "Celebrationator" (Mark Mothersbaugh); "The Inventor Song," "Pickle Shanty" (Cody Cameron); "Music Box Dancer" (Frank Mills); "Yummy Yummy Yummy" (Joe Levine, Arthur Resnick); "Get Ready for This" (Jean-Paul De Coster, Filip De Wilde); "All of Us Together" (Tim Myers); "La Da Dee" (Kevin Anyaeji, Antowoine Collins, Richking, Roman Ramirez, Cody Simpson, Keinan Warsame, Wayne Wilkins); "99 Buckets of Chum" (traditional). **p**, Kirk Bodyfelt, Chris Juen; **d**, Cody Cameron, Kris Pearn; **cast** (voiceovers), Bill Hader, Anna Faris, Will Forte, Neil Patrick Harris, Benjamin Bratt, June Christopher, Terry Crews, Elisa Gabrielli, Jackie Gonneau, Khamani Griffin, Tania Gunadi; **w**, John Francis Daley, Phil Lord, Christopher Miller, Jonathan M. Goldstein, Erica Rivinoja (based on characters created by Judi Barrett, Ron Barrett); **m**, Mark Mothersbaugh; **ed**, Stan Webb; **prod d**, Justin Thompson; **art d**, David Bleich; **spec eff**, Shawn Kirsch, Peter G. Travers.

Cold War ★★★ 2013; Hong Kong; 102m; Edko Films/Lionsgate; Color; Crime Drama; Children: Unacceptable (MPAA: R); **BD**; **DVD**. Intriguing and action-packed crime yarn begins with the Hong Kong police department, a sacrosanct security organization that has made the city one of the safest in the world. Untouchable for years, the force is attacked one night when its headquarters receives an anonymous phone call after a fully loaded police van carrying five officers and equipment disappears off the radar grid. More cryptic phone calls come in from the hijackers, and one officer begins to suspect that the thieves are aware of every crucial decision made by the police. The police execute an attack code named "Cold War," but little do they know that they've become unwitting pawns in a dangerous game involving widespread corruption within the ranks of the much-vaunted police. Violence and gutter language prohibit viewing by children. **p**, Ivy Ho, Mathew Tang, Hong Tat Cheung, Kei-Mei Goon, Yue Ren; **d&w**, Lok Man Leung as Longmond Leung, Kim-Ching Luk as Sunny Luk; **cast**, Aaron Kwok, Tony Leung Ka Fai Leung, Charlie Yeung, Ka Tung Lam, Kar Lok Chin, Andy On, Terence Yin, Aarif Rahman, Eddie Peng, Andy Lau; **c**, Jason Kwan, Kenny Tse; **m**, Peter Kam; **ed**, Chi-Leung Kwong, Hoi Wong; **prod d**, Alex Mok; **spec eff**, Cecil Cheng, Yiu Ho Cheung, Kathy Lai, King Ho Tse.

The Company You Keep ★★★ 2013; U.S.; 125m; Voltage Pictures; Sony; Color; Crime Drama; Children: Unacceptable (MPAA: R); **BD**; **DVD**. Taut crime tale sees Redford as a former 1970s Weather Underground militant known as Nick Sloan, in hiding for thirty years as Jim Grant, who has become a defense attorney near Albany, New York. He learns that Christie, an old compatriot, has been arrested in Canada for a Michigan bank robbery that went deadly back in the 1970s when a security guard was killed, and Redford is wanted as an accomplice.

David Gyasi and Jim Sturgess in *Cloud Atlas*, **2012.**

LaBeouf, an ambitious young reporter, hopes to break the case. Redford, who has been recently widowed, aims to clear his name, going on the run with Evancho, his eleven-year-old daughter. He believes Christie can clear him before the FBI catches him. Sarandon, another former Weather Underground member, is arrested in 2011. Kendrick, LaBeouf's former girlfriend, is an FBI agent, and he presses her about the case. She tells him to look up Root, an old hippie with a history of drug arrests who is an old friend of Sarandon's and a former client of Redford's. Redford checks into a New York City hotel with Evancho as the case gets national news attention. Redford leaves Evancho when she is sleeping and leaves the room key hidden in the hotel lobby, but it is found by his brother, Cooper. The FBI has been tracking Cooper and follows him to the hotel where they attempt to apprehend him, but he escapes. Redford goes to Milwaukee to see his old best friend, Nolte, who owns a lumber yard. Nolte discourages Redford from looking for Christie, but tells him to talk to Jenkins, a history professor. Jenkins refuses to help Redford, but when he learns that Redford is trying to protect his young daughter, he uses connections to track down Christie. She is in California importing marijuana into the U.S. aboard a sail boat as part of a big drug operation operated by Elliott, her boyfriend. LaBeouf goes to Michigan and meets Gleeson, a retired cop, who was the first law enforcement officer to investigate the Michigan bank robbery and who has information that could clear Redford because it would prove he was not at the robbery. The frantic manhunt and dragnet ends when Christie gives herself up and Redford is cleared of all charges before he reunites with his daughter. LaBeouf sits on a big story but refuses to expose Gleeson for his part in the robbery cover-up in order to protect Gleeson's adopted daughter, Marling. Redford, who produced, directed and stars in this thriller, provides a suspense-filled tale, and he also renders a compelling performance as a man attempting to survive a violent past. Cast performances, especially Marling and Sarandon, are also exceptional, and production values, from the crisp cinematography to the intelligent script, are high. The film saw a modest success at the box office, earning more than $14.9 million in its initial release against a budget of $5.1 million. A lot goes on in this film but it's worth following for an interesting, fast-paced story. Songs: "Islands" (Mark Satterthwaite, Clay Jones), "Traitors Gate" (Tristan Lambeth, Bob Farrell); **p**, Robert Redford, Bill Holderman, Nicolas Chartier; **d**, Redford; **cast**, Redford, Shia LaBeouf, Julie Christie, Sarah Sarandon, Nick Nolte, Chris Cooper, Brit Marling, Sam Elliott, Stanley Tucci, Terrence Howard, Brendan Gleeson, Richard Jenkins, Anna Kendrick, Jacqueline Evancho; **w**, Lem Dobbs (based on the novel by Neil Gordon); **c**, Adriano Goldman; **m**, Cliff Martinez; **ed**, Mark Day; **prod d**, Laurence Bennett; **art d**, Jeremy Stanbridge; **set d**, Carol Lavellee; **spec eff**, Jak Osmond, Adam Stern.

The Conjuring ★★★ 2013; U.S.; 112m; New Line Cinema; Color; Horror; Children: Unacceptable (MPAA: R); **BD**; **DVD**; **IV**. This tense and terrifying paranormal film is set in 1971 and is based on a true story. A young couple, the Perrons, played by Lili Taylor and Ron Livingston, and their five daughters, move into an old, rundown Rhode Island farmhouse. Livingston is a truck driver, and Taylor looks after the children at home. They are excited about living in the farmhouse until strange things begin to happen, with doors slamming shut on their own, clocks stopping, and strangest of all, the Perron family photos are destroyed. Frightened and fearing the house is haunted, the parents call in Ed and Lorraine Warren, played by Wilson and Farmiga, real-life paranormal investigators, to examine the house. The investigators soon learn that a satanic haunting permeates the house and is targeting the family living there. Farmiga and Wilson are a religious couple, dedicated professional paranormal investigators who are concerned for the souls of those victimized by satanic forces. Wilson is the only demonologist recognized outside the Catholic Church, and Farmiga is a clairvoyant, who apparently can communicate with spirits. While investigating the haunted farmhouse they also begin to fear for their own safety as they realize that they are confronting the most powerful and vengeful spirit they have ever encountered. Farmiga becomes so distraught and frightened, Wilson worries that she may be risking demonic possession herself, or insanity and even death as they prepare to perform an exorcism of the house. Well directed and acted, this film was a huge box office success, earning more than $318 million in its initial release against a budget of $20 million. Songs/Music: "Time of the Season" (Rod Argent), "Sleep Walk" (John Farina, Santo Farina, Ann Farina, Don Wolf), "In the Room Where You Sleep" (Ryan Gosling, Zach Shields), "So Cold" (Benjamin Burney), "Tubular Bells" (Mike Oldfield). *Author's Note*: Edward Warren Miney (1926-2006) and Lorraine Moran Warren (1927-), he a former police officer and self-taught demonologist, and she a clairvoyant and light trance medium, worked together as professional paranormal investigators in New England. They were best known for their involvement in the 1976 so-called Amityville Horror in which a young New York couple, George and Kathy Lutz, claimed their house was haunted by a demonic spirit. That haunting became the basis for the 1977 book *The Amityville Horror* and the 1979 and 2005 films of that name. Violence and terrifying scenes prohibit viewing by children. **p**, Rob Cowan, Tony DeRosa-Grund, Peter Safran; **d**, James Wan; **cast**, Vera Farmiga, Patrick Wilson, Lili Taylor, Ron Livingston, Shanley Caswell, Hayley McFarland, Joey King, Mackenzie Foy, Kyla Deaver, Shannon Kook, John Brotherton, Sterling Jerins; **w**, Chad Hayes; **c**, John R. Leonetti; **m**, Joseph Bishara; **ed**, Kirk Morri; **prod d**, Julie Berghoff; **art d**, Geoffrey S. Grimsman; **set d**, Sophie Neudorfer; **spec eff**, David Beavis.

The Counselor ★★★ 2013; U.S./U.K.; 117m; Chockstone Pictures; FOX; Color; Crime Drama; Children: Unacceptable (MPAA: R); **BD**; **DVD**. Taut crime yarn sees Fassbender as a respected lawyer in the Southwest who is known only as "The Counselor." Arrogant and self-possessed, he thinks he can get into the drug trafficking racket without getting caught. He meets Ganz, a diamond dealer, in Amsterdam, to buy a pricey engagement ring for Cruz, his girlfriend. Fassebender proposes marriage to her and she accepts. He meets Barden and they talk about opening a nightclub and also a drug deal, which would be Fassbender's first criminal act. Fassbender then meets with Barden's business associate, Pitt, and learns of a Mexican drug deal, but realizes that his participation would be dangerous since that country's drug cartels are unforgiving. Fassbender discards all caution and goes for the drug deal. While preparing to do the deal, Barden tells Fassbender about a device that strangles and then decapitates a victim. Fassbender then visits Perez, one of his legal clients, who is on trial for murder. Cabral, Perez's son, is a member of a cartel who was recently arrested and is in jail for speeding while being a biker or runner for the cartel. Fassbender agrees to bail him out. Meanwhile, Barden's girlfriend, Diaz, also a drug trafficker, hires Spruell to steal the drugs Barden and Fassbender are seeking. Spruell steals the drugs while using the decapitating device. The drugs, being stolen from a rival cartel, are in the form of cocaine, and Bardem plans to leave town immediately and tells Fassbender he should do the same. Fassbender calls Cruz and tells her to meet him in another state. Two cartel members posing as policemen shoot and kill Spruell in a gunfight in Texas. Cartel gunmen then kill Bardem and kidnap Cruz. Fassbender believes Cruz is being held in Mexico, so he goes there while hoping to rescue her, but he receives a DVD at his hotel showing her body being dumped into a landfill. Diaz has failed to steal the drugs, so she tracks Pitt to London and there hires Dormer to seduce him and steal his bank codes that can lead her to the drug money. In the process, cartel members kill Pitt by using the decapitating device. Diaz then meets with her banker, Visnjic, and explains how she wants the drug money delivered to her, convinced that she has outwitted the drug cartel, or so she thinks. The film earned more than $71 million in its initial release against a budget of more than $25 million. Songs: "Theory of Fudu" (Jonathan Miguez Vazquez), "Don't Owe You a Thang" (Gary Clark, Jr.), "Roll Up" and "I Love My Sex" (Alessandro Benassi, Benny Benassi, V.C. Bratu, A. Pignagnoli), "Sweet Georgia Brown" (Ben Bernie, Kenneth Casey, Maceo Pinkard), "La Frekuencia" (Nils Leske), "Zapata Se Queda" (Lila Downs, Paul Cohen), "Santa Fe" (Zach Condon), "Together" (Rabon Brunnings, Fabian Lenssen, Clyde Sergio Narain), "Woman, When I've Raised Hell" (Josh T. Pearson), "Territorio" (Camilo Lara), "De Donde Vengo You" (Gabriel Martinez, Miguel Martinez, Carlos Valencia). Graphic violence, grisly images, strong sexual content and gutter language prohibit viewing by children. **p**, Ridley Scott, Steve Schwartz, Paula Mae Schwartz, Nick Wechsler; **d**, Scott; **cast**, Michael Fassbender, Brad Pitt, Penelope Cruz, Cameron Diaz, Javier Bardem, John Leguizamo, Rosie Perez, Goran Visnjic, Natalie Dormer, Dean Norris, **w**, Cormac McCarthy, **c**, Dariusz Wolski; **m**, Daniel Pemberton; **ed**, Pietro Scalia; **prod d**, Arthur Max; **art d**, Alex Cameron, Alejandro Fernandez, Ben Munro, Tom Weaving; **set d**, Sonja Klaus; **spec eff**, Stefano Pepin, Matthew Horton, Charley Henley, Richard Stammers.

Creed ★★★ 2015; U.S.; 132m; MGM/WB; Color; Sports Drama; Children: Unacceptable (MPAA: PG-13); **BD**; **DVD**. In this action-packed seventh installment of the "Rocky" boxing franchise, Stallone again plays Rocky Balboa. He is now too old to fight so he becomes the manager of a young up-and-coming boxer, Jordan. In a flashback, we meet Jordan as a teenager in a Los Angeles juvenile detention center who has been arrested for illegal street fighting. An orphan going from one institution to another, he is visited by Mary Anne Creed, who is played by Rashad, and who tells him he is the illegitimate son of her late husband, former heavyweight boxing champion Apollo Creed. Flashing forward to the present day, Jordan is now in his twenties and living with Rashad, intending against her wishes to go to Tijuana to engage in illegal weekend prize fights. He first goes to Philadelphia to train with Stallone, the man he knows best knew his father's boxing skills. Stallone has been a restaurant owner and frequently visits the grave of his late wife. He needs coaxing to return to the boxing game, but Jordan is persuasive and Stallone agrees to train him. Jordan soon starts a romance with Thompson, a hearing-impaired musician and neighbor. Jordan wins a tough and bloody match and news spreads about his famous parentage. Bellew, the British light-heavyweight champion, decides to fight him in Liverpool, thinking to cash in on the publicity and win easily over the novice fighter. In true "Rocky" fashion, the film ends with a big prizefight, this time a young contender, Jordan, like the "Rocky" of old, hopeful of upsetting the champion with the help of Stallone who relishes being back in the fight, if only as a manager. Though well acted and carefully directed, the script (which was not written by Stallone) provides a rather thin story line with little character development. The film did modest box office, earning more than $46.3 million in its initial release against a budget of $35 million. Violence, gutter language and sexuality prohibit viewing by children. **p**, Robert Chartoff, William

Brad Pitt in *The Counselor*, 2013.

Chartoff, Sylvester Stallone, Kevin King Templeton, David Winkler, Irwin Winkler; **d**, Ryan Coogler; **cast**, Stallone, Michael B. Jordan, Tessa Thompson, Phylica Rashad, Andre Ward, Tony Bellew, Ritchie Coster, Jacob "Stitch" Duran, Graham McTavish, Michael Buffer, Jim Lampley, Liev Schreiber (HBO boxing match narrator); **w**, Coogler, Aaron Covington (based on a story by Coogler and characters created by Stallone); **c**, Maryse Alberti; **m**, Ludwig Goransson; **ed**, Claudia Castello, Michael P. Shawver; **prod d**, Hannah Beachler; **art d**, Jesse Rosenthal; **set d**, Amanda Carroll; **spec eff**, Patrick Edward White, Kurt Wunder.

Crimson Peak ★★★ 2015; U.S.; 119m; Legendary Pictures/UNIV; Color; Horror; Children: Unacceptable (MPAA: R); **BD**; **DVD**; **IV**. Exciting visuals highlight this genuinely frightening film. Wasikowska is bored living with Beaver, her doting industrialist father in 1900s Buffalo, New York. She has several suitors and is conflicted about which of them to accept: Hunnam, a childhood friend who is a colorless ophthalmologist, and Hiddleston, a handsome but penniless British baronet with the foreboding name of Sharpe, who has come to Buffalo looking for a rich but innocent bride. Hiddleston needs money to finance a contraption that digs clay out of his estate in England. Accompanying him is Chastain, his weird sister. Wasikowska chooses Hiddleston, and, after their marriage, he takes her to his ancestral British estate, a crumbling pile of stone that is called Crimson Peak. She soon senses that the place is haunted by ghostly and ghastly spirts. Feeding her apprehensions is Wasikowska's lively imagination. She would like to write novels, especially tales of the supernatural, and believes in ghosts. She also believes that her late mother, Jones, visited her from the beyond when she was a young girl and had warned her to "Beware of Crimson Peak." Soon after her marriage, her father is brutally murdered when his skull is crushed. Wasikowska soon begins to sense the spirits of women whom she believes were Hiddleston's past wives. She begins to see these specters through closed doors and rising from the floors. Ghosts hardly trouble her, but Wasikowska begins to think something is wrong between Hiddleston and Chastain, then becomes more troubled when she coughs up blood. Wasikowska begins searching for answers among the questions she has about Hiddleston and the enigmatic Chastain, who has become a mystery to her. Wasikowska explores the mansion by candlelight in this beautifully photographed and richly costumed but mostly unromantic Gothic romance populated by ghosts that only its heroine takes seriously. She nevertheless learns that Hiddleston and Chastain have had a long-standing incestuous relationship and that they have poisoned three of Hiddleston's previous wives in order to obtain their inheritances and to keep funding Hiddleston's madman inventions. Hunnam, back in the U.S., has learned all of this and goes to England, resolved to save

Jared Leto and Matthew McConaughey in *Dallas Buyers Club*, 2013.

Wasikowska. When he arrives, however, he is attacked and almost killed by Chastain, but is saved and hidden by Hiddleston, who has now fallen in love with his wife and has no intention of killing her. Chastain, realizing this, kills her brother and then attempts to murder Wasikowska. Hiddleston's ghost, however, comes to Wasikowska's aid and helps her kill the berserk Chastain. Hunnam and Wasikowska then depart to make a life together while Chastain dominates the decrepit mansion as the most terrifying and resident ghost. The eerie sets and startling photography sustain tensions and suspense, overcoming the stereotypical characters. The film enjoyed a modest box office success, earning more than $74 million in its initial release against a budget of $55 million. Song: "Red Right Hand" (Mick Harvey, Nick Cave, Thomas Wydler). Violence, sexual content and gutter language prohibit viewing by children. **p**, Guillermo del Toro, Callum Greene, Jon Jashni, Thomas Tull; **d**, del Toro; **cast**, Mia Wasikowska, Charlie Hunnam, Jessica Chastain, Tom Hiddleston, Doug Jones, Burn Gorman, Jim Beaver, Leslie Hope, Javier Botet, Sofia Wells, Jim Watson; **w**, del Toro, Matthew Robbins; **c**, Dan Laustsen; **m**, Fernando Velazquez; **ed**, Bernat Vilaplana; **prod d**, Thomas E. Sanders; **art d**, Brandt Gordon; **set d**, Jeffrey A. Melvin, Shane Vieau; **spec eff**, Michael Innanen.

The Croods ★★★ 2013; U.S.; 98m; DreamWorks/FOX; Color; Animated Comedy; Children: Cautionary (MPAA: PG); **BD**; **DVD**. Beautifully animated prehistoric comedy in which the cave the world's first family lives is destroyed, compelling its members to make a journey to find a new home. They travel across a spectacular landscape and discover an amazing new world filled with fantastic creatures. The adventure changes their outlook on life and the world they live in. Eep Crood (Stone voiceover) is a cave girl whose family is part of the *Homoerectus* classification living in the hardscrabble environment of the Stone Age with her overprotective father (Cage voiceover), her kind mother (Keener voiceover), her grandmother (Leachman voiceover), and her younger siblings Duke and Thom. Stone lives a sheltered life protected by her father until one night she sees a light outside the cave. Defying Cage's rule against going out after dark, she follows the light and meets a Neanderthal boy (Reynolds voiceover), who is an inventive idealist, and his pet sloth (Sanders voiceover). Reynolds introduces Stone to fire and explains that he is escaping what he calls "The End," saying that a cataclysm is coming that could destroy Stone and her family. She refuses to go with Reynolds, but he gives her a shell to use as a horn to call him if she needs him. Cage, looking for Stone, eventually finds her and grounds her for breaking the rules. On their way back to the cave, an earthquake causes its destruction, revealing a tropical wilderness. They are forced to escape into the wilderness when a predator attacks them, and Cage looks for a new cave where the family can live. Stone uses the horn to call for help when a feline cat and piranhakeets send them running. Reynolds comes to their rescue using a torch to keep the piranhakeets from attacking. After their scary first encounter with fire, Stone's family realizes Reynolds' value to their survival and Cage asks Reynolds to guide them toward a mountain that he thinks will provide refuge. Reynolds introduces Stone and her family to shoes so they can walk over sharp terrain. That makes Cage jealous of Reynolds, causing him to create his own innovations, including a "rug," calling it that because it rhymes with his name. His inventions prove to be useless, and the family decides go with Reynolds to a place he calls Tomorrow. At the mountain, Cage attacks Reynolds when the others refuse to join Cage in a cave where he wants them to settle. Cage and Reynolds engage in a tussle and get caught in a tar pit. Reynolds reveals that his family died in such a pit. Cage finally realizes his mistakes about Reynolds and they make amends. Fleeing to the peak of the mountain, the family is cut off from land of Tomorrow by an explosion, but Cage deduces that his family is safer following the sun and throws them across a gorge, then sharing a brief invention he calls a "hug" with Stone. Cut off from his family, Cage seeks shelter in a cave and fashions an airship out of a skeleton, using the wings of the dead piranha birds as a means to fly across the chasm with some friendly animals he has encountered. Reunited with his family, they hug each other. Cage gains a new perspective on life, and is no longer an overbearing and overprotective parent. Later, the Croods live on the land and have settled on a vast beach where every day they can follow the light to Tomorrow land. Pixar again provides amazing and startling visuals, and its digital enhancements are at the appealing center of the story, as the plot and characters are nothing more than adolescent imaginings (as befitting any unsophisticated caveman). The film received an Oscar nomination as Best Animated Film and it had a great success at the box office, earning more than $587.2 million in its initial release against a budget of $135 million. Songs: "Tusk" (Lindsey Buckingham), "Shine Your Way" (Alan Silvestri, Glen Ballard, Kirk De Micco, Chris Sanders). *Author's Note*: This film was planned for production as early as 2005, but was put on hold when director-writer Sanders went into production for **How to Train Your Dragon**, 2010. Frightening action presents caution for viewing by children. **p**, Kristine Belson, Jane Hartwell; **d&w**, Kirk De Micco, Chris Sanders (based on a story by De Mico, Sanders, John Cleese; **cast** (voiceovers), Nicolas Cage, Emma Stone, Ryan Reynolds, Catherine Keener, Cloris Leachman, Clark Duke, Randy Thom, Chris Sanders; **c**, Yong Duk Jhun; **m**, Alan Silvestri; **ed**, Darren T. Holmes; **prod d**, Christophe Lautrette; **art d**, Paul Duncan, Dominique Louis; **spec eff**, Markus Manninen.

Dallas Buyers Club ★★★ 2013; U.S.; 117m; Truth Entertainment; Focus Features; Color; Biographical Drama; Children: Unacceptable (MPAA: R); **BD**; **DVD**. This riveting biopic is based on true events involving Ron Woodroof (1950-1992), who is played by McConaughey. He is a Dallas, Texas, electrician who is diagnosed as being HIV-positive and given thirty days to live. A drug-taking, woman-loving, homophobic man, he starts taking the Food and Drug Administration-approved AZT, the only legal HIV drug allowed in America, but the drug nearly kills him. He learns of some other HIV-fighting drugs in Mexico, so he goes there, obtains these unapproved drugs, and, after three months, seems to feels better. He then poses as a priest to get the drugs past border inspectors and starts selling them in America to other HIV victims. With the help of Leto, a transsexual HIV-positive patient, he creates "The Dallas Buyers Club," charging $400 a month for membership, and it becomes widely popular. The Dallas club becomes the first of dozens which then form across the country to provide its paying members with these alternative treatments. The clubs, growing in numbers and members, are brought to the attention of the FDA and pharmaceutical companies which wage war on them and McConaughey. His struggle to live lasts 2,191 days until he dies on Sept. 12, 1992, six years after he was diagnosed with the HIV virus. Morose and somewhat depressing, this film and its woeful message is highlighted by a stunning performance from McConaughey, who is empathetic and compelling as a man struggling to overcome a dooming fate. McConaughey received an Oscar for Best Actor, while Leto received an Oscar as Best Supporting Actor. The film also received an Oscar for Best Makeup and Hairstyling (Adruitha Lee, Robin Mathews). The film did well at the box office, earning more than $55.2 million in its initial release against a budget of $5 million. Songs: "Purple" and "Sweet Thang" (Johnny Otis); "Ruby, Don't Take Your Love to Town" (Mel Tillis); "The Fool" (Lee Hazlewood); "El Adios Del Soldado" (Carlos Periguez); "Follow Me" (Amanda Lear, Anton Monn); "Obsession" (Michael Des Barres, Holly Knight); "Life Is Strang," "Ballrooms of Mars," "Main Man" (Marc Bolan); "Prelude" (Alexandra Streliski); "City of Angels" (Jared Leto); "Following Morning," "Hell and Back," "Ready to Be Called On," "Life of the Party," "The Walker," "Shudder to Think," "Stayin' Alive," "Romance Languages," "Mexican Mariachi" (Federico Ferrandina, Stefano Torossi); "Wrong Path," "Hit the Road" (Stephen Edwards). Pervasive gutter language, strong sexual content, nudity and drug use prohibit viewing by children. **p**, Robbie Brenner, Rachel Winter, Michael Sledd; **d**, Jean-Marc Vallee; **cast**, Matthew McConaughey, Jared Leto, Jennifer Garner, Steve Zahn, Dallas Roberts, Kevin Rankin, Denis O'Hare, Jane McNeill, Griffin Dunne, James DuMont, Juliet Reeves London; **w**, Craig Borten, Melisa Wallack; **c**, Yves Belanger; **ed**, Martin Pensa, Jean-Marc Vallee; **prod d**, John Paino; **art d**, Javiera Varas; **set d**, Robert Covelman; **spec eff**, Katie Riggs, Daniel Coupal.

Danny Collins ★★★ 2015; U.S.; 106m; Big Indie Pictures/Bleeker Street Media; Color; Comedy/Drama; Children: Unacceptable (MPAA: R); **BD**; **DVD**; **IV**. This good musical biopic is based on the life of a 1970s rock star singer. Pacino plays Collins, who is aging but cannot give up his drinking and drugs. His manager, Plummer, finds a letter encouraging Pacino as a singer that was undelivered to him forty years earlier and written by John Lennon. Pacino reads it and decides to change his life. He goes to New Jersey and meets his grown son, Cannavale, whom he had never seen before. Less happily, he learns that his young fiancé is cheating on him and has been sleeping with another man in his house. Pacino forgives her and then gives them his blessing, magnanimously allowing them stay in the house. Pacino then checks into a hotel in New Jersey where he is recognized as a former star and is befriended by Bening, the hotel manager. She is twenty years younger than he but Pacino nevertheless tries to recapture his youth by attempting a romance with her. He also becomes friends with Peck, a valet, and front-desk clerk Benoist. These heartwarming experiences enable Pacino to start to lead a healthier, better life. Though Pacino is very long in the tooth (seventy-five when this film was released), he nevertheless renders an empathetic performance as a man whose time is over and must now reform his wastrel ways to enjoy what little time is left for him. Bening and Cannavale are exceptional in their roles while Fogelman presents an intelligent, somewhat melodramatic script that he directs with a firm hand. The film did not do well at the box office (possibly indicating Pacino's waning star power), earning $8.2 million in its initial release against a budget of $10 million. Songs/Music: "Mary" (Ryan Adams); "Hey Baby Doll" (Ciaran Gribbin, Greg Agar); "Working Class Hero," "Whatever Gets You Through the Night," "Imagine," "Hold On," "Beautiful Boy," "Nobody Told Me," "#9 Dream," "Cold Turkey," Love," "Instant Karma" (John Lennon); "Happy Go Lucky" (Stephen Lang, Marc Ferrari); "Itsy Bitsy Spider" (traditional); "Another Lonely Night" (Daniel May); "The Rip Tide" (Zach Condon); "It Was Over" (Scott Nickoley, Ronald Dunlap, Stephen Lang); "Don't Look Down" (Ryan Adams, Don Was); "Musical Chairs" (Joey Stevens, Itaru De La Vega); "Brandenburg Concerto No. 3, lst Movement" (Johann Sebastian Bach); "Piano Sonata in C Major, Andante 5" (Wolfgang Amadeus Mozart). *Author's Note*: This film was thinly based upon a letter that

Christian Bale as Batman in *The Dark Knight Rises*, 2012.

John Lennon (1940-1980), and his common-law wife Yoko Ono (1933-), sent to British folk singer Steve Tilston (1950-). Gutter language, drug use and some nudity prohibit viewing by children. **p**, Nimitt Mankad, Jessie Nelson; **d&w**, Dan Fogelman; **cast**, Al Pacino, Annette Bening, Jennifer Garner, Bobby Cannavale, Christopher Plummer, Katarina Cas, Giselle Eisenberg, Melissa Benoist, Josh Peck, Brian Thomas Smith; **c**, Steve Yedlin; **m**, Ryan Adams, Theodore Shapiro; **ed**, Julie Monroe; **prod d**, Dan Bishop; **art d**, Christopher Brown; **spec eff**, Nickolas Crist, David Gaddie.

The Dark Knight Rises ★★★ 2012; U.S./U.K.; 165m; WB; Color; Adventure/Fantasy; Children: Unacceptable (MPAA: PG-13); **BD**; **DVD**. In this action-loaded sequel to **Batman Begins**, 2005, and **The Dark Knight**, 2008, Gotham City is quiet eight years after the fall of the Joker and Harvey Dent, but that peace is soon to be shattered by Bane, played by Hardy, a militant mercenary, who arrives and plans a campaign of terror to destroy the city. Bruce Wayne as Batman, played by Bale, again comes out of retirement to save Gotham. Bale's allies are again his butler Alfred Pennyworth, portrayed by Caine, Police Commissioner James Gordon, essayed by Oldman, and Lucius Fox, played by Freeman, while the film introduces a dangerous cat burglar, Hathaway. The film begins when Batman has disappeared and Bruce Wayne has become a recluse. Cat burglar Hathaway obtains Bruce's fingerprints from his home, and then kidnaps Cullen, a congressman, before disappearing. Hathaway gives Bruce's fingerprints to Gorman, an assistant to Bruce's business rival, Mendelsohn, in the hope of having her criminal record erased. Gorman double-crosses Hathaway, but she uses the congressman's stolen cell phone to alert police to their location. Commissioner Gordon (Oldman) and the police find the congressmen and then pursue Gorman's men into the sewers while Hathaway flees. A masked man called Bane (Hardy) lures Caine, but he escapes and is found by Gordon-Levitt, a former patrol officer who has deduced Batman's true identity from their similar backgrounds. Oldman promotes Gordon-Levitt to detective and has him reporting directly to him. Wayne Enterprises becomes unprofitable after Bruce Wayne discontinued his fusion reactor project when he learned that the core could be weaponized. Later, Hardy attacks the Gotham Stock Exchange, using Wayne's fingerprints in a transaction that bankrupts Wayne. Fearing that Mendelsohn, Hardy's employer, would gain access to the reactor, Bruce Wayne asks Wayne Enterprises board member Cotillard to take over his company. After being promised the software to erase her criminal record, Hathaway agrees to take Batman to Hardy, but instead she leads him into Hardy's trap. Hardy reveals that he intends to fulfill Ra's Al Ghul's (Neeson) mission to destroy Gotham with the League of Shadows remnant. He delivers a crippling blow to Batman's back before taking him

Matthew Modine in *The Dark Knight Rises*, 2012.

to a foreign prison-like place where escape is virtually impossible. The inmates tell Bruce the story of Ra's Al Ghul's child, born in the prison and cared for by a fellow prisoner before escaping, the only prisoner ever to have done so. Bruce Wayne assumes that the child is his own. Meanwhile, Hardy lures Gotham police underground and collapses the exits. He kills Mayor Garcia, played by Carbonell, and forces an abducted physicist, Aboutboul, to convert the reactor core into a nuclear bomb. Hardy releases the prisoners of Blackgate Penitentiary, initiating a revolution. The wealthy and powerful have their property expropriated, are dragged from their homes, and given show trials presided over by Murphy, where any sentence means likely death. Bruce Wayne, after months of recovery and retraining, escapes from the prison and enlists Hathaway, Gordon-Levitt, Cotillard, Oldman, and Freeman, to help stop the nuclear bomb's detonation. While police and Hardy's forces clash, Batman defeats Hardy, but Cotillard intervenes and stabs Batman, and is identified as Talia Al Guhl, daughter of Ra's Al Ghul. Cotillard escapes the prison aided by her fellow prisoner and protector, Hardy. She plans to complete her father's work by detonating the bomb and destroying Gotham, but Oldman blocks the bomb's signal, preventing remote detonation. Cotillard leaves to find the bomb while Hardy prepares to kill Batman, but Hathaway kills Hardy using the Batpod. Batman pursues Hathaway in the Bat, an aircraft developed by Freeman, hoping to bring the bomb back to the reactor where it can be stabilized. Cotillard's truck crashes, but she remotely destroys the reactor before dying. With no way to stop the detonation, Batman uses the Bat to take the bomb over the bay, where it blows up. Batman is presumed to be dead and is honored as a hero. With Bruce also presumed dead, Wayne Manor is left to the city to become an orphanage, and Wayne's remaining estate is left to Caine. Freeman discovers that Bruce had fixed the Bat's autopilot, and Oldman finds the Bat-signal refurbished. While visiting Florence, Italy, Caine witnesses Bruce and Hathaway together. Gordon-Levitt resigns from the police force and inherits the Bat Cave. As was the case with its predecessors, this film presents almost nonstop incredible action that will rivet even the most jaded viewer and the acting is universally exceptional where director Nolan does a good job handling the complex story line. The special effects are outstandingly and brilliantly choreographed with the real-life action. The film proved to be a mega box office hit, earning more than $1,085 billion in its initial release against a budget of $230 million. Songs: "The Star-Spangled Banner" (Francis Scott Key, John Stafford Smith), "Pavann for a Dead Princess" (Maurice Ravel), "Roses From the South" (Johann Strauss Jr.). *Author's Note*: The release of this film was marred when a deranged killer, James Egan Holmes (1987-), who, during a July 20, 2012, midnight showing of this film at the Century 16 Theater in Aurora, Colorado, entered that theater and used automatic weapons to kill twelve

people and wound fifty-eight others. He was sentenced to prison for life with no possibility of parole. Intense violence, sexuality and gutter language prohibit viewing by children. **p**, Christopher Nolan, Charles Roven, Emma Thomas, Jordan Goldberg; **d**, Nolan; **cast**, Christian Bale, Tom Hardy, Anne Hathaway, Gary Oldman, Michael Caine, Marion Cotillard, Morgan Freeman, Matthew Modine, Brett Cullen, Alon Moni Aboutboul, Ben Mendelsohn, Cillian Murphy, Burn Gorman, Nestor Carbonell; **w**, Christopher Nolan, Jonathan Nolan (based on a story by Christopher Nolan, David S. Goyer, and character of Batman created by Bob Kane; **c**, Wally Pfister; **m**, Hans Zimmer; **ed**, Lee Smith; **prod d**, Nathan Crowley, Kevin Kavanaugh; **art d**, Toby Britton, Kate Grimble, Zack Grobler, Jonathan Kevin Ong, Tom Still, Gerald Sullivan, Su Whitaker, Dean Wolcott, Robert Woodruff; **set d**, Paki Smith; **spec eff**, Chris Corbould, Andrew Smith, Jeff Brink.

Dawn of the Planet of the Apes ★★★ 2014; U.S.; 130m; Chernin Entertainment; FOX; Color; Science Fiction; Children: Unacceptable (MPAA: PG-13); **BD**; **DVD**. To-notch entry in the series, this film begins with a prologue stating that a virus caused the collapse of human civilization following martial law, civil unrest, and the economic collapse of every country in the world. Ten years later, Caesar, played by Serkis, a common chimpanzee and leader of the apes, leads and governs a new generation of apes in Muir Woods. While walking in the forest, his son Blue Eyes, played by Thurston, and Ash, played by Shaw, son of another ape leader, Rocket, played by Notary, come upon a human, Acevedo, who panics and shoots Shaw, wounding him. Acevedo calls for the rest of his small party of armed survivors, led by Clarke, while Thurston calls for the other apes. Serkis orders the humans to leave. The remaining humans living in San Francisco, genetically immune to the virus, are living in a guarded tower within the ruined city. Prompted by Koba, played by Kebbell, who holds a grudge against the humans for his mistreatment, Serkis brings a large group of apes to the city where he says that, while the apes do not want war, they will fight to defend their home. He then demands that the humans stay in their territory and says the apes will stay in theirs. Clarke convinces his fellow human leader, Oldman, to give him three days to reconcile with the apes to gain access to a hydroelectric dam in their territory, which could provide long-term power to the city. But Oldman does not trust the apes and accesses an abandoned armory to provide weapons to survivors. Clarke then travels into the Ape Village, but is captured by gorilla guards who take him to Serkis. After a tense discussion, Serkis allows Clarke to work on the dam's generator, if they will surrender their guns. As Clarke, his wife, Russell, and their son work on the generator, they bond with the apes. Mutual distrust on both sides gradually fades, but then Acevdeo threatens Serkis' sons with a concealed shotgun. Both sides reconcile as Russell is allowed to treat Serkis' ill wife, Greer, with antibiotics. Meanwhile, Kebbell discovers the armory and questions Serkis' loyalty to the apes, taunting him about his "love" for the humans. Serkis responds by beating Kebbell, but, since he does not kill other apes, he chooses to forgive him. Kebbell then returns to the army, steals an assault rifle, and murders two human guards. He then kills Acevdeo, stealing his lighter and cap. Eventually, the dam is repaired and restores power to San Francisco. Celebrating, Kebbell sets fire to the apes' home. Then, unseen any anyone else, Kebbell and Serkis confront each other and Kebbell shoots Serkis in the chest, causing him to fall from the settlement's main tree. Kebbell then takes charge and orders the apes to war against the humans. Clarke's group goes into hiding as Kebbell leads the apes into the city where they raid the armory and charge the tower gates. Despite heavy casualties, the apes breach the gates using a hijacked tank and overrun the tower and imprison all the humans while Oldman flees underground. Shaw refuses Kebbell's orders to kill unarmed humans, citing Serkis' teachings, so Kebbell kills him and imprisons all those who are known to be loyal to Serkis. Clarke's group finds Serkis barely alive, and take him to his former home in San Francisco. He reveals to Clarke that Kebbell shot him, realizing that his notion that all apes are better than humans was naïve. Entering the city to find medical supplies so Russell can operate on Serkis, Clarke encounters Thurston, who decided to spare Kebbell's life, and takes him to Serkis' house. Thurston then returns to the tower, freeing the caged humans and the apes loyal to Serkis. Clarke leads the apes to the tower unseen, and then encounters Oldman, who tells him that his men have made radio contact with more human survivors at a military base up north, and who are on their way to help fight the apes. The freed apes join Serkis and confront Kebbell at the summit of the tower. As Serkis and Kebbell fight, Clarke fails to prevent Oldman from detonating a bomb beneath the tower. The explosion kills Oldman and part of the tower falls. Serkis overpowers Kebbell, knocking him to the edge of the tower. Kebbell reminds Serkis that apes do not kill apes, but Serkis proclaims that Kebbell is no longer an ape and lets him fall to his death. Clarke then informs Serkis of the impending arrival of human military reinforcements. They lament the lost opportunity for peace, and Serkis tells Clarke that the humans will never forgive the apes for the war the apes started and tells him to leave with his family for safety. They acknowledge their mutual friendship, and, as Clarke leaves, Serkis stands before a mass of apes who await the coming battle with the humans. The centerpiece for this action-packed film is its astounding special effects that sustain riveting attention throughout. The film was nominated for an Oscar for Best Visual Effects. It was a great success at the box office, earning more than $710.6 million in its initial release against a budget of $170 million. Songs: "The Weight" (Robbie Robertson); "Ain't That a Stinger" (Griffith Giacchino). Violence prohibits viewing by children. **p**, Peter Chernin, Dylan Clark, Rick Jaffa, Amanda Silver, Thomas M. Hammel; **d**, Matt Reeves; **cast**, Andy Serkis, Gary Oldman, Keri Russell, Judy Greer, Angela Kerecz, Jason Clarke, Toby Kebbell, Karin Konoval, Nick Thurston, Terry Notary, Doc Shaw, Kodi Smit-McPhee, Kevin Rankin, Christopher Berry; **w**, Jaffa, Silver, Mark Bomback (based on the novel *La planete des singes* by Pierre Boulle and characters created by Jaffa, Silver); **c**, Michael Seresin; **m**, Michael Giacchino; **ed**, William Hoy, Stan Salfas; **prod d**, James Chinlund; **art d**, Aaron Haye, William O. Hunter, Naaman Marshall; **set d**, Amanda Moss Serino; **spec eff**, Matt Kutcher, Alex Burdett.

Dead Man Down ★★★ 2013; U.S.; 118m; Color; Crime Drama; Children: Unacceptable (MPAA: R); **BD**; **DVD**. Farrell gives a stoic performance as a young gangster whose wife and daughter were murdered by gangster chief Howard. He works his way into the mob boss' gang, intending to kill that boss for the murders two years earlier. Meanwhile, Rapace, a woman whose face is disfigured and is living in an apartment across from Farrell, watches him closely before meeting him. She tells Farrell she has a video of him killing a man and intends to go to the police with it unless he kills the drunk driver who caused the accident that disfigured her. Farrell believes some Jamaicans led by Howard are sending him death threats. Farrell kidnaps Biberi, the brother of an Albanian crime boss who had helped Howard kill Farrell's wife and daughter. Farrell plans to kill Biberi and his men and Howard and his men all at the same time. He kills Biberi's brother, then sets a trap for his enemies, but learns that Rapace has been kidnapped and is being kept at Howard's house. Farrell crashes his truck into the house, and, in a wild gunfight, Rapace escapes with him and they kiss on a subway ride to safety. The plot is improbable and the action reckless, but Farrell, Rapace and the rest of the cast render solid performances in this somewhat outlandish but memorable film noir entry. The film did not fare well at the box office, earning more than $18 million in its initial release against a budget of $30 million. Songs: "Freak" (Kenn Haunstoft), "Eblouie par la nuit" (Raphael Haroche), "What Are You Gonna Do" (Peter Smith, Peter Schultz), "Jun Bay" (Baldwin Chiu), "A Fine Mess" (Girard Knox), "Cka Me Ka Syni" (Rovena Stefa), "Life in Mono" (Martin Virgo, John Barry); Violence, gutter language and sexuality prohibit viewing by children. **p**, Neal H. Moritz, J.H. Wyman; **d**, Niels Arden Oplev; **cast**, Colin Farrell, Noomi Rapace, F. Murray Abraham, Terrence Howard, Dominic

Christian Bale and Michael Caine in *The Dark Knight Rises,* **2012.**

Cooper, Isabelle Huppert, Luis Da Silva Jr., Declan Mulvey, Stu Bennett, John Cenatiempo; **w**, Wyman; **c**, Paul Cameron; **m**, Jacob Groth; **ed**, Timothy A. Good, Frederic Thoraval; **prod d**, Niels Sejer; **art d**, Jesse Rosenthal; **set d**, Chryss Hionis; **spec eff**, Drew Jiritano, Stalin Saravanan, Scott Shapiro.

Dear White People ★★★ 2014; U.S.; 100m; UNIV; Color; Comedy; Children: Unacceptable (MPAA: PG-13); **BD**; **DVD**. Offbeat satire is set at a prestigious mostly white Ivy League university. Thompson, a biracial student who hosts a school radio show, announces an African-American-themed party thrown by white students, opening with: "Dear white people." This is followed by a satire of stories by four black students, who react to the party as riots break out. The television reality show "Black Face/White Place" follows the events on campus. Meanwhile, black misfit Williams is asked to join the school's white newspaper staff to cover the controversy, although he knows little about black culture. The satire explores racial identity in "post-racial" America. Although the humor is sometimes forced and lowbrow, many amusing scenes are present to sustain interest. The film did poorly at the box office, earning about $4 million in its initial release. Song: "Stalker" (Andy Allo). **p**, Justin Simien, Effie Brown, Ann Le, Julia Lebedev, Angel Lopez, Lena Waithe; **d&w**, Simien; **cast**, Tessa Thompson, Tyler James Williams, Teyonah Parris, Brandon P. Bell, Kyle Gallner, Dennis Haysbert, Peter Syvertsen, Brandon Alter, Brittany Curran, Justin Dobies; **c**, Topher Osborn; **m**, Kathryn Bostic; **ed**, Phillip J. Bartell; **prod d**, Bruton Jones; **art d**, Cheri Anderson; **set d**, Melissa Pritchett; **spec eff**, Patrick Clancey.

Delivery Man ★★★ 2013; U.S.; 105m; DreamWorks/Disney; Color; Comedy; Children: Unacceptable (MPAA: PG-13); **BD**; **DVD**. Hectic, impossible comedy has Vaughn as a delivery man for his parents' butcher shop; he is pursued by thugs to whom he owes $80,000, and Smulders, his girlfriend, is pregnant with his child. Twenty years earlier, as a college student needing money, Vaughn had donated to a sperm bank and over a year had fathered more than 500 children. Now his offspring want to know who their father is, but he had signed a confidentiality agreement preventing his identity from being revealed. They go to court to contest the agreement, and he meets some of these offspring without identifying himself. Pratt, a lawyer friend, defends him at the trial and helps him to win the lawsuit. He sues the sperm bank for damages, receives $200,000, pays off his debt, and then reveals his identity on Facebook. Smulders gives birth to their child, he proposes to her at the hospital, and many of his children appear to call him Father. The outlandish story is matched by some outlandish performances that sustain interest throughout. The film had moderate success at the box

Kate Winslet in *Divergent*, 2014.

office, earning more than $51 million in its initial release against a budget of $26 million. Songs: "Someday" (Julian Casablancas), "Little Hands" (Phillip Larue, Jeremy Bose), "Light of Love" (Marc Bolan), "So Shy" (Richard Myhill), "Thunderstruck" (Angus Young, Malcolm Young), "My Fallen Angel" (Clifton David Broadbridge), "Friday Night Forever" (Wolfgang Black, Dan Gautreau), "Into the Pool" (Mark Revell), "Ten Ton" (Jett Royal), "Wonderful, Glorious" (Mark O. Everett, Chet Lyster, Koool G Murder, Derek Brown), "The Ghost of the Violin" (Ted Snyder, Bert Kalmar), "Love to Get Used" (Matthew Pond), "Strike It Up" (Daniele Davoli, Mirko Limoni, Valerio Semplici), "100 Other Lovers" (Nick Urata), "Real Real Gone" (Van Morrison). Thematic material, sexual content, some drug material, brief violence and gutter language prohibit viewing by children. **p**, Andre Rouleau; **d**, Ken Scott; **cast**, Vince Vaughn, Chris Pratt, Cobie Smulders, Adrzej Blumenfeld, Simon Delaney, Bobby Moynihan, Dave Patten, Adam Chanler-Berat, Britt Robertson, Jack Reynor; **w**, Scott, Martin Petit; **c**, Eric Edwards; **m**, Jon Brion; **ed**, Priscilla Nedd-Friendly; **prod d**, Ida Random; **art d**, Mark Newell; **set d**, Sara Parks; **spec eff**, Drew Jiritano, Eli Jarra, Matt Anderson.

Diplomacy ★★★ 2014; France/Germany; 84m; Film Oblige/Gaumont/Blueprint Film/Zeitgeist Films; Color; War Drama; Children: Unacceptable; **BD**; **DVD**; **IV**. Absorbing historical tale begins when Nazi Germany's Chancellor Adolf Hitler (1889-1945) gives orders that Paris should not fall into the hands of the enemy as Allied troops advance on the French capital in the summer of 1944 during World War II (1939-1945). He orders the iron-willed and loyal Nazi governor of Paris, Gen. Dietrich von Choltitz (1894-1955), played by Arestrup, to destroy the city by burning it to the ground. This results in a war of wills between Arestrup and Swedish consul general Raoul Nordling (1881-1962), essayed by Dussollier, who is living in Paris and pleads with him to save the city and its historic buildings, monuments, and art treasures. The film shows no fighting, but presents an intriguing battle of wits between the two men as Dussollier uses a secret staircase into Arestrup's suite at the Hotel le Meurice. There, Dussollier tries the diplomatic patience of Arestrup who has already had his men place explosives at every bridge and major monument in the city, including the Eiffel Tower and the Louvre art museum. The two men reminisce about their lives before the war as they parry each other's diplomacy. Dussollier's ace card is telling Arestrup that his children and grandchildren will never forgive him for being the man who destroyed the City of Light. Arestrup finally relents and agrees to disobey Hitler by retreating from the city without damaging it. The Allies liberated Paris from German occupation on August 25, 1944. Arestrup and Dussollier are superb as they fence and parry over the survival of one of the world's great cities while all of the film's pro-

duction values are outstanding. This film saw a moderate success at the box office, earning more than $4 million in its initial release. Song/Music: "Symphony No, 7, Allegretto" (Ludwig van Beethoven), "J'ai deux amours" (Georges Koger, Henri Varna, Vincent Scotto). *Author's Note*: This subject was treated in some length in another superior war drama, **Is Paris Burning?**, 1966, where Gert Frobe played Choltitz and Orson Welles enacted the role of Nordling. Choltitz was early on persuaded not to destroy Paris, but did not give the order to set the city afire until the very last moment when Allied forces were already entering the city. The German commander was calculating to the very last as a way of preventing his own execution on Hitler's orders (he surrendered immediately to advance Allied elements) while also knowing that most of his troops had already deserted the city and fled with retreating German forces. The preservation and recouping of the Louvre's great art treasures that had been looted by the Nazis was also depicted in **The Train**, 1965, and **The Monuments Men**, 2014. (In German; English subtitles.) **p**, Marc de Bayser, Frank Le Wita, Amelie Latscha, Felix Moeller, Olivier Pere; **d**, Volker Schlondorff; **cast**, Andre Dussollier, Niels Arestrup, Burghart Klaussner, Robert Stadlober, Charlie Nelson, Jean-Marc Roulot, Stefan Wilkening, Thomas Arnold, Lucas Prisor, Attila Borlan; **w**, Cyril Gely, Schlondorff (adapted from the play by Gely); **c**, Michel Amathieu; **m**, Jorg Lemberg; **ed**, Virginie Bruant; **prod d**, Jacques Rouxel; **set d**, Philippe Turlure; **spec eff**, Guy Monbillard.

The Disappearance of Eleanor Rigby ★★★ 2014; U.S.; 89m; Unison Films/Weinstein Company; Color; Drama/Romance; Children: Unacceptable (MPAA: R); **BD**; **DVD**. The title of this intriguing tale represents the collective title of three films, **Him**, **Her**, and **Them**, written and directed by Ned Benson, his first feature film project. All three films follow the same time period but are told from the differing perspectives of a young married couple, McAvoy and Chastain, who live in New York. **Him** looks at their relationship from McAvoy's angle, while **Her** follows Chastain's, who plays Eleanor. McAvoy spends his days working in his restaurant, while his wife, Chastian, returns to college for further education. During the course of their daily lives, they encounter a life-changing event that threatens the stability of their marriage. They must try to understand each other as they cope with loss and try to reclaim the life and love they once had. There is a haunting elegance to this well-made tale, and McAvoy and Chastian shine in their roles. The film did not do as well as expected at the box office, earning less than $1 million in its initial release against a budget of $3 million. Song: "The Lucky One" (Tomas Costanza, Jacqueline Willard, Ashley Levy, Nikki Thompson, Mike London). Gutter language and drug use prohibit viewing by children. **p**, Ned Benson, Jessica Chastain, Cassandra Kulukundis, Todd J. Labarowski, Emanuel Michael; **d&w**, Benson; **cast**, James McAvoy, Chastain, Ciaran Hinds, Bill Hader, Viola Davis, William Hurt, Isabelle Huppert, Archie Panjabi, Ryan Eggold, Jess Weixler; **c**, Christopher Blauvelt; **m**, Son Lux; **ed**, Kristina Boden; **prod d**, Kelly McGehee; **set d**, Sheila Bock; **spec eff**, Drew Jiritano, Lynzi Grant, Vico Sharabani.

Disconnect ★★★ 2013; U.S.; 115m; LD Entertainment; Color; Drama; Children: Unacceptable (MPAA: R); **BD**; **DVD**. Inventive story sees four people collide through their use of electronic devices that upset their professional and personal lives. Although they are ordinary people struggling to connect in today's wired society, the modern apparatus that is controlling their lifestyles is altered in unpredictable ways. Bateman is a hardworking lawyer, who spends more time on his cell phone than he communicates with his family. Patton and Skarsgard are married, who, through the use of their dominating electronic communications, come to realize how much they love each other after their identifications are stolen. Riseborough is a television reporter covering a story on a teenage boy who perversely gets sexual highs on an adults-only website. How their lives connect is often implausible, but the lively tale from Stern and the strong performances form the cast under Rubin's firm direction provides considerable enjoyment. The film earned more than $3.4 million in its initial release. Songs: "Keep Everybody Swarm' (Michael Willison, Jodie Lynn Zeitler, David Scott Lucas), "Club Bud Dance" (Adam Zelkind), "Sail" (Aaron Bruno), "Gil" and"Fifteen" (A. Falvo, P. Conlon, A. Alcala, J. Nitti), "Restless Youth" (Lawrence Gririch, Michael Ray, Jon Schockness, Nick Spreigl, Tait Taylor, Julia Thomas, Wesley Watkins), "On the Nature of Daylight" and "Written on the Sky" (Max Richter), "Birthday Boy" (Karl Snyder, Edna Snyder), "Tisk Tisk" (Earl James Halborg, Martijn Hendrik, Bernard Bolster, William Murphy), "Ni Su Nave" and "Like a Dog" (Jayme Ivison), "American Dream" (Asa Taccone, Matthew Compton, Danger Mouse), "Foondafloe" (Adam Zelkind), "Very Busy People" (Eric Victorino, Giovanni Giusti), "Tornado" (Jon Thor Brigisson). Sexual content, graphic nudity, gutter language, violence and drug use involving teenagers prohibit viewing by children. **p**, William Horberg, Mickey Liddell, Jennifer Monroe as Jennifer Hilton, Lynn Givens; **d**, Henry Alex Rubin; **cast**, Jason Bateman, Hope Davis, Frank Grillo, Alexander Skarsgard, Paula Patton, Andrea Riseborough, Michael Nyqvist, Max Thieriot, Colin Ford, Jonah Bobo; **w**, Andrew Stern; **c**, Ken Seng; **m**, Max Richter; **ed**, Lee Percy; **prod d**, Dina Goldman; **art d**, Jennifer De-hghan; **set d**, Amanda Carroll; **spec eff**, Shane Gross, Jeff Wozniak.

Divergent ★★★ 2014; U.S.; 139m; Red Wagon Entertainment/Summit Entertainment; Color; Science Fiction; Children: Unacceptable (MPAA: PG-13); **BD**; **DVD**. Good sci-fi entry sees teenagers living in a futuristic world and ultra-conformist society that is divided by factions based on virtues and where each must make a choice of what faction to join for the rest of their life. A group decides on a faction, but must live through a very competitive initiation process to live out the choice they have made. They undergo extreme physical and intense psychological tests that transform them all. Woodley, a girl in one group, has a deadly secret. She is a Divergent, which means she doesn't fit into any one group. Should anyone discover her true nature, it would mean her certain death. She learns that there is a growing conflict over destroying Divergent humans, but she nevertheless risks her life by exposing her true character in order to save those she loves. This offbeat story presents some fine character development, and Woodley renders an outstanding perform-ance. The film did very well at the box office, earning more than $288.9 million in its initial release against a budget of $85 million. Songs: "Beating Heart," "Dead in the Water," "My Blood" (Ellie Goulding); "I Won't Let You Go" (Gary Lightbody); "Find You." Intense violence, thematic elements and sensuality prohibit viewing by children. **p**, Lucy Fisher, Pouya Shahbazian, Douglas Wick; **d**, Neil Burger; **cast**, Shailene Woodley, Kate Winslet, Tony Goldwyn, Ray Stevenson, Ashley Judd, Theo James, Miles Teller, Ansel Elgort, Zoe Kravitz, Maggie Q, Jai Courtney; **w**, Evan Dougherty, Vanessa Taylor (based on the novel by Veronica Roth); **c**, Alwin H. Kuchler; **m**, Junkie XL; **ed**, Richard Fran-cis-Bruce; **prod d**, Andy Nicholson; **art d**, Chris Cleek, A. Todd Hol-land, Patrick M. Sullivan Jr.; **set d**, Anne Kuljian; **spec eff**, Yves De Bono.

Django Unchained ★★★ 2012; U.S.; 165m; Weinstein/COL; Color; Western; Children: Unacceptable (MPAA: R); **BD**; **DVD**. This fine se-quel to **Django**, 1966, is set two years before the American Civil War (1861-1865), where Waltz, a former German dentist who hates slavery buys the freedom of a slave, Django, who is played by Foxx, intending to make him his deputy in bounty hunting. Waltz is determined to cap-ture two vicious outlaw brothers, and with Foxx's help, the mission is accomplished. Waltz then rewards Foxx for his heroic services by free-ing him. Together they ride off to hunt down more of the South's most wanted and dangerous criminals. Their pursuit of outlaws leads them to the estate of DiCaprio, a ruthless plantation owner, who is holding Foxx's long-lost wife, Washington, captive as a slave. DiCaprio has a favorite slave, Jackson, an Uncle Tom who acts as his butler and chief of staff, while Jackson deludes himself into believing that he is not

Don Johnson in *Django Unchained*, 2012.

black. The sadistic DiCaprio enjoys after-dinner entertainment by hav-ing two slaves fight each other to the death, resulting in a brutal blood-bath. The fight ends with one winning and DiCaprio dropping a hammer on the floor next to the victor who uses it on his almost-dead opponent. In a film that is very violent and contains a lot of racial tension, one scene involves hooded Ku Klux Klan members who offer a bit of black comedy relief by complaining that they cannot see through the slits in their hoods. Waltz and Foxx have their hands full to rescue Foxx's wife and bring DiCaprio to justice or his grave, but they nevertheless to defeat this monster in human form. The acting is superior throughout this rather clichéd but well-mounted production, and the characters are almost stereotypes out of *Uncle Tom's Cabin* but are uniquely updated to more twisted and fascinating characterizations under Tarantino's weirdly cre-ative direction. DiCaprio, as a man oozing evil, steals every scene. Tarantino became a political activist for the Black Lives Matter organ-ization in 2015, and his racial politics are manifested in this film. Waltz, who renders a captivating performance, received an Oscar as Best Sup-porting Actor. Lavishly produced on a $100 million budget, the film was a great box office success, earning more than $425.4 million in its initial release. Songs/Music: "Django Theme Song" (music: Luis Bacalov; lyrics: Franco Migliacci, Robert Merlin); "Rito Finale" (from **The Fam-ily**); "The Braying Mule," "Norme con ironie," "The Big Risk," "Mi-nacciosamente Lotano," "Dopo la congiura," "Un monumento" (from **Hellbenders**); "Sister Sara's Theme" (from **Two Mules for Sister Sara** by Ennio Morricone); "Main Titles (theme song from **Lo Chiamavano King**); "Town of Silence," "La Corsa," "Blue Dark Waltz" (Luis Bacalov); "Gavotte" (Grace Collins); "Freedom" (Elayna Boynton, Kelvin Wooten, Anthony Hamilton); "I Got a Name" (Charles Fox, Nor-man Gimble); "Dies Irae, Requiem" (from **Battle Royale** by Giuseppe Verdi); "I giorni dell'ira" (from **Day of Anger** by Riz Ortolani); "100 Black Coffins" (Jamie Fox, Rick Ross); "Trackers Chant" (Quention Tarantino); "Nicaragua" (Jerry Goldsmith); "Ancora Qui" (Morricone, Elisa Toffoli); "Fur Elise" (Ludwig van Beethoven); "The Payback" (James Brown, Fred Wesley, John Starks); "Untouchable" (Kasseem Dean, Yafeu Fula, Anthony Henderson, Tupac Shakur, Hussein Fatal); "Freedom" (Richie Havens); "Who Did That to You?" (John Legend); "Ain't No Grave" (Johnny Cash, Claude Ely); "To Old to Die Young" (Dege Legg); "Trinity: Titoli" (from **My Name Is Trinity** by Franco Micalizzi, Harold Stott); "Will the Circle Be Unbroken" (Ada R. Haber-shon, Charles Gabriel); "In the Sweet By-and-By" (1868; music: J.P. Webster; lyrics: S. Fillmore Bennett). *Author's Note*: Some of the the-matic elements for this unusual tale can be seen in a more comedic pro-duction, **Skin Game**, 1972, where James Garner plays a bounty hunter who consistently recaptures the same runaway slave, Louis Gossett Jr., collecting a reward for the capture and then rescuing Gossett repeatedly

Joseph Gordon-Levitt in *Don Jon*, 2013.

from hanging. The two continue this chase-and0capture routine and share the profits of their scam. There are many historical inaccuracies in this film, especially where DiCaprio perversely satisfies himself by having his slaves fighting to the death in gladiatorial battles. No such event in the Ante-Bellum South during the plantation era was ever documented and is nothing more than a figment of Tarantino's vivid and offbeat imagination (he wrote the script as well as directed). No slave owner in the Old South would ever waste what he knew to be valuable property by having his slaves kill each other. Intense graphic violence throughout, gutter language (repeated use of the word "nigger") and nudity prohibit viewing by children. **p**, Reginald Hudlin, Pilar Savone, Stacey Sher; **d&w**, Quentin Tarantino; **cast**, Jamie Foxx, Christoph Waltz, Leonardo DiCaprio, Kerry Washington, Samuel L. Jackson, Don Johnson, Franco Nero, Bruce Dern, Tom Wopat, James Russo, Walton Goggins, Dennis Christopher, Russ Tamblyn, Don Stroud, Robert Carradine, Michael Parks; **c**, Robert Richardson; **ed**, Fred Raskin; **prod d**, J. Michael Riva; **art d**, David Klassen, Page Buckner; **set d**, Leslie Pope; **spec eff**, John McLeod.

Don Jon ★★★ 2013; U.S.; 90m; Voltage Pictures/Relativity Media; Color; Comedy/Romance; Children: Unacceptable; MPAA: R; **BD**; **DVD**. Entertaining romantic comedy begins with Jon Martello, played by Gordon-Levitt), who is a handsome young New Jersey man, and who appears to have it all. He has a comfortable bachelor apartment, a nice car, and is dedicated to his parents and church. Because he scores with women every weekend, his friends call him "Don Jon" (after Don Juan, a legendary great lover as described in the celebrated poem by Lord [George Gordon] Byron [1788-1824]). Gordon-Levitt develops unrealistic expectations about women by naively watching pornography on his computer and decides he wants to find happiness and intimacy with one woman he would truly love. This pursuit ends with him learning important lessons of life and love as he gets into relationships with two very different women, Johansson and Moore. He is especially drawn to Johansson, a beautiful old-fashioned girl who grew up watching romantic Hollywood movies and who is determined to find her Prince Charming. Gordon-Levitt and Johansson both have to struggle against a media culture full of false fantasies in order to find true intimacy together. Gordon-Levitt, Johansson and Moore are standouts in their roles while being supported by an equally talented cast. The film was popular at the box office, earning more than $30.5 million in its initial release against a budget of $3 million. Songs: "Bout That Life" (DeYon Dobson, Lawrence Young, Antoine Vick), "BB by Two Nyte" (Sean Thomas, Lawrence Neal Young III, Myles Annie Plancq), "The Mighty Don" (Ryan Lott, Nathan Johnson), "Money Talks" (Amon Flanagan, Christopher Carpenter), "Baby Break It Down" (Lawrence Young, Alfred Gip-

son), "Give Yourself Up" (Kathy Sledge, Adam Barta), "Hit the Floor B" (Andrew David Lee, Loopmasters and UtkuS), "Sport News 2" (Ian Anderson), "Horse Show" (Gerhard Trede), "Pre Meditation" (De La Main), "PGM Clown Town" (David Robert Phillips), "Some Like It Hot" (Matty Malneck, Isidore Diamond), "Addiction" (Malcolm Kirby Jr.), "Bang Up" (Daniel Lenz), "The Grind" (Adam Longlands), "The Party Starts Now" (Dan Book, Alexei Misoul, Scott Stallone, Steven Stern), "Squasher" (Danny Saber), "BB Take a Picture" (DeYon Dobson, Alfred Gipson, Richie Pena, Sigfrido Diaz), "Good Vibrations" (Amir Q. Shakir, Mark Wahlberg, Donnie Wahlberg, Dan Hartman), "Making It Hot" and "Don Jon's Radio Ad 1, 2, 3" (Jeffrey Sudakin), "100 Dollar Bills" (Beat Mekanic, Deonata Moore, Christian Salyer as Cadence Blaze), "Thong Song" (Sisqo), "Hey Shorty" (Allen Maldonado, Christian Salyer as Cadence Blaze), "Bass Junkie" (Derek Yopp, Jujuan Gailey, Andrew John Kim), "Good Morning World" (Jimmy Kaleth), "Lazy Bones" (Che Kropp), "Queen Desire" (Raymond Weil), "Would You Do the Same for Me" (Lee Baker, Laura Vane). Strong graphic sexual material and dialogue, nudity, gutter language and drug use prohibit viewing by children. **p**, Ram Bergman, Jeff Franks; **d&w**, Joseph Gordon-Levitt; **cast**, Gordon-Levitt, Scarlett Johansson, Julianne Moore, Tony Danza, Glenne Headly, Brie Larson, Rob Brown, Jeremy Luke, Italia Ricci, Lindsey Broad, Amanda Perez, Sarah Dumont, Sloane Avery; **c**, Thomas Kloss; **m**, Nathan Johnson; **ed**, Lauren Zuckerman; **prod d**, Meghan C. Rogers; **art d**, Elizabeth Cummings; **set d**, Cindy Coburn; **spec eff**, Kundan Basnet, Jamison Scott Goei, Karen E. Goulekas, Jan Krupp.

Dope ★★★ 2015; U.S.; 103m; Forest Whitaker's Significant Productions/Open Road Films; Color; Comedy/Crime/Drama; Children: Unacceptable (MPAA: R); **BD**; **DVD**. In this good coming-of-age comedy-drama, Moore, whose main interest is mathematics, survives in the tough neighborhood of Inglewood, California (part of L.A.) and is known as The Bottoms, a run-down area inhabited by savage gangsters and drug dealers. While interviewing and taking tests for his senior year in college, his dream is to attend Harvard University. He is sidetracked into an underground party where he is influenced by drug dealers and addicts. This leads him to into drugs, but Moore ultimately finds his true self and begins to realize his potential in the legitimate world. Moore gives an outstanding performance as do the rest of the cast in this unsavory but intriguing tale. The film produced $18 million at the box office in its initial release against a shoestring budget of $700,000. Songs: "Hip Hop Hooray" (Vincent Brown, Keir Gist, Anthony Criss, Ernie Isley, O'Kelly Isley, Ronald Isley, Rudolph Isley, Christopher Jasper); "Go Head," "New Money," "Can't Bring Me Down," Don't Get Deleted," "It's My Turn Now" (Pharrell Williams); "Woo-Hah! Got You All in Check" (Trevor Smith, Arthur MacDermot); "The Choice Is Yours" (James Alexander, Ben Cauley, Allen Jones, William McLean, John Smith, Andres Titus, Johnny Hammond); "I'm Your Drug" (Mike Larson); "I Wanna Rock" (Luther Campbell, Harry Wayne Casey, Richard Finch); "Poppin' Off" (Jesse Rankins, Eddie Smith III, Jonathan Wells); "The Boy" (Casey Jones, Chauncey Hollis, Raymond Martin, Rashad Muhammad, Chris E. Martin); "Go!" (Q Tip, Karen Orzolek, Dave Taylor, Santi Zinner, Huy Battarel); "Buggin' Out" (Kamaal Fareed, Malik Taylor, Ali Jones-Muhammad); "Juice (Know the Ledge)" (Eric Barrier, William Griffin); "The World Is Yours" (Peter Phillips, Nasir Jones); "Dirty Feeling" (Zoe Kravitz, James Levy); "Freak on a Leash" (Reginald Arvizu, Jonathan Davis, James Shaffer, David Silveria, Brian Welch); "Home Is Where the Hatred Is" (Gil Scott-Heron); "Rebirth of Slick (Cool Like Dat)" (Ishmael R. Butler, Mary Ann Vierra); "Bitch Better Have Money" (Jason Lewis); "Slam" (Jason Mizell, Tyrone Taylor, Kirk Jones, Chylow M. Parker, Fred Jr. Scruggs); "Lord Pretty Flacko Jodye 2" (Rakim Mayers, Mario Loving, Nesbitt Wesonga Jr.); "Know What I Want" (Karly Loaza, Jason Fleming); "Rebel Without a Pause" (Carlton Reidenhour, Eric Sadler, James Boxley, Norman Rogers); "Gas" (Moors); "Cocaina Shawty (Kap G, Pharrell Williams); "The Humpty Dance" (George Jr. Clinton, William Collins, Walter Morrison). Excessive violence, drug content, teen mayhem, gutter language, sexuality and nudity prohibit viewing by children. **p**, Nina Yang Bongiovi, Forest Whitaker, Mimi Valdes, Caron Veazey; **d&w**, Rick Famuyiwa; **cast**, Shameik Moore, Rakim Mayers, Blake Anderson, Bruce Beatty, Julian Brand, Quincy Brown, Kiersey Clemons, Kimberly Elise, Rick Fox, Ricky Harris; **c**, Rachel Morrison; **m**, Germaine Franco; **ed**, Lee Haugen; **prod d**, Scott Falconer; **art d**, Lawson Brown; **set d**, Christine Eyer; **spec eff**, Larry Fioritto, Steve Newquist, Sam Dean.

Draft Day ★★★ 2014; U.S.; 109m; Summit Entertainment; Color; Sports Drama; Children: Unacceptable (MPAA: PG-13); **BD**; **DVD**. Exciting football tale sees Costner as the general manager of the Cleveland Browns football team. He must fight to land the number one draft pick after a thirteen-year unlucky streak that could cost him his job. On the fictional 2014 NFL draft day, the number one pick is a University of Wisconsin quarterback, Pence, the current Heisman Trophy winner. Costner is holding the seventh pick. His father had coached the Browns, but was fired by Costner and died a week before the draft. Costner is given the opportunity to trade the first overall draft pick, held by a fictionalized Seattle Seahawks whose general manager is St. Esprit and his boss-owner, McBride. Before the pick, Costner learns that his girlfriend, Garner, is pregnant with his child. She also works for the Browns as a lawyer, and is concerned about the team's salary cap. St. Esprit offers the number one pick to Costner, but he declines. However, later he accepts it after being told to "make a splash" by Browns owner Langella. The Browns can now trade their three first-round draft picks over the next three years to the Seahawks in exchange for the top pick. Costner believes this is a good deal for his team. However, it angers many Seahawks fans who want Pence to play for their team and they take to social media to say how displeased they are with Costner and demand that McBride fire him. The Browns head coach, Leary, also is angered, because he wanted to draft running back Crews for his system offense, and the current quarterback Welling, who led the team to a 5-1 start the previous year, before being injured. News leaks out, tweeted by Boseman, a defensive player for Ohio State, who wants to play for the Browns and advises Costner to re-watch a tape of him sacking Pence four times in one game, to see what Pence does next. Costner also turns down a proposed trade from the Buffalo Bills and an inquiry from the Kansas City Chiefs about the availability of Welling. Coming to the draft, the only downside to Pence seems to be two incidents that reflect on his honesty, a twenty-first birthday party ruckus-robbery, where Pence reportedly lied to the Washington Redskins about reading a playbook they sent him. When the Browns are to make their first overall pick, Costner sends in the choice of Boseman without the rest of the head office's knowledge. While Welling appears to be relieved of the choice for Boseman, Langella angrily leaves the draft in New York City to fly back to Cleveland to confront Costner. Pence has what appears to be an anxiety attack and leaves by the back door, but is coaxed back to the draft by his agent. Pence's appeal steadily drops in the draft, but he is still available for the sixth pick, held by the Jacksonville Jaguars. Costner talks the rookie general manager of that team into giving him the sixth overall pick in trade for the next three years of the Browns' second-round draft picks. Langella is furious with Costner for passing over Pence for Boseman, but Costner tells him he had his reasons for picking Boseman and manages to convince Langella to let him do his job. Costner then calls St. Esprit, who wants Pence badly, and secures all three first-round draft picks back for the sixth pick. Seattle takes Pence which allows Costner to also select Crews and thereby making coach Leary happy. The draft is looked upon as a success for the Browns, and Opening Day 2014 shows a pregnant Garner still with Costner. The team prepares for the game with all Browns players, including Boseman, St. Esprit, and Welling, in high spirits and eager for the season to begin. Although professional football executives criticized

Xavier Samuel in *Drift*, 2013.

this film as not actually depicting the conduct of an NFL team leading up to and during the draft, the drama of the story is well told. Further, exceptional performances are rendered by Costner, Langella, Pence, Garner, Boseman, St. Esprit and the rest of the cast, while production values are high. The film earned more than $29.5 million in its initial release against a budget of $25 million. Songs: "NFL on Fox Theme" (Phil Garrod, Reed Hayes, Scott Schreer), "Reno" (Michael Joseph Hewitt, Craig A. Rose, Kent S. Ross, Michael Matthew Turallo), "Born to Rise" (Alexander Francis Barry, Mark Kasprzyk, Julian Tomarin). ***Author's Note***: Other films depicting actual NFL teams include **The Blind Side**, 2009 (Baltimore Ravens); **Crazylegs**, 1953 (Cleveland Browns, Los Angeles Rams, Chicago Bears); **Heaven Can Wait**, 1978 (Los Angeles Rams); and **Invincible**, 2006 (Philadelphia Eagles, New York Giants, Cincinnati Bengals). Excessive gutter language and sexual references prohibit viewing by children. The film was originally rated by the MPAA as R, but Lionsgate, the producing company appealed and the rating was changed to PG-13, which routinely shows how the MPAA rating system is ineffective. **p**, Ivan Reitman, Ali Bell, Joe Medjuck, Gigi Pritzker, **d**, Reitman; **cast**, Kevin Costner, Jennifer Garner, Frank Langella, Sam Elliott, Josh Pence, Tom Welling, Ellen Burstyn, Patrick St. Esprit, Rosanna Arquette, Denis Leary, Terry Crews, Chadwick Boseman, Kevin Dunn; **w**, Scott Rothman, Rajiv Joseph; **c**, Eric Steelberg; **m**, John Debney; **ed**, Dana E. Glauberman, Sheldon Kahn; **prod d**, Stephen Altman; **art d**, John Bucklin, Gregory A. Weimerskirch; **set d**, Maria Nay; **spec eff**, Richard Fike, Ryan Flick.

Drift ★★★ 2013; Australia; 153m; World-Wide-Mind Films/Wrekin Hill Entertainment/Lionsgate; Color; Sports Drama; Children: Unacceptable (MPAA: R); **BD**; **DVD**. Exciting tale, based on a true story in 1970s Australia, begins with surfer brothers Andy Kelly, age twenty-eight, and Jimmy, twenty-two. They have one great passion: riding big waves. When they were boys, their mother left Sydney to go to Margaret River, a sleepy coastal town with some of the world's most challenging and dangerous waves. Over the next dozen years, the brothers perfect their surfing skills in the waters there, always searching for the perfect surfboard ride. More free-spirited Jimmy, played by Samuel, is a gifted surfer and innovator, but starts to slip toward a life of crime to help get the family out of debt. Andy, played by Pollard, quits his job and bets his younger brother's surf inventions and his own business abilities and launches a backyard surf equipment business. The brothers rethink surfboard design and make homemade wetsuits, selling their wares out of their van. They are encouraged by new friends, including Worthington, a surfing photographer, and Brandt, his beautiful Hawaiian surfer companion, to whom both brothers are attracted. Then things take a downturn as the brothers get involved with a local drug dealer and they must

Mr. O'Hare (Rob Riggle voiceover) in *Dr. Seuss' The Lorax,* 2012.

struggle to get themselves out of their own dilemma. Set in breathtaking surfing locations, the film was inspired by the true story of Australia's legendary surf ware innovators while chronicling the rise of surf brands and expansion of the laidback surf attitude into a global lifestyle. This well-crafted and superbly acted film also tells a tale of courage and the will to survive against all odds. The film saw a moderate success at the box office, earning more than $11 million in its initial release. Songs: "Johnny B. Goode" (Chuck Berry), "The Jump" (Michael Yezerski, Nathaniel Joyce), "Run Through the Jungle" (John Fogerty), "Rock and Roll Part 2" (Gary Glitter, Mike Leander), "Turn Up Your Radio" (Douglas Ford, James Keays), "Sunshine" (Michael Yezerski), "I Don't Need You No More" (Peter Wolf, Seth Justman), "I'm Alive" (Peter Howe), "Govinda" (Crispian Mills, Alonza Bevan, Paul Winter-Hart, Jay Darlington), "Only Good for Conversation" (Sixto Rodriguez), "Gold on the Ceiling" (Dan Auerbach, Patrick Carney, Brian Burton), "20th Century Boy" (Marc Bolan), "Endless Summer" (Heather Shannon, Hayley McGlone, Nikolas Kaloper, Samuel Lockwood). *Author's Note*: Other films profiling surfers include **Back to the Beach**, 1987; **The Big Bounce**, 2004; **Big Wednesday**, 1978; **Blue Crush**, 2002; **Blue Juice**, 1995; **Chairman of the Board**, 1998; **Chasing Mavericks**, 2012; **The Cove**, 2009; **Don't Make Waves**, 1967; **The Drifter**, 2009; **First Love**, 2010; **Isolated**, 2013; **Jaws**, 1975; **Jaws 2**, 1978; **John from Cincinnati**, 2007- (TV series); **Laguna Beach: The Real Orange County**, 2002-2006 (TV series); **Lilo & Stitch**, 2002; **Local Boys**, 2002; **Loch Ness**, 1996; **Muscle Beach Party**, 1964; **North Shore**, 1987; **Off the Lip**, 2004; **Open Water**, 2004; **Open Water 2**, 2006; **Point Break**, 1991; **The Prince and the Surfer**, 1999; **Psycho Beach Party**, 2000; **Ride the Wild Surf**, 1964; **A Scene at the Sea**, 1991; **Shout for Joy**, 1983; **Soul Surfer**, 2011; **Surf Ninjas**, 1993; **Surf School**, 2006; **Surf's Up**, 2007; **Teen Beach Movie**, 2013 (made-for-TV); **There Goes My Baby**, 1994; and **Without a Paddle**, 2004. Gutter language and drug content prohibit viewing by children. **p**, Tim Duffy, Michele Bennett, Myles Pollard; **d**, Ben Nott, Morgan O'Neill; **cast**, Sam Worthington, Xavier Samuel, Jeremy Piven, Lesley-Ann Brandt, Robyn Malcolm, Myles Pollard, Sean Keenan, Steve Bastoni, Aaron Glenane, Laura Fairclough, Ben Mortley, David Bowers; **w**, O'Neill (based on a story by O'Neill and Duffy); **c**, Geoffrey Hall; **m**, Michael Yezerski; **ed**, Marus D'Arcy; **prod d**, Clayton Jauncey; **art d**, Emma Fletcher; **set d**, Christine Lynch; **spec eff**, Matthew Gidney.

Dr. Seuss' The Lorax ★★★ 2012; U.S.; 86m; Illumination Entertainment/UNIV; Color; Animated Comedy; Children: Cautionary (MPAA: PG); **3-D**; **BD**; **DVD**. Entertaining animated tale begins with Efron, an idealistic twelve-year-old boy living in the walled city of Thneed-Ville where everything, including the air, is artificial and made of plastic,

metal, or synthetics. He has a crush on Swift, a girl who wishes she could see a real tree. Efron's grandmother, White, tells him the legend of the Once-ler (Helms voiceover), who remembers trees and will describe them for fifteen cents, a nail, and the shell of an old snail. Efron leaves the city to find Helms, who, because of his greed, devastated the land and became a hermit. Efron finds that the world outside of Thneed-Ville is a contaminated wasteland. He gets the necessary items to give to Helms, but the mayor of Thneed-Ville (Riggle voiceover) is also a greedy man and pressures Efron to come back and stay in town so as not to endanger his bottled oxygen business that capitalizes on the devastated environment. White helps Efron escape the city and he finds Helms, who tells him how his greed led to his and the area's undoing. Helms further tells Efron that the Lorax, who loves and protects trees and the environment, sent the animals of the region to find a better place, then departed into the sky. Helms gives Efron the last seed that can grow a tree. Helms does this in hopes of reminding everyone about the importance of nature and the importance of not destroying it. The seed is planted and Swift kisses Efron on the cheek. Time passes and trees grow again, the animals return and the natural environment begins to return. Based on the book and television show, this well-animated story was filmed in 3-D. The film was a great success at the box office, earning more than $348.8 million in its initial release against a budget of $70 million. Songs: "Thneedville," "These Trees," "Everybody Needs a Thneed," "Let It Grow," "This Is the Place," "You Need a Thneed" (John Powell, Cinco Paul); "The Hustle" (Van McCoy); "O'Hare Air Jingle" (Chad Fisher); "Happy Birthday to You" (Mildred J. Hill, Patty Smith Hill); "Mission Impossible Theme" (Lalo Schifrin); "How Bad Can I Be?" (John Powell, Cinco Paul, Kool Kojak); "Let It Grow/Celebrate the World" (Christopher Stewart, Ester Dean, John Powell, Cinco Paul, Aaron Pearce III). Strong language cautions viewing by children. **p**, Janet Healy, Christopher Meledandri; **d**, Chris Renaud, Kyle Balda; **cast** (voiceovers), Zac Efron, Danny DeVito, Ed Helms, Betty White, Taylor Swift, Rob Riggle, Jenny Slate, Nasim Pedrad, Elmarie Wendel, Joel Swetow, Michael Beattie; **w**, Cinco Paul, Ken Daurio (based on the book by Dr. Seuss (Ted Geisel); **m**, John Powell; **ed**, Claire Dodgson, Steven Liu, Ken Schretzmann; **prod d**, Yarrow Cheney; **art d**, Eric Guillon; **spec eff**, Maxime Bray, Celine Allegre, Romain Privat de Fortunie.

The Drop ★★★ 2014; U.S.; 106m; Chernin Entertainment/FOX; Color; Crime Drama; Children: Unacceptable (MPAA: R); **BD**; **DVD**. Chilling thriller begins with Hardy, a bartender working at a neighborhood tavern in Brooklyn called Cousin Marv's that is run by Marv (Gandolfini). The tavern operates as a "drop" bar where criminals launder money. Gandolfini becomes angry at some men honoring the tenth anniversary of a man being murdered. On his way home, Hardy finds a badly beaten pit bull inside a garbage can. Rapace, who lives in the nearby house, sees that the dog is injured, and helps Hardy tend to its needs. She says that because it's a pit bull, it will be put down at the shelter if its owner doesn't come for it, so he calls the dog Rocco and takes it to a church where he does not notice Ortiz, a watchful parishioner who is a detective. The bar is then robbed by two gunmen, and, during the robbery, Hardy notices that one of the gunmen has a broken watch. Ortiz shows up to investigate and Hardy shows him the watch. This upsets Gandolfini, who knows that the Chechens are going to be angry that their money has been stolen. The next day, Aronov, a leader of the Chechen mob, wants to know why the police know about the broken watch, and tells Gandolfini to find the money. Hardy and Rapace grow fonder about each other as they take care of Rocco. Hardy then meets Schoenaerts, who says Rocco is a nice-looking dog. Gandolfini, who lives with his sister, is told by her that a collection agency has been calling because they need to pay for their ill father's life support. She suggests that they should take him off of the life support, but he objects. Gandolfini then meets up with one of the robbers, which reveals that Gandolfini orchestrated the robbery of his own bar. Schoenaerts then shows up at Hardy's house and demands the dog back. He takes Hardy's umbrella and leaves. On his way to the bar, a man stops Gandolfini to ask directions, which makes Gandolfini believe he is being followed. He tells Hardy that Schoenaerts is a local thug, who claims to have killed the man mentioned earlier. They then find a bag near a garbage area that contains the arm with the broken watch and all the stolen money. Hardy disposes of the arm while Gandolfini returns the money to the Chechens. They tell him that his bar will be the drop bar for the night of the Super Bowl. Gandolfini finds the other robber and, while driving, tells Hardy that they are going to rob the bar again during the night of the big football game. The car's trunk pops open and Gandolfini tells the robber inside to get out and shut it. When he does, Gandolfini runs him over, killing him. Schoenaerts then stops by and asks Hardy about Rapace. Hardy asks him how he knows Schoenaerts and he says they used to date each other. Hardy goes home and sees Rocco, but his umbrella is there, too, making him believe that Schoenaerts has been in his house. Gandolfini meets with Schoenaerts to recruit him to rob the bar after the Super Bowl. Gandolfini calls in sick the day of the game, and Hardy asks if he's planning on doing something they can't clean up this time. Hardy takes $10,000 hidden in his basement with him to the bar, along with Rocco, for the Super Bowl evening. He puts the money behind the bar, next to a pistol. Schoenaerts breaks into Rapace's home and forces her to go to the bar with him. While they are there, Gandolfini calls Schoenaerts and warns him not to underestimate seemingly gentle Hardy. Gandolfini then lines the trunk of his car with plastic and drives to the bar, parking nearby and waiting. Different mob members drop off money throughout the evening, and the bar eventually clears except for Schoenaerts and Rapace. She warns Hardy that Schoenaerts plans to shoot him. Schoenaerts tells Hardy to open the safe at 2 a.m. and Hardy tells the story of the dead man… Gandolfini had once been a loan shark, but had a gambling problem. The man owed Gandolfini a lot of money, but won a casino jackpot and was able to pay Gandolfini back. In order to cover Gandolfini's own debts, no one could know that he was paid back. Hardy was the one who murdered the man, not Schoenaerts, who had claimed to have been the killer. Hardy then shoots Schoenaerts dead and tells Rapace that she is safe now and can go. Outside, while approaching his car, Gandolfini sees the man who had earlier asked for directions. Gandolfini senses that his time is now up, as the man shoots him in the head. The Chechens arrive and dispose of Schoenaerts' body. Aronov also arrives and tells Hardy he is the new Marv, and will be operating the drop bar. The next day, Ortiz appears at the bar and questions Hardy about the disappearance of Schoenaerts. Ortiz also tells Hardy that he knows Schoenaerts could not have killed the man because Schoenaerts was in a psychiatric ward at the time. Hardy and Rocco go to Rapace's home so he can apologize for the night at the bar. He asks her to take a walk with him and Rocco, and she agrees, but first insists that she get a coat. She walks away on a sidewalk leading to the rear of the house and disappears. She does not return and suddenly Hardy hears footsteps approaching and that is where this enigmatic and very strange tale ends. Brutal and permeated with disgustingly offensive language (as befit the lowlife characters, but will insult mainstream audiences), the film is nevertheless well made and the acting from all is superior. The film did not do well at the box office, earning more than $18.7 million in its initial release against a budget of $12.6 million. Song: "Survival of the Fittest" (Robert DeLong). *Author's Note*: The overweight Gandolfini, who had made his mark as the foul-mouthed Mafia boss in the HBO TV series **The Sopranos**, died of a heart attack in a hotel room in Rome, Italy, on June 19, 2013, at age fifty-one, fifteen months before this film was released in the U.S. Vile gutter language and violence prohibit viewing by children. **p**, Peter Chernin, Dylan Clark, Mike Larocca; **d**, Michael R. Roskam; **cast**, Tom Hardy, James Gandolfini, Noomi Rapace, Elizabeth Rodriguez, Matthias Schoenaerts, James Frecheville, Erin Darke, Patricia Squire, John Oritz, Michael Esper; **w**, Dennis Lehane (based on his short story "Animal Rescue"); **c**, Nicolas Karakatsanis; **m**, Marco Beltrami, Raf Keunen; **ed**, Christopher Tellefsen; **prod**

Mr. O'Hare (Rob Riggle voiceover) in *Dr. Seuss' The Lorax*, 2012.

d, Therese DePrez; **art d**, Michael Ahern; **set d**, Mila Khalevich; **spec eff**, Drew Jiritano, Eran Dinur.

The DUFF ★★★ 2015; U.S.; 101m; CBS Films/Lionsgate; Color; Comedy; Children: Unacceptable (MPAA: PG-13); **BD**; **DVD**. Entertaining comedy sees Whitman as a somewhat overweight high school senior whose self-image is strongly damaged when Thorne, a classmate, begins labeling everyone. Thorne and the other prettier, more popular girls at school start calling her "DUFF" which stands for "Designated Ugly Fat Friend." She has a crush on Eversman, a guitar-playing student, and her closest friends are Samuels and Santos. To help her change her image, she hopes to enlist the aid of the school's football star, Amell. She reluctantly goes to Thorne's party to talk to Amell, but he learns that she is the one who is called "The Duff." Amell explains to Whitman that the name merely refers to someone who is less popular in a group. She learns that Thorne and others are calling her "The Duff" so they can win from her the friendship of Samuels and Santos. Things look up for Whitman after discovering that Amell's science teacher, Wylde, has threatened to stop efforts to get a college football scholarship for him if he fails his midterm exam. Whitman tells Amell she will help him study to pass the exam if he will help her to stop being called "The Duff." This leads to her getting a date with Eversman, and she learns that he has been calling her the derogatory name too, so as to get friendly with her two best friends. Whitman loses interest in Eversman, and the film ends at a homecoming dance where Thorne is crowned homecoming queen. Whitman then tells Thorne off in front of everyone and says that everyone is a "DUFF" of some kind to some people. Amell is named homecoming king, but declines the honor and, instead, kisses Whitman. The crowd cheers as the film ends with Whitman going to go to Northwestern University and Amell to Ohio State on a football scholarship. It is understood that they will remain friends, or even develop a deeper relationship. This good coming-of-age story sees good performances from Whitman, Thorne, Amell and the rest of the cast, all of whom are desperately seeking approval from their peers even though they all know they will soon enter a more open society where they will be on their own to establish their own singular identities. The film did well at the box office, particularly through the support of teenage viewers, earning more than $43.5 million in its initial release against a budget of more than $8.5 million. Songs/Music: "Kill the Band" (Tom Holkenberg, Joost van Bellen), "I Own It" (Angel Haze, Andrew Wallace, Autumn Rowe), "Do Ya" (Merrill Nisker), "Amazing!" (Jen DeMartino, Richard Gradone), "Your Finger Tips" (Ali Theodore, Susan Paroff, Sarai Howard, Julian Harris, Richard Fiocca), "Heavy Mood" (Kiana Alarid, Neely Jenkins, Nick White, Derek Pressnall, Jamie Pressnall), "Boom Clap" (Charlotte Aitchison, Fredrik Berger, Patrik Berger, Stefan

Jim Carrey and Jeff Daniels in *Dumb and Dumber To,* **2014.**

Graslund), "Let Me See You Get Low" and "Make That Booty Pop" (Ali Theodore, Jordan Yeager), "Made In Gold" (Evan Bogart, Dilesh Haria, Julia Michaels, Spencer Nezey, Greg Ogan, Lindy Robbins, Nova Rockafeller, Sam Watters), "Jealous" (Nicholas Jonas, Nolan Lambroza, Simon Wilcox), "Bad Reputation" (Joan Jett, Kenny Laguna, Ritchie Codell, Marty Kupersmith), "All the Girls" (Patrick Sturrock), "Wakeup makeup" (Tsugumi Takashi), "Watch Me" (Ali Theodore, Jordan Yaeger, Sergio Cabral, Sarai Howard), "Sexy Silk" (Jack Hammer, Justin Broad, Paul Herman, Jessica Cornish, Aston Millard), "#Selfie" (Andrew Taggart), "Baby Got Back" (Anthony Ray), "Big Round Booty" (Ali Theodore, Jordan Jaeger, Sergio Cabral, Sarai Howard), "Symphony No. 9, Finale: Presto-Allegro assai" (Ludwig van Beethoven), "Say My Name" (Jim Jammy, Rodger Dodgers), "Nothing Left to Lose" (Karl Kimmel), "How Come You Don't Want Me" (Jack Antonoff, Tegan Rain Quin, Sara Keirsten Quin), "All I Need Is You" (Christian Cabrerizo, Brent Paschke, Peter McGinnis), "I Love You" (Nicole Yun, Daniel Cundiff), "All Night" (Brian Lee, Jonathan Sloan, Luke Steele, Aino Jawo, Caroline Hjelt, Elof Loelv, Nick Littlemore), "Give Life Back to Music" (Thomas Bangalter, Guy-Manuel De Homem-Christo, Paul Jackson Jr., Nile Rodgers), "If It's Not You" (Koen Mestrum, Tuen Pranger, Danny Schmittler, Ian Walsh), "Ready to Go" (William Abers, Ulises Bella, Justin Poree, Asdru Sierra, Raul Pacheco, Jiro Yamaguchi), "Perfect World" (James Mercer, Brian Burton), "Somebody to You" (Kristian Lundin, Savan Kotecha, Carl Anthony Falk), "Favorite Record" (Andrew Hurley, Patrick Stump, Joseph Trohman, Peter Wentz). Crude and sexual material throughout, gutter language and wild teen partying prohibit viewing by children. **p**, Susan Cartsonis, McG (Joseph McGinty Nichol), Mary Viola; **d**, Ari Sandel; **cast**, Mae Whitman, Bella Thorne, Robbie Amell, Bianca A. Santos, Skyler Samuels, Romany Malco, Nick Eversman, Chris Wylde, Ken Jeong, Allison Janney; **w**, Josh A. Cagan (based on the novel by Kody Keplinger); **c**, David Hennings; **m**, Dominic Lewis; **ed**, Wendy Greene Bricmont; **prod d**, Aaron Osborne; **spec eff**, Sarah McCulley, James Yates.

Dumb and Dumber To ★★★ 2014; U.S.; 110m; UNIV; Color; Comedy; Children: Unacceptable (MPAA: PG-13); **BD**; **DVD**. Twenty years have passed since Carrey's and Daniels' first adventure together and Carrey has been hospitalized and has been in a coma all those years. His younger friend, Daniels, visits and changes Carrey's diaper and doo-doo bag, then learns that Carrey has not really been in a coma and that this prolonged ruse is just his latest and endless prank. They then discover that Daniels has a twelve-year-old daughter, Melvin, who was given up for adoption at birth by her mother, Turner, who was Daniels' girlfriend at the time. Daniels wants to reconnect with Melvin, so he

and Carrey go on a road trip to find her. This leads to another wild adventure, compounded with mayhem through their mutual stupidity as they visit Melvin's adoptive parents and then become involved in a marital intrigue that has them going to El Paso for a conference of science geniuses. The exaggerated manic manipulations of Carrey and Daniels are shuddering wonders to behold as they often appear to be victims of St. Vitus Dance or epileptic fits, but their grand zaniness nevertheless sustains lowbrow humor and funny-bone interest throughout. Their mindless and outlandish adolescent behavior proved appealing to unsophisticated young audiences that made this film a box office success, and the film earned almost $170 million in its initial release against a budget of $40 million. Songs: "Woody Woodpecker" (Walter Greene), "Back at the Party" and "Go Go" (William "Billy" Goodrum). **p**, Riza Aziz, Bobby Farrelly, Peter Farrelly, Joey McFarland, Bradley Thomas, Charles B. Wessler, J.B. Rogers; **d**, Bobby Farrelly, Peter Farrelly; **cast**, Jim Carrey, Jeff Daniels, Kathleen Turner, Bill Murray, Tembi Locke, Rob Riggle, Laurie Holden, Rachel Melvin, Steve Tom, Don Lake, Patricia French, **w**, Sean Anders, Mike Cerrone, Bobby Farrelly, Peter Farrelly, John Morris, Bennett Yellin; **c**, Matthew F. Leonetti; **m**, Empire of the Sun; **ed**, Steven Rasch; **prod d**, Aaron Osborne; **set d**, Jennifer M. Gentile; spec eff, Russell Tyrrell.

The East ★★★ 2013; U.S./U.K.; 116m; Scott Free Productions/FOX Searchlight; Color; Spy Drama; Children: Acceptable; MPAA: PG-13; **BD**; **DVD**. Deftly paced espionage tale has Marling, a former FBI agent, as a successful operative for an elite private intelligence firm in Washington, D.C., that is headed by Clarkson. The attractive Marling is assigned to infiltrate an anarchist group, The East, known for perpetrating covert attacks on major corporations. Under the pretext of going to Dubai, she is dropped off at Dulles Airport by her boyfriend, Ritter. Instead of going through security check, Marling goes to the arrivals section and takes a cab to a motel. There she goes undercover to become a traveler and, disguised, begins a search for The East, hoping to locate their headquarters and feed information about them to Clarkson so Clarkson can protect her corporate clients. Marling becomes attracted to Skarsgard, a member of The East, which causes her to question the morality of her undercover duty when she learns from him that she is working for Clarkson in an anti-environmental action against corporations. She takes part in their next adventure, called a "jam," and learns that each member of The East has been personally damaged by corporate chemical polluting activities involving dumping chemicals into waterways. Marling wants Skarsgard to run away with her, but he insists they go together to complete the final jam against Clarkson's agents. At first reluctant, Marling finally agrees, and they go by car to the last jam. Skarsgard drives them to Clarkson's headquarters outside Washington, D.C., and reveals that he has always suspected her of being a Clarkson agent. He wants Marling to obtain a list of Clarkson's agents worldwide. Marling confronts Clarkson about the firm's activities, Skarsgard leaves the country, and Marling has the list of agents. Marling then contacts the other Clarkson agents and tries to change their minds about their undercover activities in polluting the world's waterways, and to join her in ecological activism. The idealistic motive to have a cleaner earth does not reside within the grim realism of espionage, this naïve ambition damaging the dense plot of an otherwise intriguing and well-acted tale. Songs: "Four Songs from the Fountain of Youth" (Johannes Brahms), "Doc's Song" (Rostam Batmangli), "Spiegel im Spiegel" (Arvo Part), "About Today" (Matt Berninger, Aaron Dessner), "Bad Dr. Blues" (Sedef Seren), "Divertimento No. 1" (Wolfgang Amadeus Mozart), "Buffalo Gals" (1844; John Hodges). Thematic elements, violence, disturbing images, sexual content and partial nudity prohibit viewing by children. **p**, Ridley Scott, Tony Scott, Brit Marling, Michael Costigan, Jocelyn Hayes, Jonathan McCoy; **d**, Zal Batmanglij; **cast**, Marling, Alexander Skarsgard, Patricia Clarkson, Julia Ormond, Ellen Page, Toby

Kebbell, Shiloh Fernandez, Aldis Hodge, Danielle Macdonald, Hillary Baack, Jason Ritter; **w**, Batmanglij, Brit Marling; **c**, Roman Vasyanov; **m**, Halli Cauthery, Harry Gregson-Williams; **ed**, Andrew Weisblum, Bill Pankow; **prod d**, Alex DiGerlando; **art d**, Nikki Black; **set d**, Cynthia Anne Slagter; **spec eff**, Jack Lynch, Roger Nall.

Edge of Tomorrow ★★★ 2014; U.S.; 113m; WB; Color; Science Fiction; Children: Unacceptable (MPAA: PG-13); **BD**; **DVD**. Cruise is exceptional playing a U.S. Army major who has never been in combat and is assigned to a virtual suicide mission. The task is the result of an alien race striking Earth in an unrelenting assault, believed to be unbeatable by any army in the world. Cruise is killed within minutes of battle, and finds himself in a time loop that forces him to relive the same brutal combat over and over again, fighting and dying again, and again. It is a time-changing trick of the aliens. However, with each battle Cruise becomes more skillful in battle while fighting alongside Blunt, a female Special Forces warrior. As might be expected, they also become romantically involved, although only she is alive. Through a series of learning battles, Cruise learns that the alien force is hidden with the pyramid at the Louvre in Paris. He infiltrates the pyramid and sets off an explosive device that destroys the aliens and himself, which destroys the constant battle loops and his own mimicking demise. He is now returned to the present with the alien threat no longer real and where he is greeted with respect by his subordinates, except for Blunt, who makes a sarcastic remark about him. This only causes Cruise to laugh, who has retained the memory of the war that has now never existed, as well as his experience with her and we are left to wonder about their future relationship together. Complex and clever, the myriad battle loops sometimes present confusing continuity, but the special effects and the exceptional production values are so vividly presented that interest is maintained throughout. The film was a huge box office success, earning more than $369.2 million in its initial release against a budget of $178 million. Songs: "Massive Mellow" (Daniel Lenz), "Railroad Track" (Willy Moon, Curtis Lundy), "Trip Into the Light" (Jeremy Lubin, Stephen Lubin, Craig Bonich, Patrick Meyer, Nathan Post), "Love Me Again" (Steve Booker, John Newman). Excessive violence, gutter language and brief suggestive material prohibit viewing by children. **p**, Jason Hoffs, Gregory Jacobs, Tom Lasssally, Jeffrey Silver, Erwin Stoff, Tim Lewis, Kim Winther; **d**, Doug Liman; **cast**, Tom Cruise, Emily Blunt, Brendan Gleeson, Bill Paxton, Jonas Armstrong, Noah Taylor, Tony Way, Kick Gurry, Franz Drameh, Dragomir Mrsic; **w**, Christopher McQuarrie, Jez Butterworth, John-Henry Butterworth (base on the novel *All You Need Is Kill* by Hiroshi Sakurazaka); **c**, Dion Beebe; **m**, Christophe Beck; **ed**, James Herbert, Laura Jennings; **prod d**, Oliver Scholl; **art d**, Alastair Bullock; **set d**, Elli Griff; **spec eff**, Jess Lewington, Dominick Tuohy.

Elysium ★★★ 2013; U.S.; 109m; TriStar/Sony; Color; Science Fiction; Children: Unacceptable (MPAA: R); **BD**; **DVD**. In this sequel to **District 9**, 2009, Earth is ruined by overpopulation, pollution, and disease in the year 2154. The wealthiest survivors live on an idyllic space station orbiting Earth called Elysium. Damon, a former car thief working in a factory assembling robots in rundown Los Angeles, is better off than most because he has a job while others are poor and destitute, governed by brutal robot police who arrest indiscriminately. A radiation accident at the factory gives Damon an overdose of the lethal surge and leaves him with only a few days to live. He will die unless he can get to Elysium where he has learned that healing pods can solve all medical problems in seconds. He asks Moura, a former criminal colleague, to help him get to Elysium. Moura runs a racket smuggling the sick and infirm to Elysium and the healing pods. Moura agrees to help Damon if he will perform one last job, to kidnap billionaire contractor Fichtner and download his brain so they can steal his secrets. To achieve this goal, Moura gives Damon a brain implant and, since Damon is weak from the radiation, affixes a metal skeleton into his body which makes Damon a hybrid of human and techno-man. Meanwhile, on Elysium, we meet

Emily Blunt in *Edge of Tomorrow*, 2014.

Foster, its ruthless defense secretary, who uses force to benefit the rich, even shooting down refugees from Earth, who try to land there in space craft. Damon manages to download Fichtner's brain and learns his secrets of sustaining life. Foster then has her "take no hostages" henchman (Copley) go after Damon, and the hunt-and-chase is on. Damon accomplishes his mission, manages to get to Elysium and there confronts Foster and her ruthless cohorts, defeating them, but at the willful cost of his own life. His sacrifice sees Elysium sending a huge fleet of medical ships to Earth to restore the health of humans living on that afflicted planet to end this exciting sci-fi saga. Though mesmerizing special effects dominate this film, as one might expect from its genre, the superior acting nevertheless rises above the dazzling visuals to impact the viewer with an empathetic drama of human survival. This film was a success at the box office, earning more than $286.1 million in its initial release against a budget of $115 million. Songs/Music: "Ghost" (Lorn as Marcos Ortega), "Robot Eater" (Patrick McKay), "The Pining Pt2" (Chris Clark), "We Got More" (Brendon Angelides), "Metropolis" (Alexander Lloyd), "Piano Concerto No. 8 in C Minor 'Pathetique' adagio cantabile, Piano Concerto No, 4. in G Major, rondo vivace" (Ludwig van Beethoven), "Suite for Solo Cello No. 1" (Johann Sebastian Bach), "Kou Kou" (Roderick Jackson), "Twitch/It Grows and Grows" (Benjamin Stefanski), "Bio Techno" (Audio Android), "Loner" (William Bevan), "New World Disorder" (Yoann Hebert), "Six Degrees" (Brett Bigden, Simon Shreeve), "Stjernekiggeri" (Mike Sheridan), "Sierre Leone" (Simon Attwell, Peter Cohen, Jesse Cooper, Neil John Francis Hawks, Zolani Mahola, Julio Sigauque, Kyla-Rose Smith), "Elysium" (Ryan Amon), "Down to Earth" (Peter Gabriel, Thomas Newman). Consistent gore and violence and gutter language throughout prohibit viewing by chiidren. **p**, Bill Block, Neill Blomkamp, Simon Kinberg, Stacy Perskie; **d&w**, Blomkamp; **cast**, Matt Damon, Jodie Foster, Sharlto Copley, Alice Braga, Diego Luna, Wagner Moura, William Fichtner, Brandon Auret, Josh Blacker, Emma Tremblay, Jose Pablo Cantillo; **c**, Trent Opaloch; **m**, Ryan Amon; **ed**, Julian Clarke, Lee Smith; **prod d**, Philip Ivey; **art d**, Don Macaulay; **set d**, Peter Lando, Ide Foyle, Gena Vazquez; **spec eff**, John MacCuspie.

Emperor ★★★ 2012; U.S./Japan; 105m; Krasnoff Foster Productions/Lionsgate; Color; War Drama; Children: Unacceptable (MPAA: PG-13); **BD**; **DVD**. Absorbing wartime tale begins when the Japanese surrender at the end of World War II (1939-1945), where General Douglas MacArthur (1880-1964), played by Jones, becomes the *de facto* ruler of Japan as Supreme Commander for Allied Powers of the occupying forces. Jones must decide whether Emperor Hirohito (1901-1989), played by Kataoka, should be executed as a war criminal, or if he was innocent of planning and executing the war. Jones assigns a member of

Matt Damon in *Elysium*, 2013.

his staff, U.S. General Bonner Fellers (1896-1973), played by Fox, to investigate the part the emperor played in the war. Fox meets with advisors to the emperor, but is rebuked by the Japanese people. Frustrated in his investigation, Fox arranges a meeting between the emperor and the supreme commander in which the emperor's perception of human dignity is presented. This leads to the supreme commander deciding against executing the emperor, which changes the course of history and the peacetime future of the two nations. During his investigation, Fox searches for Hatsune, a female Japanese exchange student he met years earlier and for whom he had romantic feelings while they were both in the United States. It is Fox's investigation that occupies the main story, an intriguing quest for the truth from Japanese militarists who have long ago abandoned honesty in order to advance their lofty careers and shield their endless wartime atrocities. Fox, for instance, interviews Hino, who plays General Hideki Tojo (1884-1948), asking him to give him three names that will exonerate the emperor. Hino, who had been Japan's prime minister (1941-1944) and is a condemned war criminal, gives Fox only one name, Fumimaro Konoe (1891-1945), played by Nakamura, and who was Tojo's predecessor as prime minister, but Fox gets little information from him, and Nakamura, rather than report to American authorities for trial as a war criminal, commits suicide. Fox learns that Kataoka (Hirohito) made the final decision to surrender to the Allied forces, defying the militarists who wanted to continue the war, even after the U.S. had dropped two atom bombs on Hiroshima and Nagasaki. Further, Fox learns that a right-wing military cabal reportedly attempted a coup to overthrow the emperor for his decision by invading the Imperial palace, but they were all overwhelmed and killed. In the end, Jones accepts Fox's claim that Hirohito had no part in Japan's military aggressions and both men meet. Kataoka tells Jones that he should be punished and not his country. Jones tells Kataoka that he does not intend to punish either Japan or its emperor and only wants to discuss the reconstruction of Kataoka's war-devastated country. The story is well told with a strong script, and the acting from the entire cast is superior while the period production values are superlative. This film had a moderate success at the box office, earning more than $14.6 million in its initial release. *Author's Note*: The question of Hirohito's guilt in beginning the war in the Far East has long been in debate. Where this film seeks to exonerate the emperor, many other credible sources insist that Hirohito was the chief architect in Japan's wartime aggressions and that its militarists were simply stooges playing totemic roles who pretended to have wrested control of the government. The Tanaka Memorial, or Tanaka Plan, which allegedly originated in 1927 and was prepared by Japan's then prime minister, Giichi Tanaka (1964-1929), was presented, at the emperor's request, to Hirohito as a wartime schedule on how to conquer the Far East by first taking over Manchuria and

parts of Mongolia and then mainland China and, subsequently, the Southeast island countries. Though some (including all Japanese historians still seeking to protect Japan's image as well as that of its emperor, Hirohito) claim the Tanaka Memorial was a forgery, Japan's actual aggressions in Manchuria, Mongolia and China religiously followed the timeline set forth in that plan. No original copy was ever located when the U.S. took control of Japan following WWII, but it was then believed that the authorities had destroyed all traces of the Memorial in order to protect Hirohito, who, in Japan's predominantly Shinto religion, was a god living on Earth. Learned scholar David Bergamini (1928-1983), published a massive and brilliant work, *Japan's Imperial Conspiracy* (1971), which, through exhaustive research and documentation, pinpointed Hirohito as a ruler who was behind all of the military actions enacted by Japan in WWII, beginning with that country's encroachment into Manchuria in 1931. It further documents how Hirohito shielded his identity as the architect of war in the Far East by insidiously establishing mock military cabals that ostensibly wrested control of the government from him but who were nevertheless obsequiously obedient to his dictates as the god-emperor of Japan. Moreover, the book extensively documents how real Japanese political opponents to Hirohito's plan of aggression were routinely assassinated in the 1930s by, again, those bogus military cabals, but under the secret direction of Hirohito. A number of historians, chiefly Japanese, have attempted to discredit Bergamini's superlative work, but it nevertheless remains as a credible documentation that convincingly underscore's Hirohito's guilt and responsibility. It was reported that Hirohito did meet with MacArthur to offer his apology for the war and taking full responsibility for it, but another report has it that when Hirohito arrived to make that apology, MacArthur refused to see the defeated emperor. Five years before his death, on September 6, 1984, Hirohito stated to China's Prime Minister Chun Doo-hwan (b. 1931): "It is indeed regrettable that there was an unfortunate past between us [Japan and China] for a period in this century and I believe that it should not be repeated again." This was the closest thing Hirohito ever came to any kind of apology which, of course, was no apology at all but an ambiguous statement that infers that Japan and China had had some kind of difficult misunderstanding, and where he, Hirohito, took no responsibility for his country's wartime actions. His equivocating statement to Chun Doo-hwan was typical of Hirohito's face-saving conduct throughout his protected life and only supports the well-researched documentation by Bergamini and others that he was culpable for WWII in the Far East. Through such clever machinations, the emperor escaped the violent fates of his fellow dictators, Adolf Hitler (1889-1945; suicide) and Benito Mussolini (1883-1945; assassinated), who had, like Hirohito, sought to conquer the world and were politically and militarily united through the Tripartite Act (of September 27, 1940 where Japan, Germany and Italy signed that military alliance, which Hirohito sanctioned). MacArthur, this author believes, knew full well of Hirohito's real guilt, rightly surmising that Japan's die-hard militarists would have ignored Hirohito's decision to surrender had he not possessed actual supreme authority in Japan. However, to keep that country stabilized when he took control of that country, MacArthur decided not to prosecute that god-emperor as the war criminal he most likely was, and not the titular puppet he positioned himself to be. Other actors depicting General Douglas MacArthur in other films include **America: Call to Greatness**, 1995 (made-for-TV; James Huston); **An American Guerrilla in the Philippines**, 1950 (Robert Barrat); **Code Breakers**, 2005 (made-for-TV; Jeremy Akerman); **Collision Course: Truman vs. MacArthur**, 1976 (made-for-TV; Henry Fonda); **The Court Martial of Billy Mitchell**, 1955 (Dayton Lummis); **Death of a Soldier**, 1986 (Jon Sidney); **Farewell to the King**, 1989 (John Bennett Perry); **In Pursuit of Honor**, 1995 (made-for-TV; James Sikking); **Inchon**, 1982 (Laurence Olivier); **Korea: The Unknown War**, 1988 (TV series; Charlton Heston); **The Korean War**, 2001 (TV series; Frank Novak); **The Last Bastion**, 1984 (TV series; Robert Vaughn); **MacArthur**, 1977 (Gregory Peck); **The**

Republic, 1998 (Istemi Betil); **The Sun**, 2005 (Robert Dawson); **They Were Expendable**, 1945 (Robert Barrat); **Truman**, 1995 (made-for-TV; Daniel von Bargen); **Voyagers!**, 1982-1983 (TV series; "Sneak Attack," 1983 episode: Frank Marth); and **The World Wars**, 2014 (TV miniseries; Prescott Hathaway as young MacArthur; Daniel Martin Berkey as elder MacArthur). Other actors have essayed Hirohito in other films that include **Danger Five**, 2011- (TV series; "Kill Men of the Rising Sun," 2012 episode; Paul Muscat); **Dante's Inferno**, 2007 (Scott Adsit); **Hiroshima**, 1995 (made-for-TV; Naohiko Umewaka); **Japan's Longest Day**, 1967 (Hakuo Matsumoto); **The Last Emperor**, 1987 (Lingmu Zhang); **MacArthur**, 1977 (John Fujioka); **Monarch of the Moon**, 2005 (Kenzo Lee); **Star Spangled Rhythm**, 1942 (Richard Loo); and **The Sun**, 2005 (Issei Ogata). Other actors portraying Hideki Tojo in other films include **Ano senso w aka—Nichibei kaisen to Tojo Hideki**, 2008 (made-for-TV; Takeshi Kitano); **Blood on the Sun**, 1945 (Robert Armstrong); **Daitoa senso to kokusai saiban**, 1959 (Kanjuro Arashi); **Gekido no showashi 'Gunbatsu,'** 1970 (Keiju Kobayashi); **Histeria!**, 1998-2000 (TV series; "World War II," 1999 episode; Rob Paulsen); **The Imperial Japanese Empire**, 1982 (Tetsuro Tanba); **Pride: The Fateful Moment—Japan**, 2001 (Masahiko Tsugawa); and **Tora! Tora! Tora!**, 1970 (Asao Uchida). Violence, gutter language and smoking prohibit viewing by children. **p**, Gary Foster, Russ Krasnoff, Yoko Narahashi, Eugene Nomura, Tim Coddington; **d**, Peter Webber; **cast**, Matthew Fox, Tommy Lee Jones, Eriko Hatsune, Takataroi Kataoka, Aaron Jackson, Shohei Hino, Toshiyuki Nishida, Masayoshi Haneda, Kaori Momoi, Colin Moy, Masatoshi Nakamura, Masato Ibu; **w**, Vera Blasi, David Klass (based on the book by Shiro Okamoto); **c**, Stuart Dryburgh; **m**, Alex Heffes; **ed**, Chris Plummer; **prod d**, Grant Major; **art d**, Jill Cormack; **set d**, Daniel Birt; **spec eff**, Richard Schuler, Julian Dimsey.

Enemy ★★★ 2014; Canada/Spain; 90m; Rhombus Media/A24; Color; Mystery; Children: Unacceptable (MPAA: R); **BD**; **DVD**. Strange but obsessively interesting tale begins with Adam (Gyllenhaal), a mild but depressed and bearded college history professor. He sees a movie in which an actor playing Anthony (also Gyllenhaal), is a bellboy and who is his exact double, except that he has no beard. He then assumes the character of the film, this behavioral change troubling his girlfriend, Laurent. Adam stalks the actor, visiting the office where he works and calling him at his home. Anthony's pregnant wife, Gadon, confuses the two men, unable to determine which one is her spouse. The two men realize they are perfect copies of each other although Adam is reserved and Anthony is more sexually aggressive. Adam becomes attracted to Gadon and they go to bed together in a hotel room. She senses he is different, but nevertheless stays with him. She then discovers he is not her husband because he is not wearing a wedding ring. They fight and, while arguing in a car, the auto crashes and Anthony and Gadon are both killed. The following day, Adam dresses in Anthony's clothes intending to begin life as his dead double. Weird tale takes much from the concepts of Franz Kafka, but nevertheless sustains interest throughout. Songs: "The Cheater" (John Krenski), "Not So Much to Be Loved as to Love" (Jonathan Richman), "After the Lights Go Out" (John C. Stewart). Strong sexual content, graphic nudity and gutter language prohibit viewing by children. **p**, M.A. Faura, Niv Fichman, Sari Friedland, Luc Dery; **d**, Denis Villeneuve; **cast**, Jake Gyllenhaal, Melanie Laurent, Sarah Gadon, Isabella Rossellini, Joshua Peace, Tim Post, Kedar Brown, Darryl Dinn, Misha Highstead, Megan Mann; **w**, Javier Gullon (based on the novel by Jose Saramago); **c**, Nicolas Bolduc; **m**, Danny Bensi, Saunder Jurriaans; **ed**, Matthew Hannam; **prod d**, Patrice Vermette; **art d**, Sean Breaugh; **set d**, Jim Lambie; **spec eff**, Laetitia Seguin.

Ephraim's Rescue ★★★ 2013; U.S.; 138m; ImageMovers/EPH Film/Excel Entertainment; Color; Biographical Drama; Children: Unacceptable (MPAA: PG); **BD**; **DVD**. This well-made inspirational film is based on the life of Ephraim Knowlton Hanks (1826-1896), a promi-

Edward Woodward in the TV series *The Equalizer*, 1985-1989.

nent member of the 19th-Century Church of Jesus Christ of Latter-Day Saints. A Mormon pioneer and a well-known leader in the early settlement of Utah, Hanks is exceptionally played by Southam. The film begins with Southam, a grizzled frontiersman, riding hard up to a farmhouse before he restores the health to a woman who had been presumed dead for hours. He then rides away while his story unfolds. The film follows his adventures as an early Utah settler, who, in 1856, played a dramatic role in rescuing Mormon emigrants from Illinois trapped by early winter snow storms in the Rocky Mountains while attempting to reach Salt Lake City. Southam becomes known as the rescuer of the Martin handcart company of Mormon pioneers (men and women who pulled wheeled carts by hand which contained their belongings). He hunts and provides buffalo meat to the starving party, which Southam finds remarkable because he had traveled that region many times and has never before seen so many buffaloes in the area, and he and the survivors come to believe that the Lord has sent the beasts in answer to their prayers. Many moving and traumatic moments detail how the Mormons survived through Southam's aid, although one of the more horrific scenes involves his mandatory amputation of arms and legs with his hunting knife, albeit the survivors claimed that they felt no pain when experiencing these life-threatening operations. Song: "My Kindness Shall Not Depart from Thee" (Rob Gardner). Written and directed by Christensen, the creative force behind another inspirational Mormon film **17 Miracles** (2011). **p**, T. C. Christensen, Steven A. Lee, Ron Tanner; **d&w**, Christensen; **cast**, Darin Southam, Richard Benedict, Charley Boon, Travis Eberhard, James Gaisford, Jeremy Hoop, Ally Ioannides, Rick Macy, Christopher Robin Miller, Clara Susan Morey II; **c**, Christensen; **ed**, Tanner Christensen; **prod d**, Roger Crandall; **spec eff**, Tanner Christensen.

The Equalizer ★★★ 2014; U.S.; 132m; COL; Color; Crime Drama; Children: Unacceptable (MPAA: R); **BD**; **DVD**. Hard-hitting vigilante film sees Washington as a man who believes he has put his mysterious past behind him and has now dedicated himself to beginning a new and peaceful life. When he meets Moretz, a girl under the control of ultra-violent Russian gangsters, he changes his mind and decides to help her. Armed with hidden skills that allow him to serve vengeance against anyone who would brutalize the helpless, Washington comes out of his self-imposed retirement and finds his desire for justice reawakened. If someone has a problem, if the odds are stacked against them, if they have nowhere or no one else to turn to, he will help because he has become The Equalizer. To defeat the Russian mobsters, Washington gets help from former CIA operatives Pullman and Leo. He compels corrupt cop Harbour, who has been working with the Russians by flooding his car with carbon monoxide, and Harbour reveals the whereabouts of one

Arnold Schwarzenegger and Sylvester Stallone in *Escape Plan*, 2013.

of the money-laundering operations operated by Russian mob boss Kulich. Washington destroys the place and then confronts the Russian mobsters, killing one after another. He then trails Kulich to his lair in Moscow and electrocutes him to death while the mob boss is taking a shower. Returning to Boston, he finds that Moretz has reformed and is no longer a prostitute and has a legitimate job. Washington then advertises his services and decides to answer another call for help from the Equalizer. Though this superhero tale is implausible and Washington's exploits are cartoon-like, the action is well choreographed and Washington does a good job keeping a straight face as he overcomes all odds and obstacles. The film was popular with younger inner-city audiences craving violent action (and there is plenty of it through some nifty special effects), earning more than $192 million at the box office in its initial release against a budget of $55 million. Songs: "Sixteen" (Jay Hawkins, Chris Ellul, Kelvin Swaby, Dan Taylor, Spencer Page); "Turn Up Tonight" (Fancy Hagood, Nathan Barlowe, Jesse Frasure); "Friendship Train" (Barrett Strong, Norman Whitfield); "Give 'Em What They Love" (Janelle Monae Robinson, Nathaniel Irvin III, Terrence Brown); "Hit It & Run" (Kaleb Rollins, Marc Soto, Scott Harris, Emily Warren); "Silver" (Zach Abels, Jeremy Freedman, Mike Margott, Jesse Rutherford); "Rocksteady" (Simone Cogo); "2 Kaiser" (Sebastian Ugowski, Siarhei Parkhomenka, Azad Azadpour); "El Rey De La Calle" (Danny Richard Osuna); "Alonzo Perez" (Juan Antonio Gonzalez Rodriguez);, "Midnight Train to Georgia" (James Weatherly); "Vengeance," "Graven Image" (Zack Hemsey); "New Dawn Fades" (Ian Curtis, Peter Hook, Stephen Morris, Bernard Sumner); "Guts Over Fear" (Eminem, Emile Haynie, Sia Furler, Luis Resto); "Valse-Scherzo, Op. 34," "Swan Lake Finale," "Violin Concerto in D Major, Op. 35" (Pyotr Ilyich Tchaikovsky). Excessive gore and violence, gutter language and some sexual references prohibit viewing by children. Not related to a 1985 film with the same name. **p**, Todd Black, Jason Blumenthal, Tony Eldridge, Mace Neufeld, Alex Siskin, Michael Sloan, Steve Tisch, Denzel Washington, Richard Wenk, Lance Johnson; **d**, Antoine Fuqua; **cast**, Washington, Bill Pullman, Melissa Leo, Marton Csokas, Chloe Grace Moretz, David Harbour, Haley Bennett, David Meunier, Johnny Skourtis, Alex Veadov, Vladimir Kulich; **w**, Wenk (based on the television series by Michael Sloan, Richard Lindheim); **c**, Mauro Fiore; **m**, Harry Gregson-Williams; **ed**, John Fefoua; **prod d**, Naomi Shohan; **art d**, David Lazan; **set d**, Leslie E. Rollins; **spec eff**, Jack Lynch, Judson Bell, Herve Desroches.

Ernest & Celestine ★★★ 2014; France/Belgium; 80m; La Parti Films/Gkids; Color; Animated Comedy/Drama; Children: Cautionary (MPAA: PG); **BD**; **DVD**. Impressively made animated tale depicts an unlikely friendship between a bear, Ernest (Whitaker voiceover), and a young mouse, Celestine (Brunner voiceover). Celestine lives in an underground orphanage where she is constantly read horror stories about evil bears by an orphanage guardian (Loop voiceover). She doesn't believe the stories and draws pictures of nice bears who befriend mice, while other rodents mock her for it. All mice are raised to be dentists, and one day Celestine is sent outside into the bear world to collect lost teeth from under bear cubs' pillows. On this adventure she meets Ernest, who is a starving hobo and, at first, wants to eat her. She shows him a cellar full of candy and a friendship forms between them as they find shelter in a secluded cabin. Others find their friendship frightening and try to keep them apart, but the affectionate bond is strong enough to overcome the obstacles placed between them and their friendship becomes a role model that brings about a better understanding between both species. A lot of good entertainment mixes an effective message about how to overcome prejudice. The film was nominated for Best Animated Feature. Released in English and French versions, the film did moderate box office, earning more than $6.2 million in its initial release. Songs: "Ernest's Song" and "The Song of Ernest and Celestine" (Thomas Fersen, Vincent Courtois). Some frightening moments caution viewing by children. (French version has English subtitles.) **p**, (French version) Didier Brunner, Henri Megalon, Stephan Roelants, Vincent Tavier; (English version) Eric Beckman, David Jesteadt, Michael Sinterniklaas); **d**, Stephane Aubier, Vincent Patar, Benjamin Renner; **cast** (voiceovers), Forest Whitaker, Lambert Wilson, Pauline Brunner, Mackenzie Foy, Lauren Bacall, Paul Giamatti, William H. Macy, Patrice Melennec, Anne-Marie Loop, Brigitte Virtudes; **w**, Daniel Pennac (based on the book by Gabrielle Vincent); **m**, Vincent Courtois; **prod d**, Zaza, Zyk; **spec eff**, Marc Ume.

Escape Plan ★★★ 2013; U.S.; 115m; Summit Entertainment; Color; Crime Drama; Children: Unacceptable (MPAA: R); **BD**; **DVD**. Clever crime caper begins with Stallone as a former prosecutor and owner of a Los Angeles security firm that tests maximum security prisons to see if they are escape proof. He is drawn to such work after his wife and child have been murdered by an escaped convict he had successfully prosecuted. CIA agent Balfe offers him and his business partner, D'Onofrio, a deal worth several million dollars to test a top-secret prison and see if it is escape proof. Stallone and his colleagues are not told where the prison is, to lessen the risk of outside help while escaping from it. Stallone reluctantly agrees and allows himself to be arrested in New Orleans as a Spanish terrorist. His captors remove a tracking microchip from his arm, implanted so authorities could trace his whereabouts, and he is drugged when taken to prison, so his colleagues do not know where he has been taken. Stallone arrives at an area of glass cells with no windows so he cannot see where he is imprisoned. He meets Schwarzenegger, also an inmate, and they stage a fight that will allow Stallone to study the prison's solitary confinement section. Stallone opens the floor of his cell which leads to a downward passageway, following it to learn that the prison is inside of a cargo ship in the middle of an ocean, so it is impossible to escape. Meanwhile, Stallone's friends, Ryan and Jackson, become suspicious when Stallone's paycheck for the job is frozen, and learn that the prison he is in is code-named "The Tomb," owned by an organization with connections to a security provider. Stallone and Schwarzenegger use a makeshift sexton to learn the ship's latitude and conclude that they are in the Atlantic Ocean near Morocco. They convince Caviezel, the warden, that a riot is about to break out in one of the prison's cell blocks. This ruse draws security guards to the riot cell block while Stallone and Schwarzenegger run to the deck. The prison's electrical system is shut down, but Stallone manages to get the system working again as a helicopter gets into a gunfight with the ship's crew. Schwarzenegger boards the helicopter as Stallone is sent to the ship's bottom by an automated water system. The helicopter picks up Stallone, but when Caviezel shoots at him and Schwarzenegger, Stallone shoots and kills Caviezel. The escapees then land safely on a beach in Morocco to end this thriller. A clever script presents a lot of plot twists that sustain interest while old pros Stallone and Schwarzenegger entertainingly reprise their musclebound personas of yore. This action-loaded film did well at the box office, earning more than $137 million in its initial release against a budget of $50 million. Songs: "Don't Sleep" (Ali Theodore, Lordkim Allah), "Show Me What You Got" (Willie Clarke), "Head Held High" and "Drum Circle 2" (Alex Heffes), "Piano Sonata No. 2 (Joseph Bonn). Violence and gutter language prohibit viewing by children. **p**, Robbie Brenner, Mark Canton, Remington Chase, Randall Emmett, Kevin King-Templeton, Brandon Grimes; **d**, Mikael Hafstrom; **cast**, Sylvester Stallone, Arnold Schwarzenegger, Jim Caviezel, Faran Tahir, Amy Ryan, Sam Neill, Vincent D'Onofrio, Vinnie Jones, Matt Gerald, Curtis "50 Cent" Jackson, Caitriona Balfe; **w**, Miles Chapman, Jason Keller as Arnell Jesko (based on a story by Chapman); **c**, Brendan Galvin; **m**, Alex Heffes; **ed**, Elliot Greenberg; **prod d**, Barry Chusid; **art d**, James A. Gelarden; **set d**, Bradford Johnson; **spec eff**, Michael Lantieri.

Everest ★★★ 2015; UK/U.S./Ireland; 121m; Working Title Films/UNIV; Color; Adventure; Children: Unacceptable (MPAA: PG-13); **BD**; **DVD**. Based on true events, this exciting film (released in both Imax and 3-D) excitingly chronicles the disastrous 1996 attempt to reach the summit of Mount Everest, the highest mountain in the world. Expeditions from several countries arrive in March of that year, one of which is led by Clarke, who is from New Zealand. He is one of three guides for Adventure Consultants, a team that includes Brolin, a Texas doctor, who is an experienced climber; Hawkes, a mailman with ambition to climb Everest; and Mori, a Japanese climber, who had reached six of the seven summits on previous expeditions and wants to become the oldest woman to reach the top. Gyllenhaal, a well-known sportsman, is the chief guide for Mountain Madness. The climbers meet Watson at base camp where she is the manager of the climb and later communicates with the climbers by way of a walkie-talkie radio. After a harrowing ascent, Clarke reaches the summit while Mori plants the flag of Japan in the snow at the top, but then freezes to death there. As some others struggle to reach the top, a severe snowstorm strikes the mountain as well as subzero temperatures,and they die from falls or hypothermia. Before long, Brolin reaches the summit, but has to be rescued by helicopter, becoming the expedition's only survivor. He returns home to his wife, Knightley, but has lost both hands and his nose to severe frostbite. The lensing provides eye-popping mountain vistas while all the players render standout performances in this gritty and grueling test of strength and courage. The film was a great success at the box office, earning more than $202 million in its initial release against a budget of $55 million. Song: "Yeh Ladki Haye Allah" (Kabhi Khushi Kabi Gham). *Author's Note*: Actors Gyllenhaal and Brolin trained extensively for their mountain-climbing roles by scaling the Santa Monica Mountains prior to production. The film was shot in Nepal, in and around Everest. The cast and crew suffered from freezing weather during the production, but none were injured. A second unit taking follow-up shots in the preproduction period on the mountain, however, lost sixteen Sherpa guides who were engulfed them in an avalanche. Other films depicting mountain-climbing include **The Abominable Snowman**, 1957 (Yeti); **The Ascent**, 1994; **Aguirre: The Wrath of God**, 1972; **Alive**, 1993 (Andes Mountains); **The Ascent**, 1994: **Auntie Mame**, 1958 (Matterhorn); **Bergwind**, 1963; **Beyond the Edge**, 2014 (Everest; Edmund Hillary and Tenzing Norgay); **Beyond the Rocks**, 1922; **Blind Husbands**, 1919 (Dolomites); **The Blue Light**, 1934; **Bridal Suite**, 1939; **The Bulldog Breed**, 1960; **Canoa**, 1976; **Cast Away**, 2000; **The Challenge**, 1939 (ill-fated 1865 climb on Matterhorn); **Cliffhanger**, 1993; **The Climb**, 1986; **The Climb**, 2002; **Courage Mountain**, 1990; **Death Hunt**, 1981; **Demon of the Himalayas**, 1935; **The Devil's Brigade**, 1968; **Devil's Pass**, 2013; **Drums in the Deep South**, 1951; **The Eiger Sanction**, 1975; **The Endless Knot**, 2007; **Everest**, 2007 (TV miniseries); **A Farewell to Arms**, 1932; **A Farewell to Arms**, 1957; **Final Ascent**, 2000 (made-for-TV); **Five Days One Summer**, 1982 (Swiss Alps); **The**

Domhnall Gleeson and Alicia Vikander in *Ex Machina*, 2015.

Giant of the Dolomites, 1927; **The Girl from the Chartreuse**, 2005; **The Gold Rush**, 1925 (Alaska); **Goodbye, Mr. Chips**, 1939; **Goodbye, Mr. Chips**, 2002; **Gran Paradiso**, 2000; **The Great Leap**, 1927; **The Guns of Navarone**, 1961; **High Ice**, 1980 (made-for-TV); **Himalaya**, 2016; **The Holy Mountain**, 1927; **The Holy Mountain**, 1973; **Into Thin Air: Death on Everest**, 1997 (made-for-TV); **Kleine Scheidegg**, 1937 (Swiss Alps); **K2**, 1992; **Letter from an Unknown Woman**, 1948; **The Longest Day**, 1962 (climbing Pointe du Hoc, a 100-foot cliff, during the 1944 Normandy invasion); **Lost Continent**, 1951; **Lost Horizon**, 1937 (Himalayas); **Love and Bullets**, 1979 (Matterhorn); **Lowlands**, 1981; **Magic Boy**, 1961; **Man Beast**, 1956 (Yeti); **Midnight Eagle**, 2007; **Mount Hakkoda**, 2014 (ill-fated Japanese military exercise in 1902); **The Mountain**, 1956; **The Mountain Calls**, 1938 (ill-fated 1865 climb on Matterhorn); **Mountain Crystal**, 1949; **The Mountaineers**, 1925; **Mountains on Fire**, 1931 (shot in the Dolomites); **Nanga Parbat**, 2010 (ill-fated 1970 climb); **Never Again as Before**, 2005; **Nim's Island**, 2008; **North Face**, 2008 (Eiger in the Bernese Alps); **127 Hours**, 2011; **Operation Edelweiss**, 1954; **The Passage**, 1979 (Pyrenees); **Pathfinder**, 1988; **The Peak Scaler**, 1937; **The Place of the Dead**, 1997; **Premier de Cordee**, 1999 (made-for-TV); **Private Lives**, 1931; **The Rebel**, 1933 (Austrian Alps); **Road to Utopia**, 1946; **S.O.S. Iceberg**, 1934 (Bernina Alps); **Sacred Waters**, 1932; **Sacred Waters**, 1962; **Scream of Stone**, 1991 (Cerro Torre); **Secret Agent**, 1936; **Seven Years in Tibet**, 1997; **She**, 1935; **Shoot to Kill**, 1988; **The Silent Barrier**, 1920; **Snowbound**, 1949; **The Son of the White Mountain**, 1933; **The Squaw Man**, 1914; **Stars at Noon**, 1959; **Storm and Sorrow**, 1990 (made-for-TV); **Storm over Mont Blanc**, 1932; **Struggle for the Matterhorn**, 1929; **Survival Quest**, 1988; **Third Man on the Mountain**, 1959; **The Treasure of the Sierra Madre**, 1948; **Vertical Limit**, 2000; **The Vulture Wally**, 1921; **The Werewolf of London**, 1935 (Tibetan Mountains); **What Lies Above**, 2004; **Where Eagles Dare**, 1969; **White Fang**, 1991 (Alaskan Gold Rush); **The White Hell of Pitz Palu**, 1930; **The White Hell of Pitz Palu**, 1953; **The White Tower**, 1950 (role model for Matterhorn); **Wide Country**, 1962-1963 (TV series; "A Cry from the Mountain," 1963 episode); **A Wife Confesses**, 1961; **With a Friend Like Harry**, 2001 (Matterhorn); and **Yevade Subramanyam**, 2015 (Everest). Images showing intense peril prohibit viewing by children. **p**, Nicky Kentish Barnes, Tim Bevan, Liza Chasin, Eric Fellner, Evan Hayes, Brian Oliver, Tyler Thompson, David Breashears; **d**, Baltasar Kormakur; **cast**, Jake Gyllenhaal, Naomo Mori, John Hawkes, Keira Knightley, Josh Brolin, Jason Clarke, Martin Henderson, Emily Watson, Robin Wright, Sam Worthington, Elizabeth Debicki, Justin Salinger, Ang Phula Sherpa, Thomas M. Wright; **w**, William Nicholson, Simon Beaufoy; **c**, Salvatore Totino; **m**, Dario Marianelli; **ed**, Mick Audsley; **prod d**, Gary Freeman;

Christian Bale as Moses in *Exodus: Gods and Kings,* 2014.

art d, Tom Still, Alessandro Santucci; **set d**, Raffaella Giovannetti; **spec eff**, Richard Van Den Bergh, Jonathan Bullock.

Ex Machina ★★★ 2015; U.K./U.S.; 108m; DNA Films/A24; Color; Science Fiction; Children: Unacceptable (MPAA: R); **BD**; **DVD**. Gleeson is a young computer programmer for the world's most popular Internet search engine. He wins a contest for a one-week visit to the estate of Isaac, the owner of the Internet company. It is a high-security, secluded estate where the only person there besides Isaac is Mizuno, his housemaid, who was hired by Isaac for security reasons because she does not speak English. Isaac tells Gleeson he has built a beautiful humanoid robot called Ava (Vikander), the "machine" of the film's title. Isaac has programmed Vikander with personal information he has pirated from billions of users of his Internet company. Isaac wants Gleeson to test Vikander to see if she is human enough to fall in love. Gleeson agrees and, in daily talks with Vikander, the two become romantically interested in each other. Gleeson is attracted to her robotic body and human-appearing face. She is confined to an apartment where they meet daily, and she tells him she wants to be with him. She says she can trigger power outages, and, during one of them, they could escape together. Isaac overhears this during a power outage while using a battery-operated listening device. Vikander tells Gleeson that Isaac is a liar and cannot be trusted. She got that right, because Isaac is planning to reprogram her and end her charming personality. Gleeson then discovers that Mizuno is also a robot. When Gleeson and Vikander meet next, she cuts the power and plans to escape with Gleeson. The robotic chips are down now, and Mizuno stabs Isaac, but he survives, only to be killed by Vikander. Before dying, Isaac has locked all the doors, and Gleeson is trapped inside Vikander's apartment as she boards a helicopter to escape and enter the world, pretending to be a human, although she remains a robot to the core of her hard drive. This eerie tale is well written and presents some stunning performances from the cast, its programmed characters reminiscent of another superior science fiction outing, **Blade Runner**, 1982. The film did well at the box office, earning more than $37 million in its initial release against a budget of $15 million. Songs/Music: "Piano Sonata No. 21 (Franz Schubert), "Unaccompanied Cello Suite No. 1" (Johann Sebastian Bach), "Bunsen Burner" (Anthony Tombling, Jr.), "Ghostbusters" (Ray Erskine), "Enola Gay" (Andrew McCluskey), "Get Down Saturday Night" (Oliver Cheatham), "Husbands" (Thompson, Hassan, Milton, and Camille Berthomier). Graphic nudity, gutter language, sexual references and violence prohibit viewing by children. **p**, Andrew Macdonald, Allon Reich; **d&w**, Alex Garland; **cast**, Domhnall Gleeson, Oscar Isaac, Alicia Vikander, Corey Johnson, Sonoya Mizuno, Claire Selby, Symara Templeman, Gana Bayarsaikhan, Tiffany Pisani; **c**, Rob Hardy; **m**, Geoff Barrow, Ben Salis-

bury; **ed**, Mark Day; **prod d**, Mark Digby; **art d**, Katrina Mackay, Denis Schnegg; **set d**, Michelle Day; **spec eff**, Richard Conway.

Exodus: Gods and Kings ★★★ 2014; U.K./U.S./Spain; 142m; Chernin Entertainment/FOX; Color; Biblical Drama; Children: Unacceptable (MPAA: R); **BD**; **DVD**. Superb retelling of the story of Moses and the exodus of the Hebrews from Egypt is depicted in sweeping detail, and where outstanding performances permeate this memorable saga. Set in 1300 B.C. Egypt, Moses, who is played by Bale, is an army general and a member of the royal family. He is sent to the city of Pithom to meet with Mendelsohn, a viceroy who oversees the Hebrew slaves. Arriving there, Bale is appalled by the terrible living conditions among the captives. He meets Kingsley, who reveals to Bale his true heritage, that he is the child of Hebrew parents who was sent by his sister Miriam (Fitzgerald), to be raised by Pharaoh's daughter. The story is overheard and reported to Mendelsohn. Pharaoh Turturro (Seti I) dies shortly after Bale returns to Memphis, and Edgerton becomes the new Pharaoh (Rameses II, 1303-1213 B.C.). Mendelsohn arrives to reveal Bale's true identity, but Fitzgerald denies being Moses' sister. Bale then reveals that he really is a Hebrew and Edgerton sends him into exile. In the desert, Bale meets a woman, Valverde (Zipporah), and her father, Jethro (Malikyan). Moses becomes a shepherd, marries Valverde, and they have a son, Hewetson. Nine years later, Bale is told that God resides on Mount Horeb (Mount Sinai) and he is drawn to the mountain when chasing some sheep up its slopes. He is engulfed in a mudslide and buried except for his face. He sees a burning bush and a boy named Malak (Andrews), Bale believing Andrews to be an angel or messenger of God. He is told by Andrews to go forth and save the Hebrews from Egyptian slavery. Bale reveals his past to Zipporah and states that God has ordained him to save his people. Bale returns to Egypt and trains the Hebrew slaves how to fight, but, after Edgerton threatens to kill Hebrew slaves at random, Bale gives himself up. The arrogant Edgerton dismisses him as harmless, believing Bale to be nothing more than an annoyance. When Edgerton refuses to release the Hebrews, Bale, as instructed by Andrews, then threatens that ten plagues will fall on Egypt unless Edgerton frees the Hebrews. Plagues do fall on Egypt, but Edgerton refuses Bale's demand. The plagues, from locusts to burning hailstorms, all but ruin the Egyptian economy and bring widespread starvation and unrest. Edgerton comes to believe that Bale's God has, indeed, worked these hardships upon Egypt, and while ruminating at night in his palace, threatens God with his own plague, insisting that his own powers as Pharaoh can match and overcome that of any god. He states that all the first-born of the Hebrews will be put to death. Bale learns of this through Andrew and is told to warn the Hebrews. Bale has the Hebrews mark the doors of their houses with the blood of lambs, so that the Tenth Plague, Death itself, will pass over these dwellings, and strike, instead the first-born of all Egyptian households. The plague sweeps through the city and Egyptian first-born die, including Edgerton's own son. Stunned that the God of Israel has proven to be all powerful, Edgerton, carrying his mummified son in his arms, goes to Bale and tells him and all the Hebrews to go, to leave Egypt and not return. As Bale leads the Hebrews from Egypt, he is told that Edgerton has changed his mind and is now pursuing the Hebrews with his army, riding chariots and horses, and intent upon recapturing and enslaving the Hebrews once more. Bale arrives at the Red Sea, realizing that his way is blocked. He then hurls his old Egyptian sword into the sea and then sees the waters of the sea begin to recede. He calls out to the Hebrews to follow him as he wades into the receding waters and all do. The waters recede as the Hebrew fugitives cross the dry bed of the sea, only to see in the distance the arriving forces of Edgerton. Bale and a small group of mounted Hebrews then ride back toward the approaching Egyptians, but they know they are no match for Edgerton's powerful forces. As the fugitives reach the far bank of the Red Sea, Bale and his followers see a huge wave rushing forward to recover the bed of the sea. Edgerton and his forces rush forward, but then turn back when seeing the oncoming wall of water, which crashes forward, engulfing the Egyptians and destroying them. Bale manages to survive the rush of water, rejoining his people. On the far bank, Edgerton wanders along the coastline, seeing nothing but the corpses of his troops. Bale leads the Hebrews back to Midian where he reunites with Zipporah and his son. At Mount Sinai, as the wayward Hebrews prepare to worship the Golden Calf, Bale climbs the mountain and, at the instructions of Andrew, chisels on the stone the Ten Commandments, taking these Heavenly edicts to his people where Bale tells them to love each other and God and to worship only God. He is seen riding in a cart with the Ten Commandments (the Ark) as he and his followers search for their promised land. Finally seen as an old man, Bale sees in the crowd of Hebrews following the cart the boy Andrews, who smiles at him to end this superlative biblical saga. Scott directs this epic with his usual great skill and attention to historical detail. Unlike the glossy images as earlier presented by Cecil B. DeMille in his silent and talking versions of the story, Scott presents a very gritty image of that ancient era, one where poverty and filth is everywhere and all but the royal occupants of the Pharaoh's palace, struggle to survive incredible hardships in their crude and primitive lifestyles. The scenes of the plagues are marvels to behold, from the bloodying of the Nile to the swarms of insects and death-dealing diseases. Most spectacular is the crossing of the Hebrews of the Red Sea. The waters are not parted in an instant, but slowly recede as they are invaded by wading Hebrews led by Bale. This is where Scott employs the theory often held that a low tide allowed the fugitives to escape their pursuers, who were then engulfed, as Scott shows with titanic images of onrushing walls of water, when the sea's high tide returned. The acting from all, particularly Bale and Edgerton, is riveting from the first frame to the last, and the script faithfully and intelligently follows the Old Testament's passages of Exodus to describe this unforgettable story. All of the production values, from sets and costumes, to the startling photography and moving score, are excellent. The film was a box office success, earning more than $248 million in its initial release against a budget of $140 million. *Author's Note*: Scott stated he positioned the parting of the Red Sea in accordance with what he believed happened at that time, a tsunami that occurred about 3000 B.C., following an underwater earthquake off the Italian coast. The director implies in these stunning scenes that the parting of the water was more of a natural phenomenon than through an instant miracle, but that parting of the sea at the very moment the Hebrews needed just such a phenomenon is nevertheless nothing short of that miracle. A great deal of computer enhancement was employed in the scenes showing the Exodus and the Red Sea scenes, where digital special effects literally provided 400,000 individuals cross that sea. The film was shot on location in England, in Morocco, Almeria and, for the Red Sea sequences, Fuerteventura, an island in the Canary Islands off the coast of Africa. Many other actors have profiled Moses in many other films, including **After Six Days**, 1920 (Guido Guiducci); **Are We Civilized?**, 1934 (Alin Cavin); **BBC Sunday-Night Theatre**, 1950-1959 (TV series; "The Green Pastures," 1958 episode: James Clarke); **The Bible**, 2013 (TV miniseries, "Exodus," 2013 episode: Joe Forte as young Moses; William Houston as older Moses); **The Cradle of God**, 1926 (Victor Vina); **Exodus**, 2008 (Jack and Stephen Greenhough as Baby Moses); **Greatest Heroes of the Bible**, 1978-1979 (TV series; several episodes: John Marley); **The Green Pastures**, 1936 (Frank H. Wilson); **The Green Pastures**, 1959 (made-for-TV; Frederick O'Neal); **Herod and Marianne**, 1965 (made-for TV; Wolf Schlamminger); **History of the World: Part I**, 1981 (Mel Brooks); **In the Beginning**, 2000 (made-for-TV; Billy Campbell); **Moise**, 1984 (made-for-TV; Samuel Ramey); **Moon of Israel**, 1924 (Henry Mar); **Moses**, 1995 (made-for-TV; Ben Kingsley); **Moses and Aaron**, 1975 (Gunter Reich); **Moses the Lawgiver**, 1974 (TV miniseries; Burt Lancaster as adult Moses, William Lancaster as young Moses); **Moses und Aaron**, 2006 (made-for-TV; Franz Grundheber); **Moses and Aaron**, 2009 (made-for-TV; Dale Duesing); **The Old Testament Scriptures**, 1958 (TV series; Thayer Roberts); **The Prince of Egypt**, 1998 (Val Kilmer voiceover;

Edward Burns and Connie Britton in *The Fitzgerald Family Christmas*, 2012.

Amick Byram singing voice); **Son of God**, 2014 (William Houston); **The Story of Mankind**, 1957 (Francis X. Bushman); **The Ten Commandments**, 1923 (Theodore Roberts); **The Ten Commandments**, 1956 (Charlton Heston); **The Ten Commandments**, 2006 (made-for-TV; Dougray Scott); **The Ten Commandments**, 2007 (Christian Slater voiceover); and **The Ten Commandments: The Musical**, 2006 (Val Kilmer). Violence prohibits viewing by children. **p**, Ridley Scott, Peter Chernin, Mark Huffam, Michael Schaefer, Jenno Topping, Adam Somner; **d**, Ridley Scott; **cast**, Christian Bale, Joel Edgerton, Aaron Paul, Sigourney Weaver, Ben Kingsley, John Turturro, Indira Varma, Ben Mendelsohn, Maria Valverde, Emun Elliott, Kevork Malikyan, Anton Alexander, Isaac Andrews; **w**, Steven Zaillian (based on a story by Bill Collage, Adam Cooper); **c**, Dariusz Wolski (3-D); **m**, Alberto Iglesias; **ed**, Billy Rich; **prod d**, Arthur Max; **art d**, Marc Homes; **set d**, Celia Bobak; **spec eff**, Neil Corbould, Victoria Stokes, Pau Costa.

The Face of Love ★★★ 2014; U.S.; 92m; Mockingbird Pictures/IFC Films; Color; Drama/Romance; Children: Unacceptable (MPAA: PG-13); **BD**; **DVD**. Pleasant romance has Bening as a widow still grieving over the death of her beloved husband five year earlier. One day while visiting an art gallery she sees a man, Harris, who looks exactly like her late husband. She returns to the gallery again and again, but does not see him, until one day he is there again. She discovers he teaches art at a local college and joins the class, but makes some foolish mistakes. Harris, nevertheless, becomes intrigued by her, and they soon begin a romance. Bening is, however, emotionally disturbed and unable or just not ready to have a healthy relationship with Harris. She does not tell him he looks just like her late husband, and even hides him from her friends and family because she doesn't want anything to stop her from symbolically repossessing her dead husband in the form of Harris. The take a trip to Mexico, but Harris realizes that it is the very place where Bening spent her best moments with her former husband, his own lookalike. When he confronts her with this, Bening races to the sea in a rage. Thinking she intends to commit suicide, Harris rescues her and they spend the night together comforting each other. The relationship, however, appears hopeless and both part. A year later, Bening receives an invitation to attend an art showing of Harris' work. When she arrives, she learns that Harris has died of a heart condition he had kept from Bening. The centerpiece of the show is Harris' portrait of himself with Bening, one titled "The Face of Love." **p**, Bonnie Curtis, Julie Lynn, Jonathan McCoy; **d**, Arie Posin; **cast**, Annette Bening, Ed Harris, Robin Williams, Amy Brenneman, Jess Weixler, Linda Park, Deana Molle, Jeffrey Vincent Parise, Kim Farris, **w**, Posin, Matthew McDuffie; **c**, Anto-

Denzel Washington in *Flight*, 2012.

nio Riestra; **m**, Marcelo Zarvos; **ed**, Matt Maddox; **prod d**, Jeannine Claudia Oppewall; **art d**, Lisa Clark; **set d**, Meg Everist; **spec eff**, Josh Hakian, Shawn Schminke.

The Family ★★★ 2013; U.S./France; 111m; EuropaCorp/Relativity Media; Color; Comedy/Crime Drama; Children: Acceptable (MPAA: R); **BD**; **DVD**. After testifying against mob leaders, De Niro, a Mafia boss, goes undercover in the witness protection program. He and his wife, Pfeiffer, and their daughter, Agron, and son, D'Leo, are relocated to a sleepy town in France. Jones, a CIA agent, tries to keep them in line, but they can't help but revert to old anti-social habits. They blow their cover by handling their problems "the family way" as Pfeiffer burns down a local grocery store after a clerk insults her French-American accent. D'Leo is accused of corruption, theft, and bribery at school, and Agron beats up a French boy, who may just have accidentally touched her arm without her permission. These and other transgressions lead to their former Mafia associates tracking them down, which gives Jones more work and headaches than he bargained for. Old scores are settled violently in a sometimes darkly humorous film that sees a wild climax where five hitmen are outlandishly dispatched by De Niro and his family. The mob boss and his family members then once more go undercover with new identities and at a new location, a nomadic condition that promises to routinely reoccur, given the uncontrollable and tempestuous personalities of these strange fugitives. CIA operative Jones, who has to put up with all this antic mayhem, is exceptional while playing a frustrated protective chaperone to a bunch of certifiable cuckoos. The film did well at the box office, earning more than $78 million in its initial release against a budget of $30 million. Songs: "Shine Brightly" (Don Boyette, Brittany Butler, Ted Silbert), "Mosh Pit Match" (Jono Brown, Kevin Chown, Jeff Kollman), "OC Punk" (Ed X Ray Dog), "A Hymn of Peace" (Richard Harvey), "Doce Doce" (Alfredo Bongusto, Loris Boresti), "This Is My Club" (Isaac Petit-Frere, Reginald Marquis Wilks), "O.C. Boy" (Timothy Stithem, David Jones), "After Hours" (Jim Crew), "The Greatest" (Chan Marshall), "Genius of Love" (Tina Weymouth, Chris Frantz, Adrian Belew, Stephen Stanley), "Life or Death" (Jono Brown, Jeff Kollman), "Coccinella" (Arrigo Riccardo Agosti, Piera Scoffici), "Me and My Baby" (Don Cavalli, Doncalli-Vincent Talpaert), "New York, I Love You But You're Bringing Me Down" (James Jeremiah Murphy), "Reflections" (Stanley Myers), "Rags to Riches" (Richard Adler, Jerry Ross), "Nurture" (Chris Allen), "Head of the Family" (David Gosnell), "Clint Eastwood" (Damon Albarn, Jamie Hewlett, Teren Jones), "To Binge" (Damon Albarn, Jamie Hewlett, Frederik Daniel Wallin, Yukimi Eleanora Nagano, Hakan Wirenstrand, Erik Oskar Bodin), "Pop Musik" (Robin Scott). Violence, gutter language and brief sexuality prohibit viewing by children. **p**, Luc Besson, Ryan Kavanaugh, Virginie Besson-Silla, Martin Scorsese, Jason Beckman; **d**, Besson; **cast**, Robert De Niro, Michelle Pfeiffer, Tommy Lee Jones, Dianna Agron, John D'Leo, Dominic Chianese, Vincent Pastore, Domenick Lombardozzi, Joseph Perrino, David Belle; **w**, Besson, Michael Caleo (based on the book by Tonino Benacquista); **c**, Thierry Arbogast; **m**, Evgueni Galperine, Sacha Galperine; **ed**, Julien Rey; **prod d**, Hugues Tissandier; **art d**, Gilles Boillot, Eric Dean, Dominique Moisan, Stephane Robuchon, Thierry Zemmour; **set d**, Cherish Magennis, Evelyne Tissandier; **spec eff**, Kevin Zack.

Far from the Madding Crowd ★★★★ 2015; U.K./U.S.; 119m; BBC Films/Fox Searchlight; Color; Drama/Romance; Children: Unacceptable (MPAA: PG-13); **BD**; **DVD**; **IV**. Superlative production of the fourth film version of the Hardy novel sees beautiful and independent Mulligan living on her aunt's farm in Dorset in 1870s Victorian England. Schoenaerts, a handsome new neighbor, sees her riding her horse and instantly falls in love with her. He proposes marriage, but she turns him down and says she is too independent and he would soon grow to dislike her. Schoenaerts has used all his money to invest in a sheep farm, but disaster strikes when a new sheepdog chases his entire flock off of a cliff, forcing him to become a migrant worker. Mulligan's rich uncle dies and leaves her a large farm in nearby Weatherbury. Schoenaerts goes to that farm just as its barn catches fire. He puts out the fire and Mulligan hires him as a sheepherder. The romantic plot now thickens when Sturridge, a dashing British army sergeant arrives upon the scene after his fiancée has jilted him at their wedding ceremony because he inadvertently had gone to the wrong church for the nuptials. Meanwhile, Sheen, Mulligan's neighbor, who is a very wealthy bachelor but older than she, becomes interested in her and proposes. Mulligan turns him down because she does not feel attracted to him. Schoenaerts tries to win Mulligan again, but they argue and she fires him. Her sheep become poisoned eating some bad plants and are dying of bloat, so she sends for Schoenaerts and begs him to come back. He returns to her farm, saves some of her sheep, and remains as her sheepherder. Next, Mulligan falls for Sturridge, who is very handsome in his soldier's uniform, and he tells her he is of a noble family. Schoenaerts tries to warn Mulligan that Sturridge is really a fortune-hunter and gambler, not wealthy or an honorable man, but she doesn't believe him. Sturridge makes love to Mulligan and proposes marriage, and this time she accepts. On the night of their marriage, at a party at Mulligan's farm, Sturridge tells her workers that he is now boss of the farm, not Mulligan. A fierce storm erupts on the wedding night that threatens the farm's crop, but Sturridge is too drunk to be of any help, so Schoenaerts tries to save the harvest. Mulligan helps him in the rain storm and admits she was a fool to fall for Sturridge. The callous Sturridge, while drunk, tells Mulligan that Temple, his former fiancée, was more beautiful than she and that he still loves Temple. Sturridge then sees Temple in town and she is pregnant with his baby. He promises to find her a home and asks Mulligan for some money for that purpose, but she refuses, saying she needs the money for the farm. Temple and the baby die in childbirth, and Sturridge admits to Mulligan that Temple means more to him in death than she does or ever will. Despondent, Sturridge goes into the ocean and drowns himself. Mulligan is left with her debts and may lose her farm. Sheen offers to buy it and merge her farm with his, and again proposes. Sheen throws a Christmas party at his estate and Sturridge surprisingly appears. The strutting imposter, who has faked his drowning, now demands money and insists that Mulligan sell her farm and go off with him. Sheen is enraged and shoots and kills Sturridge, then is arrested and sent to prison. Schoenaerts tells Mulligan he has decided to go to America, and leaves her and the farm. Mulligan realizes she has loved Schoenaerts all along. She goes after him and they embrace and kiss, then return to the farm together where they plan their future. Mishaps, misfortunes and misadventures permeate this melodramatic tale, but its complex and plague-beset characters are nevertheless brought to vivid life by a talented cast, who sustain viewer interest throughout while managing to charge this dusty tale with great energy. Much of that achievement should be credited to Vinterberg's firm and careful direction, which is greatly aided by stunning visuals by cinematographer Christensen. The film did well at the box office, earning more than $30 million in its initial release. The story was previously filmed as a silent in 1915, and a talkie in 1967 (starring Julie Christie), as well as a 1998 television movie. Song: "Let No Man Steal Your Thyme." Sexuality and violence prohibit viewing by children. **p**, Andrew Macdonald, Allon Reich, Anita Overland; **d**, Thomas Vinterberg; **cast**, Carey Mulligan, Matthias Schoenaerts, Tom Sturridge, Michael Sheen, Juno Temple, Tilly Vosburgh, Sam Phillips, Jessica Barden, Bradley Hall, Hilton McRae; **w**, David Nicholls (based on the novel by Thomas Hardy); **c**, Charlotte Bruus Christensen; **m**, Craig Armstrong; **ed**, Claire Simpson; **prod d**, Kave Quinn; **art d**, Julia Castle, Tim Blake, Hannah Moseley; **set d**, Niamh Coulter; **spec eff**, James Smith, Mark Holt.

A Field in England ★★★ 2013; U.K.; 90m; Film4/Drafthouse Films; B&W; Drama/Horror; Children: Unacceptable; **BD**; **DVD**. This earthy tale is set during the British Civil War in 17th-Century England, and where Shearsmith, an alchemist's assistant, flees from his strict commander, Barratt. Deserting battle, Shearsmith meets Pope and two other army deserters, Ferdinando and Glover. Together they leave the battlefield and search for an ale house. They encounter Smiley, an Irishman Shearsmith had been earlier sent to apprehend for the theft of his master's works and literature. The manipulative Smiley quickly takes charge of the group and tells them of a treasure hidden somewhere in a nearby field. After using Shearsmith to locate the treasure, Smiley tells Ferdinando and Glover to dig for it and leaves Pope to supervise. Ferdinando falls under the influence of hallucinogens while digging, and attacks Glover. Pope attempts to intervene and accidentally shoots Glover to death. Pope is forced to finish digging by himself while the others slip away unnoticed. Pope discovers that the "treasure" is nothing more than a skull. He berates Smiley who then kills him. Smiley then pursues Shearsmith and Ferdinando, who leave with Pope's weapons and return to their army camp. As their unit prepares for an attack, Glover reappears very much alive and reveals their location to Smiley. Smiley then shoots Ferdinando in the stomach, but Ferdinando returns fire and shoots Smiley in the foot. Glover then charges Smiley with a pike, but Smiley kills him with his last shot. Shearsmith takes advantage of the situation to kill Smiley and then buries his comrades in the treasure hole. Wearing Smiley's clothes, he gathers his master's stolen belongings and returns to a hedgerow where he first met Pope, Ferdinando, and Glover. As he hears battle sounds, Shearsmith wades through the hedge and is astonished to find Ferdinando and Glover waiting for him. They explain that they had all fallen victims to psychedelic traumas from the field which is magnetic. Weird and eerie, this film was shot in black-and-white, which lends visual credence to its manic mayhem and where characters routinely die only to resurface again (the weaponry of that era being very undependable in ultimately dispatching anyone). The film saw limited distribution and did little box office, but it nevertheless remains an intriguing experiment. Songs: "Chernobyl" (Benjamin John Power, Blanck Mass), "Metallic Fields" (Martin Pavey, Ben Wheatley), "Lady Anne Bothwell's Lament" (traditional). Excessive violence prohibits viewing by children. **p**, Claire Jones, Andrew Starke; **d**, Ben Wheatley; **cast**, Julian Barratt, Peter Ferdinando, Richard Glover, Ryan Pope, Reece Shearsmith, Michael Smiley, Sara Dee; **w**, Amy Jump; **c**, Laurie Rose; **m**, Jim Williams; **ed**, Wheatley, Jump; **prod d**, Andy Kelly; **spec eff**, Mark Holt, Dan Martin.

Field of Lost Shoes ★★★ 2014; U.S.; 96m; Brookwell-McNamara Entertainment/Bosch Media; War Drama; Children: Unacceptable (MPAA: PG-13); **BD**; **DVD**. Stirring tale is based on true events at the Battle of New Market, Virginia, on May 15, 1864, during the American Civil War, (1861-1865). Union army Lt. Gen. Ulysses S. Grant (1822-1885), played by Skerritt, orders troops to advance into Virginia's Shenandoah

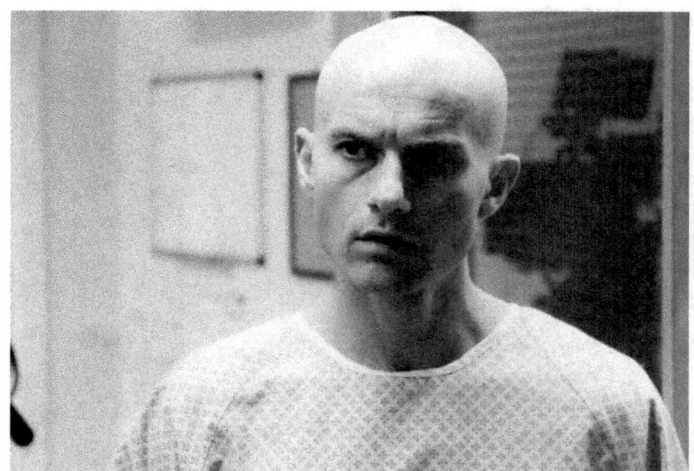

James Badge Dale in *Flight*, **2012**.

Valley to fight Confederate forces near the town of New Market. Confederate forces are small compared to the advancing Union army, so Maj. Gen. John C. Breckenridge, played by Isaacs, reluctantly orders the Corps of Cadets at the nearby Virginia Military Institute (VMI) to help defend the valley. The cadets are patriotic teenagers eager to defend the area. The battle takes place in a muddy field in which many of the institute's cadets lose their shoes. Before the battle, we learn that the institute's cadets hold no negative feelings against blacks and defend the school's beloved black cook, played by David, from persecution. They also rescue a young slave woman, who is trapped under a fallen carriage. The drama is relieved by a love story in which one of the cadets, Lloyd-Jones, becomes infatuated with local girl Mouser, whose mother, Holly, when asked after the battle if a wounded soldier is her son, replies: "They're all my sons." Arquette plays a Union colonel who shouts, "God bless the Pennsylvania boys, holding fast!" The story is moving and full of the esprit de corps exampled by those playing the indomitable cadets (revered as heroes to this day at VMI), and the battle sequences are particularly well choreographed. *Author's Note*: Ten VMI cadets were killed during the battle and forty-seven others were wounded. Their sacrifice contributed to Confederate forces being able to drive the Union soldiers out of the valley. The film was shot on location at the Virginia Military Institute, and at Powhatan and Lexington, Virginia. Violence and thematic material prohibit viewing by children. **p**, Thomas Farrell, Dave Kennedy, Kevin R. Hershberger, Joey Paul Jensen; **d**, Sean McNamara; **cast**, David Arquette, Jason Isaacs, Nolan Gould, Lauren Holly, Keith David, Tom Skerritt, Luke Benward, Zach Roerig, Gale Harold, Josh Zuckerman, Mary Mouser, Max Lloyd-Jones; **w**, Thomas Farrell, David Kennedy; **c**, Brad Shield; **m**, Frederik Wiedmann; **ed**, Jeff Canavan; **prod d**, Dawn R. Ferry; **art d**, Jeremiah Hornbaker; **set d**, Eric Hunsaker; **spec eff**, Brian Merrick.

50 to 1 ★★★ 2014; U.S.; 150m; Ten Furlongs; Color; Drama/Comedy; Children: Unacceptable (MPAA: PG-13); **BD**; **DVD**. Some misfit cowboys from New Mexico take a journey to the Kentucky Derby with their crooked-footed racehorse. Based on an inspiring true story of Mine That Bird, the ambitious boys face a series of misadventures on their way to Churchill Downs, then become underdogs as they and their horse compete with the world's racing elite. Their odds are the film's title. But Mine That Bird wins, despite the odds and becomes the 2009 Kentucky Derby winner in a stunning upset. Kane plays the horse's owner, while Ulrich plays its trainer in a good old-fashioned tale that has some very exciting moments and considerable humor. Songs: "Leavin' on Your Mind" (Lonny Ray Gregory). Suggestive material and a bar brawl prohibit viewing by children. **p&d**, Jim Wilson; **cast**, Skeet Ulrich, Christian Kane, William Devane, Madelyn Deutch, Todd Lowe, David

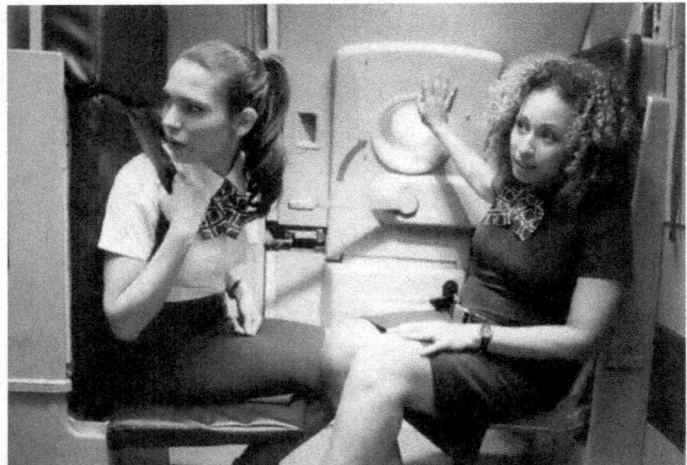

Nadine Velazquez and Tamara Tunie in *Flight*, 2012.

Atkinson, Calvin Borel, Bruce Wayne Eckelman, Hugo Perez, Eloy Casados; **w**, Wilson, Faith Conroy; **c**, Tim Suhrstedt; **m**, William Ross; **ed**, Ben Callahan; **prod d**, Guy Barnes; **set d**, Wendy Ozols-Barnes; **spec eff**, Randy E. Moore, Donnie Dean.

Fill the Void ★★★ 2012; Israel; 90m; Avi Chai Fund/Sony; Color; Drama; Children: Unacceptable (MPAA: PG); **BD**; **DVD**. This graceful and gentle film begins with Yaron, a devout eighteen-year-old Israeli girl living in Tel Aviv who looks forward to an arranged marriage with a young man she likes. However, Raz, her older sister, dies in childbirth, and Yaron is pressured to marry Klein, her late sister's husband. Unfortunately for her, it is futile to declare her independence, which is not an option in the Orthodox Haredi Jewish community where religious law, tradition, and the rabbi's word are absolute. The marriage is delayed so as not to have to deal with an empty house so soon after Raz's death. Klein begins to regularly bring his newborn son to the bereaved family's house where Yaron cares for him. Complications arise from the marriage delay and Klein thinks he may instead marry a woman he knows in Belgium. But Yaron, whose parents now agree to a marriage date set for her and Klein, agree that it may be best for the newborn boy that Yaron and Klein marry. However, Tal, the rabbi, sees that Yaron is merely agreeing to marry Klein to please her parents, so he refuses to condone the marriage. Time passes and Yaron eventually grows to love Klein. She reveals this to the rabbi and he agrees to marry the couple. The film ends with their wedding. Yaron and Klein are standouts in their sensitive roles and Burshtein directs with a careful eye to Jewish Orthodoxy, but nevertheless presents a touching tale. Song: "If I Forget Thee Jerusalem" (Yitzhak Azulay). (In Hebrew; English subtitles.) Mild thematic elements and brief smoking prohibit viewing by children. **p**, Assaf Amir; **d&w**; Rama Burshtein; **cast**, Hadas Yaron, Yiftach Klein, Irit Sheleg, Chayim Sharir, Razia Israeli, Hila Feldman, Renana Raz, Yael Tal, Michael David Weigl, Ido Samuel, Neta Moran, Melech Thal; **c**, Asaf Sudri; **m**, Yitzhak Azulay; **ed**, Sharon Elovic; **art d**, Uri Aminov.

The Fitzgerald Family Christmas ★★★ 2012; U.S.; 99m; Marlboro Road Gang Productions/Tribeca Film; Color; Drama; Children: Unacceptable (MPAA: PG-13); **BD**; **DVD**. The adult siblings of the Fitzgerald family prepare for their estranged father, Lauter, to return home for Christmas for the first time since walking out on them twenty years earlier. Edward Burns is the head of the family with six siblings. He runs the family restaurant and keeps urging the others to visit their mother, Gillette, with whom he lives. His older brother, McGlone, is about to propose to a much younger woman who it is obvious all wrong for him, while one of his younger sisters is involved with a man twice her age and who also may be wrong for her. Another sister, Heather Burns, has just broken up her own marriage by cheating with a young gardener, while Guiry, a younger brother, is just out of drug rehabilitation. Lauter wants to see his family again and has a good reason why. At Yuletide, the family is in turmoil as Lauter's wife and grown children bicker about forgiving him as they struggle with their decision to welcome him back as head of the family. Well directed and finely acted by the entire cast, this drama sustains interest throughout as the viewer anxiously awaits Lauter's approval and place within this sometimes troubled family. Songs: "Toyland" (1903; music: Victor Herbert; lyrics Glenn MacDonough); "Away in a Manger" (1895; music: William J. Kirkpatrick; 1885; lyrics [hymn]: Martin Luther). Mature themes prohibit viewing by children. **p**, Edward Burns, Michael McGlone, Aaron Lubin, William Rexer, Nicolas Newbold; **d&w**, Burns; **cast**, Burns, Kerry Bishe, Connie Britton, Heather Burns, Dara Coleman, Brian d'Arcy James, Marsha Dietlein, Noah Emmerich, Caitlin FitzGerald, Anita Gillette, Tom Guiry, Ed Lauter; **c**, William Rexer; **m**, P.T. Walkley; **ed**, Janet Gaynor; **spec eff**, Vico Sharabani, Lynzi Grant.

Flight ★★★ 2012; U.S.; 138m; ImageMovers/PAR; Color; Drama; Children: Unacceptable (MPAA: R); **BD**; **DVD**. Absorbing tale begins with computer airline pilot Washington. After a night of drugs, drinking, and sex, he is flying a plane from Orlando, Florida, to Atlanta, Georgia, when he has a drink of vodka and orange juice and the plane soon starts to fly erratically. He crashes the plane, saving the lives of 96 of the 102 people on board, but he is injured. While recuperating in a hospital, Washington learns that he may face criminal charges because his blood test showed that he was intoxicated with alcohol and cocaine while piloting the crashed plane. An investigation begins and Washington denies that substances impaired his ability to safely fly the plane, but giving up his addictions is not easy for him. If convicted of alcohol, drug, and manslaughter charges, he could be sent to prison. Goodman, his drug dealer, sneaks him out of the hospital, and Washington drives to his late father's farm where he dumps all the alcohol he has. He then allows Reilly, a young woman recovering from a drug overdose, to stay at the farm. The night before the hearing, Washington drinks and the next morning he passes out drunk, but is revived with some cocaine. At the hearing, Leo, an airline union lawyer, explains that a damaged elevator assembly jackscrew was the primary cause of the plane malfunctioning and that Washington was a hero for crash-landing the plane at an airfield. But Washington, so as not to implicate anyone else, admits he was intoxicated from the vodka-orange juice drink and that he also is intoxicated at the hearing. Washington is sentenced to prison and, after thirteen months of a five-year sentence, tells a support group of fellow inmates that he is glad to be sober and that he did the right thing in admitting his guilt at the hearing. He says he has lost his piloting license, but has not lost his way. Washington, who has had some hit-and-miss performances in recent years, provides a self-examining and sensitive character who sustains interest throughout, and he is ably supported by a strong and talented cast. The film was successful at the box office, earning more than $161.8 million in its initial release against a budget of more than $30 million. Songs: "Alcohol" (Stephen Duffy, Steven Page), "Feelin' Alright" (Dave Mason), "Under the Bridge" (Flea, John Frusciante, Anthony Kiedis, Chad Smith), "Sweet Jane" (Lou Reed), "Sympathy for the Devil" and "Gimme Shelter" (Mick Jagger, Keith Richards), "Ain't No Sunshine" (Bill Withers), "Never Get Out of These Blues Alive" (John Lee Hooker), "What's Going On" (Renaldo Benson, Alfred Cleveland, Marvin Gaye), "Going Down" (Don Nix), "With a Little Help from My Friends" (John Lennon, Paul McCartney). Drug and alcohol abuse, gutter language, sexuality, nudity and intense action prohibit viewing by children. **p**, Robert Zemeckis, Laurie MacDonald, Walter F. Parkes, Jack Rapke, Steve Starkey; **d**, Zemeckis; **cast**, Denzel Washington, Kelly Reilly, John Goodman, Nadine Velazquez, Brian Geraghty, Bruce Greenwood, Don Cheadle, Melissa Leo, Conor O'Neill, Tamara Tunie, Ravi Kapoor; **w**, John Gatins; **c**, Don Burgess; **m**, Alan Silvestri; **ed**, Jeremiah O'Driscoll; **prod d**, Nelson Coates; **art d**, David Lazan;

set d, James Edward Ferrell, Jr.; spec eff, Michael Lantieri, Andrew Miller, Ian C. McArthur.

Flowers for Fannie ★★★ 2013; U.S.; 101m; Mainstreet Productions; Vivendi Visual Entertainment; Color; Drama; Children: Unacceptable; **BD**; **DVD**. Binkley is Fannie Fairchild, an elderly woman who cannot recover emotionally from the death of her husband who was killed in World War I (1914-1918). She has found no love in her life since his death and, now facing her own mortality, realizes there is no one to put flowers on her grave. Several attempts to hire someone for the task fail because she is rude to people. She eventually finds herself under the care of Wilharm, a young woman who is both pretty and friendly. Binkley must decide to either accept love from the caregiver or continue the lonely life she has lived for so many years. While this well-enacted film is too mature for children, it is nevertheless a good faith-based Christian film. **p**, Fred Wilharm; **d&w**, Sharon Wilharm; **cast**, Patricia Binkley, Brittany Wilharm, PattiNicole Wheeler, Robert Baker Jr., David Chattam, Roger D. Eldridge, Jonathan Everett, Rob Wilds, Danny Actchley, Lois Berg.

Focus ★★★ 2015; U.S.; 107m; UNIV; Color; Comedy/Drama/Romance; Children: Unacceptable (MPAA: PG-13); **BD**; **DVD**; **IV**. This entertaining adventure begins with con artist Smith going to a nightclub where he meets beautiful Robbie, who promptly seduces him. Robbie is playing the old Badger Game, one where she pretends they have been caught lovemaking by her jealous husband. Will advises the couple never to lose focus when faced with unexpected situations. Robbie convinces Smith to be her mentor. He agrees and takes her to New Orleans where he introduces her to his associates, all experienced sharpers who operated sophisticated confidence swindles. Three years pass and Smith is working for Santoro, a billionaire motor sport team owner in Buenos Aires. Smith pretends to be a member of a rival team in a con game to win a big race. Smith and Robbie are by now romantically involved with each other. After some more con game misadventures, Smith's lung is punctured and McRaney, an associate of Robbie's, takes Smith's money while he is in the hospital. Robbie, however, saves the day and Smith's money and they leave the hospital together for what might lead to the altar as they keep their focus lovingly upon each other. Smith and Robbie give top-notch performances that overcome a somewhat lightweight script, and the on-location lush lensing of the Argentina landscape is often breathtaking. The film did well at the box office, earning almost $160 million in its initial release against a budget of more than $50 million. Songs: "I'm a Manchild" (Bruno Hovart); "Small Time" (Dale Jennings, Daniel Hastie, Joel Bowers, Sean O'Shea, Sergio Rios, Stewart Killen); "Sofa Rockers" (Wolfgang Frisch, Michael Holzgruber, Markus Kienzl, Wolfgang Schloegl); "Please!" (Alexander Ebert, Jade Allyson Castrinos, Nicolo Joseph Aglietti); "Buck It Like a Horse" (Corey Henry); "Let Me Do My Thing" (Glen Andrews, Philip Frazier III, Tyrus Chapman); "Wind It Up" (Andrew Baham, Walter Ramsey); "The Windmills of Your Mind" (music: Michel Legrand; lyrics: Alan and Marilyn Bergman); "You Don't Have to Worry" (Dorian Burton, Herman Kelley); "First Waltz" (Terrance Simien); "Let Me Go Home, Whiskey" (John Willie Henry); "Anything You Want/Not That" (Kathrin Wollermann, Richard Carr, Tim Godwin); "Meet Me in the City" (Junior Kimbrough); "Baby Please Don't Go" (Joseph Lee Williams); "Kernkraft 400" (Emanuel Guenther, Floria Sentfer); "Backatown" (Troy Andrews); "Do It Again" (Derrik Tabb); "It Takes Two" (James Brown, Robert Ginyard Jr.); "Sympathy for the Devil" (Mick Jagger, Keith Richards); "Gimme Danger" (Iggy Pop, James Williamson); "Rumbero," "Lisboa Mulata" (Pedro Goncalves, To Trips); "Chorra" (Enrique Santos Discepolo); "Today Tomorrow" (Amparo Battaglia, Sergio Martin Grasso); "Body Speaking" (Sasu Ripatti); "La Espada de Cadorna" (Mauro Alberelli, Fernando Diego Barreyro, Marla Carla Flores, Fermin Escheveste, Manuel Gonzalez Aguilar, Mateo Gonzales Aguilar, Carlos Russo); "Gerli Hood" (Ivan Diaz Mathe, Jorge Es-

Denzel Washington in *Flight*, 2012.

tebenet, Sebastian Martinez); "Rap Para Las Madres" (Maria Paz Ferreyra, Guillermo Beresnak); "Comfortable" (Benjamin Ruttner, James Patterson, Sam Harris); "Corazon de Piedra" (Alejandro Juan Medina); "Regalo," "Mismo Lado" "La Distancia" (Christian Puschel); "El Blus" (Fernando Diego Barreyro, Juan Philipe Correa, Martin Batmalle, Maxilliano Sosa, Miguel Mactas, Santiago Morales); "Trinidad" (David and Linda LaFlamme); "Love Makes the World Go Round" (Deon Jackson); "Never Le Nkemise" (Ninja, You-Landi Visser, D.J. Hi-Tek). Gutter language, sexual content and brief violence prohibit viewing by children. **p**, Denise Di Novi; **d&w**, Glenn Ficarra, John Requa; **cast**, Will Smith, Margot Robbie, Adrian Martinez, Gerald McRaney, Rodrigo Santoro, BD Wong, Brennan Brown, Robert Taylor, Dotan Bonen, Griff Furst; **c**, Xavier Grobet; **m**, Nick Urata; **ed**, Jan Kovac; **prod d**, Beth Mickle; **art d**, Kelly Curley; **set d**, Lisa K. Sessions; **spec eff**, Justin B. Johnson, Matt Kutcher.

Force Majeure ★★★ 2014; Sweden/France/Denmark/Norway; 118m; Color; Comedy/Drama; Children: Unacceptable (MPAA: R); **BD**; **DVD**. Well-made tale carefully reveals the emotional frailties of Kuhnke, a Swedish husband, while he vacations with his family at an Alpine resort. He, his wife Kongsli, and their young children, Clara and Vincent Wettergren, are staying at a ski resort when, on their second day there, they are caught in a "controlled avalanche" that strikes the resort while they are at lunch. Kuhnke panics, grabbing his cell phone and running out, leaving Kongsli to protect their children. Kuhnke returns and attempts to convince Kongsli that he is not a coward and that it was he, not she, who acted levelheaded during the incident. They disagree and it threatens their marriage while their arguing frightens their children. In a movingly cathartic scene, Kuhnke breaks down, appearing to sob as he admits not only his cowardice, but innumerable weaknesses that have harmed his marriage, including past infidelities. Kongsli accuses him of crying crocodile tears, but he later redeems himself by displaying honor and bravery to recoup some respect and a little admiration from his wife and children. Superior acting that offers impressive characterizations and dazzling landscapes of the French Alps (shot on location at the Les Arcs ski resort in Savole, France) sustains interest throughout. Not related to a 1989 film with the same title. Songs: "Concerto No. 2 in G Minor, Op. 8, Summer" (Antonio Vivaldi), "Bad Things" (Jonas Rudels), "Reload" (Sebastian Ingrosso, Thomas Olsen, Vincent Pontare, Adam Baptiste, John Lindstrom Martin, Michel Zitron), "Terror" (Allan Smith). ***Author's Note***: The title stems from a French legal term that does not make any parties responsible for actions caused by an "Act of God," such as the avalanche that occurs and so disrupts the marriage union between Kuhnke and Kongsli. Gutter language and brief nudity prohibit viewing by children. **p**, Philippe Bober, Erik Hemmendorff,

Mr. Rzykruski (Martin Landau voiceover) in *Frankenweenie,* **2012.**

Marie Kjellson, Katja Adomeit, Marina Perales, Yngve Saether; **d&w**, Ruben Ostlund; **cast**, Lisa Loven Kongsli, Johannes Bah Kuhnke, Clara Wettergren, Vincent Wettergren, Brady Corbet, Jakob Granqvist, Kristofer Hivju, Fanni Metelius, Malin Dahl; **c**, Fredrik Wenzel; **m**, Ola Flottum; **ed**, Jacob Secher Schulsinger; **prod d&art d**, Josefin Asberg; **spec eff**, Johan Harnesk.

Fort Bliss ★★★ 2014; U.S./Turkey; 116m; Yeniceri Produkcyon/Phase 4 Films; Color; Drama; Children: Unacceptable (MPAA: R); **BD**; **DVD**. Absorbing tale begins with Monaghan, who is a U.S. Army combat doctor. After performing heroically in two terms in the Afghanistan war (2001-present), she is reassigned to the military hospital in Fort Bliss, Texas. She finds that Fegley, her five-year-old son, has grown up without really knowing her and is attached to his father, Livingston, whom she has divorced and who has a new girlfriend, Chriqui. Monaghan forces her son to live with her in a cramped apartment on the army base, then in a rented house she does little to decorate. Monaghan comes to realize she is not a very good or adequate mother, frustrated easily when Fegley misbehaves. At the same time, she is a terrific soldier, getting high approval from Rodriguez, her strict commander, and Akinnagbe, a tough sergeant, as well as other members of her unit. She also tries to accept the attentions of Cardona, a handsome Mexican car mechanic. Meanwhile, she rarely sleeps, haunted by memories of her war years. Just as she starts to feel a thaw in her son's coldness toward her, Monaghan receives orders that she is to be reassigned. The film is a rare look at the private lives of service women who have to juggle their duties as wife and mother with obligations of being a soldier, and dealing with the haunting memories of service in a war zone. **p**, Claudia Myers, Patrick Cunningham, Brendan McDonald, Adam Silver, John Sullivan; **d&w**, Myers; **cast**, Michelle Monaghan, Anthony Alexander Smith, Pablo Schreiber, Emmanuelle Chriqui, Dash Mihok, Ron Livingston, John Savage, Gbenga Akinnagbe, Manolo Cardona, Fahim Fazli, Oakes Fegley; **ed**, Matt Chesse, Carsten Kurpanek; **prod d**, Krystyna Loboda; **art d**, Scott Enge; **spec eff**, Brad Kalinoski, Ben Sumner, Tinatsu Wallace.

42 ★★★★★ 2013; U.S.; 128m; Legendary Pictures/WB; Color; Biographical Drama/Sports Drama; Children: Unacceptable (MPAA: PG-13); **BD**; **DVD**. Superb biopic about the great Jackie Robinson (1919-1972), wonderfully played by Boseman, begins when he is a Negro League baseball player in 1946 who bristles at any racist remark. Branch Rickey (1881-1965), played by Ford, is a Major League team executive with a bold idea. He recruits Boseman to play for the Brooklyn Dodgers, thus breaking the unspoken color line as the first modern African American Major League player. This proves to be a terrible challenge for Boseman and his family as they experience unrelenting racist hostility both on and off the field, from players and fans alike. Boseman, whose jersey number is 42, struggles against his nature to endure such abuse without complaining. He finds allies and hope where he least expects it. The film focuses mainly on the 1947 Dodgers season as well as the 1946 season with the Montreal Royals. Boseman is first shown in 1945 with his team, the Kansas City Monarchs, their team bus stopped by a gas station where the attendant refuses to let him enter the washroom. Boseman tells his teammates they will find another station to get a fill-up, so the attendant relents. A scout for the Brooklyn Dodgers has seen potential in Boseman and sends him to Brooklyn. Dodgers team owner Ford offers him a contract for $600 a month and a $3,500 signing bonus, which Boseman accepts, after being warned he has to control his temper if he wants to play for the Dodgers. Boseman agrees and phones his girlfriend, Beharie, proposing to her, and she accepts. During spring training, Boseman makes it to the Dodgers' franchise farm team in Montreal, has a great season there, and, after training in Panama, advances to the Dodgers. There is trouble right from the start. Most of the team signs a petition refusing to play with Boseman because he is black, but manager Leo Durocher (1905-1991), essayed by Meloni, insists he will nevertheless play the new first baseman. Meloni is then suspended for other reasons, leaving the Dodgers without a manager. However, at the last moment, Burt Shotton (1994-1962), played by Gail, manage the team, telling Ford that he has no objection to having Boseman on the team. Boseman has a run-in with Phillies manager Ben Chapman (1908-1993), played by Tudyk, who calls him all sorts of racist names (including "nigger" and who ordered his pitchers to "bean" or hit Robinson when at a 3-0 count) from the dugout. So enraged is Boseman (as was the real Robinson) that he breaks his bat in the Dodgers' dugout and then leaves the field. Ford, however, stops him and urges him to control himself and, by doing so, will make a successful path for many other black players to enter the Major Leagues. Boseman agrees and returns to the game, performing so well that the Dodgers win the match. Tudyk's racist remarks give the Phillies so much bad press that, in the team's next match with the Dodgers, the Phillies owner insists that Tudyk pose with Boseman for newspaper photographers. Boseman's public image is bolstered when his teammate, Harold Peter Henry "Pee Wee" Reese (1918-1999), portrayed by Black, makes a public show of supporting him before a hostile crowd in Cincinnati. Boseman scores the winning home run against the Pittsburgh Pirates pitcher Fritz Ostermueller (1907-1957), played by Hand, who had earlier hit him in the head, and the run clinches the National League pennant for the Dodgers, sending them to the 1947 World Series, which the Dodgers lose in seven games to the New York Yankees. The movie ends saying that Boseman, and many of the Dodgers players went on to have distinguished careers including inductions into the Baseball Hall of Fame (as well as the pioneering Rickey), and also tells about other African Americans who later played in the Major Leagues, beginning with the season after Boseman debuted in the Major Leagues. The fine field action is matched by outstanding performances that are both moving and revealing. One of the many stunning scenes is where Boseman asks Ford: "Why are you doing this?" Ford explains that, in his early days, he had the opportunity to advance the career of a black baseball player, but failed to do so, and that he has decided to make up for his failure to bring racial equality to the great game of baseball. Both Boseman and Ford are outstanding in roles of two very courageous men, one literally risking his life for the sake of his race and the other risking his reputation and fortune to achieve that racial equality. The story was told years earlier in **The Jackie Robinson Story**, 1950, but never so tellingly and candidly as in this excelling sports biopic. The film did well at the box office, earning more than $97.5 million in its initial release against a budget of $40 million. Songs: "Good Rockin' Tonight" (Roy Brown), "Shame on You" (Donnell Clyde Cooley Jr.), "Moon Glow" (Irving Mills, Will Hudson, Edgar De Lange), "Begin the Beguine" (Cole Porter), "Be Honest with Me" (Gene Autry, Fred Rose), "Star-Spangled Banner" (Francis Scott Key), "Lover Man, Oh, Where Can You Be?" (James Edward Davis,

Roger Ramirez, Jimmy Sherman), "Panama" (Ernesto Lecuona), "Masabi" (Roberto Ravelo Fiol), "Moonlight Memories" (Tom Mc-Gowan), "Rose of Tralee" (Charles William Glover), "Take Me Out to the Ball Game" (Albert von Tilzer, Jack Norworth), "Straighten Up and Fly Right" (Nat "King" Cole, Irving Mills), "The Sidewalks of New York" (Charles Lawlor, James Blake), "Don't Get Around Much Anymore" (Duke Ellington, Bob Russell), "I'm Gonna Move to the Outskirts of Town" (Roy Jordan, William Westley Weldon), "Move It On Over" (Hank Williams), "The Ball Game" (Sister Mynona Carr), "Did You See Jackie Robinson Hit That Ball?" (Buddy Johnson). *Author's Note*: Black director-producer Spike Lee attempted to make a film about Robinson, but various deals did not work out. Robert Redford then thought to produce the story with himself in the role of Rickey, but that project, too, collapsed. Legendary Pictures then hired Helgeland to write and direct the film, which was distributed by Warner Brothers. Robinson's widow, Rachel Robinson, served as a consultant on the film, praising its completion and stating: "I didn't want them to make him [Jackie Robinson] an angry black man, or some stereotype, so it was important for me to be in there...I love the movie." The film was shot on location in Birmingham, Alabama; Macon, Georgia; and Chattanooga, Tennessee. Other films depicting baseball players and their teams include **Alibi Ike**, 1935 (Chicago Cubs); **Angels in the Outfield**, 1951 (Pittsburgh Pirates); **Angels in the Outfield**, 1994 (California Angels); **The Babe**, 1992 (Babe Ruth; New York Yankees); **Babe Ruth**, 1991 (made-for-TV; New York Yankees); **The Babe Ruth Story**, 1948 (New York Yankees); **Bang the Drum Slowly**, 1973 (fictional New York baseball team); **The Bingo Long Traveling All Stars & Motor Kings**; 1976 (Negro League); **Brewster's Millions**, 1985 (minor league team); **Bull Durham**, 1988 (minor league team); **Casey at the Bat**, 1927 (minor league); **Cobb**, 1994 (Ty Cobb; Detroit Tigers); **Damn Yankees**, 1958 (New York Yankees); **Damn Yankees!**, 1967 (made-for-TV; New York Yankees); **Ed**, 1996 (minor league); **Eight Men Out**, 1988 (Chicago White Sox); **Elmer the Great** (Chicago Cubs), 1933; **Everyone's Hero**, 2006 (animated; Babe Ruth; New York Yankees, Chicago Cubs); **The Fan**, 1996 (San Francisco Giants); **Fear Strikes Out**, 1957 (Jimmy Piersall; Boston Red Sox); **Field of Dreams**, 1989 (Chicago White Sox); **Fireman, Save My Child**, 1932 (St. Louis Cardinals, New York Yankees); **For the Love of the Game**, 1999 (Detroit Tigers, New York Yankees); **Hit and Run**, 1924 (minor league); **Hot Curves**, 1930 (minor league); **In the Name of the Law**, 1922 (Honus Wagner; Pittsburgh Pirates); **It Happened in Flatbush**, 1942 (Brooklyn Dodgers); **It Happens Every Spring**, 1949 (unspecified St. Louis team); **The Jackie Robinson Story**, 1950 (Brooklyn Dodgers); **Jim Thorpe—All American**, 1951 (New York Giants); **Joe Torre: Curveballs along the Way**, 1997 (made-for-TV; New York Yankees); **The Kid from Cleveland**, 1949 (Bill Veeck, Tris Speaker, Hank Greenberg; Cleveland Indians; Boston Braves); **The Kid from Left Field**, 1979 (San Diego Padres); **Kill the Umpire**, 1950 (minor Texas league); **Ladies' Day**, 1943 (minor league); **A League of Their Own**, 1992 (All-American Girls Professional Baseball League/AAGPBL); **Little Big League**, 1994 (Minnesota Twins); **Long Gone**, 1987 (made-for-cable TV; minor league); **Major League**, 1989 (Cleveland Indians); **Major League II**, 1994 (Cleveland Indians); **Major League: Back to the Minors**, 1998 (Minnesota Twins); **A Mile in His Shoes**, 2011 (made-for-TV; minor league); **Mr. Baseball**, 1992 (Japanese professional team); **Mr. Dynamite**, 1941 (minor league); **Mr. Go**, 2013 (Korean baseball team); **Mr. 3000**, 2004 (Milwaukee Brewers); **Moonlight in Havana**, 1942 (minor league); **The Natural**, 1984 (New York Knights, a fictional team, leading character based on Eddie Waitkus of the Philadelphia Phillies); **The Pride of St. Louis**, 1952 (Jerome "Dizzy" Dean; St. Louis Cardinals); **The Pride of the Yankees**, 1942 (Lou Gehrig; New York Yankees); **Rhubarb**, 1951 (Brooklyn Dodgers); **Rookie of the Year**, 1993 (Chicago Cubs); **Safe at Home**, 1962 (New York Yankees); **The Scout**, 1994 (New York Yankees); **61**, 2001 (made-for-TV; Roger Maris, Mickey Mantle; New York Yankees); **Slide, Kelly, Slide**, 1927 (New

Edgar "E" Gore (Atticus Shaffer voiceover) in *Frankenweenie*, 2012.

York Yankees); **The Slugger's Wife**, 1985 (Atlanta Braves); **Soul of the Game**, 1996 (made-for-TV; Negro League; Jackie Robinson); **Speedy**, 1928 (Babe Ruth; New York Yankees); **Stealing Home**, 1988 (minor league); **The Stratton Story**, 1949 (Monty Stratton; Chicago White Sox); **Sugar**, 2008 (minor league); **Summer Catch**, 2001 (minor league team); **Take Me Out to the Ballgame**, 1949 (minor league team); **Talent for the Game**, 1991 (California Angels); **Trouble with the Curve**, 2012 (Atlanta Braves); **Warming Up**, 1928 (minor league); **Whistling in Brooklyn**, 1943 (Brooklyn Dodgers); **A Winner Never Quits**, 1986 (made-for-TV; one-armed Pete Gray; St. Louis Browns); **The Winning Season**, 2004 (made-for-TV; Honus Wagner; Ty Cobb); and **The Winning Team**, 1952 (Grover Cleveland Alexander; Philadelphia Phillies, Chicago Cubs, St. Louis Cardinals). Thematic elements, racial slurs and gutter language prohibit viewing by children. **p**, Thomas Tull, Darryl Pryor, Jillian Zaks; **d&w**, Brian Helgeland; **cast**, Chadwick Boseman, Harrison Ford, Nicole Beharie, Brett Cullen, Christopher Meloni, Ryan Merriman, Lucas Black, Linc Hand, Andre Holland, Alan Tudyk, John C. McGinley, Max Gail, Gino Anthony Pesi; **c**, Don Burgess; **m**, Mark Isham; **ed**, Peter McNulty, Kevin Stitt; **prod d**, Richard Hoover; **art d**, Dennis Bradford, Sharon Davis, Aaron Haye; **set d**, Cindy Carr; **spec eff**, Jamie Dixon, Bryan Godwin, Justin Jones, Eric J. Robertson.

Foxcatcher ★★★ 2014; U.S.; 130m; Annapurna Pictures/Sony; Color; Biographical Drama/Crime Drama; Children: Unacceptable (MPAA: R); **BD**; **DVD**. Based on the true story of Olympic wrestling champion Mark Philip Schultz (b. 1960), played by Tatum, and how his brother Dave Schultz (1959-1996), played by Ruffalo, also an Olympic champion, was killed by paranoiac schizophrenic John du Pont (1938-2010), who is essayed by Carell. The film opens in 1996, when billionaire du Pont, in his late fifties and head of the industrial dynasty, shoots dead his friend and Olympic wrestler Ruffalo at his Pennsylvania estate where he had kept a private training camp for wrestlers called "Foxcatcher" and which was named after the family racing stable. (Du Pont had wanted to take over the Olympic wrestling team, coaching them himself and also competing as a wrestler in veteran competitions.) Ruffalo and Tatum become his star wrestlers, having won gold medals in the 1984 Los Angeles Olympics, and Carell hopes the brothers would do the same in Seoul in 1988. After shooting Ruffalo, for unexplained reasons, Carell pleads not guilty by reason of insanity, but is found guilty of third-degree murder, although mentally ill. He is sentenced to prison and dies there in 2010. This well-made film is based on the autobiography by Mark Schultz, but did poorly at the box office, earning only $18.9 million in its initial release against a budget of $24 million. Songs: "St. Stephen" (Jerry Garcia, Philip Lesh, Robert Hunter), "Fame" (Carlos Alomar,

Toshiaki (James Hiroyuki Liao voiceover) in *Frankenweenie,* **2012.**

David Bowie, John Lennon), "Fragments/Winged Creatures" (Marcelo Zarvos), "This Noble Land" (David Marsden), "This Land Is Your Land" (Woody Guthrie), "Villa del Refugio" (Raymond Brown, Jeremy Galindo, Christopher King, Andrew Miller), "Fur Alina" (Arvo Part), "Escape" (Johann Johannsson), "Soaring Eagle" (Emanuel Kallins), "Sea Lion" and "Numb" (Joshua L. Pearson), "I Thought He Was a Very Nice Gentleman" (Michael Danna), "The Times They Are A-Changin'," (Bob Dylan). Drug use and violence prohibit viewing by children. **p**, Anthony Bregman, Megan Ellison, Jon Kilik, Bennett Miller, Scott Robertson; **d**, Bennett Miller; **cast**, Channing Tatum, Mark Ruffalo, Steve Carell, Vanessa Redgrave, Sienna Miller, Anthony Michael Hall, Tara Subkoff, Brett Rice, Roger Callard, Stephanie Garvin; Mark Schultz plays a weigh-in official; **w**, E. Max Frye, Dan Futterman; **c**, Greig Fraser; **m**, Mychael Danna, Rob Simonsen; **ed**, Jay Cassidy, Stuart Levy, Conor O'Neill; **prod d**, Jess Gonchor; **art d**, Brad Ricker; **set d**, Kathy Lucass; **spec eff**, Andrea Atwater, John Bair, Jake Braver.

Frances Ha ★★★ 2012; U.S.; 86m; Pine Distributing Pictures/IFC Films; B/W; Comedy/Drama; Children: Unacceptable; (MPAA: R); **BD**; **DVD**. Entertaining tale begins with Frances, who is a twenty-seven-year-old woman, played by Greta Gerwig, who lives in New York and who is happy, but, to others, her life seems depressing. She lives with her best friend, Sumner, in her friend's apartment, until Sumner decides to move out and live with her boyfriend. Gerwig has no money and is an apprentice for a dance company, but is really not a dancer. On top of this, she and Sumner are no longer speaking to each other. Despite these distractions, Gerwig remains hopeful of her future and lives her life joyfully in the present moment. Gerwig and Sumner make up and Gerwig serves as a bridesmaid at her friend's wedding. Gerwig becomes a beginning choreographer, teaching children to dance and gets an apartment of her own and may even have a boyfriend in the bargain. Pleasant tale with some top-notch acting sustains interest throughout. The film had a modest success at the box office, earning more than $9 million in its initial limited release against a budget of $3 million. The film was shot digitally in black and white and, according to director Baumbach, in homage to the Woody Allen comedy films that were similarly produced. Songs: "Theme de Camille," "Stanislas et Camille," "La Polka Pavane," "La Valse Tordue," "Les Repos," "Negresco's Waltz," "Les Bicyclettes," "Theme de la Joie de Vivre" (Georges Delerue); "Ann Buchanan Theme" "Million Dollar Doll" (Britta Phillips, Dean Wareham); "Blue Sway" (Paul McCartney); "Modern Love" (David Bowie); "Divertimento de la Sonata a Due" (Maurice Jaubert); "Mrs. Butter's Lament" (Harry Nilsson, Bob Segarini); "Concerto for two Violins, Strings, Basso Continuo, and Orchestra in D Minor" (Johann Sebastian Bach); "Falling Off a Horse" (Felix Leband); "Rocks Off" (Mick Jagger, Keith

Richards); "Ecole Buissoniere" (Jean Constantin); "Heureux en Menage" (Antoine Duhamel); "Axis" (Joan Jeanrenaud); "Every 1's a Winner" (Hot Chocolate); "String Quartet in G Major, lst Movement" (Wolfgang Amadeus Mozart). Sexual references and gutter language prohibit viewing by children. **p**, Noah Baumbach, Scott Rudin, Rodrigo Teixeira, Lila Yacoub, Oscar Boyson, Eli Bush; **d**, Noah Baumbach; **cast**, Greta Gerwig, Mickey Sumner, Michael Esper, Josh Hamilton, Adam Driver, Michael Zegwn, Christine Gerwig, Godon Gerwig, Grace Gummer, Charlotte d'Amboise, Justine Lupe; **w**, Baumbach, Gerwig; **c**, Sam Levy; **ed**, Jennifer Lame; **prod d**, Sam Lisenco; **set d**, Hannah Rothfield.

Frank ★★★ 2014; U.K./Ireland; 95m; Runaway Fridge Productions; Magnolia Pictures; Color; Comedy/Drama/Mystery; Children: Unacceptable (MPAA: R); **BD**; **DVD**. Amusing offbeat tale sees Gleeson as a young British man who aspires to be a professional musician. He is invited to join a band whose leader is Frank (Fassbender) before a concert when Gleeson is asked if he is able to play a few chords. He manages that, and Fassbender makes him a permanent member of the band when it goes to Ireland to record an album. There Gleeson begins posting videos on the Internet of the band's rehearsal sessions, and they achieve some success through these online promotions. The public takes to the band in part because of Fassbender's gimmick of wearing a large papier-mâché head, a strange gimmick never explained, but then again, other than a lot of entertaining songs, little is explained in this shotgun but fascinating story. The film saw limited distribution and realized about $2 million at the box office in its initial release against a budget of about $1.5 million. Songs: "Endless Rolling Waves" (music: Domhnall Gleeson; lyrics: Lenny Abrahamson), "Children Building Castles in the Sand" and "Band's Playing in My Town," (Gleeson), "Lady in the Red Coat" (music: Gleeson, Stephen Rennicks; lyrics: Gleeson), "It Must Be Love" (Labi Siffre), "Little Boxes" (music: Gleeson; lyrics: Jon Ronson), "The Ginger Crouton" (music: Rennicks; lyrics: Abrahamson), "Aviary" (Rennicks), "Lone Standing Tuft" and "Breathe" (music: Rennicks; lyrics: Rennicks, Abrahamson), "Walking Down the Street" (Gleeson), "Be Still" (Rennicks), O,O,O,O,O, O" (Gleeson), "The La La La Song" (Gleeson, Rennicks, Darragh O'Kelly), "It's Just Me" (music: Rennicks, Hugh Drumm; lyrics: Abrahamson, Rennicks), "Broken" (Rennicks), "On Top of Old Smokey" (traditional), "Frank's Most Likeable Song" (music: Rennicks; lyrics: Rennicks, Jon Ronson), "Lighthouse Keeper" (Erika Eigen), "Swinging Guitar" (Rennicks), "I Love You All," "Tuft" (music: Rennicks; lyrics: Rennicks, Abrahamson). Gutter language and sexual content prohibit viewing by children. **p**, David Barron, Ed Guiney, Stevie Lee, Andrew Lowe; **d**, Leonard (Lenny) Abrahamson; **cast**, Michael Fassbender, Maggie Gyllenhaal, Domhnall Gleeson, Scoot McNairy, Moira Brooker, Paul Butterworth, Phil Kingston, Lauren Poole, Tess Harper, Bruce McIntosh; **w**, Jon Ronson, Peter Straughan (based on a character created by Chris Sievey); **c**, James Mather; **m**, Stephen Rennicks; **ed**, Nathan Nugent; **prod d**, Richard Bullock; **art d**, Tamara Conboy, Kevin Pierce; **set d**, Marcia Calosio, Jenny Oman; **spec eff**, Brendan Byrne, Ed Bruce.

Frankenweenie ★★★ 2012; U.S.; 87m; Walt Disney; B/W; Animated Comedy/Horror; Children: Cautionary (MPAA: PG); **3-D**; **BD**; **DVD**. Well-animated and very amusing horror spoof begins with a boy named Victor Frankenstein (Tahan voiceover), who is an amateur scientist making home movies and using his beloved dog Sparky in monster films. When Sparky is hit by a car and killed, Tahan is influenced by his science teacher (Landau voiceover) to reclaim his beloved pet. Landau demonstrated in class the effect of electricity on dead frogs, and Tahan uses the same technology to bring Sparky back to life, using electricity in his attic laboratory. Sparky comes back to life as a dog with bolts in his neck, a creature that frightens neighbors and causes havoc in town. Tahan has to convince his parents (Short and O'Hara voiceovers) that Sparky is still the lovable pet he always was, even though he looks like a monster. Tahan's classmates discover his laboratory and formula for bringing the dead back to life, and they use it to revive some animals, but those creatures, indeed, turn into monsters, including a vampire cat and a dead rat that becomes a were-rat. The monsters break loose and invade the town fair, causing havoc. Townspeople blame Sparky for the plague of monsters and chase him to a windmill, which the mayor (also Short voiceover) accidentally sets on fire. Tahan and Sparky enter the burning windmill to rescue Ryder, niece of the mayor (Baker voiceover), and Tahan is trapped inside. Sparky, however, proves he is true-blue by rescuing Tahan. This entertaining film, created as 3-D stop-motion animation, pays homage to the 1931 film **Frankenstein**, ends with Sparky acquiring a girlfriend in the form of Ryder's pet poodle, one that sports a hairstyle with a gray streak like Elsa Lancaster's in **The Bride of Frankenstein**, 1935. The film received an Oscar nomination as Best Animated Feature Film and it did well at the box office, earning more than $81.5 million in its initial release against a budget of $39 million. Songs: "Six Powerful Cues" (Wilfred William Burns), "Death of the Alienj 1" (Harry Bluestone, Emil Cadkin), "Savage Episode" (Lee Stevens), "Green Peppers" (Sol Lake), "Elsa's Song" (Danny Elfman, John August), "Folkloric" (Alfred Kluten), "Carousel" (Craig Austin), "Strange Love" (Karen Orzolek). *Author's Note*: This production was an extended remake of the 1984 short version. Thematic elements, scary images and frightening action cautions viewing by children. **p**, Tim Burton, Allison Abbate, Derek Frey; **d**, Burton; **cast** (voiceovers), Charlie Tahan, Martin Short, Catherine O'Hara, Martin Landau, Winona Ryder, Atticus Shaffer, Conchata Ferrell, Robert Capron, James Hiroyuki Liao, Tom Kenny, Dee Bradley Baker, Jeff Bennett, Frank Welker; **w**, John August (based on an idea by Burton and the 1984 **Frankenweenie** screenplay by Leonard Ripps); **c**, Peter Sorg; **m**, Danny Elfman; **ed**, Chris Lebenzon, Mark Solomon; **prod d**, Rick Heinrichs; **art d**, Tim Browning, Alexandra Walker; **spec eff**, Tim Ledbury, Hugh Macdonald.

Free Men ★★★ 2012; France; 99m; Pyramide Productions/Film Movement; Color; Drama/War; Children: Unacceptable; **BD**; **DVD**. Intriguing WWII (1939-1945) tale takes place during the German occupation of France in 1942. Rahim, a young Algerian immigrant, deals on the black market selling cigarettes and food to fellow Algerians in Paris. He is arrested, but. instead of going to prison, he is freed when he agrees to infiltrate the Paris Mosque and spy on its rector, Lonsdale. Lonsdale is suspected of aiding Muslim resistance agents and helping North African Jews by providing them with false exit papers and also harboring some of them. At the mosque, Rahim becomes aware of the life-threatening discrimination against Jews by the Nazis while becoming a close friend of an Algerian singer, Shalaby, whom he discovers is both Jewish and homosexual. This friendship causes Rahim to change from a politically naive black marketer into a resolute freedom fighter. Along the way in this transformation, Rahim encounters Azabal, a beautiful mystery woman, Vichy collaborators, resistance fighters, informant traitors, and others in this drama depicting the dangerous activities of Algerian and Jewish resistance fighters in France during WWII. Although much of the tale is purely fictitious, Rahim gives an outstanding performance, one that rivets from the first frame to the last. The film saw limited distribution and did poorly at the box office, earning a little more than $1 million in its initial release. Song: "Madnak Gafah Maikadoh" (Ahmed Chawky, Mohamed Abdel Wahab). *Author's Note*: There are no records to indicate that there was any organized resistance among Muslims in France during WWII, or any widespread movement by Muslims to protect or shield Jews at that time. (In French; English subtitles.) **p**, Fabienne Vonier; **d**, Ismael Ferroukhi; **cast**, Tahar Rahim, Michael Lonsdale, Mahmud Shalaby, Lubna Azabal, Christopher Buchholz, Farid Larbi, Stephane Rideau, Bruno Fleury, Francois Delaive, Jean-Pierre Becker; **w**, Ferroukhi, Alain-Michel Blanc; **c**, Jerome Almeras; **m**, Armand Amar; **ed**, Annette Dutertre; **prod d**, Thierry Francois; **set d**, Hind Ghazali, Catherine Jarrier-Prieur; **spec eff**, Berengere Dominiguez, Roxane Fechner.

Mr. Frankenstein, Victor, Sparky and Mrs. Frankenstein in *Frankenweenie*, **2012.**

Freedom ★★★ 2015; U.S.; 94m; Production One/ARC Entertainment; Color; Drama; Children: Unacceptable (MPAA: R); **BD**; **DVD**. This well-made anti-slavery film depicts two stories. Gooding Jr. is a slave in 1856, who escapes from a plantation near Richmond, Virginia. He is torn between two emotions, freedom, or revenge for his and his ancestors being slaves. He and his wife, Leal, and children, are pursued by Sadler, a relentless slave hunter, but are secreted north to Canada by members of the abolitionist Underground Railroad. A second story flashes back to 1748 when John Newton (1725-1807), played by Forcher, is captain of a slave trading ship, and which sails from Africa with a cargo of slaves bound for America. He is struggling with his faith as a Christian and his conscience transporting slaves. On board Forcher's ship is Gooding's great-grandfather whose survival depends on the fate of Newton. The voyage changes Newton's life as he creates the hymn "Amazing Grace" that inspires Gooding and millions of others in the years to come. Although there are many stereotypical images and Uncle Tom nuances invading these stories, the acting is superior and sustains interest throughout. Songs: "A City Called Heaven" (Shree Newman-Isabell), "Motherless Child" (traditional). Violence prohibits viewing by children. **p**, Timothy A. Chey, Sheila Rabizadeh; **d**, Peter Cousens; **cast**, Cuba Gooding Jr., Bernhard Forcher, William Sadler, Sharon Leal, David Rasche, Terrence Mann, Michael Goodwin, Phyllis Bash, Phillip Boykin, Diane Salinger, Tony Sheldon, Bart Shatto, Anna Sims; **w**, Timothy A. Chey, John Senczuk; **c**, Dean Cundey; **m**, James Lavino; **ed**, Ray Hubley; **prod d**, Steven Legler; **art d**, Sam Kramer; **set d**, Sergio De La Vega; **spec eff**, Rob Morganroth, Christopher Cundey.

The Frozen ★★★ 2012; U.S.; 135m; Fox Hill Productions/Ketchup Entertainment; Color; Horror; Children: Unacceptable (MPAA: R); **BD**; **DVD**. Taut tale begins with Mitchell and Morgan, a young unmarried couple on vacation. They have a harrowing snowmobile accident and are stranded in woods in freezing winter. They try to survive while waiting for help to arrive. Things go from bad to worse when Mitchell disappears, leaving Morgan on her own, not only to fight the elements, but to elude a mysterious hunter, Segan, who is tracking her through the frozen forest. Cohen, a young ghost, appears to further frighten Morgan as she wonders where Mitchell has gone. Not related to 2010 and 2013 films with the same title. Bloody images, gutter language and terror scenes prohibit viewing by children. **p**, Brian Girard, Samantha Lusk, Seth David Mitchell; **d&w**, Andrew Hyatt; **cast**, Mitchell, Sedona Cohen, Seth David Mitchell, Brit Morgan, Noah Segan; **c**, Maximilian Gutierrez; **m**, James Grundler; **ed**, David Heinz; **prod d**, Martine Hall.

Frozen ★★★ 2013; U.S.; 102m; Walt Disney; Color; Animated Fan-

Tahar Rahim in *Free Men*, 2012.

tasy; Children: Unacceptable (MPAA: PG-13); **BD**; **DVD**. This well-animated fantasy in 3-D is based in part on Hans Christian Andersen's fairy tale *The Snow Queen*. It all begins when a girl named Elsa (Menzel voiceover) is born with powers enabling her to produce ice, frost, and snow as she wishes. One night, while playing, she inadvertently injures her younger sister, Anna (Bell voiceover). They are both princesses of the land of Arendelle, and their parents, the king (LaMarche voiceover) and queen (Lee voiceover), keep them in a castle until Menzel is able to control her magical powers. Menzel, fearful that she might hurt her sister again, isolates herself alone in her room in the castle, and the two grow apart as they grow up. When they become teenagers, their parents die in a storm at sea. Menzel comes of age and is about to be crowned queen of the kingdom. Bell is allowed to leave the castle and, in town, meets Prince Hans (Fontana voiceover), who is from a warmer kingdom. They fall in love and Fontana proposes to Bell and she gladly accepts. Menzel, however, forbids them from marrying. She then flees the castle, which creates an eternal winter in the kingdom. She goes into the mountains and vows never to return to the castle, creating an ice palace where she can live alone. Bell then searches for Menzel and, on her journey to the ice palace, meets a man of ice called Kristoff (Groff voiceover) and his friendly reindeer, and she convinces them to journey with her. Along their way, they encounter Olaf (Gad voiceover), who was a snowman from the sisters' childhood, and he leads them to Menzel's ice palace. The sisters are reunited, but Menzel fears her powers may harm Bell, and accidentally strikes Bell in her heart, then orders her, Groff, and Gad to leave, while creating a gigantic snow creature called Marshmallow that chases them away from the palace. Groff notices that Bell's hair is turning white. Fearing she is in danger, he asks his adoptive family, some trolls, to help him. It is then learned that Bell's heart has been frozen by Menzel forever unless it is thawed by an act of true love. Groff hopes to accomplish this by Fontana giving Bell a kiss of true love. In a battle in the ice palace, Groff asks Menzel to end the winter and thaw Bell's heart, but she says she does not know how to do that. Fontana is then reunited with Bell, but refuses to kiss her. He then admits that he only intended to marry her so he could become king of Arendelle. Fontana leaves Bell to die, but Menzel departs her ice palace and the winter storm comes to a sudden end which allows Bell and Groff to be reunited. Bell, when seeing that Fontana is about to kill Menzel, puts herself between them and freezes solid. Menzel grieves for her sister, but, to her amazement, Bell thaws, since her willingness to sacrifice herself to save her sister was an act of true love. Menzel has learned that love can control her powers and thaws the kingdom. Fontana is exiled and the sisters are finally reconciled. The animation is top drawer, a combination of hand-drawn animation and digital enhancement, but the story line gets so complex that confusion sometimes presents itself. The film received two Oscars, one for Best Animated Feature, the other for Best Original Song ("Let It Go"). The film was a huge box office success, earning more than $1.2 billion in its initial release against a budget of $150 million. Not related to a 2010 film with the same name. Songs: "Frozen Heart," "Do You Want to Build a Snowman?," "For the First Time in Forever," "Love Is an Open Door," "Let It Go," "Reindeer Are Better than People," "In Summer," "Fixer Upper" (Kristen Anderson-Lopez, Robert Lopez); "Vuelie" (Frode Fjellheim, Christophe Beck); "Heimr Arnadalr" (Christophe Bec). **p**, Peter Del Vecho; **d**, Chris Buck, Jennifer Lee; **cast**, (voiceovers): Kristen Bell, Idina Menzel, Jonathan Groff, Josh Gad, Santino Fontana, Alan Tudyk, Ciaran Hinds, Eva Bella, Spencer Lacey Ganus, Tyree Brown, Paul Briggs, Maurice LaMarche, Jennifer Lee; **w**, Jennifer Lee (and a story by Lee, Chris Buck, Shane Morris, Dean Wellins, inspired by the fairy tale "The Snow Queen" by Hans Christian Andersen); **ed**, Jeff Draheim; **m**, Christophe Beck; **prod d**, David Womersley; **art d**, Michael Giaimo.

The Frozen Ground ★★★ 2013; U.S.; 105m; Grindstone Entertainment Group/Lionsgate; Color; Crime Drama; Children: Unacceptable (MPAA: R); **BD**; **DVD**. Based on a true story, this grim but riveting crime tale begins with Alaska National Guard officer Jack Halcombe, played by Cage. He becomes a partner of Hudgens, a seventeen-year-old girl who escaped Robert Hansen (1939-2014), a serial killer, portrayed by Cusack, and both attempt to bring him to justice. Risking his life, Cage goes on a personal manhunt to find Cusack as bodies of street girls pile up in Anchorage and the public fears who will be the killer's next victim. The film is set in a violent world of pimps, drugs, and alcohol, in an Alaska winter of constant snow. Cusack, a wary killer, knows he is being tracked and hides all of the evidence concerning his many murders, but Cage uses a clever ruse to finally obtain that evidence that sends Cusack behind bars for life. Superior performances from Cage, Cusack and Hudgens keep this riveting tale in high tension throughout. The film did not do well at the box office, earning a little more than $5.6 million in its initial release against a budget of $19.2 million, indicating that the public's taste for such gory biopics was well on the wane. Songs: "Deadlocked," "Something About You," "Summers Sweet," "At the Playground" (Joe Conte); "Take Me Home" (Robert Cutarella, Minna Walker); "I Always Tried" (Kevin Fisher); "This Is Who I Am" (Susan Hunkler, Kim Arden); "4-3-1," "Real Time" (Brad Buxer, B. Connole); "Hey" (D.R. Wilke, P. Murphy); "Heavy Metal Shuffle" (David Rubinstein, P. Bakija); "If Ever 2 Hearts Were Meant to Be" (E. Scott, R. Smith, T. Allen); "These Walls Between" (Dennis Livingston); "Fates May Lie," "One Foot in the Grave" (Josh Weekley, Steve Benton); "Walk My Way" (M. Mongelli, M. James. S. Kops); "Have a Ball" (Darin Baker); "Play Me Like a Rhythm" (R. Galpin, S. Whiteman, M. Schenker, J. Chalfant); "Triumph Over Will" (Eric Keith Jackson); "Fightin Society," "Let Me Go Crazy" (Dennis Livingston); "Smoke from a Gun" (Larry Greene, Roger Craig); "Waking All the Demons" (Stuart Hart); "Memory Finds You" (Nathan Picard); "No Angel" (Minna Walker). *Author's Note*: Hansen was captured and convicted in 1983 and sentenced to 461 years in prison, plus one life sentence, to assure that he would never be paroled. Called the "Butcher Baker" by the press, Hansen raped and murdered at least seventeen women from 1971 to 1983 in and around Anchorage, Alaska, and may have claimed as many as thirty or more victims. He died behind bars at age seventy-five on August 14, 2014. Violence, sexuality, nudity, gutter language and drug use prohibit viewing by children. **p**, Mark Ordesky, Jane Fleming, Jeff Rice, Remington Chase, Randall Emmett, 50 Cent (Curtis Jackson), Gus Furla, Brandon Grimes; **d&w**, Scott Walker; **cast**, Nicolas Cage, John Cusack, Vanessa Hudgens, Radha Mitchell, Dean Norris, Jodi Lyn O'Keefe, Katherine LaNasa, 50 Cent (Curtis Jackson), Michael McGrady, Gia Mantegna, Ryan O'Nan; **c**, Patrick Murguia; **m**, Lorne Balfe; **ed**, Sarah Boyd; **prod d**, Clark Hunter; **set d**, Monique Champagne; **spec eff**, Damian Lund, Ed Chapman.

Fruitvale Station ★★★ 2013; U.S.; 85m; UNIV; Color; Biographical Drama; Children: Unacceptable (MPAA: R); **BD**; **DVD**. This riveting tale is based on the life of Oscar Grant III (1987-2009), played by Jordan, who is a twenty-two-year-old San Francisco Bay area resident fatally shot on New Year's Day, 2009. When Jordan wakes up on the morning of December 31, 2008, he senses that something is in the air. Not sure what it is, he takes his enigmatic perception to be a sign to get a head start on his New Year's resolutions. He has resolved to be a better son to his mother whose birthday falls on New Year's Eve; being a better partner to his girlfriend, Diaz, with whom he hasn't been completely honest; and being a better father to T, their beautiful four-year-old daughter, who is portrayed by Neal. He starts out well, but as the last day of the year progresses, he realizes that change is not going to come easy. He attempts to regain a job at a grocery store where he once worked but where he has been fired. Failing at this, Jordan considers illegally selling marijuana, but discards the stash and resolves to find a legitimate job. He crosses paths with family, friends, and strangers, each exchange showing that there is much more to him than meets the eye. But it will be his final encounter of the day, with police officers at the Fruitvale BART station that shakes the Bay Area to its very core and causes the entire nation to be witnesses to the story of Oscar Grant. While riding on the train, Jordan is recognized by another ex-convict from his prison days and the two get into a scuffle. Responding to reports of a fight on a crowded Bay Area Rapid Transit train returning from San Francisco, BART police detain Jordan and several other passengers on the platform at the Fruitvale BART Station. Two officers restrain Grant. He is unarmed and lying face down, but he has allegedly resisted arrest. When Jordan seems to resist further, one of the officers shoots Jordan in the back and he is rushed to a hospital, dying the next day. The film ends with cell phone and videos by actual eyewitnesses being shown of the real incident and how widespread protests led to riots all over San Francisco over Jordan's death. Jordan is exceptional as the ill-fated Grant and he is well supported by a talented cast enacting a fascinating and well-written script. The film was shot on a shoestring budget in San Francisco and did very well at the box office, earning more than $17.4 million in its initial release. Songs: "Won't Be Right" (M. Wade, D. Newton), "Rubber Band" and "Intelligent" (Mar Keyes, William Peoples, Noah Coogler), "Hey Little Mama" (Stanley Cox, Johnny Castaneda, D. Newton, Jason Valerio), "My Fattburger" (Patrick Yandall), "Won't Be Right" (D. Newton, M. Wade), "Feelin' Myself" (Andre Hicks, Sean Thompson). *Author's Note*: BART police officer Johannes Mehserle reportedly stood, drew his gun, and shot Grant once in the back. Grant was taken to a hospital in Oakland where he died the next morning. The shooting was variously called an involuntary manslaughter and a summary execution. Mehserle was later charged with murder for the shooting, resigned from the police force, and pleaded not guilty. His defense claimed he mistakenly shot Jordan with his pistol, instead of using his Taser when he saw Jordan reaching for his waistband. A jury found Mehserle guilty of involuntary manslaughter but not guilty of second-degree murder and voluntary manslaughter. Riots broke out after the verdict and nearly eighty people were arrested. Mehserle was sentenced to two years, minus time served, then was released in 2011 and is now on parole. Violence, gutter language and drug use prohibit viewing by children. **p**, Nina Yang Bongiovi, Forest Whitaker, Sev Ohanian, Harvey Weinstein; **d&w**, Ryan Coogler; **cast**, Michael B. Jordan, Melonie Diaz, Octavia Spencer, Kevin Durand, Chad Michael Murray, Ahna O'Reilly, Ariana Neal, Keenan Coogler, Trestin George; **c**, Rachel Morrison; **m**, Ludwig Goransson; **ed**, Claudia S. Castello, Michael P. Shawver; **prod d**, Hannah Beachler; **set d**, Kris Boxell; **spec eff**, Lauren F. Ellis, Taraneh Golozar, Brittany Kikuchi, Shauna Lacoste, Ksenia Strelets.

Furious Seven ★★★ 2015; U.S./Japan/China; 131m; UNIV; Color; Crime Drama; Children: Unacceptable (MPAA: PG-13); **BD**; **DVD**. This exciting thriller is the seventh installment of the adventure series.

Dwayne Johnson in *Furious Seven*, 2015.

Diesel, Walker, and the rest of their crew become targets of Statham, a Special Forces assassin seeking revenge for the team's death of his brother, an international terrorist. This leads to the team air-dropping their cars over the Caucasus Mountains in Azerbaijan to rescue one of their members. They learn Statham is back in Los Angeles and return there to confront him. The team finally manages to have Statham arrested and locked away in a secret prison. The film ends with Walker and his wife playing with their son at a beach while the others look on, glad that Walker has decided to retire and become a full-time husband and father. Walker and Diesel recall exciting times together and say farewell as they part good friends. The story is thin but the nonstop action is eye-popping throughout. As usual, the chiefly adolescent audience that has routinely supported this action series gave enormous response at the box office where the film earned more than a whopping $1.5 billion in its initial release against a budget of $190 million. Songs: "Payback" (Alex Schwartz, Joe Khajadourian, Gregory Earley, Dominic W. Woods, Kevin Gilyard, Jordan Houston, Future, Gilbere Forte), "Off Set" (Cordale Quinn, Clifford Harris Jr., Jeff Williams, Edward Page II), "Delirious/Boneless" (Steven Aoki, Brian Collins, Aid Vllasaliu, Christopher Lake, Erin Beck, Jenson Vaughan, Whitney Phillips), "Blast Off" (Michael Anthony, Ebow Graham, David Guetta, Kaz James, Pavan Mukhi, David Lee Roth, Giorgio Tuinfort, Alex Van Halen, Edward Van Halen, Ralph Wegner), "Holler" (William Bennett, Long Phung), "Hulk and Huge Rock" (Joe Harnell), "Ay Vamos" (Alejandro Suarez, Rene Rios, Carlos Patino, Jose Balvin), "Six Days" (Josh Davis, Brian Farrell), "U Can't Tough This" (Alonzo Miller, Rick James, Kirk Burrell), "How Bad Do You Want It/Oh Yeah" (James Abrahart, Chloe Angelides, Andrew Sedar, Theodore Economou, Justin Franks, Klejdi Llupa, James Smith, Amber Streeter), "Get Low" (Steve Guess, William Grigahcine), "My Angel" (Justin Franks, Andrew Cedar, Sangsik Shin, Edwin Serrano, Geoffrey Rojas), "Firebrand" (Brian Tyler), "Turn Down for What" (Steve Guess, Jonathan Smith, William Grigahcine), "GDFR" (Dominic Woods, Justin Franks, Andrew Cedar, Mike Caren, Paulo Rodriguez, Tramar Dillard, Sylvester Allen, Harold R. Brown, Charles W. Miller, Lee Oskar, Howard E. Scott, Gerald Goldstein), "Francoise" (Pierre-Antoine Melki, Raphael Jurdin), "Happy Birthday to You" (Mildred J. Hill, Patty S. Hill), "Roses from the South" (Johann Strauss II), "Hamdulillah" (Yassin Alsalman), "I Will Return" (Jonathan Rotem, Skylar Grey, Luke Laird), "Tempest" (Chino Moreno, Stephen Carpenter, Abe Cunningham, Frank Delgado, Sergio Vega), "Meneo" (Armando Perez, Jorge Gomez, Jose Garcia, Keith Kanashiro, Roberto Testa, Robert Fernandez), "See You Again" (Justin Franks, Andrew Cedar, Charlie Puth, Cameron Thomaz), "Ride Out" (Olubowale Akintimehin, Brian Collins, Keenon Jackson, Paris Jones, DeQuantes Lamar, Michael Nguyen-Stevenson, Jamie Sanderson), "Go Hard or Go Home"

Brad Pitt in *Fury*, 2014.

(William Featherstone, Justin Featherstone, Christopher Featherstone, Paulo Rodriguez, Dominic Woods, Breyan Isaac, Cameron Thomaz, Amethyst Kelly). *Author's Note*: In real life, Walker was killed in an auto accident before release of this film. **Furious Eight** is scheduled for 2017 release. Excessive violence, mayhem, suggestive content and gutter language prohibit viewing by children. **p**, Vin Diesel, Michael Fottrell, Neal H. Moritz, Brandon Birtell; **d**, James Wan; **cast**, Diesel, Paul Walker, Jason Statham, Kurt Russell, Michelle Rodriguez, Jordana Brewster, Tyrese Gibson, Ludacris, Dwayne Johnson, Lucas Black; **w**, Chris Morgan (based on characters created by Gary Scott Thompson); **c**, Marc Spicer, Stephen F. Windon; **m**, Brian Tyler; **ed**, Leigh Folsom Boyd, Dylan Highsmith, Kirk Morri, Christian Wagner; **prod d**, Bill Brzeski; **art d**, Desma Murphy; **set d**, Danielle Berman; **spec eff**, Grant Bensley.

Fury ★★★ 2014; U.K.; 134 m; Grisbee Productions/Sony; Color; War Drama; Children: Unacceptable (MPAA: R); **BD**; **DVD**. Gritty war tale profiles in exciting detail a tank crew battling German troops to the bitter end. The setting is April 1945, the last month of the European Theater during World War II (1939-1945), as the Allies make their final push to overwhelm the diehard troops of Nazi Germany. The crew is led by Pitt, a battle-hardened U.S. Army sergeant named "Wardaddy," who commands a M4A3E8 Sherman tank called "Fury." Its five-man crew is assigned a deadly mission behind German lines. Outnumbered and outgunned, Pitt and his men face overwhelming odds in their heroic attempts to strike at the heart of Nazi Germany and must hold a crossroads until reinforcements can arrive. Prior to that assignment, Pitt and his crew enter a German town with other U.S. forces. They systematically blast its German defenders to pieces. Following their capture of the town, they find a lone German soldier alive, who cowers before them and begs for his life. Lerman, who has become a last-minute replacement with Pitt's crew and has no battle experience and has been trained only as a typist, is ordered to kill the German captive. He refuses, even though Pitt humiliates him and finally forces him to shoot the German by using Pitt's .45-caliber pistol. (Of the many implausible scenes in this otherwise well-organized action film, this sequence tests the believability of any knowledgeable viewer in that no non-commissioned officer would order such a public execution in defiance of the rules of war, and in front of scores of witnesses, knowing that he could be later charged with murder, or a war crime.) The tank crew later invades a German apartment where two women serve them a meal and where Pitt demands that the women be treated decently (as if to exonerate his earlier ruthless assassination of an unarmed prisoner). When the crew finally reaches the crossroads, it drives off a small contingent of Germans and its track is damaged so that it is now incapable of moving anywhere.

The crew decides to abandon the tank, but Pitt resolutely orders them to remain and perform their duty. Pitt and his men disguise the tank by creating small fires on and about it as if to make it appear thoroughly disabled and out of action. This ruse works as a large German force arrives at the crossroads and ignores the tank as they pass it. Pitt and his men then open fire and decimate the German troops and their mechanized vehicles, but the tank then comes under savage and incessant attack, a horrific bombardment where only Pitt and Lerman are left aside inside the tank and still fighting the enemy. When mortally wounded, Pitt orders Lerman to escape through a hatch at the bottom of the tank, which is now consumed by flames. Lerman manages to elude the Germans swarming everywhere about the tank, until he sees U.S. troops driving the Germans back in a counterattack. The loss of Pitt and his men has not been an essential sacrifice, but another seemingly waste of life to further emphasize the futility of war, which is what this jarring and well-enacted film is all about. Pitt, Lerman and the rest of the cast render stellar performances, even though most of the GIs are portrayed as savage beasts, men who have lost all sense of decency and humanity and act more as fugitives from a chain gang than disciplined soldiers. The story line leans heavily upon two classic films depicting WWII, **Sahara**, 1943, and **Saving Private Ryan**, 1998, but does not achieve the overall dramatic effects of either of these outstanding works, albeit it does provide an exciting action where the battle sequences are superbly choreographed. The film proved very successful at the box office, earning more than $211 million in its initial release against a budget of more than $68 million. Not related to the 1936 drama with the same title. Songs: "The Old Rugged Cross" (traditional), "You Always Hurt the One You Love" (Doris Fisher, Allan Roberts), "Drunk Man's Wiggle" (Jimmy Myers), "Dust Up Ragtime" and "Sunday Rag" (Eric V. Hachikian), "I Don't Mean a Thing to You" (Hal Clark), "Whoopee Ti Yi You" (traditional), "Shotgun Wedding" (Rufus Charles Shoffner), "Virgin's Slumber Song/Maria Wiegenlied" (Max Reger, John Grady), "La Legion Marche" (Karl Boegelsack, Christian Jaehrig, Wolfram Phillips). *Author's Note*: One of the last serviceable German Tiger Tanks was used in making this film, the vehicle loaned from a British museum. The film was shot on location in England. Other films depicting tanks and their crews fighting in WWII include **American Guerrilla in the Philippines**, 1950; **Back to Bataan**, 1945; **Band of Brothers**, 2001 (TV miniseries); **Battle of the Bulge**, 1965; **The Big Red One**, 1980; **Breakthrough**, 1950; **The Bridge at Remagen**, 1969; **A Bridge Too Far**, 1977; **Days of Glory**, 2006; **The Days of Rage**, 2001; **The Desert Fox: The Story of Rommel**, 1951; **The Desert Rats**, 1953; **The Devil's Brigade**, 1968; **The Fighting Rats of Tobruk**, 1951; **The Fighting Seabees**, 1944; **Five Graves to Cairo**, 1943; **Force of Arms**, 1951; **The Great Raid**, 2005; **Guadalcanal Diary**, 1943; **Halls of Montezuma**, 1950; **The Hurt Locker**, 2009; **Kelly's Heroes**, 1970; **The North Star**, 1943; **Patton**, 1970; **Play Dirty**, 1969; **Raid on Rommel**, 1971; **Sahara**, 1943; **Sahara**, 1995 (made-for-TV); **Sands of Iwo Jima**, 1949; **Saving Private Ryan**, 1998; **Sea of Sand** (AKA: Desert Patrol), 1961; **The Story of G.I. Joe**, 1945; **The Tanks Are Coming**, 1951; **To Hell and Back**, 1955; **Tobruk**, 1967; **A Walk in the Sun**, 1945; and **Windtalkers**, 2002. Excessive violence prohibits viewing by children. **p**, Bill Block, John Lesher, Ethan Smith, Alex Ott; **d&w**, David Ayer; **cast**, Brad Pitt, Shia LaBeouf, Logan Lerman, Scott Eastwood, Jon Bernthal, Xavier Samuel, Michael Pena, Jim Parrack, Eugenia Kuzmina; **c**, Roman Vasyanov; **m**, Steven Price; **ed**, Dody Dorn; **prod d**, Andrew Menzies; **art d**, Mark Scruton; **set d**, Malcolm Stone; **spec eff**, Jalila Otky, Andy Williams.

Gabbar Is Back ★★★ 2015; India; 128m; SLB Films/Viacom 18; Color; Crime Drama; Children: Unacceptable; **BD**; **DVD**. Offbeat but intriguing tale of rebellion against corruption sees Kumar as Gabbar, a loose cannon who operates his private network called "Anti-Corruption

Force." His aim is to kidnap and kill the most corrupt police officers. Police and government officials are desperate to learn the identity of the person masterminding the assassinations. Grover, a police driver, is convinced he can discover who the killer is after the assassin sends a compact disc calling himself "Gabbar," but Grover receives only uncooperative hostility from others in the police department. He becomes convinced that there is an honest police officer in each department and they can lead him to solving the case. His investigation leads him to students at the National College, who are arrested, but, even after being beaten, refuse to inform on Kumar, whom they consider to be a hero. It turns out that Kumar is both Gabbar and a police officer and he is finally exposed and arrested. He cautions students to do what he could not, subjugate his anger at corrupt police, and make change through honest means, rather than his murderous efforts. He is then hanged. Violence prohibits viewing by children. **p**, Sanjay Leela Bhansali, Shabina Khan; **d**, Radha Krishna Jagarlamudi; **cast**, Akshay Kumar, Shruti K. Haasan, Sunil Grover, Kareena Kapoor, Ishita Vyas, Shruti Bapna, Jaideep Ahlawat, Raj Singh Arora, Praveena Deshpande; **w**, Rajat Arora (based on a story by A.R. Murugadoss); **c**, Niray Shah; **m**, Sandeep Chowta, Amar Mohile; **ed**, Rajesh Pandey; **prod d**, Boishali Sinha, Tanushree Sarkar; **spec eff**, Rajeev Rajasekharan, Abrez Mohammed, Praveen Bareria.

Gangster Squad ★★★ 2013; U.S.; 113m; Langley Park Productions; WB; Color; Crime Drama; Children: Unacceptable (MPAA: R); **BD**; **DVD**. Although almost all of the scenes shown in this gangster tale present a mythical Mickey Cohen (1913-1976), played by Penn, it nevertheless provides a lot of entertaining action and offers a rich portrait of L.A. in the late 1940s. Penn is shown in Los Angeles in 1949 where he intends to control all criminal activity in the city. He buys off local judges and police and no one is willing to testify against him, except Brolin, a police sergeant and World War II veteran, who has settled with his family in what he wants to be a peaceful city. Nolte, the police chief, forms a special Gangster Squad Unit to take down Penn and picks Brolin, a police sergeant, to head the guerilla-warfare-style unit. Brolin chooses four cops: Mackie, Ribisi, Patrick and Pena, and asks a close friend, Gosling, also a police sergeant and war vet, to join them. Gosling is not interested, but later changes his mind after seeing a boy murdered by Penn's goons and he joins Brolin's team. At first, Penn thinks gang rivals in the Mafia are after him, until he realizes the cops are attempting to close down his operations. Wire-tapping leads the squad to learn the central location of Penn's wire gambling business, which is at the heart of his criminal empire. The squad burns down the business, and is then lured into a trap in the city's Chinatown by Penn's chief hitman, Garity. Gosling learns of the Chinatown ambush in time to save Brolin, but Garity escapes. Brolin's house is later fired on in a drive-by shooting, and his wife, Enos, gives birth to a son under the stress. Brolin spirits his wife and baby out of the city and continues his war against Penn. Stone, a woman friend of Penn's, tells Gosling she is willing to testify against Penn. Brolin and the squad go to the Park Plaza Hotel to arrest Penn and a shoot-out occurs in which Gosling is wounded after killing Garity. Penn escapes, but Brolin pursues him and they engage in a bare-knuckle boxing match while a crowd of people and journalists watch. Brolin wins the fight and Penn is arrested, ending his reign as crime boss, which also ends the spread of the Mafia in the Los Angeles area. Penn is sentenced to twenty-five years to life at Alcatraz, and Brolin quits the police force to live a quiet life with his wife and son. Other than the wire service Penn runs in this tale, the murders and mayhem exhibited is pure Hollywood hokum. The acting and action, however, are superior and so well presented that interest is sustained throughout. It is nevertheless true that Clarence B. Horrall (1895-1960), who was LAPD's chief of police from 1941 to 1949, did establish a "gangster squad" that concentrated on breaking up various rackets. The same story line can be seen in such films as **Bugsy**, 1991 (where Harvey Keitel is exceptional playing Cohen); **L.A. Confidential**, 1997; **Mulholland**

Sean Penn, at left, as L.A. gangster Mickey Cohen in *Gangster Squad*, 2013.

Falls, 1996, and **Mob City**, 2013 (TV miniseries). This film did well at the box office, earning more than $105 million in its initial release against a budget of more than $60 million. Songs: "The Hills of California" (Robert Hayward, Robert Staver); "Mr. Five by Five" (Gene DePaul, Don Raye); "No Baby Nobody But You" (Seger Ellis); "Perdido" (Juan Tizol); "Chicken Shack Boogie" (Lola Cullum, Amos Milburn); "Amado Mio" (Doris Fisher, Allan Roberts); "Kiss Kiss," "Jelly Wiggle Boogie" (Dan Higgins); "A Little Bird Taught Me" (Paula Watson); "Route 66" (Bobby Troup); "Big Jay's Hop," "Boogie in Front," "Blow Blow Blow" (Big Jay McNeely); "Bull Fiddle Boogie" (Charles R. Grean, Cy Coben); "Early Autumn" (Ralph Burns, Woody Herman); "Ole Buttermilk Sky" (Hoagy Carmichael, Jack Brooks); "So Tired" (Russ Morgan, Jack Stuart); "Mr. Fool" (Dave Bartholomew); "Chica Chica Boom Chick" (Harry Warren, Mack Gordon); "Apricot Flowers Blossoming" (Ma Xiaonan); "Evening Primrose" (Huang Qingshi, Li Jingjuang); "Bless You/For the Good That's in You" (Peggy Lee, Mel Torme). *Author's Note*: This author met Cohen in 1974, two years after he had been released from the federal penitentiary at Atlanta and two years before his death. He was living quietly in L.A. at that time. In my meeting with Cohen, I was accompanied by an LAPD lieutenant friend of mine, who knew Cohen, and introduced us. I had written about Cohen in my book, *Bloodletters and Badmen*, and Cohen stated that he had read those passages, telling me: "You came pretty close to the truth about me, but nobody really knows my story, except me." He went on to say: "The press and a lot of Hollywood hacks made up a lot of crap about me, claiming I bumped off more people than live in Baker, California! They claimed that I peddled drugs into L.A., and that's a lot of bull, too. Back in the old days, when Ben [Bugsy] Siegel was alive, I was in charge of his wire service that ran out of the Flamingo [the gangland-controlled wire service reporting racetrack results, which Cohen established in Siegel's Flamingo Hotel and Casino in Las Vegas] and bossed a lot of the bookies. I made too much dough and that sent me [imprisoned] away on tax evasion. The trouble is, I lived a little too much in the public eye, so the feds and cops concentrated on me, instead of the real big shots running things. I paid for all that prancing around. We all do, if you show off too much. No, all that stuff they say I did, I never did. Well, maybe a little…" Excessive violence and gutter language prohibit viewing by children. **p**, Dan Lin, Kevin McCormick, Michael Tadross, Jon Silk; **d**, Ruben Fleischer; **cast**, Sean Penn, Josh Brolin, Ryan Gosling, Nick Nolte, Mireille Enos, Troy Garity, Austin Abrams, Emma Stone, Josh Pence, Anthony Mackie, Robert Patrick, Michael Pena, Giovanni Ribisi; **w**, Will Beall (based on the book by Paul Lieberman); **c**, Dion Beebe; **m**, Steve Jablonsky; **ed**, Alan Baumgarten, James Herbert; **prod d**, Maher Ahmad; **art d**, Mark Hunstable, Timothy D. O'Brien, Dean Wolcott; **set d**, Gene Serdena; **spec eff**, Burt

The monster again on the loose in *Godzilla*, 2014.

Dalton, Bruno Van Zeebroeck, George Zamora.

Gimme Shelter ★★★ 2014; U.S.; 201m; Day Twenty-Eight Films/Roadside Attractions; Color; Drama; Children: Unacceptable (MPAA: PG-13); **BD**; **DVD**. Taut and well-acted tale begins with sixteen-year-old street-wise Hudgens, who has never had an easy life. Her mother, Dawson, is a drug addict and prostitute, both physically and verbally abusive to Hudgens, and is grooming her to follow in her vile trade. Hudgens wants more out of life and resists her mother by running away and goes in search of her father, Fraser. She had never known him because he was nineteen when he got her mother pregnant and then left. He has become a Wall Street broker and takes her in. She then learns that she has become pregnant by a teenage boy she met on the train to New York, but he now wants nothing to do with her. She is forced to leave Fraser's house because she chooses to give birth to the baby. She runs away again, but is finally taken in again by her father, a parent who loves his daughter at all costs. The story isn't much, but the acting is stunning from Hudgens, Fraser and Dawson, all convincing us that they are, indeed, the troubled characters enmeshed in an inescapable past, but, on the part of Hudgens and Fraser, having the courage and resolve to change the future for a better lifestyle. Not related to the 1970 Rolling Stones documentary of the same name. Songs: "George Jeffersons" (Chaz Wheeler, Dennis P. Coronel, Kahallie L. Oden, Wesley Paul Ivazes), "The Bottom" (Kevin Bennett, Jr.), "Turn It Up" (Jerome Hindes, Jr.), "Not Much Time Left" (Mychael Danna), "Anyway" (Bennett, Jr.), "Born to Die" (Justin Parker, Lana Del Rey), "Puttin in that Work" (Bennett, Jr.), "Price Tag" (Lukasz Gottwald, Claude Kelly, Bobby Ray Jr. Simmons, Jessica Cornish), "Unconscious" (Seth Jones, Marie Miller, Luke Sheets), "Here Comes Santa Claus (Right Down Santa Claus Lane) (Gene Autry, Oakley Haldeman), "Karen's Letter" (Edward Shearmur), "To Build a Home" (Jason Swinscoe, Patrick Wilson, Phil France), "The Prayer" (David Foster, Carole Bayer Sager). Mature thematic material involving mistreatment, drug content, violence and gutter language, all involving teens, prohibit viewing by children. p, Ron Krauss, Jeff Rice, Joshua Amir, Dylan Russell; d&w, Krauss; cast, Vanessa Hudgens, Rosario Dawson, Brendan Fraser, James Earl Jones, Dascha Polanco, Stephanie Szostak, Emily Meade, Candace Smith, Ann Dowd, Tashiana Washington; c, Alain Marcoen; m, Olafur Arnalds; ed, Marie-Helene Dozo, Mark Sult; prod d, William Ladd Skinner; art d, Stephanie Beaurain; set d, Beaurain, Cathy T. Marshall; spec eff, Drew Jiritano, Phillip Moses, Iva Petkova, Radost Yonkova.

Gimme the Loot ★★★ 2013; U.S.; 79m; Seven for Ten/Sundance Selects; Color; Comedy; Children: Unacceptable; **BD**; **DVD**. Off-the-wall comedy depicts in very natural terms two African-American teenagers from the Bronx, Hickson and Washington. They are self-styled graffiti artists whose work is messed up by a rival gang. They spend two hot summer days trying to get $500 they need to get revenge on their rivals by signing a huge apple that appears at the New York Mets' baseball field (Shea Stadium) whenever any player hits a home run. The feat would make them the most famous or notorious graffiti writers in the city, if they can pull it off. Lighthearted and even charming, the tale overcomes the miserable social setting where gangs rule the roost and where friendship is at the core of the story. Though street smart, the boys are nevertheless as naïve as any country bumpkin, which provides for considerable mirth. This film, like so many inner-city portraits, saw limited distribution. Songs: "Let's Shimmy," "Send the Holy Ghost Down" (B. Clark); "Burnin' Fire," "Good Ol' Jack," "Daffodils," Black Box," "Whattup," "So Gracefully" (Nicholas Britell); "Stardust" (1927; Hoagy Carmichael); "My Man Rockhead" (Ike Turner); "Alter-Ego" (music: Nicholas Britell; music: Matt Garelick, James A. Shiavone); "Corrido" (music: Nicholas Britell; lyrics: Mario Grullon); "Annual Moon Words" (Angus Andrews, Julian Gross, Aaron Hemphill); "Spinning and Scratching" (Fredrik Bengt Eriksson, Markus Jasper Gorsch, Johan Bo Lindwall, Josephine Ewa Linn Olausson, Nicholaus Sparding); "If It Wasn't for the Lord What Would I Do," "The Vibrator" (Jack McDuff); "I Need You Tonight," "The Lord Is My Shepherd," "I Found Jesus in Time" (traditional); "Grand Central" (music: Nicholas Britell; lyrics: Rahzel Brown Jr.); "The Collector Returns/Mount Zion" (music: Nicholas Britell; lyrics: J Nyah the Collector); "I Shall Be Released" (Bob Dylan). Mature themes and drug-dealing references prohibit viewing by children. p, Jonathan Demme, Dominic Buchanan, Natalie Difford, Jamund Washington; d&w, Adam Leon; cast, Ty Hickson, Tashiana Washington, Meeko, Zoe Lescaze, Sam Soghor, Adam Metzger, Greyson Cruz, James Harris Jr., Melvin Mogoli, Joshua Rivera, Howard Donowitz, Angelo Rodriguez, Jose Rivera; c, Jonathan Miller; m, Nicholas Britell; ed, Morgan Faust; prod d, Katie Hickman, Sam Lisenco.

Girl Most Likely ★★★ 2012; U.S.; 103m; Maven Pictures/Lionsgate; Color; Comedy; Children: Unacceptable (MPAA: PG-13); **BD**; **DVD**. Pleasant comedy sees Wiig, a failed young New York playwright, faced with mounting problems. Her career is in a tailspin and her boyfriend dumps her. She loses her writing job at a magazine and then gets evicted from her rental apartment. An attempt at suicide fails, so she leaves Manhattan and returns home to Ocean City, New Jersey, to live in what she considers to be utter failure with her dysfunctional family. Her father left the clan some years ago while her mother, Bening, is a kooky compulsive gambler and her younger brother, Fitzgerald, is a stay-at-home inventor of things no one wants. As if that wasn't bad enough, she finds a strange man, Criss, in her old bedroom and an even stranger man, Dillon, sleeping in her mother's bed. She learns the hard way that in order to rebuild her life, she must first come to love and accept both her family and her Jersey roots if she is ever going to get away from them. Songs: "Sunday Girl" (Chris Stein), "Dream Vacation" (William Risby). Sexual content and gutter language prohibit viewing by children. p, Mark Amin, Alix Madigan, Celine Rattray, Trudie Styler, Luca Borghese, Cynthia Coury, Hardy Justice; d, Shari Springer Berman, Robert Pulcini; cast, Kristen Wiig, Annette Bening, Matt Dillon, Darren Criss, Christopher Fitzgerald, June Diane Raphael, Natasha Lyonne, Bob Balaban, Sydney Lucas, Jimmy Palumbo; w, Michelle Morgan; c, Steve Yedlin; m, Rob Simonsen; ed, Robert Pulcini; prod d, Annie Spitz; set d, Shannon Finnerty; spec eff, Drew Jiritano, Shaina Holmes.

Girl on a Bicycle ★★★ 2014; U.S./Germany; 101m; Weidemann & Berg Filmproduktion/Monterey Media; Color; Comedy/Romance; Children: Unacceptable MPAA: R); **BD**; **DVD**. Entertaining and lively romance tale begins with Amato, an Italian who drives a Paris tour bus. He thinks he is in love Tschirner, a German stewardess, and proposes marriage. She accepts and becomes his fiancée. No sooner is he committed to marriage than he sees Monot, a beautiful young French woman. When Monot rides her bicycle next to Amato's bus, Considine, Amato's friend, urges him to follow Monot. Amato impulsively follows his romantic urge, and his life is soon turned upside down. He must now contend with a French "wife," a German fiancée, and two Australian children who call him "Papa." There are more than a few hilarious moments in this zany story, and Amato and the rest of the cast give rollicking performances. Songs: "It Just Takes a Moment," "Play with Me," "Last Stop Paris" (Craig Richey); "All Smiles" (Jess Penner); "New Morning" (Jo Kelly Stephenson); "Such a Wonderful" (Jody Friedman, Stephen Paul Sulikowski); "Believe in You" (Bess Rogers, Chris Kuffner); "Doesn't Get Better Than This" (Tim Myers, Joy Williams); "Happy As Can Be" (Thomas Feuer, Neal Pawley); "Sunnyside" (Austin Joseph Nicholson, Shirli McAllen); "C'est L'amour" (Rosi Golan, Boots Ottestad); "I Am Smiling," "Con Te Partiro." Sexuality, nudity and gutter language prohibit viewing by children. **p**, Max Weidemann, Quirin Berg; **d&w**, Jeremy Leven; **cast**, Vincenzo Amato, Nora Tschirner, Louise Monot, Paddy Considine, Stephane Debac, Brice Fournier, Kellie Shirley, Aurelien Cavaud, Christine Citti, Chiara de Luca, **c**, Robert Fraisse; **m**, Craig Richey; **ed**, Michael Trent; **prod d**, Jean-Michel Hugon; **art d**, Andreas Olshausen; **spec eff**, Ismat Zaidi.

The Giver ★★★ 2014; U.S.; 97m.; As Is Productions/Weinstein Co.; B/W/Color; Science Fiction; Children: Unacceptable (MPAA: PG-13); **BD**; **DVD**. Thwaites lives in a futuristic world where everyone conforms and is seemingly content, deprived of choice and what is considered to be the burden of memories. There is no hunger, suffering, or violence but also no freedom, choice, or individuality in his scientifically controlled environment. Streep, the Chief Elder of this utopia, assigns Thwaites to inherit the highly honored role of the community's Receiver of Memories and he begins training with the man currently holding that office, Bridges, known as the Giver. Through Bridges, Thwaites learns about joy and pleasure, but also pain, suffering, war, and death, which leads him to question the utopia in which he has been living. Both Bridges and Thwaites agree it is time for change, to let everyone have the right of choice, which can be accomplished by returning memories. When Thwaites experiences emotion for the first time, he falls in love with Rush, whom he had previously considered just a friend. Now he must race against time to escape his past utopian life in order to save his own and the lives of those he loves. Well made and intelligently scripted, good performances are seen by the entire cast. The story nevertheless owes much to other tales such as **Invasion of the Body Snatchers**, 1956, and its 1978 remake where humans are replaced by plant-like lookalikes that have no memories or emotions. Songs: "Silent Night" (1818; music: Franz Gruber; lyrics: Joseph Mohr), "The Holly and the Ivy" (traditional British carol), "Ordinary Human" (Ryan Tedder). **p**, Jeff Bridges, Neil Koenigsberg, Nikki Silver; **d**, Phillip Noyce; **cast**, Bridges, Meryl Streep, Alexander Skarsgard, Katie Holmes, Brenton Thwaites, Taylor Swift, Cameron Monaghan, Odeya Rush, Emma Tremblay, Katharina Damm; **w**, Michael Mitnick, Robert B. Weide (based on the novel by Lois Lowry); **c**, Ross Emery; **m**, Marco Beltrami; **ed**, Barry Alexander Brown; **prod d**, Ed Verreaux; **art d**, Christopher R. DeMuri, Catherine Palmer, Shira Hockman; **set d**, Andrew McCarthy; **spec eff**, Cordell McQueen.

God Help the Girl ★★★ 2014; U.K.; 111m; Barry Mendel/Amplify; Color; Drama/Romance; Children: Unacceptable (MPAA: PG-13); **BD**; **DVD**. Pleasing tale sees Browning as a young woman in a hospital in Glasgow, Scotland, suffering from anorexia nervosa. She escapes the psychiatric ward and starts writing songs as a way to improve her emotional stability. Songwriting leads her to meeting Alexander and Murray, two songwriters who are having relationship problems. The film follows their adventures over the course of a long, seemingly idyllic sum-

The earliest version of the monster, *Godzilla*, 1956.

mer and which ends in a final concert. The film saw limited distribution. Drug use prohibits viewing by children. **p**, Barry Mendel, Carole Sheridan; **d&w**, Stuart Murdoch; **cast**, Emily Browning, Olly Alexander, Hannah Murray, Pierre Boulanger, Cora Bisset, Sarah Swire, Mark Radcliffe, Stuart Maconie, Ann Scott-Jones, Josie Long; **c**, Giles Nuttgens; **ed**, David Arthur; **prod d**, Mark Leese; **art d**, Caroline Grebbell; **spec eff**, Perry Costello, Fiorenza Bagnariol.

Godzilla ★★★ 2014; U.S./Japan; 123m; Legendary Pictures/WB; Color; Adventure; Science Fiction; Children: Unacceptable; **3-D**; **BD**; **DVD**. Sixteen years after the scaly monster last appeared on film, this new addition to the Godzilla franchise begins in 1999 with Cranston, an American engineer, in charge of a nuclear plant beneath Mount Fuji in Japan. Tremors from an earthquake in the Philippines are felt in Japan, although some believe that the Earth's shaking is being caused by something else. The plant begins to break apart, its core is breached, and those who haven't been killed run for their lives. Fifteen years later, Cranston still has nightmares about that fatal day, and is haunted by thinking that something other than an earthquake brought down the power plant and whatever caused it has been covered up. He returns to the place where the plant was once located and finds the area to be off limits and under a quarantine. He is arrested by Japanese officials for trespassing and taken to jail, where his son, Taylor-Johnson, later bails him out. Taylor-Johnson, a U.S. Navy lieutenant and ordnance disposal technician in San Francisco, then goes to Japan to investigate his father's long-held suspicion that the tremors at the nuclear plant were not from an earthquake. Ford experiences similar ground movement, so father and son become determined to learn what is going on. They infiltrate the quarantine zone together and discover a secret facility at its center where experiments are being performed on a giant monster that feeds on nuclear radiation. It's not called Godzilla but MUTO (Massive Unidentified Terrestrial Organism) and it is said to have caused the 1999 tragedy at the plant. It is not alone, as a second variation of insect-like creatures appears. The MUTOs want to meet and mate, and Godzilla decides to make its presence known for reasons of its own. The three species of monsters plan to converge in San Francisco to get at Ford's wife, Olsen, and young son. Ford and some armed forces colleagues attempt to prevent this from happening by deploying a nuclear weapon, even though they know that the MUTOs are seemingly immune to radioactive material. The monsters arrive at San Francisco, where the monsters destroy the Golden Gate Bridge and other landmarks. Efforts to nuke the MUTO and Godzilla keep failing and, as usual, it looks like the end of mankind. However, the monsters are eventually and thankfully subdued once again and humanity saved. The story is complex and sometimes confusing, but the special effects are

Another version of the monster, *Godzilla*, 1985.

awesomely impressive and the real reason to see this futuristic tale. The film was enormously popular at the box office, earning more than $529.1 million in its initial release against a budget of $160 million. *Author's Note*: The film was several years in the making, the computer-generated special effects taking a great deal of time to achieve. The film was shot on location in Vancouver and throughout British Columbia, Canada. The Golden Gate Bridge has been destroyed in other science fiction films, including **The Core**, 2003 (radiation from Earth's disturbed core cuts the bridge in half); **It Came from Beneath the Sea**, 1955 (mammoth octopus destroys the bridge); **Megashark vs. Giant Octopus**, 2009 (giant shark bites the bridge in half); **Meteor Storm**, 2010 (made-for-TV; meteor shower destroys the bridge); **Pacific Rim**, 2013 (futuristic monsters destroy the bridge); **X-Men: The Last Stand**, 2006 (Magneto and his mutants rip away the foundation of the bridge and use the structure as a span to link San Francisco to the island of Alcatraz). **p**, Jon Jashni, Mary Parent, Brian Rogers, Thomas Tull; **d**, Gareth Edwards; **cast**, Aaron Taylor-Johnson, Juliette Binoche, Ken Watanabe, David Strathairn, Elizabeth Olsen, Bryan Cranston, Sally Hawkins, Victor Rasuk, CJ Adams, Al Sapienza; **w**, Max Borenstein (based on a story by David Callaham); **c**, Seamus McGarvey; **m**, Alexandre Desplat; **ed**, Bob Ducsay; **prod d**, Owen Paterson; **art d**, Ross Dempster, Dan Hermansen, Scott Meehan, Grant Van Der Slagt; **set d**, Elizabeth Wilcox; **spec eff**, Eric Frazier, Joel Whist.

Gone Girl ★★★ 2014; U.S.; 116m; New Regency/FOX; Color; Crime Drama; Children: Unacceptable (MPAA: R); **BD**; **DVD**. Taut thriller begins when Affleck returns from an early-morning visit to the bar he owns with his twin sister to find, on the day of his 15th wedding anniversary, that his wife, Pike, is not home. He sees signs of a struggle and calls police who suspect he might have arranged her disappearance. The film flashes back to the night they met and Pike tells him he has a "villainous chin," so he covers it with a forefinger when he tries to be sincere. Affleck has been a writer until he lost his job in Missouri and moved to Manhattan, and Pike, also unemployed, went with him. She was the inspiration for her parents' series of children's books. Police set up a hotline, launch a website, and talk to suspects. Affleck begins to feel the weight of the cops presuming he is responsible, and the media is already convicting him of kidnapping and killing his wife. He hires Perry, a celebrity lawyer, to defend him. Then entries from Pike's diary begin to surface and we learn she was not as happy in the marriage as might have been thought. Then it is revealed that Affleck has been having an affair with another woman and Pike is alive, but in hiding, trying to frame Affleck for her reported death. Pike's earlier boyfriend, Harris, agrees to hide her, but she is soon uncomfortable with his romantic advances. She murders him and returns to Affleck saying she had been

kidnapped. Affleck accepts her back despite knowing she is a murderer, because she is pregnant with their child, and even here, Pike has been deceptive as she has artificially inseminated herself with Affleck's semen from a sperm bank. The film ends with evil triumphant as the so-called happy couple announce to the world in a TV appearance that they are about to have a child. The tale is sinister from beginning to the end and Pike's riveting performance captions her corrupt and calculating persona. Pike received an Oscar nomination as Best Actress, and she is supported with outstanding performances from the rest of the cast. The film was popular at the box office, earning more than $369.3 million against a budget of $61 million. Songs: "Saved By Zero" (Adam Woods, Alfred Agius, Cyril Curnin, James West-Oram, Peter Greenall), "Wall of God" (Eddie Lundon, Gary Daly, Gary Johnson), "New York, New York" (Fred Ebb, John Kander), "Law and Order Theme" (Mike Post), "Don't Fear the Reaper" (Donald Roeser), "Defy Spaces for You" (Didier Francois Goret), "Left Ey3" (Natasia Gail Zolot, Michael Weiner, Anthony Negrete), "Lady Double Dealer" (Fernando von Arb, Chris von Rohr), "Cool Cat" (Simon Thorpe, John Donaldson), "I'm Trippin Out" (Jason DeFord), "Not Gonna Bring Me Down" (Matt Naylor, Scott Stallone, Steven Stern, Cristi Waughan), and "The Informer," "The Instigator," "Heavy Justice," "Drastic Measures," and "Cold Case" (all by Will Collins, Christpher Collins). Violence, strong sexual content, nudity and gutter language prohibit viewing by children. **p**, Cean Chaffin, Joshua Donen, Arnon Milchan, Reese Witherspoon; **d**, David Fincher; **cast**, Ben Affleck, Rosamund Pike, Neil Patrick Harris, Sela Ward, Missi Pyle, Tyler Perry, Scoot McNairy, Boyd Holbrook, Lee Norris, Carrie Coon; **w**, Gillian Flynn (based on her novel); **c**, Jeff Cronenweth; **m**, Trent Reznor, Atticus Ross; **ed**, Kirk Baxter; **prod d**, Donald Graham Burt; **art d**, Dawn Swiderski; **set d**, Douglas A. Mowat; **spec eff**, Ron Bolanowski.

The Good Dinosaur ★★★★ 2015; U.S.; 100m; Pixar/WB; Color; Animated Adventure; Children: Cautionary (MPAA: PG-13); **BD**; **DVD**. This beautifully animated tale depicts a warm-hearted story of friendship between species in the American Northwest. Arlo (Ochoa voiceover) is a small Apatosaurus who survives the extinction of dinosaurs sixty-five million years earlier and now lives in an advanced agricultural environment. He lives with his parents (Wright and McDormand voiceovers) and older and bigger siblings (Scribner and Padilla voiceovers) on the banks of a river that may be in prehistoric Wyoming where there is a family of green, long-necked dinosaurs. Ochoa feels inferior to everyone, although his father, Wright, tries to teach him the importance of bravery and setting good goals. Wright tells Ochoa that he has to earn his place in the world by doing something significant. Ochoa's big chance comes when a heavy rainstorm washes him downriver and he winds up miles from home, alone with just a small human at his side. The wild Neanderthal boy (Bright voiceover) is wary of the huge beast and, at first, they distrust each other, but slowly become friends. Bright crawls and grunts, but he and Ochoa eventually find a way to wordlessly share a sense of sorrow in their plight far from their homes. Their struggle for survival and to find their way home has them encountering various species of hostile animals, including a cobra with legs and a strange old horned Styracosauru (Sohn voiceover), then a pack of vicious raptors and a group of starved pterodactyls led by Zahn (voiceover). Ochoa and Bright escape to the mountains where they fortunately meet a friendly clan of Tyrannosaurus rex, who are like Western ranchers or cowboys. Along the way home, Ochoa gets to demonstrate his courage, most notably in befriending Bright, a being unlike himself, but with the same kind of fortitude. The digital effects are top-notch while the story line presents a very entertaining and heartfelt adventure from Pixar, the firm that made **Toy Story**, 1995, and so many other outstanding digitally enhanced productions. Though the film did well at the box office, earning more than $214.4 million, its budget of $200 million was narrowly offset. Scenes of peril, action and thematic elements caution viewing by children. **p**, Denise Ream; **d**, Peter Sohn; **cast**

(voiceovers), Jeffrey Wright, Frances McDormand, Raymond Ochoa, Jack Bright, Maleah Padilla, Sam Elliott, Anna Paquin, Ryan Teeple, Jack McGraw, Marcus Scribner, Peter Sohn, Steve Zahn; **w**, Meg LeFauve (from a story by LeFauve, Sohn, Erik Benson, Kelsey Mann, Bob Peterson; **c**, Stephen Schaffer; **m**, Jeff Danna, Mychael Danna; **spec eff**, Lou Hamou-Lhadj, Andrew Jimenez.

Good People ★★★ 2014; U.S.; 90m; Film 60/Millennium Entertainment; Color; Crime Drama; Children: Unacceptable (MPAA: R); **BD**; **DVD**. This taut thriller begins with young American couple Franco and Hudson, who move to London for a fresh start in their marriage after Hudson has a miscarriage. She is a schoolteacher and he is renovating her family's old house. They are spending too much money on the renovation and are hard up for cash when the tenant in the apartment below dies of a drug overdose. They discover a bag containing more than $200,000 in British pound notes and decide to use it to clear up their debts. Wilkinson, a detective who has been on the trail of the missing money, believes the dead man was connected to a brutal criminal, Spruell, and questions Franco and Hudson, suspecting they know something about the money. He convinces them to act as bait for the drug-peddling Spruell and his henchmen and they arrange to make the money drop with Spruell. Friel, who is Hudson's friend, is taken hostage, along with her child, by Spruell, but they escape when Wilkinson, Franco and Hudson spring a trap for him and his men. A cat-and-mouse game ensues within the old house Franco and Hudson had been renovating. Spruell, however, along with his cohorts, are eliminated one by one while the old house burns down. Franco and Hudson have done the right thing and Franco is elated when Hudson announces that she is about to have another child. The acting is superior and the tension is held high throughout via Genz's firm direction, despite the outlandish plot. The film did not do well at the box office and deserved better from reviewers that unfairly panned the film because of its traditional plotlines. Songs: "For You" (Serena Ryder, Jay Hawkins, Jon Levine), "Mansquito" excerpt (Joseph Conlan, Sophia Morizet). Bloody violence and gutter language prohibit viewing by children. **p**, Tobey Maguire, Ed Cathell III, Ben Forkner, Thomas Gammeltoft, Eric Kranzler, Avi Lerner, Sean Wheelan; **d**, Henrik Ruben Genz; **cast**, James Franco, Kate Hudson, Tom Wilkinson, Anna Friel, Omar Sy, Diarmaid Murtagh, Sam Spruell, Michael Jibson, Diana Hardcastle, Oliver Dimsdale, Lasco Atkins; **w**, Kelly Masterson (based on the novel by Marcus Sakey); **c**, Jorgen Johansson; **m**, Neil Davidge; **ed**, Paul Tothill; **prod d**, Kave Quinn; **art d**, Tim Blake, Mark Raggett; **set d**, Niamh Coulter; **spec eff**, David H. Watkins.

Goosebumps ★★★ 2015; U.S./Australia; 103m; Scholastic Entertainment/COL; Color; Animated Horror; Children: Unacceptable (MPAA: PG); **BD**; **DVD**. Teenage Minnette is unhappy about moving from a big city to a small town, but things look better when he meets Rush, the lovely girl next door. Things get complicated then when Minnette learns that Rush's father is R.L. Stine, author of scary books for children. Minnette learns that Stine, played by Black, is strange and the reason is that he is a prisoner of his own imagination, so that the monsters in his stories are real to him and he keeps them from harming readers by keeping them locked up in his books. Minnette accidentally releases the monsters from their stories, and they begin terrorizing the town. It's now up to Minnette, Rush, and Black to get them all back into the books to restore peace to the town. A lot of scary scenes and frightening monsters are produced in this computer-animated feature, and its special effects provide genuinely frightening sequences. The film was popular at the box office, earning more than $119.2 million in its initial release against a budget of more than $58 million. **p**, Deborah Forte, Neal H. Moritz; **d**, Rob Letterman; **cast**, Jack Black, Dylan Minnette, Odeya Rush, Halston Sage, Amy Ryan, Ryan Lee, Kumail Nanjiani, Jared Sandler, Jillian Bell, Ken Marino, Timothy Simons; **w**, Darren Lemke (based on the story by Scott Alexander, Larry Karaszewski, based on the books by R.L. Stine); **c**, Javier Aguirresarobe; **m**, Danny Elfman; **ed**, Jim May; **prod d**, Sean

Raymond Burr, right, reprises his 1956 role in *Godzilla*, 1985.

Haworth; **art d**, Dawn Snyder, Patrick M. Sullivan Jr., Andrew White; **set d**, Frank Galline; **spec eff**, Eric Rylander.

The Grand Budapest Hotel ★★★★ 2014; U.K./Germany; 99m; Scott Rudin Productions/Fox Searchlight; Color; Comedy/Drama; Children: Unacceptable (MPAA: R); **BD**; **DVD**. Exceptionally well-made tale depicts the fictional adventures of Gustave H., wonderfully portrayed by Fiennes, a legendary concierge at the famous but also mythical European hotel between WWI (1914-1918) and WWII (1939-1945). It also is the story of Revolori, the lobby boy, who becomes Fiennes' most trusted friend and helps Fiennes prove his innocence after being framed for murder. The film opens in the present time as a teenage girl standing in the now dilapidated hotel's courtyard reads a memoir written by Wilkinson, a man who tells of a trip to the hotel in the late 1960s when it had become rundown and had but a few guests. Wilkinson tells of when he was a young man, played by Law, and when he met the hotel's then owner, Revolori, who relates its history and gives a reason for not closing it. Revolori's story begins in 1932 during the hotel's final glory years. Located in fictional Middle European Zubrowska, the area is on the verge of World War II, but that is of little concern to Fiennes, the hotel's devoted concierge, who has an affair with a mysterious wealthy guest, Madame D, played by Swinton. She is soon afterward found dead under mysterious circumstances, and he learns that in her will she has bequeathed him a valuable painting. Her family becomes enraged, especially her son, Brody. Fiennes hides the painting in a safe at the hotel, then is arrested and framed for murdering the woman. He is imprisoned, but the hotel's new teenage lobby boy, Revolori, helps him to escape. Fiennes then teams up with Revolori to prove his innocence. They go to a mountaintop monastery where they meet Amalric, who can provide Fiennes with an alibi for the night of the murder, but they are pursued by Dafoe, an assassin, who kills Amalric. Fiennes and Revolori steal a sled and chase Dafoe as he flees the monastery. At the edge of a cliff, Revolori kills Dafvoe and rescues Fiennes. Meanwhile, the military has taken over the hotel and turned it into a bunker as war is imminent. Fiennes gets Revolori's young wife, Ronan, to retrieve the painting in the hotel, but she is discovered by Brody. A gunfight ensues before Fiennes' innocence is proven by way of a letter, penned by Amalric and which has been hidden in the painting's frame. Another version of Madame D's will is discovered in which she reveals that she was the owner of the Grand Budapest Hotel and leaves much of her fortune, the hotel, and the painting to Fiennes, making him fabulously rich. He becomes one of the hotel's regular guests and later grants Revolori ownership. Meanwhile, the war rages on. During a train trip, soldiers search Fiennes's coach and he is shot and killed during an argument. Revolori vows to continue Fiennes' legacy at the hotel, but the war takes its toll.

Ralph Fiennes in *The Grand Budapest Hotel*, 2014.

Ronan contracts a disease and dies a few years later. Revolori, now aging and devastated, tells the author of the memoir, Wilkinson, that he can't bring himself to close the hotel because it is his last link to his late wife and the best years of his life. Wilkinson later departs for South America and never returns to the hotel, leaving the hotel's and Revolori's fate unknown. In flash-forward to the present, the girl finishes reading the memoir about the hotel and leaves the courtyard. Fiennes, Revolori and the rest of the fine cast render standout performances in this haunting, sometimes eerie, tale, which is full of poignancy and a strange longing for a past that never existed. The film won Oscars for Best Original Score (Desplat); Best Production Design (Stockhausen; Summersgill, Gessler, Sullivan; set decoration: Pinnock); Best Costume Design (Milena Canonero) and Best Makeup and Hairstyling (Frances Hannon, Mark Coulier). It received Oscar nominations for Best Picture; Best Director (Anderson); Best Original Screenplay (Anderson, Guinness); Best Cinematography (Yeoman); and Best Film Editing (Pilling). The film was very successful at the box office, earning more than $174.6 million in its initial release against a budget of more than $30 million. Songs: "s'Rothe-Zauerli" (Ruedi Roth, Werner Roth), "Concerto for Lute and Plucked Strings I. Moderato" (Antonio Vivaldi), "The Linden Tree" (Pavel Vasilevich Kulikov), "Roses from the South" (Johann Strauss Jr.), "Happy Birthday to You" (Mildred J. Hill, Patty S. Hill), "Kamarinskaya" (traditional), "Svetit Mesyats" (Vasily Vasilievich Andreyev). Violence, gutter language and some sexual content prohibit viewing by children. **p**, Wes Anderson, Scott Rudin, Jeremy Dawson, Steven M. Rales, Eli Bush; **d**, Anderson; **cast**, Ralph Fiennes, Tony Revolori, Saoirse Ronan, F. Murray Abraham, Jude Law, Adrien Brody, Bill Murray, Edward Norton, Tilda Swinton, Tom Wilkinson, Willem Dafoe, Jeff Goldblum, Harvey Keitel, Owen Wilson; **w**, Anderson (based on a story by Anderson, Hugo Guinness, and inspired by the works of Stefan Zweig); **c**, Robert D. Yeoman; **m**, Alexandre Desplat; **ed**, Barney Pilling; **prod d**, Adam Stockhausen; **art d**, Steve Summersgill, Stephan O. Gessler, Gerald Sullivan; **set d**, Anna Pinnock; **spec eff**, Gerd Nefzer.

Grand Piano ★★★ 2013; Spain; 90m; Nostromo Pictures; Magnet Releasing; Color; Crime Drama; Children: Unacceptable (MPAA: R); **BD**; **DVD**. Taut thriller sees Wood as an up-and-coming concert pianist until he develops stage fright while attempting to play an unplayable piece, "La Cinquette," that causes him to break down during a performance. Five years later, he is contracted to reappear in public for a comeback performance in Chicago that will be dedicated to the memory of his late mentor, pianist-composer Patrick Godureaux, who has posthumously acquired massive media coverage due to the mysterious disappearance of his vast fortune. Wood's decision to return to performing

in public is due to encouragement from his actress-singer wife, Bishe. Just before the concert is to begin, Winter, a house usher, hands Wood a folder of sheet music that Wood greatly appreciates because he almost walked on stage without it. He opens the folder and, to his chagrin, finds the manuscript to "La Cinquette." He crumples the sheet music and throws it to the floor, then walks onstage. The concert opens with a three-movement piano concerto, which Wood plays brilliantly. However, late in the first movement, he turns over his sheet music and sees a warning that, if he plays one wrong note, he will die. He is annoyed but shrugs it off as a prank from one of the orchestra members, but, as he turns to the next page he sees another message that tells him, "Do you think I'm kidding? Look to your right." Wood looks and sees a laser dot from a sniper rifle aimed at his hand. Turning the page again, a third message warns that, if he calls for help, he will be shot between the eyes. Both frightened and confused, Wood leaves the stage and returns to his dressing room. The audience, including Bishe and her friends Leech and Egerton, are shocked. In his dressing room, Wood receives a text message that tells him to look in his backpack. He finds an earpiece there, so now he can hear and speak with his predator. The voice tells him that he is in control of the situation, and, if Wood makes any attempts to seek help, or leave the concert hall, both he and Bishe will be shot. Wood then walks back to the wings of the stage where his predator, Cusack, from a balcony box, demonstrates the power and accuracy of his high-tech silenced sniper rifle as he shoots the carpet next to the piano, with no one in the audience or the orchestra noticing. Cusack then commands Wood to return to the stage to begin the concerto's second movement. Wood desperately pulls out his cell phone and places it to his left on the piano, out of the sight of the sniper, and attempts to call Leech, who is sitting in the audience in the balcony. Leech attempts to answer by leaving his seat and tries to call Wood back. Through one sheet on the music, Wood is able to text message Leech to let him know that Bishe is in danger. Leech receives the text and goes up to the box level to alert Bishe, but Winter, the usher who handed Wood the music before the concert, stops him. Leech shows Winter the text message, but the usher, who is in league with Cusack, begins walking with him to Bishe's box. He pulls out a taser to stun Leech, then snaps his neck. Egerton goes looking for Leech, but is ambushed and killed by Winter. Cusack then tells Wood to look above him to the rafters where he sees Leech's dead body hanging over a light fixture ramp, and the shooter cautions him not to lose his focus on playing the piano or he will die. Cusack then commands Wood that, instead of performing Beethoven's "Tempest Sonata," as the conductor originally announced, he must perform the piece that caused him to have the anxiety attack five years before, which was "La Cinquette." Cusack taunts Wood about the final four bars of the piece, which caused Wood to freeze up on stage and break down, unable to complete the performance. Cusack then reveals that he is a professional locksmith, and that shorty before Patrick Godureaux's death, he was hired by the composer to design a highly complex lock inside the piano that Wood is currently playing. When the final four bars of the music are played flawlessly, the lock system is triggered and will reveal a key to a safe which contains the composer's fortune. Cusack threatens that the last four bars are difficult but crucial and that Wood's and Bish's lives are at stake. During intermission, Wood hurries backstage to try to find the manuscript he had crumpled and tossed onto the floor, only to find that the janitor burned it in the basement with the other trash. Wood anxiously listens to the piece in his dressing room and takes notes on a program to help him remember. The conductor then announces Wood's solo performance of the Beethoven sonata, but Wood interrupts him, nervously announcing that he will perform "La Cinquette" instead, which is much to the audience's delight. Cusack warns Wood to pace himself, so as not to wear himself out. Wood plays the piece completely without error, until he gets to the very last note of the piece, a solo D note toward the very low end of the keyboard, but deliberately plays the wrong note to end the piece, which infuriates Cusack. Wood retorts back that the audience doesn't know the difference, and receives a huge standing ovation, having finally conquered the almost impossible piece. Cusack swears at him, but Wood ignores him, and introduces Bishe, much to hers and the audience's surprise and announces that she will sing a song as an encore, with the conductor accompanying. She reluctantly agrees, but her singing alone on stage allows Wood time to find Cusack. Wood races to the balcony where he finds the usher's dead body and then is confronted by Cusack, who chases him up to the light fixture rafters, directly above the piano onstage. They struggle, which causes a rivet to come loose and, to the horror of the audience, Wood and Cusack both come crashing down onto the stage. Cusack lands on the piano and is killed, while Wood breaks his leg but survives. Bishe rushes to him and they embrace. Later, Wood sees the damaged piano being loaded into a shipping truck and tells Bishe that he has to finish playing the "La Cinquette" properly. Inside the truck, Wood plays the last four bars of the piece perfectly, but nothing happens. Disappointed, he starts to walk away until he hears the gears of the internal lock system begin to turn, and the sound of a metal key hitting the floor. He bends down to pick it up as the film ends. Stylishly presented, the outlandish and often confusing plot is overcome by some very good acting by Wood, Cusack and the rest of the cast. Tension is sustained throughout by the increasing tempo of the somewhat bombastic music being played and the incessant interacting murderous threats foisted upon Wood by the sadistic Cusack. (The increasing pace between the music and the dramatic events working against each other was effectively used in another and earlier harrowing concert scene used by Alfred Hitchcock in **The Man Who Knew Too Much**, 1956, one where an assassination is about to take place.) Song: "Motherless Child" (Victor Reyes). Violence and gutter language prohibit viewing by children. **p**, Rodrigo Cortes, Adrian Guerra; **d**, Eugenio Mira; **cast**, Elijah Wood, John Cusack, Kerry Bishe, Tamsin Egerton, Allen Leech, Don McManus, Alex Winter, Ricardo Alexander, Dee Wallace, Jim Arnold; **w**, Damien Chazelle; **c**, Unax Mendia; **m**, Victor Reyes; **ed**, Jose Luis Romeu; **prod d**, Javier Alvarino; **spec eff**, Javier Jal, Alex Villagrasa.

Gravity ★★★★ 2013; U.S./U.K.; 91m; WB; Color; Science Fiction; Children: Unacceptable (MPAA: PG-13); **3-D**; **BD**; **DVD**. Often riveting futuristic tale sees veteran astronaut Clooney on his last flight before retiring, accompanied by Bullock, a medical engineer on her first shuttle mission to service the Hubble Space Telescope. Mission Control in Houston warns them about a Russian missile strike on a defunct satellite that results in a cloud of debris in space. The mission is ordered aborted, and the shuttle begins reentry when communication with Houston is lost. High-speed debris strikes the shuttle and detaches Bullock from the space craft, leaving her tumbling through space. Clooney manages to recover her and they make their way back to the space shuttle, but discover it has suffered catastrophic damage and the crew is dead. They use a thruster pack to make their way to the International Space Station (ISS), which is in orbit about 900 miles away, but Clooney estimates they have only ninety minutes before the debris field completes an orbit and threatens them again. Approaching the damaged but still operational ISS, they see its crew has evacuated in one of its two Soyuz modules. The remaining Soyuz has been damaged, causing its parachute to deploy and rendering it useless for returning to Earth. Clooney decides to use it to travel to a Chinese space station 100 miles away and board one of its modules to return safely to Earth. As they fly by the ISS, Bullock's leg gets entangled in the module's parachute cords and she grabs a strap on Clooney's suit. Despite her protests, Clooney detaches himself from the tether that holds them in order to save her from drifting away from him, and she is pulled back toward the ISS while Clooney floats away into space. Bullock enters the ISS by way of an airlock, but cannot reestablish communication with Clooney and concludes that she is the sole survivor. A fire breaks out forcing her to make her way to the Soyuz. She spacewalks to release the parachute cables just as the debris completes its orbit and destroys ISS. Bullock manages to align the

George Clooney in *Gravity*, 2013.

Soyuz with the Chinese space station, but discovers that its engine has no fuel. She resigns herself to being stranded in space and shuts down the cabin's oxygen supply to commit suicide. As she begins to lose consciousness, Clooney enters the capsule and scolds her for giving up. He tells her to rig the Soyuz's landing rockets to propel the capsule toward the Chinese space station, but Bullock then realizes that Clooney is not really alive and back with her. His imaginary reappearance gives her courage to carry on and she restores the flow of oxygen and uses the landing rockets to navigate with the Chinese space station, which is rapidly going out of orbit. Unable to dock the Soyuz with the Chinese station, Bullock ejects herself by way of an explosive decompression and uses a fire extinguisher as a makeshift thruster to travel to the Chinese station. Just as the station begins to break up, Bullock enters its space capsule and she becomes determined to return to Earth whether dead or alive. Her space capsule reenters Earth's atmosphere and she hears Mission Control over the radio. The capsule lands in a lake but dense smoke from an electrical fire inside the capsule forces Bullock to evacuate immediately. She opens the capsule hatch, which allows water to enter and sink it, forcing her to swim to safety ashore. She then watches as the remains of the Chinese space station reenters the atmosphere and takes her first steps back on land. Clooney and Bullock give exceptional performances as they struggle to survive in space and where that struggle presents a fascination chronicle of survival, based upon will power and considerable imagination. The lensing is spectacular, placing the viewer into an outer space of constant uncertainty and wonder. The film won Oscars for Best Director (Cuaron); Best Cinematography (Lubezki); Best Original Score (Price); Best Film Editing (Cuaron); Best Visual Effects (Corbould, Efrem); Best Sound Editing (Glenn Fremantle); and Best Sound Mixing (Skip Lievsay, Christopher Benstead, Niv Adiri, Chris Munro). The film also received Oscar nominations for Best Picture; Best Actress (Bullock); and Best Production Design (Nicholson, Scruton; set decoration: Goodwin). The film was a huge box office success, earning more than $723.2 million in its initial release against a budget of more than $100 million. Songs: "Angels Are Hard to Find" (Hank Williams Jr.), "Mera Joota Hai Japani" (Shailendra, Shankar Jaikishan), "Sinigit Meerannguaq" (Juaaka Lyberth), "Destination Anywhere" (Christopher Benstead, Robin Baynton), "922 Anthem" (Gaurav Dayal), "Ready" (Charles Leslie Scott, Chelsea Lynne Hinshaw). Intense perilous sequences, some disturbing images and gutter language prohibit viewing by children. **p**, Alfonso Cuaron, David Heyman; **d**, Alfonso Cuaron; **cast**, George Clooney, Sandra Bullock, Paul Sharma, (voiceovers) Eric Michels, Basher Savage; **w**, Alfonso and Jonas Cuaron; **c**, Emmanuel Lubezki; **m**, Steven Price; **ed**, Alfonso Cuaron, Mark Sanger; **prod d**, Andy Nicholson; **art d**, Mark Scruton; **set d**, Rosie Goodwin; **spec eff**, Neil Corbould, Manex Efrem.

Carey Mulligan and Leonardo DiCaprio in *The Great Gatsby,* 2013.

The Great Beauty ★★★★ 2014; Italy/France; 141m; Indigo Film; Janus Films; Color; Drama; Children: Unacceptable; **BD**; **DVD**. Top-notch drama sees Servillo as a journalist who has climbed to the top in Rome for decades by capitalizing on his charm. His one and only novella is virtually forgotten, but he considers himself to be a successful novelist, although he no longer writes serious fiction, and has kept his literary image alive by writing columns about local culture. He has spent most of his time giving parties and mending fences in the social world. His life changes as he turns sixty-five years old and is confronted by his past, making him reflect on his life. He discovers for the first time that he is living in a city of fantastic beauty. He looks for inspiration and temporarily finds it in Ferilli, a beautiful stripper, but their romance is never realized. This wonderfully acted film provides an incisive and thought-provoking character study of a disillusioned man who fears his best years are already behind him, even though they were never significant in the grand scheme of things. Rome is, he decides, the great beauty of his life. Superbly directed, the film received an Oscar as Best Foreign Language Film. The film saw a modest success at the box office, earning more than $24 million in its initial release. Songs/Music: "I Lie" and "World to Come IV" (David Lang), "Far l'amore" (Franco Bracardi, Bob Sinclair as Christophe le Friant, Danielle Pace), "More Than Secret" (Matt Fitzgerald, Pete Kelly, Tom Schuzinger, Ben Ely), "Mueve la colita" (F. Attanasio, Ricky Nanni, Lorenzo Confetta, S. Attanasio, G. Attanasio), "My Heart's in the Highlands" (music: Arvo Part; lyrics: Robert Burns), "The Lamb" (John Tavener, William Blake), "Parade" (Andreas Berthling, Tomas Hallonsten, Johan Berthling), "Moody" (Scroggins Sisters), "Symphony No. 3, Lento, Cantabile Semplice" (Henryk Mikolaj Gorecki), "Take My Breath Away" (Gui Boratto), "The Beatitudes" (Victor Martynov), "Forever" (Maurizio Fabrizio, Antonello Venditti), "Pancho" (Julius Steffaro, Jack Trombey), "There Must Be an Angel/Playing with My Heart" (Annie Lennox, David A. Stewart), "Water from the Same Source" (Christian Frederickson, Rachel Grimes, Jason Noble), "Symphony in C Major, II. Adagio" (Georges Bizet), "Dies Irae" (Zbigniew Preisner), "Everything Trying" (Damien Jurado), "Discoteca" (Christian Bouyjou, Chloe Fabre, Radha Valli), "We Speak No Americano" (Renato Carosone, Nicola Salerno, Matthew Handley, Duncan MacLennan, Andrew Stanley), "Ti rubero" (Bruno Lauzi), "Beata Vicera" (Magister Perotinus), "Three Movements Perpetual, 1—Assez modere" (Francis Poulenc). (In Italian, French; English subtitles) **p**, Francesca Cima, Nicola Giuliano, Fabio Conversi, Jerome Seydoux; **d**, Paolo Sorrentino; **cast**, Toni Servillo, Carlo Verdone, Sabrina Ferilli, Carlo Buccirosso, Iaia Forte, Pamela Villoresi, Galatea Ranzi, Franco Graziosi, Giorgio Pasotti, Massimo Popolizio, Sonia Gessner, **w**, Sorrentino, Umberto Contarello (based on a story by Sorrentino); **c**, Luca Bigazzi; **m**, Lele Marchitelli; **ed**, Cristiano Travaglioli; **prod d**, Stefania

Cella; **spec eff**, Tiberio Angeloni, Franco Galiano, Massimo Giovannetti.

The Great Gatsby ★★★ 2013; Australia/U.S.; 142m; WB; Color; Crime Drama/Romance/ Children: Unacceptable (MPAA: PG-13); **3-D**; **BD**; **DVD**. The classic F. Scott Fitzgerald story receives a fourth version in this decidedly superior production. The film begins with Nick Carraway, portrayed by Maguire, a Yale University graduate and veteran of World War I (1914-1918). He is a disillusioned alcoholic in a sanitarium who talks about a man named Gatsby he says was the most hopeful man he ever met. Thompson, his doctor, suggests he write Gatsby's story as therapy, since writing calms him and brings him solace. Maguire's story takes us back to the summer of 1922 when he moves from the Midwest to New York and works as a bond salesman. He rents a cottage on Long Island in the fictional village of West Egg, next door to the mansion of Jay Gatsby, played by DiCaprio, a mysterious business millionaire who throws huge, extravagant parties at his vast estate. Maguire drives across the bay to East Egg for dinner at the mansion of his cousin Daisy Buchanan, portrayed by Mulligan, and her millionaire husband Tom, played by Edgerton, whom Maguire knew from college days. They introduce Maguire to Jordan Baker, essayed by Debicki, an attractive but cynical young golfer who Mulligan hopes to match up with Maguire. Mulligan tells Maguire that Edgerton has a mistress in a nearby industrial dumping ground between West Egg and New York City called the "valley of ashes." Soon afterward, Edgerton drives Maguire there and they stop at a garage owned by George Wilson, played by Clarke, and his wife Myrtle, portrayed by Fisher, who is the woman Mulligan claims to be Edgerton's lover. Maguire goes along with Edgerton and Fisher to an apartment in New York City which is Edgerton's and Fisher's love nest. Fisher throws a vulgar party and, after she taunts Edgerton about Daisy, he breaks her nose. Soon after that, Maguire receives an invitation to one of DiCaprio's parties at his mansion. Maguire attends the party and learns that none of the guests know who DiCaprio is or has ever met him. At the party, Maguire meets Debicki again and then, for the first time, meets DiCaprio. Maguire and DiCaprio become friends and, soon after the party, DiCaprio takes Maguire to lunch in New York City with DiCaprio's mysterious friend Meyer Wolfsheim, played by Bachchan. Later, Maguire learns from Debicki that DiCaprio has been in love with Mulligan since 1917 when he was a poor soldier about to go overseas in WWI (1914-1918) and she was from a rich Southern family. Debicki says DiCaprio is still madly in love with Mulligan, although she is married and has a young daughter by Edgerton. Unknown to Maguire, DiCaprio spends many nights looking across the bay at the green light at the end of Mulligan's dock, hoping one day to regain his lost romance with her. DiCaprio asks Maguire to arrange a tea at his cottage and invite Mulligan so they can meet again. DiCaprio and Mulligan are reunited at the tea and begin an affair. Edgerton becomes suspicious of Mulligan's and DiCaprio's feelings for each other, and then realizes they love each other. Although Edgerton is involved in an extramarital affair with Fisher, he is furious about his wife having one with DiCaprio. Edgerton suggests they all go to the Plaza Hotel in New York City on a hot summer afternoon, and Edgerton tells DiCaprio that he, Edgerton, and Mulligan have a relationship that he, DiCaprio, could never understand. Edgerton then tells Mulligan at the hotel party that DiCaprio is a criminal who made his fortune from bootlegging alcohol and other illegal activities. DiCaprio is close to hitting Edgerton when Edgerton realizes that Mulligan's loyalty, if not her love, is to him and not to DiCaprio. Edgerton believes Mulligan will stay in their marriage, so he sends her back to their home in East Egg in a car with DiCaprio. Edgerton, Maguire, and Debicki drive back to Edgerton's home in another car and en route at the valley of ashes see that DiCaprio's car has struck and killed Fisher, Edgerton's lover. Maguire learns that Mulligan was driving the hit-and-run car, not DiCaprio, but DiCaprio intends to take the blame for her. That night, DiCaprio tells Maguire of his poor background and that his real name is James Gatz, and of his associations with bootleggers. In the morning, Maguire leaves for work in New York while DiCaprio takes a swim in the outdoor pool at his mansion. Ever the romantic optimist, DiCaprio is waiting for Mulligan to call him and say she loves him more than anyone, and that she will divorce Edgerton. But the night before, Edgerton has lied to Clarke, telling him that Di-Caprio was Fisher's lover, and, the next morning, Clarke goes to Di-Caprio's mansion with a gun. DiCaprio hears the phone ring, gets out of the pool, and believes it is Mulligan calling to say she loves him and will go away with him, when Clarke shoots and kills him, then turns the gun on himself. The phone call, however, is from Maguire, and he hears two gunshots on the open line. Maguire later invites Mulligan and Edgerton to attend DiCaprio's funeral, but they say they are leaving for New York with their young daughter. Only reporters attend DiCaprio's funeral, and the media reports that DiCaprio was both the lover and murderer of Fisher. Only Maguire knows the truth, but keeps it to himself, as the story returns to the present and he finishes writing about DiCaprio, calling his memoirs "The Great Gatsby." DiCaprio and the rest of the cast give exceptional performances in this most stylish version of the Fitzgerald story, which received Oscars for Best Production Design (Martin, Drew, Turner, Gracie, Dunn); and Best Costume Design (Catherine Martin). The film was very popular at the box office, earning more than $351 million in its initial release against a budget of more than $105 million. This film is a remake of the 1926 silent film with Warner Baxter as Gatsby and Lois Wilson as Daisy, the 1949 film with Alan Ladd as Gatsby and Betty Field as Daisy, and the 1974 version with Robert Redford as Gatsby and Mia Farrow as Daisy. Paramount took the Ladd film out of circulation so as not to be compared with the Redford version, but to some critics, including this one, the Alan Ladd film and his resolute interpretation of Gatsby remains the best. (In all other versions, Gatsby is played as if he were a social dilettante, unsure of his position in life and having a feckless, indecisive personality; Fitzgerald, however, portrayed him as a strong-willed young man, utterly enigmatic, and with an almost omnipotent mindset and only Ladd captured that persona.) Songs: "Back to Back" (Amy Winehouse), "Young and Beautiful" (Lana Del Rey), "Together" (Romey Madley Croft, Oliver Dim, Jamie Smith), "No Church in the Wild" (Shawn JAY Z Carter, James Brown, Kanye West, Michael Dean, Charles Njapa, Terius Nash, Gary Wright, Phil Manzanera, Joseph Roach, Christopher Breaux), "Hearts a Mess" (Wally De Backer, William Attaway, Irving Burgie), "Let's Misbehave" (Cole Porter), "Ain't Misbehavin'" (Thomas "Fats" Waller, Harry Brooks, Andy Razaf), "St. Louis Blues" (W.C. Handy), "Love Is the Drug" (Bryan Ferry, Andrew Mackay), "New Orleans Bump/Monrovia" (Ferd "Jelly Roll" Morton), "Who Gonna Stop Me" (Shawn JAY Z Carter, Kanye West, Michael Dean, Shama Joseph, Maurice Simmonds, Joshua Kierkegaard Grant Steele), "Bang Bang" (William Adams, Sonny Bono, James P. Johnson, Cecil Mack), "A Little Party Never Killed Nobody/All We Got" (David Listenbee, Jordan Orvash, Maureen Ann McDonald, Francesca Richard, Andre Smith, Stacy Ferguson, Alexander Scott, Andrea Martin, Kamaal Fareed), "Rhapsody in Blue" (George Gershwin), "Over the Love" (Stuart Hammond, Kid Harpoon, Aaron Foulds, Florence Welch), "Still" (Lionel Richie), "Izzo/H.O.V.A." (Shawn JAY Z Carter, Kanye West, Freddie Perron, Alphonso Mizell, Berry Gordy, Deke Richards), "Empire State Of Mind/Part II/Broken Down" (Shawn JAY Z Carter, Alexander Shuckburgh, Sylvia Robinson, Bert Keyes, Alicia Augello-Cook, Angela Hunte, Jane't Sewell), "100$ Bill" (Shawn JAY Z Carter, Evan Mast), "Where the Wind Blows" (Andrea Martin, Dan Dougherty, Phil Ponce), "Crazy in Love" (Shawn JAY Z Carter, Rich Harrison, Beyonce Knowles, Eugene Record), "Oh! You Have No Idea" (Dan Dougherty, Phil Ponce), "Love Is Blindness" (U2), "Into the Past" (Joseph Ray, Daniel Stephens, Alana Watson, Craig Armstrong), "Kill and Run" (Sia Furler, Chris Braide), and "Can't Repeat the Past," and "Infinite Hope," "Daisy's Theme" (Craig Armstrong). Violent images, sexual content, smoking, partying, drinking, and gutter language prohibit viewing by children. **p**, Baz Luhrmann, Lucy Fisher, Catherine Knapman, Catherine Martin, Douglas Wick, Anton Monsted; **d**, Luhrmann; **cast**, Leonardo

Gollum (Andy Serkis voiceover) in *The Hobbit: An Unexpected Journey*, 2012.

DiCaprio, Carey Mulligan, Toby Maguire, Joel Edgerton, Callan McAuliffe, Elizabeth Debicki, Amitabh Bachchan, Jason Clarke, Richard Carter, Jack Thompson, Adelaide Clemens, Vince Colosimo, Max Cullen; **w**, Luhrmann, Craig Pearce (based on the 1925 novel by F. Scott Fitzgerald); **c**, Simon Duggan; **m**, Craig Armstrong; **ed**, Jason Ballantine, Jonathan Redmond, Matt Villa; **prod d**, Catherine Martin; **art d**, Damien Drew, Michael Turner, Ian Gracie; **set d**, Beverley Dunn; **spec eff**, Dan Oliver, Jabin Dickins, Lloyd Finnemore, Jasmin Lyford.

Guardians of the Galaxy ★★★ 2014; U.S.; 122m; Marvel/Walt Disney; Color; Science Fiction; Children: Unacceptable (MPAA: R); **BD**; **DVD**. Another action-packed comic book hero tale begins in 1988, where, after his mother's death, Pratt, a young man, is abducted from Earth by the Ravagers, a group of space pirates led by Rooker. Twenty-six years later on the planet Morag, Pratt steals an orb and is intercepted by Hounsou, a substitute to the fanatical Kree, played by Pace. Although Pratt escapes with the orb, Rooker discovers the theft and offers a bounty for his capture while Pace sends an assassin, Saldana, after him. Pratt tries selling the orb on the Nova Empire capital world, Xandar, but Saldana ambushes him and steals it. A fight develops and a pair of bounty hunters join the fight. They are the genetically engineered raccoon, Cooper, and the tree-like humanoid, Diesel. Nova Corps arrive and arrest all four and imprison them in the Kyln. There, a powerful inmate, Bautista, tries to kill Saldana because she is in league with Pace, who killed his family. Pratt talks Bautista out of killing Saldana because Saldana can bring Pace to him. Saldana then reveals that she has betrayed Pace, not willing to let him use the orb's power to destroy entire planets such as Xandar. Learning that Saldana has a buyer for the orb, she, Pratt, Cooper, Diesel, and Bautista join forces to escape from the prison. Pace now meets with Brolin, Saldana's adoptive father, to discuss her betrayal and the theft of the orb. Pratt and his accomplices, accompanied by Bautista, then escape the prison in his ship, the *Milano*, and flee to Knowhere, a remote criminal outpost in space. Bautista, while drunk, summons Pace while the rest of the group meets Saldana's contact, the collector Taneleer Tivan, played by Del Toro. He opens the orb, which reveals an Infinity Stone, a thing of great power that destroys all but the most powerful things who wield it. Del Toro's tormented assistant grabs the stone, triggering an explosion that engulfs Del Toro's archive. Pace then arrives and easily defeats Bautista, while the others flee by spaceship, pursued by Pace's followers and Saldana's sister, Gillan. Gillan destroys Saldana's ship, leaving her floating in space, and Pace's forces leave with the orb. Pratt contacts Rooker before following Saldana into space, giving her his helmet so she can survive. Rooker arrives and retrieves them. Then Cooper, Diesel, and Bautista threaten to attack Rooker's ship to rescue them, but Pratt arranges a truce by convincing

Dean O'Gorman as Fili in *The Hobbit: An Unexpected Journey*, 2012.

Rooker that they can recover the orb. The friends agree that facing Pace means certain death, yet they also understand they have to stop him from using the Infinity Stone to destroy the galaxy. Aboard Pace's flagship, the *Dark Aster*, Pace embeds the Infinity Stone in his warhammer, reserving its power for himself. He contacts Brolin, threatening to kill him after the destruction of Xandar. Hating her adoptive father, Gillan allies with Pace. Near Xandar, the *Dark Aster* is confronted by the Ravagers, the Nova Corps, and Pratt's group, with that group breaching the *Dark Aster*. While Ronan uses his warhammer to destroy the Nova Corps fleet, Bautista kills Hounsou. On the *Dark Aster*, after Saldana defeats Gillan (who escapes), she unlocks Pace's chambers, but the group finds themselves outmatched by his power until Cooper crashes the *Milano* through the *Dark Aster* and into Pace. Damaged, *Dark Aster* crash-lands on Xandar, and Diesel sacrifices himself to shield his friends. Pace comes out of the wreck and is about to destroy Xandar, but Pratt distracts him, which allows Bautista and Cooper to destroy Pace's warhammer. Pratt grabs the freed Stone, and with Saldana, Bautista, and Cooper sharing its burden, they use it to disintegrate Pace. Afterward, Pratt tricks Rooker into taking a container supposedly containing the Stone, then gives the real Stone to the Nova Corps. As the Ravagers leave Xandar, Rooker says that it all turned out well and they did not deliver Pratt to his father, according to their agreement. Pratt's group, now known as the Guardians of the Galaxy, have their criminal records erased, and Pratt learns that he is only half-human, his father being part of an ancient, unknown species. Pratt finally opens the last present he received from his mother. It is a cassette tape filled with her favorite songs. The Guardians leave in a rebuilt *Milano* together with a sapling cut from Diesel. Special effects are the chief attraction to see this outlandish sci-fi opus, and they are, indeed, spectacular, undoubtedly creating the huge stir at the box office that earned for this film more than $773.3 million in its initial release against a budget of more than $195.9 million. Song: "Hooked on a Feeling" (Francis Zambon as Mark James). Violence prohibits viewing by children. **p**, Kevin Feige, Nikolas Korda; **d**, James Gunn; **cast**, Chris Pratt, Glenn Close, Karen Gillan, Zoe Saldana, Benicio Del Toro, Lee Pace, Laura Haddock, Emmett Scanlan, and just the voices of Bradley Cooper, Vin Diesel; **w**, Gunn, Nicole Perlman (based on the comic book by Dan Abnett, Andy Lanning); **c**, Ben Davis; **m**, Tyler Bates; **ed**, Fred Raskin, Hughes Winborne; **prod d**, Charles Wood; **art d**, Ray Chan, Thomas Brown, Alan Payne, Mike Stallion; **set d**, Richard Roberts; **spec eff**, Luke Marcel, Gareth Wingrove.

The Guest ★★★ 2014; U.S.; 99m; Hollywood Film Office/ArtAffects Entertainment; Color; Crime Drama; Children: Unacceptable (MPAA: R); **BD**; **DVD**. Well-made thriller begins with Stevens, a handsome, polite and charismatic ex-GI who introduces himself to a family by claim-

ing to be a friend of their son, who died in action in the Afghanistan War (2001-). He says he has come to fulfill a promise to his fallen comrade to visit them and tell them about their son's bravery. The father, Orser, and mother, Kelley, welcome him into their home, although their teenage daughter, Monroe, and younger son, Meyer, are, at first, reluctant to accept him. Stevens soon wins over Monroe with his good looks and charm and by helping her friends. He then befriends Meyer by roughing up some teenage bullies at a roadside bar. When Orser tells Stevens he's stuck in a middle-management job, his boss mysteriously disappears, which elevates Orser to his boss' job and a substantially increased salary. Monroe argues with her boyfriend, Williamson, and soon a gun is planted in the boy's truck which implicates him in the murder of a friend. Stevens carries a switchblade knife, "just in case," which he gives to Meyer, advising him that, if someone takes it away, he should burn down their house with their family inside. Though Stevens appears to be the perfect house guest, a mysterious chain of events, including some supposedly accidental deaths in town, causes Kelley to question whether he is actually who he claims to be. She then learns that he is a murderer and is going after Monroe and Meyer because they have learned he is a psychopathic killer now intent on murdering them. Stevens murders Kelley and Orser while he is returning to the house. Monroe and Meyer then learn from Reddick, a U.S. Army officer, that Stevens is a rogue GI who has been specially programmed to kill anyone who learns of his identity. Stevens then kills Reddick and attacks Monroe and Meyer, but both successfully fight him off and ostensibly kill the berserk killer. As they sit in an ambulance nurturing wounds received from Stevens, they see firefighters emerging from the ruins of a burned-out structure and, to their horror, sees Stevens very much alive and posing as one of those firefighters. Tautly directed and well acted, this thriller generated limited returns at the box office, earning less than $2.5 million in its initial release. Excessive violence, gutter language, drug use and a scene of sexuality prohibit viewing by children. **p**, Keith Calder, Jessica Wu, Chris Harding; **d**, Adam Wingard; **cast**, Dan Stevens, Maika Monroe, Joel David Moore, Lance Reddick, Candice Patton, Ethan Embry, Brendan Meyer, Leland Orser, Sheila Kelley, Chase Williamson; **w**, Simon Barrett; **c**, Robby Baumgartner; **m**, Steve Moore; **prod d**, Thomas S. Hammock; **set d**, Susan Magestro; **spec eff**, William Boggs, Dimitri Loginowski.

Haemoo ★★★ 2014; South Korea; 111m; Lewis Pictures; Color; Crime Drama; Children: Unacceptable; **BD**; **DVD**. This beautifully photographed nautical thriller takes place in South Pacific waters in the late 1990s, shortly after the Asian financial crisis of 1997. Yun-seok Kim is the captain of an old and unseaworthy fishing ship, who is discouraged because he and his crew have failed to catch much fish on their most recent outing. The boat's owner intends to sell off the boat to get some quick money, and Yun-seok fears he soon will be out of a job. He decides to take a deal to smuggle some illegal Chinese-Korean immigrants from China to Korea. His crew is mostly interested in having relations with female immigrants on board. A small romance blossoms between Han, one of the crew, and a young woman he rescues from the sea after she falls into the briny while boarding. Meanwhile, a disgruntled crewman becomes an agitator and tries to create a mutiny as Yun-seok starts to descend into madness. The film's title translates to "sea fog," which covers the boat and becomes symbolic of its mission in which sex takes over and one aboard the boat is murdered in cold blood in front of the others. The film earned more than $11 million in its initial release against a budget of $10 million. *Author's Note*: The story is based on the real-life incident in which a Korean fishing boat crew cast the bodies of twenty-five illegal immigrants overboard in a botched smuggling operation. **p**, Joon Ho Bong, Neung-yeon Joh, Lewis Taewan Kim; **d**, Sung-bo Shim; **cast**, Yun-seok Kim, Yoo-chun Park, Ye-ri Han, Seong-kun Mun, Sang-ho Kim, Hee-jun Lee, Seung-mok Yoo, In-gi Jeong,

Kyung-Sook Jo; **w**, Sung-bo Shim, Joon Ho Bong; **c**, Kyung-pyo Hong; **ed**, Jae-beom Kim, Sang-beom Kim; **prod d**, Ha-jun Lee; **spec eff**, Chansoo Kim.

Heaven Is for Real ★★★ 2014; U.S.; 99m; Tri-Star/Sony; Color; Drama; Children: Unacceptable (MPAA: PG); **BD**; **DVD**. Based on a true story, Corum, the four-year-old son of Kinnear, a small-town Nebraska pastor, says he's experienced heaven during an emergency surgery. He says he saw the doctor, Sorel, operating and Kinnear praying in the waiting room at the hospital. Corum says he met his sister, who died when his mother, Reilly, miscarried, but he had not been told about it. In heaven, Corum also meets his great-grandfather who died thirty years before Corum was born. Then he shares with his parents details about his sister and great-grandfather that he could not have known. He also describes a rainbow-colored horse that only Jesus rides, that he met Jesus and sat in his lap, describing a "really big" God and his chair, and how the Holy Spirit "shoots down power" from heaven to help us. Some believe Corum, some do not, but the message in this Christian film is that heaven is a real place, Jesus really loves children, and that everyone should be ready for a final battle coming between God and Satan. Kinnear relates what his son has claimed to the local community, which, at first, disturbs his parishioners, but they eventually and protectively support the story. The film is told in simplistic terms by director Wallace, and the natural acting from the entire cast impresses as sincere, furthering belief in this truly inspiring story. Songs: "Come Thou Fount of Every Blessing" (Robert Robinson, John Wyeth), "Jesus Loves the Little Children" (Clare Herbert Woolston, George F. Root), "My Jesus I Love Thee" (William Ralph Featherston, Adoniram Gordon), "Amazing Grace" (John Newton), "This Little Light of Mine" (traditional), "We Will Rock You" (Brian May), "You Are Home" (Randall Wallace, Nick Glennie-Smith), "Taps" (traditional), "Compass" (Diane Warren). Thematic material including medical situations prohibit viewing by children. **p**, Joe Roth, T.D. Jakes, Andrew Wallace, Kim H. Winther; **d**, Randall Wallace; **cast**, Greg Kinnear, Kelly Reilly, Connor Corum, Thomas Hayden Church, Jacob Vargas, Nancy Sorel, Lane Styles, Margo Martindale, Jon Ted Wynne, Danso Gordon; **w**, Chris Parker (based on the book *Heaven Is for Real: A Little Boy's Astounding Story of His Trip to Heaven and Back* by Todd Burpo, Lynn Vincent); **c**, Dean Semler; **m**, Nick Glennie-Smith; **ed**, John Wright; **prod d**, Arvinder Grewal; **art d**, Larry Spittle; **spec eff**, Laird McMurray, Isaac Lipstadt.

Hellion ★★★ 2014; U.S.; 94m; Across Town Productions/Sundance Selects; Color; Comedy/Drama/Thriller; Children: Unacceptable (MPAA: R); **BD**; **DVD**. Intriguing tale begins with Wiggins, a thirteen-year-old delinquent living in southeast Texas oil refinery country. He is obsessed with motocross and heavy metal music and is forced to place his little brother, Garner, with their emotionally unstable father, Paul, and an aunt, Lewis. Paul has taken to drink after the loss of his wife, spending more time drowning his sorrows at the local bar and working on his damaged beach house than being an active parent. He must eventually take responsibility for the boys and himself and get them back home with him. Songs: "The Burning of Atlanta" (Tony Portaro), "When I Was Young" and "The Other Side of Lonesome" (Ben Nichols), "It's a Miracle" (The Names), "South of Heaven" (Jeff Hanneman), "2000 Miles" D-Why), "See You Tonight" (Contraband), "Pinball Two-Step" (Ryan J. Simon), "Hawks and Serpents" and "Battery" (James Hetfield, Lars Ulrich), "Future Shock" (Joel Grind), "Too Late to Forgive" (The Quantrells), "Arcane Montane" and "It's Still You" (Fred Cole), "Cloak of Feathers" and "The Man Who Would Be King" (Maleveller), "Metal Militia" (James Hetfield, Lars Ulrich, Dave Mustaine). Mature themes prohibit viewing by children. **p**, Jonathan Duffy, Kelly Williams, Andrew Logan; **d&w**, Kat Candler; **cast**, Aaron Paul, Juliette Lewis, Josh Wiggins, Deke Garner, Dalton Sutton, Camron Owens, Dylan Cole, Jonny Mars, Walt Roberts, Annalee Jefferies, Corby Sullivan; **c**, Brett Pawlak; **m**, Curtis Heath; **prod d**, Deneice O'Connor;

Christopher Lee as Saruman in *The Hobbit: An Unexpected Journey,* 2012.

ed, Alan Canant; **art d**, Dustin Shroff; **spec eff**, Mike Hava.

A Hijacking ★★★ 2013; Denmark; 99m; Nordisk Films/Magnolia Pictures; Color; Crime Drama; Children: Unacceptable (MPAA: R); **BD**; **DVD**. Strange but tension-filled tale begins with Asbaek as a cook aboard a Danish cargo ship. He is anxious to return to Denmark and his family as the vessel heads for harbor in the Indian Ocean. Back in Denmark, Salim, unable to close a difficult financial deal, requests help from Malling, the Copenhagen shipping company's CEO, who talks to a group of Japanese businessmen down from an adamant offer. Soon afterward, Malling learns that pirates in the Indian Ocean have hijacked one of his company's ships, one in which Asbaek is sailing. On board that ship, the crew is separated into two groups, and Asbaek is forced at gunpoint to cook a meal for the pirates. Automatic gunfire fills the night, frightening the hostages who are held for a ransom of millions of dollars. Malling hires Porter, an English hostage negotiator who has experience with pirates. His first suggestion is to use a neutral third party to handle negotiations, but Malling refuses to delegate the responsibility. Their first communication with the pirates comes when Asgar, a Somali, says he is a translator taken hostage by the pirates, and asks Asbaek to contact Malling. Malling, however, refuses to negotiate through Asbaek and hangs up. Asgar himself calls and relates the pirates' demands. Malling's counteroffer is so little that he knows the pirates will refuse, but it will open the negotiation process. Porter explains that if they give in too quickly or easily, the pirates will only renege on the deal. Weeks go by, and the pirates allow the hostages a few limited privileges such as use of the bathrooms. Asbaek and Malling attempt to befriend one of the pirates, who, as a prank, humiliates Moller. Asbaek becomes irritated over the ship's dwindling food supplies, but Asgar refuses to restock the vessel and forces Asbaek to call Malling. Malling again refuses to communicate through Asbaek and hangs up. Negotiations slowly continue and Asgar reacts reluctantly to Malling's continued low-ball offers, which he says will result in his and the crew's death unless Malling makes a realistic offer. The pirates finally allow the hostages on the deck and Asbaek catches a large fish. Both pirates and hostages celebrate together and sing sea shanties. Asbaek reveals that it is his daughter's birthday, and they all sing "Happy Birthday" to her. Asgar allows Asbaek to phone his wife, but a pirate cuts their conversation short. Asgar then demands that Asbaek's wife, Alstrup, put pressure on Malling to pay the ransom demanded by the pirates. Against Porter's advice, Malling makes a higher offer and loses his composure. Asgar, insulted by the offer, insists that the pirates will soon begin to kill some of the hostages, and a gunshot is heard as the phone connection to Alstrup goes dead. Malling begins to wonder if he is responsible for Asbaek's death. The shipping company's board of directors begins to grow impatient with Malling's

Cate Blanchett as Galadriel in *The Hobbit: An Unexpected Journey*, 2012.

negotiation and threaten to replace him with a hired negotiator if he can't close a deal with the pirates by the end of the month. Malling then receives a fax from the pirates. He asks for proof that Asbaek is still alive, which Moller supervises. Asbaek is still alive, but, because of poor treatment and psychological abuse, he is now an emotional wreck. As negotiations restart, Malling offers the pirates $2.8 million. Asgar rejects the offer, so Salim suggests that Malling pretend to add $500,000 of his own money. Asgar, by now tired of negotiating and convinced that the company cannot pay any more than what Malling has offered, finally accepts. Asgar orders the hostages to go on deck where the two separate groups see each other once more. An airplane circles several times and drops a package. The pirates are joyful as they retrieve it. Thankful that the ordeal has finally come to an end, Asbaek retrieves his wedding band, which he earlier hid when the pirates boarded the ship, and wears it publicly. As the pirates leave the ship, one grabs Asbaek's ring. When Asbaek objects, the captain, Pearson, intercedes and takes the ring from the pirate. Angry, the pirate shoots and kills Pearson. Asgar strikes the pirate and berates him. Asbaek, almost in shock from his traumatic experiences as a hostage, shows only a little emotion when he is later reunited with his family. Though the story line is complex and sometimes confusing, the intense acting by the cast sustains interest throughout. (In Danish; English subtitles.) Violence and gutter language prohibit viewing by children. **p**, Rene Ezra, Tomas Radoor; **d&w**, Tobias Lindholm; **cast**, Pilou Asbaek, Soren Malling, Dar Salim, Roland Moller, Gary Skjoldmose Porter, Abdihakin Asgar, Amalie Ihle Alstrup, Amalie Vuluff Andersen, Linda Laursen, Keith Pearson; **c**, Magnus Nordenhof Jonck; **m**, Hildur Guonadottir; **ed**, Adam Nielsen; **prod d**, Thomas Greve; **spec eff**, Martin Madsen.

The Hobbit: An Unexpected Journey ★★★ 2012; U.S./New Zealand; 169m; New Line Cinema/WB; Color; Fantasy; Children: Unacceptable (MPAA: PG-13); **BD**; **DVD**. Bilbo Baggins, portrayed by Freeman, embarks on a quest to reclaim the lost Dwarf Kingdom of Erebof from the fearsome dragon Smaug (Cumberbatch voiceover). McKellen, a wizard, enlists him in joining thirteen dwarves led by a legendary warrior, Armitage. Their journey takes them into dangerous lands teeming with goblins and other deadly creatures and sorcerers. Their goal lies to the east and the wastelands of the Lonely Mountain, but first they must escape the goblin tunnels where Freeman meets Gollum (Serkis), a creature that will change his life. Freeman finds himself alone with Serkis on the shores of an underground lake where he discovers courage he never dreamed he possessed. He obtains Serkis' precious ring that holds unexpected qualities and powers, a gold ring that is tied to the fate of all Middle Earth in ways Freeman can't begin to imagine. When arriving at the Misty Mountains, they encounter a fierce battle between stone gi-

ants and hide within a cave. They are captured by goblins, who take them to the Great Goblin (Humphries). They nevertheless escape the mountain, but are ambushed by the evil Azog (Bennett) and his minions. Armitage (as Thorin) charges at Bennett, but is overwhelmed. His life is saved by Freeman, and Bennett now has respect for Freeman as they and the dwarfs retreat to safety. In the distance they hear the sound of the awakening Smaug. Special effects dazzle in this, the first of a three-part film adaptation of the 1937 novel *The Hobbit* by J.R.R. Tolkien. Together, these productions act as prequels to the **Lord of the Rings** series: **Lord of the Rings**, 1978; **Lord of the Rings: Fellowship of the Ring**, 2001; **Lord of the Rings: The Two Towers**, 2002; and **Lord of the Rings: Return of the King**, 2003. The film received Oscar nominations for Best Production Design (Hennah), Best Special Effects (Ingram), and Best Makeup and Hairstyling. It was a staggering success at the box office, earning more than $1 billion in its initial release against a budget of more than $300 million, one of the largest grossing films of all time. Songs: "Song of the Lonely Mountain" (Neil Finn, David Donaldson, David Long, Steve Roche, Janet Roddick), "Torture Song" (Stephen Gallagher, Philippa Boyens, Fran Walsh), "Blunt the Knives" (Steve Gallagher, J.R.R. Tolkien), "Misty Mountains" (David Donaldson, David Long, Steve Roche, Janet Roddick, J.R.R. Tolkien), "The Valley of Imladris" (Howard Shore). Excessive violence and frightening images prohibit viewing by children. **p**, Peter Jackson, Fran Walsh, Carolynne Cunningham, Zane Weiner, Philippa Boyens, Eileen Moran; **d**, Peter Jackson; **cast**, Martin Freeman, Ian McKellen, Elijah Wood, Cate Blanchett, Andy Serkis, Christopher Lee, Benedict Cumberbatch, Manu Bennett, Richard Armitage, Ken Stott, Ian Holm, Barry Humphries, Graham McTavish, William Kircher; **w**, Jackson, Fran Walsh, Philippa Boyens, Guillermo del Toro (based on the novel *The Hobbit* by J.R.R. Tolkien); **c**, Andrew Lesnie; **m**, Howard Shore; **ed**, Jabez Olssen; **prod d**, Dan Hennah; **art d**, Brian Massey, Andy McLaren, Brad Mill, Simon Bright; **set d**, Simon Bright, Ra Vincent; **spec eff**, Steve Ingram.

The Hobbit: The Battle of Five the Armies ★★★ 2014; New Zealand; U.S.; 144m; New Line Cinema; MGM/WB; Color; Fantasy; Children: Unacceptable (MPAA: PG-13); **BD**; **DVD**. A 3-D sequel to **The Hobbit: The Desolation of Smaug**, 2013, this action-packed film opens with an enraged dragon, Smaug (Cumberbatch voiceover) threatening Evans, a band of dwarfs, and their hobbit burglar (Freeman) in the serpent's mountain lair, along with the wizard (McKellen). Freeman and the dwarfs watch as Cumberbatch destroys Laketown. Evans then escapes from prison and kills Cumberbatch. Now the new leader, Evans leads everyone to the ruins of Dale for safety. Freeman learns that Armitage has been infected with Cumberbatch's dragon's sickness as he searches for the Arkenstone. Five armies war in a battle in an effort to recover a treasure from Cumberbatch. Like its predecessors, this film was a great success at the box office, earning more than $956 million in its initial release against a budget of more than $250 million. **p**, Peter Jackson, Carolynne Cunningham, Fran Walsh, Philippa Boyens, Zane Weiner; **d**, Jackson; **cast**, Ian McKellen, Benedict Cumberbatch (voice only), Martin Freeman, Orlando Bloom, Cate Blanchett, Billy Connolly, Richard Armitage, Stephen Fry, Ken Stott, Graham McTavish, William Kircher, Christopher Lee, Ian Holm; **w**, Jackson, Walsh, Boyens, Guillermo del Toro (based on the novel **The Hobbit** by J.R.R. Tolkien); **c**, Andrew Lesnie; **m**, Howard Shore; **ed**, Jabez Olssen; **prod d**, Dan Hennah; **art d**, Simon Bright, Andy McLaren; **set d**, Mykyta Brazhnyk, Simon Bright, Ra Vincent; **spec eff**, Phil McLaren, Karl Chisholm, Oliver Gee.

The Hobbit: The Desolation of Smaug ★★★ 2013; U.S./New Zealand; 161m.; New Line Cinema/MGM/WB; Color; Fantasy; Children: Unacceptable (MPAA: PG-13); **BD**; **DVD**. The Hobbit adventure continues in this second of three films as the dwarfs, Bilbo (Freeman), and the wizard Gandalf (McKellen) have escaped the Misty Mountains and Freeman has gained the One Ring. They continue on their epic quest to get their gold back from the dragon, Smaug (Cumberbatch), and reclaim the lost Dwarf Kingdom of Erebor. Again, the core of attraction is the spectacular special effects. The film is a sequel to **The Hobbit: An Unexpected Journey**, 2012, and the second of a three-part film adaptation of the 1937 novel *The Hobbit* by J.R.R. Tolkien which together acts as prequels to the **Lord of the Rings** film series: **Lord of the Rings**, 1978; **Lord of the Rings: Fellowship of the Ring**, 2001; **Lord of the Rings: The Two Towers**, 2002; and **Lord of the Rings: Return of the King**, 2003. The film saw enormous success at the box office, earning more than $958 million in its initial release against a budget of $225 million. Songs: "Trumpet Fanfare" (David Donaldson, David Long, Steve Roche, Janet Roddick), "I See Fire" (Ed Sheeran). Excessive violence prohibits viewing by children. **p**, Peter Jackson, Fran Walsh, Zane Weiner, Carolynne Cunningham, Philippa Boyens; **d**, Jackson; **cast**, Ian McKellen, Benedict Cumberbatch, Cate Blanchett, Elija Wood, Stephen Fry, Billy Connolly, Ian Holm, Christopher Lee, Orlando Bloom, Martin Freeman, , Andy Serkis, Richard Armitage, Aidan Turner, Lee Pace; **w**, Jackson, Walsh, Boyens, Guillermo del Toro, (based on the novel *The Hobbit* by J.R.R. Tolkien); **c**, Andrew Lesnie; **m**, Howard Shore; **ed**, Jabez Olssen; **prod d**, Dan Hennah; **set d**, Ra Vincent; **spec eff**, Wily Tyight, Paul Verrall, Joe Letteri, Eric Saindon.

Home ★★★ 2015; U.S.; 94m; DreamWorks/FOX; Color; Animated Comedy; Children: Unacceptable; MPAA: PG; **BD**; **DVD**, **IV**. Some aliens from another planet are being pursued by an evil alien and find Earth a good place to call home, so they begin a friendly invasion led by Captain Smek (Martin voiceover). One of the aliens, Oh (Parsons voiceover), is a lovable misfit who invites the other aliens to a party at the home of humans where it now lives. Meanwhile, a preteen human girl named Tip (Rihanna voiceover) is looking for her mother (Lopez voiceover) after they have been separated during the alien invasion, leaving her only with her cat. Parsons by now has invited all the other aliens to her party but her invitations get botched and it turns out she has invited all the aliens in the galaxy to the party. More adventures follow and the aliens learn to dance and thousands of spaceships from other planets head to Earth for Parsons' party. Along the way in this comedy, Parsons and Rihanna both learn the true meaning of home. Although the script is somewhat silly, the 3-D animation is eye dazzling and the production values are superb. The film was a huge box office success, earning more than $386 million in its initial release against a budget of $135 million. Songs: "Red Balloon" (Tor Erik Hermansen, Mikkel S. Eriksen, Charlotte Aitchison, Magnus Hoiberg), "Deck the Halls" (traditional), "Slushious" (Hermansen, Eriksen, Ori Kaplan, Sebastian Arman), "Attackish Sax" (Kaplan), "Run to Me" (Jonathan Yip, Ray Romulus, Jeremy Reeves, Ray McCulloch II, Clarence Coffee Jr., "Only Girl in the World" (Hermansen, Eriksen, Crystal Johnson, Sandy Wilhelm), "Dancing in the Dark" (Hermansen, Eriksen, Ester Dean, Maureen McDonald, Robyn Fentry), "Cannonball" and "Feel the Light" (Hermanzsen, Eriksen, Kiesza Ellestad, Emile Haynie), "Peaceful Holiday" (James Clark), "Boov Death Song" (Jim Parsons), "Toward the Sun" (Tiago Carvalho, Gary Baker, Robyn Fenty), "Drop That" (Jacob Plant, Robyn Fenty), "As Real as You and Me" (Rodney Jerkins, Alisha Williams, Robyn Fenty). Some disturbing action and crude humor prohibit viewing by children. **p**, Suzanne Buirgy, Christopher Jenkins, Mireille Soria; **d**, Tim Johnson; **cast** (voiceovers), Jim Parsons, Rihanna (Robyn Fenty), Steve Martin, Jennifer Lopez, Brian Stepanek, April M. Lawrence, Stephen Kearin, Lisa Stewart, April Winchell, Nigel W. Tierney; **w**, Tom J. Astle, Matt Ember (based on the book *The True Meaning of Smekday* by Adam Rex); **m**, Lorne Balfe; **ed**, Nick Fletcher; **prod d**, Kathy Altieri; **art d**, Emil Mitev; **spec eff**, Eric Michael Miller.

Homeland ★★★ 2013; Algeria/France; 87m; Quad Productions; Color; Drama; Children: Unacceptable; **BD**; **DVD**. Absorbing tale shows Jallab in France studying to become a lawyer when he learns that his sixty-year-old father is sick and about to lose his house in Algeria. Jallab must

Meryl Streep and Jean Smart in *Hope Springs*, 2012.

travel for the first time in his life to Algeria, the country where his parents were born. He speaks only a little Arabs and does not know much about his parents or their history. He considers himself to be a Frenchman and discovers an entire new world across the Mediterranean Sea, thanks to his cousin, Debbouze. Unfortunately for Jallab, his cousin has stolen a passport for him and Jallab leaves France with it. Now Jallab must deal with Algerian and French bureaucracy while his cousin starts behaving badly in France. Not related to a 2011 film with the same title. **p**, Jamel Debbouze, Nicolas Duval-Adassovsky, Laurent Zeitoun, Yann Zenou, Benedicte Bellocq, Sousad Lamriki; **d**, Mohamed Hamidi; **cast**, Tewfik Jallab, Jamel Debbouze, Benaissa Ahouari, Fatsah Boyahmed, Abdelkader Secteur, Malik Bentalha, Fehd Benchemsi, Mourad Zaoui, Miloud Khetib, Mohamed Majd, Julie De Bona; **w**, Hamidi, Alain-Michel Blanc; **c**, Alex Lamarque; **m**, Armand Amar; **ed**, Marion Monnier; **prod d**, Arnaud Roth; **spec eff**, Seif Boutella.

The Homesman ★★★ 2014; France/U.S.; 122m; EuropaCorp/Roadside Attractions/Saban Films; Color; Western/Drama; Children: Unacceptable; MPAA: R; **BD**; **DVD**. Swank is a middle-aged, single woman in a small desert community in Nebraska. While being financially a catch, potential husbands reject her because she is headstrong and plain looking. She is active in the community and well respected by men and women. Three young women, Grummer, Otto, and Richter, show signs of insanity, and the town's minister, Lithgow, calls upon one of their husbands to escort the women to Iowa where they can be treated at a sanitarium for the mentally ill. Swank does not think the men capable of the task, so she volunteers to take the women alone, and Lithgow reluctantly agrees. Before loading the women into a wagon to start out for Iowa, Swank encounters Jones, a claim jumper, who is about to be lynched for using another man's land as his own. Jones begs Swank to help him and she wins his freedom in return for his help escorting the women (shades of **Goin' South**, 1978, where thief Jack Nicholson is rescued from the gallows by a local woman). Jones believes he is free now to leave any time he wants, but agrees to go with her on the journey to Iowa after Swank tells him that $300 is waiting for him at their destination. Jones comes in handy when they are attacked by Indians, and then one of the women wanders off and is taken in by a cowboy, but only temporarily. Soon they discover a desecrated grave of an eleven-year-old girl, and Swank wants to stop and fix up the grave, while Jones says he wants to push on. Swank says she will catch up with him and, after restoring the grave, sets out on horseback to meet up with Jones and the wagon of women. Riding all night, she falls asleep aboard the horse and, in the morning, discovers that her horse has returned her to the grave. She finally catches up with Jones and says they make a good team and suggests they marry. Lee doesn't think she is much of a beauty,

Daniel Radcliffe and snake in *Horns*, 2013.

but, when unclothed, she propositions him again. He agrees to marry her and they sleep together. The next morning, Jones is devastated when he finds that Swank has hung herself, from depression. He buries her body and lashes out at the three women, blaming them for driving Swank to kill herself. He takes the horse and leaves the three women behind in the wagon, but they follow him on foot, almost drowning in a river crossing. He returns and pledges to care for them until they arrive in Iowa. Jones seeks food and shelter for them at a hotel belonging to Spader, who says there is no room for them, despite the hotel being completely abandoned. Angry and bitter, Jones attacks Spader, but his men force Jones to leave at gunpoint. Jones leaves the hotel, then doubles back on horseback, steals Spader's roast pig dinner and shoots him in the foot. He then burns down the hotel, and kills Spader and his men. Jones finally delivers the women to Iowa, placing them in the care of Streep. He tells Streep about Swank's death, but does not say what caused it. He then suggests marriage to one of the women, but then decides against it and leaves her. Instead, he makes a headstone for Swank's grave and boards a river barge. En route to Swank's grave, Jones meets some musicians and begins taunting the men on the far bank as he dances drunkenly and shoots off his gun. As the barge departs, one of the workers kicks Swank's headstone into the river. This offbeat, even bizarre tale offers a gritty, hardscrabble portrait of pioneering and shows no mercy to its miserable characters. There is no redemption, let alone resolution, but the characters, weird as they are, nevertheless fascinate. The film did poorly at the box office, earning less than $3 million in its initial release against a budget of $16 million. Songs: "Rosalie the Prairie Flower" (George Fredrick Root), "Hist Hvor Vejen Slar enBugt" (music: J.C. Gebauer; lyrics: Hans Christian Andersen), "Flow Gently, Sweet Afton" (Robert Burns), "Weevily Wheat" (anonymous), "Take Thee This Token" (music: Marco Beltrami; lyrics: Glendon Swarthout). Violence, sexual scenes and suicide prohibit viewing by children. **p**, Luc Besson, Peter Brant, Brian Kennedy; **d**, Tommy Lee Jones; **cast**, Jones, Hilary Swank, Meryl Streep, James Spader, John Lithgow, Grace Gummer, Miranda Otto, Sonja Richter, David Dencik, Tim Blake Nelson, William Fichtner; **w**, Jones, Kieran Fitzgerald, Wesley Oliver (based on the novel by Glendon Swarthout); **c**, Rodrigo Prieto; **m**, Marco Beltrami; **ed**, Roberto Silvi; **prod d**, Merideth Boswell; **art d**, Guy Barnes; **set d**, Wendy Ozols-Barnes; **spec eff**, Blair Foord, Barry McQueary.

Hope Springs ★★★ 2012; U.S.; 100m; COL; Color; Romance; Children: Unacceptable (MPAA: PG-13); **BD**; **DVD**. Streep and Jones, a middle-aged empty-nest couple in Omaha, Nebraska, realize that their thirty-year marriage is in decline. They sleep in separate rooms, not showing any of their old love for each other. Streep reads a book written by Carell, a marriage counselor, and signs up Jones and herself for an intense week-long marriage counseling session at a coastal resort town in Maine. Jones reluctantly agrees to attend, believing that there is nothing wrong with their marriage. Over the next few days of counseling, Carell tries to help the couple understand how they have drifted apart emotionally and suggests what they can do to restart their love for one another. But even with Carell's advice, Streep and Jones find that a real challenge. Still, they spend a night in bed together at a motel for the first time in years and Streep wakes up in the morning to find Jones' arm around her. Jones arranges a dinner with Streep at a luxury inn and another night in bed together. They attempt to make love in front of a fireplace, but there is no spark in their love life. After the week is up, Carell suggests they take therapy back home in Omaha. There Streep plans to move in with a friend as the start of a permanent separation with Jones, but he enters her bedroom and they tenderly embrace. Gradually they fall into lovemaking that is warm and natural as well as quietly passionate. The old spark has ignited and, later that year, they renew their marriage vows on a beach with Carell present. The reunited couple promise to be more understanding and considerate of each other, as well as more romantic. This pleasant tale is well acted by Streep and Jones; their performances are natural and empathetic, and they sustain interest throughout by offering universally identifiable and personable characters in which hope springs eternal. This film was a great success at the box office, earning more than $114.2 million in its initial release against a budget of $30 million. Not related to a 2003 film with the same title. Songs: "Let's Stay Together" (Al Green, Willie Mitchell, Al Jackson Jr.), "Why" (Annie Lennox), "It Ain't Over 'Til It's Over" (Lenny Kravitz), "Ain't Love Somethin'" (Sam Brooker), "Highway Tune" (Daniel May, Marc Ferrari), "More, More, More" (Ingrid Michaelson), "Tormented" (Johnny Rotella, Ray Gilbert), "I Can't Face My Friends" (Johnny Rotella, Murray Schwimmer), "Glancing Lovers" (Hiram Bronkelstein), "I Don't Want to Be Your Mother" (Rachel Yamagata, Michael Viola), "Everybody Plays the Fool" (J.R. Bailey, Rudy Clark, Ken Williams), "Le diner de cons" (Vladimir Cosma), "Light in Your Eyes" (Stephan Sechi), "Lovers Eyes" (Norman Dane), "I Wish You Well" (Daniel May), "Enforcer Training" (Glenn Rueger), "Situation Quiet" (Max Steiner), "Bright Side of the Road" (Van Morrison), "You Make It Better" (Shawn Mullins, Gerry Hansen). Mature themes and sexuality prohibit viewing by children. **p**, Todd Black, Guymon Casady, Brian Bell, Lawrence Grey, Kelli Konop; **d**, David Frankel; **cast**, Meryl Streep, Tommy Lee Jones, Steve Carell, Jean Smart, Ben Rappaport, Marin Ireland, Patch Darragh, Brett Rice, Becky Ann Baker, Elisabeth Shue, Charles Techman, Mimi Rogers; **w**, Vanessa Taylor; **c**, Florian Ballhaus; **m**, Theodore Shapiro; **ed**, Steven Weisberg; **prod d**, Stuart Wurtzel; **art d**, Patricia Woodbridge; **set d**, George DeTitta Jr.; **spec eff**, J.C. Brotherhood, Nathaniel Brotherhood, John Blair.

Horns ★★★ 2013; U.S./Canada; 123m; Red Granite Pictures/Dimension Films; Color; Horror; Children: Unacceptable (MPAA: R); **BD**; **DVD**. Well-crafted horror tale begins when Temple, Radcliffe's girlfriend, is raped and murdered, and he becomes the prime suspect in her death. He successfully defends himself, but wakes up one morning after a night of drinking noticing large horns protruding from his forehead. He finds that no one but him notices the horns. While under hypnosis in a doctor's office, he dreams about himself; his brother, Anderson; his lawyer, Minghella, who also is his friend; another friend, Adamthwaite; and Garner, a girl. Minghella had introduced Radcliffe to Temple when he first noticed her in church. Temple accidentally broke the cross on her necklace, and Minghella repaired it. Realizing that Radcliffe is attracted to Temple, Minghella trades him the necklace for a cherry bomb, and Radcliffe gives the necklace back to Temple, which starts their relationship. In the present, after his dream, Radcliffe begins to embrace his horns because he senses they are giving him enhanced psychological powers so that he can manipulate the behavior of other people. At the same time, he is coming closer to learning who killed Temple. On the night she was murdered, she had ended their relationship, which left him heartbroken and suspicious that she was in love with someone else. Through skin contact, he finds that he can read Anderson's mind and discovers that Anderson drove Temple home the night she was killed, but she exited into some woods. Anderson fell asleep waiting for her to return and woke up the next morning holding a blood-stained rock. Anderson then removed any evidence linking him to her murder. Shocked to learn this, Radcliffe beats Anderson brutally, but is arrested by Adamthwaite, who is a policeman. Radcliffe notices that snakes are following him, but he can control and direct them so they attack and punish people. The next day, Radcliffe tells Minghella what has been happening. Minghella does not see Radcliffe's horns and is not affected by their influence to manipulate. Radcliffe notices that Minghella is wearing Temple's cross and tears it from him. The cross had been shielding Minghella from Radcliffe's horns, but now he succumbs to their power. In touching Minghella's skin, Radcliffe sees again the night of Temple's murder and sees in flashback how Minghella followed Temple into the woods. Minghella tells Temple that he loves her, but she rebuffed him, saying she loves only Radcliffe. Angry at hearing this, Minghella then rapes and murders Temple, and then tries to frame Anderson for the killing. In flash-forward, Radcliffe is badly beaten by Minghella, who then sets him on fire inside his car. Radcliffe escapes the flames by driving his car into some water and is presumed to have drowned. Minghella tells police that Radcliffe confessed to the murder and then committed suicide. However, Radcliffe survives the incident due to his powers, although he is badly burned and mutilated. He goes to Temple's father, who gives him a key with Radcliffe's name on it, a gift Temple had left before her death. Radcliffe wears Temple's cross, which heals his burns and removes his horns. He takes the key to his and Temple's childhood tree house and unlocks a secret storage compartment. He finds a letter from Temple saying that she had cancer and knew he was going to propose to her soon. She writes that she wanted more than anything to be his wife, but nevertheless wanted to spare him the agony of seeing her slowly die. She therefore used a pretense to sever their relationship. Although heartbroken over Temple's death, Radcliffe is overjoyed to learn that Temple still loved him. He confronts Minghella and demands he go to the police to admit raping and killing Temple. Anderson and Adamthwaite also arrive and learn that Minghella killed Temple. Minghella agrees to confess to the police, but, while Adamthwaite escorts him at gunpoint, Minghella seizes the gun. He kills Adamthwaite and badly wounds Anderson. As Minghella is about to shoot Radcliffe, Radcliffe tears Temple's cross from his neck and transforms into a satanic monster, summoning his army of snakes to kill Minghella. Radcliffe, dying from his wounds, spends his last moments with Anderson before turning into stone. In the end, Radcliffe and Temple are reunited in Heaven. Off the wall and over the top, the script is somewhat muddled and its story line misleading at times, but Radcliffe presents such a compelling and magnetic performance that he ushers the viewer quickly from one horrific scene to another. The film was not popular at the box office, earning less than $3.4 million in its initial release. Sexual content, graphic nudity, disturbing violence, including sexual assaults, gutter language and drug use prohibit viewing by children. **p**, Alexandre Aja, Riza Aziz, Joey McFarland, Cathy Schulman; **d**, Aja; **cast**, Daniel Radcliffe, Juno Temple, Kathleen Quinlan, Joe Anderson, Heather Graham, Kelli Garner, Sabrina Carpenter, James Remar, Max Minghella, David Morse; **w**, Keith Bunin (based on the novel by Joe Hill); **c**, Frederick Elmes; **m**, Robin Coudert; **ed**, Baxter; **prod d**, Allan Cameron; **art d**, Jeremy Stanbridge; **set d**, Shane Vieau; **spec eff**, Jak Osmond.

Hotel Transylvania ★★★ 2012; U.S.; 91m; COL; Color; Animated Comedy; Children: Cautionary (MPAA: PG); **BD**; **DVD**. Entertaining and well-animated tale outlandishly spoofs the vampire legend when Dracula the vampire (Sandler voiceover) builds a resort hotel in 1895 to raise his daughter (Gomez voiceover) in a safe environment away from humans. Monsters go there to vacation with their families, includ-

Quasimodo, Jonathan and Dracula in *Hotel Transylvania*, 2012.

ing Dracula's friends, the Frankenstein Monster (James voiceover) and his wife Eunice (Dresher voiceover), werewolves Wayne (Buscemi voiceover) and Wanda (Shannon voiceover), along with an invisible man named Griffin, a mummy named Murray, and Bigfoot. They arrive at the hotel to celebrate Gomez's 118th birthday, but, before the party begins, a twenty-one-year-old human named Jonathan (Samberg voiceover) is hiking in the forest when he sees the hotel. Sandler sees Samberg and disguises himself as a monster so as to hide the young human from his guests. However, Gomez sees and falls in love with Samberg, to Sandler's dismay. Even though Sandler warns her against humans, chiefly Samberg, Gomez has a mind and heart of her own. The script is funny, albeit sometimes adolescently silly, and provides many hilarious scenes while the fast-acting animation (via impressive 3-D computer creation) presents a bevy of classic horror creatures who outlandishly prove indestructible, despite their constant destruction. The film was an enormous success at the box office, earning more than $358.4 million in its initial release against a budget of $85 million. Songs: "Hush Little Baby" (traditional), "Daddy's Girl" (Adam Sandler, Robert Smigel), "Sexy and I Know It" (George Robertson, Kenneth Oliver, Skyler Gordy, Stefan Gordy, Erin Beck, David Lisenbee), "Where Did the Time Go Girl" (Smigel, Dennis White), "Sweet 118" (Andy Samberg, Stuart Hart, Trevor Simpson), "The Zing" (Adam Sandler, Robert Smigel, Dennis White), "Helpless" (Peter Tvrznik), "Problem" (Lukasz Gottwald, Henry Walter, Becky Gomez, William Adams). Crude humor and scary images cautions viewing by children. **p**, Michelle Murdocca, Lydia Bottegoni; **d**, Genndy Tartakovsky; **cast**, Adam Sandler, Andy Samberg, Selena Gomez, Kevin James, Fran Drescher, Steve Buscemi, Molly Shannon, David Spade, CeeLo Green, Jon Lovitz, Brian George, Luenell; **w**, Peter Baynham, Robert Smigel (based on a story by Todd Durham, Dan Hageman, Kevin Hageman); **m**, Mark Mothersbaugh; **ed**, Catherine Apple; **prod d**, Marcelo Vignali; **art d**, Ron Lukas, Noelle Triaureau; **spec eff**, Natalie DeJohn.

Hotel Transylvania 2 ★★★ 2015; U.S.; 89m; COL/Sony; Color; Animated Comedy; Children: Cautionary (MPAA: PG); **BD**; **DVD**. In this entertaining and well-made sequel to the 2012 film, the Drac Pack (short for Dracula) are enjoying their afterlife at Hotel Transylvania. Dracula (Sandler, voiceover) has relaxed his policy of monsters-only as guests, so humans are now welcome. However, he is worried that his grandson Dennis (Blinkoff voiceover), who is half-human and half-vampire, isn't showing signs that he is even half a vampire. Grandfather Drac (Offerman voiceover) enlists the aid of his friends to put Blinkoff through a "monster-in-training" boot camp. But little does Offerman know that his vampire father, Vlad (Brooks voiceover), is about to pay a family visit to the hotel. When Brooks discovers that his great-grandson

Elizabeth Banks and Jennifer Lawrence in *The Hunger Games*, 2012.

Blinkoff is not a pure-blooded vampire and humans are now welcome at the hotel, bat wings start to flutter, flap and fly. The animation, like the original, is superb and the monster sight gags are consistently funny and appealing. This film outdid the original's success at the box office, earning more than $456.2 million in its initial release against a budget of more than $80 million. Songs: "I'm in Love with a Monster" (Harmony Sanuels, Carmen Reece, Sara Mancuso, Edgar Etienne, Ericka Coulter), "Johnny's Girl" (Keith Baxter, Adam Sandler, Robert Smigel), "Daddy's Girl" (Sandler, Smigel), "GDFR" (Thomas Allen, Harold R. Brown, Mike Caren, Andrew Cedar, Morris Dickerson, Tramar Dillard, Justin Franks, Gerald Goldstein, LeRoy L. Jordan, Lee Oskar, Charles W. Miller, Paulo Rodriguez, Howard E. Scott, Dominic Woods), "Twinkle, Twinkle, Little Star" (Jane Taylor), "Suffer, Suffer, Scream in Pain" (Taylor, Sandler, Smigel), "Worth It" (Brian Collins, Mikkel Eriksen, Tor Hermansen, Ori Kaplan, Priscilla Renea), "Rollin'" (Adam McLeer, Michael McLeer, Russ-T Cobb), "Friends Forever" (Keith Baxter, Leonard Capizzi, Bobby Pickett), "Nutsy Koo Koo" (Lodge Webster, Sandler, Smigel), "Phantom" (Baxter, Sandler, Smigel). Scary images and crude humor cautions viewing by children. **p**, Michelle Murdocca, Skye Lyons; **d**, Genndy Tartakovsky; **cast** (voiceovers), Adam Sandler, Steve Buscemi, Mel Brooks, David Spade, Andy Samberg, Dana Carvey, Selena Gomez, Kevin James, Keegan-Michael Key, Asher Blinkoff, Fran Drescher, Molly Shannon, Megan Mullally, Nick Offerman; **w**, Robert Smigel, Sandler; **m**, Mark Mothersbaugh; **ed**, Catherine Apple; **prod d**, Michael Kurinsky; **art d**, Steve Lumley.

The Hundred-Foot Journey ★★★ 2014; India/United Arab Emirates/U.S.; 122 m; Amblin Entertainment/Touchstone; Color; Drama; Children: Unacceptable (MPAA: PG); **BD**; **DVD**. The Indian Kadam family has owned a restaurant in Mumbai for several years and the second-oldest son, Hassan, portrayed by Dayal, is being trained to take over his mother's (Chawla) role as its main cook. All is going well until a mob firebombs the restaurant because of an election dispute. Puri, the family's patriarch and others are able to get patrons to safety, but Chawla is killed in the fire. The family leaves the dangerous city and moves to London but do not find a place to open a new restaurant so they move on to mainland Europe. Traveling by van, while crossing the border between Switzerland and France, the brakes fail near the village of Saint-Antonin-Noble-Val. They meet lovely young Le Bon, and she offers help in finding an auto repair shop and guest house, telling them she is a chef at an upscale French restaurant called Le Saule Pleueur, which translates into "The Weeping Willow." Le Bon takes the family to her apartment and feeds them. Puri thinks the village would be a good place to open a restaurant and learns of an abandoned restaurant building just outside of town that is available for purchase. Believing this to be divine

providence, Puri decides to renovate it into an Indian restaurant called "Maison Mumbai." However, the building is right across the street from the Weeping Willow, which is only a hundred feet away. Mirren, its widowed owner, is afraid of competition so she tries to sabotage the Kadams by buying up all the locally available produce needed to cook their entres on opening night. A veritable Cold War breaks out between Puri and Mirren and that peaks on Bastille Day, the day when Mirren's chefs and two others vandalize Puri's restaurant by spray-painting the outer wall and firebombing the interior. Dayal catches the vandals in the act of painting and burning, and scares them off, but his hands are badly burned in the fire. The next day, Mirren meets with her chefs and asks if they know the words to "La Marseillaise." She cites lines from the French national anthem about equality, justice, and fraternity, and fires the chef responsible for the vandalism, then cleans up the graffiti herself. Dayal then learns that Mirren's policy is to hire potential chefs by taste-testing an omelet they prepare for her, and asks if he may cook an omelet for her from his special recipe. She agrees, but because his hands are injured, he asks her to help him make the omelet. She does and, after tasting it, concedes that he could be a great chef and invites him to work in her restaurant. At first, he is against the move, but Puri reluctantly agrees. Dayal's cooking becomes popular with customers and the Weeping Willow wins its second Michelin Star, an honor only bestowed on a few restaurants in Europe. This attracts national attention to Dayal's skills as a chef, and he is offered a job in Paris. He accepts and Puri and Mirren eventually become friends and begin a romantic affair. Dayal's work in Paris receives critical acclaim, and there is talk that there will be a third Michelin Star for the Paris restaurant. However, his mind is distracted by homesickness for his family and for Le Bon, whom he had been romancing. He decides to return home and reunites with her, then invites her to join him in buying an interest in Mirren's restaurant, along with operational control. Dayal believes this will help Mirren's restaurant earn its third Michelin Star. That night, Dayal and Le Bon prepare dinner for his family at Mirren's restaurant, and they anticipate an evening of romance and fine dining in the courtyard of Maison Mumbai. Superior acting, especially Mirren's sterling essay, and firm direction provide an entertaining domestic tale while highlighting some delightful cuisine along the way. The film was a success at the box office, earning more than $88.9 million in its initial release against a budget of $22 million. *Author's Note*: The film was jointly produced by Steven Spielberg's DreamWorks Company and Oprah Winfrey's Harpo Company. The film was shot on location in southern France, the Netherlands and in Paris. Thematic elements, some violence, gutter language and brief sexuality prohibit viewing by children. **p**, Oprah Winfrey, Steven Spielberg, Juliet Blake, Raphael Benoliel; **d**, Lasse Hallstrom; **cast**, Helen Mirren, Charlotte Lebon, Rohan Chand, Manish Dayal, Om Puri, Juhi Chawla, Amit Shah, Michel Blanc, Farzana Dua Elahe, Dillon Mitra; **w**, Steven Knight (based on the book by Richard C. Morais); **c**, Linus Sandgren; **m**, A.R. Rahman; **ed**, Andrew Mondshein; **prod d**, David Gropman; **set d**, Marie-Laure Valla; **spec eff**, Tony Kenny, Janson Raymond Kenny, Hudson Kenny.

The Hunger Games ★★★ 2012; U.S.; 142m; Color Force/Lionsgate; Color; Science-Fiction; Children: Unacceptable (MPAA: PG-13); **BD**; **DVD**. This grim tale begins in futuristic Panem, a nation ruled by Sutherland, a despot who orders that each year two teenage representatives from each of twelve districts be selected by lottery to take part in a fight-to-the death ritual called The Hunger Games. The deadly games are in part retribution for a previous rebellion against his authority. In the games, twenty-four participants are forced to eliminate the others while Panem citizens are forced to watch these ritualistic blood-baths, not unlike ancient Roman slaughters against Christians. Prim, a sixteen-year-old girl, played by Shields, is selected to be District 12's female representative, but her older sister Katniss, essayed by Lawrence, volunteers to take her place. Lawrence and her male teammate, Hutcherson, are to fight stronger, bigger opponents, some of whom have trained their entire lives for the battle. The gory, blood-soaked action is spectacular and mesmerizing, and the film provides superior production values, particularly its special effects, but this and its three sequels are not for the sensitive viewer or those with faint hearts. Reminiscent of many the stunning and combative Roman arena film of old (**Barabbas**, 1962; **Demetrius and the Gladiators**, 1954; **Gladiator**, 2000; **The Last Days of Pompeii**, 1935; **Quo Vadis**, 1913 and 1951; **The Sign of the Cross**, 1932; **Spartacus**, 1960;), there is a marked absence of shame or remorse for its wanton bloodletting, and this film and its sequels somewhat sadistically or perversely play to its widespread inhuman cruelty and savagery. The film was a huge box office success, earning more than $694 million in its initial release against a budget of $78 million. This film was the first in a series, followed by **Hunger Games: Catching Fire**, 2013; **Hunger Games: Mockingjay—Part 1**, 2014; and **Hunger Games: Mockingjay—Part 2**, 2015. Songs/Music: "Deep in the Meadow" (music: T Bone Burnett, Simone Burnett; lyrics: Suzanne Collins), "Farewell" (Evgueni Galperine), "Horn of Plenty" (Win Butler, Regine Chassagne), "War" (Gabriel Hubert, Saiph Graves, Amal Hubert, Tycho Cohran, Jafar Graves, Uttama Hubert, Seba Graves, Tank Graves), "Sediment" (Laurie Spiegel), "A Warp on Her Abdomen" (Chas Smith), "Three Movements for Orchestra Mvt. 1" (Steve Reich), "Akkt Varo Hljott" (Olafur Arnalds), "Marissa Flashback" (Thomas Rowlands), "Abraham's Daughter" (Win Butler, Regine Chassagne, T Bone Burnett), "Safe and Sound" (Taylor Swift, John Paul White, Joy Williams, T Bone Burnett), "Kingdom Come" (John Paul White, Joy Williams). Intense violence and disturbing images, all involving teenagers, prohibit viewing by children. **p**, Nina Jacobson, Jon Kilik, Diana Alvarez, Martin Cohen, Louis Phillips, Aldric La'auli Porter, Bryan Unkeless; **d**, Gary Ross; **cast**, Jennifer Lawrence, Josh Hutcherson, Stanley Tucci, Woody Harrelson, Donald Sutherland, Wes Bentley, Willow Shields, Liam Hemsworth, Elizabeth Banks, Sandra Lafferty, Paula Malcomson, Rhoda Griffis; **w**, Ross, Billy Ray, Suzanne Collins (based on the novel by Collins); **c**, Tom Stern; **m**, James Newton Howard; **ed**, Christopher S. Capp, Stephen Mirrione, Juliette Welfling; **prod d**, Philip Messina; **art d**, John Collins, Robert Fechtman, Paul G. Richards; **set d**, Larry Dias; **spec eff**, Steve Cremin, William D. Lee.

The Hunger Games: Catching Fire ★★★ 2013; U.S.; 146m; Color Force/Lionsgate; Color; Science Fiction; Children: Unacceptable (MPAA: PG-13); **BD**; **DVD**; **IV**. In a futuristic society called Panem, teenage Lawrence and her male partner Hutcherson have won the 74th Hunger Games, a ritual in which teenagers are pitted against each other in battle to win or die. A year later the country is in revolution against the games as they are about to go on a victory tour to visit all the districts of Panem. Sutherland, the blood-seeking despotic president who invented the cruel game and made it the law for all teens to enter it by lottery, tells them they must stop the uprising that their victory caused and that threatens his rule. Now all of their lives are at stake again. Again, Lawrence is outstanding in her action-filled role, and the "games," albeit always emotionally disturbing, are well-choreographed. The film was a staggering success, earning more than $865 million in its initial release against a budget of $130 million. Songs: "Atlas" (Guy Berryman, Jon Buckland, Will Champion, Chris Martin), "Silhouettes" (Of Monster and Men)," and "Gale Song" (Jeremy Caleb Fraites, Wesley Schultz, Neyla Pekarel), "Who We Are" (Daniel Reynolds, Daniel Sermon, Ben McKee, Joshua Mosser, Alexander Grant). Intense violence and action, frightening images, thematic elements, suggestive situations and gutter language prohibit viewing by children. **p**, Nina Jacobson, Jon Kilik, Aldric La'auli Porter, Bryan Unkeless; **d**, Francis Lawrence; **cast**, Jennifer Lawrence, Josh Hutcherson, Woody Harrelson, Liam Hemsworth, Donald Sutherland, Stanley Tucci, Jack Quaid, Taylor St. Clair, Sandra Lafferty, Paula Malcomson, Willow Shields; **w**, Michael deBruyn, Simon Beaufoy (based on the novel *Catching Fire* by Suzanne Collins); **c**, Jo Willems; **m**, James Newton Howard; **ed**,

Jennifer Lawrence in *The Hunger Games*, 2012.

Alan Edward Bell; **prod d**, Philip Messina; **art d**, John Collins; **set d**, Larry Dias; **spec eff**, Steve Cremin, William D. Lee.

The Hunger Games: Mockingjay—Part 1 ★★★ 2014; U.S.; 123m; Color Force/Lionsgate; Color; Science Fiction; Children: Unacceptable (MPAA: PG-13); **BD**; **DVD**; **IV**. In the futuristic land of Panem, the notorious and deadly Hunger Games in which teenagers fight to the death have been destroyed by the victory of Lawrence and her partner Hutcherson. Together with their friends Hemsworth, Claflin, and Wright, they enter District 13 of Panem to take part in a rebellion against the games' originator, Panem President Sutherland. They battle the oppressive Sutherland under the name "Mockingjay," the symbol of the rebellion. Again, spectacular action and special effects dominate this tale, its bloody violence nevertheless visually disturbing. The film, like its predecessors and successor, was a hit at the box office, earning more than $755 million in its initial release against a budget of $125 million. Songs: "The Hanging Tree" (Suzanne Collins, Jeremiah Caleb Fraites, Wesley Schultz), "Yellow Flicker Beat" (Ella Yelich-O'Connor, Joel Little). Intense violence and action, frightening images, thematic elements, suggestive situations and gutter language prohibit viewing by children. **p**, Nina Jacobson, Jon Kilik, Bryan Unkeless; **d**, Francis Lawrence; **cast**, Jennifer Lawrence, Josh Hutcherson, Woody Harrelson, Liam Hemsworth, Donald Sutherland, Philip Seymour Hoffman, Julianne Moore, Stanley Tucci, Willow Shields, Sam Claflin, Elizabeth Banks, Jeffrey Wright; **w**, Peter Craig, Danny Strong (based on an adaptation by Suzanne Collins from her novel *Mockingjay*); **c**, Jo Willems; **m**, James Newton Howard; **ed**, Alan Edward Bell, Mark Yoshikawa; **prod d**, Philip Messina; **art d**, David Scheunemann, Dan Webster; **set d**, Larry Dias; **spec eff**, Steve Cremin, William D. Lee.

The Hunger Games: Mockingjay—Part 2 ★★★ 2015; U.S.; 137m; Color Force/Lionsgate; Color; Science Fiction; Children: Unacceptable (MPAA: PG-13); **BD**; **DVD**. This action-loaded sequel to **The Hunger Games: Mockingjay—Part 1**, 2014, the fourth film in the series, presents an off-handed condemnation of war. The film takes place in a post-apocalyptic future in the nation of Panem where boys and girls between the ages of twelve and eighteen must take part in the Hunger Games, a televised annual event in which the young "tributes" must fight to the death until there is only one survivor. Katniss, portrayed by Lawrence, a teenager, is joined by her district's male tribute, Hutcherson, to take part in the Hunger Games under the guidance of the former victor, Harrelson. The last episode ended with Hutcherson trying to choke Lawrence to death. Part 2 opens with Lawrence bruised and battered, recovering from her injuries and trying to help Hutcherson, who has been brainwashed and programmed to kill her and end her role in the

Laura Linney and Bill Murray as President Franklin D. Roosevelt in *Hyde Park on the Hudson*, 2012.

revolt against ruthless President Snow, essayed by the always crack-brained Sutherland. She wants to kill him, but Moore wants Lawrence out of the way so she can be the person and inspiration behind the uprising, called the Mockingjay (routinely battling mutant zombies with mouths like piranhas). Lawrence, however, has other plans, and winds up serving in a brigade called the Star Squad, its members being in the field for propaganda purposes, but who are still in danger. As resistance fighters enter the capital, Sutherland orders his Hunger gamers to booby-trap the city, resulting in great violence and an ending that is both highly emotional and dark. Lawrence shines as a young adult heroine who fights for her family, friends, and a peaceful future. Like its predecessors, this film enjoyed a great box office success, earning more than $623.5 million in its initial release against a budget of $160 million. Song: "Deep in the Meadow" (music: T Bone Burnett, Simone Burnett). Intense, gory violence and some thematic material prohibit viewing by children. **p**, Nina Jacobson, Jon Kilik, Christoph Fisser, Henning Molfenter, Bryan Unkleless, Charlie Woebcken; **d**, Francis Lawrence; **cast**, Jennifer Lawrence, Josh Hutcherson, Liam Hemsworth, Woody Harrelson, Donald Sutherland, Stanley Tucci, Philip Seymour Hoffman, Julianne Moore, Willow Shields, Sam Claflin, Elizabeth Banks; **w**, Peter Craig, Danny Strong (based on an adaptation by Suzanne Collins of her novel *Mickingjay*); **c**, Jo Willems; **m**, James Newton Howard; **ed**, Alan Edward Bell, Mark Yoshikawa; **prod d**, Philip Messina; **art d**, Dan Webster, David Scheunemann; **set d**, Larry Dias, Mark Rosinski; **spec eff**, Gerd Nefzer, Steven Cremin.

Hyde Park on the Hudson ★★★ 2012; U.S.; 94m; Daybreak Pictures/Focus Features; Color; Biographical Drama; Children: Unacceptable (MPAA: R); **BD**; **DVD**. This good biopic is set in the Hudson Valley, New York, in July 1939, focusing upon U.S. President Franklin D. Roosevelt (1882-1945), who is wonderfully played by Murray. He is visited at his family's country estate at Hyde Park by a distant cousin, Margaret "Daisy" Suckley (1891-1991), played by Linney. She arrives to help him relax, but they soon become platonic lovers. Their relationship causes discomfort when British King George VI (1895-1952), played by West, and Queen Elizabeth (1900-2002), played by Colman, visit Hyde Park for a weekend. West and Colman visit on hopes Murray can bolster American support for the United Kingdom on the eve of World War II (1939-1945) which broke out less than three months later. West discovers American fast food by eating his first hot dog (which the Roosevelts served to the royal couple with mustard, onions and relish). West and Colman are uncertain how to react to Murray's and Linney's delicate romantic situation while Linney comes to realize there is a lot more to the President and his life than she realized. Murray's wife, Eleanor Roosevelt (1884-1962), played by

Williams, turns a tolerant eye not only to Murray's emotional attentions to Linney, but to his devoted secretary, Marguerite "Missy" LeHand (1898-1944), played by Marvel, who has also maintained a longstanding platonic relationship with the President. Meanwhile, West discloses his apprehensions concerning his stuttering speech, but Murray reassures him that such an inability is not a liability with the British public any more than Murray's (Roosevelt's) inability to walk (Roosevelt had been stricken by infantile paralysis and was confined to a wheelchair and wore ten-pound iron braces on his legs) has taken any toll with the American public. The public does not observe their handicaps, Murray wisely points out to West, because "it is not what they want to see." The night that West and Colman arrive to visit the President, Linney sees Murray and Marvel sharing some intimate moments. Shocked, she is later told by Marvel that she and Marvel are not the only women who have become emotionally involved with the President, mentioning other women and stating that Linney, like Marvel and Williams, must accept these shared relationships. The following day, West and Colman pose with Murray and Williams, West successfully eats a hot dog while news photographers take pictures. Linney states in voiceover how the picnic cemented a strong relationship between the U.S. and Great Britain. She later concedes that she has accepted what affection she can have from Murray as she watches him become frail over the years, but that everyone "still [looked] to him, still seeing whatever it was they wanted to see." Murray gives a powerful and compelling performance of one of America's greatest presidents, who was emotionally dependent upon several women while he guided the U.S. through the hazardous years of WWII (1939-1945), but who was, as Ernest Hemingway once wrote, "strong at the broken places." Linney, Williams and Marvel are also exceptional in their roles as the women who loved FDR, and West gives an impressive performance of George VI. The production values that accurately reflect the period are high while Michell directs with a firm hand. The film saw a modest return at the box office, earning more than $11 million in its initial release. Songs: "Moonlight Serenade" (Glenn Miller, Mitchell Parish), "I Don't Want to Set the World on Fire" (Bernie Benjamin, Eddie Durham, Sol Marcus, Edward Saller), "If I Didn't Care" (Jack Lawrence), "Thunder Song," and "Benny's Song," "Chief Mountain Song," and "Squaw Mountain" (Jonathan Brewer). *Author's Note*: The most egregious liberties taken in this film involve the sexually implied relationship between FDR and Suckley. At one point, in 1935, the two were on an outing and the President kissed her, but the relationship, to all reliable accounts never went any further. Moreover, FDR requested that the affectionate letters Suckley wrote to him be destroyed by her, but she nevertheless held on to some of them, which were found after her death in 1991 and used as the basis for this film. The film was shot on location in England where Roosevelt's Hyde Park residence was recreated. Many other actors have portrayed FDR in many other films, including **Action in the North Atlantic**, 1943 (Art Gilmore); **Albert Einstein**, 1990 (TV series; Ernst Heise); **Annie**, 1982 (Edward Herrmann); **Annie**, 1999 (made-for-TV; Dennis Howard); **Back Stairs at the White House**, 1979 (TV miniseries; John Anderson); **Beau James**, 1957 (Dick Nelson); **The Beginning or the End**, 1947 (Godfrey Tearle); **Bertie and Elizabeth**, 2002 (made-for-TV; Robert Hardy); **Churchill: The Hollywood Years**, 2004 (Henry Goodman); **Cradle Will Rock**, 1999 (himself in archive footage); **Crossings**, 1986 (TV miniseries; Jack Denton); **Day One**, 1989 (made-for-TV; Donald Ogden Stiers); **De Gaulle**, 2006 (TV series; Robert Hardy); **Edge of Darkness**, 1943 (voiceover of Jack Young); **Einstein**, 1984-1985 (TV miniseries; Gerard Buhr); **Eleanor and Franklin**, 1976 (made-for-TV; Edward Herrmann); **Eleanor and Franklin: The White House Years**, 1977 (made-for-TV; Edward Herrmann); **Enola Gay: The Men, the Mission, the Atomic Bomb**, 1980 (made-for-TV; Stephen Roberts); **The Fall of Berlin**, 1952 (Oleg Frelikh); **F.D.R.**, 1965 (TV miniseries; Charleton Heston voiceover); **F.D.R.: A One-Man Show**, 1987 (Chris Elliott); **F.D.R.: The Last**

Year, 1980 (made-for-TV; Jason Robards Jr.); **F.D.R.: The Man in the White House**, 1982 (made-for-TV; Robert Vaughn); **The First Front**, 1949 (Nikolai Cherkasov); **First to Fight**, 1967 (Stephen Roberts); **For All: Springboard to Victory**, 1998 (Guaracy Picado); **Freedom to Speak**, 1982 (TV miniseries; Laurence Luckinbill); **The Great Battle**, 1973 (Stanislaw Jaskiewicz); **Ike: The War Years**, 1979 (TV miniseries; Stephen Roberts): **Into the Storm**, 2009 (made-for-TV; Len Cariou); **J. Edgar**, 2011 (David A. Cooper); **J. Edgar Hoover**, 1987 (made-for-TV; David Ogden Stiers); **Katastrofa w Gibraltarze**, 1984 (Andrzej Krasicki); **The Kennedys of Massachusetts**, 1990 (TV miniseries; Josef Sommer); **Kingfish: The Story of Huey P. Long**, 1995 (made-for-TV; Bob Gunton); **The Last Bastion**, 1984 (TV miniseries; Warren Mitchell); **The Long Days of Summer**, 1980 (made-for-TV; Stephen Roberts); **MacArthur**, 1977 (Dan O'Herlihy); **Mission to Moscow**, 1943 (Jack Young); **Murrow**, 1986 (made-for-TV; Robert Vaughn); **Pearl Harbor**, 2001 (Jon Voight); **The Pigeon That Took Rome**, 1962 (Dick Nelson; scenes deleted); **The Private Files of J. Edgar Hoover**, 1977 (Howard Da Silva); **The Revenge of Al Capone**, 1989 (made-for-TV; Donald Craig); **The Right Man**, 1960 (made-for-TV; Art Carney); **Roosevelt and Truman**, 1977 (made-for-TV; Art Evans); **Spies**, 1992 (made-for-TV; Chris Nubel); **Sunrise at Campobello**, 1960 (Ralph Bellamy); **This Is the Army**, 1943 (Jack Young); **Truman**, 1995 (made-for-TV; Lee Richardson, and himself, archive footage, funeral procession); **The Untouchables**, 1959-1963 (TV series; "The Unhired Assassin, Part II," 1960 episode: Paul Frees); **The Untouchables**, 1993-1994 (TV series; "Radical Solution," 1993 episode: Richard Henzel); **The Victors and the Vanquished**, 1949 (Nikolai Cherkasov); **Victory**, 1984 (Algimantas Masiulis); **Voyagers!**, 1982-1983 (TV series; Nicholas Pryor); **War and Remembrance**, 1988 (TV miniseries; Ralph Bellamy); **Warm Springs**, 2005 (made-for-TV; Kenneth Branagh); **Winchell**, 1998 (made-for-TV; Christopher Plummer); **The Winds of War**, 1983 (TV miniseries; Ralph Bellamy); **World War Two: Behind Closed Doors**, 2008 (TV series; Bob Gunton); **World War II: When Lions Roared**, 1994 (made-for-TV; John Lithgow); **Yalta**, 1984 (made-for-TV; Robert Rimbaud); **Yankee Doodle Dandy**, 1942 (Jack Young). Brief sexuality prohibits viewing by children. **p**, David Aukin, Kevin Loader; **d**, Roger Michell; **cast**, Bill Murray, Laura Linney, Samuel West, Olivia Colman, Elizabeth Marvel, Olivia Williams, Elizabeth Wilson, Martin McDougall, Andrew Havill, Eleanor Bron, Nancy Baldwin; **w**, Richard Nelson (based on the journal of Margaret Suckley); **c**, Lol Crawley; **m**, Jeremy Sams; **ed**, Nicolas Gaster; **prod d**, Simon Bowles; **art d**, Hannah Moseley, Mark Raggett; **set d**, Celia Bobak; **spec eff**, Chris Reynolds, Adam Gascoyne, Tim Caplan.

Ice Age: Continental Drift ★★★ 2012; U.S.; 88m; Blue Sky Studios; FOX; Color; Animated Adventure; Children: Cautionary (MPAA: PG); **BD**; **DVD**. In this fifth entry in the entertaining series, after their continent is set adrift, friends Manny, a wooly mammoth (Romano voiceover); Diego, a smilodon (Leary voiceover); and Sid (Leguizamo voiceover), a lazy ground sloth, undertake another adventure. They use an iceberg as a ship and battle sea creatures and pirates. It all starts when Scrat, a saber-toothed squirrel (Wedge voiceover) causes Pangaea to break apart and Romano and his wife Ellie (Latifah voiceover) have to deal with their teenage daughter Peaches (Palmer voiceover), who can't get along with anyone. Palmer's friend Louis, a mole hog (Gad voiceover), tries warning her when she comes near a mammoth to whom she is attracted. Meanwhile, Leguizamo's family returns to leave his elderly grandmother Granny (Sykes voiceover) before abandoning them. Palmer meets up with her boyfriend, and this leads to an estrangement between mother and daughter. Then Romano is trapped on a moving iceberg with Leguizamo and Leary. At the same time, a giant shift of land nears Latifah, Palmer and the rest of those on land, and they start

Diego and Shira in *Ice Age: Continental Drift*, 2012.

for a land bridge. Wedge then finds an acorn whose treasure map leads him to an island. A giant crab forces Romano, Leguizamo, and Leary farther from land where they find Sykes asleep on the iceberg. They are soon captured by some pirates on a floating iceberg, and their captain Gutt (Dinklage voiceover) tries to enlist them into his crew. When they refuse, Dinklage threatens to kill them, but they escape and sink his ship. Dinklage's first mate, a female saber-toothed tiger named Shira (Lopez voiceover) joins them. Dinklage takes revenge on Romano for sinking his ship by planning an attack. Romano counteracts with a plan to steal Dinklage's new ship to return home. Lopez leaves Dinklage and remains to try to protect the others from him. Wedge is then swallowed by a shark. Sailing home on the current, Leary, Leguizamo, and Sykes are threatened by monstrous sirens, but Romano manages to save them. Romano, Leguizamo, Leary, and Sykes finally return home, but find the land bridge was destroyed in an earthquake and that Dinklage and his pirate crew got there first and captured Latifah and Palmer. A battle follows between the herd and the pirates and Dinklage tries to kill Palmer, but she outwits him and also saves her mother. Romano wins in a duel with Dinklage on an ice floe and reunites with his family and friends. A siren then eats Dinklage alive. Their home has been destroyed, so the herd sails to an island which will be their new home. The animation, like its predecessors, is superbly crafted, and the characters amuse and delight throughout, and the script is often more witty than silly. The film was a great success at the box office, earning more than $877 million in its initial release against a budget of $95 million. Songs: "Chasing the Sun" (Elliott Gleave, Alex James Smith), "Master of the Seas" (Adam Schlesinger), "Candy Man" (Leslie Bricusse, Anthony Newley), "We Are" (Ester Dean), "Symphony No. 9 in D Major, Op. 125" (Ludwig van Beethoven), "America the Beautiful" (Samuel A. Ward). Mild crude humor and perilous action cautions viewing by children. **p**, John C. Donkin, Lori Forte; **d**, Steve Martino, Michael Thurmeier; **cast** (voiceovers), Ray Romano, Leary, Leguizamo, Jennifer Lopez, Queen Latifah, Aziz Ansari, Joy Behar, Christopher Campbell, Alain Chabat, Ester Dean, Peter Dinklage, Karen Disher, Jason Fricchione; **w**, Michael Berg, Jason Fuchs (based on a story by Berg, Lori Forte); **c**, Renato Falcao; **m**, John Powell; **ed**, Christopher Campbell, James Palumbo, David Ian Salter; **art d**, Nash Dunnigan; **set d**, Isaac Holze; **spec eff**, Daniel Abramovich, Inna Agujen, Ilan Gabai.

Ida ★★★ 2013; U.S.; 107m; Opus Film/Music Box Films; B/W; Drama; Children: Unacceptable (MPAA: PG-13); **BD**; **DVD**; **IV**. Absorbing tale set in 1962 Poland sees Trzebuchowska, a young orphan girl, brought up by nuns in a Catholic convent where she becomes a novice. At eighteen, before taking her final vows to become a nun, she must see her only living relative, Kulesza. She learns from her that her

Benedict Cumberbatch in *The Imitation Game,* 2014.

parents were Jews and had been victims of the Nazi Holocaust in World War II (1939-1945), but she does not know if they survived. She goes in search of learning the fate of her parents and then struggles with her decision to become a nun, a harrowingly emotional journey that tests her faith and future. She finds Kulesza, her "aunt," a hard-drinking, promiscuous communist, who had taken her in when she was a child and the woman leads her to others where it is revealed that her family was slaughtered by Poles fearful of being accused of hiding Jews and possibly to rob them of their believed wealth. In the course of her wanderings, Trzebuchowska meets an affable, young saxophonist and has a one-night assignation with him, rejecting his marriage proposal and then donning her habit and moving on, undecided at the end whether to return to the convent or not. Trzebuchowska gives a startling performance as a person who is wholly displaced in a world that engulfs her into the grim past of the Holocaust. The film saw a modest success at the box office, earning more than $11 million in its initial release. Songs: "Serduszko puka w rytnie cha-cha" (music: Romuald Zylinski; lyrics: Janusz Odrowaz-Wisniewski); 'Jupiter' Symphony No. 41 in C Major" (1788; Wolfgang Amadeus Mozart); "Rodnye glaza," "O Jmmy Joe," "Nie placz, kiedy odjade" (music: Marino Marini; lyrics: Wanda Sieradzka de Ruig); "Rudy rydz" (music: Boguslaw Klimczuk; lyrics: Jacek Bochenski); "Big boogie-woogie" (music: Leszek Bogdanowicz; lyrics: Michaj Burano); "Love in Portofino" (music: Fred Buscaglione; lyrics: Agnieszka Osiecka); "21 mila baci" (musoc: Adriano Celentano; lyrics: Fucio Fulci, Piero Vivarelli); "Naima," "Equinox" (John Coltrane); "Alabama " (music: Romuald Zylinski; lyrics: Bogdan Choinski; lyrics: Jan Galkowski); "The Inernationale" (music: Pierre Degeyter; lyrics:Eugene Pottier); "Ich Ruf Zu Herr Jesu Christ" (Johann Sebastian Bach). Thematic elements, some sexuality and smoking prohibit viewing by children. (In French; English subtitles.) **p**, Eric Abraham, Piotr Dzieciol, Ewa Puszcynska, Christian Falkenberg Husum; **d**, Pawel Pawlikowski; **cast**, Agata Trzebuchowska, Agata Kulesza, Dawid Ogrodnik, Jerzy Trela, Adam Szyszkowski, Halina Skoczynska, Joanna Kulig, Dorota Kuduk, Natalia Lagiewczyk, Afrodyta Weselak; **w**, Pawlikowski, Rebecca Lenkiewicz; **c**, Ryszard Lenczewski, Lukasz Zal; **m**, Kristian Selin Eidnes Andersen; **ed**, Jaroslaw Kaminski; **prod d**, Marcel Slawinski, Katarzyna Sobanska; **art d**, Jagna Dobesz; **spec eff**, Slawomir Maslanka, Piotr Nowacki, Robert Stasz, Michal Truszkowski.

Identity Thief ★★★ 2013; U.S.; 111m; Aggregate Films/UNIV; Color; Comedy/Crime Drama; Children: Unacceptable (MPAA: R); **BD**; **DVD**. Amusing tale sees Bateman as a mild-mannered Denver businessman who gets a phone call from a woman confirming his name and other identifying information. Soon afterward, he gets a call from a spa in Florida reminding him of his appointment and then learns that his credit cards have been maxed out. Bateman leaves his wife, kids, and job to go to Miami and track down the woman, McCarthy, who has stolen his identity. This takes him into run-ins with bounty hunters and discovering more about himself and McCarthy than he ever expected. This bit of entertaining fluff did well at the box office, earning more than $174 million in its initial release against a budget of $35 million. Songs: "Bad Girls" (Maya Arulpragasam, Marcella Araica, Nate "Danja" Hills), "Off the Wall" (Ali Theodore), "Shake It" (Ali Theodore, Aaron Sandlofer, Alana Da Fonseca, Julian Michael Davis), "Swagger Jagger" (Andre Davidson, Sean Davidson, Autumn Rowe, Andrew Harr, Jermaine Jackson, Cher Lloyd, Clarence Coffe Jr., Marcus Lomax), "I'm Gonna Be Me/500 Miles" (Charles Stobo Reid, Craig Morris Reid), "Right Thurr" (Howard "Chingy" Bailey, Shamar Daugherty, Alonzo Lee), "Milkshake" (Pharrell Williams, Chad Hugo), "Ain't Mesin 'Round" (Gary Clark Jr.), "The Payback" (James Brown, Fred Wesley, John Starks), "Barracuda" (Ann Wilson, Nancy Wilson, Michael DeRosier, Roger Fisher), "With No Siesta" (Ali Theodore, Joseph Katsaros, Julian Michael Davis), "It's the End of the Road" (Christopher Lennertz, Todd Bozung), "Shake Ya Ass" (Pharrell Williams, Chad Hugo, Michael Mystikal Tyler), "Good Intent" (Kimbra Johnson, Francois Tetaz), "The Walker" (Michael Fitzpatrick, Noelle Scaggs, Joseph Scott Karnes, James Midhi King, Jeremy Ruzumna, John Wicks), "I Eat Boys Like You for Breakfast" (Stefan Tornby, Ida Siversten), "Habanera" from the opera "Carmen" (Georges Bizet), "Happy Birthday to You" (Mildred J. Hill, Patty S. Hill). Sexual content and gutter language prohibit viewing by children. **p**, Jason Bateman, Pamela Abdy, Scott Stuber, Mary Rohlich; **d**, Seth Gordon; **cast**, Bateman, Melissa McCarthy, Jon Favreau, Amanda Peet, Tip "T.I." Harris, Genesis Rodriguez, Morris Chestnut, John Cho, Robert Patrick, Eric Stonestreet; **w**, Craig Mazin (based on a story by Jerry Eeten, Craig Mazin); **c**, Javier Aguirresarobe; **m**, Christopher Lennertz; **ed**, Peter Teschner; **prod d**, Shepherd Frankel; **art d**, Andrew Max Cahn; **set d**, Maria Nay; **spec eff**, John S. Baker, Jeremy Hays, Olcun Tan, Thomas Tannenberger.

The Imitation Game ★★★ 2014; U.K./U.S.; 113m; Black Bear Pictures/Weinstein Company; Color; Biographical Drama; Spy Drama; Children: Unacceptable; **BD**; **DVD**. Based on the life of legendary cryptanalyst Alan Turing (1912-1954), played by Cumberbatch, the film follows his and his team of code breakers at Britain's top-secret Government Code and Cypher School at Bletchley Park to decipher the Nazi German code during the darkest days of World War II (1939-1945). The code breakers, a group of scholars, mathematicians, linguists, chess champions, and intelligence officers, have a powerful ally in Prime Minister Winston Churchill (1874-1965), who authorizes providing any resources they need. The film covers key periods of the cryptanalyst's life, from his unhappy teenage years at a boarding school to his secret wartime work on the revolutionary electro-mechanical device that was capable of breaking 3,000 Enigma-generated naval codes a day, and his post-war decline following his conviction for gross indecency, a onetime British criminal offence stemming from his having admitted to being in a homosexual relationship. Cumberbatch proves exceptional in his essay of the sensitive and gifted Turing, and he is well-supported by a talented cast in what is an intelligently written, tension-filled tale that sustains interest throughout. The film did exceptionally well at the box office, earning more than $227.8 million in its initial release against a budget of $14 million. Songs: "Opportunity" (Alexander Norris, Stuart A. Hart, Scott Lean), "Eddie's Boogie" (Eddie Palermo), "Time to Go" (Andrew Snitzer, Tom Gloia), "Coffee Meditation" (Milan Svoboda), "Jive Time" (Cathy Bielawski). *Author's Note*: The film takes considerable liberties with the actual historical facts, chiefly attributing the creation of the computer that broke the German Enigma Code to Turing when that was a collaborative effort on the part of a large team of code experts. Leech, who plays John Cairncross (1913-1995), was part of that brilliant code-breaking team and who copied all the information gotten at Bletchley and drove such top secrets packed in boxes in the back seat of a car to London where he delivered these secrets to the Soviet embassy (that provided that car). Cairncross later acted as a double Soviet agent when working in London for MI6 and only years later admitted his treason. He was, in exchange for his information, not prosecuted and even given a safe and well-paying job in Rome where he worked for the United Nations. For more details on Cairncross and Turing, see my book, *Spies: A Narrative Encyclopedia of Dirty Tricks & Double Dealing from Biblical Times to the Present* (M. Evans, 1997; Cairncross: page 126; Turing: page 486). **p**, Nora Grossman, Ido Ostrowsky, Teddy Schwarzman, Peter Heslop; **d**, Morten Tyldum; **cast**, Benedict Cumberbatch, Keira Knightley, Matthew Goode, Mark Strong, Charles Dance, Allen Leech, Tuppence Middleton, Rory Kinnear, Hayley Joanne Bacon, Steven Waddington; **w**, Graham Moore (based on the book *Alan Turing: The Enigma* by Andrew Hodges); **c**, Oscar Faura; **m**, Alexandre Desplat; **ed**, William Goldenberg; **prod d**, Maria Djurkovic; **art d**, Nick Dent; **spec eff**, Jason Troughton.

The Immigrant ★★★ 2014; U.S.; 120m; Keep Your Head/Weinstein Co.; Color; Drama/Romance; Children: Unacceptable (MPAA: R); **BD**; **DVD**. Powerful portrait records the corruption and seedy lifestyles imposed upon young females migrating to the U.S. in the early 1920s. Cotillard and her sister, Sarafyan, leave their native Poland in 1921 to go by ship to New York to seek a better life in America after their home has been destroyed during World War I (1914-1918). At Ellis Island, Sarafyan is quarantined because of her lung disease. Cotillard is about to be deported, when a young man, Phoenix, notices she is beautiful and speaks fluent English, so he bribes a police officer to let her go, then takes her to his house. He knows she needs money to live on and help her hospitalized sister, so he lets her dance at a theater while becoming her pimp as he compels her into prostitution. Along the way, he becomes romantically interested in her. While looking for relatives in Manhattan, Cotillard is arrested as an illegal immigrant and she is again almost deported. Taken back to Ellis Island, Cotillard watches a performance by Renner, a magician, who gives her a white rose. The next day, Renner gets her released and she again meets Phoenix at the theater where she danced, learning that Renner is Phoenix's brother. Renner asks Cotillard to assist him in a mind-reading trick, but the audience hoots at the act, labelling her a trollop, a reputation she has earned through Phoenix's pimping. The uproar ends in a brawl between Phoenix and Renner. Phoenix later gets Cotillard to join his other girls in showing themselves off in Central Park as a way of enticing patrons to purchase their sexual favors. Renner has by now fallen in love with Cotillard, which creates more conflict between him and Phoenix, one of which has Phoenix jailed overnight. Both men then try to help Cotillard get her sister out of the hospital. In a confrontation between her and the two men, Renner pulls out an unloaded gun and aims it at Phoenix. To defend himself, Phoenix stabs Renner to death. Phoenix then goads Cotillard into helping him dump Renner's body in the street at night, but a prostitute at odds with Cotillard tells police Cotillard killed Renner. Phoenix hides Cotillard, but police find them and severely beat him, then take a large amount of money Phoenix has been carrying. Phoenix tells her that he would have used the money to help her sister. Cotillard then makes contact with her aunt, who agrees to loan the money needed to bribe an Ellis Island authority so Sarafyan can be released. After accomplishing this, Phoenix gives the sisters train tickets to Jersey City. As the sisters leave, Phoenix tells them he intends to stay in New York and confess to police about having killed Renner in self-defense. Cotillard, Phoenix and Renner all provide compelling performances in what is otherwise a soapy melodrama that presents what appears to be an almost a verbatim story line from a classic silent film, **Traffic in Souls**, 1913. The prosaic and somewhat predictable tale (young, defenseless women imperiled by cruel villains) is nevertheless presented with such panache and verve that it all becomes absorbingly empathetic. The film fared poorly at the box office, earning less than $6 million in its initial release against a budget of $16 million. Not related to the 1917 Charles Chaplin film with

Samuel Joslin, Oaklee Pendergast, Tom Holland, Ewan McGregor and Naomi Watts in *The Impossible*, 2012.

the same title. Songs: "Buffalo Girls" (traditional), "A Rag Time Episode," and "La Rondine, Act III" (Giacomo Puccini), "Accordion Polka" (Dory Bavarsky), "Sing that Melody" (Keith Nichols), "Funeral Canticle" (John Tavener, Mother Thekla), "Old Folks at Home" (Stephen Foster), "The Gypsy in Me" (Ken Morrison), "The Voyage of the Nancy Lee" (H.O. Morrison), "Ma Mere L'Oye" (Maurice Ravel), "Il Trovatore" (Giuseppe Verdi), "Jazz Piano Rag" (Richard Geere), "The Girl of the Golden West" (music: Giacomo Puccini; lyrics: Guelfo Civinini, Carlo Zangarini). Sexual content, nudity and gutter language prohibit viewing by children. **p**, James Gray, Anthony Katagas, Greg Shapiro, Christopher Woodrow; **d**, Gray; **cast**, Marion Cotillard, Joaquin Phoenix, Jeremy Renner, Angela Sarafyan, Dagmara Dominczyk, Jicky Schnee, Yelena Solovey, Maja Wampuszyc, Ilia Volok; **w**, Gray, Richard Menello; **c**, Darius Khondji; **m**, Christopher Spelman; **ed**, John Axelrad, Kayla Emter; **prod d**, Happy Massee; **art d**, Pete Zumba; **set d**, David Schlesinger; **spec eff**, Drew Jiritano, Andrew Mortelliti.

The Impossible ★★★ 2012; Spain; 114m; Apaches Entertainment; Summit Entertainment; Color; Drama; Children: Unacceptable (MPAA: PG-13); **BD**; **DVD**. Exciting disaster film with astounding special effects opens when Watts, an English doctor, and her Scottish husband, McGregor, and their sons, Holland, Joslin, and Pendergast, spend Christmas 2004 holiday in Khao Lak, Thailand. After settling in at a villa on the coastline of the Indian Ocean and exchanging gifts, they take a swim in the villa's pool with some other tourists. They think they are in an island paradise until a noise in the distance becomes a roar. A tsunami has struck the region, triggered by an Indian Ocean earthquake, and there is no time to escape. Watts and her eldest son, Holland, are swept one way while McGregor and the youngest son, Joslin, are swept in another direction. They don't know what has become of their other son, five-year-old Pendergast. Watts and Holland barely survive and locals find them and take them to a hospital. Hospital staff workers mistakenly believe that Watts, severely injured, has died and Holland is taken to a tent where children are held. Surgery is performed on Watts and she is eventually reunited with Holland. Elsewhere, McGregor, Joslin, and Pendergast have survived the tsunami, although McGregor is injured. McGregor puts Joslin and Pendergast in a vehicle that takes tourists to a safe place, and he then begins searching for Watts and Holland. He later loses track of Joslin and Pendergast, but Mohring, a tourist, also separated from his family, joins McGregor in looking for both their families. After an extensive search, they find their families at the hospital where Watts and Holland are being nursed. Both families are reunited and Watts has surgery to a leg. Next day, Watts, McGregor and their sons board an ambulance airplane to Singapore. Well acted, the tale is based on the experiences of Maria Belon and her family, which is told

Samuel Joslin, Ewan McGregor and Oaklee Pendergast in *The Impossible*, **2012.**

in an intelligent script while marvelous special effects provide astonishing disaster scenes. Geraldine Chaplin gives a good cameo portrait when playing an old woman in the film. Watts dominates the film with a harrowing portrait of a woman frantic over the lives of her family members, an essay so riveting that it earned her an Oscar nomination as Best Actress. The film was a resounding success at the box office, earning more than $180.3 million in its initial release against a budget of $45 million. Songs: "IYLM" (1995, For Fiesta), "Kamalani" (1995, Larry Rivera). *Author's Note*: The tsunami seen in this film was created in a huge water tank in Spain where the film was shot on location. Real water surges, combined with special effects, were shot in slow motion to achieve the exciting disaster scenes. Watts and Holland spent more than five weeks in that water tank to achieve their involvement in the disaster scenes. The sixteen-year-old Holland described his experience as "brutal." Other films depicting tsunamis or tidal waves include **The Abyss**, 1989; **Aftershock**, 2012; **Akira**, 1988; **Atlantis: The Lost Empire**, 2001; **Bait**, 2012; **Bruce Almighty**, 2003; **The Day after Tomorrow**, 2004; **Deathwave**, 2009; **End Day**, 2005 (made-for-TV); **Escape from L.A.**, 1996; **Godzilla**, 2014; **Gorath**, 1962; **Hereafter**, 2010; **Himizu**, 2014 (based on the 2011 Tohoku earthquake and tsunami); **Homeland**, 2014 (based on the 2011 Tohoku earthquake and tsunami); **Immortals**, 2011; **Isle of Forgotten Sins**, 1943; **Japan Sinks**, 2006; **Krakatoa, East of Java**, 1969; **Land of Hope**, 2012 (based on the 2011 Tohoku earthquake and tsunami); **The Last Wave**, 1978; **Lost City Raiders**, 2008 (made-for-TV); **Malibu Shark Attack**, 2009 (made-for-TV); **Mind Games**, 2004; **The Omen**, 2006; **Orange County**, 2002; **Pirates**, 1998; **Pompeii**, 2014; **Ponyo**, 2008; **The Poseidon Adventure**, 1972; **Rescue from Gilligan's Island**, 1978 (made-for-TV); **Reunion**, 2013 (based on the 2011 Tohoku earthquake and tsunami); **San Andreas**, 2015; **The Sorcerer and the White Snake**, 2013; **The Ten Avatars**, 2008; **Tidal Wave**, 1973; **Tidal Wave**, 2009; **Tokyo Fiancée**, 2014; **Tomorrowland**, 2015; **Tsunami**, 2005 (made-for-TV); **Tsunami: The Aftermath**, 2006 (made-for-cable; based on the 2004 Indian Ocean tsunami); **A View to Kill**, 1985; **Vinyan**, 2008; **When Dinosaurs Ruled the Earth**, 1970; and **Wonderful Town**, 2007. Intense realistic disaster sequences, disturbing injury images and brief nudity prohibit viewing by children. **p**, Belen Atienza, Alvaro Augustin, Ghislain Barrois, Enrique Lopez Lavigne; **d**, Juan Antonio Bayona; **cast**, Naomi Watts, Ewan McGregor, Tom Holland, Samuel Joslin, Oaklee Pendergast, Sonke Mohring, Geraldine Chaplin, Marta Etura, Ploy Jindachote, Jomjaoi Sae-Limh, Johan Sundberg; **w**, Sergio G. Sanchez (based on writings by Maria Belon); **c**, Oscar Faura; **m**, Fernando Velazquez; **ed**, Elena Ruiz, Bernat Vilaplana; **prod d**, Eugenio Caballero; **art d**, Didac Bono; **set d**, Pilar Revuelta; **spec eff**, Pau Costa, Javier H. Moneo, Felix Berges, Javier Garcia.

In Secret ★★★ 2014; U.S.; 107m; LD Entertainment/Roadside Attractions; Color; Drama; Children: Unacceptable (MPAA: R); **BD**; **DVD**. This fascinating tale begins in a poor section of 1860s Paris where Olsen, a beautiful but sexually repressed young woman, is trapped in a loveless marriage to her sickly cousin, Felton, by her dominating aunt, Lange. She works days as a clerk in a small shop and, at night, watches Lange play dominoes with an oddball group of people. Olsen meets Isaac, an alluring friend of Felton's, who seduces her, and their secret affair leads to tragedy. While Olsen goes on a lake outing with Felton and Isaac, tragedy and murder overwhelm the trio. While Felton falls into the lake, Isaac, instead of saving him, causes him to drown while beating him as Felton hopelessly thrashes about in the water. Lange is so overwhelmed at the death of her son that she is paralyzed by a stroke, even though she suspects foul play by Olsen and Isaac. Believing that they have drawn suspicion upon themselves and not wanting to be apprehended by the police, Olsen and Isaac take their own lives. They drink champagne in front of Lange, their glasses purposely laced with poison, and both succumb in front of the startled Lange. Morose, and even depressing, fascinating interest in this grim tale is nevertheless sustained throughout via the fine performances from Olsen, Isaac, Felton and Lange. The film did not fare well at the box office, earning less than $500,000 in its initial release against a budget of $2 million. Sexual content and violent images prohibit viewing by children. **p**, William Horberg, Mickey Liddell, Lynn Givens; **d**, Charlie Stratton; **cast**, Elizabeth Olsen, Oscar Isaac, Tom Felton, Jessica Lange, Shirley Henderson, Matt Lucas, Mackenzie Crook, John Kavanagh, Lily Laight, Matt Devere; **w**, Stratton (based on the novel *Therese Raquin* by Emile Zola and the play by Neal Bell); **c**, Florian Hoffmeister; **m**, Gabriel Yared; **ed**, Celia Haining, Leslie Jones, Paul Tothill; **prod d**, Uli Hanisch; **art d**, Jasna Dragovic, Tibor Lazar, Kai Koch; **spec eff**, Muhamed M'Barek, Michael Fechner.

In the Heart of the Sea ★★★★ 2015; U.S.; 121m; Cott Productions; WB; Color; Adventure; Children: Unacceptable (MPAA: PG-13; **BD**; **DVD**. This fascinating and superbly made film presents an exciting tale about a real whaling ship that was attacked and sunk by a gigantic whale that inspired the Herman Melville novel *Moby Dick*. In November 1820 the whaling ship *Essex*, out of Nantucket and crewed by twenty-one men, is on a whale-hunting voyage in the Pacific Ocean. The ship is captained by George Pollard, portrayed by Walker, while his first mate is Owen Chase, played by Hemsworth; second mate Matthew Joy, essayed by Murphy; and cabin boy Thomas Nickerson, played by Holland. The ship is savagely attacked by a huge sperm whale with a human-like sense of rage and vengeance, sinking the ship and leaving its men stranded at sea in small boats. They are pushed to the limit to stay alive, braving storms, starvation, panic and despair, all of which questions their deepest religious beliefs. No other Nantucket ship had ever been rammed by a whale and sunk. No crew in open boats had ever been that far from land and survived. The ship's small boats are a thousand miles from the nearest land, the Marquesas Islands, home to cannibals where, if they reach it, they dare not land. With limited food and water, at the mercy of the elements, as Walker and Owen search for direction on the open sea, they also battle their own anger and vengeance to somehow bring the great whale down. Some are rescued at sea while others drift to a landfall. Holland ends the tale with narration that describes how Hemsworth returned to the sea as a captain and Walker also captained a ship, but only to vainly hunt for the gigantic whale and kill it. He finally retired, living out his bitter memories. Meanwhile, Whishaw, who plays Herman Melville (1819-1891), a member of the crew, begins to write his novel, *Moby Dick*, with the words: "Call me Ishmael…" Howard directs this sea saga with great skill, producing many harrowing moments as he chronicles the actual events with vivid accuracy and where the cast members are standouts in their roles. Though the film did well at the box office, earning more than $83.6 million in its initial release, it did not offset its budget of more than $100 million. *Author's Note*: The film was shot in England and the Canary Islands off the coast of Spain. A huge tank was constructed where the ocean-going scenes occur. The film is reminiscent of many sea classics, such as **The Sea Beast**, 1926, and **Moby Dick**, 1956 (and that film's many remakes), but it stands strongly on its own superior production values as a singularly impressive story. The film was shot on location in England and in the Canary Islands. Intense sequences of peril, violence and thematic material prohibit viewing by children. **p**, Ron Howard, Brian Grazer, Joe Roth, Will Ward, Paula Weinstein, William M. Connor; **d**, Howard; **cast**, Chris Hemsworth, Ben Whishaw, Cillian Murphy, Tom Holland, Charlotte Riley, Brendan Gleeson, Frank Dillane, Paul Anderson, Benjamin Walker, Michele Fairlley; **w**, Charles Leavitt (based on the story by Leavitt, Rick Jaffa, Amanda Silver from the book *In the Heart of the Sea: The Tragedy of the Whaleship Essex* by Nathaniel Philbrick); **c**, Anthony Dod Mantle; **m**, Roque Banos; **ed**, Daniel P. Hanley, Mike Hill; **prod d**, Mark Tildesley; **art d**, Christian Huband, Niall Moroney; **set d**, Dominic Capon; **spec eff**, Mark Holt, James Davis III, Manex Efrem.

Inside Llewyn Davis ★★★ 2013; U.S./France; 105m; Mike Zoss Productions/CBS Films; Color; Drama; Children: Unacceptable (MPAA: R); **BD**; **DVD**. Intriguing drama sees a week in the life of Isaac, a young folk singer-songwriter in the Greenwich Village folk scene during the winter of 1961. With his guitar, he faces a cold New York season, struggling to make it as a musician against many obstacles, some of which are of his own making. He's very handsome, but self-destructive, getting only small gigs in folk clubs and is beaten in an alley behind one of them. He has nowhere to live and sleeps in the apartments of anyone who will put up with him. His relationship with Mulligan, a foulmouthed female folk singer, goes nowhere, like the nomadic Isaac. Though the story is bleak and uninspiring, the many songs presented lighten the tale, as does Isaac's empathetic performance. Designed as a black comedy, the story is so thin that it becomes a chronicle of haggard survival in the waning days of the Beat Generation's dominance in Greenwich Village. The film saw a modest success at the box office, earning more than $32.9 million in its initial release against a budget of $11 million. Songs: "Hang Me, Oh Hang Me," "Dink's Song," "Old MacDonald," "The Death of Queen Jane" (traditonal); "Farewell" (Bob Dylan); "Requiem in D Minor, Lacrimosa Dies" (Wolfgang Amadeus Mozart); "The Last Thing on My Mind" (Tom Paxton); "Please Please Mr. Kennedy" (Ed Rush, Geore Cromarty, T Bone Burnett, Justin Timberlake, Joel Coen, Ethan Coen); "Five Hundred Miles" (Hedy West); "Ballade No. 2 in F Minor, Op. 38" (Frederic Chopin); "Piano Sonata No., 15 in D Major, Op. 28, Pastorale" (Ludwig van Beethoven); "Leaving the Cat" (Todd Kasow); "Green, Green Rocky Road" (Len Chandler, Robert Kaufman); "Symphony No. 4, Sehr Behaglich" (Gustav Mahler); "Cocaine" (Gary Davis); "The Old Triangle" (Brendan Behan); "Shoals of Herring" (Ewan MacColl); "Storms Are on the Ocean" (A.P. Carter); "3 Romances, Op. 18, No. 2 in F Sharp Major" (Robert Schumann). *Author's Note*: The film is loosely based on the posthumously published memoir *The Mayor of MacDougal Street* by Dave Van Ronk (1936-2002), a minor musician on that long-ago scene. Gutter language and sexual references prohibit viewing by children. **p**, Ethan Coen, Joel Coen, Scott Rudin; **d&w**, Ethan Coen, Joel Coen; **cast**, Oscar Isaac, Carey Mulligan, John Goodman, Justin Timberlake, F. Murray Abraham, Garrett Hedlund, Ricardo Cordero, Adam Driver, Max Casella, Ethan Phillips; **c**, Bruno Delbonnel; **prod d**, Jess Gonchor; **art d**, Deborah Jensen; **set d**, Susan Bode; **spec eff**, Alex Lemke.

Inside Out ★★★★ 2015; U.S.; 107m; Pixar/UNIV; Color; Animated Comedy/Drama; Children: Cautionary (MPAA: PG-13); **3-D, BD**; **DVD, IV**. This ambitious three-dimensional computer animated adventure probes the mind of Dias, an eleven-year-old Minnesota girl where five emotions lead her through life as she moves to San Francisco with her parents (Lane and MacLachlan voiceovers) after her father gets a

Naomi Watts and Tom Holland in *The Impossible*, 2012.

new job there. The emotions are joy (Poehler voiceover), sadness (Smith voiceover), fear (Hader voiceover), anger (Black voiceover), and disgust (Kaling voiceover). Dias' emotions live in her conscious mind in compartments called Headquarters where they influence her thoughts and actions by way of a control console. Her new memories are stored in colored orbs that go into storage all during her days and nights. Dias' most important memories are in a hub in Headquarters and power five so-called islands that reflect a different part of her personality. The dominant emotion is joy (Poehler) which keeps her happy, but she does not understand the purpose of the emotion sadness (Smith). Dias becomes distressed when her belongings get lost in Texas while en route to San Francisco and sadness (Smith) starts to enter her emotions. She becomes sad on her first day at her new school and cries in front of the class. This upsets all of Dias' emotions and they fall into a so-called "memory dump" where memories are forgotten. Anger (Black) then takes over her emotions and she wants to run away to Minnesota believing she can achieve new core memories there. Now joy and sadness find Dias' imaginary childhood friend, Bing Bong (Kind voiceover), and the three of them ride a train of thought to help her. Dias is about to board a bus for Minnesota, which sends joy into the memory dump along with Bing Bong. This all leads to Dias telling her parents that she misses her old home in Minnesota. Joy and sadness work together to create a happier memory for Dias, and a year later she has adapted to her new home. All her emotions now work in harmony to help her to be content. The story is both poignant and provocative, and Poehler, Kind and Smith do outstanding work. The animation from Pixar, the premiere producer of such films, is marvelous to behold, visually stunning in rich colors and with the kind of image detail only found in the best animated productions. The film was a staggering success at the box office, earning more than $856 million in its initial release against a budget of $175 million. Songs: "Grim Grinning Ghosts" (Buddy Baker, Xavier Atencio), "Exotico Speedo" (Laurent Lombard). Mild thematic elements and some hazardous action scenes caution viewing by children. **p**, Jonas Rivera; **d**, Pete Docter, Ronnnmie Del Carmen; **cast** (voiceovers), Amy Poehler, Bill Hader, Diane Lane, Kyle MacLachlan, Phyllis Smith, Richard Kind, Lewis Black, Mindy Kaling, Kaitlyn Dias, Paula Poundstone, Bobby Moynihan, Paula Pell, Frank Oz; **w**, Docter, Meg LeFauve, Josh Cooley (based on a story by Docter, Del Carmen); **m**, Michael Giacchino; **ed**, Kevin Nolting; **prod d**, Ralph Eggleston; **art d**, Bert Berry; **spec eff**, Leon JeongWook Park.

Interstellar ★★★ 2014; U.S./U.K.; 169m; Legendary Pictures/PAR; Color; Science Fiction; Children: Unacceptable (MPAA: PG-13); **BD**; **DVD**. Absorbing sci-fi tale sees an Earth not able to sustain humanity in the near future as crops are stricken by blight and dust storms, and

Anne Le Ny, Francois Cluzet and Omar Sy in *The Intouchables*, 2012.

the world has regressed into an agrarian society. McConaughey, a former NASA test pilot and engineer, becomes a farmer and lives with his family, which includes his son, Affleck, ten-year-old daughter Foy, and father-in-law Lithgow. Foy believes their house is haunted by a ghost trying to communicate to her. McConaughey discovers that the would-be ghost is an unknown form of intelligence sending them code messages by means of gravitation that alters the dust on the floor to resemble messages in Morse code. The messages direct them to a secret NASA installation led by Caine, a professor. Caine reveals to McConaughey that a wormhole has been discovered in the solar system that is orbiting Saturn and that the only chance humanity has for survival is to traverse through the wormhole so as to colonize new worlds in another galaxy. NASA scientists come to believe that extra-dimensional beings are communicating with them and have provided the wormhole to save humanity. McConaughey is assigned to pilot *Endurance*, an experimental spacecraft, to follow the Lazarus Mission, a series of manned capsules sent through the wormhole to survey a dozen planets to determine if any have long-term sustainability. The data from Lazarus gives NASA three potential habitable planets: Miller, Edmunds, and Mann, named after astronauts who carried out the surveys. Once the planets' viability is confirmed, humans will follow aboard the NASA facility which is a huge space station. McConaughey's decision to join *Endurance* breaks Foy's heart because they will be separated and they depart under strained relations. McConaughey joins Caine's daughter, Hathaway, physicist Gyasi, geographer Bentley, and two robots on a two-year space journey to the wormhole before crossing over into the new galaxy. While traversing the wormhole, Hathaway encounters an extra-dimensional presence that she thinks has created the wormhole to save humanity. After traversing the wormhole, *Endurance* follows a signal left by Miller's expedition, but they soon encounter a problem. The candidate planet to inhabit is near Gargantuan, a nearby rotating black hole, and, due to its gravitational pull, time on the planet is slower than that on Earth. Also, giant tidal waves race across its surface. Bentley is killed by one of the tidal waves as the crew tries to retrieve Miller's data recording instrument, and their departure is delayed by an hour. When they return, they discover that twenty-three years have passed for Gyasi on *Endurance*. Back on Earth, McConaughey's daughter is now an adult as Chastain, who has joined NASA and attempts to solve a physics problem that has troubled Caine for years. It is the question of how humans can escape Earth's gravitational pull *en masse*. Caine's health begins to fail and he admits that he solved the necessary equation decades earlier, but realized that he needed data from a singularity behind a black hole to complete it. This leads Caine to conclude that there is no hope that humanity can escape Earth, but puts his faith in a "population bomb," a mass repopulation project using fertilized embryos to start humankind over, sacri-

ficing Earth in the process. With much valuable resources used in the long mission to retrieve Miller's data, *Endurance* is forced to choose between following the other potential life-sustaining planets Mann or Edmunds. By now, McConaughey and Hathaway are at odds, with him accusing her of being compromised by her emotional attachment to Edmunds. She responds by accusing him of being compromised by his desire to see his family again, because *Endurance* can reach both planets only if they give up on returning to Earth to use the population bomb. The crew seeks out Mann, who is portrayed by Damon, finding him frozen on an icy ammonia-saturated planet, and they manage to revive him. However, Damon has forged the data about the viability of his planet so the *Endurance* would arrive to end his isolation. When McConaughey decides to return to Earth, Damon murders Gyasi and attempts to kill McConaughey before fleeing to *Endurance* with the shuttle, intending to take the population bomb to Edmunds' planet instead. Hathaway rescues McConaughey and they chase Damon, but are not able to prevent him from improperly docking with *Endurance*. However, Damon is killed when the airlock depressurizes. McConaughey then manages to get a damaged *Endurance* under control for the flight back to Earth. McConaughey and Hathaway now plan to pilot the spacecraft to Gargantua's event horizon and jettison a robot into it to gather data on the singularity behind the black hole, which they can relay to Earth. Once the robot transmits the data back to them, they will be able to set a course to Edmunds' planet. McConaughey releases his shuttle into Gargantua in order to reduce the *Endurance*'s weight, which enables Hathaway to escape the gravitational pull. Before his craft is destroyed, McConaughey ejects and comes to a halt in an extra-dimensional space where time is not linear. He then realizes that the extra-dimensional beings are in fact a future form of humanity that has evolved to the point of transcending time and space. They have come back in time to create the wormhole to ensure humanity's survival. Now equipped with the robot's data on the singularity, McConaughey communicates with Chastain across the dimensional barrier from inside a tesseract through gravitational waves, making him the "ghost" from her childhood. With this information, Chastain is able to complete Caine's equation, allowing Earth's population to be evacuated *en masse*. McConaughey, his mission now complete, is transported back to Earth through the wormhole and is rescued by a NASA ship. He wakes up aboard the NASA station orbiting Saturn, which now serves as a place to marshal the remainder of humanity to cross the wormhole, and is reunited with Chastain. She convinces him to go to Hathaway, who has located the remains of Edmunds' expedition and which asserts that Edmund is a planet that can sustain human life. The complex tale (which takes some story impetus from **When Worlds Collide**, 1951) is cleverly sorted out by a stunning cast of characters, all of whom are well enacted, and the amazing special effects sustain interest throughout. The film was a resounding success at the box office, earning more than $675.1 million in its initial release against a budget of $165 million. Intense perilous action and gutter language prohibit viewing by children. **p**, Christopher Nolan, Lynda Obst, Emma Thomas; **d**, Nolan; **cast**, Matthew McConaughey, Anne Hathaway, Michael Caine, Casey Affleck, Topher Grace, Jessica Chastain, Wes Bentley, David Gyasi, John Lithgow, Mackenzie Foy, Ellen Burstyn, William Devane, Matt Damon (uncredited); **w**, Christopher Nolan, Jonathan Nolan; **c**, Hoyte Van Hoytema; **m**, Hans Zimmer; **ed**, Lee Smith; **prod d**, Nathan Crowley; **art d**, Dean Wolcott; **set d**, Gary Fettis, Paul Healy, Gena Vazquez; **spec eff**, Scott R. Fisher, James Paradis.

The Interview ★★★ 2014; U.S.; m; COL; Color; Comedy; Children: Unacceptable; MPAA: PG-13; **BD**; **DVD**. In the most controversial film of the year, Franco is the host of a cable tabloid television show produced by Rogen. They learn that a fan is North Korean dictator Kim Jong-Un, played by Park, so they decide to go to Pyongyang and interview him for their show. Before departing for North Korea the FBI sends an agent, Caplan, to get their help in assassinating him, giving them a fast-acting poison that can be transferred by shaking his hand. What happens in Pyongyang could test the genius of James Bond, but Franco and Rogen do not belong anywhere in 007's league in this farcical comedy that the North Koreans did not think was very funny. Franco and Rogen are standouts as they bumble their way toward an impossible mission. Not related to the 1998 film of the same name. The film did poorly at the box office, earning less than $11.3 million in its initial release against a budget of $44 million. Songs: "Yuna's Song" (Sujin Nam, Dan Sterling), "The Interview Freestyle" (Eminem), "Medicine Ball" (Eminem, Mark Batson, Andre Young, Dawaun Parker, Trevor Lawrence Jr.), "Coleen" (Spencer Page, Kelvin Swaby, Daniel Taylor), "New York Soul" (Ray Barretto, Louis Cruz), "Cowboy on the Run" (Jay Chou, Jun Lang Huang), "Conquest" (Corky Robbins), "Get Up/Ratthe" (Paul V. Baumer, Jae Choung, Virman Coquia, Koen Groeneveld, Maarten Hoogstraten, Hugo Langras, Kevin Nishimura, James Roh, Addy Van Der Zwan, Nate Walker), "Yeah!" (Lil Jon as Jonathan Smith, Sean Garrett, Patrick Smith, Christopher Bridges, James Phillips, LaMarquis Jefferson), "I'm Afraid of Americans/Nine Inch Nails VI Mix" (David Bowie, Brian Eno), "Walk On By" (Burt Bacahach, Hal David), "Pon De Floor" (Vybz Kartel as Adidja Palmer, Thomas Pentz, Dave Taylor, Nick Van De Wall), "A Milli" (Dwayne Carter, Shondrae Crawford, Kamaal Ibn John Freed, Ali Shaheed Jones-Muhammad), "Firework" (Katy Perry, Esther Dean, Mikkel Eriksen, Tor Hermansen, Sandy Wilhelm), "Got Your Money" (Chad Hugo, Russell Jones, Pharrell Williams), "Payday/May Day Remix" (Yoonmirae, Tiger JK, Anne One), "Pixie Promenade" (Lyle Workman), "Welcome to the Jungle" (W. Axl Rose, Izzy Stradlin, Saul Hudson, Duff McKagan, Steven Adler), "The Moon Which Loves the Sun" (Zion), "Bam Bam" (Winston Riley), "Wind of Change" (Klaus Meine). **p**, Evan Goldberg, Seth Rogen, James Weaver, Alex McAtee; **d**, Goldberg, Rogen; **cast**, James Franco, Rogen, Randall Park, Lizzy Caplan, Diana Bang, Tommy Chang, Charles Rahi Chun, Dominique Lalonde, Timothy Simons, Steve Chang; **w**, Goldberg, Rogen, Dan Sterling; **c**, Brandon Trost; **m**, Henry Jackman; **ed**, Zene Baker; **prod d**, Jon Billington; **art d**, James Steuart; **set d**, Johanne Hubert; **spec eff**, Jak Osmond, Joe Greenberg.

Into the White ★★★ 2012; Norway/Sweden; 100m; Zentrope International Norway/Magnolia Films; Color; War Drama; Children: Unacceptable (MPAA: R); **BD**; **DVD**. Based on true events during World War II (1939-1945), this action-packed film begins when three German airmen, Lukas, Kross and Hoff, shoot down a British warplane. In the battle, their own plane crashes in the winter wilderness of Norway. The Germans struggle through a snowstorm until they reach shelter in an abandoned hunters' cabin. Soon after they arrive, survivors of the plane they have shot down, British pilot Nieboer and gunner Grint, arrive and become prisoners of the Germans. The bitter enemies, however, soon realize that they have to put their political feelings aside and team up to survive in the winter wilderness, which ends with all becoming friends. The acting is superior as are the production values while the script is intelligent and the direction from Naess is resolute. The film did not do well at the box office, earning a little more than $700,000 in its initial release. Songs: "Over the Rainbow" (1939; music: Harold Arlen; lyrics: E.Y. "Yip" Harburgh), "Forget Me Not" (Peter Godfrey), "Deutschlandlied" (music: Joseph Haydn; lyrics: August Heinrich Hoffman von Fallersleben). Gutter language prohibits viewing by children. **p**, Peter Aalbaek Jensen, Valerie Saunders, Jessica Ask, Madeleine Ekman, Maria Kopf; **d**, Petter Naess; **cast**, Florian Lukas, David Kross, Stig Henrik Hoff, Lachlan Nieboer, Rupert Grint, Kim Haugen, Knut Joner, Morten Faldaas, Sondre Krogtoft Larsen; **w**, Naess, Ole Meldgaard, Dave Mango; **ed**, Frida Eggum Michaelsen; **c**, Daniel Voldheim; **prod d**, Udo Kramer; **art d**, Stefan Hauck; **spec eff**, Soren Skov Haraldsted, Hummer Hoimark.

Into the Woods ★★★ 2014; U.S.; 124m; Lucamar Productions/Disney; Color; Fantasy; Children: Unacceptable (MPAA: PG); **BD**; **DVD**. Based

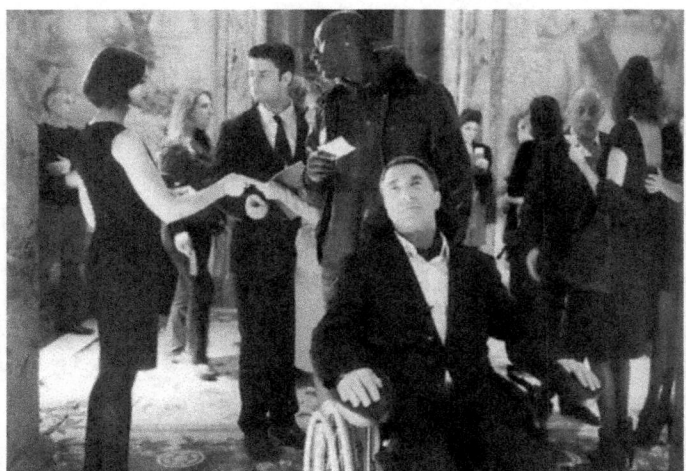
Omar Sy and Francois Cluzet in *The Intouchables,* 2012.

on the 1987 Broadway musical by Stephen Sondheim and James Lapine, this lively fantasy combines several Brothers Grimm fairy tales into a story about a baker, Corden, and his wife, Blunt, who learn that they have been cursed childless by Streep, a witch. They must embark into the woods to find the objects needed to break the spell and begin a family. Fairy tale characters they meet in the woods include Little Red Riding Hood (Crawford), Cinderella (Kendrick), Prince Charming (Pine), the Big Bad Wolf (Depp), Jack and the Beanstalk (Huttlestone), and Rapunzel (Mauzy). The film begins as a lively irreverent fantasy musical but eventually becomes a meaningful tale about responsibility, the problems that arise from making wishes, and the legacy that we leave our children. Not related to the 2008, 2011, or 2012 films with the same title. Well made and cleverly presented, this film did extremely well at the box office, earning more than $213 million in its initial release against a budget of $50 million. Songs: "Into the Woods," "Cinderella at the Grave," "Hello, Little Girl," "Rapunzel's Song," "The Cow as White as Milk," "I Know Things Now," "A Very Nice Price," "Giants in the Sky," "Agony," It Takes Two," "Stay with Me," "On the Steps of the Palace," "Careful My Toe," "Witch's Lament," "Any Moment," "Moments in the Woods," "Your Fault," "Last Midnight," "No More," "No One Is Alone," "Children Will Listen" (all by Stephen Sondheim). Thematic elements, perilous action and some suggestive material prohibit viewing by children. **p**, John DeLuca, Rob Marshall, Callum Mc-Dougall, Marc Platt, Angus More Gordon; **d**, Marshall; **cast**, Meryl Streep, Johnny Depp, Anna Kendrick, Chris Pine, Emily Blunt, James Corden, Mackenzie Mauzy, Lilla Crawford, Daniel Huttlestone; Lucy Punch, Tracey Ullman, Billy Magnussen; **w**, James Lapine, Stephen Sondheim (based on the book by Lapine); **c**, Dion Beebe; **m**, Stephen Sondheim; **ed**, Wyatt Smith; **prod d**, Dennis Gassner; **art d**, Andrew Bennett, Benn Collins, Chris Lowe, Mary Mackenzie; **set d**, Anna Pinnock; **spec eff**, Stefano Pepin.

The Intouchables ★★★ 2012; France; 112m; Quad Productions/Weinstein Co.; Color; Comedy/Drama; Children: Unacceptable (MPAA: R); **BD**; **DVD**. Entertaining and heartwarming tale begins with Cluzet, who is an aristocratic, wealthy white man in Paris, a widower without children and who becomes a quadriplegic after a paragliding accident. He advertises for a companion-caregiver and chooses Sy, a rude young African man who served six months in jail for robbery, and who is on a one-month trial period. Sy moves into Cluzet's mansion, and, over the course of the month, he and Cluzet become unlikely close friends. Sy absorbs some culture, discovering modern art, opera, and takes up painting. Cluzet hosts a private concert of classical music in his mansion on his birthday and that also reaches Sy. The caretaker learns that Cluzet has a slight relationship with Briere, a young woman who lives in

Omar Sy in *The Intouchables*, 2012.

Dunkirk, and encourages him to meet her, but Cluzet is afraid of her reaction when seeing him in a wheelchair. Sy gets Cluzet to talk to Briere on the phone and urges him to send a photo of himself in the wheelchair. Instead, Cluzet sends a photograph of how he looked before his accident. Briere agrees to meet Cluzet, but he is too apprehensive, so he goes off with Sy in his private jet to show Sy what a paragliding weekend is like. Sy's younger cousin is in gang trouble and takes refuge in Cluzet's mansion. Cluzet senses Sy's need to help his cousin, so he releases him from his job as caretaker. Sy leaves and returns to his old friends, but also helps his cousin. Cluzet hires a few replacements for Sy, but he is unhappy with all of them. Sy returns and takes Cluzet to the seaside where, to Cluzet's surprise, Briere appears. It seems that she doesn't mind that Cluzet is a quadriplegic, and the film ends with Sy smiling at Cluzet, then saying farewell and walking away. Cluzet and Sy render top-flight performances in this heartfelt story, one that carefully develops its empathetic characters while showing emotional recovery through care and understanding, one which is richly reminiscent of **Driving Miss Daisy**, 1989. The film was a resounding success at the box office, earning more than $426.6 million in its initial release against a budget of more than $10.8 million. Songs: "Fly," "Una Mattina," "L'Origine Nascolta," "Writing Poems," "Cache Cache," "Senza Respiro" (Ludovico Einaudi); "September" (Maurice White, Alice Willis, Al McKay); "Nocturne in Si bemol" (Frederic Chopin); "Ave Maria" (Franz Schubert); "The Ghetto" (Donny Hathaway, Leroy Hutson); "Nein langer trag ich night die Qualen" from the opera "Die Freischutz" (Carl Maria von Weber); "You're Goin' Miss Your Candyman" (Terence Callier, Phyllis Braxton); "L'estate: Adagio," "Spring," "Concerto for 2 Violins and Orchestra" (Antonio Vivaldi); "Colombine Overture Burlesque" (Georg Philipp Telemann); "Concerto Grosso" (George Frideric Handel); "Prelude, Suite Violincello no, 1," "Suite in 2: Badinerie," "Concerto in F" (Johann Sebastian Bach); "Feeling Good" (Leslie Bricusse, Anthony Newley); "Le vol dui Bourdon" (Nikolai Rimsky-Korsakov); "Boogie Wonderland" (Jonathan Lind, Alice Willis); "Ein Maedchen oder Weibchen" from the opera "The Magic Flute" (Wolfgang Amadeus Mozart); "Les Indes galantes" (Jean-Philippe Rameau). Gutter language and drug use prohibit viewing by children. **p**, Nicolas Duval Adassovsky, Laurent Zeitoun, Yann Zenou; **d&w**, Olivier Nakache, Eric Toledano; **cast**, Francois Cluzet, Omar Sy, Audrey Fleurot, Anne Le Ny, Josephine de Meaux, Clotilde Mollet, Alba Gaia Bellugi, Cyril Mendy, Salimata Kamate, Absa Diatou Toure, Gregoire Oestermann; **c**, Mathieu Vadepied; **m**, Ludovico Einaudi; **ed**, Dorian Rigal-Ansous; **prod d**, Francois Emmanuelli; **art d**, Olivia Bloch-Laine; **spec eff**, Teurlai Aurelien.

Iron Man 3 ★★★ 2013; U.S./China; 130m; Marvel Studios/Para-

mount/Walt Disney Pictures; Color; Science Fiction; Children: Unacceptable (MPAA: PG-13); **BD**; **DVD**. This well-made third entry in the Marvel comics Iron Man series has brilliant industrialist Tony Stark/Iron Man, played by Downey Jr., up against a terrorist called Mandarin, essayed by Kingsley, who is bent on taking over the world (no one seems to settle for North America anymore). Downey recalls a New Year's Eve party in 1999 where he met Hall, a scientist and inventor of Extremis, an experimental regenerative treatment that allows recovery from crippling injuries. Pearce, a disabled scientist, offers Downey and Hall positions in his company, but Downey rejects the offer, which humiliates Pearce. Years later, Downey's experiences during the alien invasion of New York City are causing him to have panic attacks. He builds several dozen Iron Man suits, which causes problems with his girlfriend, Paltrow, who objects to him becoming a superhero again. By now a series of bombings by Kingsley leaves intelligence agencies puzzled by a lack of forensic evidence. Downey's best friend, security chief Favreau, becomes badly injured in a terrorist attack, causing Downey to send Kingsley a televised threat. Kingsley responds by destroying Downey's home with helicopter gunships. Hall, who arrives to warn Downey, survives the attack, along with Paltrow. Downey escapes in an Iron Man suit and goes to rural Tennessee, following a flight plan from his investigation into Kingsley. Downey's experimental armor does not have enough power allowing him to return to California, and the rest of the world thinks he is dead, killed in the attack on his home. Downey teams up with Simpkins, a precocious ten-year-old boy, and they investigate the remains of a local explosion that has the earmarks of a Kingsley attack. Downey discovers that the "bombings" were triggered by soldiers subjected to Extremis, which, at this stage of development, can cause some subjects to explosively reject it. The explosions have been falsely attributed to a terrorist plot so as to actually cover up Extremis' flaws. Downey witnesses Extremis firsthand when Kingsley's agents Szostak and Dale attack him. With Simpkins' help, Downey uses improvised weapons to trace Kingsley's headquarters. Inside, he discovers Kingsley is actually a British actor named Trevor Slattery, who claims he knows nothing about the terrorist activities carried out in his name. Pearce then reveals he is the real Mandarin, using Kingsley as a cover. Pearce kidnaps Paltrow and subjects her to Extremis in order to get Downey to help fix the flaws in Extremis. Pearce then kills Hall when she has a change of heart about the plan. Downey then learns that Pearce intends to attack Sadler, the U.S. President, aboard Air Force One. Downey saves some passengers and crew, but cannot stop Pearce from kidnapping Sadler and destroying the plane. Pearce is then traced to a damaged oil tanker where he intends to kill Sadler on live television. Ferrer, the Vice President, will become a puppet leader and follow Pearce's orders in exchange for Extremis to cure his young daughter's disability. Downey goes to save Paltrow while Cheadle saves Sadler. Downey summons his Iron Man suits to provide air support. Cheadle secures Sadler and takes him to safety, while Downey discovers Paltrow has survived the Extremis procedure. Before Downey can save Paltrow, a rig collapses around them and she falls to her apparent death. Downey confronts Pearce and traps him in an Iron Man suit that self-destructs, but fails to kill him. Paltrow, her Extremis powers enabling her to survive her fall, intervenes and kills Pearce. Downey then has each Iron Man suit destroyed as a sign of his devotion to Paltrow, while Ferrer is arrested. With Downey's help, Paltrow's Extremis effects are stabilized. Downey then undergoes surgery to remove shrapnel embedded near his heart. He throws his obsolete chest arc reactor into the sea, thinking he always will be Iron Man. Elaborate and complex to the point of some confusion, the film is saved and interest is sustained throughout via explosive and obsessive action, along with some good performances from Downey, Pearce, Paltrow and Kingsley. The marvelous special effects (produced by no less than seventeen companies), of course, are the centerpiece of this fast-moving and exciting sci-fi tale. The film received an Oscar nomination for Best Visual Effects (Townsend, Williams, Nash, Sudick). Like almost all such recent films focusing upon eye-popping special effects, this film saw an overwhelming success at the box office, earning more than $1.215 billion in its initial release against a budget of $200 million. Songs: "Blue/Da Ba Dee" (Gianfranco Randone, Maurizio Lobina, Massimo Gabutti), "Jingle Bells" (James Pierpont), "Mambo No. 5/A Little Bit of Monika" (Perez Prado, Lou Bega, Zippy Davids), "Santa Claus Is Back in Town" (Jerry Leiber, Mike Stoller), "Auld Lang Syne" (traditional), "We Are the Champions" (Armath, J. Deja), "Some Kind of Joke" (Aaron R. Bruno), "O Christmas Tree" (traditional), "Ready Aim Fire" (Imagine Dragons, Alex da Kid). Intense science-fiction action and violence and brief suggestive material prohibit viewing by children. **p**, Kevin Feige; **d**, Shane Black; **cast**, Robert Downey Jr., Gwyneth Paltrow, Don Cheadle, Guy Pearce, Ben Kingsley, Rebecca Hall, Jon Favreau, James Badge Dale, Stephanie Szostak, Paul Bettany (voice only); **w**, Black, Drew Pearce (based on the comic book by Stan Lee, Don Heck, Larry Lieber, Jack Kirby, and the *Extremis* television miniseries written by Warren Ellis, Adi Granov); **c**, John Toll; **m**, Brian Tyler; **ed**, Peter S. Elliot, Jeffrey Ford; **prod d**, Bill Brzeski; **art d**, Desma Murphy; **set d**, Danielle Berman; **spec eff**, Christopher Townsend, Guy Williams, Erik Nash, Daniel Sudick.

Jack Reacher ★★★ 2012; U.S.; 130m; Skydance/PAR; Color; Crime; Mystery; Children: Unacceptable; MPAA: PG-13; **BD**; **DVD**. Harrowing tale begins when five people are randomly shot dead by an expert sniper in Pittsburgh, who fires only six shots to kill his victims. The viewer sees all five shootings and is left to wonder about the identity of the mass murderer. A suspect is arrested within a few hours and a strong case is made to prove he is the killer. The suspect is comatose so he does not confess to the crimes, and instead writes the words, "Get Jack Reacher." Reacher, who is played by Cruise, is a former U.S. Army investigator, who has become a crusader for justice and who ignores the law to deal with criminals. Cruise sees the message on television and goes to Pittsburgh where he contacts Pike, the suspect's beautiful young defense attorney, who is also the daughter of the district attorney, Jenkins, who is prosecuting the suspect. At first, Cruise and Pike find no reason to doubt the evidence against her client. Then Cruise notices some minor details that lead him to suspect the arrested man is being framed and he suspects that a man only known as "The Zed," essayed by Herzog, is the real sniper. Oyelowo plays a police detective who becomes involved in the case while Duvall is the owner of a gun range that Cruise meets during his investigation. Herzog is revealed as the real sniper, a heartless villain who threatens to beat one of his victims to death and drink his blood from a boot, but he is nevertheless and thankfully brought to justice. Well crafted and tension filled, this crime saga sees top performances from Cruise and the rest of the cast, but its bloodletting may be too unsettling for sensitive viewers. The film was a box office success, earning more than $218.3 million in its initial release against a budget of $60 million. Songs: "Jump Around" (Larry Muggerud, Erik Schrody), "The Fightin' Side of Me" (Merle Haggard), "Young Americans" (David Bowie), "Little By Little" (Melvin London). Excessive violence, gutter language and drug material prohibit viewing by children. **p**, Tom Cruise, Don Granger, Gary Levinsohn, Paula Wagner; **d&w**, Christopher McQuarrie (based on the book *One Shot* by Lee Child); **cast**, Cruise, Rosamund Pike, Robert Duvall, Richard Jenkins, David Oyelowo, Werner Herzog, Jai Courtney, Vladimir Sizov, Joseph Sikora, Michael Raymond-James, Alexia Fast, Josh Helman; **c**, Caleb Deschanel; **m**, Joe Kraemer; **ed**, Kevin Stitt; **prod d**, Jim Bissell; **art d**, Christa Munro, Gregory Weimerskirch; **set d**, Douglas Mowat; **spec eff**, Kevin Hannigan.

Jack the Giant Slayer ★★★ 2013; U.S.; 114m; New Line Cinema/WB; Color; Fantasy; Children: Unacceptable (MPAA: PG-13); **BD**; **DVD**. Wonderfully made retelling of the fairy tale begins in the

Tom Cruise and Robert Duvall in *Jack Reacher*, 2012.

kingdom of Cloister where Jack, a young farm boy, ably played by Hoult, is fascinated by the legend of Erik, an ancient king who defeated an army of invading giants from a realm in the sky by controlling them with a magical crown. At the same time, a princess, Tomlinson, becomes fascinated by the same legend. Ten years pass and Jack goes into town to sell his horse in order to save the farm owned by his uncle, Fairbank. There he sees Tomlinson and saves her from some hooligans. Meanwhile, her father the king, played by McShane, discovers that Lowe, a monk, has robbed him in his castle. Lowe offers Hoult some magic beans he has stolen from McShane as collateral for Hoult's horse. Back at the castle, Tomlinson quarrels with McShane because she wants to explore the kingdom, but he wants her to stay and marry a nobleman, Tucci. When returning home, Fairbank scolds Hoult for being foolish in trading the horse for some beans and throws them on the floor, then leaves the house. Tomlinson by now has sneaked out of the castle and seeks shelter from the rain in Hoult's house. Some rain leaks into the house and falls on one of the beans. It takes root and grows into a huge beanstalk that carries the house and Tomlinson skyward as Hoult falls to the ground. Hoult, Tucci, and Tucci's assistant, Bremner, volunteer to rescue the missing princess, joining McShane's knights, led by McGregor, and his second in-command, Marsan, and they all climb the beanstalk in search of Tomlinson. As they climb, evil Tucci and Bremner cut a safety rope, intentionally killing some of the knights. Reaching the top of the beanstalk, the climbers discover the realm of a two-headed giant, played by Nighy and Kassir, and split up into two groups. Hoult, McGregor, and Marsan make up one group, while Tucci and Bremner make up the other. In doing so, Tucci forcibly takes the remaining magic beans from Hoult, although Hoult manages to save one. Nighy and Kassir trap Hoult and his friends and take McGregor and Marsan prisoner, while Hoult escapes. Two other giants then emerge and one of them eats Bremner. Tucci saves himself by putting on a magic crown. Hoult follows Nighy and Kassir to their stronghold where one of them has killed Marsan. Hoult finds imprisoned Tomlinson and McGregor; as they are about to be killed, Tucci enters and enslaves the giants with his magic crown. He tells the giants they will attack the Cloister at dawn and gives them permission to eat McGregor. Hoult rescues Tomlinson and McGregor as one of the giants is about to cook McGregor. The three friends make for the beanstalk where Hoult causes the giant guarding it to fall to his death. Seeing this, McShane knows he now cannot save his daughter and reluctantly orders the beanstalk cut down so as to avoid an invasion of Cloister by the giants. Hoult and Tomlinson start climbing down the beanstalk while McGregor confronts Tucci and kills him. Nighy and Kassir take the magic crown before McGregor can get it, and McGregor escapes down the beanstalk after his friends. The trio all survive a fall after the giants cut down the beanstalk. Everyone returns

Jai Courtney in *Jack Reacher*, 2012.

safely home, but Hoult warns that the giants are using Tucci's beans to create another beanstalk to descend to Earth and attack Cloister. This is exactly what happens when Nighy and Kassir sew a bean into a stream in their sky domain. Another beanstalk quickly grows, allowing the giants to use it to descend to Earth. Hoult sees the giants landing and gives the alarm, wildly riding his horse after the royal caravan. McShane and Tomlinson are alerted and they and their escorts ride pell-mell toward the castle, as does Hoult. They arrive at the castle just in time, crossing the drawbridge just as the thundering giants arrive outside the bastion. McGregor fills the surrounding moat with oil and sets it on fire. The giants and the defenders battle for the drawbridge, the giants attempting to pull it down while McGregor and his troops attempt to hold it away from the burning moat. In the battle, Nighy and Kassir fall into the burning moat and appear to drown, but they survive and enter the castle through an underground passageway as the remaining giants continue to attack the castle. In the siege that follows, Hoult and Tomlinson are captured inside the castle by Nighy and Kassir, but Hoult throws the final bean down the throat of the two-headed giant, which causes a beanstalk to rip its body apart. The remaining giants finally tear down the drawbridge and enter the main courtyard where the defenders are now at the mercy of the towering invaders. Hoult, however, has taken the magic crown from the slain two-headed giant, which he wears when confronting the giants and which enables him to send the invaders back up to their realm. All ends well as Hoult and Tomlinson marry and tell the story of their adventure with the giants to their children. As time passes, the magic crown is crafted into St. Edward's Crown and is secured in the Tower of London. The special effects used throughout this thoroughly entertaining film are wonderfully presented, including the menacing giants, all brutish and ugly creatures with no redeeming virtues (they are shown chewing on captured humans as snacks, which may or may not have been influenced by **King Kong**, 1933, where that beast is shown routinely chewing up natives on its island), and, as such, are truly frightening creatures. The film was a success at the box office, earning more than $250.7 million in its initial release against a budget of more than $200 million. Songs: "In the Gardens of Ginger Pig," "Ginger Pig's Duet," "Ginger Pig's Magical Flute" (Lior Rosner); "Panto Giganticus" (Kristopher Gee). Intense scenes of fantasy violence, some frightening images and some gutter language prohibit viewing by children. **p**, David Dobkin, Ori Marmur, Patrick McCormick, Neal H. Moritz, Bryan Singer; **d**, Singer; **cast**, Nicholas Hoult, Eleanor Tomlinson, Ewan McGregor, Stanley Tucci, Eddie Marsan, Ewen Bremner, Ian McShane, Christopher Fairbank, Simon Lowe, Bill Nighy, John Kassir; **w**, Darren Lemke, Christopher McQuarrie, Dan Studney (based on a story by Lemke, David Dobkin); **c**, Newton Tomas Sigel; **m**, John Ottman; **ed**, Bob Ducsay, **prod d**, Gavin

Bocquet; **art d**, Mark Harris, Phil Harvey, Rod McLean, Peter Russell, Gary Tomkins; **set d**, Richard Roberts; **spec eff**, Carmila Gittens, Dominic Tuohy.

Jalaibee ★★★ 2015; Pakistan; 117m; Ary Films/Redrum Films; Color; Crime Drama; Children: Unacceptable; **DVD**. The title of this film means "twist," and there are many of them in this well-made and intriguing caper story. Two friends, Taimoor, and Safina, both orphans, are deeply and dangerously in debt to a Mafia group called the Unit. While trying to find ways to repay the debt before thugs come to collect it and might kill them, they find themselves in even worse shape than they imagined. Their dilemma has been caused by Khan, another gangster, and his partner, Uzair Jaswal, who want revenge against the Mafia boss known as the King, the man who has killed their father and forced their mother to commit suicide when they were boys. Now they intend to kidnap and kill the King. Jaffar, the King's front man, is in a tight spot, caught between collecting the debt from Taimoor and Safina and handling the kidnapping while holding the city in fear. Taimoor and Safina plan to repay the debt they owe by robbing a local casino. To do this they get the help of Sharhadi, a bar dancer, who seduces the owner of the club. While this is going on, Imam, the daughter of Hassan, a wealthy industrialist who is a leading contender for the seat of prime minister of Pakistan, becomes enmeshed in a separate intrigue. It is indeed a dangerous mess the friends are in, but they manage to right wrongs while surviving their enemies. The film had a modest success at the U.S. box office, earning about $1 million in its initial limited release against a budget of about $980,000. Song: "Jee Raha" (Umair Jaswal, Sarmad Ghafoor). **p**, Eman Syed; **d&w**, Yasir Jaswal; **cast**, Danish Taimoor, Ali Safina, Wiqar Ali Khan, Zhalay Sharhadi, Adnan Jaffar, Sabeeka Imam, Sajid Hasan, Uzair Jaswal, Salmaan Shaukat; **c**, Mo Azmi; **ed**, Rizwan A.Q.; **prod d**, Nida Khan, Khurram Syed; **set d**, Aqueel ur Rehman.

Joe ★★★★ 2013; U.S.; 117m; UNIV; Color; Drama; Children: Unacceptable (MPAA: R); **BD**; **DVD**. Cage gives a riveting performance as an ex-convict in this well-made tale. He meets Sheridan, a fifteen-year-old boy, and, although an unlikely role model for the boy, finds himself choosing between redemption and ruin. Cage plays a man who is a drinker and gambler. His only companion is a mean bulldog. He has been in a long feud with Blevins, a local bully, a confrontation that keeps escalating. He employs some day laborers to work a business poisoning trees for a local lumber company. Sheridan asks him for a job, and Cage learns he is living in an abandoned house with his mother, sister, and father, Poulter, a heavy drinker who beats Sheridan, taking anything his son earns. Cage tries to help the boy at his own risk and, while doing so, becomes the better man Cage has always wanted to be, but at a consummate sacrifice. The grim tale is well acted by the entire cast and the script is both intelligent and provocative. The film did not fare well at the box office, earning less than $2.4 million in its initial release against a budget of more than $4 million. Songs: "Annihilate" (Weston Gage), "Force of Evil" (Miles Whittaker, Sean Canty), "Keeping Man" (Lance LaGault), "You Knew Joe?" (Chris Hrasky, Michael James, Munaf Rayani, Mark Smith), "For Anyone's Sake" (Ryan Bingham). Violence, disturbing material, gutter language and strong sexual content prohibit viewing by children. **p**, David Gordon Green, Lisa Muskat, Derrick Tseng, Christopher Woodrow, Alexander Uhlmann, Atilla Salih Yucer; **d**, Green; **cast**, Nicolas Cage, Tye Sheridan, Adriene Miscler, Ronnie Gene Blevins, Heather Kafka, Sue Rock, Robert Johnson, Dana Freitag, Lazaro Solares, Gary Poulter; **w**, Gary Hawkins (based on the novel by Larry Brown); **c**, Tim Orr; **m**, Jeff McIlwain; **ed**, Colin Patton; **prod d**, Chris L. Spellman; **set d**, Helen Britten; **spec eff**, Damian Lund, Justin Paul Warren.

John Carter ★★★ 2012; U.S.; 132m; Walt Disney; Color; Science Fiction; Children: Unacceptable; MPAA: PG-13; **BD**; **DVD**. In a futuristic story by Burroughs, author of the Tarzan books, a veteran of the U.S. Civil War (1861-1865), John Carter, played by Kitsch, is asked by the Army to join up again, but he refuses because he is against all wars, preferring to try to lead a normal life as a civilian in New York City in 1881. He is jailed for refusing, and escapes, but then is pursued. Fighting off some Indians, Kitsch hides in a cave where he meets someone who possesses a mysterious medallion. When Kitsch touches the medal he is transported to a strange land where he has unusual powers, including the ability to leap to very high heights, defying the laws of gravity, and he finds that he can travel far distances through the air. He meets others, including a woman who helps him to learn that he is now living on Mars and the planet is about to be invaded. Some evil creatures are bent on infiltrating and destroying the planet and its inhabitants. Kitsch has had more than his fill of war and considers the human race to be a "war species," and that "war is a shameful thing," but he now must resolve the dilemma of whether he wants to help save the people of Mars by aiding them in their war against the invaders, or ignore their plight. The pulpy space adventure provides a lot of exciting action, and the special effects are outstanding. The film was successful at the box office, earning more than $284 million in its initial release, but it failed to earn back a budget of more than $300 million (including promotion). *Author's Note*: The story was originally serialized in a pulp magazine in 1912 and it was later adapted in 1935 as a crude stop-action cartoon that was rejected as outlandish by film distributors. Intense violence prohibits viewing by children. **p**, Lindsey Collins, Jim Morris, Colin Wilson; **d**, Andrew Stanton; **cast**, Taylor Kitsch, Lynn Collins, Samantha Morton, Wilem Dafoe, James Purefoy, Thomas Haden Church, Mark Strong, Ciaran Hinds, Dominic West, Bryan Cranston, Polly Walker; **w**, Mark Andrews, Michael Chabon, Andrew Stanton (based on the story "A Princess of Mars" by Edgar Rice Burroughs); **c**, Dan Mindel; **m**, Michael Giacchino; **ed**, Eric Zumbrunnen; **prod d**, Nathan Crowley; **art d**, David Allday, James Hambidge, Naaman Marshall; **set d**, Paki Smith; **spec eff**, Tom Murtag, Peter Notley.

John Wick ★★★★ 2014; China/Canada/U.S.; 107m; 87 Eleven/Summit Entertainment; Color; Crime Drama; Children: Unacceptable (MPAA: R); **BD**; **DVD**. In New York City, Reeves' wife dies of cancer and shortly afterward he gets a posthumous gift from her. It is a puppy named Daisy, and there is a letter saying she wants him to keep the dog to help him cope with losing her. At first, he is indifferent to Daisy, but soon comes to love the puppy as they spend days driving in his vintage 1969 Mustang. Reeves encounters three young members of a Russian gang at a gas station and their leader, Allen, wants to buy his car, but Reeves refuses to sell and makes a snide remark at Allen before leaving. The gang members follow Reeves to his home, break in at night, and attack him. He watches, unable to stop them, as they kill Daisy and then steal his car. The next day, Allen attempts to have the car modified by Leguizamo, owner of a chop shop, but he refuses to take work on it because he recognizes the car as belonging to Reeves. Then Reeves visits Leguizamo, who tells him that Allen is the son of Nyqvist, head of the Russian crime syndicate in New York. He then lends Reeves another car. Leguizamo, we learn, works for Nyqvist. Nyqvist then upbraids Allen and explains that Reeves is his best assassin, nicknamed the "Boogeyman," and that, before taking a break to care for his dying wife five years earlier, helped Nyqvist gain control of his syndicate by singlehandedly killing off the competition. Reeves wants retribution against Allen, but Nyqvist, to protect Allen, sends a hit squad to Reeves' house to execute him. Reeves, however, kills the entire squad. Nyqvist then puts a $2 million bounty on Reeves' head and offers it to Dafoe, a veteran assassin, who is Reeves' mentor, and he grudgingly accepts. Reeves hides out at the Continental, a hotel that caters to assassins with the rule that no business can be conducted on its premises. Nyqvist learns where Reeves is and doubles the bounty. Reeves then learns from the hotel's owner, McShane, that Nyqvist has Allen protected at his night club, the Red Circle. Reeves goes there and kills Allen's friend, Moore. Reeves

White apes attacking in *John Carter*, 2012.

is subdued by Bernhardt, Nyqvist's henchman, and Allen escapes. Reeves returns to the Continental to treat his wounds, and is attacked by Palicki, a female assassin and former acquaintance of Reeves, who has taken the contract to kill him. Reeves subdues Palicki and forces her to reveal where Nyqvist's money is hidden and he then takes her with a neighbor and friend, Peters, to await her punishment for breaking the hotel rules. Palicki is able to break free and kills Peters. Reeves goes to a church that is a front for Nyqvist's hidden money, eliminates all the guards, and burns Nyqvist's money, as well as his computer hard drives and recordings that contain evidence against government officials that Nyqvist uses as blackmail against city politicians. When Nyqvist and more of his henchmen arrive at the church, Reeves ambushes them and kills more of them before being subdued by Bernhardt. Reeves is tied up and Nyqvist taunts him for causing trouble over a dog. He leaves Reeves to be tortured and killed by Bernhardt and another henchman, but Dafoe, having decided to protect Reeves, kills the henchman, thus allowing Reeves to break free and kill Bernhardt. Reeves then intercepts Nyqvist's car and forces him to reveal where Allen is as well as grudgingly cancelling the bounty on him. Reeves goes to the safe house where Allen is hiding and kills all of the guards before killing Allen. Palicki sees that Reeves and Dafoe have been working together and tells Nyqvist, who has Dafoe tortured and killed in his home over his betrayal. Nyqvist then contacts Reeves about Dafoe's death and lures him to his (Nyqvist's) home where Palicki is waiting to ambush Reeves. Before she can do that, she gets called to a meeting with McShane, who revokes her membership to the Continental for breaking the rules and has her executed. McShane then calls Reeves to inform him that a helicopter is on its way to the harbor to take Nyqvist away. Reeves hurries to the harbor and executes Nyqvist's remaining henchmen, then gets into a fist fight with Nyqvist on the dock. Nyqvist pulls a knife on Reeves and, as they fight, Reeves is wounded but takes the knife and stabs Nyqvist in the side of the neck. Nyqvist, before dying, warns Reeves he will see him again. Reeves is taken to a veterinary hospital where his wound is treated and then takes a pit-bull out of one of the cages for a walk on the boardwalk where he had his last date with his wife. There is no sense of morality or justice in this action-packed thriller, where human life is less valued than that of a canine. The plotline is fuzzy and the characters often confusing, but the tension is maintained throughout, keeping viewers in suspense over whether or not Reeves will survive an army of assassins out to destroy him. The film was successful at the box office, earning more than $86 million in its initial release against a budget of $20 million. Excessive violence prohibits viewing by children. **p**, Chad Stahelski, Basil Iwanyk, David Leitch, Eva Longoria, Mike Witherill, Keanu Reeves; **d**, Stahelski; **cast**, Reeves, Willem Dafoe, Ian McShane, Bridget Moynahan, Adrianne Pal-

Dominic West in *John Carter*, 2012.

icki, Jason Isaacs, Bridget Regan, Alfie Allen, Lance Reddick, Dean Winters, David Patrick Kelly; **w**, Derek Kolstad; **c**, Jonathan Sela; **m**, Tyler Bates, Joel J. Richard; **ed**, Elisabet Ronaldsdottir; **prod d**, Jeremy Jonathan White, Dan Leigh; **art d**, C.J. Simpson; **set d**, Susan Bode; **spec eff**, Drew Jiritano, R. Bruce Steinheimer.

Journey to the West: Conquering the Demons ★★★ 2014; China; 107m; Bingo Movie Development/Magnet Releasing; Color; Fantasy; Children: Unacceptable (MPAA: PG-13); **BD**; **DVD**. This offbeat but fascinating tale is set in 16th-Century China where a young village girl plays by a river and her father frightens her by pretending to be a fish demon. He is then killed by a mysterious water creature. Min Hun, a Taoist priest, kills a giant manta ray and insists the demon is now dead. Zhang, a Buddhist demon hunter, appears to warn that the animal is not the real demon, but he is ignored. The demon emerges again and kills some villagers, but Zhang is able to beach the fish-like demon, which then turns into a man. Zhang then opens a book of nursery rhymes and begins singing to the man. The man feels harassed and attacks Zhang, but a young woman, Miss Duan (Qui), appears and captures the demon in her cloth, turning the demon into a puppet. Zhang reveals to Qui that his master, Sihan, had taught him a humanist approach to use the nursery rhymes to coax goodness out of demons, but Qui laughs at that tactic. Zhang is disillusioned, but then meets up again with Sihan and bemoans his lack of ability in comparison to more aggressive demon-hunters such as Qui. Sihan reaffirms his philosophy of trying to reform evil demons and sends Zhang off again, telling him to find "enlightenment." A couple then enters an empty restaurant, but the chef becomes a pig demon and kills them. Zhang goes to the same restaurant, but this time it is filled with people. He sees that the people are only an illusion and recognizes them as reanimated corpses of the demon's victims, as well as seeing the demon's nine-pronged weapon. Zhang battles with one of the corpses, but Qui arrives and destroys them all. Qui then battles the demon, during which the restaurant collapses and Zhang and Qui leave as the demon is momentarily injured. Qui then develops a strong liking for Zhang after being impressed by his selfless ideals. She wants to kiss him, but he flees, not wanting to deal with romance in his quest for enlightenment. Zhang's master advises him to tame the Monkey King demon (Bo) that has been trapped by Buddha, to subdue the pig demon. That night, Zhang is captured by a gang that also had subdued Qui. It is later revealed to be a ploy arranged by Qui to trick Zhang into sexual intercourse. When Zhang again rejects her, Qui has him imprisoned. The pig demon reappears and injures Qui, but is chased off by three rivaling demon hunters. Qui mistakes Zhang's concern for her injuries as romantic attraction to her. But Zhang again refuses her and she destroys his book of nursery rhymes and he then leaves. Zhang travels for several days before he discovers a hole where Bo has been trapped in for 500 years. Bo tells Zhang to use a dancer under the full moon as bait. Qui appears and volunteers to dance. The pig demon appears then and falls into Bo's hole, turning into a miniature pig, which Qui then turns into a puppet. Qui gives both the fish and pig puppets to Zhang and offers her golden ringed weapon as an engagement ring, but he again rejects her. She returns his nursery rhyme book to him and then departs. Zhang, however, does not realize the book has accidentally been turned into a sutra, as a result of Qui, who cannot read, mixing up the words. Bo tricks Zhang into removing the seal on his prison. The three demon hunters appear, to catch Bo, but he kills them in a brutal fight. Zhang then begins to pray to Buddha and, in retaliation, Bo scalps the hair from his head. Qui arrives to save Zhang, but Bo mortally injures her. Zhang finally tells Qui that he loves her. Bo destroys her body, but Zhang reads chants from the sutra, summoning Buddha to defeat Bo. Zhang then places Qui's golden ring atop Bo as his iconic restrictive headband. Zhang tells his master, Sihan, that his suffering, because of losing Qui, has helped him to achieve enlightenment. Zhang is then instructed to journey west for the Buddhist sutras of Leiyin Temple, and it is shown that the water demon, pig demon, and Monkey King have been tamed and turned into humans. As they hike across the desert, Zhang looks across the sand and sees an image of Qui. Excessive violence, bloody images, sexual content and partial nudity prohibit viewing by children. (In Mandarin; English subtitles.) **p**, Ivy Kong, Zhang Daju, Wang Zhong Lei; **d**, Stephen Chow, Derek Kwok; **cast**, Zhang Wen, Qi Shu, Bo Huang, Show Luo, Shing-Cheung Lee, Bingqiang Chen, Sihan Cheng, Xing Yu, Zhengyu Lu, Chi Ling Chiu; **w**, Chow, Kwok, Xin Huo, Yun Wang, Fung Chih Chiang, Lu Zheng Yu, Lee Sheung Shing, Y.Y. Kong (based on the 16th-century novels by Wu Cheng'en); **c**, Sung Fai Choi; **m**, Raymond Wong; **ed**, Chai Wai Chan; **prod d**, Bruce Yu; **art d**, Eric Lam; **spec eff**, Ken Law, Jing Kun Zhan.

Joy ★★★ 2015; U.S.; 124m; Anapurna Pictures/FOX; Color; Biographical Drama; Children: Unacceptable (MPAA: PG-13); **BD**; **DVD**. Absorbing tale, based on real events, chronicles four generations of the family of Joy Mangano (1956-), played by Lawrence, and her Italian-American relatives, as well as her invention of the Miracle Mop, which establishes a business dynasty for them all. The road to riches is not, however, without its potholes, such as betrayal, treachery, loss of innocence, and various bumpy adventures with love. Lawrence's courage and determination overcome all obstacles in her rise to wealth and fame. Excessive gutter language prohibits viewing by children. The film earned more than $54.8 million in its initial release, but failed to offset its budget of $60 million. **p**, John Davis, Megan Ellison, Jonathan Gordon, Ken Mok, David O. Russell, Michele Ziegler; **d**, David O. Russell; **cast**, Jennifer Lawrence, Bradley Cooper, Robert De Niro, Diane Ladd, Isabella Rossellini, Donna Mills, Elisabeth Rohm, Edgar Ramirez, Dascha Polanco, Drena De Niro; **w**, Russell (based on a story by Russell, Annie Mumolo); **c**, Linus Sandgren; **m**, David Campbell, West Dylan Thordson; **ed**, Alan Baumgarten, Jay Cassidy, Tom Cross, Christopher Tellefsen; **prod d**, Judy Becker; **art d**, Peter Rogness; **set d**, Heather Loeffler; **spec eff**, Christopher Walsh.

The Judge ★★★ 2014; U.S.; 141m; WB; Color; Drama; Children: Unacceptable (MPAA: R); **BD**; **DVD**. Taut tale begins with Downey Jr., a successful Chicago defense attorney in the process of getting a divorce and who is in a custody battle for the guardianship of his daughter. His brother, D'Onofrio, calls to say that their mother has died, so Downey leaves his home to fly to his family. Downey goes to Carlinville, Indiana, for his mother's funeral and reunites with his brothers, D'Onofrio, who owns a car tire shop, and Strong, who appears to be slightly mentally handicapped. Downey also sees his father, Duvall, who is a local judge. The morning after the funeral, Downey notices damage to Duvall's car and wonders about it. On the flight back to Chicago, D'Onofrio calls Downey with the news that their father is being questioned by police in a fatal hit-and-run accident. It is learned that Duvall ran over a man he had sentenced to thirty days in jail and who then went on to kill a sixteen-year-old girl. Duvall had given the man a light sentence because he reminded him of Downey. Duvall stands trial, but Downey is not immediately chosen to represent him, despite being the most suitable choice. An inexperienced lawyer is chosen instead, but Duvall then employs Downey. Downey says he will take the case to improve his *pro bono* quota. Duvall's account of the accident has some flaws, but they may have to do with the chemotherapy he has been undergoing, which he has kept secret from his family. Thornton, the prosecutor, seeks a first degree murder conviction, but Duvall is found only guilty of voluntary manslaughter, but is nonetheless sent to prison. He serves his sentence and is released on compassionate parole after seven months. He and Downey are next seen fishing at an old watering hole where Duvall tells Downey he is the best lawyer he has ever seen, and then dies. After the funeral, Downey notices that the courtroom flag is flying at half-staff, as Downey had expected if his father had been found guilty. Downey's daughter is also there, which means he has won the custody battle. Downey takes his father's hat to his bench in the courthouse, spins Duvall's chair, and when the chair stops it faces him, as if to invite him to take his father's place. First-rate performances are seen from Downey, Duvall and the rest of the cast in this intriguing story where one is never quite clear about Duvall's guilt or intent on killing a child murderer. The script is well written, and director Dobkin does a good job fully developing his characters, albeit they are less empathetic than what one might wish. Duvall received an Oscar nomination as Best Supporting Actor. The film was successful at the box office, earning more than $84.4 million in its initial release against a budget of more than $50 million. Gutter language and sexual references prohibit viewing by children. **p**, David Dobkin, Susan Downey, David Gambino; **d**, Dobkin; **cast**, Robert Downey Jr., Robert Duvall, Billy Bob Thornton, Vincent D'Onofrio, Leighton Meester, Vera Farmiga, Ian Nelson, Dax Shepard, Ken Howard, Balthazar Getty; **w**, Nick Schenk, Bill Dubuque (based on a story by Dobkin, Schenk); **c**, Janusz Kaminski; **m**, Thomas Newman; **ed**, Mark Livolsi; **prod d**, Mark Ricker; **art d**, Shadya H. Ballug, David Swayze; **set d**, Rena DeAngelo; **spec eff**, Gary Chandler, Katherine Filtranti.

Jurassic World ★★★★ 2015; U.S./China; 107m; UNIV; Amblin; UNIV; Color; Science Fiction; Children: Unacceptable (MPAA: PG-13); **3-D**; **BD**; **DVD**. Some twenty-two years after the original Jurassic Park failed, the new Jurassic World dinosaur theme park opens for business on an island, its star attraction being a new genetically engineered dinosaur. The film opens as brothers Robinson and Simpkins visit their aunt, Howard, who is the park's operations manager. The boys go on a tour with her assistant. They learn that the new dinosaur is a combination of *Tyrannosaurus rex* and the DNA of some other predatory dinosaurs as well as some modern-day animals. Chief geneticist Wong keeps the exact genetic engineering makeup classified. Pratt, the park's dinosaur expert, warns Howard that one of the dinosaurs, the *Indominus*, is very dangerous because it is not socialized to get along with other animals. *Indominus* proves it is a troublesome dinosaur by trying to escape its enclosure. Pratt and Howard enter the enclosure but *Indominus* ambushes them, then escapes into the island's interior. Pratt wants it hunted down and killed, but a containment unit is sent to capture the dinosaur alive. The creature kills most of the team sent to capture it, and Howard orders the northern part of the island to be evacuated. Robinson and Simpkins ignore their aunt's evacuation order and go off to explore a restricted area. The *Indominus* attacks their vehicle, but they escape without injury and find the ruins of the original Jurassic Park's visitor center. They repair an old jeep and drive back to the Jurassic World resort area. Pratt and Howard follow them and narrowly escape being overtaken by the *Indominus*, which keeps continues its mayhem, breaking into the park's pterosaur aviary. The *Indominus* is hunted by helicopter, but the prehistoric birds cause the helicopters to crash, killing

Lynn Collins and Taylor Kitsch in *John Carter*, 2012.

all those aboard. Robinson and Simpkins arrive to find Pratt and Howard safe while armed soldiers subdue the pterosaurs. D'Onofrio then assumes charge of the park and uses raptors to track the runaway *Indominus*, and Pratt joins him on the hunt as they follow the scent of the dinosaur into the jungle. D'Onofrio then says he plans to create more genetically modified dinosaurs as weapons, but a raptor breaks into his laboratory and kills him. The raptors then attack the *Indominus* and it kills two of them. Howard then sends the park's *T. Rex* to do battle with the *Indominus*, but the *rex* is nearly killed, then saved by surviving raptors who force *Indominus* to enter a lagoon where it drowns. The humans are evacuated to the mainland and the island is given back to the dinosaurs while Robinson and Simpkins rejoin their parents and Pratt and Howard decide to marry. The startling special effects action (computer-generated imagery) is amazing. They provide consistent tension and considerable viewer angst throughout as the prehistoric monsters stalk human beings, who are so stupid as to be on this dangerous island, but that's the attractive and exciting nature of this beastly story. As expected, the film was a colossal box office success, earning more than $1.6 billion in its initial worldwide release against a budget of more than $150 million (the largest grossing film for 2015, and the third-largest grossing film in film history). A sequel is planned for 2018 release. Songs: "Have Yourself a Merry Little Christmas" (1944: Hugh Martin, Ralph Blane), "Sunrise O'er Jurassic World" (Mick Giacchino), "The Ever Elusive Future" (Jimmy Buffett, Mac McAnally, Eric Darken). Excessive violence and peril prohibit viewing by children. **p**, Patrick Crowley, Frank Marshall; **d**, Colin Trevorrow; **cast**, Chris Pratt, Bryce Dallas Howard, Irrfan Khan, Vincent D'Onofrio, Ty Simpkins, Nick Robinson, Jake Johnson, Omar Sy, BD Wong, Judy Greer, Lauren Lapkus, Brian Tee; **w**, Rick Jaffa, Amanda Silver, Trevorrow, Derek Connolly (based on a story by Jaffa, Silver, and characters created by Michael Crichton); **c**, John Schwartzman; **m**, Michael Giacchino; **ed**, Kevin Stitt; **prod d**, Ed Verreaux; **art d**, Aaron McBride; **set d**, Ronald R. Reiss; **spec eff**, Michael Meinardus, Mark McCreery.

Justice Is Mind ★★★ 2014; U.S.; 153m; Affidavit Productions/Ashton Times; Color; Crime Drama; Children: Unacceptable; **BD**; **DVD**. Gripping crime yarn begins with Aldershoff, a successful restaurant owner, who is happily married. All is well in his life until he collapses from what is believed to be a cerebral hemorrhage. He is hospitalized and his wife, Rapoport, learns that he has been seeing a neurologist about headaches he has had since he was a boy. His doctor, Fournier, persuades Aldershoff to undergo a new procedure, an FVMRI, like a MRI, that reads long-held memory in video form. The test reveals that Aldershoff shot and killed two people on his farm. Aldershoff then goes to trial for the murders, but does not remember them. His father, Sewell, sees tel-

Thomas Doret in *The Kid with a Bike*, 2012.

evision coverage of the trial and falls ill, recalling having had that same memory of murder. Rapoport is then in a desperate search to learn what happened so as to clear Aldershoff of the crimes before he is found guilty. He may be convicted for a crime that his brain recalls but one of which he has no recollection. The acting from Aldershoff, Rapoport and the rest of the cast in this thriller is exceptional, as is the clever script and director-writer Lund sustains suspense and tension to the final scene. Mature subject matter prohibits viewing by children. **p**, Jessica Killam, Arnold Peter, Mary Wexler; **d&w**, Mark Lund; **cast**, Vernon Aldershoff, Robin Ann Rapoport, Kim Gordon, Paul Lussier, Michele Mortensen, Carlyne Fournier, Richard Sewell, Mary Wexler, Chara Victoria Gannett, Jesse Mangan; **c**, Jeremy Blaiklock; **m**, Daniel Elek-Diamanta; **ed**, Jared Skolnick; **spec eff**, Adam Starr.

The Kid with a Bike ★★★ 2012; Belgium/France/Italy; 87m; Les Films du Fleuve/Sundance Select; Color; Drama; Children: Unacceptable (MPAA: PG-13); **BD**; **DVD**. Touching tale sees Doret as an abandoned eleven-year-old boy whose mother has died and his father, Renier, leaves him at an orphanage and goes off for a life on his own in a small town. Doret goes to the places where he knows his father is living, visiting a bar and a pastry shop, then the apartment his father had lived in, hoping to find him and his bike, which has been stolen. He sees a boy riding his bike and learns that Renier sold it to him. Doret buys the bike back and then meets De France, a kindly hairdresser, who takes him into her home on weekends. He is stubborn and remains aloof from her, instead becoming involved with a young crook, Di Mateo, who leads him into petty crimes. Doret never finds his father, but eventually bonds with De France to see a more promising life. Doret, De France and Renier give exceptional performances in this prosaic story (shot in Belgium in fifty-five days). The film saw a modest success at the box office, earning more than $5 million in its initial release. (In French; English subtitles.) Songs/Music: "Gravity" (Didier Dauvrin, Raphael Mancini, Frederic Migeot, Adam Aldridge, Pierre Constant, Xaxier Lesenfans), "Just a Day in the Life" (John Hunter Jr., Jonathan Slott, Nicholas Seeley), "DDTO1 et DDTO2" (SRG), "Adagio un poco mosso" from "Piano Concerto No. 5" (Ludwig van Beethoven). Thematic elements, violence, gutter language and smoking prohibit viewing by children. **p**, Jean-Pierre Dardenne, Luc Dardenne, Denis Freyd, Andrea Occhipinti; **d&w**, Jean-Pierre Dardenne, Luc Dardenne; **cast**, Thomas Doret, Cecile De France, Jeremie Renier, Fabrizio Rongione, Egon Di Mateo, Olivier Gourmet, Baptiste Sornin, Samuel De Rijk, Carl Jadot, Claudy Delfosse; **c**, Alain Marcoen; **ed**, Marie-Helene Dozo; **prod d**, Igor Gabriel.

Kill the Messenger ★★★ 2014; U.S.; 112m; Bluegrass Films/Focus Features; Color; Biographical Drama/Crime Drama; Children: Unacceptable (MPAA: R); **BD**; **DVD**. Journalist Gary Webb (1955-2004), played by Renner, comes upon a story that not only leads to the origins of America's crack drug epidemic, but also alleges that the CIA (U.S. Central Intelligence Agency) was well aware of the dealers who were smuggling cocaine into the United States, the agency supporting this covert enterprise and using the profits to arm Nicaraguan rebels in that country. Despite warnings to stop his investigation, Renner keeps digging and uncovers a conspiracy with explosive implications. As a result of his findings, his family, career, and life come under lethal threat. The story is tautly presented, and Renner is outstanding in the role of the dogged investigative reporter. Unfortunately, the film did poorly at the box office, earning a little more than $2.5 million in its initial release against a budget of $5 million. Songs: "Street Legal/The Face of the Crowd" (Nathan Johnson), "Cumbia de Guerra (Reinery Diaz). *Author's Note*: Webb worked for the San Jose *Mercury News*, which later admitted in print the editorial shortcomings of Webb's series of articles about the CIA's covert actions. He quit the paper in 1997 and published a book on his series the following year. He committed suicide in 2004. Gutter language and drug content prohibit viewing by children. **p**, Pamela Abdy, Naomi Despres, Jeremy Renner, Scott Stuber; **d**, Michael Cuesta; **cast**, Renner, Robert Patrick, Jena Sims, Robert Pralgo, Hajji Golightly, Ted Huckabee, Mary Elizabeth Winstead, Lucas Hedges, Rosemarie DeWitt, Kai Schmoll, Matt Lintz, Parker Douglas; **w**, Peter Landesman (based on the books *Dark Alliance* by Gary Webb and *Kill the Messenger* by Nick Schou); **c**, Sean Bobbitt; **m**, Nathan Johnson; **ed**, Brian A. Kates; **prod d**, John Paino; **art d**, Scott G. Anderson; **set d**, Nicole LeBlanc; **spec eff**, Wayne Beauchamp.

Killing Them Softly ★★★ 2012; U.S.; 97m; Plan B Entertainment/Weinstein Co.; Color; Crime Drama; Children: Unacceptable; MPAA: R; **BD**; **DVD**. Tension-filled thriller begins with a high-stakes poker game run by Liotta for the mob in 2008. The ambiguous setting might be New Orleans or just outside New York City, and the game is held up by two men wearing hoods who get away with all the money. The theft is the brain child of Curatola, who believes it will be blamed on Liotta and who has a previous record of stealing from the mob in card games. Curatola hires two ex-convicts, Mendelsohn and McNairy, to hit the card game, which digs into the mob's wallet. Since mob business is on the down curve, like everything else in the economy, Pitt, a hit man, is hired to bump off the two men. Pitt is dangerous, but likes to kill softly, thus the film's title. Pitt does his job and more killings follow and another one of Liotta's card games is raided. Mob leaders must now decide what to do with Liotta, either have Pitt kill him or just have him beaten to a pulp. All of the underworld doings transpire during the 2008 presidential campaign, ending with Barack Obama's election and victory speech as Pitt demands payment from Liotta with the implication that, failing to receive that payment, Liotta will forfeit with his life; the film ends abruptly, with Liotta's fate left unresolved. Pitt, Liotta and the rest of the cast are convincing in their brutal roles, and the script is well constructed (with a good understanding of lowlife underworld behavior and parlance) and firmly directed by Dominik. The film saw a modest success at the box office, earning more than $37.9 million in its initial release against a budget of more than $15 million. Excessive violence, sexual references, pervasive gutter language and drug use prohibit viewing by children. **p**, Dede Gardner, Anthony Katagas, Brad Pitt, Paula Mae Schwartz, Steve Schwartz, Matt Budman, Will French, Stephen Roberts, Douglas Saylor Jr., Roger Schwartz; **d&w**, Andrew Dominik (based on the novel *Cogan's Trade* by George V. Higgins), **cast**, Pitt, James Gandolfini, Ray Liotta, Sam Shepard, Ben Mendelsohn, Richard Jenkins, Vincent Curatola, Trevor Long, Scoot McNairy, Max Casella, Linara Washington; **c**, Grieg Fraser; **ed**, Brian A. Kates, John Paul Horstmann; **prod d**, Patricia Norris; **set d**, Leslie Morales; **spec eff**, Bob Riggs.

The Kings of Summer ★★★ 2013; U.S.; 95m; Big Beach Films/CBS Films; Color; Comedy; Children: Unacceptable (MPAA: PG-13); **BD**; **DVD**. This amusing tale begins with Robintson, a boy nearing adolescence, who is frustrated by the attempts of his single parent father, Offerman, to manage his life. He breaks away by escaping to a clearing in some woods with his best friend, Basso, and a strange boy, Arias, and they start to build a house, free from responsibility and parents (they think). Once their makeshift home in the woods is finished, the three boys find themselves masters of their own destiny, alone in the woods, but learn that even that life of supposed freedom has its drawbacks. Robinson claims himself and Arias to be hunters, while Basso goes off to harvest. Several weeks pass and Robinson and Arias are missing, and news about their disappearance is seen on many television news channels. Basso and Robinson fall out when Robinson invites the girl he has a crush on, Moriarty, to visit the house they have constructed. She takes a liking to Basso and they begin a relationship. Robinson teams with Arias in a Monopoly game against Basso, and they trade land and buy hotels, leading Basso to lose the game. Robinson and Basso get into a fight and accuse Moriarty of having broken up their friendship, sending her out of their home in the woods in despair. Basso goes after Moriarty and comforts her with a kiss. Robinson then tells Arias to leave the house and is left there alone. A month passes and Robinson is still living alone in the woods. Needing money, he hunts for his own food, eventually killing and eating a rabbit. Not disposing of the rabbit's body properly, a snake enters the house. Moriarty, meanwhile, goes to Offerman and tells him she can take him to Robinson. When they arrive at the house in the woods they find Robinson cornered by a snake that may be venomous. Arias then barges in and swings a machete at the snake, but is bitten and collapses, violently ill. His friends have Arias rushed to the hospital and he survives and tells Robinson that he saw Heaven and, if he had it to do all over again, he would do the same thing. Then he changes his mind. Robinson's and Basso's parents drive them home and the boys look at each other from the cars carrying them to their separate ways. The film ends with a view of the house the boys built, and after the credits, Arias is seen residing in the house in the woods. The adolescent cast members give credible performances of bumbling youths attempting to make their own lifestyles but without much adult reasoning to make things work well and a lot of genuine humor results. It's a simple coming-of-age story told in such prosaic terms that the characters all become sincerely alive. This independently made film saw limited distribution, earning a little more than $1.3 million in its initial release. Songs: "Cowboy Song" (Brian Downey, Phil Lynott); "The Youth" (Ben Goldwasser, Andrew Van Wyngarden); "17" (Trevor Powers); "Golden Clouds" (Thomas Fehlmann, Duncan Alexander, Robert Paterson, Lee Scratch Perry, Steve Reich); "Pickpocket," "How I Rise," "Loose Bands" (Kevin Writer, Douglas James); "Take Me Out to the Ball Game" (Jack Norworth, Albert von Tilzer). Gutter language and teen drinking prohibit viewing by children. **p**, Tyler Davidson, John Hodges, Peter Saraf, Eric Hollenbeck, Robert Ruggeri, Susan Wasserman; **d**, Jordan Vogt-Roberts; **cast**, Nick Robinson, Gabriel Basso, Moises Arias, Nick Offerman, Erin Moriarty, Craig Cackowski, William Sonnie, Nathan Keyes, Christoffer Carter, Megan Mullally, Priscilla Kaczuk; **w**, Chris Galletta; **c**, Ross Riege; **m**, Ryan Miller; **ed**, Terel Gibson; **prod d**, Tyler B. Robinson; **art d**, Jennifer Klide; **set d**, Carmen Navis; **spec eff**, Richard Fike.

Kingsman: The Secret Service ★★★ 2015; U.K.; 129m; FOX; Color; Spy Drama; Children: Unacceptable (MPAA: R); **BD**; **DVD**. This action-loaded film is based on a comic book of that name in which Firth, the head of a top secret spy organization, recruits Egerton, a London street-wise boy, into its training program. Firth thinks Egerton, whose late father, Davies, worked for his spy organization, could help him and also be saved from a life of crime since he had been arrested for car theft. Firth also feels obligated to help Egerton because the boy's father sacrificed his life to save a member of his team. The film follows

Richard Jenkins in *Killing Them Softly,* 2012.

Egerton's training in the secret service as Jackson, a mad technology genius, poses a worldwide threat with his plan to solve the problem of climate change by way of a worldwide killing spree. Jackson kidnaps Hamill, a professor, along with Davenport, one of Firth's agents, who is killed in a rescue attempt by Boutella, a Jackson henchwoman. Firth locates Hamill, but a computer chip implanted in Hamill's head explodes and he is killed. Firth eventually tracks Jackson to a church in Kentucky, which has been involved in hate crimes. A fight breaks out, and Firth is the only survivor, but, soon afterward, Jackson kills Firth after revealing to him his mass murder plan. Egerton confronts Jackson, who tells him he plans to kill off all but a few people he believes are worthy of living. Egerton then joins forces with other secret service agents, including one who pilots a high-altitude balloon, to strike a missile to destroy Jackson's deadly satellite. The satellite is destroyed but Jackson has another. After more adventure, Egerton kills Boutella and then kills Jackson to end the crazed scientist's misguided climate control plan. The comic book story line and its often silly characters (where stereotypical villain Jackson again goes way over the top) are nevertheless redeemed through a lot of mesmerizing action and startling special effects that sustain interest throughout. The film saw great success at the box office, earning more than $414.4 million in its initial release against a budget of more than $81 million. Excessive violence, gutter language and some sexual content prohibit viewing by children. Songs/Music: "Money for Nothing" (Mark Knofler, Sting), "Bonkers" (Dylan Mills, Armand van Helden), "Feel the Love" (Piers Aggett, Kesi Dryden, Amir Izadkhah, John Newman), "Free Bird" (Allen Collins, Ronnie Van Zant), "Give It Up" (Deborah Career, Harry Wayne Casey), "Slave to Love" (Bryan Ferry), "Get Ready for It" (Gary Barlow, Howard Donald, Mark Owen, Steve Robson), "Heavy Crown" (Iggy Azalea, Jon Turner, Jon Shave, George Astasio, Jason Pebworth, Ellie Goulding, Salt Wives), "Pomp and Circumstance" (Edward Elgar). **p**, Matthew Vaughn, Adam Bohling, David Reid, Jane Goldman; **d**, Vaughn; **cast**, Colin Firth, Samuel L. Jackson, Taron Egerton, Michael Caine, Mark Hamill, Jack Davenport, Sofia Boutella, Mark Strong, Jonno Davies, Alex Nikolov, Samantha Womack, Velibor Topic; **w**, Vaughn, Jane Goldman (based on the comic book *The Secret Service* by Mark Millar, Dave Gibbons); **c**, George Richmond; **m**, Henry Jackman, Matthew Margeson; **ed**, Eddie Hamilton, Jon Harris; **prod d**, Paul Kirby; **art d**, Andy Thomson; **set d**, David Morison, Jennifer Williams, Naomi Moore; **spec eff**, Anna Krawczyk, Neil Corbould.

Kon-Tiki ★★★ 2013; U.K./Norway/Denmark/Germany/Sweden; 118m; RPC (Recorded Pictures Co.)/Weinstein Co.; Color; Adventure; Children: Unacceptable (MPAA: PG-13); **BD**; **DVD**. This compelling tale chronicles the 1947 journey across the Pacific Ocean on a self-made

Melanie Laurent in *La Rafle,* 2012.

balsa wood raft by Norwegian explorer Thor Heyerdahl (1914-2002), who is ably played by Hagen. His journey with five men was to prove that people from South America could have settled Polynesia in pre-Columbian times. After financing the trip with loans, they set off from South America on a 101-day trip across 4,300 miles of ocean while the world waits for the results, and they eventually arrive in the Tuamotu Islands. The film tells about the origin of the idea, preparations, and events on the trip. The raft, Kon-Tiki, was named after the Incan sun god, Viracocha. Heyerdahl filmed the adventure, which won a 1951 Academy Award for the best documentary and was titled **Kon Tiki**, and his book about the expedition was translated into seventy languages and sold more than 50 million copies worldwide. The film did well at the box office, earning more than $22.8 million in its initial release against a budget of more than $15.5 million. *Author's Note*: Today, most anthropologists do not believe that South Americans were the original settlers in Polynesia, as Heyerdahl believed. A disturbing violent sequence prohibits viewing by children. **p**, Aage Aaberge, Jeremy Thomas; **d**, Joachim Ronning, Espen Saandberg; **cast**, Pal Sverre Hagen, Anders Baasmo Christiansen, Tobias Santelmann, Gustaf Skarsgard, Odd-Magnus Williamson, Jakob Oftebro, Agnes Kittelsen, Peter Wight, Amund Hellum Noraker, Eilif Hellum Noraker; **w**, Peter Skavlan, Allan Scott (based on the book by Thor Heyerdahl); **c**, Geir Hartly Andreassen; **m**, Johan Soderqvist; **ed**, Per-Erik Eriksen, Martin Stoltz; **prod d**, Karl Juliusson; **art d**, Lek Chaiyan Chunsuttiwat; **set d**, Louise Drake af Hagelsrum; **spec eff**, Ivo Jivkov, Hege Anita Berg, Mattias Lindahl, Martin Madsen.

La Rafle ★★★ 2012; France/Germany/Hungary; 115m; Legende Films/Menemsha Films; Color; War Drama; Children: Unacceptable; **BD**; **DVD**. Gritty tale based on true events, this film tells of the plight of Jews in Paris during the Nazi occupation in World War II (1939-1945). Candidly depicted are the mass arrests (Rafle or Roundup) of 13,000 French Jews by Vichy French police collaborating with the Nazis in July 1942. Jews are herded into a sports arena in Paris, but the majority of them are then sent by train to be exterminated at Auschwitz in the Holocaust. The film follows the Schmuel Weismann family, Gad Elmaleh playing the father, Raphaelle Agogue playing the mother; and Hugo Leverdez playing their eleven-year-old son Joseph, who, along with his pals, has no idea about the fate of his parents or himself or the others rounded up. Reno plays a kindly Jewish doctor, who stays with his patients, and Laurent essays a nurse who tries to help the family. The family is briefly held in a French internment camp, where Reno and Laurent arrive to tend to the sick inmates suf-

fering from the poor diet and harsh conditions at the camp. The parents are then ordered to ostensibly leave by train to work in the East for the Germans, but this is a ruse as the Nazis are shipping these victims to extermination camps. Reno is ordered to go with the parents, but he persuades Laurent, who wants to accompany him, not to leave the children. She remains behind and grows ill. Then the children are told that they will be leaving by train to rejoin their parents, but the truth is that the parents have already been murdered en masse, and the children are to follow them to the extermination camps. Leverdez and a friend distrust the officials and, using money his parents have earlier hidden, escape through barbed wire just before the children are shipped by train from the city. Laurent, learning of the Nazi plot, runs to the station, but finds in anguish that the train and its tragic victims have already departed. After the war ends, Laurent searches for the children she had nursed. To her joy, she finds Leverdez, who is about to be adopted by a family. Closing credits state that thousands more Jews were, in fact, hidden from the Gestapo by brave Parisians, preventing them from being exterminated. The cast members are all standouts in their roles and tension is sustained throughout under the firm direction of Bosch. Songs/Music: "Paris" (Andre Bernheim), "Tout en flanant" (Louis Poterat), "Quand un vicomte" (music: Mireille; lyrics: Jean Nohain), "L'or du Rhin" (Richard Wagner), "La Savane Op. 3" (Louis Moreau Gottschalk), "Waltz, posthume en la mineur" (Frederic Chopin), "Concerto de l'adieu" (Georges Delerue), "Tombe du ciel" (music: Charles Trenet, Albert Lasry; lyrics: Trenet), "Concerto for Violin and Orchestra" (Philip Glass), "Insensiblement" (Paul Misraki), "Automne" (traditional), "Etats d'ame" (Jerome Lemonnier), "La mort d'Ase from Peer Gynt" (Edvard Grieg), "Clair de Lune" (Claude Debussy), "Operation Terminated" from the 2008 film **Valkyrie** (John Ottman). *Author's Note*: Bosch became interested in making this film after she found Joseph Weismann, and other Holocaust survivors and their stories provided the core of the film's story line. The film was shot in Paris in 2009 within thirteen weeks and also in Hungary where an old Nazi concentration camp was reconstructed. (In French; English subtitles.) **p**, Alain Goldman, Catherine Morisse; **d&w**, Rose Bosch; **cast**, Hugo Leverdez, Melanie Laurent, Sylvie Testud, Jean Reno, Raphaelle Agogue, Anne Brochet, Denis Menochet, Mathieu Di Concerto, Romain Di Concerto, Oliver Cywie; **c**, David Ungaro; **m**, Christian Henson; **ed**, Aurelien Dupont, Yann Malcor; **art d**, Alexis McKenzie Main; **set d**, Clemence Boussicot; **spec eff**, Laszlo Pinter.

Labor Day ★★★ 2014; U.S.; 111m; Indian Paintbrush/PAR; Color; Drama; Children: Unacceptable (MPAA: PG-13); **BD**; **DVD**. This absorbing story begins when Winslet, who is a depressed single mother, and her thirteen-year-old son, Griffith, offer a ride to Brolin, an injured, bloody man, in 1987. He is an escaped convict from a local jail and police are searching for him. Winslet and Griffith gradually learn his true story, that he is a Vietnam veteran who returned home and married his pregnant girlfriend, Monroe, who soon gave birth. A year later, Brolin and Monroe have an argument and she unintentionally reveals that Brolin is not the child's father. He accidentally pushes her against a radiator and she is killed. At the same time, the baby drowns and Brolin is jailed, charged with Monroe's murder. Winslet and Brolin fall in love during his escape and plan to go to Canada with Griffith. They begin packing, planning to leave on Labor Day. Meanwhile, Griffith becomes friends with a mature woman, Fleming, and goes to see her one more time before leaving with Winslet and Brolin. Fleming manipulates Griffith into thinking his mother and Brolin are going to abandon him and he reveals Brolin's past. On the morning they are about to leave for Canada, Griffith takes a note to his father's house and leaves it in his mailbox. While Griffith is walking home, Van Der Beek, a cop, offers him a ride home, and Van Der Beek becomes suspicious of the car in the driveway packed with belongings and a house nearly empty, but he leaves without investigating. Winslet goes to the bank to take out her money, and when she returns to the house a neighbor gives her some cinnamon rolls and becomes suspicious about Brolin. Griffith's father finds the note and calls the house to ask what is going on. Before Brolin can escape with Winlset and Griffith, police arrive and are going to arrest Brolin. He ties up Winset and Griffith so they will not be charged with harboring a fugitive, then surrenders to police. Years later, Griffith has grown to be an adult, played by Maguire, who is a successful banker, and he is contacted by Brolin, who is getting out of jail. Griffith tells Brolin that Winslet has not remarried and Winslet and Brolin meet again at her home and the viewer is left to wonder if these old lovers will reunite. Winslet, Brolin, and, especially, Griffith, render top-flight performances in this tale of star-crossed lovers and ironic circumstances that destroys hope and promise. The film had a modest success at the box office, earning more than $20.2 million in its initial release against a budget of more than $18 million. Songs/Music: "I'm Going Home" (Arlo Guthrie), "Life of Leisure" (Keith Mansfield), "True News Bump" (Galen Shostac), "I'm in the Mood for Love" (music: Jimmy McHugh; lyrics: Dorothy Fields), "Studio XIX" (Celedonio Romero), "Here Before" (Vashti Bunyan), "End Title from **Close Encounters of the Third Kind**" (John Williams), "All I Have to Do Is Dream" (Boudleaux Bryant), "It Ain't Necessarily So" (music: George Gershwin; lyrics: Ira Gershwin), "Exercises in B Minor, Allegretto" (Fernando Sor), "Romance de los Pinos" (Frederico Moreno Torroba). Thematic material, brief violence and sexuality prohibit viewing by children. **p**, Jason Reitman, Helen Estabrook, Lianne Halfon, Russell Smith, Nicole C. Taylor, Jason Blumenfeld; **d&w**, Reitman (based on the novel by Joyce Maynard); **cast**, Kate Winslet, Josh Brolin, Tobey Maguire, Gattlin Griffith, Tom Lipinski, Maika Monroe, Clark Gregg, James Van Der Beek, J.K. Simmons, Brooke Smith; **c**, Eric Steelberg; **m**, Rolfe Kent; **ed**, Dana E. Glauberman; **prod d**, Steve Saklad; **art d**, Mark Robert Taylor; **set d**, Tracey A. Doyle; **spec eff**, Jeremy Dominick, Christopher Walsh, Seth Kleinberg.

Laggies ★★★ 2014; U.S.; 99m; Anonymous Content/A24; Color; Comedy/Romance; Children: Unacceptable; MPAA: R; **BD**; **DVD**. Knightley is exceptional in this well-made coming-of-age film. She is a beautiful but headstrong and immature twenty-eight-year-old woman, who is conflicted about her feelings about marrying and growing up. When she attends her tenth-year high school reunion, Webber, her longtime school sweetheart, surprises her by proposing she marry him. She accepts his engagement ring, but has cold feet about going to the altar. Knightley's classmates have all married and are mothers, but the thought of becoming an adult so frightens her that she leaves Webber and the reunion and wanders into the city. She joins up with Moretz, who is sixteen and out on a night of drinking with her teenage friends, and gets drunk with them. The next day, Knightley tells Webber she is going to spend the week at a career seminar, but it is just an excuse to put off a decision about marrying him. Instead, she spends more time with Moretz because she is also unhappy at home. Moretz's parents have been separated for several years, and she lives with her lawyer father, Rockwell. Knightley asks Moretz if she can move into her house and stay a week, but Rockwell is, at first, against it, then changes his mind and develops romantic feelings for Knightley and says she can stay longer, but Knightley declines. Moretz sees Rockwell kissing Knightley and she approves of their relationship. Knightley and Rockwell later have sex together. Moretz asks Knightley to drive her to see her mother, Mol, because she hasn't seen her in some time, and Knightley does. Moretz then finds Knightley's engagement ring, and Knightley admits she is engaged to her high school boyfriend. They then go shopping for a prom dress for Moretz while being taken to stores in a car driven by Webber. He has been drinking because his parents disapprove of him marrying Knightley. He accidentally crashes the car, and when police arrive, Knightley tells them she was driving, as she feels sorry for Webber. Police find alcohol on Knightley's breath and arrest her for DUI, compelling Knightley's father, Garlin, to go to the jail to bail her out. Knightley finally breaks off her engagement to Webber and goes to

Gary Oldman in *Lawless*, 2012.

Moretz's house and tells Rockwell she loves him. He lets her in the house to begin a relationship, but that is left uncertain since he is still married. The film's title apparently refers to Knightley and the others lagging behind in maturity. Songs: "Such Great Heights" (Benjamin Gibbard, Jimmy Tamborello), "Get Go/Breakdown" (Alice Russell, Alex Cowan), "Home Free" (Louis Yoelin, Daniel Brecher), "Canon in D" (Johann Pachelbel), "If I'm Not Made for You/If You're Not the One" (Daniel Bedingfield), "It Was Always You" (Joel Wachbrit, Richard Levinson), "Super Diana" (Reg Tilsley), "Easy" (Frank McDonald, Chris Rae), "Gymnopedie" (Erik Satie), "Etude No. 3" (Frederic Chopin), "Dang Diggy Dang" (Charlie G. Bethel, Kheedim Oh, Utkarsh Ambudkar), "Night Light" (Beteh Thornley, Jess Furman), "The House Party" (Matthew Harris), "Party Time" (Barrington Lawrence Jr., Brendan Nadel Woodard), "Under the Lights" (Jake Hanner, Casey Hanner, John Churton), "Never" (Eli Lishinsky), "April Fool" (Jeff Anderson, Garrett Croxon, Brady Harvey, Jessi Reed), "In the Town" and "La Tracicion" (Javier Fioramonti, Tony Herschmann), "Sure as Spring" (Shana Cleveland, La Luz), "Anarchy" (John Hyde), "Black Velvet" (Keith Papworth), "Camiliano" (Peter Reno), "Can't Stay" (Orville Neeley Bateman III), "Summer Air" (Jason Brewer), "That Feeling" (Matthew Rhodes, Sarah Graziani), "It's Never Too Late" (Benjamin Gibbard). **p**, Kevin Scott Frakes, Steve Golin, Alix Madigan, Myles Nestel, Raj Brinder Singh, Rosalie Swedlin, Lacey Leavitt; **d**, Lynn Shelton; **cast**, Keira Knightley, Chloe Grace Moretz, Sam Rockwell, Mark Webber, Ellie Kemper, Jeff Garlin, Gretchen Mol, Eric Riedmann, Kaitlyn Dever, Daniel Zovatto; **w**, Andrea Seigel; **c**, Benjamin Kasulke; **m**, Benjamin Gibbard; **ed**, Nat Sanders; **prod d**, John Lavin; **art d**, Schuyler Telleen; **set d**, Tania Kupczak; **spec eff**, Stephen Klineburger, Jamison Huber, Connor Meechan.

The Last of Robin Hood ★★★ 2014; U.S.; 94m; A+E/Samuel Goldwyn; Color; Biographical Drama; Children: Unacceptable; (MPAA: PG-13); **BD**; **DVD**. Sad but absorbing tale is based on the story of Beverly Aadland (1942-2010), a teenage movie starlet, who became the last girlfriend of legendary movie star Errol Flynn (1909-1959). In 1957, Aadland, who is played by Fanning, is working at Warner Brothers studios with a fake birth certificate saying she is eighteen when, in fact, she is only fifteen, and meets Flynn, who is played by Kline. They began a relationship that her mother, Florence, played by Sarandon, encourages, hoping it will help her daughter's film career. The affair between Fanning and Kline takes them from Los Angeles to New York, Africa, and then to Cuba where Kline gets approval from rebels to make a pro-Castro propaganda film starring Fanning. Sarandon, with high movie ambitions for Fanning, enjoys the media attention until it all comes crashing down when Kline dies in Fanning's arms in Vancouver,

Shia LeBeouf and Mia Wasikowska in *Lawless*, 2012.

Canada. Kline does a credible job playing Flynn, but no one could really capture that actor's inimitable charm and charisma, while Fanning is a standout as the naïve and manipulated teenager seeking fame at the ruthless urging of Sarandon, who is superb as her ambitious matriarch. The film did poorly at the box office, earning less than $300,000 in its initial release. Songs: "Un Cantoa Mi Cuba," "Flynn's Cocktail," "Midday Promenade" (Carlos Jose Alvarez). *Author's Note*: Flynn died in Vancouver where he was trying to lease his yacht, as he was in dire need of cash. He suffered pain and was treated by a doctor, but a short time later, when Aadland checked on him, he was discovered dead from a heart attack, October 14, 1959. Sean Flynn, grandson of Errol Flynn, has a bit part as a studio grip in this film. Sexuality and gutter language prohibit viewing by children. **p**, Declan Baldwin, Pamela Koffler, Christine Vachon; **d&w**, Richard Glatzer, Wash Westmoreland; **cast**, Kevin Kline, Susan Sarandon, Dakota Fanning, Patrick St. Esprit, Sean Flynn, Max Casella, Bryan Batt, Matt Kane, Jane McNeill, Ben Winchell, Jason Davis; **c**, Michael Simmonds; **ed**, Robin Katz; **prod d**, Jade Healy; **art d**, Alexandra West; **set d**, Adam Willis; **spec eff**, Matt Fleming, Thomas Tannenberger.

The Last Ride ★★★ 2012; Australia; 90m; Australia Film Finance Corp./Music Box Films; Color; Drama; Children: Unacceptable; **BD**; **DVD**. Offbeat father-and-son tale begins when Weaving becomes wanted by Australian police for committing a violent crime. He escapes into the outback with Russell, his ten-year-old son. They travel by foot until Weaving steals an SUV. They survive by eating canned beans or shooting rabbits and roasting them, or stealing food and sleeping outdoors by a campfire. Weaving does not tell Russell why they are traveling, but, in flashbacks, we see the boy trying to sort out his father's dilemma. They stay awhile at a national park and into and out of small towns. One night, Russell shoplifts some sparklers from a gas station, and he and Weaving set them afire for fun. They meet Hegh, a kind woman, and Russell bonds with her, hoping they will stay with her, but Weaving wants no additional company and they move on. Russell does not understand why they are living as they are and tells Weaving he is not a proper father. Weaving strikes him and then abandons Russell as he drives away without him. Russell walks on alone in the wilderness. When he breaks down and cries, Weaving suddenly returns and orders Russell back into the car and they drive on to an uncertain future. Weaving and Russell give outstanding performances as self-imposed outcasts in an uninviting world, where a sense of evocative loneliness permeates almost every scene. Theirs is a compelling story, even though its conclusion remains unresolved. The film saw limited distribution and did not fare well at the box office. Songs: "Black Diamond" (Tom Russell), "I Get a Longing to Hear Hank Sing the Blues" (M. McCormick, J. Mur-

phy), "Pharaoh's Dream" and "Hawa Al Nahar" (Joseph Tawadros), "Indescribably Blue" (Pete Holinari), "Sugar Town" (Lee Hazlewood), "Home" (I. Mae, C. Lee-Williams). **p**, Antonia Barnard, Nick Cole; **d**, Glendyn Ivin; **cast**, Hugo Weaving, Tom Russell, Anita Hegh, John Brumpton, Kelton Pell, Sonya Suares, Loren Taylor as Loren Horsley, Adam Morgan, Chrissie Page; **w**, Mac Gudgeon (based on the novel by Denise Young); **c**, Greig Fraser; **m**, Paul Charlier; **ed**, Jack Hutchings; **prod d**, Josephine Ford; **spec eff**, Jon Holmes.

The Last Stand ★★★ 2013; U.S.; 107m; Di Bonaventura Pictures/Lionsgate; Color; Crime Drama; Children: Unacceptable (MPAA: R); **BD**; **DVD**. In his first film in ten years, Schwarzenegger plays a sheriff of a small border town on the U.S. side of Mexico. He is bored fighting what little crime is there, after having lost his post with the LAPD, following a bungled operation that left his partner crippled. One night, international drug lord Noriega makes a daring escape from FBI custody in Las Vegas and speeds away in a modified Chevrolet Corvette C6 ZR1, taking Rodriguez, a female FBI agent, as his hostage while he drives at 200 mph for the Mexican border. FBI agent Whitaker has a blockade set up in a small city in Arizona, but Noriega mows down the police officers and clears the road for him to continue his getaway. Back in the border town, Schwarzenegger dispatches deputies Gilford and Alexander to visit a local farmer, Stanton, who has mysteriously missed his usual milk delivery at a diner in town. Stanton is found murdered and a trail of tire tracks leads to Noriega's henchman, Stormare, and his goons, who are placing a mobile assault bridge across a canyon that marks the U.S.-Mexican border. Schwarzenegger and his deputies barricade the main road into the town, and, in an ensuing gunfight, Schwarzenegger and a deputy shoot down most of the thugs with a Vickers machine gun mounted on the back of a school bus. Noriega finally arrives in town in his Corvette, smashing through the barricade of cars as Schwarzenegger and his deputies shoot at it. Noriega pushes Rodriguez out of the car and then speeds through a cornfield. Schwarzenegger races after him in a car he has borrowed from the mayor, Menchaca, and both cars collide with a tractor. Dazed, Noriega tries escaping on foot, but Schwarzenegger meets him at the bridge over the canyon. Noriega attempts to bribe Schwarzenegger to let him go, but it doesn't work. Both men wrestle on the bridge and Noriega slashes Schwarzenegger with a push dagger, but Schwarzenegger is victorious, handcuffing Noriega and taking him back to town. Rodriguez is also arrested, for having taken a bribe from Noriega and aiding in his escape. The film ends with Menchaca looking at what's left of his car, and Schwarzenegger warning him about having parked it in a fire lane. Although the script offers a lot of stereotypical drug tale characters, the action is superlative and the moral message sound as justice triumphs. The film had success at the box office, earning more than $48 million in its initial release against a budget of $45 million. Songs: "Cortez Extraction," "Jerry Dies and So," "Canyon Shootout" (Lee Seong Hyeon as Mowg); "Blue Moon Revisited/Song for Elvis" (Richard Rodgers, Lorenz Hart), "Angel from Heaven" (Paul Cary); "I'll Pretend" (Glen Morris); "I Ain't Superstitious" (Willie Dixon), Excessive violence and gutter language prohibit viewing by children. **p**, Lorenzo di Bonaventura, Udi Nedivi; **d**, Kim Jee-woon; **cast**, Arnold Schwarzenegger, Forest Whitaker, Eduardo Noriega, Harry Dean Stanton, Genesis Rodriguez, Titos Menchaca, Peter Stormare, Richard Dillard, Luis Guzman, Sonny Landham, Jaimie Alexander, Mathew Greer, Johnny Knoxville, Chris Browning; **w**, Andrew Knauer; **c**, Ji-yong Kim; **m**, Mowg; **ed**, Steven Kemper; **prod d**, Franco-Giacomo Carbone; **art d**, James F. Oberlander; **set d**, Carla Curry; **spec eff**, Josh Hakian, Stuart Lashley, Chris LeDoux, Gregory D. Liegey, Mike Uguccioni.

A Late Quartet ★★★ 2012; U.S.; 105m; Opening Night Productions; Entertainment One; Color; Musical Drama; Children: Unacceptable (MPAA: R); **BD**; **DVD**. Walken, the cellist and oldest member of a Manhattan classical music ensemble, the Fugue String Quartet, that has been successful for a quarter of a century, learns that he is in the early stages of Parkinson's disease and decides it is time for him to retire. His decision has a profound effect on the others in the group as they voice long repressed resentments and desires. Hoffman, for instance, would like to become the lead violinist and replace Ivanir. At the same time, Ivanir is having an affair with Poots, the daughter of two married violin members of the group, Hoffman and Keener. The dramas unfold as the group rehearses and performs Beethoven's String Quartet No. 14, a piece for which they have become famous and which could be Walken's final performance. The offbeat story is nevertheless absorbing as it fuses some fine classical music with the dramatic events of those performing that music, and the cast members shine in their intriguing roles. The film saw limited distribution, which caused its poor box office performance, earning a little more than $1.5 million in its initial release. Music: "City Nights" (Uri Caine), "Bulerias Del Encuentro" (Cristian Puig), "String Quartet No. 12 in C# Minor, Op. 131" (Ludwig van Beethoven), "String Quartet in F Minor, Op,. 20/5, 3rd Movement" (Franz Joseph Haydn), "Zigeunerweisen/Gypsy Airs" (Pablo de Sarasate), "Salty Air" (Jonathan Dagan), "Cello Suite No. 4, Prelude and Allemande" (Johann Sebastian Bach), "The Blue Danube" (Johann Strauss Jr.), "Marietta's Song from Die Tote Stadt/The Dead City" (Erich Wolfgang Korngold). Gutter language and some sexuality prohibit viewing by children. **p**, Vanessa Coifman, David Faigenblum, Emanuel Michael, Tamar Sela, Mandy Tagger Brockey, Yaron Zilberman, Annabelle Quezada; **d**, Zilberman; **cast**, Philip Seymour Hoffman, Christopher Walken, Catherine Keener, Imogen Poots, Mark Ivanir, Madhur Jaffrey, Liraz Charhi, Wallace Shawn, Pamela Quinn, Brooklyn Parkinson Group; **w**, Zilberman, Seth Grossman (based on a story by Zilberman); **c**, Frederick Elmes; **m**, Angelo Badalamenti; **ed**, Yuval Shar; **prod d**, John Kasarda; **art d**, Rumiko Ishii; **set d**, Susan Ogu; **spec eff**, Alex Frisch, Vico Sharabani.

Lawless ★★★ 2012; U.S.; 116m; Weinstein Company; Color; Crime/Drama; Children: Unacceptable (MPAA: R); **BD**; **DVD**. Three brothers control the bootleg moonshine trade in Franklin County, Virginia, in 1931 during the Prohibition era (1920-1933) when the making, selling, and consumption of alcoholic beverages were against the law of the land. Hardy plays the oldest brother, so tough that when his throat is slit open he holds the wound together and walks in a snowstorm to a hospital. LaBeouf, the youngest, is aching to prove himself to his siblings, but is really a coward. Clarke, the middle brother, is the most dangerous of the trio. These hardened bootleggers shoot anyone who threatens their backwoods kingdom, which consists of a liquor shop, restaurant, and gas station. Pearce, a federal agent from Chicago, ignores their fierce reputation and goes after them. Pearce, who dresses like a foppish dandy and wears dress gloves, has a fatalistic attitude about his goal as he works with the local sheriff to shut the brothers' business down or kill them, if necessary. Into this dangerous backwoods world comes Chastain, a mystery woman from Chicago, who becomes a waitress and manages the brothers' bootlegging business while being Hardy's girlfriend. (Her role is reminiscent of the role played by Dimitra Arliss in **The Sting**, 1973, and who essays a waitress in a cheap restaurant, but who is really a top assassin for the mob.) LaBeouf and a preacher's pretty daughter, Wasikowska, fall for each other just as events come to a climax. That bloody finale of the war between the brothers and Pearce and local lawmen takes place as they face each other on a road outside of town and trade bullets in a wild exchange of gunfire. Although this film does not match the crime classics of the 1930s (**Little Caesar**, 1931; **The Public Enemy**, 1931; **Scarface**, 1932), it presents an accurate and chilling portrait of the reckless, almost suicidal bootleggers of the Depression era. The period is well presented in accurately drawn sets, costuming and score while Hillcoat provides an overall haunting image of a desperate age where all seems as forlorn and doomed as seen in another outstanding film on that gun crazy age, **Road to Perdition**, 2002. The film did well at the box office, earning more

Dane DeHaan and Guy Pearce in *Lawless,* **2012.**

than $53.6 million in its initial release against a budget of $26 million. Songs: "Fire and Brimstone" (Link Wray as Fred Lincoln Wray Jr.); "Night of Canakkale," "He Is All" (David Sardy, Jordan Tappis); "Fire in the Blood," "Cosmonaut," "Hymn," "End Crawl" (Nick Cave, Warren Ellis); "Midnight Run" (Marc Copely, James Bernard Dolan, Adam Levy); "Sweet Truth," "The Morning After" (David Sardy); "Detroit" (Philip Doddridge); "So You'll Aim Towards the Sky" (Jason Lytle); "Wave Storm" (Blake Mills); "Burnin' Hell" (Bernard Besman, John Lee Hooker); "The Snake Song" (Townes Van Zandt); "White Light/White Heat" (Lou Reed); "The Telephone Girl" (Orville Reed); "The Cuckoo Bird" (traditional); "Sure 'Nuff 'Yes I Do" (Herb Bermann, Don Van Vliet). Excessive violence, gutter language, sexuality and nudity prohibit viewing by children. **p**, Michael Benaroya, Megan Ellison, Lucy Fisher, Douglas Wick, John Allen, Matthew Budman; **d**, John Hillcoat; **cast**, Tom Hardy, Shia LaBeouf, Jason Clarke, Guy Pearce, Jessica Chastain, Mia Wasikowska, Dane DeHaan, Chris McGarry, Tim Tolin, Gary Oldman, Lew Temple, Marcus Hester, Noah Taylor; **w**, Nick Cave (based on the novel *The Wettest County in the World* by Matt Bondurant); **c**, Benoit Delhomme; **m**, Nick Cave, Warren Ellis; **ed**, Dylan Tichenor; **prod d**, Chris Kennedy; **art d**, Gershon Ginsburg; **set d**, Maria Nay; **spec eff**, David Fletcher.

Le Week-End ★★★ 2014; U.K./France; 93m; Film 4/Music Box Films; Color; Comedy/Drama; Children: Unacceptable (MPAA: R); **BD**; **DVD**. Well-written tale sees Broadbent and Duncan, a middle-aged British couple, going to Paris for a weekend to observe their 30th wedding anniversary. He is a college lecturer and she a school teacher. Broadbent still loves Duncan, but she has had a seven-year itch for at least twenty-three years. As soon as they arrive in the City of Light, where they had honeymooned three decades earlier, Duncan becomes dissatisfied with everything. She insists on moving to a more luxurious hotel in Paris and makes it plain that she would like to dump Broadbent for a more exciting husband. They run into Goldblum, his old college friend, a successful writer, who has a new young wife. When Broadbent and Duncan attend a party hosted by Goldblum, their perspectives on life dramatically alter, and Duncan concludes that life has cheated her out of happiness. The performances from Broadbent and Duncan are stunningly charming, producing a bittersweet image of aging lovers struggling to define the actual identity of their long relationship. There is no perfection in any marriage and here we see a couple wanting to preserve or, at least, find the best of their imperfect union. It is the desire or the lack of it for that perfection that holds together or destroys any marriage, and it is the survival of that desire that is tested here to the breaking point. Unfortunately, the film did poorly at the box office, earning more than $2 million in its initial release. Songs: "Clair de lune"

Isabelle Allen and Hugh Jackman in *Les Miserables*, 2012.

(music: Claude Debussy), "Like a Rolling Stone" (Bob Dylan), "Pink Moon" and "Road" (Nick Drake), "Vero Valse" (Rene Briaval), "Apres moi" (Bernie Bennett), "Invitatorium Hodie Exultandum." Gutter language and sexual content prohibit viewing by children. **p**, Kevin Loader, Bertrand Faivre; **d**, Roger Michell; **cast**, Lindsay Duncan, Jim Broadbent, Jeff Goldblum, Igor Gotesman, Olivier Audibert, Sophie-Charlotte Husson, Etienne Dalibert, Mauricette Laurence, Gabriel Mailhebiau, Violaine Baccon; **w**, Hanif Kureishi; **c**, Nathalie Durand; **m**, Jeremy Sams; **ed**, Kristina Hetherington; **prod d**, Emmanuelle Duplay; **spec eff**, Adam Gascoyne, Tim Caplan.

Legend ★★★ 2015; U.K./France; 131m; ACE (Anton Capitol Entertainment)/UNIV; Color; Crime Drama; Children: Unacceptable (MPAA: R); **BD**; **DVD**. Hard-hitting, new adaptation of the lives and careers of Ronald "Ronnie" and Reginald "Reggie" Kray, identical twins who were two of the most notorious criminals in British history. This film chronicles the development of their organized crime empire in the East End of London and how they thrived during the 1950s and 1960s. Ronnie (1933-1995) and Reggie (1933-2000), were involved in armed robberies, arson, protection rackets, assaults, and the murders of at least two other gangsters. The film depicts how the deadly twins became owners of a nightclub and mixed with politicians and movie stars, becoming celebrities themselves, for their crimes, until they were arrested and imprisoned for life in 1969. Their lives were earlier filmed as **The Krays**, 1990. The script faithfully follows the facts, and the period is shown in authentic-looking sets and costumes while the cast members render standout performances. The film fared well at the box office, earning more than $38.7 million in its initial release against a budget of more than $25 million. Rated R for strong violence, language, some sexual and drug material. **p**, Tim Bevan, Chris Clark, Quentin Curtis, Eric Fellner, Brian Oliver, Jane Robertson; **d&w**, Brian Helgeland (based on the book *The Profession of Violence: The Rise and Fall of the Kray Twins* by John Pearson); **cast**, Tom Hardy, Christopher Eccleston, David Thewlis, Nicholas Farrell, Paul Anderson, Joshua Hill, Emily Browning, Colin Morgan, Tara Fitzgerald, Adam Fogerty, Mel Raido; **c**, Dick Pope; **m**, Carter Burwell; **ed**, Peter McNulty; **prod d**, Tom Conroy; **art d**, Patrick Rolfe, Gareth Cousins, Marco Anton Restivo; **set d**, Crispian Sallis; **spec eff**, Neal Champion.

The Lego Movie ★★★ 2014; Australia/U.S./Denmark; 100m; WB; Color; Animated Adventure; Children: Unacceptable (MPAA: PG-13); **BD**; **DVD**; **3-D**. Emmet (Pratt voiceover), an ordinary Lego construction worker mini-figure, finds a magic brick that will reveal some higher truth. He and some friends then journey to find the Piece of Resistance that is capable of stopping an evil Lord Business (Ferrell

voiceover) from taking over Lego World. Lego people across the universe use creative forces to build machines and weapons to fight the forces of Ferrell. Lego characters involved include Superman, Batman, Wonder Woman, **Star Wars** characters, and others. Mindless characters, goofy (but often very amusing) mayhem and a pubescent script adds up to another blockbuster at the box office where this film earned more than $469 million in its initial release against a budget of $60 million. Songs: "Everything Is Awesome" (music: Shawn Patterson, Joshua Bartholomew, Lisa Harriton; lyrics: Akiva Schaffer, Andy Samberg, Jorma Taccone), "War Cry" (Collin Hegna, Carl Werner), "Jag in a Jungle" (Luke Andrew Smith, Shaun Libman), "Get Ready for This" (Filip De Wilde, Jean-Paul DeCoster, Ray Slijngaard, Simon Harris), "Star Wars/Blockade Runner" and "Jabba the Hutt" (John Williams), "How Ya Gonna Keep 'Em Down on the Farm" (Joe Young, Sam Lewis, Walter Donaldson), "Double Dare Theme" (Edd Kalehoff), "Untitled Self Portrait" (Mark Mothersbaugh, Will Arnett, Phil Lord, Christopher Miller). Roughhouse action and crude humor prohibit viewing by children. **p**, Roy Lee, Dan Lin, Igor Khait, John Powers Middleton; **d**, Phil Lord, Christopher Miller; **cast** (voiceovers), Chris Pratt, Will Arnett, Will Ferrell, Liam Neeson, Channing Tatum, Billy Dee Williams, Shaquille O'Neal, Morgan Freeman, Dave Franco, Elizabeth Banks, Craig Berry, Anthony Daniels, Will Forte; **w**, Lord, Miller (based on a story by Dan Hageman, Kevin Hageman, Lord, Miller) **c**, Barry Peterson, Pablo Plaisted; **m**, Mark Mothersbaugh; **ed**, David Burrows, Chris McKay; **prod d**, Grant Freckelton; **art d**, Jay Pelissier; **set d**, Danielle Berman; **spec eff**, Matt Akey.

Les Miserables ★★★★ 2012; U.S./U.K.; 158m; UNIV; Color; Drama/Musical; Children: Unacceptable (MPAA: PG-13); **BD**; **DVD**. The oft-told classic tale of Jean Valjean, portrayed by Jackman, begins when he is released on parole by prison guard Javert, essayed by Crowe, in 1815 after Jackman has served a nineteen-year sentence for stealing a loaf of bread and numerous escape attempts. Because of his parole status, Jackman is forced to leave every town. Wilkinson, a bishop, however, offers him food and shelter, but Jackman steals his silver and flees. He is apprehended, but Wilkinson tells the authorities the silver was not stolen, but was a gift he bestowed upon Jackma. Officers release Jackman, who, startled by Wilkinson's forgiveness, then vows to start an honest life by assuming a new identity, where he dedicates his efforts to help others. Eight years later, Jackman becomes a beloved factory owner and mayor of a small town. One of his factory workers, Hathaway, is dismissed for sending some company money to her illegitimate daughter, Allen, who lives with an unscrupulous couple, Carter and Cohen, and their daughter, Barks. Desperate to support Allen, Hathaway becomes a prostitute. Later, Jackman learns that a man believed to be him when he was a criminal has been arrested, so he reveals his identity to a court at the man's trial. Hathaway is dying, and Jackman promises he will look after her daughter. Crowe arrives to take Jackman into custody for parole violation and prison breaks, but Jackman jumps into a river to escape again. He pays Carter and Cohen, two swindling innkeepers, to allow him to take Allen and promises to be like a father to her, then takes her to Paris. Javert follows them there, determined to finally put Jackman away in prison for good as an escaped convict, but again Jackman escapes. Nine years pass and, in 1832, there is widespread poverty in Paris, and teenage revolutionary students, including Redmayne and Huddlestone, plan a rebellion against the French monarchy. Redmayne falls in love with Hathaway's daughter, now grown as Seyfried. A gang led by Carter and Cohen attempts to capture Jackman for ransom, but Jackman is warned and flees, unaware that Seyfried loves Redmayne. The students begin their revolt, and Crowe poses as a rebel in order to infiltrate the underground organization and collect information that will send its members to prison, but he is found out and captured. Crowe is about to be executed by Jackman when, instead, Jackman frees him and shoots his pistol at a wall so that students will think he has killed him. The rebels are almost all killed in a battle at a barricade, but Jackman carries wounded Redmayne to a doctor. Soon afterward, Crowe returns and has Jackman at gunpoint on a ledge overlooking the Seine, but Crowe then has misgivings about how he has hounded Jackman for years and, remembering that Jackman saved his life, and unable to live with his nagging conscience, commits suicide by leaping into the river. Jackman then tells the recovering Redmayne his past and says he will now leave because his presence endangers Seyfried, but asks Redmayne not to reveal his past to her. Redmayne and Seyfried marry. Jackman is dying in a convent and gives Seyfried a letter telling her of his past, and then has a vision of Hathaway taking him to Heaven, joining the spirits of those who fought and died at the barricade. Several versions of this tale have been filmed, and Fredric March's 1935 portrayal of Jean Valjean is considered to be an unmatchable classic portrait of this unforgettable antihero, as well as Charles Laughton's equally unforgettable essay of the savagely dogged detective, Javert. Jackman, however, as well as the dynamic Crowe, come very close to the 1935 portrayals with intensely powerful performances. Hathaway, as the doomed trollop attempting to preserve a safe life for her child, gives a compassionate and memorable performance, so effective that it deservedly won for her an Oscar as Best Actress. Seyfried, Allen, Wilkinson, Carter, Cohen, Barks, and Huddlestone are also exceptional in their memorable characters. The sets and costuming are exceptionally in period, but the cinematography and editing are often distracting if not annoying as hand-held cameras erratically record the action for too many prolonged sequences and abrupt jump cuts jar the disrupt the story line, as well as the continuity. The film includes almost all of the songs (which are sung in recitative) appearing in the original 1980 stage musical. The film also won Oscars for Best Makeup and Hairstyling (Lisa Westcott and Julie Dartnell) and Best Sound Mixing (Andy Nelson, Mark Paterson, Simon Hayes). The film received Oscar nominations for Best Picture; Best Actor (Jackman); Best Original Song ("Suddenly"); Best Production Design (Stewart; set decoration: Lynch-Robinson); and Best Costume Design (Paco Delgado). The film saw enormous success at the box office, earning more than $441.8 million in its initial release against a budget of $61 million. Songs: "Suddenly," "Master of the House," "At the End of Each Day," "I Dreamed a Dream," "The Confrontation," "Castle on a Cloud," "Stars," "ABC Café/Red and Black," "A Heart Full of Love," "On My Own," "One Day More!," "Bring Him Home," "Javert's Suicide," "Empty Chairs at Empty Tables," "Epilogue," "Valjean Arrested, Valjean Forgiven," "Valjean's Soliloquy," "The Runaway Cart," "Lovely Ladies," "Fantine's Arrest," "Who Am I?," "Come to Me," "Look Down," "The Final Battle," "The Robbery/Javert's Intervention," "Eponine's Errand," "Attack on the Rue Plumet," "In My Life," "Beggars at the Feast," "Drink with Me," "Do You Hear the People Sing?," "Little People/Javert's Arrival," "A Little Fall of Rain," "The Night of Anguish," "Turning," "The Sewers," "On Parole," "The Bishop," "The Bargain," "The Thenardier Waltz of Treachery," "Building the Barricade," "Every Day/A Heart Full of Love," "The Death of Gavroche," "The Wedding" (Herbert Kretzmer, Claude-Michel Sconberg, Alain Boublil). *Author's Note*: The film was based on the Broadway musical and novel by Victor Hugo. The classic story was filmed previously not as a musical but a drama in 1919 as a silent film, and as talkies in 1935, 1952, 1958, 1982, 1995, 1998, and 2000. **p**, Tim Bevan, Eric Fellner, Debra Hayward, Cameron Mackintosh, Bernard Bellew, Raphael Benoliel; **d**, Tom Hooper; **cast**, Hugh Jackman, Russell Crowe, Anne Hathaway, Eddie Redmayne, Amanda Seyfried, Helena Bonham Carter, Sacha Baron Cohen, Aaron Tveit, Samantha Barks, Daniel Huttlestone, Colm Wilkinson, Tim Downie, Georgie Glen, Andrew Havill; **w**, Herbert Kretzmer, Alain Boublil, William Nicholson, Claude-Michel Schonberg (based on the stage musical by Boublil, Schonberg, and the novel by Victor Hugo); **c**, Sammy Cohen; **ed**, Chris Dickens, Melanie Oliver; **prod d**, Eve Stewart; **art d**, Gary Jopling, Hannah Moseley, Grant Armstrong, Su Whitaker; **set d**, Anna Lynch-Robinson; **spec eff**, Mark Holt, Mike Kelt.

Eddie Redmayne and Amanda Seyfried in *Les Miserables*, 2012.

Leviathan ★★★ 2014; Russia; 140m; Curzon Film World/Sony; Color; Drama; Children: Unacceptable (MPAA: R); **BD**; **DVD**. Taut tale begins outside a small coastal town by the Barents Sea, where whales sometimes come to its bay, and where Serebryakov, lives with his wife, Lyadova, and their teenage son, Pokhodaev. They are haunted by a local corrupt mayor, Madyanov, who is trying to take away their land, house, and a small auto repair shop. To save their homes, Serebrayakov calls his old army friend, Vdovichenkov, an attorney in Moscow. Together they fight Madyanov by gathering incriminating and embarrassing evidence that proves his corruption. Lyadova is then discovered having an affair with a local man, both beaten by Serebryakov. Lyadova vanishes from her home and is later found dead, and Madyanov has Serebryakov arrested. He is charged with killing his wife, convicted and sent to prison while the now homeless Pokhodaev is taken in by friends. Madyanov gloats over his enemy's plight and, after Serebryakov's house has been torn down, Madyanov sits in a new cathedral he has donated to the local bishop, who sermonizes to parishioners while Madyanov sits triumphantly in that new church. Serebryakov had consulted a priest when all of his problems confronted him, and the priest told him that, if he showed the patience of Job, he would be rewarded with happiness. Just the opposite, however, has happened as this rather grim but compelling film comes to an end. The acting from the entire cast is superior as are the production values, but the film nevertheless did not enjoy a box office success, earning less than $3.4 million in its initial release. Not related to a 1989 film with the same title. Song: "Akhnaten, Act 1, Prelude: Refrain, Verse 1, Verse 2" (Philip Glass). (In Russian/English subtitles.) Gutter language, sexuality and graphic nudity prohibit viewing by children. **p**, Aleksandr Rodnyanskiy; **d**, Andrey Zvyagintsev; **cast**, Vladimir Vdovichenkov, Elena Lyadova, Aleksey Serebrayakov, Roman Madyanov, Anna Ukolova, Sergey Pokhodaev, Kristina Pakarina, Aleksey Rozin, Lesya Kudryashova; **w**, Zyvagintsev, Oleg Negin; **c**, Mikhail Krichman; **prod d**, Andrey Ponkratov; **spec eff**, Dimitry Tokoyakov.

The Liberator ★★★★ 2014; Venezuela/Spain; 119m; Cohen Media Group; Color; Biographical Drama; Children: Unacceptable; **BD**; **DVD**. Well-made biopic chronicles Simon Bolivar's historic campaign to end three centuries of Spanish rule over much of South America. The film opens in 1828 when Bolivar (1783-1830), played by Ramirez, frantically escapes an assassination attempt. He is then shown in flashback to his early life. He is born to a wealthy, aristocratic Venezuelan family, but, at an early age, he is tutored by professor and mentor Don Simon Rodriguez, portrayed by Francisco Denis, who encourages him to fight for their country's liberation from Spain. When he is sixteen, Ramirez is sent to Spain to be educated, and there begins his ambition to free his country from Spanish rule. Ramirez marries at a young age to Valverde,

Tiger and Suraj Sharma in *Life of Pi*, 2012.

who soon dies of yellow fever. Ramirez then uses his wealth to organize a private army and begins liberating South America. He leads his army in more than 100 battles against the Spanish empire, riding horseback more than 70,000 miles and leading campaigns that covers twice the territory conquered by Alexander the Great (356-323 BC). Ramirez's army never conquers; it liberates the people. He becomes president of a short-lived republic now called *Gran Colombia*, parts of which would become Ecuador, Panama, Peru, Guyana, Brazil, and Bolivia, which was named after him. The film ends with the liberator's death implying he was murdered, perhaps by poisoning, but, in real life, he died in bed at the age of forty-seven. Ramirez is superb in playing the heroic Bolivar, and the sweep of action is often breathtaking while the astounding facts of this tale are faithfully presented. **p**, Alberto Arvelo, Winfried Hammacher, Ana Loehnert, Jose Luis Escolar; **d**, Alberto Arvelo; **cast**, Edgar Ramirez, Francisco Denis, Erich Wildpret, Maria Valverde, Juana Acosta, Imanol Arias, Leandro Arvelo, Marta Garcia de Polavieja, Jon Bermudez, Dacio Caballero, Alejandro Furth; **w**, Timothy J. Sexton; **c**, Xavi Gimenez; **m**, Gustavo Dudamel; **ed**, Tariq Anwar; **prod d**, Paul D. Austerberry; **art d**, Benjamin Fernandez, Felix Lariviere-Charron; **set d**, Philippe Turlure; **spec eff**, Pau Costa.

Life of Crime ★★★ 2013; U.S.; 94m; Abbolita Productions/Lionsgate; Color; Comedy; Children: Unacceptable (MPAA: R); **BD**; **DVD**. Compulsively funny crime farce sees Aniston as the wife of wealthy Robbins, but, after she is kidnapped, he doesn't want to pay her ransom because he is close to dumping her for a younger woman, Fisher. The bumbling kidnappers, Bey and Hawkes, are left with plan B, but have no idea what that should be while their time is running out and Aniston is making their lives a living nightmare. Songs: "X Marks the Spot" and "Hearts on Ice" (Jordan Galland), "I Can't Change It" (Brett Boyett). Gutter language, sexual content and violence prohibit viewing by children. **p**, Ashok Amritraj, Elizabeth Destro, Ellen Goldsmith-Vein, Jordan Kessler, Michael Siegel, Lee Stollman, Wendy Benge, Peter Pietrangeli; **d&w**, Daniel Schechter (based on the novel *The Switch* by Elmore Leonard); **cast**, Jennifer Aniston, Tim Robbins, Will Forte, John Hawkes, Mark Boone Junior, Kevin Cannon, Isla Fisher, Jenna Nye, Leonard Robinson, Margaret Rossini; **c**, Eric Alan Edwards; **m**, The Newton Brothers (John Andrew Grush, Taylor Stewart); **prod d**, Inbal Weinberg; **art d**, Lisa Myers; **set d**, Jasmine E. Ballou; **spec eff**, Drew Jiritano, Mike Uguccioni.

Life of Pi ★★★★★ 2012; U.S./Taiwan; 127m; FOX 2000; Color; Adventure/Drama/Fantasy; Children: Unacceptable (MPAA: PG); **3-D**; **BD**; **DVD**. Superlative tale chronicles the adventures of Sharma, a sixteen-year-old Indian boy, who is the son of Hussain, a zookeeper. He survives a shipwreck in which his family dies, and is stranded in the Pacific Ocean on an inflatable lifeboat with a Bengal tiger as the only other occupant. The film starts with a writer, Spall, meeting an Indian man, Irrfan Khan, who knows about an adventure for a good book. Khan recalls his past, when Hussain named him Piscine after a swimming pool in France, but, as a child, Sharma changed it to Pi. As a child he took a great interest in animals at his father's zoo, especially a Bengal tiger named Richard Parker. Sharma is brought up as a Hindu but, at age twelve, he is introduced to Christianity and then to Islam, following all three religions because he "just wants to love God." Sharma comes to love the tiger like a pet, but Hussain warns him that tigers are killers, while his mother, Tabu, supports his desire to learn and use his imagination. As a teenager, Sharma meets a girl, Sainath, at a dance class and they fall in love. When Sharma is sixteen, Hussain decides to relocate the family to Winnipeg, Manitoba, Canada, taking the zoo animals with them and intending to sell them later. Sharma and his parents are aboard a Japanese freighter in the Pacific Ocean when it flounders in a storm and Sharma watches helplessly as it sinks and his parents and the crew drown. After the storm, Sharma finds himself in a lifeboat with an injured zebra, orangutan, hyena, but the animals soon die in accidents. The tiger is the only animal survivor and it eats the bodies of the others. Sharma keeps his distance from the tiger by building a small raft and staying in it as the tiger remains on the lifeboat. After a while, Sharma trains the tiger to be friendly to him and realizes that, by doing this, he is keeping them both alive. Weeks pass and Sharma and the tiger are half dead when they reach an island with edible plants, fresh water pools, and a large number of meerkats. Sharma and the tiger eat and drink to regain their strength, but he discovers the island is inhabited by cannibals, so he and the tiger return to sea in the lifeboat. Eventually, the lifeboat reaches the coast of Mexico, but Sharma is heartbroken when his friend, the tiger, leaves him and disappears into the jungle. Sharma is rescued and taken to a hospital where he regains his strength. Insurance agents for the Japanese freighter interview him, but do not believe him when he tells them how he survived in a lifeboat with a Bengal tiger. He tells the writer a less fantastic account of his adventure, this time sharing the lifeboat not with a tiger but with his mother, a Buddhist sailor, Wang, and a cook, Depardieu, who kills Wang and eats him and uses him as fishing bait. Later, Tabu takes Sharma to safety on a smaller raft where Depardieu stabs her and throws her overboard. Then Sharma takes the knife and kills Depardieu. Spall isn't sure which of Sharma's stories to believe, but believes there are parallels between them: the orangutan was Sharma's mother, the zebra was the sailor, the hyena was the cook, and Richard Parker the Bengal tiger, was Sharma himself. Sharma asks which story he prefers, and Spall says it is the one with the tiger because it "is the better story". Sharma thanks him and says, "And so it goes with God." Spall stays for dinner with Pi (Irrfan Khan) and his family and the film ends with the tiger walking away into the jungle as Sharma said it had, but without looking back and disappearing behind the dense foliage. This finely acted and photographed allegorical film is wonderfully constructed with live action and computerized scenes showing the interaction between Sharma and the tiger. The brilliant many-hued cinematography that records their survival of countless hazards on the roiling sea, first as enemies, then as friends, is utterly mesmerizing. The film won Oscars for Best Director (Lee); Best Original Score (Danna); Best Cinematography (Miranda); and Best Visual Effects (Westenhofer, Rocheron, De Boer, Elliott). The film received Oscar nominations for Best Picture; Best Adapted Screenplay (Magee); Best Original Song ("Pi's Lullaby"); Best Sound Editing (Eugene Gearty, Philip Stockton); Best Sound Mixing (Ron Bartlett, D.M. Hemphill, Drew Kunin); Best Production Design (Gropman; set decoration: Pinnock); and Best Film Editing (Squyres). The was a huge success at the box office, earning more than $609 million in its initial release against a budget of $160 million. Songs: "Pi's Lullaby" (Mychael Danna, Bombay Jayashri), "Sous le ciel de Paris" (Hubert Giraud, Jean Drejac), "Anandi's Dance" (Sheejith Krishna, Padmini Ramachandran), "Tum Aa Gaye Ho Noor Aa" (Dev Raul Burman, Gulzar), "Tiruppukal" (Arunagirinathar). Highly emotional thematic content throughout and frightening action sequences and peril prohibit viewing by children. **p**, Ang Lee, Gil Netter, David Womark, David Lee; **d**, Ang Lee; **cast**, Suraj Sharma, Irrfan Khan, Rafe Spall, Gerard Depardieu, Ayush Tandon, Gautam Belur, Adil Hussain, Tabu, Ayaan Khan, Andrea Di Stefano, James Saito, Jun Naito, Elie Alouf; **w**, David Magee (based on the novel by Yann Martel); **c**, Claudio Miranda; **m**, Mychael Danna; **ed**, Tim Squyres; **prod d**, David Gropman; **art d**, Al Hobbs, Dan Webster; **set d**, Anna Pinnock, Terry Lewis; **spec eff**, Bill Westenhofer, Guillaume Rocheron, Erik-Jan De Boer, Donald R. Elliott, Louis Craig, Jean-Martin Desmarais.

Like Father, Like Son ★★★★ 2013; Japan; 121m; Amuse/Sundance; Color; Drama; Children: Unacceptable; **BD**; **DVD**. Compelling story sees Fukuyama, a workaholic architect, and his wife, Ono, happily married and living in a high-rise luxury apartment. Life seems blissful until they get a phone call from a hospital. They are told that their six-year-old son, Ninomiya, is not theirs, and that the hospital gave them the wrong baby. The hospital says the infants were accidentally switched at birth by a careless nurse. Ninomiya was really born to Maki and her husband, Furanki, who were also unaware that the son, Hwang, is the child of Fukuyama and Ono. The two married couples are opposites. Fukuyama and Ono are reserved and have money, while Maki and Furanki are freewheeling, loud, boisterous, and are not well off. Their sons also have grown up differently, Ninomiya in privilege, and Hwang in a working-class environment. The hospital recommends exchanging the boys as soon as possible. But Fukuyama is obsessed with his lineage and the success he has planned for his son, and is against the hospital's idea to give him up. Ono is troubled about what is best for both boys, while Fukuyama starts to question himself, whether he has really been a father to Ninomiya all these years. Fukuyama and Ono have pushed Ninomiya to excel, preparing him for an admission interview to an elite school, having him take piano lessons, and limiting his play time. Hwang has no such great expectations for the future but has been brought up to be a more normal, carefree boy who loves his two siblings. The film ends on a gentle note, without answering the dilemma, but it is sensed that the boys and the parents have the right sons in the right homes. The intelligent script, and gifted acting and direction provide an absorbing story that sustains interest throughout. The film did well at the box office, earning more than $31 million in its initial release. Not related to 1987 and 2005 films with the same title. **p**, Kaoru Matsuzaki, Hijiri Taguchi; **d&w**, Hirokazu Koreeda; **cast**, Masaharu Fukuyama, Machiko Ono, Yoko Maki, Riri Furanki, Jun Fubuki, Shogen Hwang, Arata Iura, Kirin Kiki, Jun Kunimura, Megumi Morisaki; **c**, Mikiya Takimoto; **m**, Takeshi Matsubara, Junichi Matsumoto, Takashi Mori; **ed**, Hirokazu Koreeda; **prod d**, Keiko Mitsumatsu.

Lincoln ★★★★★ 2012; U.S.; 150m; DreamWorks/Touchstone; Color; Biographical Drama/War Drama; Children: Unacceptable (MPAA: PG-13); **BD**; **DVD**. This wonderful film focuses upon the final four months of the administration and life of U.S. President Abraham Lincoln (1809-1865), who is masterfully essayed by Day-Lewis. As the American Civil War (1861-1865) nears its end in January 1865, Day-Lewis tries to get the U.S. House of Representatives to pass a historic and highly controversial 13th Amendment to the U.S. Constitution, ratifying and turning into law his Emancipation Proclamation, which freed the slaves and forever banned slavery from the United States (the Proclamation was issued as an executive order by Lincoln more than a year earlier on January 1, 1863). Day-Lewis races against time in this endeavor because peace can come at any time, and, if it does before the amendment is passed, Southern states returning to the Union will vote against it, defeating and abrogating the Proclamation. Day-Lewis must get enough votes from Congress before peace arrives. Yet, he is torn because an early peace would save thousands of lives, so he is engaged in a crisis of conscience:

Daniel Day-Lewis as President Abraham Lincoln in *Lincoln*, 2012.

end slavery or end the war. Support for and against the amendment hinge on volatile Republican and Democrat politics. Day-Lewis sends his most trusted political minions to contact the members of the U.S. Congress who are most likely to vote against the amendment in an effort to change their minds, and these intriguing segments depict in graphic and repugnant detail how many of those politicians display their blatant bigotry and racial hatred toward blacks. (The two most erstwhile lobbyists are marvelously played by Spader, who plays Republican operator William N. Bilbo, 1815-1867, and Nelson, who essays Democratic lobbyist Richard Schell, 1810-1879.) Meanwhile, Republican Party leader Francis Preston Blair (1791-1876), played by Holbrook, pressures Day-Lewis to end the war, pointing out that emissaries from the Confederate States of America (led by its vice president, Alexander H. Stephens, 1812-1883, played by Haley) have arrived at a neutral meeting place to discuss the peace terms. Day-Lewis (as did Lincoln) artfully avoids entering negotiations by not officially recognizing these emissaries under the assumption that they do not represent a legitimate government in the U.S., using this clever tactic to stall negotiations so that the 13th Amendment can be passed by the Republican-controlled Congress. Day-Lewis knows well that by stalling the peace efforts, he is risking the loss of more lives on both sides of the conflict, but he nevertheless proceeds with his hazardous political ploy in order to have his freeing of the slaves order officially sanctioned. He meanwhile hides his intentions and actions from all but a few of his closest confidantes and even these intimate supporters are left largely in the dark about his thinking. Day-Lewis must also contend with the strong objections from his wife, Mary Todd Lincoln (1818-1882), played by Field, over their oldest son, Robert Todd Lincoln (1843-1926), who is played by Gordon-Leaitt, from entering the Union army. Field is beside herself with worry over Gordon-Levitt's safety, believing that he may be killed in the closing days of the war. Gordon-Levitt, who has grown to manhood (Robert Lincoln was then twenty-one-years old) then confronts his father, insisting that he be allowed to enter the army and serve as any other young man of his generation. He feels embarrassed and degraded by being protected through the authority of his father and defies Day-Lewis, saying that he will enter the army with or without his permission. Day-Lewis becomes so overwrought at this decision (which, he knows, will make a nervous wreck of his wife) that he strikes Gordon-Lewis, who sullenly walks away, stating that he intends to immediately enlist. (Robert Lincoln did enter the army as an officer, but was assigned a staff position so that he would be kept from combat and was present at the surrender of Robert E. Lee, 1807-1870, at Appomattox Courthouse on April 9, 1865.) At the same time Day-Lewis is undergoing his personal and political crises, Jones, who plays the eccentric U.S. congressman Thaddeus Stevens, 1792-1868, the leader of the abolitionist

Tommy Lee Jones as Thaddeus Stevens in *Lincoln*, 2012.

Republicans, fanatically intimidates fellow members of Congress to vote for the Amendment, using any ploy at his disposal, including naked threats to destroy the political careers of those who oppose the Amendment. (Jones was never better in presenting a blood-chilling performance of this strange and dogged American politician whose underhanded political tactics were as savage as a scheming Machiavelli.) The opposition to the Amendment is led by Pace, who essays Democratic leader from New York Fernando Wood, 1812-1881), leader of NYC's powerful political machine, Tammany Hall, and one-time mayor of New York City, who, with his allies, showed a decided support for the Confederacy in order to sustain its profitable cotton trade. Pace and his supporters use the same vicious tactics employed by Jones in order to defeat the Amendment, threatening the destruction of any member of Congress not voting with them. In the final vote at Congress, Field attends the proceedings, but her feelings about the Amendment mixed as she comes from a southern family that has given its allegiance to the Confederacy and her loved ones have died fighting the Union that Day-Lewis so desperately has preserved. Sitting at her side in the gallery is Reuben, who plays Elizabeth Keckley (1818-1907), who was the black seamstress and reportedly one of the closest confidantes of Mary Todd Lincoln. (It is questionable that Keckley actually appeared with the First Lady in that gallery at the time when the Amendment was voted upon; she later wrote a book about her relationship with Mrs. Lincoln, its publication causing Mary Lincoln to cease their friendship as Mrs. Lincoln believed Keckley had betrayed her confidences, as well as misrepresented their relationship). While Day-Lewis agonizes over the outcome of the vote, members of Congress struggle with their consciences when delivering their decisions. Enough of them, however, radically change their views to support the Amendment, which narrowly passes. Day-Lewis' great Emancipation Proclamation is now the law of the land. The story moves forward two months to show Day-Lewis visiting the battlefield at Petersburg, Va., where he talks with Union General Ulysses S. Grant (1822-1885), played by Harris. Shortly after, on April 9, 1865, the war ends at Appomattox Courthouse, Va., where Harris receives the surrender of Confederate General Robert E. Lee (1807-1870), played by Boyer. Five days later, Day-Lewis is at a meeting with members of his cabinet on the evening of April 14, 1865, to discuss future measures to grant blacks the right to vote, when he is reminded that his wife, Field, is waiting to go to Ford's Theater and see a play. That night, while Thomas "Tad" Lincoln (1853-1871), played by McGrath, is watching a children's play, "Aladdin and the Wonderful Lamp" at Grover's Theater, a man announces that the President has been shot. The next morning, Day-Lewis (Lincoln) is pronounced dead. The film ends with a flashback to the President delivering his second inaugural address on March 4, 1865. Day-Lewis is utterly fascinating as he essays a very human and down-to-earth Abraham Lincoln, using all of his political wiles to advance the great causes of winning the war and preserving the Union while, at the same time bringing about the end (in the U.S.) of one of the world's greatest evils, slavery. In his portrait, unlike any other, we see a Lincoln exhausted with the chores of a wartime president, but one who summons enough energy and courage to deal with the seemingly overwhelming social evils of his day. He is compassionate and generous of thought, but, to achieve his lofty goals, he is also as petty as any other conniving politician and even devious in his methods. Unlike the Olympian figure of Lincoln shown in many previous films, Day-Lewis recreates a Lincoln who is very real and vulnerable, normally prone to impulsive anger, while, at the same time, maintaining an almost ethereal, spiritual persona that captures the complete attention of the viewer. His is a magnificent performance that deservedly won for him an Oscar as Best Actor. The sterling cast sees excellent performances from Field, Jones, Spader, Gordon-Levitt, Pace, Holbrook, and the rest of the cast members, who superbly and accurately capture their memorable characters under the firm direction of master filmmaker Spielberg. Also stunning are the authentic sets and costumes that so well reprise the Civil War period, all visually presented in gritty lensing from the gifted Kaminski, and Williams' evocative score perfectly matches the dramatically changing moods of the chaotic historical events and those ardent activists who shaped them. In addition to the Oscar going to Day-Lewis, the film also won an Oscar for Best Production Design (Carter; set decoration: Erickson). It received Oscar nominations for Best Picture; Best Director (Spielberg); Best Supporting Actor (Jones); Best Supporting Actress (Field); Best Adapted Screenplay (Kushner); Best Original Score (Williams); Best Cinematography (Kaminski); Best Film Editing (Kahn); Best Sound Mixing (Andy Nelson, Gary Rydstrom, Ronald Judkins); and Best Costume Design (Joanna Johnston). The film was a great success at the box office, earning more than $275.3 million in its initial release against a budget of more than $65 million. Songs: "We Are Coming, Father Abra'am" (traditional); "Quintet No. 1. in B-Flat Major" (Wolfgang Amadeus Mozart); "Three Forks of Hell," "Last of Sizemore," "They Swung John Brown to a Sour Apple Tree" (traditional); "O Nuit d'Amour" (from the opera "Faust" by Charles Gounod); "Battle Cry of Freedom" (traditional); "Overture to Egmont" (Ludwig van Beethoven). *Author's Note*: When Spielberg offered the role to Day-Lewis, the actor turned it down, saying that it was "preposterous" for him to undertake a part involving the iconic Lincoln. The gifted Liam Neeson was then hired for the part and he studied hard for the role. He then withdrew, stating that he was too old to play Lincoln (he was then fifty-eight and Lincoln, at the time of the setting, was fifty-five). Day-Lewis was again approached and he accepted the role. The film was shot on location in Virginia, chiefly in Richmond, where the exteriors and interiors of the State Capitol were used to represent the U.S. Capitol in Washington, D.C., and where the State House was remodeled to make it appear to be the U.S. House of Representatives of Lincoln's era. Although there are some minor liberties taken about the actual events of that period, the film remarkably stays close to the truth of those times and the colorful personalities who inhabited them. Lincoln has been portrayed by many other actors in many other films, including **Abe Lincoln: Freedom Fighter**, 1978 (Allen Williams); **Abe Lincoln in Illinois**, 1940 (Raymond Massey); **Abe Lincoln in Illinois**, 1945 (made-for-TV: Stephen Courtleigh); **Abe Lincoln in Illinois**, 1964 (made-for-TV; Jason Robards Jr.); **Abraham Lincoln**, 1930 (Walter Huston); **Abraham Lincoln: Vampire Hunter**, 2012 (Benjamin Walker as adult Lincoln; Lux Haney-Jardine as young Lincoln); **Action Family**, 1986 (made-for-TV; Drummond Erskine); **The Adams Chronicles**, 1976 (TV miniseries; Stephen D. Newman); **Alcoa Presents: One Step Beyond**, 1959-1961 (TV series; "The Day the World Wept: The Lincoln Story," 1960 episode: Barry Atwater); **America: A Call to Greatness**, 1995 (made-for-TV; Raymond Baker); **American Inventory**, 1951-1952 (TV series; "Abe Lincoln's Story,"1952 episode: Crahan Denton); **Apache Ambush**, 1955 (James Griffith); **Appointment with Destiny**,

1971-1973 (TV series; "Surrender at Appomattox, 1972 episode: Joseph Leisch Jr.); **Are We Civilized?**, 1934 (Frank McGlynn Sr.); **The Battle Cry of Peace**, 1915 (William J. Ferguson); **The Big Picture**, 1989 (Richard Blake); **Bill and Ted's Excellent Adventure**, 1989 (Robert Barron); **The Birth of a Nation**, 1915 (Joseph Henabery); **The Blue and the Gray**, 1982 (TV miniseries; Gregory Peck); **Captains and Kings**, 1976 (TV series; Ford Rainey); **Carl Schurz**, 1968 (Christian Rode); **Cavalcade of America**, 1952-1957 (TV series; "Moonlight Witness," 1954 episode: Bruce Bennett; "New Salem Story," 1953 episode: James Griffith; "The Palmetto Conspiracy," 1955 episode: Richard Hale); **The Civil War**, 1990 (TV miniseries; Sam Waterston voiceover); **The Conspirator**, 2011 (Gerald Bestrom); **Courage of the West**, 1937 (Albert Russell); **The Crisis**, 1916 (Sam D. Drane); **Cybill**, 1995-1998 (TV series; "It's for You, Mr. Lincoln," 1996 episode: Charles L. Brame); **The Day Lincoln Was Shot**, 1998 (made-for-TV; Lance Henriksen); **Days That Shook the World**, 2003-2013 (TV series; "Terror Made in America: Assassination of Abraham Lincoln...," 2004 episode: Jim Babel); **The Dramatic Life of Abraham Lincoln**, 1924 (George A. Billings as adult Lincoln; Danny Hoy as a young Lincoln); **Dream West**, 1986 (TV miniseries; F. Murray Abraham); **The DuPont Show of the Month**, 1957-1961 (TV series; "The Lincoln Murder Case," 1961 episode: Drummond Erskine); **The Faking of the President**, 1976 (William J. Daprato); **FDR: A One Man Show**, 1987 (made-for-TV; Drummond Erskine); **Ford Star Jubilee**, 1955-1956 (TV series; "The Day Lincoln Was Shot," 1956 episode: Raymond Massey); **The Fortune Cookie**, 1966 (John Anderson); **G. E. True Theater**, 1953-1962 (TV series: "Prologue to Glory," 1956 episode: John Ireland); **The Great Battles of the Civil War**, 1994 (TV miniseries; Charlton Heston); **The Great John Ericsson**, 1938 (John Ericsson); **The Great Man's Whiskers**, 1973 (made-for-TV; Dennis Weaver); **Guardian of the Wilderness**, 1976 (Ford Rainey); **Hands Up!**, 1926 (George A. Billings); **Happy Gilmore**, 1996 (Charles L. Brame); **The Heart of Lincoln**, 1915 (Francis Ford); **The Heart of Maryland**, 1927 (Charles Edward Bull); **Hearts in Bondage**, 1936 (Frank McGlynn Sr.); **Her Country's Call**, 1917 (Benjamin Chapin); **Histeria!**, 1998-2000 (TV series; four 1998 segments: Maurice LaMarche); **How the West Was Won**, 1962 (Raymond Massey); **In the Days of Buffalo Bill**, 1922 (Joel Day); **The Iron Horse**, 1924 (Charles Edward Bull); **Ironclads**, 1991 (made-for-TV; James Getty); **Lincoln**, 1974-1975 (TV series; Hal Holbrook); **Lincoln**, 1988 (TV miniseries; Sam Waterston); **Lincoln**, 1992 (made-for-TV; Jason Robards Jr.); **Lincoln: American Mastermind**, 2009 (made-for-TV; Fritz Klein); **Lincoln and the War Within**, 1992 (made-for-TV; Jason Robards Jr.); **The Lincoln Conspiracy**, 1977 (John Anderson); **The Lincoln Cycle**, 1917 (Benjamin Chapin); **The Lincoln-Douglas Debates**, 1976 (made-for-TV; Scott Mandrell); **Lincoln-Douglas Galesburg Debate**, 1994 (made-for-TV; Michael Krebs); **The Lone Ranger**, 1938 (Frank McGlynn Sr.); **The Littlest Rebel**, 1935 (Frank McGlynn Sr.); **Lost River: Lincoln's Secret Weapon**, 2009 (Fritz Klein); **Lux Video Theater**, 1950-1959 (TV series; "Abe Lincoln in Illinois," 1951 episode: Raymond Massey); **The Mad Empress**, 1939 (Mexican version of **Juarez**, 1939; Frank McGlynn Sr.); **Madame Who**, 1918 (Clarence Barr); **Medic**, 1954-1956 (TV series; "Black Friday," 1955 episode: Austin Green); **Mister Lincoln**, 1981 (made-for-TV; Roy Dotrice); **My Own United States**, 1918 (Gerald Day); **New Mexico**, 1951 (Hans Conried); **North and South, Book II**, 1986 (TV miniseries; Hal Holbrook); **Of Human Hearts**, 1938 (John Carradine); **Omnibus**, 1952-1961 (TV series; "Mr. Lincoln," five parts, 1952-1953: Royal Dano); **Out of This World**, 1987-1991 (TV series; "Honest Evie," 1989 episode: Robert Barron); **The Perfect Tribute**, 1991 (made-for-TV; Jason Robards Jr.); **Philco-Goodyear Television Playhouse**, 1948-1956 (TV series; "Ann Rutledge," 1950 episode: Stephen Courtleigh); **The Plainsman**, 1936 (Frank McGlynn Sr.); **Police Squad!**, 1982 (TV series; many segments: Rex Hamilton); **Prince of Players**, 1955 (Stanley Hall); **The Prisoner of Shark Island**, 1936 (Frank McGlynn Sr.); **Pulitzer Prize Playhouse**, 1950-1952 (TV series;

Sally Field as Mary Todd Lincoln in *Lincoln*, 2012.

"Abe Lincoln in Illinois," 1950 episode: Raymond Massey); **Red Dwarf**, 1988- (TV series; "Meltdown," 1991 episode: Jack Klaff); **The Right Man**, 1960 (made-for-TV; Richard Boone); **The Rivalry**, 1975 (made-for-TV; Arthur Hill); **Riverboat**, 1959-1961 (TV series; "No Bridge on the River," 1960 episode: Sandy Kenyon); **Rock Island Trail**, 1950 (Jeff Corey); **San Antoine**, 1953 (Richard Hale); **Saving Lincoln**, 2013 (Tom Amandes); **Schlitz Playhouse**, 1951-1959 (TV series; "Washington Incident," 1956 episode: Mark Stevens); **Screen Director's Playhouse**, 1955-1956 (TV series; "Lincoln's Doctor's Dog," 1955 episode: Robert Ryan); **The Secret Diary of Desmond Pfeiffer**, 1998 (TV series; four segments: Dann Florek); **The Slacker's Heart**, 1917 (Benjamin Chapin); **Stage to Tucson**, 1950 (James Griffith); **The Story of Mankind**, 1957 (Austin Green); **Studio One in Hollywood**, 1948-1958 (TV series; "Abraham Lincoln," 1952 episode: Robert Pastene); **Sunday Showcase**, 1959-1961 (TV series; "An American Heritage: Shadow of a Soldier," 1960 episode: Ford Rainey); **Tad**, 1995 (made-for TV; Kris Kristofferson); **The Tall Target**, 1951 (Leslie Kimmell); **Telephone Time**, 1956-1958 (TV series; "The Stepmother," 1956 episode: Ronnie Lee); **They've Killed President Lincoln!**, 1971 (made-for-TV; Joseph Leisch Jr.); **This Is America, Charlie Brown**, 1988 (TV miniseries; "The Smithsonian and the Presidency," 1989 episode: Frank Welker); **The Time Tunnel**, 1966-1967 (TV series; "The Death Trap," 1966 episode: Ford Rainey); **Trailin' West**, 1936 (Robert Barrat); **Treasure of the Aztecs**, 1965 (Jeff Corey); **TV Reader's Digest**, 1955-1956 (TV series; "How Chance Made Lincoln President," 1955 episode: Richard Gaines); **Twilight Zone**, 1959-1964 (TV series; "The Passerby," 1961 episode: Austin Green); **Two Fisted Justice**, 1931 (Joseph Mills); **Virginia City**, 1940 (Victor Kilian); **Voyagers!**, 1982-1983 (TV series; "The Day the Rebs Took Lincoln," 1982 episode: John Anderson); **Weird Science**, 1994-1996 (TV series; "Community Property," 1996 episode: Gary Bullock); **Wells Fargo**, 1937 (Frank McGlynn Sr.); **Western Gold**, 1937 (Frank McGlynn Sr.); **Woman with a Sword**, 1952 (made-for-TV; Henry Sharp); **Wrongfully Accused**, 1998 (Mark Francis); **You Are There**, 1953-1957 (TV series; "The Emancipation Proclamation," 1955 episode: Jeff Morrow; "The Gettysburg Address," 1953 episode: Paul Tripp; "The Nomination of Abraham Lincoln," 1954 episode: Jeff Morrow); **Young Mr. Lincoln**, 1939 (Henry Fonda); **Zoolander**, 2001 (Charles L. Brame). Violence, carnage and gutter language prohibit viewing by children. **p**, Steven Spielberg, Kathleen Kennedy, Kristie Macosko Krieger, Adam Somner; **d**, Spielberg; **cast**, Daniel Day-Lewis, Sally Field, David Strathairn, Joseph Gordon-Levitt, James Spader, Hal Holbrook, Tommy Lee Jones, John Hawkes, Jackie Earle Haley, Lee Pace, Bruce McGill, Jared Harris, Gulliver McGrath, Joseph Cross, Gloria Reuben, Tim Blake Nelson, Christopher Boyer; **w**, Tony Kushner (based in part on the book *Team*

Daniel Day-Lewis and Joseph Gordon-Levitt in *Lincoln*, 2012.

of Rivals: The Political Genius of Abraham Lincoln by Doris Kearns Goodwin); **c**, Janusz Kaminski; **m**, John Williams; **ed**, Michael Kahn; **prod d**, Rick Carter; **art d**, Curt Beech, David Clrank, Leslie McDonald; **set d**, Jim Erickson, Charles Maloy, Peter T. Frank; **spec eff**, Steve Cremin, Gavin Miljkovich, Ben Morris.

Listen Up Philip ★★★ 2014; U.S.; 108m; Sailor Bear/Tribecca Films; Color; Drama; Children: Unacceptable; **BD**; **DVD**. Absorbing story begins with Schwartzman, a young novelist who is angry as he awaits publication of his second novel. He is indifferent about promoting his new novel and has relationship problems with Moss, his photographer girlfriend. He lives in a noisy city so when his idol, Pryce, offers him the use of his isolated summer home as a refuge, Schwartzman finally gets the peace and quiet to focus on the subject that means most to him, himself. This introspective tale sees an intense performance from Schwartzman that chillingly reveals a self-serving lifestyle and no little narcissism. **p**, Joshua Blum, Toby Halbrooks, James M. Johnston, David Lowery, Katie Stern, Michaela McKee; **d&w**, Alex Ross Perry; **cast**, Jason Schwartzman, Elisabeth Moss, Krysten Ritter, Jonathan Pryce, Jess Weixler, Kate Lyn Sheil, Dree Hemingway, Josephine de La Baume, Daniel London, Joanne Tucker, Eric Bogosian (narrator); **c**, Sean Price Williams; **m**, Keegan DeWitt; **ed**, Robert Greene; **prod d**, Scott Kuzio; **art d**, Fletcher Chancey; **set d**, Nora Mendis, Molly Ann Walker.

Little Boy ★★★ 2015; Mexico/U.S.; 100m; Metanoia Films/Open Road Films; Color; War Drama; Children: Cautionary (MPAA: PG-13); **BD**; **DVD**; **IV**y This inspiring Christian-themed story begins with a boy praying that his father will return safely from WWII (1939-1945). The title refers both to the boy's height, since he is short, and to the code name for the atomic bomb that was dropped on Hiroshima on August 6, 1945. Set in the 1940s, a seven-year-old boy, Salvati, becomes fearful when his auto mechanic father, Rapaport, goes into the U.S. Army to fight the Japanese. Salvati's mother, Watson, and older brother Henrie also fear for Rapaport's safety, but Salvati does something about it. He gets advice from Wilkinson, a priest who convinces him that the power to bring his father back home safely may be within himself. Salvati discovers the *Bible* verse, "Truly I tell you, if you have faith as small as a mustard seed, you can say to this mountain, 'Move from here to there,' and it will move." This helps him to become determined to get enough faith to bring his father home. Wilkinson tells Salvati that faith is useless to anyone who harbors hatred. Salvati, like millions of others in those war years, hates the Japanese for starting the war. Wilkinson advises Salvati to befriend a Japanese man, Tagawa. Salvati reluctantly tries to do this and gradually learns from him to stand up to those who bully him at school about his height. Rapaport is then reported to be missing

in action, making Salvati and his mother and brother even more fearful for Rapaport's safety. Rapaport is captured and sent to a Japanese POW camp as Salvati prays for a miracle to end the war so his father will come home again. The miracle happens with the explosion of the atomic bomb on Hiroshima, but Salvati later learns that his father died in a gunfight to liberate the camp. This report proves to be false, however, when the film ends with Salvati learning that his father did survive the war, because another prisoner had stolen Rapaport's boots and dog-tags, so Rapaport had been misidentified among the dead. Salvati's prayers and faith bring his father home safely after all. Many critics of the film were harsh about the happy ending, which did not ring true to them, but they ignored the fact that this is a Christian-inspirational film. They also ignored the fact that all events do not end on a dire or miserable note and that happy endings are a matter of countless records. It is also a matter of record that the dropping of the atomic bomb, irrespective of the number of Japanese lives lost to that terrible weapon, abrogated the Allied need to invade a then fanatical Japan and, in the process, saved millions of lives, including Japanese. Salvati and the rest of the cast provide standout performances in a well-written story that will appeal to any sensitive viewers believing that faith can, indeed, move mountains. The film had a modest success at the box office, earning more than $17.4 million in its initial release against a budget of more than $20 million. Song: "O'Hare Air Jungle" (Chad Fischer). Mature thematic material and violence cautions viewing by children. **p**, Alejandro Monteverde, Leo Severino, **d**, Monteverde; **cast**, Jakob Salvati, Emily Watson, Ben Chaplin, Tom Wilkinson, Ali Landry, Kevin James, David Henrie, Michael Rapaport, Ted Levine, Eduardo Verastegui, Cary-Hiroyuki Tagawa, Toby Huss; **w**, Monteverde, Pepe Portillo; **c**, Andrew Cadelago; **m**, Stephan Altman, Mark Foster; **ed**, Meg Ramsay, Joan Sobel, Fernando Villena; **prod d**, Bernardo Trujillo; **art d**, Carlos Benassini, Francisco Blanc, Marco Niro; **set d**, Jay Aroesty, Jorge Barba.

Locke ★★★ 2013; UK/U.S.; 85m; IM Global/A24; Color; Drama; Children: Unacceptable (MPAA: R); **BD**; **DVD**. Ivan Locke, played by Hardy, is a good British family man and successful construction foreman working in Birmingham, England. Before he must supervise a large concrete pour, he receives a phone call that changes his life. Colman, a colleague with whom he had a one-night stand seven months before, tells him that she has gone into premature labor with his child. Despite his job responsibilities and, although his wife and sons are eagerly awaiting his arrival at home to watch an important football game, Hardy drives to London to be with Colman during childbirth. The unusual drama consists almost entirely of scenes of Hardy in his car driving to London, phoning his boss and a coworker to ensure that the concrete pour is successful. He also phones his wife, Wilson, to confess his infidelity, and calls Colman to reassure her during her labor. Hardy's confession to his wife is revealed to be a reaction to his own father, who abandoned him as a child. During the two-hour drive to London, Hardy is fired from his job, kicked out of his house by his wife, and asked by his older son to return home. Also by phone, he coaches his assistant, Scott, how to prepare the concrete pour, despite several major setbacks. He also imagines his father is in the back seat of his car and has several conversations with him. When he is close to the hospital in London, Hardy learns of the birth of his daughter and that she and Colman are fine, even though otherwise, his life has become a disaster. This unconventional film sees an outstanding performance from Hardy, a tour de force essay that fully develops and exposes his character, his failings and virtues, all at once and in a very moving and empathetic way. This fine film enjoyed only a modest success at the box office, earning more than $5 million at the box office in its initial release against a budget of $5 million. *Author's Note*: The film was almost entirely shot within a BMW X5 as it was being driven along England's M6 Motorway while it was being carried on a flatbed truck and was shot in real-time as were the scenes where Hardy talks with unseen others on the phone. Gutter language prohibits viewing by children. **p**, Paul Webster, Guy Heeley, Charles Auty,

Stephen Fuss, Sarah Micciche, Andrew Warren, Lesley Wise; **d&w**, Steven Knight; **cast**, Tom Hardy, (voices only) Olivia Colman, Ruth Wilson, Andrew Scott, Ben Daniaels, Tom Holland, Bill Milner, Danny Webb, Alice Lowe, Silas Carson, Lee Ross, Kirsty Dillon; **c**, Haris Zambarloukos; **m**, Dickon Hinchcliffe; **ed**, Justine Wright; **spec eff**, James Devlin, Humayun Mirza.

The Lone Ranger ★★★ 2013; U.S.; 149m; Walt Disney; Color; Western; Children: Unacceptable (MPAA: PG-13); **BD**; **DVD**. Cook, a boy who idolizes a legend known as the Lone Ranger, visits a sideshow at a San Francisco fair in 1933. There Cook meets Tonto, who is played by Depp, an odd and elderly Comanche Native American who poses as a mannequin. Depp tells Cook about his earlier Old West adventures with the Lone Ranger, who is played by Hammer. In flashback, the viewer sees 1869 Colby, Texas, where idealistic young lawyer John Reid (Hammer) returns home by way of the as-yet uncompleted Transcontinental Railroad, which is managed by rail tycoon Wilkinson. Unknown to Hammer, the train also is carrying Tonto and an outlaw, Butch Cavendish, portrayed by Fichtner, who is being transported to his hanging after being captured by Dan Reid (Dale), Hammer's Texas Ranger brother. Fichtner's gang rescues him and derails the train. Depp is then jailed. Dale deputizes Hammer as a Texas Ranger and, with six other rangers at their side, they pursue Fichtner and his gang. Fichtner and his men ambush and kill Hammer, Dale and the other rangers pursuing them in a canyon, and Fichtner cuts out and eats Dale's heart. Depp escapes from jail and comes across the dead Rangers and buries them. While doing this, a white spirit horse appears and awakens Hammer as a "spirit walker," and Depp tells Hammer that he, Hammer, cannot be killed in battle. He also tells him that Rippy, one of the Rangers, betrayed Dale, and is working for Fichtner. Hammer, whom everyone but Depp believes to be dead, dons a mask to hide his identity. Depp gives Hammer a silver bullet made from the fallen Rangers' badges and tells him to kill Fichtner with it. At a brothel, Carter informs them about Dale's and Rippy's fight over a cursed silver rock. Meanwhile, Fichtner's men, disguised as Comanche Indians, raid frontier towns. Hammer and Depp arrive after raiders abduct Wilson, Dale's widow, and son, Prince. Rippy feels guilty and tries to help the captives escape, but Wilkinson shoots him dead. Wilkinson claims the raiders are hostile Comanche raiders and sends Pepper, a U.S. Cavalry captain and his unit to wipe out the Indians, his reason being to keep the Indians from interfering with the railroad they oppose. Indians capture Hammer and Depp after the friends find railroad tracks in Indian territory. Hammer and Depp manage to talk the chief into only burying them in sand up to their heads, from which they nevertheless escape. They go to the silver mine where they capture Fichtner and Depp urges Hammer to shoot and kill Fichtner with the silver bullet, but he refuses. Depp knocks Fichtner unconscious and brings him to Wilkinson and Pepper. Wilson and her son Prince are then taken hostage while Hammer is taken back to the silver mine to be executed. Depp rescues them and they escape as the Comanche attack, but are massacred by the cavalry. Hammer realizes that Wilkinson is too powerful to be taken lawfully, so he dons his Lone Ranger mask. At the site of the union of the Transcontinental Railroad, Wilkinson reveals his true plan to his investors, a scheme to take complete control of the railroad and use the mined silver to achieve more wealth and power. To that end, Wilkinson summarily shoots and kills some of the investors who object, cowing the rest into submission. Depp and Hammer steal some nitroglycerin and destroy a railroad bridge. With Carter's help, Depp steals the train with the silver. Wilkinson, Fichtner, and Pepper pursue him in a second train on which Wilson and Prince are being held captive. Riding his white horse Silver, Hammer pursues both trains. During a furious rail chase and fights on both trains, Wilkinson and Pepper are killed when the carriages in which they are riding collide. Wilson and Prince are rescued, and Wilkinson is buried beneath the silver ore after the train plunges off the broken bridge and into the river below. Hammer is called a hero, his Lone Ranger identity not revealed, and he is offered

Daniel Day-Lewis, Stephen McKinley Henderson and Joseph Gordon-Levitt in *Lincoln,* **2012.**

a law enforcement position, but he declines. He and Depp ride off on another adventure. As they reach a magnificent butte, Hammer revels in accepting his permanent identity as the heroic Lone Ranger and rears his white horse, shouting: "Hi-Yo! Silver!" Depp gives him a reproving scowl and says: "Don't ever do that again." With that they gallop off to legendary fame. In flash-forward to 1933, Cook, the boy at the San Francisco fair, questions Depp about the truth of his tale, and Depp gives him a silver bullet, telling him to decide for himself as he leaves the fair to meet his old friend, Hammer. Depp was never better than in his role of the enigmatic Tonto, close-mouthed, taciturn and resolute in the belief that he is a powerful mystic that knows everything and where he is guessing at events to come at almost every turn (and where Hammer repeatedly calls him a posturing fake). Hammer is a standout at the unbeatable Lone Ranger, a hero of heroes. There is a good deal of dark tongue-in-cheek humor that cleverly spoofs the beloved genre, and there is no end to spectacular eye-popping action, greatly aided by wonderfully conceived special effects. The battle on the two trains and where Hammer rides Silver atop and through the rollicking train cars while exchanging bullets with his adversaries is a sight to behold. Wilkinson, one of the most prolific aging character actors in the business (acutely reminiscent of John Houseman), is again superb as a consummate villain, and the rest of the cast members are also standouts in their roles. The film received Oscar nominations for Best Visual Effects (Alexander, Brozenich, Williams, Frazier) and Best Makeup and Hairstyling (Joel Harlow, Gloria Pasqua-Casny). The film enjoyed a great success at the box office, earning more than $260.5 million in its initial release against a budget of more than $225 million. Songs: "Blayton Races" (Trevor Thornton), "Tumbling Tumbleweeds" (Bob Nolan, Gordon V. Thompson), "William Tell Overture" (Gioachino Rossini), "After the Battle of Aughrim" (Hans Zimmer, Ann Marie Calhoun), "Hanson Place/Shall We Gather at the River" (traditional), "I'm Leaving You" (Bobby Johnston), "Mean-Ass Cattle" and "Traffic Circle" (Brian Satterwhite), "Celeste Aida" (Giuseppe Verdi), "The Glendy Burk" (traditional), "Battle Hymn of the Republic" (traditional), "Red's Theater of the Absurd" (Jack White), "Beautiful Dreamer" (Stephen Foster), "The Girl in the Flying Trapeze" (traditional/Jack White), "Dixie" (traditional), "Stars and Stripes Forever" (John Philip Sousa), "Marse Henry March" (Geoff Zanelli), "The Star Spangled Banner" (Francis Scott Key), "Swan Lake Op. 20, Suite I" (Pyotr Ilyich Tchaikovsky), "Bugle Charge" (traditional). *Author's Note:* Columbia Pictures first thought to produce this film as early as 2002, but the project was put on hold until 2008 when Disney decided to produce the film and signed Depp for the role of Tonto. Hammer was signed for the role of the Lone Ranger a short time before the film went into production in 2012, and where it was shot on location in Utah, New Mexico, Colorado, Arizona,

Mark Wahlberg, Taylor Kitsch, Emile Hirsch and Ben Foster in *Lone Survivor,* **2013.**

Texas and California. Other actors playing the Lone Ranger in other films include **The Legend of the Lone Ranger**, 1952 (Clayton Moore); **The Legend of the Lone Ranger**, 1981 (Klinton Spilsbury); **The Lone Ranger**, 1938 (serial; Lee Powell); **The Lone Ranger**, 1949-1957 (TV series; Clayton Moore); **The Lone Ranger**, 1956 (Clayton Moore); **The Lone Ranger**, 1966-1969 (TV series; Michael Rye); **The Lone Ranger**, 2003 (made-for-TV; Chad Michael Murray); **The Lone Ranger**, 2013 (Armie Hammer); and **The Lone Ranger Rides Again**, 1939 (serial; Robert Livingston). Intense violence and suggestive material prohibit viewing by children. **p**, Jerry Bruckheimer, Gore Verbinski; **d**, Verbinski; **cast**, Johnny Depp, Armie Hammer, William Fichtner, Tom Wilkinson, Ruth Wilson, Helena Bonham Carter, James Badge Dale, Bryant Prince, Barry Pepper, Mason Cook; **w**, Justin Haythe, Ted Elliott, Terry Rosio (based on their story and characters created by Fran Striker); **c**, Bojan Bazelli; **m**, Hans Zimmer; **ed**, James Haygood, Craig Wood; **prod d**, Jess Gonchor, Mark "Crash" McCreery; **art d**, Naaman Marshall, Iain McFadyen, James F. Oberlander, Domenic Silvestri; **set d**, Cheryl Carasik; **spec eff**, Tim Alexander, Gary Brozenich, Edson Williams, John Frazier.

Lone Survivor ★★★ 2013; U.S.; 121m; Emmett/Furla Films/UNIV; Color; War Drama; Children: Unacceptable (MPAA: R); **BD**; **DVD**. This action-packed war tale is based on the true adventures of Marcus Luttrell (b. 1975), A U.S. Navy SEAL. In Afghanistan in late June 2005, Taliban leader Ahmad Shah, portrayed by Azami, is responsible for killing more than twenty U.S. Marines, as well as villagers and refugees who were aiding American forces. In response to the killings, a U.S. Navy SEALs unit is ordered to execute a counterinsurgent mission to capture Azami. As part of the mission, a four-man SEAL reconnaissance and surveillance team is given the task of locating Azami. The SEAL unit includes team leader Michael Murphy, played by Kitsch; snipers Marcus Luttrell, portrayed by Wahlberg, and Matt Axelson, essayed by Foster; and communications specialist Danny Dietz, played by Hirsch. The team enters the Hindu Kush region of Afghanistan where they make a trek through the mountains. They begin to have communications problems that will play a critical role in events that follow. Arriving at their designated location, the team is accidentally discovered by an elderly shepherd and two teenage goat herders. Wahlberg convinces his comrades that they will incite backlash if they kill the three herders, so the team decides to release them and abort the mission. Before they can escape, however, they are discovered by Taliban forces. They manage to kill several Taliban soldiers, but find themselves to be heavily outnumbered and at a significant tactical disadvantage. Each of the team members suffers serious injuries during the firefight, and, in an attempt to flee from the insurgents, they jump off the edge of a cliff. Despite their injuries, the team runs through some woods. Hirsch begins to lose consciousness and shouts questions to Wahlberg, unwittingly revealing the team's position to the Taliban. Kitsch and Foster jump off another cliff to flee from the Taliban fighters. Wahlberg tries to carry Hirsch down the mountain, but Hirsch is shot in the shoulder. The impact forces Wahlberg to lose his grip and fall forward off the cliff. Hirsch remains dying at the top of the cliff and is taken into custody by the Taliban insurgents. Kitsch decides to try climbing back up the cliff to get a phone signal in order to call in support forces by satellite phone. Foster and Wahlberg shoot at the Taliban fighters to provide Kitsch with cover. When Kitsch finally reaches higher ground, he is able to alert the SEAL base of his team's location and ask for emergency assistance just before he is shot dead by Taliban fighters. A quick reaction force team boards two helicopters and heads for the location to rescue the remaining members of the SEAL team. Taliban insurgents shoot down one of the helicopters, killing eight Navy SEALs and eight Special Operations aviators who were on board. The second helicopter is forced to turn back. After witnessing the attack, Wahlberg and the badly injured Foster are left behind. Foster finds cover but is killed when he leaves his hiding place to attack some approaching insurgents. When the Taliban discover Wahlberg, one of the insurgents fires a rocket-propelled grenade whose impact causes Wahlberg to land at the bottom of a rock crevice where he is able to hide from the Taliban. He finds a little water and submerges himself only to find upon surfacing that a local villager, Mohammad Gulab, played by Suliman, has discovered his location. Suliman takes Wahlberg into his care, returning with him to his village, and there attempts to hide him in his home. Suliman then sends a mountain man to the nearest American air base to alert officials there of Wahlberg's location. Taliban fighters arrive at the village to capture and kill Wahlberg, but Suliman and other villagers intervene, threatening to kill the fighters if they harm Wahlberg. The fighters leave, but later return to punish the villagers for protecting Wahlberg. He and Suliman are able to fend off several fighters during an ensuing attack. The remaining Taliban fighters are chased off by American forces who arrive by helicopter and take Wahlberg to safety, the lone survivor of the harrowing mission. The film ends with a four-minute photo montage of the real-life Marcus Luttrell, Mohammad Gulab, and the fallen soldiers who died during the mission. Wahlberg, Kitsch, Hirsch and Foster shine in their heroic roles, and director Berg presents a gritty, uncompromising portrait of war to startling effect in every chilling scene. In addition to an intelligent script, the lensing is also exceptional, and the harrowing battle sequences are superbly choreographed. The film received Oscar nominations for Best Sound Editing (Wylie Stateman), and Best Sound Mixing (Andy Koyama, Beau Borders, David Brownlow). The film was a success at the box office, earning more than $154.8 million in its initial release against a budget of more than $49 million. Songs: "Canned Heat" (Sola Akingbola, Wallis Buchanan, Simon Katz, Jason Kay, Toby Smith, Derrick McKenzie), "Heroes" (David Bowie, Brian Eno), "Aerials" (Christopher Franzen). Excessive violence and pervasive gutter language prohibit viewing by children. **p**, Sarah Aubrey, Randall Emmett, Akiva Goldsman, Norton Herrick, Stephen Levinson, Barry Spikings, Mark Wahlberg, Dama Claire, Brandon Grimes, Petra Holtorf; **d&w**, Peter Berg (based on the book by Marcus Luttrell, Patrick Robinson); **cast**, Wahlberg, Taylor Kitsch, Emile Hirsch, Ben Foster, Eric Bana, Yousuf Azami, Ali Suliman, Alexander Ludwig, Rich Ting, Dan Bilzerian; **c**, Tobias Schliessler; **m**, Steve Jablonsky, Explosions in the Sky; **ed**, Colby Parker Jr.; **prod d**, Tom Duffield; **art d**, Steve Cooper; **set d**, Ron Reiss; **spec eff**, William Aldridge, Bruno Van Zeebroeck.

The Longest Ride ★★★ 2015; U.S.; 139m; FOX; Color; Drama/Romance; Children: Unacceptable (MPAA: PG-13); **BD**; **DVD**. Intriguing star-crossed love affair involves Eastwood, a former champion bull rider, and Robertson, a college student. He is trying to make a comeback while she is about to begin her dream job in the art world of New York City. Their divergent paths and interests test their relationship while a secondary love story enters the picture. That creates inspiration for East-wood and Robertson as they meet Alda, who has been deeply in love with his wife for many years and they remain together. The love stories intertwine as they span generations to explore the challenges and re-wards of enduring love. To a rodeo bull rider, love may be the longest and most rewarding ride. Eastwood wins his last ride and then retires from the rodeos forever, telling Robertson that he would rather be with her. Moreover, when Eastwood attends an auction of Alda's paintings, he purchases one of them, a portrait of Chaplin, Alda's wife, both of them by now dead. Eastwood then learns to his surprise that he has in-herited all of Alda's priceless works in buying the one portraying Chap-lin, as decreed in Alda's will. This pleasing tale sees fine performances from the entire cast and presents a story that will warm the heart of any viewer. The film performed well at the box office, earning almost $70 million in its initial release against a budget of more than $34 million. Songs: "Get Free" (Craig Nicholls), "Games" (Nili Ohayon, Jonathan Levy), "Show Pony" (Eric Christopher Owen, Kevin Michael McKe-own), "Terrorize" and "Dimebag Damage" (Zack Tempest), "Small Stuff" (Dan Robinson, Benn Cutarelli), "Sleep with a Stranger" and "The Ceiling" (Barry Dean, Luke Laird, Nikki Lane), "Backwoods Company" (Taylor Burns, Ricky Young, Joel King, Leroy Wulfmeier), "Got It Bad for Yah" (Matthew Masurka, Danielle Parente), "I Feel a Sin Comin' On" (Miranda Lambert, Ashley Monroe, Angaleena Pres-ley), "Blue Eyes" (Matthew Vasquez), "Real Man" (David Henzerling, John Covington, Robert Mason, John Colby), "Reverberocket" (John Hott, Bryan Harvey), "Double Up" (Zach Danziger), "Learn It All Again Tomorrow" (Ben Harper), "Chattanooga Choo Choo" (music: Harry Warren; lyrics: Mack Gordon), "Danger: Love at Work" (music: Harry Revel; lyrics: Mack Gordon), "Hi-Ya Love" (music: Ralph Rainger; lyrics: Leo Robin), "Partypocalypse" (David Whiteside, Dawn Jordan), "On Tonight" (Josh Abbott, Sunny Helms), "Dancing to the Radio" (Adan Jodorowsky), "Warm Water" (Jillian Banks, Orlando Higginbot-tom), "Desire" (Ryan Adams), "Love Like This" (Stephen Garrigan, Vincent May, Mark Prendergast), "Deeply" (King Britt, Natasha Kmeto), "Gotta Get It On" (Carlos Nino), "Hot Tub Love" (James Brad-dell, Kier Fraser), "The Sky in Ione" and "Fighter Strike" (Ted Caplan), "Keep Moving" (Andrew Stockdale), "The Curse" (Matt Vandervan-der), "Dead in Your Tracks" (Brian Tichy), "Wildfire" (Stephen Robson, Harry Draper, Jack Stedman, Lisa Scinta). *Author's Note*: Scott East-wood is the real-life son of Clint Eastwood and looks like a younger version of him, and he offers on the screen the same kind of empathetic persona his father has exhibited over many decades. The film was shot in North Carolina, where action shots of an actual rodeo were incorpo-rated into its scenes. For other films about rodeos, see Subject Index, Rodeos and Rodeo Performers. Sexuality, partial nudity and violent ac-tion prohibit viewing by children. **p**, Marty Bowen, Wyck Godfrey, Theresa Park, Nicholas Sparks, H.H. Cooper; **d**, George Tillman, Jr.; **cast**, Britt Robertson, Scott Eastwood, Alan Alda, Jack Huston, Oona Chaplin, Melissa Benoist, Lolita Davidovich, Elea Oberon, Kate Forbes, Tiago Riani, Danny Vinson; **w**, Craig Bolotin (based on the novella by Nicholas Sparks); **c**, David Tattersall; **m**, Mark Isham; **ed**, Jason Bal-lantine; **prod d**, Mark Garner; **art d**, Geoffrey S. Grimsman; **set d**, Chuck Potter; **spec eff**, Ken Gorrell, Joe Pancake.

The Longest Week ★★★ 2014; U.S.; 86m; Armian Pictures/Gravitas Ventures; Color; Comedy/Romance; Children: Unacceptable (MPAA: PG-13); **BD**; **DVD**. Pleasant romantic comedy focuses upon Bateman, who is an aimless young man living a life of leisure in his parents' pres-tigious Manhattan hotel. His princely lifestyle evaporates when a di-vorce acrimoniously separates his parents, leaving him broke and homeless. He moves in with Crudup, a friend, and meets Wilde, the woman of his dreams, only to find that she is already dating Crudup. The trio romantically maneuvers until Bateman and Wilde come to-gether, but theirs is not a lasting union. Clever and amusing, the storyline and characters owe much to Woody Allen's brilliant **Annie Hall**, 1977,

Scott Eastwood in *The Longest Ride,* 2015.

but there is much to appreciate and enjoy for its own entertaining sake and Crudup, Wilde and Bateman shine as empathetic persons. Sexual content and smoking prohibit viewing by children. **p**, Neda Armian, Uday Chopra; **d**, Peter Glanz; **cast**, Jason Bateman, Olivia Wilde, Billy Crudup, Jenny Slate, Erin Darke, Tony Roberts, Barbara Schultz, An-thony Laciura, Jayce Bartok, Steve Witting; **w**, Glanz (based on a story by Glanz, Juan Iglesias); **c**, Ben Kutchins; **m**, Jay Israelson; **ed**, Sarah Flack; **prod d**, Rick Butler; **set d**, Amy Williams; **spec eff**, Jonathan Podwil.

Lore ★★★ 2012; Germany/Australia/U.K.; 109m; Rohfilm/Music Box Films; Color; Drama; Children: Unacceptable; **BD**; **DVD**. Taut tale takes place in Germany at the close of World War II (1939-1945), where Wagner, the head of a once-prominent German family, and his wife, Lardi, flee their once-luxurious home in southwestern Germany because they fear the approaching Allied forces will punish or execute them for having been high-level Nazis, who were aware of the Nazi genocide of Jews. They leave behind their teenage daughter Lore, played by Rosendahl, and four younger children, telling her to lead them to Hagen, their grandmother, who lives in Husum, near Hamburg, beyond the Black Forest. Their arduous journey takes place on foot, some 900 miles, through dense and muddy woods. In the woods, they meet a young Jewish man, Malina, who survived a concentration camp, and he becomes their guardian. Malina gets them passage on a train to Ham-burg but is stopped by Russian soldiers, who ask for his passport. He has none, so he leaves the train to avoid being arrested. Rosendahl and her siblings finally reach their grandmother's house, and she feeds and gives them shelter. Hagen tells them not to be ashamed of their parents. Rosendahl, however, has learned from Malina and others on the journey that Hitler was not the god she thought he had been, but had been a monster that led Germany to ruin while he and others instigated the ex-termination of Jews. The tale teaches visually with impressionistic im-ages but without lecturing, and the acting is uniformly above average as is the firm direction and the sound script. Songs/Music: "Junge will Marschieren" (traditional), "Marschmusic: Von Finnland bis zum Schwarzen Meer/In Finland By the Black Sea" (traditional), "Ich hatte einen Kameraden/I Have a Comrade" (Ludwig Uhland), "Der Mond ist Aufgegagen" (Paul Gerhardt), "Bruderchen, komm tanz mit mir/Brother, Come Dance with Me" (Engelbert Humperdinck), "Match Box Blues" (Blind Lemon Jefferson), "Ein Mannlein steht in Walde" (August von Fallersleben), "Don't Bring Lulu" (1925; Lew Brown, Ray Henderson, Billy Rose); **p**, Benny Drechse, Karsten Stoter, Liz Watts, Paul Welsh; **d**, Cate Shortland; **cast**, Saskia Rosendahl, Kai Malina, Nele Trebs, Mike Weidner, Ursina Lardi, Hans-Jochen Wagner, Nick Leander Holaschke, Andre Frid, Mika Seidel, Sven Pippig, Philip

Tom Hardy in *Mad Max: Fury Road*, 2015.

Wiegratz; **w**, Shortland, Robin Mukherjee (based on the *novel The Dark Room* by Rachel Seiffert); **c**, Adam Arkapaw; **m**, Max Richter; **ed**, Veronika Jenet; **prod d**, Silke Fischer; **art d**, Jochen Dehn; **spec eff**, Geoff Aitken, John Durney, Rod Wallwork.

Love and Mercy ★★★ 2015; U.S.; 121m; River Road Entertainment; Roadside Attractions; Color; Biographical Drama; Children: Unacceptable (MPAA: PG-13); **BD**; **DVD**. Fascinating biopic portrays the life and artistry of Brian Wilson (b. 1942), songwriter, singer, and co-founder of the top rock group the Beach Boys in the 1960s and one of the most influential creative forces in popular music. Portrayed by Dano in youth and Cusack in old age, he is shown to be paying a heavy price for fame with drugs and alcohol as he tries to please his abusive father. His demons drive him to a nervous breakdown that has long-lasting psychological effects. As Dano, success causes him to suffer a jarring panic attack and he quits concert touring with the Beach Boys and everyone else. He retreats to a studio where, now unhinged, he plans to create the greatest musical album, one consisting of pet sounds. In the 1980s, as Cusack, he was able to function, but just barely, while he is under the domination Giamatti, who plays Dr. Eugene Landy (1934-2006), a destructive psychotherapist. This treatment, however, enables him to fall in love with Banks, who sells Cadillacs. She becomes aware of Giamatti's abuse and tries to break Cusack from his dependence on drugs as well as the rather sinister control Giamatti wields over him. Though the film is reminiscent of many patient-therapist tales, especially **Whirlpool**, 1949 (where self-styled psychologist Jose Ferrer manipulates troubled Gene Tierney into believing she is a murderer), the story presents its own unique Svengali interpretations and many chilling scenes. Cusack is outstanding as the willing victim who thinks his therapist is his only grip on reality; the gifted Giamatti is superb as the mind-controlling guru (he has never failed to give a stunning performance), and Banks is a standout as a positive rescuer, who can only combat the evils of insanity and drug abuse with the power of her limitless love. In addition to a mesmerizing dramatic portrait, the film also details the brilliantly innovative techniques Wilson employed when originally making his marvelous recordings. The film did well at the box office, earning more than $26 million in its initial release. The film contains many songs performed on soundtrack by the Beach Boys. Songs: "Surfin' U.S.A." (Chuck Berry); "Don't Worry Baby" (Brian Wilson, Roger Christian); "Surfer Girl," "Pet Sounds," "Love and Mercy," "Hang on to Your Ego," "Sloop John B," "The Element: Fire (Mrs. O'Leary's Cow)," "Til I Die"" (Brian Wilson), "I Get Around," "Fun, Fun, Fun," "I'm Waiting for the Day," "Good Vibrations" (Brian Wilson, Mike Love); "Songbird" (Kenny Gorelick); "These Dreams" (Martin Page, Bernard Taupin); "Nowhere to Run" (Brian Holland, Edward Holland Jr., Lamont

Dozier); "The In Crowd" (Bill Page); "On the Wings of Love" (Jeffrey Osborne, Petr Schless); "Nights in White Satin" (Justin Hayward); "God Only Knows," "You Still Believe in Me," "Caroline, No," "Don't Talk/Put Your Head on My Shoulder" (Brian Wilson, Tony Asher); "Wouldn't It Be Nice" (Wilson, Love, Asher); "I Live for the Sun" (Rick Henn); "Heart Full of Soul" (Graham Gouldman); "You Don't Have to Say You Love Me" (Giuseppe Donaggio, Simon Napier-Bell, Vito Pallavinci, Vicki Wickham); "Surf's Up," "Heroes & Villains," "Do You Like Worms" (Wilson, Van Dyke Parks); "In My Room" (Wilson, Gary Usher); "Day By Day" (Sammy Cahn, Axel Stordhahl, Paul Weston); "One Kind of Love" (Wilson, Scott Bennett); "Black Hole," "End Date," "Believe," "Silhouette," "Headphones," "Knives and Forks," "Deep End," "Baby No Morph," "Bed Montage," "Into Mercy," (Atticus Ross); "Be My Baby" (Jeff Barry, Ellie Greenwich, Phil Spector). Thematic elements, drug content and gutter language prohibit viewing by children. **p**, Bill Pohlad, Claire Rudnick Polstein, John Wells; **d**, Pohlad; **cast**, John Cusack, Paul Dano, Elizabeth Banks, Paul Giamatti, Jake Abel, Kenny Wormald, Graham Rogers, Joanna Going, Bill Camp, Brett Davern, Tyson Ritter, Nick Gehlfuss, Erin Darke; **w**, Michael Alan Lerner, Oren Moverman (based on the life of Brian Wilson); **c**, Robert D. Yeoman; **m**, Atticus Ross; **ed**, Dino Jonsater; **prod d**, Keith P. Cunningham; **art d**, Andrew Max Cahn, Luke Freeborn; **set d**, Maggie Martin; **spec eff**, Anthony Simonaitis.

Love Is All You Need ★★★ 2012; Denmark/Sweden/Italy/France/Germany; 116m; Zentropa Productions/Sony; Color; Comedy/Romance; Children: Unacceptable (MPAA: R); **BD**; **DVD**. Entertaining romantic tale sees Dyrholm as a young Danish woman who has just completed cancer treatments. She walks in on her husband, who is in bed with his young coworker. Disenchanted with her marriage, she travels alone to her daughter's wedding in Italy where she meets the groom's widowed father, Brosnan, and immediately makes a bad first impression. At a seaside villa where Brosnan once lived with his wife, conflicts arise between the bridal couple before the wedding, which is called off. First impressions fly out the window, and Dyrholm sees a chance for a new life with Brosnan after he relocates in Italy and Dyrholm goes after him. The film produced more than $10 million from the box office in its initial release against a budget of more than $7 million. Songs: "That's Amore" (Harry Warren, Jak Brooks), "Sara Perche Ti Amo" (Dario Farina), "Tintarella di Luna" (Mina), "Buona Serea Signorina" (Sigman/De Rose), "Happy Birthday" (Mildred J. Hill, Patty S. Hill), "I dag er det Oles fodselsdag" (Otto Mikkelsen). Sexuality, nudity and gutter language prohibit viewing by children. **p**, Sisse Graum Jorgensen, Vibeke Windelov, Remi Burah, Lionello Cerri, Madeleine Ekman, Maria Kopf, Peter Nadermann, Charlotte Pedersen, Martin Persson, Cesar Petrillo, Vieri Razzini, Marianne Slot, Sigrid Strohmann, Meinolf Zurhorst; **d**, Susanne Bier; **cast**, Trine Dyrholm, Pierce Brosnan, Sebastian Jessen, Molly Blixt Egelind, Marco D'Amore, Stina Ekblad, Line Kruse, Paprika Steen, Birthe Neumann, Kim Bodnia; **w**, Anders Thomas Jensen (based on a story by Jensen, Bier); **c**, Morten Soborg; **m**, Johan Soderqvist; **ed**, Pernille Bech Christensen, Morten Egholm; **prod d**, Peter Grant; **art d**, Tamara Marini; **spec eff**, Hummer Hoimark, Lars Werner Nielsen Lalo.

The Love Punch ★★★ 2014; U.K./France; 94m; Process Media; Ketchup Entertainment; Color; Comedy; Children: Unacceptable (MPAA: PG-13); **BD**; **DVD**. Pleasant comedy begins with a bickering divorced British couple, Thompson and Brosnan, who have two children and resort to drastic efforts when Brosnan loses his retirement money after his company is sold to Lafitte, a corrupt French businessman. They go to Paris where Lafitte blatantly admits that he has swindled them. In retaliation, they plan to steal a diamond worth $10 million, the amount taken by the underhanded Lafitte, and which he plans to give to his intended, Bourgoin, but, along the way, Brosnan and Thompson have second thoughts about their divorce as they bond to achieve sweet revenge.

The film had a weak showing at the box office, earning less than $5 million in its initial release. **p,** Jean-Charles Levy, Clement Miserez, Tim Perell, Nicola Usborne; **d&w,** Joel Hopkins; **cast,** Emma Thompson, Pierce Brosnan, Timothy Spall, Tuppence Middleton, Laurent Lafitte, Marisa Berenson, Celia Imrie, Louise Bourgoin, Sabine Crossen, Christopher Craig, Jordan Jones; **c,** Jerome Almeras; **m,** Jean-Michel Bernard; **ed,** Susan Littenberg; **prod d,** Patrick Durand; **art d,** Fanny Stauff; **spec eff,** Cyrille Bonjean.

Low Down ★★★ 2014; U.S.; 114m; Bona Fide Productions/Oscilloscope Pictures; Color; Biographical Drama; Children: Unacceptable (MPAA: R); **BD; DVD.** Well-made biopic takes a longing look at the life of modern jazz pianist Joe Albany (Joseph Alboni, 1924-1988), played by Hawkes, from the perspective of his young daughter Amy, who is played by Fanning, as she watches him contend with his drug addiction during the 1960s and 1970s jazz scene. Good performances are seen all around in a story that has been often told, but here sees a lot of new twists and turns. (Albeit it is very reminiscent of **Too Much, Too Soon,** 1958, where Dorothy Malone, as Diana Barrymore, sees her legendary father, John Barrymore, magnificently played by Errol Flynn, disintegrate under the ravages of alcohol.) This film saw limited distribution, but deserved a wider audience. Drug use, gutter language and sexual content prohibit viewing by children. **p,** Albert Berger, Mindy Goldberg, Ron Yerxa; **d,** Jeff Preiss; **cast,** John Hawkes, Taryn Manning, Elle Fanning, Glenn Close, Lena Headey, Peter Dinklage, Burn Gorman, Tim Daly, Caleb Landry Jones, Ronnie Rodriguez; **w,** Topper Lilien, Amy Albany (based on her memoir); **c,** Christopher Blauvelt; **m,** Ohad Talmor; **ed,** Michael Saia; **prod d,** Elliott Hostetter; **art d,** Mark Robert Taylor; **set d,** Chilly Nathan; **spec eff,** Steve Tozzi.

The Lunchbox ★★★★ 2014; India/France/Germany/U.S.; 104m; Sikhya Entertainment/Sony; Color; Drama/Romance; Children: Unacceptable (MPAA: PG); **BD; DVD.** A mistaken delivery in Mumbai's famously efficient lunchbox delivery system connects a young housewife, Kaur, to an older man, Khan, in the waning years of his life as they build a fantasy world together through notes in the lunchbox. Khan has been grieving since his wife died, and Kaur wants to win the attention and affection of her husband Vaid by cooking delicious meals for him. Because of a rare mix-up, the lunchbox Kaur had prepared for her husband gets delivered instead to Khan. Realizing the mistake, Kaur writes Khan a note about it. This leads to an exchange of notes in the lunchbox and Kaur learns that her husband is having an affair, so she writes to Khan about it and says she wants to move to Bhutan where she is told people are known to be happy. Khan considers moving there with her and writes back about that. Kaur replies, saying she would like to meet him first. They arrange to meet at a food center, but Khan does not show up. Disappointed, the next day Kaur sends him an empty lunchbox. Khan sends her a lunchbox note saying he did not meet with her because he thought himself too old for her, and suggests that she go to Bhutan alone and find a new life. Kaur learns where Khan works and goes to meet him, but when there she learns he has left and is going to Nashik. He goes there, but returns to Mumbai and searches for Kaur, but we do not learn if these two frustrated love-hungry people ever meet to find happiness. This offbeat love story is somewhat frustrating, but intrigues as two characters, both superbly enacted, grope for each other's affections while examining their own lives. This expertly directed and well-written film saw a modest success at the box office, earning more than $15 million in its initial release against a budget of more than $3.3 million. Thematic material and smoking prohibit viewing by children. **p,** Anurag Kashyap, Guneet Monga, Arun Rangachari, Shahnaab Alam, Marc Baschet, Benny Drechsel, Nina Lath Gupta, Sunil John, Siddarth Roy Kapur, Nittin Keni, Cedomir Kolar, Vivek Rangachari, Karsten Stoter, Danis Tanovic; **d&w,** Ritesh Batra; **cast,** Irrfan Khan, Nimrat Kaur, Nakul Vaid, Nawazuddin Siddiqui, Lillete Dubey, Bharati Achrekar, Yashvi Puneet Nagar, Denzil Smith, Shruti Bapna, Lokesh Raj; **c,**

Ambyr Childers, Rami Malek and Philip Seymour Hoffman in *The Master,* **2012.**

Michael Simmonds; **m,** Max Richter; **ed,** John F. Lyons; **prod d,** Shruti Gupte; **set d,** Akshi Kapoor; **spec eff,** Abhishek Goel, Prasad Patel.

Macbeth ★★★★ 2015 (U.K./France/U.S.; 113m; See-Saw Films/Weinstein; Color; Drama/War; Children: Unacceptable (MPAA: R); **BD; DVD.** This well-made and very faithful new filming of the legendary Shakespeare play opens with three witches plotting to meet with the melancholy Dane, Macbeth, wonderfully portrayed by Fassbender. We then see a wounded sergeant report to King Duncan of Scotland, essayed by Thewlis, that Macbeth, the Thane of Glamis, and his friend Banquo, played by Considine, have been victorious in defeating the combined armies of Norway and Ireland. Fassbender and Constantine are seen recalling their victorious battle before they are greeted by the witches, who tell them some prophesies, including that Fassbender will soon be king. The witches then vanish, and Fassbender learns that the Thane of Cawdor is to be put to death for treason and Fassbender will take his place and title. This fulfills the first of the witches' prophesies. Fassbender's mother, Lady Macbeth, played by Cotillard, now wants him to murder the king, so he can be crowned in his place. He agrees and they plot to get Thewlis drunk and kill him, planning to blame his murder on two chamberlains. Fassbender stabs Thewlis, and the next morning the monarch's body is discovered. Fassbender then murders the chamberlains to keep them from claiming they are innocent of the crime. Through these brutal actions, Fassbender becomes King of Scotland. Considine is now uneasy because the witches had predicted that, while he would never become king, his descendants would. Fassbender also becomes uneasy, remembering that prophesy. Fassbender now plots to have Considine murdered so he hires three assassins to do the job. They succeed in killing Considine, but his young son escapes, so now Fassbender feels insecure as long as the son lives. At a banquet in the palace, Considine's ghost appears and sits in Fassbender's place, but only Fassbender can see the spirit. Guests panic when they see Fassbender ranting at an empty chair and think he has gone mad. Cotillard assures everyone that he is only temporarily afflicted with a malady. Fassbender visits the three witches, and they foretell more events to relieve his fears about his future. Cotillard, mentally disturbed with guilt, begins sleepwalking and, while in a trance, tries to wash the blood of her victims off of her hands. She has gone mad. Fassbender has meanwhile had the wife and children of another nobleman, Macduff, played by Harris, murdered, so Harris vows revenge. Harris leads an invasion of Fassbender's palace with the support of Scottish nobles who have become unnerved by the king's murderous behavior. Before the invasion, Fassbender receives news that Cotillard has committed suicide. Fassbender descends into

Madisen Beaty and Joaquin Phoenix in *The Master*, 2012.

near-madness while trying to defend himself and his rule. He continues to fight even though he feels doomed. Harris kills and beheads him, thus fulfilling the third prophesy of the witches that Fassbender would not remain king for a prolonged period. Although this version of the classic drama is the most sumptuously mounted and its production values are most impressive, Fassbender's exceptional performance challenges but cannot surpass that of Orson Welles in the 1948 version. Nevertheless, this is most likely the most effective and telling version of that great tragedy, where the invasion of madness into human minds is chillingly depicted in mesmerizing scenes. The film, unhappily, did not do as well as expected at the box office, earning more than $11.3 million in its initial release against a budget of almost $20 million. Violence prohibits viewing by children. **p**, Iain Canning, Laura Hastings-Smith, Emile Sherman, Andrew Warren; **d**, Justin Kurzel; **cast**, Michael Fassbender, Marion Cotillard, Sean Harris, Elizabeth Debicki, David Thewlis, Jack Reynor, Paddy Considine, David Hayman, Rebecca Benson, Lynn Kennedy, Maurice Reeves; **w**, Jacob Koskoff, Michael Lesslie, Todd Louiso (based on the play by William Shakespeare); **c**, Adam Arkapaw; **m**, Jed Kurzel; **ed**, Chris Dickens; **prod d**, Fiona Crombie; **art d**, Nick Dent; **set d**, Alice Felton; **spec eff**, Mike Kelt.

Mad Max: Fury Road ★★★ 2015; Australia/U.S.; 120m; Kennedy Miller Mitchell/WB; Color; Adventure/Science Fiction; Children: Unacceptable (MPAA: PG-13); **BD**; **DVD**, **IV**. In this new and exciting entry in the Mad Max series, Earth becomes a desert wasteland and civilization barely survives after a nuclear holocaust. One of the survivors, Max, portrayed by Hardy, is captured by an army of thugs called the War Boys and taken to the citadel of their leader, Joe, played by Keays-Byrne. Hardy is imprisoned and made a universal blood donor to keep alive sick War Boys. Meanwhile, one of Keays-Byrne's lieutenants called Furiosa, essayed by Theron, is sent to obtain gasoline for the army's vehicles. En route, she learns that Keays-Byrne has five wives, women he chose strictly to bear him children, and that the women are missing. Keayes-Byrne now pursues Theron with his army, having Hardy strapped to his car so he can keep supplying blood. Hardy escapes and helps Theron. Some menacing bikers now pursue them as Theron tells Hardy they are escaping to a peaceful land called the "Green Place" that she remembers from her childhood. They drive through swamps and deserts until they find the "Green Place," but discover that it is no longer what Theron remembered and is now unfit for human life. They then ride across salt flats to search for another land of refuge, but eventually they return to the citadel. There they are attacked by Keays-Byrne and his army, but Keays-Byrne is killed. Hardy, Theron, and the missing wives are all welcomed by the now-friendly War Boys, but Hardy decides to go away to be on his own again, a res-

olute nomad in a desolate and uninviting world. Like its predecessors, the viewer is offered in this updated action-loaded tale the same kind of grim, cruel world inhabited by lethal maniacs. And, again, like its predecessors, breathtaking special effects action dominates the dire story line. Only smidgeons of decency emerge from a few of its characters, but all are well-enacted in a soundly constructed tale. The spectacular action is superbly choreographed, but it is nevertheless an artistic dance of death a la Hieronymus Bosch. The film was nominated for ten Oscars, including Best Picture and Best Director. It was a smash hit at the box office, its mostly teenage audience flocking to theaters where it earned more than $375.8 million in its initial release against a budget of more than $150 million. Songs/Music: "Elegy for Rosa," "Refugee's Theme Symphonic Variation No. 1 (Ellini Karaindrou), "Requiem Mass, Das Irae" (Guiseppe Verdi), "Teardrop" Intense violence throughout and disturbing images prohibit viewing by children. **p**, George Miller, Doug Mitchell, P.J. Voeten; **d**, Miller; **cast**, Tom Hardy, Charlize Theron, Nicholas Hoult, Hugh Keays-Byrne, Josh Helman, Nathan Jones, Zoe Kravitz, Riley Keough, Abbey Lee, Courtney Eaton, Rosie Huntington-Whiteley; **w**, Miller, Brendan McCarthy, Nick Lathouris; **c**, John Seale; **m**, Tom Holkenborg; **ed**, Margaret Sixel; **prod d**, Colin Gibson; **art d**, Shira Hockman, Jacinta Leong; **set d**, Katie Sharrock, Lisa Thompson; **spec eff**, Dan Oliver, Andy Williams.

Magic in the Moonlight ★★★ 2014; U.S.; 97m; Dippermouth/Sony; Color; Comedy/Romance; Children: Unacceptable (MPAA: PG-13); **BD**; **DVD**. Exciting romantic comedy begins in 1928 Berlin where Firth is a worldwide famous illusionist known as Wei Ling Soo. After performing his magic act and walking off the stage, we see that he is really an Englishman named Stanley. He is not a very pleasant person, berating his employers and even well-wishers. He is greeted in his dressing room by old friend and fellow illusionist McBurney, who asks him to go with him to the Cote d'Azur of France where he believes a wealthy American family has been taken in by a clairvoyant and mystic, Stone. The family's son, Linklater, has fallen in love with Stone, and his sister, Leerhsen, and brother-in-law, Shamos, fear that Linklater is going to propose marriage to Stone. McBurney admits to Firth that he has not been able to discover the secrets behind Stone's tricks and the more he watches her perform them, the more he believes she may really have supernatural powers. He asks Firth, who has exposed charlatan mystics in the past, to help him prove Stone is a fraud. They travel to the French Riviera and go to the mansion where the family resides, and Firth is soon amazed to see Stone go into a trance and reveal highly personal details about him and his family. Firth then witnesses a séance where Stone communicates with the rich family's deceased patriarch. A candle floats upward from the table, and McBurney grabs it to try to learn what trick Stone has performed. However, he cannot discover her secret. Firth then spends some time with Stone and takes her to visit his aunt, Atkins. On the drive there they are caught in a heavy rain storm and end up at an observatory that Firth had visited as a child. After the storm passes, they open the observatory's roof and gaze at the stars. While visiting Atkins and holding her pearls, Stone tells Firth details of Atkins' one great love affair. That convinces Firth that Stone really has mystic powers and is so taken by her unfettered perceptions that he now looks at the world with new eyes. Stone asks Firth if he has any romantic feelings for her, but he says he has not, which disappoints her. The next day, Firth holds a press conference to tell the world that he had been debunking mystics as fakes, but has met one who is genuine. The news conference is interrupted by news that Atkins has been in a car accident. He rushes to the hospital where she was taken and, while in a waiting room, considers turning to prayer in hopes of her life being spared. He begins praying for a miracle to save her life, but then is unable to go through with it. His cold reasoning rejects prayer while he is consumed with the idea that Stone does not possess supernatural powers. He sets out once more to prove that she is a fraud. Firth overhears Stone and Linklater talking about their parts in an elaborate ruse, and uses a trick from his stage act, which leads him to discover how Stone has been able to learn so much about him and Atkins. Linklater, who has by now fallen in love with Stone, had told her about Atkins' great love. Firth now knows that Stone is a charlatan out to swindle the rich family. Atkins recovers from her injury, and Firth comes to realize he is nevertheless in love with Stone and asks her to marry him. She rejects him, saying she is going to marry Linklater. She then changes her mind, accepts Firth's proposal, and the film happily ends (as do all satisfying romantic comedies) with a loving embrace and a kiss. Firth and Stone shine in this romantic cat-and-mouse tale, which is evocative of the pleasant comedies of the 1930s of which director Allen is so fond (and where he has always found such rich story line grist). The magic tricks are impressively presented, recalling the eerie séances shown in such films as **Houdini**, 1953, and **Ministry of Fear**, 1944, while the crisp lensing and delightful score (sprinkled with Allen's favorite tunes from songsmiths Porter, Rodgers and others) add much to the production values, as do the faithful period costumes and sets. It isn't **Annie Hall**, but nevertheless delivers the kind of warm-hearted entertainment that has so effectively enriched audiences over the decades. The film fared well at the box office, earning more than $32.3 million in its initial release against a budget of more than $16.8 million. Songs: "You Do Something to Me" (Cole Porter), "Adoration of the Earth" from "The Rite of Spring" (Igor Stravinsky), "Bolero" (Maurice Ravel), "Molto Vivace" from "Symphony No. 9 in D Minor" (Ludwig van Beethoven), "It's All a Swindle" (Mischa Spoliansky, Marcellus Schiffer), "Moritat" (Kurt Weill), "Dancing with Tears in My Eyes" (Joseph A. Burke), "Thou Swell" (music: Richard Rodgers; lyrics, Lorenz Hart), "Big Boy" (Milton Ager), "I'm Always Chasing Rainbows" (music: Fredric Chopin, Harry Carroll; lyrics: Joseph McCarthy), "Sorry" (Raymond Klages), "The Sheik of Araby" (music: Ted Snyder; lyrics: Harry B. Smith, Francis Wheeler), "Who" (music: Jerome Kern; lyrics: Oscar Hammerstein II, Otto Harbach), "Chinatown, My Chinatown" (William Jerome, Jean Schwartz), "Remember Me" (Sonny Miller), "Charleston" (James P. Johnson, R.C. McPherson), "Sweet Georgia Brown" (Ben Bernie, Kenneth Casey, Maceo Pinkard), "You Call It Madness, but I Call It Love" (Con Conrad, Gladys DuBois, Russ Colombo, Paul Gregory), "At the Jazz Band Ball" (Larry Shields, Anthony S. Barbaro, D. James LaRocca, Edwin B. Edwards), "It All Depends On You" (Lew Brown, B.G. DeSylva, Ray Henderson), "I'll Get By, As Long As I Have You" (Fred E. Ahlert, Roy Turk). Smoking and brief suggestive comments prohibit viewing by children. **p**, Letty Aronson, Stephen Tenenbaum, Edward Walson, Raphael Benoliel, Helen Robin; **d&w**, Woody Allen; **cast**, Colin Firth, Emma Stone, Eileen Atkins, Marcia Gay Harden, Simon McBurney, Hamish Linklater, Jacki Weaver, Catherine McCormack, Jeremy Shamos, Erica Leerhsen; **c**, Darius Khondji; **ed**, Alisa Lepselter; **prod d**, Anne Seibel; **set d**, Jille Azis; **spec eff**, Andrew Lim, Laurens Ehrmann.

Maleficent ★★★ 2014; U.S.; 97m; Moving Picture Company/Walt Disney Pictures; Color; Adventure; Children: Unacceptable (MPAA: PG-13); **BD**; **DVD**; **3-D**. This visually exciting live-action film is based on the 1959 animated film **Sleeping Beauty** in which the villainess Maleficent, portrayed by Jolie, reveals the events that hardened her heart at the christening of Princess Aurora and that drove her to curse the baby, only to later realize Aurora may hold the key to peace in the land. Driven by revenge for not being invited to the christening, which was an accident, she has a fierce desire to protect the moors over which she presides. She curses baby Aurora, the human king's daughter. As Aurora grows to be Fanning she is caught in the middle of the conflict between the forest kingdom she has grown to love and the human kingdom that holds her legacy. Jolie realizes that Aurora may hold the secret to security and happiness in the land and is forced to take drastic actions that will change both the forest and human worlds forever. Jolie is exceptional as she embodies the very essence of the antagonistic Maleficent, and the marvelous special effects hold visual sway for the

Joaquin Phoenix in *The Master*, 2012.

viewer. The film received an Oscar nomination for Best Costume Design (Anna B. Sheppard). The film saw a huge success at the box office, earning more than $785.5 million in its initial release against a budget of more than $180 million. Song: "Once Upon a Dream" (Sammy Fain, Jack Lawrence). Violence and frightening images prohibit viewing by children. **p**, Joe Roth, Scott Michael Murray; **d**, Robert Stromberg; **cast**, Angelina Jolie, Elle Fanning, Imelda Staunton, Juno Temple, Brenton Thwaites, Ella Purnell, Hannah New, Sharlto Copley, Lesley Manville; **w**, Linda Woolverton, John Lee Perrault (based on the story "La Belle au bois dormant" by Charles Perrault and the story "Little Briar Rose" by Jacob and Wilhelm Grimm, and the 1959 motion picture **Sleeping Beauty**, story adapted by Erdman Penner, screenplay by Joe Rinaldi, Winston Hibler, Bill Peet, Ted Sears, Ralph Wright, Milt Banta, Peter Capaldi; **c**, Dean Semler; **m**, James Newton Howard; **ed**, Chris Lebenzon, Richard Pearson; **prod d**, Dylan Cole, Gary Freeman; **art d**, Frank Walsh, David Allday; **set d**, Lee Sandales; **spec eff**, Michael Dawson.

Man of Steel ★★★ 2013; U.S./Canada/U.K.; 143m; WB; Color; Science Fiction; Children: Unacceptable (MPAA: PG-13); **BD**; **DVD**. Superior retelling of the Superman story has British actor Cavill in the tights and cape. The planet Krypton's unstable core is expected to doom the planet and those on it, while its ruling council is under the threat of rebel General Zod, portrayed by Shannon, and his supporters. Scientist Jor-El, essayed by Crowe, and his wife send their newborn son Kal-El on a spacecraft to Earth with a genetic code in his cells that will preserve the planet's race. Shannon and his followers murder Crowe, but are captured and banished from the planet as Krypton explodes shortly thereafter, freeing them. Infant Kal-El arrives on Earth in Kansas and is adopted by Jonathan and Martha Kent, Costner and Lane, who name him Clark. As he becomes a teenager as Sprayberry, Costner advises him not to use his superhuman powers or society will reject him, but the boy gradually learns to use them to help others. Costner dies and, as Kal-El grows to maturity as Cavill, he works several jobs under assumed names. While investigating a Krypton scout spaceship in the Arctic, Cavill meets newspaper reporter Lois Lane, essayed by Adams, who is covering the story. Cavill saves her life in a superhuman way but, when she reports it to her editor, Perry White (Fishburne), the hard-nosed newspaperman rejects her claims that Cavill is superhuman. This prompts Adams to investigate Cavill, and she traces him back to Kansas. He tells her about his alien origin, but she promises to keep his spectacular past a secret. By this time, Shannon has learned that Cavill is on Earth and threatens war against humans unless Cavill surrenders himself to him with the genetic code he carries. Cavill agrees, and Shannon reveals that he intends to transform Earth into a new Krypton, eliminating

Joaquin Phoenix in *The Master*, 2012.

all humans in the process and then repopulate Earth with genetical-lyengineered Kryptonians from the code Cavill carries in him. This all ends with a spectacular battle in which Cavill kills Shannon and then becomes a reporter on the paper for which Adams works, where he devotes himself to continue his fight against crime under the cover of being a human newspaper reporter. Cavill is convincing as the superhero and he receives strong support from a gifted cast, with the amazing special effects depicting his spectacular feats excitingly carrying the viewer on a wild visual ride from the first frame to the last. The film religiously maintains the convenient stereotyped characters (and where no further development is imaginable), and it was a megahit at the box office, earning more than $668 million in its initial release against a whopping budget of $225 million. Songs: "Ring of Fire" (June Carter Cash, Merle Killgore), "Seasons" (Chris Cornell), "The Long Walk" (Marco Beltrami, Buck Sanders). *Author's Note*: The film was shot on location in Chicago, Illinois, and elsewhere in the state, as well as in California. In addition to the digitally enhanced and double negative techniques employed to achieve the marvelous special effects, handheld cameras were liberally used to give the film a visually jittery or nervous-wracked effect. Superman has been portrayed by many actors in many films, including **Adventures of Superman**, 1952-1958 (TV series; George Reeves); **The Batman Superman Movie: World's Finest**, 1997 (animated made-for-TV; Tim Daly voiceover); **Justice League**, 2001-2006 (animated TV series; George Newbern); **Lois & Clark: The New Adventures of Superman**, 1993-1997 (TV series; Dean Cain); **The New Adventures of Superman**, 1966-1970 (animated TV series; Bob Hastings voiceover); **Smallville**, 2001-2011 (TV series; Tom Welling); **Superboy**, 1988-1992 (TV series; Gerard Christopher); **Superman**, 1941-1943 (serial; Bud Collyer); **Superman**, 1948 (serial; Kirk Alyn); **Superman**, 1978 (Christopher Reeve); **Superman**, 1988 (animated TV series; Beau Weaver voiceover); **Superman and the Mole-Men**, 1951 (George Reeves); **Superman: Requiem**, 2011 (Martin Richardson); **Superman Returns**, 2006 (Brandon Routh); **Superman: The Last Son of Krypton**, 1996 (animated made-for-TV; Tim Daly); **Superman IV: The Quest for Peace**, 1987 (Christopher Reeve); **Superman III**, 1983 (Christopher Reeve); **Superman II**, 1981 p, (Christopher Reeve); **Superman**, 1996-2000 (Animated TV series; Tim Daly voiceover); and **Young Justice**, 2010- (TV series; Nolan North). Excessive violence and gutter language prohibit viewing by children. Christopher Nolan, Charles Roven, Deborah Snyder, Emma Thomas, Wesley Coller; **d**, Zack Snyder; **cast**, Henry Cavill, Kevin Costner, Diane Lane, Russell Crowe, Amy Adams, Laurence Fishburne, Michael Shannon, Dylan Sprayberry, Harry Lennix, Antje Traue, Richard Schiff; **w**, David S. Goyer (based on a story by Goyer, Nolan and characters created by Jerry Siegel, Joe Shuster); **c**, Amir Mokri; **m**, Hans Zimmer; **ed**, David Bren-

ner; **prod d**, Alex McDowell; **art d**, Chris Farmer, Kim Sinclair; **set d**, Anne Kuljian; **spec eff**, Allen Hall, Scott Kodrik, Joel Whist.

Maps to the Stars ★★★ 2014; Canada/U.S./Germany/France; 111m; Prospero Pictures/Focus Films; Color; Drama; Children: Unacceptable (MPAA: R); **BD**; **DVD**. Absorbing drama begins with the Weiss family, which makes up a Hollywood dynasty. Cusack, the father, is an analyst and acting coach who has made a fortune with his self-help manuals. The mother, Williams, looks after the career of their son, Bird, a 13-year-old child star. One of Cusack's clients, Moore, is an actress with ambitions of shooting a remake of a movie that made her mother, Gadon, famous. Gadon has since died but visions of her come to haunt Moore at night. Bird has just been released from a rehab program for drug abuse that he joined when he was nine years old. His sister, Wasikowska, has recently been released from a sanatorium where she was treated for criminal pyromania. She has befriended Pattison, a limousine driver who is also an aspiring actor (and what resident of Southern California is not?). The film cleverly and incisively chronicles the ups and downs of this disparate group, each one of them a socially ruptured duck that will make any viewer feel superior and thankful for having residence beyond Tinsel Town. The film did not do well at the box office, earning a little more than $4 million in its initial release against a budget of $13 million. Songs: "Na Na Hey Hey Kiss Him Goodbye" (Gary De Carlo, Paul Leka, Dale Frashuer), "Hell Blazer" (Supafly, Omar G). *Author's Note*: Carrie Fisher plays herself in the film, a brief cameo appearance made on behest of a friend in the cast. Excessive violence, sexual content, graphic nudity, gutter language and drug use prohibit viewing by children. **p**, Said Ben Said, Martin Katz, Michel Merkt, Alfred Hurmer; **d**, David Cronenberg; **cast**, Julianne Moore, Robert Pattinson, John Cusack, Mia Wasikowska, Carrie Fisher, Sarah Gadon, Olivia Williams, Amanda Brugel, Niamh Wilson, Evan Bird; **w**, Bruce Wagner; **c**, Peter Suschitzky; **m**, Howard Shore; **ed**, Ronald Sanders; **prod d**, Carol Spier; **art d**, Edward Bonutto, Elinor Rose Galbraith; **set d**, Sandy Lindstedt, Peter P. Nicolakakos; **spec eff**, Jon Campfens, Peter Denomme, Beau Parsons, Brent Pate.

The Martian ★★★★ 2015; U.S.; 141m; Genre Films/FOX; Color; Science Fiction; Children: Unacceptable (MPAA: PG-13); **BD**; **DVD**. Outstanding sci-fi adventure begins when a NASA spacecraft, *Hermes*, travels on a manned mission to Mars and lands on the Red Planet. Upon landing, the space explorers encounter a violent sandstorm that forces them to evacuate their landing site and return to Earth. One crew member, Damon, is believed to have died in the storm while outside the spacecraft and when studying the terrain for possible plant or human life. Presuming him to be dead, the mission's commander, Chastian, leaves him behind. However, Damon wakes up to discover that he has been abandoned and alone on the inhospitable and airless planet. He begins a desperate attempt to survive until he hopefully can be rescued, once NASA realizes he is not aboard the Hermes when it returns to Earth. Fortunately for Damon, he is the spaceship's botanist, so he is able to feed himself with potatoes he grows and fertilizes with his own excrement. NASA realizes that Damon has been left behind on Mars, and Chastain and other space employees, including former mission members Pena, Mara, Stan, Hennie, as well as other NASA engineers and trouble-shooters Daniels, Bean, Ejiofer, Wong, Davis and Glover, work on a plan to rescue him. Damon expects to be rescued within three years, if he can obtain enough food and water. NASA officials Bean and Wong decide to send a probe to Mars to supply Damon so he can last four years until another spacecraft can reach him. However, the probe explodes upon launching. Meanwhile, Damon's crops die in an explosive disaster and his supply of food is drastically reduced. China comes to NASA's aid by sending a booster rocket to Mars while NASA intensifies its efforts to send a rescue craft for Damon. He now manages to get some damaged equipment from the original spacecraft into an orbit around Mars while NASA, with Chastain and a crew of another spaceship, attempt to reach him. Damon manages to come close enough for Chastain to catch him in her orbiting craft. Damon is finally saved and becomes an instructor for new NASA astronauts in training. Damon is riveting as the desperate space survivor as the story details how he fends for himself to preserve life and limb on a hostile planet. The special effects (now the preeminent requirement for any Hollywood film funding) are superbly effective and convincing and guarantee to eye-dazzle viewers from first frame to last. The film had a huge box office success, earning more than $597.6 million in its initial release against a budget of more than $108 million. *Author's Note*: The film was especially timely because, in the autumn of 2015, NASA scientists released satellite photos of Mars that indicate that the planet has water and therefore may sustain some sort of plant life. Gutter language, injury images and brief nudity prohibit viewing by children. **p**, Ridley Scott, Mark Huffam, Simon Kinberg, Michael Schaefer, Aditya Sood; **d**, Scott; **cast**, Matt Damon, Jeff Daniels, Sean Bean, Jessica Chastain, Kristen Wiig, Michael Pena, Kate Mara, Sebastian Stan, Aksel Hennie, Chiwetel Ejiofor, Mackenzie Davis, Donald Glover; **w**, Drew Goddard (based on the book by Andy Weir); **c**, Dariusz Wolski; **m**, Harry Gregson-Williams; **ed**, Pietro Scalia; **prod d**, Arthur Max; **art d**, Marc Homes, Samy Keilani; **set d**, Celia Bobak, Zoltan Horvath; **spec eff**, Neil Corbould, Steven Warner.

The Master ★★★ 2012; U.S.; 144m; Weinstein Co.; Color; Drama; Cult; Children: Unacceptable (MPAA: R); **BD**; **DVD**. Offbeat but absorbing drama sees Phoenix as a sex-obsessed alcoholic U.S. Navy veteran of World War II (1939-1945), who is struggling to adjust to civilian life. He works as a portrait photographer at a department store but is fired for getting into a drunken fight with a customer, then works on a cabbage farm but is dismissed after making moonshine that poisons an elderly migrant worker. He then stows away on the yacht of Hoffman, leader of a religious movement known as "The Cause," who accepts him into the cult. Phoenix likes the movement and begins traveling with Hoffman along the East Coast to spread his teachings. Hoffman indoctrinates Phoenix in what he calls "Processing," a psychological questioning aimed at helping Phoenix conquer past traumas. Phoenix reveals that his father is dead and his mother is in an institution, and he may have had an incestuous relationship with an aunt. He also abandoned the young woman he loved, Beaty, who corresponded with him during the war. Phoenix beats up a man who questions Hoffman's methods and then other members of the cult become concerned about his drinking and seemingly uncontrollable temper. Adams, who is Hoffman's wife, tells Phoenix that he must stop drinking or leave the movement. Phoenix agrees, but has no such intention. Hoffman is soon afterward arrested for practicing medicine illegally, and Phoenix is arrested for assaulting some police officers. Phoenix breaks down in jail and accuses Hoffman of being a fake. They reconcile after being released from jail, but Cause members suspect Phoenix of being insane or an undercover agent. Hoffman writes a book about the movement, but when its publisher doubts its teachings, Phoenix physically attacks him. Phoenix is then assigned to ride a motorcycle at high speed in the desert near Phoenix, Arizona, but, instead of returning, he abandons the cult. He rides away in search of Beaty, thinking they might be reconciled, but then learns that she has married and is living in Alabama. While sleeping in a movie theater, Phoenix then goes to Hoffman, but is told that either he stays with the program or he must leave it for good. Phoenix leaves and has sex with a woman he meets in a bar. The film ends with Phoenix curling up on a beach next to a sand sculpture of a woman that he imagined during the war. There is nothing normal or average about this tale or its off-kilter characters, all of them strangers to mainstream society and few of them empathetic, especially the always intense Phoenix. He nevertheless rivets in a captivating portrayal of an unredeemable veteran of a war of redemption, his powerful portrayal earning him an Oscar as Best Actor. Hoffman and Adams are also superb in their roles of manipulating gurus, their portraits earning them Oscars as Best Supporting Actor and Best

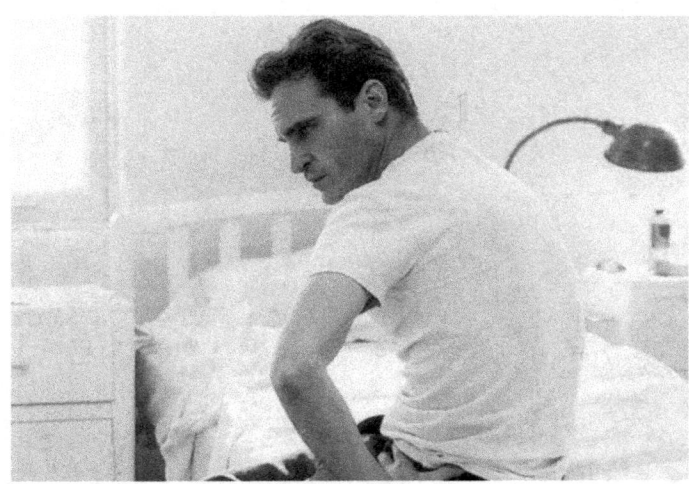

Joaquin Phoenix in *The Master,* 2012.

Supporting Actress. There have been many outstanding films portraying how WWII veterans adjusted to civilian life, including **The Best Years of Our Lives**, 1946 and **Till the End of Time**, 1946, but these films depict more normally adjusted men yearning simply for jobs and families. This entry more befits a much darker portrait that can be found in **Crossfire**, 1947, where, among returning veterans, is seen a murderous bigot lurking within the ranks of otherwise decent and upstanding men. Phoenix's repugnant character belongs with such moral misfits, a wholly self-serving person with an overcharged libido and no values whatsoever. The self-appointed message-givers he turns to in his feeble attempt to make something of his miserable life are equally unsavory (and more aptly apply to the phony pundits palavering gibberish in the drug-swamped 1970s). The film is nevertheless worth viewing if for no other reason than to marvel at Phoenix's startling anti-social performance. The film yielded $28.3 million in its initial release against a budget of more than $32 million. No relation to two other films with the same title in 1980 and 1992. Songs: "Don't Sit Under the Apple Tree/With Anyone Else But Me" (Lew Brown, Charles Tobias, Sam H. Stept); "Dancers in Love" (Duke Ellington); "I'll Go No More A-Rovin'" (traditional); "On a Slow Boat to China" (Frank Loesser); "Children of the Family," "Celebration Solaire" (Eban Schletter); "No Other Love" (Bob Russell, Paul Weston); "Baton Sparks," "Overtones" "Able-Bodied Seamen," "Time Hole" "Atomic Healer," "Application 45 Version 1," "Sweetness of Freddie" (Jonny Greenwood); "Get Thee Behind Me Satan" (Irving Berlin); "Dahil Sa Iyo" (Mike Velarde as Miguel Vilarde Jr.); "Sweet Sue, Just You" (Victor Young, Will J. Harris); "You Go to My Head" (Haven Gillespie, J. Fred Coots); "Lotus Blossom" (Billy Strayhorn); "A-Tisket A-Tasket" (Van Alexander, Ella Fitzgerald); "The Deep Boo Sea" (Winston Sharples); "Changing Partners" (Larry Coleman Jr., Joe Darion). Sexual content, graphic nudity and gutter language prohibit viewing by children. **p**, Paul Thomas Anderson, Megan Ellison, Daniel Lupi, JoAnne Sellar, Will Weiske, Albert Chi; **d&w**, Anderson; **cast**, Joaquin Phoenix, Laura Dern, Price Carson, Mike Howard, Patty McCormack, Mimi Cozzens, Charley Morgan, Christopher Evan Welch, Barlow Jacobs, David Warshofsky; **c**, Mihai Malaimare Jr.; **m**, Jonny Greenwood; **ed**, Leslie Jones, Peter McNulty; **prod d**, David Crank, Jack Fisk; **set d**, Amy Wells; **spec eff**, Michael Lantieri, Andy Foster, Dan Glass, Chelsea Kammeyer, Gregory D. Liegey.

McFarland, USA ★★★ 2015; U.S.; 129m; Mayhem Pictures/Walt Disney; Color; Sports Drama; Children: Unacceptable (MPAA: PG); **BD**; **DVD**; **IV**. This intriguing story begins with high school football coach Costner, who is seen lambasting his players for a poor half of a game in Boise, Idaho, in 1987. Losing his temper, he throws a shoe with cleats at a player and is fired. He moves with his wife, Bello, and two daugh-

Michael Stuhlbarg, Will Smith and Josh Brolin in *Men in Black 3*, 2012.

ters, Saylor and Fisher, to McFarland, California, a mostly Hispanic town. During their first night in town, a Latino makes a pass at Saylor, so Costner and his family leave. Costner becomes a high school life-science teacher and assistant football coach. He assembles a team of boys, who have various problems; they play a game in Palo Alto, but the team loses. Costner takes the blame and encourages the team to work harder. Meanwhile, townspeople organize a party for Saylor when she turns fifteen, and Costner begins to take a liking to the local inhabitants. Costner is offered a coaching job with the Palo Alto district as state championships begin. McFarland wins and Costner decides to turn down the Palo Alto job and remain in McFarland where he and his family have become happy, finding a home with loving people who have welcomed them into their hearts. Costner does a fine job essaying a hard-case coach whose bark is chipped away through the kindness and thoughtfulness of others. He receives strong support by a talented cast, and the story is moved along at a brisk pace under Caro's firm direction. The film did well at the box office, earning more than $47.5 million in its initial release against a budget of $17 million. Songs: "Cheer" (John F. Burns); "America" (Enrique Franco); "War Is Coming! War Is Coming!," "Me and Baby Brother" (Sylvester Allen, Harold Brown, Morris Dickerson, LeRoy Jordan, Charles W. Miller, Lee Oskar, Howard E. Scott); "Make It Rain" (Carlton J. Smith); "Impala Creeper" (Raney Shockne); "In My '64" (Mark Pistel, Chuck Prophet, Happy Sanchez); "Stand Up" (Cameron Graves, Carl Graves); "Vato Loco" (Happy Sanchez, Karl Perazzo, Marc Pinate); "Llevatela" (Edel Ramirez); "Give It Up" (Chris Gerniottis); "Si Se Puedo" (Manuel Palafox, Mingo Cervantes, Enrique Mendoza, Jesse Luna, Ray Comacho); "Turn the Stars Upside Down" (Jack Conrad, Donald Goodman); "Watermelon Man" (Herbie Hancock);"Rafael el Colombiano" (Andy Gonzalez, John Salazar); "Function Underground" (Leonard Michael Lenaburg); "Flashlight" (William Collins, George Clinton, Jr., Bernard Worrell); "Ahora te Puedes Marchar" (Mike Hawker, Ivor Raymonde, Luis Gomez Roldan); "Mala" (German Baratto Callejas, Scott Gerow); "Whittier Blvd." (George Dominguez, John Figuerova, William Garcia, Benjamin Lopez, Roy Marquez, Romeo Parado, Jose Rendon, George Salazar); "La Mananitas," "La Gavilan," "El Vals de las Mariposas" (Daniel De La Campa); "Suavecito" (Richard Bean, Pablo Tellez, Abel Zarate); "I'm Still Here" (Clifford Curry); "The Star Spangled Banner" (music: John Stafford Smith; lyrics" Francis Scott Key); "Juntos/Together" (Juan Luis Guerra). Thematic material, some violence and gutter language prohibit viewing by children. **p**, Mark Ciardi, Gordon Gray; **d**, Niki Caro; **cast**, Kevin Costner, Ramiro Rodriguez, Carlos Pratts, Johnny Ortiz, Rafael Martinez, Hector Duran, Sergio Avelar, Michael Aguero, Diana Maria Riva, Omar Leyva; **w**, Christopher Cleveland, Bettina Gilois, Grant Thompson (based on a story by Cleveland, Gilois); **c**, Adam Arkapaw; **m**, An-

tonio Pinto; **ed**, David Coulson; **prod d**, Richard Hoover; **art d**, Karen Steward; **spec eff**, James D. Schwalm.

Men in Black 3 ★★★ 2012; U.S.; 106m; COL; Color; Science Fiction; Children: Unacceptable (MPAA: PG-13); **BD**; **DVD**; **3D**. Another good outing for the exciting action-loaded sci-fi series begins in 2008, where Boris the Animal, played by Clement, last of the malevolent Boglodites that consumed all planets in their path in earlier films in the series, escapes from a lunar prison. Clement seeks vengeance on Men in Black Agent K, portrayed by Jones, who shot off his left arm and jailed him in 1969. Clement confronts Jones and his partner Agent J, essayed by Smith, telling Jones he is "already dead" before fleeing. Smith searches the Men in Black database when Jones refuses to discuss his past and discovers that Clement committed several murders in 1969 before being captured by Jones. Jones then deployed the "ArcNet" shield around Earth that prevented a Boglodite invasion and starved the race to extinction. Agent O, played by Thompson, the new head of MBI, tells Smith not to investigate deeper. That night, as Jones talks with Smith on the phone, Jones vanishes. Smith arrives at MIB headquarters looking for Jones, but finds no one there who can remember that Jones ever existed. Thompson shows Smith a memorial statue of Jones, who was killed by Clement in 1969. Further discussion reveals the chocolate-milk cravings and headaches Smith is experiencing are signs of the presence of a "temporal fracture," or a break in the time line. From warnings of approaching Boglodite warships, Smith deduces that Clement time-traveled to July 16, 1969, and succeeded in killing Jones, thereby preventing the ArcNet from ever being installed. In an effort to keep Jones alive for the future, Smith time-travels to the day before Jones is scheduled to be killed by Clement. At Coney Island in 1969, where the first MIB murder took place, Smith finds the 1969 Boris and tries to shoot him, but is knocked out by young K. Smith is taken to 1969 MIB headquarters for questioning and watches in disbelief as Jones flirts with the 1969 Agent O (Thompson). Jones prepares to neutralize Smith until Smith reveals his mission, convincing Jones to accept his help in stopping Clement. They follow clues to Stuhlbarg, a fifth-dimensional being who sees multiple time lines simultaneously and is the current possessor of the ArcNet. At "The Factory" studio party hosted by Andy Warhol (played by Hader), who is revealed to be an MIB agent, the 1969 Clement flees, but not before promising a gift and leaving a hint about a miracle game. Smith remembers that a "miracle game" of the 1969 World Series took place in Shea Stadium. There they find Stuhlbarg, who tells the time line vision of "his favorite moment in human history" when the underdog New York Mets win the World Series. Before Griffin can give them the ArcNet, the 1969 Clement kidnaps him. Smith and Jones pursue and rescue Stuhlbarg and the ArcNet, but the 1969 Clement escapes and meets his 2008 counterpart. Smith, Jones, and Stuhlbarg jet-pack to Cape Canaveral, Florida, where the ArcNet must be attached to the Apollo 11 rocket so it can be deployed in space. Military police stop them, but Stuhlbarg shows Colter, a skeptical colonel, a glimpse of the future, convincing him of the agents' importance, and Colter assists them in reaching the launch site. As the agents climb up the rocket's launch tower, both the 1969 Clement and 2008 Clement attack them. Using his time-travel device, Smith evades an attack by 2008 Boris' left arm, knocking him off the launch tower. The ArcNet is attached and deploys successfully, with 2008 Boris being incinerated by the launching rocket's exhaust. Jones and Smith both escape to ground zero by way of zip line baskets. Once back on the ground, the younger Clement attacks Jones, only to mortally wound the colonel who has jumped in front of Jones to save him. Jones kills Clement since Smith had told him not to take him alive. The colonel's young son, Martin, runs to him, but is stopped by Jones, who uses the neutralizer on the boy and tells him his father is a hero. Looking on from afar, Smith recognizes Martin's pocket watch as it is identical to the one he carries with him. He realizes that Martin is actually himself, the colonel, Colter, his father, and that Jones has been watching over him all his life. Smith returns to 2008 with the time line restored, joins Jones at a diner for pie, and thanks him for all his care. As they leave, Stuhlbarg, who has been sitting nearby, says that this is now his new favorite moment in human history. The rollicking action of this well-made film is only surpassed by the many comedic moments (where Smith generally lampoons the outlandish exploits of the aliens, the MIB agents and his own far-out pursuits). He, Jones and the rest of the cast are perfect in their futuristic roles, working well with the superbly organized special effects that dominate this well-crafted production. The film saw a huge success at the box office, earning more than $624 million in its initial release against a budget of more than $215 million. Songs: "Toccata-Carpimus Noctem" (Johann Sebastian Bach), "Love Is Strange" (Sylvia Robinson, Mickey Baker, Bo Diddley as Ellas McDaniel), "2000 Light Years from Home" (Mick Jagger, Keith Richards), "Pictures of Matchstick Men" (Francis Rossi), "I'm Waiting for the Man" (Lou Reed), "A Summer Song" (Chad Stuart, Keith Noble, Clive Metcalfe), "Empire State of Mind" (Jay-Z as Shawn Carter, Alicia Augello-Cook, Angela Hunte, Bert Keys, Sylvia Robinson, Janet Sewell, Al Shuckburgh), "Back in Time" (Armando Christian Perez, Marc Kinchen, Adrian Trejo, Urales Vargas, Sylvia Robinson, Mickey Baker, Bo Diddley as Ellas McDaniel), "Strange Brew" (Eric Clapton, Gail Collins, Felix Pappalardi), "I'm an Old Cowhand" (Johnny Mercer), "Theo's Dream" (Karen Hua Qi Han Ottosson), "Amazing Grace" (John Newton), "Baseball Stomp" and "Three Cheers" (Adam Blau), "Happy Birthday to You" (Patty S. Hill, Mildred J. Hill). Excessive violence and brief suggestive content prohibit viewing by children. **p**, Steven Spielberg, Laurie MacDonald, Walter F. Parkes, Joyce Cox, Riyoko Tanaka; **d**, Barry Sonnenfeld; **cast**, Will Smith, Tommy Lee Jones, Josh Brolin, Emma Thompson, Jemaine Clement, Michael Stuhlbarg, Mike Colter, Michael Chernus, David Rasche, Bill Hader; **w**, Etan Cohen (based on the Malibu comic by Lowell Cunningham); **c**, Bill Pope; **m**, Danny Elfman; **ed**, Don Zimmerman; **prod d**, Bo Welch; **art d**, W. Steven Graham, Maya Shimoguchi; **set d**, Susan Bode; **spec eff**, Jeff Brink, Mark Hawker.

Miles Ahead ★★★ 2015; U.S.; 100m; Bifrost Pictures/Sony; Color; Biographical Drama; Children: Unacceptable; **BD**; **DVD**.T This well-made biopic is loosely based on the life and music of black jazz musician Miles Davis (1926-1991), who is superbly played by Cheadle. An American jazz trumpeter, bandleader, composer, and artist, he became considered to be one of the most influential and innovative musicians of the 20th Century. The film does not cover his early years when he was born to a well-to-do family in East St. Louis and his early years as a musician, but begins when Cheadle goes to New York to start a band. The film follows an interview Cheadle has with a *Rolling Stone* magazine reporter, McGregor, to dramatize his musical rise to fame and fortune. He leads his first musical group in 1949, already taking jazz to new dimensions that begins to be called "cool jazz," although he rejected the term "jazz" and instead called his sound "social music." While he himself is black, he brings to his group musicians regardless of race, as long as they can play well. He marries, but the relationship deteriorates when his wife, Corinealdi, leaves him due to his drug addiction, violence and rampant infidelities. The latter part of the film focuses on his efforts to retrieve an unheard music session tape in the late 1970s that falls into the hands of an unscrupulous record producer, Stuhlbarg. While he gains fame and fortune, he fights a heroin addiction for four years after finally conquering drugs. The film takes a sudden and unexpected turn as the camera cuts to a wild car chase in which Cheadle leaps from a vehicle amid gunfire, before abruptly cutting to his Manhattan apartment in the 1970s where he retreats from medical problems, drug use, and a creative block that nearly ends his career and life. The music of Davis provides the background for many of the scenes. Davis was also an abstract painter, and his life comes together in this film like one of his abstract paintings, abandoning continuity and a cohesive story line. Cheadle nevertheless provides a compelling portrait of this gifted man. The film saw limited distribution. **p**, Don Cheadle, Robert Ogden Barnum, Pamela

Tom Cruise, at right, in *Mission Impossible—Rogue Nation*, 2015.

Hirsch, Darryl Porter, Daniel Wagner, Vince Wilburn Jr., Lenore Zerman; **d**, Cheadle; **cast**, Cheadle, Ewan McGregor, Michael Stuhlbarg, Lakeith Lee Stanfield, Emayatzy Corinealdi, Morgan Wolk, Austin Lyon, William Willet, Chris Hahn, Jeffrey Grover; **w**, Cheadle, Steven Baigelman (based on a story by Cheadle, Baigelman, Stephen J. Rivele, Christopher Wilkinson); **c**, Roberto Schaefer; **m**, Robert Glasper; **ed**, John Axelrad, Kayla Emter; **prod d**, Hannah Beachler; **art d**, Korey Washington; **set d**, Helen Britten; **spec eff**, Amy Bradford, Richard Fike.

Million Dollar Arm ★★★ 2014; U.S.; 124m; Walt Disney Pictures; Color; Biography/Drama/Sports; Children: Unacceptable (MPAA: PG-13); **BD**; **DVD**. Absorbing sports drama is based on a true story involving a once-successful sports agent, Hamm. He and his partner, Mandvi, will have to close down their business unless Hamm finds a way out soon. Hamm watches a cricket game being played on television in India and decides to go there and find the next baseball pitching star. He goes to Mumbai with a scout, Arkin, and schedules a televised reality show competition, "The Million Dollar Arm," in which 40,000 contestants compete against two teenage finalists, Sharma and Mittal. The teenagers win the competition and Hamm brings them to the U.S. to train with legendary pitching coach Paxton. The goal is to get the teenagers to sign with a major league baseball team. But the game proves difficult for the Indian boys to learn and they also must learn American culture, as well as teach Hamm the true meaning of teamwork and commitment. Hamm, for his part, persuades the excited teenagers to relax when they try out for the Pittsburgh Pirates and both hurl accurate pitches at 90 mph and both are signed to the team. The teenage recruits so influence Hamm that he gradually becomes more of a nice guy and part of a family. The film is closely reminiscent of **The Scout**, 1994, but nevertheless offers its own unique and rewarding story with top-flight performances from the cast. The film did well at the box office, earning more than $39.2 million in its initial release against a budget of more than $25 million. Song: "Can't Hold Us" (Macklemore [Benjamin Haggerty], Ray Dalton, Ryan Lewis). *Author's Note*: The film was shot on location in Mumbai; Atlanta, Georgia; and California. Gutter language and suggestive content prohibit viewing by children. **p**, Joe Roth, Mark Ciardi, Gordon Gray, Michael Mandt, Neil Mandt, Tabrez Noorani; **d**, Craig Gillespie; **cast**, Jon Hamm, Alan Arkin, Bill Paxton, Madhur Mittal, Suraj Sharma, Lake Bell, Aasif Mandvi, Al Sapienza, Autumn Dial, Tzi Ma; **w**, Thomas McCarthy; **c**, Gyula Pados; **m**, A.R. Rahman; **ed**, Tatiana S. Riegel; **prod d**, Barry Robison; **art d**, Mark Robins, Jeremy Woolsey; **set d**, Jeanette Scott; **spec eff**, Sean Thigpen, David Van Dyke.

A Million Ways to Die in the West ★★★ 2014; U.S.; 116m; Bluegrass Films/UNIV; Color; Western; Children: Unacceptable (MPAA: R); **BD**;

Ian McKellen as Sherlock Holmes in *Mr. Holmes,* 2015.

DVD. This offbeat but fascinating oater begins in 1882 in the town of Old Stump, Arizona. MacFarlane is a cowardly young sheep farmer, who is dumped by Seyfried, the girl he loves, after he refuses to participate in a duel. He decides to leave for San Francisco, believing the frontier is not the right place for him. Meanwhile, Neeson, an infamous outlaw, robs and kills an old prospector for a nugget of gold. He orders Jones, one of his companions, to escort his wife, Theron, to Old Stump to lie low while he continues his work as a bandit. Jones and Theron arrive in Old Stump as two siblings intending to start a farm, but Jones shoots a man in a saloon and is arrested. MacFarlane saves Theron from being crushed by two of the saloon brawlers, and they begin a relationship. They go to a county fair at which Seyfried's new boyfriend, foppish Harris, challenges MacFarlane to a shooting contest. Harris wins, but Theron defeats him and then teaches MacFarlane how to shoot. Jones breaks out of jail and murders the sheriff, Linn, after he sees Theron and MacFarlane kissing and reports it to Neeson. The savage outlaw demands to know who kissed his wife, but when no one has the courage to tell him, he shoots Reynolds, a cowboy. Neeson then says he will continue killing people until the man who kissed Theron duels with him at noon the next day. Neeson then gets Theron to reveal the name of the man who kissed her, MacFarlane, and then attempts to have sex with her, but she knocks him cold and escapes. Theron goes to MacFarlane's farm, but Neeson pursues her there, capturing her while MacFarlane escapes. MacFarlane is next captured by a tribe of Native Americans who threaten to burn him alive. However, they spare him after he reveals that he can speak their tongue. They give him some hallucinogenic food which ignites flashing memories back to his birth and through traumatic events of his boyhood. He then realizes that he loves Theron and returns to Old Stump and faces off with Neeson in a gun match. He wounds Neeson with a bullet poisoned with rattlesnake venom, but Neeson shoots MacFarlane's gun out of his hand. Neeson then succumbs to the poison and dies. Seyfried attempts to win back MacFarlane, but he rejects her and, instead, resumes a relationship with Theron. MacFarlane also receives bounty money for killing Neeson and uses it to buy more sheep, deciding to be a rancher after all. MacFarlane is excellent as a reluctant hero while Theron and Seyfried serve as attractive vamps enticing him into torrid romance. Neeson steals the show as the wild man outlaw, his brutal and cruel performance equaling the chilling western maniac played by Aldo Ray in **Welcome to Hard Times**, 1967, or the bloodthirsty gunslinger essayed by Gene Hackman in **The Quick and the Dead**, 1995. Silly, clever and sometimes touching, the script has its characters speaking in modern terms that would have puzzled any resident of the Old West. Much of this content, intentional or not, is rooted to an offhand spoof of westerns and the uncouth and unsophisticated people who bumped along their dusty trails. The film did well at the box office, earning more than $87.2 million in its initial release against a budget of more than $40 million. Songs: "If You've Only Got a Moustache" (Stephen Foster, Seth MacFarlane, Alec Sulkin, Wellesley Wild), "Tarzan Boy" (Maurizio Bassii, Naimy Hackett), "A Million Ways to Die" (music: Joel McNelley; lyrics: Seth MacFarlane), "Back to the Future (theme)" (Alan Silvestri). Crude and sexual content, gutter language, excessive violence and drug use prohibit viewing by children. **p**, Seth MacFarlane, Jason Clark, Scott Stuber; **d**, MacFarlane; **cast**, Liam Neeson, Charlize Theron, Amanda Seyfried, MacFarlane, Neil Patrick Harris, Giovanni Ribisi, Sarah Silverman, Wes Studi, Evan Jones, Preston Bailey; **w**, MacFarlane, Alec Sulkin, Wellesley Wild; **c**, Michael Barrett; **m**, Joel McNeely; **ed**, Jeff Freeman; **prod d**, Stephen J. Lineweaver; **art d**, Peter Borck, Bryan Felty, Mark Hansen; **set d**, Carla Curry; **spec eff**, Todd Minobe, Blair Clark.

Minions ★★★ 2015; U.S.; 91m; Illumination Enterprises/UNIV; Color; Computer Animated Comedy; Children: Cautionary (MPAA: PG-13); **BD**; **DVD**; **IV**. Entertaining tale begins at the beginning of time when the first forms of life are single-celled yellow organisms that evolve through the ages into minions. They are not powerful and obey orders of stronger-willed leaders. The Minions in this film are continuously unsuccessful at keeping their masters, from Tyrannosaurus Rex to Napoleon I. They keep finding themselves without someone to serve, so they fall into a deep depression. One Minion, called Kevin (Coffin voiceover) has a plan. Together with a teenage rebel (Coffin voiceover), and lovable little Bob (Coffin voiceover), he ventures out into the world to find a new boss for them and the other Minions. Their hazardous journey leads them to a super-villain, Scarlet Overkill (Bullock voiceover). They travel from icy Antarctica to New York City in the 1960s, ending in present-day London where they must face their biggest challenge yet, which is to save all Minions from annihilation. The innovative animation provides an amazing visual journey through the Minions' world, even though the script is rather mindless and even pubescent, but that, too, works well for its kindergarten plot. The film saw a gigantic box office success, earning more than $1.157 billion in its initial release against a budget of more than $74 million. Songs/Music: "Happy Together" (Gary Bonner, Alan Gordon); "We Wish You a Merry Christmas," "Aura Lee" (traditional); "19th Nervous Breakdown" (Mick Jagger, Keith Richards); "The Saint," from the 1962 television series (Edwin Astley); "Bewitched" (Howard Greenfield, Jack Keller); "The Dating Game" (Chuck Barris, David Mook); "Ride of the Valkyries" (Richard Wagner); "I'm a Man" (Steve Winwood, Jimmy Miller); "Break on Through/To the Other Side" (John Densmore, Robby Krieger, Ray Manzarek, Jim Morrison); "Make 'Em Laugh" (Arthur Freed, Nacio Brown); "Purple Haze" (Jimi Hendrix); "Peter and the Wolf" (Pyotr Ilyich Tchaikovsky); "Hair" (Galt MacDermot, James Rado, Gerome Ragni); "Rule Britannia" (Thomas Augustine Arne, James Thomson); "You Really Got Me" (Ray Davies); "The Letter" (Wayne Carson Thompson); "Pomp and Circumstance" (Edward Elgar); "My Generation" (Pete Townshend); "The Monkees Theme" (Bobby Hart, Tommy Boyce); "Love Me Do," "Got to Get You Into My Life," "Revolution" (John Lennon, Paul McCartney); "Rocky Road to Dublin" (Ronnie Drew, Barney McKenna, Luke Kelly, Ciaran Bourke, John Sheehan); "Taps" (traditional); "Eruption" (Michael Anthony, David Lee Roth, Alex Van Halen, Edward Van Halen); "Mellow Yellow" (Donovan Leitch). Harrowing action and rude humor cautions viewing by children. **p**, Jack Healey, Christopher Meledandri; **d**, Kyle Balda, Pierre Coffin; **cast** (voiceovers), Sandra Bullock, Jon Hamm, Michael Keaton, Geoffrey Rush, Steve Carell, Peter Coffin, Katy Allison Janney, Steve Coogan, Jennifer Saunders, Katy Mixon, Michael Beattie; **w**, Brian Lynch; **c**, Claire Dodgson; **m**, Heitor Pereira; **ed**, Claire Dodgson; **art d**, Olivier Adam; **spec eff**, Valerie Gabriel, Olivier Schmitt.

Miss Julie ★★★ 2014; Norway/U.K.; 129m; Maipo Film/COL TriStar; Color; Drama; Children: Unacceptable (MPAA: PG-13); **BD**; **DVD**.

Taut, strange tale begins over a midsummer night in 1890, where Chastain, the unsettled daughter of an Anglo-Irish aristocratic family in Sweden, encourages Farrell, her father's valet, to seduce her. She is attracted to him because he is handsome, well mannered, well read, and well traveled. Most of the action takes place in the kitchen of her father's mansion where Farrell's fiancée, Morton, cooks and sometimes naps while he and Chastain talk. Their relationship that night rapidly escalates into love and is consummated. Chastain and Farrell then quarrel until he convinces her that the only way for her to escape her predicament is to commit suicide. Though there is a claustrophobic and stagey look throughout, the intense performances from Chastain and Farrell are exceptionally captivating. The film did poorly at the box office and did not recoup its budget of more than $5.5 million. Mature and sexual material prohibits viewing by children. **p**, Oliver Dungey, Teun Hilte, Synnove Horsdal, Rita Dagher, Tristan Lynch, Aoife O'Sullivan; **d&w**, Liv Ullmann (based on the play by August Strindberg); **cast**, Jessica Chastain, Colin Farrell, Samantha Morton, Nora McMenamy; **c**, Mikhail Krichman; **ed**, Michal Leszczylowski; **prod d**, Caroline Amies; **art d**, Heather Greenlees; **spec eff**, Nick Morton, Michael Woods.

Mission Impossible—Rogue Nation ★★★ 2015; U.S./Hong Kong/China; 131m; PAR; Color; Spy Drama; Children: Unacceptable; MPAA: PG-13; **BD**; **DVD**; **IV**. Another exciting entry in the series sees Crruise, an Impossible Missions Force (MI6) agent, obtain a nerve gas being sold to terrorists. He is certain he can prove the existence of an international crime organization known as the Syndicate, which the Central Intelligence Agency (CIA) thinks does not exist. Cruise is then captured by the Syndicate, but, with the help of Ferguson, a female MI6 agent who is a mole in the Syndicate, he escapes torture led by Syndicate member Vinter, played by Hulten. Meanwhile there is a power struggle between CIA director Baldwin and IMF field operations director Renner as Baldwin wants the IMF disbanded and to become part of the CIA. Cruise has escaped the Syndicate but remains a fugitive six months later. He enlists the aid of Pegg, a former IMF colleague, to attend the opera "Turndot" in Vienna to search for Harris, whom he suspects is the Syndicate's leader. Next, Wickham, the Austrian chancellor, is killed when a bomb planted on his car explodes. The Syndicate now hunts Cruise to a power station in Morocco. Ferguson betrays fellow Syndicate members by stealing a ledger with the names of all the group's members. The other Syndicate members pursue Ferguson, who returns to London intending to use the file to conclude her mission to infiltrate the Syndicate. All this ends with the Syndicate being identified and exposed. Harris and his associates are arrested, and Cruise and the IMF continues for further adventures and sequels to the popular film franchise. Cruise is hard-hitting and effective as the uncompromising agent and he is supported strongly by a stellar cast while the stunning action is almost nonstop. The film was a huge success at the box office, earning more than $682.3 million in its initial release against a budget of more than $150 million. Music: "Popolo di Pechino, Ali Tuoi Piedi Ci Prostriam," "Nessun Dorma" from the opera "Turandot" (music: Giacomo Puccini; lyrics: Giuseppe Adami, Renato Simoni), "The Plot" (from the 1966 television series "Mission Impossible," by Lalo Schifrin), "Symphony No. 3, Eroica" (Ludwig van Beethoven), "The Marriage of Figaro" (Wolfgang Amadeus Mozart). Excessive violence, and brief partial nudity prohibit viewing by children. **p**, J.J. Abrams, Bryan Burk, Tom Cruise, David Ellison, Don Granger; **d**, Christopher McQuarrie; **cast**, Cruise, Alec Baldwin, Jeremy Renner, Simon Pegg, Rebecca Ferguson, Ving Rhames, Sean Harris, Simon McBurney, Jingchu Zhang, Tom Hollander, Jens Hulten; **w**, McQuarrie (based on a story by McQuarrie, Drew Pearce (and the television series by Bruce Geller); **c**, Robert Elswit; **m**, Joe Kraemer; **ed**, Eddie Hamilton; **prod d**, James D. Bissell; **art d**, Paul Inglis; **set d**, John Bush, Abdenabi Izlaguen; **spec eff**, Jess Lewington, Elia P. Popov.

Gabriel Rush, Edward Norton and Chandler Frantz in *Moonrise Kingdom,* **2012.**

Mistaken ★★★ 2013; U.K.; 75m; Take Home Productions; Color; Crime Drama; Children: Unacceptable (MPAA: R); **BD**; **DVD**. Taut thriller begins when Roberts arrives back in London from a business trip to see his fiancée, but he has no idea how hard his life is to become. His fiancée is murdered by a professional hit man, and Roberts narrowly escapes alive from his home. Not having any idea why he too is targeted, he seeks help from his best friend, Nash, a detective. They investigate together and both narrowly escape being killed, becoming involved in events beyond their imagination or control. Roberts discovers something in his past that may be the cause of it all. Violence prohibits viewing by children. **p**, Anthony Roberts, Jamie Nash; **d**, Roberts; **cast**, Roberts, Nash, Daniel Poli, Mat Hall, Simon Harvey, James Harvey, James DiPietro, Christina Oliver, Lana Burton, Claire Gin-Sing (voice), Joanna Thomas, Tony Cook; **w**, Roberts, Zac Stone; **c**, Roberts; **m**, Dominik Hauser; **ed**, Roberts; **prod d**, Mat Hall; **spec eff**, Roberts.

Mr. Holmes ★★★ 2015; U.K./U.S.; 104m; AI Films/Roadside Attractions; Color; Mystery; Children: Unacceptable (MPAA: PG-13); **BD**; **DVD**; **IV**. Absorbing whodunit brings the legendary Sherlock Holmes (at age ninety-three), superbly played by McKellen, back to his dangerous sleuthing. Long-retired from his private detective pursuits, McKellen is living at a remote farmhouse in Sussex with his housekeeper, Linney, and her young son Roger, played by Parker. He is unhappy about his former partner Doctor Watson's fictionalization of his last case and decides to write down his own version of events. However, he finds it difficult to chronicle his own exploits as he cannot recall all of its details. McKellen begins to have paternal feelings for Parker as they work together in caring for bees in the farmhouse's apiary. Parker's questions restore McKellen's memories about the case, which is then shown in flashback. About thirty years earlier, Kennedy had asked McKellen to find out why his wife, Morahan, had changed so much after suffering two miscarriages. McKellen follows Morahan about London and discovers that she has been forging checks in Kennedy's name and cashing them, looking at details of his will, and buying poison. It all looks to him as if she is planning to kill Kennedy in order to inherit his money and property. He also thinks she will commit suicide with the poison. McKellen urges her to return to her husband, but, instead, Morahan kills herself by throwing herself in front of a speeding train. McKellen blames himself for her death and retires. In more flashbacks, McKellen goes to Japan and befriends Sanada, whose father had abandoned him. Back in the present, Linney decides to leave McKellen's service and take a job at a hotel in Portsmouth, planning to take Parker with her, but her move is delayed by tensions between her and Parker. McKellen and Linney find Parker unconscious near the house, having been bitten by bees, and the boy is rushed to a hospital. In anger,

Frances McDormand and Bruce Willis in *Moonrise Kingdom,* **2012.**

Linney attempts to burn down the apiary and blames McKellen for only caring about the bees. McKellen helps her burn down the wasp's nest, and Parker recovers. McKellen then tells Linney that he plans to leave the house to her and Parker upon his death. McKellen's thoughts about his last case lead him to realize that Doctor Watson's embellishments of that case were done as a kindness to Kennedy. Linney agrees that she and Parker will remain with McKellen, and the film ends with McKellen remembering a Japanese tradition. That ritual involves placing a ring of stones that helps bereaved people to remember their deceased loved one. McKellen is wonderful as a doddering but still functioning Holmes, and his acute sense of deduction is still in evidence as he collects the memories of the past to heal the emotional problems of the present. The popularity of the Holmes character has not waned as indicated by the success this film saw at the box office, where it earned more than $28.1 million in its initial release. Thematic elements, disturbing images and smoking prohibit viewing by children. **p**, Iain Canning, Anne Carey, Emile Sherman, Luca Borghese, Jack Morrissey, Paul Ritchie, Greg Yolen; **d**, Bill Condon; **cast**, Ian McKellen, Laura Linney, Milo Parker, Hiroyuki Sanada, Hattie Morahan, Patrick Kennedy, Roger Allam, Philip Davis, Frances de la Tour, Charles Maddox; **w**, Jeffrey Hatcher (based on the novel *A Slight Trick of the Mind* by Mitch Cullin and characters created by Arthur Conan Doyle); **c**, Tobias A. Schliessler; **m**, Carter Burwell; **ed**, Virginia Katz; **prod d**, Martin Childs; **art d**, Jonathan Houlding, James Wakefield; **set d**, Charlotte Watts; **spec eff**, Neal Champion, Alistair Anderson.

Mr. Peabody & Sherman ★★★ 2014; U.S.; 92m; DreamWorks/FOX; Color; Animated Adventure; Children: Unacceptable (MPAA: PG); **BD**; **DVD**. This amusing and very entertaining animated adventure tale is based on the long-standing television series. Mr. Peabody (Burrell voiceover) is a business tycoon, inventor, scientist, Olympic medal winner, and a genius who is also a dog. His invention, a time machine, takes him and his adopted boy Sherman (Charles voiceover) back in time to engage in historical events with famous people of the past. But Charles causes problems when he breaks the rules of time travel by altering some events, and then must try to restore history and save the future. One of their adventures takes them to 18th-Century France, where they become involved with Marie Antoinette, and another time journey lands them in ancient Egypt. All the while, Burrell must deal with the complexities of being a father when Charles wants to do things on his own. The animation is exceptional and registered well at the box office where the film earned more than $275.7 million in its initial release against a budget of more than $145 million. Songs: "Pause" (Armando Perez, Urales Vargas, Ari Kalimi, Abdelouahid Ben, Adrian Santalla), "Beautiful Boy/Darling Boy" (John Lennon), "Rhapsody in Blue" (George

Gershwin), "Tezka Radost" (Ondrej Smeykal), "Purple Haze" (Jimi Hendrix), "Aquarela do Brasil" (Ary Barroso), "Way Back When" (Adam M. Roth, Fredrik Eriksson, Sebastian Fritze), "Kid" (Peter Andre). Harrowing action and brief rude humor prohibit viewing by children. **p**, Denise Nolan Cascino, Alex Schwartz; **d**, Rob Minkoff; **cast** (voiceovers), Ty Burrell, Max Charles, Stephen Colbert, Dennis Haysbert, Lauri Fraser, Guillaume Aretos, Patrice A. Musick, Ariel Winter, Karan Brar, Joshua Rush, Allison Janney; **w**, Craig Wright, Robert Ben Garant, Thomas Lennon, Michael McCullers (based on the television series produced by Jay Ward); **m**, Danny Elfman; **ed**, Michael Andrews; **prod d**, Zachary Gold, Laura C. Denton, Scott Sakamoto, Carlyn Siegler; **art d**, Walt Dohrn; **spec eff**, Naveen Kumar Bolla, Ken Ball.

Mr. Turner ★★★ 2014; U.K./France/Germany; 150m; Film4/Focus Features/Sony; Color; Biography/Drama/History; Children: Unacceptable (MPAA: R); **BD**; **DVD**. Provocative production chronicles the last quarter century in the life and work of the eccentric Victorian era British landscape painter J.M.W. Turner (1775-1851), who is played by Timothy Spall. Born Joseph Mallard William Turner, the son of a London barber, he becomes regarded by many as the greatest landscape painter of the 19th Century. His paintings bring him early attention for their luminosity and romantic imagery and in a style that begins in realism but later precedes Impressionism. Spall becomes both wealthy and famous, and is a professor of perspective at the Royal Academy of Art. As he becomes famous, his mother is committed to a mental institution and his father, Jesson, moves in with him and becomes his studio assistant and manager. Spall then begins to travel to the European continent where he creates hundreds of drawings and water colors, many inspired by masterworks in art museums. During these years, Spall travels more, is the house guest of British aristocracy, spends time in brothels, and is both admired and reviled by the public and royalty. Often at odds with the Royal Academy of Art for his odd artistic ways, his unpredictable nature is exampled when, at one time, he has himself strapped to the mast of a sailing ship so he can paint a snowstorm. In his later years Spall becomes profoundly depressed by the death of Jesson and takes for granted a housekeeper who loves him, but sometimes he has indifferent sex with her. He then has a close relationship with a landlady with whom he lives incognito at a seaside cottage in Chelsea where he dies. Spall does an outstanding job of essaying this enigmatic and very creative man, one who is totally absorbed in himself and his art, as its the case with many such artists. The film received Oscar nominations for Best Cinematography (Pope); Best Original Score (Yershon); Best Production Design (Davies; set decoration: Watts); and Best Costume Design (Jacqueline Durran). The film saw a modest success at the box office, earning more than $17.8 million in its initial release. Songs: "Dido's Lament" from the opera "Dido and Aenas" (1689; music: Henry Purcell; lyrics: Nahum Tate), "Piano Concerto No. 8 in C Minor, Op. 13/Sonata Pathetique" (1798-1799; Ludwig van Beethoven). Sexual content prohibits viewing by children. **p**, Georgina Lowe; **d&w**, Mike Leigh; **cast**,Timothy Spall, Paul Jesson, Dorothy Atkinson, Maarion Bailey, Karl Johnson, Ruth Sheen, Sandy Foster, Amy Dawson, Lesley Manville, Martin Savage; **c**, Dick Pope; **m**, Gary Yershon; **ed**, Jon Gregory; **prod d**, Suzie Davies; **art d**, Dan Taylor; **set d**, Charlotte Watts; **spec eff**, Peter Kersey.

The Monuments Men ★★★ 2014; U.S./Germany; 144m; Smokehouse Pictures/COL/FOX; Color; War Drama; Children: Unacceptable (MPAA: R); **BD**; **DVD**. Intriguing tale takes place during World War II (1939-1945), where experts compete with each other to recoup the masterpiece artworks stolen by the Nazis. The Allied nations, including the U.S. government, form a group of international art experts, including art historians and museum curators, to go behind enemy lines to hunt down and recover hundreds if not thousands of famous works of art that were stolen and then hidden by the Nazis. They are to do this before Adolf Hitler (1889-1945) can have them destroyed under his direct order as the war is ending. The title refers to the art recovery group (the Monuments, Fine Arts, and Archives Program) that is to find the art and return it to their rightful owners. The ragtag and aging art experts make their way into enemy territory before realizing how difficult and hazardous their task presents. The film presents some many harrowing moments, but one, where a Nazi youth is found firing on some of the art detectives, is a blatant lift scene from **The Bridge at Remagen**, 1969, where a preteen Nazi youth fires upon GIs and who is then killed to the disgust of his slayers, albeit the youth is allowed to live in this version. Though the acting is superior, many of the players are woefully miscast, especially Goodman, Murray, Giamatti and Balaban, who are far too old for the characters they enact and where Goodman (age sixty-three) and Murray (age sixty-five) are so obese that they ridiculously waddle in their uniforms when appearing in combat (such butt-sprung and belly-bloated individuals would have most certainly been killed had they ever dared to appear on a real battlefield). The race to save the great artworks is shown not only between the Allies and the Nazis out to destroy them, but between the U.S. experts and Soviet forces, the latter wanting to seize and hoard these priceless works as did the Nazis. A treasure trove of such artworks are found in a cavern beneath a mountain, and the U.S. experts manage to seize and take them to their own lines before Russian troops arrive to find the underground facility empty. Clooney, as one of the American art experts, and Blanchett, as a conscientious German woman who aids the Americans in locating the looted artworks, are exceptional in their roles, as is Damon, the young U.S. officer who persuades Blanchett to cooperate in the search for the stolen masterpieces. The sets, props and costumes are faithful to the period and the lensing is excellent, but there are far too many characters clogging up the continuity and story line (as if producer-director Clooney was compelled to hire all of his schmoozing Hollywood cronies). The film was a success at the box office (mostly due to the star attraction of Damon, Clooney and Blanchett), earning more than $155 million in its initial release against a budget of $70 million. Another and far superior film, **The Train**, 1965, also depicts the Nazi looting of European artworks in WWII, chiefly the classic paintings of French artists. A bizarre comedic effort, **A Night in Casablanca**, 1946, touches upon the same theme, but where the Nazis are attempting to recoup some stolen treasure, only to be foiled by the zany Marx Brothers. Songs: "Night and Day" (Cole Porter), "You Always Hurt the One You Love" (Doris Fisher, Allan Roberts), "Have Yourself a Merry Little Christmas" (Ralph Blane, Hugh Martin). Excessive violence and smoking prohibit viewing by children. **p**, George Clooney, Grant Heslov, Christoph Fisser, Henning Molfenter, Charlie Woebcken; **d**, Clooney; **cast**, Clooney, Matt Damon, Cate Blanchett, Bill Murray, Hugh Bonneville, Jean Dujardin, Michael Brandner, John Goodman, Bob Balaban, Dimitri Leonidas, Diarmaid Murtagh; **w**, Clooney, Heslov (based on the book *The Monuments Men: Allied Heroes, Nazi Thieves, and the Greatest Treasure Hunt in History* by Robert Edsel and Bret Witter); **c**, Phedon Papamichael; **m**, Alexandre Desplat; **ed**, Ruy Diaz, Stephen Mirrione; **prod d**, James D. Bissell; **art d**, Helen Jarvis, Cornelia Ott, David Scheunemann; **set d**, Bernhard Henrich; **spec eff**, Sam Conway, Gerd Nefzer.

Mood Indigo ★★★ 2014; France/Belgium; 131m; Brio Films/Drafthouse Films; Color/B/W; Comedy/Drama; Children: Unacceptable; **BD**; **DVD**. Entertaining tale presents a charming but surreal Paris where a wealthy bachelor, Duris, devotes his time to developing a cocktail-making piano he calls a "pianoctail" and eating food prepared by Sy, his trusty chef. Sy has a new American girlfriend while Duris goes to a party in hopes of falling in love. Duris meets Tautou and, while dancing to Duke Ellington's song "Mood Indigo," they begin a romance. Their whirlwind courtship is tested when Tautou falls ill from an unusual malady and a flower begins to grow in her lungs. To save her, Duris discovers that the only cure is to surround Tautou with a never-ending supply of fresh flowers. Song: "Mood Indigo" (Duke Ellington). (In French; English subtitles.) **p**, Luc Bossi, Genevieve Lemal, Arlette Zyl-

Chandler Frantz and Edward Norton in *Moonrise Kingdom,* **2012.**

berberg, **d**, Michel Gondry; **cast**, Romain Duris, Audrey Tautou, Gad Elmaleh, Omar Sy, Aissa Maiga, Charlotte Le Bon, Sacha Bourdo, Vincent Rottiers, Philippe Torreton, Laurent Lafitte; **w**, Gondry, Bossi (adapted from the novel by Boris Vian); **c**, Christophe Beaucarne; **m**, Etienne Charry; **ed**, Marie-Charlotte Moreau; **prod d**, Stephane Rosenbaum; **art d**, Pierre Renson; **spec eff**, Julien Poncet de la Grave.

Moonrise Kingdom ★★★ 2012; U.S.; 94m; Indian Paintbrush/Focus Features; Color; Comedy/Drama/Romance; Children: Unacceptable (MPAA: PG-13); **BD**; **DVD**. Charming coming-of-age story has Gilman as a twelve-year-old orphan boy, who is attending a summer camp led by Norton on a New England island in 1965. Hayward, a girl his age, lives on the island with her father, Murray, and mother, McDormand (who are both attorneys) and three younger brothers. Gilman and Hayward had met the previous summer and had written to each other since. They fell in love as pen pals and made a secret pact to run away together. Gilman brings camping equipment and Hayward brings six books, her cat, and a record player. They spend several days and nights hiking and camping in the wilderness, heading for a secluded cove on the island that they call Moonrise Kingdom. They set up camp there, go swimming, and later dance in their underwear and kiss. A search for them results in Norton finding them at the cove. Hayward's parents take her home and forbid her to see Gilman again. Gilman stays with a police captain, Willis, while waiting for a social worker, Swinton, to come and place him in a "juvenile refuge" because his foster parents refuse to take him back. Friends at the camp decide to help Gilman and Hayward run away again, but the young lovers are caught on a church steeple during a hurricane and flood. The steeple is destroyed, but they survive. Willis decides to become Gilman's legal guardian, which allows the boy to stay on the island and remain in contact with Hayward. Gilman paints a landscape of the cove at Willis' home and then slips out a window as Hayward and her brothers are called to dinner. It looks like the teenage lovers will stay reunited, as most viewers may hopefully envision. The well-written script received an Oscar nomination at Best Original Screenplay (Anderson, Coppola), and the film enjoyed a solid success at the box office, earning more than $68.2 million in its initial release against a budget of more than $16 million. Songs: "Khaki Scout Marches/Camp Ivanhoe Medley" (Mark Mothersbaugh); "Young People's Guide to the Orchestra," "Playful Pizzicato from Simple Symphony," "Noye, Take Thou Thy Company," "A Midsummer Night Dream," "Songs from Friday Afternoon" (Benjamin Britten); "Kaw-Liga" (1952, Fred Rose, Hank Williams); "Heroic Weather Conditions," (Alexandre Desplat); "Long Gone Lonesome Blues," "Ramblin' Man," "Cold, Cold Heart" (Hank Williams); "Voliere" from "Carnival of the Animals," "Noye's Fuddle" (Camille Saint-Saens);, "Le temps du

Kara Hayward in *Moonrise Kingdom,* **2012.**

l'amour" (Andre Salvet, Jacques Dutronc); "An die Musik" (Franz Schubert), "Soave sia il vento" from the opera "Cosi fan tutti" (Wolfgang Amadeus Mozart). Sexual content and smoking prohibit viewing by children. **p**, Scott Rudin, Wes Anderson, Jeremy Dawson, Steven Rales, Eli Bush, Lila Yacoub; **d**, Wes Anderson; **cast**, Jared Gilman, Kara Hayward, Edward Norton, Bruce Willis, Bill Murray, Frances McDormand, Tilda Swinton, Jason Schwartzman, Bob Balaban, Lucas Hedges, Charlie Kilgore, Andreas Sheikh, Chandler Frantz; **w**, Anderson, Roman Coppola; **c**, Robert D. Yeoman; **m**, Alexandre Desplat; **ed**, Andrew Weisblum; **prod d**, Adam Stockhausen; **art d**, Gerald Sullivan; **set d**, Kris Moran; **spec eff**, John Ruggieri, Colleen Bachman, Dan Schrecker.

Monsieur Lazhar ★★★ 2012; Canada; 94m; Micro-Scope/Music Box; Color; Drama; Children: Unacceptable (MPAA: PG-13); **BD**; **DVD**. Absorbing drama begins when an elementary schoolteacher in Montreal, Canada, commits suicide and her replacement is Lazhar, played by Fellag, who is an Algerian illegal immigrant recovering from the deaths of his wife and two children in an arson attack in Algeria. He has no teaching qualification and previously ran a restaurant. The film focuses on his relationships with students and faculty and how the students come to terms with their former teacher's suicide. Neron, one of the students, blames himself for the suicide. Eventually, Fellag's refuge status and lack of teaching qualifications are found out and he is fired, and is about to be deported. He asks permission to teach one more day and has his students make up a fable he wrote, which is a metaphor of his tragic past life in Algeria and the loss of his family in a fire. He has tried to help the students cope with their experience with death, but is forced to leave. Before he goes, Nelisse, his favorite student, gives him a farewell hug. This prosaic story has no great message, but deals with emotional problems in a satisfying manner where old wounds are mended through understanding and genuine empathy. The film received an Oscar nomination as Best Foreign Language Film. The film saw a modest success at the box office, earning more than $6.6 million in its initial release. Mature thematic material, a disturbing image and brief gutter language prohibit viewing by children. (In French; English subtitles.) **p**, Luc Dery, Kim McCraw; **d&w**, Philippe Falardeau (based on "Bazhir Lazhar," a one-character play by Evelyne de la Cheneliere); **cast**, Mohamed Fellag, Emilien Neron, Sophie Nelisse, Marie-Eve Beauregard, Vincent Millard, Seddik Benslimane, Louis-David Leblanc, Gabriel Verdier, Marianne Soucy-Lord, Danielle Proulx; **c**, Roland Plante; **m**, Martin Leon; **ed**, Stephane Lafleur; **prod d**, Emmanuel Frechette; **set d**, Josee Arseneault; **spec eff**, Guillaume Murray, Sebastien Moreau.

A Most Violent Year ★★★ 2014; U.S.; 107m; Before the Door Pic-

tures/A24 Films; Color; Crime Drama; Children: Unacceptable (MPAA: R); **BD**; **DVD**. Tense crime thriller is set during the winter of 1981, one of the most violent years in New York City's history. The film focuses upon the lives of an immigrant, Isaac, and his wife, Chastain, as they face harrowing barriers in trying to expand the business they bought from his wife's gangster father. The business is under investigation by district attorney Oyelowo, a harassing probe that becomes an obstacle in Isaac's efforts to buy land he needs to expand. His truck drivers are beaten up and their vehicles are stolen. Isaac's lawyer, Brooks, and wife, Chastain, find that their lives are in danger. Isac and Nivola, who is Isaac's super-rich friend and competitor, then suddenly clash as Isaac doggedly continues to pursue the American businessman's dream of riches, despite the increasing risks involved. Isaac, Chastain and the rest of the cast deliver standout performances in this suspense-filled tale, which is firmly directed by Chandor, who takes considerable pains to fully develop his characters. The film deserved a better fate at the box office, where it earned only $6 million in its initial release against a budget of more than $20 million. Songs: "Inner City Blues/Make Me Wanna Holler" (Marvin Gaye, James Nyx), "America for Me" (Alex Ebert), "Me and the Blues" (Ray Bryant), "Una Lacrima Sul Viso" (Giulio Rapetti Mogol, Roberto Satti). Excessive violence prohibits viewing by children. **p**, Neal Dodson, Anna Gerb; **d&w**, J.C. Chandor; **cast**, Oscar Isaac, Jessica Chastain, Albert Brooks, David Oyelowo, Alessandro Nivola, Elyes Gabel, Catalina Sandino Moreno, Peter Gerety, Christopher Abbott, Ashley Williams, John Procaccino; **c**, Bradford Young; **ed**, Ron Patane; **prod d**, John P. Goldsmith; **art d**, Doug Huszti; **set d**, Melanie J. Baker; **spec eff**, Mark Russell, Naz Shams, Vadim Turchin, Jeff Wozniak.

A Most Wanted Man ★★★ 2014; U.K./U.S./Germany; 121m; Ink Factory/Roadside Attractions; Color; Spy Drama; Children: Unacceptable (MPAA: R); **BD**; **DVD**. Gritty espionage tale begins when Hoffman goes to the German port city of Hamburg's Islamic community. Both German and U.S. security agents take a close interest in him and attempt to learn if he is an oppressed victim or a terrorist. Hamburg is terrorism focused because it was where Mohammed Atta and his collaborators planned the September 11, 2001, terrorist attacks on New York and Washington. Hoffman actually runs a secret antiterrorism team that seeks to develop sources within the Islamic community that would lead them to high-profile terrorist suspects. He is continually hampered by Bock, a Hamburg intelligence chief whose style is to arrest first and ask questions later. Their latest bone of contention is Dobrygin, a 26-year-old half-Chechen, half-Russian immigrant, who had been tortured and imprisoned in his native countries. Dobrygin quickly connects with McAdams, a human-rights attorney, who agrees to help him claim his inheritance which is worth tens of millions of Euros. Bock wants to arrest Dobrygin before he can make contact with Islamic terrorist cells, while Hoffman isn't sure Dobrygin is a terrorist. Hoffman gives a compelling performance of a much harassed secret agent who spends most of his time sidestepping danger while he gropes for answers in a world of shadows. Songs: "To Hell with Poverty" (Dave Allen, Hugo H. Burnham, Andrew Gill, John King), "Sea of Love" (Philip Paptiste, George Khoury), "Everyone Says Hi" (David Bowie), "Der Mussolini" (Robert Gorl, Gabi Delgado-Lopez), "Down Man" (Jan Akkerman, Kaz Lux), "Falling" (Roy Orbison), "Hoist That Rag" (Kathleen Brennan, Tom Waits). *Author's Note*: This was Hoffman's last film. He was found dead at the age of forty-six in the bathroom of his Manhattan apartment on February 2, 2014. A heavy drug user, heroin and other drugs were found in evidence and a syringe still inserted in Hoffman's arm, his death an obvious overdose. Gutter language prohibits viewing by children. **p**, Andrea Calderwood, Simon Cornwell, Stephen Cornwell, Gail Egan, Malte Grunert, Solveig Fina; Helge Sasse; **d**, Anton Corbijn; **cast**, Philip Seymour Hoffman, Grigoriy Dobrygin, Rainer Bock, Willem Dafoe, Rachel McAdams, Robin Wright, Daniel Bruhl, Mehdi Dehbi, Kostja Ullmann, Nina Hoss, Martin Wuttke; **w**, Andrew Bovell (based on the novel by John le Carre); **c**, Benoit Delhomme; **m**, Herbert Gronemeyer; **ed**, Claire Simpson; **prod d**, Sebastian T. Krawinkel; **art d**, Sabine Engelberg; **set d**, Yesim Zolan; **spec eff**, Jean-Michel Boublil, Malte Sarnes.

Mud ★★★ 2013; U.S.; 130m; Everest Entertainment/Lionsgate; Color; Drama; Children: Unacceptable (MPAA: PG-13); **BD**; **DVD**. Tense coming-of-age tale begins with Sheridan, a fourteen-year-old boy who lives on a houseboat on the banks of a river in Arkansas with his father, McKinnon, and mother, Paulson. He and his best friend, Lofland, also fourteen, and who lives with an uncle, Shannon, go off by small boat to an island on the Mississippi River, where Lofland has previously seen a boat suspended high up in some trees after a recent flood. They climb the tree and get into the boat and find fresh bread and footprints there. When they return to their boat, they find the same footprints in their boat. They soon meet McConaughey, a strange young man who calls himself "Mud." He tells them that he killed a man who made his girlfriend, Witherspoon, pregnant and then pushed her down a flight of stairs so that she would miscarry. The boys decide to help McConaughey by getting the boat down from the tree in exchange for his pistol. Baker, who is the father of McConaughey's victim, is searching for him, and McConaughey goes to an old friend, Shepard, for help, but Shepard refuses to lend a hand. The boys help McConaughey repair the boat from the tree and they find Witherspoon, but she has meanwhile taken up with another man. McConaughey falls into a creek and is bitten by water moccasins. The boys get him to a hospital on the mainland where an employee recognizes McConaughey from wanted posters. During a shootout with police McConaughey shoots some of them and then flees. Shepard finds McConaughey, who has been wounded in the shootout, and treats his wounds. Meanwhile, Sheridan's parents separate and they lose their houseboat. Despite these troubles, Sheridan looks forward to the future with optimism, although he is uncertain about whether McConaughey is alive or not. McConaughey is last seen traveling in the repaired boat with Shepard as they head down the Mississippi River to a getaway in the Gulf of Mexico. Sheridan and Lofland are exceptional as lads as adventurous as Tom Sawyer and Huckleberry Finn (and they manifest many of the classic characteristics of those lovable errant boys who inspired writer-director Nichols to produce this film). McConaughey, Shepard and the rest of the cast give strong support in a strange but intriguing and well-written tale. The film did well at the box office, earning more than $28.8 million in its initial release against a budget of more than $10 million. Songs: "May Pearl" (Jeff McIlwain); "Everything You Need," "Davy Brown," "The Kid," "Take You Away," "Snake Bite" (Ben Nichols); "Help Me, Rhonda" (Brian Wilson, Mike Love); "Alice Wading," "This Night," "In Fall" (Warren Ellis, Mick Turner, Jim White); "Sunday Beer," "Too Loud for Louisville" (Corey Bacon, Alan Disaster, Matt Floydm, Jon Rice); "The Steez" (Cassidy Howell); "One Beer Closer" (Dillon O'Brian). Violence, sexual references, gutter language, smoking and thematic material prohibit viewing by children. **p**, Lisa Maria Falcone, Sarah Green, Aaron Ryder; **d&w**, Jeff Nichols, **cast**, Matthew McConaughey, Reese Witherspoon, Sam Shepard, Tye Sheridan, Jacob Lofland, Sarah Paulson, Ray McKinnon, Joe Don Baker, Paul Sparks, Michael Shannon, Johnny Cheek, Bonnie Sturdivant, Stuart Greer; **c**, Adam Stone; **m**, David Wingo; **ed**, Julie Monroe; **prod d**, Richard A. Wright; **art d**, Elliott Glick; **set d**, Fontaine Beauchamp Fontaine; **spec eff**, Everett Byrom III, Jason Schugardt.

Muppets Most Wanted ★★★ 2014; U.S.; 112m; Walt Disney Pictures; Color; Musical Comedy; Children: Cautionary (MPAA: PG); **BD**; **DVD**. Entertaining entry (eighth Muppet film made) sees the Muppets go on a world tour just as Constantine (Vogel voiceover), the world's number one criminal who is a dead ringer for Kermit (Whitmire voiceover) escapes from a Siberian gulag. He makes contact with Badguy (Gervais voiceover), the tour's general manager, who also is Vogel's subordinate. The Muppets perform in Berlin while Miss Piggy

Kara Hayward, Jared Gilman and Jason Schwartzman in *Moonrise Kingdom*, **2012.**

(Jacobson voiceover) keeps hinting that Whitmire marry her. Whitmire is overtaken by a hooded Vogel, who puts a mole on Whitmire's right cheek, which makes him resemble Vogel. Whitmire is then arrested and taken to the gulag in his place. Vogel then joins the Muppets and they all believe him to be Whitmire, except the doubting Animal (Jacobson voiceover). While the Muppets are performing, Vogel and Gervais sneak off to a nearby museum to steal some paintings. Meanwhile, Whitmire's several attempts to escape the gulag are stopped by a guard (Fey voiceover), who orders him to help put on an annual prison show. After the art theft, a French Interpol agent, Burrell, and CIA agent, Jacobson, join forces to find the thieves. Vogel and Gervais then send the Muppets to Madrid as part of a plot to steal the crown jewels of Great Britain. While performing in Madrid, Vogel and Gervais attempt to steal the crown jewels but their bumbling efforts go awry. The Muppets go on to Dublin where Fozzie Bear (Jacobson voiceover) realizes the resemblance between Whitmire and Vogel and, while on a train, realizes that Vogel is posing as Whitmire and that Gervais and Vogel are working together to steal jewels. Vogel sees that he has been found out and attacks the Muppets, but Animal (Jacobson voiceover) fights him off and goes off to rescue Whitmire from the gulag. In Dublin, Vogel proposes to Miss Piggy (Jacobson voiceover) and she accepts him for a wedding to take place at the Tower of London, which Vogel intends to use as a distraction while the crown jewels are to be stolen by Gervais. Fozzie (Jacobson voiceover) and Animal (Jacobson voiceover) arrive at the gulag and tell Whitmire about Vogel's plan. They escape during the prison show and head for London. While the wedding is about to begin, Gervais steals the crown jewels, but Whitmire stops the ceremony and reveals that Vogel is an imposter and the brains behind the jewel thefts. Vogel escapes by helicopter, taking Miss Piggy (Jacobson voiceover) with him, but Whitmire intercepts them by using a "Muppet ladder" to stop the helicopter. Vogel and Gervais are arrested and the Muppet tour ends at the Siberian gulag where Vogel is part of the prison show. There is a lot of entertaining mayhem, innovative gags and clever tunes to satisfy even the most jaded viewer, albeit this helter-skelter entry does not quite match some of the earlier productions. The film performed well at the box office, earning more than $80 million in its initial release against a budget of more than $50 million. Songs: "We're Doing a Sequel," "I'm Number One," "The Big House, "I'll Get What You Want/Cockatoo in Malibu," "Interrogation Song," "Something So Right," "Together Again," "Life's a Happy Song" (Bret McKenzie); "The Muppet Show Theme" (Jim Henson, Sam Pottle); "Working in the Coal Mine" (Allen Toussaint); "Moves Like Jagger" (Adam Levine, Beno Blanko, Ammar Malik, Karl Schuster); "Macarena" (Antonio Romero, Rafael Ruiz); "We Run the Night," "Melrose Plaza" (Homer Greencastle); "Long Train Runnin'" (Charles Thomas Johnston); "I

Jared Gilman in *Moonrise Kingdom*, 2012.

Hope I Get It" (Marvin Hamlish, Ed Kleban); "Blue Danube Waltz" (Johann Strauss Jr.); "Dance of the Sugar Plum Fairy" (Pyotr Ilyich Tchaikovsky); "My Heart Will Go On' (James Horner, Will Jennings); "Rainbow Connection" (Kenny Ascher, Paul Williams); "Water Music" George Frederic Handel); "The Muppets Pit Band Again," "Total Mayhem" (Ed Mitchell, Steve Morrell); "Toreador Suite from Carmen" (Georges Bizet); "Gulag Piano" (Neil Carter); "Jesu, Joy of Man's Desiring" (Johann Sebastian Bach); "End of the Road" (Kenneth Edmonds, L.A. Reid, Daryl Simmons); "Bridal Chorus from Lohengrin" (Richard Wagner); "A Chorus Line" (music: Marvin Hamlisch; lyrics: Edward Kleban). Some harrowing action cautions viewing by children. **p**, David Hoberman, Todd Lieberman, Bill Barretta, Angus More Gordon; **d**, James Bobin; **cast**, Ricky Gervais, Matt Vogel, Tina Fey, Ty Burrell, and (voiceovers) Steve Whitmire, Eric Jacobson, Dave Goelz, Bill Barretta, Peter Linz, and (live guest performers) Tony Bennett, Hugh Bonneville, Celine Dion, Lady Gaga, Salma Hayek, Tom Hollander, Frank Langella, Ray Liotta, James McAvoy, Miranda Richardson, Stanley Tucci, Christoph Waltz; **w**, Bobin, Nicholas Stoller (based on Muppets characters created by Jim Henson); **c**, Don Burgess; **m**, Christophe Beck; **ed**, James Thomas; **prod d**, Eve Stewart; **art d**, Grant Armstrong, Andrew Max Cahn, Julia Castle, Hannah Moseley, James F. Truesdale; **set d**, Anna Lynch-Robinson; **spec eff**, Jane Gootnick, James D. Schwalm, Victoria Albanese, Sean Mathiesen, Fay McConkey, Adam McInnes, Nick Ocean.

Mustang ★★★ 2015; Turkey/France/Qatar/Germany; 97m; CG Cinema/Cohen Media Group; Color; Drama; Children: Unacceptable; (MPAA: PG-13); **BD**; **DVD**. Solid and provocative drama begins when school lets out for the summer in a present-day village in Turkey. Teenage Sensoy and her four older sisters, Doguslu, Iscan, Sunguroglu and Akdogan) walk to the beach with some classmates, both male and female, and engage in some innocent horseplay. Some on-looking adults perceive the girls' actions as immoral and report it to their guardians. The girls are in the care of an uncle and grandmother, Koldas, who confine them to the house which becomes like a prison to them because they are free-spirited girls. Their grandmother instructs them on how to become good cooks and housekeepers in order to become subservient wives in marriages that will be arranged for them. The girls now consider themselves to be living in what Sensoy calls "a wife factory," and she becomes determined to save her and her sisters from the lives their guardians want for them. They then attempt to find inventive ways to make their futures happier. Sensoy and the rest of her siblings are standouts in their roles in this well-crafted coming-of-age tale that also mixes themes from **The Stepford Wives**, 1975. The film saw limited distribution and fared poorly at the box office where it earned less than $2 mil-

lion in its initial release. Not related to 1955, 1959, or 1973 films with the same name. Mature thematic material, sexual content and rude gestures prohibit viewing by children. (In Turkish; English subtitles.) **p**, Charles Gillibert, Patrick Andre, Frank Henschke, Anja Uhland, Mine Vargi; **d**, Deniz Gamze Erguven; **cast**, Gunes Sensoy, Doga Zeynep Doguslu, Elit Iscan, Tugba Sunguroglu, Ilayda Akdogan, Nihal G. Koldas, Ayberk Pekcan, Bahar Kerimoglu, Burak Yigit, Erol Afsin; **w**, Erguven, Alice Winocour; **c**, David Chizallet, Ersin Gok; **m**, Warren Ellis; **ed**, Mathilde Van de Moortel; **art d**, Serdar Yemisci.

My All American ★★★ 2015; U.S.; 118m; Anthem Productions/Clarius Entertainment; Color; Sports Drama; Children: Unacceptable (MPAA: PG); **BD**; **DVD**. Based on true events, Wittrock plays Freddie Joe Steinmark (1949-1971), whose dream is to play college football, but is considered to be too small by general athletic standards. His father trains him hard, and Wittrock is noticed by Darrell Royal, played by Eckhart, the legendary football coach at the University of Texas, who helps him win a scholarship to attend the University in Austin. Wittrock takes his high school sweetheart, Bolger, along. Wittrock joins the football team and is put through a grueling practice schedule. During the football season that fall, while Wittrock played safety, the U of T's team rises in the charts, giving the Longhorns a chance to improve on their previous year's mediocre record. They do that by winning the national championship in 1969. However, two days after the Longhorns win "The Game of the Century" against the 1969 Arkansas Razorbacks, Wittrock suffers a leg injury and X-rays reveal a bone tumor just above his left knee. The cancer is said to be malignant and his leg has to be amputated at the hip. He is well enough twenty days later to stand on the sidelines with his team as Texas defeats Notre Dame in the 1970 Cotton Bowl on New Year's Day. His fight against cancer inspires the U.S. Congress to write the National Cancer Act of 1971, beginning America's "war on cancer." In 1971, Wittrock writes his autobiography titled *I Play to Win*. He proved that by living his courageous life, which is candidly presented in this well-enacted and well-directed film. Sadly, this film saw limited distribution and earned less than $2.3 million at the box office in its initial release against a budget of $20 million. ***Author's Note***: Steinmark died of cancer on June 6, 1971, at age twenty-two. **p**, Paul Schiff, Kell Cahoon, Lawrence M. Kopeikin; **d**, Angelo Pizzo; **cast**, Aaron Eckhart, Finn Wittrock, Sarah Bolger, Rett Terrell, Juston Street, Robin Tunney, Tracey Ely, MacKenzie Meehan, Donny Boaz, Emily Grace Dunn, Todd Allen; **w**, Pizzo (based on the book *Courage beyond the Game: The Freddie Steinmark Story* by Jim Dent); **c**, Frank G. DeMarco; **m**, John Paesano; **ed**, Dan Zimmerman; **prod d**, Bruce Curtis; **art d**, Rodney Becker; **set d**, Gabriella Villarreal; **spec eff**, Everett Byrom III.

My Brother the Devil ★★★ 2012; U.K.; 111m; Rooks Nest/Paladin; Color; Drama; Children: Unacceptable (MPAA: R); **BD**; **DVD**. Taut tale sees two teenage brothers, sons of Egyptian Muslim immigrants, living in their family's modest East London flat. Elsayed idolizes his handsome older brother, Floyd, and wants to be like him. But Floyd is a member of a local gang and deals in drugs in part to make money so that Elsayed can go to college and lead a more honest life (shades of **Invisible Stripes**, 1939, and **The Sons of Katie Elder**, 1965). Floyd would like to get a job, but has no work record. The gang Floyd is in seeks revenge on their rivals, and Elsayed wants to join them. It isn't going to be easy, but Floyd does everything he can to save Elsayed from falling into the same crime pit that has swallowed his life. Elsayed and Floyd are standouts in their roles, working with an intelligent script and a talented director, Hosaini. This award-winning film saw limited distribution, earning a little more than $1.2 million in its initial release. Drug use prohibits viewing by children. **p**, Julia Gidzinskaya, Gayle Griffiths, Michael Sackler; **d&w**, Sally El Hosaini; **cast**, James Floyd, Fady Elsayed, Said Taghmaoui, Aymen Hamdouchi, Ashley Thomas, Anthony Welsh, Arnold Oceng, Letitia Wright, Amira Ghazalla, Elarica Gallacher, Nasser Memarzia; **c**, David Raedeker; **m**, Stuart Earl; **ed**, Iain

Kitching; **prod d**, Stephane Collonge; **art d**, Pedro Moura; **spec eff**, Scott McIntyre, Dominic Thomson.

My Lucky Star ★★★ 2013; China; 114m; Bona International/China Lion; Color; Comedy/Romance; Children: Unacceptable; **BD**; **DVD**. Entertaining story has Zhang, a bored travel agent and aspiring comic book artist, dreaming of her ideal man, invariably drawing him into her art. She wins an all-expenses-paid trip to Singapore, where she accidentally becomes involved in a diamond theft. Wang, a secret agent, investigates and falls in love with her while suspecting she holds the key to recovering a gem that could destroy the world, it if falls into the wrong hands. Zhang and Wang give delightful performances in this romantic romp, which did well at the box office, earning more than $22.7 million in its initial release against a budget of more than $8 million. Not related to the 1938 film with the same title. Song: "Love a Little." (In Chinese; English subtitles.) **p**, Second Chan, William Cheng, Ming Beaver Kwei, Ling Lucas, Ziyi Zhang, Ryan Wong; **d**, Dennie Gordon; **cast**, Ziyi Zhang, Leehom Wang, Terri Kwan, Ryan Zheng, Jack Kao, Chen Yao, Ruby Lin, Hua Liu, Ada Choi, Morris Hsiang Jung, Brian Thomas Burrell; **w**, Amy Snow, Chris Chow, Hai Huang, Yao Meng (based on a story by Gordon, Snow, Kwei); **c**, Armando Salas; **m**, Nathan Wang; **ed**, Zack Arnold, Ka-Fai Cheung; **prod d**, Chan; **spec eff**, Sing-Choong Foo,

---

NH10 ★★★ 2015; India; 115m; Clean Slate Productions; Color; Crime Drama; Children: Unacceptable; **DVD**. Well-made thriller sees Anushka Sharma and Bhoopalam living and working in Gurgaon when, one night, Sharma leaves a party and is attacked by some ruffians. She is traumatized by the attack and Bhoopalam blames himself for not being with her when the assault took place. He tries to redeem himself by treating her to a luxurious desert holiday. While stopping on a highway for dinner at a restaurant, they see some hoodlums pick up a young girl. Bhoopalam, feeling guilty for not being there earlier for Sharma, goes after the molesters, despite the danger. The film's title refers to National Highway 10 in India. Top-notch acting and a well-written script provide a tension-filled chiller. The film saw a modest box office success, earning about $5 million in its initial release against a budget of almost $2 million. *Author's Note*: The story is loosely based on the honor killing of two Indian newlyweds in 2007 that was ordered by a religious caste-based council that prohibited marriage against societal norms. Violence prohibits viewing by children. **p**, Vikas Bahl, Anurag Kashyap, Krishika Lulla, Vikramaditya Motwane, Anushka Sharma, Karnesh Sharma; **d**, Navdeep Singh; **cast**, Anushka Sharma, Neil Bhoopalam, Ravi Beniwal, Siddarth Bharadwaj, Tushar Grover, Ravi Jhankal, Darshan Kumaar, Krishan Kumar, Deepti Naval, Tanya Purohit, Kanchan Sharma; **w**, Sudip Sharma; **c**, Arvind Kannabiran; **m**, Karan Gour; **ed**, Jabeen Merchant; **prod d**, Mustafa Stationwala; **spec eff**, Sriranjan Rath.

Night at the Museum: Secret of the Tomb ★★★ 2014; U.S./U.K.; 97m; FOX; Color; Comedy; Children: Unacceptable (MPAA: PG); **BD**; **DVD**. In this third entertaining installment of the series, Stiller serves as an overnight security guard at the Museum of Natural History in New York City. As expected, he has further encounters with exhibits of famous people and animals on display that come to life and wreak havoc because of an ancient curse. One by one, statues of famous people of the past and primeval beasts come to life and trash the museum. He tries to restore order with the help of Teddy Roosevelt (1858-1919), essayed by Williams. Stiller has his personal problems to solve as well. He is divorced, unable to keep a stable job, and has failed at many business ventures. Raver, his ex-wife, believes he is a bad example for their ten-year-old son, Gisondo, and Stiller now fears that the boy respects Rudd, his future stepfather, a successful bond trader, more than him. The action (or superb special effects mayhem) is almost nonstop and dazzles the viewer while Stiller continues to impress with his mopey character that,

Melanie Griffith in *Night Moves*, 1975.

at the last minute, miraculously restores order to the institution while redeeming himself in the eyes of his loving son. The film was a great success at the box office, earning more than $363.2 million in its initial release against a budget of more than $127 million. Song: "Boogie Wonderland" (Jon Lind, Allee Willis). *Author's Note*: Shortly after their cameo appearances in this film, Williams died at his own hands, a suicide by hanging, while the beloved Rooney died peacefully in his sleep at the age of ninety-three. Some harrowing action, crude humor and gutter language prohibit viewing by children. **p**, Chris Columbus, Shawn Levy; **d**, Levy; **cast**, Ben Stiller, Robin Williams, Dan Stevens, Ben Kingsley, Dick Van Dyke, Owen Wilson, Mickey Rooney, Rebel Wilson, Steve Coogan, Rachel Harris, Ricky Gervais, Rami Malek, Mizuo Peck; **w**, David Guion, Michael Handelman (based on a story by Guion, Handelman, Mark Friedman and characters created by Robert Ben Garant, Thomas Lennon); **c**, Guillermo Navarro; **m**, Alan Silvestri; **ed**, Dean Zimmerman; **prod d**, Martin Whist; **art d**, Nigel Evans, Catherine Ircha; **set d**, Peter Lando; **spec eff**, Mike Splatt, Jayme Smith.

The Night Before ★★★ 2015; U.S.; 101m; COL; Color; Comedy; Children: Unacceptable (MPAA: R); **BD**; **DVD**. Laugh-filled comedy sees Gordon-Levitt, Rogen, and Mackie, who have been friends since childhood, holding a reunion every Christmas Eve for a decade, spending it in laughs and debauchery. Gordon-Levitt has to overcome feelings of sadness because his parents were killed in a drunk-driving accident on Christmas Eve ten years earlier. Mackie is soon to be a father, and Rogen is becoming a popular athlete, so he now thinks to be on his best behavior after their final Christmas fling. Now the friends are entering adulthood, they realize their prankish tradition is coming to an end, so they decide to make it one holiday night they will never forget. They set out to find the Nutcracker Ball, the biggest and wildest of all Christmas parties with booze, drugs, and sex, which winds them all behind the proverbial eight ball. All ends well, however, and the following Yuletide, the friends wind up singing a Christmas song to Mackie's newborn child, the baby so delighted by this paternal serenade that the infant claps in appreciation to end this mirthful film. The cleverly written script sees some standout performances from the energetic cast, all guided well under Levine's firm direction. The film, shot on location in NYC, saw a solid success at the box office, earning more than $52 million in its initial release against a budget of more than $25 million. Not related to the 1988 film. Songs: "Light Up" (Akrivi Nikokiridou), "Wrecking Ball." Drug use, gutter language, strong sexual content and graphic nudity prohibit viewing by children. **p**, Evan Goldberg, Seth Rogen, James Weaver; **d**, Jonathan Levine; **cast**, Joseph Gordon-Levitt, Seth Rogen, Anthony Mackie, James Franco, Miley Cyrus, Jillian Bell, Michael Shannon, Helene Yorke, Ilana Glazer, Aaron Hill, Tracy Morgan; **w**,

Tom Cruise in *Oblivion*, **2013.**

Levine, Kyle Hunter, Ariel Shaffir, Evan Goldberg (based on a story by Levine); **c**, Brandon Trost; **m**, Marco Beltrami, Miles Hankins; **ed**, Zene Baker; **prod d**, Annie Spitz; **set d**, Chryss Hionis; **spec eff**, Nathen Cavins, Joe Heffernan, Robert J. Scupp.

Night Moves ★★★ 2013; U.S.; 112m; Maybach Film Productions; Cinedigm; Color; Crime Drama; Children: Unacceptable (MPAA: PG-13); **BD**; **DVD**. Three radical environmentalists look to explode a hydroelectric dam they feel is endangering the environment. Eisenberg and Fanning, two ecology terrorists, buy a boat and tow it a long distance to meet Sarsgaard, an ex-Marine. They buy fertilizer, assemble a bomb, and load it onto their boat. In the dark of night, they take the boat to the dam, arm the bomb, and then escape. The bomb goes off, and Sarsgaard tells the others goodbye and drives away. Eisenberg and Fanning are then stopped by police, but manage to evade suspicion. Eisenberg then returns to the farm where he lives and works. Others on the farm talk about the explosion and the media reports that a man who was camping near the dam has gone missing. Sarsgaard phones Eisenberg and tells him that Fanning is worried. Concerned that she will go to the police, Eisenberg agrees to talk to her. Fanning admits she feels guilty about the dam bombing and admits that she is thinking of going to the police. They argue and she leaves Sarsgaard, and he tells Eisenberg that Fanning needs to be silenced. Then those living on the farm grow suspicious, believing that Eisenberg was involved in the bombing, and they ask him to leave. He then learns that the body of the missing man has been found. He surprises Fanning at the spa where she works, and she attacks him and runs off. Eisenberg later finds her in a sauna and brutally strangles her. Eisenberg then calls Sarsgaard and, in tears, tells him that Fanning is dead. Sarsgaard tells Eisenberg they cannot communicate with each other again and tells him to vanish. Eisenberg destroys his phone and asks for a job application in a camping supplies store, ending this strange, uncompromising story of crime begetting crime (and where, as is wont in most recent Hollywood films, the criminal remains unpunished for the crimes). The film saw a miserable box office performance and is not related to a 1975 film of the same title. Songs: "Bulletproof" (Hayley Taylor), "San Francisco Street" (Rai Thistlethwayte, Jeff Trott), "The Reflection of You" (Jon Philpot, Joseph Blodget Stickney, Adam Stewart Wills, Michael Darius Wofford). Gutter language and nudity prohibit viewing by children. **p**, Saemi Kim, Neil Kopp, Chris Maybach, Anish Savjani, Rodrigo Teixeira, Vincent Savino; **d**, Kelly Reichardt; **cast**, Jesse Eisenberg, Dakota Fanning, Peter Sarsgaard, Alia Shawkat, Logan Miller, Kai Lennox, Katherine Waterston, James Le Gros, Taber Charles Burns, Autumn Nidalmia; **w**, Reichardt, Jonathan Raymond; **c**, Christopher Blauvelt; **m**, Jeff Grace; **ed**, Kelly Reichardt; **prod d**, Elliott Hostetter; **art d**, Almitra Corey; **set d**, Virginia Yount; **spec eff**, Craig Waxman.

Nightcrawler ★★★ 2014; U.S.; 117m; Bold Films/Open Road Films; Color; Crime Drama; Children: Unacceptable (MPAA: R); **BD**; **DVD**. Gritty crime tale sees petty thief Gyllenhaal desperate for work. He comes upon the underground world of Los Angeles freelance crime journalism. He sees some freelance camera crews that videotape car crashes, fires, and shootings. He then works his way into the dangerous and dog-eat-dog world of "nightcrawling'" where each police siren wail equals a possible windfall of money by selling on-the-spot crime films to television stations. Gyllenhaal is aided by Russo, a beautiful female veteran of local television news, and he begins to make good money while covering unsavory stories but then becomes the star of his own harrowing story. Though the film smacks of Joe Pesci's enterprising, freelancing photojournalist in **The Public Eye**, 1992, or Danny De-Vito's crime-peddling yellow journalist in **L.A. Confidential**, 1997, it nevertheless presents its own identity, and Gyllenhaal excels as a lusty peddler of any seamy and repugnant street story. The story obliquely illustrates how newspapers and TV stations no longer employ their own reliable and professional crime photographers (as seen in such films as **Picture Snatcher**, 1933, or **-30-**, 1959), but rely largely upon photographic street scavengers to provide them with sensational images. The film did very well at the box office, earning more than $50.3 million in its initial release against a budget of more than $8.5 million. Songs: "City of Angels" and "Doubt Me" (Jared MacGill, James Paxton). Violence, bloody images and gutter language prohibit viewing by children. **p**, Jennifer Fox, Tony Gilroy, Jake Gyllenhaal, David Lancaster, Michel Litvak, Stephanie Wilcox; **d&w**, Dan Gilroy; **cast**, Gyllenhaal, Rene Russo, Bill Paxton, Ann Cusack, Anne McDaniels, Riz Ahmed, Kevin Rahm, Kathleen York, Eric Lange, Jamie McShane, Michael Hyatt; **c**, Robert Elswit; **m**, James Newton Howard; **ed**, John Gilroy; **prod d**, Kevin Kavanaugh; **art d**, Naaman Marshall; **set d**, Meg Everist; **spec eff**, Joe Pancake, Elia P. Popov.

99 Homes ★★★ 2015; U.S.; 112m; Noruz Films/Broad Green Pictures; Color; Drama; Children: Unacceptable (MPAA: R); **BD**; **DVD**. Taut tale sees Garfield as a construction laborer in Orlando, Florida, in 2010. He is a single parent with a nine-year-old son, Lomax. When he loses his job, he can no longer pay the mortgage on his house and is evicted by Shannon, a merciless real estate agent who is court-appointed to repossess homes by a bank holding the mortgages. Shannon shows no sympathy for families being evicted as he serves them notice while backed up by armed sheriff's deputies. He also takes a cut from the eventual repossession sale, which will be at a bargain rate. Garfield moves his mother, Dern, and Lomax into a motel that is both shabby and unsafe, but it is all he can afford. He gets a bright idea and goes to work for Shannon in hopes of finding a way to get his house back. This backfires as cynical Shannon instructs him in how to be successful in business in today's hard, cruel world. He says he does it by white collar scamming and stealing from banks and the government, thereby getting rich. Shannon pulls no punches, telling Garfield, "America doesn't bail out losers. America was built by bailing out winners." He says government rigs America to be "a nation of the winners, for the winners, and by the winners." Garfield enters the world of greed and soon makes good money, but the riches bug has bitten him and he wants more. When Shannon orders him to evict families from their homes for not keeping up with mortgage payments, as has been his earlier fate, Garfield becomes bothered by a nagging conscience, but he nevertheless does what he is asked. Despite feelings of guilt, Garfield slips down the slope of greed and marginal honesty, telling himself it is all necessary so that he can properly house his mother and son, although greed now may be his primary objective and he is willing to swim with the greedy realtor gators such as Shannon. Garfield becomes the slavish minion of the manipulative Shannon and wittingly delivers a forged document to the court where an eviction ordered by Shannon is being tried. When police arrive to evict the homeowner, a former friend of Garfield's, conscience finally seizes and compels Garfield to publicly blurt that the homeowner's lawsuit is correct and that he was responsible for providing a forged document in order to dispossess the homeowner. Garfield is arrested on the spot, but the smug Shannon, the real guilty party, is seen to go off without punishment or retribution, proving that crime does, in real estate, pay and pay well. Garfield, Shannon, Dern and Lomax, along with the rest of a fine supporting cast, are standouts as the troubled and troubling characters. There is little empathy for the evicted victims shown in this film, no more than those being shown driven from their dust-consumed farms by bulldozing workers in **The Grapes of Wrath**, 1940. Unfortunately, the film did poorly at the box office, earning about $1.7 million in its initial release against a budget of more than $8 million. Gutter language, sexual references and a brief violent image prohibit viewing by children. **p**, Ashok Amritraj, Ramin Bahrani, Andrew Garfield, Justin Nappi, Kevin Turen; **d**, Bahrani; **cast**, Andrew Garfield, Laura Dern, Michael Shannon, Noah Lomax, Clancy Brown, Tim Guinee, Nicole Barre, J.D. Evermore, Juan Gaspard; **w**, Bahrani, Amir Naderi (based on a story by Bahrani, Bahareh Azimi); **c**, Bobby Bukowski; **m**, Antony Partos, Matteo Zingales; **ed**, Bahrani; **prod d**, Alex DiGerlando; **art d**, Christina Eunji Kim; **set d**, Monique Champagne; **spec eff**, Edward Joubert.

No ★★★ 2012; Chile/U.S./France/Mexico; 118m; Fabula/Sony; Color; Drama; Children: Unacceptable (MPAA: R); **BD**; **DVD**. Tense tale sees Bernal as a young advertising executive who is chosen to defeat military dictator Augusto Pinochet (1915-2006) in Chile when, after fifteen years in power, a referendum is called in 1988 to decide if the despot will get another eight years as president. With limited resources and constant scrutiny of Pinochet's watchers, Bernal is approached by the "No" side committee to devise a bold plan to win the election and free their country from oppression and have an open democratic presidential election the next year. Bernal's plan is to launch a campaign stressing positive concepts such as "happiness." The campaign takes place over twenty-seven nights of television advertisements in which each side has fifteen minutes to present its point of view. The humanistic "No" campaign defeats the opposition's "Yes" message, one that is unimaginative and impersonal while employing doctored positive economic statistics. Bernal then adds Hollywood celebrity spots in the "No" commercials and street concert rallies that are so popular with the public that even police attacks cannot discourage its supporters. On the day of the referendum, it appears as if the "Yes" side has the lead, but the final results turn out to be firmly on the "No" side. Government troops surrounding the "No" headquarters withdraw as news comes that the Chilean senior military command has forced Pinochet to concede his defeat. Bernal goes back to his normal advertising work in a new democratic Chile. Bernal gives a riveting performance as an inventive advertising man turned crusader, and the gritty lensing adds much to the taut story. The film received an Oscar nomination for Best Foreign Language Film, but it did poorly at the box office, earning less than $2.5 million in its initial release. Songs: "La alegria ya viene" (Sergio Bravo, Jaime de Aguirre), "Vuelvo" (Patricio Manns, Horacio Salinas), "No lo quiero" (Isabel Parra). Gutter language prohibits viewing by children. **p**, Daniel Marc Dreifuss, Juan de Dios Larrain, Pablo Larrain; **d**, Pablo Larrain; **cast**, Gael Garcia Bernal, Alfredo Castro, Luis Gnecco, Nestor Cantillana, Antonio Zegers, Marcial Tagle, Pascal Montero, Jaime Vadell, Elsa Poblete, Diego Munoz; **w**, Pedro Peirano (based on a play by Antonio Skarmeta); **c**, Sergio Armstrong; **m**, Carlos Cabezas; **ed**, Andrea Chignoli; **art d**, Estefania Larrain; **set d**, Maria Eugenia Hederra; **spec eff**, Ismael Cabrera.

Noah ★★★★ 2014; U.S.; 138m; PAR; Color; Adventure/Drama; Children: Unacceptable (MPAA: PG-13); **BD**; **DVD**. This finely crafted historical tale takes its story from the Bible, one wherein God instructs Noah, played by Crowe, to build an ark to rescue his family and two of each kind of animal and bird before an apocalyptic flood engulfs the Earth. Crowe, a bearded, middle-aged vegetarian, obeys the command,

Gerard Butler in *Olympus Has Fallen*, 2013.

telling his wife, Connelly, and his adopted daughter, Watson. There is romantic interest from Noah's three sons, Booth, Lerman and Carroll, who are estranged from the rest of the family. God is disappointed in his creation of man, while Noah is considered to be the last good man on Earth, so he is to build an ark to preserve the world's animal and bird life while the wicked will be swept away in a flood, forcing humanity to make a new start. Noah is a determined survivalist so he follows his instructions and builds the ark and gathers the species needed, but also is an environmentalist who also collects what is needed and can be used. He and his immediate family are joined by his grandfather Methuselah, played by Hopkins, and they are visited by "the Watchers," so-called Nephilin who are fallen angels and who take the form of ferocious-looking rock people (voiced by Nolte, Margolis and Langella). They help Noah do the heavy construction in building the ark. They also keep outcasts and misfits from going aboard the ark, particularly a group led by Winstone, who is a descendant of Cain, the world's first murderer, slayer of his own brother, Abel. Winstone becomes a stowaway on the ark, which creates a crisis in Noah's family. The film does not show Noah gathering the animals for the voyage, and they go to sleep immediately upon boarding, so as to avoid internecine conflict and to concentrate on Noah's efforts to fulfill his mission. After the flood, the ark reaches land where Noah's family members are to repopulate the world. Crowe and the rest of the supporting cast members are standouts in their biblical roles, and the film presents astounding special effects to show the world-encompassing flood. The film saw a huge box office success (mostly due to it marvelous visuals), earning more than $362.6 million in its initial release against a budget of more than $125 million. Songs: "Father Song," "Mercy Is" (Patti Smith, Lenny Kaye, Russell Crowe); "Mercy Is" (Smith, Kaye). *Author's Note*: Much of the film was shot on location in southern Iceland and in New York State where the set representing the Ark was constructed. The film was banned in many countries in the Middle East as it was thought that the script wen against Islamic teachings. Noah has been enacted by many actors in many other films, including **After Six Days**, 1920 (Augusto Mastripietri); **The Bible: In the Beginning...**, 1966 (John Huston); **Disintegration**, 2007 (Larry Flournoy); **The Flood**, 1962 (made-for-TV; Sebastian Cabot); **Genesis: The Creation and the Flood**, 1994 (Omero Antonutti); **Greatest Heroes of the Bible**, 1978- (TV series; "The Story of Noah," two episodes in 1978: Lew Ayres); **The Green Pastures**, 1936 (Eddie "Rochester" Anderson); **The Green Pastures**, 1959 (made-for-TV; Eddie "Rochester" Anderson); **Mary's Incredible Dream**, 1976 (made-for-TV; Ben Vereen); **Noah**, 1946 (made-for-TV; Michael Hordern); **Noah**, 1998 (Tony Danza); **Noah**, 2012 (Michael Keaton); **Noah's Ark**, 1928 (Paul McAllister); **Noah's Ark**, 1999- (TV miniseries; Jon Voight); **Omnibus**, 1952-1961 (TV series; "The Horn Blows at Midnight," 1953

Akshay Kumar in *OMG: Oh My God,* **2012.**

episode; Rolfe Sedan); **The Passion**, 1999- (TV series; David Mahoney); **Son of God**, 2014 (David Rintoul); and **Testament: The Bible in Animation**, 1996- (TV series; Joss Ackland voiceover). Violence, disturbing images and brief suggestive content prohibit viewing by children. **p**, Darren Aronofsky, Scott Franklin, Arnon Milchan, Mary Parent, Amy Herman; **d**, Aronofsky; **cast**, Russell Crowe, Jennifer Connelly, Ray Winstone, Anthony Hopkins, Emma Watson, Nick Nolte, Logan Lerman, Douglas Booth, Mark Margolis, (voiceover) Frank Langella; **w**, Aronofsky, Ari Handel; **c**, Matthew Libatique; **m**, Clint Mansell; **ed**, Andrew Weisblum; **prod d**, Mark Friedberg; **art d**, Dan Webster, Alex DiGerlando, Atli Geir Gretarsson, Deborah Jensen; **set d**, Nicholas Di-Blasio, Debra Schutt; **spec eff**, Burt Dalton, Haukur Karlsson.

Northmen: A Viking Saga ★★★ 2014; Switzerland, Germany, South Africa; 97m; Elite Filmproduktion; Color; Adventure; Children: Unacceptable (MPAA: R); **BD**; **DVD**. Action-oriented adventure sees a group of Vikings stranded behind enemy lines on the coast of Alba as their longboat sinks in a storm. Their only chance of survival is to find a way to a Viking settlement over unfamiliar and hostile country they have never before seen. Their ordeal becomes a race for their lives when the King of Alba sends his most feared mercenaries in pursuit of them. However, after the Vikings meet a kind Christian monk, who wields a mean sword (a la Friar Tuck in the Robin Hood legend), their prospects improve. He helps them and the hunters become the hunted as the Vikings set deadly traps and slay their pursuers in a final and deadly battle. The film saw limited distribution and earned only a little more than $2.8 million in its initial release. Excessive violence prohibits viewing by children. **p**, Marco Del Bianco, Karin G. Dietrich, Ralph S. Dietrich, Daniel Hoeltschi, Frank Kaminski, Bertha Spieker, Ulrich Stiehm, Giselher Venzke, Rolf Wappenschmitt; **d**, Claudio Fah; **cast**, Ed Skrein, Ryan Kwanten, James Norton, Tom Hopper, Charlie Murphy, Leo Gregory, Ken Duken, Johan Hegg, Anatole Taubman, Nic Rasenti; **w**, Matthias Bauer, Bastian Zach, Claudio Fah, Adrian Jelcik; **c**, Lorenzo Senatore; **m**, Marcus Trumpp; **ed**, Adam Recht; **prod d**, Shane Bunce, Tom Hannam; **art d**, Jonathan Hely-Hutchinson, Patrick O'Connor; **set d**, Henry du Rand; **spec eff**, Marco Del Bianco, Frank Kaminski.

The November Man ★★★ 2014; U.S.; 108m; Das Films/Relativity Media; Color; Spy Drama; Children: Unacceptable (MPAA: R); **BD**; **DVD**. Exciting espionage tale has Brosnan, a former CIA operative known as "The November Man," enjoying a quiet life in retirement in Switzerland when he brought back into action by an old colleague, Smitrovich, on a very personal mission. He soon finds himself protecting social worker Kurylenko, who is a potential source as to the whereabouts of a key witness. He then becomes the target of Bracey, his

former CIA protégé, after Brosnan uncovers the truth about the origins of the Chechen War (1994-1996; 1999-2009) in Russia that resulted in the deaths of thousands of innocent people. With growing suspicions of a CIA cover-up, there is no one Brosnan can trust, no rules to follow, and no holds barred. With Kurylenko's help, Brosnan discovers that Smitrovich was part of the cover-up and manages to expose him, but not before he overcomes harrowing dangers and almost impossible odds. The action is non stop as Brosnan does a fine job as a secret agent who is no secret to his enemies, and firm direction from Donaldson (who had worked with Brosnan in **Dante's Peak**, 1997) assures suspense and tension throughout. The film did well at the box office, earning more than $34.8 million in its initial release against a budget of more than $15 million. Songs: "Die This Way" (Marco Beltrami, Tyson Lozensky), "Keep It Up" (Makao), "Gnossienne No. 3" (Erik Satie), "Ticking Bomb" (Aloe Blacc, Adam Schmalholz, Antonio Armano, Timothy James Price). Excessive violence, including a sexual assault, gutter language, sexuality and nudity prohibit viewing by children. **p**, Sriram Das, Beau St. Clair, Keith Arnold, Steve Shapiro; **d**, Roger Donaldson; **cast**, Pierce Brosnan, Luke Bracey, Will Patton, Patrick Kennedy, Olga Kurylenko, Bill Smitrovich, Amila Terzimehic, Lazar Ristovski, Mediha Musliovic, Eliza Taylor, Caterina Scorsone, Akie Kotabe; **w**, Michael Finch, Karl Gajdusek (based on the book *There Are No Spies* by Bill Granger); **c**, Romain Lacourbas; **m**, Marco Beltrami; **ed**, John Gilbert; **prod d**, Kevin Kavanaugh; **art d**, Jasna Dragovic; **set d**, Meg Everist; **spec eff**, Muhamed M'Barek, Jason Troughton.

Now You See Me ★★★ 2013; U.S.; 115m; Summit Entertainment; Color; Crime Drama; Children: Unacceptable (MPAA: PG-13); **BD**; **DVD**. Absorbing cape film sees four musicians respond to a mysterious summons at an address having dangerous secrets within. A year later, they are the Four Horsemen, famous stage illusionists, who end their Las Vegas show with a bank robbery that is apparently very real. The mystery is not easy to solve, even when attempted by Freeman, a professional illusion exposer. A strange investigation follows in which nothing is what it seems, with illusions, dark secrets, and hidden agendas as everyone involved finds that the closer they look, the less they discover. The acting is top notch and is only triumphed by some of the illusionist wizardry presented and well choreographed by director Leterrier. The film had a huge success at the box office, earning more than $351.7 million in its initial release against a budget of $75 million. Songs: "Codec" (Anton Zaslavski), "Ash Wednesday Sunrise" and "Cineramascope" (Ben Ellman, Robert Joseph Mercurio, Stanton Emery Moore, Jeffrey H. Raines, Richard Vogel), "Goodnight Benny" (Ronald Paul Curcio Jr.), "Let's Take a Stroll on the Boardwalk" (Mark Gasbarro), "Entertainment" (Thomas Pablo Croquet, Christian Mazzalai, Laurent Mazzalai, Frederic Jean Joseph Moulin). Violence, gutter language and sexual content prohibit viewing by children. **p**, Bobby Cohen, Alex Kurtzman, Roberto Orci; **d**, Louis Leterrier; **cast**, Morgan Freeman, Jesse Eisenberg, Mark Ruffalo, Woody Harrelson, Dave Franco, Michael Caine, Isla Fisher, Melanie Laurent, Michael J. Kelly, Jose Garcia; **w**, Ed Solomon, Boaz Yakin, Edward Ricourt (based on a story by Yakin and Ricourt); **c**, Mitchell Amundsen, Larry Fong; **m**, Brian Tyler; **ed**, Robert Leighton, Vincent Tabaillon; **prod d**, Peter Wenham; **art d**, Kim Jennings, Scott Plauche, Thomas Valentine; **set d**, Beauchamp Fontaine Hebb; **spec eff**, Jeff Brink, Guy Clayton Jr.

Oblivion ★★★ 2013; U.S.; 124m; UNIV; Color; Science Fiction; Children: Unacceptable (MPAA: PG-13); **BD**; **DVD**. Exciting sci-fi tale begins in 2077, where Cruise is one of the last drone repairmen stationed on Earth after the planet was destroyed 60 years earlier during a war against alien invaders known as "Scavs" (short for Scavengers). They destroyed the Moon, causing massive earthquakes and tsunamis on Earth before launching their invasion. They were defeated by nuclear weapons, which left most of the planet irradiated and uninhabitable. The few surviving humans migrated to a colony on Titan, which is powered by using sea water energy from Earth. Cruise is based in northeastern United States with his partner and lover Riseborough, who work as a team to maintain autonomous drones that defend power stations from a few remaining Scav bandits. They receive their orders from Leo, their mission commander, who is located on a space station orbiting Earth, and expect to join her in two weeks. Cruise's and Riseborough's memories had been erased for security reasons, but he has dreams about meeting a mystery woman at the Empire State Building in a time before the war, a rendezvous that took place before he was born. Scav drones invade again, and Cruise rescues Kurylenko, recognizing her as the woman from his dreams. She says her ship, the *Odyssey*, was on a NASA mission, and she and Cruise recover the ship's flight recorder. They are captured by Scavs, who are humans led by Freeman and who are living in a mountain complex. Cruise takes Kurylenko to the ruins of the Empire State Building where she reveals she was his wife before the alien war. More action leads to Cruise coming face-to-face with a clone of himself. He fights and defeats the clone and it all ends with Cruise deactivating the remaining Scav drones around the world. Cruise does a credible job as a futuristic man attempting to regain his memory, identity and the woman he loves in an action-packed tale where special effects dazzle throughout. The thin story and the underdevelopment of characters is overcome through the mesmerizing visuals lavishing this production. The film was a great success at the box office, earning more than $286.2 million in its initial release against a budget of $120 million. A 1994 film with the same title had a different plot. Songs: "Ramble On" (Robert Plant, Jimmy Page), "A Whiter Shade of Pale" (Keith Reid, Gary Brooker, Matthew Fisher), "Oblivion" (Anthony Gonzalez, Susanne Sundfor). Violence, gutter language, sensuality and nudity prohibit viewing by children. **p**, Joseph Kosinski, Peter Chernin, Dylan Clark, Duncan Henderson, Mike Larocca, R.J. Mino, Bruce Franklin, Steve Gaub; **d**, Kosinski; **cast**, Tom Cruise, Morgan Freeman, Nikolaj Coster-Waldau, Melissa Leo, Zoe Bell, Abigail Lowe, Isabelle Lowe, Olga Kurylenko, Andrea Riseborough, David Madison; **w**, Karl Gajdusek, Michael Arndt as Michael deBruyn (based on a graphic novel story by Kosinski); **c**, Claudio Miranda; **m**, Anthony Gonzalez, Joseph Trapanese; **ed**, Richard Francis-Bruce; **prod d**, Darren Gilford; **art d**, Kevin Ishioka, Mark W. Mansbridge; **set d**, Ronald R. Reiss; **spec eff**, Michael Meinardus.

Olympus Has Fallen ★★★ 2013; U.S.; 119m; Millennium Films; FilmDistrict; Color; Crime Drama; Children: Unacceptable (MPAA: R); **BD**; **DVD**. Action-loaded thriller begins when terror strikes the White House after Eckhart, the U.S. President, unwittingly invites Yune, the prime minister of North Korea, and his delegation to discuss mounting hostilities between the two countries. Eckhart does not know that Yune and his minions plan to kidnap him and his young son, Jacobsen, and steal the Secret Service Code named "Olympus." As the meeting begins, a heavily armed military transport plane descends on the White House, and Secret Service agents take Eckhart and Jacobsen to his command bunker for safety. The plane is downed on the White House mall, and armed terrorists enter the White House and infiltrate Eckhart's bunker. Yune demands that America remove its forces from the demilitarized zone between North and South Korea, move the U.S. 7th Naval Fleet out of that area, and surrender three Secret Service codes to a fail-safe program called Cerberus, which will disable the U.S. nuclear arsenal against North Korea. The acting president, Freeman (who is the Speaker of the House of Representatives), is about to agree to Yune's demands when he learns that Butler has infiltrated the White House, which is under siege by the North Koreans. Butler and the Secret Service team then have the near impossible job of saving Eckhart and Jacobsen, reclaiming the White House, and recovering the Olympus code. The premise that U.S. security at the White House is so frail (undoubtedly inspired by the bevy of White House lawn invaders over recent years) that such

Logan Lerman in *The Perks of Being a Wallflower*, 2012.

an organized act of terrorism could take place challenges credibility, but the outstanding acting from Eckhart, Jacobsen, Yune, and that fine character actor Freeman, brings considerable belief to an otherwise fantastic tale. The wild action is well coordinated and the lensing is a standout. The film was a success at the box office, earning more than $161 million in its initial release against a budget of more than $70 million. Another film that year, **White House Down**, 2013, covers much the same story line but is a much inferior production. Song: "Christmas with the Man I Love" (Andrew Peter Kingslow, Sarah Dowling). Violence and gutter language throughout prohibit viewing by children. **p**, Gerard Butler, Ed Cathell III, Antoine Fuqua, Danny Lerner, Alan Siegel; **d**, Fuqua; **cast**, Butler, Aaron Eckhart, Morgan Freeman, Angela Bassett, Melissa Leo, Dylan McDermott, Ashley Judd, Robert Forster, Rick Yune, Radha Mitchell, Finley Jacobsen, Cole Hauser, Phil Austin; **w**, Creighton Rothenberger, Katrin Benedikt; **c**, Conrad W. Hall; **m**, Trevor Morris; **ed**, John Refoua; **prod d**, Derek R. Hill; **art d**, Karen Steward; **set d**, Cathy T. Marshall; **spec eff**, Jack Lynch.

OMG: Oh My God ★★★ 2012; India; 125m; Grazing Goat Pictures; Color; Comedy; Children: Cautionary; **BD**; **DVD**. Delightfully humorous satire begins with Rawal, who is an atheist Hindi, and who sells idols of Hindu gods and makes up stories about them in selling them at his shop in Mumbai, India. Rawal's outlandish method of peddling his wares greatly displeases his God-fearing wife, Salim. Then a localized earthquake destroys his shop but does not damage anything else. He is refused monetary relief from his insurance company because they say their coverage does not include natural calamities, and that the adjusters consider Rawal's damaged shop to be an "act of God." Rawal desperately files a lawsuit against God, accusing Him of willfully destroying his property and claiming that He is liable to pay him for the damages. Since God has no known address, he sends a notice to all those he knows who proclaim their faith in God. The case goes to court, and Rawal argues it against neighbors and others who are believers in God, although, being an atheist and in order to win the case, he must prove that God does exist and caused the quake that destroyed his business. He tries proving that by calling Catholic priests, Muslim Mullahs, and other religious leaders to the stand as defense witnesses. Hussain, the presiding judge, then demands written proof that the disaster was an act of God. The trial causes Rawal to read more about religion and faith that challenges his atheism. Whether he wins or loses his case, Rawal advises everyone to search for God in themselves, not in statues. Rawal is delightful in his role as a non-believer impaled on his own petard, compelling himself to confirm the existence of what he does not believe exists. The film did well at the box office, earning more than $18 million in its initial release against a budget of more than $3 million. Song: "Go

Emma Watson in *The Perks of Being a Wallflower,* 2012.

Go Govinda (Himesh Reshammiya). **p**, B.K. Modi, Ashvini Yardi; **d**, Umesh Shukla; **cast**, Paresh Rawal, Akshay Kumar, Subna Salin, Om Puri, Yousef HussainKhan, Mithun Chakraborty, Apoorva Avora, Arun Bali, Puja Gupta, Murli Mishra, Govind Namdeo, Krunal Pandit; **w**, Shukla, Bhavesh Mandalia; **c**, Sethu Sriram; **m**, Himesh Reshammiya; **ed**, Rajesh Panchal, Tushar Shivan; **spec eff**, V. Gouri Shankar Rao.

One Chance ★★★ 2014; U.K./U.S.; 103m; Relevant Entertainment; Weinstein; Color; Biographical Drama/Musical; Children: Unacceptable (MPAA: PG-13); **BD**; **DVD**. Entertaining biopic based on the life and career of Paul Potts (1970-), who is played by Cordon, a shy, bullied London shop assistant by day and an amateur opera tenor by night who became a sensation after being chosen for and then winning the British television reality show "Britain's Got Talent." His opera ambitions nearly cost him his marriage, but we see in this well-written story how his ambition to exercise his wonderful talent triumphs in the end. The film earned $10.9 million in its initial release but did not offset its budget of more than $12 million. Songs: "Allegro Con Brio from Symphony No. 5 in G Minor," "Confutatis maledictis from Requiem in D Minor, K. 626" (Wolfgang Amadeus Mozart); "Che Gelida Manina from La Boheme," "O Soave Fanciulla from La Boheme," "Quando M'en Vo from La Boheme" (music: Giacomo Puccini; lyrics: Luigi Illica, Giuseppe Giacosa); "Golden Retriever" (Bunford, Ciaran, Ieuan, Pruce, Rhys); "YMCA" (Henri Belolo, Jacques Morali, Victor Edward Willis); "Vesti la Giubba from Pagliacci" (Ruggero Leoncavallo); "Waltz Op. 69 No. 2 for Clarinet and Strings" (Frederick Chopin); "Italian Dance" (Andy Georges); "Let It Be Me" (Ray Lamontagne); "I Love Thee/Ich Liebe Dich" (music: Edward Grieg; lyrics: Henry G. Chapman); "Come On Eileen" (James Paterson, Kevin Rowland, Kevin Adams); "Never Gonna Give You Up" (Aitkin, Waterman, Stock); "Come and Get It" (Ryan Spraker, Michael Isvara Montgomery); "Nessun Dorma from Turnadot" (Giacomo Puccini); "Farewell to Earth from Aida," "Gloria all'Egritto from Aida," "Celeste Aida from Aida" (music: Giuseppe Verdi; lyrics: Antonio Ghislanzoni); "Rewind" (Kelly Jones); "Something to Believe In," "Con Te Partiro" (Franco Sartori, Lucio Quarantotto); "Do Re Mi" (music: Richard Rodgers; lyrics: Oscar Hammerstein III);, "Britain's Got Talent Theme" (Jorgenson, Love); "Sweeter Than Fiction" (Jack Antonoff, Taylor Swift). Gutter language and some sexual material prohibit viewing by children. **p**, Simon Cowell, Michael Menchel, Kris Thykier, Brad Weston, Jane Hooks; **d**, David Frankel; **cast**, James Corden, Alexandra Roach, Julie Walters, Colm Meaney, Mackenzie Crook, Valeria Bilello, Trystan Gravelle, Sion Tudor Owen, Jemima Rooper, Alex Macqueen; **w**, Justin Zackham; **c**, Florian Ballhaus; **m**, Theodore Shapiro; **ed**, Wendy Greene Bricmont; **prod d**, Martin Childs; **art d**, James Wakefield, Nick Dent; **set d**, Celia Bobak; **spec eff**, Neal Champion, Eric J. Robertson, Wilson Cameron.

The 100-Year-Old Man Who Climbed Out the Window and Disappeared ★★★ 2014; Sweden/Russia/U.K./France/Spain; 114m; NICE FLX Pictures/Music Box Films; Color; Comedy; Children: Unacceptable (MPAA: R); **BD**; **DVD**. Rollicking comedy sees Gustafsson as a retired explosives expert, who is a centenarian living in a retirement home. He suddenly decides to leave and see what life still holds in store for him by climbing out a window and into an adventure he never could have imagined. Through flashbacks we learn that he has met some important people of the 20th Century (shades of **Forrest Gump**, 1994), including Gustafsson's fighting on the side of Spain's dictator Francisco Franco (1892-1975) in the Spanish Civil War (1936-1939). In flash-forward, Gustafsson goes further into the future as he sells nuclear secrets to the Soviets. In between, he inherits a suitcase full of money, deals with a dangerous gang of motorbikers, angry mobsters, and even goes up against a rogue elephant. Along the way we see that Gustafsson has a knack for interfering with and slightly altering historical events. Gustafsson is outstanding in his man-of-all-ages role, and many of his outrageous predicaments present some very amusing comedic moments. The film received an Oscar nomination for Best Makeup and Hairstyling (Love Larson, Eva Von Bahr). The film was also a great hit at the box office, earning more than $50 million in its initial release against a budget of more than $9.1 million. Violence and gutter language prohibit viewing by children. **p**, Felix Herngren, Malte Forssell, Henrik Jansson-Schweizer, Patrick Nebout; **d**, Herngren; **cast**, Robert Gustafsson, Iwar Winklander, David Wiberg, Mia Skaringer, Jens Hulten, Binaca Cruzeiro, Alan Ford, Sven Lonn, David Shackleton, Georg Nikoloff; **w**, Herngren, Hans Ingemansson (based on the novel by Jonas Jonasson); **c**, Goran Hallberg; **m**, Matti Bye; **ed**, Henrik Kallberg; **prod d**, Mikael Varhelyi; **art d**, Christian Olander, Piroska Szabady; **spec eff**, Ferenc Deak, Johan Harnesk, Gyula Kransyanszky.

The One I Love ★★★ 2014; U.S.; 97m; RaDiUS; Color; Drama; Children: Unacceptable (MPAA: R); **BD**; **DVD**. Eerie and often chilling tale begins with Duplass and Moss, a young couple having marital problems. They are in marriage counseling for familiar reasons. He cheated on her and they don't communicate very well so they are not having sex anymore. They wish they were like they used to be and where they had great sex together. Danson, their marriage counselor, suggests that they go on a "retreat" together for a weekend because he has had success sending other couples to the same place. Duplass and Moss agree and go on a weekend to a big old house on a large property with a swimming pool and guest house. There are no other guests and there is no one checking on them. They explore the grounds where they get the eerie feeling someone is watching them. That night, alone in the house, they make dinner, drink wine, and smoke pot, all of which helps them to relax with each other. Afterward they have sex together, but, the next morning, Moss has no memory of it. Strange things then begin to go on in the guest house which frightens them so they flee the property, but then return thinking Danson is causing the strange goings-on there. They had told him they would be open to new experiences, but fear the worst. They periodically have satisfying sex with one another, and then have no recollection of their trysts. At one point Moss cooks eggs and bacon for Duplass, who finds it strange that she has prepared a meal where she formerly hated even the smell of bacon. They finally discover that they have been romancing their dopplegangers, these twin-like creatures disappearing and reappearing. Realizing that they are being somehow manipulated by other world lookalikes through Danson's weird therapy, they flee the house and return to Danson's office to demand explanations. They find that office empty, except for a piano. Going home, they decide to make a go of their marriage on their own. When Duplass wakes up the next morning, however, and asks Moss what she will be making for breakfast, she tells him bacon and eggs. Duplass stares in horror, believing that he is now living with his wife's lookalike (and the implication that Moss has gone off with Duplass' other world twin). Duplass and Moss render outstanding performances as a couple wanting to fall in love again but challenged with the terror-filled thought that each other has been replaced by a total stranger (which, in real life, is often the case). The script is clever and, and providing many twists and turn to keep the viewer's tension and interest to the fadeout. Unfortunately, the film did not do well at the box office, earning less than $1 million in its initial release. Songs: "Bye Bye Baby" (Little Hat Jones), "Piano Concerto No. 21, 2nd movement" (Wolfgang Amadeus Mozart), "Roses Grow Thorns" (Matraca Berg, Mary Steenburgen), "It Ain't Like That" (Nik Freitas), "Ashes to the Wind" (MiWi), "Dedicated to the One I Love" (Ralph Bass, Lowman Pauling). Gutter language, sexuality and drug use prohibit viewing by children. **p**, Mel Eslyn; **d**, Charlie McDowell; **cast**, Mark Duplass, Elisabeth Moss, Ted Danson, Kiana Cason, Kaitlyn Dodson, Lori Farrar, Marlee Matlin, Tim Peddicord, Ryan Pederson, Mary Steenburgen (voice); **w**, Justin Lader; **c**, Doug Emmett; **m**, Danny Bensi, Saunder Jurriaans; **ed**, Jennifer Lilly; **prod d**, Theresa Guleserian; **art d**, Erika Toth; **spec eff**, Stefan Scherperel.

Oslo, August 31st ★★★ 2012; Norway; 95m; Don't Look Now/Strand Releasing; Color; Drama; Children: Unacceptable; **BD**; **DVD**. Top-drawer drama has Lie, a talented novelist, suffering from a writer's block as he is under pressure from previous literary successes to repeat his triumphs. A recovering drug addict at a treatment center, he considers committing suicide. His girlfriend, Olava, and an old drug buddy, Brenner, cannot retrieve him from his mental tailspin as he believes that life holds nothing for him. The film follows one day in his life in Oslo, after which he returns to the treatment center. Lie is outstanding as the drug-controlled writer struggling to free himself from his addiction and he receives strong support from Olava and Brenner as he attempts to live a better lifestyle. The intelligent script lends much to the acting and the strong direction from Trier, all of which provide a sometimes emotionally wrenching experience, but one rich with empathy. Songs: "Too Long/Steam Machine" (Thomas Bangalter, Guy-Manuel de Homem-Christo); "Dying Hipster," "Exit Ghost," "Everyman" (Torgny Amdam); "Lamentation" (The White Birch). Drug use prohibits viewing by children. (In Norwegian; English subtitles.) **p**, Hans-Jorgen Osnes, Yngve Saether; **d**, Joachim Trier; **cast**, Anders Danielsen Lie, Hans Olav Brenner, Ingrid Olava, Anders Borchgrevink, Andreas Braaten, Malin Crepin, Petter Width Kristiansen, Emil Lund, Tone Beate Mostraum, Renate Reinsve; **w**, Trier, Eskil Vogt (based on the novel *Le Feu Follet* by Pierre Drieu La Rochelle); **c**, Jakob Ihre; **m**, Torgny Amdam, Ola Flottum; **ed**, Olivier Bugge Coutte; **prod d**, Jorgen Stangebye Larsen; **art d**, Solfrid Kjetsa; **spec eff**, Raymond Gangstad, Kjetil Haugen.

Out of the Furnace ★★★ 2013; U.S./U.K.; 116m; Appian Way/Relativity Media; Color; Crime Drama; Children: Unacceptable (MPAA: R); **BD**; **DVD**. Taut crime yarn has Bale and his younger brother Affleck living in the poor Rust Belt, dreaming of escaping and finding better lives. In a cruel twist of fate, Bale, while driving home drunk, hits and kills some people and is convicted of manslaughter and imprisoned. Affleck, an inveterate gambler always indebted to bookies, chiefly Dafoe, a ruthless loan shark and bar owner, and he becomes involved with one of the most ruthless and violent criminal gangs in the Northeast. While Bale is in prison he learns that his father, Shepard, has died, and his wife, Saldana, has left him. When Bale is released from prison he has to make a choice between possibly losing his own freedom or risk it to seek justice for his brother. In order to pay off his debts, Affleck, a four-tour Iraq veteran, participates in bloody bare-knuckle fistfights (a la Charles Bronson in **Hard Times**, 1975), but makes so little money in these dangerous matches that he is unable to repay Dafoe. A fixed fight is then set up by Dafoe where Affleck is compelled to take a dive, so that he no longer owes money to Dafoe and Dafoe, in turn, will no longer owe anything to financial backer and gangster Harrelson. Following the fight, however, Harrelson kills Dafoe and then murders Af-

Erin Wilhelmi, Logan Lerman and Mae Whitman in *The Perks of Being a Wallflower,* 2012.

fleck. That night, Bale finds a letter from Affleck telling him that he is quitting the fights and that he wants to work with Bale in the mill where Bale is employed, something Bale has urged all along. Learning how Affleck has been murdered, Bale entices Harrelson to a meeting where he shoots him several times, killing him. He then returns home and is shown sitting at his kitchen room table as this grim film ends. Bale gives a riveting performance as a protective older brother who cannot prevent the self-destruction of the sibling he loves, and Affleck is outstanding as that errant youth; Dafoe and Harrelson are exceptional in their villainous roles. Though well-scripted and firmly directed, this film did not do well at the box office, earning less than $15.5 million in its initial release against a budget of more than $22 million. Songs: "Release" (Eddie Vedder, Jeff Ament, Stone Gossard, Dave Krusen, Mike McCready). Excessive violence, gutter language and drug interest prohibit viewing by children. **p**, Michael Costigan, Leonardo DiCaprio, Ryan Kavanaugh, Jennifer Davisson Killoran, Ridley Scott, Tony Scott, Danny Dimbort, Ken Halsband, Michael Ireland, Jamie Marshall, John Ridley; **d**, Scott Cooper; **cast**, Christian Bale, Casey Affleck, Sam Shepard, Woody Harrelson, Willem Dafoe, Forest Whitaker, Boyd Holbrook, Tom Bower, Charles David Richards, Zoe Saldana; **w**, Cooper, Brad Ingelsby; **c**, Masanobu Takayanagi; **m**, Dickon Hincliffe; **ed**, David Rosenbloom; **prod d**, Therese DePrez; **art d**, Gary Kosko; **set d**, Merissa Lombardo; **spec eff**, Ray Bivins, Ann-Marie Blommaert, Cat Counsell.

Oz the Great and Powerful ★★★ 2014; U.S.; 130m; Walt Disney; Sony; Color; Fantasy; Children: Cautionary (MPAA: PG); **3-D**; **PG**; **BD**; **DVD**. This good prequel to **The Wizard of Oz**, 1939, takes place twenty years earlier in 1905 Kansas. Oscar "Oz" Diggs, played by Franco, is a magician in a traveling circus. Holmes, the circus strongman, learns that Franco has flirted with his wife, Wynne, and, as a storm approaches the area, goes to attack him. Franco escapes in a hot air balloon that is lifted into a tornado that takes him to the mythical Land of Oz. There he encounters three witches, Weisz, Kunis and Williams, who are in a power struggle to rule Oz and do not believe he is the wizard foretold to rule the land instead of one of them. Franco has to learn which of the witches is good or bad before they can kill him. While resolving conflicts with the witches, he becomes king of Oz, using a hidden smoke machine and image projector to make everyone believe he is, indeed, a powerful wizard. He gives gifts to those who help him, then takes the only good witch, Glinda (Williams) behind the curtain hiding his projector and kisses her. Along the way to the happy ending there are castle seizes, battles with flying monkeys, baboons, and a host of other dazzling wonders. Franco is a standout as the wizard and he receives strong support by the gifted Williams, Weisz and Kunis. The sets

Logan Lerman, Mae Whitman, Ezra Miller and Erin Wilhelmi in *The Perks of Being a Wallflower,* **2012.**

and costumes are marvelous to behold as are the eye-popping special effects. The film enjoyed a great success at the box office, earning more than $493.3 million in its initial release against a budget of more than $215 million. Songs: "Almost Home" (Simone Porter, Justin Gray, Lindsey Ray, Tor Erik Hermansen, Mikkel Eriksen, Mariah Carey), "The Munchkin Welcome Song" (music: Danny Elfman; lyrics: David Lindsay-Abaire), "Oz's Magic Show Piano" (David Reinstein), "Shofar" (Roberto Juan Rodriguez). Frightening action, scary images and brief rough language prohibit viewing by children. **p**, Joe Roth, K.C. Hodenfield, W. Mark McNair, Tamara Watts Kent; **d**, Sam Raimi; **cast**, James Franco, Rachel Weisz, Michelle Williams, Mila Kunis, Zach Braff, Bill Cobbs, Joey King, Tony Cox, Stephen R. Hart, Abigail Spencer, Tim Holmes, Toni Wynne; **w**, Mitchell Kapner, David Lindsay-Abaire (based on a story by Kapner and the *Oz* books of L. Frank Baum); **c**, Peter Deming; **m**, Danny Elfman; **ed**, Bob Murawski; **prod d**, Robert Stromberg; **art d**, Andrew L. Jones, Iain McFadyen, Meghan C. Rogers, Domenic Silvestri, John Lord Booth III, Todd Cherniawsky; **set d**, Nancy Heigh; **spec eff**, John Frazier, Scott Stokdyk, Daniel P. Rosen.

Pacific Rim ★★★ 2013; U.S.; 132m; WB/ Color; Adventure/Science Fiction; Children: Unacceptable (MPAA: PG-13); **BD**; **DVD**. Action-packed sci-fi tale begins when a war starts with monstrous creatures known as Kaiji that will take millions of lives and use up human resources for many years. To fight back against the monsters, a special type of weapon is devised in the form of massive robots called Jaegers that are controlled simultaneously by two pilots whose minds are locked together. But even the Jaegers prove to be nearly defenseless against the relentless Kaiju. Near to defeat, the forces defending mankind desperately turn to two unlikely heroes, Hunnam, a washed-up former pilot, and Kikuchi, a rookie trainee. They are to drive a legendary but seemingly obsolete Jaeger from previous action and they become mankind's last hope against the end of the world. Loading the Jaeger with a nuclear device, the two manage to escape before exploding it, destroying all the invaders and surviving when they find themselves splashing in the Pacific Ocean. The story line often ignores cohesiveness and continuity and there is a senselessness to the constant mayhem, but the special effects (the star of almost every film made in the last decade) provide a wondrous light show. The film was a megahit, earning more than $411 million in its initial release against a budget of more than $190 million. Songs: "Just Like Your Tenderness" (Liang Hong Zhi), "Drift" (Blake Perlman, RZA, Damin Djawadi). Excessive violence and gutter language prohibit viewing by children. **p**, Guillermo del Toro, Jon Jashni, Mary Parent, Thomas Tull, Jillian Zaks; **d**, del Toro; **cast**, Charlie Hun-

nam, Diego Klattenhoff, Idris Elba, Rinko Kikuchi, Charlie Day, Burn Gorman, Max Martini, Robert Kazinsky, Clifton Collins Jr., Ron Perlman, Brad William Henke, Larry Joe Campbell; **w**, del Toro, Travis Beacham (based on a story by Beacham); **c**, Guillermo Navarro; **m**, Ramin Djawadi; **ed**, Peter Amundson, John Gilroy; **prod d**, Andrew Neskoromny, Carol Spier; **art d**, Elinor Rose Galbraith, Richard L. Johnson, Andrew Li, Sandra Tanaka; **set d**, Peter Nicolakakos; **spec eff**, Stephen Wallace, Skyler Wilson.

Paranormal Activity: The Ghost Dimension ★★★ 2015; U.S.; 88m; Blumhouse Productions/PAR; Color; Horror; Children: Unacceptable (MPAA: R); **BD**; **DVD**. In this well-made fifth installment of the horror series which is filmed in 3-D to enhance the eerie effects, the story goes back to 1988 when two sisters, Csengery and Brown, watch as a man's spine is crushed by an unknown force. Foote, the girls' grandmother, takes them to a dark room where a man they cannot see tells them about someone named Tobi, who is played by Steger, and that he has a plan for them. In flash-forward it is twenty-five years later in the year 2013 when a young married couple, Murray and Shaw, move into a new house with their daughter, George, who is seven years old. As they prepare for Christmas, the family is joined by Murray's brother, Gill, and Shaw's best friend, Dudley. Murray and Gill are rummaging in the garage where they find an old video camcorder and some VHS tapes dating back to the late 1980s. The tapes are videos of Csengery and Brown with their mother and her boyfriend in 1988, while others show the sisters engaging in supernatural events with Steger. When Murray and Gill look through the lens of the camera they see paranormal activity happening around them. The tapes are home videos that record the lives of Csengery and Brown who lived in the house at that time. Strange things then begin to happen in the house as George starts to talk to a shadowy figure calling himself Tobi (Steger), and the camera records apparitions that none of those in the house can see with the naked eye. Murray learns that their house was built on the same lot where Csengery and Brown used to live before their house burned down in 1992. Murray and Shaw become more concerned for George's safety so they call in Kwaric, a Catholic priest, to investigate the strange goings-on. During Kwaric's search of the house, George attacks him and Kwaric becomes convinced that Steger is a demon connected to a cult called the Midwives. Murray researches the cult and learns that its members killed a family in Nevada, who were related to a boy named Hunter (Lovekamp), and who was born on the same day as George. Most disturbing, Murray learns that George's blood is needed to finish the transformation of Lovekamp into a human being. George then meets with Steger, who leads her into a room into which she disappears. Murray and Shaw find George and take her to a hotel. Kwaric returns to the house in an attempt to exorcise it, and the mysterious force haunting the house begins to shake the building violently. Steger then strangles Kwaric and drags him away. Murray traps the demon, covers it in a white sheet, and recites a prayer concluding an exorcism. George returns to being a normal little girl, and the demon seems to have finally left the house. Dudley then throws up, spewing hot blood over Gill, and they are both burned to death. George then flees the house and, in going after her, Murray is killed, impaled by a large arm that strikes him in the chest. George and Shaw then travel back in time to go to Csengery's and Brown's house in 1988 where they find Csengery threatened by Steger. Shaw pleads with Steger to spare Csengery's life, but he snaps Csengery's neck and her body is tossed at the video camera. George then identifies Tobi (Steger) and walks off with him as the camera ends and so does the movie, conveniently allowing for yet another sequel in the series. The story is sometimes confusing as its continuity abruptly changes, but the intense performances from cast members and the startling visuals sustain chilling interest throughout. The film did well at the box office, earning more than $78 million in its initial release against a budget of more than $10 million. Earlier films in the series were **Paranormal Activity**, 2007; **Paranormal Activity 2**, 2010; **Paranormal Activity 3**, 2011; and **Paranormal**

Activity: The Marked Ones, 2014. Songs: "Painting Shadows," "Blackout" (Chester Bennington); "Jingle Bells," "We Wish You a Merry Christmas," "Joy to the World," "We Three Kings," "Deck the Halls," "Holiday Bells" (traditional). Gutter language and horror violence and gore prohibit viewing by children. **p**, Jason Blum, Oren Peli; **d**, Gregory Plotkin; **cast**, Chris J. Murray, Brit Shaw, Ivy George, Dan Gill, Olivia Taylor Dudley, Chloe Csengery, Jessica Brown, Don McManus, Michael Krawic, Hallie Foote, Aiden Lovekamp, Cara Pifko, Mark Steger; **w**, Jason Pagan, Andrew Deutschman, Adam Robitel, Gavin Heffernan (based on a story by Pagan, Deutschman, Brantley Aufil, and the 2007 film **Paranormal Activity** written by Oren Peli); **c**, John Rutland; **ed**, Michel Aller; **prod d**, Nathan Amondson; **art d**, Nick Ralbovsky; **spec eff**, Linda Drake, Kevin Field, Tarun Kripalani, Eddie Pasquarello.

Parkland ★★★ 2013; U.S.; 93m; American Film Co./Exclusive Media Group; Color; Drama; Children: Unacceptable (MPAA: PG-13); **BD**; **DVD**. Anguishing tale depicts the chaotic events at Parkland Hospital in Dallas, Texas, after the assassination of U.S. President John F. Kennedy (1917-1963), portrayed by Stimely, on November 22, 1963. The film focuses on the perspectives of some of the key hospital staff members as well as others. Of particular note is Abraham Zapruder (1905-1970), played by Giamatti, a clothing salesman whose video camera filmed the presidential motorcade at the time Kennedy was shot. Another key person is James Hosty (1924-2011), essayed by Livingston, an FBI agent who earlier that morning received a flyer blasting JFK for treason. Inside the hospital, staff members can hardly grasp the horror to come when they learn that the blood-soaked President is being wheeled into the operating room. Young Dr. Charles Carrico (Efron) is so overcome with shock at what he sees, a nurse has to help him back to reality shouting, "Doctor, this is the President!" The emergency room becomes crowded with medics giving orders and moving about as they try to save the life of the man on the operating table. Members of the Secret Service watch anxiously through a window in the door, medics stand in disbelief, and First Lady Jacqueline Kennedy (1929-1994), played by Steffens, paces one side of the room in a daze, her gloved hands still clutching pieces of the President's skull and brain matter, which she had retrieved from the car in which the President was shot. The film does not cover the apprehension and murder of assassin Lee Harvey Oswald (1939-1963), played by Strong, who is shown only peripherally, but centers on the events at Parkland where the President dies and how Vice President Lyndon B. Johnson (1908-1973), played by McGraw, rises to power by becoming President. The script is well written and faithfully follows the dire events on that black day in Dallas, and cast members give convincing and often riveting performances under the firm direction of Landesman, who does a fine job coordinating the chaotic events. Where such films as **JFK**, 1991, explore the background and subsequent events in the Kennedy assassination, this film is the only production to concentrate on the events occurring at Parkland. The film did not do as well as expected at the box office, earning less than $1.5 million in its initial release against a budget of more than $10 million. Assassination and bloody sequences of emergency room trauma procedures, violent images, gutter language and smoking throughout prohibit viewing by children. **p**, Tom Hanks, Gary Goetzman, Matt Jackson, Bill Paxton, Nigel Sinclair, Jillian Longnecker; **d&w**, Peter Landesman; **cast**, Zac Efron, Marcia Gay Harden, Tom Welling, Ron Livingston, Paul Giamatti, Billy Bob Thornton, Kat Steffens, James Badge Dale, Brett Stimely, Jackie Earle Haley, Colin Hanks, Mark Duplass, Jeremy Strong, Sean McGraw; **c**, Barry Ackroyd; **m**, James Newton Howard; **ed**, Leo Trombetta; **prod d**, Bruce Curtis; **art d**, Rodney Becker; **spec eff**, Scott Gordon, Maru Buendia-Senties.

The Past ★★★ 2013; France/Italy/Iran; 130m; Memento Films/Sony; Color; Drama; Children: Unacceptable (MPAA: PG-13); **BD**; **DVD**. Well-made tale begins when Mosaffa returns to Paris from his native

Ezra Miller and Emma Watson in *The Perks of Being a Wallflower*, 2012.

Iran to join his wife, Bejo, in finalizing their divorce after being separated for four years. She intends to marry Rahim, an Arab owner of a laundry in Paris whose wife is in a coma from shock after she tried to commit suicide. Mosaffa and Bejo have three children, two of whom are Bejo's from a previous marriage. The relationship of the older daughter, Burlet, and Bejo has become strained because Burlet thinks that Bejo is the cause of the comatose state afflicting Rahim's wife. Burlet also disapproves of Bejo's relationship with Rahim. Romantic affairs become even more complicated and strained when Burlet reveals something terrible that she has committed. Taut tale provides considerable tension through some fine character studies achieved through the fine cast. The film saw limited distribution, earning more than $12.1 million in its initial release against a budget of more than $11 million. Mature thematic material and gutter language prohibit viewing by children. (In French; English subtitles.) **p**, Alexandre Mallet-Guy; **d&w**, Asghar Farhadi; **cast**, Berenice Bejo, Ali Mosaffa, Tahar Rahim, Pauline Burlet, Elyes Aguis, Jeanne Jestin, Sabrina Ouazani, Babak Karimi, Valeria Cavalli, Aleksandra Klebanska, Jean-Michel Simonet, Pierre Guerder; **c**, Mahmoud Kalari; **m**, Evgueni Galperine, Youli Galperine; **ed**, Juliette Welfling; **prod d**, Claude Lenoir; **spec eff**, Jean-Cristophe Magnaud, Philippe Hubin.

The Peanuts Movie ★★★★ 2015; U.S.; 93m; FOX; Color; Animated Adventure; Children: Recommended (MPAA: G); **BD**; **DVD**. The Peanuts gang appears in their first movie, filmed in 3-D animation and where the beloved characters are all here employing their delightful antics with two main plots: Charlie Brown (Schnapp voiceover) has his usual feelings of inferiority while having a crush on his new next-door neighbor, the Little Red-Haired Girl (Capaldi voiceover). His erstwhile beagle pal Snoopy (Melendez voiceover) mounts his dog house to take control of his imaginary airplane and search the skies for his nemesis, the German ace pilot of World War I, the Red Baron, then engages him in aerial dogfights. Along the way, Lucy (Miller voiceover) pines for pianist Schroeder (Johnston voiceover) whose mind and heart belong to Beethoven. The film begins in winter so we see snowflakes and ice skaters and then Capaldi arrives at school and Schnapp does what little he can to make her like him. Miller is of no help to him, but Melendez as Snoopy is a very active supporter. He gets his pal Woodstock (Melendez voiceover), after an abandoned typewriter is found in a dump, to write a romance in which he saves a beautiful French poodle, Fifi (Chenoweth voiceover) from the clutches of the Red Baron. The film introduces the Peanuts gang to new audiences while reminding those who have read the strip for more than fifty years why these endearing characters fascinate. Schnapp struggles to fly his kite as Charlie Brown, and Miller as Lucy fools him again as he tries to kick a football and of-

Happy high school graduates in *The Perks of Being a Wallflower,* **2012.**

fers psychological advice for five cents. Miller convinces Schnapp that, if he really wants to impress Capaldi, he has to show her that he is a winner, not the loser he thinks himself to be. He tries to do this at a school dance, but proves hopeless on the dance floor. We also follow short adventures by Linus (Garfin, voiceover), Peppermint Patty (Schultheis voiceover), and Pig pen (Tecce voiceover). Through it all, Melendez comes to realize he has some self-worth after all. Lucy narrates Snoopy's WWI saga, and, when she finishes, she throws the manuscript at the viewer, declaring that it is the very worst story she has ever read. While Hollywood drowns in a sea of violent and special effects productions, this wonderfully computer-animated tale refreshes with the simplistic hijinks and frolics of heart-touching children who have more positive (and hilariously amusing) statements to make about life than all the thundering pundits of our harassing era. The cast members are superb in their voiceover roles, and the stunningly detailed animation is strongly supported by a lively and provocative score from Beck (with contributions from jazz musician and composer David Benoit, who is remembered for his own version of "Linus and Lucy"). The public responded well to this prosaic, laugh-producing film at the box office, where it earned more than $231.7 million in its initial release against a budget of more than $99 million. Songs/Music: "Skating," "Linus and Lucy" (Vince Guaraldi); "Moonlight Sonata," "Symphony No. 5, allegro con brio" (Ludwig van Beethoven); "Pomp and Circumstance" (Edward Elgar); "William Tell Overture" (Gioachino Rossini); "Jungle Jump" (Laurence Cottle); "Bamboleo" (Wjalhoul Bouchikhi, Nicolas Reyes, Tonino Baliardo, Simon Diaz); "The Chicken Dance" (Werner Thomas, Terry Rendall); "Better When I'm Dancin'" (Meghan Trainor, Thaddeus Dixon); "Stuck to You" (Nikka Costa, Justin Stanley); "Good to Be Alive" (Meghan Trainor, Ryan Trainor); "That's What I Like" (Jamie Sanderson, Breyan Isaac, Miles Beard, Vincent Venditto, Teemu Brunila, Tramar Dillard, Thomas Troelsen, James Marinos, Mike Skill, Wally Palamarchuk, Frederick Hibbert); "Christmas Time Is Here" (Vince Guaraldi, Lee Mendelson); "Roses from the South" (George Wilson); "Mister Softee/Jingle and Chimes," "Parade, Marching Band." **p**, Paul Feig, Bryan Schulz, Craig Schulz, Michael J. Travers, Cornelius Uliano; **d**, Steve Martino; **cast** (voiceovers), Noah Schnapp, Alex Garfin, Noah Johnston, Bill Melendez, Hadley Belle Miller, Venus Schultheis, A.J. Tecce, Trombone Shorty, Rebecca Bloom, Anastasia Bredikhina, Francesca Capaldi, Kristin Chenoweth, Micah Revelli; **w**, Bryan Schulz, Craig Schulz, Cornelius Uliano (based on the *Peanuts* comic strip by Charles M. Schulz); **c**, Renato Falcao; **m**, Christophe Beck; **prod d**, Anthony Nisi, Lauren Conway Weber; **ed**, Randy Trager; **art d**, Nash Dunnigan; **spec eff**, Bill Houston Ball, Matt Roach.

The People vs. Fritz Bauer ★★★★ 2015; Germany; 105m; Zero One

Films/Cohen Media Group; Color; Biographical Drama; Children: Unacceptable; **BD**; **DVD**. This moving dramatization presents the true story of Fritz Bauer (1903-1968), played by Klaussner, an attorney general of the German state of Hessen who, in 1957, wants to hunt down Adolf Eichmann (1906-1962), who is played by Schenk. Eichmann was the infamous Nazi called the "architect of the Holocaust" in which millions of Jews were executed during World War II (1939-1945). The film recounts the events of the attorney general in initiating the Auschwitz Trials in Frankfurt, Germany. Bauer was an active socialist in the 1920s and, in the early 1930s was arrested and imprisoned in a concentration camp for his opposition to the Nazis. He was released in 1935 and later migrated to Sweden. Following the war, Bauer is shown returning to Germany where he becomes active in politics and the judicial system, where he provides information to Israeli intelligence (Mossad) that brings about the arrest of Eichmann, who is taken to Israel, tried and condemned for his key role in the oppression of the Jews known as the Holocaust. The film is presented as a docudrama, and Klaussner and Schenk are convincing in their compelling and chilling roles. The film saw limited distribution upon its initial release. Songs: "Inkognito," "Ich bin ein Mann." *Author's Note*: The title of this film refers to the animosity Bauer fearlessly incurred from Germans who did not want Bauer hunting down Nazi criminals to, in their minds, further embarrass and stigmatize the country. Bauer is little known internationally, but Eichmann remains one of that country's most notorious mass murderers. Adolf Eichmann has been portrayed by many actors in many other films, including **Armstrong Circle Theatre**, 1950-1963 (TV series; "Engineer of Death: The Eichmann Story," 1960 episode: Frederick Rolf); **The Aryan Couple**, 2004 (Steve Mackintosh); **BBC Play of the Month**, 1965-1983 (TV series; "The Joel Brand Story," 1960 episode; Anton Diffring); **Conspiracy**, 2001 (made-for-TV; Stanley Tucci); **The Final Solution: The Wannsee Conference**, 1984 (made-for-TV; Gerd Bockmann); **Good**, 2008 (Steven Elder); **Holocaust**, 1978 (TV miniseries; Tom Bell); **The House on Garibaldi Street**, 1979 (made-for-TV; Alfred Burke); **The Man in the Glass Booth**, 1975 (role model for Maximilian Schell); **The Man Who Captured Eichmann**, 1996 (made-for-TV; Robert Duvall); **Mother Night**, 1996 (Henry Gibson); **Murderers among Us: The Simon Wiesenthal Story**, 1989 (made-for-TV; Janos Gosztonyi); **Operation Eichmann**, 1961 (Werner Klemperer); **Perlasca: The Courage of a Just Man**, 2005 (made-for-TV; Tamas Puskas); **Reinhard Heydrich: Manager des Terrors**, 1977 (made-for-TV; Wolgang Rau); **Walking with the Enemy**, 2013 (Charles Hubbell); **Wallenberg: A Hero's Story**, 1985 (made-for-TV; Kenneth Colley); and **War and Remembrance**, 1988 (TV miniseries; Milton Johns). **p**, Thomas Kufus, Barbara Buhl, Christoph Friedel, Jorg Himstedt, Georg Steinert; **d**, Lars Kraume; **cast**, Burghart Klaussner, Michael Schenk, Ronald Zehrfeld, Robert Atzorn, Sebastian Blomberg, Christopher Buchholz, Stefan Gebelhoff, Cornelia Groschel, Rudiger Klink; **w**, Kraume, Olivier Guez; **c**, Jens Harant; **m**, Christoph M. Kaiser, Julian Maas; **ed**, Barbara Gies; **prod d**, Cora Pratz; **spec eff**, Volker Lorig.

The Perks of Being a Wallflower ★★★ 2012; U.S.; 102m; Summit Entertainment; Color; Drama/Romance; Children: Unacceptable (MPAA: PG-13); **BD**; **DVD**. Well-made coming-of-age tale has Lerman as an introverted and shy fifteen-year-old high school sophomore in a Pittsburgh suburb in the early 1990s. He is a troubled youth who must deal with his first love, Watson, his favorite aunt's suicide, and his own mental illness. He is introverted and has trouble finding the right people to be with, until two seniors, a girl named Sam (Watson) and her stepbrother, Miller, take him under their wings. They introduce Lerman to their world, which is totally new to Lerman and involves drugs, alcohol, and sex with both genders, since Miller is secretly dating a closeted football player at the school. Lerman develops a crush on Watson, who was sexually abused as a child and is uncertain that Lerman's feelings for her are genuine. Meanwhile, Rudd, Lerman's English teacher, notices that, while he is a wallflower socially, Lerman has a strong interest in writing, so he encourages Lerman to make some literary achievements. The complicated lives of these teenagers end with Lerman being in a mental hospital where he writes about it all. He recovers, leaves the hospital, and his friends Watson and Miller visit him at home, so all is now well with them. Lerman, Watson, Miller, Rudd and the rest of the cast are convincing in their roles as Chbosky directs his own story with a firm hand and at a brisk pace. The film did well at the box office, earning more than $33.4 million in its initial release against a budget of more than $13 million. Songs: "Could It Be Another Change" (Sean Kelly); "Courted" (Michael Brook); "Asleep" (Steven Morrissey, Johnny Marr); "Odessa Hip Hop" (Rob Walker); "Teen Age Riot" (Kim Gordon, Thurston Moore, Lee Ranaldo, Steven Shelley); "Rally the Funk" (Keith Horn, Doug Bossi); "Love Him" (Ali Theodore, Alana Da Fonseca, Zach Danziger, Joseph Katsaros); "Come On Eileen" (Kevin Adams, James Paterson, Kevin Rowland); "What You've Got" (Gabriele Morgan, Gar Robertson); "Low" (David Charles Lowery, David Faragher, John Hickman); "Falling Elevators" (Mark Griffin); "Tugboat" (Damon Krukowski, Michael Dean Wareham, Naomi Yang); "No New Tale to Tell" (Daniel Ash, Kevin Haskins, David Jay); "Here" (Stephen Malkmus, Scott Kannberg); "Heroes" (David Bowie, Brian Eno); "All Out of Love" (Clive Davis, Graham Russell); "Dear God" (Andy Partridge); "Don't Dream It" (Richard O'Brien); "Temptation" (Gillian Lesley Gilbert, Peter Hook, Stephen Paul David Morris, Bernard Sumner); "Seasick, Yet Still Docked" (Steven Morrissey, Alain Whyte); "Bust a Move" (Matt Dike, Luther Rabb, Marvin Young, Jim Walters); "Christmas/Baby Please Come Home" (Jeff Barry, Phil Spector, Ellie Greenwich); "Sam & Charlie's Piano Theme" (Stephen Chbosky); "Away in a Manger" (traditional); "The Angel Gabriel" (traditional); "Hot Wax" (Alex Silverman); "Ye Olde Backlash" (Mark Stevan Kramer, Ann Magnuson); "Don't Dream It's Over" (Neil Finn); "Toucha Toucha Touch Me" (Richard O'Brien); "Eternity with You" (Robert Carr, Johnny Mitchell), "Evensong" (Don Peris, Karen Peris); "Pretend We're Dead" (Donita Sparks); "Counting Backwards" (Kristin Hersh); "Jefferson," "Pouter," "Lincoln" (Michael Brook); "Araby" (John Croslin, Kim Longacre); "Pearly Dew Drops Drop" (Elizabeth Fraser, Robin Guthrie, Simon Raymonde); "It's Time" (Imagine Dragons). Mature thematic material, drug and alcohol use, sexual content and fighting, all involving teens, prohibit viewing by children. **p,** Lianne Halfon, John Malkovich, Russell Smith, Gillian Brown; **d&w,** Stephen Chbosky (based on his novel); **cast,** Logan Lerman, Emma Watson, Ezra Miller, Paul Rudd, Dylan McDermitt, Kate Walsh, Patrick de Ledebur, Johnny Simmons, Brian Balzerini, Tom Kruszewski, Nina Dobrev, Nicholas Braun, Julia Garner; **c,** Andrew Dunn; **m,** Michael Brook; **ed,** Mary Jo Markey; **prod d,** Inbal Weinberg; **art d,** Gregory Weimerskirch; **set d,** Merissa Lombardo; **spec eff,** Russell Tyrrell.

Philomena ★★★ 2013; U.K./U.S./France; 98m; BBC Films/Weinstein/FOX; Color; Drama; Children: Unacceptable (MPAA: PG-13); **BD; DVD.** Intriguing tale begins with Coogan, a journalist, who is approached by the daughter of Dench to write a story about her mother. Coogan meets with Dench and hears her story, one where she describes in painful detail how she was forced to give up her child, Anthony, fifty years earlier. Coogan decides to investigate. The film flashes back to 1951 when Dench becomes pregnant at a fair and her father sends her to a Catholic abbey in Ireland. She gives birth there, but is forced to work in the laundry for four years to pay off the cost of her stay. Without her knowing, the nuns adopt her son out to a couple. Over the next fifty years, Dench keeps her son's birth a secret from her family, but visits the convent periodically in an effort to locate her child. The nuns keep telling her they are unable to help her find him because adoption records were lost in a fire years earlier. Later, at a pub, locals tell Coogan that the convent deliberately destroyed the records in a bonfire, and that most of the children had been sold to rich Americans. Dench and Coogan go to the United States to search for her son. They learn that he grew up to become a lawyer and a senior official in the administrations

Pirates at sea in *The Pirates! Band of Misfits,* 2012.

of Presidents Ronald Reagan (1911-2004) and George H.W. Bush (1924-). They then learn Dench's son died nine years earlier. Dench persists in meeting people who knew her son and discover that he was gay and died of AIDS. Dench and Coogan visit her son's sister, Winningham, who also was adopted at the same time from the convent and learn that her son's lover was Hermann. Dench meets Herman and learns that her son had always wondered about his birth mother and had visited the convent in Ireland several times in order to learn more about her. Dench and Coogan then learn that the nuns had told her son that she had abandoned him and they had lost contact with her. Finally, they learn that her son is buried in the convent's graveyard. The film ends at the convent where Coogan confronts Jefford, a nun who had been present when Dench's son tried to find her. Jefford is unrepentant, saying that losing her son was Dench's penance for the sin of having given birth out of wedlock. Coogan tells Jefford she should apologize to Dench, but Dench instead forgives Jefford. She then asks to see her son's grave. Coogan then tells Dench he will not publish the story, but Dench tells him to go ahead because "people should know what happened here." The taut tale is touching and disturbing as it indicts Catholic nuns who otherwise have always been shown in a sympathetic light, but are depicted here as draconian and manipulating creatures, if not outright sinister individials imposing their religious credo upon the lives of helpless victims of circumstance. The acting from all is superior and the tale is well directed by Frears. The film did extremely well at the box office, earning more than $100 million in its initial release against a budget of more than $12 million. Songs: "Mother of God Here I Stand" (John Tavener, Mikhail Lermontov), "Nocturne in F-Sharp, Op. 15, No. 2" (Frederic Chopin), "Panis Angelicus" (music: Cesar Franck; lyrics: St. Thomas Aquinas). Gutter language, thematic elements and sexual references prohibit viewing by children. **p,** Steve Coogan, Tracey Seaward, Gabrielle Tana; **d,** Stephen Frears; **cast,** Judi Dench, Steve Coogan, Mare Winningham, Barbara Jefford, Ruth McCabe, Peter Hermann, Sean Mahon, Anna Maxwell Martin, Michelle Fairley, Wunmi Mosaku; **w,** Coogan, Jeff Pope (based on the book *The Lost Child of Philomena Lee* by Martin Sixsmith); **c,** Robbie Ryan; **m,** Alexandre Desplat; **ed,** Valerio Bonelli; **prod d,** Alan MacDonald; **art d,** Leslie McDonald, Sarah Stuart, Rod McLean; **set d,** Barbara Herman-Skelding; **spec eff,** Manex Efrem.

The Pirate Fairy ★★★ 2014; U.S.; 78m; DisneyToon Studios/Walt Disney; Color; Animated Fantasy; Children: Acceptable (MPAA: G); **BD; DVD.** Delightful animated fantasy begins with Zarina (Hendricks voiceover), a misunderstood fairy dust keeper, who steals Pixie Hollow's Blue Pixie Dust and flies away to join forces with the pirates of Skull Rock. Tinker Bell (Whitman voiceover) and her friends set off on a jour-

Pirates admiring their own wanted poster in *The Pirates! Band of Misfits*, 2012.

ney to get the magical dust back and return it to their rightful place. However, during their pursuit of Hendricks, Whitman's world is turned upside down. She and her friends find that their respective talents have been switched and they have to race against time to retrieve the Blue Pixie Dust and return home to save Pixie Hollow. The animation is outstanding and the voiceover acting top notch in another winner from Disney aimed at children and adults alike. The film was very successful at the box office, earning almost $65 million in its initial release. Songs: "Who I Am" (Adam Watts, Andy Dodd); "The Frigate That Flies" (music: Gaby Alter; lyrics: Alter, Itamar Moses); "Weightless" (Natasha Bedingfield, Stephen Kipner, Wayne Wilkins, Andre Merritt); "Following the Leader" (Oliver Wallace, Ted Sears, Winston Hibler); "Never Smile at a Crocodile" (Frank Churchill, Jack Lawrence); "What If There Was Pink?," "Zarina the Alchemist," "Zarina Visits Tink," "Four Seasons Opening Ceremony," "Captain Zarina," "James Betrays Zarina," "A Very Familiar Coat," "Fairy Dusted Festival." **p**, Jenni Magee-Cook; **d**, Peggy Holmes; **cast**, (voiceovers) Mae Whitman, Christina Hendricks, Angelica Huston, Tom Hiddleston, Lucy Liu, Raven-Symone, Megan Hilty, Pamela Adlon, Angela Bartys, Jim Cummings, Carlos Ponce; **w**, Jeffrey M. Howard, Kate Kondell (based on a story by Holmes, Howard, John Lasseter, Roberts Gannaway, Lorna Cook, Craig Gerber; **m**, Joel McNeely; **spec eff**, Ashwin C. John.

The Pirates! Band of Misfits ★★★ 2012; U.K./U.S.; 188m; COL; Color; Animated Adventure; Children: Unacceptable (MPAA: PG); **3-D**; **BD**; **DVD**. Exciting action is seen in this adventure tale, beginning in 1837, where a pirate captain (Grant voiceover) has been frustrated for years because he has not been able to win the coveted Pirate of the Year Award in Victorian England. He and his crew enter a race to pillage the most booty, their competitors being Black Bellamy (Piven voiceover), Peg Leg Hastings (Henry voiceover), and Cutlass Liz (Hayek voiceover). Grant soon encounters scientist Charles Darwin (1809-1882; Tennant voiceover), who tells Grant that his prized parrot could lead them to the treasure for which they are searching. Their adventures take them to an encounter with pirate-hating Queen Victoria (1819-1901; Staunton voiceover). Grant has to choose between being crowned Pirate of the Year or remaining faithful to his loyal crew. Top-drawer animation coupled to a witty script that provides a lot of comedy sustains interest throughout. The film received an Oscar nomination as Best Animated Feature and saw considerable success at the box office, earning more than $123 million in its initial release against a budget of more than $55 million. Songs: "Rule Britannia" (Thomas Augustine Arne, James Thomson), "Fiesta" (Jem Finer, Shane MacGowan, Edmund Koetscher, Rudi Lindt), "Swords of a Thousand Men" (Edward Tudorpole), "Train to Skaville" (Leonard Winston Dillon), "Sailing Out

on the Ocean" (traditional), "London Calling" (Mick Jones, Joe Strummer, Paul Simonon, Topper Headon), "Blow the Man Down" (traditional), "Also Sprach Zarathustra" (Richard Strauss), "The Girl from Ipanema" (Antonio Carlos Jobim, Vinicius de Moraes, Normal Gimbel), "Waiting for the Robert E. Lee" (Lewis F. Muir), "I'm Not Crying" (Jemaine Clement, Bret McKenzie), "Ranking Full Stop" (David Steele, David Wakeling, Everett Morton, Roger Charley, Andrew Cox), "Morgenblatter (Morning Newspaper)" (Johann Strauss, Jr.), "You Can Get It If You Really Want" (Jimmy Cliff), "Alright" (Daniel Goffey, Gareth Coombes, Michael Quinn). Crude humor and gutter language prohibit viewing by children. **p**, Peter Lord, Julie Lockhart, David Sproxton; **d**, Lord, Jeff Newitt; **cast** (voices of), Hugh Grant, Imelda Staunton, David Tennant, Jeremy Piven, Salma Hayek, Lenny Henry, Brian Blessed, Martin Freeman, Russell Tovey, Brendan Gleeson, Anton Yelchin, Ben Whitehead; **w**, Gideon Defoe (based on his book *The Pirates! In an Adventure with Scientists*); **c**, Frank Passingham; **m**, Theodore Shapiro; **ed**, Justin Krish; **prod d**, Norman Garwood; **art d**, Sarah Hauldren, Phil Lewis, Matt Sanders, Matt Perry; **spec eff**, Melanie Callaghan.

Pitch Perfect ★★★ 2012; U.S.; 112m; Brownstone Productions/UNIV; Color; Musical Comedy; Children: Unacceptable (MPAA: PG-13); **BD**; **DVD**. Entertaining songfest presents a singing group of beautiful college girls known as the Barden Bellas who become popular until they fail their final examinations and are forced to regroup. A new recruit is Kendrick, an independent freshman and an aspiring disc jockey with no interest in college life. After she meets Astin, from an all-male singing group at the college, she has a new outlook and helps the Bellas find their new look and sound so they once again become popular. The story line is thin as shaved ham, but the songs rollick and please throughout. The film proved to a startling sleeper hit at the box office, earning more than $115.4 million in its initial release against a budget of more than $17 million. Its sequel, **Pitch Perfect 2**, 2015, far surpassed the success of the original. Songs: "Don't Stop the Music" (Michael Jackson, Mikkel S. Eriksen, T.E. Hermansen, Frankie Storm), "Let It Whip" (Reginald Andrews, Ndugu Chancler), "Since U Been Gone" (Lukasz Gottwald, Max Martin), "Cups" (A.P. Carter, Luisa Gerstein), "Mickey" (Michael Chapman, Nicolas Ghinn), "The Sign" (Buddha, Malin Berggren, Kenny Berggren, Joker), "Right Round" (Lukasz Gottwald, Allan Grigg, Flo Rida as Tramar Dillard, Phil Lawrence, Bruno Mars, Jimmy Franks, Timothy Lever, Michael Percy, Peter Burns, Stephen Coy), "Just the Way You Are" (Khari Chain, Peter Hernandez, Bruno Mars, Philip Lawrence, Ari Levine, Cassius D. Kalb as Khalil Walton, Flo Rida as Tramar Dillard), "Party in the U.S.A." (Jessie J., Lukasz Gottwald, Claude Kelly), "Bright Lights Bigger City" (Benjamin Heward Allen III, Tony Reyes, CeeLo Green as Thomas Decarlo Callaway), "Price Tag" (Jessica Cornish), Lukasz Gottwald, Claude Kelly, Bobby Simmons Jr.), "212" (Jef Martens, Azealia Banks), "Bust A Move" (Marvin Young, Matt Dike, Michael Ross, Luther James Rabb, Jim Walters), "Carry on Wayward Son" (Kerry Livgren), "Lost in It" (Michael Corcoran, Eric Goldman), "Punching in a Dream" (Aaron Short, Alisa Xayalith, Thomas B. Powers), "Keep You" (Natalie Bergman, Elliott Bergman), "Don't Move" (Sarah Barthel, Josh Carter), "Yitanium" (David Guetta, Giorgio Tuinfort, Nick Van De Wall, Sia Furler), "I'm Gonna Be/500 Miles" (Charlie Reid, Craig Reid), "Before We Fall in Love" (Jason French Muniz, Daniel Mestanza, Colton Fisher, Jason Rabinowitz), "Keep Your Head Up" (Andy Grammer), "Starships" (Wayne Hector, Carl Anthony Falk, Nicki Minaj as Onika Tanya Maraj, Rami Tacoub, RedOne as Nadir Khayat), "Turn the Beat Around/Love to Hear Percussion" (Peter Jackson Jr., Gerald Jackson), "Rome" (Christopher Keating, Ira Tuton, Anand Wilder), "Like a Virgin" (Tom Kelly, Billy Steinberg), "Hit Me with Your Best Shot" (Edward Schwartz), "It Must Have Been Love" (Per Gessle), "S & M" (Sandy Wilhelm, Ester Dean, T.E. Hermansen, Mikkel S. Eriksen), "Let's Talk About Sex" (Herbie Azor), "I'll Make Love to You" (Kenneth "Babyface" Edmonds), "Feels Like the First Time" (Michael L.

Jones), "No Diggity" (Chauncey Hannibal, Teddy Riley, William Stewart, Richard Vick, Queen Pen as Lynise Walters, Bill Withers), "Bulletproof" (Eleanor Jackson, Benedict Langimaid), "Release Me" (Anders Hansson, Sharon Vaughn, Agnes Carlsson), "Don't You Forget About Me" (Keith Forsey, Steve Schiff), "Booty Wurk/One Cheek at a Time" (Faheem Najm, Christopher Brown, Bryan Levar Jones, Joseph Williams, Tramaine Michael Winfrey, Orlando Woods Jr.), "Hip Hop 911" (Richard Vick), "Sobre Las Olas/Over the Waves" (Juventino Rosas), "Blame It on the Boogie" (Clark Michael George Jackson, Rich David John Jackson, Elmar Krohn, Hans Kampschroer, Thomas Meyer), "Open Season" (Jack Milas, Oliver Chang), "Get You Off" (Michael Corcoran, Eric Goldman, Jodan Infinity Suecof), "Chelsea Dagger" (Jon Fratelli), "Whoomp!/There It Is" (Stephen Gibson, Cecil Glenn), "Just a Dream" (Nelly as Cornell Hayes, James Scheffer, Rico Love as Richard Butle Jr., Frank Romano), "Final Countdown" (Joey Tempest), "Magic" (Rivers Cuomo, Lukasz Gottwald, Bobby Simmons Jr.), "Give Me Everything" (Pitbull as A. Perez, Ne-Yo as S. Smith, N. Wall), "We Came to Smash/In a Black Tuxedo" (Martin Solveig as Martin Picandet, Julien Jabre, Dev as Devin Tailes), "2123 vs Bust a Move" (Jef Martens, Azealia Banks, Marvin Young, Matt Dike, Michael Ross, Luther James Rabb, Jim Walters), "Bella Regionals: The Sign/Eternal Flame/Turn the Beat Around" (Buddha, Malin Berggren, Jenny Berggren, Joker, Susanna Hoffs, Thomas F. Kelly, Billy Steinberg, Peter Jackson Jr., Gerald Jackson). Sexual material, gutter language and drug references prohibit viewing by children. **p**, Elizabeth Banks, Paul Brooks, Max Handelman, Jeff Levine; **d**, Jason Moore; **cast**, Anna Kendrick, Skylar Astin, Ben Platt, Brittany Snow, Anna Camp, Rebel Wilson, Alexis Knapp, Ester Dean, Hana Mae Lee, Kelley Alice Jakle, Wanetah Walmsley, Shelley Regner; **w**, Kay Cannon (based on the book by Mickey Rapkin); **c**, Julio Macat; **m**, Christophe Beck, Mark Kilian; **ed**, Lisa Zeno Churgin; **prod d**, Barry Robison; **art d**, Jeremy Wollsey; **set d**, David Hack; **spec eff**, Ken Gorrell, Matthew Zaff.

Pitch Perfect 2 ★★★ 2015; U.S.; 115m; Brownstone Productions; UNIV; Color; Comedy/Music; Children: Unacceptable (MPAA: PG-13); **BD**; **DVD**. This sequel to the blockbuster musical comedy **Pitch Perfect**, 2012, follows the further adventures of the fictional Barden University's all-girl a capella singing group, the Bellas. The film became an instant hit with the public, especially teenage girls, becoming the highest-grossing music comedy film of all time. The story begins three years after the first film, with the Barden Bellas now led by Kendrick and Snow. The Bellas have won national championships for three years in a row. While at the top of their game, they stumble at a Lincoln Center concert in New York City for President Barack Obama (1961-) when a wardrobe problem exposes Wilson's private parts and the group is reprimanded by being barred from appearing on the national a capella circuit. Kendrick manages to make a deal that will get the group reinstated if they win the upcoming world championship of a capella. In this pursuit they are joined by a freshman, Steinfeld, who writes songs for the group. Meanwhile, Kendrick has begun an internship with a recording studio without telling the others. On her first day there she watches as her self-centered boss, Key, lashes out at his assistant, which becomes her baptism into the world of a ruthless music factory. Kendrick has aspirations of becoming a song producer and scores with a Christmas album song and is given the chance to send demonstration copies to Key. In flashback, we see preparations for the a capella world championships, where two more new members join the group, Borg and Sorensen. The Bellas go to a retreat where they can practice and hopefully put to rest some personal differences among members. At the retreat, which is like an a capella boot camp, the girls learn to work together and trust each other more as a team. Their work together impresses Key and he encourages their future as a group. The senior members of the group graduate from the university and they and the younger members go off to Copenhagen, Denmark, for the world a capella finals. They are a sensation and win the championship, which

Charles Darwin and Pirate Captain in *The Pirates! Band of Misfits,* **2012.**

restores their reputation. The remaining younger members of the Bellas now have to recruit new members to keep the group alive into the next year, thus the leaving way open for another sequel, which is scheduled for release in 2017. The film set a record at the box office by becoming the largest grossing production for a musical comedy, earning more than $287.1 million in its initial release against a budget of more than $29 million. Songs: "The Marine's Hymn" and "Hail to the Chief" (traditional), "We Got the World" (Caroline Hjelt, Aino Jawo, Elof Loelv), Nicole Louise Morier, Tove Lo, Linus Eklow), "Timber" (Kesha Sebert, Henry Walter, Lukasz Gottwald, Charles Carter, Waung Hankerson, Roger Parkeer, Steve Arrington, Armando Christian Perez, Pebe Sebert, Breyan Stanley Isaac, Greg Irrico, Aaron Davis Arnold, Jamie Sanderson, Keri Oskar, Lee Oskar, Priscilla Renea Hamilton), "America the Beautiful" (Katherine Lee Bates, Samuel A. Ward), "Wrecking Ball" (Mozella, Henry Walter, Lukasz Gottwald, Sacha Skarbek, Stephan Richard Moccio), "Bang Bang" (Savan Kotecha, Rickard Goransson, Max Martin, Onika Tanya Maraj), "If You Leave Me Now" (Peter P. Cetera), "Lollipop" (Michael Holbrook Penniman), "Change Your Life" (Amethyst Amelia Kelly), Clifford Harris, Nasri Atweh, Adam Messinger, Lovy Longomba, Natalie Sims, Svetha Roa), "Flashlight" (Sam Smith, Sia Furler, Christian Guzman, Jason Moore), "Sunshine" (Klas Ahlund, Joakim Ahlund, Patrik Arve, Natalie Ann Marie Cole), "Fist Pump, Jump Jump" (Alexander Papaconstantinou, Nadir Khayat, Deongelo Holmes, Eric Jackson Jr., Isaac Hayes III), "Uprising" (Matthew James Bellamy), "Tsunami" (Alexandre Van Den Hoef, Christopher Van Den Hoef, John James Borger Jr., Niles Hollowell-Dhar), "A Different Beat" (Ian Farquharson, Thomas Andrew Searle Barnes, Perrie Louise Edwards, Iain James, Peter Norman, Cullen Kelleher, Benjamin Alexander Kohn, Jesy Nelson, Leigh Anne Pinnock, Ayak Thiik, Jade Amelia Thirlwall), "Winter Wonderland" (Felix Bernard, Richard B. Smith), "Here Comes Santa Claus/Right Down Santa Claus Lane" (Gene Autry, Oakley Haldeman), "Trumpets" (Jonathan David Bellion, Jason Koel Desrouleaux), "Can You Feel It" (Bob Mair, Nick Vincent), "Thong Song" (Mark Andrews, Bob Robinson, Desmond Child, Joseph Longo, Marquis T. Collins, Robi Rosa, Tim Kelley), "Shake Your Booty" (Harry Wayne Casey, Richard Raymond Finch), "Low" (Howard Simmons, Korey Roberson, Montay Humphrey, Tramar Dillard, Faheem Najm), "Bootylicious" (Beyonce Knowles, Falonte D. Moore, Rob Fusari, Stephanie Nicks), "Baby Got Back" (Anthony L. Ray), "Like You Were Dying" (Timothy Nichols, Craig M. Wiseman), "Before He Cheats" (Josh Kear, Christopher G. Tompkins), "A Thousand Miles" (Vanessa Carlton), "We Are Never Ever Getting Back Together" (Taylor Swift, Johan Schuster, Max Martin), "What's Love Got to Do with It" (Terry Britten, Graham Lyle), "This Is How We Do It" (Montell Jordan, Ricky Walters, Oji Pierce), "Doo Wop/That Thing"

Mr. Bobo in *The Pirates! Band of Misfits*, **2012.**

(Lauryn Hill), "Poison" (Elliott Straite), "Scenario" (John W. Davis, Bryan Higgins, James Jackson, Ali Shaheed Jones-Muhammad, Trevor Smith, Malik Izaak Taylor, Kamall Fareed), "Insane in the Brain" (Louis M. Freese, Larry Muggerud, Senen Reyes), "Jump" (Leroy Bonner, Berry Gordy Jr., Marshall E. Jones, Jermaine Dupri, Ralph Middlebrooks, Alphonso Mizell, Walter Morrison, Norman Napier, Freddie J. Perren, Marvin Pierce, Deke Richards, Gregory A. Webster, Andrew Noland), "There Is Only Room for You" (Mansa Wakili, Sylvie Simhon, Colton Fisher, Jason Rabinowitz), "Promises" (Alana Watson, Daniel Stephens, Joseph Ray, Sonny Moore), "Problem" (Jeff Bhasker, Natalia Cappuccini, Sky Montique, Natalie Noemi Hersom, Guillaume Doubet), "Stars" (Andrew Macken, Thomas Macken), "Tom" (Scott Cutler, Anne Pereven, Phil Thornalley), "Boogie Woogie Bugle Boy" (Hughie Prince, Don Raye), "You Can't Hurry Love" (Brian Holland, Edward Holland Jr., Lamont Dozier), "Lady Marmalade" (Kenny Nolan, Robert Crewe), "Mmbop" (Isaac Clarke Hanson, Jordan Taylor Hanson, Zachary Walkeer Hanson), "My Lovin'/You're Never Gonna Get It" (Denzil Foster, Thomas McElroy), "Cups" (A.P. Carter, Luisa Gerstein, Heloise Tunstall-Behrens), "We Belong" (Daniel Anthony Novarro, David Eric Lowen), "Good Time" (Armando Christian Perez, Eric Frederic, Thomas Troelsen, Andreas Schuller, James John Abrahart Jr.), "Let's Go" (Caroline Hjelt, Alexander Reuterskiold, Marcus Sepehrmwnesh, Yijs Verwest, Oscar Thomas Holter), "Any Way You Want It" (Neal Schon, Steve Perry), "My Songs Know What You Did In the Dark/Light Em Up" (Andrew Hurley, Butch Walker, John Hill, Joseph Trohman, Patrick Stump, Peter Wentz), "All I Do Is Win" (Johnny Mollings, Leonardo Mollings, William Roberts, Calvin Broadus, Christopher Bridges, Faheem Najm, Khaled Mohammed Khaled), "Run the World/Girls" (Beyonce Knowles, Dave Taylor, Adidja Palmer, Nick van de Wall, Terius Nash, Thomas Pentz), "Where Them Girls At" (Michael Caren, George Tuinfort, Jared Cotter, Juan Salinas, Oscar Salinas, Tramar Dillard, David Guetta, Onika Tanya Maraj, Sandy Wilhem), "Crazy Youngsters" (Ester Dean, Deandria Dean), "All of Me" (Toby Gad, John Stephens), "Heartbreak Dream" (Peter Thomas Walsh, Jessica Newham). Some suggestive scenes, partial nudity and gutter language prohibit viewing by children. **p**, Elizabeth Banks, Paul Brooks, Max Handelman, Kay Cannon, Jeff Levine; **d**, Banks; **cast**, Anna Kendrick, Brittany Snow, Rebel Wilson, Hailee Steinfeld, Keegan-Michael Key, Elizabeth Banks, Skylar Astin, Hana Mae Lee, Ester Dean, Chrissie Fit, Birgitte Hjort Sorensen, Flula Borg, Adam DeVine, Ben Platt, John Michael Higgins; **w**, Kay Cannon, Mickey Rapkin; **c**, Jim Denault; **m**, Mark Mothersbaugh; **ed**, Craig Alpert; **prod d**, Toby Corbett; **art d**, Nate Jones; **set d**, Monique Champagne; **spec eff**, Richard Allen Slinker Jr., Jase Warrington.

The Place beyond the Pines ★★★ 2013; U.S.; 140m; Sidney Kimmel

Entertainment/Focus Features; Color; Crime Drama; Children: Unacceptable (MPAA: R); **BD**; **DVD**. Tense crime yarn begins with Gosling, who is a motorcycle daredevil riding with a traveling circus and who has been living with Mendes, a single mother caring for their young son. She has a new boyfriend, Ali, and Gosling wants to care for their son. Gosling does not earn much money with the circus so he supplements his income by robbing banks. He finds that easy pickings until Cooper, a rookie New York City cop, gets on his trail. Cooper and his bride have a baby boy and he hopes that finding the bank robber will get him a promotion in a corrupt police department. Fifteen years pass and both men's sons, DeHaan and Cohen, meet as sixteen-year-old high school students and the sins of the past begin to haunt the boys. Their only refuge is found in the place beyond the pines. The acting, lensing and score are all superior and provide suspense throughout in this well-made thriller. The film saw limited distribution, earning more than $35.5 million in its initial release against a budget of more than $15 million. Songs: "Miserere Mei" (Gregorio Allegri); "Don't Go Please Stay" (music: Burt Bacharach; lyrics: Bob Hilliard); "Maneater" (Sara Allen, Daryl Hall, John Oates); "Che" (Martin Rev, Alan Vega); "Fratres for Cello and Piano," "Fratres for Violin and Percussion" (Arvo Part); "Contrapostive," "The Weight orf Consequences," "The Snow Angel," "Lodo March" (Mike Patton); "Dancing in the Dark" (Bruce Springsteen); "Get on My Hype" (Marvin Watson); "Trap Door" (Heather Marie Marlatt, John Alexander Holland, John Merlo Donoghue); "Fall Back" (Yonas); "Ninna Nanna per Adulteri" (Ennino Morricone); "Fools Rhythm" (Amon Tobin); "Bank Robbert Blues," "A Bad Decision," "We Shouldn't Be Here," "The Air of Betrayal," "And Then It Hit Me," "Dread," "Return What Isn't Yours," "Descending Dread," "Insidious Air" (Jim Helton); "Borriquito" (Pedro Pubil Calaf); "The Wolves" (Justin Vernon). Gutter language, violence, teen drug and alcohol use and a sexual reference prohibit viewing by children. **p**, Sidney Kimmel, Lynette Howell, Alex Orlovsky, Jamie Patricof, Carrie Fix; **d**, Derek Cianfrance; **cast**, Ryan Gosling, Bradley Cooper, Ray Liotta, Craig Van Hook, Eva Mendes, Olga Merediz, Anthony Angelo Pizza Jr., Mahershala Ali, Rev. John Facci, Ben Mendelsohn, Bruce Greenwood; **w**, Cianfrance, Ben Coccio, Darius Marder (based on a story by Cianfrance, Coccio; **c**, Sean Bobbitt; **m**, Mike Patton; **ed**, Jim Helton, Ron Patane; **prod d**, Inbal Weinberg; **art d**, Michael Ahern; **set d**, Jasmine Ballou.

Predestination ★★★ 2014; Australia; 97m; BlackLab Entertainment; Sony; Color; Science Fiction; Children: Unacceptable (MPAA: R); **BD**; **DVD**. The adventures of Temporal Agent Hawke begin when he is sent on a series of time-travel missions which are meant to ensure the continuation of his law enforcement career for all eternity. On his final assignment, he must pursue the one criminal called "Fizzle Bomber," who has eluded him throughout time, and Hawke must further disarm an explosive rigged by the terrorist in 1970s New York. The explosion blows up in Hawke's face, requiring massive reconstruction surgery that leaves him with a handsome face. Working as a bartender, Hawke meets Snook, a tough-appearing male patron who identifies himself as "the Unmarried Mother," his byline for stories he writes for magazines. Snook recalls in flashbacks the moment of his birth when he was born a girl named Jane and left on the doorstep of a Cleveland orphanage in 1945. Growing into her teens, she is bullied by other children and fights back with unusual physical ability and excels in studies, making her an ideal candidate for Space Corps, a 1960s-era government program to put women into outer space. The true purpose of this insidious program, however, is to provide comfort women as a service for male astronauts. Viewers of the time-travel film also meet the enigmatic Mr. Robertson (Taylor), who becomes a guiding influence in Snook's life as Jane. Hawke, as the Temporal Agent, offers Snook, as the Unmarried Mother, the opportunity to go back in time and alter his/her past. Weird and off the wall, this tale must have been hatched while scriptwriters were imbibing spiked sake; all of its characters are unappealing, but the action zips along with special effects that dazzle the eye, visuals that otherwise redeem this bizarre tale. Snook gives a compelling performance as a person undecided and constantly vexed about his/her gender. The film saw very limited distribution, earning only about $4.3 million in its initial release. Songs: "1970/I Feel Alright" (Scott Asheton, Ronald Asheton, Iggy Pop as James Osterberg, David Alexander), "Is It Over" (Emma Bosworth, Tim Buckley), "I'm My Own Grandpa" (Dwight Latham, Moe Jaffe). Violence, sexuality, nudity and gutter language prohibit viewing by children. **p**, Paddy McDonald, Tim McGahan; **d&w**, Michael Spierig, Peter Spierig (based on the story "All You Zombies" by Robert A. Heinlein); **cast**, Ethan Hawke, Noah Taylor, Sarah Snook, Christopher Kirby, Madeleine West, Freya Stafford, Jim Knobeloch, Elise Jansen, Cate Wolfe, Hayley Butcher, Alexis Fernandez, Christopher Stollery; **c**, Ben Nott; **m**, Peter Spierig; **ed**, Matt Villa; **prod d**, Matthew Putland; **set d**, Vanessa Cerne; **spec eff**, Brian Pearce.

Prem Ratan Dhan Payo ★★★ 2015; India.; 164m; Urajshi Productions; Color; Drama/Romance; Children: Unacceptable; **BD**; **DVD**. This entertaining romantic Bollywood film owes a lot to *The Prisoner of Zenda*, the 1894 novel by Anthony Hope and its many film versions in 1913, 1915, 1922, 1952 (best made in 1937 with Ronald Colman and Madeleine Carroll). Khan plays a rather cold prince who recovers from an assassination attempt four days before he is to be crowned king. He is replaced by a more warm-hearted look-alike (also played by Khan). His younger brother, Mukesh, has ambitions of becoming king, so he hatches a plot to do away with the rightful heir to the throne. The prince's double falls in love with the beautiful princess, Kapoor, who is to marry the real prince, and vice versa. Khan manages to not only survive attempts on his life, but foils the villains in the process, preserving the throne for his doppleganger, while, unfortunately sacrificing his romance with the stunning Kapoor. Sumptuously mounted and well-acted by Khan and Kapoor, this thoroughly exciting and satisfying production was a megahit as a Bollywood production, earning more than $64 million in its initial release against a budget of more than $16 million, proving to be one of the all-time grossers of its genre from India. Songs: "Prem Leela," Jalte Dije," "Jalte Diye," "Jab Tum Chalo," "Halo Re," "Tod Tadaiyya," "Bachpan Kahan," "Murli Ki Taanon Si," "Aaj Unse Kehna Hai" (Irshad Kamil). The film's title means "Got the Treasure of Love." (In Hindi; English subtitles) **p**, Ajit Kumar Barjatya, Kamal Kumar Barjatya, Rajkumar Barjatya; **d&w**, Sooraj R. Barjaty; **cast**, Salmon Khan, Sonam Kapoor, Neil Nitin Mukesh, Arman Kohli, Anupam Kher, Deepak Dodriyal, Swara Bashkar, Samaira Rao, Prem Khan, Mohamed Alinour; **c**, Manikandan; **m**, Sanjoy Chowdhury, Himesh Reshammiya; **ed**, Sanjay Sankla; **prod d**, Nitin Chandrakant Desai, Prasad Sutar.

The Prince ★★★ 2014; U.S.; 93m; Emmett/Furla Films/Grindstone; Color; Crime Drama; Children: Unacceptable (MPAA: R); **BD; DVD**. Taut and tense crime tale has Patric as a retired Las Vegas crime lord and widowed father, who discovers that his college-age daughter, Mantegna, has gone missing. He gets help from Cusack, a violent former crime buddy and from Lowndes, one of Mantegna's school friends, to track her down, while, at the same time, finds himself targeted by some underworld killers he manages to dispatch. This leads him to Jackson, a drug dealer known as "The Pharmacy" and who has been supplying college girls with heroin. However, the real villain is Willis, a crime boss whose wife and young daughter had been blown up in a car bomb planted by Patric some years earlier in a deadly mistake that nonetheless has prompted Willis to doggedly seek revenge. In a final showdown where Willis holds Mantegna hostage, Patric confronts his old nemesis, dispatching Rain, who is Willis' right-hand hitman, and, with Mantegna's help, as well as Willis, so that father and daughter are reunited for a bloody but happy ending. The plot is thick with melodrama and the characters are somewhat predictable, but the performances are convincingly intense and, on the part of Patric and Mantegna, considerably empathetic to sustain viewer interest to the finale. The film saw a mod-

Ester Dean, Anna Kendrick and Alexis Knapp in *Pitch Perfect*, 2012.

est success at the box office, earning no more than $18 million in its initial release. Song: "Back to You" (Jesse Pruett). Drug content, violence and gutter language prohibit viewing by children. **p**, Randall Emmett, George Furla, Adam Goldworm, Ho-Sung Pak, Fred Song, Dama Claire, Gus Furla, Timothy C. Sullivan; **d**, Brian A. Miller; **cast**, Bruce Willis, John Cusack, Jason Patric, Gia Mantegna, Jessica Lowndes, Jonathon Schaech, Rain, Courtney B. Turk, Don Harvey, Jaylen Moore, Natalie Light, Tim Fields; **w**, Andre Fabrizio, Jeremy Passmore; **c**, Yaron Levy; **m**, The Newton Brothers (John Andrew Grush, Taylor Stewart); **ed**, Rick Shaine; **prod d**, Nate Jones; **art d**, Michelle Jones; **set d**, John Richoux.

Prisoners ★★★ 2013; U.S.; 146m; Alcon Entertainment/WB; Color; Crime Drama; Children: Unacceptable (MPAA: R); **BD**; **DVD**. Taut crime tale begins when Bello, the six-year-old daughter of Jackman, a Boston carpenter, and her best friend are kidnapped on Thanksgiving. Jackman comes in conflict with Gyllenhaal, a young, brash detective who is in charge of the investigation. After searching, Jackman learns about an old recreational vehicle owned by Dano. Feeling that the law is failing in the search, Jackman captures Dano, whom he believes is the kidnapper. He wants to learn what Dano did with the girls, whom he is convinced are still alive. But the further Jackman goes to get Dano to confess, the closer he comes to losing his soul. Jackman, Gyllenhaal and Dano are exceptional in the roles and where director Villeneuve sustains high tension and suspense throughout. The film received an Oscar for Best Cinematography (Deakens) and saw considerable success at the box office, earning more than $122.1 million in its initial release against a budget of more than $46 million. Songs: "Put Your Hand in the Hand" (Gene MacLellan), "Escape" (Johann Johannsson), "Codex" (Thomas Yorke, Jonathan Greenwood, Colin Greenwood, Edward O'Brien, Philip Selway). Disturbing violent content, including torture, and gutter language throughout prohibit viewing by children. **p**, Kira Davis, Broderick Johnson, Adam Kolbrenner, Andrew A. Kosgove, Stephen P. Wegner; **d**, Denis Villeneuve; **cast**, Hugh Jackman, Jake Gyllenhaal, Viola Davis, Melissa Leo, Maria Bello, Paul Dano, Terene Howard, Dylan Minnette, Len Cariou, Jane McNeill, Brad James; **w**, Aaron Guzikowski; **c**, Roger A. Deakins; **m**, Johann Johannsson; **ed**, Joel Cox, Gary D. Roach; **prod d**, Patrice Vermette; **art d**, Paul D. Kelly; **set d**, Frank Galline; **spec eff**, Thomas Little, Tim Walkey, Vincent Cirelli.

Prometheus ★★★ 2012; U.S./UK; 124m; FOX; Color; Science Fiction; Children: Unacceptable (MPAA: R); **BD**; **DVD**. This exciting 3-D science sci-fi yarn is set in 2093 when some space explorers, including archaeologists, are on an undisclosed mission aboard a space ship called

Adam DeVine, Utkarsh Ambudkar, Skylar Astin and Michael Viruet in *Pitch Perfect*, 2012.

Prometheus. (In Greek mythology, Prometheus was a clever trickster, who gave the human race the gifts of fire and metalwork.) The explorers reach a planet far from Earth with no plant life or breathable atmosphere, but see what they believe to be evidence of civilization, a naked human-like animal that stalks a high ridge with nearby flowing water. Some of the space visitors are members of the Weyland Corporation and believe the planet is where the human race originated. The visitors next see traces leading to a pyramid, and most of the film then takes place under the pyramid and within the visiting spaceship. Rapace, a scientist in the group, wears a cross symbolizing that she is a Christian and believes life had a divine origin. Marshall-Green, her boyfriend, accuses her of dismissing the scientific theories of evolution. Within the pyramid the group finds alien humanoids in suspended animation, and a test of their DNA shows these artifacts are of the human race. Rapace, when alone on the space ship, discovers she is pregnant with an alien, but destroys it with robot surgery. Theron is a member of the Weyland Corporation that financed the spaceship which is piloted by Elba, both contributing problems for the space researchers. The group speculates that the humanoids came to Earth, but cannot surmise the reason for their visit. They explore the pyramid, and one of their crew, Fassbender, who is an android, thinks he can explain everything they encounter, although much of what they find remains enigmatic. The film is visually stunning and builds suspense through some fine acting, but the ending is as unsatisfying as the conclusions of **2001: A Space Odyssey**, 1968; and its sequel, **2010**, 1984, as one might expect as it gropingly attempts to define the source of humanity within the history of the universe. The film was nevertheless a huge box office hit (thanks mostly to its special effects), earning more than $403.4 million in its initial release against a budget of more than $130 million. Songs/Music: "Theme from *Alien*" (Jerry Goldsmith), "O Come All Ye Faithful" (traditional), "Love the One You're With" (Stephen Stills). Violence, intense images and gutter language prohibit viewing by children. Not related to 1921 or 1998 films with the same name. **p**, Ridley Scott, David Giler, Walter Hill, Mary Richards; **d**, Scott; **cast**, Michael Fassbender, Noomi Rapace, Charlize Theron, Guy Pearce, Idris Elba, Patrick Wilson, Logan Marshall-Green, Sean Harris, Rafe Spall, Emun Elliott, Benedict Wong, Kate Dickie; **w**, Jon Spaihts, Damon Lindelof, Dan O'Banon, Ronald Shusett; **c**, Dariusz Wolski; **m**, Marc Streitenfeld; **ed**, Pietro Scalia; **prod d**, Arthur Max; **art d**, John King; **set d**, Sonja Klaus; **spec eff**, Jack George, James Grummitt, Jignesh Mehta.

Quartet ★★★ 2013; U.K.; 98m; Headline Films/Weinstein Co.; Color; Comedy/Drama; Children: Unacceptable (MPAA: PG-13); **BD**; **DVD**.

Well-enacted tale from Hoffman (in his directorial debut) sees three former opera stars, Collins, Courtenay and Connolly, living in a home for retired British musicians. Each year on October 10 they take part in a concert to observe the birthday of composer Giuseppe Verdi (1813-1901) that can raise money to keep the home open. Smith, who had been married to Courtenay, arrives and disrupts the event, acting like a diva, but refusing to sing because critics years earlier had not praised her singing. She had been unfaithful to Courtenay in their marriage, but their relationship mellows during the course of the day and she admits to others that she still loves him, which he overhears. The show must go on and it does, breathing new life into the residents, proving that old age and art go together like fish and chips. This delightful, heartwarming film ends with Courtenay asking Smith to marry him again as they step onto the stage before their performance and she whispers her acceptance. The acting is superb and the robust music wonderful and energetically delivered straight to the heart of opera lovers. The dramatic and singing scenes are all carefully and lovingly organized and presented by Hoffman, who shows that he has a decided gift at helming films. The film proved to be extraordinarily successful at the box office for a story rooted to opera, earning almost $60 million in its initial release against a budget of more than $11 million. Songs: "Libiamo ne'lieti calci" (from the opera "La Traviata," by Giuseppe Verdi), "La donna e mobile" and "Caro nome" (from the opera "Rigoletto" by Giuseppe Verdi, Francesco Maria Piave), "Fantasia for Clarinet" (Donato Lovreglio), "Czardas" (Vittorio Monti), "Who Is Sylvia" (Franz Schubert), "Pass Out" (Patrick Okogwu, Labrinth as Timothy McKenzie, Marc Williams), "Flowers That Bloom in the Spring" and "Three Little Maids from School" (from "The Mikado" by Arthur Sullivan and William S. Gilbert), "So, Please You Sir, We Much Regret" (from "The Mikado" by Arthur Sullivan and William S. Gilbert), "Toccata and Fugue in D Minor" (Johann Sebastian Bach), "The Swan" (from "The Carnival of the Animals" by Camille Saint-Saens), "Ayo Listen Up" (Mikis Michaelides, Doc Brown), "Colombia Cumbia" (Javier Fioramonti, Toby Herschmann), "Minuet from String Quintet in E" (Luigi Boccherini), "Military Symphony No. 100 in G" (Joseph Haydn), "So Tell Aunt Rhody" (traditional), "Are You Havin' Any Fun" (Sammy Fain, Jack Yellen), "Ah! Qual colpo in aspettato" (from "The Barber of Saville" by Gioachino Rossini), "Happy Birthday" (Mildred J. Hill, Patty S. Hill), "Vissi d'arte" (from the opera "Tosca" by Giacomo Puccini, Luigi Illica, Giuseppe Giacosa), "Underneath the Arches" (Bud Flanagan, Chesney Allen), "Sunrise String Quartet" (Joseph Haydn). ***Author's Note***: According to Hoffman, Harwood based his play and film script on the 1984 documentary "Tosca's Kiss". The retirement home in the film was patterned after the Casa di Riposo per Musicisti for gifted musicians founded by Verdi. Ironically, Smith had appeared in another film titled **Quartet**, 1981, that is wholly unrelated to this story. Gutter language and suggestive humor prohibit viewing by children. **p**, Finola Dwyer, Stewart Mackinnon; **d**, Dustin Hoffman; **cast**, Maggie Smith, Tom Courtenay, Billy Connolly, Pauline Collins, Michael Gambon, Sheridan Smith, Andrew Sachs, Gwyneth Jones, Trevor Peacock, David Ryall, Michael Byrne; **w**, Ronald Harwood (based on his play); **c**, John de Borman; **m**, Dano Marianelli; **ed**, Barney Pilling; **prod d**, Andrew McAlpine; **art d**, Ben Smith; **set d**, Sarah Whittle; **spec eff**, Chris Reynolds, Shanaullah Umerji.

The Railway Man ★★★ 2014; Australia/U.K./Switzerland; 116m; Archer Street Productions/Lionsgate/Weinstein Co.; Color; War Drama; Children: Unacceptable (MPAA: R); **BD**; **DVD**. Tough and uncompromising true story sees Firth playing Eric Lomax (1919-2012), a British officer captured by the Japanese at the fall of Singapore during World War II (1939-1945). He is sent to a Thai prisoner of war camp where he and other prisoners are forced to work on the Thai-Burma Railway north of the Malay Peninsula. During his time in the camp, he is tortured for building a radio from spare parts with which he plans to get help to escape (in reality, the radio was simply used to boost morale). Years afterward, still suffering from the psychological trauma of his wartime experiences, and with the help of his wife, Kidman, and best friend, Skarsgard, Firth decides to find and confront one of his former captors, who had escaped prosecution as a war criminal. He returns to the scene of his torture after he has tracked down the Japanese officer, Sanada, in an attempt to rid himself of a lifetime of bitterness and hate toward him. In addition to an intelligent script and firm direction, the acting is superior from Firth and Sanada, as well as the rest of the cast. The graphically displayed brutality and various tortures depicted, however, will unnerve many sensitive viewers. Although the film is reminiscent of **The Bridge on the River Kwai**, 1957, it presents its own unique and chilling story line. The film saw a modest success at the box office, earning more than $22 million in its initial release against a budget of more than $18 million. Music: "Prelude from the Gadfly Suite" (Dimitri Shostakovich), "Rasputin" (Farian, Jat, Reyam). Disturbing POW violence prohibits viewing by children. **p**, Chris Brown, Bill Curbishley, Andy Paterson, Annalise Davis; **d**, Jonathan Teplitzky; **cast**, Colin Firth, Nicole Kidman, Stellan Skarsgard, Hiroyuki Sanada, Michael MacKenzie, Jeremy Irvine, Jeffrey Daunton, Tom Stokes, Bryan Probets, Tom Hobbs; **w**, Frank Cottrell Boyce, Paterson (from the book by Eric Lomax); **c**, Garry Phillips; **m**, David Hirschfelder; **ed**, Martin Connor; **prod d**, Steven Jones-Evans; **art d**, Nicki McCallum; **set d**, Nicki Gardiner; **spec eff**, Daniel Houweling, Clint Ingram, Kevin Chisnall, Helen Kok, James Rogers.

Reclaim ★★★ 2014; U.S.; China/Malaysia/U.S.; 96m; Grindstone Entertainment Group/Lionsgate; Color; Crime Drama; Children: Unacceptable (MPAA: R); **BD**; **DVD**. After their newly adopted daughter goes missing in a small Asian town while they are traveling, an American couple, Phillippe and Lefevre, try to discover the truth of her disappearance and the dangerous secret behind the adoption agency they trusted. Risking their lives, they will discover just what being a parent means and how far they will go to recoup their missing child. In the process, they not only expose a scamming adoption agency, but become victims of child traffickers who think to hold them hostage for ransom. This taut crime tale is well enacted and sees firm direction from White, who sustains suspense throughout, albeit the story line is a bit predictable. Violence and gutter language prohibit viewing by children. **p**, Brian R. Etting, Josh H. Etting, Mike Gabrawy, Gary Hamilton, Robert Luketic, Fredrik Malmberg, Silvio Muraglia, Ian Sutherland, Adrian Teh, Wang Yan; **d**, Alan White; **cast**, John Cusack, Ryan Philippe, Rachelle Lefevre, Jacki Weaver, Luis Guzman, Briana Roy, Jandres Burgos, Veronica Fay Foo, Alex Cintron, Millie Ruperto; **w**, Luke Davis, Carmine Gaeta; **c**, Scott Kevan; **m**, Inon Zur; **ed**, Scott D. Hanson, Doobie White; **prod d**, Meghan C. Rogers; **art d**, Elizabeth Cummings; **set d**, Glenda Rosa; **spec eff**, Shelley Madison.

Red Lights ★★★ 2012; Spain/U.S.; 113m; Nostromo Pictures/Millennium Entertainment; Color; Drama/Mystery; Children: Unacceptable (MPAA: R); **BD**; **DVD**. Well-made thriller sees Weaver, a psychologist, and Murphy, her phychic assistant, as specialists in debunking fraudulent paranormal phenomena. De Niro, a famous psychic, shows up in public after many years of absence, and Murphy becomes obsessed with determining whether or not De Niro is a fraud, while Weaver is skeptical of paranormal phenomena in general. As Murphy investigates De Niro strange events occur, electronic devices exploding and dead birds suddenly appearing. Then Murphy's laboratory is vandalized. Murphy attributes these weird events to De Niro as his way of subverting Murphy's investigation of his paranormal activities. Murphy manages to expose De Niro's fraudulent psychic performances but it is then learned that Murphy also possesses paranormal powers that have caused many of the inexplicable events shown throughout the story. Eerie and chilling, this well-written tale sees standout performances from Murphy, De Niro, Weaver and the rest of the cast. The film did limited box office, earning

Rebel Wilson and Anna Camp in *Pitch Perfect,* **2012.**

less than $13.6 million in its initial release against a budget of more than $14 million. Not related to the 2004 film with the same name. Gutter language and violence prohibit viewing by children. **p**, Rodrigo Cortes, Adrian Guerra, Manuel Monzon, Christina Piovesan; **d&w**, Cortes; **cast**, Sigourney Weaver, Cillian Murphy, Robert De Niro, Toby Jones, Joley Richardson, Elizabeth Olsen, Craig Roberts, Leonardo Sbaraglia, Adriane Lenox, Garrick Hagon; **c**, Xavi Gimenez; **m**, Victor Reyes; **ed**, Cortes; **prod d**, Anton Laguna; **art d**, Edward Bonutto; **set d**, Rob Hepburn; **spec eff**, Anthony S. Ciccarelli, Marcos Sagasta.

The Reluctant Fundamentalist ★★★ 2013; U.S./U.K./Qatar; 130m; Cine Mosaic/IFC Films; Color; Drama; Children: Unacceptable (MPAA: R); **BD**; **DVD**. Exciting thriller begins with Richardson, who is an American professor at Lahore University and who is kidnapped in 2011 after going to a movie theater. A ransom video is sent to a local newspaper demanding release of 690 detainees from a Muslim concentration camp in Kot Lakhpat and a large amount of money for children of Waziristan. Schreiber, an American journalist who is an undercover CIA informant in Pakistan, arranges a café interview with Ahmed, a colleague of Richardson's whom he suspects of being involved in the abduction. Ahmed begins the interview calling attention to his admiration for the American equal playing field in economic advancement. He is from the higher echelon of people (at one time attending Princeton on a scholarship) who increasingly find themselves left out of the economic progress. His father, Puri, is a famous poet, and his mother, Azmia, a housewife. After graduating Princeton, we see Ahmed working at a top Wall Street valuation firm where he meets Hudson, a lovely American photographer, in Central Park. They meet again at a party at the home of Sutherland, an associate of his employer, and begin a relationship. The terrorist attacks on the World Trade Center take place on September 11, 2001, while Ahmed is in Manila on business. When he returns to the United States he is strip-searched at the airport in New York City. Both his attitude toward the U.S. seems to change as well as his relationship with Hudson, who still has feelings for a former boyfriend. While valuating a publisher in Istanbul, Ahmed finds the company to be worthless, but then discovers they had translated into Turkish and published some of his father's poetry, so he realizes that the company has preserved culture that is priceless. Despite Sutherland's protests, Ahmed resigns from the Wall Street firm and ends his relationship with Hudson. Now a foreigner without a job and his work visa about to expire in two weeks, Ahmed returns to Lahore where he finds that foreign professors are leaving the country in large numbers. He is hired as a lecturer and voices dissatisfaction with U.S. intrusion in Pakistan that catches the attention of suspected al Qaeda members who raid his office and his parents' home, threatening them. While Ahmed and Schreiber talk in the café,

Jeremy Sisto in _Robot & Frank_, 2012.

protestors gather outside and Schreiber gets periodic pressure from the CIA to get information from Ahmed about the location of the kidnapped professor. Protests grow more hostile and Ahmed says he has heard of a butcher shop which may lead to information about the kidnapping, but contact is lost before information can be phoned to the CIA operatives working with Schreiber. Then Schreiber becomes suspicious when seeing Ahmed texting, although Ahmed says he was merely communicating with his parents. Schreiber now believes the only way to safety is to use Ahmed as a shield, venturing into the hostile crowded street outside the café. Attempts are made to keep the crowd stable, but things get worse and Schreiber is hustled to the ground and his gun goes off and a bullet strikes Shah, one of Ahmed's militant students. A militant sniper then shoots Schreiber and CIA agents remove him. Schreiber then learns that Richardson died while a captive earlier that day, and that Ahmed had rejected working with the suspected mastermind behind the kidnapping. The text message Ahmed had sent was to his sister, Shafi. Schreiber recuperates in a hospital, recalling Ahmed's words: "Looks can be deceiving. I am a lover of America, although I have been raised to be very Pakistani." The intense acting between Ahmed and Schreiber, as well as Richardson and Sutherland, and the mounting suspense created by the gifted director, Nair, sustains interest throughout in this well-made thriller. The film did poorly at the box office, earning a little more than $2 million in its initial release against a budget of more than $15 million. Songs: "Kangna" (traditional), "Bum Phutta" (Ali Azmat), "Scottish" (Robert Walter), "Rich and Well" (Jacques Slade, Lamar Van Sciver, Frank Greenfield), "No More Dues Aml" (Jerry Kalaf), "Measure of Me" (Amy Elizabeth Ray), "Aaj Mausam bada Beimaan Hai" (Anad Bakshi, Pyarelal Sharma), "Kaindey Ney Naina" (Wazie Afzal), "Dil Jalaane Ki Baat" (music: Moshin Razaa; lyrics: Javed Qureshi), "Raga Misra Mand" (Ali Akbar Khan, Nikhil Banerjee), "Mori Araj Suno" (music: Atif Aslam, Michael Andrews; lyrics: Faiz Ahmed Faiz), "Bol" (Peter Gabriel). Gutter language, violence and brief sexuality prohibit viewing by children. **p**, Lydia Dean Pilcher, Ami Boghani, Anadil Hossain, Robin Sweet; **d**, Mira Nair; **cast**, Riz Ahmed, Kate Hudson, Liv Schreiber, Kiefer Sutherland, Om Puri, Shabana Azmi, Martin Donovan, Nelsan Ellis, Haluk Bilginer, Meesha Shafi, Imaad Shah, Chris Smith, Ashwath Bhatt; **w**, William Wheeler, Ami Boghani, Mohsin Hamid (based on the novel by Hamid); **c**, Declan Quinn; **m**, Michael Andrews; **ed**, Shimit Amin; **prod d**, Michael Carlin; **spec eff**, Matt Mehring, Shakhabat Hussain, Robert Vazquez.

Renoir ★★★ 2013; France; 111m; Fidelite Films/Samuel Goldwyn; Color; Biographical Drama; Children: Unacceptable; MPAA: R; **BD**; **DVD**. This well-made biopic is set on the French Riviera in the summer of 1915, Jean Renoir (1894-1979), son of the Impressionist painter Pierre-Auguste Renoir (1841-1919), returns home to convalesce after being wounded in World War I (1914-1918). Bouquet plays Pierre-August Renoir and Rottiers plays Jean Renoir. Theret, a beautiful young woman who is Bouquet's model, enchants and inspires both him and Rottiers, although Rottiers feels a strong need to go back to the war. A somewhat languid tale, it is nevertheless redeemed through the warm father-son relationship as demonstrated by Bouquet and Rottiers and where Renoir's stunning paintings are richly depicted. The film saw limited distribution and did poorly at the box office, earning only $5.8 million in its initial release against a budget of more than $6 million. Songs: "Shimmy Dedee," "No Time Blues," "Everybody Shimmies Now" (Joe Gold, E.J. Porray, E. West). _Author's Note_: Director Bourdos employed Guy Ribes, an art forger, to recreate many of the Renoir masterpieces on screen in live action. Jean Renoir did not follow his father into a career in art, but became a great filmmaker, most noted for **Grand Illusion**, 1937, and **The Rules of the Game**, 1939. Art-related nudity and brief gutter language prohibit viewing by children. (In French; English subtitles) **p**, Olivier Delbosc, Marc Missonnier; **d**, Gilles Bourdos; **cast**, Michel Bouquet, Vincent Rottiers, Christa Theret, Thomas Doret, Romane Bohringer, Michele Gleizer, Laurent Poitrenaux, Annelise Heimburger, Sylviane Goudal, Solene Rigot, Emmanuelle Lepoutre; **w**, Bourdos, Jerome Tonnerre, Michel Spinosa (based on a work by Jacques Renoir); **c**, Mark Ping Bing Lee; **m**, Alexandre Desplat; **ed**, Yannick Kergoat; **prod d**, Benoit Barouh.

Retreat ★★★ 2012; U.K.; 90m; Magnet Films/Samuel Goldwyn; Color; Horror; Children: Unacceptable (MPAA: R); **BD**; **DVD**. Tense thriller begins when the marriage of Newton, a journalist, and Murphy, an architect, begins to fail after their first child is stillborn. In an effort to reconcile, they leave their home in London and go to remote but beautiful Blackholme Island off the west coast of Scotland. The cottage they rent is the only house on the island and it is owned by Yuill, who lives on the mainland. They had previously spent happy times at Fairweather Cottage on the idyllic island, the only house there, and arrive by ferry boat on a cold autumn day. Freezing winds blow over the island and, when Newton and Murphy are in the cottage, the generator explodes and injures one of Murphy's arms. Without electricity, they use the cottage's Citizen Band radio to contact Yuill, who says he will be right out by ferry to help them. While waiting for Yuill's arrival, a heavy rainstorm sweeps over the island, and Bell, a young man in army fatigues, is washed up on shore in a semi-conscious state. He comes to and says he is a British soldier, a private, and then reveals he carries a deadly message, while also carrying a gun. Bell tells them they are among the lone survivors of a deadly disease spreading worldwide that causes people to choke on their blood and die. He advises them to remain in the cottage and gets Murphy's help in boarding up the door and windows. Murphy is now distrustful of Bell and tries to escape the cottage, but Bell locks him and Newton in a bedroom. Murphy escapes through a skylight and goes to the pier where he finds the bodies of Yuill and Yuill's wife. Murphy returns to the cottage for his wife and manages to get Bell's gun away from him. As Newton ties Bell's hands behind him, Murphy begins to choke on his own blood. He and Newton both now realize that the disease is real and, to spare him from a slow and agonizing death, Newton shoots and kills Murphy. Bell then tells Newton he was experimented on at a British military hospital, but was released without realizing he was a carrier of the deadly disease. Bell also says he infected his wife with the disease and he killed her to save her from a terrible death, then he flew to Blackholme Island to quarantine himself. Over the CB radio, they hear a military broadcast reporting that a vaccine has been found for the blood disease, but Bell does not believe it. He tells Newton that the military are lying and they will not be allowed off the island. Newton now does not believe Bell and thinks he is insane and bent on killing her. Though there are continuity breaks in the somewhat predictable story, the acting from the entire cast is superior, and Tibbetts, a former film editor, shows considerable skills in his directorial debut and does a good job hurrying this chilling tale to its startling conclusion. Violence prohibits viewing by children. **p**, Gary Sinyor; **d**, Carl Tibbetts; **cast**, Cillian Murphy, Thandie Newton, Jamie Bell, Jimmy Yuill, Marilyn Mantle, **w**, Tibbetts, Janice Hallett; **c**, Chris Seager; **m**, Ilan Eshkeri; **ed**, Jamie Trevill; **spec eff**, Charlotte Collings.

The Reunion ★★★ 2013; Sweden; 88m; French Quarter Film/Mouse-Trap Films; Color; Drama; Children: Unacceptable (MPAA: PG-13); **BD**; **DVD**. Anna Odell (1973-), a famous artist played by Andreis, does not get an invitation to her class reunion. She then makes a film about what could have happened if she had attended the reunion and confronted those who had bullied her at school. Later, she shows her imagined confrontation to her former classmates and documents their reactions. This clever comeuppance tale sees Andreis shine as a woman using her talent to overcome the bitter memories of an abusive past. Not related to a 2012 film with the same title. Songs: "Let X It Tango" (Laurie Anderson), "The War Is Over." Mature subject matter prohibits viewing by children. (In Swedish; English subtitles.) **p**, Mathilde Dedye, Gunnar Carlsson, Mikael Frisell, Hans Vermeij; **d&w**, Anna Odell; **cast**, Sandra Andreis, Kamila Benhamza, Anders Berg, Jimmy Carlberg, Erik Ehn, Niklas Engdahl, Per Fenger-Krog, Jimmy Forsen, Robert Fransson, Sara Karlsdotter; **c**, Ragna Jorming; **ed**, Kristin Grundstrom; **art d**, Madeleine Norling, Eva Torsvall.

The Revenant ★★★★ 2015; U.S.; 156m; New Regency Pictures/FOX; Color; Adventure/Drama; Children: Unacceptable (MPAA: R); **BD**; **DVD**. Visually exciting throughout, this unusual tale presents a gripping American frontier survival story based on true events of the early 1820s. DiCaprio plays Hugh Glass (1780-1833), a Pennsylvania-born frontiersman and fur trapper who became an explorer of the uncharted Upper Missouri River in present-day Montana, North Dakota, South Dakota, and the Platte River area of Nebraska. On an 1823 expedition, his fellow explorers, and traders, including John S. Fitzgerald, played by Hardy, leave him to die without food or weapons, but he veritably crawls his way 200 miles to Fort Kiowa in South Dakota, surviving attacks by a grizzly bear and Native Americans of the Arikara tribe who shoot DiCaprio in the leg. The tribe is searching for the daughter of its leader who was kidnapped and will kill anyone in their way. The expedition is low on food as winter slows their way, so its leader, Gleeson, orders his men to return to their home base at Fort Kiowa. Hardy does not want to go back, so he encourages the others to disobey Gleeson whom he does not trust, while he also does not like DiCaprio. While the others debate about returning to the fort, DiCaprio is off alone when he is attacked by a grizzly bear. (The scenes involving this fantastic fight between man and beast is one of the most ferocious ever put on film.) The expedition then splits up, with some following Gleeson and others going with Hardy. With the Indians threatening in the area and DiCaprio so badly mauled that he may not survive, Hardy agrees to the dangerous task of staying with DiCaprio until he dies of his wounds and then burying him on the promise that DiCaprio's parents will reward them. Staying with DiCaprio is Poulter (playing famed trail blazer Jim Bridger, 1804-1881) and DiCaprio's half-breed son, Goodluck. Hardy soon tires of caring for DiCaprio and kills Goodluck by burying him alive as DiCaprio is immobile and unable to intervene. Hardy and Poulter then head back to Fort Kiowa, leaving DiCaprio near death. DiCaprio summons an almost inhuman life force to not only survive but get revenge on Hardy for killing his son, so he undertakes the nearly impossible journey through snow and across mountains to the fort which gives the film its title, meaning someone who returns to life after dying or being long absent. The unrelenting and grim hardship endured by these almost superhuman frontiersmen is graphically depicted in this robust and action-loaded film under Inarritu's energetic direction. DiCaprio presents a tour de force performance of one of those pioneers possessed of inspiring endurance and he is superbly supported by fellow cast mem-

Susan Sarandon, Frank Langella and robot in *Robot & Frank*, 2012.

bers. The lensing of the unwelcoming landscape is lavish and stunning. The film deservedly received twelve Oscar nominations, including those for Best Picture, Best Director (Inarritu); Best Actor (DiCaprio) and Best Supporting Actor (Hardy). The film enjoyed a great box office success, earning more than $223.6 million in its initial release against a budget of more than $135 million. Not related to 2009 or 2012 films of the same name. Songs/Music: "Arikara Elder," "Miss McLeod's Reel" (traditional); "Qilyuan," "Become Ocean," "The Place Where You Go to Listen" (John Luther Adams); "Jetsun Mila, excerpt" (Eliane Radique); "Harakiri Opening," "Taboos" (Ryuichi Sakamoto); "Stoukur," "Whitten" (Hildur Guonadott); "Messiaen: Oraison" (Olivier Messiaen); "Glacier" (Sakamoto, Skuli Sverrisson, Ren Takada); "Op. 1-1" (Ryoji Ikeda); "Duoon" (Carsten Nicolai, Sakamoto); "Viisari" (Vladislav Delay); "Lachrimae," "Viaton" (Bryce Dessner); "Haloid Xerrox Copy I and II," "Xerrox Spiegel," "Xerrox Spark" (Carsten Nicolai). ***Author's Note***: Glass's ordeal was previously depicted in **Man in the Wilderness**, 1971, with Richard Harris. Violence, including gory images, a sexual assault, gutter language and brief nudity prohibit viewing by children. **p**, Steve Golin, Alejandro G. Inarritu, David Kanter, Arnon Milchan, Mary Parent, Keith Redmon, James W. Skotchdopole, Alexander Dinelaris, Nicolas Giacobone, Scott Robertson, Alex G. Scott; **d**, Inarritu; **cast**, Leonardo DiCaprio, Tom Hardy, Domhnall Gleeson, Lukas Haas, Will Poulter, Forrest Goodluck, Paul Anderson, Kristoffer Joner, Joshua Burge, Duane Howard, Melaw Nakehk'o, Fabrice Adde, Arthur RedCloud; **w**, Inarritu, Mark L. Smith (based in part on the novel by Michael Punke); **c**, Emmanuel Lubezki, **m**, Carsten Nicolai as Alva Noto, Ryuichi Sakamoto; **ed**, Stephen Mirrione; **prod d**, Jack Fisk; **art d**, Michael Diner, Isabelle Guay, Laurel Bergman; **set d**, Hamish Purdy; **spec eff**, David Benediktson, Stewart Bradley, Brad Zehr.

Rio 2 ★★★ 2014; U.S.; 101m; Blue Sky/FOX; Color; Animated Adventure/Comedy; Children: Acceptable (MPAA: G); **BD**; **DVD**. In this good sequel to **Rio**, 2011, Blu (Eisenberg voiceover) and his wife Jewel (Hathaway voiceover), and their three children leave their peaceful home life in Rio de Janeiro and journey to the Amazon rain forest. There they encounter various creatures that are born to be wild. They soon meet Hathaway's long-lost macaw father (Garcia voiceover), who is having problems fitting in with a tribe of other macaws. Their Amazon habitat then comes under threat and the family's old nemesis, Nigel the cockatoo (Clement voiceover), is after them for revenge. Like the 2011 original, this sequel presents wonderfully created computer animated scenes where the action is dazzling and nonstop as the tropical birds perform their delightful antics and even put on a musical show. The script is also as brilliantly witty and funny as the original, and the actors'

Frank Langella and robot in *Robot & Frank*, 2012.

voiceovers perfectly match their characters. Also, like the original, this sequel was a megahit at the box office, earning more than $500 million in its initial release against a budget of more than $103 million. Songs: "What Is Love" (Janelle Monae, Nathaniel Irvin III, Roman Irvin); "Rio Rio" (Ester Dean, Carlinhos Brown, Mikael Mutti, B.o.B); "Beautiful Creatures," "Welcome Back," "O Vida" (Carlinhos Brown, John Powell, Sergio Mendes); "It's a Jungle Out There" (Philip Lawrence); "Don't Go Away" (Flavia Maia); "Batucada Familia," "I Will Survive" (Freddie Perren, Dino Fekaris); "Bola Viva" (Carlinhos Brown); "Favo de Mel" (music: Sergio Mendes, Carlinhos Brown, Mikael Mutti, John Powell; lyrics: Siedah Garrett). **p**, Bruce Anderson, John C. Donkin; **d**, Carlos Saldanha; **cast** (voiceovers), Jesse Eisenberg, Anne Hathaway, Andy Garcia, Jamie Foxx, Kristin Chenoweth, Jemaine Clement, Rodrigo Santoro, Leslie Mann, Amandla Stenberg; **w**, Saldanha, Don Rhymer (based on characters created by Saldanha); **c**, Renato Falcao; **m**, John Powell; **set d**, Isaac Holze; **spec eff**, Rhett Collier.

Robot & Frank ★★★ 2012; U.S.; 89m; Dog Run Pictures/State 6 Films; Color; Comedy/Crime Drama; Children: Unacceptable (MPAA: PG-13); **BD**; **DVD**. Inventive and amusing crime caper begins with Frank, played by Langella, who is an aging ex-convict and retired jewel thief living alone. Langella is suffering from increasing dementia, which bothers his successful attorney son, Marsden. Too busy with his practice and a family of his own, Marsden has tired of making weekly visits to see Langella. Marsden, however, is reluctant to put his father into full-time hospital care, so he buys a domestic robot (Sarsgaard voiceover) to be Langella's constant companion. The robot is programmed to provide Langella with therapeutic care, including fixed daily routing and memory-enhancing activities, which includes gardening. Langella is at first leery of the robot's intrusion into his lifestyle, but eventually accepts his new partner, especially after he realizes that the robot is not programmed to distinguish between legal recreational activities and criminal pursuits. Langella, a career criminal, now happily realizes that his mechanical housemate can now assist him in picking locks. They commit a robbery together so that Langella can win the affection of Sarandon, the local librarian, by stealing an antique copy of *Don Quixote* from the library shelves. The library is being renovated and turned into a community center because of declining public interest in print media. Meanwhile, Tyler, Langella's daughter, who is away on a philanthropic trip in Turkmenistan, hears about the robot and returns, attempting to convince her father to get rid of the machine, which she thinks is an unethical machine. Langella insists on keeping the robot, and he and the robot commit another caper, filching jewels from Strong, the rich young developer who is supervising at the renovation of the library. Police become suspicious and question Langella, monitoring him

while he claims that he is innocent and while he pretends to be seriously ill so that Marsden will visit him again. Covering his criminal tracks, Langella is now faced with the decision of whether or not to wipe out the memory of his robot, even though he knows he is losing his own memory. Langella returns to the library where he discovers that Sarandon is his ex-wife, which he had forgotten. He then returns home where the robot convinces him to wipe its holographic memory, because it is not a person and its sole reason for existence is to help Langella. Then Langella is then sent to a "Brain Center" where he received help in coping with his dementia. Police do not recover the jewels, but Langella comes clean by explaining in a note to Marsden that the gems are hidden under the tomato plants in the garden that the robot cultivated. Langella gives a wonderful and entertaining performance as a foxy old man who is still clever enough to employ modern technology in order to cling to his errant ways. He is well supported by the gifted Sarandon and Marsden, and Tyler provides a refreshing essay as a caring but suspicious daughter. The film saw very limited distribution and only produced a little more than $3.3 million at the box office in its initial release against a small budget of more than $2.5 million. Songs: "Ahhh" (Sam Bisbee), "Swear" (inc.) "Fell On Your Head" (Francis and the light) "Fugue in C Minor, K. 546" and "Requiem Mass" (Wolfgang Amadeus Mozart). Gutter language prohibits viewing by children. **p**, Lance Acord, Jackie Kelman Bisbee, Sam Bisbee, Galt Niederhoffer, Erika Hampson, Cody Ryder; **d**, Jake Schreier; **cast**, Frank Langella, James Marsden, Liv Tyler, Peter Sarsgaard (voice of robot), Susan Sarandon, Jeremy Strong, Jeremy Sisto, Rachael Ma, Bonnie Bentley, Dario Barosso, Joshua Ormond; **w**, Christopher Ford; **c**, Matthew J. Lloyd; **m**, Francis and the Lights; **ed**, Jacob Craycroft; **prod d**, Sharon Lomofsky; **art d**, Lisa Myers; **set d**, Michelle Schluter-Ford.

Room ★★★★ 2015; Ireland/Canada; 118m; Element Pictures/A24; Color; Drama; Children: Unacceptable (MPAA: R); **BD**; **DVD**. Superbly made tale begins with Larson, who, for some unknown reason, keeps herself and her five-year-old son Jack, played by Tremblay, living in a backyard one-room shed, an area ten square feet with no windows. Larson calls their living quarters "Room" and gives her son loving care within the confines of the shed, which becomes their total world. Larson had lived for seventeen years in the outside world before coming to the room after Tremblay was born. Apparently, the world had become too stressful for Larson, and she chose to shut herself and her son off from it. She tells Tremblay that the room is all there is in the world and there is nothing outside. Tremblay becomes increasingly curious about what is outside their room and finally convinces Larson to leave. This brings them into what for them may be the scariest place imaginable... the outside world. Larson's parents had separated during those years. Her father, Macy, lives on the other side of the country, and her mother, Allen, lives with a friend, McCamus. They do finally leave the room, and Larson finds that the world has changed a great deal in the five years she has lived in the shed. It has become more stressful, but she will have to cope with it, and try as best she can to help her son do the same as the story of their sequestered lives in the room becomes fodder for television news and talk shows. The prosaic story relates a sensitive tale with deeply empathetic characters superbly enacted by Larson, Tremblay and the rest of the cast, and Abrahamson directs with great skill and energy. The film received Oscar nominations for Best Picture, Best Director (Abrahamson), and Best Adapted Screenplay (Donoghue). The film saw limited distribution, earning only $9.1 million at the box office in its initial release against a budget of more than $6 million. Gutter language prohibits viewing by children. **p**, David Gross, Ed Guiney; **d**, Lenny Abrahamson; **cast**, Brie Larson, Jacob Tremblay, Joan Allen, William H. Macy, Amanda Brugel, Megan Park, Wendy Crewson, Sean Bridgers, Kate Drummond, Chantelle Chung; **w**, Emma Donoghue (based on her novel); **c**, Danny Cohen; **m**, Stephen Rennicks; **ed**, Nathan Nugent; **prod d**, Ethan Tobman; **art d**, Michelle Lannon; **set d**, Mary Kirkland; **spec eff**, Ed Bruce, Alan Collins, Kenneth Coyne.

Rosewater ★★★ 2014; U.S.; 103m; Busboy Productions/Open Road Films; Color; Drama; Children: Unacceptable (MPAA: R); **BD**; **DVD**. Based on true events, Maziar Bahri, played by Bernal, is a London-based journalist who is detained in Iran for more than 100 days in 2009 due to an interview he got regarding the country's presidential election. The interview is shown on *The Daily Show* with Jon Stewart on U.S. television in 1996, one in which an actor pretends to be a spy. Iranian authorities suspect that Bernal is in touch with an American spy and he is arrested and kept a prisoner. While his pregnant fiancée, Agh-dashloo, waits for him, Bernal spends five months at Evin Prison while being brutally interrogated. The only feature of his savage interrogator, Bodnia, that Bernal can remember (as he is blindfolded during the interrogations) is that Bodnia smells of rosewater. This chilling tale uncompromisingly shows in detail the brutality and oppression of the tyrannical Iranian regime. Bernal is riveting in his empathetic role as a helpless captive, and Bodnia is equally impressive as his torturing interrogator. The film saw limited distribution and did poorly at the box office, earning no more than $3.2 million in its initial release against a budget more than twice that amount. Songs: "New Bloom," "Vagheyi" (Mahdyar Aghajani). Violence and brutality prohibit viewing by children. **p**, Gigi Pritzker, Scott Rudin, Jon Stewart, Will Weiske; **d**, Jon Stewart; **cast**, Gael Garcia Bernal, Shohreh Agh-dashloo, Kim Bodnia, Golshifteh Farahani, Dimitri Leonidas, Jason Jones, Andrew Gower, Haluk Bilginer, Nasser Faris, Numan Acar; **w**, Stewart (based on the book *Then They Came for Me: A Family's Story of Love, Captivity, and Survival* by Maziar Bahri, Aimee Molloy); **c**, Bobby Bukowski; **m**, Howard Shore; **ed**, Jay Rabinowitz; **prod d**, Gerald Sullivan; **art d**, Samy Keilani; **set d**, Karim Kheir, Nasser Zoubi; **spec eff**, Michael Huber.

A Royal Affair ★★★★ 2012; Denmark/Norway/Czech Republic; 137m; Zentrope Entertainments/Magnolia Pictures; Color; Drama/Romance; Children: Unacceptable (MPAA: R); **BD**; **DVD**. Sumptuous historical romance is set in 1767, where British Princess Caroline Mathilde (1751-1775), played by Vikander, is married to mentally ill King Christian VII of Denmark (1749-1806), played by Folsgaard. While Folsgaard falls under the influence of a young German doctor, Johann Struensee (1737-1772), played by Mikkelsen, Vikander falls in love with the self-assured physician. Mikkelsen, an idealist, becomes the royal physician and persuades Folsgaard to make sweeping social and politically enlightened reforms. Mikkelsen becomes the most powerful man in the country, but the secret love affair becomes a tragedy when palace conservative enemies of Folsgaard use the protected romance to their advantage. Dencik, playing Denmark's powerful statesman Ove Hoegh-Gulberg (1731-1808), objects to the widespread reforms and plots against Mikkelsen, disclosing the fact to Folsgaard that his wife has sired a child through the secret affair she has been conducting. He persuades the heartbroken Folsgaard to send Vikander into exile while sentencing Mikkelsen to death. Following Mikkelsen's execution by beheading, the insidious Dencik becomes the regent of Denmark. The sets and costumes of this historical saga are superb and accurate to their period while the acting, particularly from Mikkelsen, Vikander, Folsgaard and Dencik, is outstanding under the firm direction of Arcel. The rewarding production received an Oscar nomination as Best Foreign Language Film. The film saw limited distribution, earning about $7.6 million at the box office in its initial release. Songs: "Trio Sonata No. 6" (Christoph Willibald Gluck), "Water Music" and Suite No. 1" (George Frideric Handel), "Sinfonia No. 4" (Johann Adolf Scheibe), "Symphony in A Major" (Karl Dittersdorf), "Trio Sonata in B Flat Major" (Antonio Vivaldi), "Harpsichord Concerto No. 1" (Johann Palschau). Sexual content and some violent images prohibit viewing by children. (In Danish; English subtitles.) **p**, Meta Louise Foldager, Sisse Graum Jorgensen, Louise Vesth, Jessica Ask, Gillian Berrie, Anna Duffield, Madeleine Ekman, Maria Kopf, Pavel Muller, Charlotte Pedersen, Martin Persson; **d**,

Alicia Vikander as Queen Caroline Mathilda in *A Royal Affair*, 2012.

Nikolaj Arcel; **cast**, Alicia Vikander, Mads Mikkelsen, Mikkel Boe Folsgaard, Trine Dryholm, David Dencik, Thomas W. Gabrielsson, Cyron Bjorn Melville, Bent Mejding, Harriet Walter, Laura Bro; **w**, Arcel, Rasmus Heisterberg (based on the novel *Prinsesse af blodet* by Bodil Steensen-Leth); **c**, Rasmus Videbaek; **m**, Cyrille Aufort, Gabriel Yared; **ed**, Kasper Leick, Mikkel E.G. Nielsen; **prod d**, Niels Sejer; **art d**, Martin Kurel; **spec eff**, Jeppe N. Christensen, Esben Syberg.

Run All Night ★★★ 2015; U.S.; 114m; Energy Entertainment/WB; Color; Crime Drama; Children: Unacceptable (MPAA: R); **BD**; **DVD**, **IV**. Tough crime tale sees Neeson as an alcoholic and a professional hit man in Brooklyn, who is known as "The Gravedigger." He had been a loyal employee of Harris until Harris marks Neeson's estranged son, Kinnaman, for death by the mob. Now Neeson has to go against Harris to save his son's life. Kinnaman is a limousine driver, married and with children. Complicating family matters, Harris' son, Holbrook, is both ambitious and a troublemaker. Holbrook makes arrangements with Albanese drug dealers on Christmas Day, but Harris refuses to take part in the deal. By coincidence, Kinnaman drives the Albanese in his limo to Holbrook's house where Holbrook kills them. Holbrook then pursues Kinnaman because he was a witness. Neeson learns of it all and kills Holbrook, but now Harris seeks revenge and puts a contract on both Neeson and Kinnaman. Neeson and Kinnaman are then hunted by Harris' mobsters, as well as a deadly hit man, and corrupt police officers. Neeson's only chance to protect his son is the support of D'Onofrio, an honest detective who has been after Neeson for years. Neeson now realizes that he may have to sacrifice himself in order to save his son's life. Neeson gives a riveting performance as do the rest of the cast in this hard-hitting thriller, one where the action is well coordinated by director Collet-Serra, who moves the story along at a fast clip. The film did well at the box office, earning more than $71.6 million in its initial release against a budget of more than $50 million. Songs: "Christmas Auld Lang Syne" (Curtis Mann, Frank Military), "You Spin Me 'Round Like a Record" (Michael Percy, Peter Jozeppi Burns, Stephen Coy, Timothy Lever), "Nasty" (Nasir Jones, Salaam Remi), "No Way Out" (Edsel Dope, Virus), "Fairytale of New York" (Jeremy Finer, Shane MacGowan). Rated R for strong violence, language, sexual references, drug use. **p**, Roy Lee, Michael Tadross, Brooklyn Weaver; **d**, Jaume Collet-Serra; **cast**, Liam Neeson, Ed Harris, Joel Kinnaman, Boyd Holbrook, Vincent D'Onofrio, Bruce McGill, Genesis Rodriguez, Lois Smith, Common, Beau Knapp, Patricia Kalember, Daniel Stewart Sherman; **w**, Brad Ingelsby; **c**, Martin Ruhe; **m**, Tom Holkenborg; **ed**, Dirk Westervelt; **prod d**, Sharon Seymour; **art d**, Deborah Jensen; **set d**, Chryss Hionis; **spec eff**, Jeff Brink.

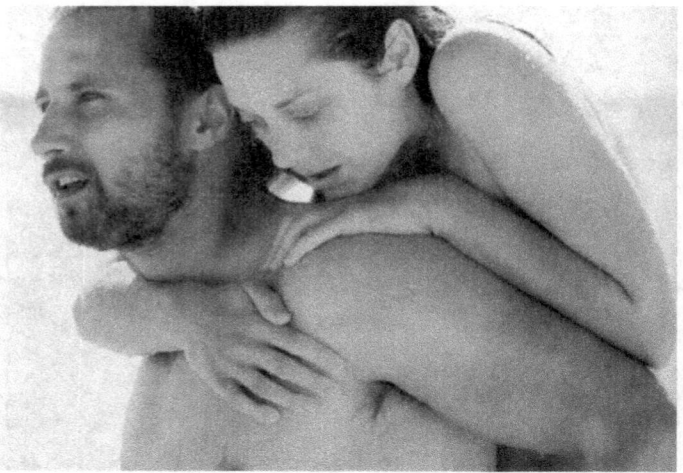

Matthias Schoenaerts and Marion Cotillard in *Rust and Bone,* **2012.**

Run & Jump ★★★ 2014; Ireland/Germany; 145m; Samson Films/IFC Films; Color; Comedy/Drama; Children: Unacceptable; **BD**; **DVD**. Entertaining tale begins in an Irish village where Peake is the upbeat, red-haired and attractive wife of MacLiam, a thirty-eight-year-old stroke victim. Peake takes him home after he has been in a coma for a month and four months in recovery. Accompanying them is Forte, a handsome, young American psychologist who will live with the couple and their two children for a few months and record MacLiam's progress for a book he is writing. MacLiam, a formerly skilled carpenter, withdraws into building useless wooden spheres instead of the fine furniture he previously constructed and marketed. He ignores Peake and their children and avoids personal contact with them. Forte becomes drawn to Peake and her teenage son, Morris, and younger daughter, and also becomes helpful to the children, taking over as the male head of the house. Even MacLiam begins to rely on Forte, and the family's dependency on the young psychologist becomes troublesome to friends and Peake's in-laws. Peake, Forte, MacLiam and the cast members render standout performances in this enriching and rewarding story of emotional recovery and family stability. Songs: "Born Natty," "No Nextel," "Doogie Hauser" (Jonathan Sanford, Lauren Nagel). Mature themes and sexual references prohibit viewing by children. **p**, Tamara Anghie, Asdtrid Kahmke, Philipp Kreuzer; **d**, Steph Green; **cast**, Maxine Peake, Edward MacLiam, Will Forte, Sharon Horgan, Clare Barrett, Ciara Gallagher, Ri Galway, Kelby Guilfoyle, Michael Harding, Joseph Kelly; **w**, Green, Ailbhe Keogan; **c**, Kevin Richey; **m**, Sebastian Pille; **ed**, Nathan Nugent; **prod d**, Stephen Daly; **art d**, Briana Hegarty; **spec eff**, Markus Hagemeier, Thomas Menz.

Rust and Bone ★★★★ 2012; France/Belgium; 120m; Why Not Productions/Sony; Color; Drama/Romance; Children: Unacceptable (MPAA: R); **BD**; **DVD**. Superior drama is set in Belgium where Schoenaerts, a former prizefighter with aspirations of becoming a martial arts champion, becomes a single parent and is put in charge of his young son, Verdure. He leaves Belgium to go to Antibes to live with his sister and her husband. There he becomes a nightclub bouncer and saves Cotillard from a brawler, and they become attracted to each other. Cotillard, who trains killer whales at a marine park, is attacked by a whale and loses both her legs above the knee. After surgery, she is fitted with prosthetic legs and, while at a rehabilitation hospital, learns to walk on them. She is mainly confined to a wheelchair, but Schoenaerts nevertheless remains attracted to her and becomes her caretaker. She becomes depressed and discouraged about her recovery, but Schoenearts will not give up on her or allow her to give up on herself, sometimes carrying her to the beach. They eventually have sex, but neither is sure that it means they are in love. Meanwhile, Schoenaerts and Verdure play on

an icy lake, but Verdure falls through and Schoenaerts fractures his hands while pounding on the ice to recover Verdure. Nonethelesss he enters a kick boxing contest to make money and to make a name for himself in that sport. Cotillard attends a martial arts bout that Schoenaerts wins in a bloody match, and then he fights again a few hours later in another even bloodier match. Schoenaerts becomes a physical wreck while trying to retain his championship, and it is emotionally very difficult on both him and Cotillard. She is uncertain that she can cope with his new career, which strains their relationship. While Verdure is recovering in the hospital, Schoenaerts phones Cotillard and tells her he loves her. The film ends with Schoenaerts winning a major kick boxing event in Warsaw, and he and Verdure are joined by Cotillard for a happy ending. This powerful drama sees mesmerizing performances from Cotillard (Best Actress Oscar winner for playing French singer Edith Piaf in **La vie en Rose**, 2007), and Schoenaerts, one of Europe's leading young film actors in the early 2000s. The script is intelligent, and gifted director Audiard helms with considerable skill, fully developing his characters and maintaining a quick pace and sustaining suspense throughout. The film did well at the box office, earning more than $25.8 million in its initial release against a budget of more than $20 million. Songs: "I Follow Rivers" (Lykke Li); "The Wolves" (Bon Iver); "Firework" (Katy Perry, Esther Dean, Mikkel Eriksen, Tor Hermansen, Sandy Wilhelm); "Love Shack" (Kate Pierson, Fred Schneider, Keith Strickland, Cindy Wilson); "State Trooper" (Bruce Springsteen); "Wash" (Justin Vernon); "Out of Clubzz," "Sexy Phone Girls; Fantasies," "Yo Hommies," "Jim" (Mike Kourtzer); "Back to the Future," "Tonight I'm a Superstar" (Lola Zaidline, Philippe Lees); "The Real Thing" (John Anderson, Klas Wahl); "I Like to Move It" (Erick Morillo, Mark Quashie); "On the Floor" (Carsten Wegener, Timo Hohnholz); "Evidently Chickentown" (John Cooper Clarke, Martin Hannett, Stephen Hopkins); "Candy Bar" (Aaron Gilbert); "Night Music" (Shahrooz Raoofi); "Entertainment dans la Meer" (Evgueni Galperine, Sasha Galperine); "With You" (Alexis Benjamin Taylor, Mehdi Faveeris-Essadi, Henry Smithson); "Reckless with Your Love" (Alexander III, Dinamo Azari, Starving Yet Full); "All the Days I've Missed You" (Colin Stetson); "Firewater" (James Dixon, Thomas Grace, David Maclean, Vincent Neff). Sexual content, graphic nudity, violence and gutter language prohibit viewing by children. **p**, Jacques Audiard, Martine Cassinelli, Pascal Caucheteux, Gregorie Sorlat, Jean-Pierre Dardenne, Luc Dardenne, Alix Raynaud; **d**, Audiard; **cast**, Marion Cotillard, Matthias Schoenaerts, Armand Verdure, Celine Sallette, Corinne Masiero, Bouli Lanners, Jean-Michael Correia, Mourad Frarema, Yannick Choirat, **w**, Audiard, Thomas Bidegain (based on a story by Craig Davidson); **c**, Stephane Fontaine; **m**, Alexandre Desplat; **ed**, Juliette Welfling; **prod d**, Michel Barthelemy; **art d**, Yann Megard; **set d**, Boris Piot; **spec eff**, Julien Poncet de la Grave.

St. Vincent ★★★ 2014; U.S.; 143m; Chernin Entertainment/Weinstein Co.; Color; Comedy; Children: Unacceptable (MPAA: PG-13); **BD**; **DVD**. Murray is wonderful as an aging Vietnam vet, who smokes, gambles and abrasively fights back at a world he thinks has been kicking him around. He lives in retirement at Sheepshead Bay, Brooklyn, and regularly visits his wife, Mitchell, who resides in a nursing home and suffers from Alzheimer's. Murray does her laundry and, when visiting her, pretends to be her doctor as Mitchell no longer recognizes him as her husband. Murray's only friends are his pet cat, Felix, and Watts, a Russian-born sex worker, who is pregnant and lives alone. When a new neighbor moves in next door, Murray's thirty-year-old Chrysler Lebaron is damaged by a tree branch unloosed by a moving van. Murray then demands payment for damage to his car from new neighbor McCarthy, a single mother with a twelve-year-old son, Lieberher. He soon realizes that McCarthy has her own deep troubles as she works as a medical technician while supporting her son, her marriage ruined by a cheating husband. Moreover, Lieberher has trouble at the Catholic school he attends where he is bullied and, on his first day, his house keys and phone are stolen from his locker. He arrives home but cannot enter it and asks Murray if he can stay with him until his mother returns home from work. Murray agrees and becomes the boy's babysitter, but for a fee. While Lieberher, an outgoing and friendly boy, begins a good relationship with his teacher, O'Dowd, he looks forward to seeing Murray, who picks him up at school. Murray, however, has some strange habits, taking the boy with him to bars and racetracks. Murray and Lieberher soon bond, and Murray teaches the boy how to defend himself so well that when a bully attempts to punish him, Lieberher promptly breaks the bully's nose. The boy, in turn, teaches Murray how to mature. The two win considerable cash with a winning racetrack ticket, and this allows Murray to pay off some of his debts. Murray uses the rest of the money on gambling, hoping to win more so that he can continue to pay for Mitchell's nursing home upkeep as he is behind in payments. He has been borrowing heavily from loan sharks Howard and O'Connor, and when they come to collect, they take his wife's jewelry and Murray suffers a stroke; he is left immobile on the floor as the thieves flee. While Murray his hospitalized, McCarthy, Watts and Lieberher tend to him, but, after he learns that Mitchell has died, he becomes inconsolably depressed and explosively irritable. Adsit, who is Lieberher's father and an attorney, learns that his son has been chumming around with Murray and gets a court order that prohibits the boy from again seeing Murray. Lieberher, however, refuses to give up on Murray and chooses him as the subject for his school project, "Saints among Us," where he interviews everyone he can find who knows and talks favorably about Murray to compile his report which is widely acclaimed. Watts then has her baby, and Murray returns home where he is seen having dinner with her, McCarthy and Lieberher to end this satisfying and heartwarming film. The acting is superior in this domestic tale, which sometimes narrowly sidesteps mawkish sentimentality and is skillfully delivered by Melfi (who debuts as a director with his first theatrically released feature); the script is both witty and sensitive, allowing for all of the characters to be fully developed. The film did well at the box office, earning more than $54.8 million in its initial release against a budget of more than $13 million. Songs: "Draggin' the Line" (Tommy James, Robert King), "Somebody to Love" (Darby Slick), "You Da One" (Mark Victor, John Staryand, Adam Smeaton), "One Toke Over the Line" (Michael Brewer, Tom Shipley), "Further On" (Chris Henderson), "Start a War" (Matthew Berninger, Aaron Dessner), "Molodaya Luna" (Vechyaslav Samarin), "Try Loving Me" (Willie Cooper), "Welcome Home" (Benjamin Cooper), "Stripper Pole" (Chris Bull, DeAngelo Samuel), "I Fought the Law" (Sonny Curtis), "It Makes You Feel So Bad" (Bill Swicegood), "Wheel of Fortune Bonus Clock" (Frankie Blue Sposato), "Shelter from the Storm" (Bob Dylan). Mature thematic material, sexual content, gutter language, and alcohol and tobacco use prohibit viewing by children. **p,** Theodore Melfi, Peter Chernin, Fred Roos, Jenno Topping; **d&w,** Melfi; **cast,** Bill Murray, Naomi Watts, Jaeden Lieberher, Melissa McCarthy, Donna Mitchell, Chris O'Dowd, Terrence Howard, James Andrew O'Connor, Nate Corddry, Scott Adsit, Kimberly Quinn; **c,** John Lindley; **m,** Theodore Shapiro; **ed,** Sarah Flack, Peter Teschner; **prod d,** Inbal Weinberg; **art d,** Michael Ahern; **set d,** Jaswmine E. Ballou.

San Andreas ★★★ 2015; U.S./Australia/Canada; 113m; Village Roadshow/WB; Color; Adventure; Children: Unacceptable (MPAA: PG-13); **3D; BD; DVD; IV.** Stunning disaster tale begins when Giamatti, a seismologist at California Tech, and Lee, a professor associate, are at Hoover Dam researching the predictability of earthquakes. A fault that was previously unknown ruptures, creating a 7.1 magnitude earthquake that collapses the dam and kills Lee. Giamatti then discovers that the San Andreas Fault is shifting and could cause a catastrophic earthquake, destroying cities along the fault line. Among those called to duty in the approaching disaster is Johnson, a Los Angeles Fire Department Air Rescue pilot. He is in the process of a divorce from his wife, Gugino, and planning a trip to San Francisco with their daughter,

Armand Verdure and Matthias Schoenaerts in *Rust and Bone,* 2012.

Daddario. Their trip is cancelled and Daddario goes with Gugino's boyfriend, Gruffudd, to the city by the bay. Gugino is lunching with Gruffudd's sister, Minogue, when the fault slips and starts a quake registering 9.1 magnitude, and Minogue and others die as buildings collapse and fires break out everywhere. Johnson saves Gugino from a collapsing building, and they escape the crumbling and burning city in his helicopter. The copter fails and he lands it at a mall in Bakersfield, where widespread panic and looting is happening. Johnson steals a truck and he and Gugino escape, then meet a couple who own an airplane and who trade it for the truck. Johnson and Gugino fly to San Francisco and find the city in flames, engulfed in what is now a massive 9.6 earthquake. Now a tsunami strikes in the bay, and the desperate couple make their way through the flooded city. They and Daddario survive and go to a disaster relief camp where Johnson and Gugino reconcile as San Francisco and the area recover from one of the world's worst earthquakes. Although there is little time for character development in the many subplots, the story nevertheless offers some of the most awesome disaster scenes ever put on film, thanks to the talents of special effects experts. The successive quakes, tsunami and fires are extremely well coordinated to show the ravages of the earth and loss of life in their carnage-producing process. The film was a megahit at the box office, earning more than $473.8 million in its initial release against a budget of more than $110 million. Songs: "Style" (Ali Payami, Johan Schuster, Max Martin, Taylor Swift), "Up on the Hollow Hill" (Robert Plant, Justin Adams, Liam Tyson, John Baggott, William Fuller), "Archipelago" (Will Holland), "California Dreamin'" (John Phillips, Michelle Phillips). Intense disaster action and mayhem throughout and gutter language prohibit viewing by children. **p,** Beau Flynn, Hiram Garcia; **d,** Brad Peyton; **cast,** Dwayne Johnson, Paul Giamatti, Carla Gugino, Alexandra Daddario, Ioan Gruffudd, Archie Panjabi, Hugo Johnstone-Burt, Art Parkinson, Will Yun Lee, Kylie Minogue, Colton Haynes; **w,** Carlton Cuse (based on a story by Andre Fabrizio, Jeremy Passmore); **c,** Steve Yedlin; **m,** Andrew Lockington; **ed,** Bob Ducsay; **prod d,** Barry Chusid; **art d,** Charlie Revai; **set d,** Lisa Thompson, Michael Westerman; **spec eff,** Leeanne Brooks, Joe Pancake, Geoff Heron, Brian Cox.

Saving Lincoln ★★★ 2013; U.S.; 147m; Pictures from the Fringe/Lake Street Pictures; Color; Biographical Drama; Children: Unacceptable (MPAA: R); **BD; DVD.** Based on true events, this highly stylized biopic depicts the close friendship between President Abraham Lincoln (1809-1865) and U.S. Marshal Ward Hill Lamon (1828-1893). They were law partners in Springfield, Illinois, before Lincoln, played by Amandes, ran for office. Joke-telling, banjo-playing Lamon, played by Coco, appoints himself Lincoln's bodyguard and witnesses every as-

Judi Dench, Bill Nighy and Celia Imrie in *The Second Best Exotic Marigold Hotel,* **2015.**

pect of his presidency, including calming him at times of stress. He saves Lincoln from repeated attempts on his life, including the plot to kill Lincoln in Maryland while the president was traveling to Washington, D.C., after his first election. Lamon worked with Allan Pinkerton (1819-1884), founder of the Pinkerton Detective Agency, to thwart that plan (this attempt on Lincoln's life by a southern cabal is depicted in **The Tall Target**, 1951). Fearing the president was always in mortal danger, Lamon, at times, slept by Lincoln's bedroom door wearing a brace of pistols. Lamon was away from Washington on a mission to Richmond, Virginia, the night Lincoln was assassinated on April 14, 1865. The film also depicts Lincoln's anguish over the countless casualties of the Civil War (1861-1865). He must also contend with and settle conflicts with members of his cabinet, particularly those from his Secretary of War, Edwin M. Stanton, 1814-1869, played by Craighead, and those in the U.S. Congress. The most devastating blow to Lincoln proves to be the death of his son, Willie (William Wallace Lincoln, 1850-1862), who is played by Nelson, and how Lincoln found it all but impossible to console his wife, Mary Todd Lincoln (1818-1882), who is played by Miller. Amandes, Coco, Miller and the rest of the cast members are standouts in their roles, all convincingly portraying their historical characters, which, under Litvak's firm direction, are fully developed and prove fascinating throughout. The script is top notch, and the inventive lensing and dynamic score strongly support the tale, while the period costumes and sets are impressively accurate to that traumatic era, having been created through the CineCollage Process (using contemporary photos of Lincoln's day) and which was created by Litvak. **p**, Reuben Lim, Judy Kim, Michael David Lynch, Matthew Stasior, Alan Noel Vega; **d**, Salvador Litvak; **cast**, Tom Amandes, Penelope Ann Miller, Lea Coco, Bruce Davison, Elijah Nelson, Creed Bratton, Saidah Arrika Ekulona, Josh Stamberg, Robert Craighead, Lew Temple, Michael Maize; **w**, Litvak, Nina Davidovich; **c**, Alexandre Naufel; **m**, Mark Adler; **ed**, Josh Noyes; **prod d**, Rachel Myers, Gabor Norman; **art d**, Jeffrey Givens; **set d**, Julie Ziah; **spec eff**, Ryan Bauer, Daniel Land, Catherine Tate.

Saving Mr. Banks ★★★ 2013; U.S./U.K./Australia; 125m; Ruby Films/Walt Disney; Color; Biographical Drama; Children: Unacceptable (MPAA: PG-13); **BD**; **DVD**. Well-crafted biopic dwells on the twenty-year pursuit by Walt Disney (1901-1966) to acquire the film rights to P.L. Travers' (Pamela L. Travers, 1899-1996) 1934 novel, *Mary Poppins*. Disney is aptly played by Hanks while Thompson gives a marvelous essay of Travers. From the beginning, Thompson fears that a Hollywood movie will ruin her beloved character, a magical nanny. But, as the book stops selling and she needs money in 1961, Thompson agrees to leave her home in California and go to Los Angeles and hear

Hanks' plans for the movie. He offers her an impressive preproduction schedule for a top film that promises to be faithful to her book and its memorable characters, but Thompson still hesitates and refuses to sign a contract. When she learns that there is to be animated sequences in the film to support its live action characters, she balks and ends her negotiations, returning to England. By that time, Thompson has reflected upon her difficult childhood in Australia, especially regarding her father, who became the inspiration for Mr. Banks. That unsympathetic character is the father in her book. He is a rules-bound Victorian patriarch, and very strict with his children. He tries his utmost to discourage their imagination, the very source of energy that produces their magical governess. Hanks refuses to take no for an answer and follows Thompson to London. When meeting her again, he tells her of his own difficult childhood and how he overcame bitter memories of his youth through the therapy of his very busy work. This helps Thompson to put the past behind her and she finally agrees to let Hanks film the book. The result is **Mary Poppins**, 1964, which becomes a huge box office hit, and one of the most endearing films in cinematic history. The acting is superb, particularly the scenes with Hanks and Thompson and those where the planning of the movie is presented, offering exciting revelations that deal with Disney's techniques and imaginative applications. In addition, Giamatti, who plays an empathetic limousine driver taking Thompson everywhere in her Hollywood visit, gives a warmhearted performance as Thompson's protector, one gently guiding Thompson through Disney's world, one to which Giamatti is nevertheless wholly devoted. The film received an Oscar nomination for Best Original Score (Newman) and proved to be a box office hit, earning more than $112.5 million in its initial release against a budget of more than $35 million. Songs: "Chim Chim Cheree," "Wonderful World of Color," "Supercalifragilisticexpialidocius," "A Spoonful of Sugar," "Feed the Birds, "A Man Has Dreams," " Fidelity Fiduciary Bank," "Let's Go Fly a Kite," "Jolly Holiday," "Step in Time," "Mary Poppins Medley: A Spoonful of Sugar, Jolly Holiday, Feed the Birds" (Richard M. and Robert B. Sherman); "One Mint Julep" (Rudolph Toombs); "Big Noise from Winnetka" (Ray Bauduc, Bob Haggart, Bob Crosby, Gil Rodin); "Lassie Main Title" (Les Baxter); "Heigh-Ho" (Frank Churchill, Larry Morey); "This Is Not Goodbye," "A Kiss Under the Stars" (Marc Ferrari, Daniel May); "Estudiantina," "Blaydon Races," "Men of Harlech," "A Dream Is a Wish Your Heart Makes" (Al Hoffman, Jerry Livingston, Mack David); "Zip-A-Dee-Doo-Dah" (Allie Wrubel, Ray Gilbert). Thematic elements and some unsettling images prohibit viewing by children. **p**, Ian Collie, Alison Owen, Philip Steuer; **d**, John Lee Hancock; **cast**, Tom Hanks, Emma Thompson, Colin Farrell, Paul Giamatti, Ruth Wilson, Rachel Griffiths, Annie Rose Buckley, Bradley Whitford, Jason Schwartzman, B.J. Novak, Victoria Summer; **w**, Kelly Marcel, Sue Smith; **c**, John Schwartzman; **m**, Thomas Newman; **ed**, Mark Livolsi; **prod d**, Michael Corenblith; **art d**, Lauren E. Polizzi; **set d**, Susan Benjamin; **spec eff**, J.D. Schwalm, Alexandre Cancado, Vincent Cirelli.

The Second Best Exotic Marigold Hotel ★★★★ 2015; U.K./U.S.; 122m; Blueprint Pictures/FOX Searchlight; Color; Comedy/Drama; Children: Cautionary (MPAA: PG); **BD**; **DVD**, **IV**. This delightful sequel to **The Best Exotic Marigold Hotel**, 2011, lives up to its promise and more. Patel, the energetic but ineffectual proprietor of the hotel, is about to be married to his love, Desai, and his hotel, now run by British expatriate Smith, is flourishing. With only one room left to be rented to Gere and his wife, Greig, Patel dreams of opening another hotel, one for "the elderly and beautiful." Meanwhile, other guests at the Marigold keep themselves busy. Dench and Nighy are also working at the hotel, while Pickup and Hardcastle are in an on-again, off-again relationship, and Imrie keeps two wealthy suitors guessing. The hotel would come undone if not for Smith, its indomitable co-manager with Patel. Pickup then becomes alarmed when a taxi driver mistakenly believes that Pickup wanted him to arrange a fatal accident for his lover, Hardcastle, only to discover that Hardcastle has been cheating on him with other men. Smith meanwhile receives bad news after a recent medical checkup, but she keeps this to herself as she prevents Patel from ruining his own wedding to Desai, that ceremony finally taking place to everyone's joy and jubilation. The acting from Patel, Smith, Dench, Nighy, Pickup and the rest of the cast members is outstanding in this warm-hearted tale, where director Madden does a good job of seamlessly weaving all of the subplots into a cohesive, fast-moving and utterly delightful story. The film was, like its predecessor, a hit at the box office, earning more than $86 million in its initial release against a budget of more than $10 million. Songs: "Move It On Over" (Hank Williams), "Death by Lift Shaft" (music: Pritam Chakraborty; lyrics: Irshaad Kamil, "Plastic Bubble" (Steve Adams, David Brogan, Zachary Gill, Daniel Lebowitz), "Shwas-Uchhashwas/The Beginning" (Zakir Hussain), "Balma" (music: Himesh Reshammiya; lyrics: Sameer Anjaan), "Wedding Mantra" (traditional), "Strangers in the Night" (music: Bert Kaempfert; lyrics: Charles Singleton, Eddie Snyder), "Mehndi Tharo" (traditional), "Aila Re Aila" (music: Pritam Chakraborty; lyrics: Nitin Raikwar), "Jhoom Barabar Jhoom, JBJ" (Gulzar, Shankar Mahadevan, Aloysuis Peter Mendosa, Ehsaan Noorain). Gutter language and suggestive comments prohibit viewing by children. **p**, Graham Broadbent, Pete Czernin, Pravesh Sahni; **d**, John Madden; **cast**, Judi Dench, Maggie Smith, Penelope Wilton, Dev Patel, David Strathairn, Bill Nighy, Celia Imrie, Ronald Pickup, Diana Hardcastle, Subhrajyoti Barat, Fiona Mollison, Richard Gere; Gary Tantony; **w**, Ol Parker (based on a story by Madden, Parker); **c**, Ben Smithard; **m**, Thomas Newman; **ed**, Victoria Boydell; **prod d**, Martin Childs; **set d**, Ed Turner; **spec eff**, Thomas Proctor.

The Secret World of Arrietty ★★★ 2012; U.S.; 125m; UNIV; Color; Animated Fantasy; Children: Acceptable (MPAA: G); **BD**; **DVD**. This delightful animated feature presents the four-inch-tall Clock family living in secret under the floorboards of a house in the country where they make their own home. Their peaceful life changes when their fourteen-year-old daughter Arrietty (Mendler voiceover) is discovered by a sad, sickly boy (Henrie voiceover) who comes to live in the house with his aunt and her snooping housekeeper (Burnett voiceover). Mendler and Henrie become friends but Mendler's father (Arnett voiceover) does not trust humans, while Burnett is determined to catch the little people. To survive, the Clock family must contend with pest control people and a family cat that is forever hunting them. There were several versions of this gentle, charming film for children and the whole family, but this version is one of the best. The film proved to be a huge box office hit, earning more than $145 million in its initial release. The story was filmed earlier in live-action as **The Borrowers**, 1977. Songs: "Arrietty's Song," "The Neglected Garden," "Our House Below," "Dollhouse," "Sho's Lament," "Sho no Waltz," "Spiller," "Rain," "The Wild Waltz," "An Uneasy Feeling," "With You," "The House Is in Silence," "Sho's Song," "Goodbye My Friend," "I Will Never Forget You," "Tears in My Eyes" (Cecile Corbel). (In Japanese and English.) **p**, Toshio Suzuki, Soledad Gatti-Pascual; **d**, Hiromasa Yonebayashi; **cast** (voices of), Carol Burnett, Will Arnett, Bridgit Mendler, David Henrie, Saoirse Ronan, Tom Holland, Luke Allen-Gale, Phyllida Law, Tatsuya Fujiwara, Tomokazu Miura, Kirin Kiki, Peter Jason, Mirai Shida, Dale Sison; **w**, Hayao Miyazaki, Keiko Niwa (based on the novel *The Borrowers* by Mary Norton); **c**, Atsushi Okui; **m**, Cecile Corbel; **ed**, Rie Matsuhara; **art d**, Yoji Takeshige, Noboru Yoshida.

Seeking a Friend for the End of the World ★★★ 2012; U.S./Singapore/Malaysia/Indonesia; 101m; Focus Features; Color; Comedy; Drama; Children: Unacceptable (MPAA: R); **BD**; **DVD**. Offbeat comedy begins when a threatened cataclysmic event brings out the worst in many people. News spreads that a huge asteroid is going to hit Earth in three weeks and blow it to kingdom come. This causes the wife of a mild insurance salesman, Carell, to leave him, so she can spend her last days with a man she really loves. Carell routinely returns to his now

Arietty (Bridgit Mendler voiceover), and Shawn (David Henrie voiceover) in *The Secret World of Arietty,* 2012.

empty NYC apartment and attempts to continue working, but everyone is now abandoning their work, participating in illegal drug use and conducting wild affairs while others commit suicide. Moreover, the impending disaster causes people to loot stores for big-screen television sets, hold orgies, and get their children baptized. Carell then meets Knightley, a beautiful young woman who lives next door, and they decide to take a road trip together. She will reunite with her parents while he will search for his long-lost high school girlfriend he now believes is the love of his life. On their road trip to Carell's hometown in Delaware, Carell and Knightley encounter Petersen, who has hired a hit man to shoot him, and a survivalist who thinks the emergency things he has amassed will save his life. It becomes a road trip without end, even though the world does not and, as suspected, Carell and Knightley grow to love one another and become a happy couple. Carell and Knightley shine in their frantic roles, and the rest of the cast members are standouts as characters going off the deep end as most people panic and where many comedic moments are mixed with tragedies. Scafaria, in her directorial debut, does a fine job balancing traumatic and touching scenes (such as the tender sequence where a couple gets married on a beach in defiance of the apocalypse, and which calms and encourages Carell and Knightley into their own romance). The film fared poorly at the box office, earning more than $9.6 million in its initial release against a budget of more than $10 million. Songs: "Wouldn't It Be Nice" (Tony Asher, Mike Love, Brian Wilson), "The Cherry Tree" (Steve Sidwell), "Bopology" (Ray Davies), "Devil Inside" (Mike Hutchencen, Andrew Farriss), "Dance Hall Days" (Darren Costin, Nick Feldman, Jack Hues), "Home to Sacramento" (Arthur Nix), "Cinco de Hiphop" (Christian Salyer as Cadence Blaze, Francisco Santacruz), "OOH" (Scott Hoffman, Jake Shears as Jason Sellards, Del Marquis as Derek Gruen), "New Day" (Alan Galvin, Eamon Gilson, Amanda Eustace, Alan Condon), "Pastel Lights" (John Mudd, Brad Dale), "Everybody Have Fun Tonight" (Nick Feldman, Jack Hues, Peter Wolf), "Sex Tourists" (Nicholas Stumpf, Lawrence Stumpf), "On My Radio" (Noel Davies), "My Time to Shine" (Byron Simpson, Eothen Alspatt, David Del Conte), "Set Adrift on Memory of Bliss" (Gary Kemp, Steve Cordes), "In the Time of My Ruin" (Charles Thompson), "Let's Go Out Tonight" (Dave Goodman, Blake Colie, David Lee Wilder, Dan Ubick, Davey Chegwidden, Alex Desert, Deston Berry, Malik Asu Moore, Christopher Shakespeare, Steve Kaye, Dan Mastle, Sergio Rios), "Cavaleade" (Roger Renaud), "Tijuana Ride" (Paul Williams), "This Guy's in Love with You" (Burt Bacharach, Hal David), "Air That I Breathe" (Albert Hammond, Michael Hazelwood), "The Sun Ain't Gonna Shine Anymore" (Bob Crewe, Bob Gaudio), "Stay with Me" (George Weiss, Jerry Ragovoy). Sexual references, drug use and brief violence prohibit viewing by children. **p**, Steve Golin, Joy Gorman, Steven M. Rales, Mark Roybal, Kelli

Patton Oswalt and Steve Carell in *Seeking a Friend for the End of the World,* **2012.**

Konop; **d&w**, Lorene Scafaria; **cast**, Steve Carell, Keira Knightley, Martin Sheen, William Petersen, Nancy Carell, Mark Moses, Roger Aaron Brown, Rob Huebel, Tonita Castro, Leslie Murphy, Connie Britton, Rob Corddry; **c**, Tim Orr; **m**, Jonathan Sadoff, Rob Simonsen; **ed**, Zene Baker; **prod d**, Chris L. Spellman; **set d**, Kathy Lucas; **spec eff**, Don Frazee.

Selma ★★★ 2014; U.K./U.S.; 128m; Cloud Eight Films; Harpo Films/PAR; Color; Biographical Drama; Children: Unacceptable (MPAA: PG-13); **BD**; **DVD**; **IV**. This well-crafted dramatization depicts the epic civil rights campaign of Martin Luther King, Jr. (1929-1968), played by Oyelowo, and his followers to secure equal voting rights by marching for three months in 1965 from Selma to Montgomery, Alabama, against violent opposition. During the march, peaceful protesters are whipped in the street by policemen, but continue their nonviolent march. In one scene, a black woman, played by Winfrey, is treated with contempt as she fills out a voter registration card. Police and FBI harassment is constant and a vicious attack by police on protestors as they cross the Edmund Pettus Bridge near Selma puts viewers inside the brutal battle of the marchers. The historic march led to President Lyndon B. Johnson (1908-1973), played by Wilkinson, signing the Voting Rights Act of 1965, one of the most significant victories for the civil rights movement. The acting from all is superior and the script intelligent and faithful to the historic events of that period. The film received an Oscar for Best Original Song ("Glory"; John Stephens, Lonnie Lynn, Che Smith) and received an Oscar nomination for Best Picture. The film saw success at the box office, earning more than $66.8 million in its initial release against a budget of more than $20 million. Songs: "One Morning Soon" (traditional), "House of the Rising Sun" (Duane Eddy), "Easy Street" (Allan Rankin Jones), "Walk with Me" (Ralph Bass), "Precious Lord Take My Hand" (Rev. Thomas A. Dorsey), "Why Am I Treated So Bad" (Roebuck Staples), "Ole Man Trouble" (Otis Redding), "Masters of War" (Bob Dylan), "Keep On Pushing" (Curtis Mayfield), "Time Brings About a Change" (Jimmy Outler), "I Got the New World In My View" and "Don't You Want My Lovin" (Kenneth Gamble, Leon Huff), "You Ain't Got But One Life to Live" (traditional), "Day-O" (William Attaway, Irving Burgie), "Yesterday Was Hard On All of Us" (Finian Greenall, Guy Whittaker, Tim Thornton), "Bamboo Flute Blues" (Yusef Lateef), "Glory" (John Stephens, Lonnie Lynn, Che Smith), "This Little Light of Mine/Freedom Now Chant/Come By Here" Medley (traditional). Disturbing thematic material including violence, a suggestive moment and gutter language prohibit viewing by children. **p**, Christian Colson, Dede Gardner, Jeremy Kleiner, Oprah Winfrey; **d**, Ava DuVernay; **cast**, David Oyelowo; Carmen Ejogo, Tom Wilkinson, Tim Roth, Cuba Gooding Jr., Oprah Winfrey, Jim France, Dylan Baker, Clay Chap-

pell, Giovanni Ribisi, Martin Sheen; **w**, Paul Webb; **c**, Bradford Young; **ed**, Spencer Averick; **art d**, Kim Jennings; **set d**, Elizabeth Keenan; **spec eff**, Caius Man, Scott Willis.

'71 ★★★★ 2014; U.K.; 99m; Crab Apple Films/Roadside Attractions; Color; Drama; Children: Unacceptable (MPAA: R); **BD**; **DVD**. This entry gives a chilling portrait of the Irish "Troubles," a time of both strong religious and patriotic differences in Northern Ireland. The title refers to a huge wooden "71" standing near the Botanic Gardens in south Belfast, Ireland, erected for the Ulster 71 Exposition that observed the fifty years of the Northern Irish state. The Troubles conflict began in 1968 and continued for more than thirty years to 1998 and the Belfast "Good Friday" agreement that year. It was mainly a bloody political war with strong ethnic and Catholic-Protestant conflicts. Unionist-royalists were mostly Protestants, who considered themselves to be British and wanted Northern Ireland to remain within the United Kingdom. Nationalist-republicans, mostly Roman Catholic, viewed themselves as Irish and wanted to leave the United Kingdom and join a United Ireland. More than 3,500 people were killed in the conflict. The Troubles is humanized by a fictitious story featuring O'Connell, who plays a soldier from Derbyshire and who is sent to Belfast as the situation there in Northern Ireland comes close to anarchy as the people revolt. O'Connell and his comrades find themselves in a wild street battle and he becomes separated from his squad. As night falls, he has to make his way home through occupied territory. Most of the film takes place on his journey through the long night that is fraught with danger as he has a drink in a loyalist pub and Republicans want his life, and O'Connell feels that he is living precariously on a dangerous planet. O'Connell manages to return to his barracks, but not without many dangerous encounters that almost take his life and where he must use lethal force to survive. The film is presented as a harrowing journey to safety, and O'Connell gives a powerful and compelling performance, strongly supported by a talented cast and well directed by the skillful Demange. The film did poorly at the box office (undoubtedly due to the waning interest in the genre, which had been often filmed), earning less than $3 million in its initial release. Songs: "The Sky Is Crying" (Elmore James), "You Better Move On" (Arthur Alexander), "Right or Wrong" (Wanda Jackson), "Cry to Me" (Bert Berns), "Gwely Mernana" (Richard D. James), "Walking the Streets in the Rain" (G. Prendergast, Jack Harrigan, Teresa Conlon), "My Autumns Done Gone" (Lee Hazelwood), "Burning Bridges" (Walter Scott). Excessive violence, disturbing images and gutter language throughout prohibit viewing by children. **p**, Robin Gutch, Angus Lamont; **d**, Yann Demange; **cast**, Jack O'Connell, Jack Lowden, Paul Popplewell, Adam Nagaitis, Joshua Hill, Ben Williams-Lee, Jonah Russell, Harry Verity, Peter McNeil O'Connor, Sam Reid, James McArdle; **w**, Gregory Burke; **c**, Tat Radcliffe; **m**, David Holmes; **ed**, Chris Wyatt; **prod d**, Chris Oddy; **art d**, Kat Hale, Nigel Pollock; **set d**, Kate Guyan.

Shadow Dancer ★★★ 2012; U.K./Ireland; 101m; UNIV; Color; Spy Drama; Children: Unacceptable (MPAA: R); **BD**; **DVD**. Taut tale is set in Belfast, Ireland, where Riseborough, a young girl, witnesses the death of her brother at the hands of Belfast violence in 1973. Twenty years later, in 1993, she is a single mother and has grown into a tentative operative for the underground IRA (Irish Republican Army), although her recent mission to bomb a London subway is left undone when she decides not to trigger the explosive device in her purse. She is arrested and placed in the care of Owen, a British MI5 intelligence agent. Owen urges her to become an informant so as to assure a future of freedom for her young son, reminding her that she could go to prison for twenty-five years. She cautiously agrees to become an informant and returns home to an undercover IRA cell in Belfast. Its leader, Wilmot, grows suspicious of her loyalty when their first strike against the British is thwarted by outside forces, an operation code-named Shadow Dancer. Unsure of her position in the cell, Riseborough grows distrustful of both sides. She watches as Owen breaks his vow of nonviolence, while Wilmot is determined to find and kill the mole that is disrupting his plans. Riseborough is faced with betraying her brothers, who are active IRA members, or protecting her son, while fearing her family will learn she may have informed on them. Riseborough, Owen and Wilmot deliver compelling performances while lethal violence looms and erupts all about them in this effective thriller, which is well directed by Marsh. The film performed poorly at the box office, earning about $2.2 million in its initial release. Song: "Night Whispers" (Simon Tinsdale, Joel Bevan, George Robertson). Gutter language and violent content prohibit viewing by children. **p**, Chris Coen, Ed Guiney, Andrew Lowe, Camille Gatin; **d**, James Marsh; **cast**, Clive Owen, Andrea Riseborough, Barry Barnes, Maria Laird, Ben Smyth, Brid Brennan, Jamie Scott, Bradley Burke, Ian Patterson, Michael McElhatton, Gillian Anderson, David Wilmot, Alan O'Neill, Gary Lydon; **w**, Tom Bradby (based on his novel); **c**, Rob Hardy; **m**, Dickon Hinchliffe; **ed**, Jinx Godfrey; **spec eff**, Paul Byrne, Sheila Wickens, Katie Roehrick, Sean Farrow.

Shaun the Sheep Movie ★★★ 2015; U.K./France; 85m; StudioCanal; Lionsgate; Color; Animated Adventure/Comedy; Children: Cautionary (MPAA: PG); **BD**; **DVD**; **IV**. Entertaining stop-action animated tale has Shaun (Fletcher voiceover) as a bored and mischievous sheep living with a flock at Mossy Bottom Farm. He decides to take a day off from work and leave the farm, achieving this feat by tricking the farmer (Sparkes voiceover) into going to sleep while counting sheep. Sparkes goes to sleep in a caravan that accidentally rolls away into the city. His dog Bitzer (also Sparkes voiceover) goes after him, ordering the sheep to stay on the farm until he gets back. The farmer (Sparkes) is hit on the head and hospitalized. He suffers amnesia and leaves the hospital, then goes into a ritzy hair salon where he cuts a celebrity's hair the way he would shear a sheep. The celebrity actually likes the new haircut, and Sparkes becomes famous as a hair stylist. Meanwhile, back at the farm, Fletcher and the other sheep go to the city in buses, but Fletcher is captured by Djalili, an animal control worker. Fletcher and Bitzer (Sparkes) are reunited in the animal shelter and escape with the help of a dog named Slip (Hands voiceover). When they find farmer Sparkes, he does not recognize them, causing the distraught Fletcher to devise a plan to get farmer Sparkes back to his farm where he hopes Sparkes will regain his memory. Djalili, by this time, pursues them, intending to kill the sheep. Once back at the farm, Fletcher and friends hide from Djalili in a shed, which Djalili intends to push into a rock quarry. Farmer Sparkes wakes up, regaining his memory, and he and Fletcher and the other sheep drive Djalili away. Farmer Sparkes celebrates by having Fletcher and the sheep take the next day off from work. Fletcher is happy again at the farm while the animal control center is turned into an animal protection center. Djalili loses his job but finds another in which he wears a chicken suit to entice people to come to a restaurant. The wacky style of comedy is nonstop and provides some rollicking laughter in almost every scene as humans imitate the antics of the endearing animals. The script is witty and the stop-action animation is cleverly depicted with a lot of surprising sequences, all of which provides a pleasing viewing experience. The film received an Oscar nomination for Best Animated Feature and proved to be a box office hit, earning more than $96.7 million in its initial release against a budget of more than $25 million. Songs: "Feels Like Summer" (Ilan Eshkeri, Nick Hodgson, Tim Wheeler), "Shaun the Sheep—Life's a Treat" (Mark Thomas), "Search for the Hero" (Paul Heard, Michael Pickering), "Rocks" (Bobby Gillespie, Robert Young, Andrew Innes), "More Wheels Cha Cha" (Norman Petty, Richard Stephens, Jimmy Torres), "Big City" (Eshkeri, Hodgson), "Stranger Adagio for Barbers" (John Matthews, Stuart Bruce), "Bad to the Bone" (George Thorogood), "I'm a Wonderful Thing, Baby" (Kid Creole as August Darnell, Peter Schott), "Home" (Dave Grohl, Taylor Hawkins, Christopher Shiflett, Nate Mendel), "Amazing Adventures of Morph" (Andy Clark), "House of Fun" (Michael Barson, Lee Thompson), "Shaun the Sheep—Life's a Treat (Rizzle Kicks Remix)" (Mark

Adam Brody in *Seeking a Friend for the End of the World*, **2012.**

Thomas Jordan Stephens, Harley Sylvester, Ben Cullum). Crude humor cautions viewing by children. **p**, Paul Kewley, Julie Lockhart; **d**, Mark Burton, Richard Starzak; **cast** (voiceovers), Justin Fletcher, John Sparkes, Omid Djalili, Richard Webber, Kate Harbour, Tim Hands, Andy Nyman, Simon Greenall, Emma Tate, Sean Connolly, Henry Burton; **w**, Burton, Starzak (based on characters created for a television series by Nick Park); **c**, Charles Copping, Dave Alex Riddett; **m**, Ilan Eshkeri; **ed**, Sim Evan-Jones; **prod d**, Matt Perry; **spec eff**, Ella Askew, Melanie Byrne, Howard Jones.

Short Peace ★★★ 2014; Japan; 68m; Bandai Visual Co./Eleven Arts; Color; Animated Fantasy; Children: Unacceptable; **BD**; **DVD**. Well-made episodic film presents in exiting animation a series of fascinating stories that begins with a man traveling alone and where he encounters strange spirits in an abandoned shrine. A second tale presents lovers, honor, and firefighting in ancient Japan and a third story profiles a mysterious white bear that defends a royal family from a red demon. (In Japanese; English subtitles.) **p**, David Del Rio; **d**, Hiroaki Ando, Hajime Katoki, Shuhei Morita, Katsuhiro Ohtomo; **cast**, "Tsukomo" segment: Koichi Yamadera, Midori Yuki, Takeshi Kusao; "Hi no yojin" segment: Saori Hayami, Seiichi Morita, Yu Kobayashi, Taro Ishida, Masaaki Emori; "Opening" segment: Fuka Haruna, Miyu Nakamura; **m**, Minilogue; **spec eff**, Shuji Shinoda, Koichi Yoshino.

Sicario ★★★ 2015; U.S.; 121m; Black Label Media/Lionsgate; Color; Crime Drama; Children: Unacceptable (MPAA: R); **DVD**; **IV**. Taut crime tale has Brolin, a U.S. government official, enlisting idealistic FBI Weapons and Tactics Team agent Blunt to assist in a joint task force tracking down an anonymous drug lord. The drug czar is operating at the border between the United States and Mexico. We first meet Blunt in Arizona, in a hideout run by a Mexican drug cartel where dozens of decomposing corpses are stuffed in the drywall of a home belonging to an arm of the cartel. Blunt becomes a member of a team tracking the drug operations of Del Toro as his cartel travels back and forth across the U.S.-Mexican border, using one cartel boss (Saracino) to flush out a bigger cartel run by Cedillo. After members of Blunt's team are murdered by the cartel's hitmen, she makes it her private mission to eradicate the killers, albeit Brolin urges her to restrain herself as the procedures no longer involve justice or morality, only keeping the peace between government agencies and the waring cartels. Blunt, irrespective of the life-threatening hazards, goes her own way and metes out the kind of old-fashioned justice that remains at the core of her beliefs. The script and lensing are superior as is the acting from the entire cast, although the story line sometimes becomes muddled in its attempt to separate the various hit men representing the separate drug cartels. The film was a

Bradley Cooper in *Silver Linings Playbook*, 2012.

success at the box office, earning more than $80.6 million in its initial release against a budget of more than $30 million. Not related to the 1995 film by the same title. *Author's Note*: The title for this thriller, Sicario, is a Spanish word referring to a hired killer in Latin American drug cartels. These professional hit men performed contract work for other drug cartels, often operating as an armed wing in exchange for various benefits, and operating in Mexico, the U.S. south, and Central America. Founded in 1988, it was reportedly later disbanded. Excessive violence, grisly images, gutter language and drug references prohibit viewing by children. **p**, Basil Iwanyk, Thad Luckinbill, Trent Luckinbill, Edward McDonnell, Molly Smith; **d**, Denis Villeneuve; **cast**, Emily Blunt, Josh Brolin, Benicio Del Toro, Victor Garber, Jon Bernthal, Daniel Kaluuya, Jeffrey Donovan, Raoul Trujillo, Julio Cedillo, Hank Rogerson; **w**, Taylor Sheridan; **c**, Roger Deakins; **m**, Johann Johannsson; **ed**, Joe Walker; **prod d**, Patrice Vermette; **art d**, Paul D. Kelly, Bjarne Sletteland; **set d**, Jan Pascale; **spec eff**, Stan Blackwell.

Silver Linings Playbook ★★★★ 2012; U.S.; 122m; Weinstein Co.; Color; Comedy/Drama/Romance; Children: Unacceptable (MPAA: R); **BD**; **DVD**. Outstanding romantic comedy-drama sees Cooper as a young man with a bipolar disorder who is released from a psychiatric hospital and moves back in with his parents, De Niro and Weaver. He is determined to win back his estranged wife, Bee, but she has obtained a restraining order against him. He tells his therapist, Kher, that he had come home from teaching high school to find her in the shower with another man, so he beat her lover severely. While looking for his wife, he meets Lawrence, who is recently widowed, and she tells him she will help him get his wife back if he enters a dance competition with her. They become more than dance partners as they practice. Meanwhile, we learn that Cooper's wife, Bee, has moved away and De Niro is out of work and engaging in illegal bookmaking to get enough money to start a restaurant. Cooper becomes a victim when racist thugs attack him and is arrested, but he is later released. He and Lawrence perform their dance routine and see that Bee is in the audience. It all ends with Cooper and Lawrence dancing off into a future together while the always hopeful De Niro continues to find ways to buy his restaurant. The story is uncomplicated, but so touchingly down-to-earth that its empathetic characters endear throughout. Cooper, Lawrence and the rest of the cast are impressively convincing in their well-developed roles as director Russell skillfully guides this warm hearted tale to its happy conclusion. Lawrence deservedly won an Oscar as Best Actress, and the film received Oscar nominations for Best Picture; Best Director (Russell); Best Actor (Cooper); Best Supporting Actor (De Niro); Best Supporting Actress (Weaver); Best Screenplay (Russell); and Best Film Editing (Cassidy). The film was a huge hit at the box office, earning more than

$236.4 million in its initial release against a budget of more than $21 million. Songs: "Fell in Love with a Girl" (Jack White), "Goodnight Moon" (Lawrence McVinnie, Ambrosia Parsley), "My Cherie Amour" (Stevie Wonder, Henry Crosby, Sylvia Moy), "Unsquare Dance" (Dave Brubeck), "Buffalo" (Joe Newman, Gus Unger-Hamilton, Gwil Sainsbury, Thom Green), "Girl from the North Country" (Bob Dylan), "Maria" (Leonard Bernstein), "Hustle and Cuss" (Jack Lawrence, Alison Mosshart), "Brahms' Lullaby" (Johannes Brahms), "What Is and What Should Never Be" (Jimmy Page, Robert Plant), "The Moon of Manakoora" (Alfred Newman, Frank Loesser), "Now I'm a Fool" (Joshua Homme, Jesse Hughes), "Fly, Eagles Fly" (Charles Borrelli, Roger Courtland), "Hello Operator" (Jack White), "Hey Big Brother" (Dino Fekaris, Nickolas Zesses), "Always Alright" (Zachary Cockrell, Heath Fogg, Brittany Howard, Steven Johnson), "Silver Lining" (Diane Warren), "Rain in My Eyes" (Joan Shaw), "Hard to Find" (William Kimball), "Monster Mash" (Leonard L. Capizzi, Robert Pickett), "Don't You Worry 'Bout a Thing" (Stevie Wonder), "Willie Willie" (Will Schaefer), "Sweet Cadence" (Gordon Henderson), "Have Yourself a Merry Little Christmas" (Ralph Blane, Hugh Martin), "Amore A Forza" (Piero Piccioni), "Popeye's Clog" (Evan Lurie), "Guarapiranga" (Tomaz Di Cunto), "Caesaroni's Tango" (Andrea Guerra), "Sway" (Norman Gimbel, Pablo Beltran Ruiz, Luis Demetrio), "Devil Tango" (Evan Lurie), "Misty" (Johnny Burke, Erroll Garner). Gutter language, sexual content and nudity prohibit viewing by children. **p**, Bruce Cohen, Donna Gigliotti, Jonathan Gordon, Mark Kamine; **d&w**, David O. Russell (based on the novel by Matthew Quick); **cast**, Bradley Cooper, Jennifer Lawrence, Robert De Niro, Jacki Weaver, Chris Tucker, Anupam Kher, John Ortiz, Brea Bee, Shea Whigham, Julia Stiles, Paul Herman, Dash Mihok, Matthew Russell, Cheryl Williams; **c**, Masanobu Takayanagi; **m**, Danny Elfman; **ed**, Jay Cassidy, Crispin Struthers; **prod d**, Judy Becker; **art d**, Jesse Rosenthal; **set d**, Heather Loeffler; **spec eff**, Mike Myers, Drew Jiritano, Ed Mendez, Ian Markiewicz.

Skyfall ★★★★ 2012; U.K./U.S.; 143m; Eon Productions/COL; Color; Spy Drama; Children: Unacceptable (MPAA: PG-13); **3-D**; **BD**; **DVD**. Outstanding espionage tale (the twenty-second entry in the series of twenty-three to this writing of 2015) sees a superb performance from Craig in his third outing as spy hero James Bond. The film opens in Istanbul, Turkey, where Craig is accompanied by Eve Moneypenny, played by Harris, both chasing Rapace, a ruthless mercenary who has stolen a computer hard drive containing information on undercover agents operating in terrorist organizations by NATO states. Rapace and Craig battle atop a speeding train, where Harris accidentally shoots Craig and Rapace escapes. Craig falls into a river and is presumed dead. Craig's boss, Dench, playing M, the head of British Military Intelligence (MI6), comes under political pressure to retire Fiennes, the chairman of the Intelligence and Security Committee. Dench then narrowly escapes death in an explosion in her office as several employees are killed, compelling her to relocate to emergency offices underground. Craig, however, is very much alive, having survived his fall into the river, and he returns to London and Dench approves his return to work. Shrapnel taken from Craig's shoulder identifies Rapace, who is traced to Shanghai where he plans an assassination. Craig is assigned to learn the identity of Rapace's employer, recover the stolen hard drive, and kill Rapace. Craig doggedly tracks down his nemesis, finding him atop a skyscraper where Rapce assassinates his targeted victim. Craig then confronts Rapace and they get into a fierce fight where Rapace falls to his death before Craig can learn the identity of his boss. Searching Rapace's belongings, Craig finds a gambling chip intended as payment for the assassination and that leads him to Macau. There Craig meets Marlohe whom he saw at the assassination in Macau, and asks to meet her employer, the same person who directed Rapace's lethal operations. Marlohe warns Craig that he is about to be killed by her bodyguards, but says she will help him if he kills her employer. Craig defeats the bodyguards and joins Marlohe on her boat. They travel to an isolated island off the coast of Macau where they are taken prisoner by the crew and turned over to Bardem, a former MI6 officer, who had worked under Dench, and who has become a cyberterrorist, heading his own network of agents. Bardem kills Marlohe, but Craig overpowers his guards and captures him, to take him to Dench in London. Bardem escapes custody in London, and Craig chases him through a network of tunnels beneath the city. Bardem attacks Dench at a public inquiry into her handling of the stolen hard drive. Craig joins Fiennes and Harris in repelling Bardem's attack, and Dench is taken to safety by her aide, Kinnear. Craig drives Dench to Skyfall, his family estate and childhood home in Scotland, where he lays a trap for Bardem. Craig leaves an electronic trail for Bardem to follow. Craig and Dench are met by Finney, the Skyfall gamekeeper, and they set booby traps in the house. Bardem's men arrive before him and Craig, Dench, and Finney fight off their attack, although Dench is wounded. Bardem arrives by helicopter to lead a second attack, but Craig sends Dench and Finney off to safety through a secret tunnel that leads to a chapel on the estate. Bardem's assault is conducted by a helicopter, dropping grenades and firing a machine gun mounted on the craft, but Craig detonates gas canisters with a stick of dynamite, which allows him to escape through the same tunnel to the chapel. The blast causes the helicopter to crash, destroying the house and killing most of Bardem's men. Bardem survives and finds Dench and Finney in the chapel, but Craig arrives and throws a knife into Bardem's back, killing him. Dench then dies from her wounds. After Dench's funeral, Harris retires from field work to become secretary for the new head of MI6, Fiennes, who assumes the title of M. The action in this well-crafted thriller is almost nonstop and its frenetic, eye-dazzling scenes are expertly choreographed. Craig, Harris, Dench and Fiennes are all standouts as MI6 heroes while Rapace and Bardem are scene-stealers as insidious villains worthy of every hateful hiss. The film received Oscars for Best Original Song ("Skyfall"; Adele Atkins, Paul Epworth) and Best Sound Editing (Per Hallberg, Karen Baker Landers). It received Oscar nominations for Best Cinematography (Deakins); Best Original Score (Newman); and Best Sound Mixing (Stuart Wilson, Scott Millan, Greg P. Russell). The film was a megahit at the box office, earning more than $1.1 billion in its initial release against a budget of more than $150 million, becoming the fourteenth film to gross more than $1 billion. Songs: "Skyfall" (Adele Atkins, Paul Epworth), "Boum!" (Charles Trenet), "Boom Boom" (John Lee Hooker), "Konyali" (Huseyin Turkmenler), "CNN Breaking News Theme 2" (Herb Avery), "Moonlight" (Jun Chen), "The Name's Bond... James Bond" (Monty Norman). *Author's Note*: This film marked the gifted Dench's final appearance as M. The film was shot in 128 days on location in London and inside the Old Vic Tunnels near Waterloo Station, as well as in Turkey. In addition to this production, the James Bond films to date include **Casino Royale**, 1967; **Diamonds Are Forever**, 1971; **Dr. No**, 1962; **For Your Eyes Only**, 1981; **From Russia with Love**, 1963; **GoldenEye**, 1995; **Goldfinger**, 1964; **License to Kill**, 1989; **Live and Let Die**, 1973; **The Living Daylights**, 1987; **The Man with the Golden Gun**, 1974; **Moonraker**, 1979; **Never Say Never Again**, 1963; **Octopussy**, 1963; **On Her Majesty's Secret Service**, 1969; **Spectre**, 2015; **The Spy Who Loved Me**, 1977; **Thunderball**, 1965; **Tomorrow Never Dies**, 1997; **A View to a Kill**, 1965; **The World Is Not Enough**, 1999; **You Only Live Twice**, 1967. Intense violence, sexuality, gutter language and smoking prohibit viewing by children. **p**, Barbara Broccoli, Michael G. Wilson, Andrew Noakes, David Pope; **d**, Sam Mendes; **cast**, Daniel Craig, Judi Dench, Javier Bardem, Ralph Fiennes, Albert Finney, Naomie Harris, Berenice Lim Marlohe, Ben Whishaw, Rory Kinnear, Ola Rapace, Helen McCrory, Nicholas Woodeson, Bill Buckhurst; **w**, Neal Purvis, Robert Wade, John Logan (based on characters created by Ian Fleming); **c**, Roger Deakins; **m**, Thomas Newman; **ed**, Stuart Baird; **prod d**, Dennis Gassner; **art d**, Neal Callow, Dean Clegg, James Foster, Mark Harris, Marc Homes, Paul Inglis, Jason Knox-Johnston, Chris Lowe; **set d**, Anna Pinnock; **spec eff**, Asregadoo Arundi, Steve Begg, Hugh Macdonald, Jonathan Neill, Edson Williams, Angela Barson.

Ralph Fiennes in *Skyfall*, 2012.

Sleeping with Other People ★★★ 2015; U.S.; 101m; Gloria Sanchez Productions/IFC Films; Color; Comedy/Romance; Children: Unacceptable (MPAA: R); **BD**; **DVD**. Offbeat romantic comedy sees Sudeikis and Brie making up a very odd couple to fall in love, especially since Sudeikis is a flagrant womanizer and Brie habitually cheats on her lovers. The film opens in a college dorm where Brie has been stood up by her latest beau. Sudeikis comes along to calm her and they wind up sleeping together on the roof. Twelve years pass and both of them have been sleeping with other people. Brie still has a crush on the college boy who jilted her, but has since gotten married. Sudeikis still has not found the girl of his dreams, although he has slept with most of his prospects. They meet once again and become attracted to each other, forming a platonic relationship that blossoms into a romance that shows some positive signs of lasting. Brie and Sudeikis are outstanding in their roles as wholly selfish people who become less self-centered as they begin to romantically focus upon one another. The script is clever, and director Headland moves this very amusing tale along at a brisk pace. Even though the outcome is predictable, the film satisfies throughout as these two romantic clucks begin to click in unison. Songs/Music: "Get Over It" (Damian Kulash); "We Bounce" (Eric V. Hachikian); "Don't Blow It" (Thomas Carroll, Aaron Hatch, Andrew Petersen, Anthony Petersen); "Ganhou O Meu Caracao" (Alana Da Fonseca, John McCurry, Ali Theodore); "Palmreader," "Minimum Wage," "Wolf-Like Howls from the Bathhouse" (Sonny Smith); "Oblivious," "UTBTS" (Charles Brand, Rick Schaier, Brandon Lee, Algernon Quashie); "Spring Flowering" (Rudy Khan, Anton Nevski, Pierre Arrachart); "Love Me" (Jerry Leiber, Mike Stoller); "As Lon as You Are Mine" (John Morrical, Michael Schenk); "Pachuquin" (Enzo Villaparedes, Daniel Indart, Sara Traina); "Jingle Bells" (traditional); "BAP U" (Dylan Engen Ragland); "Christmas with You" (Joe Lervold, Clifford Goldmacher); "Welcome to the Terrordome" (Chuck D, Keith Shocklee); "Remedy" (Matthew Depauw, Nicholas Fotinakes, Travis Hawley, Rico D. Rodriguez, Aaron J. Rubin, Michael Van Kranenburg); "Like the Clappers" (Paul Reeves); "Open Season" "Bridge" (Oliver Chang, Jackson Milas); "Modern Love" (David Bowie); "Moonlight Sonata" (Ludwig van Beethoven); "As Long as I Got You" (Julia Cavazos, Joleen Belle, Joachim Svare); "China Tea" (Rudy Khan, Anton Nevski, Pierre Arrachart); "Double Vision" (Nathan William Jerde, Jered Burl Gummere, Brian Case, Melissa Ann Elias); "The Unexpected" (Joe Lervold, Lisa Aschmann); "Come On" (Mikhael Paskalev); "People and So On" (Joakim Christopher Sveningsson, Daniel Johansson); "Fuck It and Whatever" (Jake Rabinbach). Sexual content, gutter language and drug use prohibit viewing by children. **p**, Jessica Elbaum, Will Ferrell, Sidney Kimmel, Adam McKay, Kathryn Dean, Mark Mikutowicz, Dylan Tarason; **d&w**, Leslye Headland; **cast**, Alison Brie, Jason Sudeikis, Jordan Carlos, Margarita

Daniel Craig in *Skyfall*, 2012.

Levieva, Amanda Peet, Charles Cain, Adam Brody, Michael Cyril Creighton, Billy Eichner, Jason Mantzoukas, Margaret Odette; **c**, Ben Kutchins; **m**, Andrew Feltenstein; **ed**, Paul Frank; **prod d**, Amy Williams; **art d**, Gonzalo Cordoba; **spec eff**, Eric J. Robertson.

Slow West ★★★★ 2015; U.K./New Zealand; 84m; See-Saw Films; A24; Color; Western; Children: Unacceptable (MPAA: R); **BD**; **DVD**. Adventure-filled western begins with Smit-McPhee, a young upper-class Scotsman who goes to America to look for Pistorius, the woman he loves, and runs into some men who are pursuing an Indian with intensions of killing him. While the pursuers question him, Fassbender, a bounty hunter, kills the group's leader. Smit-McPhee then pays Fassbender to give him protection while he searches for Pistorius. At a trading post, Fassbender sees a poster offering a bounty of $2,000 for Pistorius and her father, McCann. Smit-McPhee does not see the poster so he does not know that Pistorius and McCann are wanted by the law. Fassbender now plans to use Smit-McPhee as a lure to find them. A man called Victor the Hawk, played by Wright, who is also a bounty hunter, has also seen the wanted poster and sets out to capture the fugitives. At the trading post, Smit-McPhee and Fassbender witness an attempted robbery by a Swedish couple that results in the post's owner and the Swedish man being killed. Leaving the post, Smit-McPhee and Fassbender discover the Swedish couple's children waiting outside, so Smit-McPhee gives them some clothes and food and then leaves with Fassbender. In flashbacks, we learn that Pistorius only cared for Smit-McPhee as a brother. We also learn that Smit-McPhee's uncle, a Scottish lord, was accidentally killed by Pistorius' father during an argument, which results in her and her father fleeing to America, their actions creating the bounty placed on their heads. Smit-McPhee now leaves Fassbender and goes on alone in his search for Pistorius, still not knowing she is wanted by the law. Smit-McPhee then meets Robertt, a writer who accompanies him. Robertt then robs Smit-McPhee and steals his horse. Fassbender then finds Smit-McPhee and returns his horse and belongings, saying he came upon Robertt. They then meet Mendelsohn, leader of a gang to which Fassbender once belonged. Mendelsohn steals their guns while the two sleep, and as they go on together, Fassbender tells Smit-McPhee about the bounty on Pistorius and her father. It all ends in several gunfights, with the final shootout between Mendelsohn and Smit-McPhee; both fatally shoot each other, and Pistorius is briefly reunited with Smit-McPhee. She tells Fassbender that Smit-McPhee truly loved her, and Fassbender remains with her and the orphaned children of the Swedish couple. Grim and uncompromising, the film does not flinch from the everyday hardscrabble lifestyle of the Old West, or the routine brutalities inherent in the savage natures of its unsophisticated inhabitants. Smit-McPhee and Fassbender are standouts in their roles,

one coming from a cultivated and genteel society, the other as crude and unthinking as the world in which both attempt to survive. Songs: "The Minstrel's Song" (Bryan Michael Mills, John Maclean), "Jupiter and Mars" (Mills, Nicholas Munro), "Theme from The Orkestra of the Dead" (Mills), "Mbanza Congo" (Passi Jo), "Aeolian Arietta" (Lone Pigeon), "Slow West" (Django Django). Violence and gutter language prohibit viewing by children. **p**, Iain Canning, Rachel Gardner, Conor McCaughan, Emile Sherman; **d&w**, John Maclean; **cast**, Kodi Smit-McPhee, Michael Fassbender, Ben Mendelsohn, Aorere Paki, Hayden Frost, Caren Pistorius, Kieran Charnock, Edwin Wright, Joseph Passi, Andrew Robertt; **c**, Robbie Ryan; **m**, Jed Kurzel; **ed**, Roland Gallois, Jon Gregory; **prod d**, Kim Sinclair; **art d**, Sarah Finlay, Ken Turner; **set d**, Amber Richards; **spec eff**, Perry Costello, Steve Ingram.

Snow White and the Huntsman ★★★ 2012; U.K./U.S.; 127m; Roth Films/UNIV; Color; Adventure/Fantasy; Children: Unacceptable (MPAA: PG-13); **BD**; **DVD**. The visual effects are amazing in this live-action fantasy that begins when Queen Eleanor, played by Ross, wishes she had a daughter as white as snow, as red as blood, and as strong and defiant as the rose she finds blooming in the snow. She gives birth to Snow White, portrayed by Stewart, who becomes Princess of the Kingdom of Tabor. Soon afterward, Ross falls ill and dies. Her husband, King Magnus, essayed by Huntley, marries beautiful Ravenna, played by Theron, not knowing she is an evil sorceress. On their wedding night, she kills him because she believes all men exploit women for their beauty but then discard them. Theron then takes control of the kingdom. Regan, a duke who resists Theron's rule, escapes the castle with his teenage son, Claflin, but is unable to take Stewart to safety because she is captured by Theron's brother, Spruell, who locks her away in the castle's north tower. Theron's mother had cast a spell on her that allowed her to keep her beauty forever, but Theron learns from her magic mirror that, after Stewart comes of age, Stewart will be more beautiful and Theron will die. Theron orders Spruell to bring Stewart to her, but she escapes into the nearby Dark Forest where Theron has no power. Hemsworth, portraying Eric the Huntsman, a widower and drunkard living in the forest, is brought to Theron, who orders him to lead Spruell in finding Stewart. He refuses until Theron threatens to kill him, and, to inspire Hemsworth to cooperate, promises him that she will revive his dead wife. Hemsworth finds Stewart in the forest, but refuses to turn her over to Spruell until he is sure that Theron will keep her promises to him. Spruell tells Hemsworth that Theron cannot bring back the dead, and that he is a fool. Stewart promises Hemsworth gold if he will escort her to Regan's castle while Spruell gathers a band of men to find her. Regan learns that Stewart is alive and somewhere in the Dark Forest. Claflin, who has known and loved Stewart since they were children, leaves the castle to find her and joins Spruell's men as a bowman so he can find her, although he has no loyalty to Spruell. Stewart and Hemsworth leave the forest and come upon a huge troll who attacks him, but Stewart saves Hemsworth by charming the troll. Next, they encounter some women in boats who take them to a fishing village where women live who have disfigured themselves in order to escape Theron by not challenging her beauty. While there, Hemsworth finally learns that Stewart is the princess. He leaves her in the care of the women, but returns when the village is burned down by Spruell's men. Stewart and Hemsworth evade them and meet a band of eight dwarves. One of them, Muir, played by Hoskins, is blind but senses that Stewart is the daughter of King Magnus and the only person who can defeat Theron and end her evil reign. The dwarves are attacked by Spruell and his men, but Hemsworth kills Spruell after learning that Spruell admits to having murdered Hemsworth's wife. Claflin then defeats Spruell's men while another dwarf, Gus, played by Gleeson, sacrifices himself by taking an arrow meant for Stewart. Claflin then joins Stewart and Hemsworth in journeying to Regan's castle. Theron meanwhile disguises herself and tempts Stewart into eating a poisoned apple, but flees when Claflin and Hemsworth identify her disguise as an old crone. Stewart, however, has eaten the deadly apple and falls into a deep sleep and appears to be dead. At Regan's castle, Hemsworth kisses Stewart, thinking she is dead and because she reminds him of his wife. His kiss breaks the spell and Stewart awakens. Stewart then leads Regan and his army to battle Theron. The dwarves travel by sewer to Theron's castle and open the gates allowing Regan's army to invade the castle. Theron is about to kill Stewart when Stewart remembers a defensive tactic Hemsworth had used on an enemy and uses it to kill Theron. Regan and his army are victorious and peace returns to the kingdom as Stewart is crowned the new queen. Richly mounted and wonderfully enacted by the entire cast, this film provides much menace and mendacity in its mesmerizing action through dazzling special effects, but it cannot match the endearing charm of the Disney classic, **Snow White and the Seven Dwarfs**, 1937. The film was a great success at the box office, earning more than $396 million in its initial release against a budget of more than $170 million. Songs: "Breath of Life," "Gone" (Ioanna Gika), "What Will You Do?" (June Tabor, Maddy Prior), "Preab San OI" (traditional). Intense sequences of violence and action and brief sexuality prohibit viewing by children. **p**, Sam Mercer, Palak Patel, Joe Roth, Sarah Bradshaw; **d**, Rupert Sanders; **cast**, Kristen Stewart, Chris Hemsworth, Charlize Theron, Sam Claflin, Sam Spruell, Ian McShane, Bob Hoskins, Brian Gleeson, Ray Winstone, Nick Frost, Eddie Marsan, Toby Jones, Johnny Harris, Vincent Regan, Noah Huntley, Liberty Ross; **w**, Evan Daugherty, John Lee Hancock, Hossein Amini (based on a screen story by Daugherty and the fairy tale by the Brothers Grimm); **c**, Greig Fraser; **m**, James Newton Howard; **ed**, Conrad Buff IV, Neil Smith; **prod d**, Dominic Watkins; **art d**, Andrew Ackland-Snow, Alastair Bullock, John Frankish, Oliver Goodier, Stuart Rose, David Warren; **set d**, Fainche MacCarthy; **spec eff**, Neil Corbould, Michael Dawson.

Snowpiercer ★★★ 2014; South Korea/Czech Republic/U.S./France; 126m; SnowPiercer/Anchor Bay; Color; Science Fiction; Children: Unacceptable (MPAA: R); **BD**; **DVD**. Exciting sci-fi tale begins when global warming in the future causes an ice age killing nearly all living on Earth. The only survivors are living on a massive train called the Snowpiercer that travels on a globe-spanning track and is powered by a perpetual motion engine. A class system is in place on the train, with elites living in the front end and the poor living in the tail. In 2031, the tail inhabitants prepare for a new series of rebellions. Guards arrive periodically to deliver protein blocks for food and take some of the children, who are dying of starvation. During one of these visits, Evans leads the tail inhabitants in a revolt, forcing their way through several train cars to the prison section. There they release prisoner Namgoong Minsoo, played by Song, the man who built the security system that controls the doors dividing each car, and Ko, his clairvoyant daughter. They offer Song some uncut Kronole, a drug to which he and his daughter are addicted, as payment for unlocking each of the remaining doors on the train. One of the cars is filled with armed men. Under orders from Swinton, second in command on the train, after Harris, the men battle Evans' forces, but Evans and his forces prevail and he captures Swinton, although, in the process, he is forced to sacrifice his second-in-command, Bell. Swinton agrees to lead the group through the high-class cars in exchange for her life. While in the school car the teacher points out seven frozen rebels through a window. She and a henchman then use machine guns to slaughter many of Evans' followers, while also executing his mentor, Hurt. Evans takes revenge by killing Swinton. Then he and his few remaining followers, including Kang-ho and Ah-sung, continue through the train, discovering the extravagant luxury in which the elites have been living while the poor starved in squalor. One of Swinton's henchmen, Franco the Elder, played by Ivanov, kills the rest of Evans' followers, before the henchman is seemingly killed. Evans resolves to complete his mission, accompanied by Song and Ko. The three of them move through the remaining cars where the elites are partying on Kronole. Song steals much of his Kronole from the drugged revelers. As they arrive at the engine door, Song suggests they use the collected Kro-

Charlize Theron in *Snow White and the Huntsman*, 2012.

nole, made from explosive chemical waste, to blow open the side of the train and escape into the outside. Kang-ho explains that every year, the train has passed a crashed plane buried in snow that has become less hidden with each passing year, suggesting that Earth is warming again and that survival outside is now possible. Evans explains why he must confront Harris, creator of the train, and his leading associates. When the tail dwellers first boarded the train, they were deprived of food, water, and supplies, and where crowded conditions forced them to turn to cannibalism. Before the introduction of the protein blocks, Evans had kidnapped an infant, Bell, to eat him, and killed his mother, before Hurt cuts off his own arm and offers it in Bell's place. Kang-ho resolves to use the explosive, but the engine door opens and Song is shot and wounded by Harris' assistant, Levie, who forces Evans inside. Evans confronts Harris, who explains that the revolution was orchestrated between him and Hurt to achieve population control, necessary to maintaining balance aboard the train for supplies, but Evans was too successful and Harris's own losses became too great, so he executed Hurt as punishment. Harris says he is getting old and wants Evans to replace him as the train's overseer. While in the tail, Harris' henchmen execute about a quarter of its inhabitants. Meanwhile, Song and Ko fight off the irate people partying. Ah-sung gets inside the engine room and pulls up the floor to reveal that Harris is using the tail children as slave labor to replace the train's failing components. Outraged, Evans sacrifices an arm to block the train gears, freeing one of the boys, Reis. Ko recovers the explosive from Levie and ignites it, before retreating into the engine with Song. The damaged engine door fails to close, and Evans and Song sacrifice themselves to shield Ko and Reis from the resulting explosion. The sound wave from the blast causes an avalanche in the surrounding mountains that derails the train, destroying many of the cars and killing everyone inside of them. Ko and Reis step out into the snow and, in the distance, they see a polar bear, indicating that life exists outside the train and that there is hope for the human race, which has, through the ice age, become almost inhuman in thought and deed. The plot is so complex that few viewers will be able to make a lot of cohesive sense of its story line, but the overwhelming and almost nonstop action overwhelms to the point where none of that seems to matter. This chilling actioner was a box office hit, producing more than $86.8 million in its initial release against a budget of more than $40 million. Songs: "Strange Brew" (Eric Clapton, Felix Pappalardi, Gail Collins), "Goldberg Variations, Air and Variations Nos. 1-30 BMW 988" (Johann Sebastian Bach), "Midnight the Stars and You" (James Campbell, Harry Woods, Reginald Connelly). Bloody gore, excessive violence, drug content and gutter language prohibit viewing by children. **p**, Tae-sung Jeong, Tae-hunJeong, Steven Nam, Chan-wook Park, Jisun Back, Robert Berenacchi, Dooho Choi, Francis Chung, David Minkowski,

Chris Hemsworth and Kristen Stewart in *Snow White and the Huntsman*, **2012.**

Tae-joon Park, Matthew Stillman; **d**, Joon Ho Bong; **cast**, Chris Evans, Kang-ho Song, Ah-sung Ko, Ed Harris, John Hurt, Tilda Swinton, Jamie Bell, Octavia Spencer, Ewen Bremner, Alison Pill, Luke Pasqualino, Vlad Ivanov; **w**, Bong, Kelly Masterson (based on a screen story by Bong and the graphic novel *Le Transperceneige* by Jacques Lob, Benjamin Legrand, Jean-Marc Rochette); **c**, Kyung-pyo Hong; **m**, Marco Beltrami; **ed**, Steve M. Choe, Changju Kim; **prod d**, Ondrej Nekvasil; **art d**, Stefan Kovacik; **set d**, Beata Brendtnerova; **spec eff**, Pavel Sagner.

Southpaw ★★★ 2015; U.S.; 124m; Escape Artists/Weinstein; Color; Sports Drama; Children: Unacceptable (MPAA: R); **BD**; **DVD**. In this walloping sports tale, New York City boxer Gyllenhaal suffers an eye injury while successfully defending his world light heavyweight title. His wife, McAdams, convinces him to retire as a champion. Later, at a charity event, he is confronted by Gomez, and, in a brawl that follows, McAdams is accidentally shot and killed by Gomez's brother, who escapes. Despondent, Gyllenhaal takes to drink and drugs, learns where the killer is hiding out and goes there, but finds only Ora, the man's wife, a drug addict. Gyllenhaal goes back into the ring, but attacks a referee after losing a fight and is suspended and is now heavy in debt. He is arrested for drunk driving and loses custody of his daughter, Laurence, who is put in the care of Harris, a Child Protective Services officer. This causes Gyllenhaal to sober up, but it is too late and Laurence rejects him. Gyllenhaal then gets a job at a gym owned by Whitaker and talks him into becoming his manager for a comeback against champion Gomez. Laurence watches Gyllenhaal's comeback fight on closed circuit television in the stadium's locker room with Harris. Gyllenhaal is close to losing the fight when he knocks down Gomez with a powerful left uppercut with his right hand (the southpaw of the film's title). Gyllenhaal regains his title in a split decision and is reunited with Laurence as all ends well. The acting by Gyllenhaal, Laurence and Ora is exceptional, as is the well-choreographed boxing matches. The film was very successful at the box office, earning more than $91.6 million in its initial release against a budget of more than $25 million. Songs: "Beast" (Charles Caripides, Robert Bailey), "We Dem Boyz" (Carmen Thomaz, Maurice Brown, Noel Fisher, Kemion Cooks), "RNS" (Joe Budden, Joel Ortiz, Dominick Wickliffe, Abraham Orellana, Betty Mabry, Fred Muhlbock), "Perfect Day" (Kari Kimmel, Joseph Corcoran), "That's All Over, Baby" (Joe C. Jones, Percy Jones, Willie Otis Munson), "Toe 2 Toe" (John Paul Gosney, Buddy Long), "The Boys Are Back" (Johnny Pakfar, Shane Ellis), "Kings Never Die" (Eminem [Marshall Mathers], Luis Resto, Khalil Abdul-Rahman, Erik Alcock, Chin Injeti, Liz Rodrigues), "Ain't Worried" (Ali Theodore Dee, Jordan Yaeger), "Wicked Games" (Abel Tesfaye, Doc McKinney, Carlo Montagnese, Rainer

Blanchaer), "Lover's Glance" (Homer Greencastle), "Notorious Thugs" (Christopher Wallace, Sean Puffy Combs, Bryon McCane, Steve Howse, Anthony Henderson, Steven Jordan), "Turn the Sunshine On" (Kyler England, Cathy Heller, Matthew Puckett), "Phenomenal" (Marshall Mathers, Luis Resto, Mario Resto), "Walk" (Marcus Merriett, Alvin Merriett), "Wise Man" (Frank Ocean, Malay), "Cry for Love," "This Corner," "What About the Rest of Us," "All I Think About," "Drama Never Dies," "Mode." Excessive violence and gutter language prohibit viewing by children. **p**, Todd Black, Jason Blumenthal, Antoine Fuqua, Alan Riche, Peter Riche, Kat Samick, Steve Tisch, Jerry Ye; **d**, Fuqua; **cast**, Jake Gyllenhaal, Forest Whitaker, Rachel McAdams, Oona Laurence, 50 Cent, Skylan Brooks, Naomie Harris, Victor Ortiz, Beau Knapp, Miguel Gomez, Dominic Colon; **w**, Kurt Sutter; **c**, Mauro Fiore; **m**, James Horner; **ed**, John Refoua; **prod d**, Derek R. Hill; **art d**, Gregory A. Weimerskirch; **set d**, Merissa Lombardo; **spec eff**, Jason Trosky.

Spare Parts ★★★ 2015; U.S.; 83m; UNIV; Color; Drama; Children: Unacceptable (MPAA: PG-13); **BD**; **DVD**. This inspirational science film based on true events sees four Hispanic students, all illegal immigrants from Mexico, attending Carl Hayden High School in Phoenix, Arizona. They brazenly enter the 2004 national underwater robotics competition with only $800 and some spare automobile parts. With determination and encouragement from their parents and a new science teacher, Lopez, who knows nothing about robotics, they win over heavy competition from some highly funded university teams. Their work together forms friendships that may last their entire lives. All the cast members are standouts in their empathic roles, and the well-written script, along with robust direction from McNamara, sustains interest throughout. The film, unfortunately, did not do well at the box office, earning about $3.6 million in its initial release. Songs: "Guerrero/Can't Stop Now" (Andres Levin, Ileana Padron, Filip Mitrovic, Debi Nova, Pete Ho, Oscar Botello, Alan Montalvo, Fedrico Ruiz), "Kick Drum" (Jessica Patterson, Leonard Patterson, Greg Camp), "Stinky Jam" (Andres Levin), "Robot" (Diego Traverso, Santiego Marreero, David Stabilito, Esteban Lopez, Nicholas Femczylo), "Miles to Go" (Mateo Stevens, Erik Janson, Felix Samuel Harris Jr.), "Bang Data" (Juan Manuel Caipo, Jorge Guerrero, David Ivan Lopez), "Good As Gone" (Mark Seliger), "Here We Go" and "Place in the Sun" (Willy Abers, Ulises Bella, Raul Pacheco, Justin Poree, Karl Porter, Asdru Sierra, Jabulani Smith-Freeman, Jiro Yamaguchi), "Escrbeme Pronto" (Holger Beier, Camilo Lara), "Back in Town" and "Desconocido" (Mateo Stevens, Erik Janson), "Break Our Bones" (J.J. Hodari), "Dip Chick" (Ivan Corraliza), "Waiting on California" (Ruwanga Samath, Vincent Berry II, Brandon Hicks), "Whatch Like About Me" (Ileana Padron), "Brand New Day" (Mackenzie Bourg, Battleroy, Ruwanga Samath, Ozzy Doniz), "Tu Me Haces Falta" (Cucurucho Valdes), "Once You Leave" (Ruwanga Samath, Greg Cahn, Alexander Yang, Oscar Doniz), "Guerrero Finale" (Andres Levin, Debi Nova), "You're Not the Only One" (Andres Levin, Claudia Brant). Violence and gutter language prohibit viewing by children. **p**, David Alpert, Rick Jacobs, Leslie Kolins Small, George Lopez, Ben Odell, Paul Michael Perez; **d**, Sean McNamara; **cast**, George Lopez, Marisa Tomei, Jamie Lee Curtis, Carlos PenaVega, Jose Julian, David Del Rio, Oscar Gutierrez, Alessandra Rosaldo, J.R. Villarreal, Aubrey Miller; **w**, Elissa Matsueda (based on the *Wired* magazine article "La Vida Robot" by Joshua Davis); **c**, Richard Wong; **m**, Andres Levin; **ed**, Maysie Hoy; **prod d**, Robb Wilson King; **set d**, Susan Magestro; **spec eff**, Randy E. Moore.

Sparkle ★★★ 2012; U.S.; 156m; Akil Production Co./Sony; Color; Drama/Music; Children: Unacceptable (MPAA: PG-13); **BD**; **DVD**. A fictional musical drama inspired by the Supremes, the female singing group during the 1960s that remains America's most successful vocal group. The Supremes' rise to fame was different than in this film and members did not have a drug problem, but one of this film's vocalists does. Three African American teenage sisters in Detroit, Michigan, form an all-girl singing group in the late 1950s. The girls are Sparks playing 19-year-old "Sparkle," Ejogo, and Sumpter. Houston plays their mother. Sparks attends a concert in which her eldest sister, ten years older than she and called "Sister," played by Ejogo, is one of the singers. Ejogo is noticed by Luke who thinks she has talent. When the girls return home, they are joined by their middle sister "Dee," who is 24 years old, played by Sumpter, and their mother (Houston), who is overprotective of the girls and disapproves of them staying out late going to pop concerts or taking up careers in entertainment. Luke tries to get the three sisters to form a singing group and becomes attracted to Sparks, a relationship of which Houston disapproves. Luke's associate, Hardwick, becomes attracted to Ejogo, but then another associate, Epps, who works as a comic, develops a romantic interest in her as well, creating a conflict between the two men. The girls agree to become a singing act and are a big success with an audience which especially takes to Ejogo whose performance is very sexy. The girls then get singing engagements in Detroit. Houston hosts a dinner party whose guests include her minister (Beach), and at this occasion Ejogo reveals that she and Epps have become engaged. Epps loses it at the dinner, making rude remarks and insulting guests, and an argument ensues between Epps, Ejogo, and Houston. Ejogo sides with Epps, so Houston sends her packing. The girls' singing group rises in popularity and becomes the opening act for Aretha Franklin on her television show. They are being considered by Columbia Records until it is revealed that Ejogo has developed a cocaine problem, and they lose the chance for a contract with the song publisher. Luke then proposes to Sparks but she turns him down. All three sisters then have an argument with Epps, and Sumpter hits him with a hot fire rod, and he dies. Ejogo assumes responsibility for Epps' death and is charged with manslaughter. Her arrest makes nationwide newspaper headlines. While Ejogo is in prison, Sumpter then departs to enroll in a medical college, and Sparks moves out of the house to take an apartment. Sparks tries to rekindle her chances of a Columbia recording contract and she learns that she can get it if she performs well as a solo singer at a concert. Sparks has the jitters before going on stage at the concert, but Luke calms her with a piece of cake to celebrate her 20th birthday, and then proposes to her. Sparkle then sings a song she dedicates to Ejogo. The audience loves her and she also finally gets Houston's approval as a professional singer, she will get the Columbia contract, and is on her way to fame and happiness. Songs: "I'm a Man" (CeeLo Green as Thomas DeCarlo Callaway, Kevin Risto, Wayne Nugent, Charlie Gambetta); "Yes I Do" (Guordan Banks, Warren Felder, Andrew Wansel); "Soul Finger" (James Alexander, Ronnie Caldwell, Ben Cauley, Carl Cunningham, Phalon R. Jones Jr., Jimmy King); "We're Back" (Peter Nashel, Andy Farber); "Sunshine of Your Love" (Jack Bruce, Pete Brown, Eric Patrick Clapton); "Hooked on Your Love," "Jump," "Something He Can Feel," "Look Into Your Heart" (Curtis Mayfield); "Sing a Simple Song" (Sylvester Stewart); "If" (Aloe Blacc, Leon Michels, Nicholas Anthony Movshon, Jeffrey Scott Silverman); "Love Makes a Woman" (Carl Davis, Eugene Record, William Nelson Sanders, Gerald Marvin Sims); "Moanin'," (Bobby Timmons); "Shadow of a Memory" (Theodore Goodloe, Kenneth Goodloe, Joe C. Jones); "You Taught Me to Love Again " (Tommy Dorsey, Henri Woode, Charles Carpenter); "Sweet Thing" (Frankie Brown, Robert Lee); "Special Occasion" (Alfred Cleveland, William Robinson Jr.); "Running" (Charles Harmon, Claude Kelly); "Mercy, Mercy, Mercy" (Josef Zawinul); "Please Accept My Prayer" (Shirley Ann Lee, James E. Lee); "You're All I Need to Get By" (Nickolas Ashford, Valerie Simpson), "Night Life" (Willie Nelson, Paul Buskirk, Walter M. Breeland); "When You Gonna Get Respect/When You Haven't Cut Your Process Yet" (Hank Ballard, James Brown, Buddy Hobgood); "His Eye Is On the Sparrow" (Civilla Martin, Charles Gabriel); "These Boots Are Made for Walkin'," (Lee Hazlewood); "Feeling Good" (Leslie Bricusse, Anthony Newley); "One Wing," "Love Will," "Celebrate" (R. Kelly). Rated PG-13 for mature thematic content involving domestic abuse and drug material, some violence, language, smoking. Houston died three

Jake Gyllenhaal in *Southpaw,* 2015.

months after completing work on the film. Made earlier with the same title in 1976, but not related to the 2007 British film of the same name. **p**, Salim Akil, Mara Brock Akil, Debra Martin Chase, T.D. Jakes, Curtis Wallace, Derrick Williams; **d**, Salim Akil; **cast**, Jordin Sparks, Whitney Houston, Derek Luke, Mike Epps, Carmen Ejogo, Tika Sumpter, Omari Hardwick, CeeLo Green, Curtis Armstrong, Terrence Jenkins, Tamela Mann, Michael Beach, Brely Evans; **w**, Mara Brock Akil (based on a story by Howard Rosenman, Joel Schumacher); **c**, Anastas Michos; **m**, Salaam Remi; **ed**, Terilyn A. Shropshire; **prod d**, Gary Frutkoff; **art d**, Gary Myers; **set d**, Tina Tottis; **spec eff**, Bob Sturgess, Russell Tyrrell.

Special Forces ★★★ 2012; France/U.K.; 109m; Easy Company/Entertainment One; Color; War Drama; Children: Unacceptable (MPAA: R); **BD**; **DVD**. Powerfully told and intense tale begins with Kruger, a French journalist, and her colleague, Nebbou, who are in Afghanistan covering the story of a woman who was sold to a man when she was a child. Kruger and Nebbou are abducted by Degan, a Taliban leader who tries to force them to read a message to Western powers. This results in the president of France sending six Special Forces agents to rescue the captives being held in a fortress in Pakistan. The team, led by Hounsou, consists of Magimel, Personnaz, Menochet, Figlarz, and Alivon. They manage to free Kruger and Nebbou but in the process lose their radios. This leaves them all to cross the war-ravaged land to save their lives. In an escape through the mountains all but Hounsou and Magimel of the Special Forces are killed by Degan's soldiers. Kruger and Nebbou reach a road where friendly forces rescue them and the surviving Special Forces team. The action is excitingly presented throughout, and suspense and tension fills almost every scene. Songs: "E=MC2" (Dan Donovan, Don Letts, Mick Jones), "Pick Your God or Devils" (Niddi O., Robin Foster). Gutter language and violence prohibit viewing by children. **p**, Thierry Marro, Benoit Ponsaille; **d**, Stephane Rybojad; **cast**, Diane Kruger, Medhi Nebbou, Dijmon Hounsou, Raz Degan, Raphael Personnaz, Benloit Magimel, Dennis Menochet, Alain Figlarz, Alain Alivon, Tcheky Karyo, Morjana Alaoui, **w**, Rybojad, Emmanuelle Collomp, Michael Cooper; **c**, David Jankowski; **m**, Xavier Berthelot; **ed**, Erwan Pecher, Stephane Rybojad; **prod d**, Christophe Jutz; **set d**, Jutz; **spec eff**, Jeremie Abrial.

The Spectacular Now ★★★ 2013; U.S.; 95m; 21 Laps Entertainment/A24; Color; Comedy/Drama/Romance; Children: Unacceptable (MPAA: R); **BD**; **DVD**. Teller is a seemingly happy and content high school senior who likes working at a men's clothing store but has no grand plans for his future, preferring to take today and all tomorrows as they come. His girlfriend Larson tires of his aimless and irresponsible ways and his penchant for only living in the present moment. Larson

Mike Epps and Carmen Ejogo in *Sparkle*, 2012.

dumps him and Teller starts drinking. One night, he gets drunk and wakes up on a lawn of a lovely teenage girl, Woodley, wondering who she is and how he got there. Woodley says she reads Japanese science-fiction magazines and thinks a lot about having a happy future. Despite him living for today and she focusing on the future, they are drawn to each other. When Teller seeks advice and comfort from his father, Chandler, he finds that Chandler is as shiftless and selfish as himself. Woodley, meanwhile, is struck by a car, but suffers only a broken arm, after she is ordered from a car driven by Teller and after she has tried to comfort him over the disconnect between him and his father. Teller continues to foul up his life and, while drunk, crashes his car. He goes to his mother, Leigh, confessing that he is just like his self-centered father, a rather worthless human being. She tells him that he is nothing like Chandler and that he has a great and loving heart. Bolstered by Leigh's support, Teller reforms and stops drinking before he applies for college. He then drives to see Woodley, finding her as she leaves a high school class, and they tenderly behold one another as the film ends. A simple coming-of-age tale of two high school seniors, the story is presented in such an endearing manner and with such totally innocent performances from Teller and Woodley that it does not fail to charm and entertain throughout. Almost any viewer will identify with Teller and Woodley as they will see their own fumbling and groping past in this very natural and genuine story that is skillfully presented by director Ponsoldt. The film earned more than $6.9 million in its initial release against a budget of more than $2.5 million. Songs: "Live Fast, Love Hard, Die Young" (Joe Allison), "Dolce ed Ostinato" (Piero Umiliani), "New Theory" (Ernest Greene), "Private Comfort" (Roberto Benozzo, Massimo Salvagnini, Andrea Valfre), "Go Hard" (Jesse Leon McMullen), "Baby" (Donnie Charles Emerson, Joseph Glen Emerson), "Wild Nights" (David Timothy Cooper, Jonathan William Messenger, Georgie G. Rodriguez Jr., Christopher Ray Sanchez), "Farming Man" (Michael Hendrix), "The Riff" (Mitchell Dancik, Danny Rubin), "Need Someone to Love" (Winfred Lorenzo Lovett), "Bright Whites" (Ishibashi Kaoru). Alcohol use, gutter language, and some sexuality, all involving teenagers, prohibit viewing by children. **p**, Michelle Krumm, Andrew Lauren, Shawn Levy, Tom McNulty, Dan Cohen, Billy Rosenberg; **d**, James Ponsoldt; **cast**, Miles Teller, Shailene Woodley, Brie Larson, Masam Holden, Dayo Okeniyi, Kyle Chandler, Jennifer Jason Leigh, Nicci Faires, Ava London, Whitney Goin; **w**, Scott Neustadter, Michael H. Weber (based on the novel by Tim Tharp); **c**, Jess Hall; **m**, Rob Simonsen; **ed**, Darrin Navarro; **prod d**, Linda Sena; **set d**, Jess Royal; **spec eff**, Matthew Bramante, Gresham Lochner.

Spectre ★★★★ 2015; U.S./U.K.; 150m; Eon/B24/COL/MGM/COL; Color; Spy Drama; Children: Unacceptable (MPAA: PG-13); **DVD**; **IV**.

Exciting espionage tale is the 24th James Bond film in the series and the fourth with the enigmatic Craig as O07. A cryptic message to British Military Intelligence 6 (MI6) sparks events that see Craig coming face to face with the evil organization known as Spectre. Fiennes, the newly appointed M, continues fighting government pressures that threaten MI6's future as Bond learns that the only way to uncover the web of conspiracy to end MI6 is to protect Seydoux, the beautiful and innocent daughter of a powerful enemy. Craig follows a trail of clues from England to Mexico, Italy, Austria, and Morocco as he has to often bend the law in order to confront an enemy from his past. Waltz plays a mysterious figure within Spectre who claims to have a personal connection to Bond. In Austria, Craig finds old enemy Christensen, who had headed Quantum, a subsidiary of Spectre, but who is now dying of thallium poisoning. Christensen begs Craig to protect his daughter, Seydoux, who has been marked for death by Christensen's old enemies. He tells Craig that Seydoux can lead him to the top echelons of Spectre before Christensen commits suicide. Craig locates Seydoux, but she is abducted by Spectre assassin Bautista, who has previously attempted to kill Craig. After Craig rescues her, they travel by train to a hotel in Tangiers. En route, Bautista attacks them, but, in a wild struggle, the assassin is thrown from the speeding train. Upon arrival, Craig and Seydoux are taken to a Spectre stronghold where Craig is tortured. Both, however, manage to escape, but not before they destroy the stronghold. They have learned that Spectre is staging worldwide terrorist acts in order to control governments and increase its power. When returning to London, Seydoux tells Craig that she wants no part of espionage and leaves him. Meanwhile, Waltz, who plays old nemesis Ernst Stavro Blofeld, and was long thought to be dead, is very much alive and is heading Spectre in its attempt to dominate the world. Seydoux and Craig are both kidnapped by Spectre agents, and Q (MI6's Quartermaster), played by Whishaw, prevents other agents from using online applications to bring about widespread destruction. Further, Scott, a member of the British government who is treasonously operating as a secret Spectre agent, confronts M (Fienes) and both violently struggle until Scott plunges to his death. Craig, by this time, has been held captive with Seydoux and is taken to the old MI6 building, which is scheduled for demolition. Waltz confronts Craig, telling him that he has three minutes of life left as the building is about to be exploded. Craig, however, breaks free, and, with Seydoux in tow, escapes the destruction of the building through underground tunnels and finally in a fast boat. Seeing Waltz escaping by air, Craig shoots down the helicopter carrying Waltz, which crashes into Westminster Bridge. As the stunned Waltz crawls from the wreckage of the copter, Craig confronts him, but, instead of taking his life, turns him over to Fiennes, who arrests the villain. Craig and Seydoux then depart together. The action sequences are spectacularly shown with amazingly performed stunts while the lensing also superbly supports the outstanding acting by Craig, Seydoux, Fiennes, Bautista, Christensen and the rest of the cast members. The film received an Oscar nomination for Best Original Song ("Writings on the Wall"; Smith). The film was a megahit at the box office, earning more than $877.5 million in its initial release against a budget of more than $250 million. Song: "Writings on the Wall" (Sam Smith). Intense action, violence, disturbing images, sexuality and gutter language prohibit viewing by children. **p**, Barbara Broccoli, Daniel Craig, Michael G. Wilson, Andrew Noakes, Stacy Perskie, David Pope; **d**, Sam Mendes; **cast**, Craig, Christoph Waltz, Ralph Fiennes, Ben Whishaw, Andrew Scott, Rory Kinnear; Naomie Harris, Lea Seydoux, Monica Bellucci, Dave Bautista, Jesper Christensen, Stephanie Sigman, **w**, John Logan, Neal Purvis, Robert Wade, Jez Butterworth (based on a story by Logan, Purvis, Wade, and characters created by Ian Fleming); **c**, Hjoyte Van Hoytema; **m**, Thomas Newman; **ed**, Lee Smith; **prod d**, Dennis Gassner; **art d**, Chris Lowe; **set d**, Anna Pinnock, Danieal Rojas; **spec eff**, Chris Corbould, Franco Ragusa.

Spotlight ★★★★ 2015; U.S.; 128m; Anonymous Content/Open Road

Films; Color; Drama/History; Children: Unacceptable (MPAA: R); **BD**; **DVD**. Riveting drama is based on the true events involving the *Boston Globe* newspaper's "Spotlight" team of investigators looking into allegations of sexual abuse in the city's Roman Catholic diocese. In 2001, the paper's new Jewish editor, Marty Baron (1954-), played by Schreiber, assigns the paper's team of journalists to investigate the allegations against a defrocked priest who has been accused of molesting more than eighty boys. Keaton, who plays Spotlight editor Walter "Robby" Robinson, leads the team made up of Michael Rezendes (Ruffalo), Matt Carroll (James), and Sacha Pfeiffer (McAdams). Their investigation is not only very sensitive because of allegations against the church in a largely Catholic city, but also because the father of the *Globe*'s deputy managing editor, Ben Bradlee Jr., portrayed by Slatterly, risked his job as editor of the *Washington Post* in investigating the Watergate scandal of the 1970s. In that scandal, Republican politicians broke into the Democratic National Committee's headquarters at the Watergate office complex in Washington, D.C., which led to the resignation of President Richard Nixon (1913-1994) in 1974. For more than a year, the Spotlight team interviews alleged victims and tries to have sensitive Church documents unsealed so they can read them in an effort to provide proof of a cover-up of sexual abuse within the Roman Catholic Church in Boston. By 2002, the *Globe* publishes almost 600 articles on child sex-abuse allegations against Catholic priests and Church cover-ups that followed. Widespread sexual abuse of boys by dozens of priests in the Boston area made worldwide news and led to investigations of pedophilia by priests in other cities and nations. Along those found to be involved in the cover-up were Boston archbishop Bernard Francis Law (1931-), played by Cariou, and the plaintiff's lawyer Eric MacLeish, essayed by Crudup. Law, who reportedly covered up the scandal and transferred suspected priests from parish to parish, resigned in 2002 and was reassigned to Rome. The Spotlight team won a Pulitzer Prize for its sensational expose that drew worldwide attention. Although this film saw considerable criticism from Catholic officials as being too harsh in recreating the exposé of the myriad pedophile offenses committed by errant priests, this uncompromising and hard-hitting production is both credible and viewer worthy. Keaton is exceptional as the relentless crusader Robinson and receives great support from a fine cast. The film earned more than $34.3 million in its initial release against a budget of more than $20 million. Songs: "These Exiled Years" (Flogging Molly), "Bean's Blues" (Coleman Hawkins), "Cocinando Suave" (Ray Barretto). Gutter language and sexual references prohibit viewing by children. **p**, Blye Pagon Faust, Steve Golin, Nicole Rocklin, Michael Sugar, Kate Churchill, Youtchi von Lintel; **d**, Tom McCarthy; **cast**, Mark Ruffalo, Michael Keaton, Rachel McAdams, Billy Crudup, Liev Schreiber, Stanley Tucci, John Slattery, Brian d'Arcy James, Elena Wohl, Gene Amoroso, Doug Murray, Sharon McFarlane; **w**, McCarthy, Josh Singer; **c**, Masanobu Takayanagi; **m**, Howard Shore; **ed**, Tom McArdle; **prod d**, Stephen H. Carter; **art d**, Michaela Cheyne; **set d**, Shane Vieau; **spec eff**, Kayla Cabral, Coli Davies, Neishaw Ali.

Spy ★★★ 2015; U.S.; 119m; Chernin Entertainment/FOX; Color; Comedy; Children: Unacceptable (MPAA: PG-13); **BD**; **DVD**, **IV**. In this very funny takeoff on James Bond films, providing both action and laughs, roly-poly McCarthy is a desk-bound Central Intelligence Agent working for Law, a, slim, handsome, and sexy CIA agent for whom she has a big crush. She protects Law from danger by using sophisticated technology and a near-invisible ear piece. Law's luck and McCarthy's help runs out when he is killed by Byrne, a Bulgarian arms dealer. McCarthy then convinces her boss, Janney, to take a chance and let her undertake her first undercover field assignment to help bring Byrne and her associates in arms dealing to justice and avenge Law's assassination. The plot takes light turns when McCarthy dons a towering hairdo and poses as Byrne's bodyguard, trading insults as they dislike each other. McCarthy now meets Statham, a rogue agent who takes an immediate

Tika Sumpter, Carmen Ejogo and Jordin Sparks in *Sparkle*, 2012.

jealous dislike to her. More misadventures and hijinks follow until McCarthy manages to kill everyone responsible for Law's murder to bring this humorous spy thriller to a satisfying close. This slaphappy spy spoof sees a wonderfully amusing performance from McCarthy, and Byrne is equally humorous as a berserk femme fatale. The film was a great hit at the box office, earning more than $235.7 million in its initial release against a budget of more than $65 million. Songs/Music: "Who Can You Trust" (Theodore Shapiro, Craig Wedren), "Sandbar" (Terje Olsen), "Kris" (Leyla Safai, Benjamin Pollock), "Mickey" (Michael Chaplan, Nicholas Chinn), "Brazil" (Ary Barroso), "Spy Party" (Audrey Danilko), "Bounce" (Mark Hadfield, Mike Di Scala, Iggy Azalea, Oladayo Olatunji, Jochem G. Paap, Talay Riley, Natalie Sims), "I'm a Diva/Need Nobody" (Jeffrey Carson, Asani Charles, Nicole Brandy), "Mondaine" and Double or Nothing" (Ran Galor, Gad Emile Zeitune), "Go!" (Kamaal Fareed, Karen Orzolek, Nicholas Zinner, Santi White, David Taylor, Guy Batterel, Jean-Pierre Massiera), "Cold Blooded" (Ida Maria, Anthony Rossomando), "Mi Mi Mi" (Maxim Fadeev, Olga Seryabkina), "Twisted" (Curtis Jackson, Jovan Woods, Anthony Caines), "King of the Night" (Gin Wigmore, Julian Thomas Hamilton, Gary Clark), "Cola Song" (Breyan Stanley Isaac, Andreas Scheen Shuller, Jose Osorio, Andrew Frampton, Thomas Rozdilsky), "Bad Seed Rising" (Mason Gainer, Aiden Marceron, Francheska Pastor, Louey Peraza, Scott Stevens), "Waltz No. 1" (Antonin Dvorak), "String Quartet in G Major, 2nd Movement" (Wolfgang Amadeus Mozart). Gutter language, violence, sexual content and brief graphic nudity prohibit viewing by children. **p**, Paul Feig, Peter Chernin, Michele Colombo, Jessie Henderson, Jenno Topping; **d&w**, Feig; **cast**, Melissa McCarthy, Rose Byrne, Jude Law, Jason Statham, Raad Rawi, Jessica Chaffin, Miranda Hart, Sam Richardson, Katie Dippold, Jaime Pacheco, Romain Apelbaum; **c**, Robert D. Yeoman; **m**, Theodore Shapiro; **ed**, Melissa Bretherton, Brent White; **prod d**, Jefferson Sage; **art d**, Tom Brown, Bence Erdely; **set d**, Kelly Berry; **spec eff**, Yves De Bono.

Stalingrad ★★★ 2014; Russia; 131m; Art Pictures Studio/COL; Color; War Drama; Children: Unacceptable (MPAA: R); **BD**; **3-D**; **DVD**. Taut tale sees a small band of Russian soldiers taking refuge in a bombed-out building across the square from a Nazi installation during the World War II (1939-1945) battle of Stalingrad (August 23, 1942-February 2, 1943). These five Soviet soldiers include a famous tenor, a marksman, and an officer in the Worker Peasant Army, who take pot shots at any Germans daring to venture into the open. The five men fight to hold a strategic building in the devastated city against a ruthless enemy. Their efforts lead them to become deeply connected to two Russian women who are living in the city. Smolnikova, a young Russian woman, wanders around in the building and lives traumatized in its ruins, and several

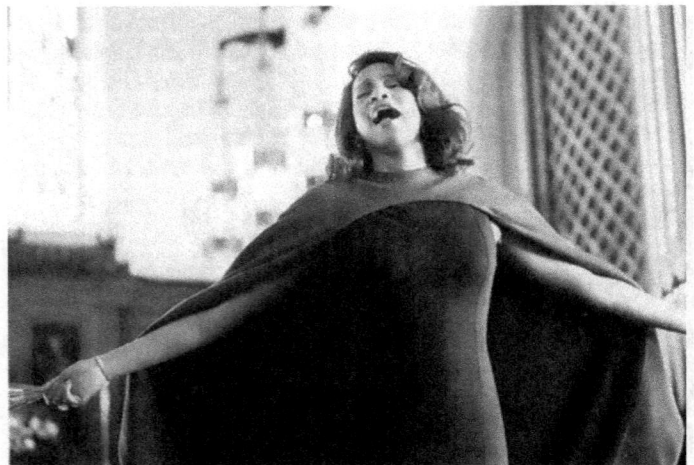

Whitney Houston in *Sparkle,* **2012.**

of the Red Army soldiers are attracted to her. Meanwhile, a handsome Nazi captain, Kretschmann, has an affair with a Russian blonde, Studilina, against the objections of his commanding officer and local citizens who disapprove of her fraternizing with the enemy. Realizing that the Russian soldiers occupy a pivotal position, the Germans, with heavy reinforcements, storm the building the Soviets occupy, killing them one by one. Fyodorov desperately sends out a radio message to have Russian planes destroy the building just as Kretschmann finds him. They both fatally shoot each other. The message, however, is received and Soviet planes fly over the building, bombing it into rubble as Smolnikova witness its destruction and weeps. This gripping film sees outstanding performances from the entire cast while director Bondarchuk expertly orchestrates the fascinating battle action. The film saw success at the box office, earning more than $68 million in its initial release against a budget of more than $30 million. Other films about the battle of Stalingrad with that title were released in 1943, 1989, and 1993; the battle also extensively profiled in **Enemy at the Gates**, 2001. (In Russian; German/English subtitles.) Violence prohibits viewing by children. **p**, Sergey Melkumov, Aleksandr Rodnyanskiy, Dimitriy Rudovskiy, Steve Schklair; **d**, Fedor Bondarchuk; **cast**, Thomas Kretschmann, Mariya Smolnikova, Yanina Studilina, Pyotr Fyodorov, Sergey Bondarchuk, Dimitriy Lysenkov, Andrey Smolyakov, Aleksey Barabash, Oleg Volku, Heiner Lauterbach; **w**, Sergey Snezhkin, Ilya Tilkin; **c**, Maksim Osadchiy; **m**, Angelo Badalamenti; **ed**, Igor Litoninskiy; **art d**, Sergei Ivanov; **spec eff**, Seth William Meier, Ilya Sherstobitov.

Stand Up Guys ★★★ 2012; U.S.; 95m; Lionsgate; Color; Comedy; Children: Unacceptable (MPAA: R); **BD**; **DVD**. Offbeat crime spoof begins when Pacino is released from prison after twenty-eight years behind bars, and his friend Walken, a former partner in crime, meets him outside the gates with his car (not unlike that of Dan Aykroyd waiting outside a prison to pick up John Belushi, his recently released brother in **The Blues Brothers**, 1980). Finally out of prison, Pacino is not really a free man because Margolis, the local mob czar, is dedicated to having him killed because he blames Pacino for his son's death in a robbery years earlier. Pacino does not know it, but Margolis has hired Walken to kill him before morning. Pacino, unaware it may be his last night alive, wants to celebrate being out of prison by partying. He wants some Viagra so he and Walken break into a pharmacy. After midnight, they pick up Arkin, who drove the getaway car on their earlier robberies. They drive to a whorehouse where they help a woman in distress, bury a body, and eat at a café where the waitress excites Pacino. As the sun comes up, Pacino now realizes that Walken has been hired to kill him. Life was fun while it lasted, but it may now be over. Played for laughs (and there are many of them, especially via the antics of the gifted

Arkin), the film lampoons professional criminals and mob bosses, but the story runs a bit thin at times. The intense acting from the veteran players, however, sustains interest throughout. The film was not a success at the box office, earning no more than $3.3 million in its initial release against a budget of more than $15 million. Songs: "Hard Times" (Curtis Mayfield), "Fooled Around and Fell in Love" (Elvin Bishop), "Cooler Couleur" (Ashley Bates, Sam Genders, Rebecca Jacobs, Mike Lindsay, Martin Bradley-Smith, Philip David Winter, Francesco Berbaglie, Julie Budet, Tanguy Destable, Andrea Fratangelo, John Hill, Jean-Francois Perrier, Dave Taylor), "Stand Up" and "Papa Was Stoned" (Steve Raskin, Rob Myes, Jon Horvath, Sid Barcelona), "When Something Is Wrong with My Baby" (Isaac Hayes, David Porter), "How Long" (Charles Bradley, Thomas Branneck, Daniel Foder, David Guy, Homer Steinweiss, Leon Michels), "Love from Above" (Raney Shockne, Jeeve), "Insomnia" (James Calvin Wilsey), "Hoochie Coochie Man" (Willie Dixon), "Get Down with It" (Bobby Marchan), "Sock It to 'Em J B" (Clay Dunn, Rex Garvin, Pete Holman), "Old Habits Die Hard" and "Not Running Anymore" (Jon Bon Jovi), "Give It Back" (David Guy, Sharon Jones, Thomas R. Brenneck), "Bright Lights" (Gary Clark Jr.). Gutter language, sexual content, violence and drug use prohibit viewing by children. **p**, Sidney Kimmel, Gary Lucchesi, Tom Rosenberg, Jim Tauber; **d**, Fisher Stevens; **cast**, Al Pacino, Christopher Walken, Alan Arkin, Julianna Margulies, Mark Margolis, Lucy Punch, Addison Timlin, Vanessa Ferlito, Katheryn Winnick, Bill Burr; **w**, Noah Haidle; **c**, Michael Grady; **m**, Lyle Workman; **ed**, Mark Livolis; **prod d**, Maher Ahmad; **art d**, Thomas T. Taylor; **set d**, Kathy Lucas; **spec eff**, Bart Dion.

Star Trek: Into the Darkness ★★★ 2013; U.S.; 132m; PAR; Color; Science Fiction; Children: Unacceptable (MPAA: PG-13); **BD**; **DVD**. This exciting twelfth film in the **Star Trek** movie series begins when the *USS Enterprise* is called back home in 2259, a year after the events in the previous installment. Kirk, played by Pine, and his crew find an unstoppable force of terror from within their own organization, one that has detonated the fleet, leaving the world in a state of crisis. Having a personal score to settle, Pine leads a manhunt to a war zone to capture a one-man weapon of mass destruction. Pine and his crew study a primitive culture on the planet Nibiru. Kirk and his first officer, Commander Spock, essayed by Quinto, save the planet's inhabitants from an extinction-threatening volcanic eruption, but Pine refuses to obey a prime directive by exposing the ship to the native inhabitants. Returning to Earth, Pine loses command of the *Enterprise* and Greenwood, an admiral, is reinstated as its commanding officer with Pine demoted to first officer. For his part in the incident, Quinto is reassigned to another spaceship. An officers' meeting is called to discuss the bombing of a Section 31 installation in London that has been perpetrated by the renegade Starfleet operative John Harrison, played by Cumberbatch. He attacks the meeting in a jumpsuit, killing Greenwood. Pine disables the jumpsuit, but Cumberbatch uses a portable transporter to escape to Kronos, home world of the rebel Klingons. Admiral Weller orders the *Enterprise* to destroy Cumberbatch and his henchmen, arming it with seventy-two prototype photon torpedoes, shielded and untraceable to sensors. On its way to Kronos, the *Enterprise* suffers an unexpected coolant leak which disables its warp capabilities. Pine leads a team with Quinto onto the planet where they are ambushed by Klingon patrols. Cumberbatch dispatches the Klingons, but then surrenders after learning of the number of torpedoes locked on his location. Cumberbatch then reveals his own true identity as Khan, a genetically engineered superhuman awaked from a 300-year suspended animation to develop advanced weapons for war against the Klingon Empire. Cumberbatch reveals that the *Enterprise's* warp drive had been sabotaged, intending for the Klingons to destroy the ship after firing on Kronos, giving him an apparent moral justification to go to war with the Klingon Empire. The *Enterprise* is intercepted by a larger Federation warship, the *USS Vengeance*, commanded by Weller, who demands that Pine deliver Cumberbatch. But the *Enterprise*, with a hastily repaired warp drive, flees to Earth to expose Weller. After the *Vengeance* intercepts and disables his ship, Pine offers to exchange Cumberbatch and the cryogenic pods for the lives of his crew. Weller then orders the *Enterprise*'s destruction. The *Vengeance* suddenly loses power, having been sabotaged by Pegg, who infiltrated the ship after following coordinates relayed by Cumberbatch through Pine. Meanwhile, after capturing the bridge, Cumberbatch overpowers Pine, killing Weller and seizing control of the *Vengeance*. Cumberbatch demands that Quinto return his crew in exchange for the *Enterprise* officers, and Quinto complies, but removes Cumberbatch's frozen crew and arms the warheads. Cumberbatch betrays their agreement by critically damaging the *Enterprise*, but the *Vengeance* is disabled when the torpedoes detonate. Pine is beamed aboard the *Enterprise* and, with both starships caught in Earth's gravity, they plummet toward the surface. Pine enters the radioactive reactor chamber to realign the warp core, saving the ship at the cost of his life. Cumberbatch crashes the *Vengeance* into San Francisco in an attempt to destroy Starfleet's headquarters. Cumberbatch survives the crash and flees, but Quinto transports down in pursuit. Urban discovers that Cumberbatch's blood has regenerative properties that may save Pine. Quinto captures Cumberbatch and Pine is revived. Nearly a year later, Pine speaks at the re-dedication ceremony of the *Enterprise* and recalls the sacrifices made by the victims of Weller's treachery where he recited the "where no man has gone before" monologue. Cumberbatch is sealed in his cryogenic pod and stored with his compatriots, while the recommissioned *Enterprise* departs on a five-year exploratory mission with Pine again in command. Though the story line goes over familiar ground, the action is spectacular and the special effects are dazzling while the acting from the entire cast presents convincing characters. The film was a great hit at the box office, earning more than $467.4 million in its initial release against a budget of more than $185 million. Songs: "Theme from 'Star Trek' Television Series" (Alexander Courage, Gene Roddenberry), "Body Movin'/Fat Boy Slim Remix" (Mario Caldato Jr., Michael Diamond, Adam Horovitz, Tito Puente, Adam Yauch), "Everybody Wants to Go to Heaven" (Don Nix), "The Growl" (J.J. Adams, Charles Scott), Anne Preven, Kassia Conway), "Ritual" (Gerald Fried), "The Dark Collide" (Robert Conley, Penelope Austin). Excessive violence prohibits viewing by children. **p**, J.J. Abrams, Bryan Burk, Alex Kurtzman, Damon Lindelof, Roberto Orci, Tommy Gormley, Tommy Harper, Michelle Rejwan, Ben Rosenblatt; **d**, Abrams; **cast**, Chris Pine, Zachary Quinto, Benedict Cumberbatch, Zoe Saldana, Karl Urban, Simon Pegg, John Cho, Anton Yelchin, Bruce Greenwood, Peter Weller, Alice Eve, Noel Clarke; **w**, Orci, Kurtzman, Lindelof (based on the television series "Star Trek" by Gene Roddenberry); **c**, Daniel Mindel; **m**, Michael Giacchino; **ed**, Maryann Brandon, Mary Jo Markey; **prod d**, Scott Chambliss; **art d**, Ramsey Avery; **set d**, Karen Manthey; **spec eff**, Burt Dalton.

Star Wars: Episode VII—The Force Awakens ★★★★ 2015; U.S.; 135m; Lucasfilm/Walt Disney; Color; Science Fiction; Children: Unacceptable (MPAA: PG-13); **BD**; **DVD**. This exciting film takes up the Star Wars story thirty years after the original trilogy that ended with **Return of the Jedi**, 1983, ignoring the plots of the films following that one and creating new adventures and characters. Luke Skywalker, played by Hamill; Han Solo, essayed by Ford; and Princess Leia, portrayed by Carrie Fisher; having defeated the Galactic Empire, face a new menace from Kylo Ren, played by Driver, and his army of storm troopers. Fisher continues to be the leader of the Resistance, although older and tougher. The dark force of the enemy is now called the First Order, which is bent on establishing a more fascist control over the universe, assembling huge rallies with thousands of soldiers that remind viewers of those of Adolf Hitler (1889-1945) during World War II (1939-1945). The First Order is a new army of space terrorists that surfaced after the evil Empire, about three decades after the Battle of Endor. Doing battle with the First Order are the good people behind a rebel movement called the Resistance. Ridley is a new heroine called Rey,

Christopher Walken, Alan Arkin and Al Pacino in *Stand Up Guys*, 2012.

who is a white female survivor on the remote planet of Jakku and who pilots the *Millennium Falcon* airship. Boyega plays Finn, a black man and former storm trooper, who had been brainwashed into serving the First Order and hopes for redemption by betraying his First Order masters, led by Driver, the new and very cruel Dark Lord of the universe. Driver flies into a rage and wields his light saber when subordinates report bad news such as a temporary victory by the Resistance. Isaac plays Poe Dameron, a Resistance officer captured by the First Order, but who manages to hide a top-secret map inside a small droid that he sends to a desert planet. There, a human scavenger, Ridley, reads the message from Isaac and learns where to find the last of the Jedi knights, Luke Skywalker (Hamill), who had gone missing. Boyega escapes the First Order with Isaac's help, and crash-lands on Jakku where he joins up with Ridley, who didn't think she needed rescuing. Ridley and Boyega take the Millennium Falcon into space and Han Solo (Ford) turns up to claim his old space ship. Ford joins Ridley and Boyega, who are amazed and delighted to meet the legendary space outlaw. Ford assures them it is all true… the Force, the Jedi, Darth Vader. They then join Fisher and she and Ford engage in some playful banter. In subsequent adventures, Ridley and Boyega are attacked by frightening creatures with sharp teeth and tentacles. The Death Star, destroyed at the end of the original **Star Wars** film, is replaced by a larger armed planet, and the cantina in the first film is now a watering hole managed by Nyong'o, who passes on to Ridley some vital information about the Force. The film ends with an opening to a sequel involving further adventures of its two main characters, Ridley and Boyega. Like its predecessors, this entry offers a panorama of startling space action where special effects amaze in almost every scene and where the star-studded cast members not only reprise their legendary roles but continue to satisfy with rewarding performances. This film broke box office records, earning more than $1.95 billion in its initial release against a budget of more than $200 million. Excessive violence prohibits viewing by children. **p**, J.J. Abrams, Bryan Burk, Kathleen Kennedy, Tommy Gormley, Laurence Kasdan, Michelle Rejwan, Ben Rosenblatt, John Swartz; **d**, Abrams; **cast**, Daisy Ridley, John Boyega, Oscar Isaac, Lupita Nyong'o, Max von Sydow, Andy Serkis, Billie Lourd, Adam Driver, Gwendoline Christie, Domhnall Gleeson, Simon Pegg, Warwick Davis, and reprising their roles from the first **Star Wars** films: Mark Hamill as Luke Skywalker, Carrie Fisher as Princess Leia, Harrison Ford as Han Solo, Peter Mayhew as Chewbacca, Kenny Baker as R2-D2, Anthony Daniels as C-3PO; **w**, Abrams, Lawrence Kasdan, Michael Arndt (based on characters created by George Lucas); **c**, Dan Mindel; **m**, John Williams; **ed**, Maryann Brandon, Mary Jo Markey; **prod d**, Rick Carter, Darren Gilford; **art d**, Neil Lamont, Gary Tomkins, Alastair Bullock, **set d**, Lee Sandales; **spec eff**, Chris Corbould, Lynne Corbould.

Kathryn McCormick and Ryan Guzman in *Step Up Revolution,* **2012.**

Starred Up ★★★ 2013; U.K.; 106m; Sigma Films/Tribecca Film/Fox Searchlight; Color; Prison Drama; Children: Unacceptable; **BD**; **DVD**. Taut crime tale sees O'Connell as a troubled and explosively violent nineteen-year-old who is transferred to an adult prison where he finally meets his match, a man who also happens to be his estranged father, Mendelsohn. O'Connell's temper quickly finds him enemies in both prison authorities and fellow inmates. His already volatile relationship with his father is pushed past the breaking point. He is approached by Friend, a volunteer psychotherapist who runs an anger management group for prisoners. Torn between gang politics, prison corruption, and a glimmer of something better, O'Connell finds himself in a fight for his own life, unsure if his father is there to protect him or to join in punishing him. O'Connell is riveting in his role as a young rebel struggling with a decision that can alter his life, and Mendelsohn is equally intriguing as an enigmatic father not wanting to recognize his own offspring. The film saw limited distribution and did poorly at the box office, earning no more than $3 million in its initial release. *Author's Note*: The film was written by Asser, a volunteer prison system therapist dealing with some of England's most violent criminals, and is an uncompromising portrayal of a dehumanizing life behind bars. The film's title is a term used to describe the early transfer of a criminal from a young offender institution to an adult prison. **p**, Gillian Berrie, Brian Coffey; **d**, David Mackenzie; **cast**, Jack O'Connell, Gilly Gilchrist, Frederick Schmidt, Edna Caskey, Darren Hart, Raphael Sowole, Duncan Airlie James, Anthony Welsh, David Ajala; **w**, Jonathan Asser; **c**, Michael McDonough; **ed**, Jake Roberts, Nick Emerson; **prod d**, Tom McCullagh; **art d**, Gillian Devenney.

Step Up Revolution ★★★ 2012; U.S.; 99m; Offspring Entertainment; Summit Entertainment; Color; Drama/Music/Romance; Children: Unacceptable (MPAA: PG-13); **BD**; **DVD**. This lively 3-D dance film, fourth in the **Step Up** series, sees a group called The Mob disrupt traffic and shut off Ocean Drive in Miami by dancing on top of cars to loud rock music. Their leaders, Guzman, Gabriel and Boss, then watch their "flashmob" performance on television news in a restaurant kitchen where they work. They then go to a hotel beach club where they work but pretend to be guests. McCormick, a lovely young aspiring professional dancer whose father owns the hotel, is impatient to get a drink at the club so she takes over as bartender. Guzman is attracted to her and orders a beer from her. She says it's on the house, then goes to the beach to dance with him, but leaves when she notices Dewey, one of Gallagher's business partners. The next day, McCormick and Gallagher argue during breakfast at the hotel, and she sees that their waiter is Guzman. She leaves her father and goes into the ballroom and begins a hot dance. Guzman watches and she tells him she wants to audition for a

top dance group at the Winwood Dance Academy Company where she is a pupil. Guzman encourages her to dance more lively and contemporarily, inviting her to visit him at the Miami Museum of Fine Arts. She rendezvous there and sees the statues come to life in movements choreographed by The Mob as Guzman admits that he is a member of that group. McCormick then becomes a member of The Mob and dances at a restaurant where she becomes the main attraction. McCormick then meets the other members of The Mob who tell her they are hoping to win a contest if they can get ten million watchers on YouTube. They celebrate at a café where McCormick and Guzman do a sizzling Hispanic dance together. They then go on a boat that Guzman has chartered, sleeping together that night and finding a mutual bond in that neither of their mothers approve of their dancing. They then return to the café, which is owned by Guzman's uncle, Sanchez, who tells them that Gallagher, a building millionaire, plans to develop the area by tearing down the bar, Guzman's home and that of his sister, among other things. McCormick is angered and goes off to confront Gallagher. She learns of a meeting to decide if Gallagher will go through with his plan. The Mob dances at the meeting, which draws more than a million viewers on YouTube. McCormick then has a falling out with Guzman, so she quits her partnering dance routine to do only a solo. Her dance fails and she tells Guzman she is going to back to work for Gallagher at his hotel, fulfilling a promise to him that she would do that if she failed as a professional dancer by the end of summer. Guzman and Gabriel are then arrested for being members on charges of disrupting traffic. Sanchez bails them out and they, including McCormick, perform another disturbance to stop the development. Gallagher sees how happy his daughter is and changes his mind, deciding to cancel the development plan. McCormick and Guzman embrace and Gallagher arranges for them and the other Mob members to dance in his marketing firm's television commercials, the film ending with The Mob making those performances. The story line is somewhat confusing and the continuity out of kilter, but the dancing ensembles and piercing music (for those who prefer cacophony to melodic sound) will entertain fans throughout. None of the dancers display the stunning grace of Fred Astaire and Ginger Rogers, or the precision and agility of Gene Kelly and Cyd Charisse, but they nevertheless entertain throughout with frenetic and exhausting movements that prove their considerable acrobatic skills. The film was a hit at the box office, earning more than $140.4 million in its initial release against a budget of more than $33 million. Other films in the series were **Step Up**, 2006; **Step Up 2: The Streets**, 2008; and **Step Up All In**, 2014. Songs/Music: "Goin' In" (Kamahl Listenbee, David Quinones, Joseph Angel, Coleridge Tillman, Tramar Dillard, Michael Warren); "Let's Go" (Michael Altha, Travis Barker, Twista, Lil Jon, Trevor Smith, Kevin Bivona); "Hands in the Air" (Timothy Mosley, Ne-Yo, Keithin Nichimura, Virma Coquia, Bilah Hajji, Jean Claude Sindres, John Mamann, Nadir Khayat, Yohanne Simon, Nate Walker); "Live My Life," "Bad Girls" (Maya Arulpragasam, Nate Hills, Marcella Araica); "Get Loose," "Rhythm" (Ricky Luna, Sohanny Rose); "Wait" (Anthony Gonzalez, Yann Gonzalez, Justin Meldal-Johnsen); "Feel Alive" (Jaime Munson, Dallas Koehlke, Stacy Ferguson); "U Don't Like Me" (Lil Jon, Thomas Wesley Penrtz, Dave Taylor); "This Is the Life," "Bring It Back" (Markus Roberts, Harold Demetrius Duncan, Danquez Woods, Lakeem Mattox); "Dance Without You" (Skylar Grey, Alex da Kid), "Hear Me Coming" (Jasiel Robinson, Benny Tillman, Carlos Thornton); "Undone" (Haley Reinhart, Maureen McDonald, Rune Westberg); "Dancing" (Elisa Toffoli); "How You Like Me Now?" (Artester Christian, Kelvin Swaby, Dan Taylor, Spencer Page, Chris Ellul); "Let It Roll" (Earl King, Raphael Judrin, Pierre-Antoine Melki, Axel Hedford, Tramar Dillard, Mike Caren, Antonio Clarence Mobley, Breyan Isaac); "Words" (Alex da Kid, Skylar Grey); "Buyou" (Matthew Burnett, J. Cole, Keri Hilson, Polow Da Don, Matthew Samuels, Bei Maejor); "Ocean Blvd," Atmos 126," "Gimme Some," "Hotel 1," "Martini Zone," "AM Prelude" (Daniel DiPrima, Alex Marlowe); "Ropa Vieja" (Steve Linsey, Daniel Freiberg); "Whip My Hair" (Ronald Jackson,

Janae Ratliff); "Secrets" (Alexa Woodward); "Aquarium" (Jason Chung); "String Quartet No. 8 in C Minor, Op. 110" (Dimitri Shostakovich); "String Quartet No. 17 in B flat major" (Wolfgang Amadeus Mozart); "Moca" (Chris Clark); "Prituri Se Planinata" (Sonja Drakulich, Danny Beall); "Aqui Esta La Clava," "Este Mi Ritmo" (Steve Linsey, Daniel Freiberg); "In This Shirt" (James McDermott); "Ants" (Edward Randolf Ma); "To Build a Home" (Patrick Wilson, Jason Swinscoe, Phil France, Stella Page); "Fortune Days" (Edward Ma, Justin Boreta, Josh Lawrence Mayer); "Jungle Ship" (Donald Ray Dantzler Jr.); "Death Metal" (Mark Jackson, Ian Scott); "Robo Cop" (Ricky Lane); "Drup It," "Shut the Lights" (Ricky Luna); "Pyramid Song" (Edward Thomas Yorke, Jonathan Greenwood, Colin Greenwood, Edward John O'Brien, Philip James Selway); "Monday" (Steve Nelepa, Justin Boreta, Edward Ma, Joshua Mayer). Suggestive dancing and gutter language prohibit viewing by children. **p**, Erik Feig, Jennifer Gibgot, Garrett Grant, Adam Shankman, Patrick Wachsberger; **d**, Scott Speer; **cast**, Kathryn McCormick, Ryan Guzman, Peter Gallagher, Misha Gabriel, Michael Langebeck, Stephen Boss, Claudio Pinto, Nicole Dabeau, Chris Charles, Tommy Dewey, Mario Ernesto Sanchez; **w**, Amanda Brody, Duane Adler; **c**, Karsten Gopinath; **m**, Aaron Zigman; **ed**, Matthew Friedman, Avi Youabian; **prod d**, Carlos Menendez; **art d**, Charles Daboub Jr., Caleb Mikler; **set d**, Helen Britten; **spec eff**, Bruce E. Merlin.

Steve Jobs ★★★ 2015; U.S.; 122m; Legendary Pictures/UNIV; Color; Biographical Drama; Children: Unacceptable (MPAA: R); **BD**; **DVD**. Not really a film of the life and work of Jobs (1955-2001), played by Fassbender, the film focuses more on the work and the steps Jobs took in becoming the co-founder of the Apple computer with Steve Wozniak (1950-), who is played by Rogen. The production is rather a backstage farce in three acts as the viewer follows the creation of their revolutionary technology by two disparate geniuses. The film opens in 1984 at De Anza Community College in Cupertino, California, where Fassbender unveils the first-ever Macintosh. Software developer Andy Hertzfeld (1953-), portrayed by Michael Stuhlbarg, is desperately trying to get the computer to say "Hello" to the audience, upon Fassbender's insistence. Fassbender's personal problems then surface when Waterston, his ex-girlfriend, shows up at the ceremony with her five-year-old daughter, accusing Fassbender of being the father, which he denies. Waterston nevertheless demands money from him. Winslet plays his trusted friend, who tries to manage Fassbender's moods and perfectionist personality, trying to get him to behave better around everyone who criticizes him. Rogen frequently feels left out of the computer's success story that began in a garage owned by Fassbender's parents. The film then shifts to 1988 when the Macintosh has lost its following and Fassbender is fired from Apple, but is working on his new company, NeXT which would sell for an astronomical $6,500. The setting is now the San Francisco Opera House as Fassbender and Rogen argue about the uncertain future of NeXT and Apple. Fassbender now feuds with John Sculley (1939-), played by Daniels, the Apple CEO who fired him three years earlier. Apple has by now foundered since Fassbender has gone, and now Daniels is on his way out of the company. The third and final act of the computer drama is set in 1998 at Davies Symphony Hall in San Francisco in 1998 when Fassbender, now forty-three, has been restored to leadership at Apple and is about to launch the iMac while working on the iPod which will be unveiled three years later. Fassbender is as obstinate as ever and has another confrontation with Rogen. There is a lot of arguing between the two Steves in this film, which is really more of a dramatic tutorial about corporate maneuvering and machinations than an incisive or revealing biopic. The viewer nevertheless learns about their differing personalities which somehow allowed them to work together to launch the Computer Age. As Wozniak aptly urged Jobs: "You can be decent and gifted at the same time." Fassbender and Winslet are outstanding, each deservedly receiving Oscar nominations for Best Actor and Best Supporting Actress. The film earned more than $30.7

Ryan Guzman in *Step Up Revolution*, 2012.

million in its initial release against a budget of more than $30 million. Jobs was also profiled in another biopic, **Jobs**, 2013. Gutter language prohibits viewing by children. **p**, Danny Boyle, Guymon Casady, Christian Colson, Mark Gordon, Scott Rudin, Jason Sack; **d**, Boyle; **cast**, Michael Fassbender, Kate Winslet, Seth Rogen, Jeff Daniels, Sarah Snook, Katherine Waterston, Michael Stuhlbarg, Perla Haney-Jardine, John Ortiz, Vanessa Ross; **w**, Aaron Sorkin (based on the book *Steve Jobs* by Walter Isaacson); **c**, Alwin H. Kuchler; **m**, Daniel Pemberton; **ed**, Elliot Graham; **prod d**, Guy Hendrix Dyas; **art d**, Luke Freeborn, Peter Borck; **set d**, Gene Serdena; **spec eff**, Adam Gascoyne, Helen Streeter.

Still Alice ★★★ 2014; U.S./France; 101m; BSM Studio/Sony; Color; Drama; Children: Unacceptable (MPAA: PG-13); **BD**; **DVD**; **IV**. Moore gives an outstanding performance as the title character in this absorbing drama. She is a fifty-year-old linguistics professor, happily married to Baldwin and mother of their grown children, Parrish and Stewart. While she is physically healthy, she begins to suffer from an early onset of Alzheimer's disease. The malady surfaces during a lecture to a class when she cannot remember the word "lexicon," and her failing memory startles her. She puts the experience out of her mind and shortly afterward does very well in playing a word game. Then she finds herself getting lost while jogging in Manhattan, although she lives there and is familiar with the route she takes. Fearing something strange is going on, Moore visits a neurologist and, after examining her, confirms what she fears most, telling her she is in the early stages of Alzheimer's. It is a rare strain that is familial, meaning that her children are also at risk of contracting the disease. Moore anguishes as her mind deteriorates while she misplaces things and they are found in unlikely places where she has put them. As she struggles to reinforce her identity to herself, Baldwin is caring and patient with her, painfully seeing his wife losing her mind day by day. To maintain his own peace of mind he immerses himself in his work. Moore and her daughter Stewart, a twenty-something actress, had been estranged, but Moore's illness brings about a reconciliation as she relies on her more and more. As Moore's condition deteriorates, Stewart asks her mother several times, "What's it like for you?" Moore, in this heart-wrenching scene, struggles with an answer to her daughter's question. Does she still feel she is Alice, or is she someone else? The film attempts to describe the symptoms of Alzheimer's, and Moore does an outstanding job in depicting how that debilitating that disease can be. She deservedly won an Oscar as Best Actress for her portrayal of a middle-aged woman suffering from the dreaded mental disease. The film, due to Moore's riveting performance, was a box office hit, earning more than $43 million in its initial release against a budget of more than $5 million. Songs: "Roamin' Round" and

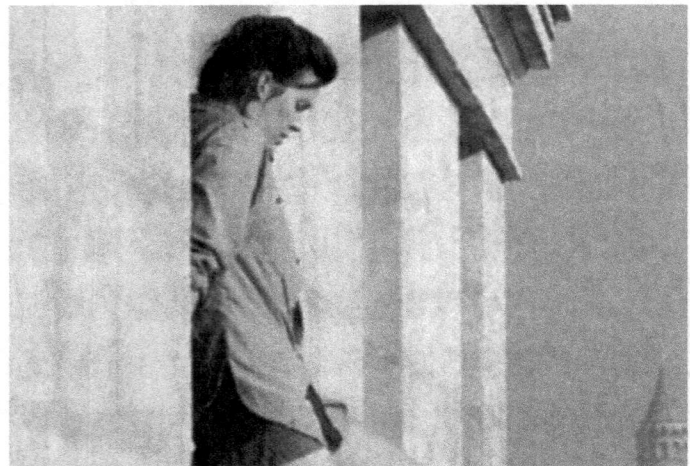

Maggie Grace in *Taken 2*, 2012.

"Jazzy Jingle Bells" (Carlos Jose Alvarez), "Ode to Cannonball" (Guy Barker), "Lucky Man" (John Courtney Morrison, Erika Sharpe, John Holt, Tyrone Evans, Howard Barrett), "God Rest Ye Merry Gentlemen" (traditional), "Dead Sound" (Sune Wagner), "Cello Suite No. 1 in G Major" (Johann Sebastian Bach), "Brand New Start" (Haroula Rose), "Everything with You" (Kip Berman, Kurt Feldman, Alexander Naidus, Peggy Wang), "In Dulci Jublio" (Robert Lucas Pearsall), "We Three Kings" (John Henry Hopkins Jr.), "Veneer" (Fil OK), "If I Had a Boat" (Lyle Lovett), "My Heart" (Emil Svanangen). Mature thematic material, gutter language and a sexual reference prohibit viewing by children. **p**, James Brown, Pamela Koffler, Lex Lutzus, Declan Baldwin, Elizabeth Gelfand Stearns; **d&w**, Richard Glatzer, Wash Westmoreland (based on the novel by Lisa Genova); **cast**, Julianne Moore, Alec Baldwin, Kate Bosworth, Shane McRae, Hunter Parrish, Kristen Stewart, Stephen Kunken, Seth Gilliam, Orlagh Cassidy, Erin Drake; **c**, Denis Lenoir; **m**, Ilan Eshkeri; **ed**, Nicolas Chaudeurge; **prod d**, Tommaso Ortino; **set d**, Susan Perlman; **spec eff**, Joseph Mulvanerty, Lucien Harriot.

Still Mine ★★★ 2013; Canada; 102m; Mulmur Feed Co./Samuel Goldwyn Films; Color; Drama/Romance; Children: Unacceptable (MPAA: PG-13); **BD**; **DVD**. Touching tale sees the stable lives of an octogenarian couple, Cromwell and Bujold, are about to change when they are unable to make a living any longer from their small farm in coastal New Brunswick, Canada. Bujold shows signs of early dementia, and their existing home no longer suits her condition. Over the objections of their two children, who reside in the area and who would prefer standard care for Bujold, Cromwell decides to build a one-story house on the property where he and Bujold can live out their lives. He knows how to build, having been a master shipbuilder who learned construction from his father. He plans to mill lumber from the trees on the farm and goes ahead with the process of getting building permits. He builds the house to exacting standards of centuries ago but encounters one roadblock after another including opposition from Potts, a local government bureaucrat, who contests Cromwell's right to build the house. The performances from Cromwell and Bujold are powerful and memorable, wholly representing the dignity and respect embodied in the elderly, as well as the love that endures within these two aging and empathetic people. The film saw limited distribution and did little box office, earning no more than $1.1 million in its initial release. Song: "After the Storm" (Benjamin Lovett, Edward Dwane, Marcus Mumford, Winston Marshall). Thematic material, brief sexuality and partial nudity prohibit viewing by children. **p**, Michael McGowan, Jody Colero, Tamara Deverell, Avi Federgreen, **d&w**, McGowan; **cast**, James Cromwell, Genevieve Bujold, Campbell Scott, Chuck Shamata, Ronan Rees, Julie Stewart, Rick

Roberts, George R. Robertson, Hawksley Workman, Joe Pingue; **c**, Brendan Steacy; **m**, Hugh Marsh, Don Rooke, Michelle Willis; **ed**, Roderick Deogrades; **prod d**, Deverell; **art d**, David Gruer, Marc Kuitenbrouwer.

Straight Outta Compton ★★★ 2015; U.S.; 147m; Circle of Confusion/UNIV; Color; Biographical Drama; Children: Unacceptable; MPAA: R; **BD**; **DVD**. Five young musicians write and perform songs that express their anger and frustration about life in the mid-1980s in and around Los Angeles, their compositions continuing until 1991. They include Ice Cube (Jackson Jr.), Dr. Dre (Corey Hawkins), Eazy-E (Mitchell), DJ Yella (Brown Jr.), and MC Ren (Hodge). These five enterprising musicians are from the suburb of Compton where middle-class blacks live. The musicians become a worldwide sensation for their "hip-hop" and "gangsta rap" music with angry lyrics in a group called N.W.A. (Niggaz Wit Attitudes) under manager Jerry Heller (Giamatti). Though the music is blaringly loud and the lyrics often offensive and even repulsive, the acting is superior, and the gifted Giamatti as the manager tolerates all the abuse to put these talented people across. The film was a huge hit at the box office, earning more than $200.4 million in its initial release against a budget of more than $28 million. Songs: "Straight Outta Compton" (Ice Cube as O'Shea Jackson, M.C. Ren as Lorenzo Patterson, Eazy-E as Eric Wright, Dr. Dre as Andre Young), "Talking to My Diary" (Slim the Mobster as Anthony Johnson, Sly Jordan, Dr. Dre as Andre Young, Russell Brown, Mario Johnson), "Everybody Loves the Sunshine" (Roy Ayres), "Jam-Master Jay" (Darryl McDaniels, Jason Mizell, Joseph Simmons, Russell Simmons, Lawrence Smith), "Everybody Wants to Rule the World" (Roland Orzabal, Chris Hughes, Ian Stanley), "More Bounce to the Ounce" (Roger Troutman), "Just Another Day" (Jayceon Terdrell, Stat Quo, Asia Bryant), "Al Naafiysh/The Soul" (Jerry Calliste Jr.), "I Didn't Mean to Turn You On" (James Harris III, Terry Lewis), "Weak at the Knees" (Steve Arrington, Charles Carter, Waung Hankerson, Roger Parker), "Gangsta Gangsta" and "Dopeman" (William DeVaughn, O'Shea Jackson, Lorenzo Patterson, Eric Wright, Andre Young, Leroy Bonner, Marshall Jones, Ralph Middlebrooks, Walter Morrison, Norman Napier, Andrew Noland, Marvin Pierce, Gregory Webster, Steve Arrington, Charles Carter, Waung Hankerson, Roger Parker), "Love You Down" (Melvin Riley Jr.), "Computer Love" (Shirley Murdock, Roger Troutman, Larry Troutman), "Atomic Dog" (George Clinton Jr., Garry Shider, David Spradley), "The Boyz-N-the-Hood" (O'Shea Jackson, Eric Wright, Andre Young), "Closer to Home/I'm Your Captain" (Mark Farner), "Not Just/Knee Deep" (George Clinton Jr., Philippe Wynn), "Dopeman" (Leroy Bonner, O'Shea Jackson, Andrew Young, Marshall Jones), "Quiet on Tha Set" (Patterson, Young), "Express Yourself" (Charles W. Wright), "Fuck tha Police" (Jackson, Patterson, Harry Whitaker, Young), "We Want Eazy" (George Clinton Jr., Bootsy Collins, Maceo Parker, Eric Wright), "Black Jay" (Jamie Laboz), "C'mon Babe" (Luther Campbell, David Hobbs, Michael Ross, Chris Wong Won), "8 Ball" (Jackson, Young, Larry Troutman, Roger Troutman), "Red Wine" (Martin Santiago), "Ruder Thump" (Jason Ruder), "The Nigga Ya Love to Hate" (Eric Sadler, O'Shea Jackson, Clinton Jr., Garry Shider, David Spradley, Steven Arrington, Charles Carter, Waung Hankerson, Roger Parker, Buddy Hank), "Flash Light" and "Mothership Connection/Star Child" (Clinton Jr., Bootsy Collins, Bernard Worrell), "Real Niggaz" (Antoine Carraby, Lorenzo Patterson, Eric Wright, Andre Young), "No Vaseline" (Jackson, Clinton Jr., Shider, Spradley, Reginald Hargis, Edward Irons, Raymond Ransom, Anthony Wheaton), "Appetite for Destruction" (Tracy Curry, Jerry Long, Patterson, Young), "Deep Cover" (Calvin Broadus, Colin Wolfe, Andre Young), "Nothin' But a 'G' Thang" (Broadus, Leon Haywood, Frederick Knight), "One Nation Under a Groove" (Clinton Jr., Shider, Walter Morrison), "Neighborhood Sniper" (Michael Bell, Gregory Hutchinson, Jerry Long, Paul Turner), "Hail Mary" (Tupac Shakur, Rufus Lee Cooper, Katari Cox, Joseph Paquette, Yafeu Fula, Bruce Washington, Tyrone Wrice), "California

Love" (Larry Troutman, Roger Trautman, Ronnie Hudson, Mikel Hooks, Joe Cocker, Chris Stainton), "What Would U Do" (Ricardo Brown, Delmar Arnaud, Dwight Williams, Calvin Broadus, Jewell Caples), "Flava in Ya Ear" (Craig Mack, Osten Harvey), "C.R.E.A.M" (Dennis Coles, Robert Diggs, Gary Grice, Lamont Hawkins, Isaac Hayes, Jason Hunter, Russell Jones, David Porter, Clifford Smith, Corey Woods), "Barking in Compton" (Becky Barksdale). Offensive gutter language, strong sexuality, nudity, violence and drugs prohibit viewing by children. **p**, Matt Alvarez, Scott Bernstein, Dr. Dre, F. Gary Gray, Ice Cube, Tomica Woods-Wright; **d**, Gray; **cast**, Paul Giamatti, O'Shea Jackson Jr., Corey Hawkins, Jason Mitchell, Neil Brown Jr., Aldis Hodge, Marlon Yates Jr., R. Marcos Taylor, Carra Patterson, Alexandra Shipp; **w**, Jonathan Herman, Andrea Berloff (based on a story by S. Leigh Savidge, Alan Wenkus, Andrea Berloff); **c**, Matthew Libatique; **m**, Joseph Trapanese; **ed**, Billy Fox, Michael Tronick; **prod d**, Shane Valentino; **art d**, Christopher Brown; **set d**, Christopher Carlson; **spec eff**, Eric Frazier, Eric Rylander.

Summer in February ★★★ 2014; U.K.; 100m; CrossDay Productions/Tribeca Film; Color; Biographical Drama/Romance; Children: Unacceptable; **BD**; **DVD**. Fascinating story is based on activities and romances of artists at the Newlyn School on the beautiful Cornish coast in northern England on the eve of World War I (1914-1918). Action focuses on the Lamorna Group in that small town which includes Alfred (A.J.) Munnings, played by Cooper, and Laura and Harold Knight, essayed by Morahan and Dingwall, who, years later, became very important artists. Romantic feelings develop between the anti-Modernist Munnings and an aspiring new artist, Florence Carter-Wood, portrayed by Browning. His best friend is Gilbert Evans, played by Stevens, who is the land agent in charge of the Lamorna Valley estate. Cooper is a self-centered young womanizer and drinker, while Stevens is more stable, a thoughtful and sincere young man. Both become attracted to Browning, but she is more aware of Cooper's feelings for her. Stevens is about to propose to her, but Cooper beats him to it, not really knowing how deep Stevens' feelings are for Browning. Before Stevens can ask Browning to marry him, Cooper proposes to Browning and she, unexpectedly and perhaps not really knowing Cooper, says yes to him. Before they marry, Browning begins to have second thoughts about Cooper, realizing he is a callous womanizer, but she nevertheless marries him. On their wedding night, she is so distraught about the marriage that she goes to her room and swallows some arsenic, intending to kill herself. She rushes out among the wedding guests and is taken to a hospital where she recovers. The marriage has not been consummated and Browning does not give herself to Cooper in the months that follow. During this period, she falls in love with Stevens, who gives her the gentle but deep affection she has not found in Cooper. Stevens cannot help himself and, in giving compassionate friendship to Browning, gives her love besides, and she returns his love. Cooper is unable to win back Browning's love, and the situation prompts Stevens to absent himself by taking a three-year assignment to help the poor and starving in Africa. After he leaves, Browning is noticeably pregnant and Cooper knows the child she is bearing is not his because he and Browning have never consummated their marriage. At an artists' costume ball, Cooper notices that Browning is with child and goes into a rage in front of everyone, calling her a whore and realizing she is bearing Stevens' child. Browning drinks arsenic again and dies. The film ends three years later with Stevens returning to Lamorna as a British soldier and laying flowers at Browning's grave. Their love had been a short, doomed summer in winter, as the title suggests. In an epilog, we learn that Munnings (Cooper) became a famous artist and president of the Royal Academy of Art, while Stevens remained in Lamorna the rest of his life with a painting of Browning riding a horse that Cooper had painted of her and then left for Stevens before going off to London to become a famous artist. This beautifully lensed tale is wonderfully enacted by Browning, Cooper and Stevens, all fully capturing the sensitive triangle of the star-crossed

Liam Neeson in *Taken 2*, 2012.

lovers. The pre-World War I period is accurately and stunningly represented in superb sets and costumes. Songs: "Siren's Lullaby" and "In Perfect Starlight" (Benjamin Wallfisch, Joanna Wallfisch), "After the Ball" (Charles K. Harris). **p**, Jeremy Cowdrey, Pippa Cross, Janette Day, Dan Stevens; **d**, Christopher Menaul; **cast**, Dominic Cooper, Stevens, Emily Browning, Hattie Morahan, Max Deacon, Shaun Dingwall, Michael Maloney, Tom Ward-Thomas, Joshua James, Nicholas Farrell; **w**, Jonathan Smith; **c**, Andrew Dunn; **m**, Benjamin Wallfisch; **ed**, Chris Gill, St. John O'Rorke; **prod d**, Sophie Becher; **art d**, James Morrall, Dan Taylor; **set d**, Stella Fox; **spec eff**, Bob Hollow.

Taken 2 ★★★ 2012; France; 92m; EuropaCorp/FOX; Color; Crime Drama; Children: Unacceptable (MPAA: PG-13); **BD**; **DVD**. In this sequel to the 2008 film **Taken**, the funerals of Albanian mobsters killed by CIA agent Neeson in the first film are shown being held in Tropoje, Albania. Serbedzija, the mob boss whose son was electrocuted by Neeson, vows to capture Neeson and bring him to the graves of his son. Serbedzija's men track down Rabourdin, a corrupt French intelligence officer who was in the first film, and torture him in an attempt to learn Neeson's whereabouts. They end up bribing another official for the information. Grace, Neeson's teenage daughter, and his ex-wife, Janssen, who is having marital problems with her second husband, surprise Neeson by joining him in Istanbul where he is stationed and has just completed a three-day security assignment. The day after their reunion, Neeson and Janssen go out for lunch while Grace goes swimming in the pool at their hotel. Neeson realizes he and Janssen are being followed, and, after a wild chase by Serbedzija's men, they capture Janssen. Before Neeson can surrender to the kidnappers to try to rescue Janssen, he telephones Grace and warns her to get to safety and wait for further instructions. Grace hurries to Neeson's hotel room and enters it through a window along a ledge. The men pursuing her shoot another hotel guest and two security guards, but fail to find her as she hides in a closet. The would-be abductors flee when an alarm is sounded. Neeson gives himself up to the kidnappers and wakes up with his hands tied to a pole in the basement of an old house. He finds a cell phone and calls Grace, instructing her to go the American embassy and tell them what happened, but she begs for a chance to rescue him and her mother. Under Neeson's guidance by phone she opens his suitcase containing weapons, and throws two grenades onto a deserted rooftop parking lot. By timing the seconds of the explosions, Neeson is able to successfully learn the location where he is being held captive. Meanwhile, the Albanian mobsters bring in a struggling Janssen. One takes a knife and makes a small cut to her throat before hanging her upside-down by chains. They then

Sarah Fischer, Chanty Sok, Ted, Kristina Ellery and Katelyn Lorren in *Ted*, 2012.

tell Neeson to watch her bleed out and die before they kill him. The mobsters leave them and Neeson undoes his chains, takes Janssen down, and calls Grace to tell her to detonate two more grenades so he can determine where he has now been taken. This enables Neeson to guide Grace close enough to his location so that she can see steam he sends up a chimney to mark his precise position. Grace tosses a gun down the chimney and Neeson uses it to kill the mobsters in the building, then saves Grace from a thug pursuing her on the hotel rooftop. Meanwhile, Janssen is taken away by her captors. Neeson steals a taxi and follows the kidnappers, then leaves Grace in the taxi while he goes to rescue Janssen. She is being taken to a van, and Neeson shoots at it, but fails to save her. He returns to the taxi and Grace drives to the U.S. embassy. A chase and shootout with the police and the kidnappers end when Neeson drives the taxi with Grace and crosses a railroad track just moments before the car carrying their pursuers is hit by a train. Neeson leaves Grace at the U.S. embassy and retraces the route to Serbedzija's hideout. Confronting him there, Neeson suspects that, if he kills Serbedzija, the mobster's two remaining sons will seek revenge on him, so he offers to let Serbedzija live if he gives his word to end the vendetta. Serbedzija agrees, Neeson lowers his gun and is about to walk way, when Serbedzija seizes the gun and attempts to shoot Neeson, only to discover that Neeson had removed the cartridge from the pistol's chamber. After a struggle with Neeson, Serbedzija is impaled on a towel hook by Neeson. Neeson then picks up Janssen and leaves. Three weeks later, Neeson and his family are at a dinner back home on the Los Angeles coast and having milkshakes to celebrate Grace's passing her high school driving test. They are joined by her boyfriend, Grimes, and Grace jokingly asks her father not to shoot "this one." The action in this thriller is stunningly genuine and presents harrowing excitement throughout while Neeson, Grace, Janssen are superb as the victims of Serbedzija, who plays one of the most insidious villains ever to slink across the screen. The film was a megahit at the box office, earning more than $376.1 million in its initial release against a budget of more than $43 million. Songs: "A Real Hero" (David Grellier, Austin Garrick, Bronwyn Griffin), "Tick of the Clock" (Johnny Jewel), "Babasaz" (Ozgur Sakar, Pat Jabbar), "Too Close" (Alex Clare), "Handyman" (Henry Wikstrom, Steve Martin), "Let Me" (Phoebe Tolmer), "Dream Come True" (Alan Ett), "Bosumus" (Mavi Saz, Mahzuni Serif), "Violonizm" (Yann Mace, Luc Leroy), "Optum Ewa" (Mace, Leroy), "Dadaklarinda Arzu" (Sevim Ozham, Saadettin Oktenay), "Dertler Benim Olsun" (Orhan Gencebay), "Belly Dancer" (Daghan Baydur, Wzra Baydur, Sarah Baydur), "Come Out to LA" (Hart/Dudas). Intense violence and action and some sensuality prohibit viewing by children. **p**, Luc Besson; **d**, Olivier Megaton; **cast**, Liam Neeson, Maggie Grace, Famke Janssen, D.B. Sweeney, Rade Sherbedzija, Olivier Rabourdin, Leland Orser, Jon Gries, Luke Grimes;

w, Besson, Robert Mark Kamen (based on characters they created). **c**, Romain Lacourbas; **m**, Nathaniel Mechaly; **ed**, Camille Delamarre, Vincent Tabaillon; **prod d**, Sebastien Inizan; **art d**, Nanci Roberts, Atilla Yilmaz; **spec eff**, Philippe Hubin, Donn Markel, Jean-Christophe Magnaud.

Tanu Weds Manu Returns ★★★ 2015; India; 128m; Eros International/KVH Media Group; Color; Comedy/Drama/Romance; Children: Unacceptable; **BD**; **DVD**. After living in London four years into their marriage, an Indian couple, Tanu (Ranaut) and Manu (Madhavan), find that their love for one another has fled. They are opposites who no longer feel any attraction toward one another. Ranaut expected Madhavan to be more exciting, but he merely wanted a quiet life with a docile wife. While they both regret their marriage, Madhavan's old friend, Dobriyal, is happy about his impending nuptials. Ranaut and Madhavan decide to give their marriage one last chance by going to Dobriyal's wedding in Kanpur. There Ranaut meets a neighbor and they start seeing each other, while Madhavan flirts with a university student who looks a lot like Ranaut. This romantic menagerie is further confused as Ranaut says of her husband, "I think I love him, but I've stopped liking him." Despite this, Ranaut and Madhavan manage to save their marriage by falling in love with one another again, and for the same reasons that sparked their initial romance. Gentle and delightful tale sees superior performances from Ranaut and Madhavan, along with the rest of the cast. The film performed well at the box office, earning more than $36 million in its initial release against a budget of $$5.8 million. Mature material prohibits viewing by children. **p**, Sunil Lulla; **d**, Aanand Rai; **cast**, Kangana Ranaut, Madhavan (Madhavan Ranganathan), Jimmy Shergill, Deepak Dobriyal, Mohammed Zeeshan Ayyub, Swara Bhaskar, Eijaz Khan, Manu Rishi Chadha, Alex Jaep; **w**, Himanshu Sharma; **c**, Chirantan Das; **m**, Krsna Solo, **ed**, Hemal Kothari; **spec eff**, Praveen Bareria, Mahesh Baria.

Ted ★★★ 2012; U.S.; 106m; UNIV; Color; Comedy/Fantasy; Children: Unacceptable (MPAA: R); **BD**; **DVD**. John Bennett, portrayed by Manley, is a lonely boy in Boston in 1985. His parents, Garman and Borstein, give him a teddy bear to which he immediately becomes emotionally attached, calling it Ted, and wishing it could become alive. A shooting star passing over the house makes his dream come true. Twenty-seven years later (2012), Bennett, now played as an adult by Wahlberg, works at a car rental and has kept up his strong bond of friendship with Ted (voice of MacFarlane), but Kunis, his girlfriend, is jealous of the stuffed but very much alive teddy bear. She fears that Ted, with whom Wahlberg drinks and uses drugs, is holding him mentally captive as a child. Wahlberg and Kunis do not marry, but live together, and, on their fourth anniversary, come home to find Ted with five hookers, one of whom has defecated on the floor during a game of Truth or Dare. Kunis wants Wahlberg to try to live without Ted, so Wahlberg gets Ted an apartment and a job at a grocery store where Ted soon has sex with Barth, a new cashier at the store. While walking in a park, Wahlberg and Ted encounter Ribisi and his spoiled, obnoxious son, Mincks, and Ribisi offers to buy Ted, but Wahlberg refuses. Wahlberg and Kunis go to a party hosted by her boss, McHale, who has a crush on her. Ted phones Wahlberg and tells him that Sam J. Jones, the actor who played the lead in **Flash Gordon** (1980), their favorite film from childhood, is attending a housewarming party at Ted's house. Wahlberg and Ted have some drinks and drugs with Jones but a fight begins with Ted's neighbor, Wu, whom Jones mistakes for Emperor Ming from the old movie. Kunis has had enough of Wahlberg's obsession with Ted so she leaves him. Wahlberg, meanwhile, tells Ted to stay away from him and takes up residence in a hotel. A week later, McHale asks Kunis for a date and she accepts, hoping to get over Wahlberg. Ted goes to Wahlberg's hotel room and they get into a fight. They reconcile and decide to interrupt a Norah Jones concert that Kunis is attending with McHale, but Wahlberg is booed off the stage as he tries to sing to Kunis. More misadventures follow and Ted winds up at Fenway Park where, in a fight with Ribisi and Mincks, Mincks accidentally tears Ted in half. Wahlberg and Kunis try to piece Ted back together and Ted tells them they need each other more than they need him, which breaks the magic spell that gave him life and he is now an ordinary but much worn-out teddy bear once more. Wahlberg and Kunis marry and the best man is Ted, who has come back to life after Kunis wishes it. It appears that these slaphappy and emotionally bound together humans are going to be a happy threesome... maybe. Although some may find the humor crude or even offensive, there is a certain lowlife charm to this wacky tale, not unlike that of frolicking peasants oafishly amusing themselves with mud fights that passed for festivals in the Dark Ages. The story is somewhat mindless (taking a large leaf from the great comedy **Harvey**, 1950, where James Stewart's drinking buddy in an invisible six-foot rabbit), but the adult cast members do a good job enacting their adolescent to pubescent roles. The film even managed to receive an Oscar nomination for Best Original Song ("Everybody Needs a Best Friend" Murphy and MacFarlane). This coarse and loutish comedy widely appealed to present-day unsophisticated audiences, earning more than $549 million at the box office in its initial release against a budget of $51 million. Songs: "I Think We're Alone Now" (Ritchie Cordell); "Only Wanna Be with You" (Mark Bryan, Dean Felber, Darius Rucker, Jim Sonefeld); "Come Away with Me" (Norah Jones); "All Time High" (John Barry, Tim Rice); "Oh My Little Sixpence" (traditional); "Staying Alive" (Barry Gibb, Robin Gibb, Maurice Gibb); "Song for the Young Folk" (Thomas Newsom); "Flash's Theme" (Brian May); "Thunder Buddies" (Alec Sulkin, Wellesley Wild, Seth MacFarlane); "Kiss Kiss" (Chris Brown, Faheem Najm); "The Imperial March," "Raiders of the Lost Ark," The Key" (John Williams); "Find Myself Again," "Isabelle" (Tim Mercer, Chris Bird, Kevin Burt, Rob McGary); "Knight Rider" (Glen Larson, Stuart Phillips); "Soldier" (Denzell Cameron, Ruwanga "Ru" Samath); "Football Fight" (Freddie Mercury); "Sin," "Crush" (Tim Mercer, Mike Burdge, Scott Garapolo); "Get Free" (Franz Stahl, Peter Stahl); "Sexy Little Thing" (K.C. Booker, D'Andre Johnson); "The Hero" (Brian May); "Saving Ted/Lori's Wish," "Everybody Needs a Best Friend" (Walter Murphy, Seth MacFarlane). Crude and sexual content, gutter language, and drug use prohibit viewing by children. **p**, Seth MacFarlane, Jason Clark, John Jacobs, Scott Stuber, Eric Heffron, Mark Kamine; **d**, MacFarlane; **cast**, Mark Wahlberg, Mila Kunis, Tom Skerritt, Joel McHale, Giovanni Ribisi, Patrick Warburton, Matt Walsh, Jessica Barth, Sam J. Jones, Norah Jones, narrated by Patrick Stewart, and MacFarlane as the voice of Ted; **w**, MacFarlane, Alec Sulkin, Wellesley Wild (from a story by MacFarlane); **c**, Michael Barrett; **m**, Walter Murphy; **ed**, Jeff Freeman; **prod d**, Stephen Lineweaver; **art d**, E. David Cosier; **set d**, Kyra Friedman; **spec eff**, James Ochoa, Judson Bell.

Ted 2 ★★★ 2015; U.S.; 115m; UNIV; Color; Comedy/Fantasy; Children: Unacceptable (MPAA: R); **BD**; **DVD**. In this entertaining sequel to **Ted**, 2012, Wahlberg and his wife are divorced because she refuses to accept his teddy bear (MacFarlane, voiceover) as a live person, which Wahlberg thinks it is. He marries Barth, but their marriage is also in trouble because she wants to have a child, but he cannot and Barth is infertile because of her drug use. They solve their problem by deciding to adopt. Wahlberg wants to adopt his old teddy bear (MacFarlane), and the case goes to court where the teddy is declared property and not a person. Wahlberg's marriage to Barth is then annulled. Wahlberg turns for help from Freeman, a civil rights lawyer, who manages in court to convince jurors that the teddy (MacFarlane) feels emotions including empathy. Wahlberg and Barth get remarried, adopt a baby boy, and all ends well with teddy remaining part of the family. The cast does a good job with an implausible and decidedly sophomoric tale, and Wahlberg is a standout (as he was in the original 2012 rendition of this goofy fantasy). Freeman, too, is exceptional as a lawyer who takes his ridiculous legal chores as serious, albeit this fine character actor is overexposed, having appeared in four films in 2013; six films in 2014; five films in

Laura Vandervoort in *Ted*, 2012.

2015; and six films in 2016. His persona has begun to wear; you would think that, at his age of seventy-eight, he might want to ease back a bit. Although this film did not do the mega millions gleaned by its predecessor, it nevertheless earned a healthy $216.7 million at the box office in its initial release against a budget of more than $68 million. Songs: "Celebration" (Robert Bell, Ronald Bell, George Brown, Eumir Deodato, Robert Mickens, Claydes Smith, J.T. Taylor, Dennis Thomas, Earl Toon), "Steppin' Out with My Baby" (Irving Berlin), "Law and Order, Main Title" (Mike Post), "Down and Out" (Tim Mercer, Pete Risano, Joe Russillo), "Tiny Dancer" (Elton John, Bernie Taupin), "One Foot in Front of the Other" (Marc Levinthal, Scott Wilk), "Gonna Fly Now" (Carol Connors, Bill Conti, Ayn Robbins), "At This Moment" (Billy Vera), "Angry Birds Theme" (Ari Pulkkinen), "Ride with Me" (Eldra DeBarge, William Randall, Jason Epperson, Cordell Haynes, Etterlene Jordan, Lavell Webb), "Mess Around" (Ahmet Ertegun), "Knight Rider/Main Title" (Glen Larson, Stuart Phillips), "New York" (1953: Ken Darby, Lionel Newman), "Sweet Caroline" (Neil Diamond), "I Think We're Alone Now" (Ritchie Cordell), "Mean O' Moon" (music: Walter Murphy; lyrics: Seth MacFarlane). Crude and sexual content, gutter language and drug use prohibit viewing by children. **p**, Jason Clark, John Jacobs, Seth MacFarlane, Scott Stuber, Mark Kamine, John Wiseman; **d**, MacFarlane; **cast**, Mark Wahlberg, MacFarlane (voiceover), Amanda Seyfried, Morgan Freeman, Sam J. Jones, Dennis Haysbert, Giovanni Ribisi, Jessica Barth, Tom Brady, Liam Neeson, Patrick Warburton, Jay Leno, Patrick Stewart (narrator). Leno and Neeson have minor guest roles. **w**, MacFarlane, Alec Sulkin, Wellesley Wild; **c**, Michael Barrett; **m**, Walter Murphy; **ed**, Jeff Freeman; **prod d**, Stephen J. Lineweaver; **art d**, Peter Borck; **set d**, Kyra Friedman Curcio; **spec eff**, John Ruggieri, J.D. Schwalm.

10 Days in a Madhouse ★★★ 2015; U.S.; 111m; Pendragon Pictures; Tricoast Worldwide/Café Pictures; Color; Biographical Drama; Children: Unacceptable (MPAA: R). Nellie Bly (Elizabeth Cochran Seaman; 1864-1922) is well enacted by Barry, who becomes one of the first female investigative reporters in America when going to work for Joseph Pulitzer's New York *World* in 1887. Her first assignment is to feign insanity and have herself committed to the Women's Lunatic Asylum at Blackwell's Island, a hellhole for mentally deranged females. Barry, like the rest of the hapless inmates at this miserable institution, is subjected to terrible food and dirty drinking water, and refuse and garbage is strewn everywhere, including the eating areas, while legions or disease-carrying rats scurry about unmolested. Barry and others are subjected to consistently harsh treatment (the inmates were compelled to sit on hard benches and were often doused by freezing buckets of water to get them to move about, and slept in filthy bug-ridden beds). Physical abuse

Ted and Sam J. Jones in *Ted*, 2012.

is seen from an uncaring and callous medical staff of selfish doctors and sadistic nurses. The nightmare conditions actually threaten Barry's sanity as she endures punishments and offenses, but she is thankfully released at the request of her newspaper after ten torturous days. Barry writes a scathing series of articles exposing the terrible conditions on Blackwell Island that becomes a sensation. Her exposé prompts NYC officials to launch an investigation that soon brings about reforms (the budget for NYC's Department of Charities and Corrections was immediately increased to $850,000 to provide better food, equipment and medical supplies, and treatment and diagnoses quickly improved). Barry is outstanding as the courageous Bly, her memorable performance (despite critical detractors) being a shuddering one, where the viewer shares her fears as she and others endure incredible abuse and while one senses that her sanity will, indeed, become permanently impaired. Hines does a good job in helming this tense film, capturing the mounting tension of its horrific tale from frame to frame. This film was shot on a shoestring budget, but nevertheless presents authentic period-looking sets, saw limited distribution, although it deserved a much larger theatrical audience. It earned only $14.6 million at the box office in its initial release against a budget of $12 million. *Author's Note*: Barry was selected for her role out of a reported 8,000 applicants and only after two months when she had moved from Colorado to Los Angeles to pursue an acting career. Not coincidentally, she bears an almost identical appearance to the real Nellie Bly; her fine acting ability is a bonus. The film was shot on location in Eugene, Oregon, in an abandoned mental institution with no heating or lighting, which perfectly duplicated the conditions of Blackwell Island in 1887. Ironically, this area was the same used for another film exploring mental illness, **One Flew over the Cuckoo's Nest**, 1975. The series of articles made Bly famous, and she went on to expose political corruption, medical malpractice and other social evils by going undercover to get her stories, and who emulated the Jules Verne story by going around the world in seventy-two days in 1889. Part of her startling expose about Blackwell Island included the following lines: "I would like the expert physicians, who are condemning me for my action [of feigning insanity to infiltrate the asylum], which have proven their ability, to take a perfectly sane and healthy woman, shut her up and make her sit from 6 a.m. to 8 p.m. on straight-back benches, do not allow her to talk or move during these hours, give her no reading and let her know nothing of the world or its doings, give her bad food and harsh treatment, and see how long it will take to make her insane?" Other actresses playing Bly in other films include **The Adventures of Nellie Bly**, 1981 (made-for-TV; Linda Purl); **The Barbara Stanwyck Show**, 1960- (TV series; "Little Big Mouth," 1961 episode: Barbara Stanwyck); **The Dinah Shore Chevy Show**, 1956-1963 (TV series; "Around the World with Nellie Bly,"

1960 episode: Janet Blair, released in 1960 as a separate TV movie); **Frankie and Johnny**, 1936 (Lilyan Tashman); **Frankie and Johnny**, 1966 (Nancy Kovack); **Voyagers!**, 1982-1983 (TV series; "Jack's Back," 1983 episode: Julia Duffy). **p**, Susan Goforth, Marcy Levitas Hamilton, Strathford Hamilton, Donovan Le, Jessica Burgoyne, Jesse Zesbaugh; **d**, Timothy Hines; **cast**, Caroline Barry, Christopher Lambert, Kelly Le Brock, Julia Chantrey, Alexandra Callas, David Mitchum Brown, Natalia Davidenko, Jess Campbell, Andi Morrow, Katie Singleton, Everette Scott Ortiz, Christopher Beeson, Goforth; **w**, Hines (based on *Ten Days in a Madhouse* by Nellie Bly); **c**, Aaron Anderson; **m**, Jamie Hall; **ed**, Avril Beukes, Stephen Eckelberry; **prod d**, Lori Francia, Ezra Hamill, Adem Opa; **set d**, Hillary Matheny; **spec eff**, Terrence Giang, Adam Lima, Vincent Febriyanto Mak.

That Awkward Moment ★★★ 2014; U.S.; 94m; Treehouse Pictures; Focus Features; Color; Comedy/Romance; Children: Unacceptable (MPAA: R); **BD**; **DVD**. Three male best friends in their twenties living in New York City are Efron and Teller, both book cover designers at a publishing house, and Jordan, an emergency room doctor. Efron and Teller are happy swinging bachelors with girlfriends, while Jordan's wife, Lucas, wants a divorce. All three men pledge to remain single together. Unknown to the others, Jordan tries to revive his marriage, while Efron gets chummy with a new girl, Poots, and Teller becomes interested in a pick-up, Davis. The three yuppies have to make up their minds whether they will continue with their fraternal pledge to each other or go their own ways with women pulling at their heartstrings. Though somewhat contrived, there are enough humorous moments to entertain throughout. The film did good box office, earning more than $40.5 million in its initial release against a budget of more than $8 million. Songs: "Closed Shades" and "We'll Be Gone by Then" (John Helmuth, Sean Lee), "After Dark," "Drones" (Brandon Duhon, Rodney Connell), "Down on Life" (Ellinor Olovsdotter, Tommy Tysper), "Morning Sun" (Stephen Docker, Gerard Sidhu), "Amoureux" and "Feathers and Gold" (Robert Vogel), "Heartbeat" (Elizabeth Berg, Jason Boesel, Alex Greenwald, Stephen Runion, James Valentine), "The Captain's Blues" (Sam Zeines), "After You've Gone" (Creamer, Layton), "I Don't Recall" (Steven John Gregoropoulos, Becky Stark, Ron Rege Jr., Jeff Rosenberg, Damian Kulash Jr.), "So Good at Being in Trouble" (Ruban Nielson), "Tales and Truths" (Andrew Scarborough, Jeffret Scarborough), "Walking Backwards" (Tyler Burkum, Thad Cockrell, Jeremy Lutito), "Won't You Come Home" (Devendra Barnhart), "That Old Familiar Feeling" (Daniel May, Marc Ferrari), "Still Life" (Faris Adam Derar Badwan, Rhys Timothy Webb, Joseph Patrick Spurgeon, Joshua Mark Hayward. Tom Furse Cowan), "Still Not a Player" (Michele Williams, Japhe Tejeda, Rodney Jerkins, Brenda Gordon Russell, Jolyon W. Skinner, Joe L. Thomas). Semi-nudity and sexuality prohibit viewing by children. **p**, Scott Aversano, Justin Nappi, Andrew O'Connor, Kevin Turen, Andrew Fierberg, Ray Marshall; **d&w**, Tom Gormican; **cast**, Zac Efron, Miles Teller, Michael B. Jordan, Imogen Poots, Mackenzie Davis, Jessica Lucas, Addison Timlin, Josh Pais, Evelina Turen, Karen Ludwig; **c**, Brandon Trost; **m**, David Torn; **ed**, Shawn Paper, Greg Tillman; **prod d**, Ethan Tobman; **set d**, Deirdre Brennan; **spec eff**, Francesco Panzieri, Daniel Apodaca, Jonathan Jelkin.

The Theory of Everything ★★★★ 2014; U.K.; 123m; Working Title Films/Focus Features; Color; Biographical Drama; Children: Unacceptable (MPAA: PG-13); **BD**; **DVD**. Often fascinating film about the relationship between brilliant physicist Stephen William Hawking (1942-), played by Redmayne, and his second wife, Jane Wilde Hawking, played by Jones, from whom he was divorced in 2006. Hawking, wheelchair-bound, suffers from a Motor Neurone disease related to ALS (amyotrophic lateral sclerosis), keeping him confined to a wheelchair. Almost entirely paralyzed, he communicates through a speech generating device. He is divorced twice, with three children. Redmayne gives a powerful performance, one that earned him an Oscar as Best Actor. The film also received Oscar nominations for Best Picture; Best Actress (Jones); Best Adapted Screenplay (McCarten); and Best Original Score (Johannsson). The film did well at the box office, earning more than $123.7 million in its initial release against a budget of $15 million. Thematic material and suggestive matter prohibit viewing by children. **p**, Tim Bevan, Lisa Bruce, Eric Fellner, Anthony McCarten, Richard Hewitt; **d**, James Marsh; **cast**, Eddie Redmayne, Felicity Jones, Emma Watson, David Thewlis, Charlie Cox, Harry Lloyd, Simon McBurney, Adam Godley, Maxine Peake, Charlotte Hope, Tom Prior, Enzo Cilenti; **w**, Anthony McCarten (based on the book *Traveling to Infinity: My Life with Stephen* by Jane Hawking); **c**, Benoit Delhomme; **m**, Johann Johannsson; **ed**, Jinx Godfrey; **prod d**, John Paul Kelly; **set d**, Claire Nia Richards; **spec eff**, Mark Holt.

13 Minutes ★★★ 2015; Germany; 114 m; Lucky Bird Pictures/Sony; Color; Drama/Biographical Drama; Children: Unacceptable (MPAA: R); **BD**; **DVD**. Based on true events, this well-crafted film dramatizes the failed attempt by Georg Elser (1903-1945), played by Friedel, to assassinate Adolf Hitler (1889-1945), who is played by Schenk. In flashback, we see Friedel as a carpenter who builds furniture and later wooden propellers for small airplanes. In 1938, he works in the shipping department of an arms company producing fuses and detonators. He becomes a member of a leftist labor union and the Communist Party, having opposed the Nazi regime in 1933 and considering Hitler to be the downfall of Germany. Friedel decides to construct a bomb and assassinate Hitler (Schenk) when the Nazi leader is to speak at the Munich beer hall on the anniversary of his failed attempt to take over the Bavarian government in 1923. However, Schenk cut his 1939 speech at the beer-hall short, thirteen minutes before Elser's bomb explodes. By that time, Schenk and his group of high-ranking Nazi officials have left the beer hall. The bomb brings down the ceiling and roof, killing seven and injuring sixty-three others. Friedel is captured and executed in Dachau in 1945, just before Allied troops reached the concentration camp where he was held. Both Friedel and Schenk give riveting performances in this taut film where tension mounts throughout. (In German; English subtitles) *Author's Note*: Elser's assassination attempt was also profiled in the 1989 film **Seven Minutes**. Disturbing violence and some sexual reference prohibit viewing by children. **p**, Boris Ausserer, Fred Breinersdorfer, Oliver Schundler, Gotz Bolten, Manfred Hattendorf, Philipp Hoepp, Michael Schmidl, Andreas Schretmuller, Claudia Simionescu, Christine Strobl; **d**, Oliver Hirschbiegel; **cast**, Christian Friedel, Katharina Schuttler, Udo Schenk, Burghart Klaussner, Johann von Bulow, Felix Eitner, David Zimmerschied, Rudiger Klink, Simon Licht, Cornelia Kondgen; **w**, Leonie-Claire Breinersdorfer, Fred Breinersdorfer; **c**, Judith Kaufmann; **m**, David Holmes; **ed**, Alexander Dittner; **prod d**, Benedikt Herforth, Thomas Stammer; **art d**, Astrid Poeschke; **set d**, Daniele Drobny; **spec eff**, Dirk Lange.

This Is Happening ★★★ 2015; U.S.; 84m; Paladin/Seed&Spark; Color; Comedy/Drama; Children: Unacceptable (MPAA: PG-13); **BD**; **DVD**. Wolk and Sumner are standouts as an estranged brother and sister whose father, Nelson, sends them to escort the siblings' grandmother, Leachman, to an assisted living facility. Wolk is handsome, but ineffectual, and Sumner is a small-time drug dealer who stashes some marijuana in the trunk of their car. They go to Leachman's house where she learns of their plan to institutionalize her, so she escapes in their car, taking her dead stuffed dog along, while the marijuana is in the trunk. Leachman eludes the siblings after several misadventures by all three, until they track her down. The clue to her whereabouts is that Leachman and Sumner order the same strange breakfast combination at restaurants: mayonnaise and pancakes. It all ends with them finding Leachman and depositing her safely at the facility for the elderly. The independent film is a comedic exercise in learning how to understand your family in order to understand yourself, and, in the process, provides many hilarious moments. Leachman is exceptional as the madcap grandmother, who re-

Eddie Redmayne in *The Theory of Everything*, 2014.

fuses to go gentle into that docile rest home. Drug use and wild antics prohibit viewing by children. **p**, Ryan Jaffe, Lisa Barrett McGuire, Scott Einziger, Matthew Weinberg, Corey Bobker, Benjamin Friedberg; **d&w**, Jaffe; **cast**, James Wolk, Mickey Sumner, Kenny Apel, Rene Auberjonois, Cloris Leachman, Judd Nelson, J DOC Farrow, Zarin Khan, Shabana Shah, Emily Tremaine, Mike Wade; **c**, Ryan Meyer; **m**, Adam Crystal; **ed**, Dylan Firshein; **prod d**, Jessica Mahnke; **art d**, Morgan McShea.

This Is the End ★★★ 2013; U.S.; 104m; UNIV; Color; Comedy/Fantasy/Horror; Children: Unacceptable (MPAA: R); **BD**; **DVD**. Showbiz is broadly parodied in this frantic film. It begins with partygoers in Los Angeles, all of the actors playing themselves at a wild party in a house in Los Angeles, desperately doing drugs and having sex as the biblical apocalypse begins. Outside there are explosions, car crashes, and mass chaos, but inside the house the party goes on. A powerful earthquake erupts and the partygoers begin to fear for their lives, boarding up the doors and windows and rationing food and drugs. A large crack opens up in the earth and some of them are killed. The remaining partygoers band together to attempt to survive the end of the world, only to find that they are all too stupid and superficial to survive, unless they discover the only way out. They distract their fears by filming a homemade sequel to **Pineapple Express**, 2008, in which most of them have appeared. One of them, Hill, becomes possessed by a demon and finds himself to be supernaturally strong. Then they are chased by a demonic bull, but, during an exorcism attempt, a fire destroys the house, kills Hill, and only four are left to flee outdoors. One of the survivors, Robinson, volunteers to sacrifice himself to let the others escape from a large winged demon. Satan then appears, preparing to consume two of the survivors, Rogen and Baruchel, when Rogen sacrifices himself to save Baruchel. Then Satan is taken by the Lord. In Heaven, Robinson, who is now an angel, welcomes his two friends and says they are in a paradise where any wish comes true. Baruchel wishes that the Backstreet Boys rock band would reunite, and the movie ends with the band performing "Everybody" for a raucous heavenly party. There is little sense to the manic tale where anarchy and lowlife crude behavior reigns in every scene and every actor is allowed to go over the top, a stunning exercise in unbridled mayhem. The film did good box office, earning more than $126 million in its initial release against a budget of $32 million. Songs: "Everybody" (Max Martin, Denniz Pop), "Step Into a World/Rapture's Delight" (Deborah Harry, Chris Stein, Harry Palmer), "A Joyful Process" (George S. Clinton, Bernie Worrell), "Girls Girls $" (Theophilus London, Joakim Ahlund), "Tipsy" (Jerrell Jones, Joe Kent, Mark Williams), "Easy Fix" (Kristine Flaherty, Dave McCracken), "Disco 2000" (Nick Banks, Jarvis Cocker, Candida Doyle, Stephen

Jay Galloway in *Trouble with the Curve*, 2012.

Mackey, Russell Senior, Mark Webber), "Love In the Old Days" (James Franco, Tim O'Keefe, Matt Everett), "She Got That Too" and "Take Yo Panties Off" (Craig Robinson), "Go Outside" (Madeline Follin McKenna, Ryan Michael Mattos), "Please Save My Soul" (Kyle Hunter, Ariel Shaffir, Jason Stone), "Spiteful Intervention" (Kevin Barnes), "War Pigs" (Ozzy Osbourne, Tony Iommi, Terence Butler, Bill Ward), "Ruff Ryder's Anthem" (Swizz Beatz, DMX), "When the She—Goes Down" (Lawrence Dickens, Louis Freeze, Larry Muggerud), "Gangnam Style" (Jai-sang Park, Gun Hyung Yoo), "Paper Planes" (Mathangi Arulpragasam, Topper Headon, Mick Jones, Thomas Pentz, Paul Simonon, Joe Strummer), "The Next Episode" (Andre Young, Melvin Bradford, Brian Anthony Bailey, Calvin Broadus, David Axelrod), "Hole in the Earth" (Chino Moreno, Stephen Carpenter, Chi Cheng, Abe Cunningham, Frank Delago), "Watchu Want" (Jesse Shatkin, Jaime Garfield McPherson), "I Will Always Love You" (Dolly Parton), "Spirit in the Sky" (Norman Greenbaum), "The End of the Beginning" (Ozzy Osbourne, Tony Iommi, Terence Butler), "Toccata and Fugue in D Minor" (Johann Sebastian Bach). Crude and sexual content, brief graphic nudity, gutter language, drug use and some violence prohibit viewing by children. **p**, Seth Rogen, Evan Goldberg, James Weaver; **d**, Rogen, Goldberg; **cast**, Rogen, James Franco, Jay Baruchel, Paul Rudd, Emma Watson, Channing Tatum, Craig Robinson, Jonah Hill, Danny McBride, Michael Cera, Rihanna, Jason Segel, Brian Huskey, Backstreet Boys (Nick Carter, Brian Littrell, Howie Dorough, Kevin Scott Richardson, AJ McLean); **w**, Rogen, Goldberg (based on their story and the short film **Jay and Seth vs. the Apocalypse** by Jason Stone); **c**, Brandon Trost; **m**, Henry Jackman; **ed**, Zene Baker; **prod d**, Chris L. Spellman; **art d**, William Ladd Skinner; **set d**, Helen Britten; **spec eff**, Eric Frazier, Craig Tex Barnett, Durk Tyndall, Robert Caban.

Thor: The Dark World ★★★ 2013; U.S.; 112m; Marvel Entertainment/Disney; Color; Science Fiction; Children: Unacceptable (MPAA: R); **BD**; **DVD**. In this sequel to **Thor** (2011), thousands of years ago, an evil race called the Dark Elves tries to send the universe into darkness with a weapon called the Aether. Warriors from Asgard stop them, but their leader Malekith, played by Eccleston, escapes to wait for a future chance to do his evil. In the present day, Jane Foster, portrayed by Portman, awaits the return of heroic Thor, essayed by Hemsworth, although they have not seen each other for two years. Meanwhile, Hemsworth attempts to bring peace to the nine realms of the universe. Portman investigates a wormhole, but is sucked into it. Back on Asgard, Hemsworth wants to return to Earth, but his father, Hopkins, refuses to let him make the trip. Hemsworth then learns that Portman has vanished. He returns to Earth just as Portman reappears. Some police officers try to arrest Portman, but an unknown energy force repells them. Hemsworth then rescues

and brings Portman to Asgard and the scene is set for a sequel. The action is almost nonstop, and special effects are packed into every scene of this sci-fi opus. The film was a mega-blockbuster at the box office, earning more than $644.6 million in its initial release against a budget of more than $170 million. Songs: "We Cakin' Up" (Xzibit), "The Lobby Lounge" (Robert G. Cressey), "Golden Song" (Sarah Jane Cion), "Jade" (Eric Speier), "Captain America March" (Alan Silvestri), "We Are the Champions" (Armath and Deja), "Theme from the movie **Caged Heat** (1985; Mike Post). Intense violence and suggestive content prohibit viewing by children. **p**, Kevin Feige; **d**, Alan Taylor; **cast**, Chris Hemsworth, Natalie Portman, Anthony Hopkins, Stellan Skarsgaard, Christopher Eccleston, Ray Stevenson, Rene Russo, Tom Hiddleston, Idris Elba, Kat Dennings, Jaimie Alexander; **w**, Christopher Yost, Christopher Markus, Stephen McFeely (based on a story by Don Payne, Robert Rodat, and the comic book characters by Stan Lee, Larry Lieber, Jack Kirby); **c**, Kramer Morgenthau; **m**, Brian Tyler; **ed**, Dan Lebental, Wyatt Smith; **prod d**, Charles Wood; **art d**, Ray Chan, Thomas Brown, Jordan Crockett, Matthew Robinson, Mike Stallion, Mark Swain; **set d**, Guoni Lindal Benediktsson, John Bush; **spec eff**, Eggert Ketilsson, Stephane Ceretti, Jake Morrison, Alex Wuttke.

3 Bahadur ★★★ 2015; Pakistan; 94m; SOC Films/ARI Films; Color; Adventure/Family/Comedy/Drama; Children: Unacceptable; **BD**; **DVD**. The title of this film 3-D animated film from Pakistan means three brave ones. The film opens as three eleven-year-old friends, Yaseen, Zuhab Khan and Shahid, are at a festival in their neighborhood in a fictional town called Roshan Basti (Town of Light). A little girl is kidnapped by an old man named Mangu, portrayed by Khalid Ahmed, but she is rescued and Ahmed hides in a cave where a terrible creature gives him evil powers. Ahmed and his goons then terrorize the town. The three young friends are granted powers including advanced speed, hearing, and intelligence which enable them to defeat Ahmed and his henchmen. This involves obtaining a demonic key, one that they find and throw into a black hole. This ends Ahmed's powers and the three young friends have restored peace to their town. This lively animated outing is packed with adventurous action, but its mature subject matter prohibits viewing by children. The film earned about $660,000 at the box office in its initial release against a budget of more than $150,000. **p**, Sharmeen Obaid-Chinoy, Salman Iqbal, Jerjees Seja; **d**, Chinoy; **cast**, Muneeba Yaseen, Hanzala Shahid, Zuhab Khan, Khalid Ahmed, Behroze Sabzwari, Alyy Khan, Kulsoom Aftab Ahmed, Farhan Ahmad Qadri; **w**, Kamran Khan (from Khan's story); **c**, Kamran Khan; **ed**, Husain Qaizar; **art d**, Syed Salman Nasir.

To the Wonder ★★★ 2012; U.S.; 112m; Brothers K Productions/Magnolia Pictures; Color; Drama/Romance; Children: Unacceptable (MPAA: R); **BD**; **DVD**. Affleck, an American visiting in Paris, France, meets Kurylenko, a single mother, and they fall deeply in love. He wants her to come home with him to rural Minnesota and bring her little daughter with her. She agrees, but soon after they begin a life together, they have a falling out. Affleck then begins seeing McAdams, an American girl he once loved, and the romantic feelings he had for Kurylenko leave him. Bardem, a priest from Europe, arrives in the area to become pastor of a new church. He is having a crisis of faith as he visits prisoners, and the poor, the ill and the illiterate in his parish. The lives of these young people become intertwined with Bardem's, as everyone seeks happiness. Affleck seeks it in his feelings for Kurylenko and McAdams, and Bardem in his seeking for faith in God. Kurylenko then confesses to Affleck that she is having sex with a carpenter and they say goodbye at an airport as she departs with her daughter to return to Paris. The somewhat depressing ending nevertheless underscores the reality of the well-crafted story, and Affleck, Kurylenko, McAdams and Bardem are standouts in their roles. Director Malick delivers a beautifully photographed film, but his message is somewhat somber. The film did not do well at the box office, earning only about $2.7 million in its initial release. Songs: "The Isle of the Dead" (Sergei Rachmaninoff); "Troops

Advance" "Cosmic Beam Take 5," "McKron Freaks" (Francesco Lupica, Lee Scott); "Prophecy of the Village Kremna" (Arsenije Jovanovic); "Symphony No, 3" (Henryk Gorecki); "Harold in Italy" (Hector Berlioz); "Parsifal, Prelude to Act One" (Richard Wagner); "The Seasons" (Joseph Haydn); "Ancient Airs and Dances" (Ottorino Respighi); "The Medusa Song" (Tatiana Chiline); "June/Barcarolle" (Pyotr Ilyich Tchaikovsky); "So Go" (Lauren Marie Mikus); "Ou tu t'endors" (Michael Tuccio); "Bartlesville Fight Song," "Symphony No. 9/From the New World" (Antonin Dvorak); "Miss Mary Mack" (traditional); "Lahaul Valley" (David Parsons); "Quadrpospazzes" (Thee Oh Sees); "Symphony No. 3" (Henryk Gorecki); "The Little Grey Wolf" (traditional); "Unto Us a Child Is Born/Christmas Cantata No 142" (Johann Sebastian Bach); "Cantus Arcticus" (Einojuhani Rautavaara); "Frates for Eight Cellos" (Arvo Part); "Piano Concerto No, 2" (Dimitri Shostakovich); "Now Now" (St. Vincent); "Cosmic Beam Drone No. 1" (Francesco Lupica); "Cosmic Beam Take 1" (Lupica, Lee Scott). Sexuality and nudity prohibit viewing by children. **p**, Sarah Green, Nicolas Gonda, Hans Graffunder, Sandhya Shardanand; **d&w**, Terrence Malick; **cast**, Ben Affleck, Olga Kurylenko, Rachel McAdams, Javier Bardem, Tatiana Chiline, Romina Mondello, Tony O'Gans, Charles Baker, Marshall Bell, Jamie Conner; **c**, Emmanuel Lubezki; **m**, Hanan Townshend; **ed**, A.J. Edwards, Keith Fraase, Shane Hazen, Christopher Roldan, Mark Yoshikawa; **prod d**, Jack Fisk; **art d**, David Crank; **set d**, Jeanette Scott; **spec eff**, Philippe Majdalani, Patrick Clancey, Andrew Francis.

Tomorrowland ★★★ 2015; U.S./Spain; 131m; Walt Disney Pictures/Walt Disney; Color; ScienceFiction; Children: Unacceptable (MPAA: PG-13); **BD**; **DVD**: IV. This futuristic adventure film opens with Robinson, playing a boy named Walker who is an inventor visiting the 1964 New York World's Fair. A mysterious girl gives him a magical pin, and he takes it to a ride at the fair that is a portal to another dimension. The film then flashes forward to the present time, and we meet Walker again, now a grown man played by Clooney, who has become disillusioned with the world. He meets Robertson, a sixteen-year-old girl, who loves science and is the daughter of NASA engineer McGraw, who is soon to lose his job at Cape Canaveral when the agency closes it. Robertson tries to sabotage the agency's attempts to dismantle the launch pad, but is arrested for vandalism. Someone gives her a metal pin that immediately transports her to a better world with a shiny futuristic city. Her efforts to find the origins of the pin lead her to a ten-year-old robotic girl, Cassidy, who has an English accent and is adept at martial arts. She also meets Clooney, who is depressed and waiting for the apocalypse. Clooney begins a dangerous mission with Robertson, who wants to learn the secrets of a mysterious place somewhere in time Robertson calls "Tommorowland," a happy land which exists only in her imagination. The film's villain is Laurie, who talks endlessly about fantasies that are poisoning everyone's minds and news stories of mayhem and disasters the news media spews forth each day. Their journey takes them from one thrilling adventure to another through unknown dimensions into the future. What they must do when they get to their promised land will change the world and them forever. The story is a bit complex, but the cast members are empathetic and the special effects dazzling. The film did well at the box office, earning more than $209 million in its initial release against a budget of $190 million. Songs: "There's a Great Big Beautiful Tomorrow" and "It's a Small World" (Robert B. Sherman, Richard M. Sherman), "I Got Mine" (Dan Auerbach, Patrick Carney), "Sadie" (Theodore Tyler), "Star Wars Main Theme" (John Williams), "The End Is Coming" (Bobby Huff, James Slater). Violence, peril, thematic elements, and gutter language prohibit viewing by children. **p**, Brad Bird, Jeffrey Chernov, Damon Lindelof; **d**, Bird; **cast**, George Clooney, Hugh Laurie, Britt Robertson, Raffey Cassidy, Tim McGraw, Kathryn Hahn, Keegan-Michael Key, Chris Bauer, Thomas Robinson, Pierce Gagnon, Judy Greer; **w**, Bird, Lindelof (based on a story by Bird, Lindelof, Jeff Jensen); **c**, Claudio Miranda;

Amy Adams and Justin Timberlake in *Trouble with the Curve,* 2012.

m, Michael Giacchino; **ed**, Walter Murch, Craig Wood; **prod d**, Scott Chambliss; **art d**, Ramsey Avery, Don Macaulay; **set d**, Lin MacDonald; **spec eff**, Mike Vezina, Brad Zehr.

Tracks ★★★ 2014; Australia; 112m; See-Saw Films/Weinstein Co.; Color; Biographical Drama; Children: Unacceptable (MPAA: PG-13); **BD**; **DVD**. Based on the memoirs of Robyn Davidson, who is played by Wasikowska, the film follows her nine-month 1,700-mile journey across the deserts of West Australia to the Indian Ocean in 1977 with her dog and four camels. *National Geographic* photographer Rick Smolan records her adventurous odyssey, capturing stunning landscapes and seldom-seen wonders of the Outback. Unfortunately, this film did not do well at the box office, earning less than $5 million in its initial release against a budget of more than $12 million. Thematic elements, some partial nudity, disturbing images and gutter language prohibit viewing by children. **p**, Iain Canning, Emile Sherman, Antonia Barnard, Julie Ryan; **d**, John Curran; **cast**, Mia Wasikowska, Lily Pearl, Philip Dodd, Fiona Press, Daisy Walkabout, Rainer Bock, Felicity Steel, John Flaus, Ian Conway, Evan Casey, David Pearce; **w**, Marion Nelson (based on the book by Robyn Davidson); **c**, Mandy Walker; **m**, Garth Stevenson; **ed**, Alexandre de Francheschi; **prod d**, Melinda Doring; **spec eff**, Peter Stubbs, Tim O'Brien.

Transcendence ★★★ 2014; U.K./China/U.S.; 119m; Alcon Entertainment/WB; Color; Action/Drama/Science Fiction; Children: Unacceptable; MPAA: PG-13; **BD**; **DVD**. Depp is an artificial intelligence research scientist who downloads his mind into a computer in creating a machine that possesses sentience and collective intelligence. Extremists opposing technological advancement target him, but their actions drive him harder to achieve his goal. He also wants to become part of the new technology, but this is questioned by his wife, Hall, and his best friend, Bettany, who are also researchers. His main goal is to acquire knowledge so he can possess power, and he seems to be unstoppable in that pursuit. In the end, Depp causes irreparable damage to his family and friends but sacrifices his life to save others, claiming that his goal was to make right the wrongs done to the world ecosystems. The dialog is occasionally trite and Depp's usual deadpan performance disappoints, but the marvelous special effects, sets and overall ambience of this intriguing tale sustains viewership to the finale. Financially, the film broke even, earning $103 million at the box office in its initial release against a budget of $100 million. Songs: "Genesis" (Jorma Kaukonen), "Happy Birthday to You" (Mildred Hill, Patty Hill). Violence, bloody images, gutter language and sensuality prohibit viewing by children. **p**, Kate Cohen, Broderick Johnson, Andrew A. Kosove, Annie Marter, Marisa Polvino, Aaron Ryder, David Valdes, Yolanda T. Cochran, Regency

John Goodman, Amy Adams and Clint Eastwood in *Trouble with the Curve*, 2012.

Boies, Scott Andrew Robertson; **d**, Wally Pfister; **cast**, Johnny Depp, Morgan Freeman, Paul Bettany, Kate Mara, Rebecca Hall, Cillian Murphy, Cole Hauser, Clifton Collins Jr., Josh Stewart, Xander Berkeley; **w**, Jack Paglen; **c**, Jess Hall; **m**, Mychael Danna; **ed**, David Rosenbloom; **prod d**, Chris Seagers; **art d**, Dawn Swiderski; **set d**, Gene Serdena; **spec eff**, Scott R. Fisher.

Trash ★★★ 2015; U.K./Brazil; 124m; O2 Filmes/Focus World; Color; Adventure/Comedy/Crime; Children: Unacceptable (MPAA: R); **BD**; **DVD**. Three teenage homeless boys, Tevez, Luis and Weinstein, go trash-hunting in the slums of Rio de Janeiro and find a wallet at their local dump. Corrupt and brutal police arrive and offer a big reward for the return of the wallet, so the boys suspect it possesses great value. The boys find themselves to be innocent victims in a city plagued by corruption. Rather than turn over the wallet to authorities for a reward, the friends seek the confidence of a priest, Sheen, and a social worker, Mara, but this further puts their freedom and perhaps their lives in danger. Well crafted and with standout performances from the cast, the film unfortunately did mediocre box office, earning less than $6 million in its initial release. Not related to the 1970 Andy Warhol film of the same name. Songs: "Pe Na Estrada" (Claudio Passavanti), "A Minha Menina" (Jorge Ben), "Baiana" (Barbatuques, Danubio, Ricardo Lima, Smoking London). Violence and gutter language prohibit viewing by children. **p**, Tim Bevan, Eric Fellner, Kris Thykier; **d**, Stephen Daldry, Christian Duurvoort; **cast**, Rickson Tevez, Eduardo Luis, Martin Sheen, Wagner Moura, Rooney Mara, Selton Mello, Christiane Amanpour, Andre Ramiro, Nelson Xavier, Jesuita Barbosa; **w**, Richard Curtis, Felipe Braga (based on the novel by Andy Mulligan); **c**, Adriano Goldman; **m**, Antonio Pinto; **ed**, Elliot Graham; **prod d**, Tule Peak; **art d**, Pedro Equi; **spec eff**, Sergio Farjalla Jr.

Trouble with the Curve ★★★ 2012; U.S.; 111m; WB; Color; Sports Drama; Children: Unacceptable (MPAA: PG-13); **BD**; **DVD**. Eastwood is a baseball scout for a team he thinks should retire. He asks them to let him do more scouting to prove he can lead them to be a winning team. His friend Goodman asks Eastwood's estranged daughter, Adams, if she will go with Eastwood to make sure he is up to the task because his eyes are failing. Adams puts her job on hold and travels with Eastwood to North Carolina, asking why he pushed her out of his life. In North Carolina, Eastwood meets Timberlake, a scout for another team who was a promising player Eastwood once scouted. Timberlake and Adams become attracted to each other while Eastwood tries to decide if Timberlake can be the winning new player for his team. Eastwood's grizzled persona works well with the effervescent Adams in this well-written, introspective drama that has the added attraction of some very

good baseball scenes. The film failed to return its investment, earning less than $50 million in its initial release against a budget of $60 million. Songs: "Don't Owe You a Thing" (Gary Clark Jr.), "Blues with a Feeling" (Walter Jacobs), "Beach Dream" (Adam Wilson Kittredge, Jocelyn Greenwood, Piers Henwood, Antonio Alana Freybe-Smith, Luca Stephen Renshaw), "You Are My Sunshine" (Jimmie Davis), "Heartbreaker" (James Leithauzser, Matthew Barrick, Paul Maroon, Peter Bauer, Walter Martin), "Chicken Fried" (Zac Brown, Wyatt Durrette), "Long Cool Woman in a Black Dress" (Allan Clarke, Roger Cook, Roger Greenaway), "On My Way" (Greg Camp, Randy Brown, Colby Pollard, Joe Hester), "Prison Bound Blues" (Josh White), "The Long Waltz Home" (Casey Cook), "Cotton-Eyed Joe" (traditional), "Everythang and Mo" (Robert R. Page, Samuel Favers), "Distance" (Christina Perri, David Hodges). ***Author's Note***: Eastwood had vowed that he would no longer appear as an actor in films after making **Gran Torino**, 2008, stating that he would only direct films in the future. The producers of this film, however, convinced Eastwood to return to the screen in this outing. Gutter language, sexual references, thematic material and smoking prohibit viewing by children. **p**, Clint Eastwood, Robert Lorenz, Michele Weisler, Tim Moore; **d**, Lorenz; **cast**, Eastwood, Justin Timberlake, Amy Adams, John Goodman, Clifton Guterman, Carla Fisher, Chelcie Ross, Raymond Anthony Thomas, Ed Lauter, George Wyner, Bob Gunton, Jack Gilpin, Scott Eastwood; **w**, Randy Brown; **c**, Tom Stern; **m**, Marco Beltrami; **ed**, Joel Cox, Gary Roach; **prod d**, James J. Murakami; **art d**, Patrick M. Sullivan Jr.; **set d**, Gary Fettis; **spec eff**, Steve S. Riley, Ryan Riley, Dominic V. Ruiz.

Trumbo ★★★★ 2015; U.S.; 121m; Groundswell/Bleeker Street Media; Color; Biographical Drama; Children: Unacceptable (MPAA: R); **BD**; **DVD**. This provocative and fascinating film, based on the career of screenwriter Dalton Trumbo (1905-1976), sees an outstanding performance from Cranston, who plays the controversial writer. Cranston writes the stories or screenplays for such hits as **Kitty Foyle**, 1940, and **A Guy Named Joe**, 1943, courageously holding to his principles when accused of being a member of the Communist Party in 1947. He is among a group of ten Hollywood actors, writers, and others accused by the U.S. House Un-American Activities Committee in a political witch hunt instigated by Republican Senator Joseph McCarthy (1908-1957) of Wisconsin, and FBI chief J. Edgar Hoover (1895-1972). For Cranston's refusal to name those who were Communists in Hollywood, he is blacklisted, prohibited from writing for the movies, and, when charged with contempt of Congress, is sent to prison. Cranston becomes one of the most famous (infamous to his enemies) of those blacklisted and called "The Hollywood Ten." Others were screenwriters Alvah Bessie, Lester Cole, Ring Lardner Jr., Albert Maltz, Samuel Ornitz, director Edward Dmytryk, director and screenwriter Herbert Biberman, and producer and screenwriter Adrian Scott. Many others were blacklisted earlier, most of whom were not communists, but had become non-active members of the Communist Party early in their careers. The film follows Cranston over the years during which he has a loving and supportive wife, superbly played by Lane, but is hounded by Hollywood gossip columnist Hedda Hopper, expertly enacted by Mirren, whose crusade is to stamp out communism in Hollywood. She takes up a vitriolic campaign against Cranston after he becomes a staunch supporter of a labor dispute between the Conference of Studio Unions and Hollywood studio heads. Cranston is released from jail after eleven months, but is still banned from screenwriting in Hollywood. However, he wins Academy Awards for screenplays he writes under pen names, **The Brave One**, 1956, and **Roman Holiday**, 1987 (awarded posthumously). He also writes scripts for B films such as **Gun Crazy**, 1950, under false names and finds work in Europe. In one scene at the hearings, Cranston attacks actor John Wayne, played by Elliott, for being a shirker during World War II (1939-1945) by staying out of military service while making films that had him winning the war almost singlehandedly. (In this savage attack, Trumbo was decidedly wrong in that Wayne was too old for military service and was deemed physically unfit to serve and it is a matter of record that Wayne tried many times to enlist.) In another scene at the hearings, left-leaning actor Edward G. Robinson, enacted by Stuhlbarg, names some he calls Communists in order to steer political criticism away from himself. The film also depicts actor Kirk Douglas, portrayed by O'Gorman, assigning Cranston to write the screenplay for his epic film, **Spartacus**, 1960, and is bold enough to give Cranston on-screen credit for his writing, thus publicly ending Cranston's Hollywood blacklisting. Cranston deservedly received an Oscar nomination as Best Actor for his stunning performance as Trumbo, and director Roach presents a faithful portrait of this memorable and gifted writer. The film did not do well at the box office, earning $8.2 million in its initial release against a budget of more than $15 million. *Author's Note*: This author met Trumbo a few years before his death, and his wrath against those who had blacklisted him was still white hot, telling me: "I understood the politicians who were out to make hay with the political straw of our lives [he and other industry workers]. Those jackals were obvious. It was the Hollywood moguls who buckled under the pressure from those politicians who were the real villains in those days. They were a gutless bunch without any sense of personal honor or courage. All of them feared that their studios would lose money. So they threw us into the Washington garbage heap. Everybody ran like hell from us, except a few brave souls, like Kirk Douglas, who stood up to those bullies. Those were very lonely days." Other films profiling the blacklisting of that era include **Chaplin**, 1992; **Dash and Lilly**, 1999 (made-for-TV; based on the lives of Lillian Hellman and Dashiell Hammett, the latter having been imprisoned and blacklisted for previous communist activities); **Fear on Trial**, 1975 (made-for-TV; based on blacklisted TV/radio personality John Henry Faulk); **The Front**, 1976; **Good Night, and Good Luck**, 2005; **Guilty by Suspicion**, 1991; **The Majestic**, 2001; **Marathon Man**, 1976; **One of the Hollywood Ten**, 2000; and **The Way We Were**, 1973. Gutter language and sexual references prohibit viewing by children. **p**, Kevin Kelly Brown, Monica Levinson, Michael London, Nimitt Mankad, John McNamara, Shivani Rawat, Janice Williams, Michelle Graham; **d**, Jay Roach; **cast**, Bryan Cranston, Diane Lane, Helen Mirren, Michael Schulberg, David Maldonado, Richard Portnow, John Getz, David James Elliott, Madison Wolfe, Alan Tudyk, Dean O'Gormon, Christian Berkel; **w**, John McNamara (based on the book *Dalton Trumbo* by Bruce Cook); **c**, Jim Denault; **m**, Theodore Shapiro; **ed**, Alan Baumgarten; **prod d**, Mark Ricker; **art d**, Jesse Rosenthal, Lisa Marinaccio; **set d**, Cindy Carr; **spec eff**, Bob Riggs.

The Turin Horse ★★★ 2012; Hungary/France/Germany, Switzerland/U.S.; 146m; TT Filmmuhely/Cinema Guild; B/W; Drama; Children: Unacceptable; **BD**; **DVD**. Gritty, fascinating tale opens with Derzsi, an elderly coachman who cannot get his old horse to move during a rainstorm in the city of Turin, Italy. In frustration, he whips the animal, causing a man, Kormos, to throw his arms around the horse's neck to protect it before falling to the street. Derzsi takes the horse to its stable where it is dried off and fed. In the next six days, Derzsi and his daughter, Bok, barely exist in their hardscrabble dwelling as the horse declines in health, and even the well they use at their small stone house outside of Turin runs dry. The little family and the horse continue to survive, but their miserable lifestyle reflects the grim indifference of the world. The film, which is well crafted and enacted, is based on a real-life experience of German philosopher Friedrich Nietzsche (1844-1900). According to his biographers, while traveling alone in Italy in 1889 when he was forty-four years old, he saw a coachman whipping an old horse in a public square during a rainstorm in Turin. He threw his arms around the neck of the horse to protect it and then he collapsed. In less than a month, Nietzsche was diagnosed with a serious mental illness that would render him speechless and confine him to bed for the next eleven years until his death. It is uncertain how or if witnessing the horse beating caused his breakdown, and what happened to the horse is

Erika Bok in *The Turin Horse*, 2012.

fictionalized in this somber tale. The film is reflective of Nietzsche's existential philosophy and is decidedly allegorical about the pointlessness of life and the finality of death. Pervasive hopelessness prohibits viewing by children. **p**, Martin Hagemann, Juliette Lepoutre, Marie-Pierre Macia, Gabor Teni, Ruth Waldburger; **d**, Bela Tarr, Agnes Hranitzky; **cast**, Janos Derzsi, Erika Bok, Mihaly Kormos, Mihaly Raday (narrator); **w**, Tarr, Laszlo Krasznahorkai; **c**, Fred Kelemen; **m**, Mihaly Vig; **ed**, Hranitzky; **prod d**, Kata Czigler; **spec eff**, Zoltan Pataki.

12 Years a Slave ★★★★ 2013; U.S./U.K.; 134m; Regency Enterprises; FOX; Color; Biographical Drama; Children: Unacceptable (MPAA: R); **BD**; **DVD**. This superbly made film is based on a true story of a black man's struggle for survival and freedom in the years before the U.S. Civil War (1861-1865). In 1841, Solomon Northrup, who is played by Ejiofor, is a free African American man working as a violinist, living in Sarasota Springs, New York, with his wife and two children. Two men, McNairy and Killam, offer him a two-week job as a musician if he will travel with them to Washington, D.C. He agrees, but when they arrive there, they drug him and he wakes up in chains, to be sold into slavery. He is shipped to New Orleans, renamed "Platt," and called a runaway slave from Georgia. Repeatedly beaten, Ejiofor is eventually bought by a plantation owner, Cumberbatch, a relatively decent master. Ejiofor designs a waterway for transporting logs across a swamp, and his master gives him a violin in gratitude. However, Dano, the plantation overseer, resents Ejiofor and verbally harasses him. Dano attacks him and when Ejiofor fights back, Dano and his friends attempt to lynch him, causing Ejiofor to hang by his tiptoes in the noose for many hours. Cumberbatch tells him that, in order to save his life, he must sell him to a cotton plantation owner, Fassbender. Ejiofor cannot convince Cumberbatch that he is a free man, and Fassbender proves to be a cruel master, believing the Bible says it is his right to abuse his slaves. The slaves working for Fassbender must pick at least 200 pounds of cotton every day or be beaten. Nyong'o, a young female slave, picks more than 500 pounds daily and is praised by Fassbender, who becomes obsessed with her beauty and rapes her. Fassbender's wife, Paulson, becomes jealous of Nyong'o and frequently humiliates and attacks her. Fassbender repeatedly rapes Nyong'o and she wishes to die, asking Ejiofor to kill her, but he refuses. A plague of cotton worms devastates the plantation, which Fassbender blames on the slaves, sent there by God, so he leases them to a nearby plantation for the season. While there, Ejiofor wins favor by playing the violin at the plantation owner's wedding anniversary celebration, and is allowed to keep some money he is given for performing. When returning to the Fassbender plantation, Ejiofor pays a white field hand, Dillahunt, to mail a letter to his friends in New York, but is betrayed when the worker keeps the money and burns the letter. Ejiofor then helps

Janos Derzsi in *The Turin Horse*, 2012.

build a gazebo with Pitt, a Canadian laborer, who is opposed to slavery and urges Fassbender to have some compassion toward his slaves. Then Nyong'o goes missing and, after she returns, she explains that she went to get a bar of soap from a neighbor, Woodard. Fassbender has her stripped, tied to a post, and Paulson forces Ejiofor to whip her. Ejiofor agrees reluctantly, but gives Nyong'o a mild whipping, until Fassbender takes the whip away and savagely lashes her. Ejiofor confides in Pitt that he was kidnapped and asks Pitt to get a letter to his friends in Sarasota Springs. Pitt agrees, at the risk of his life. Huguley, the local sheriff, arrives and asks Ejiofor about his past life in New York. Convinced Ejiofor was wrongfully enslaved, he takes him away to become a free man again. After being enslaved for twelve years, Ejiofor returns to his family and finds that his daughter has given him a grandson, named after him. The film stunningly presents an authentic antebellum South, with all of its inhumanity and cruelties, and he cast members render unforgettable performances, particularly Ejiofor, Nyong'o, Fassbender, Cumberbatch and Paulson. The pervasive sense of Ejiofor's hopeless situation is ameliorated through his marvelous expressions of faith that he will eventually see his freedom through his indomitable will to survive. Ridley's distinctive and memorable script excellently defines Northup's character and captures in full the desperation of the slave era, albeit it owes allegiance to **Solomon Northup's Odyssey** [aka: **Half Slave, Half Free**], 1984 (made-for-TV) and the carefree but nevertheless hapless characters immortalized by writer Harriet Beecher Stowe in her classic *Uncle Tom's Cabin* (1852). The widescreen photography, which lends itself to the actual epic proportions of the story, is impressively and inventively presented by talented cinematographer Bobbitt. The euphonic score from Zimmer ideally fuses western classic music with folk songs of the period. The film won an Oscar as Best Picture, as well as Best Supporting Actress (Nyong'o), and Best Adapted Screenplay (Ridley). The film received Oscar nominations for Best Director (McQueen); Best Actor (Ejiofor); Best Supporting Actor (Fassbender); Best Film Editing (Walker); Best Production Design (Stockhausen, Stein, and Set Decoration: Baker); and Best Costume Design (Patricia Norris). The film was a box office hit, earning more than $187 million in its initial release against a budget of $22 million. Songs/Music: "My Lord Sunshine," "The Old Promenade," "Cotton Song," "Yarney's Waltz," "O Teach Me Lord," "Roll Jordan Roll" (Nicholas Britell); "The Devil's Dream," "Money Musk," "Miller's Reel" (Britell, Tim Fain); "Trio in B-Flat" (Franz Schubert); "Run Nigger Run" (John A. Lomax, Alan Lomax); "Awake on Foreign Shores" (Colin Stetson); "Apache Blessing Song" (Chesley Wilson); "John" (John Davis). *Author's Note*: This was the first film that won an Oscar as Best Picture where its director, the gifted McQueen, was a black man, a precedent long in coming. The story came into development when McQueen partnered with

writer Ridley to produce a working script that impressed actor Pitt, whose company initially financed the production. The high literary quality of the language and dialects spoken in the film must be credited to dialect coach Michael Buster, who combined the style of speech as shown in books depicting the South and published in the pre-Civil War era and the alliterative prose exhibited in the King James Bible. The film was shot in seven weeks on four antebellum plantations just north of New Orleans, Louisiana, the very location where Northup had been enslaved for twelve years. Norris' historically authentic-looking costumes were elaborately researched, and she managed to find and match some clothes actually worn by slaves of that period. Unlike the more glossy and glamourized portraits of the Old South as seen in the studio productions of the 1930s-1950s, this film does not romanticize that harsh era, but presents a true image of its most likely landscapes and lifestyles, uncompromising and unforgettable. Other films depicting slaves and slavery of the Old South include **Abe Lincoln in Illinois**, 1940; **Abraham Lincoln**, 1930; **Amistad**, 1997; **Band of Angels**, 1957; **Belle Starr**, 1941; **The Birth of a Nation**, 1915; **Burn!**, 1969; **Cold Mountain**, 2003; **The Color Purple**, 1985; **Dark Command**, 1940; **Enslavement; The True Story of Fanny Kemble**, 2000 (made-for-TV); **The Foxes of Harrow**, 1947; **Gettysburg**, 1993; **Glory**, 1989; **Gods and Generals**, 2003; **Gone with the Wind**, 1939; **The Gorgeous Hussy**, 1936; **Hearts Divided**, 1936; **Her Purchase Price**, 1919; **The Horse Soldiers**, 1959; **Huckleberry Finn**, 1931; **Huckleberry Finn** [aka: **The Adventures of Huckleberry Finn**], 1939; **I Am Slave**, 2011; **Jezebel**, 1938; **John Paul Jones**, 1959; **Journey to Shiloh**, 1968; **The Legend of Nigger Charley**, 1972; **Lincoln**, 2012; **The Littlest Rebel**, 1936; **Mandingo**, 1975; **New Moon**, 1940; **North and South**, 1985 (TV miniseries); **Northwest Passage**, 1940; **The Patriot**, 2000; **The Prisoner of Shark Island**, 1936; **Ride with the Devil**, 1999; **Roots**, 1977 (TV miniseries); **Roots: The Gift**, 1988 (made-for-TV); **Santa Fe Trail**, 1940 (John Brown); **Savannah**, 2013; **The Scalphunters**, 1968; **Seven Angry Men**, 1955 (John Brown); **1776**, 1972; **Skin Game**, 1971; **The Slave Hunters**, 2010 (TV miniseries); **Slavers**, 1980; **Slaves**, 1969; **Solomon Northup's Odyssey** [aka: **Half Slave, Half Free**], 1984 (made-for-TV); **Song of Freedom**, 1936; **Souls at Sea**, 1937; **Tennessee Johnson**, 1942; **They Died with Their Boots On**, 1941; **Topsy and Eva**, 1927; **Uncle Tom's Cabin**, 1914; **Uncle Tom's Cabin**, 1918; **Uncle Tom's Cabin**, 1927; **Uncle Tom's Cabin**, 1969; and **Way Down South**, 1939. Violence, cruelty, some nudity and brief sexuality prohibit viewing by children. p, Steve McQueen, Brad Pitt, Dede Gardner, Anthony Katagas, Jeremy Kleiner, Arnon Milchan, Bill Pohlad; d, McQueen; cast, Chiwetel Ejiofor, Lupita Nyong'o, Pitt, Benedict Cumberbatch, Michael Fassbender, Sarah Paulson, Alfre Woodard, Scott McNairy, Paul Dano, Paul Giamatti, Garret Dillahunt, Taran Killam, Jay Huguley; w, John Ridley (based on the book by Solomon Northup); c, Sean Bobbitt; m, Hans Zimmer; ed, Joe Walker; prod d, Adam Stockhausen; art d, David Stein; set d, Alice Baker; spec eff, David Nash, James Gorman.

Two Days, One Night ★★★ 2014; Belgium/France/Italy; 95m; Les Films du Fleuve/Sundance; Unacceptable (MPAA: PG-13); **BD**; **DVD**. Cotillard is exceptional in playing a young Belgian wife and mother of two children who is unpopular with co-workers and management at the company for which she works. Her co-workers agree to a pay bonus in exchange for working her shift after her temporary absence. She is put on medical leave for depression, having a weekend to convince her co-workers to give up their bonuses so she can keep her job. She goes to each worker to plead for her job, painful interviews that show how hard-pressed each worker truly is and where each is struggling to survive. The workers assemble later to vote on keeping Cotillard as a fellow employee, but, of the sixteen employees, only eight vote to have her remain. The tie is broken by her employer, who says she can keep her job, but only at the expense of another worker, who will be dismissed, this worker having voted in her favor. Cotillard bravely refuses this arrangement as she has now regained enough confidence to face the future and find another job. This is a little often-seen dilemma story, but it becomes inviting and even inspirational through Cotillard's outstanding performance. The film saw mediocre box office, earning less than $10 million in its initial release. Songs: "La nuit n'en finit plus" (Jacques Plante), "Gloria" (Van Morrison), "Kili Watch" (Gus Derse, Glen Powell), "Lunch Pop" (Olivier Hauregard). Mature thematic elements prohibit viewing by children. (In French; English subtitles.) **p**, Jean-Pierre Dardenne, Luc Dardenne, Denis Freyd, Peter Bouckaert; **d&w**, Jean-Pierre Dardenne, Luc Dardenne; **cast**, Marion Cotillard, Fabrizio Rongione, Catherine Salee, Baptiste Sornin, Pili Groyne, Simon Caudry, Lara Persain, Alain Eloy, Myriem Akheddiou, Fabrienne Sciascia; **c**, Alain Marcoen; **ed**, Marie-Helene Dozo; **prod d**, Igor Gabriel.

The Two Faces of January ★★★ 2014; UK/U.S./France; 96m; Timnick Films/Studio Canal; Color; Crime Drama; Children: Unacceptable; **BD**; **DVD**. An American couple, Mortensen and Dunst, tour Greece in 1962 and visit the Acropolis in Athens where they meet Isaac, a tour guide who scams tourists. The couple invites Isaac to dinner and he accepts, impressed by their wealth and attractiveness. Mortensen is on the run for operating a Ponzi scheme in the U.S., and when a local police detective visits him, Mortensen kills him. Isaac is persuaded by Mortensen to help him and Dunst hide the officer's body, and the three of them then flee the city. They arrive in Crete where they take hotel rooms under assumed names, and Dunst begins to flirt with Isaac. Seeing this, Mortensen, enraged, throws a heavy storage container at Isaac, but it misses its mark, striking and killing Dunst. Both men flee in separate directions as they are equally sought as Dunst's killer. Mortensen flees to Paris and then to Marseille where he plans to take boat passage back to the U.S. He gets drunk in a bar, however, and is mugged and robbed, then arrested when police identify him as a wanted man. While in custody, Mortensen makes a break for freedom and is mortally shot. Before dying, he confesses to the two killings he has committed. Isaac, who has been on his trail and has also been arrested, is then set free, promising to visit Mortensen's grave, still perplexed about the enigmatic man and strange woman who had so imperiled his life. Though this film owes much to the plotline of **The Talented Mr. Ripley**, 1999, it nevertheless presents its own oddball and fascinating story line, and Mortensen, Dunst and Isaac are standouts in their peculiar roles and deep tension genuinely mounts from frame to frame. **p**, Tim Bevan, Eric Fellner, Robyn Slovo, Tom Sternberg, Caroline Hewitt; **d**, Hossein Amini; **cast**, Viggo Mortensen, Kirsten Dunst, Oscar Isaac, Daisy Bevan, Yigit Ozsener, Ozan Tas, Nikos Mavrakis, Prometheus Alefer, Brian Niblett, James Sobol Kelly; **w**, Amini (based on the novel by Patricia Highsmith); **c**, Marcel Zyskind; **m**, Alberto Iglesias; **ed**, Nicolas Chaudeurge, Jon Harris; **prod d**, Michael Carlin; **art d**, Patrick Rolfe, Alex Baily; **set d**, Dominic Capon; **spec eff**, Stuart Lashley.

2 Guns ★★★ 2013; U.S.; 109m; UNIV; Color; Crime/Comedy; Children: Unacceptable (MPAA: PG-13); **BD**; **DVD**. Washington is effective as an undercover DEA government agent, who takes advantage of gunman Wahlberg's idea to rob a bank so as to arrest a mob boss. The caper nets them more money than they expected, while Washington's forces fail to stop their getaway. Wahlberg is really a U.S. Navy intelligence agent who shoots Washington and takes the money. The two men then find themselves involved in corrupt rivalries as they are hunted and blackmailed for the loot on both sides of the law. They now have to work together to find a way out. Though somewhat clichéd, the film provides enough action and taut scenes to sustain interest throughout, albeit Washington's persona seems to be part of the clichés as he reprises the same role over and over again. Songs: "Divorciada" (Andrew Gonzales), "Sacrifice" (Nicholas McCarrell), "Entregate" (Matt Hirt, Marc Ferrari, Francisco Rodriguez), "Crazy Things" (Nicholas McCarrell, Nicole Leidinger), "Mi Corazon Mi Amor" (Lionel Wendling), "Two Against One" and "All the Blues I Need" (Jai Josefs), "Are You Ready

Kirsten Dunst in *The Two Faces of January,* **2014.**

for Me?" (Dave Bassett, Tim Myers). Violence, gutter language and brief nudity prohibit viewing by children. **p**, Andrew Cosby, Randall Emmett, George Furla, Norton Herrick, Marc Platt, Ross Richie, Adam Siegel, Brandon Grimes, Jeff Rice; **d**, Baltasar Kormakur; **cast**, Denzel Washington, Mark Wahlberg, Paula Patton, Edward James Olmos, Bill Paxton, James Marsden, Robert John Burke, Greg Sproles, Fred Ward, Patrick Fischler; **w**, Blake Masters (based on the Boom! Studios graphic novels by Steven Gant); **c**, Oliver Wood; **m**, Clinton Shorter; **ed**, Michael Tronick; **prod d**, Beth Mickle; **art d**, Kevin Hardison; **set d**, Leonard Spears; **spec eff**, James Lorimer, Ron Trost, Eric Kimelton.

Jack O'Connell in *Unbroken*, 2014.

Unbroken ★★★★ 2014; U.S.; 137m; 3 Arts Entertainment/UNIV; Color; Biographical Drama; Children: Unacceptable; MPAA: PG-13; **BD**; **DVD**. This fine dramatization profiles the life of Louis Zamperini (1917-2014), played by O'Connell, a 1936 Olympic 5000-meter distance runner who joined the U.S. Army Air Corps in September 1941, four months before the Japanese attack on Pearl Harbor December 7. He was commissioned a second lieutenant, serving as a bombardier during World War II (1939-1945). His Consolidated B-24 Liberator bomber is on a mission to search for some pilots missing in a raid and it crashes into the ocean 850 miles south of Oahu, Hawaii. He is among three survivors of eight men aboard and they become adrift at sea on a life raft, subsisting on rainwater and small fish eaten raw, threatened by sharks and strafed by Japanese planes. One of O'Connell's two crewmates, Francis McNamara, played by Writtrock, dies after thirty-three days at sea. On their forty-seventh day adrift at sea, O'Connell and Russell Phillips played by Gleeson, reach an island in the Marshall Islands held by the Japanese and are captured and sent to a prisoner of war camp at Ofuna. At the camp, O'Connell runs afoul of a sadistic guard, Mutsuhiro Watanabe (1918-2003), played by Ishihara (Miyavi), a corporal nicknamed "Bird" (as in bird of prey) by POWs. Ishihara viciously beats O'Connell, ostensibly prompted by jealousy over O'Connell's Olympic status. At one point, however, O'Connell is given a reprieve and taken to comfortable quarters in Tokyo where he is allowed to speak over the radio to announce to his relatives that he is alive and well as a prisoner in Japan. While he is later eating in a spacious restaurant, O'Connell is asked by Japanese intelligence agents (Kempei Tai, Japanese secret police), to make another radio announcement, and they present him with a script that indicts the U.S. as an aggressor nation, along with other propaganda. O'Connell, after reading the script, tells his hosts that he cannot read such statements. They then threaten to send him back to an oppressive POW camp unless he cooperates. They point out what appears to be some U.S. Army officers sitting at a far table and enjoying a lavish lunch, telling O'Connell that these men have cooperated and have made such statements and they are now enjoying a luxurious life. (One might as-

sume that these were actors to convince O'Connell to join him in betraying his country.) O'Connell, however, utterly refuses to become a propaganda tool for the Japanese and he is transferred to a POW camp in northern Japan where, to his horror, he again meets Ishihara, who is now a sergeant and who resumes his sadistic punishment against O'Connell. The brutal treatment Ishihara exacts against O'Connell is savage and unrelenting, but O'Connell displays his will to live and defies Ishihara by standing up to these horrific tortures. O'Connell finally embarrasses his tormentor by standing for hours with a huge beam of wood on his shoulders, refusing to collapse under its terrible weight. (It was the custom for Japanese guards to mercilessly beat POWs until they collapsed and screamed in pain and where that punishment would renew. Those who did not shout out and remained standing under such beatings were left alone by the guards after a certain number of required blows were administered.) O'Connell amazingly survives the incredible hardships of his POW camp until the war's end in 1945. Ishihara, who (as was Watanabe in real life) is listed as one of the most wanted Japanese war criminals, disappears. At first listed as missing at sea, O'Connell finally returns home in California to a hero's welcome. He marries and, remembering how his faith in God enabled him to survive, becomes an Evangelical Christian speaker, forgiving his captors, even Ishihara. O'Connell returns to Japan and tries to visit Ishihara, who has escaped punishment through U.S. amnesty. Ishihara (like Watanabe), however, refuses to see O'Connell, and this is where this superbly crafted film ends. O'Connell is wholly empathetic in the role of the courageous Zampirini, underplaying his character with quiet resolve, a pensive characterization that marvelously counterbalances the overt and brutal acts of his oppressors, especially that of Ishihara, who also gives a horrific portrayal as an utterly bestial human monster. Actress Jolie directs this film with an unerring eye to detail while seamlessly presenting the tale with vigor, wisely inserting scenes that relax the unsettling tension that nevertheless mounts to the crescendo of O'Connell's ultimate defiance at the risk of his life. She is both brilliant and unflinching in her portrayal of man's inhumanity to man, and O'Connell, Ishihara and the rest of the cast present outstanding performances that convince the viewer of their characters' authenticity. The script is realistic and the dialog natural while Deakins' cinematography wonderfully captures the broad and bloody saga of war and the misery of the POW lifestyle. Desplat's score is as bold and brash as the spectacular scenes it underscores with lower register definition. The film received Oscar nominations for Best Cinematography (Deakins); Best Sound Editing (Becky Sullivan, Andrew DeCristofaro); and Best Sound Mixing (Jon Taylor, David Lee, Frank A. Montano). The film was a hit at the box office, earning more than $163.4 million in its initial release against a budget of more than $65 million. Song: "Miracles" (Guy Berryman, Jon Buckland, Will Champion, Chris Martin). ***Author's Note***: A few days before his eighty-first birthday, former Olympian Zampirini ran a leg in the torch relay at the Winter Olympics in January 1998 at Nagano, Japan, ironically close to the very POW camp housing him in WWII. At that time, he attempted to see Watanabe, but the former Japanese war criminal refused to meet with the man he had so horribly abused more than a half century earlier. After Japan surrendered and the U.S. occupied that country, General Douglas MacArthur (1880-1964) listed Watanabe as number twenty-three in importance of Japanese war criminals. Watanabe had subjected many POWs to savage punishments. He forced a man with only undergarments to sit in freezing weather for four days. He tied a sixty-five-year-old prisoner to tree and kept him there for several days. He ordered another prisoner to report to him every day to be punched in the face for three weeks. He selected an appendectomy patient upon which to practice judo, leaping upon and kicking this patient's abdomen. He reportedly caused the permanent disfigurement and deaths of several prisoners. By that time, Watanabe went into hiding, being moved about and shielded by cronies of Japan's old military regime. To establish a permanent peace with Japan, U.S. officials, years later, granted amnesty to those war criminals still being sought and Watanabe emerged from hiding. He had been using an alias as a flourishing businessman. He never admitted his atrocities and this film was initially banned in Japan, but later released to a very limited number of theaters. Many Japanese nationalists denounced this film as false and even branded it "immoral," but the staggering amount of documented evidence proving the atrocities chronicled in this film and elsewhere is profound and wholly substantiated. Sadly, Zampirini never saw this film about his heroic ordeal, dying of pneumonia in his Los Angeles home at the age of ninety-seven on July 2, 2014, five months before this outstanding film was released. Other films depicting Allied POWs held in Japanese prison camps include **Back to Bataan**, 1945 (begins with the spectacular raid against the Japanese POW camp at Cabanatuan, Luzon, Philippines, where more than 500 prisoners were rescued on April 30, 1945); **Battle of the Coral Sea**, 1959 (base on the USS *Perch*, a submarine that was depth-charged by Japanese ships and captured in 1942, its crew held in a Japanese prison camp, along with Australian POWs, and where some escape); **The Bridge on the River Kwai**, 1957 (British troops in a Japanese POW camp in Burma, 1942-1943); **The Camp on Blood Island**, 1958 (Japanese POW camp holding British captives in Malaya); **Empire of the Sun**, 1987 (Allied prisoners in Shanghai, 1939-1945); **The Great Raid**, 2005 (details the spectacular raid against a Japanese POW camp at Cabanatuan, Luzon, Philippines, where more than 500 prisoners were rescued on April 30, 1945); **King Rat**, 1965 (Allied POWs in Malaysia); **The Longest Hundred Miles**, 1967 (Allied prisoners in the Philippines); **Merry Christmas, Mr. Lawrence**, 1983 (British soldiers in a Japanese POW camp); **Paradise Road**, 1997 (Allied female POWs held in a Japanese prison camp); **The Purple Heart**, 1944 (Doolittle Raid against Japan, April 18, 1942; U.S. airmen tried for the attack held in a Japanese prison); **The Railway Man**, 2014 (British captives in Japanese POW camp, who are used as laborers to build the Thai-Burma Railway); **Return from the River Kwai**, 1989 (British POWs in Burma); **The Secret of Blood Island**, 1965 (British soldiers in a Japanese POW camp aid a female agent to escape); **7 Women from Hell**, 1961 (Allied women captives in a Japanese POW camp); **Three Came Home**, 1950 (British male and female captives in Japanese POW camps); **Women of Valor**, 1986 (made-for-TV; U.S. Army nurses captured on Bataan and Corregidor, who are held as POWs in a Japanese prison camp). Violence, brutality and gutter language prohibit viewing by children. **p**, Matthew Baer, Angelina Jolie, Erwin Stoff, Clayton Townsend, Joseph P. Reidy, **d**, Jolie; **cast**, Jack O'Connell, Domhnall Gleeson, Garrett Hedlund, Takamasa Ishihara (Miyavi), Finn Wittrock, Jai Courtney, Maddalena Ischiale, Vincenzo Amato; **w**, Joel Coen, Ethan Coen, Richard LaGravenese, William Nicholson (based on the book by Laura Hillenbrand); **c**, Roger Deakins; **m**, Alexandre Desplat; **ed**, William Goldenberg, Tim Squyers; **prod d**, Jon Hutman; **art d**, Charlie Revai, Bill Booth, Jacinta Leong; **set d**, Lisa Thompson; **spec eff**, Leanne Brooks, Brian Cox, Clint Ingram.

Unfinished Song ★★★ 2012; U.K./Germany; 93m; Steel Mill Pictures/Weinstein Co.; Color; Comedy/Drama/Music; Children: Unacceptable (MPAA: PG-13); **BD**; **DVD**. Stamp is a shy, grumpy London pensioner who nevertheless deeply loves his ailing wife, Redgrave. To please her, he reluctantly attends her local unconventional senior's church choir, but he is not impressed by some of its contemporary songs, some of which he finds distasteful. When the choir, led by Arterton, arrives at his home to serenade the terminally ill Redgrave, Stamp takes exception. Redgrave grows so ill that she can no longer serve in the choir, and Stamp attempts to share her passion for performing in her place by joining the choir. Stamp is surprised to see that his attendance is therapeutic in that this helps him to reconcile with his estranged son, Eccleston. At the same time, the choir director, Arterton, persuades him that he can find a new joy in life as he undertakes both a personal and musical journey into self-discovery that will prepare him for a life without Redgrave. Sensitive and telling, this film is wonderfully enacted by Stamp and Redgrave, and Arterton and Eccleston give strong support to a moving story. Director Williams carefully presents this heartwarm-

Kirsten Bell in *Veronica Mars,* 2014.

ing story while avoiding mawkish pitfalls, and he fully develops its appealing characters. The film earned about $7 million in its initial release. Songs: "True Colours" (Tom Kelly, Billy Steinberg), "The Most Beautiful Girl" (Rory Bourke, Billy Sherrill, Norris Wilson), "Lullaby/Goodnight My Angel" (Billy Joel), "Unfinished Songs" (Diane Warren), "Nowhere to Run" (1965; Lamont Dozier, Brian Holland, Edward Holland Jr.), "You Are the Sunshine of My Life" (1972; Stevie Wonder), "All These Years" and "Cabbage" (Paul Osborne, Spencer Chrisham, Torq Pagdin), "Ain't Nobody" (1983; David Wolinski), "How Do You Speak to an Angel" (1952; music: Jule Styne; lyrics: Bob Hilliard), "Love Shack" (1989; Fred Schneider, Keith Strickland, Cynthia Wilson), "Crazy" (2006; Thomas Decarlo Callaway, Brian Joseph Burton, Gianfranco Reverberi, Gian Piero Reverberi), "Opera of Love" (2012; Daniel Steer), "Let's Talk About Sex" (1990; Herbie Azor), "Ace of Spades" (1980; Fast Eddie Clarke, Lemmy, Philip John Taylor), "Something's Got a Hold on Me" (1962; Etta James, Leroy Kirkland, Pearl Woods), "Mohair Sam" (Dallas Frazier), "Cabbage" (Paul Osborne). *Author's Note*: Though the setting is London, the film was shot in about seven weeks on location at Durham and Newcastle upon Tyne. Sexual references and rude gestures prohibit viewing by children. **p**, Ken Marshall, Philip Moross, Christopher Billows, Rachel Dargavel, Jens Meurer; **d&w**, Paul Andrew Williams; **cast**, Terence Stamp, Vanessa Redrave, Gemma Arterton, Christopher Eccleston, Barry Martin, Taru Devani, Anne Reid, Elizabeth Counsell, Ram John Holder, Denise Rubens; **c**, Carlos Catalan; **m**, Laura Rossi; **ed**, Daniel Farrell; **prod d**, Sophie Becher; **art d**, Keith Slote; **set d**, Stella Fox; **spec eff**, Hayden Jones, Jonathan Privett.

Veronica Mars ★★★ 2014; U.S.; 107m; WB; Color; Mystery; Children: Unacceptable (MPAA: PG-13); **BD**; **DVD**. A few years after teenage private detective Mars, played by Bell, gives up that "Nancy Drew" sideline, she returns to her hometown for her 10th high school reunion. There she learns that her former boyfriend, Dohring, now a U.S. Navy lieutenant, is accused of murdering his girlfriend, who became a pop star, and her murder may be connected to the death of that woman's best friend, a woman last seen on a boat at sea nine years earlier. Bell also reunites with her father, Colantoni, the town's former sheriff, who has become a private investigator, and tells her how corrupt his replacement, O'Connell, has become. Though she does not intend to stay long in her hometown, she begins to investigate the case. With the help of Colantoni, she begins to unearth clues that prove that Dohring has been framed while she begins a romance with the accused young man. Further, Colantoni, while getting information from one of O'Con-

Paul Rudd and Jennifer Aniston in *Wanderlust*, 2012.

nell's deputies, is critically injured and the deputy killed. Bell decides that the pop star was murdered because she threatened to identify the killer of her best friend many years earlier. She not only entraps the mastermind behind the killings, but lures him to a basement where she knocks him unconscious with a golf club and then awaits police to make the arrest. Having solved the crime, Bell decides to remain in town and take over her father's private investigations into local corruption. Lively whodunit sees an exceptional performance from Bell, and she receives strong support from a talented cast. The inventive script provides many darkly amusing scenes, and is both witty and intelligent. Unfortunately, this film did poorly at the box office, earning a little more than $3.5 million in its initial release against a budget of $6 million. Songs: "We Used to Be Friends" (Takashi Hirose, Jon Lee, Grant Nicholas, Courtney Taylor-Taylor), "Go Captain and Pinlighter" (Chad R. Matheny), "All the Drunks Say Amen" (John Croslin), "Holding My Breath" and "All Around and Away We Go" (Ubdhav Gupta, Andrea Estella, Eric Cardona, Gabel D'Amico, Bryan Ujueta), "Face Off" (Jason Katalbas, Jason Rabinowitz, Colton Fisher), "If You Wanna Shine" (Kyle Andrews, Neil Mason, Lauren Ross), "Criminal" (Dan Auerbach, Evan Bogart, Bernard Freeman, Freddie Gibbs, Evan Ingersoll, Brendan Joyce, Jonathan Keller, Richard Parry, Zsuzsanna Ward, Charles Worth), "She's Bad" (Salim B. Akram, Santiago Araujo, Fredna Baakye, Sheel M. Dave, Jayson Dezuzio, Maxwell G. Masser, Richard P. Thompson), "Chicago" (Sufjan Stevens), "I Got You Babe" (Sonny Bono), "The Cut" (Erica Quitzow), "We Own the Club" (Joe Faraci), "Dangerous" (Daniel Armbruster, Alan Wilkis), "Unafraid" (Jon Dee Graham), "Crystal Ball" (Kyle Adrews), "Stick Up" (Max Schneider, Jacob Scott Sinclair, John Colley), "Never Give In" (Ben Braun, Ian Mackintosh), "Catch Me If You Can" (Drew Lerdal), "Hyperflowers" (Jose Diogo, Santos Tornada), "Analog Girls" (Matt Masurka), "True to You" (John Clayton), "Happy at Your Gate" (Erika Spring Forster), "Prosthetic Love" (Kyle Morton), "Second Chances" (Gregory Alan Isakov, Ilan Isakov), "You'll Never Find Another Love Like Mine" (Kenny Gamble, Leon Huff), "O Canada" Sexuality, drug use, violence and gutter language prohibit viewing by children. **p**, Rob Thomas, Dan Etheridge, Danielle Stokdyk; **d**, Thomas; **cast**, Kristen Bell, Jason Dohring, Jerry O'Connell, Jamie Lee Curtis, Enrico Colantoni, Martin Starr, Chris Lowell, Percy Daggs III, Tina Majorino, Ryan Hansen, Ryan Lane; **w**, Thomas, Diane Ruggiero (based on a story by Thomas); **c**, Ben Kutchins; **m**, Josh Kramon; **ed**, Daniel Gabbe; **prod d**, Jeff Schoen; **art d**, Elizabeth Cummings; **set d**, Cindy Coburn; **spec eff**, Chris Nelson, Jacob Eaton, Gary Oldroyd, Renee Reizman.

Victor Frankenstein ★★★ 2015; U.S.; 109m; Davis Entertainment; FOX; Color; Horror; Children: Unacceptable (MPAA: PG-13); **BD**; **DVD**. This inventive horror entry takes a new approach in the telling of the Frankenstein story, one told from the perspective of Igor Strausman, played by Radcliffe, the troubled young assistant to a young medical student, Victor Von Frankenstein, who is played by McAvoy. Radcliffe becomes an eyewitness to the procedure by which McAvoy creates his monster. They share a noble desire to aid humanity through their groundbreaking research into immortality by creating life from parts of dead bodies. McAvoy, however, becomes obsessed with his work, and only Radcliffe can bring him back from the brink of madness. Nevertheless, McAvoy cannot be stopped, and his obsession has horrifying consequences in bringing to life his monster, Dance, who renders a truly frightening performance as the creature. Although this outing does not compare with the classic films about the monster, it nevertheless provides an incisive and fresh approach to what is an undying subject. The film earned more than $32 million in its initial release against a budget of more than $40 million. Macabre images, violence and sequence of destruction prohibit viewing by children. **p**, John Davis, Mairi Bett; **d**, Paul McGuigan; **cast**, Daniel Radcliffe, James McAvoy, Charles Dance, Jessica Brown Findlay, Bronson Webb, Daniel Mays, Spencer Wilding, Robin Pearce, Andrew Scott, Callum Turner, Di Botcher, Will Keen, Alistair Petrie; **w**, Max Landis (based on his story and characters created by Mary Shelley in her novel *Frankenstein*); **c**, Fabian Wagner; **m**, Craig Armstrong; **ed**, Andrew Hulme, Charlie Phillips; **prod d**, Eve Stewart; **art d**, Grant Armstrong, Oliver Carroll, Tom Weaving; **set d**, Michael Standish; **spec eff**, Paul Dimmer.

The Walk ★★★ 2015; U.S.; 123m; ImageMovers/Sony; Color; Adventure; Children: Unacceptable (MPAA: PG-13); **BD**; **DVD**. Based on true events, French high-wire walker Philippe Petit, played by Gordon-Levitt, recruits a team of people to help him realize his dream, to walk the long void between the World Trade Center towers, 110 stories above Wall Street in New York City. Guided by his mentor Papa Rudy, portrayed by Kingsley (who aids in providing expert knot-tying and rope rigging), and helped by some international recruits, he and his associates overcome long odds, betrayals, dissension, and many close calls to conceive and execute their plan. At first, Gordon-Levitt is evicted from his home because he is thought to be a loafer with no job or income and earns meager tips while juggling as a street performer. He goes to a circus where he practices his juggling and is seen by Kingsley, who takes him under his avuncular wing. He meets Le Bon, an attractive girl who, like himself, is a street performer, and the two have a romance, and Gordon-Levitt tells her of his dream to someday walk a wire between the Twin Towers in NYC. She encourages that dream, but, in his first trial, Gordon-Levitt falls into a lake. He next successfully scrambles over the heights of Notre Dame Cathedral in Paris, but is arrested for his daring feat. Undaunted, Gordon-Levitt, along with Le Bon and his supporters, travels to NYC to attempt his historic walkover between the two towers on a cable. In what is a breathtaking sequence, Gordon-Levitt and his crew manage to string the cable between the Twin Towers on the morning of August 7, 1974, and the twenty-four-year-old wire walker successfully walks the cable between the two towers while thousands in the streets below cheer and urge him onward and as police order him to desist and even threaten to remove him with a helicopter. His performance takes forty-five minutes, using a custom-made 26-foot long cable and a 55-pound balancing pole. Not only does Gordon-Levitt (as did Petit) successfully walk the cable from one tower to the next, but he walks back again, and even kneels to his audience and, at one point, lies down on the cable. Following his stunning performance, Gordon-Levitt is arrested, but he is soon released on his promise that he will not again attempt another such hazardous feat. The film ends with the manager of the Twin Towers giving him a free pass to the observation decks of both towers, the camera closing on the pass, and where the expiration date has been crossed out and replaced with the word "Forever." The acting is superior and the photography (Imax and 3D) is amazing, albeit anyone with a fear of heights might want to pause before viewing this astounding film (one which, most likely, would never have been produced by director Alfred Hitchcock, who was deathly afraid of heights). The film did well at the box office, earning more than $61 million in its initial release against a budget of more than $35 million. *Author's Note*: Police dropped all charges against Petit in exchange for his performing a high-wire performance in Central Park for children. Since then this accomplished aerialist has performed wire walking as part of official celebrations in the U.S. and abroad. Other films depicting high-wire or tight-rope walkers include **Berserk**, 1967; **Billy Rose's Jumbo**, 1962; **Boot Hill**, 1969; **Butch and Sundance: The Early Days**, 1979; **Capricious Summer**, 1968; **The Circus**, 1928; **Circus Girl**, 1937; **Circus World**, 1964; **The Dark Tower**, 1943; **Delightfully Dangerous**, 1945; **Elvira Madigan**, 1967; **Fixer Dugan**, 1939; **The Flame of New Orleans**, 1941; **Flesh and Fantasy**, 1943; **The Great Wallendas**, 1978 (made-for-TV); **The Greatest Show on Earth**, 1952; **Here Come the Girls**, 1953; **Homicide for Three**, 1948; **Invitation to the Dance**, 1956; **King of the Carnival**, 1955; **La Strada**, 1956; **The Little Adventuress**, 1938; **Little Big Top**, 2006; **Looking for Cheyenne**, 2005; **Madagascar 3: Europe's Most Wanted**, 2012; **The Monster**, 1925; **My Friend Joe**, 1996; **New York Stories**, 1989; **Obsession**, 1997; **One from the Heart**, 1981; **Pippi on the Run**, 1977; **The Pirate**, 1948; **Ring of Fear**, 1954; **Road to Rio**, 1947; **Roseanna's Grave**, 1997; **Save the Green Planet**, 2003; **Starstruck**, 1982; **Still Life**, 2006; **The Story of Three Loves**, 1953; **Swashbuckler**, 1976; **Tarzan's Desert Mystery**, 1943; **The Twelve Tasks of Asterix**, 1976; and **Van Helsing**, 2004. Thematic elements involving peril, gutter language, brief drug references and smoking prohibit viewing by children. **p**, Robert Zemeckis, Jack Rapke, Tom Rothman, Steve Starkey; **d**, Zemeckis; **cast**, Joseph Gordon-Levitt, Ben Kingsley, Charlotte Le Bon, Martin Lefebvre, Philippe Bertrand, Patrick Baby, Soleyman Pierini, Marie Turgeon; **w**, Zemeckis, Christopher Browne (based on the book *To Reach the Clouds* by Petit); **c**, Dariusz Wolski; **m**, Alan Silvestri; **ed**, Jeremiah O'Driscoll; **prod d**, Naomi Shohan; **art d**, Felix Lariviere-Charron; **set d**, Ann Smart; **spec eff**, Ryal Cosgrove.

A Walk among the Tombstones ★★★ 2014; U.S.; 113m; 1984 Private Defense Contractors/UNIV; Color; Crime Drama; Children: Unacceptable (MPAA: R); **BD**; **DVD**. Neeson is a former New York City police detective, who is now a recovering alcoholic and is haunted by regrets both professional and personal. He feels guilty over his services as a NYPD detective. In one instance, a young girl was killed in crossfire during a gunfight when he pursued robbers in a tavern holdup. While attending an Alcoholics Anonymous meeting, he is introduced to Stevens, a fellow addict who is a Brooklyn drug trafficker. Stevens hires him to find two men who abducted and then killed his wife. Stevens has already paid for her ransom, but, after the kidnappers led him to a car to see his wife's butchered body inside the trunk, he now wants bloody revenge. Neeson takes on the case as an unlicensed private detective and tracks suspects through the boroughs, reading up on old cases in the New York City Public Library archives and simply wandering the streets. He is helped in his investigation by Bradley, a homeless teenager who sleeps in the library and does Internet research. This leads them to discover that a pattern is in place where for months two kidnappers have been targeting the wives of drug dealers, who are unlikely to go to the police, despite always viciously killing their captors once payment of ransom has been received. They later learn that the kidnapper-killers are a gay couple, Harbour and Thompson, whose motives for the violence are never revealed. The film ends with a shootout in which the killers are themselves killed. Though the script is somewhat predictable, its usual twists and turns provide mounting tension throughout. Further, Neeson, Bradley and rest of the cast members render superior performances and are believable while enacting their lowlife characters. The film saw healthy returns at the box office, earning more than $58.8 mil-

Alan Alda in *Wanderlust*, 2012.

lion in its initial release against a budget of more than $28 million. Songs: "Atlantis" (Donovan Leitch), "Carrie-Anne" (Alan Clarke, Tony Hicks, Graham Nash), "Crank" (Dror Mohar), "Black Hole Sun" (Chris Cornell). Excessive violence, disturbing images, gutter language and brief nudity prohibit viewing by children. **p**, Tobin Armbrust, Danny DeVito, Brian Oliver, Michael Shamberg, Stacey Sher, Christopher Goode, Jillian Longnecker, Steven Chester Prince; **d&w**, Scott Frank (based on the novel by Lawrence Block); **cast**, Liam Neeson, Dan Stevens, David Harbour, Adam David Thompson, Brian Bradley, Maurice Compte, Patrick McDade, Laura Birn, Eric Nelsen, Razsane Jammal, Al Nazemian; **c**, Mihai Malaimare Jr.; **m**, Carlos Rafael Rivera; **ed**, Jill Savitt; **prod d**, David Brisbin; **art d**, Jonathan Arkin; **set d**, Cherish M. Hale; **spec eff**, Jeff Brink, Kevin Zack.

The Wall ★★★ 2012; Austria/Germany; 108m; Coop99 Filmproduktion/Music Box Films; Color; Drama/Fantasy; Children: Unacceptable; **DVD**. Gedeck finds herself inexplicably cut off from all human contact when an invisible, unyielding wall suddenly surrounds the countryside. Accompanied by her dog, the woman becomes immersed in a world untouched by civilization and ruled by the laws of nature. She approaches a farmhouse, but cannot reach it, two of its occupants seeming to be frozen in time. She finds a cow and leads it along with her, realizing that the animal is a burden, but will nevertheless provide milk. She then locates a car and attempts to drive it from the area, but it crashes into the invisible wall, preventing her from going further. Gedeck accepts her isolated fate, gathering wood for fires at night and planting potatoes. During the warm days of the summer, she crosses off each day on a calendar, following the routine of her former, normal life. In the fall, she harvests the potato crop. As winter approaches, she climbs to a high lodge and takes refuge there, along with the cow, and a cat. The cat gives birth to kittens and the cow delivers a calf. The following spring, Gedeck sees a man in the distance killing the calf and her dog with an ax and she shoots and kills the stranger, rolling his body over a cliff. She, the cow and the cat then retreat to the lodge to spend another winter season and where she ends her written narrative since she has run out of paper upon which to write. This film is a poetic and beautifully photographed production about isolation and nature in which Gedeck gives a tour de force performance, translating her situation through a diary that she keeps, documenting the events of the strange event, a film that is part adventurous survival and part existential allegory, with a dash of psychological horror. This offbeat experimental film did poorly at the box office, earning $1.2 million in its initial release, but it is worth the watching. Not related to the 1983 film with the same name. **p**, Wasiliki Bleser, Rainer Kolmel, Antonin Svoboda, Bruno Wagner; **d**, Julian Polsler; **cast**, Martina Gedeck, Karl Heinz Hackl, Ulrike Beimpold, Julia Gschnitzer,

Paul Rudd and Joe Lo Truglio in *Wanderlust*, **2012.**

Hans-Michael Rehberg, Wolfgang M. Bauer; **w**, Polsler (based on the novel by Marlen Haushofer); **c**, Markus Fraunholz, Martin Gschlacht, Bernhard Keller, Helmut Pirnat, Hans Selikovsky, Richi Wagner; **ed**, Thomas Kohler, Bettina Mazakarini; **prod d**, Hajo Schwarz; **spec eff**, Nina Knott, Marco Pelzel.

Wanderlust ★★★ 2012; U.S.; 98m; A Hot Dog/UNIV; Color; Comedy; Children: Unacceptable (MPAA: R); **BD**; **DVD**; **IV**. Aniston has ambitions of becoming a filmmaker, so she persuades her husband, Rudd, to buy a high-priced Manhattan loft apartment where she will work on a documentary about the lives of penguins. She hopes to sell the film to HBO to pay for the apartment and filming equipment. HBO rejects the film and, because of a poor economy in the country, they sell the apartment at a big financial loss. Rudd loses his job and can't find a new one. Marino, Rudd's brother, offers him a job with his company in Atlanta, so he and Aniston drive there. On the way, they stop for a night at a hotel called the Elysium, which they discover is a haven for hippies and vegetarians. They see Truglio, a naked man, running toward their car in the parking lot, and Rudd gets there first to try to get him and Aniston away, but, in doing so, the car overturns. The hotel owners invite the distraught couple to stay, but they go on to Atlanta. There, Rudd has an argument with arrogant Marino and decides he can't work with his brother, so he and Aniston return to the Elysium. They take a room there and Aniston likes the place because the hippies practice free love, but Rudd disapproves. Meanwhile, Aniston flirts with a hippie and a free-loving girl tries to seduce Rudd. They become enmeshed with these sex-crazed wackos, but finally bring their lives to some order when they write a book together, a thriller, that becomes a success. Anything that can go wrong certainly does in this hectic comedy, where Aniston and Rudd are as much the same kind of impossible victims as Jack Lemmon and Sandy Dennis in **The Out of Towners**, 1970. Aniston and Rudd, however, inadvertently create much of their own self-styled mayhem in what is nevertheless a very funny, albeit crude story. The film earned more than $21.6 million in its initial release, failing to recoup its $35 million budget. Not related to a 2001 film with the same title. Songs: "Get Your Body," "Higher and Higher," "Old Enough," "Black Water," "Jesus Is Just Alright," "Ways of the Wind," (Craig Wedren, Theodore Shapiro); "Bushlands" (Murray Burns, Colin Bayley); "Driver 8," "Home," "Two Princes," "Underdog," "Save the Land," "I Come Tumblin'," "Never Been to Spain," "Hazy World" (Dominic Glover, Gary James Crockett, Jay Stuart Glover); "Just Don't" (Robert Lester Hardenbrook); "Stella Theme," "Stoned A" (Paul Lenart); "The Big Reunion" (Dan Radlauer); "Groovy Times," "The Real Housewives of Atlanta Theme"); "The Beat Goes On," "Love Take Me Down To the Streets"); "Requiem" (George Andersen); "Two Princes" (Spin Doctors).

Sexual content, graphic male and female frontal nudity, gutter language and drug use prohibit viewing by children. **p**, Judd Apatow, Ken Marino, Paul Rudd, David Wain; **d**, Wain; **cast**, Paul Rudd, Jennifer Aniston, Marino, Justin Theroux, Alan Alda, Malin Akerman, Joe Lo Truglio, Kathryn Hahn, Kerri Kenney-Silver, Lauren Ambrose, Michaela Watkins, Wain; **w**, Wain, Marino; **c**, Michael Bonvillain; **m**, Craig Wedren; **ed**, David Moritz, Robert Nassau; **prod d**, Aaron Osborne; **art d**, Erin Cochran; **set d**, Jennifer M. Gentile; **spec eff**, Robert Vazquez, Eric A . Martin.

Welcome to Me ★★★ 2015; U.S.; 87m; Bron/Alchemy; Color; Comedy/Drama; Children: Unacceptable (MPAA: R); **BD**; **DVD**, **IV**. Wiig is a young woman with a borderline personality disorder who has her television on night and day for years, and wins $86 million dollars in a lottery. She wants the world to know who she is, so she appears on a television show but is cut off when she begins talking about her personal sexual life. Wiig angrily recoils by spending some of her money to pay two brothers, Marsden and Bentley, who are would-be TV producers, to helm her own television show called "Welcome to Me," intending the show to be autobiographical and spontaneous. This leads to a relationship with co-producer Bentley and they have sex together. The offbeat television show starts out badly, but then becomes popular, although it alienates her from her best friend, Cardinelli, when she states on the show that Cardellini is fat. Mann, a graduate student, interviews Wiig about her sudden fame and they have sex in a limousine, which is secretly recorded and aired. She shows how dogs are neutered live on her show and this is the last straw for Bentley and he quits. The show is then served with lawsuits for slander and Wiig loses all but $7 million of her lottery money. She suffers a nervous breakdown at a casino by walking naked among the stunned patrons. She is hospitalized, but later released and hosts a telethon to find owners for the dogs she has had neutered, then apologizes to everyone, including Cardellini, and to thank her for being her best friend, giving her all that is left of her lottery money. She then goes home and turns off the television she has had on night and day for more than eleven years. Offbeat and often hilariously disturbing, the moral lesson of this film is that money not only corrupts but can easily send its owners to an asylum. Wiig gives a bravura performance of a disturbed woman who becomes even more disturbed after riches and weird fame engulf her. Her ridiculous antics provide both mirth and sorrow in this well-crafted and incisively written tale. Songs: "Where Is My Mind," "Happy Talk," "Brubecking," "Bossa Me," "Girl," "Wes Time," "The Happiest Girl in the Whole U.S.A.," Good Dreams," "Catch a Falling Star," "Sun," "This Is My Time," "Django," "Ozma," "I'll Be Around," "ESP Switch" (David Robbins). Sexual content, some graphic nudity, gutter language and brief drug use prohibit viewing by children. **p**, Jessica Elbaum, Will Ferrell, Aaron L. Gilbert, Marina Grasic, Adam McKay, Kristen Wiig; **d**, Shira Piven; **cast**, Kristen Wiig, James Marsden, Joan Cusack, Tim Robbins, Wes Bentley, Linda Cardellini, Loretta Devine, Jennifer Jason Leigh, Thomas Mann, Alan Tudyk, Mitch Silpa, Jeremy Piven (voice only); **w**, Eliot Lawrence; **c**, Eric Alan Edwards; **m**, David Robbins; **ed**, Josh Salzberg, Kevin Tent; **prod d**, Clayton Hartley; **art d**, Andres Cubillan; **set d**, Jan Pascale; **spec eff**, Josh Hakian, Chris Cline.

The Well-Digger's Daughter ★★★ 2012; France; 107m; Les Films Alain Sarde/Kino Lorber; Color; Drama; Children: Unacceptable; MPAA: R; **BD**; **DVD**. Auteuil, a hardworking well-digger, is left a widower when his wife dies and leaves him with six daughters in the south of France before World War I (1914-1918). A wealthy woman takes an interest in his second oldest daughter, Berges-Frisbey, and pays for her to come to Paris and attend a convent school. Berges-Frisbey returns home when she is eighteen to help Auteuil with her siblings. Auteuil hopes she will marry his longtime employee, Merad, who takes her to town in his small new car where she meets Duvauchelle, the handsome son of the owner of a general store. Berges-Frisbey and Duvauchelle fall in love at first sight, but they are from different social classes. His parents, Azema and Darroussin, reject her as being the daughter of a well-digger. No matter, the young people are in love and she becomes pregnant as Duvauchelle is called into service by the French air force and sent to Africa. Berges-Frisbey thinks she has been abandoned, so she tells Merad about her condition and he offers to marry her. She turns down the offer, a selfless act in that she believes one of her younger sisters is in love with Merad. Berges-Frisbey goes to live with his sister where she gives birth to a son. Meanwhile, Berges-Frsibey is further abandoned by Duvauchelle's parents, who refuse to acknowledge her child as being fathered by their son. A happy ending is seen, however, when Duvauchelle, who was thought to have been shot down and killed by the Germans, returns from a POW camp to realize that he has a son, and he reunites with the woman who has waited for him. This sensitive tale is well directed and enacted; the story line is predictable but shown in such tenderly prosaic terms that it endears throughout. Songs: "Core 'n Grato" (Carolli, Sisca), "J'ai reve d'une fleur" and "Foolin' Myself" (Crescenzo, Scotto), "La Marseillaise," "Marche des enfants de troupe" (Armand Tournel), "Le Commandant" (Willy Haag); In French. English subtitles; a remake of the 1940 French film and based on the novel by Marcel Pagnol). Mature themes prohibit viewing by children. **p**, Alain Sarde; **d&w**, Daniel Auteuil (based on the novel by Marcel Pagnol); **cast**, Auteuil, Astrid Berges-Frisbey, Nicolas Duvauchelle, Jean-Pierre Darroussin, Kad Merad, Sabine Azema, Emilie Cazenave, Marie-Anne Chazel, Coline Bosso, Chloe Malarde, Brune Coustellier; **c**, Jean-Francois Robin; **m**, Alexandre Desplat; **spec eff**, Thierry Delobel, Annabelle Troukens, Virginie Wintrebert.

West of Thunder ★★★ 2012; U.S.; 123m; Sunka Wakan Dragonfly Film Studios/Indican Pictures; Color; Western; Children: Unacceptable (MPAA: PG-13); **BD**; **DVD**. Taut western set in 1899 South Dakota, nine years after the Massacre of Wounded Knee, sees the Lakota people on Pine Ridge Reservation fearful about a mysterious stranger, Davies, who arrives at a small town on the outskirts of the reservation. Strange events in town make the residents fear he is a supernatural demon seeking retribution and revenge. The tribe's respected spiritual leader, Little Thunder, played by Conroy, has his own thoughts about the mystery man. A deadly cat-and-mouse game is played as the Indians must decide to eliminate this stranger or live with him in peace and risk what they think might be a terrible retribution. Violence prohibits viewing by children. **p**, Avi Bar-Lev, Jody Marriott Bar-Lev; **d**, Jody Marriott Bar-Lev, Steve Russell; **cast**, Dan Davies, Corbin Conroy, Clifford Henry, Steve Garcia, Larry Swalley, Albert Red-Bear, Michael Worth, Raffaello Degruttola, Chrispian Belfrage, Sadie Kaye; **w**, Jody Marriott, Bar-Lev, Davies; **c**, Steve Russell, John Stanier; **m**, Deni Bonet, Neville Farmer, Ian Hatton, Juan Mesteth, Albert Red-Bear; **ed**, Russell, Stanier, Dave Thrasher; **spec eff**, Chase C. Wright.

What If ★★★ 2013; Ireland/Canada; 98m; No Trace Camping/CBS Films; Color; Comedy/Drama/Romance; Children: Unacceptable (MPAA: PG-13); **BD**; **DVD**. Radcliffe, a medical school dropout, becomes disillusioned after a series of failed relationships with women. While his roommate, Driver, seems to be finding the perfect partner, Radcliffe decides to put his love life on hold. He then meets Kazan, an animator who lives with her longtime boyfriend, Spall. Radcliffe and Kazan become immediately attracted to each other, striking up a close friendship. There is a lot of chemistry between them, leading them to wonder if the love of their lives can actually be one's best friend. The two develop a deepening romance that is ruptured when Kazan sees Radcliffe devoting most of his time to his resumed medical studies and she decides to move to an assignment in Taiwan. They have a tearful farewell but Radcliffe realizes that he loves Kazan, and, as shown in an epilogue, Radcliffe goes to Taiwan where he proposes to Kazan and she accepts. This simple love story offers predictable stopgaps, but its interest is nevertheless sustained through a clever script and top-flight act-

Paul Rudd and Jennifer Aniston in *Wanderlust*, 2012.

ing, proving to be a delightful, warmhearted tale. The film earned a little more than $7.8 million in its initial release, failing to recoup its budget of $11 million. A 2010 film with the same title has a different plot. Songs: "Walking Through the Sleeping City" (Mick Jagger, Keith Richards), "Ben Wilson Is A.L.I.V.E." (Rich Aucoin), "Best of Friends" (William Doyle, Samuel Fryer, Alexander Jesson, Jeffrey Peter Mayhew), "Wings" (Ben Gebert, Nini Fabi), "Big Bird in a Small Cage" and "Into Giants" (Patrick Watson, Mikhail Stein, Robbie Kuster, Simon Angell), "Once Upon a Time/Storybook Love" (Mark Knopfler), "Oh Saskatchewan" (Matt Masters), "Chinese Lament" (Abbas Premjee), "Our Hour" (Evan Bobrowski), "Big Noise from Winnetka" (Bob Crosby, Ray Bauduc, Bob Haggart, Gil Rodin), "Blackwind" and "Lighthouse" (Patrick Watson, Mikhail Stein, Robbie Kuster, Melanie Belair, Simon Angell), "H.O.S.H." (Holger Behn), "Piano Sonata, Opus 78, No. 25 "Cuckoo" (Ludwig van Beethoven), "Dreaming" (Adam Waito), "Wedding March" (Felix Mendelssohn-Bartholdy), "Oh No! Not The Beast Day" (Marsha Hunt, Steve Rowland, Hugh Burns), "Glen to Glen" and "Float" (Ryan Marshall Lawhon), "It" (Rich Aucoin), "Let's Get High" (Alex Ebert). Sexual content, partial nudity and gutter language prohibit viewing by children. **p**, David Gross, Macdara Kelleher, Andre Rouleau, Marc Stephenson; **d**, Michael Dowse; **cast**, Daniel Radcliffe, Zoe Kazan, Megan Park, Adam Driver, Mackenzie Davis, Rafe Spall, Lucius Hoyos, Jemima Rooper, Rebecca Northan, Jonathan Cherry; **w**, Elan Mastai (based on the play "Toothpaste and Cigars" by T.J. Dawe, Michael Rinaldi); **c**, Rogier Stoffers; **m**, A.C. Newman; **ed**, Yvann Thibaudeau; **prod d**, Ethan Tobman; **art d**, Mark Steel; **set d**, Mary Kirkland; **spec eff**, Carole Bouchard, Francine Fontaine.

What Maisie Knew ★★★ 2013; U.S.; 99m; Red Crown Productions; Millennium Entertainment; Color; Drama; Children: Unacceptable (MPAA: R); **BD**; **DVD**. Maisie, played by Aprile, is a six-year-old daughter who lives with her self-absorbed parents in an upscale Manhattan apartment. Her mother, Moore, is a slightly aging rock star, and her father, Coogan, is an art dealer glued to his cell phone. The parents constantly argue and are close to a divorce, but perky Aprile tunes everything out in her room playing with toy horses and coloring books. Coogan moves to an apartment and hires a friendly and caring nanny, Vanderham, to look after Aprile, but the employee soon becomes romantically interested in the employer. Moore and Coogan divorce and he marries Vanderham while Moore marries Skarsgard, a younger bartender. Only Skarsgard seems to care how all of this effects Aprile. Moore becomes jealous of the growing bond between Aprile and Skarsgard. Moore and Coogan come to use Aprile as a target for their bitterness, but she somehow survives, thanks to Skarsgard, her new parent. This is a gripping drama of innocence being attacked, but Aprile shows

Nicolas Duvauchelle and Astrid Berges-Frisbey in *The Well-Digger's Daughter*, 2012.

how strong she truly is to survive the family catastrophe while fiercely holding on to her innocent childhood. This is what Maisie truly learns and now knows. Though reminiscent of **Kramer vs. Kramer**, 1979, the film presents its own distinctive persona through Aprile, who gives a stellar performance. Unfortunately, this heartwarming film did little box office, earning less than $2.8 million in its initial release against a budget of $5 million. Songs: "Anesthesia" (Jose Castillo, Tyler Morrisette), "Rock-a-Bye Baby" (traditional), "Night Train" and "Hook and Line" (The Kills: Alison Mosshart, Jamie Hince), "Little Red Riding Hood" (traditional), "Low Light" (Paul Dreux Smith, Senon Williams), "Feeling of Being" (Lucy Schwartz, Sally Seltmann). Gutter language prohibits viewing by children. **p**, Daniel Crown, Daniela Taplin Lundberg, William Teitler, Charles Weinstock, Elfar Adalsteins, Mohammed Al Turki, Sam Connelly, Brad Coolidge, Melissa Collidge; **d**, Scott McGehee, David Siegel; **cast**, Julianne Moore, Alexander Skarsgard, Onata Aprile, Steve Coogan, Joanna Vanderham, Sadie Rae Lee, Jesse Stone Spadaccini, Diana Garcia Soto, Amelia Campbell, Maddie Corman, Paddy Croft; **w**, Nancy Doyne, Carroll Cartwright (based on the novel by Henry James); **c**, Giles Nuttgens; **m**, Nick Urata; **ed**, Madeleine Gavin; **prod d**, Kelly McGehee; **set d**, Susan Perlman; **spec eff**, Daniel Cohen.

When Animals Dream ★★★ 2014; Denmark; 84m; AlphaVille Productions Copenhagen/RADiUS-TWC; Color; Horror; Children: Unacceptable; **BD**; **DVD**. Genuinely frightening film begins with Suhl, a nineteen-year-old girl who is shy and avoids social contact. She lives in a remote fishing village in Denmark, and where her father, Mikkelsen, and mother, Richter, also keep to themselves. Her mother ails from a strange and unstated malady and half the time she is comatose. When conscious, she moves about in a wheelchair. Suhl becomes upset when a rash suddenly develops on her chest, and she becomes even more disturbed when hair begins to grow there. Her uncouth coworkers at a fish processing plant make insulting remarks about her, pretending that they are simply hazing her. Their cruel remarks, however, are maliciously sincere. More unnatural physical changes slowly occur in Suhl's body as she comes to suspect that her mother and father have been hiding a grim secret from her and that her mother's illness has something to do with her physical transformations. Suhl eventually realizes, as will any shocked viewer, that she is transforming into a murderous werewolf and that everyone in the village is her prey. This was Arnby's directorial debut and he presents a haunting tale where Suhl is outstanding as a gentle girl turned savage beast. (In Danish; English subtitles.) **p**, Ditte Milsted, Caroline Schluter; **d**, Jonas Alexander Arnby; **cast**, Sonia Suhl, Lars Mikkelsen, Sonja Richter, Jakob Oftebro, Mads Riisom, Gustav Giese, Esben Dalgaard, Stig Hoffmeyer, Benjamin Boe Rasmussen; **w**, Rasmus Birch; **c**, Niels Thastum; **m**, Mikkel Hess; **ed**, Peter Brandt; **prod d**, Sabine Hviid; **set d**, Trine Gram; **spec eff**, Morten Arnoldus.

When the Game Stands Tall ★★★ 2014; U.S.; 115m; Affirm Films/Sony; Color; Sports Drama; Children: Unacceptable (MPAA: PG); **BD**; **DVD**. An inspirational film based on true events, it tells the remarkable journey of legendary football coach Bob Ladouceur (1954-), played by Caviezel, who took the De La Salle High School Spartans football team in Concord, California, from obscurity to a 151-game winning streak over twelve years that shattered all records for any American sport. While coaching the game of football, Caviezel emphasizes purpose and significance rather than winning streaks and titles. But when real-life adversity leaves the team reeling, the boys must decide if the sacrifice, commitment, and teamwork they have always trusted can rebuild what is now disintegrating around them. This film received abuse from unconventional critics (who seem to have no point of reference and most likely never viewed such football classics as **Knute Rockne, All American**, 1940, or **The Iron Major**, 1943) because it follows traditional values, but it deserved better treatment and any high school football player would do well to see this heart-lifting production. The film had a modest success at the box office, earning more than $30 million against a budget of more than $15 million. Songs: "Sail" (Aaron Bruno), "Do or Die" (Jared Leto). Thematic material, a scene of violence and brief smoking prohibit viewing by children. **p**, David Zelon; **d**, Thomas Carter; **cast**, Jim Caviezel, Laura Dern, Alexander Ludwig, Michael Chiklis, Clancy Brown, Ser'Darius Blain, Stephan James, Matthew Daddario, Joe Massingill, Jessie Usher, Matthew Frias; **w**, Scott Marshall Smith (based on his story with David Zelon and the book by Neil Hayes); **c**, Michael Lohmann; **m**, John Paesano; **ed**, Scott Richter; **prod d**, Jaymes Hinkle; **art d**, Raymond Pumilia; **set d**, Kristin Bicksler; **spec eff**, Justin B. Johnson, Matt Kutcher.

Where Do We Go Now? ★★★ 2012; France/Lebanon/Egypt/Italy; 110m; Les Films des Tournelles/Sony; Color; Comedy/Drama; Children: Unacceptable (MPAA: PG-13); **BD**; **DVD**. Christians and Muslims live harmoniously for years in a small Lebanese village until television comes to town and the two religious groups watch outside news that makes them decide they are enemies, even though they do the same jobs, eat the same food, like the same music, worship the same God, and speak the same language. Some village women try to avert violence by means of some schemes that initially prove ineffective. When violence does break out, the women find themselves needing to make deeply personal sacrifices for the sake of peace. One Christian woman, Labaki, is secretly in love with a Muslim man. She and the other women break the television set and lighten the men's moods by serving them hashish brownies. Still unable to bring peace between the two groups of men, the women turn to sex, importing some exotic dancers from Ukraine. That does the trick as the men enjoy the dancers and get sexually aroused so they go back to their lives and religious harmony returns to the village. Well-crafted by director-actress Labaki, the film takes a light approach to what is otherwise a very serious problem that continues to plague the Middle East, particularly in this era of jihadist terrorism. Songs: "Danse Funebre," "La Grande Marche," "Kifou Hal Helou," "Machkal," "Pax Ukrania," "Un Air de Liberte," "Nassim," "Hashishet Albi," "Deuil de Nassim," "Kyrie Akkah," "Miracle du Flipper" (Khaled Mouzanar). Thematic drug material, some sexuality and violent images prohibit viewing by children. (In French, Arabic; English subtitles.) **p**, Nadine Labaki, Anne-Dominique Toussaint, Hesham Abdelkhalek, Romain Le Grand, Tarak Ben Ammar; **d**, Labaki; **cast**, Claude Baz Moussawbaa, Layla Hakim, Labaki, Yvonne Maalouf, Antoinette Noufaily, Julian Farhat, Ali Haidar, Kevin Abboud, Petra Saghbini, Mostafa Al Sakka, Caroline Labaki; **w**, Rodney Al Haddid, Jihad Hojeily, Labaki, Thomas Bidegain, Sam Nessim as Sam Mounier; **c**, Christophe Offenstein; **m**, Khaled Mouzannar; **ed**,

Veronique Lange; **prod d**, Cynthia Zahar; **spec eff**, Joel Pinto, Florian Chauvet.

Whiplash ★★★ 2014; U.S.; 106m; Blumhouse Productions/Sony; Color; Drama; Children: Unacceptable (MPAA: R); **BD**; **DVD**. Teller is a young New York jazz drummer who is a first-year student attending one of the best music schools in the United States under the tutelage of Simmons, the mean-minded jazz band master, who demands the best of his pupils. He is abusive to Teller, slapping him, tossing a chair at him, and insulting him about being Jewish. The mistreatment only makes Teller work harder, and he even gives up his girlfriend, Benoist, to concentrate on being a drummer, and, particularly, to please the demanding Simmons whose insistence on perfection borders on the psychopathic. Following a car accident, however, Teller performs poorly at an important stage competition and Simmons orders him from the stage. Teller explodes, attacking Simmons and is expelled from the school. Teller and his parents take revenge on Simmons by testifying against him, convincing officials that a fellow student hanged himself after suffering depression from Simmons' oppressive ways. Simmons is fired, but he later forms his own band and Teller, who has given up music, is invited to join it, and Simmons admits that he was a hard taskmaster only to force students to do their best. Teller appears with the band, but is humiliated in front of the audience when Simmons leaves him without any sheet music. Teller, however, returns to the stage and performs a spectacular routine that earns Simmons' approval, and this is where the film ends. Teller and Simmons are standouts in their antagonistic roles, and director Chazelle moves the absorbing story along at a fast and entertaining clip. Simmons received an Oscar for Best Supporting Actor and Oscars also went to Cross for Best Film Editing and Craig Mann, Ben Wilkins and Thomas Curley for Best Sound Mixing. The film did well at the box office, earning more than $49 million in its initial release against a budget of more than $3.3 million. Not related to the 1948 or 2002 films with the same name. Songs: "Overture," "When I Wake," "Casey's Song," "Fletcher's Song in Club," "No Two Words" (Justin Hurwitz); "Black Girls" (D.A. Wallach, Maxwell Drummey, Travis Barker); "Keep Me Waiting" (Drummey, Dana Williams); "Reaction" (Nicholas Britell); "lst and Nassau Band Rehearsal," "Studio Band Eavesdrop, "Overbrook Competition," Upswingin" (Tim Simonec); "Cathy's Song" (Buddy Rich); "Whiplash" (Hank Levy); "Caravan" (music: Duke Ellington; lyrics: Juan Tizol); "Intoit" (Stan Getz); "No Two Words" (Justin Hurwitz). Violence and sexual references prohibit viewing by children. **p**, Jason Blum, Helen Estabrook, David Lancaster, Michel Litvak, Nicholas Britell, Garrick Dion, Sarah Potts, Stephanie Wilcox; **d&w**, Damien Chazelle; **cast**, Melissa Benoist, Miles Teller, J.K. Simmons, Paul Reiser, Austin Stowell, Jayson Blair, Damon Gupton, April Grace, Kavita Patil, Kofi Siriboe; **c**, Sharone Meir; **m**, Justin Hurwitz; **ed**, Tom Cross; **prod d**, Melanie Jones; **art d**, Hunter Brown; **set d**, Karuna Karmarkar; **spec eff**, Jamison Scott Goei, David Lebensfeld, Grant Miller.

White Bird in a Blizzard ★★★ 2014; France/U.S.; 91m; Desperate Pictures/Magnolia; Drama; Children: Unacceptable (MPAA: R); **BD**; **DVD**. Woodley is a seventeen-year-old girl who lives in a stifled, emotionally repressed home life when her perfect homemaker mother, Green, a beautiful but enigmatic and haunted woman, disappears. It happens just as Woodley is discovering and relishing her newfound sexuality. She barely registers her mother's absence and doesn't blame her wimpy father, Meloni, for the loss. Her mother's disappearance is almost a relief to Woodley. However, as time passes, Woodley comes to grips with how deeply the loss has affected her. Returning home on a break from college, she finds herself confronted with the truth about her mother's sudden departure and her own denial about the events surrounding it. This absorbing film sees strong performances from Woodley, Green and Meloni, while Araki guides this good domestic tale with a firm hand. Song: "Dazzle/Glamour Mix" (Siouxsie Sioux, Steven Severin, Peter Clarke as Budgie, Robert Smith). Sexual content, nudity,

Oxana Chihane, Olga Yerofyeyeva and Anneta Bousaleh in *Where Do We Go Now?*, 2012.

gutter language and drug use prohibit viewing by children. **p**, Gregg Araki, Pascal Caucheteux, Pavlina Hatoupis, Sebastien Lemerciere, Alix Madigan; **d**, Araki (based on the novel by Laura Kasischke); **cast**, Shailene Woodley, Eva Green, Christopher Meloni, Angela Bassett, Gabourey Sidibe, Shiloh Fernandez, Thomas Jane, Sheryl Lee, Dale Dickey, Jacob Artist; **c**, Sandra Valde-Hansen; **m**, Robin Guthrie; **prod d**, Todd Fjelsted; **art d**, Caity Birmingham; **set d**, Ryan Watson; **spec eff**, Kevin J. Williams, Matthew Bramante, Gresham Lochner.

Wild ★★★ 2014; U.S.; 115m; Fox Searchlight; Color; Biographical Drama; Children: Unacceptable (MPAA: R); **BD**; **DVD**; **IV**. A young woman, Cheryl Strayed (1968-), played by Witherspoon, becomes despondent after her marriage fails and her mother, Dern, dies in agony of cancer. She lives recklessly and self-destructively for several years, addicted to both drugs and sex. Feeling that her life is hopeless, she makes a dangerous decision to go alone and with no previous experience on a hiking trip of more than a thousand miles along the Pacific Crest Trail in the northwestern United States. The trail, 2,663 miles long, passes through twenty-five national forests and seven national parks and is closely aligned with the highest portion of the Sierra Nevada and Cascade mountain ranges, its northern terminus being the Oregon-Washington border with Canada and reaching south to the border with Mexico. Witherspoon's journey involves many hardships of terrain and weather, but also leads her to gain inner strength and embark on a much more positive future. This is a well-made inspirational film that nurtures the human spirit, and Witherspoon renders a powerful performance where her physical and mental sensitivities are in full and impressive display. Witherspoon deservedly received an Oscar nomination as Best Actress and Dern received an Oscar nomination as Best Supporting Actress. The film did very well at the box office, earning more than $52.5 million in its initial release against a budget of more than $15 million. Songs: "El Condor Pasa" (1913; Daniel Alomia Robles), "Love Struck Baby" (Stevie Ray Vaughan). Sexual content, nudity, drug use and gutter language prohibit viewing by children. **p**, Bruna Papandrea, Bill Pohlad, Reese Witherspoon; **d**, Jean-Marc Vallee; **cast**, Witherspoon, Laura Dern, Thomas Sadoski, Keene McRae, Michiel Huisman, W. Earl Brown, Gaby Hoffmann, Kevin Rankin, Brian Van Holt, Cliff De Young; **w**, Nick Hornby (based on the memoir "Wild: From Lost to Found on the Pacific Crest Trail" by Cheryl Strayed); **c**, Yves Belanger; **ed**, Martin Pensa, John Mac McMurphy; **prod d**, John Paino; **art d**, Javiera Varas; **set d**, Robert Covelman; **spec eff**, Bob Riggs, John S. Baker.

Wild Tales ★★★ 2014; Argentina/Spain; 122m; Comer Producciones; Sony; Color; Comedy/Drama; Children: Unacceptable (MPAA: R);

Nadine Labaki and Julien Farhat in *Where Do We Go Now?*, 2012.

BD; **DVD**. This skillfully woven film is told in six parts, each of which contains dark humor while dealing with revenge and retribution. In "Pasternak," a model and a music critic are on a plane trip when they discover they both know a man named Pasternak, who had been their lover until they dumped him. Before long they realize that the crew and all the other passengers also know Pasternak and had affairs with him. "The Rats" involves a waitress who recognizes the grumpy man she is waiting on as the loan shark who caused her father to commit suicide. She tells the cook about it and she suggests mixing some rat poison in the man's food. She refuses to take such drastic revenge on the man, but the cook nevertheless goes ahead with her lethal plan. "In Road to Hell" (aka "The Strongest"), a man is driving his new sports car on a desolate highway and shouts obscenities to the driver of a pick-up truck. Their ensuing argument is virtually historic and ends in tragedy. In "Little Bomb," a demolitions engineer goes into a bakery to pick up his daughter's birthday cake, and when he returns to his car, he finds that it is being towed for being in a no-parking space. He and the tow truck driver argue and it leads to the engineer's life being destroyed, including the ending of his marriage, so he seeks revenge on the tow truck driver and his company. In "The Proposal," a spoiled and careless teenager of a wealthy family has a fateful hit-and-run accident, running down a pregnant woman. The boy's father and his lawyer scheme to pay his gardener to tell authorities he was the reckless motorist. In the final segment, "Till Death Us Do Part," the bride at a wedding reception discovers that the groom has previously cheated on her with one of the women guests. She takes revenge on her new spouse and soon has him begging for forgiveness. Episodic films are hit-and-miss proposals, but this one consistently fascinates and entertains, thanks to a lively and inventive script and some standout performances. The film earned more than $27 million at the box office in its initial release against a budget of more than $3.3 million. Songs/Music: "Love Theme" from **Flashdance** (1983: Giorgio Moored), "Lady, Lady, Lady" (music: Moroder; lyrics: Keith Forsey), "Titanium" (David Guetta, Giorgio Tuinfort, Sia Kate Furler), "Fly Me to the Moon" (1968: Bart Howard), "Hallelujah" (music: Kobi Oshrat; lyrics: Shimrit Or), "Happy Birthday" (music: Mildred J. Hill; lyrics: Patty S. Hill), "Aire Libre." Violence, gutter language and brief sexuality prohibit viewing by children. (In Spanish; English subtitles.) **p**, Agustin Almodovar, Pedro Almodovar, Esther Garcia, Matias Mosteirin, Hugo Sigman, Axel Kushevatzky, **d&w**, Damian Szifron; **cast**, Dario Grandinetti, Maria Marull, Monica Villa, Rita Cortese, Julieta Zylberberg, Cesar Bordon, Leonardo Saraglia, Walter Donaldo, Ricardo Darin, Nancy Duplaa; **c**, Javier Julia; **m**, Gustavo Santaolalla; **ed**, Pablo Barbieri Carrea, Damian Szifron; **prod d**, Maria Clara Notari; **spec eff**, Eduardo Puga, Federico Ransenberg.

The Wind Rises ★★★ 2014; Japan; 126m; Studio Ghibli/Buena Vista; Color; Animation/Biographical Drama; Children: Unacceptable (MPAA: PG-13); **BD**; **DVD**. Fascinating biopic is based on the life of Jiro Horikoshi (1903-1982), Gordon-Levitt voiceover, who designed Japanese fighter planes for World War II (1939-1945). Gordon-Levitt dreams of designing and flying airplanes, inspired by Italian aeronautical designer Giovanni Caprioni (1886-1957), Tucci voiceover. Nearsighted from an early age and unable to become a pilot, Gordon-Levitt becomes one of the world's most innovative and accomplished airplane designers. The film follows his career from the Great Kanto Earthquake of 1923, through the 1930s Great Depression, the worldwide tuberculosis epidemic, and Japan's ill-conceived plunge into World War II. It also includes his love for Nahoko Satomi (Blunt voiceover) and friendship with colleague Honjo (Krasinski voiceover) The animation is top flight and the script provocative, cleverly and obliquely promoting the image of one who greatly aided in Japan's war of aggression. The producers must be credited in having Gordon-Levitt confess, after the end of WWII, that the planes he designed were used for Japan's aggressions. The producers wisely opted to depict this tale in animated form rather than live-action where its characters might be more sharply and critically defined in the light of Japan's ignominious WWII history. The film enjoyed a great box office success, earning more than $136.5 million in its initial release against a budget of more than $30 million. Songs: "Hikouki-gumo" (Yumi Matsutoya as Arai Yumi); "Das gibt's nur einmal" (music: Werner R. Heymann; lyrics: Robert Gilbert). Disturbing images and smoking prohibit viewing by children. **p**, Toshio Suzuki; **d&w**, Hayao Miyazaki (based on his graphic novel); **cast** (voiceovers), Joseph Gordon-Levitt, John Krasinski, Emily Blunt, Martin Short, Stanley Tucci, Mandy Patinkin, Mae Whitman, Werner Herzog, Jennifer Grey, William H. Macy; **m**, Joe Hisaishi.

The Wise Kids ★★★ 2012; U.S.; 95m; Cone Arts/Wolfe; Color; Drama; Children: Unacceptable; **DVD**; **IV**. A sensitive and heartfelt Southern-set coming-of-age story in which some high school seniors attempt to learn what their lives are going to be like when they go to college and afterward, both spiritually and secularly. The action mainly takes place in and around a Baptist church in Charleston, South Carolina. Kunz is the daughter of Rogers, the pastor, and who is consumed by doubts about her faith and fears of the future. Her best friend, Torem, is an optimistic believer in a happy future, but is shocked when learning that their friend Ross, who is a devout Christian, is trying to deal with his homosexuality. Meanwhile, Cone, the church's musical director, who has been married for eight years to Rifai, also comes to realize that he is gay and is attracted to Ross. The three friends decide on going to the same college, but remain uncertain as to their futures. This well-made tale incisively examines some serious problems that confront teenagers as they struggle to maturity. Songs: "Could Be Here" (Danielle Howle), "Kammst ou nun, Jesu from Six Schubler Chorales" (Johann Sebastian Bach); "How Deep the Father's Love for Us" (Stuart Townsend); "How to Live," "Crosswalk Stereo," "Colors" (Kyle E. Peters, Will Roberts, Brian Healey, Neil Lucas); "The Audition" Mikhail Fiksel, Seeking Wonderland); "Kaleidoscope" (Jeff Wild); "Electric Shock" (Fiksel, Seth Bockley); "O Come, O Come Emmanuel" (traditional); "Hodie Christis natus est" (Jan Pieterzoon Sweelincj); "Low, How a Rose E'er Blooming" (traditional); "Adagio, Allegro, Adagio from Concerto Grosso Opus 6, No. 8" (Archangelo Corelli); "Mission Demo" (Christina Cone). *Author's Note*: This film was shot on a shoestring budget of about $17,000 to start with and saw limited distribution. It was shot on location in director Cone's hometown of Charleston, South Carolina. Mature sexuality themes prohibit viewing by children. **p**, Stephen Cone, Laura Klein, Mitchell Crosby, Sue Redman, Monte Redman, Carolyn Redman, Tim Whitfield; **d&w**, Cone; **cast**, Molly Kunz, Allison Torem, Tyler Ross, Eric Hulsebos, Frank Stennett, Lee Armstrong, Cone, Sadie Rifai, Cynthia Pulsifer, Braxton Williams, Cliff Chamberlain; **c**, Stephanie Dufford; **m**, Mikhail Fiksel;

ed, Cone; **prod d**, Caity Birmingham; **set d**, Elsie Eubanks.

Wish I Was Here ★★★ 2014; U.S.; 120m; Worldview Entertainment; Focus Features; Color; Comedy/Drama; Children: Unacceptable (MPAA: R); **BD**; **DVD**. Braff is a struggling young actor, a husband and father, who at the age of thirty-five is still trying to discover his purpose in life, as he and his wife, Hudson, work menial jobs. His father, Patinkin, contracts cancer and can no longer afford to pay for the private education for the children. His selfish brother, Gad, is of little use, and will only babysit the children if paid money. Moreover, the public school is about to close, so Braff, with Hudson's urging, tries home-schooling his children. This labor of love becomes more enlightening than what Braff and Hudson ever expected. In teaching the children about life his way, Braff makes some major self-discoveries. Well enacted, this delightful domestic story not only entertains but examples in detail the responsibilities of parenthood. This film, unfortunately, did poorly at the box office, earning less than $5.5 million in its initial release against a budget of $6 million. Songs: "Broke Window" (Gary Jules), "Wish I Was Here" (Berryman, Buckland, Champion, Martin), "The Mute" (Ben Cooper), "Mexico" (Jay Clifford), "Tangled Up in Blue" (Bob Dylan), "Sweet Baby James" (James Taylor), "Fallen" (Cary Brothers), "Wait It Out" (Imogen Heap), "Cherry Wine" (Andrew Hozier Bryne), "The Obvious Child" (Paul Simon), "Holocene" (Justin Vernon), "Breathe In" (Gabriel Strum, Wafia Al-Rikabi), "The Shining" (Damon Gough), "Heavenly Father" (Justin Vernon), "Kilo" (Pedro D'Eyrot, Rodrigo Gorky, Charlie McCoy, Laura Taylor, Kent Westberry), "Raven's Song" (Aaron Embry), "So Now What" (James Mercer), "Mend" (Deb Talan, Steve Tannen), "No One to Let You Down" (Kenneth Hensley, Joshua Johnson, Jonathan Russell, Charity Rose Thielen, Robert Tyler Williams, Christopher Zasche). Gutter language and sexual content prohibit viewing by children. **p**, Zach Braff, Adam J. Braff, Matthew Andrews, Michael Shamberg, Stacey Sher, Amanda Bowers, Coco Francini, Adriana L. Randall; **d**, Zach Braff; **cast**, Zach Braff, Kate Hudson, Mandy Patinkin, Pierce Gagnon, Joey King, Alexander Chaplin, Jim Parsons, Josh Gad, Allan Rich, Cody Sullivan; **w**, Zach Braff, Adam J. Braff; **c**, Lawrence Sher; **m**, Rob Simonsen; **ed**, Myron I. Kerstein; **prod d**, Tony Fanning; **set d**, Beth Wooke; **spec eff**, Frank Iudica.

The Wolf of Wall Street ★★★★ 2013; U.S.; 180m; Red Granite Pictures/PAR; Color; Biographical Drama; Children: Unacceptable (MPAA: PG-13); **BD**; **DVD**. Gripping biopic presents the true story of Jordan Ross Belfort (1962-), played by the always versatile DiCaprio, from his rise as a wealthy New York City stockbroker to his fall through his involvement in crime and corruption. DiCaprio begins with a low-level job at an established Wall Street firm and is taken under the wing of company executive Mark Hanna, played by McConaughey, becoming a licensed stockbroker, then becoming retrenched due to the firm's bankruptcy following Black Monday (October 17, 1987, when the stock market crashed around the world). DiCaprio's wife, Milioti, encourages him to take a job with a Long Island firm dealing in penny stocks. He impresses his new boss with an aggressive sales pitching style and earns a small fortune for the firm and himself. DiCaprio befriends Donnie Azoff, essayed by Hill, a salesman living in DiCaprio's apartment complex, and they become partners in business along with several friends. To cover the fact that their firm is little more than a con game and scam, DiCaprio gives it the respectable name of Stratton Oakmont. FBI agent Patrick Denham, portrayed by Chandler, smells foul business practice and begins investigating the firm. DiCaprio starts an affair with Robbie that results in his divorce from Milioti. He and Robbie marry and they move into a mansion he buys and where they sail about in luxury on a yacht DiCaprio names after Robbie, and they soon have a daughter. Meanwhile, at work, DiCaprio, Hill, and their colleagues engage in non-stop debauchery and drug use. DiCaprio makes $22 million after securing control of Steve Madden Ltd. To hide his earnings, he opens a Swiss bank account with a corrupt banker, Jean Jacques Saurel, played by Du-

Frank Stennett, Tyler Ross and Stephen Cone in *The Wise Kids*, 2012.

jardin, using friends with European passports to smuggle cash into that account. The account is opened in the name of Robbie's aunt, Lumley, a British citizen, who is outside the reach of U.S. authorities. By now, DiCaprio is taking large doses of Quaaludes. He then gets a call from his private investigator, insisting that DiCaprio call him back from a pay phone. DiCaprio is told that one of his colleagues, Bernthal, has been arrested and that DiCaprio's phones are tapped. As the Quaaludes take effect on DiCaprio, he drives to his home to prevent his partner, Hill, from using his phone. But when he gets there, he finds Hill drunk, on the phone with Dujardin. They struggle and Hill, eating a piece of ham, starts choking. DiCaprio snorts some cocaine and saves Hill. DiCaprio's father, Reiner, and lawyer, Favreau, try to convince him to step down from Stratton Oakmont and escape a large number of legal penalties. DiCaprio agrees, but greed and power change his mind in the middle of his resignation speech. DiCaprio, Hill, and their wives take a yacht trip to Italy where they learn that Lumley has died, so the Swiss bank account is locked up. While Lumley left the money to DiCaprio, he must go to Switzerland the next day to sign for it. Over Robbie's objections, he sails to Monaco with her when a violent storm capsizes the boat. They are rescued and taken by plane to Geneva, but the plane is destroyed by a seagull flying into the engine, exploding, and killing three people. DiCaprio considers it a sign from God and decides to sober up. Two years pass and Chandler arrests DiCaprio during the filming of an infomercial after Dujardin informs on him to the FBI. DiCaprio attempts to deal with the government by giving evidence on his colleagues in exchange for leniency. Robbie expects him to get a heavy prison sentence, so she says she will file for divorce, demanding custody of their two children. DiCaprio throws a tantrum, gets high on drugs, and, while driving, crashes his car in his driveway during an attempt to escape with one of the children. DiCaprio is then arrested for failing to go through with his government informant deal. The FBI then raids and shuts down Stratton Oakmont. DiCaprio cooperates with the government and receives a reduced sentence of thirty-six months in a minimum security federal prison in Nevada. Upon his release, DiCaprio is reduced to making a living by hosting seminars on sales techniques in New Zealand. (The final comeuppance for DiCaprio is not dissimilar to that of the arrogant Ray Liotta, in Scorsese's **Goodfellas**, 1990, where Liotta grows rich through bloody underworld thefts and drug deals, only to turn informant and wind up as an insignificant nonentity on the federal dole.) DiCaprio is outstanding as the meteoric Belfort, his performance incisively (and frighteningly) expressing his character's exploding vanity and drug-chained carelessness as great wealth surfaces in his life, along with all the dark demands of avarice leading to the destruction of his moral decency, marriage and freedom. He is blessed with wonderfully talented supporting cast members, who also render startling perform-

Tyler Ross and Jacob Leinbach in *The Wise Kids*, 2012.

ances, and the unpredictably gifted Scorsese this time restrains his natural bent to go over the top as he diligently guides this utterly obsessive tale to its jail-destined conclusion. So excessive are DiCaprio's indulgences in drugs and riches that, rather than glorify such profligate conduct, Scorsese darkly satirizes this extravagant character's self-serving lifestyle with razor-sharp words and images, leaving no sensible person the ability to admire this man. There are evidences that Scorsese was influenced by another outstanding film about stockbrokers, **Wall Street**, 1987, but he nevertheless presents a much more insidious scenario that scathingly and uncompromisingly portrays his main characters as worthless human beings. All of them are essentially dull and inwardly vacuous people glorifying themselves through money and power, earning our pity if not contempt. The film, not unexpectedly, received many Oscar nominations, including Best Picture; Best Director (Scorsese); Best Actor (DiCaprio); Best Supporting Actor (Hill), and Best Adapted Screenplay (Winter). The film was a megahit at the box office, earning more than $392 million in its initial release against a budget of more than $100 million. Songs: "Stratton Oakmont," "Exotic Vacations," "Infomercial" (Theodore Shapiro); "Dust My Broom" (Elmore James, Robert Johnson); "Lifestyles of the Rich and Famous Score" (Michael Karp); "Dust My Blues" (Joe Bihari, Elmore James); "Spoonful" (Willie Dixon); "Mercy, Mercy, Mercy" (Josef Zawinul); "Hit Me with Your Rhythm Stick" (Ian Dury, Charles Jankel); "Bang! Bang!" (Jimmy Sabater, Joe Cuba); "Tear It Down" (Clyde McCoy, Raymond Leveen); "Movin' Out/Anthony's Song" (Billy Joel); "Surrey with the Fringe on Top" (music: Richard Rodgers; lyrics" Oscar Hammerstein II); "Road Runner" (Bo Diddley as Ellas McDaniel); "Stars and Stripes Forever" (John Philip Sousa); "Smokestack Lightning" (Charles Burnett as Howlin' Wolf); "Double Dutch" (Trevor Horn, Petrus Manelli, Malcolm McLaren); "Cloudburst" (Jimmy Harris, Jon Hendricks, Leroy Kirkland); "Insane in the Brain" (Louis Freeze, Larry Muggerud, Senen Reyes); "King Arthur, Act3: What Power Thou Art" (Henry Purcell); "Steve Madden 'Chick Walker' Commercial" (Human); "Never Say Never" (Benjamin Bossi, Larry Carter, Debora Iyall, Peter Woods, Frank Zincavage); "There Is No Greater Love" (Isham Jones, Marty Symes); "Boom Boom" (John Lee Hooker); "C'est si bon" (music: Ange Henri Betti; lyrics: Andrew Hornez); "Give Me Luv" (Jean-Phillippe Aviance, Victor Imbres); "Uncontrollable Urge" (Mark Mothersbaugh); "Moonlight in Vermont" (John Blackburn, Karl Suessdorf); "Pretty Thing" (Willie Dixon); "In the Bush" (Patrick Adams, Sandora Cooper); "Can't Help Falling in Love" (Luigi Creatore, Hugo Peretti, George Weiss); "Goldfinger" (John Barry, Leslie Bricusse, Anthony Newley); "Baby Got Back" (Anthony Ray); "Everlong" (Dave Grohl); "The Oompa Loompa Song" (Bricusse, Newley); "Hey Leroy, Your Mama's Callin' You" (Jimmy Castor, John Pruit); "Sloop John B" (Brian Wilson);

"Boom Boom Boom" (Lamar Hula Mahone, Keith D. Mayberry); "I Need You Baby/Mona" (McDaniel); "Meth Lab Zoso Sticker" (Joie Calio, Phil Leavitt); "Flying High"and "Get Us Down" from "Family Matters" (Bennett Salvay, Jesse Frederick); "I'm Popeye the Sailor Man" (Sammy Lerner); "I Don't Want to Walk Without You" (Frank Loesser, Jule Styne); "Dream Lover" (Clifford Grey, Victor Schertzinger); "Popeye Meets Hercules Score" (Winston Sharples); "One Step Beyond" (Cecil Campbell); "Hip Hop Hooray" (Vincent Brown, Anthony Criss, Keir Gist, Ernie Isley, Marvin Isley, O'Kelly Isley, Ronald Isley, Rudolph Isley, Christopher Jasper); "Wednesday Night Prayer Meeting" (Charles Mingus); "Gloria" (Giancarlo Bigazzi, Umberto Tozzi); "Ca plane pour moi" (Lou De Prijck, Yves Maurice A. Lacomblez); "Cast Your Fate to the Wind" (Vince Guaraldi); "Mrs. Robinson" (Paul Simon); "The Money Chant" (Robbie Robertson, Matthew McConaughey). ***Author's Note***: Warner Brothers acquired the film rights for Belfort's book for $1 million and originally slated Scorsese to direct with DiCaprio in the starring role. That studio eventually dumped the project and it was undertaken by the independent Red Granite Pictures that arranged for Paramount to distribute the film in North America and Japan, this studio ironically being the first studio to bid on the project. Hill, who received an Oscar nomination as Best Supporting Actor, later complained that he received only $60,000 for his performance while DiCaprio, who served as a producer and star, received a payment of $10 million, grimly illustrating the standard excesses of the in-place and disproportionate star system of today where almost all substantial budgets for significant theatrically released films are gobbled up by a scant number of top stars, which sharply reflects the blatant greed depicted in this biting-the-hand-that-feeds-you film. Other films depicting stockbrokers, stock manipulators and Wall Street include **The Abandonment**, 1916; **All My Loved Ones**, 1999; **All of It**, 1998; **American Psycho**, 2000; **Any Woman**, 1925; **The April Fools**, 1969; **Bernie**, 2011; **The Bet**, 2006; **Blood Will Tell**, 1917; **The Bonfire of the Vanities**, 1990; **The Boss' Wife**, 1986; **Bruiser**, 2000; **Bucking Broadway**, 1917; **Bull**, 2000- (TV series); **Bull's Market**, 1970; **The Cheat**, 1915; **City Limits**, 1934; **Dealers**, 1989; **Derailed**, 2005; **A Dispatch from Reuters**, 1940; **Don't Tell the Wife**, 1937; **Each Pearl a Tear**, 1916; **East of Ludgate Hill**, 1937; **Fast and Loose**, 1939; **The First 9 ½ Weeks**, 1998; **The Flash of Fate**, 1918; **Forbidden Fruit**, 1915; **From Headquarters**, 1915; **Gone, but Not Forgotten**, 2003; **Good Advice**, 2001; **A Good Year**, 2006; **Hiding Out**, 1987; **Hitch**, 2005; **I Melt with You**, 2011; **In Between**, 1994; **In Your Wildest Dreams**, 1991; **Johnny Apollo**, 1940; **Joshua**, 2007; **Jungle 2 Jungle**, 1997; **Kiss the Bride**, 2002; **The Log of the Black Pearl**, 1975 (made-for-TV); **Lucky Losers**, 1950; **The Marriage of a Young Stockbroker**, 1971; **The Match King**, 1932 (based on the life of Swedish stock swindler Ivar Kreuger); **Maurice**, 1997; **Memoirs of an Invisible Man**, 1992; **Million Dollar Weekend**, 1948; **Modern Husbands**, 1919; **Net Worth**, 2001; **New Faces of 1937**, 1937; **Nicholas Nickleby**, 2002; **Night at the Museum**, 2006; **The Ninth Guest**, 1934; **Overnight**, 2007; **Paris Interlude**, 1934; **The Path of Darkness**, 1916; **The Patient in Room 18**, 1938; **Penguin Pool Murder**, 1932; **The Plunger**, 1920; **The Pursuit of Happiness**, 2006; **Quicksilver**, 1986; **Reaching for the Moon**, 1930; **The Rich Are Always with Us**, 1932; **Rumpole of the Bailey**, 1978-1992 (TV series); **Runaway Jury**, 2003; **The Scarlet Road**, 1918; **Second Chance**, 1972 (made-for-TV); **The Secretary**, 1995 (made-for-TV); **Seize the Day**, 1986; **Soldiers of Fortune**, 2012; **A Soul for Sale**, 1918; **Stavisky**, 1974 (French stock swindler Serge Stavisky); **Steambath**, 1973 (made-for-TV); **The Strong Way**, 1917; **Surviving the Game**, 1994; **Swingtown**, 2008; **These Glamour Girls**, 1939; **They're Off**, 1918; **Times Square Playboy**, 1936; **To Honor and Obey**, 1917; **The Toast of New York**, 1937 (profiles stock manipulator James "Big Jim" Fisk Jr.); **12 Angry Men**, 1957; **25th Hour**, 2002; **Two for the Money**, 2005; **Universal Groove**, 2007; **Urbania**, 2000; **Van Gogh**, 1991; **Wall Street**, 1987; **The Wall Street Mystery**, 1931; **A Wall Street Tragedy**, 1916; **Wash-**

ington Square, 1997; **The Way of a Man with a Maid**, 1918; **The White Raven**, 1917; **The Wife He Bought**, 1918; **Wildness of Youth**, 1922; **Wolves of Wall Street**, 2002; and **You Can't Fool Your Wife**, 1923. Strong sexual content, graphic nudity, drug use, gutter language and violence prohibit viewing by children. **p**, Martin Scorsese, Leonardo DiCaprio, Riza Aziz, Joey McFarland, Emma Tillinger Koskoff, Richard Baratta, Ted Griffin; **d**, Scorsese; **cast**, DiCaprio, Matthew Mc-Conaughey, Jonah Hill, Margot Robbie, Kyle Chandler, Rob Reiner, Jon Bernthal, Jon Favreau, Jean Dujardin, Joanna Lumley, Cristin Milioti; **w**, Terence Winter (based on the book by Jordan Belfort); **c**, Rodrigo Prieto; **ed**, Thelma Schoonmaker; **prod d**, Bob Shaw; **art d**, Chris Shriver, Ellen Christiansen; **spec eff**, Drew Jiritano.

The Wolverine ★★★ 2013; U.S.; 126m; FOX; Color; Adventure; Children: Unacceptable (MPAA: R); **BD**; **DVD**. In modern-day Japan, Wolverine, played by Jackman, a mutant who cannot die and is a member of the similar X-Men, is in an unfamiliar world as he faces his ultimate nemesis, Sanada, a Yakuza crime boss, in a life-or-death battle that will leave him changed forever. He is vulnerable for the first time and pushed to his physical and emotional limits as he confronts not only lethal samurai steel but also an inner struggle against his own mortality. Despite incredible barriers and odds, Jackman wins all these battles and emerges more powerful than before. Along the way there is some love interest as Sanada's beautiful daughter, Okamoto, who is adept in karate and knife-throwing, and who is torn between her love for Jackman and her duty to Sanada. The nonstop action and the amazing special effects offered in this spectacular tale will edify any and all action-hero fans. The film was a megahit at the box office, earning more than $414.9 million in its initial release against a budget of more than $120 million. The film is the sixth in the "X-Men" series and a sequel to **X-Men: The Last Stand**, 2006; other films were **X-Men**, 2000; **X-Men: 2**, 2003, **X-Men: Origins: Wolverine**, 2009; **X-Men: First Class**, 2011. Songs: "Requiem KV 626 (Wolfgang Amadeus Mozart), "Symphony in D Minor, Movement 1" (Cesar Franck), "Dragon Dance" (Luke Steele, Hugh Jardon), "Calling Occupants of Interplanetary Craft" (Terry Edward Draper, John William Woloschuck), "Sono Tokiga Kurumade" (DJ Pmx, K Dub Shine), "Onna, Kanashi, Otona" (Yoshiko Miura, Tsunku), "Six Feet Under" (Roland Pierrehumbert, Fred Gudit, Michel Demierre, Boris De Piante, Lionel Blanc, Juerg Naegeli, Jacques Marion), "Low" (David Lowery, John Hickman), "Cielo Estrellado" (Kensuke Mitome, Gouta Wakabayashi), "Ikigai" (Michio Yamagami, Tsuyoshi Shibuya), "Person in Power" (George Mathews, Gilde Flores). Intense violence prohibits viewing by children. **p**, Hugh Jackman, John Palermo, Hutch Parker, Lauren Shuler Donner; **d**, James Mangold; **cast**, Jackman, Famke Janssen, Will Yun Lee, Tao Okamoto, Hiroyuki Sanada, Brian Tee, Svetlana Khodchenkova, Rila Fukushima, Luke Webb, Hal Yamanouchi; **w**, Mark Bomback, Scott Frank; **c**, Ross Emery; **m**, Marco Beltrami; **ed**, Michael McCusker; **prod d**, Francois Audouy; **art d**, Rika Nakanishi, Michael Turner, Ian Gracie; **spec eff**, Brian Cox, Mitchell Cox, Leanne Brooks, Louis Craig.

Woman in Gold ★★★ 2015; U.K.; 109m; Origin Productions/Weinstein; Color; Drama; Children: Unacceptable (MPAA: PG-13); **BD**; **DVD**; **IV**. Based on a true story, Mirren plays Maria Altmann (1916-2011), a Jewish woman who fled Vienna, Austria, sixty years before the film begins. It is her story of attempting to reclaim wealthy family possessions including art works that had been seized by the Nazis just before the start of WWII (1939-1945). Among the family's stolen treasures was a portrait of her beloved aunt, "Portrait of Adele Bloch-Bauer 1" painted by Gustave Klimt, a friend of the family which also owned four others by the artist that were stolen by the Nazis. Living in Los Angeles as the film begins, Mirren enlists Reynolds, a young lawyer, to help her, but they face many obstacles because the Austrian government considers the artworks now to be their own national treasures because they had

Leonardo DiCaprio in *The Wolf of Wall Street*, 2013.

never left Austria. The film contains several flashbacks as Mirren recalls Nazi suppression and looting of Jews in Vienna when she was a girl (played by Maslany) and how, when escaping, she is forced to abandon her parents. In flash-forward, Mirren is seen attending her sister's funeral, and, among her things, she finds letters from the 1940s that reveal the Nazi theft of family possessions including the Klimt portrait of their aunt, who had since become known as the "Woman in Gold" because of the painting. Austria's minister and art director fight efforts to reclaim the work, saying it has become part of Austria's national identity and they claim that the aunt willed it to Austria, but that proves to be false. Mirren and Reynolds spend nearly ten years in their struggle and take their case to the U.S. Supreme Court which rules in Mirren's favor in 2004. Mirren recovers the painting which she sold for $135 million to Ronald Lauder in 2006 and is now on permanent display at his Neue Galerie in New York City. Mirren is exceptional in her role, as is Reynolds, her dedicated representative, in their uphill battle to reclaim their prized possessions. The film is reminiscent of **The Monuments Men**, 2014, released a year earlier, where dedicated art experts at the end of WWII make a desperate effort to reclaim the great European artworks stolen by the Nazis before and during WWII. This film was a success at the box office, earning more than $61.6 million in its initial release against a budget of more than $11 million. Songs/Music: "Persuasion Theme" (Martin Phipps), "It" (Marcos D'Cruze), "O Mary Don't You Weep" (traditional), "Sherele Dance" and "Mizinke Oysgegebn" (M.M. Warshawsk), "Prayer from Jewish Life" (Ernest Bloch), "Verklarte Nacht, Op. 4" (Arnold Schoenberg), "Carousels and Clowns" (Anthony Sadler, Gaynor Sadler). Thematic elements and brief gutter language prohibit viewing by children. **p**, David M. Thompson, Kris Thykier, Joanie Blaikie, Peter Heslop; **d**, Simon Curtis; **cast**, Helen Mirren, Ryan Reynolds, Charles Dance, Elizabeth McGovern, Jonathan Pryce, Frances Fisher, Mortiz Bleibtreu, Tom Schilling, Daniel Bruhl, Katie Holmes, Tatiana Maslany; **w**, Alexi Kaye Campbell (based on the life story of Maria Altmann, E. Randol Schoenberg); **c**, Ross Emery; **m**, Hans Zimmer, Martin Phipps; **ed**, Peter Lambert; **prod d**, Jim Clay; **art d**, Dominic Masters, Caty Maxey; **set d**, **spec eff**, Mark Holt.

Woodlawn ★★★ 2015; U.S.; 123m; Crescent City Productions/Pure-Flix Cinema; Color; Sports Drama; Children: Unacceptable (MPAA: PG); **BD**; **DVD**. This inspiring Christian film, based on true events, begins when racial tensions surface both on and off the football field at Woodlawn High School in Birmingham, Alabama, when it is integrated in the early 1970s. Bishop, the team's coach, enlists the help of Astin, a motivational speaker, to heal relations among the players. He scores points by telling the team that Jesus is the way, the truth, and the life. Castille, one of the black players, becomes very valuable to the team

Hugh Jackman in *The Wolverine*, 2013.

and is instrumental in resolving the racial differences of the players. Castille, who renders an exceptional performance, plays Tony Curtis Nathan (1956-), running back for the team and who later became a coach. Voight, too, is a standout when playing legendary University of Alabama football coach Paul "Bear" Bryant (1913-1983) as are Bishop and Astin, the latter having had great experience with football when starring in the excellent sports film **Rudy**, 1993. The film earned $14.4 million in its initial release against a budget of more than $25 million. Thematic elements, racial tension and violence prohibit viewing by children. **p**, Kevin Downes, Daryl C. Lefever, Bill Marsilii, Justin Tolley, Josha Walsh; **d**, Andrew Erwin, Jon Erwin; **cast**, Sean Astin, Caleb Castille, Jon Voight, Nic Bishop, Sherri Shepherd, C. Thomas Howell, Joy Brunson, Lance E. Nichols, Kevin Sizemore, Brett Rice, DeVon Franklin; **w**, Jon Erwin, Quinton Peeples; **c**, Kristopher Kimlin, **m**, Paul Mills; **ed**, Brent McCorkle; **prod d**, Jaymes Hinkle; **set d**, David Hack; **spec eff**, John Baker, Mack Chapman.

The Words ★★★ 2012; U.S.; 102m; Also Known As Pictures/CBS Films; Color; Drama; Children: Unacceptable (MPAA: PG-13); **BD**; **DVD**; **IV**. Quaid is a novelist who has become an overnight sensation for writing a bestseller about a struggling young writer, Cooper, who, while on his honeymoon in Paris with his wife, Saldana, finds a briefcase in an antique shop. Inside the case he finds a manuscript about a young American soldier's doomed romance with a French woman at the end of WWII (1939-1945). (The viewer may rightly guess that the soldier is Ernest Hemingway and that Hemingway wrote the story before he became famous.) In flashback, we see Cooper retyping the manuscript and it is published, having a huge success. Cooper then meets the true author of the work, Irons, who is known as The Old Man, and, surprisingly, is not upset that Cooper has stolen his work. Irons, nevertheless, wants Cooper to face the Pandora's Box moral consequences of stealing another writer's manuscript. That will, if achieved, make Cooper realize he really is only a mediocre writer. In flashback, we see Irons as Barnes, a young soldier stationed in Paris during the close of WWII, falling in love with French waitress Arnezeder. They marry, but after they lose their infant child and Arnezeder misplaces Barnes' brilliant manuscript on a Paris metro, they divorce. It is that very lost manuscript that Cooper plagiarizes In flash-forward, Cooper meets with Irons, who now works in a NYC plant nursery and attempts to make amends with payment and recognition that Irons is the true author of the book. Irons, however, refuses, saying that all of this would only ruin them both and that Cooper should live with his mistake and move on with his life, just as he has done. Troubled to the last frame of this dilemma-crowded film, Cooper confesses his guilt and regrets about the work that has made him rich and famous to his loving wife. Sal-

dana, however, assures Cooper that they are going to be fine. Though many critics slammed this film for being too intellectual and literary for audiences, it deserved a better fate as it does a good job examining conscience and morality in committing plagiarism (something lost on the Internet where such thieving is blatant as evidenced in the massive lifting exhibited by Wikipedia and other such ersatz source sites). Good performances are rendered by Quaid, Cooper, Saldana, Irons, Barnes, Arnezeder and the rest of the cast, while the story is inventive, revealing, and entertaining throughout. The film earned more than $13.2 million in its initial release against a budget of more than $6 million. Songs: "La Marseillaise" (Claude Joseph Rouget De Lisle), "Dodo, L'enfante, Do" (traditional), "Harry Hops" (Cory Wong). *Author's Note*: As earlier stated, the lost-and-found manuscript on which this story is based stems from a suitcase of manuscripts Ernest Hemingway (1899-1961) lost early in his budding career. Actually, Hemingway's first wife, Elizabeth Hadley Richardson (1891-1979), planned to take all of his manuscripts before joining him in Switzerland, but misplaced the suitcase packed with those manuscripts, including all copies and carbons, in a Paris train station (the Gare de Lyon) in December 1922. Only two of Hemingway's stories, "Up in Michigan," and "My Old Man," which were inaccessible to the thoroughly packing Hadley, survived. This is exactly what happens in one of the flashbacks in this film. When this author met Hemingway and asked him about this tragic loss, he shrugged it off as an insignificant incident, stating: "It was juvenilia—young, rough stuff I had not cleaned up. Some ideas, some scenes I might have used somewhere, sometime, but I did not feel any great loss about those missing scripts. I have a good memory and I could recall what I needed to remember in the writing that went forward in those days. Poor Hadley—she wept and wept over that. Her tears were more precious than any of those missing stories." Ironically, the actor playing that early Hemingway role model (Irons as a youth) in this film, Ben Barnes, bears the same last name as Hemingway's hero in his first significant novel, Jake Barnes, in *The Sun Also Rises*, 1925. This film was shot on location in Montreal, Canada, as its locale ideally served for both the Paris and NYC settings of this story. Gutter language and smoking prohibit viewing by children. **p**, Michael Benaroya, Tatiana Kelly, Jim Young, Rose Ganguzza, James Lejsek, Ben Sachs; **d&w**, Brian Klugman, Lee Sternthal; **cast**, Bradley Cooper, Jeremy Irons, Dennis Quaid, John Hannah, Zoe Saldana, Ben Barnes, Nora Arnezeder, Zeljko Ivanek, Michael McKean, J.K. Simmons, Olivia Wilde, James Babson, Klugman, Sternthal; **c**, Antonio Calvache; **m**, Marcel Zarvos; **ed**, Leslie Jones; **prod d**, Michele Laliberte; **set d**, Frederique Bolte; **spec eff**, Bill Rivard, Louis Craig.

Words and Pictures ★★★ 2013; U.S.; 111m; Latitude Productions; Roadside Attractions; Color; Comedy/Drama/Romance; Children: Unacceptable (MPAA: PG-13); **BD**; **DVD**. Owen, a high-spirited English teacher, and Binoche, a new, stoic art teacher, become attracted to one another at an upscale prep school in Maine, but have a strong disagreement. They clash about which is more powerful in teaching techniques, words or pictures. It ends up with a competition at the school in which students decide which is more important, while the two teachers struggle with their own personal demons as they try to connect with each other. Further, the couple must face their own personal dilemmas; Owen's job is at risk because he is an alcoholic, and Binoche, a perfectionist who is indifferent to the personal needs of her students, can't paint as she would like because of rheumatoid arthritis. Owen organizes the words and pictures competition among the students, and the school administrators are so impressed with his plan that they decide to keep him on staff. Owen then pursues Binoche, who invites him to her home, but he quickly over-drinks her vodka and drunkenly crashes into and ruins her best painting. Moreover, Owen admits that he has plagiarized a poem from his own son and Binoche cannot forgive him, ordering him from her sanctuary. Owen recoups Binoche's affection and his own integrity by stating to the school board his plagiarism and then resigns. He asks only that he stay on for the remaining season so that he can organize the Words and Pictures assembly and he is granted his wish; it is seen that he and Binoche will have a strong relationship in the future. Owen and Binoche are standouts in this delightful film, which is cleverly written, the script being witty and intelligent. The film earned about $3.3 million in its initial release. Songs: "Jungle Drum" (Emilara Torrini, Daniel Carey), "Hope" (Joey Calderazzo), "The Stars Are Out Tonight" (David Bowie), "Waiting for My Real Life to Begin" (Colin Hay, Thomas Mooney), "You Bring the Sun Out" (Jessy Dixon, Tom Snow), "I Am a Small Poem" (Paul Grabowsky, Gerald DiPago), "Doubly" and "Minor Three" (Grabowsky). Sexual material, including nude sketches, mature thematic material and gutter language prohibit viewing by children. **p**, Curtis Burch, Gerald Di Pego, Fred Schepisi, Gary Cogill, Frankey Dey; **d**, Schepisi; **cast**, Clive Owen, Juliette Binoche, Bruce Davison, Valerie Tian, Navid Negahban, Amy Brenneman, Adam DiMarco, Josh Ssettuba, Janet Kidder, Christian Scheider, Keegan Connor Tracy; **w**, Gerald Di Pego as Gerald Dipego; **c**, Ian Baker; **m**, Paul Grabowsky; **ed**, Peter Honess; **art d**, Kendelle Elliott, James Steuart; **set d**, Hamish Purdy.

World War Z ★★★ 2013; U.S./Malta; 116m; PAR; Color; Horror; Children: Unacceptable (MPAA: PG-13); **BD**; **DVD**. Action-loaded tale begins with Pitt, who is a former United Nations investigator and is content with his wife, Enos, and family. The world is suddenly plagued by a mysterious infection turning large human populations into rampaging, mindless zombies. After barely escaping the zombies, Pitt is sent on a mission to investigate the devastating disease. He goes on a harrowing trip around the world, braving dangers to find answers to solve the mystery before the plague brings an end to civilization. Pitt is exceptional as he battles the ghastly zombies (a genre running thin through overuse), and the special effects take the prize in sustaining tension and high-fright throughout. The film was a megahit at the box office, earning more than $540 million in its initial release against a budget of more than $190 million. Songs: "The 2nd Law: Isolated System," "Follow Me" (Matthew Bellamy); "Villa del Refugio" (Jeremy Gallindo, Christopher Royal King, Ramond Brown); "Go" (Kari Kimmel); "Salaam" (Mosh Ben-Ari). Frightening zombie sequences, violence and disturbing images prohibit viewing by children. **p**, Brad Pitt, Ian Bryce, Dede Gardner, Jeremy Kleiner; **d**, Marc Forster; **cast**, Pitt, Mireille Enos, Matthew Fox, Daniella Kertesz, James Badge Dale, Ludi Boeken, Fana Mokoena, David Morse, Elyes Gabel, Peter Capaldi, Ruth Negga, Sterling Jerins; **w**, Matthew Michael Carnahan, Drew Goddard, Damon Lindelof (based on a story by Carnahan, J. Michael Straczynski and the novel by Max Brooks); **c**, Ben Seresin, Robert Richardson; **m**, Marco Beltrami; **ed**, Roger Barton, Matt Chesse; **prod d**, Nigel Phelps; **art d**, Ben Collins, James Foster, Matthew Gray, Jon Billington, Alan Gilmore; **set d**, Jennifer Williams; **spec eff**, Neil Corbould, Gabor Kiszelly.

The World's End ★★★ 2013; U.K.; 109m; Big Talk Productions; Focus Features; Color; Science Fiction; Children: Unacceptable (MPAA: R); **BD**; **DVD**. Five friends in England reunite twenty years after attempting a major evening of pub-crawling when one of them, Pegg, becomes obsessed with attempting the drinking marathon again. He drags his reluctant friends to their hometown once gain to reach the pub they visited years earlier, called The World's End. In trying to reconcile the past and present, they all realize the real struggle for them is for the future, not just their destinies, but the fate of the human race. They learn that one of them has been replaced by androids and come to think the others have also been replicated, until they find that the four are still human beings. They eventually learn to live with the systematic conversion of humans to androids from alien Nighy, who tells them that the android invasion of Earth was essential in bringing the turbulent planet into harmony with the confederation of planets throughout the universe. The implausibility of this story is accented by its clever script that presents many comedic moments to prove what fools all mortals

Simon Pegg, Nick Frost, Eddie Marsan and Paddy Considine in *The World's End,* **2013.**

be, and the cast members give zesty performances that fascinate throughout. The film saw a healthy return from the box office, earning more than $46 million in its initial release against a budget of more than $20 million. Songs: "Alabama Song/Whisky Bar" (music: Kurt Weill; lyrics: Bertolt Brecht), "Summer's Magic" (Luc Aulivier, Jacques Charriere, Serge Danot, Alain LeGrand, Mark Summers), "The Only Rhyme That Bites" (Andrew Barker, Nicky Lockett, Graham Massey, Jerome Moross, Darren Partington, Martin Price), "Loaded" (Bobby Gillespie, Andrew Innes, Robert Young), "There's No Other Way" (Damon Albarn, Graham Coxon, Steven James, David Roundtree), "I'm Free" (Mick Jagger, Keith Richards), "Step On" (Christos Demetriou, John Kongos), "So Young" (Brett Anderson, Bernard Butler), "Old Red Eyes Is Back" (Paul Heaton, David Rotheray), "Come Home" (Timothy Booth, James Glennie, James Gott), "The Only One I Know" (Jon Baker, Martin Victor Blunt, Jon Brookes, Timothy Burgess, Robert James Collins), "Do You Remember the First Time?" Nick Banks, Jarvis Cocker, Candida Doyle, Stephen Mackey, Russell Senior), "What You Do to Me" (Norman Blake, Gerard Love, Raymond McGinley, Brendan O'Hare), "Fools Gold" (Ian Brown, John Squire), "Get a Life" (Hayden Browne, Beresford Romeo), "This Is How It Feels" (Clinton Booth, Craig Hill, Thomas Hingley, Graham Lambert, Martyn Walsh), "Wear Your Love Like Heaven" (Rex Brough, Kevin Clark, B.B. Cunningham, Gary McEwen, Donald Weeks), "Set Adrift on Memory Bliss" (Attrell Cordes, Gary Kemp), "Step Back in Time" (Stock Aiken Waterman), "Join Our Club" (Bob Stanley, Peter Wiggs), "Here's Where the Story Ends" (David Gavurin, Harriet Wheeler), "20 Seconds to Comply" (Richard Brown), "This Corrosion" (Andrew Eldritch), "Happy Hour" (Ian Peter Cullimore, Paul Heaton). Gutter language, sexual references and drinking prohibit viewing by children. **p**, Tim Bevan, Eric Fellner, Nira Park, Mairi Bett; **d**, Edgar Wright; **cast**, Simon Pegg, Thomas Law, Zachary Bailess, Jasper Levine, James Tarpey, Luke Bromley, Sophie Evans, Samantha White, Rose Reynolds, Richard Hadfield; **w**, Simon Pegg, Wright; **c**, Bill Pope; **m**, Steven Price; **ed**, Paul Machliss; **prod d**, Marcus Rowland; **art d**, Peter Dorme, Nick Gottschalk; **set d**, Sara Wan; **spec eff**, Chris Reynolds, Frazer Churchill, Genevieve Claire.

X-Men: Days of Future Past ★★★ 2014; U.S./U.K.; 131m; Marvel Entertainment/FOX; Color; Science Fiction; Children: Unacceptable (MPAA: PG-13); **BD**; **DVD**. The X-Men send Wolverine, portrayed by Jackman, to the past in a desperate attempt to change history and prevent an event that results in doom for both humans and mutants. The plot alternates between the year 1980 and the future year of 2013. In the future, Sentinels rule the United States and mutants are hunted and placed in

Jennifer Ehle in *Zero Dark Thirty*, 2012.

internment camps. Having conquered North America, the Sentinels turn their attention to mutants and other super humans around the world. On the eve of a feared nuclear holocaust, the few remaining X-Men led by Jackman send the mind of Kitty Pryde, played by Page, backward through time to possess the body of her younger self and to prevent a pivotal event in mutant-human history, the assassination of a senator by the newly reassembled Brotherhood of Evil Mutants, led by Mystique, who is essayed by Lawrence. Working with the present-day X-Men, Page's future self succeeds in her mission and is pulled back to her own time, while her present-day self is returned without memory of any interim adventure. The world of 2013 is not shown again in the story, and the present-day X-Men are left to wonder whether their future has been averted or simply delayed. Tension-filled throughout, the nonstop action is accented by spectacular special effects that dazzle and amaze from the first frame to the last. Not unexpectedly, the film received an Oscar nomination for Best Visual Effects, the first time any entry of the series received an Academy Award nomination. This seventh installment of the X-Men series saw an enormous box office success, becoming the highest-grossing entry in the series when earning more than $747.9 million in its initial release against a budget of more than $200 million. Songs: "The First Time Ever I Saw Your Face" (Ewan MacColl), "The Price Is Right Theme" (Robert Israel), "Hello Hooray" (Rolf Peter Kempf), "Sanford and Son Theme (The Streetbeater)" (Quincy Jones), "Time in a Bottle" (Jim Croce), "Stop au nom de l'amour" (Brian Holland, Lamont Dozier, Edward Holland, Jr.), "C'est si bon" (Andre Hornez, Henri Betti), "Time Reverse/Future" (Alexander Courage), "King Cotton" (Harry Bluestone), "Hail to the Chief" (James Sanderson), "Star Spangled Banner" (Francis Scott Key), "Dixie Chicken" (Lowell George, Martin Kibbee). Violence, suggestive material, nudity, and gutter language prohibit viewing by children. **p**, Bryan Singer, Simon Kinberg, Hutch Parker, Lauren Shuler Donner; **d**, Singer; **cast**, Hugh Jackman, Patrick Stewart, Halle Berry, Ian McKellen, James McAvoy, Anna Paquin, Evan Peters, Jennifer Lawrence, Michael Fassbender, Peter Dinklage; **w**, Kinberg (based on a story by Kinberg, Jane Goldman, Matthew Vaughn); **c**, Newton Thomas Sigel; **m**, John Ottman; **ed**, John Ottman; **prod d**, John Myhre; **art d**, Michele Laliberte, Vincent Gingras-Liberali, Felix Lariviere-Charron; **set d**, Gordon Sim; **spec eff**, Cameron Waldbauer.

Yennai Arindhaal ★★★ 2015; India; 168m; Sri Sathya Sai Movies; Color; Crime Drama; Children: Unacceptable; **DVD**. Shetty is in Boston and becomes ill on an airplane as she sits next to Kumar. The following day, she is in a coffee shop when Vijay, a criminal, tries to

abduct her, but Kumar overpowers Vijay to prevent the abduction. In flashback to Madras in 1989, we see a criminal kill Kumar's father, Nasser. Kumar then gets into trouble with the law and winds up in a prison cell with Vijay. They manage to escape, and this leads to a series of kidnappings and killings which ends with Vijay admitting he killed Nasser and some others. Vijay and Kumar get into a fight that Kumar wins. Kumar then drags the wounded Vijay out of a house and allows his associates in crime to kill him for his past betrayals. Offbeat and even bizarre, this film presents many unexpected twists and turns that will keep the viewer's attention until its violent end. Songs: "Yaen Ennai," "Mazhai Vara Pogudhae," "Unakkenna Venum Sollu," "Yennai Arindhaal," "Adhaaru Adhaaru," "Maya Bazaar," "Idhayathai Vedho Ondru" (Thamarai). Excessive violence prohibits viewing by children. **p**, Aishwarya, A.M. Rathnam; **d**, Gautham Menon; **cast**, Ajith Kumar, Arun Vijay, Trishna Krishnan, Anushka Shetty, Vivek, Baby Anikha, Ashish Vidyarthi, Suman, Avinash, Parvathy Nair, Selva Stunt, George Vishnu, Cell Murugan; **w**, Menon, Thiagarajan Kumararaja, Shridhar Raghavan; **c**, Dan Macarthur; **m**, Harris Jayaraj; **ed**, Anthony; **art d**, Rajeevan; **spec eff**, Rv Balajai.

Zero Dark Thirty ★★★ 2012; U.S.; 157m; COL; Color; Historical Drama; Thriller; Children: Unacceptable (MPAA: R); **BD**; **DVD**. This well-crafted film presents the ten-year hunt for al-Qaeda terrorist leader Osama bin Laden after the September 2001 attacks in the United States and his death at the hands of the U.S. Navy SEAL Team 6 in May 2011. The film's title is spy language for "half past midnight," the time of bin Laden's death. Most of the film follows Maya, played by Chastain, a CIA agent at the U.S. embassy in Pakistan. She does not believe the terrorist is hiding in a cave in Afghanistan, as the media insists, but that he is living in almost open sight, and she deals with opposition to this theory. She goes through mountains of data and tries to locate Abu Ahmed and use him to find bin Laden and survives the 2008 bombing of the Islamabad Marriott Hotel and an attack against her when she is shot at in her car. Ehle, her friend and fellow officer, is killed the following year in an attack on Camp Chapman. The CIA traces phone calls that lead them to a compound in Abbottabad, Pakistan, near the Pakistan Military Academy. The CIA puts the compound under heavy surveillance for several months, confident that bin Laden is there. The CIA is tasked with producing a plan to capture or kill bin Laden if it can be confirmed that he is hiding in the compound. When that seems likely to be true, two U.S. stealth helicopters secretly enter Pakistan and deposit the SEAL team to raid the compound. The raid is approved and executed on May 2, 2011, during which one of the helicopters crashes and the SEALS team kills a number of people within the compound, among them a man on the top floor, who is identified as bin Laden. The SEALS team takes the terrorist's body to a U.S. base in Jalalabad, Afghanistan, where Chastain confirms it is that of bin Laden. She then boards a military transport plane to return to the U.S. and is its only passenger. The pilot asks where she wants to be flown but she does not reply, but begins to weep over her life-threatening odyssey to track down one of the world's worst mass murderers. The decade-long ordeal to find bin Laden is finally over and he is dead. Chastain is a standout in her role as the relentless CIA operative seeking justice, and who is strongly supported by the rest of the talented cast members, all working from a taut script that provides tension throughout under the firm direction of Bigelow. The action sequences are particularly well orchestrated, especially in the raid against the terrorist's compound. Paul N.J. Ottosson received an Oscar for Best Sound Editing. The film also received Oscar nominations for Best Picture; Best Actress (Chastain); Best Original Screenplay (Boal); and Best Film Editing (Goldenberg; Tichenor). The film was a great success at the box office, earning more than $132.8 million in its initial release against a budget of more than $40 million. Songs: "Need You Now" (Hillary Scott, Josh Kear, Dave Haywood, Charles Kelley),

"Move Ya Body" (Lionel Bermingham, Elijah Wells, Cordel Burell, Natalie Albino, Nicole Albino, Luis Diaz), "Pavlov's Dogs" (Charles Maggio, Keith Huckins, Andrew Gormley, Nick Forte, Chris Laucella), "Pyaar Hai Tumse" (Amir Jamal, Nasir Hussain, Nasir Ali Nasir), "Night Song" (Nusrat Fateh Ali Khan), "Rise Up" (Seren Reyes, Louise Freese, Demrick Shelton Ferm, Tom Morello), "Murder" (Jimmy Gnecco). Excessive violence, including brutal disturbing images, and gutter language prohibit viewing by children. **p**, Kathryn Bigelow, Mark Boal, Megan Ellison, Stephanie Antosca, Matthew Budman, Jonathan Leven; **d**, Bigelow; **cast**, Jessica Chastain, Jason Clarke, James Gandolfini, Jennifer Ehle, John Barrowman, Stephen Dillane, Reda Kateb, Kyle Chandler, Harold Perrineau, Jeremy Strong, Fares Fares, Scott Adkins, Mark Strong, Lauren Shaw; **w**, Mark Boal; **c**, Greig Fraser; **m**, Alexandre Desplat; **ed**, William Goldenberg, Dylan Tichenor; **prod d**, Jeremy Hindle; **art d**, Ben Collins, Rod McLean; **set d**, Lisa Chugg; **spec eff**, Blair Foord, Neil Corbould, David Brighton, David Watkins, J.D. Schwalm.

The Zero Theorem ★★★ 2014; U.S./Romania/U.K.; 107m; Voltage Pictures/Amplify; Color; Science Fiction; Children: Unacceptable (MPAA: R); **BD**; **DVD**. The film begins with Waltz, an eccentric and reclusive computer genius living in a futuristic corporate world and suffering from existential anxiety as he waits for a phone call explaining the meaning of life. Under the instruction of a shadowy figure known only as "Management" (Damon), Waltz works to solve the "Zero Theorem," a mathematical formula derived from the Big Crunch theory of the creation of the universe. The fate of the universe as a black hole is believed to show that life has no purpose. Waltz's workplace is a burned-out chapel that serves as his home, and he is interrupted by visits from Thierry, a seductive woman, and Damon's teenage son, Hedges, both purposely sent to distract him. Offbeat, even weird, this film seeks to find with Earth-trapped logic a concrete answer to the "Big Bang Theory," where there is none, but nevertheless provides considerable fascination in the quest for what is otherwise God. This film did not do well at the box office, earning a little more than $1.2 million in its initial release against a budget of between $8 and $13 million. Songs: "Creep" (Thom Yorke), "Chapel of Love" (Jeff Barry, Ellie Greenwich, Phil Spector). *Author's Note*: Any and all scientists advancing the "Big Bang Theory" have only shrugged when asked where the "Bang" originated. None want to confront the fact that something cannot come from nothing and that the source of that "Bang" had to be supernatural rather than natural, which revealingly admits (as did Thomas Aquinas, the foremost proponent of natural theology) the existence of God. Gutter language, some sexuality and nudity prohibit viewing by children. **p**, Nicolas Chartier, Dean Zanuck, Christoph Waltz, Chris Curling, Zev Foreman, Phil Robertson, Andreea Stanculeanu; **d**, Terry Gilliam; **cast**, Waltz, Matt Damon, Rupert Friend, Melanie Thierry, David Thewlis, Ben Whishaw, Tilda Swinton, Lucas Hedges, Sanjeev Bhaskar; **w**, Pat Rushin; **c**, Nicola Pecorini; **m**, George Fenton; **ed**, Mick Audsley; **prod d**, David Warren; **art d**, Adrian Curelea; **set d**, Jille Azis, Gina Stancu; **spec eff**, Nick Allder, Adrian Popescu.

ALTERNATE TITLES

Note: Titles in this index apply to only entries profiled in this work and are shown in boldface, these boldfaced titles being the most popularly used as U.S. releases.

Abandoned Woman; see **Abandoned**, 1949.

Abbott and Costello Meet the Ghosts; see **Abbott and Costello Meet Frankenstein**, 1948.

Able Seaman Brown; see **Sailor of the King**, 1953.

Accused; see **Mark of the Hawk**, 1958.

Ace in the Hole; see **The Big Carnival**, 1951.

Adalen Riots; see **Adalen 31**, 1969.

Adventures of Huckleberry Finn; see **Huckleberry Finn**, 1939.

Adventures of Jack London; see **Jack London**, 1943.

The Adventures of Quentin Durward; see **Quentin Durward**, 1955.

The Adventuress; see **I See a Dark Stranger**, 1946.

The Affairs of Sally; see **The Fuller Brush Girl**, 1950.

African Fury; see **Cry, the Beloved Country**, 1952.

After You; see **Apres vous**, 2003.

The Age of Beauty; see **Belle epoque**, 1992.

Age of Gold; see **L'age d'or**, 1979.

Akira Kurosawa's Dreams; see **Dreams**, 1990.

Alexander Graham Bell, see **The Story of Alexander Graham Bell**, 1939

Ali—Fear Eats the Soul; see **Fear Eats the Soul**, 1974.

All Dogs Go to Heaven 2: Charlie's New Adventure, see **All Dogs Go to Heaven 2**, 1996

All That Money Can Buy; see **The Devil and Daniel Webster**, 1941.

All the Mornings of the World; see **Tous les matins du monde**, 1991.

All the Way; see **The Joker Is Wild**, 1957.

Amelie from Montmartre; see **Amelie**, 2001.

The Amorous General; see **Waltz of the Toreadors**, 1962.

An Affair of the Heart; see **Body and Soul**, 1947.

An Autumn Tale; see **Autumn Tale**, 1998.

Andrews' Raiders; see **The Great Locomotive Chase**, 1956.

Angel Street; see **Gaslight**, 1940.

Angels and the Pirates; see **Angels in the Outfield**, 1951.

Animal House; see **National Lampoon's Animal House**, 1978.

Anne and Muriel; see **Two English Girls**, 1972.

Annie's Coming Out; see **A Test of Love**, 1985.

Antonia; see **Antonia's Line**, 1995.

The Anxious Years; see **The Dark Journey**, 1937.

The Army of Shadows; see **L'armee des ombres**, 1969.

At Good Old Siwash; see **Those Were the Days**, 1940.

Atertraffen; see **The Reunion**, 2013.

Atlantic City U.S.A.; see **Atlantic City**, 1981.

The Atomic Monster; see **Man-Made Monster**, 1941.

Atomic Rocketship; see **Flash Gordon**, 1936.

Bachelor Knight; see **The Bachelor and the Bobby-Soxer**, 1947.

Bad Man of Wyoming; see **Wyoming**, 1940.

The Bad Sleep Well; see **Warui yatsu hodo yoku nemuru**, 1963.

The Bailiff; see **Sansho, the Bailiff**, 1969.

The Bank Detective; see **The Bank Dick**, 1940.

Banner in the Sky; see **Third Man on the Mountain**, 1959.

Barnacle Bill; see **All at Sea**, 1958.

The Battle for Anzio; see **Anzio**, 1968.

The Battle of Midway; see **Midway**, 1976.

Battle Stripe; see **The Men**, 1950.

The Battling Bellhop; see **Kid Galahad**, 1937.

Beauty of the Day; see **Belle de jour**, 1968.

Beggars Opera; see **The Three Penny Opera**, 1931.

Behind the Iron Curtain; see **The Iron Curtain**, 1948.

Betrayed; see **When Strangers Marry**, 1944.

The Big Heart; see **The Miracle on 34th Street**, 1947.

The Big North; see **The Wild North**, 1952.

Billy Rose's Diamond Horseshoe; see **Diamond Horseshoe**, 1945.

The Birds and the Bees; see **Three Daring Daughters**, 1948.

Birds of a Feather; see **La cage aux folles**, 1979.

Birthmark; see **The Omen**, 1976.

The Bitch; see **La chienne**, 1975.

The Black Book, see **Reign of Terror**, 1949.

Blazing Arrows; see **Fighting Caravans**, 1931.

Blonde Bombshell; see **Bombshell**, 1933.

A Blonde in Love; see **Loves of a Blonde**, 1966.

Blood Oath; see **Prisoners of the Sun**, 1991.

Blood on My Hands; see **Kiss the Blood off My Hands**, 1948.

Blood of the Vampires; see **Curse of the Vampires**, 1970.

The Boat; see **Das Boot**, 1982.

Bosambo; see **Sanders of the River**, 1935.

Both Ends of the Candle; see **The Helen Morgan Story**, 1959.

The Boys from County Clare; see **The Boys and Girls from County Clare**, 2005.

Brigham Young; see **Brigham Young: Frontiersman**, 1940.

Brink of Hell; see **Toward the Unknown**, 1956.

Brotherhood of the Yakuza; see **The Yakuza**, 1975.

Build My Gallows High; see **Out of the Past**, 1947.

Cabiria; see **Nights of Cabiria**, 1957.

Café of the Seven Sinners; see **Seven Sinners**, 1940.

Caine, see **Shark!**, 1969.

Calling Northside 777; see **Call Northside 777**, 1948.

Canaris, Master Spy; see **Canaris**, 1955.

Captain Horatio Hornblower, R.N.; see **Captain Horatio Hornblower**, 1951.

The Card, see **The Promoter**, 1952.

Cardigan's Last Call; see **State's Attorney**, 1932.

Cargo of Innocents; see **Stand By for Action**, 1942.

Carmen; see **Bizet's Carmen**, 1984.

Caribbean Holiday; see **One Night in the Tropics**, 1940.

Carrington V.C.; see **Court Martial**, 1954.

The Cars That Eat People; see **The Cars That Ate Paris**, 1974.

The Castaway; see **The Cheaters**, 1945.

Castle of Doom; see **Vampyr**, 1932.

The Castle of the Spider's Web; see **Throne of Blood**, 1961.

The Cave Dwellers; see **One Million B.C.**, 1940.

Cave Man; see **One Million B.C.**, 1940.

Chained to Yesterday; see **Limbo**, 1972.

Charley's American Aunt; see **Charley's Aunt**, 1941.

Chicago, Chicago; see **Gaily, Gaily**, 1969.

Chocolate; see **Chocolat**, 1989.

The City Jungle; see **The Young Philadelphians**, 1959.

City Sentinel; see **The Beast of the City**, 1932.

The Clansman; see **The Birth of a Nation**, 1915.

Clean Slate; see **Coup de torchon**, 1981.

Cobweb Castle; see **Throne of Blood**, 1961.

Code Name: Trixie; see **The Crazies**, 1973.

Cody Banks; see **Agent Cody Banks**, 2003.

Colossus 1980; see **Colossus: The Forbin Project**, 1969.

ComDads; see **Le gai savoir**, 1984.

The Comedian Harmonists; see **The Harmonists**, 1997.

Confessions of a Cheat; see **The Story of a Cheat**, 1938.

The Contact Man; see **Alias Nick Beal**, 1949.

Convention City; see **Sons of the Desert**, 1933.

Crazy; see **C.R.A.Z.Y.**, 2005.

Creatures of Evil; see **Curse of the Vampires**, 1970.

The Crime of the Century; see **Walk East on Beacon**, 1952.

Crimes of Dr. Mabuse; see **The Testament of Dr. Mabuse**, 1943.

The Criminal; see **The Concrete Jungle**, 1962.

The Crown Caper; see **The Thomas Crown Affair**, 1968.

Cry for Me, Billy; see **Count Your Bullets**, 1972.

Cutter's Way; see **Cutter and Bone**, 1981.

The Damned; see **These Are the Damned**, 1965.

Dance of the Vampires; see **My Neck**, 1967.

Dangerous Age; see **Wild Boys of the Road**, 1933.

Dangerous Female; see **The Maltese Falcon**, 1931.

The Dark Avenger; see **The Warriors**, 1955.

Dark Eyes of London; see **The Human Monster**, 1940.

The Dark Page; see **Scandal Sheet**, 1952.

The Darkest Hour; see **Hell on Frisco Bay**, 1956.

Dead End; Cradle of Crime; see **Dead End**, 1937.

Deadline; see **Deadline—U.S.A.**, 1952.

Defense of the Realm; see **Defence of the Realm**, 1985.

The Demi-Paradise; see **Adventure for Two**, 1945.

Demon Planet; see **Planet of the Vampires**, 1966.

Desperate Siege; see **Rawhide**, 1951.

Devil in the Castle; see **Daredevil in the Castle**, 1969.

The Devil Takes the Count; see **The Devil Is a Sissy**, 1936.

Diamonds and Crime; see **Hi Diddle Diddle**, 1943.

Diary of Oharu; see **Life of Oharu**, 1964.

The Disappearance of Garcia Lorca; see **Death in Granada**, 1996.

The Dividing Line; see **The Lawless**, 1950.

The Doctor from Seven Dials; see **Corridors of Blood**, 1962.

Doctor Sleep; see **Close Your Eyes**, 2002.

Doctor Zhivago; see **Dr. Zhivago**, 1965.

Doppelganger; see **Journey to the Far Side of the Sun**, 1969.

The Double; see **Kagemusha**, 1980.

Down Went McGinty; see **The Great McGinty**, 1940.

Dr. Strangelove: Or How I Learned to Stop Worrying and Love the Bomb; see **Dr. Strangelove**, 1964.

Dracula; see **Bram Stoker's Dracula**, 1992.

Dream of Life; see **Life Begins**, 1932.

The Drum; see **Drums**, 1938.

The Earth Will Tremble; see **La Terra Trema**, 1947.

East of Shanghai; see **Rich and Strange**, 1932.

East of the Rising Sun; see **Malaya**, 1950.

The Easy Way; see **Room for One More**, 1952.

Edgar Allan Poe's Conqueror Worm; see **The Conqueror Worm**, 1968.

El, This Passion Torments; see **El**, 1955.

The Electric Man; see **Man-Made Monster**, 1941.

Elizabeth and Essex; see **The Private Lives of Elizabeth and Essex**, 1939.

Elizabeth the Queen; see **The Private Lives of Elizabeth and Essex**, 1939.

Elizabeth: The Virgin Queen; see **Elizabeth**, 1998.

Elser; see **13 Minutes**, 2015.

Emperor of the North; see **Emperor of the North Pole**, 1973.

End as a Man; see **The Strange One**, 1957.

Enemies of the Public; see **The Public Enemy**, 1931.

Escape in the Dark; see **The Littlest Horse Thieves**, 1977.

Essex and Elizabeth; see **The Private Lives of Elizabeth and Essex**, 1939.

Everybody's Cheering; see **Take Me Out to the Ball Game**, 1949.

Evil Mind; see **The Clairvoyant**, 1935.

Expedition Moon; see **Rocketship X-M**, 1950.

The Experiment; see **Das Experiment**, 2001.

Eye of Evil; see **The 1,000 Eyes of Dr. Mabuse**, 1966.

Eyes without a Face; see **Horror Express**, 1972.

The Face; see **The Magician**, 1959.

Face to the Wind; see **Count Your Bullets**, 1972.

Fake Faces; see **Let 'Em Have It**, 1935.

The Fall of Lola Montes; see **Lola Montes**, 1955.

Fall of the House of Usher; see **House of Usher**, 1960.

Falstaff; see **Chimes at Midnight**, 1967.

False Witness; see **Circle of Deceit**, 1982.

Fanatic; see **Die, Die, My Darling**, 1965.

Farewell, My Lovely; see **Murder, My Sweet**, 1944.

Fashions; see **Fashions of 1934**, 1934.

Federico Fellini's 8 ½; see **8 ½**, 1963.

Fellini's Intervista; see **Intervista**, 1987.

The Fifth Chair; see **It's in the Bag**, 1945.

Fighting Command; see **We've Never Been Licked**, 1943.

The Fighting Seventh; see **Little Big Horn**, 1951.

The Fighting Sullivans; see **The Sullivans**, 1944.

Finally Sunday; see **Confidentially Yours**, 1983.

Fine and Dandy; see **The West Point Story**, 1950.

The First Great Train Robbery; see **The Great Train Robbery**, 1979.

The First of the Few; see **Spitfire**, 1943.

The First Rebel; see **Allegheny Uprising**, 1939.

Fistful of Dynamite; see **Duck, You Sucker!**, 1972.

Five Against the House; see **5 Against the House**, 1955.

Flight Commander; see **The Dawn Patrol**, 1930.

Fog; see **A Study in Terror**, 1966.

Forbidden Alliance; see **The Barretts of Wimpole Street**, 1934.

Forbidden Love; see **Freaks**, 1937.

The Forbin Project; see **Colossus: The Forbin Project**, 1969.

Forever in Love; see **Pride of the Marines**, 1945.

The Forsyte Saga; see **That Forsyte Woman**, 1949.

Forward March; see **Doughboys**, 1930.

The Four Hundred Blows; see **The 400 Blows**, 1959.

Fraternally Yours; see **Sons of the Desert**, 1933.

Free to Live; see **Holiday**, 1938.

Frenzy; see **Torment**, 1947.

Full House; see **O. Henry's Full House**, 1952.

Gang War; see **Odd Man Out**, 1947.

Gaol Birds; see **Pardon Us**, 1931.

The Gay Divorce; see **The Gay Divorcee**, 1934.

The Gay Mrs. Trexel; see **Susan and God**, 1940.

Gentleman for a Day; see **Union Depot**, 1932.

Geordie; see **Wee Geordie**, 1956.

Georgia's Friends; see **Four Friends**, 1981.

The Ghost of John Holling; see **Mystery Liner**, 1935.

The Ghost Steps Out; see **The Time of Their Lives**, 1946.

A Girl for Joe; see **Force of Arms**, 1951.

Girl in Pawn; see **Little Miss Marker**, 1934.

Girl of the Year; see **The Petty Girl**, 1950.

The Girl Was Young; see **Young and Innocent**, 1938.

The Girls He Left Behind; see **The Gang's All Here**, 1943.

Girls in Uniform; see **Maedchen in Uniform**, 1932.

Give Me Your Hand My Love; **The Life and Loves of Mozart**, 1959.

Godard's Passion; see **Passion**, 1982.

Going Ape; see **Where's Poppa?**, 1970.

Golden Marie; see **Casque d'or**, 1956.

The Golden Trail; see **Riders of the Whistling Skull**, 1937.

Golden Virgin; see **The Story of Esther Costello**, 1957.

The Golem; see **The Gholem**, 1937.

The Good Guys Always Win; see **The Outfit**, 1973.

The Good Marriage; see **Le beau marriage**, 1982.

Good Morning Doctor; see **You Belong to Me**, 1941.

Good Old School Days; see **Those Were the Days**, 1940.

Goodbye to the Hill; see **Paddy**, 1970.

A Gorgeous Girl Like Me; see **Such a Gorgeous Kid Like Me**, 1973.

Gorillas in the Mist; see **Gorillas in the Mist: The Story of Diane Fossey**, 1988.

The Gov'nor; see **Mr. Hobo**, 1936.

The Grace Moore Story; see **So This Is Love**, 1953.

The Great Schnozzle; see **Palooka**, 1934.

Grip of Fear; see **Experiment in Terror**, 1962.

The Gun Runners; see **Santiago**, 1956.

Guns a' Blazing; see **Law and Order**, 1932.

Guns in the Afternoon; see **Ride the High Country**, 1962.

Guns, Sin and Bathtub Gin; see **The Lady in Red**, 1979.

Guy with a Grin; see **No Time for Comedy**, 1940.

Hallelujah, I'm a Tramp; see **Hallelujah, I'm a Bum!**, 1933.

A Handful of Clouds; see **Doorway to Hell**, 1930.

Hands of Orlac; see **Mad Love**, 1935.

Handsome Serge; see **Le beau serge**, 1959.

Happy Go Lucky; see **Hallelujah, I'm a Bum!**, 1933.

Happy Knowledge; see **Le gai savoir**, 1968.

Happy Landing; see **Flying High**, 1931.

Happy Times; see **The Inspector General**, 1949.

Harmony Parade; see **Pigskin Parade**, 1936.

Harry Black; see **Harry Black and the Tiger**, 1958.

He Will Bring Out the Devil in You; see **Horns**, 2013.

A Heart in Winter; see **Un Coeur en Hiver**, 1992.

The Heart of New York; see **Hallelujah, I'm a Bum!**, 1933.

Hemingway's Adventures of a Young Man; see **Adventures of a Young Man**, 1962.

Hey Sailor; see **Here Comes the Navy**, 1934.

Hidden; see **Cache**, 2005.

High Heels; see **Docteur Popaul**, 1972.

Highway to Freedom; see **Joe Smith, American**, 1942.

His Other Woman; see **Desk Set**, 1957.

Hitler: A Film from Germany; see **Our Hitler: A Film from Germany**, 1980.

Hitler's Hangman; see **Hitler's Madman**, 1943.

H.M.S. Defiant; see **Damn the Defiant!**, 1962.

Holiday; see **Jour de fete**, 1952.

Hollywood Cowboy; see **Hearts of the West**, 1975.

Home at Seven; see **Murder on Monday**, 1953.

The Honorable Mr. Wong; see **The Hatchet Man**, 1932.

Hopalong Cassidy Enters; see **Hopalong Cassidy**, 1935.

Hoppity Goes to Town; see **Mr. Bug Goes to Town**, 1941.

A Horse Called Phar Lap; see **Phar Lap**, 1984.

The Hot One; see **Corvette Summer**, 1978.

Hot Spot; see **I Wake Up Screaming**, 1942.

The Hounds of Zaroff; see **The Most Dangerous Game**, 1932.

How to Steal a Diamond in Four Easy Lessons; see **The Hot Rock**, 1972.

The Human Beast; see **La belle humaine**, 1938.

Hypnotic; see **Close Your Eyes**, 2002.

I Am a Fugitive from the Chain Gang; see **I Am a Fugitive from a Chain Gang**, 1932.

I Call First, J.R.; see **Who's That Knocking at My Door?**, 1968.

I Married a Communist; see **The Woman on Pier 13**, 1950.

I Married a Nazi; see **The Man I Married**, 1940.

I Shall Return; see **An American Guerrilla in the Philippines**, 1951.

I Was Faithless; see **Cynara**, 1932.

I Was Monty's Double; see **Hell, Heaven or Hoboken**, 1958.

If You Feel Like Singing; see **Summer Stock**, 1950.

Imaginary Sweetheart; see **Professional Sweetheart**, 1933.

In the Woods; see **Rashomon**, 1951.

Indiscretion; see **Christmas in Connecticut**, 1945.

Innocence Is Bliss; see **Miss Grant Takes Richmond**, 1949.

Intermezzo; see **Intermezzo: A Love Story**, 1939.

The Invaders; see **The 49th Parallel**, 1941.

The Iron Kiss; see **The Naked Kiss**, 1964.

Island Escape; see **No Man Is an Island**, 1962.

Isn't Life a Bitch?; **La Chienne**, 1975.

It Happened One Summer; see **State Fair**, 1946.

It Hurts Only When I Laugh; see **Only When I Laugh**, 1981.

It Shouldn't Happen to a Vet; see **All Things Bright and Beautiful**, 1979.

It's Hot in Hell; see **A Monkey in Winter**, 1962.

It's My Life; see **My Life to Live**, 1963.

J.R.; see **Who's That Knocking at My Door?**, 1968.

Jail Birds; see **Pardon Us**, 1931.

The James Brothers; see **The True Story of Jesse James**, 1957.

Jealousy; see **Variety**, 1925.

Jennie; see **Portrait of Jennie**, 1949.

Jenny Lind; see **A Lady's Morals**, 1930.

Joan Medford Is Missing; see **House of Horrors**, 1946.

Joe Palooka; see **Palooka**, 1934.

John Huston's The Dead; see **The Dead**, 1987.

The Joy of Learning; see **Le gai savoir**, 1968.

Jungle Fighters; see **The Long and the Short and the Tall**, 1961.

Justice for Sale; see **Night Court**, 1932.

Kaidan; see **Kwaidan**, 1965.

The Kidnappers; see **The Little Kidnappers**, 1954.

Killer on a Horse; see **Welcome to Hard Times**, 1967.

Kiss My Butterfly; see **I Love You, Alice B. Toklas**, 1968.

Knight without Armour; see **Knight without Armor**, 1937.

The Lady Dances; see **The Merry Widow**, 1934.

Lady Hamilton; see **That Hamilton Woman**, 1941.

The Lady Killers; see **The Ladykillers**, 1956.

Lady with a Lamp; see **Lady with the Lamp**, 1951.

The Lament of the Path; see **Pather Panchali**, 1955.

Larceny Lane; see **Blonde Crazy**, 1931.

The Last 4 Days; see **Last Days of Mussolini**, 1974.

The Last Illusion; see **The Fallen Idol**, 1949.

The Last Stage; see **The Last Stop**, 1949.

Last Ten Days of Adolf Hitler; see **The Last Ten Days**, 1956.

The Last Will of Dr. Mabuse; see **The Testament of Dr. Mabuse**, 1943.

Lazy Bones; see **Hallelujah, I'm a Bum!**, 1933.

L'espoir; see **Man's Hope**, 1947.

Lest We Forget; see **Hangmen Also Die**, 1943.

The Life and Death of Colonel Blimp; see **Colonel Blimp**, 1945.

Life for Ruth; see **Walk in the Shadow**, 1966.

Lights Out; see **Bright Victory**, 1951.

A Lion in the Streets; see **A Lion Is in the Streets**, 1953.

Lion of Sparta; see **The 300 Spartans**, 1962.

Live Today for Tomorrow; see **An Act of Murder**, 1948.

Lock Your Doors; see **The Ape Man**, 1943.

The Lone Wolf's Daughter; see **The Lone Wolf Spy Hunt**, 1939.

The Lonely Hearts Killer; see **The Honeymoon Killers**, 1969.

The Long Arm; see **The Third Key**, 1957.

Long Walk Home; see **Rabbit-Proof Fence**, 2003.

The Lorax; see **Dr. Seuss' The Lorax**, 2012.

The Loudest Whisper; see **The Children's Hour**, 1961.

Love and Sacrifice; see **America**, 1924.

Love, Sin and Bathtub Gin; see **The Lady in Red**, 1979.

Lovely to Look At; see **Thin Ice**, 1937.

The Lullaby; see **The Sin of Madelon Claudet**, 1931.

MacDonald of the Canadian Mounties; see **Pony Soldier**, 1952.

The Mad Cage; see **La cage aux folles**, 1979.

Mad Dog; see **Mad Dog Morgan**, 1976.

Mad Max II; see **The Road Warrior**, 1982.

The Mad Monk; see **Rasputin and the Empress**, 1932.

Mademoiselle France; see **Reunion in France**, 1942.

The Magnificent Seven; see **The Seven Samurai**, 1956.

The Magnificent Showman; see **Circus World**, 1964.

Man and His Mate; see **One Million B.C.**, 1940.

A Man Called Sullivan; see **The Great John L.**, 1945.

The Man from C.O.T.T.O.N.; see **Gone Are the Days!**, 1963.

The Man from the Follies Bergere; see **Follies Bergere**, 1935.

Man Hunt; see **Manhunt**, 1941.

A Man Is Ten Feet Tall; see **Edge of the City**, 1957.

Man of Bronze; see **Jim Thorpe—All American**, 1951.

The Man on America's Conscience; see **Tennessee Johnson**, 1942.

The Man Who Came Back; see **Swamp Water**, 1941.

The Man Who Cheated Life; see **The Student of Prague**, 1929.

The Man Who Lost His Way; see **Crossroads**, 1942.

The Man with Thirty Sons; see **The Magnificent Yankee**, 1950.

Maneater; see **Shark**, 1970.

Manhunt; see **From Hell to Texas**, 1958.

March of the Wooden Soldiers; see **Babes in Toyland**, 1934.

Marching Along; see **Stars and Stripes Forever**, 1952.

Marco Polo; see **Marco the Magnificent**, 1966.

Marie Du Port; see **La Marie du Port**, 1951.

Marie Walewska; see **Conquest**, 1937.

Married but Single; see **This Thing Called Love**, 1940.

Masks; see **Persona**, 1967.

Master of Lassie; see **The Hills of Home**, 1948.

Matchstick Men; see **Matchstick Man**, 2003.

A Matter of Life and Death; see **Stairway to Heaven**, 1946.

McKlusky; see **White Lightning**, 1973.

Meet Me Tonight; see **Tonight at 8:30**, 1953.

Meet Miss Marple; see **Murder She Said**, 1961.

Meet Whiplash Willie; see **The Fortune Cookie**, 1966.

Melville Goodwin, U.S.A.; see **Top Secret Affair**, 1957.

Merry Wisdom; see **Le gai savoir**, 1968.

Microscopia; see **Fantastic Voyage**, 1966.

Midshipman Easy; see **Men of the Sea**, 1951.

Miracle in the Sand; see **Three Godfathers**, 1936.

The Miracle of Fatima; see **The Miracle of Our Lady of Fatima**, 1952.

Miracle of Life; see **Our Daily Bread**, 1934.

Mishima: A Life in Four Chapters; see **Mishima**, 1985.

Miss Fane's Baby; see **Miss Fane's Baby Is Stolen**, 1934.

A Modern Hero; see **Knute Rockne—All American**, 1940.

The Modern Miracle; see **The Story of Alexander Graham Bell**, 1939.

The Molester; see **Never Take Candy from a Stranger**, 1961.

Mon oncle, see **My Uncle**, 1958.

Mon oncle d'Amerique, see **My American Uncle**, 1980.

The Monster Show; see **Freaks**, 1937.

Montenegro—Or Pigs and Pearls; see **Montenegro**, 1981.

Morgan: A Suitable Case for Treatment; see **Morgan**, 1966.

The Moving Target; see **Harper**, 1966.

Mozart; see **The Life and Loves of Mozart**, 1959.

Mr. Ashton Was Indiscreet; see **The Senator Was Indiscreet**, 1947.

Mr. Bean's Holiday, see **Mr. Bean's Vacation**, 2007.

Mr. Jordan; see **Here Comes Mr. Jordan**, 1941.

Mr. Toad's Wild Ride; see **The Wind in the Willows**, 1997.

Mr. V; see **Pimpernel Smith**, 1942.

The Murder in Thornton Square; see **Gaslight**, 1944.

Murder, Inc.; see **The Enforcer**, 1951.

The Murderers Are amongst Us; see **Murderers among Us**, 1948.

Muriel (1963), see Muriel, or The Time of Return, 2007.

My Enemy the Sea; see **Alone on the Pacific**, 1964.

My Family; see **My Family/Mi Familia**, 1995.

My Favourite Year; see **My Favorite Year**, 1982.

My Hero; see **A Southern Yankee**, 1948.

My Love Letters; see **Love Letters**, 1983.

My Main Man from Stony Island; see **Stony Island**, 1978.

My Night with Maud; see **My Night at Maud's**, 1970.

My Soul Runs Naked; see **Ratfink**, 1965.

The Mysterious Mr. Moto; see **Mysterious Mr. Moto**, 1938.

The Mysterious Mr. Wong; see **Mysterious Mr. Wong**, 1935.

Naked Revenge; see **Count Your Bullets**, 1972.

The Naked Truth; see **Your Past Is Showing**, 1958.

The Nark; see **La Balance**, 1982.

Nathaniel Hawthorne's Twice Told Tales; see **Twice Told Tales**, 1963.

Nature's Mistakes; see **Freaks**, 1937.

The Nelson Touch; see **Corvette K-225**, 1943.

Never Give an Inch; see **Sometimes a Great Notion**, 1971.

Never Take Sweets from a Stranger; see **Never Take Candy from a Stranger**, 1961.

The New Adventures of Don Juan; see **Adventures of Don Juan**, 1949.

New York; see **Hallelujah, I'm a Bum!**, 1933.

Nicholas Nickelby; see **Nicholas Nickleby**, 2002.

Night Flight from Moscow; see **The Serpent**, 1973.

The Night Has Eyes; see **Terror House**, 1942.

A Night of Terror; see **Love from a Stranger**, 1937.

Night of the Demon; see **Curse of the Demon**, 1958.

Night of the Flesh Eaters; see **Night of the Living Dead**, 1968.

The Night They Invented Striptease; see **The Night They Invaded Minsky's**, 1968.

Night Train to Munich; see **Night Train**, 1940.

Nine Days a Queen; see **Lady Jane Grey**, 1936.

Nine Hours to Live; see **Nine Hours to Rama**, 1963.

No Highway; see **No Highway in the Sky**, 1951.

North West Frontier; see **Flame over India**, 1960.

Nosferatu, the Vampyre; see **Nosferatu: The Vampire**, 1979.

Not against the Flesh; see **Vampyr**, 1932.

O.H.M.S.; see **You're in the Navy Now**, 1951.

Obsession; see **The Hidden Room**, 1949.

October; see **Ten Days That Shook the World**, 1928.

The O'Flynn; see **The Fighting O'Flynn**, 1949.

Oh, Charlie; see **Hold That Ghost**, 1941.

Oh Doctor; see **Hit the Ice**, 1943.

Oh! For a Man; see **Will Success Spoil Rock Hunter?**, 1957.

On the Stroke of Nine; see **Murder on the Campus**, 1934.

One against Seven; see **Counter-Attack**, 1945.

One Born Every Minute; see **The Flim-Flam Man**, 1967.

One Fatal Hour; see **Five Star Final**, 1931.

One for the Book; see **The Voice of the Turtle**, 1947.

One Hundred Percent Pure; see **The Girl from Missouri**, 1934.

One Man Mutiny; see **The Court-Martial of Billy Mitchell**, 1955.

Only the Best; see **I Can Get It for You Wholesale**, 1951.

Only the French Can; see **French Cancan**, 1956.

Operation Cicero; see **5 Fingers**, 1952.

The Optimist; see **Hallelujah, I'm a Bum!**, 1933.

The Optimists of Nine Elms; see **The Optimists**, 1973.

Oriental Dream; see **Kismet**, 1944.

O'Rourke of the Royal Mounted; see **Saskatchewan**, 1954.

Our Hitler; see **Our Hitler: A Film from Germany**, 1980.

Panic on the Trans-Siberian Express; see **Horror Express**, 1972.

Paris Underground; see **Touchez pas au Grisbi**, 1960.

The Passionate Friends; see **One Woman's Story**, 1949.

Patton—Lust for Glory; see **Patton**, 1970.

Patton: A Salute to a Rebel; see **Patton**, 1970.

Paula; see **Framed**, 1947.

Pearl of the South Pacific; see **South Sea Woman**, 1953.

Perfect Strangers; see **Vacation from Marriage**, 1945.

A Perfect Weekend; see **The St. Louis Kid**, 1934.

Personal Column; see **Lured**, 1947.

Personal Velocity: Three Portraits; see **Personal Velocity**, 2002.

Pete 'n' Tillie: see **Pete and Tillie**, 1972.

Phar Lap: Heart of a Nation; see **Phar Lap**, 1984.

The Phoenix Story; see **The Phenix Story**, 1955.

The Plainsmen; see **The Raiders**, 1964.

Planet of Blood; see **Planet of the Vampires**, 1966.

Poe's Tales of Terror; see **Tales of Terror**, 1962.

Polly Fulton; see **B.F.'s Daughter**, 1948.

Pookie; see **The Sterile Cuckoo**, 1969.

The Poor Little Rich Girl; see **Poor Little Rich Girl**, 1936.

Portrait in Smoke; see **Wicked as They Come**, 1957.

Potemkin; see **The Battleship Potemkin**, 1925.

Power and Glory; see **The Power and the Glory**, 1933.

Pride of Kentucky; see **The Story of Seabiscuit**, 1949.

Private Fears in Public Places; see **Coeurs**, 2006.

The Private Wore Skirts; see **Never Wave at a WAC**, 1952.

Profession: Reporter; see **The Passenger**, 1975.

PT Raiders; see **The Ship That Died of Shame**, 1956.

Purlie Victorious; see **Gone Are the Days!**, 1963.

Queen of Destiny; see **Sixty Glorious Years**, 1938.

Rain; see **Baran**, 2001.

The Rake's Progress; see **Notorious Gentleman**, 1945.

Rat Fink; see **Ratfink**, 1965.

Rebel with a Cause; see **The Loneliness of the Long Distance Runner**, 1962.

Record of a Living Being; see **I Live in Fear**, 1967.

The Red Beret; see **Paratrooper**, 1954.

The Red Head; see **Poil de Carotte**, 1932.

The Refugee; see **Three Faces West**, 1940.

Rehearsal for a Crime; see **The Criminal Life of Archibald de la Cruz**, 1962.

Return of the Bad Men; see **The Return of the Badmen**, 1948.

Reunion; see **Reunion in France**, 1942.

The Revenge of Milady; see **The Four Musketeers**, 1975.

Revolt; see **Ran**, 1985.

Rhodes of Africa; see **Rhodes**, 1936.

Riff-Raff; see **Riffraff**, 1936.

The Rise of Catherine the Great; see **Catherine the Great**, 1934.

The Road; see **La Strada**, 1956.

Road to Frisco; see **They Drive by Night**, 1940.

Road to Perdition; see **The Road to Perdition**, 2002.

Roaring Timbers; see **Come and Get It**, 1936.

Robin and Marian; see **Robin and Marion**, 1976.

Robinson Crusoe, see **The Adventures of Robinson Crusoe**, 1954.

Rocket Ship; see **Flash Gordon**, 1936.

Rome: Open City; see **Open City**, 1946.

Rommel—Desert Fox; see **The Desert Fox: The Story of Rommel**, 1951.

Rosemarie; see **Rosemary**, 1960.

Rough Company; see **The Violent Men**, 1955.

'Round Midnight; see **Round Midnight**, 1986.

The Roundup; see **La Rafle**, 2012.

Rudyard Kipling's Jungle Book; see **Jungle Book**, 1942.

Sabotage Agent; see **Adventures of Tartu**, 1943.

The Saboteur; see **Morituri**, 1956.

The Saboteur: Code Name Morituri; see **Morituri**, 1956.

Sabrina Fair; see **Sabrina**, 1954.

Saddle in the Wind; see **Saddle the Wind**, 1958.

The Saga of the Road; see **Pather Panchali**, 1955.

St. Martin's Lane; see **Sidewalks of London**, 1940.

The Saint's Return; see **The Saint's Girl Friday**, 1954.

Salerno Beachhead; see **A Walk in the Sun**, 1945.

Salute to Courage; see **Nazi Agent**, 1942.

Sam Marlow, Private Eye; see **The Man with Bogart's Face**, 1980.

Samurai, Loyal 47 Ronin; see **Chushingura**, 1963.

Saraband for Dead Lovers; see **Saraband**, 1949.

Sardonicus; see **Mr. Sardonicus**, 1961.

Satyricon; see **Fellini Satyricon**, 1969.

The Scar; see **Hollow Triumph**, 1948.

Scarface, Shame of a Nation; see **Scarface**, 1932.

Screenplay; see **Antonia & Jane**, 1991.

Secrets; see **Secrets of the Lone Wolf**, 1941.

The Settlers; see **The New Land**, 1973.

Seven Bad Men; see **Rage at Dawn**, 1955.

Seven Waves Away; see **Abandon Ship!**, 1957.

Seven Women; see **7 Women**, 1966.

The Shadow Versus: The Thousand Eyes of Dr. Mabuse; see **The 1,000 Eyes of Dr. Mabuse**, 1966.

The Shadow Warrior; **Kagemusha**, 1980.

Shadows of the Past, see **Abilene**, 1999.

She Got What She Asked for; see **Yesterday, Today, and Tomorrow**, 1964.

Sherlock Holmes; see **The Adventures of Sherlock Holmes**, 1939.

Sherlock Holmes and the Scarlet Claw; see **The Scarlet Claw**, 1944.

Shoeshine; see **Shoe Shine**, 1947.

Shoot the Pianist; see **Shoot the Piano Player**, 1962.

The Shop on High Street; see **The Shop on Main Street**, 1966.

Single-Handed; see **Sailor of the King**, 1953.

The Sin of Harold Diddlebock; see **Mad Wednesday**, 1950.

Sinners Go to Hell; see **No Exit**, 1962.

The Sins of Lola Montes; see **Lola Montes**, 1955.

The Sixth of June; see **D-Day the Sixth of June**, 1956.

The Sky is Yours; see **Le ciel est a vous**, 1957.

Smilin' Through; see **Smiling Through**, 1932.

Smilin' Through; see **Smiling Through**, 1941.

Smoke Jumpers, see **Red Skies of Montana**, 1952.

So Big; see **So Big!**, 1932.

So Bright the Flame; see **The Girl in White**, 1952.

Soil; see **Earth**, 1930.

Soldier in Love; see **Fanfan the Tulip**, 1962.

Soldiers of the Air; see **Thunder Birds**, 1942.

Someone Is Killing the Great Chefs of Europe; see **Who Is Killing the Great Chefs of Europe?**, 1978.

Something Like the Truth; see **The Offense**, 1973.

Song for Marion; see **Unfinished Song**, 2012.

A Song for You; see **My Song for You**, 1935.

The Song of Bernadette; see **Song of Bernadette**, 1943.

The Song of the Road; see **Pather Panchali**, 1955.

Sons of the Legion; see **Sons of the Desert**, 1933.

The Sound Barrier; see **Breaking the Sound Barrier**, 1952.

Space Soldiers; see **Flash Gordon**, 1936.

Spaceship to the Unknown; see **Flash Gordon**, 1936.

Spirit of the People; see **Abe Lincoln in Illinois**, 1940.

The Spy in Black; see **U-Boat 29**, 1939.

The Star Said No; see **Callaway Went Thataway**, 1951.

Step Up 4: Miami Heat; see **Step Up Revolution**, 2012.

The Stolen Children; see **Stolen Children**, 1992.

The Stoolie; see **The Fingerman**, 1963.

The Storm Within; see **Les parents terribles**, 1950.

The Story of a Divorce; see **Payment on Demand**, 1951.

The Story of Cinderella; see **The Slipper and the Rose**, 1976.

The Story of Dr. Ehrlich's Magic Bullet; see **Dr. Ehrlich's Magic Bullet**, 1940.

The Story of Robin Hood and His Merrie Men; see **The Story of Robin Hood**, 1952.

The Story without a Name; see **Without Warning**, 1952.

The Strange Affair of Uncle Harry; see **Uncle Harry**, 1945.

Strange Case of Madeleine; see **Madeleine**, 1950.

Strange Deception; see **The Accused**, 1949.

Strange Journey; see **Fantastic Voyage**, 1966.

State Secret; see **The Great Manhunt**, 1951.

The Strange Adventure of David Gray; see **Vampyr**, 1932.

Strange Incident; see **The Ox-Bow Incident**, 1943.

Strange Interval; see **Strange Interlude**, 1932.

The Streetfighter; see **Hard Times**, 1975.

Streets of Missing Women; see **Café Hostess**, 1940.

The Strikers; see **The Organizer**, 1964.

Such a Gorgeous Kid Like Me; see **Such a Gorgeous Girl Like Me**, 1973.

Such Men Are Dangerous; see **The Racers**, 1955.

Suicide Run; see **Too Late the Hero**, 1970.

Summer Flight; see **Stolen Hours**, 1963.

Summer Madness; see **Summertime**, 1955.

Suspense; see **Fear**, 1946.

A Suitable Case for Treatment; see **Morgan**, 1966.

Summer Lightning; see **Scudda-Hoo! Scudda Hay!**, 1949.

Summer of the Seventeenth Doll; see **Season of Passion**, 1961.

S.W.A.L.K.; see **Melody**, 1971.

The Swinging Fink; see **Ratfink**, 1965.

Symphony of Love; see **Ecstasy**, 1940.

Tainted Money; see **Show Them No Mercy**, 1938.

Tales of Beatrix Potter; see **Peter Rabbit and Tales of Beatrix Potter**, 1971.

Tales of Mystery and Imagination; see **The Spirits of the Dead**, 1969.

Tammy; see **Tammy and the Bachelor**, 1957.

Tartu; see **Adventures of Tartu**, 1943.

Taste of Fear; see **Scream of Fear**, 1961.

Teen Kanya; see **Two Daughters**, 1963.

The Tempest; see **Tempest**, 1958.

A Terrible Beauty; see **The Night Fighters**, 1960.

Territory of Love; see **Close to Eden**, 1991.

Terror in the City; see **Pie in the Sky**, 1964.

That Man Mr. Jones; see **The Fuller Brush Man**, 1948.

Theatre Royal; see **The Royal Family of Broadway**, 1930.

Thelma Jordan; see **The File on Thelma Jordan**, 1950.

Theorem; see **Teorema**, 1969.

They Gave Him a Gun; see **They Gave Me a Gun**, 1937.

They Loved Life; **Kagemusha**, 1980.

They Passed This Way; see **Four Faces West**, 1948.

Thieves Highway; see **A Scandal in Paris**, 1946.

The Thing; see **The Thing from Another World**, 1951.

The Thirteen Trunks of Mr. O.F.; see **The Trunks of Mr. O.F.**, 1932.

This Land Is Mine; see **This Land of Mine**, 1943.

This Man Reuter; see **A Dispatch from Reuters**, 1940.

Thomas Crown and Company; see **The Thomas Crown Affair**, 1968.

Those Were the Happy Times; see **Star!**, 1968.

Thou Shalt Not Kill; see **The Avenging Conscience**, 1914.

The Thousand Eyes of Dr. Mabuse; see **The 1,000 Eyes of Dr. Mabuse**, 1966.

Three Bad Men in the Hidden Fortress; see **The Hidden Fortress**, 1959.

Three Colors Red, see **Red**, 1994.

Three Rascals in the Hidden Fortress; see **The Hidden Fortress**, 1959.

Three Stooges Meet the Gunslinger; see **The Outlaws Is Coming**, 1965.

Tidal Wave; see **Portrait of Jennie**, 1949.

Tiger in the Sky; see **The McConnell Story**, 1955.

The Time of Return; see **Muriel**, 1963.

Too Many Chefs; see **Who Is Killing the Great Chefs of Europe?**, 1978.

Top Job; see **Grand Slam**, 1968.

A Touch of Love; see **Thank You All Very Much**, 1969.

Trained to Kill; see **White Dog**, 1982.

Tree of Liberty; see **The Howards of Virginia**, 1940.

Truth Is Stranger; see **When Ladies Meet**, 1933.

Try and Find It; see **Hi Diddle Diddle**, 1943.

Try and Get Me; see **The Sound of Fury**, 1950.

Tudor Rose; see **Lady Jane Grey**, 1936.

The Tunnel; see **Transatlantic Tunnel**, 1935.

The Twisted Road; see **They Live by Night**, 1949.

Two Is a Happy Number; see **One Is a Lonely Number**, 1972.

Two Merry Adventurers; see **The Man Who Was Sherlock Holmes**, 1937.

Two Merry Gentlemen; see **The Man Who Was Sherlock Holmes**, 1937.

Two Texas Knights; see **Two Guys from Texas**, 1948.

U-Boat 29; see **The Spy in Black**, 1939.

Unconventional Linda; see **Holiday**, 1938.

Under the Clock; see **The Clock**, 1945.

Under the Red Robe; see **Under the Robe**, 1937.

Unearthly Stranger; see **The Unearthly Stranger**, 1964.

The Untamed West; see **The Far Horizons**, 1955.

Unto a Good Land; see **The New Land**, 1973.

The Unvanquished; see **Aparajito**, 1959.

U.S.S. Teakettle; see **You're in the Navy Now**, 1951.

Valley of Gwangi; see **Valley of the Gwangi**, 1969.

The Vampire; see **Vampyr**, 1932.

Veggie Tales: The Ballad of Little Joe; see **The Ballad of Little Joe**, 2003.

Vessel of Wrath; see **The Beachcomber**, 1938.

The Village of the Damned; see **Village of the Damned**, 1960.

Violent Streets; see **Thief**, 1981.

Viva Las Vegas; see **Meet Me in Las Vegas**, 1956.

Volcano; see **Krakatoa, East of Java**, 1969.

Wages of Fear; see **Sorcerer**, 1977.

Waiting Women; see **Secrets of Women**, 1961.

The Wanton Contessa; see **Senso**, 1968.

War Correspondent; see **The Story of G.I. Joe**, 1945.

The Way to the Stars; see **Johnny in the Clouds**, 1945.

Wedding Bells; see **Royal Wedding**, 1951.

Wedding Breakfast; see **The Catered Affair**, 1956.

Well, If You Know Me; see **Yennai Arindhaal**, 2015.

The Well-Made Marriage; see **Le beau marriage**, 1982.

We're in the Army Now; see **Pack Up Your Troubles**, 1939.

What a Man; see **Never Give a Sucker an Even Break**, 1941.

When Knighthood Was in Flower; see **The Sword and the Rose**, 1953.

When the Door Opened; see **Escape**, 1940.

When the Girls Meet the Boys; see **Girl Crazy**, 1943.

Whisper to the Wind; see **Curse of the Vampires**, 1970.

Whisky Galore; see **Tight Little Island**, 1949.

The Widow and the Gigolo; see **The Roman Spring of Mrs. Stone**, 1961.

Wild and Willing; see **Ratfink**, 1965.

Wild Flower; see **Fiorile**, 1993.

William Shakespeare's Romeo + Juliet, see **Romeo + Juliet**, 1996.

The Winged Serpent; see **Q**, 1982.

The Winston Affair; see **The Man in the Middle**, 1964.

Witchfinder General; see **The Conqueror Worm**, 1968.

Within the Law; see **Paid**, 1930.

A Woman Alone; see **Sabotage**, 1937.

The Woman Alone; see **Sabotage**, 1937.

The Woman Between; see **The Woman I Love**, 1937.

A Woman Destroyed; see **Smash-Up: The Story of a Woman**, 1947.

The Woman in His House; see **The Animal Kingdom**, 1932.

Woman of the Dunes; see **Woman in the Dunes**, 1964.

Women in Limbo; see **Limbo**, 1972.

Wooden Crosses; see **The Road to Glory**, 1936.

The World and His Wife; see **State of the Union**, 1948.

The Worlds of Gulliver; see **The 3 Worlds of Gulliver**, 1960.

Written on the Sand; see **Play Dirty**, 1969.

A Yankee in King Arthur's Court; see **A Connecticut Yankee in King Arthur's Court**, 1949.

Years without Days; see **Castle on the Hudson**, 1940.

You Can't Sleep Here; see **I Was a Male War Bride**, 1949.

The Young and the Damned; see **Los Olvidados**, 1950.

The Young and the Passionate; see **Vitelloni**, 1956.

Your Red Wagon; see **They Live by Night**, 1949.

Zazie in the Subway; see **Zazie**, 1961.

Zazie in the Underground; see **Zazie**, 1961.

Zero Hour; see **The Road to Glory**, 1936.

EVENTS

Note: The following annotated index, exclusively created by the author, shows important worldwide events throughout history appearing in theatrically released feature films (chiefly U.S. and British releases, along with notable foreign productions, showing U.S. year of release), as well as feature films made-for-TV, TV series and miniseries, but does not include shorts, documentaries or video productions. Titles of films are sequentially presented in alphabetical and chronological order and titles shown in boldface represent entries profiled in this work.

Afghan War (2001-): **Brothers**, 2009; **Charlie Wilson's War**, 2007; Lions for Lambs, 2007; Stop-Loss, 2008.

Alaskan (Klondike) Gold Rush, 1896-1899: Belle of the Yukon, 1944; **Call of the Wild**, 1935; The Call of the Wild, 1972; The Call of the Wild: Dog of the Yukon, 1997; Call of the Wild 3D, 2009; Carmen of the Klondike, 1918; The Chechacos, 1923; **The Far Country**, 1954; The Flame of the Yukon, 1926; Gold, 2013; **The Gold Rush**, 1925; Gold Rush: A Real Life Alaskan Adventure, 1998 (made-for-TV); The Grub Stake, 1923; **Jack London**, 1943; Klondike Annie, 1936; Klondike Fever, 1980; The Legend of White Fang, 1992-1994 (TV series); Lure of the Yukon, 1924; **Nikki, Wild Dog of the North**, 1961; The North Star, 1996; **North to Alaska**, 1960; **Road to Utopia**, 1946; The Spoilers, 1914; The Spoilers, 1923; **The Spoilers**, 1930; **The Spoilers**, 1942; The Spoilers, 1955; Those Redheads from Seattle, 1953; **The Trail of '98**, 1928; White Fang, 1936; **White Fang**, 1991.

American Civil War (1861-1865 and events leading up to the war and those following it during Reconstruction): **Abraham Lincoln**, 1930; Across Five Aprils, 1990 (brother against brother); The Adventures of Mickey Matson and the Copperhead Treasure, 2012; **Alvarez Kelly**, 1966 (fictional version of the September 1864 Beefsteak Raid conducted by Confederate General Wade Hampton to steal needed Union cattle during the siege of Richmond and Petersburg, Virginia); The American Civil War, 1965 (made-for-TV); American Outlaws, 2001 (border guerrillas; Frank and Jesse James); Andersonville, 1996 (made-for-TV; profiles the worst Confederate POW camp located at Andersonville, Georgia, during the Civil War); The Andersonville Trial, 1970 (made-for-TV; trial of Henry Wirz [Heinrich Hartmann Wirz, 1823-1865] commandant of the Confederate POW camp in Andersonville, Georgia, who was found guilty of murder and executed); Apache Ambush, 1955; **Arizona**, 1940 (struggle for Arizona between Union and Confederate forces); The Arizona Kid, 1939 (border guerrillas in Missouri); Arizona Raiders, 1965 (Quantrill's guerrillas); **Bad Men of Missouri**, 1941 (border guerrillas); **Band of Angels**, 1957 (slavery; Union occupation of New Orleans in 1862); Barbara Frietchie, 1915 (Barbara Fritchie, 1766-1862, based on the folk tale and the resulting John Greenleaf Whittier poem about the elderly woman who defied Confederate General Thomas Jonathan "Stonewall" Jackson, 1824-1863, and his troops when they entered Frederick, Maryland, in 1862 by boldly waving a U.S. flag and where Jackson allegedly stopped his soldiers from shooting her, all of which is considered a myth as Fritchie, then age ninety-five, was sick in bed that day, but a U.S. flag waved outside of her house that was shot to pieces by passing Rebels.); Barbara Frietchie, 1924; The Battle of Gettysburg, 1913; The Beguiled, 1971; **Belle Starr**, 1941 (fictionalized biopic of notorious prostitute and horse thief Belle Starr, aka: Myra Maybelle Shirley Reed Starr, 1848-1889; border guerrillas); Beulah Land, 1980 (TV series); Big Bend Country, 1981 (made-for-TV; Reconstruction in Tennessee); **The Birth of a Nation**, 1915 (slavery; siege of Petersburg, 1864; Ku Klux Klan); The Black Dakotas, 1954 (espionage in the West during the Civil War); The Blue and the Gray, 1982 (TV miniseries); Border River, 1954 (border guerrillas); Cheyenne Warrior, 1994 (the Civil War in the West); The Civil War, 1990 (TV miniseries); Class of

'61, 1993 (made-for-TV; West Point graduates at the beginning of the Civil War; depicts the first battle of Bull Run, July 21, 1861 in Prince William County, Virginia); **Cold Mountain**, 2003; Colorado, 1940 (border guerrillas); The Colt, 2005 (made-for-TV); Column South, 1953 (Civil War in the West); **The Conspirator**, 2011 (Lincoln conspiracy; Mary Elizabeth Jenkins Surratt, 1820-1865); **Copper Canyon**, 1950; The Copperhead, 1920 (espionage; sabotage; guerrilla warfare; Siege of Vicksburg, May 18-July 4, 1863); Copperhead, 2013 (anti-Union sentiments in upstate New York in the Civil War); Court Martial, 1928 (Belle Starr, 1848-1889); The Coward, 1915 (Confederate soldiers); The Crisis, 1916 (depicts several battles in the Civil War, including the Siege and Battle of Vicksburg, May 18-July 4, 1863); **Dances with Wolves**, 1990; **Dark Command**, 1940 (border guerrillas in Missouri and Kansas; fictionalized profile of William Clarke Quantrill, 1837-1865); Dead Birds, 2004; Deliverance Creek, 2014 (made-for-TV); The Desperados!, 1969 (Civil War in the West); Dog Jack, 2010 (slavery; Union Army); The Dramatic Life of Abraham Lincoln, 1924; Drango, 1957 (Union occupation of Georgia immediately following the war); **Drums in the Deep South**, 1951 (Sherman's March to the Sea, 1864); **Escape from Fort Bravo**, 1953 (Confederate POWs in the West); **Field of Lost Shoes**, 2014 (Battle of New Market, May 15, 1864, in the Shenandoah Valley, Virginia); Five Guns West, 1955 (espionage); The Free State of Jones, 2016 (based on Southern Unionist Newton Knight, 1837-1922); **Friendly Persuasion**, 1956; Friendly Persuasion, 1975 (made-for-TV); Gangs of New York, 2002 (NYC riot against the Union draft, July 13-16, 1863); **The General**, 1926 (fictional account of the Andrews' Raid of April 12, 1862, when several Union saboteurs stole a southern train and created havoc in northern Georgia); General Spanky, 1936; **Gettysburg**, 1993; Ghost Brigade, 1993; **Glory**, 1989 (Union Colonel Robert Gould Shaw, 1837-1863, and the 54th Massachusetts Regiment of black volunteer soldiers fighting at the Second Battle of Fort Wagner, South Carolina, on July 18, 1863); **Gods and Generals**, 2003 (Battles of Bull Run, 1861; Fredericksburg, 1862; Chancellorsville, 1863; Confederate General Thomas Jonathan "Stonewall" Jackson, 1824-1863); **The Good, the Bad and the Ugly**, 1967; **Gone with the Wind**, 1939 (Battle of Atlanta, Georgia, July 22, 1864 and the city's evacuation thereafter); **The Great Locomotive Chase**, 1956 (Andrews Raid of April 12, 1862, where Union scout James J. Andrews, 1829-1862, with twenty-one Union soldiers stole a train in northern Georgia, driving it to southern Tennessee and conducting sabotage en route before being stopped); **The Great Missouri Raid**, 1951 (border guerrillas in Missouri and Kansas; Jesse James, 1847-1882); Hands Up!, 1926 (espionage); The Heart of Maryland, 1915 (southern plantation life); The Heart of Maryland, 1921 (southern plantation life); The Heart of Maryland, 1927 (southern plantation life); Hearts in Bondage, 1936 (Battle of Hampton Roads between the CSA *Merrimack* and the USS *Monitor*, on March 8-9, 1862); Her Country's Call, 1917; Her Father's Son, 1916; Hitchin' Posts, 1920 (war on the Mississippi River); **The Horse Soldiers**, 1959 (fictional version of Union Colonel Benjamin Grierson's diversionary raid of four cavalry regiments through Mississippi to Baton Rouge, Louisiana, on April 17-May 2, 1863, during the Vicksburg Campaign); **How the West Was Won**, 1962 (Battle of Shiloh, April 6-8, 1862); How the West Was Won, 1977 (TV series); The Hunley, 1999 (made-for-TV; the ill-fated and first submarine, CSS *Hunley*, constructed by Confederates to sink Union blockading ships in Charleston, S.C. Harbor, sinking the USS *Housatonic* on February 17, 1864, with an implanted torpedo before the innovative submarine sank with its crew of eight); In the Midst of Life, 1963 (Battle of Chickamauga, September 19-20, 1863); Ironclads, 1991 (made-for-TV; Battle of Hampton Roads between the CSA *Merrimack* and the USS *Monitor*, on March 8-9, 1862); The Jayhawkers!, 1959 (guerrillas in pre-Civil War Kansas); **Jezebel**, 1938 (southern plantation life); **Journey to Shiloh**, 1968 (Battle of Shiloh, April 6-8, 1862; Confederate General Braxton Bragg, 1817-1876); Kansas Pacific, 1953 (pre-Civil War struggle to build a railroad); Kansas Raiders, 1950 (border guerrillas in Missouri and Kansas; William Clarke Quantrill, 1837-1865;

Jesse and Frank James); The Keeping Room, 2014; The Kentucky Colonel, 1920; Kill Them All and Come Back Alone, 1970; The Last Confederate: The Story of Robert Adams, 2005; The Last Frontier, 1955 (Civil War in the West); **The Last Outpost**, 1951 (Confederate and Union cavalry fighting in the West); Last Stand at Saber River, 1997 (made-for-TV); The Legend of the Golden Gun, 1979 (made-for-TV); Lincoln, 1988 (TV miniseries); **Lincoln**, 2012 (following Lincoln's Emancipation Proclamation, the passing of the U.S. Thirteenth Amendment, on January 31, 1865, officially abolishing slavery and involuntary servitude); The Lincoln Conspiracy, 1977; **The Little Colonel**, 1935; The Little Shepherd of Kingdom Come, 1920; The Little Shepherd of Kingdom Come, 1928; The Little Shepherd of Kingdom Come, 1961; **Little Women**, 1933; **Little Women**, 1949; Little Women, 1970 (TV miniseries); Little Women, 1978 (TV miniseries); **Little Women**, 1994; **The Littlest Rebel**, 1935; Love Me Tender, 1956; **Major Dundee**, 1965 (Confederates serving with Union forces in the West); The Man from Colorado, 1948; Menace on the Mountain, 1970 (made-for-TV; Civil War deserters); The Million Dollar Dixie Deliverance, 1978 (made-for-TV); Morgan's Last Raid, 1929 (Confederate General John Hunt Morgan, 1825-1864, who led daring cavalry raids through Kentucky and Tennessee during the war); My Brother's War, 2005 (brother against brother); **Mysterious Island**, 1961; **The Naked Spur**, 1953; North and South, 1985-1986 (TV miniseries; brother against brother); **Of Human Hearts**, 1938; Only the Brave, 1930 (espionage); Operator 13, 1934 (espionage); **The Outlaw Josey Wales**, 1976 (border guerrillas in Missouri and Kansas); **The Outriders**, 1950 (border guerrillas); The Overland Telegraph, 1929; Pharaoh's Army, 1995; Prairie Rose, 2006 (Union POW Camp Douglas at Chicago, Illinois, in 1862); **The Prisoner of Shark Island**, 1936 (Lincoln conspiracy, Dr. Samuel Alexander Mudd, 1833-1883); The Private History of a Campaign That Failed, 1981 (made-for-TV; testing Confederate bravery and cowardice); Quantrill's Raiders, 1958 (border guerrillas in Missouri and Kansas; William Clarke Quantrill, 1837-1865); **The Raid**, 1954 (Confederate raiders robbing two banks in St. Albans, Vermont, on October 19, 1864); Raiders of Ghost City, 1944 (serial); **Raintree County**, 1957; A Reason to Live, a Reason to Die, 1972; Rebel City, 1953 (copperheads and guerrillas in Kansas); **The Red Badge of Courage**, 1951; **Red Mountain**, 1951; Red Runs the River, 1963 (Confederate General Richard Stoddert Ewell, 1817-1882); The Redhead and the Cowboy, 1951 (espionage and guerrilla warfare in the West); The Revengers, 1972 (border guerrillas); Revolt at Fort Laramie, 1957; **Ride with the Devil**, 1999 (border guerrillas in Missouri and Kansas; Lawrence, Kansas, Massacre, August 21, 1863, where more than 180 men and boys thought to be pro-Union were killed by a Rebel guerrilla force of about 300 to 400 riders; William Clarke Quantrill, 1837-1865); Rio Lobo, 1970; **Rocky Mountain**, 1950 (Confederate guerrillas in the West); **The Romance of Rosy Ridge**, 1947 (Reconstruction in Missouri); The Rose and the Jackal, 1990 (made-for-TV; northern and southern espionage between Union detective Allan Pinkerton, 1819-1884 and Rebel spy Rose O'Neal Greenhow, 1813-1864); **Run of the Arrow**, 1957; **Santa Fe Trail**, 1940 (John Brown, 1800-1859); **Saving Lincoln**, 2013 (Lincoln conspiracy); The Scarlet Drop, 1918; Secret Service, 1919 (Northern espionage); Secret Service, 1931 (espionage); **Seraphim Falls**, 2006, **Seven Angry Men**, 1955 (John Brown, 1800-1859); The Shadow Riders, 1982 (made-for-TV); **Shenandoah**, 1965; Silver Canyon, 1951 (guerrillas in Utah); Silver River, 1948; So Red the Rose, 1935 (southern plantation life); **Sommersby**, 1993; The Soul of Nigger Charley, 1973; **A Southern Yankee**, 1948 (espionage); The Spreading Dawn, 1917; **Springfield Rifle**, 1952 (Confederate guerrillas in the West); **Swanee River**, 1939 (composer Stephen Foster, 1826-1864); **Tap Roots**, 1948 (loosely based on Southern Unionist Newton Knight, 1837-1922); The Tempest, 1998 (made-for-TV); **Tennessee Johnson**, 1942 (Battle of Chickamauga, September 19-20, 1863; Andrew Johnson, 1808-1875); **They Died with Their Boots On**, 1941 (Battles of Bull Run, 1861; Gettysburg-Hanover, Pennsylvania, July 1863; Union General George Armstrong Custer, 1839-

1876); A Time for Killing, 1967 (Confederate POWs escaping a Union camp in the West); Trailin' West, 1936 (espionage); True Women, 1997 (made-for-TV); **Two Flags West**, 1950 (Confederates serving with Union forces in the West); **Uncle Tom's Cabin**, 1927 (slavery; southern plantation life); **The Undefeated**, 1969 (Confederates migrating after the war to serve with Mexico's Emperor Maximilian I); **Virginia City**, 1940 (Confederate guerrillas in the West); War Flowers, 2012 (Confederate home front in North Carolina); The Warrens of Virginia, 1915; The Warrens of Virginia, 1924 (southern plantation life; Robert E. Lee, 1807-1870; Ulysses S. Grant [Hiram Ulysses Grant], 1822-1885); **Wells Fargo**, 1937; Western Gold, 1937 (Confederates fighting in the West); Wicked Spring, 2002 (Battle of the Wilderness, May 5-7, 1864); Yellowneck, 1955 (Confederate deserters in the Everglades); Young Bill Hickok, 1940 (Confederate guerrillas in the West); **Young Jesse James**, 1960 (border guerrillas in Missouri and Kansas; Jesse James, 1847-1882).

American Revolutionary War (1775-1783): The Adams Chronicles, 1976 (TV miniseries); All for Liberty, 2009; Amazing Grace, 2007 (British anit-slavery movement; William Wilberforce, 1759-1833; William Pitt the Younger, 1759-1806); April Morning, 1988 (made-for-TV; Battles of Concord and Lexington, Massachusetts, April 19, 1775); **America**, 1924 (Battles of Bunker Hill/Breed's Hill, 1775; Yorktown, 1781; Cherry Valley, New York Massacre, on November 11, 1778); The Bastard, 1978 (made-for-TV); Beaumarchais the Scoundrel, 1997; Benedict Arnold: A Question of Honor, 2003 (made-for-TV); The Crossing, 2000 (made-for-TV; Washington's crossing of the Delaware River and the Battle of Trenton, January 2, 1777; George Washington, 1732-1799); Daniel Boone, 1964-1970 (TV series); The Deserter, 2003; **The Devil's Disciple**, 1959 (Battle of Saratoga, September 19-October 7, 1777; British General John Burgoyne, 1722-1792); Divided Loyalties, 1990 (Cherry Valley, New York, Massacre on November 11, 1778; George Washington, 1732-1799); **Drums Along the Mohawk**, 1939 (New York frontier; Fort Dayton; Nicholas Herkimer, 1728-1777); George Washington, 1984 (TV miniseries); The Heart of a Hero, 1916 (espionage; Nathan Hale, 1755-1776; Thomas Jefferson, 1743-1826); **The Howards of Virginia**, 1940 (Shenandoah Valley, Virginia; Thomas Jefferson, 1743-1826; George Washington, 1732-1799); **Janice Meredith**, 1924 (Paul Revere's ride in 1775; Washington's crossing of the Delaware River and the Battle of Trenton, January 2, 1777; George Washington, 1732-1799); John Adams, 2008 (TV miniseries; John Adams, 1735-1826); **John Paul Jones**, 1959 (John Paul Jones, 1747-1792; Benjamin Franklin, 1706-1790; Marie Antoinette, 1755-1793; Patrick Henry, 1736-1799; Catherine the Great, 1729-1796; Louis XVI, 1754-1793; George Washington, 1732-1799; George III, 1738-1820; sea battle between the USS *Bohomme Richard* and HMS *Serapis* on September 23, 1779); **Johnny Tremaine**, 1957 (Sons of Liberty; Boston Tea Party, May 10, 1773; Battle of Concord, April 19, 1775; Paul Revere, 1734-1818; Samuel Adams, 1722-1803; Josiah Quincy, 1710-1784; Lafayette, 1963; Liberty! The American Revolution, 1997 (TV miniseries); The Little Patriot, 1995; Marie Antoinette, 2006; Mary Silliman's War, 1994 (made-for-TV); The Other Side of Victory, 1976; **The Patriot**, 2000 (loosely based on the lives of revolutionary military leader General Francis Marion, 1732-1795, known as the "Swamp Fox"; British General Charles Cornwallis, 1738-1805; British Colonel Banastre Tarleton, 1754-1833; and uses historic elements about the Battles of Cowpens, January 17, 1781 and Guilford Courthouse, March 15, 1781); Revolution, 1985 (Battle of Long Island, August 27, 1776; Valley Forge, 1777-1778); **The Scarlet Coat**, 1955 (espionage; Benedict Arnold, 1741-1801; John Andre, 1750-1780); The Seekers, 1979 (made-for-TV); **1776**, 1972 (Declaration of Independence; John Adams, 1735-1826; Benjamin Franklin, 1706-1790; Thomas Jefferson, 1743-1826); The Spirit of '76, 1917 (Cherry Valley, New York Massacre, on November 11, 1778); Sybil Ludington, 2010; Taking Liberty, 1993 (Benjamin Franklin, 1706-1790); Thomas Jefferson, 1997 (TV miniseries; Thomas

Jefferson, 1743-1826); **The Time of Their Lives**, 1946 (espionage); Valley Forge, 1975 (made-for-TV; George Washington, 1732-1799); The Young Rebels, 1970-1971 (TV series).

Battle of Bataan (WWII; Pacific Theater; Philippines Defense; January 7, 1942-April 9, 1942; Philippines; Death March): **Back to Bataan**, 1945; **Bataan**, 1943; Blood of Bataan, 1953; Bus to Bataan, 1961; **Cry Havoc**, 1943; **So Proudly We Hail**, 1943; **Somewhere I'll Find You**, 1942; Texas to Bataan, 1942; **They Were Expendable**, 1945; Women of Valor, 1986 (made-for-TV).

Battle of Corregidor (WWII; Pacific Theater; Philippines Defense; April 9, 1942-May 6, 1942): Corregidor, 1943; **So Proudly We Hail**, 1943; **They Were Expendable**, 1945; You Are There, 1953-1971 (TV series; "The Surrender of Corregidor, May 6, 1942," 1954 episode).

Battle of Guadalcanal (WWII; Pacific Theater; Operation Watchtower; August 7, 1942-Febuary 9, 1943): **Battle Cry**, 1955; **First to Fight**, 1967; **Flying Leathernecks**, 1951; **The Gallant Hours**, 1960; **Guadal-canal Diary**, 1943; **Marine Raiders**, 1944; The Pacific, 2010 (TV miniseries); **Pride of the Marines**, 1945; **South Sea Woman**, 1953; **Tarawa Beachhead**, 1958; **The Thin Red Line**, 1964; **The Thin Red Line**, 1998.

Battle of Iwo Jima (WWII; Pacific Theater; February 19, 1945-March 26, 1945): **The FBI Story**, 1959; **Flags of Our Fathers**, 2006; **Letters from Iwo Jima**, 2006; **The Outsider**, 1961; The Pacific, 2010 (TV series); **Sands of Iwo Jima**, 1949.

Battle of Midway (WWII; Pacific Theater; June 3-7, 1942): **Admiral Yamamoto**, 1968; The Eternal Zero, 2013; **Midway**, 1976; **Task Force**, 1949; War and Remembrance, 1988 (TV miniseries); **Wing and a Prayer**, 1944.

Battle of Monte Cassino (WWII; European Theater; Italy; January 17, 1944-May 18, 1944): The Battle of the Last Panzer, 1969; Die grunen Teufel von Monte Cassino, 1958; Monte Cassino, 1946; **The Story of G.I. Joe**, 1945.

Battle of Normandy (WWII; European Theater; Operation Overlord; June 6, 1944): The Americanization of Emily, 1964; **D-Day the Sixth of June**, 1956; **The Longest Day**, 1962; **Saving Private Ryan**, 1998; **36 Hours**, 1965.

Battle of Tarawa (WWII; Pacific Theater; November 20-23, 1943): **Bat-tle Cry**, 1955; **Flags of Our Fathers**, 2006; **Halls of Montezuma**, 1950; The Hi-Lo Country, 1998; **Sands of Iwo Jima**, 1949; **Tarawa Beachhead**, 1958.

Battle of the Argonne (WWI; Western Front; September 26, 1918-No-vember 11, 1918): **The Fighting 69th**, 1940; The Lost Battalion, 2001 (made-for-TV); **Pilgrimage**, 1933; **Sergeant York**, 1941.

Battle of the Bulge (WWII; European Theater; December 16, 1944-Jan-uary 25, 1945): **Attack**, 1956; Battle of the Bulge, 1965; **Battleground**, 1949; **Castle Keep**, 1969; Everyman's War, 2009; **A Midnight Clear**, 1992; **Patton**, 1970; **Saints and Soldiers**, 2005; Silent Night, 2002 (made-for-TV); The Wereth Eleven, 2011; **White Christmas**, 1954.

Battle of the Little Big Horn (Eastern Montana Territory; June 25-26, 1876; during the Great Sioux War; between approximately 2,500-3,000 Sioux and other Indian tribes and 647 members of the U.S. 7th Cavalry under the command of Lieutenant-Colonel George Armstrong Custer where Custer and 267 others in his command were killed, the remaining retreating with the Sioux victorious; also see Custer, George Armstrong,

in Historical Persons Index): Britton of the Seventh, 1916; Bugles in the Afternoon, 1952; Cheyenne, 1955-1963 (TV series; "The Broken Pledge," 1957 episode; "Glory, Gold and Custer," 1960 episode); The Court Martial of George Armstrong Custer, 1977 (made-for-TV); Crazy Horse, 1996 (made-for-TV); Custer, 1967 (TV series); Custer of Big Horn, 1926; Custer of the West, 1968; Dr. Quinn, Medicine Woman, 1993-1998 (TV series; several episodes); The Flaming Frontier, 1926; The Glory Guys, 1965; The Great Sioux Massacre, 1965; Histeria!, 1998-2000 (TV series; 1998 and 2000 episodes); Into the West, 2005 (TV miniseries); Legend, 1995 (TV series; "Custer's Next to Last Stand," 1995 episode); The Legend of Custer, 1968; The Legend of the Golden Gun, 1979 (made-for-TV); The Legend of the Lone Ranger, 1981; **Little Big Man**, 1970; **The Plainsman**, 1936; The Plainsman, 1966; The Secret Adventures of Jules Verne, 2000 (TV series; "The Rocket's Red Glare," 2000 episode); Sitting Bull, 1954; Son of the Morning Star, 1991 (made-for-TV); Stolen Women, Captured Hearts, 1997 (made-for-TV); **They Died with Their Boots On**, 1942; The Time Tunnel, 1966-1967 (TV series; "Massacre," 1966 episode); Tonka, 1958; Warpath, 1951; The Wild West, 2006-2007 (TV series; "Custer's Last Stand," 2007 episode); The World Changes, 1933; **Wyoming**, 1940.

Battle of Waterloo (Napoleonic Wars; June 18, 1815, between the forces of France and the Allies of England and Prussia, resulting in a resound-ing victory for the Allies and ending the reign of Napoleon I): Becky Sharp, 1935; **Desirée**, 1954; **Waterloo**, 1971.

The Blitz (September 7, 1940-May 21, 1941; German aerial attacks against sixteen British cities, chiefly London, in WWII, 1939-1945): **Adventure for Two**, 1945; The Bells Go Down, 1943; Bertie and Eliz-abeth, 2002 (made-for-TV); The Brighton Strangler, 1945; **The Chron-icles of Narnia: The Lion; the Witch; and the Wardrobe**, 2005; Colditz, 2005 (made-for-TV); Good Night, Mr. Tom, 1998 (made-for-TV); **The Good Shepherd**, 2006; **Hope and Glory**, 1987; **In Which We Serve**, 1942 (London); **The Locket**, 1946 (London); **Mrs. Miniver**, 1942; Murder on the Home Front, 2013 (made-for-TV); **Nightmare**, 1942; **The Return of the Vampire**, 1944 (London); Tears in the Rain, 1988 (made-for-TV); **This Above All**, 1942 (London); Till Death Do Us Part, 1972 (London); **The Time Machine**, 1960; **The Time Ma-chine**, 2002; **Waterloo Road**, 1945 (London).

Bosnian War (April 1992-December 1995): **Beautiful People**, 2000; **Before the Rain**, 1995; Behind Enemy Lines, 2001; Circles, 2013; Esma's Secret—Grbavica, 2007; For Ever Mozart, 1996; The Hunting Party, 2007; In the Land of Blood and Honey, 2011; **Interview**, 2007; Killing Season, 2013; Lana's Rain, 2002; Love, 2005; Resolution 819, 2008 (made-for-TV); Sabotage, 1996; Savior, 1998; Shot through the Heart, 1988 (made-for-TV); Unstoppable, 2004; Warchild, 2006; Wel-come to Sarajevo, 1997.

California Gold Rush (1848-1855): **The Adventures of Bullwhip Grif-fin**, 1967; **Barbary Coast**, 1935; Black Bart, 1948; California, 1947; **The Cowboys**, 1972; The Firebrand, 1962; Girl Rush, 1944; **How the West Was Won**, 1962; Jack McCall, Desperado, 1953; The Luck of the Roaring Camp, 1937; **Paint Your Wagon**, 1969; A Perilous Journey, 1953; The Raiders, 1952; **Robin Hood of El Dorado**, 1936; A Romance of the Redwoods, 1917; The Splendid Road, 1925; **Sutter's Gold**, 1936; **Wells Fargo**, 1937.

Christmas (also see Ebenezer Scrooge and Santa Claus in Fictional Characters Index): **An Affair to Remember**, 1957; All I Want for Christmas, 1991; An American Girl Holiday, 2004 (made-for-TV); Arthur Christmas, 2011; Arthur's Perfect Christmas, 2000 (made-for-TV); **Babes in Toyland**, 1934; Babes in Toyland, 1986 (made-for-TV); Bad Santa, 2003; **The Bells of St. Mary's**, 1945; The Best Man Holiday,

2013; **The Bishop's Wife**, 1947; Black Christmas, 1974; Black Nativity, 2013; A Boyfriend for Christmas, 2004 (made-for-TV); A Bride for Christmas, 2012 (made-for-TV); **Bright Eyes**, 1934; Catch a Christmas Star, 2013 (made-for-TV); A Charlie Brown Christmas, 1965 (made-for-TV); **The Cheaters**, 1945; Christmas, 2009; Christmas Angel, 2012 (made-for-TV); Christmas at Pee Wee's Playhouse, 1988 (made-for-TV); Christmas Belle, 2013 (made-for-TV); The Christmas Candle, 2013; The Christmas Card, 2006 (made-for-TV); **A Christmas Carol**, 1938; **A Christmas Carol**, 1951; A Christmas Carol, 1984 (made-for-TV); A Christmas Carol, 1999 (made-for-TV); A Christmas Carol, 2009; Christmas Carol: The Movie, 2001; Christmas Cupid, 2010 (made-for-TV); Christmas Eve, 1947; Christmas Eve, 2015; **Christmas Holiday**, 1944; A Christmas Kiss, 2011 (made-for-TV); A Christmas Kiss II, 2014 (made-for-TV); **Christmas in Connecticut**, 1945; Christmas in Connecticut, 1992 (made-for-TV); Christmas in Conway, 2013 (made-for-TV); Christmas Lodge, 2011 (made-for-TV); A Christmas Memory, 1997 (made-for-TV); Christmas on the Bayou, 2013 (made-for-TV); The Christmas Parade, 2014 (made-for-TV); The Christmas Secret, 2014 (made-for-TV); The Christmas Shoes, 2002 (made-for-TV); **A Christmas Story**, 1983; Christmas under Wraps, 2014 (made-for-TV); Christmas Vacation, 1989; Christmas Vacation 2: Cousin Eddie's Island Adventure, 2003 (made-for-TV); A Christmas Wedding Date, 2012 (made-for-TV); A Christmas Wish, 2011 (made-for-TV); Christmas with Holly, 2012 (made-for-TV); Christmas with the Kranks, 2004; **Come to the Stable**, 1949; A Cookie Cutter Christmas, 2014 (made-for-TV); Dear Santa, 2011 (made-for-TV); Deck the Halls, 2006; **Elf**, 2003; Ernest Saves Christmas, 1998; **An Evergreen Christmas**, 2014; A Fairly Odd Christmas, 2012 (made-for-TV); **The Fitzgerald Family Christmas**, 2012; Four Christmases, 2008; Fred Claus, 2007; Good Luck Charlie, It's Christmas!, 2011 (made-for-TV); Grumpy Cat's Worst Christmas Ever, 2014 (made-for-TV); Happy Christmas, 2014; A Heartland Christmas, 2010 (made-for-TV); Help for the Holidays, 2012 (made-for-TV); **Holiday**, 1938; The Holiday, 2006; Holiday Engagement, 2011 (made-for-TV); Holiday in Handcuffs, 2007 (made-for-TV); **Holiday Inn**, 1942; **The Holly and the Ivy**, 1954; **Home Alone**, 1990; **Home Alone 2: Lost in New York**, 1992; Home Alone 4, 2002 (made-for-TV); Home Alone: The Holiday Heist, 2011 (made-for-TV); How about You..., 2007; **How the Grinch Stole Christmas**, 2000; I'll Be Home for Christmas, 1998; **I'll Be Seeing You**, 1944; **It's a Wonderful Life**, 1946; Jingle All the Way, 1996; **Joyeux Noel**, 2005; **The Lemon Drop Kid**, 1951; **The Lion in Winter**, 1968; The Lion in Winter, 2003 (made-for-TV); **Love Affair**, 1939; Love at the Christmas Table, 2012 (made-for-TV); **Love Finds Andy Hardy**, 1938; **The Man Who Came to Dinner**, 1942; **Meet John Doe**, 1941; **Meet Me in St. Louis**, 1944; Merry Christmas, Drake & Josh, 2008 (made-for-TV); **Merry Christmas, Mr. Lawrence**, 1983; **A Midnight Clear**, 1992; Miracle at Sage Creek, 2005; **Miracle on 34th Street**, 1947; Miracle on 34th Street, 1994; The Mistle-Tones, 2012 (made-for-TV); The Most Wonderful Time of the Year, 2008 (made-for-TV); **The Muppet Christmas Carol**, 1992; The Nativity Story, 2006; **The Nightmare before Christmas**, 1993; The Nine Lives of Christmas, 2014 (made-for-TV); Noel, 2004; Northpole, 2014 (made-for-TV); **Nothing Like the Holidays**, 2008; The Nutcracker, 1993; **O. Henry's Full House**, 1952 ("The Gift of the Magi" sequence); **One Magic Christmas**, 1985; One Starry Christmas, 2014 (made-for-TV); Pete's Christmas, 2013 (made-for-TV); **Pocketful of Miracles**, 1961; The Polar Express, 2004; **Prancer**, 1989; A Princess for Christmas, 2011 (made-for-TV); **Remember the Night**, 1940; A Royal Christmas, 2014 (made-for-TV); Rudolph, the Red-Nosed Reindeer, 1964 (made-for-TV); Santa Claus, 1959; Santa Claus, 1985; **The Santa Clause**, 1994; Santa Claus Conquers the Martians, 1964; Santa Claus Is Comin' to Town, 1970 (made-for-TV); The Santa Clause 3: The Escape Clause, 2006; **The Santa Clause 2**, 2002; Saving Christmas, 2014; **Scrooge**, 1970; Scrooged, 1988; **The Shop around the Corner**, 1940; **Stella Dallas**, 1925; **Stella Dallas**, 1937; Surviving Christmas, 2004; This

Christmas, 2007; **The Three Godfathers**, 1916; **Three Godfathers**, 1936; **3 Godfathers**, 1948; To Grandmother's House We Go, 1992 (made-for-TV); The Tree That Saved Christmas, 2014 (made-for-TV); The Trouble with Angels, 1966; A Very Brady Christmas, 1988 (made-for-TV); **The Way of All Flesh**, 1927; **White Christmas**, 1954; The Year without a Santa Claus, 1974 (made-for-TV).

Cuban Missile Crisis (Thirteen-day confrontation between the U.S. and Soviet Union over Soviet missiles based in Cuba, October 14-28, 1962, where the Soviets, following a U.S. naval blockade, removed the missiles): An American Affair, 2009; Blast from the Past, 2009; Ginger and Rosa, 2012; The Good Shepherd, 2006; Holiday Beach, 2011; Hope, 1997 (made-for-TV); Jackie, Ethel, Joan: The Women of Camelot, 2001 (made-for-TV); Kennedy, 1983 (TV miniseries); The Kennedys, 2011 (TV miniseries); Lisanka, 2010; **Matinee**, 1993; Memories of Underdevelopment, 1973; The Missiles of October, 1974 (made-for-TV); A Single Man, 2009; The Steagle, 1971; Taken, 2002 (TV miniseries); **Thirteen Days**, 2000; **Topaz**, 1969; **X-Men: First Class**, 2011; **When Did You Last See Your Father?**, 2007.

D-Day (June 6, 1944; the Normandy Invasion of WWII): The Americanization of Emily, 1964; Band of Brothers, 2001 (TV miniseries); **The Big Red One**, 1980; The Blockhouse, 1974; D-Day 6.6.1944, 2004 (made-for-TV); **D-Day: the Sixth of June**, 1956; **The Desert Fox: The Story of Rommel**, 1951; **Fighter Squadron**, 1948; The Four Horsemen of the Apocalypse, 1962; **I See a Dark Stranger**, 1947; Ike: Countdown to D-Day, 2004 (made-for-TV); The Last Rescue, 2014; **The Longest Day**, 1962; Overlord, 1975; **Patton**, 1970; Storming Juno, 2010 (made-for-TV); Rommel, 2012 (made-for-TV); **36 Hours**, 1965; War and Remembrance, 1988 (TV miniseries).

Doolittle Raid (in WWII; aka: Tokyo Raid, April 18, 1942, when sixteen B-25 Mitchell Medium bombers bombed Tokyo and other cities in Japan in retaliation for its attack on Pearl Harbor, Hawaii, on December 7, 1941): **Destination Tokyo**, 1943; **Midway**, 1976; **Pearl Harbor**, 2001; **The Purple Heart**, 1944; **Thirty Seconds over Tokyo**, 1944; and The Twentieth Century, 1957-1966 (TV series; "The Doolittle Raid," 1957 episode).

Dunkirk Evacuation (WWII; mass evacuation of more than 300,000 [chiefly] British and French troops from the harbor and beaches of Dunkirk, between May 27 and June 4, 1940): And a Nightingale Sang, 1989 (made-for-TV); Atonement, 2007; **Battle of Britain**, 1969; **Dunkirk**, 1958; Dunkirk, 2004 (made-for-TV); Goodnight, Mr. Tom, 1998 (made-for-TV); It Happened Here, 1965; **Mrs. Miniver**, 1942; Noce blanche, 1989; **Reunion in France**, 1942; **A Yank in the R.A.F.**, 1941.

Easter (Christian Sunday celebrating the resurrection of Jesus of Nazareth; a moveable feast in that it does not fall upon a fixed date): American Psycho, 2000; Andrei Rublev, 1973; Angela's Ashes, 1999; **Annie Hall**, 1977; The Astronaut Farmer, 2006; Au revoir les enfants, 1988; The Barber of Siberia, 1998; Beyond the Gates, 2005; Bless the Child, 2000; Bugs Bunny's Easter Special, 1977 (made-for-TV); Changing Hearts, 2002; **Chocolat**, 2000; **The Color Purple**, 1985; **Cookie's Fortune**, 1999; Cover-Up, 1991; **Dark City**, 1950; Dracula Untold, 2014; Easter, 2002; **Easter Parade**, 1948; The Easter Promise, 1975 (made-for-TV); **The FBI Story**, 1959; Fools in the Mountains, 1957; For Your Consideration, 2006; Georgia O'Keefe, 2009 (made-for-TV); Hank and Mike, 2008; Happy Easter, 1984; **Holiday Inn**, 1942; Home Movie, 2008; Hop, 2011; **Household Saints**, 1993; It's the Easter Beagle, Charlie Brown!, 1974 (made-for-TV); Jesus of Nazareth, 1977 (TV miniseries); La Passion de Bernadette, 1989; Land of Storms, 2014; Le Jour se leve, 1940; The Lion of Judah, 2011; Love, 1927; Mendel, 1997; **The Mill and the Cross**, 2011; **My Dream Is Yours**, 1949; **My**

Mother's Castle, 1991; No Deposit, No Return, 1976; **Of Gods and Men**, 2011; Palm Springs Weekend, 1963; The Passion, 2008 (TV miniseries); **The Perks of Being a Wallflower**, 2012; **Peyton Place**, 1957; Pieces of Easter, 2013; The Penitent, 1988; The Proud and the Beautiful, 1953; **Rebel without a Cause**, 1955; Resurrection, 1999; Risen, 2016; Rocco and His Brothers, 1961; Saved!, 2004; Siberian Exile, 2013; Slow Burn, 2005; A Song for Martin, 2001; **Steel Magnolias**, 1989; **Sweet Bird of Youth**, 1962; They Were Five, 1936; Universal Signs, 2008; The Vicar of Dibley, 1994-2007 (TV series); The Wait, 2015; **The War Is Over**, 1968; **What Price Hollywood?**, 1932.

Father's Day (honoring fathers and father figures; third Sunday in June in the U.S.): **The Castle**, 1997; **The Diving Bell and the Butterfly**, 2007; Father's Day, 1997; **Joe Smith, American**, 1942; A Long Way Off, 2014; TV Junkie, 2006.

French and Indian War (1754-1763; waged through the American colonies controlled by the British and where French forces and their Indian allies attempted to destroy the colonial settlements and forts): The Broken Chain, 1993 (made-for-TV); Chingachgook, die grosse Schlange, 1967; Convoy of Women, 1977; Frontier Rangers, 1959; George Washington, 1984 (TV series); Hawkeye, 1994-1995 (TV series); Hawkeye and the Last of the Mohicans, 1957 (TV series); **The Last of the Mohicans**, 1920; **The Last of the Mohicans**, 1936; The Last of the Mohicans, 1971 (TV miniseries); **The Last of the Mohicans**, 1992; Net Playhouse, 1964-1972 (TV series; "Portrait of the Hero as a Young Man," 1972 episode); **Northwest Passage**, 1940; The Pathfinder, 1952; **Unconquered**, 1947; Winners of the Wilderness, 1927.

French Indochina War (1946-1954; also see Vietnam War succeeding the French Indochina War): A Captain's Honor, 1982; China Gate, 1957; Dien Bien Phu, 1992; Elevator to the Gallows, 1958; Five Gates to Hell, 1959; Jump into Hell, 1955; The Little Thief, 1988; Lost Command, 1966; **Murmur of the Heart**, 1971; Outpost in Indo-China, 1963; Outside the Law, 2010; **The Quiet American**, 1958; **Rogue's Regiment**, 1948; Shock Patrol, 1957; The 317th Platoon, 1965.

French Revolution (1789-1799): The Affair of the Necklace, 2001; BBC Night Theater, 1950-1959 (TV series; "The Scarlet Pimpernel," 1951 episode); **Black Magic**, 1949; Brotherhood of the Wolf, 2001; Dangerous Exile, 1957; Danton, 1983; The DuPont Show of the Month, 1957-1961 (TV series; "The Scarlet Pimpernel," 1960 episode); The Elusive Pimpernel, 1919; The Elusive Pimpernel, 1969 (TV miniseries); **Farewell, My Queen**, 2012; The Fighting Pimpernel, 1953; The Lady and the Duke, 2001; Lady Oscar, 1979; The Lame Devil, 1948; **La Marseillaise**, 1939; La revolution francaise, 1989 (two-part film); Let Them Eat Cake, 1999 (TV series); Madame, 1963; Madame Guillotine, 1931; Marat/Sade, 1967; Marie Antoinette: The Love of a King, 1922; **Marie Antoinette**, 1938; Marie Antoinette, 2006; Marie Antoinette, Queen of France, 1956; **Napoleon**, 1929; The Only Way, 1927; **Orphans of the Storm**, 1921; The Prisoner of Corbal, 1936; Quatre-vingt-treize, 1921; **Reign of Terror**, 1949; The Return of the Scarlet Pimpernel, 1938; Ridicule, 1996; **Scaramouche**, 1923; The Scarlet Daredevil, 1929; The Scarlet Pimpernel, 1917; **The Scarlet Pimpernel**, 1934; The Scarlet Pimpernel, 1956 (TV series); The Scarlet Pimpernel, 1982 (made-for-TV); The Scarlet Pimpernel, 1999-2000 (TV series); Start the Revolution without Me, 1970; A Tale of Two Cities, 1922; **A Tale of Two Cities**, 1935; A Tale of Two Cities, 1958; That Night in Varennes, 1983.

General Slocum (passenger steamboat built in 1890; caught fire and sank in the East River of New York City on June 15, 1904, with 1,021 of the 1342 people on board dying either by drowning or by fire): **Manhattan Melodrama**, 1934.

Gleiwitz Incident (August 31, 1939; attack by Nazi SS commandos dressed as Polish soldiers against a German radio station in Upper Silesia, which was led by saboteur Alfred Helmut Naujocks, 1911-1966; in this fake attack several Germans were ostensibly killed, these being inmates from a German concentration camp, the fake attack then used byAdolf Hitler, 1889-1945, to invade Poland, which started WWII, 1939-1945): Der Fall Gleiwtiz, 1961.

Good Friday (Christian religious holiday commemorating the crucifixion of Jesus and observed during Easter Week): **The Assassination of Jesse James by the Coward Robert Ford**, 2007; **Barabbas**, 1962; **Ben Hur: A Tale of the Christ**, 1925; **Ben-Hur**, 1959; The Day Christ Died, 1980 (made-for-TV); **Demetrius and the Gladiators**, 1954; Good Friday, 2014; The Gospel according to St. Matthew, 1964; Gospel Road: The Story of Jesus, 1973; **The Greatest Story Ever Told**, 1965; Herod the Great, 1959; Jesus, 1999 (made-for-TV); **Jesus Christ Superstar**, 1973; The Jesus Film, 1979; Jesus of Nazareth, 1977 (made-for-TV); Judas, 2004 (made-for-TV); **The King of Kings**, 1927; **King of Kings**, 1961; **The Last Days of Pompeii**, 1935; The Last Temptation of Christ, 1988; Let Joy Reign Supreme, 1975; The Living Christ Series, 1951 (TV miniseries); **The Long Good Friday**, 1982; Mary, Mother of Jesus, 1999 (made-for-TV); Mary of Nazareth, 2012 (made-for-TV); The Miracle Maker, 2000; The Passion of Christ, 2004; Perceval, 1978; Peter and Paul, 1981 (made-for-TV); **Quo Vadis**, 1913; **Quo Vadis**, 1951; Quo Vadis, 2001; Risen, 2016; **The Robe**, 1953; St. Paul, 2000 (made-for-TV); **Saint Ralph**, 2005; **The Silver Chalice**, 1954; Son of God, 2014; Taking Chance, 2009 (made-for-TV); The Visual Bible: The Gospel of John, 2003; **The Wind Journeys**, 2010.

Gulf War (1990-1991): The Big Lebowski, 1998; A Christmas Visitor, 2002 (made-for-TV); Closed Doors, 1999; **Courage under Fire**, 1996; Dawn of the World, 2008; Dead to Rights, 2003; Death of a President, 2006; The Devil's Double, 2011; Eye of the Storm, 1992; House of Saddam, 2008 (TV miniseries); In the Army Now, 1994; The Jacket, 2005; **Jarhead**, 2005; The Law of Enclosures, 2000; Live from Baghdad, 2002 (made-for-TV); The Manchurian Candidate, 2004; The One That Got Away, 1996 (made-for-TV); The Pentagon Wars, 1998 (made-for-TV); Redacted, 2007; Soldier's Girl, 2003 (made-for-TV); The Song of the Siren, 1994; **Three Kings**, 1999; Towelhead, 2007; Trooper, 2010; W., 2008; Yana's Friends, 1999.

Gunfight at the O.K. Corral (Tombstone, Arizona, Wednesday, October 26, 1881, 3 p.m.; legendary gunfight between lawman, Wyatt Earp and his brothers, along with gunfighter John H. "Doc" Holliday, and the outlaw clan of the Clanton and McLaury [or McLowery] Brothers and others, resulting in the deaths of Billy Clanton and Tom and Frank McLaury): **Doc**, 1971; **Frontier Marshal**, 1939; **Gunfight at the O.K. Corral**, 1957; **Hour of the Gun**, 1967; **Law and Order**, 1932; **My Darling Clementine**, 1946; **Sunset**, 1988 (recreation on a Hollywood set); **Tombstone**, 1993; **Tombstone: The Town Too Tough to Die**, 1942; **Wyatt Earp**, 1994.

Halloween (All Hallows' Eve; All Saints' Eve; Christian feast observed in many countries on October 31, remembering saints, martyrs and all of the faithfully departed; in modern times construed to be the night when evil spirits or the undead rise from their graves to harass, terrify and injure the living; children's trick-or-treat night): **The Addams Family**, 1991; **Adventures of Ichabod and Mr. Toad**, 1949; Affliction, 1997; All Hallows' Eve, 2013; All Hallows' Eve 2, 2015; **American Splendor**, 2003; Animals, 2012; Any Day Now, 2012; **Apollo 13**, 1995; **Arsenic and Old Lace**, 1944; Arsenic and Old Lace, 1969 (made-for-TV); Awake, 2007; **Batman Forever**, 1995; Beginners, 2010; Behind the Mask: The Rise of Leslie Vernon, 2006; Bewitched, 2005; Big Monster on Campus, 2000; The Blair Witch Project, 1999; Blood Creek, 2009; Blood of Dracula, 1957; Boo, 2005; Boy of the Streets, 1937; Breakfast with Scot, 2007; Brick, 2005; Can't Buy Me Love, 1987;

Casper, 1995; Charlie and the Chocolate Factory, 2005; A Cinderella Story, 2004; Clownhouse, 1989; The Collingswood Story, 2002; Communion, 1989; **Conrack**, 1974; Creepshow, 1982; The Crow, 1994; The Crow: City of Angels, 1996; A Daughter's Nightmare, 2014 (made-for-TV); Deadly Friend, 1986; **Dear White People**, 2014; Death Defying Acts, 2007; Diary of a Wimpy Kid, 2010; Die, Mommie, Die!, 2003; The Dog Who Saved Halloween, 2011 (made-for-TV); Donnie Darko, 2001; Double, Double, Toil and Trouble, 1993 (made-for-TV); Down to the Bone, 2004; **E.T.: The Extra-Terrestrial**, 1982; **Ed Wood**, 1994; The Effects of Magic, 1998; Ernest Scared Stupid, 1991; Everyone Says I Love You, 1998; The Exorcism of Emily Rose, 2005; **The Exorcist**, 1973; Fame, 2009; Flatliners, 1990; Flawless, 1999; Fun Size, 2012; George's Island, 1989; The Ghost of St. Michael's, 1941; Ghost Squad, 2015; Ghostwatch, 1992 (made-for-TV); Ginger Snaps, 2000; Girl vs. Monster, 2012 (made-for-TV); The Good Girl, 2002; **The Guest**, 2014; **Halloween**, 1978; Halloween, 2007; Halloween 5, 1989; Halloween IV: The Return of Michael Myers, Halloween Hell, 2014; 1988; Halloween H20: Twenty Years Later, 1998; Halloween: Resurrection, 2002; Halloween: The Curse of Michael Myers; Halloween III: Season of the Witch, 1982; The Halloween Tree, 1993 (made-for-TV); Halloween II, 1981; Halloween II, 2009; Halloweentown, 1998 (made-for-TV); Halloweentown High, 2004 (made-for-TV); Hanging Up, 2000; **Harry Potter and the Sorcerer's Stone**, 2001; Hell Night, 1981; Hellboy, 2004; Hellions, 2015; Hocus Pocus, 1993; The Hollow, 2015 (made-for-TV); The Hollywood Knights, 1984; Hone Movie, 2008; **Houdini**, 1953; House of Fears, 2007; House of 1,000 Corpses, 2003; House II: The Second Story, 1987; The Houses October Built, 2014; How High, 2001; I Am Sam, 2001; Idle Hands, 1999; If I Stay, 2014; In America, 2002; The Invasion, 2007; Jack, 1996; Jack the Bear, 1993; **Kramer vs. Kramer**, 1979; Lady in White, 1988; The Last Keepers, 2013; Liberty Heights, 1999; Lightning Bug, 2004; **The Little Girl Who Lives Down the Lane**, 1977; Locked In, 2010; Made of Honor, 2008; May, 2002; Mean Girls, 2004; **Meet Me in St. Louis**, 1944; Merlin, 1993; Midnight Masquerade, 2014 (made-for-TV); Monster House, 2006; Mozart and the Whale, 2005; The Mudge Boy, 2003; Murder Party, 2007; Must Love Dogs, 2005; **My Blue Heaven**, 1950; **My Life So Far**, 1999; My Teacher's Wife, 1999; Naomi and Ely's No Kiss List, 2015; The Next Best Thing, 2000; **Next Stop Wonderland**, 1998; Night of the Demons, 1988; Night of the Demons, 2009; Night of the Demons 2, 1994; The Night of the Headless Horseman, 1999 (made-for-TV); **The Nightmare before Christmas**, 1993; Once Bitten, 1985; **One True Thing**, 1998; Only the Lonely, 1991; Orange County, 2002; **Ordinary People**, 1980; Paper Towns, 2015; Party Monster, 2003; Pay the Ghost, 2015; Penelope, 2006; A Perfect World, 1993; Practical Magic, 1998; Rent, 2005; The Return of Dracula, 1958; Return to Halloweentown, 2006 (made-for-TV); Return to Zero, 2014; Restless, 2011; Riding the Bullet, 2004; Role Models, 2008; Saved!, 2004; **Silver Linings Playbook**, 2012; The Skeleton Twins, 2014; Speak, 2004; The Spy Next Door, 2010; **Steel Magnolias**, 1989; Step Up 3D, 2010; Summer Magic, 1963; **A Summer Place**, 1959; Tales of Halloween, 2015; They Came Together, 2014; The Third Wheel, 2002; The Town That Dreaded Sundown, 2014; **The Tree of Life**, 2011; Trick or Treats, 1982; 12 and Holding, 2005; 2 Days in New York, 2012; Twin Falls Idaho, 1999; **The Two Jakes**, 1990; Under Wraps, 1997 (made-for-TV); Unfaithfully Yours, 1984; We Need to Talk About Kevin, 2011; When Good Ghouls Go Bad, 2001 (made-for-TV); Without a Paddle, 2004; **Woman Who Came Back**, 1945; The Worst Witch, 1986 (made-for-TV); **Zodiac**, 2007.

Hanukkah (Jewish Festival of Lights): **An American Tail**, 1986; Arthur's Perfect Christmas, 2000 (made-for-TV); Christmas at Pee Wee's Playhouse, 1988 (made-for-TV); **The Diary of Anne Frank**, 1959; Die, Mommie, Die!, 2003; Eight Crazy Nights, 2002; God Is Great and I'm Not, 2001; The Hebrew Hammer, 2003; Hit and Run-away, 1999; Hitched for the Holidays, 2012 (made-for-TV); The Holiday, 2006; Holy Rollers, 2010; Imaginary Heroes, 2004; Kissing Jessica Stein, 2001; **A Majority of One**, 1961; Miracle at Moreaux, 1985 (made-for-TV); Southern Belles, 2005; Switchmas, 2012; Waiting for the Messiah, 2012; Wide Awake, 1998; Will You Marry Me?, 2008.

Holocaust (persecution and genocidal destruction of European Jews by the Nazis of Hitler's Third Reich in Germany; 1933-1945, and its survivors): Abraham's Gold, 1990; Adam Resurrected, 2008; After the Truth, 1999 (Josef Mengele); Aftermath, 2012; Aimee & Jaguar, 1999 (German resistance); All My Loved Ones, 1999 (Nazi-occupied Prague); **Amen**, 2002; And the Violins Stopped Playing, 1988; Angel of Budapest, 2011 (made-for-TV); Angry Harvest, 1986 (Jews in Silesia, 1942-1943); Anne Frank: The Whole Story, 2001 (TV miniseries); Apt Pupil, 1998; The Army of Shadows, 2006 (French Resistance and Jews in Nazi-occupied France); The Aryan Couple, 2006; **The Assissi Underground**, 1985; The Attic: The Hiding of Anne Frank, 1988 (made-for-TV); Au revoir les enfants, 1988; Auschwitz, 2011 (Nazi death camp); Bent, 1997 (Nazi concentration camp); Black Book, 2006; **The Boy in Striped Pajamas**, 2008; **The Book Thief**, 2013; Broken Promise, 2009; Conspiracy, 2001 (made-for-TV; 1942 Wannsee Nazi conference where Final Solution to the Holocaust was decided); **The Counterfeit Traitor**, 1962; **The Counterfeiters**, 2008 (Nazi Operation Bernhard); The Day the Clown Cried, 1972; Defiance, 2008 (Belarussian Resistance in WWII); Descending Angel, 1990 (made-for-TV; suspected escaped Nazi having to do with the Holocaust); The Devil's Arithmetic, 1999 (made-for-TV); **The Diary of Anne Frank**, 1959; The Diary of Anne Frank, 1967 (made-for-TV); The Diary of Anne Frank, 1980 (made-for-TV); The Diary of Anne Frank, 1987 (made-for-TV); The Diary of Anne Frank, 1995; The Diary of Anne Frank, 2009 (TV miniseries); **Divided We Fall**, 2000 (Nazi-occupied Czechoslovakia); Eichmann, 2007; **Escape**, 1940 (Nazi concentration camp); Escape from Sobibor, 1987 (made-for-TV; Nazi death camp); **Europa Europa**, 1991 (German boy tries to hide the fact that he is Jewish); **Exodus**, 1960 (Holocaust victims to Israel); **Fateless**, 2005 (Hungarian Jews in a Nazi concentration camp); The Final Solution: The Wannsee Conference, 1984 (made-for-TV); For Those I Loved, 1983 (survivor of the Holocaust in Poland); Forbidden, 1984 (smuggling Jews out of Nazi-controlled Berlin); Forget Me Not: The Anne Frank Story, 1996 (made-for-TV); From Cover to Cover, 1958 (TV series; Anne Frank); **The Garden of the Finzi-Continis**, 1976 (Jews oppressed in Italy in pre-WWII); God on Trial, 2008 (made-for-TV; Jews in a concentration camp indict God for allowing Nazi oppressions); Gloomy Sunday, 1999; Goliath Awaits, 1981 (made-for-TV); Good Evening, Mr. Wallenberg, 1993 (Swedish diplomat Raoul Wallenberg, 1912-1947?, who saved thousands of Jews during the Holocaust); **The Grey Zone**, 2002 (Auschwitz Nazi death camp); Gruningers Fall, 2015 (Paul Gruninger, Swiss police commander who forged documents that saved more than 3,600 Jewish refugees); Haven, 2001 (made-for-TV; 1,000 Jews rescued in Italy in 1944 and taken to the U.S. by American journalist Ruth Gruber, 1911-); Hidden Children, 2004 (made-for-TV; Jewish children attempting to flee the Holocaust to Palestine); The Hiding Place, 1975 (Dutch civilians hiding Jews in Holland in WWII); Holocaust, 1978 (TV miniseries); The House of Garibaldi Street, 1979 (made-for-TV; Adolf Eichmann); Hotel Lux, 2011; Inglourious Basterds, 2009; **Ida**, 2013; In Darkness, 2011; Jakob the Liar, 1999; **Judgment at Nuremberg**, 1961; **The Juggler**, 1953 (German Jew and Holocaust victims in Israel); Kapo, 1960 (Nazi concentration camp); The Keep, 1983; Korkoro, 2009; **La Rafle**, 2012 (1942 capturing of Jews in Paris by Nazis); The Last Train, 2006 (prisoners being sent to a German concentration camp in 1945); **Life Is Beautiful**, 1999 (the Holocaust in Italy); Look to the Sky, 1993 (Dutch Jews in a Nazi concentration camp); Lore, 2012 (German children fleeing the approach of Allied forces in Germany at the end of WWII and where they are protected by a young Jewish man, who has been the victim of the Holocaust); **The Man in the Glass Booth**, 1975 (Eichmann); The Man Who Captured Eichmann, 1996 (made-for-TV); Max and Helen, 1990 (made-for-TV); Memories of Anne Frank, 2010 (made-for-TV); Miracle at Midnight, 1998 (made-for-TV; rescuing Jews in Denmark during the Holocaust); Miracle at Moreaux, 1985 (made-for-TV; Catholic nuns rescue Jews at Christmas during the Nazi Holocaust); **Morituri**, 1965; Mother Night, 1996; Music Box, 1989 (man accused of being a Nazi war criminal); Naked among Wolves, 1963 (Buchenwald Nazi death camp); Naked among Wolves, 2015 (made-for-TV; Buchenwald, Nazi death camp); Never Forget, 1991 (made-for-TV); The Ninth Circle, 1960 (Jewish girl marries in Croatia to escape Nazi persecution during the Holocaust); **The Ninth Day**, 2004 (based on the diary of Catholic priest Jean Bernard, 1907-1994, who was a prisoner at Dachau, the Nazi concentration camp); The Notebook, 2013; **Nowhere in Africa**, 2001 (Jews fleeing Nazi Germany in 1930s to Kenya); Nuremberg, 2000 (TV miniseries); **The Odessa File**, 1974 (escaped Nazi war criminals); One Day You'll Understand, 2008; The Only Way, 1970 (Jews attempt to escape Denmark in 1943); Out of the Ashes, 2003 (made-for-TV; Dr. Gisella Perl, Auschwitz survivor); Passenger, 1963 (Auschwitz, Nazi death camp); **The Pawnbroker**, 1965 (embittered survivor of the Holocaust); **The People vs. Fritz Bauer**, 2015 (Eichmann role model); **The Pianist**, 2002; Playing for Time, 1980 (made-for-TV; female musicians prolonging their lives at Auschwitz by playing music); The Relief of Belsen, 2007 (Nazi concentration camp); The Ring, 1996 (made-for-TV; Nazi concentration camp); Rosenstrasse, 2003 (Jewish husbands held in Berlin during the Holocaust); Sarah's Key, 2010; **Schindler's List**, 1993 (Nazi concentration camps, including Auschwitz); **The Seventh Cross**, 1944 (escape of seven prisoners from a Nazi concentration camp in 1936); **Ship of Fools**, 1965; The Singing Forest, 2003; **Sophie's Choice**, 1982 (survivor of a Nazi concentration camp); Spring of Life, 2000 (Nazis attempting to create an Aryan race); **The Stranger**, 1946 (escaped Nazi war criminal); **Sunshine**, 2000 (a Jewish family through the 20th Century); **Sword in the Desert**, 1949 (Holocaust victims to Israel); The Third Half, 2012 (Nazi persecutions in Soviet Russia); The Third Part of the Night, 1971 (Nazi occupied Poland); Train of Life, 1998 (Jews attempting to escape to Palestine in 1941); **Triumph of the Spirit**, 1990 (Olympic boxer survives Auschwitz Nazi death camp by fighting); The Truce, 1997 (surviving Italian Jews returning from Auschwitz); The Tulse Luper Suitcases, Part 3: From Sark to Finish, 2004 (Swedish diplomat Raoul Wallenberg, 1912-1947?, who saved thousands of Jews during the Holocaust); The 25th Hour, 1967 (Jews in a Nazi concentration camp); Uprising, 2001 (made-for-TV; 1943 uprising in Warsaw's Jewish ghetto); Voyage of the Damned, 1976 (doomed Jewish refugees aboard the SS *St. Louis*); Walk on Water, 2004; Walking with the Enemy, 2013; The Wall, 1982 (made-for-TV; 1943 uprising in Warsaw's Jewish ghetto); Wallenberg: A Hero's Story, 1985 (made-for-TV; Swedish diplomat Raoul Wallenberg, 1912-1947?, who saved thousands of Jews during the Holocaust); We'll Go to the City, 1966 (the Holocaust in Italy); **The White Rose**, 1983 (German resistance in Nazi Germany); **Woman in Gold**, 2015; Wunderkinder, 2011; **The Young Lions**, 1958 (Nazi concentration camp).

Independence Day (U.S. Fourth of July, when the Declaration of Independence was signed in 1776): Asteroid, 1997 (made-for-TV); Blown Away, 1994; **Born on the Fourth of July**, 1989; The Boy in the Plastic Bubble, 1976 (made-for-TV); **Dragonwyck**, 1946; Flight of the Navigator, 1986; **The Great Escape**, 1963; Grown Ups, 2010; **Independence Day**, 1996; **Live Free or Die Hard**, 2007; **The Patriot**, 2000; **Rocky**, 1976; **1776**, 1972; **Shane**, 1953; The Spirit of '76, 1990; **Toby Tyler, or Ten Weeks with a Circus**, 1960; **A Walk on the Moon**, 1999; **Washington Square**, 1997; The Wild and the Innocent, 1959; **Yankee Doodle Dandy**, 1942.

Indianapolis 500 (since 1911, annual auto car race held yearly on Memorial Day weekend in Indianapolis, Indiana; cars racing 500 miles or 200 laps, winning with the best time): The Big Wheel, 1949; **The Crowd Roars**, 1932; Indianapolis Speedway, 1939; Road Demon, 1938;

Speedway, 1929; Ten Laps to Go, 1936; Turbo, 2013; **Winning**, 1969.

Korean War (1950-1953; films dealing directly with the war and films involving civilians, recruits and veterans of that war): All the Young Men, 1960; The Amazing Colossal Man, 1957; ...And the Earth Did Not Swallow Him, 1995; The Bamboo Prison, 1954; Battle Circus, 1953; Battle Flame, 1959; Battle Hymn, 1957; Battle Taxi, 1955; Battle Zone, 1952; Battleground 625, 2005; Before the Deluge, 1954; The Big Chase, 1954; **Big Fish**, 2003; The Blue Peter, 1957; Bombers B-52, 1957; **The Bridges at Toko-Ri**, 1954; Canon Cheol-jin's Mission, 1977; Chattahoochee, 1990; Collision Course: Truman vs. MacArthur, 1976 (made-for-TV); Combat Squad, 1953; Cry for Happy, 1961; Day Zero, 2007; Dragonfly Squadron, 1954; Field of Honor, 1986; **Fixed Bayonets!**, 1951; **Flat Top**, 1952; For the Boys, 1991; The Front Line, 2011; Geisha Girl, 1952; Give 'Em Hell, Harry!, 1975; **The Glory Brigade**, 1953; **The Great Imposter**, 1961; **Heartbreak Ridge**, 1986; A Hill in Korea, 1956; **Hold Back the Night**, 1956; The Hook, 1963; The Hunters, 1958; I Die Alone, 2013; **I Want You**, 1951; Inchon, 1982; Japanese War Bride, 1952; Jet Attack, 1958; Korea Patrol, 1951; The Korean War, 2001 (TV series); Last Exit to Brooklyn, 1989; **The Last Picture Show**, 1971; **Love Is a Many Splendored Thing**, 1955; **The Manchurian Candidate**, 1962; Marines, Let's Go, 1961; **M*A*S*H**, 1970; M*A*S*H, 1972-1983 (TV series); Mask of the Dragon, 1951; **MacArthur**, 1977; **The McConnell Story**, 1955; **Men in War**, 1957; **Men of the Fighting Lady**, 1954; Mission over Korea, 1953; The Nun and the Sergeant, 1962; **One Minute to Zero**, 1952; The Orphan, 2008; Period of Adjustment, 1962; **Pork Chop Hill**, 1959; The Price of Heaven, 1997 (made-for-TV); **Prisoner of War**, 1954; **The Rack**, 1956; **Retreat!**, 2012; **Retreat, Hell!**, 1952; The Reluctant Heroes, 1971 (made-for-TV); Sabre Jet, 1953; **Sayonara**, 1957; Sergeant Ryker, 1968; 71: Into the Fire, 2010; Shang gan ling, 1956; Sniper's Ridge, 1961; Soldiers of Innocence, 1987; **Starlift**, 1951; **The Steel Helmet**, 1951; **Submarine Command**, 1951; Tae Guk Gi: The Brotherhood of War, 2004; Taebaek sanmaek, 1994; **Take the High Ground!**, 1953; Tank Battalion, 1958; Target Zero, 1955; **Time Limit**, 1957; Tokyo File 212, 1951; **Toward the Unknown**, 1956; **War Hunt**, 1962; **War Is Hell**, 1963; A Yank in Korea, 1951; The Young and the Brave, 1963.

Le Mans Race (since 1923; 24-hour endurance race of sportscars held annually in Le Mans, France, in the second weekend of June): Blonde Comet, 1941; Journey to Le Mans, 2014; **Le Mans**. 1971; Michel Vaillant, 2003; The Reckless Lady, 1926.

Krakatoa (island in the Dutch East Indies that was chiefly a volcano and erupted on August 27, 1883, destroying the island and creating tsunamis where more than 35,000 persons were killed, one of the world's most devastating disasters): **Krakatoa: East of Java**, 1969; Krakatoa, 2008 (made-for-TV).

Long Beach, California (earthquake occurring on March 10, 1933, 6.4 on the Richter Scale, damaging much of the city, where 115 people died, mostly struck by falling debris; also see Earthquakes, Subject Index): **The Day of the Locust**, 1975; Looking for Trouble, 1934.

Malmedy (Belgium) Massacre (WWII; December 17, 1944; eighty U.S. soldiers, who had been captured by a mechanized unit of the 1st SS Panzer Division commanded by Col. Joachim Peiper [1915-1976], were bound with their hands behind their backs and then summarily shot to death in a mass execution. The bodies were discovered on January 14-15, 1945. Peiper and seventy others were tried as war criminals for the massacre in May-June 1946, and he and forty-two others received death sentences, but none were ever carried out and the defendants were all later released): Battle of the Bulge, 1965, **Judgment at Nuremberg**, 1961; **Hart's War**, 2002, and **Saints and Soldiers**, 2005.

Memorial Day (formerly Decoration Day; observed on the last Monday in May and commemorates all men and women who have died in the military service of the U.S.): **Act of Violence**, 1948; A Christmas Visitor, 2002 (made-for-TV); **Flags of Our Fathers**, 2006; Judge Priest, 1934; Memorial Day, 1983 (made-for-TV); Memorial Day, 1998; Memorial Day, 2011; Native Land, 1942; Red Hot Tires, 1935; Speedway, 1929; **They Won't Forget**, 1937.

Mexican Revolution (1866-1867, or earlier; to depose the French dictatorship of Maximilian I [Hapsburg] by the forces of Benito Juarez): Adios Sabata, 1971; Aquellos anos, 1974; Blood Red Rose, 1946; Cinco de Mayo, La Battala, 2013; The Cisco Kid, 1994 (made-for-TV); Cuando lloran los valientes, 1947; El carruaje, 1972 (TV series); El Condor, 1970; El joven Juarez, 1954; El vuelo del aguila, 1994 (TV series); The Hourglass Sanatorium, 1973; **Juarez**, 1939; Juarez and Maximilian, 1935; La Tormenta, 1967 (TV series); The Mad Empress, 1939; **Major Dundee**, 1965; Maximilian von Mexiko, 1970 (made-for-TV); Mexicanos al grito de guerra, 1943; Prariejager in Mexiko: Benito Juarez, 1988; Treasure of the Aztecs, 1966; **Two Mules for Sister Sara**, 1970; **The Undefeated**, 1969; **Vera Cruz**, 1954; Visita al Pasado, 1981; Zorro's Fighting Legion, 1939.

Mexican Revolution (1910-1920 and later): The Abandoned, 1945; Adventurous Youth, 1928; American Family, 2002-2004 (TV series; "Mexican Revolution," 2002 episode); And Starring Pancho Villa as Himself, 2003 (made-for-TV); Antonieta, 1982; Aqui esta Juan Colorado, 1947; Bandido, 1956; Bandits, 1991; Bad Man's River, 1974; Behind the Clouds, 1963; Behind the Lines, 1916 (U.S. troops in Mexico); A Bullet for the General, 1968; Café Colon, 1959; Cannon for Cordoba, 1970; Capitan de rurales, 1951; Como agua para chocalate, 1993; Companeros, 1972; Cuando Viva Viva!...es la muerte, 1961; Cuartelazo, 1977; Django 2—Il grande ritorno, 1987; Don't Turn the Other Cheek, 1974; **Duck, You Sucker**, 1972; Duelo en las montanas, 1950; El caudillo, 1968; El diablo en persona, 1973; El escapulario, 1968; El ojo de vidrio, 1969; El principio, 1973; The Five Man Army, 1970; Godfather Mendoza, 1934; The Guns of Juana Gallo, 1962; Guns of the Magnificent Seven, 1969; The Hidden One, 1957; Il lungo giorno della violenza, 1971; Impatient Heart, 1960; Killer Kid, 1967; La bandida, 1963; La cebra, 2011; La chamuscada, 1971; La constitucion, 1970; La genererala, 1971; La guerrillera de Villa, 1967; La parajera, 1945; La tormenta, 1967 (TV series); La trinchera, 1969; La Valentina, 1966; Land of Darkness, 1995; Las fuerzas vivas, 1975; Las tres pelonas, 1958; The Light of Western Stars, 1940; Los cuatro Juanes, 1966; Los de abajo, 1940; Los de abajo, 1978; Morir de pie, 1957; **Old Gringo**, 1989; 100 Rifles, 1969; Pancho Villa, 1973; Pancho Villa and Valentina, 1961; Pedro Paramo, 1967; Prision de mujeres, 1977; Prisoner 13, 1933; A Professional Gun, 1970; **The Professionals**, 1966; Pueblo en armas, 1959; Run, Man, Run, 1968; Sangre derramada, 1975; Senda de gloria, 1987 (TV series); Shadow of Pancho Villa, 1934; She Came to the Valley, 1979; Si Adelita se fuera con otro, 1948; The Soldiers of Pancho Villa, 1961; Sucedio en Jalisco, 1972; **They Came to Cordura**, 1959; Tepepa, 1979; This Was Pancho Villa, 1959; A Town Called Hell, 1972; The Treasure of Pancho Villa, 1957; Trini, 1979; Un treno per Durango, 1968; Valente Quintero, 1973; Valentin de la Sierra, 1968; **Villa Rides**, 1968; Vino el remolino y nos alevanto, 1950; Viva Benito Canales!, 1966; Viva Cangaceiro, 1970; Viva Maria!, 1965; **Viva Villa!**, 1934; **Viva Zapata!**, 1952; Vuelve Pancho Villa, 1950; Wanted: The Sundance Woman, 1976 (made-for-TV); What Am I Doing in the Middle of the Revolution, 1972; **The Wild Bunch**, 1969; Wings of the Hawk, 1953.

Monaco Grand Prix (since 1929; annual sports car race in the Principality of Monaco; cars racing seventy-eight laps with the winning time): **Cars 2**, 2011; The Challengers, 1970 (made-for-TV); Collision Course, 1989; The Good Thief, 2002; Grand Prix, 1934; Grand Prix, 1966; **The Love Bug**, 1968; The Pinchcliffe Grand Prix, 1981; Race for Glory,

1989; Race for Life, 1954; Summer Love, 1970; The Young Racers, 1963.

Mother's Day (U.S. national holiday since 1914, the second Sunday in May that honors mothers and motherhood): **The Egg and I**, 1947; Going Shopping, 2005; **Lady by Choice**, 1934; Loggerheads, 2005; The Machinist, 2004; The Merry Frinks, 1934; Missing Daughters, 1939; Mom's Night Out, 2014; Mother's Day, 1993; Mother's Day, 2010; Mother's Day, 2013 (made-for-TV); Mother's Day, 2016; My Bill, 1938; Parking, 2008; That Brennan Girl, 1946; **Three Men on a Horse**, 1936.

Nanking Massacre (Second Sino-Japanese War; Japanese troop conquering Nanking, China, were unleashed by their commanders to wantonly murder as many as 300,000 unarmed combatants and civilians, men, women and children, as well as raping tens of thousands of helpless females, from December 13, 1937 through January 1938; several individuals responsible were later convicted as war criminals and hanged): Devils on the Doorstep, 2002; Nanking, 2007.

New Year's Day (Celebrating the first day of the new year on January 1 where many make resolutions to improve their lives): Assault on Precinct 13, 2005; A Bright Shining Lie, 1998 (made-for-TV); Carole, 2015; Devils on the Doorstep, 2002; **Diner**, 1982; The Fourth Protocol, 1987; **Fruitvale Station**, 2013; Happy New Year, 1987; **I'll Be Seeing You**, 1944; In Search of a Midnight Kiss, 2007; In the Room, 2015; January 2nd, 2006; **Kwaidan**, 1965; Nanking, 2007; New Year's Day, 1989; New Year's Day, 2000; **Operation Petticoat**, 1959; **The Perks of Being a Wallflower**, 2012; **The Poseidon Adventure**, 1972; Repeat Performance, 1947; **Rocky**, 1976; The Square, 2008; The White Balloon, 1996.

New Year's Eve (Celebrating at the stroke of midnight the first day of the new year on January 1): **About a Boy**, 2002; About Last Night..., 1986; About Time, 2013; **After the Thin Man**, 1936; Aimee & Jaguar, 1999; Alaska, 2015; **An American in Paris**, 1951; And So They Were Married, 1936; Angel Heart, 1997; Another Year, 2014; **The Apartment**, 1960; Assault on Precinct 13, 2005; **Babe**, 1995; Baby Face, 1933; **Bachelor Mother**, 1939; The Bandit, 1949; **The Best of Youth**, 2003; Better Luck Tomorrow, 2002; The Big Year, 2011; Black Beauty, 1933; The Black Dahlia, 2006; Black's Game, 2012; Blast of Silence, 1961; Bless the Child, 2000; The Book of Life, 1998; Break of Hearts, 1935; The Bride Walks Out, 1936; **Bridget Jones's Diary**, 2001; The Brighton Strangler, 1945; The Broken Circle Breakdown, 2012; Burning Secret, 1988; Carnival in Moscow, 1957; **Cavalcade**, 1933; Cheers for Miss Bishop, 1941; Christine, 1983; The Company, 2003; Conviction, 2010; CQ, 2001; Cronos, 1993; Death Hunt, 1981; The Debt, 2010; Definitely, Maybe, 2008; Devils on the Doorstep, 2002; **Diner**, 1982; **The Divorcee**, 1930; Don't Tell, 2005; Elegy, 2008; End of Days, 1999; Entrapment, 1999; Factory Girl, 2006; The Facts of Life, 1960; Far from Heaven, 2002; Fireworks Wednesday, 2006; **Forrest Gump**, 1994; Four Rooms, 1995; The Fourth Protocol, 1987; Friends with Kids, 2011; Frozen Land, 2005; **Fruitvale Station**, 2013; A Gentleman after Dark, 1942; Get Crazy, 1983; **Ghostbusters II**, 1989; Ginger in the Morning, 1974; The Girl from Mandalay, 1936; **The Godfather Part II**, 1974; **The Gold Rush**, 1925; The Good Heart, 2009; Ground Control, 1988; Happiness Ahead, 1934; Happy New Year, 1973; Happy New Year, 1987; **Has Anybody Seen My Gal?**, 1952; Havana, 1990; The Heart of Me, 2002; **Holiday**, 1938; The Holiday, 2006; Holiday Affair, 1949; **Holiday Inn**, 1942; Home Movie, 2008; The Hotel New Hampshire, 1984; The Hudsucker Proxy, 1994; I Don't Kiss, 1995; If This Be Sin, 1949; Il Posto, 1963; **I'll Be Seeing You**, 1944; Imaginary Heroes, 2004; In Search of a Midnight Kiss, 2007; Indiscreet, 1931; **Iron Man 3**, 2013; It All Came True, 1998; The January Man, 1989; The Lady Consents, 1936; Lake Placid Serenade, 1944; Last Holiday, 2006; Les liaisons dangereuses, 1961; Liam, 2000; **The Long Day Closes**, 1992; A Long Way Down, 2014; **Looking for Mr. Goodbar**, 1977; A Lot Like Love, 2005; Love Laughs at Andy Hardy, 1946; **Made for Each Other**, 1939; Madhouse, 1974; **The Man I Love**, 1947; **Middle of the Night**, 1959; Midnight, 2006; Mrs. Parker and the Vicious Circle, 1994; Money Train, 1995; My Sex Life, or How I Got into an Argument, 1996; **Mystery of the Wax Museum**, 1933; New Year's Eve, 1924; New Year's Eve, 1929; New Year's Eve, 2011; **Ocean's Eleven**, 1960; **Ocean's Eleven**, 2001; On the Road, 2012; One Man's Journey, 1933; **One True Thing**, 1998; **One Way Passage**, 1932; The Overcoat, 1953; Paris 36, 2008; The Passionate Thief, 1963; **Penny Serenade**, 1941; **The Perks of Being a Wallflower**, 2012; **Peter's Friends**, 1992; The Phantom Wagon, 1940; A Place in the World, 1982; Poseidon, 2006; **The Poseidon Adventure**, 1972; The Poseidon Adventure, 2005 (made-for-TV); The Purchase Price, 1932; **Radio Days**, 1987; **Remember the Night**, 1940; Rent, 2005; Repeat Performance, 1947; Ride the Wild Surf, 1964; Rigged, 2008; Romance, 1930; **Rosemary's Baby**, 1968; **Rosewood**, 1997; The Saint Strikes Back, 1939; **The Shining**, 1980; **Show Boat**, 1951; **Show Business**, 1944; **Sleepless in Seattle**, 1993; Someone Like You…, 2001; The Spirit of Stanford, 1942; The Square, 2008; Starstruck, 1982; Starter for 10, 2006; Strange Days, 1995; Studs Lonigan, 1960; **Sunset Boulevard**, 1950; **Sunshine**, 2000; Swift Shift, 1984; **Tea with Mussolini**, 1999; Tempest, 1982; Terror Train, 1980; 'Til We Meet Again, 1940; **The Time Machine**, 1960; A Touch of Sin, 2013; **Trading Places**, 1983; **Two Lovers**, 2009; Under Western Eyes, 1936; **Underworld U.S.A.**, 1961; Velvet Goldmine, 1998; Waiting to Exhale, 1995; Whatever Works, 2009; **When Harry Met Sally**, 1989; While You Were Sleeping, 1995; The White Balloon, 1996; White Collar Blues, 1975; Winter Sleepers, 1997; Year of the Dog, 2007; **Young Guns**, 1988; **The Young Lions**, 1958.

Olympics: Ace of Aces, 1982 (1936 in Berlin, Germany); Alex, 1992 (1960 in Rome, Italy); Berlin '36, 2009 (1936 in Berlin, Germany); Bert & Dickie, 2012 (1948 in London, England); The Bob Mathias Story, 1954 (1948 in London, England; 1952 in Helsinki, Finland); **The Book Thief**, 2013 (1936 in Berlin, Germany); Breaking the Surface: The Greg Louganis Story, 1997 (made-for-TV; 1984 in Los Angeles, California; 1988 in Seoul, South Korea); **Chariots of Fire**, 1981 (1924 in Paris, France); Cool Runnings, 1993 (1988 in Calgary, Alberta, Canada); **The Cutting Edge**, 1992 (1988 in Calgary, Alberta, Canada); Dark Horse, 1990; Dawn!, 1979 (1956 in Melbourne, Australia; 1960 in Rome, Italy; 1964 in Tokyo, Japan); Four Minutes, 2005 (made-for-TV; Roger Bannister; 1952 in Helsinki, Finland); **Foxcatcher**, 2014 (1988 in Seoul, South Korea); The Gabby Douglas Story, 2014 (made-for-TV; 2012 in London, England); The Games, 1970; Ice Pawn, 1989; International Velvet, 1978; It Happened in Athens, 1962 (1896 in Athens, Greece); The Jesse Owens Story, 1984 (made-for-TV; 1936 in Berlin, Germany); **Jim Thorpe—All American**, 1951 (1912 in Stockholm, Sweden; 1932 in Los Angeles, California); Make It or Break It, 2009 (TV series); **Million Dollar Legs**, 1932 (1932 in Los Angeles, California); A Million to One, 1937; Miracle, 2004 (1980 in Moscow, Soviet Union [Russia]); Miracle on Ice, 1981 (made-for-TV; 1980 in Lake Placid, New York); Munich, 2005 (1972 in Munich, Germany); Prefontaine, 1997 (Steve Prefontaine; 1972 in Munich, Germany); Race, 2016 (Jesse Owens; 1936 in Berlin, Germany); Rowing Through, 1996 (1980 in Moscow, Soviet Union [Russia]); Run for the Dream: The Gail Devers Story, 1996 (made-for-TV; 1988 in Seoul, South Korea); Running, 1979; Running Brave, 1983 (William Mervin "Billy" Mills; 1964 in Tokyo, Japan); **Saint Ralph**, 2005 (1936 in Berlin, Germany, and 1954 Boston Marathon); The Setting Sun, 1997; Swimming Upstream, 2003 (championship swimmer Tony Fingleton, who declined an invitation to perform in the 1964 Olympics in Tokyo, Japan); Sword of Gideon, 1986 (made-for-TV; 1972 in Munich, Germany); 21 Hours at Munich, 1976 (made-for-TV; 1972 in Munich, Germany); **Unbroken**, 2014 (1936 in Berlin, Germany); **Walk Don't Run**, 1966 (1964 in Tokyo, Japan); **Wee Geordie**, 1955

(1956 in Melbourne, Australia); Wilma, 1977 (made-for-TV; Wilma Rudolph; 1960 in Rome, Italy); Without Limits, 1998 (Steve Prefontaine; 1972 in Munich, Germany).

Pearl Harbor (WWII; Oahu, Hawaii; Japanese Attack; December 7, 1941): **Admiral Yamamoto**, 1968; **Air Force**, 1943; December 7th, 1943; Eleanor and Franklin: The White House Years, 1977 (made-for-TV); **From Here to Eternity**, 1953; **In Harm's Way**, 1965, **Pearl Harbor**, 2001; Remember Pearl Harbor, 1942; **Secret Agent of Japan**, 1942; **Tora! Tora! Tora!**, 1970; War and Remembrance, 1988 (TV miniseries); We've Never Been Licked, 1943.

Philippine Insurrection (Philippine-American War; 1899-1902): **Across the Pacific**, 1926; Amigo, 2011; **The Real Glory**, 1939.

Pompeii, Italy (August 24 or October 24, 79 A.D., volcanic eruption of Vesuvius, one of the world's greatest natural disasters, destroying the towns of Pompeii and Herculaneum, where more than 1,500 bodies were later found but the actual number of fatalities may have been much more): Apocalypse Pompeii, 2014; The Last Days of Pompeii, 1913; **The Last Days of Pompeii**, 1935; The Last Days of Pompeii, 1959; The Last Days of Pompeii, 1984 (TV miniseries); **Night at the Museum: Secret of the Tomb**, 2014; Pompeii, 2014; Pompeii: The Last Day, 2003 (made-for-TV).

Rosh Hashanah (Jewish New Year): The Believer, 2001; Liberty Heights, 1999; Safe Men, 1998.

Russian Civil War (1919-1922): Admiral, 2008; And Quiet Flows the Don, 1957; Archangel, 1990; **Arsenal**, 1929; At Home among Strangers, a Stranger among His Own, 1974; Beg, 1971; Chapayev, 1934; Chekist, 1992; The Commissar, 1967; Coup de grace, 1976; Der Stille Don, 2006- (TV series); **Doctor Zhivago**, 1965; The Forty-First, 1956; **Knight without Armor**, 1937; **The Last Command**, 1928; The Red and the White, 1968; **Reds**, 1981; Reilly: Ace of Spies, 1983 (TV miniseries); A Slave of Love, 1976; **Storm over Asia**, 1930; We Are from Kronstadt, 1936; We the Living, 1942; White Sun of the Desert, 1970.

Russian Rebellion (1905): **Battleship Potemkin**, 1925; Mother, 1926; **Nicholas and Alexandra**, 1971; The Soul Keeper, 2002.

Russian Revolution (1917-1919): Admiral, 2008; **Anastasia**, 1956; Anastasia, 1997; Anastasia: The Mystery of Anna, 1986 (made-for-TV); And Quiet Flows the Don, 1957; The Assassination of Trotsky, 1972; At Home among Strangers, a Stranger among His Own, 1974; At the Mercy of Men, 1918; Billions, 1920; The Blackguard, 1925; British Agent, 1934; Chapayev, 1934; Der Stille Don, 2006- (TV series); **Doctor Zhivago**, 1965; The Fall of the Romanoffs, 1917; Flame Top, 1980; The End of St. Petersburg, 1927; The Grand Duchess and the Waiter, 1926; **Knight without Armor**, 1937; **The Last Command**, 1928; The Last Station, 2009; The Leatherneck, 1929; The Legion of Death, 1918; Meet the Prince, 1926; Mockery, 1927; My Official Wife, 1926; **Nicholas and Alexandra**, 1971; Rasputin, 1996 (made-for-TV); Rasputin, 2010; **Rasputin and the Empress**, 1932; **Rasputin the Mad Monk**, 1966; The Red Dance, 1928; **Reds**, 1981; Reilly: Ace of Spies, 1983 (TV miniseries); The Romanovs: An Imperial Family, 2000; The Rose of Blood, 1917; Russian Ark, 2002; Scarlet Dawn, 1932; The Scarlet Lady, 1928; The Song of the Flame, 1930; Tempest, 1928; **Ten Days That Shook the World** (aka: October), 1928; They Wanted Peace, 1938; Torment, 1924; Trust, 1976; Under False Colors, 1917; Under Western Eyes, 1975 (made-for-TV); The Volga Boatman, 1926; When a Girl Loves, 1924; The World and Its Woman, 1919; World and the Flesh, 1932; Zoya, 1995 (made-for-TV).

Russo-Japanese War (February 8, 1904-September 5, 1905; war between the Russian Empire and the Empire of Japan over territories in Manchuria and Korea): The Breath of the Gods, 1920; Clouds over the Hill, 2009-2011 (TV series); Emperor Meiji and the Great Russo-Japanese War, 1958; The Fall of the Empire, 2005 (TV miniseries); **Jack London**, 1943; Leonie, 2010; **Nicholas and Alexandra**, 1971; Nihonkai daikaisen, 1969; Reilly: Ace of Spies, 1983 (TV miniseries); 203 kochi, 1980.

Salem Witch Trials (1692-1693; trials of many individuals falsely accused of practicing witchcraft that resulted in the executions of twenty persons in and about Salem, Massachusetts): Burned at the Stake, 1981; Crowhaven Farm, 1970 (made-for-TV); The Crucible, 1958; **The Crucible**, 1996; The Crucible, 2014; Hocus Pocus, 1993; **I Married a Witch**, 1942; The Lords of Salem, 2002; Maid of Salem, 1937; Puritan Passions, 1923; Salem Witch Trials, 2002; The Scarecrow, 1972 (made-for-TV); The Secret Village, 2013; **Woman Who Came Back**, 1945.

Spanish-American War (April 25, 1898-August 12, 1898): Across the Pacific, 1926; **Bite the Bullet**, 1975; **The Bowery**, 1933; Cimarron, 1960; **Citizen Kane**, 1941; The Daughter of Rosie O'Grady, 1950; I Loved a Woman, 1933; A Message to Garcia, 1936; Mother Carey's Chickens, 1938; Oklahoma Renegades, 1940; **Pursued**, 1947; The Rough Riders, 1927; Rough Riders, 1997 (made-for-TV); Rustlers of Devil's Canyon, 1947; Shame, 1917; **Stars and Stripes Forever**, 1952; Sweet Adeline, 1934; Texas Trail, 1937; Tonto Basin Outlaws, 1941; Wyoming Wildcat, 1941; **Yellow Jack**, 1938.

Spanish Civil War (July 17, 1936-April 1, 1939): The Anarchist's Wife, 2009; Angel of Death, 2002; The Angel Wore Red, 1960; **Arch of Triumph**, 1948; **Arise My Love**, 1940; As Long as You Live, 1955; **Ay, Carmela!**, 1991; Behold a Pale Horse, 1964; **Belle epoque**, 1992; Bethune, 1977 (made-for-TV); Black Bread, 2011; **Blockade**, 1938; Broken Silence, 2001; Butterfly (aka: Butterly's Tongue), 2000; Carmen among the Reds, 1939; Carol's Journey, 2003; **Confidential Agent**, 1945; Cousin Angelica, 1974; **Dancing at Lughnasa**, 1998; **Death in Granada** (aka: The Disappearance of Garcia Lorca), 1997; Desire, 2002; The Devil's Backbone, 2001; Dr. Bethune (aka: Bethune: The Making of a Hero), 1993; Doomed Souls, 1975; Dragon Rapide, 1986; El Mar, 2000; En la ciudad sin limites, 2002; The End of a Mystery, 2003; Espionage Agent, 1939; **The Fallen Sparrow**, 1943; Fiesta, 1995; **For Whom the Bell Tolls**, 1943; A Forbidden God, 2013; Front of Madrid, 1939; Funf Patronenhulsen (Five Cartridges), 1960; The Girl of Your Dreams, 1998; Head in the Clouds, 2004; The Heifer, 1985; Hemingway & Gellhorn, 2012 (made-for-TV); I Am Curious (Yellow), 1969; If They Tell You I Fell, 1992; In Praise of Older Women, 1997; Ispansi!, 2011; The Keep, 1983; Land and Freedom, 1996; Las 13 rosas, 2007; The Last Circus, 2010; **The Last Train from Madrid**, 1937; Libertarias, 1996; A Life Sold, 1976; Little Ashes, 2008; The Long Holidays of 1936, 1976; Long Live Death, 1971; The Long Winter, 1992; Lovers of the Arctic Circle, 1999; The Madness, 1976 (made-for-TV); Madrid, 1987; The Man of the Legion, 1940; The Mirror, 1983; **The 100-Year-Old Man Who Climbed Out of the Window and Disappeared**, 2013; Painless, 2012; **Pan's Labyrinth**, 2007; Paul Robeson, 1979 (made-for-TV); **The Prime of Miss Jean Brodie**, 1969; Raza, 1942; Riders of the Dawn, 1990 (TV series); Roads to the South, 1978; Shadow of a Hero, 2015; **Ship of Fools**, 1965; The Siege of the Alcazar, 1940; Slacker, 1991; **The Sleeping Voice**, 2012; **The Snows of Kilimanjaro**, 1952; Soldiers of Salamis, 2004; Special Correspondents, 1943; **The Spirit of the Beehive** (1973); **Spitfire**, 1943; Talk of Angels, 1998; There Be Dragons, 2011; **Thunder Rock**, 1944; The Time of the Doves, 1982; The Tree of Guernica, 1976; Under a Blanket of Stars, 2014; Valentina, 1982 (made-for-TV); Voyage to Nowhere, 1986; **The War Is Over**, 1967; The War We Left Behind, 1980; **Wings of the**

Morning, 1937; Year of Enlightenment, 1988; Your Name Poisons My Dreams, 1996.

St. Bartholomew's Day Massacre (France; August 24, 1572-October 3, 1572; Catholic mob violence in France against French Calvinist Protestants or Huguenots): **Ashes of Vengeance**, 1923; **Intolerance: Love's Struggle throughout the Ages**, 1916; A Woman of Evil, 1954.

St. Valentine's Day Massacre (Chicago, Illinois; February 14, 1929): **Al Capone**, 1959; Capone, 1975 (Ben Gazzarra); **The St. Valentine's Day Massacre**, 1967; The St. Valentine's Day Massacre, 1997 (made-for-TV); **Scarface**, 1932; **Some Like It Hot**, 1959.

San Francisco Earthquake (a devastating quake, 7.8 on the Richter Scale, occurred on April 18, 1906, and great fissures appeared and resulting fires took the lives of about 3,000 people and destroying about 80 percent of the city; considered to be one of the world's greatest natural disasters; also see Earthquakes, Subject Index): Flame of the Barbary Coast, 1945; Frisco Jenny, 1932; Hell Morgan's Girl, 1917; Old San Francisco, 1927; **San Francisco**, 1936; **The Shock**, 1923; **The Sisters**, 1938; **Somebody Loves Me**, 1952; A Virtuous Vamp, 1919.

Texas Revolution (1836; including the Battle of the Alamo, February 23-March 6, 1836, and the Battle of San Jacinto, April 21, 1836): **The Alamo**, 1960; **The Alamo**, 2004; The Alamo: Thirteen Days of Glory, 1987 (made-for-TVF); Davy Crockett at the Fall of the Alamo, 1926; **Davy Crockett: King of the Wild Frontier**, 1955; The First Texan, 1956; Gone to Texas, 1986 (made-for-TV); Heroes of the Alamo, 1937; **The Last Command**, 1955; **The Man from the Alamo**, 1953; **Man of Conquest**, 1939; Martyrs of the Alamo, 1915; Texas, 1994 (made-for-TV); True Women, 1997 (made-for-TV); Two for Texas, 1998 (made-for-TV).

Thanksgiving (national holiday in Canada, celebrated on the second Monday of October and a national holiday in the U.S., celebrated on the fourth Thursday of November): About Last Night, 1986; A.C.O.D., 2013; Across the Universe, 2007; **Addams Family Values**, 1993; Alice's Restaurant, 1969; All I Want for Christmas, 2007 (made-for-TV); All You Need, 2001; Alone in the Woods, 1996; American Gangster, 2007; An American Girl Holiday, 2004 (made-for-TV); American Son, 2008; **Antwone Fisher**, 2002; Aurora Borealis, 2005; **Avalon**, 1990; Back Street, 1961; Battle Hymn, 1957; Big Eden, 2000; **The Big House**, 1930; The Blind Side, 2009; **Boyhood**, 2014; Boyz n the Hood, 1991; Brokeback Mountain, 2005; Capturing the Friedmans, 2003; Carolina, 2003; Charlie and the Chocolate Factory, 2005; The Christmas Wish, 1998 (made-for-TV); A Christmas without Snow, 1980 (made-for-TV); Cold Turkey, 2013; College Road Trip, 2008; Contagion, 2011; Convicted Woman, 1940; A Day for Thanks on Walton's Mountain, 1982 (made-for-TV); Daytrippers, 1996; Dead Presidents, 1995; The Dish & the Spoon, 2011; Don't Say a Word, 2001; The Doors, 1991; Down to the Bone, 2004; **Driving Miss Daisy**, 1989; The Dry Land, 2010; Duane Hopwood, 2005; Dutch, 1991; Easy Virtue, 2008; Enough Said, 2013; The Event, 2003; Everyone Says I Love You, 1996; A Family Thanksgiving, 2010 (made-for-TV); **Fearless**, 1993; Fifty Pills, 2006; **5 Against the House**, 1955; For Your Consideration, 2006; Four Brothers, 2005; Fracture, 2007; Free Birds, 2013; Funny People, 2009; **Giant**, 1956; The Good Mother, 1988; Grumpy Old Men, 1993; Hanging Up, 2000; **Hannah and Her Sisters**, 1986; Haven, 2001 (made-for-TV); Hit and Runaway, 1999; Holiday Engagement, 2011 (made-for-TV); Home for the Holidays, 1995; Home of the Brave, 2006; Home Sweet Home, 1981; The House of Yes, 1997; The Ice Storm, 1997; In Enemy Hands, 2004; In the Family, 2011; In Your Eyes, 2010; Kill the Irishman, 2011; Kissing Cousins, 2008; **Kit Kittredge: An American Girl**, 2008; Kristy, 2014; Life in the Fast Lane, 1998; The Lookout, 2007; Love at the Thanksgiving Day Parade, 2012 (made-for-

TV); Love Happens, 1999; Martian Child, 2007; **Miracle on 34th Street**, 1947; The Morning After, 1986; The Mosquito Coast, 1986; Music from Another Room, 1998; Must Love Dogs, 2005; The Myth of Fingerprints, 1997; New Jack City, 1991; **Next Stop Wonderland**, 1998; **Nobody's Fool**, 1994; The Object of My Affection, 1998; An Old Fashioned Thanksgiving, 2008 (made-for-TV); One Special Night, 1999 (made-for-TV); **One True Thing**, 1998; The Oranges, 2011; The Other Sister, 1999; Palo Alto, CA, 2007; Paul Blart, Mall Cop, 2009; Pieces of April, 2013; Planes, Trains & Automobiles, 1987; Prime, 2005; The Prince and Me, 2004; **Prisoners**, 2013; **Raising Arizona**, 1987; Return to Zero, 2014; **Rocky**, 1976; **The Santa Clause**, 1994; **Scent of a Woman**, 1992; Séance, 2006; Season of Change, 1994; Shopgirl, 2005; **Starting Over**, 1979; Tadpole, 2002; Smart People, 2008; Son in Law, 1993; Songs, 2004; Soul Food, 1997; Speak, 2004; **Spider-Man**, 2000; **Squanto: A Warrior's Tale**, 1994; **Sunday Dinner for a Soldier**, 1944; Thanksgiving, 2014; Thanksgiving Day, 1990 (made-for-TV); Thanksgiving Family Reunion, 2003 (made-for-TV); The Thanksgiving House, 2013 (made-for-TV); The Thanksgiving Treasure, 1973 (made-for-TV); **Three Faces West**, 1940; A Time to Remember, 2003 (made-for-TV); Tower Heist, 2011; 24 Nights, 1999; **Two Lovers**, 2009; The Ultimate Gift, 2006; Undertow, 2004; **Unhook the Stars**, 1996; **Unknown**, 2011; **The Very Thought of You**, 1944; The Vicious Kind, 2009; **Walk the Line**, 2005; A Walton Thanksgiving Reunion, 1993 (made-for-TV); The War at Home, 1996; We Own the Night, 2007; What's Cooking?, 2000; **White Palace**, 1990; **The White Ribbon**, 2009; Wide Awake, 1998; The Wiz, 1978; You're Not You, 2014; Youth in Revolt, 2009.

Titanic Sinking (April 14-15, 1912; the great ocean liner struck an iceberg in the North Atlantic Ocean during its maiden voyage from England to New York City, with a loss of 1,514 passengers and crew members and with 710 people surviving): **A Night to Remember**, 1958; **Titanic** [1943], 1950; **Titanic**, 1953; **Titanic**, 1997.

Valentine's Day (February 14; symbolized with gift-giving between loved ones; also see St. Valentine's Day Massacre, this index): And Now...Ladies and Gentlemen..., 2002; Baghban, 2003; Be My Valentine, 2013 (made-for-TV); Be My Valentine, Charlie Brown, 1975 (made-for-TV); Blonde Ambition, 2007; **Blood Work**, 2002; A Charlie Brown Valentine, 2002 (made-for-TV); Dog Park, 1998; Entropy, 1999; **Eternal Sunshine of the Spotless Mind**, 2004; **Holiday Inn**, 1942; Home Movie, 2008; **The Honeymoon Killers**, 1969; I Hate Valentine's Day, 2009; **J. Edgar**, 2011; The Lake House, 2006; **Low Down**, 2014; The Merry Gentleman, 2008; My Bloody Valentine, 2009; No Strings Attached, 2011; Obvious Child, 2014; On Valentine's Day, 1986; Petals on the Wind, 2014 (made-for-TV); **Picnic at Hanging Rock**, 1975; Raising Cain, 1982; Ruby in Paradise, 1993; Saved!, 2004; Sex and the City, 2008; **Sleepless in Seattle**, 1993; Something New, 2006; Speak, 2004; Supergirl, 1984; **Tales from the Crypt**, 1972; The Third Wheel, 2002; Valentine, 2001; A Valentine Carol, 2007 (made-for-TV); Valentine's Day, 2008 (made-for-TV); Valentine's Day, 2010; What Love Is, 2007; You're So Cupid!, 2010.

Vietnam War (1955-1975; also see French-Indochina War, this index; films dealing directly with the Vietnam War and films profiling those facing the military draft in that war and the after-effects of the war upon veterans as well as those gone missing in that war): American Beach, 1988-1991 (TV series); Air America, 1990; American Gangster, 2007; **Apocalypse Now**, 1979; Bat*21, 1988; Battle Rats, 1990; **The Beautiful Country**, 2005; Behind the Lines, 1986; Billy Jack, 1971; **Birdy**, 1984; **Born on the Fourth of July**, 1989; The Boys in Company C, 1978; Braddock: Missing in Action III, 1988; A Bright Shining Lie, 1998; Brotherhood of Death, 1976; Captain Milkshake, 1970; **Casualties of War**, 1989; Cease Fire, 1985; The Chaos Factor, 2000; **Coming Home**, 1978; Cutter's Way, 1981; Day Zero, 2007; Dead Presidents, 1995; **The Deer Hunter**, 1979; The Devastator, 1986; Dirty Deeds,

2003; Faith of My Fathers, 2005; Fighting Back, 1980 (made-for-TV); First Blood, 1982; Flight of the Intruder, 1991; Forgotten Heroes, 1990; Frankie's House, 1992 (made-for-TV); **Frost/Nixon**, 2008; **Full Metal Jacket**, 1987; Fury to Freedom, 1985; Gardens of Stone, 1987; **Getting Straight**, 1970; **Go Tell the Spartans**, 1978; Going Back, 2001 (made-for-TV); **Good Morning, Vietnam**, 1987; **The Green Berets**, 1968; Green Dragon, 2001; Greetings, 1968; Hail, Hero!, 1969; **Hair**, 1979; **Hamburger Hill**, 1987; Handsome Harry, 2009; Heaven and Earth, 1993; Hell on the Battleground, 1989; Intrusion: Cambodia, 1983; The Iron Triangle, 1989; Jacob's Ladder, 1990; Journey from the Fall, 2006; Jud, 1971; Jungle Heat, 1985; Killer Instinct, 1988; Last Flight Out, 1990 (made-for-TV); Little Boy Blue, 1998; A Lonely Place for Dying, 2008; The Losers, 1970; Love-In, 1972; **Medium Cool**, 1969; Memorial Day, 1983 (made-for-TV); **The Messenger**, 2009; Missing Brenda, 2003; Missing in America, 2005; Missing in Action, 1984; Missing in Action 2: The Beginning, 1985; A Mission to Kill, 1992; Music Within, 2007; My Father, My Son, 1988 (made-for-TV); 1969, 1988; **Nixon**, 1995; Ordinary Heroes, 1986; Path to War, 2002 (made-for-TV); Parades, 1972; The Pentagon Papers, 2003; **Platoon**, 1986; Platoon Leader, 1988; The Quiet American, 2003; Rambo, 2008; Rambo: First Blood Part II, 1985; Rambo III, 1988; **Rescue Dawn**, 2007; Rules of Engagement, 2000; A Rumor of War, 1980 (made-for-TV); **Running on Empty**, 1988; Search and Destroy, 1981; **The Siege of Firebase Gloria**, 1989; The Soldier's Story, 1983; Some Kind of Hero, 1982; **Some May Live**, 1967; Special Forces, 2012; Steele Justice, 1987; Sticks and Bones, 1973; Strike Commando, 1987; **The Stunt Man**, 1980; There Goes My Baby, 1994; **Tigerland**, 2000; Tour of Duty, 1987-1990 (TV series); The Trial of Billy Jack, 1974; Universal Soldier, 1992; Vietnam War Story, 1987 (made-for-TV); Vietnam War Story, 1987-1988 (TV series); Vietnam War Story: The Last Days, 1980 (made-for-cable TV); The War at Home, 1996; **We Were Soldiers**, 2002; When Hell Was in Session, 1979 (made-for-TV); **Who'll Stop the Rain**, 1978; Word of Honor, 2003 (made-for-TV); The Year That Trembled, 2002; **Yesterday**, 1981.

World War I (1914-1918): **Ace of Aces**, 1933 (air war; France, Western Front); **Aces High**, 1977 (air war; France; Western Front); An Accidental Soldier, 2013 (made-for-TV; Australian soldier deserts when ordered into the trenches of the Western Front); Admiral, 2008 (Russian Navy); **Adventures of a Young Man**, 1962 (ambulance corps; Italian Front); **The African Queen**, 1951; After Tonight, 1933 (Austrian espionage); **All Quiet on the Western Front**, 1930 (German infantry; France); And the Ship Sails On, 1984 (Serbian refugees); Army Surgeon, 1942 (U.S. Medical Corps); **Arsenal**, 1929 (Eastern Front); The Awakening, 1928 (French and German troops; French nursing; France; Western Front); **Barbed Wire**, 1927 (French and German infantry; France; Western Front); **The Battle Cry of Peace**, 1915 (German espionage in U.S.); Behind the Door, 1919 (German submariners; Atlantic Theater); Beneath Hill 60, 2010 (Australian sappers tunneling during the Ypres Saliant in 1914); The Better 'Ole, 1926 (British troops; France; Western Front); Beyond Victory, 1931 (U.S. troops; France; Western Front); **The Big Parade**, 1925 (U.S. infantry; France; Western Front); **Blockheads**, 1938 (U.S. infantry; France; Western Front); The Blue Eagle, 1926 (U.S. submariners); **The Blue Max**, 1966 (German aviators; France; Western Front); Body and Soul, 1931 (British aviators; France; Western Front); Born for Glory, 1935 (British and German sailors); Britannic, 2000 (made-for-cable); British Intelligence, 1940 (British and German espionage); Broken Lullaby, 1932 (French and German infantry; France; Western Front); **Captain Eddie**, 1945 (U.S. aviators; France; Western Front; Edward Rickenbacker); Captured!, 1933 (British POWs); **Cavalcade**, 1933 (British troops; France; Western Front); **Colonel Redl**, 1985 (Austrian and Russian espionage); The Common Cause, 1919 (Western Front); Company K, 2004 (U.S. Marines; France; Western Front); Convoy, 1927 (U.S. and German espionage); Crimson Romance, 1934 (German aviators; France; Western Front); **The Dark Angel**, 1935

(British soldiers; France; Western Front); **Dark Journey**, 1937 (British and German espionage); Darling Lili, 1970 (German espionage); Dawn, 1933 (German submariners; Atlantic Theater); **The Dawn Patrol**, 1930 (British aviators; France; Western Front); **The Dawn Patrol**, 1938 (British aviators; France; Western Front); Deathwatch, 2002 (British and German troops; France; Western Front); **Dishonored**, 1931 (Austrian Secret Service); **Dr. Zhivago**, 1965 (Russian forces; Eastern Front); **Doughboys**, 1930 (U.S. troops; France; Western Front); **The Eagle and the Hawk**, 1933 (British aviators; France; Western Front); The Enemy, 1927; Everything Is Thunder, 1936 (Canadian POWs); **A Farewell to Arms**, 1932 (ambulance service; Italian Front); **A Farewell to Arms**, 1957 (ambulance service; Italian Front); **The Fighting 69th**, 1940 (U.S. infantry; France; Western Front); **Flyboys**, 2006 (Lafayette Escadrille, France; Western Front); 40,000 Horsemen, 1941 (Australian cavalry; last cavalry charge at the Battle of Beersheba, 1917, in the Palestinian Campaign); **The Four Horsemen of the Apocalypse**, 1921 (France; Western Front); **Four Sons**, 1928 (U.S. and German soldiers; France; Western Front); Fraulein Doktor, 1969 (German espionage); **Gallipoli**, 1981 (Australian infantry; Turkish Front); **Grand Illusion**, 1938 (Allied POWs); **The Great Dictator**, 1940 (German artillery; France; Western Front); The Great Love, 1918 (U.S. troops; France; Western Front); The Greatest Thing in Life, 1918 (U.S. troops; France; Western Front); **Half Shot at Sunrise**, 1930 (U.S. troops; France; Western Front); **Hearts of the World**, 1918 (French and German troops; France; Western Front); **Hell Below**, 1933 (U.S. submariners in the Adriatic, 1918); Hell in the Heavens, 1934 (U.S. pilots in the Lafayette Escadrille; Western Front; France); **Hell's Angels**, 1930 (U.S. Air Corps; France; Western Front); Heroes for Sale, 1933 (U.S. infantry; France; Western Front); Hotel Imperial, 1939 (Austrian and Russian troops; Eastern Front); The Hun Within, 1918 (U.S. homefront; German espionage); In Love and War, 1996 (Ambulance service; Italian front); Inside the Lines, 1930 (German espionage, Gibraltar); **Joan the Woman**, 1916 (British troops; France; Western Front); Johnny Got His Gun, 1971 (U.S. infantry; France; Western Front); **Journey's End**, 1930 (British troops; France; Western Front); **Joyeux Noel**, 2005 (British, French, German troops fraternizing at Christmas 1914; France; Western Front); **Jules and Jim**, 1962 (France; Western Front); The Kaiser: Beast of Berlin, 1918; **King & Country**, 1964 (British infantry; France; Western Front); **Knight without Armor**, 1937 (British espionage; Russia; Eastern Front); Lafayette Escadrille, 1958 (Allied aviators; France; Western Front); **Lancer Spy**, 1937 (British and German espionage); **The Land That Time Forgot**, 1975 (German submariners); The Last Flight, 1931 (U.S. Air Corps; France; Western Front); The Last Outpost, 1935 (British troops; Middle East); **Lawrence of Arabia**, 1962 (Arab guerrillas; Arabian-Turkish Front); Legends of the Fall, 1995 (U.S. forces; France; Western Front); The Legion of the Condemned, 1928 (Lafayette Escadrille; France; Western Front); L'equipage, 1938 (aka: Flight into Darkness; French air pilots fighting in the skies over the Western Front; remade as **The Woman I Love**, 1937); **The Lighthorseman**, 1988 (Australian cavalry; last cavalry charge at the Battle of Beersheba, 1917 in the Palestinian Campaign); **Lilac Time**, 1928 (air war; Western Front); The Little American, 1917 (German troops; France; Western Front); The Lost Battalion, 2001 (made-for-TV; based on an actual battalion of U.S. troops surrounded by German forces in the Argonne Forest during the Meuse-Argonne Campaign of 1918); **The Lost Patrol**, 1934 (British troops; Mesopotamian Front); **The Lost Squadron**, 1932 (Allied and German veteran aviators); The Love Light, 1921 (Italian Front); The Mad Parade, 1931 (female canteen workers; France; Western Front); Madame Spy, 1934 (German and Russian espionage); A Man from Wyoming, 1930 (U.S. Army engineers; France; Western Front); Marianne, 1929 (France; Western Front); Marthe, 1997 (French troops; France; Western Front); **Mata Hari**, 1931 (German espionage); Mata Hari, 1985 (German espionage); Mata Hari, Agent H21, 1964 (German espionage); Mata Hari: The Red Dancer, 1927 (German espionage); Men Must Fight, 1933 (U.S. pilots; Western Front; France); The Mighty, 1929 (U.S. troops;

France; Western Front); My Four Years in Germany, 1918 (Germany's leadership); **My Son, My Son!**, 1940 (British troops; France; Western Front); **Nicholas and Alexandra**, 1971 (Russian troops; Eastern Front); **Nurse Edith Cavell**, 1939 (Belgium underground smuggling Allied soldiers out of German-occupied Brussels); **Oh! What a Lovely War**, 1969 (British troops; Western Front); **Pack Up Your Troubles**, 1932 (U.S. infantry; France; Western Front); Pack Up Your Troubles, 1939 (U.S. troops; France; Western Front); **Passchendaele**, 2008 (British-Canadian troops, Belgium; Western Front); **Paths of Glory**, 1957 (French infantry; France; Western Front); The Patriots, 1933 (Russian infantry; Eastern Front); **Random Harvest**, 1942 (British wounded; France; Western Front); **Rasputin and the Empress**, 1932 (Russian troops; Eastern Front); **The Red Baron**, 2010 (Baron Manfred von Richthofen; German aviators; France; Western Front); The Red Dance, 1928 (Russian troops; Eastern Front); Revenge of the Red Baron, 1994; Richthofen, 1929; The Riddle of the Sands, 1984 (British espionage; England); **The Road Back**, 1937 (German veterans); **The Road to Glory**, 1936 (French infantry; France; Western Front); Roaring Rails, 1924 (U.S. troops; France; Western Front); **The Roaring Twenties**, 1939 (U.S. infantry; France; Western Front); **Rosa Luxemburg**, 1987 (Spartacists against the war in Germany); Scotland Yard, 1930 (British troops; France; Western Front); Seas Beneath, 1931 (Atlantic Theater); The Secret Game, 1917 (German and Japanese espionage); **Sergeant York**, 1941 (U.S. infantry; France; Western Front); **The Serpent**, 1916 (Russian troops; Eastern Front); Seven Days Leave, 1930 (British troops; France; Western Front); **7th Heaven**, 1927 (France; Western Front); She Goes to War, 1929 (U.S. infantry; France; Western Front); **The Shopworn Angel**, 1938 (U.S. homefront); **Shoulder Arms**, 1918 (U.S. troops; France; Western Front); Shout at the Devil, 1976 (British sabotage; East Africa); The Sky Hawk, 1929 (British aviators; Western Front; France); Sons o' Guns, 1936 (U.S. troops; France; Western Front); The Spy, 1917 (U.S. and German espionage); **The Spy in Black**, 1939 (British and German espionage); **Stamboul Quest**, 1934 (German espionage; Turkish Theater); Storm at Daybreak, 1933 (Sarajevo, June 28, 1914); **The Story of Vernon and Irene Castle**, 1939 (U.S. aviators); Submarine Patrol, 1938 (Submariners; Atlantic Theater); Suicide Fleet, 1931 (U.S. sailors; Atlantic Theater); **Suzy**, 1936 (French aviators; France; Western Front); Tannenberg, 1932 (German troops; Eastern Front); **They Gave Him a Gun**, 1937 (U.S. soldiers; France; Western Front); **Three Comrades**, 1938 (German infantry; France; Western Front); Three Faces East, 1930 (British espionage); Till We Meet Again, 1936 (British espionage); **To Each His Own**, 1946 (U.S. Air Corps; France; Western Front); Today We Live, 1933 (British aviators and sailors); The Trench, 2000 (British troops; Battle of the Somme, 1916); **Two Arabian Knights**, 1927 (American POWs); The Unbeliever, 1918 (U.S. Marines; France; Western Front); The Unknown Soldier, 1926 (U.S. infantry; France; Western Front); **Von Richthofen and Brown**, 1971 (Baron Manfred von Richthofen and Roy Brown; German and British aviators; Western Front; France); **War Horse**, 2011 (British and German troops; France; Western Front); War Nurse, 1930 (U.S. aviators and nurses; France; Western Front); **War of the Worlds: Goliath**, 2012; Waterloo Bridge, 1931 (U.S. Army; France; Western Front); **Waterloo Bridge**, 1940 (British Army; France; Western Front); **Westfront 1918**, 1931 (German infantry; France); **What Price Glory**, 1926 (U.S. Marines; France, Western Front); **What Price Glory**, 1952 (U.S. Marines; France; Western Front); **The White Cliffs of Dover**, 1944 (British troops; France; Western Front); **The White Sister**, 1933 (Italian troops; Italian Front); **Wilson**, 1945 (U.S. homefront); **Wings**, 1927 (U.S.-German air corps; air war; Western Front); The Woman Disputed, 1928 (Austrian and Russian troops; Eastern Front); **The Woman I Love**, 1937 (French aviators; France; Western Front); **Wooden Crosses**, 1932 (French infantry; France; Western Front); **The World Moves On**, 1934 (U.S. home front); **Yankee Doodle Dandy**, 1942 (U.S. home front); Young Eagles, 1930 (British and German aviators; France; Western Front); **Zeppelin**, 1971 (British and German espionage).

World War II (1939-1945; European Theater): **Above Us the Waves**, 1956 (British submarine warfare); **Action in the North Atlantic**, 1943 (U.S. Liberty cargo ship in its Atlantic voyage to deliver war material to Murmansk, Russia, while being attacked by German submarines and airplanes); **The Assault**, 1986 (Dutch Resistance); **Against the Wind**, 1949 (British espionage in German-occupied Europe); **Ashes and Diamonds**, 1961 (Polish Resistance); **Attack**, 1956 (Battle of the Bulge); **Ballad of a Soldier**, 1960 (Russian troops on Eastern Front); **Battle of Britain**, 1969 (British and German air warfare over England); Battle of the Bulge, 1965 (combat between U.S. and German forces in Belgium, Germany and Luxembourg from December 16, 1944 to January 25, 1945); **Battleground**, 1949 (Bastogne and Battle of the Bulge, 1944-1945); Betrayed, 1954 (Dutch Resistance in German-occupied Netherlands); **The Big Red One**, 1980 (U.S. troops in Italy and France); **Breakthrough**, 1950 (Northern France); **The Bridge at Remagen**, 1969 (the capturing of the vital Ludendorff Bridge at Remagen, Germany in March 1945); **A Bridge Too Far**, 1977 (Operation Market Garden; U.S. and British forces attempting to capture vital bridges in the Netherlands, September 17-25, 1944); **The Cockleshell Heroes**, 1955 (British Royal Marines destroying German warships at Bordeaux, France); **Command Decision**, 1948 (U.S. Eighth Air Force air attacks over France and Germany); **Commandos Strike at Dawn**, 1942 (British troops and Norwegian guerrillas raiding Nazi bases in German-occupied Norway); **Corvette K-225**, 1943 (exploits of a Canadian convoy escort warship in the Atlantic); **Crash Dive**, 1943 (exploits of a U.S. submarine in the Atlantic as it battles German Q boats); **Cross of Iron**, 1977 (German troops fighting on the Eastern Front); **The Cross of Lorraine**, 1943 (French Resistance in German-occupied France); **The Cruel Sea**, 1953 (exploits of a British convoy escort warship in the Atlantic); **Das Boot** [aka: The Boat]; 1982 (exploits of a German submarine in the Atlantic and the Mediterranean); A Day Before Dawn, 1994 (Operation Overlord, Normandy Invasion, June 6, 1944); **D-Day; the Sixth of June**, 1956 (Operation Overlord: Normandy Invasion of June 6, 1944); **The Desert Fox: The Story of Rommel**, 1951 (Western Front); **Desperate Journey**, 1942 (British Air Force bombing Germany); **Dunkirk**, 1958 (British evacuation of more than 338,000 British and French troops from Dunkirk, France, by more than 800 ships and boats of all sizes from May 26 to June 3, 1940, during the Fall of France to German forces); **Eagle Squadron**, 1942 (R.A.F. fighter pilots battling German planes during the Battle of Britain, from July 10 to October 31, 1940); **Edge of Darkness**, 1943 (Norwegian Resistance in German-occupied Norway); **Eight Iron Men**, 1952 (U.S. troops fighting in Italy); **Enemy at the Gates**, 2001 (German and Russian snipers during the Battle of Stalingrad, August 23, 1942-February 2, 1943); **The Enemy Below**, 1957 (cat-and-mouse battle between a U.S. destroyer and a German submarine in the Atlantic); **Fighter Squadron**, 1948 (U.S. fighter pilots in England in 1943); **Fury**, 2014 (U.S. tank crew battling German troops in Germany in April 1945); **Go for Broke**, 1951 (the 442nd Regimental Combat Team of Japanese-Americans fighting in Italy and France); **A Guy Named Joe**, 1943 (U.S. bomber pilots stationed in England, where Spencer Tracy dies while sinking a mythical German aircraft carrier, his spirit later guiding a young American pilot); **The Heroes of Telemark**, 1965 (Norwegian Resistance in German-occupied Norway); **In Which We Serve**, 1942 (exploits of a British destroyer in the Atlantic and Mediterranean); **Is Paris Burning?**, 1966 (capture of Paris on August 25, 1944); **Joan of Paris**, 1942 (French Resistance in German-occupied France); **Kelly's Heroes**, 1970 (U.S. forces in France); **The Longest Day**, 1962 (Operation Overlord: Normandy Invasion of June 6, 1944); **Memphis Belle**, 1990 (crew of a B-17 on its last bombing mission over Germany in May 1943); **A Midnight Clear**, 1992 (Battle of the Bulge, 1944-1945); Miracle at St. Anna, 2008 (African American forces fighting in Italy); **Mrs. Miniver**, 1942 (British evacuation of British and French troops from Dunkirk from May 26 to June 3, 1940); **The Monuments Men**, 2014 (efforts of U.S. forces to recoup art treasures stolen by the Nazis toward the close of the war);

The North Star, 1943 (Soviet Resistance in German-occupied Russia in June 1941); **O.S.S.**, 1946 (covert operations in German-occupied France by members of the U.S. Office of Strategic Services); **One of Our Aircraft Is Missing**, 1942 (downed British bomber crew aided by Dutch Resistance); **Passage to Marseilles**, 1944 (French bomber crew in England); **Patton**, 1970 (General George Patton's military exploits in France and Germany, including his spectacular relief on December 27, 1944, of U.S. forces in besieged Bastogne); Red Tails, 2012 (African-American pilots in Italy); **Saving Private Ryan**, 1998 (Operation Overlord, Normandy Invasion of June 6, 1944, and afterward); **Saints and Soldiers**, 2005 (survivors of the Malmedy Massacre during the Battle of the Bulge, 1944-1945); **Sink the Bismarck!**, 1960 (the hunting down and destruction of the German pocket battleship by warships of the British Royal Navy on May 26-27, 1941); Stalingrad, 1992; **The Story of G.I. Joe**, 1945 (U.S. troops fighting in Italy); The Tanks Are Coming, 1951 (U.S. tank crews fighting in Germany); **13 Rue Madeleine**, 1947 (O.S.S. covert operations in German-occupied France); **To Hell and Back**, 1955 (Sicily, Italy, Southern France, the exploits of war hero Audie Murphy); Women in War, 1940 (British nurses during the Blitz); **Twelve O'Clock High**, 1949 (U.S. Eighth Air Force air attacks over France and Germany); **Uncertain Glory**, 1944 (French Resistance in German-occupied France); **Up Front**, 1951 (U.S. troops in Italy); **Valkyrie**, 2008 (plot to kill Adolf Hitler by German conspirators on July 20, 1944); **The Victors**, 1963 (a squad of U.S. GIs fighting in Italy and France); **We Dive at Dawn**, 1943 (British submarine tracking a German warship); **A Yank in the R.A.F.**, 1941 (R.A.F. fighter pilots battling German planes during the Battle of Britain, from July 10 to October 31, 1940); **The Young Lions**, 1958 (German and U.S soldiers fighting in France and Germany).

World War II (Italian Campaign, Sicily and Italy, 1943-1945): Abandoned, 1955; And Agnes Chose to Die, 1976; Anni difficili, 1950; Anzio, 1968; The Art of Getting Along, 1954; **The Assissi Underground**, 1985; Baaria, 2010; Baciami piccina, 2006; Before Him All Rome Trembled, 1947; **The Big Red One**, 1980; Blood of the Losers, 2008; **Cloak and Dagger**, 1946; Cobari, 1970; A Day for Lionhearts, 1961; **Days of Glory**, 2006; The Days of Rage, 2001; **The Devil's Brigade**, 1968; **The English Patient**, 1996; Escape by Night, 1982; Everybody Go Home!, 1962; The Fallen, 2004; The Fascist, 1965; Fighter Attack, 1953; **Force of Arms**, 1951; The Four Days of Naples, 1963; From the Clouds to the Resistance, 1979; **Generale Della Rovere**, 1961; Hidden Children, 2004 (made-for-TV); Honey Sweet Love, 1996; Hotel Meina, 2007; Il cielo cade, 2000; Il gobbo, 1963; It Happened in '43, 1960; La grande quercia, 1997; **Last Days of Mussolini**, 1974; **Life Is Beautiful**, 1999; Little Teachers, 1998; **The Man in the Gray Flannel Suit**, 1956; The Man Who Will Come, 2010; Men or Not Men, 1981; Miracle at St. Anna, 2008; Monte Cassino, 1948; Mussolini: The Untold Story, 1985 (TV series); **The Night of the Shooting Stars**, 1982; **1900**, 1977; **Open City**, 1946; **Paisan**, 1948; Passione, 2011; **Patton**, 1970; The Pigeon That Took Rome, 1962; Portrait: A Man Whose Name Was John, 1973 (made-for-TV); Private Angelo, 1949; Rosolino Paterno, soldato…, 1970; Salvo D'Acquisto, 1974; The Secret of Santa Vittoria, 1969; The Secret War of Harry Frigg, 1968; **Seven Beauties**, 1976; **The Story of G.I. Joe**, 1945; **Tea with Mussolini**, 1999; **To Hell and Back**, 1955; The Tuskegee Airmen, 1995 (African American fighter pilots); Two Anonymous Letters, 1947; The Two Marshals, 1961; **Two Women**, 1960; **Up Front**, 1951; **Von Ryan's Express**, 1965; **A Walk in the Sun**, 1945; The White Ship, 1941.

World War II (1939-1945; North African Theater): **The Big Red One**, 1980 (Battle of Kassarine Pass); **The Desert Fox: The Story of Rommel**, 1951 (Second Battle of El Alamein, 1942); **The Desert Rats**, 1953 (Tobruk, 1941); The Fighting Rats of Tobruk, 1951 (North Africa); **Five Graves to Cairo**, 1943 (British espionage and Second Battle of El Alamein, 1942); For the Boys, 1991; Immortal Sergeant, 1943 (Egypt);

Patton, 1970 (Battle of the Kasserine Pass, Tunisia Campaign, 1943; Battle of El Guettar, Tunisia Campaign, 1943); **Play Dirty**, 1969 (raid on Rommel's fuel depot by British commandos); Raid on Rommel, 1971 (Libya, 1943); **Sahara**, 1943 (battles of Gazala and Tobruk in Libya, 1942); Sea of Sand (AKA: Desert Patrol), 1961 (North Africa, 1943; British, German troops); **To Hell and Back**, 1955 (U.S. North African campaign, Sicily, Italy, Southern France); **Tobruk**, 1967 (Tobruk in Libya, 1942); **Valkyrie**, 2008 (German troops in North Africa); **The Young Lions**, 1958 (German troops in North Africa).

World War II (1939-1945; Pacific Theater): **Above and Beyond**, 1953 (atom bombing of Hiroshima, 1945); Abroad with Two Yanks, 1944 (Australia); **Admiral Yamamoto**, 1968 (Japanese Pearl Harbor Attack, December 7, 1941; Pacific, 1942-1943); Aerial Gunner, 1943 (Pacific, 1942); **Air Force**, 1943 (Japanese attack against Pearl Harbor, 1941; Philippine Defense, 1942); Ambush Bay, 1966 (Philippines, 1944); **American Guerrilla in the Philippines**, 1950 (Philippine Defense, 1942; Leyte, 1944); Attack Force Z, 1982 (Pacific island); **Australia**, 2008; Away All Boats, 1956 (Okinawa, 1945); Back Door to Hell, 1964 (Philippines, Leyte, 1944); **Back to Bataan**, 1945 (Philippine Defense, 1941-1942; Leyte invasion, 1944; begins with the spectacular raid against Japanese prison camp at Cabanatuan, Luzon, Philippines, where more than 500 prisoners were rescued on April 30, 1945); The Bamboo Blonde, 1946 (B-29 crew in the Pacific); **Bataan**, 1943 (Philippine Defense, 1941-1942); Battle at Bloody Beach, 1961 (Philippine Resistance, 1943); **Battle Cry**, 1955 (Guadalcanal, 1942; Tarawa, 1943); Battle of Blood Island, 1960 (Pacific island); Battle of the Coral Sea, 1959 (Pacific, 1942); Beach Red, 1967 (Bougainville, 1943-1944); **Beachhead**, 1954 (Choiseul Island in Bougainville Campaign, 1943-1945); **Between Heaven and Hell**, 1956 (Philippines, 1944); Blood Oath, 1990 (Laha Massacre, 1942); **Bombardier**, 1943 (Pacific, 1942); Bombs over Burma, 1943 (Burma Road, 1942); **The Bridge on the River Kwai**, 1957 (Burma, 1942-1943); The Burmese Harp [1956], 1967 (Burma, 1941-1945 from the Japanese perspective; remade as a color version in 1985); **The Caine Mutiny**, 1954 (exploits of a U.S. minesweeper in the Pacific under the command of a mentally unstable captain); The Camp on Blood Island, 1958 (Japanese POW camp holding British captives in Malaya); **China**, 1943 (China, 1941); **China Girl**, 1942 (Burma, China, 1941); **China Sky**, 1945 (Sino-Japanese War, 1937-1945); Codename: Fox, 2001 (aka: Battle of the Pacific; Oba: The Last Samurai; Japanese fighting U.S. forces on Saipan); Corregidor, 1943 (Philippine Defense, 1941-1942); **Cry Havoc**, 1943 (Bataan, Philippines, 1941-1942); Cry of Battle, 1963 (Philippine Defense, 1941-1942); The Deep Six, 1958 (Aleutian Islands); **Destination Gobi**, 1953 (Mongolia); **Destination Tokyo**, 1943 (Aleutian Islands; Honsho, Japan; Doolittle Raid against Japan, April 18, 1942); **Destroyer**, 1943 (old U.S. destroyer fighting in the Pacific); Don't Go Near the Water, 1957 (Pacific island); **Dragon Seed**, 1944 (Sino-Japanese War, 1942); **Empire of the Sun**, 1987 (Allied prisoners in Shanghai, 1939-1945); Ensign Pulver, 1964 (Pacific island); Escape from Hong Kong, 1942; The Eve of St. Mark, 1944 (Philippine Defense, 1941-1942); The Extraordinary Seaman, 1969 (fighting at sea in the Pacific); Farewell to the King, 1987 (Borneo); **Father Goose**, 1964 (coast watcher on a Pacific island); **The Fighting Seabees**, 1944 (Pacific, 1943); Fire on That Flag!, 1944 (Corregidor, Philippines); Fires on the Plain, 1963 (released in Japan in 1959; Japanese soldier attempting to survive on Leyte in February 1945; Fires on the Plain, 2014 (remake of 1959 film; Japanese soldier attempting to survive on Leyte in February 1945; **First to Fight**, 1967 (Guadalcanal, 1942); **First Yank into Tokyo**, 1945 (Honshu, Japan, 1943); **Flags of Our Fathers**, 2006 (Iwo Jima, 1945); **Flight for Freedom**, 1943 (Pacific island; fictional portrait of Amelia Earhart, 1897-1939); **Flying Leathernecks**, 1951 (Guadalcanal, 1942); **Flying Tigers**, 1942 (China, Burma, 1941); For the Boys, 1991; **The Frogmen**, 1951 (Southwestern Pacific); **From Here to Eternity**, 1953 (Japanese attack against Pearl Harbor, 1941); **The Gallant Hours**, 1960 (Guadalcanal, 1942); The

Girls of Pleasure Island, 1953 (Pacific island where Marines are building an air base in 1945); **God Is My Co-Pilot**, 1945 (China, Burma, 1941-1942); Golden Partners, 1979 (Saipan); Grave of the Fireflies, 1994 (released in Japan in 1988; animated tale of two children trying to survive the devastation of WWII in Kobe, Japan, just after the war in September 1945); Grave of the Fireflies, 2005 (made-for-TV live-action remake of 1988 film where two children try to survive the devastation of WWII in Kobe, Japan, just after the war in September 1945); **The Great Raid**, 2005 (details the spectacular raid against Japanese prison camp at Cabanatuan, Luzon, Philippines, where more than 500 prisoners were rescued on April 30, 1945); **Guadalcanal Diary**, 1943 (Battle of Guadalcanal, August 7, 1942-February 9, 1943); Guerillas in Pink Lace, 1964 (Invasion of the Philippines, 1941-1942); **Gung Ho!**, 1943 (Makin Island); **A Guy Named Joe**, 1943 (European Theater and later, a Pacific island); **Halls of Montezuma**, 1951 (Okinawa, 1945); **Heaven Knows, Mr. Allison**, 1957 (a nun and a Marine trapped on a Japanese-held island in the Pacific); **Hell in the Pacific**, 1968 (Pacific island); Hell to Eternity, 1960 (Saipan, 1944); High Barbaree, 1947 (shot-down navy pilot and companion survive at sea in the Pacific); The Highest Honor, 1984 (British POWs in Singapore in 1943); **Hiroshima mon amour**, 1959 (dropping of the atom bomb on Hiroshima, 1945; remade in 2001 as **H Story**); **Home of the Brave**, 1949 (Pacific island, 1944); Hong Kong 1941, 1984 (Japanese occupation); The Horizontal Lieutenant, 1962 (Japanese-held island); I Was an American Spy, 1951 (Philippine Defense, 1941-1944; based on the exploits of Claire Phillips, 1908-1960); **In Harm's Way**, 1965 (Japanese attack against Pearl Harbor, 1941; Solomon Islands, 1942); Island of Desire, 1952 (aka: Saturday Island; marooned on a Pacific island); Isoroku Yamamoto: The Commander-in-Chief of the Combined Fleet, 2011 (Japanese naval operations in the Pacific); Jungle Fighters, 1962 (aka: The Long and the Short and the Tall; British forces fighting in Burmese jungles during the 1942 Malayan Campaign); King Rat, 1965 (Allied POWs in Malaysia); Kokoda: 39th Battalion, 2007 (Australian forces during the Kokoda Trail Campaign, July-November 1942); **The Last Emperor**, 1987 (Sino-Japanese War, 1937-1945); **Letters from Iwo Jima**, 2006 (Japanese defenders on Iwo Jima); Lost Battalion, 1962 (guerrillas fighting in Japanese-occupied Philippines); **MacArthur**, 1977 (Gregory Peck portrays U.S. five-star general Douglas MacArthur, 1880-1964, and his campaigns in the Philippine Defense, 1941-1942, and his island-hopping campaigns, 1943-1945, and his campaigns in the Korean War); **Malaya**, 1949 (rubber smuggling in Japanese-occupied Malaya); **The Man in the Gray Flannel Suit**, 1956 (Pacific island); **Manila Calling**, 1942 (Philippine Defense, 1942); **Marine Raiders**, 1944 (Guadalcanal, 1942; Solomon Islands, 1943); **Merrill's Marauders**, 1962 (Burma, 1944); **Merry Christmas, Mr. Lawrence**, 1983 (British soldiers in a Japanese POW camp); **Midway**, 1976 (Doolittle Raid against Japan, April 18, 1942; Coral Sea and Midway, 1942); Minesweeper, 1943 (Japanese attack against Pearl Harbor, December 7, 1941); **Mister Roberts**, 1955 (Pacific island); **Mr. Winkle Goes to War**, 1944 (Pacific island); Monkey on My Back, 1957 (biopic of prizefighter Barney Ross, 1909-1967, who won the Silver Star for heroism when fighting at Guadalcanal but became addicted to drugs when treated with morphine to combat malaria); The Mountain Road, 1960 (China, 1944); The Naked and the Dead, 1958 (Pacific island); **Never So Few**, 1959 (Burma, 1943); **1941**, 1979 (California); **No Man Is an Island**, 1962 (Guam, 1941-1944); None but the Brave, 1965 (Pacific island); Not Forgotton, 2000 (Saipan); **Objective, Burma!**, 1945 (based on the 1944 raids by Merrill's Marauders in 1944); Okinawa, 1952; Once before I Die, 1966 (Philippine Defense, 1941-1942); Operation Bikini, 1963 (U.S. submarine in the Pacific); **Operation Pacific**, 1951 (based on the exploits in the Pacific of USS *Darter*, SS-227, 1943-1944); **Operation Petticoat**, 1959 (submarine operations in the Pacific); **The Outsider**, 1961 (portraying the exploits of Marine and Pima Native American Ira Hayes, 1923-1955, one of those who raised the American flag at Mount Suribachi during the battle of Iwo Jima, and who is enacted by Tony Curtis); The Pacific, 2010 (cable-TV miniseries; Guadalcanal, 1942; Peleliu, 1944; Iwo Jima, 1945); Paloh, 2003 (Japanese occupation of Malaya); Paradise Road, 1997 (Sumatra, 1941-1945); **Pearl Harbor**, 2001 (Japanese attack at Pearl Harbor, 1941); Pilot No. 5, 1943 (Java, 1942); **Pride of the Marines**, 1945 (Guadalcanal, 1942); Prisoner of Japan, 1942 (Pacific island); The Proud and the Profane, 1956 (Marines fighting in the Pacific); **PT-109**, 1963 (Tulagi in the Solomon Islands, 1943); **The Purple Heart**, 1944 (Doolittle Raid against Japan, April 18, 1942); **The Purple Plain**, 1954 (Burma); **The Railway Man**, 2014 (captives in a Japanese POW camp in Burma); Remember Pearl Harbor, 1942 (Japanese attack against Pearl Harbor, December 7, 1941); Return from the River Kwai, 1989 (British POWs in Burma); **Run Silent, Run Deep**, 1955 (Bungo Straits, Japan, 1944); Salute to the Marines, 1943 (Philippine Defense, 1941-1942); **Sands of Iwo Jima**, 1949 (Tarawa, 1943; Iwo Jima, 1945); The Secret of Blood Island, 1965 (British soldiers in a Japanese POW camp); 7 Women from Hell, 1961 (women captives in a Japanese POW camp); Shima, 2007 (Japanese war survivors on a remote island); **So Proudly We Hail!**, 1943 (Philippine Defense, Bataan and Corregidor, 1941-1942); **Somewhere I'll Find You**, 1942 (Manila, Philippine Defense, 1941-1942); **South Pacific**, 1958 (U.S. men and women stationed on a Pacific island); **South Sea Woman**, 1953 (Guadalcanal, 1942); **Stand By for Action**, 1942 (an old WWI U.S. destroyer fighting in the Pacific during 1942); The Steel Claw, 1961 (Philippine Defense, 1941-1942); Storm over the Pacific, 1960 (Japanese attack against Pearl Harbor, December 7, 1941, Battle of Midway, 1942); **The Story of Dr. Wassell**, 1944 (Java, 1942); **Submarine Command**, 1951 (Pacific, 1945; Korean War); Submarine Seahawk, 1958 (operations in the Pacific); Submarine Raider, 1942 (Japanese attack against Pearl Harbor on December 7, 1941); Suicide Battalion, 1958 (U.S. forces fighting in the Philippines); **The Sullivans** [AKA: The Fighting Sullivans] 1944 (USS *Juneau*, CL-52, sunk during action off Guadalcanal, Solomon Islands, November 13, 1942, where all five Sullivan brothers were lost); Sunset at Chaophraya, 1996 (Japanese and resistance fighters in Thailand; remade in 2013); **Tarawa Beachhead**, 1958 (Guadalcanal, 1942; Tarawa, 1943); **Task Force**, 1949 (USS *Franklin*, CV-13/AVT-8, Bonin and Mariana Islands, Peleliu, Leyte, 1944; Honshu, Japan, 1945); **They Met in Bombay**, 1941 (China, 1941); **They Were Expendable**, 1945 (Philippine Defense, 1942); **The Thin Red Line**, 1964 (Guadalcanal); **The Thin Red Line**, 1998 (Guadalcanal, 1942); **Thirty Seconds over Tokyo**, 1944 (Doolittle Raid against Japan, April 18, 1942); 36 Hours to Hell, 1969 (Pacific island); **Three Came Home**, 1950 (Battle of Borneo, 1941-1942); **To End All Wars**, 2001 (British troops in a POW camp in Burma); **Tora! Tora! Tora!**, 1970 (Japanese attack against Pearl Harbor, 1941); **Too Late the Hero**, 1970 (New Hebrides); **Torpedo Alley**, 1952 (Pacific, 1945; Korean War); **Torpedo Run**, 1958 (Philippine Defense; Honshu, Japan, Aleutian Islands, 1942); A Town Like Alice, 1958 (Japanese invasion of Malaya, 1942); **Unbroken**, 2014 (biopic of Louis Zamperini, 1917-2014, who survived several Japanese prison camps); **Up Periscope**, 1959 (Kosrae Island, Micronesia, 1944); The Wackiest Ship in the Army, 1960 (operations in the Pacific); **Wake Island**, 1942 (Wake Island Defense, 1942); **We've Never Been Licked**, 1943 (Pacific, 1942); **Windtalkers**, 2002 (Navajo Marines use their native language to communicate and confuse Japanese listeners during the Battle of Saipan, June 15-July 9, 1944); **Wing and a Prayer**, 1944 (Coral Sea, Midway, 1942); Women of Valor, 1986 (made-for-TV; U.S. nurses captured on Bataan, Philippines, in 1942 and held in a Japanese POW camp); **A Yank on the Burma Road**, 1942 (Burma, 1942); **Yesterday's Enemy**, 1959 (Burma).

World War II (sea battles in the European and Pacific Theaters): **Above Us the Waves**, 1956; **Admiral Yamamoto**, 1968; **Action in the North Atlantic**, 1943; **Air Force**, 1943; **American Guerrilla in the Philippines**, 1950; **Arise, My Love**, 1940; Away All Boats, 1956; **Back to Bataan**, 1945; Battle of the Coral Sea, 1959; **Bombardier**, 1943; **The Caine Mutiny**, 1954; **The Cockleshell Heroes**, 1955; **Corvette K-225**,

1943; **Crash Dive**, 1943; **The Cruel Sea**, 1953; **Das Boot**, 1982; **Destination Tokyo**, 1943; **Destroyer**, 1943; **The Enemy Below**, 1957; **The Eternal Sea**, 1955; Fighting Coast Guard, 1951; The Final Countdown, 1980; **Flat Top**, 1952; **49th Parallel**, 1941; **The Frogmen**, 1951; **The Gallant Hours**, 1960; **Gung Ho!**, 1943; **A Guy Named Joe**, 1943; Hellcats of the Navy, 1957; **Here Come the Waves**, 1944; In Enemy Hands, 2004; **In Harm's Way**, 1965; **In Which We Serve**, 1942; **The Incredible Mr. Limpet**, 1964; **Lifeboat**, 1944; **The Longest Day**, 1962; **Midway**, 1976; Minesweeper, 1943; **Mister Roberts**, 1955; **Mrs. Miniver**, 1942;); **Morituri**, 1965; **Murphy's War**, 1971; The Navy Comes Through, 1942; **Nazi Agent**, 1942; Okinawa, 1952; **Operation Pacific**, 1951; **Operation Petticoat**, 1959; Pacific Inferno, 1979; **Pearl Harbor**, 2001; **PT-109**, 1963; Prisoner of Japan, 1942; Pursuit of the Graf Spee, 1957; Remember Pearl Harbor, 1942; **Run Silent, Run Deep**, 1955; The Sea Chase, 1955; **Sealed Cargo**, 1951; **The Silver Fleet**, 1945; **Sink the Bismarck!**, 1960; South Sea Woman, 1953; **Stand By for Action**, 1942; Storm over the Pacific, 1960; **The Story of Dr. Wassell**, 1944; **Submarine Command**, 1951; Submarine Raider, 1942; Submarine Seahawk, 1958; **Submarine X-1**, 1969; **The Sullivans**, 1944; **Task Force**, 1949; **They Came to Blow Up America**, 1943; **They Were Expendable**, 1945; **Thirty Seconds over Tokyo**, 1944; **Tora! Tora! Tora!**, 1970; **Torpedo Alley**, 1952; **Torpedo Run**, 1958; **U-571**, 2000; **Under Ten Flags**, 1960; **Up Periscope**, 1959; **We Dive at Dawn**, 1943; **Wing and a Prayer**, 1944.

Yom Kippur (Jewish Day of Atonement): The Believer, 2001; The Conrad Boys, 2006; Enemies: A Love Story, 1989; Garden State, 2004; God Is Great and I'm Not, 2001; **The Jazz Singer**, 1927; Killer: A Journal of Murder, 1995; **The Lost Weekend**, 1945; **Marathon Man**, 1976; Mendel, 1997; My Sex Life, or How I Got Into an Argument, 1996; Pi, 1998; A Price Above Rubies, 1998.

FICTIONAL PERSONS

Note: The following annotated index, exclusively created by the author, shows fictional and supernatural persons appearing in theatrically released feature films (chiefly U.S. and British releases, along with notable foreign productions, showing U.S. year of release), as well as feature films made-for-TV, TV series and miniseries, but does not include shorts, documentaries or video productions. Persons are presented alphabetically by first name and titles of films are sequentially presented in alphabetical and chronological order. Titles shown in boldface represent entries profiled in this work, with the actor or actress enacting the character shown in parenthesis following each entry.

A.J. Raffles (Arthur J. Raffles; gentleman jewel thief in London, who adeptly evades detection by Scotland Yard as he filches the gems of the rich, as first depicted in Ernest William Hornung's 1898 short story "The Ides of March"): Raffles, The Gentleman Thief, 2001 (made-for-TV; Nigel Havers); Mr. Justice Raffles, 1921 (Gerald Ames); Raffles, 1925 (House Peters); **Raffles**, 1930 (Ronald Colman); **Raffles**, 1939 (David Niven); Raffles, 1975- (TV series; Anthony Valentine); the Amateur Cracksman, 1917 (John Barrymore); The Return of Raffles, 1932 (George Barraud).

Abel Magwitch (aka: The Convict; Provis; Mr. Campbell; escapee from a prison ship aided by youthful orphan Pip and who later becomes Pip's secret benefactor in Charles Dickens' 1861 novel *Great Expectations*): Great Expectations, 1917 (Frank Losee); Great Expectations, 1934 (Henry Hull); **Great Expectations**, 1946 (Finlay Currie); Great Expectations, 1959- (TV series; Jerold Wells); Great Expectations, 1967- (TV series; John Tate); Great Expectations, 1974 (made-for-TV; James Mason); Great Expectations, 1981- (TV miniseries; Stratford Johns); Great Expectations, 1989- (TV miniseries; Anthony Hopkins); Great Expectations, 1999 (made-for-TV; Bernard Hill); Great Expectations, 2011 (TV miniseries; Ray Winstone); Great Expectations, 2012 (Ralph Fiennes); Great Expectations, 2013 (Christopher Ellison); Playdate, 1961-1964 (TV series; "Great Expectations," two episodes in 1962: Tony Van Bridge); Robert Montgomery Presents, 1950-1957 (TV series; "Great Expectations," two episodes in 1954: Jacques Aubuchon); Store forventninger, 1922 (Emil Helsengreen).

Abraham Van Helsing (Dutch physician and vampire hunter depicted in the 1897 gothic horror novel *Dracula* by Bram Stoker): **Bram Stoker's Dracula**, 1992 (Anthony Hopkins); The Brides of Dracula, 1960 (Peter Cushing); Broadway on Showtime, 1979- (TV series; "Passion of Dracula," 1980 episode: Malachi Throne); Count Dracula, 1973 (Herbert Lom); Count Dracula, 1977 (made-for-TV; Frank Finlay); Dawn of Dracula, 2013 (Marlena Midnite as Victoria Van Helsing); Die Hard Dracula, 1998 (Bruce Glover); Don Dracula, 1982 (animated TV series; Junpei Takiguchi); **Dracula**, 1931 (Edward Van Sloan); Dracula, 1931 (Spanish version; Eduardo Arozamena); Dracula, 1972 (made-for-TV; Hermann Hartmann); Dracula, 1973 (made-for-TV; Nehemiah Persoff); Dracula, 1974 (made-for-TV; Nigel Davenport); **Dracula**, 1979 (Laurence Olivier); Dracula, 2007 (made-for-TV; David Suchet); Dracula, 2010 (Ken Pohl); Dracula, 2013-2014 (TV series; Thomas Kretschmann); Dracula A.D., 1972 (Peter Cushing); Dracula: A Chamber Musical, 2000 (made-for-TV; Michael Fletcher); **Dracula: Dead and Loving It**, 1995 (Mel Brooks); Dracula: The Dark Prince, 2013 (Jon Voight); Dracula 3D, 2013 (Rutger Hauer); Dracula 3000, 2004 (Casper Van Dien); Dracula 2000, 2000 (Christopher Plummer); **Dracula's Daughter**, 1936 (Edward Van Sloan); Dreaming Dracula, 2014 (Simon Klinkertz); Fatal Kiss, 2002 (Victor Lundin); Gothica, 2013 (made-for-TV; Janet Montgomery as Grace Van Helsing); **Horror of Dracula**, 1958 (Peter Cushing); The Legend of the 7 Golden Vampires, 1979 (Peter Cushing); Love at First Bite, 1979 (Richard Ben-

Anthony Hopkins as vampire hunter Abraham Van Helsing in *Bram Stoker's Dracula*, **1992.**

jamin); Modern Vampires, 1998 (made-for-TV; Rod Steiger as Frederick Van Helsing); The Monster Squad, 1987 (Jack Gwillim); Mystery and Imagination, 1966-1970 (TV series; "Dracula," 1968 episode: Bernard Archard); Nadja, 1995 (Peter Fonda, who also plays Dracula); Nosferatu the Vampyre, 1979 (Walter Ladengast); Penny Dreadful, 2014 (TV series; David Warner); The Satanic Rites of Dracula, 1978 (Peter Cushing); Son of Dracula, 1974 (Dennis Price); Sundown: The Vampire in Retreat, 1990 (Bruce Campbell); Tales from the Crypt, 1989-1996 (TV series; "The Reluctant Vampire," 1991 episode: Michael Berryman as Rupert Van Helsing); Terror of Dracula, 2012 (Terry Wade); Transylvania Twist, 1989 (Ace Mask as Victor Von Helsing); **Van Helsing**, 2004 (Hugh Jackman); Van Helsing: The Vampire Hunter, 2012 (Matthew Ferguson); Virtual Murder, 1992- (TV series; "A Dream of Dracula," 1992 episode: Ronald Fraser); Way of the Vampire, 2005 (Rhett Giles); Young Dracula, 2006- (TV series; Terence Maynard).

Achilles (Greek warrior in Greek mythology and foremost warrior in Trojan War): BBC Sunday-Night Theatre, 1950-1959 (TV series; "Troilus and Cressida," 1954 episode: Geoffrey Toone); The Death of Socrates, 2010 (Anthony Walmlsey); Die schone Helena, 1979 (made-for-TV; Harald Serafin); The Further Adventures of Cupid and Eros, 2010- (TV series; Bradford Anderson); Fury of Achilles, 1962 (Gordon Mitchell); Hector the Mighty, 1972 (Mike Forrest [Michael Forrest]); Helen of Troy, 1924 (Carlo Aldini); Helen of Troy, 1956 (Stanley Baker); Helen of Troy, 2003 (TV miniseries; Joe Montana); Hercules, 1998-1999 (TV series; Dom Irrera voiceover); Ich log die Wahrheit, 1971 (made-for-TV; Frank Hoffmann); King Priam, 1985 (made-for-TV; Neil Jenkins); La belle Helene, 1996 (made-for-TV; Steve Davislim); La Belle Helene, 2000 (Eric Huchet); L'odissea, 1991 (made-for-TV; Maurizio Seimandi); The Loves of Hercules, 1960 (Gil Vidal); The Odyssey, 1997- (TV series; Richard Truett); Penthesilea, 1963 (made-for-TV; Heinz Baumann); The Private Life of Helen of Troy, 1927 (Bert Sprotte); Romulus the Great, 1965 (made-for-TV; Alexander Engel); Romulus the Great, 1969 (made-for-TV; Ejner Federspiel); Royal Children, 1950 (Walter Kottenkamp); Tantalus: Behind the Mask, 2001 (made-for-TV; Robert Petkoff); Theatre Night, 1985- (TV series; "Iphigenia at Aulis," 1990 episode: Graham Sinclair); The Three Stooges Meet Hercules, 1962 (Lewis Charles); Troilus & Cressida, 1981 (made-for-TV; Kenneth Haigh); Troilus und Cressida, 1964 (made-for-TV; Erich Aberle); Troilus und Cressida, 1966 (made-for-TV; Dennis Marks); Troilus und Cressida, 1969 (made-for-TV; Hubert Suschka); Troilus und Cressida, 1981 (made-for-TV; Kenneth Haigh); The Trojan Horse, 1962 (Arturo Dominici); **Troy**, 2004 (Brad Pitt); **Ulysses**, 1955 (Piero Lulli).

Gregory Peck as Ahab in *Moby Dick*, 1956.

Adolf Kramer (the kindly grandfather who raises Heidi, a young girl in the Swiss Alps, as depicted in the 1881 novel by Swiss author Johanna Spyri): Courage Mountain, 1990 (Jan Rubes); A Gift for Heidi, 1958 (Douglas Fowley); **Heidi**, 1937 (Jean Hersholt); Heidi, 1954 (Heinrich Gretler); Heidi, 1959 (TV series; Mark Dignam); Heidi, 1968 (Gustav Knuth); Heidi, 1968 (made-for-TV; Michael Redgrave); Heidi, 1974 (TV miniseries; Hans Meyer); Heidi, 1993 (Jason Robards Jr.); Heidi, 2001 (Paolo Villaggio); Heidi, 2005 (Max von Sydow); Heidi, 2015 (Bruno Ganz); Heidi Grows Up, 1954 (TV miniseries; Roger Maxwell); Heidi and Peter, 1955 (Thomas Klameth); The New Adventures of Heidi, 1978 (made-for-TV; Burl Ives); Heidi's Song, 1982 (animated musical; Lorne Greene voiceover).

Agamemnon (Greek king in Greek mythology and commander of the Greek army during the Trojan War): The Adventures of Ulysses, 1968 (TV miniseries; Rolf Boysen); Agamemnon, 1967 (made-for-TV; Matti Orovisto); BBC Sunday-Night Theatre, 1950-1959 (TV series; "Troilus and Cressida," 1954 episode: Joseph O'Conor); Electra, 1962 (Theodoros Dimitriou); Electra, 1981 (Rolf Boysen); The Face of Love, 1954 (made-for-TV; Paul Whitsun-Jones); Fury of Achilles, 1962 (Mario Petri); The Greeks: A Journey in Space and Time, 1980- (TV series; "Heroes and Men," 1980 episode: T.P. McKenna); Hector the Mighty, 1972 (Aldo Giuffre/Edward Mannix voiceover); Helen of Troy, 1924 (Karl Wustenhagen); Helen of Troy, 1956 (Robert Douglas); Helen of Troy, 2003- (TV miniseries; Rufus Sewell); Helen, Yes...Helen of Troy, 1974 (Michael Forest); Ich log die Wahrheit, 1971 (made-for-TV; Klausjurgen Wussow); Iphigenie en Aulide, 2002 (made-for-TV; Christopher Robertson); La belle Helene, 1951 (made-for-TV; John Hargreaves); La belle Helene, 1996 (made-for-TV; Oliver Widmer); La Belle Helene, 1999 (made-for-TV; Victor Braun); La Belle Helene, 2000 (made-for-TV; Laurent Naouri); The Legend of Hercules, 2012 (Luke Newberry); **Mr. Peabody & Sherman**, 2014 (Patrick Warburton voiceover); NET Playhouse, 1964-1972 (TV series; "The Prodigal," 1969 episode: Roy Poole); The Odyssey, 1997 (TV series; Yogo Voyagis); Orestea, 1975 (made-for-TV; Massimo Foschi); Oresteia, 1979 (TV miniseries; Denis Quilley); The Oresteia, 2001 (Greg Teachout); Sacrifice to the Wind, 1954 (made-for-TV; Andrew Cruickshank); Tantulus: Behind the Mask, 2001 (Greg Hicks); **Time Bandits**, 1981 (Sean Connery); Troilus & Cressida, 1981 (made-for-TV; Vernon Dobtcheff); Troilus und Cressida, 1964 (made-for-TV; Wilhelm Grimm); Troilus und Cressida, 1969 (made-for-TV; Heinz Rippert); Troilus & Cressida, 1981 (made-for-TV; Vernon Dobtcheff); The Trojan Horse, 1962 (Nerio Bernardi); **Troy**, 2004 (Brian Cox); **Ulysses**, 1955 (Andrea Bosic).

Ahab (fictional character in Herman Melville's sea saga *Moby Dick*, a novel published in 1851): Animated Epics: Moby Dick, 2000 (Rod Steiger voiceover); **Moby Dick**, 1930 (John Barrymore); Moby Dick, 1954 (made-for-TV; Victor Jory); **Moby Dick**, 1956 (Gregory Peck); Moby Dick, 1978 (Jack Aranson); Moby Dick, 1998 (TV miniseries; Patrick Stewart); Moby Dick, 2010-2011 (TV miniseries; William Hurt); Moby Dick, 2013 (Jay Hunter Morris); Moby Dick Rehearsed, 1955 (Orson Welles); The Pagemaster, 1994 (George Hearn voiceover); **The Sea Beast**, 1926 (John Barrymore); Tales of the Gold Monkey, 1982-1983 (TV series; "Shanghaied," 1982 episode: Guy Stockwell).

Ajax (Greek warrior in Greek mythology, slain during the Trojan War): BBC Sunday-Night Theatre, 1950-1959 (TV series; "Troilus and Cressida," 1954 episode: Michael Brennan); Der trojanisch krieg findet nicht statt, 1964 (made-for-TV; Walter Buschhoff); The Face of Love, 1954 (made-for-TV; Alan Tilvern); Helen of Troy, 1956 (Maxwell Reed); Helen of Troy, 2003- (TV miniseries; Alex Mizzi); Helen, Yes...Helen of Troy, 1974 (Pietro Torrisi); Hercules: The Brave and the Bold, 2013 (Ted Burke); Hercules: The Legendary Journeys, 1995-1999 (TV series; 'War Wounds," 1998 episode; Peter McCauley); Hercules: The Brave and the Bold, 2013 (Ted Burke); ITV Play of the Week, 1955-1974 (TV series; "Tiger at the Gate," 1960 episode; Bryan Pringle); Le guerre de Troie n'aura pas lieu, 1967 (made-for-TV; Jacques Seiler); Lisistrata, 2002 (Javier Gurruchaga); **Mr. Peabody & Sherman**, 2014 (Al Rodrigo voiceover); Play of the Week, 1959-1961 (TV series; "Tiger at the Gate," 1960 episode: Mike Kellin); The Private Life of Helen of Troy, 1927 (Mario Carillo); Troilus & Cressida, 1981 (made-for-TV; Anthony Pedley); Troilus und Cressida, 1964 (made-for-TV; Heinz Theo Branding); Troilus und Cressida, 1969 (made-for-TV; Peter Kuiper); Troilus & Cressida, 1981 (made-for-TV; Anthony Pedley); The Trojan Horse, 1962 (Mimmo Palmara); **Troy**, 2004 (Tyler Mane).

Aladdin (fictional character of Arabic folktales, included in *One Thousand and One Nights*): Abbacadabra, 1983 (made-for-TV; Joost Timp); Aladdin, 1951 (made-for-TV; David Jacobs); Aladdin, 1967 (made-for-TV; Fred Grades); Aladdin, 1990 (Brent Sudduth); **Aladdin**, 1992 (Scott Weinger voiceover); Aladdin, 1992 (Cam Clarke); Aladdin, 1992 (Nick Stoter); Aladdin, 1994-1995 (TV series; Scott Weinger voiceover); Aladdin, 2000 (made-for-TV; Ed Byrne); Aladdin, 2001 (made-for-TV; Kelli Marie); Aladdin and His Lamp, 1952 (Johnny Sands); Aladdin and His Magic Lamp, 1967 (Boris Bystrov); Aladdin and His Magic Lamp, 1970 (Gaston Guez voiceover); Aladdin and His Wonderful Lamp, 1917 (Francis Carpenter); Aladdin and His Wonderful Lamp, 1966 (made-for-TV; Angela Richards); Aladdin and the Death Lamp, 2012 (made-for-TV; Darren Shahlavi); Aladdin and the Forty Thieves, 1984 (made-for-TV; Sarah Greene); Aladdin and the Magic Lamp, 1982 (Christopher Atkins voiceover); Aladdin and the Marvelous Lamp, 1958 (Antonio Espino); Aladdin on Ice, 1975 (made-for-TV; Reg Park); Aladdin on Ice, 1995 (made-for-TV; Kurt Browning); **Arabian Nights**, 1942 (John Qualen); Arabian Nights, 2000 (TV miniseries; Jason Scott Lee); Christmas Night of One Hundred Stars, 1986 (TV special; Anita Harris); The Desert Hawk, 1950 (Jackie Gleason); Hercules, 1998-1999 (TV series; "Hercules and the Arabian Night," 1999 episode; Scott Weinger voiceover); ITV Play of the Week, 1955-1974 (TV series; "Aladdin," 1967 episode; Cliff Richard); Magi: The Kingdom of Magic, 2013- (TV series; Erica Mendez, Kaori Ishihara voiceovers); Magi: The Labyrinth of Magic, 2012- (TV series; Erica Mendez voiceover); The Magic of Aladdin, 1989 (Jeff Hyslop); One Arabian Night, 1923 (Lionelle Howard); **1001 Arabian Nights**, 1959; The Red Skelton Hour, 1951-1971 (TV series; "Fairy Tales for Old Children," 1968 episode: Cyril Ritchard); Shirley Temple's Storybook, 1958-1961 (TV series; "The Land of Green Ginger," 1958 episode: Anthony Eustrel); Thief of Damascus, 1952 (Robert Clary); **A Thousand and One Nights**, 1945 (Cornel Wilde); The Wizard of Baghdad, 1960 (Bill Mumy); The Wonders of Aladdin, 1961 (Donald O'Connor).

Alan Breck (adventurer and Jacobite created by Robert Louis Stevenson in his 1886 novel *Kidnapped*, who champions youth David Balfour in his efforts to secure his rightful inheritance): Kidnapped, 1917 (Robert Cain); **Kidnapped**, 1938 (Warner Baxter); Kidnapped, 1948 (Dan O'Herlihy); Kidnapped, 1952- (TV series; Patrick Troughton); Kidnapped, 1956- (TV series; Patrick Troughton); Kidnapped, 1960 (Peter Finch); Kidnapped, 1963- (TV miniseries; Roddy McMillan); Kidnapped, 1970 (Thomas Weisgerber); **Kidnapped**, 1971 (Michael Caine); Kidnapped, 1978- (TV miniseries; David McCallum); Kidnapped, 1986 (animated version; Tom Burlinson voiceover); Kidnapped, 1995 (made-for-TV; Armand Assante).

Alan-a-Dale (fictional character and follower of Robin Hood): The Adventures of Robin Hood, 1955-1960 (TV series; Richard Coleman; John Schlesinger); The Bandit of Sherwood Forest, 1946 (Leslie Denison); A Challenge for Robin Hood, 1968 (Eric Flynn); The Legend of Robin Hood, 1968- (TV series; Noel Harrison); Long Live Robin Hood, 1971 (Mark Damon); **Robin Hood**, 1922 (Lloyd Talman); Robin Hood, 1953- (TV miniseries; John Breslin); **Robin Hood**, 1973 (Roger Miller voiceover); Robin Hood, 2006-2009 (TV series; Joe Armstrong); **Robin Hood**, 2010 (Alan Doyle); Rogues of Sherwood Forest, 1950 (Lester Matthews); Son of Robin Hood, 1959 (George Coulouris); **The Story of Robin Hood** [aka: The Story of Robin Hood and His Merrie Men] 1952 (Elton Hayes); Sword of Sherwood Forest, 1961 (Dennis Lotis); Tales of Robin Hood, 1951 (Bruce Lester); Young Robin Hood, 1991-1992 (animated TV series; Michael O'Reilly voiceover).

Alfred Davidson (fire and brimstone missionary who converts Sadie Thompson, a South Seas prostitute, to religion, only to succumb to the pleasures of the flesh by seducing her and then committing suicide, as depicted in W. Somerset Maugham's short story, "Rain," as well as the 1923 play): **Miss Sadie Thompson**, 1953 (Jose Ferrer); **Rain**, 1932 (Walter Huston); **Sadie Thompson**, 1928 (Lionel Barrymore); W. Somerset Maugham, 1969-1970 (TV series; "Rain," 1970 episode: Michael Bryant).

Ali Baba (fictional character of Arabic folktales, included in *One Thousand and One Nights*): Aladdin and the Forty Thieves, 1984 (made-for-TV; Todd Carty); Ali Baba and the Forty Thieves, 1918 (George Stone); **Ali Baba and the Forty Thieves**, 1944; Ali Baba and the Forty Thieves, 1954 (Fernandel); Ali Baba and the Forty Thieves, 1971 (Sadri Alisik); The Arabian Nights: Adventures of Sinbad, 1975- (TV series; Niko Macoulis); Arabian Nights, 2000- (TV miniseries; Rufus Sewell); The Dinah Shore Chevy Show, 1956-1963 (TV series; "Arabian Nights," 1960 episode: John Hoyt); Magi: The Kingdom of Magic, 2013- (TV series; Yuki Kaji voiceover); Magi: The Labyrinth of Magic, 2012- (TV series; Erik Scott Kimerer voiceover); The Seven Tasks of Ali Baba, 1963 (Rod Flash); Shirley Temple's Storybook, 1958-1961 (TV series; "Ali Baba and the Forty Thieves," 1958 episode: Nehemiah Persoff); Son of Ali Baba, 1952 (Morris Ankrum); The Sword of Ali Baba, 1965 (Peter Mann); Thief of Damascus, 1952 (Philip Van Zandt).

Alice (fictional character from the 1865 novel by British author Lewis Carroll): Adventures in Wonderland, 1992-1994 (TV series; Elisabeth Harnois); Alice, 2009 (TV miniseries; Caterina Scorsone); Alice at the Palace, 1982 (made-for-TV; Meryl Streep); Alice in Wonderland, 1915 (Viola Savoy); Alice in Wonderland, 1931 (Ruth Gilbert); **Alice in Wonderland**, 1933 (Charlotte Henry); Alice in Wonderland, 1949 (Carol Marsh in live action and in voiceover as a puppet of Alice); **Alice in Wonderland**, 1951 (Kathryn Beaumont voiceover); Alice in Wonderland, 1955 (made-for-TV; Gillian Barber); Alice in Wonderland, 1966 (made-for-TV; Anne-Marie Mallik); Alice in Wonderland, 1976 (Monica von Reust); Alice in Wonderland, 1982 (made-for-TV; Annie Enneking); Alice in Wonderland, 1985 (made-for-TV; Natalie Gregory); Alice in Wonderland, 1985 (TV series; Giselle Andrews); Alice in Wonderland,

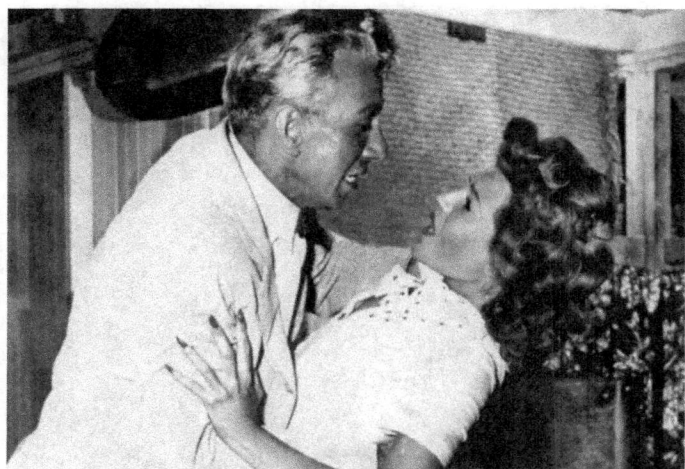

Jose Ferrer (as Alfred Davidson) and Rita Hayworth in *Miss Sadie Thompson*, 1953.

1986 (made-for-TV; four 30-minute segments; Kate Dorning); Alice in Wonderland, 1999 (made-for-TV; Tina Majorino); **Alice in Wonderland**, 2010 (Mia Wasikowska); Alice in Wonderland or What's a Nice Kid Like You Doing in a Place Like This?, 1966 (animated made-for-TV; Janet Waldo, Doris Drew Allen as Alice's singing voice); Alice through the Looking Box, 1960 (made-for-TV; Jeannie Carson); Alice through the Looking Glass, 1966 (made-for-TV; Judi Rolin); Alice through the Looking Glass, 1973 (made-for-TV; Sarah Sutton); Alice through the Looking Glass, 1973 (TV series; Carol Hollands); Alice through the Looking Glass, 1987 (made-for-TV; Janet Waldo voiceover); Alice through the Looking Glass, 1998 (made-for-TV; Kate Beckinsale; little Alice, Charlotte Curley); Alice's Adventures in Wonderland, 1956 (made-for-TV; Lisa Barnett); Alice's Adventures in Wonderland, 1972 (Fiona Fullerton); Alice's Adventures in Wonderland, 2011 (made-for-TV; Lauren Cuthbertson); Alice's Adventures in Wonderland and tthrough the Looking Glass, 1948 (made-for-TV; Margaret Barton); A Dream of Alice, 1982 (made-for-TV; Jenny Agutter); Dreamchild, 1985 (Coral Browne; Amelia Shankley as little Alice); The Ford Theatre Hour, 1948-1951 (TV series; "Alice in Wonderland," 1950 episode; Iris Mann); Great Performances, 1971- (TV series; "Alice in Wonderland," 1983 episode; Kate Burton); Kraft Theatre, 1947-1958 (TV series: "Alice in Wonderland," 1954 episode: Robin Morgan); Miyuki-chan in Wonderland, 1995- (TV miniseries; Mariko Kouda); Once upon a Time in Wonderland, 2013 (TV series; Sophie Lowe); Unsuk Chin: Alice in Wonderland, 2007 (Sally Matthews); The Wednesday Play, 1964-1970 (TV series; "Alice," 1965 episode: Deborah Watling).

Allan Quartermain (indefatigable white hunter in Africa as depicted in H. Rider Haggard's 1885 novel of adventure, *King Solomon's Mines*): Allan Quartermain and the Lost City of Gold, 1987 (Richard Chamberlain); King Solomon's Mines, 1919 (Albert Lawrence); **King Solomon's Mines**, 1937 (Cedric Hardwicke); **King Solomon's Mines**, 1950 (Stewart Granger); King Solomon's Mines, 1985 (Richard Chamberlain); King Solomon's Mines, 1986 (made-for-TV; Arthur Dignam); King Solomon's Mines, 2004 (made-for-TV; Patrick Swayze); King Solomon's Treasure, 1979 (John Colicos); The League of Extraordinary Gentlemen, 2003 (Sean Connery); Watusi, 1959 (George Montgomery as Harry Quartermain, son of Allan).

Amphitryon (king and general in Greek mythology): Amphitryon, 1935 (Willy Fritsch); Amphitryon, 1961 (made-for-TV; Rolf Boysen); Amphitryon, 1978 (made-for-TV; Klaus-Dieter Klebsch); Amphitryon, 1981 (made-for-TV; Christian Kohlund); Amphitryon, 2003 (made-for-TV; Eric Ruf); Amphitryon 38, 1963 (made-for-TV; Hannes Messemer);

Greta Garbo as the fallen lady in *Anna Christie*, 1931.

Hercules, 1997 (Hal Holbrook voiceover).

Amy March (one of four teenage sisters who finds romance as she and her siblings mature in a Massachusetts household during the American Civil War as profiled in Louisa May Alcott's timeless novel *Little Women*, 1868-1869): The Ford Theatre Hour, 1948-1951 (TV series; "Little Women," 1949 episode: June Lockhart); Good Wives, 1958 (TV series; Jill Dixon); Great Performances, 1971- (TV series; "Little Women," 2001 episode: Margaret Lloyd); Jo's Boys, 1959 (TV series; Susan Maryott); Little Women, 1917 (Daisy Burrell); Little Women, 1918 (Florence Flynn); **Little Women**, 1933 (Joan Bennett); **Little Women**, 1949 (Elizabeth Taylor); Little Women, 1950- (TV series; Susan Stephen); Little Women, 1958 (TV series; Sylvia Davies); Little Women, 1958 (made-for-TV; Zina Bethune); Little Women, 1970 (TV miniseries; Janina Faye); Little Women, 1978 (TV miniseries; Ann Dusenberry); **Little Women**, 1994 (Kirsten Dunst as younger Amy; Samantha Mathis as older Amy); Matinee Theatre, 1955-1958 (TV series; "Little Women," 1956 episode: June Ashton); NBC Special Treat, 1975-1986 (TV series; "Little Women," 1976 episode: Judith Fugate); Studio One in Hollywood, 1948-1958 (TV series; "Little Women: Jo's Story," 1950 episode: Lois Hall; "Little Women: Meg's Story," 1950 episode: Lois Hall).

Andromeda (beautiful princess in Greek mythology saved from the sea monster Cretus by Perseus, who married her): **Clash of the Titans**, 1981 (Judi Bowker); **Clash of the Titans**, 2010 (Alexa Davalos); Mythic Warriors: Guardians of the Legend, 1998- (TV series; Caroly Larson); Persee, 2004 (made-for-TV; Marie Lenormand); Perseus against the Monsters, 1963 (Anna Ranalli); Wrath of the Titans, 2012 (Rosamund Pike).

Anna Christie (onetime prostitute who returns home and attempts to live a better life and find a future with a loving man, a character created by playwright Eugene O'Neill in his 1922 Pulitzer Prize-winning play): **Anna Christie**, 1923 (Blanche Sweet); **Anna Christie**, 1931 (Greta Garbo in her first talking role); Anna Christie, 1946 (made-for-TV; Monica McGrath); Anna Christie, 1957 (made-for-TV; Diane Cilento); Anna Christie, 1964 (made-for-TV; Anja Pohjola); Anna Christie, 1965 (made-for-TV; Violeta Antier); Celanese Theatre, 1951-1952 (TV series; "Anna Christie," 1952 episode; June Havoc); Estudio 1, 1965-1984 (TV seris; "Anna Christie," 1976 episode; Maria del Puy); Theatre Parade, 1936-1938 (TV series; "Anna Christie," 1937 episode: Flora Robson).

Anna Karenina (ill-starred heroine in Leo Tolstoy's classic 1878 novel): Anna Karenina, 1914 (Mariya Germanova); Anna Karenina, 1915 (Betty

Nansen); Anna Karenina, 1918 (Iren Varsanyi); Anna Karenina, 1919 (Lya Mara); **Anna Karenina**, 1935 (Greta Garbo); **Anna Karenina**, 1948 (Vivien Leigh); Anna Karenina, 1961 (made-for-TV; Claire Bloom); Anna Karenina, 1967 (Tatyana Samoylova); Anna Karenina, 1974 (TV miniseries; Lea Massari); Anna Karenina, 1977 (TV miniseries; Nicola Pagett); Anna Karenina, 1979 (ballet; Maya Plisetskaya); Anna Karenina, 1985 (made-for-TV; Jacqueline Bisset); Anna Karenina, 1997 (Sophie Marceau); Anna Karenina, 2000 (TV miniseries; Helen McCrory); Anna Karenina, 2009 (TV miniseries; Tatyana Drubich); **Anna Karenina**, 2012 (Keira Knightley); Anna Karenina, 2013 (TV miniseries; Vittoria Puccini); Love, 1927 (Greta Garbo).

Aphrodite (Greek goddess of love, pleasure, beauty and procreation; Venus in Roman mythology): The Adventures of Hercules II, 1985 (Margit Evelyn Newton): The Affairs of Aphrodite, 1970 (Antoinette Maynard); **Clash of the Titans**, 1981 (Ursula Andress); **Clash of the Titans**, 2010 (Agyness Deyn); Hercules, 1998-1999 (TV series; Lisa Kudrow voiceover); Hercules: The Brave and the Bold, 2013 (Angie Bilyeu); Mythic Warriors: Guardians of the Legend, 1998- (TV series; Wendy Lands); Myths, 2009- (TV series; Ana Mulvoy-Ten); Percy Jackson & the Olympians: The Lightning Thief, 2010 (Serinda Swan); The Private Life of Helen of Troy, 1927 (Alice Adair); Xena: Warrior Princess, 1995-2001 (TV series; Alexandra Tydings).

Apollo (Greek god of music, prophecy and truth, son of Zeus): The Affairs of Aphrodite, 1970 (Walt Phillips); Biblioteca di Studio Uno: Odissea, 1964 (made-for-TV; Giorgio Favretto); **Clash of the Titans**, 2010 (Luke Evans); Hercules, 1998-1999 (TV series; Keith David voiceover); The Illiac Passion, 1968 (Philip Merker); Immortals, 2011 (Corey Sevier); Mythic Warriors: Guardians of the Legend, 1998- (TV series; Jesse Collins); Night Life of the Gods, 1935 (Ray Corrigan); Percy Jackson & the Olympians: The Lightning Thief, 2010 (Dimitri Lekkos); Rome in a Day, 2008 (Andrew L. Salmonson); The Triumph of Venus, 1918 (Donald MacDonald); Wrath of the Titans, 2012 (Freddy Drabble); Young Hercules, 1998-1999 (TV series; Scott Michaelson).

Apple Annie (Damon Runyon character, a Broadway alcoholic who sells apples to high rollers): **Bloodhounds of Broadway**, 1952 (Bee Humphries); **Lady for a Day**, 1933 (May Robson); Ledi na den, 2002 (Marina Neyolova); Miracles—Mr. Canton and Lady Rose, 1989 (Ya-Lei Kuei); **Pocketful of Miracles**, 1961 (Bette Davis).

Aquaman (aka: Arthur Curry; fictional comic book superhero): The All-New Super Friends Hour, 1977-1978 (animated TV series; Norman Alden voiceover); Batman: The Brave and the Bold, 2008-2011 (animated TV series; John DiMaggio voiceover); Challenge of the Super Friends, 1978- (animated TV series; William Callaway voiceover); Justice League, 2001-2006 (TV series; Scott Rummell voiceover); Super Friends, 1973-2011 (animated TV series; Norman Alden voiceover); Super Friends, 1980-1983 (animated TV series; William Callaway voiceover); Super Friends: The Legendary Super Powers Show, 1984- (animated TV series; William Callaway voiceover); The Super Powers Team: Galactic Guardians, 1985- (animated TV series; William Callaway voiceover); Superman, 1996-2000 (TV series; Miguel Ferrer voiceover); The Superman/Aquaman Hour of Adventure, 1967-1968 (TV series; Marvin Miller); The World's Greatest Super Friends, 1979- (animated TV series; William Callaway voiceover); Young Justice, 2010- (animated TV series; Phil LeMarr voiceover).

Aramis (character in the fictional works of Alexander Dumas pere): Animated Three Musketeers, 1987 (TV series; Eiko Yamada); At Sword's Point, 1952 (Dan O'Herlihy as Aramis Jr.); Biblioteca di Studio Uno: I tre moschettieri, 1964 (made-for-TV; Tata Giocobetti); D'Artagnan, 1969 (TV miniseries; Adriano Amidei Migliano); D'Artagnon, 1991 (made-for-TV; Pierre Val); D'Artagnan amoureux, 1977 (TV miniseries;

Serge Maillat); D'Artagnan et les trois mousquetaires, 2005 (Gregori Derangere); D'Artanyan i tri mushketyora, 1979 (TV series; Igor Starygin); De drie Musketiers, 1968 (made-for-TV; Roger Sterckx); Die Drie Musketiere, 2013 (Pavel Barshak); Family Classics: The Three Musketeers, 1960 (made-for-TV; Tim O'Connor); The Four Charlots Musketeers, 1974 (Georges Mansart); The Four Musketeers, 1963 (Betto Di Paolo); **The Four Musketeers**, 1975 (Richard Chamberlain); The Gay Swordsman: The Glorious Musketeers, 1974 (Michel Duchaussoy voiceover); I tre moschettieri, 1991 (made-for-TV; Teo Teocoli); **The Iron Mask**, 1929 (Gino Corrado); Knights of the Queen, 1958 (Paul Campbell); La loca historia de los tres mosqueteros, 1983 (Josema Yuste); Lady in the Iron Mask, 1952 (Judd Holdren); Les 3 Mousquetaires, 1953 (Jacques Francois); Les trois mousquetaires, 1959 (made-for-TV; Hubert Noel); Les trois mousquetaires ou L'escrime ne paie pas, 1979 (made-for-TV; Jean-Renaud Garcia); Les trois mousquetaires: Premiere epoque—Les ferrets de la reine, 1961 (Jacques Toja); The Magnavox Theater, 1950 (TV series; "The Three Musketeers," 1950 episode: Keith Richards); **The Man in the Iron Mask**, 1939 (Miles Mander); Milady and the Three Musketeers, 2004 (made-for-TV; Eric Ruf); **The Musketeer**, 2001 (Nick Moran); The Musketeers, 2014 (TV series; Santiago Cabrera); Os tres Mosqueteiros, 1957 (TV series; Astrogilda Filho; Rogerio Marcico); Three and a Half Musketeers, 1957 (Wolf Ruvinskis); The Three Musketeers, 1916 (C. [Claude] N. Mortensen); **The Three Musketeers**, 1921 (Eugene Pallette); Three Musketeers, 1932 (Jean-Lous Allibert); The Three Musketeers, 1935 (Onslow Stevens); The Three Musketeers, 1939 (John King); **The Three Musketeers**, 1948 (Robert Coote); The Three Musketeers, 1954 (TV series; Paul Hansard); The Three Musketeers, 1966 (TV miniseries; Gary Watson); **The Three Musketeers**, 1974 (Richard Chamberlain); **The Three Musketeers**, 1993 (Charlie Sheen); The Three Musketeers, 2007 (Peter Gantzler voiceover); The Three Musketeers, 2011 (Luke Evans); Vengeance of the Three Musketeers, 1961 (Jacques Toja); Vingt ans apres, 1922 (Pierre de Guingand); Tri musketyri, 1983 (TV miniseries; Victor Preiss); Tri mushketera, 2013 (Pavel Barshak); Young Blades, 2001 (Callum Blue).

Ares (Greek god of war; Mars in Roman mythology): Immortals, 2011 (Daniel Sharman); Hercules, 1998-1999 (TV series; Jay Thomas voiceover); Xena: Warrior Princess, 1995-2001 (TV series; Kevin Smith); Young Hercules, 1998-1999 (TV series; Kevin Smith).

Artemis (Greek goddess of the hunt; Diana in Roman mythology): **Clash of the Titans**, 2010 (Nathalie Cox); Hercules: The Brave and the Bold, 2013 (Chamane Barbatti); Mythic Warriors: Guardians of the Legend, 1998- (TV series; Elizabeth Hanna); Percy Jackson & the Olympians: The Lightning Thief, 2010 (Ona Grauer).

Artful Dodger (a fictional character in the Charles Dickens novel *Oliver Twist*, a street urchin, who is a member of a ring of pickpocketing boys in 19th-Century London, England): The ABC Saturday Superstar Movie, 1972-1974 (animated TV series; "Oliver and the Artful Dodger," two 1972 episodes: Michael Bell); Escape of the Artful Dodger, 2001- (TV series; Luke O'Loughlin); The Further Adventures of Oliver Twist, 1980- (TV series; John Fowler); Oliver & Company, 1988 (Billy Joel voiceover); Oliver Twist, 1916 (Raymond Hatton); **Oliver Twist**, 1922 (Edouard Trebaol); Oliver Twist, 1933 (Sonny Ray); **Oliver Twist**, 1951 (Anthony Newley); Oliver Twist, 1962 (TV miniseries; Melvyn Hayes); **Oliver!**, 1968 (Jack Wild); Oliver Twist, 1974 (animated version; Davy Jones voiceover); Oliver Twist, 1982 (made-for-TV; Martin Tempest); Oliver Twist, 1985 (TV miniseries; David Garlick); Oliver Twist, 1997 (made-for-TV; Elijah Wood); Oliver Twist, 1999 (TV miniseries; Alex Crowley); **Oliver Twist**, 2005 (Harry Eden); Oliver Twist Jr., 1921 (Scott McKee).

Arthur (legendary king who held court at the Round Table in Camelot in 6th-Century Britain): The Adventures of Sir Galahad, 1949 (serial;

Sean Connery (as King Arthur) and Richard Gere in *First Knight*, 1995.

Nelson Leigh); The Adventures of Sir Lancelot, 1956-1957 (TV series; Ronald Leigh-Hunt/Bruce Seton); Arthur of the Britons, 1972-1973 (TV series; Oliver Tobias); Arthur the King, 1985 (made-for-TV; Malcolm McDowell); Arthur's Quest, 1999 (made-for-TV; Eric Christian Olsen/Robby Seager as young Arthur); The Black Knight, 1954 (Anthony Bushell); **Camelot**, 1967 (Richard Harris as adult Arthur, Nicolas Beauvy as Arthur as a boy); Camelot, 1982 (made-for-TV; Richard Harris); Camelot, 2011 (TV miniseries; James Campbell Bower); Carry On Laughing!, 1975 (TV series; Kenneth Connor); **A Connecitcut Yankee**, 1931 (William Farnum); A Connecticut Yankee, 1955 (made-for-TV; Boris Karloff); A Connecticut Yankee in King Arthur's Court, 1921 (Charles Clary); **A Connecticut Yankee in King Arthur's Court**, 1949 (Sir Cedric Hardwicke); A Connecticut Yankee in King Arthur's Court, 1989 (made-for-TV: Michael Gross); Crystal Cave, 1996 (made-for-TV; Martin Sheen); **Dragonheart**, 1996 (John Guilgud voiceover); **Excalibur**, 1981 (Nigel Terry); **First Knight**, 1995 (Sean Connery); Gawain and the Green Knight, 1991 (made-for-TV; Marc Warren); Ginevra, 1992 (Gerhard Theuring); Guinevere, 1994 (made-for-TV; Sean Patrick Flanery); Highway to Heaven, 1984-1989 (TV series; "A Divine Madness," 1984 episode: Ron Moody); Into the Labyrinth, 1981-1982 (TV series; "Excaliber," 1982 episode: Ewen Solon); Jake's Journey, 1988 (made-for-TV; Peter Cook); A Kid in King Arthur's Court, 1995 (Joss Ackland); **King Arthur**, 2004 (Clive Owen; Shane Murray-Corcoran as young Arthur); King Arthur: The Young Warlord, 1975 (Oliver Tobias); A Knight in Camelot, 1998 (made-for-TV; Michael York); **Knights of the Round Table**, 1953 (Mel Ferrer); Lancelot of the Lake, 1970 (made-for-TV; Tony Taffin); Lancelot of the Lake, 1974 (Vladimir Antolek-Oresek); **The Last Legion**, 2007 (Rory James as the young Arthur); The Legend of King Arthur, 1979 (TV series; Andrew Burt); The Legend of Prince Valiant, 1991-1994 (TV series; Efrem Zimbalist Jr.); Merlin, 1998 (TV miniseries; Paul Curran); Merlin: The Return, 2000 (Parick Bergin); The Mists of Avalon, 2001 (made-for-TV; Edward Atterton); **Monty Python and the Holy Grail**, 1975 (Graham Chapman); Morte d'Arthur, 1980 (made-for-TV; Jeremy Brett); Once Upon a Classic, 1976-1979 (TV series: "A Connecticut Yankee in King Arthur's Court," 1978 episode: Richard Basehart); Perceval, 1978 (Marc Eyraud); Ponds Theater, 1953-1957 (aka: Kraft Theater; TV series; "A Connecticut Yankee in King Arthur's Court," 1954 episode; Jack Livesey); **Prince Valiant**, 1954 (Brian Aherne); Prince Valiant, 1997 (Edward Fox); Quest for Camelot, 1998 (Pierce Brosnan/Steve Perry singing voice); Robin Hood, 1984-1986 (TV series; "The Inheritance," 1986 episode, James Woodward/Hywel Bennett voiceover); Siege of the Saxons, 1963 (Mark Dignam); Studio One in Hollywood, 1948-1958 (TV series: "A Connecticut Yankee in King Arthur's Court," 1952 episode: Boris Karloff; "I Do," 1952 episode: John Shellie; "No Place

Helen Gahagan (as Ayesha) and Randolph Scott in *She*, 1935.

to Run," 1958 episode: Addison Richards); **The Sword and the Stone**, 1963 (Rickie Sorensen voiceover); Sword of Lancelot, 1963 (Brian Aherne); Sword of the Valiant: The Legend of Sir Gawain and the Green Knight, 1984 (Trevor Howard); The Time Tunnel, 1966-1967 (TV series; "Merlin the Magician," 1967 episode: Jim McMullan); Unidentified Flying Oddball, 1979 (Kenneth More); Waxworks II: Lost in Time, 1992 (John Ireland); A Young Connecticut Yankee in King Arthur's Court, 1996 (Nick Mancuso).

Athena (Greek goddess of the arts and patron of Greek heroes; Minerva in Roman mythology): The Adventures of Hercules II, 1985 (Carlotta [Carla Ferrigno] Green): **Clash of the Titans**, 1981 (Susan Fleetwood); **Clash of the Titans**, 2010 (Izabella Miko); Hercules, 1983 (Delia Boccardo); Goddess of Love, 1988 (made-for-TV; Jordana Capra); Hercules, 1998-1999 (TV series; Jane Leeves voiceover); Hercules: The Brave and the Bold, 2013 (Chelsea Zotta); Immortals, 2011 (Isabel Lucas); Mythic Warriors: Guardians of the Legend, 1998- (TV series; Lally Cadeau, Wendy Thatcher); Myths, 2009- (TV series; Jade Ewen); Percy Jackson & the Olympians: The Lightning Thief, 2010 (Melina Kanakaredes); The Private Life of Helen of Troy, 1927 (Helen Fairweather); Wrath of the Titans, 2012 (Kathryn Carpenter); Young Hercules, 1998-1999 (TV series; Jane Fullerton-Smith).

Athos (Character in the fictional works of Alexander Dumas pere): Animated Three Musketeers, 1987 (TV series; Akira Kamiya); Biblioteca di Studio Uno: I tre moschettieri, 1964 (made-for-TV; Virgilio Savona); D'Artagnan, 1969 (TV miniseries; Francois Chaumette); D'Artagnon, 1991 (made-for-TV; Andre Obadia); D'Artagnan amoureux, 1977 (TV miniseries; Yves Lefebvre); D'Artagnan et les trois mousquetaires, 2005 (Heino Ferch); D'Artanyan i tri mushketyora, 1979 (TV series; Venyamin Smekhov); De drie Musketiers, 1968 (made-for-TV; Erik Maes); Die Drie Musketiere, 2013 (Yuriy Chursin); Family Classics: The Three Musketeers, 1960 (made-for-TV; Barry Morse); The Four Charlots Musketeers, 1974 (Yvan Tanguy); The Four Musketeers, 1963 (Ferdinando Poggi); **The Four Musketeers**, 1975 (Oliver Reed); The Glorious Musketeers, 1974 (Michel Elias voiceover); I tre moschettieri, 1991 (made-for-TV; Francesco Salvi); **The Iron Mask**, 1929 (Leon Bary); Knights of the Queen, 1958 (Domenico Modugno); La loca historia de los tres mosqueteros, 1983 (Millan Salcedo); Lady in the Iron Mask, 1952 (Steve Brodie); Les 3 Mousquetaires, 1953 (Jean Martinelli); Les trois mousquetaires, 1959 (made-for-TV; Jean Chevrier); Les trois mousquetaires ou L'escrime ne paie pas, 1979 (made-for-TV; Serge Maillat); Les trois mousquetaires: Premiere epoque—Les ferrets de la reine, 1961 (Georges Descrieres); The Magnavox Theater, 1950 (TV series; "The Three Musketeers," 1950 episode: John Hubbard); **The**

Man in the Iron Mask, 1939 (Bert Roach); Mask of the Musketeers, 1963 (Giacomo Rossi-Stuart); Milady and the Three Musketeers, 2004 (made-for-TV; Guillaume Depardieu); **The Musketeer**, 2001 (Jan-Gregor Kremp); The Musketeers, 2014 (TV series; Tom Burke); Os tres Mosqueteiros, 1957 (TV series; Walter Stuart); Three and a Half Musketeers, 1957 (Luis Aldas); The Three Musketeers, 1916 (Alfred Hollingsworth); **The Three Musketeers**, 1921 (Leon Bary); Three Musketeers, 1932 (Henri Rollan); The Three Musketeers, 1935 (Paul Lukas); The Three Musketeers, 1939 (Douglas Dumbrille); The Three Musketeers, 1945 (Roberto Airaldi); **The Three Musketeers**, 1948 (Van Heflin); The Three Musketeers, 1954 (TV series; Roger Delgado); The Three Musketeers, 1966 (TV miniseries; Jeremy Young); **The Three Musketeers**, 1974 (Oliver Reed); **The Three Musketeers**, 1993 (Kiefer Sutherland); The Three Musketeers, 2007 (Lars Bom voiceover); The Three Musketeers, 2011 (Matthew Macfedyen); Vengeance of the Three Musketeers, 1961 (Georges Descrieres); Vingt ans apre, 1922 (Henri Rollan); Tri musketyri, 1983 (TV miniseries; Alois Svehlik); Tri mushketera, 2013 (Yuriy Chursin); Young Blades, 2001 (Scott Hickman).

Atlas (Greek god condemned to hold upon his shoulders earth and sky): Hercules in New York, 1970 (Dennis Tinerino); Jason and the Argonauts, 2000 (TV miniseries; Joseph Gatt); The Storyteller: Greek Myths, 1990- (TV miniseries; Pat Roach); Ulysses 31, 1981-1982 (TV series; Jean-Claude Ballard).

August A. Topaze (mild-mannered, honest teacher, who is used by crooked politicians and becomes a colossal swindler in Marcel Pagnol's satirical 1928 play): Mr. Topaze [aka: I Like Money], 1962 (Peter Sellers); **Topaze**, 1933 (John Barrymore); Topaze, 1935 (Louis Jouvet); Topaze, 1936 (Alexandre Arnaudy); Topaze, 1952 (Fernandel); Topaze, 1960 (TV miniseries; Marcos Zucker); Topaze, 1963 (made-for-TV; Allan Edwall); Topaze, 1988 (TV miniseries; Raul Solnado); Topaze, 1994 (made-for-TV; Francis Perrin).

Aunt Polly (character in the books of Mark Twain): The Adventures of Huckleberry Finn, 1955 (made-for-TV; Elizabeth Patterson); The Adventures of Mark Twain, 1985 (Marley Stone voiceover); **The Adventures of Tom Sawyer**, 1938 (May Robson); The Adventures of Tom Sawyer, 1960 (TV series; Betty Hardy); The Adventures of Tom Sawyer, 1986 (Jane Harders voiceover); The Adventures of Tom Sawyer and Huckleberry Finn, 1982 (made-for-TV; Yekaterina Vasilyeva); Climax!, 1954-1958 (TV series; "Adventures of Huckleberry Finn," 1955 episode: Elizabeth Patterson); Huck and Tom, 1918 (Edythe Chapman); Huckleberry Finn, 1920 (Edythe Chapman); Huckleberry Finn, 1931 (Clara Blandick); Huckleberry Finn, 1975 (made-for-TV; Sarah Selby); Huckleberry Finn and His Friends, 1979-1980 (TV series; Brigitte Horney); Les aventures de Tom Sawyer, 1968 (TV miniseries; Lina Carstens); The New Adventures of Huckleberry Finn, 1968-1969 (TV series; Anne Bellamy); The Secret Adventures of Tom Sawyer and Huck Finn, 1982 (made-for-TV; Allyn Ann McLerie); Shirley Temple's Storybook, 1958-1961 (TV series; "Tom and Huck," 1960 episode: Janet Blair); Tom and Huck, 1995 (Amy Wright); Tom Sawyer, 1917 (Edythe Chapman); **Tom Sawyer**, 1930 (Clara Blandick); **Tom Sawyer**, 1973 (Celeste Holm); Tom Sawyer, 1973 (made-for-TV; Jane Wyatt); Tom Sawyer, 2011 (Heike Makatsch); Tom Sawyer & Huckleberry Finn, 2015 (Christine Kaufmann); Tom Sawyer, Detective, 1938 (Clara Blandick); Wishbone, 1995-1999 (TV series; "A Tail in Twain," two 1995 episodes: Sharon Bunn).

Auntie Mame (Mame Dennis; eccentric, madcap woman epitomizing the wild antics of the 1920s as depicted in the 1955 novel by Patrick Dennis, who based this charming character on his own eccentric aunt, Marion Tanner): **Auntie Mame**, 1958 (Rosalind Russell); Mame, 1974 (Lucille Ball).

Ayesha (aka: She; a 2,000-year-old beautiful woman who attains everlasting life by walking through the flame of youth while ruling a mythical African kingdom as depicted in H. Rider Haggard's 1887 novel *She, A History of Adventure*): She, 1916 (Alice Delysia); She, 1917 (Valeska Suratt); She, 1925 (Betty Blythe); **She**, 1935 (Helen Gahagan); She, 1965 (Ursula Andress); The Vengeance of She, 1968 (Olga Schoberova); She, 2005 (Ophelie Winter).

Bacchus (Dionysus; Greek god of alcohol): The Bacchae, 2002 (Rich Werner); Death in Venice, 1990 (made-for-TV; Alan Opie voiceover); Hercules, 1998-1999 (TV series; Dom DeLuise voiceover); Mythic Warriors: Guardians of the Legend, 1998- (TV series; Stephen Ouimette); Night Life of the Gods, 1935 (George Hassell); Percy Jackson & the Olympians: The Lightning Thief, 2010 (Luke Camilleri); Percy Jackson: Sea of Monsters, 2013 (Stanley Tucci); Rome in a Day, 2008 (Seth Gorden); Vamping Venus, 1928 (Russ Powell); Xena: Warrior Princess, 1995-2001 (TV series; Anthony Ray Parker); Young Hercules, 1998-1999 (TV series; Kevin Smith).

Baron Munchausen (fictional character based on the tall tales by German nobleman and teller of such fantasy stories, Baron Hieronymus Carl Friedrich von Munchausen, 1720-1797): The Adventures of Baron Munchausen, 1943 (Hans Albers); The Adventures of Baron Munchausen, 1982 (TV series; Sergei Tseits); **The Adventures of Baron Munchausen**, 1989 (John Neville); Baron Munchausen, 1940 (Vlasta Burian); Der Schuft der den Munchausen schrieb, 1979 (made-for-TV; Ferdy Mayne); Hollywood Party, 1934 (Jack Pearl); Les fabuleuses aventures du legendaire Baron de Munchausen, 1979 (Dominique Paturel); Meet the Baron, 1933 (Henry Kolker, Jack Pearl); Moon Madness, 1984 (Dominique Paturel voiceover); The Outrageous Baron Munchausen, 1964 (Milos Kopecky).

Bat Girl (aka: Barbara Gordon; fictional comic book character in the Batman series): Batgirl: Year One, 2009- (animated TV series; Kate Higgins); Batman, 1966-1968 (TV series; Yvonne Craig); The Batman, 2004-2008 (TV series; Danielle Judovits voiceover); **Batman and Robin**, 1997 (Alicia Silverstone); Batman: The Animated Series, 1992-1995 (TV series; Melissa Gilbert voiceover); Batman: The Brave and the Bold, 2008-2011 (animated TV series; Mae Whitman voiceover); The Batman/Superman Hour, 1968-1969 (animated TV series; Jane Webb voiceover); Birds of Prey, 2002-2003 (TV series; Dina Meyer); Gotham Girls, 2000- (TV series; Tara Strong); The New Adventures of Batman, 1977-1978 (animated TV series; Melendy Britt voiceover); The New Batman Adventures, 1997-1999 (TV series; Tara Strong voiceover); The Sky Has Fallen, 2009 (Amanda Russell); Super Best Friends Forever, 2012- (animated TV series; Tara Strong voiceover).

Batman (aka: Bruce Wayne; fictional comic book character): The All-New Super Friends Hour, 1977-1978 (animated TV series; Olan Soule voiceover); Batman, 1943 (serial; Lewis Wilson); Batman, 1966-1968 (TV series; Adam West); **Batman**, 1989 (Michael Keaton); The Batman, 2004-2008 (TV series; Rino Romano voiceover); Batman and Robin, 1949 (serial; Robert Lowery); **Batman and Robin**, 1997 (George Clooney); **Batman Begins**, 2005 (Christian Bale); Batman Beyond, 1999-2001 (TV series; Kevin Conroy voiceover); **Batman Forever**, 1995 (Val Kilmer); **Batman: Mask of the Phantasm**, 1993 (Kevin Conroy voiceover); **Batman Returns**, 1992 (Michael Keaton); Batman Revealed, 2012 (Dave Stewart); Batman: The Animated Series, 1992-1995 (TV series; Kevin Conroy voiceover); Batman: The Brave and the Bold, 2008-2011 (animated TV series; Diedrich Bader voiceover); The Batman/Superman Hour, 1968-1969 (animated TV series; Olan Soule voiceover); The Batman Superman Movie: World's Finest, 1997 (made-for-TV; Kevin Conroy voiceover); Batman: The Movie, 1966 (Adam West); Batman The Movie, 1999 (made-for-TV; Kevin Conroy voiceover); Batman v Superman: Dawn of Justice, 2016 (Ben Affleck); Batman with Robin the Wonder Boy, 1969 (TV series; Olan Soule

John Neville as Baron Munchausen in *The Adventures of Baron Munchausen*, **1989.**

voiceover); Challenge of the Super Friends, 1978- (animated TV series; Olan Soule voiceover); **The Dark Knight**, 2008 (Christian Bale); The Dark Knight Falls, 2015 (Mark Hendricks); **The Dark Knight Rises**, 2012 (Christian Bale); Gotham, 2014- (TV series; David Mazouz); Justice League, 2001-2006 (TV series; Kevin Conroy voiceover); Legends of the Superheroes, 1979 (TV series; Adam West); **The Lego Movie**, 2014 (Will Arnett voiceover); The New Adventures of Batman, 1977-1978 (animated TV series; Adam West voiceover); The New Batman Adventures, 1997-1999 (TV series; Kevin Conroy voiceover); Super Friends, 1973-2011 (animated TV series; Olan Soule voiceover); Super Friends, 1980-1983 (animated TV series; Olan Soule voiceover); Super Friends: The Legendary Super Powers Show, 1984- (animated TV series; Adam West voiceover); The Super Powers Team: Galactic Guardians, 1985- (animated TV series; Adam West voiceover); Superman, 1996-2000 (TV series; Kevin Conroy voiceover); The World's Greatest Super Friends, 1979- (animated TV series; Olan Soule voiceover); Young Justice, 2010- (animated TV series; Bruce Greenwood voiceover).

Beau Geste (Michael "Beau" Geste; British hero in the Foreign Legion appearing in the 1924 adventure novel *Beau Geste* by P.C. Wren): **Beau Geste**, 1926 (Ronald Colman; Maurice Murphy as young Beau); **Beau Geste**, 1939 (Gary Cooper; Donald O'Connor as young Beau); Beau Geste, 1966 (Guy Stockwell); Beau Geste, 1982- (TV miniseries; Benedict Taylor; Paul Hawkins as young Beau); The Last Remake of Beau Geste, 1977 (Michael York; Philip Bollard and Nicholas Bridge as young Beau in separate ages).

Becky Sharp (gold-digging social-climbing female who seduces upper-class men to advance herself in the satirical 1847-1848 novel *Vanity Fair* by William Makepeace Thackeray): BBC Sunday-Night Theatre, 1950-1959 (TV series; "Vanity Fair," 1950 episode; Belle Chrystall); Becky Sharp, 1935 (Miriam Hopkins); The Goodyear-Philco Television Playhouse, 1948-1956 (TV series; "Becky Sharp," 1949 episode: Claire Luce); La fiera delle vanita, 1967- (TV miniseries; Adriana Asti); Novela, 1963-1978 (TV series; "La feria de las vanidades," 1973 episode: Fiorella Faltoyano); Vanity Fair, 1915 (Minnie Maddern Fiske); Vanity Fair, 1923 (Mabel Ballin); Vanity Fair, 1932 (Myrna Loy); Vanity Fair, 1956-1957 (TV series; Joyce Redman); Vanity Fair, 1961 (TV series; Diane Cilento); Vanity Fair, 1967- (TV miniseries; Susan Hampshire); Vanity Fair, 1987- (TV series; Eve Matheson); Vanity Fair, 1998 (TV miniseries; Natasha Little); Vanity Fair, 2004 (Reese Witherspoon).

Becky Thatcher (character in the books of Mark Twain): The Adventures of Mark Twain, 1985 (Michele Mariana voiceover); **The Adventures**

Angela Lansbury, Karolyn Grimes and George Sanders (as Bel Ami) in *The Private Affairs of Bel Ami*, 1947.

of Tom Sawyer, 1938 (Ann Gillis); The Adventures of Tom Sawyer, 1960 (TV series; Janina Faye); The Adventures of Tom Sawyer, 1980 (TV series; Kelko Han voiceover); The Adventures of Tom Sawyer, 1986 (Jane Harders voiceover); The Adventures of Tom Sawyer and Huckleberry Finn, 1982 (made-for-TV; Mariya Mironova); Back to Hannibal: The Return of Tom Sawyer and Huckleberry Finn, 1990 (made-for-TV; Megan Follows); Huck and Tom, 1918 (Clara Horton); Huckleberry Finn, 1920 (Thelma Salter); Huckleberry Finn, 1931 (Mitzi Green); Huckleberry Finn and His Friends, 1979-1980 (TV series; Holly Findlay); Les aventures de Tom Sawyer, 1968 (TV miniseries; Lucia Ocrain); The New Adventures of Huckleberry Finn, 1968-1969 (TV series; Lu Ann Haslam); Sawyer and Finn, 1983 (made-for-TV; P.J. Soles); Shirley Temple's Storybook, 1958-1961 (TV series; "Tom and Huck,' 1960 episode: Ruthie Robinson); Tom and Huck, 1995 (Rachel Leigh Cook); Tom Sawyer, 1917 (Clara Horton); **Tom Sawyer**, 1930 (Mitzi Green); **Tom Sawyer**, 1973 (Jodie Foster); Tom Sawyer, 1973 (made-for-TV; Karen Pearson); Tom Sawyer, 2011 (Magali Greif); Tom Sawyer & Huckleberry Finn, 2015 (Katherine McNamara); The United States Steel Hour, 1953-1963 (TV series; "Tom Sawyer," 1956 episode: Bennye Gatteys); Wishbone, 1995-1999 (TV series; "A Tail in Twain," two 1995 episodes: Shea Fowler).

Bel Ami (aka: George Duroy; character created by Guy de Maupassant, an unscrupulous rogue who exploits women to rise in 19th-Century Parisian society): Bel Ami, 1939 (Willi Forst); Bel Ami, 1947 (Armando Calvo); Bel Ami, 1955 (Jean Danet); Bel Ami, 1968 (made-for-TV; Helmut Griem); Bel Ami, 1971- (TV series; Robin Ellis); Bel Ami, 1979- (TV series; Corrado Pani); Bel Ami, 1983- (TV series; Jacques Weber); Bel Ami, 2005 (made-for-TV; Sagamore Stevenin); Bel Ami, 2012 (Robert Pattinson); Bel Ami Der Frauenheld von Paris, 1955 (Johannes Heesters); **The Private Affairs of Bel Ami**, 1947 (George Sanders).

Beth March (one of four teenage sisters who finds romance as she and her siblings mature in a Massachusetts household during the American Civil War as profiled in Louisa May Alcott's timeless novel, *Little Women*, 1868-1869): The Ford Theatre Hour, 1948-1951 (TV series; "Little Women," 1949 episode: Peggy Ann Garner; Patricia Kirkland); Good Wives, 1958 (TV series; Diana Day); Great Performances, 1971- (TV series; "Little Women," 2001 episode: Stacey Tappan); Little Women, 1917 (Muriel Meyers); Little Women, 1918 (Lillian Hall); **Little Women**, 1933 (Jean Parker); **Little Women**, 1949 (Margaret O'Brien); Little Women, 1950- (TV series; Norah Gorsen); Little Women, 1958 (TV series; Diana Day); Little Women, 1958 (made-for-TV; Margaret O'Brien); Little Women, 1970 (TV miniseries; Sarah Craze); Little Women, 1978 (TV miniseries; Eve Plumb); **Little**

Women, 1994 (Claire Danes); Matinee Theatre, 1955-1958 (TV series; "Little Women," 1956 episode: Arianne Ulmer); NBC Special Treat, 1975-1986 (TV series; "Little Women," 1976 episode: Susan Pillarre); Studio One in Hollywood, 1948-1958 (TV series; "Little Women: Jo's Story," 1950 episode: June Dayton; "Little Women: Meg's Story," 1950 episode: June Dayton).

Bill Sykes (or "Sikes"; a fictional character in the Charles Dickens novel *Oliver Twist*, a murderous criminal operating in 19th-Century London, England): The DuPont Show of the Month, 1957-1961 (TV series; "Oliver Twist," 1959 episode: Tom Clancy); Oliver & Company, 1988 (Robert Loggia voiceover); Oliver Twist, 1912 (Mortimer Martine); Oliver Twist, 1916 (Hobart Bosworth); Oliver Twist, 1919 (Gyula Szoreghy); **Oliver Twist**, 1922 (George Siegmann); Oliver Twist, 1933 (William "Stage" Boyd); **Oliver Twist**, 1951 (Robert Newton); Oliver Twist, 1962 (TV miniseries; Peter Vaughan); **Oliver!**, 1968 (Oliver Reed); Oliver Twist, 1982 (made-for-TV; Tim Curry); Oliver Twist, 1985 (TV miniseries; Michael Attwell); Oliver Twist, 1997 (made-for-TV; David O'Hara); Oliver Twist, 1999 (TV miniseries; Andy Serkis); **Oliver Twist**, 2005 (Jamie Foreman); Oliver Twist, 2007 (TV series; Tom Hardy); Oliver Twist Jr., 1921 (G. Raymond Nye).

Blue Fairy (a fairy who enables a wooden marionette to transform into a real boy, a fictional character in the 1883 children's novel *The Adventures of Pinocchio* by Italian author Carlo Collodi): The Adventures of Pinocchio, 1972 (TV miniseries; Gina Lollobrigida); Geppetto, 2000 (made-for-TV; Julia Louis-Dreyfus); Geppetto's Secret, 2005 (Claudia Christian); Happily Ever After: Fairy Tales for Every Child, 1995-2000 (TV series; "Pinocchio," 1997 episode: Della Reese); The New Adventures of Pinocchio, 1999 (Gemma Gregory); **Pinocchio**, 1940 (Evelyn Venable voiceover); Pinocchio, 1957 (made-for-TV; Fran Allison); Pinocchio, 1965 (made-for-TV; Jodi Williams); Pinocchio, 1968 (made-for-TV; Anita Gillette); Pinocchio, 1969 (Marianne Wunscher); Pinocchio, 1978 (Vittoria Febbi voiceover); Pinocchio, 1978 (TV series; Rhoda Lewis); Pinocchio, 2002 (Nicoletta Braschi); Pinocchio, 2008 (made-for-TV; Violante Placido); Pinocchio, 2012 (Lucrezia Marricchi voiceover); Pinocchio and the Emperor of the Night, 1987 (Rickie Lee Jones voiceover); Welcome Back Pinocchio, 2007 (Emanuela Rossi).

Bob Cratchit (meek-mannered clerk who slaves for miserly businessman Ebenezer Scrooge in Charles Dickens' 1843 novella, *A Christmas Carol*): The Alcoa Hour, 1955-1957 (TV series; "The Stingiest Man in Town," 1956 episode; Martyn Green); **A Christmas Carol**, 1938 (Gene Lockhart); A Christmas Carol, 1950 (made-for-TV; John Ruddock); **A Christmas Carol**, 1951 (Mervyn Johns); A Christmas Carol, 1977 (made-for-TV; Clive Merrison); A Christmas Carol, 1979 (musical; Don Torcerson); A Christmas Carol, 1981 (made-for-TV; Mark Murphey); A Christmas Carol, 1982 (made-for-TV; J. Patrick Martin); A Christmas Carol, 1984 (made-for-TV; David Warner); A Christmas Carol, 1999 (made-for-TV; Richard E. Grant); A Chirstmas Carol, 2000 (made-for-TV; Michael Maloney); A Christmas Carol, 2009 (animated; Gary Oldman voiceover); A Christmas Carol, 2015 (Dave Hudson); A Christmas Carol at Ford's Theatre, 1979 (made-for-TV; Geoff Garland); A Christmas Carol: The Concert, 2013 (made-for-TV; Scott Coulter); A Christmas Carol: 50thAnniversary, 2015 (James Betteridge); Christmas Carol: The Movie, 2001 (animated; Rhys Ifans voiceover); A Christmas Carol: The Musical, 2004 (made-for-TV; Edward Gower); Dickensian, 2015- (TV series; Robert Wilfort); A Diva's Christmas Carol, 2000 (made-for-TV; Brian McNamara); Ebenezer, 1998 (made-for-TV; Albert Schultz); Fireside Theatre, 1949-1955 (TV series; "A Christmas Carol," 1951 episode: Norman Barrs); General Electric Theater, 1953-1962 (TV series; "The Trail to Christmas," 1957 episode; Sam Edwards); The Gospel According to Scrooge, 1983 (made-for-TV; Robert Whitesel); Mr. Magoo's Christmas Carol, 1962 (made-for-TV; Jack Cassidy); Mr. Scrooge, 1964 (made-for-TV; Alfie Bass); Mr. Scrooge to See You, 2013

(Ken T. Williams); Ms. Scrooge, 1997 (made-for-TV; John Bourgeois); **The Muppet Christmas Carol**, 1992 (Steve Whitmire voiceover as Kermit the Frog); The Philco-Goodyear Television Playhouse, 1948-1956 (TV series; "A Christmas Carol," 1948 episode: James MacColl); Ponds Theatre, 1953- (TV series; "A Christmas Carol," 1953 episode: Harry Townes); The Right to Be Happy, 1916 (John Cook); Scrooge, 1935 (Donald Calthrop); **Scrooge**, 1970 (David Collings); Scrooge, 1978 (made-for-TV; Ray Hunt); Shower of Stars, 1954-1958 (TV series; "A Christmas Carol," 1954 and 1956 episodes; Bob Sweeney); The Stingiest Man in Town, 1978 (animated made-for-TV; Sonny Melendrez voiceover).

Bors (legendary knight in the King Arthur legend in 6th-Century Britain, who quested for the Holy Grail): The Adventures of Sir Galahad, 1949 (serial; Charles King); **King Arthur**, 2004 (Ray Winstone); The Legend of King Arthur, 1979 (TV series; Godfrey James); **Monty Python and the Holy Grail**, 1975 (Terry Gilliam); Morte d'Arthur, 1980 (made-for-TV; Roy Jones).

Bulldog Drummond (Hugh Drummond; ex-WWI British officer turned sleuth and first appearing in H.C. McNeile's *Bulldog Drummond*, 1920): Alias Bulldog Drummond [aka: Bulldog Jack], 1935 (Atholl Fleming); Arrest Bulldog Drummond, 1939 (John Howard); Bulldog Drummond, 1923 (Carlyle Blackwell); Bulldog Drummond, 1929 (Ronald Colman); Bulldog Drummond at Bay, 1937 (John Lodge); Bulldog Drummond at Bay, 1947 (Ron Randell); Bulldog Drummond Comes Back, 1937 (John Howard); Bulldog Drummond Escapes, 1937 (Ray Milland); Bulldog Drummond in Africa, 1938 (John Howard); **Bulldog Drummond Strikes Back**, 1934 (Ronald Colman); Bulldog Drummond Strikes Back, 1947 (Ron Randell); Bulldog Drummond's Bride, 1939 (John Howard); Bulldog Drummond's Peril, 1938 (John Howard); Bulldog Drummond's Revenge, 1937 (John Howard); Bulldog Drummond's Secret Police, 1939 (John Howard); Bulldog Drummond's Third Round, 1925 (Jack Buchanan); Calling Bulldog Drummond, 1951 (Walter Pidgeon); The Challenge, 1948 (Tom Conway); Deadlier Than the Male, 1967 (Richard Johnson); The Return of Bulldog Drummond, 1934 (Ralph Richardson); Rheingold Theatre, 1953-1957 (TV series; "Bulldog Drummond and the Ludlow Affair," 1957 episode; Robert Beatty); Some Girls Do, 1969 (Richard Johnson); Temple Tower, 1930 (Kenneth MacKenna); 13 Lead Soldiers, 1948 (Tom Conway).

Buzz Lightyear (animated spaceman toy character): **Toy Story**, 1995 (Tim Allen); Toy Story 3, 2010 (Tim Allen voiceover); Toy Story 2, 1999 (Tim Allen voiceover).

Camille (ill-starred beautiful courtesan portrayed in the Alexander Dumas novel of 1848): Armchair Theatre, 1956-1974 (TV series; "The Lady of Camellias," 1958 episode: Ann Todd); Camille, 1917 (Theda Bara); Camille, 1921 (Alla Nazimova); Camille, 1926 (Norma Talmadge); **Camille**, 1937 (Greta Garbo); Camille, 1984 (made-for-TV; Greta Scacchi); Festival, 1963-1964 (TV series; "The Lady of the Camellias," 1964 episode: Billie Whitelaw); La dama de las camelias, 1944 (Lina Montes); La dame aux camelias, 1935 (Yvonne Printemps); La dame aux camelias, 1953 (Micheline Presle); La dame aux camelias, 1962 (made-for-TV; Yori Bertin); La dame aux camelias, 1972 (made-for-TV; Ludmilla Tcherina); La dame aux camelias, 1998 (made-for-TV; Cristiania Reali); La signora delle camelie, 2005 (made-for-TV; Francesca Neri); The Lady of the Camellias, 1976- (TV series; Kate Nelligan); Lady of the Camelias, 1981 (Caria Fracci); Marguerite Gautier, 1963 (made-for-TV; Andrea Domburg); The Philco-Goodyear Television Playhouse, 1948-1956 (TV series; "Camille," 1948 episode: Judith Eveyln).

Captain America (aka: Steve Rogers; fictional comic book superhero): The Adventures of the Spirit, 1963 (TV miniseries; Bob Burns); Agent

Chris Evans as Captain America in *Captain America: The First Avenger,* 2011.

Carter, 2015 (TV series; Walker Roach as radio actor Captain America); **The Avengers**, 2012 (Chris Evans); **Avengers: Age of Ultron**, 2015 (Chris Evans); Avengers Assemble!, 2010- (TV series; Kevin Spooner); The Avengers: Earth's Mightiest Heroes, 2010-2012 (TV series; Brian Bloom); Captain America, 1944 (serial; Dick Purcell); Captain America, 1966 (TV series; Sandy Becker); Captain America, 1979 (made-for-TV; Reb Brown); Captain America, 1990 (Matt Salinger); **Captain America: The First Avenger**, 2011 (Chris Evans); **Captain America: The Winter Soldier**, 2014 (Chris Evans); Captain America II: Death Too Soon, 1979 (made-for-TV; Reb Brown); Heroes Crossing, 2010 (Checc Musolino); The Marvel Super Heroes, 1966 (TV series; Sandy Becker); Spider-Man, 1994-1998 (TV series; David Hayter); The Super Hero Squad Show, 2009-2011 (TV series; Tom Kenny).

Captain Marvel (fictional comic book superhero): Adventures of Captain Marvel, 1941 (serial; Tom Tyler); The Avengers: Earth's Mightiest Heroes, 2010-2012 (TV series; Roger Craig Smith); Batman: The Brave and the Bold, 2008-2011 (animated TV series; John DeVito voiceover); Heroes Crossing, 2010 (Jeremy Martin); The Kid Super Power Hour with Shazam!, 1981-1982 (TV series; Barry Gordon); Legends of the Superheroes, 1979 (TV series; Garret Craig); The Secrets of ISIS, 1975-1976 (TV series; John Davey); Shazam!, 1974-1977 (TV series; Jackson Bostwick, John Davey); The Super Hero Squad Show, 2009-2011 (TV series; Ty Burrell); Young Justice, 2010- (animated TV series; Chad Lowe voiceover).

Captain Hook (fictional character created by Scottish playwright J. M. Barrie in his 1904 play, "Peter Pan, or The Boy Who Wouldn't Grow Up)": The Adventures of Peter Pan, 1989 (TV series; Chikao Ohtsuka); **Finding Neverland**, 2004 (Tim Potter); **Hook**, 1991 (Dustin Hoffman); Neverland, 2003 (Gary Kelley); Neverland, 2011 (TV series; Rhys Ifans); Once upon a Time, 2011- (TV series; Colin O'Donoghue); Peter Pan, 1924 (Ernest Torrence); **Peter Pan**, 1953 (Hans Conreid voiceover); Peter Pan, 1955 (Cyril Ritchard); Peter Pan, 1960 (made-for-TV; Cyril Ritchard); Peter Pan, 1976 (made-for-TV; Danny Kaye); Peter Pan, 2000 (made-for-TV; Paul Schoeffler); Peter Pan, 2003 (Jason Isaacs); Peter Pan and the Pirates, 1990-1991 (TV series; Tim Curry); Return to Never Land, 2002 (Corey Burton voiceover).

Captain Nemo (aka: Dakkar; the egotistical anti-war scientific genius created by Jules Verne in his 1870 novel *Twenty Thousand Leagues under the Sea*): The Amazing Captain Nemo, 1978 (made-for-TV; Jose Ferrer); Captain Nemo, 1975 (Vladislav Dvorzhetsky); Captain Nemo and the Underwater City, 1970 (Robert Ryan); Das Phantom des grossen Zeltes, 1954 (Helmut von Hofe); JV: The Extraordinary Adventures of

Dorothy Dandridge (as a modern-day Carmen) and Harry Belafonte in *Carmen Jones*, 1954.

Jules Verne, 2013- (animated TV series; Hope Brown voiceover); The League of Extraordinary Gentlemen, 2003 (Naseeruddin Shah); The Mysterious Island, 1929 (Lionel Barrymore); Mysterious Island, 1951 (Leonard Penn); **Mysterious Island**, 1961 (Herbert Lom); The Mysterious Island, 1974 (Omar Sharif); Mysterious Island, 1995 (TV series; John Bach); Mysterious Island, 2005 (Patrick Stewart); Mysterious Island, 2012 (Mark Sheppard as young Nemo; William Morgan Sheppard as old Nemo); Nemo taucht auf, 1965 (made-for-TV; Hubert Suschka); Tales of Tomorrow, 1951-1953 (TV series; "Twenty Thousand Leagues under the Sea," two 1952 episodes: Thomas Mitchell); 20,000 Leagues under the Sea, 1916 (Allen Holubar); **20,000 Leagues under the Sea**, 1954 (James Mason); 20,000 Leagues under the Sea, 1997 (made-for-TV; Ben Cross); 20,000 Leagues under the Sea, 1997 (made-for-TV; Michael Caine); The Undersea Adventures of Captain Nemo, 1974- (TV series; Len Carlson).

Carmen (seducing femme fatale, who is killed by her lover, and depicted in the 1845 novella by Prosper Merimee and in the 1875 opera by Georges Bizet): Carmen, 1915 (Theda Bara); Carmen, 1915 (Geraldine Farrar); Carmen, 1918 (Pola Negri); Carmen, 1926 (Raquel Meller); Carmen, 1932 (Marguerite Namara); Carmen, 1946 (Vivianne Romance); Carmen, 1969 (Grace Bumbry); Carmen, 1980 (made-for-TV; Teresa Berganza); Carmen, 1983 (Laura del Sol); Carmen, 1984 (Julia Migenes); Carmen, 1987 (made-for-TV; Agnes Baltsa); Carmen, 1989 (made-for-TV; Maria Ewing); Carmen, 1999 (made-for-TV; Charlotte Hellekant); Carmen, 2002 (Anne Sofie von Otter); Carmen, 2003 (Paz Vega); Carmen, 2003 (Olga Filippovna); Carmen, 2003 (made-for-TV; Marina Domashenko); Carmen, 2004 (made-for-TV; Beatrice Uria-Monzon); Carmen, Baby, 1967 (Uta Levka); Carmen de la Ronda [aka: A Girl Against Napoleon], 1962 (Sara Montiel); Carmen di Trastevere, 1962 (Giovanna Ralli); **Carmen Jones**, 1954 (modern-day version; Dorothy Dandridge); Carmen on Ice, 1990 (made-for-TV; Katarina Witt); The Loves of Carmen, 1927 (Dolores del Rio); The Loves of Carmen, 1948 (Rita Hayworth); Nights in Andalusia, 1938 (Imperio Argentina); Pride and Vengeance, 1967 (Tina Aumont); U-Carmen eKhayelitsha, 2005 (Pauline Malefane).

Cat and the Fiddle (Mother Goose character): **Babes in Toyland**, 1934 (Pete Gordon).

Cat Woman (fictional comic book character): Batman, 1966-1968 (TV series; Julie Newmar; Eartha Kitt); The Batman, 2004-2008 (TV series; Gina Gershon voiceover); **Batman Returns**, 1992 (Michelle Pfeiffer); Batman Revealed, 2012 (Kelly Weston); Batman: The Brave and the Bold, 2008-2011 (animated TV series; Nika Futterman voiceover); Bat-

man: The Movie, 1966 (Lee Meriwether); Batman: The Animated Series, 1992-1995 (TV series; Adrienne Barbeau voiceover); Gotham Girls, 2000- (TV series; Adrienne Barbeau); The New Batman Adventures, 1997-1999 (TV series; Adrienne Barbeau voiceover).

Caterpillar (fictional character from the 1865 novel Alice's Adventures in Wonderland by British author Lewis Carroll): Adventures in Wonderland, 1992-1994 (TV series; Wesley Mann); Alice, 2009 (TV miniseries; Harry Dean Stanton); Alice in Wonderland, 1931 (Jimmy Rosen); **Alice in Wonderland**, 1933 (Ned Sparks); **Alice in Wonderland**, 1951 (Richard Haydn voiceover); Alice in Wonderland, 1955 (made-for-TV; Noel Leslie); Alice in Wonderland, 1966 (made-for-TV; Michael Redgrave); Alice in Wonderland, 1976 (Roberto Granados); Alice in Wonderland, 1982 (made-for-TV; Jason McLean); Alice in Wonderland, 1985 (made-for-TV; Sammy Davis Jr.); Alice in Wonderland, 1985 (TV series; John Barron); Alice in Wonderland, 1986 (made-for-TV; four 30-minute segments; Roy Macready); Alice in Wonderland, 1999 (made-for-TV; Ben Kingsley); **Alice in Wonderland**, 2010 (Alan Rickman); Alice through the Looking Box, 1960 (made-for-TV; Donald Pleasence); Alice's Adventures in Wonderland, 1972 (Ralph Richardson); Alice's Adventures in Wonderland, 2011 (made-for-TV; Eric Underwood); Alice's Adventures in Wonderland and Through the Looking Glass, 1948 (made-for-TV; Cameron Miller); Dreamchild, 1985 (Steve Whitmire, Frank Middlemass); Great Performances, 1971- (TV series; Fritz Weaver); Kraft Theatre, 1947-1958 (TV series; "Alice in Wonderland," 1954 episode; Chandler Cowles); Once upon a Time in Wonderland, 2013 (TV series; Iggy Pop); Unsuk Chin: Alice in Wonderland, 2007 (Stefan Schneider); The Wednesday Play, 1964-1970 (TV series; "Alice," 1965 episode; Keith Campbell).

Catherine Earnshaw (Cathy; beautiful star-crossed lover of Heathcliff, a poor boy who becomes rich, but loses the woman of his heart when she tragically dies, her ghost haunting him thereafter until they are reunited at death as depicted in Emily Bronte's 1847 novel, *Wuthering Heights*): BBC Sunday-Night Theatre, 1950-1959 (TV series; "Wuthering Heights," 1953 episode: Yvonne Mitchell); Broadway Television Theatre, 1952-1954 (TV series; "Wuthering Heights," 1953 episode; Meg Mundy); The DuPont Show of the Month, 1957-1961 (TV series; "Wuthering Heights," 1958 episode: Yvonne Furneaux; Patty Duke as young Cathy); Heathcliff, 1997 (made-for-TV; Helen Hobson); Matinee Theatre, 1955-1958 (TV series; "Wuthering Heights," 1955 episode: Peggy Webber; Shelley Fabares as young Cathy; "Wuthering Heights," 1957 episode: Barbara Rush; Reba Waters as young Cathy); Wuthering Heights, 1920 (Ann Trevor; Colette Brettel; Baby Twinkles [Florence Hunter] as young Cathy); **Wuthering Heights**, 1939 (Merle Oberon; Sarita Wooten [Wooton] as young Cathy); Wuthering Heights, 1948 (made-for-TV; Katharine Blake); Wuthering Heights, 1962 (made-for-TV; Claire Bloom); Wuthering Heights, 1967 (TV series; Angela Scoular; June Liversedge as young Cathy); Wuthering Heights, 1970 (Anna Calder-Marshall); Wuthering Heights, 1978 (TV miniseries; Kay Adshead; Maria Swailes; Francesca Gerrard); Wuthering Heights, 1983 (Irasema Dilian); Wuthering Heights, 1992 (Juliette Binoche; Jessica Hennell as young Cathy); Wuthering Heights, 1998 (made-for-TV; Orla Brady; Kadie Savage as young Cathy); Wuthering Heights, 2009 (TV miniseries; Charlotte Riley; Rebecca Night; Alexandra Pearson as young Cathy); Wuthering Heights, 2012 (Kaya Scodelario; Shannon Beer as young Cathy).

Cesar (owner of a Marseilles quayside bistro who befriends Fanny, a fish-seller deserted by her seafaring lover): **Cesar**, 1936 (Raimu); **Fanny**, 1948 (Raimu); **Fanny**, 1961 (Charles Boyer); Fanny, 2008 (made-for-TV; Gilles David); Fanny, 2014 (Daniel Auteuil); La trilogie Marseillaise: Cesar, 2000 (made-for-TV; Roger Hanin); La trilogie Marseillaise: Fanny, 2000 (made-for-TV; Roger Hanin); La trilogie Marseillaise: Marius, 2000 (made-for-TV; Roger Hanin); **Marius**, 1933 (Raimu); Marius, 2014 (Daniel Auteuil); Pagnol, 1977 (TV series; Ko van Dijk); Port of Seven Seas, 1938 (Wallace Beery).

Charles Darnay (one of the chief protagonists in the 1859 novel *A Tale of Two Cities* by Charles Dickens): The DuPont Show of the Month, 1957-1961 (TV series; "A Tale of Two Cities," 1958 episode: Denholm Elliott); The Only Way, 1927 (Frederick Cooper); The Only Way, 1948 (made-for-TV; Hatton Duprez); The Plymouth Playhouse, 1953 (TV series; "A Tale of Two Cities," two 1953 episodes: Carleton Young); A Tale of Two Cities, 1917 (William Farnum); **A Tale of Two Cities**, 1935 (Donald Woods); A Tale of Two Cities, 1957 (TV miniseries; Edward de Souza); A Tale of Two Cities, 1958 (Paul Guers); A Tale of Two Cities, 1958 (made-for-TV; Alexander Young); A Tale of Two Cities, 1965 (TV series; Nicholas Pennell); A Tale of Two Cities, 1980 (TV miniseries; Paul Shelley); A Tale of Two Cities, 1980 (made-for-TV; Chris Sarandon); A Tale of Two Cities, 1989 (TV miniseries; Xavier Deluc).

Charles Dreyfus (French police commissioner of the Paris Surete who is inadvertently harassed, embarrassed and compromised by his bumbling subordinate, Inspector Clouseau; see Inspector Clouseau, this index): Curse of the Pink Panther, 1983 (Herbert Lom); The Pink Panther, 2006 (Kevin Kline); The Pink Panther 2, 2009 (John Cleese); **The Pink Panther Strikes Again**, 1976 (Herbert Lom); **The Return of the Pink Panther**, 1975 (Herbert Lom); **Revenge of the Pink Panther**, 1978 (Herbert Lom); **A Shot in the Dark**, 1964 (Herbert Lom); Trail of the Pink Panther, 1982 (Herbert Lom).

Charlie Chan (clever Chinese detective, the fictional creation of Earl Derr Biggers, first appearing in the 1925 *Saturday Evening Post* serial): The Amazing Chan and the Chan Clan, 1972 (animated TV series; Key Luke voiceover); Behind That Curtain, 1929 (E.L. Park); The Black Camel, 1931 (Warner Oland); Black Magic, 1944 (Sidney Toler); Castle in the Desert, 1942 (Sidney Toler); Charlie Chan and the Curse of the Dragon Queen, 1981 (Peter Ustinov); Charlie Chan at Monte Carlo, 1937 (Warner Oland); Charlie Chan at the Circus, 1936 (Warner Oland); Charlie Chan at the Olympics, 1937 (Warner Oland); **Charlie Chan at the Opera**, 1936 (Warner Oland); **Charlie Chan at the Race Track**, 1936 (Warner Oland); Charlie Chan at the Wax Museum, 1940 (Sidney Toler); Charlie Chan at Treasure Island, 1939 (Sidney Toler); **Charlie Chan Carries On**, 1931 (Warner Oland); Charlie Chan in Black Magic, 1944 (Sidney Toler); **Charlie Chan in Egypt**, 1935 (Warner Oland); Charlie Chan in Honolulu, 1938 (Sidney Toler); Charlie Chan in London, 1934 (Warner Oland); Charlie Chan in Panama, 1940 (Sidney Toler); Charlie Chan in Paris, 1935 (Warner Oland); Charlie Chan in Reno, 1939 (Sidney Toler); Charlie Chan in Rio, 1941 (Sidney Toler); Charlie Chan in Shanghai, 1935 (Warner Oland); Charlie Chan in the City of Darkness, 1939 (Sidney Toler); Charlie Chan in the Secret Service, 1944 (Sidney Toler); Charlie Chan on Broadway, 1937 (Warner Oland); Charlie Chan's Chance, 1932 (Warner Oland); Charlie Chan's Courage, 1934 (Warner Oland); Charlie Chan's Greatest Case, 1933 (Warner Oland); Charlie Chan's Murder Cruise, 1940 (Sidney Toler); **Charlie Chan's Secret**, 1936 (Warner Oland); The Chinese Cat, 1944 (Sidney Toler); The Chinese Parrot, 1927 (Sojin Kamiyama); The Chinese Ring, 1947 (Roland Winters); Dangerous Money, 1946 (Sidney Toler); Dark Alibi, 1946 (Sidney Toler); Dead Men Tell, 1941 (Sidney Toler); Docks of New Orleans, 1948 (Roland Winters); Eran trece [Spanish version of Charlie Chan Carries On], 1931 (Manuel Arbo); The Feathered Serpent, 1948 (Roland Winters); The Golden Eye, 1948 (Roland Winters); The House without a Key, 1926 (serial; George Kuwa); The Jade Mask, 1945 (Sidney Toler); Murder over New York, 1940 (Sidney Toler); The Mystery of the Golden Eye, 1948 (Roland Winters); The New Adventures of Charlie Chan, 1957 (TV series; J. Carrol Naish); The Red Dragon, 1946 (Sidney Toler); The Return of Charlie Chan, 1979 (made-for-TV; Ross Martin); The Scarlet Clue, 1945 (Sidney Toler); Shadows over Chinatown, 1946 (Sidney Toler); The

Keye Luke (as son Lee Chan) and Warner Oland (as Charlie Chan) in *Charlie Chan at the Opera,* 1936.

Shanghai Chest, 1948 (Roland Winters); The Shanghai Cobra, 1945 (Sidney Toler); Sky Dragon, 1949 (Roland Winters); The Trap, 1947 (Sidney Toler).

Charon (or Kharon; in Greek mythology; the skeletal ferryman who takes the souls of recently deceased to the world of the dead): Atlantis, 2013-2015 (TV series; "Pandora's Box," 2013 episode: Trevor Allan Davies); Dante 01, 2008 (Gerald Laroche); Dante's Inferno, 2007 (Michael Coleman); Hellhounds, 2009 (Theodore Danetti, Arthur Grosser); Hercules, 1998-1999 (animated TV series; John Kassir); Hercules in the Underworld, 1994 (made-for-TV; Michael Hurst); Hercules: The Legendary Journeys, 1995-1999 (TV series; Michael Hurst); Highway to Hell, 1992 (Kevin Peter Hall); Hulk and the Agents of S.M.A.S.H., 2013 (TV series; "The Tale of Hercules," 2013 episode: Fred Tatasciore); MythQuest, 2001 (TV series; 2001 episode: Richard Strange); Percy Jackson & the Olympians: The Lightning Thief, 2010 (Julian Richings); A Storyteller: Greek Myths, 1990- (TV miniseries; Trevor Peacock); A TV Dante, 1989- (TV miniseries; Robert Eddison); Orpheus & Eurydice, 2000 (Joseph Gatt); Sabrina: The Teenage Witch, 1996-2003 (TV series; 2001 episode: E. J. Callahan); Xena: Warrior Princess, 1995-2001 (TV series; Michael Hurst); Young Hercules, 1998-1999 (TV series; Michael Hurst).

Cheshire Cat (fictional character from the 1865 novel Alice's Adventures in Wonderland by British author Lewis Carroll): Adventures in Wonderland, 1992-1994 (TV series; Richard Kuhlman); Alice at the Palace, 1982 (made-for-TV; Rodney Hudson); Alice in Wonderland, 1931 (Tom Corless); **Alice in Wonderland**, 1933 (Richard Arlen); Alice in Wonderland, 1949 (Felix Aylmer voiceover); **Alice in Wonderland**, 1951 (Sterling Holloway voiceover); Alice in Wonderland, 1976 (Ruben Fraga); Alice in Wonderland, 1982 (made-for-TV; Leslye Orr); Alice in Wonderland, 1985 (made-for-TV; Telly Savalas); Alice in Wonderland, 1986 (made-for-TV; four 30-minute segments; Michael Wisher); Alice in Wonderland, 1999 (made-for-TV; Whoopi Goldberg); **Alice in Wonderland**, 2010 (Stephen Fry); Alice in Wonderland or What's a Nice Kid Like You Doing in a Place Like This?, 1966 (animated made-for-TV; Sammy Davis Jr.); Alice's Adventures in Wonderland, 1972 (Roy Kinnear); Alice's Adventures in Wonderland and through the Looking Glass, 1948 (made-for-TV; Morris Sweden); Great Performances, 1971- (TV series; Geoffrey Holder); Kraft Theatre, 1947-1958 (TV series; "Alice in Wonderland," 1954 episode: Arthur Treacher); Miyuki-chan in Wonderland, 1995- (TV miniseries; Ai Orikasa); Unsuk Chin: Alice in Wonderland, 2007 (Pia Komsi, Julia Rempe).

Chingachgook (chief and last living survivor of the extinct Mohican In-

Robert Barrat (as Chingachgook), Randolph Scott (Hawkeye) and Philip Reed (Uncus) in *The Last of the Mohicans*, 1936.

dian tribe, a branch of the Delaware Indians, a character in James Fenimore Cooper's *Leatherstocking Tales*): The Deerslayer, 1978 (made-for-TV; Ned Romero); Fall of the Mohicans, 1965 (Jose Marco); Hawkeye, 1994- (TV series; Rodney A. Grant); Hawkeye and the Last of the Mohicans, 1957- (TV series; Lon Chaney Jr.); Hawkeye, the Pathfinder, 1973- (TV miniseries; John Abineri); **The Last of the Mohicans**, 1920 (Theodore Lorch); The Last of the Mohicans, 1932 (Hobart Bosworth); **The Last of the Mohicans**, 1936 (Robert Barrat); The Last of the Mohicans, 1971 (TV miniseries; John Abineri); The Last of the Mohicans, 1975 (animated made-for-TV; John Doucette voiceover); Last of the Mohicans, 1977 (made-for-TV; Ned Romero); **The Last of the Mohicans**, 1992 (Russell Means); The Leatherstocking Tales, 1984 (TV miniseries; Roger Hill); Pathfinder, 1996 (made-for-TV; Graham Greene).

Cinderella (folk character from the story *The Little Glass Slipper*; also see Fairy Godmother, Prince Charming, this index): Carry On Christmas, 1969 (made-for-TV; Barbara Windsor); Christmas at Walt Disney World, 1978 (TV special; Danielle Spencer); Christmas Night of One Hundred Stars, 1986 (TV special; Janet Dibley); Cinderella, 1914 (Mary Pickford); Cinderella, 1947 (Yanina Zhejmo); Cinderella, 1947 (TV miniseries; Julia Bretton); **Cinderella**, 1950 (Ilene Woods voiceover); Cinderella, 1950 (made-for-TV; Sally Ann Howes, Lois Green); Cinderella, 1957 (made-for-TV; Julie Andrews); Cinderella, 1958 (made-for-TV; June Thorburn); Cinderella, 1965 (made-for-TV; Lesley Ann Warren); Cinderella, 1966 (Rita-Maria Nowotny); Cinderella, 1969 (Antoinette Sibley); Cinderella, 1977 (Cheryl Smith); Cinderella, 1986 (made-for-TV; Francoise Joullie); Cinderella, 1989 (made-for-TV; Petra Vigna); Cinderella, 1997 (made-for-TV; Brandy Norwood); Cinderella, 2000 (made-for-TV; Marcella Plunkett); Cinderella, 2000 (made-for-TV; Sam Janus [Samantha Womack]); Cinderella, 2010 (made-for-TV; Emilia Schule); Cinderella, 2011 (made-for-TV; Aylin Tezel); **Cinderella**, 2015 (Lily James); Cinderella...Frozen in Time, 1994 (made-for-TV; Dorothy Hamill); Cinderella; The Shoe Must Go On, 1986 (made-for-TV; Cheryl Baker); Cinderella: Single Again, 2000 (Sarah Chalke); Cinderella 3D, 2012 (Alexandra Lamy voiceover); Faerie Tale Theatre, 1982-1987 (TV series; "Cinderella," 1985 episode; Jennifer Beals); The Glass Slipper, 1955 (Leslie Caron); Great Performances, 1971- (TV series; "Cinderella," 1985 episode: Evelyn Cisneros); Happily Ever After: Fairy Tales for Every Child, 1995-2000 (TV series; "Cinderella," 1995 episode: Daphne Zuniga); Hey Cinderella!, 1969 (made-for-TV; Belinda Montgomery); A Kiss for Cinderella, 1925 (Betty Bronson); A Kiss for Cinderella, 1959 (made-for-TV; Jeannie Carson); Once upon a Brothers Grimm, 1977 (made-for-TV; Stephanie Steele); Once upon a Time, 1973- (TV series; Adrienne Posta); The Sleeping Princess, 1939 (made-for-TV; Elizabeth Miller); The Wonderful World of the Brothers Grimm, 1962 (Pamela Baird); **The Slipper and the Rose**, 1976 (Gemma Craven).

Circe (goddess of magic, sorceress, witch, enchantress in Greek mythology; also see Ulysses, this index): Atlantis, 2013- (TV series; Lucy Cohu); Biblioteca di Studio Uno: Odissea, 1964 (made-for-TV; Elena Sedlak); Circe, the Enchantress, 1924 (Mae Murray); Gladiators of Rome, 2013 (Daniela Abbruzzese); Hercules, 1983 (Mirella D'Anelo); Hercules, 1998-1999 (TV series; "Hercules and the Song of Circe," 1998 episode; Idina Menzel voiceover); Mythic Warriors: Guardians of the Legend, 1998- (TV series; "Ulysses and Circe," 1998 episode; Torri Higginson); Odissea, 1968 (TV miniseries; Juliette Mayniel); The Odyssey, 1997- (TV series; Bernadette Peters); Olympus, 2015- (TV series; Brenda McDonald); Toast with the Gods, 1995 (Tifani Bless); **Ulysses**, 1955 (Silvana Mangano); Vamping Venus, 1928 (Louise Fazenda).

Constance Bonacieux (fictional character; ill-fated lover of French swordsman D'Artagnan in the works of Alexander Dumas pere): Animated Three Musketeers, 1987 (TV series; Noriko Hidaka); Biblioteca di Studio Uno: I tre moschettieri, 1964 (made-for-TV; Jenny Luna); D'Artagnan, 1969 (TV miniseries; Paloma Matta); D'Artagnan, 1991 (made-for-TV; Mona Heftre); D'Artagnan et les trois mousquetaires, 2005 (Diana Amft); D'Artanyan i tri mushketyora, 1979 (TV series; Irina Alfyorova); De drie Musketiers, 1968 (made-for-TV; Gerda Marchand); Die Drie Musketiere, 2013 (Anna Starshenbaum); Family Classics: The Three Musketeers, 1960 (made-for-TV; Felicia Farr); The Four Charlots Musketeers, 1974 (Josephine Chaplin); The Four Musketeers, 1963 (Carla Marlier); **The Four Musketeers**, 1975 (Raquel Welch); The Glorious Musketeers, 1974 (Anna Gaylor voiceover); I tre moschettieri, 1991 (made-for-TV; Pamela Prati); **The Iron Mask**, 1929 (Marguerite De La Motte); La loca historia de los tres mosqueteros, 1983 (Adriana Ozores); Les quatre mousquetaires, 1934 (Mona Sem); Les trois mousquetaires ou L'escrime ne paie pas, 1979 (made-for-TV; Nicole Jamet); Les trois mousquetaires: Premiere epoque—Les ferrets de la reine, 1961 (Perrette Pradier); Milady and the Three Musketeers, 2004 (made-for-TV; Julie Depardieu); The Musketeers, 2014 (TV series; Tamla Kari); Os tres Mosqueteiros, 1957 (TV series; Maria Valeria); Three and a Half Musketeers, 1957 (Rosa Arenas); The Three Musketeers, 1916 (Rhea Mitchell); **The Three Musketeers**, 1921 (Marguerite De La Motte); The Three Musketeers, 1932 (Blanche Montel); The Three Musketeers, 1935 (Heather Angel); **The Three Musketeers**, 1948 (June Allyson); The Three Musketeers, 1954 (TV series; Clare Austin); The Three Musketeers, 1966 (TV miniseries; Kathleen Breck); **The Three Musketeers**, 1974 (Raquel Welch); **The Three Musketeers**, 1993 (Julie Delpy); The Three Musketeers, 2007 (Lene Maria Christiansen voiceover); The Three Musketeers, 2011 (Gabriella Wilde); Tri mushketera, 2013 (Anna Starshenbaum); Vengeance of the Three Musketeers, 1961 (Perrette Pradier).

The Corsican Brothers (Lucien and Mario Franchi, fictional Siamese twins separated at birth who live separate lives but who are emotionally and spiritually joined and who later reunite to suppress a tyrant, first appearing in Alexander Dumas' 1845 novel): Bandits of Corsica [akaA: The Return of the Corsican Brothers], 1953 (Richard Greene in dual roles); Double Impact, 1991 (modern-day version; Jean-Claude Van Damme in dual roles); The Corsican Brothers, 1917 (Henry Krauss in dual roles); The Corsican Brothers, 1920 (Dustin Farnum in dual roles); The Corsican Brothers, 1938 (Pierre Brasseur, Jacques Erwin); **The Corsican Brothers**, 1941 (Douglas Fairbanks Jr. in dual roles); The Corsican Brothers, 1955 (Antonio Vilar in dual roles); The Corsican Brothers, 1985 (made-for-TV; Trevor Eve); The Corsican Brothers, Lions of Corsica, 1961 (Geoffrey Horne in dual roles).

Cosmo Topper (meek-mannered banker who encounters two lively ghosts bent on liberating him from his hen-pecking wife and humdrum lifestyle as created in Thorne Smith's enormously popular 1926 novel): **Topper**, 1937 (Roland Young); Topper, 1953-1955 (TV series; Leo G. Carroll); Topper, 1979 (made-for-TV; Jack Warden); **Topper Returns**, 1941 (Roland Young); **Topper Takes a Trip**, 1938 (Roland Young).

The Cowardly Lion (a lion that is afraid of everything and becomes a devoted companion to Dorothy, a young girl from Kansas transported to a strange world in L. Frank Baum's iconic 1900 novel, *The Wonderful Wizard of Oz*): Journey Back to Oz, 1972 (animated; Milton Berle voiceover); The Muppets' Wizard of Oz, 2005 (Eric Jacobson as Fozzie Bear voiceover); The New Wizard of Oz, 1914 (Fred Woodward); Off to See the Wizard, 1967-1968 (animated TV series; Mel Blanc); The Wiz, 1978 (Ted Ross); The Wizard of Oz, 1925 (Spencer Bell); **The Wizard of Oz**, 1939 (Bert Lahr); The Wizard of Oz, 1982 (animated; Thick Wilson voiceover); The Wizard of Oz, 1990-1991 (animated TV series; Charles Adler voiceover); The Wizard of Oz in Concert: Dreams Come True, 1995 (made-for-TV; Nathan Lane); The Wizard of Oz on Ice, 1996 (made-for-TV; Mark Richard Farrington); The Wizard of the Emerald City, 1994 (Vyacheslav Nevinnyy).

Cupid (Roman god of love; Eros in Greek mythology): The Illiac Passion, 1968 (Philip Fagan); In Performance, 1978- (TV series; "Orpheus in the Underworld," 1983 episode: Elizabeth Gale); Jacques Offenbach: Orpheus in the Underworld, 1997 (made-for-TV; Marie-Noelle de Callatay); Orphee aux enfers, 1997 (made-for-TV; Cassandre Berthon); Orpheus in der Unterwelt, 1975 (Mona Boxberger); The Triumph of Venus, 1918 (Bonnie Marie).

Cyrano de Bergerac (long-nosed, unlucky-at-love swordsman and poet created by playwright Edmond Rostand in 1897; also see Roxane, this index): BBC Play of the Month, 1965-1983 (TV series; 'Cyrano de Bergerac," 1968 episode: Eric Porter); Cyrano de Bergerac, 1923 (Pierre Magnier); Cyrano de Bergerac, 1946 (Claude Dauphin); **Cyrano de Bergerac**, 1950 (Jose Ferrer); Cyrano de Bergerac, 1960 (made-for-TV; Daniel Sorano); Cyrano de Bergerac, 1962 (made-for-TV; Christopher Plummer); Cyrano de Bergerac, 1975 (made-for-TV; Guus Hermus); Cyrano de Bergerac, 1978 (made-for-TV; Denis Ganio); Cyrano de Bergerac, 1985 (made-for-TV; Derek Jacobi); Cyrano de Bergerac, 1986 (made-for-TV; Josep Maria Flotats); **Cyrano de Bergerac**, 1990 (Gerard Depardieu); Cyrano de Bergerac, 2000 (made-for-TV; Klaus Maria Brandauer); Cyrano de Bergerac, 2007 (made-for-TV; Michel Vuillermoz); Cyrano de Bergerac, 2008 (Placido Domingo); Cyrano et d'Artagnan, 1964 (Jose Ferrer); Great Performances, 1971- (TV series; "Cyrano de Bergerac," 1974 episode: Peter Donat; "Cyrano de Bergerac," 2008 episode: Kevin Kline); The Philco-Goodyear Television Playhouse, 1948-1956 (TV series; "Cyrano de Bergerac," 1949 episode; Jose Ferrer); Producers' Showcase, 1954-1957 (TV series; "Cyrano de Bergerac," 1955 episode: Jose Ferrer); Schlitz Playhouse, 1951-1959 (TV series; "The Sword," 1957 episode; Fredd Wayne).

Daisy Buchanan (spoiled wife of millionaire who dallies with former lover Jay Gatsby, a romantic bootlegger of the 1920s, a character in the classic 1925 novel, *The Great Gatsby*, by pantheon author F. Scott Fitzgerald): **The Great Gatsby**, 1926 (Lois Wilson); **The Great Gatsby**, 1949 (Betty Field); **The Great Gatsby**, 1974 (Mia Farrow); The Great Gatsby, 2001 (made-for-TV; Mira Sorvino); **The Great Gatsby**, 2013 (Carey Mulligan); Playhouse 90, 1956-1961 (TV series; "The Great Gatsby," 1958 episode: Jeanne Crain); Robert Montgomery Presents, 1950-1957 (TV series; "The Great Gatsby," 1955 episode; Phyllis Kirk).

D'Artagnan (great swordsman and character in the fictional works of Alexander Dumas pere): Animated Three Musketeers, 1987 (TV series;

Jose Ferrer (as Cyrano) and Mala Powers (as Roxane) in *Cyrano de Bergerac,* **1950.**

Miguel Guilherme); At Sword's Point, 1952 (Cornel Wilde as D'Artagnan Jr.); Biblioteca di Studio Uno: I tre moschettieri, 1964 (made-for-TV; Alberto Lupo); Cyrano et d'Artagnan, 1964 (Jean-Pierre Cassel); D'Artagnan, 1969 (TV miniseries; Dominque Paturel); D'Artagnan, 1991 (made-for-TV; Christophe Malavoy); D'Artagnan amoureux, 1977 (TV miniseries; Nicolas Silberg); D'Artagnan et les trois mousquetaires, 2005 (Vincent Elbaz); D'Artanyan i tri mushketyora, 1979 (TV series; Mikhail Boyarskiy); De drie Musketiers, 1968 (made-for-TV; Senne Rouffaer); Die Drie Musketiere, 2013 (Rinal Mukhametov); Family Classics: The Three Musketeers, 1960 (made-for-TV; Maximilian Schell); The Four Charlots Musketeers, 1974 (Jean Valmont); The Four Musketeers, 1963 (Georges Riviere); **The Four Musketeers**, 1975 (Michael York); The Glorious Musketeers, 1974 (Francis Perrin voiceover); I tre moschettieri, 1991 (made-for-TV; Marco Columbro); Il colpo segreto di d'Artagnan, 1963 (George Nader); **The Iron Mask**, 1929 (Douglas Fairbanks Sr.); Knights of the Queen, 1958 (Jeff Stone); La loca historia de los tres mosqueteros, 1983 (Jose Martinez Blanco voiceover); Lady in the Iron Mask, 1952 (Louis Hayward); Les quatre mouquetaires, 1934 (Rittche); Les 3 Mousquetaires, 1953 (Georges Marchal); Les trois mousquetaires, 1959 (made-for-TV; Jean-Paul Belmondo); Les trois mousquetaires ou L'escrime ne paie pas, 1979 (made-for-TV; Francis Perrin); Les trois mousquetaires: Premiere epoque—Les ferrets de la reine, 1961 (Gerard Barry); The Magnavox Theater, 1950 (TV series; "The Three Musketeers," 1950 episode: Robert Clarke); **The Man in the Iron Mask**, 1939 (Warren William); Mask of the Musketeers, 1963 (Tony Zamperla); Milady and the Three Musketeers, 2004 (made-for-TV; Florent Pagny); **The Musketeer**, 2001 (Justin Chambers; Max Dolbey as young D'Artagnan); The Musketeers, 2014 (TV series; Luke Pasqualino); Os tres Mosqueteiros, 1957 (TV series; Jose Parisi); Three and a Half Musketeers, 1957 (Tin Tan [German Valdes]); The Three Musketeers, 1916 (Orrin Johnson); **The Three Musketeers**, 1921 (Douglas Fairbanks Sr.); Three Musketeers, 1932 (Aime Simon-Girard); The Three Musketeers, 1935 (Walter Abel); The Three Musketeers, 1939 (Don Ameche); The Three Musketeers, 1945 (Armando Bo); **The Three Musketeers**, 1948 (Gene Kelly); The Three Musketeers, 1954 (TV series; Laurence Payne); The Three Musketeers, 1966 (TV miniseries; Jeremy Brett); **The Three Musketeers**, 1974 (Michael York); The Three Musketeers, 1986 (made-for-TV; Ivar Kants voiceover); **The Three Musketeers**, 1993 (Chris O'Donnell); The Three Musketeers, 2007 (Nicolaj Kopernikus voiceover); The Three Musketeers, 2011 (Logan Lerman); Vengeance of the Three Musketeers, 1961 (Garard Barray); Vingt ans apres, 1922 (Jean Yonnel); Tri musketyri, 1983 (TV miniseries; Jan Censky); Tri mushketera, 2013 (Rinal Mukhametov); Young Blades, 2001 (Hugh Dancy).

Walter Huston (as Scratch), Edward Arnold (Webster) and James Craig in *The Devil and Daniel Webster*, 1941.

David Balfour (youth created by Robert Louis Stevenson in his 1886 novel, *Kidnapped*, and who becomes involved in many adventures while attempting to secure his rightful inheritance): Kidnapped, 1917 (Raymond McKee); **Kidnapped**, 1938 (Freddie Bartholomew); Kidnapped, 1948 (Roddy McDowall); Kidnapped, 1952- (TV series; John Fraser); Kidnapped, 1956- (TV series; Leo Maguire); Kidnapped, 1960 (James MacArthur); Kidnapped, 1963- (TV miniseries; Ian Cullen); Kidnapped, 1970 (Werner Kanitz); **Kidnapped**, 1971 (Lawrence Douglas); Kidnapped, 1978- (TV miniseries; Ekkehardt Belle); Kidnapped, 1986 (animated version; Matthew Fargher voiceover); Kidnapped, 1995 (made-for-TV; Brian McCardie); Kidnapped, 2005 (made-for-TV; James Anthony Pearson).

David Copperfield (youth who endures cruelty and kindness as he grows to manhood, one of Charles Dickens' best-known fictional characters, albeit partly autobiographical, and first appearing in the 1850 novel of the same name): Armchair Theatre, 1956-1974 (TV series; "Young David," 1959 episode; Martin Stephens); David Copperfield, 1913 (Reginald Sheffield as the boy; Kenneth Ware as the man); David Copperfield, 1922 (Martin Herzberg as the boy; Gorm Schmidt as the man); **David Copperfield**, 1935 (Freddie Bartholomew as the boy; Frank Lawton as the man); David Copperfield, 1958 (TV series; Marcio Trunkl); David Copperfield, 1965 (TV miniseries; Giancarlo Giannini); David Copperfield, 1966- (TV series; Ian McKellen); David Copperfield, 1970 (made-for-TV; Alistair Mackenzie as the boy; Robin Phillips as the man); David Copperfield, 1974- (TV miniseries; Jonathan Kahn as the boy; David Yelland as the man); David Copperfield, 1986- (TV miniseries; David Dexter as the boy; Colin Hurley as the man); David Copperfield, 1993 (animated made-for-TV; Julian Lennon); David Copperfield, 1999- (TV miniseries; Daniel Radcliffe as the boy; Ciaran McMenamin as the man); David Copperfield, 2000 (made-for-TV; Max Dolbey as the boy; Hugh Dancy as the man); David Copperfield, 2009 (made-for-TV; Christian Frasacco as the boy; Giorgio Pasotti as the man); Fredric March Presents Tales from Dickens, 1958- (TV series; several 1958 episodes: Martin Stephens; several 1959 episodes: William Russell); Robert Montgomery Presents, 1950-1957 (TV series; "David Copperfield," 1954 episode: David Cole).

Desdemona (character in "Othello," by William Shakespeare, c.1601, the wife of military leader Othello, who is wrongly accused of adultery and murdered by her jealous husband): BBC Sunday-Night Theatre, 1950-1959 (TV series; "Othello," 1950 episode: Joan Hopkins); **A Double Life**, 1947 (Signe Hasso portraying an actress on stage as Desdemona); Encounter [General Motors Presents], 1952-1961 (TV series; "Othello," 1953 episode: Peggi Loder); Masterpiece Playhouse, 1950-

(TV series; "Othello," 1950 episode; Olive Deering); Otello, 1948 (made-for-TV; Licia Albanese); Otello, 1958 (Rosanna Carteri); Otello, 1959 (made-for-TV; Gabriella Tucci); Otello, 1962 (made-for-TV; Renata Tebaldi); Otello, 1965 (made-for-TV; Sena Jurinac); Otello, 1974 (Mirella Freni); Otello, 1976 (made-for-TV; Mirella Freni); **Otello**, 1986 (Katia Ricciarelli); Otello, 2012 (Zvetelina Vassileva); Othello, 1914 (Cesira Lenard); Othello, 1918 (Ellen Korth); Othello, 1923 (Ica von Lenkeffy); Othello, 1937 (made-for-TV; Diana Wynward); **Othello** [1952], 1955 (Suzanne Cloutier); Othello, 1955 (made-for-TV; Rosemary Harris); Othello, 1958 (made-for-TV; Carine Christian); Othello [1955], 1960 (Irina Skobtseva); Othello, 1962 (made-for-TV; Francine Berge); Othello, 1965 (made-for-TV; Frances McDonald); **Othello**, 1965 (Maggie Smith); Othello, 1968 (made-for-TV; Heidelinde Weis); Othello, 1969 (made-for-TV; Chris Lomme); Othello, 1979 (made-for-TV; Patricia Lesieur); Othello, 1980 (Audrey Branker); Othello, 1981 (made-for-TV; Penelope Wilton); Othello, 1989 (made-for-TV; Joanna Weinberg); **Othello**, 1995 (Irene Jacob); The Philco-Goodyear Television Playhouse, 1948-1956 (TV series; "Othello," 1953 episode: Olive Deering).

Devil (Lucifer; Nick; Old Nick; Satan; Scratch): The Acid Eaters, 1968 (Buck Kartalian); Angel and the Devil, 1946 (Enzo Biliotti); Angel Heart, 1987 (Robert De Niro); **Angel on My Shoulder**, 1946 (Claude Rains); Angels in the Infield, 2000 (made-for-TV; Colin Fox); **Alias Nick Beal**, 1949 (Ray Milland); The Anti-Christ [aka: Tempter], 1978 (Carla Gravina); Army from Hell, 2014 (Richard Mason); Back from Hell, 1993 (Don Reum); Bait, 1954 (Cedric Hardwicke); Band of Drivers, 2011 (Robert Poirier); Beauty and the Devil, 1952 (Michel Simon); Bedazzled, 1967 (Peter Cook); Bedazzled, 2000 (Elizabeth Hurley, Lex Lang); Beyond the Door [aka: The Devil within Her], 1975 (Juliet Mills); The Big Show-Off, 1945 (Paul Hurst); Blue Exorcist: The Movie, 2012 (Hiroshi Kamiya); Boardwalk, 1979 (Roger Campo); The Book of Life, 1998 (Thomas J. Ryan); Boston Blackie and the Law, 1946 (Eugene Borden); Brimstone and Treacle, 1982 (Sting); **Cabin in the Sky**, 1943 (Rex Ingram as Lucifer Jr.); The Chosen One, 2007 (Tim Curry); **Cinderella**, 1950 (June Foray); The Company of Wolves, 1984 (Terence Stamp); Constantine, 2005 (Peter Stormare); Crossroads, 1986 (Robert Judd); Damien: Omen II, 1978 (Jonathan Scott-Taylor); **Damn Yankees**, 1958 (Ray Walston); Damned on Earth, 2014 (Mika Metz); **Dante's Inferno**, 1935 (Noble Johnson, Ray Corrigan, Paul Schwegler, Aloha Porter); Dante's Inferno, 2007 (Paul Zaloom); **Deconstructing Harry**, 1997 (Dan Moran, Billy Crystal); Deep Breath, 2001 (Damien Odoul); Demon, Demon (aka: The Devil within Her; made-for-TV), 1975 (Juliet Mills); **The Devil and Daniel Webster** (aka: All That Money Can Buy), 1941 (Walter Huston); The Devil and Max Devlin, 1981 (Bill Cosby); The Devil and the Ten Commandments, 1963 (Claude Rich); The Devil in Love, 1968 (Vittorio Gassman, Mickey Rooney); The Devil Knows Why, 2003 (Oldrich Kaiser); The Devil May Well Laugh, 1960 (Walter Morath); The Devil with Hitler, 1942 (Alan Mowbray); The Devil's Advocate, 1997 (Al Pacino); The Devil's Carnival, 2012 (Terrance Zdunic); The Devil's Envoys, 1947 (Jules Berry); The Devil's Eye, 1961 (Stig Jarrel); The Devil's Messenger, 1962 (Lon Chaney, Jr.); The Devil's Partner, 1958 (Ed Nelson); The Devil's Rain, 1975 (Ernest Borgnine); The Devil's Three Golden Hairs, 1977 (Dieter Franke); The Devil's Toy, 1916 (Edwin Stevens); The Devil's Wedding Night, 1973 (Sarah Bay); Dirty Work, 1998 (Adam Sandler); Do or Die, 1921 (J.P. McGowan); Dr. Faustus, 1968 (Andreas Teuber); Dr. Faustus, 1983 (Bruce Gray); Doctor Faustus, 2012 (Nigel Cooke, Arthur Darvill); Don Juan in Hell, 1960 (made-for-TV; George C. Scott); **Don't Tempt Me**, 2001 (Gael Garcia Bernal); End of Days, 1999 (Gabriel Byrne); Enter the Devil, 1978 (Ivan Rassimov); The Entrance, 2006 (Frank Cassini); The Evil, 1978 (Victor Buono); **The Exorcist**, 1973 (Linda Blair possessed by a demon; Mercedes McCambridge as voiceover of demon); Exorcist: The Beginning, 2004 (Rupert Degas); The Exorcist III, 1990 (Colleen Dewhurst as voiceover of demon); The Exorcist II:

The Heretic, 1977 (Linda Blair possessed by a demon); Fatty Drives the Bus, 1999 (Scot Robinson); Faust, 1926 (Emil Jannings); Faust, 1952 (Michael Langdon); Faust, 1963 (Gustaf Gruendgens); Faust, 1964 (Roban Cody); Faust, 1967 (Jorj Voicu); Faust, 1980 (Monica Buford); Faust, 1982 (made-for-TV; Peter Fitz); Faust and the Devil, 1950 (Italo Tajo); Faustina, 1958 (Fernando Fernan Gomez); Feel the Motion, 1985 (Kurt Raab); The First and Last, 1996 (David Anthony Pizzuto); Flame and the Devil, 1952 (Aldo Silvani); **Flesh and Fantasy**, 1943 (Lane Chandler); The Gate of Fallen Angels, 2009 (Wolfgang Meyer); Ghost Rider, 2007 (Peter Fonda); G-Men from Hell, 2000 (Robert Goulet); Goblins and Good Luck 2, 2001 (Karel Gott); Going to Glory…Come to Jesus, 1946 (John Watts); **The Greatest Story Ever Told**, 1965 (Donald Pleasence); Harry and Harriet, 1992 (Charles Gray); Hatchet County, 2012 (Christy Johnson, Gregg Frucci); The Haunted, 2015 (Tyler Lueck); Haxan: Witchcraft through the Ages, 1922 (Benjamin Christiansen); **Heaven Can Wait**, 1943 (Laird Cregar); Heaven Is Hell, 2014 (Jack Schultz); The Heavenly Play, 1944 (Emil Fjellstrom); Holocaust 2000, 1978 (Simon Ward); House of Fallen, 2008 (Jeff Wincott); I Am Suzanne!, 1933 (Lionel Belmore); I Dream of Dracula, 2003 (Paul Dougherty); The Imaginarium of Doctor Parnassus, 2009 (Tom Waits); The Immortal Edward Lumley, 2013 (Mike Burnell); Inquisition, 1978 (Paul Naschy); Island of Swans, 1983 (Conny Hege); It Is Hell with the Princess, 2009 (Martin Stransky); The Jersey Devil, 2014 (Jack Mulcahy); Journey of Redemption, 2002 (Jules Willcox); The Joys of Jezebel, 1970 (Christopher Stone); **The Kid**, 1921 (Jack Coogan Sr.); **The King of Kings,** 1927 (Alan Brooks); **King of Kings**, 1961 (Ted de Corsia voiceover); The Knight of the Night, 1953 (Jean Servais); The Last Temptation of Christ, 1988 (Leo Marks); Leaves from Satan's Book (aka: Blade of Satan's Bog, silent), 1920 (Helge Nissen); Laugh Killer Laugh, 2015 (Jim Fletcher); Legend, 1985 (Tim Curry); Les visiteurs du soir, 1947 (Jules Berry); Letters from My Windmill, 1954 (Daxley); Little Nicky, 2000 (Harvey Keitel); Macario, 1961 (Jose Galvez); **Mad Max Beyond Thunderdome**, 1985 (Adam Willits); Marguerite of the Night, 1956 (Yves Montand); Martyr, 2006 (Christopher Dane); The Master and Margaret, 1980 (Alain Cuny); Meet Mr. Lucifer, 1953 (Stanley Holloway); Men Cry Bullets, 1999 (Jon Simanton); Midstream, 1929 (Leslie Brigham); The Milky Way, 1970 (Pierre Clementi); Mr. Frost, 1990 (Jeff Goldblum); The Night before Christmas, 1961 (Gregori Millyar); Night Train to Terror, 1985 (Tony Giorgio); Oh, God! You Devil, 1982 (George Burns); **The Omen**, 1976 (Harvey Stephens); Once Upon a Midnight Dreary, 2003 (Mike M. Burke); One Day Like Rain, 2007 (Alec Nemser); One Day with the Devil, 1945 (Andres Solar); One Hell of a Christmas, 2002 (Erik Holmey); One Hell of a Guy, 2000 (Michael York); Original Sin, 2001 (Thomas Jane); The Passion of the Christ, 2004 (Rosalinda Celentano); Peer Gynt, 1981 (made-for-TV; Didier Sandre); Petey Wheatstraw, 1977 (G. Tito Shaw); **The Phantom of the Opera**, 1925 (Alexander Bevani); The Phantom of the Opera, 1983 (made-for-TV; Ferenc Beganyi); The Phantom of the Opera, 1989 (John Ghavan); The Phantom of the Opera, 1998 (Tibor Nemes); The Photograph, 2003 (Marc Jeffreys); The Picture of Dorian Gray, 1916 (A.B. Imeson); The Private Lives of Adam and Eve, 1960 (Mickey Rooney); The Prophecy, 1995 (Viggo Mortensen); Ricky 6, 2000 (Gerald Wong); Ring of Darkness, 1979 (Ezio Miani); **San Francisco**, 1936 (Tudor Williams in stage performance); Satan's Touch, 1984 (Paul Davies); Scratch Harry, 1969 (Mio Domani); Second Time Lucky, 1984 (Robert Helpmann); The Sentinel, 1977 (Burgess Meredith); Shortcut to Happiness, 2004 (Jennifer Love Hewitt); Six Gun Savior, 2016 (Eric Roberts); A Smile in the Dark, 1991 (Helen Shaver); The Soldier's Tale, 1965 (Robert Helpmann); The Soldier's Tale, 1984 (Max von Sydow); The Soldier's Tale, 2010 (made-for-TV; Matthew Hart); Sons of Perdition, 2007 (David Simon); The Sorrows of Satan (silent), 1926 (Adolphe Menjou); South Park: Bigger, Larger & Uncut, 1998 (TV series; Frey Parker); Spawn, 1997 (Frank Welker); **Spirits of the Dead**, 1969 (Marina Yaru); The Story of Mankind, 1957 (Vincent Price); Suing the Devil, 2011 (Malcolm McDowell); The Suitcase, 2009 (Riley); Switch,

Warren Beatty as Dick Tracy in *Dick Tracy,* 1990.

1991 (Bruce Martyn Payne); **Tales from the Crypt**, 1972 (Ralph Richardson); Tales from the Hood, 1995 (Clarence Williams III); Tenacious D in the Pick of Destiny, 2006 (Dave Grohl); Thank You Satan, 1989 (Annie Legrand); **Three Sisters**, 1974 (Harry Fielder); Time Bandits, 1981 (David Warner); Torture Garden, 1968 (Burgess Meredith); Touched by an Angel, 1994-2003 (TV series; "In the Name of God," 1995 episode; John Schneider; "Breaking Bread," 1998 episode: Todd Rulapaugh); The Tragedy of Man, 2011 (Matyas Usztics); The Undead, 1957 (Richard Devon); Up in Smoke, 1957 (Byron Foulger); Under the Sun of Satan, 1989 (Philippe Pallut); Vengeance of the Zombies, 1973 (Paul Naschy); Wishful Thinking, 2010 (Amelie Blanc); **The Witches of Eastwick**, 1987 (Jack Nicholson).

Diana (Roman goddess of the hunt; Artemis in Greek mythology): Hercules in New York, 1970 (Diane Goble); In Performance, 1978- (TV series; "Orpheus in the Underworld," 1983 episode: Isobel Buchanan); Jacques Offenbach: Orpheus in the Underworld, 1997 (made-for-TV; Sonja Theodoridou); Night Life of the Gods, 1935 (Irene Ware); Orphee aux enfers, 1997 (made-for-TV; Virginie Pochon); Orpheus in der Unterwelt, 1975 (Helga Piur); Orpheus in the Underworld, 1961 (made-for-TV; Suzanne Steele); Rome in a Day, 2008 (Diana Butler); The Temple of Venus, 1923 (Helen Vigil); The Triumph of Venus, 1918 (Phyllis Beveridge).

Dick Tracy (tough, intelligent police detective created by comic strip artist Chester Gould in 1931): Dick Tracy, 1937 (serial; Ralph Byrd); Dick Tracy, 1945 (Morgan Conway); Dick Tracy, 1950-1952 (TV series; Morgan Conway); **Dick Tracy**, 1990 (Warren Beatty); Dick Tracy Meets Gruesome, 1947 (Morgan Conway); Dick Tracy Returns, 1938 (serial; Ralph Byrd); The Dick Tracy Show, 1961- (animated TV series; Everett Sloane voiceover); Dick Tracy Special, 2010 (made-for-TV; Warren Beatty); Dick Tracy vs. Crime Inc., 1941 (serial; Ralph Byrd); Dick Tracy vs. Cueball, 1946 (Morgan Conway); Dick Tracy's Dilemma, 1947 (Morgan Conway); Dick Tracy's G-Men, 1939 (serial; Ralph Byrd); The Famous Adventures of Mr. Magoo, 1964-1965 (TV series; "Mr. Magoo's Dick Tracy and the Mob," 1965 episode; Everett Sloane).

Dodo Bird (fictional character from the 1865 novel Alice's Adventures in Wonderland by British author Lewis Carroll): **Alice in Wonderland**, 1933 (Polly Moran); **Alice in Wonderland**, 1951 (Bill Thompson voiceover); Alice in Wonderland, 1966 (made-for-TV; Finlay Currie); Alice in Wonderland, 1985 (made-for-TV; Shelley Winters); Alice in Wonderland, 1986 (made-for-TV; four 30-minute segments; Ian Wallace); Alice in Wonderland, 1999 (made-for-TV; Pat Bayliss); **Alice in**

John Barrymore as the great lover, Don Juan, in *Don Juan*, 1926.

Wonderland, 2010 (Michael Gough); Alice's Adventures in Wonderland, 1972 (William Ellis).

Dolly Levi (scheming, but affable matchmaker, this character created by Thornton Wilder in his 1955 play, "The Matchmaker"): **Hello, Dolly!**, 1969 (Barbra Streisand); **The Matchmaker**, 1958 (Shirley Booth).

Don Juan (fictional character, a notorious libertine and romancer of countless women, invariably of noble birth, who first appears in a 14th-Century play): **Adventures of Don Juan**, 1949 (Errol Flynn); **Amadeus**, 1984 (Karel Fiala while performing as Don Giovanni in "Don Giovanni"); Armchair Theatre, 1956-1974 (TV series; "Death of Satan," 1958 episode; Alan Badel); BBC Play of the Month, 1965-1983 (TV series; "Don Juan in Hell," 1971 episode: Christopher Plummer); CBC Summer Theatre, 1955- (TV series; "The Return of Don Juan," 1955 episode: Patrick Macnee); **The Devil's Eye**, 1961 (Jarl Kulle); Die chinesische Mauer, 1965 (made-for-TV; Heinz Baumann); Don Juan, 2003 (Andrzej Seweryn); Don Juan ou Le festin de Pierre, 1965 (made-for-TV; Michel Piccoli); Don Giovanni, 1960 (made-for-TV; Mario Petri); Don Giovanni, 1961 (made-for-TV; Dietrich Fischer-Dieskau); Don Giovanni, 1967 (made-for-TV; Giorgio Albertazzi); Don Giovanni, 1970 (made-for-TV; Carmelo Bene); Don Giovanni, 1974 (made-for-TV; Ben Martin); Don Giovanni, 1977 (made-for-TV; Sherrill Milnes); Don Giovanni, 1978 (made-for-TV; Benjamin Luxon); Don Giovanni, 1979 (Ruggero Raimondi); Don Giovanni, 1982 (made-for-TV; Michael Devlin); Don Giovanni, 1987 (Hakan Hagegard); Don Giovanni, 1987 (made-for-TV; Samuel Ramey); Don Giovanni, 1987 (made-for-TV; Thomas Allen); Don Giovanni, 1990 (Eugene Perry); Don Giovanni, 1991 (Jeffrey Black); Don Giovanni, 1995 (made-for-TV; Gilles Cachemaille); Don Giovanni, 1997 (made-for-TV; Simon Keenlyside); Don Giovanni, 1999 (made-for-TV; Carlos Alvarez); Don Giovanni, 2000 (Bryn Terfel); Don Giovanni, 2001 (Rodney Gilfry); Don Giovanni, 2003 (made-for-TV; Peter Mattei); Don Giovanni, 2007 (made-for-TV; Simon Keenlyside); Don Giovanni, 2008 (made-for-TV; Simon Kennelyside); Don Giovanni, 2009 (made-for-TV; Christopher Maltman); Don Giovanni, 2010 (Mariusz Kwiecien); Don Giovanni, 2010 (made-for-TV; Gerald Finley); Don Giovanni, 2011 (Teddy Tahu Rhodes); Don Giovanni, 2011 (made-for-TV; Peter Mattei); Don Juan, 1922 (Hans Adalbert Schlettow); **Don Juan**, 1926 (John Barrymore); Don Juan, 1946 (made-for-TV; David King-Wood); Don Juan [aka: The Loves of Don Juan], 1950 (Antonio Vilar); Don Juan, 1956 (Cesare Danova; Alfred Poell singing voice for Don Juan); Don Juan, 1956 (Erno Crisa); Don Juan, 1965 (made-for-TV; Will Quadflieg); Don Juan, 1972 (made-for-TV; Horst Drinda); Don Juan, 1973 (made-for-TV; Henning Moritzen); Don Juan, 1978 (made-for-TV; Josep Maria Flotats);

Don Juan, 1987 (made-for-TV; Thorsten Flinck); Don Juan, 1997- (TV miniseries; Jose Coronado); Don Juan, 1998 (Jacques Weber); Don Juan, 2011 (Nick Cordero); Don Juan in Hell, 1960 (made-for-TV; Hurd Hatfield); Don Juan in Hell, 1991 (Fernando Guillen); Don Juan, My Dear Ghost (1990; Juan Luis Galiardo); Don Juan (Or If Don Juan Were a Woman), 1976 (Brigitte Bardot); Don Juan revient de guerre, 1968 (made-for-TV; Jean Rochefort); Don Juan Tenorio, 1922 (Fortunio Bonanova); Don Juan Tenorio, 1937 (Rene Cardona); Don Juan Tenorio, 1952 (Enrique Diosdado); Don Juan tulee sodasta, 1967 (made-for-TV; Helge Herala); The Errol Flynn Theatre, 1956 (TV series; "1000th Night of Don Juan," 1956 episode; Errol Flynn); Great Performances, 1971- (TV series; "Don Giovanni Unmasked," 2001 episode; Dmitri Hvorostovsky); I, Don Giovanni, 2009 (Borja Quiza); ITV Play of the Week, 1955-1974 (TV series; "Don Juan in Hell," 1962 episode: Alan Badel); La dame fantome, 1968 (made-for-TV; Gamil Ratib); La rebellion de los fantasmas, 1949 (Rudy del Moral); Loves of Don Juan, 1942 (Adriano Rimoldi); Men Think Only of That, 1954 (Jean-Marie Amato); The Metropolitan Opera Presents, 1977- (TV series; "Don Giovanni," 1978 episode: James Morris; "Don Giovanni," 1990 episode: Samuel Ramey); Mozart's Don Giovanni, 1955 (Cesare Siepi); Nights and Loves of Don Juan, 1971 (Robert Hoffmann); Omnibus, 1952-1961 (TV series; "The Last Night of Don Juan," 1953 episode: Fredric March); The Private Life of Don Juan, 1934 (Douglas Fairbanks Sr.); The Wednesday Play, 1964-1970 (TV series; "The Snow Ball," 1966 episode: Patrick Allen).

Don Quixote (fictional character, a deluded self-appointed knight out to achieve impossible deeds of valor who is profiled in Miguel de Cervantes' 1605 novel, *The Ingenuous Gentleman Don Quixote of La Mancha*): BBC Play of the Month, 1965-1983 (TV series; "The Adventures of Don Quixote," 1973 episode: Rex Harrison); CBS Television Workshop, 1952- (TV series; "Don Quixote," 1952 episode: Boris Karloff); Der Mann von La Mancha, 1994 (made-for-TV; Karl Merkatz); Don de la mancha, 1980 (TV miniseries; Kenji Utsumi, Theodore Lehmann); Don Kikhot, 1961 (Nicolai Cherkassov); Don Quichotte, 2000 (Samuel Ramey); Don Quichotte, 2010 (made-for-TV; Jose van Dam); Don Quijote de la Mancha, 1949 (Rafael Rivelles); Don Quijote de la Mancha, 1978 (TV series; Fernando Fernan Gomez); Don Quijote de la Mancha, 1991-1992 (TV series; Fernando Rey); Don Quijote von der Mancha, 1965 (TV miniseries; Josef Meinrad); Don Quixote, 1915 (DeWolf Hopper Sr.); Don Quixote, 1923 (Jerrold Robertshaw); **Don Quixote** [aka: The Adventure of Don Quixote], 1934 (Feodor Chaliapin); **Don Quixote**, 1973 (Robert Helpmann); Don Quixote, 1992 (Francisco Reiguera, Pepe Mediavilla voiceover); Don Quixote, 2000 (made-for-TV; John Lithgow); Don Quixote, Knight Errant, 2002 (Juan Luis Galiardo); Don Quixote of La Mancha, 1987 (animated made-for-TV; Robert Helpmann voiceover); Don Quixote: The Ingenious Gentleman of La Mancha, 2015 (Carmen Argenziano); The DuPont Show of the Month, 1957-1961 (TV series; "I, Don Quixote," 1959 episode; Lee J. Cobb); Great Performances, 1971- (TV series; "Monsieur Quixote," 1987 episode: Alec Guinness); La rebellion de los fantasmas, 1949 (Luis G. Barreiro); Man of La Mancha, 1972 (Peter O'Toole); Parade of Stars, 1983 (made-for-TV; Richard Kiley).

Dorian Gray (profligate and perverse handsome young British man of wealth whose ravages of aging is transferred to his hidden portrait while he remains youthful as depicted in the 1890 novel by Oscar Wilde): Armchair Theatre, 1956-1974 (TV series; "The Picture of Dorian Gray," 1961 episode: Jeremy Brett); Az elet kiralya, 1918 (Norbert Dan); BBC Play of the Month, 1965-1983 (TV series; "The Picture of Dorian Gray," 1976 episode: Peter Firth); Das Bildnis des Dorian Gray, 1917 (Bernd Aldor); Dorian, 2004 (Ethan Erikson); Dorian Gray, 1970 (Helmut Berger); Dorian Gray, 2009 (Ben Barnes); Dorian Gray im Spiegel der Boulevardpresse, 1984 (Veruschka von Lehndorff); El retrato de Dorian Gray, 1969- (TV series; Enrique Alvarez Felix); Golden Showcase,

1961- (TV series; "The Picture of Dorian Gray," 1961 episode: John Fraser); Gothica, 2013 (made-for-TV; Christopher Egan); Great Performances, 1971- (TV series; "Feasting with Panthers," 1974 episode; Richard Kavanaugh); Le portrait de Dorian Gray, 1977 (Patrice Alexsandre); The League of Extraordinary Gentlemen, 2003 (Stuart Townsend); Penny Dreadful, 2014 (TV series; Reeve Carney); **The Picture of Dorian Gray**, 1945 (Hurd Hatfield); The Picture of Dorian Gray, 1973 (made-for-TV; Shane Briant); The Picture of Dorian Gray, 2005 (Josh Duhamel); The Picture of Dorian Gray, 2007 (David Gallagher); Portret Doriana Greya, 1968 (made-for-TV; Valeri Babyatinksy); The Sins of Dorian Gray, 1983 (Belinda Bauer); Three Shadows, 2010 (Kevin Shayer).

Dormouse (fictional character from the 1865 novel Alice's Adventures in Wonderland by British author Lewis Carroll): Adventures in Wonderland, 1992-1994 (TV series; John Lovelady); Alice, 2009 (TV miniseries; Nancy Robertson); Alice at the Palace, 1982 (made-for-TV; Michael Jeter); Alice in Wonderland, 1915 (Louis Merkle); Alice in Wonderland, 1931 (Raymond Schultz); **Alice in Wonderland**, 1933 (Jackie Searl); Alice in Wonderland, 1949 (Joyce Grenfell voiceover); **Alice in Wonderland**, 1951 (James MacDonald voiceover); Alice in Wonderland, 1955 (made-for-TV; Alice Pearce); Alice in Wonderland, 1966 (made-for-TV; Wilfred Lawson); Alice in Wonderland, 1982 (made-for-TV; Marin Osterberg); Alice in Wonderland, 1985 (made-for-TV; Arte Johnson); Alice in Wonderland, 1985 (TV series; Royce Mills); Alice in Wonderland, 1986 (made-for-TV; four 30-minute segments; Elisabeth Sladen); Alice in Wonderland, 1999 (made-for-TV; Nigel Plaskitt; Dave Barclay); **Alice in Wonderland**, 2010 (Barbara Windsor); Alice in Wonderland or What's a Nice Kid Like You Doing in a Place Like This?, 1966 (animated made-for-TV; Don Messick); Alice through the Looking Box, 1960 (made-for-TV; Ronnie Corbett); Alice's Adventures in Wonderland, 1972 (Dudley Moore); Alice's Adventures in Wonderland, 2011 (made-for-TV; James Wilkie); Alice's Adventures in Wonderland and through the Looking Glass, 1948 (made-for-TV; Charles Wade); The Ford Theatre Hour, 1948-1951 (TV series; "Alice in Wonderland," 1950 episode: Tiny Schrimp); Kraft Theatre, 1947-1958 (TV series; "Alice in Wonderland," 1954 episode: Joe E. Marks); Unsuk Chin: Alice in Wonderland, 2007 (Guy de Mey); The Wednesday Play, 1964-1970 (TV series; "Alice," 1965 episode: Peter Bartlett).

Dorothy (Dorothy Gale; young girl from Kansas who is whisked by a tornado into a strange world in L. Frank Baum's iconic 1900 novel, *The Wonderful Wizard of Oz*): Journey Back to Oz, 1972 (animated; Liza Minnelli voiceover); The Muppets' Wizard of Oz, 2005 (Ashanti); The New Wizard of Oz, 1914 (Violet MacMillan); Off to See the Wizard, 1967-1968 (animated TV series; June Foray voiceover); 20th Century Oz, 1976 (Joy Dunstan); The Wiz, 1978 (Diana Ross); The Wizard of Oz, 1925 (Dorothy Dwan); **The Wizard of Oz**, 1939 (Judy Garland); The Wizard of Oz, 1982 (animated; Aileen Quinn voiceover); The Wizard of Oz, 1990-1991 (animated TV series; Liz Georges voiceover); The Wizard of Oz in Concert: Dreams Come True, 1995 (made-for-TV; Jewel [Kilcher]); The Wizard of Oz on Ice, 1996 (made-for-TV; Oksana Baiul; Shanice voiceover of Dorothy); The Wizard of the Emerald City, 1994 (Yekaterina Mikhaylovskaya).

Dracula (fictional character created by writer Bram Stoker in his 1897 novel *Dracula*; Also see Subject Index, Reincarnation): **Abbott and Costello Meet Frankenstein**, 1948 (Bela Lugosi); The ABC Saturday Night Superstar Movie, 1972-1974 (TV series; "The Mad, Mad, Mad Monsters," animated 1972 episode: Allen Swift voiceover); About Adam, 2000 (Mark Smith); Ahkea Khots, 1961 (Yechoon Lee); Andy Warhol's Dracula (aka: Blood for Dracula), 1974 (Udo Kier); Awake, 2007 (David Harbour); Batman Dracula, 1964 (Jack Smith); Batman Fights Dracula, 1967 (Dante Rivero); Billy the Kid vs. Dracula, 1966 (John Carradine); Black Sunday, 1960 (Barbara Steele); Blacula, 1972

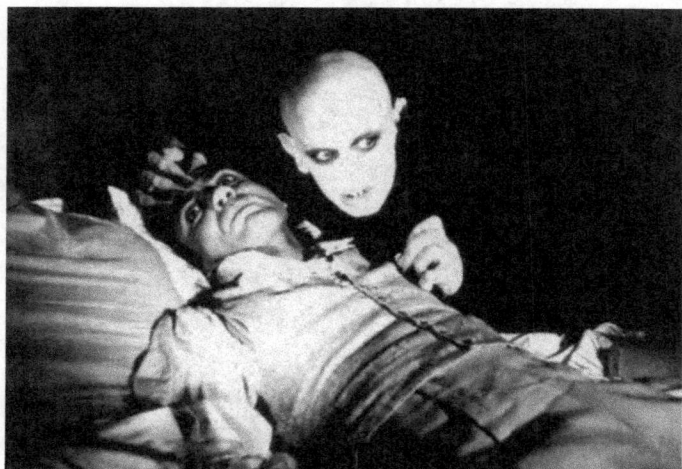

Klaus Kinski (as Dracula) in *Nosferatu the Vampyre*, 1979.

(Charles Macaulay); Blood, 1974 (Hope Stansbury as Dracula's daughter); Blood for Dracula, 1974 (Udo Kier); Blood of Dracula's Castle, 1969 (Alexander D'Arcy); Bonnie & Clyde vs. Dracula, 2008 (Russell Friend); Bram Stoker's Dracula, 1974 (made-for-TV; Jack Palance); **Bram Stoker's Dracula** (aka: Dracula), 1992 (Gary Oldman); The Brides of Dracula, 1960 (David Peel); Buffy the Vampire Slayer, 1992 (Rutger Hauer); Carry On Chistmas, 1969 (made-for-TV; Peter Butterworth); Count Dracula, 1973 (Christopher Lee); Count Dracula's Great Love, 1974 (Paul Naschy); The Creeps, 1997 (Phil Fondacaro); The Curse of Dracula, 1979 (TV series; Michael Nouri); Dark Prince: The True Story of Dracula, 2000 (Rudolf Martin); Deadly Hands of Kung Fu, 1977 (Hsi Chang); Die Hard Dracula, 1998 (Ernest M. Garcia); Doctor Dracula, 1978 (John Carradine); Dr. Terror's Gallery of Horrors, 1967 (Mitch Evans); **Dracula**, 1931 (Bela Lugosi); Dracula, 1931 (Spanish version of 1931 U.S. release; Carlos Villarias); Dracula, 1972 (made-for-TV; Werner Vielhaber); Dracula, 1973 (made-for-TV; Norman Welsh); **Dracula**, 1979 (Frank Langella); Dracula, 1980 (animated made-for-TV; Kenji Utsumi voiceover); Dracula, 2002 (made-for-TV; Patrick Bergin); Dracula, 2007 (made-for-TV; Marc Warren); Dracula, 2013- (TV series; Jonathan Rhys Meyers); Dracula A.D. 1972, 1972 (Christopher Lee); Dracula and Son, 1979 (Christopher Lee); Dracula contra Frankenstein, 1972 (Howard Vernon); **Dracula: Dead and Loving It**, 1995 (Leslie Nielsen); Dracula in Istanbul, 1953 (Atif Kaptan); Dracula in Pakistan, 1967 (Rehan); **Dracula Has Risen from the Grave**, 1969 (Christopher Lee); Dracula: Pages from a Virgin's Diary, 2003 (Wei-Qiang Zhang); **Dracula: Prince of Darkness**, 1966 (Christopher Lee); Dracula Reborn, 2012 (Stuart Rigby); Dracula Rising, 1993 (Zahari Vatahov); The Dracula Saga, 1973 (Narciso Ibanez Menta); Dracula: The Dark Prince, 2013 (Luke Roberts); Dracula (The Dirty Old Man), 1969 (Vince Kelley); Dracula: The Series, 1990-1991 (TV series; Geordie Johnson); Dracula 3D, 2013 (Thomas Kretschmann); Dracula II: Ascension, 2003 (Stephen Billinton); Dracula 2000, 2000 (Gerard Butler); Dracula 2012, 2013 (Sudheer Sukumaran); Dracula Untold, 2014 (Luke Evans as Vlad Tepes, role model for Dracula); Dracula vs. Frankenstein (aka: Blood of Frankenstein), 1971 (Zandor Vorkov); **Dracula's Daughter**, 1936 (Gloria Holden); Dracula's Death, 1921 (Paul Askonas); Dracula's Dog (aka: Zoltan: Hound of Dracula), 1978 (Michael Pataki); Dracula's Family Visit, 2006 (Harrie Huijs); Dracula's Guest, 2008 (Andrew Bryniarski); Drakula halala, 1921 (Paul Askonas); Embrace of the Vampire, 1995 (Martin Kemp); The Empire of Dracula, 1967 (Eric del Castillo); The Fearless Vampire Killers, 1967 (Ferdy Mayne); Frankenstein and Me, 1997 (Conner Vandeer); Frankenstein's Aunt, 1987 (Ferdy Mayne); Freckled Max and Spook, 1987 (Ferdy Mayne); Ghost in the Water, 1982 (made-for-TV; Daniel D'Arcy); The Great Bear Scare, 1983 (animated made-for-TV; Louis

Beaker, Bunsen Honeydew and Michael Caine (as Ebenezer Scrooge) in *The Muppet Christmas Carol*, 1992.

Nye voiceover); Guess What Happened to Count Dracula?, 1970 (Des Roberts); Haunted, 1993 (David Markwart); The Hilarious House of Frankenstein, 1971 (TV series; Billy Van); Hope, 2001 (made-for-TV; Dennis Meyer); **Horror of Dracula** (aka: Dracula), 1958 (Christopher Lee); Hotel Transylvania, 2012 (animated; Adam Sandler voiceover); **House of Dracula**, 1945 (John Carradine); **House of Frankenstein**, 1944 (John Carradine); House of the Wolf Man, 2009 (Michael R. Thomas); Hysterical, 1983 (Charlie Callas); Jonathan (aka: Jonathan: Vampire Sterben Nicht), 1970 (Paul Albert Krumm); Killer Barbys vs. Dracula, 2005 (Enrique Sarasola); La fille de Dracula (aka: Dracula's Daughter), 1972 (Howard Vernon); Ladies Night, 1983 (Henry Flores); Lady Dracula, 1977 (Stephen Boyd); Lake of Dracula, 1973 (Shin Kishida); The Legend of the 7 Golden Vampires, 1979 (John Forbes-Robertson); Love at First Bite, 1979 (George Hamilton); Mad Monster Party?, 1967 (animated feature; Allen Swift voiceover); Mark of the Vampire, 1935 (Bela Lugosi); Matinee Theater, 1955-1958 (TV series; "Dracula," two 1956 episodes: John Carradine); Modern Vampires, 1998 (made-for-TV; Robert Pastorelli); Monster Mash: The Movie, 1995 (Anthony Crivello); Monster Squad, 1976 (TV series: Henry Polic II); The Monster Squad, 1987 (Duncan Regehr); Mystery and Imagination, 1966-1970 (TV series; "Dracula," 1968 episode: Denholm Elliott); Nadja, 1994 (Peter Fonda); Never on a Sunday, 2006 (Axel Ricco); Night of the Vampire Hunter, 2000 (Nicole Muller); Night People, 2006 (Alastair Bruce); Nocturna, 1979 (John Carradine); **Nosferatu**, 1922 (Max Schreck); **Nosferatu the Vampyre**, 1979 (Klaus Kinski); Old Dracula (aka: Old Drac; Vampira), 1975 (David Niven); One More Time, 1970 (Christopher Lee); Renfield the Undead, 2011 (John Stevens); The Return of Dracula, 1958 (Francis Lederer); The Return of the Vampire, 1944 (Bela Lugosi); Saint Dracula 3D, 2012 (Mitch Powell); The Satanic Rites of Dracula, 1978 (Christopher Lee); Scars of Dracula, 1970 (Christopher Lee); Shadow of the Vampire, 2000 (William Dafoe); Son of Darkness: To Die For II, 1991 (Michael Praed); **Son of Dracula**, 1943 (Lon Chaney, Jr.); Son of Dracula, 1974 (Dan Meaden); Taste the Blood of Dracula, 1970 (Christopher Lee); Terror of Dracula, 2012 (Anthony D.P. Mann); To Die For, 1989 (Brendan Hughes); Vampire City, 2009 (Wolf Morrison); Vampires, 1998 (Thomas Ian Griffith); **Van Helsing**, 2004 (Richard Roxburgh); Vlad (aka: The True Life of Dracula), 1982 (role model for Dracula; Stefan Sileanu); Vlad, 2003 (role model for Dracula; Francesco Quinn); Vlad Tepes, 1979 (role model for Dracula; Stefan Sileanu); Waxwork, 1988 (Miles O'Keeffe); Way of the Vampire, 2005 (Paul Logan); The Worst Crime of Them All! (aka: Mondo Keyhole), 1966 (Pluto Felix).

Duchess (fictional character from the 1865 novel Alice's Adventures in Wonderland by British author Lewis Carroll): Alice in Wonderland,

1931 (Mabel Wright); **Alice in Wonderland**, 1933 (Alison Skipworth); Alice in Wonderland, 1949 (Joyce Grenfell voiceover); Alice in Wonderland, 1955 (made-for-TV; Bobby Clark); Alice in Wonderland, 1966 (made-for-TV; Leo McKern); Alice in Wonderland, 1982 (made-for-TV; Gary Briggle); Alice in Wonderland, 1985 (made-for-TV; Martha Raye); Alice in Wonderland, 1986 (made-for-TV; four 30-minute segments; Claire Davenport); Alice in Wonderland, 1999 (made-for-TV; Elizabeth Spriggs); Alice's Adventures in Wonderland, 1972 (Peter Bull).

Duck (fictional character from the 1865 novel Alice's Adventures in Wonderland by British author Lewis Carroll): Alice in Wonderland, 1966 (made-for-TV; Mark Allington); Alice in Wonderland, 1985 (made-for-TV; Charles Dougherty); Alice in Wonderland, 1986 (made-for-TV; four 30-minute segments; Jill Goldstone; Crispin Letts); Alice in Wonderland, 1999 (made-for-TV; Ken Campbell); Alice's Adventures in Wonderland, 1972 (Brian Tripping).

Dulcinea (fictional character, an idealized woman unseen in Miguel de Cervantes' 1605 novel about the deluded knight Don Quioxte, *The Ingenuous Gentleman Don Quixote of La Mancha*): BBC Play of the Month, 1965-1983 (TV series; "The Adventures of Don Quixote," 1973 episode: Rosemary Leach); CBS Television Workshop, 1952- (TV series; "Don Quixote," 1952 episode; Grace Kelly); Der Mann von La Mancha, 1994 (made-for-TV; Dagmar Hellberg); Don de la mancha, 1980 (TV miniseries; Mami Koyama); Don Quichotte, 2000 (Carmen Oprisanu); Don Quichotte, 2010 (made-for-TV; Silvia Tro Santafe); Don Quijote von der Mancha, 1965 (TV miniseries; Maria Saavedra); Don Quixote, 1915 (Fay Tincher); Don Quixote, 1923 (Minna Leslie); **Don Quixote** [aka: The Adventure of Don Quixote], 1934 (Renee Valliers); **Don Quixote**, 1973 (Lucette Aldous); Don Quixote, 2000 (made-for-TV; Vanessa Williams); Don Quixote, Knight Errant, 2002 (Marta Etura); Don Quixote: The Ingenious Gentleman of La Mancha, 2015 (Vera Cherny); The DuPont Show of the Month, 1957-1961 (TV series; "I, Don Quixote," 1959 episode: Colleen Dewhurst); Man of La Mancha, 1972 (Sophia Loren).

Duncan Heyward (heroic British major who is in love with Alice Munro and sacrifices his life to save hers in the 1826 novel *The Last of the Mohicans* by James Fenimore Cooper): Fall of the Mohicans, 1965 (Jack Taylor); **The Last of the Mohicans**, 1920 (Henry Woodward); The Last of the Mohicans, 1932 (Walter Miller); **The Last of the Mohicans**, 1936 (Henry Wilcoxon); The Last of the Mohicans, 1971 (TV miniseries; Tim Goodman); The Last of the Mohicans, 1975 (animated made-for-TV; Paul Hecht voiceover); Last of the Mohicans, 1977 (made-for-TV; Andrew Prine); **The Last of the Mohicans**, 1992 (Steve Waddington).

Eaglet (fictional character from the 1865 novel Alice's Adventures in Wonderland by British author Lewis Carroll): Alice in Wonderland, 1966 (made-for-TV; Nicholas Evans); Alice in Wonderland, 1985 (made-for-TV; Billy Braver); Alice in Wonderland, 1999 (made-for-TV; Heathcote Williams); Alice's Adventures in Wonderland, 1972 (Ray Edwards).

Ebenezer Scrooge (cold-hearted miser and wealthy British businessman who hates Christmas, the central character in Charles Dickens' 1843 novella, *A Christmas Carol*): The Alcoa Hour, 1955-1957 (TV series; "The Stingiest Man in Town," 1956 episode: Basil Rathbone); A Carol for Another Christmas, 1964 (made-for-TV; Sterling Hayden); Carry On Christmas, 1969 (made-for-TV; Sidney James); **A Christmas Carol**, 1938 (Reginald Owen); A Christmas Carol, 1943 (made-for-TV; William Podmore); A Christmas Carol, 1947 (made-for-TV; John Carradine); A Christmas Carol, 1950 (made-for-TV; Bransby Williams); **A Christmas Carol**, 1951 (Alastair Sim); A Christmas Carol, 1977 (made-for-TV; Michael Hordern); A Christmas Carol, 1979 (musical; Jim Bullock); A Christmas Carol, 1981 (made-for-TV; William Paterson); A Christmas Carol, 1982 (made-for-TV; Richard Hilger); A Christmas

Carol, 1984 (made-for-TV; George C. Scott); A Christmas Carol, 1999 (made-for-TV; Patrick Stewart); A Chirstmas Carol, 2000 (made-for-TV; Ross Kemp); A Christmas Carol, 2009 (animated; Jim Carrey voiceover); A Christmas Carol, 2015 (Anthony D.P. Mann); A Christmas Carol at Ford's Theatre, 1979 (made-for-TV; Ron [Ronald] Bishop); A Christmas Carol: The Concert, 2013 (made-for-TV; Michael Aaron Linder [Lindner]); A Christmas Carol: 50th Anniversary, 2015 (Tom Killam); Christmas Carol: The Movie, 2001 (animated; Simon Callow voiceover); A Christmas Carol: The Musical, 2004 (made-for-TV; Kelsey Grammer); Dickensian, 2015- (TV series; Ned Dennehy); A Diva's Christmas Carol, 2000 (made-for-TV; Vanessa Williams); Ebenezer, 1998 (made-for-TV; Jack Palance); Fireside Theatre, 1949-1955 (TV series; "A Christmas Carol," 1951 episode; Ralph Richardson); General Electric Theater, 1953-1962 (TV series; "The Trail to Christmas," 1957 episode; John McIntire); The Gospel according to Scrooge, 1983 (made-for-TV; Robert Buchanan); Kraft Theatre, 1947-1958 (TV series; "A Christmas Carol," 1952 episode: Malcolm Keen); Mr. Magoo's Christmas Carol, 1962 (made-for-TV; Jim Backus); Mr. Scrooge, 1964 (made-for-TV; Cyril Ritchard); Mr. Scrooge to See You, 2013 (David Ruprecht); Ms. Scrooge, 1997 (made-for-TV; Cicely Tyson); **The Muppet Christmas Carol**, 1992 (Michael Caine); The Philco-Goodyear Television Playhouse, 1948-1956 (TV series; "A Christmas Carol," 1948 episode: Dennis King); Ponds Theatre, 1953- (TV series; "A Christmas Carol," 1953 episode; Noel Leslie); The Right to Be Happy, 1916 (Rupert Julian); Scrooge, 1935 (Seymour Hicks); **Scrooge**, 1970 (Albert Finney); Scrooge, 1978 (made-for-TV; Warren Graves); Scrooged, 1988 (Buddy Hackett); Shower of Stars, 1954-1958 (TV series; "A Christmas Carol," 1954 and 1956 episodes: Fredric March); The Stingiest Man in Town, 1978 (animated made-for-TV; Walter Matthau voiceover).

Edmund Dantes (wrongly imprisoned young man, who escapes to find riches that enable him to take revenge against his enemies, created by Alexander Dumas [the elder] in his adventure novel *The Count of Monte Cristo*, 1844): The Count of Monte Cristo, 1913 (James O'Neill); The Count of Monte Cristo, 1917-1918 (Leon Mathot in fifteen short episodes produced in France); **The Count of Monte Cristo**, 1934 (Robert Donat); The Count of Monte Cristo, 1943 (Mexican production with Arturo de Cordova); The Count of Monte Cristo, 1943 (French production with Pierre Richard-Willm); The Count of Monte Cristo, 1953 (Jorge Mistral); The Count of Monte Cristo, 1954 (French production with Jean Marais); The Count of Monte Cristo, 1956 (TV series with George Dolenz); Count of Mont Cristo, 1964- (TV series; Alan Badel); The Count of Monte Cristo, 1975 (made-for-TV movie with Richard Chamberlain); The Count of Monte Cristo, 1998 (TV miniseries with Guillaume Depardieu); **The Count of Monte Cristo**, 2002 (James Caviezel); The DuPont Show of the Month, 1957-1961 (TV series; "The Count of Monte Cristo," 1958 episode: Hurd Hatfield); El Conde de Montecristo, 1954 (Argentine production with Jorge Mistral); Monte Cristo, 1922 (John Gilbert); Monte Cristo, 1929 (French production with Jean Angelo); The Return of Monte Cristo [aka: Monte Cristo's Revenge], 1946 (Louis Hayward); The Return of Monte Cristo,1968 (Paul Barge); The Son of Monte Cristo, 1940 (Louis Hayward as Edmund Dantes Jr.); The Story of the Count of Monte Cristo, 1961 (Louis Jourdan); Sword of the Avenger, 1948 (loosely based on the Dumas story with Ramon Del Gado playing a Dantes role model); Sword of Venus [AKA: Island of Monte Cristo], 1953 (Robert Clarke); Treasure of Monte Cristo, 1949 (Glenn Langan); The Wife of Monte Cristo, 1946 (Martin Kosleck).

Eliza Doolittle (Cockney flower girl transformed into a grand lady, her character created in George Bernard Shaw's 1912 play, "*Pygmalion*"): BBC Play of the Month, 1965-1983 (TV series, "Pygmalion," 1973 episode: Lynn Redgrave); BBC Sunday-Night Theater, 1950-1959 (TV series; "Pygmalion," 1956 episode: Pat Kirkwood); Celebrity Play-

Telly Savalas as criminal mastermind Ernst Stavro Blofeld in *On Her Majesty's Secret Service*, 1969.

house, 1981 (TV series, "Pygmalion," 1981 episode; Twiggy); The Makeover, 2013 (made-for-TV; David Walton as Elliot Doolittle in a gender switch); **My Fair Lady**, 1964 (Audrey Hepburn); My Fair Lady; Minha Linda Senhora, 2004 (made-for-TV; Anabela); My Fair Zombie, 2013 (Sacha Gabriel); National Theatre Live: 50 Years on Stage, 2013 (made-for-TV; Rosalie Craig); Pygmalion, 1935 (Jenny Jugo); Pygmalion, 1937 (Lily Bouwmeester); **Pygmalion**, 1938 (Wendy Hiller); Pygmalion, 1948 (made-for-TV; Margaret Lockwood); Pygmalion, 1954 (made-for-TV; Kay Hammond); Pygmalion, 1956 (made-for-TV; Agnes Fink); Pygmalion, 1957 (made-for-TV; Margret Homeyer); Pygmalion, 1958 (made-for-TV; Konstantsiya Royek); Pygmalion, 1963 (made-for-TV; Julie Harris); Pygmalion, 1968 (made-for-TV; Harriet Andersson); Pygmalion, 1976 (made-for-TV; Mary Dresselhuys); Pygmalion, 1983 (made-for-TV; Margot Kidder).

Emma Bovary (ill-starred heroine of Gustav Flaubert's debut novel of 1856, a beautiful, selfish doctor's wife who lives beyond her means and conducts many adulterous affairs, her life ending in tragedy): Madame Bovary, 1934 (Valentine Tessier); Madame Bovary, 1937 (Pola Negri); Madame Bovary, 1947 (Mecha Ortiz); **Madame Bovary**, 1949 (Jennifer Jones); Madame Bovary, 1964- (TV series; Nyree Dawn Porter); Madame Bovary, 1968 (made-for-TV; Elfriede Irrall); Madame Bovary [aka: Play the Game of Leave the Bed], 1969 (Edwige Fenech); Madame Bovary, 1974 (made-for-TV; Nicole Courcel); Madame Bovary, 1975- (TV miniseries; Francesca Annis); Madame Bovary, 1978- (TV miniseries; Carla Gravina); Madame Bovary, 1991 (Isabelle Huppert); Madame Bovary, 2000 (made-for-TV; Frances O'-Connor); Madame Bovary, 2014 (Mia Wasikowska); Unholy Love, 1932 (Lila Lee).

Ernst Stavro Blofeld (power-mad villain in Ian Fleming's James Bond thrillers): **Diamonds Are Forever**, 1971 (Charles Gray); **For Your Eyes Only**, 1981 (John Hollis; Robert Rietty voiceover); **From Russia with Love**, 1963 (Anthony Dawson; Eric Pohlmann voiceover); Never Say Never Again, 1983 (Max von Sydow); **On Her Majesty's Secret Service**, 1969 (Telly Savalas); **Spectre**, 2015 (Christoph Waltz); **Thunderball**, 1965 (Anthony Dawson; Eric Pohlmann voiceover); **You Only Live Twice**, 1967 (Donald Pleasence).

Esmeralda (beautiful street waif and heroine in Victor Hugo's classic 1831 novel, *The Hunchback of Notre Dame*): The Darling of Paris, 1917 (Theda Bara); The Hunchback, 1997 (made-for-TV; Salma Hayek); **The Hunchback of Notre Dame**, 1923 (Patsy Ruth Miller); **The Hunchback of Notre Dame**, 1939 (Maureen O'Hara); The Hunchback of Notre Dame, 1956 (Gina Lollobrigida); The Hunchback of Notre Dame,

Charles Boyer, Leslie Caron (as Fanny) and Maurice Chevalier in *Fanny,* **1961.**

1966 (TV series; Gay Hamilton); The Hunchback of Notre Dame, 1977 (made-for-TV; Michelle Newell); The Hunchback of Notre Dame, 1982 (made-for-TV; Lesley Anne Down); The Hunchback of Notre Dame, 1986 (animated made-for-TV; Angela Punch McGregor voiceover); **The Hunchback of Notre Dame**, 1996 (animated; Demi Moore voiceover); The Magical Adventures of Quasimodo, 1996- (animated TV series; Eleanor Noble voiceover); Notre-Dame de Paris, 1996 (made-for-TV; Isabelle Guerin); Notre-Dame de Paris, 1999 (made-for-TV; Helene Segara); Notre-Dame de Paris, 2002 (made-for-TV; Lola Ponce); Robert Montgomery Presents, 1950-1957 (TV series; "The Hunchback of Notre Dame," two-part episodes, 1954: Celia Lipton).

Estella (the beautiful adopted daughter of eccentric Miss Havisham in Charles Dickens' 1861 novel, *Great Expectations*, and who is seemingly incapable of loving Pip, the young man who loves her): Great Expectations, 1917 (Louise Huff); Great Expectations, 1934 (Jane Wyatt; Anne Howard as young Estella); **Great Expectations**, 1946 (Valerie Hobson; Jean Simmons as young Estella); Great Expectations, 1959- (TV series; Helen Lindsay; Sandra Michaels as young Estella); Great Expectations, 1967- (TV series; Francesca Annis); Great Expectations, 1974 (made-for-TV; Sarah Miles); Great Expectations, 1981- (TV miniseries; Sarah-Jane Varley; Patsy Kensit as young Estella); Great Expectations, 1989- (TV miniseries; Kim Thomson); Great Expectations, 1999 (made-for-TV; Justine Waddell; Gemma Gregory as young Estella); Great Expectations, 2011 (TV miniseries; Vanessa Kirby; Izzy Meikle-Small as young Estella); Great Expectations, 2012 (Holliday Grainger; Helena Barlow as young Estella); Great Expectations, 2013 (Grace Rowe); Playdate, 1961-1964 (TV series; "Great Expectations," two episodes in 1962: Michael Learned; Wendy Wolff as young Estella); Robert Montgomery Presents, 1950-1957 (TV series; "Great Expectations," two episodes in 1954: Nina Reader); Store forventninger, 1922 (Olga D'Org [Belajeff]; Esther Kjaer Jensen as young Estella).

Etienne Javert (French police inspector who interminably hounds escaped convict Jean Valjean in the 1862 novel *Les Miserables* by Victor Hugo): Les Miserables, 1913 (Henri Etievant); Les Miserables, 1917 (Hardee Kirkland); **Les Miserables**, 1935 (Charles Laughton); Les Miserables, 1936 (Charles Vanel); Les Miserables, 1952 (Hans Hinrich); **Les Miserables**, 1952 (Robert Newton); Les Miserables, 1958 (Bernard Blier); Les Miserables, 1967- (TV series; Anthony Bate); Les Miserables, 1972- (TV miniseries; Bernard Fresson); Les Miserables, 1978 (made-for-TV; Anthony Perkins); Les Miserables, 1982 (Michel Bouquet); **Les Miserables**, 1995 (Philippe Khorsand); **Les Miserables**, 1998 (Geoffrey Rush); Les Miserables, 2000- (TV miniseries; John Malkovich); Los miserables, 1943 (Antonio Bravo); Los miserables, 1973- (TV series; Anto-

nio Passy); Soul of Humanity, 1926 (Jean Toulout).

Fagin (a fictional character in the Charles Dickens novel *Oliver Twist*; a criminal Svengali who trains and operates a ring of young boys as pickpockets in 19th-Century London, England): The DuPont Show of the Month, 1957-1961 (TV series; "Oliver Twist," 1959 episode; Eric Portman); Escape of the Artful Dodger, 2001- (TV series; Chris Baz); The Further Adventures of Oliver Twist, 1980- (TV series; David Swift); Oliver & Company, 1988 (Dom DeLuise voiceover); Oliver Twist, 1916 (Tully Marshall); Oliver Twist, 1919 (Laszlo Z. Molnar); **Oliver Twist**, 1922 (Lon Chaney Sr.); Oliver Twist, 1933 (Irving Pichel); **Oliver Twist**, 1951 (Alec Guinness); Oliver Twist, 1960 (TV series; Jaime Barcellos); Oliver Twist, 1962 (TV miniseries; Max Adrian); **Oliver!**, 1968 (Ron Moody); Oliver Twist, 1974 (animated version; Les Tremayne voiceover); Oliver Twist, 1982 (made-for-TV; George C. Scott); Oliver Twist, 1985 (TV miniseries; Eric Porter); Oliver Twist, 1997 (made-for-TV; Richard Dreyfuss); Oliver Twist, 1999 (TV miniseries; Robert Lindsay); **Oliver Twist**, 2005 (Ben Kingsley); Oliver Twist, 2007 (TV series; Timothy Spall); Oliver Twist Jr., 1921 (Clarence Wilson).

Fairy Godmother (folk character from the story *The Little Glass Slipper*): Hey Cinderella!, 1969 (made-for-TV; Frankie Howerd); Cinderella, 1914 (Inez Ranous); Cinderella, 1947 (TV miniseries; Timara Kirova); **Cinderella**, 1950 (Verna Felton voiceover); Cinderella, 1950 (made-for-TV; Brenda Ralston); Cinderella, 1957 (made-for-TV; Edie Adams); Cinderella, 1958 (made-for-TV; Mary Mackenzie); Cinderella, 1965 (made-for-TV; Celeste Holm); Cinderella, 1966 (Renee Stobrawa); Cinderella, 1969 (Georgina Parkinson); Cinderella, 1977 (Sy Richardson); Cinderella, 1986 (made-for-TV; Genevieve Raynaud); Cinderella, 1997 (made-for-TV; Whitney Houston); Cinderella, 2000 (made-for-TV; Julian Clary); **Cinderella**, 2015 (Helena Bonham Carter); Cinderella...Frozen in Time, 1994 (made-for-TV; Catherine Foulkes); Cinderella; The Shoe Must Go On, 1986 (made-for-TV; Faith Brown); Cinderella: Single Again, 2000 (Mary McDonald); Faerie Tale Theatre, 1982-1987 (TV series; "Cinderella," 1985 episode: Jean Stapleton); Happily Ever After: Fairy Tales for Every Child, 1995-2000 (TV series; "Cinderella," 1995 episode: Liz Torres); Hey Cinderella!, 1969 (made-for-TV; Joyce Gordon); A Kiss for Cinderella, 1925 (Esther Ralston); A Kiss for Cinderella, 1959 (made-for-TV; Mary Jones); Once upon a Brothers Grimm, 1977 (made-for-TV; Corinne Conley); **The Slipper and the Rose**, 1976 (Annette Crosbie).

The Falcon (Gay Stanhope Falcon; Gay Laurence; Gay Lawrence; Tom Lawrence; Michael Waring; sophisticated private detective invariably involved in high-society crimes, created by Michael Arlen and first appearing in the pages of *Town & Country*, 1940): A Date with the Falcon, 1941 (George Sanders); Appointment with Murder, 1948 (John Calvert); Devil's Cargo, 1948 (John Calvert); **The Falcon and the Co-Eds**, 1943 (Tom Conway); The Falcon in Danger, 1943 (Tom Conway); The Falcon in Hollywood, 1944 (Tom Conway); **The Falcon in Mexico**, 1944 (Tom Conway); The Falcon in San Francisco, 1945 (Tom Conway); The Falcon Out West, 1944 (Tom Conway); The Falcon Strikes Back, 1943 (Tom Conway); **The Falcon Takes Over**, 1942 (George Sanders); The Falcon's Adventure, 1946 (Tom Conway); **The Falcon's Alibi**, 1946 (Tom Conway); **The Falcon's Brother**, 1942 (George Sanders; Tom Conway); The Gay Falcon, 1941 (George Sanders); Search for Danger, 1949 (John Calvert).

Fanny (young fish seller in Marseilles, who loses her lover and marries an elderly man so her unborn child will have a father, and who is later reunited with the man she loves): **Cesar**, 1936 (Orane Demazis); **Fanny**, 1948 (Orane Demazis); **Fanny**, 1961 (Leslie Caron); Fanny, 2008 (made-for-TV; Marie-Sophie Ferdane); Fanny, 2014 (Victoire Belezy); La trilogie Marseillaise: Cesar, 2000 (made-for-TV; Gaela Le Devehat); La trilogie Marseillaise: Fanny, 2000 (made-for-TV; Gaela Le Devehat);

La trilogie Marseillaise: Marius, 2000 (made-for-TV; Gaela Le Deve-hat); **Marius**, 1933 (Orane Demazis); Marius, 2014 (Victoire Belezy); Pagnol, 1977 (TV series; Ganci Geraedts); Port of Seven Seas, 1938 (Maureen O'Sullivan).

Father Brown (mild-mannered priest from Essex, England, created by G.K. Chesteron in his 1911 short story, a gentle sleuth more interested in the redemption of criminals than their arrest and conviction): Das schwarze Schaf, 1960 (Heinz Ruhmann); **The Detective**, 1954 (Alec Guinness); Detective, 1964-1969 (TV series; "The Quick One," 1964 episode: Mervyn Johns); Er kanns nicht lassen, 1962 (Heinz Ruhmann); Father Brown, 1974- (TV series; Kenneth More); Father Brown, 2013- (TV series; Mark Williams); Father Brown, Detective, 1934 (Walter Connolly); G.K. Chesterton: The Apostle of Common Sense, 2000- (TV series; several episodes: Kevin O'Connor); I racconti di Padre Brown, 1970- (TV series; Renato Rascel); Pater Brown, 1966-1972 (TV series; Josef Meinrad); Pfarrer Braun, 2003- (TV series; Ottfried Fischer); Sanctuary of Fear, 1979 (made-for-TV; Bernard Hughes); Sei delitti per padre Brown, 1988- (TV miniseries; Emrys James); Theater of the Word, Inc., 2009- (TV series; "The Honor of Israel Gow," 2009 episode; Kevin O'Brien).

Faust (Georges Faust; a learned scholar in German legend, refined by Goethe in 1808, who makes a pact with the Devil, exchanging his soul for unlimited knowledge and pleasure, the character used under different names but with the same plotline in more modern versions): **Alias Nick Beal**, 1949 (Thomas Mitchell as a ruthlessly ambitious politician); Beauty and the Devil, 1953 (Gerard Philipe; Michel Simon as aging Faust); Bedazzled, 1967 (Dudley Moore as a young man seeking the perfect woman); Bedazzled, 2000 (Brendan Fraser as a young man seeking the perfect woman); **Damn Yankees**, 1958 (Tab Hunter as an ambitious baseball player); The Damnation of Faust, 1986 (Curtis Rayam); The Damnation of Faust, 2011 (made-for-TV; Peter Hoare); **The Devil and Daniel Webster** [aka: All That Money Can Buy], 1941 (James Craig as a greedy New England farmer); Doctor Faustus, 1961- (TV series; Alan Dobie); Doctor Faustus, 1968 (Richard Burton); Faust, 1926 (Gosta Ekman); Faust, 1960 (Will Quadflieg); Faust, 1964 (Robert Towner); Faust, 1975 (made-for-TV; Nicolai Gedda); Faust, 1980 (Brian Abbott); Faust, 1982 (Bernhard Minetti); Faust, 1985 (made-for-TV; Francisco Araiza); Faust, 1986 (made-for-TV; Alfredo Kraus); Faust, 1996 (made-for-TV; Ulf Dohlsten); Faust, 1994-1997 (TV series; Heiner Lauterbach); Faust, 2000 (Mark Frost); Faust, 2004 (made-for-TV; Robert Alagna); Faust, 2009 (Matthew Greene); Faust, 2010 (James Warke voiceover); Faust, 2013 (Johannes Zeiler); Faust and the Devil, 1950 (Gino Mattera); The Fiery Angel, 1993 (made-for-TV; Sergei Alexashkin); La damnation de Faust, 1999 (made-for-TV; Paul Groves); Lesson Faust, 1995 (Peter Cepek); Marguerite of the Night, 1955 (Jean Francoise Calve); Mephisto, 1982 (Gyorgy Banffy); Midstream, 1929 (Louis Alvarez); Mon Faust, 1970 (made-for-TV; Pierre Fresnay); Original Sin, 2001 (James Have as stage Faust); **The Phantom of the Opera**, 1925 (Edward Cecil as stage Faust); The Phantom of the Opera, 1983 (made-for-TV; Pal Kovacs).

Fay Cheyney (attractive and clever jewel thief, a female character created by Frederick Lonsdale in his 1926 play, "The Last of Mrs. Cheyney): Broadway Television Theatre, 1952-1954 (TV series; "The Last of Mrs. Cheyney," 1953 episode; Vicki Cummings); Frau Cheneys Ende, 1961 (Lilli Palmer); ITV Play of the Week, 1955-1974 (TV series; "The Last of Mrs. Cheyney," 1956 episode: Margaret Lockwood); The Last of Mrs. Cheyney, 1929 (Norma Shearer); The Last of Mrs. Cheyney, 1937 (Joan Crawford); The Law and the Lady, 1951 (Greer Garson); Mrs. Cheneys Ende, 1957 (made-for-TV; Sonja Sutter); Mrs. Cheneys Ende, 1965 (made-for-TV; Johanna von Koczian).

Fish Footman (fictional character in the 1865 novel Alice's Adventures

Ronald Colman and Madeleine Carroll (as Princess Flavia) in *The Prisoner of Zenda,* **1937.**

in Wonderland by British author Lewis Carroll): Alice in Wonderland, 1903 (8-minute short; Norman Whitten); Alice in Wonderland, 1955 (made-for-TV; Michael Enserro); Alice in Wonderland, 1982 (made-for-TV; Jerome Wallin); Alice in Wonderland, 1985 (made-for-TV; Scotch Byerly); Alice in Wonderland, 1999 (made-for-TV; Hugh Lloyd); Alice's Adventures in Wonderland, 1972 (Peter O'Farrell).

Flavia (consort to the king of mythical Ruritania and falls in love with a pretender to the throne in Anthony Hope's 1894 adventure novel, *The Prisoner of Zenda*): **The Prisoner of Zenda**, 1922 (Alice Terry); **The Prisoner of Zenda**, 1937 (Madeleine Carroll); **The Prisoner of Zenda**, 1952 (Deborah Kerr); The Prisoner of Zenda, 1979 (Lynne Frederick); The Prisoner of Zenda, 1984- (TV miniseries; Victoria Wicks); Rupert of Hentzau, 1915 (Jane Gail); Rupert of Hentzau, 1964- (TV series; Barbara Shelley).

Frankenstein (household name of fictional mad scientist depicted in Mary Shelley's 1818 novel, or his relatives or others, who continued his ghoulish labors to create life from dead human tissue or other matter): The ABC Saturday Night Superstar Movie, 1972-1974 (TV series; 'The Mad, Mad, Mad Monsters," animated 1972 episode: Baron Henry von Frankenstein: Bob McFadden voiceover); Arabela, 1979 (TV series; Dr. Frankenstein: Vit Olmer); Blood, 1974 (Baron von Frankenstein: Lawrence Seelars); **The Bride of Frankenstein**, 1945 (Henry Frankenstein: Colin Clive); Casanova Frankenstein, 1975 (Dr. Frankenstein: Gianrico Tedeschi); **The Curse of Frankenstein**, 1957 (Victor Frankenstein: Peter Cushing); Dr. Frankenstein on Campus, 1970 (Viktor Frankenstein: Robin Ward); Dracula vs. Frankenstein, 1971 (aka: Blood of Frankenstein; Dr. Frankenstein: J. Carroll Naish); The Erotic Rites of Frankenstein, 1973 (Doctor Frankenstein: Denis [Dennis] Price); The Evil of Frankenstein, 1964 (Baron Frankenstein: Peter Cushing); Flesh for Frankenstein, 1974 (Baron Frankenstein: Udo Kier); **Frankenstein**, 1931 (Henry Frankenstein: Colin Clive); Frankenstein, 1984 (made-for-TV; Victor Frankenstein: Robert Powell); Frankenstein, 1987 (made-for-TV; Victor Frankenstein: Carl Beck); Frankenstein, 1992 (made-for-TV; Dr. Victor Frankenstein: Patrick Bergin); Frankenstein, 1994 (Victor Frankenstein: Kenneth Branagh); Frankenstein, 2004 (TV miniseries; Victor Frankenstein: Alec Newman); Frankenstein, 2007 (made-for-TV; Dr. Victoria Frankenstein: Helen McCrory); Frankenstein, 2011 (Victor Frankenstein: Lee Godwin); Frankenstein and the Monster from Hell, 1974 (Victor Frankenstein: Peter Cushing); Frankenstein: Birth of a Monster, 2003 (made-for-TV; Victor Frankenstein: Ronan Vibert); **Frankenstein Created Woman**, 1967 (Baron Frankenstein: Peter Cushing); Frankenstein: Day of the Beast, 2011 (Victor Frankenstein: Adam Stephenson); Frankenstein General Hospi-

Elsa Lanchester and Boris Karloff (as the Frankenstein Monster) in *The Bride of Frankenstein*, 1935.

tal, 1988 (Dr. Bob Frankenstein: Mark Blankfield); Frankenstein Island, 1981 (Dr. Frankenstein: John Carradine); Frankenstein Meets the Space Monster, 1965 (Robert Reilly); **Frankenstein Meets the Wolf Man**, 1943 (Elsa Frankenstein: Ilona Massey); **Frankenstein Must Be Destroyed**, 1970 (Baron Frankenstein: Peter Cushing); Frankenstein—1970, 1958 (Victor Frankenstein: Boris Karloff); Frankenstein 90, 1984 (Victor Frankenstein: Jean Rochefort); Frankenstein Rising, 2010 (Victor Frankenstein: Domiziano Arcangeli); Frankenstein: The College Years, 1991 (made-for-TV; Vincent Hammond); Frankenstein: The True Story, 1973 (made-for-TV; Leonard Whiting); Frankenstein Unbound, 1990 (Victor Frankenstein: Raul Julia); Frankenstein's Aunt, 1987 (TV series; Henry Frankenstein: Bolek Polivka); Frankenstein's Cat, 2007-2008 (TV series; animated: Dr. Frankenstein: Keith Wickham voiceover); Frankenstein's Daughter, 1958 (Sandra Knight); Frankenstein's Great Aunt Tillie, 1984 (Victor Frankenstein; Donald Pleasence); Frankenstein's Wedding, 2011 (made-for-TV; Victor Frankenstein: Andrew Gower); Frankenweenie, 1984 (Victor Frankenstein: Barret Oliver); Freckled Max and Spooks, 1987 (Henry Frankenstein: Bolek Polivka); The Ghost Busters, 1975 (TV series; "Dr. Whatsisname," 1975 episode: Dr. Frankenstein: Bernie Kopell); **The Ghost of Frankenstein**, 1942 (Henry Frankenstein: Colin Clive; Ludwig Frankenstein: Cedric Hardwicke); The Horror of Frankenstein, 1971 (Victor Frankenstein: Ralph Bates); **The House of Frankenstein**, 1944 (Dr. Niemann: Boris Karloff); I, Frankenstein, 2014 (Victor Frankenstein: Aden Young); I Was a Teenage Frankenstein, 1957 (Professor Frankenstein: Whit Bissell); Jesse James Meets Frankenstein's Daughter, 1966 (Dr. Rudolph Frankenstein: Steven Geray; Dr. Maria Frankenstein: Narda Onyx); Lady Frankenstein, 1973 (Baron Frankenstein: Joseph Cotten); Mad Monster Party?, 1967 (animated comedy; Baron Boris von Frankenstein: Boris Karloff voiceover); Monster Mash: The Movie, 1995 (Dr. Victor Frankenstein: Bobby Pickett); Once upon a Time, 1973 (TV series; Victor Frankenstein: Geoffrey Bayldon); One More Time, 1970 (Dr. Frankenstein: Peter Cushing); Pastel de sangre, 1971 (Victor Frankenstein: Angel Carmona Ristol); The Revenge of Frankenstein, 1958 (Dr. Victor Stein: Peter Cushing); Son of Dracula, 1974 (The Baron: Freddie Jones); **Son of Frankenstein**, 1939 (Wolf von Frankenstein: Basil Rathbone); Tales of Tomorrow, 1951-1953 (TV series; "Frankenstein," 1952 episode: Victor Frankenstein: John Newland); Terror of Frankenstein, 1977 (Victor Frankenstein: Leon Vitali); The Transformers, 1984-1987 (TV animated series; "Autobot Spike," 1985 episode: Dr. Victor Frankenstein: Frank Welker voiceover); **Van Helsing**, 2004 (Dr. Victor Frankenstein: Samuel West); **Victor Frankenstein**, 2015 (James McAvoy as Victor Frankenstein); Waxworks II: Lost in Time, 1992 (Baron von Frankenstein: Martin Kemp); The Wide World of Mystery, 1973-1978 (TV series; two 1973 episodes: Victor Frankenstein: Robert

Foxworth); **Young Frankenstein**, 1974 (Dr. Frederick Frankenstein: Gene Wilder).

Frankenstein Monster (fictional character in the 1818 novel by Mary Shelley): **Abbott and Costello Meet Frankenstein**, 1948 (Glenn Strange); The ABC Saturday Night Superstar Movie, 1972-1974 (TV series; 'The Mad, Mad, Mad Monsters," animated 1972 episode: Allen Swift voiceover); Andy Warhol's Frankenstein, 1973 (Srdjan Zelenovic; Miomir Aleksic); Big Monster on Campus, 2000 (Matthew Lawrence); Billy Frankenstein, 1998 (Brian Carrillo); Blood: The Last Vampire, 2009 (Joey Anaya; Khary Payton); The Bride, 1985 (Clancy Brown); **The Bride of Frankenstein**, 1935 (Boris Karloff); Carry On Christmas, 1969 (made-for-TV; Bernard Bresslaw); Casanova Frankenstein, 1975 (Aldo Maccione); **Casino Royale**, 1967 (David Prowse); The Creeps, 1997 (Thomas Wellington); **The Curse of Frankenstein**, 1957 (Christopher Lee); Dracula vs. Frankenstein, 1971 (aka: Blood of Frankenstein; John Bloom); The Erotic Rites of Frankenstein, 1973 (Fernando Bilbao); The Evil of Frankenstein, 1964 (Kiwi Kingston); Flesh for Frankenstein, 1974 (Srdjan Zelenovic); **Frankenstein**, 1931 (Boris Karloff); Frankenstein, 1984 (made-for-TV; David Warner); Frankenstein, 1987 (made-for-TV; Chris Sarandon); Frankenstein, 1992 (made-for-TV; Randy Quaid); Frankenstein, 2004 (made-for-TV; Vincent Perez); Frankenstein, 2004 (TV miniseries; Luke Goss); Frankenstein, 2007 (made-for-TV; Julian Bleach); Frankenstein, 2011 (Dean Gangle); Frankenstein and the Monster from Hell, 1974 (David Prowse); Frankenstein and the Werewolf Reborn!, 2005 (Ethan Wilde); Frankenstein: Birth of a Monster, 2003 (made-for-TV; David Schofield); Frankenstein Conquers the World, 1966 (Koji Furuhata; young Frankenstein: Sumio Nakao); **Frankenstein Created Woman**, 1967 (Robert Morse); Frankenstein: Day of the Beast, 2011 (Tim Krueger); Frankenstein General Hospital, 1988 (Irwin Keyes); Frankenstein Meets the Space Monster, 1965 (Bruce Glover); **Frankenstein Meets the Wolf Man**, 1943 (Bela Lugosi); **Frankenstein Must Be Destroyed**, 1970 (brain: George Pravda; body: Freddie Jones); Frankenstein—1970, 1958 (Mike Lane); Frankenstein 90, 1984 (Eddy Mitchell); Frankenstein Reborn!, 1998 (Ethan Wilde); Frankenstein Reborn!, 2005 (Joel Hebner); Frankenstein Rising, 2010 (Randal Malone); Frankenstein: The True Story, 1973 (made-for-TV; Michael Sarrazin); Frankenstein Unbound, 1990 (Nick Brimble); Frankenstein vs. the Creature from Blood Cove, 2005 (Lawrence Furbish); Frankenstein's Aunt, 1987 (TV series; Gerhard Karzel); Frankenstein's Daughter, 1958 (Harry Wilson); Frankenstein's Great Aunt Tillie, 1984 (Miguel Angel Fuentes); Frankenstein's Monster, 2013 (Matt Risoldi); Frankenstein's Planet of Monsters!, 1995 (Mike Brunelle); Frankenstein's Wedding, 2011 (made-for-TV; David Harewood); Frankenweenie, 1984 (Sparky); The Ghost Busters, 1975 (TV series; "Dr. Whatsisname," 1975 episode: Bill [William] Engesser); **The Ghost of Frankenstein**, 1942 (Lon Chaney, Jr.); Gothic, 1987 (Kiran Shah); Haunted, 1993 (David Sanders); **Hellzapoppin'**, 1941 (Dale Van Sickel); The Horror of Frankenstein, 1971 (Dave [David] Prowse); **House of Dracula**, 1945 (Glenn Strange); **The House of Frankenstein**, 1944 (Glenn Strange); House of Frankenstein, 1997 (made-for-TV; Peter Crombie); House of the Wolf Man, 2009 (Craig Dabbs); I, Frankenstein, 2014 (Aaron Eckhart); I Was a Teenage Frankenstein, 1957 (Gary Conway); Jesse James Meets Frankenstein's Daughter, 1966 (Cal Bolder); Lady Frankenstein, 1973 (Peter Whiteman); Life without Soul, 1915 (Percy Darrell Standing); Mary Shelley's Frankenstein, 1994 (Robert De Niro); Mr. Stitch, 1995 (made-for-TV; Wil Wheaton); Monster Brawl, 2011 (Robert Maillet); Monster Mash: The Movie, 1995 (Deron McBee); Monster Squad, 1976 (TV series; Mike Lane); Monstrosity, 1988 (Haal Borske); Munster, Go Home!, 1966 (Fred Gwynne); Necropolis, 1970 (Bruno Corazzari); The Prey, 1984 (Carel Struycken); The Revenge of Frankenstein, 1958 (Michael Gwynn); The Rocky Horror Picture Show, 1975 (Peter Hinwood); Son of Dracula, 1974 (Morris Bush); **Son of Frankenstein**, 1939 (Boris Karloff); Spider-Man and His Amazing Friends, 1981-1986 (TV series;

Walker Edmiston); Tales of Tomorrow, 1951-1953 (TV series; "Frankenstein," 1952 episode: Lon Chaney Jr.); Terror of Frankenstein, 1977 (Per Oscarsson); **Van Helsing**, 2004 (Shuler Hensley); **Victor Frankenstein**, 2015 (Charles Dance); Waxworks II: Lost in Time, 1992 (Stefanos Miltsakakis); The Wide World of Mystery, 1973-1978 (TV series; two 1973 episodes: Bo Svenson); **Young Frankenstein**, 1974 (Peter Boyle).

Friar Tuck (fictional character, a rotund, feisty priest and swordsman aligned with Robin Hood): **The Adventures of Robin Hood**, 1938 (Eugene Pallette); The Adventures of Robin Hood, 1955-1960 (TV series; Alexander Gauge); The Bandit of Sherwood Forest, 1946 (Edgar Buchanan); Beyond Sherwood Forest, 2009 (made-for-TV; Bill Dow); A Challenge for Robin Hood, 1968 (James Hayter); Il Magnifico Robin Hood, 1970 (Jim Clay); **Ivanhoe**, 1952 (Sebastian Cabot); Ivanhoe, 1970- (TV miniseries; Barry Linehan); Ivanhoe, 1982 (made-for-TV; Tony Haygarth); Ivanhoe, 1997- (TV miniseries; Ron Donachie); The Legend of Robin Hood, 1968- (TV series; Walter Slezak); The Legend of Robin Hood, 1975 (TV miniseries; Tony Caunter); Long Live Robin Hood, 1971 (Mario Adorf); The Men of Sherwood Forest, 1954 (Reginald Beckwith); NBC Children's Theatre, 1963-1973 (TV series; "Robin Hood," 1964 episode: Billy Rollo); The New Adventures of Robin Hood, 1997-1999 (TV series; Martyn Ellis); Prince of Thieves, 1948 (Alan Mowbray); The Revenge of Ivanhoe, 1965 (Renato Terra); **Robin and Marian**, 1976 (Ronnie Barker); **Robin Hood**, 1922 (Willard Louis); Robin Hood, 1953- (TV miniseries; Wensley Pithey); **Robin Hood**, 1973 (Andy Devine voiceover); Robin Hood, 1984-1986 (TV series; Phil Rose); Robin Hood, 1991 (Jeff Nuttall); Robin Hood, 2006-2009 (TV series; David Harewood); Robin Hood en zijn schelmen, 1962 (Michel Odekerken); Robin Hood: Ghosts of Sherwood 3D, 2012 (Kai Borchardt); Robin Hood: The Noble Robber, 1966 (Stanislav Ledinek); **Robin Hood: Prince of Thieves**, 1991 (Michael McShane); Rogues of Sherwood Forest, 1950 (Billy House); **The Story of Robin Hood** [aka: The Story of Robin Hood and His Merrie Men], 1952 (James Hayter); Sword of Sherwood Forest, 1961 (Niall MacGinnis); Tales of Robin Hood, 1951 (Ben Welden); The Time Tunnel, 1966-1967 (TV series; "The Revenge of Robin Hood," 1966 episode: Ronald Long); Wolfshead: The Legend of Robin Hood, 1973 (Kenneth Gilbert); Young Robin Hood, 1991-1992 (animated TV series; Harry Standjofski voiceover).

Frog Footman (fictional character in the 1865 novel Alice's Adventures in Wonderland by British author Lewis Carroll): Alice in Wonderland, 1903 (8-minute short; Cecil M. Hepworth); Alice in Wonderland, 1955 (made-for-TV; Gilbert Mack); Alice in Wonderland, 1982 (made-for-TV; Stephen Polk); Alice in Wonderland, 1985 (made-for-TV; Robert Axelrod); Alice's Adventures in Wonderland, 1972 (Ian Trigger); Alice in Wonderland, 1999 (made-for-TV; Peter Eyre); Alice's Adventures in Wonderland, 1972 (Michael Reardon).

Fu Manchu (criminal mastermind created in 1912 by British author Sax Rohmer, appeared in more than two dozen shorts in the 1920s and enacted by H. Agar Lyons before the character appeared in feature films): The Adventures of Fu Manchu, 1956- (TV series; Glen Gordon); The Blood of Fu Manchu, 1968 (Christopher Lee); The Brides of Fu Manchu, 1966 (Christopher Lee); The Castle of Fu Manchu, 1972 (Christopher Lee); Comedy Playhouse, 1961- (TV series; "Elementary My Dear Watson," 1973 episode: Larry Martyn); The Fiendish Plot of Dr. Fu Manchu, 1980 (Peter Sellers); Daughter of the Dragon, 1931 (Warner Oland); Drums of Fu Manchu, 1940 (serial; Henry Brandon); The Face of Fu Manchu, 1965 (Christopher Lee); **The Mask of Fu Manchu**, 1932 (Boris Karloff); **The Mysterious Dr. Fu Manchu**, 1929 (Warner Oland); Paramount on Parade, 1930 (Warner Orland in cameo appearance as Fu Manchu); The Return of Fu Manchu, 1930 (Warner Oland); The Seven Vampires, 1986 (Wilson Grey); The

Warner Oland as Fu Manchu in *The Mysterious Dr. Fu Manchu*, 1929.

Vengeance of Fu Manchu, 1968 (Christopher Lee).

Gabriel (Archangel): The Becoming, 2012 (Jonathan Windt); Bedtime Fairy Tales for Crocodiles, 2003 (Baltimore Beltran); The Bible, 2013- (TV miniseries; Eddie Elks); Celestial Hunt, 2013 (Harvey Malkin voiceover); The Discovery of Heaven, 2003 (Jeroen Krabbe); Dominion, 2014- (TV series; Carl Beukes); Faust, 1960 (Christian Rode); Folio, 1955-1959 (TV series; "The Nativity," 1956 episode: William Needles); Gabriel, 2007 (Andy Whitfield); **Gabriel over the White House** (1933); **The Green Pastures**, 1936 (Oscar Polk); The Green Pastures, 1957 (made-for-TV; Terry Carter); Halleluja!, 2005-2008 (TV series; Gregory Caers); The Hill, 1960 (made-for-TV; Henry Comor); Joyful Hour, 1960 (made-for-TV; Basil Tellou); Laudes Evangelii, 1961 (made-for-TV; Gerard Ohn); Liliom, 1930 (Harvey Clark); The Littlest Angel, 1969 (made-for-TV; Cab Callaway); Lucifer, 1966 (Guido de Moor); Lucifer, 1981 (Ton Lutz); Mary and Joseph: A Story of Faith, 1979 (made-for-TV; Peter Dykstra); Mary, Mother of Jesus, 1999 (made-for-TV; John Light); The Nativity Story, 2006 (Alexander Siddig); The Nativity, 2010 (TV miniseries; John Lynch); Nostradamus, 1994 (Daniel Dresner); **The Nun's Story**, 1959 (Colleen Dewhurst in a sanatorium); On Earth as It Is in Heaven, 1995 (Enrique San Francisco); The Prophecy II, 1998 (Christopher Walken); Raging Angels, 1995 (Deron McBee); The Second Greatest Story Ever Told, 1994 (made-for-TV; Malcolm McDowell); The Three Wise Men, 1976 (Jorge Sanchez Fogarty voiceover); Wandering, 2011 (Aram Sukiasyan); Wingless, 2009 (Karel Zima).

Galahad (legendary knight in the legend of King Arthur in 6th-Century Britain, who quested for the Holy Grail): The Adventures of Sir Galahad, 1949 (serial; George Reeves); **A Connecticut Yankee in King Arthur's Court**, 1949 (Richard Webb); **King Arthur**, 2004 (Hugh Dancy); Merlin, 1998 (TV miniseries; Justin Girdler); **Monty Python and the Holy Grail**, 1975 (Michael Palin); **Prince Valiant**, 1954 (Richard Webb); Prince Valiant, 1997 (Peri Callimanopulos); A Young Connecticut Yankee in King Arthur's Court, 1996 (Paul Hopkins).

Gawain (legendary knight in King Arthur's Round Table in 6th-Century Britain): The Adventures of Sir Galahad, 1949 (serial; Rick Vallin); The Adventures of Sir Lancelot, 1956-1957 (TV series; Andrew Crawford); Arthur the King, 1985 (made-for-TV; Patrick Ryecart); Camelot, 2011 (TV miniseries; Clive Standen); **Excalibur**, 1981 (Liam Neeson); **First Knight**, 1995 (Robert Gwyn Davin); Gawain and the Green Knight, 1973 (Murray Head); Gawain and the Green Knight, 1991 (made-for-TV; Jason Durr); Guinevere, 1994 (made-for-TV; Martin East); **King Arthur**, 2004 (Joel Edgerton); **Knights of the Round Table**, 1953

Martin Landau as the puppet-maker Geppetto in *The Adventures of Pinocchio,* **1996.**

(Robert Urquhart); Lancelot of the Lake, 1974 (Humbert Balsan); The Legend of King Arthur, 1979 (TV series; Geoffrey Bateman); The Legend of Prince Valiant, 1991-1994 (TV series; Tim Curry); Merlin, 1998 (TV miniseries; Sebastian Roche); Merlin: The Return, 2000 (Anthony Bishop); The Mists of Avalon, 2001 (made-for-TV; Noah Huntley); Morte d'Arthur, 1980 (made-for-TV; Roland Alexander); Perceval, 1978 (Andre Dussollier); **Prince Valiant**, 1954 (Sterling Hayden); Prince Valiant, 1997 (Anthony Hickox); Sword of Lancelot, 1963 (George Baker); Sword of the Valiant: The Legend of Sir Gawain and the Green Knight, 1984 (Miles O'Keefe; voiceover by Peter Firth); Unidentified Flying Oddball, 1979 (John Le Mesurier).

Geppetto (a woodcarver who creates a marionette that transform into a real boy, a fictional character in the 1883 children's novel *The Adventures of Pinocchio* by Italian author Carlo Collodi): The Adventures of Pinocchio, 1947 (Augusto Contardi); The Adventures of Pinocchio, 1972 (TV miniseries; Nino Manfredi); **The Adventures of Pinocchio**, 1996 (Martin Landau); Geppetto, 2000 (made-for-TV; Drew Carey); Geppetto's Secret, 2005 (Tom Bosley); The New Adventures of Pinocchio, 1960-1961 (TV series; Stan Francis); The New Adventures of Pinocchio, 1999 (Martin Landau); Once Upon a Time, 2011 (TV series; Tony Amendola); **Pinocchio**, 1940 (Christian Rub voiceover); Pinocchio, 1957 (made-for-TV; Walter Slezak); Pinocchio, 1968 (made-for-TV; Burl Ives); Pinocchio, 1976 (made-for-TV; Danny Kaye); Pinocchio, 1978 (Roberto Bertea voiceover); Pinocchio, 1978 (TV series; Derek Smith voiceover); Pinocchio, 2002 (Carlo Giuffre); Pinocchio, 2008 (made-for-TV; Bob Hoskins); Pinocchio, 2012 (Mino Caprio voiceover); Pinocchio, 2013 (TV miniseries; Mario Adorf); Pinocchio and His Magic Show, 1976 (John H. Fields voiceover); Pinocchio and the Emperor of the Night, 1987 (Tom Bosley voiceover); Pinocchio 3000, 2004 (Howard Ryshpan); Pinocchio's Christmas, 1980 (made-for-TV; George S. Irving); **Shrek**, 2001 (Chris Miller voiceover); **Shrek Forever After**, 2010 (Chris Miller voiceover).

Gervaise (tragic heroine in Emile Zola's 1877 novel, *L'Assommoir*, a destitute young laundress, the mother of Nana who struggles to survive poverty and who takes to drink after her alcoholic husband goes insane in the slums of mid-19th-Century Paris, to which she finally and tragically succumbs): Drink, 1917 (Irene Brown; Joan Morgan as young Gervaise); L'Assommoir, 1921 (Louise Storza; Jean Jabely as young Gervaise); L'Assommoir, 1933 (Line Noro); Gervaise, 1957 (Maria Schell).

Gideon (a devious cat that inveigles a wooden marionette into trouble before that puppet transforms into a real boy, a fictional character in the

1883 children's novel *The Adventures of Pinocchio* by Italian author Carlo Collodi): The Adventures of Pinocchio, 1972 (TV miniseries; Franco Franchi); The New Adventures of Pinocchio, 1999 (Sarah Alexander); **Pinocchio**, 1940 (Mel Blanc voiceover); Pinocchio, 2002 (Max Cavallari); Pinocchio, 2008 (made-for-TV; Rupert Degas).

Gigi (attractive young Parisian girl groomed to be a mistress for a wealthy man, who comes to love her and eventually marries her, a character created in the 1944 novella by French author Colette): Gigi, 1950 (Daniele Delorme); **Gigi**, 1958 (Leslie Caron; Betty Wand singing voice for Gigi); Gigi, 1987 (made-for-TV; Anne Jacquemin); Mademoiselle Gigi, 2006 (made-for-TV; Juliette Lamboley).

Glinda (Good witch of the North who helps Dorothy, a young girl from Kansas transported to a strange world in L. Frank Baum's iconic 1900 novel, *The Wonderful Wizard of Oz*): Journey Back to Oz, 1972 (animated; Rise Stevens voiceover); The Muppets' Wizard of Oz, 2005 (Eric Jacobson as Miss Piggy voiceover); **Oz the Great and Powerful**, 2013 (Michelle Williams); 20th Century Oz, 1976 (Robin Ramsay); The Wiz, 1978 (Lena Horne); **The Wizard of Oz**, 1939 (Billie Burke); The Wizard of Oz, 1982 (animated; Wendy Thatcher voiceover); The Wizard of Oz, 1990-1991 (animated TV series; B.J. Ward voiceover); The Wizard of Oz in Concert: Dreams Come True, 1995 (made-for-TV; Natalie Cole).

God (The Almighty; Supreme Being): Animated Stories from the Bible, 1987-2005 (TV series; Daniel A. Keeler voiceover); The Ark, 2007 (Ron von Paulus); Army from Hell, 2014 (Joe Estevez); The Bible: In the Beginning, 1966 (John Huston voiceover); A Box of Faith, 2015 (Savanah McMahon); Bruce Almighty, 2003 (Morgan Freeman); Death's Wearing High Heels, 2009 (Lorena Sanchez); Evan Almighty, 2007 (Morgan Freeman); **Exodus: Gods and Kings**, 2014 (Isaac Andrews, an eleven-year-old boy, who is God's messenger and/or speaks for God to Moses); Faust, 2010 (Jules Hartley voiceover); Futurama, 1999-2013 (TV series; Billy West); Good Show, 1993 (TV series; Marcos Mundstock); **The Green Pastures**, 1936 (Rex Ingram); Half Past Original, 2012- (TV series; Carl-Mar Moller); Joey, 1982 (made-for-TV; David Fox); Let There Be Light, 1998 (Pierre Arditi voiceover); Macario, 1961 (Jose Luis Jimenez); **Oh, God!**, 1977 (George Burns); Oh, God!: Book II, 1980 (George Burns); Oh, God! You Devil, 1982 (George Burns); On Earth as It Is in Heaven, 1995 (Fernando Fernan Gomez); The Phantom Wagon, 1940 (Rene Genin); **The Prince of Egypt**, 1998 (Val Kilmer voiceover); Robot Chicken, 2005- (animated TV series; Seth Green voiceover); The Sandman, 2011 (Rick Kerrigan); A Soul for Sale, 1915 (Austin Camp); **Strange Cargo**, 1940 (Ian Hunter); Switch, 1991 (Richard Prevost, Linda Gary); Tattooed, 2008 (Ricky Warwick); **The Ten Commandments**, 1956 (Donald Hayne voiceover); Touched by an Angel, 2015 (Jerry Lynch); The Young Ones, 1982-1984 (TV series; two 1984 episodes with Alan Freeman as God).

Goldilocks (fairytale character from the story of *Goldilocks and the Three Bears*): Christmas Night of One Hundred Stars, 1986 (TV special; Sarah Payne); Dora the Explorer, 2000- (TV series; "What Happened Next," 2004 episode: Kailani Coba); Faerie Tale Theatre, 1982-1987 (TV series; "Goldilocks and the Three Bears," 1984 episode: Tatum O'Neal); Happily N'Ever After, 2009 (Kate Higgins voiceover); Jack and the Beanstalk, 1998 (Morwenna Banks).

Green Arrow (fictional comic book superhero): The Batman, 2004-2008 (TV series; Chris Hardwick voiceover); Batman: The Brave and the Bold, 2008-2011 (animated TV series; James Arnold Taylor voiceover); Justice League, 2001-2006 (TV series; Kin Shriner voiceover).

Green Knight (legendary foe of King Arthur in 6th-Century Britain): Gawain and the Green Knight, 1991 (made-for-TV; Malcolm Storry);

Knights of the Round Table, 1953 (Niall MacGinnis); **Monty Python and the Holy Grail**, 1975 (Terry Gilliam); Sword of the Valiant: The Legend of Sir Gawain and the Green Knight, 1984 (Sean Connery).

Green Lantern (fictional comic book superhero): The All-New Super Friends Hour, 1977-1978 (animated TV series; Michael Rye voiceover); Justice League, 2001-2006 (TV series; Dermot Mulroney voiceover); Challenge of the Super Friends, 1978- (animated TV series; Michael Rye voiceover); Justice League, 2001-2006 (TV series; Phil LeMarr voiceover); Legends of the Superheroes, 1979 (TV series; Howard Murphy); **The Lego Movie**, 2014 (Jonah Hill voiceover); The Super Powers Team: Galactic Guardians, 1985- (animated TV series; Michael Rye voiceover); Superman, 1996-2000 (TV series; Michael P. Greco voiceover); The Superman/Aquaman Hour of Adventure, 1967-1968 (TV series; Gerald Mohr).

Gryphon (fictional character from the 1865 novel Alice's Adventures in Wonderland by British author Lewis Carroll): Alice in Wonderland, 1931 (Charles Silvern); **Alice in Wonderland**, 1933 (William Austin); Alice in Wonderland, 1955 (made-for-TV; J. Pat O'Malley); Alice in Wonderland, 1966 (made-for-TV; Malcolm Muggeridge); Alice in Wonderland, 1976 (Paulino Andrada); Alice in Wonderland, 1985 (made-for-TV; Sid Caesar); Alice in Wonderland, 1985- (TV series; Windsor Davies); Alice in Wonderland, 1986 (made-for-TV; four 30-minute segments; Brian Miller); Alice in Wonderland, 1999 (made-for-TV; Donald Sinden; Adrian Getley; Robert Tygner; Dave Barclay); Alice's Adventures in Wonderland, 1972 (Spike Milligan); Alice's Adventures in Wonderland and through the Looking Glass, 1948 (made-for-TV; Dennis Bowen); Alicja, 1982 (Dominic Guard); Dreamchild, 1985 (Ron Mueck); Great Performances, 1971- (TV series; "Alice in Wonderland,' 1983 episode; Swen Swenson); The Wednesday Play, 1964-1970 (TV series; "Alice," 1965 episode: Frank Shelley).

Guinevere (legendary queen of King Arthur in 6th Century Britain): The Adventures of Sir Galahad, 1949 (serial; Marjorie Stapp); The Adventures of Sir Lancelot, 1956-1957 (TV series; Jane Hylton); Arthur the King, 1985 (made-for-TV; Rosalyn Landor); The Black Knight, 1954 (Jean Lodge); **Camelot**, 1967 (Vanessa Redgrave); Camelot, 1982 (made-for-TV; Meg Bussert); Camelot, 2011 (TV miniseries; Tamsin Egerton); Carry On Laughing!, 1975 (TV series; Joan Sims); A Connecticut Yankee in King Arthur's Court, 1989 (made-for-TV: Emma Samms); **Excalibur**, 1981 (Cherie Lunghi); **First Knight**, 1995 (Julia Ormond); Gawain and the Green Knight, 1991 (made-for-TV; Marie Francis); Guinevere, 1994 (made-for-TV; Sheryl Lee); **King Arthur**, 2004 (Keira Knightley); A Knight in Camelot, 1998 (made-for-TV; Amanda Donohoe); **Knights of the Round Table**, 1953 (Ava Gardner); Lancelot of the Lake, 1970 (made-for-TV; Marie-Christine Barrault); Lancelot of the Lake, 1974 (Laura Duke Condominas); The Legend of King Arthur, 1979 (TV series; Felicity Dean); The Legend of Prince Valiant, 1991-1994 (TV series; Samantha Egger); Merlin, 1998 (TV miniseries; Lena Headey); Merlin: The Return, 2000 (Julie Hartley); Morte d'Arthur, 1980 (made-for-TV; Barbara Kellerman); Perceval, 1978 (Marie-Christine Barrault); **Prince Valiant**, 1954 (Jarma Lewis); Sword of Lancelot, 1963 (Jean Wallace); The Time Tunnel, 1966-1967 (TV series; "Merlin the Magician," 1967 episode: Lisa Jak); A Young Connecticut Yankee in King Arthur's Court, 1996 (Lisa Flores).

Gustave Flambeau (an arch criminal and nemesis of Father Brown in G.K. Chesterton's stories; see Father Brown, this index): Das schwarze Schaf, 1960 (Siegfried Lowitz); **The Detective**, 1954 (Peter Finch); Father Brown, 1974- (TV series; Dennis Burgess); Father Brown, 2013- (TV series; John Light); Father Brown, Detective, 1934 (Paul Lukas); I racconti di Padre Brown, 1970- (TV series; Arnoldo Foa); Pater Brown, 1966-1972 (TV series; Ingold Platzer); Theater of the Word, Inc., 2009-

Keira Knightley as Guinevere in *King Arthur*, 2004.

(TV series; "The Honor of Israel Gow," 2009 episode: Julian Ahlquist). Gypo Nolan (towering, dim-witted Irish thug who betrays his best friend to the British during the Irish Civil War and is hunted by the IRA in Dublin as depicted in Liam O'Flaherty's 1925 novel, *The Informer*): The Informer, 1929 (Lars Hansen); **The Informer**, 1935 (Victor McLaglen); Uptight, 1968 (Julian Mayfield).

Hades (in Greek mythology; god of the underworld or, in modern perception, hell; Pluto in Roman mythology): **Clash of the Titans**, 2010 (Ralph Fiennes); **Hercules**, 1997 (James Woods voiceover); Hercules, 1998-1999 (TV series; James Woods voiceover); Hercules in the Underworld, 1994 (made-for-TV; Mark Ferguson); Hercules: The Brave and the Bold, 2013 (Bryan Kreutz); The Illiac Passion, 1968 (Carlos Anduze); Mythic Warriors: Guardians of the Legend, 1998- (TV series; Norm Spencer); Myths, 2009- (TV series; Christopher Hughes); Percy Jackson & the Olympians: The Lightning Thief, 2010 (Steve Coogan); Persephone, 1952 (made-for-TV; Lewis Stringer); Wrath of the Titans, 2012 (Ralph Fiennes); Young Hercules, 1998-1999 (TV series; Erik Thomson).

Hamlet (Prince of Denmark, the tragic son of a murdered king who sets out to avenge his father's death, the best known and most popular character of the brilliant plays by William Shakespeare): The DuPont Show of the Month, 1957-1961 (TV series; "Hamlet," 1959 episode: John Neville); An Englishman Abroad, 1984 (made-for-TV; Mark Wing-Davey); Great Performances, 1971- (TV series; "Hamlet," 1990 episode: Kevin Kline); Hamlet, 1913 (Johnston Forbes-Robertson); Hamlet, 1917 (Ruggero Ruggeri); Hamlet, 1921 (Asta Nielsen); Hamlet, 1947 (made-for-TV; John Byron); **Hamlet**, 1948 (Laurence Olivier); Hamlet, 1954 (made-for-TV; Maurice Evans); Hamlet, 1955 (made-for-TV; Bengt Ekerot); Hamlet, 1959 (made-for-TV; William Job); Hamlet, 1960 (made-for-TV; Maximilian Schell); Hamlet, 1961 (TV series; Barry Foster); Hamlet, 1964 (made-for-TV; Alfredo Alcon); Hamlet, 1964 (Richard Burton); Hamlet, 1966 (Innokenti Smoktunovski); **Hamlet**, 1969 (Nicol Williamson); Hamlet, 1970 (Ian McKellen); Hamlet, 1973 (Rick McKenna); Hamlet, 1976 (Anthony Meyer; David Meyer); Hamlet, 1979 (made-for-TV; Michel Hermon); Hamlet, 1983 (made-for-TV; Laszlo Galffi); Hamlet, 1985 (made-for-TV; Tero Jartti); Hamlet, 1990 (made-for-TV; Gerard Desarthe); **Hamlet**, 1990 (Mel Gibson); Hamlet, 1992 (made-for-TV; Heikki Kinnunen); Hamlet, 1994 (made-for-TV; Michael Schenk); **Hamlet**, 1996 (Kenneth Branagh); Hamlet, 2000 (Thomas Hampson); Hamlet, 2000 (Ethan Hawke); Hamlet, 2000 (made-for-TV; Campbell Scott); Hamlet, 2004 (made-for-TV; Michal Czernecki); Hamlet, 2005 (Stephen Cavanagh); Hamlet, 2007 (Wilson [William] Belchambers); Hamlet, 2009 (David Melville); Hamlet, 2009 (made-for-

Clint Eastwood as "Dirty Harry" Callahan in *Magnum Force*, 1973.

TV; David Tennant); Hamlet, 2014 (Bruce Ramsay); Hamlet, 2015 (Travis Wilker); Hamlet, 2015 (Maxine Peake); Hamlet at Elsinore, 1964 (made for TV; Christopher Plummer); Hamlet, Prince of Denmark, 1980 (made-for-TV; Derek Jacobi); Hamlet, Prince of Denmark, 1997 (Gary Paul Wright); Hamlet: The Series, 2014 (TV series; Kitty Mortland); ITV Play of the Week, 1955-1974 (TV series; "Hamlet," 1956 episode: Paul Scofield); ITV Saturday Night Theatre, 1969- (TV series; "Hamlet," 1970 episode: Richard Chamberlain); Khoon Ka Khoon, 1935 (Sohrab Modi); Rosencrantz & Guildenstern Are Dead, 1991 (Iain Glen).

Hank Martin (fictional character in Mark Twain's 1889 fantasy novel, *A Connecticut Yankee in King Arthur's Court*): **A Connecticut Yankee**, 1931 (Will Rogers); A Connecticut Yankee in King Arthur's Court, 1921 (Harry Myers); **A Connecticut Yankee in King Arthur's Court**, 1949 (Bing Crosby); Once upon a Classic, 1976-1979 (TV series: "A Connecticut Yankee in King Arthur's Court," 1978 episode: Paul Rudd); Studio One in Hollywood, 1948-1958 (TV series: "A Connecticut Yankee in King Arthur's Court," 1952 episode: Thomas Mitchell).

Harry Callahan (rugged SFPD inspector who doggedly tracks down crimiminals irrespective of police policies and regulations, all played by Clint Eastwood): **The Dead Pool**, 1988; **Dirty Harry**, 1971; **The Enforcer**, 1976; **Magnum Force**, 1973; **Sudden Impact**, 1983.

Harry Faversham (British officer who sets put to prove his courage after he is accused of cowardice by his friends and lover in A.E.W. Mason's 1902 adventure novel, *The Four Feathers*): Four Feathers, 1915 (Howard Estabrook; Ogden Child Jr. as young Harry); The Four Feathers, 1921 (Harry Ham; Roger Livesey as young Harry); The Four Feathers, 1929 (Richard Arlen; Philippe De Lacy as young Harry); **The Four Feathers**, 1939 (John Clements; Clive Baxter as young Harry); Storm over the Nile, 1955 (Anthony Steel; Paul Streather as young Harry); The Four Feathers, 1978 (made-for-TV; Beau Bridges; Alexander Bird and Jonathan Scott-Taylor in separate ages as young Harry); The Four Feathers, 2002 (Heath Ledger).

Harry Morgan (tough hero in Ernest Hemingway's 1937 novel, *To Have and Have Not*): **The Breaking Point**, 1950 (John Garfield); The Gun Runners, 1958 (Audie Murphy as Sam Martin, role model of Harry Morgan); Lux Video Theatre, 1950-1959 (TV series; "To Have and Have Not," 1957 episode: Edmond O'Brien); **To Have and Have Not**, 1944 (Humphrey Bogart).

Harry Palmer (unenthusiastic British agent who manages to triumph in spite of himself, a character created by spy writer Len Deighton in his 1962 novel, *The Ipcress File*): Billion Dollar Brain, 1967 (Michael Caine); Bullet to Beijing, 1998 (made-for-TV; Michael Caine); **Funeral in Berlin**, 1966 (Michael Caine); **The Ipcress File**, 1965 (Michael Caine); Midnight in St. Petersburg, 1998 (made-for-TV; Michael Caine); Spy Story, 1976 (Michael Petrovitch).

Harry Potter (youth wizard who, along with friends, attends the Hogswart School of Witchcraft and Wizardry and who battles an evil professor bent on world domination, created by British author J.K. Rowling): **Harry Potter and the Chamber of Secrets**, 2002 (Daniel Radcliffe); **Harry Potter and the Deathly Hallows Part 1**, 2010 (Daniel Radcliffe); **Harry Potter and the Deathly Hallows Part 2**, 2011 (Daniel Radcliffe); **Harry Potter and the Goblet of Fire**, 2005 (Daniel Radcliffe); **Harry Potter and the Half-Blood Prince**, 2009 (Daniel Radcliffe); Harry Potter and the Order of the Phoenix, 2007 (Daniel Radcliffe); **Harry Potter and the Prisoner of Azkaban**, 2004 (Daniel Radcliffe); **Harry Potter and the Sorcerer's Stone**, 2001 (Daniel Radcliffe).

Hawkeye (Nathaniel "Natty" Bumppo; indefatigable pioneer, scout and Indian fighter who was raised by the Mohican tribe, a wilderness hero created by author James Fenimore Cooper in his pentalogy of novels titled the *Leatherstocking Tales*; this character is most likely based on real-life pioneer Daniel Boone): The Deerslayer, 1978 (made-for-TV; Steve Forrest); Fall of the Mohicans, 1965 (Luis Induni); Hawkeye, 1994- (TV series; Lee Horsley); Hawkeye and the Last of the Mohicans, 1957- (TV series; John Hart); Hawkeye, the Pathfinder, 1973- (TV miniseries; Paul Massie); The Iroquois Trail, 1950 (Robert Montgomery); **The Last of the Mohicans**, 1920 (Harry Lorraine); The Last of the Mohicans, 1932 (Harry Carey); **The Last of the Mohicans**, 1936 (Randolph Scott); The Last of the Mohicans, 1971 (TV miniseries; Kenneth Ives); The Last of the Mohicans, 1975 (animated made-for-TV; Mike Road voiceover); Last of the Mohicans, 1977 (made-for-TV; Steve Forrest); The Last of the Mohicans, 1987 (animated made-for-TV; John Waters voiceover); **The Last of the Mohicans**, 1992 (Daniel Day-Lewis); Last of the Redmen, 1947 (Michael O'Shea); The Leatherstocking Tales, 1984 (TV miniseries; Cliff De Young); The Pathfinder, 1996 (made-for-TV; Kevin Dillon).

Heathcliff (Brooding anti-hero and star-crossed lover of Catherine Earnshaw in Emily Bronte's 1847 novel, *Wuthering Heights*): BBC Sunday-Night Theatre, 1950-1959 (TV series; "Wuthering Heights," 1953 episode: Richard Todd); Broadway Television Theatre, 1952-1954 (TV series; "Wuthering Heights," 1953 episode: William Prince); The DuPont Show of the Month, 1957-1961 (TV series; "Wuthering Heights," 1958 episode: Richard Burton); Heathcliff, 1997 (made-for-TV; Cliff Richard); Matinee Theatre, 1955-1958 (TV series; "Wuthering Heights," 1955 episode: Richard Boone; Sammy Ogg as young Heathcliff; "Wuthering Heights,' 1957 episode: Tom Tryon; Johnny Crawford as young Heathcliff); Wuthering Heights, 1920 (Milton Rosmer; Albert Brantford as young Heathcliff); **Wuthering Heights**, 1939 (Laurence Olivier; Rex Downing as young Heathcliff); Wuthering Heights, 1948 (made-for-TV; Kieron Moore); Wuthering Heights, 1962 (made-for-TV; Keith Michell); Wuthering Heights, 1967 (TV series; Ian McShane; Dennis Golding as young Heathcliff); Wuthering Heights, 1970 (Timothy Dalton); Wuthering Heights, 1978 (TV miniseries; Ken Hutchison; Dale Tarry and Robin Glynn as young Heathcliff); Wuthering Heights, 1983 (Jorge Mistral); Wuthering Heights, 1992 (Ralph Fiennes; Jon Howard as young Heathcliff); Wuthering Heights, 1998 (made-for-TV; Robert Cavanah; Terry Clynes as young Heathcliff); Wuthering Heights, 2009 (TV miniseries; Tom Hardy; Declan Wheeldon as young Heathcliff); Wuthering Heights, 2012 (James Howson; Solomon Glave as young Heathcliff).

Hebe (Greek goddess of youth; daughter of Zeus and Hera; Juventus in

Roman mythology): Hercules: The Brave and the Bold, 2013 (Elizabeth Renee); Night Life of the Gods, 1935 (Geneva Mitchell); Rome in a Day, 2008 (Cathy Bennett); The Triumph of Venus, 1918 (Ruth Bradley).

Hector (Trojan prince in Greek mythology and greatest fighter in the Trojan War): BBC Sunday-Night Theatre, 1950-1959 (TV series; "Troilus and Cressida," 1954 episode: William Squire); Der trojanisch krieg findet nicht statt, 1957 (made-for-TV; Jurgen Goslar); Der trojanisch krieg findet nicht statt, 1964 (made-for-TV; Rolf Boysen); The Face of Love, 1954 (made-for-TV; Hugh Sinclair); Fury of Achilles, 1962 (Jacques Bergerac); Hector the Mighty, 1972 (Frank Latimore voiceover); Helen of Troy, 1924 (Carl de Vogt); Helen of Troy, 1951 (Stig Jarrel); Helen of Troy, 1956 (Harry Andrews); Helen of Troy, 2003 (TV miniseries; Daniel Lapaine); ITV Play of the Week, 1955-1974 (TV series; "Tiger at the Gates," 1960 episode: Keith Mitchell); King Priam, 1985 (made-for-TV; Omar Ebrahim); Le guerre de Troie n'aura pas lieu, 1967 (made-for-TV; Daniel Ivernel); The Odyssey, 1997- (TV series; Derek Lea); Play of the Week, 1959-1961 (TV series; "Tiger at the Gate," 1960 episode: Donald Davis); The Private Life of Helen of Troy, 1927 (George Kotsonaros); Troilus & Cressida, 1981 (made-for-TV; John Shrapnel); Troilus und Cressida, 1964 (made-for-TV; Hans Hackermann); Troilus und Cressida, 1969 (made-for-TV; Kurt Heintel); **Troy**, 2004 (Eric Bana).

Heidi (young and effervescent orphan girl who lives in the Swiss Alps under the care of her gentle grandfather, first appearing in the 1881 novel by Swiss author Johanna Spyri, one of the most widely read children's books ever written): Courage Mountain, 1990 (Juliette Caton); A Gift for Heidi, 1958 (Sandy Descher); **Heidi**, 1937 (Shirley Temple); Heidi, 1954 (Elsbeth Sigmund); Heidi, 1956 (TV series; Verinha Darci); Heidi, 1959 (TV series; Sara O'Connor); Heidi, 1968 (Eva Maria Singhammer); Heidi, 1968 (made-for-TV; Jennifer Edwards); Heidi, 1974 (TV miniseries; Emma Blake); Heidi, 1978- (TV series; Katia Polletin); Heidi, 1993 (Noley Thornton); Heidi, 2001 (Cornelia Groschel); Heidi, 2005 (Emma Bolger); Heidi, 2015 (Anuk Steffen); Heidi: A Girl of the Alps, 1974- (animated made-for-TV; Kazuko Sugiyama voiceover); Heidi Grows Up, 1954 (TV miniseries; Julia Lockwood; Ann Summers); Heidi and Peter, 1955 (Elsbeth Sigmund); Heidi's Song, 1982 (animated musical; Margery Gray voiceover); The New Adventures of Heidi, 1978 (made-for-TV; Katy Kurtzman).

Helen of Troy (in Greek mythology; abducted by Paris of Troy, creating the Greek-Trojan War): **The Awful Truth**, 1937 (Betty Douglas); BBC Sunday-Night Theatre, 1950-1959 (TV series; "Troilus and Cressida," 1954 episode; Helen Shingler); Der trojanisch krieg findet nicht statt, 1957 (made-for-TV; Margit Saad); Der trojanisch krieg findet nicht statt, 1964 (made-for-TV; Ruth-Maria Kubitschek); Doctor Faustus, 1968 (Elizabeth Taylor); Eneide, 1971 (TV series; Annabella Incontrera); The Face of Love, 1954 (made-for-TV; Joan Miller); Helen of Troy, 1924 (Edy Darclea); Helen of Troy, 1951 (Eva Dahlbeck); Helen of Troy, 1956 (Rossana Podesta); Helen of Troy, 2003 (made-for-TV: Sienna Guillory); Helen, Yes…Helen of Troy, 1974 (Christa Linder); Hercules, 1998-1999 (TV series; Jodi Benson voiceover); Hercules: The Brave and the Bold, 2013 (Kinesha Holt); Ich log die Wahrheit, 1971 (made-for-TV; Inken Sommer); ITV Play of the Week, 1955-1974 (TV series; "Tiger at the Gates," 1960 episode: Carole Lesley); King Priam, 1985 (made-for-TV; Anne Mason); La belle Helene, 1996 (Vesselina Kasarova); La belle Helene, 2000 (Felicity Lott); Las troyanas, 1963 (Erna Martha Bauman); Le guerre de Troie n'aura pas lieu, 1967 (made-for-TV; Caroline Cellier); The Lion of Thebes, 1964 (Yvonne Furneaux); Loves of Three Queens, 1954 (Hedy Lamarr); Mythic Warriors: Guardians of the Legend, 1998- (TV series; "Ulysses and the Trojan Horse," 1999 episode; Kristina Nicoll voiceover); The Pharaoh Project, 2001 (Suzanne Turner); Play of the Week, 1959-1961 (TV se-

Louis Wolheim and John Barrymore (as Henry Jekyll) in *Dr. Jekyll and Mr. Hyde,* **1920.**

ries; "Tiger at the Gate," 1960 episode: Patricia Cutts); The Private Life of Helen of Troy, 1927 (Maria Corda); The Story of Mankind, 1957 (Dani Crayne); Tantalus: Behind the Mask, 2001 (Annalee Jefferies); The Time Tunnel, 1966-1967 (TV series; "Revenge of the Gods," 1966 episode: Dee Hartford); Toto all'inferno, 1955 (Mara Werlen); Troilus & Cressida, 1981 (made-for-TV; Ann Pennington); Troilus und Cressida, 1964 (made-for-TV; Marlies Hoffmann); Troilus und Cressida, 1966 (made-for-TV; Mary Payne); Troilus und Cressida, 1969 (made-for-TV; Margot Trooger); The Trojan Horse, 1962 (Hedy Vessel); The Trojan Women, 1971 (Irene Papas); The Trojan Women, 2004 (Shelley Delayne); **Troy**, 2004 (Diane Kruger).

Henry Higgins (Professor Henry Higgins; chauvenistic educator of dialects who transforms an uncouth Cockney flower girl into a grand lady, his character created in George Bernard Shaw's 1912 play, "*Pygmalion*"): BBC Play of the Month, 1965-1983 (TV series, "Pygmalion," 1973 episode: James Villiers); BBC Sunday-Night Theater, 1950-1959 (TV series; "Pygmalion," 1956 episode: Keith Michell); Celebrity Playhouse, 1981 (TV series, "Pygmalion," 1981 episode: Robert Powell); The Makeover, 2013 (made-for-TV; Julia Stiles as Hannah Higgins in a gender switch); **My Fair Lady**, 1964 (Rex Harrison); My Fair Lady; Minha Linda Senhora, 2004 (made-for-TV; Carlos Quintas); My Fair Zombie, 2013 (Lawrence Evenchick); National Theatre Live: 50 Years on Stage, 2013 (made-for-TV; Alex Jennings); Pygmalion, 1935 (Gustaf Grundgens); Pygmalion, 1937 (Johan De Meester); **Pygmalion**, 1938 (Leslie Howard); Pygmalion, 1948 (made-for-TV; Ralph Michael); Pygmalion, 1954 (made-for-TV; John Clements); Pygmalion, 1956 (made-for-TV; Axel von Ambesser); Pygmalion, 1957 (made-for-TV; Heinz Hinze); Pygmalion, 1958 (made-for-TV; Mikhail Tsaryov); Pygmalion, 1963 (made-for-TV; James Donald); Pygmalion, 1968 (made-for-TV; Gunnar Bjornstrand); Pygmalion, 1976 (made-for-TV; Coen Flink); Pygmalion, 1983 (made-for-TV; Peter O'Toole).

Henry Jekyll (Dr. Henry Jekyll, fictional character who transforms from a good persona into an evil one called Edward Hyde, as portrayed in the 1886 novel *The Strange Case of Dr. Jekyll and Mr. Hyde* by Robert Louis Stevenson): Abbott and Costello Meet Dr. Jekyll and Mr. Hyde, 1953 (Boris Karloff); The ABC Saturday Night Superstar Movie, 1972-1974 (TV series; "The Mad, Mad, Mad Monsters," animated 1972 episode: Allen Swift voiceover); Daughter of Dr. Jekyll, 1957 (Gloria Talbot); Der Januskopf [aka: Janus-Faced], 1920 (role model for Conrad Veidt); **Dr. Jekyll and Mr. Hyde**, 1920 (John Barrymore); **Dr. Jekyll and Mr. Hyde**, 1931 (Fredric March); **Dr. Jekyll and Mr. Hyde**, 1941 (Spencer Tracy); Dr. Jekyll and Mr. Hyde, 1956 (TV series; Dennis Price); Dr. Jekyll and Mr. Hyde, 1973 (made-for-TV; Kirk Douglas);

Peter Ustinov (as Agatha Christie's sleuth Hercule Poirot) in *Death on the Nile,* 1978.

Dr. Jekyll and Mr. Hyde, 1980 (made-for-TV; David Hemmings); Dr. Jekyll and Mr. Hyde, 1986 (made-for-TV; Max Meldrum voiceover); Dr. Jekyll and Mr. Hyde, 2000 (Adam Baldwin); Dr. Jekyll and Mr. Hyde, 2003 (made-for-TV; John Hannah); Dr. Jekyll and Mr. Hyde, 2008 (made-for-TV; Dougray Scott); Dr. Jekyll and Sister Hyde, 1971 (Dr. Jekyll: Ralph Bates; Sister Hyde: Martine Beswick); Dr. Jekyll's Dungeon of Death, 1979 (James Mathers); Edge of Sanity, 1989 (Tony Perkins); Experiment in Evil, 1959 (role model for Jean-Louis Barrault); I, Monster, 1971 (role model for Christopher Lee); Jekyll, 2007 (Matt Keeslar); Jekyll and Hyde, 1990 (made-for-TV; Michael Caine); Jekyll & Hyde, 2015 (TV series; Tom Bateman); Jekyll and Hyde: The Musical, 2001 (David Hasselhoff); Jekyll and Hyde…Together Again, 1982 (Mark Blankfield); The League of Extraordinary Gentlemen, 2003 (Jason Flemyng); The Man with Two Faces, 2008 (James Ian Mair); Mary Reilly, 1996 (John Malkovich); Matinee Theatre, 1955-1958 (TV series; "Dr. Jekyll and Mr. Hyde," 1957 episode: Douglass Montgomery); Mr. Black, Mr. Hyde, 1976 (Bernie Casey); Nightmare Classics, 1989- (TV series; "Dr. Jekyll and Mr. Hyde," 1989 episode: Anthony Andrews); **The Nutty Professor**, 1963 (role model for Jerry Lewis); **The Nutty Professor**, 1996 (role model for Eddie Murphy); The Pagemaster, 1994 (Leonard Nimoy voiceover); The Son of Dr. Jekyll, 1951 (Louis Hayward); The Strange Case of Dr. Jekyll and Mr. Hyde, 1950 (made-for-TV; Dr. Jekyll: Alan Judd; Mr. Hyde: Desmond Llewelyn); The Strange Case of Dr. Jekyll and Mr. Hyde, 1968 (made-for-TV; Jack Palance); The Strange Case of Dr. Jekyll and Mr. Hyde, 2006 (Tony Todd); Suspense, 1949-1954 (TV series; "Dr. Jekyll and Mr. Hyde," 1949 episode: Ralph Bell; "Dr. Jekyll and Mr. Hyde," 1951 episode; Basil Rathbone); The Two Faces of Dr. Jekyll, 1961 (Paul Massie); **Van Helsing**, 2004 (Henry Jekyll: Stephen H. Fisher; Edward Hyde: Robbie Coltrane); Waxworks II: Lost in Time, 1992 (Michael Viela).

Hephaestus (Greek god of fire, volcanoes and forging of iron; Vulcan in Roman mythology): Hercules, 1998-1999 (TV series; Kevin Michael Richardson voiceover); Percy Jackson & the Olympians: The Lightning Thief, 2010 (Conrad Coates); Young Hercules, 1998-1999 (TV series; Jason Hoyte).

Hera (Greek goddess of women, one of three sisters to Zeus and also the wife of Zeus; Juno in Roman mythology): The Adventures of Hercules II, 1985 (Maria Rosario Omaggio): **Clash of the Titans**, 1981 (Claire Bloom); **Clash of the Titans**, 2010 (Nina Young); Goddess of Love, 1988 (made-for-TV; Betsy Palmer); Hercules, 1983 (Rosanna Podesta); **Hercules**, 1997 (Samantha Eggar voiceover); Hercules, 1998-1999 (TV series; Samantha Eggar voiceover); Hercules: The Brave and

the Bold, 2013 (Camille Marolf); Hercules: The Legendary Journeys—Hercules and the Circle of Fire, 1994 (made-for-TV; Joy Watson voiceover); **Jason and the Argonauts**, 1963 (Honor Blackman); Jason and the Argonauts, 2000 (TV miniseries; Olivia Williams); Mythic Warriors: Guardians of the Legend, 1998- (TV series; Janet-Laine Green); Myths, 2009- (TV series; Scarlett Sabet); Percy Jackson & the Olympians: The Lightning Thief, 2010 (Erica Cerra); The Private Life of Helen of Troy, 1927 (Virginia Thomas); Young Hercules, 1998-1999 (TV series; Elizabeth Hawthorne).

Hercule Poirot (incisive and meticulous Belgian detective created by Agatha Christie who appears in more than forty of her novels and dozens of short stories): Alibi, 1931 (Austin Trevor); The Alphabet Murders, 1965 (Tony Randall); Agatha Christie: Poirot, 1989-2013 (TV series; David Suchet); Appointment with Death, 1988 (Peter Ustinov); Black Coffee, 1931 (Austin Trevor); Black Coffee, 1973 (made-for-TV; Horst Bollmann); Dead Man's Folly, 1986 (made-for-TV; Peter Ustinov); **Death on the Nile**, 1978 (Peter Ustinov); Evil under the Sun, 1982 (Peter Ustinov); General Electric Theater, 1953-1962 (TV series; "Hercule Poirot," 1962 episode: Martin Gabel); Lord Edgware Dies, 1934 (Austin Trevor); Murder by the Book, 1986 (made-for-TV; Ian Holm); Murder in Three Acts, 1986 (made-for-TV; Peter Ustinov); **Murder on the Orient Express**, 1974 (Albert Finney); Murder on the Orient Express, 2001 (made-for-TV; Alfred Molina); **Revenge of the Pink Panther**, 1978 (Andrew Sachs); The Strange Case of the End of Civilization as We Know It, 1977 (Dudley Jones); Thirteen at Dinner, 1985 (made-for-TV; Peter Ustinov).

Hercules (aka: Heracles, son of God Zeus in Greek mythology possessing great strength): The Adventures of Hercules II, 1985 (Lou Ferrigno); The Conqueror of Atlantis, 1965 (Kirk Morris); Conquest of Mycene, 1963 (Gordon Scott); The Fury of Hercules, 1963 (Brad Harris); Greek Gods and Goddesses: Jason and the Argonauts, 2004 (made-for-TV; Nick Brimble); Helen of Troy, 1951 (Ake Soderblom); Herakles, 1966 (made-for-TV; Martti Kuisma); Hercules, 1959 (Steve Reeves); Hercules, 1983 (Lou Ferrigno); **Hercules**, 1997 (Tate Donovan voiceover); Hercules, 1998-1999 (TV series; Tate Donovan voiceover); Hercules, 2005- (TV miniseries; Paul Telfer; Jamie Croft as young Hercules); Hercules, 2014 (Dwayne Johnson); Hercules against the Barbarians, 1964 (Mark Forest); Hercules against Rome, 1964 (Sergio Ciani); Hercules against the Moon Men, 1964 (Sergio Ciani); Hercules Against the Sons of the Sun, 1964 (Mark Forest); Hercules and the Amazon Women, 1994 (made-for-TV; Kevin Sorbo; Peter Malloch as young Hercules); Hercules and the Captive Women, 1963 (Reg Park); Hercules and the Haunted World, 1964 (Reg Park); Hercules and the Princess of Troy, 1965 (made-for-TV; Gordon Scott); Hercules and the Tyrants of Babylon, 1964 (Peter Lupus); Hercules and the Valley of Woe, 1961 (Frank Gordon); Hercules in New York, 1970 (Arnold Schwarzenegger); Hercules in the Maze of the Minotaur, 1994 (made-for-TV; Kevin Sorbo); Hercules in the Underworld, 1994 (made-for-TV; Kevin Sorbo); Hercules Reborn, 2014 (John Hennigan); Hercules Returns, 1993 (Des Mangan); Hercules' Revenge, 1960 (Mark Forest); Hercules, Samson & Ulysses, 1965 (Kirk Morris); Hercules the Avenger, 1965 (Reg Park); Hercules: The Brave and the Bold, 2013 (Eric Ober as adult Hercules); Hercules the Invincible, 1964 (Dan Vadis); Hercules: The Legendary Journeys—Hercules and the Circle of Fire, 1994 (made-for-TV; Kevin Sorbo); Hercules: The Legendary Journeys—Hercules and the Lost Kingdom, 1994 (made-for-TV; Kevin Sorbo); Hercules Unchained, 1960 (Steve Reeves); Hercules vs. the Giant Warriors, 1964 (Dan Vadis); **Jason and the Argonauts**, 1963 (Nigel Green); Jason and the Argonauts, 2000- (TV series; Brian Thompson); Jason and the Heroes of Mount Olympus, 2001- (TV series; Pat Fraley); The Legend of Hercules, 2014 (Kellan Lutz); The Loves of Hercules, 1960 (Mickey Hargitay); The Magnificent Gladiator, 1964 (Mark Forest); The Mighty Hercules, 1963-1966 (TV series; Jimmy Tapp voiceover); Miciste il vendicatore dei Maya, 1964 (Kirk Morris); Mythic Warriors: Guardians of the Legend, 1998- (TV series; Lawrence Bayne); Samson and the Mighty Challenge, 1964 (Sergio Ciani); Space Sentinels, 1977 (TV series; George DiCenzo); The Three Stooges Meet Hercules, 1962 (Samson Burke); The Thracian Horses, 1946 (made-for-TV; Andrew Cruickshank); Ulysses against Hercules, 1962 (Mike Lane); Vamping Venus, 1928 (Joe Bonomo); Xena: Warrior Princess, 1995-2001 (TV series; Kevin Sorbo); Young Hercules, 1998-1999 (TV series; Ryan Gosling).

Hermes (Greek god, son of Zeus and messenger of the gods; Mercury in Roman mythology): **Clash of the Titans**, 2010 (Alexander Siddig); **Hercules**, 1997 (Paul Shaffer voiceover); Hercules, 1998-1999 (TV series; Paul Shaffer voiceover); Hercules: The Brave and the Bold, 2013 (Jeremy Jex); **Jason and the Argonauts**, 1963 (Michael Gwynn); Mythic Warriors: Guardians of the Legend, 1998- (TV series; Richard Clarkin, Stephen Bogaert); Percy Jackson & the Olympians: The Lightning Thief, 2010 (Dylan Neal); Percy Jackson: Sea of Monsters, 2013 (Nathan Fillion); Persephone, 1952 (made-for-TV; Peter Symcox).

Huckleberry Finn (character in the books of Mark Twain): The Adventures of Huck Finn, 1993 (Elijah Wood); The Adventures of Huckleberry Finn, 1955 (made-for-TV; Charles Taylor); **The Adventures of Huckleberry Finn**, 1960 (Eddie Hodges); The Adventures of Huckleberry Finn, 1973 (Roman Madyanov); The Adventures of Huckleberry Finn, 1981 (made-for-TV; Kurt Ida); The Adventures of Huckleberry Finn, 1984 (made-for-TV; Simon Hinton voiceover); **The Adventures of Mark Twain**, 1944 (Gene Holland); The Adventures of Mark Twain, 1985 (Gary Krug voiceover); The Adventures of Tom Sawyer, 1960 (TV series; Mark Strotheide); **The Adventures of Tom Sawyer**, 1938 (Jackie Moran); The Adventures of Tom Sawyer, 1980 (TV series; Kazuyo Aoki voiceover); The Adventures of Tom Sawyer, 1986 (Scott Higgins voiceover); The Adventures of Tom Sawyer and Huckleberry Finn, 1982 (made-for-TV; Vladislav Galkin [as Vladik Sukhachyov]); Aventures de Tom Sawyer, 1953 (TV series; Joao Manuel); Back to Hannibal: The Return of Tom Sawyer and Huckleberry Finn, 1990 (made-for-TV; Mitchell Anderson); Climax!, 1954-1958 (TV series; "Adventures of Huckleberry Finn," 1955 episode: Charles Taylor); Excursion, 1953 (TV series; "The Adventures of Huckleberry Finn," 1953 episode: Clifford Tatum Jr.); Fantasy Island, 1977-1984 (TV series; "The Angel's Triangle/Natchez Bound," 1982 episode: Adam Rich); Huck and the King of Hearts, 1994 (Chauncey Leopardi); Huck and Tom, 1918 (Robert Gordon); Huckleberry Finn, 1920 (Lewis Sargent); Huckleberry Finn, 1931 (Junior Durkin); **Huckleberry Finn** [aka: The Adventures of Huckleberry Finn], 1939 (Mickey Rooney); Huckleberry Finn, 1967 (made-for-TV; Martin Lartigue); Huckleberry Finn, 1974 (Jeff East); Huckleberry Finn, 1975 (made-for-TV; Ron Howard); Huckleberry Finn and His Friends, 1979-1980 (TV series; Ian Tracey); Mark Twain: Beneath the Laughter, 1979 (made-for-TV; Steve Stark); The New Adventures of Huckleberry Finn, 1968-1969 (TV series; Michael Shea); The Secret Adventures of Tom Sawyer and Huck Finn, 1982 (made-for-TV; Anthony Michael Hall); Sawyer and Finn, 1983 (made-for-TV; Michael Dudikoff); Shirley Temple's Storybook, 1958-1961 (TV series; "Tom and Huck," 1960 episode: Teddy Rooney); Tom and Huck, 1995 (Brad Renfro); Tom Sawyer, 1917 (Robert Gordon); **Tom Sawyer**, 1930 (Junior Durkin); **Tom Sawyer**, 1973 (Jeff East); Tom Sawyer, 1973 (made-for-TV; Jeff Tyler); Tom Sawyer, 2011 (Leon Seidel); Tom Sawyer & Huckleberry Finn, 2015 (Jake T. Austin); Tom Sawyer, Detective, 1938 (Donald O'Connor); The United States Steel Hour, 1953-1963 (TV series; "Tom Sawyer," 1956 episode: Jimmy Boyd; "The Adventures of Huckleberry Finn," 1957 episode: Jimmy Boyd); Wishbone, 1995-1999 (TV series; "A Tail in Twain," two 1995 episodes: Christopher Reagan Ammons [as Reagan Ammons]).

Humpty-Dumpty (fictional character from the 1865 novel Alice's Ad-

Tommy Kelly (Tom Sawyer) and Jackie Moran (Huckleberry Finn) in *The Adventures of Tom Sawyer,* **1938.**

ventures in Wonderland by British author Lewis Carroll): **Alice in Wonderland**, 1933 (W.C. Fields); Alice in Wonderland, 1955 (made-for-TV; Karl Swenson); Alice in Wonderland, 1976 (Bruno Llacer); Alice in Wonderland, 1982 (made-for-TV; George Muschamp); Alice in Wonderland, 1985 (made-for-TV; Jonathan Winters); Alice in Wonderland or What's a Nice Kid Like You Doing in a Place Like This?, 1966 (animated made-for-TV; Allan Melvin); Alice through the Looking Box, 1960 (made-for-TV; Harry Secombe); Alice through the Looking Glass, 1966 (made-for-TV; Jimmy Durante); Alice through the Looking Glass, 1973 (made-for-TV; Freddie Jones); Alice through the Looking Glass, 1987 (made-for-TV; George Gobel voiceover); Alice through the Looking Glass, 1998 (made-for-TV; Desmond Barrit); Alice's Adventures in Wonderland and through the Looking Glass, 1948 (made-for-TV; Jack Howarth); Geppetto's Secret, 2005 (Bill Ratner); Great Performances, 1971- (TV series; Richard Woods); Happily Ever After: Fairy Tales for Every Child, 1995-2000 (TV series; Denzel Washington); Happily N'Ever After, 2009 (Kelly Brewster voiceover); Mother Goose: A Rappin' 'n' Rhymin' Special, 1997 (made-for-TV; Denzel Washington); Mother Goose Rock 'n' Rhyme, 1990 (made-for-TV; Howie Mandel); Miyuki-chan in Wonderland, 1995- (TV miniseries; Masako Katsuki); Puss in Boots, 2011 (Zach Galifianakis); Theatre Parade, 1936-1938 (TV series; 1937 episode: Esme Percy).

Iago (character in "Othello," by William Shakespeare, c. 1601, an insidious aide to Othello who hates his master and plants suspicion in his master's mind that another aide is having an affair with Othello's wife): BBC Sunday-Night Theatre, 1950-1959 (TV series; "Othello," 1950 episode: Stephen Murray); Encounter [General Motors Presents], 1952-1961 (TV series; "Othello," 1953 episode: Joseph Furst); Masterpiece Playhouse, 1950- (TV series; "Othello," 1950 episode: Alfred Ryder); Otello, 1948 (made-for-TV; Leonard Warren); Otello, 1958 (Renato Capecchi); Otello, 1959 (made-for-TV; Tito Gobbi); Otello, 1962 (made-for-TV; William Dooley); Otello, 1965 (made-for-TV; Norman Mittelmann); Otello, 1974 (Peter Glossop); Otello, 1976 (made-for-TV; Piero Cappuccilli); **Otello**, 1986 (Justino Diaz); Otello, 2012 (Marco Vratogna); Othello, 1914 (Riccardo Tolentino); Othello, 1923 (Werner Krauss); Othello, 1937 (made-for-TV; Henry Oscar); **Othello** [1952], 1955 (Micheal MacLiammoir); Othello, 1955 (made-for-TV; Paul Rogers); Othello, 1958 (made-for-TV; Howard Vernon); Othello [1955], 1960 (Andrei Popov); Othello, 1962 (made-for-TV; Jean Topart); Othello, 1965 (made-for-TV; Keith Lee); **Othello**, 1965 (Frank Finlay); Othello, 1968 (made-for-TV; Stefan Wigger); Othello, 1969 (made-for-TV; Senne Rouffaer); Othello, 1979 (made-for-TV; Michel Duchaussoy); Othello, 1980 (Richard Dixon); Othello, 1981 (made-for-TV; Bob Hoskins); Othello, 1989 (made-for-TV; Richard Haddon Haines); **Oth-**

Pierce Brosnan (as James Bond) and Joe Don Baker in
GoldenEye, **1995.**

ello, 1995 (Kenneth Branagh); The Philco-Goodyear Television Play-house, 1948-1956 (TV series; "Othello," 1953 episode: Walter Matthau).

Icarus (in Greek mythology who vainly flew too high on man-made wings and fell to his death): Hercules, 1998-1999 (TV series; French Stewart voiceover); The Illiac Passion, 1968 (Wayne Weber).

Injun Joe (fictional character in the books of Mark Twain): The Adventures of Huckleberry Finn, 1955 (made-for-TV; Sol Gorss); **The Adventures of Tom Sawyer**, 1938 (Victor Jory); The Adventures of Tom Sawyer, 1960 (TV series; John Bennett); The Adventures of Tom Sawyer, 1986 (Michael Pate voiceover); The Adventures of Tom Sawyer and Huckleberry Finn, 1982 (made-for-TV; Talgat Nigmatulin); Climax!, 1954-1958 (TV series; "Adventures of Huckleberry Finn," 1955 episode: Sol Gorss); Huck and Tom, 1918 (Frank Lanning); Huckleberry Finn and His Friends, 1979-1980 (TV series; Alex Diakun); Les aventures de Tom Sawyer, 1968 (TV miniseries; Jacques Bilodeau); The New Adventures of Huckleberry Finn, 1968-1969 (TV series; Ted Cassidy); Shirley Temple's Storybook, 1958-1961 (TV series; "Tom and Huck," 1960 episode: Paul Stevens); **Tom Sawyer**, 1930 (Charles Stevens); **Tom Sawyer**, 1973 (Henry O'Brien); Tom Sawyer, 1973 (made-for-TV; Vic Morrow); Tom Sawyer, 2011 (Benno Furmann); Tom Sawyer & Huckleberry Finn, 2015 (Kaloian Vodenicharov); The United States Steel Hour, 1953-1963 (TV series; "Tom Sawyer," 1956 episode: Matt Mattox).

Inspector Clouseau (Jacques Clouseau; bumbling French detective with the Paris Surete, who falls afoul of every object and structure in his pursuit of criminals, so mangling and botching his investigations that he drives his superior, Charles Dreyfus, to the brink of insanity; see Charles Dreyfus, this index): Curse of the Pink Panther, 1983 (Roger Moore); Inspector Clouseau, 1968 (Alan Arkin); **The Pink Panther**, 1964 (Peter Sellers); The Pink Panther, 2006 (Steve Martin); The Pink Panther 2, 2009 (Steve Martin); **The Pink Panther Strikes Again**, 1976 (Peter Sellers); **The Return of the Pink Panther**, 1975 (Peter Sellers); **Revenge of the Pink Panther**, 1978 (Peter Sellers); **A Shot in the Dark**, 1964 (Peter Sellers); Trail of the Pink Panther, 1982 (Peter Sellers).

Ivanhoe (fictional Saxon knight in the service of Richard I of England; also see Richard I in Historical Persons index): The Ballad of the Valiant Knight Ivanhoe, 1983 (Peteris Gaudins); Dark Knight, 2000- (TV series; Ben Pullen); **Ivanhoe**, 1952 (Robert Taylor); Ivanhoe, 1958- (TV series; Roger Moore); Ivanhoe, 1970- (TV miniseries; Eric Flynn); Ivanhoe, 1982 (made-for-TV; Anthony Andrews); Ivanhoe, 1986 (made-for-TV; Lewis Fitz-Gerald voiceover); Ivanhoe, 1997- (TV miniseries; Steven

Waddington); The Revenge of Ivanhoe, 1965 (Clyde Rogers [Rik Van Nutter]; Rainer Brandt voiceover).

Invisible Man (fictional character first appearing in H.G. Wells' 1897 novella, *The Invisible Man*): **Abbott and Costello Meet Frankenstein**, 1948 (Vincent Price voiceover); Abbott and Costello Meet the Invisible Man, 1951 (Arthur Franz); The ABC Saturday Night Superstar Movie, 1972-1974 (TV series; "The Mad, Mad, Mad Monsters," animated 1972 episode: Allen Swift voiceover); Attack of the 60 Foot Centerfold, 1995 (Tony Clay); Dragon Ball, 1995-2003 (animated TV series; two 2002 episodes; Chuck Huber); H.G. Wells' Invisible Man, 1958-1960 (TV series; Tim Turner, Johnny Scripps); **Hotel Transylvania**, 2012 (David Spade voiceover); **Hotel Transylvania 2**, 2015 (David Spade voiceover); Invisible Agent, 1942 (Jon Hall); **The Invisible Man**, 1933 (Claude Rains); The Invisible Man, 1975-1976 (TV series; David Mc-Calum); The Invisible Man, 1984 (TV miniseries; Pip Donhagy); The Invisible Man, 1998 (made-for-TV; Kyle MacLachlan); The Invisible Man, 2000-2002 (TV series; Vincent Ventresca); The Invisible Man, 2014 (TV miniseries; John Hightower); **The Invisible Man Returns**, 1940 (Vincent Price); The Invisible Man's Revenge, 1944 (Jon Hall); Lois & Clark: The New Adventures of Superman, 1993-1997 (TV series; "I'm Looking through You," 1993 episode: Leslie Jordan, Bob Mc-Cracken); The League of Extraordinary Gentlemen, 2003 (Tony Curran); Mad Monster Party, 1967 (Allen Swift voiceover); Memoirs of an Invisible Man, 1992 (Chevy Chase).

J. Worthington Foulfellow (aka: "Honest John"; a sly fox who inveigles a wooden marionette into trouble before that puppet transforms into a real boy, a fictional character in the 1883 children's novel *The Adventures of Pinocchio* by Italian author Carlo Collodi): The Adventures of Pinocchio, 1972 (TV miniseries; Ciccio Ingrassia); The New Adventures of Pinocchio, 1999 (Simon Schatzberger); **Pinocchio**, 1940 (Walter Catlett voiceover); Pinocchio, 2002 (Bruno Arena); Pinocchio, 2008 (made-for-TV; Toni Bertorelli; Jimmy Hibbert voiceover).

Jabberwocky (fictional character from the 1865 novel Alice's Adventures in Wonderland by British author Lewis Carroll): Alice in Wonderland, 1985 (made-for-TV; Tom McLoughlin); **Alice in Wonderland**, 2010 (Christopher Lee); Alice through the Looking Glass, 1966 (made-for-TV; Jack Palance); Alice through the Looking Glass, 1987 (made-for-TV; Mr. T. voiceover); The Alphabet Conspiracy, 1959 (Dolores Starr); The Care Bears Adventure in Wonderland, 1987 (Keith Hampshire voiceover); Jabberwocky, 1977 (Peter Salmon voiceover); Once upon a Time in Wonderland, 2013- (TV series; Peta Sergeant).

Jack in the Box (Mother Goose character): **Babes in Toyland**, 1934 (Charles Bimbo; Buster Brodie); Babes in Toyland, 1986 (made-for-TV; Pipo Sosman); The Magic Land of Mother Goose, 1967 (Ebenezer Lifting); The Mouse and His Child, 1977 (Robert Ridgely voiceover).

James Bond (heroic British MI5 espionage agent with code name 007, a secret service character created by novelist Ian Fleming): The Amazing Dr. G., 1968 (George Hilton); Casino Royale, 1967 (David Niven); **Casino Royale**, 2006 (Daniel Craig); Deadly Hands of Kung Fu, 1977 (Alexander Grand); **Diamonds Are Forever**, 1971 (Sean Connery); **Die Another Day**, 2002 (Pierce Brosnan); **Dr. No**, 1962 (Sean Connery); **For Your Eyes Only**, 1981 (Roger Moore); **From Russia with Love**, 1963 (Sean Connery); Goldeneye, 1989 (made-for-TV; Reg Gadney); **GoldenEye**, 1995 (Pierce Brosnan); **Goldfinger**, 1964 (Sean Connery); **License to Kill**, 1989 (Timothy Dalton); Live and Let Die, 1973 (Roger Moore); The Living Daylights, 1987 (Timothy Dalton); Mad Mission 3: Our Man from Bond Street, 1984 (Jean Mersant); The Man with the Golden Gun, 1974 (Roger Moore); **Moonraker**, 1979 (Roger Moore); Never Say Never Again, 1983 (Sean Connery); Octopussy, 1983 (Roger Moore); **On Her Majesty's Secret Service**, 1969 (George Lazenby);

Quantum of Solace, 2008 (Daniel Craig); **Skyfall**, 2012 (Daniel Craig); **Spectre**, 2015 (Daniel Craig); **The Spy Who Loved Me**, 1977 (Roger Moore); That Woman, 1966 (Hans-Joachim Ketzlin); **Thunderball**, 1965 (Sean Connery); Tomorrow Never Dies, 1997 (Pierce Brosnan); A View to a Kill, 1985 (Roger Moore); **You Only Live Twice**, 1967 (Sean Connery).

James Moriarty (Professor James Moriarty; fictional character and criminal mastermind, as well as nemesis of Sherlock Holmes in the stories by Arthur Conan Doyle; also see John H. Watson, Sebastian Moran and Sherlock Holmes, this index): **The Adventure of Sherlock Holmes' Smarter Brother**, 1975 (Leo McKern); **The Adventures of Sherlock Holmes**, 1939 (George Zucco); The Adventures of Sherlock Holmes, 1984-1985 (TV series; Eric Porter); The Adventures of Sherlock Holmes and Dr. Watson, 1980 (TV series; Viktor Yevgrafov); Elementary, 2012- (TV series; Natalie Dormer as Jamie Moriarty); Hands of a Murderer, 1990 (Anthony Andrews); The Hound of London, 1994 (made-for-TV; Jack Macreath); **Mr. Holmes**, 2015 (John Sessions); The Return of Sherlock Holmes, 1929 (Harry T. Morey); The Return of Sherlock Holmes, 1986-1988 (TV series; Eric Porter); **The Seven-Per-Cent Solution**, 1976 (Laurence Olivier); Sherlock, 2002 (made-for-TV; Vincent D'Onofrio); Sherlock Holmes, 1916 (Ernest Maupain); **Sherlock Holmes**, 1922 (Gustav von Seyffertitz); Sherlock Holmes, 1932 (Ernest Torrence); Sherlock Holmes, 2011 (Daniel Rios); **Sherlock Holmes: A Game of Shadows**, 2011 (Jared Harris); Sherlock Holmes and the Deadly Necklace, 1962 (Hans Sohnker); **Sherlock Holmes and the Secret Weapon**, 1942 (Lionel Atwill); Sherlock Holmes' Fatal Hour, 1931 (Norman McKinnel); Sherlock Holmes in New York, 1976 (made-for-TV; John Huston); Sherlock Holmes in the 22nd Century, 1999-2001 (TV series; Richard Newman); Silver Blaze (aka: Murder at the Baskervilles), 1937 (Lyn Harding); The Triumph of Sherlock Holmes, 1935 (Lyn Harding); The Valley of Fear, 1916 (Booth Conway); **Without a Clue**, 1988 (Paul Freeman); **The Woman in Green**, 1945 (Henry Daniell).

Jane Eyre (heroine in Charlotte Bronte's 1847 novel): Jane Eyre, 1921 (Mabel Ballin); Jane Eyre, 1934 (Virginia Bruce; Jean Darling as young Jane); **Jane Eyre**, 1944 (Joan Fontaine; Peggy Ann Garner as young Jane); Jane Eyre, 1956 (TV series; Daphne Slater); Jane Eyre, 1957 (TV miniseries; Ilaria Occhini); Jane Eyre, 1958 (made-for-TV; Mia Goossen); Jane Eyre, 1961 (made-for-TV; Sally Ann Howes); Jane Eyre, 1963 (TV series; Ann Bell); Jane Eyre, 1968 (Hristina Sylva); Jane Eyre, 1970 (made-for-TV; Susannah York; Sara Gibson as young Jane); Jane Eyre, 1973- (TV miniseries; Sorcha Cusack; Juliet Waley as young Jane); Jane Eyre, 1996 (Charlotte Gainsbourg; Anna Paquin as young Jane); Jane Eyre, 1997 (made-for-TV; Samantha Morton; Laura Harling as young Jane); Jane Eyre, 2006- (TV miniseries; Ruth Wilson; Georgie Henley as young Jane); **Jane Eyre**, 2011 (Mia Wasikowska; Amelia Clarkson as young Jane); Dead Ringers, 2002-2007 (TV series; 2004 episode: India Fisher); Guiding Light, 1952-2009 (TV series; 1981 episode: Lisa Brown); Kraft Theatre, 1947-1958 (TV series; "Jane Eyre," 1951 episode; Kathleen Crowley); Matinee Theatre, 1955-1958 (TV series; "Jane Eyre," 1957 episode: Joan Elan); Monodrama Theater, 1952- (TV series; "Jane Eyre," 1953 episode: Jan Sherwood); Orphan of Lowood, 1926 (Evelyn Holt); Studio One in Hollywood, 1948-1958 (TV series; "Jane Eyre," 1949 episode: Mary Sinclair); "Jane Eyre," 1952 episode: Katharine Bard); Woman and Wife, 1918 (Alice Brady).

Jason (in Greek mythology, a hero who led the Argonauts in search of the Golden Fleece): **Jason and the Argonauts**, 1963 (Todd Armstrong; Tim Tuner voiceover); Jason and the Argonauts, 2000 (TV miniseries; Jason London); Jason and the Heroes of Mount Olympus, 2001- (animated TV series; Miles Marsico voiceover); Mythic Warriors: Guardians of the Legend, 1998- (TV series; David Orth; Kevin Duhaney as young Jason); Young Hercules, 1998-1999 (TV series; Chris Conrad).

Orson Welles and Joan Fontaine (as Jane Eyre) in *Jane Eyre,* **1944.**

Jay Gatsby (romantic, wealthy gangster-bootlegger of the 1920s who loves a married woman from afar, meeting a tragic and ironic death, a character created by pantheon author F. Scott Fitzgerald in his classic 1925 novel, *The Great Gatsby*): **The Great Gatsby**, 1926 (Warner Baxter); **The Great Gatsby**, 1949 (Alan Ladd); **The Great Gatsby**, 1974 (Robert Redford); The Great Gatsby, 2001 (made-for-TV; Toby Stephens); **The Great Gatsby**, 2013 (Leonardo DiCaprio); Playhouse 90, 1956-1961 (TV series; "The Great Gatsby," 1958 episode: Robert Ryan); Robert Montgomery Presents, 1950-1957 (TV series; "The Great Gatsby," 1955 episode: Robert Montgomery).

Jean Passepartout (loyal, bumbling servant to Phileas Fogg, a British gentleman who makes an impossible wager that he can go around the world in eighty days, first depicted in the 1873 adventure novel, *Around the World in Eighty Days*, by Jules Verne): Around the World in Eighty Days, 1919 (Eugen Rex); **Around the World in 80 Days**, 1956 (Cantinflas); Around the World in Eighty Days, 1972-1973 (TV series; Ross Higgins); Around the World in 80 Days, 1989 (TV miniseries; Eric Idle); Around the World in 80 Days, 2004 (Jackie Chan); De reis om de wereld in 80 dagen, 1957- (TV series; Cyriel Van Gent); Die Reise um die Erde in 80 Tagen, 1963 (made-for-TV; Uwe-Detlev Jessen); Le Tour du monde en 80 jours, 1975 (TV miniseries; Pierre Trabaud); Le tour du monde en 80 jours, 1979 (made-for-TV; Roger Pierre); Le tour du monde en 80 jours, 1980 (TV series; Charles Caunant); The Secret Adventures of Jules Verne, 2000 (TV series; Michel Courtemanche).

Jean Valjean (French peasant who steals a loaf of bread and endures living hell in prison until escaping, but who is doggedly tracked by police inspector Javert in the 1862 novel *Les Miserables* by Victor Hugo): Les Miserables, 1913 (Henry Krauss); Les Miserables, 1917 (William Farnum); **Les Miserables**, 1935 (Fredric March); Les Miserables, 1936 (Harry Baur); Les Miserables, 1952 (Gino Cervi); **Les Miserables**, 1952 (Michael Rennie); Les Miserables, 1958 (Jean Gabin); Les Miserables, 1967- (TV series; Frank Finlay); Les Miserables, 1972- (TV miniseries; Georges Geret); Les Miserables, 1978 (made-for-TV; Richard Jordan); Les Miserables, 1982 (Lino Ventura); **Les Miserables**, 1995 (Jean-Paul Belmondo); **Les Miserables**, 1998 (Liam Neeson); Les Miserables, 2000- (TV miniseries; Gerard Depardieu); Los miserables, 1943 (Domingo Soler); Los miserables, 1973- (TV series; Sergio Bustamante); Medallion Theatre, 1953-1954 (TV series; "The Bishop's Candlesticks," 1953 episode: Victor Jory); Novela, 1963-1978 (TV series; "Los miserable," eighteen episodes in 1971: Jose Calvo); Soul of Humanity, 1926 (Gabriel Gabrio); Your Show Time, 1949- (TV series; "The Bishop's Experiment," 1949 episode: Leif Erickson).

Winona Ryder (as Jo March) in *Little Women*, 1994.

Jim (black slave and character in the books of Mark Twain): The Adventures of Huck Finn, 1993 (Courtney B. Vance); **The Adventures of Huckleberry Finn**, 1960 (Archie Moore); The Adventures of Huckleberry Finn, 1973 (Feliks Imokuede); The Adventures of Huckleberry Finn, 1981 (made-for-TV; Brock Peters); The Adventures of Huckleberry Finn, 1984 (made-for-TV; Alistair Duncan voiceover); **The Adventures of Mark Twain**, 1944 (Frederick Spencer); The Adventures of Tom Sawyer, 1980 (TV series; Ikuo Nishikawa voiceover); The Adventures of Tom Sawyer and Huckleberry Finn, 1982 (made-for-TV; Behailu Mengesha); Back to Hannibal: The Return of Tom Sawyer and Huckleberry Finn, 1990 (made-for-TV; Paul Winfield); Excursion, 1953 (TV series; "The Adventures of Huckleberry Finn," 1953 episode: Sugar Ray Robinson); Huckleberry Finn, 1920 (George Reed); Huckleberry Finn, 1931 (Clarence Muse); **Huckleberry Finn**, 1939 (aka: The Adventures of Huckleberry Finn; Rex Ingram); Huckleberry Finn, 1974 (Paul Winfield); Huckleberry Finn, 1975 (made-for-TV; Antonio Fargas); Huckleberry Finn and His Friends, 1979-1980 (TV series; Blu Makuma); Les aventures de Tom Sawyer, 1968 (TV miniseries; Serge Nubret); Sawyer and Finn, 1983 (made-for-TV; Stack Pierce); Tom Sawyer, 2011 (Jaymes Butler as John the Slave).

Jim Hawkins (British youth working in his mother's seaside inn who discoves a treasure map that leads to a great adventure in Robert Louis Stevenson's 1883 novel, *Treasure Island*): The Adventures of Ben Gunn, 1958- (TV series; John H. Watson); The Adventures of Long John Silver, 1955- (TV; Kit Taylor); The DuPont Show of the Month, 1957-1961 (TV series; "Treasure Island," Richard O'Sullivan); The Legends of Treasure Island, 1993-1995 (TV series; John Hasler); Long John Silver, 1954 (Kit Taylor); Muppet Treasure Island, 1996 (Kevin Bishop); National Theatre Live: Treasure Island, 2015 (Patsy Ferran); Pirates of Treasure Island, 2006 (Tom Nagel); Return to Treasure Island, 1986 (TV miniseries; Christopher Guard); Return to Treasure Island, 1988 (animated; Valery Bessarab voiceover); Return to Treasure Island, 1996 (made-for-TV; Dean O'Gorman); Schatteneiland, 1957- (TV series; Alex Wilequet); Shirley Temple's Storybook, 1958-1961 (TV series; "The Return of Long John Silver," 1961 episode; Tim O'Connor); Studio One in Hollywood, 1948-1958 (TV series; "Treasure Island," 1952 episode: Peter Avarmo); Treasure Island, 1918 (Francis Carpenter); Treasure Island, 1920 (Shirley Mason); **Treasure Island**, 1934 (Jackie Cooper); **Treasure Island**, 1950 (Bobby Driscoll); Treasure Island, 1951- (TV series; John Quayle); Treasure Island, 1957- (TV series; Richard Palmer); Treasure Island, 1968- (TV series; Michael Newport); Treasure Island, 1972 (Kim Burfield); Treasure Island, 1973 (animated; Davy Jones voiceover); Treasure Island, 1977 (TV miniseries; Ashley Knight); Treasure Island, 1978 (animated TV series; Mari Shimizu

voiceover); Treasure Island, 1982 (made-for-TV; Piers Eady); Treasure Island, 1990 (made-for-TV; Christian Bale); Treasure Island, 1995 (made-for-TV; Gregory Hall); Treasure Island, 2001 (Kevin Zegers); Treasure Island, 2007 (Francois Goeske); Treasure Island, 2012 (Toby Regbo); Treasure Island in Outer Space, 1987 (TV miniseries; Itaco Nardulli).

Jiminy Cricket (a talking cricket who becomes the friend and conscience of a marionette that transforms into a real boy, a fictional character in the 1883 children's novel *The Adventures of Pinocchio* by Italian author Carlo Collodi): The Adventures of Pinocchio, 1947 (Cristina Pagliarini); **The Adventures of Pinocchio**, 1996 (David Doyle voiceover); A Disney Channel Christmas, 1983 (made-for-TV; Eddie Carroll); DTV "Doggone" Valentine, 1987 (made-for-TV; Eddie Carroll); DTV Valentine, 1986 (made-for-TV; Eddie Carroll); Fun and Fancy Free, 1947 (Cliff Edwards); The Mickey Mouse Club, 1955-1958 (TV series; Cliff Edwards); Once upon a Time, 2011 (TV series; Raphael Sbarge); **Pinocchio**, 1940 (Cliff Edwards voiceover); Pinocchio, 2002 (Peppe Barra); Pinocchio, 2008 (made-for-TV; Luciana Littizzetto); Pinocchio, 2013 (TV miniseries; Anke Engelke); Walt Disney's Wonderful World of Color, 1959-1992 (TV series; Cliff Edwards, Eddie Carroll).

Jo March (one of four teenage sisters who finds romance as she and her siblings mature in a Massachusetts household during the American Civil War as profiled in Louisa May Alcott's timeless novel, *Little Women*, 1868-1869): The Ford Theatre Hour, 1948-1951 (TV series; "Little Women," 1949 episode: Meg Murdy); Good Wives, 1958 (TV series; Annabelle Lee); Great Performances, 1971- (TV series; "Little Women," 2001 episode: Stephanie Novacek); Jo's Boys, 1959 (TV series; Annabelle Lee); Little Women, 1917 (Ruby Miller); Little Women, 1918 (Dorothy Bernard); **Little Women**, 1933 (Katharine Hepburn); **Little Women**, 1949 (June Allyson); Little Women, 1950- (TV series; Jane Hardie); Little Women, 1958 (TV series; Andree Melly); Little Women, 1958 (made-for-TV; Jeannie Carson); Little Women, 1970 (TV miniseries; Angela Down); Little Women, 1978 (TV miniseries; Susan Dey); **Little Women**, 1994 (Winona Ryder); Matinee Theatre, 1955-1958 (TV series; "Little Women," 1956 episode: Judith Braun); NBC Special Treat, 1975-1986 (TV series; "Little Women," 1976 episode: Susan Hendl); Studio One in Hollywood, 1948-1958 (TV series; "Little Women: Jo's Story," 1950 episode: Mary Sinclair; Nancy Marchand; "Little Women: Meg's Story," 1950 episode: Nancy Marchand).

John Henry (U.S. folklore hero, legendary steel driver): **Tall Tale: The Unbelievable Adventures of Pecos Bill**, 1995 (Roger Aaron Brown); Tall Tales and Legends, 1985-1988 (TV series; "John Henry," 1986 episode: Danny Glover).

John H. Watson (Dr. Watson, close companion to Sherlock Holmes; fictional character appearing in the four novels and fifty-six short stories about super detective Sherlock Holmes by Arthur Conan Doyle; also see James Moriarty, Sebastian Moran, and Sherlock Holmes, this index): **The Adventures of Sherlock Holmes**, 1939 (Nigel Bruce); The Adventures of Sherlock Holmes, 1984-1985 (TV series; David Burke); The Adventures of Sherlock Holmes and Dr. Watson, 1980 (TV series; Vitali Solomin); The Baker Street Boys, 1983 (TV series; Hubert Rees); The Case of Marcel Duchamp, 1984 (Raymond Francis); The Case of the Whitechapel Vampire, 2002 (made-for-TV; Kenneth Welsh); The Casebook of Sherlock Holmes, 1991-1993 (TV series; Edward Hardwicke); Crazy House, 1943 (Nigel Bruce); The Crucifer of Blood, 1991 (made-for-TV; Richard Johnson); Der Hund von Baskerville, 1929 (George Seroff); **Dressed to Kill**, 1946 (Nigel Bruce); Elementary, 2012- (TV series; Lucy Liu as Dr. Joan Watson); Hands of a Murderer, 1990 (John Hillerman); The Hound of the Baskervilles, 1915 (Alwin Neuss); The Hound of the Baskervilles, 1932 (Frederick Lloyd); The Hound of the Baskervilles, 1937 (Fritz Odemar); **The Hound of the Baskervilles,**

1939 (Nigel Bruce); **The Hound of the Baskervilles**, 1959 (Andre Morell); The Hound of the Baskervilles, 1972 (made-for-TV; Bernard Fox); The Hound of the Baskervilles, 1980 (Dudley Moore); The Hound of the Baskervilles, 1981 (made-for-TV; Vitali Solomin); The Hound of the Baskervilles, 1982 (TV miniseries; Terence Rigby); The Hound of the Baskervilles, 1983 (made-for-TV; Donald Churchill); The Hound of the Baskervilles, 1988 (made-for-TV; Edward Hardwicke); The Hound of the Baskervilles, 2000 (made-for-TV; Kenneth Welsh); The Hound of the Baskervilles, 2003 (made-for-TV; Ian Hart); The Hound of London, 1994 (made-for-TV; John Scott-Paget); **The House of Fear**, 1945 (Nigel Bruce); Incident at Victoria Falls, 1992 (made-for-TV; Patrick Macnee); The Man Who Was Sherlock Holmes, 1937 (aka: Two Merry Adventurers; Heinz Ruhmann impersonating Dr. Watson); The Memoirs of Sherlock Holmes, 1994 (TV series; Edward Hardwicke); **Mr. Holmes**, 2015 (Colin Starkey); **Murder by Decree**, 1979 (James Mason); **The Pearl of Death**, 1944 (Nigel Bruce); **The Private Life of Sherlock Holmes**, 1970 (Colin Blakely); **Pursuit to Algiers**, 1945 (Nigel Bruce); The Return of Sherlock Holmes, 1929 (H. Reeves-Smith); The Return of Sherlock Holmes, 1987 (made-for-TV; Margaret Colin as Jane Watson); The Return of Sherlock Holmes, 1986-1988 (TV series; Edward Hardwicke); The Royal Scandal, 2001 (made-for-TV; Kenneth Welsh); **The Scarlet Claw**, 1944 (Nigel Bruce); **The Seven-Per-Cent Solution**, 1976 (Robert Duvall); Sherlock, 2002 (made-for-TV; Roger Morlidge); Sherlock Holmes, 1916 (Edward Fielding); **Sherlock Holmes**, 1922 (Roland Young); Sherlock Holmes, 1932 (Reginald Owen); Sherlock Holmes, 1951 (TV miniseries; Raymond Francis); Sherlock Holmes, 1954-1955 (TV series; Howard Marion-Crawford); Sherlock Holmes, 1964-1968 (TV series; Nigel Stock); Sherlock Holmes, 1967-1968 (TV series; Paul Edwin Roth); **Sherlock Holmes**, 2009 (Jude Law); Sherlock Holmes, 2011 (Charles Simon); **Sherlock Holmes: A Game of Shadows**, 2011 (Jude Law); Sherlock Holmes and a Study in Scarlet, 1983 (Earle Cross voiceover); Sherlock Holmes and Dr. Watson: The Bloody Inscription, 1979 (made-for-TV; Vitali Solomin); Sherlock Holmes and the Baker Street Irregulars, 2007 (made-for-TV; Bill Paterson); Sherlock Holmes and the Baskerville Curse, 1983 (Earle Cross voiceover); Sherlock Holmes and the Case of the Silk Stocking, 2004 (made-for-TV; Ian Hart); Sherlock Holmes and the Deadly Necklace, 1962 (Thorley Walters); Sherlock Holmes and the Leading Lady, 1991 (made-for-TV; Patrick Macnee); Sherlock Holmes and the Masks of Death, 1984 (made-for-TV; John Mills); Sherlock Holmes and the Missing Rembrandt, 1932 (Ian Fleming); **Sherlock Holmes and the Secret Weapon**, 1942 (Nigel Bruce); Sherlock Holmes and the Shadow Watchers, 2011 (Terry Wade); Sherlock Holmes and the Sign of Four, 1983 (Earle Cross voiceover); Sherlock Holmes and the Valley of Fear, 1983 (Earle Cross voiceover); **Sherlock Holmes and the Voice of Terror**, 1942 (Nigel Bruce); **Sherlock Holmes Faces Death**, 1943 (Nigel Bruce); Sherlock Holmes' Fatal Hour, 1931 (Ian Fleming); Sherlock Holmes in China, 1994 (Zhongquan Xu); Sherlock Holmes in New York, 1976 (made-for-TV; Patrick Macnee); **Sherlock Holmes in Washington**, 1943 (Nigel Bruce); Sherlock Holmes in the 22nd Century, 1999-2001 (TV series; John Payne); The Sign of Four: Sherlock Holmes' Greatest Case, 1932 (Ian Hunter); The Sign of Four, 1983 (made-for-TV; David Healy); The Sign of Four, 1988 (made-for-TV; Edward Hardwicke); The Sign of Four, 2001 (made-for-TV; Kenneth Welsh); Silver Blaze (aka: Murder at the Baskervilles), 1937 (Ian Fleming); **The Speckled Band**, 1931 (Athole Stewart); **The Spider Woman**, 1944 (Nigel Bruce); The Strange Case of the End of Civilization as We Know It, 1977 (Arthur Lowe); A Study in Scarlet, 1933 (Warburton Gamble); **A Study in Terror**, 1966 (Donald Houston); **Terror by Night**, 1946 (Nigel Bruce); The Three Garridebs, 1937 (made-for-TV; William Podmore); Touha Sherlocka Holmese, 1971 (Vaclav Voska); The Triumph of Sherlock Holmes, 1935 (Ian Fleming); The Valley of Fear, 1916 (Arthur M. Cullin); **Without a Clue**, 1988 (Ben Kingsley); **The Woman in Green**, 1945 (Nigel Bruce); The Xango from Baker Street, 2002 (Anthony O'Donnell); **Young Sherlock Holmes**,

Nigel Bruce (as Dr. John H. Watson) and Basil Rathbone (as Sherlock Holmes) in *Sherlock Holmes Faces Death*, 1943.

1985 (Alan Cox; older Watson in voiceover: Michael Hordern).

The Joker (fictional evil character in the Batman series): Batman, 1966-1968 (TV series; Cesar Romero); **Batman**, 1989 (Jack Nicholson); The Batman, 2004-2008 (TV series; Kevin Michael Richardson voiceover); **Batman: Mask of the Phantasm**, 1993 (Mark Hamill voiceover); The Batman/Superman Hour, 1968-1969 (animated TV series; Larry Storch voiceover); Batman: The Animated Series, 1992-1995 (TV series; Mark Hamill voiceover); Batman: The Brave and the Bold, 2008-2011 (animated TV series; Jeff Bennett voiceover); The Batman Superman Movie: World's Finest, 1997 (made-for-TV; Mark Hamill voiceover); The New Batman Adventures, 1997-1999 (TV series; Mark Hamill voiceover); Superman, 1996-2000 (TV series; Mark Hamill voiceover).

Judah Ben-Hur (Jewish prince and merchant in Jerusalem in the time of Jesus Christ, a fictional protagonist in the 1880 novel by Lew Wallace titled: *Ben-Hur: A Tale of the Christ*): **Ben-Hur: A Tale of the Christ**, 1925 (Raymond Novarro); **Ben-Hur**, 1959 (Charlton Heston); Ben Hur, 2010 (TV miniseries; Joseph Morgan).

Jules Maigret (pensive, pipe-smoking Paris detective created by French author Georges Simenon in 1931 and who appeared in dozens of short stories and novels): Afera Saint-Fiacre, 1963 (made-for-TV; Ljuba Tadic); BBC Play of the Month, 1965-1983 (TV series; "Maigret at Bay," 1969 episode: Rupert Davies); BBC Sunday-Night Theatre, 1950-1959 (TV series; "Maigret and the Lost Life," 1959 episode: Basil Sydney); Cecile Is Dead, 1944 (Albert Prejean); Enter Inspector Maigret, 1966 (Heinz Ruhmann); Full House, 1952 (Michel Simon); Inspector Maigret, 1958 (Jean Gabin); La tete d'un homme, 1933 (Harry Baur); Le inchieste del commissario Maigret, 1964- (TV series; Gino Cervi); Les enquetes du commissaire Maigret, 1967-1990 (TV series; Jean Richard); Liberty Bar, 1960 (made-for-TV; Louis Arbessier); Maigret, 1959-1963 (TV series; Rupert Davies); Maigret, 1964-1968 (TV series; Jan Teulings); Maigret, 1988 (made-for-TV; Richard Harris); Maigret, 1991 (TV series; Bruno Cremer); Maigret, 1992- (TV series; Michael Gambon); Maigret a Pigalle, 1966 (Gino Cervi); Maigret and the Old Lady, 1974 (Boris Tenin); Maigret and the St. Fiacre Case, 1959 (Jean Gabin); Maigret: De kruideniers, 1964 (made-for-TV; Kees Brusse); Maigret dirige l'enqute, 1955 (Maurice Manson); Maigret: La trappola, 2004 (made-for-TV; Sergio Castellitto); Maigret: L'ombra cinese, 2004 (made-for-TV; Sergio Castellitto); Maigret Sets a Trap, 2016 (made-for-TV; Rowan Atkinson); Maigret voit rouge, 1963 (Jean Gabin); Maigret's Dead Man, 2016 (made-for-TV; Rowan Atkinson); Majestic Hotel Cellars, 1945 (Albert Prejean); **The Man on the Eiffel Tower**, 1949 (Charles Laughton); Night at the Crossroads, 1932 (Pierre Renoir); Pic-

Claire Danes (as Juliet) in *Romeo + Juliet*, 1996.

pus, 1943 (Albert Prejean); Signe Furax, 1981 (Jean Richard); Suspense, 1949-1954 (TV series; "The Old Lady of Bayeux," 1952 episode: Luis Van Rooten); The Trap, 1950- (TV series; "Stan, the Killer," 1950 episode; Herbert Berghof); The Yellow Dog, 1932 (Abel Tarride).

Juliet (fictional character and star-crossed lover of Romeo in William Shakespeare's 1597 play "Romeo and Juliet"; see Romeo, this index): BBC Play of the Month, 1965-1983 (TV series; "Romeo and Juliet," 1967 episode: Kika Markham); BBC Sunday-Night Theatre, 1950-1959 (TV series; "Romeo and Juliet," 1955 episode; Virginia McKenna); The Hollywood Review of 1929, 1929 (Norman Shearer); Kraft Theatre, 1947-1958 (TV series; "Romeo and Juliet," 1954 episode: Susan Strasberg); The Philco-Goodyear Television Playhouse, 1948-1956 (TV series; "Romeo and Juliet," 1949 episode: Patricia Breslin); Producers' Showcase, 1954-1957 (TV series; "Romeo and Juliet," 1957 episode: Claire Bloom); Romeo and Juliet, 1916 (Beverly Bayne); Romeo and Juliet, 1916 (Theda Bara); **Romeo and Juliet**, 1936 (Norma Shearer); Romeo and Juliet, 1947 (made-for-TV; Rosalie Crutchley); **Romeo and Juliet**, 1954 (Susan Shentall); Romeo and Juliet, 1956 (Galina Ulanova); Romeo and Juliet, 1962 (TV series; Jane Asher); Romeo and Juliet, 1965 (Angela Scoular); Romeo and Juliet, 1966 (ballet; Margot Fonteyn); **Romeo and Juliet**, 1968 (Olivia Hussey); Romeo and Juliet, 1976 (made-for-TV; Ann Hasson); Romeo and Juliet, 1978 (made-for-TV; Rebecca Saire); Romeo & Juliet, 1982 (ballet; Carla Fracci); Romeo and Juliet, 1984 (British Royal Ballet at Covent Garden; Alessandra Ferri); Romeo & Juliet, 1993 (Megan Follows); Romeo & Juliet, 1994 (Geraldine Somerville); Romeo and Juliet on Ice, 1983 (made-for-TV; Dorothy Hamill); Romeo & Juliet: Sealed with a Kiss, 2006 (animated animal version; Tricia Trippett voiceover); **Romeo + Juliet**, 1996 (Claire Danes); Shakespeare: The Animated Tales, 1992-1994 (TV miniseries; "Romeo and Juliet," 1992 episode: Clare Holman voiceover).

Juno (Roman goddess of women, wife of Jupiter; Hera in Greek mythology): Hercules in New York, 1970 (Tanny McDonald); In Performance, 1978- (TV series; "Orpheus in the Underworld," 1983 episode: Honor Blackman); Jacques Offenbach: Orpheus in the Underworld, 1997 (made-for-TV; Jacqueline van Quaille); Orphee aux enfers, 1997 (made-for-TV; Lydie Pruvot); Orpheus in der Unterwelt, 1975 (Lisa Macheiner); Orpheus in der Unterwelt, 2007 (made-for-TV; Inge Meysel); Platee, 1977 (made-for-TV; Suzanne Sarrocca); Platee, 2000 (made-for-TV; Doris Lamprecht); Rome in a Day, 2008 (Nina Gorden); The Temple of Venus, 1923 (Marilyn Boyd); The Triumph of Venus, 1918 (Beatrice Armstrong); Vamping Venus, 1928 (Janet MacLeod); Vulcan, Son of Giove, 1962 (Yvonne Sire).

Jupiter (or Jove; Roman god; father of the gods; Zeus in Greek mythology): Amphitryon, 1935 (Willy Fritsch); Amphitryon, 1961 (made-for-TV; Peter Pasetti); Amphitryon, 1978 (made-for-TV; Hartmut Puls); Amphitryon, 1981 (made-for-TV; Christian Rode); Amphitryon, 2003 (made-for-TV; Jean-Pierre Michael); Amphitryon 38, 1963 (made-for-TV; Hermann Lenschau); In Performance, 1978- (TV series; "Orpheus in the Underworld," 1983 episode; Denis Quilley); Jacques Offenbach: Orpheus in the Underworld, 1997 (made-for-TV; Dale Duesing); Jason and the Heroes of Mount Olympus, 2001- (animated TV series; Tom Bosley voiceover); Orphee aux enfers, 1997 (made-for-TV; Laurent Naouri); Orpheus in der Unterwelt, 1975 (Rolf Hoppe); Orpheus in der Unterwelt, 2007 (made-for-TV; Toni Blankenheim); Orpheus in the Underworld, 1961 (made-for-TV; Eric Shilling); Platee, 1977 (made-for-TV; Roger Soyer); Platee, 2000 (made-for-TV; Vincent Le Texier); Rome in a Day, 2008 (Andrew Russell Stewart); The Triumph of Venus, 1918 (John Fedris); Vamping Venus, 1928 (Gustav von Seyffertitz); Vulcan, Son of Giove, 1962 (Furio Meniconi).

Katharina (tempestuous man-eating beauty who is tamed and married by Petruchio in William Shakespeare's 1594 play, "The Taming of the Shrew"): BBC Sunday-Night Theatre, 1950-1959 (TV series; "The Taming of the Shrew," 1952 episode: Margaret Johnston); Great Performances, 1971- (TV series; "Kiss Me Kate," 2003 episode: Rachel York); Kate: The Taming of the Shrew, 2004 (Daniela Cavallini); Katharine and Petruchio, 1939 (made-for-TV; Margaretta Scott); **Kiss Me Kate**, 1953 (Kathryn Grayson); Kiss Me Kate, 1968 (made-for-TV; Carol Lawrence); La bisbetica domata, 1942 (Lilia Silvi); La fierecilla domada, 1956 (Carmen Sevilla); Shakespeare: The Animated Tales, 1993-1994 (TV series; "The Taming of the Shrew," 1994 episode: Amanda Root); Studio One in Hollywood, 1948-1958 (TV series; "The Taming of the Shrew," 1950 episode: Lisa Kirk); The Taming of the Shrew, 1929 (Mary Pickford); The Taming of the Shrew, 1956 (made-for-TV; Lilli Palmer); The Taming of the Shrew, 1962 (made-for-TV; Brigid Lenihan); **The Taming of the Shrew**, 1967 (Elizabeth Taylor); The Taming of the Shrew, 1973 (made-for-TV; Carol MacReady); The Taming of the Shrew, 1976 (made-for-TV; Fredi Olster); The Taming of the Shrew, 1980 (made-for-TV; Sarah Badel); The Taming of the Shrew, 1982 (made-for-TV; Sharry Flett); The Taming of the Shrew, 1988 (made-for-TV; Goldie Semple).

Kay (legendary knight and foster brother of King Arthur in 6th Century Britain): The Adventures of Sir Galahad, 1949 (serial; Jim Diehl); The Adventures of Sir Lancelot, 1956-1957 (TV series; David Morrell/Brian Worth); Camelot, 2011 (TV miniseries; Peter Mooney); A Connecticut Yankee, 1955 (made-for-TV; John Conte); **A Connecticut Yankee in King Arthur's Court**, 1949 (George Cathrey); **Excalibur**, 1981 (Niall O'Brien); **First Knight**, 1995 (Christopher Villiers); The Legend of Prince Valiant, 1991-1994 (TV series; Jameson Parker); The Mists of Avalon, 2001 (made-for-TV; Honza Klima); **Prince Valiant**, 1954 (Tom Conway); Prince Valiant, 1997 (Zach Galligan); **The Sword and the Stone**, 1963 (Norman Alden voiceover); Sword of Lancelot, 1963 (Joseph Tomelty).

Kim (Kimball O'Hara; Irish-born orphan boy who becomes a secret agent for the British in India during the days of Victorian colonialism, a character created by Rudyard Kipling in his 1901 novel, *Kim*): **Kim**, 1950 (Dean Stockwell); Kim, 1955 (TV series; David Jose); Shirley Temple's Storybook, 1958-1961 (TV series; "Kim," 1960 episode: Tony Haig); Kim, 1984 (made-for-TV; Ravi Sheth).

King of Hearts (fictional character from the 1865 novel Alice's Adventures in Wonderland by British author Lewis Carroll): Alice in Wonderland, 1931 (N. R. Cregan); **Alice in Wonderland**, 1933 (Alec B. Francis); Alice in Wonderland, 1949 (David Reed voiceover); **Alice in Wonderland**, 1951 (Dink Trout voiceover); Alice in Wonderland, 1955 (made-for-TV; Hiram Sherman); Alice in Wonderland, 1966 (made-for-TV; Peter Sellers); Alice in Wonderland, 1982 (made-for-TV; Oliver Osterberg); Alice in Wonderland, 1985 (made-for-TV; Robert Morley); Alice in Wonderland, 1986 (made-for-TV; four 30-minute segments; Brian Oulton); Alice in Wonderland, 1999 (made-for-TV; Simon Russell Beale); Alice's Adventures in Wonderland, 1972 (Dennis Price).

Knave of Hearts (fictional character from the 1865 novel Alice's Adventures in Wonderland by British author Lewis Carroll): Alice in Wonderland, 1931 (Patrick Glasgow); Alice in Wonderland, 1955 (made-for-TV; Tom Bosley); Alice in Wonderland, 1966 (made-for-TV; Peter Eyre); Alice in Wonderland, 1982 (made-for-TV; Michael De Leon); Alice in Wonderland, 1985 (made-for-TV; James Joseph Galante); Alice in Wonderland, 1986 (made-for-TV; four 30-minute segments; Mark Bassenger); Alice in Wonderland, 1999 (made-for-TV; Jason Flemyng); **Alice in Wonderland**, 2010 (Crispin Glover); Alice's Adventures in Wonderland, 1972 (Rodney Bewes).

Lady de Winter (Charater in the fictional works of Alexander Dumas pere): Animated Three Musketeers, 1987 (TV series; Fumi Hirano); Biblioteca di Studio Uno: I tre moschettieri, 1964 (made-for-TV; Lucia Mannucci); D'Artagnan, 1969 (TV miniseries; D'Artagnan, 1991 (made-for-TV; Valerie Zarrouk); Antonella Lualdi); D'Artagnan et les trois mousquetaires, 2005 (Emmanuelle Beart); D'Artanyan i tri mushketyora, 1979 (TV series; Margarita Terekhova); De drie Musketiers, 1968 (made-for-TV; Chris Lomme); Die Drie Musketiere, 2013 (Ekaterina Vilkova); Family Classics: The Three Musketeers, 1960 (made-for-TV; Patricia Cutts); The Four Charlots Musketeers, 1974 (Karin Petersen); The Four Musketeers, 1963 (Lisa Gastoni); **The Four Musketeers**, 1975 (Faye Dunaway); The Glorious Musketeers, 1974 (Perrette Pradier voiceover); I tre moschettieri, 1991 (made-for-TV; Marina Morgan); **The Iron Mask**, 1929 (Dorothy Revier); La loca historia de los tres mosqueteros, 1983 (Nadiuska); Les 3 Mousquetaires, 1953 (Yvonne Sanson); Les trois mousquetaires, 1959 (made-for-TV; Gaby Sylvia); Les trois mousquetaires ou L'escrime ne paie pas, 1979 (made-for-TV; Maria Laborit); Les trois mousquetaires: Premiere epoque— Les ferrets de la reine, 1961 (Mylene Demongeot); The Magnavox Theater, 1950 (TV series; "The Three Musketeers," 1950 episode: Kristine Miller); Milady and the Three Musketeers, 2004 (made-for-TV; Arielle Dombasle); The Musketeers, 2014 (TV series; Maimie McCoy); Os tres Mosqueteiros, 1957 (TV series; Vida Alves); Three and a Half Musketeers, 1957 (Martha Valdes); **The Three Musketeers**, 1921 (Barbara La Marr); Three Musketeers, 1932 (Edith Mera); The Three Musketeers, 1939 (Binnie Barnes); **The Three Musketeers**, 1948 (Lana Turner); The Three Musketeers, 1954 (TV series; Adrienne Corri); The Three Musketeers, 1966 (TV miniseries; Mary Peach); **The Three Musketeers**, 1974 (Faye Dunaway); The Three Musketeers, 1986 (made-for-TV; Kate Fitzpatrick voiceover); **The Three Musketeers**, 1993 (Rebecca De Mornay); The Three Musketeers, 2007 (Maria Stokholm voiceover); The Three Musketeers, 2011 (Milla Jovovich); Tri mushketera, 2013 (Ekaterina Vilkova); Vengeance of the Three Musketeers, 1961 (Mylene Demongeot); Vingt ans apres, 1922 (Pierrette Madd); Tri musketyri, 1983 (TV miniseries; Hana Maciuchova).

Lady Macbeth (power-crazed wife of a Scottish nobleman who drives him to murder in order to acquire the throne, a character appearing in William Shakespeare's 1606 play): BBC Play of the Month, 1965-1983 (TV series; "Macbeth," 1975 episode: Janet Suzman); Crimson Curtain, 1952 (Monelle Valentin); Folio, 1955-1959 (TV series; "Macbeth," 1955 episode: Katharine Blake); Great Performances, 1971- (TV series; "Macbeth," 2010 episode: Kate Fleetwood); Kraft Theatre, 1947-1958 (TV series; "Macbeth," 1950 episode: Uta Hagen); Macbeth, 1913 (Violet Vanbrugh); Macbeth, 1915 (Georgette Leblanc); Macbeth, 1916 (Constance Collier); Macbeth, 1946 (Jain Wilimorsky); **Macbeth**, 1948 (Jeanette Nolan); Macbeth, 1949 (made-for-TV; Ruth Lodge); Macbeth,

Rebecca De Mornay (as Lady de Winter) in *The Three Musketeers,* **1993.**

1954 (made-for-TV; Judith Anderson); Macbeth, 1959 (made-for-TV; Maria Casares); Macbeth, 1961 (made-for-TV; Zoe Caldwell); Macbeth, 1965 (made-for-TV; Terri Aldred); Macbeth, 1966 (made-for-TV; Ruth Meyers); Macbeth, 1968 (made-for-TV; Lois Nettleton); Macbeth, 1970 (TV series; Barbara Leigh-Hunt); **Macbeth**, 1971 (Francesca Annis); Macbeth, 1972 (made-for-TV; Josephine Barstow); Macbeth, 1974 (made-for-TV; Veronika Bayer); Macbeth, 1975 (made-for-TV; Valeria Moriconi); Macbeth, 1976 (made-for-TV; Shirley Verrett); Macbeth, 1978 (made-for-TV; Violeta Gindeva); Macbeth, 1982 (made-for-TV; Maureen Anderman); Macbeth, 1983 (made-for-TV; Jane Lapotaire); Macbeth, 1987 (made-for-TV; Mara Zampieri); Macbeth, 1987 (Verdi opera version; Shirley Verrett); Macbeth, 1993 (made-for-TV; Cynthia Makris); Macbeth, 1997 (Helen Baxendale); Macbeth, 1998 (Dawn Winarski); Macbeth, 1998 (made-for-TV; Greta Scacchi); Macbeth, 2001 (made-for-TV; Harriet Walter); Macbeth, 2002 (made-for-TV; Paoletta Marrocu); Macbeth, 2004 (Pam Bradley); Macbeth, 2006 (made-for-TV; Sylvie Valayre); Macbeth, 2009 (made-for-TV; Violeta Urmana); Macbeth, 2011 (Liudmyla Monastyrska); Macbeth, 2013 (Shannon Michelle Parsons); Macbeth, 2014 (Samantha Spiro); **Macbeth**, 2015 (Marion Cotillard); Macbeth the Movie, 2009 (Kat Olsson); A Performance of Macbeth, 1979 (made-for-TV; Judi Dench); The Philco-Goodyear Television Playhouse, 1948-1956 (TV series; "Macbeth," 1949 episode; Joyce Redman); Studio One in Hollywood, 1948-1958 (TV series; "Macbeth," 1951 episode; Judith Evelyn).

Lady of the Lake (legendary spirit inhabiting a magical lake in the King Arthur legend of 6th-Century Britain): The Adventures of Sir Galahad, 1949 (serial; Lois Hall); **Excalibur**, 1981 (Hilary Joyalie); Gargoyles, 1994- (TV series; "Pendragon," 1996 episode: B.J. Ward); Kaamelott, 2004 (TV series; Audrey Fleurot); Merlin, 1998- (TV miniseries; Miranda Richardson); Merlin, 2008-2012 (TV series; Georgia Moffett); Merlin's Apprentice, 2006- (TV miniseries; Miranda Richardson); Prince Valiant, 1997 (Jodie Kidd); Throg, 2004 (Lori Power).

Laertes (Father of Ulysses [Odysseus] and king of Ithaca in Greek mythology): The Giants of Thessaly, 1963 (Paolo Gozlino); Hercules, Samson & Ulysses, 1965 (Andrea Fantasia); Hercules Unchained, 1960 (Andrea Fantasia); Jason and the Argonauts, 2000- (TV miniseries; Charles Cartmell); Odissea [aka: The Adventures of Ulysses], 1968 (TV miniseries; Branko Kovacic); Odysseus, 2013- (TV series; Carlo Brandt); **Ulysses,** 1955 (Gualtiero Tumiati).

Lampwick (an errant boy who turns into a donkey while accompanying a wooden marionette that transforms into a real boy, a fictional character in the 1883 children's novel *The Adventures of Pinocchio* by Italian au-

Janet Leigh and Paul Newman (as Lew Harper) in *Harper,* **1966.**

thor Carlo Collodi): **The Adventures of Pinocchio**, 1996 (Corey Carrier); The New Adventures of Pinocchio, 1999 (Ben Ridgeway); **Pinocchio**, 1940 (Frankie Darro voiceover); Pinocchio, 2013 (TV miniseries; Arved Friese).

Lancelot (legendary knight of King Arthur's Round Table in 6th-Century England): The Adventures of Sir Galahad, 1949 (serial; Hugh Prosser); The Adventures of Sir Lancelot, 1956-1957 (TV series; William Russell); Arthur the King, 1985 (made-for-TV; Rupert Everett); **Camelot**, 1967 (Franco Nero); Camelot, 1982 (made-for-TV; Richard Muenz); A Connecticut Yankee in King Arthur's Court, 1921 (Wilfred McDonald); **A Connecticut Yankee in King Arthur's Court**, 1949 (Henry Wilcoxon); **Excalibur**, 1981 (Nicholas Clay); **First Knight**, 1995 (Richard Gere as adult Lancelot; Ryan Todd as young Lancelot); Ginevra, 1992 (Serge Maggiani); Guinevere, 1994 (made-for-TV; Noah Wyle); **King Arthur**, 2004 (Ioan Gruffudd; Elliot Henderson-Boyle as young Lancelot); A Knight in Camelot, 1998 (made-for-TV; James Coombes); **Knights of the Round Table**, 1953 (Robert Taylor); Lancelot of the Lake, 1970 (made-for-TV; Gerard Falconetti); Lancelot of the Lake, 1974 (Luc Simon); The Legend of King Arthur, 1979 (TV series; David Robb); Merlin, 1998 (TV miniseries; Jeremy Sheffield); Merlin: The Return, 2000 (Adrian Paul); The Mists of Avalon, 2001 (made-for-TV; Michael Vartan); **Monty Python and the Holy Grail**, 1975 (John Cleese); Morte d'Arthur, 1980 (made-for-TV; David Robb); **Prince Valiant**, 1954 (Don Megowan); Sword of Lancelot, 1963 (Cornel Wilde); A Young Connecticut Yankee in King Arthur's Court, 1996 (Ian Falconer).

Lear (King Lear; aging British monarch wanting to end his days in peace, but who is hounded into madness through the machinations of his three daughters as depicted in William Shakespeare's "King Lear"): An Angel Comes to Brooklyn, 1945 (Frank Pharr); BBC Play of the Month, 1965-1983 (TV series; "King Lear," 1975 episode: Michael Hordern); Great Performances, 1971- (TV series; "King Lear," 1974 episode; James Earl Jones; "King Lear," 2008 episode: Ian McKellen); King Lear, 1916 (Frederick Warde); King Lear, 1948 (made-for-TV; William Devlin); **King Lear**, 1971 (Paul Scofield); King Lear, 1974 (TV series; Patrick Magee); King Lear, 1975 (Juri Jarvet); King Lear, 1982 (made-for-TV; Michael Hordern); King Lear, 1983 (made-for-TV; Laurence Olivier); King Lear, 1999 (Brian Blessed); King Lear, 2008 (Ian McKellen); Omnibus, 1951-1962 (TV series; "King Lear," 1953 episode; Orson Welles).

Lemon Drop Kid (a racetrack tipster created by Damon Runyon, who must raise $10,000 to pay off mobsters or face the consequences by

Christmastime): **The Lemmon Drop Kid**, 1934 (Lee Tracy); **The Lemmon Drop Kid**, 1951 (Bob Hope).

Lew Harper (Lew Archer; private detective created by mystery writer Ross Macdonald): **The Drowning Pool**, 1975 (Paul Newman); **Harper** [aka: The Moving Target], 1966 (Paul Newman).

Lex Luthor (fictional evil character in the Superman series): Atom Man vs. Superman, 1950 (serial; Lyle Talbot); The Batman/Superman Hour, 1968-1969 (animated TV series; Jackson Beck voiceover); Challenge of the Super Friends, 1978- (animated TV series; Stan Jones voiceover); Superman IV: The Quest for Peace, 1987 (Gene Hackman); The Batman Superman Movie: World's Finest, 1997 (made-for-TV; Clancy Brown voiceover); Justice League, 2001-2006 (TV series; Clancy Brown, Kenji Nomura voiceovers); Smallville, 2001-2011 (TV series; Michael Rosenbaum); Super Friends: The Legendary Super Powers Show, 1984- (animated TV series; Stan Jones voiceover); **Superman**, 1978 (Gene Hackman); Superman, 1988 (Animated TV series; Michael Bell voiceover); Superman, 1996-2000 (TV series; Clancy Brown voiceover); **Superman II**, 1981 (Gene Hackman); Young Justice, 2010- (animated TV series; Mark Rolston voiceover).

Little Bo Peep (Mother Goose character): **Babes in Toyland**, 1934 (Charlotte Henry); Babes in Toyland, 1961 (Ann Jillian); The Bride Goes Wild, 1948 (Jean Dean); **Champagne for Caesar**, 1950 (Rose Plummer); **Dante's Inferno**, 1935 (Gale Goodson); Fairy Tales, 1978 (Angela Aames); Halloween with the New Addams Family, 1977 (made-for-TV; Patrick Campbell); Happily N'Ever After, 2009 (Gina K. Bowes voiceover); Madam Satan, 1930 (Mary Carlisle); The Magic Land of Mother Goose, 1967 (Linda Lee); Mother Goose Rock 'n' Rhyme, 1990 (made-for-TV; Shelley Duvall); The Pied Piper of Astroworld, 1968 (made-for-TV; Lesley Gore); **Toy Story**, 1995 (Annie Potts voiceover); **Toy Story 2**, 1999 (Annie Potts voiceover).

Little Boy Blue (Mother Goose character): **Babes in Toyland**, 1934 (Johnny Downs); Babes in Toyland, 1961 (Kevin Corcoran); Puss in Boots, 2011 (Latifa Ouaou voiceover).

Little Jack Horner (Mother Goose character): **Babes in Toyland**, 1934 (Sumner Getchell).

Little John (fictional character and erstwhile companion of Robin Hood): **The Adventures of Robin Hood**, 1938 (Alan Hale); The Adventures of Robin Hood, 1955-1960 (TV series; Archie Duncan; Rufus Cruikshank); The Bandit of Sherwood Forest, 1946 (Ray Teal); Beyond Sherwood Forest, 2009 (made-for-TV; Mark Gibbon); A Challenge for Robin Hood, 1968 (Leon Greene); Il Magnifico Robin Hood, 1970 (Chris Huerta); Il trionfo di Robin Hood, 1962 (Samson Burke); Ivanhoe, 1997- (TV miniseries; David Nicholls); The Legend of Robin Hood, 1968- (TV series; Bruce Yarnell); The Legend of Robin Hood, 1975 (TV miniseries; Conrad Asquith); Long Live Robin Hood, 1971 (Nello Pazzafini); The Men of Sherwood Forest, 1954 (Leslie Linder); NBC Children's Theatre, 1963-1973 (TV series; "Robin Hood," 1964 episode: Jack Hollander); The New Adventures of Robin Hood, 1997-1999 (TV series; Richard Ashton); Prince of Thieves, 1948 (Walter Sande); **Robin and Marian**, 1976 (Nicol Williamson); **Robin Hood**, 1922 (Alan Hale); Robin Hood, 1953- (TV miniseries; Kenneth MacKintosh); **Robin Hood**, 1973 (Phil Harris voiceover); Robin Hood, 1984-1986 (TV series; Clive Mantle); Robin Hood, 1991 (David Morrissey); Robin Hood, 2006-2009 (TV series; Gordon Kennedy); **Robin Hood**, 2010 (Kevin Durand); Robin Hood: Ghosts of Sherwood 3D, 2012 (Kane Hodder); **Robin Hood: Men in Tights**, 1993 (Eric Allan Kramer); **Robin Hood: Prince of Thieves**, 1991 (Nick Brimble); Rogues of Sherwood Forest, 1950 (Alan Hale); Son of Robin Hood, 1959 (George Woodbridge); **The Story of Robin Hood** [aka: The Story of Robin Hood and His Merrie Men], 1952 (James Robertson Justice); Sword of Sherwood Forest, 1961 (Nigel Green); Tales of Robin Hood, 1951 (Wade Crosby); The Time Tunnel, 1966-1967 (TV series; "The Revenge of Robin Hood," 1966 episode: John Alderson); Wolfshead: The Legend of Robin Hood, 1973 (Dan Meaden); Young Robin Hood, 1991-1992 (animated TV series; Terrence Scammell voiceover).

Little Miss Muffett (Mother Goose character): **Babes in Toyland**, 1934 (Alice Dahl); Happily Ever After: Fairy Tales for Every Child, 1995-2000 (TV series; Lauren Tom).

Lone Ranger (fictional character of the Old West first appearing in a 1933 radio broadcast by Detroit's WXYZ): The Legend of the Lone Ranger, 1952 (Clayton Moore); The Legend of the Lone Ranger, 1981 (Klinton Spilsbury); The Lone Ranger, 1938 (serial; Lee Powell); The Lone Ranger, 1949-1957 (TV series; Clayton Moore); **The Lone Ranger**, 1956 (Clayton Moore); The Lone Ranger, 1966-1969 (TV series; Michael Rye); The Lone Ranger, 2003 (made-for-TV; Chad Michael Murray); **The Lone Ranger**, 2013 (Armie Hammer); The Lone Ranger Rides Again, 1939 (serial; Robert Livingston).

Lois Lane (fictional character in the Superman series): Adventures of Superman, 1952-1958 (TV series; Noel Neill; Phyllis Coates); Atom Man vs. Superman, 1950 (serial; Noel Neill); The Batman, 2004-2008 (TV series; Dana Delany voiceover); The Batman Superman Movie: World's Finest, 1997 (made-for-TV; Dana Delany voiceover); Batman: The Brave and the Bold, 2008-2011 (animated TV series; Sirena Irwin voiceover); Justice League, 2001-2006 (TV series; Dana Delany voiceover); Lois & Clark: The New Adventures of Superman, 1993-1997 (TV series; Teri Hatcher); Smallville, 2001-2011 (TV series; Erica Durance); Superman, 1948 (serial; Noel Neill); **Superman**, 1978 (Margot Kidder); Superman, 1988 (Animated TV series; Ginny McSwain voiceover); Superman, 1996-2000 (TV series; Dana Delany voiceover); Superman and the Mole-Men, 1951 (Phyllis Coates); Superman IV: The Quest for Peace, 1987 (Margot Kidder); **Superman III**, 1983 (Margot Kidder); **Superman II**, 1981 (Margot Kidder); The Superman/Aquaman Hour of Adventure, 1967-1968 (TV series; Julie Bennett, Joan Alexander).

Long John Silver (one-legged pirate on crutches and with a parrot on his shoulder screeching "pieces of eight!" as depicted in the classic 1883 adventure novel *Treasure Island* by Robert Louis Stevenson): The Adventures of Ben Gunn, 1958- (TV series; Peter Wyngarde); The Adventures of Long John Silver, 1955- (TV; Robert Newton); The DuPont Show of the Month, 1957-1961 (TV series; "Treasure Island," Hugh Griffith); The Legends of Treasure Island, 1993-1995 (TV series; Richard E. Grant); Long John Silver, 1954 (Robert Newton); Muppet Treasure Island, 1996 (Tim Curry); National Theatre Live: Treasure Island, 2015 (Arthur Darvill); Pirates of Treasure Island, 2006 (Lance Henriksen); Return to Treasure Island, 1986 (TV miniseries; Brian Blessed); Return to Treasure Island, 1988 (animated; Armen Dzhigarkhanyan voiceover); Return to Treasure Island, 1996 (made-for-TV; Stig Eldred); Schatteneiland, 1957- (TV series; Dries Wieme); Shirley Temple's Storybook, 1958-1961 (TV series; "The Return of Long John Silver," 1961 episode: James Westerfield); Studio One in Hollywood, 1948-1958 (TV series; "Treasure Island," 1952 episode: Francis L. Sullivan); Treasure Island, 1918 (Violet Radcliffe); Treasure Island, 1920 (Charles Ogle); **Treasure Island**, 1934 (Wallace Beery); **Treasure Island**, 1950 (Robert Newton); Treasure Island, 1951- (TV series; Bernard Miles); Treasure Island, 1957- (TV series; Bernard Miles); Treasure Island, 1968- (TV series; Peter Vaughan); Treasure Island, 1972 (Orson Welles); Treasure Island, 1973 (animated; Richard Dawson voiceover); Treasure Island, 1977 (TV miniseries; Alfred Burke); Treasure Island, 1978 (animated TV series; Genzo Wakayama voiceover); Treasure Island, 1982 (made-for-TV; Bernard Miles); Treasure Island, 1990 (made-

Orson Welles (as Macbeth) in *Macbeth,* **1948.**

for-TV; Charlton Heston); Treasure Island, 1995 (made-for-TV; Hetty Baynes as Long Jane Silver); Treasure Island, 2001 (Jack Palance); Treasure Island, 2007 (Tobias Moretti); Treasure Island, 2012 (Eddie Izzard); Treasure Island in Outer Space, 1987 (TV miniseries; Anthony Quinn).

Lorna Doone (kidnapped daughter of a Scottish nobleman who is raised by an outlaw clan, the heroine of British author Richard Doddridge Blackmore's 1869 novel): Lorna Doone, 1920 (Bertie Gordon); Lorna Doone, 1922 (Madge Bellamy); Lorna Doone, 1934 (Victoria Hopper; Alexis France as young Lorna); Lorna Doone, 1951 (Barbara Hale; Gloria Petroff as young Lorna); Lorna Doone, 1963 (TV miniseries; Jane Merrow); Lorna Doone, 1976 (TV miniseries; Emily Richard); Lorna Doone, 1990 (made-for-TV; Polly Walker; Claire Madden as young Lorna); Lorna Doone, 2000 (made-for-TV; Amelia Warner; Katie Pitts-Drake as young Lorna); Once upon a Classic, 1976-1979 (TV series; "Lorna Doone," 1976; Emily Richard).

Macbeth (ambitious Scottish nobleman who commits murder to become king, his lethal deeds encouraged by his power-mad wife, Lady Macbeth, characters appearing in William Shakespeare's 1606 play): BBC Play of the Month, 1965-1983 (TV series; "Macbeth," 1975 episode: Eric Porter); Crimson Curtain, 1952 (Pierre Brasseur); Folio, 1955-1959 (TV series; "Macbeth," 1955 episode: Barry Morse); Great Performances, 1971- (TV series; "Macbeth," 2010 episode: Patrick Stewart); Kraft Theatre, 1947-1958 (TV series; "Macbeth," 1950 episode: E.G. Marshall); Macbeth, 1913 (Michael Bourchier); Macbeth, 1915 (Severin-Mars); Macbeth, 1916 (Herbert Beerbohm Tree); Macbeth, 1946 (David Bradley); **Macbeth**, 1948 (Orson Welles); Macbeth, 1949 (made-for-TV; Stephen Murray); Macbeth, 1954 (made-for-TV; Maurice Evans); Macbeth, 1959 (made-for-TV; Daniel Sorano); Macbeth, 1961 (made-for-TV; Sean Connery); Macbeth, 1965 (made-for-TV; Wyn Roberts); Macbeth, 1966 (made-for-TV; Andrew Keir); Macbeth, 1968 (made-for-TV; Earle Hyman); Macbeth, 1970 (TV series; Michael Jayston); **Macbeth**, 1971 (Jon Finch); Macbeth, 1972 (made-for-TV; Kostas Paskalis); Macbeth, 1974 (made-for-TV; Hans Schulze); Macbeth, 1975 (made-for-TV; Glauco Mauri); Macbeth, 1976 (made-for-TV; Piero Cappuccilli); Macbeth, 1978 (made-for-TV; Lyubomir Kiselichki); Macbeth, 1982 (made-for-TV; Philip Anglim); Macbeth, 1983 (made-for-TV; Nicol Williamson); Macbeth, 1987 (made-for-TV; Renato Bruson); Macbeth, 1987 (Verdi opera version; Leo Nucci); Macbeth, 1993 (made-for-TV; Jorma Hynninen); Macbeth, 1997 (Jason Connery); Macbeth, 1998 (Stephen J. Lewis); Macbeth, 1998 (made-for-TV; Sean Pertwee); Macbeth, 2001 (made-for-TV; Antony Sher); Macbeth, 2002 (made-for-TV; Thomas Hampson); Macbeth, 2004 (Gary

Olivia de Havilland (as Maid Marian) and Errol Flynn (as Robin Hood) in *The Adventures of Robin Hood,* **1938.**

Saderup); Macbeth, 2006 (made-for-TV; Leo Nucci); Macbeth, 2009 (made-for-TV; Dimitris Tiliakos); Macbeth, 2011 (Simon Keenlyside); Macbeth, 2013 (Evan William Miller); Macbeth, 2014 (Joseph Millson); **Macbeth**, 2015 (Michael Fassbender); Macbeth the Movie, 2009 (Chris Canfield); A Performance of Macbeth, 1979 (made-for-TV; Ian McKellen); The Philco-Goodyear Television Playhouse, 1948-1956 (TV series; "Macbeth," 1949 episode: Walter Hampden); Studio One in Hollywood, 1948-1958 (TV series; "Macbeth," 1951 episode: Charlton Heston).

The Mad Hatter (fictional character from the 1865 novel Alice's Adventures in Wonderland by British author Lewis Carroll): Adventures in Wonderland, 1992-1994 (TV series; John Hoffman); Alice, 2009 (TV miniseries; Andrew Lee Potts); Alice at the Palace, 1982 (made-for-TV; Richard Cox); Alice in Wonderland, 1915 (William Tilden); Alice in Wonderland, 1931 (Leslie T. King); **Alice in Wonderland**, 1933 (Edward Everett Horton); Alice in Wonderland, 1949 (Raymond Bussieres voiceover); **Alice in Wonderland**, 1951 (Ed Wynn voiceover); Alice in Wonderland, 1955 (made-for-TV; Mort Marshall); Alice in Wonderland, 1966 (made-for-TV; Peter Cook); Alice in Wonderland, 1976 (Nano Gruberg); Alice in Wonderland, 1982 (made-for-TV; Carl Beck); Alice in Wonderland, 1985 (made-for-TV; Anthony Newley); Alice in Wonderland, 1985 (TV series; Eric Sykes); Alice in Wonderland, 1986 (made-for-TV; four 30-minute segments; Pip Donaghy); Alice in Wonderland, 1999 (made-for-TV; Martin Short); **Alice in Wonderland**, 2010 (Johnny Depp); Alice in Wonderland or What's a Nice Kid Like You Doing in a Place Like This?, 1966 (animated made-for-TV; Harvey Korman); Alice through the Looking Box, 1960 (made-for-TV; Ron Moody); Alice through the Looking Glass, 1973 (TV series; Jonathan Cecil); Alice's Adventures in Wonderland, 1956 (made-for-TV; Patrick Cargill); Alice's Adventures in Wonderland, 1972 (Robert Helpmann); Alice's Adventures in Wonderland, 2011 (made-for-TV; Steven McRae); Dreamchild, 1985 (Michael Walter, Tony Haygarth); The Ford Theatre Hour, 1948-1951 (TV series; "Alice in Wonderland," 1950 episode; Richard Waring); Great Performances, 1971- (TV series; "Alice in Wonderland," 1983 episode: Andre Gregory); Kraft Theatre, 1947-1958 (TV series; "Alice in Wonderland," 1954 episode; Art Carney); Miyuki-chan in Wonderland, 1995- (TV miniseries; Emi Shinohara); Unsuk Chin: Alice in Wonderland, 2007 (Dietrich Henschel); The Wednesday Play, 1964-1970 (TV series; "Alice," 1965 episode: John Bailey).

Madame Therese Defarge (ruthless French revolutionary who schemes to send persons to the guillotine, a character in the 1859 novel, *A Tale of Two Cities,* by Charles Dickens): The DuPont Show of the Month, 1957-1961 (TV series; "A Tale of Two Cities," 1958 episode: Agnes

Moorehead); History of the World: Part I, 1981 (Cloris Leachman); The Only Way, 1927 (Jean Jay); The Only Way, 1948 (made-for-TV; Roger Snowden); The Plymouth Playhouse, 1953 (TV series; "A Tale of Two Cities," two 1953 episodes: Judith Evelyn); A Tale of Two Cities, 1917 (Rosita Marstini); **A Tale of Two Cities**, 1935 (Blanche Yurka); A Tale of Two Cities, 1957 (TV miniseries; Margaretta Scott); A Tale of Two Cities, 1958 (Rosalie Crutchley); A Tale of Two Cities, 1958 (made-for-TV; Amy Stuart); A Tale of Two Cities, 1965 (TV series; Rosalie Crutchley); A Tale of Two Cities, 1980 (TV miniseries; Judy Parfitt); A Tale of Two Cities, 1980 (made-for-TV; Billie Whitelaw); A Tale of Two Cities, 1989 (TV miniseries; Kathy Kriegel).

Madame X (tragic mother and wife who loses her family and sinks to degradation and is later defended in a murder charge by her own son, who does not know she is his mother, as depicted in Alexandre Brisson's melodramatic 1910 play): Madame X, 1916 (Dorothy Donnelly); Madame X, 1920 (Pauline Frederick); Madame X, 1929 (Ruth Chatterton); Madame X, 1937 (Gladys George); **Madame X**, 1966 (Lana Turner); Madame X, 1981 (made-for-TV; Tuesday Weld).

Magua (villainous and bloodthirsty chief of the Huron Indian tribe who creates wholesale massacres of British colonists and troops in the 1826 novel *The Last of the Mohicans* by James Fenimore Cooper): Fall of the Mohicans, 1965 (Jose Manuel Martin); **The Last of the Mohicans**, 1920 (Wallace Beery); The Last of the Mohicans, 1932 (Bob Kortman); **The Last of the Mohicans**, 1936 (Bruce Cabot); The Last of the Mohicans, 1971 (TV miniseries; Philip Madoc); The Last of the Mohicans, 1975 (animated made-for-TV; Frank Welker voiceover); Last of the Mohicans, 1977 (made-for-TV; Robert Tessier); **The Last of the Mohicans**, 1992 (Wes Studi); Last of the Redmen, 1947 (Buster Crabbe).

Maid Marian (fictional character; woman loved by folklore outlaw hero Robin Hood): **The Adventures of Robin Hood**, 1938 (Olivia de Havilland); The Adventures of Robin Hood, 1955-1960 (TV series; Bernadette O'Farrell; Patricia Driscoll); The Adventures of Robin Hood, 1985 (made-for-TV; Helen Morse voiceover); Beyond Sherwood Forest, 2009 (made-for-TV; Erica Durance); A Challenge for Robin Hood, 1968 (Gay Hamilton); Il Magnifico Robin Hood, 1970 (Antonella Murgia); Il trionfo di Robin Hood, 1962 (Gia Scala); Into the Labyrinth, 1981-1982 (TV series; "Robin," 1981 episode: Patricia Driscoll); The Legend of Robin Hood, 1975 (TV miniseries; Diane Keen); Long Live Robin Hood, 1971 (Silvia Dionisio); The Men of Sherwood Forest, 1954 (Eileen Moore); NBC Children's Theatre, 1963-1973 (TV series; "Robin Hood," 1964 episode: Lynda Day George); The New Adventures of Robin Hood, 1997-1999 (TV series; Barbara Griffin); Prince of Thieves, 1948 (Patricia Morison); **Robin and Marian**, 1976 (Audrey Hepburn); **Robin Hood**, 1922 (Enid Bennett); Robin Hood, 1953- (TV miniseries; Josee Richard); **Robin Hood**, 1973 (Monica Evans voiceover); Robin Hood, 1984-1986 (TV series; Judi Trott); Robin Hood, 1991 (Uma Thurman); Robin Hood, 2006-2009 (TV series; Lucy Griffiths); **Robin Hood**, 2010 (Cate Blanchett); Robin Hood en zijn schelmen, 1962 (Phia Bours); Robin Hood: Ghosts of Sherwood 3D, 2012 (Ramona Kuen); **Robin Hood: Men in Tights**, 1993 (Amy Yasbeck); **Robin Hood: Prince of Thieves**, 1991 (Mary Elizabeth Mastrantonio); Rogues of Sherwood Forest, 1950 (Diana Lynn); **The Story of Robin Hood** [aka: The Story of Robin Hood and His Merrie Men], 1952 (Joan Rice); Sword of Sherwood Forest, 1961 (Sarah Branch); Tales of Robin Hood, 1951 (Mary Hatcher); Wolfshead: The Legend of Robin Hood, 1973 (Ciaran Madden); Young Robin Hood, 1991-1992 (animated TV series; Anik Matern voiceover, Liz MacRae voiceover); The Zany Adventures of Robin Hood, 1984 (made-for-TV; Morgan Fairchild).

March Hare (fictional character from the 1865 novel Alice's Adventures in Wonderland by British author Lewis Carroll): Adventures in Wonderland, 1992-1994 (TV series; Reece Holland); Alice at the Palace,

1982 (made-for-TV; Mark Linn-Baker); Alice in Wonderland, 1931 (Meyer Berensen); **Alice in Wonderland**, 1933 (Charles Ruggles); **Alice in Wonderland**, 1951 (Jerry Colonna voiceover); Alice in Wonderland, 1955 (made-for-TV; Robert Casper); Alice in Wonderland, 1966 (made-for-TV; Michael Gough); Alice in Wonderland, 1976 (Sally Cutting); Alice in Wonderland, 1982 (made-for-TV; Tom Dunn); Alice in Wonderland, 1985 (made-for-TV; Roddy McDowall); Alice in Wonderland, 1985 (TV series; Michael Bentine); Alice in Wonderland, 1986 (made-for-TV; four 30-minute segments; Neil Fitzwilliam); Alice in Wonderland, 1999 (made-for-TV; Francis Wright; Adrian Getley; Robert Tygner); **Alice in Wonderland**, 2010 (Paul Whitehouse); Alice's Adventures in Wonderland, 1972 (Peter Sellers); Alice's Adventures in Wonderland and through the Looking Glass, 1948 (made-for-TV; Anthony Oliver); Alice in Wonderland or What's a Nice Kid Like You Doing in a Place Like This?, 1966 (animated made-for-TV; Daws Butler); Alice through the Looking Box, 1960 (made-for-TV; Bernard Bresslaw); Alice through the Looking Glass, 1973 (made-for-TV; Stephen Moore); Alice's Adventures in Wonderland, 2011 (made-for-TV; Ricardo Cervera); Great Performances, 1971- (TV series; "Alice in Wonderland," 1983 episode: Zeliko Ivanek); Kraft Theatre, 1947-1958 (TV series; "Alice in Wonderland," 1954 episode; Fredd Wayne); Unsuk Chin: Alice in Wonderland, 2007 (Andrew Watts); The Wednesday Play, 1964-1970 (TV series; "Alice," 1965 episode: John Saunders).

Marius (adventurous French sailor from Marseilles who deserts his lover Fanny but is later reunited with her and their child): **Cesar**, 1936 (Pierre Fresnay); **Fanny**, 1948 (Pierre Fresnay); **Fanny**, 1961 (Horst Buchholz); Fanny, 2008 (made-for-TV; Stephane Varupenne); Fanny, 2014 (Raphael Personnaz); La trilogie Marseillaise: Cesar, 2000 (made-for-TV; Eric Poulain); La trilogie Marseillaise: Fanny, 2000 (made-for-TV; Eric Poulain); La trilogie Marseillaise: Marius, 2000 (made-for-TV; Eric Poulain); **Marius**, 1933 (Pierre Fresnay); Marius, 2014 (Raphael Personnaz); Pagnol, 1977 (TV series; Peter Romer); Port of Seven Seas, 1938 (John Beal).

Mars (Roman god of war; Ares in Greek mythology): Castor et Pollux, 1991 (made-for-TV; Bernard Deletre); In Performance, 1978- (TV series; "Orpheus in the Underworld," 1983 episode: John Fryatt); Mars: God of War, 1962 (Roger Browne); Orpheus in der Unterwelt, 1975 (Werner Senftleben); Orpheus in der Unterwelt, 2007 (made-for-TV; Franz Grundheber); Rome in a Day, 2008 (Luke Butler); The Triumph of Venus, 1918 (Karl Dane); Vamping Venus, 1928 (Guinn "Big Boy" Williams); Vulcan, Son of Giove, 1962 (Roger Browne).

Mary Quite Contrary (Mother Goose character): **Babes in Toyland**, 1934 (Marie Wilson); Babes in Toyland, 1961 (Annette Funicello); Babes in Toyland, 1986 (made-for-TV; Jill Schoelen); Hercules: The Legendary Journeys, 1995-1999 (TV series; Elizabeth Hawthorne); Mother Goose Rock 'n' Rhyme, 1990 (made-for-TV; Katey Sagal).

Medea (in Greek mythology, a sorceress and niece of Circe, later a wife to Jason): **Jason and the Argonauts**, 1963 (Nancy Kovack; Eve Haddon voiceover); Jason and the Argonauts, 2000 (TV miniseries; Jolene Blalock); Mythic Warriors: Guardians of the Legend, 1998- (TV series; Sally Cahill).

Medusa (in Greek mythology a gorgon or monster, half woman, half snake with a headful of hair as snakes and with the power to kill those who looked upon her hideousness): **Clash of the Titans**, 2010 (Natalia Vodianova); Hercules, 1998-1999 (TV series; Jennifer Love Hewitt voiceover); Hercules: The Brave and the Bold, 2013 (Julie Graue); Mythic Warriors: Guardians of the Legend, 1998- (TV series; Jennifer Dale); Percy Jackson & the Olympians: The Lightning Thief, 2010 (Uma Thurman); Persee, 2004 (made-for-TV; Olivier Laquerre); The Storyteller: Greek Myths, 1990- (TV miniseries; "Perseus and the Gor-

Natalia Vodianova (as Medusa) in *Clash of the Titans*, 2010.

gon," 19991 episode: Frances Barber).

Meg March (one of four teenage sisters who finds romance as she and her siblings mature in a Massachusetts household during the American Civil War as profiled in Louisa May Alcott's timeless novel, *Little Women*, 1868-1869): The Ford Theatre Hour, 1948-1951 (TV series; "Little Women," 1949 episode; Kim Hunter); Good Wives, 1958 (TV series; Kate Cameron); Great Performances, 1971- (TV series; "Little Women," 2001 episode: Joyce DiDonato); Jo's Boys, 1959 (TV series; Kate Cameron); Little Women, 1917 (Mary Lincoln); Little Women, 1918 (Isabel Lamon); **Little Women**, 1933 (Frances Dee); **Little Women**, 1949 (Janet Leigh); Little Women, 1950- (TV series; Sheila Shand Gibbs); Little Women, 1958 (TV series; Kate Cameron); Little Women, 1958 (made-for-TV; Florence Henderson); Little Women, 1970 (TV miniseries; Jo Rowbottom); Little Women, 1978 (TV miniseries; Meredith Baxter); **Little Women**, 1994 (Trini Alvarado); Matinee Theatre, 1955-1958 (TV series; "Little Women," 1956 episode: Diane Jergens); NBC Special Treat, 1975-1986 (TV series; "Little Women," 1976 episode: Anna Arago); Studio One in Hollywood, 1948-1958 (TV series; "Little Women: Jo's Story," 1950 episode: Peg Hellias; "Little Women: Meg's Story," 1950 episode: Mary Sinclair).

Menelaus (King of Sparta in Greek mythology and husband of Helen of Troy, who was one of the Greek leaders in the Trojan War): Adam and Eve, 1949 (Enzo Biliotti); BBC Sunday-Night Theatre, 1950-1959 (TV series; "Troilus and Cressida," 1954 episode: John Vere); Helen of Troy, 1924 (Friedrich Ulmer); Helen of Troy, 1951 (Max Hansen); Helen of Troy, 1956 (Niall MacGinnis); Helen, Yes…Helen of Troy, 1974 (Pupo De Luca); La belle Helene, 1996 (Volker Vogel); La belle Helene, 2000 (Michel Senechal); Las troyanas, 1963 (Antonio Medellin); The Lion of Thebes, 1964 (Alberto Lupo); Loves of Three Queens, 1954 (Robert Beatty); Mythic Warriors: Guardians of the Legend, 1998- (TV series; "Ulysses and the Trojan Horse," 1999 episode: Colin Fox); The Odyssey, 1997- (TV series; Nicholas Clay); The Private Life of Helen of Troy, 1927 (Lewis Stone); Sacrifice to the Wind, 1954 (made-for-TV; Douglas Wilmer); Troilus & Cressida, 1981 (made-for-TV; Bernard Brown); Troilus und Cressida, 1964 (made-for-TV; Hans Gunther Muller); Troilus und Cressida, 1969 (made-for-TV; Joseph Saxinger); The Trojan Horse, 1962 (Nando Tamberlani); The Trojan Women, 1971 (Patrick Magee); **Troy**, 2004 (Brendan Gleeson); Xena: Warrior Princess, 1995-2001 (TV series; Ken Blackburn).

Mercury (Roman god and messenger of the gods; Hermes in Greek mythology): Amphitryon, 1978 (made-for-TV; Gunter Ringe); Amphitryon, 1981 (made-for-TV; Klaus Hohne); Amphitryon, 2003 (made-for-

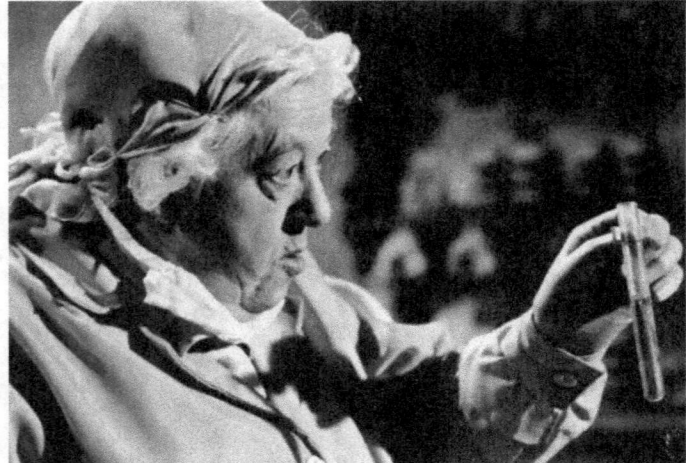

Margaret Rutherford (as sleuth Miss Marple) in *Murder Ahoy,* **1964.**

TV; Jerome Pouly); Biblioteca di Studio Uno: Odissea, 1964 (made-for-TV; Giustino Durano); Goddess of Love, 1988 (made-for-TV; Benjamin Schick); Hercules Returns, 1993 (Frank Thring); Hercules in New York, 1970 (Dan Hamilton); In Performance, 1978- (TV series; "Orpheus in the Underworld," 1983 episode: Christopher Gable); Jacques Offenbach: Orpheus in the Underworld, 1997 (made-for-TV; Franck Cassard); Jason and the Heroes of Mount Olympus, 2001- (animated TV series; S. Scott Bullock voiceover); L'odissea, 1991 (made-for-TV; Gigi Sammarchi); Night Life of the Gods, 1935 (Paul Kaye); Orphee aux enfers, 1997 (made-for-TV; Ethienne Lescroart); Orpheus in der Unterwelt, 1975 (Fred Delmare); Persee, 2004 (made-for-TV; Colin Ainsworth); Platee, 2000 (made-for-TV; Yann Beuron); The Triumph of Venus, 1918 (A. Freeland); Vamping Venus, 1928 (Spec O'Donnell); Vulcan, Son of Giove, 1962 (Isarco Ravaioli).

Merlin (legendary magician in the court of King Arthur in 6th-Century Britain): The Adventures of Sir Galahad, 1949 (serial; William Fawcett); The Adventures of Sir Lancelot, 1956-1957 (TV series; Cyril Smith); Arthur the King, 1985 (made-for-TV; Edward Woodward); Arthur's Quest, 1999 (made-for-TV; Arye Gross); Batman: The Brave and the Bold, 2008-2011 (animated TV series; David McCallum voiceover); **Camelot**, 1967 (Laurence Naismith); Camelot, 1982 (made-for-TV; James Valentine); Camelot, 2011 (TV miniseries; Joseph Fiennes); Carry On Laughing!, 1975 (TV series; Peter Butterworth); **A Connecticut Yankee**, 1931 (Brandon Hurst); A Connecticut Yankee, 1955 (made-for-TV; Leonard Elliott); A Connecticut Yankee in King Arthur's Court, 1921 (William V. Mong); **A Connecticut Yankee in King Arthur's Court**, 1949 (Murvyn Vye); A Connecticut Yankee in King Arthur's Court, 1989 (made-for-TV: Rene Auberjonois); Crystal Cave, 1996 (made-for-TV; Robert Guillaume); **Excalibur**, 1981 (Nicol Williamson); Guinevere, 1994 (made-for-TV; Donald Pleasence); Guinevere Jones, 2002 (TV series; Ted Hamilton); A Kid in King Arthur's Court, 1995 (Ron Moody); **King Arthur**, 2004 (Stephen Dillane); King Arthur and the Knights of Justice, 1992-1993 (TV series; Jim Byrnes voiceover); A Knight in Camelot, 1998 (made-for-TV; Ian Richardson); **Knights of the Round Table**, 1953 (Felix Aylmer); Lancelot of the Lake, 1970 (made-for-TV; Claude Santelli); **The Last Legion**, 2007 (Ben Kingsley); The Legend of King Arthur, 1979 (TV series; Robert Eddison); The Legend of Prince Valiant, 1991-1994 (TV series; Alan Oppenheimer); The Magic Land of Mother Goose, 1967 (Roy Huston); Merlin, 1993 (Rodney Wood); Merlin, 1998 (TV miniseries; Sam Neill as adult Merlin; Daniel Brocklebank as young Merlin); Merlin, 2008-2012 (TV series); Merlin: The Return, 2000 (Rik Mayall); Mr. Merlin, 1981-1982 (TV series; Bernard Hughes); The Mists of Avalon, 2001 (made-for-TV; Michael Byrne); Once upon a Classic, 1976-1979 (TV series: "A Connecticut Yankee in King Arthur's Court," 1978 episode: Roscoe Lee Browne); Quest for Camelot, 1998 (John Gielgud); **7 Faces of Dr. Lao**, 1964 (Tony Randall); Siege of the Saxons, 1963 (John Laurie); Studio One in Hollywood, 1948-1958 (TV series: "A Connecticut Yankee in King Arthur's Court," 1952 episode: Salem Ludwig); **The Sword and the Stone**, 1963 (Karl Swenson voiceover); Sword of Lancelot, 1963 (Mark Dignam); The Time Tunnel, 1966-1967 (TV series; "Merlin the Magician," 1967 episode: Christopher Cary as adult Merlin; Dennis Christopher as young Merlin); Unidentified Flying Oddball, 1979 (Ron Moody); A Young Connecticut Yankee in King Arthur's Court, 1996 (Michael York).

Messala (Roman soldier, official and chariot-racer in Jerusalem in the time of Jesus Christ, a fictional character in the 1880 novel by Lew Wallace entitled: *Ben-Hur: A Tale of the Christ*): **Ben-Hur: A Tale of the Christ**, 1925 (Francis X. Bushman); **Ben-Hur**, 1959 (Stephen Boyd); Ben Hur, 2010 (TV miniseries; Stephen Campbell Moore).

Michael (Archangel): The Becoming, 2012 (Nicholas Alexander); Bedtime Fairy Tales for Crocodiles, 2003 (Arturo Rios); Celestial Hunt, 2013 (John Donahue); Celestial Run, 2012 (John Donahue); Centurian A.D., 2015 (Kevin Caliber); The Curse of El Charro, 2005 (James Intfeld); Dominion, 2014- (TV series; Tom Wisdom); Faust, 1960 (Karl-Heinz von Hassel); Good Satan, 2012 (Ari Zagaris); In Media Res, 2011 (Mark Edward Lewis); Joan of Arc, 2003 (made-for-TV; Marcel Jakubovie); Lucifer, 1966 (Kees Coolen); Lucifer, 1981 (Alexander Van Heteren); **Michael**, 1996 (John Travolta); Mostly Dead, 2014 (Dean Puleo); On Angel's Wings, 2014 (Robert Michael Szot); The Prophecy II, 1998 (Eric Roberts); Supernatural, 2005- (TV series; Richard Speight Jr.); Valeri Fox, 2014- (TV series; Steven D. Moyer); Wandering, 2011 (Kami Libaridyan); Xena: Warrior Princess, 1995-2001 (TV series; Charles Mesure).

Mike Hammer (hard-boiled private detective created by author Mickey Spillane in his 1947 novel, *I, the Jury*): The Girl Hunters, 1963 (Mickey Spillane); Come Die with Me: A Mickey Spillane's Mike Hammer Mystery, 1994 (made-for-TV; Robert Estes); I, the Jury, 1953 (Biff Elliot); I, the Jury, 1982 (Armand Assante); **Kiss Me Deadly**, 1955 (Ralph Meeker); Margin for Murder, 1981 (made-for-TV; Kevin Dobson); Mike Hammer, 1958-1959 (TV series; Darren McGavin); Mike Hammer: Murder Takes All, 1989 (made-for-TV; Stacy Keach); Mike Hammer, Private Eye, 1997-1999 (TV series; Stacy Keach); More Than Murder, 1984 (made-for-TV; Stacy Keach); Murder Me, Murder You, 1983 (made-for-TV; Stacy Keach); My Gun Is Quick, 1957 (Robert Bray); The New Mike Hammer, 1984-1989 (TV series; Stacy Keach); The Return of Mickey Spillane's Mike Hammer, 1986 (made-for-TV; Stacy Keach).

Miles Herndon (character in the children's novel, *The Prince and the Pauper*, 1881, by Mark Twain, a soldier-of-fortune who rescues Edward VI of England after he exchanges identities with his lookalike, a fictional urchin boy named Tom Canty): The Adventures of the Prince and the Pauper, 1969 (Gene Bua); Crossed Swords, 1978 (Oliver Reed); The DuPont Show of the Month, 1957-1961 (TV series; "The Prince and the Pauper," 1957 episode: Christopher Plummer); The Prince and the Pauper, 1915 (William Sorelle); The Prince and the Pauper, 1920 (Franz Everth); **The Prince and the Pauper**, 1937 (Errol Flynn); The Prince and the Pauper, 1976 (TV series; Barry Stokes); The Prince and the Pauper, 1977 (Oliver Reed); The Prince and the Pauper, 1996 (TV series; six episodes: James Purefoy); The Prince and the Pauper, 2000 (made-for-TV; Aidan Quinn); Shirley Temple's Storybook, 1958-1960 (TV series; "The Prince and the Pauper," 1960 episode: Gig Young); Walt Disney's Wonderful World of Color, 1954-1992 (TV series; "The Prince and the Pauper: The Pauper King," 1962 episode: Guy Williams; "The Prince and the Pauper: The Merciful Law of the King," 1962 episode:

Guy Williams; "The Prince and the Pauper: Long Live the Rightful King," 1962 episode: Guy Williams).

Minerva (Roman goddess of the arts and patron of Roman heroes; Athena in Greek mythology): Castor et Pollux, 1991 (made-for-TV; Claire Brua); Jacques Offenbach: Orpheus in the Underworld, 1997 (made-for-TV; Laurence Misonne); L'odissea, 1991 (made-for-TV; Sylva Koscina); Orphee aux enfers, 1997 (made-for-TV; Alketa Cela); Rome in a Day, 2008 (Cathy Bennett).

Miss Havisham (wealthy, embittered and aging spinster who constantly wears the fading wedding dress she wore long earlier when jilted at the altar and who lives in a ruined mansion as portrayed in Charles Dickens' 1861 novel, *Great Expectations*): Great Expectations, 1917 (Grace Barton); Great Expectations, 1934 (Florence Reed); **Great Expectations**, 1946 (Martita Hunt); Great Expectations, 1959- (TV series; Marjory Hawtrey); Great Expectations, 1967- (TV series; Maxine Audley); Great Expectations, 1974 (made-for-TV; Margaret Leighton); Great Expectations, 1981- (TV miniseries; Joan Hickson); Great Expectations, 1989- (TV miniseries; Jean Simmons); Great Expectations, 1999 (made-for-TV; Charlotte Rampling); Great Expectations, 2011 (TV miniseries; Gillian Anderson); Great Expectations, 2012 (Helena Bonham Carter); Great Expectations, 2013 (Paula Wilcox); Playdate, 1961-1964 (TV series; "Great Expectations," two episodes in 1962: Cathleen Nesbitt); Robert Montgomery Presents, 1950-1957 (TV series; "Great Expectations," two episodes in 1954: Estelle Winwood); Store forventninger, 1922 (Marie Dinesen).

Miss Jane Marple (clever spinster sleuth created by mystery writer Agatha Christie and who first appeared in her short story, "The Tuesday Night Club," published in *The Royal Magazine*, December 1927): Agatha Christie's Miss Marple, 1984- (TV miniseries; Joan Hickson); The Alphabet Murders, 1965 (Margaret Rutherford); A Caribbean Mystery, 1983 (made-for-TV; Helen Hayes); Goodyear Playhouse, 1951-1957 (TV series; "A Murder Is Announced," 1956 episode: Gracie Fields); Masterpiece Theatre, 1980- (TV series; several episodes; Joan Hickson); **The Mirror Crack'd**, 1980 (Angela Lansbury); Mord im Pfarrhaus, 1970 (made-for-TV; Inge Langen); **Murder Ahoy**, 1964 (Margaret Rutherford); **Murder at the Gallop**, 1963 (Margaret Rutherford); **Murder by Death**, 1976 (spoof of great detectives; Elsa Lancaster as Miss Jessica Marbles); **Murder Most Foul**, 1964 (Margaret Rutherford); Murder with Mirrors, 1985 (made-for-TV; Helen Hayes); **Murder She Said**, 1961 (Margaret Rutherford).

Mr. Moto (wily Japanese detective and secret agent created by U.S. author John P. Marquand in his 1935 novel, *Your Turn, Mr. Moto*; the character lost all popularity in America after Japan attacked the U.S. military installations at Pearl Harbor on December 7, 1945; Peter Lorre, who played the character in most of the films, hated playing the role as he repeatedly told this author): Mr. Moto in Danger Island, 1939 (Peter Lorre); Mr. Moto Takes a Chance, 1938 (Peter Lorre); Mr. Moto Takes a Vacation, 1939 (Peter Lorre); **Mr. Moto's Gamble**, 1938 (Peter Lorre); **Mr. Moto's Last Warning**, 1939 (Peter Lorre); **The Mysterious Mr. Moto**, 1938 (Peter Lorre); The Return of Mr. Moto, 1965 (Henry Silva); Thank You, Mr. Moto, 1938 (Peter Lorre); **Think Fast, Mr. Moto**, 1937 (Peter Lorre).

Mock Turtle (fictional character from the 1865 novel Alice's Adventures in Wonderland by British author Lewis Carroll): Alice in Wonderland, 1931 (Gus Alexander); **Alice in Wonderland**, 1933 (Cary Grant); Alice in Wonderland, 1955 (made-for-TV; Burr Tillstrom); Alice in Wonderland, 1966 (made-for-TV; John Gielgud); Alice in Wonderland, 1976 (Marta Larreina); Alice in Wonderland, 1985 (made-for-TV; Ringo Starr); Alice in Wonderland, 1985 (TV series; Bernard Cribbins); Alice in Wonderland, 1986 (made-for-TV; four 30-minute segments; Roy

Dick Baldwin, Peter Lorre (as Mr. Moto) and Keye Luke in *Mr. Moto's Gamble*, 1938.

Skelton); Alice in Wonderland, 1999 (made-for-TV; Gene Wilder); Alice's Adventures in Wonderland, 1972 (Michael Hordern); Alice's Adventures in Wonderland and through the Looking Glass, 1948 (made-for-TV; Gordon Bell); Dreamchild, 1985 (Steve Whitmire, Alan Bennett); Great Performances, 1971- (TV series; "Alice in Wonderland," 1983 episode: Donald O'Connor); Kraft Theatre, 1947-1958 (TV series; "Alice in Wonderland," 1954 episode: James Barton); The Wednesday Play, 1964-1970 (TV series; "Alice," 1965 episode: Norman Scace).

Mordred (or Modred; legendary evil knight, supposedly illegitimate son of King Arthur in 6th-Century Britain): The Adventures of Sir Galahad, 1949 (serial; Leonard Penn); Arthur the King, 1985 (made-for-TV; Joseph Blatchley); **Camelot**, 1967 (David Hemmings); Camelot, 1982 (made-for-TV; Richard Backus); **Excalibur**, 1981 (Robert Addie as adult Mordred; Charley Boorman as young Mordred); Into the Labyrinth, 1981-1982 (TV series: "Excalibur," 1982 episode, Pavel Douglas); **Knights of the Round Table**, 1953 (Stanley Baker); Lancelot of the Lake, 1974 (Patrick Bernard); The Legend of King Arthur, 1979 (TV series; Steve Hodson); Merlin, 1998 (TV miniseries; Jason Done); Merlin: The Return, 2000 (Craig Sheffer); The Mists of Avalon, 2001 (made-for-TV; Hans Matheson; Elias Zerael Bauer as the young Mordred); Morte d'Arthur, 1980 (made-for-TV; Nickolas Grace); Sword of Lancelot, 1963 (Michael Meacham); Unidentified Flying Oddball, 1979 (Jim Dale).

Morgan le Fay (or Morgana; legendary evil sorceress in the court of King Arthur in 6th-Century Britain): The Adventures of Sir Galahad, 1949 (serial; Pat Barton); Arthur the King, 1985 (made-for-TV; Candice Bergen); Arthur's Quest, 1999 (made-for-TV; Catherine Oxenberg); Camelot, 2011 (TV miniseries; Eva Green); **A Connecticut Yankee**, 1931 (Myrna Loy); A Connecticut Yankee, 1955 (made-for-TV; Gale Sherwood); A Connecticut Yankee in King Arthur's Court, 1921 (Rosemary Theby); **A Connecticut Yankee in King Arthur's Court**, 1949 (Virginia Field); A Connecticut Yankee in King Arthur's Court, 1989 (made-for-TV: Jean Marsh); **Excalibur**, 1981 (Helen Mirren as adult Morgana; Barbara Byrne as young Morgana; Kay McLaren as aged Morgana); Guinevere, 1994 (made-for-TV; Brid Brennan); **Knights of the Round Table**, 1953 (Anne Crawford); The Legend of King Arthur, 1979 (TV series; Maureen O'Brien); The Legend of Prince Valiant, 1991-1994 (TV series; Patty Duke/Diana Muldaur); Merlin, 1998 (TV miniseries; Helena Bonham Carter as adult Morgana; Alice Hamilton as young Morgana); Merlin: The Return, 2000 (Grethe Fox); The Mists of Avalon, 2001 (made-for-TV; Julianna Margulies/Tamsin Egerton as the young Morgana); Prince Valiant, 1997 (Joanna Lumley); Sword of the Valiant: The Legend of Sir Gawain and the Green Knight, 1984

Boris Karloff (as the Mummy) and Zita Johann in *The Mummy,* 1932.

(Emma Sutton); A Young Connecticut Yankee in King Arthur's Court, 1996 (Theresa Russell).

Mother Goose (Mother Goose character): **Babes in Toyland**, 1934 (Virginia Karns); Babes in Toyland, 1961 (Mary McCarty); Barney & Friends, 1992-2009 (TV series; Sandy Walper, Barbara Lowin); The Bride Goes Wild, 1948 (Estelle Etterre); Christmas Night of One Hundred Stars, 1986 (TV special; Christopher Biggins); Happily Ever After: Fairy Tales for Every Child, 1995-2000 (animated TV series; Whoopi Goldberg); Higglety Pigglety Pop!, 1985 (Deborah Rees); The Magic Land of Mother Goose, 1967 (Judith Snow); A Modern Mother Goose, 1917 (Rachel James); Mother Goose, 1959 (Frankie Howerd); Mother Goose, 1965 (made-for-TV; Terry Scott); Mother Goose and Friends, 2005- (TV series; Jolene Patrick); Mother Goose and Grimm, 1991-1993 (TV series; Mitzi McCall); Mother Goose Rock 'n' Rhyme, 1990 (made-for-TV; Jean Stapleton); The New Adventures of Mother Goose, 1995 (made-for-TV; Sally Struthers); Off to See the Wizard, 1967-1968 (TV series; Maureen O'Hara); The Rake's Progress: 1994 (Linda Ormiston); The Rake's Progress, A Fable, 1979 (made-for-TV; Nuala Willis); Shirley Temple's Storybook, 1958-1961 (TV series; "Mother Goose," 1958 episode; Elsa Lanchester); Super Why!, 2007- (TV series; Marsha Mason); The Wacky World of Mother Goose, 1967 (Margaret Rutherford).

Mother Hubbard (Mother Goose character): **Babes in Toyland**, 1934 (Alice Cooke); Happily Ever After: Fairy Tales for Every Child, 1995-2000 (animated TV series; Marla Gibbs); Mother Goose Rock 'n' Rhyme, 1990 (made-for-TV; Elayne Boosler).

Mouse (fictional character from the 1865 novel Alice's Adventures in Wonderland by British author Lewis Carroll): **Alice in Wonderland**, 1933 (Raymond Hatton); Alice in Wonderland, 1966 (made-for-TV; Alan Bennett); Alice in Wonderland, 1985 (made-for-TV; Sherman Hemsley); Alice in Wonderland, 1985 (TV series; Mary Miller); Alice in Wonderland, 1986 (made-for-TV; four 30-minute segments; Ysanne Churchman); Alice in Wonderland, 1999 (made-for-TV; Ken Dodd); Alice's Adventures in Wonderland, 1972 (Davy Kaye); Great Performances, 1971- (TV series; "Alice in Wonderland," 1983 episode: Nathan Lane).

Mr. Bumble (arrogant and self-important master of the workhouse in Charles Dickens' 1837 novel, *Oliver Twist*): The ABC Saturday Superstar Movie, 1972-1974 (TV series; "Oliver and the Artful Dodger," two 1927 episodes: Ronald Long); The DuPont Show of the Month, 1957-1961 (TV series; "Oliver Twist," 1959 episode: Robert Morley); The Further Adventures of Oliver Twist, 1980- (TV series; Harold Innocent);

Oliver!, 1968 (Harry Secombe); Oliver Twist, 1916 (Harry L. Rattenberry); **Oliver Twist**, 1922 (James Marcus); Oliver Twist, 1933 (Lionel Belmore); **Oliver Twist**, 1951 (Francis L. Sullivan); Oliver Twist, 1962- (TV miniseries; Willoughby Goddard); Oliver Twist, 1982 (made-for-TV; Timothy West); Oliver Twist, 1985- (TV miniseries; Godfrey James); Oliver Twist, 1999- (TV miniseries; David Ross); Oliver Twist, 2002- (TV miniseries; Michael Segerstrom); **Oliver Twist**, 2005 (Jeremy Swift); Oliver Twist, 2007- (TV miniseries; Gregor Fisher).

The Mummy (character in horror films; an ancient Egyptian priest most usually named Imhotep or Kharis, who is resurrected to bring havoc and death to the living): The Curse of the Mummy's Tomb, 1964 (Dickie Owen); Day of the Mummy, 2014 (Brandon deSpain as Neferu, the Mummy); Monster Force, 1994 (TV series; Robert Bockstael as Imhotep); **The Mummy**, 1932 (Boris Karloff as Imhotep and the Mummy); The Mummy, 1959 (Christopher Lee as Kharis and the Mummy); **The Mummy**, 1999 (Arnold Vosloo as Imhotep); **The Mummy Returns**, 2001 (Arnold Vosloo as Imhotep); The Mummy: Secrets of the Medjai, 2001- (animated TV series; Jim Cummings voiceover as Imhotep); **The Mummy: Tomb of the Dragon Emperor**, 2008 (Jet Li as Emperor Han who has been transformed into a mummy); The Mummy's Curse, 1944 (Lon Chaney Jr. as Kharis); The Mummy's Ghost, 1944 (Lon Chaney Jr. as Kharis); **The Mummy's Hand**, 1940 (Tom Tyler as Kharis); The Mummy's Kiss, 2003 (Sasha Peralto); The Mummy's Tomb, 1942 (Lon Chaney Jr. as Kharis); Saturday the 14th Strikes Back, 1988 (Joseph Ruskin as Kharis; Michael Berryman as the Mummy).

Mycroft Holmes (fictional charcter; the older brother of Sherlock Holmes in the stories of Arthur Conan Doyle): The Adventures of Sherlock Holmes, 1984-1985 (TV series; Charles Gray); The Adventures of Sherlock Holmes and Dr. Watson, 1980 (TV series; Boris Klyuev); Hands of a Murderer, 1990 (Peter Jeffrey); Incident at Victoria Falls, 1992 (made-for-TV; Jerome Willis); The Memoirs of Sherlock Holmes, 1994 (TV series; Charles Gray); **The Private Life of Sherlock Holmes**, 1970 (Christopher Lee); The Return of Sherlock Holmes, 1986-1988 (TV series; Charles Gray); The Royal Scandal, 2001 (made-for-TV; R. H. Thomson); **The Seven-Per-Cent Solution**, 1976 (Charles Gray); Sherlock Holmes, 1967-1968 (TV series; Hans Crossy); Sherlock, 2002 (made-for-TV; Richard E. Grant); **Sherlock Holmes: A Game of Shadows**, 2011 (Stephen Fry); Sherlock Holmes and Dr. Watson: The Bloody Inscription, 1979 (made-for-TV; Boris Klyuev); Sherlock Holmes and the Leading Lady, 1991 (made-for-TV; Jerome Willis); **A Study in Terror**, 1966 (Robert Morley).

Nana (the alluring prostitute daughter of Gervaise in Emile Zola's 1880 novel): Nana, 1926 (Catherine Hessling); Nana, 1934 (Anna Sten); Nana, 1944 (Lupe Velez); Nana, 1955 (Martine Carol); Nana, 1968 (TV miniseries; Katherine Schofield); Nana, 1981 (TV miniseries; Veronique Genest); Nana, 1985 (Irma Serrano); Nana, 1999 (made-for-TV; Francesca Dellera); Nana, 2001 (made-for-TV; Lou Doillon).

Neptune (Roman god of the seas; Poseidon in Greek mythology): Goddess of Love, 1988 (made-for-TV; Kay E. Kuter); L'odissea, 1991 (made-for-TV; Sergio Vastano); Night Life of the Gods, 1935 (Robert Warwick); The Temple of Venus, 1923 (Robert Klein); Vulcan, Son of Giove, 1962 (Omero Gargano).

Nick Adams (character appearing in the short stories of Ernest Hemingway, loosely based upon the author's early life): **Adventures of a Young Man**, 1962 (Richard Beymer); **The Killers**, 1946 (Phil Brown).

Nick Charles (suave, heavy-drinking detective in the stories by Dashiell Hammett; William Powell in all): **After the Thin Man**, 1936; **Another Thin Man**, 1939; **Shadow of the Thin Man**, 1941; **Song of the Thin**

Man, 1947; **The Thin Man**, 1934; **The Thin Man Goes Home**, 1945.

Ninotchka (attractive female Soviet enoy to Paris who falls in love with a wealthy American): **Ninotchka**, 1939 (Greta Garbo); Ninotchka, 1960 (made-for-TV; Maria Schell); Ninotchka, 1965 (made-for-TV; Ruth Leuwerik); Ninotschka sucht Fruhling, 1973 (made-for-TV; Catrin Hennig); **Silk Stockings**, 1957 (Cyd Charisse).

Nora Charles (character, wife of Nick Charles, in the stories by Dashiell Hammett; Myrna Loy in all): **After the Thin Man**, 1936; **Another Thin Man**, 1939; **Shadow of the Thin Man**, 1941; **Song of the Thin Man**, 1947; **The Thin Man**, 1934; **The Thin Man Goes Home**, 1945.

Old Woman Who Lives in the Shoe (fairy tale character): Happily N'Ever After, 2009 (Jennie Fahn voiceover); Mother Goose Rock 'n' Rhyme, 1990 (made-for-TV; Deborah Harry); The 7D, 2014 (TV series; Tress MacNeille).

Old King Cole (Mother Goose character): **Babes in Toyland**, 1934 (Kewpie Morgan); Birthday Party, 1947-1949 (TV series; Ted Brown); Fairy Tales, 1978 (Bob Leslie); Happily N'Ever After, 2009 (Kelly Brewster voiceover); The Magic Land of Mother Goose, 1967 (David Hammond); Mother Goose Rock 'n' Rhyme, 1990 (made-for-TV; Little Richard).

Oliver Twist (a fictional character in the Charles Dickens novel *Oliver Twist*, an orphaned boy who falls in with a gang of pickpockets in 19th-Century London, England): The ABC Saturday Superstar Movie, 1972-1974 (animated TV series; "Oliver and the Artful Dodger," two 1972 episodes; Gary Marsh); The DuPont Show of the Month, 1957-1961 (TV series; "Oliver Twist," 1959 episode; Richard Thomas); Escape of the Artful Dodger, 2001- (TV series; Rowan Witt); The Further Adventures of Oliver Twist, 1980- (TV series; Daniel Murray); Oliver & Company, 1988 (Joey Lawrence voiceover); Oliver Twist, 1916 (Marie Doro); Oliver Twist, 1919 (Tibor Lubinszky); **Oliver Twist**, 1922 (Jackie Coogan); Oliver Twist, 1933 (Dickie Moore); **Oliver Twist**, 1951 (John Howard Davies); Oliver Twist, 1955 (TV series; Adriano Stuart); Oliver Twist, 1960 (TV series; Osmar Prado); Oliver Twist, 1962 (TV miniseries; Bruce Prochnik); **Oliver!**, 1968 (Mark Lester); Oliver Twist, 1974 (animated version; Josh Albee voiceover; Billy Simpson singing voice); Oliver Twist, 1982 (made-for-TV; Richard Charles); Oliver Twist, 1985 (TV miniseries; Ben Rodska); Oliver Twist, 1997 (made-for-TV; Alex Trench); Oliver Twist, 1999 (TV miniseries; Sam Smith); **Oliver Twist**, 2005 (Barney Clark); Oliver Twist, 2007 (TV series; William Miller); Oliver Twist Jr., 1921 (Harold Goodwin).

Orpheus (legendary Greek poet and musician): The Illiac Passion, 1968 (Jack Smith); In Performance, 1978- (TV series; "Orpheus in the Underworld," 1983 episode: Alexander Oliver); Jacques Offenbach: Orpheus in the Underworld, 1997 (made-for-TV; Alexandru Badea); Jason and the Argonauts, 2000 (TV miniseries; Adrian Lester); Mythic Warriors: Guardians of the Legend, 1998- (TV series; Tony Rosato); Myths, 2009- (TV series; Charles Mnene); Orphee aux enfers, 1997 (made-for-TV; Yann Beuron); Orpheus in der Unterwelt, 1975 (Wolfgang Greese); Orpheus in der Unterwelt, 2007 (made-for-TV; Kurt Marschner); Orpheus in the Underworld, 1961 (made-for-TV; Kevin Miller); Rome in a Day, 2008 (Luke Butler); Young Hercules, 1998-1999 (TV series; Kieren Hutchison).

Othello (character in "Othello," by William Shakespeare, c. 1601, a noble Moor who is consumed by murderous rage that his wife, Desdemona, is carrying on an affair with another, a falsehood spread by Othello's traitorous aide, Iago, causing Othello to murder his innocent wife, and, when discovering his error, commits suicide): BBC Sunday-Night Theatre, 1950-1959 (TV series; "Othello," 1950 episode; Andre Morell);

William Powell (as Nick Charles), Myrna Loy (as Nora Charles) and Asta in *The Thin Man*, 1934.

A Double Life, 1947 (Ronald Colman portraying an actor on stage as Othello); Encounter [General Motors Presents], 1952-1961 (TV series; "Othello," 1953 episode; Lorne Greene); Masterpiece Playhouse, 1950- (TV series; "Othello," 1950 episode; Torin Thatcher); Otello, 1948 (made-for-TV; Ramon Vinay); Otello, 1958 (Mario Del Monaco); Otello, 1959 (made-for-TV; Mario Del Monaco); Otello, 1962 (made-for-TV; Hans Beirer); Otello, 1965 (made-for-TV; Wolfgang Windgassen); Otello, 1974 (Jon Vickers); Otello, 1976 (made-for-TV; Placido Domingo); **Otello**, 1986 (Placido Domingo); Otello, 2012 (Johan Botha); Othello, 1914 (Paolo Colaci); Othello, 1918 (Beni Montano); Othello, 1923 (Emil Jannings); Othello, 1937 (made-for-TV; Ralph Richardson); **Othello** [1952], 1955 (Orson Welles); Othello, 1955 (made-for-TV; Gordon Heath); Othello, 1958 (made-for-TV; Peter Pasetti); Othello [1955], 1960 (Sergei Bondarchuk); Othello, 1962 (made-for-TV; Daniel Sorano); Othello, 1965 (made-for-TV; Raymond Westwell); **Othello**, 1965 (Laurence Olivier); Othello, 1968 (made-for-TV; Wolfgang Reichmann); Othello, 1969 (made-for-TV; Bert Struys); Othello, 1979 (made-for-TV; Roger Hanin); Othello, 1980 (Yaphet Kotto); Othello, 1981 (made-for-TV; Anthony Hopkins); Othello, 1989 (made-for-TV; John Kani); **Othello**, 1995 (Laurence Fishburne); The Philco-Goodyear Television Playhouse, 1948-1956 (TV series; "Othello," 1953 episode: Torin Thatcher).

Panisse (good-hearted widower and elderly sailmaker who marries Fanny, a fish seller in Marseilles who is deserted by her sailor lover): **Cesar**, 1936 (Fernand Charpin); **Fanny**, 1948 (Fernand Charpin); **Fanny**, 1961 (Maurice Chevalier); Fanny, 2008 (made-for-TV; Andrzej Seweryn); Fanny, 2014 (Jean-Pierre Darroussin); La trilogie Marseillaise: Cesar, 2000 (made-for-TV; Henri Tisot); La trilogie Marseillaise: Fanny, 2000 (made-for-TV; Henri Tisot); La trilogie Marseillaise: Marius, 2000 (made-for-TV; Henri Tisot); **Marius**, 1933 (Fernand Charpin); Marius, 2014 (Jean-Pierre Darroussin); Pagnol, 1977 (TV series; Jan Teulings); Port of Seven Seas, 1938 (Frank Morgan).

Paris (Trojan prince in Greek mythology who stole Helen and precipated the Trojan War): The Affairs of Aphrodite, 1970 (Robi Courtney); BBC Sunday-Night Theatre, 1950-1959 (TV series; "Troilus and Cressida," 1954 episode: Simon Lack); Dertrojanisch krieg findet nicht statt, 1964 (made-for-TV; Karl Walter Diess); The Face of Love, 1954 (made-for-TV; Brian Worth); Fury of Achilles, 1962 (Roberto Risso); Helen of Troy, 1924 (Vladimir Gajdarov); Helen of Troy, 1951 (Per Grunden); Helen of Troy, 1956 (Jacques Sernas); ITV Play of the Week, 1955-1974 (TV series; "Tiger at the Gates," 1960 episode; John Bonney); King Priam, 1985 (made-for-TV; Howard Haskin); La belle Helene, 1996 (Deon van der Walt); La belle Helene, 2000 (Yann Beuron); Le guerre

Kirk Douglas (as Ulysses) and Silvana Mangano (as Penelope) in *Ulysses*, 1955.

de Troie n'aura pas lieu, 1967 (made-for-TV; Yves Lefebvre); Mythic Warriors: Guardians of the Legend, 1998- (TV series; "Ulysses and the Trojan Horse," 1999 episode; John Ralston): Myths, 2009- (TV series; Tommy Knight); Play of the Week, 1959-1961 (TV series; "Tiger at the Gate," 1960 episode: Patrick Horgan); The Private Life of Helen of Troy, 1927 (Ricardo Cortez); The Time Tunnel, 1966-1967 (TV series; "Revenge of the Gods," 1966 episode: Paul Carr); Troilus & Cressida, 1981 (made-for-TV; David Firth); Troilus und Cressida, 1964 (made-for-TV; Norbert Hansing); Troilus und Cressida, 1969 (made-for-TV; Wolfgang Schwarz); The Trojan Horse, 1962 (Warner Bentivegna); **Troy**, 2004 (Orlando Bloom).

Paul Bunyan (U.S. folklore hero; a mythical gigantic lumberjack): **Tall Tale: The Unbelievable Adventures of Pecos Bill**, 1995 (Oliver Platt).

Pecos Bill (U.S. folklore hero, a cowboy of the Old West capable of incredible feats): The Mysterious Rider, 1938 (Douglas Dumbrille); On the High Card, 1921 (Charles E. Graham); **Tall Tale: The Unbelievable Adventures of Pecos Bill**, 1995 (Patrick Swayze); Tall Tales & Legends, 1985-1988 (TV series; "Pecos Bill," 1986 episode: Steve Guttenberg); Walt Disney's Wonderful World of Color, 1954-1992 (TV series; "The Golden Horseshoe Revue," 1962 episode: Wally Boag as a performing Pecos Bill).

Pegasus (in Greek mythology, a divine white-winged stallion able to fly anywhere): **Clash of the Titans**, 1981; Hercules, 1998-1999 (TV series; Frank Welker voiceover).

Penelope (loyal wife of Greek warrior Ulysses [Odysseus] in Greek mythology): Biblioteca di Studio Uno: Odissea, 1964 (made-for-TV; Lucia Mannucci); Dante's Inferno, 2007 (Tami Sagher); Hercules Unchained, 1960 (Patrizia Della Rovere); Il ritorno d'Ulisse in patria, 1980 (Trudeliese Schmidt); Odissea, 1968 (TV miniseries; Irene Pappas); Hercules: The Legendary Journeys, 1995-1999 (TV series; Jacqueline Collen, Tammy Barker); Mythic Warriors: Guardians of the Legend, 1998- (TV series; four episodes; Julie Lemieux); Odysseus, 2013 (TV series; eight episodes: Caterina Murino); Odysseus: Voyage to the Underworld, 2008 (Leah Gibson); The Odyssey, 1997- (TV series; Greta Scacchi); Penelope, 2009 (Natalie Finderle); Penelope oder Die Lorbeemaske, 1959 (made-for-TV; Susanne von Almassy); The Return of Ulysses to His Homeland, 1973 (made-for-TV; Janet Baker); **Ulysses**, 1955 (Silvana Mangano).

The Penguin (aka: Oswald Cobblepot; fictional evil character in the Batman series): Batman, 1966-1968 (TV series; Burgess Meredith); The

Batman, 2004-2008 (TV series; Tom Kenny voiceover); **Batman Returns**, 1992 (Danny DeVito); Batman Revealed, 2012 (Chris Clark); Batman: The Brave and the Bold, 2008-2011 (animated TV series; Stephen Root voiceover); The New Batman Adventures, 1997-1999 (TV series; Paul Williams voiceover); Superman, 1996-2000 (TV series; Paul Williams voiceover).

Pepe le Moko (infamous Parisian jewel thief hiding out in the Casbah, a citadel for criminals in Algiers, Algeria, but who dooms himself when leaving his sanctuary for the love of a woman): **Algiers**, 1938 (Charles Boyer); **Casbah**, 1948 (Tony Martin); **Pepe le Moko** [1937], 1941 (Jean Gabin); Toto le Moko, 1948 (Carlo Ninchi).

Percival (or Perceval; legendary knight of King Arthur's Round Table in 6th-Century Britain, who quested for the Holy Grail): **Excalibur**, 1981 (Paul Geoffrey); Guinevere, 1994 (made-for-TV; Andrius Bobrovas); **Knights of the Round Table**, 1953 (Gabriel Woolf); Perceval, 1978 (Fabrice Luchini).

Percy Blakeney (aka: The Scarlet Pimpernel; heroic character and protagonist in the novels and stories by Baroness Emma Orczy, beginning with her first 1792 novel, *The Scarlet Pimpernel*): BBC Night Theater, 1950-1959 (TV series; "The Scarlet Pimpernel," 1951 episode: James Carney); The DuPont Show of the Month, 1957-1961 (TV series; "The Scarlet Pimpernel," 1960 episode: Michael Rennie); The Elusive Pimpernel, 1919 (Cecil Humphreys); The Elusive Pimpernel, 1969 (TV miniseries; Anton Rodgers); The Fighting Pimpernel, 1953 (David Niven); The Return of the Scarlet Pimpernel, 1938 (Barry K. Barnes); The Scarlet Daredevil, 1929 (Matheson Lang); The Scarlet Pimpernel, 1917 (Dustin Farnum); **The Scarlet Pimpernel**, 1934 (Leslie Howard); The Scarlet Pimpernel, 1956 (TV series; Marius Goring); The Scarlet Pimpernel, 1982 (made-for-TV; Anthony Andrews); The Scarlet Pimpernel, 1999-2000 (TV series; Richard E. Grant).

Persephone (in Greek mythology a goddess and the daughter of Zeus): The Illiac Passion, 1968 (Beverly Grant); Percy Jackson & the Olympians: The Lightning Thief, 2010 (Rosario Dawson).

Perseus (mythical great Greek hero and son of the god Zeus, who, in his adventures, overwhelmed monsters, rescuing Andromeda and marrying her): **Clash of the Titans**, 1981 (Harry Hamlin); **Clash of the Titans**, 2010 (Sam Worthington; Otto Farrant as young Perseus); Hercules: The Brave and the Bold, 2013 (Jordan Lambay); Mythic Warriors: Guardians of the Legend, 1998- (TV series; Robin Dunne, Noah Reid as young Perseus); Night Life of the Gods, 1935 (Pat DiCicco); Persee, 2004 (made-for-TV; Cyril Auvity); Perseus against the Monsters, 1963 (Richard Harrison); The Storyteller: Greek Myths, 1990- (TV miniseries; "Perseus and the Gorgon," 1991 episode; Jeremy Gilley, Oscar Webb as a young Perseus); Wrath of the Titans, 2012 (Sam Worthington).

Peter Pan (fictional character created by Scottish playwright J. M. Barrie, 1860-1937, who first appears as only one character in a chapter in Barrie's 1902 novel for adults, The Little White Bird, 1902, and as the leading character in his 1904 play, "Peter Pan, or The Boy Who Wouldn't Grow Up"): The Adventures of Peter Pan, 1989 (TV series; Noriko Hidaka); Fairy Tale: A True Story, 1997 (Anna Chancellor); **Finding Neverland**, 2004 (Kelly Macdonald); Happy Birthday, Peter Pan, 2005 (TV special; Rupert Grint voiceover; Jeremy Sumpter); **Hook**, 1991 (Robin Williams as an adult; and Ryan Francis, Jewell Newlander Hubbard, Max Hoffman and Matthew Van Ginkel as Peter in various stages as a boy); The New Adventures of Peter Pan, 2012 (TV series; Mehani Taric); Neverland, 2003 (Rick Sparks); Neverland, 2011 (TV series; Charlie Rowe); Once upon a Time, 2011- (TV series; Robbie Kay); One Hour in Wonderland, 1950 (made-for-TV; Bobby Driscoll); Peter Pan, 1924 (Betty Bronson); **Peter Pan**, 1953 (Bobby Driscoll voiceover); Peter Pan, 1955 (Mary Martin); Peter Pan, 1960 (made-for-TV; Mary Martin); Peter Pan, 1962 (made-for-TV; Michael Ande); Peter Pan, 1976 (made-for-TV; Mia Farrow); Peter Pan, 2000 (made-for-TV; Cathy Rigby); Peter Pan, 2003 (Jeremy Sumpter); Peter Pan and the Pirates, 1990-1991 (TV series; Jason Marsden); Return to Never Land, 2002 (Blayne Weaver voiceover); **Shrek**, 2001 (Michael Galasso voiceover); Too Many Kisses, 1925 (Harpo Marx, as the Village Peter Pan); The Walt Disney Christmas Show, 1951 (made-for-TV; Bobby Driscoll).

Peter Piper (British fictional character in tongue-twisting nursery rhyme): Mother Goose Rock 'n' Rhyme, 1990 (made-for-TV; Harry Anderson).

Petruchio (clever lover who tames and marries the tempestuous, man-eating Katharina in William Shakespeare's 1594 play, "The Taming of the Shrew"): BBC Sunday-Night Theatre, 1950-1959 (TV series; "The Taming of the Shrew," 1952 episode: Stanley Baker); Great Performances, 1971- (TV series; "Kiss Me Kate," 2003 episode; Brent Barrett); Kate: The Taming of the Shrew, 2004 (Neri Marcore); Katharine and Petruchio, 1939 (made-for-TV; Austin Trevor); **Kiss Me Kate**, 1953 (Howard Keel); Kiss Me Kate, 1968 (made-for-TV; Robert Goulet); La bisbetica domata, 1942 (Amedeo Nazzari); La fierecilla domada, 1956 (Alberto Closas); Shakespeare: The Animated Tales, 1993-1994 (TV series; "The Taming of the Shrew," 1994 episode: Nigel Le Vaillant); Studio One in Hollywood, 1948-1958 (TV series; "The Taming of the Shrew," 1950 episode: Charlton Heston); The Taming of the Shrew, 1929 (Douglas Fairbanks Sr.); The Taming of the Shrew, 1956 (made-for-TV; Maurice Evans); The Taming of the Shrew, 1962 (made-for-TV; Ron Haddrick); **The Taming of the Shrew**, 1967 (Richard Burton); The Taming of the Shrew, 1973 (made-for-TV; John Bell); The Taming of the Shrew, 1976 (made-for-TV; Mark Singer); The Taming of the Shrew, 1980 (made-for-TV; John Cleese); The Taming of the Shrew, 1982 (made-for-TV; Len Cariou); The Taming of the Shrew, 1988 (made-for-TV; Colm Feore).

Phantom of the Opera (disfigured and demented musician who haunts the underground caves beneath the Paris Opera and aids a beautiful, young prima donna, as depicted in Gaston Leroux's 1911 novel): Das Phantom der Oper, 1916 (Nils Olaf Crisander); **The Phantom of the Opera**, 1925 (Lon Chaney Sr.); **Phantom of the Opera**, 1943 (Claude Rains); **The Phantom of the Opera**, 1962 (Herbert Lom); The Phantom of the Opera, 1983 (made-for-TV; Maximilian Schell); The Phantom of the Opera, 1988 (made-for-TV; Aiden Grennell); The Phantom of the Opera, 1989 (Robert Englund); The Phantom of the Opera, 1990 (made-for-TV; Charles Dance); The Phantom of the Opera, 1998 (Julian Sands); **The Phantom of the Opera**, 2004 (Gerard Butler); Phantom of the Paradise, 1974 (William Finlay).

Phileas Fogg (indefatigable Englishman who wagers £20,000 with fellow members of the elitist Reform Club in London that he can go around the world in eighty days and, despite all obstacles, and, with the help of his loyal servant, Jean Passepartout, achieves his near-impossible goal and wins the bet; first depicted in the 1873 adventure novel, *Around the World in Eighty Days*, by Jules Verne): Around the World in Eighty Days, 1919 (Conrad Veidt); **Around the World in 80 Days**, 1956 (David Niven); Around the World in Eighty Days, 1972-1973 (TV series; Alistair Duncan); Around the World in 80 Days, 1989 (TV miniseries; Pierce Brosnan); Around the World in 80 Days, 2004 (Steve Coogan); De reis om de wereld in 80 dagen, 1957- (TV series; Senne Rouffaer); Die Reise um die Erde in 80 Tagen, 1963 (made-for-TV; Alfred Muller); Le Tour du monde en 80 jours, 1975 (TV miniseries; Jean Le Poulain); Le tour du monde en 80 jours, 1979 (made-for-TV; Daniel Ceccaldi); Le tour du monde en 80 jours, 1980 (TV series; Jean Pellotier); The Secret Adventures of Jules Verne, 2000

Dorothy Malone and Humphrey Bogart (as Philip Marlowe) in
The Big Sleep, **1946.**

(TV series; Michael Praed).

Philip Marlowe (hard-boiled private detective created by author Raymond Chandler in his 1939 novel, *The Big Sleep*): **The Big Sleep**, 1946 (Humphrey Bogart); The Big Sleep, 1978 (Robert Mitchum); The Brasher Doubloom, 1947 (George Montgomery); Climax!, 1954-1958 (TV series; "The Long Goodbye," 1954 episode: Dick Powell); **Farewell, My Lovely**, 1975 (Robert Mitchum); **Lady in the Lake**, 1947 (Robert Montgomery); **The Long Goodbye**, 1973 (Elliott Gould); **Marlowe**, 1969 (James Garner); Marlowe, 1983 (made-for-TV; Jose Jorge Duarte); Marlowe, 2007 (made-for-TV; Jason O'Mara); **Murder, My Sweet**, 1944 (Dick Powell); Omnibus, 1967-2003 (TV series; "Raymond Chandler: Down These Mean Streets a Man Must Go," 1969 episode; Edward Judd); Philip Marlowe, 1959-1960 (TV series; Philip Carey); Philip Marlowe, Private Eye, 1983-1986 (TV series; Powers Boothe); Poodle Springs, 1998 (made-for-TV; James Caan); Robert Montgomery Presents, 1950-1957 (TV series; "The Big Sleep," 1950 episode: Zachary Scott).

Philo Vance (suave private detective created by S.S. Van Dine in his 1926 novel, *The Benson Murder Case*): The Benson Murder Case, 1930 (William Powell); The Bishop Murder Case, 1930 (William Powell); Calling Philo Vance, 1940 (James Stephenson); **The Canary Murder Case**, 1929 (William Powell); The Casino Murder Case, 1935 (Paul Lukas); The Dragon Murder Case, 1934 (Warren William); The Garden Murder Case, 1936 (Edmund Lowe); Gracie Allen Murder Case, 1939 (Warren William); **The Greene Murder Case**, 1929 (William Powell); **The Kennel Murder Case**, 1933 (William Powell); Night of Mystery, 1937 (Grant Richards); Paramount on Parade, 1930 (William Powell); Philo Vance, 1974- (TV miniseries; Giorgio Albertazzi); Philo Vance Returns, 1947 (William Wright); Philo Vance's Gamble, 1947 (Alan Curtis); Philo Vance's Secret Mission, 1947 (Alan Curtis); The Scarab Murder Case, 1937 (Wilfrid Hyde White); Vyvrazdeni rodiny Greenu, 2002 (made-for-TV; Jiri Dvorak).

Pied Piper (fairy tale character in German legends, who lures rats away from towns with his magic pipe or flute, and also lures children with him after townsfolk refuse to pay him for his services; as early as 1300 in Hamelin, Germany): Ever After High-Legacy Day: A Tale of Two Tales, 2013 (made-for-TV; Cam Clarke voiceover); Happily N'Ever After, 2009 (Doug Erholtz voiceover); The Pied Piper, 1972 (Donovan voiceover); The Pied Piper of Astroworld, 1968 (made-for-TV; Soupy Sales); The Pied Piper of Hamelin, 1918 (Paul Wegener); The Pied Piper of Hamelin, 1926 (Edward Sorley); The Pied Piper of Hamelin, 1957 (made-for-TV; Van Johnson).

Pinocchio (Jonathan Taylor Thomas voiceover) in *The Adventures of Pinocchio*, 1996.

Pink Panther (fictional animated cartoon character shown in the credits of comedy films and in the TV series featuring the bumbling French detective Inspector Clouseau, the character also appearing in its own series of animated shorts): Curse of the Pink Panther, 1983 (Roger Moore as Inspector Clouseau); Inspector Clouseau, 1968 (Alan Arkin as Inspector Clouseau); **The Pink Panther**, 1964 (Peter Sellers as Inspector Clouseau); The Pink Panther, 1993-1996 (TV series); The Pink Panther, 2006 (Steve Martin as Inspector Clouseau); The Pink Panther Show, 1969-1976 (animated TV series); The Pink Panther 2, 2009 (Steve Martin as Inspector Clouseau); **The Pink Panther Strikes Again**, 1976 (Peter Sellers as Inspector Clouseau); **The Return of the Pink Panther**, 1975 (Peter Sellers as Inspector Clouseau); **Revenge of the Pink Panther**, 1978 (Peter Sellers as Inspector Clouseau); **A Shot in the Dark**, 1964 (Peter Sellers as Inspector Clouseau); Son of the Pink Panther, 1993; and Trail of the Pink Panther, 1982 (Peter Sellers as Inspector Clouseau).

Pinocchio (a wooden marionette that transforms into a real boy, a fictional character in the 1883 children's novel *The Adventures of Pinocchio* by Italian author Carlo Collodi): Abbacadabra, 1983 (made-for-TV; Nico Haak); The Adventures of Pinocchio, 1947 (Alessandro Tomei); The Adventures of Pinocchio, 1972 (TV miniseries; Andrea Balestri); The Adventures of Pinocchio, 1988 (Danielle Romeo); **The Adventures of Pinocchio**, 1996 (Jonathan Taylor Thomas voiceover); Disney's House of Mouse, 2001-2003 (animated TV series; Michael Welch); Geppetto's Secret, 2005 (Nika Futterman); Geppetto's Workshop, 1980- (TV series; Stephanie Silver); Geppetto, 2000 (made-for-TV; Seth Adkins); Happily Ever After: Fairy Tales for Every Child, 1995-2000 (TV series; "Pinocchio," 1997 episode: Will Smith); The New Adventures of Pinocchio, 1960-1961 (TV series; Joan Fowler); The New Adventures of Pinocchio, 1999 (Gabriel Thomson); Once Upon a Time, 2011 (TV series; Eion Bailey); **Pinocchio**, 1940 (Dickie Jones voiceover); Pinocchio, 1957 (made-for-TV; Mickey Rooney); Pinocchio, 1965 (made-for-TV; John Joy); Pinocchio, 1968 (made-for-TV; Peter Noone); Pinocchio, 1969 (Uwe Thielisch); Pinocchio, 1976 (made-for-TV; Sandy Duncan); Pinocchio, 1978 (Roberta Paladini voiceover); Pinocchio, 1978 (TV series; Rosemary Miller voiceover); Pinocchio, 2002 (Roberto Benigni); Pinocchio, 2008 (made-for-TV; Robbie Kay); Pinocchio, 2012 (Gabriele Caprio voiceover); Pinocchio, 2013 (TV miniseries; Moritz Russ, Aaron Kissiov); Pinocchio and His Magic Show, 1976 (Ellen Prince voiceover); Pinocchio and the Emperor of the Night, 1987 (Scott Grimes voiceover); Pinocchio in Outer Space, 1965 (Peter Lazar); Pinocchio 3000, 2004 (Sonja Ball); Pinocchio's Christmas, 1980 (made-for-TV; Todd Porter); **Shrek**, 2001 (Cody Cameron voiceover); **Shrek Forever After**, 2010 (Cody Cameron voiceover); Shrek 4-D, 2009 (Cody Cameron voiceover); **Shrek the Third**, 2007 (Cody Cameron voiceover); **Shrek 2**, 2004 (Cody Cameron voiceover); Welcome Back Pinocchio, 2007 (Federico Bebi); **Who Framed Roger Rabbit**, 1988 (Peter Westy voiceover).

Pip (Philip Pirrip; an orphan and apprentice blacksmith who becomes a refined gentleman through the aid of a secret benefactor in Charles Dickens' 1861 novel, *Great Expectations*): Great Expectations, 1917 (Jack Pickford); Great Expectations, 1934 (Phillips Holmes; George P. Breakston as young Pip); **Great Expectations**, 1946 (John Mills; Anthony Wager as young Pip); Great Expectations, 1959- (TV series; Dinsdale Landen; Colin Spaull as young Pip); Great Expectations, 1967- (TV series; Gary Bond; Christopher Guard and Douglas Mann as young Pitt); Great Expectations, 1974 (made-for-TV; Michael York; Simon Gipps-Kent as young Pip); Great Expectations, 1981- (TV miniseries; Gerry Sundquist; Paul Davies Prowles and Graham McGrath as young Pip); Great Expectations, 1989- (TV miniseries; Anthony Calf; Martin Harvey as young Pip); Great Expectations, 1999 (made-for-TV; Ioan Gruffudd; Gabriel Thomson as young Pip); Great Expectations, 2011 (TV miniseries; Douglas Booth; Oscar Kennedy as young Pip); Great Expectations, 2012 (Jeremy Irvine; Toby Irvine as young Pip); Great Expectations, 2013 (Paul Nivison; Taylor Jay-Davies as young Pip); Playdate, 1961-1964 (TV series; "Great Expectations," two episodes in 1962: Douglas Rain; Rex Hagon as young Pip); Robert Montgomery Presents, 1950-1957 (TV series; "Great Expectations," two episodes in 1954: Roddy McDowall; Rex Thompson as young Pip); Store forventninger, 1922 (Harry Komdrup; Budd Martin [Martin Herzberg] as young Pip).

Pluto (in Roman mythology; god of the underworld or, in modern perception, hell; Hades in Greek mythology): Hercules in New York, 1970 (Michael Lipton); In Performance, 1978- (TV series; "Orpheus in the Underworld," 1983 episode: Emile Belcourt); Orpheus in der Unterwelt, 1975 (Kurt Marschner; Achim Wichert); Orpheus in der Unterwelt, 2007 (made-for-TV; William Workman); Orpheus in the Underworld, 1961 (made-for-TV; Jon Weaving).

Popeye Doyle (Jimmy Doyle; tough and uncompromising NYPD detective): **The French Connection**, 1971 (Gene Hackman); **French Connection II**, 1975 (Gene Hackman); Popeye Doyle, 1986 (made-for-TV; Ed O'Neill).

Popeye (Popeye the Sailor Man; spinach-eating muscular cartoon character since the 1930s, chiefly appearing in cartoon shorts): The All-New Popeye Hour, 1978-1979 (animated TV series; Jack Mercer voiceover); Popeye, 1980 (Robin Williams; Jack Mercer voiceover in animated prologue); Popeye and Son, 1987 (animated TV series; Maurice LaMarche voiceover).

Porfiri Petrovich (wily Russian detective who plays cat-and-mouse with a killer to await his expected confession in Fyodor Dostoyevsky's classic 1866 novel, *Crime and Punishment*): Crime and Punishment, 1917 (Robert Cummings); **Crime and Punishment**, 1935 (Harry Baur); **Crime and Punishment**, 1935 (Edward Arnold); Crime and Punishment, 1948 (Sigurd Wallen); Crime and Punishment, 1951 (Carlos Lopez Moctezuma); Crime and Punishment, 1956 (Jean Gabin); Crime and Punishment, 1970 (Innokenty Smoktunovsky); Crime and Punishment, 1971 (made-for-TV; Jean Topart); Crime and Punishment, 1979 (TV miniseries; Timothy West); Crime and Punishment, 1998 (made-for-TV; Ben Kingsley); Crime and Punishment, 2002 (made-for-TV; Ian McDiarmid); Crime and Punishment, 2002 (John Hurt); Crime and Punishment, USA, 1959 (Frank Silvera); Crime et chatiment, 1955 (made-for-TV; Pierre Mondy); Pickpocket, 1959 (Jean Pelegri); Raskolnikoff, 1959 (Paul Verhoeven); Raskolnikow, 1953 (made-for-TV; Hans Stiebener [Stiebner]); Ten Great Writers of the

Modern World, 1988 (TV miniseries; "Fyodor Dostoyevsky's 'Crime and Punishment,'" Timothy Spall).

Porthos (Character in the fictional works of Alexander Dumas pere): At Sword's Point, 1952 (Moroni Olsen; Alan Hale Jr. as Porthos Jr.); Biblioteca di Studio Uno: I tre moschettieri, 1964 (made-for-TV; Felice Chiusano); D'Artagnan, 1969 (TV miniseries; Rolf Arndt); D'Artagnon, 1991 (made-for-TV; Denis Brandon); D'Artagnan amoureux, 1977 (TV miniseries; Jacques Le Carpentier); D'Artagnan et les trois mousquetaires, 2005 (Gregory Gadebois); D'Artanyan i tri mushketyora, 1979 (TV series; Valentin Smirnitskiy); De drie Musketiers, 1968 (made-for-TV; Herman Bruggen); Die Drie Musketiere, 2013 (Aleksey Makarov); Family Classics: The Three Musketeers, 1960 (made-for-TV; John Colicos); The Four Charlots Musketeers, 1974 (Gib Grossac); The Four Musketeers, 1963 (Andrea Aureli); **The Four Musketeers**, 1975 (Frank Finlay); The Glorious Musketeers, 1974 (Claude Bertrand voiceover); I tre moschettieri, 1991 (made-for-TV; Gerry Scotti); Il colpo segreto di d'Artagnan, 1963 (Mario Petri); **The Iron Mask**, 1929 (Tiny Sandford); Knights of the Queen, 1958 (Sebastian Cabot); La loca historia de los tres mosqueteros, 1983 (Fernando Conde); Lady in the Iron Mask, 1952 (Alan Hale Jr.); Les 3 Mousquetaires, 1953 (Gino Cervi); Les trois mousquetaires, 1959 (made-for-TV; Daniel Sorano); Les trois mousquetaires ou L'escrime ne paie pas, 1979 (made-for-TV; Remy Kirch); The Magnavox Theater, 1950 (TV series; "The Three Musketeers," 1950 episode: Mel Archer); **The Man in the Iron Mask**, 1939 (Alan Hale); Mask of the Musketeers, 1963 (Livio Lorenzon); Milady and the Three Musketeers, 2004 (made-for-TV; Frederic Longbois); **The Musketeer**, 2001 (Steve Speirs); The Musketeers, 2014 (TV series; Howard Charles); Os tres Mosqueteiros, 1957 (TV series; Fernando Baleroni); Three and a Half Musketeers, 1957 (Marcelo [Chavez]); The Three Musketeers, 1916 (Edward Kenny); **The Three Musketeers**, 1921 (George Siegmann); Three Musketeers, 1932 (Thomy Bourdelle); The Three Musketeers, 1935 (Moroni Olsen); The Three Musketeers, 1939 (Russell Hicks); The Three Musketeers, 1945 (Francisco Pablo Donadio); **The Three Musketeers**, 1948 (Gig Young); The Three Musketeers, 1954 (TV series; Paul Whitsun-Jones); The Three Musketeers, 1966 (TV miniseries; Brian Blessed); **The Three Musketeers**, 1974 (Frank Finlay); **The Three Musketeers**, 1993 (Oliver Platt); The Three Musketeers, 2007 (Lars Hjortshoj voiceover); The Three Musketeers, 2011 (Ray Stevenson); Vengeance of the Three Musketeers, 1961 (Bernard Woringer); Vingt ans apres, 1922 (Charles Martinelli); Tri musketyri, 1983 (TV miniseries; Jiri Krampol); Tri mushketera, 2013 (Aleksey Makarov); Young Blades, 2001 (Anthony Strachan).

Poseidon (Greek god of the seas, creator of earthquakes; Neptune in Roman mythology): The Adventures of Hercules II, 1985 (Ferdinando Poggi); **Clash of the Titans**, 1981 (Jack Gwillim); **Clash of the Titans**, 2010 (Danny Huston); Hercules, 1998-1999 (TV series; Jason Alexander voiceover); Hercules: The Brave and the Bold, 2013 (Joe McGettigan); The Illiac Passion, 1968 (Andy Warhol); Immortals, 2011 (Kellan Lutz); Mythic Warriors: Guardians of the Legend, 1998- (TV series; Frank Diakowsky); Percy Jackson & the Olympians: The Lightning Thief, 2010 (Kevin McKidd); Wrath of the Titans, 2012 (Danny Huston).

Priam (King of Troy in Greek mythology): Der trojanisch krieg findet nicht statt, 1964 (made-for-TV; Albrecht Schoenhals); Fury of Achilles, 1962 (Fosco Giachetti); Helen of Troy, 1956 (Sir Cedric Hardwicke); ITV Play of the Week, 1955-1974 (TV series; "Tiger at the Gates," 1960 episode: Robert Eddison); King Priam, 1985 (made-for-TV; Rodney Macann); Le guerre de Troie n'aura pas lieu, 1967 (made-for-TV; Henri Nassiet); Troilus & Cressida, 1981 (made-for-TV; Esmond Knight); Troilus und Cressida, 1964 (made-for-TV; Franz Gesien); Troilus und Cressida, 1969 (made-for-TV; Rudolf Kalvius); The Trojan

Oliver Pratt (as Porthos) in *The Three Musketeers*, 1993.

Horse, 1962 (Carlo Tamberlani); **Troy**, 2004 (Peter O'Toole).

Prince Charming (folk character from the story *The Little Glass Slipper*): American Playhouse, 1981- (TV series; "Into the Woods," 1991 episode: Robert Westenberg); Cinderella, 1914 (Owen Moore); Cinderella, 1947 (Aleksey Konsovksy); Cinderella, 1947 (TV miniseries; Jean Kent); **Cinderella**, 1950 (Mike Douglas voiceover); Cinderella, 1950 (made-for-TV; Joy Nichols); Cinderella, 1957 (made-for-TV; Jon Cypher); Cinderella, 1958 (made-for-TV; John Fabian); Cinderella, 1965 (made-for-TV; Stuart Damon); Cinderella, 1966 (Rudiger Lichti); Cinderella, 1969 (Anthony Dowell); Cinderella, 1977 (Brett Smiley); Cinderella, 1986 (made-for-TV; Stephane Vessier); Cinderella, 1989 (made-for-TV; Stephan Meyer-Kohlhoff); Cinderella, 1997 (made-for-TV; Paolo Montalban); Cinderella, 2000 (made-for-TV; Gideon Turner); Cinderella, 2000 (made-for-TV; Alexander Armstrong); Cinderella, 2010 (made-for-TV; Max Felder); Cinderella, 2011 (made-for-TV; Florian Bartholomai); **Cinderella**, 2015 (Richard Madden); Cinderella...Frozen in Time, 1994 (made-for-TV; Andrew Naylor); Cinderella; The Shoe Must Go On, 1986 (made-for-TV; Michael Howe); Cinderella 3D, 2012 (Antoine de Caunes voiceover); Faerie Tale Theatre, 1982-1987 (TV series; "Cinderella," 1985 episode: Matthew Broderick); The Glass Slipper, 1955 (Michael Wilding); Happily Ever After: Fairy Tales for Every Child, 1995-2000 (TV series; "Cinderella," 1995 episode: Jimmy Smits); Hey Cinderella!, 1969 (made-for-TV; Robin Ward); Once upon a Brothers Grimm, 1977 (made-for-TV; John McCook); Once upon a Time, 1973- (TV series; Rula Lenska); The Sleeping Princess, 1939 (made-for-TV; Robert Helpmann); **The Slipper and the Rose**, 1976 (Richard Chamberlain).

Prince Charming (fairy tale character in the story about Sleeping Beauty created by the Brothers Grimm, who brings to life a beautiful princess in a comatose sleep by kissing her): Dornroschen, 1917 (Harry Liedtke); Faerie Tale Theatre, 1982-1987 (TV series; "Sleeping Beauty," 1983 episode: Christopher Reeve); Great Performances, 1971- (TV series; "The Sleeping Beauty," 1995 episode: Zoltan Solymosi); Once upon a Brothers Grimm, 1977 (made-for-TV; John Clifford); Producer's Showcase, 1954-1957 (TV series; "The Sleeping Beauty," 1955 episode: Michael Somes); **Sleeping Beauty**, 1959 (Bill Shirley); Sleeping Beauty, 1965 (Gert Reinholm); Sleeping Beauty, 1971 (Burkhard Mann); Sleeping Beauty, 1987 (Nicholas Clay); The Sleeping Beauty, 1987 (made-for-TV; Robin Cousins); The Sleeping Beauty, 2003 (made-for-TV; Gael Lambiotte); The Sleeping Beauty, 2007 (made-for-TV; Frederico Bonelli); Sleeping Beauty, 2008 (made-for-TV; Moritz Schulze); The Sleeping Princess, 1939 (made-for-TV; Robert Helpmann).

Quasimodo (Tom Hulce voiceover) in *The Hunchback of Notre Dame*, 1996.

Prince Charming (fairy tale character from *Snow White and the Seven Dwarfs* by the Brothers Grimm, 1812): American Playhouse, 1981- (TV series; "Into the Woods," 1991 episode;); Happily Ever After, 1993 (Michael Horton); Mirror Mirror, 2012 (Armie Hammer); Schneewittchen, 2009 (made-for-TV; Nicolas Artajo); The Seven Dwarfs to the Rescue, 1951 (Roberto Risso); Snow White, 1916 (Creighton Hale); Snow White, 1961 (Wolf-Dieter Panse); Snow White, 1989 (James Ian Wright); Snow White, 2009 (Sergio Diaz); **Snow White and the Seven Dwarfs**, 1937 (Harry Stockwell voiceover); Snow White and the Seven Dwarfs, 1955 (Niels Clausnitzer); Snow White and the Three Stooges, 1961 (Edson Stroll); Snow White Live, 1980 (made-for-TV; Richard Bowne).

Prince Charming (fairy tale character in the Rapunzel tales as told by the Brothers Grimm as early as 1812): American Playhouse, 1981- (TV series; "Into the Woods," 1991 episode: Chuck Wagner); Faerie Tale Theatre, 1982-1987 (TV series; "Rapunzel," 1983 episode: Jeff Bridges); Happily Ever After: Fairy Tales for Every Child, 1995-2000 (TV series; "Rapunzel," 1995 episode: Duane Martin); Into the Woods, 2014 (Billy Magnussen); Rapunzel, 2009 (made-for-TV; Jaime Ferkic); Rapunzel or the Magic of Tears, 1988 (made-for-TV; Dirk Schoedon); Shirley Temple's Storybook, 1958-1961 (TV series; "Rapunzel," 1958 episode: Don Dubbins); Tangled, 2010 (Zachary Levi).

Prince Karl (aka: Prince Karl Heinrich or Karl Heinz; fictional royal hero of the 1924 operetta by Sigmund Romberg): Alt Heidelberg, 1923 (Paul Hartmann); Alt Heidelberg, 1959 (Christian Wolff); Alt Heidelberg, 1959 (made-for-TV; Gotz von Langheim); Old Heidelberg, 1915 (Wallace Reid); **The Student Prince**, 1954 (Edmund Purdom; Mario Lanza singing voice); **The Student Prince in Old Heidelberg**, 1927 (Ramon Novarro).

Prince Valiant (fictional character in comic strip created by Hal Foster in 1937, who is involved in adventures during the time of King Arthur in 6th-Century Britain): The Legend of Prince Valiant, 1991-1994 (TV series; Robby Benson); **Prince Valiant**, 1954 (Robert Wagner); Prince Valiant, 1997 (Stephen Moyer).

Professor Challenger (George Edward Challenger; fictional explorer-scientist in Arthur Conan Doyle's *Lost World*, 1912): King of the Lost World, 2005 (Bruce Boxleitner); **The Lost World**, 1925 (Wallace Beery); The Lost World, 1960 (Claude Rains); The Lost World, 1992 (John Rhys-Davies); The Lost World, 1998 (made-for-TV; Armin Shimerman); The Lost World, 1998 (Patrick Bergin); The Lost World, 1999 (made-for-TV; Patrick McCauley); The Lost World, 2001 (made-for-TV; Bob Hoskins); The Lost World, 1999-2002 (TV series; Peter McCauley).

Prometheus (a Titan in Greek mythology, a deity that stole fire from Olympus and gave it to mankind): Hercules: The Legendary Journeys—Hercules and the Circle of Fire, 1994 (made-for-TV; Mark Ferguson); The Illiac Passion, 1968 (Richard Beauvais).

Quasimodo (pathetically deformed and horrfiic-looking protagonist in Victor Hugo's classic 1831 novel, *The Hunchback of Notre Dame*): The Darling of Paris, 1917 (Glen White); **Hotel Transylvania**, 2012 (Jon Lovitz); The Hunchback, 1997 (made-for-TV; Mandy Patinkin); **The Hunchback of Notre Dame**, 1923 (Lon Chaney Sr.); **The Hunchback of Notre Dame**, 1939 (Charles Laughton); The Hunchback of Notre Dame, 1956 (Anthony Quinn); The Hunchback of Notre Dame, 1966 (TV series; Peter Woodthorpe); The Hunchback of Notre Dame, 1977 (made-for-TV; Warren Clarke); The Hunchback of Notre Dame, 1982 (made-for-TV; Anthony Hopkins); The Hunchback of Notre Dame, 1986 (animated made-for-TV; Tom Burlinson voiceover); **The Hunchback of Notre Dame**, 1996 (animated; Tom Hulce voiceover); The Magical Adventures of Quasimodo, 1996- (animated TV series; Daniel Brochu voiceover); Notre-Dame de Paris, 1996 (made-for-TV; Nicolas Le Riche); Notre-Dame de Paris, 1999 (made-for-TV; Garou); Notre-Dame de Paris, 2002 (made-for-TV; Gio Di Tonno); Robert Montgomery Presents, 1950-1957 (TV series; "The Hunchback of Notre Dame," two-part episodes, 1954: Robert Ellenstein).

Queen of Hearts (fictional character from the 1865 novel Alice's Adventures in Wonderland by British author Lewis Carroll): Alice in Wonderland, 1931 (Vie Quinn); **Alice in Wonderland**, 1933 (May Robson); Alice in Wonderland, 1949 (Pamela Brown voiceover); **Alice in Wonderland**, 1951 (Verna Felton voiceover); Alice in Wonderland, 1955 (made-for-TV; Ronald Long); Alice in Wonderland, 1966 (made-for-TV; Alison Leggatt); Alice in Wonderland, 1976 (Marta Serrano); Alice in Wonderland, 1982 (made-for-TV; Julee Cruise); Alice in Wonderland, 1985 (made-for-TV; Jayne Meadows); Alice in Wonderland, 1985 (TV series; Joan Sanderson); Alice in Wonderland, 1986 (made-for-TV; four 30-minute segments; Janet Henfrey); Alice in Wonderland, 1999 (made-for-TV; Miranda Richardson); Alice in Wonderland or What's a Nice Kid Like You Doing in a Place Like This?, 1966 (animated made-for-TV; Zsa Zsa Gabor); Alice through the Looking Box, 1960 (made-for-TV; Adele Leigh); Alice's Adventures in Wonderland, 1956 (made-for-TV; Violet Gould); Alice's Adventures in Wonderland, 1972 (Flora Robson); Alice's Adventures in Wonderland, 2011 (made-for-TV; Zenaida Yanowksky); Alice's Adventures in Wonderland and through the Looking Glass, 1948 (made-for-TV; Sybil Arundale); Great Performances, 1971- (TV series; "Alice in Wonderland," 1983 episode: Eve Arden); Kraft Theatre, 1947-1958 (TV series; "Alice in Wonderland," 1954 episode: Blanche Yurka); Unsuk Chin: Alice in Wonderland, 2007 (Gwyneth Jones).

Raphael (Archangel): Faust, 1960 (Konrad Krauss); The Fish and the Angel, 1953 (made-for-TV; Joseph O'Conor); Gabriel, 2007 (Jack Campbell); Good Satan, 2012 (Jake Wesley Stewart); Jacob's Ladder, 2003-2004 (TV series; Billy Engel); Joseph Haydn: The Creation, 1990 (made-for-TV; Michael George); The Littlest Angel, 1969 (made-for-TV; Cris Alexander); Lucifer, 1966 (Julien Schoenaerts); Lucifer, 1981 (Sigrid Koetse); The Prophecy II, 1998 (William Prael); Supernatural, 2005- (TV series; Demore Barnes); Tobias and the Angel, 1938 (made-for-TV; Tyrone Guthrie); Tobias and the Angel, 1939 (made-for-TV; Robert Eddison); Xena: Warrior Princess, 1995-2001 (TV series; Tamati Rice).

Rapunzel (German fairytale character, part of the Grimm Brothers collections as early as 1812): American Playhouse, 1981- (TV series; "Into the Woods," 1991 episode: Pamela Winslow); Faerie Tale Theatre, 1982-

1987 (TV series; "Rapunzel," 1983 episode: Shelley Duvall); Happily Ever After: Fairy Tales for Every Child, 1995-2000 (TV series; "Rapunzel," 1995 episode; Tisha Campbell-Martin); Into the Woods, 2011 (Alice Fearn); Into the Woods, 2014 (Mackenzie Mauzy); Once upon a Time, 2011- (TV series; Alexandra Metz); Our Most Beautiful Love Stories, 2012- (Christine Gwillim); Rapunzel, 2009 (made-for-TV; Luis Wietzorek); Rapunzel or the Magic of Tears, 1988 (made-for-TV; Sylvia Wolff); Shirley Temple's Storybook, 1958-1961 (TV series; "Rapunzel," 1958 episode: Carol Lynley); **Shrek the Third**, 2007 (Maya Rudolph); Tangled, 2010 (Mandy Moore); Timeless Tales from Hallmark, 1990- (TV series; "Rapunzel," 1990 episode: Linda Purl).

Red King (fictional character from the 1865 novel Alice's Adventures in Wonderland by British author Lewis Carroll): Alice in Wonderland, 1955 (made-for-TV; Don Somers); Alice in Wonderland, 1985 (made-for-TV; Patrick Culliton); Alice through the Looking Glass, 1966 (made-for-TV; Robert Coote); Alice through the Looking Glass, 1998 (made-for-TV; Michael Medwin).

Red Queen (sometimes a separate character in films or the same character as the Queen of Hearts; fictional character from the 1865 novel Alice's Adventures in Wonderland by British author Lewis Carroll): Adventures in Wonderland, 1992-1994 (TV series; Armelia McQueen); Alice at the Palace, 1982 (made-for-TV; Debbie Allen); **Alice in Wonderland**, 1933 (Edna Mae Oliver); Alice in Wonderland, 1955 (made-for-TV; Elsa Lanchester); Alice in Wonderland, 1985 (made-for-TV; Ann Jillian); **Alice in Wonderland**, 2010 (Helena Bonham Carter); Alice through the Looking Glass, 1966 (made-for-TV; Agnes Moorehead); Alice through the Looking Glass, 1973 (made-for-TV; Judy Parfitt); Alice through the Looking Glass, 1987 (made-for-TV; Janet Waldo voiceover); Alice through the Looking Glass, 1998 (made-for-TV; Sian Phillips); Alice's Adventures in Wonderland and through the Looking Glass, 1948 (made-for-TV; Louise Hampton); Once upon a Time in Wonderland, 2013 (TV series; Emma Rigby).

Richard Hannay (Canadian businessman who is wrongly accused of murder and who is ensnared in a lethal spy ring as he attempts to vindicate himself as depicted in the 1915 novel, *The Thirty-Nine Steps*, by John Buchan): Hannay, 1988-1989 (TV series; Robert Powell); **The 39 Steps**, 1935 (Robert Donat); The 39 Steps, 1960 (Kenneth More); The Thirty-Nine Steps, 1978 (Robert Powell); The 39 Steps, 2008 (made-for-TV; Rupert Penry-Jones); The Three Hostages, 1952- (TV series; Patrick Barr); The Three Hostages, 1977 (Barry Foster).

The Riddler (fictional evil character in the Batman series): Batman, 1966-1968 (TV series; Frank Gorshin); The Batman, 2004-2008 (TV series; Robert Englund voiceover); **Batman Forever**, 1995 (Jim Carrey); Batman: The Brave and the Bold, 2008-2011 (animated TV series; John Michael Higgins voiceover); Challenge of the Super Friends, 1978- (animated TV series; Michael Bell voiceover); Legends of the Superheroes, 1979 (TV series; Frank Gorshin).

Robin (aka: Dick Grayson; fictional comic book character and sidekick to Batman): The All-New Super Friends Hour, 1977-1978 (animated TV series; Casey Kasem voiceover); Batman, 1943 (serial; Douglas Croft); Batman, 1966-1968 (TV series; Burt Ward); The Batman, 2004-2008 (TV series; Evan Sabara voiceover); Batman and Robin, 1949 (serial; Johnny Duncan); **Batman and Robin**, 1997 (Chris O'Donnell); **Batman Forever**, 1995 (Chris O'Donnell); Batman Revealed, 2012 (Derek Mindler); The Batman/Superman Hour, 1968-1969 (animated TV series; Casey Kasem voiceover); Batman: The Animated Series, 1992-1995 (TV series; Loren Lester voiceover); Batman: The Brave and the Bold, 2008-2011 (animated TV series; Jeremy Shada voiceover); Batman: The Movie, 1966 (Burt Ward); Batman with Robin the Wonder Boy, 1969 (TV series; Casey Kasem voiceover); Challenge of the Super

Russell Crowe (as Robin Hood) in *Robin Hood*, 2010.

Friends, 1978- (animated TV series; Casey Kasem voiceover); Legends of the Superheroes, 1979 (TV series; Burt Ward); The New Adventures of Batman, 1977-1978 (TV series; Burt Ward voiceover); The New Batman Adventures, 1997-1999 (TV series; Mathew Valencia, Loren Lester voiceovers); Super Friends, 1973-2011 (animated TV series; Casey Kasem voiceover); Super Friends, 1980-1983 (animated TV series; Casey Kasem voiceover); Super Friends: The Legendary Super Powers Show, 1984- (animated TV series; Casey Kasem voiceover); The Super Powers Team: Galactic Guardians, 1985- (animated TV series; Casey Kasem voiceover); Superman, 1996-2000 (TV series; Mathew Valencia voiceover); The World's Greatest Super Friends, 1979- (animated TV series; Casey Kasem voiceover); Young Justice, 2010- (animated TV series; Jesse McCartney, Cameron Bowen voiceovers).

Robin Hood (fictional character; heroic outlaw in British folklore): **The Adventures of Robin Hood**, 1938 (Errol Flynn); The Adventures of Robin Hood, 1955-1960 (TV series; Richard Greene); The Adventures of Robin Hood, 1985 (made-for-TV; Robert Colby voiceover); The Ballad of the Valiant Knight Ivanhoe, 1983 (Boris Khmelnitsky); The Bandit of Sherwood Forest, 1946 (Russell Hicks; Cornel Wilde as the son of Robin Hood); Beyond Sherwood Forest, 2009 (made-for-TV; Robin Dunne); A Challenge for Robin Hood, 1968 (Barrie Ingham); Il Magnifico Robin Hood, 1970 (George Martin); Il trionfo di Robin Hood, 1962 (Don Burnett); Into the Labyrinth, 1981-1982 (TV series; "Robin," 1981 episode: Tony Wright); **Ivanhoe**, 1952 (Harold Warrender); Ivanhoe, 1970- (TV miniseries; Clive Graham); Ivanhoe, 1982 (made-for-TV; David Robb); Ivanhoe, 1986 (made-for-TV; Robert Colby voiceover); Ivanhoe, 1997- (TV miniseries; Aden Gillett); The Legend of Robin Hood, 1968- (TV series; David Watson); The Legend of Robin Hood, 1975 (TV miniseries; Martin Potter); Long Live Robin Hood, 1971 (Giuliano Gemma); The Men of Sherwood Forest, 1954 (Don Taylor); NBC Children's Theatre, 1963-1973 (TV series; "Robin Hood," 1964 episode: Dan Ferrone); The New Adventures of Robin Hood, 1997-1999 (TV series; Matthew Porretta, John Bradley); Once upon a Time, 2011- (TV series; Sean Maguire); One Hysterical Night, 1929 (Slim Summerville as a lunatic in an asylum believing himself to be the famous outlaw); Prince of Thieves, 1948 (Jon Hall); Richard the Lionheart, 1962 (TV series; Ronald Howard); **Robin and Marian**, 1976 (Sean Connery); **Robin Hood**, 1922 (Douglas Fairbanks Sr.); Robin Hood, 1953- (TV miniseries; Patrick Troughton); Robin Hood, 1970 (Carlos Quiney); **Robin Hood**, 1973 (Brian Bedford voiceover); Robin Hood, 1984-1986 (TV series; Michael Praed; Toby Lee as young Robin); Robin Hood, 1991 (Patrick Bergin); Robin Hood, 2006-2009 (TV series; Jonas Armstrong); **Robin Hood**, 2010 (Russell Crowe; Jack Downham as young Robin); Robin Hood and the Pirates, 1960 (Lex

Aidan Quinn (as Robinson Crusoe) in *Crusoe*, 1989.

Barker); Robin Hood en zijn schelmen, 1962 (Henk Van Der Linden); Robin Hood: Ghosts of Sherwood 3D, 2012 (Martin Thon); **Robin Hood: Men in Tights**, 1993 (Cary Elwes); **Robin Hood: Prince of Thieves**, 1991 (Kevin Costner); Robin Hood: The Noble Robber, 1966 (Hans von Borsody; Manfred Heidmann voiceover); Rogues of Sherwood Forest, 1950 (John Derek); **The Story of Robin Hood** [aka: The Story of Robin Hood and His Merrie Men], 1952 (Richard Todd); Sword of Sherwood Forest, 1961 (Richard Greene); Tales of Robin Hood, 1951 (Robert Clarke; David Stollery, Robin as a boy); **Time Bandits**, 1981 (John Cleese); The Time Tunnel, 1966-1967 (TV series; "The Revenge of Robin Hood," 1966 episode: Donald Harron); Wolfshead: The Legend of Robin Hood, 1973 (David Warbeck); Young Robin Hood, 1991-1992 (animated TV series; Thor Bishopric voiceover); The Zany Adventures of Robin Hood, 1984 (made-for-TV; George Segal).

Robinson Crusoe (young British squire who is shipwrecked on an island and must make a life for himself for twenty years with only a dog, a cat and, eventually, a young native he names Friday, as depicted in Daniel DeFoe's 1719 adventure novel): The Adventures of Robinson Crusoe, 1922 (Harry Myers); **The Adventures of Robinson Crusoe** [aka: Robinson Crusoe], 1954 (Dan O'Herlihy); The Adventures of Robinson Crusoe, 1964- (TV miniseries; Michael Chevalier, Erich Bludau, Lee Payant, Curt Ackermann, Robert Hoffmann); As Aventuras de Robinson Crusoe, 1978 (Costinha); BBC Play of the Month, 1965-1983 (TV series; "Robinson Crusoe," 1974 episode: Stanley Baker); **Crusoe**, 1989 (Aidan Quinn); Crusoe, 2008-2009 (TV series; Philip Winchester); Ein Robinson, 1940 (Herbert A.E. Bohme); Lt. Robin Crusoe, U.S.N., 1966 (Dick Van Dyke); Man Friday, 1976 (Peter O'Toole); Miss Robinson Crusoe, 1954 (Amanda Blake); Mr. Robinson Crusoe, 1932 (Douglas Fairbanks Sr.); Robinson Crusoe, 1927 (M.A. Wetherell); Robinson Crusoe, 1947 (Pavel Kadochnikov); Robinson Crusoe, 1970 (Hugo Stiglitz); Robinson Crusoe, 1973 (Leonid Kuravlyov); Robinson Crusoe, 1974 (Ion Caramitru voiceover); Robinson Crusoe, 1980 (TV series; Nolle Versyp); Robinson Crusoe, 1997 (Pierce Brosnan); Robinson Crusoe, 2003 (made-for-TV; Pierre Richard).

Roderick Raskolnikov (Roskolnikov; intellectual crime writer and killer whose conscience haunts and nags him into the confession of a murder in Fyodor Dostoyevsky's classic 1866 novel, *Crime and Punishment*): Crime and Punishment, 1917 (Derwent Hall Caine); Crime and Punishment, 1927 (Gregori Chmara); **Crime and Punishment**, 1935 (Pierre Blanchar); **Crime and Punishment**, 1935 (Peter Lorre); Crime and Punishment, 1948 (Hampe Faustman); Crime and Punishment, 1951 (Roberto Canedo); Crime and Punishment, 1956 (Robert Hossein);

Crime and Punishment, 1970 (Georgy Taratorkin); Crime and Punishment, 1971 (made-for-TV; Francois Marthouret); Crime and Punishment, 1979 (TV miniseries; John Hurt); Crime and Punishment, 1998 (made-for-TV; Patrick Dempsey); Crime and Punishment, 2002 (made-for-TV; John Simm); Crime and Punishment, 2002 (Crispin Glover); Crime and Punishment, USA, 1959 (George Hamilton); Crime et chatiment, 1955 (made-for-TV; Roger Crouzet); Pickpocket, 1959 (Martin LaSalle); Raskolnikoff, 1959 (Hartmut Reck); Raskolnikow, 1953 (made-for-TV; Paul Edwin Roth); Ten Great Writers of the Modern World, 1988 (TV miniseries; "Fyodor Dostoyevsky's 'Crime and Punishment,'" Douglas Hodge).

Romeo (fictional character and star-crossed lover of Juliet in William Shakespeare's 1597 play "Romeo and Juliet"; see Juliet, this index): BBC Play of the Month, 1965-1983 (TV series; "Romeo and Juliet," 1967 episode: Hywel Bennett); BBC Sunday Night Theatre, 1950-1959 (TV series; "Romeo and Juliet," 1955 episode: Tony Britton); The Hollywood Review of 1929, 1929 (John Gilbert); Kraft Theatre, 1947-1958 (TV series; "Romeo and Juliet," 1954 episode: Liam Sullivan); The Philco-Goodyear Television Playhouse, 1948-1956 (TV series; "Romeo and Juliet," 1949 episode: Kevin McCarthy); Producers' Showcase, 1954-1957 (TV series; "Romeo and Juliet," 1957 episode: John Neville); Romeo and Juliet, 1916 (Francis X. Bushman); Romeo and Juliet, 1916 (Harry Hilliard); **Romeo and Juliet**, 1936 (Leslie Howard); Romeo and Juliet, 1947 (made-for-TV; John Bailey); **Romeo and Juliet**, 1954 (Laurence Harvey); Romeo and Juliet, 1956 (Yuri Zhdanov); Romeo and Juliet, 1962 (TV series; David Weston); Romeo and Juliet, 1965 (Clive Francis); Romeo and Juliet, 1966 (ballet; Rudolf Nureyev); **Romeo and Juliet**, 1968 (Leonard Whiting); Romeo and Juliet, 1976 (made-for-TV; Christopher Neame); Romeo and Juliet, 1978 (made-for-TV; Patrick Ryecart); Romeo & Juliet, 1982 (ballet; Rudolf Nureyev); Romeo and Juliet, 1984 (British Royal Ballet at Covent Garden; Wayne Eagling); Romeo & Juliet, 1993 (Antoni Cimolino); Romeo & Juliet, 1994 (Jonathan Firth); Romeo and Juliet on Ice, 1983 (made-for-TV; Brian Pockar); Romeo & Juliet: Sealed with a Kiss, 2006 (animated animal version; Daniel Trippett voiceover); **Romeo + Juliet**, 1996 (Leonardo DiCaprio); Shakespeare: The Animated Tales, 1992-1994 (TV miniseries; "Romeo and Juliet," 1992 episode: Linus Roache voiceover).

Rooster Cogburn (fictional U.S. marshal who shoots first and talks later, a colorful lawman serving in the Indian Territory of the Old West where he heroically bests bandits and villains against all odds): **Rooster Cogburn**, 1975 (John Wayne); **True Grit**, 1969 (John Wayne); True Grit, 1978 (made-for-TV; Warren Oates); **True Grit**, 2010 (Jeff Bridges).

Roxanne (the beautiful cousin of long-nosed swordsman and poet Cyrano de Bergerac, created by playwright Edmond Rostand in 1897, a woman Cyrano believes he cannot win because of his protruding nose and therefore recites in hiding his sonnets of love to her for another suitor): BBC Play of the Month, 1965-1983 (TV series; "Cyrano de Bergerac," 1968 episode: Suzanne Neve); Cyrano de Bergerac, 1923 (Linda Moglia);): Cyrano de Bergerac, 1946 (Ellen Bernsen); **Cyrano de Bergerac**, 1950 (Mala Powers); Cyrano de Bergerac, 1960 (made-for-TV; Francoise Christophe); Cyrano de Bergerac, 1962 (made-for-TV; Hope Lange); Cyrano de Bergerac, 1975 (made-for-TV; Lies Franken); Cyrano de Bergerac, 1978 (made-for-TV; Evelyne Desutter); Cyrano de Bergerac, 1985 (made-for-TV; Sinead Cusack); Cyrano de Bergerac, 1986 (made-for-TV; Rosa Cadafalch); **Cyrano de Bergerac**, 1990 (Anne Brochet); Cyrano de Bergerac, 2000 (made-for-TV; Barbara Auer); Cyrano de Bergerac, 2007 (made-for-TV; Francoise Gillard); Cyrano de Bergerac, 2008 (Sondra Radvanosky); Great Performances, 1971- (TV series; "Cyrano de Bergerac," 1974 episode: Marsha Mason; "Cyrano de Bergerac," 2008 episode: Jennifer Garner); The Philco-Goodyear Television Playhouse, 1948-1956 (TV series; "Cyrano de

Bergerac," 1949 episode: Frances Reid); Producers' Showcase, 1954-1957 (TV series; "Cyrano de Bergerac," 1955 episode: Claire Bloom); Schlitz Playhouse, 1951-1959 (TV series; "The Sword," 1957 episode:Niki Dantine).

Rudolph Rassendyll (lookalike cousin to the king of mythical Ruritania who saves his relative's crown and life by impersonating him in Anthony Hope's 1894 adventure novel, *The Prisoner of Zenda*, this character invariably played as dual roles): The DuPont Show of the Month, 1957-1961 (TV series; "The Prisoner of Zenda," 1961 episode: Christopher Plummer); The Prisoner of Zenda, 1915 (Henry Ainley); **The Prisoner of Zenda**, 1922 (Lewis Stone); **The Prisoner of Zenda**, 1937 (Ronald Colman); **The Prisoner of Zenda**, 1952 (Stewart Granger); The Prisoner of Zenda, 1979 (Peter Sellers); The Prisoner of Zenda, 1984- (TV miniseries; Malcolm Sinclair); Rupert of Hentzau, 1915 (Henry Ainley); Rupert of Hentzau, 1923 (Bert Lytell); Rupert of Hentzau, 1957 (made-for-TV; John Westbrook); Rupert of Hentzau, 1964- (TV series; George Baker).

Rumpelstiltskin (fairy tale character in German lore, a hideous-looking imp who can spin gold from straw): Faerie Tale Theatre 1982-1987 (TV series; "Rupelstiltskin," 1982 episode: Herve Villechaize); Happily N'Ever After, 2006 (Michael McShane); Happily N'Ever After 2, 2009 (David Lodge); Once upon a Brothers Grimm, 1977 (made-for-TV; Clive Revill); Rumpelstiltskin, 1955 (Werner Kruger); Rumpelstiltskin, 1987 (Billy Barty); Rumpelstiltskin, 1995 (Max Grodenchik); 7 Dwarves: The Forest Is Not Enough, 2006 (Axel Neumann); The Seventh Dwarf, 2015 (Darius Hammersmith); Shirley Temple's Storybook, 1958-1961 (TV series; "Rupelstiltskin," Shaike Ophir); **Shrek Forever After**, 2010 (Walt Dohrn); **Shrek the Third**, 2007 (Conrad Vernon); The Wonderful World of the Brothers Grimm, 1962 (Arnold Stang).

Rupert of Hentzau (conspirator to seize the throne in mythical Ruitania and one of the master villains in literature, created in Anthony Hope's 1894 adventure novel, *The Prisoner of Zenda*): **The Prisoner of Zenda**, 1922 (Ramon Novarro); **The Prisoner of Zenda**, 1937 (Douglas Fairbanks Jr.); **The Prisoner of Zenda**, 1952 (James Mason); The Prisoner of Zenda, 1979 (Stuart Wilson); The Prisoner of Zenda, 1984- (TV miniseries; Jonathon Morris); Rupert of Hentzau, 1915 (Gerald Ames); Rupert of Hentzau, 1964- (TV series; Peter Wynegarde).

Sadie Thompson (prostitute of the South Seas who finds redemption through a fanatical missionary only to be further disillusioned when seduced by him, as depicted in W. Somerset Maugham's short story, "Rain," as well as the 1923 play): **Miss Sadie Thompson**, 1953 (Rita Hayworth); **Rain**, 1932 (Joan Crawford); **Sadie Thompson**, 1928 (Gloria Swanson); W. Somerset Maugham, 1969-1970 (TV series; "Rain," 1970 episode: Carroll Baker).

Sagramore (legendary knight in King Arthur's Round Table in 6th-Century England): **Camelot**, 1967 (Peter Bromilow); **A Connecticut Yankee**, 1931 (Mitchell Harris); A Connecticut Yankee in King Arthur's Court, 1921 (George Siegmann); **A Connecticut Yankee in King Arthur's Court**, 1949 (William Bendix); **First Knight**, 1995 (Tom Lucy); A Knight in Camelot, 1998 (made-for-TV; Robert Addie); Once upon a Classic, 1976-1979 (TV series: "A Connecticut Yankee in King Arthur's Court," 1978 episode: Fredrick Coffin); Perceval, 1978 (Gilles Raab); Studio One in Hollywood, 1948-1958 (TV series: "A Connecticut Yankee in King Arthur's Court," 1952 episode: Barry Kroeger).

Sally Bowles (amoral but optimistic cabaret singer in 1930s Berlin created in the books of Christopher Isherwood): **Cabaret**, 1972 (Liza Minnelli); Cabaret, 1993 (made-for-TV; Jane Horrocks); I Am a Camera, 1955 (Julie Harris); To cabare, 1979 (made-for-TV; Aliki Vougiouklaki).

Liza Minnelli (as Sally Bowles) in *Cabaret*, **1972.**

Sam Spade (hard-boiled San Francisco private detective created by Dashiell Hammett, first appearing in the 1930 novel *The Maltese Falcon*): **The Black Bird**, 1975 (George Segal as Sam Spade Jr.); **The Life of Riley**, 1949 (Howard Duff as the voice of Sam Spade on the radio); **The Maltese Falcon**, 1931 (Ricardo Cortez); **The Maltese Falcon**, 1941 (Humphrey Bogart); **Murder by Death**, 1976 (spoof of great detectives; Peter Falk as Sam Diamond); **Satan Met a Lady**, 1936 (Warren William as Ted Shane); **Revenge of the Pink Panther**, 1978 (Lon Satton, Rosita Yarboy, Keith Hodiak, Pepsi Maycock); The Strange Case of the End of Civilization as We Know It, 1977 (Mike O'Malley).

Sancho Panza (fictional character, a self-indulging squire who aids deluded knight Don Quioxte to ostensibly achieve impossible deeds of valor and who is profiled in Miguel de Cervantes' 1605 novel, *The Ingenuous Gentleman Don Quixote of La Mancha*): BBC Play of the Month, 1965-1983 (TV series; "The Adventures of Don Quixote," 1973 episode: Frank Finlay); CBS Television Workshop, 1952- (TV series; "Don Quixote," 1952 episode: Jimmy Savo); Der Mann von La Mancha, 1994 (made-for-TV; Helmut Wallner); Don de La Mancha, 1980 (TV miniseries; Setsuo Wakui, Clifton Wells); Don Quichotte, 2000 (Jean-Philippe Lafont); Don Quichotte, 2010 (made-for-TV; Werner Van Mechelen); Don Quijote de La Mancha, 1949 (Juan Calvo); Don Quijote de La Mancha, 1978 (TV series; Antonio Ferrandis); Don Quijote de la Mancha, 1991-1992 (TV series; Alfredo Landa); Don Quijote von der Mancha, 1965 (TV miniseries; Roger Carel); Don Quixote, 1915 (Max Davidson); Don Quixote, 1923 (George Robey); **Don Quixote** [aka: The Adventure of Don Quixote], 1934 (George Robey); **Don Quixote**, 1973 (Ray Powell); Don Quixote, 1992 (Akim Tamiroff, Juan Carlos Ordonez voiceover); Don Quixote, 2000 (made-for-TV; Bob Hoskins); Don Quixote, Knight Errant, 2002 (Carlos Iglesias); Don Quixote: The Ingenious Gentleman of La Mancha, 2015 (Horatio Sanz); The DuPont Show of the Month, 1957-1961 (TV series; "I, Don Quixote," 1959 episode: Eli Wallach); Great Performances, 1971- (TV series; "Monsieur Quixote," 1987 episode: Leo McKern); La rebellion de los fantasmas, 1949 (Francisco Pando); Man of La Mancha, 1972 (James Coco).

Santa Claus (Chris Cringle; Father Christmas; Kris Kringle; Le Pere Noel; Saint Nicholas; Saint Nick; Santa; jovial gift-giving mythical figure appearing at Christmastime, endeared to children everywhere): The Alcoa Hour, 1955-1957 (TV series; "Night," 1957 episode: William Hansen); All I Want for Christmas, 1991 (Leslie Nielsen); Amen, 1986-1991 (TV series; "Miracle on 134th Street," two 1990 episodes: William Windom); The Arrangement, 1969 (Stephen Coit); Arthur Christmas, 2011 (Jim Broadbent); Asphalt Girl, 1964 (Hiroshi Hirano); **Babes in**

Eric Lloyd and Tim Allen (as Santa Claus) in *The Santa Clause*, 1994.

Toyland, 1934 (Ferdinand Munier); Babes in Toyland, 1954 (made-for-TV; Dave Garroway); The Boy Who Saved Christmas, 1998 (Colin McClean); A Boyfriend for Christmas, 2004 (made-for-TV; Charles Durning); Broadway Serenade, 1939 (Sydney Jarvis); Bundle of Joy, 1956 (Paul Maxey); The Case for Christmas, 2011 (made-for-TV; George Buza); **The Cheaters**, 1945 (Jack Daley); The Christmas Dragon, 2014 (Adam Johnson); Christmas Dream, 2000 (made-for-TV; Gary Russell); A Christmas Eve Miracle, 2015 (William "Bus" Riley); Christmas in Wonderland, 2007 (Matthew Walker); The Christmas List, 1997 (made-for-TV; Percy Hayes); Christmas on the Bayou, 2013 (Edward Asner); Christmas Reunion, 1994 (made-for-TV; James Coburn); **A Christmas Story**, 1983 (Jeff Gillen); Christmas Story, 2008 (Hannu-Pekka Bjorkman); The Christmas That Almost Wasn't, 1966 (Alberto Rabaglioti); A Christmas Wedding Tail, 2011 (made-for-TV; Keith Dobbins); The Christmas Wife, 1988 (made-for-TV; Bill Lynn); **The Chronicles of Narnia: The Lion; the Witch; and the Wardrobe**, 2005 (James Cosmo); The Coca-Cola Kid, 1985 (David Bracks, Ian Nimmo, Scott J. Ateah, Chris Hession, Bernard Ledger); Come See the Paradise, 1990 (David MacIntyre); The Comic Book Christmas Caper, 1990 (Ned Beatty); A Country Christmas, 2013 (Abraham Benrubi); Dear Santa, 1998 (Bennett Curland); Deck the Halls, 2005 (made-for-TV; Rob Morton); Defending Santa, 2013 (Bill Lewis); A Different Kind of Christmas, 1996 (made-for-TV; Bruce Kirby); Double Dynamite, 1951 (Virgil Johnson, Charles Coleman); Elmo's Christmas Countdown, 2007 (made-for-TV; Kevin James); Eloise at Christmastime, 2003 (made-for-TV; Tom Tumminello); Ernest Saves Christmas, 1988 (Douglas Seale); Exclusive, 1937 (Pat West); A Fairly Odd Christmas, 2012 (made-for-TV; Donavon Stinson); Farewell, Mr. Kringle, 2010 (made-for-TV; William Morgan Sheppard); Finding Mrs. Claus, 2012 (made-for-TV; Will Sasso); A Flintstone Christmas, 1977 (made-for-TV; Hal Smith); The Ford Television Theatre, 1952-1957 (TV series; "Remembrance Day," 1956 episode: George Cisar): Fred Claus, 2007 (Theo Stevenson, Paul Giamatti); Gay Blades, 1946 (Matt McHugh); Get Santa, 2014 (Jim Broadbent); The Gift of Love: A Christmas Story, 1983 (made-for-TV; James Dodds); Good Sam, 1948 (Tom Dugan); The Good Shepherd, 2006 (Sjoerd Dejong); Great Performances, 1971- (TV series; "The Nutcracker," 2001 episode: Richard Ramsey); The Great Santa Claus Switch, 1970 (made-for-TV; Art Carney); The Greatest Store in the World, 1999 (made-for-TV; Ricky Tomlinson); Grumpy Cat's Worst Christmas Ever, 2014 (made-for-TV; Russell Peters); Happy Holidays, 2008 (Nicole Anderson); Help for the Holidays, 2012 (made-for-TV; Steve Larkin); Her Highness and the Bellboy, 1945 (Charles Morton); Highway Patrol, 1954-1959 (TV series; "Christmas Story," 1956 episode: Elmore Vincent); Holiday Affair, 1949 (Frank Johnson); Holiday in Your Heart, 1997 (made-for-TV; John William Galt); **Holiday**

Inn, 1942 (Bud Jamison); A Holiday to Remember, 1995 (made-for-TV; Don McManus); **Home Alone**, 1990 (Ken Hudson Campbell); Homeless for the Holidays, 2009 (Russ Bruzek); How the Toys Saved Christmas, 1996 (Neil Shee voiceover); How to Marry a Billionaire: A Christmas Tale, 2000 (made-for-TV; Hamilton Camp); I Saw Mommy Kissing Santa Claus, 2001 (Dane Stevens, Sonny Carl Davis); In the Nick of Time, 1991 (made-for-TV; Lloyd Bridges); It's Christmas, 2007 (Harace Carpenter); The Jack Benny Program, 1950-1965 (TV series; "Christmas Show," 1960 episode; Paul Maxey); The Jim Backus Show, 1960-1961 (TV series; "Sad Sack Santa," 1961 episode; J. Pat O'Malley); Jingle All the Way, 1996 (James Belushi); Journey to the Christmas Star, 2012 (Andreas Cappelen); Julie's Christmas Special, 1973 (made-for-TV; Peter Ustinov); The Kid Who Loved Christmas, 1990 (Jimmy Carville); Lake Placid Serenade, 1944 (Ferdinand Munier); Last Christmas, 1999 (made-for-TV; Mark Benton); Le pere Noel, 2014 (Tahar Rahim); **The Lemon Drop Kid**, 1951 (Bob Hope, Harry Tyler); **Les Misérables**, 2012 (Peter Mair, Jack Chissick); The Life and Adventures of Santa Claus, 1985 (made-for-TV; Earl Hammond; J.D. Roth as young Santa); Life Begins at Eight-Thirty, 1942 (Alec Craig); Life with Mikey, 1993 (Christopher Durang); Like Father, Like Santa, 1998 (made-for-TV; William Hootkins); The Lion, the Witch & the Wardrobe, 1988 (TV miniseries; Bert Parnaby); Little Brother, Big Trouble: A Christmas Adventure, 2012 (Gary Mountaine); The Loretta Young Show, 1953-1961 (TV series; "Time and Yuletide," 1954 episode: Forrest Lewis); Love That Brute, 1950 (Tiny Timbrell); Magic Silver, 2009 (Knut Walle); Magic Silver II, 2011 (Knut Walle); The Magic Snowflake, 2013 (Michael Sorich, Benoit Allemane, Vincent Grass); The Man in the Santa Claus Suit, 1979 (made-for-TV; Fred Astaire); The Marvelous History of St. Bernard, 1952 (made-for-TV; Tom Bosley); Mary Christmas, 2002 (made-for-TV; Tom Bosley); **Millions**, 2005 (Harry Kirkham); The Miracle of the White Reindeer, 1960 (Hal Smith); **Miracle on 34th Street**, 1947 (Edmund Gwenn as the real Santa Claus; Percy Helton as drunken Santa Claus); Miracle on 34th Street, 1959 (made-for-TV; Ed Wynn); Miracle on 34th Street, 1973 (made-for-TV; Sebastian Cabot); Miracle on 34th Street, 1994 (Richard Attenborough); Mister Scrooge to See You, 2013 (Torry Martin); Mr. St. Nick, 2002 (made-for-TV; Kelsey Grammer); Mrs. Santa Claus, 1996 (made-for-TV; Charles Durning); A Muppets Christmas: Letters to Santa, 2008 (made-for-TV; Richard Griffiths); The Munsters' Scary Little Christmas, 1996 (made-for-TV; Mark Mitchell); Musical Comedy Time, 1950-1951 (TV series; "Babes in Toyland," 1950 episode: Robert Weede); Must Be Santa, 1999 (made-for-TV; Arnold Pinnock); A Nanny for Christmas, 2010 (Keith Dobbins); The Night before Christmas, 1994 (J. Michael Oliva); The Night Before the Night before Christmas, 2010 (made-for-TV; R.D. Reid); The Night They Saved Christmas, 1984 (made-for-TV; Art Carney); **The Nightmare before Christmas**, 1993 (Edward Ivory); North Station, 2002 (Benoit Briere); Northpole: Open for Christmas, 2015 (made-for-TV; Donovan Scott); **O. Henry's Full House**, 1952 (Fred Kelsey); Once upon a Christmas, 2000 (made-for-TV; Douglas Campbell); One Magic Christmas, 1985 (Jan Rubes); **One True Thing**, 1998 (John Deyle); Our First Christmas, 2008 (made-for-TV; Richard Riehle); Paris, Palace Hotel, 1956 (Rene Genin); Peter in Magicland, 1990 (Walter Reichelt); The Polar Express, 2004 (Tom Hanks); **Prancer**, 1989 (Michael Constantine); A Princess for Christmas, 2011 (made-for-TV; Iovu Costel); The Proud and the Profane, 1956 (Alvin Greenman); **Road to Utopia**, 1946 (Ferdinand Munier); Ruby and Rata, 1990 (Peter Sharp); Rudolph and Frosty's Christmas in July, 1979 (Mickey Rooney); Rudolph, the Red-Nosed Reindeer, 1964 (made-for-TV; Stan Francis); Rudolph the Red-Nosed Reindeer: The Movie, 1998 (John Goodman); Rudolph's Shiny New Year, 1976 (made-for-TV; Paul Frees); Saint Ralph, 2005 (Robert Smith); **St. Vincent**, 2014 (Nicholas Wuehrmann); Santa and Pete, 1999 (made-for-TV; Hume Cronyn); Santa and the Ice Cream Bunny, 1972 (Jay Ripley); Santa and the Three Bears, 1970 (Hal Smith voiceover); Santa Baby, 2006 (made-for-TV; George Wendt); Santa Baby 2: Christmas Maybe, 2009 (made-for-TV; Paul Sorvino);

Santa Claus, 1960 (Jose Elias Moreno); Santa Claus, 1985 (David Huddleston); The Santa Claus Brothers, 2001 (made-for-TV; Bryan Cranston); Santa Claus Conquers the Martians, 1964 (John Call); Santa Claus Is Comin' to Town, 1970 (made-for-TV; Mickey Rooney voiceover); **The Santa Clause**, 1994 (Tim Allen); The Santa Clause 3: The Escape Clause, 2006 (Tim Allen); **The Santa Clause 2**, 2002 (Tim Allen); The Santa Trap, 2002 (made-for-TV; Dick Van Patten); Santa vs. Claus, 2008 (made-for-TV; Stephen Hughes); Santa Who?, 2000 (made-for-TV; Leslie Nielsen); Santa's Apprentice, 2015 (Michael Sorich, Shane Jacobson, Benoit Allemane); Santa's Christmas Circus, 1966 (John Bilyeu); Santa's Magic Book, 1996 (made-for-TV; Buz McKim); Scrooged, 1988 (Al "Red Dog" Weber); Secret Santa, 2003 (made-for-TV; John A. Keim); Single Santa Seeks Mrs. Claus, 2004 (made-for-TV; John Wheeler, Austin Miles); The Story of Santa Claus, 1996 (Edward Asner voiceover); Studio 57, 1954-1958 (TV series; "Christmas Every Day," 1954 episode: Harry Bartell); Surviving Christmas, 2004 (Tumbleweed); Tall, Dark and Handsome, 1941 (Arthur Thalasso); A Thousand Men and a Baby, 1997 (made-for-TV; Joe Bays); To Grandmother's House We Go, 1992 (made-for-TV; Rick Poltaruk); 'Twas the Night, 2001 (made-for-TV; Jefferson Mappin); The 20th Century Fox Hour, 1955-1957 (TV series; "Miracle on 34th Street," 1955 episode; Thomas Mitchell); Twice Upon Christmas, 2001 (made-for-TV; Matthew Walker); The Ultimate Christmas Present, 2000 (made-for-TV; John B. Lowe); A Very Cool Christmas, 2004 (made-for-TV; George Hamilton); The Walt Disney Christmas Show, 1951 (made-for-TV; Don Barclay); Walt Disney's Wonderful World of Color, 1954-1992 (TV series; "Holiday Time at Disneyland," 1962 episode; Paul Maxey; "Lefty, the Dingaling Lynx," 1971 episode: James L. Wilson); When Santa Fell to Earth, 2011 (Alexander Scheer); Wonderful Adventures of Nils, 1962 (Manne Grunberger); The Year without a Santa Claus, 1974 (made-for-TV; Mickey Rooney); Yogi's First Christmas, 1980 (made-for-TV; Hal Smith voiceover).

Scaramouche (fictional stock clown character in Italian and French comedies, usually a boasting and cowardly buffoon): The Adventures of Scaramouche, 1964 (Gerard Barray); La grande avventura di Scaramouche, 1972 (Christian Hay); The Loves and Times of Scaramouche, 1976 (Michael Sarrazin); Marion Delorme, 1967 (made-for-TV; Marcel Champel); Moliere, 1980 (Mario Gonzales); **Scaramouche**, 1923 (Ramon Novarro); **Scaramouche**, 1952 (Henry Corden; Stewart Granger); Scaramouche, 1960 (made-for-TV; Klaus Salin); Scaramouche, 1965 (TV miniseries; Dominico Modugno).

The Scarecrow (straw-filled scarecrow that comes alive and becomes a devoted companion to Dorothy, a young girl from Kansas transported to a strange world in L. Frank Baum's iconic 1900 novel, *The Wonderful Wizard of Oz*): Journey Back to Oz, 1972 (animated; Mickey Rooney voiceover); The Muppets' Wizard of Oz, 2005 (Steve Whitmore as Kermit the Frog voiceover); The New Wizard of Oz, 1914 (Frank Moore); Off to See the Wizard, 1967-1968 (animated TV series; Daws Butler voiceover); The Wiz, 1978 (Michael Jackson); The Wizard of Oz, 1925 (Larry Semon); **The Wizard of Oz**, 1939 (Ray Bolger); The Wizard of Oz, 1982 (animated; Billy Van voiceover); The Wizard of Oz, 1990-1991 (animated TV series; David Lodge voiceover); The Wizard of Oz in Concert: Dreams Come True, 1995 (made-for-TV; Jackson Browne); The Wizard of Oz on Ice, 1996 (made-for-TV; Victor Petrenko).

Sebastian Moran (Colonel Sebastian Moran; fictional character and criminal mastermind and nemesis of Sherlock Holmes in the stories written by Arthur Conan Doyle; also see James Moriarty, John Watson, Sherlock Holmes, this index): The Adventures of Sherlock Holmes and Dr. Watson, 1980 (TV series; Nikolai Kryukov); The Baker Street Boys, 1983- (TV series; Michael Godley); Elementary, 2012- (TV series; Vinnie Jones); Detective Conan: The Phantom of Baker Street, 2002 (Jou Fujimoto); Murdoch Mysteries, 2008- (TV series; "A Study in Sher-

Christopher Plummer (as Sherlock Holmes) and James Mason (as Dr. Watson) in *Murder by Decree*, 1979.

lock," 2013 episode: Steve Boyle); No Place Like Holmes, 2010- (TV series; Mark Saint John Ridley); The Return of Sherlock Holmes, 1929 (Donald Crisp); The Return of Sherlock Holmes, 1986-1988 (TV series; Patrick Allen); Sherlock Holmes, 1951 (TV miniseries; Eric Maturin); **Sherlock Holmes: A Game of Shadows**, 2011 (Paul Anderson); Sherlock Holmes' Fatal Hour, 1931 (Louis Goodrich); Silver Blaze (aka: Murder at the Baskervilles), 1937 (Arthur Goulett); **Terror by Night**, 1946 (Alan Mowbray); The Triumph of Sherlock Holmes, 1935 (Wilfrid Caithness); **Without a Clue**, 1988 (Tim Killick).

Sherlock Holmes (brilliant private detective in four novels and fifty-six short stories by Arthur Conan Doyle, first appearing in publication in 1887 in the short story "A Study in Scarlet," Beeton's Christmas Annual, London): **The Adventure of Sherlock Holmes' Smarter Brother**, 1975 (Douglas Wilmer); **The Adventures of Sherlock Holmes**, 1939 (Basil Rathbone); The Adventures of Sherlock Holmes, 1984-1985 (TV series; Jeremy Brett); The Adventures of Sherlock Holmes and Dr. Watson, 1980 (TV series; Vasily Livanov); The Baker Street Boys, 1983 (TV series; Roger Ostime); Batman: The Brave and the Bold, 2008-2011 (animated TV series; Ian Buchanan voiceover); The Case of Marcel Duchamp, 1984 (Guy Rolfe); The Case of the Whitechapel Vampire, 2002 (made-for-TV; Matt Frewer); The Casebook of Sherlock Holmes, 1991-1993 (TV series; Jeremy Brett); Crazy House, 1943 (Basil Rathbone); The Crucifer of Blood, 1991 (made-for-TV; Charlton Heston); Der Hund von Baskerville, 1929 (Carlyle Blackwell); The Double-Barreled Detective Story, 1965 (Jerome Raphael); **Dressed to Kill**, 1946 (Basil Rathbone); Elementary, 2012- (TV series; Jonny Lee Miller); Hands of a Murderer, 1990 (Edward Woodward); The Hound of the Baskervilles, 1932 (Robert Rendel); The Hound of the Baskervilles, 1937 (Bruno Guttner); **The Hound of the Baskervilles**, 1939 (Basil Rathbone); **The Hound of the Baskervilles**, 1959 (Peter Cushing); The Hound of the Baskervilles, 1972 (made-for-TV; Stewart Granger); The Hound of the Baskervilles, 1980 (Peter Cook); The Hound of the Baskervilles, 1981 (made-for-TV; Vasili Livanov); The Hound of the Baskervilles, 1982 (TV miniseries; Tom Baker); The Hound of the Baskervilles, 1983 (made-for-TV; Ian Richardson); The Hound of the Baskervilles, 1988 (made-for-TV; Jeremy Brett); The Hound of the Baskervilles, 2000 (made-for-TV; Matt Frewer); The Hound of the Baskervilles, 2003 (made-for-TV; Richard Roxburgh); The Hound of London, 1994 (made-for-TV; Patrick Macnee); **The House of Fear**, 1945 (Basil Rathbone); Incident at Victoria Falls, 1992 (made-for-TV; Christopher Lee); Lelicek in the Service of Sherlock Holmes, 1932 (Mac Fric); The Man Who Was Sherlock Holmes, 1937 (aka: Two Merry Adventurers; Hans Albers impersonating Holmes); The Memoirs of Sherlock Holmes, 1994 (TV series; Jeremy Brett); **Mr. Holmes**, 2015 (Ian

George Sanders (as Simon Templar) in *The Saint Strikes Back*, 1939.

McKellen); **Murder by Decree**, 1979 (Christopher Plummer); The Other Side, 1992 (made-for-TV; Richard E. Grant); Pater Brown, 1966-1972 (TV series; Gerhard Dorfer); **The Pearl of Death**, 1944 (Basil Rathbone); **The Private Life of Sherlock Holmes**, 1970 (Robert Stephens); **Pursuit to Algiers**, 1945 (Basil Rathbone); The Return of Sherlock Holmes, 1929 (Clive Brook); The Return of Sherlock Holmes, 1987 (made-for-TV; Margaret Colin as Michael Pennington); The Return of Sherlock Holmes, 1986-1988 (TV series; Jeremy Brett); The Royal Scandal, 2001 (made-for-TV; Matt Frewer); **The Scarlet Claw**, 1944 (Basil Rathbone); **The Seven-Per-Cent Solution**, 1976 (Nicol Williamson); Sherlock, 2002 (made-for-TV; James D'Arcy; Stefan Veronca as young Holmes); Sherlock Holmes, 1916 (William Gillette); **Sherlock Holmes**, 1922 (John Barrymore); Sherlock Holmes, 1932 (Clive Brook); Sherlock Holmes, 1951 (TV miniseries; Alan Wheatley); Sherlock Holmes, 1954-1955 (TV series; Ronald Howard); Sherlock Holmes, 1964-1968 (TV series; Perter Cushing; Douglas Wilmer); Sherlock Holmes, 1967-1968 (TV series; Eric Schellow); **Sherlock Holmes**, 2009 (Robert Downey Jr.); Sherlock Holmes, 2011 (Kevin Glaser); **Sherlock Holmes: A Game of Shadows**, 2011 (Robert Downey Jr.); Sherlock Holmes and a Study in Scarlet, 1983 (Peter O'Toole voiceover); Sherlock Holmes and Dr. Watson: The Bloody Inscription, 1979 (made-for-TV; Vasily Livanov); Sherlock Holmes and the Baker Street Irregulars, 2007 (made-for-TV; Jonathan Pryce); Sherlock Holmes and the Baskerville Curse, 1983 (Peter O'Toole voiceover); Sherlock Holmes and the Case of the Silk Stocking, 2004 (made-for-TV; Rupert Everett); Sherlock Holmes and the Deadly Necklace, 1962 (Christopher Lee); Sherlock Holmes and the Leading Lady, 1991 (made-for-TV; Christopher Lee); Sherlock Holmes and the Masks of Death, 1984 (made-for-TV; Peter Cushing); Sherlock Holmes and the Missing Rembrandt, 1932 (Arthur Wontner); **Sherlock Holmes and the Secret Weapon**, 1942 (Basil Rathbone); Sherlock Holmes and the Shadow Watchers, 2011 (Anthony D. P. Mann); Sherlock Holmes and the Sign of Four, 1983 (Peter O'Toole voiceover); Sherlock Holmes and the Valley of Fear, 1983 (Peter O'Toole voiceover); **Sherlock Holmes and the Voice of Terror**, 1942 (Basil Rathbone); **Sherlock Holmes Faces Death**, 1943 (Basil Rathbone); Sherlock Holmes' Fatal Hour, 1931 (Arthur Wontner); Sherlock Holmes in China, 1994 (Alex Vanderpor); **Sherlock Holmes in New York**, 1976 (made-for-TV; Roger Moore); **Sherlock Holmes in Washington**, 1943 (Basil Rathbone); Sherlock Holmes in the 22nd Century, 1999-2001 (TV series; Jason Gray-Stanford); Sherlock Holmes Returns, 1993 (made-for-TV; Anthony Higgins); The Sign of Four: Sherlock Holmes' Greatest Case, 1932 (Arthur Wontner); The Sign of Four, 1983 (made-for-TV; Ian Richardson); The Sign of Four, 1988 (made-for-TV; Jeremy Brett); The Sign of Four, 2001 (made-for-TV; Matt Frewer); Silver Blaze (aka: Murder at the Baskervilles), 1937 (Arthur Wontner); **The Speckled Band**, 1931 (Raymond Massey); **The Spider Woman**, 1944 (Basil Rathbone); The Strange Case of the End of Civilization as We Know It, 1977 (John Cleese as Arthur Sherlock Holmes); A Study in Scarlet, 1933 (Reginald Owen); **A Study in Terror**, 1966 (John Neville); **Terror by Night**, 1946 (Basil Rathbone); Testimony, 1988 (Rodney Litchfield); **They Might Be Giants**, 1971 (role model for George C. Scott); The Three Garridebs, 1937 (made-for-TV; Louis Hector); Touha Sherlocka Holmese, 1971 (Radovan Lukavsky); The Triumph of Sherlock Holmes, 1935 (Arthur Wontner); The Valley of Fear, 1916 (H.A. Saintsbury); **Without a Clue**, 1988 (Michael Caine); **The Woman in Green**, 1945 (Basil Rathbone); The Xango from Baker Street, 2002 (Joaquim de Almeida); Young Sherlock, 1981 (TV series; Guy Henry); **Young Sherlock Holmes**, 1985 (Nicholas Rowe).

Sheriff of Nottingham (fictional character and dedicated foe of Robin Hood): **The Adventures of Robin Hood**, 1938 (Melville Cooper); The Adventures of Robin Hood, 1955-1960 (TV series; Alan Wheatley); The Bandit of Sherwood Forest, 1946 (Lloyd Corrigan); A Challenge for Robin Hood, 1968 (John Arnatt); Into the Labyrinth, 1981-1982 (TV series; "Robin," 1981 episode: Conrad Phillips); The Legend of Robin Hood, 1968- (TV series; Steve Forrest); The Legend of Robin Hood, 1975 (TV miniseries; Paul Darrow); The Men of Sherwood Forest, 1954 (Leonard Sachs); NBC Children's Theatre, 1963-1973 (TV series; "Robin Hood," 1964 episode: Sorrell Brooke); **Robin and Marian**, 1976 (Robert Shaw); **Robin Hood**, 1922 (William Lowery); Robin Hood, 1953- (TV miniseries; David Kossoff); **Robin Hood**, 1973 (Pat Buttram voiceover); Robin Hood, 2006-2009 (TV series; Keith Allen); **Robin Hood**, 2010 (Matthew Macfadyen); Robin Hood: Ghosts of Sherwood 3D, 2012 (Tom Savini); **Robin Hood: Men in Tights**, 1993 (Roger Rees); **Robin Hood: Prince of Thieves**, 1991 (Alan Rickman); **The Story of Robin Hood** [aka: The Story of Robin Hood and His Merrie Men], 1952 (Peter Finch); Sword of Sherwood Forest, 1961 (Peter Cushing); Tales of Robin Hood, 1951 (Tiny Stowe); Young Robin Hood, 1991-1992 (animated TV series; A.J. Henderson voiceover).

Silas Barnaby (Mother Goose character): **Babes in Toyland**, 1934 (Henry Brandon); Babes in Toyland, 1954 (made-for-TV; Jack E. Leonard); Babes in Toyland, 1961 (Ray Bolger); Babes in Toyland, 1986 (made-for-TV; Richard Mulligan); Babes in Toyland, 1997 (Christopher Plummer voiceover); Shirley Temple's Storybook, 1958-1961 (TV series, "Babes in Toyland," 1960 episode: Jonathan Winters).

Simon Templar (aka: The Saint; suave amateur detective created by British-Chinese author Leslie Charteris, appearing first in a 1928 novel): CBS Summer Playhouse, 1987-1989 (TV series; "The Saint in Manhattan," 1987 episode: Andrew Clarke); The Dance of Death, 1960 (Felix Marten); The Fiction Makers, 1967 (Roger Moore); The Return of the Saint, 1978-1979 (TV series; Ian Ogilvy); The Saint, 1962-1969 (TV series; Roger Moore); The Saint, 1997 (Val Kilmer); The Saint, 2016 (made-for-TV; Adam Rayner); The Saint and the Brave Goose, 1979 (Ian Ogilvy); The Saint: Fear in Fun Park, 1989 (made-for-TV; Simon Dutton); **The Saint in London**, 1939 (George Sanders); **The Saint in New York**, 1938 (Louis Hayward); **The Saint in Palm Springs**, 1941 (George Sanders); The Saint Lies in Wait, 1966 (Jean Marais); The Saint Meets the Tiger, 1941 (Hugh Sinclair); **The Saint Strikes Back**, 1939 (George Sanders); The Saint: The Big Bang, 1989 (made-for-TV; Simon Dutton); The Saint: The Blue Dulac, 1989 (made-for-TV; Simon Dutton); The Saint: The Brazilian Connection, 1989 (made-for-TV; Simon Dutton); The Saint: The Software Murders, 1989 (made-for-TV; Simon Dutton); The Saint: Wrong Number, 1989 (made-for-TV; Simon Dutton); **The Saint's Double Trouble**, 1940 (George Sanders); **The Saint's Girl Friday**, 1954 (Louis Hayward); **The Saint's Vacation**, 1941 (Hugh Sinclair); True Crimes: The First 72 Hours, 2003- (TV series; "The Saint," 2003 episode: Garth Hewitt); Vendetta for the Saint, 1969 (Roger Moore).

Simple Simon (Mother Goose character): **Babes in Toyland**, 1934 (Charley Rogers); Happily N'Ever After, 2009 (Doug Erholtz voiceover).

Sinbad (aka: Sinbad the Sailor; fictional seaman and hero of Middle Eastern origin): The Adventures of Sinbad, 1996-1998 (TV series; Zen Gesner); **Arabian Nights**, 1942 (Shemp Howard); The Arabian Nights: Adventures of Sinbad, 1975- (TV series; Ian Odle); Babes in Bagdad, 1952 (Sebastian Cabot); Captain Sinbad, 1963 (Guy Williams); The Desert Hawk, 1950 (Joe Besser); The Dinah Shore Chevy Show, 1956-1963 (TV series; "Arabian Nights," 1960 episode: John Vivyan); The Freedom Force, 1978- (TV miniseries; Michael Bell); **The Golden Voyage of Sinbad**, 1974 (John Phillip Law); **Invitation to the Dance**, 1956 (Gene Kelly in dance number); Magi: The Kingdom of Magic, 2013- (TV series; Matthew Mercer); Magi: The Labyrinth of Magic, 2012 (TV series; Matthew Mercer); The Magic Lamp, 1956 (animated; Gene Kelly); **The 7th Voyage of Sinbad**, 1958 (Kerwin Matthews); Sinbad, 2012- (TV series; Elliot Knight); **Sinbad and the Eye of the Tiger**, 1977 (Patrick Wayne); Sinbad and the Minotaur, 2011 (made-for-TV; Manu Bennett); Sinbad: Beyond the Veil of Mists, 2000 (Brendan Fraser); **Sinbad: Legend of the Seven Seas**, 2003 (Brad Pitt voiceover); Sinbad of the Seven Seas, 1989 (Lou Ferrigno); Sinbad: The Battle of the Dark Knights, 1998 (Richard Grieco); **Sinbad the Sailor**, 1947 (Douglas Fairbanks Jr.); Son of Sinbad, 1955 (Dale Robertson); Thief of Damascus, 1952 (Lon Chaney Jr.); The Wizard of Bagdad, 1960 (Frank Logan).

Sleeping Beauty (aka: Princess Aurora; fairy tale character created by the Brothers Grimm, a beautiful, young princess in a state of deep sleep as a result of a curse and who is awakened by a kiss from Prince Charming): American Playhouse, 1981- (TV series; "Into the Woods," 1991 episode: Maureen Davis); Dornroschen, 1917 (Mabel Kaul); Faerie Tale Theatre, 1982-1987 (TV series; "Sleeping Beauty," 1983 episode: Bernadette Peters); Great Performances, 1971- (TV series; "The Sleeping Beauty," 1995 episode: Viviana Durante); The Magic Land of Mother Goose, 1967 (Linda Appleby); Once upon a Brothers Grimm, 1977 (made-for-TV; Joanna Kirkland); Producer's Showcase, 1954-1957 (TV series; "The Sleeping Beauty," 1955 episode: Margot Fonteyn); Shirley Temple's Storybook, 1958-1961 (TV series; "The Sleeping Beauty," 1958 episode: Anne Helm); Sleeping Beauty, 1949 (Tuula Usva); **Sleeping Beauty**, 1959 (Mary Costa); Sleeping Beauty, 1965 (Angela von Leitner); Sleeping Beauty, 1971 (Juliane Koren); Sleeping Beauty, 1987 (Tahnee Welch); The Sleeping Beauty, 1987 (made-for-TV; Rosalynn Sumners); Sleeping Beauty, 1999 (made-for-TV; Vanessa de Ligniere); The Sleeping Beauty, 2003 (made-for-TV; Sofiane Sylve); The Sleeping Beauty, 2007 (made-for-TV; Alina Cojocaru); Sleeping Beauty, 2008 (made-for-TV; Anna Hausburg); The Sleeping Princess, 1939 (made-for-TV; Margot Fonteyn).

Snow White (fairy tale character from *Snow White and the Seven Dwarfs* by the Brothers Grimm, 1812): American Playhouse, 1981- (TV series; "Into the Woods," Cindy Robinson); Christmas Night of One Hundred Stars, 1986 (TV special; Dana); Faerie Tale Theatre, 1982-1987 (TV series; "Snow White and the Seven Dwarfs," 1984 episode: Elizabeth McGovern); Happily Ever After, 1993 (Irene Cara); Happily Ever After: Fairy Tales for Every Child, 1995-2000 (TV series; "Snow White," 1995 episode: Elaine Bilstad); Happily N'Ever After, 2009 (Helen Niedwick voiceover); Into the Woods, 2011 (Sophie Caton); Mirror Mirror, 2012 (Lily Collins); Schneewittchen, 2009 (made-for-TV; Laura Berlin); The Seven Dwarfs to the Rescue, 1951 (Rossana Podesta); 7 Dwarves: The Forest Is Not Enough, 2006 (Katy Karrenbauer); **Shrek the Third**, 2007 (Amy Poehler); Snow White, 1916 (Amy Ehrlich); Snow White, 1916 (Marguerite Clark); Snow White, 1961 (Doris Weikow); Snow White, 1989 (Sarah Patterson; Nicola Stapleton playing Snow White as a child); Snow White, 2009 (Nagisa Shirai); Snow White and Rose Red, 1966 (Rosemarie Seehofer); **Snow White and the Huntsman**, 2012 (Kristen

Sinbad (Brad Pitt voice) and Marina (Catherine Zeta-Jones voice) in *Sinbad: Legend of the Seven Seas*, 2003.

Stewart); **Snow White and the Seven Dwarfs**, 1937 (Adriana Caselotti voiceover); Snow White and the Seven Dwarfs, 1955 (Elke Arendt); Snow White and the Three Stooges, 1961 (Carol Heiss); Snow White Live, 1980 (made-for-TV; Mary Jo Salerno); The Wonderful World of the Brothers Grimm, 1962 (True Ellison).

Spider-Man (aka: Peter Parker; U.S. comic book character, a superhero crime-fighter): The Amazing Spider-Man, 1977-1979 (TV series; Nicholas Hammond); The Amazing Spider-Man, 2012 (Andrew Garfield); **The Amazing Spider-Man 2**, 2014 (Andrew Garfield); The Avengers: Earth's Mightiest Heroes, 2010-2012 (TV series; Drake Bell); The Spectacular Spider-Man, 2008-2009 (TV series; Josh Keaton); Spider-Man, 1967-1970 (TV series; Paul Soles); Spider-Man, 1981-1987 (TV series; Ted Schwartz); Spider-Man, 1994-1998 (TV series; Christopher Daniel Barnes); **Spider-Man**, 2002 (Tobey Maguire); Spider-Man, 2003 (TV series; Neil Patrick Harris); Spider-Man and His Amazing Friends, 1981-1986 (TV series; Dan Gilvezan); Spider-Man: Lost Cause, 2014 (Joey Lever); The Spider-Man Saga: 2015- (TV series; Mark Ricci); **Spider-Man 2**, 2004 (Tobey Maguire); Spider-Man Unlimited, 1999-2001 (TV series; Rino Romano); Ultimate Spider-Man, 2012- (TV series; Drake Bell).

Stephen Orlac (gifted concert pianist who suffers a mutilating accident and has the hands of a murderer grafted to his arms, these hands causing him to become a horrific killer): Des voix dans la nuit—Les mains de Orlac, 1991 (made-for-TV; Jacques Bonnaffe); Hands of a Stranger, 1962 (James Stapleton [James Noah]); The Hands of Orlac, 1924 (Conrad Veidt); The Hands of Orlac, 1964 (Mel Ferrer); **Mad Love**, 1935 (Colin Clive).

Stromboli (original story name is Mangiafuoco; the manager of a marionette theater who holds captive a wooden marionette that transforms into a real boy, a fictional character in the 1883 children's novel *The Adventures of Pinocchio* by Italian author Carlo Collodi): The Adventures of Pinocchio, 1947 (Erminio Spalla); The Adventures of Pinocchio, 1972 (TV miniseries; Lionel Stander); The Adventures of Pinocchio, 1996 (Udo Kier); Geppetto, 2000 (made-for-TV; Brent Spiner); The New Adventures of Pinocchio, 1999 (Udo Kier); **Pinocchio**, 1940 (Charles Judels voiceover); Pinocchio, 1972 (Michele Gammino); Pinocchio, 2002 (Franco Javarone); Pinocchio, 2006 (Will Kemp); Pinocchio, 2008 (made-for-TV; Maurizio Donadoni); Pinocchio, 2012 (Rocco Papaleo); Pinocchio, 2013 (TV miniseries; Ulrich Tukur); **Shrek the Third**, 2007 (Chris Miller voiceover); Walt Disney's Wonderful World of Color, 1954-1992 (TV series; "Disney on Parade," 1971 episode: Thuri Ravenscroft).

Christopher Reeve (as Superman) in *Superman,* **1978.**

Stygian Witches (three haggard sisters in Greek mythology who share one eye and one tooth and possess great powers): **Clash of the Titans**, 1981 (Freda Jackson, Anna Manahan, Flora Robson).

Superman (aka: Clark Kent; U.S. comic book character created in 1933, a crime fighter having superhuman powers): Adventures of Superman, 1952-1958 (TV series; George Reeves); The All-New Super Friends Hour, 1977-1978 (animated TV series; Danny Dark voiceover); Atom Man vs. Superman, 1950 (serial; Kirk Alyn); The Batman, 2004-2008 (TV series; George Newbern voiceover); The Batman/Superman Hour, 1968-1969 (animated TV series; Bud Collyer, Bob Hastings voiceovers); The Batman Superman Movie: World's Finest, 1997 (animated made-for-TV; Tim Daly voiceover); Batman: The Brave and the Bold, 2008-2011 (animated TV series; Roger Rose voiceover); Batman v Superman: Dawn of Justice, 2016 (Henry Cavill); Challenge of the Super Friends, 1978- (animated TV series; Danny Dark voiceover); Justice League, 2001-2006 (animated TV series; George Newbern); **The Lego Movie**, 2014 (Channing Tatum voiceover); Lois & Clark: The New Adventures of Superman, 1993-1997 (TV series; Dean Cain); **Man of Steel**, 2013 (Henry Cavill); The New Adventures of Superman, 1966-1970 (Animated TV series; Bob Hastings voiceover); Smallville, 2001-2011 (TV series; Tom Welling); Superboy, 1988-1992 (TV series; Gerard Christopher); Super Friends, 1973-2011 (animated TV series; Danny Dark voiceover); Super Friends, 1980-1983 (animated TV series; Danny Dark voiceover); Super Friends: The Legendary Super Powers Show, 1984- (animated TV series; Danny Dark voiceover); The Super Powers Team: Galactic Guardians, 1985- (animated TV series; Danny Dark voiceover); Superman, 1941-1943 (serial; Bud Collyer); Superman, 1948 (serial; Kirk Alyn); **Superman**, 1978 (Christopher Reeve; Jeff East as young Clark Kent); Superman, 1988 (animated TV series; Beau Weaver voiceover); Superman and the Mole-Men, 1951 (George Reeves); Superman IV: The Quest for Peace, 1987 (Christopher Reeve); Superman: Requiem, 2011 (Martin Richardson); **Superman Returns**, 2006 (Brandon Routh); Superman: The Last Son of Krypton, 1996 (Animated made-for-TV; Tim Daly); Superman IV: The Quest for Peace, 1987 (Christopher Reeve); **Superman III**, 1983 (Christopher Reeve); **Superman II**, 1981 (Christopher Reeve); Superman, 1996-2000 (animated TV series; Tim Daly voiceover); The Superman/Aquaman Hour of Adventure, 1967-1968 (TV series; Bud Collyer); The World's Greatest Super Friends, 1979- (animated TV series; Danny Dark voiceover); Young Justice, 2010- (TV series; Nolan North).

Svengali (insidious Hungarian music teacher who uses his hypnotic powers to transform a beautiful model into a singing superstar as depicted in the 1895 novel *Trilby* by George du Maurier): BBC Play of the Month, 1965-1983 (TV series; "Trilby," 1976 episode: Alan Badel); Saturday Playhouse, 1958-1961 (TV series; "Trilby," 1959 episode; Stephen Murray); Studio One in Hollywood, 1948-1958 (TV series; "Trilby," 1950 episode: Arnold Moss); Svengali, 1914 (Ferdinand Bonn); Svengali, 1927 (Paul Wegener); **Svengali**, 1931 (John Barrymore); Svengali, 1955 (Donald Wolfit); Svengali, 1983 (made-for-TV; Peter O'Toole); Three Tales of Terror, 1912 (Paul Askonas); Trilby, 1914 (Herbert Beerbohm Tree); Trilby, 1915 (Wilton Lackaye); Trilby, 1923 (Arthur Edmund Carewe); Trilby, 1947 (made-for-TV; Abraham Sofaer).

Sydney Carton (one of the chief protagonists in the 1859 novel *A Tale of Two Cities* by Charles Dickens): The DuPont Show of the Month, 1957-1961 (TV series; "A Tale of Two Cities," 1958 episode: James Donald); The Only Way, 1927 (John Martin Harvey); The Only Way, 1948 (made-for-TV; Andrew Osborn); The Plymouth Playhouse, 1953 (TV series; "A Tale of Two Cities," two 1953 episodes: Wendell Corey); A Tale of Two Cities, 1917 (William Farnum); **A Tale of Two Cities**, 1935 (Ronald Colman); A Tale of Two Cities, 1957 (TV miniseries; Peter Wyngarde); A Tale of Two Cities, 1958 (Dirk Borgarde); A Tale of Two Cities, 1958 (made-for-TV; John Cameron); A Tale of Two Cities, 1965 (TV series; John Wood); A Tale of Two Cities, 1980 (TV miniseries; Paul Shelley); A Tale of Two Cities, 1980 (made-for-TV; Chris Sarandon); A Tale of Two Cities, 1989 (TV miniseries; James Wilby).

Tarzan (fictional character of a jungle man raised by apes, created by author Edgar Rice Burroughs, 1875-1950, in his 1912 magazine story and subsequent 1914 novel in book form): The Adventures of Tarzan, 1921 (Elmo Lincoln); Adventures of Tarzan, 1985 (Hemant Birje); At Long Last Love, 1975 (Bill Couch); Bons baisers de Tarzan, 1974 (made-for-TV; Luis Rego); **The Death of Tarzan**, 1968 (Rudolf Hrusinsky); Diamonds, 2000 (Val Bisiglio); **Greystoke: The Legend of Tarzan, Lord of the Apes**, 1984 (Christopher Lambert); Green Inferno, 1973 (Richard Yesteran [Jose Luis Ayesteran]); The Hollywood Knights, 1980 (Gary Prendergast); The Journey to Paris, 1999 (Olivier Gourmet); The Legend of Tarzan, 2001-2003 (TV series; Michael T. Weiss voiceover); The New Adventures of Tarzan, 1935 (Herman Brix [Bruce Bennett]); The Revenge of Tarzan, 1920 (Gene Pollar); The Romance of Tarzan, 1920 (Elmo Lincoln); The Son of Tarzan, 1920 (P. Dempsey Tabler); Tansan vs. Tansan, 1963 (Vic Vargas); Tarzan, 1966-1968 (TV series; Ron Ely); Tarzan, 1991-1994 (TV series; Wolf Larson); Tarzan, 2013 (Kellan Lutz voiceover); **Tarzan and His Mate**, 1934 (Johnny Weissmuller); Tarzan and Jane, 2002 (Michael T. Weiss voiceover); Tarzan and Jane Regained...Sort Of, 1964 (Taylor Mead); Tarzan and King Kong, 1965 (Randhava); Tarzan and the Amazons, 1945 (Johnny Weissmuller); Tarzan and the Brown Prince, 1972 (Steve Hawkes); Tarzan and the Golden Lion, 1927 (James Pierce); Tarzan and the Great River, 1967 (Mike Henry); Tarzan and the Huntress, 1947 (Johnny Weissmuller); Tarzan and the Jungle Boy, 1968 (Mike Henry); Tarzan and the Kawana Treasure, 1974 (Richard Yesteran [Jose Luis Ayesteran]); Tarzan and the Leopard Woman, 1946 (Johnny Weissmuller); Tarzan and the Lost City, 1998 (Casper Van Dien); Tarzan and the Lost Safari, 1957 (Gordon Scott); Tarzan and the Mermaids, 1948 (Johnny Weissmuller); Tarzan and the She-Devil, 1953 (Lex Barker); Tarzan and the Slave Girl, 1950 (Lex Barker); Tarzan and the Super 7, 1978-1980 (TV series; Robert Ridgely voiceover); Tarzan and the Trappers, 1960 (made-for-TV; Gordon Scott); Tarzan and the Valley of Gold, 1966 (Mike Henry); Tarzan and the Valley of Lust, 1970 (Duane Prodd); Tarzan Comes to Delhi, 1965 (Dara Singh); Tarzan en la gruta del oro, 1972 (Steve Hawkes); Tarzan en las minas del rey Solomon, 1974 (David Carpenter); **Tarzan Escapes**, 1936 (Johnny Weissmuller); **Tarzan Finds a Son!**, 1939 (Johnny Weissmuller); Tarzan Goes to India, 1962 (Jock Mahoney); Tarzan in Manhattan, 1989 (Joe Lara); Tarzan in Istanbul, 1952 (Tamer Balci); Tarzan, Lord of the Jungle,

1976-1978 (TV series; Robert Ridgely voiceover); **Tarzan of the Apes**, 1918 (Elmo Lincoln); **Tarzan the Ape Man**, 1932 (Johnny Weissmuller); Tarzan the Ape Man, 1959 (Denny Miller); Tarzan the Ape Man, 1981 (Miles O'Keefe); Tarzan: The Epic Adventures, 1996 (TV series; Joe Lara); Tarzan the Fearless, 1933 (Buster Crabbe); Tarzan the Magnificent, 1960 (Gordon Scott); Tarzan the Mighty, 1928 (Frank Merrill); Tarzan the Tiger, 1929 (Frank Merrill); Tarzan Triumphs, 1943 (Johnny Weissmuller); Tarzan's Desert Mystery, 1943 (Johnny Weissmuller); Tarzan's Fight for Life, 1958 (Gordon Scott); **Tarzan's Greatest Adventure**, 1959 (Gordon Scott); Tarzan's Hidden Jungle, 1955 (Gordon Scott); Tarzan's Magic Fountain, 1949 (Lex Barker); Tarzan's New York Adventure, 1942 (Johnny Weissmuller); Tarzan's Peril, 1951 (Lex Barker); Tarzan's Revenge, 1938 (Glenn Morris); Tarzan's Savage Fury, 1952 (Lex Barker); **Tarzan's Secret Treasure**, 1941 (Johnny Weissmuller); **Tarzan's Three Challenges**, 1963 (Jock Mahoney).

Thetis (Greek goddess of water, mother of Achilles): **Clash of the Titans**, 1981 (Maggie Smith); The Temple of Venus, 1923 (Senorita Consuella).

Thief of Bagdad (inventive thief who undergoes wondrous adventures as depicted in the 1924 novel, *The Thief of Bagdad*, by Achmed Abdullah, elements derived from the fables in *One Thousand and One Nights*): The Princess and the Cobbler, 1993 (animated; Ed E. Carroll); **The Thief of Bagdad**, 1924 (Douglas Fairbanks Sr.); **The Thief of Bagdad**, 1940 (Sabu); The Thief of Baghdad, 1961 (Steve Reeves); The Thief of Baghdad, 1978 (made-for-TV; Frank Finlay).

The Tin Man (Tin Woodman; man made of tin that comes alive and becomes a devoted companion to Dorothy, a young girl from Kansas transported to a strange world in L. Frank Baum's iconic 1900 novel, *The Wonderful Wizard of Oz*): Journey Back to Oz, 1972 (animated; Danny Thomas voiceover); The New Wizard of Oz, 1914 (Pierre Couderc); The Wiz, 1978 (Nipsey Russell); The Wizard of Oz, 1925 (Oliver Hardy); **The Wizard of Oz**, 1939 (Jack Haley); The Wizard of Oz, 1982 (animated; John Stocker voiceover); The Wizard of Oz, 1990-1991 (animated TV series; Hal Rayle voiceover); The Wizard of Oz in Concert: Dreams Come True, 1995 (made-for-TV; Roger Daltrey); The Wizard of Oz on Ice, 1996 (made-for-TV; Bob Frank); The Wizard of the Emerald City, 1994 (Evgeny Gerasimov).

Tinker Bell (fictional character, a fairy created by Scottish playwright J.M. Barrie in his 1904 play "Peter Pan, or The Boy Who Wouldn't Grow Up"): The Adventures of Peter Pan, 1989 (TV series; Sumi Shimamato); **Hook**, 1991 (Julia Roberts); Neverland, 2003 (Kari Wahlgren); Peter Pan, 1924 (Virginia Brown Faire); Peter Pan, 2003 (Ludivine Sagnier); Peter Pan and the Pirates, 1990-1991 (TV series; Debi Derryberry).

Tiny Tim (crippled but optimistic young boy, the son of a meek-mannered clerk who slaves for miserly businessman Ebenezer Scrooge in Charles Dickens' 1843 novella, *A Christmas Carol*): The Alcoa Hour, 1955-1957 (TV series; "The Stingiest Man in Town," 1956 episode: Dennis Kohler); **A Christmas Carol**, 1938 (Terry Kilburn); A Chirstmas Carol, 1950 (made-for-TV; Thomas Moore); **A Christmas Carol**, 1951 (Glyn Dearman); A Christmas Carol, 1977 (made-for-TV; Timothy Chasin); A Christmas Carol, 1979 (musical; Kirk Hanson); A Christmas Carol, 1981 (made-for-TV; Tyson Thomas); A Christmas Carol, 1984 (made-for-TV; Anthony Walters); A Christmas Carol, 1999 (made-for-TV; Ben Tibber); A Christmas Carol, 2000 (made-for-TV; Ben Tibber); A Christmas Carol, 2009 (animated; Gary Oldman voiceover); A Christmas Carol, 2015 (Devon Murray-Powell); A Christmas Carol at Ford's Theatre, 1979 (made-for-TV; John Morgal); A Christmas Carol: 50th Anniversary, 2015 (Bradley Bundlie); A Christmas Carol: The Musical, 2004 (made-for-TV; Jacob Moriarty); Dickensian, 2015- (TV series;

Maureen O'Sullivan (as Jane), Cheetah and Johnny Weissmuller (as Tarzan) in *Tarzan and His Mate*, 1934.

Zaak Conway); A Diva's Christmas Carol, 2000 (made-for-TV; Joshua Archambault); Ebenezer, 1998 (made-for-TV; Joshua Silberg); Fireside Theatre, 1949-1955 (TV series; "A Christmas Carol," 1951 episode: Robert Hay-Smith); General Electric Theater, 1953-1962 (TV series; "The Trail to Christmas," 1957 episode: Dennis Holmes); The Gospel according to Scrooge, 1983 (made-for-TV; Melanie Burve); Mr. Magoo's Christmas Carol, 1962 (made-for-TV; Joan Gardner); Mr. Scrooge, 1964 (made-for-TV; Neil Culleton); Mr. Scrooge to See You, 2013 (Matt Koester); Ms. Scrooge, 1997 (made-for-TV; William Greenblatt); **The Muppet Christmas Carol**, 1992 (Jerry Nelson voiceover); The Right to Be Happy, 1916 (Francis [Frankie] Lee); Scrooge, 1935 (Philip Frost); **Scrooge**, 1970 (Richard Beaumont); Scrooge, 1978 (made-for-TV; Colin Graves); Shower of Stars, 1954-1958 (TV series; "A Christmas Carol," 1954 and 1956 episodes; Christopher Cook); The Stingiest Man in Town, 1978 (animated made-for-TV; Bobby Rolofson voiceover).

Tom Canty (character in the children's novel *The Prince and the Pauper*, 1881, by Mark Twain, a boy who exchanges identities with the prince of England, Edward VI): The Adventures of the Prince and the Pauper, 1969 (Barry Pearl); Crossed Swords, 1978 (Mark Lester); The DuPont Show of the Month, 1957-1961 (TV series; "The Prince and the Pauper," 1957 episode: Johnny Washbrook); The Prince and the Pauper, 1915 (Marguerite Clark); The Prince and the Pauper, 1920 (Tibi Lubinszky); **The Prince and the Pauper**, 1937 (Billy Mauch); The Prince and the Pauper, 1943 (Mariya Barabanova); The Prince and the Pauper, 1976 (TV series; Nicholas Lyndhurst); The Prince and the Pauper, 1977 (Mark Lester); The Prince and the Pauper, 1996 (TV series; six episodes: Philip Sarson); The Prince and the Pauper, 2000 (made-for-TV; Robert Timmins); Shirley Temple's Storybook, 1958-1960 (TV series; "The Prince and the Pauper," 1960 episode: Peter Lazer); Walt Disney's Wonderful World of Color, 1954-1992 (TV series; "The Prince and the Pauper: The Pauper King," 1962 episode: John Scully; "The Prince and the Pauper: The Merciful Law of the King," 1962 episode: John Scully; "The Prince and the Pauper: Long Live the Rightful King," 1962 episode: John Scully).

Tom Jones (wild country boy who womanizes his way from the West Country to London in Henry Fielding's 1749 novel): The Bawdy Adventures of Tom Jones, 1976 (Nicky Henson); Tom Jones, 1917 (Langhorn Burton); **Tom Jones**, 1963 (Albert Finney); Tom Jones, 1996 (made-for-TV; Greg Fedderly).

Tom Sawyer (character in the books of Mark Twain): The Adventures of Huckleberry Finn, 1955 (made-for-TV; Robert Hyatt [Bobby Hyatt]); The Adventures of Huckleberry Finn, 1981 (made-for-TV; Dan Mona-

Tweedledee and Tweedledum (Matt Lucas voice for both) in *Alice in Wonderland,* **2010.**

han); **The Adventures of Mark Twain**, 1944 (Michael Miller); The Adventures of Mark Twain, 1985 (Chris Ritchie voiceover); **The Adventures of Tom Sawyer**, 1938 (Tommy Kelly); The Adventures of Tom Sawyer, 1960 (TV series; Fred Smith); The Adventures of Tom Sawyer, 1980 (TV series; Masako Nozawa voiceover); The Adventures of Tom Sawyer, 1986 (Simon Hinton voiceover); The Adventures of Tom Sawyer and Huckleberry Finn, 1982 (made-for-TV; Fyodor Stukov [as Fedya Stukov]); Climax!, 1954-1958 (TV series; "Adventures of Huckleberry Finn," 1955 episode: Robert Hyatt); Aventures de Tom Sawyer, 1953 (TV series; David Jose); Back to Hannibal: The Return of Tom Sawyer and Huckleberry Finn, 1990 (made-for-TV; Raphael Sparge); Huck and Tom, 1918 (Jack Pickford); Huckleberry Finn, 1920 (Gordon Griffith); Huckleberry Finn, 1931 (Jackie Coogan); Huckleberry Finn, 1967 (made-for-TV; Pascal Duffard); Huckleberry Finn and His Friends, 1979-1980 (TV series; Sammy Snyders); Les aventures de Tom Sawyer, 1968 (TV miniseries; Roland Demongeot); The New Adventures of Huckleberry Finn, 1968-1969 (TV series; Kevin Schultz); Huckleberry Finn, 1975 (made-for-TV; Don Most [as Donny Most]); Rascals and Robbers: The Secret Adventures of Tom Sawyer and Huck Finn, 1982 (made-for-TV; Patrick Creadon); Sawyer and Finn, 1983 (made-for-TV; Peter Horton); Shirley Temple's Storybook, 1958-1961 (TV series; "Tom and Huck," 1960 episode: David Ladd); Tom and Huck, 1995 (Jonathan Taylor Thomas); Tom Sawyer, 1917 (Jack Pickford); **Tom Sawyer**, 1930 (Jackie Coogan); Tom Sawyer, Detective, 1938 (Billy Cook); **Tom Sawyer**, 1973 (Johnny Whitaker); Tom Sawyer, 1973 (made-for-TV; Josh Albee); Tom Sawyer, 2011 (Louis Hofmann); Tom Sawyer & Huckleberry Finn, 2015 (Joel Courtney); The United States Steel Hour, 1953-1963 (TV series; "Tom Sawyer," 1956 episode: John Sharpe).

Tom Thumb (five-inch heroic youth created in a 16th-Century fable): Cendre, 2014 (Ray Pan); Elle voit des nains partout!, 1982 (Martin Lamotte); Rugrats, 1990-2006 (TV series; "Rugrats Tales from the Crib: Three Jacks and a Beanstalk," 2006 episode: Don Lake); Snow White: The Sequel, 2007 (Sasha Supera); **Tom Thumb**, 1958 (Russ Tamblyn); Tom Thumb, 1958 (Cesareo Quesadas); Tom Thumb, 1976 (Titoyo); Tom Thumb and Little Red Riding Hood, 1962 (Cesareo Quesadas).

Tonto (fictional Indian sidekick character to the Lone Ranger of the Old West first appearing in a 1933 radio broadcast by Detroit's WXYZ): The Legend of the Lone Ranger, 1952 (Jay Silverheels); The Legend of the Lone Ranger, 1981 (Michael Horse); The Lone Ranger, 1938 (serial; Chief Thundercloud); The Lone Ranger, 1949-1957 (TV series; Jay Silverheels); **The Lone Ranger**, 1956 (Jay Silverheels); The Lone Ranger, 1966-1969 (TV series; Shepard Menken); The Lone Ranger, 2003

(made-for-TV; Nathaniel Arcand); **The Lone Ranger**, 2013 (Johnny Depp); The Lone Ranger Rides Again, 1939 (serial; Chief Thundercloud).

Troilus (Trojan prince, son of Priam, in Greek mythology): Le guerre de Troie n'aura pas lieu, 1967 (made-for-TV; Gerald Robard); Troilus und Cressida, 1964 (made-for-TV; Karl-Heinz Pelzer); Troilus und Cressida, 1966 (made-for-TV; Andrew Murray); Troilus und Cressida, 1969 (made-for-TV; Gerd Seid).

Tweedledee (fictional character from the 1865 novel Alice's Adventures in Wonderland by British author Lewis Carroll): Adventures in Wonderland, 1992-1994 (TV series; Harry Waters Jr.); **Alice in Wonderland**, 1933 (Roscoe Karns); **Alice in Wonderland**, 1951 (J. Pat O'Malley voiceover); Alice in Wonderland, 1955 (made-for-TV; Don Hanmer); Alice in Wonderland, 1982 (made-for-TV; Matthew Brassill); Alice in Wonderland, 1985 (made-for-TV; Eydie Gorme); Alice in Wonderland, 1999 (made-for-TV; George Wendt); **Alice in Wonderland**, 2010 (Matt Lucas); Alice through the Looking Box, 1960 (made-for-TV; Bernie Winters); Alice through the Looking Glass, 1966 (made-for-TV; Dick Smothers); Alice through the Looking Glass, 1973 (made-for-TV; Raymond Mason); Alice through the Looking Glass, 1987 (made-for-TV; Jonathan Winters voiceover); Alice through the Looking Glass, 1998 (made-for-TV; Marc Warren); Alice's Adventures in Wonderland, 1972 (Frank Cox); Alice's Adventures in Wonderland and through the Looking Glass, 1948 (made-for-TV; James Hayter); The Ford Theatre Hour, 1948-1951 (TV series; "Alice in Wonderland," 1950 episode: Biff McGuire); Great Performances, 1971- (TV series; "Alice in Wonderland," 1983 episode: Alan Weeks); Kraft Theatre, 1947-1958 (TV series; "Alice in Wonderland," 1954 episode; Carl White); Once upon a Time in Wonderland, 2013 (TV series; Ben Cotton, Matty Finochio).

Tweedledum (fictional character from the 1865 novel by British author Lewis Carroll): Adventures in Wonderland, 1992-1994 (TV series; Robert Barry Fleming); **Alice in Wonderland**, 1933 (Jack Oakie); **Alice in Wonderland**, 1951 (J. Pat O'Malley voiceover); Alice in Wonderland, 1955 (made-for-TV; Ian Martin); Alice in Wonderland, 1982 (made-for-TV; Gary Costello); Alice in Wonderland, 1985 (made-for-TV; Steve Lawrence); Alice in Wonderland, 1999 (made-for-TV; Robbie Coltrane); **Alice in Wonderland**, 2010 (Matt Lucas); Alice through the Looking Box, 1960 (made-for-TV; Mike Winters); Alice through the Looking Glass, 1966 (made-for-TV; Tom Smothers); Alice through the Looking Glass, 1973 (made-for-TV; Anthony Collin); Alice through the Looking Glass, 1987 (made-for-TV; Jonathan Winters voiceover); Alice through the Looking Glass, 1998 (made-for-TV; Gary Olsen); Alice's Adventures in Wonderland, 1972 (Freddie Cox); Alice's Adventures in Wonderland and through the Looking Glass, 1948 (made-for-TV; Ian Wallace); Great Performances, 1971- (TV series; "Alice in Wonderland," 1983 episode: Andre De Shields); Kraft Theatre, 1947-1958 (TV series; "Alice in Wonderland," 1954 episode; Iggie Wolfington); Once upon a Time in Wonderland, 2013 (TV series; Ben Cotton, Matty Finochio).

Two Face (aka: Harvey Dent; fictional evil character in the Batman series): **Batman Forever**, 1995 (Tommy Lee Jones); Batman Revealed, 2012 (Tim Nugent); Batman: The Animated Series, 1992-1995 (TV series; Richard Moll voiceover); Batman: The Brave and the Bold, 2008-2011 (animated TV series; James Remar voiceover); The New Batman Adventures, 1997-1999 (TV series; Richard Moll voiceover).

Ulysses (aka: Odysseus; hero of Greek mythology): Adventures from the Book of Virtues, 1996-2000 (TV series; "Perseverance," 1997 episode: Mark Harmon); BBC Sunday-Night Theatre, 1950-1959 (TV series; "Troilus and Cressida," 1954 episode: Walter Hudd); Biblioteca di Studio Uno: Odissea, 1964 (made-for-TV; Felice Chiusano); Dante's

Inferno, 2011 (Anthony Alabi voiceover); Der trojanisch krieg findet nicht statt, 1957 (made-for-TV; Wolfgang Priess); Der todiche Schlag, 1975 (made-for-TV; Hannes Messemer); Der trojanisch krieg findet nicht statt, 1964 (made-for-TV; Hannes Messemer); Doctor Who, 1963-1989 (TV series; several episodes: Ivor Salter); Eine Odyssee, 2010 (made-for-TV; Max Nehrig); El viaje de Penelope, 2010 (Glauca); Furkesz tortenetei, 1983 (TV series; four episodes: Tibor Bitskey); Fury of Achilles, 1962 (Piero Lulli); Hector the Mighty, 1972 (Giancarlo Giannini/Andy Luotto voiceover); Helen of Troy, 1924 (Otto Kronburger); Helen of Troy, 1956 (Torin Thatcher); Helen of Troy, 2003 (made-for-TV; Nigel Whitmey); Hercules, 1959 (Gabriele Antonini); Hercules, 1998-1999 (TV series; 1998 and 1999 episodes: Steven Weber); Hercules and the Princess of Troy, 1965 (made-for-TV; Mart Hulswit); Hercules Unchained, 1960 (Gabriele Antonini); Hercules, Samson & Ulysses, 1965 (Enzo Cerusico); Ich log die Wahrheit, 1971 (made-for-TV; Walter Kohut); Il ritorno d'Ulisse in patria, 1980 (Werner Hollweg); Il ritorno d'Ulisse in patria, 1985 (made-for-TV; Thomas Allen); Il ritorno d'Ulisse in patria, 2002 (made-for-TV; Dietrich Henschel); Il ritorno d'Ulisse in patria, 2002 (made-for-TV; Kresimir Spicer); ITV Play of the Week, 1955-1974 (TV series; "Tiger at the Gates," 1960 episode: Charles Gray); Le guerre de Troie n'aura pas lieu, 1967 (made-for-TV; Michel Etcheverry); Le guerre de Troie n'aura pas lieu, 1981 (made-for-TV; Jean Piat); L'odissea, 1991 (made-for-TV; Andrea Roncato); L'odyssee, 2003 (made-for-TV; Francois Papineau); **Mr. Peabody and Sherman**, 2014 (Tom McGrath voiceover); Mythic Warriors, Guardians of the Legend, 1998-2000 (TV series; four episodes: Roger Honeywell); Myths, 2009 (TV series; Jamie Doyle); O Canto das Sereias, 1990 (TV miniseries; Jose de Abreu); Odissea, 1968 (TV miniseries; Bekim Fehmiu); Odysseia sto diadiktio, 2009-2010 (TV series; Dimosthenis Halkiopoulos); Odysseus, 2013 (TV series; eight episodes: Alessio Boni); Odysseus auf Ogygia, 1968 (made-for-TV; Alexander Kerst); Odysseus: Voyage to the Underworld, 2008 (Arnold Vosloo); The Odyssey, 1997 (TV series; Armand Assante); Operazione Odissea, 1999 (made-for-TV; Daniele Liotti); Penelope, 2009 (Frano Maskovic); Penelope oder Die Lorbeemaske, 1959 (made-for-TV; Max Eckard); Penthesilea, 1963 (made-for-TV; Hannsgeorg Laubenthal); Play of the Week, 1959-1961 (TV series; "Tiger at the Gate," 1960 episode: Martin Gabel); The Private Life of Helen of Troy, 1927 (Tom O'Brien); The Return of Ulysses to His Homeland, 1973 (made-for-TV; Benjamin Luxon); Sacrifice to the Wind, 1954 (made-for-TV; John Justin); Seinto Seiya: Tenkai-hen joso—Overture, 2004 (Hiroki Takahashi voiceover); Tantalus: Behind the Mask, 2001 (made-for-TV; Alan Dobie); The Three Stooges Meet Hercules, 1962 (John Cliff); The Time Tunnel, 1966-1967 (TV series; "Revenge of the Gods,' 1966 episode: John Doucette); Troilus & Cressida, 1981 (made-for-TV; Benjamin Whitrow); Troilus und Cressida, 1964 (made-for-TV; Manfred Heidmann); Troilus und Cressida, 1966 (made-for-TV; Derek Seaton); Troilus und Cressida, 1969 (made-for-TV; Arno Assmann); Troilus und Cressida, 1981 (made-for-TV; Benjamin Whitrow); The Trojan Horse, 1962 (John Drew Barrymore); **Troy**, 2004 (Sean Bean); Ulysse est revenu, 1978 (made-for-TV; Maxence Mailfort); **Ulysses**, 1955 (Kirk Douglas); Ulysses against Hercules, 1962 (Georges Marchal); Ulysses 31, 1981-1982 (TV series; twenty-seven episodes: Matt Berman [English version]); Xena: Warrior Princess, 1995-2001 (TV series; "Ulysses," 1997 episode: John D'Aquino).

Uncus (son of Chingachgook, the last living survivor of the extinct Mohican Indian tribe, a branch of the Delaware Indians, a character in James Fenimore Cooper's *Leatherstocking Tales*): Fall of the Mohicans, 1965 (Daniel Martin); **The Last of the Mohicans**, 1920 (Alan Roscoe); The Last of the Mohicans, 1932 (Frank Coghlan Jr.); **The Last of the Mohicans**, 1936 (Phillip Reed); The Last of the Mohicans, 1971 (TV miniseries; Richard Warwick); The Last of the Mohicans, 1975 (animated made-for-TV; Casey Kasem voiceover); Last of the Mohicans, 1977 (made-for-TV; Don Shanks); **The Last of the Mohicans**, 1992

Uma Thurman (as Venus) and Oliver Reed (as Vulcan) in *The Adventures of Baron Munchausen,* **1989.**

(Eric Schweig); Last of the Redmen, 1947 (Rick Vallin).

Uther Pendragon (legendary king of Britain and the father of King Arthur): Camelot, 2011 (TV miniseries; Sebastian Koch); **Excalibur**, 1981 (Gabriel Byrne); Merlin, 1998 (TV miniseries; Mark Jax); The Mists of Avalon, 2001 (made-for-TV; Mark Lewis Jones).

Venus (Roman goddess of love, pleasure, beauty and procreation; Aphrodite in Greek mythology): **The Adventures of Baron Munchausen**, 1989 (Uma Thurman); The Brave and the Bold, 2013 (Sereniti Stewart); Castor et Pollux, 1991 (made-for-TV; Sandrine Piau); Goddess of Love, 1988 (made-for-TV; Vanna White); Hercules in New York, 1970 (Erica Fitz); In Performance, 1978- (TV series; "Orpheus in the Underworld," 1983 episode: Felicity Palmer); The Illiac Passion, 1968 (Tally Brown); Jacques Offenbach: Orpheus in the Underworld, 1997 (made-for-TV; Michele Patzakis); Jason and the Heroes of Mount Olympus, 2001- (animated TV series; Tifanie Christun voiceover); L'odissea, 1991 (made-for-TV; Wendy Windham); Mars: God of War, 1962 (Michele Bailly); Night Life of the Gods, 1935 (Marda Deering); One Touch of Venus, 1948 (Ava Gardner); Orphee aux enfers, 1997 (made-for-TV; Maryline Fallot); Orpheus in der Unterwelt, 1975 (Gisela Bestehorn); Orpheus in der Unterwelt, 2007 (made-for-TV; Urszula Koszut); Romulus and the Sabines, 1961 (Rosanna Schiaffino); The Temple of Venus, 1923 (Celeste Lee); The Tinted Venus, 1921 (Maud Cressall); The Triumph of Venus, 1918 (Betty Lee); Vamping Venus, 1928 (Thelma Todd).

Vulcan (Roman god of fire, volcanoes and forging of iron; Hephaestus in Greek mythology): **The Adventures of Baron Munchausen**, 1989 (Oliver Reed); **Clash of the Titans**, 1981 (Pat Roach); Goddess of Love, 1988 (made-for-TV; Sid Haig); The Triumph of Venus, 1918 (Percy Standing); Vamping Venus, 1928 (Fred O'Beck); Vulcan, Son of Giove, 1962 (Rod Flash); Young Hercules, 1998-1999 (TV series; Jason Hoyte).

Walrus (fictional character from the 1865 novel Alice's Adventures in Wonderland by British author Lewis Carroll): Adventures in Wonderland, 1992-1994 (TV series; Ken Page); Alice, 2009 (TV miniseries; David "Squatch" Ward); **Alice in Wonderland**, 1951 (J. Pat O'Malley voiceover); Alice in Wonderland, 1955 (made-for-TV; Mark Breaux); Alice in Wonderland, 1982 (made-for-TV; Tucker McCrady); Alice in Wonderland, 1985 (made-for-TV; Karl Malden); Alice in Wonderland, 1999 (made-for-TV; Peter Ustinov); Alice through the Looking Box, 1960 (made-for-TV; Glen Melville); Alice through the Looking Glass, 1973 (made-for-TV; Bruce Purchase); Alice through the Looking Glass, 1998 (made-for-TV; Brian Gilks).

Margaret Hamilton (as the Wicked Witch), melting in *The Wizard of Oz*, 1939.

White King (fictional character from the 1865 novel Alice's Adventures in Wonderland by British author Lewis Carroll): **Alice in Wonderland**, 1933 (Ford Sterling); Alice in Wonderland, 1982 (made-for-TV; Stephen Boe); Alice in Wonderland, 1985 (made-for-TV; Harvey Korman); Alice through the Looking Glass, 1966 (made-for-TV; Ricardo Montalban); Alice through the Looking Glass, 1973 (made-for-TV; Richard Pearson); Alice through the Looking Glass, 1987 (made-for-TV; Alan Dinehart voiceover); Alice through the Looking Glass, 1998 (made-for-TV; Geoffrey Palmer); Alice's Adventures in Wonderland and through the Looking Glass, 1948 (made-for-TV; Harold Scott).

White Knight (fictional character from the 1865 novel by Alice's Adventures in Wonderland British author Lewis Carroll): Alice, 2009 (TV miniseries; Matt Frewer); **Alice in Wonderland**, 1933 (Gary Cooper); Alice in Wonderland, 1955 (made-for-TV; Reginald Gardiner); Alice in Wonderland, 1982 (made-for-TV; Stephen Boe); Alice in Wonderland, 1985 (made-for-TV; Lloyd Bridges); Alice in Wonderland, 1999 (made-for-TV; Christopher Lloyd); Alice in Wonderland or What's a Nice Kid Like You Doing in a Place Like This?, 1966 (animated made-for-TV; Bill Dana); Alice through the Looking Glass, 1973 (made-for-TV; Geoffrey Bayldon); Alice through the Looking Glass, 1987 (made-for-TV; Alan Young voiceover); Alice through the Looking Glass, 1998 (made-for-TV; Ian Holm); Alice's Adventures in Wonderland and through the Looking Glass, 1948 (made-for-TV; Anthony Sharp); Great Performances, 1971- (TV series; "Alice in Wonderland," 1983 episode; Richard Burton); Kraft Theatre, 1947-1958 (TV series; "Alice in Wonderland," 1954 episode; Ernest Truex); Once upon a Time in Wonderland, 2013 (TV series; Ben Wilkinson).

White Queen (fictional character from the 1865 novel Alice's Adventures in Wonderland by British author Lewis Carroll): **Alice in Wonderland**, 1933 (Louise Fazenda); Alice in Wonderland, 1955 (made-for-TV; Eva Le Gallienne); Alice in Wonderland, 1985 (made-for-TV; Carol Channing); **Alice in Wonderland**, 2010 (Anne Hathaway); Alice through the Looking Glass, 1966 (made-for-TV; Nanette Fabray); Alice through the Looking Glass, 1973 (made-for-TV; Brenda Bruce); Alice through the Looking Glass, 1987 (made-for-TV; Phyllis Diller voiceover); Alice through the Looking Glass, 1998 (made-for-TV; Penelope Wilton); Alice's Adventures in Wonderland and through the Looking Glass, 1948 (made-for-TV; Ann Codrington); Great Performances, 1971- (TV series; "Alice in Wonderland," 1983 episode: Maureen Stapleton).

White Rabbit (fictional character from the 1865 novel Alice's Adventures in Wonderland by British author Lewis Carroll): Adventures in

Wonderland, 1992-1994 (TV series; Patrick Richwood); Alice, 2009 (TV miniseries; Alan Gray); Alice in Wonderland, 1915 (Herbert Rice); Alice in Wonderland, 1931 (Ralph Hertz); **Alice in Wonderland**, 1933 (Skeets Gallagher); Alice in Wonderland, 1949 (Ernest Milton voiceover); **Alice in Wonderland**, 1951 (Bill Thompson voiceover); Alice in Wonderland, 1955 (made-for-TV; Martyn Green); Alice in Wonderland, 1966 (made-for-TV; Wilfred Brambell); Alice in Wonderland, 1976 (Carlos Lorca); Alice in Wonderland, 1982 (made-for-TV; Wendy Lehr); Alice in Wonderland, 1985 (made-for-TV; Red Buttons); Alice in Wonderland, 1985 (TV series; Paul Eddington); Alice in Wonderland, 1986 (made-for-TV; four 30-minute segments; Jonathan Cecil); Alice in Wonderland, 1999 (made-for-TV; Kiran Shah; Richard Coombs voiceover); **Alice in Wonderland**, 2010 (Michael Sheen); Alice in Wonderland or What's a Nice Kid Like You Doing in a Place Like This?, 1966 (animated made-for-TV; Howard Morris); Alice through the Looking Box, 1960 (made-for-TV; Spike Milligan); Alice's Adventures in Wonderland, 1956 (made-for-TV; Michael Segal); Alice's Adventures in Wonderland, 1972 (Michael Crawford); Alice's Adventures in Wonderland, 2011 (made-for-TV; Edward Watson); Alice's Adventures in Wonderland and through the Looking Glass, 1948 (made-for-TV; Roddy Hughes); Great Performances, 1971- (TV series; "Alice in Wonderland," 1983 episode: Austin Pendleton); Kraft Theatre, 1947-1958 (TV series; "Alice in Wonderland," 1954 episode: Joseph Walsh); Once upon a Time in Wonderland, 2013 (TV series; John Lithgow); Unsuk Chin: Alice in Wonderland, 2007 (Andrew Watts).

Wicked Witch of the West (evil witch who attempts to acquire the magic slippers worn by Dorothy, a young girl from Kansas transported to a strange world in L. Frank Baum's iconic 1900 novel, *The Wonderful Wizard of Oz*): Journey Back to Oz, 1972 (animated; Ethel Merman voiceover); The Muppets' Wizard of Oz, 2005 (Eric Jacobson as Miss Piggy voiceover); **Oz the Great and Powerful**, 2013 (Mila Kunis); The Wiz, 1978 (Mabel King); **The Wizard of Oz**, 1939 (Margaret Hamilton); The Wizard of Oz, 1982 (animated; Elizabeth Hanna voiceover); The Wizard of Oz, 1990-1991 (animated TV series; Tress MacNeille voiceover); The Wizard of Oz in Concert: Dreams Come True, 1995 (made-for-TV; Debra Winger).

Will Scarlet (fictional character and follower of Robin Hood): **The Adventures of Robin Hood**, 1938 (Patric Knowles); The Adventures of Robin Hood, 1955-1960 (TV series; Paul Eddington; Ronald Howard); The Bandit of Sherwood Forest, 1946 (John Abbott); Beyond Sherwood Forest, 2009 (made-for-TV; Richard de Klerk); A Challenge for Robin Hood, 1968 (Douglas Mitchell); Il Magnifico Robin Hood, 1970 (Luciano Conti); The Legend of Robin Hood, 1968- (TV series; Harvey Jason); The Legend of Robin Hood, 1975 (TV miniseries; Miles Anderson); Long Live Robin Hood, 1971 (Manuel Zarzo); The Men of Sherwood Forest, 1954 (John Van Eyssen); NBC Children's Theatre, 1963-1973 (TV series; "Robin Hood," 1964 episode: Joey Trent); Prince of Thieves, 1948 (Syd Saylor); **Robin Hood**, 2010 (Scott Grimes); **Robin and Marian**, 1976 (Denholm Elliott); **Robin Hood**, 1922 (Maine [Bud] Geary); Robin Hood, 1953- (TV miniseries; Philip Guard); Robin Hood, 1984-1986 (TV series; Ray Winstone); Robin Hood, 1991 (Owen Teale); Robin Hood, 2006-2009 (TV series; Harry Lloyd); Robin Hood: Ghosts of Sherwood 3D, 2012 (Dennis Zachmann); **Robin Hood: Men in Tights**, 1993 (Matthew Porretta); **Robin Hood: Prince of Thieves**, 1991 (Christian Slater); Rogues of Sherwood Forest, 1950 (Billy Bevan); Son of Robin Hood, 1959 (Jack Lambert); **The Story of Robin Hood** [aka: The Story of Robin Hood and His Merrie Men], 1952 (Anthony Forwood); Tales of Robin Hood, 1951 (Robert Bice); Young Robin Hood, 1991-1992 (animated TV series; Sonja Ball voiceover).

The Wizard of Oz (a shifty, palavering charlatan, who pretends to be an all-powerful wizard and who is challenged by Dorothy, a young girl from Kansas transported to a strange world in L. Frank Baum's iconic 1900 novel, *The Wonderful Wizard of Oz*): Journey Back to Oz, 1972 (animated; Bill Cosby voiceover); The Muppets' Wizard of Oz, 2005 (Jeffrey Tambor); The New Wizard of Oz, 1914 (J. Charles Haydon); **Oz the Great and Powerful**, 2013 (James Franco); 20th Century Oz, 1976 (Graham Matters); The Wiz, 1978 (Richard Pryor); The Wizard of Oz, 1925 (Charles Murray); **The Wizard of Oz**, 1939 (Frank Morgan); The Wizard of Oz, 1982 (animated; Lorne Greene voiceover); The Wizard of Oz, 1990-1991 (animated TV series; Alan Oppenheimer voiceover); The Wizard of Oz in Concert: Dreams Come True, 1995 (made-for-TV; Joel Grey); The Wizard of Oz on Ice, 1996 (made-for-TV; Bobby McFerrin); The Wizard of the Emerald City, 1994 (Viktor Pavlov).

Wolf Larsen (sea captain with a superman complex depicted in Jack London's 1904 novel, *The Sea Wolf*): Barricade, 1950 (Raymond Massey); Legend of the Sea Wolf, 1978 (Chuck Connors); The Sea Wolf, 1913 (Hobart Bosworth); The Sea Wolf, 1920 (Noah Beery); The Sea Wolf, 1926 (Ralph Ince); The Sea Wolf, 1930 (Milton Sills); **The Sea Wolf**, 1941 (Edward G. Robinson); The Sea Wolf, 1990- (TV series; Liubomiras Laucevicius); The Sea Wolf, 1993 (made-for-TV; Charles Bronson); The Sea Wolf, 2008 (made-for-TV; Thomas Kretschmann); Sea Wolf, 2009 (TV miniseries; Sebastian Koch); The Seawolf, 1971 (TV miniseries; Raimund Harmstorf); Wolf Larsen, 1958 (Barry Sullivan).

Wolf Man (Lawrence Talbot, a fictional character afflicted by lycanthropy that transforms him into a werewolf): **Abbott and Costello Meet Frankenstein**, 1948 (Lon Chaney Jr.); Frankenstein and the Werewolf Reborn!, 2005 (Robin Downes); **Frankenstein Meets the Wolf Man**, 1943 (Lon Chaney Jr.); Frankenstein's Aunt, 1987 (TV series; Flavio Bucci); **House of Dracula**, 1945 (Lon Chaney Jr.); **The House of Frankenstein**, 1944 (Lon Chaney Jr.); House of the Wolf Man, 2009 (Billy Bussey); Monster Brawl, 2011 (R. J. Skinner); Monster Squad, 1976 (TV series; Buck Kartalian); Transylvania 6-5000, 1985 (Donald Gibbs); **The Wolf Man**, 1941 (Lon Chaney Jr.); The Wolf Man, 2010 (Benicio Del Toro).

Wonder Woman (aka: Diana Prince; fictional comic book superhero character): The All-New Super Friends Hour, 1977-1978 (animated TV series; Shannon Farnon voiceover); Batman: The Brave and the Bold, 2008-2011 (animated TV series; Vicki Lewis voiceover); Challenge of the Super Friends, 1978- (animated TV series; Shannon Farnon voiceover); Heroes Crossing, 2010 (Tere Lee); Justice League, 2001-2006 (TV series; Susan Eisenberg voiceover); **The Lego Movie**, 2014 (Cobie Smulders voiceover); Super Friends, 1973-2011 (animated TV series; Shannon Farnon voiceover); Super Friends, 1980-1983 (animated TV series; Shannon Farnon voiceover); Super Friends: The Legendary Super Powers Show, 1984- (animated TV series; Constance Cawlfield voiceover); The Super Powers Team: Galactic Guardians, 1985- (animated TV series; B.J. Ward voiceover); Superman, 1988 (animated TV series; Mary McDonald-Lewis voiceover); Wonder Woman, 1974 (made-for-TV; Cathy Lee Crosby); Wonder Woman, 1975-1979 (TV series; Lynda Carter); Wonder Woman, 2013- (animated TV series; Susan Eisenberg voiceover); The World's Greatest Super Friends, 1979- (animated TV series; Shannon Farnon voiceover).

Woody (animated cowboy doll character): **Toy Story**, 1995 (Tom Hanks voiceover); **Toy Story 3**, 2010 (Tom Hanks voiceover); **Toy Story 2**, 1999 (Tom Hanks voiceover).

Zaroff (Count Zaroff, an insane Cossack aristocrat who rules a remote island and hunts human beings to the death for sport, as depicted in the1924 short story "The Most Dangerous Game" [aka: "The Hounds of Zaroff"] by Richard Connell): A Game of Death, 1945 (Edgar Barrier

Laurence Olivier (as Zeus) in *Clash of the Titans*, 1981.

as Erich Kreiger); Johnny Allegro, 1949 (role model for George Macready); Kill or Be Killed, 1950 (role model for George Coulouris); **The Most Dangerous Game**, 1932 (Leslie Banks); The Most Dangerous Game, 2015 (Eric Etebari); **Run for the Sun**, 1956 (Trevor Howard as Browne); To Kill a Clown, 1972 (role model for Alan Alda).

Zeus (father of the gods residing on Mount Olympus in Greek mythology; Jupiter in Roman mythology): The Adventures of Hercules II, 1985 (Claudio Cassinelli): Biblioteca di Studio Uno: Odissea, 1964 (made-for-TV; Umberto D'Orsi); **Clash of the Titans**, 1981 (Laurence Olivier); **Clash of the Titans**, 2010 (Liam Neeson); Conan the Destroyer, 1984 (Matt Conner); The Enchanted Castle, 1979- (TV series; "Feast of Magic," 1979 episode: Alastair Hunter); Goddess of Love, 1988 (made-for-TV; John Rhys-Davies); Hercules, 1983 (Claudio Cassinella); **Hercules**, 1997 (Rip Torn voiceover); Hercules, 1998-1999 (TV series; Corey Burton voiceover); Hercules and the Amazon Women, 1994 (made-for-TV; Anthony Quinn); Hercules in New York, 1970 (Ernest Graves); Hercules in the Maze of the Minotaur, 1994 (made-for-TV; Anthony Quinn); Hercules in the Underworld, 1994 (made-for-TV; Anthony Quinn); Hercules: The Brave and the Bold, 2013 (Brayden Patterson); Hercules: The Legendary Journeys—Hercules and the Circle of Fire, 1994 (made-for-TV; Anthony Quinn); Hercules: The Legendary Journeys—Hercules and the Lost Kingdom, 1994 (made-for-TV; Anthony Quinn); The Illiac Passion, 1968 (Paul Swan); Immortals, 2011 (Luke Evans); **Jason and the Argonauts**, 1963 (Niall MacGinnis); Jason and the Argonauts, 2000 (TV miniseries; Angus Macfayden); Mighty Aphrodite, 1995 (Kent Blocher voiceover); The Mighty Hercules, 1963-1966 (TV series; Jimmy Tapp voiceover); Mythic Warriors: Guardians of the Legend, 1998- (TV series; Gary Krawford); Myths, 2009- (TV series; Josh Bowman); Percy Jackson & the Olympians: The Lightning Thief, 2010 (Sean Bean); Persephone, 1952 (made-for-TV; Noel Carey); The Temple of Venus, 1923 (Frank Keller); The Thracian Horses, 1946 (made-for-TV; Rupert Davies); Ulysses 31, 1981-1982 (TV series; Vlasta Vrana); Wondrous Myths & Legends, 1999- (TV series; Ian James Corlett); Wrath of the Titans, 2012 (Liam Neeson).

GREAT LAST LINES

Note: The following annotated index, exclusively created by the author, offers some of the great last lines delivered in theatrically released feature films (chiefly U.S. and British releases, along with notable foreign productions, showing U.S. year of release). All titles shown in boldface represent entries profiled in this work.

Above Suspicion, 1943: Fred MacMurray (after he and wife Joan Crawford escape Nazis in Bavarian Alps and are about to enter Italy): "Well, how about some spaghetti?"

The Adventures of Don Juan, 1948; Errol Flynn: "My dear friend, there's a little bit of Don Juan in every man, but since I am Don Juan, there must be more of it in me."

The Adventures of Robin Hood, 1938; Errol Flynn (to Ian Hunter, playing King Richard the Lionheart of England, who has ordered Flynn to marry Maid Marian): "May I obey all your commands with equal pleasure, Sire!"

Alien, 1979; Sigourney Weaver (recording her final report just before getting into a hibernation chamber on a small spacecraft with her cat after battling a deadly alien monster on a distant planet): "Final report of the commercial starship *Nostromo*. Third officer reporting. The other members of the crew—Kane, Lambert, Parker, Brett, Ash, and Captain Dallas—are dead. Cargo and ship destroyed. I should reach the frontier in about six weeks. With a little luck, the network will pick me up. This is Ripley, last survivor of the *Nostromo*, signing off. Come on, cat."

Amelia, 2009; Hilary Swank (as Amelia Earhart; voiceover): "All the things I never said for so very long, look up, they're in my eyes. Everyone has oceans to fly, as long as you have the heart to do it. Is it reckless? Maybe. But what do dreams know of boundaries? I think about the hands that I have held, the places I've seen, the vast lands whose dirt is caked on the bottom of my shoes. The world has changed me."

Angels with Dirty Faces, 1938; Pat O'Brien (as a priest to street boys who have idolized a gangster just put to death in the electric chair and who was O'Brien's boyhood friend, and who, in their youth, had been captured by police and set on a path of crime while O'Brien escaped): "Let's go and say a prayer for a boy who couldn't run as fast as I could."

Annie Hall, 1977; Woody Allen: (describing his ended up-and-down relationship with Diane Keaton, the girl of the title name): "But it was great seeing Annie again…and I thought about that old joke, you know…this guy goes to a psychiatrist and says 'Doc, my brother's crazy. He thinks he's a chicken.' And the doctor says 'Well, why don't you turn him in.' And the guys says 'I would, but I need the eggs.' Well, I guess that's pretty much now how I feel about relationships. You know, they're totally irrational and crazy and absurd, but I guess we keep going through it…because…most of us need the eggs."

The Apartment, 1960; Shirley MacLaine (to Jack Lemmon, who had declared his love for her and before they play cards): "Shut up and deal."

Apollo 13, 1995; Tom Hanks (as Jim Lovell, narrating): "And, as for me, the seven extraordinary days of Apollo 13 were my last in space. I watched other men walk on the moon and return safely, all from the confines of Mission Control, or our house in Houston. I sometimes catch myself looking at the moon, remembering our changes of fortune in our long voyage, thinking of the thousands of people who worked to bring the three of us home. I look up at the moon and wonder: When will we be going back, and who will that be?"

Arsenic and Old Lace, 1944; Garry Owen (frustrated cab driver who has waited hours for a fare outside of a house where darkly comedic murder and mayhem has occurred): "I'm not a cab driver. I'm a coffeepot!"

The Assassination of Jesse James by the Coward Robert Ford, 2007; Narrator: "There would be no eulogies for Bob. No photographs of his body would be sold in sundries stores, no people would crowd the streets in the rain to see his funeral cortege, no biographies would be written about him, no children named after him, no one would ever pay twenty-five cents to stand in the room he grew up in. The shotgun would ignite, Ella Mae would scream, but Robert Ford would only lay on the floor and look at the ceiling, the light going out of his eyes before he could find the right words."

The Aviator, 2004; Leonardo DiCaprio (as Howard Hughes): "The way of the future…The Way of the future…The way of the future…"

Bananas, 1971; Howard Cossell (sports commentator describing the bedroom antics of wacky comedian Woody Allen and wife Louise Lasser as if covering an important sports event): "It's hard to tell what may happen in the future. But they may live happily ever after. Again, they may not. Be assured of this, though. Wherever the action is, we will be there with ABC's Wild World of Sports to cover it. Now, on behalf of Nancy and Fielding Mellish and all the others who have made this possible, this is Howard Cossell thanking you for joining us and wishing you a most pleasant good night."

Bataan, 1943; Robert Taylor (the last survivor of a small U.S. infantry unit in the Philippines in WWII, who has dug his own grave next to those of his men and is firing at advancing Japanese troops with a machine gun): "Come and get it!…We're still here!…We'll always be here!…"

Bell, Book and Candle, 1958; Kim Novak (having lost her powers as a witch by falling in love with James Stewart, who asks her to stop crying): "I don't think I can. I am only human."

The Best Years of Our Lives, 1946; Dana Andrews (former WWII Army Air Force officer struggling to adjust to civilian life while proposing to Teresa Wright, the woman he loves): "You know what it will be, Peggy. It may take us years to get anywhere. We'll have no money, no decent place to live. We'll have to work—get kicked around."

The Big Carnival (aka: Ace in the Hole), 1951; Kirk Douglas (as an opportunistic newspaperman): "I'm a thousand-dollar-a-day newspaperman. You can have me for nothing."

The Big Sleep, 1946; Humphrey Bogart: "What's wrong with you?"; Lauren Bacall: "Nothing you can't fix."

The Birth of a Nation, 1915; title card written by director D.W. Griffith: "Liberty and Union, one and inseparable, now and forever!"

Blade Runner, 1982; Harrison Ford (a futuristic police detective talking about the android woman he loves): "Tyrell had told me that Rachel was special: no termination date. I didn't know how long we had together. Who does?"

Blood on the Sun, 1945; James Cagney (as a U.S. journalist in pre-WWII Tokyo, who has discovered the Tanaka Plan that reveals Japan's secret schedule for world domination): "Sure, forgive your enemies. But first, get even."

Bolero, 1934; William Frawley (holding George Raft, who has just died of a heart attack in a nightclub after dancing a frantic Bolero): "He was too good for this joint!"

The Bourne Legacy, 2012; Rachel Weisz (as Dr. Marta Shearing): "Are we lost?"; Jeremy Renner (as Aaron Cross): "No, I was just looking at our options."; Weisz: "Oh, I was kind of hoping we were lost."

Boys Town, 1938; Spencer Tracy (as Father Edward Joseph Flanagan, founder of the orphanage called Boys Town in Douglas County, Nebraska): "This is no bad boy."

Braveheart, 1995; Narrator: "In the year of our Lord 1314, patriots of Scotland, starving and outnumbered, charged the fields of Bannockburn. They fought like warrior poets. They fought like Scotsmen and won their freedom."

The Bridges at Toko-Ri, 1954; Fredric March (as an admiral on board an aircraft carrier during the Korean War): "Where do we get such men? They leave this ship and they do their job. Then they must find this speck somewhere lost on the sea. When they find it, they have to land on its pitching deck. Where do we get such men?" Voice on loudspeaker: "Launch jets!"

Brother Orchid, 1940; Edward G. Robinson (a former gangster who has become a monk in a monastery): "This…this is the real class!"

Butch Cassidy and the Sundance Kid, 1969; Paul Newman (as Cassidy, to Robert Redford as Sundance when they are pinned down by hundreds of police and troops in a Bolivian village and are about to be killed but Redford has told Newman that famed U.S. lawman Joe Lefors is not present among their attackers): "Oh, good. For a moment there, I thought we were in trouble."

Cabaret, 1972; Joel Grey (master of ceremonies at the Kit-Kat Club in Berlin, which is now controlled by Nazi storm troopers): "Ladies and gentlemen, where are your troubles now? Forgotten? I told you so. We have no troubles here. Here, life is beautiful. The girls are beautiful. Even the orchestra is beautiful. *Auf wiedersehen*! *A bientot*!"

The Cabinet of Dr. Caligari, 1921; title card (about a killer somnambulist): "I think I know how to cure him now."

Caddyshack, 1980; Rodney Dangerfield: "Hey, everybody! We're gonna get laid!"

The Candidate, 1972; Robert Redford (an attractive but utterly shallow politician who has been elected to the U.S. Senate from California after a driving, insidious and manipulative campaign and who has no idea of what his new post entails or the reason why he has run for office): "What do we do now?"

Cape Fear, 1962; Gregory Peck (to Robert Mitchum, a sadistic killer who has menaced Peck and his family and who has been captured by Peck): "You're going to live a long life—in a cage! That's where you belong. And that's where you're going. And this time, for life! Bang your head against the walls! Count the years, the months, the hours until the day you rot!"

Casablanca, 1942: Humphrey Bogart (to Claude Rains, the police prefect who has shielded Bogart and who must now both flee to a Free French garrison): "Louis, I think this is the beginning of a beautiful friendship."

Champion, 1949; Arthur Kennedy (generously white-washing his cor-

rupt prizefighting brother, who has just died of injuries in the ring): "I'll give you a statement…He was a champion. He went out like a champion. He was a credit to the fight game…to the very end."

Charlotte's Web, 1973; (narration): "Wilbur never forgot Charlotte. Although he loved her children and grandchildren dearly, none of the new spiders ever quite took her place in his heart. She was in a class by herself. It's not often when someone comes along who is a true friend and a good writer. Charlotte was both."

A Christmas Carol, 1938; Reginald Owen [as Scrooge]: "God bless us, every one!"

City Lights, 1931; title card: "Yes, I can see now."

Clash of the Titans, 1981; Laurence Olivier (as Zeus on Mount Olympus): "As long as man shall walk on earth and search the night sky in wonder, they will remember the courage of Perseus forever. Even if we, the gods, are abandoned, or forgotten, the stars will never fade, never. They will burn to the end of time."

The Curious Case of Benjamin Button, 2008; Brad Pitt (as Benjamin Button): "Some people are born to sit by a river. Some get struck by lightning. Some have an ear for music. Some are artists. Some swim. Some know buttons. Some know Shakespeare. Some are mothers. And some people dance."

The Dark Knight, 2008; Gary Oldman (as Lt. James Gordon): "Because he's the hero Gotham deserves, but not the one it needs right now. So, we'll hunt him because he can take it, because he's not our hero. He's a silent guardian, a watchful protector, a dark knight."

Desperate Journey, 1942; Errol Flynn (escaping Germany in a stolen enemy plane during WWII): "Now for Australia and a crack at those Japs!"

Detour, 1945; Tom Neal (though innocent, wanted and on the run for the murder of a scheming woman that inveigled him into crime): "Yes, fate or some mysterious force can put the finger on you and me for no good reason at all."

Dinner at Eight, 1933; Marie Dressler: "Oh, my dear, that's something you need never to worry about."

D.O.A., 1950; Roy Engel (a police captain to whom Edmond O'Brien tells how he has been fatally poisoned by a stealthy murderer, and, after O'Brien collapses dead in the police office, Engel tells a subordinate how to make out the report): "Better make it 'Dead on Arrival.'"

Dr. Strangelove…1964; Peter Sellers (as a deformed former Nazi scientist, one of three characters he plays, and where he finally leaves his wheelchair, to say to the U.S. President, whom he also plays): "Mein Fuehrer, I can walk!"

Dracula's Daughter, 1936; Edward Van Sloan: "She was beautiful when she died…a hundred years ago."

Edison: The Man, 1940; Spencer Tracy [as Thomas Alva Edison]: "What man's mind can conceive, man's character can control. Man must learn that, and then we needn't be afraid of tomorrow. And man will go forward toward more light."

Foreign Correspondent, 1940; Joel McCrea (a newspaper correspondent broadcasting from London, England, as the city is under a bombing attack by German planes): "I can't read the rest of this speech because the lights have gone out, so I'll just have to talk off the cuff. All that noise you hear isn't static. It's death coming to London. Yes, they're coming here now. You can hear the bombs falling on the streets and homes. Don't tune me out—hang on—this is a big story, and you're part of it. It's too late now to do anything except to stand in the dark and let them come. It feels as if the lights are all out everywhere except in America. Keep those lights burning. Cover them with steel! Ring them with guns! Build a canopy of battleships and bombing planes around them! Hello, America! Hang on to your lights! They're the only lights left in the world!"

The Front Page, 1931 and its 1974 remake; Adolphe Menjou and Walter Matthau (playing the scheming editor of a Chicago newspaper and who has given his watch as a memento to his prized reporter leaving town to be married and whom he schemes to have back on his staff by having that reporter arrested when calling police to make the following report): "The son-of-a-bitch stole my watch!"

Gandhi, 1982; Ben Kingsley (as Gandhi): "When I despair, I remember that all through history the way of truth and love has always won. There have been tyrants and murderers, and, for a time, they can seem invincible, but, in the end, they always fail. Think of it. Always."

Giant, 1956; Rock Hudson (to wife Elizabeth Taylor): "You want to know something, Leslie. If I live to be ninety, I'm never gonna be able to figure you out."

Golden Boy, 1939; William Holden: "Papa, I've come home!"

Gone with the Wind, 1939; Clark Gable (as Rhett Butler): "Frankly, my dear, I don't give a damn."; Vivien Leigh (as Scarlett O'Hara): "Well, tomorrow *is* another day!"

The Good Earth, 1937; Paul Muni: "O-Lan, you are the earth!"

Good Night and Good Luck, 2005; David Strathairn (as Edward R. Murrow): "Good night and good luck."

The Goodbye Girl, 1977; (over the phone as Marsha Mason learns that her room renter actor Richard Dreyfuss loves her and is returning to her and while she retrieves the guitar he has left behind, asking her to restring it and while she holds it, crying, and telling him that she loves him): Richard Dreyfuss: "Never mind that. You're rusting my guitar."

Goodfellas, 1990; Ray Liotta (voiceover, sourly commenting on his mundane life in the witness protection program): "Today, everything is different. There's no action. I have to wait around like everyone else. Can't even get decent food. Right after I got here, I ordered some spaghetti with marinara sauce and I got egg noodles and ketchup. I'm an average nobody. I get to live the rest of my life like a schnook."

Grand Hotel, 1932; Lewis Stone (hotel physician, who is oblivious to the dramatic events that have just occurred at the hotel): "Grand Hotel... always the same...people come, people go...nothing ever happens... Grand Hotel."

The Grapes of Wrath, 1940; Jane Darwell (as Ma Joad, head of an Okie family that has survived innumerable hardships in the Great Depression): "That's what makes us tough. Rich fellas come up and they die, and their kids ain't no good, and they die out. Bet we keep a-coming. We're the people that live. They can't wipe us out. They can't lick us. And we'll go on forever, Pa, 'cause we're the people!"

The Great Gatsby, 2013; Tobey Maguire (as Nick Carraway, voiceover): "I remembered how we'd all come to Gatsby's and guessed

at his corruption, while he stood before us concealing his incorruptible dream. The moon rose higher and, as I stood there brooding on the old unknown world, I thought of Gatsby's wonder when he first picked out the green light at the end of Daisy's dock. He had come such a long way, and his dream must have seemed so close that he could hardly fail to grasp it. But he did not know that it was already behind him. Gatsby believed in the green light, the orgastic future that year by year recedes before us. It eluded us then, but that's no matter. Tomorrow we will run faster, stretch out our arms farther...And then one fine morning...So we beat on, boats against the current, borne back ceaselessly into the past."

The Great Ziegfeld, 1936; William Powell (as dying showman Florenz Ziegfeld): "I've got to have more steps. I need more steps. I've got to get higher...higher!"

A Guy Named Joe, 1943; Spencer Tracy (as the spirit of a dead American pilot who has become the temporary guardian angel of the woman he loved on earth and the young man who has replaced him in her heart): "That's my girl...and that's my boy."

High Society, 1956; Louis "Satchmo" Armstrong: "End of story."

The Horn Blows at Midnight, 1945; Jack Benny (a horn player who falls from his chair on a bandstand after dreaming that he was an angel ordered to blow Gabriel's horn to end the world): "Elizabeth, I just had the craziest dream. You know, if you saw it in the movies, you'd never believe it."

The Hucksters, 1947; Clark Gable (to Deborah Kerr after walking out on a high-paying advertising job): "Now we're starting out with an even nothing in the world. It's neater that way."

The Hunchback of Notre Dame, 1939; Charles Laughton (as Quasimodo while sitting next to a stone gargoyle in one of the church towers): "Why was I not made of stone like thee?"

The Hurricane, 1937; Raymond Massey (the French governor of an island obliterated by a hurricane, who sees through his telescope a wanted native fleeing with his family far out to sea, but, because the native has saved his wife's life, abandons all notions of pursuit and capture, with a benevolently lying statement to his wife, Mary Astor): "Yes, it's only a floating log."

I Am a Fugitive from a Chain Gang, 1932; Paul Muni (as he retreats into darkness from the woman he loves): "I steal!"

In a Lonely Place, 1950; Gloria Grahame (after ending her affair with a tempestuous writer): "I lived a few weeks while you loved me. Goodbye, Dix."

The Incredible Shrinking Man, 1957; Grant Williams (narration): "All this vast majesty of creation, it had to mean something. And then I meant something, too. Yes, smaller than the smallest, I meant something, too. To God there is no zero. I still exist!"

Indiscreet, 1958; Cary Grant to Ingrid Bergman, who accepts his proposal and is crying: "Don't cry, Anna. I love you. Everything will be all right. You'll like being married. You will. You'll see. Yes."

Jaws, 1975; (after they have lost their boat and killed a giant shark in a life-and-death battle and are floating toward shore): Roy Scheider: "I used to hate the water..." Richard Dreyfuss: "I can't imagine why."

Jurassic Park, 1993; Sam Neill: "Hammond, after careful consideration, I have decided *not* to endorse your park."; Richard Attenborough: "So have I."

King Kong, 1933; Robert Armstrong: "Oh, no, it wasn't the airplanes. It was Beauty [that] killed the beast."

L.A. Confidential, 1997; Kim Basinger: "Some men get the world. Others get ex-hookers and a trip to Arizona."

The Lady from Shanghai, 1948; Orson Welles: "Well, everybody is somebody's fool. The only way to stay out of trouble is to grow old, so I guess I'll concentrate on that. Maybe I'll live so long that I'll forget her. Maybe I'll die trying."

The Last Hurrah, 1958; Spencer Tracy (as an old-fashioned politician on his deathbed when a reformer suggests that he would have changed his life or political decisions): "Like hell I would!"

The Last of the Mohicans, 1992; Russell Means: "Great Spirit and the Maker of all life. A warrior goes to you swift and straight as an arrow shot into the sun. Welcome him and let him take his place at the council fire of my people. He is Uncus, my son. Tell them to be patient and ask death for speed for they are all there but one, I, Chingachgook, last of the Mohicans."

The Life of Emile Zola, 1937; Morris Carnovsky (as Anatole France at Zola's funeral): "He was a moment of the conscience of man."

Little Caesar, 1931; Edward G. Robinson (as a ruthless gangster dying from police bullets): "Mother of Mercy! Is this the end of Rico?"

The Longest Day, 1962; Richard Beymer (a GI lost after landing in Normandy on June 6, 1944, and rhetorically asking downed and wounded R.A.F. pilot Richard Burton which side was victorious): "I wonder who won."

Lost Horizon, 1937; Hugh Buckler: "Here's my hope that Robert Conway will find his Shangri-La...Here's my hope that we all find our Shangri-La."

The Lost Weekend, 1945; Ray Milland (recovering alcoholic ending the film with a cautionary narrative): "I wonder how many others that are like me, poor bedeviled guys on fire with thirst...such comical figures to the rest of the world as they stagger blindly towards another binge, another bender, another spree."

Love Story, 1970; Ryan O'Neal: "Love means never having to say you're sorry."

The Magnificent Seven, 1960; Yul Brynner (gunfighter leaving a small Mexican village after defending it from a horde of bandits): "The old man was right. Only the farmers won. We lost. We always lose."

Magnum Force, 1973; Clint Eastwood (watching his corrupt police superior drive away only to be killed by a bomb explosion Eastwood knew was hidden in the car): "A man's got to know his limitations."

The Maltese Falcon, 1941; Humphrey Bogart (as detective Sam Spade, carrying and describing the statuette of a falcon): "The stuff that dreams are made of."

The Man Who Knew Too Much, 1956; James Stewart (to some family friends waiting in their hotel room after he and wife Doris Day have harrowingly rescued their son from kidnappers): "I'm sorry that we were gone so long, but we had to go over and pick up Hank."

The Manchurian Candidate, 1962; Frank Sinatra (about Laurence Harvey, who had been mentally programmed as an assassin by his Communist captors during the Korean War and how Harvey truly earned his Congressional Medal of Honor): "Made to commit acts too unspeakable to be cited here by an enemy that had captured his mind and soul. He freed himself at last and, in the end, heroically and unhesitatingly gave his life to save his country. Raymond Shaw...Hell!...Hell!"

Manila Calling, 1942; Lloyd Nolan (an American who has joined the Filipino guerrillas in resisting the Japanese that have invaded the Philippines in WWII, and while calling the U.S. via radio): "This is Manila calling—and I ain't no Jap!"

The Mark of Zorro, 1940; Tyrone Power: "We're going to marry and raise fat children and watch our vineyards grow!"

Meet John Doe, 1941; James Gleason (addressing a powerful kingpin): "There are, Norton. The people! Try and lick that!"

Midnight Run, 1988; (after bounty hunter Robert De Niro asks a cabdriver at L.A. Airport if he can change a $1,000 bill): Bob Maroff/cabdriver: "What are you, a comedian? Get out of here, you bum!"; De Niro (to himself): "Looks like I'm walking."

The Misfits, 1961; Clark Gable (to Marilyn Monroe): "Just head for that big star straight on. The Highway's under it. It'll take us right home."

Mrs. Miniver, 1942; Henry Wilcoxon (minister preaching from a bombed-out church in England): "This is the people's war. It is our war. Fight it then. Fight it with all that is in us, and may God defend the right."

Mr. Roberts, 1955; Jack Lemmon: "Captain, it is I, Ensign Pulver, and I just threw your stinking palm tree overboard. Now what's all this crud about no movies tonight?"

Moby Dick, 1956; Richard Basehart (voiceover narration): "The drama's done. All are departed away. The great shroud of the sea rolls over the *Pequod*, her crew and Moby Dick. I only am escaped, alone, to tell thee."

My Little Chickadee, 1940; (as two film icons exchange their trademark lines): W.C. Fields: "You must come up and see me sometime."; Mae West: "Oh, yeah, yeah, I'll do that, my little chickadee."

The Naked City, 1948; (narration): 'There are eight million stories in the naked city. This has been one of them."

The Natural, 1984; Sports Announcer (after Robert Redford hits a game-winning home run and goes around the bases as the ball strikes an arc light that creates a series of showering and dazzling explosions): "And it's spinning away, way back up, high into the right field! That ball is still going! It's way back, high up in there! He did it! Hobbs did it!"

Network, 1976; (narrator): "This was the story of Howard Beale, the first known instance of a man who was killed because he had lousy ratings."

The Night of the Hunter, 1955; Lillian Gish (about the children in her care she has protected from a murderous maniac, and children everywhere): "They abide and they endure."

No Country for Old Men, 2007; Tommy Lee Jones: "And in the dream, I knew that he was goin' on ahead and he was fixin' to make a fire somewhere out there in all that dark and all that cold. And I knew that whenever I got there, he'd be there. And then I woke up."

Now, Voyager, 1942; Bette Davis: "Don't let's ask for the moon—we have the stars."

An Officer and a Gentleman, 1982; Lisa Blount (when seeing Richard Gere, who has graduated officer training school in the U.S. Navy and who returns to retrieve Blount's close friend and the woman Gere loves, Debra Winger, from her factory job, kissing her and carrying her from the place): "Way to go, Paula! Way to go!"

The Old Man and the Sea, 1958; (Spencer Tracy narration, quoting the end of Ernest Hemingway's great novella): "Up the road in his shack the old man was sleeping again. He was still sleeping on his face, and the boy was sitting by him, watching him. The old man was dreaming about the lions."

The Outlaw Josey Wales, 1976; Clint Eastwood: "I guess we all died a little in that damn war."

Patton, 1970; George C. Scott (narrating as General George S. Patton): "For over a thousand years, Roman conquerors returning from the wars enjoyed the honor of a triumph, a tumultuous parade…The conqueror rode in a triumphant chariot, the dazed prisoners walking in chains before him. Sometimes his children, robed in white, stood with him in the chariot, or rode the trace horses. A slave stood behind the conqueror holding a golden crown and whispering in his ear a warning that all glory is fleeting."

The Petrified Forest, 1936; Bette Davis (quoting French poet Francois Villon in her farewell to dying lover Leslie Howard): "'This is the end for which we twain are met.'"

The Plainsman, 1936; Jean Arthur (as Calamity Jane, kissing Gary Cooper, who plays gunfighter Wild Bill Hickok and who has just been killed): "That's one kiss you won't wipe off."

Platoon, 1986; Charlie Sheen (voiceover): "But be that as it may, those of us who did make it have an obligation to build again, to teach to others what we know, and to try with what's left of our lives to find a goodness and meaning to our lives."

Play Misty for Me, 1971; Clint Eastwood (a hip California disc jockey playing a record for a rejected, berserk woman who has repeatedly tried to kill him and his girlfriend and who originally called in to have him play the title song): "And now, here's a pretty one for lonely lovers on a cool, cool night. It's the great Earl Garner classic, 'Misty.' And this one is especially for Evelyn."

Poppy, 1936; W.C. Fields: "Never give a sucker an even break."

The Prestige, 2006; Michael Caine: "Now you're looking for the secret. But you won't find it, of course, because you're not really looking. You don't really want to work it out. You want to be fooled."

The Pride of the Yankees, 1942; Gary Cooper (as New York Yankees first baseman Lou Gehrig, who has been stricken with an incurable disease, and quoting Gehrig's own words in his farewell speech at Yankee Stadium): "People all say that I've had a bad break, but today…Today I consider myself the luckiest man on the face of the earth."

The Princess Bride, 1987; Fred Savage (the grandson to whom this story has been read by his grandfather): "Grandpa, maybe you could come over and read it again to me tomorrow."; Peter Falk (the grandfather): "As you wish."

The Producers, 1967; Zero Mostel (directing chorus dancers to kick higher in a rehearsal of a prison show): "Higher, you animals, higher. We open in Leavenworth [Penitentiary] Saturday night!"

The Professionals, 1966; Lee Marvin (an adventurer, who has released the wife of Ralph Bellamy, a wealthy man, to her lover and after Bellamy has called him an "S.O.B."): "Yes, sir. In my case, an accident of birth, but, you, sir, you are a self-made man."

Prometheus, 2012; Noomi Rapace (as Elizabeth Shaw; voiceover): "Final report of the vessel *Prometheus*. The ship and her entire crew are gone. If you're receiving this transmission, make no attempt to come to the point of its origin. There is only death here now, and I am leaving it behind. It is New Year's Day, the year of our Lord, 2094. My name is Elizabeth Shaw, the last survivor of the *Prometheus*. And I am still searching."

Psycho, 1960; Tony Perkins (in custody for murder, sitting in a straitjacket, eyes nervously searching the jail cell, now psychologically transformed into his own mother's persona): "I'm not even going to swat that fly. I hope they are watching. They'll see and they'll know and they'll say: 'Why she wouldn't even harm a fly.'"

Pygmalion, 1938 and its 1964 remake **My Fair Lady**; Leslie Howard and Rex Harrison: "Where the devil are my slippers, Eliza?"

Radio Days, 1987; Narrator: "I never forgot that New Year's Eve when Aunt Bea awakened me to watch 1944 come in. And I've never forgotten any of those people, or any of the voices we used to hear on the radio. Although the truth is, with the passing of each New Year's Eve, those voices do seem to grow dimmer and dimmer."

Rain, 1932; Joan Crawford: "I'm sorry for everybody in the world, I guess."

The Right Stuff, 1983; Narrator: "The Mercury Program was over. Four years later Gus Grissom was killed, along with astronauts White and Chaffee, when fire swept through their Apollo capsule. But on that glorious day in May 1963, Gordo Cooper went higher, farther and faster than any other American—twenty-two complete orbits around the world. He was the last American ever to go into space alone. And, for a brief moment, Gordo Cooper became the greatest pilot anyone had ever seen."

Road to Perdition, 2002; Tyler Hoechlin (as Michael Sullivan Jr. voiceover): "When people ask me if Michael Sullivan was a good man, or if there was just no good in him at all, I always give the same answer. I just tell them: 'He was my father.'"

The Roaring Twenties, 1939; Gladys George (holding the body of slain gangster James Cagney while identifying the dead man to a cop arriving upon the scene): "He used to be a big shot!"

Robin and Marian, 1976; Sean Connery (as Robin Hood, to Nicol Williamson, playing Little John, and about to shoot an arrow, the spot where it falls to be his burial spot as well as that of lifelong lover Marian): "Give me my bow. Where this falls, John, put us close, and leave us there."

Sahara, 1943; Humphrey Bogart (holding the dog tags of those in his contingent who died while fighting a German mechanized battalion and after hearing that British troops have stopped German forces in a major battle): "They'd want to know…They stopped them at El Alamein!"

Sands of Iwo Jima, 1949; John Agar (as he and other Marines watch the American flag being raised atop Mount Suribachi at Iwo Jima): "There she goes. All right! Saddle up! Let's get back in the war."

Saving Private Ryan, 1998; Harrison Young (as old Ryan): "Tell me I am a good man."; Kathleen Byron (as old Mrs. Ryan): "You are."

The Searchers, 1956; John Wayne: "Let's go home, Debbie."

Sergeant York, 1941; Gary Cooper: "The Lord sure does move in mysterious ways."

Seven Brides for Seven Brothers, 1954; (A preacher performing a mass marriage ceremony): "I now pronounce you men and wives."

The Shanghai Gesture, 1942; Mike Mazurki (a towering Chinese doorman outside a lavish casino, who ironically repeats a line that has earlier mocked him from a powerful Anglo patron, Walter Huston and who leaves the casino at the end of the film with his life in ruins): "You likee Chinese New Year?"

The Shawshank Redemption, 1994; Morgan Freeman (voiceover): "I find that I am so excited that I can barely sit still or hold a thought in my head. I think it's the excitement only a free man can feel, a free man at the start of a long journey whose conclusion is uncertain. I hope I can make it across the border. I hope to see my friend and shake his hand. I hope the Pacific is as blue as it has been in my dreams. I hope."

Ship of Fools, 1965; Michael Dunn (a philosophical dwarf and one of the passengers on an ocean liner sailing to Nazi-controlled Germany, delivering his lines directly to the audience): "Oh, I can just hear you saying; 'What has all this to do with us?' Nothing."

Sleeper, 1973; Woody Allen: "Sex and death, two things that come once in a lifetime. But, at least after death, you're not nauseous."

Some Like It Hot, 1959; Joe E. Brown (a daffy millionaire, who is smitten with Jack Lemmon, and, despite the fact that Lemmon removes his wig to reveal that he has been impersonating a woman and declares that he is a man): "Well, nobody's perfect!"

Spider-Man, 2002; Tobey Maguire (as Peter Parker/Spider-Man): "Whatever life holds in store for me, I will never forget these words: 'With great power comes great responsibility.' This is my gift…my curse. Who am I? I'm Spider-Man."

Stagecoach, 1939; George Bancroft: "I'll buy you a drink."; Thomas Mitchell: "Just one."

Stalag 17, 1953; Robert Strauss (remarking about the recent escape of a fellow inmate from a German POW camp in WWII): "Maybe he just wanted to steal our wire-cutters. Did you ever think of that?"

Stand by Me, 1986; Richard Dreyfuss (The Writer writing the following words on a computer): "I never had any friends later on like the ones I had when I was twelve. Jesus, does anyone?"

A Star Is Born, 1937 and its 1954 remake; Janet Gaynor, and Judy Garland: "Hello, everybody. This is Mrs. Norman Maine!"

Star Trek VI: The Undiscovered Country, 1991; William Shatner (as Captain James T. Kirk; voiceover): "This is the final cruise of the Star-

ship *Enterprise* under my command. The ship and her history will shortly become the care of another crew. To them and their posterity we will commit our future. They will continue the voyages we have begun and journey to all the undiscovered countries, boldly going where no man…where no one has gone before."

The Sting, 1973; (two con artists after having successfully swindled a vicious NYC gangster out of a fortune in a sham betting parlor in Chicago): Paul Newman: "You're not going to stick around for your share?" Robert Redford: "Naw, I'd only blow it."

The Strawberry Blonde, 1941; James Cagney: "When I want to kiss my wife, I'll kiss her anytime, anyplace, anywhere. That's the kind of hairpin I am!"

A Streetcar Named Desire, 1951; Marlon Brando: "Hey, Stella! Hey, Stella!"

The Sullivans (aka: The Fighting Sullivans), 1944; Selena Royle (as the mother of the five Sullivan boys, who all died together as sailors in battle in the Pacific during WWII and after launching a new destroyer named after them, as she remarks to her husband, Thomas Mitchell): "Tom, our boys are afloat again!"

Sunset Boulevard, 1950; Gloria Swanson (as faded silent film star Norma Desmond, after killing her gigolo lover, and while newspaper cameras record her descent on a staircase inside her mansion before she goes into police custody and, in her demented state, believes she is again starring in a movie): "All right, Mr. DeMille, I'm ready for my close-up…"

Superman, 1978; Christopher Reeve (as Superman and after delivering returning dangerous criminals to prison and where the warden thanks him): "No, sir! Don't thank me, Warden. We're all part of the same team. Good night!"

A Tale of Two Cities, 1935; Ronald Colman (just before he mounts the stairs of a scaffold to be guillotined after having taken the place of another person during the French Revolution): "It's a far, far better thing I do than I have ever done. It's a far, far better rest I go to than I have I have ever known."

Them!, 1954; Edmund Gwen (as a scientist): "When Man entered the Atomic Age, he opened a door into a new world. What we will find in that new world nobody can predict."

There Will Be Blood, 2007; Daniel Day-Lewis (as a ruthless oil baron who has just murdered a manipulative preacher): "I'm finished!"

The Thief of Bagdad, 1924; title card: "Happiness must be earned!"

The Thief of Bagdad, 1940; Sabu (as the thief Abu): "You've got what you wanted…Now I am going to get what I want—some fun and adventure!"

The Thing from Another World, 1951; Douglas Spencer (a newspaper reporter who has witnessed an attack from a space alien near the North Pole and is talking from that outpost via radio): "Every one of you listening to my voice, tell the world. Tell this to everybody, wherever they are. Watch the skies, everywhere, keep looking. Keep watching the skies!"

Things to Come, 1936; Raymond Massey (a futuristic leader who has just sent a colony of humans into space by rocket ship): "All the universe or nothingness…which shall it be…which shall it be?"

The 39 Steps, 1935; Wylie Watson (as a dying Mr. Memory, who has just related a complicated top secret to Scotland Yard detectives): "Thank you, sir. Thank you. I'm glad it's off my mind. Glad."

A Thousand Clowns, 1965; Jason Robards Jr. (a non-conformist who is returning to a full-time job he dislikes in order to keep custody of his nephew and while loudly addressing the neighborhood in NYC street at morning with no one responding): "Campers, I can't think of anything to say."

Tight Spot, 1955; Ginger Rogers (who has been marked for death and identifying herself as she takes the witness stand in a trial to testify against a mob boss): "Gang buster!"

To Catch a Thief, 1955; Grace Kelly (to a not-too-happy Cary Grant after she sees his mountaintop villa): "So this is where you live. Oh, Mother will love it up here."

To Each His Own, 1946; John Lund (to Olivia de Havilland): "I think this is our dance, Mother."

Tombstone, 1993; Robert Mitchum (as narrator): "Wyatt and Josephine embarked upon a series of adventures. Up or down, thin or flush, in forty-seven years they never left each other's side. Wyatt Earp died in Los Angeles in 1929. Among the pallbearers at his funeral were early western movie stars William S. Hart and Tom Mix. Tom Mix wept."

Toy Story 2, 1999; Tom Hanks (as Woody): "Besides, when it all ends, I'll have old Buzz Lightyear to keep me company—for infinity and beyond."

True Grit, 1969; John Wayne (as Rooster Gogburn): "Well, come and see a fat old man sometime!"

2010: The Year We Made Contact, 1984; Narrator: "You can tell your children of the day when everyone looked up and realized that we were only tenants in this world. We have been given a new lease, and a warning, from the landlord."

Unforgiven, 1992; Clint Eastwood (shouting to hiding inhabitants as he leaves the town of Big Whiskey in a rainstorm): "You better bury Ned right! You better not cut up or otherwise harm no whores, or I'll come back and kill every one of you sons-of-bitches!"

The Untouchables, 1987; Kevin Costner (playing Prohibition Agent Elliot Ness, who, when asked what he will do when Prohibition is repealed, replies): "I think I'll have a drink."

Viva Villa!, 1934; Wallace Beery (dying as Francesco "Pancho" Villa): "Forgive me? Johnny—what I done wrong?"

The War of the Worlds, 1953; Sir Cedric Hardwicke (voiceover narration): "The Martians had no resistance to the bacteria in our atmosphere to which we have long since become immune. Once they had breathed our air, germs, which no longer affect us, began to kill them. The end came swiftly. All over the world, their machines began to stop and fall. After all that men could do had failed, the Martians were destroyed and humanity was saved by the littlest things, which, God in His wisdom, had put upon this earth."

White Heat, 1949; James Cagney (a ruthless gangster engulfed in flames from an exploding gas tank): "Made it, ma! Top of the world!"; John Archer (an FBI agent, who, with others, watches the gangster being blown to pieces): "Codie Jarrett. He finally got to the top of the world

and it blew right up in his face."

The Wild Bunch, 1969; Edmond O'Brien (to Robert Ryan, the last two survivors of a misanthropic U.S. outlaw band, and where he proposes that Ryan join him and others in joining the rebels in the Mexican Revolution): "Well, me and the boys here, we got some work to do. You wanna come along? It ain't like it used to be, but it'll do."

The Wizard of Oz, 1939; Judy Garland (after returning to her Kansas farm and family from the magical country of Oz): "There's no place like home!"

Woman of the Year, 1942; Spencer Tracy (returning from off-camera scene with Katharine Hepburn's unctuous secretary, Gerald, who wanted her to launch a battleship with a bottle of champagne, and after the crashing sound of the bottle has been heard): "I've just launched Gerald."

The Women, 1939; Norma Shearer (deciding to fight for the man she loves at the cost of her pride): "No pride at all. That's a luxury a woman in love can't afford."

A Yank in the R.A.F., 1941; Tyrone Power (wounded and getting off a boat after being shot down in WWII and where a nurse passes him, asking him to call her up as he reunites with his always forgiving girlfriend Betty Grable, stating to Grable): "I know…I'm a worm."

Young Frankenstein, 1974; Madeline Kahn (singing, as she consummates her marriage to a gigantic monster turned gentleman Peter Boyle): "Ah, sweet mystery of life, at last I've found you!"

Young Mr. Lincoln, 1939; Henry Fonda (as a young Abraham Lincoln and after having won a murder case that freed two innocent young men, telling a friend that he is going to take a stroll in the Illinois countryside): "No, I think I might go on a piece…maybe to the top of that hill."

HISTORICAL PERSONS

Note: The following annotated index, exclusively created by the author, shows significant historical persons appearing in theatrically released feature films (chiefly U.S. and British releases, along with notable foreign productions, showing U.S. year of release), as well as feature films made-for-TV, TV series and miniseries, but does not include shorts, documentaries or video productions. Persons are presented alphabetically by last and first name and titles of films are sequentially presented in alphabetical and chronological order. Titles shown in boldface represent entries profiled in this work, with the actor or actress enacting the historical person shown in parenthesis following each entry.

Aaron (In Old Testament Bible; older brother of Moses): The Bible, 2013 (TV miniseries, "Exodus," 2013 episode: Louis Hilyer); **Exodus: Gods and Kings**, 2014 (Andrew Tarbet); **The Green Pastures**, 1936 (David Bethea); In the Beginning, 2000 (made-for-TV; David Threlfall); Moses, 1995 (made-for-TV; David Suchet); Moses and Aaron, 1975 (Louis Devos); Moses and Aaron, 2009 (made-for-TV; Andreas Conrad); Moses the Lawgiver, 1974 (TV miniseries; Anthony Quayle); Moses und Aaron, 2006 (made-for-TV; Thomas Moser); **The Prince of Egypt**, 1998 (Jeff Goldblum voiceover); **The Ten Commandments**, 1923 (James Neill); **The Ten Commandments**, 1956 (John Carradine);The Ten Commandments, 2006 (made-for-TV; Linus Roache); The Ten Commandments, 2007 (Christopher Gaze voiceover); The Ten Commandments: The Musical, 2006 (Nicholas Rodriguez).

Abel (Biblical person, one of two sons born to Adam and Eve; murdered by his brother Cain): After Six Days, 1920 (Mario Cionci); The Bible: In the Beginning..., 1966 (Franco Nero); The Cradle of God, 1926 (Gabriel de Gravone); Genesis: The Creation and the Flood, 1994 (B. Haddan Mohammed); **The Green Pastures**, 1936 (Duke Upshaw); La biblia en pasta, 1984 (Alberto de Gregorio); The Last Eve, 2005 (Chul Jeong); The Making of...And God Spoke, 1994 (Andy Dick); **Noah**, 2014 (Arnar Dan); SuperBook, 1981-1982 (animated TV series; "My Brother's Keeper: Cain and Abel," 1982 episode: Hal Studer); Year One, 2009 (Paul Rudd).

Abel, Rudolf (Vilyam Fisher; c.1903-1971; Soviet spymaster and KGB colonel operating in the U.S., captured by the FBI in 1957 and imprisoned, later exchanged for Gary Francis Powers, 1929-1977, pilot of the CIA U-2 spy plane, which was shot down by the Soviets on May 1, 1960, by one of eight ground-to-air missiles, on February 10, 1962, at the Glienicke Bridge in Berlin, Germany): **Bridge of Spies**, 2015 (Mark Rylance); Francis Gary Powers: The True Story of the U-2 Spy Incident, 1976 (made-for-TV; Nehemiah Persoff in role model for Abel). For more information on Abel, see my book, *Spies: A Narrative Encyclopedia of Dirty Tricks and Double Dealing from Biblical Times to Today* (M. Evans, 1997; illustrated pages: 13-17).

Abernathy, Ralph David Sr. (1926-1990; U.S. black civil rights leader): All the Way, 2016 (made-for-TV; Dohn Norwood); Betty and Coretta, 2013 (made-for-TV; Benz Antoine); Boycott, 2001 (made-for-TV; Terrence Howard); Hoover vs. the Kennedys: The Second Civil War, 1987 (made-for-TV; Charles Woods Gray); King, 1978- (TV miniseries; Ernie Lee Banks); **Selma**, 2014 (Colman Domingo); The Vernon Johns Story, 1994 (made-for-TV; Michael Howell).

Abraham (Founding father of the Israelites): Abraham, 1993 (TV miniseries; Richard Harris); Abraham en Samuel, 1989 (made-for-TV; Pol Goossen); Animated Stories from the Bible, 1987-2005 (TV series; "Abraham and Isaac," 1992 episode: Oscar Rowland); The Bible, 2013- (TV miniseries; "In the Beginning," 2013 episode: Gary Oliver); Bible Battles, 2005 (made-for-TV; Ray Porter); The Bible: In the Beginning,

Estelle Taylor (Miriam), James Neill (Aaron) and Theodore Roberts (Moses) in *The Ten Commandments*, 1923.

1966 (George C. Scott); The Cradle of God, 1926 (Gabriel Signoret); Greatest Heroes of the Bible, 1978- (TV series; two 1982 episodes: Gene Barry); **The Green Pastures**, 1936 (Billy Cumby); In the Beginning, 2000 (made-for-TV; Martin Landau); It Is Written, 1956- (TV series; "Lessons from a Vacant Lot," 2008 episode: Larry Marko); Jacob, The Man Who Fought with God, 1977 (Fosco Giachetti); Matinee Theatre, 1955-1958 (TV series; "The Story of Sarah," 1957 episode: Tom Tryon); Mysteries and Miracles, 1965- (TV series; "Guilds and Pageants," 1965 episode: Ralph Nossek); The Old Testament Scriptures, 1958 (TV series; Bruce Wendell); The Real Old Testament, 2003 (Sam Lloyd); Restitution, 1918 (Frank Whitson); Son of God, 2014 (Gary Oliver); SuperBooks, 1981-1982 (animated TV series; Ray Owens, George Gonneau); Testament: The Bible in Animation, 1996- (TV series; "Abraham," 1996 espisode: Robert Hardy); Year One, 2009 (Hank Azaria).

Acheson, Dean (Dean Gooderham Acheson; 1893-1971; U.S. attorney, statesman and 51st U.S. Secretary of State): Collision Course: Truman vs. MacArthur, 1976 (made-for-TV; Barry Sullivan); Die Kuba-Krise, 1969 (made-for-TV; Ernst Fritz Furbringer); The Flood, 1962 (made-for-TV; Jacques d'Amboise); Kennedy, 1983- (TV miniseries; George Martin); **MacArthur**, 1977 (Art Fleming); The Missiles of October, 1974 (made-for-TV; John Dehner); Tail Gunner Joe, 1977 (made-for-TV; Alan Hewitt); Truman, 1995 (made-for-TV; Ramak Ramsey); Spies, Lies and the Superbomb, 2007 (TV miniseries; Ben Tyler); **Thirteen Days**, 2000 (Len Cariou); Truman, 1995 (made-for-TV; Remak Ramsey).

Adam (Biblical person, the first human being made by God): Adam and Eve, 1958 (Carlos Baena); The Adventures of Mark Twain, 1985 (John Morrison voiceover); After Six Days, 1920 (Umberto Semprebene); The Bible, 2013- (TV miniseries; "In the Beginning," 2013 episode; Paul Knops); The Bible: In the Beginning, 1966 (Michael Parks); The Cradle of God, 1926 (Pierre Daltour); Genesis: The Creation and the Flood, 1994 (Sabir Aziz); **The Green Pastures**, 1936 (Rex Ingram); The Green Pastures, 1959 (made-for-TV; Earle Hyman); In the Beginning, 2000 (made-for-TV; Sendhil Ramamurthy); Jacob: The Man Who Fought with God, 1977 (Giuseppe Addobbati); The Jersey Devil, 2014 (Roy Nowlin); The Making Of "...And God Spoke,"1994 (Andrew Simmons); **Noah**, 2014 (Adam Griffith); The Private Lives of Adam and Eve, 1960 (made-for-TV; Martin Milner); The Real Old Testament, 2003 (Andy Hirsch); Restitution, 1918 (Eugene Corey); The Sin of Adam and Eve, 1973 (Jorge Rivero); Son of God, 2014 (Paul Knops); Testament: The Bible in Animation, 1996- (TV series; "Creation and the Flood," 1996 espisode: Simon Harris); Year One, 2009 (Harold Ramis).

Anthony Hopkins (as John Quincy Adams) in *Amistad*, 1997.

Adams, Abigail Smith (1744-1818; First Lady and wife of U.S. President John Adams): The Adams Chronicles, 1976 (TV miniseries; Leora Dana; Kathryn Walker); The American Revolution, 1994 (made-for-TV; Michael Learned voiceover); The American Woman: Portraits of Courage, 1976 (made-for-TV; Joanna Miles); Daniel Boone, 1964-1970 (TV series; "Taking the Southbound Stage," 1967 episode: Mabel Albertson); General Electric Theater, 1953-1962 (TV series; "Adam's Apples," 1960 episode: Christine White); George Washington, 1984 (TV miniseries; Christine Estabrook); Ichabod and Me, 1961- (TV series; many episodes: Christine White); John Adams, 2008- (TV miniseries; Laura Linney); Liberty! The American Revolution, 1997 (TV miniseries; Donna Murphy); Profiles in Courage, 1964-1965 (TV series; "John Adams," 1964 episode: Phyllis Love); 1776, 1972 (Virginia Vestoff); Sleepy Hollow, 2013- (TV series; Michelle Trachtenberg); Sons of Liberty, 2015- (TV series; Daisy Lewis); A Woman for the Ages, 1952 (made-for-TV; Sylvia Field).

Adams, Charles (1770-1800; U.S. attorney and second son of John Adams, second U.S. President; died of alcoholism): The Adams Chronicles, 1976 (TV miniseries; J.C. Powell; Philip Anglim).

Adams, Charles Francis (1807-1886; U.S. politician, diplomat and editor; grandson of John Adams, second U.S. President and son of John Quincy Adams, sixth President of the U.S.): The Adams Chronicles, 1976 (TV miniseries; John Beal; Thomas A. Stewart; Rodman Flender; Steven Krey); American Experience, 1988- (TV series; Nicholas Purcell); John Adams, 2008- (TV miniseries; Kevin Trainor).

Adams, Franklin Pierce (1881-1960; U.S. columnist and poet; member of the Algonquin Round Table): Mrs. Parker and the Vicious Circle, 1994 (Chip Zien).

Adams, George Washington (1801-1829; U.S. attorney and politician; eldest son of John Quincy Adams, sixth President of the U.S.; reportedly had a manic depressive personality and who struggled with alcoholism; he allegedly committed suicide when leaping from the ship *Benjamin Franklin*, which was sailing in Long Island Sound, on June 9, 1829): The Adams Chronicles, 1976 (TV miniseries; David Elliott; Peter Coffield).

Adams. John (1735-1826; U.S. politician and founding father; second U.S. President): The Adams Chronicles, 1976 (TV miniseries; George Grizzard); The American Revolution, 1994 (made-for-TV; William Daniels); The American Woman: Portraits of Courage, 1976 (made-for-TV; Frank Langella); The Beautiful Mrs. Reynolds, 1918 (Jack Dru-

mier); Benjamin Franklin, 2002 (TV miniseries; Peter Donaldson); Cavalcades of America, 1952-1957 (TV series; "Poor Richard," 1952 episode: Dabbs Greer; "John Yankee," 1953 episode: Whitfield Connor); Daniel Boone, 1964-1970 (TV series; "Taking the Southbound Stage," 1967 episode: Torin Thatcher); Family Ties, 1982-1989 (TV series; "Philadelphia Story," 1985 episode: Ben Piazza); Founders or Traitors?, 2007 (made-for-TV; Steve Holloway); George Washington, 1984 (TV miniseries; Hal Holbrook); George Washington II: The Forging of a Nation, 1986 (made-for-TV; Paul Collins); Histeria!, 1998-2000 (animated TV series; "The Thomas Jefferson Program,' 1998 episode: Billy West voiceover); John Adams, 2008- (TV miniseries; Paul Giamatti); **John Paul Jones**, 1959 (Robert Ayres); Liberty! The American Revolution, 1997 (TV miniseries; Peter Donaldson); Liberty's Kids: Est. 1776, 2002-2003 (animated TV series; five 2002 episodes; Billy Crystal); A More Perfect Union: America Becomes a Nation, 1989 (Ivan Crosland); Profiles in Courage, 1964-1965 (TV series; "John Adams," 1964 episode: David McCullum); Pursuit of Honor: The Rise of George Washington, 2006 (Timothy McCarthy); The Rebels, 1979 (made-for-TV; William Daniels); The Revolution, 2006- (TV series; five 2007 episodes; Tony Scheinman); Samuel Adams, 2014 (Ronald Duthweiler); **1776**, 1972 (William Daniels); Sons of Liberty, 2015- (TV miniseries; Henry Thomas); Swing Out, Sweet Land, 1970 (made-for-TV; William Shatner); A Woman for the Ages, 1952 (made-for-TV; John Boruff); You Are There, 1953-1971 (TV series; "The Boston Tea Party, December 12, 1773," 1953 episode: Whit Bissell; "Washington Crosses the Delaware, December 25, 1776," 1955 episode: Howard Wendell).

Adams, John Quincy (1767-1848; U.S. politician and sixth President of the U.S.): The Adams Chronicles, 1976 (TV miniseries; Mark Winkworth; Steve Austin; Steven Grover; Marcel Trenchard; David Birney; William Daniels); **Amistad**, 1997 (Anthony Hopkins); Enslavement: The True Story of Fanny Kemble, 2000 (made-for-TV; Colin Fox); John Adams, 2008 (TV miniseries; Ebon Moss-Bachrach; Steven Hinkle as young John Quincy Adams); Profiles in Courage, 1964-1965 (TV series; "John Quincy Adams," 1965 episode: Douglas Campbell); A Woman for the Ages, 1952 (made-for-TV; William Daniels).

Adams, Samuel (1722-1823; political philosopher and one of the Founding Fathers of the U.S.): The Adams Chronicles, 1976 (TV miniseries; W.B. Brydon); **America**, 1924 (Lee Beggs); The American Revolution, 2014- (TV series; Jody Matzer); The Bastard, 1978 (made-for-TV; William Daniels); Founding Fathers, 2000- (TV miniseries; Beau Bridges); Freedom to Speak, 1982 (TV miniseries; Mason Adams); George Washington, 1984 (TV miniseries; Richard Fancy); John Adams, 2008- (TV miniseries; Danny Huston); **Johnny Tremain**, 1957 (Rusty Lane); Profiles in Courage, 1964-1965 (TV series; "John Adams," 1964 episode; Gene Lyons); Samual Adams, 2014 (made-for-TV; Jack E. Curenton); Sleepy Hollow, 2013- (TV series; "The Midnight Ride," 2013 episode: Allen O'Reilly); Sons of Liberty, 2015- (TV series; Ben Barnes); Thomas Jefferson, 1997 (TV miniseries; Philip Bosco voiceover); You Are There, 1953-1971 (TV series; "The Boston Tea Party [December 12, 1773]," 1953 episode: E.G. Marshall; Herbert Rudley; "Paul Revere's Ride [April 18, 1775], 1954 episode: E. G. Marshall).

Adamson, Joy (Friederike Victoria Gessner; 1910-1980; Austrian-born naturalist, artist and author, chiefly noted for her African experiences in raising wild animals such as lions; murdered by Paul Nakware Ekai, a discharged laborer in Adams' employ, who was sent to prison instead of being executed as he was ruled a minor when committing the crime): **Born Free**, 1966 (Virginia McKenna); Born Free, 1974 (TV series; Diana Muldaur); The Joy Adamson Story, 1980 (herself in 45-minute documentary made-for-TV); **Living Free**, 1972 (Susan Hampshire); Psychobitches, 2012- (TV series; 2013 episode: Julia Davis); To Walk with Lions, 1999 (Honor Blackman).

Adler, Polly (Pearl "Polly" Adler; 1900-1962; U.S. prostitute and madam): A House Is Not a Home, 1964 (Shelley Winters); Mrs. Parker and the Vicious Circle, 1994 (Gisele Rousseau). Note: For detailed information on Adler, see my *Encyclopedia of World Crime*, Volume I (CrimeBooks, Inc., 1990; illustrated pages 31-32).

Adonis, Joe (Giuseppe Antonio Doto; 1902-1971; Italian-born U.S. gangster aligned with Charles "Lucky" Luciano in NYC rackets): **Bugsy**, 1991 (Lewis Van Bergen); Lansky, 1999 (made-for-TV; Sal Landi).

Afraid of Horses (AKA: Young Man Afraid of Horses; 1836-1900; a chief of the Oglala Sioux who participated in Red Cloud's war against the U.S. government): The Gun That Won the West, 1955 (Michael Morgan); Redigo, 1963- (TV series; "The Hunters," 1963 episode: Perry Lopez); The Travels of Jaimie McPheeters, 1963-1964 (TV series; "The Day of the Pawnees," two 1963 episodes: Howard Caine).

Agrippina (Julia Agrippina; Agrippina the Younger; 15-59 A.D.; Roman empress, wife of Claudius, mother of Nero): A.D., 1985 (TV miniseries; Ava Gardner); Agrippina, 1985 (made-for-TV; Barbara Daniels); The Caesars, 1968- (TV miniseries; Caroline Blakiston); Caligula, 1980 (Lori Wagner); Caligula and Messalina, 1981 (Francoise Blanchard); I, Claudius, 1976- (TV miniseries; Fiona Walker; Barbara Young); Imperium: Nerone, 2004 (made-for-TV; Laura Morante); Messalina, Empress of Rome, 1977 (Lori Wagner); Nero, 1979 (made-for-TV; Lola Muthel); Nero and the Burning of Rome, 1954 (Paola Barbara); Nerone, 1977 (Paola Borboni); Nerone e Agrippina, 1918 (Maria Caserini); Nerone e Messalina, 1953 (Paola Barbara); Nero's Mistress, 1962 (Gloria Swanson); Warrior Queen, 2003 (Frances Barber).

Aguinaldo, Emilio (1869-1964; Filipino insurrectionist leader and great patriot of the Philippines): **Across the Pacific**, 1926 (Charles Stevens); Ang Paglilitis kay Andres Bonifacio, 2010 (Lance Raymundo); Baler, 2008 (Mengie Ngo); Bonifacio: Ang unang pangulo, 2014 (Jun Nayra); El Presidente, 2012 (Cesar Montano); Emilio Aguinaldo, 2000 (Jorge Estregan); Heneral Luna, 2015 (Mon Confiado); Katipunan, 2013 (TV miniseries; Nico Antonio); Tirad Pass: The Story of Gen. Gregoria del Pilar, 1997 (Joel Torre); Virgin Forest, 1985 (Roy Lachica).

Aguirre, Lope de (1510-1561; Spanish conquistador): **Aguirre, The Wrath of God**, 1977 (Klaus Kinski); El Dorado, 1988 (Omero Antonutti).

Aiken, Frederick Augustus (1832-1878; U.S. attorney who was one of the defense counsels for Mary Surratt in the conspiracy trial involving the assassination of President Abraham Lincoln): **The Conspirator**, 2011 (James McAvoy); The Killing of Mary Surratt, 2009 (Erik Sundquist).

Aitken, William Maxwell (aka: Max; 1st Baron Beaverbrook; 1879-1964): Above and Beyond, 2006 (TV miniseries; Kenneth Welsh); Bomber Harris, 1989 (made-for-TV; Phil Brown); Churchill's Secret, 2016 (made-for-TV; Matthew Marsh); Edward & Mrs. Simpson, 1978- (TV miniseries; Ed Devereaux); The Gathering Storm, 1974 (made-for-TV; Robert Beatty); The Last Bastion, 1984 (TV series; Robin Cuming); The Life and Times of David Lloyd George, 1981- (TV series; Ed Devereaux); **The Magic Box**, 1952 (Robert Beatty); Menzies and Churchill at War, 2008 (made-for-TV; Chris Waters); Number 10, 1983- (TV miniseries; Christian Rodska); War and Remembrance, 1988 (TV miniseries; Howard Cain); Winston Churchill: The Wilderness Years, 1981- (TV miniseries; Phil Brown).

Alaric I (370-410 A.D.; King of the Visgoths): Ancient Rome: The Rise and Fall of an Empire, 2006 (TV series; Mark Lockyer); Les evasions

Van Johnson (John Alden) and Dawn Addams (Priscilla Mullins) in *Plymouth Adventure*, 1952.

celebres, 1972- (TV series; Guy Fox); Revenge of the Barbarians, 1960 (Cesare Fantoni).

Albee, Edward Franklin II (1857-1930; U.S. theatrical producer): **Yankee Doodle Dandy**, 1942 (Minor Watson).

Alcott, Louisa May (1832-1888; U.S. author best known for her 1868 novel *Little Women*): Mary Cassatt: An American Impressionist, 1999 (made-for-TV; Danette Mackay).

Alden, John (1599-1687; crew member of the Mayflower on the historic 1620 voyage, who remained in Plymouth, marrying passenger Priscilla Mullins): The Courtship of Myles Stanish, 1923 (Charles Ray); The Mayflower, 2006 (made-for-TV; Shann Whynot-Young); Mayflower: The Pilgrims' Adventure, 1979 (made-for-TV; Michael Beck); **Plymouth Adventure**, 1952 (Van Johnson); TV Reader's Digest, 1955-1956 (TV series; "The Voyage of Captain Tom Jones, Pirate," John Stephenson).

Alexander I (1777-1825; Czar of Russia): The Adams Chronicles, 1976 (TV miniseries; Christopher Lloyd); Attack from the Sea, 1954 (Mikhail Navanov); Congress Dances, 1932 (Willy Fritsch); Congress of Love, 1966 (Curt Jurgens); Dancing on Graves, 1950 (Leif Wager); Der kongress tanzt, 1957 (Rudolf Prack); Die Abrechnung 1963 (made-for-TV; Wolfgang Buttner); Die schone Lugnerin, 1959 (Jean-Claude Pascal); 1812, 1944 (N. Timchenko); Frauen, die Geschichte machten, 2013 (TV series; Gabor Biedermann); Grafinya Sheremeteva, 1994 (made-for-TV; Boris Plotnikov); Helmikuum manifesti, 1939 (Leo Lahteenmaki); ITV Play of the Week, 1955-1974 (TV series; "War and Peace," 1963 episode: Tim Pearce); Konigin Luise, 1957 (Bernhard Wicki); La lumiere des justes, 1979- (TV miniseries; Mike Marshall); Luise, Queen of Prussia, 1932 (Vladimir Gajdarov); Marschall Vorwarts, 1932 (Carl Auen); Napoleon, 1955 (Constantin Nepo); Napoleon, 2002- (TV miniseries; Toby Stephens); Napoleon and Love, 1974- (TV miniseries; Jonathan Newth); Napoleon at St. Helena, 1929 (Alfred Gerasch); Nezrimyy puteshestvennik, 1999 (Vasily Lanovoy); Queen Luise, 1959 (Bernhard Wicki); Scharnhorst, 1978- (TV miniseries; Peter Bause); **War and Peace**, 1956 (Savo Raskovitch); **War and Peace**, 1968 (Viktor Murganov); War and Peace, 1972-1973 (TV miniseries; Donald Douglas); War and Peace, 2007 (TV miniseries; Igor Kostolevskiy); War and Peace, 2016 (TV miniseries; Ben Lloyd-Hughes); Zvezda plenitelnogo schastya, 1975 (Boris Dubensky).

Alexander II (1818-1881; Czar of Russia; assassinated): Adorable Sinner, 1963 (Curt Jurgens); Assassin of the Tsar, 1993 (Yury Belyayev);

Richard Burton (Alexander of Macedon) and Claire Bloom in *Alexander the Great,* **1956.**

The Cossacks, 1960 (Massimo Girotti); Heroes of Shipka, 1956 (Ivan Kononenko-Kozelsky); Hogaktningsfullt J.L. Runeberg, 1979 (Rune Sandlund); Katia, 1939 (John Loder); Lyubov imperatora, 2002 (Georgi Taratorkin); Michael Strogoff, 1960 (Louis Arbessier); Michel Strogoff, 1926 (Vladimir Gajdarov); Sofiya Perovskaya, 1968 (Vladislav Strzhelchik); The Soldier and the Lady, 1937 (Paul Harvey); Tainstvennyy uznik, 1986 (Aleksandr Lazarev); Turetsky Gambit, 2005 (Evgeny Lazarev); Valtiopeli, 1863, 2013 (made-for-TV; Valtteri Simonen). Note: For detailed information on the assassination of Alexander II, see my two-volume work *The Great Pictorial History of World Crime*, Volume I (History, Inc., 2004; illustrated pages 49-53).

Alexander III (c. 1100-1181; Catholic Pope): **Becket**, 1964 (Paolo Stoppa); Meriota, die Tanzerin, 1922 (Max Devrient); Una vita scellerata, 1990 (Ted Rusoff).

Alexander III (1845-1894; Czar of Russia, father of Nicholas II): The Barber of Siberia, 1998 (Nikita Mikhalkov); Bialy mazur, 1979 (Wladyslaw Strzelczyk); Bismarck's Dismissal, 1942 (Walther Sussenguth); Das Geheimnis um Johann Orth, 1936 (Fritz Alberti); Edward the King, 1975 (TV miniseries; Bruce Purchase); Fall of Eagles, 1974 (TV miniseries; Tony Jay); Roman imperatora, 1994 (Sergei Kudimov).

Alexander III of Macedon (aka: Alexander the Great; 356-323 B.C.; Macedonian king and conqueror): Alexander, 2004 (Colin Farrell); Alexander; Hero of Heroes, 2007 (Hawk Younkins); Alexander the Great, 1941 (Prithviraj Kapoor); **Alexander the Great**, 1956 (Richard Burton); Alexander the Great, 1968 (made-for-TV; William Shatner); Alexander the Great, 2006 (animated; Mark Adair-Rios voiceover); BBC Sunday-Night Theatre, 1950-1959 (TV series; "Adventure Story," 1950 episode: Andrew Osborn); Einer wird gewinnen, 1964- (TV series; 1968 episode: Thomas Reiner); Goliath and the Rebel Slave, 1963 (Gabriele Antonini); Off to See the Wizard, 1967-1968 (animated TV series; William Shatner voiceover); Reign: The Conqueror, 1997 (animated TV series; Andrew Philpot, Sonny Chang, Boo Su Han; Toshihiko Seki); The Search for Alexander the Great, 1981 (TV miniseries; Nicholas Clay); Witness to Yesterday, 1998 (TV series; "Alexander the Great," 1998 episode: Paul Gross); Young Alexander the Great, 2010 (Sam Heughan).

Alexander VI (1431-1503; Roderic Leoncoli de Borja; Pope of the Catholic Church, 1492-1503; notorious for his libertinism and nepotism, as well as corrupt political practices in advancing the careers of his offspring, notably his unscrupulous son, Cesare Borgia and his scheming daughter, Lucrezia Borgia): The Borgia, 2006 (Lluis Homar); Borgia,

2011 (TV series; John Dorman); The Borgias, 1981 (TV miniseries; Adolfo Celi); The Borgias, 2011 (TV series; Jeremy Irons); Les Borgia ou le sang dore, 1977 (made-for-TV; Julien Guiomar); Lucrezia Borgia, 1928 (Albert Bassermann); Lucrezia Borgia, 1937 (Roger Karl); Lucrezia Borgia, 1968 (Leon Askin); Lucrezia giovane, 1974 (Ettore Manni); Meriota, die Tanzerin, 1922 (Max Devrient).

Alexander, Edward Porter (1835-1910; U.S. military officer and engineer and general in the Confederate Army of Northern Virginia during the American Civil War): **Gettysburg**, 1993 ([James] Patrick Stuart); **Gods and Generals**, 2003 (James Patrick Stuart); Sunday Showcase, 1959-1961 (TV series; "An American Heritage: Gentleman's Decision," 1961 episode: Mark O'Daniels).

Alexander, Grover Cleveland (aka: "Alexander the Great," "Old Pete"; American baseball player, legendary pitcher; 1887-1950): **The Winning Team**, 1952 (Ronald Reagan).

Alexander, Harold (1891-1969; British field marshal in WWII): Churchill and the Generals, 1979 (made-for-TV; Terence Alexander); Dunkirk, 2004 (made-for-TV; Kevin McNally); **Patton**, 1970 (Gerald Flood).

Alexandra (1872-1918; Empress of Russia; assassinated); A carne osszeeskuvese, 1977 (made-for-TV; Eva Ruttkai); Anastasia: The Mystery of Anna, 1986 (made-for-TV; Claire Bloom); Assassin of the Tsar, 1993 (Olga Antonova); BBC Play of the Month, 1965-1983 (TV series; "Rasputin," 1971 episode: Isabel Dean); Edward the King, 1975- (TV series; two episodes: Meriel Brook); Fall of Eagles, 1974 (TV miniseries; "Tell the King the Sky Is Falling," 1974 episode: Gayle Hunnicutt); The Fall of the Romanovs, 1917 (Nance O'Neil); Into Her Kingdom, 1926 (Elinor Vanderveer); It Was a Gay Ballnight, 1939 (Zarah Leander); The Last Days Before the War, 1932 (Lucie Hoflich); The Legion of Death, 1918 (Grace Aide); The Lost Prince, 2004 (made-for-TV; Ingeborga Dapkunaite); **Nicholas and Alexandra**, 1971 (Janet Suzman); The Night They Killed Rasputin, 1962 (Gianna Maria Canale); 1914, the Last Days before the War, 1932 (Lucie Hoflich); **Oh! What a Lovely War**, 1969 (Pamela Abbott); Raspoutine, 2011 (made-for-TV; Fanny Ardant); Rasputin, 1939 (Marcelle Chantal); Rasputin, 1954 (Isa Miranda); Rasputin, 1966 (made-for-TV; Anneliese Romer); Rasputin, 1967 (Dorothee Blanck); **Rasputin**, 1985 (Velta Line); Rasputin, 1996 (made-for-TV; Greta Scacchi); Rasputin, 2011 (Diana Dell'Erba); **Rasputin and the Empress**, 1932 (Ethel Barrymore); Rasputin and the Holy Devil, 1928 (Diana Karenne); Rasputin, Demon with Women, 1932 (Hermine Sterler); Rasputin, the Black Monk, 1917 (role model for Florence Beresford); **Rasputin: The Mad Monk**, 1966 (Rene Asherson); Rasputins Liebesabenteuer, 1929 (Diana Karenne); The Romanovs: An Imperial Family, 2000 (Lynda Bellingham); Russian Ark, 2002 (Anna Aleksakhina); The Successor, 1996 (Anna Zapryagalova); Tsar Nikolay II, 1917 (Vera Orlova). Note: For detailed information on the assassination of Alexandra, Nicholas II and their family, see my two-volume work *The Great Pictorial History of World Crime*, Volume II (History, Inc., 2004; illustrated pages 79-83).

Alexandra of Denmark (1844-1925; Queen consort of Edward VII of Great Britain): All the King's Men, 2000 (made-for-TV; Maggie Smith); Edward the King, 1975- (TV series; Helen Ryan); **The Elephant Man**, 1980 (Helen Ryan); The Elephant Man, 1982 (made-for-TV; Glenn Close); **Her Majesty Mrs. Brown**, 1997 (Sara Stewart); Lillie, 1978- (TV miniseries; Ann Firbank); The Lost Prince, 2004 (made-for-TV; Bibi Andersson); The Memoirs of Sherlock Holmes, 1994 (TV series; "The Mazarin Stone," 1994 episode: Helen Ryan); **Murder by Decree**, 1979 (Pamela Abbott); Passion, 1999 (Julia Blake); The Waltz Dream, 1925 (Mady Christians).

Alexei Nikolaevich (1904-1918; Alexei Romanov; son of Czar Nicholas II; heir to the Russian throne; assassinated): Anastasia: The Mystery of Anna, 1986 (made-for-TV; Christian Bale); Assassin of the Tsar, 1993 (Aleksei Logunov); BBC Play of the Month, 1965-1983 (TV series; "Rasputin," 1971 episode: Jonathan Moore); Die Brandstifter Europas, 1926 (K. Loibner); Edward the King, 1975 (TV series; "Dearest Prince" and "The Invisible Queen," 1975 episodes: Bruce Purchase); Fall of Eagles, 1974 (TV miniseries; "Tell the King the Sky Is Falling," 1974 episode: Piers Flint-Shipman [Frederick Alexander]); The Fall of the Romanovs, 1917 (Lawrence Johnson); Into Her Kingdom, 1926 (Byron Sage); The Lost Prince, 2004 (made-for-TV; Kostya Severov; San Page as younger Alexei); **Nicholas and Alexandra**, 1971 (Roderic Noble); Rasputin, 1939 (Jean Claudio); Rasputin, 1996 (made-for-TV; Freddie Findlay); **Rasputin and the Empress**, 1932 (Tad Alexander); Rasputin, the Black Monk, 1917 (Bertram Grassby); **Rasputin: The Mad Monk**, 1966 (Robert Duncan); The Romanovs: An Imperial Family, 2000 (Vladimir Grachyov);The Successor, 1996 (Yaroslav Primachenko). Note: For detailed information on the assassination of Alexei and his family, see my two-volume work *The Great Pictorial History of World Crime*, Volume II (History, Inc., 2004; illustrated pages 79-83).

Alexiev, Michael (1857-1918; Russian general of the Imperial Russian Army and commander-in-chief of all armed forces under the Russian Provisional Government; died of a heart attack while fighting Bolshevik forces in the Russian Civil War): Fall of Eagles, 1974 (TV miniseries; "Tell the King the Sky Is Falling," 1974 episode: Nigel Stock); **Nicholas and Alexandra**, 1971 (Roy Dotrice); The Romanovs: An Imperial Family, 2000 (Yuri Kayurov).

Alfonso de Aragon (1417-1495; Italian nobleman): The Borgia, 2006 (Giorgio Marchesi); Borgia, 2011 (TV series; Raimund Wallisch); The Borgias, 2011-2013 (TV series; Sebastian De Souza); Les Borgia ou le sang dore, 1977 (made-for-TV; Herve Bellon); Lucrece Borgia, 1956 (Massimo Serato); Lucrezia Borgia, 1937 (Max Michel); Lucrezia giovane, 1974 (Fred Robsahm).

Alfonso d'Este (1476-1534; Italian nobleman, Duke of Ferrara and patron of Renaissance artists who married the notorious Lucrezia Borgia, his second wife): Borgia, 2011 (TV series; Andrew Hawley); The Borgias, 1981 (TV miniseries; Keith Washington); Bride of Vengeance, 1949 (John Lund); Lucrezia Borgia, 1980 (made-for-TV; Stafford Dean); Lucrezia Borgia, 1994 (made-for-TV; Giampierro Fortebraccio); Pleasant Nights, 1966 (Luigi Vannucchi); **Prince of Foxes**, 1947 (James Carney); The Profession of Arms, 2001 (Giancarlo Belelli); Satanas, 1920 (Ernst Stahl-Nachbaur).

Alfonso XII (1857-1885; king of Spain): Alfonso XII y Maria Cristina, 1960 (Vicente Parra); El marques de Salamanca, 1948 (Jacinto San Emeterio); Ramon y Cajal, 1982 (TV series; Vicente Parra); Restauracio, 1990 (made-for-TV; Pere Ponce); Where Are You Going, Alfonso XII?, 1959 (Vicente Parra).

Almond, Edward (1892-1979; U.S. lieutenant general): Inchon, 1982 (James T. Callahan).

Amann, Max (German soldier who served in a sergeant in WWI and was Adolf Hitler's immediate superior and was one of his only friends; later promoted by Hitler to control and suppress media in Germany that was hostile to Hitler's dictatorship; convicted as a war criminal following WWII and imprisoned for ten years; died in poverty in Munich; 1891-1957): Hitler: The Rise of Evil, 2003 (made-for-TV; Marek Vasut).

American Horse (1840-1908; Oglala Lakota chief of the Sioux Nation who opposed Crazy Horse's war against the U.S. government in 1876-1877): Bury My Heart at Wounded Knee, 2007 (made-for-TV; Morris

Ingrid Berman (as Anastasia) and Yul Brynner in *Anastasia*, 1956.

Birdyellowhead).

Ames, Adelbert (1835-1933; U.S. soldier and politician; Union general during the American Civil War and a radical Republican): **Gods and Generals**, 2003 (Matt Letscher).

Ames, Aldrich Hazen (1941- ; U.S. CIA counterintelligence agent who spied for the Soviets and is currently serving a life prison sentence): Aldrich Ames: Traitor Within, 1998 (made-for-TV; Timothy Hutton).

Anastasia, Albert (aka: Mad Hatter; 1902-1957; U.S. gangster, board member of the U.S. crime syndicate and close ally of Louis "Lepke" Buchalter): Bonanno: A Godfather's Story, 1999 (made-for-TV; Maurizio Terrazzano); Climax!, 1954-1958 (TV series; "Albert Anastasia—His Life and Death," 1958 episode; Eli Wallach); Johnny Ryan, 1990 (made-for-TV; Joe Greco); Lansky, 1999 (made-for-TV; Nick Corello); Lepke, 1975 (Gianni Russo); **Murder, Inc.**, 1960 (Howard I. Smith); My Brother Anastasia, 1973 (Richard Conte); **The Valachi Papers**, 1972 (Fausto Tozzi). Note: For detailed information on Anastasia, see my book *World Encyclopedia of Organized Crime* (Paragon House, 1992; illustrated pages 27-31).

Anastasia Nikolaevna (1901-1918; Anastasia Romanov; Grand Duchess of Russia; daughter of Czar Nicholas II; assassinated): **Anastasia**, 1956 (Ingrid Bergman); Anastasia, 1997 (Meg Ryan, Kirsten Dunst voiceovers; Liz Callaway, Lacey Chabert singing voiceover); Anastasia: The Mystery of Anna, 1986 (made-for-TV; Jennifer Dundas); Assassin of the Tsar, 1993 (Olga Borisova); Clothes Make the Woman, 1928 (Eve Southern); Dulce Anastasia, 1977 (made-for-TV; Graciela Borges); Fall of Eagles, 1974 (TV miniseries; "Tell the King the Sky Is Falling," 1974 episode: Pippa Vickers); The Lost Prince, 2004 (made-for-TV; Algina Lipskyte [Lipskis]); **Nicholas and Alexandra**, 1971 (Fiona Fullerton); Northern Exposure, 1990-1995 (TV series; "Zarya," 1994 episode; Tushka Bergen); Rasputin, 1996 (made-for-TV; Patricia Kovacs); **Rasputin and the Empress**, 1932 (Anne Shirley); The Romanovs: An Imperial Family, 2000 (Olga Budina); The Successor, 1996 (Cristina Vichev). Note: For detailed information on the assassination of the Romanov family, see my two-volume work *The Great Pictorial History of World Crime*, Volume II (History, Inc., 2004; illustrated [eight images] pages 79-83).

Andersen, Hans Christian (1805-1875; Danish author of stories, plays and poems, celebrated for his fairy tales): The Daydreamer, 1966 (Paul O'Keefe); Die schwedische Nachtigall, 1953 (Joachim Gottschalk); 1864, 2014 (TV series; Stig Hoffmeyer); H.C. Andersen's The Long

Danny Kaye (as Hans Christian Andersen) in *Hans Christian Andersen*, 1953.

Shadow, 1998 (animated; Jesper Klein voiceover); **Hans Christian Andersen**, 1952 (Danny Kaye); Hans Christian Andersen: My Life as a Fairy Tale, 2003 (made-for-TV; Kieran Bew); The Little Mermaid, 1992-1994 (TV series; Mark Hamill); Magic Town, 1968 (Jorgan Weel); Mister Blot's Academy, 1984 (Lembit Ulfsak); Mr. H.C. Andersen, 1950 (animated; Ashley Glynne voiceover); Once upon a Time, 2005 (made-for-TV; Henrik Koefoed); The Red Shoes, 1983 (made-for-TV; Stephen Boe); Song of Norway, 1970 (Richard Wordsworth); Tales from a Flying Trunk, 1979 (Murray Melvin); Young Andersen, 2005 (Simon Dahl Thaulow).

Anderson, Anna (1896-1984; claimant to the title and identity of Russian Grand Duchess of Russia Anastasia): Anastasia: The Czar's Last Daughter, 1956 (Lilly Palmer); Anastasia: The False Czar's Daughter, 1928 (Camilla von Hollay); Anastasia: The Mystery of Anna, 1986 (made-for-TV; Amy Irving); BBC Sunday-Night Theatre, 1950-1959 (TV series; "Anastasia," 1953 episode: Mary Kerridge).

Anderson, Marian (1897-1993; U.S. African-American contralto and one of the most celebrated singers of the 20th Century): Eleanor and Franklin: The White House Years, 1977 (made-for-TV; Barbara Smith Conrad).

Anderson, William T. (AKA: Bloody Bill; 1839-1864; Confederate guerilla leader during the American Civil War): Bronco, 1958-1962 (TV series; "Shadow of Jesse James," 1960 episode: Lasse Hellman); Jesse James Under the Black Flag, 1921 (F. G. McCabe); Kansas Raiders, 1950 (Scott Brady); **The Outlaw Josey Wales**, 1976 (John Russell); **Woman They Almost Lynched**, 1953 (Paul Livermore).

Andersson, Elsa (1897-1922; Swedish aviatrix;): As White as in Snow, 2001 (Amanda Ooms).

Andre, John (1750-1780; British major and spy in the American Revolutionary War, 1775-1783; in league with American traitor Benedict Arnold in an effort to seize the fort at West Point, New York, in July 1780; captured and hanged as a spy on orders of General George Washington): Benedict Arnold: A Question of Honor, 2003 (made-for-TV; John Light); Daniel Boone, 1964-1970 (TV series; "Fort West Point," 1967 episode: Bill Fletcher); George Washington, 1984 (TV miniseries; Randy Anderson); I Spy, 1955- (TV series; "Betrayal at West Point," 1956 episode: Louis Edmonds); The Revolution, 2006- (TV series; "Treason and Betrayal," 2007 episode: Jorge Marcos); **The Scarlet Coat**, 1955 (Michael Wilding); TURN: Washington's Spies, 2014- (TV series; many episodes; J.J. Feild); You Are There, 1953-1971 (TV series;

"The Treason of Benedict Arnold," 1953 episode: John Gabriel). Note: For detailed information on Andre, see my book *Spies: A Narrative Encyclopedia of Dirty Tricks & Double Dealing from Biblical Times to Today* (M. Evans, 1997; illustrated pages 35-40).

Andrew (Saint Andrew; one of the twelve Apostles of Jesus): Acts of the Apostles, 1969 (TV miniseries; Hedi Novira); Animated Stories from the New Testament, 1987- (TV series; Bruce Winant voiceover); Apostle Peter and the Last Supper, 2012 (Leon Melas); The Big Fisherman, 1959 (Rhodes Reason); Color of the Cross, 2006 (Andrea Scarduzio); Color of the Cross 2: The Resurrection, 2008 (Andrea Scarduzio); Crown of Thorns, 1934 (silent; Edward Kandl); Darkness into Light, 2016 (Andrew Harwood Mills); The Day Christ Died, 1980 (made-for-TV; Dov Gottesfeld); Day of Triumph, 1954 (Touch Connors/Mike Connors); 40 Nights, 2016 (Stetson Bloomfield); The Gospel according to Matthew, 1993 (Hannes Muller); The Gospel according to St. Matthew, 1966 (Alfonso Gatto); The Gospel of John, 2014 (Abdelaziz N'Mila); The Gospel of Luke, 2015 (Abdelaziz N'Mila); Gospel Road: A Story of Jesus, 1973 (Lyle Nicholson); The Great Commandment, 1939 (Harold Minjir); **The Greatest Story Ever Told**, 1965 (Burt Brinckerhoff); Il messia, 1975 (Rouf Ben Yaghlane); Imperium: Saint Peter, 2005 (Manrico Gammarota); Jesus [aka: The Jesus Film], 1979 (Gad Roll); Jesus, 2000 (made-for-TV; Gilly Gilchrist); **Jesus Christ Superstar**, 1973 (Richard Molinare); Jesus of Nazareth, 1942 (Armando Velasco); Jesus of Nazareth, 1977 (TV miniseries; Tony Vogel); Judas, 2004 (made-for-TV; Rory Kinnear); **The King of Kings**, 1927 (David Imboden); **King of Kings**, 1961 (Tino Barrero); Kristo, 1996 (Conrad Poe); The Last Supper: Thirteen Men of Courage, 2007 (made-for-TV; John Torres); The Last Temptation of Christ, 1988 (Gary Basaraba); The Living Christ Series, 1951 (TV miniseries; William Henry; Harry Lauter); Matthew: 26:17, 2005 (Andrew Archibeque); Mary, 2005 (Ettore D'Alessandro); Mary, Mother of the Son of God, 2003 (Nilvan Santos); The Milky Way, 1969 (Christian Van Cau); The Miracle Worker, 2000 (Ewan Stewart); The Passion, 2008 (TV miniseries; Eoin Geoghegan); The Passover Plot, 1976 (Daniel Ades); The Power of the Resurrection, 1958 (Warren Parker); The Testaments: Of One Fold and One Shepherd, 2000 (David Alan Else); The Visual Bible: The Gospel of John, 2003 (Tristan Gemmill).

Angleton, James Jesus (1917-1987; U.S. Associated Deputy Director of Counterintelligence for the CIA): Agent of Influence, 2002 (made-for-TV; Douglas MacLeod); Cambridge Spies, 2003 (TV miniseries; John Light); The Company, 2007 (TV miniseries; Michael Keaton); The Good Shepherd, 2006 (Matt Damon); Yuri Nosenko, KGB, 1986 (Josef Sommer). Note: For detailed information on Angleton, see my book, *Spies: A Narrative Encyclopedia of Dirty Tricks & Double Dealing from Biblical Times to Today* (M. Evans, 1997; illustrated pages 41-42).

Anne of Austria (1601-1666; Queen consort of France, wife of Louis XIII): Animated Three Musketeers, 1987 (TV series; Mari Okamoto); At Sword's Point, 1952 (Gladys Cooper); Biblioteca di Studio Uno: I tre moschettieri, 1964 (made-for-TV; Nilla Pizzi); Cardinal Richelieu, 1935 (Katharine Alexander); Cinq-Mars, 1981 (made-for-TV; Pascale Audret); Cyrano et d'Artagnan, 1964 (Laura Valenzuela); D'Artagnan, 1969 (TV miniseries; Eleonora Rossi Drago); D'Artagnan, 1991 (made-for-TV; Alex Pandev); D'Artagnan et les trois mousquetaires, 2005 (Stefania Rocca); D'Artanyan i tri mushketyora, 1979 (TV series; Alisa Freyndlikh); De drie Musketiers, 1968 (made-for-TV; Vera Veroft); Die Drie Musketiere, 2013 (Mariya Mironova); Family Classics: The Three Musketeers, 1960 (made-for-TV; Joan Tetzel); The Four Musketeers, 1963 (Beatrice Altariba); **The Four Musketeers**, 1975 (Geraldine Chaplin); I tre moschettieri, 1991 (made-for-TV; Iva Zanicchi); La loca historia de los tres mosqueteros, 1983 (Paloma Hurtado); Les quatre mouquetaires, 1934 (Esther Deltenre); Le camera explore le temps, 1957-1966 (TV series; "La conjuration de Cinq-Mars," 1962 episode:

Eleonore Hirt); Les trois mousquetaires ou L'escrime ne paie pas, 1979 (made-for-TV; Claire Maurier); Les trois mousquetaires: Premiere epoque—Les ferrets de la reine, 1961 (Francoise Christophe); The Magnavox Theater, 1950 (TV series; "The Three Musketeers," 1950 episode: Marjorie Lord); **The Man in the Iron Mask**, 1939 (Doris Kenyon); Mazarin, 1978 (TV miniseries; Martine Sarcey); **The Musketeer**, 2001 (Catherine Deneuve); The Musketeers, 2014 (TV series; Alexandra Dowling); Panache, 1976 (made-for-TV; Amy Irving); The Queen and the Cardinal, 2009 (made-for-TV; Alassandra Martines); Richelieu, 1914 (Edythe Chapman); Richelieu, 1977 (TV miniseries; Marie-Christine Demarest); Richelieu, la pourpre et la sang, 2013 (made-for-TV; Cecile Bois); Richelieu ou La journee des dupes, 1983 (made-for-TV; Sophie De La Rochefoucauld); The Three Musketeers, 1916 (Dorothy Dalton); **The Three Musketeers**, 1921 (Mary MacLaren); Three Musketeers, 1932 (Andree Lafayette); The Three Musketeers, 1935 (Rosamond Pinchot); The Three Musketeers, 1939 (Gloria Stuart); **The Three Musketeers**, 1948 (Angela Lansbury); The Three Musketeers, 1954 (TV series; Veronica Hurst); The Three Musketeers, 1966 (TV miniseries; Carole Potter); Under the Red Robe, 1923 (Mary MacLaren); **The Three Musketeers**, 1974 (Geraldine Chaplin); **The Three Musketeers**, 1993 (Gabrielle Anwar); The Three Musketeers, 2007 (Nastja Arcel voiceover); The Three Musketeers, 2011 (Juno Temple); Vengeance of the Three Musketeers, 1961 (Francoise Christophe); Vingt ans apres, 1922 (Marguerite Moreno); Tri musketyri, 1983 (TV miniseries; Marta Vancurova); Tri mushketera, 2013 (Mariya Mironova); Versailles, 2015- (TV series; Dominique Blanc).

Anne of Cleves (1515-1557; Queen of England; fourth wife of Henry VIII): BBC Sunday-Night Theatre, 1950-1959 (TV series; "The Rose without a Thorn," 1953 episode: Christie Humphrey); Heinrich VIII und seine Frauen, 1968 (made-for-TV; Gerda Gmelin); Henry VIII, 2003 (made-for-TV; Pia Girard); Henry VIII and His Six Wives, 1972 (Jenny Bos); La jument du roi, 1972 (made-for-TV; Francoise Seigner); **The Private Life of Henry VIII**, 1933 (Elsa Lanchester); The Six Wives of Henry VIII, 1970- (TV miniseries; Elvi Hale); The Six Wives of Henry VIII, 2001 (TV miniseries; Catherine Siggins); The Tudors, 2007-2010 (TV series; Joss Stone).

Anselmi, Albert (1883-1929; Sicilian assassin-for-hire in the employ of Chicago crime czar Al Capone, and who, with his partner John Scalisi, murdered more than a dozen persons, including bootleggers Charles Dion O'Banion, Earl "Hymie" Weiss and the seven victims of the George "Bugs" Moran gang in what became known as the St. Valentine's Day Massacre of 1929; he, along with his partner Scalisi, and confederate Joseph "Hop Toad" Giunta, were all murdered by Capone after they tried to usurp his underworld fiefdom): **Al Capone**, 1959 (Steve Gravers); Playhouse 90, 1956-1961 (TV series; "Seven Against the Wall," 1958 episode; Tito Vuolo); **The St. Valentine's Day Massacre**, 1967 (Rico Cattani). Note: For detailed information on Anselmi, see my book, *World Encyclopedia of Organized Crime* (Paragon House, 1992; illustrated pages 33-36).

Anthony, Susan Brownell (1820-1906; U.S. civil rights leader and feminist): The American Adventure, 1982 (Tricia Buttrill voiceover); The American Parade, 1974 (TV miniseries; "We the Women," 1974 episode; Leora Dana); The American Woman: Portraits of Courage, 1976 (made-for-TV; Lois Nettleton); You Are There, 1953-1971 (TV series; "The Trial of Susan B. Anthony [June 18, 1873]," 1955 episode; Carmen Mathews); Under This Sky, 1979 (Collin Wilcox Paxton).

Antony, Marc (Mark Antony; 83 B.C.-30 B.C.; Roman general and politician): Ancient Rome: The Rise and Fall of an Empire, 2006 (TV series; Alex Ferns); Antoine et Cleopatre, 1967 (Francois Chaumette); Antonio e Cleopatra, 1965 (made-for-TV; Enrico Maria Salerno); Antonius und Cleopatra, 1963 (Peter Pasetti); Antony and Cleopatra, 1913

John Gielgud and Charlton Heston (as Marc Antony) in *Julius Caesar*, 1970.

(Amleto Novelli); Antony and Cleopatra, 1951 (Robert Speaight); Antony and Cleopatra, 1959 (made-for-TV; Keith Eden); Antony and Cleopatra, 1973 (Charlton Heston); Antony and Cleopatra, 1975 (made-for-TV; Richard Johnson); Antony and Cleopatra, 1981 (made-for-TV; Colin Blakely); Antony and Cleopatra, 1984 (made-for-TV; Timothy Dalton); Antony and Cleopatra, 2015 (Geraint Wyn Davies); BBC Play of the Month, 1965-1983 (TV series; "Julius Caesar," 1969 episode: Robert Stephens); BBC Sunday-Night Theatre, 1950-1959 (TV series; "Julius Caesar," two 1951 episodes: Anthony Hawtrey); Caesar, 2003 (made-for-TV; Jay Rodan); Caesar Must Die, 2012 (Antonio Frasca); Caesar the Conqueror, 1963 (Bruno Tocci); Carry On Cleo, 1964 (Sidney James); Cleopatra, 1943 (Badr Lama); Cleopatra, 1912 (Charles Sindelar); Cleopatra, 1917 (Thurston Hall); **Cleopatra**, 1934 (Henry Wilcoxon); Cleopatra, 1962- (TV series; Tarcisio Meira); **Cleopatra**, 1963 (Richard Burton); Cleopatra, 1999 (TV miniseries; Billy Zane); Cleopatra, 2007 (Bruno Garcia); The Destiny of Rome, 2011 (TV miniseries; Pawel Delag); Empire, 2005 (TV miniseries; Vincent Ragan); Festival, 1960- (TV series; "Julius Caesar," 1960 episode: William Shatner); Histeria!, 1998-2000 (animated TV series; "Return to Rome," 1998 episode: Fred Travalena voiceover); An Honourable Murder, 1960 (Philip Saville); The Ides of March, 1961 (made-for-TV; Dennis Mitchell); Imperium: Augustus, 2003 (made-for-TV; Massimo Ghini); Julius Caesar, 1938 (made-for-TV; D.A. Clarke-Smith); Julius Caesar, 1949 (made-for-TV; Raymond McDonell); Julius Caesar, 1950 (Charlton Heston); **Julius Caesar**, 1953 (Marlon Brando); Julius Caesar, 1963- (TV series; Patrick Allen); Julius Caesar, 1966 (made-for-TV; Peter Donat); **Julius Caesar**, 1970 (Charlton Heston); Julius Caesar, 1979 (made-for-TV; Keith Michell); Julius Caesar, 2011 (Ryan Jay Jones); Julius Caesar, 2012 (made-for-TV; Ray Fearon); Julius Caesar, 2014 (Michael Parks); Legions of the Nile, 1959 (Georges Marchal); The Notorious Cleopatra, 1970 (Johnny Rocco); Rome, 2005-2007 (TV series; James Purefoy); Serpent of the Nile, 1953 (Raymond Burr); Shakespeare: The Animated Tales, 1992-1994 (TV series; "Julius Caesar," 1994 episode: Jim Carter voiceover); The Spread of the Eagle, 1963- (TV miniseries; Keith Michell); The Story of Mankind, 1957 (Helmut Dantine); Studio One in Hollywood, 1948-1958 (TV series; "Julius Caesar," two 1949 episodes: Richard Hart; Philip Bourneuf; "Julius Caesar," 1955 episode; Alfred Ryder); Toto and Cleopatra, 1963 (Toto as Marc Antony); Two Nights with Cleopatra, 1964 (Ettore Manni); World Theatre, 1959- (TV miniseries; "Julius Caesar," 1959 episode: William Sylvester); Xena: Warrior Princess, 1995-2001 (TV series; John O'Leary in one 1995 episode; Manu Bennett in one 2000 episode).

Apache Kid (Haskay-bay-nay-ntyl; c. 1860-c. 1919; White Mountain

Elizabeth Taylor (as Cleopatra) and Roddy McDowall (as Augustus) in *Cleopatra,* **1963.**

Apache scout and later renegade and outlaw): Apache Warrior, 1957 (Michael Carr); Stories of the Century, 1954- (TV series; "Apache Kid," 1955 episode; Kenneth Alton). Note: For detailed information on the Apache Kid, see my book, *Encyclopedia of Western Lawmen and Outlaws* (Paragon House, 1992; illustrated pages 10-11).

Aristotle (384-322 B.C.; Greek philosopher and scientist): Alexander, 2004 (Christopher Plummer); Alexander; Hero of Heroes, 2007 (Terrence Evans); Alexander the Great, 1941 (Shakir); **Alexander the Great**, 1956 (Barry Jones); Mon couer est rouge, 1977 (Maud Rimbaud); Reign: The Conqueror, 1997 (animated TV series; John Rafter Lee; John Wesley; Nachi Nozawa); Walt Disney's Wonderful World of Color, 1954-1992 (TV series; "Beyond Witch Mountain," 1982 episode: Efrem Zimbalist Jr.); Young Alexander the Great, 2010 (Christopher Cazenove).

Armistead, Lewis Addison (1817-1863; Confederate general in the Army of Northern Virginia during the American Civil War; mortally wounded in Pickett's Charge on July 3, 1863): **Gettysburg**, 1993 (Richard Jordan); **Gods and Generals**, 2003 (John Prosky).

Armstrong, Neil Alden (1930- ; U.S. astronaut, first man to walk on the moon); Apollo 11, 1996 (Jeffrey Nordling); **Apollo 13**, 1995 (Mark Wheeler); The Challenger Disaster, 2013 (made-for-TV; Stephen Jennings); From Earth to the Moon, 1998 (TV miniseries; Tony Goldwyn); **Men in Black 3**, 2012 (Jared Johnston); Moonshot, 2009 (made-for-TV; Daniel Lapaine).

Arnaud, Charles Auguste (1825-1883; French sculptor, who went insane before dying horribly in a railway accident): Paradise Found, 2003 (Chris Haywood).

Arnim, Hans-Jurgen von (1889-1962; German general in WWII): The Biggest Battle, 1978 (Bill Vanders).

Arnold, Benedict (1741-1801; heroic general in the Continental Army during the American Revolutionary War, 1775, 1783, largely credited with the victory over the British at Saratoga in 1777, but who turned traitor, defecting to the British after failing to turn over the fort at West Point, New York, in July 1780 and later fighting on the side of the British; his name is synonymous with treason): The American Revolution, 1994 (made-for-TV; Kelsey Grammer voiceover); Benedict Arnold: A Question of Honor, 2003 (made-for-TV; Aidan Quinn); Cavalcade of America, 1952-1957 (TV series; "The Betrayal," 1953 episode: Dan O'Herlihy); George Washington, 1984 (TV miniseries;

Stephen Macht); The Green Mountain Boys, 1955 (made-for-TV; Barry Kroger [Kroeger]); I Spy, 1955- (TV series; "Betrayal at West Point," 1956 episode: Otto Hulett); The Philco-Goodyear Television Playhouse, 1948-1956 (TV series; "Pride's Way," 1953 episode: Shepperd Strudwick); The Plot to Kidnap General Washington, 1952 (made-for-TV; Guy Spaull); The Revolution, 2006- (TV series; James Karcher); **The Scarlet Coat**, 1955 (Robert Douglas); TURN: Washington's Spies, 2014 (TV series; Owain Yeoman); Where Do We Go From Here?, 1945 (John Davidson); You Are There, 1953-1971 (TV series; "The Treason of Benedict Arnold," 1953 episode: Richard Dysart). Note: For detailed information on Benedict Arnold, see my book *Spies: A Narrative Encyclopedia of Dirty Tricks & Double Dealing from Biblical Times to Today* (M. Evans, 1997; illustrated pages 44-51).

Arnold, Henry H. (Henry Harley Arnold; aka: "Hap"; 1886-1950; American five-star general of the army and general of the air force, commanding general of the U.S. Army Air Force in WWII; pioneer in aviation): **The Court Martial of Billy Mitchell**, 1955 (Robert Brubaker); **The Glenn Miller Story**, 1954 (Barton MacLane).

Arnold, Margaret Shippen ("Peggy"; 1760-1804; wife of American traitor Benedict Arnold): Benedict Arnold: A Question of Honor, 2003 (made-for-TV; Flora Montgomery); George Washington, 1984 (TV miniseries; Megan Gallahger); The Philco-Goodyear Television Playhouse, 1948-1956 (TV series; "Pride's Way," 1953 episode: Stella Andrew); You Are There, 1953-1971 (TV series; "The Treason of Benedict Arnold," 1953 episode: Jennifer Darling). Note: For detailed information on Margaret Arnold, see my book *Spies: A Narrative Encyclopedia of Dirty Tricks & Double Dealing from Biblical Times to Today* (M. Evans, 1997; illustrated pages 44-51).

Arnold, Samuel (1834-1906; convicted of conspiring to kidnap and/or assassinate U.S. President Abraham Lincoln in 1865 and sent to prison for life; pardoned by U.S. President Andrew Johnson in 1869): The Lincoln Conspiracy, 1977 (Ben Jones).

Attila the Hun (d. 453; ruthless ruler of the Huns in Europe): Attila, 1954 (Anthony Quinn): Attila, 1985 (made-for-TV; Yevgeni Nesterenko); Attila, 1991 (made-for-TV; Samuel Ramey); Attila, 2001 (made-for-TV; Samuel Ramey); Attila, 2001- (TV miniseries; Gerard Butler; Rollo Weeks as young Attila); Attila, 2010 (made-for-TV; Giovanni Battista Parodi); Attila, 2013 (Chris Cole); Attila flagella di Dio, 1982 (Diego Abatantuono); Attila: The Scourge of God, 1918 (Febo Mari); Highway to Hell, 1992 (Ben Stiller); **Night at the Museum**, 2006 (Patrick Gallagher); **Night at the Museum: Battle of the Smithsonian**, 2009 (Patrick Gallagher); Sign of the Pagan, 1954 (Jack Palance); Tarkan, 1969 (Oktar Durukan); Tarkan: The Gold Medallion, 1972 (Kamran Usluer).

Attucks, Crispus (1723-1770; U.S. citizen and first victim slain in the Boston Massacre of March 5, 1770, in Boston, Massachusetts, at the hands of British troops): Samuel Adams, 2014 (made-for-TV; Will Green); Swing Out, Sweet Land, 1970 (made-for-TV; Greg Morris); You Are There, 1953-1971 (TV series; "The Boston Tea Party [December 12, 1773]," 1953 episode: Roy Glenn).

Atzerodt, George Andreas (1835-1865; U.S. carriage repairman, who was one of the four main conspirators in the 1865 assassination of President Abraham Lincoln and who was convicted and executed by hanging): **The Conspirator**, 2011 (John Michael Weatherly); The Day Lincoln Was Shot, 1998 (made-for-TV; Kirk B.R. Woller); Days That Shook the World, 2003-2013 (TV series; "Terror Made in America: Assassination of Abraham Lincoln...," 2004 episode: Robert Wagner); The Killing of Mary Surratt, 2009 (Brian Rife); The Lincoln Conspiracy, 1977 (Bill Dial). Note: For detailed information on Atzerodt, see my book *The Great Pictorial History of World Crime*, Volume I (History, Inc., 2004; illustrated pages 26-44).

Audisio, Walter (AKA: Valerio; 1909-1973; Communist partisan and politician who personally murdered Italian dictator Benito Mussolini and his mistress, Clara Petacci): **Last Days of Mussolini**, 1977 (Franco Nero).

Audubon, John James (1785-1851; French-American ornithologist, naturalist and painter): The Adventures of Jim Bowie, 1956-1958 (TV series; Robert Cornthwaite; Harry Bartell); **The Iron Mistress**, 1952 (George Voskovec).

Augustine I of Mexico (Augustin de Iturbide; 1783-1824; Emperor of Mexico): Gritos de muerte y libertad, 2010 (TV series; Daniel Gimenez Cacho); Heroes de Carne y Hueso, 2010 (TV series; Ruben Zamora); **Juarez**, 1939 (Mickey Kuhn); La antorcha encendida, 1996 (TV series; Rene Casados); Los caudillos, 1968 (TV series; Jose Loza); Morelos, 2012 (Andres Montiel).

Augustus (Octavius; Augustus; 63 B.C.-14 A.D.; Roman emperor and founder of the Roman Empire): Ancient Rome: The Rise and Fall of an Empire, 2006 (TV miniseries; "Revolution," 2006 episode: James Hillier); Antonio e Cleopatra, 1965 (made-for-TV; Daniele Tedeschi); Antony and Cleopatra, 1913 (Ignazio Lupi); Antony and Cleopatra, 1973 (John Castle); Antony and Cleopatra, 1975 (made-for-TV; Corin Redgrave); Antony and Cleopatra, 1984 (made-for-TV; Anthony Geary); Antony and Cleopatra, 2015 (Ben Carlson); BBC Play of the Month, 1965-1983 (TV series; "Julius Caesar," 1969 episode: John Alderton); BBC Sunday-Night Theatre, 1950-1959 (TV series; "Julius Caesar," two 1951 episodes: Richard Bebb; "Prelude to Glory," 1954 episode: Willoughby Goddard); The Caesars, 1968- (TV miniseries; "Augustus," 1968 episode: Roland Culver); Caligula, 1975 (made-for-TV; Joris Collet); Cleopatra, 1912 (Mr. Paul); Cleopatra, 1917 (Henri De Vries); **Cleopatra**, 1934 (Ian Keith); **Cleopatra**, 1963 (Roddy McDowall); Cleopatra, 1999 (TV miniseries; Rupert Graves); Cleopatra, 2007 (Taumaturgo Ferreira); The Destiny of Rome, 2011 (TV miniseries; Andy Gillet); Empire, 2005 (TV miniseries; Santiago Cabrera); Herod the Great, 1960 (Massimo Girotti); I, Claudius, 1937 (Roy Emerton); I, Claudius 1976 (TV miniseries; Brian Blessed); Imperium: Augustus, 2003 (made-for-TV; Peter O'Toole as adult Augustus; Benjamin Sadler as young Augustus); Julius Caesar, 1938 (made-for-TV; Douglas Matthews); Julius Caesar, 1950 (Bob Holt); **Julius Caesar**, 1953 (Douglass Watson); Julius Caesar, 1963- (TV series; Michael Graham); **Julius Caesar**, 1970 (Richard Chamberlain); Julius Caesar, 1979 (made-for-TV; Garrick Hagon); Julius Caesar, 2011 (Miles Yekinni); Julius Caesar, 2012 (made-for-TV; Ivanno Jeremiah); Julius Caesar, 2014 (Salvatore Capuano); Legions of the Nile, 1959 (Alfredo Mayo); **Night at the Museum**, 2006 (Steve Coogan); **Night at the Museum: Battle of the Smithsonian**, 2009 (Steve Coogan); **Night at the Museum: Secret of the Tomb**, 2014 (Steve Coogan); Rome, 2005-2007 (TV series; Simon Woods); Serpent of the Nile, 1953 (Michael Fox); Shakespeare: The Animated Tales, 1992-1994 (TV series; "Julius Caesar,"1994 episode: Andrew Wincott voiceover); Son of Cleopatra, 1964 (Alberto Lupo); The Spread of the Eagle, 1963- (TV miniseries; "The Monument: Antony and Cleopatra," 1963 episode: David William); Studio One in Hollywood, 1948-1958 (TV series; "Julius Caesar," 1955 episode: Michael Tolan); The Viking Queen, 1967 (Andrew Keir); World Theatre, 1959- (TV miniseries; "Julius Caesar," 1959 episode: Jeremy Burnham); Xena: Warrior Princess, 1995-2001 (TV series; Mark Warren in two 2000 episodes; Colin Moy in one 2000 episode).

Austen, Jane (1775-1817; British author): **Becoming Jane**, 2007 (Anne Hathaway); Miss Austen Regrets, 2008 (made-for-TV; Olivia Williams); Northanger Abbey, 2007 (made-for-TV; Geraldine James voiceover);

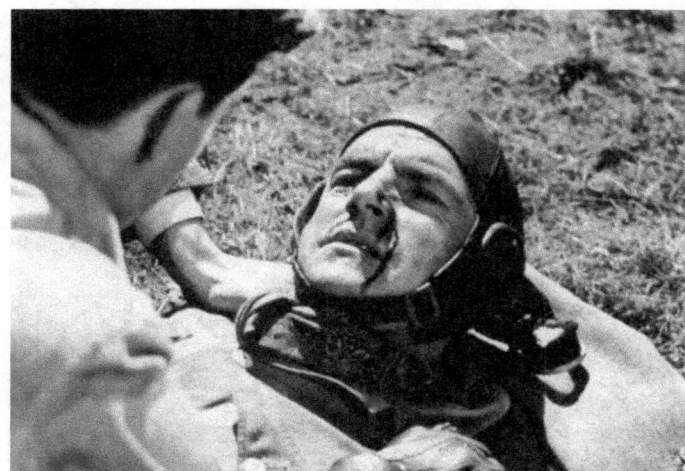

Kenneth More (as RAF ace Douglas Bader) in *Reach for the Sky*, 1957.

Pride and Prejudice, 1952 (TV miniseries; Thea Holme).

Austin, Stephen Fuller (1793-1836; U.S. pioneer and one of the founders of the Republic of Texas): American Playhouse, 1981 (TV series; "Seguin," 1982 episode: Robert Viharo); Death Valley Days, 1952-1970 (TV series; "Trial at Belle's Springs," 1964 episode: David McLean; "Here Stands Bailey," 1969 episode: John Carter); The First Texan, 1956 (Dayton Lummis); Gone to Texas, 1986 (made-for-TV; James Stephens); Heroes of the Alamo, 1937 (Earle Hodgins); **The Last Command**, 1955 (Otto Kruger); **Man of Conquest**, 1939 (Ralph Morgan); Texas, 1994 (made-for-TV; Patrick Duffy).

Aylward, Gladys (1902-1970; heroic British evangelical Christian missionary to China): **The Inn of the Sixth Happiness**, 1958 (Ingrid Bergman).

Azev, Yevno (1860-1918; Russian spymaster; a double agent for the Bolsheviks and the Imperial Russian police): Azev: Le tsar de nuit, 1975 (made-for-TV; Pierre Santini); Fall of Eagles, 1974 (TV miniseries; Victor Winding); Imperiya pod udarom, 2000- (TV miniseries; Vladimir Bogdanov); Lockspitzel Asew, 1935 (Fritz Rasp); The Rider Named Death, 2004 (Dmitry Dyuzhev). Note: For detailed information on Azev, see my book *Spies: A Narrative Encyclopedia of Dirty Deeds & Double Dealing from Biblical Times to Today* (M. Evans, 1997; illustrated pages 54-61).

Bacon, Francis (1561-1626; British statesman, scientist and author): Churchill's People, 1974 (TV series; "A Rich and Beautiful Empire," 1974 episode: John Nettleton); Elizabeth I, 2005 (TV miniseries; Will Keen); Elizabeth R, 1971- (TV miniseries; "Sweet England's Pride," 1971 episode: John Nettleton); ITV Play of the Week, 1955-1974 (TV series; "In the Shadow of the Axe," 1958 episode: Derek Godfrey); Master Shakespeare, Strolling Player, 1916 (Robert Whittier); **The Private Lives of Elizabeth and Essex**, 1939 (Donald Crisp); Queen Elizabeth, 1912 (Jean Chameroy); The Virgin Queen, 2005 (TV miniseries; Neil Stuke); You Are There, 1953-1971 (TV series; "The First Command Performance of Romeo and Juliet [1597]," 1954 episode: Kendall Clark).

Bader, Douglas (1910-1982; British RAF ace in WWII): **Reach for the Sky**, 1957 (Kenneth More).

Baker, Josephine (1906-1975; U.S. African-American dancer in France): Federico Garcia Lorca Noir Despair, 2013 (Vianna Asencio); Frida, 2002 (Karine Plantadit—Bageot); Great Performances, 1971 (TV series; "Harlem in Montmartre: A Paris Jazz Story," 2009 episode: Quincy

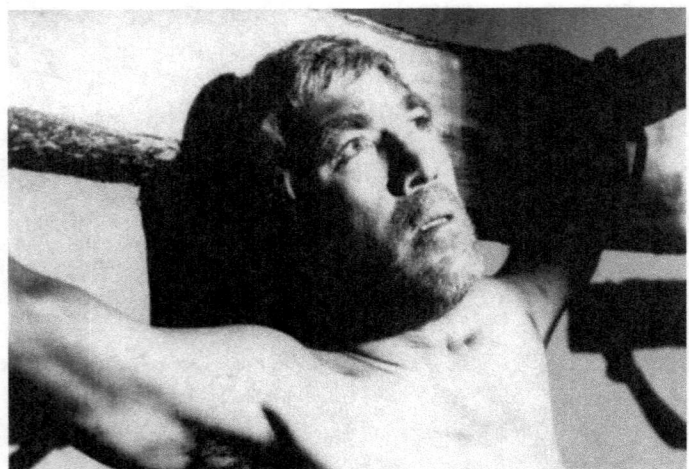

Anthony Quinn (as Barabbas) in *Barabbas,* **1962.**

Tyler Bernstine); JK, 2006 (TV miniseries; Quiteria Chagas); The Josephine Baker Story, 1991 (made-for-TV; Lynn Whitfield); La rumba, 1987 (Vivian Reed); Les enfants du pays, 2006 (Maud Rakotondravohitra); **Midnight in Paris**, 2011 (Sonia Rolland); Parade of Stars, 1983 (made-for-TV; Debbie Allen); Return to Babylon, 2013 (Rolonda Watts); Two, 2002 (Tim Fischer); Winchell, 1998 (made-for-TV; Victoria Gabrielle Platt).

Baker, Lafayette Curry (1826-1868; U.S. military officer and head of the Union Secret Service [Intelligence Service] during the American Civil War, who was involved with capturing the conspirators in the 1865 assassination of President Abraham Lincoln; devious and self-serving, Baker, following his dismissal, claimed that U.S. Department of War Secretary Edwin M. Stanton had a hand in the murder of Lincoln; he was dismissed from his post for spying on U.S. President Andrew Johnson and it was later claimed that he had been murdered to silence him): The Lincoln Conspiracy, 1977 (John Dehner); You Are There, 1953-1957 (TV series; "The Capture of John Wilkes Booth," 1953 episode: Tyler McVey). Note: For detailed information on Lafayette Baker, see my book *The Great Pictorial History of World Crime*, Volume I (History, Inc., 2004; illustrated pages 26-44).

Baker, Luther Byron (1839-1896; U.S. detective and younger brother of Lafayette Baker, head of the U.S. Secret Service [Intelligence Service] during the American Civil War, and who was reportedly in charge of the U.S. cavalry unit that tracked down and killed John Wilkes Booth, assassin of President Abraham Lincoln): The Lincoln Conspiracy, 1977 (J. Don Ferguson); You Are There, 1953-1957 (TV series; "The Capture of John Wilkes Booth," 1953 episode: Paul Hahn). Note: For detailed information on Luther Baker, see my book *The Great Pictorial History of World Crime*, Volume I (History, Inc., 2004; illustrated pages 26-44).

Baldwin, Raymond Earl (1893-1986; U.S. politician, U.S. senator [Ct.] and 72nd and 74th governor of Connecticut): Tail Gunner Joe, 1977 (made-for-TV; Herb Volland).

Ball, George (1909-1994; U.S. diplomat and 7th U.S. ambassador to the United Nations): Path to War, 2002 (made-for-TV; Bruce McGill).

Ball, Lucille (1911-1989; U.S. comedienne and actress): Abbott and Costello in Hollywood, 1945 (herself); **Best Foot Forward**, 1943 (herself); Hollywood Babylon, 1992-1993 (TV series; "Lucy & Desi/Fatty Arbuckle," 1992 episode: Barbara Gates Wilson); **J. Edgar**, 2011 (Jennipher Foster); Lucy, 2003 (made-for-TV; Rachel York; Madeline Zima as teenage Lucy); Lucy & Desi: Before the Laughter, 1991 (made-for-

TV; Frances Fisher); The Scarlett O'Hara War, 1980 (made-for-TV; Gypsi DeYoung); Spending Nights with Joan, 1998 (made-for-TV; Angelika Thomas); **Thousands Cheer**, 1943 (herself); Timecop, 1997- (TV miniseries; "Stalker," 1997 episode: Suzanne LaRusch); A Woman of Distinction, 1950 (herself); **Ziegfeld Follies**, 1945 (herself).

Balthazar (Biblical person in the Gospel of Matthew in the New Testament, one of three Wise Men, who came to worship the birth of Jesus): Amahl and the Night Visitors, 1951 (made-for-TV; Leon Lishner); **Ben-Hur**, 1959 (Finlay Currie); **Ben-Hur: A Tale of the Christ**, 1925 (Charles Belcher); The Christmas Toy, 1986 (made-for-TV; Jerry Nelson); Family Theatre, 1949-1958 (TV series; "A Star Shall Rise," 1952 episode; Raymond Burr); The Fourth King, 1997 (made-for-TV; Joachim Fuchsberger); **The Greatest Story Ever Told**, 1965 (Mark Lenard); **King of Kings**, 1961 (Edric Connor); Mary, Mother of Jesus, 1999 (made-for-TV; Artur Kalid); The Nativity Story, 2006 (Eriq Ebouaney); Son of God, 2014 (Patrice Naiambana); The Three Wise Men, 1976 (animated; Armando Coria Sr. voiceover); The 3 Wise Men, 2003 (animated; Imanol Arias voiceover).

Balzac, Honore de (1799-1850; French novelist and playwright): Balzac: A Passionate Life, 2000 (made-for-TV; Gerard Depardieu); Eugene Sue, 1974 (made-for-TV; Jacques Ferriere); George Sand, une femme libre, 1995 (made-for-TV; Andre Marcon); The Life of Giuseppe Verdi, 1940 (Gabriel Gabrio); Mauvais genre, 1997 (Francoise Dukrate); Mon couer est rouge, 1977 (Francoise Dukrate); Notorious Woman, 1974 (TV miniseries; Peter Woodthorpe); Prometheus: The Life of Balzac, 1975- (TV miniseries; Nicky Henson); **A Song to Remember**, 1945 (Peter Cusanelli).

Barabbas (Hebrew criminal and outlaw who was released at the urgings of a mob instead of Jesus): Barabbas, 1953 (Ulf Palme); **Barabbas**, 1962 (Anthony Quinn); Barabbas, 2013 (made-for-TV; Billy Zane); Barabbas, 2014 (Timothy Gilbert); Day of Triumph, 1954 (Anthony Warde); The Final Inquiry, 2006 (Giacomo Gonnella); Give Us Barabbas!, 1961 (made-for-TV; James Daly); **The Greatest Story Ever Told**, 1965 (Richard Conte); Jesus, 2000 (made-for-TV; Claudio Amendola); Jesus, Mary and Joseph, 1972 (Rene Dupeyron); Jesus of Nazareth, 1977 (TV miniseries; Stacy Keach); Judas, 2004 (made-for-TV; Adil Abdelouahed); **The King of Kings**, 1927 (George Siegmann); **King of Kings**, 1961 (Harry Guardino); Kristo, 1996 (Ricky Davao); The Life and the Passion of Christ, 2005 (made-for-TV; Cesar Rodriguez); Maria's Hours, 1979 (Jose Manuel Bissau); The Miracle Maker, 2000 (Tim McInnerny); Neither Are We Enemies, 1970 (made-for-TV; Harris Yulin); The Passion, 2008 (TV miniseries; Stephen Graham); The Passion, 2013 (made-for-TV; Thomas Dekker); The Passion, 2014 (made-for-TV; Glenn Helder); The Passion of the Christ, 2004 (Pietro Sarubbi); Pontius Pilot, 1967 (Livio Lorenzon); Secondo Ponzio Pilato, 1987 (Roberto Herlitzka); Son of God, 2014 (Fraser Ayres); Story of Judas, 2015 (Mohamad Aroussi); The Sword and the Cross, 1958 (Andrea Aureli); Tertterituokio, 1962- (TV series; "Barabbas," 1967 episode: Pekka Laiho); The Trial of Christ, 1962 (Wolf Ruvinskis); Which Will Ye Have!, 1949 (Niall MacGinnis); Wine of Morning, 1955 (Al Carter).

Barker, Arthur (aka: Dock; 1899-1939; U.S. bank robber, kidnapper and killer; member of the Barker Brothers or Barker-Karpis gang): Bloody Mama, 1970 (Clint Kimbrough); The F.B.I. Story: The FBI versus Alvin Karpis, Public Enemy Number One, 1974 (made-for-TV; Charles Cyphers); Guns Don't Argue, 1957 (Lash La Rue); The Kansas City Massacre, 1975 (made-for-TV; Gary Sandy); Ma Barker's Killer Brood, 1960 (Gary Ammann as a boy; Ronald Foster as a man); Murder in the First, 1995 (Michael Melvin); **Public Enemies**, 2009 (Steve Key); The Untouchables, 1959-1963 (TV series; Peter Baldwin); **White Heat**, 1949 (role model for James Cagney). Note: For detailed information on Arthur Barker, see my books *Bloodletters and Badmen: A Narrative En-*

cyclopedia of American Criminals from the Piligrims to the Past (M. Evans, 1973-2015; illustrated pages 43-51; *Encyclopedia of World Crime*, Volume I (CrimeBooks, Inc., 1990; illustrated pages 235-243).

Barker, Fred (d. 1935; U.S. bank robber, kidnapper and killer; member of the Barker Brothers or Barker-Karpis gang): **The FBI Story**, 1959 (Alan Craig); The F.B.I. Story: The FBI versus Alvin Karpis, Public Enemy Number One, 1974 (made-for-TV; Gary Lockwood); Guns Don't Argue, 1957 (Sam Edwards); The Kansas City Massacre, 1975 (made-for-TV; Hunter von Leer); Ma Barker's Killer Brood, 1960 (Michael Smith as a boy; Eric Morris as a man); **Public Enemies**; 2009 (Lance Baker); The Untouchables, 1959-1963 (TV series; Joe Di Reda). Note: For detailed information on Fred Barker, see my books, *Bloodletters and Badmen: A Narrative Encyclopedia of American Criminals from the Piligrims to the Past* (M. Evans, 1973-2015; illustrated pages 43-51; *Encyclopedia of World Crime*, Volume I (CrimeBooks, Inc., 1990; illustrated pages 235-243).

Barker, Ma (Arizona Donnie Clark Barker; 1873-1935; mother of the notorious Barker brothers, robbers and killers and for which she was reportedly their mentor in crime, although members of the gang emphatically denied her having such a role): Big Bad Mama, 1974 (role model for Angie Dickinson); Bloody Mama, 1970 (Lisa Linsky as girl; Shelley Winters as woman); **The FBI Story**, 1959 (Jane Crowley); The F.B.I. Story: The FBI versus Alvin Karpis, Public Enemy Number One, 1974 (made-for-TV; Eileen Heckart); Gang Busters, 1952- (TV series, two 1952 episodes: Jean Harvey); Guns Don't Argue, 1957 (Jean Harvey); Ma Barker's Killer Brood, 1960 (Lurene Tuttle); **Queen of the Mob**, 1940 (role model for Blanche Yurka); Spirits of St. Paul: The Gangster Era, 2012 (Carol Vnuk); The Untouchable Family, 1988 (Caridad Sanchez); The Untouchables, 1959-1963 (TV series; "Ma Barker and Her Boys," 1959 episode: Claire Trevor); **White Heat**, 1959 (role model for Margaret Wycherly); The Witness, 1960-1961 (TV series; "Ma Barker," 1961 episode: Joan Blondell). Note: For detailed information on Ma Barker, see my books *Bloodletters and Badmen: A Narrative Encyclopedia of American Criminals from the Piligrims to the Past* (M. Evans, 1973-2015; illustrated pages 43-51; *Encyclopedia of World Crime*, Volume I (CrimeBooks, Inc., 1990; illustrated pages 235-243).

Barksdale, William (1821-1863; U.S. lawyer, newspaper editor, secessionist and Confederate general during the American Civil War): **Gettysburg**, 1993 (Charles Lester Kinsolving).

Barnes, Djuna (1892-1982; U.S. author in France): The Fly Room, 2014 (Erika Fae); **Midnight in Paris**, 2011 (Emmanuelle Uzan).

Barnes, Pancho (Florence Lowe "Pancho" Barnes; 1901-1975; U.S. pioneer aviatrix and stunt pilot): Pancho Barnes, 1988 (made-for-TV; Valerie Bertinelli); **The Right Stuff**, 1982 (Kim Stanley).

Barnum, Phineas Taylor (1810-1891; U.S. showman celebrated for promoting hoaxes, establishing the circus that eventually became the Ringling Brothers and Barnum and Bailey Circus and for coining the phrase: "There's a sucker born every minute"): A.J.'s Time Travelers, 1995- (TV series; "P.T. Barnum," 1995 episode: Dell Yount); Barnum!, 1986 (made-for-TV; Michael Crawford); Branded, 1965-1966 (TV series; "The Greatest Coward on Earth," 1965 episode: Pat O'Brien); Broadway Broke, 1923 (Macklyn Arbuckle); The Folklorist, 2012- (TV series; Kevin Murphy); Gangs of New York, 2002 (Roger Ashton-Griffiths); The Great John Ericsson, 1938 (Gosta Bodin); The Greatest Showman on Earth, 2017 (Hugh Jackman); High, Wide and Handsome, 1937 (Raymond Brown); Jenny Lind, 1931 (Andre Berley); A Lady's Morals, 1930 (Wallace Beery); Mentors, 1998-2005 (TV series; "Humbug," 2002 epiosde: Heath Lamberts); **The Mighty Barnum**, 1934 (Wallace Beery); P.T. Barnum, 1999 (made-for-TV; Beau Bridges; Jor-

Warren Beatty (as Clyde Barrow) shoots it out with police in *Bonnie and Clyde,* **1967.**

dan Bridges as young Barnum); The Restless Gun, 1957-1959 (TV series; "More Than Kin," 1958 episode; Robert Carson); Those Fantastic Flying Fools, 1967 (Burl Ives); You Are There, 1953-1971 (TV series; "P.T. Barnum Presents Jenny Lind [September 11, 1850]," 1955 episode; Ray Collins). Note: For detailed information on Barnum, see my book, *Zanies: The World's Greatest Eccentrics* (New Century Publishers, 1982; illustrated pages 18-22).

Barrie, J. M. (Sir James Matthew Barrie; 1860-1937; Scottish playwright, notable for his 1904 play "Peter Pan, or The Boy Who Wouldn't Grow Up"): **Finding Neverland**, 2004 (Johnny Depp); The Lost Boys, 1978 (TV series; Ian Holm); Mary White, 1977 (made-for-TV; Donald Moffat); The Young Visitors, 1984 (Alec McCowen).

Barrow, Clyde Chestnut (1909-1934; U.S. robber and killer, who was killed with his mistress and co-robber and killer, Bonnie Parker, on May 23, 1934): The Barrow Gang, 1995 (Anthony Snow); **Bonnie and Clyde**, 1967 (Warren Beatty); Bonnie & Clyde, 2013- (TV miniseries; Emile Hirsch); Bonnie and Clyde: The Real Story, 1992 (Dana Ashbrook); The Bonnie Parker Story, 1958 (Jack Hogan); Gang Busters, 1952- (TV series; Baynes Barron); Guns Don't Argue, 1957 (Baynes Barron); Lois & Clark: The New Adventures of Superman, 1993-1997 (TV series; "That Old Gang of Mine," 1994 episode: Joseph Gian); Lovers on the Run: The Complete Story of Bonnie & Clyde, 2015 (Marty Laquidara); Man, Moment, Machine, 2005-2007 (TV series; "Hunting Bonnie and Clyde," 2005 episode: Michael Fleck); The Other Side of Bonnie and Clyde, 1968 (Lucky Mosley); Paper Moon, 1974-1975 (TV series; "Bonnie and Clyde," 1974 episode: Robert F. Lyons); Poor Devil, 1973 (made-for-TV; Clyde Ventura); Top Kids, 1987 (made-for-TV; Dale Midkiff). Note: For detailed information on Barrow, see my books *Bloodletters and Badmen: A Narrative Encyclopedia of American Criminals from the Piligrims to the Past* (M. Evans, 1973-2015; illustrated pages 51-57; *Encyclopedia of World Crime*, Volume I (CrimeBooks, Inc., 1990; illustrated pages 250-263).

Barrymore, John (1882-1942; U.S. stage, screen and radio actor whose performance of "Hamlet" is considered one of the greatest): Barrymore, 2012 (Christopher Plummer); It Happened in Hollywood, 1937 (John Bohn); My Wicked, Wicked Ways: The Legend of Errol Flynn, 1985 (made-for-TV; Barrie Ingham); Playmates, 1941 (himself); **The Royal Family of Broadway**, 1930 (role model for Fredric March); **Too Much, Too Soon**, 1958 (Errol Flynn); **W.C. Fields and Me**, 1976 (Jack Cassidy); The Young Indiana Jones Chronicles, 1992-1993 (TV series; one 1993 episode: Brent Young). Note: For detailed information on Barrymore, see my book *Zanies: The World's Greatest Eccentrics* (New Cen-

Susan Hayward as Bathsheba in *David and Bathsheba*, 1951.

tury Publishers, 1982; illustrated pages 22-27).

Bartholomew (aka: Nathaniel; Saint Bartholomew; one of the twelve Apostles of Jesus): Acts of the Apostles, 1969 (TV miniseries; Bouraoui); Animated Stories from the New Testament, 1987- (TV series; Robert Axelrod voiceover); Apostle Peter and the Last Supper, 2012 (Thomas Colby); Crown of Thorns, 1934 (silent; Leo Reuss/Lionel Royce); The Day Christ Died, 1980 (made-for-TV; Samuele Cerri); Family Theatre, 1949-1958 (TV series; "Triumphant Hour," 1953 episode: Michael Hale); The Gospel according to Matthew, 1993 (Jacques De Klerk); The Gospel according to St. Matthew, 1966 (Guido Cerretani); The Gospel of John, 2014 (Mohamed N'Mila); The Gospel of Luke, 2015 (Mohamed N'Mila); Gospel Road: A Story of Jesus, 1973 (Stuart Stark); **The Greatest Story Ever Told**, 1965 (Peter Mann); Il messia, 1975 (Fadhel Jaziri); Jesus [aka: The Jesus Film], 1979 (Michael Warshaviak); Jesus, 2000 (made-for-TV; Mohammed Taleb); Jesus of Nazareth, 1977 (TV miniseries; John Eastham); Judas, 2004 (made-for-TV; Aziz El Hattab); **The King of Kings**, 1927 (Clayton Packard); Kristo, 1996 (Romy Romulo); The Last Supper: Thirteen Men of Courage, 2007 (made-for-TV; Jeff Perry); Mary, Mother of the Son of God, 2003 (Eugenio Bretas); The Passion, 2008 (TV miniseries; Eugene Wood); The Power of the Resurrection, 1958 (Mark Mitchell); Risen, 2016 (Stephen Hagan/Joe Manjon); The Visual Bible: The Gospel of John, 2003 (Elliot Levey).

Basilone, John (1916-1945; U.S. Marine who was awarded the Congressional Medal of Honor for mowing down hundreds of assulating Japanese during the battle of Guadalcanal in 1942, and who died heroically in the Battle for Iwo Jima in 1945): **First to Fight**, 1967 (role model for Chad Everett); The Pacific, 2010 (cable-TV miniseries; Jon Seda).

Bass, Samuel (aka: Sam; 1851-1878; U.S. Old West outlaw and train robber): The Fabulous Texan, 1947 (Jim Davis); **Bad Man's Territory**, 1946 (Nestor Paiva); Calamity Jane and Sam Bass, 1949 (Howard Duff); Colt .45, 1957-1960 (TV series; "The Saga of Sam Bass," 1959 episode: Alan Hale Jr.); Deadwood '76, 1965 (Rex Marlow); Death Valley Days, 1952-1970 (TV series; "The Informer Who Cried," 1967 episode: Ed Bakey); Hawkeye and the Last of the Mohicans, 1957- (TV series; Timothy Neufeld); Maverick, 1957-1962 (TV series; "Full House," 1959 episode: Kelly Thordsen); Outlaw Women, 1952 (Leonard Penn); Outlaws, 1960-1962 (TV series; "Sam Bass," 1961 episode: Jack Chaplain); Skin Game, 1971 (Fred Carson); The Slowest Gun in the West, 1960 (made-for-TV; Lee Van Cleef); Stories of the Century, 1954- (TV series; "Sam Bass," 1954 episode: Don Haggerty); The Tales of Allen, Texas,

2003-2006 (TV series; "A Short History of Allen, Texas," 2003 episode: "The Sam Bass Gang," 2006 episode: Thomas Joyce for both); Tales of Wells Fargo, 1957-1962 (TV series; "Sam Bass," 1957 episode: Chuck Connors); The Texas Rangers, 1951 (William Bishop); Trackdown, 1957-1959 (TV series; "End of an Outlaw," 1957 episode: John Anderson); Wagon Train,1957-1965 (TV series; "The Maggie Hamilton Story," 1960 episode: Orville Sherman). Note: For detailed information on Bass, see my book *Encyclopedia of Western Lawmen and Outlaws* (Paragon House, 1992; illustrated pages 26-29).

Bassett, Charles (aka: Charlie Bassett; c.1847-1896; U.S. lawman in Dodge City, Kansas, deputy under Wyatt Earp): **Gunfight at the O.K. Corral**, 1957 (Earl Holliman). Note: For detailed information on Bass, see my book, *Encyclopedia of Western Lawmen and Outlaws* (Paragon House, 1992; illustrated pages 20-30).

Bathory, Elizabeth (1560-1614; Hungarian countess and serial killer, who practiced witchcraft and had young girls in her province routinely murdered so that she could bathe in their blood, believing that such baths would prolong her life; between eighty and 650 victims were claimed by Bathory and her murderous servants; several servants were tried and executed, but Bathory was never brought to trial; this demented woman was bricked into a set of rooms in her castle with small openings for ventilation and through which food was given to her; she died four years later on August 24, 1614): Bathory, 2011 (Maria Heller); Bathory, Countess of Blood, 2008 (Anna Friel); The Bathory Legend, 2010 (TV series; Andrea Toreki); Bloodbath, 1999 (Susannah Devereux); Chastity Bites, 2013 (Louise Griffiths); The Countess, 2009 (Julie Delpy; Paula Hartman at age six; Ella-Maria Gollmer at age eleven); Countess Dracula, 1972 (Ingrid Pitt); The Crusaders #357: Experiment in Evil!, 2008 (Christine Robert); Curse of the Devil, 1977 (Maria Silva); Daughters of Darkness, 1971 (Delphine Seyrig); Deadly Women 2005-2010 (TV series; "Obsession," 2005 episode: Georgina Anderson); Dracula's Curse, 2006 (Christina Rosenberg); Elizabeth Bathory, 2014 (Tilke Hill); Eternal, 2005 (Elizabeth Kane); Frankenstein's Aunt, 1987 (TV series; Mercedes Sampietro); Freckled Max and Spooks, 1987 (Mercedes Sampietro); Hellboy Animated: Blood and Iron, 2007 (made-for-TV; Erzsebet Ondrushko); La mort mystererieuse de Nina Chereau, 1988 (made-for-TV; Maud Adams); The Legend of Blood Castle, 1974 (Lucia Bose); Mama Dracula, 1980 (Louise Fletcher); Metamorphosis, 2010 (Adel Kovats); Mondo Weirdo, 1990 (Miranda Mariaux); Necropolis, 1970 (Viva Auder); Night Fangs, 2005 (Marina Muzychenko); Night of the Werewolf, 1985 (Julia Saly); Shock House, 2011 (MaryAnne Edwards); Stay Alive, 2006 (Maria Kalinina); Thirst, 1979; Tomb of the Werewolf, 2004 (Michelle Bauer); Vampire Secrets, 2006 (made-for-TV; Christa Bella); The Werewolf vs. the Vampire Woman, 1972 (Patty Shepard). Note: For detailed information on Bathory, see my two-volume work, *The Great Pictorial History of World Crime*, Volume II (History, Inc., 2004; illustrated pages 1021-1022).

Bathsheba (Wife of Uriah the Hittite and wife of David, King of Judah and Israel, mother of Solomon, who succeeded David): And David Wept, 1971 (made-for-TV; Rosalind Elias); Battles B.C., 2009 (TV series; "David: Giant Slayer," 2009 episode: Berenice Noriega); The Cradle of God, 1926 (Gina Relly); David, 1924 (Georgette de Nove); David, 1997 (made-for-TV; Sheryl Lee); **David and Bathsheba**, 1951 (Susan Hayward); General Electric Theater, 1953-1962 (TV series; "Absolom, My Son," 1959 episode: Patricia Medina); Greatest Heroes of the Bible, 1978- (TV series; "The Judgment of Solomon," 1978 episode: Carol Lawrence); King David, 1985 (Alice Krige); Koning David, 1965 (made-for-TV; Ellen Vogel); The Queen of Sheba, 1921 (Genevieve Blinn); Rei Davi, 2012 (TV series; Renata Dominguez); So This Is Marriage?, 1924 (Mabel Julienne Scott); Solomon, 2000 (made-for-TV; Anouk Aimee); **Solomon and Sheba**, 1959 (Maruchi Fresno); The Story of David, 1976 (made-for-TV; Jane Seymour).

Bayerlein, Fritz (1899-1970; German general in WWII; served under Field Marshal Erwin Rommel in the Africa Corps): **The Desert Fox**, 1951 (George Macready).

Bayes, Nora (1880-1928; U.S. singer, comedian and actress): Shine on Harvest Moon, 1944 (Ann Sheridan); **Yankee Doodle Dandy**, 1942 (Frances Langford); Ziegfeld: The Man and His Women, 1978 (made-for-TV; Inga Swenson).

Bazaine, Francois Achille (1811-1888; French general and marshal of France): Aquellos anos, 1974 (Farnesio de Bernal); **Juarez**, 1939 (Donald Crisp); Juarez and Maximillian, 1935 (Alfredo del Diestro); Maximilian von Mexiko, 1970 (made-for-TV; Josef Dahmen); Prariejager in Mexiko: Benito Juarez, 1988 (Werner Ehrlicher); Treasure of the Aztecs, 1966 (Jean-Roger Caussimon).

Bean, Roy (aka: Judge; Phantly Roy Bean, Jr.; 1825-1903; U.S. saloon-keeper and justice of the peace in Texas): Colt .45, 1957-1960 (TV series; "Law West of the Pecos," 1959 episode: Frank Ferguson); Death Valley Days, 1952-1970 (TV series; "A Sense of Justice," 1966 episode: Tom Skerritt); The Gambler Returns: The Luck of the Draw, 1991 (made-for-TV; Brad Sullivan); Hell Town, 1985 (made-for-TV; Warren Vanders); Judge Roy Bean, 1956-1957 (TV series; Edgar Buchanan); Judge Roy Bean, 1971 (Pierre Perret); **The Life and Times of Judge Roy Bean**, 1972 (Paul Newman); Lillie, 1978 (TV miniseries: Tommy Dugan); Lives and Deaths of the Poets, 2011 (Jim Epstein); Streets of Laredo, 1995 (TV miniseries; Ned Beatty); A Time for Dying, 1982 (Victor Jory); **The Westerner**, 1940 (Walter Brennan). Note: For detailed information on Bean, see my book *Encyclopedia of Western Lawmen and Outlaws* (Paragon House, 1992; illustrated pages 30-32).

Beauharnais, Josephine de (1763-1814; wife of Napoleon Bonaparte and Empress of France): Amoureuse Josephine, 1974 (made-for-TV; Evelyne Dandry); The Battle of Austerlitz, 1960 (Martine Carol); **Desiree**, 1954 (Merle Oberon); Destinee, 1926 (Ady Cresso); The Fighting Eagle, 1927 (Julia Faye); I cavalieri dell'illusione, 1954 (Hedy Lamarr); I grandi camaleonti, 1964- (TV miniseries; Valentina Cortese); Imperial Venus, 1972 (Micheline Presle); La camera explore le temps, 1957-1966 (TV series; three episodes, 1957-1962; Anne Caprile); La sposa dei re, 1938 (Norma Nova); The Loves and Times of Scaramouche, 1976 (Ursula Andress); Loves of Three Queens, 1954 (Hedy Lamarr); Mlle. Desiree, 1948 (Lise Delamare); Madame Recamier, 1920 (Johanna Mund); Madame Sans-Gene, 1925 (Suzanne Talba); **Napoleon**, 1927 (Gina Manes); Napoleon, 1955 (Michele Morgan); Napoleon, 2002 (TV miniseries; Isabella Rossellini as Josephine); Napoleon and Josephine: A Love Story, 1987 (TV miniseries; Jacqueline Bisset); Napoleon and Love, 1974 (TV miniseries; Billie Whitelaw); Napoleon et l'Europe, 1991- (TV series; Beatrice Agenin); Napoleone, 1951 (Marisa Merlini); Omnibus, 1952-1961 (TV series; "The Love Story of Napoleon," 1953 episode; Pamela Mason); Pamela, 1945 (Gisele Casadesus); **The Pearls of the Crown**, 1938 (Jacqueline Delubac); A Royal Divorce, 1926 (Gertrude McCoy); A Royal Divorce, 1938 (Ruth Chatterton); The Sea Pirate, 1967 (Monica Randall); The Story of Mankind, 1957 (Marie Windsor).

Beaumarchais, Pierre (1732-1799; French playwright, composer, inventor, spy and revolutionary): Beaumarchais, 1969 (made-for-TV; Helmut Wildt); Beaumarchais the Scoundrel, 1997 (Fabrice Luchini); Ce diable d'homme, 1978- (TV miniseries; Gerard Caillaud); Clavigo, 1970 (made-for-TV; Friedholm Ptok); Clavigo, 1978 (made-for-TV; Gunter Schoss); Daniel Boone, 1964-1970 (TV series; "Beaumarchais," 1967 episode: Maurice Evans); Enigmas de l'histoire, 1956-1957 (TV series; "Le chevalier d'Eon," 1957 episode: Jacques Mauclair); Exzellenz Unterrock, 1921 (Albert Steinruck); Figaro-ci, Figaro-la, 1972 (made-for-TV; Jean-Francois Poron); The Ghosts of Versailles, 1992

Paul Newman (as Roy Bean) in *The Life and Times of Judge Roy Bean,* **1972.**

(made-for-TV; Hakan Hagegard); **The Great Garrick**, 1937 (Lionel Atwill); If Paris Were Told to Us, 1956 (Aime Clariond); L'enfant des Lumieres, 2002 (TV miniseries; Michel Feller); Louis XV, le soleil noir, 2008 (made-for-TV; Boris Alestchenkoff); Louis XVI: The Man Who Didn't Want to Be King, 2011 (made-for-TV; Sylvain Clama); **Napoleon**, 1927 (Henri Beaulieu); Nicolas Le Floch, 2008 (TV series; Sebastien Thiery); Royal Affairs in Versailles, 1957 (Bernard Dheran); Sara, 1975 (made-for-TV; Jacques Sereys). Note: For detailed information on Beaumarchais, see my book *Spies: A Narrative Encyclopedia of Dirty Tricks & Double Dealing from Biblical Times to Today* (M. Evans, 1997; pages 81-83).

Beauregard, Pierre Gustav Toutant (1818-1893; U.S. military officer and Confederate general during the American Civil War): Carolina, 1934 (Andre Cheron); The Great Adventure, 1963-1964 (TV series; "The Treasure Train of Jefferson Davis," 1963 episode: Byron Morrow).

Beck, Ludwig (1880-1944; German general in WWII who participated in the 1944 attempt to kill Adolf Hitler; suicide): Alcoa Theatre, 1957-1960 (TV series; "Operation Spark," 1959 episode; Grandon Rhodes); Claus Graf Stauffenberg, 1970 (made-for-TV; Wolfgang Buttner); Countdown to War, 1989 (made-for-TV; Stephen Moore); Days of Betrayal, 1973 (Gerhard Rachold); Der Fall der Generale, 1966 (made-for-TV; Fritz Tillmann); Die Stunde der Offiziere, 2004 (made-for-TV; Jurgen Schornagel); General Oster—Verrater oder Patriot?, 1970 (made-for-TV; Wolfgang Buttner); The Great Battle, 1973 (TV series; W. Wieland); I Spy, 1955-1957 (TV series; "Canaris Story": Robert Dryden); It Happened on July 20th, 1955 (Karl Ludwig Diehl); Operation Valkyrie, 2004 (made-for-TV; Remo Girone; Joachim Hoppner voiceover); Operation Walkure, 1971 (made-for-TV; Rolf Muller; Gerard Ferat in French version); The Plot to Assassinate Hitler, 1955 (Werner Hinz); The Plot to Kill Hitler, 1990 (made-for-TV; Ian Richardson); **Valkyrie**, 2008 (Terence Stamp); War and Remembrance, 1988 (TV miniseries; Justin Berlin); War and Remembrance, 1988- (TV miniseries; Justin Berlin); The Wednesday Play, 1964-1970 (TV series; "The July Plot," 1964 episode: Cyril Luckham). Note: For detailed information on the 1944 assassination attempt on Hitler, see my book *The Great Pictorial History of World Crime*, Volume I (History, Inc., 2004; illustrated pages 138-148).

Beck, Martha Jule (1920-1951; U.S. serial killer, who, with Raymond Fernandez, 1914-1951, bilked and murdered as many as twenty women in marital scams where Fernandez married these victims and then looted their assets before killing them; both were executed on March 8, 1951): **The Honeymoon Killers**, 1969 (Shirley Stoler); Lonely Hearts, 2006

Dolores Del Rio (as Jeanne Bécu/Madame Du Barry) in *Madame Du Barry,* **1934.**

(Salma Hayek). Note: For detailed information on Beck and her co-killer, Raymond Fernandez, see my book *The Great Pictorial History of World Crime,* Volume I (History, Inc., 2004; illustrated pages 239-243).

Becket, Thomas (Saint Thomas of Canterbury; 1119-1170; British Catholic clergyman): Becket, 1923 (Frank R. Benson); **Becket**, 1964 (Richard Burton); Becket odor Die Ehre Gottes, 1962 (made-for-TV; Heinz Baumann); The Devil's Crown, 1978- (TV series; Jack Shepherd); Mord im Dom, 1962 (made-for-TV; Gerd Brudern); Murder in the Cathedral, 1952 (John Groser); Theatre Parade, 1936-1938 (TV series; "Murder in the Cathedral," 1936 episode: Robert Speaight); Who Killed Thomas Becket?, 2004 (made-for-TV; Guy Henry). Note: For detailed information on Becket's assassination, see my eight-volume work, *Enclopedia of World Crime,* Volume I (CrimeBooks, Inc., 1990; illustrated page 310).

Becu, Jeanne (Madame du Barry; 1743-1793; French royal courtesan and mistress of King Louis XV): **Black Magic**, 1949 (Margot Grahame); Die Dubarry, 1951 (Sari Barabas); DuBarry, 1915 (Mrs. Leslie Carter); Du Barry Was a Lady, 1943 (Lucille Ball); Du Barry, Woman of Passion, 1930 (Norma Talmadge); George White's 1935 Scandals, 1935 (Lois Eckert); Hat, Coat, and Glove, 1934 (Margaret Hamilton); Louis XV, le soleil noir, 2009 (made-for-TV; Coralie Revel); The Loves of Madame Dubarry, 1938 (Gitta Alpar); Madame Du Barry, 1917 (Theda Bara); Madame DuBarry, 1919 (Pola Negri); Madame Du Barry, 1934 (Dolores Del Rio); Madame du Barry, 1954 (Martine Carol); **Marie Antoinette**, 1938 (Gladys George); Marie Antoinette, 1975 (TV miniseries; Michele Grellier); Marie Antoinette, 2006 (Asia Argento); Marie Antoinette, 2006 (made-for-TV; Helene Florent); **The Pearls of the Crown**, 1938 (Simone Renant); Remontons les Champs-Elysees, 1939 (Ariane Pathe); The Rose of Versailles, 1979-1980 (animated TV series; Yoshiko Kimiya); The Seats of the Mighty, 1914 (Marjorie Bonner [Brenner]); Shadow of the Guillotine, 1956 (Anne Carrere); Todo un caballero, 1947 (Maruja Grifell); Une maison, une histoire, 1980 (TV series; "Marie-Antoinette," 1980 episode: Beatrice Constantini).

Beethoven, Ludwig von (1770-1827; German composer): Animated Hero Classics, 1991-2005 (TV series; "Beethoven," 2005 episode: William Dennis Hunt; Michael Henwright as young Beethoven); Beethoven, 2005 (TV miniseries; Paul Rhys); Beethoven Lives Upstairs, 1992 (made-for-TV; Neil Munro); Bill & Ted's Excellent Adventure, 1989 (Clifford David); Das Leben des Beethoven, 1927 (Fritz Kortner); Der Martyrer seines Herzens, 1918 (Fritz Kortner); Eroica, 1951 (Ewald Balser); Franz Schuberts letzte Liebe, 1926 (Theodor Weiser); Immortal

Beloved, 1994 (Gary Oldman); **The Life and Loves of Beethoven**, 1937 (Harry Baur); The Life of Wolfgang Amadeus Mozart [aka: The Mozart Story], 1948 (Rene Deltgen); Liszt Ferenc, 1982 (TV miniseries; Han Wolfgang Zeiger); Napoleon, 1955 (Erich von Stroheim); New Wine, 1941 (Albert Bassermann); Rossini, 1948 (Memo Benassi); Walt Disney's Wonderful World of Color, 1954-1992 (TV series; "The Magnificent Rebel," two 1962 episodes: Karlheinz Bohm); You Are There, 1953-1971 (TV series; "The Torment of Beethoven [October 6, 1802]," 1955 episode: Lorne Greene).

Behan, Johnny (1844-1912, U.S. western lawman): Appointment with Destiny, 1971-1973 (TV series; "Showdown at O.K. Corral," 1972 episode: Robert Tindall); **Gunfight at the O.K. Corral**, 1957 (role model for Frank Faylen); **Hour of the Gun**, 1967 (role model for Frank Faylen); I Married Wyatt Earp, 1983 (made-for-TV; John Bennett Perry); The Life and Legend of Wyatt Earp, 1955-1961 (TV series; seventeen episodes: Steve Brodie); **Tombstone**, 1993 (Jon Tenney); The Wild West, 2006-2007 (TV miniseries; "The Gunfight at the O.K. Corral," 2007 episode: Nigel Lindsay); **Wyatt Earp**, 1994 (Mark Harmon); Wyatt Earp: Return to Tombstone, 1994 (made-for-TV; Steve Brodie); You Are There, 1953-1971 (TV series; "The Gunfight at the O.K. Corral [October 26, 1881]," 1955 episode: Paul Birch).

Bell, Alexander Graham (1847-1922; U.S. inventor, engineer and scientist; in 1876, he was granted a patent for the electromagnetic transmission of vocal sound by electric current, a family-held monopoly for this invention): Alexander Graham Bell: The Sound and the Silence, 1993 (made-for-TV; John Bach); The American Adventure, 1982 (Joe Rohde voiceover); Antonio Meucci, 1940 (Nerio Bernardi); Cook and Peary: The Race to the Pole, 1983 (made-for-TV; Don Robinson); Histeria!, 1998-2000 (animated TV series; "Inventors Hall of Fame: Part I," 1998 episode: Jeff Bennett voiceover); Man, Moment, Machine, 2005-2007 (TV series; "Alexander Graham Bell and the Astonishing Telephone," 2006 episode: Chris Hamilton); Meucci, 2005 (made-for-TV; James Weber Brown); Netherbeast Incorporated, 2007 (Bill Lippincott); **The Story of Alexander Graham Bell**, 1939 (Don Ameche); The Story of Mankind, 1957 (Jim Ameche); Strings of Steel, 1926 (Alphonse Martell); The Talking Wire, 1955 (made-for-TV; Peter Hanson); Titans, 1981-1982 (TV series, "Alexander Graham Bell," 1981 episode: Patrick Watson); Voyagers!, 1982-1983 (TV series; "Barriers of Sound," 1983 episode: Kip Gilman); The Winds of Kitty Hawk, 1978 (made-for-TV; John Randolph).

Benchley, Robert Charles (1889-1945; U.S. writer and actor, witty member of the Algonquin Round Table): **Duffy's Tavern**, 1945 (himself); Mrs. Parker and the Vicious Circle, 1994 (Campbell Scott).

Bennion, Mervyn Sharp (1887-1941; U.S. naval officer and captain of the USS *West Virginia*, who was killed during the Japanese sneak attack on Pearl Harbor on December 7, 1941, and who, though mortally wounded, remained at his post; posthumously awarded the Congressional Medal of Honor): **Pearl Harbor**, 2002 (Peter Firth).

Benny, Jack (1894-1974; U.S. comedian, actor, violinist): Angels with Angles, 2005 (Whitney Rydbeck); **Beau James**, 1957 (himself); Buck Benny Rides Again, 1940 (himself); Christmas Carol, 1978 (made-for-TV; Rich Little); The Great Lover, 1949 (himself); **Gypsy**, 1962 (himself); **Hollywood Canteen**, 1944 (himself); **It's in the Bag!**, 1945 (himself); Love Thy Neighbor, 1940 (himself); Mr. Broadway, 1933 (himself); Parade of Stars, 1983 (made-for-TV; Rich Little); **Somebody Loves Me**, 1952 (himself); **Without Reservations**, 1946 (himself).

Benteen, William Frederick (1834-1898; U.S. military officer who survived the 1876 Custer Massacre): Bugles in the Afternoon, 1952 (Walter Coy); Custer of the West, 1968 (Jeffrey Hunter); Custer's Last Stand,

1936 (serial; Lafe McKee); **7th Cavalry**, 1956 (Michael Pate); Son of the Morning Star, 1991 (made-for-TV; David Strathairn); Tonka, 1958 (Herbert Rudley).

Berengaria of Navarre (c.1165-1230; Queen of England and wife of Richard I [Richard the Lionheart]): **The Crusades**, 1935 (Loretta Young); The Devil's Crown, 1978 (TV series; Zoe Wanamaker); El Naser Salah el Dine, 1983 (Laila Taher); **King Richard and the Crusaders**, 1954 (Paula Raymond); Richard the Lionheart, 1962 (TV series; Sheila Whittingham); Richard the Lion-Hearted, 1923 (Kathleen Clifford); The Talisman, 1980- (TV series; Joanne Pearce).

Berg, Alan (1934-1984; U.S. radio talk show host for Denver's KOA station; a radical liberal on the far left, he alienated ultra-conservatives through his acid-tongued ridiculing of them; he was murdered by David Lane and Bruce Pierce, two members of the the racist group The Order, and who were sent to prison for life): Betrayed, 1988 (Richard Libertini); Brotherhood of Murder, 1999 (made-for-TV; Rob LaBelle); **Talk Radio**, 1989 (Eric Bogosian).

Beria, Lavrenti (1899-1953; Russian head of the Soviet secret police [NKDV] under Joseph Stalin): Archangel, 2005 (made-for-TV; Ervand Arzumanyan); Children of the Revolution, 1996 (Paul Livingston); The Girl in the Kremlin, 1957 (Aram Katcher); The Forgotten King, 2013 (Temo Barbaqadze); Hotel Lux, 2011 (Krzysztof Dracz); The Inner Circle, 1991 (Bob Hoskins); Lost in Siberia, 1991 (Valentin Graft); **The 100-Year-Old Man Who Climbed Out of the Window and Disappeared**, 2014 (Tzvet Lazar); An Ordinary Execution, 2010 (Gilles Gaston-Dreyfus); Playhouse 90, 1956-1961 (TV series; "The Plot to Kill Stalin," 1958 episode: E.G. Marshall); Red Monarch, 1983 (made-for-TV; David Suchet); Spies, Lies and the Superbomb, 2007 (TV miniseries; Boris Isarov); Stalin, 1992 (made-for-TV; Roshan Seth); Staline est morte, 1981 (made-for-TV; Jean Le Poulain). Note: For detailed information on Beria, see my book, *Spies: A Narrative Encyclopedia of Dirty Tricks & Double Dealing from Biblical Times to Today* (M. Evans, 1997; illustrated pages 91-92).

Berlin, Irving (U.S. composer; 1888-1989): **De-Lovely**, 2004 (Keith Allen); **This Is the Army**, 1943 (himself); Ziegfeld: The Man and His Women, 1978 (made-for-TV; David Levy).

Berlioz, Hector (1803-1869; French composer): Il etait un musicien, 1978- (TV series; "Monsieur Berlioz," 1978 episode; Daniel Riviere); La symphonie fantastique, 1947 (Jean-Louis Barrault); La vie de Berlioz, 1983 (TV miniseries; Daniel Mesguich); Liszt Ferenc, 1982 (TV miniseries; Jozsef Szekhelyi); Lisztomania, 1975 (Murray Melvin); Moi, Hector Berlioz, 2003 (made-for-TV; Assassi as young Berlioz; Yann de Monterno as older Berlioz); Ok tudjak mi a szerelem, 1964 (Imre Sinkovits); Paganini, 1923 (Jean Nadolovitch); Paganini, 1976- (TV miniseries; Agostino De Berti).

Bernadette: see Soubirous, Bernadette.

Bernadotte, Jean-Baptiste (1763-1844; French marshal under Napoleon; later Charles XIV, John of Sweden, king of Sweden and Norway): **Desiree**, 1954 (Michael Rennie); Heroische Komodie, 1962 (made-for-TV; Alexander Kerst); Madame Sans-Gene, 1925 (Raoul Villiers); Mlle. Desiree, 1948 (Jacques Varennes); Napoleon, 1955 (Jacques Dumesnil).

Bernhardt, Sarah (1844-1923; French stage and early film actress): Amelia, 2002 (Beatrice Agenin); Around the World in 80 Days, 1989 (TV miniseries; Lee Remick); De memoires, van Sarah Bernhardt, 1981 (made-for-TV; Yvonne Lex); Death Valley Days, 1952-1970 (TV series; "The Paper Dynasty," 1964 episode: Michele Montau); If Paris Were

Jack Buetel (Billy the Kid) and Walter Huston (Doc Holliday) in *The Outlaw,* **1943.**

Told to Us, 1956 (Jeanne Boitel); The Incredible Sarah, 1976 (Glenda Jackson); Laurier, 1984- (TV miniseries; Helene Loiselle); Le souffleur de l'affair, 2014 (Clotilde Hesme); Lillie, 1978 (TV miniseries; "Let Them Say," 1978 episode: Cheryl Campbell); Masterpiece Theatre: Sons and Lovers, 1981- (TV miniseries; 1981 episode: Ann Heffernan); Of Penguins and Peacocks, 2000 (made-for-TV; Liliane Montevecchi); Parade of Stars, 1983 (made-for-TV; Jeanne Moreau); Proudly I Love, 1953 (made-for-TV; Sarah Churchill); The Rest Is Silence, 2008 (Mara Nicolescu); Sangue do Meu Sangue, 1969- (TV series; Nathalia Timberg); Sarah, 2003 (made-for-TV; Fanny Ardant); Sarah Bernhardt: Une etoile un plein jour, 2006 (made-for-TV; Telephone Time, 1956-1958 (TV series; "Recipe for Success," 1958 episode: Edith Barrett); Three Waltzes, 1939 (Colette Regis); You Are There, 1953-1971 (TV series; "The Final Performance of Sarah Bernhardt [November 30, 1922]," 1955 episode: Jeanette Nolan); The Xango from Baker Street, 2002 (Maria de Madeiros).

Bernstein, Carl (1944- ; U.S. journalist and investigative reporter who, with Bob Woodward, exposed the Watergate scandal in a series of articles written for the Washington *Post*, and who won a Pulitzer Prize): **All the President's Men**, 1976 (Dustin Hoffman); Dick, 1999 (Bruce McCulloch).

Berthier, Louis-Alexander (1753-1815; French soldier and marshal of France under Napoleon I): 1812, 1944 (Yevgeny Kaluzhsky); Mlle. Desiree, 1948 (Jean Davy); Napoleon, 1955 (Louis Arbessier); Napoleon and Love, 1974- (TV miniseries; Ronald Hines); War and Peace, 1972-1974 (TV miniseries; John Breslin); War and Peace, 1991 (made-for-TV; Andrei Khramtsov); **Waterloo**, 1971 (Giorgio Sciolette).

Bertrand, Henri Gatien (1773-1844; French soldier and general; marshal of France under Napoleon I): Eagle in a Cage, 1972 (Richard Waring); Napoleon, 1955 (Jean Marchat); Napoleon at St. Helena, 1930 (Philippe Heriat); **Waterloo**, 1971 (Boris Molchanov).

Bethmann-Hollweg, Theobald von (1856-1921; German politician, statesman and Chancellor of the German Empire, 1909-1917): Europas letzter Sommer, 2012 (made-for-TV; Frank Roth); Fall of Eagles, 1974 (TV miniseries; Peter Copley); The Great Victory, Wilson or the Kaiser? The Fall of the Hohenzollerns, 1919 (Karl Dane); In the Employ of the Secret Service, 1931 (Friedrich Keyssler); The Kaiser, the Beast of Berlin, 1918 (Lon Chaney Sr.); Me und Gott, 1918 (Jim Welch); 1914, The Last Days before the War, 1932 (Albert Bassermann); My Four Years in Germany, 1918 (Karl Dane); 37 Days, 2014 (TV miniseries; Ludger Pistor); To Hell with the Kaiser!, 1918 (Karl Dane).

Charles Laughton as Captain William Bligh in *Mutiny on the Bounty*, 1935.

Bierce, Ambrose (Ambrose Gwinnett Bierce; 1842-1913; U.S. writer): Ah! Silenciosa, 1999 (Jim Beaver); Ambrose Bierce: Civil War Stories, 2006 (made-for-TV; Campbell Scott); Death Valley Days, 1952-1970 (TV series; "The Paper Dynasty," 1964 episode: James Lanphier); **Old Gringo**, 1989 (Gregory Peck).

Big Elk (1770-1846 or 1853; chief of the Omaha tribe on the upper Missouri River): **Brigham Young: Frontiersman**, 1940 (Chief John Big Tree).

Billington, John (c. 1580-1630; one of the passengers sailing on the historic 1620 voyage of the *Mayflower* to Plymouth Rock and who became the colony's first convicted murderer after slaying a fellow Pilgrim, John Newcomen; Billington was hanged): **Plymouth Adventure**, 1952 (John Sherman).

Billy the Kid (William H. Bonney; William Henry McCarty Jr.; Henry Antrim; 1859-1881; U.S. outlaw and gunfighter, who reportedly killed twenty-one persons before age twenty-one): Another Man, Another Chance, 1977 (Tony Crupi); Bill & Ted's Excellent Adventure, 1989 (Dan Shor); Billy the Kid, 1925 (Franklyn Farnum); Billy the Kid, 1930 (Johnny Mack Brown); **Billy the Kid**, 1941 (Robert Taylor); Billy the Kid, 1964 (Jack Taylor); Billy the Kid, 1989 (made-for-TV; Val Kilmer); **Billy the Kid**, 2013 (Christopher Bowman); Billy the Kid in Santa Fe, 1941 (Bob Steele); Billy the Kid in Texas, 1940 (Bob Steele); Billy the Kid Outlawed, 1940 (Bob Steele); Billy the Kid Returns, 1938 (Roy Rogers); Billy the Kid: Showdown in Lincoln County, 2015 (Christopher Bowman); Billy the Kid Trapped, 1942 (Buster Crabbe); Billy the Kid vs. Dracula, 1966 (Chuck Courtney); Billy the Kid Wanted, 1941 (Buster Crabbe); Billy the Kid's Fighting Pals, 1941 (Bob Steele); Billy the Kid's Gun Justice, 1940 (Bob Steele); Billy the Kid's Range War, 1941 (Bob Steele); Billy the Kid's Round-Up, 1941 (Buster Crabbe); Billy the Kid's Smoking Guns, 1942 (Buster Crabbe); Birth of a Legend: Billy the Kid & the Lincoln County War, 2011 (Robert Shrimplin); Blazing Frontier, 1943 (Buster Crabbe); The Boy from Oklahoma, 1954 (Tyler MacDuff); Bronco, 1958-1962 (TV series; "Death of an Outlaw," 1960 episode: Stephen Joyce); Buffalo Bill Jr., 1955-1956 (TV series; "Trail of the Killer," 1955 episode: Chuck Courtney); Cattle Stampede, 1943 (Buster Crabbe); **Chisum**, 1970 (Geoffrey Deuel); Colt .45, 1957-1960 (TV series; "Amnesty," 1959 episode: Robert Conrad); Copperhead, 2008 (made-for-TV; Keith Stone); Dirty Little Billy, 1972 (Michael J. Pollard); The Fourth Horseman, 1932 (Paul Shawhan); Fugitive of the Plains, 1943 (Buster Crabbe); A Girl Is a Gun, 1971 (Jean-Pierre Leaud); Histeria!, 1998-2000 (animated TV series; "The Wild West," 1998 episode: Luke Ruegger voiceover); Horse Opera, 1993

(made-for-TV; Jonathan Moore); The Hunter's Moon, 2009 (Austin Lord); I Shot Billy the Kid, 1950 (Don "Red" Barry); I'll Kill Him and Return Alone, 1967 (Peter Lee Lawrence); The Kid from Texas, 1950 (Audie Murphy); The Kid Rides Again, 1943 (Buster Crabbe); Law and Order (aka: Billy the Kid's Law and Order), 1942 (Buster Crabbe); The Law vs. Billy the Kid, 1954 (Scott Brady); **The Left Handed Gun**, 1958 (Paul Newman); **The Life and Times of Judge Roy Bean**, 1972 (Mark Headley); Lucky Luke, 2009 (Michael Youn); The Mysterious Rider, 1942 (Buster Crabbe); Omnibus, 1952-1961 (TV series; one 1953 episode: John Kriza); The Outlaw, 1943 (Jack Buetel); **The Outlaws Is Coming!**, 1965 (Johnny Ginger); The Parson and the Outlaw, 1957 (Anthony Dexter); **Pat Garrett and Billy the Kid**, 1973 (Kris Kristofferson); The Philco-Goodyear Television Playhouse, 1948-1956 (TV series; "The Death of Billy the Kid," 1955 episode: Paul Newman); Purgatory, 1999 (made-for-TV; Donnie Wahlberg); Redemption, 2009 (Owen Conway); The Renegade, 1943 (Buster Crabbe); **Return of the Bad Men**, 1948 (Dean White); Sheriff of Sage Valley, 1942 (Buster Crabbe); Son of Billy the Kid, 1949 (William Perrot); Stories of the Century, 1954- (TV series; "Billy the Kid," 1954 episode: Richard Jaeckel); Strange Lady in Town, 1955 (Nick Adams); The Tall Man, 1960-1962 (TV series; Clu Gulager); The Time Tunnel, 1966-1967 (TV series; "Billy the Kid," 1967 episode: Robert Walker Jr.); Timemaster, 1995 (George Pilgrim); Western Cyclone, 1943 (Buster Crabbe); The Wild West, 2006- (TV miniseries; "Billy the Kid," 2006 episode; David Leon); **Young Guns**, 1988 (Emilio Estevez); **Young Guns II**, 1990 (Emilio Estevez).

Bismarck, Otto von (1815-1898; German statesman and first chancellor of the German Empire): Berlin 1885: The Division of Africa, 2011 (made-for-TV; Jacques Spiesser); Bischof Ketteler, 1969 (made-for-TV; Detlof Kruger); Bismarck, 1914 (Franz Ludwig); Bismarck, 1940 (Paul Hartmann); Bismarck, 1990 (TV miniseries; Uwe Ochsenknecht); Bismarck 1862-1898, 1927 (Franz Ludwig; Ralph Ludwig as young Bismarck); Bismarck's Dismissal, 1942 (Emil Jannings); Carl Peters, 1941 (Friedrich Otto Fischer); Die Unbesiegbaren, 1953 (Walter Brandt); Disraeli: Portrait of a Romantic, 1978- (TV miniseries; Brewster Mason); Edward the King, 1975- (TV series; Brewster Mason); 1864, 2014 (TV series; Rainer Bock); Emile Waldteufel, 1981 (made-for-TV; Patrick Burgel); Fall of Eagles, 1974 (TV miniseries; Curt Jurgens); Ferdinand Lassalle, 1918 (Herr Braun); The Great Victory, Wilson or the Kaiser? The Fall of the Hohenzollerns, 1919 (Henry Carvill); The Hourglass Sanatorium, 1973 (Czeslaw Piaskowski); Invincible Mr. Disraeli, 1963 (made-for-TV; Peter von Zerneck); Ludwig: Requiem for a Virgin King, 1980 (Peter Przygodda); Ludwig II, 1922 (Josef Schreiber); Ludwig II: Glanz und Ende eines Konigs, 1959 (Friedrich Domin); Made in Germany, 1957 (Heinz Klevenow); Preussen uber alles—Bismarcks deutsche Einigung, 1971 (TV miniseries; Heinz Klevenow); The Prime Minister, 1942 (Lyn Harding); **Royal Flash**, 1975 (Oliver Reed); Sisi, 2009 (made-for-TV; Dieter Kirchlechner); Spy of Napoleon, 1936 (Lyn Harding); To Hell with the Kaiser!, 1918 (Henry Carvill); Unser Haus in Kamerun, 1961 (Kenneth Spencer).

Blackbeard (Edward Teach; Edward Thatch; c.1680-1718; notorious pirate of the West Indies and the eastern coast of the American colonies): Anne of the Indies, 1951 (Thomas Gomez); Black Sails, 2014- (TV series; Ray Stevenson); Blackbeard, 2006 (TV miniseries; Angus Macfadyen); Blackbeard; Terror at Sea, 2006 (made-for-TV; James Purefoy); Blackbeard the Pirate, 1952 (Robert Newton); Blackbeard's Ghost, 1968 (Peter Ustinov); The Boy and the Pirates, 1960 (Murvyn Vye); The Buccaneers, 1956-1957 (TV series; Terence Cooper in two 1956 episodes; George Margo in one 1956 episode); Captain Kidd and the Slave Girl, 1954 (Michael Ross); Captain Z-Ro, 1955- (TV series; "Blackbeard the Pirate," 1956 episode: John Trigonis); Crossbones, 2014- (TV series; John Malkovich); Double Crossbones, 1951 (Louis Bacigalupi); **Pirates of the Caribbean: On Stranger Tides**, 2011 (Ian McShane); Rogue's

Gallery, 2005- (TV series; Vic Reeves); True Caribbean Pirates, 2006 (made-for-TV; Patrick Lander); TV Reader's Digest, 1955-1956 (TV series; "The End of Blackbeard the Pirate," 1955 episode: Jeff Morrow); Voyage to the Bottom of the Sea, 1964-1968 (TV series; "The Return of Blackbeard," 1967 episode: Malachi Throne). For detailed information on Blackbeard, see my two-volume work *The Great Pictorial History of World Crime*, Volume II (History, Inc., 2004; illustrated pages 1290-1293).

Blair, Francis Preston (1791-1876; U.S. journalist and adviser to U.S. presidents, including Abraham Lincoln): **Gods and Generals**, 2003 (Malachy McCourt); **Lincoln**, 2012 (Hal Holbrook).

Blair, Montgomery (1813-1883; U.S. politician and 20th U.S. Postmaster General; older brother of Francis Preston Blair Jr.): The Dramatic Life of Abraham Lincoln, 1924 (Joseph Mills); **Lincoln**, 2012 (Byron Jennings); **Saving Lincoln**, 2013 (Lew Temple).

Blamey, Thomas (Sir Thomas Albert Blamey; 1884-1951; Australian general in WWI and WWII and the only Australian military commander ever to achieve the rank of field marshal): Behind the Legend, 1972-1975 (TV series; John Frawley); **MacArthur**, 1977 (Gerald Peters).

Bligh, William (1754-1817; British captain of the HMS *Bounty*, which was seized by mutineers led by first mate Fletcher Christian on April 29, 1879; Bligh and others were set adrift in an open boat, sailing 3,618 miles to the island of Timor): Bligh, 1992- (TV series; Michael Veitch); **The Bounty**, 1984 (Anthony Hopkins); Captain James Cook, 1987- (TV miniseries; David Whitney); General Electric Theater, 1953-1962 (TV series; "The Bounty Court Martial," 1955 episode: Francis L. Sullivan); In the Wake of the Bounty, 1933 (Mayne Lynton); The Man Who Shot the Albatross, 1972 (made-for-TV; Leo McKern); The Mutiny on the Bounty, 1916 (George Cross); **Mutiny on the Bounty**, 1935 (Charles Laughton); **Mutiny on the Bounty**, 1962 (Trevor Howard); Mutiny on the Bounty, 2011 (made-for-TV; Mark Chinnery); Rogue Nation, 2009 (TV series; "Honour among Thieves," 2009 episode: John Wood); Sara Dane, 1982 (made-for-TV; Micheal Duffield); Stormy Petrel, 1960- (TV series; Brian James); The Timeless Land, 1980- (TV series; Ray Barrett); You Are There, 1953-1971 (TV series; "Mr. Christian Seizes the Bounty [April 28, 1789]," 1956 episode: Jacques Aubuchon). Note: For detailed information on the mutiny on board the *Bounty*, see my eight-volume work *Encyclopedia of World Crime*, Volume III (CrimeBooks, Inc., 1990; illustrated pages 2269-2270).

Blixen, Karen (Baroness Karen von Blixen-Finecke; 1885-1962; Danish author who described her life in Kenya in her best-selling 1937 book of memoirs, *Out of Africa*): The Adventures of Picasso, 1978 (Ove Sprogoe); **Out of Africa**, 1985 (Meryl Streep).

Blood, Thomas (1618-1680; British colonel who, along with confederates, attempted to steal the crown jewels from the Tower of London on May 9, 1671; he was captured and imprisoned but later pardoned by Charles II, who admired his daring): Colonel Blood, 1934 (Frank Cellier); The Joseph Cotten Show: On Trial, 1956-1959 (TV series; "The Trial of Colonel Blood," 1957 episode: Michael Wilding); Rogue's Gallery, 2005- (TV series; Vic Reeves); Theft Royal, 1956 (made-for-TV; William Devlin). For detailed information on Thomas Blood and the theft of the Crown Jewels, see my two-volume work *The Pictorial History of World Crime*, Volume II (History, Inc., 2004; illustrated pages 1330-1332).

Blucher, Gebhard von (1742-1819; German soldier and field marshal in the Napoleonic Wars): Hundred Days, 1935 (Eduard von Winterstein); The Iron Duke, 1935 (Franklin Dyall); Marschall Vorwarts, 1932 (Paul

Klaus Maria Brandauer and Meryl Streep (as Karen Blixen) in *Out of Africa*, **1985.**

Wegener); **Waterloo**, 1971 (Sergo Zakariadze).

Blumentritt, Gunther von (1892-1967; German general in WWII): A Bridge Too Far, 1977 (Hans von Borsody); **The Longest Day**, 1962 (Curt Jurgens); Operation Walkure, 1971 (made-for-TV; Helmut Oeser).

Blunt, Anthony Frederick (aka: Sir Anthony Blunt; 1907-1983; British art historian who, after being offered immunity, confessed to being a Soviet spy and member of the notorioius "Cambridge Five" in 1963; he was stripped of his knighthood in 1979 after Prime Minister Margaret Thatcher exposed his treasonous espionage): Cambridge Spies, 2003 (TV miniseries; Samuel West); Screen One, 1985-2002 (TV series; "A Question of Attribution," 1991 episode: James Fox); Screen Two, 1985-2002 (TV series; "Blunt," 1987 episode: Ian Richardson). Note: For detailed information on Blunt, see my book *Spies: A Narrative Encyclopedia of Dirty Tricks & Double Dealing from Biblical Times to Today* (M. Evans, 1997; illustrated pages 107-109).

Bly, Nellie (Elizabeth Cochran Seaman; 1864-1922; pioneer investigative reporter who exposed political corruption, medical malpractice and other social evils by going undercover to get her stories, and who emulated the Jules Verne story by going around the world in seventy-two days in 1889): The Adventures of Nellie Bly, 1981 (made-for-TV; Linda Purl); The Barbara Stanwyck Show, 1960- (TV series; "Little Big Mouth," 1961 episode: Barbara Stanwyck); The Dinah Shore Chevy Show, 1956-1963 (TV series; "Around the World with Nellie Bly," 1960 episode: Janet Blair, released in 1960 as a separate TV movie); Frankie and Johnny, 1936 (Lilyan Tashman); Frankie and Johnny, 1966 (Nancy Kovack); **10 Days in a Madhouse**, 2015 (Caroline Barry); Voyagers!, 1982-1983 (TV series; "Jack's Back," 1983 episode; Julia Duffy).

Bo Diddley (Elias Otha Bates; 1928-2008; U.S. singer, songwriter and guitarist who pioneered rock 'n' roll music): Country Blue, 1975 (Concho Evans); Eddie and the Cruisers: Eddie Lives!, 1989 (Al Ward); Mr. Rock 'n' Roll: The Alan Freed Story, 1999 (made-for-TV; Michael Dunston); Vinyl, 2016 (TV series; Kareem Bunton); Who Do You Love, 2010 (Robert Randolph).

Boleyn, Anne (1501/1507-1536; Queen of England): Anna Bolena, 1984 (made-for-TV; Joan Sutherland); Anna Bolena, 2011 (made-for-TV; Anna Netrebko); Anna Boleyn, 1920 (Henny Porten); **Anne of the Thousand Days**, 1969 (Genevieve Bujold); BBC Sunday-Night Theatre, 1950-1959 (TV series; "The White Falcon," 1956 episode: Jeanette Sterke); Catalina de Inglaterra, 1951 (Mary Lamar); Complete and Utter History of Britain, 1969 (TV series; "Perkin Warbeck to Bloody

Irene Pappas, director Charles Jarrott, Genevieve Bujold (as Anne Boleyn) in *Anne of the Thousand Days*, 1969.

Mary,"1969 episode: Melinda Mays); God's Outlaw, 1986 (Oona Kirsch); Heinrich VIII. und seine Frauen, 1968 (made-for-TV; Christine Wodetzky); Henry VIII, 1979 (made-for-TV; Barbara Kellerman); Henry VIII, 1991 (made-for-TV; Lucile Vignon); Henry VIII, 2003 (made-for-TV; Helena Bonham Carter); Henry VIII and His Six Wives, 1972 (Charlotte Rampling); Henry VIII: Mind of a Tyrant, 2009 (TV series: Sophie Hunter); The Last Days of Anne Boleyn, 2013 (made-for-TV; Tara Breathnach); The Madness of Henry VIII, 2006 (made-for-TV; Iona Flora); **A Man for All Seasons**, 1966 (Vanessa Redgrave); Monarch, 2000 (Jean Marsh); Nunca me hagan eso, 1957 (Noemi Barreiro); Omnibus, 1952-1961 (TV series; "The Trial of Anne Boleyn," 1952 episode: Lilli Palmer); The Other Boleyn Girl, 2003 (made-for-TV; Jodhi May); The Other Boleyn Girl, 2008 (Natalie Portman); **The Pearls of the Crown**, 1938 (Barbara Shaw); **The Private Life of Henry VIII**, 1933 (Merle Oberon); A Royal Love, 2016 (Samantha Haitsma); The Six Wives of Henry VIII, 1970 (TV miniseries; Dorothy Tutin); The Six Wives of Henry VIII, 2001 (TV miniseries; Julia Marsen); The Third Testament, 2010 (Kristina Candelarie); The Tudors, 2007-2010 (TV series; Natalie Dormer); The Twisted Tale of Bloody Mary, 2008 (made-for-TV; Lisa Marie Kennedy); Where Thunder Reigns, 2016 (Lauren Falconer); Wolf Hall, 2015 (TV miniseries; Claire Foy); You Are There, 1953-1971 (TV series: "The Crisis of Anne Boleyn [May 16, 1536]," 1954 episode: Beatrice Straight); **Young Bess**, 1953 (Elaine Stewart).

Boleyn, Mary (1499-1543; English courtier in the court of Henry VIII, reportedly a one-time mistress of Henry VIII and who gave birth to two illegitimate children by him; sister of Anne Boleyn, queen consort of England): **Anne of the Thousand Days**, 1969 (Valerie Gearon); Henry VIII, 2003 (made-for-TV; Clare Cameron); The Other Boleyn Girl, 2003 (made-for-TV; Natascha McElhone); The Other Boleyn Girl, 2008 (Scarlett Johansson); A Royal Love, 2016 (Nikki Olthof); The Six Wives of Henry VIII, 1970 (TV miniseries; "Ann Boleyn," 1970 episode: Hilary Mason); The Tudors, 2007-2010 (TV series; Perdita Weeks); Wolf Hall, 2015 (TV miniseries; Charity Wakefield).

Bonaparte, Jerome-Napoleon (1784-1860; French politician; youngest brother of Napoleon I and king of Westphalia): Eugenia de Montijo, 1944 (Guillermo Marin); Glorious Betsy, 1928 (Conrad Nagel); The Little Napoleon, 1923 (Paul Heidemann); Madame, 1963 (Carlo Giuffre): Miss Bonaparte, 1942 (Guillaume de Sax); **Napoleon**, 1927 (Roger Chantal); Napoleon, 1955 (Claude Arlay).

Bonaparte, Joseph-Napoleon (1768-1844; elder brother of Napoleon I; king of Naples, King of Spain as Jose I): **Desiree**, 1954 (Cameron

Mitchell); The Firefly, 1937 (Stanley Price); Goya's Ghosts, 2007 (Julian Wadham); Josephine ou la comedie des ambitions, 1979- (TV miniseries; Fabrizio Jovine); La sposa dei re, 1938 (Emilio Cigoli); Mlle. Desiree, 1948 (Aime Clariond); Murat, 1975- (TV miniseries; Diego Michelotti); **Napoleon**, 1927 (Georges Lampin); Napoleon, 1955 (Robert Manuel); Napoleon, 2002 (TV miniseries; Ennio Fastastichini); Napoleon and Josephine: A Love Story, 1987- (TV miniseries; Anthony Higgins); Napoleon and Love, 1974- (TV miniseries; Edward de Souza); Napoleon Bonaparte, 1935 (Georges Lampin); Napoleone a Sant'Elena, 1973- (TV miniseries; Marcello Tusco); A Royal Divorce, 1938 (John Laurie).

Bonaparte, Louis-Napoleon (1778-1846; brother of Napoleon I; king of Holland): **Desiree**, 1954 (Larry Crane); Josephine ou la comedie des ambitions, 1979- (TV miniseries; Jose Lifante); Napoleon, 1955 (Gilbert Gil); Napoleon and Josephine: A Love Story, 1987- (TV miniseries; Jeremy Brudenell); A Royal Divorce, 1938 (David Farrar).

Bonaparte, Lucien (1775-1840; French nobleman and younger brother of Napoleon I): The Ace of Spades, 1925 (Aaron Edwards); The Battle of Austerlitz, 1960 (Rossano Brazzi); **Desiree**, 1954 (Richard van Cleemput); Josephine ou la comedie des ambitions, 1979- (TV miniseries; Raymond Aquaviva); **Napoleon**, 1927 (Sylvio Cavicchia); Napoleon, 1955 (Serge Reggiani); Napoleon and Josephine: A Love Story, 1987- (TV miniseries; Colin Bruce); Napoleon Bonaparte, 1935 (Sylvio Cavicchia).

Bonifacio, Andres (1863-1897; Filipino insurrectionist who fought for Philippines independence): Ang Paglilitis kay Andres Bonifacio, 2010 (Alfred Vargas); **Back to Bataan**, 1945 (Anthony Quinn as the grandson of Andres Bonifacio); Bayani, 1992 (Julio Diaz); Bonifacio: Ang unang pangulo, 2014 (Robin Padilla); El Presidente, 2012 (Cesar Montano); Ilustrado, 2014- (TV series; Sid Lucero); Indio, 2013- (TV series; Jolo Revilla); Jose Rizal, 1998 (Gardo Versoza); Katipunan, 2013 (TV miniseries; Sid Lucero); Supemo, 2012 (Alfred Vargas).

Bonnet, Stede (AKA: The Gentleman Pirate; c. 1688-1718; British-born businessman turned pirate in waters off Barbados and who worked with fellow pirate Blackbeard; he was executed by hanging): True Caribbean Pirates, 2006 (made-for-TV; Andrew Block).

Bonny, Anne (Bonney; c. 1702-1782; female pirate of the Caribbean): Abbott and Costello Meet Captain Kidd, 1952 (Hillary Brooke); Anne of the Indies, 1951 (Jean Peters); Black Sails, 2014- (TV series; Clara Paget); Captain Kidd and the Slave Girl, 1954 (Sonia Sorel); Double Crossbones, 1951 (Hope Emerson); Pirates, 1998 (Lorna Bennett); **The Spanish Main**, 1945 (Binnie Barnes); True Caribbean Pirates, 2006 (made-for-TV; Michelle Michaels).

Boone, Daniel (1734-1820; U.S. pioneer, explorer and frontiersman): Captain Z-Ro, 1955- (TV series; "Daniel Boone," 1955 episode; Billy Hicks); Daniel Boone, 1936 (George O'Brien); Daniel Boone, 1964-1970 (TV series; Fess Parker); Daniel Boone, Frontier Trail Rider, 1966 (Fess Parker); Daniel Boone thru the Wilderness, 1926 (Roy Stewart); Daniel Boone, Trail Blazer, 1956 (Bruce Bennett); The Great Adventure, 1963-1964 (TV series; two 1964 episodes: Peter Graves); The Great Meadow, 1931 (John Miljan); In the Days of Daniel Boone, 1923 (Charles Brinley); Mentors, 1998-2005 (TV series; "The Rescue," 1999 episode; Roddy Piper); The Miracle Rider, 1935 (serial; Jay Wilsey); Young Daniel Boone, 1950 (David Bruce); Walt Disney's Wonderful World of Color, 1954-1992 (TV series; two 1960 episodes and two 1961 episodes; all with Dewey Martin as Boone); Young Dan'l Boone, 1977- (TV series; Rick Moses).

Booth, Asia (1835-1888; U.S. poet and sister of actors Edwin Booth and

John Wilkes Booth): **Prince of Players**, 1955 (Elizabeth Sellars); They've Killed President Lincoln!, 1971 (made-for-TV; Grayce Grant).

Booth, Edwin (1833-1893; U.S. performer, considered to be the greatest actor of his era; older brother of assassin John Wilkes Booth; ironically Edwin Booth saved the life of Lincoln's oldest son, Robert, from being killed by a train in Jersey City, New Jersey, in late 1864): Bonanza, 1959-1973 (TV series; "The Actress," 1963 episode: John Rodney); Branded, 1965-1966 (TV series; "The Stage of Fools," 1966 episode: Martin Landau); Bronco, 1958-1962 (TV series; "The Prince of Darkness," 1961 episode: Efrem Zimbalist Jr.); Colt .45, 1957-1960 (TV series; "The Man Who Loved Lincoln," 1959 episode: Robert McQueeney); Death Valley Days, 1952-1970 (TV series; "His Brother's Keeper," 1960 episode: Harry Townes); **Prince of Players**, 1955 (Richard Burton as adult Edwin Booth; Christopher Cook as young Edwin Booth); Wagon Train, 1957-1965 (TV series; "The Will Santee Story," 1961 episode: John Crawford).

Booth, John Wilkes (1838-1865; U.S. actor and assassin of President Abraham Lincoln): **Abraham Lincoln**, 1930 (Ian Keith); Bedazzled, 2000 (Julian Firth); **The Birth of a Nation**, 1915 (Raoul Walsh); **The Conspirator**, 2011 (Toby Kebbell); The Day Lincoln Was Shot, 1998 (made-for-TV; Rob Morrow); Days That Shook the World, 2003-2013 (TV series; "Terror Made in America: Assassination of Abraham Lincoln…," 2004 episode: Donald William Jayroe); The Dramatic Life of Abraham Lincoln, 1924 (William F. Moran); The Farmer Takes a Wife, 1935 (Philip Cooper); Ford Star Jubilee, 1955-1956 (TV series; "The Day Lincoln Was Shot," 1956 episode: Jack Lemmon); **Gods and Generals**, 2003 (Chris Conner); In the Days of Buffalo Bill, 1922 (William F. Moran); Lincoln, 1988 (made-for-TV; Glenn Faigen); The Lincoln Conspiracy, 1977 (Bradford Dillman); Look Away, 1987 (made-for-TV; Jeff Kizer); The Ordeal of Dr. Mudd, 1980 (made-for-TV; Bill Gribble); Passions, 1999-2008 (TV series; episode 1,625: Mark St. Amant); The Philco-Goodyear Television Playhouse, 1948-1956 (TV series; "The Story of Mary Surratt," 1949 episode: Kent Smith); **Prince of Players**, 1955 (John Derek); **The Prisoner of Shark Island**, 1936 (Francis McDonald); Saturday the 14th Strikes Back, 1988 (Jeff Winkless); Telephone Time, 1956-1958 (TV series; "The Quality of Mercy," 1958 episode: Michael Emmet); They've Killed President Lincoln!, 1971 (made-for-TV; Robert Leonard); Westinghouse Desilu Playhouse, 1958-1960 (TV series; "The Case for Dr. Mudd," 1958 episode: Don Harron); You Are There, 1953-1957 (TV series; "The Capture of John Wilkes Booth," 1953 episode: Michael O'Connell); Zane Grey Theater, 1956-1961 (TV series; "The Ghost," 1959 episode: Alexander Davion); Zoolander, 2001 (James Marsden). Note: For detailed information on Booth and the Lincoln assassination, see my two-volume work *The Great Pictorial History of World Crime*, Volume I (History, Inc., 2004; illustrated [47 images] pages 26-44).

Booth, Junius Brutus Sr. (1796-1852; U.S. actor, father of actors Edwin Booth and John Wilkes Booth, considered to be the greatest actor of his era; he reportedly went insane): Copper, 2012- (TV series; two 2012 episodes: Andrew Jackson); The Farmer Takes a Wife, 1935 (Robert Warwick); **Prince of Players**, 1955 (Raymond Massey).

Borden, Lizzie (1860-1927; U.S. spinster, accused of murdering her mother and father, but acquitted): Alfred Hitchcock Presents, 1955-1962 (TV series; "The Older Sister," 1956 episode: Carmen Mathews); Armstrong Circle Theatre, 1950-1963 (TV series: "Legend of Murder: The Untold Story of Lizzie Borden," 1961 episode: Clarice Blackburn); The Legend of Lizzie Borden, 1973 (Elizabeth Montgomery); Lizzie Borden Took an Axe, 2014 (Christina Ricci); Saturday the 14th Strikes Back, 1988 (Lauren Peterson); Second Verdict, 1976- (TV series; "Lizzie Borden," 1976 episode: Rosemary Leach); Suspense, 1949-1954 (TV series; "The Legend of Lizzie," 1953 episode: Katharine Bard); Terror in the

Jean Peters as Anne Bonny in *Anne of the Indies*, 1951.

Wax Museum, 1973 (Judy Wetmore). For detailed information on Borden, see my two-volume work *The Great Pictorial History of World Crime*, Volume I (History, Inc., 2004; illustrated pages 1203-1212).

Borgia, Cesare (1475-1507; Italian nobleman and son of Pope Alexander VI and brother of the notorious Lucrezia Borgia; a ruthless politician and military leader, who is credited with a number of murders in his effort to gain lands and power): The Black Duke, 1964 (Cameron Mitchell); The Borgia, 2006 (Sergio Peris-Mencheta); Borgia, 2011 (TV series; Mark Ryder); The Borgias, 1981 (TV miniseries; Oliver Cotton); The Borgias, 2011-2013 (TV series; Francois Arnaud); Bride of Vengeance, 1923 (Conrad Veidt); Bride of Vengeance, 1949 (Macdonald Carey); Caterina Sforza, la leonessa di Romagna, 1959 (Erno Crisa); Der Schatten, 1961 (made-for-TV; Edwin Marian); **Don Juan**, 1926 (Warner Orland); Giovanni de Medici: The Leader, 1940 (Erwin Klietsch); Leonardo, 2003 (made-for-TV; James Frain); Les Borgia ou le sang dore, 1977 (made-for-TV; Jean-Claude Bouillon); The Life of Leonardo Da Vinci, 1971 (TV series; Federico Pietrabruna); Les Borgia ou le sang dore, 1977 (made-for-TV; Jean-Claude Bouillon); Lucrece Borgia, 1956 (Pedro Armendariz); Lucrezia Boria, 1928 (Conrad Veidt); Lucrezia Borgia, 1937 (Gabriel Gabrio); Lucrezia Borgia, 1968 (Lou Castel); Lucrezia Borgia; or Plaything of Power, 1923 (Russell Thorndike); Lucrezia giovane, 1974 (Massimo Foschi); L'uomo che ride, 1966 (AKA: The Man with the Golden Mask; Edmund Purdom); The Mask of Cesare Borgia, 1941 (Osvaldo Valenti); Meriota, die Tanzerin, 1922 (Oscar Beregi Sr.); The Nights of Lucretia Borgia, 1960 (Franco Fabrizi); O Falcao Negro, 1954 (TV series; Fernando Baleroni); **Prince of Foxes**, 1947 (Orson Welles); The Power of the Borgias, 1920 (Enrico Piacentini); Prisoner in the Tower of Fire, 1953 (Rossano Brazzi).

Borgia, Lucrezia (1480-1519; Italian noblewoman; daughter of Pope Alexander VI and sister of Cesare Borgia, a political and military adventurer and conqueror, who was married several times so that her family could gain lands and power and is portrayed as femme fatale in history, even as a poisoner involved in many murderous schemes): The Black Duke, 1964 (Gloria Osuna); The Borgia, 2006 (Maria Valverde); Borgia, 2011 (TV series; Isolda Dychauk); The Borgias, 1981 (TV miniseries; Anne-Louise Lambert); The Borgias, 2011-2013 (TV series; Holliday Grainger); Bride of Vengeance, 1923 (Liane Haid); Bride of Vengeance, 1949 (Paulette Goddard); Caterina Sforza, la leonessa di Romagna, 1959 (Caprice Chantal); Conspiracy of the Borgias, 1959 (Constance Smith); **Dante's Inferno**, 1935 (Leone Lane); **Don Juan**, 1926 (Estelle Taylor); The Eternal Sin, 1917 (Florence Reed); Les Borgia ou le sang dore, 1977 (made-for-TV; Maureen Kerwin); Lucrece

Tyrone Power and Orson Welles (as Cesare Borgia) in *Prince of Foxes,* 1949.

Borgia, 1956 (Martine Carol); Lucrezia Boria, 1928 (Liane Haid); Lucrezia Borgia, 1937 (Edwige Feuillere); Lucrezia Borgia, 1940 (Isa Pola); Lucrezia Borgia, 1968 (Olga Schoberova/Olinka Berova); Lucrezia Borgia, 1977 (made-for-TV; Joan Sutherland); Lucrezia Borgia, 1990 (Lucia Prato); Lucrezia Borgia, 1994 (Francesca Benedetti); Lucrezia Borgia, 2002 (made-for-TV; Mariella Devia); Lucrezia Borgia, 2007 (made-for-TV; Dimitra Theodossiou); Lucrezia Borgia, 2009 (made-for-TV; Edita Gruberova); Lucrezia Borgia, 2013 (Renee Fleming); Lucrezia Borgia; or Plaything of Power, 1923 (Nina Vanna); Lucrezia giovane, 1974 (Simonetta Stefanelli); L'uomo che ride, 1966 (aka: The Man with the Golden Mask; Lisa Gastoni); Meriota, die Tanzerin, 1922 (Nora Gregor); The Nights of Lucretia Borgia, 1960 (Belinda Lee); O Falcao Negro, 1954 (TV series; Marly Bueno); Pleasant Nights, 1966 (Maria Grazia Buccella); Satanas, 1920 (Else Berna); A Season of Giants, 1990 (made-for-TV; Danja Gazzara); The Secret Nights of Lucrezia Borgia, 1982 (Sirpa Lane); Terror in the Wax Museum, 1973 (Rosa Huerta); Witness to Yesterday, 1970- (TV series; "Lucrezia Borgia," 1976 episode: Alexandra Bastedo).

Borgia, Rodrigo, see Alexander VI.

Bormann, Martin (1900-1945; German Nazi politician and private secretary of Adolf Hitler): The Bunker, 1981 (made-for-TV; Michael Lonsdale); Churchill: The Hollywood Years, 2004 (Phil Cornwell); Downfall, 2004 (Thomas Thieme); Eyes That Kill, 1947 (Robert Berkeley); The Great Battle, 1969- (TV series; Joachim Pape); Hitler, 1962 (Stan Jones); Hitler: The Last Ten Days, 1973 (Mark Kingston); Inside the Third Reich, 1982 (made-for-TV; Derek Newark); ITV Sunday Night Theatre, 1969- (TV series; "The Death of Adolf Hitler," 1973 episode: Ed Devereaux); The Last Ten Days, 1955 (Curt Eilers); Le Bunker, 1972 (made-for-TV; Francois Chaumette); The Motorola Television Hour, 1953-1954 (TV series; "The Last Days of Hitler," 1954 episode: Arnold Moss); The Search for the Evil One, 1967 (Henry Brandon); War and Remembrance, 1988 (TV miniseries; Wolfgang Reichmann).

Bothwell, 4th Earl: see Hepburn, James

Bowie, James (1796-1836; U.S. frontiersman): The Adventures of Jim Bowie, 1956-1958 (TV series; Scott Forbes); The Alamo, 1960 (Richard Widmark); The Alamo, 2004 (Jason Patric); The Alamo: Thirteen Days to Glory, 1987 (made-for-TV; James Arness); Comanche Territory, 1950 (Macdonald Carey); Davy Crockett at the Fall of the Alamo, 1926 (Bob Fleming); Davy Crockett: King of the Wild Frontier, 1955 (Kenneth Tobey); The First Texan, 1956 (Jeff Morrow); Gone to Texas, 1986 (made-for-TV; Michael Beck); Heroes of the Alamo, 1937 (Roger

Williams); Into the Labyrinth, 1981-1982 (TV series; "Alamo," 1981 episode: Norman Bowler); The Iron Mistress, 1952 (Alan Ladd); Kit & Co., 1974 (Hans Lucke); The Last Command, 1955 (Sterling Hayden); The Man from the Alamo, 1953 (Stuart Randall); Man of Conquest, 1939 (Robert Armstrong); Martyrs of the Alamo, 1915 (Alfred Paget); Texas, 1994 (made-for-TV; David Keith); The Time Tunnel, 1966-1967 (TV series; "The Alamo," 1966 episode: Jim Davis); Two for Texas, 1998 (made-for-TV; Peter Coyote); Walt Disney's Wonderful World of Color, 1954-1992 (TV series; "Davy Crockett at the Alamo," 1955 episode: Kenneth Tobey).

Braddock, Edward (1695-1755; British general and commander-in-chief of the thirteen American colonies during the French and Indian War, 1754-1765): George Washington, 1984 (TV miniseries; James Mason); In the Days of Daniel Boone, 1923 (Herschel Mayall); Winners of the Wilderness, 1927 (Will Walling).

Braddock, James J. (1905-1974; U.S. prizefighter and World Heavyweight Champion, 1935-1937): Cinderella Man, 2005 (Russell Crowe); Joe and Max, 2002 (made-for-TV; Frank Shattuck).

Bradford, Dorothy (d. 1620; wife of Piligrim leader William Bradford; she apparently fell from the Mayflower and drowned while her husband was away with a party exploring the Plymouth Rock area shortly after the ship arrived): The Mayflower, 2006 (made-for-TV; Erin Raftery); Plymouth Adventure, 1952 (Gene Tierney).

Bradford, William (1590-1657; one of the leaders of the Pilgrims landing at Plymouth Rock in 1620): The Courtship of Myles Stanish, 1923 (Norval MacGregor); The Mayflower, 2006 (made-for-TV; Sam Redford); Plymouth Adventure, 1952 (Leo Genn).

Bradlee, Benjamin C. (b. 1921; U.S. newspaper editor of the Washington Post): All the President's Men, 1976 (Jason Robards Jr.); Dick, 1999 (G. D. Spradlin); The Kennedys, 2011- (TV series; Steve Cumyn).

Bradley, Omar M. (1893-1981; U.S. solider and five-star U.S. Army general in WWII and thereafter): Collision Course: Truman vs. MacArthur, 1976 (made-for-TV; John Larch); Great Events of the 20th Century: Series II, 2005 (TV series; Jeff Gordon); Ike: Countdown to D-Day, 2004 (made-for-TV; James Remar); Ike: The War Years, 1979 (TV miniseries; Richard Herd); Is Paris Burning?, 1966 (Glenn Ford); The Longest Day, 1962 (Nicholas Stuart); MacArthur, 1977 (Fred Stuthman); Man, Moment, Machine, 2005-2007 (TV series; "Patton and the Desperate Tank Attack," 2006 episode: John White); Never Wave at a WAC, 1953 (himself); Patton, 1970 (Karl Malden); War and Remembrance, 1988- (TV miniseries; Leo Gordon).

Brady, James Buchanan (aka: Diamond Jim; 1856-1917; U.S. businessman and financier): Broadway to Hollywood, 1933 (Robert Greig); Death Valley Days, 1952-1970 (TV series; "Diamond Jim Brady," 1963 episode: Howard Keel); Diamond Jim, 1935 (Edward Arnold); Diamond Jim: Skulduggery in Samantha, 1965 (made-for-TV; Dale Robertson); The Gambler Returns: The Luck of the Draw, 1991 (made-for-TV; Dion Anderson); The Gentleman from Louisiana, 1936 (Charles C. Wilson); Lillian Russell, 1940 (Edward Arnold); Lillie, 1978- (TV miniseries; David Healy); Maverick, 1957-1962 (TV series; "One of Our Trains Is Missing," 1962 episode: Barry Kelley); Somewhere in Time, 1980 (Don Melvoin); Ziegfeld: The Man and His Women, 1978 (made-for-TV; Leon Charles).

Brahms. Johannes (1833-1897; German composer and pianist): Der Fall des Robert Schumann, 1990 (made for TV: Martin Ehrbacher); Geliebte Clara, 2008 (Malik Zidi; singing voice: Manuel Straube); Robert Schumann—Clara Wieck—Johannes Brahms, 2006 (made-for-TV; Sebastian

Mirow); Rosen aud dem Suden, 1934 (Hugo Werner-Kahle); **Song of Love**, 1947 (Robert Walker); The Strauss Family, 1972 (TV miniseries; Laurence Carter); Traumerei, 1944 (Ullrich Haupt).

Brandon, Charles (1484-1545; British nobleman; 1st Duke of Suffolk; close friend of Henry VIII): Henry VIII, 1979 (made-for-TV; Lewis Fiander); Henry VIII and His Six Wives, 1972 (Brian Blessed); The Six Wives of Henry VIII, 1970- (TV miniseries; "Catherine of Aragon," 1970 episode: Raymond Adamson); A Royal Love, 2016 (Torsten Colijn); **The Sword and the Rose**, 1953 (Richard Todd); The Tudors, 2007-2010 (TV series; Henry Cavill); **When Knighthood Was in Flower**, 1922 (Forrest Stanley); Wolf Hall, 2015- (TV miniseries; Richard Dillane).

Brant, Joseph (1743-1897; Mohawk chief in the American Revolutionary War, 1775-1783; led, with British officer Walter Butler, 1752-1781, a guerrilla force of British loyalists and Iroquois Indians into Cherry Valley, New York, on November 11, 1778, where they massacred about thirty non-combatants, including women and children): **America**, 1924 (Riley Hatch); Divided Loyalties, 1990 (Jack Langedijk); The Spirit of '76, 1917 (Dark Cloud).

Bratton, Rufus S. (Rufus Sumter Bratton; 1892-1958; American Army intelligence officer, who determined Japanese sneak attack against Pearl Harbor on December 7, 1941): **Tora! Tora! Tora!**, 1970 (E. G. Marshall).

Brauchitsch, Walther (Heinrich Alfred Hermann Walther von Brauchitsch; 1881-1948; German field marshal in WWII): Days of Betrayal, 1973 (Werner Wieland); War and Remembrance, 1988 (TV miniseries; Wolfgang Preiss); The Winds of War, 1983- (TV miniseries; Wolfgang Preiss).

Braun, Eva (1912-1945; German mistress and wife of Adolf Hitler): Adolf and Marlene, 1977 (Ila von Hasperg); The Bunker, 1981 (made-for-TV; Susan Blakely); Churchill: The Hollywood Years, 2004 (Miranda Richardson); Downfall, 2004 (Juliane Kohler); The Empty Mirror, 1999 (Camilla Soeberg); The Fall of Berlin, 1952 (M. Novakova); Gandhi to Hitler, 2011 (Neha Dhupia); The Great Battle, 1969- (TV series; Angelika Waller); Hitler, 1962 (Maria Emo); Hitler: A Film from Geermany, 1980 (Johannes Buzalski); Hitler: The Last Ten Days, 1973 (Doris Kunstmann); Hitler: The Rise of Evil, 2003 (made-for-TV; Zoe Telford); Inside the Third Reich, 1982 (made-for-TV; Renee Soutendijk); ITV Sunday Night Theatre, 1969- (TV series; "The Death of Adolf Hitler," 1973 episode: Caroline Mortimer); **La Rafle**, 2012 (Franziska Schubert); The Last Ten Days, 1955 (Lotte Tobisch); Le Bunker, 1972 (made-for-TV; Claude Winter); Loose Cannons, 1990 (Margaret Klenck); The Motorola Television Hour, 1953-1954 (TV series; "The Last Days of Hitler," 1954 episode: Lotte Stavisky); **The Producers**, 1967 (impersonation by Rene Taylor); Rogue Male, 1977 (made-for-TV; Shirley Dynevor); The Search for the Evil One, 1967 (Anna-Lisa); War and Remembrance, 1988 (TV miniseries; Kirstie Pooley); The Winds of War, 1983- (TV series; Kirstie Pooley).

Braun, Wernher von (1912-1977; German aerospace engineer, who invented the Nazi V-2 rocket in WWII, and the U.S. Saturn V): Der Raketenmann Wernher von Braun, 2009 (made-for-TV; Johann Hillmann, Ludwig Blochberger, Daniel Rohr); From the Earth to the Moon, 1998 (TV miniseries; Norbert Weisser); I Aim at the Stars, 1960 (Curt Jurgens); Lloyd in Space, 2001- (TV series; "Caution: Wormhole!," 2001 episode: Tony Jay); October Sky, 1999 (Joe Digaetano); Peenemunde, 1970 (made-for-TV; Dieter Kirchlechner); Space Race, 2005- (TV series; Richard Dillane); Voyagers!, 1982-1983 (TV series; "Pursuit," 1983 episode: David Olivier).

Alan Ladd (as Jim Bowie), Virginia Mayo and Richard Carlyle in *The Iron Mistress*, **1952.**

Breckinridge, John Cabell (1821-1875; U.S. lawyer and politician; general in the Confederacy during the American Civil War): The Great Adventure, 1963-1964 (TV series; "The Treasure Train of Jefferson Davis," 1963 episode: Tim O'Connor); Lost River: Lincoln's Secret Weapon, 2009 (Steve McKee).

Brewster, William (1568-1644; preacher and one of the leaders of the Pilgrims landing at Plymouth Rock in 1620): The Courtship of Myles Standish, 1923 (Joseph J. Dowling); The Mayflower, 2006 (made-for-TV; Keith Bartlett); Mayflower: The Pilgrims' Adventure, 1979 (made-for-TV; Richard Crenna); **Plymouth Adventure**, 1952 (Barry Jones).

Brezhnev, Leonid (1906-1982; USSR general secretary of the Central Committee of the Communist Party): Brezhnev, 2005- (TV series; Artur Vakha); Dick, 1999 (Len Doncheff); The Final Days, 1989 (made-for-TV; Boris Sichkin); **Nixon**, 1995 (Boris Sichkin); Squaring the Circle, 1984 (made-for-TV; Frank Middlemass).

Brice, Fanny (1891-1951; U.S. singer, comedienne and actress on the U.S. stage and in movies): **The Cotton Club**, 1984 (Rosalind Harris); **Funny Girl**, 1968 (Barbra Streisand); **Funny Lady**, 1975 (Barbra Streisand); Parade of Stars, 1983 (made-for-TV; Dorothy Loudon); Ziegfeld: The Man and His Women, 1978 (made-for-TV; Catherine Jacoby).

Bridger, Jim (James Felix "Jim" Bridger; 1804-1881; U.S. frontiersman and trailblazer): Along the Oregon Trail, 1947 (Will Wright); Bridger, 1976 (made-for-TV; James Wainwright); **Brigham Young: Frontiersman**, 1940 (Arthur Aylesworth); **The Covered Wagon**, 1923 (Tully Marshall); Death's Dealer, 1971 (Leonard Mann); **Fighting Caravans**, 1931 (Tully Marshall); Fighting with Kit Carson, 1933 (Tully Marshall); The Gun That Won the West, 1955 (Dennis Morgan); Incredible Rocky Mountain Race, 1977 (made-for-TV; Jack Kruschen); Kit Carson, 1928 (Nelson McDowell); **Kit Carson**, 1940 (Raymond Hatton); Kit Carson and the Mountain Men, 1977 (made-for-TV; Gregg Palmer); **Pony Express**, 1953 (Porter Hall); **The Revenant**, 2015 (Will Poulter); **Tomahawk**, 1951 (Van Heflin); Unknown Valley, 1933 (Edward LeSaint); Wagon Train, 1957-1965 (TV series; "The Flint McCullough Story," 1959 episode: Theodore Newton; "The Jim Bridger Story," 1961 episode: Karl Swenson).

Brocius, William (aka: Curly Bill; 1845-1882; U.S. Old West cowboy, gunman and outlaw): Death Valley Days, 1952-1970 (TV series; "A Mule...Like the Army's Mule," 1968 episode: Robert Yuro); The Deputy, 1959-1961 (TV series; "The Big Four," 1959 episode: Gerald

Leo Gen (as William Bradford) and Gene Tierney (as Dorothy Bradford) in *Plymouth Adventure*, 1952.

Milton); Gunslingers, 2014- (TV miniseries; Justin Ramsey); The High Chaparral, 1967-1971 (TV series; "Shadow of the Wind," 1969 episode: Charles Bail); **Hour of the Gun**, 1967 (Jon Voight); The Life and Legend of Wyatt Earp, 1955-1961 (TV series; sixteen episodes: William Phipps); **Tombstone**, 1993 (Powers Boothe); Tombstone Territory, 1957- (TV series; two 1957 episodes: one 1958 episode: Robert Foulk for all); **Tombstone: The Town Too Tough to Die**, 1942 (Edgar Buchanan); The Toughest Gun in Tombstone, 1958 (Lane Bradford); Wanted: Dead or Alive, 1958-1961 (TV series; "Bad Gun," 1959 episode: Harry Bellaver); **Wyatt Earp**, 1994 (Lewis Smith); Wyatt Earp: Return to Tombstone, 1994 (made-for-TV; William Phipps); Note: For detailed information on Brocius, see my book *Encyclopedia of Western Lawmen and Outlaws* (Paragon House, 1992; page 53).

Brodie, Steve (1861-1901; U.S. daredevil who reportedly leaped from NYC's Brooklyn Bridge in 1886 and survived, becoming a legend and opening a successful saloon in the city): **The Bowery**, 1933 (George Raft); **Park Row**, 1952 (George O'Hanlon).

Brodie, William (aka: Deacon Brodie; 1741-1788; cabinetmaker and deacon of the carpenter guild in Edinburgh, Scotland where he also masterminded a burglary ring; he was executed by hanging; his dual life inspired Robert Louis Stevenson to author *Dr. Jekyll and Mr. Hyde*): Deacon Brodie, 1997 (made-for-TV; Billy Connolly); Rogue's Gallery, 2005- (TV series; Vic Reeves). Note: For detailed information on Brodie, see my two-volume work, *The Great Pictorial History of World Crime*, Volume I (History, Inc., 2004; illustrated pages 249-253).

Broun, Heywood Campbell Sr. (1888-1939; U.S. writer and newspaper columnist; member of the Algonquin Round Table): Mrs. Parker and the Vicious Circle, 1994 (Gary Basaraba); **The Private Files of J. Edgar Hoover**, 1977 (as "Heywood Brown"; John Bay).

Brown, Grace (U.S. sweetheart of Chester Gillette, murdered by him in 1906): **An American Tragedy**, 1931 (role model for Sylvia Sidney); **A Place in the Sun**, 1951 (role model for Shelley Winters).

Brown, John (1800-1859; U.S. abolitionist, executed by hanging for attempting to lead a black revolt in the South): **Abe Lincoln in Illinois**, 1940 (John Cromwell); Bad Blood: The Border War That Triggered the Civil War, 2007 (made-for-TV; Chris Glaze); The Blue and the Gray, 1982 (TV miniseries; Sterling Hayden); The Great Adventure, 1963-1964 (TV series, "The Night Raiders," 1964 episode: Jack Klugman); John Brown, 1960 (made-for-TV; Richard Flink); North and South, 1985 (TV series; five episodes: Johnny Cash); **Santa Fe Trail,** 1940

(Raymond Massey); **Seven Angry Men**, 1955 (Raymond Massey); Skin Game, 1971 (Royal Dano); Touched by Fire: Bleeding Kansas, 2005 (made-for-TV; Darren Biggs/Clayton Crenshaw); The War That Made America, 2006 (TV series; Jeffrey Grover).

Brown, Margaret (nee Tobin; aka: "Molly"; 1867-1932; U.S. wealthy woman from Colorado noted for her heroic behavior as a survivor of the sinking of the RMS *Titantic*, on April 15, 1912, and who was known as "The Unsinkable Molly Brown"): French and Saunders, 1987- (TV series; "Titanic," 1998 episode: Harriet Thorpe); **A Night to Remember**, 1958 (Tucker McGuire); S.O.S. Titanic, 1979 (made-for-TV; Cloris Leachman); Telephone Time, 1956-1958 (TV series; "The Unsinkable Molly Brown," 1957 episode: Cloris Leachman); **Titanic**, 1953 (role model for Thelma Ritter, who plays a feisty woman named Maude Young); Titanic, 1996 (TV series; Merilu Henner); **Titanic**, 1997 (Kathy Bates); Titanic, 2012 (TV miniseries; Linda Kash); **The Unsinkable Molly Brown**, 1964 (Debbie Reynolds); Voyager from the Unknown, 1982 (Fionnula Flanagan); Voyagers!, 1982-1983 (TV series; "Voyagers of the Titanic," 1983 episode: Fionnula Flanagan).

Brown, Oliver (d. 1859; U.S. abolitionist and son of John Brown, killed at Harper's Ferry, Virginia during Brown's abortive slave rebellion): **Santa Fe Trail**, 1940 (Alan Baxter); **Seven Angry Men**, 1955 (Larry Pennell).

Brown, Roy (1893-1944; Canadian fighter pilot who is credited with shooting down German ace Manfred von Richthofen in WWI): **The Red Baron**, 2010 (Joseph Fiennes); **Von Richthofen and Brown**, 1971 (Don Stroud).

Browning, Elizabeth Barrett (1806-1861; U.S. poet): **The Barretts of Wimpole Street**, 1934 (Norma Shearer); **The Barretts of Wimpole Street**, 1957 (Jennifer Jones); The Barretts of Wimpole Street, 1982 (made-for-TV; Jane Lapotaire); BBC Sunday-Night Play, 1960-1963 (TV series; "The Barretts of Wimpole Street," 1961 episode: Gwen Watford); BBC Sunday-Night Theatre, 1950-1959 (TV series; "The Barretts of Wimpole Street," 1951 episode: Pauline Jameson); Carry On Christmas, 1969 (made-for-TV; Hattie Jacques); Front Row Center, 1955-1956 (TV series; "The Barretts of Wimpole Street," 1955 episode: Geraldine Fitzgerald); Late Night Theatre, 1972-1974 (TV series; "Dear Love," 1974 episode: Geraldine McEwan); Love Story, 1952 (made-for-TV; Beatrice Straight); Ponds Theater, 1953- (TV series; "The Barretts of Wimpole Street," 1953 episode: Valerie Cossart); Producers' Showcase, 1954-1957 (TV series; "The Barretts of Wimpole Street," 1956 episode: Katharine Cornell); The Prudential Family Playhouse, 1950-1951 (TV series; "The Barretts of Wimpole Street," 1950 episode; Helen Hayes); Robert and Elizabeth, 1965 (made-for-TV; June Bronhill); Telephone Time, 1956-1958 (TV series: "Mr. and Mrs. Browning," 1956 episode: Leora Dana).

Browning, Robert (1812-1889; U.S. poet): **The Barretts of Wimpole Street**, 1934 (Fredric March); **The Barretts of Wimpole Street**, 1957 (Bill Travers); The Barretts of Wimpole Street, 1982 (made-for-TV; Jeremy Brett); BBC Sunday-Night Play, 1960-1963 (TV series; "The Barretts of Wimpole Street," 1961 episode: John Neville); BBC Sunday-Night Theatre, 1950-1959 (TV series; "The Barretts of Wimpole Street," 1951 episode: Griffith Jones); Carry On Christmas, 1969 (made-for-TV; Frankie Howerd); Front Row Center, 1955-1956 (TV series; "The Barretts of Wimpole Street," 1955 episode: Robert Douglas); Late Night Theatre, 1972-1974 (TV series; "Dear Love," 1974 episode: Keith Michell); Love Story, 1952 (made-for-TV; Tom Helmore); Ponds Theater, 1953- (TV series; "The Barretts of Wimpole Street," 1953 episode: Alexander Scourby); Producers' Showcase, 1954-1957 (TV series; "The Barretts of Wimpole Street," 1956 episode: Anthony Quayle); The Prudential Family Playhouse, 1950-1951 (TV series; "The Barretts of Wimpole Street," 1950 episode: Robert Pastene); Robert and Elizabeth, 1965 (made-for-TV; Keith Michell); Telephone Time, 1956-1958 (TV series: "Mr. and Mrs. Browning," 1956 episode: Scott Forbes).

Brummell, George Bryan (Beau Brummell; 1778-1840): BBC Sunday-Night Theatre, 1950-1959 (TV series; "Beau Brummell," 1954 episode: Peter Cushing); **Beau Brummel**, 1924 (John Barrymore); **Beau Brummell**, 1954 (Stewart Granger); Beau Brummell: This Charming Man, 2006 (made-for-TV; James Purefoy); Mrs. Fitzherbert, 1950 (Barry Morse).

Brutus, Marcus Junius (85-42 B.C.; Roman politician and leader of the asssassins who murdered Julius Caesar): Asterix and Obelix Meet Cleopatra, 2002 (animated; Victor Loukianenko voiceover); Asterix and Obelix vs. Caesar, 1999 (animated; Didier Cauchy voiceover); Asterix at the Olympic Games, 2008 (Benoit Poelvoorde); BBC Play of the Month, 1965-1983 (TV series; "Julius Caesar," 1969 episode: Frank Finlay); BBC Sunday-Night Theatre, 1950-1959 (TV series; "Julius Caesar," two 1951 episodes: Patrick Barr); Carry On Cleo, 1964 (Brian Oulton); Caesar, 2003 (made-for-TV; Ian Duncan); Caesar Must Die, 2012 (Salvatore Striano); **Cleopatra**, 1934 (Arthur Hohl); **Cleopatra**, 1963 (Kenneth Haigh); Cleopatra, 1999 (TV miniseries; Sean Pertwee); Conflict, 1966-1969 (TV series; "Julius Caesar," 1966 episode: Jeremy Kemp); The Destiny of Rome, 2011- (TV miniseries; Cedric Brenner); Empire, 2005 (TV miniseries; James Frain); Hercules: The Legendary Journeys, 1995-1999 (TV series; "Love on the Rocks," 1999 episode: Hori Ahipene); An Honourable Murder, 1960 (Norman Wooland); Julius Caesar, 1914 (Antonio Nazzari); Julius Caesar, 1938 (made-for-TV; Sebastian Shaw); Julius Caesar, 1949 (made-for-TV; James Maxwell); Julius Caesar, 1950 (David Bradley); **Julius Caesar**, 1953 (James Mason); Julius Caesar, 1963- (TV series; William Squire); **Julius Caesar**, 1970 (Jason Robards Jr.); Julius Caesar, 1979 (made-for-TV; Richard Pasco); Julius Caesar, 2011 (Jordan Daws); Julius Caesar, 2012 (made-for-TV; Paterson Joseph); Julius Caesar, 2014 (Michael Golding); The Notorious Cleopatra, 1970 (Larry Martinelli); Rome, 2005-2007 (TV series; Tobias Menzies); Serpent of the Nile, 1953 (Robert Griffin); Shakespeare: The Animated Tales, 1992-1994 (TV series; "Julius Caesar," 1994 episode: David Robb voiceover); The Spread of the Eagle, 1963- (TV miniseries; Paul Eddington); Studio One in Hollywood, 1948-1958 (TV series; "Julius Caesar," two 1949 episodes: Robert Keith; "Julius Caesar," 1955 episode: Philip Bourneuf); Theatre 625, 1964-1968 (TV series; "All the Conspirators: The Ides of March," 1964 episode: Alexander Davion); Xena: Warrior Princess, 1995-2001 (TV series; seven episodes: David Franklin; Darren Young); You Are There, 1953-1971 (TV series; "The Assassination of Julius Caesar [March 15, 44 B.C.]," shown in 1953 and 1955: Michael Pate for both).

Bryan, William Jennings (1860-1925; U.S. politician, fundamentalist): Alleged, 2010 (Fred Dalton Thompson); Captains and Kings, 1976- (TV series; Byron Webster); Cross of Fire, 1989 (made-for-TV; Christopher Curry); God in America, 2010- (TV series; Kenneth Tigar); **Inherit the Wind**, 1960 (role model for Fredric March); The Right Man, 1960 (made-for-TV; Martin Gabel); Profiles in Courage, 1964-1965 (TV series; "Oscar W. Underwood," 1964 episode: Tol Avery); **Silver Dollar**, 1932 (Niles Welch); TV Reader's Digest, 1955-1956 (TV series; "The Sad Death of a Hero," 1955: Douglass Dumbrille); **Wilson**, 1944 (Edwin Maxwell); You Are There, 1953-1971 (TV series; "William Jennings Bryan's Presidential Nomination [July 8, 1896]," 1956 episode: Ainslie Pryor).

Bryant, Charles (AKA: Black Face Charlie; d. 1891; U.S. western outlaw, member of the Dalton and Doolin gangs): **Bad Man's Territory**, 1946 (Glen McCarthy).

Bryant, Louise (1885-1936; U.S. Marxist-anarchist writer and common-

Eric Blore and Edward Arnold (as Diamond Jim Brady) in *Diamond Jim*, 1935.

law wife of socialist writer John Reed): **Reds**, 1981 (Diane Keaton); V dni oktyabrya, 1958 (Galina Vodyanitskaya).

Buchalter, Louis (aka: Lepke; 1897-1944; U.S. gangster in Prohibition, who controlled the NYC garment industry and was a board member of the U.S. crime syndicate, the only such national crime cartel boss to be executed): **The Enforcer**, 1951 (role model for Everett Sloane); Gangster Wars, 1981 (Ron Max); The Lawless Years, 1959-1961 (TV series; John Vivyan); Lepke, 1975 (Tony Curtis as adult Buchalter; Barry Miller as young Buchalter); **Murder, Inc.**, 1960 (David J. Stewart). Note: For detailed information on Buchalter, see my book *World Encyclopedia of Organized Crime* (Paragon House, 1992; illustrated [6 images] pages 69-73).

Buchanan, James (1791-1868; U.S. politician and fifteenth President of the U.S.): The Rose and the Jackal, 1990 (made-for-TV; Jeff Corey).

Buckner, Simon Bolivar (1823-1914; U.S. military officer and Confederate general in the American Civil War): Sunday Showcase, 1959-1961 (TV series; "An American Heritage: Shadow of a Soldier," 1960 episode: Henderson Forsythe).

Buddha (563-483 B.C.; sage and teacher most likely in northeastern India): Are We Civilized?, 1934 (Conrad Seideman); Journey to the West, 2010- (TV series; Yan-fei Zhu); Looking for Buddha, 2001 (Peter Nilsson); Monkey, 1978-1980 (TV series; Cecile Chevreau); Monkey Magic, 1998- (animated TV series; Scott McNeil); Saiyuki, 1961 (Kunihisa Takeda); Saiyuki, 1993 (made-for-TV; Kaoru Yachigusa); Shaka, 1963 (Peter Fernandez); Tobe! Songoku, 1977-1979 (TV series; Sen Hara); Wishbone, 1995-1999 (TV series; "Barking at Buddha,"1998 episode: John William Galt).

Buffalo Bill: see Cody, William Frederick.

Buford, John Jr. (1826-1863; U.S. military officer and Union general during the American Civil War): **Gettysburg**, 1993 (Sam Elliott).

Bulow, Hans von (1830-1894; German composer, conductor and pianist): Ferdinand Lassalle, 1918 (Bodo Serp); Lisztomania, 1975 (Andrew Reilly); Ludwig, 1973 (Mark Burns); Magic Fire, 1956 (Erik Schumann); Wagner, 1983 (TV series; Miguel Herz-Kestranek); Wahnfried, 1987 (Peter Matic).

Bundy, McGeorge (1919-1996; U.S. politician and 6th U.S. National Adviser to President John F. Kennedy and President Lyndon B. Johnson;

Jennifer Jones (as Elizabeth Browning), Virginia McKenna and John Gielgud in *The Barretts of Wimpole Street*, 1957.

he was instrumental in escalating U.S. involvement in the Vietnam War): JFK: Seven Days That Made a President, 2013 (made-for-TV; Ray Nedzel); Kennedy, 1983 (TV miniseries; Albert Stratton); The Kennedys, 2011 (TV series; Dan Lett); Lee Daniels, the Butler, 2013 (David Jensen); The Missiles of October, 1974 (made-for-TV; James Olson); Path to War, 2002 (made-for-TV; Cliff De Young).

Bunuel, Luis (1900-1983; Spanish director and filmmaker): Buneul and King Solomon's Table, 2001 (Pere Arguillue); Dali, 1991 (Dimiter Guerasimof); Dali, etre Dieu, 2002 (made-for-TV; Lolo Herrero); El ministerio del tiempo, 2015- (TV series; Jordi Coll); Federico Garcia Lorca Noir Despair, 2013 (Ibrahim Faal); Little Ashes, 2009 (Matthew McNulty); Lorca, muerte de un poeta, 1987-1988 (TV series; two 1987 episodes: Tito Valverde); **Midnight in Paris**, 2011 (Adrien de Van); Miroslava, 1993 (Esteban Placido Mealaza); One Hundred and One Nights, 1999 (Francisco Rabal); Severo Ochoa: La conquista de un Nobel, 2001- (TV miniseries; Manuel Martinez); Surrealissimo: The Scandalous Success of Salvador Dali, 2002 (made-for-TV; Matt Lucas).

Buntline, Ned (Edward Zane Carroll Judson Sr.; 1821-1886; U.S. publisher, journalist and publicist): **Annie Oakley**, 1935 (Dick Elliott); **Buffalo Bill**, 1944 (Thomas Mitchell); Buffalo Bill and the Indians, 1976 (Burt Lancaster); Colt .45, 1957-1960 (TV series; "A Legend of Buffalo Bill," 1959 episode: C. Lindsay Workman); The Life and Legend of Wyatt Earp, 1955-1961 (TV series; Lloyd Corrigan).

Burgdorf, Wilhelm Emanuel (1895-1945; German general and dedicated Nazi under Adolf Hitler): **The Desert Fox: The Story of Rommel**, 1951 (Everett Sloane); Downfall, 2005 (Justus von Dohnanyi); Hitler: The Last Ten Days, 1973 (Joss Ackland); **Is Paris Burning?**, 1966 (Peter Jacob); ITV Sunday Night Theatre, 1969- (TV series; "The Death of Adolf Hitler," 1973 episode: Hector Ross); The Last Ten Days, 1955 (Erik Frey); Rommel, 2012 (made-for-TV; Peter Kremer).

Burgess, Guy Francis de Moncy (1911-1963; British intelligence officer turned traitor and spy for the Soviets, defecting to the USSR in 1951): Another Country, 1984 (Rupert Everett); Cambridge Spies, 2003 (TV miniseries; Tom Hollander); An Englishman Abroad, 1984 (made-for-TV; Alan Bates); Goodnight Sweetheart, 1993-1999 (TV series; "Between the Devil and the Deep Blue Sea," 1995 episode; Tim Dutton); Kim Philby war der dritte Mann, 1969 (made-for-TV; Harald Juhnke); Philby, Burgess and Maclean, 1977 (made-for-TV; Derek Jacobi); Screen Two, 1985-2002 (TV series; "Blunt," 1987 episode: Anthony Hopkins). Note: For detailed information on Burgess, see my book *Spies: A Narrative Encyclopedia of Dirty Tricks & Double Dealing from*

Biblical Times to Today (M. Evans, 1997; illustrated pages 119-122).

Burgoyne, John (1722-1792; British general who surrendered at Saratoga in 1777 during the American Revolutionary War, 1775-1783): **The Devil's Disciple**, 1959 (Laurence Olivier); Liberty! The American Revolution, 1997 (TV miniseries; Terrence Mann); Theatre Night, 1985 (TV series; "The Devil's Disciple," 1987 episode: Ian Richardson).

Burke, Billie (Mary "Billie" Burke; 1884-1970; U.S. actress): **The Great Ziegfeld**, 1936 (Myrna Loy); Ziegfeld: The Man and His Women, 1978 (made-for-TV; Samatha Eggar).

Burke, Edmund (1729-1797; Irish politician and statesman in British Parliament who supported the American revolutionaries and Catholic emancipation in England): **America**, 1924 (Will S. Rising).

Burke, William (1792-1829; Irish-born laborer turned murderer in Edinburgh, Scotland, where, in 1828, he, along with William Hare, murdered at least sixteen persons, selling the cadavers to an unwitting Dr. Robert Knox for his anatomy studies; Burke was hanged after his partner, Hare, informed on him): The Alfred Hitchcock Hour, 1962-1965 (TV series; "The McGregor Affair," 1964 episode: Arthur Malet); The Anatomist, 1939 (made-for-TV; W.G. Fay); The Anatomist, 1956 (made-for-TV; Diarmuid Kelly); The Body Snatcher, 1945 (role model for Boris Karloff); Burke and Hare, 1972 (Derren Nesbitt); Burke and Hare, 2010 (Simon Pegg); The Doctor and the Devils, 1985 (role model for Jonathan Pryce); The Flesh and the Fiends, 1961 (George Rose); Horror Maniacs, 1953 (role model for Tod Slaughter); Mystery and Imagination, 1966-1970 (TV series; "The Body Snatcher," 1966 episode: John Garrie). Note: For detailed information on Burke and Hare, see my two-volume work *The Great Pictorial History of World Crime*, Volume II (History, Inc., 2004; illustrated [11 images] pages 1023-1028).

Burns, William J. (1861-1932; U.S. private detective, headed the Burns Detective Agency; director of the U.S. Bureau of Investigation [BOI, 1921-1924], predecessor of the FBI): J. Edgar Hoover, 1987 (made-for-TV; Erik Holland); The Murder of Mary Phagan, 1988 (TV mini-series; Paul Dooley). Note: For detailed information on Burns, see my eight-volume work *Encyclopedia of World Crime*, Volume I (CrimeBooks, Inc., 1990; illustrated pages 553-554); see Burns' involvement in the Leo Frank case in my book *"I Am Innocent!": A Comprehensive Encyclopedic History of the World's Wrongly Convicted Persons* (Da Capo Press, 2008; illustrated [10 images] pages 315-329); see Burns' involvement in the 1910 union terrorst explosion of the Los Angeles *Times* Building in my two-volume work *The Great Pictorial History of World Crime*, Volume II (History, Inc., 2004; illustrated [10 images] pages 1501-1506).

Burnside, Ambrose Everett (1824-1881; U.S. military officer and Union general during the American Civil War): **Gods and Generals**, 2003 (Alex Hyde-White).

Burr, Aaron (1756-1836; U.S. politician and adventurer; third vice-president of U.S. under Thomas Jefferson; charged with treason in 1807 and acquitted; lived in England for some time before returning to the U.S. to practice law and died in obscurity): The Beautiful Mrs. Reynolds, 1918 (Arthur Ashley); Daniel Boone, 1964-1970 (TV series; "The Aaron Burr Story," 1965 episode: Leif Erikson); Magnificent Doll, 1947 (David Niven); Mistress of the White House, 1952 (made-for-TV; David Orrick [McDearmon]); My Own United States, 1918 (Charles Graham); Studio One in Hollywood, 1948-1958 (TV series; "Rachel," 1956 episode: Everett Sloane); You Are There, 1953-1971 (TV series; one 1953 episode; Walter Coy; two 1954 episodes; Richard Waring).

Burr, Theodosia (1783-1813; U.S. housewife and daughter of U.S. Vice President Aaron Burr who was lost at sea at age twenty-nine): The Beautiful Mrs. Reynolds, 1918 (Betty K. Peterson).

Burton, Richard Francis (1821-1890; British explorer in Asia, Africa and the Americas): **Mountains of the Moon**, 1990 (Patrick Bergin); The Search for the Nile, 1971- (TV miniseries; Kenneth Haigh).

Butler, Fanny Kemble (1809-1893; British-born author, who married Georgia plantation owner Pierce Mease Butler and kept a diary of slave conditions: her celebrated anti-slavery journal was published in 1863 during the American Civil War, by which time she had separated from her husband): Enslavement: The True Story of Fanny Kemble, 2000 (made-for-TV; Jane Seymour).

Butler, Frank E. (1852-1926; U.S. marksman appearing in Wild West shows and husband of sharpshooter Annie Oakley): **Annie Get Your Gun**, 1950 (Howard Keel); Annie Get Your Gun, 1957 (made-for-TV; John Raitt); Annie Get Your Gun, 1967 (made-for-TV; Bruce Yarnell); Tall Tales and Legends, 1985-1988 (TV series; "Annie Oakley," 1985 episode: Cliff De Young); **Annie Oakley**, 1935 (Preston Foster).

Butler, Walter (1752-1781; loyalist and British officer in the American Revolutionary War, 1775-1783, who, with Mohawk Chief Joseph Brant, 1743-1807, led a guerrilla force of British loyalists and Iroquois Indians into Cherry Valley, New York, on November 11, 1778, where they massacred about thirty non-combatants, including women and children): **America**, 1924 (Lionel Barrymore); Divided Loyalties, 1990 (Paul Gross); The Spirit of '76, 1917 (George Chesebro).

Byrnes, James F. (1882-1972; U.S. politician and 49th U.S. Secretary of State, 1945-1947): Day One, 1989 (made-for-TV; Hume Cronyn); Hiroshima, 1995 (made-for-TV; Ken Jenkins); Race for the Bomb, 1987 (TV series; Robert Barr); Separate But Equal, 1991 (made-for-TV; John McMartin); Truman at Potsdam, 1976 (made-for-TV; Barry Morse).

Byron, George Gordon (Lord Byron; 1788-1824; British poet): Armchair Theatre, 1956-1974 (TV series; "Death of Satan," 1958 episode: Barry Hirst); The Bad Lord Byron, 1949 (Dennis Price); **Beau Brummel**, 1924 (George Beranger); **Beau Brummell**, 1954 (Noel Willman); Beau Brummell: This Charming Man, 2006 (made-for-TV; Matthew Rhys); Biography, 1970- (TV series; "Byron," 1970 episode: Keith Barron); **The Bride of Frankenstein**, 1935 (Gavin Gordon); Byron, 2005 (made-for-TV; Jonny Lee Miller); Byron: Ballad for a Daemon, 1992 (Manos Vakousis); CBC Summer Theatre, 1955- (TV series; "The Return of Don Juan," 1955 episode: Alan Nunn); Encounter, 1952-1961 (TV series; "The Return of Don Juan," 1957 episode: Richard Easton); The Finest Gift, 1955 (made-for-TV; Tod Andrews); Frankenstein: Birth of a Monster, 2003 (made-for-TV; Stephen Mangan); Gothic, 1987 (Gabriel Byrne); Haunted Summer, 1988 (Philip Anglim); Helter Skelter, 1949 (Dennis Price); Highlander, 1992-1998 (TV series; "The Modern Prometheus," 1997 episode: Jonathan Firth); I Remember Nelson, 1982 (TV series; Sylvester Morand); Lady Caroline Lamb, 1972 (Richard Chamberlain); The Last Rose of Summer, 1937 (Malcolm Graham); The Life of Lord Byron, 1922 (Howard Gaye); Lives and Deaths of the Poets, 2011 (Lou Zammichieli); Pandaemonium, 2001 (Guy Lankester); The Poetry Hall of Fame, 1993 (made-for-TV; Neil Hunt); Roger Corman's Frankenstein Unbound, 1990 (Jason Patric); The Romantics, 2011 (TV miniseries; "Eternity," 2011 episode: Joseph Millson); Rowing in the Wind, 1988 (Hugh Grant); Screenplay, 1986-1993 (TV series; "Dead Poets' Society," 1992 episode; Alex Jennings); Shelley, 1972 (made-for-TV; Peter Bowles).

Caesar, Julius (Gaius Julius Caesar; 100 B.C.-44 B.C.; Roman general and politician): Ancient Rome: The Rise and Fall of an Empire, 2006

Preston Foster (as Frank E. Butler) and Barbara Stanwyck (as Annie Oakley) in *Annie Oakley,* 1935.

(TV series; Sean Pertwee); Androcles and the Lion, 1938 (made-for-TV; Michael Martin Harvey); Androcles and the Lion, 1946 (made-for-TV; Ernest Thesiger); Androcles and the Lion, 1951 (Raymond Lovell); Androcles and the Lion, 1952 (Maurice Evans); Androcles and the Lion, 1967 (made-for-TV; Noel Coward); Antony and Cleopatra, 1959 (made-for-TV; Kevin Miles); Asterix and Caesar, 1985 (animated; Serge Sauvion voiceover); Asterix and Obelix: God Save Britannia, 2012 (Fabrice Luchini); Asterix and Obelix Meet Cleopatra, 2002 (animated; Alain Chabat voiceover); Asterix and Obelix vs. Caesar, 1999 (animated; Gottfried John voiceover); Asterix at the Olympic Games, 2008 (Alain Delon); Asterix Conquers America, 1994 (animated; Robert Party voiceover); Asterix in Britain, 1986 (animated; Serge Sauvion voiceover); The Battle for Rome, 2006 (TV miniseries; Sean Pertwee); BBC Play of the Month, 1965-1983 (TV series; "Julius Caesar," 1969 episode: Maurice Denham); BBC Sunday-Night Theatre, 1950-1959 (TV series; "Julius Caesar," two 1951 episodes; Walter Hudd); Brutus, 1981 (made-for-TV; Kornel Gelley); Caesar, 2003 (made-for-TV; Jeremy Sisto); Caesar against the Pirates, 1962 (Gustavo Rojo); **Caesar and Cleopatra**, 1946 (Claude Rains); Caesar and Cleopatra, 1970 (made-for-TV; Wolf Kaiser); Caesar and Cleopatra, 1976 (made-for-TV; Alec Guinness); Caesar and Cleopatra, 2009 (Christopher Plummer); Caesar Must Die, 2012 (Giovanni Arcuri); Caesar the Conqueror, 1963 (Cameron Mitchell); Caesar und Cleopatra, 1964 (made-for-TV; Paul Verhoeven); Caesar und Cleopatra, 1969 (made-for-TV; O.E. Hasse); Carry On Cleo, 1964 (Kenneth Williams); Cleopatra, 1917 (Fritz Leiber); **Cleopatra**, 1934 (Warren William); **Cleopatra**, 1963 (Rex Harrison); Cleopatra, 1970 (Louis Waldon); Cleopatra, 1999 (TV miniseries; Timothy Dalton); Cleopatra, 2007 (Miguel Falabella); The Cleopatras, 1983 (TV miniseries; Robert Hardy); Conflict, 1966-1969 (TV series; "Julius Caesar," 1966 episode: Antony Viccars as the ghost of Caesar); Empire, 2005 (TV miniseries; Colm Feore); General Electric Theater, 1953-1962 (TV series; "Caesar and Cleopatra," 1959 episode: Maurice Evans); Giants of Rome, 1964 (Alessandro Sperli); Hercules: The Legendary Journeys, 1995-1999 (TV series; "Render Unto Caesar," 1998 episode: Karl Urban); Histeria!, 1998-2000 (animated TV series; two 1998 episodes: and one 1999 episode: Fred Travalena voiceover); An Honourable Murder, 1960 (John Longden); The Ides of March, 1961 (made-for-TV; Brian James); Imperium: Augustus, 2003 (made-for-TV; Gerard Klein); Jules Cesar, 2011 (Lawrence Zazzo); Julius Caesar, 1914 (Amleto Novelli); Julius Caesar, 1938 (made-for-TV; Ernest Milton); Julius Caesar, 1949 (made-for-TV; George Bliss); Julius Caesar, 1950 (Harold Tasker); **Julius Caesar**, 1953 (Louis Calhern); Julius Caesar, 1963- (TV series; Gerald Young); Julius Caesar, 1966 (made-for-TV; Budd Knapp); **Julius Caesar**, 1970 (John Gielgud); Julius Caesar, 1979 (made-for-TV; Charles Gray); Julius Caesar, 1984 (made-for-TV; Janet

Richard Chamberlain as Lord Byron in *Lady Caroline Lamb*, 1973.

Baker); Julius Caesar, 2007 (made-for-TV; Andreas Scholl); Julius Caesar, 2011 (Magnus Erland McCullagh); Julius Caesar, 2012 (made-for-TV; Jeffery Kissoon); Julius Caesar, 2014 (Benjamin Moore); The Notorious Cleopatra, 1970 (Jay Edwards); Producers' Showcase, 1954-1957 (TV series; "Caesar and Cleopatra," 1956 episode: Cedric Hardwicke); A Queen for Caesar, 1962 (Gordon Scott); Rome, 2005-2007 (TV series; Ciaran Hinds); Shakespeare: The Animated Tales, 1992-1994 (TV series; "Julius Caesar,' 1994 episode: Joss Ackland voiceover); **Spartacus**, 1960 (John Gavin); Spartacus, 2004 (made-for-TV; Richard Dillane); Spartacus: War of the Damned, 2010-2013 (TV series; Todd Lasance); The Spread of the Eagle, 1963- (TV miniseries; Barry Jones); The Story of Mankind, 1957 (Reginald Sheffield); Studio One in Hollywood, 1948-1958 (TV series; "Julius Caesar," two 1949 episodes; William Post Jr.; "Julius Caesar," 1955 episode: Theodore Bikel); Theatre 625, 1964-1968 (TV series; "The Ides of March," 1964 episode; Douglas Wilmer); World Theatre, 1959- (TV miniseries; "Julius Caesar," 1959 episode: Robert Perceval); Xena: Warrior Princess, 1995-2001 (TV series; five episodes: Karl Urban); You Are There, 1953-1971 (TV series; "The Assassination of Julius Caesar [March 15, 44 B.C.]," shown in 1953 and 1955: Russ Conway for both).

Cagliostro (Joseph Balsamo; 1743-1795; Italian hypnotist, charlatan, swindler and practioner of witchcraft): The Adventures of Baron Munchausen, 1943 (Ferdinand Marian); The Affair of the Necklace, 2001 (Christopher Walken); Barbarina, the King's Dancer, 1932 (Paul Otto); **Black Magic**, 1949 (Orson Welles); Cagliostro, 1929 (Hans Stuwe); Cagliostro, 1977; The Case of Becky, 1921 (Montagu Love); The Castle of Cagliostro, 1991 (Michael McConnohie); The Erotic Rites of Frankenstein, 1973 (Howard Vernon); Formula of Love, 1984 (Nodar Mgaloblishvili); Francis the First [1937], 1947 (Alexandre Mihalesco); Joseph Balsamo, 1973 (TV series; Gert Gunther Hoffmann); Kaliostro, 1918 (Fryderyk Jarossy); La comtesse de Charny (Jean-Francois Garreaud); L'araignee, 1981 (Yann Le Bonniec); Le Chevalier D'Eon, 2006- (TV series; Nobuyuki Kobushi); Les gloutonnes, 1975 (Howard Vernon); The Mystic Tales of Nikolas Winter, 2012 (Mihran Konanyan); Queen's Necklace, 1947 (Pierre Dux); Return of the Moonwalker, 2013 (Mike Maria); Royal Affairs in Versailles, 1957 (Gino Cervi); Subversion, 1979 (Daniel Emilfork); The Three Musketeers, 2011 (Til Schweiger); Thriller, 1960-1962 (TV series; "The Prisoner in the Mirror," 1961 episode; Henry Daniell); Vagen till Klockrike, 1953 (Kenne Fant).

Caiaphas (aka; Caiphus; Hebrew high priest who reportedly conspired to have Jesus killed): Behold the Man, 1935 (Charles Granval); Color

of the Cross, 2006 (Elya Baskin); Day of Triumph, 1954 (Robert Freud); The Gospel according to St. Matthew, 1966 (Rudolfo Wilcock); The Gospel of Mark, 2015 (Ramdane Aala); **The Greatest Story Ever Told**, 1965 (Martin Landau); Il messia, 1975 (John Karlsen); Jesus, 1979 (Ori Levy); Jesus, 2000 (made-for-TV; Christian Kohlund); Jesus Christ Superstar, 1972 (made-for-TV; Peter North); **Jesus Christ Superstar**, 1973 (Bob Bingham); Jesus of Nazareth, 1942 (Rafael Maria de Labra); Jesus of Nazareth, 1977 (TV miniseries; Anthony Quinn); Judas, 2004 (made-for-TV; Bob Gunton); **The King of Kings**, 1927 (Rudolph Schildkraut); **King of Kings**, 1961 (Guy Rolfe); The Life of Jesus Christ, 2011- (TV miniseries; Dave Nilson); The Living Bible, 1952 (TV series; Dean Fredericks); The Living Christ Series, 1951 (TV series; Lawrence Dobkin); The Passion, 2008 (TV miniseries; Ben Daniels); The Pilgrimage Play, 1949 (C. Montagu Shaw); The Power of the Resurrection, 1958 (Robert Cornthwaite).

Cain (In Bible, one of two sons of Adam and Eve, who murdered his good brother, Abel): After Six Days, 1920 (Bruto Castellani); The Bible: In the Beginning..., 1966 (Richard Harris); The Cradle of God, 1926 (Gaston Rieffler); Genesis: The Creation and the Flood, 1994 (Annabi Abdelialil); **The Green Pastures**, 1936 (Al Stokes); La biblia en pasta, 1984 (Juan Munoz Alegrias); The Last Eve, 2005 (Brian Kahn); The Making of...And God Spoke, 1994 (Lou Ferrigno); **Noah**, 2014 (Johannes Haukur Johannesson); Year One, 2009 (David Cross).

Calamity Jane (Martha Jane Canary; 1852-1903; U.S. frontierswoman, scout and prostitute; falsely claimed to have been married to James Butler "Wild Bill" Hickok): Badlands of Dakota, 1941 (Frances Farmer); Bonanza, 1959-1973 (TV series; "Calamity Over the Comstock," 1963 episode; Stefanie Powers); Buffalo Girls, 1995 (made-for-TV; Anjelica Huston); A Calamity Called Jane, 1966 (TV episode of Death Valley Days; Fay Spain); **Calamity Jane**, 1953 (Doris Day); Calamity Jane, 1963 (made-for-TV; Carol Burnett); Calamity Jane, 1984 (made-for-TV; Jane Alexander); Calamity Jane, 1987 (made-for-TV; Maria do Ceu Guerra); Calamity Jane: Wild West Legend, 2015 (Kay Campbell); Calamity Jane and Sam Bass, 1949 (Yvonne De Carlo); Caught, 1931 (Louise Dresser); Custer's Last Stand, 1936 (serial; Helen Gibson); Deadwood, 2004-2006 (TV series; Robin Weigert); Deadwood Dick, 1940 (serial; Marin Sais); Death Valley Days, 1952-1970 (TV series; "A Calamity Called Jane," 1966 episode: Fay Spain); Gunslingers, 2014- (TV miniseries; Rachel Katherine Ross); Jane B. for Agnes V., 1988 (Jane Birkin); The Legend of Calamity Jane, 1997 (TV series; Barbara Scaff); Lucky Luke, 1984 (animated TV series; Micheline Dax voiceover); Lucky Luke, 2009 (Sylvie Testud); My Old Kentucky Home, 1922 (Lucy Fox); The New Adventures of Lucky Luke, 2001- (TV series; Isabelle Mangini); Overland Trail, 1960- (TV series; "First Stage to Denver," 1960 episode: Sue George); **The Paleface**, 1948 (Jane Russell); **The Plainsman**, 1936 (Jean Arthur); The Plainsman, 1966 (Abby Dalton); **The Raiders**, 1963 (Judi Meredith); Schlitz Playhouse, 1951-1959 (TV series; "The Pussyfootin' Rocks," 1952 episode: Joan Blondell); Seven Hours of Gunfire, 1965 (Gloria Milland); **Tall Tale: The Unbelievable Adventures of Pecos Bill**, 1995 (Catherine O'Hara); The Texan Meets Calamity Jane, 1950 (Evelyn Ankers); This Is the West That Was, 1974 (made-for-TV; Kim Darby); Two Gangsters in the Wild West, 1964 (Olimpia Cavalli); Two Sons of Trinity, 1972 (Anny Degli Uberti); **Wild Bill**, 1995 (Ellen Barkin); **Wild Bill Hickok**, 1923 (Ellen Grey Terry); The Wild West, 1993 (TV series; Conchata Ferrell); Young Bill Hickok, 1940 (Sally Payne).

Calhoun, John C. (1782-1850; seventh vicepresident of the U.S.; Southern politician): The Adams Chronicles, 1976 (TV miniseries; Robert Phalen); **Amistad**, 1999 (Arliss Howard); Andrew Jackson, 2007 (made-for-TV; Steven T. Bartlett); The Gorgeous Hussy, 1936 (Frank Conroy); The Great Adventure, 1963-1964 (TV series; "The Testing of Sam Houston," 1964 episode: David White); You Are There, 1953-1971

(TV series; "Daniel Webster's Sacrifice to Save the Union [March 7, 1850])," 1956 episode: Carl Benton Reid).

Calico Jack (John "Jack" Rackham; 1682-1720; British pirate operating in the Bahamas and off Cuba): Black Sails, 2014- (TV series; Toby Schmitz); Captain Kidd and the Slave Girl, 1954 (Robert Long); The Secret of the Black Falcon, 1961 (Walter Barnes); True Caribbean Pirates, 2006 (made-for-TV; David Joseph Boyd); White Slave Ship, 1962 (Armand Mestral). Note: For detailed information on Rackham, see my two-volume work *The Great Pictorial History of World Crime*, Volume II (History, Inc., 2004; illustrated pages 1298-1300).

Caligula (12-41 A.D.; Roman emperor known for his cruelty and murders): Caligula, 1980 (Malcolm McDowell); A.D., 1985 (TV miniseries; John McEnery); A.D.: The Bible Continues, 2015 (TV series; Andrew Gower); The Caesars, 1968 (TV series; Ralph Bates); Caligola, 2004 (Flavio Sciole); Caligula, 1966 (made-for-TV; Horst Frank); Caligula, 1975 (made-for-TV; Frans Maas); Caligula, 1989 (Malcolm McDowell); Caligula, 1996 (Szabolcs Hajdu); Caligula and Messalina, 1982 (Vladimir Brajovic); Caligula: 1400 Days of Terror, 2012 (made-for-TV; Lowell Byers); **Demetrius and the Gladiators**, 1954 (Jay Robinson); I, Claudius, 1937 (Emlyn Williams); I, Claudius, 1976- (TV miniseries; John Hurt); Imperium: Nero, 2004 (made-for-TV; John Simm); Messalina vs. the Son of Hercules, 1964 (Charles Borromel); **The Robe**, 1953 (Jay Robinson); Rome '78, 1978 (David McDermott); Xena: Warrior Princess, 1995-2001 (TV series; Alexis Arquette).

Callas, Maria (1923-1977; Greek operatic soprano, one of the most famous divas of the opera): Adriana, 2004 (Antonio Moco); Callas e Onassis, 2005 (made-for-TV; Luisa Ranieri); **Callas Forever**, 2002 (Fanny Ardant); Grace of Monaco, 2014 (Paz Vega); Jackie Bouvier Kennedy Onassis, 2000 (made-for-TV; Leslie Cottle); Onassis: The Richest Man in the World, 1988 (made-for-TV; Jane Seymour); Pasolini, the Hidden Truth, 2013 (Stars in Their Eyes, 1990- (TV series; "Live Grand Final," 2000 episode: Nicola Kirsch).

Canaris, Wilhelm Franz (1887N1945; German admiral and head of the Abwehr, German military intelligence, 1935-1944, who actively plotted to kill Adolf Hitler and who was executed by Nazis): BBC Play of the Week, 1977- (TV series; "True Patriot," 1977 episode: Richard Hurndall); **Canaris** (aka: Deadly Decision), 1958 (O. E. Hasse); **The Eagle Has Landed**, 1977 (Anthony Quayle); General Oster—Verrater oder Patriot?, 1970 (made-for-TV; Dieter Borsche); Hunt the Kaiser's Cruisers, 2006 (made-for-TV; Steffen Schroeder); I Spy, 1955-1957 (TV series; "Canaris Story": Harold Vermilyea); **The Man Who Never Was**, 1956 (Wolf Frees); The Red Orchestra, 1989 (Jurgen Mash); Sekret Enigmy, 1979 (Tadeusz Szaniecki); **The Two-Headed Spy**, 1959 (Walter Hudd); Voyage of the Damned, 1976 (Denholm Elliott); When Heroes Die, 1970 (Rafael Cores). Note: For detailed information on Canaris, see my book *Spies: A Narrative Encyclopedia of Dirty Tricks & Double Dealing from Biblical Times to Today* (M. Evans, 1997; illustrated pages 126-136).

Canby, Edward Richard Sprigg (U.S. military officer and general, assassinated by Modoc leader Captain Jack during peace talks; 1817-1873): **Drum Beat**, 1954 (Warner Anderson).

Cantor, Eddie (1892-1964; U.S. actor, comedian, singer, dancer, composer): Boardwalk Empire, 2010- (TV series: seven episodes: Stephen DeRosa); The Eddie Cantor Story, 1953 (Keefe Brasselle); **The Great Ziegfeld**, 1936 (Buddy Doyle); It Happened in Hollywood, 1937 (Franky [Frankie] Farr); Pretty Ladies, 1925 (Jimmie [James] Quinn); The Rat Pack, 1998 (made-for-TV; Greg Berg); **Thank Your Lucky Stars**, 1943 (himself); Ziegfeld: The Man and His Women, 1978 (made-for-TV; Richard Shea).

Keefe Brasselle (as Eddie Cantor) in *The Eddie Cantor Story*, 1953.

Capone, Alphonse (aka: Scarface; 1899-1947; Chicago crime boss): **Al Capone**, 1959 (Rod Steiger); **The Babe**, 1992 (Bernie Gigliotti); Baby Face Nelson, 1996 (F. Murray Abraham); Boardwalk Empire, 2010- (TV series; thirty-seven episodes: Stephen Graham); Bonanno: A Godfather's Story, 1999 (made-for TV; Lou Vani); Bronx Barbes, 2003 (Thomas Guei); Capone's Boys, 2002 (Julian Littman); Capone, 1975 (Ben Gazzarra); Dillinger and Capone, 1995 (F. Murray Abraham); **The Finger Points**, 1931 (role model for Clark Gable); Frank Nitti: The Enforcer, 1988 (made-for-TV; Vincent Guastaferro); Gangster Wars, 1981 (Louis Giambalvo); The George Raft Story, 1961 (Neville Brand); In Suspicious Circumstances, 1991- (TV series; "No Witnesses, No Case," 1993 episode: Marcus D'Amico); Kiss of Death, 1997 (Kurt Andon); **Little Caesar**, 1931 (role model for Edward G. Robinson); The Little Worm, 1999 (Vincent Riotta); The Lost Capone, 1990 (made-for-TV; Eric Roberts); Mobsters, 1991 (Titus Welliver); **Night at the Museum: Battle of the Smithsonian**, 2009 (John Bernthal); **Party Girl**, 1958 (role model for Lee J. Cobb); Playhouse 90, 1956-1961 (TV series; "Seven against the Wall," 1958 episode: Paul Lambert); Poor Devil, 1973 (made-for-TV; Buddy Lester); **The Purple Gang**, 1960 (Saverio LoMedico); **The Racket**, 1928 (role model for Louis Wolheim); The Revenge of Al Capone, 1989 (made-for-TV; Ray Sharkey); **Road to Perdition**, 2002 (Anthony LaPaglia; scenes deleted); **The St. Valentine's Day Massacre**, 1967 (Jason Robards Jr.); The St. Valentine's Day Massacre, 1997 (made-for-TV; Joe Hanna); **Scarface**, 1932 (role model for Paul Muni); The Scarface Mob, 1959 (made-for-TV; Neville Brand); **The Secret Six**, 1931 (role model for Wallace Beery); Sizzle, 1981 (made-for-TV; Robert Costanzo); **Some Like It Hot**, 1959 (role model for George Raft); **Underworld**, 1927 (some characteristics serving as a role model for George Bancroft); The Untouchables, 1959-1963 (TV series; Neville Brand); **The Untouchables**, 1987 (Robert De Niro); The Verne Miller Story, 1988 (Thomas G. Waites). Note: For comprehensive details on Capone and the Chicago gangs and gangsters of the 1920s, as well as the St. Valentine's Day Massacre, see my works *Bloodletters and Badmen* (M. Evans, 1973, 1995; Capone: pages 119-130; McGurn: pages 408-411; Moran: pages 439-444; O'Bannion: 472-478; Weiss: pages 662-666); *Encyclopedia of Organized Crime* (Paragon House, 1992; Capone: pages 78-98; Burke: pages 74-75; McGurn: pages 259-261; Moran: pages 288-291; O'Bannion: pages 304-310; St. Valentine's Day Massacre: pages 343-347; Weiss: pages 402-403), and *The Great Pictorial History of World Crime* (History, Inc., 2004; Capone et al.: illustrated pages 503-541).

Captain Jack (Kintpuach; 1837-1873; chief of the Modoc Native American tribe; murderer and renegade, hanged): **Drum Beat**, 1954 (Charles

Edward G. Robinson (in role model of Al Capone) and Maurice Black in *Little Caesar*, 1931.

Bronson).

Carlota of Mexico (Carlotta; Charlotte of Belgium; 1840-1927; Empress of Mexico and wife of Maximilian I, Emperor of Mexico): Aquellos anos, 1974 (Helena Rojo); Cheyenne, 1955-1963 (TV series; "Border Affair," 1957 episode: Joy Page); El carruaje, 1972 (TV series; Nelly Meden); El vuelo del aguila, 1994 (TV series; Laura Flores); Goodyear Playhouse, 1951-1957 (TV series; "Crown of Shadows," 1952 episode: Felicia Montealegre); Imperial Cavalry, 1942 (Medea de Novara); **Juarez**, 1939 (Bette Davis); Juarez and Maximillian, 1935 (Medea de Novara); La Paloma, 1938 (Medea de Novara); The Mad Empress, 1939 (Medea de Novara); Maximilian von Mexiko, 1970 (made-for-TV; Christine Wodetzky); Prariejager in Mexiko: Benito Juarez, 1988 (Sabine Unger); A Rainha Louca, 1967- (TV series; Nathalia Timberg); Universum History, 2013- (TV series; "Maximilian von Mexiko—Der Traum vom Herrschen," 2014 episode: Viktoria Hillisch); Unter der Dornenkrone—Mexikos kaisertragodie, 1921 (Lys Andersen).

Carnegie, Andrew (1835-1919; Scottish-American industrialist and leading steel magnate in the U.S.): The American Adventure, 1982 (Walker Edmiston voiceover); Freedom to Speak, 1982 (TV miniseries; Edward Herrmann); How We Got Here, 2015 (TV series; "Steel Builds the Metropolis," 2015 episode: C. J. Irwin); Murdoch Mysteries, 2008 (TV series; "The Murdoch Sting," 2014 episode: Philip Craig); Our American Heritage, 1959-1961 (TV series; "Millionaire's Mile," 1960 episode: David Wayne).

Carroll, Lewis (Charles Lutwidge Dodgson; 1832-1898; British author of children's fantasy books, notably *Alice's Adventures in Wonderland*, 1865, and its sequel, **Through the Looking Glass**, 1871): Alice in Wonderland, 1949 (Stephen Murray voiceover); Alice in Wonderland, 1985- (TV series; Robert Peters); Alice in Wonderland, 1986- (TV series; David Leonard); Alice through the Looking Glass, 1973 (TV series; Cyril Fletcher); Alice's Adventures in Wonderland, 1956 (made-for-TV; Barry Letts); Alice's Adventures in Wonderland, 1972 (Michael Jayston); Alice's Adventures in Wonderland, 2011 (made-for-TV; Edward Watson); Alice's Adventures in Wonderland and through the Looking Glass, 1948 (made-for-TV; James McKecknie); Dreamchild, 1985 (Ian Holm).

Carson, Kit (Christopher Houston Carson; aka: "Kit"; U.S. frontiersman and Indian fighter; 1809-1868): The Adventures of Kit Carson, 1951-1955 (TV series; Bill Williams); Along the Oregon Trail, 1947 (Forrest Taylor); Bridger, 1976 (made-for-TV; Ben Murphy); **The Covered Wagon**, 1923 (Guy Oliver); Fighting with Kit Carson, 1933 (Johnny Mack Brown); Kit Carson, 1928 (Fred Thomson); **Kit Carson**, 1940 (Jon Hall); Kit Carson and the Mountain Men, 1977 (made-for-TV; Christopher Connelly); Kit Carson over the Great Divide, 1925 (Jack Mower); Lawless Plainsman, 1942 (Forrest Taylor); Overland with Kit Carson, 1939 (Bill Elliott); The Painted Stallion, 1938 (Sammy McKim).

Caruso, Enrico (1873-1921; famed Italian tenor and opera singer): Caruso, 2012 (made-for-TV; Gianluca Terranova); **The Great Caruso**, 1951 (Mario Lanza as an adult; Peter Edward Price as a boy); Great Performances, 1971- (TV series; "Melba," 1988 episode: Anson Austin); The Great Quake, 2006 (made-for-TV; Norman McIsaac); **The Immigrant**, 2014 (Joseph Calleja); My Cousin, 1918 (himself); **Pay or Die**, 1960 (Howard Caine); Screen Directors Playhouse, 1955-1956 (TV series; "The Day I Met Caruso," 1956 episode: Lotfi Mansouri); The Splendid Romance, 1919 (himself); The Untouchables, 1993-1994 (TV series; pilot, part one, 1993 episode: Dale Calandra); The Young Caruso, 1953 (Ermanno Randi as an adult; Maurizio Di Nardo as a boy).

Carver, John (1584-1621; leader of the Pilgrims who drew up the pact signed by all passengers on the historic 1620 voyage of the *Mayflower* to Plymouth Rock and who became the first governor of the New Plymouth Colony): The Courtship of Myles Standish, 1923 (Sam De Grasse); **Plymouth Adventure**, 1952 (Paul Cavanagh).

Casanova, Giacomo (1725-1798; Italian adventurer and author, known for his notorious womanizing and romances he celebrated in his written works and who also served as a spy for several masters): The Adventures of Baron Munchausen, 1943 (Gustav Waldau); Adventures of Casanova, 1948 (Arturo de Cordorva); Cagliostro, 1977 (Massimo Girotti); Casanova, 1919 (Alfred Deesy); Casanova, 1928 (Michael Bohnen); Casanova, 1934 (Ivan Mozzhukhin); Casanova, 1971- (TV miniseries; Frank Finlay); Casanova, 1981 (made-for-TV; Walter Koeninger); Casanova, 1987 (made-for-TV; Richard Chamberlain); **Casanova**, 2005 (Heath Ledger; Eugene Simon as Casanova as a boy); Casanova, 2005- (TV miniseries; David Tennant); Casanova, 2005 (made-for-TV; Thomas Heinze); Casanova, 2015 (Diego Luna); Casanova's Big Night, 1954 (Vincent Price); Casanova's Last Stand, 2007 (Patrick Bergin); C'est arrive a Paris, 1977 (made-for-TV; Jean-Pierre Andreani); Fellini's Casanova, 1977 (Donald Sutherland); Giacomo Casanova, 2004 (made-for-TV; Robert Hunger-Buhler); Goodbye, Casanova, 2000 (Gian-Carlo Scandiuzzi); How Women Love, 1922 (Templar Saxe); I, Don Giovanni, 2009 (Tobias Moretti); Il giovane casanova, 2002 (made-for-TV; Stefano Accorsi); It's a Woman's World, 1964- (TV series; "Virginia," 1964 episode; Ray Brooks); Last Rose from Casanova, 1966 (Felix Le Breux); The Loves of Casanova, 1929 (Ivan Mozzhukhin); Loves of Casanova, 1948 (Georges Guetary); Men Think Only of That, 1954 (Edmond Tamiz); The Mysterious Rider, 1948 (Vittorio Gassman); Sins of Casanova, 1957 (Gabrielle Ferzetti); Some Like It Cool, 1979 (Tony Curtis); That Night in Varennes, 1983 (Marcello Mastroianni); Theatre 625, 1964-1968 (TV series; "The Magicians: The Incantation of Casanova," 1967 episode: Jeremy Brett); Till the End of the World, 1963 (Didi Perego); A Touch of the Casanovas, 1975 (made-for-TV; Stuart Damon). Note: For detailed information on Casanova's espionage activities, see my book, *Spies: A Narrative Encyclopedia of Dirty Tricks & Double Dealing from Biblical Times to Today* (M. Evans, 1997; illustrated pages 139-140).

Cassatt, Mary Stevenson (1844-1926; U.S. painter and printmaker): Mary Cassatt: An American Impressionist, 1999 (made-for-TV; Amy Brennerman).

Cassidy, Butch (Robert Leroy Parker; U.S. Old West outlaw, bank and train robber; 1866-1908?): Adios Companeros, 1971 (Jack Betts); Badman's Country, 1958 (Neville Brand); Blackthorn, 2011 (Nikolaj Coster-

Waldau); Bronco, 1958-1962 (TV series; "The Equalizer," 1962 episode: Steve Brodie); Buffalo Bill, Jr., 1955-1956 (TV series; "Redskin Gap," 1955 episode: Harry Lauter); Butch and Sundance: The Early Days, 1979 (Tom Berenger); **Butch Cassidy and the Sundance Kid**, 1969 (Paul Newman); **Cat Ballou**, 1965 (Arthur Hunnicutt); Deadwood Pass, 1933 (Slim Whitaker); The Dream Chasers, 1982 (Jarion Monroe); Frontier Doctor, 1958- (TV series; "The Outlaw Legion," 1958 episode; Joe Sawyer); Gambler V: Playing for Keeps, 1994 (made-for-TV; Scott Paulin); Goodnight for Justice: Queen of Hearts, 2008 (made-for-TV; Kerry James); The Legend of Butch and Sundance, 2006 (made-for-TV; David Clayton Rogers); The Maverick Queen, 1956 (Howard Petrie); Mentors, 1998-2005 (TV series; "Dusty Trails," 2002 episode: John Pyper-Ferguson); Return of the Gunfighter, 1967 (John Crawford); Stories of the Century, 1954- (TV series; "The Wild Bunch of Wyoming"; 1954 episode: Joe Sawyer); Tales of Wells Fargo, 1957-1962 (TV series; "Butch Cassidy," 1958 episode; Charles Bronson); The Texas Rangers, 1951 (John Doucette); The Three Outlaws, 1956 (Neville Brand); Wyoming Renegades, 1954 (Gene Evans). Note: For detailed information on Cassidy, see my book *Encyclopedia of Western Lawmen and Outlaws* (Paragon House, 1992; illustrated pages 67-70; and the two-volume work, *The Great Pictorial History of World Crime*, Volume II (History, Inc., illustrated [9 images] pages 1362-1368).

Castle, Irene (1893-1969; U.S. dancer who partnered with her husband Vernon): La vie revee de Vincent Scotto, 1973 (made-for-TV; Therese Moreux); Parade of Stars, 1983 (made-for-TV; Sandy Duncan); **The Story of Vernon and Irene Castle**, 1939 (Ginger Rogers).

Castle, Vernon (1887-1918; U.S. dancer who partnered with his wife Irene; killed in an air crash while serving in the U.S. Army Air Force at the end of WWI): La vie revee de Vincent Scotto, 1973 (made-for-TV; Luis Diaz); Parade of Stars, 1983 (made-for-TV; Don Correia); **The Story of Vernon and Irene Castle**, 1939 (Fred Astaire).

Catherine de Medici (1519-1589; Italian nobleman, queen consort of France as the wife of Henry II): **Ashes of Vengeance**, 1923 (Josephine Crowell); **Dante's Inferno**, 1935 (Juana Sutton); Diane, 1956 (Marisa Pavan); Elizabeth R, 1971- (TV miniseries; "Shadow in the Sun," 1971 episode: Margaretta Scott); Gallant Ladies, 1990 (Laura Betti); Henry, King of Navarre, 1924 (Stella St. Audrie); If Paris Were Told to Us, 1956 (Germaine Dermoz); **Intolerance: Love's Struggle throughout the Ages**, 1916 (Josephine Crowell); La camera explore le temps, 1957-1966 (TV series; two episodes in 1960: Maria Meriko); La reine Margot, 1961 (made-for-TV; Alice Sapritch); The Loves of Mary, Queen of Scots, 1923 (Irene Rooke); Mary, Queen of Scots, 1971 (Katherine Kath); Nostradamus, 1994 (Amanda Plummer); Nostradamus, 2006 (made-for-TV; Kerry Fox); **The Pearls of the Crown**, 1938 (Marguerite Moreno); Princess of Cleves, 1961 (Lea Padovani); Queen Margot, 1994 (Virna Lisa); Reign, 2013- (TV series; Megan Follows); Sir Francis Drake, 1961- (TV series; "Mission to Paris," 1962 episode: Pamela Brown); The Tournament, 1928 (Blanche Bernis); A Woman of Evil, 1954 (Francoise Rosay).

Catherine of Aragon (Katherine of Aragon; 1485-1536; Queen of England, wife of Henry VIII): Anna Boleyn, 1921 (Hedwig Pauly-Winterstein); **Anne of the Thousand Days**, 1969 (Irene Papas); BBC Sunday-Night Theatre, 1950-1959 (TV series; "The White Falcon," 1956 episode: Margaretta Scott); Catalina de Inglaterra, 1951 (Maruchi Fresno); Forever Amber, 1947 (Lillian Molieri); Heinrich VIII und seine Frauen, 1968 (made-for-TV; Eva Katharina Schultz); Henry VIII, 1979 (made-for-TV; Claire Bloom); Henry VIII, 1991 (made-for-TV; Michele Command); Henry VIII, 2003 (made-for-TV; Assumpta Serna); Henry VIII and His Six Wives, 1972 (Frances Cuka); Henry VIII: Mind of a Tyrant, 2009 (TV series: Siobhan Hewlett); Isabel, 2011-2014 (TV series; Natalia Rodriguez); The Madness of Henry VIII, 2006 (made-for-

Lucille Bremer and Arturo de Cordova (as Casanova) in *The Adventures of Casanova*, 1948.

TV; Georgeta Marin); Monarch, 2000 (Jean Marsh); The Other Boleyn Girl, 2003 (made-for-TV; Yolanda Vasquez); The Other Boleyn Girl, 2008 (Ana Torrent); **The Pearls of the Crown**, 1938 (Rosine Derean); A Royal Love, 2016 (Tamara van Sprundel); The Six Wives of Henry VIII, 1970- (TV miniseries; "Catherine of Aragon," 1970 episode: Annette Crosbie); The Six Wives of Henry VIII, 2001 (TV miniseries; two episodes: Annabelle Dowler); **The Sword and the Rose**, 1953 (Rosalie Crutchley); Theatre 625, 1964-1968 (TV series; "The Queen and the Welshman," 1966 episode: Dorothy Tutin); The Tudors, 2007-2010 (TV series; Maria Doyle Kennedy); **When Knighthood Was in Flower**, 1922 (Theresa Maxwell Conover); Wolf Hall, 2015 (TV miniseries; Joanne Whalley); Wolf Hall, 2015 (TV miniseries; Joanne Whalley).

Catherine the Great (Catherine II; 1729-1796; Empress of Russia); Admiral Ushakov, 1954 (Olga Zhiznyeva); The Adventures of Baron Munchausen, 1943 (Brigitte Horney); The Captain's Daughter, 2001 (Olga Antonova); Catherine of Russia, 1963 (Hildegard [Hildegarde] Knef [Neff]); Catherine the Great, 1996 (made-for-TV; Catherine Zeta-Jones); Catherine the Great, 2005 (made-for-TV; Emily Bruni); The Chess Player, 1930 (Marcelle Charles Dullin); Chess Player, 1939 (Francoise Rosay); Cossacks in Exile, 1939 (L. Biberowich); The Eagle, 1925 (Louise Dresser); Ekaterina, 2014- (TV series; Marina Alekandrova); Forbidden Paradise, 1924 (Pola Negri); Grafinya Sheremeteva, 1994 (made-for-TV; Lidya Fedoseeva-Shukshina); Great Catherine, 1948 (made-for-TV; Gertrude Lawrence); Great Catherine, 1958 (made-for-TV; Sydney Sturgess); Great Catherine, 1969 (Jeanne Moreau); **John Paul Jones**, 1959 (Bette Davis); The Loves of Casanova, 1929 (Suzanne Bianchetti); Meeting of the Minds, 1977-1981 (TV series; "Catherine the Great," 1981 episode: Jayne Meadows); Pugachev, 1980 (Vija Artmane); The Queen of Spades, 1999 (made-for-TV; Inga Rappaport); The Ring of the Empress, 1930 (Lil Dagover); The Rise of Catherine the Great, 1934 (Elizabeth Bergner); **A Royal Scandal**, 1945 (Tallulah Bankhead); Russia, 1986 (TV miniseries; Valentina Azovskaya); Russian Ark, 2002 (Maria Kuznetsova/Natalia Nikulenko); **The Scarlet Empress**, 1934 (Marlene Dietrich); **Seven Faces**, 1929 (Salka [Viertel] Stenermann); Shadow of the Eagle, 1950 (Binnie Barnes); Tempest, 1959 (Viveca Lindfors); Tsigni pitsisa, 1984 (Nina Yurasova); Wednesday Theater, 1951-1953 (TV series; "Great Catherine," 1953 episode: Mary Ellis); Young Catherine, 1991 (made-for-TV; Julia Ormond).

Cauchon, Pierre (1371-1442; French bishop who headed the tribunal judging Joan of Arc): BBC Play of the Month, 1965-1983 (TV series; "St. Joan," 1968 episode: Maurice Denham); Der Fall Jeanne d'Arc, 1966 (made-for-TV; Carl Lange); Jeanne d'Arc, 1973 (made-for-TV;

Jeff Daniels as Joshua Lawrence Chamberlain in *Gettysburg,* **1993.**

Robert Lombard); Jeanne la Pucelle II: Les prisons, 1994 (Alain Ollivier); Jeanne oder Die Lerche, 1966 (made-for-TV; Erwin Linder); Joan of Arc, 1914 (Arturo Garzes); **Joan of Arc**, 1948 (Francis L. Sullivan); Joan of Arc, 1999 (made-for-TV; Peter O'Toole); Joan of Arc, 2003 (made-for-TV; Vladimir Marek); Joan of Arc, 2005 (made-for-TV; Francis Dumaurier); Joan the Woman, 1916 (Theodore Roberts); The Lark, 1957 (made-for-TV; Boris Karloff); The Lark, 1958 (made-for-TV; Frank Gatliff); **The Messenger: The Story of Joan of Arc**, 1999 (Timothy West); **The Miracle of the Bells**, 1948 (Franz Roehn); NBC Television Opera Theater, 1950-1964 (TV series; "The Trial at Rouen," 1956 episode: Hugh Thompson); **The Passion of Joan of Arc**, 1928 (Eugene Silvain); Saint Joan, 1946 (made-for-TV; Lewis Casson); Saint Joan, 1957 (Anton Walbrook); Saint Joan, 1967 (made-for-TV; Maurice Evans); Sainte Jeanne, 1969 (made-for-TV; Michel Etcheverry); The Story of Mankind, 1957 (Henry Daniell); The Trial of Joan of Arc, 1965 (Jean-Claude Fourneau).

Cavell, Edith (1865-1915; British nurse who heroically saved the lives of countless soldiers on both sides of WWI and is credited in smuggling more than 200 Allied soldiers from German-occupied Belgium before she was arrested and shot by a German firing squad, which aroused the anger of Germany's foes, and she became a cause celebre in recruiting volunteers for the British Army; she was commemorated by the Church of England in its Calendar of Saints): All Star Review, 1950- (TV series; 1953 episode:v Tallulah Bankhead); Dawn, 1928 (Sybil Thorndyke); The Great Victory, Wilson or the Kaiser? The Fall of the Hohenzollerns, 1919 (Margaret McWade); ITV Play of the Week, 1955-1974 (TV series; "...And Humanity," 1958 episode: Flora Robson); Nurse and Martyr, 1915 (Cora Lee); Nurse Cavell, 1948 (made-for-TV; Nancy Price); **Nurse Edith Cavell**, 1939 (Anna Neagle); The Velvet Glove, 1977- (TV series; "Happy in War," 1977 episode: Lynn Farleigh); The Woman the Germans Shot, 1918 (Julia Arthur; Amy Dennis as young Edith Cavell). Note: For detailed information on Cavell, see my book, *Spies: A Narrative Encyclopedia of Dirty Tricks & Double Dealing from Biblical Times to Today* (M. Evans, 1997; illustrated pages 142-143).

Cervantes, Miguel de (1547-1616; Spanish poet, playwright and novelist, noted for his creation of the delusionary knight, Don Quixote, who is colorfully depicted in his 1605 novel, *The Ingenuous Gentleman Don Quixote of La Mancha*): Cervantes, 1981 (TV series; Julian Mateos); Der Mann von La Mancha, 1994 (made-for-TV; Karl Merkatz); Don Quijote de La Mancha, 1978 (TV series; Rafael de Penagos); Don Quijote de La Mancha, 1991-1992 (TV series; Jose Luis Pellicena); Don Quijote von der Mancha, 1965 (TV miniseries; Wolfgang Kieling); The

DuPont Show of the Month, 1957-1961 (TV series; "I, Don Quixote," 1959 episode; Lee J. Cobb): Man of La Mancha, 1972 (Peter O'Toole); Parade of Stars, 1983 (made-for-TV; Richard Kiley); Sir Francis Drake, 1961- (TV series; "Gentlemen of Spain," 1962 episode: Nigel Davenport); Young Rebel, 1969 (Horst Buchholz).

Chamberlain, Joshua Lawrence (1828-1914; Union general in the American Civil War; college professor and governor of the state of Maine, 1867-1871): **Gettysburg**, 1993 (Jeff Daniels); **Gods and Generals**, 2003 (Jeff Daniels).

Chanel, Coco (Gabrielle Bonheur Chanel; 1883-1971; French fashion designer and creator of Chanel brand of perfumes and other products): Chanel; Solitaire, 1981 (Marie-France Pisier); **Coco before Chanel**, 2009 (Audrey Tautou); Coco Chanel, 2008 (made-for-TV; Rosabell Laurenti Sellers; Shirley MacLaine as older Coco; Barbora Bobulova as younger Coco); Coco Chanel & Igor Stravinsky, 2010 (Anna Mouglalis); The Man Who Lived at the Ritz, 1989 (made-for-TV; Leslie Caron); Opium, 2013 (Audrey Marnay).

Chaney, Lon (Lon Chaney Sr.; 1883-1930; U.S. actor; chiefly in silent films as startling characters): **Man of a Thousand Faces**, 1957 (James Cagney).

Chapin, Charles (1858-1930; U.S. editor of the New York *World*, who was convicted of second-degree murder in the killing of his wife, Nellie, on the night of September 16, 1918, as she slept in her bed at the Hotel Cumberland; he claimed his was a mercy killing in that he was bankrupt and did not want his wife to live in poverty and that she was also ailing at that time; he was sent to prison for twenty years briefly editing the prison newspaper and cultivating rose beds for the warden, which led him to be called "The Rose Man of Sing Sing"): **Scandal Sheet**, 1931 (role model for George Bancroft). Note: For detailed information on Chapin, see my book *Murder among the Mighty* (Delacorte Press, 1983; illustrated pages 69-74).

Chaplin, Charles (Charles Spencer Chaplin; 1889-1977; U.K. comedian, film actor, director, producer and composer; celebrated for his comic character "The Little Tramp" in silent films): The Cat's Meow, 2002 (Eddie Izzard); Chaplin, 1992 (Hugh Downey Jr.); Cobb, 1994 (Brian Patrick Mulligan); **The Cotton Club**, 1984 (Gregory Rozakis); The Hearst and Davies Affair, 1985 (made-for-TV; Lorne Kennedy); Hollywood Babylon, 1972 (Myron Griffin); It Happened in Hollywood, 1937 (Eugene DeVerdi); Magnum, P.I., 1980-1988 (TV series; "The Case of the Red-Faced Thespian," 1984 episode: Larry Manetti); The Scarlett O'Hara War, 1980 (made-for-TV; Clive Revill); Shanghai Knights, 2003 (Aaron Taylor-Johnson); Silent Life, 2016 (Prida Moreza); Wonderworks: Young Charlie Chaplin, 1989- (TV series; Joe Geary).

Chapman, Annie (Elizabeth Ann Smith; c. 1841-1888; British prostitute and murder victim of Jack the Ripper): From Hell, 2001 (Katrin Cartlidge); Jack the Ripper, 1988 (TV series; Deirdre Costello); Love Lies Bleeding, 1999 (Michaela Hans); **Murder by Decree**, 1979 (June Brown); The Outer Limits, 1995-2002 (TV series; "Ripper," 1999 episode: Deni DeLory); **A Study in Terror**, 1966 (Barbara Windsor). For detailed information on this and the other Ripper murders, see my two-volume work *The Great Pictorial History of World Crime*, Volume II (History Inc., 2004; illustrated pages 1180-1203).

Chapman, Eddie (1914-1997; British safecracker who offered his services to Nazi Germany as a spy in England, but who became a heroic double agent for England in WWII): Studio One in Hollywood, 1948-1958 (TV series; "The Eddie Chapman Story," 1955 episode: Roy Dean); **Triple Cross**, 1967 (Christopher Plummer). Note: For detailed information on Chapman, see my book *Spies: A Narrative Encyclopedia* *of Dirty Tricks & Double Dealing from Biblical Times to Today* (M. Evans, 1997; illustrated pages 146-148).

Chapman, John (aka: Johnny Appleseed; 1774-1845; U.S. pioneer nurseryman, planting apple trees in large areas of Pennsylvania, Ohio, Indiana, Illinois and West Virginia, as well as Ontario, Canada): Tall Tales and Legends, 1985-1988 (TV series; "Johnny Appleseed," Martin Short); Walt Disney's Wonderful World of Color, 1954-1992 (TV series; "Four Fabulous Characters," 1957 episode: Dennis Day).

Charles I (1600-1649; King of England, Scotland and Ireland; executed under orders from Oliver Cromwell, who usurped the throne): The Boy Who Would Be King, 2004 (made-for-TV; Alex Gavin; Edward Petherbridge as Charles I voice); By the Sword Divided, 1983- (TV series; Jeremy Clyde); Cromwell, 1970 (Alec Guinness); The Devil's Whore, 2008- (TV series; Peter Capaldi); ITV Play of the Week, 1955-1974 (TV series; "The Killing of the King," 1959 episode: Paul Rogers); The Last King, 2003 (TV miniseries; Martin Turner); The Return of the Musketeers, 1989 (Bill Paterson); The Royal Oak, 1923 (Henry Victor); Thirty-Minute Theatre, 1965-1973 (TV series; "Revolutions: Cromwell," 1970 espisode: Kenneth Colley); The Trial of the King Killers, 2005 (Miles Richardson); The Vicar of Bray, 1937 (Hugh Miller).

Charles II (1630-1685; King of England, Ireland and Scotland): Admiral, 2016 (Charles Dance); And So to Bed, 1949 (made-for-TV; Austin Trevor); The Adventurer, 1920 (Harry Southard); BBC Play of the Month, 1965-1983 (TV series; "In Good King Charles' Golden Days," 1970 episode: John Gielgud); BBC Sunday-Night Theatre, 1950-1959 (TV series; "The Portugal Lady," 1952 episode: Eric Berry; "Ninety Sail," 1954 episode: Reginald Tate); Bonnie Prince Charlie, 1923 (Lewis Gilbert); Border Warfare, 1990- (TV series; "Towards the Union," 1990 episode: Robin Begg); The Boy Who Would Be King, 2004 (made-for-TV; Russell Saunders; Martin Colton as young Charles II; Mark Lockyer as Charles II voice); Broadside, 2009 (made-for-TV; Thomas Arnold); By the Sword Divided, 1983- (TV series; "Restoration," 1985 episode: Simon Treves); Cardboard Cavalier, 1949 (Anthony Hulme); The Children of Green Knowe, 1986- (TV series; Iain Rettray); The Children of the New Forest, 1964- (TV series; David Cargill); Churchill's People, 1974- (TV series; "A Bill of Mortality," 1975 episode: Denis Quilley); Colonel Blood, 1934 (Allan Jeayes); Complete and Utter History of Britain, 1969- (TV series; "James the McFirst to Oliver Cromwell," 1969 episode: Michael Palin); Courageous Mr. Penn, 1943 (Dennis Arundell); D'Artagnan, 1969 (TV miniseries; Roberto Bisacco); The Diary of Samuel Pepys, 1958- (TV series; Douglas Wilmer); England, My England, 1995 (Simon Callow); The Exile, 1947 (Douglas Fairbanks Jr.); Father Came Too!, 1964 (Peter Jones); The First Churchills, 1969- (TV series; "Plot, Counter-Plot," 1971 episode: James Villiers); Forever Amber, 1947 (George Sanders); Fortunes of Captain Blood, 1950 (Curt Bois); The Glorious Adventure, 1922 (William Luff); The Great Fire, 2014 (TV miniseries; Jack Huston); Helter Skelter, 1949 (Jon Pertwee); **Hudson's Bay**, 1941 (Vincent Price); The Joseph Cotten Show: On Trial, 1956-1959 (TV series; "The Trial of Colonel Blood," 1957 episode:: Henry Daniell); The King's Thief, 1955 (George Sanders); The Lady and the Highwayman, 1989 (made-for-TV; Michael York); The Last King, 2003 (TV miniseries; Rufus Sewell); Let's Make Up, 1956 (David Farrar); The Libertine, 2006 (John Malkovich); Looking About, 1961-1962 (TV series; "Oakapple Day," 1962 episode: Nicholas Courtney); Lorna Doone, 1951 (Lester Matthews); Mistress Nell, 1915 (Owen Moore); The Moonraker, 1958 (Gary Raymond); Mysteries at the Castle, 2014- (TV series; "House That Saved a King; Joan of Arc; Hamilton Sex Scandal," 2015 episode: Justin Colon); Nell Gwyn, 1926 (Randle Ayrton); Nell Gwyn, 1935 (Cedric Hardwicke); New Worlds, 2014- (TV miniseries; Jeremy Northam); The Private Life of Samuel Pepys, 2003 (made-for-TV; Nathaniel Parker); Restoration, 1996 (Sam Neill); The Royal Oak, 1923 (Henry Victor); Stage Beauty,

George Sanders (as Charles II) and Linda Darnell in *Forever Amber,* **1947.**

2004 (Rupert Everett); Theatre Parade, 1936-1938 (TV series; "Thank You Mr. Pepys," 1938 episode: Barry K. Barnes); Theft Royal, 1956 (made-for-TV; Derek Godfrey); The Trial of the King Killers, 2005 (Miles Richardson); Versailles, 2015- (TV series; Daniel Lapaine); The Vicar of Bray, 1937 (K. Hamilton Price); Voyage of the "Surprise," 1956 (made-for-TV; John Richmond); The Wicked Lady, 1983 (Mark Burns); Young Blades, 2005- (TV series; Michael Boisvert).

Charles VII (1403-1461; Dauphin and later king of France): An Age of Kings, 1960 (TV series; "Henry VI, Part 1: The Red Rose and the White," 1960 episode: David Andrews); Heinrich VI—Der Krieg der Rosen 1. Teil, 1969 (made-for-TV; Nicolaus Haenel); If Paris Were Told to Us, 1956 (Paul Colline); Jeanne la Pucelle 1: Les batailles, 1994 (Jean-Luc Petit); Jeanne d'Arc, le pouvoir de l'innocence, 1989 (made-for-TV; Christophe Odent); Jeanne la Pucelle II: Les prisons, 1994 (Andre Marcon); Jeanne oder Die Lerche, 1966 (made-for-TV; Fritz Wepper); Joan of Arc, 1935 (Gustaf Grundgens); **Joan of Arc**, 1948 (Jose Ferrer); Joan of Arc, 1999 (made-for-TV; Neil Patrick Harris); Joan of Arc, 2003 (made-for-TV; Jan Apolenar); Joan the Woman, 1916 (Raymond Hatton); The Lark, 1957 (made-for-TV; Eli Wallach); The Maid of Orleans, 1993 (made-for-TV; Oleg Kulko); **The Messenger: The Story of Joan of Arc**, 1999 (John Malkovich); Mysteries at the Castle, 2014- (TV series; "House That Saved a King; Joan of Arc; Hamilton Sex Scandal," 2015 episode: Seth Clayton); National Red Cross Pageant, 1917 (Guy Favieres); Saint Joan, 1957 (Richard Widmark); Saint Joan, 1958 (made-for-TV; Kenneth Williams); Saint Joan, 1967 (made-for-TV; Roddy McDowall); Saint Joan the Maid, 1929 (Jean Debucourt); Sainte Jeanne, 1969 (made-for-TV; Francois Marthouret).

Chase, Salmon P. (1808-1873; U.S. politician and 6th chief justice of the U.S. Supreme Court): The Dramatic Life of Abraham Lincoln, 1924 (Charles Smiley); In the Days of Buffalo Bill, 1922 (Alfred Hollingsworth); Lincoln, 1988 (made-for-TV; John McMartin); Lost River: Lincoln's Secret Weapon, 2009 (Afmuth Dave); **Saving Lincoln**, 2013 (Josh Stamberg); **Tennessee Johnson**, 1942 (Montagu Love).

Chato (1854-1934; U.S. Native American; Apache warrior): Apache Warrior, 1957 (George Keymas); Chato's Land, 1972 (Charles Bronson); **Geronimo: An American Legend**, 1993 (Steve Reevis); Taza, Son of Cochise, 1954 (Eugene Igleslas); Walk the Proud Land, 1954 (Eugene Igleslas).

Chevalier d'Eon (Charles Genevieve Louis Auguste d'Eon de Beaumont; 1728-1810; French aristocrat, diplomat and spy who conducted

Cornel Wilde (as Fredric Chopin) and Merle Oberon (as George Sand) in *A Song to Remember*, 1945.

espionage for decades while impersonating a woman): Beaumarchais the Scoundrel, 1997 (Claire Nebout); Enigmas de l'histoire, 1956-1957 (TV series; "Le chevalier d'Eon," 1957 episode: Marcelle Ransom-Herve); Exzellenz Unterrock, 1921 (Marion Regler); Figaro-ci, Figaro-la, 1972 (made-for-TV; Jacques Destoop); Le chevalier D'Eon, 2006- (TV series; David Matranga; Yuuki Tai; Akio Nojima; Ted Pfister); Le secret du Chevalier d'Eon, 1959 (Andree Debar); Marquis d'Eon, der Spion der Pompadour, 1929 (Liane Haid); Nicolas Le Floch, 2008- (TV series; "L'Affaire Nicolas Le Floch," 2009 episode; Philippe Demarle). Note: For detailed information on Chevalier d'Eon, see my book, *Spies: A Narrative Encyclopedia of Dirty Tricks & Double Dealing from Biblical Times to Today* (M. Evans, 1997; illustrated [3 images] pages 173-174).

Chiang Kai-shek (1887-1975; Chinese leader and chairman of the Nationalist Government of China): Back to 1942, 2012 (Daoming Chen); The Birth of New China, 1989 (Feihu Sun); Bonds of Blood, 1997-1998 (TV series; Zhen Yu Lei); Collision Course: Truman vs. MacArthur, 1976 (made-for-TV; Richard Loo); Eastern Battlefield, 2015- (TV miniseries; Xiao Wei Ma); The Founding of a Republic, 2009 (Guoli Zhang); Hemingway & Gellhorn, 2012 (made-for-TV; Larry Tse); John Rabe, 2009 (Dong Fu Lin); The Soong Sisters, 1997 (Hsing-Kuo Wu).

Chikatilo, Andrei Romanovich (aka: Butcher of Rostov; Rostov Ripper; 1936-1994; USSR cannibal and serial killer who murdered at least fifty-two women and children from 1978 to 1990; executed on February 14, 1994): Citizen X, 1995 (made-for-TV; Jeffrey DeMunn). For more details on Chikatilo, see my two-volume work, *The Great Pictorial History of World Crime*, Volume I (History, Inc., 2004; pages 317-318).

Chisum, John Simpson (1824-1884; U.S. cattle baron in New Mexico and involved with the Lincoln County War): Birth of a Legend: Billy the Kid & the Lincoln County War, 2011 (David Morley); Bronco, 1958-1962 (TV series; "Death of an Outlaw," 1960 episode: Harry Swoger); **Chisum**, 1970 (John Wayne); Death Valley Days, 1952-1970 (TV series; "Paid in Full," 1965 episode: Michael Constantine); **Pat Garrett and Billy the Kid**, 1973 (Barry Sullivan); San Antone, 1953 (Roy Roberts); **Young Guns II**, 1990 (James Coburn).

Chivington, John Milton (1821-1894; U.S. military officer, who fought for the Union in the American Civil War and perpetrated the heinous Sand Creek Massacre in the Colorado Territory on November 29, 1864, where he and his 700 troopers slaughtered mostly defenseless women and children of the Cheyenne and Arapaho tribes, murdering between seventy to 163 Indians): Into the West, 2005 (TV miniseries; Tom Berenger).

Chopin, Frederic (1810-1849; Polish composer, notable for his patriotic composition "Polanise"): Bohemian Rapture, 1948 (aka: Housle a sen; Vaclav Voska); Chopin—Bilder einer Trennung, 1993 (Stephan Wolf-Schonberg); Chopin: Desire for Love [aka: Chopin; Pragnienie milosci], 2004 (Piotr Adamczyk); Coup de Grace, 1978 (Bruno Thost); Die lachende Grille, 1926 (Alfred Abel); Ein Winter auf Mallorca, 1982 (made-for-TV; Krystian Martinek); Farewell, 1935 (aka: La chanson de l'adieu; Un amour de Frederic Chopin; Jean Servais); Farewell Waltz, 1934 (Wolfgang Liebeneiner); George and Fanchette, 2010 (made-for-TV; Fabrice Pruvost); George Sand, 1958 (TV series; Egidio Eccio); George Who?, 1973 (Pierre Kalinovski); Heinrich Heine, 1978 (made-for-TV; Claus Bantzer); **Impromptu**, 1991 (Hugh Grant); International, 1969 (aka: Jutrzenka; Christopher Sandford); La note bleue, 1991 (Janusz Olejniczak); La rebellion de los fantasmas, 1949 (Francisco Valera); La Valse de l'adieu, 1928 (Pierre Blanchar); Liszt Ferenc, 1982 (TV miniseries; Laszlo Galffi); Lisztomania, 1975 (Ken [Kenneth] Colley); Nocturne in Scotland, 1951 (made-for-TV; Hugh Burden); Nocturno der Liebe, 1919 (Conrad Veidt); Notorious Woman, 1974 (TV miniseries; George Chakiris); Pontcarral, colonel d'empire, 1942 (Jean Chaduc); Prelude, 1952 (made-for-TV; Alan Shayne); Preludio, A Vida de Chopin, 1962 (TV series; Claudio Marzo); **A Song to Remember**, 1945 (Cornel Wilde); **Song without End**, 1960 (Alex [Alexander] Davion); The Strange Case of Delphina Potocka or the Mystery of Chopin, 1999 (Paul Rhys); Szerelmes szivek, 1944 (Gyula Benko); Titans, 1981-1982 (TV series; Andrea Martin); Toute la ville en parle, 2000 (made-for-TV; Maurice Mons); **Young Chopin**, 1952 (Czeslaw Wollejko).

Christian, Fletcher (1764-1793; British first mate on the HMS *Bounty*, who led a mutiny and seized command of the ship from Captain William Bligh on April 29, 1879, setting Bligh and others in a open boat before eventually settling on the island of Pitcairn): **The Bounty**, 1984 (Mel Gibson); In the Wake of the Bounty, 1933 (Errol Flynn); The Mutiny on the Bounty, 1916 (Wilton Power); **Mutiny on the Bounty**, 1935 (Clark Gable); **Mutiny on the Bounty**, 1962 (Marlon Brando); Mutiny on the Bounty, 2011 (made-for-TV; Steve Ryan); You Are There, 1953-1971 (TV series; "Mr. Christian Seizes the Bounty [April 28, 1789]," 1956 episode: Russell Johnson). Note: For detailed information on the mutiny on board the *Bounty*, see my eight-volume work *Encyclopedia of World Crime*, Volume III (CrimeBooks, Inc., 1990; illustrated pages 2269-2270).

Christie, John Reginald Halliday (1899-1953; British serial killer who killed his wife, Ethel, along with seven other women at his home at 10 Rillington Place, Notting Hill, London, England, from 1943 to 1953; he was executed by hanging on July 15, 1953): Fred Dinenage Murder Casebook, 2011- (TV series; "John Christie," 2011 episode: Paul Ramshaw); Gnade fur Timothy Evans, 1969 (made-for-TV; Friedrich G. Beckhaus); **10 Rillington Place**, 1971 (Richard Attenborough); 13 Steps Down, 2012 (TV series; two 2012 episodes: Mark Lambert). For more details on Christie, see my books *Encyclopedia of World Crime*, Volume I (A-C) (CrimeBooks, 1990; illustrated pages 705-708); *World Encyclopedia of 20th Century Murder* (Paragon House, 1992; illustrated pages: 118-122); *The Great Pictorial History of World Crime*, Volume II (History, Inc., 2004; illustrated pages 1105-1108).

Christina, Queen of Sweden (1626-1689; Queen regnant of Sweden, 1632-1654; abdicated her throne): The Abdication, 1974 (Liv Ullmann); Christina, 1988 (made-for-TV; Andreas Unge as young Christina; Birgitta Svenden as older Christina); Comenius, 1975 (made-for-TV; Kornelia Boje); Fridericus Rex, 1823 (Erna Morena); The Girl King, 2015 (Malin Buska); Konigin Christine, 1970 (made-for-TV; Elfriede Kuzmany); **Queen Christina**, 1933 (Greta Garbo); Vasasagan, 1998 (made-for TV; Nina Togner Fex).

Christy, Edwin Pearce (1815-1862; U.S. theatrical producer and theater owner noted for his traveling troupe of singers known as Christy's Minstrels, white singers who performned in blackface and sang mostly the songs composed by Stephen Collins Foster): Harmony Lane, 1935 (William Frawley); I Dream of Jeanie, 1952 (Ray Middleton); **Sewanee River**, 1939 (Al Jolson).

Chuichi Nagumo (1887-1944; Japanese admiral who commanded the task force that made the sneak attack against Pearl Harbor on December 7, 1941): **Midway**, 1976 (James Shigeta); **Tora! Tora! Tora!**, 1970 (Eijiro Tono); War and Remembrance, 1988 (TV miniseries; Danny Kamekona).

Churchill, Winston (Winston Leonard Spencer Churchill; 1874-1965; British statesman and prime minister of Great Britain): Above and Beyond, 2006 (TV miniseries; Joss Ackland); **Above Us the Waves**, 1956 (Peter Cavanagh); Absolutely Modern, 2013 (John Apicella); The Adventures of Picasso, 1978 (Sune Mangs); Allegiance, 2005 (Mel Smith); **An American in Paris**, 1951 (Dudley Field Malone); Annie: A Royal Adventure, 1995 (made-for-TV; David King); The Battle of Sutjeska, 1973 (Orson Welles); Bertie and Elizabeth, 2002 (made-for-TV; David Ryall); Bomber Harris, 1989 (made-for-TV; Robert Hardy); Bullet for Heydrich, 2013 (Richard Syms); Callas e Onassis, 2005 (made-for-TV; Gerry George); **Captains of the Clouds**, 1942 (Miles Mander); Casablanca Express, 1989 (John Evans); Castles in the Sky, 2014 (Tim McInnerny); Churchill, 2016 (Brian Cox); Churchill and the Generals, 1981 (made-for-TV; Timothy West); Churchill: 100 Days That Saved Britain, 2015 (made-for-TV; Robert Hardy); Churchill: The Hollywood Years, 2004 (Christian Slater); Churchill: When Britain Said No, 2015 (made-for-TV; Christian Rodska); Churchill's First World War, 2013 (made-for-TV; Adam James); Days of Betrayal, 1973 (Jan Vitek); The Days That Made History, 2009- (TV series; Christian Rodska); De Gaulle, 2006- (TV series; David Ryall); Deadline Gallipoli, 2015 (TV miniseries; Simon Maiden); **The Desert Fox**, 1955 (voiceover of Jack Moyles); Dieppe, 1993 (made-for-TV; W.B. Brydon); Dunkirk, 2004 (made-for-TV; Simon Russell Beale); **The Eagle Has Landed**, 1977 (Leigh Dilley); Edward & Mrs. Simpson, 1978 (TV miniseries; Wensley Pithey); Edward the King, 1975 (TV series; Christopher Strauli); F.D.R.: The Last Year, 1980 (made-for-TV; Wensley Pithey); The Fall of Berlin, 1952 (Viktor Stanitsyn); The Gathering Storm, 1974 (made-for-TV; Richard Burton); The Gathering Storm, 2002 (made-for-TV; Albert Finney); The Great Battle, 1973 (Yuri Durov); The Great Escape II: The Untold Story, 1988 (made-for-TV; Ronald Lacey); Heyday!, 2006 (made-for-TV; Frank Holden); Hiroshima, 1995 (made-for-TV; Timothy West); Hiroshima, 2005 (made-for-TV; Robert Austin); Honey Sweet Love…, 1994 (John Evans); Ike: Countdown to D-Day, 2004 (made-forTV; Ian Mune); Ike: The War Years, 1979 (TV miniseries; Wensley Pithey); Inglourious Basterds, 2009 (Rod Taylor); Into the Storm, 2009 (made-for-TV; Brendan Gleeson); Jennie: Lady Randolph Churchill, 1974 (TV miniseries; Warren Clarke); **The King's Speech**, 2010 (Timothy Spall); Kurtulus, 1994 (TV miniseries; Simon Ward); The Last Bastion, 1984 (TV miniseries; Timothy West); Le bourreau des coeurs, 1983 (Rene Douglas); The Life and Times of David Lloyd George, 1981 (TV series; William Hootkins); A Man Called Intrepid, 1979 (TV miniseries; Nigil Stock); **The Man Who Never Was**, 1956 (Peter Sellers voiceover); Masterpiece Theatre: Lord Mountbatten—The Last Viceroy, 1986 (TV miniseries; Malcolm Terris); Matinee Theatre, 1955-1958 (TV series; "Savrola," 1956 episode; David Frankham); Menzies and Churchill at War, 2008 (made-for-TV; Charles "Bud" Tingwell); **Mission to Moscow**, 1943 (Dudley Field Malone); Moi, general de Gaulle, 1990 (made-for-TV; Donald Pleasence); National Theatre Live: The Audience, 2013 (Edward Fox); Number 10, 1983 (TV miniseries; Terence Harvey); Onassis: The Richest Man in the World, 1988 (made-for-TV;

Mel Gibson (as Fletcher Christian) in *The Bounty*, 1984.

Thorley Walters); **Operation Crossbow**, 1965 (Patrick Wymark); Peenemunde, 1970 (made-for-TV; Alfred Schieske); Queen of the Desert, 2015 (Christopher Fulford); Regal Cavalcade, 1935 (C.M. Hallard); The Siege 1922 (2013; Mario Rosenstock); The Siege of Sidney Street, 1961 (Jimmy Sangster); Sinking of the Lusitania: Terror at Sea, 2007 (made-for-TV; Martin Le Maitre); The Sound of Spying, 2014 (John Apicella); Stalingrad, 1990 (Ronald Lacey); Suez 1956, 1979 (made-for-TV; Wensley Pithey); 37 Days, 2014 (TV miniseries; Nicholas Asbury); The Treaty, 1991 (made-for-TV; Julian Fellowes); Truman at Potsdam, 1976 (made-for-TV; John Houseman); Two Men Went to War, 2004 (David Ryall); The Unforgettable Year: 1919, 1952 (Viktor Stanitsyn); Wallis & Edward, 2005 (made-for-TV; David Calder); War and Remembrance, 1988 (TV miniseries; Robert Hardy); The Winds of War, 1983 (TV miniseries; Howard Lang); Winston Churchill: The Valiant Years, 1960-1963 (TV series; Richard Burton); Winston Churchill: The Wilderness Years, 1981 (TV series; Robert Hardy); The Woman He Loved, 1988 (made-for-TV; Robert Hardy); The Woman I Love, 1972 (made-for-TV; Henry Oliver); World War Two: Behind Closed Doors, 2008-2009 (TV series; Paul Humpoletz); World War II: When Lions Roared, 1994 (made-for-TV; Bob Hoskins); Yalta, 1984 (made-for-TV; Bernard Fresson); **Young Winston**, 1972 (Simon Ward as mature Churchill; Russell Lewis as Churchill at age seven; Michael Anderson as Churchill at age thirteen).

Cinq-Mars (Henri Coiffier de Ruze; 1620-1642; French nobleman who conspired against Cardinal Richelieu): Cinq-Mars, 1981 (made-for-TV; Paul Blain); Cyrano et d'Artagnan, 1964 (Julian Mateos); Le camera explore le temps, 1957-1966 (TV series, "La conjuration de Cinq-Mars," 1962 episode: Guy Moigne); Richelieu, 1977 (TV miniseries; Jean-Louis Broust); Richelieu, la pourpre et la sang, 2013 (made-for-TV; Pierre Boulanger).

Claiborne, Billy (William F. Claiborne; 1860-1882; U.S. gunfighter and outlaw, a member of the Clanton-McLowery [McLaury] gang, who survived the gunfight at the O.K. Corral in Tombstone, Arizona, but who was killed in another Tombstone gunfight on November 14, 1882, by "Buckskin" Frank Leslie): Stories of the Century, 1954 (TV series; "Doc Holliday," 1954 episode: Rocky Shahan); **Tombstone**, 1993 (Wyatt Earp); The Wild West, 2006-2007 (TV miniseries; "The Gunfight at the O.K. Corral," 2007 episode: Clark Webb); **Wyatt Earp**, 1994 (Kris Kamm). Note: For detailed information on Claiborne, see my book, *Encyclopedia of Western Lawmen and Outlaws* (Paragon House, 1992; illustrated pages 75-77).

Claiborne, William C.C. (c. 1773-1817; U.S. politician and first gover-

Theda Bara (as Cleopatra) in *Cleopatra*, 1917.

nor of Louisiana, 1812-1816): **The Buccaneer**, 1938 (Douglass Dumbrille); The Buccaneer, 1958 (E. G. Marshall); The Pirate and the Lawyer, 1955 (made-for-TV; Douglass Dumbrille); War of 1812, 2012 (made-for-TV; Todd Norris).

Clanton, Billy (1862-1881; U.S. outlaw; killed in the gunfight at the O.K. Corral in Tombstone, Arizona, on October 26, 1881): Appointment with Destiny, 1971-1973 (TV series; "Showdown at O.K. Corral," 1972 episode: John O'Connor White); Bullets Don't Argue, 1964 (Horst Frank); Cowboys, 2009 (TV miniseries; "Gunfight at the O.K. Corral," 2009 episode: Benjamin Joel Caron); **Doc**, 1971 (Bruce M. Fischer); **Gunfight at the O.K. Corral**, 1957 (Dennis Hopper); **Hour of the Gun**, 1967 (Walter Gregg); I Married Wyatt Earp, 1983 (made-for-TV; Tom Assalone); The Life and Legend of Wyatt Earp, 1955-1961 (TV series; many episodes: Ralph Reed); **My Darling Clementine**, 1946 (John Ireland); Pistols 'n' Petticoats, 1966-1967 (TV series; "Shootout at O'Day Corral," 1966 episode: Bruce Watson as "Billy Blanton"); Stories of the Century, 1954 (TV series; "Doc Holliday," 1954 episode: Joe Phillips); **Sunset**, 1988 (Denney Pierce); **Tombstone**, 1993 (Thomas Haden Church); Tombstone Territory, 1957- (TV series; "Pick Up the Gun," 1958 episode: Tom Pittman); **Tombstone: The Town Too Tough to Die**, 1942 (James Ferrara); Wagon Train, 1957-1965 (TV series; "The Silver Lady," 1965 episode: Dave Cass [David S. Cass Sr.]); **Wyatt Earp**, 1994 (Gabriel Folse); Wyatt Earp: Return to Tombstone, 1994 (made-for-TV; Ralph Reed); You Are There, 1953-1957 (TV series; "The Gunfight at the O.K. Corral," 1955 episode: Edward McNally). Note: For detailed information on Clanton, see my book *Encyclopedia of Western Lawmen and Outlaws* (Paragon House, 1992; illustrated pages 75-77).

Clanton, Ike (Joseph Isaac Clanton; 1847-1887; U.S. rancher and outlaw, opponent with others against the Earp faction in Tombstone, Arizona): Appointment with Destiny, 1971-1973 (TV series; "Showdown at O.K. Corral," 1972 episode: Thomas Hunter); Arizona Bushwhackers, 1968 (James Craig); Cowboys, 2009 (TV miniseries; "Gunfight at the O.K. Corral," 2009 episode: Jim Cegan); Days That Shook the World, 2003- (TV series; "Rule of the Gun," 2006 episode: Dan Gunther); Death Valley Days, 1952-1970 (TV series; "After the O.K. Corral," 1964 episode: William Tannen); The Deputy, 1959-1961 (TV series; "The Big Four," 1959 episode; Charles Fredericks); **Doc**, 1971 (Michael Witney); **Gunfight at the O.K. Corral**, 1957 (Llye Bettger); Gunslingers, 2014- (TV miniseries; "The Tombstone Vendetta," 2014 episode: Jonathan David Dixon); **Hour of the Gun**, 1967 (Robert Ryan); I Married Wyatt Earp, 1983 (made-for-TV; Charles Benton); The Life and Legend of Wyatt Earp, 1955-1961 (TV series; many episodes:

Rayford Barnes); **My Darling Clementine**, 1946 (Grant Withers); Pistols 'n' Petticoats, 1966-1967 (TV series; "Shootout at O'Day Corral," 1966 episode: Charles Maxwell as "Ike Blanton"); Stories of the Century, 1954 (TV series; "Doc Holliday," 1954 episode: Frank Richards); Tales of Wells Fargo, 1957-1962 (TV series; "The Target," 1957 episode: Kelo Henderson); **Tombstone**, 1993 (Stephen Lang); **Tombstone: The Town Too Tough to Die**, 1942 (Victor Jory); The Toughest Gun in Tombstone, 1958 (Gerald Milton); Walt Disney's Wonderful World of Color, 1954-1992 (TV series; "Texas John Slaughter: Range War at Tombstone," 1959 episode: James Westerfield); The West, 2016 (TV miniseries; two 2016 episodes: Michael Chmiel); The Wild West, 2006- (TV series; "The Gunfight at the O.K. Corral," 2007 episode: Christopher Fulford); **Wyatt Earp**, 1994 (Jeff Fahey); Wyatt Earp: Return to Tombstone, 1994 (made-for-TV; Rayford Barnes); Wagon Train, 1957-1965 (TV series; "The Silver Lady," 1965 episode; Rex Holman); You Are There, 1953-1957 (TV series; "The Gunfight at the O.K. Corral," 1955 episode: DeForest Kelley). Note: For detailed information on Clanton, see my book *Encyclopedia of Western Lawmen and Outlaws* (Paragon House, 1992; illustrated pages 75-77).

Clanton, Newman Haynes (1816-1881; U.S. rancher, rustler and outlaw; father of the Clanton brothers): The Life and Legend of Wyatt Earp, 1955-1961 (TV series; many episodes: Trevor Bardette); **My Darling Clementine**, 1946 (Walter Brennan); Wagon Train, 1957-1965 (TV series; "The Silver Lady," 1965 episode: Denver Pyle); Wyatt Earp: Return to Tombstone, 1994 (made-for-TV; Trevor Bardette). Note: For detailed information on Clanton, see my book *Encyclopedia of Western Lawmen and Outlaws* (Paragon House, 1992; illustrated pages 75-77).

Clark, James (Albert Kachellek; 1887-1929; U.S. gangster and bootlegger and a member of the George "Bugs" Moran gang, one of the seven victims of Chicago's notorious 1929 St. Valentine's Day Massacre): Playhouse 90, 1956-1961 (TV series; "Seven against the Wall," 1958 episode: George Keymas); **The St. Valentine's Day Massacre**, 1967 (Kurt Kreuger). Note; For detailed information on Clark and the St. Valentine's Day Massacre, see my books *World Encyclopedia of Organized Crime* (Paragon House, 1992, illustrated pages 343-347; and *The Great Pictorial History of World Crime*, Volume I (History, Inc., 2004; [under Capone] illustrated pages 503-541).

Clark, William (1770-1838; U.S. soldier and explorer): Death Valley Days, 1952-1970 (TV series; "The Girl Who Walked the West," 1967 episode: Don Matheson); **The Far Horizons**, 1955 (Charlton Heston); Lewis and Clark, 2016- (TV miniseries; Matthias Schoenaerts); **Night at the Museum**, 2006 (Martin Sims); The Seekers, 1979 (made-for-TV; Ed Harris); Voyagers!, 1982-1983 (TV series; "Old Hickory and the Pirate," 1982 episode: Michael Bond); You Are There, 1953-1971 (TV series; "Lewis and Clark Expedition," 1971 episode: John Cullum).

Clary, Desiree (Bernadine Eugenie Desiree Clary; 1777-1860; one-time fiancée of Napoleon I; queen of Sweden and Norway, consort of Charles XIV, Jean Bernadotte): Mlle. Desiree, 1948 (Gaby Morlay); **Desiree**, 1954 (Jean Simmons); Napoleon, 1955 (Dany Robin).

Claudius (10 B.C.-54 A.D.; Roman emperor): A.D., 1985 (TV miniseries; Richard Kiley); The Affairs of Messalina, 1952 (Memo Benassi); The Caesars, 1968 (TV series; Freddie Jones); The Caesars, 1968- (TV miniseries; Freddie Jones); Caligula, 1980 (Giancarlo Badessi); Caligula and Messalina, 1981 (Antonio Passalia); **Demetrius and the Gladiators**, 1954 (Barry Jones); Fire over Rome, 1965 (Franco Fantasia); I, Claudius, 1937 (Charles Laughton); I, Claudius, 1976 (TV miniseries; Derek Jacobi); Imperium: Nero, 2004 (made-for-TV; Massimo Dapporto); The Last Days of Pompeii, 1913 (Vitale De Stefano); Messalina, 1924 (Augusto Mastripietri); Messalina, 1960 (Marcello Giorda); Messalina, Empress of Rome, 1977 (Vittorio Caprioli); Messalina vs. the

Son of Hercules, 1964 (Philippe Hersent); Roma rivoule Cesare, 1974 (made-for-TV; Daniel Olbrychski); The Secret under the Rose, 2006 (Dimitri Diatchenko); Slave of Rome, 1961 (Giacomo Rossi Stuart); Warrior Queen, 2003 (Jack Shepherd); Woman, 1918 (Paul Clerget).

Clemenceau, Georges Benjamin (1841-1929; French politician, statesman and prime minister of France, 1917-1920): Affare Dreyfus, 1959 (made-for-TV; Konrad Mayerhoff); Affare Dreyfus, 1968- (TV miniseries; Richard Munch); Bluebeard, 1963 (Raymond Queneau); Clemenceau, 2012 (made-for-TV; Didier Bezace); The Crown Prince, 2005 (**The Dreyfus Case**, 1931 (Leonard Shepherd); The Dreyfus Case, 1940 (Paul Bildt); Emile Zola ou La conscience humaine, 1978- (TV miniseries; Andre Valmy); Entente cordialle, 1939 (Jacques Baumer); Fall of Eagles, 1974 (TV miniseries; John Bennett); Folio, 1955-1959 (TV series; "Betrayal," 1955 episode: Charles Jarrott); Great Performances, 1971- (TV series; "A Dangerous Man: Lawrence after Arabia," 1992 episode: Arnold Diamond); I Accuse!, 1958 (Peter Illing); Jean Jaures: Vie et mort d'un socialiste, 1980 (made-for-TV; Dominique Zardi); Jules Ferry, 1981 (made-for-TV; Jacques Campin); La belle epoque de Gaston Coute, 1979 (made-for-TV; Henri Delmas); Les hommes nouveaux, 1936 (Gustave Gallet); Les samedis de l'histoire, 1977- (TV series; Yves Brainville); The Life and Times of David Lloyd George, 1981- (TV series; Michael Anthony); **The Life of Emile Zola**, 1937 (Grant Mitchell); Lux Video Theatre, 1950-1959 (TV series; "The Life of Emile Zola," 1955 episode: Guy Sorel); My 1919, 1999 (Gerard Thirion); The Tiger, 1936 (made-for-TV; William Devlin); The Tiger Brigades, 1973-1983 (TV series; Raoul Curet); Why America Will Win, 1918 (Johnny Hennessey); **Wilson**, 1944 (Marcel Dalio).

Clemens, Samuel Langhorne: see Twain, Mark.

Cleopatra (Cleopatra VII; last queen or pharaoh of Egypt; 69 B.C.-30 B.C.): Antoine et Cleopatre, 1967 (made-for-TV; Judith Magre); Antonio e Cleopatra, 1965 (made-for-TV; Valeria Valeri); Antonius und Cleopatra, 1963 (made-for-TV; Lola Muthel); Antony and Cleopatra, 1913 (Gianna Terribili-Gonzales); Antony and Cleopatra, 1951 (Pauline Letts); Antony and Cleopatra, 1959 (made-for-TV; Bettine Kauffman); Antony and Cleopatra, 1973 (Hildegard Neil); Antony and Cleopatra, 1975 (made-for-TV; Janet Suzman); Antony and Cleopatra, 1981 (made-for-TV; Jane Lapotaire); Antony and Cleopatra, 1984 (made-for-TV; Lynn Redgrave); Antony and Cleopatra, 2015 (Yanna McIntosh); Asterix and Cleopatra, 1969 (animated; Micheline Dax voiceover); Asterix and Obelix Meet Cleopatra, 2002 (animated; Diane Neal voiceover); Caesar, 2003 (made-for-TV; Samuela Sardo); **Caesar and Cleopatra**, 1946 (Vivien Leigh); Caesar und Cleopatra, 1964 (made-for-TV; Uta Sax); Caesar und Cleopatra, 1970 (made-for-TV; Angelica Domrose); Caesar and Cleopatra, 1976 (made-for-TV; Genevieve Bujold); Caesar and Cleopatra, 2009 (Nikki M. James); Carry On Cleo, 1965 (Amanda Barrie); Casar und Cleopatra, 1969 (made-for-TV; Violetta Ferrari); Cleopatra, 1943 (Amina Rizk); Cleopatra, 1912 (Helen Gardner); Cleopatra, 1917 (Theda Bara); **Cleopatra**, 1934 (Claudette Colbert); Cleopatra, 1962- (TV series; Solange); **Cleopatra**, 1963 (Elizabeth Taylor); Cleopatra, 1970 (Viva); Cleopatra, 1999- (TV miniseries; Leonor Varela); Cleopatra, 2007 (Alessandra Negrini); The Cleopatras, 1983 (TV miniseries; Michelle Newell); **Dante's Inferno**, 1935 (Lorna Low); Dante's Inferno, 2007 (animated; Janet Varney); The Destiny of Rome, 2011 (TV miniseries; Leatitia Eido); Legions of the Nile, 1959 (Linda Cristal); General Electric Theater, 1953-1962 (TV series; "Caesar and Cleopatra," 1959 episode: Piper Laurie); The Great Egyptians, 1998- (TV miniseries; Tamsin Greig); Highway to Hell, 1992 (Amy Stiller); The Ides of March, 1961 (made-for-TV; Carole Potter); Imperium: Augustus, 2003 (made-for-TV; Anna Valie); Jules Cesar, 2011 (Natalie Dessay); Julius Caesar, 1984 (made-for-TV; Valerie Masterson); Julius Caesar, 2007 (made-for-TV; Inger Dam-Jensen); Legions of the Nile, 1960 (Linda Cristal); The Notorious Cleopatra, 1970 (Loray White);

Jessica Lange (as Patsy Cline) in *Sweet Dreams,* **1985.**

Producers' Showcase, 1954-1957 (TV series; "Caesar and Cleopatra," 1956 episode: Claire Bloom); A Queen for Caesar, 1962 (Pascale Petit); Rome, 2005-2007 (TV series; Lyndsey Marshal); Serpent of the Nile, 1953 (Rhonda Fleming); The Spread of the Eagle, 1963- (TV miniseries; Mary Morris); The Story of Mankind, 1957 (Virginia Mayo); Toto and Cleopatra, 1963 (Magali Noel); Two Nights with Cleopatra, 1964 (Sophia Loren); Witness to Yesterday, 1970- (TV series; "Cleopatra," 1974 episode: Jayne Meadows); Xena: Warrior Princess, 1995-2001 (TV series; one 1997 episode: Gina Torres; one 2000 episode: Josephine Davison); You Are There, 1953-1971 (TV series; "The Death of Cleopatra [30 B.C.]," 1953 episode: Kim Stanley).

Cline, Patsy (1932-1963; U.S. pop and country singer, killed in a plane crash at age thirty): Big Dreams & Broken Hearts: The Dottie West Story, 1995 (made-for-TV; Tere Myers); **Coal Miner's Daughter**, 1980 (Beverly D'Angelo); Crazy, 2008 (Mandy Barnett); Sweet Dreams, 1985 (Jessica Lange).

Clinton, Henry (1730-1795; British general during the American Revolutionary War, 1775-1783): George Washington, 1984 (TV miniseries; Barry Ingham); I Spy, 1955- (TV series; "Betrayal at West Point," 1956 episode: Ralph Sumpter); **The Scarlet Coat**, 1955 (Paul Cavanagh).

Clive, Robert (Clive of India; 1725-1774; British soldier and major general who established British domination of India): BBC Sunday-Night Theatre, 1950-1959 (TV series; "Clive of India," 1956 episode: Marius Goring); **Clive of India**, 1935 (Ronald Colman); Flame of Calcutta, 1953 (Paul Cavanagh); The Hidden Master, 1940 (Peter Cushing).

Cochise (1805-1874; chief of the Chiricahua Apache tribe): The Adventures of Rin Tin Tin, 1954-1959 (TV series; Dean Fredericks in one 1955 episode; X Brands in two 1956 episodes); The Battle at Apache Pass, 1952 (Jeff Chandler); Bonanza, 1959-1973 (TV series; "The Honor of Cochise," 1961 episode: Jeff Morrow); **Broken Arrow**, 1950 (Jeff Chandler); Broken Arrow, 1956-1960 (TV series; Michael Ansara); Conquest of Cochise, 1953 (John Hodiak); **Fort Apache** (Miguel Inclan); 40 Guns to Apache Pass, 1967 (Michael Keep); Geronimo, 1993 (made-for-TV; August Schellenberg); The High Chaparral, 1967-1971 (Michael Keep; Paul Fix; Nino Cochise); **The Last Outpost**, 1951 (Chief Yowlachie); Taza, Son of Cochise, 1954 (Jeff Chandler); TV's Reader's Digest, 1955-1956 (TV series; "Cochise: Greatest of the Apaches," 1956 episode: Richard Gaines); Valley of the Sun, 1942 (Antonio Moreno).

Cody, Louisa Frederici (wife of U.S. Western scout, pioneer and show-

Jeff Chandler (as Cochise) and James Stewart (as Tom Jeffords) in *Broken Arrow*, 1950.

man, William Frederick "Buffalo Bill" Cody; 1843-1921): **Buffalo Bill**, 1944 (Maureen O'Hara).

Cody, William Frederick (aka: Buffalo Bill; Western scout, pioneer and showman; 1846-1917): **Annie Get Your Gun**, 1950 (Louis Calhern); Annie Get Your Gun, 1957 (made-for-TV; William O'Neal); Annie Get Your Gun, 1967 (made-for-TV; Rufus Smith); **Annie Oakley**, 1935 (Moroni Olsen); Badman's Country, 1958 (Malcolm Atterbury); Battling with Buffalo Bill, 1931 (Tom Tyler); **Buffalo Bill**, 1944 (Joel McCrea); Buffalo Bill (1965), 1983 (Gordon Scott); Buffalo Bill and the Indians, 1976 (Paul Newman); Buffalo Bill in Rome, 1949 (Enzo Fiermonte); Buffalo Bill in Tomahawk Territory, 1952 (Clayton Moore); Buffalo Bill Rides Again, 1947 (Richard Arlen); Buffalo Girls, 1995 (made-for-TV; Peter Coyote); Calamity Jane, 1984 (made-for-TV; Ken Kercheval); Circus Boy, 1956-1958 (TV series; "The Return of Buffalo Bill," 1957 episode: Dick Foran); Cody of the Pony Express, 1950 (Dickie Moore); Colt .45, 1957-1960 (TV series; "A Legend of Buffalo Bill," 1959 episode: Britt Lomond); Death Valley Days, 1952-1970 (TV series; "The Grand Duke," 1959 episode: John Lupton; "Two-Gun Nan," 1958 episode: William O'Neal); Don't Touch the White Woman!, 1974 (Michel Piccoli); Fighting with Buffalo Bill, 1826 (Edmund Cobb); Flaming Frontiers, 1938 (John Rutherford); **Hidalgo**, 2004 (J. K. Simmons); The Hour-Glass Sanitorium, 1973 (Andrzej Herder); In the Days of Buffalo Bill, 1922 (Duke R. Lee); **The Iron Horse**, 1924 (George Waggner); Kenny Rogers as the Gambler, Part III: The Legend Continues, 1987 (made-for-TV; Jeffrey Jones); King of the Bullwhip, 1950 (Tex Cooper); The Last Frontier, 1926 (Jack Hoxie); The Last Ride of the Dalton Gang, 1979 (made-for-TV; Buff Brady); Law of the Golden West, 1949 (Monte Hale); The Legend of the Golden Gun, 1979 (made-for-TV; R. L. Tolbert); The Legend of the Lone Ranger, 1981 (Ted Flicker); Little House on the Prairie, 1974-1983 (TV series; "For the Love of Blanche," 1983 episode: Eddie Quillan); Lonesome Dove: The Series, 1994-1995 (TV series; Dennis Weaver); The Miracle Rider, 1935 (Tex Cooper); Outlaw Express, 1938 (Carlyle Moore Jr.); Overland Mail, 1942 (Bob Baker); **The Plainsman**, 1936 (James Ellison); The Plainsman, 1966 (Guy Stockwell); The Pony Express, 1925 (John Fox Jr.); **Pony Express**, 1953 (Charlton Heston); **The Raiders**, 1963 (Jim McMullan); Riding with Buffalo Bill, 1954 (Marshall Reed); Seven Hours of Gunfire, 1965 (Clyde Rogers/Rik Van Nutter); Tall Tales and Legends, 1985-1988 (TV series; "Annie Oakley," 1985 episode: Brian Dennehy); This Is the West That Was, 1974 (made-for-TV; Matt Clark); Thundering Romance, 1924 (Jay Wilsey); Voyagers!, 1982-1983 (TV series; "Sneak Attack," 1983 episode: Ike Eisenman; "Buffalo Bill and Annie Play the Palace," 1983 episode: Robert Donner); **Wild Bill**, 1995 (Keith Carradine); The World Changes, 1933 (Douglas Dumbrille); With

Buffalo Bill on the U.P. Trail, 1926 (Roy Stewart); Wyoming, 1928 (William Fairbanks); Young Buffalo Bill, 1940 (Roy Rogers); The Young Riders, 1989-1992 (TV series; Stephen Baldwin).

Cohan, George Michael (1878-1942; U.S. composer, entertainer and producer): After the Ball, 1957 (Mark Baker); Bob Hope Presents the Chrysler Theater, 1963-1967 (TV series; "The Seven Little Foys," 1964 episode: Mickey Rooney); The Ed Sullivan Show, 1948-1971 (TV series; "Toast of the Town," 1968 episode: Joel Gray); George M!, 1970 (made-for-TV; Joel Gray); The Kraft Music Hall, 1967-1971 (TV series; "Give My Regards to Broadway," 1967 episode: Bobby Darin); Parade of Stars, 1983 (made-for-TV; David Cassidy); Producer's Showcase, 1954-1957 (TV series; "Mr. Broadway," 1957 episode: Mickey Rooney); **The Seven Little Foys**, 1955 (James Cagney); **Yankee Doodle Dandy**, 1942 (James Cagney).

Cohen, Mickey (Meyer Harris "Mickey" Cohen; 1913-1976; U.S. gangster headquartered in Los Angeles, a lieutenant of crime boss Benjamin "Bugsy" Siegel): **Bugsy**, 1991 (Harvey Keitel); Fallen Angels, 1993-1995 (TV series; "Since I Don't Have You," 1993 episode: James Woods); **Gangster Squad**, 2013 (Sean Penn); **L.A. Confidential**, 1997 (Paul Guilfoyle); Mob City, 2013- (TV series; several episodes; Jeremy Luke); The Rat Pack, 1998 (made-for-TV; Alan Woolf); Shakedown on the Sunset Strip, 1988 (made-for-TV; Harris Laskawy). Note: For detailed information on Cohen, see my book *World Encyclopedia of Organized Crime* (Paragon House, 1992; illustrated pages 106-107).

Cohn, Harry (1891-1958; U.S. movie mogul and head of Columbia Studio): RKO 281, 1999 (made-for-TV; Joseph Long); **The Godfather**, 1972 (role model for John Marley); Marilyn and Me, 1991 (made-for-TV; Thomas Wagner); Rita Hayworth: The Love Goddess, 1983 (made-for-TV; Michael Lerner); This Year's Blonde, 1980 (made-for-TV; Vic Tayback); The Three Stooges, 2000 (made-for-TV; Linal Haft); Two Hours in the Dark, 2010 (Keith Flippen).

Cohn, Roy Marcus (American attorney and chief counsel to Sen. Joseph McCarthy during the 1950s federal probes into communist activities in the U.S.; 1927-1986): Angeles in America, 2004 (made-for-TV; Donald Maxwell); Angels in America, 2003 (TV miniseries; Al Pacino); Citizen Cohn, 1992 (made-for-TV; James Woods as an adult Cohn; Brandon Danziger as young Cohn); Judgment: The Trial of Julius and Ethel Rosenberg, 1974 (made-for-TV; Harvey Jason); Onassis: The Richest Man in the World, 1988 (made-for-TV; Garrick Hagon); The Real American; Joe McCarthy, 2012 (Trystan Gravelle); Robert F. Kennedy and His Times, 1985 (TV miniseries; Joe Pantoliano); Tail Gunner Joe, 1977 (made-for-TV; George Wyner).

Coll, Vincent (aka: "Mad Dog"; 1908-1932; U.S. gangster, bootlegger and kidnapper based in NYC): Bonanno: A Godfather's Story, 1999 (made-for-TV; Matt Holland); **The Cotton Club**, 1984 (role model for Nicolas Cage); The Gangster Chronicles, 1981- (TV series; David Wilson); Hit the Dutchman, 1992 (Christopher Bradley); The Lawless Years, 1959-1961 (TV series; "The Mad Dog Coll Story," two 1961 episodes; Robert Sampson); Mad Dog Coll, 1993 (Christopher Bradley); Mobsters, 1991 (Nicolas Sadler); Portrait of a Mobster, 1960 (Joseph Gallison); **The Rise and Fall of Legs Diamond**, 1960 (Richard Gardner); The Untouchables, 1959-1963 (TV series; "Vincent 'Mad Dog' Coll," 1959 episode: Clu Gulager). Note: For detailed information on Coll, see my book *World Encyclopedia of Organized Crime* (Paragon House, 1992; illustrated [8 images] pages 107-110).

Collins, Floyd (1887-1925; pioneer cave explorer): **The Big Carnival**, 1951 (role model for Richard Benedict).

Colosimo, James (aka: Big Jim; 1878-1920; Chicago crime boss): **Al**

Capone, 1959 (Joe De Santis); **The Babe**, 1992 (Michael Nicolosi); Boardwalk Empire, 2010- (TV series; two episodes: Frank Crudele); Capone, 1975 (Frank Campanella); In Suspicious Circumstances, 1991- (TV series; "No Witnesses, No Case," 1993 episode; Peter Banks); **Little Caesar**, 1931 (role model for Stanley Fields); The Young Indiana Jones Chronicles, 1992-1993 (TV series; "Young Indiana Jones and the Mystery of the Blues," 1993 episode: Raymond Serra). Note: For detailed information on Colosimo, see my books *World Encyclopedia of Organized Crime* (Paragon House, 1992; illustrated pages 112-116); and the two-volume work *The Great Pictorial History of World Crime*, Volume I (History, Inc., 2004; illustrated pages 490-496).

Columbus, Christopher (1451-1506; Italian explorer, navigator and colonizer): Are We Civilized?, 1934 (Bert Lindley); Bye Bye Columbus, 1991 (made-for-TV; Daniel Massey); Carry on Columbus, 1992 (Jim Dale); Christopher Columbus, 1923 (Fred Eric); Christophe Columb, 1916 (Georges Wague); Christophe Columb, 1975 (made-for-TV; Victor Garrivier); **Christopher Columbus**, 1949 (Fredric March); Christopher Columbus, 1985 (TV miniseries; Gabriel Byrne); Christopher Columbus: The Discovery, 1992 (Georges Corraface); Columbus: The Lost Voyage, 2007 (made-for-TV; Olegar Federo); Cristobal Colon, 1943 (Julio Villarreal); Cristobal Colon, 1982 (Andres Pajares); Dawn of America, 1951 (Antonio Vilar); 1492: Conquest of Paradise, 1992 (Gerard Depardieu); The Glory of America, 1996 (TV miniseries; Bill Morris); Isabel, 2011- (TV series; Julio Manrique); How I Discovered America, 1949 (Erminio Macario); Juana la loca...de vez en cuando, 1983 (Juanito Navarro); The Magic Voyage, 1992 (voiceovers: Dom DeLuise, Donald Arthur, Michael Habeck); The Man with the Cloak Full of Holes, 1946 (F. Wyndham Goldie); **Night at the Museum**, 2006 (Pierfrancesco Favino); The Queen's Admiral, 1951 (made-for-TV; Joseph O'Conor); The Story of Mankind, 1957 (Anthony Dexter); True Adventures of Christopher Columbus, 1992 (TV series; Patrick Barlow); Where Do We Go from Here?, 1945 (Fortunio Bonanova).

Comstock, Anthony (1844-1915; politician and social reformer upholding the strict morality and values of the Victorian era): The American Woman: Portraits of Courage, 1976 (made-for-TV; George Rose); Choices of the Heart: The Margaret Sanger Story, 1995 (made-for-TV; Rod Steiger); The Roots of Roe, 1993 (made-for-TV; Jason Robards Jr. voiceover).

Condon, Joseph Francis (d. 1945; U.S. physician and, in 1932, the go-between with the kidnapper of Charles Lindbergh, infant son of famed aviator Charles A. Lindbergh, and who later identified the voice of that kidnapper as Bruno Richard Hauptmann as the man to whom he delivered ransom money): Crime of the Century, 1996 (made-for-TV; Bert Remsen); The Lindbergh Kidnapping Case, 1976 (made-for-TV; Joseph Cotten); Second Verdict, 1976 (TV series; "The Lindbergh Kidnapping," 1976 episode: Robert Henderson). Note: For detailed information on the Lindbergh kidnapping, see my two-volume work *The Great Pictorial History of World Crime*, Volume I (History, Inc., 2004; illustrated [34 images] pages 643-663).

Conger, Everton Judson (1834-1918; U.S. officer who helped capture John Wilkes Booth following the assassination of Abraham Lincon in 1865; became a U.S. district judge in the Montana Territory): The Lincoln Conspiracy, 1977 (Frank Schuller); You Are There, 1953-1957 (TV series; "The Capture of John Wilkes Booth," 1953 episode: DeForest Kelley).

Constantine (Constantine the Great; 272-337 A.D.; Roman emperor): Ancient Rome: The Rise and Fall of an Empire, 2006 (TV series; "Constantine," 2006 episode: David Threlfall); The Battle for Rome, 2006 (TV series; David Threlfall); **Constantine and the Cross**, 1962 (Cornel

Louis Calhern (as Buffalo Bill Cody), Betty Hutton and Howard Keel in *Annie Get Your Gun,* **1950.**

Wilde); En touto nika, 1973- (TV series; Kostas Karras).

Cook, Frederick (1865-1940; U.S. physician and explorer who claimed to have been the first person to reach the North Pole in 1908; his claims were later refuted; U.S. Navy officer and explorer Robert E. Peary is credited with that discovery in 1909): Cook and Peary: The Race to the Pole, 1983 (made-for-TV; Richard Chamberlain); The Last Place on Earth, 1985 (TV miniseries; two 1985 episdoes: Brian Dennehy).

Coolidge, Calvin (John Calvin Coolidge Jr.; 1872-1933; American politician and 30th President of the U.S.): Backstairs at the White House, 1979- (TV miniseries; three 1979 episodes: Ed Flanders); **The Court Martial of Billy Mitchell**, 1955 (Ian Wolfe); For the Greater Glory, 2012 (Bruce McGill).

Corbett, Boston (Thomas P. Corbett; 1832-1894; presumed dead; U.S. soldier who was part of the 1865 search party pursuing John Wilkes Booth (assassin of President Abraham Lincoln) and who reportedly fatally shot Booth; later judged insane and institutionalized but escaped to live as a hermit in the woods of Minnesota and reportedly died in the Great Hinckley Fire of September 1, 1894): The Hunt for Lincoln's Assassin, 2007 (Karl Bittner); Psychic History, 2005 (made-for-TV; Jeffrey F. Smith); You Are There, 1953-1957 (TV series; "The Capture of John Wilkes Booth," 1953 episode: Bing Russell). Note: For detailed information on Lincoln and his assassination, see my two-volume work, *The Great Pictorial History of World Crime*, Volume I (History, Inc., 2004; illustrated [47 images] pages 26-44).

Corbett, James John (aka: Gentleman Jim; 1866-1933; U.S. prizefighter and heavyweight champion of the world): Annie Oakley, 1954-1957 (TV series; "Annie Rings the Bell," 1956 episode; Britt Lomond); City of Bad Men, 1953 (John Daheim); Edison: The Wizard of Light, 1998 (made-for-TV; Joseph Clark); General Electric Theater, 1953-1962 (TV series; "The Return of Gentleman Jim," 1955 episode; George Montgomery); **Gentleman Jim**, 1942 (Errol Flynn); **The Great John L**, 1945 (Rory Calhoun); The Man from the Golden West, 1913 (himself); **Tom Horn**, 1980 (Steve Oliver); You Are There, 1953-1971 (TV series; "The Birth of Modern Boxing: The John L. Sullivan-James J. Corbett Battle [September 7, 1892]," 1955 episode: Pat Conway).

Corday, Charlotte (1768-1793; French patriot and assassin of Jean-Paul Marat): Charlotte Corday, 1914 (Constance Crawley); Charlotte Corday, 1919 (Lya Mara); Charlotte Corday, 2008 (made-for-TV; Emilie Dequenne); The Hourglass Sanatorium, 1973 (Jolanta Jackowska); Jean-Paul Marat, 1967 (made-for-TV; Hilkka Ostman); Liberte, egalite, choucroute, 1985 (Mimi Coutelier); **Napoleon**, 1927 (Marguerite

George Montgomery (as Davy Crockett) and Erik Rolfe in *Davy Crockett, Indian Scout,* **1950.**

Gance); Saint-Just ou La force des choses, 1975 (made-for-TV; Dominique Erlanger). Note: For detailed information on Corday and her assassination of Marat, see my two-volume work *The Great Pictorial History of World Crime*, Volume I (History, Inc., 2004; illustrated [4 images] pages 13-15).

Cornwallis, Charles (1735-1805; British general during the American Revolutionary War): Cavalcade of America, 1952-1957 (TV series; "The Absent Host," 1954 episodeV Leo Britt); George Washington, 1984 (TV miniseries; John Horton); Lafayette, 1963 (Jack Hawkins); **Janice Meredith**, 1924 (Tyrone Power Sr.); Liberty! The American Revolution, 1997 (TV miniseries; Daniel Gerroll); **The Patriot**, 2000 (Tom Wilkinson); TURN: Washington's Spies, 2014- (TV series; Jessejames Locorriere); Walt Disney's Wonderful World of Color, 1954-1992 (TV series, "The Swamp Fox: A Case of Treason," 1960 episode; "The Swamp Fox: Redcoat Strategy," 1960 episode: Robert Douglas for both); The Year of the French, 1982- (TV miniseries; Donald Bisset).

Cortes, Hernan (1485-1547; Spanish conquistador who destroyed the Aztec Empire and made most of Mexico the property of the king of Castile): **Captain from Castile**, 1947 (Cesar Romero); Carlos, Rey Emperador, 2015-2016 (TV series; Jose Luis Garcia Perez); A Day in Their Lives: Conquistador, 2001 (made-for-TV; Laurent Malaquais); The Golden Years, 1992 (made-for-TV; Robert Powell); The Other Conquest, 2000 (Inaki Aierra); Pafnucio Santo, 1977 (Jorge Humberto Robles); The Road to El Dorado, 2000 (animated; Jim Cummings voiceover); The Time Tunnel, 1966-1967 (TV series; "Idol of Death," 1967 episode: Anthony Caruso); You Are There, 1953-1971 (TV series; "The Conquest of Mexico [1519]," 1953 episode: John Baragrey).

Cosell, Howard William (Howard William Cohen; 1918-1995; sports radio and TV broadcaster): Ali, 2001 (Jon Voight); Ali: An American Hero, 2000 (made-for-TV; Earl Boen); American Brawler, 2016 (Jay Willick); **Broadway Danny Rose**, 1984 (himself); Hands of Stone, 2016 (Robb Skyler); King of the World, 2000 (made-for-TV; Darryl Cox); The Last Punch, 2016 (Ernest Orozco); Monday Night Mayhem, 2002 (made-for-TV; John Turturro); When Billie Beat Bobby, 2001 (made-for-TV; Fred Willard).

Costello, Frank (Francesco Castiglio; aka: the Prime Minister; 1891-1973; U.S. gangster and board member of the U.S. national crime syndicate): **Bugsy**, 1991 (Carmine Caridi); The Gangster Chronicles, 1981- (TV series; James Andronica); Gangster Wars, 1981 (James Andronica); Johnny Ryan, 1990 (made-for-TV; Victor Argo); Kingfish: A Story of Huey P. Long, 1995 (made-for-TV; Kirk Baltz); Lansky, 1999 (made-

for-TV; Tom La Grua); Mobsters, 1991 (Costas Mandylor); My Brother Anastasia, 1973 (Feodor Chaliapin Jr.). Note: For detailed information on Costello, see my book *World Encyclopedia of Organized Crime* (Paragon House, 1992; illustrated pages 122-125).

Cota, Norman (1893-1971; U.S. Army major-general in WWII, led troops at Omaha Beach during the Allied invasion of Normandy on June 6, 1944, in WWII): Cavalcade of America, 1952-1957 (TV series; "The Major of St. Lo," 1956 episode: Frank Gerstle); **The Longest Day**, 1962 (Robert Mitchum).

Cotten, Joseph (Joseph Cheshire Cotten Jr.; 1905-1994; U.S. actor): Malice in Wonderland, 1985 (made-for-TV; Tim Robbins); RKO 281, 1999 (made-for-TV; Angus Wright).

Coward, Noel (1899-1973; British actor and playwright): Absolutely Modern, 2013 (John Jack Rodgers); BBC2 Play of the Week, 1977- (TV series; "Exiles," 1977 episode: Ned Sherrin); Daphne, 2007 (made-for-TV; Malcolm Sinclair); Dieppe, 1993 (made-for-TV; John Mezon); Goldeneye, 1989 (made-for-TV; Julian Fellowes); Goodnight Sweetheart, 1993-1999 (TV series; David Benson); Ian Fleming: Bondmaker, 2005 (made-for-TV; Pip Torrens); Ike: The War Years, 1979 (TV miniseries; Francis Matthews); The Meaning of Life, 1983 (Eric Idle); The Sound of Spying, 2014 (John Jack Rodgers); **Star!**, 1968 (Daniel Massey); You Rang, M'Lord?, 1988-1993 (TV series; "Royal Flush," 1990 episode; Guy Siner).

Cowley, Samuel P. (1899-1934; U.S. FBI agent; killed in gunfight with bank robber Baby Face Nelson): Dillinger, 1973 (Roy Jensen); Dillinger, 1991 (made-for-TV; Joe Guzaldo); **The FBI Story**, 1959 (Bob Peoples); The Kansas City Massacre, 1975 (made-for-TV; John Karlen); Melvin Purvis: G-Man, 1974 (made-for-TV; Steve Kanaly); **Public Enemies**, 2009 (Richard Short). Note: For detailed information on Cowley and Nelson, see my eight-volume work, *Encyclopedia of World Crime*, Volume III (CrimeBooks, Inc., 1990; illustrated [9 images] pages 2301-2304).

Cnockhaert, Martha (AKA: Marthe McKenna; 1892-1966; Belgium spy for the U.K. during WWI and later the author of many spy novels): **I Was a Spy**, 1934 (Madeleine Carroll).

Crabtree, Lotta (1847-1924; U.S. actress, entertainer and comedienne): Death Valley Days, 1952-1970 (TV series; "Lotta Crabtree," 1954 episode: Gloria Jean); Golden Girl, 1951 (Mitzi Gaynor).

Cranmer, Thomas (1489-1556; British Archbishop of Canterbury, led Reformation): Anna Boleyn, 1920 (Friedrich Kuhne); BBC Sunday-Night Theatre, 1950-1959 (TV series; "The Rose without a Thorn," 1953 episode: Maurice Colbourne; "The White Falcon," 1956 episode: Marius Goring); Elizabeth R, 1971-1972 (TV miniseries; "The Lion's Club," 1971 episode: Bernard Hepton); Henry VIII, 1979 (made-for-TV; Ronald Pickup); Henry VIII, 2003 (made-for-TV; Michael Maloney); Henry VIII and His Six Wives, 1972 (Bernard Hepton); La jument du roi, 1972 (made-for-TV; Pierre Negre); A Man for All Seasons, 1957 (made-for-TV; John Wood); **A Man for All Seasons**, 1966 (Cyril Luckham); A Man for All Seasons, 1988 (made for TV; Milton Cadman); Marie Tudor, 1966 (made-for-TV; Michel Etcheverry); The Other Boleyn Girl, 2008 (Bill Wallis); The Prince and the Pauper, 1977 (Richard Hurndall); **The Private Life of Henry VIII**, 1933 (Lawrence Hanray); The Rose without a Thorn, 1947 (made-for-TV; Keith Pyott); Rose without a Thorn, 1958 (made-for-TV; Moray Powell); The Six Wives of Henry VIII, 1970 (TV miniseries; Bernard Hepton); The Six Wives of Henry VIII, 2001 (TV miniseries; Christopher Reeks); Thomas More, 1964 (made-for-TV; Franz Gary); The Tudors, 2007-2010 (TV series; Hans Matheson); Where Thunder Reigns, 2016 (Julian Cavendish); Wolf Hall, 2015 (TV miniseries; Will Keen); **Young Bess**, 1953 (Lumsden Hare).

Crawford, Joan (1904-1977; U.S. film actress, winner of the Academy Award for Best Actress for her performance in **Mildred Pierce**, 1945 and would receive two more Oscar nominations as Best Actress for performances in 1947 and 1952): **Hollywood Canteen**, 1944 (herself); **It's a Great Feeling**, 1949 (herself); Mommie Dearest, 1981 (Faye Dunaway); The Scarlett O'Hara War, 1980 (made-for-TV; Barrie Youngfellow); Spending Nights with Joan, 1998 (made-for-TV; Nadja Tiller).

Crazy Horse (c. 1840-1877; U.S. Native-America; Oglala Lakota [Sioux] war chief, who led warriors to defeat the command of Colonel George Armstrong Custer at the Battle of the Little Bighorn on June 25-26, 1876, in eastern Montana Territory): Branded, 1965-1966 (TV series; sixteen episodes: Michael Dante); **Buffalo Bill**, 1944 (Chief Thundercloud); Cheyenne, 1955-1963 (TV series; 'Gold, Glory and Custer—Requiem," 1960 episode: Keith Richards); Chief Crazy Horse, 1955 (Victor Mature); Crazy Horse, 1996 (made-for-TV; Michael Greyeyes); Custer, 1967 (TV series; sixteen episodes; Michael Dante); Custer's Last Stand, 1936 (serial; High Eagle); Fighting Pioneers, 1935 (Guate Mozin); The Great Sioux Massacre, 1965 (Iron Eyes Cody); Guestward Ho!, 1960- (TV series; "The Honorary Indian," 1961 episode: Milton Frome); Hell Town, 1985 (made-for-TV; Zitto Kazann); Incredible Rocky Mountain Race, 1977 (made-for-TV; Mike Mazurki); Into the West, 2005 (TV miniseries; Tatanka Means); The Legend of Custer, 1968 (Michael Dante); **The Outlaws Is Coming**, 1965 (Murray Alper); Overland Trail, 1960- (TV series; "Escort Detail," 1960 episode: John Marley); Sitting Bull, 1954 (Iron Eyes Cody); Son of the Morning Star, 1991 (made-for-TV; Rodney A. Grant); Stories of the Century, 1954- (TV series; "Chief Crazy Horse," 1954 episode: George Keymas); **They Died with Their Boots On**, 1941 (Anthony Quinn); The Time Tunnel, 1966-1967 (TV series; "Massacre," 1966 episode: Christopher Dark); The West, 2016 (TV miniseries; Will Strongheart); **The White Buffalo**, 1977 (Will Sampson); The Wild West, 2006- (TV series; "Custer's Last Stand," 2007 episode: Mo Brings Plenty).

Crippen, Hawley Harvey (1862-1910; American-born physician practicing in London, who murdered his wife, Cora Henrietta Crippen, for the love of another woman, Ethel Le Neve; he was executed by hanging): **The Black Bird**, 1975 (Signe Hasso); The Closer, 2005-2012 (TV series; many episodes: James Avery); Deadly Advice, 1996 (Hywel Bennett); Detective, 1964-1969 (TV series; "Crime of Passion," 1968 episode: Bernard Hepton); Dr. Crippen, 1942 (Rudolf Fernau); Dr. Crippen, 1964 (Donald Pleasence); Lady Killers, 1980-1981 (TV series; "Miss Elmore," 1981 episode: John Fraser); The Last Remake of Beau Geste, 1977 (Roland MacLeod); The Last Secret of Dr. Crippen, 2004 (Terry Francis); Shadow of the Noose, 1989- (TV series; "Sentence of Death," 1989 episode: David Hatton); **The Suspect**, 1944 (role model for Charles Laughton); Theatre Royal, 1955- (TV series; "The Case of Dr. Crippen," 1956 episode: Eric Portman); **We Are Not Alone**, 1939 (role model for Paul Muni). Note: For detailed information on Crippen, see my book *World Encyclopedia of 20th Century Murder* (Paragon House, 1992; illustrated [9 images] pages 145-152).

Crittenden, Thomas Theodore (1832-1909; U.S. politician, governor of Missouri, 1881-1885): **The Assassination of Jesse James by the Coward Robert Ford**, 2007 (James Carville); Frank and Jesse, 1995 (Jackie Stewart); The Last Days of Frank and Jesse James, 1986 (made-for-TV; Ed Evans).

Crockett, David (1786-1836; U.S. politician and frontiersman): The Adventures of Jim Bowie, 1956-1958 (TV series; "A Night in Tennessee," 1958 episode: George Dunn); **The Alamo**, 1960 (John Wayne); **The Alamo**, 2004 (Billy Bob Thornton); The Alamo: Thirteen Days to Glory, 1987 (made-for-TV; Brian Keith); Alias Jesse James, 1959 (Fess

Anthony Quinn (as Chief Crazy Horse) in *They Died with Their Boots On,* **1941.**

Parker); Davy Crockett, 1916 (Dustin Farnum); **Davy Crockett and the River Pirates**, 1956 (Fess Parker); Davy Crockett at the Fall of the Alamo, 1926 (Cullen Landis); Davy Crockett, Indian Scout, 1950 (George Montgomery); **Davy Crockett: King of the Wild Frontier**, 1955 (Fess Parker); The First Texan, 1956 (James Griffith); Heroes of the Alamo, 1937 (Lane Chandler); **The Last Command**, 1955 (Arthur Hunnicutt); **The Man from the Alamo**, 1953 (Trevor Bardette); **Man of Conquest**, 1939 (Robert Barrat); Martyrs of the Alamo, 1915 (Allan Sears); The Miracle Rider, 1935 (Bud Geary); The Painted Stallion, 1938 (Jack Perrin); Tall Tales and Legends, 1985-1988 (TV series; "Davy Crockett," 1986 episode: Mac Davis); Texas, 1994 (made-for-TV; John Schneider); Walt Disney's Wonderful World of Color, 1954-1992 (TV series; "Davy Crockett at the Alamo," 1955 episode: Fess Parker).

Cromwell, Oliver (1600-1658; British military and political leader who usurped the monarchy of Charles I, bringing about his death and becoming Lord Protector of the Commonwealth of England, Scotland and Ireland; he was executed when the Royalists took power in 1658): By the Sword Divided, 1983- (TV series; Peter Jeffrey); Cardboard Cavalier, 1949 (Edmund Willard); Carry On Laughing!, 1975- (TV series; "The Sobbing Cavalier," 1975 episode: Peter Butterworth); The Children of the New Forest, 1955- (TV series; "The Flight," 1955 episode: Warren Mitchell); Churchill's People, 1975- (TV series; "The Agreement of the People," 1975 episode: Bernard Hepton); Complete and Utter History of Britain, 1969- (TV series; "James the McFirst to Oliver Cromwell," 1969 episode: Terry Jones); **The Conqueror Worm**, 1968 (Patrick Wymark); Cromwell, 1970 (Richard Harris); The Devil's Whore, 2008- (TV series; Dominic West); The Fighting Blade, 1923 (Frederick Burton); Helter Skelter, 1949 (Bill Fraser); ITV Play of the Week, 1955-1974 (TV series; "The Killing of the King," 1959 episode: John Phillips); The Moonraker, 1958 (John Le Mesurier); Omnibus, 1967-2003 (TV series; "Paradise Restored," 1972 episode: Bernard Hepton); The Return of the Musketeers, 1989 (Alan Howard); The Royal Oak, 1923 (Henry Ainley); The Silver Swan, 1952- (TV series; "Roger," 1953 episode: Oliver Burt); The Tavern Knight, 1920 (Booth Conway); Thirty-Minute Theatre, 1965-1973 (TV series; "Revolutions: Cromwell," 1970 espisode: Leslie Sands); The Trial of the King Killers, 2005 (Ian Redford); The Vicar of Bray, 1937 (George Merritt); Woodstock, 1973- (TV series; Jerome Willis); Young Blades, 2005- (TV series; Jerry Wasserman).

Cromwell, Thomas (1485-1540; British lawyer, statesman and minister under Henry VIII; executed): **Anne of the Thousand Days**, 1969 (John Colicos); BBC Sunday-Night Theatre, 1950-1959 (TV series; "The

Jean Arthur and John Miljan (as General George Armstrong Custer) in *The Plainsman*, 1936.

White Falcon," 1956 episode: Rupert Davies); Carlos, Rey Emperador, 2015-2016 (TV series; Ferran Audi); Carry on Henry VIII, 1971 (Kenneth Williams); A Clockwork Blue, 1972 (Ed Kelly [John Vincent]); God's Outlaw, 1986 (Terrence Hardiman); Henry VIII, 1979 (made-for-TV; John Rowe); Henry VIII, 2003 (made-for-TV; Danny Webb); Henry VIII and His Six Wives, 1972 (Donald Pleasence); La jument du roi, 1972 (made-for-TV; Jacques Harden); The Madness of Henry VIII, 2006 (made-for-TV; Alexandru Georgescu); **A Man for All Seasons**, 1966 (Leo McKern); A Man for All Seasons, 1988 (made for TV; Benjamin Whitrow); The Other Boleyn Girl, 2003 (made-for-TV; Ron Cook); The Other Boleyn Girl, 2008 (Iain Mitchell); **The Private Life of Henry VIII**, 1933 (Franklin Dyall); The Six Wives of Henry VIII, 1970 (TV miniseries; Wolf Morris); The Six Wives of Henry VIII, 2001 (TV miniseries; three episodes: David Fleeshman); Thomas More, 1964 (made-for-TV; Werner Schumacher); The Tudors, 2007-2010 (TV series; James Frain); The Twisted Tale of Bloody Mary, 2008 (made-for-TV; Bertie Welland); Where Thunder Reigns, 2016 (Phil Baker); Wolf Hall, 2015 (TV miniseries; Mark Rylance).

Crook, George (1828-1890; U.S. Army officer in the American Civil War and general in the Indian wars): Chief Crazy Horse, 1955 (James Millican); Geronimo, 1962 (Lawrence Dobkin); **Geronimo: An American Legend**, 1993 (Gene Hackman); Crazy Horse, 1996 (made-for-TV; John Finn); Hondo and the Apaches, 1968 (made-for-TV; William Bryant); Indian Uprising, 1952 (Fay Roope); Mr. Horn, 1979 (made-for-TV; Jack Starrett); Taza, Son of Cochise, 1954 (Robert Burton); The Trial of Standing Bear, 1988 (made-for-TV; George Riddle).

Crowley, James Harold (aka: "Jim"; 1902-1986; American football player and coach; halfback of the famed "Four Horsemen" backfield at Notre Dame, 1922-1924): **Knute Rockne All American**, 1940 (William Bryne).

Culpepper, Thomas (1514-1541; British courtier in the reign of Henry VIII, one of the king's favorites, and reportedly the lover of Catherine Howard, Henry's fifth wife): BBC Sunday-Night Theatre, 1950-1959 (TV series; "The Rose without a Thorn," 1953 episode: Tony Britton); Henry VIII, 2003 (made-for-TV; Joseph Morgan); Henry VIII and His Six Wives, 1972 (Robin Sachs); **The Private Life of Henry VIII**, 1933 (Robert Donat); The Rose without a Thorn, 1947 (made-for-TV; John Bryning); The Six Wives of Henry VIII, 1970 (Ralph Bates); The Six Wives of Henry VIII, 2001 (TV miniseries; Sergio Corvino); The Tudors, 2007-2010 (TV series; Torrance Coombs).

Cummings, Jim (or Cummins; 1847-1929; U.S. guerrilla with Quantrill

in Civil War and member of the James-Younger outlaw gang): **The Great Missouri Raid**, 1951 (Ethan Laidlaw).

Curda, Karel (1911-1947; Czech resistance fighter who betrayed his fellow spies after they assassinated Reinhard Heydrich, Nazi governor of Czechoslovakia, in June 1942; he was given a new identity and became a Nazi spy, but was tracked down after WWII and executed for treason): Anthropoid, 2016 (Jiri Simek); Atentat, 1965 (Josef Vinklar); **Operation Daybreak**, 1975 (Martin Shaw); Operation Silver, 2007 (made-for-TV; Radim Spacek).

Curie, Marie (1867-1934; Polish-born and naturalized French physicist and chemist who discovered radium and was the first woman to receive the Nobel Prize for her pioneering research in radioactivity): Einstein, 1985- (TV miniseries; Anny Romand); **Madame Curie**, 1943 (Greer Garson); Marie Curie, 1977 (TV miniseries; Jane Lapotaire); Marie Curie, une femme honorable, 1991 (TV miniseries; Marie-Christine Barrault); Marie Curie, une femme sur le front, 2014 (made-for-TV; Dominique Reymond); The Quantum Suicide of Sophie Miller, 2013 (Clare Johnson); Race for the Bomb, 1987 (TV miniseries; Hugette Faget); You Are There, 1953-1971 (TV series; "Pierre and Marie Curie Discover Radium, January 12, 1902," 1955 episode: Jaclynne Greene); Young Einstein, 1989 (Odile Le Clezio).

Curie, Pierre (1859-1906; French physicist who, with his wife, Marie Curie, pioneered research in radioactivity and who received the Nobel Prize in 1903, along with his wife, for the discovery of radium and other achievements): **Madame Curie**, 1943 (Walter Pidgeon); Marie Curie, 1977 (TV miniseries; Nigel Hawthorne); Marie Curie, une femme honorable, 1991 (TV miniseries; Roger Van Hool); Marie Curie, une femme sur le front, 2014 (made-for-TV; Fabio Zenoni); You Are There, 1953-1971 (TV series; "Pierre and Marie Curie Discover Radium, January 12, 1902," 1955 episode: Michael Emmet).

Curtis, Charles (1860-1936; U.S. Native American [Kaw-Osage-Pottawatomie] politician and 31st vice president of the U.S.): **Jim Thorpe—All American**, 1951 (himself, newsreel footage).

Custer, Elizabeth Bacon (aka: "Libbie" 1842-1933; U.S. author and lecturer and wife of General George Armstrong Custer): Custer of the West, 1968 (Mary Ure); The Great Sioux Massacre, 1965 (Nancy Kovack); Son of the Morning Star, 1991 (made-for-TV; Rosanna Arquette); **They Died with Their Boots On**, 1942 (Olivia de Havilland).

Custer, George Armstrong (1839-1876; U.S. military officer; Union general and later Indian fighter who was killed and a large portion of his command of the 7th Cavalry wiped out at the Battle of the Little Big Horn on June 25-26, 1876, in eastern Montana Territory): Badlands of Dakota, 1941 (Addison Richards); Bob Hampton of Placer, 1921 ([T.D.] Dwight Crittenden); Britton of the Seventh, 1916 (Ned Finley); Buffalo Girls, 1995 (made-for-TV; John Diehl); Bugles in the Afternoon, 1952 (Sheb Wooley); Cheyenne, 1955-1963 (TV series; "The Broken Pledge," 1957 episode: Whit Bissell; "Glory, Gold and Custer," 1960 episode: Barry Atwater); Class of '61, 1993 (made-for-TV; Josh Lucas); The Court Martial of George Armstrong Custer, 1977 (made-for-TV; James Olson); Crazy Horse, 1996 (made-for-TV; Peter Horton); Custer, 1967 (TV series; Wayne Maunder); Custer of Big Horn, 1926 (John Beck); Custer of the West, 1968 (Robert Shaw); Dr. Quinn, Medicine Woman, 1993-1998 (TV series; several episodes: Jason Leland Adams); Don't Touch the White Woman!, 1974 (Marcello Mastroianni); The Flaming Frontier, 1926 (Dustin Farnum); **Fort Apache**, 1948 (role model for Henry Fonda); The Glory Guys, 1965 (role model for Andrew Duggan); The Great Sioux Massacre, 1965 (Philip Carey); Histeria!, 1998-2000 (animated TV series; 1998 and 2000 episodes: Rob Paulsen voiceover); Into the West, 2005 (TV miniseries; Jonathan Scarfe); Legend, 1995 (TV series; "Custer's Next to Last Stand," 1995 episode: Alex Hyde-White); The Legend of Custer, 1968 (Wayne Maunder); The Legend of the Golden Gun, 1979 (made-for-TV; Keir Dullea); The Legend of the Lone Ranger, 1981 (Lincoln Tate); **Little Big Man**, 1970 (Richard Mulligan); **Night at the Museum: Battle of the Smithsonian**, 2009 (Bill Hader); **The Plainsman**, 1936 (John Miljan); The Plainsman, 1966 (Leslie Nielsen); Sabrina, the Teenage Witch, 1996-2003 (TV series; "Present Perfect," 2003 episode: Robertson Dean); **Santa Fe Trail**, 1940 (Ronald Reagan); The Secret Adventures of Jules Verne, 2000 (TV series; "The Rocket's Red Glare," 2000 episode: Kris Holden-Ried); Sitting Bull, 1954 (Douglas Kennedy); Son of the Morning Star, 1991 (made-for-TV; Gary Cole); Stolen Women, Captured Hearts, 1997 (made-for-TV; William Shockley); **They Died with Their Boots On**, 1942 (Errol Flynn); The Time Tunnel, 1966-1967 (TV series; "Massacre," 1966 episode: Joe Maross); Tonka, 1958 (Britt Lomond); Warpath, 1951 (James Millican); The Wild West, 2006-2007 (TV series; "Custer's Last Stand," 2007 episode: Toby Stephens); The World Changes, 1933 (Clay Clement); **Wyoming**, 1940 (aka: Bad Man Paul Kelly).

Custer, Thomas Ward (1845-1876; U.S. military officer and brother of George Armstrong Custer, who was killed in the 1876 Custer Massacre): The Great Sioux Massacre, 1965 (John Napier); Son of the Morning Star, 1991 (made-for-TV; Tim Ransom).

Dali, Salvador (1904-1989; Spanish artist): The Adventures of Picasso, 1978 (Ulf von Zweigbergk); Buneul and King Solomon's Table, 2001 (Alan Enfedaque Perez); Dali, 1991 (Lorenzo Quinn); Dali, etre Dieu, 2002 (made-for-TV; Pau Quintana); El ministerio del tiempo, 2015 (TV series; Enrique Alcides); Federico Garcia Lorca Noir Despair, 2013 (Alexi Carpentieri); **Hugo**, 2011 (Ben Addis); Little Ashes, 2009 (Robert Pattison); Lives and Deaths of the Poets, 2011 (Patrick Michael Strange); Lorca, muerte de un poeta, 1987-1988 (TV series; two 1987 episodes: Fernando Lopez Veloso); **Midnight in Paris**, 2011 (Adrien Brody); Persistence of Memory, 2014 (Jason Nicola); Severo Ochoa: La conquista de un Nobel, 2001- (TV miniseries; Arturo Valls); Surrealissimo: The Scandalous Success of Salvador Dali, 2002 (made-for-TV; Ewen Bremner).

Dalton, Emmett (1871-1937; U.S. western outlaw): Beyond the Law, 1918 (himself); The Daltons Ride Again, 1945 (Alan Curtis); Death Valley Days, 1952-1970 (TV series; "Three Minutes to Eternity," 1963 episode: Tom Skerritt); Jesse James vs. the Daltons, 1954 (William Tannen); The Last Day, 1975 (made-for-TV; Tim Matheson); The Last Ride of the Dalton Gang, 1979 (made-for-TV; Larry Wilcox); Montana Belle, 1952 (Ray Teal); Outlaws, 1960-1962 (TV series; "The Daltons Must Die," two 1961 episodes: William Tennant); **Return of the Bad Men**, 1948 (Lex Barker); Stories of the Century, 1954- (TV series; "The Dalton Gang," 1954 episode: Robert Bray); Tales of Wells Fargo, 1957-1962 (TV series; "The Daltons," 1959 episode: Harry Harvey Jr.); **When the Daltons Rode**, 1940 (Frank Albertson). Note: For detailed information on Emmett Dalton, see my book *Encyclopedia of Western Lawmen and Outlaws* (Paragon House, 1992; illustrated pages 94-101).

Dalton, Frank (1860-1888; U.S. western lawman, brother to the four outlaw Daltons): Beyond the Law, 1918 (Emmett Dalton); The Dalton That Got Away, 1960 (Quintin Bulnes); The Last Ride of the Dalton Gang, 1979 (made-for-TV; Don Collier); Outlaws, 1960-1962 (TV series; "The Daltons Must Die," two 1961 episodes: Robert Lansing). Note: For detailed information on Frank Dalton, see my book, *Encyclopedia of Western Lawmen and Outlaws* (Paragon House, 1992; illustrated pages 94-101).

Dalton, Gratton (aka: Grat; 1861-1892; U.S. western outlaw): **Bad Man's Territory**, 1946 (Phil Warren); Belle Starr, 1980 (made-for-TV;

Broderick Crawford (as outlaw Bob Dalton) strikes a sheriff in *When the Daltons Rode*, 1940.

Alan Vint); Beyond the Law, 1918 (William [R.] Dunn); The Dalton That Got Away, 1960 (Zachary Milton); The Daltons Ride Again, 1945 (Lon Chaney [Jr.]); Death Valley Days, 1952-1970 (TV series; "Three Minutes to Eternity," 1963 episode: Jim Davis); Jesse James vs. the Daltons, 1954 (John Cliff); The Last Day, 1975 (made-for-TV; Richard Jaeckel); The Last Ride of the Dalton Gang, 1979 (made-for-TV; Randy Quaid); Montana Belle, 1952 (Rory Mallinson); Outlaws, 1960-1962 (TV series; "The Daltons Must Die," two 1961 episodes: Charles S. Carlson); **Return of the Bad Men**, 1948 (Michael Harvey); Stories of the Century, 1954- (TV series; "The Dalton Gang," 1954 episode: Fess Parker); **When the Daltons Rode**, 1940 (Brian Donlevy). Note: For detailed information on Gratton Dalton, see my book *Encyclopedia of Western Lawmen and Outlaws* (Paragon House, 1992; illustrated pages 94-101).

Dalton, Robert (aka: Bob; 1869-1892; U.S. western outlaw): **Bad Man's Territory**, 1946 (Steve Brodie); Belle Starr, 1980 (made-for-TV; Jesse Vint); Beyond the Law, 1918 (Emmett Dalton); The Cimarron Kid, 1952 (Noah Beery Jr.); The Dalton That Got Away, 1960 (Felix Moreno); The Daltons Ride Again, 1945 (Kent Taylor); Death Valley Days, 1952-1970 (TV series; "Three Minutes to Eternity," 1963 episode; Forrest Tucker); Jesse James vs. the Daltons, 1954 (James Griffith); The Last Day, 1975 (made-for-TV; Robert Conrad); The Last Ride of the Dalton Gang, 1979 (made-for-TV; Cliff Potts); Montana Belle, 1952 (Scott Brady); Outlaws, 1960-1962 (TV series; "The Daltons Must Die," two 1961 episodes: Larry Pennell); **Return of the Bad Men**, 1948 (Walter Reed); Stories of the Century, 1954- (TV series; "The Dalton Gang," 1954 episode: Myron Healey); Tales of Wells Fargo, 1957-1962 (TV series; "The Daltons," 1959 episode: Don Kelly); **When the Daltons Rode**, 1940 (Broderick Crawford). Note: For detailed information on Robert Dalton, see my book *Encyclopedia of Western Lawmen and Outlaws* (Paragon House, 1992; illustrated pages 94-101).

Dalton, William (aka: Bill; William Marion Dalton; 1866-1894; U.S. western outlaw): **Bad Man's Territory**, 1946 (William Moss); Jesse James vs. the Daltons, 1954 (Bill Phipps); The Last Ride of the Dalton Gang, 1979 (made-for-TV; Mills Watson); Stories of the Century, 1954- (TV series; "The Dalton Gang," 1954 episode: John Mooney). Note: For detailed information on William Dalton, see my book *Encyclopedia of Western Lawmen and Outlaws* (Paragon House, 1992; illustrated pages 94-101).

Dante (Dante Alighieri; 1265-1321; Italian poet): Dante, 2014 (Palmerio Sortino); Dante's Inferno, 1924 (Lawson Butt); Dante's Inferno, 2007 (Dermot Mulroney); Dante's Inferno, 2011 (animated; Joe Thomas

Susan Hayward and Gregory Peck (as David, King of Israel) in *David and Bathsheba*, **1951.**

voiceover); A TV Dante, 1989- (TV miniseries; Bob Peck, Francisco Reyes).

Danton, Georges-Jacques (1759-1794; French politician and a leader of the French Revolution): Arme Bitos, 1962 (made-for-TV; Leo de Hartogh); BBC Play of the Month, 1965-1983 (TV series; "Danton's Death,' 1978 episode; Norman Rodway); Captain of the Guard, 1930 (Richard Cramer); Charlotte Corday, 1914 (Henry [Harry] Griffith); Danton, 1921 (Emil Jannings); Danton, 1931 (Fritz Kortner); Danton, 1932 (Jacques Gretillat); Danton, 1983 (Gerard Depardieu); Dantons Tod, 1963 (made-for-TV; Wolfgang Reichmann); The Days That Made History, 2009- (TV series; Franck de la Personne); La camera explore le temps, 1957-1966 (TV series; two episodes in 1964; Jacques Ferriere); La mort de Danton, 1970 (made-for-TV; Georges Wilson); La revolution francaise, 1989 (Klaus Maria Brandauer); Les diamants de la victoire, 2010 (made-for-TV; Pierre Laplace); Liberte, egalite, choucroute, 1985 (Olivier de Kersauzon); Manon Roland, 1989 (made-for-TV; Niels Arestrup); **Marie Antoinette**, 1938 (Wade Crosby); **Napoleon**, 1927 (Alexandre Koubitzky); **Orphans of the Storm**, 1921 (Monte Blue); **Reign of Terror**, 1949 (Wade Crosby); Saint-Just ou La force des choses, 1975 (made-for-TV; Herve Sand); **Scaramouche**, 1923 (George Siegman); Shadow of the Guillotine, 1956 (Yves Brainville); Threatre 625, 1964-1968 (TV series; "Poor Bitos," 1965 episode; Patrick Allen); Une femme dans la revolution, 2013 (TV miniseries; Gregory Gadebois); Valmy, 1967 (made-for-TV; William Sabatier); World Theatre, 1959- (TV miniseries; "Danton's Death," 1959 episode; Patrick Wymark).

Darin, Bobby (Walden Robert Cassotto; 1936-1973; U.S. singer and actor): Beyond the Sea, 2004 (Kevin Spacey).

Darius III (380-330 B.C.; king of Persia, defeated by Alexander the Great and murdered by his cousin, Bessus, who was executed by Alexander): Alexander, 2004 (Raz Degan); Alexander; Hero of Heroes, 2007 (Tyler Ostrander); **Alexander the Great**, 1956 (Harry Andrews); Alexander the Great, 2006 (animated; Chris Coppola voiceover); BBC Sunday-Night Theatre, 1950-1959 (TV series; "Adventure Story," 1950 episode: John Gabriel); Die Perser, 1966 (made-for-TV; Adolf Peter Hoffmann); The Giant of Marathon, 1960 (Daniele Vargas); Hercules, 1998-1999 (animated TV series; Emeril Lagasse); Les perses, 1961 (made-for-TV; Rene Arrieu); Reign: The Conqueror, 1997 (animated TV series; Carlos Ferro; Koichi Yamadera); 300: Rise of an Enpire, 2014 (Igal Naor).

Darnley, Lord: see Stuart, Henry.

Darrow, Clarence (1857-1938; U.S. attorney and legendary criminal defense lawyer): Alleged, 2010 (Brian Dennehy, which reenacts Chicago's Loeb and Leopold murder case in 1924); **Anatomy of a Murder**, 1959 (role model for James Stewart who defends a U.S. Army officer in a murder case loosely based upon the 1932 Massie murder case in Hawaii, where Darrow was the defense attorney for a U.S. Navy officer accused of murder); Clarence Darrow, 1974 (made-for-TV; Henry Fonda); **Compulsion**, 1959 (role model for Orson Welles, the attorney defending two wealthy young thrill killers based upon Chicago's Loeb and Leopold murder case in 1924); Darrow, 1991 (made-for-TV; Kevin Spacey); Freedom to Speak, 1982- (TV miniseries; Mason Adams); G.E. True, 1962 (TV series; "Defendant Clarence Darrow," 1963 episode: Tol Avery); God in America, 2010- (TV series; Richard Easton); **Inherit the Wind**, 1960 (role model for Spencer Tracy, which is based on Tennessee's sensational 1925 "Monkey Trial"); Swoon, 1992 (Robert Read, which reenacts Chicago's Loeb and Leopold murder case in 1924); TV Reader's Digest, 1955-1956 (TV series; "The Sad Death of a Hero," 1955: Carl Benton Reid). Note: For detailed information on Darrow, see the eight-volume *Encyclopedia of World Crime*, Volume II (Crime-Books, Inc., 1990; illustrated [18 images] pages 872-877); *World Encyclopedia of 20th Century Murder* (Paragon House, 1992; Leopold and Loeb: illustrated [12 images] pages 353-362; Thomas Massie: illustrated [8 images] pages 395-399; and the two-volume work, *The Great Pictorial History of World Crime* (History, Inc., 2004; Leopold and Loeb; illustrated [30 images] 840-857 pages; Thomas Massie: illustrated [12 images] 867-873 pages).

Darwin, Charles (1809-1882; British naturalist and geologist famed for his theory of evolution): BBC Sunday-Night Play, 1960-1963 (TV series; "Fury in Petticoats," 1961 episode: Peter Barkworth); Creation, 2010 (Paul Bettany); The Darwin Adventure, 1972 (Nicholas Clay); Darwin's Daughter, 2002 (made-for-TV; Pip Torrens); The Voyage of Charles Darwin, 1978- (TV series; Malcolm Stoddard); Young Einstein, 1989 (Basil Clarke).

Dathan (Israelite leader in the Old Testament): **The Ten Commandments**, 1923 (Lawson Butt); **The Ten Commandments**, 1956 (Edward G. Robinson); The Ten Commandments, 2007 (Lee Tockar voiceover).

Daugherty, Harry M. (Harry Micajah Daugherty; 1860-1941; U.S. politician and kingmaker; 51st U.S. Attorney General): Boardwalk Empire, 2010- (TV series; seven episodes: Christopher McDonald); J. Edgar Hoover, 1987 (made-for-TV; Paul Kent).

David (1040 B.C.-970 B.C.; King of Judah and Israel): Absolon, 1986 (made-for-TV; Augusto Benedico); And David Wept, 1971 (made-for-TV; Sherrill Milnes); Animated Stories from the Bible, 1987-2005 (TV series; "Solomon," 1995 episode: Ray Porter voiceover as young King David; Sandy McCullum voiceover as old King David); The Cradle of God, 1926 (Lucien Dalsace); David, 1997 (made-for-TV; Nathaniel Parker; Gideon Turner as young David); **David and Bathsheba**, 1951 (Gregory Peck; Leo B. Pessin as young David); David and Goliath, 1960 (Ivica Pajer); David & Goliath, 2005 (Spencer Forsey); David and Goliath, 2015 (Miles Sloman); General Electric Theater, 1953-1962 (TV series; "Absolom, My Son," 1959 episode: Burl Ives; "The Stone," 1959 episode: Tony Curtis); Greatest Heroes of the Bible, 1978- (TV series; "The Judgment of Solomon," 1978 episode: John Carradine; "David and Goliath," 1978 episode: Roger Kern); King David, 1985 (Richard Gere; Ian Sears as young David); Koning David, 1965 (made-for-TV; Johan Schmitz); The Queen of Sheba, 1921 (George Nichols); Saul e David, 1968 (Gianni Garko; Marco Paoletti as young David); The Shepherd King, 1923 (Nerio Bernardi); Solomon, 2000 (made-for-TV; Max von Sydow); **Solomon and Sheba**, 1959 (Finlay Currie); Son of God, 2014 (Jassa Ahluwalia as young David; Langley Kirkwood as King David); The Story of David, 1976 (made-for-TV; Timothy Bottoms); A

Story of David: The Hunted, 1962 (Jeff Chandler); Testament: The Bible in Animation, 1996 (TV series; Paul McGann voiceover).

DaVinci, Leonardo (1452-1519; Italian Renaissance sculptor, painter, inventor, architect, mathematician, engineer and writer): The Age of Man, 2007 (Roman Duris); Behold the Man, 1949 (made-for-TV; Mark Didnam); Borgia, 2011- (TV series; Paul Rhys); The Borgias, 1981- (TV miniseries; Malcolm Hayes); Captain Z-Ro, 1955- (TV series; "Leonardo DaVinci," 1956 episode: Sydney Walker); Carlos, Rey Emperador, 2015-2016 (TV series; Carlos Alvarez-Novoa); Da Vinci's Demons, 2013-2015 (TV series; Tom Riley); History of the World: Part I, 1981 (Art Metrano); Leonardo, 2003 (made-for-TV; Mark Rylance); Leonardo, 2011- (TV series; Jonathan Bailey); Leonardo: A Dream of Flight, 1998 (made-for-TV; Brent Carver); Les Borgia ou Le sang dore, 1977 (made-for-TV; Henri Serre); The Life of Leonardo DaVinci, 1971- (TV series; Philippe Leroy as adult Leonardo; Alberto Fiorini as young Leonardo; Renato Cestie as Leonardo at age six; Marco Mazzoni as Leonardo at age five); Man, Moment, Machine, 2005-2007 (TV series; "DaVinci and the Handgun," 2006 episode: Stephan Smith Collins); **Mr. Peabody & Sherman**, 2014 (Stanley Tucci); A Season of Giants, 1990 (made-for-TV; John Glover); Sword of Freedom, 1957- (TV series; two 1957 episodes with Andrew Keir as DaVinci; one 1957 episode with Edward Atienza as DaVinci); Witness to Yesterday, 1970- (TV series; "Leonardo da Vinci," 1974 episode: Patrick Watson).

Davies, Marion (1897-1961; U.S. film actress and mistress of media magnate William Randolph Hearst): **The Cat's Meow**, 2002 (Kirsten Dunst); Cradle Will Rock, 1999 (Gretchen Mol); The Hearst and Davies Affair, 1985 (made-for-TV; Virginia Madsen); RKO 281, 1999 (made-for-TV; Melanie Griffith); Winston Churchill: The Wilderness Years, 1981- (TV miniseries; "Down and Out," 1981 episode: Merrie Lynn Ross).

Davis, David (1815-1886; U.S. politician and Associate Justice of the U.S. Supreme Court; a close friend of President Abraham Lincoln): Lincoln, 1974-1975 (TV series; Richard Dysart); **Saving Lincoln**, 2013 (Joe Ochman).

Davis, Howell (c. 1690-1719; Welsh pirate operating in the Caribbean Sea and Atlantic Ocean): True Caribbean Pirates, 2006 (made-for-TV; Andrew Simpson). Note: For detailed information on Davis, see my two-volume work, *The Great Pictorial History of World Crime*, Volume II (History, Inc., 2004; illustrated page 1296).

Davis, Jefferson (U.S. politician and first and only President of the Confederacy during the American Civil War; 1808-1889): Abrham Lincoln: Vampire Hunter, 2012 (John Rothman); The Adventures of Jim Bowie, 1956-1958 (TV series; "The Brothers," 1958 episode: Charles McArthur); C.S.A.: Confederate States of America, 2004 (Brian Paulette); Carolina, 1934 (Roy Watson); Cavalcade of America, 1952-1957 (TV series; "What Might Have Been," 1953 episode: Ross Ford); The Civil War, 1990 (TV miniseries; Horton Foote voiceover); The Great Adventure, 1963-1964 (TV series; "The Treasure Train of Jefferson Davis," 1963 episode: Michael Rennie); The Great John Ericsson, 1938 (John Hilke); The Heart of Maryland, 1927 (Francis Ford); Hearts in Bondage, 1936 (Erville Alderson); Lost River: Lincoln's Secret Weapon, 2009 (Gregory Sweet); North and South, Book II, 1986 (TV miniseries; Lloyd Bridges); The Rebel, 1959-1961 (TV series; "Mission—Varina," 1961 episode: Richard Gaines); **Santa Fe Trail**, 1940 (Erville Alderson); A Special Friendship, 1987 (made-for-TV; Tom Aldredge); **Tennessee Johnson**, 1942 (Morris Ankrum); **Virginia City**, 1940 (Charles Middleton); You Are There, 1953-1957 (TV series; "The Gettysburg Address," 1953 episode: Joseph Vance).

Davis, Miles (1926-1991; U.S. jazz musician): **Miles Ahead**, 2015 (Don

Kirsten Dunst (as Marion Davies) in *The Cat's Meow*, 2002.

Cheadle).

Davis, Richard Harding (U.S. journalist and author; 1864-1916): **Jack London**, 1943 (Morgan Conway); The Spanish-American War: First Intervention, 2007 (made-for-TV; Mike Agresta).

Davis, Varina (Varina Banks Howell Davis; 1826-1906; wife of Jefferson Davis, first and only President of the Confederate States of America): C.S.A.: Confederate States of America, 2004 (Lauralei Linzay); The Great Adventure, 1963-1964 (TV series; "The Treasure Train of Jefferson Davis," 1963 episode: Katharine Bard); The Rebel, 1959-1961 (TV series; "Mission—Varina," 1961 episode: Frieda Inescort); A Special Friendship, 1987 (made-for-TV; Patricia Elliott).

De Bono, Emilio (1866-1944; Italian fascist leader and marshal, strong supporter of Italian dictator Benito Mussolini, until usurping him with others and for which he was executed): Mussolini: The Untold Story, 1985 (TV miniseries; George Coulouris).

De Choiseul-Praslin, Charles (1804-1847; French duke who murdered his wife, Francoise, duchess de Choiseul-Praslin over his love for family governess, Henriette Deluzy-Desportes; he poisoned himself to death while facing a murder trial): **All This and Heaven Too**, 1940 (Charles Boyer). Note: For detailed information on the Duke de Praslin, see my two-volume work *The Great Pictorial History of World Crime*, Volume II (History, Inc., illustrated [8 images] pages 803-807).

De Choiseul-Praslin, Fanny (French duchess and murder victim; d. 1847): **All This and Heaven Too**, 1940 (Barbara O'Neil). Note: For detailed information on the De Praslin case, see my two-volume work, *The Great Pictorial History of World Crime*, Volume II (History, Inc., 2004; illustrated [8 images] pages 802-807).

De Gaulle, Charles (1890-1970; French general during WWII and President of France): Accuse Mendes France, 2011 (made-for-TV; Didier Raymond); The Army of Shadows, 2006 (Adrien Cayla-Legrand); Churchill and the Generals, 1979 (made-for-TV; Jacques Boudet); **The Day of the Jackal**, 1973 (Adrien Cayla-Legrand); The Days That Made History, 2009- (TV series; Michel Vuillermoz); De Gaulle, 2006- (TV series; Bernard Farcy); The Escape, 1978 (Adrien Cayla-Legrand); Farewell De Gaulle, Farewell, 2009 (made-for-TV; Pierre Vernier); Francis Gary Powers: The True Story of the U-2 Spy Incident, 1976 (made-for-TV; Marcel Hillaire); Grace of Monaco, 2014 (Andre Penvern); I Have Understood You: De Gaulle 1958-1962, 2010 (Patrick Chesnais); Ike: Countdown to D-Day, 2004 (made-for-TV; George

Hedy Lamarr (as Delilah) and George Sanders in *Samson and Delilah*, 1949.

Shevtsov); Ike: The War Years, 1979 (TV miniseries; Vernon Dobtcheff); Jackie Bouvier Kennedy Onassis, 2000 (made-for-TV; Marcel Sabourin); Jacqueline Bouvier Kennedy, 1981 (made-for-TV; Maurice Marsac); Jean Moulin, une affaire francaise, 2003 (made-for-TV; Jacques Boudet); Kiss Me General, 1966 (Adrien Cayla-Legrand); La guerre du royal palace, 2012 (made-for-TV; Didier Raymond); La resistance, 2008- (TV miniseries; Francois Clavier); Le bourreau des coeurs, 1983 (Adrien Cayla-Legrand); Le general a disparu, 1983 (made-for-TV; Georges Audoubert); The Missiles of October, 1974 (made-for-TV; Ron Feinberg); Moi, general de Gaulle, 1990 (made-for-TV; Henri Serre); Petain, 1993 (Pascal Brunner); Pierre Brossolette ou les passagers de la lune, 2015 (made-for-TV; Bernard Alane); Pope John XXIII, 2002 (made-for-TV; Pavel Popandov); The World Wars, 2014- (TV miniseries; Michael Perrie Jr.).

De Lesseps, Ferdinand (1804-1894; French diplomat and developer of the Suez Canal): Eugenia de Montijo, 1944 (Manuel Soto); L'homme de Suez, 1983 (TV miniseries; Guy Marchand); **Suez**, 1938 (Tyrone Power).

Dean, Jerome Herman (Jay Hanna Dean; AKA: "Dizzy Dean"; 1910-1974; American baseball player and pitcher): **The Pride of St. Louis**, 1952 (Dan Dailey).

Dean, John (John Wesley Dean III; American attorney and White House Counsel to U.S. President Richard M. Nixon; 1938-): Blind Ambition, 1979 (TV miniseries; Martin Sheen); Dick, 1999 (Jim Breuer); The Final Days, 1989 (made-for-TV; Gregg Henry); **Nixon**, 1995 (David Hyde Pierce); Will: The Autobiography of G. Gordon Liddy, 1982 (made-for-TV; Peter Retray).

Decatur, Stephen (U.S. naval officer; commodore who established the first U.S. Navy after defeating the Barbary pirates; ardent patriot known for his boast: "My country right or wrong!"; killed in a duel; 1779-1820): Haunted History, 1999- (TV series; "Washington," 1999 episode: Kryztov Lindquist); My Own United States, 1918 (Fred Herzog); You Are There, 1953-1971 (TV series; "Decatur's Raid at Tripoli [February 16, 1894])," 1956 episode: John Baer).

Dee, Sandra (1942-2005; U.S. actress): Beyond the Sea, 2004 (Kate Bosworth).

Degas, Edgar (1834-1917; French artist): Degas and the Dancer, 1999 (made-for-TV; Thomas Jay Ryan); Gauguin the Savage, 1980 (made-for-TV; Ian Richardson); Great Performances, 1971- (TV series; "Degas

and the Dance," 2004 episode: Brian Bedford; Peter Badger); The Impressionists, 2006- (TV miniseries; Aden Gillett); Lautrec, 1999 (Victor Garrivier); Mary Cassatt: An American Impressionist, 1999 (made-for-TV; Thomas Jay Ryan); Mas alla del color: La vida de Gauguin y Degas, 1958- (TV miniseries; Estaban Serrador); **Midnight in Paris**, 2011 (Francois Rostain); Oviri, 1986 (Yves Barsacq); The Phantom of the Opera, 1999 (Ferenc Deak B.).

Delilah (In the Bible, a Philistine woman of great beauty who betrayed Israeli strongman Samson for money): The Cradle of God, 1926 (Musidora); Greatest Heroes of the Bible, 1978- (TV series; "Samson and Delilah," 1978 episode: Ann Turkel); Hercules, Samson & Ulysses, 1965 (Liana Orfei); Samson, 1914 (Kathleen Kerrigan); **Samson and Delilah**, 1949 (Hedy Lamarr); Samson and Delilah, 1984 (made-for-TV; Belinda Bauer); Samson and Delilah, 1987 (Suzzanna); Samson and Delilah, 1996 (made-for-TV; Elizabeth Hurley); Samson and Delilah, 2007 (Klara Uleman); Samson and Delilah, 2008 (Olga Borodino); Samson & Delilah, 2009 (Marissa Gibson); Samson et Delila, 1981 (made-for-TV; Shirley Verrett); Samson et Delila, 2002 (made-for-TV; Olga Borodino); Samson und Delila, 1922 (Maria Corda).

Delmas, Delphin Michael (1844-1928; flamboyant California criminal defense attorney best noted for his defense of Harry Kendall Thaw, a multi-millionaire, who shot and killed famed NYC architect Stanford White in 1906 in front of horrified spectators at the rooftop theater of NYC's Madison Square Garden, ostensibly over his jealousy of White's former association with his wife, former showgirl Evelyn Nesbit): **The Girl in the Red Velvet Swing**, 1955 (Luther Adler); **Ragtime**, 1981 (Pat O'Brien). Note: For detailed information on Delmas and his defense of Thaw, see my two-volume work *The Great Pictorial History of World Crime*, Volume II (History, Inc., 2004; illustrated [17 images] pages 819-826).

Delorme, Marion (1613-1650; French courtesan who had affairs with many notable men, including Cinq-Mars): The Captain, 1946 (Sophie Desmarets); Cinq-Mars, 1981 (made-for-TV; Elisabeth Margoni); Cyrano et d'Artagnan, 1964 (Dahlia Lavi [Daliah Lavi]); Le camera explore le temps, 1957-1966 (TV series, "La conjuration de Cinq-Mars," 1962 episode: Nadine Alari); Le prix de l'honneur, 2003 (made-for-TV; Alexandra Vandernoot); The Man Who Sold Himself, 1925 (Vivian Gibson); Marion Delorme, 1967 (made-for-TV; Francoise Fabian); My Leopold, 1955 (Rita Paul); Revient le jour, 1999 (made-for-TV; Marie Ravel); Richelieu, 1914 (Edna Maison).

Deluzy-Desportes, Henriette (aka: Henrietta Field; 1813-1875; French governess and lover of Charles de Choiseul-Praslin, over which the duke murdered his wife in 1847; she left France and relocated in the U.S.): **All This and Heaven Too**, 1940 (Bette Davis). Note: For detailed information on the Deluzy-Desportes and De Praslin case, see my two-volume work *The Great Pictorial History of World Crime*, Volume II (History, Inc., 2004; illustrated [8 images] pages 802-807).

Dempsey, Jack (U.S. prizefighter and World Heavyweight Champion, 1919-1926; 1895-1983): Boardwalk Empire, 2010- (TV series: two episodes: Devin Harjes); Dempsey, 1983 (made-for-TV; Treat Williams); Joe and Max, 2002 (made-for-TV; Daniel Hugh Kelly); Mr. Broadway, 1933 (himself); Off Limits, 1953 (himself); Sweet Surrender, 1935 (himself).

DeSylva, George Gard (aka: Buddy; 1895-1950; U.S. composer, film producer and record executive): The Best Things in Life Are Free, 1956 (Gordon MacRae); **Rhapsody in Blue**, 1945 (Eddie Marr).

Devereux, Robert (or Devereaux; 1565-1601; English nobleman; 2nd

Earl of Essex; lover of Elizabeth I, who attempted to seize the throne and was executed for treason): Elizabeth R, 1971-1972 (TV miniseries; two episodes: Robin Ellis); Elizabeth the Queen, 1968 (made-for-TV; Charlton Heston); Gloriana, 1984 (made-for-TV; Anthony Rolfe-Johnson); Gloriana, 2000 (made-for-TV; Tom Randle); ITV Play of the Week, 1955-1974 (TV series; "In the Shadow of the Axe," 1958 episode: Laurence Payne); **The Private Lives of Elizabeth and Essex**, 1939 (Errol Flynn); Roberto Devereux, 1997 (made-for-TV; Giuseppe Sabbatini); Queen Elizabeth, 1912 (Lou Tellegen); The Virgin Queen, 2005 (TV miniseries; Hans Matheson).

Dew, Walter (1863-1947; British police inspector for the London Metropolitan Police, who investigated the Jack the Ripper murders of 1888 and who apprehended notorious wife killer Dr. Hawley Harvey Crippen in 1910): Detective, 1964-1969 (TV series; "Crime of Passion," 1968 episode: Glynn Edwards); Dr. Crippen, 1942 (Rene Deltgen); Dr. Crippen, 1964 (John Arnatt); Lady Killers, 1980-1981 (TV series; "Miss Elmore," 1981 episode: Alan Downer); The Last Secret of Dr. Crippen, 2004 (David Broughton Davis); **The Suspect**, 1944 (role model for Stanley Ridges); Theatre Royal, 1955- (TV series; "The Case of Dr. Crippen," 1956 episode: Philip Lennard). Note: For detailed information on Dew and the Crippen case, see my book *World Encyclopedia of 20th Century Murder* (Paragon House, 1992; illustrated [9 images] pages 145-152).

Dewey, George (U.S. admiral; 1837-1917): **The Battle Cry of Peace**, 1915 (himself in archive footage); **This Is My Affair**, 1937 (Robert McWade).

Diamond, Jack (AKA: Legs; 1897-1931; U.S. racketeer and bootlegger based in NYC): Gangster Wars, 1981 (Robert F. Lyons); Hit the Dutchman, 1992 (Will Kempe); The Lawless Years, 1959-1961 (TV series; Robert Ellenstein; Charles Cooper); Mad Dog Coll, 1993 (Will Kempe); **Murder, Inc.**, 1960 (Richard Everhart); The Outfit, 1993 (Josh Mosby); Portrait of a Mobster, 1960 (Ray Danton); **The Rise and Fall of Legs Diamond**, 1960 (Ray Danton); The Untouchables, 1959-1963 (TV series; Steven Hill). Note: For detailed information on Diamond, see my book *World Encyclopedia of Organized Crime* (Paragon House, 1992; illustrated [11 images] pages 134-139).

Diaz, Porfirio (1830-1915; Mexican patriot, revolutionary and dictator): Aquellos anos, 1974 (Alfredo Torres); Azahares para tu boda, 1950 (Antonio R. Frausto); Bodas de odio, 1983 (TV series; Jose Luis Padilla); Cananea, 1978 (Victor Junco); Cinco de Mayo: La Battala, 2013 (Pascacio Lopez); Cuartelazo, 1977 (Carlos Castanon); El carruaje, 1972 (TV series; Salvador Sanchez); El carruaje, 1972 (TV series; Salvador Sanchez); El encanto del aguila, 2011 (Ignacio Lopez Tarso); El vuelo del aguila, 1994 (TV series; Manuel Ojeda, Humberto Zurita, Fabian Robles); **Juarez**, 1939 (John Garfield); Juarez and Maximillian, 1935 (Antonio R. Frausto); The Kaiser, the Beast of Berlin, 1918 (Pedro Sose); La Constitucion, 1970 (TV series; Miguel Manzano); The Land of Refuge, 2008 (Walter Flores); The Mad Empress, 1939 (Earl Gunn); Mexikanische Revolution, 1968 (made-for-TV; Ernst Fritz Furbringer); My Memories of Mexico, 1944 (Antonio R. Frausto); Over the Waves, 1950 (Antonio R. Frausto); Toda una vida, 1981 (TV series; Jose Luis Padilla); **Viva Zapata!**, 1952 (Fay Roope); Zapata—El sueno del hero, 2004 (Justo Martinez).

Dickens, Charles (1812-1870; British writer and social critic): American Playhouse, 1981- (TV series; "Any Friend of Nicholas Nickleby Is a Friend of Mine," 1982 episode: Fred Gwynne); An Audience with Charles Dickens, 1996 (made-for-TV; Simon Callow); Bonanza, 1959-1973 (TV series; "A Passion for Justice," 1963 episode: Jonathan Harris); The CBS Festival of Lively Arts for Young People, 1973-1981 (TV series; "The Secret of Charles Dickens," 1978 episode: Alan Badel);

Lawrence Tierney (as Dillinger) being shot to death in Chicago, 1934, in *Dillinger*, 1945.

Charles Dickens' World of Christmas, 1974 (made-for-TV; Stephen Murray); A Christmas Carol, 1982 (made-for-TV; Marshall Borden); Christmas Carol: The Movie, 2001 (animated; Simon Callow voiceover); A Christmas Carol, 2013 (Laurence Foster); A Christmas Carol, 2015 (Colin Baker); Desperate Romantics, 2009- (TV series; Mark Heap); Devotion, 1946 (Reginald Sheffield); Dickens, 2002- (TV series; Anton Lesser); Dickens of London, 1976 (TV miniseries; Roy Dotrice); Dicky Monteith, 1922 (Kenelm Foss); Early Travellers in North America, 1992 (TV series; four 1992 episodes: Adrian Rawlins); Fireside Theatre, 1949-1955 (TV series; "A Christmas Carol," 1951 episode; Alan Napier); Goodyear Theatre, 1957-1960 (TV series; "Lost and Found," 1957 episode: Jack Lemmon); The Great Inimitable Mr. Dickens, 1970 (made-for-TV; Anthony Hopkins); Hans Christian Andersen: My Life as a Fairy Tale, 2003 (made-for-TV; Simon Callow); The Hero of My Life, 1970 (made-for-TV; Michael Jayston); The Invisible Woman, 2013 (Ralph Fiennes); London, 2004 (made-for-TV; Anton Lesser); The Loves of Edgar Allan Poe, 1942 (Morton Lowry); The Magic of Charles Dickens, 1967 (made-for-TV; Emlyn Williams); Mr. Dickens of London, 1967 (made-for-TV; Michael Redgrave); Mr. H.C. Andersen, 1950 (Edward Sullivan); Mysteries at the Castle, 2014- (TV series; "Irish Heist; Dickens Affair; Prince of Porcelain," 2015 episode: Jonathan Mastrojohn); The Mystery of Charles Dickens, 2000 (made-for-TV; Simon Callow); The Night before Christmas Carol, 2010 (made-for-TV; David Zum Brunnen); Oliver Twist, 1916 (W.S. Van Dyke); Omnibus, 1952-1961 (TV series; "A Tale of Two Cities," 1953 episode: Joseph Schildkraut); Once upon a Time, 1918 (Kenelm Foss); Theatre Box, 1981- (TV series; "You Must Believe All This," 1981 episode; Patrick Malahide); Voyagers!, 1982-1983 (TV series; "The Day the Rebs Took Lincoln," 1982 episode: Alex Hyde-White); What the Dickens!, 1983 (made-for-TV; Ben Cross).

Dietrich, Marlene (1901-1992; German-U.S. film actress): Adolf and Marlene, 1977 (Margit Carstensen); Edith es Marlene, 1992 (made-for-TV; Judit Hernadi); **La Vie en Rose**, 2007 (Caroline Silhol); Marlene, 2000 (Katja Flint); Piaf, 2010 (made-for-TV; Paula Sá),

Dillinger, John Herbert (U.S. bank robber and Public Enemy Number One, reportedly killed outside a movie theater in Chicago on July 22, 1934, by FBI agents led by Melvin Purvis; 1903-1934?): Baby Face Nelson, 1957 (Leo Gordon); Baby Face Nelson, 1996 (Martin Kove); Dillinger, 1945 (Lawrence Tierney); Dillinger, 1973 (Warren Oates); Dillinger and Capone, 1995 (Martin Sheen); **The FBI Story**, 1959 (Scott Peters); Guns Don't Argue, 1957 (Myron Healey); The Kansas City Massacre, 1975 (made-for-TV; William Jordan); The Lady in Red, 1979 (Robert Conrad); **The Private Files of J. Edgar Hoover**, 1977

Alec Baldwin (as Jimmy Doolittle) in *Pearl Harbor*, 2001.

(Reno Carrel); **Public Enemies**, 2009 (Johnny Depp); **Young Dillinger**, 1965 (Nick Adams). Note: For detailed information on Dillinger, see my books *Dillinger: Dead or Alive?*, 1970 (Regnery, 1970) and *The Dillinger Dossier* (December Press, 1983); and my two-volume work *The Great Pictorial History of World Crime*, Volume II (History, Inc., 2004; illustrated [63 images] pages 1374-1423).

Disraeli, Benjamin (1804-1881; first Earl of Beaconsfield; British statesman and prime minister of the United Kingdom, 1874-1880): Disraeli, 1918 (Dennis Eadie); **Disraeli**, 1929 (George Arliss); Disraeli: Portrait of a Romantic, 1978 (TV miniseries; Ian McShane); Edward the King, 1975- (TV series; John Gielgud); The Edwardians, 1972 (TV miniseries; Vernon Dobtcheff); The Ghosts of Berkeley Square, 1947 (Abraham Sofaer); Happy and Glorious, 1952- (TV series; Ernest Milton); **Her Majesty, Mrs. Brown**, 1997 (Antony Sher); Heroes of Shipka, 1956 (Vladmir Taskin); Invincible Mr. Disraeli, 1963 (made-for-TV; Trevor Howard); Jennie: Lady Randolph Churchill, 1974 (TV miniseries; Patrick Troughton); Lillie, 1978 (TV miniseries; John Gabriel); Meet Me at the Fair, 1953 (Robert Shafto); Mr. Gladstone, 1947 (made-for-TV; Sydney Tafler); **The Mudlark**, 1950 (Alec Guinness); Network First: Victoria and Albert, 1997- (TV miniseries; Michael Culver); Number 10, 1983- (TV miniseries; Richard Pasco); The Prime Minister, 1942 (John Gielgud); Queen of Destiny, 1940 (Derrick De Marney); Queen Victoria's Empire, 2001- (TV series; Elliot Levey); Robert Montgomery Presents, 1950-1957 (TV series; "Victoria Regina," 1951 episode: Robert Harris); **Suez**, 1938 (Miles Mander); Victoria Regina, 1961 (made-for TV; Basil Rathbone); Victoria Regina, 1964 (TV miniseries; Max Adrian); **Victoria the Great**, 1937 (Hugh Miller; Derrick De Marney as young Disraeli).

Donovan, James B. (James Britt Donovan, 1916-1970; U.S. attorney and political negotiator who arranged for the exchanging of KGB colonel and spymaster Rudolf Abel, who was operating in the U.S., captured by the FBI in 1957, and imprisoned, and Gary Francis Powers, 1929-1977, pilot of the CIA U-2 spy plane, which was shot down by the Soviets on May 1, 1960, by one of eight ground-to-air missiles, on February 10, 1962, the dramatic exchange taking place at the Glienicke Bridge in Berlin, Germany, on February 10, 1962; U.S. student Frederic Pryor was also exchanged at a separate Berlin checkpoint): **Bridge of Spies**, 2015 (Tom Hanks); Francis Gary Powers: The True Story of the U-2 Spy Incident, 1976 (made-for-TV; James Gregory).

Donovan, William J. (aka: Wild Bill; 1883-1959; U.S. soldier; major in U.S. Army in WWI, the only person to receive U.S. highest awards: Congressional Medal of Honor, Distinguished Service Cross, Distinguished Service Medal, and National Security Medal; also awarded the Silver Star and the Purple Heart; became the chief of OSS [Office of Strategic Services] in WWII, the precursor of the CIA, and is considered to be the "Father of American Intelligence"): **The Fighting 69th**, 1939 (George Brent). Note: For detailed information on Donovan, see my book *Spies: A Narrative Encyclopedia of Dirty Tricks & Double Dealing from Biblical Times to Today* (M. Evans, 1997; illustrated pages 183-188).

Doolin, William (aka: "Bill"; 1858-1896; U.S. western outlaw): **Bad Man's Territory**, 1946 (Carl Eric Hansen); The Cimarron Kid, 1952 (Audie Murphy); Death Valley Days, 1952-1970 (TV series; "Three Minutes to Eternity," 1963 episode: Lew Brown); **The Doolins of Oklahoma**, 1949 (Randolph Scott); The Last Ride of the Dalton Gang, 1979 (made-for-TV; Bo Hopkins); **Return of the Bad Men**, 1948 (Robert Armstrong). Note: For detailed information on Doolin, see my book *Encyclopedia of Western Lawmen and Outlaws* (Paragon House, 1992; illustrated pages 106-107).

Doolittle, James Harold (aka: Jimmy; 1896-1993; U.S. aviation pioneer and U.S. Army Air Force major general, who led the celebrated Doolittle Raid against Tokyo and other Japanese cities on April 18, 1942, in retaliation for the Japanese sneak attack at Pearl Harbor on December 7, 1941): Pancho Barnes, 1988 (made-for-TV; Vince Davis); **Pearl Harbor**, 2001 (Alec Baldwin); **Thirty Seconds over Tokyo**, 1944 (Spencer Tracy).

Dorsey, Hugh Manson (1871-1948; U.S. attorney, prosecutor in the 1913 Leo Frank murder trial and 62nd governor of Georgia): The Murder of Mary Phagan, 1988 (TV miniseries; Richard Jordan); The People v. Leo Frank, 2009 (Steve Coulter); **They Won't Forget**, 1937 (role model for Claude Rains). Note: For detailed information on Dorsey and the Leo Frank case, see my book *"I Am Innocent!": A Comprehensive Encyclopedic History of the World's Wrongly Convicted Persons* (Da Capo Press, 2008; illustrated [10 images] pages 315-329).

Douglas, Stephen (1813-1861; Stephen Arnold Douglas; U.S. politician and U.S. senator from Illinois, 1847-1861): **Abe Lincoln in Illinois**, 1940 (Gene Lockhart); Abe Lincoln in Illinois, 1964 (made-for-TV; Jack Bittner); **Abraham Lincoln**, 1930 (E. Alyn Warren); The Dramatic Life of Abraham Lincoln, 1924 (William Humphrey); Lincoln, 1988 (made-for-TV; Robin Gammell); Lincoln: American Mastermind, 2009 (made-for-TV; James Miller); The 20th Century Fox Hour, 1955-1957 (TV series; "Springfield Incident," 1957 episode: Walter Coy); **Young Mr. Lincoln**, 1939 (Milburn Stone).

Douglas, Thomas Clement (aka: "Tommy"; 1904-1986; Canadian politician and Baptist minister): Prairie Giant: The Tommy Douglas Story, 2006 (TV miniseries; Michael Thierriault); Trudeau, 2002 (made-for-TV; Eric Peterson); Trudeau II: Maverick in the Making, 2005 (made-for-TV; Eric Peterson).

Douglass, Frederick (1818-1895; U.S. African-American abolitionist, author and statesman): The American Parade, 1974- (TV miniseries; "We the Women," 1974 episode: Fred Morsell); The Civil War, 1990 (TV miniseries; Morgan Freeman voiceover); Copper, 2012- (TV series; "Aileen Aroon," 2013 episode: Eamonn Walker); Freedom, 2014 (Byron Utley); Freedom to Speak, 1982 (TV miniseries; James Earl Jones); **Glory**, 1989 (Raymon St. Jacques); ITV Play of the Week, 1955-1974 (TV series; "Gallows Glorious!," 1959 episode; Andre Dakar); Lincoln, 1988 (made-for-TV; Cleavon Little); Lincoln, 1992 (made-for-TV; Ossie Davis); North and South, 1985- (TV miniseries; Robert Guillaume); Profiles in Courage, 1964-1965 (TV series; "Frederick Douglass," 1965 episode: Robert Hooks); The North Star, 2016 (Keith David); Swing Out, Sweet Land, 1970 (made-for-TV; Roscoe Lee Brown).

Dowding, Hugh (1882-1970; RAF air marshal in WWII); **Battle of Britain**, 1969 (Laurence Olivier); **Reach for the Sky**, 1957 (Charles Carson); The Winds of War, 1983- (TV miniseries; Patrick Allen).

Doyle, Arthur Conan (1859-1930; Scottish physician and author, creator of the fictional detective Sherlock Holmes): Arthur & George, 2015- (TV series; Martin Clunes); The Edwardians, 1972 (TV miniseries; Nigel Davenport); Enigmes de l'histoire, 1956-1957 (TV series; "Le mystere de la Mary Celeste," 1956 episode: Gaston Rey); FairyTale: A True Story, 1997 (Peter O'Toole); **Finding Neverland**, 2004 (Ian Hart); The Great Houdini, 1976 (made-for-TV; Peter Cushing); Houdini, 1998 (made-for-TV; David Warner); Houdini, 2014- (TV miniseries; David Calder); Houdini and Doyle, 2016- (TV miniseries; Stephen Mangan); Mr. Selfridge, 2013- (TV series; John Sessions); Murder Rooms: Murdoch Mysteries, 2008- (TV series; Geraint Wyn Davies); Mysteries at the Castle, 2014- (TV series; Merritt Matthew Chase); Mysteries of the Real Sherlock Holmes, 2000-2001 (TV series; Charles Edwards); Mysteries at the Castle, 2014- (TV series; "House That Saved a King; Joan of Arc; Hamilton Sex Scandal," 2015 episode: Luke Young); 1914-1918, 1996- (TV miniseries; Ian Richardson); Omnibus, 1952-1961 (TV series; "The Fine Art of Murder," 1956 episode: Dennis Hoey); The Other Side, 1992 (made-for-TV; Frank Finlay); Reichenbach Falls, 2007 (made-for-TV; Richard Wilson); The Stamp of Greatness, 1985-1987 (TV series; "Sir Arthur Conan Doyle: The Man Who Was Sherlock Holmes," 1986 episode; Iain Cuthbertson); The Strange Case of Sherlock Holmes & Arthur Conan Doyle, 2005 (made-for-TV; Douglas Henshall); Walt Disney's Wonderful World of Color, 1954-1992 (TV series; "Young Harry Houdini," 1987 episode; Roy Dotrice). Note: For detailed information on Doyle's obsession with spiritualism, see my book, *Zanies: The World's Greatest Eccentrics* (New Century Publishers, 1982; illustrated pages 113-116).

Drake, Francis (Sir Francis Drake; 1540-1596; English admiral and explorer during the Elizabethan era): Drake's Venture, 1980 (made-for-TV; John Thaw); Elizabeth I, 2005- (TV miniseries; two 2005 episodes: David Delve); Elizabeth R, 1971- (TV miniseries; "The Enterpise of England," 1972 episode; John Woodvine); Father Came Too!, 1964 (Fred Emney); The Immortal Voyage of Captain Drake, 2009 (made-for-TV; Adrian Paul); Seven Seas to Calais, 1963 (Rod Taylor); Sir Francis Drake, 1961- (TV series; Terence Morgan); Sir Francis Drake: The Queen's Pirate, 2008 (Scott Gorman).

Dreyfus, Alfred (1859-1935; French officer wrongly convicted of espionage who became a cause celebre): Affare Dreyfus, 1968 (TV miniseries; Karl Michael Vogler); **The Dreyfus Case**, 1931 (Cedric Hardwicke); The Dreyfus Case, 1940 (Fritz Kortner); Folio, 1955-1959 (TV series; "Betrayal," 1955 episode; Eric House); The Hourglass Sanatorium, 1973 (Wladyslaw Sitko); I Accuse!, 1958 (Jose Ferrer); L'affaire Dreyfus, 1995 (made-for-TV; Thierry Fremont); L'affare Dreyfus, 1968 (made-for-TV; Vincenzo de Toma); **The Life of Emile Zola**, 1937 (Joseph Schildkraut); Prisoner of Honor, 1991 (made-for-TV; Kenneth Colley); You Are There, 1953-1957 (TV series; "The Dreyfus Case," 1953 episode: E.G. Marshall). Note: For detailed information on the sensational Dreyfus case, see my book *"I Am Innocent!": A Comprehensive Encyclopedic History of the World's Wrongly Convicted Persons* (Da Capo Press, 2008; illustrated [16 images] pages 1-8).

Duchin, Eddy (Edwin Frank "Eddy" Duchin; 1909-1951; pianist and bandleader): **The Eddy Duchin Story,** 1956 (Tyrone Power).

Dull Knife (aka; Morning Star; c.1810-1883; chief of Northern Cheyenne, prominent in the Indian Wars where he aligned his tribe with the Lakota Sioux in 1876 when Custer's command was wiped out at the Little Big Horn; in 1878 led his tribe in a legendary journey from its imposed reservation in Oklahoma back to the homelands of Nebraska,

Tyrone Power (as musician Eddy Duchin) in *The Eddy Duchin Story,* **1956.**

known as the Northern Cheyenne Exodus): **Cheyenne Autumn**, 1964 (Gilbert Roland); Chief Crazy Horse, 1955 (Pat Hogan).

Dulles, Allen Welsh (1893-1969; U.S. intelligence officer with the OSS in WWII and later first chief of the U.S. Central Intelligence Agency/CIA): American Playhouse, 1981- (TV series; "Concealed Enemies," 1984 episode: George Hamlin); **Bridge of Spies**, 2015 (Peter McRobbie); The Commission, 2007 (Jack Betts); The Company, 2007- (TV miniseries; Cedric Smith); Dark Skies, 1996-1997 (TV series; "We Shall Overcome," 1996 episode: Mike Kennedy; "The Warren Ommission," 1997 episode: Mike Kennedy); Day One, 1989 (made-for-TV; Terrence Labrosse); Francis Gary Powers: The True Story of the U-2 Spy Incident, 1976 (made-for-TV; Lew Ayres); The Great Battle, 1969- (TV series; Otto Busse); Kennedy, 1983- (TV miniseries; George Hamlin); The Kennedys, 2011 (TV series; "Bay of Pigs," 2011 episode: Allan Royal); The Real American: Joe McCarthy, 2012 (Tim Ahern). Note: For detailed information on Dulles, see my book *Spies: A Narrative Encyclopedia of Dirty Tricks & Double Dealing from Biblical Times to Today* (M. Evans, 1997; illustrated [4 images] pages 196-200).

Dumas, Alexander (AKA: Dumas pere; 1802-1870; French novelist who authored many adventure tales, including *The Count of Monte Cristo*, 1844, and *The Three Musketeers*, 1844): **Black Magic**, 1949 (Barry Kroeger); Dumas, 2010 (Gerard Depardieu); Ego Hugo, 1973 (made-for-TV; Eric Thompson); Enigmes de l'histoire, 1956-1957 (TV series; six episodes in 1956-1957: Andre Valmy); Eugene Sue, 1974 (made-for-TV; Guy Verda); The Four Charlots Musketeers, 1974 (Jacques Legras); Garibaldi the General, 1987- (TV miniseries; Meme Perlini); La loca historia de los tres mosqueteros, 1983 (Fernando Conde); La misere et la gloire, 1965 (made-for-TV; Claude Brasseur); La symphonie fantastique, 1947 (Georges Gosset); The Man in the Iron Mask, 1998 (William Richert); Marie Dorval, 1973 (made-for-TV; Maurice Barrier); Miss Bonaparte, 1942 (Andre Carnege); **The Musketeer**, 2001 (Bertrand Witt); Pontcarral, colonel d'empire, 1942 (Robert Christides); The Secret Adventures of Jules Verne, 2000- (TV series; "The Cardinal's Design," 2000 episode: John Rhys-Davies); The Secret of Monte-Cristo, 1948 (Rene Wilmet); Young Blades, 2005- (TV miniseries; "Secrets," 2005 episode: Winston Rekert).

Dunant, Henry (Jean Henri Dunant; 1828-1910; French social activist and businessman who was instrumental in founding the Red Cross and was the first recipient of the Nobel Peace Prize): Henry Dunant: Red on the Cross, 2006 (made-for-TV; Thomas Jouannet); Man to Men, 1949 (Jean-Louis Barrault).

Katharine Hepburn (role modeled on Amelia Earhart) in *Christopher Strong,* **1933.**

Duncan, Isadora (1877-1927; U.S. interpretive dancer who performed risqué routines with little silken garments but was the rage of Europe until a long-flowing silk scarf around her neck got caught in the spokes of a sports car and, when it drove off, broke her neck): The Dancer, 2016 (Lily-Rose Melody Depp); Isadora, 1968 (Vanessa Redgrave).

Dundee, Angelo (1921-2012; U.S. boxing trainer): Ali, 2001 (Ron Silver); Ali: An American Hero, 2000 (made-for-TV; Martin Ferrero); American Brawler, 2016 (Christopher Picone); The Greatest, 1977 (Ernest Borgnine); Hands of Stone, 2016 (Joe Urla); King of the World, 2000 (made-for-TV; John Ventimiglia); The Last Punch, 2016 (Billy Woods).

Duroc, Gerard (French soldier and General under Napoleon I; 1772-1813): **Conquest**, 1937 (George Houston); Napoleon, 1955 (Jean Chevrier).

Dysmas (or Dismas; Saint Dismas in the Eastern Orthodox Church; the penitent thief who was crucified and died with Jesus at Golgotha Hill outside Jerusalem, who reportedly asked that Jesus forgive him for his sins and was told that he would be with Jesus in Heaven; d. 33 A.D.): **Ben-Hur**, 1959 (Lord Layton); The Cross, 2001 (Joe Demonico); Day of Triumph, 1954 (Renny McEvoy); The Easter Experience, 2007- (TV series; Garret Patton); **The Greatest Story Ever Told**, 1965 (Richard Bakalyan); The Jesus Film 1979 (Oshik Levi); Jesus: The Desire of Ages, 2014 (Kevin Fox); **The King of Kings**, 1927 (Clarence Burton); King of Kings, 1961 (Luis Prendes); Kristo, 1996 (Christopher De Leon); The Passion of Christ, 2004 (Sergio Rubini); Pontius Pilate, 1967 (Claudio Scarchilli); Which Will Ye Have!, 1949 (Robert Long).

Earhart, Amelia (1897-1937; U.S. legendary aviatrix who mysteriously disappeared on a 1937 around-the-world flight; declared dead January 5, 1939): **Amelia**, 2009 (Hilary Swank as adult Amelia; Ryann Shayne as young Amelia); Amelia Earhart, 1976 (made-for-TV: Susan Clark); Amelia Earhart: The Final Flight, 1994 (made-for-TV: Diane Keaton); Attack of the Show!, 2005- (TV series; 2010 episode: Tara Platt); Cataclysmo and the Battle for Earth, 2008 (Jai Khalsa); Child Star: The Shirley Temple Story, 2001 (made-for-TV: Lucy Taylor); **Christopher Strong**, 1933 (role model for Katharine Hepburn); The 5th Quadrant, 2002 (TV series: "You're Breaking My Earhart," 2002 episode: Howard Jerome); **Flight for Freedom**, 1943 (role model for Rosalind Russell); The Folklorist, 2012- (TV series; "Cuban Missile Crisis, American Army of Two, the Grasshopper and the Ant, Amelia Earhart," 2013 episode: Liz Flemke); Histeria!, 1998-2000 (animated TV series; "Around the World in a Daze," 1998 episode: Laraine Newman

voiceover); Inside, 2007- (TV series; "The Real Amelia Earhart," 2009 episode: Rebecca Broussard); The Lancaster Miller Affair, 1990 (TV miniseries: Kathy Gordon); **Night at the Museum: Battle of the Smithsonian**, 2009 (Amy Adams); Pancho Barnes, 1988 (made-for-TV; Nance Williamson); Resolution: A Portrait of Amelia Earhart, 2012 (Kathy Rentz); Star Trek: Voyager, 1995-2001 (TV series; "The 37's," 1995 episode: Sharon Lawrence); Witness to Yesterday, 1998 (TV series; "Amelia Earhart," 1998 episode: Martha Burns); The Wright Stuff, 2005-2006 (TV series; Jackie Katzman); You Are There, 1953-1957 (TV series; "The Mystery of Amelia Earhart," 1971 episode: Geraldine Brooks). Note: For detailed information on Earhart, see my book *Among the Missing: An Anecdotal History of Missing Persons from 1800 to the Present* (Simon and Schuster, 1978; illustrated [5 images] pages 211-227).

Earp, James (1841-1926, western saloonkeeper and brother of Wyatt Earp, sometimes portrayed as a lawman): **Gunfight at the O. K. Corral**, 1957 (Martin Milner); **My Darling Clementine**, 1946 (Don Garner); **Wyatt Earp**, 1994 (David Andrews). Note: For detailed information on the Earp Brothers, see my book *Encyclopedia of Western Lawmen and Outlaws* (Paragon, 1992; illustrated [18 images] pages 110-121).

Earp, Morgan (1851-1882, western lawman): **Gunfight at the O. K. Corral**, 1957 (DeForest Kelley); **Hour of the Gun**, 1967 (Sam Melville); I Married Wyatt Earp, 1983 (made-for-TV; Josef Rainer); **My Darling Clementine**, 1946 (Ward Bond); **Tombstone**, 1993 (Bill Paxton); Wagon Train, 1957-1965 (TV series; "The Silver Lady," 1965 episode: Michael Burns); The Wild West, 2006-2007 (TV miniseries; "The Gunfight at the O.K. Corral," 2007 episode: Chad Grimes); **Wyatt Earp**, 1994 (Linden Ashby); Wyatt Earp: Return to Tombstone, 1994 (made-for-TV; Ray Boyle); You Are There, 1953-1957 (TV series; "The Gunfight at the O.K. Corral," 1955 episode: John Larch). Note: For detailed information on the Earp Brothers, see my book *Encyclopedia of Western Lawmen and Outlaws* (Paragon, 1992; illustrated [18 images] pages 110-121).

Earp, Virgil (1843-1905, western lawman): The Arizonian, 1935 (role model for James Bush); Buffalo Bill, Jr., 1955-1956 (TV series; "First Posse," 1955 episode: Russ Scott); **Gunfight at the O. K. Corral**, 1957 (John Hudson); **Hour of the Gun**, 1967 (Frank Converse); I Married Wyatt Earp, 1983 (made-for-TV; Ron Manning); **Masterson of Kansas**, 1954 (Donald Murphy); **My Darling Clementine**, 1946 (Tim Holt); Stories of the Century, 1954 (TV series; "Doc Holliday," 1954 episode: Russell Custer); **Tombstone**, 1993 (Sam Elliott); Wagon Train, 1957-1965 (TV series; "The Silver Lady," 1965 episode: Don Galloway); The Wild West, 2006-2007 (TV miniseries; "The Gunfight at the O.K. Corral," 2007 episode: Joe Jones); **Wyatt Earp**, 1994 (Michael Madsen); Wyatt Earp: Return to Tombstone, 1994 (made-for-TV; John Anderson); You Are There, 1953-1957 (TV series; "The Gunfight at the O.K. Corral," 1955 episode: John Alderson). Note: For detailed information on the Earp Brothers, see my book *Encyclopedia of Western Lawmen and Outlaws* (Paragon, 1992; illustrated [18 images] pages 110-121).

Earp, Wyatt (Wyatt Berry Stapp Earp; 1848-1929; western lawman): The Adventures of Young Indiana Jones: Hollywood Follies, 1994 (made-for-TV; Leo Gordon); Alias Jesse James, 1959 (Hugh O'Brien); Alias Smith and Jones, 1971-1973 (TV series; "Which Way to the O.K. Corral?," 1972 episode: Cameron Mitchell); Alien Nation, 1989-1990 (TV series; "Spirit of '95," 1990 episode: Mark Thomas Miller); Appointment with Destiny, 1971-1973 (TV series; "Showdown at O.K. Corral," 1972 episode: David H. Vowell); Any Last Words?, 2012 (Scott Jefferies); The Arizonian, 1935 (role model for Richard Dix); Badman's Country, 1958 (Buster Crabbe); Bat Masterson, 1958-1961 (TV series; Ron Hayes); Buffalo Bill, Jr., 1955-1956 (TV series; "First Posse," 1955 episode: Walter Reed); **Cheyenne Autumn**, 1964 (James Stewart); Dawn at Socorro, 1954 (role model for James Millican); Deadwood, 2004-2006 (TV cable series; Gale Morgan Harold); Death Valley Days, 1952-1970 (TV series; "After the O.K. Corral," 1964 episode; Jim Davis); **Doc**, 1971 (Harris Yulin); Doctor Who, 1963-1989 (TV series; John Alderson); **Dodge City**, 1939 (role model for Errol Flynn); Four Eyes and Six-Guns, 1992 (made-for-TV; Fred Ward); Frontier Marshal, 1934 (George O'Brien as "Michael Wyatt"); **Frontier Marshal**, 1939 (Randolph Scott); The Gambler Returns: The Luck of the Draw, 1991 (made-for-TV; Hugh O'Brien); Goldrush: A Real Life Alaskan Adventure, 1998 (made-for-TV; David Longworth); Gun Belt, 1953 (James Millican); **Gunfight at the O. K. Corral**, 1957 (Burt Lancaster); Gunmen of Rio Grande, 1965 (Guy Madison); Guns of Paradise, 1988-1990 (TV series; Hugh O'Brien); Hannah's Law, 2012 (made-for-TV; Greyston Holt); Horse Opera, 1993 (made-for-TV; Rik Mayall); **Hour of the Gun**, 1967 (James Garner); I Married Wyatt Earp, 1983 (made-for-TV; Bruce Boxleitner); **Law and Order**, 1932 (role model for Walter Huston); The Life and Legend of Wyatt Earp, 1955-1961 (TV series; Hugh O'Brien); **Masterson of Kansas**, 1954 (Bruce Cowling); Maverick, 1957-1962 (TV series; "Marshal Maverick," 1962 episode: Med Flory); **My Darling Clementine**, 1946 (Henry Fonda); The Outlaws Is Coming, 1965 (Bill Camfield); Pistols 'n' Petticoats, 1966-1967 (TV series; "Shootout at O.K. Corral," 1966 episode: Roy Engel); The Secret World of Eddie Hodges, 1960 (made-for-TV; Hugh O'Brien); **Sunset**, 1988 (James Garner); Stories of the Century, 1954 (TV series; "Doc Holliday," 1954 episode: James Craven); **Tombstone**, 1993 (Kurt Russell); **Tombstone: The Town Too Tough to Die**, 1942 (Richard Dix); Wagon Train, 1957-1965 (TV series; "The Silver Lady," 1965 episode: Don Collier); **Wichita**, 1955 (Joel McCrea); **Wild Bill Hickok**, 1923 (Bert Lindley); The Wild West, 2006-2007 (TV miniseries; "The Gunfight at the O.K. Corral," 2007 episode: Liam Cunningham); **Winchester '73** (Will Geer); **Wyatt Earp**, 1994 (Kevin Costner); Wyatt Earp: Return to Tombstone, 1994 (made-for-TV; Hugh O'Brien); Wyatt Earp's Revenge, 2012 (Val Kilmer as old Earp; Shawn Roberts as Earp in 1878); You Are There, 1953-1957 (TV series; "The Gunfight at the O.K. Corral," 1955 episode: Robert Bray). For more details on Wyatt Earp, see my book *Encyclopedia of Western Lawmen & Outlaws* (Paragon House, 1992; pages 110-121).

Eaton, John Henry (1790-1856; U.S. senator from Tennessee, 1829-1831; close friend of U.S. President Andrew Jackson, and whose wife, Peggy Eaton, was the center of controversy in what was called the Petticoat Affair): The Gorgeous Hussy, 1936 (Franchot Tone).

Eaton, Peggy (Margaret O'Neill Eaton; 1799-1879; wife of U.S. Senator John Henry Eaton and whose marital life was surrounded with controversy in that she may have had an affair with Eaton that caused her first husband, John B. Timberlake, to commit suicide; she was befriended and protected by U.S. President Andrew Jackson in what was called the Petticoat Affair where Washinton socialites attempted to socially ostracize Mrs. Eaton): The Gorgeous Hussy, 1936 (Joan Crawford).

Ebert, Friedrich (1871-1925; German politician and first President of Germany): Bruder, nicht schiessen!, 1989 (made-for-TV; Gunter Schubert); Der Gewaltfrieden, 2010 (made-for-TV; Jurgen Tarrach); Die Flucht nach Holland, 1967 (made-for-TV; Paul Dahlke); Ernst Thalmann—Sohn seiner Klasse, 1954 (Karl Weber); Europas letzter Sommer, 2012 (made-for-TV; Jurgen Tarrach); Fall of Eagles, 1974 (TV miniseries; Peter Schofield); Friedrich Ebert—Geburt einer Republik, 1969 (made-for-TV; Kurd Pieritz); Friedrich Ebert und Gustav Stressemann, 1969 (made-for-TV; Kurd Pieritz); Solange Leben in mir ist, 1965 (Kurt Dunkelmann).

Eckert, Thomas (1825-1910; U.S. soldier and union chief of the War Department Telegraph Staff during the American Civil War): Der Tod

Bruce Cabot and Errol Flynn (role modeled on Wyatt Earp) in *Dodge City*, **1939.**

des Prasidenten, 1967 (Friedhelm Lehmann); The Lincoln Conspiracy, 1977 (Patrick Wright); **Saving Lincoln**, 2013 (David Dastmalchian); They've Killed President Lincoln!, 1971 (made-for-TV; Michael Fairman); You Are There, 1953-1957 (TV series; "The Capture of John Wilkes Booth," 1953 episode: Mack Williams).

Eddowes, Catherine (1842-1888; British prostitute and murder victim of Jack the Ripper): The Collector, 2004-2006 (TV series; Ibolya Bolyos); From Hell, 2001 (Lesley Sharp); Jack the Ripper, 1988 (TV series; Hilary Sesta); **Murder by Decree**, 1979 (Hilary Sesta); **A Study in Terror**, 1966 (Kay Walsh). For detailed information on this and the other Ripper murders, see my two-volume work *The Great Pictorial History of World Crime*, Volume II (History Inc., 2004; illustrated pages 1180-1203).

Eden, Anthony (1897-1977; British statesman and prime minister of the U.K., 1955-1957): Churchill and the Generals, 1981 (made-for-TV; Richard Easton); Churchill's Secret, 2016 (made-for-TV; Alex Jennings); Dunkirk, 2004 (made-for-TV; Jack Fortune); Edward & Mrs. Simpson, 1978- (TV miniseries; Hugh Fraser); The Gathering Storm, 1974 (made-for-TV; Michael Elwyn); ITV Playhouse, 1967- (TV series; "Hess," 1978 episode: Paul Darrow); The Last Bastion, 1984 (TV series; John Hamblin); Menzies and Churchill at War, 2008 (made-for-TV; Tim Hughes); **Mission to Moscow**, 1943 (Clive Morgan); National Theatre Live: The Audience, 2013 (Michael Elwyn); The Queen, 2009- (TV series; "Margaret," 2009 episode: Robert Bathurst); Suez 1956, 1979 (made-for-TV; Michael Gough); Truman at Potsdam, 1976 (made-for-TV; Dennis Burgess); Upstairs Downstairs, 2010-2012 (TV series; Anthnony Calf); Winston Churchill: The Wilderness Years, 1981- (TV miniseries; three 1981 episodes: Tony Mathews); World War Two: Behind Closed Doors, 2008-2009 (TV series; Simon Thorp); Yalta, 1984 (made-for-TV; Didier Flamand).

Edison, Thomas Alva (1847-1931; U.S. inventor and businessman): The Adventures of Young Tom Edison, 2008 (made-for-TV; Randy Rossilli); Bill and Ted's Bogus Journey, 1991 (Hal Landon Sr.); **Edison the Man**, 1940 (Spencer Tracy); Edison: The Wizard of Light, 1998 (made-for-TV; Kenneth Welsh); General Electric Theater, 1953-1962 (TV series, "Edison the Man," 1954 episode: Burgess Meredith); The Hourglass Sanatorium, 1973 (Stanislaw Tylczynski); Let There Be Light: Nicola Tesla, 2005 (made-for-TV; Robert Goss); Lights of Old Broadway, 1925 (Frank Glendon); Nikola Tesla, 1977 (TV series; three episodes: Buzancic); Tall Tales and Legends, 1985-1988 (TV series; "Annie Oakley," 1985 episode: John Achorn); Tom Edison: The Boy Who Lit Up the World, 1979 (made-for-TV; David Huffman); The Young Indiana Jones

Patrick McGoohan (as Edward I) in *Braveheart,* **1995.**

Chronicles, 1992-1993 (TV series; "Princeton, February 1916," 1993 episode: Richard K. Olsen); **Young Tom Edison**, 1940 (Mickey Rooney).

Edward I (Edward Longshanks; 1239-1307; King of England and remembered for his oppressive military subjugation of Wales and Scotland): **The Black Rose**, 1950 (Michael Rennie); **Braveheart**, 1995 (Patrick McGoohan); Churchill's People, 1974- (TV series; "The Wallace," 1975 episode: Stephen Murray).

Edward IV (1442-1483; King of England): An Age of Kings, 1960- (TV series; Julian Glover); Britain's Bloody Crown, 2016 (TV series; Tom Durant); The Eternal Strife, 1915 (Roy Travers); The Golden Spur, 1959- (TV series; Michael Kilgarriff); The Hollow Crown, 2012 (TV miniseries; Geoffrey Streatfeild); The Life and Death of King Richard III, 1912 (Robert Gemp); **Richard III**, 1956 (Cedric Hardwicke); Richard IIII, 1973 (made-for-TV; Jozsef Gati); Richard III, 1983 (made-for-TV; Brian Protheroe); Richard III, 1986 (Marc Betton); Richard III, 1995 (John Wood); Richard III, 2005 (John Rackham); Richard III, 2007 (Walter Williamson); **Tower of London**, 1939 (Ian Hunter); Tower of London, 1962 (Justice Watson); The War of the Roses, 1965- (TV series; Roy Dotrice); The White Queen, 2013 (TV miniseries; nine episodes: Max Irons).

Edward VI (1537-1553; King of England): The Adventures of the Prince and the Pauper, 1969 (Kenny Morse); Crossed Swords, 1978 (Mark Lester); The DuPont Show of the Month, 1957-1961 (TV series; "The Prince and the Pauper," 1957 episode: Rex Thompson); Elizabeth R, 1971-1972 (TV miniseries; "The Lion's Club," 1971 episode: Jason Kemp); Henry VIII, 2003 (made-for-TV; Hugh Mitchell); Nine Days a Queen, 1936 (Desmond Tester); The Prince and the Pauper, 1915 (Marguerite Clark); The Prince and the Pauper, 1920 (Tibi Lubinszky); **The Prince and the Pauper**, 1937 (Robert J. Mauch); The Prince and the Pauper, 1943 (Mariya Barabanova); The Prince and the Pauper, 1976 (TV series; Nicholas Lyndhurst); The Prince and the Pauper, 1977 (Mark Lester); The Prince and the Pauper, 1996 (TV series; six episodes: Philip Sarson); The Prince and the Pauper, 2000 (made-for-TV; Jonathan Timmins); Shirley Temple's Storybook, 1958-1960 (TV series; "The Prince and the Pauper," 1960 episode: Peter Lazer); The Six Wives of Henry VIII, 2001 (TV miniseries; Matt Kane); **Tower of London**, 1939 (Ronald Sinclair); The Tudors, 2007-2010 (TV series; Eoin Murtagh); Walt Disney's Wonderful World of Color, 1954-1992 (TV series; "The Prince and the Pauper: The Pauper King," 1962 episode: John Scully; "The Prince and the Pauper: The Merciful Law of the King," 1962 episode: John Scully); **Young Bess**, 1953 (Rex Thompson).

Ehrlich, Paul (1854-1915; German physician and scientist who developed the first effective medicinal treatment for syphilis): **Dr. Ehrlich's Magic Bullet**, 1940 (Edward G. Robinson).

Eichmann, Adolf (1906-1962; German officer and SS commander considered to be one of the major organizers of the Holocaust; caught by Israelis in South America, tried in Israel and executed for war crimes): Armstrong Circle Theatre, 1950-1963 (TV series; "Engineer of Death: The Eichmann Story," 1960 episode: Frederick Rolf); The Aryan Couple, 2004 (Steve Mackintosh); BBC Play of the Month, 1965-1983 (TV series; "The Joel Brand Story," 1960 episode: Anton Diffring); Conspiracy, 2001 (made-for-TV; Stanley Tucci); Death Is My Trade, 1977 (Walter Czaschke); The Final Solution: The Wannsee Conference, 1984 (made-for-TV; Gerd Bockmann); Good, 2008 (Steven Elder); Good Evening, Mr. Wallenberg, 1993 (Laszlo Soos); Holocaust, 1978 (TV miniseries; Tom Bell); The House on Garibaldi Street, 1979 (made-for-TV; Alfred Burke); **The Man in the Glass Booth**, 1975 (role model for Maximilian Schell); The Man Who Captured Eichmann, 1996 (made-for-TV; Robert Duvall); Mother Night, 1996 (Henry Gibson); Murderers among Us: The Simon Wiesenthal Story, 1989 (made-for-TV; Janos Gosztonyi); Operation Eichmann, 1961 (Werner Klemperer); **The People vs. Fritz Bauer**, 2015 (Michael Schenk); Perlasca: The Courage of a Just Man, 2005 (made-for-TV; Tamas Puskas); Reinhard Heydrich: Manager des Terrors, 1977 (made-for-TV; Wolfgang Rau); Walking with the Enemy, 2013 (Charles Hubbell); Wallenberg: A Hero's Story, 1985 (made-for-TV; Kenneth Colley); War and Remembrance, 1988 (TV miniseries; Milton Johns).

Einstein, Albert (1879-1955; German-born theoretical physicist, who developed the theory of relativity): Albert Einstein, 1990- (TV series; Talivaldis Abolins; Siegfried Voss); Albert Schweitzer, 2009 (Armin Rohde); The Beginning or the End, 1947 (Ludwig Stossel); Day One, 1989 (made-for-TV; Peter Boretski); Einstein, 1985- (TV miniseries; Ronald Pickup); Einstein, 2008 (made-for-TV; Vincenzo Amato); Einstein: Light to the Power of 2, 1996 (made-for-TV; Paul Soles); Einstein: The Man behind the Genius, 1982 (made-for-TV; Stven Polinsky); Ende der Unschuld, 1991 (made-for-TV; Fred Duren); **Mr. Peabody & Sherman**, 2014 (Mel Brooks voiceover); A Man Called Intrepid, 1979 (TV miniseries; Joseph Golland); **Night at the Museum: Battle of the Smithsonian**, 2009 (Eugene Levy); Race for the Bomb, 1987 (TV miniseries; Denis Manuel); Robert Montgomery Presents, 1950-1957 (TV series; "Portrait of a Man," 1956 episode; Robert Ellenstein); Titans, 1981-1982 (TV series; "Albert Einstein," 1981 episode: John Marley); Young Einstein, 1989 (Yahoo Serious).

Eisenhower, Dwight David (1890-1969; American five-star general and 34th President of the U.S.): The Arrow, 1997 (made-for-TV; Michael Moriarty); Backstairs at the White House, 1979 (TV miniseries; four 1979 episodes: Andrew Duggan); Battleground: The Art of War, 2005 (TV series; "The Battle of the Bulge," 2005 episode: Chuck Kelley); Churchill, 2016 (John Slattery); Churchill and the Generals, 1981 (made-for-TV; Richard Dysart); Day One, 1989 (made-for-TV; Gary Reineke); D-Day 6.6.1944, 2004 (made-for-TV; David Lyon); **The Desert Fox**, 1951 (himself in newsreel footage); Dieppe, 1993 (made-for-TV; Marc Strange); Francis Gary Powers: The True Story of the U-2 Spy Incident, 1976 (made-for-TV; James Flavin); Histeria!, 1998-2000 (TV series; "Horray for Presidents," 1998 episode: Jeff Bennett); Ike, 1986 (made-for-TV; E.G. Marshall); Ike: Countdown to D-Day, 2004 (made for TV; Tom Selleck); Ike: The War Years, 1979 (TV miniseries; Robert Duvall); **J. Edgar**, 2011 (Gunner Wright); J. Edgar Hoover, 1987 (made-for-TV; Andrew Duggan); The Korean War, 2001 (TV series; Harrison Young); The Last Days of Patton, 1986 (made-for-TV; Richard Dysart); Lee Daniels' The Butler, 2013 (Robin Williams); **The Long Gray Line**, 1955 (Harry Carey Jr.); **The Longest Day**, 1962 (Henry Grace); Man, Moment, Machine, 2005-2007 (TV series; "Patton and the Desperate Tank Attack," 2006 episode: Greg Greenwood); **The Monuments Men**, 2014 (Werner Braunschadel); My Science Project, 1985 (Robert Beer); **The Right Stuff**, 1983 (Robert Beer); Suez 1956, 1979 (made-for-TV; Michael Turner); Suez: A Very British Crisis, 2006 (made-for-TV; Patrick Malahide); Tail Gunner Joe, 1977 (made-for-TV; Andrew Duggan); Ten Days to D-Day, 2004 (made-for-TV; Paul Haley); War and Remembrance, 1988 (TV miniseries; E. G. Marshall).

Eleanor of Aquitaine (c. 1122-1204; Queen Consort of England and France): The Adventures of Robin Hood, 1955-1960 (TV series; 1955 and 1956 episodes: Jill Esmond); BBC Sunday-Night Theatre, 1950-1959 (TV series; "The Life and Death of King John," 1952 episode: Una Venning); Becket, 1923 (Mary Clare); **Becket**, 1964 (Pamela Brown); The Bruce, 1996 (Hildegard Neil); The Devil's Crown, 1978- (TV series; Jane Lapotaire); Ivanhoe, 1958- (TV series; two episodes; Phyllis Neilson-Terry); Ivanhoe, 1997- (TV miniseries; Sian Phillips); King John, 1984 (made-for-TV; Mary Morris); The Legend of Robin Hood, 1975 (TV miniseries; Yvonne Mitchell); **The Lion in Winter**, 1968 (Katharine Hepburn); The Lion in Winter, 2003 (made-for-TV; Glenn Close); The New Adventures of Robin Hood, 1997-1999 (TV series; Tusse Silberg); Richard the Lionheart, 1962- (TV series; three 1962 episodes: Prudence Hyman; one 1963 episode: Joan Haythorne); Richard the Lionheart: Rebellion, 2013 (Debbie Rochon); Robin Hood: The Noble Robber, 1966 (Margit Saad); Robin Hood, 2006-2009 (TV series; Lynda Bellingham); **Robin Hood**, 2010 (Eileen Atkins); **The Story of Robin Hood** [aka: The Story of Robin Hood and His Merrie Men], 1952 (Martitia Hunt); The Zany Adventures of Robin Hood, 1984 (made-for-TV; Janet Suzman).

Eliot, T. S. (Thomas Stearns Eliot; 1888-1965; American-born British poet, playwright and critic): **Midnight in Paris**, 2011 (David Lowe); Tom & Viv, 1994 (Willem Dafoe).

Elisabeth of Austria (1837-1898; Empress of Austria and wife of Emperor Franz Joseph I): BBC Sunday-Night Theatre, 1950-1959 (TV series; "The Masque of Kings," 1955 episode: Joan Heath; "The Mayerling Affair," 1956 episode: Margaretta Scott); The Crown Prince, 2006 (made-for-TV; Sandra Ceccarelli); Der Kronprinz, 1989 (made-for-TV; Mijou Kovacs); Der Tag danach, 1965 (made-for-TV; Marianne Schonauer); Kaiserin Elisabeth von Osterreich, 1921 (Carla Nelsen); Kaiserin Elisabeth von Osterreich, 1972 (made-for-TV; Marisa Mell); Kaiserwalzer, 1956 (Maria Holst); The King Steps Out, 1936 (Grace Moore); Konigswalzer, 1936 (Carola Hohn); Kronprinz Rudolfs letzte Liebe, 1959 (Lil Dagover); Ludwig II, 1922 (Gina Puch-Klitsch); The Masque of Kings, 1946 (made-for-TV; Mary Newcomb); **Mayerling**, 1937 (Gabrielle Dorziat); Mayerling, 1968 (Ava Gardner); The Only Girl, 1934 (Mady Christians); Princess Sisi, 1997 (animated TV series; Terri Hawkes voiceover); Producers' Showcase, 1954-1957 (TV series; "Mayerling," 1957 episode: Diana Wynyard); The Secret of Mayerling, 1951 (Marguerite Jamois);); Sissi, 1955 (Romy Schneider); Sisi, 2009 (made-for-TV; Cristiana Capotondi); Sisi and the Kaiser, 1991 (Vanessa Wagner); Sisi: The Fateful Years, 1957 (Romy Schneider); Sisi: The Young Empress, 1956 (Romy Schneider); The Song in the Forest, 1950 (Joyce Carey).

Elizabeth I (1533-1603; Queen of England and Ireland): Border Warfare, 1990 (made-for-TV; Juliet Cadzow); Dorothy Vernon of Haddon Hall, 1924 (Clare Eames); Drake the Pirate, 1936 (Athene Seyler); Drake's Venture, 1980 (made-for-TV; Charlotte Cornwell); **Elizabeth**, 1998 (Cate Blanchett); Elizabeth, 2000 (made-for-TV; Imogen Slaughter; Saskia Blackwell; Karen Archer); Elizabeth I, 2005 (TV miniseries; Helen Mirren); Elizabeth R, 1971-1972 (TV miniseries; six episodes: Glenda Jackson); Elizabeth Rex, 2004 (made-for-TV; Diane D'Aquila); **Elizabeth: The Golden Age**, 2007 (Cate Blanchett); Elizabeth the Queen, 1968 (made-for-TV; Judith Anderson); The Eternal Strife, 1915

Katharine Hepburn (as Eleanor of Aquitaine) and Peter O'-Toole (as Henry II) in *The Lion in Winter,* **1968.**

(Maud Yates); **Fire Over England**, 1937 (Flora Robson); Gloriana, 1984 (made-for-TV; Sarah Walker); Gloriana, 2000 (made-for-TV; Josephine Barstow); Gunpowder, Treason & Plot, 2004 (made-for-TV; Catherine McCormack); The Heart of the Queen, 1940 (Maria Koppenhofer); Henry VIII, 2003 (made-for-TV; Lorna Lacey); The Hourglass Sanatorium, 1973 (Zofia Bajuk); I Married an Angel, 1942 (Edwina Coolidge); ITV Play of the Week, 1955-1974 (TV series; "In the Shadow of the Axe," 1958 episode: Catherine Lacey); Jubilee, 1978 (Jenny Runacre); Loves and Adventures in the Life of Shakespeare, 1914 (Aimee Martinek); The Loves of Mary, Queen of Scots, 1923 (Ellen Compton); Maria Stuart, 1963 (made-for-TV; Elfriede Kuzmany); Maria Stuart, 1980 (made-for-TV; Gisela Leipert); Maria Stuart, 2008 (made-for-TV; Paula Dombrowski); **Mary of Scotland**, 1936 (Florence Eldridge); Mary, Queen of Scots, 1971 (Glenda Jackson); Mary Stuart, 1982 (made-for-TV; Rosalind Plowright); O Principe E o Mendigo, 1972 (TV series; Adriana de Goes; Suzana Goncalves); The Other Boleyn Girl, 2008 (Maisie Smith); **The Pearls of the Crown**, 1938 (Yvette Pienne); Play of the Week, 1959-1961 (TV series; "Mary Stuart," 1960 episode: Eva Le Galliene); The Prince and the Pauper, 1977 (Lalla Ward); The Prince and the Pauper, 1996 (TV series; six episodes: Elizabeth Ann O'Brien); **The Private Lives of Elizabeth and Essex**, 1939 (Bette Davis); Queen Elizabeth, 1912 (Sarah Bernhardt); The Queen's Traitor, 1967 (TV series; Susan Engel); Regal Cavalcade, 1935 (Athene Seyler); Reign, 2013- (TV series; Rachel Skarsten); Roberto Devereux, 1997 (made-for-TV; Alexandrina Pendatchanska); **The Sea Hawk**, 1940 (Flora Robson); Seven Seas to Calais, 1963 (Irene Worth); Shakespeares Sonette, 2009 (made-for-TV; Jurgen Holtz); Shirley Temple's Storybook, 1958-1960 (TV series; "The Prince and the Pauper," 1960 episode: Portland Mason); The Story of Mankind, 1957 (Agnes Moorehead); Time Flies, 1944 (Olga Lindo); Titans, 1981-1982 (TV series; Frances Hyland); **Tower of London**, 1939 (Barbara O'Neil); The Tudors, 2007-2010 (TV series; Laoise Murray; Claire Macaulay; Kate Dugan); The Virgin Queen, 1923 (Diana Manners); **The Virgin Queen**, 1955 (Bette Davis); The Virgin Queen, 2005 (TV miniseries; Anne-Marie Duff); **Young Bess**, 1953 (Jean Simmons).

Elizabeth II (Queen of Great Britain; 1926-): The Amazing Mrs. Pritchard, 2006- (TV series; Dilys Laye); Bertie and Elizabeth, 2002 (made-for-TV; Elisabeth Dermot Walsh; Naomi Martin as young Elizabeth); Charles and Diana: A Royal Love Story, 1982 (made-for-TV; Margaret Tyzack); Charles and Diana: Unhappily Ever After, 1992 (made-for-TV; Amanda Walker); Churchill: The Hollywood Years, 2004 (Neve Campbell); The Crown, 2016- (TV series; Claire Foy); Diana: Her True Story, 1993 (made-for-TV; Anne Stallybrass); Fergie & Andrew: Behind the Palace Doors, 1992 (made-for-TV; Iris Russell); Her

Rosalind Ivan (role modeled on murder victim Belle Elmore) in *The Suspect*, 1944.

Majesty, 2001 (Rachel Wallis); If It's Tuesday, It Still Must Be Belgium, 1987 (made-for-TV; Jeannette Charles); Johnny English, 2003 (Prunella Scales); King Ralph, 1991 (Alison McGuire); **The King's Speech**, 2010 (Freya Wilson); Mad Mission 3: Our Man from Bond Street, 1984 (Huguette Funfrock); My Government and I, 2000 (made-for-TV; Beth Boyd); **The Naked Gun: From the Files of Police Squad**, 1988 (Jeannette Charles); National Theatre Live: The Audience, 2013 (Helen Mirren); **The Queen**, 2006 (Helen Mirren); The Queen, 2009- (TV series; Diana Quick; Barbara Flynn; Susan Jameson; Emilia Fox; Samantha Bond); The Royal Romance of Charles and Diana, 1982 (made-for-TV; Dana Wynter); Spitting Image, 1984-1986 (TV series with puppets enacting public figures; Kate Robbins voiceover; Forwell Flax voiceover); William & Catherine: A Royal Romance, 2011 (made-for-TV; Jane Alexander); The Women of Windsor, 1992 (made-for-TV; Carolyn Sadowska).

Elizabeth of Russia (1709-1762; Empress of Russia): Catherine of Russia, 1963 (Tina Lattanzi); Catherine the Great, 1996 (made-for-TV; Jeanne Moreau); Catherine the Great, 2005 (made-for-TV; Diana Dumbrava); Ekaterina, 2014- (TV series; Yuliya Aug); The Rise of Catherine the Great, 1934 (Flora Robson); **The Scarlet Empress**, 1934 (Louise Dresser); Young Catherine, 1991 (made-for-TV; Vanessa Redgrave).

Ellsworth, Elmer Ephraim (1837-1861; U.S. military officer; close friend of Abraham Lincoln; he was the first recorded casualty in the American Civil War): Lincoln, 1974-1975 (TV series; David Huffman); Lincoln, 1988 (made-for-TV; Tim Guinee); **Saving Lincoln**, 2013 (Adam Croasdell); Tad, 1995 (made-for-TV; Billy Worley).

Elmore, Belle (Corrine "Cora" Turner; Kunigunde Mackamotski; d. 1910; profligate music hall singer who was murdered by her husband, Dr. Hawley Harvey Crippen, over his love for mistress Ethel Le Neve): Detective, 1964-1969 (TV series; "Crime of Passion," 1968 episode: Pauline Delany [Delaney]); Dr. Crippen, 1942 (Anja Elkoff); Dr. Crippen, 1964 (Coral Browne); Lady Killers, 1980-1981 (TV series; "Miss Elmore," 1981 episode: Joan Sims voiceover); The Last Secret of Dr. Crippen, 2004 (Heather Coombs); **The Suspect**, 1944 (role model for Rosalind Ivan); Theatre Royal, 1955- (TV series; "The Case of Dr. Crippen," 1956 episode: Margot Grahame); **We Are Not Alone**, 1939 (role model for Flora Robson). Note: For detailed information on Belle Elmore and her murder by Crippen, see my book *World Encyclopedia of 20th Century Murder* (Paragon House, 1992; illustrated [9 images] pages 145-152).

Elser, Johann Georg (1903-1945; German carpenter with communist leanings who attempted to assassinate Adolf Hitler on November 8, 1939, by planting a bomb at the Burgerbraukeller (a beerhall) in Munich where Hitler and other high-ranking Nazi members were meeting to commemorate their 1923 Beer Hall Putsch; Hitler escaped injury, but eight others were killed and more than sixty of those attending were injured when the bomb exploded; Elser was executed at Dachau concentration camp on April 9, 1945): Der Attentater, 1969 (Fritz Hollenbeck); Seven Minutes, 1989 (Klaus Maria Brandauer); **13 Minutes**, 2015 (Christian Friedel).

Emma, Lady Hamilton (Amy Lyon; 1765-1815; mistress to British admiral Horatio Nelson): Bequest to the Nation, 1973 (Glenda Jackson); The Devine Lady, 1929 (Corinne Griffith): Emma Hamilton, 1976 (Michele Mercier); Eugenia de Montijo, 1944 (Dionesia Lahera); I Remember Nelson, 1982 (TV series; Geraldine James); Lady Hamilton, 1921 (Liane Haid); Luisa Sanfelice, 1942 (Hilde Sessak); Luisa Sanfelice, 2004 (made-for-TV; Marie Baumer); Nelson, 1918 (Malvina Longfellow); Nelson, 1926 (Gertrude McCoy); Nelson's Trafalgar, 2005 (made-for-TV; Jennifer Guy); The Romance of Lady Hamilton, 1919 (Malvina Longfellow); **That Hamilton Woman**, 1941 (Vivien Leigh).

Ericsson, John (1803-1889; Swedish-American inventor of the steam engine): The Great John Ericsson, 1938 (Victor Sjostrom); Ironclads, 1991 (made-for-TV; Fritz Weaver).

Erlanger, A. L. (1859-1930; U.S. theatrical producer): **Yankee Doodle Dandy**, 1942 (George Barbier).

Etting, Ruth (1897-1978; U.S. ballad singer and actress): **Love Me or Leave Me**, 1955 (Doris Day).

Eugénie (1826-1920; Eugénie de Montijo; empress consort of France, wife of Napoleon III): Amazing Monsieur Fabre, 1951 (Espanita Cortez); Aquellos anos, 1974 (Marcela Lopez Rey); Bernadette, 1989 (Marie-Brigitte Andrei); Bismarck, 1940 (Lil Dagover); The Countess of Castiglione, 1942 (Maria Pia Spini); The Diving Bell and the Butterfly, 2007 (Emma de Caunes); El carruaje, 1972 (TV series; Ofelia Montesco); Emile Waldteufel, 1981 (made-for-TV; Edmee Deniau); Eugenia de Montijo, 1944 (Amparito Rivelles); Fanatisme, 1934 (Andree Lafayette); Her People, 1928 (Suzanne Bianchetti); In Performance, 1978- (TV series; "Orpheus in the Underworld," 1983 episode: Honor Blackman); **Juarez**, 1939 (Gale Sondergaard); Katia, 1939 (Genia Vaury); La Castiglione, 1975 (made-for-TV; Maria Teresa Letizia); La forteresse assiegee, 2006 (made-for-TV; Virginie Ledoyen); La valse de Paris, 1950 (Raymonde Allain); L'homme de Suez, 1983 (TV miniseries; Maria Rosaria Omaggia); The Mad Empress, 1939 (Evelyn Brent); Mademoiselle Midnight, 1924 (Clarissa Selwynne); Maximilian von Mexiko, 1970 (made-for-TV; Katharina Matz); Ottocento, 1959-1960 (TV miniseries; Lea Padovani); **The Pearls of the Crown**, 1938 (Marguerite Moreno/Raymonde Allain); Preussen uber alles—Bismarcks deutsche Einigung, 1971 (TV miniseries; Tatjana Iwanow); Sisi, 2009 (TV miniseries; Andrea Osvart); **The Song of Bernadette**, 1943 (Patricia Morison); Spy of Napoleon, 1936 (Joyce Bland); **The Story of Louis Pasteur**, 1936 (Iphigenie Castiglione); **Suez**, 1938 (Loretta Young); Three Waltzes, 1939 (Jeanne Helbling); Violettes imperiales, 1932 (Suzanne Bianchetti); Violettes imperiales, 1952 (Simone Valere).

Eve (Biblical person; first human female created by God from Adam's rib): Adam and Eve, 1958 (Christiane Martel); The Adventures of Mark Twain, 1985 (Carol Edelman voiceover); After Six Days, 1920 (Ada Marucelli); The Bible, 2013- (TV miniseries; "In the Beginning," 2013 episode: Darcie Lincoln); The Bible: In the Beginning, 1966 (Ulla Bergryd); The Cradle of God, 1926 (Francine Mussey); Genesis: The Creation and the Flood, 1994 (Haddou Zoubida); **The Green Pastures**, 1936 (Myrtle Anderson); In the Beginning, 2000 (made-for-TV; Terri

Seymour); The Jersey Devil, 2014 (Rosie Gunther); The Making Of "... And God Spoke," 1994 (Christy Taylor); **Noah**, 2014 (Ariane Rinehart); The Private Lives of Adam and Eve, 1960 (made-for-TV; Mamie Van Doren); The Real Old Testament, 2003 (Kelle McQuinn); Restitution, 1918 (Lois Gardner); The Sin of Adam and Eve, 1973 (Kandy); Son of God, 2014 (Darcie Lincoln); Testament: The Bible in Animation, 1996- (TV series; "Creation and the Flood," 1996 espisode: Simon Harris); Year One, 2009 (Rhoda Griffis).

Every, Herny (Evory; Avery; aka; Long Ben; c. 1659- ; British pirate of the Atlantic and Indian oceans): Captain Kidd and the Slave Girl, 1954 (Richard Kartan); The King's Pirate, 1967 (Guy Stockwell). Note: For detailed information on Every, see my two-volume work, *The Great Pictorial History of World Crime*, Volume II (History, Inc., 2004; illustrated [3 images] pages 1280-1283).

Ewell, Richard Stoddert (1817-1872; U.S. military officer and lieutenant general in the Confederate army of Northern Virginia during the American Civil War): **Gettysburg**, 1993 (Tim Scott); **Gods and Generals**, 2003 (Jonathan Demers).

Exner, Judith Campbell (1934-1999; U.S. woman who made unsubstantiated claims that she had been the secret mistress of U.S. President John F. Kennedy, but was a known consort of Mafia bosses Sam Giancana and John Roseli): Hoover vs. the Kennedys: The Second Civil War, 1987 (made-for-TV; Brioni Farrell); The Kennedys, 2011 (TV series; Megan Vincent); Power and Beauty, 2002 (made-for-TV; Natasha Henstridge); The Rat Pack, 1998 (made-for-cable TV; Michelle Grace); The Sopranos, 1998-2007 (TV series; "In Camelot," 2004 episode: role model for Polly Bergen).

Faithfull, Starr (1906-1931; U.S. socialite remembered for her mysterious drowning, her death at age twenty-five remaining unsolved and which many believe was a homicide): **Butterfield 8**, 1960 (role model for Elizabeth Taylor). Note: For detailed information on Faithfull, see my two-volume work *The Great Pictorial History of World Crime*, Volume II (History, Inc., 2004; illustrated [6 images] pages 1234-1238).

Fawkes, Guy (1570-1606; British insurgent who led the Gunpowder Plot to overthrow the government; executed; celebrated in England on Guy Fawke's Day on November 5 when he is hanged or burned in effigy): BBC Sunday-Night Theatre, 1950-1959 (TV series; "Gunpowder, Treason & Plot," 1953 episode: Joseph O'Conor); Carry on Henry VIII, 1971 (Bill Maynard); Father Came Too!, 1964 (Joseph Brady); Gunpowder 511: The Greatest Terror Plot, 2014 (made-for-TV; Jamie Maclachlan); Gunpowder Guy, 1953 (made-for-TV; William Devlin); The Gunpowder Plot: Exploding the Legend, 2005 (made-for-TV; Henry Douthwaite); Gunpowder, Treason & Plot, 2004 (made-for-TV; Michael Fassbender); Guy Fawkes, 1923 (Matheson Lang); Jamie, 1971- (TV series; "Remember, Remember," 1971 episode; William Marlowe); Traitors, 1990 (made-for-TV; David Chittenden).

Ferdinand II of Aragon (1452-1516; Spanish monarch): The Black Sword, 1976 (Juan Ribo); The Broken Crown, 2016 (Rodolfo Sancho); Bye Bye Columbus, 1991 (made-for-TV; Alex Jennings); Carry on Columbus, 1992 (Leslie Phillips); Christophe Columb, 1916 (Marcel Verdier); **Christopher Columbus**, 1949 (Francis Lister); Christopher Columbus, 1985 (TV miniseries; Nicol Williamson); Christopher Columbus: The Discovery, 1992 (Tom Selleck); Columbus, 1923 (Robert Gaillard); Cristobal Colon, 1943 (Jose Baviera); Cristobal Colon, 1982 (Luis Varela); 1492: Conquest of Paradise, 1992 (Fernando Garcia Rimada); Isabel, 2011- (TV series; Rodolfo Sancho); Mad Love, 2002 (Hector Colome); Requiem por Granada, 1991- (TV series; Pedro Diez del Corral); Richelieu, 1977 (TV miniseries; Hans Caninenberg); True Adventures of Christopher Columbus, 1992- (TV

Jo Van Fleet (as Big Nose Kate Fisher) and Kirk Douglas (as Doc Holliday) in *Gunfight at the O.K. Corral,* **1957.**

series; Tim Piggott-Smith).

Fermi, Enrico (U.S. physicist, who worked with J. Robert Oppenheimer and others to develop the atomic bomb in WWII; 1901-1954): The Beginning or the End, 1947 (Joseph Calleia); Day One, 1989 (made-for-TV; Tony Shalhoub); Ende der Unschuld, 1991 (made-for-TV; Hermann Treusch); **Fat Man and Little Boy**, 1989 (Franco Cutietta); Mexikanische Revolution, 1968 (made-for-TV; P. Walter Jacob); Oppenheimer, 1980 (TV miniseries; Edward Hardwicke); Race for the Bomb, 1987 (TV miniseries; Pier Paolo Capponi); War and Remembrance, 1988 (TV miniseries; Frank Foti Jr.).

Fernandez, Raymond Martinez (1914-1951; U.S. serial killer, who, with Martha Jule Beck, 1920-1951, bilked and murdered as many as twenty women in marital scams where Fernandez married these victims and then looted their assets before killing them; both were executed on March 8, 1951): **The Honeymoon Killers**, 1969 (Tony Lo Bianco); Lonely Hearts, 2006 (Jared Leto). Note: For detailed information on Fernandez and his co-killer, Martha Beck, see my book *The Great Pictorial History of World Crime*, Volume I (History, Inc., 2004; illustrated pages 239-243).

Fields, W.C. (1880-1946; comedian and juggler): Barnaby, 1965 (Sorrell Brooke); Angels with Angles, 2005 (David Springhorn); Christmas Carol, 1978 (made-for-TV; Rich Little as Scrooge as W.C. Fields); **Follow the Boys**, 1944 (himself); Get Smart, 1965-1970 (TV series; "House of Max," two 1970 episodes: Bill Oberlin); Good Vibrations, 1992 (TV miniseries; Mark Mitchell); Happy Days, 1970- (TV series; 1970 episode: Bill Oberlin); **The I Don't Care Girl**, 1953 (Harmon Stevens); It Happened in Hollywood, 1937 (James May); Lives and Deaths of the Poets, 2011 (Lanny Slusher); The Mad, Mad, Mad Comedians, 1970 (made-for-TV; Paul Frees); Mae West, 1982 (made-for-TV; Chuck McCann); **The Rocketeer**, 1991 (Bob Leeman); Sensations of 1945 (himself); Train Ride to Hollywood, 1975 (Bill Oberlin); **W.C. Fields and Me**, 1976 (Rod Steiger). Note: For detailed information on Fields, see my book *Zanies: The World's Greatest Eccentrics* (New Century Publishers, 1982; illustrated pages 124-134).

Fierro, Rodolfo (1880-1915; Mexican revolutionary and officer in the army of Pancho Villa, known as "The Butcher" because of the many executions of federal soldiers he committed): Ah! Silenciosa, 1999 (Chico Hernandez); And Starring Pancho Villa as Himself, 2003 (made-for-TV: Damian Alcazar); El centauro Pancho Villa, 1967 (Carlos Lopez Moctezuma); El encanto del aguila, 2011 (Jorge de los Reyes); Let's Go with Pancho Villa, 1939 (Alfonso Sanchez Tello); Mexikanische Revo-

James Mason, center, as French novelist Gustave Flaubert, in
***Madame Bovary*, 1949.**

lution, 1968 (made-for-TV; Wolfgang Volz); Pancho Villa and Valentina, 1960 (Carlos Lopez Moctezuma); Villa Rides, 1968 (Charles Bronson); This Was Pancho Villa, 1957 (Carlos Lopez Moctezuma); **Viva Villa!**, 1934 (role model for Leo Carrillo); Wanted: The Sundance Woman, 1976 (made-for-TV; Hector Elias); Zapata: Amor en rebeldia, 2004 (TV miniseries; Alejandro Calva). Note: For detailed information on Fierro and Villa, see my two-volume work *The Great Pictorial History of World Crime*, Volume I (History, Inc., 2004; illustrated [9 images] pages 91-94).

Fischetti, Charles (1891-1951; U.S. gangster and lieutenant of Chicago crime boss Al Capone): Capone, 1975 (Joe De Nicola); Playhouse 90, 1956-1961 (TV series; "Seven against the Wall," 1958 episode: Joe De Santis); **The St. Valentine's Day Massacre**, 1967 (Paul Richards).

Fisher, Kate (Mary Katherine Horony-Cummings; AKA: Big Nose Kate; 1850-1940; U.S. prostitute and common-law wife of gunfighter John H. "Doc' Holliday): **Gunfight at the O.K. Corral**, 1957 (Jo Van Fleet); **Tombstone**, 1993 (Joanna Pacula); **Wyatt Earp**, 1994 (Isabella Rossellini).

Fitzgerald, F. Scott (1896-1940; U.S. author; known as the great chronicler of the Jazz Age and author of the classic novel *The Great Gatsby*, 1925): **Beloved Infidel**, 1959 (Gregory Peck); A Dream of Living, 1975 (made-for-TV; David Hemmings); F. Scott Fitzgerald and the Last of the Belles, 1974 (made-for-TV; Richard Chamberlain); F. Scott Fitzgerald in Hollywood, 1976 (made-for-TV: Jason Miller); Fitzgerald, 2002 (made-for-TV; Jeremy Irons); Hollywood Detective, 1991 (TV series; "The Muse," 1991 episode: Ian Buchanan); Lives and Deaths of the Poets, 2011 (Boris Alexander); Magnum, P.I., 1980-1988 (TV series; "The Case of the Red-Faced Thespian," 1984 episode: John McCook); **Midnight in Paris**, 2011 (Tom Hiddleston); Mrs. Parker and the Vicious Circle, 1994 (Malcolm Gets); Omnibus, 1967-2003 (TV series; "F. Scott Fitzgerald: The Dream Divided," 1969 episode: Edward Woodward); Perfidi incanti, 1985 (made-for-TV; Tomas Arana); Zelda, 1993 (made-for-TV; Timothy Hutton).

Fitzgerald, Zelda (1900-1948; Zelda Sayre, artist-writer and eccentric wife of F. Scott Fitzgerald): A Dream of Living, 1975 (made-for-TV; Annie Lambert); F. Scott Fitzgerald and the Last of the Belles, 1974 (made-for-TV; Blythe Danner); F. Scott Fitzgerald in Hollywood, 1976 (made-for-TV: Tuesday Weld); Fitzgerald, 2002 (made-for-TV; Sissy Spacek); Magnum, P.I., 1980-1988 (TV series; "The Case of the Red-Faced Thespian," 1984 episode: Laurette Spang); **Midnight in Paris**, 2011 (Alison Pill); Omnibus, 1967-2003 (TV series; "F. Scott Fitzger-

ald: The Dream Divided," 1969 episode: Lelia Goldoni); Zelda, 1993 (made-for-TV; Natasha Richardson).

Flaubert, Gustave (1821-1880; French writer and novelist): George Sand, 1981- (TV miniseries; Alberto Lionello); Guy de Maupassant, 1982 (Louis Navarre); If Paris Were Told to Us, 1956 (Robert Manuel); Madame Bovary, 1947 (Ricardo Galache); **Madame Bovary**, 1949 (James Mason); Notorious Woman, 1974 (TV miniseries; James Cossins); Pour Elisa, 1983 (made-for-TV; Olivier Brunhes).

Fleming, Ian Lancaster (1908-1964; British naval intelligence officer and author, famous for his spy novels profiling super secret agent James Bond, code name 007): Age of Heroes, 2011 (James D'Arcy); Fleming: The Man Who Would Be Bond, 2014- (TV miniseries; Dominic Cooper); Goldeneye, 1989 (made-for-TV; Charles Dance); Ian Fleming: Bondmaker, 2005 (made-for-TV; Ben Daniels); Spymaker: The Secret Life of Ian Fleming, 1990 (made-for-TV; Jason Connery). Note: For detailed information on Fleming, see my book, *Spies: A Narrative Encyclopedia of Dirty Deeds & Double Dealing from Biblical Times to Today* (M. Evans, 1997; page 216).

Fletcher, Frank Jack (U.S. admiral in WWII; 1885-1973): **Midway**, 1976 (Robert Webber); **Pearl Harbor**, 2002 (Tomas Arana).

Floyd, Charles Arthur (aka: "Pretty Boy"; 1904-1934; U.S. bank robber and outlaw): A Bullet for Pretty Boy, 1970 (Fabian); Dillinger, 1973 (Steve Kanaly); **The FBI Story**, 1959 (Bob Peterson); Guns Don't Argue, 1957 (Doug Wilson); The Kansas City Massacre, 1975 (made-for-TV; Bo Hopkins); **Pretty Boy Floyd**, 1960 (John Ericson); **Public Enemies**, 2009 (Channing Tatum); The Story of Pretty Boy Floyd, 1974 (made-for-TV; Martin Sheen); The Verne Miller Story, 1988 (Andrew Robinson); **Young Dillinger**, 1965 (Robert Conrad). Note: For detailed information on Floyd, see my eight-volume work, *Encyclopedia of World Crime*, Volume II (CrimeBooks, 1990; illustrated [7 images] pages 1182-1188).

Flynn, William J. (1867-1928; U.S. law enforcement official; director, 1919-1921, of the U.S. Bureau of Investigation, precursor to the Federal Bureau of Investigation/FBI): **No God, No Master**, 2012 (David Straithairn). Note: For detailed information on Flynn, see my eight-volume work, *Encyclopedia of World Crime*, Volume II (CrimeBooks, Inc., 1990; pages 1188-1189).

Foch, Ferdinand (1851-1929; French field marshal and Allied supreme commander on the Western Front in WWII): Clemenceau, 2012 (made-for-TV; Jean-Yves Gautier); Der Gewaltfrieden, 2010 (made-for-TV; Serge Avedikian); The Great Victory, Wilson or the Kaiser? The Fall of the Hohenzollerns, 1919 (Herman Gerold); Screenplay, 1971- (TV series; "Gossip from the Forest," 1979 episode: Hugh Burden); **Sergeant York**, 1941 (Jean Del Val); Why America Will Win, 1918 (Johnny Fox).

Fokker, Anthony (1890-1939; Dutch aviation pioneer who manufactured fighter planes for the German air force in WWI and prior to WWII): De Vliegende Hollander, 1957 (Ton Kuyl); **The Red Baron**, 2010 (Karsten Kaie); **Von Richthofen and Brown**, 1971 (Hurd Hatfield).

Ford, Charles Wilson (aka: Charley; 1857-1884; U.S. Old West outlaw and member of James gang; he and his brother Robert Ford assassinated Jesse James): **The Assassination of Jesse James by the Coward Robert Ford**, 2007 (Sam Rockwell); Frank and Jesse, 1995 (Alexis Arquette); **The Great Missouri Raid**, 1951 (Louis Jean Heydt); Gunfire, 1950 (Gaylord Pendleton); Hondo, 1967 (TV series; "Hondo and the Judas," 1967 episode: Fritz Ford); **I Shot Jesse James**, 1949 (Tom Noonan); **Jesse James**, 1939 (Charles Tannen); Jesse James' Hidden Treasure, 2009 (made-for-TV; Cole Dresser); Jesse James: Legend, Outlaw,

Terrorist, 2005 (made-for-TV; Glen Vaughan); **The Long Riders**, 1980 (Christopher Guest); **The Return of Frank James**, 1940 (Charles Tannen); The Return of Jesse James, 1950 (Tom Noonan); Tales of Wells Fargo, 1957-1962 (TV series; "Jesse James," 1957 episode: Christian Drake); **The True Story of Jesse James**, 1957 (Frank Gorshin). For detailed information on the Ford brothers, see my book *Encyclopedia of Western Lawmen and Outlaws* (Paragon House, 1992; illustrated [4 images] pages 128-130).

Ford, Gerald Rudolph (Leslie Lynch King Jr.; 1913-2006; U.S. politician; 38th President of the U.S.): The Commission, 2007 (Corbin Bernsen); Dark Skies, 1996-1997 (TV series: "The Warren Omission," 1997 episode: Drew Snyder).

Ford, Robert (aka: Bob; 1862-1892; U.S. Old West outlaw and, along with his brother Charles, assassinated Jesse James): **The Assassination of Jesse James by the Coward Robert Ford**, 2007 (Casey Affleck); Frank and Jesse, 1995 (Jim Flowers); Goodyear Playhouse, 1951-1957 (TV series; "Missouri Legend," 1956 episode: Thomas A. Carlin); The Great Jesse James Raid, 1953 (Jim Bannon); **The Great Missouri Raid**, 1951 (Whit Bissell); Gunfire, 1950 (Roger Anderson); Hell's Crossroads, 1957 (Robert Vaughn); Hondo, 1967 (TV series; "Hondo and the Judas," 1967 episode: Roy Jensen); **I Shot Jesse James**, 1949 (John Ireland); Jesse James, 1927 (Harry Woods); **Jesse James**, 1939 (John Carradine); Jesse James' Hidden Treasure, 2009 (made-for-TV; Corey Prechtel); Jesse James: Legend, Outlaw, Terrorist, 2005 (made-for-TV; Ben Cornish); Jesse James vs. the Daltons, 1954 (Rory Mallison); Jesse James' Women, 1954 (Michael Carr); The Last Days of Frank and Jesse James, 1986 (made-for-TV; Darrell Wilks); **The Long Riders**, 1980 (Nicholas Guest); **The Return of Frank James**, 1940 (John Carradine); The Return of Jesse James, 1950 (Clifton Young); Stories of the Century, 1954-1955 (TV series; "Frank and Jesse James," 1954 episode: Tyler McDuff); Tales of Wells Fargo, 1957-1962 (TV series; "Jesse James," 1957 episode: Robert Jordan); A Time for Dying, 1982 (J. N. Roberts); **The True Story of Jesse James**, 1957 (Carl Thayler); You Are There, 1953-1957 (TV series; "The Capture of Jesse James," 1953 episode: James Dean). For detailed information on the Ford brothers, see my book *Encyclopedia of Western Lawmen and Outlaws* (Paragon House, 1992; illustrated [4 images] pages 128-130).

Foster, Stephen Collins (1826-1864; U.S. composer known for his songs about the Old South): Harmony Lane, 1935 (Douglas Montgomery); I Dream of Jeanie, 1952 (Bill Shirley); Plantation Melodies, 1945 (a short; Craig Stevens); **Sewanee River**, 1939 (Don Ameche); Sumer Storm, 2004 (Barry W. Levy); TV Reader's Digest, 1955-1956 (TV series; "Dear Friends and Gentle Hearts," 1955 episode: Johnny Johnston).

Fouche, Joseph (1750-1820; French statesman and minister of police under Napoleon I): The Battle of Austerlitz, 1960 (Lucien Raimbourg); The Death Agony of the Eagles, 1922 (Ernst Legal); **Desiree**, 1954 (Sam Gilman); Die Tochter Napoleons, 1922 (Heinrich Peer); **The Duellists**, 1978 (Albert Finney); Hundred Days, 1935 (Gustaf Grundgens); La camera explore le temps, 1957-1966 (TV series; one 1958 episode: Renaud Mary); L'aiglonne, 1922 (Andre Marnay); Le souper, 1992 (Claude Brasseur); The Lost King, 1958- (TV series; Michael Goodliffe); Madame, 1963 (Renaud Mary); Madame Recamier, 1920 (Hermann Bottcher); Madame Sans-Gene, 1925 (Guy Favieres); Madame Sans-Gene, 1941 (Aime Clariond); Madame Sans-Gene, 1960 (made-for-TV; Renaud Mary); Madame Sans-Gene, 1981 (made-for-TV; Alain Mottet); Madame Sans-Gene, 2002 (made-for-TV; Philippe Volter); Mlle. Desiree, 1948 (Noel Roquevert); **Napoleon**, 1927 (Faviere); Napoleon, 1955 (Jean Dubucourt); Napoleon, 2002 (TV miniseries; Gerard Depardieu); Napoleon and Josephine: A Love Story, 1987- (TV miniseries; Stephen Jenn); Napoleon and Love, 1974- (TV miniseries; John Franklyn-Robbins); Napoleon et l'Europe, 1991- (TV series; Jerzy

Christopher Guest (as Charlie Ford) and Nicholas Guest (as Bob Ford) in *The Long Riders*, 1980.

Kryszak); 100 Days of Napoleon, 1936 (Enzo Biliotti); **Reign of Terror**, 1949 (Arnold Moss); The Rothschilds, 1940 (Bernhard Minetti); Saint-Just ou La force des choses, 1975 (made-for-TV; Marc Mazza); Sea Devils, 1953 (Jacques B. Brunius); Schulmeister, espion de l'empereur, 1971-1974 (TV series; Henri Virlojeux); War and Peace, 1972-1973 (TV miniseries; one 1972 episode: Morris Perry); **Waterloo**, 1971 (Rodolfo Lodi). Note: For detailed information on Fouche, see my book *Spies: A Narrative Encyclopedia of Dirty Deeds & Double Dealing from Biblical Times to Today* (M. Evans, 1997; illustrated pages 217-219).

Foy, Eddie (Eddie Foy Sr.; born Edwin Fitzgerald; 1856-1928; U.S. actor, comedian and dancer in vaudeville often appearing on stage with his seven children); Benny, from Panama, 1934 (Eddie Foy Jr.); Bob Hope Presents the Chrysler Theatre, 1963-1967 (TV series; "The Seven Little Foys," 1964 episode: Eddie Foy Jr.); **Frontier Marshal**, 1939 (Eddie Foy Jr.); **My Darling Clementine**, 1946 (role model for Alan Mowbray); Producers' Showcase, 1954-1957 (TV series; "Mr. Broadway," 1957 episode: Eddie Foy Jr.); **The Seven Little Foys**, 1955 (Bob Hope); **Tombstone**, 1993 (role model for Billy Zane); **Wilson**, 1944 (Eddie Foy Jr.); **The Woman of the Town**, 1943 (Charley Foy); **Yankee Doodle Dandy**, 1942 (Eddie Foy Jr.).

Frame, Janet Paterson (1924-2004; New Zealand writer): **An Angel at My Table**, 1990 (Kerry Fox; Alexia Keogh as adolescent Janet; Karen Fergusson as teenage Janet).

Francis of Assisi (Giovanni di Pietro di Bernardone; 1182-1226; Roman Catholic friar and saint; patron of animals): Anthony: Warrior of God, 2006 (Michele Melega); Brother Sun, Sister Moon, 1972 (Graham Faulkner); Chiara Francesco, 2007 (made-for-TV; Ettore Bassi); Cotolay, 1966 (Vicente Parra); Francesco, 1989 (Mickey Rourke); Francesco, 2005 (made-for-TV; Raoul Bova); Francis of Assisi, 1961 (Bradford Dillman); Francis of Assisi, 1966 (made-for-TV; Lou Castel); La tragica notte di Assisi, 1964 (Carlo Giustini); Light Time, 1960-1964 (TV series; Rolf Forsberg); The Flowers of St. Francis, 1952 (Nazario Gerardi); **Millions**, 2005 (Enzo Cilenti); The Passion of St. Francis, 1934 (Alberto Pasquali); Pranchiyettan and the Saint, 2010 (Jesse Fox Allen); Reluctant Saint: Francis of Assisi, 2003 (made-for-TV; Robert Sean Leonard); Saint Francois d'Assise, 1983 (made-for-TV; Jose van Dam).

Frank, Anne (1929-1945; Teenage Jewish girl, who, along with her family, was hidden in an attic in Amsterdam, the Netherlands, during WWII, to avoid Nazi extermination during the Holocaust; she was eventually captured and died in a German concentration camp): Anne Frank: The

Millie Vitale and Bob Hope (as Eddie Foy Sr.) in *The Seven Little Foys*, 1955.

Whole Story, 2001 (TV miniseries; Hannah Taylor); Anne Frank's Diary, 1999; The Attic: The Hiding of Anne Frank, 1988 (made-for-TV; Lisa Jacobs); **The Diary of Anne Frank**, 1959 (Millie Perkins); The Diary of Anne Frank, 1967 (made-for-TV; Diana Devila); The Diary of Anne Frank, 1980 (made-for-TV; Melissa Gilbert); The Diary of Anne Frank, 1987 (made-for-TV; Katharine Schlesinger); The Diary of Anne Frank, 1995 (Rena Takahashi); The Diary of Anne Frank, 2009 (TV miniseries; Ellie Kendrick); Forget Me Not: The Anne Frank Story, 1996 (made-for-TV; Jenny Krochmal); From Cover to Cover, 1958 (TV series; episode 1.5, 1958: Carole Austin); Memories of Anne Frank, 2010 (made-for-TV; Rosabell Laurenti Sellers).

Frank, Leo Max (1884-1915; American-Jewish businessman; wrongly convicted of murder and lynched): The Murder of Mary Phagan, 1988 (TV miniseries; Peter Gallagher); The People v. Leo Frank, 2009 (Will Janowitz); **They Won't Forget**, 1937 (role model for Edward Norris). Note: For detailed information on the Leo Frank case, see my book, *"I Am Innocent!": A Comprehensive Encyclopedic History of the World's Wrongly Convicted Persons* (Da Capo Press, 2008; illustrated [10 images] pages 315-329).

Franklin, Benjamin (1706-1790; U.S. inventor, author, politician and a leader of the American Revolution): The Adams Chronicles, 1976 (TV miniseries; Robert Symonds); The American Adventure, 1982 (Dal McKennon voiceover); The American Revolution, 1994 (made-for-TV; Charles Durning voiceover); The Bastard, 1978 (made-for-TV; Tom Bosley); Battle of the Brave, 2004 (Colm Meaney); Beaumarchais the Scoundrel, 1997 (Jeff Nuttall); The Broken Chain, 1993 (made-for-TV; John Hagadorn); Cavalcade of America, 1952-1957 (TV series; "Night Strike," 1953 episode: Richard Garrick; "Crisis in Paris," 1955 episode; Howard St. John); Daniel Boone, 1964-1970 (TV series; "The Ben Franklin Encounter," 1965 episode: Laurie Main; "The Printing Press," 1969 episode: Fredd Wayne); Freedom to Speak, 1982 (TV miniseries; John Houseman); Hawkeye and the Last of the Mohicans, 1957- (TV series; Stan Francis); Histeria!, 1998-2000 (animated TV series; "Inventors Hall of Fame: Part I," 1998 episode: Billy West voiceover); **Janice Meredith**, 1924 (Lee Beggs); John Adams, 2008 (TV miniseries; Tom Wilkinson); **John Paul Jones**, 1959 (Charles Coburn); Lafayette, 1963 (Orson Welles); Liberty! The American Revolution, 1997 (TV miniseries; Philip Bosco); The Lives of Benjamin Franklin, 1974- (TV miniseries; "The Whirlwind," 1974 episode: Beau Bridges; "The Rebel," 1975 episode: Richard Widmark; "The Statesman," 1975 episode: Melvyn Douglas); **Lloyd's of London**, 1936 (Thomas Pogue); Louis XVI, the Man Who Didn't Want to Be King, 2011 (made-for-TV; Joe Sheridan); Matinee Theatre, 1955-1958 (TV series; "The Last Voyage,"

1957 episode: Maurice Manson); A More Perfect Union: America Becomes a Nation, 1989 (Fredd Wayne); My Lady's Slipper, 1916 (Charles Chapman); The Rebels, 1979 (made-for-TV; Tom Bosley); **The Remarkable Andrew**, 1942 (George Watts); Royal Affairs in Versailles, 1957 (Orson Welles); **1776**, 1972 (Howard Da Silva); The Spirit of '76, 1917 (Ben Lewis); Taking Liberty, 1993 (Donald Ogden Stiers); You Are There, 1953-1971 (TV series; "Benjamin Franklin's Kite Experiment [June 15, 1752]," 1956 episode: Parley Baer).

Franz Ferdinand (1863-1914; Archduke of Austria-Hungary whose 1914 assassination in Sarajevo touched off WWI): Alcoa Premiere, 1961-1963 (TV series; "The End of the World," 1961 episode: Robert Loggia); Beware of Pity, 1947 (Ken [Kenneth] Warrington); Bride of the Wind, 2001 (Werner Prinz); Das Schicksal derer von Hapsburg, 1928 (Willi Hubert); The Day That Shook the World, 1975 (Christopher Plummer); The Devil's Lieutenant, 1984 (made-for-TV; Friedrich von Thun); Fall of Eagles, 1974 (TV miniseries; "Indian Summer of an Emperor," 1974 episode; Peter Woodthorpe); Florian, 1940 (William B. Davidson); The Great Victory, Wilson or the Kaiser? The Fall of the Hohenzollerns, 1919 (Robert Harvey); I'll Tell the World, 1934 (Alec B. Francis); Kultur, 1918 (Charles Clary); Maresi, 1948 (Alfred Neugebauer); **Oh! What a Lovely War**, 1969 (Wensley Pithey); Sarajevo, 1940 (John Lodge); Sarajevo, 1955 (Ewald Balser); The Secret of Mayerling, 1951 (Jacques Dacqmine); Storm at Daybreak, 1933 (Frank Conroy); 37 Days, 2014 (TV miniseries; Simon Coury); Weltuntergang, 1984 (made-for-TV; Hans von Borsody); The Young Indiana Jones Chronicles, 1992-1993 (TV series; "Vienna, November 1908," 1993 episode: Lennart Hjulstrom).

Franz Joseph I (Emperor of Austria-Hungary; 1830-1916): The Angel with the Trumpet, 1953 (Anton Edthofer); Austeria, 1982 (A.P. [Adolf Peter] Hoffmann); BBC Sunday-Night Theatre, 1950-1959 (TV series; "The Masque of Kings," 1955 episode: Basil Sydney; "The Mayerling Affair," 1956 episode: Andre Van Gyseghem); Bismarck, 1940 (Karl Schonbock); Champagne Waltz, 1937 (Rudolph Anders); Condemned 1910, 1974 (made-for-TV; Egon von Jordan); Congress of Love, 1966 (Hannes Schiel); The Crown Prince, 2006 (made-for-TV; Klaus Maria Brandauer); Dancing Vienna, 1929 (Eugen Burg); Das Geheimnis um Johann Orth, 1936 (Paul Otto); Das Schicksal derer von Hapsburg, 1928 (Fritz Spira); The Day That Shook the World, 1975 (Otomar Korbelar); Der Kronprinz, 1989 (made-for-TV; Alfred Reiterer); Der Tag danach, 1965 (made-for-TV; Egon [von] Jordan); The Devil's Lieutenant, 1984 (made-for-TV; Guido Wieland); Die Deutschmeister, 1955 (Paul Horbiger); Die Forsterchristl, 1956 (Karl Schonbock); Die Forsterchristl, 1962 (Peter Weck); **The Emperor Waltz**, 1948 (Richard Haydn); Enigmes de l'histoire, 1956-1957 (TV series; one 1956 episode: Jean Galland); The Eternal Waltz, 1959 (Erik Frey); Europas letzter Sommer, 2012 (made-for-TV; Bernd Fischerauer); Evensong, 1934 (Frederick Leister); Fall of Eagles, 1974 (TV miniseries; Laurence Naismith); Florian, 1940 (Reginald Owen); Fruhjahrsparade, 1934 (Paul Horbiger); **The Great Waltz**, 1938 (Henry Hull); The Great Waltz, 1972 (Prince Johannes Schonburg-Hartenstein); The Hourglass Sanatorium, 1973 (Boleslaw Mierzejewski); Im weissen Rossl, 2008 (made-for-TV; Harald Serafin); Jmenem Jeho Velicenstva, 1929 (V. Pokorny); Kaiserin Elisabeth von Osterreich, 1921 (Niels Jensen); Kaiserin Elisabeth von Osterreich, 1972 (made-for-TV; Peter Frohlich); Kaisermanover, 1957 (Benno Smytt); Kaiserwalzer, 1956 (Willy Danek); The King Steps Out, 1936 (Franchot Tone); Konigswalzer, 1936 (Curt Jurgens); Kronprinz Rudolf oder: Das Geheimnis von Mayerling, 1919 (Niels Jensen); Kronprinz Rudolfs letzte Liebe, 1959 (Erik Frey); Kultur, 1918 (Al Fremont); La camera explore le temps, 1957-1966 (TV series; two episodes in 1963-1964: Rene Dary); Ludwig II, 1922 (Franz Scherer); Ludwig II: Glanz und Ende eines Konigs, 1959 (Erik Frey); The Masque of Kings, 1946 (made-for-TV; Arthur Wontner); Maximilian von Mexiko, 1970 (made-for-TV; Albert Rueprect); **Mayerling**, 1937 (Jean Dax);

Mayerling, 1968 (James Mason); Merry-Go-Round, 1923 (Anton Vaverka); My Darling is a Hunter, 1936 (Karl Ehmann); The Night Is Young, 1935 (Henry Stephenson); 1914, The Last Days before the War, 1932 (Eugen Klopfer); **Oh! What a Lovely War**, 1969 (Jack Hawkins); Preussen uber alles—Bismarcks deutsche Einigung, 1971 (TV miniseries; Albert Rueprecht); Princess Sisi, 1997 (animated TV series; Terrence Scammell voiceover); Producers' Showcase, 1954-1957 (TV series; "Mayerling," 1957 episode: Basil Sydney); Radetzkymarsch, 1965 (made-for-TV; Max Brebeck); Sarajevo, 1940 (Jean Worms); The Secret of Mayerling, 1951 (Jean Debucourt); Sherlock Holmes and the Leading Lady, 1991 (made-for-TV; Cyril Shaps); Sissi, 1955 (Karlheinz Bohm); Sisi, 2009 (made-for-TV; David Rott); Sisi and the Kaiser, 1991 (Nils Tavenier); Sisi: The Fateful Years, 1957 (Karlheinz Bohm); Sisi: The Young Empress, 1956 (Karlheinz Bohm); **The Smiling Lieutenant**, 1931 (Cornelius MacSunday); The Song in the Forest, 1950 (Allan Jeayes); Spring Parade, 1940 (Henry Stephenson); The Strauss Family, 1972 (TV miniseries; Michael Bryant; Nicholas Jones); The Third Squadron, 1926 (Fritz Spira); A Ultima Valsa, 1969 (TV series; Rubens de Falco); Universum History, 2013- (TV series; "Maximilian von Mexiko—Der Traum vom Herrschen," 2014 episode: Christian Krall); Vladyka Andrey, 2008 (Lembit Ulfsak); War and Peace, 1972 (TV miniseries; one 1972 episode: Arthur Blake); Weltuntergang, 1984 (made-for-TV; Erik Frey).

Frechette, Mary Evelyn (aka: "Billie"; 1907-1969; U.S. waitress; singer and consort of bank robber John Dillinger): Dillinger, 1973 (Michelle Phillip); Dillinger, 1991 (made-for-TV; Sherilyn Fenn); **Public Enemies**, 2009 (Marion Cotillard).

Freed, Alan (Albert James "Alan" Freed; 1921-1965; U.S. disc jockey who promoted rock 'n' roll music): American Hot Wax, 1978 (Tim McIntire); Cadillac Records, 2008 (Eric Bogosian); Great Balls of Fire!, 1989 (Robert Lesser); **La Bamba**, 1987 (Jeffrey Alan Chandler); Mr. Rock 'n' Roll: The Alan Freed Story, 1999 (made-for-TV; Judd Nelson); **Ray**, 2004 (Tom Clark); Who Do You Love, 2008 (Ian Leson).

Fremont, John C. (John Charles Fremont; U.S. military officer and frontiersman; U.S. senator from California; Union major general in American Civil War; 1813-1890): **Kit Carson**, 1940 (Dana Andrews); Kit Carson and the Mountain Men, 1977 (made-for-TV; Robert Reed); Kit Carson over the Great Divide, 1925 (Arthur Hotaling).

Freud, Sigmund (1856-1939; Austrian neurologist and founding father of psychoanalysis): A Beginner's Guide to Freud, 1989 (made-for-TV; David Kossoff); Being Eve, 2001-2002 (TV series; "Being Obsessed," 2002 episode: Stephen Lovatt); Bill & Ted's Excellent Adventure, 1989 (Rod Loomis); A Dangerous Method, 2011 (Viggo Mortensen); Dust, 2001 (Jon Ivanovski); The Empty Mirror, 1999 (Peter Michael Goetz); A Far Country, 1971 (made-for-TV; Julien Schoenaerts); Freud, 1962 (Montgomery Clift); Freud, 1984- (TV miniseries; David Suchet); Nineteen Nineteen, 1985 (Frank Finlay); Gamen, 1973 (made-for-TV; Toivo Pawlo); Hans: A Case Study, 2012 (Austin Pendleton); The Loves of Kafka, 1988 (Karel Chromik); Lovesick, 1983 (Alex Guinness); Mahler on the Couch, 2012 (Karl Markovics); Matinee Theatre, 1955-1958 (TV series; "The Ransom of Sigmund Freud," 1957 episode: Ludwig Donath); Mon couer est rouge, 1977 (Paule Zajdemann); My Name Was Sabrina Spielrein, 2003 (Helmut Vogel); Nothing More Than Everything, 2002 (Timothy J. Cox); The Oldest Story Ever Told, 2010 (Tony Fennelly); The Secret Diary of Sigmund Freud, 1984 (Bud Cort); Sherlock Holmes and the Leading Lady, 1991 (made-for-TV; John Bennett); **The Seven-Per-Cent Solution**, 1976 (Alan Arkin); Therapy for a Vampire, 2015 (Karl Fischer); The United States Steel Hour, 1953-1963 (TV series; "The Wound Within," 1958 episode: Farley Granger); You Are There, 1953-1971 (TV series: "The Secret of Sigmund Freud," 1953 episode: Whit Bissell); Young Dr. Freud, 1976 (made-for-TV; Karlheinz

Henry Stephenson, Brenda Joyce and Richard Greene (as Robert Fulton) in *Little Old New York*, 1940.

Hackl); Young Einstein, 1988 (Kim McKew); Yungermann, 2007- (TV series; Lakis Lazopoulos).

Fromm, Friedrich (1888-1945; German general who was indecisive during the 1944 attempted assassination of Adolf Hitler and was executed at Hitler's orders): Claus Graf Stauffenberg, 1970 (made-for-TV; Franz Josef Steffens); Die Stunde der Offiziere, 2004 (made-for-TV; Hermann Lause); I Spy, 1955-1957 (TV series; "Canaris Story": Ronald Dawson); It Happened on July 20th, 1955 (Carl Wery); Operation Valkyrie, 2004 (made-for-TV; Axel Milberg); Operation Walkure, 1971 (made-for-TV; Harry Kalenberg; Jacques Monod in French version); The Plot to Assassinate Hitler, 1955 (Siegfried Schurenberg); The Plot to Kill Hitler, 1990 (made-for-TV; Helmuth Lohner); **Valkyrie**, 2008 (Tom Wilkinson); The Wednesday Play, 1964-1970 (TV series; "The July Plot," 1964 episode: Joseph Furst).

Frost, David Paradine (Sir David Paradine Frost; British journalist and media personality; 1939-): **Nixon/Frost**, 2008 (Michael Sheen).

Fuchs, Klaus (1911-1988; German theoretical physicist and atomic spy for the Soviets, who stole plans for the atomic bomb from the Manhattan Project): Atom Spies, 1979 (made-for-TV; Andrew Ray); Cambridge Spies, 2003 (TV miniseries; Garrick Hagon); CrossFade, 2002 (Wilhelm Schlotterer); Day One, 1989 (made-for-TV; Lorne Brass); Klaus Fuchs, 1965 (made-for-TV; Robert Graf); Oppenheimer, 1980- (TV miniseries; Albert Welling); Race for the Bomb, 1987 (TV series; Denis Forest); Spies, Lies and the Superbomb, 2007 (TV miniseries; Marco Hofschneider). Note: For detailed information on Fuchs, see my book *Spies: A Narrative Encyclopedia of Dirty Tricks & Double Dealing from Biblical Times to Today* (M. Evans, 1997; illustrated pages 221-224).

Fulton, Robert (1765-1815; American engineer and inventor of the first commercially successful steamboat): The Battle of Austerlitz, 1960 (Orson Welles); Little Old New York, 1923 (Courtenay Foote); Little Old New York, 1940 (Richard Greene); Triton, 1968- (TV series; Robert Cawdron).

Gabaldon, Guy Louis (1926-2006; U.S. Marine, who captured more than 1,500 Japanese troops the WWII Battle of Saipan in 1944 after persuading their commander to order his troops to surrender; Gabaldon, who was raised as a foster child in Los Angeles by a Japanese family, spoke fluent Japanese and was therefore able to convince Japanese commanders to surrender; he was awarded the Navy Cross and the Silver Star): Hell to Eternity, 1960 (Jeffrey Hunter).

Doris Dudley and George Sanders (in role modeled on Paul Gauguin) in *The Moon and Sixpence*, 1942.

Gabcik, Josef (1912-1942; Czech resistance fighter, one of those who assassinated Nazi Governor Reinhard Heydrich of Czechoslovakia in June 1942, and who was trapped by German troops in a Prague church, committing suicide rather than being taken captive): Anthropoid, 2016 (Cillian Murphy); G.E. True, 1962- (TV series; "Heydrich," two 1963 episodes: Albert Paulsen); Heydrich in Prag, 1967 (made-for-TV; Fritz Wepper); HHhH, 2016 (Jack Reynor); The Key, 1971 (Vitezslav Jandak); Lidice, 2011 (Jiri Stanek); **Operation Daybreak**, 1975 (Anthony Andrews). Note: For detailed information on Gabcik and his assassination of Heydrich, see my two-volume work *The Great Pictorial History of World Crime*, Volume I (History, Inc., 2004; illustrated [9 images] pages 134-138).

Gable, Clark (1901-1960; U.S. film actor, once known as "The King of Hollywood"; husband of actress Carole Lombard): Another Chance, 1989 (Larry Pennell); Bamboo Shark, 2011 (Ralph Chelli); Blonde, 2001 (TV miniseries; Bruce Hughes/Shayne Greenman); **Callaway Went That Away**, 1951 (himself); Ginger and Fred, 1986 (Salvatore Billa); Grace Kelly, 1983 (made-for-TV; Boyd Holister); It Happened in Hollywood, 1937 (Philip Waldron); Lucy, 2003 (made-for-TV; Charles Unwin); Malice in Wonderland, 1985 (made-for-TV; Gary Wayne); Marilyn: The Untold Story, 1980 (made-for-TV; Larry Pennell); Noise Matters, 2013 (Travis Case); Quantum Leap, 1989-1993 (TV series; "Goodbye, Norma Jean—April 4, 1960," 1993 episode: Larry Pennell); RKO 281, 1999 (made-for-TV; Bobby Valentino); **The Rocketeer**, 1991 (Gene Daily); The Scarlett O'Hara War, 1980 (made-for-TV; Edward Winter); This Magic Moment, 2013 (made-for-TV; Travis Schuldt); Train Ride to Hollywood, 1975 (Jay Lawrence).

Gage, Thomas (1719-1787; British general in the early stages of the American Revolutionary War, 1775-1783): **Allegheny Uprising**, 1939 (Olaf Hytten); **America**, 1924 (W.W. Jones); Espionage, 1963-1964 (TV series; "Once a Spy," 1964 episode: Geoffrey Kenion); George Washington, 1984 (TV miniseries; Michael Allinson); **Johnny Tremain**, 1957 (Ralph Clanton); The Revolution, 2006- (TV series; Jonah Triebwasser); Samuel Adams, 2014 (made-for-TV; Stephen Beal); Sons of Liberty, 2015- (TV miniseries; Marton Csokas).

Galba (3 B.C.-69 A.D.; Roman emperor): Nero, 1922 (Nello Carotenuto); Nerone, 1977 (Aldo Fabrizi); **Quo Vadis**, 1951 (Pietro Tordi); The Ten Gladiators, 1963 (Mirko Ellis).

Galileo Galilei (1564-1642; Italian astronomer, physicist, engineer and philosopher): Galileo, 1961 (made-for-TV; James Grout); Galileo, 1968 (Cyril Cusack); Galileo, 1975 (Topol); Galileo, 1994 (Nerendra Prasad);

Galileo: Eppur Si Muove, 2011- (TV series; Massimo Gentile); Galileo: On the Shoulders of Giants, 1998 (made-for-TV; Michael Moriarty); Lamp at Midnight, 1966 (made-for-TV; Melvyn Douglas); The Life of Galileo, 1962 (made-for-TV; Ernst Schroder); The Starry Messenger, 2009 (Bob Chapman).

Gallico, Paul William (1897-1976; U.S. author, short story writer and newspaperman): A Bloody Canvas, 2008 (made-for-TV; Tim Dillard); Madison Sq. Garden, 1932 (himself); Ring of Passion, 1978 (made-for-TV; Joseph Campanella).

Gandhi, Mahatma (Mohanda Karamchand Gandhi; 1869-1948; Indian leader for India's independence who adopted a non-violent resistance to British rule): **Gandhi**, 1982 (Ben Kingsley); Gandhi, My Father, 2007 (Darshan Jariwala); Gandhi to Hitler, 2011 (Avijit Dutt); Hey Ram, 2000 (Naseeruddin Shah); Jinnah, 1998 (Sam Dastor); The Last Days of the Raj, 2007 (made-for-TV; Surendra Rajan); The Legend of Bhagat Singh, 2002 (Surendra Rajan); The Making of the Mahatmas, 1996 (Rajit Kapoor); Masterpiece Theatre: Lord Mountbatten—The Last Viceroy, 1986- (TV miniseries; Sam Dastor); **Nine Hours to Rama**, 1963 (J.S. Casshyap); You Are There, 1953-1971 (TV series; "The Sacrifice of Mahatma Gandhi," 1954 episode: Milton Selzer). Note: For detailed information on Gandhi and his assassination, see my two-volume work *The Great Pictorial History of World Crime*, Volume I (History, Inc., 2004; illustrated [7 images] pages 156-160).

Garcia Lorca, Federico (1898-1936; Spanish poet and playwright aligned with socialist causes and who was assassinated by fascists at the beginning of the Spanish Civil War, his body never found; he was closely associated with painter Salvador Dali, although Dali rejected the poet's homosexual advances): Buneul and King Solomon's Table, 2001 (Adria Collado); Dali, 1991 (Nikola Stefanov); Dali, etre Dieu, 2002 (made-for-TV; Carles Marti); **Death in Granada**, 1996 (Andy Garcia); El ministerio del tiempo, 2015 (TV series; Angel Ruiz); Federico Garcia Lorca Noir Despair, 2013 (Alvaro Ovalle); La luz con el tiempo dentro, 2015 (Edu Bulnes); La Xirgu, l'actriu, 2015 (made-for-TV; Fran Perea); Little Ashes, 2009 (Javier Beltran); Lorca, muerte de un poeta, 1987-1988 (TV series; Nickolas Grace); Martes de carnaval, 2008 (TV miniseries; Sergio Villanueva); Persistence of Memory, 2014 (Andre Champagne); Severo Ochoa: La conquista de un Nobel, 2001- (TV miniseries; Ignacio Vaquero).

Gardner, Alexander (1821-1882; Scottish-born photographer in the U.S., who was a principal photographer of President Abraham Lincoln, the American Civil War and the execution of the four conspirators found guilty in Lincoln's 1865 assassination): **The Conspirator**, 2011 (John Bankson).

Garfield, James A. (1831-1881; U.S. politician and 20th President of the U.S., 1991; assassinated): Alexander Graham Bell: The Sound and the Silence, 1993 (made-for-TV; Ian Watkin); Captains and Kings, 1976 (TV series; Richard Matheson); Netherbeast Incorporated, 2007 (Robert Wagner); The Night Riders, 1939 (Francis Sayles); No More Excuses, 1968 (Lawrence Wolf); The Prince of Power, 1969 (Van Johnson).

Garibaldi, Giuseppe (1807-1882; Italian general and politician): Anita e Garibaldi, 2013 (Gabriel Braga Nunes); Anita Garibaldi, 1952 (Raf Vallone); Anita Garibaldi, 2012 (Giorgio Pasotti); Garibaldi, 1961 (Renzo Ricci); Garibaldi the General, 1987 (TV miniseries; Franco Nero); Il generale dei briganti, 2012 (made-for-TV; Thierry Toscan); Vita di Cavour, 1967 (TV miniseries; Glauco Onorato).

Garnett, Richard Brooke (1817-1863; U.S. military officer and Brigadier General in the Confederate army of Northern Virginia during the American Civil War): **Gettysburg**, 1993 (Andrew Prine); **Gods and Gener-**

als, 2003 (Andrew Prine).

Garrett, Pat (Patrick Floyd "Pat" Garrett; 1850-1908; U.S. Old West lawman; reported killer of Billy the Kid): Badman's Country, 1958 (George Montgomery); Billy the Kid, 1930 (Wallace Beery); **Billy the Kid**, 1941 (role model for Brian Donlevy); Billy the Kid, 1989 (made-for-TV; Duncan Regehr); Billy the Kid Returns, 1938 (Wade Boteler); Bonanza, 1959-1973 (TV series; "Commitment at Angelus," 1968 episode: Ken Lynch); Bronco, 1958-1962 (TV series; "Death of an Out-law," 1960 episode: Rhodes Reason); Buffalo Bill Jr., 1955-1956 (TV series; one 1955 episode: two 1956 episodes: Keith Richards for all); Bullets Don't Argue, 1964 (Rod Cameron); Cananea, 1978 (Carlos East); **Chisum**, 1970 (Glenn Corbett); Colt .45, 1957-1960 (TV series; "Amnesty," 1959 episode: Wayne Heffley); Copperhead, 2008 (made-for-TV; Brad Greenquist); **Four Faces West**, 1948 (Charles Bickford); Frontier Doctor, 1958- (TV series; "Three Wanted Men," 1958 episode: Richard Travis); Guns of Paradise, 1988-1990 (TV series; "A Gathering of Guns," 1989 episode: John Schneider); Gunslingers, 2014 (TV minis-eries; two 2014 episodes: Jim Burleson); Histeria!, 1998-2000 (animated TV series; "The Wild West," 1998 episode: Jeff Bennett voiceover); The Hunter's Moon, 2009 (Conor O'Farrell); I Shot Billy the Kid, 1950 (Robert Lowery); I'll Kill Him and Return Alone, 1967 (Fausto Tozzi); The Kid from Texas, 1950 (Frank Wilcox); The Last Movie, 1971 (Rod Cameron); Last of the Desperados, 1955 (James Craig); The Law vs. Billy the Kid, 1954 (James Griffith); **The Left-Handed Gun**, 1958 (John Dehner); Longarm, 1988 (made-for-TV; Lee de Broux); Omnibus, 1952-1961 (TV series; one 1953 episode: Scott Douglas); The Outcasts, 1968-1969 (TV series; "The Man from Bennington," 1968 episode; Kenneth Tobey); Outcasts of the Trail, 1949 (Monte Hale); The Parson and the Outlaw, 1957 (Bob Duncan); **Pat Garrett and Billy the Kid**, 1973 (James Coburn); The Outlaw, 1943 (Thomas Mitchell); The Philco-Goodyear Television Playhouse, 1948-1956 (TV series; "The Death of Billy the Kid," 1955 episode: Frank Overton); Redemption, 2009 (Chad Grimes); Son of Billy the Kid, 1949 (Lash La Rue); Stories of the Century, 1954- (TV series; "Billy the Kid," 1954 episode: Richard Travis); The Tall Man, 1960-1962 (TV series; Barry Sullivan); The Time Tunnel, 1966-1967 (TV series; "Billy the Kid," 1967 episode: Allen Case); Wanted: Dead or Alive, 1958-1961 (TV series; "Eager Man," 1959 episode: Walter Sande); The West, 2016 (TV miniseries; Ric Mad-dox); The Wild West, 2006- (TV miniseries; "Billy the Kid," 2006 episode: Ian Porter); **Young Guns**, 1988 (Patrick Wayne); **Young Guns II**, 1990 (William Petersen). Note: For detailed information on Garrett, see my book *Encyclopedia of Western Lawmen and Outlaws* (Paragon House, 1992; illustrated [4 images] pages 133-137).

Gascoyne-Cecil, Robert (Lord Salisbury; 1830-1903; British politician and prime minister of Great Britain): Around the World in 80 Days, 2004 (David Ryall); Disraeli: Portrait of a Romantic, 1978 (TV miniseries; John Gregg); Edward the King, 1975 (TV series; Richard Vernon); En-tente cordiale, 1939 (Jean Toulout); Jack the Ripper, 1988- (TV series; David Swift); Jennie: Lady Randolph Churchill, 1974 (TV miniseries; Llewellyn Rees); **Murder by Decree**, 1979 (John Gielgud); The Prime Minister, 1942 (Leslie Perrins); Queen of Destiny, 1940 (Harvey Bra-ban); Rhodes, 1996 (TV miniseries; Michael Atkinson); **Young Win-ston**, 1972 (Laurence Naismith).

Gates, Horatio (1727-1806; former British soldier who served as a gen-eral in the Continental Army in the American Revolutionary War, 1775-1783): The Crossing, 2000 (made-for-TV; Nigel Bennett); George Washington, 1984 (TV miniseries; Jeremy Kemp); The Revolution, 2006- (TV series; Chris O'Brocto).

Gatewood, Charles B. (1853-1896; U.S. military officer in the Geronimo campaigns): **Geronimo: An American Legend**, 1993 (Jason Patric); Stories of the Century, 1954- (TV series; one 1954 episode: Brett King);

Teresa Wright and Gary Cooper (as Lou Gehrig) in *The Pride of the Yankees*, **1942.**

Zane Grey Theater, 1956-1961 (TV series; "The Last Bugle," 1960 episode: Robert Cummings).

Gauguin, Paul (1848-1903; French artist): The Eyes of Van Gogh, 2005 (Lee Godart); Finding Gauguin, 2010 (Lee Donald Taicher); Gauguin the Savage, 1980 (made-for-TV; David Carradine); Le voyage du Hol-landais, 1981 (made-for-TV; Jean-Pierre Bisson); **Lust for Life**, 1952 (Anthony Quinn); **Midnight in Paris**, 2011 (Olivier Rabourdin); Mon cher Theo Van Gogh, 1980 (made-for-TV; Alexandre Fabre); **The Moon and Sixpence**, 1942 (role model for George Sanders); Omnibus, 1967-2003 (TV series; "Van Gogh," 1990 episode: Jack Shepherd); Oviri, 1986 (Donald Sutherland); Paradise Found, 2003 (Kiefer Sutherland); Paul Gauguin, 1975 (TV miniseries; Maurice Barrier); The Savage, 1977 (made-for-TV; Leo McKern); Shadow in a Landscape, 1987 (made-for-TV; John Hug); State of the Artist, 2001 (Neil Levine); Van Gogh, 1969 (made-for-TV; Friedrich G. Beckhaus); Van Gogh; een huis voor Vincent, 2013 (TV series; Guy Rombaux); Van Gogh: Painted with Words, 2010 (made-for-TV; Aidan McArdle); **Vincent and Theo**, 1990 (Wladimir Yordanoff); Vincent Van Gogh, 1988 (made-for-TV; Pertti Sveholm); The Yellow House, 2007 (made-for-TV; John Lynch).

Gavin, James M. (James Maurice Gavin; born James Nally Ryan; aka: "Jumping Jim"; 1907-1990; U.S. Army lieutenant general; commanded 82nd Airborne Division during the Allied invasion of Normandy on June 6, 1944): **A Bridge Too Far**, 1977 (Ryan O'Neal); **The Longest Day**, 1962 (Robert Ryan).

Gehrig, Henry Lewis (aka: "Lou"; "Buster"; 1903-1941; U.S. baseball player and legendary hitter for the New York Yankees); **The Babe**, 1992 (Michael McGrady); Babe Ruth, 1991 (made-for-TV; Neal McDo-nough); Climax!, 1954-1958 (TV series; "The Lou Gehrig Story," 1956 episode: Wendell Corey); A Love Affair: The Eleanor and Lou Gehrig Story, 1977 (made-for-TV; Edward Herrmann); **The Pride of the Yan-kees**, 1942 (Gary Cooper; Douglas Croft as young Lou Gehrig); Rawhide, 1938 (himself).

General Tom Thumb (Charles Sherwood Stratton; 1838-1883; U.S. midget and stellar attraction in the P.T. Barnum exhibits): Barnum!, 1986 (made-for-TV; Paul Miller); Barnum, 1986 (made-for-TV; Sandor Raski); **The Great John L**, 1945 (George Brasno); **The Mighty Bar-num**, 1934 (George Brasno); P.T. Barnum, 1999 (made-for-TV; Josh Ryan Evans); Tad, 1995 (made-for-TV; Ed Gale).

Genghis Khan (Temujin; c. 1162-1227; Mongol conqueror and emperor of the vast Mongol Empire): Bill & Ted's Excellent Adventure, 1989

Susan Hayward and John Wayne (as Genghis Khan) in *The Conqueror*, **1956.**

(Al Leong); The Conqueror, 1956 (John Wayne); Deadliest Warrior, 2009- (TV series; Timothy May); Genghis Khan, 1950 (Manuel Conde); Genghis Khan, 1965 (Omar Sharif); Genghis Khan, 1987 (TV series; Alex Man); Genghis Khan, 1987- (TV series; Tony Liu); Genghis Khan, 1992 (Richard Tyson); Genghis Khan, 1998 (Tumen, Hude); Genghis Khan, 2004 (TV series; Ba Sen); Genghis Khan, 2005 (made-for-TV; Orgil Makhaan); Genghis Khan: The Story of a Lifetime, 2010 (Richard Tyson); Genghis Khan: To the Ends of the Earth and Sea, 2007 (Takashi Sorimachi, Christopher Sabat, Todd Haberkorn); Changez Khan, 1957 (Sheikh Mukhtar); Changez Khan, 1958 (Allauddin); The Golden Horde, 1951 (Marvin Miller); Hercules against the Barbarians, 1964 (Roldano Lupi); Hurricanes, 1993-1997 (animated TV series; several episodes: Scott McNeil); Kingdom of Conquerors, 2013 (Tumen); Mongol: The Rise of Genghis Khan, 2008 (Tadanobu Asano, Odnyam Odsuren); The Mongols, 1961 (Roldano Lupi); Saturday the 14th Strikes Back, 1988 (Tai Logo); Star Trek, 1966-1969 (TV series; "The Savage Curtain," 1969 episode: Nathan Jung); Under the Eternal Blue Sky, 1990 (Agvaantserengiin Enkhtaivan); Witness to Yesterday, 1998- (TV series; "Genghis Khan," 1998 episode: Gordon Tootoosis); You Are There, 1953-1971 (TV series; "The Rise of Genghis Khan [1203]," 1954 episode: Raymond Bramley).

Genovese, Vito (1897-1969; Italian-born U.S. gangster and head of one of NYC's five Mafia families): Bonanno: A Godfather's Story, 1999 (made-for-TV; Emidio Michetti); Boss of Bosses, 2001 (made-for-TV; Steven Bauer); **Bugsy**, 1991 (Don Carrara); The Gangster Chronicles, 1981- (TV series; Robert Davi); Gangster Wars, 1981 (Robert Davi); Lansky, 1999 (made-for-TV; Robert Miano); Lucky Luciano, 1974 (Charles Cioffi); **The Valachi Papers**, 1972 (Lino Ventura). Note: For detailed information on Genovese, see my book, *World Encyclopedia of Organized Crime* (Paragon House, 1992; illustrated [6 images] pages 182-187).

George III (1738-1820; King of Great Britain and Ireland): The Adams Chronicles, 1976 (TV miniseries; John Tillinger); **America**, 1924 (Arthur Donaldson); The American Revolution, 1994 (made-for-TV; David Warner voiceover); Barry Lyndon, 1975 (Roger Booth); BBC Sunday-Night Theatre, 1950-1959 (TV series; "The Lass of Richmond Hill," 1957 episode: George Woodbridge); **Beau Brummell**, 1954 (Robert Morley); Boswell's Life of Johnson, 1971 (made-for-TV; John Byron); Captain James Cook, 1987- (TV miniseries; Rhys Mc-Connochie); Emissaries of Peace, 2007 (made-for-TV; Andrew Miller); Enigmes de l'histoire, 1956-1957 (TV series; two episodes in 1957; Jean Berger); The Ghosts of Oxford Street, 1991 (made-for-TV; Leigh Bowery); ITV Playhouse, 1967- (TV series; "The People's Jack," 1970

episode: Richard Wilson); John Adams, 2008- (TV miniseries; Tom Hollander); **John Paul Jones**, 1959 (Eric Pohlmann); Jonathan Strange & Mr. Norrell, 2015- (TV miniseries; Edward Petherbridge); Kings and Queens, 2002- (TV miniseries; "George III," 2002 episode: Robert Stone); Liberty! The American Revolution, 1997 (TV miniseries; Alex Jennings); **The Madness of King George**, 1994 (Nigel Hawthorne); Mrs. Fitzherbert, 1950 (Frederick Valk); Monty Python's Flying Circus, 1969-1974 (TV series; "The Golden Age of Ballooning," 1974 episode; Graham Chapman); The Mutiny on the Bounty, 1916 (John Storm); Prince Regent, 1979- (TV miniseries; Nigel Davenport); Sabotage!, 2001 (Robin Soans); Rake's Progress, 1939 (made-for-TV; Albert Lieven); Sabotage!, 2001 (Robin Soans); Samuel Adams, 2014 (made-for-TV; Napoleon Ryan); The Spirit of '76, 1917 (Jack Cosgrave); TURN: Washington's Spies, 2014- (TV series; two 2015 episodes: Paul Rhys); **The Young Mr. Pitt**, 1943 (Raymond Lovell); You Are There, 1953-1971 (TV series; "William Pitt's Last Speech to Parliament," 1954 episode: E.G. Marshall).

George IV (King of Great Britain; 1762-1830): Affairs of a Rogue, 1949 (Cecil Parker); The Amateur Gentleman, 1920 (Alfred Paumier); The Amateur Gentleman, 1926 (Gino Corrado); The Amateur Gentleman, 1936 (Gilbert Davis); BBC Sunday-Night Theatre, 1950-1959 (TV series; "Beau Brummell," 1954 episode: Walter Fitzgerald; "The Scarlet Pimpernel," 1955 episode; Jack May); **Beau Brummel**, 1924 (Willard Louis); **Beau Brummell**, 1954 (Peter Ustinov); Beau Brummell: This Charming Man, 2006 (made-for-TV; Hugh Bonneville); Becky Sharp, 1935 (Olaf Hytten); Black Adder the Third, 1987 (TV series; Hugh Laurie); The First Gentleman, 1961 (made-for-TV; Charles Gray); **The House of Rothschild**, 1934 (Lumsden Hare); Lady Hamilton, 1921 (George Alexander); The Laughing Lady, 1950 (Peter Graves); The Life of Lord Byron, 1922 (Bellenden Powell); **The Madness of King George**, 1994 (Rupert Everett); **The Man in Grey**, 1946 (Raymond Lovell); Mrs. Fitzherbert, 1950 (Peter Graves); Poldark, 1996 (made-for-TV; James Saxon); **Princess Caraboo**, 1994 (John Sessions); The Romance of Lady Hamilton, 1919 (Teddy Arundell); **Saraband**, 1949 (Anthony Lang); **The Scarlet Pimpernel**, 1935 (Nigel Bruce); The Scarlet Pimpernel, 1955 (TV series; Alexander Gauge); The Scarlet Pimpernel, 1982 (made-for-TV; Julian Fellowes); The Scarlet Pimpernel, 1999 (TV miniseries; Jonathan Coy); Shaka Zulu, 1986- (TV series; Roy Dotrice); Sharpe's Regiment, 1996 (made-for-TV; Julian Fellowes); Vanity Fair, 1987- (TV series; "The Very Best of Company," 1987 episode: Peter Schofield); Vanity Fair, 1998 (TV miniseries; Roger Ashton-Griffiths); Vanity Fair, 2004 (Richard McCabe).

George V (1865-1936; King of Great Britain): All the King's Men, 1999 (made-for-TV; David Troughton); Bertie and Elizabeth, 2002 (made-for-TV; Alan Bates); Downton Abbey, 2010-2015 (TV series; one 2013 episode with Guy Williams; one 2014 episode with Jon Glover); Edward & Mrs. Simpson, 1978- (TV miniseries; Marius Goring); Edward the King, 1975- (TV series; Michael Osborne); The Fiendish Plot of Dr. Fu Manchu, 1980 (Rene Aranda); The First Black Britons, 2005 (made-for-TV; Andrew Pritchard); The Great Air Race, 1990 (made-for-TV; David Ravenswood); The Great Victory, Wilson or the Kaiser? The Fall of the Hohenzollerns, 1919 (William Gaffney); **The King's Speech**, 2010 (Michael Gambon); A King's Story, 1965 (Carleton Hobbs); Lillie, 1978- (TV miniseries; Keith Varnier); The Lost Prince, 2004 (made-for-TV; Tom Hollander); Monash: The Forgotten Anzac, 2008 (made-for-TV; William Gluth); My Boy Jack, 2007 (made-for-TV; Julian Wadham); **My Fair Lady**, 1964 (Charles Fredericks in fantasy sequence); Number 10, 1983- (TV miniseries; Neville Barber); Suffragette, 2015 (Simon Gifford); 37 Days, 2014- (TV miniseries; Patrick FitzSymons); A Thousand Skies, 1985- (TV miniseries; Andrew Gilmour); The Treaty, 1991 (made-for-TV; John Warner); W.E., 2011 (James Fox); Wallis & Edward, 2005 (made-for-TV; Clifford Rose); Whom the Gods Destroy, 1916 (Thomas R. Mills); Why America Will

Win, 1918 (Henry Warwick); Winston Churchill: The Wilderness Years, 1981- (TV miniseries; "Down and Out," 1981 episode: Guy Deghy).

Geronimo (1829-1909; Apache war leader): The Adventures of Rin Tin Tin, 1954-1959 (TV series; Charles Stevens in 1954 and 1958 episodes: Peter Mamakos in a 1958 episode); Annie Oakley, 1954-1957 (TV series; "Tagg Oakley, Sheriff," 1956 episode: Frank Richards); **Apache**, 1954 (Monte Blue); The Battle at Apache Pass, 1952 (Jay Silverheels); Bret Maverick, 1981-1982 (TV series; "Horse of Yet Another Color," 1982 episode: Ray Tracey); **Broken Arrow**, 1950 (Jay Silverheels); Broken Arrow, 1956-1960 (TV series; three 1956 episodes: Michael Pate; one 1957 episode: Charles Horvath; one 1957 episode: Ric Roman); Buffalo Bill Jr., 1955-1956 (TV series; "Fight for Geronimo," 1955 episode: Chief Thundercloud); Casey Jones, 1957- (TV series; "Run to Deadwood," 1957 episode: Don Carlos); Death Valley Days, 1952-1970 (TV series; "The White Healer," 1960 episode: Joe Bassett); **Geronimo**, 1939 (Chief Thundercloud); Geronimo, 1962 (Chuck Connors); **Geronimo: An American Legend**, 1993 (Wes Studi); Geronimo, 1993 (made-for-TV; Joseph Runningfox); Gunsmoke: The Last Apache, 1990 (made-for-TV; Joaquin Martinez); I Killed Geronimo, 1950 (Chief Thundercloud); Indian Uprising, 1952 (Miguel Inclan); **The Last Outpost**, 1951 (John War Eagle); Mr. Horn, 1979 (made-for-TV; Enrique Lucero); Son of Geronimo: Apache Avenger, 1952 (Chief Yowlachie); Stories of the Century, 1954- (TV series; "Geronimo," 1954 episode: Chief Yowlachie); Taza, Son of Cochise, 1954 (Ian MacDonald); Tombstone Territory, 1957- (TV series; "Geronimo," 1958 episode: John Doucette); Valley of the Sun, 1942 (Tom Tyler); Walk the Proud Land, 1956 (Jay Silverheels); Walt Disney's Wonderful World of Color, 1954-1992 (TV series; "Texas John Slaughter: Geronimo's Revenge," 1960 episode; "Texas John Slaughter: End of the Trail," 1961 episode; Pat Hogan for both); Zane Grey Theater, 1956-1961 (TV series; "The Last Bugle," 1960 episode: Michael Pate).

Gerstein, Kurt (1905-1945; German officer and member of the Waffen SS, chief of the Technical Disinfection Services in the Nazi death camps and who reportedly attempted to expose the genocidal efforts of the Nazis to exterminate the Jews in the Holocaust; he allegedly commited suicide): **Amen**, 2002 (Ulrich Tukur).

Gestas (or Gesmas; the unrepentant thief, or bad thief, who died on the cross with Jesus at Golgotha Hill outside of Jerusalem; his counterpart, Dismas, or the good thief, sought forgiveness and was promised Paradise): **The Greatest Story Ever Told**, 1965 (Marc Cavell); Jesus, 1979 (Kevin O'Shea); **The King of Kings**, 1927 (James Mason); **King of Kings**, 1961 (Barry Keegan).

Giancana, Sam (1908-1975; U.S. gangster and member of the organized crime cartel in Chicago): Chicago Mob Takedown, 2008 (made-for-TV; Stan Goldstein); The Kennedys, 2011 (TV series; Serge Houde); Marilyn & Bobby: Her Final Affair, 1993 (made-for-TV; Raymond Serra); Power and Beauty, 2002 (made-for-TV; Peter Friedman); The Rat Pack, 1998 (made-for-TV; Robert Miranda); Ruby, 1992 (Carmine Caridi); Sinatra, 1992 (made-for-TV; Rod Steiger); Sugartime, 1995 (made-for-TV; John Turturro). Note: For detailed information on Giancana, see my book, *World Encyclopedia of Organized Crime* (Paragon House, 1992; illustrated pages 187-188).

Gilles de Rais (Gilles de Retz; 1404-1440; French military commander during the One Hundred Years' War and one of the captains who fought with Joan of Arc; later proved to be a horrific serial killer and was executed): BBC Play of the Month, 1965-1983 (TV series; "St. Joan," 1968 episode: Philip Bond); BBC Sunday-Night Theatre, 1950-1959 (TV series; "Festival Drama: Saint Joan," 1951 episode: Bryan Johnson); Hope: The Last Paladin, 2014- (TV series; Amir Khalighi); Jeanne d'Arc, le pouvoir de l'innocence, 1989 (made-for-TV; Vincent Gau-

Chief Thundercloud as Geronimo in *Geronimo*, 1939.

thier); **Joan of Arc**, 1948 (Henry Brandon); Les proces de l'Histoire, 2011- (TV series; Laurent Desponds); **The Messenger: The Story of Joan of Arc**, 1999 (Vincent Cassel); Monstrum, 2014 (Cedrick Spinassou); Saint Joan, 1946 (made-for-TV; Geoffrey Wilmer); Saint Joan, 1957 (David Oxley); Saint Joan, 1967 (made-for-TV; Ted van Griethuysen); Saint Joan the Maid, 1929 (Philippe Heriat); Sainte Jeanne, 1969 (made-for-TV; Francois Maistre). Note: For detailed information on Gilles de Rais, see my two-volume work, *The Great Pictorial History of World Crime*, Volume II (History, Inc., 2004; illustrated [5 images] pages 1019-1021). Note: For detailed information on Gilles des Rais and his serial murders, see my two-volume work *The Great Pictorial History of World Crime*, Volume II (History, Inc., 2004; illustrated [5 images] pages 1019-1021).

Gillette, Chester (U.S. convicted murderer; executed; 1883-1908; was the role model for the tragic young man profiled in Theodore Dreiser's 1925, *An American Tragedy*, the author attending Gillette's trial): **An American Tragedy**, 1931 (role model for Phillips Holmes); **A Place in the Sun**, 1951 (role model for Montgomery Clift). Note: For detailed information on Gillette, see my book, *World Encyclopedia of 20th Century Murder* (Paragon House, 1992; illustrated [3 images] pages 233-234).

Gipp, George (American college football player at Notre Dame; 1895-1920): **Knute Rockne All American**, 1940 (Ronald Reagan).

Girty, Simon (1741-1818; U.S. renegade, captured by Seneca tribe and raised in its culture, later acted as liaison officer between Indians allied with the British during the American Revolutionary War): Daniel Boone, 1936 (John Carradine); Daniel Boone, 1964-1970 (TV series; "A Short Walk to Salem," 1964 episode: James Westerfield); Daniel Boone, Trail Blazer, 1956 (Kem Dibbs); Hawkeye and the Last of the Mohicans, 1957- (TV series; "The Morristown Story," 1957 episode: Powys Thomas); In the Days of Daniel Boone, 1923 (Duke R. Lee).

Gladkowska, Konstancja (Constantia; 1810-1889; beautiful and gifted Polish soprano who inspired Fredric Chopin and who, as a nineteen-year-old student in Warsaw, fell in love with her, but their relationship severed when he left the country): Farewell, 1935 (aka: La chanson de l'adieu; Un amour de Frederic Chopin; Janine Crispin); Farewell Waltz, 1934 (Hanna Waag); **Young Chopin**, 1952 (Aleksandra Slaska).

Gladney, Edna (Edna Browning Kahly Gladney; 1886-1961; U.S. pioneer campaigner for children's rights and better living conditions of disadvantaged children): **Blossoms in the Dust**, 1941 (Greer Garson).

Greer Garson as Edna Gladney in *Blossoms in the Dust*, 1941.

Gladstone, William Ewart (1809-1898; British politician and prime minister of Great Britain): BBC Play of the Month, 1965-1983 (TV series; "Gordon of Khartoum," 1966 episode: Charles Carson); Disraeli: Portrait of a Romantic, 1978 (TV miniseries; John Carlisle); Edward the King, 1975- (TV series; Michael Hordern); Happy and Glorius, 1952- (TV series; "1891-1900," 1952 episode: Edmund Willard); The Imperfect Lady, 1947 (Gordon Richards); Invincible Mr. Disraeli, 1963 (made-for-TV; Geoffrey Keen); Jennie: Lady Randolph Churchill, 1974 (TV miniseries; David Steuart); **Khartoum**, 1966 (Ralph Richardson); **The Lady with a Lamp**, 1951 (Arthur Young); The Life and Times of David Lloyd George, 1981- (TV series; Roland Culver); Lillie, 1978- (TV miniseries; John Phillips); Mr. Gladstone, 1947 (made-for-TV; Kynaston Reeves); Network First: Victoria and Albert, 1997- (TV miniseries; Shay Gorman); Number 10, 1983- (TV miniseries; Denis Quilley); Parnell, 1937 (Montagu Love); Parnell, 1938 (made-for-TV; Arthur Young); Parnell & the English Woman, 1991 (TV miniseries; Robert Lang); The Prime Minister, 1942 (Stephen Murray); Queen of Destiny, 1940 (Malcolm Keen); The Time Tunnel, 1966-1967 (TV series; "Night of the Long Knives," 1966 episode: Dayton Lummis); **Victoria the Great**, 1937 (Arthur Young); You Are There, 1953-1971 (TV series; "The Fall of Parnell [December 6, 1890]," 1954 episode: Patrick McGoohan); **Young Winston**, 1972 (Willoughby Gray).

Glass, Hugh (c. 1783-1833; U.S. frontiersman): Death Valley Days, 1952-1970 (TV series; "Hugh Glass Meets the Bear," 1966 episode: John Alderson); The Folklorist, 2012 (TV series; "Hugh Glass," 2014 episode: Matthias Lupri); Man in the Wilderness, 1971 (role model for Richard Harris); **Revenant**, 2015 (Leonardo DiCaprio).

Goebbels, Joseph (1897-1945; German politician and Nazi minister of propaganda under Adolf Hitler; committed suicide with wife Magda after poisoning their six children in the Fuhrer bunker to avoid capture when Soviet forces entered Berlin in 1945): Adolf and Marlene, 1977 (Ulli Lommel); Berlin Lady, 1991- (TV miniseries; Martin Maria Abram); Churchill: The Hollywood Years, 2004 (David Schneider); **Confessions of a Nazi Spy**, 1939 (Martin Kosleck); Days of Betrayal, 1973 (Fred Alexander); Der Reichstagsbrandprozess, 1967 (Heiner Schmidt); Der Rohm-Putsch, 1967 (made-for-TV; Wilfried Klaus); Devil's Mistress, 2016 (Karl Markovics); Downfall, 2004 (Ulrich Matthes); Enemy of Women, 1943 (Paul Andor [Wolfgang Zilzer]); The Empty Mirror, 1999 (Joel Grey); Ernst Thalmann—Fuhrer seiner Klasse, 1955 (Hans Stuhrmann); The Fall of Berlin, 1952 (M. Petrunkin); Gandhi to Hitler, 2011 (Nalin Singh); General Electric Theater, 1953-1962 (TV series; "Hitler's Secret," 1959 episode: Whit Bissell); George, 2013 (made-for-TV; Martin Wuttke); The Girl of Your

Dreams, 1998 (Johannes Silberschneider); Goebbels und Geduldig, 2001 (Ulrich Muhe); The Great Battle, 1973 (TV series; H. Giese); **The Great Dictator**, 1940 (role model for Henry Daniell); **The Hindenburg**, 1975 (David Mauro); Hitler, 1962 (Martin Kosleck); **The Hitler Gang**, 1944 (Martin Kosleck); Hitler: The Last Ten Days, 1973 (John Bennett); Hitler: The Rise of Evil, 2003 (made-for-TV; Justin Salinger); Inside the Third Reich, 1982 (made-for-TV; Ian Holm); Invincible, 2002 (Klaus Handl); It Happened on July 20th, 1955 (Willy Krause); ITV Sunday Night Theatre, 1969- (TV series; "The Death of Adolf Hitler," 1973 episode: Oscar Quitak); Joe and Max, 2002 (made-for-TV; Wilfried Hochholdinger); **The Last Ten Days**, 1956 (Willy Krause); Le Bunker, 1972 (made-for-TV; Jacques Duby); The Liberation of Prague, 1978 (Fred Alexander); The Man Who Lived at the Ritz, 1989 (made-for-TV; Barrie Houghton); Mosley, 1998- (TV series; "Beyond the Pale, 1998 episode: Erich Redman); Mother Night, 1996 (Zach Grenier); The Motorola Television Hour, 1953-1954 (TV series; "The Last Days of Hitler," 1954 episode: Martin Kosleck); My Fuhrer, 2007 (Sylvester Groth); The Nightmare Years, 1989- (TV miniseries; Kurtwood Smith); Operation Valkyrie, 2004 (made-for-TV; Olli Dittrich); The Plot to Kill Hitler, 1990 (made-for-TV; Jonathan Hyde); **The Producers**, 1967 (impersonation by David Patch); Propaganda, 2004 (Ulli Lothmanns); Race, 2016 (Barnaby Metschurat); Rosenstrasse, 2004 (Martin Wuttke); Seduction of the Will, 2001 (Peter Pryor); Sweetheart of the Gods, 1960 (Willy Krause); Tomorrow I'll Wake Up and Scald Myself with Tea, 1977 (Horst Giese); Uncle Adolf, 2005 (made-for-TV; Danny Webb); **Valkyrie**, 2008 (Harvey Friedman); War and Remembrance, 1988 (TV miniseries; Ian Jentle).

Goering, Hermann (1893-1946; German aviator, politician and Nazi leader; condemned to death as a war criminal; committed suicide): Ace London, 1998 (TV series; Adriano Martins); **The Battle of Britain**, 1969 (Hein Reiss); Churchill: The Hollywood Years, 2004 (Steven O'-Donnell); Days of Betrayal, 1973 (Rudolf Jurda); The Empty Mirror, 1999 (Glenn Shadix); Ernst Thalmann, 1986 (made-for-TV; Hans-Joachim Hegewald); The First Front, 1949 (M. Garkavij); **The Great Dictator**, 1940 (role model for Billy Gilbert); Hitler, 1962 (John Mitchum); **The Hitler Gang**, 1944 (Alex Pope); Hitler: The Rise of Evil, 2003 (made-for-TV; Chris Larkin); J'etais a Nuremberg, 2011 (made-for-TV; Jean-Philippe Lafont); The Magic Face, 1951 (Hermann Erhardt); The Man Who Lived at the Ritz, 1989 (made-for-TV; Joss Ackland); The Motorola Television Hour, 1953-1954 (TV series; "The Last Days of Hitler," 1954 episode: Lawrence Fletcher); The Nightmare Years, 1989- (TV miniseries; Michael Wolf); Nuremberg, 2000- (TV miniseries; Brian Cox); The Nuremberg Trial: War Crimes on Trial, 1996 (made-for-TV; Roger Grunwald); The Ogre, 1996 (Volker Spengler); Omnibus, 1967-2003 (TV series; "Dance of the Seven Veils," 1970 episode: James Mellor); **The Producers**, 1967 (impersonation by Barney Martin); Second Verdict, 1976- (TV series; "Who Burned the Reichstag?," 1976 episode: David King); **Valkyrie**, 2008 (Gerhard Haase-Hindenberg); **Von Richthofen and Brown**, 1971 (Barry Primus); War and Remembrance, 1988 (TV miniseries; Michael Wolf).

Goldman, Emma (1869-1940; U.S.-Russian anarchist leader): Choices of the Heart: The Margaret Sanger Story, 1995 (made-for-TV; Maria Vacratsis); **J. Edgar**, 2011 (Jessica Hecht); **No God, No Master**, 2012 (Mariann Mayberry); **Reds**, 1981 (Maureen Stapleton).

Goldwyn, Samuel L. (Samuel Goldfish; 1879-1974; U.S. movie mogul and head of his own production company): Malice in Wonderland, 1985 (made-for-TV; Vernon Weddle); RKO 281, 1999 (made-for-TV; Olivier Pierre); The Year's Blonde, 1980 (made-for-TV; Lee Wallace).

Goliath (giant Philistine warrior killed by David of the Israelites in the Book of Samuel, Old Testament): David, 1997 (made-for-TV; Giorgio

Francesco Palombi); **David and Bathsheba**, 1951 (Walter Talun); David and Goliath, 1960 (Aldo Pedinotti); David & Goliath, 2005 (Thurl Bailey); David and Goliath, 2015 (Jerry Sokolosky); Greatest Heroes of the Bible, 1978- (TV series; "David and Goliath," 1978 episode: Ted Cassidy); King David, 1985 (George Eastman); Saul e David, 1968 (Stefy Lang); The Shepherd King, 1923 (Samuel Balestra); Son of God, 2014 (Conan Stevens); The Story of David, 1976 (made-for-TV; Tony [Antonio] Tarruella).

Goodman, Benny (1909-1986; Benjamin David Goodman; musician; actor): **The Benny Goodman Story**, 1956 (Steve Allen); Sinatra, 1992 (made-for-TV; David A. Kimball).

Gordon, Charles George (aka: Chinese Gordon; Gordon of Khartoun; Gordon Pasha; 1833-1885; enigmatic British general who defended Khartoum against the Mahdi and was killed when the city fell, becoming a military martyr): BBC Play of the Month, 1965-1983 (TV series; "Gordon of Khartoum," 1966 episode; Alan Badel); **The Four Feathers**, 1939 (brief montage of the fall of Khartoum with unidentified actor playing Gordon being speared to death with the fall of the city); **Khartoum**, 1966 (Charleton Heston); Queen of Destiny, 1940 (Laidman Browne).

Gorky, Maxim (1868-1936; Russian writer and Soviet activist): The Childhood of Maxim Gorky, 1938 (Aleksei Lyarsky); H.G. Wells: War of the World, 2006 (made-for-TV: Jacek Koman); Lenin in 1918, 1939 (Nikolay Cherkasov); Ivan Pavlov, 1949 (Nikolay Cherekasov); My Universities, 1940 (Nikolai Valbert); On His Own, 1939 (Aleksei Lyarsky); Road to Life, 1955 (Pavel Kadochnikov); Trust, 1970 (Afanasi Kochetkov).

Gouzenko, Igor (1919-1982; Russian cipher clerk who defected from the Soviet embassy in Ottawa, Ontario, Canada, on September 5, 1945 with 109 documents showing Soviet espionage operations in the West): Atom Spies, 1979 (made-for-TV; Boris Isarov); Der Verrat von Ottawa, 1966 (made-for-TV; Werner Bruhns); **The Iron Curtain**, 1948 (Dana Andrews); Operation Manhunt, 1954 (Harry Townes). Note: For detailed information on Gouzenko, see my book, *Spies: A Narrative Encyclopedia of Dirty Tricks & Double Dealing from Biblical Times to Today* (M. Evans, 1997; illustrated pages 243-245).

Goya, Francisco (1746-1828; Spanish painter and printmaker): The Face of Spain, 1952 (Barry Kroeger); Goya, 1969- (TV series; Wolfgang Buttner); Goya, 1971 (Francisco Rabal); Goya, 1985- (TV miniseries; Enric Majo); Goya: Awakened in a Dream, 1999 (made-for-TV; Cedric Smith); Goya in Bordeaux, 2000 (Francisco Rabal); Goya's Ghosts, 2007 (Stellan Skarsgard); Great Performances, 1971- (TV series; "Goya," 1986 episode: Placido Domingo); The Naked Maja, 1959 (Anthony Franciosa).

Graham, Barbara (1923-1955; U.S. convicted thief and murderer; executed in California's gas chamber): **I Want to Live!**, 1958 (Susan Hayward); I Want to Live, 1983 (made-for-TV; Lindsay Wagner). Note: For detailed information on Barbara Graham, see my book, *World Encyclopedia of 20th Century Murder* (Paragon House, 1992; illustrated pages 242-243).

Graham, John Gilbert (aka: Jack; 1932-1957; planted bomb in his mother's suitcase on passenger plane, United Airlines Flight 629 (DC-6B), from Denver to Seattle on November 1, 1955, which killed all on board, including his mother and forty-three others to collect $37,500 in insurance money, a policy he took out just before his mother's flight; was executed as a mass murderer): **The FBI Story**, 1959 (Nick Adams). Note: For detailed information on John Gilbert Graham, see my books *World Encyclopedia of 20th Century Murder* (Paragon House, 1992; il-

Susan Hayward (as Barbara Graham) surrendering to police in *I Want to Live!*, **1958.**

lustrated pages 244-249; and the two-volume work *The Great Pictorial History of World Crime*, Volume II (History, Inc., 2004; illustrated [7 images] pages 970-976).

Graham, Sheila (1904-1988; British-born U.S. Hollywood gossip columnist): **Beloved Infidel**, 1959 (Deborah Kerr); College Confidential, 1960 (herself); F. Scott Fitzgerald in Hollywood, 1976 (made-for-TV: Julia Foster); Fitzgerald, 2002 (made-for-TV; Natalie Radford); General Electric Theater, 1953-1962 (TV series; "Nobody's Child," 1959 episode: herself); Girls Town, 1959 (herself); The Great Jewel Robber, 1950 (herself); **Impact**, 1949 (herself); Lux Video Theater, 1950-1959 (TV series; herself in two episodes); That's Right – You're Wrong, 1939 (herself).

Grant, Cary (1904-1986; British-born actor chiefly in U.S. films): Act One, 1963 (Bert Convy as Archie Leach, Grant's real name); **The Aviator**, 2004 (Michael-John Wolfe); Poor Little Rich Girl: The Barbara Hutton Story, 1987 (made-for-TV; James Read); Sophia Loren: Her Own Story, 1980 (made-for-TV; John Gavin); Touch of Pink, 2004 (Kyle MacLachlan as the spirit of Cary Grant); **Without Reservations**, 1946 (himself).

Grant, Ulysses S. (Hiram Ulysses Grant; 1822-1885; Union general, commander-in-chief of all Union armies in American Civil War and 18th President of the U.S.): **Abraham Lincoln**, 1930 (E. Alyn Warren); **The Adventures of Mark Twain**, 1944 (Joseph Crehan); The Adventures of Rin Tin Tin, 1954-1959 (TV series; "Rin Tin Tin Meets Mr. President," 1955 episode: Paul Birch; "Presidential Citation," 1956 episode; Paul Birch); **The Battle Cry of Peace**, 1915 (Paul Scardon); The Battle of Shiloh, 1913 (John Smiley); **The Birth of a Nation**, 1915 (Donald Crisp); Black Saddle, 1959-1960 (TV series; "Mr. Simpson," 1960 episode: Paul Birch); The Blue and the Gray, 1982 (TV miniseries; Rip Torn); Branded, 1965-1966 (TV series; many episodes: William Bryant); Broken Arrow, 1956-1960 (TV series, "Smoke Signal," 1957 episode: Hugh Sanders); Bury My Heart at Wounded Knee, 2007 (made-for-TV; Fred Thompson); **Centennial Summer**, 1946 (Reginald Sheffield); The Civil War, 1990 (TV miniseries; Jason Robards Jr. voiceover); Colorado, 1940 (Joseph Crehan); The Day Lincoln Was Shot, 1998 (made-for-TV; John Ashton); Days That Shook the World, 2003-2013 (TV series; "Terror Made in America: Assassination of Abraham Lincoln...," 2004 episode: Ray Mize); The Dramatic Life of Abraham Lincoln, 1924 (Walter Rodgers); **Drum Beat**, 1954 (Hayden Rorke); Emma: Queen of the South Seas, 1988- (TV miniseries; E.G. Marshall); The Fabulous Texan, 1947 (John Hamilton); The Flaming Frontier, 1926 (Walter Rodgers); Freedom Road, 1979 (made-for-TV;

Paul Newman (as prizefighter Rocky Graziano) and Pier Angeli in *Somebody Up There Likes Me,* **1952.**

John McLiam); From Earth to the Moon, 1958 (Morris Ankrum); Frontier Scout, 1938 (Jack C. Smith); **Geronimo**, 1939 (Joseph Crehan); Gold Is Where You Find It, 1938 (Walter Rodgers); The Gray Ghost, 1957- (TV series; "Ulysses S. Grant," 1957 episode: Hugh Sanders); The Heart of Maryland, 1927 (Walter Rodgers); **The Horse Soldiers**, 1959 (Stan Jones); **How the West Was Won**, 1962 (Harry Morgan); In the Days of Buffalo Bill, 1922 (John W. Morris); Jane Wyman Presents the Fireside Theatre, 1955-1958 (TV series; "Tunnel Eight," 1958 episode: Joseph Crehan); Legend, 1995- (TV series; "Legend on His President's Secret Service," 1995 episode: G.W. Bailey); The Legend of the Lone Ranger, 1981 (Jason Robards Jr.); Liberty, 1986 (made-for-TV; Alan North); The Life and Times of Grizzly Adams, 1977-1978 (TV series; "The Stranger," 1978 episode: Mark Slade); Lincoln, 1974-1975 (TV series; Norman Burton); Lincoln, 1988 (made-for-TV; James Gammon); Lincoln, 1992 (made-for-TV; Rod Steiger); **Lincoln**, 2012 (Jared Harris); Lost River: Lincoln's Secret Weapon, 2009 (James Reeves); Madame Who, 1918 (Bert Hadley); My Own United States, 1918 (Frank Murray); North and South, Book II, 1986 (TV miniseries; Anthony Zerbe); **The Nut**, 1921 (impersonation by Frank Campeau); Only the Brave, 1930 (Guy Oliver); Operator 13, 1934 (E. Alyn Warren); Overland Trail, 1960- (TV series; "Most Dangerous Gentleman," 1960 episode; Onslow Stevens); The Philco-Goodyear Television Playhouse, 1948-1956 (TV series; "This Time, Next Year," 1949 episode: Dennis King); The Red Desert, 1949 (Joseph Crehan); **Run of the Arrow**, 1957 (Emile Avery); San Antone, 1953 (Joseph Crehan); Saving Lincoln, 2013 (Peter O'Meara); The Secret Diary of Desmond Pfeiffer, 1998- (TV series; Kelly Connell); Secret Service, 1931 (E. Alyn Warren); **Silver Dollar**, 1932 (Walter Rodgers); Silver River, 1948 (Joseph Crehan); Sitting Bull, 1954 (John Hamilton); The Son of Davy Crockett, 1941 (Harrison Greene); Son of the Morning Star, 1991 (made-for-TV; Stanley Anderson); Sugarfoot, 1957-1961 (TV series; "Welcome Enemy," 1960 episode; J. Edward McKinley); Sunday Showcase, 1959-1961 (TV series; "An American Heritage: Shadow of a Soldier," 1960 episode: James Whitmore; "An American Heritage: Gentleman's Decision," 1961 episode: Kenneth Konopka); The Tempest, 1998 (made-for-TV; Jon Huffman); **Tennessee Johnson**, 1942 (Harrison Greene); **They Died with Their Boots On**, 1942 (Joseph Crehan); They've Killed President Lincoln!, 1971 (made-for-TV; Michael Tucker); To Appomattox, 2015- (TV miniseries; Jason O'Mara); **Union Pacific**, 1939 (Joseph Crehan); Wagon Train, 1957-1965 (TV series; "The Colter Craven Story," 1960 episode: Paul Birch); Walt Disney's Wonderful World of Color, 1954-1992 (TV series; "Johnny Siloh," two 1963 episodes: Hayden Rorke); The Warrens of Virginia, 1924 (Wilbur J. Fox); The Wild Wild West, 1965-1969 (TV series; many episodes; Roy Engel); Wild Wild West, 1999 (Kevin Kline); You Are There, 1953-1957 (TV series; "Grant and

Lee at Appomattox, 1953 and 1955 episodes: Roy Engel).

Graziani, Rudolfo (1882-1955; Italian fascist field marshal before and during WWII): **Last Days of Mussolini**, 1977 (Rudolfo Dal Pra); **Lion of the Desert**, 1981 (Oliver Reed).

Graziano, Rocky (Thomas Rocco Barbella; 1919-1990; U.S. prizefighter and World Middleweight Champion): The Bronx Bull, 2016 (James Russo); **Somebody Up There Likes Me**, 1956 (Paul Newman).

Greeley, Horace (1811-1872; U.S. journalist, editor and a founder of the Republican Party): **Abe Lincoln in Illinois**, 1940 (Ian Wolfe); Barnum, 1986 (made-for-TV; Rob Roy); The Best of Post, 1960- (TV series; 'Frontier Correspondent," 1961 episode: Jerome Cowan); Branded, 1965-1966 (TV series; "Headed for Doomsday," 1966 episode: Burgess Meredith); Cavalcade of America, 1952-1957 (TV series; "One Nation Indivisible,' 1953 episode; "Petticoat Doctor," 1955 episode: Edgar Buchanan for both); The Civil War, 1990 (TV miniseries; Philip Bosco voiceover); Death Valley Days, 1952-1970 (TV series; "The Great Turkey War," 1965 episode: Parley Baer); Gangs of New York, 2002 (Michael Byrne); Lincoln, 1992 (made-for-TV; Bernard Hughes); **The Mighty Barnum**, 1934 (Davison Clark); Sail to Glory, 1967 (Bert Freed); You Are There, 1953-1971 (TV series; "The Great Diamond Fraud [November 1872]," 1956 episode: Emmett Vogan).

Greene, Nathanael (1742-1786; U.S; military officer and general during the American Revolutionary War): The Crossing, 2000 (made-for-TV; David Ferry); George Washington, 1984 (TV miniseries; Scott Hylands); **The Patriot**, 2000 (Andy Stahl); The Revolution, 2006- (TV series; Tony Scheinman in two episodes; Daniel B. Martin in two episodes); **The Scarlet Coat**, 1955 (John Dehner).

Greenhow, Rose O' Neal (1814-1864; beautiful southern woman in high society at Washington, D.C., who served as a Confederate spy during the American Civil War): Clas of '61, 1993 (made-for-TV; Sue-Ann Leeds); The Rose and the Jackal, 1990 (made-for-TV; Madolyn Smith Osborne). Note: For detailed information on Greenhow, see my book, *Spies: A Narrative Encyclopedia of Dirty Tricks & Double Dealing from Biblical Times to Today* (M. Evans, 1997; illustrated pages 248-254).

Grey, Edward (Sir Edward Grey; British Foreign Secretary; 1862-1933): **Oh! What a Lovely War**, 1969 (Ralph Richardson); Regal Cavalcade, 1935 (H. Saxon-Snell).

Grey, Jane (Lady Jane Grey; 1536-1554; British noblewoman who was Queen of England from July 10 to July 19, 1553): Elizabeth R, 1971-1972 (TV miniseries; "The Lion's Club," 1971 episode: Sarah Frampton); **Lady Jane**, 1986 (Helena Bonham Carter); **Lady Jane Grey** [aka: Nine Days a Queen; Tudor Rose], 1936 (Nova Pilbeam); **The Prince and the Pauper**, 1937 (Anne Howard); The Prince and the Pauper, 1977 (Felicity Dean); The Prince and the Pauper, 1996 (TV series; four episodes: Sophia Myles); The Prince and the Pauper, 2000 (made-for-TV; Perdita Weeks); You Are There, 1953-1971 (TV series: "The Last Day of an English Queen [Lady Jane Gray, executed February 12, 1554]," 1955 episode: Gloria Talbott).

Grieg, Edward (Edvard; 1843-1907; Norwegian composer): Rikard Nordraak, 1945 (Jorn Ording); Song of Norway, 1970 (Toralv Maurstad).

Groseilliers, Medard des (1618-1696; French fur trader and explorer, who, along with Pierre-Esprit Radisson, established the Hudson's Bay Company in Canada for Charles II of England): **Hudson's Bay**, 1941 (Laird Cregar).

Groves, Leslie (1896-1970; U.S. soldier, U.S. Army major general who supervised the Manhattan Project that developed the atomic bomb in WWII): The Beginning or the End, 1947 (Brian Donlevy); Day One, 1989 (made-for-TV; Brian Dennehy); Doctor Atomic, 2007 (made-for-TV; Eric Owens); F.D.R.: The Last Year, 1980 (made-for-TV; George R. Robertson); **Fat Man and Little Boy**, 1989 (Paul Newman); Einstein, 1985- (TV miniseries; Bernard Dumaine); Enola Gay: The Men, the Mission, the Atomic Bomb, 1980 (made-for-TV; Richard Herd); Hiroshima, 1995 (made-for-TV; Richard Masur); Man, Moment, Machine, 2005-2007 (TV series; "Ultimate Weapon: Oppenheimer and the Atomic Bomb," 2005 episode: Eric Swartz); Oppenheimer, 1980 (TV miniseries; Manning Redwood); Race for the Bomb, 1987 (TV miniseries; Maury Chaykin); War and Remembrance, 1988 (TV miniseries; George Murdock).

Gunsche, Otto (1917-2003; German SS officer and Adolf Hitler's adjutant; imprisoned by the Soviets following WWII): Downfall, 2004 (Gotz Otto); Hitler: The Last Ten Days, 1973 (John Hallam).

Gusenberg, Frank (1893-1929; U.S. gangster and bootlegger, member of the George "Bugs" Moran gang who, along with his brother Peter and five others, was killed in Chicago's notorious 1929 St. Valentine's Day Massacre): Capone, 1975 (Ben Marino); Playhouse 90, 1956-1961 (TV series; "Seven against the Wall," 1958 episode; Barry Cahill); **The St. Valentine's Day Massacre**, 1967 (David Canary). Note: For detailed information on the Gusenberg brothers and the St. Valentine's Day Massacre, see my books *World Encyclopedia of Organized Crime* (Paragon House, 1992, illustrated pages 343-347; and *The Great Pictorial History of World Crime*, Volume I (History, Inc., 2004, [under Capone] illustrated pages 503-541).

Gusenbert, Peter (1888-1929; U.S. gangster and bootlegger, member of the George "Bugs" Moran gang who, along with his brother Frank and five others, was killed in Chicago's notorious 1929 St. Valentine's Day Massacre): Capone, 1975 (Martin Kove); Playhouse 90, 1956-1961 (TV series; "Seven against the Wall," 1958 episode: Dennis Cross); **The St. Valentine's Day Massacre**, 1967 (George Segal). Note: For detailed information on the Gusenberg brothers and the St. Valentine's Day Massacre, see my books *World Encyclopedia of Organized Crime* (Paragon House, 1992, illustrated pages 343-347; and *The Great Pictorial History of World Crime*, Volume I (History, Inc., 2004; [under Capone] illustrated pages 503-541).

Guzik, Jake (aka: Greasy Thumb; 1886-1956; U.S. racketeer; political fixer and banker under Capone and for the Chicago Outfit): Boardwalk Empire, 2010- (TV series: five episodes: Joe Caniano); Capone, 1975 (Peter Maloney); Playhouse 90, 1956-1961 (TV series; "Seven against the Wall," 1958 episode; Lewis Charles); **The St. Valentine's Day Massacre**, 1967 (Joseph Turkel); The Untouchables, 1959-1963 (TV series; Nehemiah Persoff); The Untouchables, 1993-1994 (TV series; Dick Sasso). Note; For detailed information on the Guzik, see my books *World Encyclopedia of Organized Crime* (Paragon House, 1992, illustrated page 198; and the two-volume *The Great Pictorial History of World Crime*, Volume I (History, Inc., 2004; [under Capone] illustrated pages 503-541).

Gwyn, Eleanor (aka: Nell; Gwynne; 1650-1687; longtime mistress of England's Charles II): BBC Play of the Month, 1965-1983 (TV series; "In Good King Charles' Golden Days," 1970 episode: Joyce Redman); BBC Sunday-Night Theatre, 1950-1959 (TV series; "The Portugal Lady," 1952 episode: Bernadette O'Farrell; "Ninety Sail," 1954 episode: Daphne Anderson); Border Warfare, 1990- (TV series; "Towards the Union," 1990 episode: Maria Miller); Cardboard Cavalier, 1949 (Margaret Lockwood); The Diary of Samuel Pepys, 1958- (TV series; Sheila Brennan); England, My England, 1995 (Lucy Speed); Father Came Too!, 1964 (Vanda Hudson); The First Churchills, 1969- (TV series;

Nicolas Cage (as Edward "Ned" Hanlan) in *The Boy in Blue*, **1986.**

"Plot, Counter-Plot," 1971 episode: Andrea Lawrence); The Glorious Adventure, 1922 (Lois Sturt); **Hudson's Bay**, 1941 (Virginia Field); The Last King, 2003 (TV miniseries; Emma Pierson); Let's Make Up, 1956 (Anna Neagle); Mistress Nell, 1915 (Mary Pickford); Nell Gwyn, 1926 (Dorothy Gish); Nell Gwyn, 1935 (Anna Neagle); Stage Beauty, 2004 (Zoe Tapper); The Wicked Lady, 1983 (Teresa Codling); Witness to Yesterday, 1970- (TV series; "Nell Gwynn," 1974 episode: Dawn Greenhalgh).

Haarmann, Fritz (1879-1925; German serial killer who preyed upon homeless children, reportedly raping and murdering at least twenty-seven young boys; beheaded): The Deathmaker, 1995 (Gotz George); Fernsehpitaval, 1957-1978 (TV series; "Der Fall Haarmann," 1960 episode: Horst Friedrich); Tenderness of the Wolves, 1973 (Kurt Raab). Note: For detailed information on Haarmann, see my book *World Encyclopedia of 20th Century Murder* (Paragon House, 1992; illustrated page 263).

Haig, Douglas (Sir Douglas Haig; 1861-1928; British soldier and field marshal in WWII who senselessly ordered ineffective massive front attacks costing hundreds of thousands of lives): Anzacs, 1985- (TV miniseries; Noel Trevarthen); Blackadder Goes Forth, 1989- (TV series; Geoffrey Palmer); Days That Shook the World, 2003- (TV series: "The Christmas Truce," 2004 episode: Charles Hunt); The Great Victory, Wilson or the Kaiser? The Fall of the Hohenzollerns, 1919 (J.H. Forsell); The Kaiser, the Beast of Berlin, 1918 (Henry A. Barrows); Monash: The Forgotten Anzac, 2008 (made-for-TV; James Shaw); **Oh! What a Lovely War**, 1969 (John Mills); Wipers Three, 1973 (made-for-TV; Noel Willman).

Haise, Fred Wallace, Jr. (U.S. astronaut; 1933-): **Apollo 13**, 1995 (Bill Paxton).

Haldeman, H. R. (Harry Robbins Haldeman; aka: "Bob"; American businessman and White House chief of staff for U.S. President Richard M. Nixon; 1926-1993): Blind Ambition, 1979 (TV miniseries; Lawrence Pressman); Dick, 1999 (Dave Foley); **J. Edgar**, 2011 (Larkin Campbell); **Nixon**, 1995 (James Woods); The Pentagon Papers, 2003 (James Downing).

Hale, Nathan (1755-1776; American spy and hero for the Continental Army during the American Revolutionary War, 1775-1783, who was hanged): The Great Adventure, 1963-1964 (TV series; "The Story of Nathan Hale," 1963 episode: Jeremy Slate); The Heart of a Hero, 1916 (Robert Warwick); You Are There, 1953-1971 (TV series; "The Fate of

Bob Burns, Julia Adams and Rock Hudson (as John Wesley Hardin) in *The Lawless Breed*, 1953.

Nathan Hale [September 22, 1776]," 1953 episode: Paul Newman); The Young Rebels, 1970-1971 (TV series; "To Hang a Hero," 1970 episode: Brandon De Wilde). Note: For detailed information on Hale, see my book *Spies: A Narrative Encyclopedia of Dirty Tricks & Double Dealing from Biblical Times to Today* (M. Evans, 1997; illustrated pages 256-257).

Hale, William K. (aka: King of the Osage Hills; U.S. businessman and Oklahoma banker, who, with relatives, engineered as many as twenty murders of Osage Indians during the oil boom in Oklahoma in order to steal their oil claims; he was convicted and sent to Leavenworth Penitentiary for life, but later paroled): **The FBI Story**, 1953 (Fay Roope as "Dwight McCutcheon").

Halsey, William F. (William Frederick Halsey Jr.; AKA: "Bull"; 1882-1959; U.S. admiral, commander of the U.S. Third Fleet in the Pacific in WWII): Battle Stations, 1956 (Jack Diamond); **The Eternal Sea**, 1955 (John Maxwell); **The Gallant Hours**, 1960 (James Cagney); **MacArthur**, 1977 (Kenneth Tobey); **Midway**, 1976 (Robert Mitchum); **Pearl Harbor**, 2001 (Glen Morshower); **Thirty Seconds over Tokyo**, 1944 (Morris Ankrum); **Tora! Tora! Tora!**, 1970 (James Whitmore); War and Remembrance, 1988 (TV miniseries; Pat Hingle); The Winds of War, 1983 (TV miniseries; "Into the Maelstrom," 1983 episode: Richard X. Slattery); You Are There, 1953-1957 (TV series; "V-J Day [September 2, 1945],"1956 episode: Dan Riss).

Hamilton, Alexander (1757-1804; U.S. politician and founding father of America; first U.S. secretary of the treasury; killed in a duel with Aaron Burr): The Adams Chronicles, 1976 (TV miniseries; Jeremiah Sullivan); Alexander Hamilton, 1931 (George Arliss); The Beautiful Mrs. Reynolds, 1918 (Carlyle Blackwell); The Crossing, 2000 (made-for-TV; Steven McCarthy); George Washington, 1984 (TV miniseries; Robert Schenkkan); George Washington II: The Forging of a Nation, 1986 (made-for-TV; Richard Bekins); Great Performances, 1971- (TV series; "The Patriots," 1976 episode: Philip LeStrange); **Janice Meredith**, 1924 (Burton McEvilly); John Adams, 2008 (TV miniseries; Rufus Sewell); Liberty! The American Revolution, 1997 (TV miniseries; Colm Feore); Magnificent Doll, 1946 (Arthur Space); A More Perfect Union: America Becomes a Nation, 1989 (Derryl Yeager); My Own United States, 1918 (Duncan McRae); Mysteries at the Castle, 2014- (TV series; "House That Saved a King; Joan of Arc; Hamilton Sex Scandal," 2015 episode: Michael Simon Hall); The Patriots, 1963 (made-for-TV; John Fraser); Swing Out, Sweet Land, 1970 (made-for-TV; Robert Hutton).

Hamilton, Emma; see Emma, Lady Hamilton.

Hamilton, John (aka: "Red"; 1899-1934; Canadian-born bank robber in U.S. and member of the Dillinger gang): Baby Face Nelson, 1957 (Anthony Caruso); Dillinger, 1991 (made-for-TV; John Philbin); Guns Don't Argue, 1957 (Robert Vanselow); **Public Enemies**; 2009 (Jason Clarke); **Young Dillinger**, 1965 (Dan Terranova). Note: For detailed information on Hamilton, see my two-volume work *The Great Pictorial History of World Crime*, Volume II (History, Inc., 2004; [under Dillinger] illustrated pages 1374-1422).

Hammett, Dashiell (Samuel Dashiell Hammett; 1894-1961; a former Pinkerton detective, and author of hard-boiled detective novels, noted for *The Maltese Falcon*, published in 1930 and depicting the sleuthing exploits of private detective Sam Spade, and *The Thin Man*, published in 1934, which profiles the sleuthing adventures of wealthy married couple Nick and Nora Charles (these works spawning several films); Hammett battled alcoholism and tuberculosis for many year while maintaining a common-law marriage with playwright Lillian Hellman; he was blacklistd in the 1950s for his communist background and refusal to cooperate with investigative agencies probing communist influence in the U.S.): The Case of Dashiell Hammett, 1982 (made-for-TV; Lyle Talbot); Citizen Cohn, 1992 (made-for-TV; Frederic Forrest); Dash and Lilly, 1999 (made-for-TV; San Shepard); **Julia**, 1977 (Jason Robards Jr.); **Hammett**, 1982 (Frederic Forrest); Magnum, P.I., 1980-1988 (TV series; "The Case of the Red-Faced Thespian," 1984 episode: Tom Selleck).

Hancock, John (1737-1793; U.S. merchant, statesman and president of the Continental Congress during the American Revolution): The Adams Chronicles, 1976 (TV miniseries; Curt Dawson); **America**, 1924 (John Dunton); Cardigan, 1922 (William Willis); Cavalcade of America, 1952-1957 (TV series; "A Strange Journey," 1955 episode: Hugh Sanders); John Adams, 2008 (TV miniseries; Justin Theroux); **John Paul Jones**, 1959 (John Phillips); Liberty! The American Revolution, 1997 (TV miniseries; Byron Jennings); The Rebels, 1979 (made-for-TV; Jim Backus); Samuel Adams, 2014 (made-for-TV; Christopher Karbo); **1776**, 1972 (David Ford); Sons of Liberty, 2015- (TV miniseries; Rafe Spall); You Are There, 1953-1971 (TV series: "Boston Tea Party [Restaged; December 16, 1773]," 1955 episode: Russ Conway).

Hancock, Winfield Scott (1824-1886; U.S. soldier and Union general during the American Civil War): **Gettysburg**, 1993 (Brian Mallon); **Gods and Generals**, 2003 (Brian Mallon); In the Days of Buffalo Bill, 1922 (Burt Frank).

Handel, George Frederick (1685-1759; German composer): A Cry of Angels, 1963 (made-for-TV; Walter Slezak); Farinelli, 1995 (Jeroen Krabbe); God Rot Turnbridge Wells!, 1985 (made-for-TV; Trevor Howard); The Great Mr. Handel, 1943 (Wilfrid Lawson); Handel—Der Film, 2009 (made-for-TV; Matthias Wiebalck); Handel's Last Chance, 1996 (made-for-TV; Leon Pownall); Honour, Profit & Pleasure, 1985 (made-for-TV; Simon Callow); Uzhin w chetyre ruki, 2000 (made-for-TV; Mikhail Kozakov).

Hands, Isreal (Basilica Hands; Caribbean pirate and first lieutenant of Blackbeard): Blackbeard, 2006 (TV miniseries; Anthony Green); Blackbeard; Terror at Sea, 2006 (made-for-TV; Mark Noble); Long John Silver, 1954 (Rod Taylor); Treasure Island, 1990 (made-for-TV; Michael Halsey); True Caribbean Pirates, 2006 (made-for-TV; Rich Skidmore).

Handy, W.C. (1873-1958; U.S. classic composer of contemporary blues): St. Louis Blues, 1958 (Nat King Cole).

Hanlan, Edward (aka: Ned; 1855-1908; Canadian sculler and polician):

The Boy in Blue, 1986 (Nicolas Cage).

Hannibal (247-181 B.C.; Carthaginian military commander): **Cabiria**, 1914 (Emilio Vardannes); For Cannae, 1962 (made-for-TV; Jorgen Reenberg); Hannibal, 1960 (Victor Mature); Hannibal, 2006 (made-for-TV; Alexander Siddig); Jupitor's Darling, 1955 (Howard Keel); Scipione l'africano, 1939 (Camillo Pilotto).

Hanssen, Robert Philip (1944- ; U.S. FBI agent who spied for Soviet Russia and who is presently serving fifteen consecutive life prison terms): **Breach**, 2007 (Chris Cooper); Master Spy: The Robert Hanssen Story, 2002 (made-for-TV; Christopher Redman; William Hurt); Robert Hanssen: Double Agent Revealed, 2007 (made-for-TV; John Doty).

Hardin, John Wesley (1853-1895; U.S. western outlaw and fast-draw gunfighter, who, by his own claim, killed more than forty men; he was shot in the back and killed in a saloon by Old John Selman, a longtime enemy): Bronco, 1958-1962 (TV series; "The Turning Point," 1958 episode: Scott Marlowe); Death Valley Days, 1952-1970 (TV series; "Preacher with a Past," 1962 episode: Neville Brand); Dirty Dingus Magee, 1970 (Jack Elam); Gunslingers, 2014 (TV miniseries; Eric C. Schneider); Judge Roy Bean, 1956- (TV series; "Gunman's Bargain," 1956 episode: Lash La Rue); **The Lawless Breed**, 1953 (Rock Hudson); The Life and Legend of Wyatt Earp, 1955-1961 (TV series; "The Time for All Good Men," 1957 episode: Phillip Pine); Luke and the Tenderfoot, 1955- (TV series; "The John Wesley Hardin Story," 1955 episode; Charles Bronson); Maverick, 1957-1962 (TV series; "Duel at Sundown," 1959 episode: James Griffith); Stories of the Century, 1954- (TV series; "John Wesley Hardin," 1954 episode: Richard Webb); Streets of Laredo, 1995 (TV miniseries; Randy Quaid); Studio One in Hollywood, 1948-1958 (TV series; "Dead of Noon," 1957 episode: Richard Boone); Tales of Wells Fargo, 1957-1962 (TV series; "John Wesley Hardin," 1957 episode: Lyle Bettger; "The Gunfighter," 1958 episode: Lyle Bettger); The Texas Rangers, 1951 (John Dehner); The Virginian, 1962-1971 (TV series; "The Sins of the Fathers," 1970 episode: Tim McIntire); Zane Grey Theater, 1956-1961 (TV series; "Trouble at Tres Cruces," 1959 episode: Brad Johnson). For detailed information on Hardin, see my book *Encyclopedia of Western Lawmen & Outlaws* (Paragon House, 1992; illustrated pages 143-150).

Hare, William (b.1804; Scottish killer who, with William Burke, killed at least sixteen persons, selling the cadavers to an unwitting Dr. Robert Knox for his anatomy studies in Edinburgh, Scotland, in 1828; escaped punishment after informing on Burke, who was hanged): The Alfred Hitchcock Hour, 1962-1965 (TV series; "The McGregor Affair," 1964 episode: Michael Pate); The Anatomist, 1939 (made-for-TV; Harry Hutchinson); The Anatomist, 1956 (made-for-TV; Michael Ripper); The Body Snatcher, 1945 (role model for Bela Lugosi); Burke and Hare, 1972 (Glynn Edwards); Burke and Hare, 2010 (Andy Serkis); The Doctor and the Devils, 1985 (role model for Stephen Rea); The Flesh and the Fiends, 1961 (Donald Pleasence); Horror Maniacs, 1953 (role model for Henry Oscar); Mystery and Imagination, 1966-1970 (TV series; "The Body Snatcher," 1966 episode: Dermot Tuohy). Note: For detailed information on Burke and Hare, see my two-volume work *The Great Pictorial History of World Crime*, Volume II (History, Inc., 2004; illustrated [11 images] pages 1023-1028).

Harlow, Jean (1911-1937; U.S. film actress): The Amazing Howard Hughes, 1992 (made-for-TV; Susan Buckner); **The Aviator**, 2004 (Gwen Stefani); Dead Hollywood Blondes, 2010 (Missi Adams); Harlow, 1965 (Carroll Baker); Harlow, 1965 (Carol Lynley); Hughes and Harlow: Angels in Hell, 1977 (Lindsay Bloom); Pulp, 1972 (Anna Pace Donnella); Stand-Ins, 1997 (Sammi Davis); Train Ride to Hollywood, 1975 (Roberta Collins).

Beau Bridges (role modeled on Ben Hecht) and pickpocket Harry Holcombe in *Gaily, Gaily*, 1969.

Harris, Clara (Clara Harris Rathbone; 1834-1883; U.S. fiancé of Major Henry Reed Rathbone, who accompanied Rathbone and was present in the presidential box at Ford's Theater on the night of April 14, 1865, when President Abraham Lincoln was mortally shot by assassin John Wilkes Booth; she later married Rathbone, who became insane and murdered her): The Day Lincoln Was Shot, 1998 (made-for-TV; Mercedes Herrero); Lincoln, 1992 (made-for-TV; Stockard Channing); The Lincoln Conspiracy, 1977 (Liz Dent); Lost River: Lincoln's Secret Weapon, 2010 (Katheleen Manhardt).

Harris, Jean Struven (1923-2012; headmistress of private girls school in Virginia who murdered her ex-lover, wealthy Dr. Herman Tarnower, in 1980; she was sentenced to life imprisonment and was paroled in 1993): Mrs. Harris, 2005 (made-for-TV; Annette Bening); The People vs. Jean Harris, 1981 (made-for-TV; Ellen Burstyn). Note: For detailed information on Harris, see my book *Murder among the Mighty* (Delacorte Press, 1983; illustrated pages 218-246); and my two-volume work *The Great Pictorial History of World Crime*, Volume II (History, Inc., 2004; illustrated [5 images] pages 902-905).

Harris, Sam H. (U.S. theatrical producer and partner of composer George M. Cohan; 1872-1941): Act One, 1963 (Sammy Smith); George M!, 1970 (made-for-TV; Red Buttons); **Yankee Doodle Dandy**, 1942 (Richard Whorf).

Harrison, Benjamin (1833-1901; U.S. politician and twenty-third President of the U.S., 1889-1893): John Adams, 2008 (TV miniseries; Ken McNaughton); **Stars and Stripes Forever**, 1952 (Roy Gordon).

Hart, Lorenz (1895-1943; U.S. lyricist and longtime partner of composer Richard Rodgers): **Words and Music**, 1948 (Mickey Rooney).

Hart, Moss (1904-1961; U.S. playwright): Act One, 1963 (George Hamilton).

Harte, Bret (Francis Brett Harte; 1836-1902; U.S. author who chronicled the wild era of the California Gold Rush, 1848-1855, a contemporary of Mark Twain and best known for his stories of the Old West): **The Adventures of Mark Twain**, 1944 (John Carradine); Salome Where She Danced, 1945 (Alan Edwards).

Hathorne, John (1641-1717; U.S. merchant and magistrate who was one of the judges at the Salem Witch trials and who never repented his harsh judgments that sent several to their death after convictions of witchcraft): **The Devil and Daniel Webster**, 1941 (H. B. Warner).

Ava Gardner and Gregory Peck (role modeled on Ernest Hemingway) in *The Snows of Kilimanjaro,* **1952.**

Hauptmann, Anna (1898-1994; German-born wife of convicted kidnapper Bruno Richard Hauptmann): Crime of the Century, 1996 (made-for-TV; Isabella Rossellini); Kidnap, 1968 (made-for-TV; Renate Grosser); The Lindbergh Kidnapping Case, 1976 (made-for-TV; Christa Lang). Note: For detailed information on the Lindbergh kidnapping, see my two-volume work *The Great Pictorial History of World Crime*, Volume I (History, Inc., 2004; illustrated [34 images] pages 643-663).

Hauptmann, Bruno Richard (1899-1936; German-born carpenter who was convicted and executed for the 1932 kidnapping-murder of Charles Lindbergh, Jr., the son of famed aviator Charles A. Lindbergh): Crime of the Century, 1996 (made-for-TV; Stephen Rea); Forensic Files, 2000- (TV series; "The Lindbergh Baby Kidnapping: Investigation Reopened," 2005 episode: Matthew R. Staley); **J. Edgar**, 2011 (Damon Herriman); Kidnap, 1968 (made-for-TV; Norbert Kappen); The Lindbergh Kidnapping Case, 1976 (made-for-TV; Anthony Hopkins); Second Verdict, 1976 (TV series; "The Lindbergh Kidnapping," 1976 episode: Peter Marinker). Note: For detailed information on Hauptmann, see my two-volume work *The Great Pictorial History of World Crime*, Volume I (History, Inc., 2004; illustrated [34 images] 643-663).

Hay, John Milton (1838-1905; U.S. secretary of state; private secretary and assistant to U.S. President Abraham Lincoln): **Abraham Lincoln**, 1930 (Cameron Prud'Homme); The Adams Chronicles, 1976 (TV miniseries; Tom Ligon); The Dramatic Life of Abraham Lincoln, 1924 (Homer Willits); Operator 13, 1934 (Franklin Parker); Rough Riders, 1997 (made-for-TV; R. Lee Ermey); Lincoln, 1988 (TV miniseries; Steven Culp); **Saving Lincoln**, 2013 (Graham Sibley); **Tennessee Johnson**, 1942 (Mark Daniels); **The Wind and the Lion**, 1975 (John Huston).

Hayes, Ira Hamilton (1923-1955; Native American; Pima Indian; U.S. Marine and hero at the 1945 battle of Iwo Jima, where he helped to raise the American flag atop Mount Suribachi): The American, 1960 (made-for-TV; Lee Marvin); **Flags of Our Fathers**, 2006 (Adam Beach); **The Outsider**, 1961 (Tony Curtis); **Sands of Iwo Jima**, 1949 (himself).

Hayes, Rutherford Birchard (U.S. politician and 19th President of the U.S.; 1822-1893): Assault at West Point: The Court-Martial of Johnson Whittaker, 194 (made-for-TV; George Martin); Bat Masterson, 1958-1961 (TV series; "General Sherman's March through Dodge City," 1958 episode: Joseph Hamilton); **Buffalo Bill**, 1944 (John Dilson).

Haywood, William Dudley (aka: Big Bill; 1869-1928; American union leader and founder of the Industrial Workers of the World [IWW or Wobblies], who employed violent tactics to achieve goals; was accused of murder, but acquitted; convicted of violating the U.S. Espionage Act and convicted of treason and imprisoned but, while out of prison on an appeal, fled to the USSR where he died): Portrait of a Rebel: The Remarkable Mrs. Sanger, 1980 (made-for-TV: Albert Salmi); **Reds**, 1981 (Dolph Sweet). Note: For detailed information on Haywood, see my two-volume work *The Great Pictorial History of World Crime*, Volume II (History, Inc., 2004; illustrated pages 1501-1506).

Hearst, Patricia Campbell (1954- ; U.S. heiress to the media empire begun by William Randolph Hearst; reportedly kidnapped in 1974 and brainwashed by radical left-wing members of the so-called Symbionese Liberaton Army/SLA, about a dozen drop-out college students and drifters, who participated in robberies and acts of terrorism; was later sent to prison, her sentence commuted by U.S. President Jimmy Carter, later receiving a pardon from U.S. President Bill Clinton): Citizen Tania, 1989 (Shannon Smith); Drunk History, 2013- (TV series; "San Francisco," 2013 episode; Kristen Wiig); The Ordeal of Patty Hearst, 1979 (made-for-TV; Lisa Eilbacher); Pafnucio Santo, 1977 (Susana Kamini); Patty Hearst, 1988 (Natasha Richardson). Note: For detailed information on Patty Hearst and the SLA, see my book *Terrorism in the 20th Century: A Narrative Encyclopedia from the Anarchists through the Weathermen to the Unabomber* (M. Evans, 1998; illustrated pages 220-228); and my two-volume work *The Great Pictorial History of World Crime*, Volume II (History, Inc., 2004; illustrated [19 images] pages 1514-1521).

Hearst, William Randolph (1863-1951; U.S. newspaper publisher and media magnate): Ambrose Bierce: Civil War Stories, 2006 (made-for-TV; Nathan Darrow); And Starring Pancho Villa as Himself, 2003 (made-for-TV; Peter Gregory); **The Cat's Meow**, 2002 (Edward Herrmann); Chaplin, 1992 (Jack Ritschel); **Citizen Kane**, 1941 (role model for Orson Welles); Death Valley Days, 1952-1970 (TV series; "The Paper Dynasty," 1964 episode: James Hampton); E! Mysteries & Scandals, 1998- (TV series; "William Randolph Hearst," 1998 episode: Harold Clousing); The Hearst and Davies Affair, 1985 (made-for-TV; Robert Mitchum); Hollywood Babylon, 1992-1993 (TV series; one 1993 episode: Robert Koons); Hollywood Mouth, 2008 (Don Yanan); Mentors, 1998-2005 (TV series; "Citizen Cates," 2001 episode: Michael Moriarty); Million Dollar Babies, 1994 (TV series; Leon Pownall); RKO 281, 1999 (made-for-TV; James Cromwell); Rough Riders, 1997 (made-for-TV; George Hamilton); Winchell, 1998 (made-for-TV; Kevin Tighe); Winston Churchill: The Wilderness Years, 1981- (TV miniseries; "Down and Out," 1981 episode: Stephen Elliott).

Hecht, Ben (1894-1964; U.S. writer, newspaperman, playwright, novelist and screenwriter, winner of the first Academy Award for an original screenplay, **Underworld**, 1927): **Gaily, Gaily**, 1969 (role model for Beau Bridges); The Young Indiana Jones Chronicles, 1992-1993 (TV series; "Young Indiana Jones and the Mystery of the Blues," 1993 episode: Mark Kiely). Note: For detailed information on Hecht, see my book *The Innovators: Sixteen Portraits of the Famous and Infamous* (Regnery Gateway, 1982; illustrated pages 122-130).

Heine, Heinrich (1797-1856; German poet, essayist and journalist): Die lachende Grille, 1926 (Max Grunberg); Ferdinand Lassalle, 1918 (Friedrich Kuhne); Heinrich Heine, 1978 (made-for-TV; Christoph Bantzer); Liszt Ferenc, 1982 (TV miniseries; Valerio Popesco).

Held, Anna (1872-1918; Polish-born actress in France and common-law wife of theatrical impresario Florenz Ziegfeld): **Gentleman Jim**, 1942 (Madeleine Lebeau); **The Great Ziegfeld**, 1936 (Luise Rainer); Ziegfeld: The Man and His Women, 1978 (made-for-TV; Barbara Parkins).

Hellman, Lillian Florence (1905-1984; U.S. playwright and screenwriter; longtime companion of writer Dashiell Hammett): Dash and Lilly, 1999 (made-for-TV; Judy Davis); **Julia**, 1977 (Jane Fonda).

Hemingway, Ernest (U.S. author, 1899-1961): **Adventures of a Young Man**, 1962 (role model for Richard Beymer); The Adventures of Picasso, 1980 (Olle Ljungberg); American Playhouse, 1981- (TV series; "Waiting for the Moon," 1987 episode: Bruce McGill); **The Breaking Point**, 1950 (role model for John Garfield); The DuPont Show of the Week, 1961 (TV series; "Hemingway," 1961 episode: Andrew Dugan); **A Farewell to Arms**, 1932 (role model for Gary Cooper); **A Farewell to Arms**, 1957 (role model for Rock Hudson); The Fearing Mind, 2000- (TV series; "Come to Papa," 2000 episode: Robert Loggia); Genius, 2016 (Dominic West); Hello Hemingway, 1990 (Modesto Alanis von der Meden); Hemingway, 1988 (TV miniseries; Stacy Keach); Hemingway and Gellhorn, 2012 (TV; Clive Owen); The Hemingway Play, 1976 (made-for-TV; Alexander Scourby); Hemingway: That Summer in Paris, 2003 (made-for-TV; Vincent Walsh); Hemingway: The Hunter of Death, 2001 (Albert Finney); In Love and War, 1996 (Chris O'Donnell); Islands of the Stream, 1977 (role model for George C. Scott); The Legendary Life of Ernest Hemingway, 1989 (Victor Garber); Lives and Deaths of the Poets, 2011 (Jonah Baker); **Midnight in Paris**, 2011 (Corey Stoll); The Moderns, 1988 (Kevin J. O'Connor); Papa, 2015 (Adrian Sparks); Shortcut to Happiness, 2003 (Bill Boylan); The Shortest Day, 1963 (Walter Pidgeon); **The Snows of Kilimanjaro**, 1952 (role model for Gregory Peck); **To Have and Have Not**, 1944 (role model for Humphrey Bogart); Tusk, 2014 (Zak Knutson); The Young Indiana Jones Chronicles, 1992-1993 (TV series; "Young Indiana Jones and the Mystery of the Blues," 1993 episode: Jay Underwood).

Henry II (1122-1189; King of England): Becket, 1923 (A.V. Bramble); **Becket**, 1964 (Peter O'Toole); Border Warfare, 1990 (made-for-TV; John Purcell); Churchill's People, 1974- (TV series; "A Sprig of Broom," 1975 episode: Clive Revill); The Devil's Crown, 1978- (TV series; Brian Cox); **The Lion in Winter**, 1968 (Peter O'Toole); The Lion in Winter, 2003 (made-for-TV; Patrick Stewart); Murder in the Cathedral, 1951 (Alexander Gauge); Richard the Lionheart, 1962- (TV series; "The King's Champion," 1962 episode: Trader Faulkner; "Long Live the King," 1962 episode: Dominic Roche); Richard the Lionheart, 2014 (Malcolm McDowell); Richard the Lionheart: Rebellion, 2015 (Derek Allen); The Trial of Andy Fothergill, 1951 (made-for-TV; Norman Mitchell); Who Killed Thomas Becket?, 2004 (made-for-TV; Rupert Wickham).

Henry V (1386-1422; King of England): An Age of Kings, 1960- (TV series; Robert Hardy); BBC Sunday-Night Theatre, 1950-1959 (TV series; "The Life of King Henry V," 1951 episode: Clement McCallin); Conflict, 1966-1969 (TV series; "Henry V," 1967 episode: Barry Foster); The Gordon Honour, 1955-1956 (TV series; "The Prisoner's Candlestick," 1956 episode: Michael Allinson); Great Performances, 1971- (TV series; "Henry V at Shakespeare's Globe," 1997 episode: Mark Rylance); **Henry V**, 1946 (Laurence Olivier); Henry V, 1953 (made-for-TV; John Clements); Henry V, 1966 (made-for-TV; Douglas Rain); Henry V, 1979 (made-for-TV; David Gwillim); **Henry V**, 1989 (Kenneth Branagh); Henry V, 2007 (Peter Babakitis); The Hollow Crown, 2012 (TV miniseries; Tom Hiddleston); The Life and Death of Sir John Falstaff, 1959- (TV series; "A New Reign," 1959 episode: Colin Jeavons); The Nearly Complete and Utter History of Everything, 1999 (made-for-TV: Martin Clunes); Regal Cavalcade, 1935 (Matheson Lang); The Shakespeare Series, 2012- (TV series; "Henry V," 2013 episode: Gregory Mikell); Shakespeare's Globe: Henry V, 2013 (Jamie Parker); Television World Theatre, 1957-1958 (TV series; "The Life of Henry V," 1957 episode: John Neville); The War of the Roses, 1965 (TV series; Michael Pennington).

Laurence Olivier as Henry V in *Henry V*, 1946.

Henry VIII (1491-1547; King of England): An Age of Kings, 1960 (TV series; "Richard III Part II: The Boar Hunt," 1960 episode: Jerome Willis); Anna Bolena, 1984 (made-for-TV; James Morris); Anna Bolena, 2011 (made-for-TV; Ildebrando D'Arcangelo); Anna Boleyn, 1920 (Emil Jannings); **Anne of the Thousand Days**, 1969 (Richard Burton); BBC Sunday-Night Theater, 1950-1959 (TV series; "The Rose without a Thorn," 1953 episode: Basil Sydney; "The White Falcon," 1956 episode: Paul Rogers); Beauty and the Beast, 1987-1990 (TV series; "Masques," 1987 episode: Frank Patton); Bewitched, 1964-1972 (TV series; two 1971 episodes: Ronald Long); Border Warfare, 1990 (made-for-TV; William Lyon); Carry on Henry VIII, 1971 (Sidney James); Catalina de Inglaterra, 1951 (Rafael Luis Calvo); Complete and Utter History of Britain, 1969 (TV series; "Perkin Warbeck to Bloody Mary,"1969 episode: Terry Jones); The DuPont Show of the Month, 1957-1961 (TV series; "The Prince and the Pauper," 1957 episode: Douglas Campbell); Elizabeth R, 1971-1972 (TV miniseries; "The Lion's Club," 1971 episode: Keith Michell); Francis the First, 1937 (Alexandre Rignault); God's Outlaw, 1986 (Keith Barron); The Golden Age, 1967 (TV series: "Henry VIII," 1967 episode: Anthony Paul); Heinrich VIII und seine Frauen, 1968 (made-for-TV; Hans Dieter Zeidler); Henry VIII, 1979 (made-for-TV; John Stride); Henry VIII, 1991 (made-for-TV; Philippe Rouillon); Henry VIII, 2003 (made-for-TV; Ray Winstone as older Henry; Sid Mitchell as young Henry); Henry VIII and His Six Wives, 1972 (Keith Michell); Henry VIII: Mind of a Tyrant, 2009 (TV series; Laurence Spellman); It Could Happen to You, 1977 (Jonathan Adams); King and Women, 1967 (made-for-TV; Jan Werich); La jument du roi, 1972 (made-for-TV; Jean Le Poulain); The Lockhavens, 2009 (Richard Lund); The Madness of Henry VIII, 2006 (made-for-TV; Dan Astileanu as adult Henry; Gabi Rauta as young Henry); A Man for All Seasons, 1957 (made-for-TV; Noel Johnson); **A Man for All Seasons**, 1966 (Robert Shaw); Marie Tudor, 1966 (made-for-TV; Michel de Re); Monarch, 2000 (T.P. McKenna); The Nearly Complete and Utter History of Everything, 1999 (made-for-TV: Brian Blessed); Nine Days a Queen, 1936 (Frank Cellier); A Man for All Seasons, 1988 (made for TV; Martin Chamberlain); O Principe E o Mendigo, 1972 (TV series; Manoel da Nobrega); Omnibus, 1952-1961 (TV series; "The Trial of Anne Boleyn," 1952 episode: Rex Harrison); The Other Boleyn Girl, 2003 (made-for-TV; Jared Harris); The Other Boleyn Girl, 2008 (Eric Bana as adult Henry; Joseph Moore as young Henry); **The Pearls of the Crown**, 1938 (Lyn Harding); The Prince and the Pauper, 1915 (Robert Broderick); The Prince and the Pauper, 1920 (Albert Schreiber); **The Prince and the Pauper**, 1937 (Montagu Love); The Prince and the Pauper, 1943 (Yuri Tolubeyev); The Prince and the Pauper, 1976 (TV series; Ronald Radd); The Prince and the Pauper, 1977 (Charlton Heston); The Prince and the Pauper, 1996 (TV series; two episodes: Keith Michell);

James Robertson Justice as Henry VIII in *The Sword and the Rose,* **1953.**

The Prince and the Pauper, 2000 (made-for-TV; Alan Bates); **The Private Life of Henry VIII**, 1933 (Charles Laughton); The Rose without a Thorn, 1947 (made-for-TV; Arthur Young); A Royal Love, 2016 (Dirk Gunther Mohr); The Six Wives of Henry VIII, 1970 (TV miniseries; Keith Michell); The Six Wives of Henry VIII, 2001 (TV miniseries; two episodes: Andy Rashleigh; two episodes: Chris Larkin); **The Sword and the Rose**, 1953 (James Robertson Justice); The Third Testament, 2010 (Justin Kamm); **Tower of London**, 1939 (Ralph Forbes as Henry Tudor); The Tudors, 2007-2010 (TV series; Jonathan Rhys Meyers); The Twisted Tale of Bloody Mary, 2008 (made-for-TV; Jason Sharp); Walt Disney's Wonderful World of Color, 1954-1992 (TV series; "The Prince and the Pauper: The Pauper King," 1962 episode: Paul Rogers; "The Prince and the Pauper: The Merciful Law of the King," 1962 episode: Paul Rogers; "The Prince and the Pauper: Long Live the Rightful King," 1962 episode: Paul Rogers); **When Knighthood Was in Flower**, 1922 (Lyn Harding); Wolf Hall, 2015 (TV miniseries; Damian Lewis); **Young Bess**, 1953 (Charles Laughton).

Henry, Patrick (1736-1799; U.S. attorney, planter, patriot, orator and a founding father of the U.S.): The Adams Chronicles, 1976 (TV miniseries; William Shust); **America**, 1924 (Frank McGlynn Jr.); Cardigan, 1922 (George Loeffler); Daniel Boone, 1964-1970 (TV series; John Hoyt in 1966 episode; Booth Colman in two 1967 episodes: Liam Sullivan in 1969 episode); The Farmer from Monticello, 1955 (made-for-TV; Tod Griffin); Founding Fathers, 2000 (TV series; Burt Reynolds); Freedom: A History of Us, 2003 (TV series; Richard Gere); Freedom to Speak, 1982- (TV miniseries; John Rubinstein); George Washington, 1984 (TV miniseries; Harry Groener); George Washington II: The Forging of a Nation, 1986 (made-for-TV; Daniel Davis); **The Howards of Virginia**, 1940 (Richard Gaines); **Janice Meredith**, 1924 (Robert Thorne); **John Paul Jones**, 1959 (Macdonald Carey); L'abolition, 2008 (made-for-TV; Quentin Ogier); Liberty! The American Revolution, 1997 (TV miniseries; James Naughton); Liberty or Death, 2007 (made-for-TV; Kevin McGranahan); A More Perfect Union, 2009 (made-for-TV; Richard Schumann); Patrick Henry, 1955 (made-for-TV; Jack Kelly); Profiles in Courage, 1964-1965 (TV series; "George Mason," 1965 episode: John Colicos); Pursuit of Honor: The Rise of George Washington, 2006 (David Biser/Alex Jenness); The Revolution, 2006- (TV series; Ian Stewart); Samuel Adams, 2014 (made-for-TV; Brent Harvey); You Are There, 1953-1971 (TV series; "The Resolve of Patrick Henry [March 23, 1775]," 1954 episode: Ainslie Pryor).

Hepburn, James (4th Earl of Bothwell; 1534-1578; Scottish clan leader and husband of Mary, Queen of Scots): Bothwell, 1970 (made-for-TV; Brian Cox); Gunpowder, Treason & Plot, 2004 (made-for-TV; Kevin

McKidd); The Haggard Falcon, 1974- (TV series; Alex Heggie); The Heart of the Queen, 1940 (Willy Birgell); La camera explore le temps, 1957-1966 (TV series; two episodes in 1962: Pierre Tabard); The Loves of Mary, Queen of Scots, 1923 (Gerald Ames); Maria Stuart, 1927 (Fritz Kortner); **Mary of Scotland**, 1936 (Fredric March); Mary, Queen of Scots, 1971 (Nigel Davenport); Mary Queen of Scots, 2013 (Sean Biggerstaff); Pulitzer Prize Playhouse, 1950-1952 (TV series; "Mary of Scotland," 1951 episode: John Emery).

Herbert, Victor August (1859-1924; U.S. cellist, composer and conductor): **The Great Victor Herbert**, 1939 (Walter Connolly); **Till the Clouds Roll By**, 1946 (Paul Maxey).

Herkimer, Nicholas (1728-1777; American revolutionary general, mortally wounded at the Battle of Oriskany on August 6, 1777): **Drums along the Mohawk**, 1939 (Roger Imhof).

Herndon, William (1818-1891; U.S. attorney and onetime law partner of Abraham Lincoln): **Abe Lincoln in Illinois**, 1940 (Alan Baxter); Abe Lincoln in Illinois, 1964 (made-for-TV; Burt Brinckerhoff); **Abraham Lincoln**, 1930 (Jason Robards Sr.); Lincoln, 1988 (made-for-TV; Jeffrey DeMunn); **Saving Lincoln**, 2013 (Michael Maize).

Herod Antipater (Herod Antipas; 20 B.C.-39 A.D.; ruler of Galilee and Perea, whose adulterous marriage to Herodias was condemned by prophet John the Baptist and who was induced to have John beheaded after his seductive step-daughter Salome, in seeking vengeance against John for her mother's sake, reportedly conducted a sensuous dance for Herod): Behold the Man, 1935 (Harry Baur); The Big Fisherman, 1959 (Herbert Lom); The Cradle of God, 1926 (Leon Mathot); The Gospel According to St. Matthew, 1966 (Francesco Leonetti); **The Greatest Story Ever Told**, 1965 (Jose Ferrer); Herod and Marianne, 1965 (made-for TV; Walter Richter); Herod the Great, 1959 (Corrado Pani); Herodias, 1911 (short; Karlmos); Il messia, 1975 (Toni Ucci); Jesus, 1979 (Richard Peterson); Jesus, 2000 (made-for-TV; Luca Barbareschi); Jesus Christ Superstar, 1972 (made-for-TV; Reg Livermore); **Jesus Christ Superstar**, 1973 (Josh Mostel); Jesus of Nazareth, 1942 (Jose Morcillo); Jesus of Nazareth, 1977 (TV miniseries; Christopher Plummer); Joseph and Mary, 2016 (Steven Love); **King of Kings**, 1961 (Frank Thring); Kristo, 1996 (Paquito Diaz); The Living Christ Series, 1951 (TV miniseries; Peter Whitney; Jo Gilbert); The Living Bible, 1952 (TV series; Nestor Paiva); Redenzione, 1919 (Luigi Rossi); Restitution, 1918 (F.A. Turner); Salome, 1918 (G. Raymond Nye); Salome, 1923 (Vincent Coleman); Salome, 1923 (Mitchell Lewis); **Salome**, 1953 (Charles Laughton); Salome, 1973 (made-for-TV; Michel Auclair); Salome, 1986 (Tomas Milian); Salome, 1990 (made-for-TV; Horst Hiestermann); Salome, 1992 (made-for-TV; Kenneth Riegel); Salome, 2013 (Al Pacino); Salome's Last Dance, 1988 (Stratford Johns); Son of God, 2014 (Rick Bacon).

Herod the Great (Roman controlled king of Judea; 73-4 B.C.): Follow the Star, 1979 (made-for-TV; Lewis Fiander); The Gospel according to St. Matthew, 1966 (Amerigo Bevilacqua); The Gospel according to Matthew, 1993 (Patrick Mynhardt); **The Greatest Story Ever Told**, 1965 (Claude Rains); Herod the Great, 1959 (Edmund Purdom); Il messia, 1975 (Vittorio Caprioli); Jesus of Nazareth, 1977 (TV miniseries; Peter Ustinov); Joseph and Mary, 2016 (Lawrence Bayne); **King of Kings**, 1961 (Gregoire Aslan); The Living Christ Series, 1951 (TV miniseries; Will Wright); Marie de Nazareth, 1995 (Marc de Jonge); Mary, 2016 (Ben Kingsley); Mary, Mother of Jesus, 1999 (made-for-TV; Hywel Bennett); Mary, the Mother of the Son of God, 2003 (Tonico Pereira); The Nativity, 2010- (TV miniseries; Ciaran Hinds).

Herodias (mother of Salome and incestuous wife of Herod II and who divorced herself from her husband while he lived and adulterously married Herod Antipas for which John the Baptist condemned her and for which John forfeited his life; 15 B.C.-49 A.D.): Behold the Man, 1935 (Elmire Vautier); The Big Fisherman, 1959 (Martha Hyer); The Cradle of God, 1926 (Rachel Devirys); The Gospel according to St. Matthew, 1966 (Franca Cupane); **The Greatest Story Ever Told**, 1965 (Marian Seldes); Herodias, 1911 (short; Jeanne Grumbach); Il messia, 1975 (Flora Carabella); Jesus, 2000 (made-for-TV; Elena Sofia Ricci); Jesus of Nazareth, 1977 (TV miniseries; Valentina Cortese); **King of Kings**, 1961 (Rita Gam); Kristo, 1996 (Sheila Ysrael); Redenzione, 1919 (Elisa Severi); Salome, 1910 (short; Laura Orette); Salome, 1923 (Christine Winthrop); Salome, 1923 (Rose Dione); **Salome**, 1953 (Judith Anderson); Salome, 1973 (made-for-TV; Madeleine Sologne); Salome, 1986 (Pamela Salem); Salome, 1990 (made-for-TV; Leonie Sinopoli); Salome, 1992 (made-for-TV; Gillian Knight); Salome, 2013 (Roxanne Hart); Salome's Last Dance, 1988 (Glenda Jackson).

Herold, David (1842-1865; U.S. conspirator in the 1865 assassination of President Abraham Lincoln, who was tried and executed by hanging): **The Conspirator**, 2011 (Marcus Hester); The Day Lincoln Was Shot, 1998 (made-for-TV; Jaimz Woolvett); The Lincoln Conspiracy, 1977 (Fred Grandy); The Ordeal of Dr. Mudd, 1980 (made-for-TV; Luke Halpin); **The Prisoner of Shark Island**, 1936 (Paul Fix); Telephone Time, 1956-1958 (TV series; "The Quality of Mercy," 1958 episode: Robert Gothie); Westinghouse Desilu Playhouse, 1958-1960 (TV series; "The Case for Dr. Mudd," 1958 episode: Tom Pittman); You Are There, 1953-1957 (TV series; "The Capture of John Wilkes Booth," 1953 episode: Art Rease). For detailed information on Herold and his participation in the Lincoln assassination, see my two-volume work, *The Great Pictorial History of World Crime*, Volume I (History, Inc., 2004; illustrated [47 images] pages 26-44).

Hess, Rudolf (Rudolf Walter Richard Hess; 1894-1987; Nazi leader under Adolf Hitler, who served as Hitler's chief confidant and secretary until inexplicably flying to England to make a separate peace and thought to be mad; replaced by Martin Bormann as Hitler's new secretary; Hess was imprisoned for life as a war criminal): Armstrong Circle Theatre, 1950-1963 (TV series; "Engineer of Death: The Eichmann Story," 1960 episode: Carroll O'Connor); Inside the Third Reich, 1982 (made-for-TV; Maurice Roeves); ITV Playhouse, 1967- (TV series; "Hess," 1978 episode: Wolf Kahler); **The Hitler Gang**, 1944 (Victor Varconi); Hitler: The Rise of Evil, 2003 (made-for-TV; James Babson); Hitler vor Gericht, 2009 (made-for-TV; Mark-Alexander Solf); J'etais a Nuremberg, 2011 (made-for-TV; Dimiter Kuzov); Nuremberg, 2000- (TV miniseries; Roc LaFortune); **La Rafle**, 2012 (Tamas Lengyel); The Nuremberg Trial: War Crimes on Trial, 1996 (made-for-TV; Roger Grunwald); Speer und er, 2005- (TV miniseries; Andre Hennicke); Wild Geese II, 1985 (Laurence Olivier); You Are There, 1953-1971 (TV series; "The Escape of Rudolf Hess," 1953 episode: Peter Cushing).

Heth, Joice (1756-1836; African-American slave exhibited by showman P.T. Barnum, who falsely claimed that she was the 161-year-old "mammy" of President George Washington): Barnum!, 1986 (made-for-TV; Sharon Benson); Barnum, 1986 (made-for-TV; Lorena Gale); **The Mighty Barnum**, 1934 (Lucille La Verne); P.T. Barnum, 1999 (made-for-TV; Lorena Gale).

Heusinger, Adolf (1897-1982; German general in WWII and later commanded West German forces): It Happened on July 20th, 1955 (Harry Hardt); Operation Valkyrie, 2004 (made-for-TV; Ludwig Boettger); **Valkyrie**, 2008 (Matthew Burton).

Heydrich, Reinhard (Reinhard Tristan Eugen Heydrich; German official, deputy leader of the SS under Heinrich Himmler during the Nazi era and one of the architects of the Holocaust; became the oppressive governor of Czechoslovakia after the German occupation and was assassi-

Allan Jones, Sandra Lee Richards, Mary Martin and Walter Connolly (as Victor Herbert) in *The Great Victor Herbert*, 1939.

nated by Czech resistance fighters; 1904-1942): Air Raid Wardens, 1943 (Don Costello); Armstrong Circle Theatre, 1950-1963 (TV series; "Engineer of Death: The Eichmann Story," 1960 episode: Alvin Epstein); **Canaris**, 1958 (Martin Held); Conspiracy, 2001 (made-for-TV; Kenneth Branagh); Edge of War, 2012- (TV series; Todd McIntyre); G.E. True, 1962- (TV series; "Heydrich, Part 1," 1963 episode: Kurt Kreuger); **Hangmen Also Die!**, 1943 (Hans Heinrich von Twardowski); Heydrich in Prague, 1967 (made-for-TV; Martin Benrath); **The Hitler Gang**, 1944 (Peter Pohlenz); **Hitler's Madman**, 1943 (John Carradine); Hitler's SS: Portrait in Evil, 1985 (made-for-TV; David Warner); Holocaust, 1978 (TV miniseries; David Warner); Interpol, 1963-1967 (TV series; "Geld, Geld, Geld," 1965 episode: Anton Diffring); Lidice, 2012 (Detlef Bothe); **Operation Daybreak**, 1975 (Anton Diffring); Operation Himmler, 1979 (made-for-TV; Eugeniusz Kujawski); Reinhard Heydrich: Manager des Terrors, 1977 (made-for-TV; Dietrich Mattausch); When Hitler Invaded Britain, 2004 (made-for-TV; Benedict Taylor). Note: For detailed information on Heydrich and his assassination, see my two-volume work *The Great Pictorial History of World Crime*, Volume I (History, Inc., 2004; illustrated [9 images] pages 134-138).

Heyer, Adam (1889-1929; U.S. accountant and business manager of the George "Bugs" Moran gang, who, along with six others, was killed in Chicago's notorious 1929 St. Valentine's Day Massacre): Playhouse 90, 1956-1961 (TV series; "Seven against the Wall," 1958 episode: Milton Frome); **The St. Valentine's Day Massacre**, 1967 (Milton Frome). Note: For detailed information on Heyer and the St. Valentine's Day Massacre, see my books, *World Encyclopedia of Organized Crime* (Paragon House, 1992, illustrated pages 343-347; and *The Great Pictorial History of World Crime*, Volume I (History, Inc., 2004; [under Capone] illustrated pages 503-541).

Hickok, James Butler (aka: Wild Bill; 1837-1876; U.S. western lawman and gunman): Aces and Eights, 1936 (Karl Hackett); **Across the Sierras**, 1941 (Bill Elliott); Adventures of Wild Bill Hickok, 1951-1958 (TV series; Guy Madison); Badlands of Dakota, 1941 (Richard Dix); Beyond the Sacramento, 1940 (Bill Elliott); Bronco, 1958-1962 (TV series: "Montana Passage," 1960 episode: Charles Cooper; "One Evening in Abilene," 1962 episode: Jack Cassidy); Buffalo Girls, 1995 (made-for-TV; Sam Elliott); Bullets for Bandits, 1942 (Bill Elliott); **Calamity Jane**, 1953 (Howard Keel); Calamity Jane, 1963 (made-for-TV; Art Lund); Calamity Jane, 1984 (made-for-TV; Frederic Forrest); Custer's Last Stand, 1936 (serial; Allen Greer): **Dallas**, 1950 (Reed Hadley); Deadwood, 2004-2006 (TV series; Keith Carradine); Deadwood Dick, 1940 (serial; Lane Chandler); Deadwood '76, 1965 (Robert Dix); Death

Gary Cooper, Leif Erickson and Reed Hadley (as Wild Bill Hickok) in *Dallas,* **1950.**

Valley Days, 1952-1970 (TV series: "A Calamity Called Jane," 1966 episode: Rhodes Reason); The Devil's Trail, 1942 (Bill Elliott); Frontier Scout, 1938 (George Houston); The Great Adventure, 1963-1964 (TV series; "Wild Bill Hickok: The Legend and the Man," 1964 episode: Lloyd Bridges); The Great Adventures of Wild Bill Hickok, 1938 (Bill Elliott); Gunslingers, 2014- (TV miniseries; Walt Willey); Hardin, 2015 (Larry Freeland); Hands across the Rockies, 1941 (Bill Elliott); I Killed Wild Bill Hickok, 1956 (Tom Brown); **The Iron Horse**, 1924 (Jack Padjan); Jack McCall, Desperado, 1953 (Douglas Kennedy): King of Dodge City, 1941 (Bill Elliott); The Last Frontier, 1926 (J. Farrell MacDonald); **The Lawless Breed**, 1953 (Robert Anderson); Legend, 1995 (TV series; William Russ); The Legend of Calamity Jane, 1997-1998 (TV series; Clancy Brown); The Legend of the Lone Ranger, 1981 (Richard Farnsworth); **Little Big Man**, 1970 (Jeff Corey); The Lone Star Vigilantes, 1942 (Bill Elliott); The Meant to Be's, 2008 (made-for-TV; Jon Eric Price); North from the Lone Star, 1941 (Bill Elliott); **The Outlaws Is Coming!**, 1965 (Paul Shannon); Overland Trail, 1960 (TV series; "Westbound Stage," 1960 episode: Adam West); Party Wagon, 2004 (animated; made-for-TV; Dan Castellaneta voiceover); **The Plainsman**, 1936 (Gary Cooper); The Plainsman, 1966 (Don Murray); **Pony Express**, 1953 (Forrest Tucker); Prairie Gunsmoke, 1942 (Bill Elliott); Prairie Schooners, 1940 (Bill Elliott); Purgatory, 1999 (made-for-TV; Sam Shepard); **The Raiders**, 1963 (Robert Culp); Roaring Frontiers, 1941 (Bill Elliott); Seven Hours of Gunfire, 1965 (Adrian Hoven); Son of the Renegade, 1953 (Ewing Miles Brown); This Is the West That Was, 1974 (made-for-TV; Ben Murphy); **The White Buffalo**, 1977 (Charles Bronson); **Wild Bill**, 1995 (Jeff Bridges); **Wild Bill Hickok**, 1923 (William S. Hart); Wild Bill Hickok Rides, 1942 (Bruce Cabot); Wild Times, 1980 (TV series; L. Q. Jones); The Wildcat of Tucson, 1940 (Bill Elliott); The World Changes, 1933 (Charles Middleton); You Know My Name, 1999 (made-for-TV; Dwayne Armitage); Young Bill Hickok, 1940 (Roy Rogers); The Young Riders, 1989-1992 (TV series; 1992 episodes: Josh Brolin). Note: For detaile information on Hickok, see my book *Encyclopedia of Western Lawmen and Outlaws* (Paragon House, 1992; illustrated [12 images] pages 155-160).

Hideki Tojo (1884-1948; Japanese general and 40th prime minister of Japan during WWII; convicted and hanged as a war criminal): **Blood on the Sun**, 1945 (Robert Armstrong); Daitoa senso to kokusai saiban, 1959 (Kanjuro Arashi); **Emperor**, 2012 (Shohei Hino); The Fateful Moment, 2001 (Masahiko Tsugawa); Histeria!, 1998-2000 (animated TV series; "World War II," 1999 episode: Rob Paulsen voiceover); The Imperial Japanese Empire, 1982 (Tetsuru Tanba); **Tora! Tora! Tora!**, 1970 (Asao Uchida); Turning Point of Showa History—The Militarists—International, 1971 (Keiju Kobayashi).

Hill, Ambrose Powell (1825-1865; U.S. military officer and lieutenant general in the Confederate army of Northern Virginia during the American Civil War): **Gettysburg**, 1993 (Patrick Falci); **Gods and Generals**, 2003 (William Sanderson); Omnibus, 1952-1961 (TV series; "Lee at Gettysburg," 1957 episode: William Smithers).

Hill, Virginia (1916-1966; U.S. organized crime associate and courier for illegal funds, best remembered as the tempestuous lover of mobster Benjamin "Bugsy" Siegel): **Bugsy**, 1991 (Annette Bening); Lansky, 1999 (made-for-TV; Peggy Jo Jacobs); The Making of the Mob: New York, 2015- (TV miniseries; Kaelan Denali Dickinson); P.S. I. Luv U, 1991- (TV series; "What's Up, Bugsy?," 1991 episode; Connie Sellecca); Virginia Hill, 1974 (made-for-TV; Dyan Cannon). Note: For detailed information on Virginia Hill, see my book *World Encyclopedia of Organized Crime* (Paragon House, 1992; illustrated pages 203-204).

Himmler, Heinrich (1900-1945; German Nazi politician, close aide to Adolf Hitler and head of SS who supervised Holocaust extermination of political, religious and military POWs): The Angels of Death Island, 2003 (Chris McNickle); The Aryan Couple, 2004 (Danny Webb); The Black Chapel, 1959 (Werner Peters); The Bunker, 1981 (made-for-TV; Michael Sheard); **A Clockwork Orange**, 1971 (himself in archival footage); Days of Betrayal, 1973 (Josef Vorel); Death Is My Trade, 1977 (Hans Korte); Downfall, 2004 (Ulrich Noethen); **The Eagle Has Landed**, 1977 (Donald Pleasence); The Empty Mirror, 1999 (himself in archive footage); The Great Battle, 1973 (Erich Thiede); Hitler, 1962 (Rick Traeger); Hitler: A Film from Germany, 1977 (Heinz Schubert); **The Hitler Gang**, 1944 (Luis Van Rooten); **Hitler's Madman**, 1943 (Howard Freeman); Hitler's SS: Portrait in Evil, 1985 (made-for-TV; John Normington); Holocaust, 1978 (TV miniseries; Ian Holm); I Aim at the Stars, 1960 (Eric Zuckmann); Inside the Third Reich, 1982 (made-for-TV; David Shawyer); Invincible, 2002 (Alexander Duda); **La Rafle**, 2012 (Thomas Darchinger); The Last Ten Days, 1955 (Erich Stuckmann); The Magic Face, 1951 (Eric Zuckmann); The Man Who Lived at the Ritz, 1989 (made-for-TV; David Shawyer); Operation Eichmann, 1961 (Luis Van Rooten); The Red Orchestra, 1989 (Bernard Charnace); Reichsfuhrer—SS, 2015 (David B. Stewart III); Reinhard Heydrich, Manager des Terrors, 1977 (made-for-TV; Franz Rudnick); The Scarlet and the Black, 1983 (made-for-TV; T.P. McKenna); Spring of Life, 2000 (Vaclav Mares); Stalingrad, 1990 (Erich Thiede); The Strange Death of Adolf Hitler, 1943 (Frederick Giermann); To Catch a King, 1984 (made-for-TV; Stephen Moore); Uncle Adolf, 2005 (made-for-TV; Michael Eaves); Uprising, 2001 (made-for-TV; Peter Faerber); **Valkyrie**, 2008 (Matthias Freihof); War and Remembrance, 1988- (TV miniseries; Dieter Wagner); When Heroes Die, 1970 (Vicente Roca); The Winds of War, 1983- (TV miniseries; "The Changing of the Guard," 1983 episode: Dieter Wagner).

Hindenburg, Paul von (1847-1934; Prussian military officer and German field marshal in WWI; president of Germany, 1925-1934; succeeded by Adolf Hitler): Darling Lili, 1970 (Niall MacGinnis); Das Attentat—Schleicher: General der letzten Stunde, 1967 (made-for-TV; Helmuth Hinzelmann); Das Lied der Matrosen, 1958 (Eduard von Winterstein); Der Gewaltfrieden, 2010 (made-for-TV; Rainer Basedow); Die Flucht nach Holland, 1967 (made-for-TV; Hans W. Hamacher); Die Machtergreifung, 2012 (made-for-TV; Rainer Basedow); Fall of Eagles, 1974 (TV miniseries; Marius Goring); Fraulein Doktor, 1969 (Walter Williams); General Electric Theater, 1953-1962 (TV series; "Hitler's Secret," 1959 episode: Raymond Massey); The Great Victory, Wilson or the Kaiser? The Fall of the Hohenzollerns, 1919 (Emil Hoch); **The Hitler Gang**, 1944 (Sig Rumann); Hitler: The Rise of Evil, 2003 (made-for-TV; Peter O'Toole); Hugenberg—Gegen die Republik, 1967 (made-for-TV; Hans W. Hamacher); The Kaiser, the Beast of Berlin, 1918 (Jay Smith); The Life of Surgeon Sauerbruch, 1954 (Friedrich Domin); My Four Years in Germany, 1918 (George Ridell); The Prussian Cur, 1918

(James Hathaway); **The Red Baron**, 2010 (Josef Vinklar); Stresemann, 1957 (Artur Malkowsky); Tannenberg, 1932 (Karl Korner); Theatre 625, 1964-1968 (TV series; "Firebrand," 1967 episode: Kenneth J. Warren); To Hell with the Kaiser!, 1918 (Emil Hoch); Why America Will Win, 1918 (Ernest Maupain); Yankee Doodle in Berlin, 1919 (Bert Roach).

Hintze, Paul von (1864-1941; German naval officer and politician; German foreign minister in last stages of WWI): The Daredevil, 1918 (Walter Dowling); Der Gewaltfrieden, 2010 (made-for-TV; Bernd Fischerauer); Die Flucht nach Holland, 1967 (made-for-TV; Ernst von Klipstein); El encanto del aguila, 2011- (TV series; Roger Cudney).

Hirohito (1901-1989; Eemperor of Japan, 1926-1989, who led war of aggression in WWII): Danger Five, 2011- (TV series; "Kill Men of the Rising Sun," 2012 episode: Paul Muscat); Dante's Inferno, 2007 (Scott Adsit); **Emperor**, 2012 (Takataro Kataoka); Hiroshima, 1995 (made-for-TV; Naohiko Umewaka); Japan's Longest Day, 1967 (Hakuo Matsumoto); The Last Emperor, 1987 (Lingmu Zhang); **MacArthur**, 1977 (John Fujioka); Monarch of the Moon, 2005 (Kenzo Lee); **Star Spangled Rhythm**, 1942 (Richard Loo); The Sun, 2005 (Issei Ogata).

Hitler, Adolf (1889-1945; German dictator and head of the Nazi Party; committed suicide): Ace London, 1998- (TV series; Alexandre Falcao); Ace of Aces, 1982 (Gunter Meisner); Adolf and Marlene, 1977 (Kurt Raab); Adolf Hitler, 1973 (Austrian made-for-TV; Franz Trager); The Adventures of Picasso, 1978 (Magnus Harenstam); Angelus, 2000 (Tadeusz Plawicki); Appointment with Destiny, 1971-1973 (TV series; "The Plot to Kill Hitler," 1971 episode: Billy Frick); **The Battle of Britain**, 1969 (Rolf Stiefel); Battleground: The Art of War, 2005- (TV series; "The Battle of the Bulge," 2005 episode: Ernst Gossner); Between Time and Timbuktu, 1972 (made-for-TV; Page Johnson); Blazing Saddles, 1974 (Ralph Manza as man in commissary playing Hitler); Blue Light, 1966- (TV series; "Invasion by the Stars," 1966 episode:Jason Wingreen); The Bunker, 1981 (made-for-TV; Anthony Hopkins); **Canaris**, 1958 (himself in archive footage); **Captain America: The First Avenger**, 2011 (James Payton); Churchill: The Hollywood Years, 2004 (Antony Sher); **Citizen Kane**, 1941 (Carl Ekberg); **A Clockwork Orange**, 1971 (himself in archival footage); Conversation with the Beast, 1996 (Armin Mueller-Stahl); Countdown to War, 1989 (made-for-TV; Ian McKellen); Crazy Adventure, 1965 (Andrew Hughes); Days of Betrayal, 1973 (Gunnar Moller); Der Rohm-Putsch, 1967 (made-for-TV; Kurt Klopsch); **The Desert Fox: The Story of Rommel**, 1951 (Luther Adler); Devil's Mistress, 2016 (Pavel Kriz); The Dirty Dozen: Next Mission, 1985 (made-for-TV; Michael Sheard); Downfall, 2004 (Bruno Ganz); **The Eagle Has Landed**, 1977 (Peter Miles); The Empty Mirror, 1999 (Norman Rodway and Hitler himself in archive footage); Ernst Thallmann, 1986 (made-for-TV; Jurgen Reuter); Ernst Thalmann—Fuhrer seiner Klasse, 1955 (Fritz Diez); Europa Europa, 1991 (Ryszard Pietruski); The Fall of Berlin, 1952 (Vladimir Savelev); The First Front, 1949 (Mikhail Astangov); For Freedom, 1940 (Bill Russell); **A Foreign Affair**, 1948 (Bobby Watson); Forever Knight, 1992-1996 (TV series; "Jane Doe," 1996 episode: Duff MacDonald); The Four Horsemen of the Apocalypse, 1962 (Bobby Watson); The Fuhrer Runs Amok, 1974 (Henri Tosit); Gandhi to Hitler, 2011 (Raghuvir Yadav); Gaten Knut Hamsun, 1996 (Gunter Bothur); The Gathering Storm, 1974 (made-for-TV; Ian Bannen); General Electric Theater, 1953-1962 (TV series; "Hitler's Secret," 1959 episode: Robert Coogan); Goebbels und Geduldig, 2001 (Jurgen Schornagel); The Great Battle, 1973 (Fritz Diez); **The Great Dictator**, 1940 (role model for Charles Chaplin); The Great Escape II: The Untold Story, 1988 (made-for-TV; Ludwig Haas); Hamsun, 1997 (Ernst Jacobi); Highlander, 1992-1998 (TV series; "The Valkyrie," 1997 episode: Patrick Keating); Highway to Hell, 1992 (Gilbert Gottfried); Hitler, 1962 (Richard Basehart); Hitler: A Film from Germany, 1977 (Heinz Schubert); Hitler: Beast of Berlin, 1939 (himself in archive footage): Hitler: Dead or Alive,

Anne Baxter and Glenn Ford (as golfer Ben Hogan) in *Follow the Sun*, **1951.**

1942 (Bob Watson); **The Hitler Gang**, 1944 (Bobby Watson); Hitler Superstar, 1974 (made-for-TV; Buster Larsen); Hitler: The Last Ten Days, 1973 (Alec Guinness); Hitler: The Rise of Evil, 2003 (made-for-TV; Robert Carlyle); Hitler's SS: Portrait in Evil, 1985 (made-for-TV; Colin Jeavons); Hitler vor Gericht, 2009 (made-for-TV; Johannes Zimer); If Winter Comes, 1947 (Winston Severn); **Indiana Jones and the Last Crusade**, 1989 (Michael Sheard); Inside the Third Reich, 1982 (made-for-TV; Derek Jacobi); **Is Paris Burning?**, 1966 (Billy Frick); It Happened on July 20th, 1955 (Rolf Neuber); ITV Sunday Night Theatre, 1969- (TV series; "The Death of Adolf Hitler," 1973 episode: Frank Finlay); Joe and Max, 2002 (made-for-TV; Rolf Kanies); King of Hearts, 1967 (Philippe de Broca); King of the Olympics: The Life and Loves of Avery Brundage, 1988 (made-for-TV; Oskar Freitag); La guerre du royal palace, 2012 (made-for-TV; Philippe Ambrosini); **La Rafle**, 2012 (Udo Schenk); **The Last Ten Days**, 1956 (Albin Skoda); The Liberation of Prague, 1978 (Gunnar Moller); Little Nicky, 2000 (Christopher Carroll); Loose Cannons, 1990 (Ira Lewis); Ludwig: Requiem for a Virgin King, 1980 (Johannes Buzalski); The Madmen of Mandoras, 1963 (Bill Freed); The Magic Face, 1951 (Luther Adler); **Man Hunt**, 1941 (Carl Ekberg); The Man Who Crossed Hitler, 2011 (made-for-TV; Ian Hart); Margin for Error, 1943 (Ludwig Donath's voiceover for Hitler's voice) Max, 2002 (Noah Taylor); Meet the People, 1944 (Frederick Giermann); Mein Kampf, 1991 (made-for-TV; Gotz Schubert); Mein Kampf, 2010 (Tom Schilling); **The Miracle of Morgan's Creek**, 1944 (Bobby Watson); Mirage, 2005 (Boban Krstevski); Miss V from Moscow, 1942 (himself in archive footage); **The Monuments Men**, 2014 (James Payton); Mosley, 1998- (TV series; "Beyond the Pale," 1998 episode: Reinhard Michaels); The Motorola Television Hour, 1953-1954 (TV series; "The Last Days of Hitler," 1954 episode: Philip Bourneuf); Mussolini and I, 1985 (made-for-TV; Kurt Raab); Mussolini: The Untold Story, 1985 (TV miniseries; Gunnar Moller); My Fuhrer, 2007 (Helge Schneider); Nazi Apocalypse, 2012 (James Rep); Nazty Nuisance, 1943 (Bobby Watson); **Night Train to Munich**, 1940 (Billy Russell); 1914-1918, 1996- (TV miniseries; Liam Neeson); Omnibus, 1967-2003 (TV series; "Dance of the Seven Veils," 1970 episode: Kenneth Colley); On the Double, 1961 (Bobby Watson); Once upon a Honeymoon, 1942 (Carl Ekberg); 100 Years of Adolf Hitler, 1989 (Udo Kier); Operation Himmler, 1979 (made-for-TV; Ryszard Pietruski); Operation Valkyrie, 2004 (made-for-TV; Udo Schenk); **Our Hitler: A Film from Germany**, 1980 (Heinz Schubert); Passions, 1999-2008 (TV series; episode 1,625: Benton Jennings); Petain, 1993 (Ludwig Haas); The Plot to Kill Hitler, 1990 (made-for-TV; Mike Gwilym); **The Producers**, 1967 (impersonation by Dick Shawn); Race, 2016 (Adrian Zwicker); Reichsfuhrer—SS, 2015 (Richard Adams); Ring of Passion, 1978 (made-for-TV; Barry Dennen); Robert Montgomery Presents, 1950-1957 (TV series; "The Week the

Cesar Romero (as John H. "Doc" Holliday) in *Frontier Marshal*, 1939.

World Stood Still," 1957 episode: George Patelis); Rogue Male, 1977 (made-for-TV; Michael Sheard); Rommel, 2012 (made-for-TV; Johannes Silberschneider); The Search for the Evil One, 1967 (Pitt Herbert); Seduction of the Will, 2001 (Greg Wood); Shining Through, 1992 (Ludwig Haas); Shortcut to Happiness, 2003 (John Unruh); Speer und er, 2005- (TV miniseries; Tobias Moretti); Stalag Luft, 1993 (made-for-TV; Sam Kelly); Stalingrad, 1990 (Akhim Petri); **Star Spangled Rhythm**, 1942 (Tom Dugan); The Story of Mankind, 1957 (Bobby Watson); The Strange Death of Adolf Hitler, 1943 (Ludwig Donath); Strangers in Paradise, 1984 (Ulli Lommel); Theatre 625, 1964-1968 (TV series; "Firebrand," 1967 episode: David J. Grahame); They Saved Hitler's Brain, 1968 (made-for-TV; Bill Freed); **13 Minutes**, 2015 (Udo Schenk); Thirty-Minute Theatre, 1965-1973 (TV series; 'These Men are Dangerous: Hitler," 1969 episode: Kenneth Colley); Thomas the Restless One, 1967 (Bent Christensen); Time Demon, 1996 (Jean-Francois Gallotte); The Time Tunnel, 1966-1967 (TV series; "The Kidnappers," 1967 episode: Bob May); **To Be or Not to Be**, 1942 (role model for Tom Dugan); To Be or Not to Be, 1983 (Roy Goldman); To Catch a King, 1984 (made-for-TV; Fulton Mackay); Tomorrow I'll Wake Up and Scald Myself with Tea, 1977 (Frantisek Vicena); The Twilight Zone, 1959-1964 (TV series; "He's Alive," 1963 episode: Curt Conway); **The Two-Headed Spy**, 1959 (Kenneth Griffith); Uncle Adolf, 2005 (made-for-TV; Ken Stott); Undercovers Hero, 1975 (Peter Sellers); **Valkyrie**, 2008 (David Bamber); The Victors and the Vanquished, 1950 (Mikhail Astangov); War and Remembrance, 1988 (TV miniseries; Steven Berkoff); The Wednesday Play, 1964-1970 (TV series; "And Did Those Feet?," 1965 episode: Carl Jaffe); What Did You Do in the War, Daddy?, 1966 (Carl Ekberg); Which Way to the Front?, 1971 (Sidney Miller); The Wife Takes a Flyer, 1942 (Carl Ekberg); The Winds of War, 1983- (TV miniseries; Gunter Meisner); Winston Churchill: The Wilderness Years, 1981- (TV miniseries; Gunter Meisner); The World Wars, 2014- (TV miniseries; Hugh Scully): You Are There, 1953-1971 (TV series; "The Rise of Adolf Hitler [September 9, 1938]," 1953 episode: Paul Richards). Note: For detailed information on Hitler, see my two-volume work *The Great Pictorial History of World Crime*, Volume I (History, Inc., 2004; illustrated [20 images] pages 138-148).

Hoepner, Erich (1886-1944; German general in WWII; member of the plot to kill Hitler in 1944; executed): Operation Valkyrie, 2004 (made-for-TV; Ronald Nitschke); Operation Walkure, 1971 (made-for-TV; Ernst Dietz); The Plot to Assassinate Hitler, 1955 (Hans Zesch-Ballot); The Wednesday Play, 1964-1970 (TV series; "The July Plot," 1964 episode: Charles Lloyd Pack).

Hofacker, Caesar von (1896-1944; German officer who was part of the

1944 plot to assassinate Adolf Hitler): Die Stunde der Offiziere, 2004 (made-for-TV; Hubertus Hartmann); **The Desert Fox: The Story of Rommel**, 1951 (Paul Cavanagh); Operation Walkure, 1971 (made-for-TV; Gotz von Langheim).

Hoffa, James Riddle (aka: "Jimmy"; 1913-1975?; U.S. union boss of the Teamster's Union; reportedly murdered and disappeared, body never recovered): Blood Feud, 1983 (made-for-TV; Robert Blake); **Hoffa**, 1992 (Jack Nicholson); The Jesse Owens Story, 1984 (made-for-TV; Tom Bosley); Marilyn & Bobby: Her Final Affair, 1993 (made-for-TV; Thomas Wagner); Robert F. Kennedy and His Times, 1985- (TV miniseries; Trey Wilson).

Hoffman, Harold Giles (1896-1954; U.S. politician and governor of the State of New Jersey, 1935-1938): Crime of the Century, 1996 (made-for-TV; Michael Moriarty); Second Verdict, 1976 (TV series; "The Lindbergh Kidnapping," 1976 episode: Shane Rimmer).

Hoffmann, Heinrich (1885-1957; German photographer, who was Adolf Hitler's personal photographer): Hitler: The Last Ten Days, 1973 (Simon Ward); Hitler: The Rise of Evil, 2003 (made-for-TV; Rod Grover).

Hogan, William Ben (1912-1997; U.S. professional golfer, considered one of the greatest players of the sport): Curb Your Enthusiasm, 2000- (TV series; "The End," 2005 episode: Robert Pine); **Follow the Sun**, 1951 (Glenn Ford; Harold Blake as teenager Ben Hogan).

Holbein, Hans (Hans Holbein the Younger; c. 1497-1543; German artist and printmaker): **The Pearls of the Crown**, 1938 (James Craven); **The Private Life of Henry VIII**, 1933 (John Turnbull); The Tudors, 2007-2010 (TV series; Peter Gaynor).

Holiday, Billie (Eleanora Fagan; 1915-1959; U.S. black singer of jazz and blues): **Lady Sings the Blues**, 1972 (Diana Ross); Sinatra, 1992 (made-for-TV; Leata Galloway); Stars in Their Eyes, 1990- (TV series; Deborah Christopher); Touched by an Angel, 1995-2003 (TV series; "God Bless the Child," 2000 episode: Paula Jai Parker).

Holliday, John H. (John Henry "Doc" Holliday; 1851-1887; former dentist, western gambler and gunfighter): Alias Smith and Jones, 1971-1973 (TV series; "Which Way to the O.K. Corral?" and "The Ten Days That Shook Kid Curry," both 1972 episodes with Bill Fletcher); The American West, 2016- (TV miniseries; Edgar Fox); Appointment with Destiny, 1971-1973 (TV series; "Showdown at O.K. Corral," 1972 episode: Tim James); The Arizonian, 1935 (role model for Preston Foster); Bonanza, 1959-1973 (TV series; "Calamity over the Comstock," 1963 episode; Christopher Dark); Buffalo Bill, Jr., 1955-1956 (TV series; "First Posse," 1955 episode: James Griffith); **Cheyenne Autumn**, 1964 (Arthur Kennedy); Colt .45, 1957-1960 (TV series; "The Devil's Godson," 1959 episode: Adam West); Dawn at Socorro, 1954 (role model for Rory Calhoun); Death Valley Days, 1952-1970 (TV series; "The Quiet and the Fury," 1964 episode: Skip Homeier; "Doc Holliday's Gold Bars," 1966 episode: Warren Stevens); **Doc**, 1971 (Stacy Keach); Doc Holliday's Revenge, 2014 (William McNamara); Doctor Who, 1963-1989 (TV series; four 1966 episodes: Anthony Jacobs); Fireside Theatre, 1949-1955 (TV series; "Let the Cards Decide," 1953 episode: Dabbs Greer); **Frontier Marshal**, 1939 (Cesar Romero); **Gunfight at the O. K. Corral**, 1957 (Kirk Douglas); Gunslingers, 2014- (TV miniseries; Andrew DeCarlo); Hannah's Law, 2012 (made-for-TV; Ryan Kennedy); **Hour of the Gun**, 1967 (Jason Robards Jr.); I Married Wyatt Earp, 1983 (made-for-TV; Jeffrey DeMunn); Law for Tombstone, 1937 (Harvey Clark); Lawman, 1958-1962 (TV series; "The Wayfarer," 1959 episode: Adam West); The Legend of Hell's Gate: An American Conspiracy, 2011 (Jamie Thomas King); The Life and Legend of Wyatt Earp, 1955-1961 (TV series; Douglas Fowley); **Masterson of Kansas**, 1954 (James Griffith); Maverick, 1957-1962 (TV series; seven episodes: Peter Breck); **My Darling Clementine**, 1946 (Victor Mature); The Outlaw, 1943 (Walter Huston); Pistols 'n' Petticoats, 1966-1967 (TV series; "Shootout at O'Day Corral," 1966 episode: Don Beddoe); Purgatory, 1999 (made-for-TV; Randy Quaid); Stagecoach, 1987 (made-for-TV; Willie Nelson); Stories of the Century, 1954 (TV series; "Doc Holliday," 1954 episode: Kim Spalding); Sugarfoot, 1957-1961 (TV series; "Trial of the Canary Kid," 1959 episode; Adam West); Tales of Wells Fargo, 1957-1962 (TV series; "Doc Holliday," 1959 episode: Martin Landau); The Tall Man, 1960-1962 (TV series; "Rovin' Gambler," 1961 episode: Robert Lansing); **Tombstone**, 1993 (Val Kilmer); Tombstone Territory, 1957- (TV series; "Doc Holliday in Durango," 1958 episode: Gerald Mohr); **Tombstone: The Town Too Tough to Die**, 1942 (Kent Taylor); Wagon Train, 1957-1965 (TV series; "The Silver Lady," 1965 episode: Henry Silva); The Wild West, 2006- (TV series; "The Gunfight at the OK Corral," 2006 episode: George Asprey); **Wyatt Earp**, 1994 (Dennis Quaid); Wyatt Earp: Return to Tombstone, 1994 (made-for-TV; Douglas Fowley); Wyatt Earp's Revenge, 2012 (Wilson Bethel); You Are There, 1953-1957 (TV series; "The Gunfight at the O.K. Corral," 1955 episode:Barry Atwater); Zane Grey Theater, 1956-1961(TV series; "Man of Fear," 1958 episode: Dewey Martin). Note: For detailed information on Holliday, see my book *Encyclopedia of Western Lawmen and Outlaws* (Paragon House, 1992; illustrated pages 162-165).

Holly, Buddy (Charles Hardin Holley; 1936-1959; U.S. singer and songwriter who pioneered rock 'n' roll music): **The Buddy Holly Story**, 1978 (Gary Busey); Crossing Jordan, 2001-2007 (TV series; one 2004 episode: Patrick Fabian); **La Bamba**, 1987 (Marshall Crenshaw); Lives and Deaths of the Poets, 2011 (Gordon Gantt); Mr. Rock 'n' Roll: The Alan Freed Story, 1999 (made-for-TV; Joe W. Davis); Screen Two, 1985-2002 (TV series; "Words of Love," 1989 episode: Pancho Russell); Stars in Their Eyes, 1990- (TV series; 1991 episode: Marc Robinson; 1999 episode: Alan Clennall); The Young Ones, 1982-1984 (TV series; "Oil," 1982 episode: Ronnie Golden).

Holmes, Oliver Wendell, Jr. (1841-1935; U.S. officer in American Civil War; professor of law at Harvard Law School and Associate Justice of the U.S. Supreme Court, the longest-serving justice and one of the most widely cited justices of that esteemed court): Henry Hill, 1999 (IO [Tillett] Wright); **The Magnficent Yankee**, 1950 (Louis Calhern); The Magnificent Yankee, 1965 (made-for-TV; Alfred Lunt); Shadow Chasers, 1985- (TV series; "Let's Make a Deal," 1986 episode: Oliver Clark); Sunday Showcase, 1959-1960 (TV series; "Our American Heritage: Autocrat and Son," 1960 episode: Christopher Plummer); The Touch of Steel, 1955 (made-for-TV; Jan Merlin).

Holt, Joseph (1807-1894; Judge Advocate General of the U.S. Army who presided over the 1865 conspiracy trials in the assassination of President Abraham Lincoln): The Ordeal of Dr. Mudd, 1980 (made-for-TV; Lawrence Montaigne); **The Conspirator**, 2011 (Danny Huston); **The Prisoner of Shark Island**, 1936 (Frank Shannon); Westinghouse Desilu Playhouse, 1958-1960 (TV series; "The Case for Dr. Mudd," 1958 episode: Simon Scott).

Hood, John Bell (1831-1879; U.S. military leader and lieutenant general in the Confederate army of Tennessee during the American Civil War): **Gettysburg**, 1993 (Patrick Gorman); **Gods and Generals**, 2003 (Patrick Gorman); Omnibus, 1952-1961 (TV series; "Lee at Gettysburg," 1957 episode: Wesley Lau); **Santa Fe Trail**, 1940 (George Haywood).

Hoover, J. Edgar (John Edgar Hoover; 1895-1972; American bureaucrat and chief of the Federal Bureau of Investigation/FBI): All the Way, 2016

Louis Calhern (as Oliver Wendell Holmes Jr.) in *The Magnificent Yankee,* 1950.

(made-for-TV; Stephen Root); **Bananas**, 1971 (Dorthi Fox, a black actress, cast by comedian Woody Allen to mock Hoover's dislike for blacks and to enforce rumors that Hoover was a cross-dresser or transvestite, none of which was ever supported in fact; Hoover died a year after this film was released); American Playhouse, 1981-1994 (TV series; "Concealed Enemies," 1984 episode: Raymond Serra); Baby Face Nelson, 1996 (Jack Knight); The Big Story, 1949-1958 (TV series; "The Cat," 1953 episode: Russell Hardie); Blind Ambition, 1979 (TV miniseries; Logan Ramsey); Blood Feud, 1983 (made-for-TV; Ernest Borgnine); Boardwalk Empire, 2010- (TV series; two episodes: Eric Laden); **The Brink's Job**, 1978 (Sheldon Leonard); Chaplin, 1992 (Kevin Dunn); Citizen Cohn, 1992 (made-for-TV; Pat Hingle); The Commission, 2007 (Steve Eastin); Dark Skies, 1996-1997 (TV series: "We Shall Overcome," 1996 episode: Wayne Tippit; "The Warren Omission," 1997 episode: Wayne Tippit); Don't Ask, Don't Tell, 2002 (Steve Lippe); **The FBI Story**, 1959 (Will J. White; himself); The F.B.I. Story: The FBI versus Alvin Karpis, Public Enemy Number One, 1974 (made-for-TV; Harris Yulin); **G-Men**, 1935 (role model for Addison Richards, who plays the FBI leader under the name of Bruce J. Gregory); Hoover, 2000 (Ernest Borgnine); Hoover vs. the Kennedys: The Second Civil War, 1987 (made-for-TV; Jack Warden); **The House on 92nd Street**, 1945 (himself); **J. Edgar**, 2011 (Leonardo DiCaprio); J. Edgar Hoover, 1987 (made-for-TV; Treat Williams); Kennedy, 1983 (TV miniseries; Vincent Gardenia); The Kennedys, 2011 (TV series; Enrico Colantoni); King, 1978 (TV miniseries; Dolph Sweet); Lepke, 1975 (Erwin Fuller); A Man Called Intrepid, 1979 (TV miniseries; Ken James); Marilyn & Bobby: Her Final Affair, 1993 (made-for-TV; Richard Dysart); Mr. Rock 'n' Roll: The Alan Freed Story, 1999 (made-for-TV; Aron Tager); **Nixon**, 1995 (Bob Hoskins); **No God, No Master**, 2012 (Sean McNall); Panther, 1995 (Richard Dysart); **The Private Files of J. Edgar Hoover**, 1977 (Broderick Crawford as an older Hoover; James Wainwright as a younger Hoover); **Public Enemies**; 2009 (Billy Crudup); The Revenge of Al Capone, 1989 (made-for-TV; Jordan Charney); Robert F. Kennedy and His Times, 1985 (TV miniseries; Ned Beatty); **Selma**, 2014 (Dylan Baker); Sins of the Father, 2002 (made-for-TV; Tom McBeath); Timequest, 2000 (Larry Drake); Unnatural History, 2010 (TV series; "Public School Enemies," 2010 episode: Brad Borbridge); X Files, 1993-2002 (TV series; "Musings of a Cigarette Smoking Man," 1996 episode: David Fredericks). For further information on Hoover, see my book: *Citizen Hoover: A Critical Study of the Life and Times of J. Edgar Hoover and His FBI* (Nelson-Hall, 1962).

Hopkins, Harry Lloyd (U.S. 8th secretary of commerce and close adviser to U.S. President Franklin D. Roosevelt; 1890-1946): Cradle Will Rock, 1999 (Bob Balaban); Eleanor and Franklin: The White House

Sterling Hayden (as Admiral John M. Hoskins) and Hayden Rorke in *The Eternal Sea*, 1955.

Years, 1977 (made-for-TV; Donald Moffat); World War II: When Lions Roared, 1994 (made-for-TV; Ed Begley Jr.); War and Remembrance, 1988 (TV miniseries; William Schallert).

Hopper, Hedda (1885-1966; U.S. actress, writer and syndicated columnist covering Hollywood, fierce competitor with the other reigning gossip columnist of that day, Louella Q. Parsons): Breakfast in Hollywood, 1946 (herself); The Corpse Came C.O.D., 1947 (herself); Goodyear Playhouse, 1951-1957 (TV series; herself as hostess in 1953); Malice in Wonderland, 1985 (made-for-TV; Jane Alexander); The Patsy, 1964 (herself); **Pepe**, 1960 (herself); The Right Approach, 1961 (herself); RKO 281, 1999 (made-for-TV; Fiona Shaw); **Sunset Boulevard**, 1950 (herself).

Horn, Tom (Thomas Horn Jr.; aka: "Tom"; 1860-1903; U.S. frontiersman, scout; range detective and convicted murderer; hanged in Cheyenne, Wyoming on November 20, 1903): Bad Men of Tombstone, 1949 (Barry Sullivan); Dakota Lil, 1950 (George Montgomery); Death Valley Days, 1952-1970 (TV series; "Perilous Cargo," 1958 episode: Gregg Palmer); Fort Utah, 1967 (John Ireland); **The Missouri Breaks**, 1976 (Horn is the role model for Marlon Brando's character); Mr. Horn, 1979 (made-for-TV; David Carradine); Stories of the Century, 1954-1955 (TV series; "Tom Horn," 1954 episode: Louis Jean Heydt); Tales of Wells Fargo, 1957-1962 (TV series; "Tom Horn," 1959 episode: Les Johnson); **Tom Horn**, 1980 (Steve McQueen); Zane Grey Theater, 1956-1961 (TV series; "The Last Bugle," 1960 episode: Michael Hinn). Note: For detailed information on Horn, see my book, *Encyclopedia of Western Lawmen and Outlaws* (Paragon House, 1992; illustrated pages 165-167).

Hornsby, Rogers (aka: "The Rajah"; American baseball player, legendary infielder and hitter; manager and coach; 1896-1963): **The Winning Team**, 1952 (Frank Lovejoy).

Hoskins, John Madison (1898-1964; U.S. Navy admiral, who, while commanding the aircraft carrier USS *Princeton*, in 1944 in the Pacific, lost his foot in an explosion, but remained at his post): **The Eternal Sea**, 1955 (Sterling Hayden).

Houdini, Harry (Ehrich Weiss; 1874-1926; celebrated magician, escape artist and stuntman): Alfred Hitchcock Presents, 1985-1989 (TV series; "Houdini on Chanel 4," 1988 episode: Jan Filips); Cremaster 2, 1999 (Norman Mailer); Death Defying Acts, 2007 (Guy Pearce); FairyTale: A True Story, 1997 (Harvey Keitel); The Great Houdini, 1976 (made-for-TV; Paul Michael Glaser); **Houdini**, 1953 (Tony Curtis); Houdini,

1998 (made-for-TV; Johnathon Schaech; Emile Hirsch as young Houdini); Houdini, 2014- (TV miniseries; Adrien Brody); Houdini and Doyle, 2016- (TV miniseries; Michael Weston); A Night at the Magic Castle, 1990 (Arte Johnson); Parade of Stars, 1983 (made-for-TV; Alan Alan); **Ragtime**, 1981 (Jeffrey DeMunn); The Right Eye, 2015 (made-for-TV; Abed Azizi); Walt Disney's Wonderful World of Color, 1954-1992 (TV series; "Young Harry Houdini," 1987 episode: Wil Wheaton).

Houston, Samuel (1793-1863; American solider and politician): The Adventures of Jim Bowie, 1956-1958 (TV series; Denver Pyle); **The Alamo**, 1960 (Richard Boone); **The Alamo**, 2004 (Dennis Quaid); The Alamo: Thirteen Days to Glory, 1987 (made-for-TV; Lorne Greene); Carry On Cowboy, 1965 (Sydney Bromley); The Conqueror, 1917 (William Farnum); Death Valley Days, 1952-1970 (TV series; "The Girl Who Walked with a Giant," 1958 episode: "Davy's Friend," 1962 episode: Stephen Chase); Down Rio Grande Way, 1942 (Paul Newlan); The First Texan, 1956 (Joel McCrea); Frontier, 1955-1956 (TV series; "The Voyage of Captain Castle," 1956 episode: Trevor Bardette); Gone to Texas, 1986 (made-for-TV; Sam Elliott); The Great Adventure, 1963-1964 (TV series; "The Testing of Sam Houston," 1964 episode: Robert Culp); Heroes of the Alamo, 1937 (Edward Piel); The Honorable Sam Houston, 1975 (Robert Stack); **The Last Command**, 1955 (Hugh Sanders); Lone Star, 1952 (Moroni Olsen); **The Man from the Alamo**, 1953 (Howard Negley); **Man of Conquest**, 1939 (Richard Dix); Martyrs of the Alamo, 1915 (Tom Wilson); Men of Texas, 1942 (William Farnum); Profiles in Courage, 1964-1965 (TV series; "Sam Houston," 1964 episode: J.D. Cannon); Pulitzer Prize Playhouse, 1950-1952 (TV series; "The Raven," 1950 episode: Zachary Scott); The Ranger and the Lady, 1940 (Davison Clark); Telephone Time, 1956-1958 (TV series; "Sam Houston's Decision," 1957 episode: Don Taylor); Texas, 1994 (made-for-TV; Stacy Keach); Texas Rising, 2015- (TV miniseries; Bill Paxton); True Women, 1997 (made-for-TV; John Schneider); Two for Texas, 1998 (made-for-TV; Tom Skerritt); Voyagers!, 1982-1983 (TV series; "The Trial of Phineas Bogg," 1983 episode; Bill McLaughlin); You Are There, 1953-1971 (TV series; "The Burning of the Alamo," and "The Defense of the Alamo," 1953 episodes: Philip Bosco).

Howard, Catherine (1523-1542; Queen of England and fifth wife of Henry VIII): BBC Sunday-Night Theatre, 1950-1959 (TV series; "The Rose without a Thorn," 1953 episode: Barbara Jefford); Carry on Henry VIII, 1971 (Monika Dietrich); Heinrich VIII. und seine Frauen, 1968 (made-for-TV; Monika Peitsch); Henry VIII 2003 (made-for-TV; Emily Blunt); Henry VIII and His Six Wives, 1972 (Lynne Frederick); Kings and Queens, 2002- (TV miniseries; "Henry VIII," 2002 episode: Kate Loustau); Monarch, 2000 (Jean Marsh); **The Private Life of Henry VIII**, 1933 (Binnie Barnes); The Rose without a Thorn, 1947 (made-for-TV; Victoria Hopper); The Six Wives of Henry VIII, 1970 (TV miniseries; Angela Pleasence); The Six Wives of Henry VIII, 2001 (TV miniseries; Michele Abrahams); The Tudors, 2007-2010 (TV series; Tamzin Merchant); **Young Bess**, 1953 (Dawn Addams).

Howard, Oliver O. (1830-1909; U.S. military officer; Union general in American Civil War and general in Indian campaigns): **Broken Arrow**, 1950 (Basil Ruysdael); **Gods and Generals**, 2003 (Richard Bekins); I Will Fight No More Forever, 1975 (made-for-TV; James Whitmore); **The Last Wagon**, 1956 (Carl Benton Reid).

Howe, Louis McHenry (1871-1936; U.S. reporter and early political adviser to U.S. President Franklin D. Roosevelt): Eleanor and Franklin, 1976 (made-for-TV; Ed Flanders); Eleanor and Franklin: The White House Years, 1977 (made-for-TV; Walter McGinn); The Kennedys of Massachusetts, 1990 (TV miniseries; Bill Moor); **Sunrise at Campobello**, 1960 (Hume Cronyn).

Howe, William (1729-1814; British general and commander-in-chief of all British forces during the American Revolutionary War, 1775-1783): The Heart of a Hero, 1916 (Herbert Evans); The Rebels, 1979 (made-for-TV; Wilfrid Hyde-White); Valley Forge, 1975 (made-for-TV; Harry Andrews).

Huerta, Victoriano (Jose Victoriano Huerta Marquez; aka: The Jackal; 1850-1916; Mexican general and 35th president of Mexico): And Starring Pancho Villa as Himself, 2003 (made-for-TV; Jose Concepcion Macias); Cuartelazo, 1977 (Bruno Rey); El encanto del aguila, 2011 (Mario Zaragoza); El vuelo del aguila, 1994 (TV series; Bruno Rey); La estampida, 1959 (Joaquin Roche); Let's Go with Pancho Villa, 1939 (Paco Martinez); Mexikanische Revolution, 1968 (made-for-TV; Heinz Klevenow); Villa Rides, 1968 (Herbert Lom); **Viva Zapata!**, 1952 (Frank Silvera); Zapata: Amor en rebeldia, 2004 (TV miniseries; Joaquin Garrido); Zapata—El sueno del hero, 2004 (Jesus Ochoa).

Huggins, Miller James (American baseball player and manager; 1879-1929): **The Babe**, 1992 (Joe Ragno); **The Babe Ruth Story**, 1948 (Fred Lightner); **The Pride of the Yankees**, 1942 (Ernie Adams).

Hughes, Howard (Howard Robard Hughes Jr.; 1905-1976; U.S. business tycoon; aviator, engineer and filmmaker): The Amazing Howard Hughes, 1977 (made-for-TV; Tommy Lee Jones); **The Aviator**, 2004 (Leonardo DiCaprio); Dark Skies, 1996-1997 (TV series; "Dreamland," 1996 episode: Madison Mason); **Diamonds Are Forever**, 1971 (role model for Jimmy Dean); Fallen Angels, 1993-1995 (TV series; "Since I Don't Have You," 1993 episode: Tim Matheson); The Hoax, 2006 (Milton Buras); Hughes and Harlow: Angels in Hell, 1977 (Victor Holchak); Man, Moment, Machine, 2005-2007 (TV series; "Howard Hughes and the Spruce Goose," 2005 episode: Danny Swartz); **Melvin and Howard**, 1980 (Jason Robards Jr.); **One of the Hollywood Ten**, 2000 (Lars Hanson); Pancho Barnes, 1988 (made-for-TV; David Kockinis); The Rocketeer, 1991 (Terry O'Quinn); Rules Don't Apply, 2016 (Warren Beatty); **Tucker: The Man and His Dream**, 1988 (Dean Stockwell); Undercover History, 2006- (TV series; "Howard Hughes Revealed," 2007 episode: Jordan Romano).

Hugo, Victor (Victor Marie Hugo; 1802-1885; French poet, dramatist and novelist): Balzac: A Passionate Life, 2000 (made-for-TV; Gert Voss); The Count of Monte Cristo, 1956- (TV series; "Victor Hugo," 1956 episode: Keith Richards); Ego Hugo, 1973 (made-for-TV; Anthony Bate, Simon Taylor, Brian Cox); If Paris Were Told to Us, 1956 (Emile Drain and Claude Veriot); La Malibran, 1944 (Jean Chaduc); La misere et la gloire, 1965 (made-for-TV; Jean-Marie Fertey); La symphonie fantastique, 1947 (Julien Bertheau); The Life and Music of Giuseppe Verdi, 1957 (Guido Celano); The Life of Giuseppe Verdi, 1938 (Henri Rollan); Liszt Ferenc, 1982 (TV miniseries; Jean-Michel Noirey); Lives and Deaths of the Poets, 2011 (Steve Leventhal); Mauvais genre, 1997 (Francois Perrot); Prometheus: The Life of Balzac, 1975- (TV miniseries; Peter Sallis); **Suez**, 1938 (Victor Varconi); Toute la ville en parle, 2000 (made-for-TV; Alain Frerot).

Hull, Cordell (American statesman and 47th U.S. secretary of state; 1871-1955): **Sergeant York**, 1941 (Charles Trowbridge); **Tora! Tora! Tora!**, 1970 (George Macready).

Hunter, David 1802-1886; U.S. soldier and Union general during the American Civil War; a radical abolitionist, he was the president of the tribunal that presided over the trials of the conspirators in the assassination of President Abraham Lincoln): **The Conspirator**, 2011 (Colm Meaney); **The Prisoner of Shark Island**, 1936 (Paul McVey).

Hunter, Fred (1899-1982; U.S. bank and train robber and colleague of Public Enemy No. One Alvin "Old Creepy" Karpis): **The FBI Story**, 1959 (Angelo De Meo); **J. Edgar**, 2011 (Eric Larkin).

Clark Gable, Moroni Olsen (as Sam Houston) and Broderick Crawford in *Lone Star*, 1952.

Isabella I of Castile (1451-1504; Spanish monarch): The Black Sword, 1976 (Maribel Martin); The Broken Crown, 2016 (Michelle Jenner); Bye Bye Columbus, 1991 (made-for-TV; Harriet Walter); Carry on Columbus, 1992 (June Whitfield); Christophe Columb, 1916 (Leontine Massart); Christophe Columb, 1975 (made-for-TV; Brigitte Fossey); **Christopher Columbus**, 1949 (Florence Eldridge); Christopher Columbus, 1985 (TV miniseries; Faye Dunaway); Christopher Columbus: The Discovery, 1992 (Rachel Ward); 1492: Conquest of Paradise, 1992 (Sigourney Weaver); Columbus, 1923 (Dolores Cassinelli); Cristobal Colon, 1943 (Consuelo Frank); Cristobal Colon, 1982 (Fiorella Faltoyano); Dawn of America, 1951 (Amparo Rivelles); El concel de la reina, 1946 (Mary Carrillo); Fuenteovejuna, 1947 (Lina Yegros); Isabel, 2011- (TV series; Michelle Jenner); Juana la loca…de vez en cuando, 1983 (Lola Flores); Mad Love, 2002 (Susi Sanchez); The Magic Voyage, 1992 (voiceovers: Samantha Eggar, Beate Hasenau); Requiem por Granada, 1991- (TV series; Marita Marschall); True Adventures of Christopher Columbus, 1992- (TV series; Miranda Richardson).

Isabella II (1830-1904; Queen of Spain): **Amistad**, 1999 (Anna Paquin); El marques de Salamanca, 1948 (Carlota Bilbao); El ministerio del tiempo, 2015 (TV series; "Tiempo de venganza," 2015 episode: Carmen Sanchez); Where Are You Going, Alfonso XII?, 1959 (Mercedes Vecino).

Isoroku Yamamoto (1884-1943; Japanese admiral who planned the sneak attack on Pearl Harbor, December 7, 1941): **Admiral Yamamoto**, 1968 (Toshiro Mifune); **The Gallant Hours**, 1960 (James T. Goto); Gateway to Glory, 1970 (Shogo Shimada); The Imperial Navy, 1983 (Keiju Kobayashi); Isoroku Yamamoto, 2011 (Koji Yakusho); **Midway**, 1976 (Toshiro Mifune); Operation Kamikaze, 1953 (Denjiro Okochi); **Pearl Harbor**, 2002 (Mako); **Tora! Tora! Tora!**, 1970 (Soh Yamamura); Turning Point of Showa History: The Militarists, 1971 (Toshiro Mifune); War and Remembrance, 1988 (TV miniseries; Seth Sakai).

Ivan IV (Ivan the Terrible; 1530-1584; emperor of Russia): Einstein, 2002 (Oleg Maslennikov); Heaven, 1999 (Dominique Levesque); **Ivan the Terrible**, 1947 (Nikolay Cherkasov); Ivan the Terrible, 1976 (Yuri Vladimirov); **Night at the Museum: Battle of the Smithsonian**, 2009 (Christopher Guest); Terror in the Wax Museum, 1973 (Paul Wilson); Tsar, 2009 (Pyotr Mamonov); Tsar Ivan the Terrible, 1991 (Kakhi Kavsadze); **Waxworks**, 1929 (Conrad Veidt); The Wings of a Serf, 1928 (Leonid Leonidov).

Jack the Ripper (serial killer who stalked and savagely murdered five or more prostitutes in the West End of London in 1888; the fiend was never

Lionel Barrymore (as President Andrew Jackson) and Clark Gable in *Lone Star*, 1952.

apprehended): Bridge across Time, 1985 (Paul Rossilli); Edge of Sanity, 1989 (Anthony Perkins); From Hell, 2001; Hands of the Ripper, 1972; Jack the Ripper, 1960 (Ewon Solon); Jack the Ripper, 1973 (TV miniseries); Jack the Ripper, 1979 (Klaus Kinski); Jack the Ripper, 1988 (TV series); **The Lodger**, 1928 (Ivor Novello); **The Lodger**, 1944 (Laird Cregar); Lulu, 1980 (Udo Kier); **Man in the Attic**, 1953 (Jack Palance); **Murder by Decree**, 1979 (Peter Jonfield); **Pandora's Box**, 1929 (Gustav Diesel); The Phantom Fiend, 1935 (Ivor Novello); The Ripper, 1997 (Samuel West); Room to Let, 1950 (Valentine Dyall); **The Ruling Class**, 1972; Seven Murders for Scotland Yard, 1971; **A Study in Terror**, 1966 (John Fraser); **Time after Time**, 1979 (David Warner); Waxwork, 1988; Waxwork II: Lost in Time, 1992 (Alex Butler); **Waxworks**, 1929 (Werner Krauss). Note: For detailed information on Jack the Ripper and his London murders, see my two-volume work *The Great Pictorial History of World Crime*, Volume II (History, Inc., 2004; illustrated [38 images] pages 1181-1203).

Jackson, Andrew (aka: "Old Hickory"; 1767-1845; U.S. military officer and general during the War of 1812; seventh President of the U.S.): Bad Blood: The Border War That Triggered the Civil War, 2007 (made-for-TV; Robert Eckhoff); Bridger, 1976 (made-for-TV; John Anderson); **The Buccaneer**, 1938 (Hugh Sothern); The Buccaneer, 1958 (Charlton Heston); **Davy Crockett: King of the Wild Frontier**, 1955 (Basil Ruysdael); The Eagle and the Sea, 1926 (George Irving); **The Fighting Kentuckian**, 1949 (Steve Darrell); First Ladies Diaries: Rachel Jackson, 1975 (made-for-TV; Gerald Gordon); The First Texan, 1956 (Carl Benton Reid); The Frontiersman, 1927 (Russell Simpson); Gone to Texas, 1986 (made-for-TV; G. D. Spradlin); The Gorgeous Hussy, 1936 (Lionel Barrymore); The Great Adventure, 1963-1964 (TV series; "The Pirate and the Patriot," 1964 episode: John Anderson); Lone Star, 1952 (Lionel Barrymore); **Man of Conquest**, 1939 (Edward Ellis); My Own United States, 1918 (F. C. Earle); The Pirate and the Lawyer, 1955 (made-for-TV; Tom Duggan); Pirates of Treasure Island, 2006 (Thomas Downey); **The President's Lady**, 1953 (Charlton Heston); Privateer, 2009 (Corin Nemec); **The Remarkable Andrew**, 1942 (Brian Donlevy); Voyagers!, 1982-1983 (TV series; "Old Hickory and the Pirate," 1982 episode: Lance LeGault); The Wedding of Lilli Marlene, 1953 (Robert Ayres); War of 1812, 1999 (TV miniseries; Richard Clarkin).

Jackson, Rachel (Rachel Donelson Robards Jackson; 1767-1828; U.S. First Lady and wife of President Andrew Jackson): First Ladies Diaries: Rachel Jackson, 1975 (made-for-TV; Fran Brill); The Frontiersman, 1927 (Lillian Leighton); The Gorgeous Hussy, 1936 (Beulah Bondi); **The President's Lady**, 1953 (Susan Hayward).

Jackson, Thomas Jonathan (1824-1863; aka: "Stonewall"; U.S. military officer and Confederate lieutenant general under Robert E. Lee in the Army of Northern Virginia during the American Civil War): **Abe Lincoln in Illinois**, 1940 (Erville Alderson); Carolina, 1934 (John Webb Dillon); Cavalcade of America, 1952-1957 (TV series; "The Pirate's Choice," 1953 episode: Morris Ankrum); **Gods and Generals**, 2003 (Stephen Lang); North and South, 1985- (TV miniseries; Bill Eudaly); Red Runs the River, 1963 (Jack Buttram).

Jacob (in the Old Testament, patriarch of the Hebrew people): After Six Days, 1922 (Alessandro Virgili); Animated Stories from the Bible, 1987-2005 (Neil Vipond); Greatest Heroes of the Bible, 1978- (TV series; "Joseph in Egypt," 1978 episode: Walter Brooke; "Jacob's Challenge," 1979 episode: Barry Williams); **The Green Pastures**, 1936 (Ivory Williams); In the Beginning, 2000 (made-for-TV; Frederick Weller); Jacob, 1994 (made-for-TV; Matthew Modine); The Jews Are Coming, 2014- (TV series; Yossi Marshek); Joseph, 1995 (made-for-TV; Martin Landau); Joseph and the Amazing Technicolor Dreamcoat, 1972 (made-for-TV; Alex McAvoy); Joseph and the Amazing Technicolor Dreamcoat, 1991 (made-for-TV; Aubrey Woods); Joseph 2000, 2000 (made-for-TV; Mark Kilsby); Joseph in the Land of Egypt, 1932 (Ben Adler); The New Media Bible: Book of Genesis, 1979 (Eiran Baniel); Rachel's Man, 1975 (Leonard Whiting); The Red Tent, 2014- (TV miniseries; Iain Glen); Shalom Pharao, 1982 (animated; Wolf Harnisch voiceover); The Story of Jacob and Joseph, 1974 (made-for-TV; Keith Michell); The Story of Joseph and His Brethren, 1962 (Finlay Currie); Testament: The Bible in Animation, 1996- (TV series; "Joseph," 1996 episode: Gerald James voiceover).

James I (James VI) (1566-1625; King of England and Scotland): Elizabeth, 2000 (made-for-TV; Wayne Opie); Elizabeth I, 2005- (TV miniseries; Ewen Bremner); Gunpowder 511: The Greatest Terror Plot, 2014 (made-for-TV; Ken Drury); The Gunpowder Plot: Exploding the Legend, 2005 (made-for-TV; Stuart Liddle); Guy Fawkes, 1923 (Jerrold Robertshaw); The Mayflower, 2006 (made-for-TV; Peter Lovstrom).

James the Greater (d. 44 A.D.; St. James the elder; one of the twelve Apostles of Jesus and brother of John the Apostle): Acts of the Apostles, 1969 (TV miniseries; Missoume); A.D., 1985 (TV miniseries; Philip Anthony); A.D.: The Bible Continues, 2015 (TV series; Alastair Mackenzie); Apostle Peter and the Last Supper, 2012 (Shawn Savage); The Big Fisherman, 1959 (Tom Troupe); The Book of Acts Series, 1957 (Guy Prescott); Color of the Cross, 2006 (Shervin Davatgar); Color of the Cross 2: The Resurrection, 2008 (Seven Stewart); The Cross, 2001 (Ravinder Toor); Crown of Thorns, 1934 (silent; Max Kronert); The Day Christ Died, 1980 (made-for-TV; Brian Coburn); The Gospel according to Matthew, 1993 (Charlton George); The Gospel according to St. Matthew, 1966 (Luigi Barbini); Gospel Road: A Story of Jesus, 1973 (John Paul Kay); **The Greatest Story Ever Told**, 1965 (David Sheiner); The Holy Family, 2006 (made-for-TV; Massimiliano Varrese); Il messia, 1975 (Mark Lombardo); Jesus [aka: The Jesus Film], 1979 (Yitzhak Ne'eman); Jesus, 2000 (made-for-TV; Fabio Sartor); **Jesus Christ Superstar**, 1973 (Robert LuPone); Jesus of Nazareth, 1942 (Ramon G. Larrea); Jesus of Nazareth, 1977 (TV miniseries; Jonathan Muller); Judas, 2004 (made-for-TV; Enzo Sequillino Jr.); Judas' Kiss, 1954 (Arturo Fernandez); **The King of Kings**, 1927 (James Neill); Kristo, 1996 (Edgar Mande); The Last Supper: Thirteen Men of Courage, 2007 (made-for-TV; Winton Nicholson); The Last Temptation of Christ, 1988 (John Lurie); Matthew 26:17, 2005 (Jay Seals); Mary, Mother of the Son of God, 2003 (Leon Goes); The Passion, 2008 (TV miniseries; Dean Lennox Kelly); The Passion of Christ, 2004 (Chokri Ben Zagden); Paul of Tarsus, 1960 (TV series; Richard Leech, John Graham); Peter and Paul, 1981 (made-for-TV; Denis Lill); The Power of the Resurrection, 1958 (Booth Colman); Risen, 2016 (Alberto Ayala); St. Paul, 2000 (made-for-TV; Christian Brendel); The Testaments: Of One Fold and

One Shepherd, 2000 (Bruce Newbold); The Time Machine: St. Peter—The Rock, 2002 (made-for-TV; Charlie David); The Visual Bible: The Gospel of John, 2003 (Alex Karzis); The Young Messiah, 2016 (Finn Ireland).

James, Frank (Alexander Franklin James; U.S. western outlaw; 1843-1915): The Adventures of Frank and Jesse James, 1948 (Steve Darrell); Alias Jesse James, 1959 (Jim Davis); American Outlaws, 2001 (Gabriel Macht); **The Assassination of Jesse James by the Coward Robert Ford**, 2007 (Sam Shepard); **Bad Man's Territory**, 1946 (Tom Tyler); Belle Starr, 1980 (made-for-TV; Gary Combs); **Best of the Badmen**, 1951 (Tom Tyler); Bitter Heritage, 1958 (made-for-TV; Franchot Tone); Days of Jesse James, 1939 (Harry Worth); Frank and Jesse, 1995 (Bill Paxton); **The Great Missouri Raid**, 1951 (Wendell Corey); **The Great Northfield, Minnesota Raid**, 1972 (John Pearce); Gunfire, 1950 (Don "Red" Barry); Hell's Crossroads, 1957 (Douglas Kennedy); Hondo, 1967 (TV series; "Hondo and the Judas," 1967 episode: John Agar); **I Shot Jesse James**, 1949 (Tom Tyler); The James Brothers of Missouri, 1949 (Robert Bice); Jesse James, 1927 (James Pierce); **Jesse James**, 1939 (Henry Fonda): Jesse James at Bay, 1941 (Al Taylor); Jesse James' Hidden Treasure, 2009 (made-for-TV; Bill Armstrong); Jesse James' Women, 1954 (Jack Buetel); Kansas Raiders, 1950 (Richard Long); The Last Days of Frank and Jesse James, 1986 (made-for-TV; Johnny Cash); The Legend of Jesse James, 1965-1966 (TV series; Allen Case); **The Long Riders**, 1980 (Stacy Keach); Outlaw Treasure, 1955 (Robert Hinkle); Playhouse 90, 1956-1961 (TV series, "Bitter Heritage," 1958 episode: Franchot Tone); **The Return of Frank James**, 1940 (Henry Fonda); The Return of Jesse James, 1950 (Reed Hadley); Stories of the Century, 1954-1955 (TV series; "Frank and Jesse James," 1954 episode: Richard Travis); A Time for Dying, 1982 (Willard Willingham); **The True Story of Jesse James**, 1957 (Jeffrey Hunter); Two Gangsters in the Wild West, 1964 (Tony Casale); **Woman They Almost Lynched**, 1953 (James Brown); Yancy Derringer, 1958-1959 (TV series; "Outlaw at Liberty," 1959 episode: Lee Van Cleef); **Young Jesse James**, 1960 (Robert Dix); The Young Riders, 1989-1992 (TV series; Jamie Walters). Note: For detailed information on Frank and Jesse James, see my books *Encyclopedia of Western Lawmen and Outlaws* (Paragon House, 1992; illustrated [33 images] pages 172-189; and the two-volume work *The Great Pictorial History of World Crime*, Volume II (History, Inc., 2004; illustrated [29 images] pages 1342-1359).

James, Jesse (Jesse Woodson James; 1847-1882; western outlaw): The Adventures of Frank and Jesse James, 1948 (Clayton Moore); Alias Jesse James, 1959 (Wendell Corey); American Outlaws, 2001 (Colin Farrell); Another Man, Another Chance, 1977 (Christopher Lloyd); **The Assassination of Jesse James by the Coward Robert Ford**, 2007 (Brad Pitt); **Bad Man's Territory**, 1946 (Lawrence Tierney); **Bad Men of Missouri**, 1941 (Alan Baxter); Belle Starr, 1980 (made-for-TV; Michael Cavanaugh); **Best of the Badmen**, 1951 (Lawrence Tierney); Bronco, 1958-1962 (TV series; "Shadow of Jesse James," 1960 episode: James Coburn); Buffalo Bill, Jr., 1955-1956 (TV series; "Legacy of Jesse James," 1955 episode: Boyd Stockman); Days of Jesse James, 1939 (Donald Barry; Don "Red" Barry); **Fighting Man of the Plains**, 1949 (Dale Robertson); Frank & Jesse, 1995 (Rob Lowe); Goodyear Playhouse, 1951-1957 (TV series; "Missouri Legend," 1956 episode: Robert Preston); The Great Jesse James Raid, 1953 (Willard Parker); **The Great Missouri Raid**, 1951 (MacDonald Carey); **The Great Northfield, Minnesota Raid**, 1972 (Robert Duvall); Hell's Crossroads, 1957 (Henry Brandon); Hondo, 1967 (TV series; "Hondo and the Judas," 1967 episode: Ricky Nelson); Horse Opera, 1993 (made-for-TV; Stewart Copeland); **I Shot Jesse James**, 1949 (Reed Hadley); The Intruders, 1970 (made-for-TV; Stuart Margolin); The James Brothers of Missouri, 1949 (Keith Richards); Jesse James, 1927 (Fred Thomson); **Jesse James**, 1939 (Tyrone Power); Jesse James as the Outlaw, 1921 (Jesse James Jr.); Jesse James at Bay, 1941 (Roy Rogers); Jesse James'

Gene Tierney and Henry Fonda (as Frank James) in *The Return of Frank James,* **1940.**

Hidden Treasure, 2009 (made-for-TV; Jeff Elsey); Jesse James: Legend, Outlaw, Terrorist, 2005 (made-for-TV; Daniel Lennox); Jesse James Meets Frankenstein's Daughter, 1966 (John Lupton); Jesse James Rides Again, 1947 (Clayton Moore); Jesse James under the Black Flag, 1921 (Jesse James Jr.); Jesse James' Women, 1954 (Don "Red" Barry); Kansas Raiders, 1950 (Audie Murphy); The Kansan, 1943 (George Reeves); The Last Days of Frank and Jesse James, 1986 (made-for-TV; Kris Kristofferson); The Last Ride of the Dalton Gang, 1979 (made-for-TV; Harris Yulin); The Legend of Hell's Gate: An American Conspiracy, 2011 (Lukas Behnken); The Legend of Jesse James, 1965-1966 (TV series; Christopher Jones); **The Long Riders**, 1980 (James Keach); Lucky Luke, 2009 (Melvil Poupaud); The Outlaws Is Coming!, 1965 (Wayne Mack); Outlaw Treasure, 1955 (Harry Lauter); Playhouse 90, 1956-1961 (TV series, "Bitter Heritage," 1958 episode: James Drury); Purgatory, 1999 (made-for-TV; John David Souther); **The Remarkable Andrew**, 1942 (Rod Cameron); **The Return of Frank James**, 1940 (Tyrone Power, opening scene only); Stories of the Century, 1954-1955 (TV series; "Frank and Jesse James," 1954 episode: Lee Van Cleef); Tales of Wells Fargo, 1957-1962 (TV series; "Jesse James," 1957 episode: Hugh Beaumont); A Time for Dying, 1982 (Audie Murphy); **The True Story of Jesse James**, 1957 (Robert Wagner); Two Gangsters in the Wild West, 1964 (Tony Di Mitri); **Woman They Almost Lynched**, 1953 (Ben Cooper); Yancy Derringer, 1958-1959 (TV series; "Outlaw at Liberty," 1959 episode: Brett King); You Are There, 1953-1957 (TV series; "The Capture of Jesse James," 1953 episode: John Kerr); **Young Jesse James**, 1960 (Ray Stricklyn); The Young Riders, 1989-1992 (TV series; Christopher Pettiet). Note: For detailed information on Frank and Jesse James, see my books *Encyclopedia of Western Lawmen and Outlaws* (Paragon House, 1992; illustrated [33 images] pages 172-189; and the two-volume work *The Great Pictorial History of World Crime*, Volume II (History, Inc., 2004; illustrated [29 images] pages 1342-1359).

James, Jesse E. (Jesse Edward James; son of U.S. outlaw Jesse James; 1875-1951): Bitter Heritage, 1958 (made-for-TV; James Drury); Frank and Jesse, 1995 (William Michael Evans); The Great Jesse James Raid, 1953 (Tommy Walker); **The Long Riders**, 1980 (Kalen Keach).

James, Zerelda (Zerelda Elizabeth Cole James Simms Samuel; mother of outlaws Jesse and Frank James; 1825-1911): Alias Jesse James, 1959 (Mary Young); Frank and Jesse, 1995 (Mari Askew); **The Great Missouri Raid**, 1951 (Anne Revere); Jesse James, 1927 (Mary Carr); **Jesse James**, 1939 (Jane Darwell); The Legend of Jesse James, 1965-1966 (TV series; Ann Doran); **The Long Riders**, 1980 (Fran Ryan); **The True Story of Jesse James**, 1957 (Agnes Moorehead); **Young Jesse James**, 1960 (Sheila Bromley).

Martha Scott, Richard Carlson (as Thomas Jefferson) and Cary Grant in *The Howards of Virginia*, 1940.

James, Zerelda (Zerelda Amanda Mimms James; aka: "Zee"; first cousin and wife of outlaw Jesse James; 1845-1900): American Outlaws, 2001 (Ali Larter); **The Assassination of Jesse James by the Coward Robert Ford**, 2007 (Mary-Louise Parker); Days of Jesse James, 1939 (Dorothy Sebastian); Frank and Jesse, 1994 (Maria Pitillo); The Great Jesse James Raid, 1953 (Barbara Woodell); Hell's Crossroads, 1957 (Jean Howell); **I Shot Jesse James**, 1949 (Barbara Woodell); Jesse James, 1927 (Nora Lane); **Jesse James**, 1939 (Nancy Kelly); Jesse James as the Outlaw, 1921 (Marguerite Hungerford); Jesse James under the Black Flag, 1921 (Marguerite Hungerford); The Last Days of Frank and Jesse James, 1986 (made-for-TV; Margaret Gibson); **The Long Riders**, 1980 (Savannah Smith Boucher); **The True Story of Jesse James**, 1957 (Hope Lange); **Young Jesse James**, 1960 (Jacklyn O'-Donnell).

James the Lesser (Saint James the Minor; one of the twelve Apostles of Jesus): Acts of the Apostles, 1969 (TV miniseries; Zoviten); A.D., 1985 (TV miniseries; Colin Haigh); Apostle Peter and the Last Supper, 2012 (Matthew Bacis); Behold the Man, 1935 (Andre Lannes); Color of the Cross, 2006 (Malik Barnhardt); Crown of Thorns, 1934 (silent; Herr Magnus); The Day Christ Died, 1980 (made-for-TV; Jean-Paul Boucher); Day of Triumph, 1954 (George Sawaya); The Gospel according to Matthew, 1993 (Tony Joubert); The Gospel according to St. Matthew, 1966 (Marcello Galdini); **The Greatest Story Ever Told**, 1965 (Michael Anderson Jr.); Il messia, 1975 (Slim Mzali); Jesus, 1979 (Leonid Weinstein); Jesus, 2000 (made-for-TV; Abedelouhahad Mouaddine); Jesus of Nazareth, 1977 (TV miniseries; Sergio Nicolai); **The King of Kings**, 1927 (Charles Requa); Kristo, 1996 (Dindo Arroyo); The Last Supper: Thirteen Men of Courage, 2007 (made-for-TV; Nathan Atkinson); The Passion, 2008 (TV miniseries; Thomas Buchanan); Peter and Paul, 1981 (made-for-TV; Nicholas Savalas); The Power of the Resurrection, 1958 (Harry Jackson).

Jefferson, Thomas (1743-1826; U.S. politician and 3rd President of the U.S.): The Ace of Spades, 1925 (John Herdman); The Adams Chronicles, 1976 (TV miniseries; Albert Stratton); Alexander Hamilton, 1931 (Montagu Love); **America**, 1924 (Frank Walsh); The American Adventure, 1982 (Robert Easton voiceover); The American Parade, 1974- (TV series; "We the Women," 1974 episode: Barry Ford); Barbary Pirate, 1949 (Holmes Herbert); The Beautiful Mrs. Reynolds, 1918 (Al Hart); Cavalcade of America, 1952-1957 (TV series; "Experiment at Monticello," 1953 episode: Grandon Rhodes; "A Strange Journey," 1954 episode: Walter Coy); The Du Pont Story, 1950 (Grandon Rhodes); Equal Justice under the Law, 1977 (made-for-TV; James Noble); **The Far Horizons**, 1955 (Herbert Heyes); The Farmer from

Monticello, 1955 (made-for-TV; Rhodes Reason); George Washington II: The Forging of a Nation, 1986 (made-for-TV; Jeffrey Jones); The Great Adventure, 1963-1964 (TV series; "Plague," 1964 episode: John Dehner); Great Performances, 1971- (TV series; "Brother to Dragons," 1974 episode: James Eichelberger; "The Patriots," 1976 episode; Robert Murch); The Heart of a Hero, 1916 (Charles Jackson); Hearts Divided, 1936 (George Irving); **The Howards of Virginia**, 1940 (Richard Carlson as adult Jefferson; Buster Phelps as Jefferson at age eleven); Jack of All Trades, 2000- (TV series; Charles Pierard); **Janice Meredith**, 1924 (Lionel Adams); Jefferson in Paris, 1995 (Nick Nolte); John Adams, 2008- (TV miniseries; Stephen Dillane); Liberty! The American Revolution, 1997 (TV miniseries; Campbell Scott); The Loves of Edgar Allan Poe, 1942 (Gilbert Emery); Magnificent Doll, 1947 (Grandon Rhodes); Mistress of the White House, 1952 (made-for-TV; Frederic Warriner); A More Perfect Union: America Becomes a Nation, 1989 (Scott Wilkinson); My Own United States, 1918 (P. R. Scammon); Old Louisiana, 1937 (Allan Cavan); Our American Heritage, 1959-1961 (TV series; "Divided We Stand," 1959 episode: Ralph Bellamy); Patrick Henry, 1955 (made-for-TV; John Lupton); The Patriots, 1963 (made-for-TV; Charlton Heston); Profiles in Courage, 1964-1965 (TV series; "John Quincy Adams," 1965 episode: Alan Hewitt); The Rebels, 1979 (made-for-TV; Kevin Tighe); **The Remarkable Andrew**, 1942 (John Emery); The Revolution, 2006- (TV series; "Declaring Independence," 2007 episode: Ben Beckley; "A President and His Revolution," 2007 episode: Jason Audette); **1776**, 1972 (Ken Howard); Sally Hemings: An American Scandal, 2000 (made-for-TV; Sam Neill); Sunday Showcase, 1959-1960 (TV series; "Our American Heritage: Not Without Honor," 1960 episode: Ralph Bellamy); Swing Out, Sweet Land, 1970 (made-for-TV; Hugh O'Brien); Thomas Jefferson, 1997 (TV miniseries; Sam Waterston voiceover); Walt Disney's Wonderful World of Color, 1954-1992 (TV series; "The Liberty Story," 1957 episode: Hans Conried); The Will of the People, 2008 (made-for-TV; Bill Barker); You Are There, 1953-1971 (TV series; "The Resolve of Patrick Henry [March 23, 1775]," 1954 episode: Michael Emmet; "The Vote That Made Jefferson President," 1954 episode: E.G. Marshall; "Eli Whitney Invents the Cotton Gin [May 27, 1793]," 1955 episode: Walter Coy; "Lewis and Clark Expedition," 1971 episode: Addison Powell).

Jeffords, Thomas Jonathan (aka: Tom; 1832-1914; U.S. Army scout and Indian agent): **Broken Arrow**, 1950 (James Stewart); Broken Arrow, 1956-1960 (TV series; John Lupton); TV's Reader's Digest, 1955-1956 (TV series; "Cochise, Greatest of the Apaches," 1956 episode: Rhodes Reason); The 20th Century-Fox Hour, 1955-1957 (TV series; "Broken Arrow," 1956 episode: John Lupton).

Jerome, William Travers (1859-1934; district attorney for New York County, 1902-1909, who prosecuted multi-millionaire Harry Kendall Thaw for his wanton murder of esteemed architect Stanford White in 1906): **The Girl in the Red Velvet Swing**, 1955 (John Hoyt). Note: For detailed information on Jerome and his prosecution of Thaw, see my two-volume work *The Great Pictorial History of World Crime*, Volume II (History, Inc., 2004; illustrated [17 images] pages 819-826).

Jesus (Jesus of Nazareth; 7-2 B.C.-30-36 A.D.; in Christian religion the Son of God): The Adventures of God, 2000 (Daniel Freire); Animated Stories from the New Testament, 1987- (TV series; Ivan Crossland voiceover); Apostle Peter and the Last Supper, 2012 (Bruce Marchiano); The Apostle Peter: Redemption, 2016 (Joseph Mesiano); Appointment with Destiny, 1971-1973 (TV series; "The Crucifixion of Jesus," 1972 episode: Rob Greenblatt); Are We Civilized?, 1934 (Charles Requa); **Barabbas**, 1962 (Rocco Roy Mangano); Barabbas, 2013 (made-for-TV; Marco Foschi); Barabbas, 2014 (Nathan Farnor); Behold the Man [aka: Golgotha], 1935 (Robert Le Vigan); Behold the Man!, 1951 (Charles P. Carr); **Ben-Hur: A Tale of the Christ**, 1925 (Claude Payton); **Ben Hur**, 1959 (Claude Heater, face not shown); Ben Hur, 2010 (TV miniseries; Julian Casey); Boyz Nite Out/Girlz Nite In, 2012 (Jason Decker); Christus, 1914 (Alessandro Rocca); Civilization, 1916 (George Fisher); **A Clockwork Orange**, 1971 (Jeremy Curry); Color of the Cross, 2006 (Jean-Claude La Marre as adult Jesus; Alex Collins as young Jesus); Color of the Cross 2: The Resurrection, 2008 (Jean-Claude La Marre); The Cradle of God, 1926 (Jean Bradin); The Cross, 2001 (adult Jesus: Larry Salberg; young Jesus: Aaron Fisher); Crown of Thorns, 1934 (silent; Gregori Chmara); The Day Christ Died, 1980 (made-for-TV; Chris Sarandon); Day of Triumph, 1954 (Robert Wilson); The Disciple, 2010 (Joel West); Family Theatre, 1949-1958 (TV series; "Triumphant Hour," 1953 episode: Basil Tellou); The Final Inquiry, 2006 (Fabrizio Bucci); The Friends of Jesus—Judas, 2001 (made-for-TV; Danny Quinn); The Garden of Eden, 1998 (Kim Rossi Stuart); God-spell, 1973 (Victor Garber); The Gospel according to Matthew, 1993 (Bruce Marchiano); The Gospel according to St. Matthew, 1966 (Enrique Irazoqui); The Gospel of John, 2014 (Selva Rasalingam); The Gospel of Luke, 2015 (Selva Rasalingam); The Gospel of Mark, 2015 (Selva Rasalingam); Gospel Road: The Story of Jesus, 1973 (Robert Elfstrom); The Great Commandment, 1939 (Irving Pichel voiceover); Great Performances, 1971- (TV series; "La Pastorela," 1991 episode: Henry Vasquez; Jorge Galvan; "Jesus Christ, Superstar," 2001 episode: Glenn Carter); **The Greatest Story Ever Told**, 1965 (Max von Sydow); Hail Mary, 1985 (Malachi Jara Kohan); **Heaven Is for Real**, 2014 (Mike Mohrhardt); History of the World: Part I, 1981 (John Hurt); The Holy Family, 2006 (made-for-TV; Brando Pacitto); Il messia, 1975 (adult Jesus: Pier Maria Rossi; Jesus as a child: Mustapha Ferchiou); Incident in Judaea, 1991 (made-for-TV; Mark Rylance); Imperium: Saint Peter, 2005 (made-for-TV; Johannes Brandrup); **Intolerance: Love's Struggle throughout the Ages**, 1916 (Howard Gaye); Jesus, 1979 (Brian Deacon); Jesus, 1999 (Arnaud Giovaninetti); Jesus, 2000 (made-for-TV; adult Jesus: Jeremy Sisto; Jesus as a child: Josh Maguire; Jesus at age six: Miles C. Hobson); Jesus Christ Superstar, 1972 (made-for-TV; Trevor White); **Jesus Christ Superstar**, 1973 (Ted Neeley); Jesus—Der Film, 1986 (Michael Brynntrup); The Jesus Film, 1979 (Brian Deacon); Jesus, Maria y Jose, 1972 (Jose Alberto Castro); Jesus, nuestro Senor, 1971 (Claudio Brook); Jesus of Nazareth, 1942 (Jose Cibrian); Jesus of Nazareth, 1977 (TV miniseries; Robert Powell); Jesus: The Desire of Ages, 2014 (Paul Presly [Spadaro]); Johnny Got His Gun, 1971 (Donald Sutherland); Joseph and Mary, 2016 (Joseph Mesiano; Lucius Hoyos as Jesus as a boy); Joseph of Nazareth, 2000 (made-for-TV; Jurij Gentilini); Judas, 2004 (made-for-TV; Jonathan Scarfe); Juudas Iskariot, 1977 (made-for-TV; Lars Svedberg); **The King of Kings**, 1927 (H. B. Warner); **King of Kings**, 1961 (Jeffrey Hunter); Kristo, 1996 (Mat Ranillo III); La Passion, 1978 (made-for-TV; Alain Claessens); Last Days in the Desert, 2015 (Ewan McGregor); The Last Supper: Thirteen Men of Courage, 2007 (made-for-TV; Von Mclaughlin); The Last Temptation of Christ, 1988 (Willem Dafoe); The Lawton Story, 1949 (Millard Coody); The Life of Jesus Christ, 2011- (TV miniseries; John Foss); The Living Christ Series, 1951 (TV miniseries; Robert Wilson as adult Jesus; Crisy Larson as baby Jesus); The Living Bible, 1952 (TV series; Nelson Leigh); The Man Born to Be King, 1961 (made-for-TV; John Colicos); A Man Dies, 1969 (made-for-TV; Ugo Prinsen); Marie de Nazareth, 1995 (Didier Bienaime); Mary, 2005 (Matthew Modine); Mary Magdalene, 2000 (made-for-TV; Danny Quinn); Mary, Mother of Jesus, 1999 (made-for-TV; Gabor Gulyas as baby Jesus; Toby Bailiff as young Jesus; Christian Bale as adult Jesus); Mary, Mother of the Son of God, 2003 (Luigi Baricelli; Bruno Cariati as Jesus as a child); Mary's Song, 2010 (Eric Ashworth as Jesus as a boy); The Messenger, 1955 (made-for-TV; Jonathan Swift as the boy Jesus); The Miracle Maker, 2000 (Ralph Fiennes); The Passion, 2008 (TV miniseries; Joseph Mawle); The Passion of Christ, 2004 (James Caviezel); The Passover Plot, 1976 (Zalman King); The Pilgrimage Play, 1949 (Nelson Leigh); Pontius Pilate, 1967 (John Drew Barrymore); The Power of the Resurrection, 1958 (Jon Shepodd); **Quo Vadis**, 1951 (Robin Hughes

James Stewart (center as Indian scout Tom Jeffords) in *Broken Arrow*, 1950.

voiceover); The Redeemer, 1959 (Luis Alvarez); Redenzione, 1919 (Alberto Pasquali); Restitution, 1918 (Howard Gaye as adult Jesus; Harold Quintin Driscoll as young Jesus); **The Robe**, 1953 (Donald C. Klune; face not shown; voiceover by Cameron Mitchell); Son of God, 2014 (Diogo Morgado); The Son of God, 2016 (Bruno Alcon); The Testaments: Of One Fold and One Shepherd, 2000 (Tomas Kofod); The Thorn, 1971 (John Bassberger); The Twice Born Woman, 1921 (Alberto Pasquali); A Vida de Jesus Cristo, 1971 (Hemir Valvassori); The Visitor, 1980 (Franco Nero); The Visual Bible: The Gospel of John, 2003 (Henry Ian Cusick); The Wednesday Play, 1964-1970 (TV series; "Son of Man," 1969 espisode: Colin Blakely); Which Will Ye Have!, 1949 (Lewis String voiceover); The World of Don Camillo, 1984 (Allan Arbus); The Young Messiah, 2016 (Adam Greaves-Neal).

Joan of Arc (c. 1412-1431; French heroine in the Hundred Years' War and saint): An Age of Kings, 1960 (TV series; "Henry VI, Part 1: The Red Rose and the White," 1960 episode: Eileen Atkins); BBC Sunday-Night Theatre, 1950-1959 (TV series; "The Lark," 1956 episode: Hazel Penwarden); Bill & Ted's Excellent Adventure, 1989 (Jane Wiedlin); Conflict, 1966-1969 (TV series; "Saint Joan," 1966 episode: Janet Suzman); Daughters of Destiny, 1954 (Michele Morgan); Der Fall Jeanne d'Arc, 1966 (made-for-TV; Kathrin Schmid); Giovanna d'Arco al rogo, 1954 (Ingrid Bergman); Heinrich VI.—Der Krieg der Rosen 1. Teil, 1969 (made-for-TV; Rita Leska); If Paris Were Told to Us, 1956 (Sylviane Contis); Jane B. for Agnes V., 1988 (Jane Birkin); Jeanne au bucher, 1966 (made-for-TV; Edith Scob); Jeanne d'Arc au bucher, 1993 (made-for-TV; Marthe Keller); Jeanne d'Arc au bucher, 2007 (Sylvie Testud); Jeanne d'Arc au bucher, 2012 (made-for-TV; Marion Cotillard); Jeanne D'Arc auf dem Scheiterhaufen, 1960 (made-for-TV; Margot Trooger); Jeanne d'Arc, le pouvoir de l'innocence, 1989 (made-for-TV; Cecile Magnet); Jeanne la Pucelle I - Les batailles, 1994 (Sandrine Bonnaire); Jeanne la Pucelle II—Les prisons, 1994 (Sandrine Bonnaire); Jeanne oder Die Lerche, 1956 (made-for-TV; Liselotte Pulver); Jeanne oder Die Lerche, 1966 (made-for-TV; Elisabeth Schwarz); Joan of Arc, 1914 (Maria Jacobini); Joan of Arc, 1935 (Angela Sollaker); **Joan of Arc**, 1948 (Ingrid Bergman); Joan of Arc, 1952 (made-for-TV; Sarah Churchill); Joan of Arc, 1999 (TV series; Leelee Sobieski); Joan of Arc, 2003 (made-for-TV; Lucie Bila); Joan the Woman, 1916 (Geraldine Farrar); Lamp unto My Feet, 1948-1979 (TV series; "Triumph of St. Joan," 1959 episode: Lee Venora); The Lark, 1957 (made-for-TV; Julie Harris); The Lark, 1958 (made-for-TV; Beverley Dunn); Les chats bottes, 1971 (Andree Lalonde); The Maid of Orleans, 1993 (made-for-TV; Nina Rautio); **The Messenger: The Story of Joan of Arc**, 1999 (Milla Jovovich); **The Miracle of the Bells**, 1948 (Alida Valli, playing an actress essaying Joan of Arc in a film); Miracoloni, 1981 (Nadia Cassini);

H.B. Warner (standing center as Jesus of Nazareth) in *The King of Kings,* **1927.**

Mysteries at the Castle, 2014- (TV series; "House That Saved a King; Joan of Arc; Hamilton Sex Scandal," 2015 episode: Elisa Marti); Nachalo, 1970 (Inna Churikova); National Red Cross Pageant, 1917 (Ina Claire); NBC Television Opera Theater, 1950-1964 (TV series; "The Trial at Rouen," 1956 episode: Elaine Malbin); Omnibus, 1952-1961 (TV series; "Saint Joan," 1955 episode: Kim Hunter); **The Passion of Joan of Arc**, 1929 (Maria Falconetti); R.C.M.P., 1959-1960 (TV series; "Battle of the Innocents," 1960 episode: Denyse St-Pierre); Saint Joan, 1946 (made-for-TV; Ann Casson); Saint Joan, 1957 (Jean Seberg); Saint Joan, 1958 (made-for-TV; Siobhan McKenna); Saint Joan, 1967 (made-for-TV; Genevieve Bujold); Saint Joan the Maid, 1929 (Simone Genevois); Sainte Jeanne, 1969 (made-for-TV; Dominique Labourier); Shine, Shine, My Star, 1970 (Elena Proklova); The Silence of Joan, 2011 (Clemence Poesy); The Story of Mankind, 1957 (Hedy Lamarr); **The Trial of Joan of Arc**, 1965 (Florence Carrez); The Vertical Smile, 1973 (Violaine Doucy); You Are There, 1953-1957 (TV series; "The Final Hours of Joan of Arc," 1953 episode: Kim Stanley).

Jodl, Alfred (Alfred Josef Ferdinand Jodl; 1890-1946; German general and dedicated Nazi under Adolf Hitler in WWII; executed as war criminal): The Bunker, 1981 (made-for-TV; Tony Steedman); **The Desert Fox: The Story of Rommel**, 1951 (Jack Baston); Downfall, 2004 (Christian Redl); The Fall of Berlin, 1952 (Vladimir Pokrovsky); The Great Battle, 1969- (TV series; Werner Dissel); Hitler, 1962 (Walter Kohler); Hitler: The Last Ten Days, 1973 (Philip Stone); Ike: The War Years, 1970 (TV miniseries; Wolfgang Preiss); **Is Paris Burning?**, 1966 (Hannes Messemer); ITV Sunday Night Theatre, 1969- (TV series; "The Death of Adolf Hitler," 1973 episode: Tony Steedman); The Last Ten Days, 1956 (Otto Schmole); **The Longest Day**, 1962 (Wolfgang Lukschy); Nuremberg, 2000 (TV miniseries; Bill Corday); **Patton**, 1970 (Richard Munch); The Victors and the Vanquished, 1950 (V. Svoboda); War and Remembrance, 1988 (TV miniseries; Joachim Hansen); The Winds of War, 1983- (TV series; Joachim Hansen).

Joffre, Joseph (1852-1931; French general and commander-in-chief in WWI): Generale—Anatomie der Marneschlacht, 1977 (made-for-TV; Siegfried Wischnewski); The Kaiser, the Beast of Berlin, 1918 (Harry Holden); Lest We Forget, 1918 (Henry Smith); The Young Indiana Jones Chronicles, 1992-1993 (TV series; "Verdun, September 1916," 1992 episode: Bernard Fresson).

John (Saint John; one of the twelve Apostles of Jesus and one of the four Evangelists; 6-100 A.D.): Animated Stories from the New Testament, 1987- (TV series; John Runnels voiceover); Apostle Peter and the Last Supper, 2012 (Russell Wolfe); The Apostle Peter: Redemption,

2016 (Matthew Wittig); Barabbas, 1953 (Segol Mann); **Barabbas**, 1962 (Nino Segurini); Color of the Cross, 2006 (Akiva David); The Cross, 2001 (Greg Serano); Crown of Thorns, 1934 (silent; Hans Heinrich von Twardowski); Day of Triumph, 1954 (Keith Richards); The Disciple, 2010 (Giovanni Bosso Cox); Family Theatre, 1949-1958 (TV series; "Hill Number One: A Story of Faith and Inspiration," 1951 episode: James Dean; "Triumphant Hour," 1953 episode: Thayer Roberts); 40 Nights, 2016 (Eddie Kaulukukui); The Gospel according to Matthew, 1993 (Kevin Smith); The Gospel according to St. Matthew, 1966 (Giacomo Morante); The Gospel of John, 2014 (Mourad Zaoui); The Gospel of Luke, 2015 (Mourad Zaoui); Gospel Road: A Story of Jesus, 1973 (Gelles LaBlanc); **The Greatest Story Ever Told**, 1965 (John Considine); Il messia, 1975 (Luis Suarez); Jesus [aka: The Jesus Film], 1979 (Shmuel Tal); Jesus, 2000 (made-for-TV; Ian Duncan); **Jesus Christ Superstar**, 1973 (Richard Orbach); Jesus of Nazareth, 1942 (Rafael Medina); Jesus of Nazareth, 1977 (TV miniseries; John Duttine); Judas, 2004 (made-for-TV; Harry Peacock); **The King of Kings**, 1927 (Joseph Striker); **King of Kings**, 1961 (Bud Strait); Kristo, 1996 (Michael Locsin); The Last Supper: Thirteen Men of Courage, 2007 (made-for-TV; Keith Thacker); The Last Temptation of Christ, 1988 (Michael Been); The Life of Jesus Christ, 2011- (TV miniseries; Spencer M.N. Oberan); Mary, Mother of Jesus, 1999 (made-for-TV; Michael Mears); Mary, 2005 (Roy-Oronzo Casalini); Mary, Mother of the Son of God, 2003 (Thiago Martens); Matthew 26:17, 2005 (Meng Johnson); Mysteries and Miracles, 1965- (TV series; "The Crucifixion," 1965 episode: Anthony Gardner); The Passion, 2008 (TV miniseries; Jamie Sives); The Passion of Christ, 2004 (Christo Jivkov); Paul of Tarsus, 1960 (made-for-TV; Stuart Hutchison); Peter and Paul, 1981 (made-for-TV; Yannis Voglis/Giannis Voglis); The Pilgrimage Play, 1949 (Gene Cates); The Power of the Resurrection, 1958 (Stephen Joyce); Risen, 2016 (Mish Boyko); St. John in Exile, 1986 (Dean Jones); St. Paul, 2000 (made-for-TV; Giorgio Pasotti); Salome, 2002 (Javier Toca); Son of God, 2014 (Sebastian Knapp); The Testaments: Of One Fold and One Shepherd, 2000 (Thomas Hughes); The Time Machine: St. Peter—The Rock, 2002 (made-for-TV; Derek Baynham); The True Mistery of the Passion, 1960 (made-for-TV; Anthony Valentine); The Visual Bible: The Gospel of John, 2003 (Stuart Bunce).

John (John Lackland; 1166-1216; king of England): **The Adventures of Robin Hood**, 1938 (Claude Rains); The Adventures of Robin Hood, 1955-1960 (TV series; Donald Pleasence; Hubert Gregg); The Ballad of the Valiant Knight Ivanhoe, 1983 (Algimantas Masiulis); **The Crusades**, 1935 (Ramsay Hill); Dark Knight, 2000- (TV series; Cameron Rhodes); Il Magnifico Robin Hood, 1970 (Frank Brana); **Ivanhoe**, 1952 (Guy Rolfe); Ivanhoe, 1958- (TV series; Andrew Keir); Ivanhoe, 1970- (TV miniseries; Tim Preece); Ivanhoe, 1982 (made-for-TV; Ronald Pickup); Ivanhoe, 1997- (TV miniseries; Ralph Brown); The Legend of Robin Hood, 1968- (TV series; Roddy McDowall); The Legend of Robin Hood, 1975 (TV miniseries; David Dixon); **The Lion in Winter**, 1968 (Nigel Terry); Long Live Robin Hood, 1971 (Daniele Dublino); Richard the Lionheart, 1962 (TV series; Trader Faulkner); **Robin and Marian**, 1976 (Ian Holm); **Robin Hood**, 1922 (Sam De Grasse); **Robin Hood**, 1973 (Peter Ustinov voiceover); Robin Hood, 1984-1986 (TV series; Philip Davis); Robin Hood, 1991 (Edward Fox); Robin Hood, 2006-2009 (TV series; Toby Stephens); **Robin Hood**, 2010 (Oscar Isaac); **Robin Hood: Men in Tights**, 1993 (Richard Lewis); Rogues of Sherwood Forest, 1950 (George Macready); **The Story of Robin Hood** [aka: The Story of Robin Hood and His Merrie Men], 1952 (Hubert Gregg); The Time Tunnel, 1966-1967 (TV series; "The Revenge of Robin Hood," 1966 episode: John Crawford); The Zany Adventures of Robin Hood, 1984 (made-for-TV; Roddy McDowall); Young Robin Hood, 1991-1992 (animated TV series; Michael Rudder voiceover).

John the Baptist (Hebrew itinerant preacher and prophet; executed on orders to Herod Antipater after his stepdaughter, Salome, seeking vengeance against John for his condemnation of her mother's adulterous marriage to Herod, reportedly induced Herod into issuing that order after she performed a sensuous dance for him; d. 31 A.D.): The Big Fisherman, 1959 (Jay Barney); The Cradle of God, 1926 (Eric Barclay); The Cross, 2001 (George Ghali); Day of Triumph, 1954 (John Stephenson); The Gospel according to St. Matthew, 1966 (Mario Socrate); The Gospel Road, 1973 (Larry Lee); **The Greatest Story Ever Told**, 1965 (Charlton Heston); Herodias, 1911 (short; Jean-Marie de l'Isle); Il messia, 1975 (Carlos de Carvalho); Jesus, 1979 (Eli Cohen); Jesus, 2000 (made-for-TV; David O'Hara); Jesus of Nazareth, 1942 (Miguel Manzano); Jesus of Nazareth, 1977 (TV miniseries; Michael York); **King of Kings**, 1961 (Robert Ryan); Kristo, 1996 (Gabby Concepcion); The Living Christ Series, 1951 (TV miniseries; Lawrence Dobkin);); Mary Magdalene, 2000 (made-for-TV; Benjamin Sadler); The Passover Plot, 1976 (Harry Andrews); The Pilgrimage Play, 1949 (John Parrish); Salome, 1918 (Albert [Alan] Roscoe); Salome, 1923 (Nigel de Brulier); **Salome**, 1953 (Alan Badel); Salome, 1973 (made-for-TV; Jean-Paul Zehnacker); Salome, 1992 (made-for-TV; Michael Devlin); Salome, 2013 (Kevin Anderson); Salome's Last Dance, 1988 (Douglas Hodge); Son of God, 2014 (Daniel Percival); The Visual Bible: The Gospel of John, 2003 (Scott Handy).

Johnson, Andrew (1808-1875; U.S. politician and 17th President of the U.S): Cavalcade of America, 1952-1957 (TV series; "The Arrow and the Bow," 1953 episode; Sean McClory); CBS Summer Playhouse, 1987-1989 (TV series; "The Johnsons Are Home," 1988 episode: John Zarchen); **The Conspirator**, 2011 (Dennis Clark); Der Tod des Prasidenten, 1967 (Rainer Geldern); In the Days of Buffalo Bill, 1922 (Harry Myers); The Ordeal of Dr. Mudd, 1980 (made-for-TV; Bill Hindman); Profiles in Courage, 1964-1965 (TV series; "Andrew Johnson," 1965 episode: Walter Matthau); **Tennessee Johnson**, 1942 (Van Heflin).

Johnson, Claudia (aka: Lady Bird; 1912-2007; wife of U.S. President Lyndon B. Johnson): All the Way, 2016 (made-for-TV; Melissa Leo); Path to War, 2002 (made-for-TV; Felicity Huffman); Robert F. Kennedy and His Times, 1985 (TV miniseries; Danna Hansen).

Johnson, Lyndon B. (Lyndon Baines Johnson; 1908-1973; U.S. politician and 36th President of the U.S.): All the Way, 2016 (made-for-TV; Bryan Cranston); Blood Feud, 1983 (made-for-TV; Forrest Tucker); Hoover vs. the Kennedys: The Second Civil War, 1987 (made-for-TV; Richard Anderson); **J. Edgar**, 2011 (himself in archive footage); J. Edgar Hoover, 1987 (made-for-TV; Rip Torn); The Kennedys, 2011 (TV series; Don Allison); King, 1978 (TV miniseries; Warren J. Kemmerling); **The Private Files of J. Edgar Hoover**, 1977 (Andrew Duggan); Path to War, 2002 (made-for-TV; Michael Gambon); RFK, 2002 (made-for-TV; James Cromwell); Robert F. Kennedy and His Times, 1985 (TV miniseries; G. D. Spradlin); **Selma**, 2014 (Tom Wilkinson); Timequest, 2000 (Barry Corbin).

Jolson, Al (1886-1950; U.S. singer-actor-entertainer): The Best Things in Life Are Free, 1956 (Norman Brooks); Boyz Nite Out/Girlz Nite In, 2012 (Myles Nye); Ellis Island, 1984 (TV series; Jonathan Burn); Harlow, 1965 (Buddy Lewis); The Joe Longthorne Show, 1988-1991 (Joe Longthorne); **Jolson Sings Again**, 1949 (Larry Parks); **The Jolson Story**, 1946 (Larry Parks); Parade of Stars, 1983 (made-for-TV; Larry Kert); The Perfect Blue, 1997 (Matthew Finch); Regal Cavalcade, 1935 (Harry Brunning); Sweet Adeline, 1934 (Johnny Eppilite); Yanks Go Home, 1976-1977 (TV series; "Rossi Keeps His Cool," 1976 episode: Bernard Wrigley).

Jones, Christopher (1570-1622; captain of the *Mayflower* that made the historic 1620 voyage to Plymouth Rock): Mayflower: The Pilgrims' Adventure, 1979 (made-for-TV; Anthony Hopkins); **Plymouth Adventure**, 1952 (Spencer Tracy); TV Reader's Digest, 1955-1956 (TV series; "The

Ingrid Bergman (as Joan of Arc) in *Joan of Arc*, 1948.

Voyage of Captain Tom Jones, Pirate," 1955 episode: Louis Hayward).

Jones, John Paul (1747-1792; U.S. naval officer and admiral who was the father of the U.S. Navy): Cavalcade of America, 1952-1957 (TV series; "Night Strike," 1953 episode: Glenn Langan); **John Paul Jones**, 1959 (Robert Stack); The Stamp of Greatness, 1985-1987 (TV series; Jack McKenzie).

Joplin, Scott (1868-1917; U.S. composer and pianist, called the "King of Ragtime Writers"): Scott Joplin, 1977 (made-for-TV; Billy Dee Williams); That's So Raven, 2003-2007 (TV series; "True Colors," 2005 episode: Orlando Brown).

Joseph (in the Old Testament; eleventh son of Jacob and a patriarch of the Hebrew people): After Six Days, 1922 (Lucio Flamma); Animated Stories from the Bible, 1987-2005 (Brian Nissen); The Gospel of Mark, 2015 (Abdellatif Chaouqi); Greatest Heroes of the Bible, 1978- (TV series; "Joseph in Egypt," 1978 episode: Sam Bottoms); Hail Mary, 1985 (Thierry Rode); In the Beginning, 2000 (made-for-TV; Eddie Cibrian); Jacob, 1994 (made-for-TV; Emma Hall); The Jews Are Coming, 2014- (TV series; Yaniv Biton); Joseph, 1995 (made-for-TV; Paul Mercurio; Rinaldo Rocco as young Joseph; Timur Yusef as Joseph as a child); Joseph and Mary, 2016 (Kevin Sorbo); Joseph and the Amazing Technicolor Dreamcoat, 1972 (made-for-TV; Gary Bond); Joseph and the Amazing Technicolor Dreamcoat, 1991 (made-for-TV; Jason Donovan); Joseph in the Land of Egypt, 1914 (James Cruze); Joseph in the Land of Egypt, 1932 (Joseph Green); Joseph 2000, 2000 (made-for-TV; Jerome Winterburn); The New Media Bible: Book of Genesis, 1979 (Jonathan Sagall); The Red Tent, 2014- (TV miniseries; Will Tudor); Shalom Pharao, 1982 (animated; Helmuth Lohner voiceover); Slave of Dreams, 1995 (made-for-TV; Adrian Pasdar); The Story of Jacob and Joseph, 1974 (made-for-TV; Tony Lo Bianco); The Story of Joseph and His Brethren, 1962 (Geoffrey Horne); Testament: The Bible in Animation, 1996- (TV series; "Joseph," 1996 episode: Anton Lesser voiceover; Robert Harper as young Joseph voiceover).

Joseph (saint; husband of Mary, who gave birth to Jesus; d.18 A.D.): Behold the Man, 1935 (Marcel Chabrier); **Ben-Hur: A Tale of the Christ**, 1925 (Winter Hall); Color of the Cross, 2006 (Mark Winn); The Cradle of God, 1926 (Andre Roanne); The Gospel according to St. Matthew, 1966 (Marcello Morante); **The Greatest Story Ever Told**, 1965 (Robert Loggia); Herod and Marianne, 1965 (made-for TV; Richard Lauffen); Il messia, 1975 (Yatsugi Khelil); Jesus, 1979 (Joseph Shiloach); Jesus, 2000 (made-for-TV; Armin Mueller-Stahl); Jesus, Maria y Jose, 1972 (Guillermo Murray); Jesus of Nazareth, 1977 (TV

John Alexander, Larry Parks (as Al Jolson) and William Demarest in *The Jolson Story*, 1946.

miniseries; Yorgos Vogiatzis); Joseph of Nazareth, 2000 (made-for-TV; Tobias Moretti); **King of Kings**, 1961 (Gerard Tichy); The Living Christ Series, 1951 (TV miniseries; John Alvin); Marie de Nazareth, 1995 (Francis Lalanne); Mary, Mother of Jesus, 1999 (made-for-TV; Joseph Threlfall); Mary's Song, 2010 (James Constantine); Restitution, 1918 (Frederick Vroom); Son of God, 2014 (Joe Coen); The Young Messiah, 2016 (Vincent Walsh).

Joseph (Chief Joseph; U.S. Nez Perce chief; 1840-1904): Gunsmoke, 1955-1975 (TV series; "Chief Joseph," 1965 episode: Victor Jory; I Will Fight No More Forever, 1975 (made-for-TV; Ned Romero); The Life and Legend of Wyatt Earp, 1955-1961 (TV series; "The Gatling Gun," 1958 episode: Richard Garland).

Joseph II (Austrian Holy Roman Emperor; 1741-1790): **Amadeus**, 1984 (Jeffrey Jones); Eternal Melodies, 1940 (Claudio Gora); Forsterchristl, 1931 (Paul Richter); The Life and Loves of Mozart, 1959 (Elfie Weissenbock); The Life of Wolfgang Amadeus Mozart [aka: The Mozart Story], 1948 (Curt Jurgens); Mozart, 1936 (Frederick Leister); Mozart, 1982- (TV miniseries; Daniel Ceccaldi); Vergesst Mozart, 1985 (investigates Mozart's mysterious death; Zdenek Hradilak).

Josephine: see Beauharnais, Josephine de.

Joshua (1355-1235 B.C.; in Old Testament Bible; Israeli leader): **Exodus: Gods and Kings**, 2014 (Aaron Paul); **The Green Pastures**, 1936 (Reginald Fenderson); Moses, 1995 (made-for-TV; Enrico Lo Verso); Moses the Lawgiver, 1974 (TV miniseries; Aharon Ipale); **The Ten Commandments**, 1956 (John Derek); The Ten Commandments, 2007 (Matt Hill voiceover); The Ten Commandments: The Musical, 2006 (Adam Lambert).

Joyce, William (aka: Lord Haw-Haw; 1906-1946; American-born British traitor who became a Nazi, migrated to Germany to broadcast propaganda over the Nazi airways during WWII; convicted of treason and executed by hanging): Passport to Destiny, 1944 (Gavin Muir); **Twelve O'Clock High**, 1949 (Barry Jones voiceover).

Juarez, Benito (Benito Pablo Juarez Garcia; 1806-1872; Mexican attorney and president of Mexico): Aquellos anos, 1974 (Jorge Martinez de Hoyos); Cinco de Mayo, la Battala, 2013 (Noe Hernandez); The Cisco Kid, 1994 (made-for-TV; Luis Valdez); El carruaje, 1972 (TV series; Jose Carlos Ruiz); El joven Juarez, 1954 (Humberto Almazan); El vuelo del aguila, 1994 (TV series; Ernesto Gomez Cruz); The Hourglass Sanatorium, 1973 (Emir Buczacki); **Juarez**, 1939 (Paul Muni); Juarez and

Maximillian, 1935 (Froylan B. Tenes); La Tormenta, 1967 (TV series; Jose Carlos Ruiz); The Mad Empress, 1939 (Jason Robards Sr.); Maximilian von Mexiko, 1970 (made-for-TV; Dieter Borsche); Mexicanos al grito de guerra, 1943 (Miguel Inclan); Prariejager in Mexiko: Benito Juarez, 1988 (Helmut Schellhardt); Treasure of the Aztecs, 1966 (Fausto Tozzi); Visita al Pasado, 1981 (Ernesto Gomez Cruz); Zorro's Fighting Legion, 1939 (Carleton Young).

Judas Iscariot (AKA: Jude; Apostle of Jesus, who betrayed him to the Romans for thirty pieces of silver and committed suicide; d. 33 A.D.): Apostle Peter and the Last Supper, 2012 (David [Knox] Collier); Behold the Man, 1935 (Lucas Gridoux); Color of the Cross, 2006 (Johann John Jean); Color of the Cross 2: The Resurrection, 2008 (Gerald Webb); The Cross, 2001 (Agustin Rodriguez); Crown of Thorns, 1934 (silent; Alexander Granach); Day of Triumph, 1954 (James Griffith); The Friends of Jesus—Judas, 2001 (made-for-TV; Enrico Lo Verso); The Gospel according to St. Matthew, 1966 (Otello Sestili); The Gospel of Mark, 2015 (El Housseine Dejjiti); The Great Commandment, 1939 (Marc Loebell); **The Greatest Story Ever Told**, 1965 (David McCallum); Herod and Marianne, 1965 (made-for TV; Arno Gorke); Il messia, 1975 (Raouf Ben Amor); Jesus, 1979 (Eli Danker); Jesus, 2000 (made-for-TV; Thomas Lockyer); Jesus Christ Superstar, 1972 (made-for-TV; Jon English); **Jesus Christ Superstar**, 1973 (Carl Anderson); Jesus of Nazareth, 1942 (Jose Pidal); Jesus of Nazareth, 1977 (TV miniseries; Ian McShane); Joseph of Nazareth, 2000 (made-for-TV; Omar Lahlou); Judas, 2004 (made-for-TV; Johnathon Schaech); Juudas Iskariot, 1977 (made-for-TV; Ville-Veikko Salminen); **The King of Kings**, 1927 (Joseph Schildkraut); **King of Kings**, 1961 (Rip Torn); Kristo, 1996 (Rez Cortez); The Last Supper: Thirteen Men of Courage, 2007 (made-for-TV; Keith Allen); The Life of Jesus Christ, 2011- (TV miniseries; Adam Johnson); The Living Christ Series, 1951 (TV miniseries; Keith Richards; Gayne Whitman); The Living Bible, 1952 (TV series; Jan Arvan); The Passion, 2008 (TV miniseries; Paul Nicholls); The Passion of Christ, 2004 (Luca Lionello); The Pilgrimage Play, 1949 (Leonard Penn); The Power of the Resurrection, 1958 (Jan Arvan); **The Robe**, 1953 (Michael Ansara); Son of God, 2014 (Joe Wredden); The Twice Born Woman, 1921 (Eduardo Napoleoni); The Visual Bible: The Gospel of John, 2003 (Alan Van Sprang).

Julius II (Pope; 1443-1513): **The Agony and the Ecstasy**, 1965 (Rex Harrison); The Borgia, 2006 (Eusebio Poncela); Borgia, 2011- (TV series; Dejan Cukic); The Borgias, 1981- (TV miniseries; Alfred Burke); The Borgias, 2011-2013 (TV series; Colm Feore); The Cardinal, 1936 (F.B.J. Sharp); The Conclave, 2006 (Matthias Koeberlin); Inside the Vatican, 1993 (TV miniseries; Remo Remotti); La fornarina, 1944 (Pio Campa); Michelangelo—Il cuore e la pietra, 2012 (made-for-TV; Ugo Innamorati); Raphael: A Mortal God, 2004 (made-for-TV; T.P. McKenna); A Season for Giants, 1991 (made-for-TV; F. Murray Abraham).

Junge, Gertraud (aka: "Trudl"; 1920-2002; German office worker and personal secretary of Adolf Hitler in his last days): The Bunker, 1981 (made-for-TV; Sarah Marshall); Downfall, 2004 (Alexandra Maria Lara); Gandhi to Hitler, 2011 (Jasleen); Hitler: The Last Ten Days, 1973 (Ann Lynn); ITV Sunday Night Theatre, 1969- (TV series; "The Death of Adolf Hitler," 1973 episode: Wanda Moore); Uncle Adolf, 2005 (made-for-TV; Stacy Hart).

Kafka, Franz (1883-1924; German writer of existentialistic works): Einstein, 1985- (TV miniseries; Andras Balint); Full Moon Fables, 2004 (Paul Morella); Kafka, 1991 (Jeremy Irons); Labyrinth, 1991 (Christopher Chaplin); The Loves of Kafka, 1988 (Jorge Marrale); Marie Soleil, 1964 (Claude Darget); Milena, 1991 (Philip Anglim); Night Angel, 1931 (E. Lewis Waller); Northern Exposure, 1990-1995 (TV series; "Cicely," 1992 episode: Rob Morrow); The Young Indiana Jones Chronicles,

1992-1993 (TV series; "Prague, August 1917," 1993 episode: Tim McInnerny).

Kahn, Gus (Gustav Gerson Kahn; 1886-1941; U.S. German-born lyricist of many popular songs, including "Pretty Baby," "It Had to Be You" and "I'll See You in My Dreams"): **I'll See You in My Dreams**, 1951 (Danny Thomas).

Kahr, Gustav Ritter von (1862-1934; German right-wing politician instrumental in putting down Hitler's 1923 insurrection in Munich, Germany [Beer Hall Putsch], and who was murdered by the Nazis ten years later on June 30, 1934, when Hitler and other Nazi leaders exterminated major oppositional leaders in what was later called "The Night of the Long Knives"): **The Hitler Gang**, 1944 (Ludwig Donath); Hitler: The Rise of Evil, 2003 (made-for-TV; Terrence Harvey); Hitler vor Gericht, 2009 (made-for-TV; Alexander Held).

Kaltenborn, Hans von (H.V. Kaltenborn; American radio commentator; 1878-1965): **The Babe Ruth Story**, 1948 (himself); **Mr. Smith Goes to Washington**, 1939.

Karpis, Alvis (aka: "Creepy"; 1907-1979; Canadian bank and train robber and kidnapper; member of the notorious Barker gang): Birdseye, 2002 (Pato Hoffmann); **The FBI Story**, 1959 (George Khoury); The F.B.I. Story: The FBI versus Alvin Karpis, Public Enemy Number One, 1974 (made-for-TV; Robert Foxworth); Gangbusters, 1952- (TV series; two 1952 episodes: Paul Dubov); Guns Don't Argue, 1957 (Paul Dubov); **J. Edgar**, 2011 (Manu Intiraymi); The Kansas City Massacre, 1975 (made-for-TV; Morgan Paull); Ma Barker's Killer Brood, 1960 (Paul Dubov); **The Private Files of J. Edgar Hoover**, 1977 (Brad Dexter); **Public Enemies**, 2009 (Giovanni Ribisi). Note: For detailed information on Karpis, see my books *Bloodletters and Badmen: A Narrative Encyclopedia of American Criminals from the Piligrims to the Past* (M. Evans, 1973-2015; illustrated pages 350-355; *Encyclopedia of World Crime*, Volume I (CrimeBooks, Inc., 1990; illustrated [10 images] pages 1763-1766).

Katherine of Aragon: see Catherine of Aragon.

Kaufman, George S. (1889-1961; U.S. playwright, producer, humorist and critic; member of the Algonquin Round Table): Act One, 1960 (Jason Robards Jr.); Mrs. Parker and the Vicious Circle, 1994 (David Thornton).

Keaton, Buster (Joseph Frank Keaton; 1895-1966; U.S. actor and comedian, prominent comedic star in the silent era): The Buster Keaton Story, 1957 (Donald O'Connor); The Devil's Muse, 2007 (Will Keenan); **Hollywood Cavalcade**, 1939 (himself); Lucy, 2003 (made-for-TV; Ian Mune); **Sunset Boulevard**, 1950 (himself).

Keats, John (1795-1821; British romantic poet): Bright Star, 2009 (Ben Whishaw); John Keats: His Life and Death, 1973 (John Stride); The Romantics, 2006- (TV miniseries; Nicholas Shaw); Screenplay, 1986-1993 (TV series; "Dead Poets' Society," 1992 episode: Dexter Fletcher); Solo, 1970- (TV series; Ian McKellen).

Keckley, Elizabeth Hobbs (1818-1907; U.S. former slave, activist, author and confidante of First Lady Mary Todd Lincoln): Lincoln, 1988 (TV miniseries; Ruby Dee); **Lincoln**, 2012 (Gloria Reuben); Look Away, 1987 (made-for-TV; Madge Sinclair); **Saving Lincoln**, 2013 (Saidah Arrika Ekulona).

Keene, Laura (1826-1873; British actress who was performing on stage at Ford's Theater on the night of April 14, 1865, when U.S. President Abraham Lincoln was assassinated by John Wilkes Booth): **The Birth

Spencer Tracy (as Christopher Jones) and Lloyd Bridges in *Plymouth Adventure*, **1952.**

of a Nation, 1915 (Olga Grey); The Day Lincoln Was Shot, 1998 (made-for-TV; O'Mara Leary); They've Killed President Lincoln!, 1971 (made-for-TV; Cynthia Thomas).

Keitel, Wilhelm (1882-1946; German field marshal and dedicated Nazi under Adolf Hitler; executed as a war criminal): Claus Graf Stauffenberg, 1970 (made-for-TV; Heinrich Gies); Die Stunde der Offiziere, 2004 (made-for-TV; Wilfried Pucher); **The Desert Fox**: **The Story of Rommel**, 1951 (John Hoyt); Downfall, 2004 (Dieter Mann); The First Front, 1949 (Nikolai Komissarov); The Great Battle, 1973 (Gerd Michael Henneberg); Hitler, 1962 (Karl Esmond); Hitler: The Last Ten Days, 1973 (Gabriele Ferzetti); It Happened on July 20th, 1955 (Jochen Hauer); Operation Valkyrie, 2004 (made-for-TV; Christian Doermer); The Plot to Assassinate Hitler, 1955 (Georg Gutlich); The Plot to Kill Hitler, 1990 (made-for-TV; Kenneth Colley); **The Two-Headed Spy**, 1959 (Richard Grey); **Valkyrie**, 2008 (Kenneth Cranham); War and Remembrance, 1988 (TV miniseries; John Malcolm).

Keller, Helen (1880-1968; U.S. political activist and lecturer, the first deaf and blind person to earn a college degree): Adventures from the Book of Virtues, 1996- (animated TV series; "Patience," 1998 episode: Kath Soucie voiceover); Alexander Graham Bell: The Sound and the Silence, 1993 (made-for-TV; Rhondee Beriault); All That Remains, 2016 (Susan Jameson); Animated Hero Classics, 1991-2005 (TV series; "Helen Keller," 1996 episode: Elizabeth Daily voiceover); Anna dei miracoli, 1968 (made-for-TV; Cinzia De Carolis); Deliverance, 1919 (Ann Mason; Etna Ross as young Helen); Ghostlight, 2003 (Maryette Charlton); Helen Keller and Her Teacher, 1970 (Peri Weinstein); Helen Keller: The Miracle Continues, 1984 (made-for-TV; Mare Winningham); Helen Keller vs. Nightwolves, 2015 (Lin Shayne; Jessie Wiseman as young Helen); Mentors, 1998-2005 (TV series; "Breakthrough," 2002 episode: Emily Nash); **The Miracle Worker**, 1962 (Patty Duke); The Miracle Worker, 1979 (made-for-TV; Melissa Gilbert); The Miracle Worker, 2000 (made-for-TV; Hallie Kate Eisenberg); Monday After the Miracle, 1998 (made-for-TV; Moira Kelly); Playhouse 90, 1956-1961 (TV series; "The Miracle Worker," 1957 episode: Patty McCormack).

Kellerman, Annette Marie Sarah (1887-1975; Australian professional swimmer, vaudeville star and actress who introduced the one-piece swimming suit for women): **Million Dollar Mermaid**, 1952 (Esther Williams); Queen of the Sea, 1918 (herself); Venus of the South Seas, 1924 (Shona Royale).

Kelly, George (George Celino Barnes; aka: "Machine Gun"; 1895-1954; U.S. bank robber and kidnapper): Baker's Half-Dozen, 1967-1976 (TV

Frank Lovejoy (as Walter Donaldson) and Danny Thomas (as Gus Kahn) in *I'll See You in My Dreams,* **1951.**

series; "The Guy Fawkes Night Massacre," 1967 episode: Hal Galili); **The FBI Story**, 1959 (Stacy Keach Sr.); Ma Barker's Killer Brood, 1960 (Victor Lundin); Machine-Gun Kelly, 1958 (Charles Bronson); Melvin Purvis: G-MAN, 1974 (Harris Yulin); **Public Enemies**; 2009 (Tommy Dallace). Note: None of the films shown here provide dependable data on Kelly and his criminal acts. For reliable and detailed information on Kelly, see my two-volume work *The Great Pictorial History of World Crime*, Volume I (History, Inc., illustrated [15 images] pages 665-672).

Kelly, Grace (1929-1982; U.S. actress of great beauty who married Prince Ranier III and became the Princess of Monaco): Grace Kelly, 1983 (made-for-TV; Cheryl Ladd; Christina Applegate as young Grace); Grace of Monaco, 2014 (Nicole Kidman); Star Witness, 1995 (made-for-TV; Charlene Tilton; Meg Register).

Kelly, Mary Jane (c.1863-1888; British prostitute and last know murder victim of Jack the Ripper): From Hell, 2001 (Heather Graham); Jack the Ripper, 1988 (TV series; Lysette Anthony); Love Lies Bleeding, 1999 (Andrea Miltner); **Murder by Decree**, 1979 (Susan Clark); The Outer Limits, 1995-2002 (TV series; "Ripper," 1999 episode: Mary Ann Skoll); **A Study in Terror**, 1966 (Edina Ronay); The Ripper, 1997 (made-for-TV; Karen Davitt). For detailed information on this and the other Ripper murders, see my two-volume work *The Great Pictorial History of World Crime*, Volume II (History Inc., 2004; illustrated pages 1180-1203).

Kemper, James Lawson (1823-1895; Confederate general in the American Civil War): **Gettysburg**, 1993 (Royce Applegate); **Gods and Generals**, 2003 (Royce Applegate).

Kennedy, Edward Moore (aka: "Ted"; 1932-2009; U.S. Senator from Massachusetts, 1962-2009; younger brother of U.S. President John F. Kennedy and U.S. Attorney General Robert F. Kennedy): J.F.K.: Reckless Youth, 1993 (made-for-TV; Jared Cook; Fraser McGregor; Seth Gabrielse); Jackie Bouvier Kennedy Onassis, 2000 (made-for-TV; Jacob Richmond); The Kennedys of Massachusetts, 1990 (TV miniseries; Ryan Shaughnessy); RFK, 2002 (made-for-TV; Kevin Hare); Robert Kennedy and His Times, 1985 (TV miniseries; James Read); A Woman Named Jackie, 1991 (TV miniseries; Dylan Price).

Kennedy, Ethel (1928- ; U.S. wife of U.S. Attorney General Robert F. Kennedy): Blood Feud, 1983 (made-for-TV; McKee Anderson); Hoover vs. the Kennedys: The Second Civil War, 1987 (made-for-TV; Linda Goranson); Jackie, Ethel, Joan: The Women of Camelot, 2001 (made-

for-TV; Lauren Holly); The Kennedys, 2011 (TV series; Kristin Booth); RFK, 2002 (made-for-TV; Marnie McPhail); Robert Kennedy and His Times, 1985 (TV miniseries; Veronica Cartwright); A Woman Named Jackie, 1991 (TV miniseries; Kathleen McNenny).

Kennedy, Eunice (Eunice Kennedy Shriver; 1921-2009; U.S. political and pro-life activist and sister of U.S. President John F. Kennedy and U.S. Attorney General Robert F. Kennedy): J.F.K.: Reckless Youth, 1993 (made-for-TV; Melody Johnson; Nancy McClure); The Kennedys of Massachusetts, 1990 (TV miniseries; Halina Radosz); Robert Kennedy and His Times, 1985 (TV miniseries; Elizabeth Norment).

Kennedy, Jacqueline (Jacqueline "Jackie" Bouvier Kennedy Onasis; 1929-1994; U.S. First Lady, wife of President John F. Kennedy): The Greek Tycoon, 1978 (role model for Jacqueline Bisset); The Hoax, 2006 (Elizabeth Marley); Hoover vs. the Kennedys: The Second Civil War, 1987 (made-for-TV; Jennifer Dale); Jackie Bouvier Kennedy Onassis, 2000 (made-for-TV; Joanne Whalley); Jackie, Ethel, Joan: The Women of Camelot, 2001 (made-for-TV; Jill Hennessy); Jacqueline Bouvier Kennedy, 1981 (made-for-TV; Jaclyn Smith); Kennedy, 1983 (TV miniseries; Blair Brown); The Kennedys, 2011 (TV series; Katie Holmes); Onassis: The Richest Man in the World, 1988 (made-for-TV; Francesca Annis); Power and Beauty, 2002 (made-for-TV; Katie Griffin); Robert F. Kennedy and His Times, 1985 (TV miniseries; Juanin Clay); Ruby, 1992 (Mary Chris Wall); Timequest, 2000 (Caprice Benedetti).

Kennedy, Jean Ann (Jean Ann Kennedy Smith; 1928- ; U.S. ambassador to Ireland, 1993-1998; and sister to U.S. President John F. Kennedy and U.S. Attorney General Robert F. Kennedy): J.F.K.: Reckless Youth, 1993 (made-for-TV; Deanna Way; Shileen Paton; Cherry Winfield); The Kennedys of Massachusetts, 1990 (TV miniseries; Danielle Schonback); Robert Kennedy and His Times, 1985 (TV miniseries; Dorothy Fielding); A Woman Named Jackie, 1991 (TV miniseries; Marianna Bishop).

Kennedy, John F. (John Fitzgerald Kennedy; aka: "Jack"; 1917-1963; U.S. politician and 35th President of the U.S.): The Greek Tycoon, 1978 (role model for James Franciscus); Hoover vs. the Kennedys: The Second Civil War, 1987 (made-for-TV; Robert Pine); J. Edgar Hoover, 1987 (made-for-TV; Art Hindle); J.F.K.: Reckless Youth, 1993 (made-for-TV; Patrick Dempsey); Jackie Bouvier Kennedy Onassis, 2000 (made-for-TV; Tim Matheson); Jackie, Ethel, Joan: The Women of Camelot, 2001 (made-for-TV; Daniel Hugh Kelly); Jacqueline Bouvier Kennedy, 1981 (made-for-TV; James Franciscus); Johnny, We Hardly Knew Ye, 1977 (made-for-TV; Paul Rudd); Kennedy, 1983 (TV miniseries; Martin Sheen); The Kennedys of Massachusetts, 1990 (TV miniseries; Steven Weber); The Kennedys, 2011 (TV series; Greg Kinnear); King, 1978 (TV miniseries; William Jordan); **Parkland**, 2013 (Brett Stimely); Power and Beauty, 2002 (made-for-TV; Kevin Anderson); **The Private Files of J. Edgar Hoover**, 1977 (William Jordan); **PT 109**, 1963 (Cliff Robertson); The Rat Pack, 1998 (made-for-TV; William Petersen); RFK, 2002 (made-for-TV; Martin Donovan); Robert Kennedy and His Times, 1985 (TV miniseries; Cliff De Young); Ruby, 1992 (Gerard David; Kevin Wiggins); Timequest, 2000 (Victor Slezak); A Woman Named Jackie, 1991 (TV miniseries; Stephen Collins).

Kennedy, Joseph P, Jr. (1915-1944; U.S. pilot and son of wealthy businessman Joseph P. Kennedy Sr.; killed in action in WWII): J.F.K.: Reckless Youth, 1993 (made-for-TV; Loren Dean); The Kennedys of Massachusetts, 1990 (TV miniseries; Campbell Scott); Young Joe, the Forgotten Kennedy, 1977 (made-for-TV; Peter Strauss; Lance Kerwin as Joe, age fourteen).

Kennedy, Joseph P, Sr. (1888-1969; U.S. movie producer, multi-millionaire banker and businessman; onetime U.S. ambassador to England,

1938-1940; and father of U.S. President John F. Kennedy and U.S. Attorney General Robert F. Kennedy): Blood Feud, 1983 (made-for-TV; Duncan Ross); Hoover vs. the Kennedys: The Second Civil War, 1987 (made-for-TV; Barry Morse); J.F.K.: Reckless Youth, 1993 (made-for-TV; Terry Kinney); Jackie Bouvier Kennedy Onassis, 2000 (made-for-TV; Tom Skerritt); Jackie, Ethel, Joan: The Women of Camelot, 2001 (made-for-TV; Harve Presnell); Jacqueline Bouvier Kennedy, 1981 (made-for-TV; Stephen Elliott); Johnny, We Hardly Knew Ye, 1977 (made-for-TV; William Prince); The Kennedys of Massachusetts, 1990 (TV miniseries; William Petersen); The Kennedys, 2011 (TV series; Tom Wilkinson); The Rat Pack, 1998 (made-for-TV; Dan O'Herlihy); RFK, 2002 (made-for-TV; David Gardner); Robert Kennedy and His Times, 1985 (TV miniseries; Jack Warden); Upstairs Downstairs, 2010-2012 (TV series; William Hope); A Woman Named Jackie, 1991 (TV miniseries; Josef Sommer); Young Joe, the Forgotten Kennedy, 1977 (made-for-TV; Stephen Elliott).

Kennedy, Patricia (Patricia Kennedy Lawford; 1924-2006; U.S. wife of film actor Peter Lawford and sister of U.S. President John F. Kennedy and U.S. Attorney General Robert F. Kennedy): J.F.K.: Reckless Youth, 1993 (made-for-TV; Hailey Goldberg); The Kennedys of Massachusetts, 1990 (TV miniseries; Kristen Lee Kelly); Robert Kennedy and His Times, 1985 (TV miniseries; Mimi Kennedy).

Kennedy, Robert F. (Robert Francis Kennedy; aka: "Bobby"; 1925-1968; U.S. politician, U.S. senator [N.Y.] and 64th U.S. attorney general): Blood Feud, 1983 (made-for-TV; Cotter Smith); Bobby, 2006 (Dave Fraunces); Citizen Cohn, 1992 (made-for-TV; David Marshall Grant); Dark Skies, 1996-1997 (TV series: "The Warren Omission," 1997 episode: James F. Kelly); Hoover vs. the Kennedys: The Second Civil War, 1987 (made-for-TV; Nicholas Campbell); **J. Edgar**, 2011 (Jeffrey Donovan); J. Edgar Hoover, 1987 (made-for-TV; James F. Kelly); J.F.K.: Reckless Youth, 1993 (made-for-TV; Victor Erdos; John David Wood); Jackie Bouvier Kennedy Onassis, 2000 (made-for-TV; Andrew McCarthy); Jackie, Ethel, Joan: The Women of Camelot, 2001 (made-for-TV; Robert Knepper); Jacqueline Bouvier Kennedy, 1981 (made-for-TV; James F. Kelly); The Kennedys of Massachusetts, 1990 (TV miniseries; Randle Mell); The Kennedys, 2011 (TV series; Barry Pepper); King, 1978 (TV miniseries; Cliff De Young); Marilyn & Bobby: Her Final Affair, 1993 (made-for-TV; James F. Kelly); **The Private Files of J. Edgar Hoover**, 1977 (Michael Parks); The Rat Pack, 1998 (made-for-TV; Zeljko Ivanek); RFK, 2002 (made-for-TV; Linus Roache); Robert Kennedy and His Times, 1985- (TV miniseries; Brad Davis); Sugartime, 1995 (made-for-TV; Peter Krantz); Tail Gunner Joe, 1977 (made-for-TV; Sam Chew Jr.); Timequest, 2000 (Vince Grant); A Woman Named Jackie, 1991 (TV miniseries; Tim Ransom).

Kennedy, Rose (1890-1995; U.S. socialite, wife of wealthy businessman Joseph P. Kennedy and mother of U.S. President John F. Kennedy): J.F.K.: Reckless Youth, 1993 (made-for-TV; Diana Scarwid); Jackie Bouvier Kennedy Onassis, 2000 (made-for-TV; Diane Baker); Jackie, Ethel, Joan: The Women of Camelot, 2001 (made-for-TV; Charmion King); Jacqueline Bouvier Kennedy, 1981 (made-for-TV; Eve Roberts); Johnny, We Hardly Knew Ye, 1977 (made-for-TV; Shirley Rich); Kennedy, 1983 (TV miniseries; Geraldine Fitzgerald); The Kennedys, 2011 (TV series; Diana Hardcastle); The Kennedys of Massachusetts, 1990 (TV miniseries; Annette O'Toole); RFK, 2002 (made-for-TV; Corinne Conley); Robert Kennedy and His Times, 1985- (TV miniseries; Beatrice Straight); Upstairs Downstairs, 2010-2012 (TV series; Nancy Crane); A Woman Named Jackie, 1991 (TV miniseries; Rosemary Murphy); Young Joe, the Forgotten Kennedy, 1977 (made-for-TV; Gloria Stroock).

Kenny, Elizabeth (1880-1952; aka: Sister Kenny; Australian pioneering nurse who developed the practice of physical therapy to initially treat

Donald O'Connor (as Buster Keaton) in *The Buster Keaton Story*, **1957.**

and retard polio): **Sister Kenny**, 1946 (Rosalind Russell).

Kerensky, Alexander (1881-1970; Russian politician and Prime Minister of Russia): Admiral, 2009 (Viktor Verzhbitsky); Fall of Eagles, 1974 (TV miniseries; Jim Norton); The Fall of the Romanovs, 1917 (W. Francis Chapin); The Legion of Death, 1918 (H. L. Swisher); Lenin in October, 1937 (A. Kovalevsky); Lenin, You Rascal, You, 1972 (Per Goldschmidt); **Nicholas and Alexandra**, 1971 (John McEnery); October (Ten Days That Shook the World), 1928 (Nikolay Popov); Rasputin, the Black Monk, 1917 (Henry Hull); **Reds**, 1981 (Oleg Kerensky); The Romanovs: An Imperial Family, 2000 (Mikhail Efremov).

Kern, Jerome (1885-1945; U.S. composer of popular and theatrical music, notably "Showboat"): The Lost Boys, 1978- (TV series; "An Awfully Big Adventure," 1978 episode: Oliver Gilbert); **Till the Clouds Roll By**, 1946 (Robert Walker).

Ketchum, Thomas E. (aka: Black Jack; 1863-1901; U.S. Old West outlaw, bank and train robber): Badman's Country, 1958 (Fred Graham); Blackjack Ketchum, Desperado, 1956 (Howard Duff); Stories of the Century, 1954- (TV series; "Black Jack Ketchum," 1954 episode: Jack Elam). Note: For detailed information on Ketchum, see my book *Encyclopedia of Western Lawmen and Outlaws* (Paragon House, 1992; illustrated pages 198-200).

Khrushchev, Nikita (1894-1971; first secretary of the Communist Party of Soviet Russia): American Genius, 2015- (TV series; "Space Race," 2015 episode: Tim Duquette); Children of the Revolution, 1996 (Dennis Watkins); **Enemy at the Gates**, 2001 (Bob Hoskins); Francis Gary Powers: The True Story of the U-2 Spy Incident, 1976 (made-for-TV; Thayer David); Georg, 2006 (made-for-TV; Sergey Fetisov); The Kennedys, 2011- (TV series; "Cuban Missiles," 2011 episode; Eugene Lipinski); Miles from Home, 1988 (Larry Poling); The Missiles of October, 1974 (made-for-TV; Howard Da Silva); Passions, 1999-2008 (TV series; episode 1,625: Alex Rodine); Playhouse 90, 1956-1961 (TV series; 'The Plot to Kill Stalin," 1958 episode; Oskar Holmolka); Red Monarch, 1983 (made-for-TV; Brian Glover); Stalin, 1992 (made-for-TV; Murray Ewan); Staline est morte, 1981 (made-for-TV; Yves Brainville); Stalingrad, 1990 (Vadim Lobanov); Suez 1956, 1979 (made-for-TV; Aubrey Morris); Zotz!, 1962 (Albert Glasser); Zukhov, 2012 (TV series; Aleksandr Potapov).

Kichisaburo Nomura (1877-1964; Japanese admiral and ambassador to the U.S. shortly before the sneak attack against Pearl Harbor on December 7, 1941): **Pearl Harbor**, 2002 (himself in archive footage); **Tora!**

Esther Williams (as Annette Kellerman) in a water extravaganza in *Million Dollar Mermaid*, 1952.

Tora! Tora!, 1970 (Shogo Shimada).

Kidd, William (Captain Kidd; 1645-1701; Scottish sailor and privateer who has hanged for piracy): Abbott and Costello Meet Captain Kidd, 1952 (Charles Laughton); Against All Flags, 1952 (Robert Warwick); Blackbeard, 2006- (TV miniseries; Love Nystrom); Captain Kidd, 1945 (Charles Laughton); Captain Kidd and the Slave Girl, 1954 (Anthony Dexter); Double Crossbones, 1951 (Alan Napier); George's Island, 1989 (Gary Reineke); The Gold Bug, 2009 (Spike Carpenter); The Great Adventures of Captain Kidd, 1954 (John Crawford); Mystic Nights and Pirate Fights, 1998 (T.J. Glenn; Glen Michaels); Sweethearts of the U.S.A., 1944 (Edmund Cobb as the ghost of Captain Kidd). Note: For detailed information on Kidd, see my two-volume work *The Great Pictorial History of World Crime*, Volume II (History, Inc., 2004; illustrated [10 images] pages 1283-1289).

Kieffer, Philippe (1899-1962; French military commander at Sword Beach and who led the attack at Ouistreham during the Allied invasion of Normandy on June 6, 1944): **The Longest Day**, 1962 (Christian Marquand).

Kijuro Shidehara (Japanese diplomat, pacifist and prime minster of Japan, 1945-1946 during U.S. occupation; 1872-1951): **MacArthur**, 1977 (Yuki Shimoda).

Kimmel, Husband E. (Husband Edward Kimmel; 1882-1968; U.S. four-star admiral and commander-in-chief of the U.S. Pacific Fleet at Pearl Harbor during Japanese sneak attack on December 1, 1941; removed from his command): **In Harm's Way**, 1965 (role model for Franchot Tone); **Pearl Harbor**, 2002 (Colm Feore); **Tora! Tora! Tora!**, 1970 (Martin Balsam).

King, Coretta Scott (1927-2006; U.S. activist and wife of Dr. Martin Luther King): All the Way, 2016 (made-for-TV; Hilary Ward); Betty and Coretta, 2013 (made-for-TV; Angela Bassett); Boycott, 2001 (made-for-TV; Carmen Ejogo); King, 1978 (TV miniseries; Cicely Tyson); **Selma**, 2014 (Carmen Ejogo).

King, Don (1931- ; U.S. boxing promoter): Ali, 2001 (Mykelti Williamson); American Brawler, 2016 (Anthony Asse); Don King: Only in America, 1997 (made-for-TV; Ving Rhames); Hands of Stone, 2016 (Reg E. Cathey); The Last Punch, 2016 (Keith David).

King, Ernest Joseph (1878-1956; U.S. fleet admiral (five-star) of the U.S. Navy during WWII): **The Gallant Hours**, 1960 (Tyler McVey);

Hiroshima, 1995 (made-for-TV; James Bradford); The Last Bastion, 1984- (TV miniseries; Tim Robertson); **MacArthur**, 1977 (Russell D. Johnson); War and Remembrance, 1988 (TV miniseries; John Dehner); The Winds of War, 1983- (TV miniseries; John Dehner).

King, Martin Luther, Jr. (1929-1968; U.S. clergyman and civil rights activist): Ali, 2001 (LeVar Burton); All the Way, 2016 (made-for-TV; Anthony Mackie); American Playhouse, 1981- (TV series; "The Meeting," 1989 episode: Jason Bernard); Betty and Coretta, 2013 (made-for-TV; Malik Yoba); The Boy King, 1986 (made-for-TV; Fred Perron); Boycott, 2001 (made-for-TV; Jeffrey Wright); Crazy in Alabama, 1999 (Dudley F. Craig II); Freedom Song, 2000 (made-for-TV; Jeff Coopwood); Hoover vs. the Kennedys: The Second Civil War, 1987 (made-for-TV; Leland Gantt); **J. Edgar**, 2011 (himself in archive footage); Kennedy, 1983- (TV miniseries; Charles Brown); King, 1978 (TV miniseries; Paul Winfield); Lee Daniels' The Butler, 2013 (Nelsan Ellis); Path to War, 2002 (made-for-TV; Curtis McClarin); Prince Jack, 1985 (Robert Guillaume); **The Private Files of J. Edgar Hoover**, 1977 (Raymond St. Jacques); The Rosa Parks Story, 2002 (made-for-TV; Dexter King); **Selma**, 2014 (David Oyelowo); Selma, Lord, Selma, 1999 (made-for-TV; Clifton Powell); Timequest, 2000 (Reuben Yabuku); The Twilight Zone, 2002-2003 (TV series; "Memphis," 2003 episode: Efosa Otoumagie); Unconquered, 1989 (made-for-TV; Larry Riley); The Vernon Johns Story, 1989 (made-for-TV; Eric Ware). Note: For detailed information on King and his assassination, see my two-volume work *The Great Pictorial History of World Crime*, Volume I (History, Inc., 2004; illustrated [20 images] pages 171-180).

Kingston, William (Sir William Kingston; 1476-1540; British soldier and constable of the Tower of London during the reign of Henry VIII): Anna Boleyn, 1920 (Joseph Klein); **Anne of the Thousand Days**, 1969 (Esmond Knight); **The Private Life of Henry VIII**, 1933 (William Heughan).

Kipling, Rudyard (1865-1936; British short story writer, poet and novelist): **The Adventures of Mark Twain**, 1944 (Paul Scardon); Early Travellers in North America, 1992- (TV series; three 1992 episodes; Richard Lintern); **Gunga Din**, 1939 (Reginald Sheffield); **The Man Who Would Be King**, 1975 (Christopher Plummer); My Boy Jack, 2007 (David Haig); Shirley Temple's Storybook, 1958-1961 (TV series; "The Black Sheep," 1960 episode: Dennis Kohler); The Time Tunnel, 1966-1967 (TV series; "The Night of the Long Knives," 1966 episode: David Watson); Une maison, une histoire, 1980- (TV series; "Kipling," 1980 episode: Peter Birrel).

Kissinger, Henry Alfred (American statesman and 56th U.S. secretary of state; 1923-): Dick, 1999 (Saul Rubinek); **Nixon**, 1995 (Paul Sorvino).

Kitchener, Herbert (1st Earl of Kitchener; 1850-1916; British field marshal and early commandere-in-chief in WWI; drowned when en route to Russia aboard the HMS *Hampshire*, which exploded when striking a German mine): Around the World in 80 Days, 2004 (Ian McNeice); **Breaker Morant**, 1980 (Alan Cassell); Deadline Gallipoli, 2015- (TV miniseries; John Bell); Entente cordial, 1939 (Jean Galland); Gallipoli, 2015- (TV miniseries; Lachy Hulme); How Kitchener Was Betrayed, 1921 (Fred Paul); The Life and Times of David Lloyd George, 1981- (TV series; "Well, We're In," 1981 episode: Richard Beale); **Khartoum**, 1966 (Peter Arne); Outback, 1989 (Robert Davis); Paul Kruger, 1956 (Joel Herholdt); The Regiment, 1971- (TV series; "Ambush," 1973 episode: Terence Bayler); Six Dates with Barker, 1971- (TV series; "1915: Lola," 1971 episode: Valentine Dyall); That Englishwoman: An Account of the Life of Emily Hobhouse, 1990 (John Whiteley); Uncle Kruger, 1941 (Franz Schafheitlin); **Young Winston**, 1972 (John Mills).

Kluge, Gunther von (1882-1944; German field marshal in WWII; plotted to kill Hitler and committed suicide): Alcoa Theatre, 1957-1960 (TV series; "Operation Spark," 1959 episode: John Hoyt); BBC Sunday-Night Theatre, 1950-1959 (TV series; "Treason," 1959 episode: Clifford Evans); Die Stunde der Offiziere, 2004 (made-for-TV; Michael Hanemann); The Great Battle, 1973 (Hannjo Hasse); Operation Walkurie, 1971 (made-for-TV; Louis Arbessier); **Triple Cross**, 1966 (Paul Mesnier).

Knox, Henry (1750-1806; bookdealer, patriot and colonel in the Continental army under George Washington; in charge of artillery): The Adams Chronicles, 1976- (TV miniseries; Michael Egan); The Bastard, 1978 (made-for-TV; Alex Henteloff); George Washington II: The Forging of a Nation, 1986 (made-for-TV; Farnham Scott); John Adams, 2008 (TV miniseries; Del Pentecost); Liberty! The American Revolution, 1997 (TV miniseries; John Ellison Conlee); The Patriots, 1963 (made-for-TV; Herbert Nelson); The Rebels, 1979 (made-for-TV; John Chappell).

Knox, John (1514-1572; Scottish clergyman and leader of the Protestant Reformation): Border Warfare, 1990 (made-for-TV; Derek Anders); Gunpowder, Treason & Plot, 2004 (made-for-TV; Gary Lewis); The Heart of the Queen, 1940 (Ernst Stahl-Nachbaur); Here I Stand, 1977- (TV series; "Knox," 1977 episode: Fulton Mackay); The Loves of Mary, Queen of Scots, 1923 (Edward Sorley); Maria Stuart, Teil 1 und 2, 1927 (Franz Blei); **Mary of Scotland**, 1936 (Moroni Olsen); Mary, Queen of Scots, 1971 (Robert James); Nine Days a Queen, 1936 (John Laurie); Scotland's Story, 1984- (TV series; "Mary and an End to the French Connection," 1984 episode: Bill Simpson).

Knox, Robert (1792-1862; Scottish anatomist, ethnologist and physician, who purchased stolen bodies for his studies prior to the Anatomy Act of 1832, not knowing that some of these cadavers were murder victims supplied by killers William Burke and William Hare; Knox used sixteen such corpses as dissection material for his well-attended anatomy classes in Edinburgh, Scotland, in 1828; Hare turned state's evidence and Burke was hanged; Knox was not prosecuted, but his reputation badly damaged): The Alfred Hitchcock Hour, 1962-1965 (TV series; "The McGregor Affair," 1964 episode: John Hoyt); The Anatomist, 1939 (made-for-TV; Andrew Cruickshank); The Anatomist, 1956 (made-for-TV; Alastair Sim); The Body Snatcher, 1945 (role model for Henry Daniell); Burke and Hare, 1972 (Harry Andrews); Burke and Hare, 2010 (Tom Wilkinson); The Doctor and the Devils, 1985 (role model for Timothy Dalton); The Flesh and the Fiends, 1961 (Peter Cushing); Horror Maniacs, 1953 (role model for Arnold Bell); Mystery and Imagination, 1966-1970 (TV series; "The Body Snatcher," 1966 episode: Ian Holm). Note: For detailed information on Knox and Burke and Hare, see my two-volume work The Great Pictorial History of World Crime, Volume II (History, Inc., 2004; illustrated [11 images] pages 1023-1028).

Knox, William Franklin (aka: "Frank"; 1874-1944; U.S. newspaper editor, publisher and 46th U.S. secretary of the navy during WWII): **Pearl Harbor**, 2002 (Tom Everett); **Tora! Tora! Tora!**, 1970 (Leon Ames).

Koenig, Mark Anthony (American baseball player; 1904-1993): **The Babe Ruth Story**, 1948 (himself); **The Pride of the Yankees**, 1942 (himself).

Krueger, Walter (1881-1967; U.S. soldier, who rose from the rank of private to a four-star general; commanded the Sixth U.S. Army in the Southwest Pacific under the command of General of the Army Douglas MacArthur during WWII): **MacArthur**. 1977 (Everett Cooper).

Timothy Dalton (in role modeled on Dr. Robert Knox) in *The Doctor and the Devils*, 1985.

Krupa, Gene (1909-1973; U.S. musician and spectacular drummer): The Gene Krupa Story, 1959 (Sal Mineo).

Kubis, Jan (1913-1942; Czech resistance fighter, one of those who assassinated Nazi Governor Reinhard Heydrich of Czechoslovakia in June 1942, and who was trapped by German troops in a Prague church, committing suicide rather than being taken captive): Anthropoid, 2016 (Jamie Dornan); G.E. True, 1962- (TV series; "Heydrich," two 1963 episodes: Walter Linden); HHhH, 2016 (Jack O'Connell); Lidice, 2011 (Patrik Stanek); **Operation Daybreak**, 1975 (Timothy Bottoms). Note: For detailed information on Kubis and his assassination of Heydrich, see my two-volume work The Great Pictorial History of World Crime, Volume I (History, Inc., 2004; illustrated [9 images] pages 134-138).

Kublai Khan (1215-1294; Chinese emperor): **The Adventures of Marco Polo**, 1938 (George Barbier); Doctor Who, 1963-1989 (TV series; two 1964 episodes with Martin Miller as Kublai Khan); The Four Assassins, 1981 (Tung Chun Li); Into the Labyrinth, 1981-1982 (TV series; "Xanadu," 1982 episode: Peter Copley); Marco, 1973 (Zero Mostel); Marco Millions, 1939 (made-for-TV; Robert Harris); Marco Polo, 1982- (TV miniseries; Ruocheng Ying); Marco Polo, 2007 (made-for-TV; Brian Dennehy); Marco Polo, 2015- (TV series; Benedict Wong); Marco Polo: The Return to Xanadu, 2001 (animated; Michael Kostroff voiceover); **Marco the Magnificent**, 1966 (Anthony Quinn); Voyagers!, 1982-1983 (TV series; "The Travels of Marco…and Friends," 1982 episode: Key Luke).

Kurten, Peter (Kuerten; 1883-1931; aka: The Monster of Dusseldorf; The Vampire of Dusseldorf; German serial killer who murdered at least a dozen women and girls and who admitted that he attempted to drink his victims' blood after slaying them; he was beheaded): Conceptions of Murder, 1970 (TV series; "Peter and Maria," 1970 episode: Nigel Green); **M**, 1933 (role model for Peter Lorre); **M**, 1951 (role model for David Wayne); Normal the Dusseldorf Ripper, 2009 (Milan Knazko); The Secret Killer [AKA: The Vampire of Dusseldorf], 1965 (Robert Hossein). Note: For detailed information on Kurten, see my two-volume work, The Great Pictorial History of World Crime, Volume II (History, Inc., 2004; illustrated [12 images] pages 1085-1089).

Kutuzov, Mikhail (1745-1813; Russian soldier and field marshal of the Russian Empire): 1812, 1944 (Aleksei Dikij); Gusarskaya ballada, 1963 (Igor Ilyinsky); ITV Play of the Week, 1955-1974 (TV series; "War and Peace," 1963 episode: Steve Plytas); Scharnhorst, 1978 (TV series; Hans Maus); Voyna i mir IV: Pierre Bezukhov, 1967 (Boris Zakhavna); Voyna i mir III: 1812 god, 1967 (Boris Zakhava); **War and Peace**, 1956 (Oscar

Oscar Homolka (as Field Marshal Mikhail Kutuzov) and Mel Ferrer in *War and Peace*, 1956.

Homolka); **War and Peace**, 1968 (Boris Zakhava); War and Peace, 1972-1973 (TV miniseries; Frank Middlemass); War and Peace, 1991 (made-for-TV; Nikolai Okhotnikov); War and Peace, 2007 (TV miniseries; Vladimir Ilin).

La Guardia, Fiorello (1882-1947; U.S. politician and three-term mayor of NYC, 1934-1945): The Amazing Howard Hughes, 1977 (made-for-TV; Sorrell Brooke); **The Court Martial of Billy Mitchell**, 1955 (Phil Arnold); Hizzoner!, 1984 (made-for-TV; Tony Lo Bianco); Iron Jawed Angels, 2004 (made-for-TV; Vinny Genna); Madeline, 1989-2001 (animated TV series; Jim Byrnes voiceover); **The Pride of the Yankees**, 1942 (Dave Manley).

La Hire (Etienne de Vignolles; 1390-1443; French military commander during the Hundred Years' War and close comrade of Joan of Arc): Animated Hero Clasics, 1991-2005 (TV series; "Joan of Arc," 1996 episode: Robert Cottrell); BBC Play of the Month, 1965-1983 (TV series; "St. Joan," 1968 episode: Jack Watson); BBC Sunday-Night Theatre, 1950-1959 (TV series; "Festival Drama: Saint Joan," 1951 episode: Richard Warner); Jeanne d'Arc, le pouvoir de l'innocence, 1989 (made-for-TV; Claude Brosset); Jeanne la Pucelle 1—Les batailles, 1994 (Stephane Boucher); Jeanne la Pucelle II—Les prisons, 1994 (Stephane Boucher); **Joan of Arc**, 1948 (Ward Bond); Joan of Arc, 1999 (TV miniseries; Peter Strauss); Joan of Arc, 2003 (made-for-TV; Peter Kolar); Joan the Woman, 1916 (Hobart Bosworth); The Lark, 1957 (made-for-TV; Bruce Gordon); **The Messenger: The Story of Joan of Arc**, 1999 (Richard Ridings); Ordeal by Fire, 1957 (made-for-TV; Patrick Troughton); Saint Joan, 1957 (Patrick Barr); Saint Joan, 1967 (made-for-TV; Dana Elcar); Saint Joan the Maid, 1929 (Fernand Mailly); Sainte Jeanne, 1969 (made-for-TV; Gerard Dournel).

Lafayette, Marquis de (Gilbert du Motier; 1757-1834; French nobleman and politician during the American and French revolutions): **America**, 1924 (Paul Doucet); The Bastard, 1978 (made-for-TV; Ike Eisenmann); Cavalcade of America, 1952-1957 (TV series; "Plume of Honor," 1954 episode: Maurice Marsac); Daniel Boone, 1961-1970 (TV series; "Perilous Journey," 1965 episode: Albert Carrier); The Days That Made History, 2009- (TV series; Patrice Juiff); Jefferson in Paris, 1995 (Lambert Wilson); George Washington, 1984 (TV miniseries; Philip Casnoff); **The Howards of Virginia**, 1940 (Rafael Storm); Hundred Days, 1935 (Peter Erkelenz); **Janice Meredith**, 1924 (Nicolai Koesberg); La Malibran, 1944 (Jacques Varennes); Lafayette, 1963 (Michel Le Royer); The Lame Devil, 1948 (Jacques Varennes); Liberty! The American Revolution, 1997- (TV series: "The World Turned Upside Down: 1778-1783," 1997 episode: Sebastian Roche); Louis XVI, the Man Who

Didn't Want to Be King, 2011 (made-for-TV; Romain Deroo); Magnificent Doll, 1946 (Larry Steers); **Marie Antoinette**, 1938 (Robert Burton); Marie Antoinette, 1975- (TV series; Francois Dunoyer); Marie Antoinette—Das Leben einer Konigin, 1929 (Georg H. Schnell); **Napoleon**, 1927 (Boudreau); One Step Beyond, 1959-1961 (TV series; "Night of Decision," 1961 episode; Donald Buka); **The Patriot**, 2000 (Michael Neeley); The Rebels, 1979 (made-for-TV; Marc Vahanian); **Reign of Terror**, 1949 (Wilton Graff); Shadow of the Guillotine, 1956 (Guy Trejan); Sleepy Hollow, 2013- (TV series; "Incident at Stone Manor," 2016 episode: Matthew Luret); The Spirt of Lafayette, 1919 (Earl Schenck); TURN: Washington's Spies, 2015- (TV series, "Providence," 2015 episode: Brian Wiles); Valley Forge, 1975 (made-for-TV; Victor Garber); The Young Rebels, 1970-1971 (Philippe Forquet).

Lafitte, Jean (1776-1823; French pirate and privateer operating in the Gulf of Mexico in the early 19th Century): The Adventures of Jim Bowie, 1956-1958 (TV series; Peter Mamakos; Val Dufour); Andrew Jackson, 2007 (made-for-TV; Ulf Bjorlin); Bonanza, 1959-1973 (TV series; "The Gentleman from New Orleans," 1964 episode: John Dehner); **The Buccaneer**, 1938 (Fredric March); The Buccaneer, 1958 (Yul Brynner); Cavalcade of America, 1952-1957 (TV series; "The Pirate's Choice," 1953 episode: William Bishop); The Eagle of the Sea, 1926 (Ricardo Cortez); The Great Adventure, 1963-1964 (TV series; "The Pirate and the Patriot," 1964 episode: Ricardo Montalban); Last of the Buccaneers, 1950 (Paul Henreid); The Millionaire Pirate, 1919 (Monroe Salisbury); The Pirate and the Lawyer, 1955 (made-for-TV; Ray Danton); Privateer, 2009 (Nathan Grubbs); Swiss Family Robinson, 1975-1976 (TV series; Frank Langella); Voyagers!, 1982-1983 (TV series; "Old Hickory and the Pirate," 1982 episode: James Carroll Jordan). Note: For detailed information on Lafitte, see my two-volume work, *The Great Pictorial History of World Crime*, Volume II (History, Inc., 2004; illustrated [6 images] pages 1307-1310).

Lamb, Caroline (Lady Carolinne Lamb; 1785-1828; British aristocrat and novelist most known for her affair with Lord Byron; she was married to William Lamb who later became prime minister of England): The Bad Lord Byron, 1949 (Joan Greenwood); Byron, 2005 (made-for-TV; Camilla Power); Lady Caroline Lamb, 1972 (Sarah Miles); The Life of Lord Byron, 1922 (Mary Clare).

Lamon, Ward Hill (1828-1893; U.S. attorney and close friend and self-appointed bodyguard of President Abraham Lincoln, who was absent on the night of April 14, 1865, when Lincoln was mortally shot by assassin John Wilkes Booth at Ford's Theater in Washington, D.C.): Lincoln, 1988 (made-for-TV; Patrick Rowe); The Lincoln Conspiracy, 1977 (Len Wayland); **Saving Lincoln**, 2013 (Lea Coco).

LaMotta, Jake (1921- ; U.S. prizefighter and world middleweight champion): The Bronx Bull, 2016 (William Forsythe; Mojean Aria as young Jake LaMotta); **Raging Bull**, 1980 (Robert De Niro).

Landru, Henri Desire (aka: Bluebeard; 1869-1922; French serial killer who murdered at least eleven women to obtain their assets; he was executed by guillotine on February 25, 1922): Bluebeard, 1963 (Charles Denner); Bluebeard's Ten Honeymoons, 1960 (George Sanders); Charlie Chan at the Wax Museum, 1940 (exhibit); Desire Landru, 2005 (made-for-TV; Patrick Timsit); Landru: The Bluebeard of Paris, 1923 (Wilhelm Sichra); Men Think Only of That, 1954 (Edmund Tamiz); **Monsieur Verdoux**, 1947 (role model for Charles Chaplin). Note: For detailed information on Landru, see my two-volume work, *The Great Pictorial History of World Crime*, Volume II (History, Inc., 2004; illustrated [15 images] pages 1073-1079).

Langsdorff, Hans (1894-1939; German naval officer and captain of the German pocket battleship *Admiral Graf Spee*, which, after the vessel was badly damaged by British warships in the Battle of the River Platte, he scuttled the ship and committed suicide): Pursuit of the Graf Spee [aka: The Battle of the River Platte], 1957 (Peter Finch).

Langtry, Lillie (Lily Langtry; Emilie Charlotte Le Breton; aka: The Jersey Lily; 1853-1929; British-born actress who successfully toured the U.S., becoming the idol of self-styled Western judge Roy Bean): Edward the King, 1975 (TV series; two episodes: Francesca Annis); Gambler V: Playing for Keeps, 1994 (made-for-TV; Dixie Carter); Incident at Victoria Falls, 1992 (made-for-TV; Jenny Seagrove); **The Life and Times of Judge Roy Bean**, 1972 (Ava Gardner); Lillie, 1978 (TV miniseries; Francesca Annis); Oscar, 1985 (TV series; Catherine Strauss); The Trials of Oscar Wilde, 1960 (Naomi Chance); **The Westerner**, 1940 (Lilian Bond).

Lansdowne, Zachary (1888-1925; U.S. Navy officer and aviator who commanded the dirigible USS *Shenandoah*, and was killed when that lighter-than-air craft crashed on September 3, 1925): **The Court Martial of Billy Mitchell**, 1955 (Jack Lord).

Lansky, Meyer (1902-1983; U.S. gangster in NYC; board member and banker for the U.S. crime syndicate): Boardwalk Empire, 2010- (TV series; twenty-three episodes: Anatol Yusef); **Bugsy**, 1991 (Ben Kingsley); Donzi: The Legend, 2001 (Edward Asner); **The Godfather: Part II**, 1974 (role model for Lee Strasberg who plays "Hyman Roth"); Johnny Ryan, 1990 (made-for-TV; Lansky, 1999 (made-for-TV; Richard Dreyfuss; Joshua Praw and Ryan Merriman as Lansky as a boy); The Lost City, 2005 (Dustin Hoffman); The Making of the Mob: New York, 2015- (TV series; Ian Bell); Mob City, 2013 (TV series; Patrick Fischler; Jeff Baine as young Lansky); Mobsters, 1991 (Patrick Dempsey); Passion and Paradise, 1989 (made-for-TV; Sam Malkin); The Untouchables, 1993-1994 (TV series; Marc Grapey). Note: For detailed information on Lansky, see my books *World Encyclopedia of Organized Crime* (Paragon House, 1992; illustrated [11 images] pages 232-237) and the two-volume work, *The Great Pictorial History of World Crime*, Volume I (History, Inc., 2004; illustrated [10 images] pages 569-575).

Laval, Pierre (1883-1945; French politician and prime minister of France, 1942-1945; following WWII, he was convicted of high treason in collaborating with the Nazis, and executed by firing squad): **La Rafle**, 2012 (Jean-Michel Noiry); **Mission to Moscow**, 1943 (Alex Chivra); Petain, 1993 (Jean Yanne).

Lawrence, Gertrude (1898-1952; British actress, singer, dancer and musical comedy performer): Daphne, 2007 (Janet McTeer); Ike: The War Years, 1979 (TV series; Patricia Michael); ITV Sunday Night Drama, 1959-1980 (TV series; "Remember Jack Buchanan," 1980 episode: Cheryl Kennedy); **Stage Door Canteen**, 1943 (herself); **Star!**, 1968 (Julie Andrews).

Lawrence, Marjorie (Marjorie Florence Lawrence; 1907-1979; Australian operatic soprano, especially noted for her interpretation of operas by Richard Wagner): **Interrupted Melody**, 1955 (Eleanor Parker; singing vocals by Eileen Farrell).

Lawrence, T. E. (aka: Lawrence of Arabia; 1888-1935; British archeologist, diplomat and military officer who led Arab forces to victory in the Middle East during WWI): BBC Play of the Month, 1965-1983 (TV series; "Ross," 1970 episode: Ian McKellen); The English Harem, 2005 (made-for-TV; Andrew Havill); Great Performances, 1971- (TV series; "A Dangerous Man: Lawrence after Arabia," 1992 episode: Ralph Fiennes); **Lawrence of Arabia**, 1962 (Peter O'Toole); Lawrence of Arabia, 1969 (made-for-TV; Ugo Pagliai); Queen of the Desert, 2016 (Robert Pattinson); Voyagers!, 1982-1983 (TV series; "Worlds Apart,"

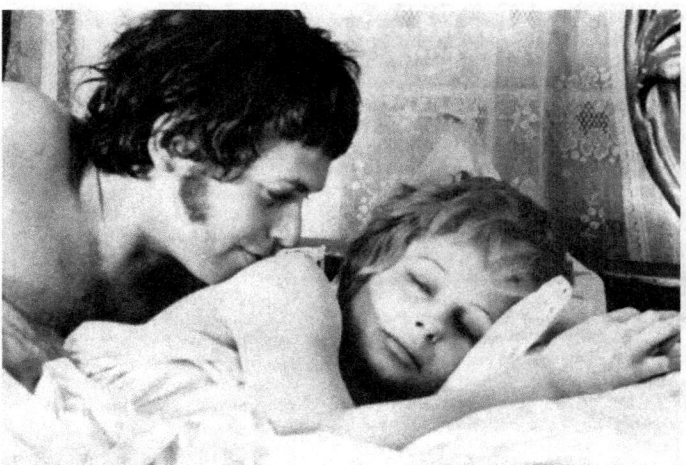

Jon Finch and Sarah Miles (as Lady Caroline Lamb) in *Lady Caroline Lamb,* **1972.**

1982 episode: Judson Scott); The Young Indiana Jones Chronicles, 1992-1993 (TV series; one 1992 episode with Joseph Bennett; two 1993 episodes with Douglas Henshall). For detailed information on Lawrence, see my book *Spies: A Narrative Encyclopedia of Dirty Tricks & Double Dealing from Biblical Times to Today* (M. Evans, 1997; illustrated pages 315-316).

Lazarus of Bethany (Saint Lazarus, who was reportedly restored to life by Jesus after having been dead for four days, one of the miracles of Jesus as recorded in the gospel of Saint John): Barabbas, 1953 (Georg Arlin); **Barabbas**, 1962 (Michael Gwynn); Barabbas, 2012 (Lorenzo Balducci); The Final Inquiry, 2006 (Giulio Base); **The Greatest Story Ever Told**, 1965 (Michael Tolan); **The King of Kings**, 1927 (Kenneth Thomson); Kristo, 1996 (Tonton Guitierrez); Jesus, 2000 (made-for-TV; Peter Gevisser); The Last Temptation of Christ, 1988 (Tomas Arana); The Living Christ Series, 1951 (TV miniseries; Bing Russell); The Miracle Maker, 2000 (Robert Duncan); Son of God, 2014 (Anas Chenin); The Son of God, 2016 (Norberto Arcusin).

Le Neve, Ethel (Ethel Clara Neave; 1883-1967; British typist who became the mistress of Dr. Hawley Harvey Crippen and over whom Crippen murdered his wife in 1910; the couple fled to the U.S., with Le Neve dressed as a boy, but they were arrested upon arrival; she was exonerated at Crippen's trial): Detective, 1964-1969 (TV series; "Crime of Passion," 1968 episode: Marion [Marian] Diamond); Dr. Crippen, 1942 (Gertrud Meyen); Dr. Crippen, 1964 (Samantha Eggar); Lady Killers, 1980-1981 (TV series; "Miss Elmore," 1981 episode: Hannah Gordon); The Last Secret of Dr. Crippen, 2004 (Tamara Ellis); **The Suspect**, 1944 (role model for Ella Raines); Theatre Royal, 1955- (TV series; "The Case of Dr. Crippen," 1956 episode: Priscilla Morgan); **We Are Not Alone**, 1939 (role model for Jane Bryan). Note: For detailed information on Le Neve, see my book *World Encyclopedia of 20th Century Murder* (Paragon House, 1992; illustrated [9 images] pages 145-152).

Ledbetter, Huddie (1888-1949; U.S. folk and blues musician): **Leadbelly**, 1976 (Roger E. Mosley).

Lee, Arthur (1740-1792; U.S. physician, diplomat and spy during the American Revolution): Beaumarchais the Scoundrel, 1997 (Dominic Gould); **Janice Meredith**, 1924 (Joe Raleigh); **John Paul Jones**, 1959 (MacDonald Parke).

Lee, Gypsy Rose (Rose Louise Hovick; 1911-1970; U.S. burlesque performer): **Gypsy**, 1962 (Natalie Wood); Gypsy, 1993 (Cynthia Gibb).

Lee, Richard Henry (1732-1794; U.S. statesman and member of the

Robert De Niro (as prizefighter Jake LaMotta) in *Raging Bull*, 1980.

Continental Congress; signer of the Declaration of Independence): **America**, 1924 (P.R. Scammon); George Washington, 1984 (TV miniseries; J. Kenneth Campbell); A More Perfect Union: America Becomes a Nation, 1989 (Bruce Eaton); **1776**, 1972 (Ron Holgate).

Lee, Robert E. (Robert Edward Lee; 1807-1870; U.S. military leader and commander-in-chief of the Confederate army of Northern Virginia during the American Civil War): **Abe Lincoln in Illinois**, 1940 (George Irving); **Abraham Lincoln**, 1930 (Hobart Bosworth); **The Birth of a Nation**, 1915 (Howard Gaye); The Blue and the Gray, 1982 (TV miniseries; Robert Symonds); Carolina, 1934 (John Elliott); The Civil War, 1990 (TV miniseries; George Black voiceover); The Dramatic Life of Abraham Lincoln, 1924 (Jim Welch); **Gettysburg**, 1993 (Martin Sheen); **Gods and Generals**, 2003 (Robert Duvall); The Great John Ericsson, 1938 (Yngve Nyqvist); The Heart of Maryland, 1927 (Jim Welch); In the Days of Buffalo Bill, 1922 (Lafayette McKee); **Lincoln**, 2012 (Christopher Boyer); North and South, Book II, 1986 (TV miniseries; William Schallert); Omnibus, 1952-1961 (TV series; "Lee at Gettysburg," 1957 episode: James Daly); Only the Brave, 1930 (John Elliott); Operator 13, 1934 (John Elliott); The Rebel, 1959-1961 (TV series; "Johnny Yuma at Appomatox," 1960 episode: George Macready); **Run of the Arrow**, 1957 (Frank Baker); Salome Where She Danced, 1945 (John Litel); **Santa Fe Trail**, 1940 (Moroni Olsen); Seminole Uprising, 1955 (Richard H. Cutting); Sunday Showcase, 1959-1961 (TV series; "An American Heritage: Shadow of a Soldier," 1960 episode: John Baragrey; "An American Heritage: Gentleman's Decision," 1961 episode: Dean Jagger); The Warrens of Virginia, 1924 (J. Barney Sherry); You Are There, 1953-1957 (TV series; "Grant and Lee at Appomattox, 1953 and 1955 episodes: Paul Birch).

Lee, Robert E, Jr. (1843-1914; U.S. planter and author; son of General Robert E. Lee, who served as an officer in the Confederate army of Northern Virginia during the American Civil War): **Gods and Generals**, 2003 (Jeremy Beck).

Lees, Robert James (1849-1931; British spiritualist, medium, writer and preacher of the Victorian era, who reportedly knew the identity of Jack the Ripper, the enigmatic killer of the Whitechapel murders of 1888): **Murder by Decree**, 1979 (Donald Sutherland).

LeHand, Marguerite (1898-1944; aka: "Missy"; U.S. private secretary to U.S. President Franklin D. Roosevelt): Eleanor and Franklin: The White House Years, 1977 (made-for-TV; Priscilla Pointer); Hyde Park on Hudson, 2012 (Elizabeth Marvel); **Sunrise at Campobello**, 1960 (Jean Hagen).

Leigh-Mallory, Trafford (1892-1944; British air marshal in WWII): **The Battle of Britain**, 1969 (Patrick Wymark); Dieppe, 1993 (made-for-TV; Benedict Campbell).

LeMay, Curtis (1906-1990; U.S. pilot and four-star general of the U.S. Air Force who commanded air forces in the Pacific Theater of WWII; engineered the Berlin Airlift and later commanded Strategic Air Command [SAC]): **Above and Beyond**, 1953 (Jim Backus); Dante's Inferno, 2007 (Matt Besser); Enola Gay: The Men, the Mission, the Atomic Bomb, 1980 (made-for-TV; Than Wyenn); Hiroshima, 1995 (made-for-TV; Cedric Smith); Kennedy, 1983- (TV miniseries; Barton Heyman); Man, Moment, Machine, 2005-2007 (TV series; "JFK and the Crisis Crusader," 2007 episode: John White); The Missiles of October, 1974 (made-for-TV; Robert P. Lieb); Race for the Bomb, 1987- (TV series; Lloyd Bochner); Thirteen Days, 2000 (Kevin Conway); **The Wild Blue Yonder**, 1951 (William Witney).

Lenin, Vladimir (1870-1924; Marxist leader of the Bolshevik-communist revolution in Russia): British Agent, 1934 (Tenen Holtz); Die Brandstifter Europas, 1926 (Eugen Dumont); Dimitrije Tucovic, 1973 (TV series; Milos Zutic); Ernst Thalmann—Sohn seiner Klasse, 1954 (Peter Schorn); Fall of Eagles, 1974 (TV miniseries; Patrick Stewart); ITV Television Playhouse, 1955-1967 (TV series; "Blood on the Snow," 1958 episode: Donald Pleasence); Lenin in October, 1937 (Boris Shchukin); Lenin in Paris, 1981 (Yury Kayurov); Lenin: The Train, 1988 (made-for-TV; Ben Kingsley); Lenin, You Rascal, You, 1972 (Peter Steen); The Man with the Gun, 1938 (Maxim Shtraukh); New Horizons, 1939 (Maxim Shtraukh); **Nicholas and Alexandra**, 1971 (Michael Bryant); Northern Exposure, 1990-1995 (TV series; "Zarya," 1994 episode: Christopher Neame); October [Ten Days That Shook the World], 1928 (Vasili Nikandrov); **Oh! What a Lovely War**, 1969 (John Gabriel); **Reds**, 1981 (Roger Sloman); Reilly: Ace of Spies, 1983- (TV miniseries; Kenneth Cranham); The Romanovs: An Imperial Family, 2000 (Alexander Filippenko); Stalin, 1992 (made-for-TV; Maximilian Schell); **Ten Days That Shook the World**, 1928 (Vasili Nikandrov); They Wanted Peace, 1938 (K. Myuffke); Thirty-Minute Theatre, 1965-1973 (TV series; "Revolutions: Lenin," 1970 episode: Lee Montague); Trust, 1970 (Kirill Lavrov); V dni oktyabrya, 1958 (V. Chestnokov); Witness to Yesterday, 1998- (TV series; "Vladimir Lenin," 1998 episode: Michael Ironside); The World Wars, 2014- (TV series; C. Conrad Cady).

Leonowens, Anna (1831-1915, who served as governess and teacher to the harem of thirty-nine wives and concubines and eighty-two children of Mongkut, king of Siam, present-day Thailand): Anna and the King, 1972- (TV series; Semantha Eggar); Anna and the King, 1999 (Jodie Foster); **Anna and the King of Siam**, 1946 (Irene Dunne); **The King and I**, 1956 (Deborah Kerr); The King and I, 1999 (animated; Miranda Richardson voiceover; Christiane Noll singing voice).

Leopold, Nathan, Jr. (1904-1971; wealthy homosexual Chicago youth who, along with partner Richard Loeb, committed what both thought would be the "perfect murder" when kidnapping and killing 14-year-old Bobby Franks in May 1924; he was paroled in 1958): **Compulsion**, 1959 (role model for Dean Stockwell); **Rope**, 1948 (role model for Farley Granger); Swoon, 1992 (Craig Chester). Note: For detailed information on Leopold and Loeb, see my books *World Encyclopedia of 20th Century Murder* (Paragon House; 1992; illustrated [12 images] pages 353-362), and *The Great Pictorial History of World Crime*, Volume II (History, Inc., 2004; illustrated [31 images] pages 840-858).

Lepke: see Buchalter, Louis.

Leslie, Maxwell Franklin (aka: Max; 1902-1985; U.S. admiral, who led a squadron of carrier-based bombers during the Battle of Midway and was instrumental in destroying several Japanese carriers in what was the decisive naval battle of WWII): **Midway**, 1976 (Monte Markham).

Lewis, Jerry Lee (1935- ; U.S. rock 'n' roll and country singer): Mr. Rock 'n' Roll: The Alan Freed Story, 1999 (made-for-TV; James C. Victor).

Lewis, Meriwether (1774-1809; U.S. explorer and soldier): Death Valley Days, 1952-1970 (TV series; 'The Girl Who Walked the West," 1967 episode; Dick Simmons); **The Far Horizons**, 1955 (Fred MacMurray); Lewis and Clark, 2016- (TV miniseries; Casey Affleck); **Night at the Museum**, 2006 (Martin Christopher); The Seekers, 1979 (made-for-TV; Skip Riley); Voyagers!, 1982-1983 (TV series; "Old Hickory and the Pirate," 1982 episode: Bill McLaughlin); You Are There, 1953-1971 (TV series; "Lewis and Clark Expedition," 1971 episode: Earl Hindman).

Liddil, Dick (James Andrew Liddil; 1852-1901; U.S. western outlaw; member of the James-Younger gang): **The Assassination of Jesse James by the Coward Robert Ford**, 2007 (Paul Schneider); **The Great Missouri Raid**, 1951 (Alan Wells); The Last Days of Frank and Jesse James, 1986 (made-for-TV; Andy Stahl).

Liddy, G. Gordon (George Gordon Battle Liddy; 1930- ; Amercian attorney, FBI agent and chief director of the 1972 Watergate burglaries for which he was convicted and imprisoned): Blind Ambition, 1979 (TV miniseries; William Daniels); Dick, 1999 (Harry Shearer); **Nixon**, 1995 (John Diehl).

Liebknecht, Karl (1871-1919; German socialist, who co-founded the Spartacist League and the Communist Party of Germany with Rosa Luxemburg and who was, with Luxemburg, assassinated by right-wing members of the Freikorps): Bruder, nicht schiessen!, 1989 (made-for-TV; Klaus-Peter Thiele); Der Fall Liebknecht-Luxemburg, 1969 (made-for-TV; Richard Lauffen); Ernst Thalmann—Sohn seiner Klasse, 1954 (Martin Florchinger); Europas letzter Sommer, 2012 (made-for-TV; Uwe Poppe); Jahreswechsel Zeitenwechsel, 1988 (made-for-TV; Ernst Meincke); **Rosa Luxemburg**, 1987 (Otto Sander); Solange Leben in mir ist, 1965 (Horst Schulze); Trotz alledem!, 1972 (Horst Schulze). Note: For detailed information on the assassination of Liebknecht and Luxemburg, see my two-volume work *The Great Pictorial History of World Crime*, Volume I (History, Inc., 2004; illustrated [4 images] pages 118-120).

Lillie, Gordon William (1860-1942; aka: Pawnee Bill; U.S. businessman and showman and onetime partner with Buffalo Bill's Wild West Show): **Annie Get Your Gun**, 1950 (Edward Arnold); Annie Get Your Gun, 1967 (made-for-TV; Jack Dabdoub).

Lincoln, Abraham (American politician; 1809-1865; 16th President of the U.S.): Abe Lincoln: Freedom Fighter, 1978 (Allen Williams); **Abe Lincoln in Illinois**, 1940 (Raymond Massey); Abe Lincoln in Illinois, 1945 (made-for-TV; Stephen Courtleigh); Abe Lincoln in Illinois, 1964 (made-for-TV; Jason Robards Jr.); **Abraham Lincoln**, 1930 (Walter Huston); Abraham Lincoln: Vampire Hunter, 2012 (Benjamin Walker as adult Lincoln; Lux Haney-Jardine as young Lincoln); Action Family, 1986 (made-for-TV; Drummond Erskine); The Adams Chronicles, 1976 (TV miniseries; Stephen D. Newman); Alcoa Presents: One Step Beyond, 1959-1961 (TV series; "The Day the World Wept: The Lincoln Story," 1960 episode: Barry Atwater); America: A Call to Greatness, 1995 (made-for-TV; Raymond Baker); American Inventory, 1951-1952 (TV series; "Abe Lincoln's Story,"1952 episode: Crahan Denton);

Ella Raines (role modeled on Ethel Le Neve) with Charles Laughton in *The Suspect*, 1944.

Apache Ambush, 1955 (James Griffith); Appointment with Destiny, 1971-1973 (TV series; "Surrender at Appomattox," 1972 episode: Joseph Leisch Jr.); Are We Civilized?, 1934 (Frank McGlynn Sr.); Batman: The Brave and the Bold, 2008-2011 (animated TV series; Peter Renaday voiceover); **The Battle Cry of Peace**, 1915 (William J. Ferguson); The Big Picture, 1989 (Richard Blake); Bill and Ted's Excellent Adventure, 1989 (Robert Barron); **The Birth of a Nation**, 1915 (Joseph Henabery); The Blue and the Gray, 1982 (TV miniseries; Gregory Peck); Captains and Kings, 1976 (TV series; Ford Rainey); Carl Schurz, 1968 (Christian Rode); Cavalcade of America, 1952-1957 (TV series; "Moonlight Witness," 1954 episode: Bruce Bennett; "New Salem Story," 1953 episode: James Griffith; "The Palmetto Conspiracy," 1955 episode: Richard Hale); The Civil War, 1990 (TV miniseries; Sam Waterston voiceover); **The Conspirator**, 2011 (Gerald Bestrom); Courage of the West, 1937 (Albert Russell); The Crisis, 1916 (Sam D. Drane); Cybill, 1995-1998 (TV series; "It's for You, Mr. Lincoln," 1996 episode: Charles L. Brame); The Day Lincoln Was Shot, 1998 (made-for-TV; Lance Henriksen); Days That Shook the World, 2003-2013 (TV series; "Terror Made in America: Assassination of Abraham Lincoln...," 2004 episode: Jim Babel); The Dramatic Life of Abraham Lincoln, 1924 (George A. Billings as adult Lincoln; Danny Hoy as young Lincoln); Dream West, 1986 (TV miniseries; F. Murray Abraham); The DuPont Show of the Month, 1957-1961 (TV series; "The Lincoln Murder Case," 1961 episode: Drummond Erskine); The Faking of the President, 1976 (William J. Daprato); FDR: A One Man Show, 1987 (made-for-TV; Drummond Erskine); Ford Star Jubilee, 1955-1956 (TV series; "The Day Lincoln Was Shot," 1956 episode: Raymond Massey); **The Fortune Cookie**, 1966 (John Anderson); G. E. True Theater, 1953-1962 (TV series: "Prologue to Glory," 1956 episode: John Ireland); The Great Battles of the Civil War, 1994 (TV miniseries; Charlton Heston); The Great John Ericsson, 1938 (John Ericsson); The Great Man's Whiskers, 1973 (made-for-TV; Dennis Weaver); Guardian of the Wilderness, 1976 (Ford Rainey); Hands Up!, 1926 (George A. Billings); Happy Gilmore, 1996 (Charles L. Brame); The Heart of Lincoln, 1915 (Francis Ford); The Heart of Maryland, 1927 (Charles Edward Bull); Hearts in Bondage, 1936 (Frank McGlynn Sr.); Her Country's Call, 1917 (Benjamin Chapin); Histeria!, 1998-2000 (animated TV series; four 1998 segments: Maurice LaMarche voiceover); **How the West Was Won**, 1962 (Raymond Massey); In the Days of Buffalo Bill, 1922 (Joel Day); **The Iron Horse**, 1924 (Charles Edward Bull); Ironclads, 1991 (made-for-TV; James Getty); **The Lego Movie**, 2014 (Orville Forte voiceover); Lincoln, 1974-1975 (TV series; Hal Holbrook); Lincoln, 1988 (TV miniseries; Sam Waterston); Lincoln, 1992 (made-for-TV; Jason Robards Jr.); **Lincoln**, 2012 (Daniel Day-Lewis); Lincoln: American Mastermind, 2009 (made-for-TV; Fritz Klein); Lincoln and the War Within,

Henry Fonda (as Abraham Lincoln) in *Young Mr. Lincoln,* **1939.**

1992 (made-for-TV; Jason Robards Jr.); The Lincoln Conspiracy, 1977 (John Anderson); The Lincoln Cycle, 1917 (Benjamin Chapin); The Lincoln-Douglas Debates, 1976 (made-for-TV; Scott Mandrell); Lincoln-Douglas Galesburg Debate, 1994 (made-for-TV; Michael Krebs); The Lone Ranger, 1938 (Frank McGlynn Sr.); **The Littlest Rebel**, 1935 (Frank McGlynn Sr.); Lost River: Lincoln's Secret Weapon, 2009 (Fritz Klein); Lux Video Theater, 1950-1959 (TV series; "Abe Lincoln in Illinois," 1951 episode: Raymond Massey); The Mad Empress, 1939 (Mexican version of **Juarez**, 1939; Frank McGlynn Sr.); Madame Who, 1918 (Clarence Barr); Medic, 1954-1956 (TV series; "Black Friday," 1955 episode: Austin Green); Mister Lincoln, 1981 (made-for-TV; Roy Dotrice); My Own United States, 1918 (Gerald Day); New Mexico, 1951 (Hans Conried); North and South, Book II, 1986 (TV miniseries; Hal Holbrook); **Of Human Hearts**, 1938 (John Carradine); Omnibus, 1952-1961 (TV series; "Mr. Lincoln," five parts, 1952-1953: Royal Dano); Out of This World, 1987-1991 (TV series; "Honest Evie," 1989 episode: Robert Barron); The Perfect Tribute, 1991 (made-for-TV; Jason Robards Jr.); Philco-Goodyear Television Playhouse, 1948-1956 (TV series; "Ann Rutledge," 1950 episode: Stephen Courtleigh); **The Plainsman**, 1936 (Frank McGlynn Sr.); Police Squad!, 1982 (TV series; many segments: Rex Hamilton); **Prince of Players**, 1955 (Stanley Hall); **The Prisoner of Shark Island**, 1936 (Frank McGlynn Sr.); Pulitzer Prize Playhouse, 1950-1952 (TV series; "Abe Lincoln in Illinois," 1950 episode: Raymond Massey); Red Dwarf, 1988- (TV series; "Meltdown," 1991 episode: Jack Klaff); The Right Man, 1960 (made-for-TV; Richard Boone); The Rivalry, 1975 (made-for-TV; Arthur Hill); Riverboat, 1959-1961 (TV series; "No Bridge on the River," 1960 episode: Sandy Kenyon); Rock Island Trail, 1950 (Jeff Corey); San Antoine, 1953 (Richard Hale); **Saving Lincoln**, 2013 (Tom Amandes); Schlitz Playhouse, 1951-1959 (TV series; "Washington Incident," 1956 episode: Mark Stevens); Screen Director's Playhouse, 1955-1956 (TV series; "Lincoln's Doctor's Dog," 1955 episode: Robert Ryan); The Secret Diary of Desmond Pfeiffer, 1998 (TV series; four segments: Dann Florek); The Slacker's Heart, 1917 (Benjamin Chapin); Stage to Tucson, 1950 (James Griffith); The Story of Mankind, 1957 (Austin Green); Studio One in Hollywood, 1948-1958 (TV series; "Abraham Lincoln," 1952 episode: Robert Pastene); Sunday Showcase, 1959-1961 (TV series; "An American Heritage: Shadow of a Soldier," 1960 episode: Ford Rainey); Tad, 1995 (made-for TV; Kris Kristofferson); **The Tall Target**, 1951 (Leslie Kimmell); Telephone Time, 1956-1958 (TV series; "The Stepmother," 1956 episode: Ronnie Lee); They've Killed President Lincoln!, 1971 (made-for-TV; Joseph Leisch Jr.); This Is America, Charlie Brown, 1988 (TV miniseries; "The Smithsonian and the Presidency," 1989 episode: Frank Welker); The Time Tunnel, 1966-1967 (TV series; "The Death Trap," 1966 episode: Ford Rainey); Trailin' West, 1936

(Robert Barrat); Treasure of the Aztecs, 1965 (Jeff Corey); TV Reader's Digest, 1955-1956 (TV series; "How Chance Made Lincoln President," 1955 episode: Richard Gaines); Twilight Zone, 1959-1964 (TV series; "The Passerby," 1961 episode: Austin Green); Two Fisted Justice, 1931 (Joseph Mills); **Virginia City**, 1940 (Victor Kilian); Voyagers!, 1982-1983 (TV series; "The Day the Rebs Took Lincoln," 1982 episode: John Anderson); Weird Science, 1994-1996 (TV series; "Community Property," 1996 episode: Gary Bullock); **Wells Fargo**, 1937 (Frank McGlynn Sr.); Western Gold, 1937 (Frank McGlynn Sr.); Woman with a Sword, 1952 (made-for-TV; Henry Sharp); Wrongfully Accused, 1998 (Mark Francis); You Are There, 1953-1957 (TV series; "The Emancipation Proclamation," 1955 episode: Jeff Morrow; "The Gettysburg Address," 1953 episode: Paul Tripp; "The Nomination of Abraham Lincoln," 1954 episode: Jeff Morrow); **Young Mr. Lincoln**, 1939 (Henry Fonda); Zoolander, 2001 (Charles L. Brame). Note: For detailed information on Lincoln and his assassination, see my two-volume work, *The Great Pictorial History of World Crime*, Volume I (History, Inc., 2004; illustrated [47 images] pages 26-44).

Lincoln, Mary Todd (1818-1882; First Lady and wife of U.S. President Abraham Lincoln): **Abe Lincoln in Illinois**, 1940 (Ruth Gordon); Abe Lincoln in Illinois, 1964 (made-for-TV; Kate Reid); **Abraham Lincoln**, 1930 (Kay Hammond); Abrham Lincoln: Vampire Hunter, 2012 (Mary Elizabeth Winstead); **The Birth of a Nation**, 1915 (Alberta Lee); The Blue and the Gray, 1982 (TV miniseries; Janice Carroll); **The Conspirator**, 2011 (Marshell Canney); The Day Lincoln Was Shot, 1998 (made-for-TV; Donna Murphy); Days That Shook the World, 2003-2013 (TV series; "Terror Made in America: Assassination of Abraham Lincoln...," 2004 episode: Cathy Scearce); Der Tod des Prasidenten, 1967 (Marianne Wischmann); The Dramatic Life of Abraham Lincoln, 1924 (Nell Craig); Ford Star Jubilee, 1955-1956 (TV series; "The Day Lincoln Was Shot," 1956 episode: Lillian Gish); The Heart of Maryland, 1927 (Madge Hunt); The Last of Mrs. Lincoln, 1976 (made-for-TV; Julie Harris); Lincoln, 1974-1975 (TV series; Sada Thompson); Lincoln, 1988 (TV miniseries; Mary Tyler Moore); **Lincoln**, 2012 (Sally Field); The Lincoln Conspiracy, 1977 (Frances Fordham); Look Away, 1987 (made-for-TV; Ellen Burstyn); Lost River: Lincoln's Secret Weapon, 2009 (Georgia Goodwin); **Prince of Players**, 1955 (Sarah Padden); **The Prisoner of Shark Island**, 1936 (Leila McIntyre); **Saving Lincoln**, 2013 (Penelope Ann Miller); They've Killed President Lincoln!, 1971 (made-for-TV; Dorothea Hammond); **Young Mr. Lincoln**, 1939 (Marjorie Weaver).

Lincoln, Robert Todd (1843-1926; first and oldest son of U.S. President Abraham Lincoln): Abe Lincoln in Illinois, 1964 (made-for-TV; Tom Slater); The Day Lincoln Was Shot, 1998 (made-for-TV; Wil Wheaton); Days That Shook the World, 2003-2013 (TV series; "Terror Made in America: Assassination of Abraham Lincoln...," 2004 episode: J. Lublinkhof); The Last of Mrs. Lincoln, 1976 (made-for-TV; Michael Cristofer); Lincoln, 1974-1975 (TV series; James Carroll Jordan); Lincoln, 1988 (TV miniseries; Gregory Cooke); **Lincoln**, 2012 (Joseph Gordon-Levitt); Lost River: Lincoln's Secret Weapon, 2009 (Benjamin Heflin); They've Killed President Lincoln!, 1971 (made-for-TV; Greg Nickerson).

Lincoln, Thomas (1853-1871; AKA: "Tad"; fourth and youngest son of Abraham and Mary Lincoln): **Abe Lincoln in Illinois**, 1940 (Henry Blair); **Abraham Lincoln**, 1930 (Gordon Thorpe); The Day Lincoln Was Shot, 1998 (made-for-TV; Adam Lamberg); Days That Shook the World, 2003-2013 (TV series; "Terror Made in America: Assassination of Abraham Lincoln...," 2004 episode: Lucas Varsano); The Dramatic Life of Abraham Lincoln, 1924 (Newton Hall); The Last of Mrs. Lincoln, 1976 (made-for-TV; Bobby Benson); Lincoln, 1974-1975 (TV series; John Levin); Lincoln, 1988 (made-for-TV; Troy Sweeney); **Lincoln**, 2012 (Gulliver McGrath); **Saving Lincoln**, 2013 (Joshua Rush).

Lincoln, William Wallace (1850-1862; aka: "Willie"; third son of Abraham and Mary Lincoln): **Abe Lincoln in Illinois**, 1940 (Sonny Bupp); Abe Lincoln in Illinois, 1964 (made-for-TV; Casey Peters); Abraham Lincoln: Vampire Hunter, 2012 (Cameron M. Brown); The Dramatic Life of Abraham Lincoln, 1924 (Michael D. Moore); Lincoln, 1974-1975 (TV series; Michael-James Wixted); Lincoln, 1988 (made-for-TV; Paul Welch); **Lincoln**, 2012 (Chase Edmonds); **Saving Lincoln**, 2013 (Elijah Nelson).

Lind, Jenny (1820-1887; Johanna Maria Lind; aka: "Swedish Nightingale"; esteemed opera singer of the 19th Century): Barnum!, 1986 (made-for-TV; Christina Collier); Barnum, 1986 (made-for-TV; Hanna Schygulla); Come to the Window, 1954 (made-for-TV; Jan Clayton); Die schwedische Nachtigall, 1941 (Ilse Werner); The Great John Ericsson, 1938 (Helga Gorlin); H.C. Andersen, 2005 (made-for-TV; Gisela Stille); H.C. Andersen's The Long Shadow, 1998 (animated; Tammi Øst); Here Comes the Brides, 1968-1970 (TV series; "The Fetching of Jenny," 1969 episode: Mala Powers); Jenny Lind, 1931 (Grace Moore); A Lady's Morals, 1930 (Grace Moore); Matinee Theatre, 1955-1958 (TV series; "The Legend of Jenny Lind," 1956 episode: Dorothy Kirsten); **The Mighty Barnum**, 1934 (Virginia Bruce; Francia White singing voiceover); Mr. H.C. Andersen, 1950 (June Elvin); Once upon a Time, 2005 (made-for-TV; Malin Christensson); P.T. Barnum, 1999 (made-for-TV; Jayne Heitmeyer); The Silver Swan, 1952 (TV series; "Gerald," 1953 episode: Elsie Morison); You Are There, 1953-1971 (TV series; "P.T. Barnum Presents Jenny Lind [September 11, 1850]," 1955 episode: Leni Landry).

Lindbergh, Anne Morrow (Anne Spencer Morrow Lindbergh; 1906-2001; author and wife of famed aviator Charles A. Lindbergh): Forensic Files, 2000- (TV series; "The Lindbergh Baby Kidnapping: Investigation Reopened," 2005 episode: Sara Pauley); Kidnap, 1968 (made-for-TV; Christa Ruth Oenicke); The Lindbergh Kidnapping Case, 1976 (made-for-TV; Sian Barbara Allen). Note: For detailed information on the Lindbergh kidnapping, see my two-volume work *The Great Pictorial History of World Crime*, Volume I (History, Inc., 2004; illustrated [34 images] pages 643-663).

Lindbergh, Charles A. (U.S. aviation pioneer and pilot who was the first to fly solo nonstop across the Atlantic Ocean from Long Island, New York, to Paris, France, on May 20-21, 1927, a distance of 3,600 miles; 1902-1974): Crime of the Century, 1996 (made-for-TV; Scott N. Stevens); Freedom to Speak, 1982 (TV miniseries; John Rubenstein); **J. Edgar**, 2011 (Josh Lucas); Kidnap, 1968 (made-for-TV; Rolf Becker); The Lindbergh Kidnapping Case, 1976 (made-for-TV; Cliff De Young); Second Verdict, 1976 (TV series; "The Lindbergh Kidnapping," 1976 episode: Burnell Tucker); Secret Lives of Charles Lindbergh, 2009 (made-for-TV; Chase Otley); **The Spirit of St. Louis**, 1957 (James Stewart); Touched by an Angel, 1994-2003 (TV series; "Godspeed," 1999 episode: Ned Vaughn); Voyagers!, 1982-1983 (TV miniseries; "An Arrow Pointing East," 1982 episode: Jonathan Frakes). Note: For detailed information on the Lindbergh kidnapping, see my two-volume work *The Great Pictorial History of World Crime*, Volume I (History, Inc., 2004; illustrated [34 images] pages 643-663).

Lingle, Alfred Jr. (aka: Jake; 1891-1930; U.S. newspaperman and leg reporter for the Chicago *Tribune* who was on the secret payroll of crime boss Al Capone as an informer and who was ordered killed by Capone when he switched allegiance to rival gangster George "Bugs" Moran): **Al Capone**, 1959 (role model for Martin Balsam); The Lady in Red, 1979 (Robert Hogan).

Lister, Joseph (1827-1912; British surgeon and pioneer of antiseptic surgery who employed Louis Pasteur's scientific methods in microbiology in advocating sterile surgery): **The Story of Louis Pasteur**, 1936 (Hal-

Dirk Bogarde (as Franz Liszt) in *Song Without End*, 1960.

liwell Hobbes).

Liszt, Franz (1811-1886; Hungarian composer): Anni, 1948 (Eugen Preiss); At the Order of the Czar, 1954 (Jacques Francois); Chopin. Pragnienie milosci, 2004 (Michal Konarski); A Dream of Love, 1939 (Ian Colin; Bertram Wallis as Liszt in old age); Dreams of Love, 1937 (Ferenc Taray); Dreams of Love, 1954 (Pierre Richard-Willm); Erkel, 1952 (Ivan Darvas); Farewell, 1935 (aka: La chanson de l'adieu; Un amour de Frederic Chopin; Daniel Lecourtois); Farewell Waltz, 1934 (Hans Schlenck); George Sand, 1958- (TV series; Maria Fernanda); George Who?, 1973 (Maxence Mailfort); Hungarian Rhapsody, 1954 (Paul Hubschmid); **Impromptu**, 1991 (Julian Sands); La musique de l'amour: Robert et Clara, 1995 (made-for-TV; Alexander Cherednik); La Valse de l'adieu, 1928 (Jacques Maury); La vie de Berlioz, 1983 (TV miniseries; Peter Trokan); Liebestraume, 1935 (Franz Herterich); Liszt Ferenc, 1982 (TV miniseries; Ivan Darvas; Geza Hegedus D.; Tomas Bolba; Bela Simon); Lisztomania, 1975 (Roger Daltrey); Liszt's Rhapsody, 1996 (made-for-TV; Geordie Johnson); The Loves of Liszt, 1975 (aka: Szerelmi almok—Liszt; Imre Sinkovits); **Lola Montes**, 1959 (Will Quadflieg); Magic Fire, 1956 (Carlos Thompson); Man of Music, 1953 (aka: Glinka; Svyatoslav Richter); Moi, Hector Berlioz, 2003 (made-for-TV; Nicolas Cardonna); Paganini, 1923 (Gustav Frohlich); **Phantom of the Opera**, 1943 (Fritz Lieber); Pontcarral, colonel d'empire, 1942 (Marc Dantzer); Prelude, 1952 (made-for-TV; Chester Stratton); **Song of Love**, 1947 (Henry Daniell); Song of Norway, 1970 (Henry Gilbert); **A Song to Remember**, 1945 (Stephen Bekassy); **Song without End**, 1960 (Dirk Bogarde); **Suez**, 1938 (Brandon Hurst); Szekszardi mise, 2001 (made-for-TV; Tibor Kenderesi); Traumerei, 1944 (Emil Lohkamp); Wagner, 1983 (TV series; Ekkehard Schall); Wahnfried, 1987 (Anton Diffring); Wenn die Musik nicht war, 1937 (Luis Rainer); Z meho zivota, 1955 (Stepan Bulejko).

Little Big Man (prominent in 1870s; Oglala Lakota warrior of the Sioux nation and top lieutenant to Sioux war leader Crazy Horse, and was reportedly responsible for the death of Crazy Horse in 1877): Chief Crazy Horse, 1955 (Ray Danton); Crazy Horse, 1996 (made-for-TV; Zahn McClarnon).

Little Wolf (c. 1820-1904; sub-chief of Northern Cheyenne, who aided Chief Dull Knife in the Northern Cheyenne Exodus of 1878 when the tribe left its imposed reservation in Oklahoma to return to its homelands in Nebraska): **Cheyenne Autumn**, 1964 (Ricardo Montalban).

Lloyd George, David (1863-1945; British politician, statesman and prime minister, 1916-1922): Anzacs, 1985- (TV miniseries; Rhys Mc-

John Dall (role modeled on Richard Loeb), James Stewart and Farley Granger in *Rope,* **1948.**

Connochie); British Agent, 1934 (George C. Pearce); Clemenceau, 2012 (made-for-TV; Leslie Clack); Deadline Gallipoli, 2015- (TV miniseries; Rob Macpherson); Edward the King, 1975- (TV series; Geoffrey Beevers); The Edwardians, 1972 (TV miniseries; Anthony Hopkins); Friedrich Ebert und Gustav Stressemann, 1969 (made-for-TV; Walter Janssen); The Gathering Storm, 1974 (made-for-TV; Edward Evans); Great Performances, 1971- (TV series; "A Dangerous Man: Lawrence after Arabia," 1992 episode; Bernard Lloyd); The Great Victory, Wilson or the Kaiser? The Fall of the Hohenzollerns, 1919 (J.C. Dunn); A Horseman Riding By, 1978- (TV series; Michael Forrest); Kurtulus, 1994- (TV miniseries; T.P. McKenna); The Last Bastion, 1984 (TV series; Ralph Cotterill); The Life and Times of David Lloyd George, 1981- (TV series; Philip Madoc); Lloyd George, 1973 (made-for-TV; Anthony Hopkins); The Life Story of David Lloyd George, 1918 (Norman Page); The Lost Prince, 2003 (made-for-TV; Ron Cook); Mosley, 1998 (TV series; Windsor Davies); Nancy Astor, 1982- (TV miniseries; Brian Hawksley); 1914-1918, 1996 (TV miniseries; Ian Richardson); Number 10, 1983- (TV miniseries; John Stride); Paris 1919: Un traite pour la paix, 2009 (made-for-TV; Nicholas Hawtrey); Regal Cavalcade, 1935 (Esme Percy); Shoulder to Shoulder, 1974- (TV miniseries; Peter Geddis); The Siege 1922, 2013 (made-for-TV; Mario Rosenstock); Suffragette, 2015 (Adrian Schiller); 37 Days, 2014 (TV miniseries; Mark Lewis Jones); The Treaty, 1991 (made-for-TV; Ian Bannen); The Treaty 1921, 2011 (made-for-TV; Mario Rosenstock); Sir Basil Zaharoff— Makler des Todes, 1969 (made-for-TV; Martin Hirthe); Wipers Three, 1973 (made-for-TV; Emrys James); The Young Indiana Jones Chronicles, 1992-1993 (TV series; "Paris, May 1919," 1993 episode: Michael Kitchen); **Young Winston**, 1972 (Anthony Hopkins).

Loeb, Richard (1905-1936; wealthy homosexual Chicago youth who, along with partner Nathan Leopold, committed what both thought would be the "perfect murder" when kidnapping and killing 14-year-old Bobby Franks in May 1924; Loeb was killed by a fellow prison inmate after he attempted to sexually molest that prisoner): **Compulsion**, 1959 (role model for Bradford Dillman); **Rope**, 1948 (role model for John Dall); Swoon, 1992 (Daniel Schlachet). For detailed information on Leopold and Loeb, see my books *World Encyclopedia of 20th Century Murder* (Paragon House; 1992; illustrated [12 images] pages 353-362), and *The Great Pictorial History of World Crime*, Volume II (History, Inc., 2004; illustrated [31 images] pages 840-858).

Logan, Harvey Alexander (aka: Kid Curry; 1867-1904; U.S. Old West outlaw, bank and train robber; committed suicide before being captured by a posse): Badman's Country, 1958 (Richard Devon); Buffalo Bill, Jr., 1955-1956 (TV series; "Kid Curry—Killer, 1956 episode: Walter

Reed); Butch and Sundance: The Early Days, 1979 (John Schuck); **Butch Cassidy and the Sundance Kid**, 1969 (Ted Cassidy); Dakota Lil, 1950 (Rod Cameron); Powder River, 1953 (John Dehner); Wyoming Renegades, 1954 (George Keymas). Note: For detailed information on Logan, see my book, *Encyclopedia of Western Lawmen and Outlaws* (Paragon House, 1992; illustrated pages 212-215).

Lombard, Carole (Jane Alice Peters; 1908-1942; U.S. film actress and wife of actor Clark Gable): Gable and Lombard, 1976 (Jill Clayburgh); Lucy, 2003 (made-for-TV; Vanessa Gray); Malice in Wonderland, 1985 (made-for-TV; Denise Crosby); RKO 281, 1999 (made-for-TV; Anastasia Hille); The Scarlett O'Hara War, 1980 (made-for-TV; Sharon Gless).

London, Jack (John Griffith "Jack" London; John Griffith Chaney; U.S. author and adventurer; 1876-1916): **Jack London**, 1943 (Michael O'Shea); The Jack London Story, 1976 (TV series; Orso Maria Guerrini); Klondike Fever, 1980 (Jeff East).

Long, Huey Pierce, Jr. (1893-1935; U.S. politician; demagogue governor and later U.S. senator from Louisiana; assassinated): **All the King's Men**, 1949 (role model for Broderick Crawford); Kingfish: A Story of Huey P. Long, 1995 (made-for-TV; John Goodman; Joe Alaskey voiceover); The Life and Assassination of the Kingfish, 1977 (made-for-TV; Edward Asner); Unsolved Mysteries, 1987-2010 (TV series; 1992 episode; John McConnell).

Longstreet, James (1821-1904; U.S. military leader and lieutenant general in the Confederate army of Northern Virginia during the American Civil War): **Gettysburg**, 1993 (Tom Berenger); **Gods and Generals**, 2003 (Bruce Boxleitner); Omnibus, 1952-1961 (TV series; "Lee at Gettysburg," 1957 episode: Bruce Gordon); **Santa Fe Trail**, 1940 (Frank Wilcox); Sunday Showcase, 1959-1961 (TV series; "An American Heritage: Gentleman's Decision," 1961 episode: Jay Barney).

Looking Glass (c. 1832-1877; U.S. Native American; war chief of Nez Perce): I Will Fight No More Forever, 1975 (made-for-TV; Vince St. Cyr).

Louis VII (1120-1180; king of France): **Becket**, 1964 (John Gielgud); The Devil's Crown, 1978- (TV series; Charles Kay); Richard the Lionheart: Rebellion, 2015 (Brian Ayres).

Louis XI (1423-1483; King of France): The Beloved Rogue, 1927 (Conrad Veidt); Blood on His Sword, 1961 (Jean-Louis Barrault); The Hollow Crown, 2012- (TV series; "Charles VI Part 2," 2016 episode: Andrew Scott); The Hunchback, 1997 (made-for-TV; Nigel Terry); **The Hunchback of Notre Dame**, 1923 (Tully Marshall); **The Hunchback of Notre Dame**, 1939 (Harry Davenport); The Hunchback of Notre Dame, 1957 (Jean Tessier); If I Were King, 1920 (Fritz Lieber); **If I Were King**, 1938 (Basil Rathbone); If Paris Were Told to Us, 1956 (Sacha Guitry); La florentine, 1991- (TV miniseries; Yves Penay); Les dossiers de l'ecran, 1967-1989 (TV series; Denis Manuel); Louis XI: Shattered Power, 2011 (made-for-TV; Jacques Perrin); Louis XI, un seul roi pour la France, 1980 (Roland Monod); The Magical Adventures of Quasimodo, 1996- (animated TV series; Harry Hill voiceover); **The Messenger: The Story of Joan of Arc**, 1999 (Irving Pomepui as Louis XI at age five); Miracle of the Wolves, 1930 (Charles Dullin); **Quentin Durward**, 1955 (Robert Morley); Quentin Durward, 1971- (TV series; Michel Vitold); **The Vagabond King**, 1930 (O.P. Heggie); **The Vagabond King**, 1956 (Walter Hampden); Yolanda, 1924 (Holbrook Blinn).

Louis XII (1462-1515; king of France): Borgia, 2011 (TV series; Joseph Beattie); The Borgias, 1981 (TV miniseries; Yves Beneyton); The Borgias, 2011 (TV series; Serge Hazanavicius); Les Borgia ou le sang dore, 1977 (made-for-TV; Andre Dumas); The Life of Leonardo Da Vinci, 1971 (TV series; Christian de Tilliere); Louis XI: Shattered Power, 2011 (made-for-TV; Bruno Debrandt); **The Sword and the Rose**, 1953 (Jean Mercure); **When Knighthood Was in Flower**, 1922 (William Norris).

Louis XIII (King of France; 1601-1643): Animated Three Musketeers, 1987 (TV series; Hideyuki Tanaka); Bardelys the Magnificent, 1926 (Arthur Lubin); Biblioteca di Studio Uno: I tre moschettieri, 1964 (made-for-TV; Claudio Villa); The Captain, 1946 (Serge Emrich); Cardinal Richelieu, 1935 (Edward Arnold); Cinq-Mars, 1981 (made-for-TV; Pierre Vanek); Cyrano et d'Artagnan, 1964 (Philippe Noiret); D'Artagnan, 1969 (TV miniseries; Edoardo Toniolo); D'Artagnan, 1991 (made-for-TV; Berenard Bollet); D'Artagnan amoureux, 1977 (TV miniseries; Gabriel Cattand); D'Artagnan et les trois mousquetaires, 2005 (Tristan Ulloa); D'Artanyan i tri mushketyora, 1979 (TV series; Oleg Tabakov); De drie Musketiers, 1968 (made-for-TV; Bert Struys); The Devils, 1971 (Graham Armitage); Die Drie Musketiere, 2013 (Filipp Yankovskiy); Family Classics: The Three Musketeers, 1960 (made-for-TV; George Macready); The Four Charlots Musketeers, 1974 (Daniel Ceccaldi); The Four Musketeers, 1963 (Francesco Mule); **The Four Musketeers**, 1975 (Jean-Pierre Cassel); The Glorious Musketeers, 1974 (Fred Pasquali voiceover); I tre moschettieri, 1991 (made-for-TV; Umberto Smalia); If Paris Were Told to Us, 1956 (Louis Arbessier and Claudy Chapeland as an infant); **The Iron Mask**, 1929 (Rolfe Sedan); Le camera explore le temps, 1957-1966 (TV series, "La conjuration de Cinq-Mars," 1962 episode: Jean-Pierre Marielle); La cite crucifiee, 1974 (made-for-TV; Simon Eine); La loca historia de los tres mosqueteros, 1983 (Juanjo Menendez); Les quatre mouquetaires, 1934 (Max Moreau); Les 3 Mousquetaires, 1953 (Louis Arbessier); Les trois mousquetaires, 1959 (made-for-TV; Georges Lannes); Les trois mousquetaires ou L'escrime ne paie pas, 1979 (made-for-TV; Jean-Claude Islert); Les trois mousquetaires: Premiere epoque—Les ferrets de la reine, 1961 (Guy Trejean [Trejan]); The Magnavox Theater, 1950 (TV series; "The Three Musketeers," 1950 episode: Don Beddoe); **The Man in the Iron Mask**, 1939 (Albert Dekker); Marion Delorme, 1967 (made-for-TV; Roland Dubillard); Mazarin, 1978 (TV miniseries; Jacques Rosny); Milady and the Three Musketeers, 2004 (made-for-TV; Azucena Caamano); **The Musketeer**, 2001 (Daniel Mesguich); The Musketeers, 2014 (TV series; Ryan Gage); Panache, 1976 (made-for-TV; Harvey Solin); The Queen and the Cardinal, 2009 (made-for-TV; Philippe du Janerand); Richelieu, 1914 (James Neill); Richelieu, 1977 (TV miniseries; Jacques Rosny); Richelieu, la pourpre et la sang, 2013 (made-for-TV; Stephan Guerin-Tillie); Richelieu ou La journee des dupes, 1983 (made-for-TV; Patrick Raynal); Royal Affairs in Versailles, 1957 (Louis Arbessier); Three and a Half Musketeers, 1957 (Oscar Pulido); The Three Musketeers, 1916 (George Fisher); **The Three Musketeers**, 1921 (Adolphe Menjou); Three Musketeers, 1932 (Fernand Francell); The Three Musketeers, 1935 (Miles Mander); The Three Musketeers, 1939 (Joseph Schildkraut); The Three Musketeers, 1945 (Cesar Flaschi); **The Three Musketeers**, 1948 (Frank Morgan); The Three Musketeers, 1954 (TV series; Garard Green); The Three Musketeers, 1966 (TV miniseries; John Carlin); **The Three Musketeers**, 1974 (Jean-Pierre Cassel); **The Three Musketeers**, 1993 (Hugh O'Conor); The Three Musketeers, 2007 (Kjeld Norgaard voiceover); The Three Musketeers, 2011 (Freddie Fox); Under the Red Robe, 1923 (Ian MacLaren); **Under the Red Robe**, 1937 (Shayle Gardner); Vengeance of the Three Musketeers, 1961 (Guy Trejean [Trejan]); Tri musketyri, 1983 (TV miniseries; Peter Oliva); Tri mushketera, 2013 (Filipp Yankovskiy); Versailles, 2015- (TV series; David Stanley); Young Blades, 2001 (Ben McCosker).

Louis XIV (aka: Sun King; 1638-1715; king of France): Angelique, 2013 (David Kross); Angelique and the King, 1966 (Jacques Toja); At Sword's Point, 1952 (Peter Miles); Blanche, 2002 (Jose Garcia); The Case of Poisons, 1955 (Raymond Gerome); D'Artagnan, 1969- (TV

Harry Davenport (as Louis XI) and Cedric Hardwicke in *The Hunchback of Notre Dame,* **1939.**

miniseries; Daniel Le Roy); Famous Love Affairs, 1961 (Philippe Noiret); The Fifth Musketeer, 1979 (Beau Bridges); The First Churchills, 1969- (TV miniseries; Robert Robinson); The Further Adventures of the Musketeers, 1967- (TV series; Louis Selwyn); I Married an Angel, 1942 (John Marlowe); If Paris Were Told to Us, 1956 (Dominique Veriot as an infant); **The Iron Mask**, 1929 (William Bakewell); The Iron Mask, 1962 (Jean-Francois Poron); The King Is Dancing, 2000 (Benoit Magimel); The King's Daughter, 2016 (Pierce Brosnan); The King's Daughters, 2000 (Jean-Pierre Kalfon); La mort de Louis XIV, 2016 (Jean-Pierre Leaud); The Lady Musketeer, 2004- (TV miniseries; Freddie Sayers); The Last King, 2003- (TV miniseries; Thierry Perkins-Lyautey); Le cardinal de Retz, 1975 (Olivier Lefort); Mademoiselle Moliere, 1964 (made-for-TV; Jean Leuvrais); **The Man in the Iron Mask**, 1939 (Louis Hayward); The Man in the Iron Mask, 1968- (TV series; Nicolas Chagrin); The Man in the Iron Mask, 1977 (made-for-TV; Richard Chamberlain); The Man in the Iron Mask, 1985 (made-for-TV; Colin Friels); The Man in the Iron Mask, 1998 (Nick Richert); **The Man in the Iron Mask**, 1998 (Leonardo DiCaprio); Marie Antoinette, 1975- (TV miniseries; Francois Dyrek); Moliere, 1980 (Jean-Claude Penchenat); The Musketeers, 2014- (TV series; Ryan Gage); Mysteries at the Castle, 2014- (TV series; one 2016 episode with Gio James Bertoia as Louis XIV); The Queen and the Cardinal, 2009 (made-for-TV; Arthur Vaughan-Whitehead; Jean-Paul Comart; Cyril Descours); The Return of the Musketeers, 1989 (David Birkin); The Rise of Louis XIV, 1966 (made-for-TV; Jean-Marie Patte); Royal Affairs in Versailles, 1957 (Sacha Guitry); The Sovereign's Servant, 2007 (Dmitry Shilyaev); Star of India, 1954 (Basil Sydney); The Three Musketeers, 1969 (made-for-TV; Eric Donkin); Versailles, 2015- (TV series; George Blagden; Nathaniel Spender); Versailles: The Dream of a King, 2008 (made-for-TV; Samuel Theis); Young Blades, 2005- (TV miniseries; Robert Sheehan).

Louis XV (1710-1774; King of France): Beaumarchais the Scoundrel, 1997 (Michel Serrault); **Black Magic**, 1949 (Robert Atkins); Casanova, 1987 (made-for-TV; Jean-Pierre Cassel); Casanova, 2015 (made-for-TV; James Flynn); De baron von Munchhausen, 1970 (Henk van Ulsen); Die Marquise von Pompadour, 1936 (Kurt Gerron); Die Pompadour, 1939 (Anton Edthofer); DuBarry, 1915 (Richard Thornton); Du Barry Was a Lady, 1943 (Red Skelton); Du Barry, Woman of Passion, 1930 (William Farnum); Enigmas de l'histoire, 1956-1957 (TV series; "Le chevalier d'Eon," 1957 episode: Alain Nobis); Exzellenz Unterrock, 1921 (Jurgen Fehling); Fan Fan the Tulip, 1925 (Jacques Guilhene); Fan Fan the Tulip, 1953 (Marcel Herrand); Fanfan, 2003 (Didier Bourdon); Figaro-ci, Figaro-la, 1972 (made-for-TV; Dominique Rozan); Il giovane casanova 2002 (made-for-TV; Francois Berleand); Joseph Balsamo,

Kevin Bacon (as Jack Swigert) and Tom Hanks (as Jim Lovell) in *Apollo 13*, **1995.**

1973 (TV series; Guy Trejan); King of the Wind, 1990 (Paul Spurrier); King on Horseback, 1958 (Jean Lara); Le chevalier d'Eon, 2006- (TV series; Tetsu Inada; Jay Hickman); Le secret du chevalier d'Eon, 1959 (Jean Desailly); Louis XV, le soleil noir, 2009 (made-for-TV; Stanley Weber); Madame de Pompador: The King's Favorite, 2006 (made-for-TV; Vincent Perez); Madame Du Barry, 1917 (Charles Clary); Madame DuBarry, 1919 (Emil Jannings); The Loves of Madame Du Barry, 1938 (Owen Nares); Madame DuBarry, 1919 (Emil Jannings); Madame Du Barry, 1934 (Reginald Owen); Madame du Barry, 1954 (Andre Luguet); Madame Pompadour, 1927 (Henri Bosc); Madame Pompadour, 1996 (made-for-TV; Hans-Gunter Martens); Marie Antoinette, 1922 (Ludwig Hartau); **Marie Antoinette**, 1938 (John Barrymore); Marie Antoinette, 1975 (TV miniseries; Robert Rimbaud); Marie Antoinette, 2006 (Rip Torn); Marie Antoinette, 2006 (made-for-TV; Paul Savoie); Marquis d'Eon, der Spion der Pompadour, 1929 (Alfred Gerasch); Monsieur Beaucaire, 1924 (Lowell Sherman); Monsieur Beaucaire, 1946 (Reginald Owen); Monsieur Pompadour, 1973 (made-for-TV; Georges Guetary); Napoleon, 1955 (Maurice Escande); Napoleon, 1955 (Maurice Escande); The Rose of Versailles, 1979-1980 (animated TV series; Hisashi Katsuda); Royal Affairs in Versailles, 1957 (Jean Marais); Shadow of the Guillotine, 1956 (Aime Clariond); Versailles: The Dream of a King, 2008 (made-for-TV; Gabriel Hallali); Voltaire, 1933 (Reginald Owen); When a Man Loves, 1927 (Stuart Holmes).

Louis XVI (King of France; 1754-1793): The Adams Chronicles, 1976 (TV miniseries; Lance Davis); The Affair of the Necklace, 2001 (Simon Shackleton); Beaumarchais, 1969 (made-for-TV; Albrecht Schiemann); Beaumarchais the Scoundrel, 1997 (Dominque Besnehard); **Black Magic**, 1949 (Lee Kresel); Cagliostro, 1929 (Edmond Van Daele); Captain of the Guard, 1930 (Stuart Holmes); Chateaubriand, 2010 (made-for-TV; Frederic J. Lozet); A Clockwork Blue, 1972 (Sebastian Brook); Danton, 1931 (Ernst Stahl-Nachbaur); The Days That Made History, 2009- (TV series; Antoine Gouy); Enigmas de l'histoire, 1956-1957 (TV series; "Le chevalier d'Eon," 1957 episode: Roger Paschy); Farewell, My Queen, 2012 (Xavier Beauvois); Figaro-ci, Figaro-la, 1972 (made-for-TV; Roger Dumas); The Fighting Guardsman, 1946 (Lloyd Corrigan); History of the World: Part 1, 1981 (Mel Brooks); If Paris Were Told to Us, 1956 (Gilbert Bokanowski); **Janice Meredith**, 1924 (Edwin Argus); John Adams, 2008- (TV miniseries; "Don't Tread on Me," 2008 episode: Damien Jouillerot); **John Paul Jones**, 1959 (Jean-Pierre Aumont); La camera explore le temps, 1957-1966 (TV series; one episode in 1960: Robert Lombard; one 1962 episode: Jacques Morel); **La Marseillaise**, 1939 (Pierre Renoir); La nuit de Varennes, 1982 (Michel Piccoli); La revolution francaise, 1989 (Jean-Francois Balmer); Lady Oscar, 1979 (Terence Budd); Lafayette, 1963 (Albert Remy); L'enfant roi, 1923

(Louis Sance); The Legendary Curse of the Hope Diamond, 1975 (made-for-TV; Robert Clary); Liberte, egalite, choucroute, 1985 (Michel Serrault); Louis XV, le soleil noir, 2009 (made-for-TV; Florian Cadiou); Louis XVI, the Man Who Didn't Want to Be King, 2011 (made-for-TV; Gabriel Dufay); Madame du Barry, 1954 (Serge Grand); Madame Sans-Gene, 1925 (Louis Sance); **Marie Antoinette**, 1938 (Robert Morley); Marie Antoinette, 1975- (TV series; Jean-Michel Farcy); Marie Antoinette, 2005 (made-for-TV; Michel Fau); Marie Antoinette, 2006 (made-for-TV; Olivier Aubin); Marie Antoinette, 2006 (Jason Schwartzman); Marie Antoinette—Das Leben einer Konigin, 1929 (Viktor Schwannecke); My Lady's Slipper, 1916 (Joseph Kilgour); **Napoleon**, 1927 (Louis Sance); Napoleon, 1955 (Gilbert Bokanowski); Nicolas Le Floch, 2008- (TV series; "Le noye du Grand Canal," 2015 episode; Louis Barraud); Novela, 1963-1978 (TV series; "El collar de la reina," 1976 episode: Emiliano Redondo); **Orphans of the Storm**, 1921 (Lee Kohlmar); The Queen's Necklace, 1931 (Harry Harment); Remontons les Champs-Elysees, 1939 (Jean Hebey); Ridicule, 1996 (Urbain Cancelier); The Rose of Versailles, 1979-1980 (TV series; Yoshito Yasuhara voiceover); Royal Affairs in Versailles, 1957 (Gilbert Bokanowski); **Scaramouche**, 1923 (Edwin Argus); Shadow of the Guillotine, 1956 (Jacques Morel); **Start the Revolution without Me**, 1970 (Hugh Griffith); We Forget Everything!, 1979 (Jacques Ardouin).

Louis XVIII (1755-1824; king of France): Beaumarchais the Scoundrel, 1997 (Pierre Gerard); C'etait Marie-Antoinette, 2010 (made-for-TV; Jeremy Briffa); **The Count of Monte Cristo**, 1934 (Ferdinand Munier); The Count of Monte Cristo, 1954 (Jean Temerson); Farewell, My Queen, 2012 (Gregory Gadebois); Hundred Days, 1935 (Ernst Legal); The Iron Duke, 1935 (Alan Aynesworth); The Lame Devil, 1948 (Henry Laverne); Le comte de Monte-Cristo, 1979- (TV miniseries; Jean Turlier); Les jupons de la revolution, 1989- (TV series; "Marie Antoinette, reine d'un seul amour," 1989 episode: Vincent Solignac); The Lost King, 1958- (TV series; "Monsieur Charles Deslys," 1958 episode; Felix Felton); **Marie Antoinette**, 1938 (Albert Dekker); Marie Antoinette, 1975- (TV series; Gerard Caillaud); Marie Antoinette, 2006 (made-for-TV; Vincent Champoux); Marie Antoinette, 2006 (Sebastian Armesto); Mlle. Desiree, 1948 (Gaston Mauger); Napoleon, 1955 (Lucien Baroux); Napoleon, 2002- (TV miniseries; Andre Chaumeau); Napoleon at St. Helena, 1929 (Albert Florath); 100 Days of Napoleon, 1936 (Ernesto Marini); The Raft of the Medusa, 1998 (Andre Penvern); Remontons les Champs-Elysees, 1939 (Philippe Richard); The Rothschilds, 1940 (Hans Leibelt); Shadow of the Guillotine, 1956 (Jacques Bergerac); Talleyrand ou Le sphinx incompris, 1972 (Aram Stephan); **Waterloo**, 1971 (Orson Welles); The Wednesday Play, 1964-1970 (TV series; "Catch as Catch Can," 1964 episode: David Home); Wicked Duchess, 1949 (Gaston Mauger).

Louis, Joe (Joseph Louis Barrow; 1914-1981; U.S. prizefighter and world heavyweight champion, 1937-1949): American Gangster, 2007 (Barri K. Willerford); The Court-Martial of Jackie Robinson, 1990 (made-for-TV; Stan Shaw); Joe and Max, 2002 (made-for-TV; Leonard Roberts); **The Joe Louis Story**, 1953 (Coley Wallace); Joe Palooka, Champ, 1946 (himself); Marciano, 1979 (made-for-TV; Coley Wallace); Max Schmeling, 2012 (Yoan Pablo Hernandez); The Phynx, 1970 (himself); **Raging Bull**, 1980 (Coley Wallace); Ring of Passion, 1978 (made-for-TV; Bernie Casey) Rocky Marciano, 1999 (made-for-TV; Duane Davis); **This Is the Army**, 1943 (himself); Voyagers!, 1982-1983 (TV series; "All Fall Down," 1983 episode: Sam Scarber).

Lovell, Jim (James Arthur "Jim" Lovell, Jr.; 1928- ; U.S. NASA astronaut, who commanded the *Apollo 13* moon mission in 1970): **Apollo 13**, 1995 (Tom Hanks); From Earth to the Moon, 1998- (TV miniseries; Tim Daly); Man, Moment, Machine, 2005-2007 (TV series; "Apollo 13: Triumph on the Dark Side," 2006 episode: Argo Thompson).

Luciano, Charles (Salvatore Lucania; aka: "Lucky"; 1897-1962; Sicilian-born U.S.-based gangster, crime syndicate founder, imprisoned for prostitution and other crimes and deported): **Billy Bathgate**, 1991 (Stanley Tucci); Boardwalk Empire, 2010-2013 (TV series; Vincent Piazza); Bonanno: A Godfather's Story, 1999 (made-for-TV; Vince Corazza); Brass Target, 1978 (Lee Montague); **Bugsy**, 1991 (Bill Graham); **The Cotton Club**, 1984 (Joe Dallesandro); Fade to Black, 2006 (Daniel Cerqueira); The Gangster Chronicles, 1981 (TV series; Michael Nouri); Gangster Wars, 1981 (Michael Nouri); Goldeneye, 1989 (made-for-TV; Joseph Long); Hit the Dutchman, 1982 (Leonard Donato); Hoodlum, 1993 (Andy Garcia); A House Is Not a Home, 1964 (Cesar Romero); Lansky, 1999 (made-for-TV; Anthony LaPaglia; Paul Sincoff as younger Luciano); Le retour d'Arsene Lupin, 1989-1996 (TV series; "Requins a la Havane," 1995 episode: Carlos Cruz); Lepke, 1975 (Vic Tayback); Lucky Luciano, 1974 (Gian Maria Volonte); Mad Dog Coll, 1993 (Matt Servitto); Mafia—Die ehrenwerte Gesellschaft, 1966- (TV series; Kurd Pieritz); The Making of the Mob: New York, 2015- (TV miniseries; Rich Graff); **Marked Woman**, 1937 (role model for Eduardo Ciannelli); Mobsters, 1991 (Christian Slater); The Outfit, 1993 (Billy Drago); Passion and Paradise, 1989 (made-for-TV; Ron White); The Real Untouchables, 2001 (made-for-TV; David Viggiano); The Revenge of Al Capone, 1989 (made-for-TV; Nicholas Mele); The Untouchables, 1959-1963 (TV series; Robert Carricart); **The Valachi Papers**, 1972 (Angelo Infanti); Voyagers!, 1982-1983 (TV series; "Cleo and the Babe," 1982 episode: Michael Gregory); White Hot: The Mysterious Murder of Thelma Todd, 1991 (made-for-TV; Robert Davi); The Witness, 1960-1961 (TV series; Telly Savalas). Note: For detailed information on Luciano, see my books *World Encyclopedia of Organized Crime* (Paragon House, 1992; illustrated [15 images] pages 251-256); and the two-volume work *The Great Pictorial History of World Crime*, Volume II (History, Inc., 2004; illustrated [16 images] pages 544-551).

Ludendorff, Erich (Erich Friedrich Wilhelm Ludendorff; 1865-1937; German army officer and general in WWI): Der Gewaltfrieden, 2010 (made-for-TV; Christian Hoening); Die konterrevolution, 2011 (made-for-TV; Christian Hoening); Die Flucht nach Holland, 1967 (made-for-TV; Ernst Schroder); Fall of Eagles, 1974 (TV miniseries; Michael Bates); Foch pour vaincre, 1977 (made-for-TV; Hans Verner); Fraulein Doktor, 1969 (James Mishler); **The Hitler Gang**, 1944 (Reinhold Schunzel); Hitler: The Rise of Evil, 2003 (TV miniseries; Friedrich von Thun); Hitler vor Gericht, 2009 (made-for-TV; Peter Fricke); Lenin, You Rascal, You, 1972 (Dirch Passer); Tannenberg, 1932 (Henry Pless).

Ludwig I (1786-1768; king of Bavaria): Der Obersteiger, 1956 (Walter Janssen); Kaspar Hauser, 1993 (Dieter Laser); Komodienstadel—Die schone Munchnerin, 2008 (made-for-TV; Winfried Frey); Konig fur eine Nacht, 1950 (Willy Fritsch); Lola Montes, 1944 (Jesus Tordesillas); **Lola Montes**, 1959 (Anton Walbrook); Lola Montez, 1922 (Arnold Korff); Ludwig—Requiem for a Virgin King, 1980 (Oskar von Schab); Prinzessin Sissy, 1939 (Otto Tessler); Wagner, 1981- (TV series; Sigfrit Steiner).

Ludwig II (aka: Mad King Ludwig; 1845-1886; king of Bavaria): The Life and Works of Richard Wagner, 1913 (Ernst Reicher); Ludwig, 1973 (Helmut Berger); Ludwig, 1981 (Helmut Berger); Ludwig der Zweite, Konig von Bayern, 1930 (William Dieterle); Ludwig II, 1922 (Olaf Fjord); Ludwig II, 2012 (Sabin Tambrea; Sebastian Schipper); Ludwig II: Glanz und Ende eines Konigs, 1959 (O.W. Fischer); Ludwig—Requiem for a Virgin King, 1980 (Harry Baer); Magic Fire, 1956 (Gerhard Riedmann); Tales of a Young Scamp, 1964 (Thomas Reiner); Wagner, 1983 (TV series; Laszlo Galffi).

Luke (Luke the Evangelist; d. 84 A.D.; one of the Four Evangelists or authors of the canonical Gospels of Jesus Christ): A.D., 1985 (TV miniseries; Gerrard McArthur); Apostle Peter and the Last Supper, 2012 (Sean

Ben Kingsley (as Meyer Lansky) and Bill Graham (as Charles "Lucky" Luciano) in *Bugsy,* **1991.**

Gibney); The Disciple, 2010 (Craig Stevenson); The Holy Family, 2006 (Pablo Enrique Castillo); Jesus, 1979 (Alexander Scourby voiceover); The Life of St. Paul, 1938 (Lewis Broughton); Paul of Tarsus, 1960- (TV series; Philip Latham); Saul: The Journey to Damascus, 2014 (Sean Buhagier); The Savior, 2014 (Yussuf Abu-Warda); **The Silver Chalice**, 1954 (Alexander Scourby).

Luther, Martin (1483-1546; German professor and priest who led the Protestant Reformation): BBC Play of the Month, 1965-1983 (TV series; "Luther," 1965 episode: Alec McCowen); Emperor, 2016 (Eddie Marsan); Frere Martin, 1981 (made-for-TV; Bernard Lincot); The Lion Roar, 2014 (Jason Burkey); Luther, 1968 (made-for-TV; Robert Shaw); Luther, 1974 (Stacy Keach); The Immortal Heart, 1939 (Bernhard Minetti); Luther, 1929 (Eugen Klopfer); Luther, 1964 (made-for-TV; Terry Norris); Luther, 2003 (Joseph Fiennes); Martin Luther, 1923 (Karl Wustenhagen); Martin Luther, 1953 (Niall MacGinnis); Martin Luther, 1983 (made-for-TV; Lambert Hamel); Martin Luther, 1983- (TV series; Ulrich Thein); Martin Luther, 2002 (made-for-TV; Timothy West); Martin Luther, Heretic, 1983 (made-for-TV; Jonathan Pryce).

Luxemburg, Rosa (1871-1919; German anarchist leader; assassinated): Anita: Dances of Vice, 1987 (Eva Maria Kurz as a lunatic patient in an asylum who thinks she is Rosa Luxemburg); Bruder, nicht schiessen!, 1989 (made-for-TV; Simone von Zglinicki); Der Fall Liebknecht-Luxemburg, 1969 (made-for-TV; Edith Heerdegen); Die rote Rosa, 1966 (made-for-TV; Ursula Lingen); Dimitrije Tucovic, 1973 (TV series; Maja Dimitrijevic); Ernst Thalmann—Sohn seiner Klasse, 1954 (Judith Harms); Europas letzter Sommer, 2012 (made-for-TV; Barbara Philipp); Jahreswechsel Zeitenwechsel, 1988 (made-for-TV; Petra Kelling); Jean Jaures: Vie et mort d'un socialiste, 1980 (made-for-TV; Maud Rayer); 1914-1918, 1996 (TV miniseries; Nastassja Kinski); **Rosa Luxemburg**, 1987 (Barbara Sukowa); Solange Leben in mir ist, 1965 (Zofia Rysiowna); Trotz alledem!, 1972 (Zofia Mrozowska); Trust, 1970 (Antonina Shuranova). Note: For detailed information on the assassination of Liebknecht and Luxemburg, see my two-volume work *The Great Pictorial History of World Crime*, Volume I (History, Inc., 2004; illustrated [4 images] pages 118-120).

Lymon, Frankie (Franklin Joseph "Frankie" Lymon; U.S. singer and early rock 'n' roll performer): Mr. Rock 'n' Roll: The Alan Freed Story, 1999 (made-for-TV; LeRoy D. Brazile); Why Do Fools Fall in Love?, 1998 (Larenz Tate).

Lynn, Loretta (b. 1932; U.S. country music singer-songwriter): Big Dreams & Broken Hearts: The Dottie West Story, 1995 (made-for-TV;

Denzel Washington (as Malcolm X) in *Malcolm X,* **1992.**

herself); **Coal Miner's Daughter**, 1980 (Sissy Spacek).

Machiavelli, Niccolo (1469-1527; Italian diplomat, writer and historian): Borgia, 2011 (TV series; Thibaut Evrard); The Borgias, 1981 (TV miniseries; Sam Dastor); The Borgias, 2011-2013 (TV series; Julian Bleach); Da Vinci: The Wings of Light Muscial, 2000 (made-for-TV; Fabian Richard); Da Vinci's Demons, 2013-2015 (TV series; Eros Vlahos); Dinner in Purgatory, 1994 (James Reynard); Egmont, 1962 (made-for-TV; Peter Capell); Egmont, 1968 (made-for-TV; Gerard Vermeersch); Egmont, 1982 (made-for-TV; Jacques Francois); I, Leonardo: A Journey of the Mind, 1983 (made-for-TV; Jeremiah Sullivan); Leonardo, 2011- (TV series; Akemnji Ndifernyan); Les Borgia ou le sang dore, 1977 (made-for-TV; Gerard Berner); The Life of Leonardo Da Vinci, 1971 (TV series; Enrico Osterman); Lucrezia Borgia, 1937 (Aime Clariond); Machiavelli Rises, 2000 (Rocco Sisto); Masque of the Red Death, 1989 (Patrick Macnee); A Season of Giants, 1990 (made-for-TV; Ricky Tognazzi); Storm over Firenze, 1968 (made-for-TV; Senne Rouffaer); Sword of Freedom, 1957- (TV series; Kenneth Hyde); The Time Tunnel, 1966-1967 (TV series; "The Death Merchant," 1967 episode: Malachi Throne); Witness to Yesterday, 1998- (TV series; "Niccolo Machiavelli," 1998 episode: David Calderisi).

Maclean, Donald Duart (1913-1983; British intelligence officer turned traitor and spy for the Soviets, defecting to the USSR in 1951): Cambridge Spies, 2003 (TV miniseries; Rupert Penry-Jones); Kim Philby war der dritte Mann, 1969 (made-for-TV; Herbert Botticher); Philby, Burgess and Maclean, 1977 (made-for-TV; Michael Culver); Screen Two, 1985-2002 (TV series; "Blunt," 1987 episode: Michael McStay). Note: For detailed information on Maclean, see my book *Spies: A Narrative Encyclopedia of Dirty Tricks & Double Dealing from Biblical Times to Today* (M. Evans, 1997; illustrated pages 329-330).

Mackenzie King, William Lyon (1874-1950; Canadian politician and prime minister of Canada): Atom Spies, 1979 (made-for-TV; Patrick Barr); The King Chronicles, 1988 (TV miniseries; Sean McCann); Les grands proces, 1993- (TV series; Kenneth Welsh); Prairie Giant: The Tommy Douglas Story, 2006 (TV miniseries; Andy Jones).

Madame Chiang Kai-shek (Soong May-ling; 1898-2003; First Lady of the Republic of China and wife of Generalissimo Chiang Kai-shek): Back to 1942, 2012 (Lan Ke); Collision Course: Truman vs. MacArthur, 1976 (made-for-TV; Essie Lin Chia); Eastern Battlefield, 2015- (TV miniseries; Feihong Yu); The Founding of a Republic, 2009 (Vivian Wu); Hemingway & Gellhorn, 2012 (made-for-TV; Joan Chen); The Soong Sisters, 1997 (Vivian Wu).

Madame du Barry: see Becu, Jeanne.

Madame Pompadour: see Pompadour, Madame.

Madero, Francisco I. (1873-1913; Mexican politician, revolutionary and 33rd president of Mexico, 1911-1913; assassinated): Aqui esta Pancho Villa, 1960 (TV series; Jose Luis Jimenez); El encanto del aguila, 2011 (Gerardo Trejoluna); El vuelo del aguila, 1994 (TV series; Luis Bayardo); La Tormenta, 1967 (TV series; Jorge Arvizu); Mexikanische Revolution, 1968 (made-for-TV; Konrad Georg); Tepepa, 1979 (Francisco Sanz); Toda una vida, 1981 (TV series; Jorge Arivzu); Villa!, 1958 (Ben Wright); **Viva Villa!**, 1934 (Henry B. Walthall); Villa Rides, 1968 (Alexander Knox); **Viva Zapata!**, 1952 (Harold Gordon); Zapata, 1970 (Jorge Arivzu); Zapata—El sueno del hero, 2004 (Fernando Becerril). For detailed information on Madero and his assassination, see my two-volume work *The Great Pictorial History of World Crime*, Volume I (History, Inc., 2004; illustrated [7 images] pages 84-87).

Madison, Dolley (Dolley Payne Todd Madison; 1768-1849; First Lady of the U.S., 1809-1817, and fourth wife of U.S. President James Madison): **The Buccaneer**, 1938 (Spring Byington); Dolley Madison, 2010 (TV series; Eve Best); The Ford Television Theatre, 1954-1957 (TV series; "Footnote on a Doll," 1957 episode: Bette Davis); Magnificent Doll, 1947 (Ginger Rogers); Mistress of the White House, 1952 (made-for-TV; June Lockhart); Sally Hemings: An American Scandal, 2000 (made-for-TV; Kathryn Meisle); War of 1812, 1999 (TV miniseries; Danielle Desormeaux).

Madison, James (1751-1836; U.S. politician and 4th President of the U.S.): The Adams Chronicles, 1976 (TV miniseries; Ken Kercheval); Cavalcade of America, 1952-1957 (TV series; "Mr. Peale's Dinosaur," 1953 episode: Louis Jean Heydt); Dolley Madison, 2010 (TV series; Jefferson Mays); George Washington II: The Forging of a Nation, 1986 (made-for-TV; Guy Paul); Liberty! The American Revolution, 1997 (TV miniseries; Jefferson Mays); Magnificent Doll, 1947 (Burgess Meredith); Mistress of the White House, 1952 (made-for-TV; Frank Daly); A More Perfect Union: America Becomes a Nation, 1989 (Craig Wasson); Old Louisiana, 1937 (Ramsay Hill); The Patriots, 1963 (made-for-TV; Frank Schofield); Profiles in Courage, 1964-1965 (TV series: "George Mason," 1965 episode: Arthur Franz); Sally Hemings: An American Scandal, 2000 (made-for-TV; Reno Roop); War of 1812, 1999 (TV miniseries; Richard Fitzpatrick).

Mahdi: see Muhammad Ahmad.

Malcolm X (Malcolm Little; 1925-1965; U.S. black activist; assassinated): Ali, 2001 (Marlo Van Peebles); Ali: An American Hero, 2000 (made-for-TV; Joe Morton); American Playhouse, 1981- (TV series; "The Meeting," 1989 episode: Dick Anthony Williams); Betty and Coretta, 2013 (Lindsay Owen Pierre); Death of a Prophet, 1981 (made-for-TV; Morgan Freeman); The Greatest, 1977 (James Earl Jones); King, 1978 (TV miniseries; Dick Anthony Williams); King of the World, 2000 (made-for-TV; Gary Dourdan); **Malcolm X**, 1992 (Denzel Washington; Zakee Howze as young Malcolm); Roots: The Next Generation, 1979- (TV miniseries; Al Freeman Jr.); **Selma**, 2014 (Nigel Thatch); World in Action, 1963-1998 (TV series; "Malcolm X," 1965 episode: Barry Johnson). For detailed information on Malcolm X and his assassination, see my two-volume work *The Great Pictorial History of World Crime*, Volume I (History, Inc., 2004; illustrated [4 images] pages 169-171).

Malenkov, Georgy (1902-1988; Soviet politician and Communist Party leader in Russia): Children of the Revolution, 1996 (Steven Abbott); An Ordinary Execution, 2010 (Alain Stern); Playhouse 90, 1956-1961 (TV series; "The Plot to Kill Stalin," 1958 episode: Thomas Gomez); Red Monarch, 1983 (made-for-TV; Peter Woodthorpe); Staline est morte,

1981 (made-for-TV; Fernand Guiot).

Mantz, Albert Paul (1903-1965; U.S. aviation stunt and racing pilot and aviation pioneer; killed when flying a makeshift plane in the film The Flight of the Phoenix, 1965): Amelia Earhart, 1976 (made-for-TV: Stephen Macht); Amelia Earhart: The Final Flight, 1994 (made-for-TV: Paul Guilfoyle); Pancho Barnes, 1988 (made-for-TV; Kurt Rhoads); Resolution: A Portrait of Amelia Earhart, 2012 (Christophe Scott).

Maranzano, Salvatore (1886-1931; Sicilian-born U.S. leader of the Cosa Nostra or Mafia in NYC; assassinated): Boardwalk Empire, 2010-2014 (TV series; Giampiero Judica); Bonanno: A Godfather's Story, 1999 (made-for-TV; Edward James Olmos); The Ganster Chronicles, 1981- (TV series; Joseph Mascolo); Gangster Wars, 1981 (Joseph Mascolo); Lansky, 1999 (made-for-TV; Ron Gilbert); Mobsters, 1991 (Michael Gambon as "Faranzano");Torchwood, 2006-2011 (TV series; "Miracle Day: Immortal Sins," 2011 episode; Chris D'Annunzio); **The Valachi Papers**, 1972 (Joseph Wiseman). Note: For detailed information on Maranzano, see my book *World Encyclopedia of Organized Crime* (Paragon House, 1992; illustrated pages 276-277).

Marat, Jean-Paul (1743-1793; French journalist, politician and a leader of the French Revolution; assassinated by Charlotte Corday): Charlotte Corday, 1914 (Arthur Maude); Charlotte Corday, 2008 (made-for-TV; Bernard Blancan); Danton, 1931 (Alexander Granach); The Days That Made History, 2009- (TV series; Frederic Cuif); If Paris Were Told to Us, 1956 (Guy Rapp); Jean-Paul Marat, 1967 (Gustav Wiklund); La revolution francaise, 1989 (Vittorio Mezzogiorno); Liberte, egalite, choucroute, 1985 (Jean Yanne); Manon Roland, 1989 (made-for-TV; Pierre Clementi); Marie Antoinette—Das Leben einer Konigin, 1929 (Max Grunberg); **Napoleon**, 1927 (Antonin Artaud); A Royal Divorce, 1938 (Allan Jeayes); Saint-Just ou La force des choses, 1975 (made-for-TV; Vicky Messica); **Scaramouche**, 1923 (Roy Coulson); Shadow of the Guillotine, 1956 (Jacques Dufilho). Note: For detailed information on Marat and his assassination, see my two-volume work *The Great Pictorial History of World Crime*, Volume I (History, Inc., 2004; illustrated [4 images] pages 13-15).

Marciano, Rocky (Rocco Francis Marchegiano; 1923-1969; U.S. prizefighter and heavyweight champion): Joe and Max, 2002 (made-for-TV; Luciano Rios Robledo); Marciano, 1979 (made-for-TV; Tony Lo Bianco); Rocky Marciano, 1999 (made-for-TV; Jon Favreau; Gil Filar as young Rocky); Resurrecting the Champ, 2007 (Nick Sandow).

Maria Feodorovna (1847-1928; empress of Russia and wife of Czar Alexander III and thereafter the dowager empress): **Anastasia**, 1956 (Helen Hayes); Anastasia: The Mystery of Anna, 1986 (made-for-TV; Olivia de Havilland); Anastasia, 1997 (Angela Lansbury); BBC Play of the Month, 1965-1983 (TV series; "Rasputin," 1971 episode; Lally Bowers); BBC Sunday-Night Theatre, 1950-1959 (TV series; "Anastasia," 1953 episode: Helen Hayes); Edward the King, 1975- (TV series; "The Invisible Queen," 1975 episode: Jane Lapotaire); Fall of Eagles, 1974- (TV miniseries; "The Last Tsar," 1974 episode; Ursula Howells); Jennie: Lady Randolph Churchill, 1974- (TV miniseries; "Jennie Jerome," 1974 episode: Thorey Mountain); Kajastus, 1930 (Anielka Elter); Lyubov imperatora, 2002- (TV series; Natalya Panina); **Nicholas and Alexandra**, 1971 (Irene Worth); Rasputin, 1939 (Gabrielle Robinne).

Maria Nickolaevna (1899-1918; Marie Romanov; grand duchess of Russia, daughter of Czar Nicholas II; assassinated): Assassin of the Tsar, 1993 (Alyona Teremizova); Fall of Eagles, 1974 (TV miniseries; "Tell the King the Sky Is Falling," 1974 episode: Prue Clarke); The Lost Prince, 2004 (made-for-TV; Nastya Razduhova); **Nicholas and Alexandra**, 1971 (Candace Glendenning); Rasputin, 1996 (made-for-TV;

Helen Hayes (as Empress Maria Feodorovna), Ivan Desny and Akim Tamiroff in *Anastasia,* **1956.**

Zsofia Ivony); **Rasputin and the Empress**, 1932 (Jean Parker); The Romanovs: An Imperial Family, 2000 (Olga Vasileva); The Successor, 1996 (Natasha Inozemtseva). Note: For detailed information on the assassination of Nicholas II and his family, see my two-volume work *The Great Pictorial History of World Crime*, Volume II (History, Inc., 2004; illustrated pages 79-83).

Marie Antoinette (1755-1793; Queen of France): The Affair of the Necklace, 2001 (Joely Richardson); Arme Bitos, 1962 (made-for-TV; Do van Stek); BBC Sunday-Night Theatre, 1950-1959 (TV series; "The Magnificent Egotist," 1957 episode: Vera Fusek; "The Three Daughters of M. Dupont," 1958 episode; Olive McFarland); Beaumarchais the Scoundrel, 1997 (Judith Godreche); **Black Magic**, 1949 (Nancy Guild); Cagliostro, 1929 (Suzanne Bianchetti); Captain of the Guard, 1930 (Evelyn Hall); C'etait Marie-Antoinette, 2010 (made-for-TV; Natacha Regnier); The Count of Brechard, 1940 (Tina Lattanzi); Dave Thomas: The Incredible Time Travels of Henry Osgood, 1986 (made-for-TV; Catherine O'Hara); The Days That Made History, 2009- (TV series; Estelle Skornik); DuBarry, 1915 (Miss Robinson); Farewell, My Queen, 2012 (Diane Kruger); The Ghosts of Versailles, 1992 (made-for-TV; Teresa Stratas); I Married an Angel, 1942 (Evelyn Atchinson); If Paris Were Told to Us, 1956 (Lana Marconi); Il cavaliere di Maison Rouge [aka: The Glorious Avenger], 1954 (Renee Saint-Cyr); **Janice Meredith**, 1924 (Princess Marie de Bourbon); Jefferson in Paris, 1995 (Charlotte de Turckheim); **John Paul Jones**, 1959 (Susan [Susana] Canales); Joseph Balsamo, 1973- (TV miniseries; Eva Kinsky); The King without a Crown, 1937 (Doris Lloyd); La camera explore le temps, 1957-1966 (TV series; one 1958 episode: Annie Ducaux; one 1960 episode; Eleonore Hirt; one 1962 episode: Giselle Pascal); La comtesse de Charny, 1989 (TV miniseries; Isabelle Guiard); La Marseillaise, 1938 (Lisa Delamare); La nuit de Varennes, 1982 (Eleonore Hirt); La revolution francaise, 1989 (Jane Seymour); Lady Oscar, 1979 (Christine Bohm); Lafayette, 1963 (Liselotte Pulver); L'Autrichienne, 1990 (Ute Lemper); Le chevalier de Maison Rouge, 1963- (TV series; Annie Ducaux); Leaves from Satan's Book, 1920 (Tenna Kraft); The Legendary Chevalier De Saint-George, 2011 (made-for-TV; Marie Van Rhijn); The Legendary Curse of the Hope Diamond, 1975 (made-for-TV; Claudine Longet); Les jupons de la revolution, 1989- (TV series; "Marie Antoinette, reine d'un seul amour," 1989 episode: Emmanuelle Beart); Let Them Eat Cake!, 1999- (TV series; Elizabeth Berrington); L'ete de la revolution, 1989 (made-for-TV; Brigitte Fossey); Liberte, egalite, choucroute, 1985 (Ursula Andress); Los miserable, 1973- (TV series; Norma Jimenez Pons); Louis XVI, the Man Who Didn't Want to Be King, 2011 (made-for-TV; Raphaelle Agogue); Madame Du Barry, 1934 (Anita Louise); Madame du Barry, 1954 (Isabelle Pia); Madame

Gerard Oury and Glynis Johns (as Mary Tudor) in *The Sword and the Rose*, **1953.**

Sans-Gene, 1925 (Vicherat); Maria Theresia, 1951 (Loni von Friedl); Maria Theresia, 1980 (made-for-TV; Ingar Schulmann); **Marie Antoinette**, 1938 (Norma Shearer); Marie Antoinette, 1975 (TV miniseries; Genevieve Casile; Pascale Christoph as young Marie Antoinette); Marie Antoinette, 2005 (made-for-TV; Vahina Giocante); Marie Antoinette, 2006 (Kirsten Dunst); Marie Antoinette, 2006 (made-for-TV; Karine Vanasse); Marie Antoinette—Das Leben einer Konigin, 1929 (Diana Karenne); Marie Antoinette is niet dood, 1996 (Antje de Boeck); Mesmer, 1994 (Beatie Edney); Miss Morison's Ghosts, 1981 (made-for-TV; Anna Korwin); **Mr. Peabody & Sherman**, 2014 (Lauri Fraser voiceover); My Lady's Slipper, 1916 (Julia Swayne Gordon); **Napoleon**, 1927 (Suzanne Bianchetti); Nicolas Le Floche, 2008 (TV series; "Le noye du Grand Canal," 2015 episode: Claire Ganaye); Novela, 1963-1978 (TV series; "El collar de la reina," 1976 episode: Amparo Pamplona); One National Marking for the King, 1970 (made-for-TV; Anna Miserocchi); The Queen of Spades, 1965 (Jacqueline Monsigny); The Queen's Necklace, 1929 (Diana Karenne); Queen's Necklace, 1947 (Marion Dorian); Remontons les Champs-Elysees, 1939 (Anna Scott); Ridicule, 1996 (Mirabelle Kirkland); The Rose of Versailles, 1979-1980 (animated TV series; Miyuki Ueda voiceover); The Rose of Versailles, 2008 (animated; Ayako Kawasumi voiceover); Royal Affairs in Versailles, 1957 (Francoise Jacquier); **Scaramouche**, 1923 (Clotilde Delano); **Scaramouche**, 1952 (Nina Foch); Shadow of the Guillotine, 1956 (Michele Morgan); **Start the Revolution without Me**, 1970 (Billie Whitelaw); The Story of Mankind, 1957 (Marie Wilson); Terror in the Wax Museum, 1973 (Rickie Weir); The Time Tunnel, 1966-1967 (TV series; "Reign of Terror," 1966 episode: Monique LeMaire); Une maison, une histoire, 1980- (TV series; "Marie-Antoinette," 1980 episode: Blanche Ravalec); Witness to Yesterday, 1998- (TV series; "Marie Antoinette," 1998 episode: Cynthia Dale).

Marie de Medici (1575-1642; second wife of Henry IV of France; queen of France): The Captain, 1946 (Huguette Duflos); Captain Blood, 1960 (Lise Delamare); Cinq-Mars, 1981 (made-for-TV; Madeleine Robinson); The Days That Made History, 2009- (TV series; Chiara de Luca); Henri 4, 2010 (Gabriela Maria Schmeide); La bouquetiere des innocents, 1923 (Dany Delile); La camera explore le temps, 1957-1966 (TV series; one 1960 episode: Helene Tossy); Remontons les Champs-Elysees, 1939 (Germaine Dermoz); Richelieu, 1977 (TV miniseries; Maria Wimmer); Richelieu ou La journee des dupes, 1983 (made-for-TV; Dominque Blanchar); Young Blades, 2001 (Sian Webber).

Mark the Evangelist (Saint Mark, one of the four Evangelists who wrote the Gospels; the others being Matthew, Luke and John): Acts of the Apostles, 1969- (TV miniseries; Mohamed Ktari); The Eleventh Hour,

1962-1964 (TV series; Robert Vaughn); Imperium: Saint Peter, 2005 (made-for-TV; Marco Leonardi); **The King of Kings**, 1927 (Micky Moore); The Passion, 2008 (TV miniseries; Mark Lewis Jones); Paul of Tarsus, 1960- (TV series; David Spenser); Peter and Paul, 1981 (made-for-TV; David Gwillim); Quo Vadis, 1985- (TV miniseries; Stojan Decermic).

Marshall, George C. (George Catlett Marshall; 1880-1959; U.S. soldier, five-star general, chief of staff and 50th U.S. secretary of state); Churchill and the Generals, 1981 (made-for-TV; Joseph Cotten); Collision Course: Truman vs. MacArthur, 1976 (made-for-TV; Ward Costello); Day One, 1989 (made-for-TV; Hal Holbrook); Enola Gay; The Men, the Mission, the Atomic Bomb, 1980 (made-for-TV; Bill Morey); First Target, 2013 (Tony Vingerhoets); Hiroshima, 1995 (made-for-TV; Leon Pownall); Ike: The War Years, 1979 (TV miniseries; Dana Andrews); The Last Bastion, 1984 (TV miniseries; Reg Gillam); **MacArthur**, 1977 (Ward Costello); **Pearl Harbor**, 2001 (Scott Wilson); **Saving Private Ryan**, 1998 (Harve Presnell); Tail Gunner Joe, 1977 (made-for-TV; John Anderson); **Tora! Tora! Tora!**, 1970 (Keith Andes); Truman, 1995 (made-for-TV; Harris Yulin); War and Remembrance, 1988 (TV miniseries; Norman Burton); War of China's Fate, 1999 (made-for-TV; Francis Dumaurier); World War Two: Behind Closed Doors, 2008-2009 (TV series; Michael J. Reynolds); The World Wars, 2014 (TV miniseries; Sewell Whitney).

Marshall, John (John James Marshall; 1755-1835; U.S. chief justice of the Supreme Court): Cavalcade of America, 1952-1957 (TV series; "Decision for Justice," 1955 episode: Jeff Morrow); General Electric Theater, 1953-1962 (TV series; "Strange Witness," 1958 episode: Sidney Blackmer); John Adams, 2008- (TV miniseries; Jack Gwaltney); **The President's Lady**, 1953 (George Spaulding); **The Remarkable Andrew**, 1942 (Brandon Hurst).

Mary (saint; mother of Jesus): A.D., 1985 (TV miniseries; Millie Perkins); Behold the Man, 1935 (Juliette Verneuil); **Ben-Hur: A Tale of the Christ**, 1925 (Betty Bronson); Color of the Cross, 2006 (Debbi Morgan); The Cross, 2001 (Jenny Gago); Crown of Thorns, 1934 (silent; Henny Porten); Family Theatre, 1949-1958 (TV series; "Triumphant Hour," 1953 episode: Mary Alan Hokanson); The Final Inquiry, 2006 (Maria Pia Calzone); The Gospel according to St. Matthew, 1966 (Margherita Caruso as the younger Mary; Susanna Pasolini as the older Mary); The Gospel of Luke, 2015 (Karima Gouit); The Gospel of Mark, 2015 (Karima Gouit); **The Greatest Story Ever Told**, 1965 (Dorothy McGuire); Hail Mary, 1985 (Myriem Roussel); Herod and Marianne, 1965 (made-for TV; Antje Weissgerber); Il messia, 1975 (Mita Ungaro); **Intolerance: Love's Struggle throughout the Ages**, 1916 (Lillian Langdon); Jesus, 1979 (Rivka Neuman); Jesus, 2000 (made-for-TV; Jacqueline Bisset); Jesus, Maria y Jose, 1972 (Gayle Bedall); Jesus of Nazareth, 1942 (Aurora Walker); Jesus of Nazareth, 1977 (TV miniseries; Olivia Hussey); Jesus: The Desire of Ages, 2014 (Stephanie Gerard); Joseph and Mary, 2016 (Lara Jean Chorostecki); Joseph of Nazareth, 2000 (made-for-TV; Stefania Rivi); **The King of Kings**, 1927 (Dorothy Cumming); **King of Kings**, 1961 (Siobhan McKenna); Kristo, 1996 (Charmaine Rivera); The Lawton Story, 1949 (Darlene Bridges); The Life of Jesus Christ, 2011- (TV miniseries; Savannah Stevenson); The Living Christ Series, 1951 (TV miniseries; Eileen Rowe); Marie de Nazareth, 1995 (Myriam Muller); Mary, Mother of Jesus, 1999 (made-for-TV; Pernilla August; Melinda Kinnaman as young Mary); Mary, Mother of the Son of God, 2003 (Giovanna Antonelli); Mary's Song, 2010 (Lilly Salcedo; Carin Carmichael as older Mary); The Passion of Christ, 2004 (Maia Morgenstern); The Pilgrimage Play, 1949 (Helen Wood); The Power of the Resurrection, 1958 (Mary Patton); Restitution, 1918 (Mabel Harvey); Son of God, 2014 (Leila Mimmack as young Mary; Roma Downey as older Mary); The Visual Bible: The Gospel of John, 2003 (Diana Berriman); The Young Messiah, 2016 (Sara Lazzaro).

Mary I (1496-1533; Queen Mary Tudor; queen of England, daughter of Henry VIII; called "Bloody Mary" because of her brutal persecution of Protestants): **Anne of the Thousand Days**, 1969 (Nicola Pagett); Die Liebe und die Konigin, 1977 (made-for-TV; Inge Keller); Elizabeth R, 1971-1972 (TV miniseries; "The Lion's Club," 1971 episode: Daphne Slater); **Elizabeth**, 1998 (Kathy Burke); Henry VIII, 2003 (made-for-TV; Lara Belmont); Lady Jane, 1986 (Jane Lapotaire); **Lady Jane Grey**, 1936 (Gwen Ffrangcon-Davies); Mary Tudor, 1917 (Jeanne Delvair), Mary Tudor, 1920 (Ellen Richter); Mary Tudor, 1966 (made-for-TV; Francoise Christophe); The Other Boleyn Girl, 2008 (Constance Stride); **The Pearls of the Crown**, 1938 (Yvette Pienne); Piece of the Sky, 1958 (Lia Ferrel); The Six Wives of Henry VIII, 1970 (TV miniseries; Alison Frazer, Verina Greenlaw); **The Sword and the Rose**, 1953 (Glynis Johns); The Tudors, 2007-2010 (TV series; Sarah Bolger); The Twisted Tale of Bloody Mary, 2008 (made-for-TV; Miranda French as older Mary; Lizzie Rees as young Mary); The Tudors, 2007-2010 (TV series; Blathnaid McKeown); **When Knighthood Was in Flower**, 1922 (Marion Davies).

Mary, Queen of Scots (Mary Stuart; Mary I of Scotland; 1542-1587): BBC Play of the Month, 1965-1983 (TV series; "Mary, Queen of Scots," 1969 episode: Virginia McKenna); Border Warfare, 1990 (made-for-TV; Maria Miller); Elizabeth, 2000 (made-for-TV; Seana Montague); Elizabeth I, 2005 (TV miniseries; Barbara Flynn); Elizabeth R, 1971-1972 (TV miniseries; two episodes: Vivian Pickles); **Elizabeth: The Golden Age**, 2007 (Samantha Morton); Elizabeth R, 1971-1972 (TV miniseries; Vivian Pickles); Father Came Too!, 1964 (Hugh Lloyd); Gunpowder, Treason & Plot, 2004 (made-for-TV; Clemence Poesy); The Heart of the Queen, 1940 (Zarah Leander); La camera explore le temps, 1957-1966 (TV series; one 1962 episode: Pascale Audret); The Loves of Mary, Queen of Scots, 1923 (Fay Compton); Maria Stuart, 1963 (made-for-TV; Agnes Fink); Maria Stuart, 1980 (made-for-TV; Gertraud Kreissig); Maria Stuart, 2008 (made-for-TV; Susanne Wolff); **Mary of Scotland**, 1936 (Katharine Hepburn); Mary, Queen of Scots, 1971 (Vanessa Redgrave); Mary, Queen of Scots, 2013 (Camille Rutherford); Mary Stuart, 1974 (made-for-TV; Maria Becker); Mary Stuart, 1982 (made-for-TV; Janet Baker); Mistress of Hardwick, 1972- (TV series; Gilly McIver); Novella, 1979-1980 (TV series; Angels Moll); **The Pearls of the Crown**, 1938 (Colette Borelli/Jacqueline Delubac); Play of the Week, 1959-1961 (TV series; "Mary Stuart," 1960 episode; Signe Hasso); Princess of Cleves, 1961 (Renee-Marie Potet); Pulitzer Prize Playhouse, 1950-1952 (TV series; "Mary of Scotland," 1951 episode: Helen Hayes); The Queen's Traitor, 1967 (TV series; Stephanie Beacham); Reign, 2013- (TV series; Adelaide Kane); Seven Seas to Calais, 1963 (Esmeralda Ruspoli); Sir Francis Drake, 1961- (TV series; "Queen of Scots," 1961 episode: Noelle Middleton); A Traveller in Time, 1978- (TV series; three 1978 episodes: Heather Chasen); The Virgin Queen, 1923 (Maisie Fisher); The Virgin Queen, 2005 (TV miniseries; Joanne Whalley; Charlotte Winner); You Are There, 1953-1971 (TV series; "The Execution of Mary, Queen of Scots [February 8, 1587]," 1954 episode: Mildred Natwick).

Mary Magdalene (Mary of Bethany; Hebrew woman; follower of Jesus and, in biblical references, present at the crucifixion of Jesus and at His Resurrection; birth and death dates unknown): **Barabbas**, 1962 (Paola Pitagora); **The Battle Cry of Peace**, 1915 (Julia Swayne Gordon); Behold the Man, 1935 (Vanah Yami); Color of the Cross, 2006 (Marjan Faritous); Color of the Cross 2: The Resurrection, 2008 (Roque); The Cross, 2001 (Devon Stohl); Crown of Thorns, 1934 (silent; Asta Nielsen); Day of Triumph, 1954 (Joanne Dru); Family Theatre, 1949-1958 (TV series; "Triumphant Hour," 1953 episode: Jeanne Bates); The Final Inquiry, 2006 (Ornella Muti); The Gospel of Mark, 2015 (Leila El Fadili); **The Greatest Story Ever Told**, 1965 (Joanna Dunham); Il messia, 1975 (Antonella Fasono); Jesus, 1979 (Talia Shapira); Jesus, 2000 (made-for-TV; Debra Messing); Jesus Christ Superstar, 1972

Katharine Hepburn as Mary, Queen of Scots in *Mary of Scotland*, 1936.

(made-for-TV; Michele Fawdon); **Jesus Christ Superstar**, 1973 (Yvonne Elliman); Jesus of Nazareth, 1942 (Adriana Lamar); Jesus of Nazareth, 1977 (TV miniseries; Anne Bancroft); Jesus: The Desire of Ages, 2014 (Desiree Orozco); **The King of Kings**, 1927 (Jacqueline Logan); **King of Kings**, 1961 (Carmen Sevilla); Kristo, 1996 (Amy Austria); The Last Supper: Thirteen Men of Courage, 2007 (made-for-TV; Marianna Hare); The Lawton Story, 1949 (Hazel Lee Becker); The Living Bible, 1952 (TV series; Mary Dew); Mary, 2005 (Juliette Binoche); Mary Magdalene, 2000 (made-for-TV; Maria Grazia Cucinotta); Mary, Mother of Jesus, 1999 (made-for-TV; Simone Bendix); The Passion of Christ, 2004 (Monica Bellucci); The Pilgrimage Play, 1949 (Fiona O'Shiel); The Power of the Resurrection, 1958 (Lisa Pons); Redenzione, 1919 (Diana Karenne); Son of God, 2014 (Amber Rose Revah); The Son of God, 2016 (Marina Artigas); The Twice Born Woman, 1921 (Deyha Loti); The Visual Bible: The Gospel of John, 2003 (Lynsey Baxter); Which Will Ye Have!, 1949 (Betty Ann Davies).

Masseria, Joe (aka: Joe the Boss; 1886-1931; U.S. crime boss in NYC during Prohibition): Boardwalk Empire, 2010- (TV series: seven episodes: Ivo Nandi); Bonanno: A Godfather's Story, 1999 (made-for-TV; Tony Calabretta); The Gangster Chronicles, 1981- (TV series; Richard S. Castellano); Gangster Wars, 1981 (Richard S. Castellano); Lansky, 1999 (made-for-TV; Bill Capizzi); Mobsters, 1991 (Anthony Quinn); **The Valachi Papers**, 1972 (Alessandro Sperli). Note: For detailed information on Masseria, see my book *World Encyclopedia of Organized Crime* (Paragon House, 1992; illustrated pages 278-280).

Masterson, William Barclay (aka: "Bat" U.S.; lawman in the Old West and later newspaper sports reporter; 1853-1921): Any Last Words?, 2012 (Tom Lagleder); Appointment with Destiny, 1971-1973 (TV series; "Showdown at O.K. Corral," 1972 episode: Dan Ferrone); Badman's Country, 1958 (Gregory Walcott); Bat Masterson, 1958-1961 (TV series; Gene Barry); Bordertown, 1989-1991 (TV series; two 1990 episodes: Steve Makaj); Doctor Who, 1963-1989 (TV series; many episodes: Richard Beale); The Gambler Returns: The Luck of the Draw, 1991 (made-for-TV; Gene Barry); The Gunfight at Dodge City, 1959 (Joel McCrea); **Gunfight at the O.K. Corral**, 1957 (Kenneth Tobey); Guns of Paradise, 1988-1990 (TV series; "A Gathering of Guns," 1989 episode: Gene Barry); The Life and Legend of Wyatt Earp, 1955-1961 (TV series; Mason Alan Dinehart); **Masterson of Kansas**, 1954 (George Montgomery); The Outlaws is Coming!, 1965 (Ed T. McDonnell); Prince of the Plains, 1949 (Monte Hale); **Santa Fe**, 1951 (Frank Ferguson); **Trail Street**, 1947 (Randolph Scott); **Wild Bill Hickok**, 1923 (Jack Gardner); **Winchester '73**, 1950 (Steve Darrell); **Witchita**, 1955 (Keith Larsen); **The Woman of the Town**, 1943 (Albert Dekker);

Greta Garbo (as WWI spy Mata Hari) in *Mata Hari*, 1931.

Wyatt Earp, 1994 (Tom Sizemore); Wyatt Earp's Revenge, 2012 (Matt Dallas). Note: For detailed information on Masterson, see my book *Encyclopedia of Western Lawmen and Outlaws* (Paragon House, 1992; illustrated pages 227-229).

Mata Hari (Margaretha Gertrude Zelle MacLeod; 1876-1917; exotic Dutch dancer and WWI spy for Germany; executed by a French firing squad): Blasco Ibanez, 1997- (TV miniseries; Mabel Lozano); Der Fall Mata Hari, 1966 (made-for-TV; Louise Martini); Dossier Mata Hari, 1967- (TV miniseries; Cosetta Greco); General Electric Theater, 1953-1962 (TV series; "I Will Not Die," 1957 episode: Merle Oberon); La camera explore le temps, 1957-1966 (TV series; one 1964 episode: Francoise Fabian); Marthe Richard, 1944 (Delia Col); Mata Hari, 1920 (Asta Nielsen); **Mata Hari**, 1931 (Greta Garbo); Mata Hari, 1981- (TV miniseries; Josine Van Dalsum); Mata Hari, 1985 (Sylvia Kristel); **Mata Hari, Agent H21**, 1967 (Jeanne Moreau); Mata Hari, la vraie histoire, 2003 (made-for-TV; Maruschka Detmers); Mata Hari: The Red Dancer, 1927 (Magda Sonja); Mentors, 1998-2005 (TV series; "Secrets and Lies," 2002 episode: Joanne Kelly); Operation Mata Hari, 1968 (Carmen de Lirio); Up the Front, 1972 (Zsa Zsa Gabor); The Young Indiana Jones Chronicles, 1992-1993 (TV series; "Paris, October 1916," 1993 episode: Domiziana Giordano). Note: For detailed information on Matra Hari, see my book *Spies: A Narrative Encyclopedia of Dirty Tricks & Double Dealing from Biblical Times to Today* (M. Evans, 1997; illustrated pages 337-342).

Matisse, Henri (French artist; 1869-1954): La banda Picasso, 2012 (Tony Gaultier); **Midnight in Paris**, 2011 (Yves-Antoine Spoto); **Surviving Picasso**, 1996 (Joss Ackland); The Young Picasso: 1881-1906, 1993 (TV miniseries; Maximo Astray).

Matthew (Saint Matthew; One of the twelve Apostles of Jesus and one of the four Evangelists): A.D., 1985 (TV miniseries; David Joss Buckley); Animated Stories from the New Testament, 1987- (TV series; Tim Eisenhart voiceover); Apostle Peter and the Last Supper, 2012 (Tom Konkle); Behold the Man, 1935 (Paul Asselin); Color of the Cross, 2006 (J.R. Dziengel); Color of the Cross 2: The Resurrection, 2008 (Lature Irvin); Crown of Thorns, 1934 (silent; Walter Neumann); The Day Christ Died, 1980 (made-for-TV; Ralph Arliss); Day of Triumph, 1954 (Lawrence Dobkin); Family Theatre, 1949-1958 (TV series; "Hill Number One: A Story of Faith and Inspiration," 1951 episode: Gene Lockhart; "Triumphant Hour," 1953 episode: Sam Flint); The Gospel according to Matthew, 1993 (Richard Kiley as old Matthew; Matthew Dylan Roberts as young Matthew); The Gospel according to St. Matthew, 1966 (Ferruccio Nuzzo); The Gospel of John, 2014 (Mohamed

El Korchi); Gospel Road: A Story of Jesus, 1973 (Terrence Winston Mannock); **The Greatest Story Ever Told**, 1965 (Roddy McDowall); Il messia, 1975 (Renato Montalbano); Incident in Judaea, 1991 (made-for-TV; Frank Baker); Jesus [aka: The Jesus Film], 1979 (Mosko Alkalai); Jesus, 2000 (made-for-TV; Sebastian Knapp); Jesus of Nazareth, 1942 (Manuel Santamaria); Jesus of Nazareth, 1977 (TV miniseries; Keith Washington); Judas, 2004 (made-for-TV; Paul Haigh); **King of Kings**, 1961 (Ruben Rojo); Kristo, 1996 (Jorge Estregan); The Last Supper: Thirteen Men of Courage, 2007 (made-for-TV; Dave Dixon); The Living Christ Series, 1951 (TV miniseries; Robert Bice); Mary, 2005 (Alex Grazioli); Mary and Joseph: A Story of Faith, 1979 (made-for-TV; Lloyd Bochner); Mary, Mother of the Son of God, 2003 (Leonardo Senna); Matthew: 26:17, 2005 (Philip Shahbaz); The Miracle Maker, 2000 (Patrick Godfrey); The Nativity, 2010 (TV miniseries; Gawn Grainger); Pasion, 2007 (TV miniseries; Martin Ferro); The Passion, 2008 (TV miniseries; Daniel Evans); The Passover Plot, 1976 (Michael Baseleon); The Power of the Resurrection, 1958 (Milt Hamerman); Risen, 2016 (Manu Fullola); Son of God, 2014 (Said Bey); Testament: The Bible in Animation, 1996 (TV series; Jonathan Tafler); The Testaments: Of One Fold and One Shepherd, 2000 (Paul Mugerian).

Mattingly, Thomas Kenneth "Ken", II (U.S. astronaut; 1936-): **Apollo 13**, 1995 (Gary Sinise); From Earth to the Moon, 1998- (TV miniseries; Zeljko Ivanek); Man, Moment, Machine, 2005-2007 (TV series; "Apollo 13: Triumph on the Dark Side," 2006 episode: Shawn Kresal).

Maugham, W. Somerset (1874-1965; British playwright, novelist, short story writer and espionage agent): Lillie, 1978- (TV miniseries; Patrick Marley); **The Moon and Sixpence**, 1942 (role model for Herbert Marshall); **The Razor's Edge**, 1946 (Herbert Marshall); Ziegfeld: The Man and His Women, 1978 (made-for-TV; David Griffiths); The Winds of War, 1983- (TV miniseries; Duncan Ross). Note: For detailed information on Maugham and his espionage service for England, see my book *Spies: A Narrative Encyclopedia of Dirty Tricks & Double Dealing from Biblical Times to Today* (M. Evans, 1997; illustrated pages 342-345).

Maximilian I (1832-1867; Austrian nobleman and Emperor I of Mexico): Aquellos anos, 1974 (Paco Morayta); El carruaje, 1972 (TV series; Carlos Monden); El vuelo del aguila, 1994 (TV series; Mario Ivan Martinez); Goodyear Playhouse, 1951-1957 (TV series; "Crown of Shadows," 1952 episode: Leslie Nielsen); The Hourglass Sanatorium, 1973 (Wlodzimierz Nowak); Imperial Cavalry, 1942 (Rene Cardona); **Juarez**, 1939 (Brian Aherne); Juarez and Maximillian, 1935 (Enrique Herrera); La Paloma, 1938 (Enrique Herrera); The Mad Empress, 1939 (Conrad Nagel); Mademoiselle Midnight, 1924 (Earl Schenck); Maximilian von Mexiko, 1970 (made-for-TV; Michael Heltau); Prariejager in Mexiko: Benito Juarez, 1988 (Erwin Berner); A Rainha Louca, 1967- (TV series; Rubens de Falco); Universum History, 2013- (TV series; "Maximilian von Mexiko—Der Traum vom Herrschen," 2014 episode: Jurgen Kapaun); **Vera Cruz**, 1954 (George Macready); Unter der Dornenkrone—Mexikos kaisertragodie, 1921 (Niels Jensen).

May, Alan Nunn (1911-2003; British physicist and Soviet spy who supplied Russia with atomic secrets in WWII): Atom Spies, 1979 (made-for-TV; Edward Wilson); Der Verrat von Ottawa, 1966 (made-for-TV; Franz Rudnick). Note: For detailed information on May, see my book *Spies: A Narrative Encyclopedia of Dirty Tricks & Double Dealing from Biblical Times to Today* (M. Evans, 1997; illustrated pages 345-346).

May, John (1893-1929; U.S. strong-arm man and mechanic of the George "Bugs" Moran gang, who, along with six others, was killed in Chicago's notorious 1929 St. Valentine's Day Massacre): Capone, 1975 (Jim Galante); Playhouse 90, 1956-1961 (TV series; "Seven against the Wall," 1958 episode: Wayne Heffley); **The St. Valentine's Day Massacre**, 1967 (Bruce Dern). Note: For detailed information on May and the other victims of the St. Valentine's Day Massacre, see my book *Bloodletters and Badmen: A Narrative Encyclopedia of American Criminals from the Pilgrims to the Present* (M. Evans, 1973-2015; illustrated pages 584-586).

Mayer, Louis B. (1884-1957; movie mogul and longtime head of MGM studio in Hollywood): **The Aviator**, 2004 (Stanley DeSantis); Child Star: The Shirley Temple Story, 2001 (made-for-TV; John O'May); Gable and Lombard, 1976 (Allen Garfield); Harlow, 1965 (Jack Kruschen); Life with Judy Garland: Me and My Shadows, 2001 (made-for-TV; Al Waxman); Malice in Wonderland, 1985 (made-for-TV; Richard Dysart); Mommie Dearest, 1981 (Howard Da Silva); Rainbow, 1978 (made-for-TV; Martin Balsam); RKO 281, 1999 (made-for-TV; David Suchet); The Three Stooges, 2000 (made-for-TV; David Baldwin); Titans, 1981-1982 (TV series; Al Waxman); **Trumbo**, 2015 (Richard Portnow).

Maynard, Robert (c. 1684-1751; British Royal Navy officer who hunted and killed Blackbeard the pirate): Blackbeard, 2006 (TV miniseries; Mark Umbers); Blackbeard the Pirate, 1952 (Keith Andes); True Caribbean Pirates, 2006 (made-for-TV; Peter Bisson); TV Reader's Digest, 1955-1956 (TV series; "The End of Blackbeard the Pirate," 1955 episode: Robert Knapp).

Mazarin, Jules (Cardinal Mazarin; 1602-1661; influential French Catholic prelate): Angelique, 2013 (Rainer Frieb); Blanche, 2002 (Jean Rochefort); D'Artagnan, 1969 (TV miniseries; Gilberto Mazzi); The Further Adventures of the Musketeers, 1967- (TV series; William Dexter); If Paris Were Told to Us, 1956 (Samson Fainsilver); The Iron Mask, 1962 (Enrico Maria Salerno); The King Is Dancing, 2000 (Serge Feuillard); The King, the Squirrel and the Grass Snake, 2010- (TV series; Jean-Pol Dubois); The Lady Musketeer, 2004 (TV miniseries; Gerard Depardieu); Le camera explore le temps, 1957-1966 (TV series, "La conjuration de Cinq-Mars," 1962 episode: Georges Riquier); Le cardinal de Retz, 1975 (made-for-TV; Alain Mottet); Le chevalier Tempete, 1967- (TV series; Giani Esposito); Le roi soleil, 2006 (Pierre Forest); Le viconte de Bragelonne, 1954 (Nico Pepe); The Man in the Iron Mask, 1998 (Jeremy West); Mazarin, 1978 (TV miniseries; Francois Perier); Ninon de Lenclos, 1920 (Julius Strobl); The Queen and the Cardinal, 1935 (Robert Le Vigan); The Queen and the Cardinal, 2009 (made-for-TV; Philippe Torreton); The Return of the Musketeers, 1989 (Philippe Noiret); Richelieu, 1977- (TV miniseries; Jean Negroni); The Rise of Louis XIV, 1966 (made-for-TV; Cesar Silvagni); Royal Affairs in Versailles, 1957 (Samson Fainsilber); Richelieu, 1977 (TV miniseries; Jean Negroni); Versailles: The Dream of a King, 2008 (made-for-TV; Enrico Di Giovanni); Vingt ans apres, 1922 (Jean Perier); Young Blades, 2005- (TV miniseries; Michael Ironside).

McCall, Jack (John "Jack" McCall; aka: Crooked Nose Jack; 1853-1877; U.S. Old West murderer of Wild Bill Hickok in Deadwood): Badlands of Dakota, 1941 (Lon Chaney Jr.); Buffalo Girls, 1995 (made-for-TV; Jerry King); Deadwood, 2004-2006 (TV series; Garret Dillahunt); Deadwood Dick, 1940 (serial; Karl Hackett); Jack McCall, Desperado, 1953 (George Montgomery); Legend, 1995- (TV series; "The Life, Death, and Life of Wild Bill Hickok," 1995 episode: John Pyper-Ferguson); **The Plainsman**, 1936 (Porter Hall); **The White Buffalo**, 1977 (Martin Kove); **Wild Bill**, 1995 (David Arquette); Wild Jack, 1989- (TV miniseries; John Schneider).

MacArthur, Charles (1895-1956; U.S. screenwriter and playwright, husband of actress Helen Hayes, and often collaborator with writer Ben Hecht): Mrs. Parker and the Vicious Circle, 1994 (Matthew Broderick); The Young Indiana Jones Chronicles, 1992-1993 (TV series; "Young Indiana Jones and the Mystery of the Blues," 1993 episode: Barry Bell).

Michael Redgrave (in a role modeled on Ramsay MacDonald) in *Fame Is the Spur,* **1949.**

MacArthur, Douglas (1880-1964; U.S. five-star general; commanded Allied forces in Southwest Pacific in WWII and UN forces during the Korean War): America: Call to Greatness, 1995 (made-for-TV; James Huston); **An American Guerrilla in the Philippines**, 1950 (Robert Barrat); Code Breakers, 2005 (made-for-TV; Jeremy Akerman); Collision Course: Truman vs. MacArthur, 1976 (made-for-TV; Henry Fonda); **The Court Martial of Billy Mitchell**, 1955 (Dayton Lummis); Death of a Soldier, 1986 (Jon Sidney); **Emperor**, 2012 (Tommy Lee Jones); Farewell to the King, 1989 (John Bennett Perry); In Pursuit of Honor, 1995 (made-for-TV; James Sikking); Inchon, 1982 (Laurence Olivier); Korea: The Unknown War, 1988 (TV series; Charlton Heston); The Korean War, 2001 (TV series; Frank Novak); The Last Bastion, 1984 (TV series; Robert Vaughn); **MacArthur**, 1977 (Gregory Peck); The Republic, 1998 (Istemi Betil); The Sun, 2005 (Robert Dawson); **They Were Expendable**, 1945 (Robert Barrat); Truman, 1995 (made-for-TV; Daniel von Bargen); Voyagers!, 1982-1983 (TV series; "Sneak Attack," 1983 episode: Frank Marth); The World Wars, 2014 (TV miniseries; Prescott Hathaway as young MacArthur; Daniel Martin Berkey as elder MacArthur).

MacArthur, Jean (Jean Marie Faircloth MacArthur; 1898-2000; second wife of U.S. General of the Army Douglas MacArthur): Collision Course: Truman vs. MacArthur, 1976 (made-for-TV; Priscilla Pointer); Inchon, 1982 (Dorothy James); **MacArthur**, 1977 (Marj Dusay).

MacDonald, James Ramsay (1866-1937; British statesman and head of the Labour Party; prime minister of England, 1924; 1929-1935): Days of Hope, 1975- (TV miniseries; "1926: General Strike," 1975 episode: John Young); Fame Is the Spur, 1949 (role model for Michael Redgrave); **Gandhi**, 1982 (Terrence Hardiman); Monty Python's Flying Circus, 1969-1974 (TV series; "How Not to Be Seen," 1970 episode; Michael Palin); Mosley, 1998 (TV series; Ralph Riach); Number 10, 1983- (TV miniseries; "Underdog," 1983 episode: Ian Richardson); Winston Churchill: The Wilderness Years, 1981- (TV miniseries; Robert James).

McCarthy, Joseph Raymond (1908-1957; U.S. politician and U.S. senator [Wis.], who lead federal probes into subversive communist activities in the late 1940s and early 1950s, often called "witch hunts"): Citizen Cohn, 1992 (made-for-TV; Joe Don Baker); Der Senator, 1968 (made-for-TV; Siegfried Wischnewski); J. Edgar Hoover, 1987 (made-for-TV; Charles Hallahan); **The Private Files of J. Edgar Hoover**, 1977 (George D. Wallace); The Real American: Joe McCarthy, 2012 (John Sessions); Robert F. Kennedy and His Times, 1985 (TV miniseries; Harris Yulin); Tail Gunner Joe, 1977 (made-for-TV; Peter Boyle).

Susan Hayward (as Messalina) in *Demetrius and the Gladiators*, 1954.

Note: For detailed information on McCarthy, see my book *Spies: A Narrative Encyclopedia of Dirty Tricks & Double Dealing from Biblical Times to Today* (M. Evans, 1997; page 347).

McCarthy, Joseph Vincent (aka: "Joe"; American baseball player and manager; 1887-1978): **The Pride of the Yankees**, 1942 (Harry Harvey); **The Winning Team**, 1952 (Hugh Sanders).

McClellan, George Brinton (1826-1885; U.S. military officer and Union general in the American Civil War): Lincoln, 1974- (TV series; "The Unwilling Warrior," 1975 episode; Ed Flanders); Lincoln, 1988 (made-for-TV; David Leary); Lincoln, 1992 (made-for-TV; Stacy Keach); Lost River: Lincoln's Secret Weapon, 2010 (Stan Babola); The Mexican-American War, 2006 (made-for-TV; Ron Fallica); My Brother's War, 2005 (William Laney); North and South, 1985- (TV miniseries; Chris Douridas); **Saving Lincoln**, 2013 (Jamie Elman); To Appomattox, 2015 (TV miniseries; Jason O'Mara).

McClusky, Clarence Wade, Jr. (U.S. admiral, who led a squadron of carrier-based bombers that destroyed several Japanese carriers in the decisive battle of Midway in WWII; 1902-1976): **Midway**, 1976 (Christopher George); **Task Force**, 1949 (Bruce Bennett).

McGurn, Jack (aka: Machine Gun Jack; Vincenzo Antonio Gibaldi; 1902-1936; Chicago Capone gangster and enforcer; reported architect of Chicago's 1929 St. Valentine Day's Massacre): Capone, 1975 (Carmen Argenziano); Playhouse 90, 1956-1961 (TV series; "Seven against the Wall," 1958 episode; Paul Stevens); **The St. Valentine's Day Massacre**, 1967 (Clint Ritchie); The Untouchables, 1959-1963 (TV series; "The Eddie O'Gara Story," 1962 episode; K.L. Smith); The Verne Miller Story, 1988 (Frank Costa). Note: For detailed information on McGurn, see my book *World Encyclopedia of Organized Crime* (Paragon House, 1992; illustrated pages 259-261).

McKellar, Kenneth Douglas (American politician and U.S. senator [Tenn.]; 1869-1957): The F.B.I. Story: The FBI versus Alvin Karpis, Public Enemy Number One, 1974 (made-for-TV; Whit Bissell); **J. Edgar**, 2011 (Michael O'Neill); J. Edgar Hoover, 1987 (made-for-TV; Mills Watson); **The Private Files of J. Edgar Hoover**, 1977 (Jim Antonio); **Public Enemies**; 2009 (Ed Bruce).

McKinley, William (1843-1901; U.S. politician and 25th President of the U.S.; assassinated): The Adventures of Ociee Nash, 2003 (Daniel Burnley); Captains and Kings, 1976 (TV series; Stephen Colt); A Message to Garcia, 1936 (John Carradine); Rough Riders, 1997 (made-for-

TV; Brian Keith); **This Is My Affair**, 1937 (Frank Conroy); The Virginian, 1962-1971 (TV series; "The Land Dreamer," 1969 episode: John Daniels. Note: For detailed information on McKinley and his assassination, see my two-volume work, *The Great Pictorial History of World Crime*, Volume I (History, Inc., 2004; illustrated [9 images] pages 55-59).

McLowery, Frank (McLaury; 1848-1881; U.S. cowboy and outlaw; killed in the gunfight at the O.K. Corral in Tombstone, Arizona, on October 26, 1881): Appointment with Destiny, 1971-1973 (TV series; "Showdown at O.K. Corral," 1972 episode: Steve DeFrance); **Doc**, 1971 (James Greene); **Gunfight at the O.K. Corral**, 1957 (Mickey Simpson); **Hour of the Gun**, 1967 (David Perna); I Married Wyatt Earp, 1983 (made-for-TV; Randy Wells); The Life and Legend of Wyatt Earp, 1955-1961 (TV series; four 1961 episodes: George Wallace); Tombstone Territory, 1957- (TV series; "Pick Up the Gun," 1958 episode: Paul Comi); **Tombstone**, 1993 (Robert John Burke); **Tombstone: The Town Too Tough to Die**, 1942 (Dick Curtis); **Wyatt Earp**, 1994 (Rex Linn); Wyatt Earp: Return to Tombstone, 1994 (made-for-TV; George Wallace); You Are There, 1953-1957 (TV series; "The Gunfight at the O.K. Corral," 1955 episode; Art Rease). Note: For detailed information on Frank and Tom McLowery, see my book *Encyclopedia of Western Lawmen and Outlaws* (Paragon House, 1992; illustrated pages 75-77).

McLowery, Thomas (McLaury; 1853-1881; U.S. cowboy and outlaw; killed in the gunfight at the O.K. Corral in Tombstone, Arizona, on October 26, 1881): Appointment with Destiny, 1971-1973 (TV series; "Showdown at O.K. Corral," 1972 episode: Archie Deming Jr.); **Gunfight at the O.K. Corral**, 1957 (Jack Elam); **Hour of the Gun**, 1967 (Jim Sheppard); I Married Wyatt Earp, 1983 (made-for-TV; Joe Corcoran); The Life and Legend of Wyatt Earp, 1955-1961 (TV series; four 1961 episodes: Greg Palmer); **Tombstone**, 1993 (John Philbin); **Tombstone: The Town Too Tough to Die**, 1942 (Paul Sutton); **Wyatt Earp**, 1994 (Adam Baldwin); Wyatt Earp: Return to Tombstone, 1994 (made-for-TV; Gregg Palmer). Note: For detailed information on Frank and Tom McLowery, see my book *Encyclopedia of Western Lawmen and Outlaws* (Paragon House, 1992; illustrated pages 75-77).

McPherson, Aimee Semple (AKA: Sister Aimee; 1890-1944; U.S. evangelist): Aimee Semple McPherson, 2006 (Mimi Michaels); **Elmer Gantry**, 1960 (role model for Jean Simmons who plays Sister Sharon Falconer).

Meade, George Gordon (1815-1872; U.S. military officer and Union general during the American Civil War): The Blue and the Gray, 1982 (TV miniseries; Rory Calhoun); Bronco, 1958-1962 (TV series; "The Burning Springs," 1959 episode: Morris Ankrum); The Dramatic Life of Abraham Lincoln, 1924 (Alfred Allen); **Gettysburg**, 1993 (Richard Anderson); To Appomattox, 2015 (TV miniseries; Dwight Yoakam); **Virginia City**, 1940 (Thurston Hall).

Means, Gaston Bullock (American private detective, swindler and accused murderer; 1879-1938): Boardwalk Empire, 2010- (made-for-TV; six episodes: Stephen Root); J. Edgar Hoover, 1987 (made-for-TV; Robert Alan Browne).

Mejia, Tomas (1820-1867; Mexican general under Maximilian I): Aquellos anos, 1974 (Rodrigo Puebla); Cinco de Mayo, La battala, 2013 (Pablo Abitia); **Juarez**, 1939 (Bill Wilkerson); Juarez and Maximillian, 1935 (J. Enriquez); The Mad Empress, 1939 (Julian Rivero); Maximilian von Mexiko, 1970 (made-for-TV; Uwe Friedrichsen); Prariejager in Mexiko: Benito Juarez, 1988 (Rolf Mey-Dahl).

Melba, Nellie (Dame Nellie Melba; 1861-1931; Australian operatic soprano and one of the most famous singers of the Victorian era): Downton

Abbey, 2010- (TV series; Kiri Te Kanawa); Melba, 1953 (Patrice Munsel); Melba, 1988 (TV series; Linda Cropper, singing vocals by Yvonne Kenny).

Mencken, H.L. (1880-1956; U.S. journalist, editor and cultural critic): Alleged, 2010 (Colm Meaney); **Inherit the Wind**, 1960 (role model for Gene Kelly).

Mengele, Joseph Rudolf (1911-1979; Nazi physician who committed atrocities through medical experiments and eugenics, using captive human guinea pigs in his operations; he was called the "Angel of Death" and is credited with murdering more than 300,000 persons at the Nazi extermination camp Auschwitz in 1943-1945; using an alias following WWII, 1939-1945, he later fled to Argentina, then to Paraguay and subsequently Brazil, drowning while swimming on the Brazilian coast on February 7, 1979, and was buried under a false name): After the Truth, 1999 (Gotz George); And the Violins Stopped Playing, 1981 (Marcin Tronski); **The Boys from Brazil**, 1978 (Gregory Peck); Commando Mengele, 1987 (Howard Vernon); Danger 5, 2011- (TV series; "Lizard Soldiers of the Third Reich," 2012 episode: "Revenge of the Lizardmen," 2015 episode: played in both episodes by Robert Tompkins); The German Doctor, 2014 (Alex Brendemuhl); **The Grey Zone**, 2002 (Henry Stram); Heroes of the North, 2010-2011 (TV series; Constantine Kourtidis); The Hydric Zone, 2015- (TV series; "Rise of the Mutant Wetlands," 2015 episode; Silvio Wolf Busch); Kessler, 1981 (TV miniseries; Oscar Quitak); **Marathon Man**, 1976 (Laurence Olivier, role modeled on Joseph Mengele); Out of the Ashes, 2003 (made-for-TV; Jonathan Cake); Playing for Time, 1980 (made-for-TV; Max Wright); **Schindler's List**, 1993 (Daniel Del-Ponte); Surf Nazis Must Die, 1987 (Michael Sonye); Testees, 2008 (TV series); The Unborn, 2009 (Braden Moran); Walking the Dead, 2000- (TV series; "Yahrzeit: Part 1" and "Yahrzeit: Part 2," 2007 episodes: Carsten Hayes).

Mercer, Lucy (Lucy Page Mercer Rutherfurd; U.S. wealthy socialite, 1891-1948; she conducted a long-term secret affair with U.S. President Franklin D. Roosevelt; she was the former social secretary to Roosevelt's wife, Eleanor, 1914-1916, until Mrs. Roosevelt discovered the affair, which, despite his promise to terminate the relationship, Franklin continued surreptitiously for three more decades): Eleanor and Franklin, 1976 (made-for-TV; Linda Kelsey); Eleanor and Franklin: The White House Years, 1977 (made-for-TV; Linda Kelsey).

Mesmer, Franz Friedrich Anton (1734-1815; German physician and astronomer who developed mesmerism or hypnotism): **Black Magic**, 1949 (Charles Goldner); The Dear Augustin, 1962 (Rudolf Forster); Epidemic, 1987 (Lars von Trier); Jefferson in Paris, 1995 (Daniel Mesguich); Mesmer, 1994 (Alan Rickman; Bence Kertesz as young Mesmer); Xena: Warrior Princess, 1995-2001 (TV series; "Dreamworker," 1995 episode: Michael Daly); Wind over the City, 1996 (Zinovy Gerdt).

Messalina (Valeria Messalina; 17-48 A.D.; scheming and adulterous wife of Roman emperor Claudius): A.D., 1985 (TV miniseries; Jennifer O'Neill); The Affairs of Messalina, 1952 (Maria Felix); The Caesars, 1968- (TV miniseries; Nicola Pagett); Caligula, 1980 (Anneka Di Lorenzo); Caligula and Messalina, 1981 (Betty Roland); **Demetrius and the Gladiators**, 1954 (Susan Hayward); I, Claudius, 1937 (Merle Oberon); I, Claudius, 1976 (TV miniseries; Sheila White); Imperium: Nero, 2004 (made-for-TV; Sonia Aquino); Messalina, 1924 (Rina De Liguoro); Messalina, 1960 (Belinda Lee); Messalina, Empress of Rome, 1977 (Anneka Di Lorenzo); Messalina vs. the Son of Hercules, 1964 (Lisa Gastoni); Nero and the Burning of Rome, 1954 (Yvonne Sanson); Nerone e Messalina, 1953 (Ludmilla Dudarova); Woman, 1918 (Flora Revalles).

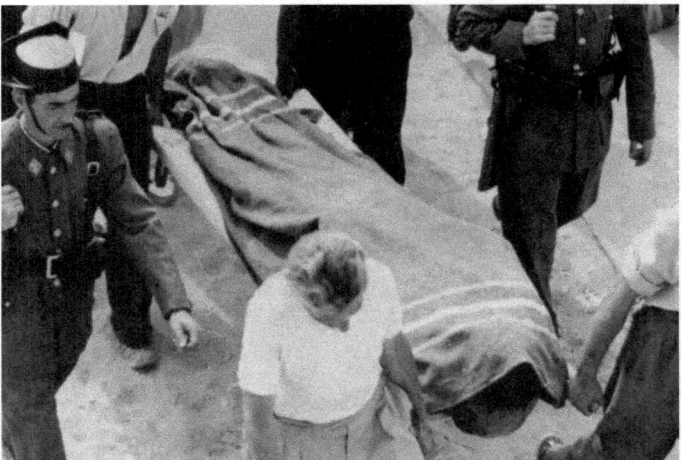

Corpse (role modeled on Glyndwr Michael) being carried in *The Man Who Never Was*, 1956.

Metternich, Klemens von (Prince Metternich; 1773-1859; German politician and statesman): BBC Sunday-Night Theatre, 1950-1959 (TV series; "L'Aiglon," 1953 episode: Andre Van Gyseghem); Bismarck, 1940 (Franz Schafheitlin); The Bridgeman, 2002 (Ivan Darvas); Congress Dances, 1932 (Conrad Veidt); Congress of Love, 1966 (Hannes Messemer); **Conquest**, 1937 (Ian Wolfe); Fanny Elssler, 1937 (Paul Hoffmann); **The House of Rothschild**, 1934 (Alan Mowbray); Hundred Days, 1935 (Kurt Junker); **Immortal Beloved**, 1994 (Barry Humphries); The Iron Duke, 1935 (Farren Soutar); **Juarez**, 1939 (Walter Kingsford); Loyalty of Love, 1937 (Luigi Cimara); The Mad Empress, 1939 (Gustav von Seyffertitz); Napoleon, 1955 (O. W. Fischer); Napoleon, 2002- (TV miniseries; Julian Sands); Napoleon and Love, 1974- (TV miniseries; "The End of Love," 1974 episode: Lewis Fiander); 100 Days of Napoleon, 1936 (Lamberto Picasso); Princess Alexandra, 1992 (made-for-TV; Jean-Jacques Moreau); A Royal Divorce, 1938 (Laurence Hanray); Serenade, 1940 (Pierre Magnier); The Strauss Dynasty, 1991- (TV miniseries; Edward Fox); The Strauss Family, 1972 (TV miniseries; John Harvey); The Strauss Dynasty, 1991- (TV miniseries; Edward Fox); Vienna Blood, 1942 (Ernst Fritz Furbringer); You Are There, 1953-1971 (TV series; "Napoleon's Return from Elba [March 7, 1815]," 1955 episode: John Mylong).

Meucci, Antonio (1808-1889; Italian inventor who created a telephonic device some years before Alexander Graham Bell was granted the patent on his telephone in 1876, but Meucci's device reportedly did not provide any electromagnetic transmission of vocal sound): Antonio Meucci, 1940 (Luigi Pavese); Antonio Meucci, 1970- (TV miniseries; Paolo Stoppa); Meucci, 2005 (made-for-TV; Massimo Ghini).

Meusel, Robert William (aka: "Bob"; American baseball player and home-run hitter for the New York Yankees, part of "Murderer's Row"; 1896-1977): **The Pride of the Yankees**, 1942 (himself).

Michael, Glyndwr (1909-1943; Welsh derelict who had swallowd rat poison and, with no known relatives, his body was passed off as an Allied officer carrying top war plans, the corpse sent from a British submarine to wash to the shores of Spain where it was examined by Nazi officials then in league with Francisco Franco's administration. The documents found with the body convinced the Nazis that the Allies planned to invade Sardinia and Greece, instead of Sicily in 1943 and they moved forces to anticipate that attack while Allied troops successfully invaded Sicily): **The Man That Never Was**, 1956 (role modeled on the corpse of Glyndwr Michael).

Michelangelo (1475-1564; Italian Renaissance artist): **The Agony and**

Charles Bickford (as Cardinal Mindszenty) and Kenneth MacDonald in *Guilty of Treason*, 1950.

the Ecstasy, 1965 (Charlton Heston); Borgia, 2011 (TV series; Danny Szam); The Cardinal, 1936 (Wilfred Fletcher); Galileo: On the Shoulders of Giants, 1998 (made-for-TV; Tony Nardi); Il magnifico avventuriero, 1963 (Andrea Bosic); Leonardo, 2003 (made-for-TV; Adam Croasdell); The Life of Leonardo Da Vinci, 1971 (TV series; Bruno Cinno); Michelangelo Buonaroti, 1977 (made-for-TV; Boris Cavazza); Michelangelo Superstar, 2005 (made-for-TV; Dan Badarau); The Tudors, 2007-2010 (TV series; "His Majesty's Pleasure," 2008 episode: James McHale); Upon This Rock, 1970 (Orson Welles voiceover); Vita de Michelangelo, 1964- (TV series; Gian Maria Volonte).

Miles, Nelson (U.S. Army military officer and general in Indian wars and the Spanish-American War; 1839-1925): Bury My Heart at Wounded Knee, 2007 (made-for-TV; Shaun Johnston); Colt .45, 1957-1960 (TV series; "The Rival Gun," 1959 episode: Stephen Chase); Comanche, 1956 (John Litel); **Geronimo: An American Legend**, 1993 (Kevin Tighe); The Great Adventure, 1963-1964 (TV series; two 1963 episodes with Kent Smith as General Miles); Mr. Horn, 1979 (made-for-TV; Stafford Morgan); Kenny Rogers as the Gambler, Part III: The Legend Continues, 1987 (made-for-TV; George Kennedy).

Miller, Clell (Cleland D. Miller; 1850-1876; U.S. Old West outlaw; member of James-Younger gang): American Outlaws, 2001 (Ty O'Neal); Frank and Jesse, 1995 (John Pyper Ferguson); **The Great Missouri Raid**, 1951 (Guy Wilkerson); **The Great Northfield, Minnesota Raid**, 1972 (R. G. Armstrong); The Legend of Jesse James, 1965-1966 (TV series; Armand Alzamora); **The Long Riders**, 1980 (Randy Quaid). Note: For detailed information on Miller, see my book *Encyclopedia of Western Lawmen and Outlaws* (Paragon House, 1992; page 232).

Miller, Don (aka: "Midnight Miller"; American football player and coach; halfback of the legendary "Four Horseman" backfield at Notre Dame, 1922-1924; 1902-1979): **Knute Rockne All American**, 1940 (William Marshall).

Miller, Edward T. (U.S. western outlaw, member of James-Younger gang; c. 1856-1881): **The Assassination of Jesse James by the Coward Robert Ford**, 2007 (Garret Dillahunt); **The Long Riders**, 1980 (Dennis Quaid).

Miller, Glenn (American musician, composer and bandleader; 1904-1944): The Big Broadcast of 1936 (himself as a trombonist in the Ray Noble Orchestra); **The Glenn Miller Story**, 1954 (James Stewart); **Orchestra Wives**, 1942 (himself); **Sun Valley Serenade**, 1941 (himself).

Miller, Marilyn (Mary Ellen Reynolds; 1898-1936; U.S. singer, dancer and actress, one of the great musical stars of the 1920s and early 1930s): **The Great Ziegfeld**, 1936 (Rosina Lawrence); Look for the Silver Lining, 1949 (June Haver); **Till the Clouds Roll By**, 1946 (Judy Garland); Ziegfeld: The Man and His Women, 1978 (Pamela Peadon).

Miller, Verne (Vernon C. Miller; 1896-1933; former South Dakota sheriff turned bank robber and killer; identified as one of the killers at the 1933 Kansas City Massacre): Baby Face Nelson, 1957 (Dan Terranova); Guns Don't Argue, 1957 (Russ Whitney); The Kansas City Massacre, 1975 (made-for-TV; Matt Clark); The Verne Miller Story, 1988 (Scott Glenn).

Mindszenty, Joseph (1892-1975; Hungarian cardinal of the Catholic Church who was imprisoned for opposing the Nazis in WWII and, later, when the Soviets seized Hungary, imprisoned and tortured by Communists; he took refuge in the U.S. embassy during the 1956 Hungarian Revolution, living there for fifteen years until allowed to leave the country, going to Austria): Guilty of Treason, 1950 (Charles Bickford); **The Prisoner**, 1955 (Alec Guinness); Studio One in Hollywood, 1948-1958 (TV series; "Cardinal Mindszenty," 1954 episode: Claude Dauphin).

Minoru Genda (Japanese naval air force officer and planner of the sneak attack at Pearl Harbor on December 7, 1941; 1904-1989): **Midway**, 1976 (Robert Ito); **Pearl Harbor**, 2002 (Cary-Hiroyuki Tagawa); **Tora! Tora! Tora!**, 1970 (Tatsuya Mihashi).

Miramon, Miguel (1832-1867; Mexican general under Maximilian I): Aquellos anos, 1974 (Hector Andremar); El carruaje, 1972 (TV series; Claudio Obregon); El vuelo del aguila, 1994 (TV series; Juan Carlos Munoz); **Juarez**, 1939 (Henry O'Neill); Juarez and Maximillian, 1935 (Roberto E. Guzman); Maximilian von Mexiko, 1970 (made-for-TV; Peter Maertens).

Miriam (sister of Moses and Aaron in the Old Testament): **The Prince of Egypt**, 1998 (Sandra Bullock voiceover; Sally Dworsky singing voice); **The Ten Commandments**, 1923 (Estelle Taylor); **The Ten Commandments**, 1956 (Olive Deering); The Ten Commandments, 2006 (made-for-TV; Susan Lynch); The Ten Commandments, 2007 (Kathleen Barr voiceover); The Ten Commandments: The Musical, 2006 (Alisan Porter).

Mitchell, John Newton (1913-1988; U.S. attorney and 67th U.S. Attorney general): Blind Ambition, 1979 (TV miniseries; John Randolph); **Nixon**, 1995 (E. G. Marshall); The Pentagon Papers, 2003 (Sean McCann).

Mitchell, William (aka: Billy; 1879-1936; U.S. Army general and considered the father of the U.S. Air Force): **The Court Martial of Billy Mitchell**, 1955 (Gary Cooper); **A Guy Named Joe**, 1943 (role model for Lionel Barrymore).

Mitsuo Fuchida (Japanese naval officer and aviator who led the first wave of warplanes in the sneak attack against Pearl Harbor, December 7, 1941; 1902-1976): **Tora! Tora! Tora!**, 1970 (Takahiro Tamura).

Moctezuma II (Montezuma; 1466-1520; Aztec king of Mexico, killed in the Spanish conquest of Hernan Cortes): Carlos, Rey Emperador, 2015-2016 (TV series; Cristhian Esquivel); The Golden Years, 1992 (made-for-TV; Ronald Pickup); La hija de Moctezuma, 2014 (Rafael Inclan); Montezuma, 1992 (Dominique Visse); The Miracle Roses, 1960 (Crox Alvarado); Visita al Pasado, 1981 (Miguel Angel Rodriguez); The Woman God Forgot, 1917 (Raymond Hatton); You Are There, 1953-1971 (TV series; "The Conquest of Mexico [1519]," 1953 episode: Juano Hernandez).

Model, Walter (1891-1945; German field marshal in WWII; committed suicide): **A Bridge Too Far**, 1977 (Walter Kohut); The Great Battle, 1973 (Peter Sturm).

Modigliani, Amedeo Clemente (1884-1920; Italian painter and sculptor): Modi, 1989 (Richard Berry); Modigliani, 2004 (Andy Garcia); Modigliani of Montparnasse, 1961 (Gerard Philipe).

Moliere (1622-1673; Jean-Baptiste Poquelin; French playwright and actor): BBC Play of the Month, 1965-1983 (TV series; "Tartuffe," 1971 episode: David Nettheim); If Paris Were Told to Us, 1956 (Gilbert Gil); Jean de la Fontaine—Le defi, 2007 (Julien Corbey); The King Is Dancing, 2000 (Tcheky Karyo); The King, the Squirrel and the Grass Snake, 2010- (TV series; Gerard Moulevrier); Le negre de Moliere, 2005 (made-for-TV; Patrick Mille); Le roi soleil, 2006 (Pierre Forest); Mademoiselle Moliere, 1964 (made-for-TV; Robert Manuel); The Man in the Iron Mask, 1998 (Dan Coplan); Marquise, 1997 (Bernard Giraudeau); Moliere, 1980 (Philippe Caubere); Moliere, 2007 (Romain Duris); Moliere pour rire et pour pleurer, 1973- (TV miniseries; Jean-Pierre Darras); Moliere spielt in Versailles, 1955 (made-for-TV; Fritz Remond Jr.); Royal Affairs in Versailles, 1957 (Fernand Gravey); Scaramouche, 1965- (TV miniseries; Gianrico Tedeschi); 1789, 1974 (Philippe Caubere); Theatre Night, 1985- (TV series; "Moliere," 1985 episode: Antony Sher); Versailles: The Dream of a King, 2008 (made-for-TV; Thierry Garet).

Molotov, Vyacheslav (Russian politician and Soviet diplomat; 1890-1986): Countdown to War, 1989 (made-for-TV; Michael Cronin); The Inner Circle, 1991 (Viktor Balabanov); **Mission to Moscow**, 1943 (Gene Lockhart); Playhouse 90, 1956-1961 (TV series; "The Plot to Kill Stalin," 1958 episode: Luther Adler); Red Monarch, 1983 (made-for-TV; Nigel Stock); Stalin, 1992 (made-for-TV; Clive Merrison); Staline est morte, 1981 (made-for-TV; Jean-Pierre Delage); World War II: When Lions Roared, 1994 (made-for-TV; Jan Triska); Yalta, 1984 (made-for-TV; Vladimir Jevtovic).

Moltke, Helmuth von (Helmuth Johann Ludwig von Moltke; Helmuth von Moltke the Younger; 1848-1916; German general and chief of staff of the German army and instrumental in planning operations that launched WWI): Europas letzter Sommer, 2012 (made-for-TV; Volker Spahr); The Great Victory, Wilson or the Kaiser? The Fall of the Hohenzollerns, 1919 (Carl De Mel); 1914, The Last Days before the War, 1932 (Wolfgang von Schwindt); **Oh! What a Lovely War**, 1969 (John Clements); Preussen uber alles—Bismarcks deutsche Einigung, 1971 (TV miniseries; Sigfrit Steiner); 37 Days, 2014 (TV miniseries; Bernhard Schutz).

Mongkut (Rama IV; 1804-1868; king of Siam, who hired Anna Leonowens as governess and teacher to his harem of thirty-nine wives and concubines and eighty-two children): Anna and the King, 1972- (TV series; Yul Brynner); Anna and the King, 1999 (Yun-fat Chow); **Anna and the King of Siam**, 1946 (Rex Harrison); **The King and I**, 1956 (Yul Brynner); The King and I, 1999 (animated; Martin Vidnovic voiceover).

Monroe, James (U.S. politician and 5th President of the U.S.; 1758-1831): The Ace of Spades, 1925 (Bert Sprotte); The Adams Chronicles, 1976 (TV miniseries; Henry Butler); Alexander Hamilton, 1931 (Morgan Wallace); The Beautiful Mrs. Reynolds, 1918 (Charles Brandt); George Washington II: The Forging of a Nation, 1986 (made-for-TV; Robert Kelly); Hearts Divided, 1936 (John Elliott); In the Days of Daniel Boone, 1923 (Jack Lewis); The Patriots, 1963 (made-for-TV; Michael Higgins).

Monroe, Marilyn (Norma Jean Mortenson; 1926-1962; U.S. actress who

Gary Cooper (as Billy Mitchell) in *The Court Martial of Billy Mitchell*, **1955.**

overdosed on drugs to end her spectacular film career): Another Chance, 1989 (Arlene Lorre); Dark Skies, 1996-1997 (TV series: "The Warren Omission," 1997 episode: Susan Griffiths); Hoover vs. the Kennedys: The Second Civil War, 1987 (made-for-TV; Heather Thomas); The Kennedys, 2011 (TV series; Charlotte Sullivan); Marilyn & Bobby: Her Final Affair, 1993 (made-for-TV; Melody Anderson); Marilyn: The Untold Story, 1980 (made-for-TV; Catherine Hicks; Tracey Gold as young Norma Jean); The Rat Pack, 1998 (made-for-TV; Barbara Niven); Timequest, 2000 (Shelley Marks); A Woman Named Jackie, 1991 (TV miniseries; Eve Gordon).

Montcalm, Louis-Joseph de (1712-1759; French soldier and general, commander of French forces in the Americas during the Seven Years' War [French and Indian War, 1754-1763]): Fall of the Mohicans, 1965 (Pastor Serrador); Hawkeye and the Last of the Mohicans, 1957- (TV series; Gregory Gaye); The Last of the Mohicans, 1932 (Mischa Auer); **The Last of the Mohicans**, 1936 (William Stack); The Last of the Mohicans, 1971 (TV miniseries; George Pravda); **The Last of the Mohicans**, 1992 (Patrice Chereau).

Montespan, Madame (Francoise-Athenais; Marquise de Montespan; French mistress of Louis XIV; 1640-1707): Royal Affairs in Versailles, 1957 (Claudette Colbert); Versailles, 2015- (TV series; Anna Brewster).

Montez, Lola (Montes; Eliza Rosanna Gilbert; Countess of Landsfeld; 1921-1861; Irish dancer and actress, who became the mistress of Ludwig I of Bavaria and who made her Countess of Landsfeld): Black Bart, 1948 (Yvonne De Carlo); The Californians, 1957-1959 (TV series; "Lola Montez," 1958 episode: Patricia Medina); Death Valley Days, 1952-1970 (TV series; "Lotta Crabtree," 1954 episode: Yvonne Cross; "Lola Montez," 1955 episode: Paula Morgan); **Golden Girl**, 1951 (Carmen D'Antonio); Lisztomania, 1975 (Anulka Dziubinska); **Lola Montes**, 1959 (Martine Carol); Lola Montez, 1944 (Conchita Montenegro); Lola Montez, 1918 (Leopoldine Konstantin); Lola Montez, die Tanzerin des Konigs, 1922 (Ellen Richter); The Loves of Liszt [AKA: Szerelmi almok—Liszt], 1975 (Larissa Trembovelskaya; Ildiko Pecsi voiceover); Ludwig—Requiem for a Virgin King, 1980 (Ingrid Caven); Midnight Madness, 1918 (Claire Du Brey); The Palace of Pleasure, 1926 (Betty Compson); **Royal Flash**, 1975 (Florinda Bolkan); Tales of Wells Fargo, 1957-1962 (TV series; "Lola Montez," 1959 episode: Rita Moreno); **Wells Fargo**, 1937 (Sheila Darcy).

Montgomery, Bernard Law (1887-1976; British field marshal in WWII): The Battle of El Alamein, 1971 (Michael Rennie); Bertie and Elizabeth, 2002 (made-for-TV; Corin Redgrave); Churchill and the Generals, 1981

Martine Carol (as Lola Montez) and Oskar Werner in *Lola Montes,* **1959.**

(made-for-TV; Ian Richardson); **The Desert Fox: The Story of Rommel**, 1951 (Trevor Ward); Dieppe, 1993 (made-for-TV; Graham Harley); Ike: Countdown to D-Day, 2004 (made-for-TV; Bruce Phillips); Ike: The War Years, 1979 (TV miniseries; Ian Richardson); Into the Storm, 2009 (made-for-TV; Patrick Malahide); Jackboots on Whitehall, 2011 (animated; Tobias Menzies voiceover); **The Longest Day**,1962 (Trevor Reid); **Patton**, 1970 (Michael Bates); Pierrepoint: The Last Hangman, 2007 (Clive Francis); War and Remembrance, 1988- (TV miniseries; Peter Dennis); The World Wars, 2014- (TV miniseries; "Never Surrender," 2014 episode: Joseph K. Bevilacqua).

Moore, Grace (aka: "Tennessee Nightingale"; 1898-1947; U.S. operatic soprano and actress of stage and film, her career and life prematurely ended by a plane crash near Copenhagen, Denmark, on January 26, 1947): **So This Is Love**, 1953 (Kathryn Grayson).

Moran, George Clarence (aka: "Bugs"; 1891-1957; Chicago crime boss of the North Side during Prohibition): **Al Capone**, 1959 (Murvyn Vye); Capone, 1975 (Robert Phillips); Early Edition, 1996-2000 (TV series; "Everybody Goes to Rick's," 2000 episode: Kevin Fry); Playhouse 90, 1956-1961 (TV series; "Seven against the Wall," 1958 episode: Dennis Patrick); **Scarface**, 1932 (role model for Boris Karloff); **The St. Valentine's Day Massacre**, 1967 (Ralph Meeker); The Untouchables, 1959-1963 (TV series; "The George 'Bugs' Moran Story," 1959 episode: Lloyd Nolan; "Arnsenal," 1962 episode: Robert J. Wilke; "The Eddie O'Gara Story," 1962 episode: Robert J. Wilke; "Doublecross," 1962 episode: Harry Morgan); The Untouchables, 1993-1994 (TV series; 'Chinatown," 1993 episode: Jack Thibeau); The Verne Miller Story, 1988 (Sean Moran). Note: For comprehensive details on Moran, his archenemy Capone and the Chicago gangs and gangsters of the 1920s, as well as the St. Valentine's Day Massacre, see my works *Bloodletters and Badmen* (M. Evans, 1973, 1995; Capone: pages 119-130; McGurn: pages 408-411; Moran: pages 439-444; O'Bannion: 472-478; Weiss: pages 662-666), *Encyclopedia of Organized Crime*, (Paragon House, 1992; Capone: pages 78-98; Burke: pages 74-75; McGurn: pages 259-261; Moran: pages 288-291; O'Bannion: pages 304-310; St. Valentine's Day Massacre: pages 343-347; Weiss: pages 402-403), and *The Great Pictorial History of World Crime* (History, Inc., 2004; Capone et al.: illustrated pages 503-541).

More, Thomas (Saint Thomas More since 1935; 1478-1535; British author, philosopher and statesman): Henry VIII and His Six Wives, 1972 (Michael Goodliffe); God's Outlaw, 1986 (Bernard Archard); Henry VIII: Mind of a Tyrant, 2009 (TV series: Ryan Kiggell); The Last Rose of Summer, 1937 (John Garrick); A Man for All Seasons, 1957 (made-

for-TV; Bernard Hepton); **A Man for All Seasons**, 1966 (Paul Scofield); A Man for All Seasons, 1988 (made for TV; Charlton Heston); A Royal Love, 2016 (Francis Cox); Thomas More, 1964 (made-for-TV; Kurt Meisel); The Tudors, 2007-2010 (TV series; Jeremy Northam); Wolf Hall, 2015 (TV miniseries; Anton Lesser).

Morgan, Helen (1900-1941; U.S. torch singer): **The Helen Morgan Story**, 1957 (Ann Blyth; singing vocals by Gogi Grant); Parade of Stars, 1983 (made-for-TV; Dinah Shore); Playhouse 90, 1956-1961 (TV series; "The Helen Morgan Story," 1957 episode: Polly Bergen).

Morgan, Henry (c. 1635-1688; Welsh buccaneer, privateer and onetime pirate who became an admiral of the British Royal Navy): **The Black Swan**, 1942 (Laird Cregar)' Blackbeard the Pirate, 1952 (Torin Thatcher); The Boy and the Pirates, 1960 (Timothy Carey); Double Crossbones, 1951 (Robert Barrat); Morgan, the Pirate, 1960 (Steve Reeves); Pirates of Tortuga, 1961 (Robert Stephens); True Caribbean Pirates, 2006 (made-for-TV; Lance J. Holt). Note: For detailed information on Morgan, see my two-volume work, *The Great Pictorial History of World Crime*, Volume II (History, Inc., 2004; illustrated [4 images] pages 1277-1279).

Morny, Charles de (Duke de Morny, 1811-1865; French statesman): Aquellos anos, 1974 (Martin LaSalle); Eugenia de Montijo, 1944 (Nicolas Novarro); Fanatisme, 1934 (Pierre Juvenet); Henry Dunant: Red on the Cross, 2006 (made-for-TV; Jeff El Eini); Her People, 1928 (Robert Guilbert); **Juarez**, 1939 (Frank Reicher); La valse de Paris, 1950 (Jacques Castelot); Miss Bonaparte, 1942 (Aime Clariond); Ottocento, 1959-1960 (TV miniseries; Diego Michelotti); Violettes imperiales, 1932 (Robert Dartois).

Moses (Hebrew leader, prophet and lawgiver; 1391-1271 B.C.): After Six Days, 1920 (Guido Guiducci); Are We Civilized?, 1934 (Alin Cavin); BBC Sunday-Night Theatre, 1950-1959 (TV series; "The Green Pastures," 1958 episode: James Clarke); The Bible, 2013 (TV miniseries, "Exodus," 2013 episode: Joe Forte as young Moses; William Houston as older Moses); The Cradle of God, 1926 (Victor Vina); Exodus, 2008 (Jack and Stephen Greenhough as Baby Moses); **Exodus: Gods and Kings**, 2014 (Christian Bale); Greatest Heroes of the Bible, 1978-1979 (TV series; several episodes: John Marley); **The Green Pastures**, 1936 (Frank H. Wilson); The Green Pastures, 1959 (made-for-TV; Frederick O'Neal); Herod and Marianne, 1965 (made-for TV; Wolf Schlamminger); History of the World: Part I, 1981 (Mel Brooks); In the Beginning, 2000 (made-for-TV; Billy Campbell); Moise, 1984 (made-for-TV; Samuel Ramey); Moon of Israel, 1924 (Henry Mar); Moses, 1995 (made-for-TV; Ben Kingsley); Moses and Aaron, 1975 (Gunter Reich); Moses the Lawgiver, 1974 (TV miniseries; Burt Lancaster as adult Moses; William Lancaster as young Moses); Moses und Aaron, 2006 (made-for-TV; Franz Grundheber); Moses and Aaron, 2009 (made-for-TV; Dale Duesing); The Old Testament Scriptures, 1958 (TV series; Thayer Roberts); **The Prince of Egypt**, 1998 (Val Kilmer voiceover; Amick Byram singing voice); Son of God, 2014 (William Houston); The Story of Mankind, 1957 (Francis X. Bushman); **The Ten Commandments**, 1923 (Theodore Roberts); **The Ten Commandments**, 1956 (Charlton Heston); The Ten Commandments, 2006 (made-for-TV; Dougray Scott); The Ten Commandments, 2007 (Christian Slater voiceover); The Ten Commandments: The Musical, 2006 (Val Kilmer).

Mosley, Oswald (1896-1980; British politician and leader of the fascist movement in England): Mosley, 1998 (TV series; Jonathan Cake).

Moulin, Jean (1899-1943; French Resistance leader in WWII killed by the Gestapo): Jean Moulin, 2002 (made-for-TV; Charles Berling); Jean Moulin, une affaire francaise, 2003 (made-for-TV; Francis Huster); La resistance, 2008 (TV miniseries; Scali Delpeyrat); Les dossiers de l'ecran, 1967-1989 (TV series; "Jean Moulin," 1977 episode: Serge Vincent); Marcel Dassault, l'homme au pardessus, 2014 (made-for-TV; Frederic Andrau); Pierre Brossolette ou les passagers de la lune, 2015 (made-for-TV; Quentin Baillot). Note: For detailed information on Moulin, see my book *Spies: A Narrative Encyclopedia of Dirty Tricks & Double Dealing from Biblical Times to Today* (M. Evans, 1997; illustrated pages 358-361).

Mozart, Wolfgang Amadeus (1756-1791; prolific Austrian composer of classical music): **Amadeus**, 1984 (Tom Hulce); Die Forsterchristl, 1931 (Oskar Carlweis); Eternal Melodies, 1940 (Gino Cervi); I, Don Giovanni, 2009 (Lino Guanciale); Jem, 1985-1988 (TV series; "Journey through Time," 1988 episode: Cam Clarke voiceover); Komponisten auf der Spur, 1994- (TV series; "Wolfgang Amadeus Mozart," 2002 episode; Ralf Bauer); La voz humana, 1986-1988 (TV series; "Mozart y Salieri," 1986 episode; Manuel Galiana); The Life and Loves of Mozart, 1959 (Oskar Werner); The Life of Wolfgang Amadeus Mozart [aka: The Mozart Story], 1948 (Hans Holt); Mozart, 1936 (Stephen Haggard); Mozart, 1975 (made-for-TV; Bernard Brocas); Mozart, 1982- (TV miniseries; Christoph Bantzer); Mozart—His Life with Music, 1985 (TV series; David Schofield); Mozart in Love, 1975 (Richard La Bonte); Mozart in viaggio verso Praga, 1974 (made-for-TV; Raoul Grassilli); Mozarts Leben, Lieben und Leiden, 1921 (Josef Zetenius); Mozart's Sister, 2010 (David Moreau); Titans, 1981-1982 (TV series; Richard Monette); Vergesst Mozart, 1985 (investigates Mozart's mysterious death; Max Tidof); Wolfgang A. Mozart, 1991 (Alexander Lutz). Note: For detailed information on the mysterious death of Mozart, see my two-volume work *The Great Pictorial History of World Crime*, Volume II (History, Inc., 2004; illustrated [8 images] pages 793-800).

Mudd, Samuel Alexander (1833-1883; U.S. physician convicted and imprisoned for aiding John Wilkes Booth, assassin of President Abraham Lincoln, albeit he may have been innocent; he helped suppress a Yellow Fever epidemic in prison that saved many lives and was pardoned by President Andrew Johnson in 1869): The Day Lincoln Was Shot, 1998 (made-for-TV; Gary Wheeler); Laramie, 1959-1963 (TV series; "Time of the Traitor," 1962 episode: Lew Ayres); The Lincoln Conspiracy, 1977 (Wallace K. Wilkinson); The Ordeal of Dr. Mudd, 1980 (made-for-TV; Dennis Weaver); **The Prisoner of Shark Island**, 1936 (Warner Baxter); Telephone Time, 1956-1958 (TV series; "The Quality of Mercy," 1958 episode: Harry Townes); Westinghouse Desilu Playhouse, 1958-1960 (TV series; "The Case for Dr. Mudd," 1958 episode: Lew Ayres); You Are There, 1953-1957 (TV series; "The Capture of John Wilkes Booth," 1953 episode: Ernest Sarracino). Note: For detailed information on Mudd and the Lincoln assassination, see my two-volume work *The Great Pictorial History of World Crime*, Volume I (History, Inc., 2004; illustrated pages 26-44).

Muhammad Ahmad (1844-1885; Sudanese religious zealot who proclaimed himself the Mahdi, the messianic redeemer of the Islamic religion and who waged war in the Sudan, overwhelming British forces at Khartoum and killing its commander, General Charles "Chinese" Gordon; he died of typhus six months after capturing the city): **Khartoum**, 1966 (Laurence Olivier).

Muhammad Ali (Cassius Marcellus Clay; 1942-2016 ; U.S. heavyweight prizefighter and champion): Ali, 2001 (Will Smith); Ali: An American Hero, 2000 (made-for-TV; David Ramsey); American Brawler, 2016 (Jerrod Paige); American Gangster, 2007 (Jerrod Paige); Don King: Only in America, 1997 (made-for-TV; Darius McCrary); The Greatest, 1977 (himself); King of the World, 2000 (made-for-TV; Terrence Howard); The Last Punch, 2016 (Karon Riley).

Mukhtar, Omar (1858-1931; Libyan tribal leader who organized resistance to Italian colonization of his country; he was captured and hanged

Charlton Heston as Moses in *The Ten Commandments*, 1956.

by Italian forces): **Lion of the Desert**, 1981 (Anthony Quinn).

Mullins, Priscilla (c.1602-1685; one of the passengers sailing on the historic voyage of the *Mayflower* in 1620 to Plymouth and who married John Alden, a member of the ship's crew): The Courtship of Myles Standish, 1923 (Enid Bennett); Mayflower: The Pilgrims' Adventure, 1979 (made-for-TV; Jenny Agutter); **Plymouth Adventure**, 1952 (Dawn Addams); TV Reader's Digest, 1955-1956 (TV series; "The Voyage of Captain Tom Jones, Pirate," 1955 episode: Kathryn Beaumont).

Mundt, Karl E. (Karl Earl Mundt; 1900-1974; U.S. politician and educator and U.S. senator [S.D.]): Tail Gunner Joe, 1977 (made-for-TV; John Chappell).

Murrieta, Joaquim (Joachim Carrillo Murrieta; c. 1829-c. 1853; California bandit and Mexican patriot): The Avenger, 1931 (Buck Jones); The Bandit Queen, 1950 (Phillip Reed); Behind the Mask of Zorro, 2005 (made-for-TV; Jesse Borrego); The Firebrand, 1962 (Valentin de Vargas); The Gay Defender, 1927 (Richard Dix); The Last Rebel, 1958 (Carlos Thompson); The Man behind the Gun, 1953 (Robert Cabal); **The Mask of Zorro**, 1998 (Victor Rivers); Murieta, 1965 (Jeffrey Hunter); **Robin Hood of El Dorado**, 1936 (Warner Baxter); Vengeance of the West, 1942 (Bill Elliott). Note: For detailed information on Murrieta, see my book *Encyclopedia of Western Lawmen and Outlaws* (Paragon House, 1992; illustrated [5 images] pages 236-238).

Musset, Alfred de (1810-1857; French poet, dramatist and novelist): Farewell Waltz, 1934 (Albert Horrmann); George Who?, 1973 (Yves Renier); **Impromptu**, 1991 (Mandy Patinkin); Notorious Woman, 1974 (TV miniseries; Shane Briant); Pontcarral, colonel d'empire, 1942 (Georges Lequesne).

Mussolini, Benito (aka: Il Duce; 1883-1945; Italian right-wing politician and dictator of Italy,1925-1943; executed along with his mistress, Clara Petacci, on April 28, 1945, by communist Italian partisans): Ace London, 1998- (TV series; "Rumo a Torento," 1998 episode: Julio Cardoso); An American Carol, 2008 (Randall Bosley); The Assassin of Rome, 1972 (Luciano Catenacci); Benito: The Rise and Fall of Mussolini, 1993- (TV miniseries; Caesar and Claretta, 1975 (made-for-TV; Robert Hardy); **Canaris**, 1958 (himself in archive footage); The Career of a Chambermaid, 1976 (Dino Baldazzi); Cesare Mori—Il prefetto di ferro, 2012 (made-for-TV; Maurizio Donadoni); Claretta Petacci, 1984 (Fernando Briamo); Countdown to War, 1989 (made-for-TV; Barrie Rutter); Dante's Inferno, 2007 (Matt Walsh); Days of Betrayal, 1973 (Vladimir Stach); Don Luigi Sturzo, 1981 (TV miniseries; Luca Biagini); **The**

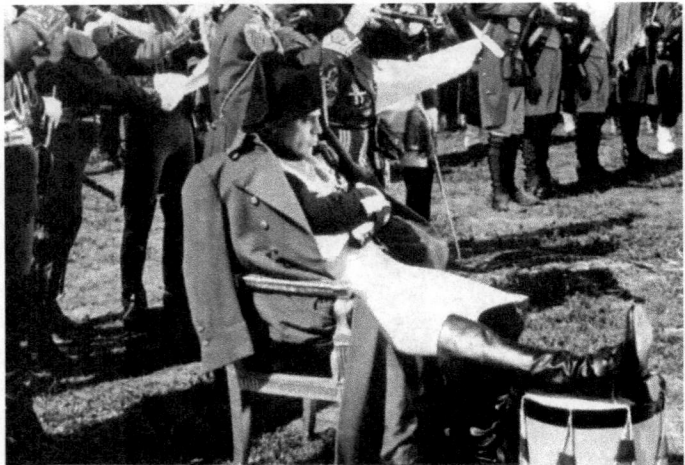

Herbert Lom as Napoleon I in *War and Peace*, 1956.

Eagle Has Landed, 1977 (himself in archive footage); The Great Battle, 1969- (TV series; Ivo Garrani); **The Great Dictator**, 1940 (role model for Jack Oakie); Histeria!, 1998-2000 (animated TV series; "World War II," 1999 episode: Jeff Bennett voiceover); Il giovane Mussolini, 1993- (TV miniseries; Antonio Banderas); **Last Days of Mussolini**, 1977 (Rod Steiger); Le bourreau des coeurs, 1983 (Gerard Couderc); **Lion of the Desert**, 1981 (Rod Steiger); Love Hollywood Style, 2006 (Harrison Held); Mafalda of Savoy, 2006 (made-for-TV; Claudio Spadaro); Maria, 1986 (Jules Bruessing); Maria Jose, l'ultima regina, 2002 (made-for-TV; Claudio Spadaro); **The Miracle of Morgan's Creek**, 1944 (Joe Devlin); Mosley, 1998 (TV series; Stephen Gressieux); Mussolini and I, 1985 (made-for-TV; Bob Hoskins); Mussolini: The Untold Story, 1985 (TV miniseries; George C. Scott); Mussulini's Daughter, 2005 (made-for-TV; Claude Brasseur); Nazis dans le metro, 1977 (Albert Medina); Passions, 1999-2008 (TV series; one 2002 episode: Dennis Garber); Playhouse 90, 1956-1961 (TV series; "The Killers of Mussolini," 1959 episode: Nehemiah Persoff); Quando c'era lui…lei!, 1978 (Eolo Capritti); **Star Spangled Rhythm**, 1942 (Paul Porcasi); **Tea with Mussolini**, 1999 (Claudio Spadaro); Ten Days to Victory, 2005 (made-for-TV; Geoffrey Greenhill); Thirty-Minute Theatre, 1965-1973 (TV series; "These Men Are Dangerous: Mussolini," 1969 episode: John Castle); The Time Tunnel, 1966-1967 (TV series; "The Ghost of Nero," 1967 episode: Nino Candido); The Winds of War, 1983- (TV miniseries; "Into the Maelstrom," 1983 episode: Enzo G. Castellari); The World Wars, 2014- (TV miniseries; Jonathan Hartman). Note: For detailed information on the assassination of Mussolini, see my two-volume work *The Great Pictorial History of World Crime*, Volume I (History, Inc., 2004; illustrated [16 images] pages 149-155).

Mussolini, Bruno (son of Italian dictator Benito Mussolini; served in the Italian air force with his brother Vittorio and was killed when his bomber accidentally crashed; 1918-1941): Mussolini: The Untold Story, 1985 (TV miniseries; Robert Downey Jr.).

Mussolini, Edda (oldest child of Italian dictator Benito Mussolini, who married Galeazzo Ciano, who was executed by her father; 1910-1995): Mussolini and I, 1985 (made-for-TV; Susan Sarandon); Mussolini: The Untold Story, 1985 (TV miniseries; Mary Elizabeth Mastrantonio).

Mussolini, Rachele (Italian mistress, wife and widow of Italian dictator Benito Mussolini; 1890-1979): Mussolini and I, 1985 (made-for-TV; Annie Girardot); Mussolini: The Untold Story, 1985 (TV miniseries; Lee Grant).

Mussolini, Vittorio (son of Italian dictator Benito Mussolini, who served

as a bomber pilot in the Italian air force during Italy's invasion of Ethiopia; he boasted of dropping bombs on helpless natives, describing them as "budding roses," and that killing people was "exceptionally good fun"; he survived WWII and became an Italian film producer, developing the careers of Federico Fellini, Roberto Rosselini and Michelangelo Antonioni, who had no compunctions in advancing their careers through the efforts of this disreputable fascist; 1916-1997): Mussolini and I, 1985 (made-for-TV; Massimo Dapporto); Mussolini: The Untold Story, 1985 (TV miniseries; Gabriel Byrne).

Napoleon I (Napoleon Bonaparte; 1769-1821; Emperor of France): The Ace of Spades, 1925 (William P. De Vaul); Adieu Bonaparte, 1985 (Patrice Chereau); The Adventures of Gerard, 1978 (Eli Wallach); **Anthony Adverse**, 1936 (Rollo Lloyd); Are We Civilized?, 1934 (William Humphrey); Austerlitz, la victoire en marchant, 2006 (made-for-TV; Bernard-Pierre Donnadieu); The Battle of Austerlitz, 1960 (Pierre Mondy); Bill & Ted's Excellent Adventure, 1989 (Terry Camilleri); **Conquest**, 1937 (Charles Boyer); **The Count of Monte Cristo**, 1934 (Paul Irving); The Count of Monte Cristo, 1954 (Julien Bertheau); **The Count of Monte Cristo**, 2002 (Alex Norton); **Desiree**, 1954 (Marlon Brando); Devil-May-Care, 1929 (William Humphrey); Eagle in a Cage, 1972 (Kenneth Haig); 1812, 1944 (Semyon Mezhinsky); 1812, 2012 (Eric Fraticelli); The Emperor's New Clothes, 2002 (Ian Holm); Glorious Betsy, 1928 (Pasquale Amato); Goya's Ghosts, 2006 (Craig Stevenson); Hary Janos, 1965 (Gyula Bodrogi); Hearts Divided, 1936 (Claude Rains); Helmikuum manifesti, 1939 (Ossi Elstela); Histeria!, 1998-2000 (animated TV series; "Inventors Hall of Fame: Part I," 1998 episode: Jeff Bennett voiceover); **The House of Rothschild**, 1934 (Louis Shapiro); Hundred Days, 1935 (Werner Krauss); Invitation to the Waltz, 1936 (Esme Percy); Josephine, 2006 (made-for-TV; Yannis Baraban); Konigen Luise, 1957 (Rene Deltgren); La camera explore le temps, 1957-1966 (TV series; one 1961 episode: Raymond Pellegrin); The Lame Devil, 1948 (Emile Drain); Le bourreau des coeurs, 1983 (Gilles Audisio); The Little Napoleon, 1923 (Egon von Hagen); **Love and Death**, 1975 (James Tolkan); The Loves and Times of Scaramouche, 1976 (Aldo Maccione); Luise, Konigin von Preussen, 1931 (Paul Gunther); Madame, 1963 (Julien Bertheau); Madame Sans-Gene, 1925 (Emile Drain); Madame Sans-Gene, 2002 (made-for-TV; Bruno Solo); Marysia i Napoleon, 1966 (Gustaw Holoubek); Mlle. Desiree, 1948 (Jean-Louis Barrault/Sacha Guitry); **Napoleon**, 1927 (Albert Dieudonne); Napoleon, 1955 (Daniel Gelin/Raymond Pellegrin); Napoleon, 2002 (TV miniseries; Christian Clavier as Napoleon); Napoleon and Josephine: A Love Story, 1987 (TV miniseries; Armand Assante); Napoleon at St. Helena, 1930 (Werner Krauss); Napoleon in Love, 1974 (TV miniseries; Ian Holm as Napoleon); Napoleon: Campaign of Russia, 2013 (TV miniseries; Marc Duret); **Night at the Museum: Battle of the Smithsonian**, 2009 (Alain Chabat); **The Pearls of the Crown**, 1938 (Jean-Louis Barrault/Emile Drain); The Purple Mask, 1955 (Robert Cornthwaite); **Reign of Terror**, 1949 (Shepperd Strudwick); Royal Affairs in Versailles, 1957 (Emile Drain); A Royal Divorce, 1938 (Pierre Blanchar); Sabotage!, 2001 (David Suchet); **Scaramouche**, 1923 (Slavko Vorkapich); **Scaramouche**, 1952 (Aram Katcher); Sea Devils, 1953 (Gerard Oury); The Sea Pirate, 1967 (Giani Esposito); The Story of Mankind, 1957 (Dennis Hopper); Sweethearts of the U.S.A., 1944 (Joseph [Joe] Kirk as the ghost of Napoleon I); Talleyrand ou Le sphinx incompris, 1972 (Denis Manuel); **Time Bandits**, 1981 (Ian Holm); **War and Peace**, 1956 (Herbert Lom); **War and Peace**, 1968 (Vladislav Strzhelcik); War and Peace, 1972-1973 (TV miniseries; Donald Swift); War and Peace, 1991 (made-for-TV; Vassily Gerelo); War and Peace, 2007 (TV miniseries; Scali Delpeyrat); War and Peace, 2016- (TV miniseries; Mathieu Kassovitz); **Waterloo**, 1971 (Rod Steiger); **The Young Mr. Pitt**, 1943 (Herbert Lom). Note: For detailed information on Napoleon I and the attempts on his life, see my two-volume work, *The Great Pictorial History of World Crime*, Volume I (History, Inc., 2004; illustrated pages 15-16).

Napoleon III (Louis Napoleon; French emperor; 1808-1873): Admiral Nakhimov, 1949 (Aleksandr Khokhlov); Amazing Monsieur Fabre, 1951 (Pierre Bertin); Aquellos anos, 1974 (Roberto Dumont); Bernadette, 1989 (Michel Duchaussoy); Bismarck, 1940 (Walter Franck); The Contessa's Secret, 1954 (Paul Meurisse); The Countess of Castiglione, 1942 (Enzo Biliotti); **A Dispatch from Reuters**, 1940 (Walter Kingsford); 1871, 1990 (Dominique Pinon); El carruaje, 1972 (TV series; Antonio Passy); El vuelo del aguila, 1994 (TV series; Luis Gimeno); Emile Waldteufel, 1981 (made-for-TV; Philippe Veys); Eugene Sue, 1974 (made-for-TV; Marcel Cuvelier); Eugenia de Montijo, 1944 (Mariano Asquerino); Fanatisme, 1934 (Lucien Rozenberg); Henry Dunant: Red on the Cross, 2006 (made-for-TV; Tom Novembre); Her People, 1928 (Daurelly); The Hourglass Sanatorium, 1973 (Jerzy Bekker); If Paris Were Told to Us, 1956 (Michel Isella); In Performance, 1978- (TV series; "Orpheus in the Underworld," 1983 episode: Denis Quilley); **Juarez**, 1939 (Claude Rains); Katia, 1939 (Georges Flateau); La Castiglione, 1975 (made-for-TV; Vincenzo De Toma); La forteresse assiegee, 2006 (made-for-TV; Francois Cluzet); La valse de Paris, 1950 (Lucien Nat); L'affaire Lourdes, 1967 (made-for-TV; Marcel Cuvelier); Lettres d'amour, 1942 (Jean Debucourt); L'homme de Suez, 1983 (TV miniseries; Armand Mestral); Lyubov imperatora, 2002 (Leonid Patsenko); The Mad Empress, 1939 (Guy Bates Post); Mademoiselle Midnight, 1924 (Paul Weigel); Man to Men, 1949 (Jean Debucourt); Maximilian von Mexiko, 1970 (made-for-TV; Siegfried Wischnewski); Mexicanos al grito de guerra, 1943 (Angel T. Sala); Nana, 1957 (Jean Debucourt); Ottocento, 1959-1960 (TV miniseries; Mario Feliciani); Pasteur, l'homme qui a vu, 2011 (made-for-TV; Eric Godon); **The Pearls of the Crown**, 1938 (Sacha Guitry); Preussen uber alles—Bismarcks deutsche Einigung, 1971 (TV miniseries; Siegfried Wischnewski); **The Song of Bernadette**, 1943 (Jerome Cowan); Spy of Napoleon, 1936 (Frank Vosper); **The Story of Louis Pasteur**, 1936 (Walter Kingsford); The Sword of Monte Cristo, 1951 (David Bond); **Suez**, 1938 (Leon Ames); Three Waltzes, 1939 (Max Maxudian); Titans, 1981-1982 (TV series; David Calderisi); Universum History, 2013- (TV series; "Maximilian von Mexiko—Der Traum vom Herrschen," 2014 episode: Dan Badarau); Verdi, 1982 (TV miniseries; Lionello Pio Di Savola); Villafranca, 1932 (Enzo Biliotti); Violettes imperiales, 1932 (Emile Drain); Violettes imperiales, 1952 (Louis Arbessier); Vita di Cavour, 1967 (TV miniseries; Sergio Graziani). Note: For detailed information on Napoleon III and the many attempts on his life, see my two-volume work *The Great Pictorial History of World Crime*, Volume I (History, Inc., 2004; illustrated [5 images] pages 16-19).

Nash, Frank (aka: "Jelly"; 1887-1933; U.S. bank robber; killed in the Kansas City Massacre of June 17, 1933): **The FBI Story**, 1959 (Herb Armstrong); The Kansas City Massacre, 1975 (made-for-TV; Mills Watson); The Verne Miller Story, 1988 (Sonny Carl David). Note: For detailed information on Nash and the Kansas City Massacre, see my two-volume work *The Great Pictorial History of World Crime*, Volume II (History, Inc., 2004; illustrated [15 images] pages 951-958).

Nash, John Forbes, Jr. (1928-2015; U.S. mathematician, Nobel laureate); **A Beautiful Mind**, 2001 (Russell Crowe).

Nation, Carrie Amelia Moore (1846-1911; U.S. leader of the temperance movement who led women into saloons to destroy bars and furniture with axes and other implements): **The Bowery**, 1933 (Lillian Harmer).

Nefertari (or Nefretiri; one of the principal wives of Ramesses I, pharoah of Egypt): **The Ten Commandments**, 1923 (Julia Faye); **The Ten Commandments**, 1956 (Anne Baxter); The Ten Commandments: The Musical, 2006 (Lauren Kennedy).

Nehru, Jawaharlal (1889-1964; Indian leader and 1st prime minister of India, 1947-1964): Food for Ravens, 1997 (made-for-TV; Roshan Seth);

Russell Crowe (as John Forbes Nash Jr.) in *A Beautiful Mind*, 2001.

Gandhi, 1982 (Roshan Seth); Hey Ram, 2000 (Raj Patra); The Last Days of the Raj, 2007 (made-for-TV; Roshan Seth); The Legend of Bhagat Singh, 2002 (Saurabh Dubey); Masterepiece Theatre: Lord Mountbatten—The Last Viceroy, 1986- (TV miniseries; Ian Richardson); Nehru: The Jewel of India, 1990 (Partap Sharma); Robert F. Kennedy and His Times, 1985 (TV miniseries; Gokul); Sardar, 1993 (Benjamin Gilani).

Nelson, Baby Face (Lester Joseph Gillis; 1908-1934; U.S. bank robber and killer; member of Dillinger gang): Baby Face Nelson, 1957 (Mickey Rooney); Baby Face Nelson, 1996 (C. Thomas Howell as adult Nelson; Michael Malota as young Nelson); Dillinger, 1973 (Richard Dreyfuss); Dillinger, 1991 (made-for-TV; Kurt Naebig); **The FBI Story**, 1959 (William Phipps); Gangbusters, 1952- (TV series; Robert Kendall); Guns Don't Argue, 1957 (Robert Kendall); The Kansas City Massacre, 1975 (made-for-TV; Elliott Street); Ma Barker's Killer Brood, 1960 (Robert Kendall); **O Brother, Where Art Thou?**, 2000 (Michael Badalucco); **Public Enemies**; 2009 (Stephen Graham); **Young Dillinger**, 1965 (John Ashley). Note: For detailed information on Nelson, see my eight-volume work *Encyclopedia of World Crime*, Volume III (CrimeBooks, Inc., 1990; illustrated [9 images] pages 2301-2304).

Nelson, Earle Leonard (1897-1928; U.S. serial killer, who strangled more than a dozen women coast-to-coast and in Canada; executed by hanging): **Shadow of a Doubt**, 1943 (role model for Joseph Cotten). For comprehensive details on Nelson, see my books *Bloodletters and Badmen: A Narrative Encyclopedia of American Criminals from the Pilgrims to the Present* (M. Evans, 1973, with updates to 2015; illustrated pages 459-464; *World Encyclopedia of 20th Century Murder* (Paragon House, 1992; illustrated pages 422-426; *The Great Pictorial History of World Crime*, Volume II (History, Inc., 2004; illustrated pages 1081-1085; *The Dark Fountain* (A&W Publishers, 1982; a novel).

Nelson, Horatio (1758-1805; British admiral in the Napoleonic Wars): Admiral Ushakov, 1954 (Ivan Solovyov); The Battle of Austerlitz, 1960 (Roland Bartrop); Bequest to the Nation, 1973 (Peter Finch); Carry On Jack, 1963 (Jimmy Thompson); The Devine Lady, 1929 (Victor Varconi): Emma Hamilton, 1968 (Richard Johnson); I Remember Nelson, 1982 (TV series; Kenneth Colley); Lady Hamilton, 1921 (Conrad Veidt); **Lloyd's of London**, 1936 (Douglas Scott as child; John Burton as adult); Luisa Sanfelice, 2004 (made-for-TV; Johannes Silberschneider); **Mutiny on the Bounty**, 1935 (Francis Lister); Napoleon and Josephine: A Love Story, 1987 (TV miniseries; Nikolas Grace); Nelson, 1918 (Eric Barker as child; Donald Calthrop as adult); Nelson, 1926 (Pat Courtney as child; Cedric Hardwicke as adult); Nelson's Trafalgar,

Joseph Cotten (as serial killer Earle Leonard Nelson) and Teresa Wright in *Shadow of a Doubt*, 1943.

2005 (made-for-TV; Simon Wright); Night at the Museum: Secret of the Tomb, 2014 (Theo Devaney); Pegasus, 1969 (made-for-TV; Terry Scully); The Romance of Lady Hamilton, 1919 (Humberston Wright); **That Hamilton Woman**, 1941 (Laurence Olivier); Trafalgar Battle Surgeon, 2005 (made-for-TV; Robert Linge); Tyrant of the Sea, 1950 (Lester Matthews); You Are There, 1953-1957 (TV series; "Lord Nelson at Trafalgar," 1954 episode: Owen Holder); **The Young Mr. Pitt**, 1943 (Stephen Haggard).

Nero (37-68 A.D.; Roman emperor): A.D., 1985 (TV miniseries; Anthony Andrews); Agrippina, 1985 (made-for-TV; David Kuebler); Ancient Rome: The Rise and Fall of an Empire, 2006 (TV series; Michael Sheen); The Apostle Peter: Redemption, 2016 (Stephen Baldwin); **Barabbas**, 1962 (Ivan Triesault); Britannicus, 1959 (made-for-TV; Daniel Ivernel); Britannicus, 1982 (made-for-TV; Jacques Bonnaffe); The Caesars, 1968 (TV series; Martin Potter); Fire Over Rome, 1965 (Vladimir Medar); History of the World: Part I, 1981 (Dom DeLuise); I, Claudius, 1976 (TV series; Christopher Biggins); Imperium: Nero, 2004 (made-for-TV; Hans Matheson as adult Nero; James Bentley as young Nero); Life of St. Paul, 1938 (George Hayes); L'incoronazione di Poppea, 1979 (Eric Tappy); L'incoronazione di Poppea, 1984 (made-for-TV; Dennis Bailey); L'incoronazione di Poppea, 1993 (made-for-TV; Richard Croft); L'incoronazione di Poppea, 1994 (made-for-TV; Brigitte Balleys); L'incoronazione di Poppea, 2000 (made-for-TV; Anne Sofie von Otter); Nero, 1922 (Jacques Gretillat); Nero and the Burning of Rome, 1954 (Gino Cervi); Nero's Mistress, 1962 (Alberto Sordi); Nerone, 1930 (Ettore Petrolini); Nerone, 1977 (Pippo Franco); Nerone, 2001 (made-for-TV; Mario Marchesi); Nerone e Agrippina, 1918 (Vittorio Rossi Pianelli); Nerone e Messalina, 1953 (Gino Cervi); Nerone e Poppea, 1982 (Piotr Stanislas); Nerone '71, 1962 (Gino Bramieri); Norman's Awesome Experience, 1988 (Enrique Latorre); O.K. Nero, 1953 (Gino Cervi); One Day with the Devil, 1945 (Hernan Vera); Per amore di Poppea, 1977 (Oreste Lionello); Peter and Paul, 1981 (made-for-TV; Julian Fellowes); Poppea, 1998 (made-for-TV; Paul Nilon); Poppeas kroning, 1978 (made-for-TV; Jonny Blanc); Poppea's Hot Nights, 1969 (Sandro Dori); **Quo Vadis?**, 1913 (Carlo Cattaneo); Quo Vadis, 1925 (Emile Jannings); **Quo Vadis**, 1951 (Peter Ustinov); Quo Vadis?, 1985 (TV miniseries; Klaus Maria Brandauer); Quo Vadis, 2001 (Michal Bajor); Restitution, 1918 (John Steppling); Satiricosissimo, 1970 (Giancarlo Badessi); The Sign of the Cross, 1914 (Sheridan Block); **Sign of the Cross**, 1932 (Charles Laughton); **The Silver Chalice**, 1954 (Jacques Aubuchon); The Story of Mankind, 1957 (Peter Lorre); Up Pompeii, 1971 (Patrick Cargill); Una casa a Roma, 1988 (made-for-TV; Toni Ucci); Warrior Queen, 2003 (Andrew Lee Potts); While Nero Fiddled, 1944 (Francis L. Sullivan).

Nesbit, Evelyn (1884-1967; alluring and sultry showgirl who was once the mistress of famed NYC architect Stanford White; later married a lunatic multimillionaire, Harry Kendall Thaw, who shot and killed White in 1906 at the rooftop theater of NYC's Madison Square Garden in front of horrified spectators over his jealousy regarding Nesbit's former association with White): **The Girl in the Red Velvet Swing**, 1955 (Joan Collins); **Ragtime**, 1981 (Elizabeth McGovern). Note: For detailed information on Nesbit, White and Thaw, see my two-volume work *The Great Pictorial History of World Crime*, Volume II (History, Inc., 2004; illustrated [17 images] pages 819-826).

Ness, Eliot (1903-1957; U.S. law enforcement official and Prohibition agent heading the Chicago office of that federal agency): The Lady in Red, 1979 (Phillip R. Allen); The Revenge of Al Capone, 1989 (made-for-TV; Scott Paulin); The Scarface Mob, 1959 (made-for-TV; Robert Stack); The Untouchables, 1959-1963 (TV series; Robert Stack); **The Untouchables**, 1987 (Kevin Costner); The Young Indiana Jones Chronicles, 1992-1993 (TV series; "Young Indiana Jones and the Mystery of the Blues," 1993 episode: Frederick Weller).

Nevsky, Alexander (1221-1263; Russian prince and warrior who achieved legendary victories over German and Swedish invaders): Aleksandr Nevskaya, 2008 (Anton Pampushny); **Alexander Nevsky**, 1938 (Nicolai Cherkasov).

Ney, Michel (1769-1815; French soldier and marshal of France under Napoleon I): 1812, 1944 (Alexander Stepanov); The Iron Duke, 1935 (Edmund Willard); Madame Sans-Gene, 1925 (Louis Vonelly); Napoleon, 2002 (TV miniseries; Alain Doutey); War and Peace, 1972-1973 (TV miniseries; John Baker); **Waterloo**, 1971 (Dan O'Herlihy).

Niccacci, Rufino (Italian priest who saved many Jewish lives in WWII; 1911-1977): **The Assissi Underground**, 1985 (Ben Cross).

Nicholas II (1868-1918; Czar of Russia; assassinated): Admiral, 2009 (Nikolai Burlyayev); Anastasia, 1997 (Rich Jones voiceover); Anastasia: The Mystery of Anna, 1986 (made-for-TV; Omar Sherif); **Arsenal**, 1929 (A. Yavdakov); Assassin of the Tsar, 1993 (Oleg Yankovsky as older Nicholas; Andrei Krivitsky as younger Nicholas); BBC Play of the Month, 1965-1983 (TV series; "Rasputin," 1971 episode: Peter Barkworth); Die Brandstifter Europas, 1926 (Heinz Hanus); Edward the King, 1975 (TV series; Michael Billington); Fall of Eagles, 1974 (TV miniseries; "Tell the King the Sky Is Falling," 1974 episode: Charles Kay); The Fall of the Romanovs, 1917 (Alfred Hickman); Helmikuum manifesti, 1939 (Arvo Kuusla); Into Her Kingdom, 1926 (H.C. Simmons); ITV Television Playhouse, 1955-1967 (TV series; "Blood on the Snow," 1958 episode: Richard Warner; "Each Wind That Blows," 1960 episode: Michael Gwynn); Kajastus, 1930 (A. Karsten); The Legion of Death, 1918 (R. O. Pennell); The Lost Prince, 2004 (made-for-TV; Ivan Marevich); **Nicholas and Alexandra**, 1971 (Michael Jayston); The Night They Killed Rasputin, 1962 (Ugo Sasso); 1914: The Last Days before the War, 1932 (Reinhold Schunzel); **Oh! What a Lovely War**, 1969 (Paul Daneman); Raspoutine, 2011 (made-for-TV; Vladimir Mashkov); Rasputin, 1939 (Jean Worms); Rasputin, 1954 (Robert Burnier); Rasputin, 1966 (made-for-TV; Wolfram Schaerf); **Rasputin**, 1985 (Anatoli Romashin); Rasputin, 1996 (made-for-TV; Ian McKellen); Rasputin, 2010 (Angelo Santamaria); **Rasputin and the Empress**, 1932 (Ralph Morgan); Rasputin and the Holy Devil, 1928 (Erwin Kalser); Rasputin, Demon with Women, 1932 (Paul Otto); Rasputin, the Black Monk, 1917 (role model for Hubert Wilke); Rasputins Liebesabenteuer, 1928 (Erwin Kalser); Razmakh krylyev, 1986 (Gennadi Glagolev); The Romanovs: An Imperial Family, 2000 (Alexander Galibin); Russian Ark, 2002 (Vladimir Baranov); The Successor, 1996 (Gennadi Glagolev); Ten Days That Shook the World, 1967 (made-for-TV; Hugh Burden); Trust, 1970 (Yury Demich); Tsar Nikolay II, 1917

(Peter Baksheyev); Trust, 1976 (Yuri Demich); Weltuntergang, 1984 (made-for-TV; Jan Niklas). Note: For detailed information on the assassination of Nicholas II and his family, see my two-volume work *The Great Pictorial History of World Crime*, Volume II (History, Inc., 2004; illustrated [8 images] pages 79-83).

Nicholas Nikolaevich (Grand Duke of Russia and cousin of Nicholas II, commanded the Russian army early in WWI; 1856-1929): Fall of Eagles, 1974 (TV miniseries; "Tell the King the Sky Is Falling," 1974 episode: John Phillips); The Fall of the Romanovs, 1917 (Charles Craig); **Nicholas and Alexandra**, 1971 (Harry Andrews); Raspoutine, 2011 (made-for-TV; Alexandr Riazantzev); Rasputin, 1939 (Georges Prieur); Suspense, 1949-1954 (TV series; "The Black Prophet," 1953 episode: Howard Ledig).

Nicolay, John George (1832-1901; U.S. biographer and secretary to President Abraham Lincoln): The Day Lincoln Was Shot, 1998 (made-for-TV; Scott Rinker); Lincoln, 1974-1975 (TV series; Michael Cristofer); Lincoln, 1988 (made-for-TV; Richard Travis); **Lincoln**, 2012 (Jeremy Strong).

Nicolas, Paul Francois Jean (Count de Barras; 1755-1829; French politician during the French Revolution): **Desiree**, 1954 (David Leonard); Napoleon, 1955 (Pierre Brasseur); **The Pearls of the Crown**, 1938 (Sacha Guitry); **Reign of Terror**, 1949 (Richard Hart); A Royal Divorce, 1938 (George Curzon).

Niemoller, Martin (1892-1984; German Lutheran leader and theologian who initially supported the Hitler regime but turned against it, resisting the Nazis; imprisoned in a concentration camp, 1937-1945 and narrowly escaped execution): **The Hitler Gang**, 1944 (Ivan Triesault).

Nietzsche, Friedrich (1844-1900; German philosopher who advanced the superman theory): Mon couer est rouge, 1977 (Mai Zetterling); Wagner, 1983 (TV series; Ronald Pickup); Wahnfried, 1987 (Christoph Waltz).

Nightingale, Florence (1820-1910; British nursing pioneer; notable for her medical contributions during the Crimean War, 1853-1856, when she introduced effective sanitary conditions that saved countless wounded combatants in that conflict): Alfresco, 1983-1984 (TV series; 1983 episode: Emma Thompson); BBC Learning: True Stories, 2012 (TV series; 2012 episode: Emily Speed; Lucinka Eisler); Big Train, 1998-2002 (TV series; 2002 episode: Amelia Bullmore); The Charles Dickens Show, 2012 (TV series; "Health," 2012 episode: Amanda Lawrence); Emergency Ward 10, 1957-1967 (TV series; "Ben Gunn's Christmas Journey," 1964 episode: Iris Russell); Florence Nightingale, 1915 (Elizabeth Risdon); Florence Nightingale, 1952 (made-for-TV; Sarah Churchill); Florence Nightingale, 1985 (Jaclyn Smith); Florence Nightingale, 2008 (made-for-TV; Laura Fraser); Histeria!, 1998-2000 (animated TV series; "Better Living through Science," 1999 episode: Tress MacNeille voiceover); The Holy Terror, 1965 (made-for-TV; Julie Harris); **The Lady with a Lamp**, 1951 (Anna Neagle); Looking About, 1961-1962 (TV series; "Florence Nightingale," 1961 episode: Clare Austin); Magic Grandad, 1993- (TV series; "Famous People: Florence Nightingale," 1994 episode: Kate Isitt); Mary Seacole: The Real Angel of the Crimea, 2005 (made-for-TV; Michelle Bunyan); Miss Nightingale, 1974 (made-for-TV; Janet Suzman); NDP Philo Café, 2006 (Jade Taylor); Palabra por palabra, 2008 (Simone Yenkinson); The Passionate Pilgrim, 1949 (made-for-TV; Betty Cooper); Queen of Destiny, 1940 (Joyce Bland); **Sixty Glorious Years**, 1938 (Joyce Bland); A Skirt through History, 1994 (TV series; "The Experiment," 1994 episode: Rosalie Crutchley); **The White Angel**, 1936 (Kay Francis); A Word in Your Eye, 1992 (TV series; 1992 episode: Helen Lederer); Wrath of Jealousy, 1936 (Fay Compton).

Kevin Costner (as Eliot Ness) in *The Untouchables*, 1987.

Nimitz, Chester M. (1885-1966; U.S. five-star fleet admiral in command of the U.S. Pacific Fleet in WWII): Black Sheep Squadron, 1976-1978 (TV series; "Flying Misfits," 1976 episode: Byron Morrow); **The Gallant Hours**, 1960 (Selmer Jackson); Hellcats of the Navy, 1957 (Selmer Jackson); **In Harm's Way**, 1965 (role model for Henry Fonda); **MacArthur**, 1977 (Addison Powell); **Midway**, 1976 (Henry Fonda); **Pearl Harbor**, 2002 (Graham Beckel); War and Remembrance, 1988 (TV miniseries; William Prince).

Nitti, Frank (aka: The Enforcer; 1886-1943; U.S. racketeer and Chicago crime boss under Al Capone; committed suicide): Capone, 1975 (Sylvester Stallone); Frank Nitti: The Enforcer, 1988 (made-for-TV; Anthony LaPaglia); Playhouse 90, 1956-1961 (TV series; "Seven Against the Wall," 1958 episode: Tige Andrews); **Public Enemies**, 2009 (Bill Camp); The Revenge of Al Capone, 1989 (made-for-TV; Alan Rosenberg); **Road to Perdition**, 2002 (Stanley Tucci); **The St. Valentine's Day Massacre**, 1967 (Harold J. Stone); The Scarface Mob, 1959 (made-for-TV; Bruce Gordon); The Untouchables, 1959-1963 (TV series; Bruce Gordon); **The Untouchables**, 1987 (Billy Drago); The Untouchables, 1993-1994 (TV series; Paul Regina). Note: For detailed information on Nitti and Capone, see my two-volume work *The Great Pictorial History of World Crime* (History, Inc., 2004; Capone et al.: illustrated pages 503-541).

Nixon, Edgar Daniel (1899-1987; U.S. black civil rights leader): The Rosa Parks Story, 2002 (made-for-TV; Von Coulter).

Nixon, Richard (Richard Milhous Nixon; 37th President of the U.S.; 1913-1994): **All the President's Men**, 1976 (himself; TV footage); Blind Ambition, 1979 (TV miniseries; Rip Torn); Dick, 1999 (Dan Hedaya); The Final Days, 1989 (made-for-TV; Lane Smith); **Frost/Nixon**, 2008 (Frank Langella); J. Edgar Hoover, 1987 (made-for-TV; Anthony Palmer); **Nixon**, 1995 (Anthony Hopkins); **The Private Files of J. Edgar Hoover**, 1977 (Richard Dixon); The Real American: Joe McCarthy, 2012 (James Garnon); Tail Gunner Joe, 1977 (made-for-TV; Richard M. Dixon).

Nixon, Thelma Catherine Ryan (aka: "Pat"; American First Lady and wife of U.S. President Richard Nixon; 1912-1993): Blind Ambition, 1979 (TV miniseries; Cathleen Cordell); Dick, 1999 (Deborah Grover); **Frost/Nixon**, 2008 (Patty McCormack); **Nixon**, 1995 (Joan Allen).

Noah (biblical character, Hebrew patriarch who built an arc or great vessel in which to house his family and the livestock of the earth against the Great Flood): After Six Days, 1920 (Augusto Mastripietri); The

Barbara Stanwyck as Annie Oakley in *Annie Oakley*, 1935.

Bible: In the Beginning…, 1966 (John Huston); Disintegration, 2007 (Larry Flournoy); The Flood, 1962 (made-for-TV; Sebastian Cabot); Genesis: The Creation and the Flood, 1994 (Omero Antonutti); Greatest Heroes of the Bible, 1978- (TV series; "The Story of Noah," two episodes in 1978: Lew Ayres); **The Green Pastures**, 1936 (Eddie "Rochester" Anderson); The Green Pastures, 1959 (made-for-TV; Eddie "Rochester" Anderson); Mary's Incredible Dream, 1976 (made-for-TV; Ben Vereen); Noah, 1946 (made-for-TV; Michael Hordern); Noah, 1998 (Tony Danza); Noah, 2012 (Michael Keaton); **Noah**, 2014 (Russell Crowe); Noah's Ark, 1928 (Paul McAllister); Noah's Ark, 1999- (TV miniseries; Jon Voight); Omnibus, 1952-1961 (TV series; "The Horn Blows at Midnight," 1953 episode: Rolfe Sedan); The Passion, 1999- (TV series; David Mahoney); Son of God, 2014 (David Rintoul); Testament: The Bible in Animation, 1996- (TV series; Joss Ackland voiceover).

Noonan, Fred (Frederick Joseph "Fred" Noonan; navigator who disappeared with Amelia Earhart; 1893-1937; declared dead on June 20, 1938): **Amelia**, 2009 (Christopher Eccleston); Amelia Earhart, 1976 (made-for-TV; Bill Vint as Fred Norman); Amelia Earhart: The Final Flight, 1994 (made-for-TV: Rutger Hauer); Inside, 2007- (TV series; "The Real Amelia Earhart," 2009 episode: Alan Ragains); Star Trek: Voyager, 1995-2001 (TV series; "The 37's," 1995 episode: David Graf); You Are There, 1953-1957 (TV series; "The Mystery of Amelia Earhart," 1971 episode: Thomas Connelly).

Noren, Irving Arnold (aka: "Irv"; American baseball and basketball player; b 1924-): **The Winning Team**, 1952 (himself).

North, Frederick (Lord North; 2nd Earl of Guilford; British politician and prime minister of Great Britain; 1732-1792): **America**, 1924 (Emil Hoch); The Bastard, 1978 (made-for-TV; John Colicos); Number 10, 1983 (TV miniseries; "Bloodline," 1983 episode: Patrick Newell); Play for Today, 1970-1984 (TV series; "The Falklands Factor," 1983 episode: John Bird); The Revolution, 2006 (TV series; Nicholas Barber); Samuel Adams, 2014 (made-for-TV; Filippo Bellucci); **Young Mr. Pitt**, 1943 (Felix Aylmer).

Northcott, Gordon Stewart (1906-1930; Canadian-born U.S. serial killer who preyed upon homeless boys at his chicken ranch in Wineville, California, during the 1920s; known to have murdered at least three boys but may have slain another half dozen; he was executed by hanging at San Quentin State Prison on October 2, 1930): **Changeling**, 2008 (Jason Butler Harner).

Nosenko, Yuri (1927-2008; Soviet colonel in the KGB, who defected to the U.S., who provided Soviet secrets but who was also thought to be a mole): Yuri Nosenko KGB, 1986 (made-for-TV; Oleg Rudnik). Note: For detailed information on Nosenko, see my book *Spies: A Narrative Encyclopedia of Dirty Tricks & Double Dealing from Biblical Times to Today* (M. Evans, 1997; illustrated pages 370-371).

Oakley, Annie (Phoebe Ann Mosley; 1860-1926; American sharpshooter and performer, chiefly in Buffalo Bill's Wild West shows): Alias Jesse James, 1959 (Gail Davis); **Annie Get Your Gun**, 1950 (Betty Hutton); Annie Get Your Gun, 1957 (made-for-TV; Mary Martin); Annie Get Your Gun, 1967 (made-for-TV; Ethel Merman); **Annie Oakley**, 1935 (Barbara Stanwyck); Annie Oakley, 1954-1957 (TV series; Gail Davis); Buffalo Bill and the Indians, 1976 (Geraldine Chaplin); Buffalo Girls, 1995 (made-for-TV; Reba McEntire); Edison: The Wizard of Light, 1998 (made-for-TV; Margery Lowe); **Hidalgo**, 2004 (Elizabeth Berridge); Mentors, 1998-2005 (TV series; "Anything You Can Do," 2001 episode: Megan Follows); Mr. I. Magination, 1949-1952 (TV series: "Annie Oakley," 1952 episode: Robin Morgan); **The Outlaws Is Coming**, 1965 (Nancy Kovack); Tall Tales and Legends, 1985-1988 (TV series; "Annie Oakley," 1985 episode: Jamie Lee Curtis); Voyagers!, 1982-1983 (TV series; "Buffalo Bill and Annie Play the Palace," 1983 episode: Diane Civita [Diane Cary]).

Oates, Lawrence (1880-1912; British explorer who died with Robert Falcon Scott on the 1912 expedition to the South Pole): Regal Cavalcade, 1935 (Austin Trevor); Scott of the Antarctic, 1949 (Derek Bond).

O'Banion, Charles Dion (or O'Bannion; aka: Dean; Deanie; 1892-1924; U.S. ganster and bootlegger in Chicago during the early 1920s, a mortal enemy of crime czar Al Capone and killed on Capone's orders): **Al Capone**, 1959 (Robert Gist); Capone, 1975 (John Orchard); **The Public Enemy**, 1931 (role model for James Cagney); **The St. Valentine's Day Massacre**, 1967 (John Agar); The Young Indiana Jones Chronicles, 1992-1993 (TV series; "Young Indiana Jones and the Mystery of the Blues," 1993 episode: Victor Slezak). Note: For detailed information on O'Banion, see my book *World Encyclopedia of Organized Crime* (Paragon House, 1992; illustrated [9 images] 304-310).

Obregon, Alvaro (Alvaro Obregon Salido; 1880-1928; Mexican general, revolutionary leader and 39th President of Mexico; assassinated): El encanto del aguila, 2011 (Carlos Corona); Mexikanische Revolution, 1968 (made-for-TV; Jurgen Goslar); Senda de Gloria, 1987 (TV series; Bruno Rey). Note: For detailed information on Obregon's assassination, see my two-volume work *The Great Pictorial History of World Crime*, Volume I (History, Inc., 2004; illustrated [4 images] pages 95-96).

Offenbach, Jacques (1819-1880; German-born French composer): Cancan und Bakarole, 1961 (made-for-TV; Helmuth Lohner); The Eternal Waltz, 1959 (Arnulf Schroder); The Great Waltz, 1972 (Dominque Weber); Hab' ich nur deine Liebe, 1953 (Egon von Jordan); Jacques Offenbach—Ein Lebensbild, 1969 (made-for-TV; Pinkas Braun); Johann Strauss: The King without a Crown, 1987 (Philippe Nicaud); La valse de Paris, 1950 (Pierre Fresnay); Les folies Offenbach, 1977- (TV miniseries; Michel Serrault); Offenbachs Geheimnis, 1996 (made-for-TV; Tamas Jordan); The Only Girl, 1934 (Julius Falkenstein); Walt Disney's Wonderful World of Color, 1954-1992 (TV series; "The Waltz King," 1963 episode: Peter Wehle).

O'Laughlin, Michael (1840-1867; U.S. conspirator in the 1865 assassination of President Abraham Lincoln; he was convicted and sent to prison for life, dying of yellow fever at Fort Jefferson in the Dry Tortugas): The Lincoln Conspiracy, 1977 (Christopher Allport).

Olbricht, Friedrich (1888-1944; German general in WWII, who participated in the 1944 attempt to kill Adolf Hitler; executed): Claus Graf Stauffenberg, 1970 (made-for-TV; Wolf Ackva); Die Stunde der Offiziere, 2004 (made-for-TV; Tilo Pruckner); The Great Battle, 1973 (Wilfried Ortmann); I Spy, 1955-1957 (TV series; "Canaris Story": John Seymour); It Happened on July 20th, 1955 (Erik Frey);); Mysteries at the Castle, 2014- (TV series; "House That Saved a King; Joan of Arc; Hamilton Sex Scandal," 2015 episode: James Feuer); Operation Valkyrie, 2004 (made-for-TV; Rainer Bock); Operation Walkure, 1971 (made-for-TV; Werner Rundshagen); The Plot to Assassinate Hitler, 1955 (Wolfgang Buttner); The Plot to Kill Hitler, 1990 (made-for-TV; Michael Byrne); **Valkyrie**, 2008 (Bill Nighy); The Wednesday Play, 1964-1970 (TV series; "The July Plot," 1964 episode: Peter Copley). Note: For detailed information on Olbricht and the 1944 attempt on Hitler's life, see my two-volume work *The Great Pictorial History of World Crime*, Volume I (History, Inc., 2004; illustrated [20 images] pages 138-148).

Olga Nikolaevna (1895-1918; Olga Romanov; grand duchess of Russia; daughter of Czar Nicholas II; assassinated): Assassin of the Tsar, 1993 (Dariya Majorova); Die Brandstifter Europas, 1926 (Charlotte Ander); Fall of Eagles, 1974 (TV miniseries; "Tell the King the Sky Is Falling," 1974 episode: Martha Nairn); The Lost Prince, 2004 (made-for-TV; Vanessa Ackerman); **Nicholas and Alexandra**, 1971 (Ania Marson); Rasputin, 1996 (made-for-TV; Yelena Malashevskaya); The Romanovs: An Imperial Family, 2000 (Yuliya Novikova); The Successor, 1996 (Yuria Kopirova). Note: For detailed information on the assassination of Nicholas II and his family, see my two-volume work *The Great Pictorial History of World Crime*, Volume II (History, Inc., 2004; illustrated [8 images] pages 79-83).

Onassis, Aristotle Socrates (1906-1975; Greek shipping magnate and second husband of Jacqueline Kennedy Onassis): Callas e Onassis, 2005 (made-for-TV; Gerard Darmon); Grace of Monaco, 2014 (Robert Lindsay); The Greek Tycoon, 1978 (role model for Anthony Quinn); Jackie Bouvier Kennedy Onassis, 2000 (made-for-TV; Philip Baker Hall); Onassis: The Richest Man in the World, 1988 (made-for-TV; Anthony Quinn; Elias Koteas as young Onassis); A Woman Named Jackie, 1991 (TV miniseries; Joss Ackland).

O'Neill, Carlotta Monterey (1888-1970; U.S. actress and wife of playwright Eugene O'Neill): American Masters, 1985- (TV series; "Eugene O'Neill: A Glory of Ghosts," 1986 episode: Zoe Caldwell); Och ge oss skuggorna, 1993 (made-for-TV; Margaretha Krook).

O'Neill, Eugene (Eugene Gladstone O'Neill; 1888-1953; U.S. playwright, Pulitzer Prize winner and recipient of the Nobel Prize for Literature): American Masters, 1985- (TV series; "Eugene O'Neill: A Glory of Ghosts," 1986 episode: Jeffrey DeMunn); American Playhouse, 1981- (TV series; "Journey into Genius," 1988 episode: Matthew Modine); Entertaining Angels: The Dorothy Day Story, 1996 (James Lancaster); Och ge oss skuggorna, 1993 (made-for-TV; Max von Sydow); **Reds**, 1981 (Jack Nicholson).

Oppenheimer, J. Robert (1904-1967; U.S. physicist and called "the father of the atomic bomb" for leading the U.S. scientists in developing that weapon in WWII): The Beginning or the End, 1947 (Hume Cronyn); Day One, 1989 (made-for-TV; David Strathairn); Doctor Atomic, 2007 (made-for-TV; Gerald Finley); Einstein: Light to the Power of 2, 1996 (made-for-TV; Tom Rack); Enola Gay: The Men, the Mission, the Atomic Bomb, 1980 (made-for-TV; Robert Walden); **Fat Man and Little Boy**, 1989 (Dwight Schultz); Hiroshima, 1995 (made-for-TV; Jeffrey DeMunn); Histeria!, 1998-2000 (animated TV series;

James Cagney (in role modeled on Dion O'Banion) and Jean Harlow in *The Public Enemy*, 1931.

"Inventors Hall of Fame: Part I," 1998 episode: Rob Paulsen voiceover); In der Sache J. Robert Oppenheimer, 1964 (made-for-TV; Charles Regnier); In der Sache J. Robert Oppenheimer, 1981 (made-for-TV; Hans-Michael Rehberg); Man, Moment, Machine, 2005-2007 (TV series; "Ultimate Weapon: Oppenheimer and the Atomic Bomb," 2005 episode: Mark Pickens); Manhattan, 2014- (TV miniseries; Daniel London); **The 100-Year-Old Man Who Climbed Out of the Window and Disappeared**, 2014 (Philip Rosch); Oppenheimer, 1980 (TV miniseries; Sam Waterston); Oppenheimerin tapaus, 1967 (made-for-TV; Matti Oravisto); The Quantum Suicide of Sophie Miller, 2013 (Kevin G. Bender); Race for the Bomb, 1987 (TV miniseries; Tom Rack); Spies, Lies and the Superbomb, 2007 (TV miniseries; Joe Jones).

Orgen, Jacob (aka: Little Augie; 1893-1927; U.S. gangster and labor racketeer during Prohibition in NYC, who was murdered by Louis "Lepke" Buchalter and Jacob "Gurrah" Shapiro): Lepke, 1975 (Jack Ackerman). Note: For detailed information on Orgen, see my book: *World Encyclopedia of Organized Crime* (Paragon House, 1992; illustrated pages 314-315).

Orlov, Alexei (1737-1808; Russian soldier and statesman; brother of Gregory Orlov and who was part of the conspiracy to assassinate Peter III): Catherine the Great, 1996 (made-for-TV; Stephen McGann); Catherine the Great, 2005 (made-for-TV; Emanuel Parvu); Shadow of the Eagle, 1950 (Richard Greene).

Orlov, Gregory (1734-1783; Russian count and lover of Catherine the Great, and who was instrumental in the assassination of Catherine's husband, Czar Peter III, 1728-1762): The Adventures of Baron Munchausen, 1943 (Waldemar Leitgeb); Catherine of Russia, 1963 (Sergio Fantoni); Catherine the Great, 1996 (made-for-TV; Mark McGann); Catherine the Great, 2005 (made-for-TV; Claudiu Bleont); The Chess Player, 1930 (Jaime Devesa); The Loves of Casanova, 1929 (Paul Guide); Pugachev, 1980 (Anatolly Azo); The Rise of Catherine the Great, 1934 (Griffith Jones); **The Scarlet Empress**, 1934 (Gavin Gordon); Young Catherine, 1991 (made-for-TV; Mark Frankel).

Orozco, Pascual (1882-1915; Mexican revolutionary leader): Pancho Villa and Valentina, 1960 (Arturo Martinez).

Osceola (Billy Powell; 1804-1838; insurgent leader of the Seminole tribe in Florida; died of disease in captivity): **Seminole**, 1953 (Anthony Quinn).

Oswald, Lee Harvey (1939-1963; U.S. political activist and reputed as-

Barbara Hale and Anthony Quinn (as Osceola) in *Seminole*, 1953.

sassin of President John F. Kennedy): Ruby, 1992 (Willie Garson); Timequest, 2000 (Jeffery Steiger).

Overton, John (1766-1833; U.S. judge and adviser to U.S. President Andrew Jackson): First Ladies Diaries: Rachel Jackson, 1975 (made-for-TV; David O'Brien); **The President's Lady**, 1953 (John McIntire).

Owens, Jesse (1913-1980; U.S. athlete and gold medal winner at the 1936 Olympics in Berlin, Germany): The Jesse Owens Story, 1984 (made-for-TV; Dorian Harewood); King of the Olympics: The Life and Loves of Avery Brundage, 1988 (made-for-TV; Ronnie Britton); Race, 2016 (Stephan James).

Paganini, Nicolo (1782-1840; Italian violinist and composer): Bohemian Rapture, 1948 (aka: Housle a sen; Karel Dostal); Die lachende Grille, 1926 (Hans Waschatko); The Magic Bow, 1947 (Stewart Granger); Moi, Hector Berlioz, 2003 (made-for-TV; Claude Jocteur); Paganini, 1923 (Conrad Veidt); **Young Chopin**, 1952 (Franciszek Jamry).

Paget, William (1506-1563; British statesman during the reign of Henry VIII): **Young Bess**, 1953 (Lester Matthews).

Pahlen, Peter Ludwig von der (1745-1826; Russian general and instrumental in the assassination of Czar Paul I): **The Patriot**, 1928 (Lewis Stone); Poor, Poor Pavel, 2003 (Oleg Yankovsky).

Paine, Lewis: see Powell, Lewis Thornton.

Paine, Thomas (1737-1809; British-born political activist and philosopher whose writings inspired the American Revolution): La nuit de Varennes, 1982 (Harvey Keitel); Liberty! The American Revolution, 1997 (TV miniseries; Roger Rees); The Romantics, 2006- (TV miniseries; Stuart Milligan); Sally Hemings: An American Scandal, 2000 (made-for-TV; Kevin Conway); That Night in Varennes, 1983 (Harvey Keitel); Witness to Yesterday, 1970 (TV series; "Tom Paine," 1974 episode: Robert Vaughn).

Paley, William (1901-1990; U.S. communications executive and head of Columbia Broadcasting System/CBS): Dark Skies, 1996-1997 (TV series; "We Shall Overcome," 1996 episode: Art Bell).

Palmer, A. Mitchell (1872-1936; American politician and 50th U.S. attorney general): **J. Edgar**, 2011 (Geoff Pierson); J. Edgar Hoover, 1987 (made-for-TV; John McLiam); **No God, No Master**, 2012 (Ray Wise).

Panin, Nikita Ivan (1718-1783; Russian nobleman and statesman, political mentor for Catherine II or Catherine the Great): The Captain's Daughter, 2001 (Mikhail Filippov).

Pankhurst, Sylvia (1882-1960; British leader of suffragette movement in Great Britain; sometimes communist): **Oh! What a Lovely War**, 1969 (Vanessa Redgrave).

Panzram, Carl (1891-1930; U.S. serial killer, arsonist, rapist, burglar; claimed to have murdered twenty-one persons, and, as a predatory homosexual, claimed to have assaulted and sodomized more than 1,000 males, boys and men; he was executed by hanging at Leavenworth Penitentiary on September 5, 1930): Killer: A Journal of Murder, 1995 (James Woods). Note: For detailed information on Panzram, see my book *World Encyclopedia of 20th Century Murder* (Paragon House, 1992; illustrated pages: 440-441).

Papen, Franz von (1879-1969; German politician and statesman who opposed the Hitler regime; later served as a foreign ambassador and intelligence chief for the German military in WWII): **Background to Danger**, 1943 (Curt Furburg); Die Machtergreifung, 2012 (made-for-TV; Mathieu Carriere); The Eagle's Eye, 1918 (serial; Paul Everton); **5 Fingers**, 1952 (John Wengraf); The Good Pope: Pope John XXIII, 2003 (made-for-TV; Erland Josephson); **The Hitler Gang**, 1944 (Walter Kingsford); Hitler: The Rise of Evil, 2003 (made-for-TV; Robert Russell); J'etais a Nuremberg, 2011 (made-for-TV; Anton Nikolov); Nuremberg, 2000 (TV miniseries; Dennis St. John); Portrait: A Man Whose Name Was John, 1973 (made-for-TV; Peter von Zerneck).

Papillon (Henry Charriere; 1906-1973; French criminal and writer who escaped from Devil's Island and who was known as Papillon, after the French word meaning "butterfly," which was tattooed on his chest): **Papillon**, 1973 (Steve McQueen).

Papin, Christine (1905-1937; French housemaid, who, along with her sister, Lea Papin, 1911-c. 2001, murdered the wife and daughter of their employer in Le Mans, France, on the night of February 2, 1933, brutally gouging out the eyes of their victims with their fingernails; Christine instigated the killings, having an obsession with eye-gouging and where she dominated her sister, Lea, both having an ongoing lesbian relationship; they were both institutionalized, Christine dying in an asylum, Lea released in 1941 and where she became a housemaid in a hotel under an assumed name): Murderous Maids, 2002 (Christine: Sylvie Testud; Lea: Julie-Marie Parmentier); Sister My Sister, 1995 (Christine: Joely Richardson; Lea: Jodhi May).

Park, Keith (1892-1975; Sir Keith Rodney Park; British air marshal in WWII): **The Battle of Britain**, 1969 (Trevor Howard).

Parker, Bonnie (Bonnie Elizabeth Parker; 1910-1934; U.S. bank robber and killer and mistress of Clyde Barrow; killed with him by a posse on May 23, 1934): The Barrow Gang, 1995 (Bethany Harper); **Bonnie and Clyde**, 1967 (Faye Dunaway); Bonnie & Clyde, 2013- (TV miniseries; Holliday Grainger); Bonnie and Clyde: The Real Story, 1992 (Tracey Needham); The Bonnie Parker Story, 1958 (Dorothy Provine); Gang Busters, 1952- (TV series; Tamar Cooper); Guns Don't Argue, 1957 (Tamar Cooper); Lois & Clark: The New Adventures of Superman, 19993-1997 (TV series; "That Old Gang of Mine," 1994 episode: Amy Hathaway); Lovers on the Run: The Complete Story of Bonnie & Clyde, 2015 (Beverly Taylor); Man, Moment, Machine, 2005-2007 (TV series; "Hunting Bonnie and Clyde," 2005 episode: Dixie Lee Sedgwick); The Other Side of Bonnie and Clyde, 1968 (Jo Enterentree); Paper Moon, 1974-1975 (TV series; "Bonnie and Clyde," 1974 episode: Linda Haynes); Public Enemies, 1941 (Wendy Barrie). Note: For detailed information on Parker, see my books *Bloodletters and Badmen: A Narra-*

tive Encyclopedia of American Criminals from the Piligrims to the Past (M. Evans, 1973-2015; illustrated pages [under Barrow, Clyde] 51-57; *Encyclopedia of World Crime*, Volume I (CrimeBooks, Inc., 1990; illustrated pages [under Barrow, Clyde] 250-263).

Parker, Dorothy (1893-1967; U.S. shortstory writer and screenwriter; known for her acerbic wit as a member of the Algonquin Round Table): Dash and Lilly, 1999 (made-for-TV; Bebe Neuwirth); F. Scott Fitzgerald in Hollywood, 1976 (made-for-TV: Dolores Sutton); Mrs. Parker and the Vicious Circle, 1994 (Jennifer Jason Leigh).

Parker, Edwin P. (1891-1983; Edwin Pearson Parker Jr.; U.S. Army general in WWII): **The Longest Day**, 1962 (Leo Genn).

Parker, Isaac Charles (aka: "The Hanging Judge"; 1838-1896; U.S. district judge for the Western District of Arkansas): **Hang 'Em High**, 1968 (role model for Pat Hingle as "Judge Fenton"); The Last Ride of the Dalton Gang, 1979 (made-for-TV; Dale Robertson); **Rooster Cogburn**, 1975 (John McIntire); **True Grit**, 1969 (James Westerfield); **True Grit**, 2010 (Jake Walker). Note: For detailed information on Parker, see my book *Encyclopedia of Western Lawmen and Outlaws* (Paragon House, 1992; illustrated pages 252-253).

Parks, Rosa Louise McCauley (1913-2005; American black social activist): The American Woman: Portraits of Courage, 1976 (made-for-TV; Jonelle Allen); Boycott, 2001 (made-for-TV; Iris Little-Thomas); The Rosa Parks Story, 2002 (made-for-TV; Angela Bassett).

Parnell, Charles Stewart (1846-1891; Irish nationalist and politician who was an influential leader in the British House of Commons in the 1880s): Captain Boycott, 1947 (Robert Donat); ITV Play of the Week, 1955-1974 (TV series; "Parnell," 1959 episode: Michael Goodliffe); Mr. Gladstone, 1947 (made-for-TV; Hector Ross); Parnell, 1937 (Clark Gable); Parnell, 1938 (made-for-TV; Wyndham Goldie); Parnell & the Englishwoman, 1991- (TV miniseries; Trevor Eve); You Are There, 1953-1971 (TV series; "The Fall of Parnell [December 6, 1890]," 1954 episode: Lorne Greene).

Parr, Catherine (1512-1548; Queen of England and sixth wife of Henry VIII): Elizabeth R, 1971-1972 (TV miniseries; "The Lion's Club," 1971 episode: Rosalie Crutchley); Heinrich VIII und seine Frauen, 1968 (made-for-TV; Hannelore Schroth); Henry VIII, 2003 (made-for-TV; Clare Holman); Henry VIII and His Six Wives, 1972 (Barbara Leigh-Hunt); King and Women, 1967 (made-for-TV; Jana Brejchova); **The Private Life of Henry VIII**, 1933 (Everley Gregg); The Six Wives of Henry VIII, 2001 (TV miniseries; six episodes: Caroline Lintott); The Tudors, 2007-2010 (TV series; Joely Richardson); **Young Bess**, 1953 (Deborah Kerr).

Parsons, Louella Q. (1881-1972; U.S. writer and syndicated newspaper columnist covering Hollywood, one of the most influential writers of media of her day): Bogie, 1980 (made-for-TV; Anne Bellamy); The Cat's Meow, 2001 (Jennifer Tilly); Climax!, 1954-1958 (TV series; "The Louella Parsons Story," 1956 episode: Teresa Wright); The Corpse Came C.O.D., 1947 (herself); The Hearst and Davies Affair, 1985 (made-for-TV; Doris Belack); **Hollywood Hotel**, 1937 (herself); **Incendiary Blonde**, 1945 (Catherine Craig); Malice in Wonderland, 1985 (made-for-TV; Elizabeth Taylor); Marilyn: The Untold Story, 1980 (made-for-TV; Priscilla Morrill); Marlene, 2000 (Sandy Martin); RKO 281, 1999 (made-for-TV; Brenda Blethyn); The Scarlett O'Hara War, 1980 (made-for-TV; Jane Kean); Shirley Temple Story, 1976 (Marta Vives); **Starlift**, 1951 (herself); **Without Reservations**, 1946 (herself); **The Woman of the Town**, 1943 (Beryl Wallace).

Pasteur, Louis (1822-1895; French chemist, who pioneered cures for

Faye Dunaway (as Bonnie Parker) in *Bonnie and Clyde, 1967*.

anthrax and hydrophobia, as well as sterilization in all surgeries): Dr. Semmelweis, 1950 (Theodor Vogeler); The Empiricist, 2003 (Oto Brezina); If Paris Were Told to Us, 1956 (Charles Lahet); Pasteur, 1922 (Charles Mosnier); Pasteur, 1935 (Sacha Guitry); Pasteur, cinq annees de rage, 1995 (made-for-TV; Bernard Fresson); Pasteur, l'homme qui a vu, 2011 (made-for-TV; Andre Marcon); **The Story of Louis Pasteur**, 1936 (Paul Muni).

Patrick, Marsena R. (1811-1888; Union general in the American Civil War): **Gods and Generals**, 2003 (Ryan Cutrona).

Patton, George S. (George Smith Patton Jr.; aka: "Old Blood and Guts"; 1885-1945; U.S. military officer and four-star general in WWII): An American Carol, 2008 (Kelsey Grammer); Battleground: The Art of War, 2005- (TV series; "The Battle of the Bulge," 2005 episode: Don Worley); The Biggest Battle, 1978 (Robert Spafford); The Brass Target, 1978 (George Kennedy); Crossroads, 1955-1957 (TV series; "The Patton Prayer," 1957 episode: Stephen McNally); Fooling Hitler, 2004 (made-for-TV; James [Carroll] Jordan); Ike: Countdown to D-Day, 2004 (made-for-TV; Gerald McRaney); Ike: The War Years, 1979 (TV miniseries; Darren McGavin); **Is Paris Burning?**, 1966 (Kirk Douglas); The Last Days of Patton, 1986 (made-for-TV; George C. Scott); The Long Way Home, 1997 (Edward Asner); Man, Moment, Machine, 2005-2007 (TV series; "Patton and the Desperate Tank Attack," 2006 episode: Dan Higgins); Margaret Bourke-White, 1989 (made-for-TV; Mitch [Mitchell] Ryan); Miracle of the Wild Stallions, 1963 (John Larch); Pancho Barnes, 1988 (made-for-TV; Robert Prentiss [Robert Manning]); **Patton**, 1970 (George C. Scott); War and Rembrance, 1988- (TV miniseries; Lawrence Dobkin); The World Wars, 2014- (TV miniseries; Dan Hartmann; Matt Dearman).

Paul (saint; Paul the Apostle; c. 5-c. 67 A.D.): Acts of the Apostles, 1969- (TV series; Edoardo Torricella); A.D., 1985 (TV miniseries; Philip Sawyer); A.D. The Bible Continues, 2015- (TV series; Emmett J. Scanlan); The Apostle Paul: The Man Who Turned the World Upside Down, 2001 (made-for-TV; Joseph Campenella; David Kieran); The Cradle of God, 1926 (Leon Mathot); Dinner in Purgatory, 1994 (Edward Halsted); The Emissary: A Biblical Epic, 1997 (Garry Cooper); The Final Inquiry, 2006 (Fernando Guillen Cuervo); Imperium: Nero, 2004 (made-for-TV; Pierre Vaneck); Imperium: Saint Peter, 2005 (made-for-TV; Daniele Pecci); Jesus, 1999 (made-for-TV; Tom Novembre); Jesus of Nazareth, 1977 (TV miniseries; Oliver Smith); The Last Temptation of Christ, 1988 (Harry Dean Stanton); The Life of St. Paul, 1938 (Neal Arden); Life of St. Paul Series, 1949 (Nelson Leigh); Paul of Tarsus, 1960- (TV series; Patrick Troughton); Peter and Paul, 1981 (made-for-TV; Anthony

Robert Donat (as Charles Stewart Parnell) in *Captain Boycott,* **1947.**

Hopkins); **Quo Vadis**, 1951 (Abraham Sofaer); Quo Vadis, 2001 (Zbigniew Walerys); Rome, 2005-2007 (TV series; Nuccio Siano); St. Paul, 2000 (made-for-TV; Johannes Brandrup); Saul: The Journey to Damascus, 2014 (Kyle Schmid); Wine of Morning, 1955 (Vincent Cervera).

Paul I (1754-1801; Russian czar; thought to be mad and assassinated): Assa, 1987 (Dmitry Dolinin); Grafinya Sheremeteva, 1994 (made-for-TV; Yury Berkin); **The Patriot**, 1928 (Emil Jannings); Poor, Poor Pavel, 2003 (Viktor Sukhorukov). Note: For detailed information on Paul I and his assassination, see my two-volume work *The Great Pictorial History of World Crime*, Volume I (History, Inc., 2004; illustrated page 12).

Paul III (1468-1549; Catholic Pope): Carlos, Rey Emperador, 2015-2016 (TV series; Francisco Olmo); The Tudors, 2007-2010 (TV series; Peter O'Toole).

Paulus, Friedrich Wilhelm Ernst (1890-1957; German field marshal in WWII, who surrendered his army at Stalingrad in 1943 to the Soviets): The First Front, 1949 (Vladimir Gajdarov); War and Remembrance, 1988 (TV miniseries; Paul Glawion).

Pavlova, Anna (1881-1931; Russian ballerina): Anna Pavlova, 1983- (TV series; Galina Belyaeva); Beneath the Czar, 1914 (Claire Whitney); Diary for My Lovers, 1987 (Erika Szegedi); Mr. Selfridge, 2013 (TV series; Natalia Kremen); Pavlova: A Tribute to the Legendary Ballerina, 1982 (made-for-TV; Amanda McKerrow; Jolinda Melendez); The Prime of Miss Jean Brodie, 1978 (TV series; "Dorothy and Juliet," 1978 episode: Andrea Durant); Regal Cavalcade, 1935 (Pearl Argyle); **Tonight We Sing**, 1953 (Tamara Toumanova); Une femme, une epoque, 1978- (TV series; "Anna Pavlova," 1978 episode: France Dougnac).

Pearson, Drew (1897-1969; American journalist, syndicated columnist and radio commentator): The Real American: Joe McCarthy, 2012 (Morgan Deare); Tail Gunner Joe, 1977 (made-for-TV; Robert F. Simon).

Peary, Robert E. (1856-1920; U.S. Navy officer and explorer, who is credited with being the first to reach the North Pole in 1909, despite the claims of explorer Frederick Cook, who said he found the Pole a year earlier): Cook and Peary: The Race to the Pole, 1983 (made-for-TV; Rod Steiger); Glory & Honor, 1988 (made-for-TV; Henry Czerny).

Peel, Robert (1788-1850; British statesman and twice prime minister of the United Kingdom): Disraeli: Portrait of a Romantic, 1978 (TV miniseries; Antony Brown); Edward the King, 1975- (TV series; Michael Barrington); Invincible Mr. Disraeli, 1963 (made-for-TV; Eric Berry);

Number 10, 1983- (TV miniseries; "The Iron Duke," 1983 episode: Peter Gale); The Prime Minister, 1942 (Nicholas Hannen); Queen of Destiny, 1940 (Charles Carson); Queen Victoria's Empire, 2001- (TV series; Martin Wady); Victoria & Albert, 2001 (made-for-TV; Alec McCowen); **Victoria the Great**, 1937 (Charles Carson); **The Young Victoria**, 2009 (Michael Maloney).

Peiper, Joachim (1915-1976; German officer and colonel in the 1st SS Panzer Division, who commanded the unit that committed the Malmedy (Belgium) Massacre on December 17, 1944, in WWII where eighty U.S. captured soldiers were bound with their hands behind their backs and then summarily shot to death in a mass execution): **Battle of the Bulge**, 1965 (role model for Robert Shaw). Note: The massacre was also depicted in **Saints and Soldiers**, 2005, and alluded to in **Judgment at Nuremberg**, 1961, and in **Hart's War**, 2002.

Pekar, Henry (1939-2010; U.S. comic book writer;): **American Splendor**, 2003 (Paul Giamatti).

Pemsel, Max-Josef (1897-1985; German lieutenant general in WWII; commanded defense forces at Normandy during the Allied invasion of June 6, 1944): **The Longest Day**, 1962 (Wolfgang Priess).

Pendergast, Thomas Joseph (aka: "Tom"; 1873-1945; American corrupt political boss controlling Kansas City and Jackson County, Missouri from 1925-1939): The Kansas City Massacre, 1975 (made-for-TV; W. T. Zacha); Truman, 1995 (made-for-TV; Pat Hingle).

Pendleton, Alexander Swift (aka: "Sandie"; 1840-1864; Confederate officer in the Army of Northern Virginia during the American Civil War): **Gods and Generals**, 2003 (Jeremy London).

Penn, William (1644-1718; British entrepreneur, Quaker, philosopher and founder of the Commonwealth of Pennsylvania in colonial U.S.): Courageous Mr. Penn, 1943 (Clifford Evans).

Pepys, Samuel (1633-1703; Member of Parliament noted for his ten-year diary that recorded significant events; became chief secretary for Charles II and James II); And So to Bed, 1949 (made-for-TV; Anthony Holles); BBC Sunday-Night Theatre, 1950-1959 (TV series; "Ninety Sail," 1954 episode: Mervyn Johns); The British, 2012- (TV series; Samuel West); Colonel Blood, 1934 (Arthur Chesney); Complete and Utter History of Britain, 1969- (TV series; "James the McFirst to Oliver Cromwell," 1969 episode: Michael Palin); Cosmos: A Space Odyssey, 2014- (TV series; "When Knowledge Conquered Fear," 2014 episode: Tom Konkle); Courageous Mr. Penn, 1943 (Henry Oscar); The Diary of Samuel Pepys, 1958- (TV series; Peter Sallis); England, My England, 1995 (John Shrapnel); From Cover to Cover, 1958- (TV series; Nigel Sharpe); The Glorious Adventure, 1922 (Lennox Pawle); The Great Fire, 2014 (TV miniseries; Daniel Mays); ITV Television Playhouse, 1955-1967 (TV series; "And So to Bed," 1957 episode: George Benson); Jamie, 1971- (TV series; Michael Graham Cox); London, 2004 (made-for-TV; Philip Jackson); Magic Grandad, 1993- (TV series; John Warnaby); Nell Gwyn, 1926 (Johnny Butt); Nell Gwyn, 1935 (Esme Percy); The Private Life of Samuel Pepys, 2003 (made-for-TV; Steve Coogan); The Pyrates, 1986 (made-for-TV; John Rapley); Stage Beauty, 2004 (Hugh Bonneville); Theatre Parade, 1936-1938 (TV series; "Thank You Mr. Pepys," 1938 episode: Edmund Gwenn).

Perkins, William Maxwell Evarts (AKA: Max; 1884-1947; U.S. book editor for Scribner's, editor of F. Scott Fitzgerald, Ernest Hemingway, Thomas Wolfe and William Faulkner; considered to be the greatest book editor of the 20th Century): Fitzgerald, 2002 (made-for-TV; John Ford); Zelda, 1993 (made-for-TV; Daniel Gerroll).

Pershing, John J. (John Joseph Pershing; aka: "Black Jack": 1860-1948; American four-star general; general of the armies; led the American Expeditionary Force in WWI in France): Cannon for Cordorba, 1970 (John Russell); **The Court Martial of Billy Mitchell**, 1955 (Herbert Heyes); The Kaiser, the Beast of Berlin, 1918 (Alfred Allen); Pancho Villa, 1972 (Walter Coy); **Sergeant York**, 1941 (Joseph W. Girard); Why America Will Win, 1918 (A. Alexander as a boy; Harris Gordon as a youth; Olaf Skavian as the adult Pershing).

Petacci, Claretta (1912-1945; Italian woman and mistress of Italian dictator Benito Mussolini, who was killed with him by Italian communist partisans, their bodies displayed as hanged upside down from the girders of a Milan gas station): Caesar and Claretta, 1975 (made-for-TV; Helen Mirren); Claretta Petacci, 1984 (Claudia Cardinale); **Last Days of Mussolini**, 1977 (Lisa Gastoni); Mussolini and I, 1985 (made-for-TV; Barbara De Rossi); Mussolini: The Untold Story, 1985 (TV miniseries; Virginia Madsen); Ten Days to Victory, 2005 (made-for-TV; Geoffrey Greenhill).

Petain, Henri Philippe (1856-1951; French marshal, esteemed for his military service in WWI, but later tried and convicted of treason for his collaborationist actions with the Nazis in WWII as the puppet premier of Vichy France): Clemenceau, 2012 (made-for-TV; Daniel Martin); The Days That Made History, 2009- (TV series; Alain Mottet); **La Rafle**, 2012 (Roland Cope); Les dossiers de l'ecran, 1967-1989 (TV series; Maurice Jacquemont); Les samedis de l'histoire, 1977- (TV series; Jean Davy); Mitterrand a Vichy, 2008 (made-for-TV; Maurice Mons); Moi, general de Gaulle, 1990 (made-for-TV; Yves Brainville); Monsignor Renaud, 2000 (TV miniseries; Warren Mitchell); Petain, 1993 (Jacques Dufilho); Strange Confession, 1944 (Arthur Stenning); Un coin d'Azur, 2005 (made-for-TV; Jean-Marc Scoccimaro).

Peter (Saint Peter; Simon Peter; d. 67 A.D.; one of the twelve Apostles of Jesus and first Catholic pope): A.D., 1985 (TV miniseries; Denis Quilley); A.D. The Bible Continues, 2015- (TV series; Adam Levy); Animated Stories from the New Testament, 1987- (TV series; John Nicolaysen and Mark Hunt voiceovers); Apostle Peter and the Last Supper, 2012 (Robert Loggia as older Peter; Ryan Alosio as younger Peter); The Apostle Peter: Redemption, 2016 (John Rhys-Davies); Barabbas, 1953 (Erik Strandmark); **Barabbas**, 1962 (Harry Andrews); Barabbas, 2013 (made-for-TV; Franco Castellano); Barabbas, 2014 (Christopher Flaxman); The Big Fisherman, 1959 (Howard Keel); Caesar's Friend, 1939 (made-for-TV; Eugene Leahy); Color of the Cross, 2006 (Jacinto Taras Riddick); Color of the Cross 2: The Resurrection, 2008 (Leonard Zanders); The Cross, 2001 (Fred Toma); Crown of Thorns, 1934 (silent; Bruno Ziener); The Day Christ Died, 1980 (made-for-TV; Jay O. Sanders); Day of Triumph, 1954 (Tyler McVey); **Demetrius and the Gladiators**, 1954 (Michael Rennie); The Final Inquiry, 2006 (Enrico Lo Verso); The Friends of Jesus—Judas, 2001 (made-for-TV; Francesco Pannofino); Give Us Barabbas!, 1961 (made-for-TV; Kermit Murdock); The Gospel according to Matthew, 1993 (Gerrit Schoonhoven); The Gospel according to St. Matthew, 1966 (Settimio Di Porto); The Gospel of John, 2014 (El Mahmoudi M'Barek); The Gospel of Luke, 2015 (El Mahmoudi M'Barek); The Gospel of Mark, 2015 (El Mahmoudi M'Barek); The Gospel of Matthew, 2014 (El Mahmoudi M'Barek); Gospel Road: A Story of Jesus, 1973 (Paul L. Smith; Jonathan Sanders); **The Greatest Story Ever Told**, 1965 (Gary Raymond); The Hill, 1960 (made-for-TV; John Drainie); Il messia, 1975 (Hedi Zoughlami); Imperium: Saint Peter, 2005 (made-for-TV; Omar Sharif); Jesus, 1979 (Niko Natai); Jesus, 2000 (made-for-TV; Luca Zingaretti); **Jesus Christ Superstar**, 1973 (Philip Toubus/Paul Thomas); The Jesus Film, 1979 (Niko Nitai); Jesus of Nazareth, 1942 (Enrique G. Alvarez); Jesus of Nazareth, 1956- (TV series; Powys Thomas); Jesus of Nazareth, 1977 (TV miniseries; James Farentino); Judas, 2004 (made-for-TV; Mark Womack); Judas Iskariot, 1977 (made-for-TV; Eero Pikkarainen); Judas'

Michael Rennie (as Peter) and Victor Mature in *Demetrius and the Gladiators*, 1954.

Kiss, 1954 (Manuel Monroy); **The King of Kings**, 1927 (Ernest Torrence); **King of Kings**, 1961 (Royal Dano); Kristo, 1996 (Ruel Vernal); The Last Days of Pompeii, 1984- (TV miniseries; Malcolm Jamieson); The Last Supper: Thirteen Men of Courage, 2007 (made-for-TV; Barry Steinman); The Last Temptation of Christ, 1988 (Victor Argo); The Lawton Story, 1949 (A.S. Fischer); The Living Christ Series, 1951 (TV miniseries; Tyler McVey); Maria Magdelena, 1946 (Carlos Villarias); Mary, 2005 (Marco Leonardi); Mary, Mother of Jesus, 1999 (made-for-TV; John Shrapnel); Mary, Mother of the Son of God, 2003 (Clemente Viscaino); Matthew: 26:17, 2005 (John Abiskaron); The Miracle Maker, 2000 (Ken Stott); Paul of Tarsus, 1960- (TV series; Walter Fitzgerald; Charles Wade); The Passion, 2008 (TV miniseries; Darren Morfitt); The Passion, 2013 (made-for-TV; Jim Bakkum); The Passion of Christ, 2004 (Francesco De Vito); The Passover Plot, 1976 (William Paul Burns); Peter and Paul, 1981 (made-for-TV; Robert Foxworth); The Pilgrimage Play, 1949 (Stephen Chase); The Power of the Resurrection, 1958 (Richard Kiley); **Quo Vadis**, 1951 (Finlay Currie); Quo Vadis?, 1985- (TV miniseries; Max von Sydow); Quo Vadis, 2001 (Franciszek Pieczka); The Redeemer, 1959 (Antonio Vilar); Risen, 2016 (Stewart Scudamore); **The Robe**, 1953 (Michael Rennie); St. Paul, 2000 (made-for-TV; Ennio Fantastichini); **The Silver Chalice**, 1954 (Lorne Greene); Son of God, 2014 (Darwin Shaw); Time Machine: St. Peter—The Rock, 2002 (made-for-TV; DJ Holte); The True Mistery of the Passion, 1960 (made-for-TV; Edward Woodward); The Visual Bible: The Gospel of John, 2003 (Daniel Kash).

Peter I (Peter the Great; 1672-1725; emperor of Russia): Charles XII, 1933 (Nicolai De Seversky); Conquest of Peter the Great, 1939 (Nikolai Simonov); David Bek, 1944 (Vladimir Yershov); Honey on the Knife, 1974 (made-for-TV; Ferenc Bessenyei); How Czar Peter the Great Married Off His Moor, 1976 (Aleksey Petrenko); Peter in Paradise, 2003 (made-for-TV; Rory McCann); Peter the First, 1937 (Nikolai Simonov); Peter the Great, 1922 (Emil Jannings); Peter the Great, 1986- (TV miniseries; Denis DeMarne); Russia, 1986 (TV miniseries; Evgeny Tilicheev); Russian Ark, 2002 (Maksim Sergeyev); The Sovereign's Servant, 2007 (Andrey Sukhov).

Peter III (aka: Peter the Mad; 1728-1762; emperor of Russia; assassinated by Count Gregory Orlov with the collusion of Peter's wife, Catherine the Great or Catherine II): Catherine of Russia, 1963 (Raoul Grassilli); Catherine the Great, 1996 (made-for-TV; Hannes Jaenicke); Catherine the Great, 2005 (made-for-TV; Danut [Dan] Chirlac); Ekaterina, 2014- (TV series; Aleksandr Yatsenko); The Loves of Casanova, 1929 (Rudolf Klein-Rogge); The Man to Kill, 1979 (Zvonimir Crnko); The Rise of Catherine the Great, 1934 (Douglas Fairbanks Jr.); **The**

Fredric March (as Philip II of Macedonia) in *Alexander the Great,* **1956.**

Scarlet Empress, 1934 (Sam Jaffe); Young Catherine, 1991 (made-for-TV; Reese Dinsdale).

Pettigrew, J. Johnston (1828-1863; U.S. military officer and Confederate general during the American Civil War): **Gettysburg**, 1993 (George Lazenby).

Phagan, Mary (1899-1913; U.S. teenage girl found murdered in an Atlanta pencil factory and for which its Jewish manager, Leo Max Frank, was wrongly convicted and lynched by a mob): The Murder of Mary Phagan, 1988 (TV miniseries; Wendy J. Cooke); **They Won't Forget**, 1937 (role model for Lana Turner). Note: For detailed information on Phagan and the Leo Frank case, see my book *"I am Innocent!": A Comprehensive Encyclopedic History of the World's Wrongly Convicted Persons* (Da Capo Press, 2008; illustrated [10 images] pages 315-329).

Philby, Harold Adrian Russell (aka: "Kim"; 1912-1988; British intelligence officer turned traitor and spy for the Soviets, defecting to the USSR in 1963 and becoming an NKVD and KGB operative): Cambridge Spies, 2003 (TV miniseries; Toby Stephens); Camp X, 2014 (made-for-TV; David Straus); The Company, 2007 (TV miniseries; Tom Hollander); Escape, 1980 (TV series; "Kim Philby," 1980 episode: Richard Pasco); The Fourth Protocol, 1987 (Michael Bilton); Kim Philby war der dritte Mann, 1969 (made-for-TV; Arno Assmann); Philby, Burgess and Maclean, 1977 (made-for-TV; Anthony Bate). Note: For detailed information on Philby, see my book *Spies: A Narrative Encyclopedia of Dirty Tricks & Double Dealing from Biblical Times to Today* (M. Evans, 1997; illustrated pages 384-388).

Philip (Saint Philip; d. 80 A.D.; one of the twelve Apostles of Jesus; crucified in Hierapolis): Acts of the Apostles, 1969 (TV miniseries; Giuseppe Mannajuolo); Animated Stories from the New Testament, 1987- (TV series; Tom Cowan voiceover); Apostle Peter and the Last Supper, 2012 (Kevin Hoffmann); The Book of Acts Series, 1957 (Chris Drake); Color of the Cross, 2006 (Michael Govia); Crown of Thorns, 1934 (silent; Wilhelm Nagel); The Day Christ Died, 1980 (made-for-TV; Fabrizzio Jovine); The Gospel according to Matthew, 1993 (Ivan D. Lucas); The Gospel according to St. Matthew, 1966 (Giorgio Agamben); The Gospel of John, 2014 (Ait Youssef Youssef); The Gospel of Luke, 2015 (Ait Youssef Youssef); The Gospel of Mark, 2015 (Ait Youssef Youssef); Gospel Road: A Story of Jesus, 1973 (Steven Chernoff); **The Greatest Story Ever Told**, 1965 (David Hedison); Il messia, 1975 (Missoume); Imperium: Saint Peter, 2005 (Lakshantha Abenayake); Jesus [aka: The Jesus Film], 1979 (Kobi Assaf); Jesus, 2000 (made-for-TV; Karim Doukkali); Jesus of Nazareth, 1977 (TV

miniseries; Steve Gardner); Judas, 2004 (made-for-TV; Mouadine Abdelouahed); **The King of Kings**, 1927 (Charles Belcher); Kristo, 1996 (Nikki Martel); The Last Temptation of Christ, 1988 (Paul Herman); Mary, Mother of the Son of God, 2003 (Expedito Barriera); Mary of Nazareth, 2012 (made-for-TV; Nejib Belhassen); Matthew: 26:17, 2005 (Carl Santangelo); The Passion, 2008 (TV miniseries; Tom Ellis); The Power of the Resurrection, 1958 (George Khoury); Risen, 2016 (Stavros Demetraki); The Visual Bible: The Gospel of John, 2003 (Andrew Pifko).

Philip (Prince; Duke of Edinburgh; b. 1921; prince consort to Elizabeth II of Great Britain): Spitting Image, 1984-1986 (TV series with puppets enacting public figures; Jon Glover voiceover).

Philip II of Macedonia (382-336 B.C.; assassinated): Alexander, 2004 (Val Kilmer); Alexander; Hero of Heroes, 2007 (Kevin O'Meara); **Alexander the Great**, 1956 (Fredric March); Reign: The Conqueror, 1997 (animated TV series; John DiMaggio; Jordan Chan; Dae-kun Lee; Yoshisada Sakaguchi). For detailed information on the assassination of Philip II, see my two-volume work *The Great Pictorial History of World Crime*, Volume I (History, Inc., 2004; illustrated page 2).

Philip II of Spain (1527-1598; king of Spain): BBC Sunday-Night Theatre, 1950-1959 (TV series; "That Lady," 1954 episode: Reginald Tate); Caution to the Wind, 1980 (Julio Espi); The Conquest of America, 2005- (TV miniseries; Michael Bellino); The Conspiracy, 2008 (Juanjo Puigcorbe); Don Carlo, 1978 (made-for-TV; Yevgeni Nesterenko); Don Carlo, 1980 (made-for-TV; Paul Plishka); Don Carlo, 1984 (made-for-TV; Simon Estes); Don Carlo, 1985 (made-for-TV; Robert Lloyd); Don Carlo, 1992 (made-for-TV; Samuel Ramey); Don Carlo, 2004 (made-for-TV; Robert Lloyd); Don Carlo, 2008 (made-for-TV; Ferruccio Furlanetto); Don Carlo, 2010 (made-for-TV; Ferruccio Furlanetto); Don Carlo, 2012 (made-for-TV; Giacomo Prestia); Don Carlos, 1957 (made-for-TV; Paul Verhoeven; Raymond Hermantier); Don Carlos, 1960 (Ewald Balser); Don Carlos, 1964 (made-for-TV; Kolbjorn Buoen); Don Carlos, 1965 (made-for-TV; Nicolai Ghiaurov); Don Carlos, 1996 (made-for-TV; Jose van Dam); Don Carlos, 2005 (made-for-TV; Alastair Miles); Don Carlos—Infant von Spanien, 1963 (made-for-TV; Ernst Fritz Furbringer); Don Carlos—Infant von Spanien, 2005 (made-for-TV; Sven-Eric Bechtolf); Don Juan in Hell, 1991 (Inaki Aierra); El Greco, 1966 (Fernando Rey); **Elizabeth**, 1998 (George Antoni); Elizabeth R, 1971-1972 (TV miniseries; two episodes: Peter Jeffrey); **Elizabeth: The Golden Age**, 2007 (Jordi Molla); Emperor, 2016 (Bill Skarsgard); **Fire over England**, 1937 (Raymond Massey); In the Palace of the King, 1923 (Sam De Grasse); Jeromin, 1953 (Adolfo Marsillach); Monsieur Beaucaire, 1946 (Howard Freeman); Novela, 1963-1978 (TV series; "Gabriel de Espinosa," 1966 episode: Pedro Sempson); Reign, 2013- (TV series; Jordan Lee); **The Sea Hawk**, 1940 (Montagu Love); Seven Seas to Calais, 1963 (Umberto Raho); Sir Francis Drake, 1961- (TV series; "Visit to Spain," 1962 episode: Zia Mohyeddin); That Lady, 1955 (Paul Scofield); The Twisted Tale of Bloody Mary, 2008 (made-for-TV; Jorge Balca); The Virgin Queen, 2005 (TV miniseries; Stanley Townsend); Willem van Oranje, 1934 (Cruys Voorbergh); Young Rebel, 1969 (Fernando Rey).

Piaf, Edith (Edith Giovanna Gassion; 1915-1963; French cabaret singer): Edith and Marcel, 1984 (Evelyne Bouix); Edith es Marlene, 1992 (made-for-TV; Erzsebet Kutvolgyi); Edith Piaf: Une breve rencontre, 1993 (made-for-TV; Sophie Artur); **La vie en rose**, 2007 (Marion Cotillard); The Man Who Lived at the Ritz, 1989 (made-for-TV; Nathalie Cerda); Piaf, 1984 (made-for-TV; Jane Lapotaire); Piaf, 2010 (made-for-TV; Sonia Lisboa); **Piaf: The Early Years**, 1982 (Brigitte Ariel; singing vocals by Betty Mars); Stars in Their Eyes, 1990- (TV series; two episodes: Marie Lloyd; Esther Rantzen).

Picasso, Pablo (1881-1973; Spanish artist): The Adventures of Picasso, 1980 (Gosta Ekman; Gosta Winbergh as Picasso's singing voice); American Playhouse, 1981- (TV series; "Waiting for the Moon," 1987 episode: Adolfo Vargas); Dali, 1991 (Anani Yavashev); La banda Picasso, 2012 (Ignacio Mateos); The Legendary Life of Ernest Hemingway, 1989 (Jose Luis Gomez); A Life Lost in Colours, 2016 (Okan Bayulgen); Lives and Deaths of the Poets, 2011 (Raja Deka); **Midnight in Paris**, 2011 (Marcial de Fonzo Bo); Modi, 1989 (David Brandon); Modigliani, 2004 (Omid Djalili); Monsieur Max, 2007 (made-for-TV; Feodor Atkine; Nazim Boudjenah as young Picasso); Oscar: The Color of Destiny, 2008 (Alejandro Jornet); Paul Gauguin, 1975 (TV miniseries; Gabriel Jabbour); Persistence of Memory, 2014 (Adam Tomas Bennett); Picasso in Munich, 1997 (Herbert Achternbusch); **Surviving Picasso**, 1996 (Anthony Hopkins); The Young Indiana Jones Chronicles, 1992-1993 (TV series; "Barcelona, May 1917," 1992 episode; "Paris, September 1908," 1993 episode: both with Danny Webb as Picasso); The Young Picasso: 1881-1906, 1993 (TV miniseries; Tony Zenet).

Pickett, George Edward (1825-1875; U.S. military leader and general in the Confederate army of Northern Virginia during the American Civil War): **Gettysburg**, 1993 (Stephen Lang); **Gods and Generals**, 2003 (Billy Campbell); Omnibus, 1952-1961 (TV series; "Lee at Gettysburg," 1957 episode: Addison Powell); **Santa Fe Trail**, 1940 (William Marshall).

Picton, Thomas (1758-1815; British soldier and general in the Napoleonic Wars): **Waterloo**, 1971 (Jack Hawkins).

Pierpont, Harry (aka: "Pete"; 1902-1934; U.S. bank robber and member of Dillinger gang): Dillinger, 1973 (Geoffrey Lewis); Dillinger, 1991 (made-for-TV; Bruce Abbott); The Kansas City Massacre, 1975 (made-for-TV; Larry Manetti); **Public Enemies**, 2009 (David Wenham). Note: For detailed information on Pierpont and his activities with the Dillinger gang, see my books, *Dillinger: Dead or Alive?*, 1970 (Regnery, 1970); *The Dillinger Dossier* (December Press, 1983); and my two-volume work *The Great Pictorial History of World Crime*, Volume II (History, Inc., 2004; illustrated [63 images] pages 1374-1423).

Pilate, Pontius (d. 37-38 A.D.; prefect of Roman province of Judea, who condemned Jesus to the Cross): About Religion, 1958- (TV series; "The News on Good Friday," 1960 episode: Anthony Nichols); A.D., 1985- (TV miniseries; Anthony Zerbe); A.D. The Bible Continues, 2015- (TV series; Vincent Regan); Animated Stories from the New Testament, 1987- (TV series; Maikel Bailey voiceover); Appointment with Destiny, 1971-1973 (TV series; "The Crucifixion of Jesus," 1972 episode: Ori Levy); Barabbas, 1935 (Frank Forbes-Robertson); **Barabbas**, 1962 (Arthur Kennedy); Barabbas, 2013 (made-for-TV; Filippo Nigro); Barabbas, 2014 (Callum Noble); BBC Sunday-Night Theatre, 1950-1959 (TV series; "Spark in Judea," 1953 episode: Sebastian Shaw; "Caesar's Friend," 1954 episode: Robert Eddison); Behold the Man, 1935 (Jean Gabin); Behold the Man!, 1951 (Francis Gough); **Ben-Hur**, 1959 (Frank Thring); Ben Hur, 2010 (TV miniseries; Hugh Bonneville); Ben-Hur, 2016 (Pilou Asbaek); Caesar's Friend, 1939 (made-for-TV; D.A. Clarke-Smith); Christus, 1916 (Amleto Novelli); Color of the Cross 2: The Resurrection, 2008 (Rene Parker); The Cross, 2001 (John Koines [John Nicholas]); Crown of Thorns, 1934 (silent; Werner Krauss); The Day Christ Died, 1980 (made-for-TV; Keith Michell); Day of Triumph, 1954 (Lowell Gilmore); The Disciple, 2010 (Juanjo Puigcorbe); The Easter Stories, 1994- (TV series; "Pilate's Tale," 1994 episode: Robert Duncan); Encounter, 1952-1961 (TV series; "The Vigil," 1953 episode: Al King); Family Theatre, 1949-1958 (TV series; "Hill Number One: A Story of Faith and Inspiration," 1951 episode: Leif Erickson; "That I May See," 1951 episode; Richard Hale; "I Beheld His Glory," 1953 episode: Lowell Gilmore); The Final Inquiry, 2006 (Hristo Shopov); The Friends of Jesus—Judas, 2001 (made-for-TV; Mathieu

Hurd Hatfield (as Pontius Pilate) and Viveca Lindfors in *King of Kings,* 1961.

Carriere); The Friends of Jesus—Thomas, 2001 (made-for-TV; Mathieu Carriere); Generation of Leaves: Jesus—A Passion Play for Americans, 1970- (TV series; Kenneth Tigar); Give Us Barabbas!, 1961 (made-for-TV; Dennis King); Good Friday, 1948 (made-for-TV; Clement McCallin); The Gospel according to Matthew, 1993 (Brian O'Shaughnessy); The Gospel according to St. Matthew, 1966 (Alessandro Clerici); The Gospel of John, 2014 (Brahim Ez Zaouy); The Gospel of Luke, 2015 (Brahim Ez Zaouy); The Gospel of Mark, 2015 (Brahim Ez Zaouy); The Gospel of Matthew, 2014 (Brahim Ez Zaouy); Great Performances, 1971- (TV series; "Jesus Christ, Superstar," 2001 episode: Fred Johanson); **The Greatest Story Ever Told**, 1965 (Telly Savalas); The Hill, 1959 (made-for-TV; Esmond Knight); The Hill, 1960 (made-for-TV; Earl Grey); Il messia, 1975 (Jean Martin); Imperium: Saint Peter, 2005 (made-for-TV; Vanni Corbellini); The Inquiry, 1987 (Harvey Keitel); Jesus, 1979 (Peter Frye); Jesus, 1999 (made-for-TV; Bernard Verley); Jesus, 2000 (made-for-TV; Gary Oldman); Jesus Christ Superstar, 1972 (made-for-TV; Robin Ramsay); **Jesus Christ Superstar**, 1973 (Barry Dennen); The Jesus Film, 1979 (Peter Frye); Jesus of Nazareth, 1928 (Charles McCaffrey); Jesus of Nazareth, 1942 (Jose Baviera); Jesus of Nazareth, 1956- (TV series; Alan Wheatley); Jesus of Nazareth, 1977 (TV miniseries; Rod Steiger); Judas, 2004 (made-for-TV; Tim Matheson); Judas' Kiss, 1954 (Gerard Tichy); **The King of Kings**, 1927 (Victor Varconi); **King of Kings**, 1961 (Hurd Hatfield); Kristo, 1996 (Romero Rivera); La Passion, 1978 (made-for-TV; J.P. Sentier); La spada e la croce, 1958 (Philippe Hersent); **The Last Days of Pompeii**, 1935 (Basil Rathbone); The Last Temptation of Christ, 1988 (David Bowie); The Living Bible, 1952 (TV series; Joe McGuinn); The Living Christ Series, 1951 (TV miniseries; Lowell Gilmore); The Man Born to Be King, 1961 (made-for-TV; Geoffrey Alexander); A Man Dies, 1969 (made-for-TV; Francois Bernard); Maria Magdalena, pecadora de Magdala, 1946 (Jose Baviera); Mary, Mother of Jesus, 1999 (made-for-TV; Robert Addie); Mary, Mother of the Son of God, 2003 (Jose Wilker); Mary of Nazareth, 1995 (Jean-Marc Bory); Mary of Nazareth, 2012 (made-for-TV; Remo Girone); The Messiah Jesus, the Spirit of God, 2010 (TV series; Fath-Ali Owesi); The Miracle Maker, 2000 (Ian Holm); Neither Are We Enemies, 1970 (made-for-TV; J.D. Cannon); The Passion, 2008 (TV miniseries; James Nesbitt); The Passion, 2011 (made-for-TV; Wilbert Gieske); The Passion, 2012 (Henk Poort); The Passion, 2013 (made-for-TV; Tom Jansen); The Passion, 2014 (made-for-TV; Jack van Gelder); The Passion, 2015 (Jon van Eerd); The Passion of Christ, 2004 (Hristo Shopov); The Passover Plot, 1976 (Donald Pleasence); The People's Passion, 1999 (made-for-TV; Robert Hardy); The Pilgrimage Play, 1949 (Richard Hale); Pontios Pilatos, 1987- (TV miniseries; Kostas Kosmopoulos); Pontius Pilate, 1966 (made-for-TV; Wolfgang Preiss); Pontius Pilate, 1967 (Jean Marais);

Paul Newman, Katharine Ross (as Etta Place) and Robert Redford in *Butch Cassidy and the Sundance Kid*, 1969.

The Redeemer, 1959 (Antonio Vilar); Reina de reinas: La Virgen Maria, 1948 (Jose Baviera); Risen, 2016 (Peter Firth); **The Robe**, 1953 (Richard Boone); Robert Montgomery Presents, 1950-1957 (TV series; "The Trial of Pontius Pilate," 1957 episode: Bruce Gordon); **Salome**, 1953 (Basil Sydney); The Savior, 2014 (Ghassen Mashini); Secondo Ponzio Pilato, 1988 (Nino Manfredi); Son of God, 2014 (Greg Hicks); The Son of God, 2016 (Augustin Repetto); The Story of Judas, 2015 (Regis Laroche); Studio One in Hollywood, 1948-1958 (TV series; "Pontius Pilate," 1952 episode: Cyril Ritchard); The Testaments: Of One Fold and One Shepherd, 2000 (M. Scott Wilkinson); The True Mistery of the Passion, 1960 (made-for-TV; Ewen Solon); The Uphill to Golgotha, 1917 (Manos Filippidis); The Visual Bible: The Gospel of John, 2003 (Stephen Russell); **The Wandering Jew**, 1935 (Basil Gill); The Wednesday Play, 1964-1970 (TV series; "Son of Man," 1969 episode: Robert Hardy); Which Will Ye Have!, 1949 (Robert Harris); Wine of Morning, 1955 (Bob Jones Jr.).

Pinkerton, Allan (1819-1884; U.S. detective): American Outlaws, 2001 (Timothy Dalton); Cavalcade of America (aka: DuPont Theater), 1952-1957 (TV series; "The Palmetto Conspiracy," 1955 episode: Pierre Watkin); Der Tod des Prasidenten, 1967 (Erich Roder); The Dramatic Life of Abraham Lincoln, 1924 (W. L. McPheeters); Frank and Jesse, 1995 (William Atherton); **The Great Missouri Raid**, 1951 (role model for Ward Bond); The Heart of Maryland, 1927 (Lew Short); In the Days of Buffalo Bill, 1922 (Burton C. Law); **Jesse James**, 1939 (role model for J. Edward Bromberg, who plays a detective named Runyon); The Life and Legend of Wyatt Earp, 1955-1961 (TV series; "The Pinkertons," 1956 episode: Douglas Evans); Lincoln, 1974-1976 (TV miniseries; "The Unwilling Warrior," 1976 episode: Brendan Dillon); Lincoln, 1988 (made-for-TV; Bill Chorney); Lincoln: American Mastermind, 2009 (made-for-TV; Robert Lavery); **The Long Riders**, 1980 (role model for James Whitemore Jr.); Mentors, 1998-2002 (TV series; "The Private Eyes," 2002 episode: Nigel Bennett); Operator 13, 1934 (Sidney Toler); The Phantom of Morrisville, 1966 (Vit Olmer); The Pinkertons, 2014-2015 (TV series; Angus Macfadyen); **The Return of Frank James**, 1940 (role model for J. Edward Bromberg, who plays a detective named Runyon); The Rose and the Jackal, 1990 (made-for-TV; Christopher Reeve); **Saving Lincoln**, 2013 (Marcus Freed); Sugar Colt, 1967 (George Rigaud); **The Tall Target**, 1951 (James Harrison); The Time Tunnel, 1966-1967 (TV series; "The Death Trap," 1966 episode: R.G. Armstrong).

Pissaro, Camille (1830-1903; Danish-French impressionist painter): **Lust for Life**, 1952 (David Leonard); Omnibus, 1967-2003 (TV series; "Van Gogh," 1990 episode: Terence Baylor); Paradise Found, 2003

(Alun Armstrong); State of the Artist, 2001 (David Nation).

Pitt, William (William Pitt the Younger; 1759-1806; prime minister of Great Britain): Admiral Ushakov, 1954 (Nikolay Volkov); Amazing Grace, 2007 (Benedict Cumberbatch); **America**, 1924 (Charles Bennett); Austerlitz, la victoire en marchant, 2006 (Jonathan Sawdon); The Battle of Austerlitz, 1960 (Anthony Stuart); Battle of the Brave, 2004 (Tim Roth); **Beau Brummell**, 1954 (Paul Rogers); The Fight against Slavery, 1975 (TV miniseries; Ronald Pickup); The First Black Britons, 2005 (made-for-TV; Alister Barton); **The Madness of King George**, 1994 (Julian Wadham); Mrs. Fitzherbert, 1950 (Henry Oscar); Nelson, 1918 (Ernest Thesiger); Number 10, 1983 (TV miniseries; Jeremy Brett as adult Pitt; Daniel Matthews as Pitt as a boy); Prince Regent, 1979 (TV miniseries; David Collings); **The Scarlet Pimpernel**, 1934 (Bruce Belfrage); You Are There, 1953-1971 (TV series; "William Pitt's Last Address to Parliament," 1954 episode: Lorne Greene); **The Young Mr. Pitt**, 1943 (Robert Donat).

Pitts, Charlie (AKA: Sam Wells; d. 1876; U.S. outlaw and member of the James-Younger gang; killed in the abortive bank robbery in Northfield, Minnesota): The Great Jesse James Raid, 1953 (Richard H. Cutting); **The Great Missouri Raid**, 1951 (Bob Bray); **The Great Northfield, Minnesota Raid**, 1972 (Wayne Sutherlin); **The Long Riders**, 1980 (Tim Rossovich); Tales of Wells Fargo, 1957-1962 (TV series; "Cole Younger," 1960 episode: George Keymas); **The True Story of Jesse James**, 1957 (Mark Hickman); **Young Jesse James**, 1960 (Rayford Barnes). Note: For detailed information on Pitts and the James-Younger gang, see my two-volume work *The Great Pictorial History of World Crime*, Volume II (History, Inc., 2004; illustrated [29 images] pages 1342-1359).

Place, Etta (c. 1878-? ; U.S. schoolteacher and consort of outlaws, common-law wife of bandit Harry Longbaugh, known as the Sundance Kid): Blackthorn, 2011 (Dominique McElligott); **Butch Cassidy and the Sundance Kid**, 1969 (Katharine Ross); Gambler V: Playing for Keeps, 1994 (made-for-TV; Mariska Hargitay); The Legend of Butch & Sundance, 2006 (made-for-TV; Rachelle Lefevre); Mrs. Sundance, 1974 (made-for-TV; Elizabeth Montgomery); Wanted: The Sundance Woman, 1976 (made-for-TV; Katharine Ross).

Plehve, Vyacheslav (1846-1904; director of Russiam Imperial Police and later Russia's minister of the interior; assassinated when a revolutionary threw a bomb into his carriage in St. Petersburg on July 28, 1904): Azev: Le tsar de nuit, 1975 (made-for-TV; Francois Maistre); Fall of Eagles, 1974 (TV miniseries; "Dearest Nicky," "Absolute Beginners," 1974 episodes: Bruce Purchase); Flame Top, 1980 (Aleksandr Zakharov); Helmikuum manifesti, 1939 (Valter Toumi); Kajastus, 1930 (Uuno Montonen).

Pluskat, Werner (d. 2000; German army officer, a major commanding beach defenses at Omaha Beach in Normandy in 1944 and reportedly the first to see the Allied invasion fleet): **The Longest Day**, 1962 (Hans Christian Blech).

Pobedonostsev, Konstantin (1827-1907; reactionary Russian jurist under three czars of Imperial Russia): Helmikuum manifesti, 1939 (Eino Juurka); House of Death, 1932 (Nikolay Podgorny); Kajastus, 1930 (Topo Leistela).

Pocahontas (1595-1617; Indian maiden in Virginia who reportedly saved the life of British explorer Captain John Smith by placing her head upon his own when her father, Indian Chief Powhatan, was about to execute Smith with a war club): Animated Hero Classics, 1991-2005 (animated TV series; "Pocahontas," 1994 episode: Debra Funkhouser voiceover); Captain John Smith and Pocahontas, 1953 (Jody Lawrence); The New

World, 2005 (Q'orlanka Kilcher); Pocahontas: The Legend, 1995 (Sandrine Holt); **Pocahontas**, 1995 (animated; Irene Bedard voiceover; Judy Kuhn singing voice); Pocahontas and Captain John Smith: Love and Survival in the New World, 2009 (made-for-TV; Jessica May Foss); Pocahontas: Princess of the American Indians, 1996 (animated TV series; Emanuela Pacotto).

Poe, Edgar Allan (1809-1849; U.S. author of mystery and horror tales): A.J.'s Time Travelers, 1995- (TV series; "Edgar Allan Poe," 1995 episode: Richard Lewis); Castle of Blood, 1964 (Montgomery Glenn [Silvano Tranquilli]); The Death of Poe, 2006 (Mark Redfield); Detective, 1964-1969 (TV series; "The Murders in the Rue Morgue," 1968 episode: Charles Kay); Dickens of London, 1976- (TV series; "Nightmare," 1976 episode: Seymour Matthews); Edgar Allan Poe at West Point, 1955 (made-for-TV; John Carlyle); Extraordinary Tales, 2015 (animated; Stephen Hughes voiceover); Go to Hell, 1999 (Troy Antoine LaFaye); Het testament van Edgar Allan Poe, 1974- (TV series; Henk van Ulsen); Lives and Deaths of the Poets, 2011 (Greg Coale); The Loves of Edgar Allan Poe, 1942 (Shepperd Strudwick); **The Man with a Cloak**, 1951 (role model for Joseph Cotten); Masters of Horror, 2005- (TV series; "The Black Cat," 2007 episode: Jeffrey Combs); Mentors, 1998-2005 (TV series; "The Raven," 1995 episode: Michael Sarrazin); Night Gallery, 1969-1973 (TV series; "Cool Air/Camera Obscura/Quoth the Raven," 1971 episode: Marty Allen); Nightmares from the Mind of Poe, 2006 (Ric White); Omnibus, 1952-1961 (TV series; "The Fine Art of Murder," 1956 episode: Felix Munro); Poe, 2011 (made-for-TV; Christopher Egan); Poe: Last Days of the Raven, 2008 (Brent Fidler); The Raven, 1915 (Henry B. Walthall); The Raven, 1935 (Raine Bennett); The Raven, 2012 (John Cusack); The Spectre of Edgar Allan Poe, 1974 (Robert Walker Jr.); The Strange Case of the Cosmic Rays, 1957 (animated made-for-TV; Bill Baird and Cora Baird voiceovers); The Tell-Tale Heart, 1960 (role model for Laurence Payne as "Edgar Marsh"); Torture Garden, 1967 (Hedger Wallace); Web of the Spider, 1975 (Klaus Kinski).

Polo, Marco (1254-1324; Venetian explorer and trader): **The Adventures of Marco Polo**, 1938 (Gary Cooper); Doctor Who, 1963-1989 (TV series; two 1964 episodes with Mark Eden as Marco Polo); The Four Assassins, 1981 (Richard Harrison); Marco, 1973 (Desi Arnaz Jr.); Marco Millions, 1939 (made-for-TV; Griffith Jones); Marco Polo, 1982- (TV miniseries; Ken Marshall); Marco Polo, 2007 (made-for-TV; Ian Somerhalder); Marco Polo, 2015- (TV series; Lorenzo Richelmy); Marco Polo: The Return to Xanadu, 2001 (animated; John Matthew voiceover); **Marco the Magnificent**, 1966 (Horst Buchholz); Voyagers!, 1982-1983 (TV series; "The Travels of Marco...and Friends," 1982 episode: Paul Regina).

Pompadour, Madame de (Jeanne Antoinette Poisson; 1721-1764; French courtesan and mistress of Louis XV): Casanova, 1934 (Marcelle Denya); Casanova, 2015 (made-for-TV; Bojana Novakovic); C'est arrive a Paris, 1977 (made-for-TV; Corinne Marchand); Die Marquise von Pompadour, 1936 (Anny Ahlers); Die Pompadour, 1939 (Kathe von Nagy); Exzellenz Unterrock, 1921 (Ellen Petz); Fan Fan the Tulip, 1925 (Claude France); Fan Fan the Tulip, 1953 (Genevieve Page); Fanfan, 2003 (Helene de Fougerolles); Figaro-ci, Figaro-la, 1972 (made-for-TV; Colette Ripert); Il giovane Casanova 2002 (made-for-TV; Katja Flint); Le secret du Chevalier d'Eon, 1959 (Simone Valere); Louis XV, le soleil noir, 2009 (made-for-TV; Romane Portail); Madame de Pompador: The King's Favorite, 2006 (made-for-TV; Helene de Fougerolles); Madame Pompadour, 1927 (Dorothy Gish); Madame Pompadour, 1960 (Elfie Mayerhofer); Madame Pompadour, 1996 (made-for-TV; Noemi Nadelmann); Mandrin, 1924 (Jeanne Helbling); Mandrin, 1947 (Mona Goya); Marquis d'Eon, der Spion der Pompadour, 1929 (Agnes Esterhazy); Monsieur Beaucaire, 1924 (Paulette Duval); Nicolas Le Floch, 2008- (TV series; "L'homme au ventre de plomb," 2008 episode: Carole

Cary Grant (as Cole Porter), Ginny Simms and Monty Woolley in *Night and Day,* **1946.**

Franck); Royal Affairs in Versailles, 1957 (Micheline Presle); **Unfaithfully Yours**, 1947 (Evelyn Beresford); Voltaire et l'affaire Calas, 2007 (made-for-TV; Anne Martinet).

Pompey the Great (106-48 B.C.; Roman military and political leader): Ancient Rome: The Rise and Fall of an Empire, 2006 (TV series; John Shrapnel); Antonio e Cleopatra, 1965 (made-for-TV; Achille Millo); Antonius und Cleopatra, 1963 (made-for-TV; Hanns Ernst Jager); Antony and Cleopatra, 1972 (Freddie Jones); Antony & Cleopatra, 1981 (made-for-TV; Donald Sumpter); Antony and Cleopatra, 1984 (made-for-TV; Walter Koenig); BBC Sunday-Night Theatre, 1950-1959 (TV series; "The Tragedy of Pompey the Great," 1950 episode: James Carney); Caesar, 2003 (made-for-TV; Christopher Mondt); Caesar the Conqueror, 1963 (Carlo Tamberlani); The Caesars, 1968- (TV series; "Germanicus," 1968 episode; Lindsay Campbell); The Cleopatras, 1983- (TV miniseries; "51 BC," 1983 episode: Phillip Cade); Giants of Rome, 1964 (Piero Lulli); **King of Kings**, 1961 (Conrado San Martin); A Queen for Caesar, 1962 (Nando Angelini); Rome, 2005-2007 (TV series; Kenneth Cranham); Spartacus, 2004 (made-for-TV; George Calil); Spartacus: War of the Damned, 2010-2013 (TV series; Joel Tobeck); The Two Gladiators, 1964 (Adriano Micantoni).

Poppaea Sabina (Poppaea Augusta Sabina; 30-65 A.D.; second wife of Roman emperor Nero, who reportedly killed her after kicking her in the abdomen when she was pregnant): Ancient Rome: The Rise and Fall of an Empire, 2006 (TV series; Catherine McCormack); The Apostle Peter: Redemption, 2016 (Bobbie Phillips); Fire over Rome, 1965 (Moira Orfei); Nero and the Burning of Rome, 1954 (Jole Fierro); Nero's Mistress, 1962 (Brigitte Bardot); Nerone, 1977 (Maria Grazia Buccella); Poppeas kroning, 1978 (made-for-TV; Elisabeth Sonderstrom); **Quo Vadis**, 1951 (Patricia Laffan); Quo Vadis, 2001 (Agnieszka Wagner).

Porter, Cole (1891-1964; U.S. composer-lyricist): Cuando me vaya, 1954 (Jorge Chesterking); **De-Lovely**, 2004 (Kevin Kline); Florence Foster Jenkins, 2016 (Mark Arnold); High Society's Favorite Gigolo, 2008 (made-for-TV; Zackary McKraken); **Kiss Me Kate**, 1953 (Ron Randell); **Midnight in Paris**, 2011 (Yves Heck); **Night and Day**, 1946 (Cary Grant).

Potemkin, Gregory (1739-1791; Russian nobleman and statesman; favorite of Catherine II): Admiral Ushakov, 1954 (Boris Livanov); The Adventures of Baron Munchausen, 1943 (Andrews Engelmann); Catherine the Great, 1996 (made-for-TV; Paul McGann); Catherine the Great, 2005 (made-for-TV; Dan Badarau); Great Catherine, 1969 (Zero Mostel).

Kent Smith (as Quanah Parker), Linda Cristal and Dana Andrews in *Comanche,* **1956.**

Powell, Lewis Thornton (aka: Lewis Paine; 1844-1865; one of the conspirators in the 1865 assassination of President Abraham Lincoln and who attempted to murder U.S. Secretary of State William H. Seward and who was later convicted and executed by hanging): **The Conspirator**, 2011 (Norman Reedus); The Day Lincoln Was Shot, 1998 (made-for-TV; Titus Welliver); The Lincoln Conspiracy, 1977 (Sonny Shroyer); You Are There, 1953-1957 (TV series; "The Capture of John Wilkes Booth," 1953 episode: Claude Akins). Note: For detailed information on Powell and his involvement in the Lincoln assassination, see my two-volume work *The Great Pictorial History of World Crime*, Volume I (History, Inc., 2004; illustrated [47 images] pages 26-44).

Powers, Francis Gary (1929-1977; U.S. pilot of the CIA U-2 spy plane, which was shot down by the Soviets on May 1, 1960, by one of eight ground-to-air missiles fired; Powers was captured and held prisoner until exchanged for Soviet spy KGB spymaster Col. Vilyam Fisher [aka: Rudolf Abel; 1903-1971] on February 10, 1962, at the Glienicke Bridge in Berlin, Germany): **Bridge of Spies**, 2015 (Austin Stowell); Francis Gary Powers: The True Story of the U-2 Spy Incident, 1976 (made-for-TV; Lee Majors). Note: For detailed information on Powers and his failed U-2 spy mission, see my book *Spies: A Narrative Encyclopedia of Dirty Tricks & Double Dealing from Biblical Times to Today* (M. Evans, 1997; illustrated [5 images] pages 394-397).

Powers, Harry (1892-1932; U.S. serial killer in West Virginia; executed): **Night of the Hunter**, 1955 (role model for Robert Mitchum). Note: For detailed information on Powers, see my book *World Encyclopedia of 20th Century Murder* (Paragon House, 1992; page 456).

Priddy, Gerald Edward (1919-1980; U.S. baseball player): **The Winning Team**, 1952 (himself).

Prim, Juan (1814-1870; Spanish general and statesman): Cinco de Mayo, La Battala, 2013 (Gines Garcia Millan); Maximilian von Mexiko, 1970 (made-for-TV; Kurt Schmitt-Mainz); Mexicanos al grito de guerra, 1943 (Francisco Jambrina);

Princip, Gavrilo (1894-1918; assassin of Austrian Archduke Franz Ferdinand): Alcoa Premiere, 1961-1963 (TV series; "The End of the World," 1961 episode: Andrew Prine); Branio sam Mladu Bosnu, 2015 (TV miniseries; Milos Djurovic); The Day That Shook the World, 1975 (Irfan Mensur); Gavre Princip—Himmel unter Steinen, 1990 (Reuben Pillsbury); 1914: The Last Days before the War, 1932 (Carl Balhaus); Last Waltz in Sarajevo, 1990 (Davor Dujmovic; Tihomir Stanic); The Man Who Defended Gavrilo Princip, 2014 (Milos Djurovic); Sarajevo,

1955 (Hubert Hilten); Sarajevo, 2014 (made-for-TV; Eugen Knecht); Sarajevski atentat, 1968 (Predrag Finci); Sarajevski atentat, 1972 (made-for-TV; Milan Mihailovic); Storm at Daybreak, 1933 (Mischa Auer); 37 Days, 2014 (TV miniseries; Chris Kelly); Weltuntergang, 1984 (made-for-TV; Rudi Wanka). Note: For detailed information on Princip and the assassination of Franz Ferdinand, see my two-volume work, *The Great Pictorial History of World Crime*, Volume I (History, Inc., 2004; illustrated [10 images] pages 65-73).

Pugachev, Yemelyan (c.1742-1775; Cossack pretender to the Russian throne during the Cossack insurrection in the reign of Catherine the Great or Catherine II): The Adventures of Baron Munchausen, 1943 (Aruth Wartan); The Captain's Daughter, 2001 (Vladimir Mashkov); Catherine the Great, 1996 (made-for-TV; John Rhys-Davies); Catherine the Great, 2005 (made-for-TV; Ioan Ionescu); Pugachev, 1980 (Yevgeni Matveyev); Tempest, 1959 (Van Heflin).

Purvis, Melvin Horace, Jr. (1903-1960; U.S. FBI agent in charge of the Chicago Bureau during the early 1930s; reportedly, with others, killed Public Enemy Number One John Dillinger outside a Chicago theater on July 22, 1934, and later shot and killed that year Public Enemy Charles Arthur "Pretty Boy" Floyd in Ohio; left the Bureau under pressure from FBI Chief J. Edgar Hoover and later headed the Junior G-Man organization for Post-Toasties; committed suicide): Dillinger, 1960 (made-for-TV; Steven Hill); Dillinger, 1973 (Ben Johnson); Dillinger, 1991 (made-for-TV; Will Patton); The Kansas City Massacre, 1975 (made-for-TV; Dale Robertson); The Lady in Red, 1979 (Alan Vint); Melvin Purvis: G-MAN, 1974 (Dale Robertson); **The Private Files of J. Edgar Hoover**, 1977 (Michael Sacks); **Public Enemies**; 2009 (Christian Bale); The Story of Pretty Boy Floyd, 1974 (made-for-TV; Geoffrey Binney). For further information on Purvis, see my book *Citizen Hoover: A Critical Study of the Life and Times of J. Edgar Hoover and His FBI* (Nelson-Hall, 1962).

Putnam, George (George Palmer Putnam; 1887-1950; U.S. publisher, husband of Amelia Earhart): **Amelia**, 2009 (Richard Gere); Amelia Earhart, 1976 (made-for-TV: John Forsythe); Amelia Earhart: The Final Flight, 1994 (made-for-TV: Bruce Dern); Resolution: A Portrait of Amelia Earhart, 2012 (Christopher Kirsch).

Putnam, Israel (1718-1790; U.S. officer and general who fought with distinction in the American Revolutionary War): The Beautiful Mrs. Reynolds, 1918 (Lionel Belmore); Histeria!, 1998-2000 (animated TV series; "Super Amazing Constitutions," 1999 episode Frank Welker voiceover); Samuel Adams, 2014 (made-for-TV; Mark Bean).

Pyle, Ernie (Ernest Taylor Pyle; 1900-1945; U.S. journalist and legendary war correspondent in WWII; killed in the Pacific): **The Story of G.I. Joe**, 1945 (Burgess Meredith).

Quanah Parker (1845-1911; chief of the Comanche tribe): Comanche, 1956 (Kent Smith).

Quantrill, William Clarke (1837-1865; Confederate guerilla leader during the American Civil War): Arizona Raiders, 1965 (Fred Graham); **Dark Command**, 1940 (role model for Walter Pidgeon); **Fighting Man of the Plains**, 1949 (James Griffith); Hondo, 1967 (TV series; "Hondo and the Judas," 1967 episode: Forrest Tucker); Into the West, 2005 (TV series; "Dreams and Schemes," 2005 episode: Jon-Paul Khouri); Jesse James Under the Black Flag, 1921 (Harry Hall); Kansas Pacific, 1953 (Reed Hadley); Kansas Raiders, 1950 (Brian Donlevy); The Legend of Jesse James, 1965-1966 (TV series; Peter Whitney); The Legend of the Golden Gun, 1979 (made-for-TV; Robert Davi); Quantrill's Raiders, 1958 (Leo Gordon); **Red Mountain**, 1951 (John Ireland); Renegade Girl, 1946 (Ray Corrigan); **Ride with the Devil**, 1999 (John Ales); The

Rough Riders, 1958-1959 (TV series; "The Plot to Assassinate President Johnson," 1959 episode: Broderick Crawford); The Secret Adventures of Jules Verne, 2000 (TV series; "The Ballad of Steeley Joe," 2000 episode: Robin Wilcock); Stories of the Century, 1954- (TV series; "Quantrill and His Raiders," 1954 episode: Bruce Bennett); The Stranger Wore a Gun, 1953 (James Millican); **Woman They Almost Lynched**, 1953 (Brian Donlevy); **Young Jesse James**, 1960 (Emile Meyer).

Quirnheim, Albrecht Mertz von (1905-1944; German colonel in WWII and part of the 1944 plot to kill Adolf Hitler): Claus Graf Stauffenberg, 1970 (made-for-TV; Werner Nippen); Die Stunde der Offiziere, 2004 (made-for-TV; Florian Martens); Operation Valkyrie, 2004 (made-for-TV; David C. Bunners); Operation Walkure, 1971 (made-for-TV; Dieter Wagner); **Valkyrie**, 2008 (Christian Berkel); The Wednesday Play, 1964-1970 (TV series; "The July Plot," 1964 episode: Michael Anthony).

Radisson, Pierre-Esprit (c.1636-1710; French fur trader and explorer, who established the Hudson's Bay Company in Canada for Charles II of England): Canada: A People's History, 2000 (TV series; Gaetan Dumont); D'Iberville, 1967 (TV series; Robert Rivard). **Hudson's Bay**, 1941 (Paul Muni); Kazan, 1921 (William Ryno).

Raleigh, Walter (Sir Walter Raleigh; c.1554-1618; British soldier and explorer): Churchill's People, 1974- (TV series; "A Rich and Beautiful Empire," 1975 episode: John Turner); Elizabeth I, 2005- (TV miniseries; Ben Pullen); Elizabeth R, 1971- (TV miniseries; Nicholas Selby); Elizabeth the Queen, 1968 (made-for-TV; Michael Allinson); **Elizabeth: The Golden Age**, 2007 (Clive Owen); Gloriana, 1984 (made-for-TV; Richard Van Allan); Gloriana, 2000 (made-for-TV; Clive Bayley); ITV Play of the Week, 1955-1974 (TV series; "In the Shadow of the Axe," 1958 episode: Derek Alyward); Kenilworth, 1967- (TV series; Nigel Terry); The Merry Wives of Windsor, 1980 (made-for-TV; Jeffrey G. Forward); My Friend Walter, 1992 (Ronald Pickup); **The Private Lives of Elizabeth and Essex**, 1939 (Vincent Price); Roanoke: The Lost Colony, 2007 (James Alexander); Roberto Devereux, 1997 (made-for-TV; Davide Baroncelli); The Story of Mankind, 1957 (Edward Everett Horton); Time Flies, 1944 (Leslie Bradley); **The Virgin Queen**, 1955 (Richard Todd); The Virgin Queen, 2005 (TV miniseries; Derek Riddell); You Are There, 1953-1971 (TV series; "The First Command Performance of Romeo and Juliet [1597]," 1954 episode: Herbert Rudley).

Reles, Abraham (Abe; aka: Kid Twist; 1906-1941; U.S. gangster and member of Murder, Inc., who turned informer and was supposedly murdered while in police custody, but whose testimony nevertheless helped send U.S. crime syndicate boss Louis "Lepke" Buchalter to the electric chair four years later): Lepke, 1975 (Zitto Kazann); **Murder, Inc.**, 1960 (Peter Falk). Note: For detailed information on Reles, see my book *World Encyclopedia of Organized Crime* (Paragon House, 1992; illustrated pages 331-332).

Ramesses II (or Ramses; 1303-1213 B.C.; founding Pharoah of Egypt's 19th Dynasty and believed to be the Phaoah of the Exodus of the Israelites): The Bible, 2013 (TV miniseries, "Exodus," 2013 episode: Sean Teale as young Ramesses; Stewart Scudamore as older Ramesses); **Exodus: Gods and Kings**, 2014 (Joel Edgerton); **The Green Pastures**, 1936 (Ernest Whitman); In the Beginning, 2000 (made-for-TV; Art Malik); Moise, 1984 (made-for-TV; Jean-Philippe Lafont); Moses, 1995 (made-for-TV; Christopher Lee); Moses the Lawgiver, 1974 (TV miniseries; Mario Ferrari as Ramses II); **The Prince of Egypt**, 1998 (Ralph Fiennes voiceover); Son of God, 2014 (Stewart Scudamore); **The Ten Commandments**, 1923 (Charles de Rochefort); **The Ten Commandments**, 1956 (Yul Brynner); The Ten Commandments, 2006 (made-for-TV; Paul Rhys); The Ten Commandments, 2007

Walter Pidgeon (as William Quantrill) and Claire Trevor in *The Dark Command*, 1940.

(Alfred Molina voiceover); The Ten Commandments: The Musical, 2006 (Kevin Earley).

Remus, George (1874-1952; U.S. attorney and bootlegger during Prohibition, who became a multimillionaire): Boardwalk Empire, 2010- (TV series: eight episodes: Glenn Fleshler).

Rasputin, Gregory (1869-1916; Russian profligate monk, mystic, psychic and hypnotist, who held sway over the last Romanov dynasty until assassinated by Felix Yusupov and other monarchists): Anastasia, 1997 (Christopher Lloyd voiceover; Jim Cummings singing voiceover); BBC Play of the Month, 1965-1983 (TV series; "Rasputin," 1971 episode: Robert Stephens); A Beautiful Stranger, 1993 (Ivan Krasko); Die Brandstifter Europas, 1926 (Max Neufeld); Dornenweg einer Furstin, 1928 (Gregori Chmara); Fall of Eagles, 1974 (TV miniseries; "Tell the King the Sky Is Falling," 1974 episode: Michael Aldridge); The Fall of the Romanovs, 1917 (Edward Connelly); Forever Knight, 1989-1996 (TV series; "Strings," 1995 episode: Sam Malkin); **Going Hollywood**, 1933 (Sam McDaniel); **Nicholas and Alexander**, 1971 (Tom Baker); The Night They Killed Rasputin, 1962 (Edmund Purdom); Raspoutine, 2011 (made-for-TV; Gerard Depardieu); Rasputin, 1939 (Harry Baur); Rasputin, 1954 (Pierre Brasseur); Rasputin, 1958 (made-for-TV; Narcisco Ibanez Menta); Rasputin, 1966 (made-for-TV; Herbert Stass); Rasputin, 1967 (Gert Frobe); **Rasputin**, 1985 (Aleksey Petrenko); Rasputin, 1996 (made-for-TV; Alan Rickman); Rasputin, 2010 (Francesco Cabras); **Rasputin and the Empress**, 1932 (Lionel Barrymore); Rasputin and the Holy Devil, 1928 (Nikolai Malikoff); Rasputin, Demon with Women, 1932 (Conrad Veidt); Rasputin, the Black Monk, 1917 (Montagu Love); **Rasputin: The Mad Monk**, 1966 (Christopher Lee); Rasputins Liebesabenteuer, 1928 (Nikolai Malikoff); The Red Dance, 1928 (Demetrius Alexis); Suspense, 1949-1954 (TV series; "The Black Prophet," 1953 episode: Boris Karloff); The Successor, 1996 (Igor Solovyov); Why Russians Are Revolting, 1970 (Wes Carter). Note: For detailed information on Rasputin and his assassination, see my two-volume works *The Great Pictorial History of World Crime*, Volume I (History, Inc., 2004; illustrated [14 images] pages 73-79).

Rathbone, Henry Reed (1837-1911; U.S. military officer who was sitting in the presidential box when John Wilkes Booth mortally shot President Abraham Lincoln at Ford's Theater on the night of April 14, 1865, Lincoln dying the next morning; Rathbone attempted to subdue Booth, but was seriously wounded by the assassin who wielded a knife before escaping; he married Clara Harris, who also attended the Lincolns that night, but later went insane, murdering her and was confined in an asylum until his death): **The Conspirator**, 2011 (Andy Martin); The Day

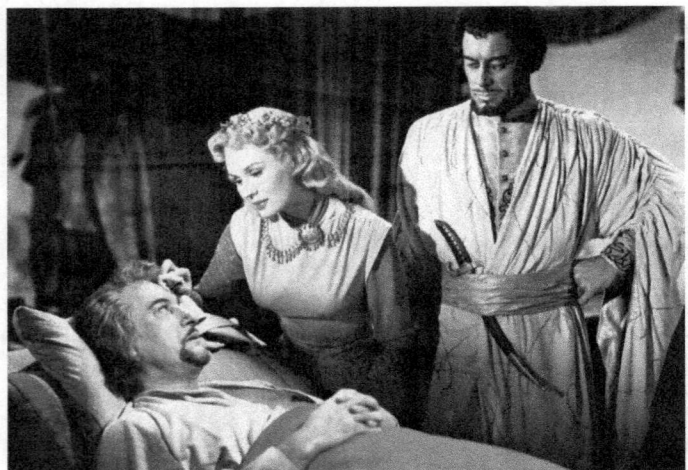

George Sanders (as Richard I), Virginia Mayo and Rex Harrison in *King Richard and the Crusaders*, 1954.

Lincoln Was Shot, 1998 (made-for-TV; Sean Baldwin); Days That Shook the World, 2003-2013 (TV series; "Terror Made in America: Assassination of Abraham Lincoln...," 2004 episode: Noah Michael Levine); The Dramatic Life of Abraham Lincoln, 1924 (Earl Schenck); The Lincoln Conspiracy, 1977 (John Cooler); **Prince of Players**, 1955 (Steve Darrell); **The Prisoner of Shark Island**, 1936 (Lloyd Whitlock).

Raubal, Geli (Angela Maria Raubal; aka: "Geli"; 1908-1931; niece of Adolf Hitler, either murdered or committed suicide after she was reportedly molested by Hitler): BBC2 Playhouse, 1973-1983 (TV series; "Journal of Bridget Hitler," 1981 episode: Nina Zuckerman); Hitler, 1962 (Cordula Trantow); **The Hitler Gang**, 1944 (Poldi Dur); Hitler: The Rise of Evil, 2003 (made-for-TV; Jena Malone); Uncle Adolf, 2005 (made-for-TV; Elaine Cassidy).

Ray, Man (Emmanuel Radnitzky; 1890-1976; U.S. visual artist, painter, fashion and portrait photographer, who resided in France and was a part of the Dada and Surrealist movements): Kiki of Montparnasse, 2013 (Matthew Geczy); The Man Who Lived at the Ritz, 1989 (made-for-TV; Richard Durden); **Midnight in Paris**, 2011 (Tom Cordier); Opium, 2013 (Virgile Bramly).

Read, Mary (or Reid; d. 1721; female pirate of the Caribbean): Pirates, 1998 (Rachel Ferjani); Queen of the Seas, 1963 (Lisa Gastoni); True Caribbean Pirates, 2006 (made-for-TV; Kimberly Adair).

Reagan, Ronald (1911-2004; U.S. actor and politician; 40th President of the U.S.): **The 100-Year-Old Man Who Climbed Out of the Window and Disappeared**, 2014 (Keith Chanter); Panther, 1995 (Ray Koch); Spitting Image, 1984-1986 (TV series with puppets enacting public figures; Chris Barrie voiceover).

Reavis, James Addison (aka: Baron of Arizona; swindler; 1843-1914): **The Baron of Arizona**, 1950 (Vincent Price).

Red Cloud (1822-1909; Oglala Lakota [Sioux] chief and warrior leader who led successful Red Cloud's War, 1866-1868): The Adventures of Champion, 1955-1956 (TV series; 'The Return of Red Cloud," 1956 episode: Alan Wells); Adventures of Wild Bill Hickok, 1951-1958 (TV series; "The Daughter of Casey O'Grady," 1958 episode: Mike Lane); Bonanza, 1959-1973 (TV series; "Warbonnet," 1971 episode: Chief Dan George); Bury My Heart at Wounded Knee, 2007 (made-for-TV; Gordon Tootoosis); Chief Crazy Horse, 1955 (Morris Ankrum); Crazy Horse, 1996 (made-for-TV; Wes Studi); Crossfire Trail, 2001 (made-for-TV; James Nicholas); The Gun That Won the West, 1955 (Robert

Bice); Hawkeye and the Last of the Mohicans, 1957 (TV series; "The Truant," 1957 episode: Eric Clavering); Hawkeye, the Pathfinder, 1973 (TV miniseries; Episode # 1.3: Drew Wood); **The Indian Fighter**, 1955 (Edward Franz); Into the West, 2005 (TV miniseries; Raoul Trujillo); Jack McCall, Desperado, 1953 (Jay Silverheels); Laredo, 1965-1967 (TV series; "Miracle at Massacre Mission," 1966 episode: Eddie Little Sky); The Last Frontier, 1955 (Manuel Donde); North of Arizona, 1935 (Artie Ortego); Outlaw Express, 1938 (Chief Many Treaties); Peter Lundy and the Medicine Hat Stallion, 1977 (made-for-TV; Ned Romero); The Return of a Man Called Horse, 1976 (Alberto Mariscal); Revolt at Fort Laramie, 1957 (Eddie Little); **Run of the Arrow**, 1957 (Frank DeKova); Seven Hours of Gunfire, 1965 (Ricardo Rodriguez); Son of the Morning Star, 1991 (made-for-TV; Nick Ramus); Spoilers of the West, 1927 (Chief Big Tree); **Tomahawk**, 1951 (John War Eagle); Wagon Train, 1957-1965 (TV series; "The Ruth Marshall Story," 1959 episode: Sam Capuano; "The Janet Hale Story," 1961 episode: Robert Warwick; "The Sam Darland Story," 1962 episode: Steven Ritch); Warrior Gap, 1925 (Len Haynes).

Reed, John (John Silas "Jack" Reed; 1887-1920; U.S. socialist and writer, author of *Ten Days That Shook the World*, an eyewitness account of the Russian Revolution; died in Russia and is buried in the Kremlin): And Starring Pancho Villa as Himself, 2003 (made-for-TV; Matt Day); Red Bells Part I: Mexico on Fire, 1982 (Franco Nero); Reed, Mexico Insurgente, 1974 (Claudio Obregon); **Reds**, 1981 (Warren Beatty); V dni oktyabrya, 1958 (A. Fyodorinov).

Reid, Frank R. (1879-1945; U.S. attorney and U.S. congressman [Ill.] and defense counsel for General Billy Mitchell during Mitchell's 1925 court martial): **The Court Martial of Billy Mitchell**, 1955 (Ralph Bellamy).

Reilly, Edward J. (b. 1884; U.S. attorney, who flamboyantly and unsuccessfully defended Bruno Richard Hauptmann, and who was convicted and executed for kidnapping and murdering Charles Lindbergh, the infant son of famed aviator Charles A. Lindbergh): Crime of the Century, 1996 (made-for-TV; John Harkins); The Lindbergh Kidnapping Case, 1976 (made-for-TV; Martin Balsam); Second Verdict, 1976 (TV series; "The Lindbergh Kidnapping," 1976 episode: Thick Wilson).

Reitsch, Hanna (1912-1979; German aviatrix and dedicated Nazi): Downfall, 2004 (Anna Thalbach); Hitler: The Last Ten Days, 1973 (Diane Cilento).

Rembrandt (1606-1669; Dutch painter): Nightwatching, 2007 (Martin Freeman); Portrait by Rembrandt, 1952 (made-for-TV; Walter Fitzgerald); **Rembrandt**, 1936 (Charles Laughton); Rembrandt, 1942 (Ewald Balser); Rembrandt, 1971 (made-for-TV; Richard Johnson); Rembrandt, 1999 (Klaus Maria Brandauer); Rembrandt: Fathers & Sons, 1999 (made-for-TV; Tom McCamus); State of the Artist, 2001 (Bruce Norris).

Remington, Fredrick (U.S. artist; 1861-1909): Rough Riders, 1997 (made-for-TV; Nick Chinlund).

Reno, Marcus Albert (1834-1889; U.S. military officer; survivor of Custer Massacre in 1876): Bugles in the Afternoon, 1952 (Nelson Leigh); Crazy Horse, 1996 (made-for-TV; Daniel O'Haco); Custer, 1967- (TV series; Alexander Davion); Custer of the West, 1968 (Ty Hardin); Custer's Last Stand, 1936 (serial; Franklyn Farnum); The Great Sioux Massacre, 1965 (Joseph Cotten); The Legend of Custer, 1968 (Alexander Davion); **7th Cavalry**, 1956 (Frank Wilcox); Son of the Morning Star, 1991 (made-for-TV; Michael Medeiros); Tonka, 1958 (Monroe Carlson).

Renoir, Pierre-Auguste (1841-1919; French artist and leader of the impressionist style of painting): Bachelor in Paris, 1952 (Anton Diffring); Lautrec, 1999 (Philippe Clay); Modi, 1989 (Feodor Chaliapin Jr.); **Renoir**, 2013 (Michel Bouquet).

Reston, James Barrett Jr. (1943- ; U.S. journalist and writer): **Frost/Nixon**, 2008 (Sam Rockwell).

Reuter, Paul Julius (1816-1899; German-born British pioneer of news reporting and telegraphy): **A Dispatch from Reuters**, 1940 (Edward G. Robinson).

Revere, Paul (1734-1818; U.S. silversmith, engraver and patriot in the American Revolution; noted for his midnight ride to give warning about British troops marching toward Concord and Lexington, Massachusetts, on the night of April 18, 1775): **America**, 1924 (Harry O'Neill); April Morning, 1988 (made-for-TV; Vlasta Vrana); The Bastard, 1978 (made-for-TV; William Shatner); Cardigan, 1922 (Austin Hume); Dawn of Our Nation, 2001 (made-for-TV; Marshall R. Teague); Hollywood Party, 1934 (Tom London); **Janice Meredith**, 1924 (Ken Maynard); **Johnny Tremaine**, 1957 (Walter Sande); One Hysterical Night, 1929 (Walter Brennan); Samuel Adams, 2014 (made-for-TV; Jose Rosete); Sleepy Hollow, 2013- (TV series; Dustin Lewis; Paul Burke); Sons of Liberty, 2015- (TV miniseries; Michael Raymond-James); You Are There, 1953-1971 (TV series; "Paul Revere's Ride [April 18, 1775])," 1954 episode: Richard Branda).

Rhodes, Cecil John (1853-1902; British businessman and prime minister of Cape Colony, 1890-1896): The Great Adventure, 1952 (Milos Kopecky); So Much to Do, 1938 (made-for-TV; Arthur Young); The Regiment, 1972- (TV series; "A Gentleman's War," 1972 episode: Leon Sinden); **Rhodes**, 1936 (Walter Huston); Rhodes, 1996- (TV miniseries; Martin Shaw); Uncle Kruger, 1941 (Ferdinand Marian); **Victoria the Great**, 1937 (Wyndham Goldie).

Ribbentrop, Joachim von (1893-1946; German politician and diplomat; Nazi foreign minister under Adolf Hitler; convicted of war crimes after WWII and hanged): Countdown to War, 1989 (made-for-TV; John Woodvine); Days of Betrayal, 1973 (Stanislav Zindulka); **The Eagle Has Landed**, 1977 (himself in archive footage); The Gathering Storm, 1974 (made-for-TV; Robert Hardy); ITV Sunday Night Theatre, 1969- (TV series; "The Death of Adolf Hitler," 1973 episode: Geoffrey Toone); Hotel Lux, 2011 (Holger Handtke); J'etais a Nuremberg, 2010 (made-for-TV; Vasil Banov); **Mission to Moscow**, 1943 (Henry Daniell); Mussolini and I, 1985 (made-for-TV; Hans-Dieter Asner); Mussolini: The Untold Story, 1985 (TV miniseries; Richard Kane); Nuremberg, 2000 (TV miniseries; Benoit Gerard); Nuremberg: Nazis on Trial, 2006- (TV miniseries; "Hermann Goering," 2006 episode: Ivaylo Geraskov); Robert Montgomery Presents, 1950-1957 (TV series; "The Week the World Stood Still," 1957 episode: Peter von Zerneck); Upstairs Downstairs, 2010-2012 (TV series; Edward Baker-Duly); The Winds of War, 1983- (TV miniseries; Anton Diffring); Winston Churchill: The Wilderness Years, 1981- (TV series; Frederick Jaeger).

Rich, Richard (1496-1567; chancellor of Great Britain; rose to power by giving perjured testimony against Thomas More): A Man for All Seasons, 1957 (made-for-TV; Leon Eagles); **A Man for All Seasons**, 1966 (John Hurt); A Man for All Seasons, 1988 (made for TV; Jonathan Hackett); Thomas More, 1964 (made-for-TV; Josef Frohlich); The Tudors, 2007-2010 (TV series; Rod Hallett).

Richard I (aka: The Lion Heart; 1157-1199; King of England; also see John [John Lackland] and Saladin in this index; and Robin Hood, in Fictional index): **The Adventures of Robin Hood**, 1938 (Ian Hunter); The Adventures of Robin Hood, 1955-1960 (TV series; five episodes: Ian Hunter); The Ballad of the Valiant Knight Ivanhoe, 1983 (Romualds

John Phillip Law (as Manfred von Richthofen) in *Von Richthofen and Brown,* **1971.**

Ancans); Churchill's People, 1974- (TV series; "Silver Giant, Wooden Dwarf," 1975 episode; Clinton Greyn); **The Crusades**, 1935 (Henry Wilcoxon); The Devil's Crown, 1978- (TV series; Michael Bryne); Doctor Who, 1963-1989 (TV series; four episodes; Julian Glover); Empires: Holy Warriors—Richard the Lionheart and Saladin, 2005 (made-for-TV; Derek Lea); **Ivanhoe**, 1952 (Norman Wooland); Ivanhoe, 1958- (TV series; "Freeing the Serfs," 1958 episode; Bruce Seton); Ivanhoe, 1982 (made-for-TV; Julian Glover); Ivanhoe, 1997- (TV miniseries; Rory Edwards); **King Richard and the Crusaders**, 1954 (George Sanders); **Kingdom of Heaven**, 2005 (Iain Glen); The Legend of Robin Hood, 1968- (TV series; Douglas Fairbanks Jr.); The Legend of Robin Hood, 1975 (TV miniseries; Michael J. Jackson); Lionheart, 1987 (Neil Dickson); Long Live Robin Hood, 1971 (Lars Bloch); The Men of Sherwood Forest, 1954 (Patrick Holt); NBC Children's Theatre, 1963-1973 (TV series; "Robin Hood," 1964 episode: Jon Cypher); Richard Lvinoe Serdtse, 1992 (Aleksandr Baluev); Richard the Lionheart, 1962 (TV series; Dermot Walsh); Richard the Lionheart, 2014 (Greg Chandler Maness); Richard the Lionheart: Rebellion, 2015 (Greg Chandler Maness); Richard the Lion-Hearted, 1923 (Wallace Beery); **Robin and Marian**, 1976 (Richard Harris); **Robin Hood**, 1922 (Wallace Beery); **Robin Hood**, 1973 (Peter Ustinov voiceover); Robin Hood, 1984-1986 (TV series; 1984 episode with John Rhys-Davies as Richard); Robin Hood, 2006-2009 (TV series; 2006 episode with Lukacs Bicskey as Richard; 2007 episode with Steven Waddington as Richard); **Robin Hood**, 2010 (Danny Huston); **Robin Hood: Men in Tights**, 1993 (Patrick Stewart); **Robin Hood: Prince of Thieves**, 1991 (Sean Connery); Rytsar Kennet, 1993 (Aleksandr Baluev); Saladin and the Great Crusades, 1963 (**The Story of Robin Hood** [AKA: The Story of Robin Hood and His Merrie Men], 1952 (Patrick Barr); The Talisman, 1980- (TV miniseries; 1980 episode: Stephan Chase); Young Ivanhoe, 1995 (made-for-TV; Marek Vasut); The Zany Adventures of Robin Hood, 1984 (made-for-TV; Robert Hardy).

Richard III (1452-1485; King of England): An Age of Kings, 1960 (TV series; "Richard III Part II: The Boar Hunt," 1960 episode: Paul Daneman; "The Rabble from Kent," 1960 episode: John Ringham); The Black Adder, 1982-1983 (TV series; "The Foretelling," 1983 episode: Peter Cook); The Black Arrow, 1951 (TV series; 1951 episode: Powys Thomas); Complete and Utter History of Britain, 1969 (TV series; 1969 episode: Wallas Eaton); The Ed Sullivan Show, 1948-1971 (TV series; 1949 episode: John Carradine); The Golden Spur, 1959 (TV series; two 1959 episodes: Oliver Reed); Hancock's Half Hour, 1956-1960 (TV series; "The Knighthood," 1959 episode: Andrew Faulds); Konig Richard III, 1964 (made-for-TV; Wolfgang Kieling); The Life and Death of King Richard III, 1912 (Frederick Warde); Masterpiece Playhouse, 1950 (TV

Minor Watson (as Branch Rickey) and Pat Flaherty in *The Jackie Robinson Story*, 1950.

series; "Richard III," 1950 episode: William Windom); Monty Python's Flying Circus, 1969-1974 (TV series; 1970 espisode: Michael Palin, Eric Idle); NOW: In the Wings on a World Stage, 2014 (Kevin Spacey); **Richard III**, 1956 (Laurence Olivier); Richard III, 1973 (made-for-TV; Peter Haumann); Richard III, 1983 (made-for-TV; Ron Cook); Richard III, 1995 (Ian McKellen); Richard III, 1996 (Aleks Shaklin); Richard III, 2008; Shakespeare: The Animated Tales, 1992-1994 (TV miniseries; "King Richard III," 1994 episode: Antony Sher); The Show of Shows, 1929 (John Barrymore); **The Tower of London**, 1939 (Basil Rathbone); Tower of London, 1962 (Vincent Price); The War of the Roses, 1965 (TV miniseries; two episodes: Ian Holm); The War of the Roses, 1989-1990 (TV series; two episodes: Colin Farrell, Andrew Jarvis); The White Queen, 2013 (TV miniseries; five episodes: Aneurin Barnard).

Richardson, I.D. (b. 1919; U.S. Navy officer who commanded PT-34, one of the PT-boats that evacuated General Douglas MacArthur, his family and staff from Corregidor in March 1941 to prevent MacArthur's capture by invading Japanese forces): **An American Guerrilla in the Philippines**, 1950 (Tyrone Power).

Richelieu, Cardinal (Armand Jean du Plessis; 1585-1642; French clergyman, nobleman and statesman): Animated Three Musketeers, 1987 (TV series; Nobuo Tanaka); At Sword's Point, 1952 (Reginald Sheffield); Bardelys the Magnificent, 1926 (Edward Connelly); Biblioteca di Studio Uno: I tre moschettieri, 1964 (made-for-TV; Gino Cervi); The Captain, 1946 (Georges Marny); Cardinal Richelieu, 1935 (George Arliss); Ce diable d'homme, 1978 (TV miniseries; Georges Descrieres); Cinq-Mars, 1981 (made-for-TV; Georges Marchal); **Cyrano de Bergerac**, 1950 (Edgar Barrier); Cyrano et d'Artagnan, 1964 (Rafael Rivelles); D'Artagnan, 1969 (TV miniseries; Raymond Jourdan); D'Artagnan, 1991 (made-for-TV; Yann Babilee); D'Artagnan amoureux, 1977 (TV miniseries; Henri Virlojeux); D'Artagnan et les trois mousquetaires, 2005 (Tcheky Karyo); D'Artanyan i tri mushketyora, 1979 (TV series; Alexander Trofimov); De drie Musketiers, 1968 (made-for-TV; Francois Bernard); Der Rote Henker, 1920 (Magnus Stifter); The Devils, 1971 (Christopher Logue); Die Drie Musketiere, 2013 (Vasiliy Lanovoy); Family Classics: The Three Musketeers, 1960 (made-for-TV; Vincent Price); The Four Charlots Musketeers, 1974 (Bernard Haller); The Four Musketeers, 1963 (Peppino De Filippo); **The Four Musketeers**, 1975 (Charlton Heston); The Glorious Musketeers, 1974 (Philippe Clay voiceover); I Spy, 1955- (TV series; "Lion of France," 1955 episode: Ian Keith); I tre moschettieri, 1991 (made-for-TV; Sergio Vastano); If Paris Were Told to Us, 1956 (Jacques Dumesnil); Il colpo segreto di d'Artagnan, 1963 (Massimo Serato); **The Iron Mask**, 1929 (Nigel De Brulier); Le camera explore le temps,

1957-1966 (TV series, "La conjuration de Cinq-Mars," 1962 episode: Pierre Asso); La cite crucifiee, 1974 (made-for-TV; Jacques Maury); La loca historia de los tres mosqueteros, 1983 (Antonio Ozores); Les mysteres de Loudun, 1976 (made-for-TV; Jean-Marie Galey); Les quatre mouquetaires, 1934 (Reginald); Les 3 Mousquetaires, 1953 (Renaud Mary); Les trois mousquetaires, 1959 (made-for-TV; Pierre Asso); Les trois mousquetaires ou L'escrime ne paie pas, 1979 (made-for-TV; Jean Danet); Les trois mousquetaires: Premiere epoque—Les ferrets de la reine, 1961 (Daniel Sorano); Louis XV, le soleil noir, 2009 (made-for-TV; Francois Berland); Madame DuBarry, 1920 (Fred Immler); Madame Du Barry, 1934 (Osgood Perkins); Madame du Barry, 1954 (Denis d'Ines); The Magnavox Theater, 1950 (TV series; "The Three Musketeers," 1950 episode: Paul Cavanagh); **The Man in the Iron Mask**, 1939 (Nigel De Brulier); Mask of the Musketeers, 1963 (Nerio Bernardi); Mazarin, 1978 (TV miniseries; Pierre Vernier); Milady and the Three Musketeers, 2004 (made-for-TV; Martin Lamotte); Monsieur Beaucaire, 1924 (John Davidson); Monsieur Vincent, 1948 (Aime Clariond); **The Musketeer**, 2001 (Stephen Rea); The Musketeers, 2014 (TV series; Peter Capaldi); Ninon de Lenclos, 1920 (Hans Lackner); Os tres Mosqueteiros, 1957 (TV series; Turibio Ruiz); Panache, 1976 (made-for-TV; Joseph Ruskin); The Queen and the Cardinal, 2009 (made-for-TV; Nicolas Vaude); Richelieu, 1914 (Murdock MacQuarrie); Richelieu, 1977 (TV miniseries; Pierre Vernier); Richelieu, la pourpre et la sang, 2013 (made-for-TV; Jacques Perrin); Richelieu ou La journee des dupes, 1983 (made-for-TV; Didier Sandre); Royal Affairs in Versailles, 1957 (Maurice Tillier); Rubens, schilder en diplomaat, 1977 (Martin Van Zundert); Three and a Half Musketeers, 1957 (Augustin Isunza); The Three Musketeers, 1916 (Walt Whitman); **The Three Musketeers**, 1921 (Nigel De Brulier); Three Musketeers, 1932 (Samson Fainsilber); The Three Musketeers, 1935 (Nigel De Brulier); The Three Musketeers, 1939 (Miles Mander); The Three Musketeers, 1945 (Miguel Moya); **The Three Musketeers**, 1948 (Vincent Price); The Three Musketeers, 1954 (TV series; William Devlin); The Three Musketeers, 1966 (TV miniseries; Richard Pasco); **The Three Musketeers**, 1974 (Charlton Heston); The Three Musketeers, 1986 (made-for-TV; Noel Ferrier voiceover); **The Three Musketeers**, 1993 (Tim Curry); The Three Musketeers, 2007 (Niels Olsen voiceover); The Three Musketeers, 2011 (Christopher Waltz); Under the Red Robe, 1915 (Jackson Wilcox); Under the Red Robe, 1923 (Robert B. Mantell); **Under the Red Robe**, 1937 (Raymond Massey); Vengeance of the Three Musketeers, 1961 (Daniel Sorano); Vingt ans apres, 1922 (Edouard de Max); Tri musketyri, 1983 (TV miniseries; Peter Kostka); Tri mushketera, 2013 (Vasiliy Lanovoy); Young Blades, 2001 (Ben Cross).

Richetti, Adam (1909-1938; U.S. bank robber, killer and criminal colleague of Charles Arthur "Pretty Boy" Floyd, and who was wrongly blamed for participating in the 1933 Kansas City Massacre): Guns Don't Argue, 1957 (Knobby Schaeffer); The Kansas City Massacre, 1975 (made-for-TV; Robert Walden); **Pretty Boy Floyd**, 1960 (Barry Newman); The Verne Miller Story, 1988 (Richard Bright). Note: For detailed information on Richetti and the Kansas City Massacre, see my two-volume work *The Great Pictorial History of World Crime*, Volume II (History, Inc., 2004; illustrated [15 images] pages 951-958).

Rickenbacker, Edward Vernon (aka: "Eddie"; "Captain Eddie"; 1890-1973; U.S. aviator and USA air force pilot in WWI, who became the top American ace, credited with twenty-six aerial victories; pioneer in commercial aviation; founded Eastern Airlines): **Captain Eddie**, 1945 (Fred MacMurray); **The Court Martial of Billy Mitchell**, 1955 (Tom McKee).

Rickey, Wesley Branch (1881-1965; American baseball executive who introduced minority players into major league baseball and created many innovations in the game): **42**, 2013 (Harrison Ford); **The Jackie Robin-**

son Story, 1950 (Minor Watson); Soul of the Game, 1996 (made-for-TV; Edward Hermann).

Richthofen, Lothar von (1894-1922; German WWI fighter pilot credited with 40 air victories and younger brother of German WWI top ace Manfred von Richthofen): **The Red Baron**, 2010 (Volker Bruch as the adult Lothar von Richthofen; Tomas Ibi as the young Lothar von Richthofen); **Von Richthofen and Brown**, 1971 (Brian Foley).

Richthofen, Manfred von (1892-1918; German air ace in WWI who shot down 80 enemy planes before being killed in an air battle): Angry Nazi Zombies, 2012 (Sam Smith); Blackadder Goes Forth, 1989 (TV series; "Private Plane," 1989 episode: Adrian Edmondson); **The Blue Max**, 1966 (Carl Schell); Darling Lili, 1970 (Ingo Morgendorf); Fantasy Island, 1977-1984 (TV series; "The Red Baron/Young at Heart," 1979 episode: Ron Ely); **The Great Waldo Pepper**, 1975 (Art Scholl); Handle with Care, 1977 (Harry Northup); **Hell's Angels**, 1930 (Wilhelm von Brincken); Man, Moment, Machine, 2005-2007 (TV series; "The Red Baron & the Wings of Death," 2006 episode: Alexander Cukor); **The Red Baron**, 2010 (Matthias Schweighofer as the adult Manfred von Richthofen; Tomas Koutnik as the young Manfred von Richthofen); Revenge of the Red Baron, 1994 (John C. McDonnell voiceover); Richthofen, 1929 (George Burghardt); **Von Richthofen and Brown**, 1971 (John Phillip Law); War of the Worlds: Goliath, 2012 (Matt Letscher voiceover).

Richthofen, Wolfram von (1895-1945; German pilot and field marshal of the Luftwaffe during WWII; cousin of the famed Manfred von Richthofen): **The Red Baron**, 2010 (Brano Holicek as the adult Wolfram von Richthofen; Albert Franc as the young Wolfram von Richthofen).

Ridgeway, Matthew B. (1895-1993; U.S. four-star general commanding U.N. forces during the Korean War): The Korean War, 2001 (TV series; S. A. Griffin).

Riefenstahl, Leni (1902-2003; German filmmaker of chiefly powerfully propagandist documentary films, most notably for Hitler and the Third Reich): The Cutting Room, 2011-2012 (TV series; Holly Greene); Kun en pige, 1995 (Renate Angelika Judes); My Fuhrer, 2007 (Marion Kracht); Newstopia, 2007- (TV series; three 2008 episodes with Julie Eckersley); The 120 Days of Bottrop, 1997 (Irmgard Freifau von Berswordt-Wallrabe); Race, 2016 (Carice van Houten); Seduction of the Will, 2001 (Hannah Dalton; Sally Mercer).

Rimsky-Korsakov, Nikolai (1844-1908; Russian composer): Monitor, 1958- (TV series; "Portrait of a Soviet Composer," 1961 episode: Boris Renevsky); Mussorgsky, 1951 (Andrei Popov); Rimsky-Korsakov, 1954 (Grigori Belov); Song of My Heart, 1948 (David Leonard); Song of Scheherazade, 1947 (Jean-Pierre Aumont).

Ringo, John Peters (Johnny; 1850-1882; U.S. Old West cowboy, gunfighter and outlaw): Death Valley Days, 1952-1970 (TV series; "The Melancholy Gun," 1963 episode: Ken Scott); **Doc**, 1971 (Fred Dennis); The Duputy, 1959-1961 (TV series; "The Big Four," 1959 episode: Henry Brandon); **Gunfight at the O. K. Corral**, 1957 (John Ireland); Gunslingers, 2014- (TV miniseries; Scott Shepherd); The High Chaparral, 1967-1971 (TV series; two 1969 episodes; Robert Viharo; Luke Askew); Johnny Oro, 1966 (Mark Damon); Johnny Ringo, 1959-1960 (TV series; Don Durant); The Last of the Fast Guns, 1958 (Lee Morgan); The Life and Legend of Wyatt Earp, 1955-1961 (TV series; fifteen episodes: Norman Alden; Britt Lomond); The Outlaws is Coming!, 1965 (Hal Fryar); Stagecoach, 1987 (made-for-TV; Kris Kristofferson); **Tombstone**, 1993 (Michael Biehn); Tombstone Territory, 1957- (TV series; "Johnny Ringo's Last Ride," 1958 episode: Myron Healey); The

Richard Todd (as Rob Roy) in *Rob Roy: The Highland Rogue,* **1954.**

Toughest Gun in Tombstone, 1958 (Jim Davis); Uccidete Johnny Ringo, 1966 (Brett Halsey); Walt Disney's Wonderful World of Color, 1954-1992 (TV series; two 1960 episodes: Allan Lane); **Wyatt Earp**, 1994 (Norman Howell); Wyatt Earp: Return to Tombstone, 1994 (made-for-TV; Norman Alden); Zane Grey Theater, 1956-1961 (TV series; "Man Alone," 1959 episode: Don Durant). Note: For detailed information on Ringo, see my book *Encyclopedia of Western Lawmen and Outlaws* (Paragon House, 1992; page 270).

Rivera, Diego (1886-1957; Mexican painter): Cantinflas, 2014 (Jose Sefami); Cradle Will Rock, 1999 (Ruben Blades); Frida, 2002 (Alfred Molina); Frida Still Life, 1988 (Juan Jose Gurrola); Modigliani, 2004 (Dan Astilean).

Rizal, Jose (1861-1896; Filipino patriot and writer; executed by the Spanish when revolution broke out in the Philippines): Bonifacio: Ang kababaihan ng Malolos, 2014 (Karl Medino); Ang unang pangulo, 2014 (Jericho Rosales); Bonifacio: Ang unang pangulo, 2014 (Robin Padilla); Jose Rizal, 1998 (Cesar Montano; Dominic Guinto as young Jose Rizal); Ilustrado, 2014- (TV series; Alden Richards); Katipunan, 2013 (TV miniseries; Nasser); The Life and Loves of Dr. Jose Rizal, 1956 (Eddie Del Mar); Rizal sa Dapitan, 1997 (Albert Martinez); 3rd World Hero, 2000 (Joel Torre; Keno Agaro and Jan Alexis Rutaquio as the younger Jose Rizal).

Rizzio, David (or Riccio; 1533-1566; Italian courtier and adviser to Mary, Queen of Scots): Gunpowder, Treason & Plot, 2004 (made-for-TV; Tadeusz Pasternak); The Heart of a Queen, 1940 (Friedrich Benfer); The Loves of Mary, Queen of Scots, 1923 (Rene Maupre); **Mary of Scotland**, 1936 (John Carradine); Mary, Queen of Scots, 1971 (Ian Holm).

Rob Roy (Robert Roy MacGregor; 1671-1734; Scottish outlaw and folk hero known as "the Scottish Robin Hood): Rob Roy, 1922 (David Hawthorne); Rob Roy, 1961- (TV series; Tom Fleming); Rob Roy, 1977- (TV series; Andrew Faulds); **Rob Roy**, 1995 (Liam Neeson); **Rob Roy: The Highland Rogue**, 1954 (Richard Todd); Rogue's Gallery, 2005- (TV series; Vic Reeves).

Robert I (Robert the Bruce; 1274-1329; 1304-1329; King of Scots): Border Warfare, 1990 (made-for-TV; Derek Anders); **Braveheart**, 1995 (Angus Macfayden); The Bruce, 1996 (Sandy Welch); Churchill's People, 1974- (TV series; "The Wallace," 1975 episode: James Cosmo); Father Came Too!, 1964 (John Bluthal); Jamie, 1971- (TV series; "Ettercap," 1971 episode: John Cairney); Strangeheart, 2003 (Brian

Will Rogers Jr. (as his father, Will Rogers Sr.) and Jane Wyman in *The Story of Will Rogers,* **1952.**

Hedenberg).

Roberts, Bartholomew (John Roberts; aka: Black Bart; 1682-1722; Welsh pirate operating in the Atlantic off the Americas and Africa; killed in battle): True Caribbean Pirates, 2006 (made-for-TV; Scott Silbor). Note: For detailed information on Roberts, see my two-volume work, *The Great Pictorial History of World Crime*, Volume II (History, Inc., 2004; illustrated pages 1296-1298).

Robespierre, Maximilien (1758-1894; French politician and a leader of the French Revolution): Arme Bitos, 1962 (made-for-TV; Paul Steenbergen); BBC Play of the Month, 1965-1983 (TV series; "Danton's Death,' 1978 episode; Ian Richardson); BBC Sunday-Night Theatre, 1950-1959 (TV series; "The Magnificent Egotist," 1957 episode: Cyril Shaps); Biography, 1970- (TV series; "Danton," 1970 episode: Alan Dobie); Captain of the Guard, 1930 (George Hackathorne); Carry On Pimpernel, 1967 (Peter Gilmore); Charlotte Corday, 2008 (made-for-TV; Franck Adrien); Danton, 1921 (Werner Krauss); Danton, 1931 (Gustaf Grundgens); Danton, 1983 (Wojciech Pszoniak); Dantons Tod, 1963 (made-for-TV; Wolfgang Buttner); Dantons Tod, 1977 (made-for-TV; Jurgen Hentsch); Dantons Tod, 1981 (Heribert Sasse); The Days That Made History, 2009- (TV series; Renaud Garnier-Fourniquet); The Elusive Pimpernel, 1919 (A.C. Fotheringham-Lysons); The Elusive Pimpernel, 1969- (TV miniseries; Jimmy Gardner); Jean Chouan, 1926 (Jean Debucourt); La camera explore le temps, 1957-1966 (TV series; three episodes, 1964-1966: Jean Negroni); La mort de Danton, 1970 (made-for-TV; Alain Mottet); La revolution francaise, 1989 (Steve Carretero); The Lady and the Duke, 2001 (Francois-Marie Banier); Lady Oscar, 1979 (Christopher Ellison); The Laughing Lady, 1950 (Charles Goldner); Liberte, egalite, choucroute, 1985 (Roland Giraud); Madam Sans-Gene, 1925 (Jose Roland); Madam Sans-Gene, 1941 (Paul Amiot); Manon Roland, 1989 (made-for-TV; Didier Sandre); Marceau ou Les enfants de la republique, 1961 (made-for-TV; Francois Marie); **Marie Antoinette**, 1938 (George Meeker); Marie Antoinette—Das Leben einer Konigin, 1929 (Georg John); **Mr. Peabody & Sherman**, 2014 (Guillaume Aretos voiceover); **Napoleon**, 1927 (Edmond Van Daele); Napoleon, 1955 (Jacques Sablon); Napoleon and Josephine: A Love Story, 1987- (TV miniseries; Marc de Jonge); **Orphans of the Storm**, 1921 (Sidney Herbert); **Reign of Terror**, 1949 (Richard Basehart); The Return of the Scarlet Pimpernel, 1938 (Henry Oscar); Royal Affairs in Versailles, 1957 (Jacques Berthier); Saint-Just ou La force des choses, 1975 (made-for-TV; Pierre Vaneck); **Scaramouche**, 1923 (Fuerburg De Garcia); The Scarlet Daredevil, 1928 (Nelson Keys); The Scarlet Pimpernel, 1982 (made-for-TV; Richard Morant); The Scarlet Pimpernel, 1999- (TV series; Ronan Vibert); The Sorcerer's Apprentice, 1977 (Jean-

Pierre Kalfon); Terror! Robespierre and the French Revolution, 2009 (made-for-TV; George Ivascu); Theatre 625, 1964-1968 (TV series; "Poor Bitos," 1965 episode: Peter Woodthorpe); Une femme dans la revolution, 2013 (TV miniseries; Alex Lutz); Valmy, 1967 (made-for-TV; Bernard Dheran); The Visitors: Bastille Day, 2016 (Nicolas Vaude); A World in Arms, 2003- (TV miniseries; Martin Hodgson); World Theatre, 1959- (TV miniseries; "Danton's Death," 1959 episode: Harold Lang).

Robinson, Jack Roosevelt (aka: "Jackie"; 1919-1972; American baseball player): Cold Case, 2003-2010 (TV series; "Colors," 2005 episode; Antonio Lewis Todd); The Court-Martial of Jackie Robinson, 1990 (made-for-TV; Andre Braugher); Everybody Hates Christ, 2005-2009 (TV series; Tico Clark in a 2006 episode; Marcus Collins in a 2007 episode); **42**, 2013 (Chadwick Boseman); **The Jackie Robinson Story**, 1950 (himself); Soul of the Game, 1996 (made-for-TV; Blair Underwood).

Robinson, Ray Charles (1930-2004; U.S. composer, singer, musician, called the "High Priest of Soul [Music]): Bamboo Shark, 2012 (Charles Middleton); **Ray**, 2004 (Jamie Foxx).

Rockefeller, John Davison (1839-1937; U.S. billionaire businessman who founded Standard Oil): Maud Rockefellers Wette, 1924 (Karl Elzer); **No God, No Master**, 2012 (David Darlow); Zorn, 1994 (Frederick Bartman).

Rockefeller, Nelson Aldrich (1908-1979; U.S. businessman and 41st vice president of the U.S.): Cradle Will Rock, 1999 (John Cusack); Frida, 2003 (Edward Norton); **Nixon**, 1995 (Edward Herrmann).

Rockwell, Porter (c.1813-1878; U.S. frontiersman, gunfighter and enforcer for the Latter Day Saints religious Mormon movement and friend of that religion's founder, Joseph Smith): The Avenging Angel, 1995 (made-for-TV; James Coburn); **Brigham Young: Frontiersman**, 1940 (John Carradine); Rockwell, 1994 (Randy Gleave); Savage Journey, 1983 (made-for-TV; Keith Gurr).

Rodes, Robert Emmett (1829-1864; Confederate general during the American Civil War): **Gettysburg**, 1993 (Graham Winton); **Gods and Generals**, 2003 (Fred Griffith).

Rodgers, Richard (1902-1979; U.S. composer): **Words and Music**, 1948 (Tom Drake).

Rodney, Caesar (1728-1784; U.S. attorney and politician; member of the Continental Congress; signer of the Declaration of Independence): John Adams, 2008- (TV miniseries; "Independence," 2008 episode: Tim Parati); **1776**, 1972 (William Hansen).

Rogers, Ginger (1911-1995; U.S. film actress): A Formulation of Rectangles, 2009 (Tyler Schlesinger); **J. Edgar**, 2011 (Jamie LeBarbier); It Happened in Hollywood, 1937 (Beatrice Coleman; Lillian Tours as a dancing Ginger Rogers).

Rogers, Will (William Penn Adair "Will" Rogers Sr.; 1879-1935; U.S. actor, humorist and social commentator): The American Adventure, 1982 (Will Rogers Jr.); The Eddie Cantor Story, 1953 (Will Rogers Jr.); **The Great Ziegfeld**, 1936 (A. A. Trimble); Look for the Silver Lining, 1949 (Will Rogers Jr.); Mrs. Parker and the Vicious Circle, 1994 (Keith Carradine); Pancho Barnes, 1988 (made-for-TV; John Hussey); **The Story of Will Rogers**, 1952 (Will Rogers Jr.); **W.C. Fields and Me**, 1976 (Buff Brady); Will Rogers: Champion of the People, 1978 (made-for-TV; Robert Hays); Will Rogers' USA, 1972 (made-for-TV; James Whitmore); You're a Sweetheart, 1937 (A.A. Trimble); Ziegfeld: The

Man and His Women, 1978 (made-for-TV; Gene McLaughlin).

Rohan, Louis de (1734-1803; French Cardinal): The Affair of the Necklace, 2001 (Jonathan Pryce); Cagliostro, 1929 (Alfred Abel); Die Halsbandaffare, 1971 (made-for-TV; Erich Auer); Joseph Balsamo, 1973- (TV miniseries; Gabriel Cattand); La camera explore le temps, 1957-1966 (TV series; "L'affaire du collier de la reine," 1962 episode: Jacques Castelot); Lady Oscar, 1979 (Gregory Floy); Le gerfaut, 1987- (TV miniseries; Herve Bellon); Les proces de l'Histoire, 2011- (TV series; Xavier Briere); Marie Antoinette, 1922 (Erich Kaiser-Titz); **Marie Antoinette**, 1938 (Bennett Parker); Marie Antoinette, 1975- (TV miniseries; Philippe March); Marie Antoinette, 2006 (made-for-TV; David La Haye); Novela, 1963-1978 (TV series; thirteen 1976 episodes with Francisco Piquer as Cardinal Rohan); The Queen's Necklace, 1929 (George Lannes); The Queen's Necklace, 1947 (Maurice Escande); Royal Affairs in Versailles, 1957 (Jean-Pierre Aumont).

Rohm, Ernst (or Roehm; 1887-1934; German soldier, politician and Nazi leader, murdered on orders of Adolf Hitler): Der Argermacher, 2003 (Dieter Winkelmann); Der Hitler/Ludendorff Prozess, 1971 (made-for-TV; Ulrich Beiger); Der Rohm-Putsch, 1967 (made-for-TV; Hans Korte); Der Teufelskreis, 1956 (Albert Garbe); Der Teufelskreis, 1982 (made-for-TV; Berthold Schulze); Die Machtergreifung, 2012 (made-for-TV; Martin Neuhaus); Hanussen, 1955 (Helmut Qualtinger); Hitler, 1962 (Barry Koeger); **The Hitler Gang**, 1944 (Roman Bohnen); Hitler: The Rise of Evil, 2003 (made-for-TV; Peter Stormare); Hitler vor Gericht, 2009 (made-for-TV; Klaus Newmann); Hitler's SS: Portrait in Evil, 1985 (made-for-TV; Michael Elphick); My Crimes after Mein Kampf, 1940 (Pierre Labry).

Romberg, Sigmund (1887-1951; Austro-Hungarian composer in U.S. known for his musicals and operettas): **Deep in My Heart**, 1954 (Jose Ferrer).

Rommel, Erwin (Erwin Johannes Eugen Rommel; 1891-1944; German field marshal in WWII): Agnostos polemos, 1971-1974 (TV series; Giorgos Kyritsis); The Battle of El Alamein, 1971 (Robert Hossein); A Bullet for Rommel, 1969 (Manuel Collado); Danger 5, 2011- (TV series; "Hitler's Golden Murder Palace," 2012 episode: Brendan Rock); D-Day 6.6.1944, 2004 (made-for-TV; Albert Welling); The Death Triangle, 1999 (Radu Banzaru); **The Desert Fox: The Story of Rommel**, 1951 (James Mason); **The Desert Rats**, 1953 (James Mason); **Five Graves to Cairo**, 1943 (Erich von Stroheim); Foxhole in Cairo, 1961 (Albert Lieven); Hitler, 1962 (Gregory Gaye); The Key to Rebecca, 1985 (made-for-TV; Robert Culp); **The Longest Day**, 1962 (Werner Hinz); Night of the Fox, 1990 (made-for-TV; Michael York); **The Night of the Generals**, 1967 (Christopher Plummer); Operation Walkure, 1971 (made-for-TV; Friedrich Siemers); **Patton**, 1970 (Karl Michael Vogler); The Plot to Kill Hitler, 1990 (made-for-TV; Helmut Griem); Raid on Rommel, 1971 (Wolfgang Preiss); Rommel, 2012 (made-for-TV; Ulrich Tukur); Rommel ruft kairo, 1959 (Paul Klinger); War and Remembrance, 1988 (TV miniseries; Hardy Kruger); When Heroes Die, 1970 (Piero Lulli).

Rommel, Manfred (1928-2013; German politician; lord mayor of Stuttgart; son of German field marshal Erwin Rommel): **The Desert Fox**, 1951 (William Reynolds); **The Longest Day**, 1962 (Michael Hinz).

Rommel, Maria Lucia (1894-1971; German wife of German field marshal Erwin Rommel): **The Desert Fox**, 1951 (Jessica Tandy); **The Longest Day**, 1962 (Ruth Hausmeister); War and Remembrance, 1988 (TV miniseries; Andrea Dahmen).

Roosevelt, Alice (Alice Lee Roosevelt Longworth; 1884-1980; oldest

Richard Boone and James Mason (as Erwin Rommel) in *The Desert Fox: The Story of Rommel*, **1951.**

child of President Theodore Roosevelt): **The Wind and the Lion**, 1975 (Deborah Baxter).

Roosevelt, Anna (1906-1975; U.S. daughter of U.S. President Franklin D. Roosevelt and First Lady Eleanor Roosevelt): Eleanor and Franklin: The White House Years, 1977 (made-for-TV; Blair Brown); **Sunrise at Campobello**, 1960 (Zina Bethune).

Roosevelt, Eleanor (Anna Eleanor Roosevelt; 1884-1962; wife of U.S. President Franklin D. Roosevelt and U.S. First Lady): **Amelia**, 2009 (Cherry Jones); Bertie and Elizabeth, 2002 (made-for-TV; Irene Richards); Eleanor and Franklin, 1976 (made-for-TV; Jane Alexander); Eleanor and Franklin: The White House Years, 1977 (made-for-TV; Jane Alexander); Hyde Park on Hudson, 2012 (Olivia Williams); **Sunrise at Campobello**, 1960 (Greer Garson); Truman, 1995 (made-for-TV; Marian Seldes); War and Remembrance, 1988 (TV miniseries; Elizabeth Hoffman).

Roosevelt, Elliott (1910-1990; U.S. Army Air Force officer and author and second son of U.S. President Franklin D. Roosevelt and First Lady Eleanor Roosevelt): Eleanor and Franklin: The White House Years, 1977 (made-for-TV; Don Howard); **Sunrise at Campobello**, 1960 (Pat Close).

Roosevelt, Franklin D. (Franklin Delano Roosevelt; AKA: "FDR"; 1882-1945; U.S. politician and 32nd President of the U.S.): **Action in the North Atlantic**, 1943 (Art Gilmore); Albert Einstein, 1990 (TV series; Ernst Heise); The American Adventure, 1982 (John Anderson voiceover); **Annie**, 1982 (Edward Herrmann); Annie, 1999 (made-for-TV; Dennis Howard); Backstairs at the White House, 1979 (TV miniseries; John Anderson); **Beau James**, 1957 (Dick Nelson); The Beginning or the End, 1947 (Godfrey Tearle); Bertie and Elizabeth, 2002 (made-for-TV; Robert Hardy); Bonanno: A Godfather's Story, 1999 (made-for-TV; Vlasta Vrana); Churchill and the Generals, 1981 (made-for-TV; Arthur Hill); Churchill: The Hollywood Years, 2004 (Henry Goodman); Cradle Will Rock, 1999 (himself in archive footage); Crossings, 1986 (TV miniseries; Jack Denton); Day One, 1989 (made-for-TV; Donald Ogden Stiers); De Gaulle, 2006 (TV series; Robert Hardy); **Edge of Darkness**, 1943 (voiceover of Jack Young); Einstein, 1984-1985 (TV miniseries; Gerard Buhr); Eleanor and Franklin, 1976 (made-for-TV; Edward Herrmann); Eleanor and Franklin: The White House Years, 1977 (made-for-TV; Edward Herrmann); Enola Gay: The Men, the Mission, the Atomic Bomb, 1980 (made-for-TV; Stephen Roberts); The Fall of Berlin, 1952 (Oleg Frelikh); F.D.R., 1965 (TV miniseries; Charlton Heston voiceover); F.D.R.: A One-Man Show, 1987

Brian Keith (as Theodore Roosevelt) in *The Wind and the Lion*, 1975.

(Chris Elliott); F.D.R.: The Last Year, 1980 (made-for-TV; Jason Robards Jr.); F.D.R.: The Man in the White House, 1982 (made-for-TV; Robert Vaughn); The First Front, 1949 (Nikolai Cherkasov); **First to Fight**, 1967 (Stephen Roberts); For All: Springboard to Victory, 1998 (Guaracy Picado); Freedom to Speak, 1982 (TV miniseries; Laurence Luckinbill); The Great Battle, 1973 (Stanislaw Jaskiewicz); **Hyde Park on Hudson**, 2012 (Bill Murray); Ike: The War Years, 1979 (TV miniseries; Stephen Roberts): Into the Storm, 2009 (made-for-TV; Len Cariou); **J. Edgar**, 2011 (David A. Cooper); J. Edgar Hoover, 1987 (made-for-TV; David Ogden Stiers); Katastrofa w Gibraltarze, 1984 (Andrzej Krasicki); The Kennedys of Massachusetts, 1990 (TV miniseries; Josef Sommer); Kingfish: The Story of Huey P. Long, 1995 (made-for-TV; Bob Gunton); The Last Bastion, 1984 (TV miniseries; Warren Mitchell); The Long Days of Summer, 1980 (made-for-TV; Stephen Roberts); **MacArthur**, 1977 (Dan O'Herlihy); **Mission to Moscow**, 1943 (Jack Young); Murrow, 1986 (made-for-TV; Robert Vaughn): **Pearl Harbor**, 2001 (Jon Voight); The Pigeon That Took Rome, 1962 (Dick Nelson; scenes deleted); **The Private Files of J. Edgar Hoover**, 1977 (Howard Da Silva); The Revenge of Al Capone, 1989 (made-for-TV; Donald Craig); The Right Man, 1960 (made-for-TV; Art Carney); Roosevelt and Truman, 1977 (made-for-TV; Art Evans); Spies, 1992 (made-for-TV; Chris Nubel); **Sunrise at Campobello**, 1960 (Ralph Bellamy); **This Is the Army**, 1943 (Jack Young); Truman, 1995 (made-for-TV; Lee Richardson, and himself, archive footage, funeral procession); The Untouchables, 1959-1963 (TV series; "The Unhired Assassin, Part II," 1960 episode: Paul Frees); The Untouchables, 1993-1994 (TV series; "Radical Solution," 1993 episode; Richard Henzel); The Victors and the Vanquished, 1949 (Nikolai Cherkasov); Victory, 1984 (Algimantas Masiulis); Voyagers!, 1982-1983 (TV series; Nicholas Pryor); War and Remembrance, 1988 (TV miniseries; Ralph Bellamy); Warm Springs, 2005 (made-for-TV; Kenneth Branagh); Winchell, 1998 (made-for-TV; Christopher Plummer); The Winds of War, 1983 (TV miniseries; Ralph Bellamy); World War Two: Behind Closed Doors, 2008 (TV series; Bob Gunton); World War II: When Lions Roared, 1994 (made-for-TV; John Lithgow); Yalta, 1984 (made-for-TV; Robert Rimbaud); **Yankee Doodle Dandy**, 1942 (Jack Young).

Roosevelt, James (1907-1991; U.S. congressman and oldest son of U.S. President Franklin D. Roosevelt and First Lady Eleanor Roosevelt): Eleanor and Franklin, 1976 (made-for-TV; Chris Lafontan); Eleanor and Franklin: The White House Years, 1977 (made-for-TV; Ray Baker); **Sunrise at Campobello**, 1960 (Tim Considine).

Roosevelt, John Aspinwall (1916-1981; U.S. Navy officer and sixth and last child of U.S. President Franklin D. Roosevelt and First Lady Eleanor Roosevelt): Eleanor and Franklin: The White House Years, 1977 (made-for-TV; Brian Patrick Clarke); **Sunrise at Campobello**, 1960 (Tom Carty).

Roosevelt, Kermit (1889-1943; U.S. explorer, soldier and son of U.S. President Theodore Roosevelt): **The Wind and the Lion**, 1975 (Chris Aller).

Roosevelt, Quentin (1897-1918; U.S. Army Air Force pilot and youngest son of U.S. President Theodore Roosevelt, who was killed in aerial combat in WWI): **The Wind and the Lion**, 1975 (Jack Cooley).

Roosevelt, Sara Ann Delano (1854-1941; U.S. housewife and mother of U.S. President Franklin D. Roosevelt, her only child): Eleanor and Franklin, 1976 (made-for-TV; Rosemary Murphy); Eleanor and Franklin: The White House Years, 1977 (made-for-TV; Rosemary Murphy); Hyde Park on Hudson, 2012 (Elizabeth Wilson); **Sunrise at Campobello**, 1960 (Ann Shoemaker).

Roosevelt, Theodore (Theodore Roosevelt, Jr.; aka: "T.R."; 1858-1919; U.S. politician and reformer; 26th President of the U.S.): The American Adventure, 1982 (Bob Boyd voiceover); Bordertown, 1989-1991 (TV series; "Four Eyes," 1990 episode: Wayne York); Bret Maverick, 1981-1982 (TV series; "Horse of Yet Another Color," 1982 episode: William Hootkins); Brighty of the Grand Canyon, 1967 (Karl Swenson); Bronco, 1958-1962 (TV series; "Yankee Tornado," 1961 episode: Peter Breck); **Buffalo Bill**, 1944 (Sidney Blackmer); Bully: An Adventure with Teddy Roosevelt, 1978 (One-man show; James Whitmore); Captains and Kings, 1976 (TV miniseries; Lee de Broux); Cavalcade of America, 1952-1957 (TV series; "The Tenderfoot," 1953 episode: Tom Brown); Circus Boy, 1956-1958 (TV series; "General Pete," 1957 episode: Ed Cassidy); **Citizen Kane**, 1941 (Thomas A. Curran); Cook and Peary: The Race to the Pole, 1983 (made-for-TV; Walter Massey); The Conquerors, 1932 (himself in archive footage); The Copperhead, 1920 (Jack Ridgway [Jack Ridgeway]); **The Curious Case of Benjamin Button**, 2008 (Ed Metzger); Cowboys from Texas, 1939 (himself in archive footage); Deadliest Warrior, 2009-2011 (TV series; "Teddy Roosevelt vs. Lawrence of Arabia," 2011 episode: Matt Allman); Eleanor and Franklin, 1976 (made-for-TV; William Phipps); Eleanor and Franklin: The White House Years, 1977 (made-for-TV; David Healy); End of the Trail, 1936 (Erle C. Kenton); Fancy Pants, 1950 (John Alexander); The Fighting Roosevelts, 1919 (Roosevelt as a boy: Francis J. Noonan; Roosevelt as a young man: Herbert Bradshaw; Roosevelt as president: E.J. Ratcliffe); The First Traveling Saleslady, 1956 (Ed Cassidy); The Ford Television Theatre, 1952-1957 (TV series; "With No Regrets," 1957 episode: Larry Thor); Freedom to Speak, 1982 (TV miniseries; Sam Waterston); The Gambler Returns: The Luck of the Draw, 1991 (made-for-TV; Claude Akins); Geronimo, 1993 (made-for-TV; Ray Geer); Gilded Lilys, 2013 (made-for-TV; Lou Carbonneau); I Loved a Woman, 1933 (E. J. Ratcliffe); I Wonder Who's Kissing Her Now, 1947 (John Merton); In Old Oklahoma, 1943 (Sidney Blackmer); Incident at Victoria Falls, 1992 (made-for-TV; Claude Akins); The Indomitable Teddy Roosevelt, 1983 (Bob Boyd); **Jack London**, 1943 (Wallis Clark); Law of the Plainsman, 1959-1960 (TV series; "The Dude," 1959 episode: Robert Vaughn); The Legend of Tarzan, 2001-2003 (TV series; "Tarzan and the Rough Rider," 2001 episode: Stephen Root); The Life and Times of Grizzly Adams, 1977-1978 (TV series; "The Tenderfoot," 1977 episode: Charles Martin Smith); Lights of Old Broadway, 1925 (Buck Black); The Magnificent Yankee, 1965 (made-for-TV; William Griffis); Meeting of the Minds, 1977-1981 (TV series; two 1977 episodes: Joe Early); My Friend Flicka, 1955-1960 (TV series; "Rough and Ready," 1956 episode: Frank Albertson); My Girl Tisa, 1948 (Sidney Blackmer); Never Kick a Man Upstairs, 1953 (made-for-TV; Sidney Blackmer); Newsies, 1992 (David James Alexander); **Night at the Museum**, 2006

(Robin Williams); **Night at the Museum: Battle of the Smithsonian**, 2009 (Robin Williams); **Night at the Museum: Secret of the Tomb**, 2014 (Robin Williams); Omnibus, 1952-1961 (TV series; "He Shall Have Power," 1960 episode: Larry Blyden); Ordeal by White House, 1952 (made-for-TV; Howard Wierum); **Ragtime**, 1981 (Robert Boyd); The Right Man, 1960 (made-for-TV; Edward G. Robinson); The Road to Galveston, 1996 (made-for-TV; Alex Morris); The Rough Riders, 1927 (Frank Hopper); Rough Riders, 1997 (made-for-TV; Tom Berenger); Silk Hat Kid, 1935 (Frankie Genardi); Sugarfoot, 1957-1961 (TV series; "Man from Medora," 1960 episode: Peter Breck); Sun Valley Cyclone, 1946 (Ed Cassidy); Sundown, 1924 (E. J. Ratcliffe); **Take Me Out to the Ball Game**, 1949 (Ed Cassidy); This Is America, Charlie Brown, 1988-1989 (TV miniseries; "The Smithsonian and the Presidency," 1989 episode: Frank Welker); **This Is My Affair**, 1937 (Sidney Blackmer); The Virginian, 1962-1971; "Riff-Raff," 1962 episode: Karl Swenson); Voyagers!, 1982-1983 (TV series; "Bully and Billy," 1982 episode: Gregg Henry); War of the Worlds: Goliath, 2012 (Jim Byrnes voiceover); Wild and Wooly, 1978 (made-for-TV; David Doyle); **The Wind and the Lion**, 1975 (Brian Keith); The Wright Stuff, 2005-2006 (TV series: Ethan Phillips); Why America Will Win, 1918 (W. E. Whittle); **Yankee Doodle Dandy**, 1942 (Wallis Clark); You Are There, 1953-1971 (TV series; "Dewey's Victory at Manila, May 1, 1898," 1955 episode: Grandon Rhodes; "Attempt to Assassinate Theodore Roosevelt, October 14, 1912," 1957 episode: Roland Winters); The Young Indiana Jones Chronicles, 1992-1993 (TV series; "British East Africa, September 1909," 1992 episode: James Gammon).

Roosevelt, Theodore III (aka: Theodore Roosevelt Jr.; 1887-1944; U.S. politician, businessman and U.S. Army general who led troops at Utah Beach during the Normandy invasion of June 6, 1944; suffered a fatal heart attack one month after the successful invasion and was awarded the Congressional Medal of Honor): **The Longest Day**, 1962 (Henry Fonda).

Rose, Billy (William "Billy" Rose; 1899-1966; U.S. theatrical impresario): **Funny Lady**, 1975 (James Caan).

Roselli, John (1905-1976; U.S. gangster and member of the U.S. crime syndicate): Bonanno: A Godfather's Story, 1999 (made-for-TV; Bruno Di Quenzio); **Nixon**, 1995 (Tony Lo Bianco); Power and Beauty, 2002 (made-for-TV; Tony Nappo); The Rat Pack, 1998 (made-for-TV; Joe Cortese); Sugartime, 1995 (made-for-TV; Sam Grana).

Rosenberg, Alfred (Alfred Ernst Rosenberg; 1893-1946; German politician and early supporter of Hitler's Nazi Party and Nazi theologian who created anti-Jewish and racial theories used to persecute minorities; held many posts in Hitler's regime and later executed as a war criminal): **The Hitler Gang**, 1944 (Tonio Selwart); Nuremberg, 2000- (TV miniseries; Alain Fournier).

Rosenberg, Ethel (Ethel Greenglass Rosenberg; 1915-1953; U.S. political activist, who, with her husband, Julius Rosenberg, was convicted of treason in covertly securing and passing top secret information about the U.S. atomic bomb to the Soviets, and was sentenced to death, executed in the electric chair at Sing Sing Prison on June 19, 1953): Angels in America, 2003- (TV miniseries; Meryl Streep); Citizen Cohn, 1992 (made-for-TV; Karen Ludwig); Les Rosenberg ne doivent pas mourir, 1975 (made-for-TV; Marie-Jose Nat).

Ross, Charlie (1885-1950; U.S. journalist and White House press secretary under U.S. President Harry S. Truman): Collision Course: Truman vs. MacArthur, 1976 (made-for-TV; John Randolph); Truman, 1995 (made-for-TV; Colm Feore).

Ross, Harold Wallace (1892-1951; U.S. journalist; founder and editor-

Ed Begley (in role model of Arnold Rothstein) and Alan Ladd in *The Great Gatsby,* **1949.**

in-chief of the *New Yorker Magazine*): **Joe Gould's Secret**, 2000 (Patrick Tovatt); Mrs. Parker and the Vicious Circle, 1994 (Sam Robards).

Rosser, Thomas L. (1836-1910; U.S. soldier and Confederate major general in the American Civil War known for his daring cavalry raids; later a railroad construction engineer and still later a U.S. brigadier general in the Spanish-American War of 1898): **Alvarez Kelly**, 1966 (role model for Richard Widmark).

Rossini, Gioachino (1792-1868; Italian composer): Die lachende Grille, 1926 (Rudulf Klein-Rogge); Lisztomania, 1975 (Ken Parry).

Roth, Lillian (1910-1980; U.S. singer and actress): **I'll Cry Tomorrow**, 1955 (Susan Hayward).

Rothschild, Mayer Amschel (1744-1812; German banker and founder of the Rothschild financial family): **The House of Rothschild**, 1934 (George Arliss); The Rothschilds, 1940 (Erich Ponto).

Rothschild, Nathaniel (1812-1870; British banker and financier): Die lachende Grille, 1926 (Eugen Burg); Disraeli: Portrait of a Romantic, 1978 (TV miniseries; David de Keyser); **The House of Rothschild**, 1934 (George Arliss); The Rothschilds, 1940 (Carl Kuhlmann).

Rothstein, Arnold (aka: Mr. Big; The Big Bankroll; 1882-1928; U.S. gambler and crime boss who reportedly fixed the 1919 World Series; his murder was never solved): Boardwalk Empire, 2010-2014 (TV series; Michael Stuhlbarg); **Eight Men Out**, 1988 (Michael Lerner); Gangster Wars, 1981 (George DiCenzo); **The Great Gatsby**, 1926 (role model for George Nash); **The Great Gatsby**, 1949 (role model for Ed Begley); **The Great Gatsby**, 1974 (role model for Howard Da Silva); **The Great Gatsby**, 2013 (role model for Amitabh Bachchan); King of the Roaring 20s: The Story of Arnold Rothstein, 1961 (David Janssen; Jimmy Baird as young Rothstein); Lansky, 1999 (made-for-TV; Stanley DeSantis); Mobsters, 1991 (F. Murray Abraham); **The Rise and Fall of Legs Diamond**, 1960 (Robert Lowery).

Rousseau, Jean-Jacques (1712-1778; French writer and philosopher): Ce diable d'homme, 1978- (TV miniseries; Jean Mourat); Jean-Jacques Rousseau, 1979 (made-for-TV; Gerard Desarthe); Joseph Balsamo, 1973- (TV miniseries; Alois Maria Giani); Le comtesse de Charny, 1989- (TV miniseries; Bernard Waver); Le siècle des lumieres, 1976 (made-for-TV; Denis Manuel); The Majordomo, 1965 (Jean Minisini); **Napoleon**, 1927 (Alberti); Narrenweisheit, 1989 (made-for-TV; Roman

Charlton Heston, Donna Reed (as Sacajawea), Herbert Heyes and Fred MacMurray in *The Far Horizons*, 1955.

Wilhelmi); Remontons les Champs-Elysees, 1938 (Andre Laurent); The Roads of Exile, 1978 (made-for-TV; Francois Simon); The Romantics, 2006- (TV miniseries; David Tennant); Royal Affairs in Versailles, 1957 (Gilbert Gil); Valmy, 1967 (made-for-TV; Marc Eyraud).

Ruby, Jack (Jacob Leon Rubenstein; 1911-1967; U.S. nightclub owner in Dallas, Texas, who killed Lee Harvey Oswald, reported assassin of President John F. Kennedy, in 1962): BBC Play of the Month, 1965-1983 (TV series; "Lee Oswald: Assassin," 1966 episode: John De Marco); Bonanno: A Godfather's Story, 1999 (made-for-TV; Michel Albert); Dark Skies, 1996-1997 (TV series; "The Warren Omission," 1997 episode: Jack Lindine); The End of a Dynasty, 1998 (Joe Adkins); Executive Action, 1973 (Oscar Oncidi); **JFK**, 1991 (Brian Doyle-Murray), JFK: The Ruby Connection, 2009 (made-for-TV; Larry Jack Dotson); Le piege americain, 2008 (Tony Calabretta); Ruby, 1992 (Danny Aiello); Ruby and Oswald, 1978 (made-for-TV; Michael Lerner); Timequest, 2000 (Alex Safi).

Rudabaugh, Dave (1854-1886; aka: Arkansas Dave; U.S. Old West outlaw and gunfighter): The Texas Rangers, 1951 (Douglas Kennedy); **Young Guns II**, 1990 (Christian Slater).

Rudolf (1858-1889; Crown Prince of Austria; committed suicide with his mistress, Baroness Mary Vetsera because they were prohibited from marrying due to her lowly social status): The Angel with the Trumpet, 1953 (Fred Liewehr); BBC Sunday-Night Theatre, 1950-1959 (TV series; "The Masque of Kings," 1955 episode: Frank Windsor; "The Mayerling Affair," 1956 episode: Keith Michell); The Crown Prince, 2006 (made-for-TV; Max von Thun); Das Geheimnis um Johann Orth, 1936 (Paul Richter); Der Kronprinz, 1989 (made-for-TV; Istvan Hirtling); Enigmes de l'histoire, 1956-1957 (TV series; one 1956 episode: Jean Paqui); Kaiserin Elisabeth von Osterreich, 1921 (Max Landa); Kaiserin Elisabeth von Osterreich, 1972 (made-for-TV; Christian Reiner); Kronprinz Rudolf oder: Das Geheimnis von Mayerling, 1919 (Rolf Randolf); Kronprinz Rudolfs letzte Liebe, 1959 (Rudolf Prack); The Masque of Kings, 1946 (made-for-TV; John Bailey); **Mayerling**, 1937 (Charles Boyer); Mayerling, 1968 (Omar Sharif); Producers' Showcase, 1954-1957 (TV series; "Mayerling," 1957 episode: Mel Ferrer); The Secret of Mayerling, 1951 (Jean Marais); The Song in the Forest, 1950 (John Byron); A Ultima Valsa, 1969 (TV series; Geraldo Del Rey).

Ruge, Friedrich Oskar (1894-1985; German navy officer): **The Desert Fox: The Story of Rommel**, 1951 (Walter Kingsford).

Rundstedt, Gerd von (Karl Rudolf Gerd von Rundstedt; 1875-1953;

German field marshal in WWII): **A Bridge Too Far**, 1977 (Wolfgang Preiss); **The Desert Fox: The Story of Rommel**, 1951 (Leo G. Carroll); The Fall of Berlin, 1952 (V. Renin); **The Longest Day**, 1962 (Paul Hartmann); Rommel, 2012 (made-for-TV; Hanns Zischler); **Triple Cross**, 1966 (Marcel Journet); War and Remembrance, 1988 (TV miniseries; Anthony Bate).

Runyon, Damon (Alfred Damon Runyon; U.S. author and newspaperman; 1880-1946): Climax!, 1954-1958 (TV series; "Mr. Runyon of Broadway," 1957 episode: Ralph Bellamy); **Daisy Kenyon**, 1947 (himself); Damon Runyon's Pueblo, 1981 (made-for-TV; Eric Austin); Dempsey, 1983 (made-for-TV; Robert Harper); Madison Sq. Garden, 1932 (himself); **The Private Files of J. Edgar Hoover**, 1977 (Jack Cassidy); Ring of Passion, 1978 (made-for-TV; Allen Garfield).

Ruppert, Jacob, Jr. (1867-1939; U.S. brewer, politician and owner of the New York Yankees): **The Babe**, 1992 (Bernard Kates).

Rusk, David Dean (1909-1994; U.S. politician and 54th U.S. secretary of state, 1961-1969): The Kennedys, 2011 (TV series; Glen Gaston); The Missiles of October, 1964 (made-for-TV; Larry Gates); Path to War, 2002 (made-for-TV; John Aylward); Thirteen Days, 2000 (Henry Strozier).

Russell, Lillian (Helen Louise Leonard; 1860-1922; U.S. singer of the Gay Nineties): Bowery to Broadway, 1944 (Louise Allbritton); David Harum, 1934 (Ruth Gillette); **Diamond Jim**, 1936 (Binnie Barnes); The Gentleman from Louisiana, 1936 (Ruth Gillette); **The Great Ziegfeld**, 1936 (Ruth Gillette); Lillian Russell, 1940 (Alice Faye); Lillie, 1978 (TV miniseries; Christina Greateaux); **My Wild Irish Rose**, 1947 (Andrea King).

Russell, Richard Brevard Jr. (1897-1971; U.S. politician; U.S. senator from Georgia): The Commission, 2007 (Martin Landau).

Rustin, Bayard (1912-1987; U.S. black socialist and civil rights leader): Boycott, 2001 (made-for-TV; Erik Dellums); Selma, 2014 (Ruben Santiago-Hudson).

Ruth, George Herman, Jr. (aka: Babe; 1895-1948; U.S. baseball player, legendary home-run hitter): A.J.'s Time Travelers, 1995- (TV series; "Babe Ruth," 1995 episode: Art LeFleur); Angels in the Infield, 2000 (made-for-TV; Paul A. MacFarlane); **The Babe**, 1992 (John Goodman); Babe Ruth, 1991 (made-for-TV; Stephen Lang); **The Babe Ruth Story**, 1948 (William Bendix; Robert Ellis playing Ruth as a boy); The Big Picture, 1989 (Walter Olkewicz); Dempsey, 1983 (made-for-TV; Michael McManus); Everyone's Hero, 2006 (animated; Brian Dennehy voiceover); Henry and Me, 2014 (animated; Chazz Palminteri); A Love Affair: The Eleanor and Lou Gehrig Story, 1977 (made-for-TV; Ramon Bieri); **The Natural**, 1984 (role model for Joe Don Baker); **The Pride of the Yankees**, 1942 (himself); **The Sandlot**, 1993 (Art LeFleur); **Speedy**, 1928 (himself); Touched by an Angel, 1994-2003 (TV series; "The Perfect Game," 2001 episode: Michael Patrick McGill); Voyagers!, 1982-1983 (TV series; "Cleo and the Babe," 1982 episode; William Lucking); Wizards of Waverly Place, 2007-2012 (TV series; "Art Museum Piece," 2008 episode; Britt Prentice). Note: For detailed information on the colorful Ruth, see my book *Zanies: The World's Greatest Eccentrics* (New Century Publishers, 1982; illustrated pages 330-335).

Rutledge, Ann Mayes (1813-1835; young woman who was reportedly Abraham Lincoln's first love): **Abe Lincoln in Illinois**, 1940 (Mary Howard); Abe Lincoln in Illinois, 1945 (made-for-TV; Alma Mansfield); Abe Lincoln in Illinois, 1964 (made-for-TV; Mildred Trares); **Abraham Lincoln**, 1930 (Una Merkel); Cavalcade of America, 1952-1957 (TV series; "New Salem Story," 1953 episode: Jeff Donnell); The Dramatic

Life of Abraham Lincoln, 1924 (Ruth Clifford); G. E. True Theater, 1953-1962 (TV series: "Prologue to Glory," 1956 episode: Joanne Woodward); Omnibus, 1952-1961 (TV series; "Mr. Lincoln," five parts, 1952-1953: Joanne Woodward); The Philco-Goodyear Television Playhouse, 1948-1956 (TV series; "Ann Rutledge," 1950 episode: Grace Kelly); **Young Mr. Lincoln**, 1939 (Pauline Moore).

Rutledge, Edward (1749-1800; U.S. politician, member of Continental Congress and signer of the Declaration of Independence): **1776**, 1972 (John Cullum).

Ryunosuke Kusaka (1893-1971; Japanese admiral and chief of staff of the combined Japanese Imperial fleet during WWII): **Tora! Tora! Tora!**, 1970 (Ichiro Reuzaki).

Saburo Kurusu (1886-1954; Japanese diplomat and special envoy to Washington, D.C., just before the sneak attack was made against Pearl Harbor on December 7, 1941): **Tora! Tora! Tora!**, 1970 (Hisao Toake); **Wake Island**, 1942 (Richard Loo).

Sacajawea (Sacagawea; c.1788-1812; Lemhi Shoshone woman and guide on the 1804-1806 Lewis and Clark expedition to the Pacific): Death Valley Days, 1952-1970 (TV series; "The Girl Who Walked the West," 1967 episode: Victoria Vetri); **The Far Horizons**, 1955 (Donna Reed); Lewis and Clark, 2016- (TV miniseries; Tanaya Beatty); **Night at the Museum**, 2006 (Mizuo Peck); **Night at the Museum: Battle of the Smithsonian**, 2009 (Mizuo Peck); You Are There, 1953-1971 (TV series; "Lewis and Clark Expedition," 1971 episode: Tenaya Torres).

Sacco, Ferdinand Nicola (1891-1927; Italian-born anarchist in the U.S., convicted and executed for robbery and murder): De zaak Sacco en Vanzetti, 1966 (made-for-TV; Wies Andersen); Der Fall Sacco und Vanzetti, 1963 (made-for-TV; Robert Freitag); L'affaire Sacco et Vanzetti, 1967 (Richard Muller); **No God, No Master**, 2012 (James Madio); Sacco & Vanzetti, 1971 (Riccardo Cucciolla); Sacco & Vanzetti, 2005 (made-for-TV; Sergio Rubini); Sacco e Vanzetti, 1977- (TV miniseries; Achille Millo); Sacco und Vanzetti, 1927 (Lutz Altcshul [Louis V. Arco]); Sunday Showcase, 1959-1960 (TV series; "The Sacco and Vanzetti Story," two 1960 episodes: Martin Balsam); The Wednesday Play, 1964-1970 (TV series; "The Good Shoemaker and the Poor Fish Peddler," 1965 episode: Bill Nagy); Windy City Heat, 2003 (made-for-TV; Wayne Wilderson). Note: For detailed information on Sacco and Vanzetti, see my eight-volume work *Encyclopedia of World Crime*, Volume IV (CrimeBooks, Inc., 1990; illustrated [8 images] 2649-2652).

Sage, Anna (Ana Cumpanas; 1889-1947; U.S. madam and operator of bordellos in Indiana and Chicago, Illinois; reportedly identified Public Enemy Number One John Dillinger to FBI agents and accompanied him to a theater where he was allegedly killed; known as the "Lady in Red," although she was wearing an orange dress that night; she was deported to Romania): Baby Face Nelson, 1957 (Lisa Davis); Dillinger, 1960 (made-for-TV; Jane Rose); Dillinger, 1973 (Cloris Leachman); Dillinger, 1991 (made-for-TV; Lucy Childs); **The FBI Story**, 1959 (Jean Willes); Gang Busters, 1952- (TV series; "Dillinger," 1952 episode: Ann Morriss); Guns Don't Argue, 1957 (Ann Morriss); The Lady in Red, 1979 (Louise Fletcher); **Public Enemies**; 2009 (Branka Katic); The Woman in Red, 1997 (Elena Albu).

Saint-Just, Louis Antoine de (1767-1794; French military and political leader during the French Revolution): Arme Bitos, 1962 (made-for-TV; Frans van der Lingen); BBC Play of the Month, 1965-1983 (TV series; "Danton's Death," 1978 episode: Michael Pennington); Biography, 1970- (TV series; "Danton," 1970 episode: David Andrews); Danton, 1921 (Robert Scholz); Danton, 1983 (Bogustaw Linda); Dan-

Virginia Mayo and Rex Harrison (as Saladin) in *King Richard and the Crusaders*, 1954.

tons Tod, 1963 (made-for-TV; Wolfgang Kieling); Dantons Tod, 1977 (made-for-TV; Henry Hubchen); Dantons Tod, 1981 (Mathieu Carriere); It Illuminates, My Dear, 1922 (William Dieterle); Jean Chouan, 1926 (Rene Vignieres); La camera explore le temps, 1957-1966 (TV series; two 1964 episodes: Denis Manuel); La mort de Danton, 1970 (made-for-TV; Denis Manuel); La revolution francaise, 1989 (Christopher Thompson); **Napoleon**, 1927 (Abel Gance); **Reign of Terror**, 1949 (Jess Barker); Saint-Just ou La force des choses, 1975 (made-for-TV; Patrice Alexandre); The Scarlet Daredevil, 1928 (Harold Huth); Terror! Robespierre and the French Revolution, 2009 (made-for-TV; George Maguire); Theatre 625, 1964-1968 (TV series; "Poor Bitos," 1965 episode: John Neville); The Tragedy of Man, 2011 (animated; Adam Lux voiceover); The Visitors: Bastille Day, 2016 (Mathieu Spinosi); World Theatre, 1959- (TV series; "Danton's Death," 1959 episode; Colin Jeavons).

Saint-Simon (Louis de Rouvroy; 1675-1755; French soldier and diplomat): Famous Love Affairs, 1961 (Palau); Richelieu, 1977 (TV miniseries; Francois Guizerix); Richelieu ou La journee des dupes, 1983 (made-for-TV; Jan-Yves Dubois); Royal Affairs at Versailles, 1954 (Jacques Francois).

Saladin (c.1137-1193; Muslim military leader of Islam; Sultan of Egypt and Syria, who warred with Richard the Lionheart in the Third Crusade): Arn: The Knight Templar, 2010- (TV miniseries; Milind Soman); Blood and Dust, 1992 (made-for-TV; Fernando Rey); **The Crusades**, 1935 (Ian Keith); Empires: Holy Warriors—Richard the Lionheart and Saladin, 2005 (made-for-TV; Hichem Rostom); **King Richard and the Crusaders**, 1954 (Rex Harrison); **Kingdom of Heaven**, 2005 (Ghassan Massoud); Richard the Lionheart, 1962 (TV series; Marne Maitland); Richard the Lionheart, 1962 (TV series; Marne Maitland); Richard the Lion-Hearted, 1923 (Charles K. Gerrard); Saladin and the Great Crusades, 1983 (Ahmed Mazhar).

Salieri, Antonio (1750-1825; Italian composer): **Amadeus**, 1984 (E. Murray Abraham); I, Don Giovanni, 2009 (Ennio Fantastichini); La voz humana, 1986-1988 (TV series; "Mozart y Salieri," 1986 episode: Joaquin Hinojosa); The Life and Loves of Mozart, 1959 ([Albin] Skoda); The Life of Wolfgang Amadeus Mozart [aka: The Mozart Story], 1948 (Wilton Graf); Mozart, 1982- (TV miniseries; Carlo Rivolta); Vergesst Mozart, 1985 (investigates Mozart's mysterious death; Winfried Glatzeder); Wolfgang A. Mozart, 1991 (Boris Rosner).

Salinger, Pierre (1925-2004; U.S. news correspondent for ABC News and former press secretary for U.S. President John F. Kennedy): Blood

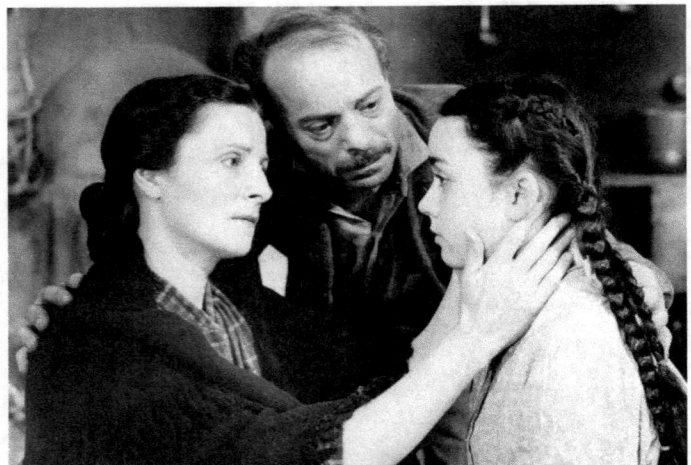

Angela Clarke, Jay Novello and Susan Whitney (as Lucia Santos) in *The Miracle of Our Lady of Fatima*, 1952.

Feud, 1983 (made-for-TV; Peter Van Norden); Robert F. Kennedy and His Times, 1985 (TV miniseries; Jeffrey Tambor); Timequest, 2000 (Greg Trzaskoma).

Salm-Salm, Agnes (Princess de Salm-Salm; 1844-1912; U.S. wife of Prussian mercenary involved in the American Civil War, 1861-1865; the Mexican Revolution, 1867-1868; and the Franco-Prussian War, 1870-1871): Juarez and Maximillian, 1935 (Matilde Palou).

Salome (14-72 A.D.; daughter of Herodias and Herod II; a voluptuous teenager who reportedly danced for Herod Antipas to persuade him to behead John the Baptist for condemning her mother's adulterous marriage): **Barabbas**, 1962 (Vera Drudi); The Cradle of God, 1926 (Stacia Napierkowska); The Cross, 2001 (Loretta Shenosky); Family Theatre, 1949-1958 (TV series; "Triumphant Hour," 1953 episode: Elizabeth Harrower); The Gospel According to St. Matthew, 1966 (Paola Tedesco); Herod and Marianne, 1965 (made-for TV; Marlene Riphahn); Herodias, 1911 (short; Maria Ventura); Il messia, 1975 (Cosetta Pichetti); Jesus, 2000 (made-for-TV; Gabriella Pession); **King of Kings**, 1961 (Brigid Bazlen); Kristo, 1996 (Lindsay Custodio); The Living Christ Series, 1951 (TV miniseries; Eugenia Paul); Mary Magdalene, 2000 (made-for-TV; Ambra Angiolini); Redenzione, 1919 (Pepa Bonafe); Salome, 1918 (Theda Bara); Salome, 1923 (Diana Allen); Salome, 1923 (Alla Nazimova); **Salome**, 1953 (Rita Hayworth); Salome, 1971 (made-for-TV; Mascha Rabben); Salome, 1972 (Donyale Luna); Salome, 1973 (made-for-TV; Ludmilla Tcherina); Salome, 1986 (adult Salome: Jo Champa; Salome as a child: Fabiana Torrente); Salome, 1990 (made-for-TV; Catherine Malfitano); Salome, 1992 (made-for-TV; Maria Ewing); Salome, 2013 (Jessica Chastain); Salome's Last Dance, 1988 (Imogene Millais-Scott).

Samson (In Bible, Israeli strongman who was betrayed by seductress Delilah to the Philistines for money): The Cradle of God, 1926 (Raoul Paoli); Greatest Heroes of the Bible, 1978- (TV series; "Samson and Delilah," 1978 episode: John Beck); Hercules in New York, 1970 (Mark Tendler); Hercules Returns, 1993 (Des Mangan); Hercules, Samson & Ulysses, 1965 (Iloosh Khoshabe); Samson, 1914 (J. Warren Kerrigan); **Samson and Delilah**, 1949 (Victor Mature); Samson and Delilah, 1984 (made-for-TV; Anthony Hamilton); Samson and Delilah, 1987 (Paul Hay); Samson and Delilah, 1996 (made-for-TV; Eric Thal); Samson and Delilah, 2007 (Charles Alvez da Cruz); Samson and Delilah, 2008 (Clifton Forbis); Samson & Delilah, 2009 (Rowan McNamara); Samson and the Mighty Challenge, 1964 (Nadir Moretti); Samson et Delila, 1981 (made-for-TV; Jon Vickers); Samson et Delila, 2002 (made-for-TV; Placido Domingo); Samson und Delila, 1922 (Al-

fredo Galoar); Son of God, 2014 (Nonso Anozie).

Samuel, Archie Peyton (1866-1875; somewhat developmentally disabled halfbrother of U.S. outlaws Frank and Jesse James; killed in explosion caused by Pinkerton agents raiding the James farmhouse, which blew off his mother's arm and earned widespread sympathy for the outlaws): Frank and Jesse, 1994 (Chad Linley); **The Long Riders**, 1980 (R. B. Thrift).

Samuel, Reuben (1828-1908; stepfather to U.S. outlaws Frank and Jesse James): Frank and Jesse, 1994 (John Stiritz); The Great Missouri Raid, 1951 (Edgar Buchanan).

Sanchez, Ilich Ramirez (aka: Carlos the Jackal; 1949- ; Marxist terrorist working for the PFLP/Popular Front for the Liberation of Palestine who, over the years, killed more than a dozen persons and injured another 150 in many terrorist attacks; her is, at this writing, serving a life term in a French prison): Death Has a Bad Reputation, 1990 (made-for-TV; Tony Lo Bianco).

Sand, George (Amantine-Lucile-Aurore Dupin; 1804-1876; French novelist and memoirist, who used a male pseudonym to identify her writings; she is best known for her romantic affair with Frederic Chopin): **Camille**, 1936 (Sibyl Harris); Canevas la ville, 1986 (Marie-Claude Deviegue); The Children of the Century, 2002 (Juliette Binoche); Chopin—Bilder einer Trennung, 1993 (Nina Hoger; Hannelore Hoger voiceover for older George Sand); Chopin: Pragnienie milosci, 2004 (Danuta Stenka); Dante's Inferno, 2007 (Laura Krafft); Die lachende Grille, 1926 (Dagny Servaes); Dreams of Love, 1954 (Mila Parely); Ein Winter auf Mallorca, 1982 (made-for-TV; Eleonore Weisgerber); Farewell, 1935 (aka: La chanson de l'adieu; Un amour de Frederic Chopin; Lucienne Le Marchand); Farewell Waltz, 1934 (Sybille Schmitz); George and Fanchette, 2010 (made-for-TV; Ariane Ascaride); George Sand, 1958 (TV series; Maria Fernanda); George Sand, 1981- (TV miniseries; Anna Proclemer); George Sand, une femme libre, 1995 (made-for-TV; Christine Citti); George Who?, 1973 (Anne Wiazemsky; Michele Simonnet; Catherine Sola; Florence Guerfy); Heinrich Heine, 1978 (made-for-TV; Ulla Berkevicz); The Hourglass Sanatorium, 1973 (Alicja Kluba); **Impromptu**, 1991 (Judy Davis); International, 1969 (aka: Jutrzenka; Lucia Bose; Nuria Espert, George Sand voiceover); La note bleue, 1991 (Marie-France Pisier); La Valse de l'adieu, 1928 (Germaine Laugier); Liszt Ferenc, 1982 (TV miniseries; Maud Rayer); Lisztomania, 1975 (Imogen Claire); Notorious Woman, 1974 (TV miniseries; Rosemary Harris); Pontcarral, colonel d'empire, 1942 (Alberte Bayol); Prelude, 1952 (made-for-TV; Sarah Churchill); Preludio, A Vida de Chopin, 1962 (TV series; Laura Cardoso); **A Song to Remember**, 1945 (Merle Oberon); **Song without End**, 1960 (Patricia Morison); The Strange Case of Delphina Potocka or the Mystery of Chopin, 1999 (Patricia Quinn).

Sanger, Margaret (Margaret Higgins Sanger; 1879-1966; American birth control activist, nurse and sex educator): Choices of the Heart: The Margaret Sanger Story, 1995 (made-for-TV; Dana Delany); Portrait of a Rebel: The Remarkable Mrs. Sanger, 1980 (made-for-TV: Bonnie Franklin); The Roots of Roe, 1993 (made-for-TV; Joanne Woodward voiceover); The Woman Rebel, 1976 (Piper Laurie).

Sansom, Odette (Odette Sansom Hallowes; 1912-1995; heroic British intelligence officer and SOE spy in WWII): **Odette**, 1951 (Anna Neagle).

Santa Anna, Antonio Lopez de (1794-1876; Mexican general and dictator): The Adventures of Jim Bowie, 1956-1958 (TV series; "Mexican Adventure," 1957 episode: Rodolfo Hoyos Jr.); **The Alamo**, 1960 (Ruben Padilla); **The Alamo**, 2004 (Emilio Echevarria); The Alamo:

Thirteen Days to Glory, 1987 (made-for-TV; Raul Julia); American Playhouse, 1981- (TV series; "Seguin," 1982 episode: Edward James Olmos); Davy Crockett at the Fall of the Alamo, 1926 (Fletcher Norton); The Eagles Cemetery, 1939 (Carlos Lopez Aldama); The First Texan, 1956 (David Silva); Gone to Texas, 1986 (made-for-TV; Richard Yniguez); Heroes of the Alamo, 1937 (Julian Rivero); His Most Serene Highness, 2000 (Alejandro Parodi); **The Last Command**, 1955 (J. Carrol Naish); **Man of Conquest**, 1939 (C. Henry Gordon); Martyrs of the Alamo, 1915 (Walter Long); **The Mask of Zorro**, 1998 (Joaquim de Almeida); The Mexican-American War, 2006 (made-for-TV; Art Bonilla); Mexicanos al grito de guerra, 1943 (Salvador Quiroz); The Red Skelton Hour, 1951-1971 (TV series; "Deadeye and the Alamo," 1961 episode: Cesar Romero); Texas, 1994 (made-for-TV; Lloyd Battista); Texas Rising, 2015 (TV miniseries; Olivier Martinez); Two for Texas, 1998 (made-for-TV; Marco Rodriguez); You Are There, 1953-1971 (TV series; "The Defense of the Alamo," 1953 episode: Manuel Sebastian).

Santos, Lucia (aka: Sister Lucia of Fatima; 1907-2005; one of three children, including her younger cousins, Jacinta and Francisco Marto, claimed to have seen the Virgin Mary on six separate occasions outside Fatima, Portugal, in 1917; on the last visitation of the Lady of Fatima, more than 50,000 persons witnessed what was described as a miracle where the sun danced, gave off multicolored lights, seemed to rush at the earth and then recede into the heavens): Aparicao, 1991 (Teresa Costa); **The Miracle of Our Lady of Fatima**, 1952 (Susan Whitney); Our Lady of Fatima, 1951 (Ines Orsini).

Savonarola, Girolamo (1452-1498; Italian Domican friar who preached republicanism and clerical integrity, denouncing corrupt members of the clergy, and establishing a large following in Florence; he defied Pope Alexander VI, was excommunicated and, along with two followers, was executed by being burned at the stake): The Borgia, 2006 (Enrique Villen); Borgia, 2011 (TV series; Iain Glen); The Borgias, 2011 (TV series; Steven Berkoff); Lucrezia Borgia, 1937 (Antonin Artaud).

Scalisi, John (1900-1929; Sicilian assassin-for-hire in the employ of Chicago crime czar Al Capone; with his partner Albert Anselmi, murdered more than a dozen persons, including bootleggers Charles Dion O'Banion, Earl "Hymie" Weiss and the seven victims of the George "Bugs" Moran gang in what became known as the St. Valentine's Day Massacre of 1929; he, along with his partner Anselmi, and confederate Joseph "Hop Toad" Giunta, were all murdered by Capone after they tried to usurp his underworld fiefdom): **Al Capone**, 1959 (Ron Soble); Playhouse 90, 1956-1961 (TV series; "Seven against the Wall," 1958 episode: Richard Sinatra); **The St. Valentine's Day Massacre**, 1967 (Richard Bakalyan). Note: For detailed information on Scalisi, see my book World Encyclopedia of Organized Crime (Paragon House, 1992; page 351).

Schell, Richard (1810-1879; U.S. politician and U.S. representative from New York, 1874-1875): **Lincoln**, 2012 (Tim Blake Nelson).

Schlabrendorff, Fabian von (1907-1980; German officer in WWII and part of the 1944 plot to kill Hitler): Die Stunde der Offiziere, 2004 (made-for-TV; Felix Eitner).

Schleicher, Kurt von (1882-1934; German general and last chancellor of Germany's Weimar Republic, who was murdered on orders of Hitler during the Night of the Long Knives, when Hitler purged many of his old political enemies): Hitler: The Rise of Evil, 2003 (made-for-TV; Christopher Ettridge).

Schmeling, Max (Maximillian Adolph Otto Siegfried "Max" Schmeling; 1905-2005; German prizefighter and world heavyweight champion,

Dustin Hoffman (as Dutch Schultz), Steven Hill and Loren Dean in *Billy Bathgate*, 1991.

1930-1932): Joe and Max, 2002 (made-for-TV; Til Schweiger); **The Joe Louis Story**, 1953 (William Thourlby); Max Schmeling, 2012 (Shaunte Knight); Ring of Passion, 1978 (made-for-TV; Stephen Macht); Rocky Marciano, 1999 (made-for-TV; Mark Simmons).

Schragmuller, Elsbeth (aka: Fraulein Doktor; 1887-1940; German espionage agent and spymaster during WWI): Fraulein Doktor, 1969 (Suzy Kendall).

Schubert, Franz (1797-1828; Austrian composer): Angeli senza paradiso, 1970 (Albano); April Blossoms, 1937 (Richard Tauber); Das Dreimaderlhaus, 1958 (Karlheinz Bohm); Du holde Kunst—Szenen um Lieder von Franz Schubert, 1961 (Kurt Heintel); Ein Walzer von Strauss, 1925 (Philipp von Zeska); Franz Schubert, 1953 (Heinrich Schweiger); Franz Schuberts letzte Liebe, 1926 (Philipp von Zeska); Jomfruburet, 1959 (made-for-TV; Hans Kurt); Komponisten auf der Spur, 1994- (TV series; "Franz Schubert," 1997 episode: Stefan Puntigam); Leise flehen meine Lieder, 1978 (made-for-TV; Christian Steyer); The Life and Loves of Beethoven, 1937 (Dalmeras); Love Time, 1934 (Nils Asther); Lover Devine, 1933 (Hans Jaray); Mit meinen heissen Tranen, 1986- (TV miniseries; "Der Wanderer," 1986 episode: Udo Samel); New Wine, 1941 (Alan Curtis); The Pretty Miller Girl, 1948 (Tino Rossi); Schubert's Dream of Spring, 1932 (Carl Joken); Schumann, Schubert und der Schnee, 2006 (made-for-TV; Ludwig Blochberger); Seine einzige Liebe, 1947 (Franz Boheim); Serenade, 1940 (Bernard Lancret); **Seven Faces**, 1929 (Paul Muni); Sinfonia d'amore, 1956 (Claude Laydu); The Temptation of Franz Schubert, 1997 (made-for-TV; Simon Russell Beale); Three Girls around Schubert, 1937 (Paul Horbiger); Unfinished Symphony, 1935 (Hans Jaray); Zenes TV szinhaz, 1970- (TV series; "Harom a kislany," 1988 episode: Janos Bandi); Zwei Herzem im Dreiviertel-Takt, 1930 (Gert Bloem).

Schultz, Dutch (Arthur Flegenheimer; 1901-1935; New York-based racketeer and bootlegger): **Billy Bathgate**, 1991 (Dustin Hoffman); **The Cotton Club**, 1984 (James Remar); The Gangster Chronicles, 1981 (TV miniseries; Jonathan Banks); Gangster Wars, 1981 (Jonathan Banks); Hit the Dutchman, 1992 (Bruce Nozick); Hoodlum, 1997 (Tim Roth); The Lawless Years, 1959-1961 (TV series; John Dennis in several 1961 episodes); Lepke, 1975 (John Durren); Mad Dog Coll, 1961 (Vincent Gardenia); Mad Dog Coll, 1993 (Bruce Nozick); **The Natural**, 1984 (James Meyer); The Outfit, 1993 (Lance Henriksen); Portrait of a Mobster, 1960 (Vic Morrow); The Revenge of Al Capone, 1989 (made-for-TV; Neil Giuntoli); **The Rise and Fall of Legs Diamond**, 1960 (role model for Jesse White); The Shadow, 1937 (Vernon Dent); Trust in Me, 1994 (Tom McBeath); The Untouchables, 1959-1963 (TV series;

Anthony Quinn and Michael Rennie (as Junipero Serra) in *Seven Cities of Gold*, 1955.

Lawrence Dobkin).

Schumann, Clara Wieck (1819-1896; German musician and composer and wife of composer Robert Schumann): Der Fall des Robert Schumann, 1990 (made for TV: Ricarda Weber as young Clara; Lili Weber-Andreae as older Clara); Geliebte Clara, 2008 (Marina Gedeck); La musique de l'amour: Robert et Clara, 1995 (made-for-TV; Isabelle Carre); Les chants de l'aube, 1981 (made-for-TV; Danielle Dubreuil); The Loretta Young Show, 1953-1961 (TV series, "The Clara Schumann Story," 1954 episode: Loretta Young); Musica—Dr. Robert Schumann, Teufelsromantiker, 1999 (made-for-TV; Bettina Kurth); Robert Schumann—Clara Wieck—Johannes Brahms, 2006 (made-for-TV; Elsa Hanewinkel); Schumann, Schubert und der Schnee, 2006 (made-for-TV; Elisabeth Trissenaar); **Song of Love**, 1947 (Katharine Hepburn); Traumerei, 1944 (Hilde Krahl).

Schumann, Robert (1810-1856; German composer): Der Fall des Robert Schumann, 1990 (made for TV: Jurgen Noll); Geliebte Clara, 2008 (Pascal Greggory; singing voice: Jacques Breuer); La musique de l'amour: Robert et Clara, 1995 (made-for-TV; Thomas Langmann); Les chants de l'aube, 1981 (made-for-TV; Yves-Marie Maurin); The Loretta Young Show, 1953-1961 (TV series; "The Clara Schumann Story," 1954 episode; George Nader); Musica—Dr. Robert Schumann, Teufelsromantiker, 1999 (made-for-TV; Michael Maertens); Robert Schumann – Clara Wieck—Johannes Brahms, 2006 (made-for-TV; Volker J. Ringe); Schumann, Schubert und der Schnee, 2006 (made-for-TV; Olaf Bar); **Song of Love**, 1947 (Paul Henreid); Traumerei, 1944 (Mathias Wieman).

Schurz, Carl Christian (1829-1906; German-born revolutionary; U.S. general in American Civil War and U.S. Senator and U.S. Secretary of the Interior): Carl Schurz, 1968 (Udo Vioff); **Cheyenne Autumn**, 1964 (Edward G. Robinson).

Schwarzkopf, Herbert Norman, Jr. (U.S. military officer; 1934-2012; four-star general of the U.S. Army): Dark Skies, 1996-1997 (TV series; "The Warren Omission," 1997 episode: Gunther Jenson).

Schwarzkopf, Herbert Norman, Sr. (1895-1958; U.S. police officer and U.S. Army major general, father of four-star U.S. Army General Herbert Norman Schwarzkopf Jr.): Crime of the Century, 1996 (made-for-TV; J.T. Walsh); **J. Edgar**, 2011 (Dermot Mulroney); The Lindbergh Kidnapping Case, 1976 (made-for-TV; Peter Donat).

Schweitzer, Albert (1874-1965; German-born theologian, philosopher and physician): The Adventures of Picasso, 1978 (Sven Lindberg); Al-

bert Schweitzer, 1987- (TV series; Wolfgang Preiss); Albert Schweitzer, 2009 (Jeroen Krabbe); Albert Schweitzer: Called to Africa, 2006 (Jeff McCarthy); BBC Sunday-Night Theatre, 1950-1959 (TV series; "It Is Midnight, Dr. Schweitzer," 1953 episode: Andre Morell); Dr. Schweitzer, 1952 (Pierre Fresnay); Schweitzer, 1990 (Malcolm McDowell).

Schwimmer, Reinhardt (d. 1929; U.S. optician and gambler, who associated as a hanger-on with the George "Bugs" Moran gang and who was killed, along with six others, in Chicago's notorious 1929 St. Valentine's Day Massacre): Playhouse 90, 1956-1961 (TV series; "Seven Against the Wall," 1958 episode: Richard Carlyle).

Scopes, John Thomas (1900-1970; U.S. teacher who was tried and convicted in 1925 of violating Tennessee's archaic Butler Act by teaching Darwin's proscribed theory of evolution): Alleged, 2010 (Jamie Kolacki); **Inherit the Wind**, 1960 (role model for Dick York); TV Reader's Digest, 1955-1956 (TV series; "The Sad Death of a Hero," 1955 episode: William Phipps).

Scott, Robert Falcon (1868-1912; British explorer who died while exploring the South Pole): Regal Cavalcade, 1935 (Frank Vosper); **Scott of the Antarctic**, 1949 (John Mills).

Scott, Winfield (1786-1866; U.S. military officer and Union general): **Abraham Lincoln**, 1930 (James Bradbury Sr.); Fields of Freedom, 2006 (Kurt Rhodes); **Gettysburg**, 1993 (Brian Mallon); **Gods and Generals**, 2003 (Brian Mallon); The Heart of Maryland, 1927 (S.D. Wilcox); Kansas Pacific, 1953 (Roy Gordon); Lincoln, 1974- (TV miniseries; "The Unwilling Warrior," 1975 episode: Robert Emhardt); Lincoln, 1988 (TV miniseries; John Houseman); Lincoln, 1992 (made-for-TV; Burgess Meredith); Lost River: Lincoln's Secret Weapon, 2009 (Wayne Strickler); North and South, Book II, 1986 (TV miniseries; Lee Anthony); One Man's Hero, 1999 (Patrick Bergin); Riverboat, 1959-1961 (TV series; "The Quota," 1960 episode: Stuart Randall); Sunday Showcase, 1959-1961 (TV series; "An American Heritage: Gentleman's Decision," 1961 episode: Robert Emhardt); **They Died with Their Boots On**, 1942 (Sydney Greenstreet); To Appomattox, 2015- (TV miniseries; Kix Brooks); War of 1812, 1999 (TV miniseries; Nigel Bennett).

Seneca (Seneca the Elder; Lucius or Marcus Annaeus Seneca; 54 B.C.-39 A.D.; Roman writer from a wealthy family): A.D., 1985 (TV miniseries; Fernando Rey); Ancient Rome: The Rise and Fall of an Empire, 2006 (TV series; Hugh Dixon); Fire over Rome, 1965 (Mario Feliciano); Imperium: Nero, 2004 (made-for-TV; Matthias Habich); Nero and the Burning of Rome, 1954 (Lamberto Picasso); Nero's Mistress, 1962 (Vittorio De Sica); Nerone, 1977 (Oreste Lionello); Peter and Paul, 1981 (made-for-TV; Valentine Dyall); Poppeas kroning, 1978 (made-for-TV; Arne Tyren); **Quo Vadis**, 1951 (Nicholas Hannen).

Serra, Junipero (1713-1784; Roman Catholic Spanish priest of the Franciscan Order who founded many missions in California): Cavalcade of America, 1952-1957 (TV series; "Gentle Conqueror," 1954 episode: Wilton Graff); **Seven Cities of Gold**, 1955 (Michael Rennie); Serra: Ever Forward, Never Back, 2013- (TV miniseries; Julio Mora).

Seti I (1294-1274 B.C.; father of Ramesses II; Pharoah of the New Kingdom Nineteenth Dynast of Egypt): **Exodus: Gods and Kings**, 2014 (John Turturro); Moon of Israel, 1924 (Adelqui Migliar); **The Prince of Egypt**, 1998 (Patrick Stewart); **The Ten Commandments**, 1956 (Cedric Hardwicke); The Ten Commandments, 2007 (Scott McNeil voiceover); The Ten Commandments: The Musical, 2006 (Aharon Impale).

Seurat, Georges Pierre (1859-1891; French artist): **Lust for Life**, 1952

(David Bond).

Sevigne, Marquise (Marie de Rabutin-Chantal; 1626-1696; French aristocrat and woman of letters): If Paris Were Told to Us, 1956 (Gisele Grandpre); Royal Affairs in Versailles, 1957 (Jeanne Boitel).

Seward, Frederick William (1830-1915; U.S. politician, son of William Henry Seward and U.S. Assistant Secretary of State): **The Conspirator**, 2011 (Brian Duffy); The Day Lincoln Was Shot, 1998 (made-for-TV; Jeremy Sisto).

Seward, William Henry (1801-1872; U.S. politician and 24th U.S. Secretary of State under President Abraham Lincoln and President Andrew Johnson; survived assassination attempt at the time Lincoln was killed): The Adams Chronicles, 1976 (TV miniseries; Alexander Clark); Bad Blood: The Border War That Triggered the Civil War, 2007 (made-for-TV; Steve Butler); The Blue and the Gray, 1982 (TV miniseries; John Vernon); Branded, 1965-1966 (TV series; "Seward's Folly," 1965 episode: Ian Wolfe); **The Conspirator**, 2011 (Glenn R. Wilder); The Day Lincoln Was Shot, 1998 (made-for-TV; John Pleshette); The Dramatic Life of Abraham Lincoln, 1924 (Willis Marks); In the Days of Buffalo Bill, 1922 (Charles Colby); The Joseph Cotten Show: On Trial, 1956-1959 (TV series; "The Freeman Case," 1957 episode: Joseph Cotten); Lincoln, 1974- (TV miniseries; "The Unwilling Warrior," 1975 episode: Lloyd Nolan; "Crossing Fox River," 1976 episode: Whit Bissell); Lincoln, 1988 (TV miniseries; Richard Mulligan); **Lincoln**, 2012 (David Strathairn); Lost River: Lincoln's Secret Weapon, 2009 (Owen McKinley); Maximilian von Mexiko, 1970 (made-for-TV; Herbert Steinmetz); North and South, Book II, 1986 (TV miniseries; William Mims); **The Plainsman**, 1936 (Charles Herzinger); **Saving Lincoln**, 2013 (Bruce Davison); Screen Directors Playhouse, 1955-1956 (TV series; "Lincoln's Doctor's Dog," 1955 episode: Howard Wendell); You Are There, 1953-1971 (TV series; "The Emancipation Proclamation [January 1, 1863]," 1955 episode: Howard Wendell).

Seymour, Jane (1508-1537; Queen of England; third wife of Henry VIII): Anna Bolena, 1984 (made-for-TV; Judith Forst); Anna Bolena, 2011 (made-for-TV; Elina Garanca); Anna Boleyn, 1920 (Aud Egede-Nissen); BBC Sunday-Night Theatre, 1950-1959 (TV series; "The White Falcon," 1956 episode: Jennifer Browne); Heinrich VIII. und seine Frauen, 1968 (made-for-TV; Karin Anselm); Henry and Anne: The Lovers Who Changed History, 2014- (TV miniseries; Fleur Keith); Henry VIII, 2003 (made-for-TV; Emelia Fox); Henry VIII and His Six Wives, 1972 (Jane Asher); Monarch, 2000 (Jean Marsh); The Other Boleyn Girl, 2003 (made-for-TV; Naomi Benson); The Other Boleyn Girl, 2008 (Corinne Galloway); **The Pearls of the Crown**, 1938 (Jacqueline Pacaud); **The Prince and the Pauper**, 1937 (Joan Valerie); **The Private Life of Henry VIII**, 1933 (Wendy Barrie); The Six Wives of Henry VIII, 1970 (TV miniseries; Anne Stallybrass); The Six Wives of Henry VIII, 2001 (TV miniseries; Charlotte Roach); The Tudors, 2007-2010 (TV series; Anita Briem); Wolf Hall, 2015 (TV miniseries; Kate Phillips).

Seymour, Thomas (1508-1549; British nobleman whose sister Jane married Henry VIII and became Queen of England): Elizabeth R, 1971-1972 (TV miniseries; "The Lion's Club," 1971 episode: John Ronane); Henry VIII, 2003 (made-for-TV; William Houston); Henry VIII and His Six Wives, 1972 (Peter Clay); Nine Days a Queen, 1936 (Leslie Perrins); The Prince and the Pauper, 1996 (TV series; six episodes: Rupert Frazer); The Six Wives of Henry VIII, 1970 (TV miniseries; John Ronane); The Six Wives of Henry VIII, 2001 (TV miniseries; Richard Felix); The Tudors, 2007-2010 (TV series; Andrew McNair); **Young Bess**, 1953 (Stewart Granger).

Seyss-Inquart, Arthur (1892-1946; Austrian-born Nazi who served under

Gwyneth Paltrow and Ralph Fiennes (as William Shakespeare) in *Shakespeare in Love,* **1998.**

Adolf Hitler; convicted and hanged as a war criminal): **The Cardinal**, 1963 (Erik Frey).

Sforza, Caterina (1462-1509; Italian noblewoman who married Giovanni de Medici): The Black Duke, 1964 (Gloria Milland); The Borgia, 2006 (Paz Vega); The Borgias, 2011 (TV series; Gina McKee); Caterina Sforza, la leonessa di Romagna, 1959 (Virna Lisi); Giovanni de Medici: The Leader, 1940 (Ethel Maggi).

Shakespeare, William (1564-1615; English businessman and playwright): Blackadder Back & Forth, 1999 (Colin Firth); Elizabeth Rex, 2004 (made-for-TV; Peter Hutt); Immortal Gentleman, 1935 (Bail Gill); **The Lego Movie**, 2014 (Jorma Taccone voiceover); Lives and Deaths of the Poets, 2011 (John Geoffrion); Loves and Adventures in the Life of Shakespere, 1914 (Albert Ward); Master Shakespeare, Strolling Player, 1916 (Lawrence Swinburne); **Shakespeare in Love**, 1998 (Ralph Fiennes); Shakespeares Sonette, 2009 (made-for-TV; Inge Keller); Sir Francis Drake, 1961- (TV series; Philip Guard); The Story of Mankind, 1957 (Reginald Gardiner); Time Flies, 1944 (John Salew); Will Shakespeare, 1978- (TV miniseries; Tim Curry); Witness to Yesterday, 1970- (TV series; "William Shakespeare," 1973 episode: Barry Morse); The Wooing of Anne Hathaway, 1938 (made-for-TV; Clement McCallin); You Are There, 1953-1971 (TV series; "The First Command Performance of Romeo and Juliet [1597]" 1954 episode: Douglass Watson).

Shapiro, Jacob (aka; "Gurrah"; 1899-1947; U.S. gangster and enforcer for U.S. crime syndicate boss Louis "Lepke" Buchalter, who got his nickname through his garbled speech when saying "gurrah" to mean "get out of here"): Lepke, 1975 (Warren Berlinger).

Shaw, George Bernard (1856-1950; Irish playwright, journalist and music and literary critic): Armchair Theatre, 1956-1974 (TV series; "Death of Satan," 1958 episode: Robert Mooney); CBC Summer Theatre, 1955- (TV series; "The Return of Don Juan," 1955 episode: Frank Peddie); Children of the Revolution, 1996 (Ken Radley); H.G. Wells: War of the World, 2006 (made-for-TV: Dermot Crowley). Note: For detailed information on Shaw, see my book *Zanies: The World's Greatest Eccentrics* (New Century Publishers, 1982; illustrated pages 336-338).

Sheba (Queen of Sheba in the Bible): The Cradle of God, 1926 (France Dhelia); The Queen of Sheba, 1921 (Betty Blythe); The Queen of Sheba, 1953 (Leonora Ruffo); The Queen of Sheba Meets the Atom Man, 1963 (Winifred Bryan); Rome '78, 1978 (Anya Phillips); Solomon, 2000 (made-for-TV; Vivica A. Fox); **Solomon and Sheba**, 1959 (Gina Lol-

John Wayne and J. Carroll Naish (as General Philip H. Sheridan) in *Rio Grande*, 1950.

lobrigida); Solomon and Sheba, 1995 (made-for-TV; Halle Berry).

Shelley, Mary Wollstonecraft (1797-1851; British novelist and writer; wife of Percy Shelley): **The Bride of Frankenstein**, 1935 (Elsa Lanchester); The Finest Gift, 1955 (made-for-TV; Mary Scott); Frankenstein: Birth of a Monster, 2003 (made-for-TV; Lucy Davenport); Gothic, 1987 (Natasha Richardson); Haunted Summer, 1988 (Alice Krige); Highlander, 1992-1998 (TV series; "The Modern Prometheus," 1997 episode: Tracy Keating); Roger Corman's Frankenstein Unbound, 1990 (Bridget Fonda); Rowing in the Wind, 1988 (Lizzy McInnerny); Screenplay, 1986-1993 (TV series; "Dead Poets' Society," 1992 episode: Emma Fielding); Shelley, 1972 (made-for-TV; Jenny Agutter).

Shelley, Percy Bysshe (1792-1822; British poet): **The Bride of Frankenstein**, 1935 (Douglas Walton); Frankenstein: Birth of a Monster, 2003 (made-for-TV; Oliver Chris); Gothic, 1987 (Julian Sands); Haunted Summer, 1988 (Eric Stoltz); Highlander, 1992-1998 (TV series; "The Modern Prometheus," 1997 episode: Christopher Staines); The Poetry Hall of Fame, 1993 (made-for-TV; Stephen Lang); Roger Corman's Frankenstein Unbound, 1990 (Michael Hutchence); The Romantics, 2011 (TV miniseries; "Eternity," 2011 episode: Blake Ritson); Rowing in the Wind, 1988 (Valentine Pelka); Screenplay, 1986-1993 (TV series; "Dead Poets' Society," 1992 episode: Alan Cumming); Shelley, 1972 (made-for-TV; Robert Powell).

Shepherd, Lemuel Cornick, Jr. (1896-1990; U.S. solider; four-star general of the USMC, who fought in WWI, WWII and the Korean War; 20th commandant of the Marine Corps): **MacArthur**, 1977 (Warde Donovan).

Sheppard, Jack (1702-1724; British thief and highwayman): Georgian Underworld, 2003- (TV series; "Invitation to a Hanging," 2003 episode: Marcus McNicoll); ITV Playhouse, 1967- (TV series; two 1968 episodes: Paul Shelley); Jack Sheppard, 1923 (Will West); Where's Jack?, 1969 (Tommy Steele).

Sheridan, Philip H. (1831-1888; U.S. soldier and Union general during American Civil War and thereafter): **Abraham Lincoln**, 1930 (Frank Campeau); Bat Masterson, 1958-1961 (TV series; "One Bullet from Broken Bow," 1959 episode: Charles Maxwell); Branded, 1965-1966 (TV series; John Pickard in three 1966 episodes; Andrew J. Fenady in one 1966 episode); Cheyenne, 1955-1963 (TV series; "Gold, Glory and Custer—Requiem," 1960 episode: Lawrence Dobkin); The Court-Martial of George Armstrong Custer, 1977 (made-for-TV; Nicolas Coster); Custer of the West, 1968 (Lawrence Tierney); Death Valley Days, 1952-

1970 (TV series; "The Grand Duke," 1959 episode: Stafford Repp); Hondo and the Apaches, 1968 (made-for-TV; Gary Merrill); **In Old Chicago**, 1937 (Sidney Blackmer); North and South, Book II, 1986 (TV miniseries; Clu Gulager); The Rebel, 1959-1961 (TV series; "Johnny Yuma at Appomattox," 1960 episode; Andrew J. Fenady); **Rio Grande**, 1950 (J. Carroll Naish); **Santa Fe Trail**, 1940 (David Bruce); Son of the Morning Star, 1991 (made-for-TV; Dean Stockwell); **They Died with Their Boots On**, 1942 (John Litel); **Union Pacific**, 1939 (Ernie Adams); Tales of Wells Fargo, 1957-1962 (TV series; "The General," 1957 episode: Paul Fix); Wagon Train, 1957-1965 (TV series; "The Danny Benedict Story," 1959 episode: Stacy Keach Sr.); You Are There, 1953-1957 (TV series; "Grant and Lee at Appomattox, 1953 and 1955 episodes: Robert Osterloh).

Sheridan, Richard Brinsley (1751-1816; Irish playwright and poet, owner of the London Theater Royal in Drury Lane): **Young Mr. Pitt**, 1943 (Max Adrian).

Sherman, Forrest P. (1896-1951; U.S. rear admiral [four-star admiral] in the U.S. Navy during WWII): **MacArthur**, 1977 (Harvey Vernon).

Sherman, Roger (1721-1793; U.S. politician and member of the Continental Congress; signer of the Declaration of Independence): A More Perfect Union: America Becomes a Nation, 1989 (H.E.D. Redford); **1776**, 1972 (Rex Robbins).

Sherman, William Tecumseh (1820-1891; U.S. military officer and lieutenantgeneral during the American Civil War): Assault at West Point: The Court-Martial of Johnson Whittaker, 1994 (made-for-TV; Val Avery); Bat Masterson, 1958-1961 (TV series; "General Sherman's March through Dodge City," 1958 episode: John Gallaudet); Branded, 1965-1966 (TV series; "A Destiny Which Made Us Brothers," 1966 episode: George Sawaya); The Civil War, 1990 (TV miniseries; Arthur Miller voiceover); Bury My Heart at Wounded Knee, 2007 (made-for-TV; Colm Feore); Cavalry Scout, 1951 (Eddy Waller); The Crisis, 1916 (Cecil Holland); **Drum Beat**, 1954 (Richard Hale); **The Horse Soldiers**, 1959 (Richard H. Cutting); **How the West Was Won**, 1962 (John Wayne); Into the West, 2005- (TV miniseries; "Hell on Wheels," 2005 episode; Joshua Bryant); Iron Horse, 1966-1968 (TV series; "Welcome for the General," 1967 episode: James Almanzar); The Life and Legend of Wyatt Earp, 1955-1961 (TV series; "When Sherman Marched through Kansas," 1958 episode: Thayer Roberts); North and South, Book II, 1986- (TV miniseries; Arlen Dean Snyder); The Oregon Trail, 1939 (Warner Richmond); Son of the Morning Star, 1991 (made-for-TV; George Dickerson); Sunday Showcase, 1959-1961 (TV series; "An American Heritage: Shadow of a Soldier," 1960 episode: George Ebeling); The Tempest, 1998 (made-for-TV; Tom Nowicki); Wagon Train, 1957-1965 (TV series; "The Colter Craven Story," 1960 episode: John Wayne); You Are There, 1953-1957 (TV series; "The Gettysburg Address," 1953 episode: Ray Walston).

Sherwood, Robert Emmet (1896-1955; U.S. playwright, screenwriter and editor, who also wrote significant speeches for President Franklin D. Roosevelt): Mrs. Parker and the Vicious Circle, 1994 (Nick Cassavetes).

Shomron, Dan (1937-2008; Israeli general and leader of the military unit that rescued the Jewish passengers held hostage at Entebbe Airport in Uganda in 1976): Operation Thunderbolt, 1978 (Arik Lavie); Raid on Entebbe, 1977 (made-for-TV; Charles Bronson); Victory at Entebbe, 1976 (made-for-TV; Harris Yulin).

Short, Elizabeth (aka: The Black Dahlia; 1924-1947; U.S. prostitute who was horrifically murdered in Los Angeles, her death remaining an unsolved homicide): American Horror Story, 2011- (TV series; Mena Suvari); The Black Dahlia, 2006 (Mia Kirshner); The Black Dahlia Haunting, 2012 (Alexis Lacona); Dark Places, 2015 (Michelle Harvey); The Devil's Muse, 2007 (Lisa Small; Lizzie Strain); Hollywood Babylon, 1992-1993 (TV series; "Chaplin & Grey/Black Dahlia," 1993 episode: Allison Bibicoff); Hunter, 1984-1991 (TV series; "The Black Dahlia," 1988 episode: Jessica Nelson); Who Is the Black Dahlia?, 1975 (made-for-TV; Lucie Arnaz). For detailed information on Short, see my two-volume work *The Great Pictorial History of World Crime*, Volume II (History, Inc., 2004; illustrated [7 images] pages 1255-1261).

Short, Walter C. (1880-1949; Walter Campbell Short; American major general commanding military defenses at Pearl Harbor during the Japanese sneak attack of December 7, 1941): **Tora! Tora! Tora!**, 1970 (Jason Robards Jr.).

Shostakovich, Dmitri (1906-1975; Russian composer and pianist): La violon de Rothschild, 1996 (Sergey Makovetsky); Testimony, 1988 (Ben Kingsley).

Sieber, Albert (aka: "Al"; 1843-1907; U.S. prospector; legendary chief of scouts of the U.S. Army during the Apache wars): **Apache**, 1954 (John McIntyre); **Arrowhead**, 1953 (role model for Charlton Heston); **Geronimo: An American Legend**, 1993 (Robert Duvall); Mr. Horn, 1979 (made-for-TV; Richard Widmark); Stories of the Century, 1954- (TV series; "Apache Kid," 1955 episode: Kenneth MacDonald).

Siegel, Benjamin (aka: Bugsy; 1906-1947; U.S. crime syndicate member who developed Las Vegas, Nevada, as a legitimate gambling center): Boardwalk Empire, 2010- (TV series: six episodes: Michael Zegen); **Bugsy**, 1991 (Warren Beatty); **The Damned Don't Cry**, 1950 (role model for Steve Cochran); E! Mysteries and Scandals, 1998- (TV series; "Bugsy Siegel," 1998 episode: Paul Sampson); The Gangster Chronicles, 1981- (TV series; Mitchell S. Benson; Joe Penny); Gangster Wars, 1981 (Joe Penny); The George Raft Story, 1961 (Brad Dexter); **The Godfather**, 1972 (role model for Alex Rocco); Haunted History, 1999- (TV series; "Hollywood," 2000 episode; Richard Cline as the ghost of Bugsy Siegel); Kill Me, Deadly, 2016 (Joe Mantegna); Lansky, 1999 (made-for-TV; Eric Roberts; Anthony Medwetz and Matthew Settle as Siegel as a boy); The Making of the Mob: New York, 2015- (TV miniseries; Jonathan C. Stewart); **The Marrying Man**, 1991 (Armand Assante); Mob City, 2013- (TV series; Edward Burns); Mobsters, 1991 (Richard Grieco); P.S.I. Luv U, 1991- (TV series; "What's Up, Bugsy?," 1991 episode: Greg Evigan); The Revenge of Al Capone, 1989 (made-for-TV; Marc Figueroa); Virginia Hill, 1974 (made-for-TV; Harvey Keitel); The Witness, 1960-1961 (TV series; "Bugsy Siegel," 1960 episode: Larry Blyden); You're So Dead, 2007 (Kyle Derek).

Simon of Cyrene (the man in the crowd along Jesus' route to his crucifixion at Golgatha who was ordered by Roman soldiers to carry Jesus' cross): Barabbas, 1953 (Hans Straat); Family Theatre, 1949-1958 (TV series; "That I May See," 1951 episode: Raymond Burr); **The Greatest Story Ever Told**, 1965 (Sidney Poitier); The Hill, 1959 (made-for-TV; Robert Adams); Jesus, 2000 (Roxanne Coyne); The Jesus Film, 1979 (Moti Boharav); Jesus: The Desire of Ages, 2014 (John Bruno); **The King of Kings**, 1927 (William Boyd); **King of Kings**, 1961 (Rafael Luis Calvo); Kristo, 1996 (Rudy Fernandez); La Passion, 1978 (made-for-TV; Frederic Santaya); Laudes Evangelii, 1961 (made-for-TV; Hans von Kusserow); Maria Magdalena, peccadora de la Magdala, 1946 (Jose Elias Moreno); The Passion, 2008 (TV miniseries; Ben Aissa El Jirari); The Passion of the Christ, 2004 (Jarreth J. Merz); Reina de reinas: La Virgin Maria, 1948 (Jose Elias Moreno); Son of God, 2014 (Idrissa Sisco); The Twice Born Woman, 1921 (George Hugo).

Simon the Zealot (Simon the Canaanite; one of the twelve apostles of Jesus): Color of the Cross, 2006 (Karim Imam); Crown of Thorns, 1923

Warren Beatty (as gangster Benjamin "Bugsy" Siegel) in *Bugsy*, 1991.

(Guido Herzfeld); The Gospel according to Matthew, 1993 (Darryl Fuchs); The Gospel according to St. Matthew, 1966 (Enzo Siciliano); The Gospel of John, 2014 (Dahabi Bouragate); The Gospel of Luke, 2014 (Dahabi Bouragate); The Gospel of Mark, 2014 (Dahabi Bouragate); The Gospel of Matthew, 2014 (Dahabi Bouragate); Great Performances, 1971- (TV series; "Jesus Christ, Superstar," 2001 episode: Tony Vincent); **The Greatest Story Ever Told**, 1965 (Robert Blake); Jesus, 1979 (Milo Rafi); Jesus Christ Superstar, 1972 (made-for-TV; Stevie Wright); **Jesus Christ Superstar**, 1973 (Larry T. Marshall/Larry Marshall); Jesus of Nazareth, 1977 (TV miniseries; Murray Salem); Kristo, 1996 (Daniel Fernando); The Last Supper: Thirteen Men of Courage, 2007 (made-for-TV; Tom Oswald); The Living Christ Series, 1951- (TV series; Michael Whalen); Mary, Mother of the Son of God, 2003 (Regis Di Sori); The Passion, 2008 (TV miniseries; Stuart Kidd); The Power of the Resurrection, 1958 (Vic Tayback).

Simpson, Wallis Warfield (1896-1986; Duchess of Windsor, divorced American woman who married Edward VIII of Great Britain after he renounced his throne to wed her, a commoner): Any Human Heart, 2010- (TV series; Gillian Anderson); Bertie and Elizabeth, 2002 (made-for-TV; Amber Sealey); A Dance to the Music of Time, 1997- (TV series; "The Thirties," 1997 episode: Mary Lincoln); Edward and Mrs. Simpson, 1978- (TV miniseries; Cynthia Harris); **The King's Speech**, 2010 (Eve Best); Passion and Paradise, 1989 (made-for-TV; Linda Griffiths); To Catch a King, 1984 (made-for-TV; Barbara Parkins); The Two Mrs. Grenvilles, 1987 (made-for-TV; Sian Phillips); Upstairs Downstairs, 2010-2012 (TV series; "The Fledgling," 2010 episode: Emma Clifford); W.E., 2011 (Andrea Riseborough); Wallis and Edward, 2005 (made-for-TV; Joely Richardson); The Woman He Loved, 1988 (made-for-TV; Jane Seymour); The Woman I Love, 1972 (made-for-TV; Faye Dunaway).

Sims, William S. (William Snowden Sims; 1858-1936; U.S. admiral who attempted to modernize the U.S. Navy in the early 20th Century): **The Court-Martial of Billy Mitchell**, 1955 (Will Wright).

Sinatra, Frank (1915-1999; U.S. singer, actor and film producer): Not the Nine O'Clock News, 1979-1982 (TV series; one 1982 episode with Philip Pope as Sinatra); The Kennedys, 2011- (TV miniseries; Chris Diamantopoulos); My Way, 2012 (Robert Knepper); The Night We Called It a Day, 2003 (Dennis Hopper); **Pepe**, 1960 (himself); Power and Beauty, 2002 (made-for-TV; John Ralston); The Rat Pack, 1998 (made-for-TV; Ray Liotta; Michael Dees singing voice); Reagan: Let's Finish the Job, 1986- (TV series; Willem Niholt); Reveille with Beverly, 1943 (himself); Sinatra, 1992 (made-for-TV; Philip Casnoff); Stealing

Frank Sinatra (playing himself) in *Till the Clouds Roll By,* **1946.**

Sinatra, 2003 (James Russo); Sugartime, 1995 (made-for-TV; Patrick Jude); Tears of a King, 2007 (Sebastian Anzaldo); **Till the Clouds Roll By**, 1946 (himself); The Tortellis, 1987- (TV series; "Frankie Comes to Dinner," 1987 episode: Alan Hugo).

Sirhan Sirhan (b. 1944; Palestinian assassin who murdered U.S. Senator and presidential candidate Robert F. Kennedy in 1968 and who, at this writing, is serving a life prison sentence): Bobby, 2006 (David Kobsantzev); The End of a Dynasty, 1998 (George N. Thompson). Note: For detailed information on Sirhan Sirhan, see my two-volume work *The Great Pictorial History of World Crime*, Volume I (History, Inc., 2004; illustrated pages 196-198).

Siringo, Charlie Angelo (1955-1928; U.S. lawman and private detective and agent for the Pinkerton Detective Agency, who pursued outlaw members of the Wild Bunch during the late 19th Century and early 20th Century): Bonanza: Under Attack, 1995 (made-for-TV; Dennis Farina); Charlie Siringo, 1976 (made-for-TV; Steve Railsback); Face to Face, 1976 (William Berger); Mrs. Sundance, 1974 (made-for-TV; L.Q. Jones); Siringo, 1995 (made-for-TV; Brad Johnson); Wanted: The Sundance Woman, 1976 (made-for-TV; Steve Forrest). Note: For detailed information on Siringo, see my book *Encyclopedia of Western Lawmen and Outlaws* (Paragon House, 1992; page 284).

Sitting Bull (1831-1890; Hunkpapa Lakota Sioux medicine man): The American West, 2016- (TV series; Mo Brings Plenty); **Annie Get Your Gun**, 1950 (J. Carrol Naish); Annie Get Your Gun, 1957 (made-for-TV; Zachary Charles); Annie Get Your Gun, 1965 (made-for-TV; Benno Hoffmann); Annie Get Your Gun, 1967 (made-for-TV; Harry Bellaver); **Annie Oakley**, 1935 (Chief Thundercloud); Branded, 1965-1966 (TV series; "Call to Glory, Part 3," 1966 episode: Felix Locher); Bronco, 1958-1962 (TV series; "Payroll of the Dead," 1959 episode: Francis McDonald); Buffalo Bill and the Indians, or Sitting Bull's History Lesson, 1976 (Frank Kaquitts); Buffalo Girls, 1995 (made-for-TV; Russell Means); Bury My Heart at Wounded Knee, 2007 (made-for-TV; August Schellenberg); Cheyenne, 1955-1963 (TV series; "The Broken Pledge," 1957 episode: Frank DeKova; "Gold, Glory and Custer—Requiem," 1960 episode: Francis McDonald); Crazy Horse, 1996 (made-for-TV; August Schellenberg); Custer of Big Horn, 1926 (Running Deer); Custer's Last Stand, 1936 (serial; Howling Wolf); Don't Touch the White Woman!, 1974 (Alain Cuny); The Flaming Frontier, 1926 (Noble Johnson); Fort Vengeance, 1953 (Michael Granger); The Gordon Honour, 1955-1956 (TV series; "The Red Indian Candlestick," 1956 episode: Peter Bull); The Great Adventure, 1963-1964 (TV series; "The Death of Sitting Bull," and "The Massacre at Wounded Knee," both

1963 episodes: and both with Anthony Caruso as Sitting Bull); The Great Sioux Massacre, 1965 (Michael Pate); Hands Up!, 1926 (Noble Johnson); In the Days of Buffalo Bill, 1922 (Chief Lightheart); Into the West, 2005 (TV miniseries; Eric Schweig); Kenny Rogers as the Gambler, Part III: The Legend Continues, 1987 (made-for-TV; George American Horse); Laramie, 1959-1963 (TV series; "Man of God," 1959 episode: Frank DeKova); Sitting Bull, 1954 (J. Carrol Naish); Sitting Bull at the Spirit Lake Massacre, 1927 (Chief Yowlachie); Son of the Morning Star, 1991 (made-for-TV; Floyd "Red Crow" Westerman); Tall Tales and Legends, 1985-1988 (TV series; "Annie Oakley," 1985 episode: Nick Ramus); The Time Tunnel, 1966-1967 (TV series; "Massacre," 1966 episode: George Mitchell); Tonka, 1958 (John War Eagle); The Wild West, 2006- (TV miniseries; "Custer's Last Stand," 2007 episode: David Enemy); Witness to Yesterday, 1970- (TV series; "Sitting Bull," 1973 episode: August Schellenberg).

Skorzeny, Otto (1908-1975; German officer who led Nazi commandos in WWII in many daring operations, including the rescuing of Italian dictator Benito Mussolini in September 1943 and infiltrating U.S. lines during the Battle of the Bulge in 1944): **The Eagle Has Landed**, 1977 (himself in archive footage); The Great Battle, 1973 (Florin Piersic); Mussolini: The Untold Story, 1985 (TV miniseries; Wolf Kahler).

Slade, Joseph Albert (aka: Jack; 1831-1864; U.S. Old West stagecoach driver, Pony Express superintendent and gunfighter): Jack Slade, 1953 (Mark Stevens); The Parson and the Outlaw, 1957 (Sonny Tufts); The Pony Express, 1925 (George Bancroft); Stories of the Century, 1955 (TV series; Greg Palmer). Note: For detailed information on Slade, see my book *Encyclopedia of Western Lawmen and Outlaws* (Paragon House, 1992; page 285).

Slaton, John M. (1866-1955; U.S. politician and 60th governor of Georgia): The Murder of Mary Phagan, 1988 (TV mini-series; Jack Lemmon); The People v. Leo Frank, 2009 (Terrence Gibney).

Slayton, Donald Kent (aka: "Deke"; 1924-1993; U.S. astronaut): **Apollo 13**, 1995 (Chris Ellis).

Smith, Alfred E. (Alfred Emanuel Smith Jr.; 1873-1944; U.S. politician and governor of the state of New York): **Beau James**, 1957 (Walter Catlett); **Sunrise at Campobello**, 1960 (Alan Bunce).

Smith, Bessie (aka: "Empress of the Blues"; 1894-1937; U.S. black jazz and blues singer): Bessie, 2015 (made-for-cable TV; Queen Latifah); Mitzi...Roaring the 1920s, 1976 (TV Special; Linda Hopkins).

Smith, Caleb Blood (1808-1864; U.S. journalist and politician; 6th U.S. secretary of the interior under President Abraham Lincoln): Lost River: Lincoln's Secret Weapon, 2009 (Daniel Webster).

Smith, Emma Hale (1804-1879; Emma Hale Smith Bidemon; first wife of Joseph Smith Jr., founder of the Latter Day Saint religious movement, a branch of Mormonism): **Brigham Young: Frontiersman**, 1940 (Claire DuBrey); Eliza and I, 1987 (Linda Bon); Emma Smith: My Story, 2008 (Katherine Nelson); How Rare a Possession: The Book of Mormon, 1987 (Scott Wilkinson); Joseph Smith: Prophet of the Restoration, 2005 (Katherine Thompson); Savage Journey, 1983 (made-for-TV; Kate Hill); The Work and the Glory, 2004 (Sarah Darling); The Work and the Glory III: A House Divided, 2006 (Melanie Hawkins); The Work and the Glory II: American Zion, 2005 (Melanie Hawkins).

Smith, Hyrum (1800-1844; one of the leaders of the Latter Day Saint religious movement, founded by his younger brother, Joseph Smith Jr., and who was murdered with his brother by a lynch mob in Carthage, Illinois, on June 27, 1844): **Brigham Young: Frontiersman**, 1940

(Stanley Andrews); Eliza and I, 1987 (Bob Manning); Emma Smith: My Story, 2008 (Dallyn Bayles); September Dawn, 2007 (Ron Webber); The Work and the Glory, 2004 (Ryan Wood).

Smith, Jess (Jesse W. Smith; 1871-1923; U.S. politician and corrupt member of the Ohio Ring in the administration of President Warren G. Harding; suicide): Boardwalk Empire, 2010- (TV series; six episodes: Ed Jewett).

Smith, John (Captain John Smith; 1580-1631; British explorer): Animated Hero Classics, 1991-2005 (TV series; "Pocahontas," 1994 episode: Jonathan Hogan voiceover); Captain John Smith and Pocahontas, 1953 (Anthony Dexter); First Landing, 2007 (made-for-TV; Josh Adamson); The New World, 2005 (Colin Farrell); **Pocahontas**, 1995 (animated; Mel Gibson voiceover); Pocahontas: The Legend, 1995 (Miles O'Keeffe); Real Housewives of the Magic Kingdom, 2010- (TV series; "Pocahontas," 2014 episode: "Cinderella," 2015 episode; Jonny Loquasto for both); Time Flies, 1944 (Roy Emerton).

Smith, Joseph, Jr. (1805-1844; Founder of the Latter Day Saint religious movement, a branch of Mormonism): Brigham, 1977 (Charles Moll); **Brigham Young: Frontiersman**, 1940 (Vincent Price); Eliza and I, 1987 (Richard Dutcher); Emma Smith: My Story, 2008 (Rick Macy); Joseph Smith: Prophet of the Restoration, 2005 (Rick Macy); Rockwell, 1994 (Scott McMillan); Savage Journey, 1983 (made-for-TV; Charles Moll); September Dawn, 2007 (Dean Cain); The Work and the Glory, 2004 (Jonathan Scarfe); The Work and the Glory III: A House Divided, 2006 (Jonathan Scarfe); The Work and the Glory II: American Zion, 2005 (Jonathan Scarfe).

Smith, Kate (Kathryn Elizabeth "Kate" Smith; 1907-1986; U.S. alto singer on radio, TV and film; celebrated for singing "God Bless America"): **This Is the Army**, 1943 (herself).

Smith, Madeleine Hamilton (1835-1928; Scottish socialite who was accused of murdering her lover in Glasgow in 1857; she was acquitted, but most believed her guilty): In Suspicious Circumstances, 1991- (TV series; "Dearest Pet," 1996 episode; Geraldine O'Rawe); **Madeleine**, 1950 (Ann Todd); Squire Mile of Murder, 1980- (TV series; "A Kiss—A Fond Embrace, Part 2," 1980 espisode: Gerda Stevenson); The World Unseen, 2007 (Grethe Fox). Note: For detailed information on Smith, see my eight-volume work *Encyclopedia of World Crime*, Volume IV (CrimeBooks, Inc., 1990; illustrated pages 2799-2800).

Smith, Margaret Chase (Margaret Madeline Chase Smith; 1897-1995; U.S. politician and U.S. senator [Maine]); Freedom to Speak, 1982 (TV miniseries; Nancy Marchand); Tail Gunner Joe, 1977 (made-for-TV; Patricia Neal).

Smith, Walter Bedell (aka: "Beetle"; 1895-1961; U.S. Army four-star general, later director of CIA and ambassador to the Soviet Union): Ike: The War Years, 1979 (TV miniseries; J. D. Cannon); The Last Days of Patton, 1986 (made-for-TV; Don Fellows); **The Longest Day**, 1962 (Alexander Knox); **Patton**, 1970 (Edward Binns).

Snook, Neta (Neta Snook Southern; 1896-1991; U.S. aviation pioneer and pilot, who was Amelia Earhart's first flying instructor): Amelia Earhart, 1976 (made-for-TV: Susan Oliver).

Socrates (470-399 B.C.; Greek philosopher): Aristophanes: The Gods Are Laughing, 1995 (made-for-TV; Eddie Izzard); Barefoot in Athens, 1966 (Peter Ustinov); Bill & Ted's Excellent Adventure, 1989 (Tony Steedman); The Death of Socrates, 2010 (Xander Berkeley and others); Diner in Purgatory, 1994 (Chris Johnston); Hercules: The Legendary Journeys, 1995-1999 (TV series; "The Apple," 1996 episode: John

Ann Todd (as Madeleine Smith) and Ivan Desny in *Madeleine*, 1950.

Smith); Histeria!, 1998-2000 (animated TV series; one 1999 episode and one 2000 episode with Maurice LaMarche as Socrates in both); Le Socrate, 1969 (Pierre Luzan); Plato's Symposium, 2015 (John Gilbert); Socrates, 1971 (made-for-TV; Jean Sylvere); Trial and Death of Socrates, 1939 (Ermete Zaconni); The War That Never Ends, 1991 (made-for-TV; Don Henderson).

Solomon (Son of David and king of Israel): Absolon, 1986 (made-for-TV; Jorge de Juan); After Six Days, 1920 (Zuppelli); Animated Stories from the Bible, 1987-2005 (TV series; "Solomon," 1995 episode: Jamie Newcomb; Matthew Best as young Solomon); The Cradle of God, 1926 (Marcel Vibert); David, 1997 (made-for-TV; Luke Elliot); Greatest Heroes of the Bible, 1978- (TV series; "The Judgment of Solomon," 1978 episode; Tom Hallick); King David, 1985 (Jason Carter; Nicholas van der Weide as young Solomon); The Kingdom of Solomon, 2010 (Amin Zendegani); The Queen of Sheba, 1921 (Fritz Leiber); The Queen of Sheba, 1953 (Gino Cervi); Solomon, 2000 (made-for-TV; Ben Cross); **Solomon and Sheba**, 1959 (Yul Brynner); Solomon and Sheba, 1995 (made-for-TV; Jimmy Smits); Song of King Solomon, 2011 (Jason Croot); You Are There, 1953-1971 (TV series; "The Plot against King Solomon [965 B.C.]," 1954 episode: Shepperd Strudwick).

Soubirous, Bernadette (1844-1879; French Saint of the Catholic Church who repeatedly saw heavenly visions at Lourdes, France, in 1858, and, at the directions of that "Lady" [Virgin Mary, mother of Jesus], dug a spring, its waters later proving to have miraculous curing powers): Aquella joven de blanco, 1965 (Cristina Galbo); Bernadette, 1989 (Sydney Penny); Bernadette of Lourdes, 1962 (Daniele Ajoret); ITV Television Playhouse, 1955-1967 (TV series; "Test of Truth," 1958 episode: Carol Wolveridge); Je m'appelle Bernadette, 2011 (Katia Miran); La vie merveilleuse de Bernadette, 1929 (Alexandra); L'affaire Lourdes, 1967 (made-for-TV; Marie-Helene Breillat); Le Miracle de Lourdes, 1926 (Pierrette Lugand); Lourdes, 2000 (made-for-TV; Angele Osinsky); **The Song of Bernadette**, 1943 (Jennifer Jones); Westinghouse Desilu Playhouse, 1958-1960 (TV series; "Song of Bernadette," 1958 episode: Pier Angeli).

Sousa, John Philip (1854-1932; U.S. composer and bandleader of patriotic march songs and who was known as the "American March King"): **Stars and Stripes Forever**, 1952 (Clifton Webb).

Spaatz, Carl Andrew (aka: "Tooey"; 1891-1974; U.S. four-star general and chief of staff of the U.S. Army Air Force in WWII): **The Court-Martial of Billy Mitchell**, 1955 (Steve Roberts); Ike: The War Years, 1979 (TV miniseries; Don Fellows).

Charles Bickford and Jennifer Jones (as the sainted Bernadette Soubirous) in *The Song of Bernadette*, 1943.

Spangler, Edmund (1825-1875; U.S. carpenter who worked at Ford's Theater in Washington, D.C., and who was convicted as a member of the 1865 conspiracy to murder President Abraham Lincoln; sent to prison for six years): **The Conspirator**, 2011 (James Kirk Sparks); The Day Lincoln Was Shot, 1998 (made-for-TV; Dan DePaola); The Dramatic Life of Abraham Lincoln, 1924 (Jack Winn); The Lincoln Conspiracy, 1977 (Jerry Fleck).

Spartacus (c. 111-71 B.C.; Thracian slave who became a gladiator and led a widespread insurrection against the Roman Republic in the Third Servile War until his forces were defeated and he was killed): Challenge of the Gladiator, 1965 (Peter Lupus); **Mr. Peabody & Sherman**, 2014 (Walt Dohrn); Up Pompeii!, 1969- (TV series; "Spartacus," 1970 episode: Shaun Curry); S.P.Q.R.: 2000 and a Half Years Ago, 1994 (Pietro Torrisi); Sins of Rome, 1954 (Massimo Girotti); Spartacus, 1913 (Mario Guaita-Ausonia); **Spartacus**, 1960 (Kirk Douglas); Spartacus, 1976 (made-for-TV; Gojko Mitic); Spartacus, 2004 (made-for-TV; Goran Visnjic); Spartacus, 2008 (made-for-TV; Carlos Acosta); Spartacus and the Ten Gladiators, 1964 (Giovanni D. Benedetto); Spartacus: Gods of the Arena, 2011- (TV miniseries; Andy Whitfield); Spartacus: War of the Damned, 2010-2013 (TV series; Liam McIntyre); Voyagers!, 1982-1983 (TV series; "Created Equal," 1982 episode: Dan Pastorini).

Spaulding, William H. (1880-1966; American football player and coach): **Knute Rockne All American**, 1940 (himself).

Speed, James (1812-1887; U.S. lawyer and 27th U.S. Attorney General): The Day Lincoln Was Shot, 1998 (made-for-TV; John Lescault); The Dramatic Life of Abraham Lincoln, 1924 (William von Hardenburg); **Lincoln**, 2012 (Richard Topol).

Speed, Joshua Fry (1814-1882; U.S. merchant and partner in a store with Abraham Lincoln): **Abe Lincoln in Illinois**, 1940 (Minor Watson); Abe Lincoln in Illinois, 1964 (made-for-TV; James Broderick); Abraham Lincoln: Vampire Hunter, 2012 (Jimmi Simpson).

Speer, Albert (1905-1981; German architect and minister of armaments in WWII): The Bunker, 1981 (made-for-TV; Richard Jordan); Downfall, 2004 (Heino Ferch); Ende der Unschuld, 1991 (made-for-TV; Hans Peter Hallwachs); Frozen Flashes, 1967 (Gerd Michael Henneberg); Gandhi to Hitler, 2011 (Nassar Abdulla); Inside the Third Reich, 1982 (made-for-TV; Rutger Hauer); ITV Sunday Night Theatre, 1969- (TV series; "The Death of Adolf Hitler," 1973 episode: Michael Lees); **The Last Ten Days**, 1956 (Erland Erlandsen); The Motorola Television Hour, 1953-1954 (TV series; "The Last Days of Hitler," 1954 episode:

Steven Geray); My Fuhrer, 2007 (Stefan Kurt); Nuremberg, 2000- (TV miniseries; Herbert Knaup); Speer und er, 2005- (TV miniseries; Sebastian Koch); **Valkyrie**, 2008 (Manfred-Anton Algrang); War and Remembrance, 1988- (TV series; Geoffrey Whitehead).

Speidel, Hans (1897-1984; German general in WWII): D-Day 6.6.1944, 2004 (made-for-TV; Tim Bentinck); **The Longest Day**, 1962 (Wolfgang Buttner); Operation Walkure, 1971 (made-for-TV; Gerd Gutbier); War and Remembrance, 1988- (TV series; Reinhard Glemnitz).

Speke, John Hanning (1827-1864; British explorer): **Mountains of the Moon**, 1990 (Iain Glen).

Spellman, Francis Joseph (1889-1967; U.S. Catholic archbishop and cardinal of New York, 1939-1967): Citizen Cohn, 1992 (made-for-TV; Daniel Benzali).

Spencer, John (1st Earl Spencer; British peer and politician; 1734-1783): **The Young Mr. Pitt**, 1943 (Stuart Lindsell).

Spruance, Raymond Ames (U.S. admiral during WWII; 1886-1969): **Pearl Harbor**, 2002 (Madison Mason); **Midway**, 1976 (Glenn Ford); War and Remembrance, 1988 (TV miniseries; G. D. Spradlin).

Stafford, Jo (Jo Elizabeth Stafford; 1917-2008; U.S. traditional pop music singer of many ballads): Girl Crazy, 1943 (herself); Sinatra, 1992 (made-for-TV; Maggie Egan).

Stagg, Amos Alonzo (American athlete and coach in multiple sports; 1862-1965): **Knute Rockne All American**, 1940 (himself).

Stalin, Joseph (1878-1953; Russian Marxist and Soviet dictator): The Airlift, 2005 (Hansjurgen Hurrig); Alexander Parkhomenko, 1942 (Semyon Goldshtab); All My Lenins, 1997 (Eduard Toman); Angelus, 2002 (Jan Bogdol); Archangel, 2005 (made-for-TV; Avtandil Makharadze); Battle of Warsaw 1920, 2011 (Igor Guzun); Bitter Harvest, 2016 (Gary Oliver); British Agent, 1934 (Joseph Mario); Children of the Revolution, 1997 (F. Murray Abraham); Countdown to War, 1989 (made-for-TV; Alex Norton); Dante's Inferno, 2007 (Bill Chott); Days of Love, 2005 (Zachi Noy); Do Not Forget, 2005- (TV series; Mikhail Polyakov); Eisenstein, 2002 (Bernard Hill); The Empty Mirror, 1999 (himself in archive footage); Ernst Thalmann—Sohn seiner Klasse, 1954 (Gerd Jaeger); F.D.R.: The Last Year, 1980 (made-for-TV; Nehemiah Persoff); The Fall of Berlin, 1950 (Mikheil Gelovani); The First Circle, 1992 (made-for-TV; F. Murray Abraham); The First Circle, 2006- (TV series; Igor Kvasha); The First Front, 1949 (Aleksei Dikij); The Forgotten King, 2013 (Kartlos Maradishvili); Fortress on the Volga, 1942 (Mikheil Gelovani); The Girl in the Kremlin, 1957 (Maurice Manson); The Great Battle, 1973 (Bukhuti Zaqariadze); H.G. Wells: War of the World, 2006 (made-for-TV: Roger Heathcott); Hiroshima, 1995 (made-for-TV; Serge Christianssens); The Inner Circle, 1991 (Aleksandr Zbruev); Into the Storm, 2009 (made-for-TV; Aleksey Petrenko); Lenin in 1918, 1939 (Mikheil Gelovani); Lenin in October, 1937 (Semyon Goldshtab); Lucky Stalin, 2001 (Chris McCawley); The Man with the Gun, 1939 (Mikheil Gelovani); **Mission to Moscow**, 1943 (Manart Kippen); Mr. Potts Goes to Moscow, 1953 (Stanislaus Zienciakiewicz); New Horizons, 1939 (Mikheil Gelovani); **Nicholas and Alexandra**, 1971 (James Hazeldine); **The 100-Year-Old Man Who Climbed Out of the Window and Disappeared**, 2014 (Algirdas Paulavicius); An Ordinary Execution, 2010 (Andre Dussollier); Playhouse 90, 1956-1961 (TV series; "The Plot to Kill Stalin," 1958 episode: Melvyn Douglas); Red Monarch, 1983 (made-for-TV; Colin Blakely); Reilly: Ace of Spies, 1983- (TV miniseries; David Burke); Screen Two, 1985-2002 (TV series; "The Kremlin, Farewell,' 1990 episode; Bernard Kay); Song of Russia, 1944 (Michael Visaroff); Stalin, 1992 (made-for-TV; Robert Duvall); Staline est morte, 1981 (made-for-TV; Jean Martinelli); Stalingrad, 1990 (Archil Gomiashvili); Stalin's Psychiatrist, 2010 (Mike J. Politis); Superman: Red Son, 2009- (TV series; Jim Meskimen); Testimony, 1988 (Terence Rigby); Thank You, Comrades, 1978 (made-for-TV; Charles Keating); They Wanted Peace, 1940 (Mikheil Gelovani); Thirty-Minute Theatre, 1965-1973 (TV series; "These Men Are Dangerous: Stalin," 1969 episode: Brian Cox); Timewatch, 1982- (TV series; "Who Killed Stalin?," 2005 episode: Jerzy Gralek); Truman at Potsdam, 1976 (made-for-TV; Jose Ferrer); V dni oktyabrya, 1958 (A. Kobaladz); The Victors and the Vanquished, 1950 (Aleksei Dikij); The Vow, 1947 (Mikheil Gelovani); War and Remembrance, 1988 (TV miniseries; Al Ruscio); Why Russians Are Revolting, 1970 (Saul Katz); The Winds of War, 1983- (TV miniseries; "Into the Maelstrom," 1983 episode: Anatoly Chaguinian); Wings of Victory, 1941 (Mikheil Gelovani); World War II: When Lions Roared, 1994 (made-for-TV; Michael Caine); Yalta, 1984 (made-for-TV; Danilo Bata Stojkovic).

Standish, Myles (1584-1656; British military officer and member of the passengers on the historic 1620 voyage of the Mayflower to Plymouth; military adviser to the Plymouth colony): The Courtship of Myles Standish, 1923 (E. Alyn Warren); Mayflower: The Pilgrims' Adventure, 1979 (made-for-TV; David Dukes); **Plymouth Adventure**, 1952 (Noel Drayton); TV Reader's Digest, 1955-1956 (TV series; "The Voyage of Captain Tom Jones, Pirate," 1956 episode: John Bryant).

Stanley, Henry Morton (1841-1904; Welsh journalist and explorer noted for his search for African missionary Dr. David Livingstone, as well as his search for the source of the Nile River): David Livingstone, 1936 (Hugh McDermott); The Explorer, 1955- (TV miniseries; Michael Aldridge); Forbidden Territory: Stanley's Search for Livingstone, 1997 (made-for-TV; Aidan Quinn); Livingstone, 1925 (Henry Walton); The Search for the Nile, 1971- (TV miniseries; two 1971 episodes with Keith Buckley as Stanley); **Stanley and Livingstone**, 1939 (Spencer Tracy); With Stanley in Africa, 1922 (George Walsh); You Are There, 1953-1971 (TV series; "When Stanley Finds Livingstone [November 10, 1871]," 1956 episode; John Craven).

Stanton, Edwin M. (1814-1869; U.S. politician and 27th U.S. secretary of war under President Abraham Lincoln and President Andrew Johnson; a radical "Black Republican" who sought to exact vengeance on the South following the American Civil War; removed from office and brought about unsuccessful impeachment proceedings against Johnson; thought by some to have taken part in the conspiracy to assassinate Abraham Lincoln): **Abraham Lincoln**, 1930 (Oscar Apfel); The Blue and the Gray, 1982 (TV miniseries; John Rolloff); **The Conspirator**, 2011 (Kevin Kline); The Day Lincoln Was Shot, 1998 (made-for-TV; Eddie Jones); Der Tod des Prasidenten, 1967 (Adolf Roland); Ford Star Jubilee, 1955-1956 (TV series; "The Day Lincoln Was Shot," 1956 episode: Raymond Bailey); The Gun That Won the West, 1955 (Richard H. Cutting); In the Days of Buffalo Bill, 1922 (William De Vaull); Ironclads, 1991 (made-for-TV; Burt Edwards); Lincoln, 1974-1975 (TV series; Bert Freed); Lincoln, 1988 (made-for-TV; Jon DeVries); **Lincoln**, 2012 (Bruce McGill); Lincoln: American Mastermind, 2009 (made-for-TV; Scott Zeiss); The Lincoln Conspiracy, 1977 (Robert Middleton); Lost River: Lincoln's Secret Weapon, 2009 (Allen Moorehead); The Ordeal of Dr. Mudd, 1980 (made-for-TV; Richard Dysart); **The Plainsman**, 1936 (Edwin Maxwell); **Saving Lincoln**, 2013 (Robert Craighead); Screen Directors Playhouse, 1955-1956 (TV series; "Lincoln's Doctor's Dog," 1955 episode; Willis Bouchey); They've Killed President Lincoln!, 1971 (made-for-TV; Robert Prosky); Touched by an Angel, 1994-2003 (TV series; "Beautiful Dreamer," 1998 episode: Jesse Bennett); You Are There, 1953-1957 (TV series; "The Capture of John Wilkes Booth," 1953 episode: Lawrence Dobkin).

Stanton, Elizabeth Cady (1815-1902; U.S. social reformer and aboli-

Clifton Webb, right (as John Philip Sousa), in *Stars and Stripes Forever,* 1952.

tionist): The American Woman: Portraits of Courage, 1976 (made-for-TV; Celeste Holm); Under This Sky, 1979 (Irene Worth).

Stark, Harold R. (Harold Rainsford Stark; 1880-1972; U.S. admiral; chief of Naval Operations at the time of the sneak attack against Pearl Harbor, December 7, 1941): **Tora! Tora! Tora!**, 1970 (Edward Andrews).

Starr, Belle (1848-1889; U.S. horse thief and prostitute): Any Last Words?, 2012 (Vaughn Taylor); **Bad Man's Territory**, 1946 (Isabel Jewell); **Belle Starr**, 1941 (Gene Tierney); Belle Starr, 1980 (made-for-TV; Elizabeth Montgomery); Belle Starr's Daughter, 1948 (Isabel Jewell); Bronco, 1958-1962 (TV series; "Shadow of Jesse James," 1960 episode: Jeanne Cooper); Court-Martial, 1928 (Betty Compson); Death Valley Days, 1952-1970 (TV series; "A Bullet for the D.A.," 1961 episode: Carole Mathews); Dr. Quinn, Medicine Woman, 1993-1998 (TV series; "Baby Outlaws," 1995 episode: Melissa Clayton); The Ghost Busters, 1975- (TV series; "They Went Thataway," 1975 episode: Brooke Tucker); Heart of Arizona, 1938 (Natalie Moorhead); **The Long Riders**, 1980 (Pamela Reed, who portrays her most accurately); Maverick, 1957-1962 (TV series; "Full House," 1959 episode; Jean Willes); Montana Belle, 1952 (Jane Russell); **The Outlaws is Coming!**, 1965 (Sally Starr); Robin Hood of the Pecos, 1941 (Sally Payne); The Rough Riders, 1958-1959 (TV series; "Double Cross," 1959 episode; Jean Willes); Schlitz Playhouse, 1951-1959 (TV series; "Way of the West," 1958 episode: Abby Dalton); Stories of the Century, 1954- (TV series; "Belle Starr," 1954 episode: Marie Windsor); Tales of Wells Fargo, 1957-1962 (TV series; "Belle Starr," 1957 episode: Jeanne Cooper); **Young Jesse James**, 1960 (Merry Anders); Zachariah, 1971 (Pat [Patricia] Quinn). Note: For detailed information on Belle Starr, see my book *Encyclopedia of Western Lawmen and Outlaws* (Paragon House, 1992; page 291).

Starr, Sam (Cherokee Indian and outlaw, prominent in 1870s; husband of Belle Starr): **Belle Starr**, 1941 (Randolph Scott); **The Long Riders**, 1980 (James Remar); Robin Hood of the Pecos, 1941 (Eddie Acuff); Stories of the Century, 1954- (TV series; "Belle Starr," 1954 episode: Ric Roman); The Traitor Within, 1942 (Don "Red" Barry).

Stauffenberg, Claus von (Claus Schenk Graf von Stauffenberg; 1907-1944; German officer who led 1944 assassination attempt on the life of Adolf Hitler): Claus Graf Stauffenberg, 1970 (made-for-TV; Horst Naumann); Die Stunde der Offiziere, 2004 (made-for-TV; Harald Schrott); **The Desert Fox: The Story of Rommel**, 1951 (Eduard Franz); Fliegen und Sturzen: Portrat der Melitta Schiller-Stauffenberg, 1974 (made-for-

Noel Drayton (left, holding gun, as Myles Standish) in *Plymouth Adventure,* **1952.**

TV; Wolfgang Arps); The Great Battle, 1973 (Alfred Struwe); Hitler, 1962 (William Sargent); I Spy, 1955-1957 (TV series; "Canaris Story": Michael Ingram); It Happened on July 20th, 1955 (Bernhard Wicki); **The Night of the Generals**, 1967 (Gerard Buhr); Ohne Kampf kein Sieg, 1966 (TV miniseries; Alfred Struwe); Operation Valkyrie, 2004 (made-for-TV; Sebastian Koch); Operation Walkure, 1971 (made-for-TV; Joachim Hansen; Jean Berger in French version); The Plot to Assassinate Hitler, 1955 (Wolfgang Preiss); The Plot to Kill Hitler, 1990 (made-for-TV; Brad Davis); **Valkyrie**, 2008 (Tom Cruise); War and Remembrance, 1988 (TV miniseries; Sky du Mont); The Wednesday Play, 1964-1970 (TV series; "The July Plot," 1964 episode: John Carson). Note: For detailed information on Stauffenberg and the 1944 assassination attempt against Hitler, see my two-volume work *The Great Pictorial History of World Crime*, Volume I (History, Inc., 2004; illustrated [20 images] pages 138-148).

Stauffenberg, Melitta von (Melitta Schiller; 1903-1945; German female test pilot for the Luftwaffe before and during WWII; sister-in-law of Claus von Stauffenberg; shot down and killed by an Allied plane on April 8, 1945): Fliegen und Sturzen: Portrat der Melitta Schiller-Stauffenberg, 1974 (made-for-TV; Cordula Trantow).

Stauffenberg, Nina (1913-2006; German wife of Claus von Stauffenberg, the German officer who led the 1944 plot to kill Adolf Hitler): Claus Graf Stauffenberg, 1970 (made-for-TV; Christine Buchegger); Operation Valkyrie, 2004 (made-for-TV; Nina Kunzendorf); The Plot to Kill Hitler, 1990 (made-for-TV; Madolyn Smith Osborne); **Valkyrie**, 2008 (Carice van Houten).

Stavisky, Serge Alexander (1886-1934; French entrepreneur and colossal swindler, chiefly of government bonds; found fatally shot in the head, which was ruled a suicide, but he was most probably murdered): Jean Galmot, aventurier, 1990 (Benoit Regent); C'est arrive a Paris, 1977 (made-for-TV; Henri-Jacques Huet); L'affare Stavisky, 1979 (TV miniseries; Pietro Biondi); **Stavisky**, 1974 (Jean-Paul Belmondo); Stavisky, l'escroc du siècle, 2015 (made-for-TV; Tomer Sisley). For detailed information on Stavisky, see my two-volume work *The Great Pictorial History of World Crime*, Volume I (History, Inc., 2004; illustrated pages 446-449).

Stein, Gertrude (U.S. writer in France; 1874-1946): The Adventures of Picasso, 1980 (Bernard Cribbins); American Playhouse, 1981- (TV series; "Waiting for the Moon," 1987 episode: Linda Bassett); Gertrude Stein, 1996 (made-for-TV; Margaretha Krook); Gertrude Stein and a Companion!, 1987 (Jan Miner); Hemingway, 1988 (TV miniseries; Re-

becca Potok); La banda Picasso, 2012 (Cristina Toma); The Legendary Life of Ernest Hemingway, 1989 (Annie Girardot); Lives and Deaths of the Poets, 2011 (Jean Burgess); **Midnight in Paris**, 2011 (Kathy Bates); The Moderns, 1988 (Elsa Raven); Modigliani, 2004 (Miriam Margolyes); Rest in Pieces, 1987 (Patty Shepard); The Young Indiana Jones Chronicles, 1992-1993 (TV series; "Paris, September 1908," 1993 episode: Ivana Prchalova). Note: For detailed information on Stein, see my book *Zanies: The World's Greatest Eccentrics* (New Century Publishers, 1982; illustrated pages 342-343).

Stein, Leo (U.S. art collector and critic, brother of Gertrude Stein, in France; 1872-1947): **Midnight in Paris**, 2011 (Laurent Claret).

Steinmark, Freddie Joe (1949-1971; U.S. college football player for University of Texas, Austin): **My All American**, 2015 (Finn Wittrock).

Stephen (Saint in New Testament; first Catholic martyr, who was stoned to death): A.D., 1985 (TV miniseries; Vincent Riotta); The Final Inquiry, 2006 (Ciro Esposito).

Stephens, Alexander (1812-1883; U.S. politician and 1st vice president of the Confederate States of America): **Lincoln**, 2012 (Jackie Earle Haley).

Stephenson, Sir William Samuel (1897-1989; Canadian businessman and spymaster during WWII): Goldeneye, 1989 (made-for-TV; Ed Devereaux); A Man Called Intrepid, 1979 (TV miniseries; David Niven).

Stern, Bill (American sports broadcaster; 1907-1971): **The Pride of the Yankees**, 1942 (himself).

Sternberg, Josef von (Jonas Sternberg; German film director who flourished in Hollywood during the early 1930s): Marlene, 2000 (Hans Werner Meyer).

Steuben, Friedrich Wilhelm von (aka: Baron von Steuben; 1730-1794; Prussian-born military officer serving under George Washington during the American Revolutionary War, 1775-1783; inspector general and major general in the Continental Army, instructing that army in drills, tactics and disciplines): George Washington, 1984 (TV miniseries; Kurt Knudson); The Hammer and the Sword, 1955 (made-for-TV; Joseph Schildkraut); The Rebels, 1979 (made-for-TV; Nehemiah Persoff).

Stevens, Thaddeus (1792-1868; U.S. politician and radical Republican; U.S. congressman from Pennsylvania): **Lincoln**, 2012 (Tommy Lee Jones); The Lincoln Conspiracy, 1977 (E. J. Andre); North and South, Book II, 1986 (TV miniseries; Lou Felder); **Tennessee Johnson**, 1942 (Lionel Barrymore).

Stilwell, Frank C. (c. 1857-1882; U.S. cowboy and outlaw, reportedly involved in the murder of lawman Morgan Earp on March 18, 1882, and who was killed by lawman Wyatt Earp in a Tuscon, Arizona, train yard on March 20, 1882, by lawman Wyatt Earp, who admitted that he lethally shot Stilwell at close range with a shotgun): **The Apple Dumpling Gang**, 1975 (Slim Pickens); Buffalo Bill, Jr., 1955-1956 (TV series; "First Posse," 1955 episode: Lane Bradford); **Hour of the Gun**, 1967 (Robert Phillips); I Married Wyatt Earp, 1983 (made-for-TV; Earl W. Smith); **Tombstone**, 1993 (Tomas Arana); The Wild West, 2006-2007 (TV miniseries; "The Gunfight at the O.K. Corral," 2007 episode: Shane Dean); **Wyatt Earp**, 1994 (John Dennis Johnston). Note: For detailed information on Stilwell, see my book *Encyclopedia of Western Lawmen and Outlaws* (Paragon House, 1992; page 293).

Stimson, Henry L. (Henry Lewis Stimson; 1867-1950; U.S. politician and statesman, 46th U.S. secretary of state and U.S. secretary of war

1911-1913; 1940-1945): The Beginning or the End, 1947 (Erville Alderson); Day One, 1989 (made-for-TV; Bernard Hughes); Enola Gay: The Men, the Mission, the Atomic Bomb, 1980 (made-for-TV; Henry Wilcoxon); **Fat Man and Little Boy**, 1989 (Walter Sullivan); **Tora! Tora! Tora!**, 1970 (Joseph Cotten); Truman, 1995 (made-for-TV; Richard Dysart).

Stolypin, Peter (1862-1911; Russian prime minister): Fall of Eagles, 1974 (TV miniseries; Frank Middlemass); **Nicholas and Alexandra**, 1971 (Eric Porter); Rasputin, 1996 (made for TV; John Wood).

Stone, Harlan Fiske (American attorney, 52nd U.S. attorney general, 12th chief justice of the U.S. Supreme Court; 1872-1946): **J. Edgar**, 2011 (Ken Howard); J. Edgar Hoover, 1987 (made-for-TV; Ford Rainey); **The Private Files of J. Edgar Hoover**, 1977 (Lloyd Nolan).

Strasser, Gregor (1892-1934; German politician and Nazi leader; murdered on Hitler's orders): Das Attentat—Schleicher: General der letzten Stunde, 1967 (made-for-TV; Gustl Bayrhammer); Die Machtergreifung, 2012 (made-for-TV; Alexander Goebel); Hitler, 1962 (John Banner); **The Hitler Gang**, 1944 (Fritz Kortner); Hitler: The Rise of Evil, 2003 (made-for-TV; Wolfgang Muller); Uncle Adolf, 2005 (made-for-TV; Robert Pugh).

Strauss, Johann II (aka: The Waltz King; 1825-1899; Austrian composer): Champagne Waltz, 1937 (Stanley Price); Dancing Vienna, 1929 (Andreas Van Horn); The Eternal Waltz, 1959 (Bernhard Wicki); **The Great Waltz**, 1938 (Fernand Gravey); The Great Waltz, 1955 (made-for-TV; Keith Andes); The Great Waltz, 1972 (Horst Buchholz); Johann Strauss: The King without a Crown, 1987 (Oliver Tobias); Rosen aud dem Suden, 1934 (Paul Horbiger); The Strauss Dynasty, 1991- (TV miniseries; Stephen McGann); The Strauss Family, 1972 (TV miniseries; Stuart Wilson); Strauss: The King of 3/4 Time, 1995 (made-for-TV; Michael Riley); Strauss: The Waltz King, 2005 (made-for-TV; Joseph Edwards); Strauss' Great Waltz, 1934 (Esmond Knight); Vienna Waltzes, 1951 (Anton Walbrook); Walt Disney's Wonderful World of Color, 1954-1992 (TV series; "The Waltz King," 1963 episode: Kerwin Mathews).

Strauss, Richard (1864-1949; German composer): Bride of the Wind, 2001 (Hans Steunzer); Das haut den starksten Zwilling um, 1971 (Ralf Wolter); Omnibus, 1967-2003 (TV series; "Dance of the Seven Veils," 1970 episode: Christopher Gable).

Streicher, Julius (1885-1946; German publisher; ardent Nazi and virulent anti-Semitic; executed as a war criminal): Hitler, 1962 (Theodore Marcuse); **The Hitler Gang**, 1944 (Alexander Granach); Nuremberg, 2000- (TV miniseries; Sam Stone).

Strickling, Howard (1896-1982; U.S. publicist and head of the publicity department of MGM Studio from the late 1920s to the early 1950s): Malice in Wonderland, 1985 (made-for-TV; Mark L. Taylor).

Stride, Elizabeth (1843-1888; British prostitute and victim of Jack the Ripper): From Hell, 2001 (Susan Lynch); Jack the Ripper, 1988 (Angela Crow); Love Lies Bleeding, 1999 (Alice Bendova); **Murder by Decree**, 1979 (Iris Fry); The Outer Limits, 1995-2002 (TV series; "Ripper," 1999 episode: Marnie Alton); **A Study in Terror**, 1966 (Norma Foster). For detailed information on this and the other Ripper murders, see my two-volume work *The Great Pictorial History of World Crime*, Volume II (History Inc., 2004; illustrated pages 1180-1203).

Strindberg, August (1849-1912; Swedish playwright, novelist and painter): Oviri, 1986 (Max von Sydow).

Eduard Franz (as Claus von Stauffenberg) in *The Desert Fox: The Story of Rommel*, 1951.

Strolin, Karl (1890-1963; German politician who plotted the assassination of Adolf Hitler): **The Desert Fox**, 1951 (Cedric Hardwicke);

Strong, George Templeton (1820-1875; U.S. attorney and diarist of the American Civil War from the Union perspective): The Civil War, 1990 (TV miniseries; George Plimpton voiceover).

Stroud, Robert Franklin (1890-1963; U.S. convicted murderer and ornithologist): **Birdman of Alcatraz**, 1962 (Burt Lancaster).

Stuart, Charles Edward (Bonnie Prince Charlie; 1720-1788; Pretender to the British throne): The Battle of Culloden, 1968 (made-for-TV; Olivier Espitalier-Noel); Bonnie Prince Charlie, 1923 (Ivor Novello); **Bonnie Prince Charlie**, 1948 (David Niven); Children in His Shadow, 2008 (Daniel Felgner); North Wind, 1950 (made-for-TV; Richard Bebb); Redgauntlet, 1959- (TV series; Brown Derby); Scotland's Story, 1984- (TV series; "The '45 and the Aftermath," 1984 episode: Ian Charleson).

Stuart, Henry (Lord Darnley; 1st Duke of Albany; 1545-1567; husband of Mary, Queen of Scots, who was mysteriously murdered): Gunpowder, Treason & Plot, 2004 (made-for-TV; Paul Nicholls); The Heart of the Queen, 1940 (Axel von Ambesser); Maria Stuart, Teil 1 und 2, 1927 (Walter Janssen); **Mary of Scotland**, 1936 (Douglas Walton); **The Pearls of the Crown**, 1938 (Derrick de Marney).

Stuart, John Ewell Brown (aka: "Jeb"; 1833-1864; lieutenant general in the confederate army of Northern Virginia, and head of Lee's cavalry during the American Civil War; killed at Yellow Tavern): **Gods and Generals**, 2003 (Joseph Fuqua); Omnibus, 1952-1961 (TV series; "Lee at Gettysburg," 1957 episode: Dickie Moore); Operator 13, 1934 (Douglass Dumbrille); **Santa Fe Trail**, 1940 (Errol Flynn).

Stuart, John Todd (1807-1885; U.S. politician and U.S. congressman; cousin of Mary Todd Lincoln, wife of President Abraham Lincoln): **Young Mr. Lincoln**, 1939 (Edwin Maxwell).

Stuhldreher, Harry (Harry Augustus Stuhldreher; American football player and coach; quarterback of the legendary "Four Horsemen" backfield of Notre Dame, 1922-1924; 1901-1965): **Knute Rockne All American**, 1940 (Nick Lukats).

Stulpnagel, Carl Heinrich (1886-1944; German general in WWII and part of the 1944 plot to assassinate Adolf Hitler): Die Stunde der Offiziere, 2004 (made-for-TV; Dieter Mann); **The Desert Fox: The Story**

Robert Redford (as the Sundance Kid) in *Butch Cassidy and the Sundance Kid*, 1969.

of Rommel, 1951 (John Goldsworthy); Operation Walkure, 1971 (made-for-TV; Friedrich Grondahl).

Stultz, Wilmer Lower (1900-1929; U.S. stunt pilot and aviation pioneer who was the pilot that flew the Fokker tri-motor plane called *Friendship* non-stop from New York to Ireland in 1928 with aviation pioneer Amelia Earhart as the first female passenger to cross the Atlantic; he was killed performing a stunt, along with two passengers the following year; Stultz, a heavy drinker, was thought to be inebriated at that time): Amelia Earhart, 1976 (made-for-TV: Jack Colvin).

Sue, Eugene (Joseph Marie Eugene Sue; 1804-1857; French novelist): Eugene Sue, 1974 (made-for-TV; Bernard Verley).

Sukarno (1901-1970; first president of Indonesia, who ruled as a dictator): **The Year of Living Dangerously**, 1982 (Mike Emperto).

Sullivan, Anne (1866-1936; aka: The Miracle Worker; U.S. blind teacher who taught deaf and mute Helen Keller how to communicate with the world): Adventures from the Book of Virtues, 1996- (animated TV series; "Patience," 1998 episode: Olivia d'Abo voiceover); Alexander Graham Bell: The Sound and the Silence, 1993 (made-for-TV; Alena McDonald); Animated Hero Classics, 1991-2005 (TV series; "Helen Keller," 1996 episode: Mary Louise Gemmill voiceover); Anna dei miracoli, 1968 (made-for-TV; Anna Proclemer); Deliverance, 1919 (Edith Lyle); Helen Keller and Her Teacher, 1970 (Barboura Morris); Helen Keller: The Miracle Continues, 1984 (made-for-TV; Blythe Danner); Helen Keller vs. Nightwolves, 2015 (Alanna Ubach); Mentors, 1998-2005 (TV series; "Breakthrough," 2002 episode: Katharine Isabelle); **The Miracle Worker**, 1962 (Anne Bancroft); The Miracle Worker, 1979 (made-for-TV; Patty Duke); The Miracle Worker, 2000 (made-for-TV; Alison Elliott); Monday after the Miracle, 1998 (made-for-TV; Roma Downey); Playhouse 90, 1956-1961 (TV series; "The Miracle Worker," 1957 episode: Teresa Wright).

Sullivan, John Lawrence (aka: Boston Strong Boy; The Great John L.; 1858-1918; U.S. prizefighter and heavyweight champion of the world): **The Bowery**, 1933 (George Walsh); **Diamond Jim**, 1935 (Bill Hoolahahn); **Gentleman Jim**, 1942 (Ward Bond); The Gentleman from Louisiana, 1936 (John Kelly); **The Great John L**, 1945 (Greg McClure); It's a Dog's Life, 1955 (Jeff York); **My Gal Sal**, 1942 (John Kelly); Tales of Wells Fargo, 1957-1962 (TV series; "The Hand That Shook the Hand," 1961 episode: Claude Akins); You Are There, 1953-1971 (TV series; "The Birth of Modern Boxing: The John L. Sullivan-James J. Corbett Battle [September 7, 1892]," 1955 episode: Jeff York).

Sullivan, William Cornelius (1912-1977; U.S. law enforcement official, chief of FBI's intelligence division): J. Edgar Hoover, 1987 (made-for-TV; Joe Regalbuto); King, 1978 (TV miniseries; Clu Gulager).

Summersby, Kay (Kathleen Helen Summersby; 1908-1975; U.S. MT Corps member and personal chauffeur for U.S. General Dwight D. Eisenhower in England during WWII; reportedly close friends but a sexual liaison is generally dismissed by scholars): D-Day 6.6.1944, 2004 (made-for-TV; Lacy Moore); Ike: The War Years, 1979 (TV miniseries; Lee Remick); War and Remembrance, 1989 (TV miniseries; Jane How).

Sumner, Charles (1811-1874; U.S. senator from Massachusetts and radical abolitionist): Bad Blood: The Border War That Triggered the Civil War, 2007 (made-for-TV; Ray Ettinger); **The Birth of a Nation**, 1915 (Sam De Grasse); Lincoln, 1988 (TV miniseries; Tom Brennan); **Lincoln**, 2012 (John Hutton); **Saving Lincoln**, 2013 (Creed Bratton).

Sundance Kid (Harry Alonzo Longbaugh or Longabauh; 1867-1908; U.S. Old West outlaw, bank and train robber): Adios Companeros, 1971 (Giancarlo Prete); Badman's Country, 1958 (Russell Johnson); Blackthorn, 2011 (Padraic Delaney); Butch and Sundance: The Early Days, 1979 (William Katt); **Butch Cassidy and the Sundance Kid**, 1969 (Robert Redford); Cheyenne, 1947 (Arthur Kennedy); Gambler V: Playing for Keeps, 1994 (made-for-TV; Brett Cullen); The Legend of Butch and Sundance, 2006 (made-for-TV; Ryan Browning); The Maverick Queen, 1956 (Scott Brady); Outlaw Trail: The Treasure of Butch Cassidy, 2006 (Michael Van Wagenen); **Return of the Bad Men**, 1948 (Robert Ryan); Return of the Gunfighter, 1967 (John Davis Chandler); Tales of Wells Fargo, 1957-1962 (TV series; "The Auction," 1957 episode: John Carlyle); The Texas Rangers, 1951 (Ian MacDonald); The Three Outlaws, 1956 (Alan Hale Jr.); Wyoming Renegades, 1954 (William Bishop); Zane Grey Theater, 1956-1961 (TV series; "Sundown at Bitter Creek, "1958 episode; Peter Breck). For detailed information on the Sundance Kid, see my book *Encyclopedia of Western Lawmen and Outlaws* (Paragon House, 1992; page 296).

Surratt, John Harrison (1844-1916; Confederate courier and spy during the American Civil War and whose mother was convicted and hanged as a conspirator in the 1865 assassination of U.S. President Abraham Lincoln; a friend of assassin John Wilkes Booth, Surratt fled to Canada, then to Italy and was finally arrested in Egypt and returned to the U.S. in 1867 for trial but was released following a mistrial and after charges of kidnapping had run out on the statute of limitations [he faced no murder charges]; went free on a $25,000 bail; he became the executive of a steamship firm): **The Conspirator**, 2011 (Johnny Simmons); The Day Lincoln Was Shot, 1998 (made-for-TV; Jason Bowcott); The Lincoln Conspiracy, 1977 (Ken Kercheval). Note: For detailed information on John Surratt and the Lincoln assassination, see my two-volume work, *The Great Pictorial History of World Crime*, Volume I (History, Inc., 2004; illustrated [47 images] pages 26-44).

Surratt, Mary (1823-1865; U.S. woman tried, convicted and executed by hanging as a part of the conspiracy to assassinate President Abraham Lincoln; she was the mother of John H. Surratt, later tried and acquitted in that conspiracy charge; many believe she was innocent): **The Conspirator**, 2011 (Robin Wright); The Day Lincoln Was Shot, 1998 (made-for-TV; Nancy Robinette); The Lincoln Conspiracy, 1977 (Mimi Honce); The Philco-Goodyear Television Playhouse, 1948-1956 (TV series; "The Story of Mary Surratt," 1949 episode: Dorothy Gish); **The Prisoner of Shark Island**, 1936 (Cecil Weston); You Are There, 1953-1957 (TV series; "The Capture of John Wilkes Booth," 1953 episode: Ellen Corby). Note: For detailed information on Mary Surratt and the Lincoln assassination, see my two-volume work *The Great Pictorial History of World Crime*, Volume I (History, Inc., 2004; illustrated [47 images] pages 26-44).

Sutherland, Richard K. (U.S. soldier and lieutenantgeneral and chief of staff for General Douglas MacArthur in the Southwest Pacific during WWII; 1893-1966): Death of a Soldier, 1986 (Michael Pate); Farewell to the King, 1989 (Michael Nissman); The Last Bastion, 1984 (TV series; Graham Rouse); **MacArthur**, 1977 (Ivan Bonar).

Sverdlov, Jakov (1885-1919; ruthless Bolshevik leader during the Russian Revolution; allegedly ordered the assassination of Czar Nicholas II and his entire family in 1918; reportedly beaten to death by workers hearing of his involvement in a plot to murder Lenin): An Extraordinary Assignment, 1966 (Alexandr Kutepov); Lenin in 1918, 1939 (Leonid Lyubashevsky); New Horizons, 1939 (Leonid Lyubashevsky); The Romanovs: An Imperial Family, 2000 (Kirill Kozakov); They Wanted Peace, 1940 (B. Poltavtsev); V dni oktyabrya, 1958 (Leonid Lyubashevsky).

Swigert, Jack (John Leonard Swigert Jr.; 1931-1982; U.S. NASA astronaut and a member of the Apollo 13 moon mission in 1970): **Apollo 13**, 1995 (Kevin Bacon); Man, Moment, Machine, 2005-2007 (TV series; "Apollo 13: Triumph on the Dark Side," 2006 episode: Jeff Ollenberger).

Symington, Stuart (William Stuart Symington; American politician, U.S. senator [Mo.], and 1st Secretary of the U.S. Air Force; 1901-1988): Tail Gunner Joe, 1977 (made-for-TV; Lin McCarthy).

Syngman Rhee (Yi Seung-man; 1875-1965; first President of the Provisional Government of the Republic of Korea): Inchon, 1982 (Kwang Nam Young).

Szabo, Violette (1921-1945; heroic French-born British SOE operative in Nazi-occupied France in WWII; captured and executed; she was posthumously awarded the George Cross): **Carve Her Name with Pride**, 1958 (Virginia McKenna).

Szilard, Leo (1898-1964; Hungarian-U.S. physicist and inventor who was instrumental in developing the atomic bomb used to end WWII): Albert Einstein, 1990- (TV series; Hansjurgen Hurrig); The Beginning or the End, 1947 (John Gallaudet); Day One, 1989 (made-for-TV; Michael Tucker); Ende der Unschuld, 1991 (made-for-TV; Jorg Gudzuhn); **Fat Man and Little Boy**, 1989 (Gerald Hiken); Oppenheimer, 1980 (TV miniseries; Gabor Vernon); Race for the Bomb, 1987 (TV miniseries; Jean-Paul Muel).

Tall Bull (U.S. Native American; Cheyenne chief; 1830-1869): **Buffalo Bill**, 1944 (Chief Many Treaties).

Tallien, Jean-Lambert (1767-1820; French politician during the French Revolution): Arme Bitos, 1962 (made-for-TV; Gijsbert Tersteeg); Danton, 1983 (Gerard Hardy); Josephine ou la comedie des ambitions, 1979- (TV miniseries; Jean-Luc Moreau); La camera explore le temps, 1957-1966 (TV series; one episode in 1964; Etienne Sevral); **Reign of Terror**, 1949 (Norman Lloyd); Saint-Just ou La force des choses, 1975 (made-for-TV; Michel Paulin); The Scarlet Daredevil, 1928 (Hadden Mason).

Tallien, Madame (1773-1835; Thérésa Cabarrus; French social personality during the French Revolution): **Desiree**, 1954 (Carolyn Jones); Madame Guillotine, 1916 (Lyda Borelli); Napoleon, 1955 (Nicole Maurey); **Reign of Terror**, 1949 (Norman Lloyd).

Tallmadge, Benjamin (1754-1835; U.S. military officer and George Washington's spymaster during the American Revolution): TURN: Washington's Spies, 2014 (TV series; Seth Numrich); You Are There,

Jason Isaacs (in role modeled on Tarleton Banastre) in *The Patriot,* **2000.**

1953-1971 (TV series; "The Treason of Benedict Arnold," 1953 episode: Lane Smith).

Talleyrand-Perigord, Charles (1754-1838; French diplomat and politician): The Battle of Austerlitz, 1960 (Jean Mercure); Congress of Love, 1966 (Paul Meurisse); **Conquest**, 1937 (Reginald Owen); **Desiree**, 1954 (John Hoyt); The Fighting Eagle, 1927 (Sam De Grasse); **The House of Rothschild**, 1934 (Georges Renavent); Hundred Days, 1935 (Alfred Gerasch); The Iron Duke, 1935 (Gibb McLaughlin); Konigin Luise, 1957 (Charles Regnier); The Lame Devil, 1948 (Sacha Guitry); Mlle. Desiree, 1948 (Jean Perier); Napoleon, 1955 (Sacha Guitry); Napoleon, 2002 (TV miniseries; John Malkovich); **The Pearls of the Crown**, 1938 (Robert Pizani); A Royal Divorce, 1938 (Frank Cellier); Talleyrand ou Le sphinx incompris, 1972 (Raymond Gerome); **The Young Mr. Pitt**, 1943 (Albert Lieven).

Tamon Yamaguchi (1882-1942; Japanese admiral who commanded part of the task force that participated in the sneak attack against Pearl Harbor on December 7, 1941; commanded aircraft carrier *Hiryu* and sank with it at the 1942 Battle of Midway): **Midway**, 1976 (John Fujioka); **Tora! Tora! Tora!**, 1970 (Susumu Fujita).

Tarleton, Banastre (1754-1833; British military officer during the American Revolutionary War): **The Patriot**, 2000 (role model for Jason Isaacs).

Tatiana Nikolaevna (1897-1918; Tatiana Romanov; Grand Duchess of Russia; daughter of Czar Nicholas II): Assassin of the Tsar, 1993 (Evgeniya Kryukova); Fall of Eagles, 1974 (TV miniseries; "Tell the King the Sky Is Falling," 1974 episode: Hetty Baynes); Into Her Kingdom, 1926 (Corinne Griffith); The Lost Prince, 2004 (made-for-TV; Holly Boyd); **Nicholas and Alexandra**, 1971 (Lynne Frederick); Rasputin, 1996 (made-for-TV; Natasha Reshetnikova); The Romanovs: An Imperial Family, 2000 (Kseniya Kachalina); The Successor, 1996 (Anna Mashina).

Taylor, Kenneth M. (Kenneth Marlar Taylor; 1919-2006; U.S. aviator and officer in the U.S. Army Air Force, who, during the Japanese sneak attack at Pearl Harbor on December 7, 1941, flew a P-40 fighter, shooting down four Japanese dive bombers before being injured in the air battle; received the Distinguished Flying Cross): **Tora! Tora! Tora!**, 1970 (Carl Reindel).

Taylor, Joseph Deems (1885-1966; U.S. composer and music critic): Mrs. Parker and the Vicious Circle, 1994 (James LeGros).

Farley Granger (as Harry Kendall Thaw) and Joan Collins in *The Girl in the Red Velvet Swing,* **1955.**

Taza (c.1843-1876; Apache chief, son of Cochise): Taza, Son of Cochise, 1954 (Rock Hudson).

Tedder, Arthur William (1890-1967; British air marshal in WWII): **Patton**, 1970 (Gerald Flood).

Teller, Edward (1908-2003; Hungarian-born U.S. theoretical physicist, called "the father of the hydrogen bomb"): Albert Einstein, 1990- (TV series; Hanns-Jorn Weber); Day One, 1989 (made-for-TV; Olek Krupa); Ende der Unschuld, 1991 (made-for-TV; Nikolas Lansky); **Fat Man and Little Boy**, 1989 (Barry Yourgrau); In der Sache J. Robert Oppenheimer, 1964 (made-for-TV; Alexander Kerst); In der Sache J. Robert Oppenheimer, 1981 (made-for-TV; Michael Degen); Oppenheimer, 1980 (TV miniseries; David Suchet); Oppenheimerin tapaus, 1967 (made-for-TV; Sakari Jurkka); Race for the Bomb, 1987 (TV miniseries; Predrag Monojlovic); Spies, Lies and the Superbomb, 2007 (TV miniseries; Mike Lawler).

Temple, Henry John (Lord Palmerston; 1784-1865; British statesman and prime minister of Great Britain): The Lame Devil, 1948 (Howard Vernon); **A Dispatch from Reuters**, 1940 (Gilbert Emery).

Temple, Shirley (1928-2014; Shirley Temple Black; U.S. child films star and actress; number one box office star in U.S., 1935-1938; 27th U.S. ambassador to Czechoslovakia, 1989-1992): **J. Edgar**, 2011 (Emily Alyn Lind).

Templeton, Fay (1865-1939; U.S. singer and actress): **Yankee Doodle Dandy**, 1942 (Irene Manning).

Terry, Alfred Howe (1827-1890; U.S. Union general in the American Civil War and in the Indian Plains wars): Don't Touch the White Woman!, 1974 (Philippe Noiret); The Great Sioux Massacre, 1965 (Frank Ferguson); Son of the Morning Star, 1991 (made-for-TV; Terry O'Quinn); Tonka, 1958 (Sydney Smith).

Terry, Ellen (1847-1928; British stage actress): Lillie, 1978- (TV miniseries; Elizabeth Power).

Tesla, Nikola (1856-1943; Serbian-American physicist, engineer and inventor; noted for his work in developing AC alternating current for electricity supply systems): Nikola Tesla, 1977- (TV series; Rade Serbedzija); The Secret Life of Nikola Tesla, 1980 (Peter Bozovic); Tesla, 1993 (made-for-TV; Svetozar Cvetkovic); War of the Worlds: Goliath, 2012 (Joey D'Auria voiceover). Note: For detailed informa-

tion on Tesla, see my book *Zanies: The World's Greatest Eccentrics* (New Century Publishers, 1982; illustrated pages 359-360).

Thaddeus (Saint Thaddeus or Saint Jude, one of the twelve Apostles of Jesus): Apostle Peter and the Last Supper, 2012 (Dominic Bogart); Color of the Cross, 2006 (Adam Green); Crown of Thorns, 1923 (Walter Werner); The Day Christ Died, 1980 (made-for-TV; Nando Paone); The Gospel according to Matthew, 1993 (Jonathan Pienaar); The Gospel according to St. Matthew, 1966 (Elio Spaziani); The Gospel of John, 2014 (Mostafa Charfaoui); The Gospel of Luke, 2015 (Mostafa Charfaoui); The Gospel of Mark, 2015 (Mostafa Charfaoui); The Gospel of Matthew, 2014 (Mostafa Charfaoui); Gospel Road: The Story of Jesus, 1973 (Ulf Pollack); **The Greatest Story Ever Told**, 1965 (Jamie Farr); Il messia, 1975 (Mohamed Ali Brikadhi); Jesus, 2000 (made-for-TV; Said Bey); Jesus, nuestro Senor, 1971 (Roy De La Serna); Jesus of Nazareth, 1977 (Mimmo Craig); **The King of Kings**, 1927 (John T. Prince); Kristo, 1996 (Tom Olivar); Matthew: 26:17, 2005 (Justin Bilancieri); Mary, Mother of the Son of God, 2003 (Gustavo Rodrigues); The Passion, 2008 (TV miniseries; Steve Morphew); The Power and the Resurrection, 1958 (Richard O'Shea); The Visual Bible: The Gospel of John, 2003 (Stephen Mapes).

Thalberg, Irving (1899-1936; U.S. film producer, chiefly for MGM Studio, who supervised many classic films of the early 1930s and who was the husband of film star Norma Shearer): The Adventures of Young Indiana Jones: Hollywood Follies, 1994 (made-for-TV; Bill Cusack); **The Last Tycoon**, 1976 (role model for Robert De Niro); The Last Tycoon, 2016 (made-for-TV; role model for Matt Bomer); **Man of a Thousand Faces**, 1957 (Robert Evans); The Silent Lovers, 1980 (made-for-TV; John Rubinstein).

Thatcher, Margaret (1925-2013; British politician and prime minister of England, 1979-1990): National Theatre Live: The Audience, 2013 (Haydn Gwynne); Spitting Image, 1984-1986 (TV series with puppets enacting public figures; Steve Nallon voiceover).

Thayer, Webster (1857-1933; U.S. jurist who presided over the Sacco-Vanzetti case and whose decided bias against the defendants was exhibited before the outcome of that trial when he reportedly stated, in crowing about denying defense motions in the case: "Did you see what I did to those anarchist bastards?"): **No God, No Master**, 2012 (James Pickering).

Thaw, Harry Kendall (1871-1947; Pittsburgh multimillionaire who shot and killed celebrated architect Stanford White in 1906 at the theater rooftop at Madison Square Garden in NYC in front of hundreds of horrified witnesses over Thaw's jealousy concerning his wife, former showgirl Evelyn Nesbit, who had once been White's mistress; Thaw was declared insane and sent to an asylum for the criminally insane from which he was later released): **The Girl in the Red Velvet Swing**, 1955 (Farley Granger); **Ragtime**, 1981 (Robert Joy). Note: For detailed information on Thaw and his murder of Stanford White, see my two-volume work *The Great Pictorial History of World Crime*, Volume II (History, Inc., 2004; illustrated [17 images] pages 819-826).

Thiers, Marie Joseph Louis Adolphe (1797-1877; French politician and second president of France, 1871-1873): **The Story of Louis Pasteur**, 1936 (Herbert Corthell).

Thomas (Saint Thomas; d. 72 A.D.; one of the twelve Apostles of Jesus; also called "Doubting Thomas" because he doubted Jesus' Resurrection until he reportedly placed his finger into Jesus' death wounds; was murdered in India where he baptized many as Christians who are now known as Saint Thomas Christians of India): Acts of the Apostles, 1969 (TV miniseries; Moncef Ben Yahia); A.D., 1985 (TV miniseries; Davyd

Harries); A.D. The Bible Continues, 2015 (Johannes Haukur); Animated Stories from the New Testament, 1987- (TV series; "He Is Risen," 2004 episode: Bruce Winant); Apostle Peter and the Last Supper, 2012 (Emilio Doorgasingh); **Barabbas**, 1962 (Jacopo Tecchi); Color of the Cross, 2006 (John-Pierre Parent); Color of the Cross 2: The Resurrection, 2008 (C. Frederick Secrease); Crown of Thorns, 1934 (silent; Emil Lind); The Day Christ Died, 1980 (made-for-TV; Leonardo Treviglio); Family Theatre, 1949-1958 (TV series; "Triumphant Hour," 1953 episode: Tudor Owen); The Friends of Jesus—Thomas, 2001 (made-for-TV; Ricky Tognazzi); The Gospel according to Matthew, 1993 (Sean Cameron Michael); The Gospel according to St. Matthew, 1966 (Rosario Migale); The Gospel of John, 2014 (Abderrahim Khira); The Gospel of Luke, 2015 (Abderrahim Khira); The Gospel of Mark, 2015 (Abderrahim Khira); Gospel Road: A Story of Jesus, 1973 (Sean Armstrong); **The Greatest Story Ever Told**, 1965 (Tom Reese); Il messia, 1975 (Moncef Ben Yahia); Jesus, 2000 (made-for-TV; Sean Harris); The Jesus Film, 1979 (Nisim Gerama); Jesus of Nazareth, 1977 (TV miniseries; Bruce Lidington); Judas, 2004 (made-for-TV; Hicham Bahloul); **The King of Kings**, 1927 (Sidney D'Albrook); **King of Kings**, 1961 (Michael Wager); Kristo, 1996 (Patrick Dela Rosa); The Last Supper: Thirteen Men of Courage, 2007 (made-for-TV; Brent Baum); The Last Temptation of Christ, 1988 (Alan Rosenberg); The Living Bible, 1952 (TV series; Thayer Thomas); The Living Christ Series, 1951 (TV miniseries; John Phillips); Marie de Nazareth, 1995 (Alain Aswani); Matthew 26:17, 2005 (Klataan Thomas); The Miracle Maker, 2000 (animated; James Frain voiceover); The Passion, 2008 (TV miniseries; Lewis Clay); The Passion of the Christ, 2004 (Adel Ben Ayed); The Power of the Resurrection, 1958 (Dan Riss); Risen, 2016 (Jan Cornet); Son of God, 2014 (Matthew Gravelle); The Visual Bible: The Gospel of John, 2003 (Andy Velasquez).

Thomson, Charles (1729-1824; U.S. secretary of the Continental Congress): **1776**, 1972 (Ralston Hill).

Thomson, Edith (Edith Jessie Graydon Thomson; 1893-1923; British murderer, executed): Another Life, 2001 (Natasha Little); A Pin to See the Peepshow, 1973- (TV series; Francesca Annis). Note: For detailed information on Thomson, see my book *World Encyclopedia of 20th Century Murder* (Paragon House, 1992; illustrated page 561).

Thorpe, James Francis (aka: "Jim"; Wa-Tho-Huk: "Bright Path"; 1888-1953; U.S. Native American [Sac and Fox], the most versatile athlete of the modern era and legendary Olympic champion): **Jim Thorpe—All American**, 1951 (Burt Lancaster); Kazan, 1921 (Ben Deeley).

Tiberius (42 B.C.-37 A.D.; Roman emperor): A.D., 1985 (TV miniseries; James Mason); Ancient Rome: The Rise and Fall of an Empire, 2006 (TV series; James D'Arcy); **Barabbas**, 1962 (Ivan Triesault); **Ben-Hur**, 1959 (George Relph); Ben Hur, 2010 (TV miniseries; Ben Cross); The Big Fisherman, 1959 (Herbert Rudley); The Caesars, 1968 (TV series; Andre Morell); Caligula, 1980 (Peter O'Toole); Columna, 1968 (Richard Johnson); Cyclops, 2008 (made-for-TV; Eric Roberts); The Final Inquiry, 2006 (Max von Sydow); I, Claudius, 1976 (TV miniseries; George Baker); Imperium: Augustus, 2003 (made-for-TV; Michele Bevilacqua); Jeff Steele and the Lost Civilization of NoyNac, 2004 (David Blanchard); **The Robe**, 1953 (Ernest Thesiger); **Salome**, 1953 (Cedric Hardwicke).

Tibbets, Paul (1915-2007; U.S. bomber pilot who flew B-29 over Hiroshima that dropped the atomic bomb in 1945): **Above and Beyond**, 1953 (Robert Taylor); The Beginning or the End, 1947 (Barry Nelson); Enola Gay: The Men, the Mission, the Atomic Bomb, 1980 (made-for-TV; Patrick Duffy).

Tilghman, William (William Matthew "Bill" Tilghman Jr.; 1854-1924;

Larry Gates and Robert Taylor (as Paul Tibbets) in *Above and Beyond*, **1953.**

U.S. lawman and gunfighter in the Old West): Wyatt Earp's Revenge, 2012 (Levi Fiehler); You Know My Name, 1999 (made-for-TV; Sam Elliott). Note: For detailed information on Tilghman, see my book *Encyclopedia of Western Lawmen and Outlaws* (Paragon House, 1992; illustrated page 303).

Tilley, Vesta (Matilda Alice Powles; 1864-1952; British music hall singer and performer and foremost male impersonator of her era): After the Ball, 1957 (Margaret Sawyer as a child; Pat Kirkwood as an adult Tilley); Lost Empires, 1986 (TV miniseries; Julia Parrott).

Timberlake, John B. (1777-1828; U.S. Navy purser and first husband of Peggy O'Neill Timberlake Eaton; he reportedly committed suicide after learning that his wife was having an affair with U.S. politician John Henry Eaton): The Gorgeous Hussy, 1936 (Robert Taylor).

Tojo Hideki (1884-1948; Japanese general and prime minister, 1941-1944; executed as a war criminal): Ano senso w aka—Nichibei kaisen to Tojo Hideki, 2008 (made-for-TV; Takeshi Kitano); **Blood on the Sun**, 1945 (Robert Armstrong); Daitoa senso to kokusai saiban, 1959 (Kanjuro Arashi); **Emperor**, 2012 (Shohei Hino); Gekido no showashi "Gunbatsu," 1970 (Keiju Kobayashi); Histeria!, 1998-2000 (animated TV series; "World War II," 1999 episode: Rob Paulsen voiceover); The Imperial Japanese Empire, 1982 (Tetsuro Tanba); Pride: The Fateful Moment—Japan, 2001 (Masahiko Tsugawa); **Tora! Tora! Tora!**, 1970 (Asao Uchida).

Toklas, Alice B. (U.S. writer and significant lesbian other to Gertrude Stein in France; 1877-1967): The Adventures of Picasso, 1980 (Wilfred Brambell); American Playhouse, 1981- (TV series; "Waiting for the Moon," 1987 episode: Linda Hunt); Gertrude Stein and a Companion!, 1987 (Marian Seldes); Hemingway, 1988 (TV miniseries; Judith Burnett); Hemingway: That Summer in Paris, 2003 (made-for-TV; Ruth Madoc-Jones); La banda Picasso, 2012 (Eszter Tompa); The Legendary Life of Ernest Hemingway, 1989 (Rita Tushingham); Lives and Deaths of the Poets, 2011 (Sheri Cohen); **Midnight in Paris**, 2011 (Therese Bourou-Rubinsztein); The Moderns, 1988 (Ali Giron); The Young Indiana Jones Chronicles, 1992-1993 (TV series; "Paris, September 1908," 1993 episode: Alice Dvorakova).

Toland, Gregg (1904-1948; U.S. cinematographer noted for his inventive lensing in such films as Citizen Kane, 1941): RKO 281, 1999 (made-for-TV; Liam Cunningham).

Tolson, Clyde Anderson (1900-1975; U.S. attorney and associate direc-

Suzanne Flon, Zsa Zsa Gabor and Jose Ferrer (as Henri Toulouse-Lautrec) in *Moulin Rouge,* 1952.

tor of the Federal Bureau of Investigation [FBI]; closest associate of FBI director J. Edgar Hoover): American Playhouse, 1981- (TV series; "Concealed Enemies," 1984 episode: Ralph Byers); Citizen Cohn, 1992 (made-for-TV; Daniel von Bargen); The Curse of Edgar, 2013 (made-for-TV; Anthony Higgins); Dark Skies, 1996-1997 (TV series: "The Warren Omission," 1997 episode: Jack Ritschel); **J. Edgar**, 2011 (Armie Hammer); J. Edgar Hoover, 1987 (made-for-TV; Robert Harper); The Kennedys, 2011- (TV series; "Bay of Pigs," 2011 episode: Kevin Jubinville); **Nixon**, 1995 (Brian Bedford); **The Private Files of J. Edgar Hoover**, 1977 (Dan Dailey); **Public Enemies**, 2009 (Chandler Williams); Robert F. Kennedy and His Times, 1985 (TV miniseries; Jack Thibeau). Note: For detailed information on Tolson, see my book *Citizen Hoover: A Critical Study of the Life and Times of J. Edgar Hoover and His FBI* (Nelson-Hall, 1972).

Tolstoy, Leo (1828-1910; Russian author): The Adventures of Young Indiana Jones: Travels with Father, 1996 (made-for-TV; Michael Gough); Anton Chekhov 1890, 2015 (Frederic Perriot); The Evil Spirit of Leo Tolstoy, 2009 (Gatis Cirulis); ITV Sunday Night Theatre, 1969- (TV series; "The Last Journey," 1972 episode: Harry Andrews); The Last Station, 2009 (Christopher Plummer); Leo Tolstoy, 1984 (Sergey Gerasimov); The Power of Dawn, 1976 (made-for-TV; Alfred Burke); A Question of Faith, 1979 (Harry Andrews); Russia, 1986 (TV miniseries; Lev Durov). Note: For detailed information on Tolstoy, see my book *Zanies: The World's Greatest Eccentrics* (New Century Publishers, 1982; illustrated pages 362-364).

Torquemado, Tomas de (Thomas of Torquemada; 1420-1498; Dominican friar, witchhunter and Grand Inquisitor of the Spanish Inquisition): Bye Bye Columbus, 1991 (made-for-TV; James Laurenson); Carry on Columbus, 1992 (James Faulkner); Christopher Columbus: The Discovery, 1992 (Marlon Brando); Cristobal Colon, de oficio…descubridor, 1982 (Quique Camoiras); Da Vinci's Demons, 2013 (TV series; "The Tower," 2013 episode: Peter Guinness); The Gospel according to God, 2004 (Golan Azulai); History of the World, Part I, 1981 (Mel Brooks); Isabel, 2011-2014 (TV series; Manel Dueso); Juana la loca…de vez en cuando, 1983 (Quique Camoiras); The Pit and the Pendulum, 1991 (Lance Henriksen); Torquemada, 1989 (Francisco Rabal).

Torrio, Johnny (1882-1957; U.S. gangster, Chicago crime boss and board member of the U.S. crime syndicate): **Al Capone**, 1959 (Nehemiah Persoff); **The Babe**, 1992 (Guy Barile); Boardwalk Empire, 2010- (TV series: thirteen episodes: Greg Antonacci); Capone, 1975 (Harry Guardino); In Suspicious Circumstances, 1991- (TV series; "No Witnesses, No Case," 1993 episode: Kieron Jecchinis); The Untouch-

ables, 1959-1963 (TV series; "Portrait of a Thief," 1960 episode: Charles McGraw); The Untouchables, 1993-1994 (TV series; Byrne Piven); The Young Indiana Jones Chronicles, 1992-1993 (TV series; "Young Indiana Jones and the Mystery of the Blues," 1993 episode: Frank Vincent). Note: For detailed information on Torrio, see my book *World Encyclopedia of Organized Crime* (Paragon House, 1992; illustrated [7 images] pages 382-389).

Toulouse-Lautrec, Henri de (1864-1901; French artist): Around the World in 80 Days, 2004 (Guillaume Siron); Der Opernball, 1971 (made-for-TV; Ernst Stankovski); The Flame Is Love, 1979 (made-for-TV; Jim Fitzgerald); The Footstep Man, 1992 (Michael Hurst); Lautrec, 1999 (Regis Royer); **Lust for Life**, 1956 (Jerry Bergen); **Midnight in Paris**, 2011 (Vincent Menjou Cortes); **Moulin Rouge**, 1952 (Jose Ferrer); Moulin Rouge!, 2001 (John Leguizamo); Moulin Rouge, a vida de Toulouse-Lautrec, 1963 (TV series; Percy Aires); Nothing Lasts Forever, 1984 (Erick Avari); Omnibus, 1967-2003 (TV series; "Van Gogh," 1990 episode: Peter O'Farrell); A Ultima Valsa, 1969 (TV series; Edson Silva); Van Gogh; een huis voor Vincent, 2013 (TV series; Louis van der Waal).

Trajan (53-117 A.D.; Roman emperor): Columna, 1968 (Amedeo Nazzari).

Travis, William Barret (1809-1836; U.S. soldier; commander of the Alamo): **The Alamo**, 1960 (Laurence Harvey); **The Alamo**, 2004 (Patrick Wilson); The Alamo: Thirteen Days to Glory, 1987 (made-for-TV; Alec Baldwin); Davy Crockett at the Fall of the Alamo, 1926 (Joe Rickson); **Davy Crockett: King of the Wild Frontier**, 1955 (Don Megowan); The First Texan, 1956 (William Hopper); Gone to Texas, 1986 (made-for-TV; William Russ); **The Last Command**, 1955 (Richard Carlson); **The Man from the Alamo**, 1953 (Arthur Space); **Man of Conquest**, 1939 (Victor Jory); Martyrs of the Alamo, 1915 (John T. Dillon); The Time Tunnel, 1966-1967 (TV series; "The Alamo," 1966 episode: Rhodes Reason); Walt Disney's Wonderful World of Color, 1954-1992 (TV series; "Davy Crockett at the Alamo," 1955 episode: Don Megowan).

Tresca, Carlo (1879-1943; Italian-born newspaper editor in the U.S., who was reportedly murdered for exposing communist schemes to overthrow the U.S. government): **No God, No Master**, 2012 (Edoardo Ballerini).

Tresckow, Henning (1901-1944; German general in WWII, part of the 1944 plot to kill Adolf Hitler): Die Stunde der Offiziere, 2004 (made-for-TV; Bernhard Schutz); The Plot to Assassinate Hitler, 1955 (Fritz Tillman); **Valkyrie**, 2008 (Kenneth Branagh).

Trimble, Isaac Ridgeway (1802-1888; U.S. military officer and Confederate general in the Army of Northern Virginia during the American Civil War): **Gettysburg**, 1993 (Morgan Sheppard); **Gods and Generals**, 2003 (Morgan Sheppard).

Trotsky, Leon (1879-1940; Russian Marxist and a leader of the Russian Revolution; assassinated): The Assassination of Trotsky, 1972 (Richard Burton); Battle of Warsaw 1920, 2011 (Krzysztof Dracz); BBC2 Playhouse, 1874-1983 (TV series; "Thank You, Comrades," 1978 episode: Derek Godfrey); British Agent, 1934 (J. Carrol Naish); Esenin, 2005 (TV miniseries; Konstantin Khabensky); Fall of Eagles, 1974 (TV miniseries; Michael Kitchen); Frida, 2002 (Geoffrey Rush); Frida Still Life, 1988 (Max Kerlow); Les dossiers de l'ecran, 1967-1989 (TV series; "Stalin-Trotsky," 1979 episode: Henri Virlojeux); **Manhattan Melodrama**, 1934 (Leo Lance); **Mission to Moscow**, 1943 (Sam Goldenberg); **Nicholas and Alexandra**, 1971 (Brian Cox); **Reds**, 1981 (Stuart Richman); The Romanovs: An Imperial Family, 2000 (Valery Kukhareshin); Seven Days, 1998-2001 (TV series; "Pilot: Part 1," 1998 episode: Endre Hules); Stalin, 1992 (made-for-TV; Daniel Massey); **Stavisky**, 1974 (Yves Peneau); Trotski in Coyoacan, 1975 (Rene Deltgen); Vrag naroda—Bukharin, 1990 (Lev Lemke); Whit Monday, 1990 (L. Shternberg); Why Russians Are Revolting, 1970 (D. F. Barry); Zina, 1986 (Philip Madoc).

Trudeau, Pierre (1919-2000; Canadian politician and prime minister): Trudeau, 2002 (made-for-TV; Colm Feore); Trudeau II: Maverick in the Making, 2005 (made-for-TV; in various ages: Dany Duval, Tobie Pellatier, Stephane Demers).

Truman, Bess (Elizabeth Virginia Wallace Truman; 1885-1982; American First Lady, wife of U.S. President Harry Truman): Collision Course: Truman vs. MacArthur, 1976 (made-for-TV; Lucille Benson); The Man from Independence, 1974 (June Dayton); Truman, 1995 (made-for-TV; Diana Scarwid).

Truman, Harry S. (1884-1972; U.S. politician and 33rd President of the U.S.): The Airlift, 2005 (made-for-TV; Jurgen Hentsch); American Genius, 2015- (TV miniseries; "Oppenheimer vs. Heisenberg," 2015 episode: David Mitchum Brown); Backstairs at the White House, 1979- (TV miniseries; Harry Morgan); The Beginning or the End, 1947 (Art Baker); Brenda Starr, 1992 (Ed Nelson); Collision Course: Truman vs. MacArthur, 1976 (made-for-TV; E. G. Marshall); Day One, 1989 (made-for-TV; Richard Dysart); Eleanor: First Lady of the World, 1982 (made-for-TV; Richard McKenzie); Enola Gay: The Men, the Mission, the Atomic Bomb, 1980 (made-for-TV; Ed Nelson); **Flags of Our Fathers**, 2006 (David Patrick Kelly); Give 'Em Hell, Harry!, 1975 (James Whitmore); Glory Alley, 1952 (Jack Gargan); Harry S. Truman: Plain Speaking, 1976 (made-for-TV; Ed Flanders); Haven, 2001 (made-for-TV; Kenneth Welsh); Hiroshima, 1995 (made-for-TV; Kenneth Welsh); Inchon, 1981 (Ed Flanders); J. Edgar Hoover, 1987 (made-for-TV; Walker Edmiston); Inchon, 1982 (Ed Flanders); Keep the Faith, Baby, 2002 (made-for-TV; Cedric Smith); The Korean War, 2001 (TV series; Harris Shore); **MacArthur**, 1977 (Ed Flanders); The Man from Independence, 1974 (Robert Vaughn); **The Monuments Men**, 2014 (Christian Rodska); **The 100-Year-Old Man Who Climbed Out of the Window and Disappeared**, 2014 (Kerry Shale); A Single Woman, 2008 (Traber Burns); Tail Gunner Joe, 1977 (made-for-TV; Robert Symonds); Truman, 1995 (made-for-TV; Gary Sinise); Truman at Potsdam, 1976 (made-for-TV; Ed Flanders); War and Remembrance, 1988- (TV miniseries; Richard Dysart); The World Wars, 2014- (TV miniseries; David Mitchum Brown).

Truman, Margaret (Mary Margaret Truman Daniel; 1924-2008; daughter of U.S. President Harry S. Truman, singer and author of mystery stories): Collision Course: Truman vs. MacArthur, 1976 (made-for-TV; Lee Kessler); The Man from Independence, 1974 (Tasha Lee); Truman, 1995 (made-for-TV; Amelia Campbell).

Truscott, Lucien (1895-1965; U.S. four-star general in WWII): Ike: The War Years, 1979 (TV miniseries; Charles H. Gray); **Patton**, 1970 (John Doucette).

Truth, Sojourner (1797-1883; U.S. African-American abolitionist and women's rights activist): The American Parade, 1974- (TV series; "We the Women," 1974 episode: Vinnette Carroll; "Sojourner," 1975 episode; Vinnette Carroll); The American Woman: Portraits of Courage, 1976 (made-for-TV; Claudia McNeil); Freedom to Speak, 1982 (TV miniseries; Lynne Thigpen).

Tubman, Harriet (Araminta Harriet Ross; 1820-1913; African-American abolitionist and Union spy during the American Civil War): Adventures from the Book of Virtues, 1996- (animated TV series; "Faith," 1997 episode: Alfre Woodard voiceover); The American Woman: Portraits of

Humphrey Bogart (center, in role model of Burton B. Turkus) in *The Enforcer*, **1951.**

Courage, 1976 (made-for-TV; Melba Moore); BBC Learning: True Stories, 2012- (TV series; Elyse Shaw); The Great Adventure, 1963-1964 (TV series; "Go Down, Moses," 1963 episode;: Ruby Dee); Mentors, 1998-2005 (TV series; "Harriet's Path," 1999 episode: Sandra Caldwell); The North Star, 2016 (Shatirah Rolle); Race to Freedom: The Underground Railroad, 1994 (made-for-TV; Alfre Woodard); A Woman Called Moses, 1978- (TV series; Cicely Tyson); Voyagers!, 1982-1983 (TV series; "Created Equal," 1982 episode: Fay Hauser).

Tucker, Sophie (1887-1966; U.S. singer, actress, entertainer and radio personality): Boardwalk Empire, 2010-2014 (TV series; "Belle Femme," 2010 episode: Kathy Brier); **Follow the Boys**, 1944 (herself); Gay Love, 1934 (herself); The George Burns and Gracie Allen Show, 1950-1958 (TV series; "Night of Vaudeville," 1956 episode: Judy Clark); **The I Don't Care Girl**, 1953 (Claire Hogan); **The Joker Is Wild**, 1957 (herself); A Love Affair: The Eleanor and Lou Gehrig Story, 1977 (made-for-TV; Lainie Kazan); Parade of Stars, 1983 (made-for-TV; Shelley Winters); **There's No Business Like Show Business**, 1954 (Isabelle Dwan).

Tukahachevsky, Mikhail (1893-1937; Russian soldier and marshal, commander-in-chief of the Red Army, 1925-1928; purged by Stalin in trumped up charges of treason, convicted and executed; shot in the back of the head): Battle of Warsaw, 2011 (Aleksandr Goshabayev); Coming Out of the Ice, 1982 (made-for-TV; Ben Cross); Der Fall Tukahachevsky, 1968 (made-for-TV; Helmut Wildt); Die Matrosen von Kronstadt, 1983 (made-for-TV; Josef Frohlich); Groza nad beloy, 1968 (Valeri Yervomichov); **Mission to Moscow**, 1943 (Ivan Triesault); Testimony, 1988 (Ronald Pickup).

Turgenev, Ivan (1818-1883; Russian writer, novelist and dramatist): BBC Sunday-Night Theatre, 1950-1959 (TV series; "The End of Summer," 1957 episode: Ferdy Mayne); Belinsky, 1953 (Litovkin); Dostoevsky, 2011- (TV miniseries; Vladimir Simonov); Dug iz Baden-Badena, 2000 (made-for-TV; Miodrag Milovanov); George Sand, 1981- (TV miniseries; Italo Dall'Orto); La note bleue, 1991 (Serge Renko); Tchaikovsky, 1970 (Bruno Frejndlikh).

Turkus, Burton B. (1902-1982; U.S. attorney and assistant district attorney for King's County, N.Y. (Brooklyn), who relentlessly investigated and prosecuted members of the notorious Murder, Inc. gang): **The Enforcer**, 1951 (role model for Humphrey Bogart); **Murder, Inc.**, 1960 (Henry Morgan).

Turner, J.M.W. (1775-1851; British landscape painter): The Genius of

Fredric March (as Mark Twain) in *The Adventures of Mark Twain,* **1944.**

Turner: Painting the Industrial Revolution, 2013 (made-for-TV; Thomas Coombes); **Mr. Turner**, 2014 (Timothy Spall).

Turner, Tina (Anna Mae Bullock; 1939- ; U.S. Afro-American singer): **What's Love Got to Do with It**, 1993 (herself).

Turpin, Dick (1705-1739; British highwayman, who was executed by hanging): The Adventures of Dick Turpin, 1929 (Kenneth McLaglen); The Bill, 1984-2010 (TV series; "Just Call Me Govnor," 1988 episode; Russell Gold); Dirk Turpin, 1925 (Tom Mix); Dick Turpin, 1934 (Victor McLaglen); Dick Turpin, 1977 (John Gaffari); Dick Turpin, 1979-1982 (TV series; Richard O'Sullivan); Dick Turpin's Ride to York, 1922 (Matheson Lang); El caballero de la noche, 1932 (Jose Mojica); The Lady and the Bandit, 1951 (Louis Hayward); Rogue's Gallery, 2005- (TV series; Vic Reeves); Walt Disney's Wonderful World of Color, 1954-1992 (TV series; "The Legend of Young Dick Turpin," two 1966 episodes: David Weston). Note: For detailed information on Turpin, see my two-volume work *The Great Pictorial History of World Crime*, Volume II (History, Inc., 2004; illustrated pages 1332-1333).

Tutankhamon (aka: King Tut; c. 1332-1323 B.C.; Egyptian pharaoh): Clementine's Enchanted Journey, 1985- (animated TV series; Francette Vernillat); The Curse of King Tut's Tomb, 2006 (made-for-TV; Francisco Bosch); Egypt, 2005 (TV miniseries; two 2005 episodes with Angelo Andreou, Alto Letto and Arkin Chandaril as Tutankhamon); Mentors, 1998-2005 (TV series; "Cursed," 2002 episode: Yani Gellman); **Mr. Peabody & Sherman**, 2014 (Zach Callison voiceover); Princess of the Nile, 1954 (Billy Curtis); The Time Crystal, 1981 (made-for-TV; Eric Greene); The Tomorrow People, 1992-1995 (TV series; "The Ramses Connection," three 1995 episodes: Adam Dean).

Twain, Mark (pseudonym for Samuel Lanhorne Clemens; 1835-1910; U.S. author): The Adventures of Huck Finn, 2012 (Christian Steyer); **The Adventures of Mark Twain**, 1944 (Fredric March as adult Twain; Jackie Brown at age twelve; Dickie Jones at age fifteen); The Adventures of Mark Twain, 1985 (James Whitmore voiceover); The American Adventure, 1982 (John Anderson voiceover); The Autobiography of Mark Twain, 2010 (Duane Mazey as old Mark Twain; Benjamin Nathan-Serio as young Mark Twain); Battle of Greed, 1937 (James Bush); The Bell Telephone Hour, 1959-1968 (TV series; "The Sounds of America," 1961 episode: Dwight Marfield); Bonanza, 1959-1973 (TV series; "Enter Mark Twain," 1959 episode: Howard Duff; "The Emperor Norton," 1966 episode: William Challee; "The Twenty-Sixth Grave," 1972 episode: Ken Howard); Broadway Broke, 1923 (Leslie King); Cavalcade of America, 1952-1957 (TV series; "Riders of the Pony Ex-

press," 1953 episode: Robert Cornthwaite); A Connecticut Yankee in King Arthur's Court, 1921 (Karl Formes); Death Valley Days, 1952-1970 (TV series; "The 275,000 Sack of Flour," 1962 episode: William Schallert; "Ten Day Millionaires," 1968 episode; Tom Skerritt); Fantasy Island, 1977-1984 (TV series; "The Angel's Triangle/Natchez Bound," 1982 episode: Stephen Shortridge); Father Murphy, 1981-1983 (TV series: "Stopover in a One-Horse Town," 1982 episode: Christopher Stone); Finding Xanadu: The Life and Films of Samuel W. Truss, 2010 (Broderick Goodnight); General Electric's All-Star Anniversary, 1978 (made-for-TV; James Stewart); Great Performances, 1971- (TV series; "Life on the Mississippi," 1980 episode: David Knell; "The Innocents Abroad," 1983 episode: Craig Wasson); Helen Keller: The Miracle Continues, 1984 (made-for-TV; Jack Warden); Huckleberry Finn, 1975 (made-for-TV; Royal Dano); Incredible Rocky Mountain Race, 1977 (made-for-TV; Christopher Connelly); Laramie, 1959-1963 (TV series; "Company Man," 1960 episode: Dabs Greer); Mark Twain: Against, 1975 (made-for-TV; Oleg Tabakov); Mark Twain and Me, 1991 (made-for-TV; Jason Robards Jr.); Mark Twain: Beneath the Laughter, 1979 (made-for-TV; Dan O'Herlihy); Nikola Tesla, 1977- (TV series; Slavko Simic); Nom-de-Plume, 1956- (TV series; "The Innocent Gunman," 1956 episode: Guy Kingsley Poynter); Playhouse 90, 1956-1961 (TV series; "The Shape of the River," 1960 episode: Franchot Tone); The Pony Express, 1925 (Charles Gerson); The Ridiculous 6, 2015 (Vanilla Ice); The Rifleman, 1958-1963 (TV series; "The Shattered Idol," 1961 episode; Kevin McCarthy); Riverworld, 2003 (made-for-TV; Cameron Daddo); Riverworld, 2010 (made-for-TV; Mark Deklin); Roughing It, 2002 (made-for-TV; James Garner); The Secret Adventures of Jules Verne, 2000 (TV series; "The Ballad of Steeley Joe," 2000 episode: Jonathan Walker); Sunday Showcase, 1959-1961 (TV series; "An American Heritage: Shadow of a Soldier," 1960 episode: Melvyn Douglas); Swing Out, Sweet Land, 1970 (made-for-TV; Bing Crosby); Tesla the Superman, 2009 (Michael Wise); Tom Sawyer & Huckleberry Finn, 2015 (Val Kilmer); Voyagers!, 1982-1983 (TV series; "Created Equal," 1982 episode: Rossie Harris); Walt Disney's Wonderful World of Color, 1954-1992 (TV series; "One Man's Dream," 1981 episode: Charles Aidman). Note: For detailed information on Twain, see my book *Zanies: The World's Greatest Eccentrics* (New Century Publishers, 1982; illustrated pages 370-374).

Tweed, George Ray (1902-1989; U.S. Navy radioman, who, along with a handful of other U.S. servicemen, evaded capture when the Japanese invaded the U.S.-held island of Guam on December 10, 1941, and survived as a guerrilla until the island was recaptured by U.S. forces in 1944 and for which he received the Legion of Merit): **No Man Is an Island**, 1962 (Jeffrey Hunter).

Tweed, William M. (aka: Boss Tweed; 1823-1878; U.S. politician and boss of Tammany Hall, the Democratic Party's corrupt political organization in NYC in the 19th Century): Gangs of New York, 2002 (Jim Broadbent); The Great Adventure, 1963-1964 (TV series; "The Man Who Stole New York City," 1963 episode: Edward Andrews); Liberty, 1986 (made-for-TV; Philip Bosco); Up in Central Park, 1948 (Vincent Price); You Are There, 1953-1971 (TV series; "The Overthrow of the Tweed Ring [November 19, 1874]," 1957 episode: Paul Maxey).

Twining, Nathan Farragut (1897-1982; U.S. military officer; U.S. Air Force general and chairman of the Joint Chiefs of Staff, 1957-1960): Dark Skies, 1996-1997 (TV series: "We Shall Overcome," 1996 episode: Arell Blanton).

Tyndale, William (1494-1536; English scholar and leader of the Protestant Reformation, known for translating the Bible into English): God's Outlaw, 1986 (Roger Rees).

Udet, Ernst (1896-1941; German fighter pilot in WWI credited with 62 victories and who helped establish the German Luftwaffe in the 1930s under the command of fellow WWI ace Hermann Goering): **The Red Baron**, 2010 (role model for Jiri Lastovka); S.O.S. Eisberg, 1933 (himself); Storm over Mont Blanc, 1930 (himself); **Von Richthofen and Brown**, 1971 (Robert La Tourneaux); White Hell of Pitz Palu, 1929 (himself).

Urbina, Tomas (c.1877-1915; Mexican revolutionary and general in the Mexican Revolution, allied with Pancho Villa and Emiliano Zapata): Villa Rides, 1968 (Robert Viharo).

Valachi, Joseph (1904-1971; U.S. gangster and member of the Cosa Nostra or Mafia): Bonanno: A Godfather's Story, 1999 (made-for-TV; Giancarlo Caltabiano as young Valachi; Michael Cianciullo as old Valachi); Ruby, 1992 (Joe Viterelli); **The Valachi Papers**, 1972 (Charles Bronson). Note: For detailed information on Valachi, see my book, *World Encyclopedia of Organized Crime* (Paragon House, 1992; page 398).

Valentino, Rudolph (1895-1926; Italian-born film star in U.S., who was the leading on-screen "Latin Lover" of the silent era): The Legend of Valentino, 1975 (made-for-TV; Franco Nero); Rodolfo Valentino—La leggenda, 2013- (TV miniseries; Gabriel Garko); The Rose Seller, 2010 (made-for-TV; Patrick Lavoie); Twilight, 1969 (Kong Sam Oeurn); Valentino, 1951 (Anthony Dexter); Valentino, 1977 (Rudolf Nureyev); The World's Greatest Lover, 1977 (Matt Collins).

Valois-Saint-Remy, Jeanne de (French adventuress and thief; 1756-1791): The Affair of the Necklace, 2001 (Hilary Swank).

Van Buren, Martin (Eighth President of the U.S.; 1782-1862): **Amistad**, 1999 (Nigel Hawthorne); The Gorgeous Hussy, 1936 (Charles Trowbridge); **Man of Conquest**, 1939 (Francis Sayles); Savage Journey, 1983 (made-for-TV; Francis L. Urry).

Van Gogh, Theo (1857-1891; Theodorus Van Gogh; art dealer and younger brother of Vincent Van Gogh): Besuch bei Van Gogh, 1985 (Hartmut Puls); The Eyes of Van Gogh, 2005 (Keith Perry); Langs de kant van de weg, 1990 (TV series; Kees Scholten); Lautrec, 1999 (Pierre Chydivar); Le voyage du Hollandais, 1981 (made-for-TV; Christian Benedetti); **Lust for Life**, 1952 (James Donald); Mon cher Theo Van Gogh, 1980 (made-for-TV; Jean Coste); Omnibus, 1967-2003 (TV series; "Van Gogh," 1990 episode: Kevin Wallace); Paul Gauguin, 1975 (TV miniseries; Jean-Jacques Moreau); Van Gogh, 1969 (made-for-TV; Til Erwig); **Van Gogh**, 1991 (Bernard Le Coq); Van Gogh; een huis voor Vincent, 2013 (TV series; Anne Prakke); Van Gogh: Painted with Words, 2010 (made-for-TV; Jamie Parker); **Vincent and Theo**, 1990 (Paul Rhys); The Yellow House, 2007 (made-for-TV; Scott Handy).

Van Gogh, Vincent (1853-1890; Dutch artist): Around the World in 80 Days, 2004 (Perry Andelin Blake); Artists' Notebooks, 1964 (TV series; Alan Dobie voiceover); Besuch bei Van Gogh, 1985 (Christian Grashof); **Dreams**, 1990 (Martin Scorsese); The Eyes of Van Gogh, 2005 (Alexander Barnett; Matthew Marchetti as young Vincent); Full Moon Fables, 2004 (Dan DePaola); Gauguin the Savage, 1980 (made-for-TV; Barrie Houghton); Histeria!, 1998-2000 (animated TV series; "Inventors Hall of Fame: Part I," 1998 episode: Frank Welker voiceover); Langs de kant van de weg, 1990 (TV series; Ids van der Krieken); Lautrec, 1999 (Karel Vingerhoets); Le voyage du Hollandais, 1981 (made-for-TV; Gerard Desarthe); **Lust for Life**, 1956 (Kirk Douglas); Medium, 2005-2011 (TV series; "Still Life," 2005 episode: Ed Baccari); Mon cher Theo Van Gogh, 1980 (made-for-TV; Gregory Knop voiceover); Moulin Rouge, a vida de Toulouse-Lautrec, 1963 (TV series; Rolando Boldrin); Omnibus, 1967-2003 (TV series; "Vincent the Dutchman," 1972 episode: Michael Gough; "Van Gogh," 1990 episode:

Kirk Douglas (with self-portrait as painter Vincent Van Gogh) in *Lust for Life,* **1956.**

Linus Roache); Out of the Box, 1998-2004 (TV series; "Mirror, Mirror," 1999 episode: Sal Viviano); Paradise Found, 2003 (Peter Varga); Paul Gauguin, 1975 (TV miniseries; Jean de Coninck); The Philco-Goodyear Television Playhouse, 1948-1956 (TV series; "The Life of Vincent Van Gogh," 1959 episode: Everett Sloane); Starry Night, 2003 (Abbott Alexander [David Abbott]); State of the Artist, 2001 (Dan DePaola); Van Gogh, 1969 (made-for-TV; Herbert Fleischmann); **Van Gogh**, 1991 (Jacques Dutronc); Van Gogh; een huis voor Vincent, 2013 (TV series; Barry Atsma); Van Gogh: Painted with Words, 2010 (made-for-TV; Benedict Cumberbatch); **Vincent and Theo**, 1990 (Tim Roth); Vincent et moi, 2001 (Tcheky Karyo); Vincent Van Gogh, 1988 (made-for-TV; Timo Torikka); The Yellow House, 2007 (made-for-TV; John Simm).

Van Lew, Elizabeth (1818-1900; U.S. spymaster for the Union army in Richmond, Virginia, during the American Civil War): A Special Friendship, 1987 (made-for-TV; Cynthia Harris).

Van Meter, Homer (U.S. bank robber and member of the Dillinger gang; 1906-1934): Baby Face Nelson, 1957 (Elisha Cook Jr.); Dillinger, 1973 (Harry Dean Stanton); Gang Busters, 1952- (TV series; Richard Crane); Guns Don't Argue, 1957 (Richard Crane); The Kansas City Massacre, 1975 (made-for-TV; Brion James); **Public Enemies**; 2009 (Stephen Dorff). Note: For detailed information on Van Meter, see my my books, *Dillinger: Dead or Alive?*, 1970 (Regnery, 1970); *The Dillinger Dossier* (December Press, 1983); and my two-volume work, *The Great Pictorial History of World Crime*, Volume II (History, Inc., 2004; illustrated [63 images] pages 1374-1423).

Vance, Zebulon Baird (1830-1894; U.S. attorney, politician and governor of South Carolina): You Are There, 1953-1957 (TV series; "The Gettysburg Address," 1953 episode: Murray Hamilton).

Vandervoort, Benjamin H. (Benjamin Hayes Vandervoort; aka: "Vandy"; 1917-1990; U.S. Army lieutenant-colonel, who led airborne troops during the Allied invasion of Normandy on June 6, 1944): **The Longest Day**, 1962 (John Wayne; Vandervoort was twenty-seven at the time of D-Day and Wayne was fifty-five when this film was made).

Vane, Charles (c. 1680-1721; British pirate operating in the Bahamas and the Atlantic; executed by hanging): Black Sails, 2014- (TV series; Zach McGowan); Blackbeard; Terror at Sea, 2006 (made-for-TV; Jack Galloway); True Caribbean Pirates, 2006 (made-for-TV; Matthew Rimmer).

Vanzetti, Bartolomeo (1888-1927; U.S. Italian immigrant and anarchist;

Irene Dunne (as Victoria I) and Alec Guinness in *The Mudlark*, 1950.

executed for robbery and murder): De zaak Sacco en Vanzetti, 1966 (made-for-TV; Henk van Ulsen); Der Fall Sacco und Vanzetti, 1963 (made-for-TV; Gunther Neutze); L'affaire Sacco et Vanzetti, 1967 (Maurice Travail); **No God, No Master**, 2012 (Alessandro Mario); Sacco & Vanzetti, 1971 (Gian Maria Volonte); Sacco & Vanzetti, 2005 (made-for-TV; Ennio Fantastichini); Sacco e Vanzetti, 1977- (TV miniseries; Franco Graziosi); Sacco und Vanzetti, 1927 (Hans Peppler); Sunday Showcase, 1959-1960 (TV series; "The Sacco and Vanzetti Story," two 1960 episodes: Steven Hill); The Wednesday Play, 1964-1970 (TV series; "The Good Shoemaker and the Poor Fish Peddler," 1965 episode: John Bailey); Windy City Heat, 2003 (made-for-TV; Scott Hartman). Note: For detailed information on Sacco and Vanzetti, see my eight-volume work *Encycloped of World Crime*, Volume IV (CrimeBooks, Inc., 1990; illustrated [8 images] 2649-2652].

Velez, Lupe (Maria Guadalupe Villalobos Velez; aka: Mexican Spitfire; 1908-1944; Mexican film actress, most popular in screwball comedies of the 1930s and early 1940s; committed suicide over a love affair): E! Mysteries & Scandals, 1998- (TV series; "Lupe Velez," 1999 episode; Letitia Robles; "Jean Spangler," 2000 episode: Letitia Robles); Lupe, 1966 (Edie Sedgwick); Marlene, 2000 (Laura Bayonas); Mr. Broadway, 1933 (herself); Return to Babylon, 2013 (Maria Conchita Alonso).

Venable, Charles Scott (1827-1900; U.S. educator and military officer who served on the staff of Confederate General Robert E. Lee from 1862 to 1865): You Are There, 1953-1957 (TV series; "Grant and Lee at Appomattox, 1953 and 1955 episodes: Dabbs Greer).

Verdi, Giuseppe (1813-1901; Italian composer): House of Ricordi, 1956 (Fosco Giachetti); I padre della patria, 1991- (TV series; "Alessandro Manzoni," 1992 episode: Pier Paolo Capponi); La famiglia Ricordi, 1995 (TV miniseries; Mariano Rigillo); The Life and Music of Giuseppe Verdi, 1957 (Pierre Cressoy); The Life of Giuseppe Verdi, 1940 (Fosco Giachetti); The Lost One, 1948 (Nerio Bernardi); Maestro der Revolution?, 1971 (made-for-TV; Karl Michael Vogler); The Teacher, 2005- (TV series; "La terza vittima," 2008 episode: Marco Bonini); Verdi, 1982 (TV miniseries; Ronald Pickup); Verdi, 1994 (made-for-TV; Bob Peck voiceover).

Verlaine, Paul-Marie (1844-1896; French poet and a member of the symbolist movement): The Flame Is Love, 1979 (made-for-TV; John Franklyn); If Paris Were Told to Us, 1956 (Antoine Balpetre); A Season in Hell, 1964 (made-for-TV; Alistair Duncan); The Time Tunnel, 1966-1967 (TV series; "Invasion," 1966 episode; Joe E. Tata); Total Eclipse,

1973 (made-for-TV; Ian Hogg); Total Eclipse, 1975 (made-for-TV; Hugo Van Den Bergh); Total Eclipse, 1995 (David Thewlis).

Vespasian (9-79 A.D.; Roman emperor): Age of Treason, 1993 (made-for-TV; Anthony Valentine); Ancient Rome: The Rise and Fall of an Empire, 2006 (TV series; Peter Firth); The Battle for Rome, 2006 (TV series; Peter Firth); I, Claudius, 1937 (Lyn Harding); Masada, 1981 (TV miniseries; Timothy West).

Vetsera, Mary (Maria Vetsera; 1871-1889; Austrian baroness and mistress of Crown Prince Rudolf who committed suicide with him at Mayerling, the Austrian royal hunting lodge, because they were prohibited from marrying due to her lowly social status): BBC Sunday-Night Theatre, 1950-1959 (TV series; "The Masque of Kings," 1955 episode: Jane Barrett; "The Mayerling Affair," 1956 episode: Mai Zetterling); The Crown Prince, 2006 (made-for-TV; Vittoria Puccini); Der Kronprinz, 1989 (made-for-TV; Adel Kovats); Enigmes de l'histoire, 1956-1957 (TV series; one 1956 episode: Pierrette Bruno); Kronprinz Rudolf oder: Das Geheimnis von Mayerling, 1919 (Thea Sandten); Kronprinz Rudolfs letzte Liebe, 1959 (Christiane Horbiger); La camera explore le temps, 1957-1966 (TV series; one 1964 episode: Danielle Palmero); **Mayerling**, 1937 (Danielle Darrieux); Mayerling, 1968 (Catherine Deneuve); Producers' Showcase, 1954-1957 (TV series; "Mayerling," 1957 episode: Audrey Hepburn); The Secret of Mayerling, 1951 (Dominique Blanchar); The Song in the Forest, 1950 (Patricia Dainton).

Victor Emmanuel II (1820-1878; King of Sardinia and King of Italy): The Hourglass Sanatorium, 1973 (Stanislaw Olczyk); Ottocento, 1959-1960 (TV miniseries; Giuseppe Pagliarini); Verdi, 1982 (TV miniseries; Dino Mattielli); Villafranca, 1932 (Annibale Betrone).

Victor Emmanuel III (1869-1947; King of Italy, who allowed Benito Mussolini to come to power and reign as a dictator): Diszmagyar, 1949 (Sandor Peti); Il delitto Matteotti, 1973 (Giulio Girola); Io e il re, 1995 (Carlo Delle Piane); Mafalda of Savoy, 2006 (made-for-TV; Carlo Dogliani); Mussolini and I, 1985 (made-for-TV; Marne Maitland); Mussolini: The Untold Story, 1985 (TV miniseries; Kenneth Colley); Quando c'era lui...lei!, 1978 (Salvatore Furnari).

Victoria I (1819-1901; Queen of Great Britain): **The Adventure of Sherlock Holmes' Smarter Brother**, 1975 (Susan Field); Adventures in Paradise, 1959-1962 (TV series; "Blueprint for Paradise," 1962 episode: Pilar Seurat); **Annie Get Your Gun**, 1950 (Evelyn Beresford); Around the World in 80 Days, 1989 (TV miniseries; Anna Massey); Around the World in 80 Days, 2004 (Kathy Bates); Balaclava, 1930 (Marian Drada); Barnum, 1986 (made-for-TV; Bronwen Mantel); The Battle of the Waltzes, 1934 (Hanna Waag); BBC Play of the Month, 1965-1983 (TV series; "Gordon of Khartoum," 1966 episode: Gladys Spencer); Bewitched, 1964-1972 (TV series; "Aunt Clara's Victoria Victory," 1967 episode: Jane Connell); Bismarck, 1940 (Marga Riffa); **Buffalo Bill**, 1944 (Evelyn Beresford); Court Waltzes, 1933 (Madeleine Ozeray); David Livingstone, 1936 (Pamela Stanley); Disraeli, 1916 (Mrs. Henry Lytton); **Disraeli**, 1929 (Margaret Mann); Disraeli: Portrait of a Romantic, 1978 (TV miniseries; Rosemary Leach); East Lynne, 1976 (made-for-TV; Shirley Steedman); Edward the King, 1975 (TV series; Annette Crosbie); The Edwardians, 1972-1973 (TV series; 'Daisy,' 1973 episode; Mollie Maureen); Entente cordiale, 1939 (Gaby Morlay); Fall of Eagles, 1974 (TV miniseries; "The English Princess," 1974 episode: Perlita Neilson; "The Last Tsar," 1974 episode: Mavis Edwards); The Flaxton Boys, 1969-1973 (TV series; "1854: The Dog," 1969 episode: Christine Ozanne); Gilbert and Sullivan, 1953 (Muriel Aked); The Great McGonagall, 1975 (Peter Sellers); The Great Victory, Wilson or the Kaiser? The Fall of the Hohenzollerns, 1919 (Fanny Cogan); Hands of a Murderer, 1990 (Honora Burke); Hans Christian Anderson: My Life as a Fairy Tale, 2003 (made-for-TV; Nina Lutjens);

Happy and Glorious, 1952 (TV series; Renee Asherson); **Her Majesty; Mrs. Brown**, 1997 (Judi Dench); Invincible Mr. Disraeli, 1963 (Kate Reid); Journey to Midnight, 1971 (Fay Compton); Journey to the Unknown, 1968 (TV series; Fay Compton); **The Lady with a Lamp**, 1951 (Anna Neagle); Let's Make Up, 1956 (Anna Neagle); Lillie, 1978 (TV miniseries; Sheila Reed); **The Little Princess**, 1939 (Beryl Mercer); Livingstone, 1925 (Blanche Graham); Marigold, 1938 (Pamela Stanley); Melba, 1953 (Sybil Thorndike); Mr. Gladstone, 1947 (made-for-TV; Ada Reeve); **The Mudlark**, 1950 (Irene Dunne); **Mystery of the Wax Museum**, 1933 (Margaret Mann as the wax effigy of Queen Victoria); Network First: Victoria and Albert, 1997- (TV miniseries; Avril Angers as older Victoria; Louise Rea); Omnibus, 1967-2002 (TV series; "Landseer: A Victorian Comedy," 1980 episode: Pamela Binns); Paul Kruger, 1956 (Gwen Ffrangcon Davies); **The Pearls of the Crown**, 1938 (Yvette Pienne); Pervirella, 1997 (Sexton Ming); **The Pirates! Band of Misfits**, 2012 (Imelda Staunton voiceover); Preussen uber alles – Bismarcks deutsche Einigung, 1971 (TV miniseries; Renate Pichler); The Prime Minister, 1942 (Fay Compton); **The Private Life of Sherlock Holmes**, 1970 (Mollie Maureen); Queen of Destiny, 1940 (Anna Neagle); Queen Victoria's Empire, 2001- (TV series; Frances McDevitt); The Ravelled Thread, 1979-1980 (TV series; "The Spy," 1980 episode: Muriel Pavlow); Rhodes, 1996 (TV miniseries; "The Price of My Blood," 1996 episode: Margaret Heale); Robert Montgomery Presents, 1950-1957 (TV series; "Victoria Regina," 1951 episode: Helen Hayes; "Victoria Regina," 1957 episode; Claire Bloom); Shadow Play, 2004 (TV series; Doreen Mantle); Shanghai Knights, 2003 (Gemma Jones); **Sixty Glorious Years**, 1938 (Anna Neagle); Sixty Years a Queen, 1913 (Blanche Forsythe); Station Jim, 2001 (made-for-TV; Prunella Scales); **The Story of Alexander Graham Bell**, 1939 (Beryl Mercer); The Story of Vickie, 1958 (Romy Schneider); The Symbol of Sacrifice, 1918 (Mrs. D. Buxton); Tall Tales and Legends, 1985-1988 (TV series; "Annie Oakley," 1985 episode: Lu Leonard); Those Fantastic Flying Fools, 1967 (Joan Sterndale-Bennett); Uncle Kruger, 1941 (Hedwig Wangel); Victoria & Albert, 2001 (made-for-TV; Victoria Hamilton); Victoria in Dover, 1936 (Jenny Jugo); Victoria in Dover, 1958 (Romy Schneider); Victoria Regina, 1961 (made-for-TV; Julie Harris); Victoria Regina, 1964 (TV miniseries; Patricia Routledge); **Victoria the Great**, 1937 (Anna Neagle); Voyagers!, 1982-1983 (TV series; "Buffalo Bill and Annie Play the Palace," 1983 episode: Lurene Tuttle); **The White Angel**, 1936 (Fay Holden); Witness to Yesterday, 1970-1976 (TV series; "Queen Victoria," 1973 episode: Kate Reid); **The Wrong Box**, 1966 (Avis Bunnage); The Yankee Clipper, 1927 (Julia Faye); **The Young Victoria**, 2009 (Emily Blunt); The Young Visitors, 2003 (made-for-TV; Janine Duvitski); Zorro in the Court of England, 1971 (Barbara Carroll). For detailed information on the assassination attempts made against Victoria I, see my two-volume work *The Great Pictorial History of World Crime*, Volume I (History, Inc., 2004; illustrated pages 20-22).

Vidocq, Eugene Francois (1775-1857; French criminal, criminologist and police official and upon whom Victor Hugo based his two main characters, Jean Valjean, an escaped criminal, and Javert, a police inspector tracking him, in his classic 1862 novel, *Les Miserables*): Adventures of Criminalistics, 1989-1993 (TV series; "Stopa," 1989 episode: Boris Rosner); Les Miserables, 1917 (role models for William Farnum and Hardee Kirkland); Les Miserables, 1927 (role models for Gabriel Gabrio and Jean Toulout); **Les Miserables**, 1935; (role models for Fredric March and Charles Laughton); Les Miserables, 1936 (role models for Harry Baur and Charles Vanel); Les Miserables, 1944 (role models for Domingo Soler and Antonio Bravo); Les Miserables, 1952 (role models for Gino Cervi and Hans Hinrich); **Les Miserables**, 1952 (role models for Michael Rennie and Robert Newton); Les Miserables, 1958 (role models for Jean Gabin and Bernard Blier); Les Miserables, 1972 (TV miniseries; role models for Georges Geret and Bernard Fresson); Les Miserables, 1978 (role models for Richard Jordan and Anthony Perkins); Les Miserables, 1982 (role models for Lino Ventura and

Wallace Beery (left, as Pancho Villa) in *Viva Villa!*, **1934.**

Michel Bouquet); Les Miserables, 1995 (role models for Jean-Paul Belmondo and Philippe Khorsand); Les Miserables, 1998 (role models for Liam Neeson and Geoffrey Rush); Les Miserables, 2012 (role models for Hugh Jackman and Russell Crowe); **A Scandal in Paris**, 1946 (George Sanders); Vidocq, 1923 (Rene Navarre); Vidocq, 1939 (Andre Brule); Vidocq, 1967 (TV series; Bernard Noel); Les nouvelles aventures de Vidocq, 1971-1973 (TV series; Claude Brasseur); **Vidocq**, 2001 (Gerard Depardieu); Vidocq, 2010 (TV series; Bruno Madinier). For detailed information about Vidocq, see my eight-volume work *Encyclopedia of World Crime*, Volume IV (CrimeBooks, Inc., illustrated pages: 3047-3049).

Villa, Pancho (Jose Doroteo Arango Arambula; 1878-1923; Mexican bandit, patriot and revolutionary leader): Ah! Silenciosa, 1999 (Carlos Roberto Majul); American Family, 2002-2004 (TV series; "Mexican Revolution," 2002 episode: Edward James Olmos); And Starring Pancho Villa as Himself, 2003 (made-for-TV: Antonio Banderas); Aqui esta Pancho Villa, 1960 (TV series; Pedro Armendariz); Between Pancho Villa and a Naked Woman, 1996 (Jesus Ochoa); Caballo prieto azabache (La tumba de Villa), 1968 (Raul "Chato" Padilla); El centauro Pancho Villa, 1967 (Jose Elias Moreno); El encanto del aguila, 2011 (Enoc Leano); El 7 leguas, 1955 (Victor Alcocer); Ethel Barrymore Theater, 1956 (TV series; "This Is Villa," 1956 episode: Akim Tamiroff); La estampida, 1959 (Jose Chavez); La muerte de Pacncho Villa, 1974 (Antonio Aguilar); La sangre de un valiente, 1993 (Antonio Aguilar); Las tres pelonas, 1958 (Jose Chavez); Let's Go with Pancho Villa, 1939 (Domingo Soler); The Life of General Villa, 1914 (Raoul Walsh as a young Villa; Pancho Villa as himself); **Old Gringo**, 1989 (Pedro Armendariz Jr.); Pancho Villa, 1972 (Telly Savalas); Pancho Villa and Valentina, 1960 (Pedro Armendariz); Pancho Villa Returns, 1950 (Leo Carrillo); Patria, 1917 (Wallace Beery); Red Bells Part I: Mexico on Fire, 1982 (Jorge Reynoso); Reed, Mexico Insurgente, 1974 (Heraclio Zepeda); Senda de Gloria, 1987 (TV series; Guillermo Gil); She Came to the Valley, 1979 (Freddy Fender); This Was Pancho Villa, 1957 (Pedro Armendariz); The Treasure of Pancho Villa, 1936 (Juan F. Triana); Villa!, 1958 (Rodolfo Hoyos); Under Strange Flags, 1937 (Maurice Black); Villa Rides, 1968 (Yul Brynner); Viva Mexico, 1980 (made-for-TV; Jose Villamor); **Viva Villa!**, 1934 (Wallace Beery); **Viva Zapata!**, 1952 (Alan Reed); Vuelve Pancho Villa, 1950 (Pedro Armendariz); Wanted: The Sundance Woman, 1976 (made-for-TV; Hector Elizondo); Why America Will Win, 1918 (George Humbert); With Villa's Veterans, 1939 (Luis Alvarez); Zapata, 1970 (David Reynoso); Zapata—El sueno del hero, 2004 (Luis Enrique Parra). For detailed information on Villa, see my two-volume work *The Great Pictorial History of World Crime*, Volume I (History, Inc., 2004; illustrated [9 images] pages 91-94).

William Farnum (as Francois Villon) in *If I Were King,* **1920.**

Villon, Francois (1431-1463?; French poet and petty criminal, who disappeared): The Beloved Rogue, 1927 (John Barrymore); C'est arrive a Paris, 1977 (made-for-TV; Jean-Luc Moreau); Francois Villon, 1950 (Serge Reggiani); Francois Villon, 1981 (made-for-TV; Jorg Pleva); Je, Francois Villon, voleur, assassin, poete, 2010 (made-for-TV; Francis Renaud); If I Were King, 1920 (William Farnum); **If I Were King**, 1938 (Ronald Colman); If Paris Were Told to Us, 1956 (Pierre Vaneck); La memoire des siecles, 1981 (TV series; Francois-Regis Marchasson); Mon couer est rouge, 1977 (Caroline Champetier); Nocny gosc, 1989 (Jacek Mikolajczak); Omnibus, 1952-1961 (TV series; "A Lodging for the Night," 1953 episode: Yul Brynner); Rheingold Theatre, 1953-1957 (TV series; "A Lodging for the Night," 1953 episode: Douglas Fairbanks Jr.); Screen Directors Playhouse, 1955-1956 (TV series; "The Sword of Villon," 1956 episode: Errol Flynn); The Triangle, 1953 (Douglas Fairbanks Jr.); **The Vagabond King**, 1930 (Dennis King); **The Vagabond King**, 1956 (Oreste Kirkop).

Virgil (70-19 B.C.; Roman poet): The Comoedia, 1981 (Richard Coleman); Dante's Inferno, 1924 (Howard Gaye); Dante's Inferno, 2007 (animated; James Cromwell voiceover); Dante's Inferno, 2011 (animated; Nevin Millan); Madoff's Inferno, 2014 (Bob Saenz); Inferno, 2016 (TV series; Ivan King); A TV Dante, 1989- (TV miniseries; John Gielgud, Fernando Bordeu).

Voltaire (Francois-Marie Arouet; 1694-1778; French historian and philosopher): Battle of the Brave, 2004 (Philippe Dormoy); BBC Play of the Month, 1965-1983 (TV series; "Candide," 1977 episode: Frank Finlay); Devine Emilie, 2007 (made-for-TV; Thierry Fremont); Die Muhle von Sanssouci, 1968 (made-for-TV; Peter Capell); Einstein's Big Idea, 2005 (made-for-TV; Anton Lesser); Frederic II, 1972 (Pierre Asso); Friedrich—Ein deutscher Konig, 2012 (made-for-TV; Karl Walter Spungala); If Paris Were Told to Us, 1956 (Jacques de Feraudy); La camera explore le temps, 1957-1966 (TV series; "L'affaire Calas," 1963 episode: Pierre Asso); The Lame Devil, 1948 (Maurice Shultz); Louis XVI, the Man Who Didn't Want to Be King, 2011 (made-for-TV; Roland Cope); Madame De Pompedour: The King's Favorite, 2006 (made-for-TV; Jean-Francois Derec); Mandrin, 1924 (Bardes); Mandrin, 1947 (Robert Pizani); Mandrin, 1962 (Georges Rouquier); Marat/Sade, 1967 (John Harwood); Monsieur Beaucaire, 1924 (Harry Lee); My Name Is Bach, 2004 (Michel Cassagne); **Napoleon**, 1927 (G. A. Martin); Royal Affairs in Versailles, 1957 (Jacques de Feraudy); Talleyrand ou Le sphinx incompris, 1972 (Renaud Mary); Theatre 625, 1964-1968 (TV series; "The Fanatics," 1968 episode; Leonard Rossiter); Voltaire, 1933 (George Arliss); Voltaire et l'affaire Calas, 2007 (made-for-TV; Claude Rich).

Voronov, Nikolai (1899-1968; Soviet field marshal in WWII): The First Front, 1949 (Vasili Merkuryev); The Victors and the Vanquished, 1949 (Vasili Merkuryev).

Voss, Werner (1897-1917; German fighter pilot credited with shooting down 48 enemy planes during WWI): **The Red Baron**, 2010 (Til Schweiger); **Von Richthofen and Brown**, 1971 (Stephen McHattie).

Wade, Benjamin Franklin (1800-1878; U.S. politician, U.S. senator and leader of the Radical Republicans during the American Civil War): Bad Blood: The Border War That Triggered the Civil War, 2007 (made-for-TV; C. J. Johnson); **Lincoln**, 2012 (Wayne Duvall); The Lincoln Conspiracy, 1977 (Dick Callinan).

Wagner, Richard (1813-1883; German composer): At the Order of the Czar, 1954 (Peter Lehmbrock); Auf den Spuren von Richard Wagners Tristan und Isolde, 1973 (made-for-TV; Kurt Buechler); Bruckners Entscheidung, 1995 (Joachim Kaiser); Celles qui aimaient Richard Wagner, 2011 (Jean-Francois Balmer); Der Clan—Die Geschichte der Familie Wagner, 2013 (Justus von Dohnanyi); Doctor Faustus, 1961- (TV series; Patrick Godfrey); Doctor Faustus, 1967 (Patrick Barwise); Faust, 1960 (Edward Marks); Faust, 1975 (made-for-TV; Jean Soumagnas); Faust, 1982 (made-for-TV; Gerd David); Faust, 2011 (Georg Friedrich); Hungarian Rhapsody, 1954 (Peter Lehmbrock); Il Mefistofele, 1989 (made-for-TV; Fabio Armiliato); The Life and Works of Richard Wagner, 1913 (Giuseppe Becce); Liszt Ferenc, 1982 (TV miniseries; Tilo Pruckner); Lisztomania, 1975 (Paul Nicholas); Liszt Ferenc, 1982- (TV miniseries; Tilo Pruckner); Ludwig, 1972 (Trevor Howard); Ludwig: Requiem for a Virgin King, 1980 (Gerhard Maerz); Ludwig II, 1922 (Eugen Preiss); Ludwig II, 2012 (Edgar Selge); Ludwig II: Glanz und Ende eines Konigs, 1959 (Paul Bildt); Magic Fire, 1956 (Alan Badel); Muchachada nui, 2007-2010 (animated TV series; Raul Cimas); **Song without End**, 1960 (Lyndon Brook); Twilight of the Gods, 2013 (Richard Franklin); Wagner, 1983 (TV series; Richard Burton); Wagner and Venice, 1982 (made-for-TV; Orson Welles); Wahnfried, 1987 (Otto Sander); Warten auf Beethoven, 1984 (made-for-TV; Giacomo Herby).

Wagner, Walter (d. 1945; German notary, who married Eva Braun and Adolf Hitler on April 29, 1945, in the dictator's bunker just before the fall of Berlin to the Soviets and before the couple committed joint suicide, she by cyanide poison, he by firing a bullet into his head): Hitler: The Last Ten Days, 1973 (Andrew Sachs).

Wainwright, Jonathan Mayhew IV (aka: "Skinny"; "Jim"; 1883-1953; U.S. Army lieutenant general, later four-star general, who surrendered Allied forces in the Philippines in 1942; recipient of the Congressional Medal of Honor; **Back to Bataan**, 1945 (John Miljan); **MacArthur**, 1977 (Sandy Kenyon).

Waldo, Rhinelander (1877-1927; New York City police commissioner): **Ragtime**, 1981 (James Cagney).

Waldron, John Charles (1900-1942; U.S. Navy lieutenant commander who led a squadron of torpedo bombers against Japanese carriers in the decisive battle of Midway in WWII; was killed in the action): **Midway**, 1976 (Glenn Corbett).

Walewska, Marie (1786-1718; Polish noblewoman and mistress of Napoleon I): **Conquest**, 1937 (Greta Garbo); Grafin Walewska, 1920 (Hella Moja); La camera explore le temps, 1957-1966 (TV series; "Marie Walewska," 1957 episode: Magali Vendeuil); Marie Walewska, 1969 (made-for-TV; Danielle Volle); Marysia i Napoleon, 1966 (Beata Tyszkiewicz); Napoleon, 1955 (Lana Marconi); Napoleon, 2002- (TV miniseries; Alexandra Maria Lara); Napoleon and Josephine: A Love Story, 1987- (TV miniseries; Wendy Stockle); Napoleon and Love,

1974- (TV miniseries; Catherine Schell); Napoleon et l'Europe, 1991- (TV series; Joanna Szczepkowska); Schulmeister, espion de l'empereur, 1971-1974 (TV series; "Avant les cent jours," 1974 episode; Francoise Giret); TV de Vangarda, 1952- (TV series; "O Grande Amor de Maria Walewska," 1958 episode: Marly Bueno).

Walker, Edwin (1909-1993; U.S. major general, who resigned after becoming involved in right-wing politics): The Korean War, 2001 (TV series; Jack Shearer).

Walker, Erwin (1918-1982; U.S. thief and killer): **He Walked by Night**, 1948 (Richard Basehart).

Walker, James J. (1891-1946; U.S. politician; mayor of NYC and composer [wrote the memorable lyrics to the 1905 song "Will You Love Me in December As You Do in May?"]; he was a colorful, liberal Democrat deeply involved with NYC's corrupt Tammany Hall political machine, and scandals in his administration eventually forced him to resign from office; a great Broadway production number, "Gentleman Jimmy" encapsulates Walker's persona in the stage musical "Fiorello!"): **Beau James**, 1957 (Bob Hope); **Zelig**, 1983 (himself in stock footage merged with live-action sequences to show actor Woody Allen socializing with him).

Walker, Walton Harris (U.S. soldier and four-star U.S. Army general in WWII and the Korean War; 1889-1950).

Wallace, George (1919-1998; U.S. politician and segregationist governor of Alabama, who later renounced segregation): George Wallace, 1997 (made-for-TV; Gary Sinise); Path to War, 2002 (made-for-TV; Gary Sinise); **Selma**, 2014 (Tim Roth); Unconquered, 1989 (made-for-TV; Bob Gunton).

Wallace Lew (Lewis "Lew" Wallace; 1827-1905; U.S. military officer; general in the American Civil War; governor of the New Mexico Territory during the notorious Lincoln County War, and author of the celebrated 1880 historical novel *Ben-Hur: A Tale of the Christ*): The Big Stampede, 1932 (Berton Churchill); Billy the Kid, 1930 (Frank Reicher); Billy the Kid, 1989 (made-for-TV; Wilford Brimley); Branded, 1965-1966 (TV series; "A Destiny Which Made Us Brothers," 1966 episode: Len Hendry); Bronco, 1958-1962 (TV series; "Death of an Outlaw," 1960 episode: Forrest Lewis); Colt .45, 1957-1960 (TV series; "Amnesty," 1959 episode: Willis Bouchey); Death Valley Days, 1952-1970 (TV series; "Shadows on the Window," 1960 episode: Dayton Lummis; "The Gold Mine on Main Street," 1968 episode: Harry Holcombe); Der Andersonville-Prozess, 1972 (made-for-TV; Alexander Hegarth); I Shot Billy the Kid, 1950 (Claude Stroud); The Kid from Texas, 1950 (Robert Barrat); Land beyond the Law, 1937 (Joe King); Law of the Plainsman, 1959- (TV series; "Amnesty," 1960 episode: Robert Warwick); The Law vs. Billy the Kid, 1954 (Otis Garth); The Little Shepherd of Kingdom Come, 1961 (Morris Ankrum); Longarm, 1988 (made-for-TV; Rene Auberjonois); **Pat Garrett and Billy the Kid**, 1973 (Jason Robards Jr.); The Philco-Goodyear Television Playhouse, 1948-1956 (TV series; "The Death of Billy the Kid," 1955 episode: Matt Crowley); Strange Lady in Town, 1955 (Ralph Moody); Tales of Wells Fargo, 1957-1962 (TV series; "Billy the Kid," 1957 episode: Addison Richards); The Tall Man, 1960-1962 (TV series; "The Great Western," 1961 episode: Frank Ferguson; "The Black Robe," 1962 episode: Robert Burton); The Wild West, 2006- (TV series; "Billy the Kid,' 2006 episode: Colin Stinton); **Young Guns II**, 1990 (Scott Wilson).

Wallace, William (d. 1305; Scottish knight and leader of the Wars of Scottish Independence): Border Warfare, 1990- (TV series; "The Greater Shall Draw the Lesser," 1990 episode: Robert Begg); **Braveheart**, 1995 (Mel Gibson); Churchill's People, 1974- (TV series; "The Wallace,"

Mel Gibson (as William Wallace) in *Braveheart*, 1995.

1975 episode; Brian Cox); Kings and Queens, 2002 (TV miniseries; "Edward I," 2002 episode: Sean Francis George); A Life More Ordinary, 2002 (Sandy Jack); Mysteries at the Castle, 2014- (TV series; "House That Saved a King; Joan of Arc; Hamilton Sex Scandal," 2015 episode: Michael D. Joseph); Strangeheart, 2003 (Matt Tobin; Joseph Burns as young Wallace).

Wallenberg, Raoul (1912-1947?; Swedish businessman and diplomat responsible for saving tens of thousands of Jews during the Holocaust in Hungary during WWII): Good Evening, Mr. Wallenberg, 1993 (Stellan Skarsgard); The Tulse Luper Suitcases, Part 3: From Sark to the Finish, 2004 (Roberto Citran); Wallenberg: A Hero's Story, 1985 (made-for-TV; Richard Chamberlain).

Wallis, Barnes Neville (1887-1979; British scientist, inventor and engineer): **The Dam Busters**, 1955 (Michael Redgrave).

Walpole, Horace (1717-1797; British historian and Whig politician): Aristocrat, 1999- (TV miniseries; Eamon Rohan); Liberty! The American Revolution, 1997 (TV miniseries; Paxton Whitehead).

Walsh, Raoul (1887-1980; U.S. pantheon film director): And Starring Pancho Villa as Himself, 2003 (made-for-TV: Kyle Chandler); It's a Great Feeling, 1949 (himself); My Wicked Wicked Ways: The Legend of Errol Flynn, 1985 (made-for-TV; Michael C. Gwynne); Rock Hudson, 1990 (made-for-TV; Lawrence Dobkin).

Walsingham, Francis (Sir Francis Walsingham; 1532-1590; secretary and spymaster for Elizabeth I of England): Elisabeth von England, 1961 (made-for-TV; Richard Bohne); **Elizabeth**, 1998 (Geoffrey Rush); Elizabeth I, 2005- (TV miniseries; Patrick Malahide); Elizabeth R, 1971-1972 (TV miniseries; three episodes: Stephen Murray); **Elizabeth: The Golden Age**, 2007 (Geoffrey Rush); **Mary of Scotland**, 1936 (Walter Byron); Mary, Queen of Scots, 1971 (Richard Warner); Queen's Champion, 1958- (TV miniseries; "The Eve of the Armada," 1958 episode: Douglas Dempster); Seven Seas to Calais, 1963 (Basil Dignam); Sir Francis Drake, 1961- (TV series; Richard Warner); The Virgin Queen, 2005 (TV miniseries; Ben Daniels); **The Sea Hawk**, 1940 (role model for Henry Daniell); Will Shakespeare, 1971- (TV series; "Dead Shepherd," 1978 episode: John Bailey). Note: For detailed information on Walsingham, see my book *Spies: A Narrative Encyclopedia of Dirty Tricks & Double Dealing from Biblical Times to Today* (M. Evans, 1997; illustrated pages 500-502).

Warde, John William (1912-1938; U.S. native of Southampton, New

Richard Basehart (in role model of John Warde) in *Fourteen Hours,* **1951.**

York, who, in an emotionally disturbed state, climbed onto the outside ledge of the seventeenth floor of NYC's Gotham Hotel, as a NYPD officer attempted to talk him back inside; a photographer spooked Warde after eleven hours when trying to take his picture and he leaped to his death before more than 10,000 horrififed spectators assembled below): **Fourteen Hours**, 1951 (role model for Richard Basehart).

Warner, Glenn Scobey (aka: "Pop"; 1871-1954; American football player and coach): **Jim Thorpe—All American**, 1951 (Charles Bickford); **Knute Rockne All American**, 1940 (himself).

Warner, Jack (Jack Leonard J.L. Warner; 1892-1978; U.S. movie mogul and head of Warner Brothers Studio): Bogie, 1980 (made-for-TV; Richard Dysart); Call Up the Stars, 1995 (made-for-TV; Jim Davidson); Gleason, 2002 (made-for-TV; Danny Wells); James Dean, 2001 (made-for-TV; Mark Rydell); James Dean: A Beautiful Soul, 2016 (Jeffrey Griffith); James Dean: Live Fast, Die Young, 1997 (made-for-TV; Mike Connors); Life, 2015 (Ben Kingsley); Life with Judy Garland: Me and My Shadows, 2001 (made-for-TV; Richard M. Davidson); Malice in Wonderland, 1985 (made-for-TV; Jason Wingreen); My Wicked Wicked Ways: The Legend of Errol Flynn, 1985 (made-for-TV; Hal Linden); The Mystery of Natalie Wood, 2004 (made-for-TV; Barry Langrishe); **One of the Hollywood Ten**, 2000 (Peter Bowles); RKO 281, 1999 (made-for-TV; Tim Woodward); This Year's Blonde, 1980 (made-for-TV; Michael Lerner); The Three Stooges, 2000 (made-for-TV; Len Kaseman).

Warren, Earl (1891-1974; U.S. politician and jurist; 14th chief justice of the U.S. Supreme Court): American Experience, 1988- (TV series; "Simple Justice," 1993 episode: Pat Hingle); **Bridge of Spies**, 2015 (Edward James Hyland); The Commission, 2007 (Alan Charof); Dark Skies, 1996-1997 (TV series: "The Warren Omission," 1997 episode: Gary Lockwood); Jackie Bouvier Kennedy Onassis, 2000 (made-for-TV; Raymond Stone); **JFK**, 1991 (Jim Garrison); Kennedy, 1983- (TV miniseries; Don MacLaughlin); The Kennedys of Massachusetts, 1990- (TV miniseries; **The Private Files of J. Edgar Hoover**, 1977 (Brooks Morton); Separate But Equal, 1991 (made-for-TV; Richard Kiley).

Warren, Joseph (1741-1775; U.S. physician and patriot in the American Revolutionary War, who was killed at the Battle of Bunker Hill [redoubt at Breed's Hill] on June 17, 1775): The Bastard, 1978 (made-for-TV; Jim Antonio); **Janice Meredith**, 1924 (Wilfred Noy).

Wasburne, Elihu Benjamin (1816-1887; U.S. congressman, radical Republican and 25th U.S. Secretary of State): Lincoln, 1988 (made-for-TV; Jerome Dempsey).

Washington, Booker T. (1856-1915; U.S. African-Ameican educator, author and orator): Having Our Say: The Delany Sisters' First 100 Years, 1999 (made-for-TV; Richard Roundtree); **Ragtime**, 1981 (Moses Gunn); The Story of Doctor Carver, 1938 (John Lester Johnson).

Washington, George (1732-1799; U.S. military officer and politician; commander-in-chief of the Continental Army during the American Revolution and first President of the U.S.; called the father of America): The Adams Chronicles, 1976 (TV miniseries; David Hooks); The Adventures of Jim Bowie, 1956-1958 (TV series; "A Night in Tennessee," 1958 episode: Anthony Ghazlo Jr.); Alexander Hamilton, 1931 (Alan Mowbray); **America**, 1924 (Arthur Dewey); An American Carol, 2008 (Jon Voight); The American Revolution, 1994 (made-for-TV; Cliff Robertson voiceover); Are We Civilized?, 1934 (Aaron Edwards); **The Battle Cry of Peace**, 1915 (Joseph Kilgour); The Beautiful Mrs. Reynolds, 1918 (George MacQuarrie); Benedict Arnold: A Question of Honor, 2003 (made-for-TV; Kelsey Grammer); Betsy Ross, 1917 (George MacQuarrie); Beyond the Mask, 2015 (John Arden McClure); The Bill of Rights, 2010 (made-for-TV; Ron Carnegie); Cavalcade of America, 1952-1957 (TV series; "The Gingerbread Man," 1953 episode: "The Strange Journey," 1954 episode: both episodes with Richard Gaines; "The Hostage," 1955 episode: Liam Sullivan); The Courtship of George Washington and Martha Curtiss1955 (made-for-TV; Marshall Thompson); The Crossing, 2000 (made-for-TV; Jeff Daniels); Daniel Boone, 1964-1970 (TV series; "Ken-Tuk-E," 1964 episode: Stephen Courtleigh; "First in War, First in Peace," 1966 episode: Ivor Barry); The Dawn of Freedom, 1916 (Joseph Kilgour); Divided Loyalties, 1990 (Alan Scarfe); First Ladies Diaries: Martha Washington, 1975 (made-for-TV; James Luisi); Gateway to the West, 1924 (Arthur Vinton); George Washington, 1984 (TV miniseries; Barry Bostwick as adult Washington; Gavin Pearce as child); George Washington II: The Forging of a Nation, 1986 (made-for-TV; Barry Bostwick); The Glory of America, 1996- (TV miniseries; Steve Brock); Great Performances, 1971- (TV series; "The Patriots," 1976 episode: Ralph Clanton); The Hammer and the Sword, 1955 (made-for-TV; Robert Warwick); Hawkeye and the Last of the Mohicans, 1957- (TV series; Rodney Bunker); **The Howards of Virginia**, 1940 (George Houston); In the Days of Daniel Boone, 1923 (Duke R. Lee); **Janice Meredith**, 1924 (Joseph Kilgour); John Adams, 2008- (TV series; David Morse); **John Paul Jones**, 1959 (John Crawford); Kraft Theatre, 1947-1958 (TV series; "Valley Forge," 1950 episode: Judson Laire); Lafayette, 1963 (Howard St. John); Liberty! The American Revolution, 1997 (TV miniseries; Stephen Lang); Marry the Girl, 1937 (William Worthington); Meet the Chump, 1941 (Charles Miller); **Mr. Peabody & Sherman**, 2014 (Jess Harnell); Monsieur Beaucaire, 1946 (Douglass Dumbrille); A More Perfect Union: America Becomes a Nation, 1989 (Michael McGuire); NET Playhouse, 1964-1972 (TV series; "Trail of Tears," 1971 episode: Pat Hingle; "Portrait of the Hero as a Young Man," 1972 episode: Rene Auberjonois); Omnibus, 1952-1961 (TV series; "He Shall Have Power," 1960 episode: Larry Gates); On Such a Night, 1937 (Lew Payton); One Step Beyond, 1959-1961 (TV series; "Night of Decision," 1961 episode: Robert Douglas); Our American Heritage, 1959-1961 (TV series; "Divided We Stand," 1959 episode: Howard St. John); **The Patriot**, 2000 (Terry Layman); The Patriots, 1963 (made-for-TV; Howard St. John); The Phantom President, 1932 (Alan Mowbray); The Plot to Kidnap General Washington, 1952 (made-for-TV; Tod Griffin); Pulitzer Prize Playhouse, 1950-1952 (TV series; "Valley Forge," 1951 episode: Albert Dekker); The Rebels, 1979 (made-for-TV; Peter Graves); **The Remarkable Andrew**, 1942 (Montagu Love); The Revolution, 2006- (TV series; Mark Collins); Samuel Adams, 2014 (made-for-TV; Steve Freudenberg); Silk Hat Kid, 1935 (Sidney Miller); Sleepy Hollow, 2013- (TV series; Mark Campbell); Sons of Liberty, 2015- (TV miniseries; Jason O'Mara); The Spirit of '76, 1917 (Noah Beery Sr.); Sunday Showcase, 1959-1960 (TV series; Our American Heritage: Not Without Honor," 1960 episode; "Our American Heritage: The Secret Rebel," 1961 episode: Howard St. John for both episodes); Swing Out, Sweet Land, 1970 (made-for-TV; Lorne Greene); Telephone Time, 1956-1958 (TV series; "The Gingerbread Man," 1956 episode; Lowell Gilmore); TURN: Washington's Spies, 2014 (TV series; Ian Kahn); **Unconquered**, 1947 (Richard Gaines); Valley Forge, 1975 (made-for-TV; Richard Basehart); When the Redskins Rode, 1951 (James Seay); Where Do We Go from Here?, 1945 (Alan Mowbray); Winners of the Wilderness, 1927 (Edward Hearn); You Are There, 1953-1971 (TV series; "The Treason of Benedict Arnold," 1953 episode: Robert Blackburn; "The Resolve of Patrick Henry [March 23, 1775]," 1954 episode; Russ Conway; "Washington's Farewell to His Officers [December 4, 1783]," 1955 episode: E.G. Marshall; "Washington Crosses the Delaware [December 25, 1776]," 1955 episode: Russ Conway); The Young Rebels, 1970-1971 (TV series; "Suicide Squad," 1970 epsisode; Myron Healey).

Washington, Martha (1731-1802; wife of George Washington, first President of the U.S.): Alexander Hamilton, 1931 (Gwendolyn Logan); The Beautiful Mrs. Reynolds, 1918 (Rose Tapley); The Courtship of George Washington and Martha Curtiss, 1955 (made-for-TV; Karen Sharpe); First Ladies Diaries: Martha Washington, 1975 (made-for-TV; Susan Browning); George Washington, 1984 (TV miniseries; Patty Duke); George Washington II: The Forging of a Nation, 1986 (made-for-TV; Patty Duke); **Janice Meredith**, 1924 (Mrs. Macklyn Arbuckle); Mistress of the White House, 1952 (made-for-TV; Pat Nye); You Are There, 1953-1971 (TV series; "Washington Crosses the Delaware [December 25, 1776]," 1955 episode; Sheila Bromley).

Watkins, Sam (Samuel Rush Watkins; 1839-1901; Confederate soldier and diarist during the American Civil War): The Civil War, 1990 (TV miniseries; Charles McDowell voiceover).

Watson, Thomas A. (1854-1934; U.S. inventor and assistant to Alexander Graham Bell): Alexander Graham Bell: The Sound and the Silence, 1993 (made-for-TV; Francis Bell); Histeria!, 1998-2000 (animated TV series; "Inventors Hall of Fame: Part I," 1998 episode: Rob Paulsen voiceover); Man, Moment, Machine, 2005-2007 (TV series; "Alexander Graham Bell and the Astonishing Telephone," 2006 episode; Jeremy Parsons); **The Story of Alexander Graham Bell**, 1939 (Henry Fonda); The Talking Wire, 1955 (made-for-TV; Burt [Bert] Masters); Voyagers!, 1982-1983 (TV series; "Barriers of Sound," 1983 episode: Linwood Boomer).

Watson, Thomas Edward (1856-1922; aka: "Tom"; American politician, racist [against blacks, Jews and Catholics], supporter of Ku Klux Klan and who engineered the framing of Leo Frank for murder in 1913; U.S. senator from Georgia, 1921-1922): The Murder of Mary Phagan, 1988 (TV miniseries; Robert Prosky).

Webster, Daniel (1782-1852; U.S. statesman; U.S. senator from Massachusetts, 1827-1841; 1845-1850; and 14th and 19th U.S. secretary of state, 1841-1843; 1850-1852): **Abe Lincoln in Illinois**, 1940 (Harry Humphries); Bridger, 1976 (made-for-TV; William Windom); Cavalcade of America, 1952-1957 (TV series; "The Last Will of Daniel Webster," 1953 episode: Ray Collins); Enslavement: The True Story of Fanny Kemble, 2000 (made-for-TV; Francois Klanfer); Freedom to Speak, 1982 (TV miniseries; William Roerick); The Gorgeous Hussy, 1936 (Sidney Toler); **The Devil and Daniel Webster**, 1941 (Edward Arnold); **The Mighty Barnum**, 1934 (George MacQuarrie); Profiles in Courage, 1964-1965 (TV series; "Thomas Corwin," 1965 episode: Lester Rawlins; "Daniel Webster," 1965 episode: Martin Gabel); Schlitz Playhouse, 1951-1959 (TV series; "Decision and Daniel Webster," 1951 episode: Walter Hampden); Shortcut to Happiness, 2004 (Anthony Hopkins); Sunday Showcase, 1959-1960 (TV series; "The Devil and Daniel

Montagu Love (second from right as George Washington) in *The Remarkable Andrew,* **1942.**

Webster," 1960 episode: Edward G. Robinson); You Are There, 1953-1971 (TV series: "Daniel Webster's Sacrifice to Save the Union [March 7, 1850]," 1956 episode: Morris Ankrum).

Weichmann, Louis J. (1842-1902; U.S. teacher, tailor, author and star witness for the prosecution in the trial of the conspirators in the 1865 assassination of President Abraham Lincoln, some believing he committed perjury in fabrications about Mary Surratt, one of the conspirators): **The Conspirator**, 2011 (Jonathan Groff); The Lincoln Conspiracy, 1977 (Howard Brunner); The Ordeal of Dr. Mudd, 1980 (made-for-TV; Greg Oliver).

Weidling, Helmuth (1891-1955; German general in WWII): Downfall, 2004 (Michael Mendl); Hitler: The Last Ten Days, 1973 (Michael Goodliffe).

Weinshank, Albert (1893-1929; U.S. business associate of Chicago gang boss George "Bugs" Moran, and who, along with six others, was killed in the notorious 1929 St. Valentine's Day Massacre): **The St. Valentine's Day Massacre**, 1967 (Joseph Campanella).

Weiss, Carl Austin Sr. (1906-1935; U.S. physician who reportedly assassinated politican demagogue Huey Pierce Long Jr., and who was killed by Long's bodyguards with an estimated sixty-two bullets; a later investigation provided serious doubts about Weiss' culpability in the Long assassination): **All the King's Men**, 1949 (role model for Shepperd Strudwick); Kingfish: A Story of Huey P. Long, 1995 (made-for-TV; Joe Chrest); Unsolved Mysteries, 1987-2010 (TV series; 1992 episode; Michael Arata). Note: For detailed information on Weiss and the assassination of Huey Long, see my two-volume work *The Great Pictorial History of World Crime*, Volume I (History, Inc., 2004; illustrated [14 images] pages 111-117).

Weiss, Earl (aka: Hymie; 1898-1926; Chicago crime underboss with Charles Dion O'Banion [or O'Bannion] and George "Bugs" Moran during Prohibition; murdered by Capone gangsters): Capone, 1975 (John Davis Chandler); **Al Capone**, 1959 (Lewis Charles); Boardwalk Empire, 2010- (TV series: three episodes: Will Janowitz); **The St. Valentine's Day Massacre**, 1967 (Reed Hadley); The Untouchables, 1959-1963 (TV series; "The Canada Run," 1962 episode: Gene Roth). Note: For detailed information on Weiss, see my book, *World Encyclopedia of Organized Crime* (Paragon House, 1992; illustrated pages 402-403).

Weiss, Mendy (Emanuel Weiss; 1906-1944; U.S. gangster in NYC and

George C. Scott, Joseph Welch (playing judge) and Ben Gazara in *Anatomy of a Murder,* **1959.**

enforcer for U.S. crime syndicate boss Louis "Lepke" Buchalter, who, along with Louis Capone and Buchalter, was executed in the electric chair at Sing Sing on March 4, 1944, for murdering Joseph Rosen, only one of their many victims, their convictions brought about by the testimony of former gang member Abe "Kid Twist" Reles and others): Lepke, 1975 (J. S. Johnson); **Murder, Inc.,** 1960 (Joseph Bernard). Note: For detailed information on Weiss, see my book, *World Encyclopedia of Organized Crime* (Paragon House, 1992; page 403).

Welch, George (1918-1954; U.S. aviator and officer in the U.S. Army Air Force, who, during the Japanese sneak attack at Pearl Harbor on December 7, 1941, flew a P-40 fighter, shooting down two Japanese dive bombers and a Zero fighter; received the Distinguished Flying Cross): **Tora! Tora! Tora!,** 1970 (Rick Cooper).

Welch, Joseph N. (Joseph Nye Welch; 1890-1960; U.S. attorney and legal counsel to the U.S. Army during the McCarthy probe into communist activities during the early 1950s): **Anatomy of a Murder**, 1959 (himself); Citizen Cohn, 1992 (made-for-TV; Ed Flanders); Tail Gunner Joe, 1977 (made-for-TV; Burgess Meredith).

Welles, Gideon (1802-1878; U.S. politician and 24th U.S. Secretary of the navy under President Abraham Lincoln and President Andrew Johnson): The Dramatic Life of Abraham Lincoln, 1924 (R. G. Dixon); Hearts in Bondage, 1936 (Irving Pichel); In the Days of Buffalo Bill, 1922 (Joseph Hazelton); Ironclads, 1991 (made-for-TV; Conrad McLaren); Lincoln, 1974- (TV miniseries; "Sad Figure, Laughing," 1975 episode: Severn Darden); Lincoln, 1992 (made-for-TV; E.G. Marshall); **Lincoln**, 2012 (Grainger Hines); **The Plainsman**, 1936 (Sydney Jarvis); They've Killed President Lincoln!, 1971 (made-for-TV; Morris Engle).

Welles, Orson (U.S. film actor-director; 1915-1985): All Star Comedy, 1982 (made-for-TV; Kenneth H. Hawryliw); Cradle Will Rock, 1999 (Angus Macfadyen); The Critic, 1994-1995 (animated TV series; Maurice LaMarche); Doctor Ray and the Devils, 2012 (Gordon Murray); **Ed Wood**, 1994 (Vincent D'Onofrio); Fade to Black, 2006 (Danny Huston); The Formulation of Rectangles, 2009 (Hunter Schlesinger); **Heavenly Creatures**, 1994 (Jean Guerin); Hemingway and Gellhorn, 2012 (made-for-TV; Malcolm Brownson); Lost Zweig, 2002 (Thelmo Fernandes); Malice in Wonderland, 1985 (made-for-TV; Eric Purcell); Man in the Chair, 2007 (Jody Ashworth); Me and Orson Welles, 2009 (Christian McKay); The Night That Panicked America, 1975 (made-for-TV; Paul Shenar); RKO 281, 1999 (made-for-TV; Liev Schreiber); Rita Hayworth: The Love Goddess, 1983 (made-for-TV; Edward Edwards); Spitting Image, 1984-1996 (TV puppet series; John Sessions voiceover);

War of the Worlds, 1988-1990 (TV series; "Eye for an Eye," 1988 episode: Frank Knight; Giovanni Paldino).

Wellington, Duke of (Arthur Wellesley; 1769-1852; British soldier, diplomat and prime minister of England): The Adventures of Gerard, 1978 (John Neville); Becky Sharp, 1935 (William Faversham); Beethoven—Days in a Life, 1976 (Joachim Pape); Black Adder the Third, 1987- (TV series; "Duel and Duality," 1987 episode: Stephen Fry); Blue Peter: Special Assignment, 1975-1981 (TV series; "The Duke of Wellington at Stratfield Sayre," 1979 episode: Tom Bell); The Chest, 2004 (Robert Boileau); The Congress Dances, 1932 (Humberston Wright); Edward the King, 1975- (TV series; "The Boy," 1975 episode: John Welsh); The Firefly, 1937 (Matthew Boulton); Goya's Ghost, 2006 (Cayetano Martinez de Irujo); Here Will I Nest, 1942 (Richard Smith); **The House of Rothschild**, 1934 (C. Aubrey Smith); Hundred Days, 1935 (Peter Voss); The Iron Duke, 1935 (George Arliss); Jonathan Strange & Mr. Norrell, 2015 (TV series; Ronan Vibert); Lady Caroline Lamb, 1973 (Laurence Olivier); Lines of Wellington, 2012 (John Malkovich); The Miracle, 1959 (Torin Thatcher); Napoleon, 1955 (Bob d'Arcy); Napoleon at St. Helena, 1929 (Gunther Hadank); Number 10, 1983- (TV miniseries; "The Iron Duke," 1983 episode: Bernard Archard); The Rothschilds, 1940 (Waldemar Leitgeb); Sabotage!, 2001 (Stephen Fry); The Scarlet and the Black, 1993 (TV miniseries; Jeremy Young); Sharpe's Battle, 1995 (made-for-TV; Hugh Fraser); Sharpe's Challenge, 2006 (made-for-TV; Hugh Fraser); Sharpe's Company, 1994 (made-for-TV; Hugh Fraser); Sharpe's Eagle, 1993 (made-for-TV; David Troughton); Sharpe's Enemy, 1994 (made-for-TV; Hugh Fraser); Sharpe's Gold, 1995 (made-for-TV; Hugh Fraser); Sharpe's Honour, 1994 (made-for-TV; Hugh Fraser); Sharpe's Mission, 1996 (made-for-TV; Hugh Fraser); Sharpe's Rifles, 1993 (made-for-TV; David Troughton); Sharpe's Siege, 1996 (made-for-TV; Hugh Fraser); Sharpe's Waterloo, 1997 (made-for-TV; Hugh Fraser); **Sixty Glorious Years** (aka: Queen of Destiny), 1938 (C. Aubrey Smith); Sixty Years a Queen, 1913 (Gilbert Esmond); Theatre 625, 1964-1968 (TV series; "Carried by the Storm," 1964 episode: Patrick Magee); Vanity Fair, 1915 (George D. Melville); Vanity Fair, 1967- (TV series; "The Celebrated Battle Scene," 1967 episode: Terry Nelson); Victoria & Albert, 2001 (made-for-TV; John Wood); **Victoria the Great**, 1937 (James Dale); **Waterloo**, 1971 (Christopher Plummer); Witness to Yesterday, 1970- (TV series; "The Duke of Wellington," 1974 episode: Christopher Plummer); **The Young Victoria**, 2009 (Julian Glover).

Wells, H.G. (1886-1946; British author noted for his futuristic tales): All Star Comedy Carnival, 1972 (made-for-TV; Jo-Jo the Dog); BBC2 Playhouse, 1973-1983 (TV series; "Fothergil," 1981 episode: John Bird); The Brazura Project, 2006- (TV series; "Sex," 2011 episode: Phillip Zachariah); Cataclysmo, 2011 (TV series; three 2011 episodes: Nate Bell); Cataclysmo and the Battle for Earth, 2008 (Nate Bell); Cataclysmo and the Time Boys, 2007 (Nate Bell); Clovek proti zkaze, 1989 (Ota Sklencka); Doctor Who, 1963-1989 (TV series; "Timelash, Part One," 1985 episode: David Chandler; "Timelash, Part Two," 1985 episode: David Chandler); Enigmes de l'histoire, 1956-1957 (TV series; "Le mystere de la Mary Celeste," 1956 episode: Robert Burnier); Father Dear Father, 1973 (Jo-Jo the Dog); H.G. Wells, War with the World, 2006 (made-for-TV: Michael Sheen); The Infinite World of H.G. Wells, 2001 (TV miniseries; Tom Ward); Lois & Clark: The New Adventures of Superman, 1993-1997 (TV series; various episodes: Terry Kisor, Hamilton Camp); Murdoch Mysteries, 2008- (TV series; "Future Imperfect," 2010 episode: Peter Mikhail); No Place Like Holmes, 2010- (TV series; "The Creature in the Rye," 2011 episode: Gene Foad); Testimony, 1988 (Brook Williams); **Time after Time**, 1979 (Malcolm McDowell); **The Time Machine**, 1960 (Rod Taylor); Warehouse 13, 2009- (TV series; many episodes: Jaime Murray).

West, Mae (1893-1980; U.S. actress and playwright known for her risqué performances in plays and in films): Angels with Angles, 2005 (Holly Farris); The Calling, 2002 (Faye Dunaway); Ernie Kovacs: Between the Laughter, 1984 (made-for-TV; Edie Adams); Finding Graceland, 1998 (Holly Farris); Hellgate, 1990 (Wendy Lazarow); Jiggs and Maggie in Court, 1948 (Sara Berner); It Happened in Hollywood, 1937 (Virginia Rendell); Mae West, 1982 (made-for-TV; Ann Jillian); Marlene, 2000 (Gloria Gray); Pulp, 1972 (Mary Caruana); Radio Pirates, 1935 (Hughie Green); The Wright Stuff, 2005-2006 (TV series: Jennifer Arcuri); Viva, 2008 (Sumiko as a Japanese Mae West). Note: For detailed information on Mae West, see my book *Zanies: The World's Greatest Eccentrics* (New Century Publishers, 1982; illustrated pages 402-407).

Westmoreland, William (1914-2005; U.S. four-star general; commanded U.S. military operations during the Vietnam War, 1964-1968; U.S, Army chief of staff, 1968-1972): A Bright Shining Lie, 1998 (made-for-TV; Kurtwood Smith); Kissinger and Nixon, 1995 (made-for-TV; Graham McPherson); Path to War, 2002 (made-for-TV; Tom Skerritt).

Wexler, Irving (aka: Waxey Gordon; 1888-1952; U.S. crime boss, prominent in NYC during Prohibition): Boardwalk Empire, 2010- (TV series; three episodes: Nick Sandow). Note: For detailed information on Wexler, see my book *World Encyclopedia of Organized Crime* (Paragon House, 1992; [under Gordon, Waxey] pages 194-195).

Weygand, Maxime (1867-1965; French officer and commander in WWI and WWII, who surrendered to the Germans in 1940 and became a part-time collaborationist in the Vichy regime, a German puppet government; cleared and released in 1948): Les samedis de l'histoire, 1977- (TV series; Rene Beriard); Moi, general de Gaulle, 1990 (made-for-TV; Andre Chazel); Petain, 1993 (Andre Thorent); Screenplay, 1971- (TV series; "Gossip from the Forest," 1979 episode: Michael Mellinger).

Whale, James (1889-1957; British director of classic horror films): Gods and Monsters, 1998 (Ian McKellen); Lives and Deaths of the Poets, 2011 (Ted Culler).

Wheeler, Earle J. (aka: "Bus"; 1908-1975; U.S. four-star general and chairman of the Joint Chiefs of Staff, 1964-1970): Path to War, 2002 (made-for-TV; Frederic Forrest).

Wheeler, Joseph (aka: "Fighting Joe"; 1836-1906; U.S. Confederate and U.S. general): Confederate Cavalry, 2014 (Danny Francis); Rough Riders, 1997 (made-for-TV; Gary Busey).

Whistler, James Abbott MacNeill (1834-1903; U.S. born artist living in England during the Gilded Age, who eschewed sentimentality and advanced the credo of "art for art's sake"): James MacNeill Whistler and the Case for Beauty, 2014 (Kevin Kline); Lillie, 1978- (TV miniseries; Don Fellows); The Lives and Deaths of the Poets, 2011 (Dave Cooperman).

White, Pearl (1889-1938; U.S. actress in the early silent screen era, invariably playing damsels in great peril and who was known as "Queen of the Serials"; chiefly performed her own spectacular stunts): **The Perils of Pauline**, 1947 (Betty Hutton).

White, Stanford (1853-1906; esteemed architect who was murdered by mad multimillionaire Harry Kendall Thaw at the rooftop theater of NYC's Madison Square Garden over Thaw's jealousy concerning his wife, former showgirl Evelyn Nesbit, who had once been White's mistress): **The Girl in the Red Velvet Swing**, 1955 (Ray Milland); **Ragtime**, 1981 (Norman Mailer). Note: For detailed information on the murder of White by Thaw, see my two-volume work *The Great Pictorial History of World Crime*, Volume II (History, Inc., 2004; illustrated [17

Ray Milland (as Stanford White) and Joan Collins in *The Girl in the Red Velvet Swing*, 1955.

images] pages 819-826).

White Bird (U.S. native American; war chief of Nez Perce; d. 1892): I Will Fight No More Forever, 1975 (made-for-TV; Frank Salsedo).

Whitman, Walt (Walter "Walt" Whitman; 1819-1892; U.S. poet and journalist): American Experience, 1988- (TV series; "Walt Whitman," 2008 episode: Chris Cooper); The American Parade, 1974- (TV series; "Song of Myself," 1976 episode: Rip Torn); The Civil War, 1990 (TV miniseries; Garrison Keillor voiceover); Whitman, 2011 (Michael J. Minor).

Whitney, Courtney (1897-1969; U.S. major general on the staff of U.S. General Douglas MacArthur during WWII and during the Occupation of Japan): Collision Course: Truman vs. MacArthur, 1976 (made-for-TV; Andrew Duggan); The Korean War, 2001 (TV series; Robert Sutton); **MacArthur**, 1977 (Dick O'Neill).

Whitney, Dorothy Ludington (1902-1982; U.S. actress who was married to attorney William Dwight Whitney): **Adam's Rib**, 1949 (Katharine Hepburn).

Wiesenthal, Simon (1908-2005; Austrian writer and Nazi hunter, a Jew who survived the Holocaust of WWII and who dedicated his life to bringing Nazis responsible for the Holocaust to justice): Max and Helen, 1990 (made-for-TV; Martin Landau); Murderers among Us: The Simon Wiesenthal Story, 1989 (made-for-TV; Ben Kingsley); **The Odessa File**, 1974 (Shmuel Rodensky).

Wilberforce, William (British politician who led abolishment of slavery; 1759-1833): Amazing Grace, 2007 (Ioan Gruffudd); The Book of Negroes, 2015- (TV miniseries; Nicholas Pauling); The Fight against Slavery, 1975- (TV miniseries; David Collings); The First Black Britons, 2005 (Rick Bacon); **The Young Mr. Pitt**, 1943 (John Mills).

Wilde, Oscar (1854-1900; Irish playwright who became notorious when identified in a lawsuit as having had homosexual affairs): Armchair Theatre, 1956-1974 (TV series; "Death of Satan," 1958 episode: Paul Whitsun-Jones); CBC Summer Theatre, 1955- (TV series; "The Return of Don Juan," 1955 episode: John Hardinge); Great Perfomances, 1971- (TV series; "Feasting with Panthers," 1974 episode: Richard Kneeland); James MacNeill Whistler and the Case for Beauty, 2014 (Jon Patrick Walker); Lillie, 1978- (TV miniseries; Peter Egan); Oscar, 1985- (TV series; Michael Gambon); **Oscar Wilde**, 1960 (Robert Morley); Oscar Wilde, 1972 (made-for-TV; Klaus Maria Brandauer); The Trials of

Jean Hagen, James Stewart (as Marsh Williams), Willis Bouchey and Wendell Corey in *Carbine Williams*, 1952.

Oscar Wilde, 1960 (Peter Finch); Salome's Last Dance, 1988 (Nickolas Grace); Wilde, 1998 (Stephen Fry).

Wilentz, David Theodore (1894-1988; U.S. attorney and attorney general for the State of New Jersey who personally and successfully prosecuted Bruno Richard Hauptmann, who was convicted and executed for the 1932 kidnapping and murder of Charles Lindbergh, the infant son of famed aviator Charles A. Lindbergh): Crime of the Century, 1996 (made-for-TV; David Paymer); The Lindbergh Kidnapping Case, 1976 (made-for-TV; David Spielberg); Second Verdict, 1976 (TV series; "The Lindbergh Kidnapping," 1976 episode: Weston Gavin). Note: For detailed information on the Lindbergh case and Hauptmann, see my two-volume work *The Great Pictorial History of World Crime*, Volume I (History, Inc., 2004; illustrated [34 images] 643-663).

Wilhelm I (1797-1888; emperor of Germany): Bismarck, 1940 (Friedrich Kayssler); Bismarck's Dismissal, 1942 (Theodor Loos); Carl Peters, 1941 (Rolf Prasch); Die Geschichte Mitteldeutschlands, 1999- (TV series; Franz Nagel); 1864, 2014- (TV series; Dieter Montag); Fall of Eagles, 1974 (TV miniseries; Maurice Denham); Johann Baptiste Lingg, 1920 (Ludwig Hartau); Ludwig—Requiem for a Virgin King, 1972 (Fridolin Werther); Preussen uber alles—Bismarcks deutsche Einigung, 1971 (TV miniseries; Dieter Borsche); Robert Koch, der Bekampfer des Todes, 1939 (Rolf Prasch); Wagner, 1981- (TV series; Siegmar Schneider).

Wilhelm II (1859-1941; Kaiser; emperor of Germany): The Adventures of Arsene Lupin, 1957 (O.E. Hasse); **Annie Get Your Gun**, 1950 (John Mylong); Archangel, 1990 (Robert Lougheed); The Birth of a Race, 1918 (Louis Dean); Bismarck, 1990- (TV series; Heikko Deutschmann); Bismarck's Dismissal, 1942 (Werner Hinz); Carl Peters, 1941 (Rolf Prasch); The Crown Prince, 2006 (made-for-TV; Robert Stadlober); Das Adlon Eine Familiensaga, 2013- (TV miniseries; Michael Schenk); Das Luftschiff, 1983 (Reinhard Straube); Die Affare Eulenburg, 1967 (made-for-TV; Hans Caninenberg); Die Deutschen, 2008- (TV miniseries; Udo Schenk); Die Deutschmeister, 1955 (Wolfgang Lukschy); Die Flucht nach Holland, 1967 (made-for-TV; Hans Caninenberg); Die letzten Tage der Menschheit, 1965 (made-for-TV; Hubert von Meyerinck); Die Unbesiegbaren, 1953 (Hanns Groth); Edward the King, 1975- (TV series; Christopher Neame); Europas letzter Sommer, 2012 (made-for-TV; Hubertus Hartmann); The Fall of the Romanovs, 1917 (Georges Deneubourg); The Great Victory, Wilson or the Kaiser? The Fall of the Hohenzollerns, 1919 (Henry Kolker); Houdini, 1998- (made-for-TV; Jack Marston); Houdini, 2014- (TV miniseries; Gyula Mesterhazy); It Is For England!, 1916 (Leonard Shepherd); Juliana, prinses van oranje,

2006-2009 (TV miniseries; Rene van Asten); The Kaiser, the Beast of Berlin, 1918 (Rupert Julian); Kaiser's Finish, 1918 (Louis Dean); The Kaiser's Last Kiss, 2016 (Christopher Plummer); Krupp: A Family between War and Peace, 2009- (TV miniseries; Michael Schenk); Krupp und Krause, 1969- (TV series; Fred Delmare); Kultur, 1918 (William Burress); The Lost Prince, 2004 (made-for-TV; David Barrass); 1914-1918, 1996 (TV miniseries; Jurgen Prochnow); A Matter of Time, 1976 (Jean Mas); Me und Gott, 1918 (Paul Weigel); **Oh! What a Lovely War**, 1969 (Kenneth More); The Prussian Cur, 1918 (Walter Lawrence); **The Red Baron**, 2010 (Ladislav Frej); Reichsgrundung: Die Nervose Grossmacht, 2012 (made-for-TV; Florian Fischer); The Riddle of the Sands, 1979 (Wolf Kahler); The Riddle of the Sands, 1987 (made-for-TV; Wigand Witting); Solange Leben in mir ist, 1965 (Harald Halgardt); 37 Days, 2014 (TV miniseries; Rainer Sellien); Those Fantastic Flying Fools, 1967 (Dan Cressy); Three Faces East, 1926 (Rupert Julian); **Von Richthofen and Brown**, 1971 (Seamus Forde); Was zu beweisen war, 1986 (made-for-TV; Martin Held); Weltuntergang, 1984 (made-for-TV; Wolfgang Hoper); Wenn Ludwig ins Manover zieht, 1967 (Dieter Borsche); Why America Will Win, 1918 (Ernest Maupain); Yankee Doodle in Berlin, 1919 (Ford Sterling).

Wilhelmina (1880-1962; Queen of the Netherlands): Beatrix, Oranje onder Vuur, 2012- (TV miniseries; Kitty Courbois); Bernhard, Scoundrel of Orange, 2010- (TV miniseries; Rick Nicolet): Bertie and Elizabeth, 2002 (made-for-TV; Helen Ryan); De Troon, 2010- (TV miniseries; Beppie Melissen); Juliana, prinses van oranje, 2006-2009 (TV miniseries; Ria Eimers); Majesty, 2010 (Nettie Blanken); Soldier of Orange, 1977 (Andrea Domburg); Wilhelmina, 2001- (TV series; Anne-Wil Blankers).

Wilkinson, Theodore Stark (1888-1946; U.S. admiral in charge of the Office of Naval Intelligence [ONI], who warned top commanders in the Pacific months before the attack on Pearl Harbor on December 7, 1941, that a Japanese attack was imminent, but did not specify Pearl Harbor): **Tora! Tora! Tora!**, 1970 (Walter Brooke).

William I (William the Conquorer; 1028-1087): Blood Royal: William the Conqueror, 1990 (made-for-TV; Michael Gambon); Hereward the Wake, 1965- (TV series; John Carson); Kings and Queens, 2002- (TV miniseries; "William the Conqueror," 2002 episode: Nick Brimble); The Nearly Complete and Utter History of Everything, 1999 (made-for-TV: James Fleet).

Williams, David Marshall (aka: Marsh; 1900-1975; U.S. moonshiner, who, while imprisoned, invented the M.1 Carbine, used widely in WWII, as well as many other weapons): **Carbine Williams**, 1952.

Wilson, Edith White Bolling Gault (wife of U.S. President Woodrow Wilson; 1872-1961): **Birdman of Alcatraz**, 1962 (Adrienne Marden); **Wilson**, 1944 (Geraldine Fitzgerald).

Wilson, Henry (Sir Henry Wilson; 1864-1922; Irish unionist politician and British field marshal): **Oh! What a Lovely War**, 1969 (Michael Redgrave); The Treaty, 1991 (made-for-TV; Liam O'Callaghan).

Wilson, Henry (Jeremiah Jones Colbath; 1812-1875; U.S. politician, U.S. senator from Massachusetts and eighteenth vice president of the U.S.): The Rose and the Jackal, 1990 (made-for-TV; Kevin McCarthy).

Wilson, Henry Lane (1857-1932; U.S. politician, diplomat and U.S. ambassador to Mexico in 1910; he documented and also meddled in the Mexican Revolution on the side of dictator Victoriano Huerta): El encanto del aguila, 2011 (Ari Brickman).

Wilson, Jackie (Jack Leroy "Jackie" Wilson Jr.; U.S. singer): Mr. Rock 'n' Roll: The Alan Freed Story, 1999 (made-for-TV; Leon).

Wilson, James (1742-1798; U.S. politician and member of the Continental Congress; signer of the Declaration of Independence): **1776**, 1972 (Emory Bass).

Wilson, Woodrow (Thomas Woodrow Wilson; 1856-1924; U.S. politician and 28th President of the U.S.): Backstairs at the White House, 1979 (TV miniseries; episode 1.1.: Robert Vaughn); The Conquerors, 1932 (himself in archive footage); The Great Victory, Wilson or the Kaiser? The Fall of the Hohenzollerns, 1919 (Fred C. Truesdell); First Ladies Diaries: Edith Wilson, 1976 (made-for-TV; Michael Kane); Freedom to Speak, 1982 (TV miniseries; Mason Adams); Frontiers of Faith, 1951-1970 (TV series; "A Dream of Earth," 1955 episode: Reynolds Evans); The Great War and the Shaping of the 20th Century, 1996 (TV miniseries; several episodes: Martin Landau); The Great Victory, Wilson or the Kaiser? The Fall of the Hohenzollerns, 1919 (Fred [Frederick] C. Truesdell); Iron Jawed Angels, 2004 (made-for-TV; Bob Gunton); The Kaiser, the Beast of Berlin, 1918 (Orlo Eastman); Nzabyvaemyy 1919 god, 1951 (L. Korsakov); **Oh! What a Lovely War**, 1969 (Frank Forsyth); Omnibus, 1952-1961 (TV series; "He Shall Have Power," 1960 episode: Harry Townes); On the Jump, 1918 (Ralph Faulkner); Polonia restituta, 1981 (Jerzy Kaliszewski); Profiles in Courage, 1964-1965 (TV series; "Woodrow Wilson," 1965 episode: Whit Bissell); The Prussian Cur, 1918 (Ralph Faulkner); **The Story of Will Rogers**, 1952 (Earl Lee); Time Squad, 2001- (TV series; "White House Weirdness" episode; Rob Paulsen); **The Wet Parade**, 1932 (himself in archive footage); **Wilson**, 1944 (Alexander Knox); Why America Will Win, 1918 (Ralph Faulkner); You Are There, 1953-1971 (TV series; "The Secret Message That Plunged America into World War I, March 1, 1917," 1955 episode: Edward Earle); You Can't Buy Everything, 1934 (Fred Lee); The Young Indiana Jones Chronicles, 1992-1993 (TV series; "Paris, May 1919," 1993 episode: Josef Sommer).

Winchell, Walter (1897-1972; U.S. syndicated gossip columnist and close friend of FBI Chief J. Edgar Hoover): **Beau James**, 1957 (himself narrating); The Bellboy, 1960 (himself narrating); The Big Story, 1949-1958 (TV series; "The Cat," 1953 episode: George Petrie); Broadway Thru a Key-Hole, 1933 (himself); Citizen Cohn, 1992 (made-for-TV; Joseph Bologna); College Confidential, 1960 (himself); **Daisy Kenyon**, 1947 (himself); Dash and Lilly, 1999 (made-for-TV; Mark Zimmerman); Dondi, 1961 (himself); **A Face in the Crowd**, 1957 (himself); The Josephine Baker Story, 1991 (made-for-TV; Craig T. Nelson); The Kraft Music Hall, 1967-1971 (TV series; "Stagedoor Johnny," 1967 episode: himself); Laughter on the 23rd Floor, 2003 (made-for-TV; Frank Proctor); Lepke, 1975 (Vaughn Meader); Love and Hisses, 1937 (himself); The Lucy Show, 1962-1968 (TV series; "Lucy the Gun Moll," 1966 episode: himself); Marilyn and Me, 1991 (made-for-TV; Michael Cavanaugh); **The Private Files of J. Edgar Hoover**, 1977 (Lloyd Gough); The Rat Pack, 1998 (made-for-TV; Michael Townsend Wright); **The Reluctant Dragon**, 1941 (Eddie Marr); The Scarlett O'Hara War, 1980 (made-for-TV; Joey Forman); Single Room Furnished, 1966 (himself); **Sorrowful Jones**, 1949 (himself, narrating); Telephone Time, 1956-1958 (TV series; "I Get along without You Very Well," 1957 episode: Winchell playing himself); **There's No Business Like Show Business**, 1954 (himself narrating); The Untouchables, 1959-1963 (TV series; Winchell narrates); Wake Up and Live, 1937 (himself); The Walter Winchell File, 1957-1958 (TV series; Winchell plays himself); The Walter Winchell Show, 1956 (TV series; himself); Wild Harvest, 1962 (himself narrating); Wild in the Streets, 1968 (himself); Winchell, 1998 (made-for-TV; Stanley Tucci). Note: For detailed information on Winchell, see my book Zanies: The World's Greatest Eccentrics (New Century Publishers, 1982; illustrated pages 410-414).

Winder, John Henry (1800-1865; U.S. military officer and general in

Lee Pace (as Fernando Wood) in *Lincoln*, 2012.

the Confederacy during the American Civil War): A Special Friendship, 1987 (made-for-TV; Josef Sommer).

Wismer, Harry (1913-1967; American sports broadcaster): **The Babe Ruth Story**, 1948 (himself).

Witherspoon, John (1723-1794; Presbyterian minister and politician; member of the Continental Congress and signer of the Declaration of Independence): **1776**, 1972 (James Noble).

Witte, Sergei (1849-1915; Russian statesman and minister): Fall of Eagles, 1974 (TV miniseries; Freddie Jones); **Nicholas and Alexandra**, 1971 (Laurence Olivier).

Witzleben, Erwin von (1881-1944; German field marshal in WWII who participated in the 1944 attempt to kill Adolf Hitler; executed): The Great Battle, 1973 (Otto Dierichs); It Happened on July 20th, 1955 (Ernst Fritz Furbringer); Operation Valkyrie, 2004 (made-for-TV; Joachim Bissmeier); Operation Walkure, 1971 (made-for-TV; Ernst Fritz Furbringer); The Plot to Assassinate Hitler, 1955 (Peter Esser); **Valkyrie**, 2008 (David Schofield).

Wolsey, Thomas (1473-1530; British Catholic cardinal): Anna Boleyn, 1920 (Adolf Klein); **Anne of the Thousand Days**, 1969 (Anthony Quayle); BBC Sunday-Night Theatre, 1950-1959 (TV series; "The White Falcon," 1956 episode: Patrick Troughton); Carlos, Rey Emperador, 2015-2016 (TV series; Blai Llopis); Carry on Henry VIII, 1971 (Terry Scott); God's Outlaw, 1986 (Willoughby Goddard); Henry VIII, 1979 (made-for-TV; Timothy West); Henry VIII, 2003 (made-for-TV; David Suchet); Henry VIII and His Six Wives, 1972 (John Bryans); Henry VIII: Mind of a Tyrant, 2009 (TV series; Roger Ashton-Griffiths); A Man for All Seasons, 1957 (made-for-TV; Peter Woodthorpe); **A Man for All Seasons**, 1966 (Orson Welles): A Man for All Seasons, 1988 (made for TV; John Gielgud); **The Pearls of the Crown**, 1938 (Percy Marmont); A Royal Love, 2016 (Tom de Jong); The Six Wives of Henry VIII, 1970 (TV miniseries; "Catherine of Aragon," 1970 episode: John Baskcomb); The Six Wives of Henry VIII, 2001 (TV miniseries; two episodes: Michael Fitzgerald); **The Sword and the Rose**, 1953 (D.A. Clarke-Smith); Thomas More, 1964 (made-for-TV; Karl Maria Schley); The Tudors, 2007-2010 (TV series; Sam Neill); **When Knighthood Was in Flower**, 1922 (Arthur Forrest); Wolf Hall, 2015 (TV miniseries; Jonathan Pryce).

Wood, Fernando (1812-1881; U.S. politician; 73rd and 75th mayor of NYC and U.S. representative from New York): **Lincoln**, 2012 (Lee Pace).

Dustin Hoffman and Robert Redford (as Bob Woodward) in *All the President's Men,* **1976.**

Wood, Leonard (U.S. Army lieutenant general; 1860-1927): **The Battle Cry of Peace**, 1915 (himself in archive footage); The Rough Riders, 1927 (Fred Lindsay); Rough Riders, 1997 (made-for-TV; Dale Dye).

Woods, Rose Mary (1917-2005; U.S. private secretary for U.S. President Richard M. Nixon): Dick, 1999 (Ana Gasteyer).

Woodville, Elizabeth (c.1437-1492; Queen consort of England, wife of Henry IV): The Life and Death of King Richard III, 1912 (Carey Lee); **Richard III**, 1956 (Mary Kerridge).

Woodward, Robert Upshur (aka: Bob; 1943- ; U.S. journalist and investigative reporter who, with Carl Bernstein, exposed the Watergate scandal in a series of articles written for the Washington *Post*, and who won a Pulitzer Prize): **All the President's Men**, 1976 (Robert Redford); Dick, 1999 (Will Ferrell); Wired, 1989 (J.T. Walsh).

Woollcott, Alexander (1887-1943; U.S. drama critic for the *New York Times*, radio commentator and member of the Algonquin Round Table): Act One, 1963 (Earl Montgomery); Backstairs at the White House, 1979 (TV miniseries; Tom Clancy); **The Man Who Came to Dinner**, 1942 (role model for Monty Woolley); Mrs. Parker and the Vicious Circle, 1994 (Tom McGowan); **Star!**, 1968 (Jock Livingston). Note: For detailed information on Woollcott, see my book *Zanies: The World's Greatest Eccentrics* (New Century Publishers, 1982; illustrated pages 418-420).

Wright, Orville (1871-1948; U.S. inventor and aviation pioneer, who, along with his brother Wilbur, constructed and flew the first airplane at Kitty Hawk, North Carolina, on December 17, 1903): The Adventures of Ociee Nash, 2004 (Sean Daniels); American Genius, 2015- (TV series; "Wright Brothers vs. Curtiss," 2015 episode: Edgar Fox; Xander Crowell as young Orville); Around the World in 80 Days, 2004 (Luke Wilson); The Conquest of the Air, 1936 (Charles Hickman); NET Playhouse, 1964-1972 (TV series; "The Wright Brothers," 1971 episode: James Keach); **Night at the Museum: Battle of the Smithsonian**, 2009 (Robert Ben Garant); Swing Out, Sweet Land, 1970 (made-for-TV; Dan Rowan); This Is America, Charlie Brown, 1988-1989 (animated TV series; "The Wright Brothers at Kitty Hawk," 1988 episode: Gregg Berger voiceover); Voyager from the Unknown, 1997 (Donald Petrie); Voyagers, 1982-1983 (Donald Petrie); Wilbur and Orville: The First to Fly, 1973 (made-for-TV; James Keach); The Winds of Kitty Hawk, 1978 (made-for-TV; David Huffman); The Wright Brothers, 1997 (Megan Murphy); The Wright Stuff, 2005-2006 (TV series; Scott Ingalls); You Are There, 1953-1971 (TV series; "The

First Flight of the Wright Brothers [December 17, 1903]," 1955 episode: William Prince).

Wright, Wilbur (1867-1912; U.S. inventor and aviation pioneer, who, along with his brother Orville, constructed and flew the first airplane at Kitty Hawk, North Carolina, on December 17, 1903): The Adventures of Ociee Nash, 2004 (Ty Pennington); American Genius, 2015- (TV series; "Wright Brothers vs. Curtiss," 2015 episode: Brian Leider; Sam Jules as young Wilbur); Around the World in 80 Days, 2004 (Owen Wilson); The Conquest of the Air, 1936 (Percy Marmont); NET Playhouse, 1964-1972 (TV series; "The Wright Brothers," 1971 episode; Stacy Keach); **Night at the Museum: Battle of the Smithsonian**, 2009 (Thomas Lennon); Swing Out, Sweet Land, 1970 (made-for-TV; Dick Martin); This Is America, Charlie Brown, 1988-1989 (animated TV series; "The Wright Brothers at Kitty Hawk," 1988 episode; Frank Welker voiceover); Voyager from the Unknown, 1997 (Ed Begley Jr.); Voyagers, 1982-1983 (Ed Begley Jr.); Wilbur and Orville: The First to Fly, 1973 (made-for-TV; Stacy Keach); The Winds of Kitty Hawk, 1978 (made-for-TV; Michael Moriarty); The Wright Brothers, 1997 (E.B. Molloy); The Wright Stuff, 2005-2006 (TV series: Ford Austin); You Are There, 1953-1971 (TV series; "The First Flight of the Wright Brothers [December 17, 1903]," 1955 episode: James Gregory).

Wriothesley, Thomas (Sir Thomas Wriothesley; 1505-1550; British aristocrat; 1st Earl of Southampton): Henry VIII and His Six Wives, 1972 (John Bennett); La jument du roi, 1972 (made-for-TV; Bernard Lavalette); **The Private Life of Henry VIII**, 1933 (Miles Mander); The Six Wives of Henry VIII, 1970 (TV miniseries; Patrick Godfrey); Wolf Hall, 2015 (TV miniseries; Joel MacCormack).

Wuornos, Aileen Carol (1956-2002; U.S. prostitute and serial killer of seven male clients between 1989 and 1990 in Florida, and who was executed by lethal injection on October 9, 2002): Monster, 2003 (Charlize Theron).

Wyatt, Thomas (1503-1542; British poet and supposed lover of Queen Anne Boleyn; charged with adultery with the queen, he was released though reportedly watched Boleyn's beheading from his cell in the Tower of London, along with five other men with whom Boleyn had had affairs): The Tudors, 2007-2010 (TV series; Jamie Thomas King); The Virgin Queen, 2005- (TV miniseries; Bryan Dick); Where Thunder Reigns, 2016 (Martin Challinor); Wolf Hall, 2015- (TV miniseries; Jack Lowden).

Yale, Frankie (Frank Yale; 1893-1928; NYC gangster during Prohibition, who reportedly acted as one of the assassins in the St. Valentine's Day Massacre): Boardwalk Empire, 2010- (TV series: four episodes: Joseph Riccobene); Capone, 1975 (John Cassavetes); The Lawless Years, 1959-1961 (TV series; "The Al Brown Story," 1959 episode; Robert Ellenstein); The Untouchables, 1959-1963 (TV series; "The Artichoke King," 1959 episode: Al Ruscio). Note: For detailed information on Yale, see my book *World Encyclopedia of Organized Crime* (Paragon House, 1992; illustrated pages 412-413).

Yates, Richard (1815-1873; U.S. politician and 13th governor of Illinois, 1861-1865, considered by many historians to be the greatest governor of the Union states during the American Civil War): Sunday Showcase, 1959-1961 (TV series; "An American Heritage: Shadow of a Soldier," 1960 episode: Allen Nourse).

Yeltsin, Boris (1931-2007; Russian politician and first president of the Russian Federation, 1991-1999): Spitting Image, 1984-1986 (TV series with puppets enacting public figures; Alistair McGowan voiceover).

Yellow Hand (d. 1876; AKA: Yellow Hair; Heova'ehe, a Cheyenne sub-chief and warrior, killed and scalped by U.S. Cavalry scout William Frederick "Buffalo Bill" Cody at the Battle of Warbonnet Creek on July 17, 1876, in northwestern Nebraska, this action later termed the "First Scalp for Custer" in retaliation for the Custer massacre by the Sioux earlier that year): **Buffalo Bill**, 1944 (Anthony Quinn); Buffalo Bill (1965), 1983 (Mirko Ellis); A Man Called Horse, 1970 (Manu Tupou); **The Plainsman**, 1936 (Paul Harvey); **Pony Express**, 1953 (Pat Hogan).

Yellow Wolf (U.S. native American; Nez Perce warrior; 1855-1935): I Will Fight No More Forever, 1975 (made-for-TV; Charles Ynfante).

Yolande of Aragon (titular queen regent of Aragon, stepmother to Charles VII of France and who initially financed the army led by Joan of Arc during the Hundred Years' War; 1384-1442): **The Messenger: The Story of Joan of Arc**, 1999 (Faye Dunaway).

York, Alvin C. (Alvin Cullem York; 1887-1964; American soldier with the rank of sergeant and one of the most decorated American soldiers in WWII, who, during the 1918 Meuse-Argonne Offensive on the Western Front in France in WWI, single-handedly destroyed thirty-two German machine gun nests, killed twenty-eight German soldiers and, with seven other American soldiers under his command, captured another 132 German troops; recipient of the Congressional Medal of Honor): **Sergeant York**, 1941 (Gary Cooper).

Young, Brigham (leader of the Latter Day Saint religious movement, a branch of Mormonism; 1801-1877): The Avenging Angel, 1995 (made-for-TV; Charlton Heston); Brigham, 1977 (Maurice Grandmaison); **Brigham Young: Frontiersman**, 1940 (Dan Jagger); Death Valley Days, 1952-1970 (TV series; "Biscuits and Billy the Kid," 1969 episode: Michael Hinn; "An Organ for Brother Brigham," 1966 episode: Byron Morrow); **Ephraim's Rescue**, 2013 (Joseph Paur); Hands Up!, 1926 (Charles K. French); NBC Television Opera Theatre, 1950-1964 (TV series; "Deseret" 1961 episode: Kenneth Smith); The 19th Wife, 2010 (made-for-TV; John Bourgeois); Rockwell, 1994 (Michael Ruud); Savage Journey, 1983 (made-for-TV; Maurice Grandmaison); September Dawn, 2007 (Terence Stamp); 17 Miracles, 2011 (J. D'Parr/Joseph Paur); The Work and the Glory II: American Zion, 2005 (Andrew Bowen).

Young, Desmond (1892-1966; British writer and British army general in WWII): **The Desert Fox**, 1951 (himself, his voice dubbed by Michael Rennie).

Younger, James Hardin (Jim; 1848-1902; U.S. western outlaw): American Outlaws, 2001 (Gregory Smith); Any Last Words?, 2012 (John Kublank); **Bad Men of Missouri**, 1941 (Arthur Kennedy); **Best of the Badmen**, 1951 (Bob Wilke); Bronco, 1958-1962 (TV series; "Shadow of Jesse James," 1960 episode: Rad Fulton/James Westmoreland); Days of Jesse James, 1939 (Carl Sepulveda); **The Great Missouri Raid**, 1951 (Bill Williams); **The Great Northfield, Minnesota Raid**, 1972 (Luke Askew); Hondo, 1967 (TV series; "Hondo and the Judas," 1967 episode: Kipp Whitman); Kansas Raiders, 1950 (Dewey Martin); The Legend of Jesse James, 1965-1966 (TV series; David Richards); **The Long Riders**, 1980 (Keith Carradine); **Return of the Bad Men**, 1948 (Tom Keene); **The True Story of Jesse James**, 1957 (Biff Elliot); **Young Jesse James**, 1960 (Johnny O'Neill). Note: For detailed information on the Younger brothers, see my book *Encyclopedia of Western Lawmen and Outlaws* (Paragon House, 1992; illustrated [9 images] pages 321-323).

Younger, John (1851-1874; U.S. outlaw with James-Younger gang): **Best of the Badmen**, 1951 (John Cliff); Frank and Jesse, 1995 (Micah Dyer); **The Long Riders**, 1980 (Kevin Brophy); **Return of the Bad**

Gary Cooper (center, returning from WWI as hero Alvin York) in *Sergeant York*, **1941.**

Men, 1948 (Robert Bray). Note: For detailed information on the Younger brothers, see my book *Encyclopedia of Western Lawmen and Outlaws* (Paragon House, 1992; illustrated [9 images] pages 321-323).

Younger, Robert Ewing (Bob; 1853-1889; U.S. western outlaw): American Outlaws, 2001 (Will McCormack); **Bad Men of Missouri**, 1941 (Wayne Morris); **Best of the Badmen**, 1951 (Jack Buetel); Bronco, 1958-1962 (TV series; "Shadow of Jesse James," 1960 episode: Bill Tennant); Days of Jesse James, 1939 (Forrest Dillon); Frank and Jesse, 1995 (Todd Field); **The Great Missouri Raid**, 1951 (Paul Lees); **The Great Northfield, Minnesota Raid**, 1972 (Matt Clark); The Intruders, 1970 (made-for-TV; Zalman King); The Legend of Jesse James, 1965-1966 (TV series; Tim McIntire); **The Long Riders**, 1980 (Robert Carradine); **The True Story of Jesse James**, 1957 (Anthony Ray); **Young Jesse James**, 1960 (Bob Palmer/Boyd Holister). Note: For detailed information on the Younger brothers, see my book *Encyclopedia of Western Lawmen and Outlaws* (Paragon House, 1992; illustrated [9 images] pages 321-323).

Younger, Thomas Coleman (Cole; 1844-1916; U.S. western outlaw): American Outlaws, 2001 (Scott Caan); **Bad Men of Missouri**, 1941 (Dennis Morgan); Belle Starr, 1980 (made-for-TV; Cliff Potts); **Best of the Badmen**, 1951 (Bruce Cabot); Bronco, 1958-1962 (TV series; "Shadow of Jesse James," 1960 episode: Richard Coogan); Cole Younger, Gunfighter, 1958 (Frank Lovejoy); Days of Jesse James, 1939 (Glenn Strange); Frank and Jesse, 1995 (Randy Travis); **The Great Missouri Raid**, 1951 (Bruce Bennett); **The Great Northfield, Minnesota Raid**, 1972 (Cliff Robertson); Hell's Crossroads, 1957 (Myron Healey); Hondo, 1967 (TV series; "Hondo and the Judas," 1967 episode: Richard Bakalyan); The Intruders, 1970 (made-for-TV; Gene Evans); Jesse James at Bay, 1941 (Chuck Morrison); Jesse James' Hidden Treasure, 2009 (made-for-TV; Jeff Prechtel); Jesse James' Women, 1954 (Sam Keller); Kansas Raiders, 1950 (James Best); The Last Ride of the Dalton Gang, 1979 (made-for-TV; Dick Autry); The Legend of Jesse James, 1965-1966 (TV series; John Milford); **The Long Riders**, 1980 (David Carradine); The Outlaws Is Coming!, 1965 (Bruce Sedley); **Return of the Bad Men**, 1948 (Steve Brodie); **The True Story of Jesse James**, 1957 (Alan Hale Jr.); **Woman They Almost Lynched**, 1953 (Jim Davis); **Young Jesse James**, 1960 (Willard Parker). Note: For detailed information on the Younger brothers, see my book *Encyclopedia of Western Lawmen and Outlaws* (Paragon House, 1992; illustrated [9 images] pages 321-323).

Yurovsky, Jacob (1878-1938; Bolshevik commander who led the execution squad that murdered Czar Nicholas II, his family and four family

William Powell (as Florence Ziegfeld) and Myrna Loy (as Billie Burke) in *The Great Ziegfeld*, **1936.**

retainers): Anastasia: The Czar's Last Daughter, 1956 (Fritz Eberth); Assassin of the Tsar, 1993 (Malcolm McDowell); **Nicholas and Alexandra**, 1971 (Alan Webb); 1914-1918, 1996- (TV miniseries; Elya Baskin); Rasputin, 1996 (made-for-TV; Gabor Koncz); The Romanovs: An Imperial Family, 2000 (Liubomiras Lauciavicius).

Yusuke Matsuoka (1880-1946; Japanese diplomat): **Tora! Tora! Tora!**, 1970 (Kazuo Kitamura).

Yusupov, Felix (1887-1967; Russian prince, assassin of Gregory Rasputin): BBC Play of the Month, 1965-1983 (TV series; "Rasputin," 1971 episode: Richard Morant); The Fall of the Romanovs, 1917 (Conway Tearle); **Nicholas and Alexandra**, 1971 (Martin Potter); The Night They Killed Rasputin, 1962 (John Drew Barrymore); Raspoutine, 2011 (made-for-TV; Filipp Yankovsky); Rasputin, 1954 (Jacques Berthier); Rasputin, 1967 (Peter McEnery); **Rasputin**, 1985 (A. Romantsov); Rasputin, 1996 (made-for-TV; James Frain); **Rasputin and the Empress**, 1932 (role model for John Barrymore); Rasputin, Demon with Women, 1932 (Karl Ludwig Diehl); Rasputin, the Black Monk, 1917 (Irving Cummings); Rasputins Liebesabenteuer, 1928 (Jack Trevor). Note: For detailed information on Felix Yusupov and the assassination of Rasputin, see my two-volume work *The Great Pictorial History of World Crime*, Volume I (History, Inc., 2004; illustrated [14 images] pages 73-78).

Yusupov, Irina (1895-1970; Russian princess and wife of Felix Yusupov): The Fall of the Romanovs, 1917 (Pauline Curley); The Night They Killed Rasputin, 1962 (Jany Clair); Raspoutine, 2011 (made-for-TV; Natalya Shvets); Rasputin, 1967 (Ira von Furstenberg). Note: For detailed information on Irina Yusupov and the assassination of Rasputin, see my two-volume work, *The Great Pictorial History of World Crime*, Volume I (History, Inc., 2004; illustrated [14 images] pages 73-78).

Zaharoff, Basil (1849-1936; mysterious munitions mogul and arms dealer, who employed lookalikes to decoy many would-be assassins): **The Mask of Dimitrios**, 1944 (role model for Zachary Scott); **Mr. Arkadin**, 1962 (role model for Orson Welles); No Greater Love, 1952 (Werner Hinz); Reilly: Ace of Spies, 1983 (TV miniseries; Leo McKern); Sir Basil Zaharoff—Makler des Todes, 1969 (made-for-TV; Richard Munch). Note: For detailed information on Zaharoff, see my book *Zanies: The World's Greatest Eccentrics* (New Century Publishers, 1982; illustrated pages 421-423).

Zangara, Giuseppe (1900-1933; U.S. assassin who attempted to kill U.S. President Franklin D. Roosevelt at a political rally in Miami, Florida,

on February 15, 1933, but who killed Chicago Mayor Anton Cermak instead; Zangara was executed within a month on March 20, 1933): The Revenge of Al Capone, 1989 (made-for-TV; Tony Amendola). Note: For detailed information on Zangara, see my two-volume work *The Great Pictorial History of World Crime*, Volume I (History, Inc., 2004; illustrated pages 108-111).

Zanuck, Darryl F. (1902-1979; U.S. writer and movie mogul, head of 20th Century Fox Studio): RKO 281, 1999 (made-for-TV; Ron Berglas).

Zapata, Emiliano (Emiliano Zapata Salazar; 1879-1919; Mexican patriot, revolutionary and general of the Liberation Army of the South; assassinated): El encanto del aguila, 2011 (Tenoch Huerta); El vuelo del aguila, 1994 (TV series; Oscar Castaneda); Lauro Punales, 1969 (Jaime Fernandez); Lucio Vazquez, 1968 (Jaime Fernandez); Mexikanische Revolution, 1968 (made-for-TV; Erik Schumann); Pafnucio Santo, 1977 (Gina Morett); Red Bells Part I: Mexico on Fire, 1982 (Jorge Luke); Santos peregrinos, 2004 (Alberto Estrella); Senda de Gloria, 1987 (TV series; Manuel Ojeda); Trini, 1979 (Iwan Tomow); Viva Mexico, 1980 (made-for-TV; Claude Juan); **Viva Zapata!**, 1952 (Marlon Brando); Zapata, 1970 (Antonio Aguilar); Zapata: Amor en rebeldia, 2004 (TV miniseries; Demian Bichir); Zapata—El sueno del heroe, 2004 (Alejandro Fernandez). For detailed information on Zapata and his assassination, see my two-volume work *The Great Pictorial History of World Crime*, Volume I (History, Inc., 2004; illustrated pages 87-89).

Zapata, Eufemio (Eufemio Zapata Salazar; 1873-1917; brother of Emiliano Zapata and a general in the Mexican Revolution): Zapata: Amor en rebeldia, 2004 (TV miniseries; Enoc Leano); **Viva Zapata!**, 1952 (Anthony Quinn).

Zaragoza, Ignacio (1829-1862; Mexican general under Benito Juarez): Aquellos anos, 1974 (Gonzalo Vega); Cinco de Mayo, La Battala, 2013 (Kuno Becker); El vuelo del aguila, 1994 (TV series; Raul Buenfil); Mexicanos al grito de guerra, 1943 (Miguel Angel Ferriz).

Zarilla, Allen Lee (aka: "Zeke"; 1919-1996; U.S. baseball player;): **The Winning Team**, 1952 (himself).

Zeitzler, Kurt (1895-1963; German general in WWII): War and Remembrance, 1988 (TV miniseries; Peter Vaughan).

Zengo Yoshida (1885-1966; Japanese admiral who opposed war against the U.S. and the sneak attack against Pearl Harbor on December 7, 1941): **Tora! Tora! Tora!**, 1970 (Junya Usami).

Zhukov, Georgy (1896-1974; Soviet field marshal in WWII): The Great Battle, 1973 (Mikhail Ulyanov).

Ziegfeld, Florenz Jr. (aka: "Flo"; 1867-1932; U.S. theatrical impresario who created the Ziegfeld Follies on Broadway): **Deep in My Heart**, 1954 (Paul Henreid); The Eddie Cantor Story, 1953 (William Forrest); Ellis Island, 1984 (TV miniseries; Julian Holloway); **Funny Girl**, 1968 (Walter Pidgeon); **The Great Ziegfeld**, 1936 (William Powell); **The Helen Morgan Story**, 1957 (Walter Woolf King); **I'll See You in My Dreams**, 1951 (William Forrest); **The Jolson Story**, 1946 (Eddie Kane); Look for the Silver Lining, 1949 (William Forrest); Polly of the Follies, 1922 (Bernard Randall); **The Story of Will Rogers**, 1952 (William Forrest); **W.C. Fields and Me**, 1976 (Paul Stewart); **Ziegfeld Follies**, 1945 (William Powell); Ziegfeld: The Man and His Women, 1978 (made-for-TV; Paul Shenar).

Ziegler, Ronald Louis (aka: "Ron"; American bureaucrat and U.S. press secretary under U.S. President Richard M. Nixon; 1939-2003): Blind Ambition, 1979 (TV miniseries; James Sloyan); **Nixon**, 1995

(David Paymer).

Zinoviev, Gregory (1883-1936; Bolshevik revolutionary and Soviet communist and a leading figure in the Russian Revolution): **Reds**, 1981 (Jerzy Kosinski).

Zola, Emile Edouard Charles Antoine (1840-1902; French journalist, author and defender of wrongly convicted Alfred Dreyfus): Affare Dreyfus, 1959 (made-for-TV; Hans Hinrich); Affare Dreyfus, 1968- (TV miniseries; Bernhard Wicki); The Dreyfus Case, 1931 (George Merritt); The Dreyfus Case, 1940 (Heinrich George); Emile Zola ou La conscience humaine, 1978- (TV miniseries; Jean Topart); Folio, 1955-1959 (TV series; "Betrayal," 1955 episode: Hugh Webster); I Accuse!, 1958 (Emlyn Williams); **The Life of Emile Zola**, 1937 (Paul Muni); Lux Video Theatre, 1950-1959 (TV series; "The Life of Emile Zola," 1955 episode; Lee J. Cobb); Prisoner of Honor, 1991 (made-for-TV; Martin Friend). Note: For detailed information on Zola and his defense of Dreyfus, see my book *"I Am Innocent": A Comprehensive Encyclopedic History of the World's Wrongly Convicted Persons* (DaCapo Press, 2008; illustrated [16 images] pages 1-8).

Zwicker, Ralph Wise (American soldier and major general; 1903-1991): Tail Gunner Joe, 1977 (made-for-TV; William Schallert).

INSTITUTIONS & ORGANIZATIONS

Note: The following annotated index, exclusively (and manually); created by the author, offers a compilation of institutions and organizations depicted in theatrically-released feature films (chiefly U.S. and British releases, along with notable foreign productions, showing U.S. year of release). All titles shown in boldface represent entries profiled in this work.

Abteilung IIIb (German military intelligence, 1889-1918): Darling Lili, 1970; **Dark Journey**, 1937; **Dishonored**, 1931; Fraulein Doktor, 1969; **Hearts of the World**, 1918; **Lancer Spy**, 1937; Mademoiselle Docteur, [1937] 1948; Mademoiselle from Armentieres, 1928; The Man Who Stayed at Home, 1915; **Mata Hari**, 1931; Mata Hari, Agent H21, 1964; Mata Hari, 1985; **Stamboul Quest**, 1934; Would You Believe It!, 1930.

Abwehr (German military intelligence, 1920-1945): **Above Suspicion**, 1943; **All through the Night**, 1942; **Arch of Triumph**, 1948; Back-Room Boy, 1942; **Background to Danger**, 1943; **Berlin Correspondent**, 1942; Betrayed, 1954; Bulldog Sees It Through, 1940; **Carve Her Name with Pride**, 1958; Circle of Deception, 1961; **Cloak and Dagger**, 1946; Clouds over Europe (aka: Foreign Sabotage; Q Planes), 1939; **Commandos Strike at Dawn**, 1942; **Confessions of a Nazi Spy**, 1939; Contraband (aka: Blackout), 1940; Cottage to Let (AKA: Bombsight Stolen), 1943; Count Five and Die, 1958; Counter-Espionage, 1942; **Decision before Dawn**, 1951; **The Desert Fox: The Story of Rommel**, 1951; **Desperate Journey**, 1942; **The Eagle Has Landed**, 1977; Enemy Agent, 1940; Enemy of Women, 1944; **Eye of the Needle**, 1981; **Eyes in the Night**, 1942; **The Falcon's Brother**, 1942; **5 Fingers**, 1952; **Foreign Correspondent**, 1940; **The 49th Parallel** (aka: The Invaders), 1942; Hidden Enemy, 1940; **The Hitler Gang**, 1944; **Hotel Reserve**, 1946; **The House on 92nd Street**, 1945; **I See a Dark Stranger**, 1947; **Journey into Fear**, 1943; **The Lady Vanishes**, 1938; The Lady Vanishes, 1979; Law and Disorder, 1940; Let George Do It! (aka: To Hell with Hitler), 1940; Lightning Conductor, 1938; The Man from Morocco, 1946; **Man Hunt**, 1941; **The Man Who Knew Too Much**, 1935; **The Man Who Never Was**, 1956; **Ministry of Fear**, 1944; **Nazi Agent**, 1942; Night Boat to Dublin, 1946; Night of the Fox, 1990 (made-for-TV); **The Night of the Generals**, 1967; **Night Train to Munich**, 1940; **Odette**, 1951; **Operation Crossbow**, 1965; **Operation Secret**, 1952; **O.S.S.**, 1946; **Pimpernel Smith**, 1942; Remember Pearl Harbor, 1942; Rogue Male, 1977; **Sabotage**, 1937; **Saboteur**, 1942; **Sealed Cargo**, 1951; The Seventh Survivor, 1942; **Sherlock Holmes and the Secret Weapon**, 1942; **Sherlock Holmes in Washington**, 1943; Shining Through, 1992; Snowbound, 1949; Sons of the Sea, 1939; Spies of the Air, 1940; Spy for a Day, 1940; Spy Ship, 1942; Squadron Leader X, 1943; **Stalag 17**, 1953; **They Came to Blow Up America**, 1943; **They Met in the Dark**, 1945; **13 Rue Madeleine**, 1947; **36 Hours**, 1965; This Was Paris, 1942; **To Be or Not to Be**, 1942; The Torso Murder Mystery (aka: Traitor Spy), 1940; Tower of Terror, 1942; **Triple Cross**, 1966; **The Two-Headed Spy**, 1959; Unseen Enemy, 1942; Waterfront, 1944; **Where Eagles Dare**, 1968; The Whip Hand, 1951; **Yellow Canary**, 1944.

Alcatraz (U.S. military prison, 1868; federal prison, 1933-1963; located in San Francisco Bay, California): **Al Capone**, 1959; Alcatraz, 2012 (TV series); Alcatraz Express, 1960 (made-for-TV); Alcatraz Island, 1937; Alcatraz: The Whole Shocking Story, 1980 (made-for-TV); **All Dogs Go to Heaven 2**, 1996; **Birdman of Alcatraz**, 1962; The Book of Eli, 2010; Dick Tracy, 1937; Electric Dreams, 1984; **The Enforcer**, 1976; **Escape from Alcatraz**, 1979; Experiment Alcatraz, 1950; Fisherman's Wharf, 1939; Half Past Dead, 2002; **The House across the Bay**, 1940; Howl, 2010; Johnny Stool Pigeon, 1949; **King of Alcatraz**, 1938; **The Last Gangster**, 1937; Murder in the First, 1995; Passport to

Alcatraz, 1940; Persons in Hiding, 1939; Pier 23, 1951; **Point Blank**, 1967; Prison Train, 1938; Rise of the Zombies, 2012 (made-for-TV); Road to Alcatraz, 1945; The Rock, 1996; Seven Miles from Alcatraz, 1943; Slaughterhouse Rock, 1988; So I Married an Axe Murderer, 1993; **Star Trek: Into Darkness**, 2013; Terror at Alcatraz, 1982 (made-for-TV); Terror on Alcatraz, 1987; Train to Alcatraz, 1948; **X-Men: The Last Stand**, 2006.

Amish (Anabaptists; Mennonites): Aaron's Way, 1988 (TV series); Amish Grace, 2010 (made-for-TV); An Amish Murder, 2013 (made-for-TV); At Close Range, 1986; Banshee, 2013- (TV series); Birch Interval, 1976; David in Wunderland, 1998; Deadly Devotion, 2013- (TV series); Deadly Reactor, 1989; Diary of the Dead, 2007; ECW One Night Stand, 2005 (made-for-TV); For Richer or Poorer, 1997; Gypsy 83, 2001; Harvest of Fire, 1996 (made-for-TV); Hitting the Nuts, 2010; Holy Matrimony, 1994; Holyman Undercover, 2010; Jesus' Son, 1999; Kaw, 2007; Kingpin, 1996; Love Finds You in Sugarcreek, 2014 (made-for-TV); Lucky Numbers, 2000; **The Night They Raided Minsky's**, 1968; North, 1994; The Outsider, 2002 (made-for-TV); Plain Truth, 2004 (made-for-TV); Road Movie, 1974; Route 30, 2007; Saving Sarah Cain, 2007; Sex Drive, 2008; The Shunning, 2011 (made-for-TV); The Stoning in Fulham County, 1988 (made-for-TV); They Call Me Renegade, 1987; **Violent Saturday**, 1955; Warlock, 1989; **Witness**, 1985.

Annapolis Naval Academy (Annapolis, Maryland; established on October 10, 1845): Annapolis, 1928; Annapolis, 2006; Annapolis Farewell, 1935; Annapolis Salute, 1937; An Annapolis Story, 1955; Faith of My Fathers, 2005 (made-for-TV); The Flying Fleet, 1929; Hello, Annapolis, 1942; Hold 'Em Navy, 1937; Men of Annapolis, 1957- (TV series); The Midshipman, 1925; Midshipman Jack, 1933; Navy Blue and Gold, 1937; **Patriot Games**, 1992; Salute, 1929; Sweetheart of the Navy, 1937; **Task Force**, 1949; Undersea Kingdom, 1936 (serial).

Baseball Teams: Alibi Ike, 1935 (Chicago Cubs); **Angels in the Outfield**, 1951 (Pittsburgh Pirates); **Angels in the Outfield**, 1994 (California Angels); **The Babe**, 1992 (Babe Ruth; New York Yankees); Babe Ruth, 1991 (made-for-TV; New York Yankees); **The Babe Ruth Story**, 1948 (New York Yankees); **Bang the Drum Slowly**, 1973 (fictional New York baseball team); **The Bingo Long Traveling All Stars & Motor Kings**, 1976 (Negro league); **Brewster's Millions**, 1985 (minor league team); **Bull Durham**, 1988 (minor league team); Casey at the Bat, 1927 (minor league); Cobb, 1994 (Ty Cobb; Detroit Tigers); **Damn Yankees**, 1958 (New York Yankees); Damn Yankees!, 1967 (made-for-TV; New York Yankees); Ed, 1996 (minor league); **Eight Men Out**, 1988 (Chicago White Sox); **Elmer the Great** (Chicago Cubs), 1933; Everyone's Hero, 2006 (animated; Babe Ruth; New York Yankees, Chicago Cubs); The Fan, 1996 (San Francisco Giants); **Fear Strikes Out**, 1957 (Jimmy Piersall; Boston Red Sox); **Field of Dreams**, 1989 (Chicago White Sox); **Fireman, Save My Child**, 1932 (St. Louis Cardinals, New York Yankees); For the Love of the Game, 1999 (Detroit Tigers, New York Yankees); **42**, 2013 (Jackie Robinson; Brooklyn Dodgers); Hit and Run, 1924 (minor league); Hot Curves, 1930 (minor league); In the Name of the Law, 1922 (Honus Wagner; Pittsburgh Pirates); It Happened in Flatbush, 1942 (Brooklyn Dodgers); **It Happens Every Spring**, 1949 (unspecified St. Louis team); **The Jackie Robinson Story**, 1950 (Brooklyn Dodgers); **Jim Thorpe—All American**, 1951 (New York Giants); Joe Torre: Curveballs along the Way, 1997 (made-for-TV; New York Yankees); The Kid from Cleveland, 1949 (Bill Veeck, Tris Speaker, Hank Greenberg; Cleveland Indians, Boston Braves); The Kid from Left Field, 1979 (San Diego Padres); Kill the Umpire, 1950 (minor Texas league); Ladies' Day, 1943 (minor league); **A League of Their Own**, 1992 (All- American Girls Professional Baseball League/AAGPBL); **Little Big League**, 1994 (Minnesota Twins); Long Gone, 1987 (made-for-cable TV; minor league); Major League, 1989 (Cleveland Indians); Major League II, 1994 (Cleveland Indians);

Major League: Back to the Minors, 1998 (Minnesota Twins); A Mile in His Shoes, 2011 (made-for-TV; minor league); **Million Dollar Arm**, 2014 (Pittsburgh Pirates); Mr. Baseball, 1992 (Japanese professional team); Mr. Dynamite, 1941 (minor league); Mr. Go, 2013 (Korean baseball team); Mr. 3000, 2004 (Milwaukee Brewers); Moonlight in Havana, 1942 (minor league); **The Natural**, 1984 (New York Knights, a fictional team, leading character based on Eddie Waitkus of the Philadelphia Phillies); **The Pride of St. Louis**, 1952 (Jerome "Dizzy" Dean; St. Louis Cardinals); **The Pride of the Yankees**, 1942 (Lou Gehrig; New York Yankees); **Rhubarb**, 1951 (Brooklyn Dodgers); Rookie of the Year, 1993 (Chicago Cubs); Safe at Home, 1962 (New York Yankees); **The Scout**, 1994 (New York Yankees); 61, 2001 (made-for-TV; Roger Maris, Mickey Mantle; New York Yankees); Slide, Kelly, Slide, 1927 (New York Yankees); The Slugger's Wife, 1985 (Atlanta Braves); Soul of the Game, 1996 (made-for-TV; Negro league; Jackie Robinson); **Speedy**, 1928 (Babe Ruth; New York Yankees); Stealing Home, 1988 (minor league); **The Stratton Story**, 1949 (Monty Stratton; Chicago White Sox); Sugar, 2008 (minor league); Summer Catch, 2001 (minor league team); **Take Me Out to the Ballgame**, 1949 (minor league team); Talent for the Game, 1991 (California Angels); **Trouble with the Curve**, 2012 (Atlanta Braves); Warming Up, 1928 (minor league); Whistling in Brooklyn, 1943 (Brooklyn Dodgers); A Winner Never Quits, 1986 (made-for-TV; one-armed Pete Gray; St. Louis Browns); The Winning Season, 2004 (made-for-TV; Honus Wagner, Ty Cobb); **The Winning Team**, 1952 (Grover Cleveland Alexander; Philadelphia Phillies, Chicago Cubs, St. Louis Cardinals).

British Royal Navy (hereafter RN): **Above Us the Waves**, 1956 (British submarines attacking the German battleship *Tirpitz* in WWII); Against All Flags, 1952 (RN battling pirates); **Amistad**, 1997 (RN and its destruction of the African slave trade); The Bounty, 1984; Battle Hell (AKA: Yangtse Incident), 1957 (based on the 1949 exploits of the HMS *Amethyst* during the Chinese Civil War); The Buccaneers, 1956-1957 (TV series); **Captain Horatio Hornblower**, 1951 (RN exploits during the Napoleonic Wars); **The Cockleshell Heroes**, 1955 (British navy commandos in kayaks in WWII); **Corvette K-225**, 1943 (RN warships escorting cargo vessels across the Atlantic in WWII); Crest of the Wave (aka: Seagulls over Sorrento), 1954 (experiments on a dangerous new torpedo); **The Cruel Sea**, 1953 (British corvette in WWII); **Fire over England**, 1937 (RN under Elizabeth I); Goldeneye, 1989 (made-for-TV); Ghostboat, 2006 (made-for-TV); Glory at Sea, 1952 (exploits of an RN destroyer in 1940 during WWII); Hell Boats, 1970 (RN battles German forces in Malta and the Mediterranean in WWII); Hell Raiders of the Deep, 1954 (Italian frogmen attacking an RN ship with limpet mines in Alexandria Harbor in WWII); **In Which We Serve**, 1942 (British destroyers in the Atlantic and Mediterranean in WWII); **Malta Story**, 1954 (RN battling German forces in the Mediterranean in WWII); **Master and Commander: The Far Side of the World**, 2003 (exploits of a British frigate during the Napoleonic Wars); **The McKenzie Break**, 1970 (RN outwitting German POWs in WWII); Men Like These, 1932 (RN submarine trapped at the bottom of the sea); **Mutiny on the Bounty**, 1935; **Mutiny on the Bounty**, 1962; The Navy Lark, 1959; Operation Disaster, 1951 (submarine trapped at the bottom of the sea); Pursuit of the Graf Spee (aka: The Battle of the River Plate), 1957 (RN warships pursue a German battleship to the River Plate); Remembrance, 1982 (RN in NATO exercises); **The Sea Hawk**, 1940 (RN under Elizabeth I); **Sailor of the King**, 1953; The Sea Chase, 1955 (RN warships chase a German freighter, after one of its members commits an atrocity on a remote British-held island); The Sea Wolves, 1980 (RN during WWII); **The Silent Enemy**, 1959 (RN agent Lionel Crabbe battles enemy frogmen in WWII); **Sink the Bismarck!**, 1960 (the destruction of the German battleship in WWII); Sink the Bismarck, 1996 (made-for-TV); **Soldier of Orange**, 1979; **The Spy in Black**, 1939 (RN during WWI); **The Spy Who Loved Me**, 1977 (nuclear British submarine is stolen); **Submarine X-1**, 1969 (midget subs in WWII); Three

Cockeyed Sailors, 1941 (Three RN sailors take over a German warship in WWII); Tomorrow Never Dies, 1997 (RN ship is sunk in an effort to set off a war); **U-47**, 1959 (exploits of German submarine commanded by Gunther Prien, who reportedly penetrated Scapa Flow in 1939 to attack RN warships); **Vacation from Marriage** (aka: Perfect Strangers), 1945; Watch Your Stern, 1961; **We Dive at Dawn**, 1943 (British submariners in WWII); When Eight Bells Toll, 1971.

Cayenne Penal Colony (French penal colony at several locations in French Guiana; aka: Devil's Island; 1852-1946): Condemned, 1929; **The Devil Doll**, 1936; Devil's Island, 1926; Devil's Island, 1939; Escape from Devil's Island, 1935; Hell on Devil's Island, 1957; I Escaped from Devil's Island, 1973; **Life of Emile Zola**, 1937; Lovers of Devil's Island, 1974; **Mysterious Mr. Moto**, 1938; **Papillon**, 1973; **Passage to Marseilles**, 1944; Schlitz Playhouse, 1951-1959 (TV series; "The Man Who Escaped from Devil's Island," 1954 episode); **Strange Cargo**, 1940; Terror of the Bloodhunters, 1962; **We're No Angels**, 1955; Women of Devil's Island, 1962.

Chain Gangs (prisons): Adios Amigo, 1976; Adventures of Don Quixote, 1933; The Badlanders, 1958; The Ballad of the Sad Café, 1991; **Bite the Bullet**, 1975; Black Cat Run, 1998 (made-for-TV); Blackmail, 1939; Boxcar Bertha, 1972; **The Buccaneer**, 1938; **Carbine Williams**, 1952; Chain Gang, 1950; Chain Gang, 1984; Chain Gang Women, 1971; Cellmates, 2011; **Convicts**, 1991; **Cool Hand Luke**, 1967; Cut-Throats Nine, 1972; **The Defiant Ones**, 1958; The Devil's 8, 1969; **Django Unchained**, 2012; **The Emperor Jones**, 1933; Fatherland, 1994 (made-for-TV); Fled, 1996; **48 Hours**, 1982; Fugitive at Large, 1939; Garden of the Dead, 1972; Girl on a Chain Gang, 1966; **Gone with the Wind**, 1939; **Hallelujah!**, 1929; Happy, Texas, 1999; Hell-Fire Austin, 1932; Hell's Highway, 1932; **I Am a Fugitive from a Chain Gang**, 1932 (based on the life of Robert Elliot Burns); Island of Fire, 1990; Judge Priest, 1934; The Killing Zone, 1991; The Laramie Kid, 1935; The Life of David Gale, 2003; The Man Who Broke 1,000 Chains, 1987 (made-for-TV; Robert Elliot Burns); Mean Dog Blues, 1978; **Nevada Smith**, 1966; **O Brother, Where Art Thou?**, 2000; One More Train to Rob, 1971; **Papillon**, 1973; **Passage to Marseilles**, 1944; Round-Up Time in Texas, 1937; Route 666, 2001; The Shadow Riders, 1982 (made-for-TV); Sing Your Song, 2011; Siringo, 1995 (made-for-TV); Slavery by Another Name, 2012 (made-for-TV); **Strange Cargo**, 1940; **Sullivan's Travels**, 1941; Superman IV: The Quest for Peace, 1987; **Take the Money and Run**, 1969; **There Will Be Blood**, 2007; 39 Stripes, 1979 (based on the life of Ed Martin, who converted to Christianity in 1944 while a convict and later established the HopeAglow prison ministries); Thunder II, 1987; **Tramp, Tramp, Tramp**, 1926; Two for Texas, 1998 (made-for-TV); **Under the Gun**, 1951.

Chinese Intelligence (MSS/Ministry of State Security, est. c. 1950): Battle beneath the Earth, 1968; Bullet to Beijing, 1997 (made-for-TV); **The Chairman**, 1969.

CIA (U.S. Central Intelligence Agency, est. 1947): **Agent Cody Banks**, 2003; Aldrich Ames: Traitor Within, 1998 (made-for-TV); **Apocalypse Now**, 1979; The A-Team, 2010; **Act of Valor**, 2012; **Argo**, 2012; Bad Company, 2002; **The Barbarian Invasions**, 2003; Black Dynamite, 2009; Body of Lies, 2008; **The Bourne Identity**, 2002; **The Bourne Ultimatum**, 2007; **The Bourne Legacy**, 2012; The Bourne Supremacy, 2004; Burn after Reading, 2008; **The Chairman**, 1969; **Charade**, 1963; **Charlie Wilson's War**, 2007; The Case of the Red Monkey (aka: Little Red Monkey), 1955; **Casino Royale**, 1967; **Casino Royale**, 2006; Columbiana, 2011; Company Business, 1991; Company Man, 2001; **Confessions of a Dangerous Mind**, 2002; Criminal, 2016; Danger Route, 1967; **The Dark Knight Rises**, 2012; **Die Another Day**, 2002; **Dr. No**, 1962; The Double Man, 1968; Erased, 2012; Escape Plan, 2013; Executive Action, 1973; Fair Game, 2010; 5 Steps to Danger, 1957;

From Paris with Love, 2010; **Goldfinger**, 1964; A Good Day to Die Hard, 2013; The Good Shepherd, 2006; **Green Zone**, 2010; **Hanna**, 2011; The Innocent, 1995 (Berlin Tunnel); Innocent Bystanders, 1973; **The In-Laws**, 1979; **The Ipcress File**, 1965; Keeping Track, 1986; The Killer Elite, 1975; Knight and Day, 2010; Laser Mission, 1989; **License to Kill**, 1989; Live and Let Die, 1973; The Living Daylights, 1987; Lockout, 2012; Madame Sin, 1972; Man on a String, 1960; Man on Fire, 2004; The Man with One Red Shoe, 1985; The Means War, 2012; Meet the Parents, 2000; **Moonraker**, 1979; **Night People**, 1954; **North by Northwest**, 1959; The November Man, 2014; The Numbers Station, 2013; Once upon a Time in Mexico, 2003; The Operative, 2000; The Osterman Weekend, 1983; Outrageous Fortune, 1987; Pineapple Express, 2008; Red, 2010; Red 2, 2013; Rendition, 2007; **Ronin**, 1998; The Russia House, 1990; Safe House, 2012; Salt, 2010; Salting the Battlefield, 2014 (made-for-TV); Scavengers, 1987; The Sell-Out, 1977; Spies Like Us, 1985; **Spy Game**, 2001; The Sum of All Fears, 2002; **Three Days of the Condor**, 1975; 3 Days to Kill, 2014; **Thunderball**, 1965; **Topaz**, 1969; **Torn Curtain**, 1966; Turks and Caicos, 2014 (made-for-TV); 2 Guns, 2013; **World War Z**, 2013; **X-Men: First Class**, 2011; Yuri Nosenko: Double Agent, 1986 (made-for-TV); **Zero Dark Thirty**, 2012.

Deuxieme Bureau (military intelligence agency for France, 1871-1940): Affare Dreyfuss, 1968- (TV miniseries); Alerte au deuxieme bureau, 1956; Deuxieme bureau contre kommandantur, 1939; Deuxieme bureau contre terroristes, 1961; **The Dreyfus Case**, 1931; The Dreyfus Case, 1940; I Accuse!, 1958; Emile Zola ou La conscience humaine, 1978- (TV miniseries); L'affaire Dreyfus, 1995 (made-for-TV); Les dossiers de l'ecran, 1967-1989 (TV series); **The Life of Emile Zola**, 1937; Lux Video Theatre, 1950-1959 (TV series; "The Life of Emile Zola," 1955 episode); **Mata Hari**, 1931; Mata Hari, Agent H21, 1964; Mata Hari, 1985; Prisoner of Honor, 1991 (made-for-TV); The Spy Catcher, 1960; Rapt au deuxieme bureau, 1958; Second Bureau, 1935.

FBI (U.S. Federal Bureau of Investigation, since 1924): After the Sunset, 2004; Ali, 2001; Aldrich Ames: Traitor Within, 1998 (made-for-TV); American Yakuza, 1993; The Americans, 2013- (TV series); Analyze That, 2002; **Analyze This**, 1999; Angela's Eyes, 2006 (TV series); Antitrust, 2001; Arlington Road, 1999; Armageddon, 1998; Arsene Lupin Returns, 1938; Art for Teachers of Children, 1995; The Art of War, 2000; The Assassination File, 1996 (made-for-TV); The Astronaut Farmer, 2007; The Atomic City, 1952; **The Aviator**, 2004; Baby for Sale, 2004 (made-for-TV); Bad Boys II, 2003; **Bananas**, 1971; Behind the Headlines, 1937; The Believer, 2001; Best Men, 1997; Betrayed, 1988; A Better Way to Die, 2000; Big House, U.S.A., 1955; Bird on a Wire, 1990; Black Dog, 1998; Black Moon Rising, 1986; Black Point, 2002; Black Widow, 1987; Blade Trinity, 2004; Bless the Child, 2000; Blood Feud, 1983 (made-for-TV); Blow, 2001; Blue Streak, 1999; Blues Brothers 2000, 1998; Boiler Room, 2000; Bones, 2005- (TV series); The Boondock Saints, 2000; Boss of Bosses, 2001; Boston Legal, 2004-2008 (TV series); **Breach**, 2007 (Robert Hanssen); Breach of Trust, 1996; **Bridge of Spies**, 2015 (Rudolf Abel; Francis Gary Powers); **The Brink's Job**, 1978; Brotherhood of Murder, 1999 (made-for-TV); Caracara, 1999 (made-for-TV); A Case of Deceit, 2012; Castle, 2009- (TV series); **Catch Me If You Can**, 2002; The Cell, 2000; Chameleon, 1996; The Chameleon, 2011; Chaos, 2005; Charlie and the Great Balloon Chase, 1981; Charlie's Angels: Full Throttle, 2003; Che Guevara, 2005; Citizen Cohn, 1992 (made-for-TV); City of Ghosts, 2003; Clay Pigeons, 1998; Clear and Present Danger, 1994; The Clearing, 2004; **The Client**, 1994; Code 11-14, 2003 (made-for-TV); Collateral, 2004; Collateral Damage, 2002; Colombiana, 2011; **Coming Home**, 1978; The Commission, 2003; Company Business, 1991; The Company You Keep, 2012; **Confessions of a Nazi Spy**, 1939; **Conspiracy Theory**, 1997; The Contender, 2000; Corky Romano, 2001; The Corruptor, 1999; Cosa Nostra: Arch Enemy of the FBI, 1967 (made-for-TV); Cover Me,

1999 (TV miniseries); **Crash**, 2004; Crime Spree, 2003; Criminal Minds, 2005- (TV series); Critical Assembly, 2003 (made-for-TV); C-16: FBI, 1997-1998 (TV series); Cumulus 9, 1992; The Dark, 1993; Dark Angel, 1990; That Darn Cat, 1997; Daughter of the Tong, 1939; Dead Silence, 1997 (made-for-TV); Deadly Impact, 2010; Death of a President, 2006; Death to Smoochy, 2002; **Deep Impact**, 1998; **The Departed**, 2006; Desert Blue, 1998; Desert Saints, 2002; **The Desperate Hours**, 1955; Desperate Hours, 1990; Did You Hear about the Morgans?, 2009; **Die Hard**, 1988; **Die Hard: With a Vengeance**, 1995; Dillinger, 1945; Dillinger, 1973; Dillinger, 1991 (made-for-TV); Direct Action, 2004; Disconnect, 2013; Dishonorable Vendetta, 2013; **Dog Day Afternoon**, 1975; Dogville, 2003; Dollhouse, 2009-2010 (TV series); Donnie Brasco, 1997; Doorways, 1993 (made-for-TV); Double Tap, 2011; **Down Three Dark Streets**, 1954; Eagle Eye, 2008; Edison, 2005; 88 Minutes, 2008; 83 Hours 'Til Dawn, 1990; The End of Violence, 1997; Entrapment, 1999; Eraser, 1996; The Event, 2010- (TV series); Every Mother's Worst Fear, 1998 (made-for-TV); Executive Action, 1973; **Experiment in Terror**, 1962; Fair Game, 2010; The Falcon and the Snowman, 1985; The Family, 2013; Family of Spies, 1990 (made-for-TV; Walker family); Fast & Furious, 2009; Fast & Furious, 2013; Fast Money, 1996; The F.B.I., 1965-1974 (TV series); FBI Code 98, 1964 (made-for-TV); FBI Girl, 1951; FBI: Negotiator, 2005 (made-for-TV); FBI Operation Yellow Viper, 1966; **The FBI Story**, 1959; The F.B.I. Story: The F.B.I. vs. Alvin Karpis, Public Enemy Number One, 1974 (made-for-TV); FBI: The Untold Stories, 1991-1993 (TV series); Federal Operator 99, 1945; 54, 1998; Feds, 1988; The Fiendish Plot of Dr. Fu Manchu, 1980; Final Approach, 2008 (made-for-TV); **Find Me Guilty**, 2006; **The Firm**, 1993; 5 Steps to Danger, 1957; Flashback, 1990; Flashforward, 2009-2010 (TV series); Flightplan, 2005; Folks!, 1992; The Following, 2013- (TV series); The Forget-Me-Not Murders, 1994 (made-for-TV); The Fourth Angel, 2001; Frailty, 2001; Framed, 2003 (made-for-TV); Francis Gary Powers: The True Story of the U-2 Spy Incident, 1976 (made-for-TV; Rudolf Abel); Free Money, 1998; **The Freshman**, 1990; The Frighteners, 1996; Fringe, 2008- (TV series); **Frost/Nixon**, 2008; Gang Busters, 1952-1955 (TV series); Gang in Blue, 1996 (made-for-TV); Gangster Squad, 2013; The Getaway, 1941; Ghost Patrol, 1936; **G-Men**, 1935; G-Men Never Forget, 1948; **The Godfather**, 1972; **The Godfather, Part II**, 1974; Golden Gate, 1994; Golgo 13, 2008-2009 (TV series); **Good Night and Good Luck**, 2005; The Good Shepherd, 2006; Government Girl, 1943; Greendale, 2003; The Grid, 2004 (TV miniseries); **The Guard**, 2011; **Guarding Tess**, 1994; Gun Crazy, 1950; Half Past Dead, 2002; The Handler, 2003-2004 (TV series); Hannibal, 2001; Hard Cash, 2002; Harsh Times, 2006; Harvest of Fire, 1996 (made-for-TV); Haven, 2004; Haven, 2010- (TV series); Head over Heels, 2001; The Heat, 2013; Heist, 2001; Hellboy, 2004; Her Desperate Choice, 1996 (made-for-TV); **The Hidden**, 1987; Hidden Agenda, 2001; **High Crimes**, 2002; High School Confidential!, 1958; Hiroshima Maiden, 1988 (made-for-TV); Hoover, 2000; Hollow Point, 1996; Hostage, 2005; House, 1986; **The House on Carroll Street**, 1988; **The House on 92nd Street**, 1945; Howl, 2010; The Hunt for the I-5 Killer, 2011 (made-for-TV); **The Hunted**, 2003; **I Was a Communist for the FBI**, 1951; I Was a Zombie for the F.B.I., 1982; I'll Get You, 1953; In Plain Sight, 2008-2012 (TV series); In the Line of Duty: Ambush in Waco, 1993 (made-for-TV); In the Line of Duty: The FBI Murders, 1988 (made-for-TV); In the Line of Duty: Hunt for Justice, 1995 (made-for-TV); **In the Line of Fire**, 1993; **Indiana Jones and the Kingdom of the Crystal Skull**, 2008; **The Informant!**, 2009; The Inside, 2005- (TV series); **The Insider**, 1999; **Insomnia**, 2002; The Insurgents, 2007; The Interpreter, 2005; **J. Edgar**, 2011; J. Edgar Hoover, 1987 (made-for-TV); Jack Ryan: Shadow Recruit, 2014; The Jackal, 1997; Johnnie Mae Gibson: FBI, 1986 (made-for-TV); Judas Kiss, 1999; The Kane Files: Life of Trial, 2010; The Kansas City Massacre, 1975 (made-for-TV); Killer Rules, 1993 (made-for-TV); The Killing Mind, 1991 (made-for-TV); King, 1978 (TV miniseries); The Kingdom, 2007; Kiss the Girls, 1997; Knight and Day, 2010; **The Last**

Gangster, 1937; The Last Mimzy, 2007; The Last Shot, 2004; The Last Stand, 2013; The Learning Curve, 2001; Layover, 2012 (made-for-TV); Letters from a Killer, 1998; Levity, 2003; Line of Fire, 2003-2004 (TV series); **Live Free or Die Hard**, 2007; Live Wire, 1992; The Lodger, 2009; The Long Kiss Goodnight, 1996; Long Wolf McQuade, 1983; Loose Cannons, 1990; A Low Down Dirty Shame, 1994; Madame Spy, 1942; Major Crimes, 2012- (TV series); Make Your Own Bed, 1944; Man at Large, 1941; **Man of Steel**, 2013; Man of the House, 2005; **Manhunter**, 1986; The Manchurian Candidate, 2004; Mao's Last Dancer, 2009; **Marie**, 1985; Marilyn & Bobby: Her Final Affair, 1993 (made-for-TV); **Married to the Mob**, 1988; Master Spy: The Robert Hanssen Story, 2002 (made-for-TV); Matilda, 1996; Maximum Risk, 1996; Melvin Purvis: G-Man, 1974 (made-for-TV); Medusa's Child, 1997 (made-for-TV); Mercury Rising, 1998; Miami Vice, 2006; Mickey Blues Eyes, 1999; **A Mighty Heart**, 2007; **Midnight Run**, 1988; Millennium, 1996-1999 (TV series); Mindhunters, 2005; The Minus Man, 1999; Miss Congeniality, 2000; **Mississippi Burning**, 1988; **Mr. & Mrs. Smith**, 2005; The Moment After, 1999; The Moment After II: The Awakening, 2006; Moment of Truth: Caught in the Crossfire, 1994; Momentum, 2003 (made-for-TV); Monk, 2002-2009 (TV miniseries); Moonshine Highway, 1996 (made-for-TV); **The More the Merrier**, 1943; **Mulholland Falls**, 1996; Murder by Numbers, 2002; Murder in My Mind, 1997 (made-for-TV); My Blue Heaven, 1990; My Mom's New Boyfriend, 2008; **My Son John**, 1952; National Treasure, 2004; National Treasure: Book of Secrets, 2007; The Negotiator, 1998; A Nero Wolfe Mystery, 2000-2002 (TV series); The Net, 1995; New York, 2009; Newsboys' Home, 1938; Next, 2007; Night Sins, 1997 (made-for-TV); **No God, No Master**, 2012; No Place to Hide, 1970; Now You See Me, 2013; Ocean's Thirteen, 2007; Olympus Has Fallen, 2013; Once upon a Time in Mexico, 2003; 1-800-Missing, 2003-2006 (TV series); Osiris, 2011- (TV series); Otis, 2008; Out of Sight, 1998; The Outer Limits, 1995-2002 (TV series); Outside Ozona, 1998; Oxygen, 1999; Paid in Full, 2002; Panther, 1995; Parker and the Box, 2011; Parkland, 2013; Passenger 57, 1992; Path to Paradise: The Untold Story of the World Trade Center Bombing, 1997 (made-for-TV); Paycheck, 2003; Payoff, 1991 (made-for-TV); **The Pelican Brief**, 1993; The People vs. Larry Flynt, 1996; A Perfect World, 1993; Persons in Hiding, 1939; Phantoms, 1998; Phenomenon, 1996; Picket Fences, 1992-1996 (TV series); **Pickup on South Street**, 1953; Players, 1997-1998 (TV series); Playing God, 1997; Point Break, 1991; The Poughkeepsie Tapes, 2009; **The President's Analyst**, 1967; **Prince of the City**, 1981; Prison Break, 2005-2009 (TV series); **The Private Files of J. Edgar Hoover**, 1977; Profiler, 1996-2000 (TV series); The Proposal, 2001; **Public Enemies**, 2009; **Public Hero No. 1**, 1935; Quick Money, 1937; **Quiz Show**, 1994; **Raising Arizona**, 1987; **Ransom**, 1996; Rapid Fire, 1992; The Rat Pack, 1988 (made-for-TV); Raw Deal, 1986; Red, 2010; Red Eye, 2005; Red 2, 2013; Red Dragon, 2002; Red Skies, 2002 (made-for-TV); Redboy 13, 1997; The Reflecting Pool, 2008; Renegade Force, 1998; Replicant, 2001; Retroactive, 1997; Robert Hanssen: Double Agent Revealed, 2007 (made-for-TV); The Rock, 1996; **Running on Empty**, 1988; Rush Hour, 1998; Sabotage, 1996; Sacrifice, 2000 (made-for-TV); **Salt**, 2010; The Salton Sea, 2002; Security Risk, 1954; Shack Out on 101, 1955; Shattered Image, 1994 (made-for-TV); Shoot to Kill, 1988; Shooter, 2007; **Sicario**, 2015; The Siege, 1998; **The Silence of the Lambs**, 1991; The Silencer, 2000; Slaughter of the Innocents, 1993; Smashing the Rackets, 1938; Smokin' Aces, 2006; Snakes on a Plane, 2006; The Sopranos, 1999-2007 (TV series); The Spanish Prisoner, 1998; Spartan, 2004; Special Agent, 1935; Special Agent K-7, 1936; **Speed**, 1994; Standoff, 1998; Standoff, 2006-2007 (TV series); The State Within, 2006 (TV series); Steal This Movie, 2000; Stealing Sinatra, 2003; Steele's Law, 1991; **The Sting**, 1973; Stone Cold, 1991; **The Stranger**, 1946; **The Street with No Name**, 1948; **The Stunt Man**, 1980; Subject: I Love You, 2011; Submarine Alert, 1943; Sudden Death, 1995; Supernatural, 2005- (TV series); Suspect Zero, 2004; **Syriana**, 2005; Tactical Force, 2011; **Take the Money and Run**, 1969; Takedown, 2000; Taken

in Broad Daylight, 2009 (made-for-TV); Tango & Cash, 1989; 10th & Wolf, 2006; **Thank You for Smoking**, 2006; **That Darn Cat!**, 1965; **Them!**, 1954; **The Thief**, 1952; 36 Hours to Kill, 1936; **Thunderheart**, 1992; Tip-Off Girls, 1938; **To Live and Die in L.A.**, 1985; To Love, Honor and Deceive, 1996 (made-for-TV); Today's F.B.I., 1981-1982 (TV series); Tower Heist, 2011; Toy Soldiers, 1991; Traitor, 2008; Transformers, 2007; Transformers: Dark of the Moon, 2011; Trapped, 2002; The Trial of Billy Jack, 1974; Troubled Waters, 2007; Trust, 2010; Turbulence, 1997; 12 Rounds, 2009; 29 Palms, 2002; Twin Peaks, 1990-1991 (TV series); 2 Guns, 2013; Two in a Crowd, 1936; Under Lock and Key, 1995; Under New Management, 2009; Universal Soldier: Day of Reckoning, 2012; Unlucky, 2011; Unstoppable, 2004; Untraceable, 2008; **The Valachi Papers**, 1972; Vanished, 1971 (made-for-TV); Vice, 2008; The Visitor, 1997-1998 (TV series); **Walk a Crooked Mile**, 1948; **Walk East on Beacon!**, 1952; War, 2007; The Watcher, 2000; Web of Lies, 2010 (made-for-TV); The Whip Hand, 1951; White Collar, 2009- (TV series); White House Down, 2013; White Sands, 1992; Who Killed Atlanta's Children?, 2000 (made-for-TV); Who?, 1975; **Who Was That Lady?**, 1960; Wild Side, 1995; Winds of Terror, 2001 (made-for-TV); The Wire, 2002-2008 (TV series); Wisdom, 1986; Without a Trace, 2002-2009 (TV series); Witness Protection, 1999 (made-for-TV); **The Wolf of Wall Street**, 2013; **The Woman on Pier 13**, 1949; Wooly Boys, 2001; Wounded, 1997; **The X Files**, 1998; The X-Files, 1993-2002 (TV series); The X-Files: I Want to Believe, 2008; The Year That Trembled, 2002; Yes Man, 2008; Yuri Nosenko: Double Agent, 1986 (made-for-TV); Zero Tolerance, 1994; **Zodiac**, 2007.

Football Teams (professional): The Blind Side, 2009 (Baltimore Ravens); Crazylegs, 1953 (Cleveland Browns, Los Angeles Rams, Chicago Bears); **Draft Day**, 2014 (Cleveland Browns; Seattle Seahawks); **Heaven Can Wait**, 1978 (Los Angeles Rams); **Invincible**, 2006 (Philadelphia Eagles, New York Giants, Cincinnati Bengals).

French Foreign Legion: Abbott and Costello in the Foreign Legion, 1950; Adventure in Sahara, 1938; Assignment Foreign Legion, 1956 (TV series); Beauties of the Night, 1954; **Beau Geste**, 1926; **Beau Geste**, 1939; Beau Geste, 1966; Beau Geste, 1982 (TV miniseries); Beau Ideal, 1931; Beau Sabreur, 1928; Beau Travail, 2000; Captain Gallant of the Foreign Legion, 1955 (TV series); Carry on in the Legion, 1968; The Curse of King Tut's Tomb, 2006 (made-for-TV); Desert Command, 1946; Desert Legion, 1953; Desert Sands, 1955; **The Desert Song**, 1943; **The Desert Song**, 1953; The Devil's in Love, 1933; Diary of a Country Priest, 1954; The Divine Woman, 1928; Don Gabriel, 1966; Drums of the Desert, 1940; Flesh and the Woman, 1958; The Flying Deuces, 1939; Follow That Camel, 1968; The Foreign Legion, 1928; Fort Algiers, 1953; Fort Saganne, 1984; Harem Girl, 1952; Hell's Island, 1930; Isabelle Eberhardt, 1991; Jungle Siren, 1942; Kiss Me Again, 1931; The Last Remake of Beau Geste, 1977; Le grand jeu, 1934; Lea, 1996; The Legion of Missing Men, 1937; Legionnaire, 1998; Les Morfalous, 1984; Lionheart, 1991; The Lost Atlantis, 1932; The Man Who Turned White, 1919; **March or Die**, 1977; **Morocco**, 1930; The Mistress of Atlantis, 1939; **The Mummy**, 1999; Old Loves and New, 1926; Operation Leopard, 1980; Outpost in Morocco, 1949; Renegades, 1930; **Rogue's Regiment**, 1948; The Sad Sack, 1957; The Sands of Time, 1998 (made-for-TV); **Secondhand Lions**, 2003; Sergeant Klems, 1971; Sergeant X of the Foreign Legion, 1960; The Silent Lover, 1926; Soldiers of Fortune, 1955-1957 (TV series); **Sorcerer**, 1977; Straight Shooter, 2001; Sweet and Sour, 1964; **Ten Tall Men**, 1951; The Three Musketeers, 1933; Timbuktu, 1959; Two Men and a Maid, 1929; Under Two Flags, 1916; Under Two Flags, 1922; **Under Two Flags**, 1936; The Unknown, 1915; Wages of Virtue, 1924; We're in the Legion Now, 1936; The Winding Stair, 1925; Women Everywhere, 1930.

Gestapo (German secret police in Nazi Germany, Italy and occupied countries, 1933-1945): **Above Suspicion**, 1943; Address Unknown,

1944; **Adventures of Tartu**, 1943; Adventures of the Flying Cadets, 1943; **Against the Wind**, 1949; Aimee & Jaguar, 1999; All My Loved Ones, 2000; 'Allo, 'Allo, 1982-1992 (TV series); **Amen**, 2002; Angry Harvest, 1986; Anne Frank: The Whole Story, 2001 (TV miniseries); **Arch of Triumph**, 1948; Arch of Triumph, 1984 (made-for-TV); Army of Crime, 2010; The Army of Shadows, 2006 (released in France in 1969); The Aryan Couple, 2004; **The Assissi Underground**, 1985; At Dawn We Die, 1943; Au revoir les enfants, 1987; Balkan Express 2, 1989; Battle for the Railway, 1978; Beast of Berlin, 1939; The Beasts of Marseilles, 1959; Before the Fall, 2008; Bent, 1997; **Berlin Correspondent**, 1942; Black Book, 2007; The Black Parachute, 1944; Bomb at 10:10, 1967; Bonhoeffer: Agent of Grace, 2000; Breakthrough, 1981; **Carve Her Name with Pride**, 1958; **Casablanca**, 1942; Circle of Deception, 1961; **Cloak and Dagger**, 1946; **Commandos Strike at Dawn**, 1942; **Confessions of a Nazi Spy**, 1939; **The Conspirators**, 1944; Count Five and Die, 1958; **The Counterfeit Traitor**, 1962; **The Counterfeiters**, 2008; **Cross of Iron**, 1977; **The Damned**, 1969; David, 1982; The Day and the Hour, 1964; **Decision bBefore Dawn**, 1951; **The Desert Fox: The Story of Rommel**, 1951; **Desperate Journey**, 1942; **The Diary of Anne Frank**, 1959; **Divided We Fall**, 2000; Dr. Petiot, 1990; **The Eagle Has Landed**, 1977; The Enemy General, 1960; Enemy of Women, 1944; **Escape**, 1940; Everyone Dies Alone, 1976; Everything Happens at Night, 1939; **The Eye of the Needle**, 1965; Fatherland, 1994 (made-for-TV); Female Agents, 2008; Flame and Citron, 2008; The Four Horsemen of the Apocalypse, 1962; **Free Men**, 2012; **Generale Della Rovere**, 1961; The Gleiwitz Case, 1961; Good, 2008; **The Great Escape**, 1963; **Hangmen Also Die**, 1943; Haven, 2001 (made-for-TV); Head in the Clouds, 2004; Higher Principle, 1960; **The Hindenburg**, 1975; **The Hitler Gang**, 1944; Hitler's Children, 1943; **Hitler's Madman**, 1943; Hitler's S.S.: Portrait of Evil, 1985 (made-for-TV); Hogan's Heroes, 1965-1971 (TV series); Holocaust, 1978 (TV miniseries); **Hotel Berlin**, 1945; **The House on 92nd Street**, 1945; I Escaped from the Gestapo, 1943; **Indiana Jones and the Last Crusade**, 1989; It Happened One Night, 1958; Jacob the Liar, 1975; Jakob the Liar, 1999; Jenny's War, 1985 (made-for-TV); Joan of Ozark, 1942; **Joan of Paris**, 1942; Joe and Max, 2002 (made-for-TV); The Key, 1971; Lacombe, Lucien, 1974; Landscape after Battle, 1978; The Last Butterfly, 1993; **The Last Metro**, 1981; The Last Train, 2006; Lili Marleen, 1981; A Life for Football, 2014 (made-for-TV); **The Lost One**, 1951; Lucie Abrac, 1999; **Man Hunt**, 1941; **The Man Who Never Was**, 1956; Massacre at Noon, 1975; Max Manus: Man of War, 2010; Mendel, 1997; Mr. Klein, 1977; Monsieur Batignole, 2003; **Morituri**, 1965; **Nazi Agent**, 1942; **Night of the Generals**, 1967; **Night Train to Munich**, 1940; **The Ninth Day**, 2004; **O.S.S.**, 1946; Once upon a Honeymoon, 1942; **Open City**, 1946; **Operation Daybreak**, 1975; **Operation Secret**, 1952; Paris Calling, 1942; Paris Underground, 1945; **The Pianist**, 2002; **Pimpernel Smith**, 1942; Red Earth, 1975; The Red Nights of the Gestapo, 1977; The Red Orchestra, 1989; **Reunion in France**, 1942; Rotation, 1950; The Savior, 1971; **Schindler's List**, 1993; Secret Command, 1944; Secret Service in Darkest Africa, 1943 (serial); Seven Minutes, 1989; **The Seventh Cross**, 1944; **Sherlock Holmes and the Secret Weapon**, 1942; **633 Squadron**, 1964; Snowbound, 1949; **Soldier of Orange**, 1979; **Sophie Scholl: The Final Days**, 2006; **Stalag 17**, 1953; Storm over Lisbon, 1944; The Strange Death of Adolf Hitler, 1943; Sunshine, 2000; **Taking Sides**, 2003; **Tea with Mussolini**, 1999; **13 Rue Madeleine**, 1947; **36 Hours**, 1965; A Time to Love and a Time to Die, 1958; **To Be or Not to Be**, 1942; **To Have and Have Not**, 1944; **The Two-Headed Spy**, 1959; U-Boat Prisoner, 1944; **U-47**, 1958; **Uncertain Glory**, 1944; **Underground**, 1941; Underground, 1996; The Unwritten Code, 1944; **Valkyrie**, 2008; **Von Ryan's Express**, 1965; Walter Defends Sarajevo, 1972; Waterfront, 1944; **When Willie Comes Marching Home**, 1950; **Where Eagles Dare**, 1969; The White Rabbit, 1967 (TV miniseries); The Wife Takes a Flyer, 1942; Women in Bondage, 1943;

The Wooden Horse, 1951; Zamach, 1959; **Zelary**, 2004.

Harvard University (Cambridge, Massachusetts; established on September 8, 1636): Accepted, 2006; Admissions, 2004; American Psycho, 2000; Angels & Demons, 2009; The Autumn Heart, 1999; Bamboozled, 2000; **Bobby Jones: Stroke of Genius**, 2004; **The Da Vinci Code**, 2006; **Dead Poets Society**, 1989; **The Departed**, 2006; **The Firm**, 1993; First Affair, 1983 (made-for-TV); The First Olympics: Athens, 1896, 1984 (TV miniseries); **Flight**, 1929; Fringe, 2008-2013 (TV series); **Giant**, 1956; **Good Will Hunting**, 1997; **The Great Debaters**, 2007; **H.M. Pulham, Esq.**, 1941; Haven, 2001 (made-for-TV); Heaven's Gate, 1980; Huddle, 1932; The Inheritor, 1973; **Joe Gould's Secret**, 2000; Lady Barnacle, 1917; Margot at the Wedding, 2007; Mr. & Mrs. Bridge, 1990; Mona Lisa Smile, 2003; My Teacher's Wife, 1999; **Mystery Street**, 1950; The Nanny Diaries, 2007; **Personal Velocity**, 2002; **Pigskin Parade**, 1936; Prozac Nation, 2001; Ruthless, 1948; School Ties, 1992; **The Secret in Their Eyes**, 2009; Seeing Other People, 2004; The Skulls, 2000; A Small Act, 2010; **The Social Network**, 2010; Soul Man, 1986; Swimming Upstream, 2003; Temple Grandin, 2010 (made-for-TV); 21, 2008; To Race the Wind, 1980 (made-for-TV); The Unbelievable Truth, 1989; Waking the Dead, 2000; The Wrong Guy, 1997; The Young Rajah, 1922.

IRA (Irish Republican Army; established 1913): Angela's Ashes, 2000; Anton, 2008; **Beloved Enemy**, 1936; The Black Windmill, 1974; **Bloody Sunday**, 2002; Blown Away, 1994; The Bombmaker, 2001 (made-for-TV); Borstal Boy, 2001; **The Boxer**, 1997; The Break, 1998; Breakfast on Pluto, 2005; **Cal**, 1984; Circle of Deceit, 1993 (made-for-TV); The Craic, 1999; **The Crying Game**, 1992; The Dawning, 1988; The Devil's Own, 1997; Disappearing in America, 2009; Divorcing Jack, 1998; **The Eagle Has Landed**, 1976; **The Enigma of Frank Ryan**, 2012; An Everlasting Piece, 2000; Exiled, 1999; Fifty Dead Men Walking, 2009; **Five Minutes of Heaven**, 2009; 48 Angels, 2007; The General, 1998; Giro City, 1984; The Glory Boys, 1984 (TV series); Guests of the Nation, 1981 (made-for-TV); Harry's Game, 1982 (TV series); Hennessy, 1975; Hidden Agenda, 1991; **Hunger**, 2008; **In the Name of the Father**, 1993; I.R.A.: King of Nothing, 2007; **I See a Dark Stranger**, 1947; In This Corner, 1985 (made-for-TV); **The Informer**, 1935; The Informant, 1998; The Jackal, 1997; Johnny Was, 2006; Liam, 2001; **The Long Good Friday**, 1982; **The Man Who Never Was**, 1956; **Michael Collins**, 1996; Midnight Man, 1997 (made-for-TV); **The Night Fighters**, 1960; **Odd Man Out**, 1947; Omagh, 2004 (made-for-TV); Ordinary Decent Criminal, 2000; **The Outsider**, 1980; **Patriot Games**, 1992; Peacefire, 2009; **The Plough and the Stars**, 1936; A Prayer for the Dying, 1987; **The Quiet Man**, 1952; **The Rising of the Moon**, 1957; Riot, 1996; **Ronin**, 1998; **Ryan's Daughter**, 1970; The Secret Invasion, 1964; **Shadow Dancer**, 2012; **Shake Hands with the Devil**, 1959; Shergar, 1999; **Some Mother's Son**, 1996; **Sword in the Desert**, 1949; Ticker, 2001; Titanic Town, 1999; **Veronica Guerin**, 2003; **When the Sky Falls**, 2000; **The Wind That Shakes the Barley**, 2007; The Year London Blew Up: 1974, 2005 (made-for-TV); **Young Cassidy**, 1965.

Indians (Native Canadians; Abenaki): **The Last of the Mohicans**, 1992; **Northwest Passage**, 1940; Severed Ways: The Norse Discovery of America, 2007.

Indians (Native Canadians; Cree): Bordertown, 1989 (TV series; "Over the Line," 1989 espisode); Brave Eagle, 1955-1956 (TV series; "Voice of the Serpent," 1955 episode); The Campbells, 1986-1990 (TV series; "Duty Bound" episode); The Canadians, 1961; **Davy Crockett: King of the Wild Frontier**, 1955; The Edge, 1997; **Northwest Mounted Police**, 1940; **Pony Soldier**, 1952; **Saskatchewan**, 1954.

Indians (U.S. Native Americans; Apache): Ambush, 1950; Amongst Vultures, 1966; The Animals, 1971; **Apache**, 1954; Apache Ambush, 1955; Apache Blood, 1975; Apache Chief, 1949; Apache Country, 1952; Apache Drums, 1951; Apache Fury, 1964; Apache Gold, 1965; The Apache Kid, 1941; The Apache Kid's Escape, 1930; Apache Rifles, 1964; Apache Territory, 1958; Apache Trail, 1942; Apache Uprising, 1965; Apache War Smoke, 1952; Apache Warrior, 1957; Apache Woman, 1955; Apachen, 1973; **Appaloosa**, 2008; **Arizona**; 1940; **Arrowhead**, 1953; The Battle at Apache Pass, 1952; Billy Two Hats, 1974; **Broken Arrow**, 1950; Buddy Goes West, 1981; Bullet for a Badman, 1964; Catlow, 1971; Chato's Land, 1972; Conagher, 1991 (made-for-TV); Cry Blood, Apache, 1970; Day of the Evil Gun, 1968; Dead Man's Walk, 1996 (TV miniseries); The Desert of the Lost, 1927; A Distant Trumpet, 1964; Doomed Fort, 1964; Dragoon Wells Massacre, 1957; El Condor, 1970; **Fort Apache**, 1948; Fort Bowie, 1958; Fort Massacre, 1958; 40 Guns to Apache Pass, 1967; **Fury at Furnace Creek**, 1948; **Garden of Evil**, 1954; **Geronimo**, 1939; Geronimo, 1962; Geronimo, 1993 (made-for-TV); **Geronimo: An American Legend**, 1993; Guns of a Stranger, 1973; Hell Hounds of the Plains, 1927; His Name Was Madron, 1970; **Hombre**, 1967; **Hondo**, 1953; I Killed Geronimo, 1950; Indian Uprising, 1952; Johnny Oro, 1966; Land Raiders, 1970; **The Last Wagon**, 1956; Lawless Plainsmen, 1942; Lone Star, 1952; Lust for Gold, 1949; Mackenna's Gold, 1969; Madron, 1970; **Major Dundee**, 1965; **The Man from Laramie**, 1955; Manitou's Shoe, 2002; Massacre Canyon, 1954; The Missing, 2003; Mr. Horn, 1979 (made-for-TV); Old Overland Trail, 1953; Old Shatterhand, 1968; One Eighth Apache, 1922; **Only the Valiant**, 1951; **Red River**, 1948; **The Ride Back**, 1957; **Ride Lonesome**, 1959; Riders of Vengeance, 1919; Rio Conchos, 1964; **Rio Grande**, 1950; Rough Riders, 1997 (made-for-TV); Savage Sam, 1963; **Sergeant Rutledge**, 1960; **Seven Men from Now**, 1956; Seven Vengeful Women, 1967; Shotgun, 1955; Soul Soldier, 1970; Southwest Passage, 1954; **Stagecoach**, 1939; **The Stalking Moon**, 1968; The Stand at Apache River, 1953; Taza, Son of Cochise, 1954; **3:10 to Yuma**, 2007; A Thunder of Drums, 1961; Tomahawk Trail, 1957; Tonio: Son of the Sierras, 1935; **Trooper Hook**, 1957; **Ulzana's Raid**, 1972; Ulzana, 1974; Una donna chiamata Apache, 1976; Winnetou, 1965; Winnetou: The Red Gentleman, 1966; **The Wonderful Country**, 1959; **Yellow Sky**, 1948.

Indians (U.S. Native Americans; Arikara): **Indian Paint**, 1965; **Revenant**, 2015.

Indians (U.S. Native Americans; Blackfoot): **Across the Wide Missouri**, 1951; Adventures from the Book of Virtues, 1996-2000 (TV series; "Perserverance," 1997 episode); **The Big Sky**, 1952; Fangs of the Arctic, 1953; The Hi-Line, 2000; Miracle in the Wilderness, 1992 (made-for-TV).

Indians (U.S. Native Americans; Cherokee): **Apache**, 1954; The Cherokee Strip, 1937; Cherokee Strip, 1940; Cherokee Uprising, 1950; Daniel Boone, 1964-1970 (TV series; "The Devil's Four," 1964 episode); Daniel Boone: Frontier Trail Rider, 1966; Destry, 1964 (TV series; "Big Deal at Little River," 1964 episode); In Old Oklahoma, 1943; Mandie and the Secret Tunnel, 2009; Net Playhouse, 1964-1972 (TV series; "Trail of Tears," 1971 episode); **The Outlaw Josey Wales**, 1976; **Red River**, 1948; Riverboat, 1959-1961 (TV series; "The Long Trail," 1960 episode); **The Undefeated**, 1969.

Indians (U.S. Native Americans; Cheyenne): Battling with Buffalo Bill, 1931; Before the White Man Came, 1920; **The Big Sky**, 1952; Brave Eagle, 1955-1956 (TV series); **Buffalo Bill**, 1944; Cavalry Scout, 1951; Cheyenne, 1947; **Cheyenne Autumn**, 1964 (Southern Cheyenne); The Cheyenne Cyclone, 1932; The Cheyenne Kid, 1930; The Cheyenne Kid, 1933; The Cheyenne Kid, 1940; Cheyenne Rides Again, 1937; Cheyenne Roundup, 1943; Cheyenne Takes Over, 1947; Cheyenne Tornado, 1935; Cheyenne Trails, 1928; Cheyenne Wildcat, 1944; Custer of

the West, 1967; Goodnight for Justice, 2011 (made-for-TV); Grayeagle, 1977; Hell on Wheels, 2011- (TV series); **The Plainsman**, 1936; Prudence and the Chief, 1970 (made-for-TV); **She Wore a Yellow Ribbon**, 1949 (Southern Cheyenne); Stagecoach West, 1960-1961 (TV series; "The Bold Whip," 1961 episode); Tales of Wells Fargo, 1957-1962 (TV series; "Renegade Raiders," 1957 episode); Treachery Rides the Range, 1936; Wagons West, 1952; **White Feather**, 1955; **Windwalker**, 1980.

Indians (U.S. Native Americans; Comanche): Comanche, 1956; Comanche, 2000; Comanche Moon, 2008 (TV miniseries); **Comanche Station**, 1960; The Comancheros, 1961; Dead Man's Walk, 1996 (TV miniseries); Fort Dobbs, 1958; The Heart of Wetona, 1919; Incident at Phantom Hill, 1966; Last of the Comanches, 1953; **The Lone Ranger**, 2013; Lone Star, 1952; Mackenzie's Raiders, 1958-1959 (TV series; "Thunder Stick," 1959 episode); McLintock!, 1963; **The Outlaw Josey Wales**, 1976; Streets of Laredo, 1995 (TV miniseries); **Red River**, 1948; The Sabre and the Arrow, 1953; **The Searchers**, 1956; The Tall Texan, 1953; Two Rode Together, 1961; White Comanche, 1968.

Indians (U.S. Native Americans; Creek): **Davy Crockett: King of the Wild Frontier**, 1955; Sunshine State, 2002.

Indians (U.S. Native Americans; Crow): Before the White Man Came, 1920; **The Big Sky**, 1952; Bury My Heart at Wounded Knee, 2007 (made-for-TV); Dreamkeeper, 2003 (made-for-TV); **Jeremiah Johnson**, 1972; John Ermine of Yellowstone, 1917; Jonah Hex, 2010; The Savage, 1952; Shanghai Noon, 2000; Triumphs of a Man Called Horse, 1983; **The White Buffalo**, 1977; **Windwalker**, 1980.

Indians (U.S. Native Americans; Huron): The Deerslayer, 1943; **Drums along the Mohawk**, 1939; Hawkeye, 1994 (TV series); Hawkeye and the Last of the Mohicans, 1957 (TV series); **The Last of the Mohicans**, 1920; **The Last of the Mohicans**, 1936; **The Last of the Mohicans**, 1992.

Indians (U.S. Native Americans; Kiowa): Belle Starr's Daughter, 1948; Dreamkeeper, 2003 (made-for-TV); **Flaming Star**, 1960; **Nevada Smith**, 1966; Prairie Thunder, 1937; The Rebel, 1959-1961 (TV series; "Yellow Hair," 1959 episode); **The Scalphunters**, 1968; Silent Tongue, 1993; Soldier Blue, 1970; They Rode West, 1954; **The Unforgiven**, 1960; War Arrow, 1953; **The War Wagon**, 1967; The Young Riders, 1989-1992 (TV series).

Indians (U.S. Native Americans; Modoc): **Drum Beat**, 1954.

Indians (U.S. Native Americans; Mohawk): Dreamkeeper, 2003 (made-for-TV); **Drums along the Mohawk**, 1939; **Frozen River**, 2008; The Great Adventures of Captain Kidd, 1953 (serial); Grey Owl, 1999; The Indian in the Cupboard, 1995; **The Last of the Mohicans**, 1920; **The Last of the Mohicans**, 1936; **The Last of the Mohicans**, 1992; **Northwest Passage**, 1940; Salem, 2014 (TV series; "The House of Pain," 2014 episode).

Indians (U.S. Native Americans; Mohican): **The Last of the Mohicans**, 1920; **The Last of the Mohicans**, 1936; **The Last of the Mohicans**, 1992; Northwest Passage, 1958-1959 (TV series; "Vengeance Trail," 1958 episode).

Indians (U.S. Native Americans; Navajo): Along the Navajo Trail, 1945; Ambush at Tomahawk Gap, 1953; **Battle Cry**, 1955; **The Big Carnival**, 1951; Black Arrow, 1944; Bodies, Rest & Motion, 1993; The Hi-Lo Country, 1998; King of the Wild Horses, 1933; **Midnight Run**, 1988; The Navajo Trail, 1945; Navajo Trail Raiders, 1949; **The Senator Was Indiscreet**, 1947; Slaughter Trail, 1951; Tonio, Son of the Sierras, 1925; **Wagon Master**, 1950; **Windtalkers**, 2002.

Indians (U.S. Native Americans; Nez Perce): **Across the Wide Missouri**, 1951; Death Valley Days, 1952-1970 (TV series; "The Thirty-Caliber Town," 1968 episode); I Will Fight No More Forever, 1975 (made-for-TV).

Indians (U.S. Native Americans; Nipissing First Nation): **Drums along the Mohawk**, 1939.

Indians (U.S. Native Americans; Oneida): **Drums along the Mohawk**, 1939.

Indians (U.S. Native Americans; Pawnee): Centennial, 1978 (TV miniseries); **Dances with Wolves**, 1990; Death Valley Days, 1952-1970 (TV series; "Bread on the Desert," 1968 episode); Dreamkeeper, 2003 (made-for-TV); **The Iron Horse**, 1924; **Little Big Man**, 1970; Pawnee, 1957; The Pride of Pawnee, 1929; The Travels of Jaimie McPheeters, 1963-1964 (TV series; "The Day of the Pawnees," two 1963 episodes); Wagon Tracks West, 1943; **Western Union**, 1941; **Westward Ho the Wagons**, 1956.

Indians (U.S. Native Americans; Pima): The American, 1960 (made-for-TV); **Flags of Our Fathers**, 2006; **The Outsider**, 1961; **Sands of Iwo Jima**, 1949.

Indians (U.S. Native Americans; Seminole): Adaptation, 2002; All About the Benjamins, 2002; Band of the Hand, 1986; Blackwater, 2007; **Distant Drums**, 1951; Drums of Destiny, 1937; Four Sheets to the Wind, 2007; Gloria's Romance, 1916; **Key Largo**, 1948; Lone Star, 1996; Naked in the Sun, 1957; Ramshackle House, 1924; **Seminole**, 1953; Seminole Uprising, 1955; Shark River, 1953; Stanley, 1972; The Substitute, 1996; Sunshine State, 2002; War Arrow, 1953; **Wind across the Everglades**, 1958.

Indians (U.S. Native Americans; Seneca): **Drums along the Mohawk**, 1939.

Indians (U.S. Native Americans; Shawnee): Brave Warrior, 1952; Davy Crockett on the Mississippi, 1976 (made-for-TV); Many Rivers to Cross, 1955; Siege at Red River, 1954.

Indians (U.S. Native Americans; Shoshone): **Bend of the River**, 1952; Death Valley Days, 1952-1970 (TV series; "The Girl Who Walked the West," 1967 episode); **The Far Horizons**, 1955; **Kit Carson**, 1940; Overland Trail, 1960 (TV series; "West of Boston," 1960 episode); **Rachel and the Stranger**, 1948; State Trooper, 1956-1959 (TV series; "The Sound of Death," 1957 episode).

Indians (U.S. Native Americans; Sioux): **Annie Get Your Gun**, 1950; **Annie Oakley**, 1935; **The Big Sky**, 1952; The Black Dakotas, 1954; **Blazing Saddles**, 1974; Buffalo Bill, 1965; Buffalo Bill and the Indians, or Sitting Bull's History Lesson, 1976; Bugles in the Afternoon, 1952; Bury My Heart at Wounded Knee, 2007 (made-for-TV); **Calamity Jane**, 1953; The Canadians, 1961; Cavalry Scout, 1951; Chief Crazy Horse, 1955; Crazy Horse, 1996 (made-for-TV); Crossfire Trail, 2001 (made-for-TV); Custer of Big Horn, 1926; Custer of the West, 1968; Custer's Last Stand, 1936 (serial); **Dances with Wolves**, 1990; A Daughter of the Sioux, 1925; Don't Touch the White Woman!, 1974; Dreamkeeper, 2003 (made-for-TV); The Flaming Frontier, 1926; The Glory Guys, 1965; The Great Sioux Massacre, 1965; The Great Sioux Uprising, 1953; Gun Fever, 1958; The Gun That Won the West, 1955; Gunman's Walk, 1958; **Hidalgo**, 2004; **The Indian Fighter**, 1955; Jack McCall, Desperado, 1953; Lakota Moon, 1992 (made-for-TV); The Last Frontier, 1926; The Legend of Walks Far Woman, 1982 (made-for-TV); Little Big Horn, 1951; **Little Big Man**, 1970; **A Man Called Horse**, 1970; The Michigan Kid, 1947; The Nebraskan, 1953; Oh! Susanna,

1951; O'Rourke of the Royal Mounted, 1954; **The Plainsman**, 1936; The Plainsman, 1966 (Leslie Nielsen); The Prairie, 1947; The Quick and the Dead, 1987 (made-for-TV); Red Tomahawk, 1967; The Return of a Man Called Horse, 1976; Revolt at Fort Laramie, 1957; Rez Bomb, 2008; Rock Island Trail, 1950; **Run of the Arrow**, 1957; **Saskatchewan**, 1954; The Savage, 1952; Seven Hours of Gunfire, 1965; Shanghai Noon, 2000; Sitting Bull, 1954; Skins, 2002; Soldier Blue, 1970; Son of the Morning Star, 1991 (made-for-TV); Stolen Women, Captured Hearts, 1997 (made-for-TV); **They Died with Their Boots On**, 1941; **Thunderheart**, 1992; Tonka, 1958; Triumphs of a Man Called Horse, 1983; The Valley of Death, 1968; Warpath, 1951; **The Way West**, 1967; **West of Thunder**, 2012; **Western Union**, 1941; **The White Buffalo**, 1977; The World Changes, 1933; Wyoming, 1940; Yellowstone Kelly, 1959.

Israeli Defense Forces (IDF): **Beaufort**, 2007.

Japanese Imperial Navy (WWII): **Admiral Yamamoto**, 1968; **Air Force**, 1943; Battle of the Coral Sea, 1959; **Destination Tokyo**, 1943; **The Gallant Hours**, 1960; **In Harm's Way**, 1965; **Midway**, 1976; **1941**, 1979; **Operation Pacific**, 1951; **Pearl Harbor**, 2001; **The Purple Heart**, 1944; **Run Silent, Run Deep**, 1958; **Stand by for Action**, 1942; **Submarine Command**, 1951; **The Sullivans** (aka: The Fighting Sullivans), 1944; **Task Force**, 1949; **They Were Expendable**, 1945; **Tora! Tora! Tora!**, 1970; **Torpedo Alley**, 1953; **Torpedo Run**, 1958; **Up Periscope**, 1959; **Wing and a Prayer**, 1944.

Kempeitai (secret police of the Imperial Japanese Army, 1881-1945, which also operated as an intelligence agency and was not dissimilar to that of the Gestapo, the German secret police during the Nazi regime of 1933-1945): **Across the Pacific**, 1942; **An American Guerrilla in the Philippines**, 1950; **Back to Bataan**, 1945; Behind the Rising Sun, 1943; Betrayal from the East, 1945; Bijo gomon, 1967; Black Dragons, 1942; **Blood on the Sun**, 1945; Bombay Clipper, 1942; Escape from Hong Kong, 1942; **First Yank into Tokyo**, 1945; **The Great Raid**, 2005; The Highest Honor, 1982; I Was an American Spy, 1951; **The Last Emperor**, 1987; **Letters from Iwo Jima**, 2006; **Manila Calling**, 1942; Prisoner of Japan, 1942; **The Purple Heart**, 1944; Remember Pearl Harbor, 1942; **Secret Agent of Japan**, 1942; **Unbroken**, 2014; Unseen Enemy, 1942; **We've Never Been Licked**, 1943.

KGB (Soviet military intelligence in Russia, 1954-1991): Agent 8¾ (aka: Hot Enough for June), 1965; The Alamut Ambush, 1988 (made-for-TV); Aldrich Ames: Traitor Within, 1998 (made-for-TV); The Americans, 2013- (TV series); Anthony Zimmer, 2005; Arctic Flight, 1952; The Assassination of Trotsky, 1972; The Assignment, 1997; Assignment: Paris, 1952; The Atticus Institute, 2015; Avalanche Express, 1979; Bang! Bang! You're Dead! (aka: Our Man in Marrakesh), 1966; The Beast of Yucca Flats, 1961; Best Defense, 1984; Billion Dollar Brain, 1967; Black Eagle, 1988; Born American, 1986; **Breach**, 2007; Bullet to Beijing, 1997 (made-for-TV); The Browning Version, 1994; Calendar, 1993; Callan, 1974; Cambridge Spies, 2003 (TV miniseries); Caravan to Vaccares, 1974; Carry On Spying, 1965; The Case of the Red Monkey (aka: Little Red Monkey), 1955; Casino Royale, 1967; Charlie Muffin, 1983 (made-for-TV); Che!, 1969; Cobra Force, 1988; Codename Kyril, 1988 (TV miniseries); Cold Front, 1989; Cold War Killers, 1986 (made-for-TV); Company Business, 1991; Comrades in Arms, 1991; Condorman, 1981; The Confession, 1990; **Confessions of a Dangerous Mind**, 2002; Cop Game, 1988; Counterspy Meets Scotland Yard, 1950; Covert Action, 1987 (made-for-TV); A Dandy in Aspic, 1968; Dead Aim, 1987; **The Deadly Affair**, 1967; A Deadly Game, 1979 (made-for-TV); Defense of the Realm, 1986; The Devil's Agent, 1962; **Die Another Day**, 2002; A Different Loyalty, 2004; **Diplomatic Courier**, 1952; **Dr. Strangelove**, 1964; The Double, 2011; The Double Man, 1968; Eastern Promises, 2007; Elling, 2002; Enigma, 1982; Escape from Terror, 1955;

Escape to Nowhere, 1973; Esenin, 2005 (TV miniseries); Est—Ouest, 2000; The Executioner, 1970; The Executioner (aka: Permission to Kill), 1975; The Experts, 1989; The Falcon and the Snowman, 1985; Family of Spies, 1990 (made-for-TV; the Walker family); Farewell, 2009; Fatal Secret, 1988; **Firefox**, 1982; **For Your Eyes Only**, 1981; Foreign Exchange, 1970 (made-for-TV); Foreign Intrigue, 1956; The Fourth Protocol, 1987; Foxbat, 1977; **From Russia with Love**, 1964; **Funeral in Berlin**, 1966; The Girl from Petrovka, 1974; The Good Shepherd, 2006; **Gorky Park**, 1983; Hamilton, 2001 (TV miniseries); Hell and High Water, 1954; High Treason, 1952; Highly Dangerous, 1951; The Human Factor, 1979; Ice Station Zebra, 1968; **Indiana Jones and the Kingdom of the Crystal Skull**, 2008; Innocent Bystanders, 1973; The Intelligence Men, 1965; Intrigue, 1988 (made-for-TV); The Jackal, 1997; Jet Attack, 1958; The Jigsaw Man, 1984 (Kim Philby); Johnny English, 2003; Johnny English Reborn (aka: Johnny English Returns), 2011; The Journey, 1959; Jumpin' Jack Flash, 1986; Karol: The Pope, the Man, 2006 (made-for-TV); Keep Your Fingers Crossed (aka: Catch Me a Spy), 1971; Keeping Track, 1986; KGB: The Secret War, 1985; **Kingsman: The Secret Service**, 2014; **The Kremlin Letter**, 1970; Ladybear, 1985 (made-for-TV); Laser Mission, 1989; Law of Corruption, 2005; Legacy, 2013 (made-for-TV); License to Kill, 1989; The Living Daylights, 1987; A Lonely Place for Dying, 2009; The Looking Glass War, 1970; Luna Park, 1992; **The Man Between**, 1953; The Man from U.N.C.L.E., 2015; Man on a String, 1960; **The Man Who Knew Too Much**, 1956; **The Manchurian Candidate**, 1962; The Manchurian Candidate, 2004; **Marathon Man**, 1976; Master Spy, 1964; Midnight in Saint Petersburg, 1996; Mirror Wars: Reflection One, 2005; **Moscow on the Hudson**, 1984; Munich, 2006; My Family Treasure, 1993; The Naked Runner, 1967; Near Mrs., 1992; Night Train to Paris, 1964; **No Way Out**, 1987; **North by Northwest**, 1959; Octopussy, 1983; Oh! Those Most Secret Agents, 1984; The Operative, 2000; Otley, 1969; Pope John Paul II, 2005; The Printing, 1990; Red Serpent, 2003; Ring of Treason (aka: Ring of Spies), 1964 (Portland Spy Ring); The Russia House, 1990; Russian Roulette, 1975; **Salt**, 2010; Scavengers, 1987; Scorpion, 1986; The Second Front, 2005; Security Risk, 1954; The Sell-Out, 1977; The Sentinel, 2006; Shoot First (aka: Rough Shoot), 1953; The Soldier, 1982; Some Girls Do, 1971; Spies Like Us, 1985; Spy Hard, 1986; The Spy Killer, 1969 (made-for-TV); Spy Story, 1976; **The Spy Who Came in from the Cold**, 1965; **The Spy Who Loved Me**, 1977; **Telefon**, 1977; **The Terminal**, 2004; Terminal Velocity, 1994; They Can't Hang Me, 1955; Tinker Tailor Soldier Spy, 1979 (TV miniseries); **Tinker Tailor Soldier Spy**, 2011; **Topaz**, 1969; **Torn Curtain**, 1966; The Trident Force, 1989; The Trouble with Spies, 1987; 23, 1998; Twist again in Moscow, 1986; Under Cover, 1991 (made-for-TV); A View to a Kill, 1985; The Violent Breed, 1984; **Walk East on Beacon!**, 1952; Where the Bullets Fly, 1967; Where the Spies Are, 1966; White Nights, 1985; Who?, 1975; Yuri Nosenko: Double Agent, 1986 (made-for-TV).

Ku Klux Klan (AKA: KKK; U.S. secret racist society since 1866; also see Lynch Mobs): **Alamo Bay**, 1985; Ambushed, 1998; Another Part of the Forest, 1948; Any Day Now, 1998-2002 (TV series); Attack on Terror: The FBI vs. the Ku Klux Klan, 1975 (made-for-TV); Bad Boys II, 2003; Betrayed, 1988; Big City, 2007; Big Stakes, 1922; **The Birth of a Nation**, 1915; The Black Klansman, 1966; **Blazing Saddles**, 1974; Boardwalk Empire, 2010- (TV series); Brotherhood of Death, 1976; The Burning Cross, 1947; Bustin' Loose, 1981; The Cabin in the Woods, 2012; **The Cardinal**, 1963; Carnage, 2011; The Chamber, 1996; Cellmates, 2011; Chiefs, 1983 (TV miniseries); **Compulsion**, 1959; Cross of Fire, 1989 (made-for-TV); Deacons for Defense, 2003 (made-for-TV); Django, 1966; Django Unchained, 2012; The Devils, 1971; A Father for Charlie, 1995 (made-for-TV); **The FBI Story**, 1959; Fletch Lives, 1989; **Fried Green Tomatoes**, 1991; Gamers, 2006; **Gone with the Wind**, 1939; Goodbye, Miss 4th of July, 1988 (made-for-TV); The Haunting in Connecticut 2: Ghosts of Georgia, 2013; Heaven & Hell:

North and South: Book III, 1994 (TV miniseries); Hoover, 2000; Hunter's Blood, 1986; I Crossed the Color Line, 1966; **The Intruder**, 1962; Jasper, Texas, 2003 (made-for-TV); Klansman, 1974; **Lady Sings the Blues**, 1972; Legion of Terror, 1936; **The Long Walk Home**, 1990; **Malcolm X**, 1992; The Mating Call, 1928; **Mississippi Burning**, 1988; Nation Aflame, 1937; Native Land, 1942; **O Brother, Where Art Thou?** 2000; Posse, 1993; **Places in the Heart**, 1984; Porky's II: The Next Day, 1983; Queen, 1993 (TV miniseries); The Right to Remain Silent, 1996 (made-for-TV); Roots: The Next Generation, 1979 (TV miniseries); **Rosewood**, 1997; Scary Movie III, 2003; Separate But Equal, 1991 (made-for-TV); Shaft, 2000; **Shock Corridor**, 1963; Sins of the Fathers, 2002 (made-for-TV); **Smile**, 1975; **Sommersby**, 1993; Sophie and the Moonhanger, 1996 (made-for-TV); **Stars in My Crown**, 1950; **Storm Warning**, 1951; The Symbol of the Unconquered, 1920; Tales from the Hood, 1995; Thurgood, 2011 (made-for-TV); ...tick... tick...tick, 1970; A Time to Kill, 1996; The Toy, 1982; Treasure of Matecombe, 1976; The Turning, 1992; Twilight of the Dogs, 1995; **Twilight Zone: The Movie**, 1983; Warm Springs, 2005 (made-for-TV); Who Killed Atlanta's Children?, 2000 (made-for-TV); The X-Files, 1993-2002 (TV series; "Milagro," 1999 episode).

Leavenworth Penitentiary (U.S. penitentiary, established in 1903 at Leavenworth, Kansas): Alcatraz Island, 1937; **Birdman of Alcatraz**, 1962; Capote, 2005; Killer: A Journal of Murder, 1995; **The St. Valentine's Day Massacre**, 1967.

Luftwaffe (German air force in WWII): **Amen**, 2002; Angels One Five, 1954; **Battle of Britain**, 1969; Battle Squadron Lutzow, 1941; Before the Fall, 2005; **Command Decision**, 1948; **Commandos Strike at Dawn**, 1942; The Crew of the Dora, 1943; Dark Blue World, 2001; **Desperate Journey**, 1942; The Devil's General, 1957; **Eagle Squadron**, 1942; **Fighter Squadron**, 1948; **The Great Escape**, 1962; **The Hindenburg**, 1975; Hogan's Heroes, 1965-1971 (TV series); **Into the White**, 2012; **The Longest Day**, 1962; Luftwaffenhelfer, 1980; **The McKenzie Break**, 1970; Mrs. Henderson Presents, 2005; **One of Our Aircraft Is Missing**, 1942; **The One That Got Away**, 1958; **Pearl Harbor**, 2001; Secret Flight, 1946; **Spitfire**, 1943; Stukas, 1941; **Twelve O'Clock High**, 1949; **Valkyrie**, 2008; The Winds of War, 1983- (TV miniseries); **A Yank in the R.A.F.**, 1941.

Massachusetts Institute of Technology (aka: M.I.T.; Cambridge, Massachusetts; established in 1861): **A Beautiful Mind**, 2001.

MGB/MVD (Soviet counterintelligence and intelligence agencies, 1946-1953): **Conspirator**, 1949; The Hunter, 1952 (TV series); **I Was a Communist for the F.B.I.**, 1951; The Innocent, 1995 (Berlin Tunnel); **The Iron Curtain**, 1948 (Igor Gouzenko); **Man on a Tightrope**, 1953; **My Son John**, 1952; Operation Manhunt, 1954 (Igor Gouzenko); Operation "The Bus," 1978; **Pickup on South Street**, 1952; **The Thief**, 1952; **Walk a Crooked Mile**, 1948; **Walk East on Beacon!**, 1952; **The Woman on Pier 13**, 1949.

MI5 (aka: Military Intelligence Service, Section Five, The Security Service; British domestic counter-intelligence agency, est. 1909): Between the Lines, 1992-1994 (TV series); Billion Dollar Brain, 1967; Bullet to Beijing, 1997 (made-for-TV); Cambridge Spies, 2003 (TV miniseries); Camp X, 2014 (made-for-TV); Clouds over Europe (aka: Foreign Sabotage; Q Planes), 1939; The Company, 2007 (TV miniseries); **Conspirator**, 1949; **The Deadly Affair**, 1967; Dick Barton at Bay, 1950; Dick Barton Strikes Back, 1949; An Englishman Abroad, 1984 (made-for-TV); Escape, 1980 (TV series); Escape to Nowhere, 1973; The Executioner, 1970; The Fourth Protocol, 1987; **Funeral in Berlin**, 1966; Goodnight Sweetheart, 1993-1999 (TV series; "Between the Devil and the Deep Blue Sea," 1995 episode); The Intelligence Men, 1965; **The Ipcress File**, 1965; Kim Philby war der dritte Mann, 1969 (made-for-TV); **Licence to Kill**, 1989; Master Spy, 1964; MI-5 (aka: Spooks), 2002-2011 (TV series); MI-5 (aka: Spooks: The Greater Good), 2015; Mortdecai, 2015; Page Eight, 2011; Philby, Burgess and Maclean, 1977 (made-for-TV); Ring of Treason (aka: Ring of Spies), 1964 (Portland Spy Ring); Salting the Battlefield, 2014 (made-for-TV); Screen Two, 1985-2002 (TV series; "Blunt," 1987 episode); **Shadow Dancer**, 2012; Shoot First (aka: Rough Shoot), 1953; Spooks, 2002-2011 (TV series); Spy, 2011- (TV series); **The Spy Who Came in from the Cold**, 1965; Tinker Tailor Soldier Spy, 1979 (TV miniseries); **Tinker Tailor Soldier Spy**, 2011; Turks and Caicos, 2014 (made-for-TV); The Writing on the Wall, 1996 (made-for-TV).

MI6 (aka: Military Intelligence Service, Section Six, SIS/Secret Intelligence Service; British intelligence agency, est. 1909): Agent 8¾ (aka: Hot Enough for June), 1965; Alex Rider: Operation Stormbreaker, 2006; Assignment K, 1968; The Black Windmill, 1974; Blue Ice, 1992; Callan, 1974; **Casino Royale**, 1967; **Casino Royale**, 2006; Charlie Muffin, 1983 (made-for-TV); A Dandy in Aspic, 1968; Danger Route, 1968; Death Has a Bad Reputation, 1990; Death Train, 1993 (made-for-TV); **Diamonds Are Forever**, 1971; Dick Barton, Special Agent, 1948; The Diplomat, 2009 (made-for-TV); **Dr. No**, 1962; Doomsday Gun, 1994 (made-for-TV); Echelon 8, 2009; **For Your Eyes Only**, 1981; Foreign Exchange, 1970 (made-for-TV); **From Russia with Love**, 1963; **GoldenEye**, 1995; **Goldfinger**, 1964; Hammerhead, 1968; Highly Dangerous, 1951; The Human Factor, 1979; The Innocent, 1995 (Berlin Tunnel); Innocent Bystanders, 1973; The Internecine Project, 1974; The Jigsaw Man, 1984 (Kim Philby); Johnny English, 2003; Johnny English Reborn (aka: Johnny English Returns), 2011; Keep Your Fingers Crossed (aka: Catch Me a Spy), 1971; Lara Croft Tomb Raider: The Cradle of Life, 2003; Lektor, 2011- (TV series); The Liquidator, 1966; **Licence to Kill**, 1989; Live and Let Die, 1973; The Living Daylights, 1987; The Looking Glass War, 1970; The Mackintosh Man, 1973; **The Man Between**, 1953; The Man with the Golden Gun, 1974; Midnight in Saint Petersburg, 1996; Mr. Nice, 2010; **Moonraker**, 1979; The Naked Runner, 1967; Never Say Never Again, 1963; No. 1 of the Secret Service, 1970; Octopussy, 1963; **On Her Majesty's Secret Service**, 1969; **Our Man in Havana**, 1959; Quantum of Solace, 2008; Red 2, 2013; The Russia House, 1990; Safe House, 2012; The 2nd Best Secret Agent in the Whole Wide World (aka: Licensed to Kill), 1965; **Skyfall**, 2012; **Spectre**, 2015; The Spy Killer, 1969 (made-for-TV); Spy Story, 1976; **The Spy Who Came in from the Cold**, 1965; **The Spy Who Loved Me**, 1977; Strike Back, 2010- (TV series); Subterfuge, 1969; Survivor, 2015; Third Falcon, 2013; **The Third Man**, 1950; **Thunderball**, 1965; Tomorrow Never Dies, 1997; A View to a Kill, 1965; **Where Eagles Dare**, 1969; **The Whistle Blower**, 1987; **The World Is Not Enough**, 1999; **You Only Live Twice**, 1967.

Mossad (intelligence and counterintelligence for Israel, est. 1949): **Charlie Wilson's War**, 2007; The Cold Light of Day, 2012; The Debt, 2010; Doomsday Gun, 1994 (made-for-TV); Escaping Tel Aviv, 2009; **Exodus**, 1960; Fair Game, 2010; **The Juggler**, 1953; Les Patriotes, 1994; Loose Cannons, 1990; **The Man in the Glass Booth**, 1975 (role model for Adolf Eichmann); The Man Who Captured Eichmann, 1986 (made-for-TV); **A Mighty Heart**, 2007; Mossad (aka: Minotaur), 1997; Munich, 2005 (1972 Munich Olympic Massacre); Operation Eichmann, 1961; OSS 117: Lost in Rio, 2009; Paradise Now, 2005; **The People vs. Fritz Bauer**, 2015; The Point Men, 2001; The Sell-Out, 1977; The Soldier, 1982; Steal the Sky, 1988 (made-for-TV); **Sword in the Desert**, 1949; Sword of Gideon, 1986 (made-for-TV; 1972 Munich Olympic Massacre); 21 Hours at Munich, 1976 (made-for-TV; 1972 Munich Olympic Massacre); Walk on Water, 2005; **World War Z**, 2013; You Don't Mess with the Zohan, 2008; **Zero Dark Thirty**, 2012.

Mounties (Northwest Mounted Police, est. 1873; Royal Canadian Mounted Police/RCMP, est. 1920): **Ace High**, 1918; Agent of Influence,

2002 (made-for-TV); Airport In, 1996; April One, 1994; Border Saddlemates, 1952; Burning Words, 1923; Cameron of the Royal Mounted, 1921; Canadian Mounties vs. Atomic Invaders, 1953; The Canadians, 1961; Clancy of the Mounted, 1933 (serial); Code of the Mounted, 1935; The Code of the Scarlet, 1928; Cold Front, 1989; Courage of the North, 1935; Covert Action, 1987 (made-for-TV); Crashing Through, 1939; Danger Ahead, 1940; Dangerous Nan McGrew, 1930; Dangers of the Canadian Mounted, 1948; Daredevils of the Clouds, 1948; The Dawson Patrol, 1978 (made-for-TV); Death Goes North, 1939; Death Hunt, 1981; Due South, 1994-1999 (TV series); Fangs of the Arctic, 1953; Fighting Mad, 1939; The Fighting Trooper, 1934; God's Country and the Man, 1937; His Fighting Blood, 1935; In the Line of Duty, 1931; **The Iron Curtain**, 1948; Jaws of Justice, 1933; Keeping Track, 1986; King of the Mounties, 1942; King of the Royal Mounted, 1940; The Man from Montreal, 1939; The Man with Nine Lives, 1940; Menace, 2008 (made-for-TV); **The Missouri Breaks**, 1976; Mrs. Mike, 1949; Murder on the Yukon, 1940; The Mysterious Pilot, 1937 (serial); North of the Rockies, 1942; Northern Frontier, 1935; **Northern Pursuit**, 1943; **Northwest Mounted Police**, 1940; Northwest Trail, 1945; On the Great White Trail, 1938; Operation Manhunt, 1954 (Igor Gouzenko); Outpost of the Mounties, 1939; Perils of the Royal Mounted, 1942; Perils of the Wilderness, 1956; Phantom Patrol, 1936; **Pony Soldier**, 1952; R.C.M.P., 1959-1960 (TV series); Renfrew of the Royal Mounted, 1937; Riders of the North, 1931; **Rose Marie**, 1936; **Rose Marie**, 1954; The Royal Mounted Patrol, 1941; The Royal Mounted Rides Again, 1945; Russian Roulette, 1975; **Saskatchewan**, 1954; Secret Patrol, 1936; Sky Bandits, 1940; The Silent Code, 1935; Sky Bandits, 1940; South of Northern Lights, 1922; Steele of the Royal Mounted, 1925; Susannah of the Mounties, 1939; Tangled Trails, 1921; Timber Terrors, 1935; The Trail Beyond, 1934; Trail of the Mounties, 1947; Trail of the Yukon, 1949; Trails of the Wild, 1935; Trial by Fire, 2000 (made-for-TV); Trooper O'Neill, 1922; Undercover Men, 1934; **The Untouchables**, 1987; What Price Vengeance, 1937; Where the North Holds Sway, 1927; **The Wild North**, 1952; Wildcat Trooper, 1936; Yukon Fight, 1940; Yukon Gold, 1952; Yukon Manhunt, 1951.

NASA (U.S. National Aeronautics and Space Administration): A.D.A.M.: The Beginning, 2013; Alien Planet, 2005 (made-for-TV); Alien Predator, 1985; Alternative 3, 1977 (made-for-TV); Another Earth, 2011; Apollo 18, 2011; Apollo 11, 1996 (made-for-TV); **Apollo 13**, 1995; Approaching the Unknown, 2016; Armageddon, 1998; The Astronaut Farmer, 2006; Battleship, 2012; Beyond, 2006 (made-for-TV); The Box, 2009; The Cape, 1996-1997 (TV series); **Capricorn One**, 1978; Challenge of the GoBots, 1984-1985 (TV series); Challenger, 1990 (made-for-TV); The Challenger Disaster, 2013 (made-for-TV); **Contact**, 1997; Countdown, 1967; **The Core**, 2003; **The Day the Earth Stood Still**, 2008; **Deep Impact**, 1998; Defense Play, 1988; **The Departed**, 2006; Die Delegation, 1970 (made-for-TV); **The Dish**, 2000; Flight of the Navigator, 1986; Frankenstein Meets the Spacemonster, 1965; From Earth to the Moon, 1998- (TV miniseries); **Gattaca**, 1997; Genesis II, 1973 (made-for-TV); **Gravity**, 2013; The Great American Moon Rock Caper, 2010; I Aim at the Stars, 1960 (Werner von Braun); I Know What I Saw, 2009 (made-for-TV); Impact, 2009- (TV miniseries); In Gold We Trust, 1990; **Interstellar**, 2014; **Into the Wild**, 2007; Invaders from Mars, 1986; The Invasion, 2007; Lifeforce, 1985; **Marooned**, 1969; **The Martian**, 2015; **Men in Black 3**, 2012; Men Into Space, 1959-1960 (TV series); Meteor, 1979; Middle Men, 2009; Moon Pilot, 1962; Moonshot, 2009 (made-for-TV); Moontrap, 1989; My Favorite Martian, 1999; Night Fright, 1967; **Night of the Living Dead**, 1968; **Oblivion**, 2013; Once upon a Spy, 1980 (made-for-TV); Passage to Mars, 2016; Pixels, 2015; Planet of the Apes, 1974- (TV series); Planetes, 2003-2004 (TV series); Project Viper, 2002 (made-for-TV); Race to Space, 2001; Red Planet, 2000; **The Right Stuff**, 1983; RocketMan, 1997; Rocket's Red Glare, 2000 (made-for-TV); Schizopolis, 1996; Shadowzone, 1990; Solar Crisis, 1990; Solaris, 2002; Space, 1985- (TV miniseries); **Space Cowboys**, 2000; SpaceCamp, 1986; Species II, 1998; Starflight: The Plane That Couldn't Land, 1983 (made-for-TV); Stowaway to the Moon, 1975 (made-for-TV); **Superman II**, 1981; Swades, 2004; Temple Grandin, 2010 (made-for-TV); The Thief Who Came to Dinner, 1973; **Tomorrowland**, 2015; Top of the Heap, 1972; Transformers: Dark of the Moon, 2011; **2001: A Space Odyssey**, 1968; **2010: The Year We Make Contact**, 1984; Unidentified Flying Oddball, 1979; **Valentin**, 2003; Walking on Air, 1987 (made-for-TV); When We Left Earth: The NASA Missions, 2008 (TV miniseries); X-15, 1961; **You Only Live Twice**, 1967.

NATO (North Atlantic Treaty Organization, since 1949): After Rubicon, 1987; Armed Hands, 2012; Barcelona, 1994; Bear Island, 1979; **The Bedford Incident**, 1965; Behind Enemy Lines, 2001; The Brain, 1969; Brent av frost, 1997; Countdown to Looking Glass, 1984 (made-for-TV); The Crown Prince, 1979; Derailed, 2002; The Disintegration, 2011; Fathom, 1967; The Fourth Protocol, 1987; G.I. Joe: The Rise of Cobra, 2009; Hammerhead, 1968; Iron Sky, 2012; Kiss Me Deadly, 2008 (made-for-TV); Lifeforce, 1985; Made in Estonia, 2003; Motforestilling, 1972; Never Say Never Again, 1983; The Package, 1989; **Private Benjamin**, 1980; Remo Williams: The Adventure Begins, 1985; **Salt**, 2010; **Skyfall**, 2012; **Thunderball**, 1965; **Topaz**, 1969; **Voyage to the Bottom of the Sea**, 1961; Zone of the Dead, 2009.

Neo-Nazism (various organizations; post-WWII): **Berlin Express**, 1948; **Cornered**, 1945; The Holcroft Covenant, 1985; **The Man in the Glass Booth**, 1975 (role model for Adolf Eichmann); **Notorious**, 1946; Notorious, 1992 (made-for-TV); **The Odessa File**, 1974; Operation Eichmann, 1961; **The Quiller Memorandum**, 1966; **The Stranger**, 1946.

Organized Crime (including Chinese tongs and triads; Chicago Outfit, Cosa Nostra, Mafia, Japanese Yakuza; Russian Mafia, the Syndicate): Above the Law, 1998; **Absence of Malice**, 1981 (Mafia); Across 110th Street, 1972 (Mafia); **Al Capone**, 1959 (Mafia); **All Dogs Go to Heaven**, 1989; American Gangster, 2007; **American Hustle**, 2013 (Mafia); American Me, 1992 (Mafia); **An American Tail**, 1986 (Russian Mafia); American Yakuza, 1993; Amish Mafia, 2012; Analyze That, 2002 (Mafia); **Analyze This**, 1999 (Mafia); **Any Which Way You Can**, 1980 (Mafia); **The Babe**, 1992; Baby Face Nelson, 1996; Bad Boys II, 2003; Bad Lieutenant: Port of Call New Orleans, 2009; The Bandit, 1998 (Mafia); The Bank Job, 2008 (Mafia); **Batman Begins**, 2005; A Better Tomorrow, 1986 (Chinese triads); **Billy Bathgate**, 1991 (NYC syndicate in early 1930s; Mafia); A Bittersweet Life, 2005 (Chinese triads); Black Hand, 1950 (Mafia); Black Rain, 1989; Boardwalk Empire, 2010- (TV series; Mafia; syndicate); Bonanno: A Godfather's Story, 1999 (made-for TV; Mafia); The Boondock Saints, 1999; The Boondock Saints II: All Saints Day, 2009; Boss of Bosses, 2001 (made-for-TV; Mafia); Bound, 1996; Brannigan, 1975 (Chicago Outfit); The Brass Target, 1978 (Mafia); **Broadway Danny Rose**, 1984 (Mafia); Bronx Barbes, 2003; Brother, 2000 (Yakuza); **The Brotherhood**, 1968 (Mafia); **Bugsy**, 1991 (NYC syndicate; Mafia); **Bullets over Broadway**, 1994 (Mafia); Capone, 1975 (Mafia); Capone's Boys, 2002 (Mafia); Carlito's Way, 1993; **Casino**, 1995 (Mafia); **Charley Varrick**, 1973 (syndicate); The Chinese Connection, 1972 (triads); City Hall, 1996 (Mafia); **The Client**, 1994; **The Cooler**, 2003 (Mafia); Cop Land, 1997; Corky Romano, 2001 (Mafia); Corleone, 2007 (TV miniseries, Mafia); The Corruptor, 1999 (Chinese triads); **The Cotton Club**, 1984 (Mafia and NYC syndicate in early 1930s); Crazy Joe, 1974 (NYC Mafia); Crime Story, 1986-1988 (TV series; Chicago Outfit); **The Dark Knight**, 2008; Dead or Alive, 1999 (Yakuza); **The Dead Pool**, 1988; The Deep, 1977; **The Departed**, 2006; **Diamonds Are Forever**, 1971 (Mafia); Dillinger and Capone, 1995 (Mafia); **Dinner Rush**, 2001 (Mafia); Domino, 2005; Donnie Brasco, 1997 (Mafia); Drive, 2011; El Narco, 2010; **Enemy of the State**, 1998; **Eraser**, 1996; Ezel, 2009- (TV series;

Mafia); **The Family**, 2013; The Fast and the Furious: Tokyo Drift, 2006 (Yakuza); **Find Me Guilty**, 2006 (Mafia); **The Finger Points**, 1931; **The Firm**, 1993; Frank Nitti: The Enforcer, 1988 (made-for-TV; Mafia; the Outfit); **The French Connection**, 1971; **French Connection II**, 1975; **The Freshman**, 1990 (Mafia); **F/X**, 1986 (Mafia); The Funeral, 1996 (Mafia); The Gambler, 1974 (Mafia); The Gang That Couldn't Shoot Straight, 1971 (Mafia); The Gangster Chronicles, 1981 (TV series; Mafia; syndicate); **Gangster Squad**, 2013; Gangster Wars, 1981; The George Raft Story, 1961; **Get Shorty**, 1995; Ghost Dog; The Way of the Samurai, 1999; **Gloria**, 1980 (Mafia); Gloria, 1999 (Mafia); **The Godfather**, 1972 (Mafia); **The Godfather: Part II**, 1974 (Mafia); The Godfather: Part III, 1990 (Mafia); Gomorrah, 2008 (Mafia); **GoodFellas**, 1990 (Mafia); Gotham, 2014 (made-for-TV); Gotti, 1996 (made-for-TV; NYC Mafia); Grosse Point Blank, 1997; Hard Boiled, 1992 (Mafia); **Hard Times**, 1975 (New Orleans syndicate); **The Hatchet Man**, 1932 (Chinese tongs); Heat, 1986 (Mafia); Heist, 2001(Mafia); Hercules in New York, 1969 (Mafia); A History of Violence, 2005 (Mafia); **Hoffa**, 1992 (Mafia); Hoodlum, 1993 (Mafia; syndicate); Hoodlum, 1997 (NYC syndicate in early 1930s); A House Is Not a Home, 1964 (Mafia; syndicate); Ichi the Killer, 2001 (Yakuza); The Italian Job, 1969 (Mafia); **JFK**, 1991; Judgment Night, 1993 (Mafia); The Juror, 1996 (Mafia); Kangaroo Jack, 2003; Kansas City, 1996 (syndicate in early 1930s); Kill the Irishman, 2011 (Mafia); **Killing Them Softly**, 2012 (Mafia); Killshot, 2008; King of New York, 1990; King of the Roaring 20's: The Story of Arnold Rothstein, 1961 (NYC syndicate; Mafia); Kiss of Death, 1995 (Mafia); Kiss of Death, 1997; Knockaround Guys, 2011; Lansky, 1999 (made-for-TV; syndicate; Mafia); The Last Action Hero, 1993; The Last Don, 1997 (TV miniseries; Mafia); The Last Dragon, 1985 (Chinese triads); Last Man Standing, 1996; Leon: The Professional, 1994; Lepke, 1975 (NYC syndicate); Lethal Weapon 3, 1992; **The Lineup**, 1958 (West Coast syndicate); **Little Caesar**, 1931; Little Odessa, 1995 (Russian Mafia); The Little Worm, 1999; **The Long Good Friday**, 1982 (British syndicate); Looper, 2012; The Lost Capone, 1990 (made-for-TV; Mafia); Lucky Luciano, 1973 (syndicate; Mafia); Mad Dog Coll, 1961 (NYC syndicate; Mafia); Mad Dog Coll, 1993 (NYC syndicate; Mafia); Mafia, 2012; **Magnum Force**, 1973 (Mafia); **Marked Woman**, 1937 (NYC syndicate; Mafia); **Married to the Mob**, 1988 (Mafia); The Mask, 1994; **Mean Streets**, 1973 (Mafia); The Mechanic, 1972 (Mafia); The Mexican, 2001; Mickey Blue Eyes, 1999 (Mafia); **Mickey One**, 1975 (syndicate; Chicago Outfit); **Midnight Run**, 1988 (Mafia); **Miller's Crossing**, 1990; Mob City, 2013; The Mob Doctor, 2012-2013 (TV series; Mafia); Mobsters, 1991 (Cosa Nostra, Mafia); The Money Train, 1995; **Mulholland Dr.**, 2001; **Murder, Inc.**, 1960 (NYC syndicate); **Murder on the Orient Express**, 1974; My Blue Heaven, 1990 (Mafia); Narrow Margin, 1990 (Mafia); New Jack City, 1991; Next of Kin, 1989; **Night at the Museum: Battle of the Smithsonian**, 2009; **On the Waterfront**, 1954; **Once upon a Time in America**, 1984 (Mafia); Oscar, 1991 (Mafia); Out for Justice, 1991; **The Outfit**, 1973; The Outfit, 1993 (NYC syndicate; Mafia); Parker, 2013; **Party Girl**, 1958; **Pay or Die**, 1960 (Black Hand; Mafia); The Perfect Dictatorship, 2014; **Point Blank**, 1967 (West Coast syndicate); Poor Devil, 1973 (made-for-TV); **Prince of the City**, 1981 (Mafia); **Prizzi's Honor**, 1985 (Mafia); A Prophet, 2009; **The Public Enemy**, 1931 (Chicago bootlegging gangs); The Punisher, 1989; The Punisher, 2004; Punisher: The War Zone, 2008; **The Purple Gang**, 1960; **The Racket**, 1928; Rapid Fire, 1992 (Mafia); Raw Deal, 1986 (Mafia); The Real Untouchables, 2001 (made-for-TV; NYC syndicate; Mafia); The Revenge of Al Capone, 1989 (made-for-TV; Mafia); **The Rise and Fall of Legs Diamond**, 1960 (NYC syndicate in early 1930s; Mafia); **Road to Perdition**, 2002 (Chicago Outfit in early 1930s; Mafia); Romeo Is Bleeding, 1993; Rounders, 1998; Rumble in the Bronx, 1995; Running Scared, 2006; **The St. Valentine's Day Massacre**, 1967 (Mafia); The St. Valentine's Day Massacre, 1997 (made-for-TV; Mafia); **Scarface**, 1932; Scarface, 1983 (Latin American drug cartels); The Scarface Mob, 1959 (made-for-TV; Mafia); **The Secret**

Six, 1931; **The Seven Ups**, 1973 (NYC syndicate); **The Shadow**, 1994; **Shaft**, 1971 (Black Mafia); Shanghai, 2010 (Chinese triads); The Sicilian, 1987 (Mafia); **The Sicilian Clan**, 1970 (Mafia); Sizzle, 1981 (made-for-TV; Mafia); Smokin' Aces, 2006; **Snatch**, 2000; Sol Madrid, 1968 (Mafia); **Some Like It Hot**, 1959; The Sopranos, 1999-2007 (TV series; Mafia); **Sorcerer**, 1977 (Mafia); The Specialist, 1994; State of Grace, 1990; **The Sting**, 1973; Stone Cold, 1991 (Mafia); The Stone Killer, 1973 (Mafia); Striptease, 1996; Suicide Kings, 1997; Super Mario Bros., 1993; Taxi Driver, 1976; **Thief**, 1981; Things to Do in Denver When You're Dead, 1995 (Mafia); **Tokyo Drifter**, 1966 (Yakuza); Toy Soldiers, 1991; True Romance, 1993; 22 Bullets, 2010; **Underworld**, 1927; Undisputed, 2002; The Untouchables, 1959-1963 (TV series; Mafia); **The Untouchables**, 1987 (Mafia); **The Valachi Papers**, 1972 (Cosa Nostra; Mafia); The Verne Miller Story, 1988; Wake of Death, 2004 (Chinese triads); **Walking Tall**, 1973; **The Way of the Dragon**, 1972 (Yakuza; tongs); White Hot: The Mysterious Murder of Thelma Todd, 1991 (made-for-TV; NYC syndicate; Mafia); The Witness, 1960-1961 (TV series; NYC syndicate; Mafia); The Whole Nine Yards, 2000; **The Wild Geese**, 1978 (Mafia); Wiseguy, 1987-1990 (TV series); Witness to the Mob, 1998 (made-for-TV; Mafia); **The Wolverine**, 2013; The Yards, 2000; **The Yakuza**, 1976; **Year of the Dragon**, 1985 (Chinese triads).

OSS (U.S. Office of Strategic Services, 1942-1945; American intelligence agency; precursor to the CIA): Action in Arabia, 1944 (George Sanders and Allied agents work to undo the Nazi efforts to unite the Arab tribes to fight for the German cause in WWII); **Background to Danger**, 1943 (George Raft workins with Allied agents in Turkey to undo clandestine operations by a Nazi spy ring run by Sydney Greenstreet); **Captain Carey, U.S.A.**, 1950 (Alan Ladd investigates hidden fascist spies in Italy in post-WWII); **Cloak and Dagger**, 1946 (where physicist Gary Cooper goes behind enemy lines in Italy for the O.S.S. to obtain information about Nazi experiments with the a-bomb); **Decision before Dawn**, 1951 (OSS operatives aid U.S. Army Intelligence in obtaining secret information behind enemy lines in Germany toward the close of WWII); The Enemy General, 1960 (OSS and French underground attempt to rescue a condemned German general); The Good Shepherd, 2007 (one man's experiences with this agency is profiled); The Last Escape, 1970 (the smuggling of German scientists involved in the V-1 and V-2 rocket program from the Soviets); **Mission Impossible—Rogue Nation**, 2015; **Never So Few**, 1959 (where OSS agents work with a native guerrilla force under the command of Frank Sinatra in Burma and China in WWII); **OSS**, 1946 (a group of U.S. agents are trained and then sent to operate secretly behind enemy lines in Nazi-occupied France in WWII); O.S.S., 1957-1958 (TV series); **Rogue's Regiment**, 1948 (an OSS agent enlistins in the French Foreign Legion to track down a Nazi bigwig, who has escaped and also joined the Legion under an alias); **13 Rue Madeleine**, 1947 (James Cagney leads a team of OSS agents behind the lines in occupied France in WWII); **Where Eagles Dare**, 1968 (Clint Eastwood, an OSS officer, joins a British team of secret agents on a mission behind the lines in Germany).

Philippine Scouts (1901-1945; U.S. Army organization made up of Filipino volunteers, who fought heroically in the Philippines in WWII): **American Guerrilla in the Philippines**, 1950; **Back to Bataan**, 1945; **Bataan**, 1943; Battle at Bloody Beach, 1951; **The Great Raid**, 2005; I Was an American Spy, 1951; **Manila Calling**, 1942; **The Real Glory**, 1939.

Pony Express (Central Overland California and Pikes Peak Express Company, 1860-1861; U.S. East-to-West communication system of a series of relay riders mounted on horseback, riding from station to station, carrying mail and other important documents): **Broken Arrow**, 1950; California Mail, 1936; Cavalcade of the West, 1936; Cody of the

Pony Express, 1950 (serial); Comin' 'Round the Mountain, 1936; Deadline, 1948; Egghead Rides Again, 1937; Flaming Frontiers, 1938; Gunslinger, 1956; Heroes of the West, 1932; **Hidalgo**, 2004; **The Iron Horse**, 1924; Iron Mountain Trail, 1953; Last of the Pony Riders, 1953; Outlaw Express, 1938; The Overland Express, 1938; Overland Mail, 1942 (serial); Peter Lundy and the Medicine Hat Stallion, 1977 (made-for-TV); Plainsman and the Lady, 1946; **Pony Express**, 1953; Pony Express, 1959 (TV series); Pony Express Days, 1940; Pony Express Rider, 1926; Pony Express Rider, 1976; Prairie Thunder, 1937; Riders of the Pony Express, 1949; Riding West, 1944; Rollin' Plains, 1938; Seven Hours of Gunfire, 1965; Silver Canyon, 1951; The Telegraph Trail, 1933; Via Pony Express, 1933; Wagons East, 1994; **Wells Fargo**, 1937; White Eagle, 1932; White Eagle, 1941; Winds of the Wasteland, 1936; Young Bill Hickok, 1940; Young Blood, 1932; The Young Riders, 1989-1992 (TV series).

Princeton University (Princeton, New Jersey; established in 1746): **Accent on Youth**, 1935; Accepted, 2006; Across the Universe, 2007; **Admission**, 2013; **A Beautiful Mind**, 2001; A Cinderella Story, 2004; The Extra Man, 2010; The First Olympics: Athens, 1896, 1984 (TV miniseries); Four Minutes, 2005 (made-for-TV); Harold & Kumar Go to White Castle, 2004; I'll Follow You Down, 2013; In Her Shoes, 2005; In Your Wildest Dreams, 1991; Infinity, 1996; Last Embrace, 1979; **Meet Me in St. Louis**, 1944; Off and Running, 2009; Runner Runner, 2013; School Ties, 1992; Spanglish, 2004; Storytelling, 2001; **What Lies Beneath**, 2000; **Wilson**, 1944; You Can't Buy Everything, 1934; **The Young Philadelphians**, 1959.

Quakers: **Alvin and the Chipmunks**, 2007; **Angel and the Badman**, 1947; Angel and the Badman, 2009 (made-for-TV); The Baroness and the Pig, 2003; Beauty's Worth, 1922; **Bedlam**, 1946; **Before Sunrise**, 1995; The Big Trees, 1952; **Cheyenne Autumn**, 1964; **Crossfire**, 1947; Down to the Sea in Ships, 1922; **Down to the Sea in Ships**, 1949; **Friendly Persuasion**, 1956; Friendly Persuasion, 1975 (made-for-TV); **Frost/Nixon**, 2008; **High Noon**, 1952; High Noon, 2000 (made-for-TV); The Lady from Cheyenne, 1941; **Nixon**, 1995; Path to War, 2002; A Prayer in the Dark, 1997 (made-for-TV); **The Scarlet Letter**, 1926; The Scarlet Letter, 1995; Seven Psychopaths, 2012; **Uncle Tom's Cabin**, 1927; The Volunteer, 1917; The Winds of Autumn, 1976.

RAF (British Royal Air Force): Angels One Five, 1954 (WWII); **Arise My Love**, 1940 (WWII); At Dawn We Die, 1943 (WWII); **Battle of Britain**, 1969 (WWII); **The Blue Max**, 1966 (WWI); **Breaking the Sound Barrier**, 1952 (post-WWII); The Brylcreem Boys, 1998 (WWII); Charlie Chan in London, 1934 (post-WWI); Charlotte Gray, 2001 (WWII); **The Dam Busters**, 1955 (WWII); Dark Blue World, 2001 (WWII); **The Dawn Patrol**, 1930 (WWI); **The Dawn Patrol**, 1938 (WWI); **Desperate Journey**, 1942 (WWII); The Devil's General, 1957 (WWII); Don't Look Now...We're Being Shot At!, 1969; **The Eagle and the Hawk**, 1933 (WWI); **Eagle Squadron**, 1942 (WWII); Fly, Dakota, Fly!, 2013 (WWII); **The Great Escape**, 1962 (WWII); High Flight, 1957 (post-WWII); I Became a Criminal (aka: They Made Me a Fugitive), 1948 (post-WWII); **I Know Where I'm Going**, 1947 (WWII); International Squadron, 1941; **Into the White**, 2012 (WWII); **Joan of Paris**, 1942 (WWII); **Johnny in the Clouds** (aka: The Way to the Stars), 1945 (WWII); The Land Girls, 1998 (WWII); Long Shadows, 2008 (post-WWII); Make Mine a Double, 1961 (WWII); Marianne & Juliane, 1981 (WWII); Monkey Warfare, 2006 (post-WWII); Mosquito Squadron, 1969 (WWII); **The Night My Number Came Up**, 1955 (post-WWII); **One of Our Aircraft Is Missing**, 1942 (WWII); **The One That Got Away**, 1958 (WWII); **Paratrooper**, 1954 (WWII); Paris Calling, 1941 (WWII); Paris Underground, 1945 (WWII); **Pearl Harbor**, 2001 (WWII); The Purple V, 1943 (WWII); Raiders in the Sky, 1953 (WWII); **The Red Baron**, 2010 (WWI); The Roses of the Desert, 2006 (WWII); Secret Flight, 1946 (WWII); Secrets of Scotland

Yard, 1944 (WWII); **633 Squadron**, 1964 (WWII); **So Well Remembered**, 1947 (WWII); **Spitfire**, 1943 (WWII); **Stairway to Heaven** (aka: A Matter of Life and Death), 1947 (WWII); Stalag Luft, 1993 (made-for-TV; WWII); Stukas, 1941 (WWII); Tears in the Rain, 1988 (made-for-TV; WWII); This England, 1941 (WWII); **Von Richthofen and Brown**, 1971 (WWI); The Wife Takes a Flyer, 1942 (WWII): The Winds of War, 1983- (TV miniseries; WWII); **The Wooden Horse**, 1951 (WWII); **A Yank in the R.A.F.**, 1941 (WWII).

Salvation Army (established in London, England, 1865; also see Subject Index, Religious Missions): **The Angel of Broadway**, 1927; **Around the World in 80 Days**, 1956; Bad Boy Bubby, 2005; Blood and Fire, 1950; The Book of Life, 1998; Come the Morning, 1993; Devil's Cargo, 1948; Elling, 2001; Even Angels Eat Beans, 1973; Excessive Force, 1993; Falling in Love, 1984; The First Deadly Sin, 1980; Fred Clause, 2007; Good Sam, 1948; **Guys and Dolls**, 1955; Hamburg: City of Vice, 1964; Heavens Above!, 1963; The Holy Child, 2001; **Honky Tonk**, 1941; Joe Hill, 1971; Judgment in Berlin, 1988; K-PAX, 2001; **Larceny, Inc.**, 1942; The Last of the Blonde Bombshells, 2000 (made-for-TV); Laughing Sinners, 1931; The Law of the Tong, 1931; **Major Barbara**, 1941; **The Man Who Never Was**, 1956; The Man without a Past, 2002; The Mystery of a Hansom Cab, 2012 (made-for-TV); **North to Alaska**, 1960; **O Lucky Man!**, 1973; **On Moonlight Bay**, 1951; On the Beach, 1959; Oranges Are Not the Only Fruit, 1989 (TV miniseries); **Pandora's Box**, 1929; Penelope, 1966; The Phantom Wagon, 1940; **A Place in the Sun**, 1951; The Power of Evil, 1916; Privilege, 1967; **The Public Enemy**, 1931; Run, Man, Run, 1968; Salvation Army, 2013; Salvation Jane, 1927; Salvation Nell, 1921; **She Done Him Wrong**, 1933 (role model); Sleepers, 1996; The Stig-Helmer Story, 2011; Strange Fascination, 1952; The Sum of Us, 1995; Surviving Christmas, 2004; The Terror, 1917; Terror Street, 1953; **The 39 Steps**, 1935; **Three Days of the Condor**, 1975; **The Time of Your Life**, 1948; Toy Mountain Christmas Special, 2006 (made-for-TV); 24 Nights, 1999; **Union Depot**, 1932; **Up the River**, 1930; The Whirlpool of Destiny, 1916; **Whistle Down the Wind**, 1961; **The Wrong Box**, 1966; The Youngest Profession, 1943; Zazie dans le metro, 1961.

San Quentin (since July 1852; California's oldest state prison): The Black Dahlia, 2006 (Elizabeth Short, victim); Cell 2455, Death Row, 1955 (Caryl Chessman; executed); Chandler, 1971; **Changeling**, 2009 (Gordon Stewart Northcott; executed); Cool Breeze, 1972; **Dark Passage**, 1947; Duffy of San Quentin, 1954; Escape from San Quentin, 1957; Felon, 2008; Hitch Hike Lady, 1935; **House of Numbers**, 1957; **I Want to Live!**, 1958 (Barbara Graham; executed); Men of San Quentin, 1942; The Prairie Home Companion, 2006; Prison Break, 1938; Prison Mutiny, 1943; **San Quentin**, 1937; San Quentin, 1946; Secret Service of the Air, 1939; Women of San Quentin, 1983 (made-for-TV).

Scotland Yard (British police agency; aka: New Scotland Yard): The Ace of Scotland Yard, 1929 (serial); **Across the Bridge**, 1957; **The Adventure of Sherlock Holmes' Smarter Brother**, 1975; **The Adventures of Sherlock Holmes**, 1939; Almost Married, 1932; The Alphabet Murders, 1966; **An American Werewolf in London**, 1981; Angels of Terror, 1971; Ask a Policeman, 1939; Basic Instinct 2, 2006; The Black Abbot, 1963; Black Limelight (aka: Footsteps in the Sand), 1939; The Black Sleep, 1956; The Black Windmill, 1974; The Blackbird, 1926; **Blackmail**, 1929; Blake of Scotland Yard, 1937 (serial); **The Blue Lamp**, 1950; Boots, 1919; Brannigan, 1975; Bulldog Drummond, 1922; Bulldog Drummond at Bay, 1947; **Bulldog Drummond Strikes Back**, 1934; Bulldog Drummond Strikes Back, 1947; Bulldog Drummond's Bride, 1939; Bulldog Drummond's Revenge, 1937; **Bunny Lake Is Missing**, 1965; Buster, 1988; The Case of the Black Parrot, 1941; The Case of the Red Monkey, 1955; The Case of the Whitechapel Vampire, 2002 (made-for-TV); A Certain Justice, 1998 (TV series); Chance Meet-

ing, 1959; **Close Your Eyes**, 2003; Code of Scotland Yard, 1948; The College Girl Murders, 1967; Cottage to Let (aka: Bombsight Stolen), 1943; Counter-Espionage, 1942; Cover Girl Killer, 1959; **Crack-Up**, 1946; Cribb, 1980-1981 (TV series); Crime over London, 1936; Crime Unlimited, 1935; Dancing with Crime, 1947; Daughter of the Dragon, 1931; Dead Eyes of London, 1961; **Dial M for Murder**, 1954; The Diamond Wizard, 1954; Dick Barton Strikes Back, 1949; Don't Open Till Christmas, 1984; **Dracula's Daughter**, 1936; **Dressed to Kill**, 1946; Drums of Fu Manchu, 1940 (serial); Drums of Fu Manchu, 1943 (feature version of serial); Eastern Promises, 2007; Eight O'Clock Walk, 1955; The Face behind the Scar, 1940; The Face of Fu Manchu, 1965; Face of the Frog, 1959; The File of the Golden Goose, 1969; **The Florentine Dagger**, 1935; For Them That Trespass, 1950; **Foreign Correspondent**, 1940; **Frenzy**, 1972; The Frog, 1937; **Gaslight**, 1944; Gaslight, 1952; Gideon of Scotland Yard, 1959; Gorilla Gang, 1968; The Green Carnation, 1954; **Hangover Square**, 1945; Harrison: Cry of the City, 1996 (made-for-TV); Haunted Honeymoon, 1940; He Who Dares, 2014; Heat of the Sun, 1998 (TV miniseries); Hideout in the Alps, 1937; Holiday Camp, 1948; **Houdini**, 1953; **The Hound of the Baskervilles**, 1939; **The Hound of the Baskervilles**, 1959; The Hound of the Baskervilles, 1972 (made-for-TV); **The House of Fear**, 1945; The House of Secrets, 1936; The Human Monster, 1939; The Hunchback of Soho, 1966; I Became a Criminal (aka: They Made Me a Fugitive), 1948; The Imperfect Lady, 1947; In the Money, 1958; Inspector Clouseau, 1968; International Lady, 1941; **The Invisible Man**, 1933; **The Invisible Man Returns**, 1940; **The Ipcress File**, 1965; **Kind Hearts and Coronets**, 1950; Jack the Ripper, 1988- (TV series); **The Jokers**, 1967; **Juggernaut**, 1974; The Last of Mrs. Cheyney, 1937; **The Lavender Hill Mob**, 1951; **Legend**, 2015; The Limping Man, 1953; **The Lodger**, 1944; London after Midnight, 1927; London Blackout Murders, 1943; London by Night, 1937; London Has Fallen, 2016; The Lone Wolf in London, 1947; The Mad Executioners, 1963; Madhouse, 1974; The Man from Planet X, 1951; Man in Hiding, 1953; **The Man Who Knew Too Much**, 1935; **The Man Who Knew Too Much**, 1956; The Man with 100 Faces, 1938; **Marie Galante**, 1934; **Midnight Lace**, 1960; **Ministry of Fear**, 1944; **The Mirror Crack'd**, 1980; Mirror Wars: Reflection One, 2005; Mrs. Pym of Scotland Yard, 1940; **Mr. Holmes**, 2015; The Monster of Blackwood Castle, 1972; The Moonstone, 1934; The Mummy's Revenge, 1973; **Murder Ahoy**, 1964; **Murder at the Gallop**, 1963; **Murder by Decree**, 1979; **Murder Most Foul**, 1964; Murder on Diamond Row, 1937; **Murder She Said**, 1961; My Lady's Garter, 1920; The Mysterious Miss X, 1939; Mystery!: Malice of Forethought, 1979- (TV series); Mystery at the Burlesque, 1949; **The Mystery of Mr. X**, 1934; New Scotland Yard, 1972-1974 (TV series); Original Sin, 1997 (TV series); **Patriot Games**, 1992; **Pearl of Death**, 1944; The Phantom Fiend, 1932; Phantom of Soho, 1974; Prison of Rio, 1988; The Private Eyes, 1980; **The Private Life of Sherlock Holmes**, 1970; **Pursuit to Algiers**, 1945; The Quartermass Experiment, 1953- (TV series); **Raffles**, 1930; **Raffles**, 1939; Raw Meat, 1972; The Runaway Bus, 1954; The Return of Dr. Fu Manchu, 1930; **The Return of the Vampire**, 1943; The Ripper, 1997 (made-for-TV); Room 13, 1964; Rough Cut, 1980; **Sabotage**, 1937; The Saint in London, 1939; Sapphire, 1959; **The Scarlet Claw**, 1944; Scotland Yard, 1930; Scotland Yard, 1941; Scotland Yard, 1960- (TV series); Scotland Yard Commands, 1937; Scotland Yard Dragnet, 1958; Scotland Yard Investigator, 1945; The Scotland Yard Mystery, 1934; Secret Venture, 1955; Secrets of Scotland Yard, 1944; Serena, 1962; **Seven Days to Noon**, 1950; Seven Murders for Scotland Yard, 1971; Shadows on the Stairs, 1941; Shanghai Knights, 2003; Sherlock Holmes, 1916; **Sherlock Holmes**, 1922; Sherlock Holmes, 1932; Sherlock Holmes, 1951 (TV miniseries); Sherlock Holmes, 1954-1955 (TV series); Sherlock Holmes, 1964-1968 (TV series); Sherlock Holmes, 1967-1968 (TV series); **Sherlock Holmes**, 2009; Sherlock Holmes, 2011; **Sherlock Holmes: A Game of Shadows**, 2011; Sherlock Holmes and a Study in Scarlet, 1983; Sherlock Holmes and Dr. Watson: The Bloody Inscription, 1979 (made-for-

TV); Sherlock Holmes and the Baker Street Irregulars, 2007 (made-for-TV); Sherlock Holmes and the Baskerville Curse, 1983; Sherlock Holmes and the Case of the Silk Stocking, 2004 (made-for-TV); Sherlock Holmes and the Deadly Necklace, 1962; Sherlock Holmes and the Leading Lady, 1991 (made-for-TV); Sherlock Holmes and the Masks of Death, 1984 (made-for-TV); Sherlock Holmes and the Missing Rembrandt, 1932; **Sherlock Holmes and the Secret Weapon**, 1942; Sherlock Holmes and the Shadow Watchers, 2011; Sherlock Holmes and the Sign of Four, 1983; Sherlock Holmes and the Valley of Fear, 1983; **Sherlock Holmes and the Voice of Terror**, 1942; **Sherlock Holmes Faces Death**, 1943; Sherlock Holmes' Fatal Hour, 1931; Sherlock Holmes in China, 1994; Sherlock Holmes in New York, 1976 (made-for-TV); **Sherlock Holmes in Washington**, 1943; Sherlock Holmes in the 22nd Century, 1999-2001 (TV series); Sherlock Holmes Returns, 1993; She-Wolf of London, 1946; Shoot On Sight, 2007; The Sign of Four: Sherlock Holmes' Greatest Case, 1932; The Sign of Four, 1983; The Sign of Four, 1988; The Sign of Four, 2001; Silver Blaze (AKA: Murder at the Baskervilles), 1937; The Sinister Monk, 1965; The Snake Woman, 1961; The Solitaire Man, 1933; South of Suez, 1940; **The Speckled Band**, 1931; **The Spider Woman**, 1944; **The Squaw Man**, 1914; The Strange Case of the End of Civilization as We Know It, 1977; The Strangler, 1942; The Strangler of Blackmoor Castle, 1963; A Study in Scarlet, 1933; **A Study in Terror**, 1966; Survivor, 2015; **The Suspect**, 1944; The Suspicions of Mr. Whicher: The Murder at Road Hill House, 2011 (made-for-TV); Sylvia of the Secret Service, 1917; A Taste of Death, 1998 (TV miniseries); The Terror, 1928; **Terror by Night**, 1946; **The Third Key**, 1957; Thirteen at Dinner, 1985 (made-for-TV); 13 Lead Soldiers, 1948; **The 39 Steps**, 1935; Three Live Ghosts, 1922; Three Live Ghosts, 1929; Three Live Ghosts, 1936; A Touch of Larceny, 1959; The Tourist, 2010; The Trygon Factor, 1966; Twinkletoes, 1926; The Undying Monster, 1942; The Unholy Night, 1929; Unnatural Causes, 1993 (made-for-TV); The Vengeance of Fu Manchu, 1967; Vengeance of the Zombies, 1973; **Victor Frankenstein**, 2015; Villain, 1971; **Walk a Crooked Mile**, 1948; The Weapon, 1956; While London Sleeps, 1926; **Witness for the Prosecution**, 1957; The Witness Vanishes, 1939; **The Woman in Green**, 1945; Women without Men, 1956.

SDECE (military intelligence service for France, from 1945): **Berlin Express**, 1948; Night Train to Paris, 1964; **Topaz**, 1969.

Sing Sing Prison (established in 1826; New York state prison located at Ossining, New York, north of New York City and next to the Hudson River): Alias Jimmy Valentine, 1915; Analyze That, 2002; And One Was Beautiful, 1940; Baby Take a Bow, 1940; Behind the Mask, 1932; **Castle on the Hudson**, 1940; Citizen Saint, 1947; A Fugitive from Matrimony, 1919; **The Helen Morgan Story**, 1957; Her Story, 1920; **Invisible Stripes**, 1939; **It's a Wonderful World**, 1939; King of New York, 1990; **Kiss of Death**, 1947; Little Miss Broadway, 1947; The Lonely Woman, 1918; Man against Women, 1932; Man on a Ledge, 2012; The Man Who Found Himself, 1915; **Manhattan Melodrama**, 1934; Maniac Cop, 1988; **Murder Man**, 1935; Naked City, 1958-1963 (TV series; "Prime of Life," 1963 episode); **The Naked Street**, 1955; Phantom of the Paradise, 1974; **Picture Snatcher**, 1933; **The Producers**, 1968; The Producers, 2005; **Scandal Sheet**, 1932; Secrets of a Nurse, 1938; Sergeant Madden, 1939; Sing Sing Nights, 1934; Strange Justice, 1932; The Supreme Sacrifice, 1916; Sworn Enemy, 1936; Three Who Loved, 1931; **20,000 Years in Sing Sing**, 1932; Two Smart People, 1936; **The Valachi Papers**, 1972; **You Can't Get Away with Murder**, 1939.

SOE (Special Operations Executive; British sabotage arm in WWII; 1940-1946): **Against the Wind**, 1949; **Carve Her Name with Pride**, 1958; Circle of Deception, 1961; Female Agents, 2008; Night of the Fox, 1990 (made-for-TV); **Odette**, 1951; **Where Eagles Dare**, 1968.

Spanish Inquisition (tribunal of the Holy Office of the Inquisition; 1478-1834; Catholic organization purging and punishing heretics and those accused of practicing witchcraft): Bye Bye Columbus, 1991; Captain Alatriste: The Spanish Musketeer, 2007; **Captain from Castile**, 1947; Carry on Columbus, 1992; **Christopher Columbus**, 1949; Christopher Columbus: The Discovery, 1992; Conquest of Paradise, 1992; Cristobal Colon, de oficio...descubridor, 1982; Cronos, 1994; Da Vinci's Demons, 2013 (TV series; "The Tower," 2013 episode); El Greco, 1966; El Greco, 2009; **Elizabeth: The Golden Age**, 2007; **Fire Over England**, 1937; Flame in the Wind, 1971; The Fountain, 2006; Game of Swords, 2006; The Gospel according to God, 2004; Goya in Bordeaux, 2000; Goya's Ghost, 2007; History of the World, Part I, 1981; The Holy Inquisition, 1975; Inquisition, 1976; Isabel, 2011-2014 (TV series); Juana la loca...de vez en cuando, 1983; Let Joy Reign Supreme, 1977; Maleficarum, 2011; Man of La Mancha, 1972; **The Pit and the Pendulum**, 1961; The Pit and the Pendulum, 1991; Torquemada, 1989; Secret Passage, 2004; **The Wandering Jew**, 1935; **The Wandering Jew**, 1949; **The Wandering Jew: The Life of Theodore Herzl**, 1923.

Special Branch (intelligence and counterintelligence division of Scotland Yard, first established as a department of London's Metropolitan Police in 1883 to deal with Irish terrorist organizations and later absorbed by Scotland Yard; subsequently each British police force established its own Special Branch): The Case of the Red Monkey (aka: Little Red Monkey), 1955; **Foreign Correspondent**, 1940; High Treason, 1952; Law and Disorder, 1940; **The Man Who Knew Too Much**, 1935; **Ministry of Fear**, 1944; **Sherlock Holmes and the Secret Weapon**, 1942; Spies of the Air, 1940; They Can't Hang Me, 1955; **Walk a Crooked Mile**, 1948.

SS (or SD; German intelligence agency of the Nazi Party; 1933-1945): **Adventures of Tartu**, 1943; **Amen**, 2002; The Angels of Death Island, 2003 (Heinrich Himmler); Anne Frank: The Whole Story, 2001- (TV miniseries); Anthropoid, 2016; Army of Crime, 2010; Armstrong Circle Theatre, 1950-1963 (TV series; "Engineer of Death: The Eichmann Story," 1960 episode); The Aryan Couple, 2004 (Heinrich Himmler; Adolf Eichmann); The Assassination, 1965 (Reinhard Heydrich); Battle of the Bulge, 1965; BBC Play of the Month, 1965-1983 (TV series; "The Joel Brand Story," 1960 episode; Adolf Eichmann); Before the Fall, 2004; Black Book, 2006; The Black Chapel, 1959 (Heinrich Himmler); **The Boy in the Striped Pajamas**, 2008; **The Boys from Brazil**, 1978; **A Bridge Too Far**, 1977; The Bunker, 1981 (made-for-TV; Heinrich Himmler); **Canaris**, 1958 (Reinhard Heydrich); **A Clockwork Orange**, 1971 (Heinrich Himmler in archive footage); **Closely Watched Trains**, 1967; Colette, 2014; **Come and See**, 1986; Conspiracy, 2001 (TV series; Reinhard Heydrich; Adolf Eichmann); **The Counterfeiters**, 2008; **The Damned**, 1969; Dark Blue World, 2001; Days of Betrayal, 1973 (Heinrich Himmler); Death Is My Trade, 1977 (Heinrich Himmler; Adolf Eichmann); **Decision before Dawn**, 1951; Defiance, 2008; **Diplomacy**, 2014; **The Dirty Dozen**, 1967; The Dirty Dozen: Deadly Mission, 1987 (made-for-TV); The Dirty Dozen: The Fatal Mission, 1988 (made-for-TV); **Divided We Fall**, 2000; Don't Look Now...We're Being Shot At!, 1969; **Downfall**, 2004 (Heinrich Himmler); **The Eagle Has Landed**, 1977 (Heinrich Himmler); The Empty Mirror, 1999 (Heinrich Himmler in archive footage); Escape from Sobibor, 1987 (made-for-TV); Fateless, 2005; Fatherland, 1994 (made-for-TV); The Final Solution: The Wannsee Conference, 1984 (made-for-TV; Adolf Eichmann); **5 Branded Women**, 1960; The Four Horsemen of the Apocalypse, 1962; **Fury**, 2014; G.E. True, 1962- (TV series; "Heydrich, Part 1," 1963 episode); **The Garden of the Finzi-Continis**, 1971; Gloomy Sunday, 1999; Good, 2008 (Adolf Eichmann); Good Evening, Mr. Wallenberg, 1990; The Good German, 2006; The Great Battle, 1973 (Heinrich Himmler); **The Grey Zone**, 2002; **The Guns of Navarone**, 1961; **Hangmen Also Die**, 1943 (Reinhard Heydrich); Heydrich in Prague, 1967 (made-for-TV); Hitler, 1962 (Heinrich Himmler); Hitler:

A Film from Germany, 1977 (Heinrich Himmler); **The Hitler Gang**, 1944 (Heinrich Himmler); Hitler: The Rise of Evil, 2003 (TV miniseries); **Hitler's Madman**, 1943 (Reinhard Heydrich; Heinrich Himmler); Hitler's SS: Portrait in Evil, 1985 (made-for-TV; Reinhard Heydrich; Heinrich Himmler); Holocaust, 1978 (TV miniseries; Heinrich Himmler; Adolf Eichmann); The House on Garibaldi Street, 1979 (made-for-TV; Adolf Eichmann); I Aim at the Stars, 1960 (Heinrich Himmler); Inside the Third Reich, 1982 (made-for-TV; Heinrich Himmler); Interpol, 1963-1967 (TV series; "Geld, Geld, Geld," 1965 episode: Reinhard Heydrich); Invincible, 2002 (Heinrich Himmler); **Is Paris Burning?**, 1966; Jacob the Liar, 1977; **Katyn**, 2008; The Keep, 1983; **La Rafle**, 2012 (Heinrich Himmler); The Last Drop, 2006; The Last Ten Days, 1955 (Heinrich Himmler); **Life Is Beautiful**, 1999; The Magic Face, 1951 (Heinrich Himmler); **The Man in the Glass Booth**, 1975 (role model for Adolf Eichmann); The Man Who Captured Eichmann, 1996 (made-for-TV; Adolf Eichmann); The Man Who Lived at the Ritz, 1989 (made-for-TV; Heinrich Himmler); Massacre in Rome, 1973; The Misfit Brigade, 1987; **Morituri**, 1965; Mother Night, 1996 (Adolf Eichmann); Murderers Among Us: The Simon Wiesenthal Story, 1989 (made-for-TV; Adolf Eichmann); The Night Porter, 1974; **The Ninth Day**, 2004; **O.S.S.**, 1946; **The Odessa File**, 1974; **Open City**, 1946; **Operation Daybreak**, 1975 (Reinhard Heydrich); Operation Eichmann, 1961 (Adolf Eichmann; Heinrich Himmler); Operation Himmler, 1979 (made-for-TV; Reinhard Heydrich; Heinrich Himmler); The Passage, 1979; **The People vs. Fritz Bauer**, 2015 (Adolf Eichmann); Perlasca: The Courage of a Just Man, 2002 (made-for-TV; Adolf Eichmann); **The Pianist**, 2002; Playing for Time, 1980 (made-for-TV); Private Schulz, 1981- (TV series); **The Reader**, 2009; Reichsfuhrer-SS, 2015 (Heinrich Himmler); The Red Orchestra, 1989 (Heinrich Himmler); Reinhard Heydrich: Manager des Terrors, 1977 (made-for-TV; Adolf Eichmann); Remember, 2015; SS-GB, 2016 (TV miniseries); Rosenstrasse, 2004; The Savior, 1971; The Scarlet and the Black, 1983 (made-for-TV; Heinrich Himmler); **Seven Beauties**, 1976; She Devils of the SS, 1973; Silent Night, 2002 (made-for-TV); **Soldier of Orange**, 1979; Spring of Life, 2000 (Heinrich Himmler); Stalag Luft, 1993 (made-for-TV); Stalingrad, 1990 (Heinrich Himmler); The Strange Death of Adolf Hitler, 1943 (Heinrich Himmler); **36 Hours**, 1965; To Catch a King, 1984 (made-for-TV; Heinrich Himmler); The Tranzit, 2009; **Triumph of the Spirit**, 1990; The Truce, 1998; The 25th Hour, 1967; Uncle Adolf, 2005 (made-for-TV; Heinrich Himmler); Uprising, 2001 (made-for-TV; Heinrich Himmler); **Valkyrie**, 2008 (Heinrich Himmler); Walking with the Enemy, 2013 (Adolf Eichmann); Wallenberg: A Hero's Story, 1985 (made-for-TV; Adolf Eichmann); War and Remembrance, 1988- (TV miniseries; Heinrich Himmler; Adolf Eichmann); When Heroes Die, 1970 (Heinrich Himmler); When Hitler Invaded Britain, 2004 (made-for-TV; Reinhard Heydrich); **Where Eagles Dare**, 1968; The Winds of War, 1983- (TV miniseries; "The Changing of the Guard," 1983 episode; Heinrich Himmler).

Stasi (East German Ministry for State Security, est. 1950): Assignment K, 1968; Barbara, 2012; Beloved Berlin Wall, 2010; Die Wahrheit uber die Stasi, 1992; The Devil's Agent, 1962; Good Bye Lenin!, 2004; Hidden Agenda, 1999; **The Lives of Others**, 2006; One Night in Berlin, 2011; The Red Cockatoo, 2006; Romeo, 2001 (made-for-TV); Shores of Hope, 2012; **The Spy Who Came in from the Cold**, 1965; Sun Alley, 2000; Two Lives, 2013.

Stateville Prison (Established in 1925; Illinois state prison for men in Crest Hill, Illinois): **Call Northside 777**, 1948; Roger Touhy, Gangster, 1944; **White Heat**, 1949.

Texas Rangers: Ahead of the Law, 1926; Alias the Bad Man, 1931; Another Pair of Aces: Three of a Kind, 1991 (made-for-TV0; Arizona Raiders, 1965; **The Ballad of Gregorio Cortez**, 1983; Bandits of Dark Canyon, 1947; Bandits of the Badlands, 1945; Battling Marshal, 1950;

Beyond the Last Frontier, 1943; The Big Show, 1936; Blood River, 1991 (made-for-TV); **Bonnie and Clyde**, 1967; Border Café, 1937; Border Devils, 1932; Border Law, 1931; Border Patrol, 1943; Border Rangers, 1950; Border Women, 1924; Borderland, 1937; The Boss of Rustler's Roost, 1928; Boss of the Rawhide, 1943; Both Barrels Blazing, 1945; Brand of the Devil, 1944; Bullet for a Bad Man, 1964; Code of the Rangers, 1972; Colorado Ranger, 1950; The Comancheros, 1961; Come on Danger!, 1932; Come On, Rangers, 1938; Crashing Through, 1949; Dead Man's Trail, 1952; Dead Man's Walk, 1996 (TV miniseries); Desert Bandit, 1941; Desert Patrol, 1938; Down Rio Grande Way, 1942; Drift Fence, 1936; Enemy of the Law, 1945; Everyman's Law, 1936; Extreme Prejudice, 1987; The Fabulous Texan, 1947; Fast Bullets, 1936; The Fighting Buckaroo, 1943; The Fighting Legion, 1930; Fighting Mustang, 1948; The Fighting Ranger, 1934; The Fighting Ranger, 1948; Fighting Valley, 1943; From Dusk Till Dawn, 1996; Frontier Fugitives, 1945; The Gallant Legion, 1948; Galloping Dynamite, 1937; **The Great Debaters**, 2007; Gun Duel in Durango, 1957; The Gun Ranger, 1936; Guns of the Pecos, 1937; Hail to the Rangers, 1943; The Hard Man, 1957; Heart of the Sunset, 1918; Hello Trouble, 1932; It Happened Out West, 1923; The Kid Ranger, 1936; Kingfisher's Roost, 1921; Laredo, 1965-1967 (TV series); Lasca of the Rio Grande, 1931; Last Man Standing, 1996; The Last of the Duanes, 1930; Last of the Duanes, 1941; Law beyond the Range, 1935; Law of the Ranger, 1937; **The Lawless Breed**, 1953; Lawless Land, 1937; The Lawless Legions, 1929; The Legend of the Lone Ranger, 1981; Lightning Guns, 1950; The Lone Ranger, 1949-1957 (TV series); **The Lone Ranger**, 2013; The Lone Ranger Rides Again, 1939; **Lone Star**, 1996; The Lone Star Ranger, 1919; The Lone Star Ranger, 1930; Lone Star Ranger, 1942; Lone Texas Ranger, 1945; Lone Wolf McQuade, 1983; Lonesome Dove, 1989 (TV miniseries); The Man from Sundown, 1939; The Man from Tumbleweeds, 1940; Man of Action, 1933; Man of the House, 2005; ,Man's Country, 1938; Marked for Murder, 1945; Masked Raiders, 1949; The Miracle Rider, 1935; My Outlaw Brother, 1951; The Mysterious Avenger, 1936; Mystery Ranch, 1932; The Navajo Trail, 1945; Once Upon a Texas Train, 1988 (made-for-TV); **The Outlaw Josey Wales**, 1976; Outlaw's Highway, 1934; Outlaws of the Red River, 1927; The Over-the-Hill Gang, 1969 (made-for-TV); The Over-the-Hill Gang Rides Again, 1970 (made-for-TV); A Perfect World, 1993; The Phantom Rider, 1936; Phantom Soldiers, 1987; Point Blank, 1998; The Ranger, 1918; Ranger Bill, 1925; Ranger Courage, 1937; The Rangers Ride, 1948; The Rangers' Round-Up, 1938; Rawhide Rangers, 1941; The Renegade Ranger, 1938; **Return of the Bad Men**, 1948; The Return of the Rangers, 1943; Return to Lonesome Dove, 1993 (TV miniseries); Ride, Ranger, Ride, 1936; Riders of the Deadline, 1943; Riders of the Lone Star, 1947; Riders of the Northland, 1942; Ridin' down the Trail, 1947; Ridin' the Cherokee Trail, 1941; Rio Grande Ranger, 1936; **Rio Rita**, 1929; **Rio Rita**, 1942; Rocky Mountain Rangers, 1940; Rollin' Plains, 1938; Sagebrush Troubadour, 1935; **The Searchers**, 1956; Seven Ways from Sundown, 1960; The Son of Sontag, 1925; Sons of Thunder, 1999 (TV series); Speedy Meade, 1919; Starlight over Texas, 1938; **Streets of Laredo**, 1949; Streets of Laredo, 1995 (TV miniseries); **The Sugarland Express**, 1974; Sundown Riders, 1948; Tales of the Texas Rangers, 1955-1959 (TV series); Texans Never Cry, 1951; Texas, 1995 (made-for-TV); The Texas Bad Man, 1932; Texas Lawmen, 1951; The Texas Ranger, 1931; Texas Ranger, 1964; **The Texas Rangers**, 1936; The Texas Rangers, 1951; The Texas Rangers, 1981 (made-for-TV); **Texas Rangers**, 2001; The Texas Rangers Ride Again, 1940; Texas Tornado, 1932; Three Guns for Texas, 1968; The Tioga Kid, 1948; Thundering Trails, 1943; Trackdown, 1957-1959 (TV series); The Trail Rider, 1925; Trail to Laredo, 1948; The Traitor, 1936; Trigger Fingers, 1924; **True Grit**, 1969; **True Grit**, 2001; Two Gun Justice, 1938; The Unknown Ranger, 1920; The Unknown Ranger, 1936; Unseen Enemies, 1926; Waco, 1952; Walker: Texas Rangers, 1993-2001 (TV series); Walker Texas Ranger 3: Deadly Reunion, 2004; Walker, Texas Ranger: Trial by Fire, 2005 (made-for-TV); West of Rainbow's End, 1938; West of Texas, 1943; West of the

Rio Grande, 1921; The Western Code, 1932; When a Man Rides Alone, 1919; Whirlwind Raiders, 1948; Without Honor, 1932; **The Wonderful Country**, 1959.

Thuggee (killer cult among Hindu and Muslim tribes in Southeast Asia, prominent for centuries until the late 19th Century; its members indiscriminately murdered countless victims as sacrifice to Kali and other gods): **Around the World in 80 Days**, 1956; Around the World in 80 Days, 1989 (made-for-TV); The Deceivers, 1988; **Gunga Din**, 1939; **Hangover Square**, 1945; Highlander, 1992-1998 (TV series; "The Wrath of Kali," 1995 episode); **Indiana Jones and the Temple of Doom**, 1984; The Stranglers of Bombay, 1959. For detailed information on Thuggee, see my two-volume work *The Great Pictorial History of World Crime*, Volume II (History, Inc., 2004; illustrated pages 1435-1447).

Tongs (Chinese secret societies; triads): Audition, 2000; Bloody Moon, 1983; Daughter of the Tong, 1939; **The Hatchet Man**, 1932; Sexton Blake and the Hooded Terror, 1938; The Tong Man, 1919; Tongs: A Chinatown Story, 1986; Touch of Death, 1988. For detailed information on Chinese tongs and triads, see my two-volume work *The Great Pictorial History of World Crime*, Volume II (History, Inc., 2004; illustrated pages 1464-1471).

United Nations (aka: UN; intergovernmental organization designed to promote international cooperation, since 1945): An American Rhapsody, 2001; The Art of War, 2000; Austin Powers: International Man of Mystery, 1997; Balibo, 2009; Batman: The Movie, 1966; Battle in Outer Space, 1959; **The Battle of Algiers**, 1967; Bear Island, 1979; **Beautiful People**, 2000; Beyond Borders, 2003; Beyond the Gates, 2005; **Black Hawk Down**, 2001; Blood Diamond, 2006; Brick Bradford, 1947 (serial); The Burma Conspiracy, 2011; Caged, 2010; Cairo Time, 2009; Che: Part One, 2008; Children of the Damned, 1964; Cold War, 1998- (TV miniseries); The Colossus of New York, 1958; **The Constant Gardener**, 2005; The Crawling Eye, 1958; Cry Uncle, 1971; Dark of the Sun, 1968; Deep Shock, 2003 (made-for-TV); Desert Flower, 2009; Diamonds, 2007 (made-for-TV); The Dictator, 2012; Eleanor, First Lady of the World, 1982 (made-for-TV); Fair Game, 2010; The Fifth Estate, 2013; The First Grader, 2010; **Flat Top**, 1952; The French Minister, 2014; The Giant Claw, 1957; A Global Affair, 1964; The Green Inferno, 2013; Gregory's Two Girls, 1999; Gypsy Magic, 1997; Happy Feet, 2006; Hill 24 Doesn't Answer, 1955; The Hostage Tower, 1980 (made-for-TV); **The Hot Rock**, 1972; **Hotel Rwanda**, 2004; The Hunting Party, 2007; **The Hurt Locker**, 2009; In the Land of Blood and Honey, 2011; **In the Loop**, 2009; Inchon, 1981; The Interpreter, 2005; Iron Sky, 2012; J.S.A.: Joint Security Area, 2000; Jack Ryan: Shadow Recruit, 2014; Journey to the Seventh Planet, 1962; Kandahar, 2001; King Kong vs. Godzilla, 1963; **The Kremlin Letter**, 1970; **Kundun**, 1997; Land of Plenty, 2004; The Last Witness, 1999 (made-for-TV); Left Behind II: Tribulation Force, 2002; Lifeforce, 1985; Live and Let Die, 1973; **Men in War**, 1957; Meteor, 1979; The Missiles of October, 1974 (made-for-TV); **Mister 880**, 1950; The Next Man, 1976; **Nighthawks**, 1981; Nightwatch, 1995; **No Man's Land**, 2001; **North by Northwest**, 1959; **On Her Majesty's Secret Service**, 1969; Operation Delta Force, 1997 (made-for-TV); **Our Man Flint**, 1966; **Pacific Rim**, 2013; A Perfect Murder, 1998; **The Poppy Is Also a Flower**, 1966; Remo Williams: The Adventure Begins, 1985; **The Rescuers**, 1977; **The Rescuers Down Under**, 1990; **Romanoff and Juliet**, 1961; Saving Jessica Lynch, 2003 (made-for-TV); Shake Hands with the Devil, 2007; Storm, 2009; Street Fighter, 1994; Superman IV: The Quest for Peace, 1987; Team America: World Police, 2004; Termination Man, 1998; **That Touch of Mink**, 1962; Thirteen Days, 2000; **Three Days of the Condor**, 1975; Tidal Wave, 1973; **Topaz**, 1969; Turtles Can Fly, 2005; The 27th Day, 1957; Two Men in Manhattan, 1959; **U.S. Marshals**, 1998; V, 1983 (TV miniseries); **Voyage to the Bottom of the Sea**, 1961; **The War Is Over**, 1967; War of the Satellites, 1958; **The War of the Worlds**, 1953; **The War of the Worlds**, 2005; **When Worlds Collide**, 1951; The Whistleblower, 2010; The World, the Flesh and the Devil, 1959; **World War Z**, 2013.

U.S. Air Force (previously known as U.S. Army Air Force): **Above and Beyond**, 1953 (WWII; Pacific Theater; atomic bomb attack against Japan); Adventure in Iraq, 1943; **Air Force**, 1943 (WWII; Pacific Theater); The Andromeda Strain, 1971; Armageddon, 1998; Attack of the Eye Creatures, 1965 (made-for-TV); Aurora: Operation Intercept, 1995; **The Aviator**, 2004; **Bataan**, 1943 (WWII; Philippines in Pacific Theater); Battle Hymn, 1957 (Korean War); **The Best Years of Our Lives**, 1946 (post-WWII); **Bombardier**, 1943 (WWII; Pacific Theater); Bombers B-52, 1957 (Korean War); **The Bourne Legacy**, 2012; **Bridge of Spies**, 2015 (U-2 affair); Broken Arrow, 1996; By Dawn's Early Light, 1990 (made-for-TV); **Captain Eddie**, 1945; Captain Newman, M.D., 1962; Captain Newman, M.D., 1972 (made-for-TV); **Captains of the Clouds**, 1942; **Catch-22**, 1970 (WWII; North African-Italian theaters); **Chain Lightning**, 1950 (test pilots); Cloverfield, 2008; **Close Encounters of the Third Kind**, 1977; **Command Decision**, 1948 (WWII; European Theater); The Cosmic Man, 1959; Countdown to Looking Glass, 1984 (made-for-TV); **The Court-Martial of Billy Mitchell**, 1955; **The Day the Earth Stood Still**, 1951; **The Day the Earth Stood Still**, 2008; **Dear Ruth**, 1947; Defense Play, 1988; **Destination Tokyo**, 1943 (WWII; Pacific Theater); The Disappearance of Flight 412, 1974 (made-for-TV); **Dr. Strangelove**, 1964 (Cold War; atomic bomb attacks); Earth vs. the Flying Saucers, 1956; **Empire of the Sun**, 1987 (WWII; Japan); **Fail Safe**, 1964 (Cold War; atomic bomb attacks); Fair Game, 2010; Falcon Down, 2001; Fighter Attack, 1953 (fighter planes in the Italian Campaign in WWII); **Fighter Squadron**, 1948 (WWII; European Theater); Flying Fortress, 1942; **Flying Tigers**, 1942 (WWII; Pacific Theater after U.S. entered war); Forever Young, 1992; The Front Line, 2011; **The Glenn Miller Story**, 1954; **God Is My Co-Pilot**, 1945 (WWII; Pacific Theater after U.S. entered war); The Good Die Young, 1954; Good Kill, 2014; **The Great Raid**, 2005 (WWII; Philippines in the Pacific Theater); Green Lantern, 2011; **A Guy Named Joe**, 1943 (WWII; mythical German aircraft carrier in European Theater; Pacific Theater); Hiroshima, 1995 (made-for-TV); Hot Shots!, 1992; The Hunters, 1958 (Korean War); Hurricane, 1974 (made-for-TV); I Dream of Jeannie, 1965-1970 (TV series); **Independence Day**, 1996; International Lady, 1941; Into the Sun, 1992; Iron Eagle, 1986; Iron Eagle II, 1988; Iron Man, 2008; **Johnny in the Clouds** (aka: Way to the Stars), 1945; Lost Continent, 1951; **Man of Steel**, 2013; **The McConnell Story**, 1955; **Memphis Belle**, 1990 (WWII; European Theater); **Midway**, 1976 (WWII; Pacific Theater; 1942 Doolittle Raid shown in opening sequence, taken from **Thirty Seconds over Tokyo**, 1944, with colored tint on old B/W footage); Missing Jane, 2004; Moon Pilot, 1962; My Favorite Martian, 1999; Never Say Never Again, 1983; **1941**, 1979 (WWII; California); **No Time for Sergeants**, 1958; **Olympus Has Fallen**, 2013; The Peacekeeper, 1997; **Pearl Harbor**, 2001 (WWII; Pacific Theater; 1942 Doolittle Raid); The Pentagon Wars, 1998 (made-for-TV); **The Perfect Storm**, 2000; The Phantom Planet, 1961; Pixels, 2015; **Planet of the Apes**, 1968; **Planet of the Apes**, 2001; Project X, 1987; **The Purple Heart**, 1944 (WWII; Pacific Theater; 1942 Doolittle Raid); Red Tails, 2012 (WWII; Italian Theater); Rendezvous with Annie, 1946; **Rescue Dawn**, 2007; **The Right Stuff**, 1983 (test pilots and astronauts); Rolling Thunder, 1977; Sabre Jet, 1953 (Korean War); **Saigon**, 1948; **Saving Private Ryan**, 1998 (WWII; 1944 Normandy Invasion); **Sayonara**, 1957 (post-WWII Japan); **Seven Days in May**, 1964; Skyline, 2010; Sole Survivor, 1970 (made-for-TV); **The Spirit of St. Louis**, 1957; The Starfighters, 1964; Steve Canyon, 1958-1960 (TV series); Storm Catcher, 1999; **Strategic Air Command**, 1955; Stealth Fighter, 1999; **Super 8**, 2011; Superman IV: The Quest for Peace, 1987; Taken, 2002- (TV miniseries); **Test Pilot**, 1938; **The Thing from Another World**, 1951; **Thirty Seconds over Tokyo**, 1944

(WWII; Pacific Theater; 1942 Doolittle Raid); **To Each His Own**, 1946 (WWI; France); **Tora! Tora! Tora!**, 1970 (WWII; Pacific Theater); **Transformers**, 2007; **Twelve O'Clock High**, 1949 (WWII; European Theater); **20 Million Miles to Earth**, 1957; **The War Lover**, 1962 (WWII; European Theater); War Nurse, 1930 (WWI; France); **The War of the Worlds**, 1953; **The War of the Worlds**, 2005; Waterloo Bridge, 1931 (WWI; France); We'll Meet Again, 1982 (TV miniseries); **The Wild Blue Yonder**, 1951 (WWII; Pacific Theater); **Wings**, 1927 (WWI; France); X-15, 1961; **X2 X-Men United**, 2003.

U.S. Army (Also see West Point): **Abraham Lincoln**, 1930 (American Civil War; Union Army); **Across the Pacific**, 1926 (Philippine-American War); **Across the Pacific**, 1942 (WWII); All the Young Men, 1960 (Korean War); **Alvarez Kelly**, 1966 (American Civil War; Union Army); **America**, 1924 (American Revolutionary War); **American Sniper**, 2014 (Iraq War); Anzio, 1968 (WWII; Italian Theater); **Apocalypse Now**, 1979 (Vietnam War); **Arizona**, 1940 (American Civil War; Union Army); **Attack**, 1956 (WWII; European Theater); **Back to Bataan**, 1945 (WWII; Pacific Theater; Philippine Defense); The Bamboo Prison, 1954 (Korean War); **Band of Angels**, 1957 (American Civil War); **Bataan**, 1943 (WWII; Pacific Theater; Philippine Defense); Battle Circus, 1953 (Korean War); Battle Flame, 1959 (Korean War); The Battle of the Bulge, 1965 (WWII; European Theater); The Battle of the Last Panzer, 1969 (WWII; Italian Theater); Battle Taxi, 1955 (Korean War); Battle Zone, 1952 (Korean War); **Battleground**, 1949 (WWII; European Theater; Bastogne); Battleground 625, 2005 (Korean War); **Belle Starr**, 1941 (American Civil War; Union Army); **The Big Parade**, 1925 (WWI; France); **The Big Red One**, 1980 (WWII; North African Theater; Italian Theater; European Theater); **The Birth of a Nation**, 1915 (American Civil War; Union Army); **Blockheads**, 1938 (WWI; France); Blood of Bataan, 1953 (WWII; Pacific Theater; Philippine Defense); **Breakthrough**, 1950 (WWII; European Theater); **The Bridge at Remagen**, 1969 (WWII; Germany); **A Bridge Too Far**, 1977 (WWII; European Theater); Bus to Bataan, 1961 (WWII; Pacific Theater; Philippine Defense); **Castle Keep**, 1969 (WWII; European Theater); **Casualties of War**, 1989 (Vietnam War); A Christmas Visitor, 2002 (made-for-TV; Gulf War); Closed Doors, 1999 (Gulf War); **Cold Mountain**, 2003 (American Civil War; Union Army); Collision Course: Truman vs. MacArthur, 1976 (made-for-TV; Korean War); Combat Squad, 1953 (Korean War); Corregidor, 1943 (WWII; Pacific Theater; Philippine Defense); **Courage Under Fire**, 1996 (Gulf War); The Crossing, 2000 (made-for-TV; American Revolutionary War); **Cry Havoc**, 1943 (WWII; Pacific Theater; Philippine Defense); **D-Day; The Sixth of June**, 1956 (WWII; European Theater; 1994 Normandy Invasion); **Dances with Wolves**, 1990 (American Civil War; Union Army); **The Deer Hunter**, 1979 (Vietnam War); **The Devil's Disciple**, 1959 (American Revolutionary War); **Doughboys**, 1930 (WWI; France); **Drums Along the Mohawk**, 1939 (American Revolutionary War); **Drums in the Deep South**, 1951 (American Civil War; Union Army); Eight Iron Men, 1952 (WWII; Italian Theater); The Enemy General, 1960 (WWII); Everyman's War, 2009 (WWII; European Theater); **Field of Lost Shoes**, 2014 (American Civil War; Union Army); **The Fighting 69th**, 1940 (WWI; France); **Fixed Bayonets!**, 1951 (Korean War); **Four Sons**, 1928 (WWI; France); **From Here to Eternity**, 1953 (WWII; Pacific Theater: 1941 Pearl Harbor attack); **Full Metal Jacket**, 1987 (Vietnam War); **Fury**, 2014 (WWII; Germany); **The General**, 1926 (American Civil War; Union Army); **Gettysburg**, 1993 (American Civil War; Union Army); **Glory**, 1989 (American Civil War; Union Army); **The Glory Brigade**, 1953 (Korean War); **Go for Broke**, 1951 (WWII; Italian Theater; European Theater); **Go Tell the Spartans**, 1978 (Vietnam War); **Gods and Generals**, 2003 (American Civil War; Union Army); **The Good, the Bad and the Ugly**, 1967 (American Civil War; Union Army); **Gone with the Wind**, 1939 (American Civil War; Union Army); **The Great Imposter**, 1961 (Korean War); **The Great Locomotive Chase**, 1956 (American Civil War; Union Army); The Great

Love, 1918 (WWI; France); The Greatest Thing in Life, 1918 (WWI; France); **The Green Berets**, 1968 (Vietnam War); **Half Shot at Sunrise**, 1930 (WWI; France); **Hamburger Hill**, 1987 (Vietnam War); **Hart's War**, 2002 (WWII); **Heartbreak Ridge**, 1986 (Korean War); A Hill in Korea, 1956; **Hold Back the Night**, 1956 (Korean War); The Hook, 1963 (Korean War); **How the West Was Won**, 1962 (American Civil War; Union Army); **The Howards of Virginia**, 1940 (American Revolutionary War); Ike: Countdown to D-Day, 2004 (made-for-TV; WWII; 1944 Normandy Invasion); Inchon, 1982 (Korean War); **Independence Day**, 1996; **Janice Meredith**, 1924 (American Revolutionary War); Johnny Got His Gun, 1971 (WWI; France); **Johnny Tremaine**, 1957 (American Revolutionary War); **Journey to Shiloh**, 1968 (American Civil War; Union Army); Legends of the Fall, 1995 (WWI; France); Liberty!, The American Revolution, 1997 (TV miniseries); **The Little Colonel**, 1935 (American Civil War; Union Army); **Little Women**, 1933 (American Civil War; Union Army); **Little Women**, 1949 (American Civil War; Union Army); **Little Women**, 1994 (American Civil War; Union Army); **The Littlest Rebel**, 1935 (American Civil War; Union Army); **The Longest Day**, 1962 (WWII; European Theater; 1944; Normandy Invasion); The Lost Battalion, 2001 (made-for-TV; WWI; France); **MacArthur**, 1977 (WWII; Pacific Theater; Korean War); A Man from Wyoming, 1930 (WWI; France); **The Manchurian Candidate**, 1962 (Korean War); **Men in War**, 1957 (Korean War); A Message to Garcia, 1936 (Spanish-American War); **A Midnight Clear**, 1992 (WWII; European Theater); **The Monuments Men**, 2014 (WWII; European Theater); **Mysterious Island**, 1961 (American Civil War; Union Army); **Of Human Hearts**, 1938 (American Civil War; Union Army); **One Minute to Zero**, 1952 (Korean War); **The Outriders**, 1950 (American Civil War; Union Army); **Pack Up Your Troubles**, 1932 (WWI; France); Pack Up Your Troubles, 1939 (WWI; France); **The Patriot**, 2000 (American Revolutionary War); **Patton**, 1970 (WWII; North African Theater; European Theater); **Pilgrimage**, 1933 (WWI; France); **Platoon**, 1986 (Vietnam War); **Pork Chop Hill**, 1959 (Korean War); **The Prisoner of Shark Island**, 1936 (American Civil War; Union Army); **Prisoner of War**, 1954 (Korean War); **The Rack**, 1956 (Korean War); **The Raid**, 1954 (American Civil War; Union Army); **Raintree County**, 1957 (American Civil War; Union Army); **The Real Glory**, 1939 (Philippine-American War); **The Red Badge of Courage**, 1951 (American Civil War; Union Army); **Retreat!**, 2012 (Korean War); **Retreat, Hell!**, 1952 (Korean War); The Reluctant Heroes, 1971 (made-for-TV; Korean War); **Ride with the Devil**, 1999 (American Civil War; Union Army); Roaring Rails, 1924 (WWI; France); **The Roaring Twenties**, 1939 (WWI; France); **Rocky Mountain**, 1950 (American Civil War; Union Army); The Rough Riders, 1927 (Spanish-American War); Rough Riders, 1997 (made-for-TV; Spanish-American War); **Saints and Soldiers**, 2005 (WWII; European Theater); **Saving Lincoln**, 2013 (American Civil War; Union Army); **Saving Private Ryan**, 1998 (WWII; 1944 Normandy Invasion); **The Scarlet Coat**, 1955 (American Revolutionary War); **Sergeant York**, 1941 (WWI; France); She Goes to War, 1929 (WWI; France); **Shoulder Arms**, 1918 (WWI; France); **The Siege of Firebase Gloria**, 1989 (Vietnam War); Silent Night, 2002 (made-for-TV; WWII; European Theater); **So Proudly We Hail**, 1943 (WWII; Pacific Theater; Philippine Defense); **Somewhere I'll Find You**, 1942 (WWII; Pacific Theater; Philippine Defense); Sons o' Guns, 1936 (WWI; France); **A Southern Yankee**, 1948 (American Civil War; Union Army); **Springfield Rifle**, 1952 (American Civil War; Union Army); **Stalag 17**, 1953 (WWII); **The Steel Helmet**, 1951 (Korean War); **The Story of G.I. Joe**, 1945 (WWII; Italian Theater); **Stripes**, 1981; **Take the High Ground!**, 1953 (Korean War); Tank Battalion, 1958 (Korean War); Target Zero, 1955 (Korean War); **Tennessee Johnson**, 1942 (American Civil War; Union Army); Texas to Bataan, 1942 (WWII; Pacific Theater; Philippine Defense); **They Died with Their Boots On**, 1941 (American Civil War; Union Army); **They Gave Him a Gun**, 1937 (WWI; France); **Three Kings**, 1999 (Gulf War); **Time Limit**, 1957 (Korean War); **The Time of Their Lives**, 1946 (American

Revolutionary War); **To Hell and Back**, 1955 (WWII; North African Theater; Italian Theater; European Theater); **Tora! Tora! Tora!**, 1970 (WWII; Pacific Theater; 1941 Pearl Harbor attack); **Two Arabian Knights**, 1927 (WWI; France); **Up Front**, 1951 (WWII; Italian Theater); **The Victors**, 1963 (WWII; Italian Theater; European Theater); **A Walk in the Sun**, 1945 (WWII; Italian Theater); War and Remembrance, 1988 (TV miniseries; WWII); **War Hunt**, 1962 (Korean War); **War Is Hell**, 1963 (Korean War); **We Were Soldiers**, 2002 (Vietnam War); **White Christmas**, 1954 (WWII); Women of Valor, 1986 (made-for-TV; WWII; Pacific Theater; Philippine Defense); A Yank in Korea, 1951; **Yellow Jack**, 1938 (Spanish-American War); You Are There, 1953-1971 (TV series; "The Surrender of Corregidor, May 6, 1942," 1954 episode; WWII; Pacific Theater; Philippine Defense); The Young and the Brave, 1963 (Korean War); **The Young Lions**, 1958 (WWII; European Theater).

U.S. Cavalry: **Abraham Lincoln**, 1930; Ambush at Cimarron Pass, 1958; **Annie Get Your Gun**, 1950; **Annie Oakley**, 1935; **Apache**, 1954; Apache Drums, 1941; Apache Rifles, 1964; Apache Territory, 1958; **Arizona**, 1940; Army Girl, 1938; **Around the World in 80 Days**, 1956; **Arrowhead**, 1953 (U.S. Cavalry during the Indian Wars); Backlash, 1956; Bad Lands, 1939; Badlands of Dakota, 1941 (Custer; 7th U.S. Cavalry); The Battle at Apache Pass, 1952; Battle of Rogue River, 1954; The Black Dakotas, 1954; Boots and Saddles, 1937; **Broken Arrow**, 1950; **Buffalo Bill**, 1944; Buffalo Soldiers, 1979 (made-for-TV); Buffalo Soldiers, 1997 (made-for-TV); Bugles in the Afternoon, 1952; Bury My Heart at Wounded Knee, 2007 (made-for-TV); Caught, 1931; Cavalier of the West, 1931; Cavalry Command, 1958; Cavalry Patrol, 1956 (made-for-TV); Cavalry Scout, 1951; **Cheyenne Autumn**, 1964 (John Ford); Chief Crazy Horse, 1955; Code of the Silver Sage, 1950; Column South, 1953; Comanche, 1956; **The Command**, 1954; Copper Sky, 1957; Custer of the West, 1967 (Custer Massacre; 7th U.S. Cavalry); Custer's Last Stand, 1936 (7th U.S. Cavalry); **Dances with Wolves**, 1990; Daredevils of the West, 1943; Day of the Evil Gun, 1968; Driftin' River, 1946; **Duel in the Sun**, 1946; End of the Trail, 1932; **Escape from Fort Bravo**, 1953; Escort West, 1959; Fighting Pioneers, 1935; The Flaming Frontier, 1926; Flaming Lead, 1939; Fool's Gold, 1947; **Fort Apache**, 1948 (John Ford; recreation of Custer Massacre); Fort Bowie, 1958; Fort Courageous, 1965; 40 Guns to Apache Pass, 1967; Frontiers of '49, 1939; **Fury at Furnace Creek**, 1948; **Geronimo**, 1939 (footage from **The Plainsman**, 1936); **Geronimo: An American Legend**, 1993; Galloping Thunder, 1946; The Glory Trail, 1936; The Great Sioux Massacre, 1965 (Custer Massacre; 7th U.S. Cavalry); The Gun That Won the West, 1955; The Hallelujah Trail, 1965; Hands across the Border, 1926; The Heart of Texas Ryan, 1917; Heart of the Sunset, 1918; Heroes of the West, 1932; **Hidalgo**, 2004; **The Horse Soldiers**, 1959 (John Ford); **How the West Was Won**, 1962; In Old Monterey, 1939; **The Iron Horse**, 1924 (John Ford); Kansas Raiders, 1950; King of the Bandits, 1947; **Kit Carson**, 1940; Landrush, 1946; The Last Frontier, 1926; The Last Frontier, 1932; The Last Frontier, 1955; **The Last Outpost**, 1951; Law and Order, 1942; Lawless Plainsmen, 1942; The Legend of Custer, 1968 (7th U.S. Cavalry); **Little Big Man**, 1970 (Custer Massacre; 7th U.S. Cavalry); **Little Big Horn**, 1951 (Custer massacre; 7th U.S. Cavalry); **The Lone Ranger**, 2013; **Major Dundee**, 1965; The Man behind the Gun, 1953; **The Man from Laramie**, 1955; The Man from Monterey, 1933; Man with the Steel Whip, 1954; The Michigan Kid, 1947; Mr. Horn, 1979 (made-for-TV; Tom Horn); New Mexico, 1951; One Little Indian, 1973; **Only the Valiant**, 1951; Oregon Passage, 1957; The Oregon Trail, 1939; **The Plainsman**, 1936 (Custer Massacre; 7th U.S. Cavalry); The Plunderers, 1948; Quincannon, Frontier Scout, 1956; The Raiders, 1963; Ranson's Folly, 1926; **The Red Badge of Courage**, 1951; (U.S. and Confederate cavalry during the Civil War); Red Tomahawk, 1967; Renegades of the Sage, 1949; Ride, Ranger, Ride, 1936; Riders of the Dark, 1928; **Rio Grande**, 1950 (John Ford); Roll Wagons

Roll, 1940; The Roundup, 1941; **Run of the Arrow**, 1957; Saddlemates, 1941; **Santa Fe Trail**, 1940; The Savage, 1952; **The Searchers**, 1956 (John Ford); **Sergeant Rutledge**, 1960; Sergeants 3, 1962; **7th Cavalry**, 1956; **She Wore a Yellow Ribbon**, 1949 (John Ford); **Shenandoah**, 1965; Shoot-Out at Medicine Bend, 1957; Siege at Red River, 1954; Silver Canyon, 1951; Sitting Bull, 1954 (Custer Massacre; 7th U.S. Cavalry); Smoke Signal, 1955; Son of the Morning Star, 1991 (made-for-TV; Custer Massacre; 7th U.S. Cavalry); **Springfield Rifle**, 1952; **Stagecoach**, 1939 (John Ford); Swing in the Saddle, 1944; Taza, Son of Cochise, 1954; Texas across the River, 1966; **There Was a Crooked Man**, 1970; **They Came to Cordura**, 1959; **They Died with Their Boots On**, 1941 (Custer Massacre; 7th U.S. Cavalry); They Rode West, 1954; A Time for Killing, 1967; **Tomahawk**, 1951; Treachery Rides the Range, 1936; Treason, 1933; **Trooper Hook**, 1957; Troopers Three, 1930; **Two Flags West**, 1950; Ulzana's Raid, 1972; **The Undefeated**, 1969; **Union Pacific**, 1939; Via Pony Express, 1933; **Virginia City**, 1940; War Arrow, 1953; **Wells Fargo**, 1937; West of Cimarron, 1941; Westbound Stage, 1939; **Western Union**, 1941; White Eagle, 1932; White Feather, 1955; **The Wild Bunch**, 1969; Wild Horse Rustlers, 1943; Wild Stallion, 1952; With Buffalo Bill on the U.P. Trail, 1926; Yellowstone Kelly, 1959.

U.S. Coast Guard: The Agronomist, 2003; **Amelia**, 2009; Assault on a Queen, 1966; The Beach Girls, 1982; The Beast from 20,000 Fathoms, 1953; Beneath the 12-Mile Reef, 1953; The Big Broadcast of 1936, 1935; Bitter Sugar, 1996; **Black Sunday**, 1977; The Boatniks, 1970; **The Breaking Point**, 1950; Casey of the Coast Guard, 1926; City without Men, 1943; Clear and Present Danger, 1994; Coast Guard, 1939; **Cocoon**, 1985; **The Company You Keep**, 2012; Daylight, 1996; Deadliest Sea, 2009 (made-for-TV); Don Winslow of the Coast Guard, 1943 (serial); **Double Jeopardy**, 1999; Fighting Coast Guard, 1951; The Finest Hours, 2016; Gambling on the High Seas, 1940; The Guardian, 2006; The Gun Runners, 1958; Harbor Command, 1957- (TV series); **The High and the Mighty**, 1954; I Still Know What You Did Last Summer, 1998; Into the Blue, 2005; Irish Whiskey Rebellion, 1972; The Island, 1980; Islander, 2006; Islands in the Stream, 1977; The Last Flight of Noah's Ark, 1980; Lethal Weapon 4, 1998; Leviathan, 1989; **Licence to Kill**, 1989; Lucky Lady, 1975; Meteor, 1979; Motor Madness, 1937; **The Navigator**, 1924; Misty, 1961; Onionhead, 1958; Pain & Gain, 2013; **The Perfect Storm**, 2000; Perils of the Coast Guard, 1926; Red Eye, 2005; Rescue from Gilligan's Island, 1978 (made-for-TV); Safe Harbor, 2009 (made-for-TV); Sea Devils, 1937; The Sea Hornet, 1951; Sea of Lost Ships, 1953; Sea Spoilers, 1936; Sea Racketeers, 1937; Sea Raiders, 1941 (serial); Sky Raiders, 1941 (serial); Smuggler's Gold, 1951; SOS Coast Guard, 1937 (serial); SOS Coast Guard, 1942; Spartan, 2004; Special Bulletin, 1983 (made-for-TV); **A Summer Place**, 1959; Super Shark, 2011; Swamp Fire, 1946; **Too Hot to Handle**, 1938; The Triangle, 2001 (made-for-TV); Twelve Miles Out, 1927; Waking the Dead, 2000; Waterfront, 1954-1956 (TV series); When Tomorrow Comes, 1939; **White Squall**, 1996; **The Woman on the Beach**, 1947; **Yours, Mine and Ours**, 1968; Yours, Mine and Ours, 2005.

U.S. House Un-American Activities Committee (HUAC; 1938-1975): **Barton Fink**, 1991; Big Jim McLain, 1952; **The Big Knife**, 1955; Career, 1959; Chaplin, 1992; Citizen Cohn, 1992 (Roy Cohn); Dash and Lilly, 1999 (made-for-TV; Dashiell Hammett and Lillian Hellman); Fear on Trial, 1975 (made-for-TV); **The Front**, 1974; **Good Night, and Good Luck**, 2005; **The Great Debaters**, 2007; Guilty by Suspicion, 1991; **The House on Carroll Street**, 1988; **I Was a Communist for the F.B.I.**, 1951; **J. Edgar**, 2011 (J. Edgar Hoover); J. Edgar Hoover, 1987 (made-for-TV); Hoover, 2000 (J. Edgar Hoover); The Lives of Others, 2006; The Majestic, 2001; **Marathon Man**, 1976; **One of the Hollywood Ten**, 2000; Paul Robeson, 1979 (made-for-TV); **The Private Files of J. Edgar Hoover**, 1977; Tail Gunner Joe, 1977 (made-for-TV; Joseph McCarthy); **Three Brave Men**, 1956; **Trumbo**, 2015;

The Way We Were, 1973.

U.S. Marines: Air Devils, 1938; **Air Force**, 1943 (Marines at Wake Island); All the Young Men, 1960 (Korean War); Ambush Bay, 1966 (WWII; Philippines); **American Beauty**, 1999; **American Sniper**, 2014 (Iraq); American Son, 2008; Annapolis, 2006; Atlanta Convoy, 1942; **Battle Cry**, 1955 (WWII; Pacific Theater; Guadalcanal; Tarawa); Battle of Los Angeles, 2011; Beach Red, 1967; **Beachhead**, 1954 (WWII; Pacific Theater; Bougainville); **Black Hawk Down**, 2001 (Somalia, 1993); **Born on the Fourth of July**, 1989; The Boys in Company C, 1978; The Brig, 1964; Busses Roar, 1942; Call Out the Marines, 1942; Charo and the Sergeant, 1976 (made-for-TV); The Cock-Eyed World, 1929; Come On, Leathernecks!, 1938; Come On, Marines!, 1934; Company K, 2004; Coronado, 1935; Corregidor, 1943 (WWII; Philippine Defense, 1941-1942); Cover-Up, 1991; Crazylegs, 1953 (Elroy Hirsch); **Cuban Love Song**, 1931; **The D.I.**, 1957; Death before Dishonor, 1987; **Devil Dogs of the Air**, 1935; Dog Tags, 2008; Down in San Diego, 1941; **A Few Good Men**, 1992; **55 Days at Peking**, 1963 (China; Boxer Rebellion, 1900); Fighting Coastguard, 1951; The Fighting Devil Dogs, 1938; The Fighting Devil Dogs, 1943; The Fighting Marines, 1935; **First to Fight**, 1967 (WWII; Pacific Theater; Guadalcanal); **Flags of Our Fathers**, 2006 (WWII; Pacific Theater; Iwo Jima); **Flight**, 1929; **Flying Leathernecks**, 1951 (WWII; Pacific Theater; Guadalcanal); The Flying Marine, 1929; **Full Metal Jacket**, 1987 (Vietnam); Fury to Freedom, 1985 (Vietnam); The Girls of Pleasure Island, 1953 (Pacific Island where Marines are building an air base in 1945); **Good Morning, Vietnam**, 1987; Green Dragon, 2001; **Guadalcanal Diary**, 1943; **Gung Ho!**, 1943 (WWII; Pacific Theater; Carlson's Makin Island Raid); A Guy, a Gal and a Pal, 1945; **Hail the Conquering Hero**, 1944; **Halls of Montezuma**, 1950 (WWII; Pacific Theater; Okinawa); **Heartbreak Ridge**, 1986; **Heaven Knows, Mr. Allison**, 1957 (WWII; Pacific Island); Hell to Eternity, 1960 (Guy Gabaldon at Saipan); Here Come the Marines, 1952; Highway Dragnet, 1954; Hot Pepper, 1933; Ice Station Zebra, 1968; **If I Had a Million**, 1932; **In Harm's Way**, 1965; Instant Justice, 1986; **The Iron Major**, 1943; Island of Desire, 1952; Isle of Destiny, 1940; **Jarhead**, 2005; Johnny Doesn't Live Here Anymore, 1944; Lady Be Careful, 1936; The Last Castle, 2001; A Line in the Sand, 2009; Loot, 1919; Lost Battalion, 1962 (WWII; Philippines); Maisie Goes to Reno, 1944; Major Payne, 1995; The Marine, 2006; **Marine Raiders**, 1944 (WWII; Pacific Theater; Guadalcanal, 1942; Solomon Islands, 1943); A Marine Story, 2010; The Marines Are Coming, 1934; The Marines Are Here, 1938; The Marines Fly High, 1940; Marines, Let's Go, 1961; Max, 2015 (Afghanistan); Memorial Day, 1983 (made-for-TV); **Miss Sadie Thompson**, 1953; Most Wanted, 1997; **1941**, 1979; None But the Brave, 1965; Operation C.I.A., 1965; **The Outsider**, 1961 (WWII; Pacific Theater; Iwo Jima; Ira Hamilton Hays); The Pacific, 2010 (TV cable series; John Basilone at Guadalcanal and Iwo Jima); Pacific Rendezvous, 1942; Parachute Jumper, 1933; **Pride of the Marines**, 1945 (WWII; Pacific Theater; Al Schmid at Guadalcanal); The Profiteer, 1919; **Rain**, 1932; Red Dawn, 2012; **Retreat, Hell!**, 1952 (Korean War); Rosie the Riveter, 1944; Rules of Engagement, 2000; **Sadie Thompson**, 1928; Safe Passage, 1994; Salute to the Marines, 1943 (WWII; Philippine Defense, 1941-1942); **Sands of Iwo Jima**, 1949 (WWII; Pacific Theater; Tarawa and Iwo Jima); Sarge Goes to College, 1947; Semper Fi, 2001 (made-for-TV); **Seven Days in May**, 1964; **The Siege of Firebase Gloria**, 1989 (Vietnam); The Singing Marine, 1937; Slave Girl, 1947; Snafu, 1945; Sniper, 1993; Sniper: Reloaded, 2011; The Soldier, 1982; Soldiers and Women, 1930; **South Sea Woman**, 1953 (WWII; Pacific Theater; Guadalcanal); Stateside, 2004; The Steel Claw, 1961 (WWII; Pacific Theater; Philippines); Step by Step, 1946; The Story without a Name, 1924; **Strangers in the Night**, 1944; Sweethearts on Parade, 1930; Taking Chance, 2009 (made-for-TV; Michael Strobl); Tell It to the Marines, 1918; **Tell It to the Marines**, 1926 (China); **The Thin Red Line**, 1964 (WWII; Pacific Theater; Guadalcanal); **The Thin Red Line**, 1998 (WWII; Pacific Theater; Guadalcanal); Thunderbolt's Tracks, 1927; **To the Shores of Tripoli**, 1942; Tribes, 1970 (made-for-TV); Tripoli, 1950; True to the Navy, 1930; The Unbeliever, 1918 (WWI; France); United States Smith, 1928; The Walking Dead, 1995 (Vietnam); **Wake Island**, 1942 (WWII; Pacific Theater); War Dogs, 1942; **The War of the Worlds**, 1953; A Warm Wind, 2011; Warrior, 2011; A Wave, a WAC and a Marine, 1944; **We've Never Been Licked**, 1943; **What Price Glory**, 1926 (WWI; France); **What Price Glory**, 1952 (WWI; France); When the Lights Go On Again, 1944; **The Wind and the Lion**, 1975 (1904 Morocco; Perdicaris Affair); **Windtalkers**, 2002 (WWII; Pacific Theater; Saipan); Women of All Nations, 1931; **Yellow Jack**, 1938.

U.S. Navy (Also see Annapolis Naval Academy): Above the Clouds, 1933; **Action in the North Atlantic**, 1943 (WWII; Atlantic Theater); The Adventures of Smilin' Jack, 1943 (serial); Agent Red, 2000 (submarine); Air Strike, 1955; **Anchors Aweigh**, 1945; Annapolis, 2006; **Antwone Fisher**, 2002; Any Mother's Son, 1997 (made-for-TV); **Apollo 13**, 1995; Arthur Takes Over, 1948; Assault on the Wayne, 1971 (made-for-TV; Cold War; nuclear submarine); The Assignment, 1997; Atlantic Convoy, 1942; Away All Boats, 1952 (WWII; Pacific Theater); Battleship, 2012; **Back to Bataan**, 1945 (WWII; Pacific Theater; Leyte, Philippines Invasion of 1944; submarine); Barbary Pirate, 1949; Barcelona, 1994; Battle of the Coral Sea, 1959 (WWII; Pacific Theater); **The Bedford Incident**, 1965 (Cold War); **The Best Years of Our Lives**, 1946 (post-WWII); Big Jim McLain, 1952; Blood and Steel, 1959; Born to Dance, 1936; **The Bourne Legacy**, 2012; **The Bridge on the River Kwai**, 1957; **The Bridges at Toko-Ri**, 1954 (aircraft carrier in Korean War); Bring on the Girls, 1945; The Bushido Blade, 1981; **The Caine Mutiny**, 1954 (minesweeper, WWII; Pacific Theater); The Caine Mutiny Court-Martial, 1988 (made-for-TV); Captain America: Civil War, 2016 (space) **Captain Phillips**, 2013 (2009 hijacking by Somali pirates); Chasers, 1992; Chip Off the Old Block, 1944; **Cinderella Liberty**, 1973; Come On, Marines!, 1934; Coronado, 1935; **Corvette K-225** (WWII; Atlantic Theater); Countdown to Looking Glass, 1984 (made-for-TV); **Cover Girl**, 1944; Cover Up, 1991; CPO Sharkey, 1976-1978 (TV series); **Crash Dive**, 1943 (WWII; Atlantic Theater); **Crimson Tide**, 1995; Danger beneath the Sea, 2001 (made-for-TV); David Harding, Counterspy, 1950; The Deep Six, 1958 (WWII; Pacific Theater); **Destination Gobi**, 1953 (WWII); **Destination Tokyo**, 1943 (submarine; aircraft carriers; USS *Hornet*, CV-8); **Destroyer**, 1943 (WWII; Atlantic Theater); Devil and the Deep, 1932 (submarine); The Devil Pays Off, 1941; **Dirigible**, 1931; **Dive Bomber**, 1941 (pre-WWII); Don Winslow of the Navy, 1942 (serial); **Don't Go Near the Water**, 1957 (WWII); Down Periscope, 1996 (submarine); Duke of the Navy, 1942; Emerald Point, N.A.S., 1983-1984 (TV series); **Empire of the Sun**, 1987 (WWII); **The Enemy Below**, 1957 (destroyer; WWII; Atlantic Theater); Ensign Pulver, 1964; Fast Life, 1932; **Father Goose**, 1964 (WWII; Pacific Theater; submarine); **A Few Good Men**, 1992; **The Fighting Seabees**, 1944; The Final Countdown, 1980 (nuclear aircraft carrier taken back in time to WWII); The First Olympics: Athens, 1896, 1984 (made-for-TV); **Flat Top**, 1952 (USS *Princeton*, CV-37; in WWII and Korean War); Flight of the Intruder, 1991 (Vietnam War); **Follow the Boys**, 1944; Follow the Boys, 1963; **Follow the Fleet**, 1936; For the Love of Mary, 1948; Free For All, 1949; Freedom Strike, 1998; G.I. Jane, 1997 (Navy Seals); **Gabriel over the White House**, 1933; A Glimpse of Hell, 2001 (made-for-TV); Godzilla, 1998; **Godzilla**, 2014; Going Under, 1990 (Cold War; submarine); Goldie, 1931; Goodbye America, 1997 (Subic Bay, Philippines); The Gorgeous Hussy, 1936; Gray Lady Down, 1978 (nuclear submarine); **Gung Ho!**, 1943 (Makin Island Raid; WWII; Pacific Theater; submarines); Handsome Harry, 2009; A Harem Knight, 1926; Hell and High Water, 1964 (Pacific; Cold War); Hell and High Water, 1954 (Cold War; submarine); **Hell Below**, 1933 (submarines); Hell below Zero, 1954; Hellcats of the Navy, 1957 (WWII; Pacific Theater; submarine); **Here Come the Waves**, 1944; **Here Comes the Navy**, 1934 (helium-filled naval airships, USS *Macon*; dirigibles); **Hit the Deck**, 1955; Homicide for Three, 1948; The Honeymoon Machine, 1961; Hostile Waters, 1997 (made-for-TV; nuclear submarines); **The House on 92nd Street**, 1945; **The Hunt for Red October**, 1990; Hurricane, 1974 (made-for-TV); I Was an American Spy, 1951; Ice Station Zebra, 1968 (nuclear submarine); In Enemy Hands, 2004 (WWII; Atlantic Theater); **In Harm's Way**, 1965 (cruisers, destroyers, PT-boats in WWII; Pacific Theater); **The Incredible Mr. Limpet**, 1964 (WWII; Pacific Theater); Intrepid, 2000; Island of Desire, 1952; Isle of Destiny, 1940; JAG, 1995-2005 (TV series; Navy's Judge Advocate General's office); **John Paul Jones**, 1959; Johnny Doesn't Live Here Anymore, 1944; **The Last Detail**, 1973; **Letters from Iwo Jima**, 2006 (WWII; Pacific Theater); **Lone Survivor**, 2013 (Navy Seals in Afghan War); Lorelei: The Witch of the Pacific Ocean, 2005 (WWII; submarine); Madame Butterfly, 1995; Madame Spy, 1942; **Marie Galante**, 1934 (Panama Canal); The Marines Are Coming, 1934; **The Master**, 2012 (post-WWII); McHale's Navy, 1962-1966 (TV series; PT-boats; WWII); McHale's Navy, 1997 (PT-boats; WWII); **Midway**, 1976 (aircraft carriers in WWII, Pacific Theater; USS *Enterprise*, CV-6; USS *Hornet*, CV-8; USS *Yorktown*, CV-5); Minesweeper, 1943; Miss V from Moscow, 1942; **Mister Roberts**, 1955 (WWII; Pacific Theater); Mister Roberts, 1984 (made-for-TV); Mother Carey's Chickens, 1938; Murder in the Fleet, 1935; Murder on the Waterfront, 1943; Mutiny, 1999 (made-for-TV; fifty Afro-American sailors court-martialed following their refusal to load munitions after the disastrous July 17, 1944, explosion in San Francisco); Navy Blues, 1929; Navy Blues, 1941; Navy Born, 1936; Navy Bound, 1951; The Navy Comes Through, 1942; Navy Seals, 1990; Navy Secrets, 1939; Navy Spy, 1937; The Navy vs. the Night Monsters, 1966; The Navy Way, 1944; NCIS, 2003- (TV series; Naval Criminal Investigative Service); NCIS: Los Angeles, 2009- (TV series; Naval Criminal Investigative Service); NCIS: New Orleans, 2014- (TV series; Naval Criminal Investigative Service); Never Say Never Again, 1983; **1941**, 1979; **No Man Is an Island**, 1962 (George Tweed; WWII; Guam in the Pacific Theater); **No Way Out**, 1987; Okinawa, 1952 (WWII; Pacific Theater); **On an Island with You**, 1948; On the Beach, 1959 (submarine); On the High Seas, 1922; **On the Town**, 1949; Operation Bikini, 1963; **Operation Pacific**, 1951 (submarine in WWII, Pacific Theater); **Operation Petticoat**, 1959 (submarine in WWII; Pacific Theater); Out of Luck, 1923; The Pacific, 2010- (TV miniseries; WWII); Pacific Rendezvous, 1942; **Pearl Harbor**, 2001 (battleships; cruisers, destroyers, aircraft carrier in WWII, Pacific Theater; USS *Hornet*, CV-8 in Doolittle Raid); The Phantom Submarine, 1940; The Philadelphia Experiment, 1984; Pixels, 2015; Prisoner of Japan, 1942; The Profiteer, 1919; **PT-109**, 1963 (John F. Kennedy; WWII; Pacific Theater); **The Purple Heart**, 1944 (aircraft carrier in WWII, Pacific Theater; USS *Hornet*, CV-8); Red Sky, 2014; **Rescue Dawn**, 2007 (Vietnam War); Rickover: The Birth of Nuclear Power, 2014; Rip Roaring Riley, 1935; Rough, Tough and Ready, 1945; **Run Silent, Run Deep**, 1958 (WWII; Pacific Theater; submarine); A Sailor-Made Man, 1921; Sailor's Lady, 1940 (battleship); Sailors on Leave, 1941; **The Sand Pebbles**, 1966 (gunboat in 1926 China); Sea Raiders, 1941 (serial); Seal Team Eight: Behind Enemy Lines, 2014; Secret Agent of Japan, 1942; She Stood Alone: The Tailhook Scandal, 1995 (made-for-TV); She's in the Army, 1942; Ship of Wanted Men, 1933; Shore Leave, 1925; The Silent Command, 1923; Slave Girl, 1947; Solar Attack, 2006 (made-for-TV); **South Pacific**, 1958 (WWII); South Pacific, 2001 (made-for-TV); Sphere, 1998 (Space); Stand By All Networks, 1942; **Stand by for Action**, 1942 (WWII); Stateside, 2004; Stealth, 2005; Stealth Fighter, 1999; **Strangers in the Night**, 1944; **Submarine**, 1928; **Submarine Command**, 1951 (in WWII and Korean War); **Submarine D-1**, 1937; **Submarine Patrol**, 1938; Submarine Seahawk, 1958 (WWII; Pacific Theater); **Submarine X-1**, 1969 (WWII; Atlantic Theater); Suicide Fleet, 1931 (WWI; Atlantic Theater); **The Sullivans** (aka: The Fighting Sullivans), 1944 (cruiser USS *Juneau*, CL-52); Supercarrier, 1998- (TV series); Sweetheart of the Fleet, 1942; Swing Fever, 1943; Swing It, Sailor!, 1938; Tahiti Honey, 1943; Tars

and Spars, 1946; Tars and Stripes, 1935; **Task Force**, 1949 (aircraft carriers in pre-WWII and WWII; Pacific Theater; USS *Enterprise*, CV-6; USS *Franklin*, CV-13; USS *Hornet*, CV-8; USS *Langley*, CV-1; USS *Saratoga*, CV-3; USS *Yorktown*, CV-5); **Tears of the Sun**, 2003 (Navy Seals in rescue mission in Nigeria); **Tell It to the Marines**, 1926 (China); **They Were Expendable**, 1945 (PT-Boats in WWII, Philippine Defense; submarine); **Thirty Seconds over Tokyo**, 1944 (aircraft carrier in WWII; Pacific Theater; USS *Hornet*, CV-8); Too Young the Hero, 1988 (made-for-TV; Calvin Graham, who enlisted in the U.S. Navy at age twelve and served in the Pacific Theater in WWII); **Top Gun**, 1986 (jet fighter pilots); **Tora! Tora! Tora!**, 1970 (WWII; Pacific Theater; Pearl Harbor attack); **Torpedo Alley**, 1952 (WWII; Korean War); **Torpedo Run**, 1958 (WWII; Pacific Theater); Trinity: Gambling for High Stakes, 1978; Tripoli, 1950; True to the Navy, 1930; Turn Back the Hours, 1928; Under Siege, 1992 (Navy Seals); Undersea Girl, 1957; Undersea Kingdom, 1936 (serial); **Up Periscope**, 1959 (WWII; Pacific Theater); **Voyage to the Bottom of the Sea**, 1961 (nuclear submarine); Voyage to the Bottom of the Sea, 1964-1968 (TV series; nuclear submarine); The Wackiest Ship in the Army, 1960; **Wake Island**, 1942 (WWII; Pacific Theater); War and Remembrance, 1988- (TV miniseries); **The Way We Were**, 1973 (WWII); Weekend Pass, 1984; We're in the Navy Now, 1926; **West Point**, 1927; **We've Never Been Licked**, 1943; The Windjammer, 1945; The Winds of War, 1983- (TV miniseries); **Wing and a Prayer**, 1944 (aircraft carrier in WWII; Pacific Theater); **The Wings of Eagles**, 1957 (jeep carriers in WWII; Pacific Theater); Wings of the Navy, 1939; Wings over Honolulu, 1937; **World War Z**, 2013; **X-Men: First Class**, 2011; Yankee Buccaneer, 1952; The Yankee Consul, 1924; Yanks Ahoy, 1943; Yellow Fin, 1951; **You're in the Navy Now**, 1951 (submarine chaser).

U.S. Secret Service (since 1865; under the U.S. Department of the Treasury until 2003): **Absolute Power**, 1997; The Amazing Dr. G, 1968; Amazon, 2000; Assassination, 1987; Behind the Mask, 1932; The Best of the Post, 1960 (TV series; "Treasury Agent," 1960 episode); **Bethlehem**, 2013; Beverly Hills Cop III, 1994; The Big Hurt, 1988; Billy the Kid's Fighting Pals, 1941; The Bodyguard, 1992; The Bogus Green, 1951 (made-for-TV); Brake, 2012; Captain Midnight, 1942; Charlie Chan in the Secret Service, 1944; Chasing Liberty, 2004; C-Man, 1949; Counterfeit, 1919; Cover Me, 1999 (TV miniseries); Dangerous Money, 1946; Dark Skies, 1929; The Day Reagan Was Shot, 2001 (made-for-TV); The Defender, 2005; **Defense of the Realm**, 1986; The Double Man, 1968; Dude Cowboy, 1941; El 13-13, 1943; Ellis Island, 1936; Fastlane, 2002-2003 (TV series); Federal Agent in Charge, 1950; The File of the Golden Goose, 1969; Finger Prints, 1931; Front-Page Detective, 1951-1953 (TV series; "Seven Seas to Danger," 1952 episode); Gang Busters, 1942; **GoldenEye**, 1995; Ground Zero, 1973; Ground Zero, 1987; Guns for Dollars, 1975; Harbor Command, 1957-1958 (TV series; "Counterfeit Money," 1957 episode; "Decoy," 1958 episode); Hackers, 1995; Heaven's Fire, 1999 (made-for-TV); In Her Line of Fire, 2006; **In the Line of Fire**, 1993; IXE-13, 1972; **The In-Laws**, 1979; Johnny English, 2003; The Kid from Amarillo, 1951; The King of the Kongo, 1929; Killers from Space, 1954; King of the Carnival, 1955; Kisses for My President, 1964; La totale!, 1991; Lawless Valley, 1948; **Lethal Weapon 4**, 1998; The Living Daylights, 1987; Lockout, 2012; The Lost Special, 1932; Luck of the Draw, 2001; Make Mine a Double, 1961; Mexican Spitfire's Elephant, 1942; **Mister 880**, 1950; Murder in the Air, 1940; Octopussy, 1983; **Olympus Has Fallen**, 2013; One Spy Too Many, 1966; OSS: Cairo, Nest of Spies, 2006; Out of Sight, 1966; Outside the Law, 1956; The Peacekeeper, 1997; Perils of the Wilderness, 1956; Pirate Submarine, 1951; The President's Man, 2000 (made-for-TV); The Revenge of Al Capone, 1989 (made-for-TV); The Scarface Mob, 1959 (made-for-TV); The Secret Life of Ian Fleming, 1990; Secret Service, 1992-1993 (TV series); The Secret Service, 2004 (made-for-TV); Secret Service of the Air, 1939; The Sentinel, 2006; Shatter, 1975; The Silent Flyer, 1926; **Skyfall**, 2012; Society Smugglers, 1939; Special

Agent 7, 1958-1959 (TV series; "The Big Top," 1959 episode; "Border Masquerade," 1959 episode; "The Gold-Plated People," 1959 episode; "The Inside Man," 1959 episode; "The Lady from Louisville," 1959 episode; "The Longshoreman," 1959 episode; "Male Order," 1959 episode; "Material Witness," 1959 episode; "The One-Armed Paperhanger," 1959 episode; "The Solid Gold Crab," 1959 episode); Special Investigator, 1936; Spy Hard, 1996; **The Spy Who Loved Me**, 1977; Stagecoach to Monterey, 1944; **Suddenly**, 1954; Suddenly, 2013; **The Tall Blonde Man with One Black Shoe**, 1973; 13 Fighting Men, 1960; **This Is My Affair**, 1937; **Thunder Road**, 1958; **T-Men**, 1947; **To Live and Die in L.A.**, 1985; Tomorrow at Seven, 1933; Torchy Gets Her Man, 1938; Trailin' West, 1936; Under Mexicali Stars, 1950; **The Undercover Man**, 1949; The Untouchables, 1959-1963 (TV series); **The Untouchables**, 1987; The Untouchables, 1993-1994 (TV series); Vantage Point, 2008; The Warning, 1927; Wayward Pines, 2014 (TV series); The West Wing, 1999-2006 (TV series; "20 Hours in L.A.," 2000 episode; "In the Shadow of Two Gunmen," 2000 episode); **The Wet Parade**, 1932; When Eight Bells Toll, 1971; **White House Down**, 2013; **The World Is Not Enough**, 1999; The World of James Bond, 1995 (made-for-TV); **X-Men: Days of Future Past**, 2014; Yancy Derringer, 1958-1959 (TV series, "Two of a Kind," 1959 episode).

Vatican (The Holy See; the Catholic Church of Rome): The Abdication, 1974; **The Agony and the Ecstasy**, 1965; **Amen**, 2002; The Bankers of God: The Calvi Affair, 2002; **Becket**, 1964; Borgia, 2011- (TV series); The Borgias, 2011-2013 (TV series); **The Cardinal**, 1963; **Casanova**, 2005; The Conclave, 2006; The Conspirators, 1969; Da Vinci's Demons, 2013-2015 (TV series); Daens, 1992; Edges of the Lord, 2001; **Elizabeth**, 1998; Escape by Night, 1960; The Final Solution: The Wannsee Conference, 1984 (made-for-TV); From a Far Country, 1981; The Godfather: Part III, 1990; God's Mighty Servant, 2011 (made-for-TV); **Il Divo**, 2008; In the Name of the Pope King, 1977; Karol: The Pope, the Man, 2006 (made-for-TV); Luther, 2003; L'Age d'Or, 1930; Lucrezia giovane, 1974; The Missing, 1999; Monsignor, 1982; **The Ninth Day**, 2004; The Order, 2003; The Omen, 2006; Pope Joan, 2009; Pope John Paul II, 2005- (TV series); The Power of Few, 2013; Revelation, 2001; **Rosemary's Baby**, 1968; Saving Grace, 1986; The Scarlet and the Black, 1983 (made-for-TV); Secret File, 2003; **The Shoes of the Fishermen**, 1968; Stephen the Great, 1975; Stigmata, 1999; The Third Solution, 1988; To Rome with Love, 2012; **Van Helsing**, 2004; The Vatican, 2013; Vatican Conspiracy, 1982; The Vatican Tapes, 2015; We Have a Pope, 2011; When in Rome, 1952; Wide Awake, 1998; **Zelig**, 1983.

Virginia Military Institute (VMI; Lexington, Virginia; established 1839); heroic charge of the cadets at the Virginia Military Institute in Virginia's Shenandoah Valley at the Battle of New Market [May 15, 1864] during the American Civil War): **Field of Lost Shoes**, 2014; **The Horse Soldiers**, 1959 (role model for cadets in this film are from a military school in Mississippi).

West Point (U.S. Military Academy, West Point, N.Y., established March 16, 1802): Arizona, 1931; Army Girl, 1938; Assault at West Point: The Court-Martial of Johnson Whittaker, 1994 (made-for-TV); Benedict Arnold: A Question of Honor, 2003 (made-for-TV); Branded, 1965-1966 (TV series; "That the Brave Endure," 1965 episode); Cadet Girl, 1941; Class of '61, 1993 (made-for-TV); Come On, Leathernecks!, 1938; A Distant Trumpet, 1964; Dress Parade, 1927; **Flirtation Walk**, 1934; **God Is My Co-Pilot**, 1945; Hold 'Em Navy, 1937; Ike, 1986 (made-for-TV); King of Diamonds, 1961-1962 (TV series; "Guided Tour de Force," 1962 episode); **Knute Rockne—All American**, 1940; The Last Castle, 2001; **The Long Gray Line**, 1955; **MacArthur**, 1977; **Rosalie**, 1937; **Santa Fe Trail**, 1940; **The Scarlet Coat**, 1955 (Benedict Arnold); The Silence, 1975 (made-for-TV); The Spirit of West Point, 1947; Ten Gentlemen from West Point, 1942; **They Died with Their**

Boots On, 1941; War of 1812, 1999 (TV miniseries); **West Point**, 1927; West Point, 1956-1957 (TV series); **The West Point Story**, 1950; Wild Stallion, 1952; Women at West Point, 1979 (made-for-TV).

Yale University (New Haven, Connecticut; established in 1701): Accepted, 2006; Admissions, 2004; American Psycho, 2000; Another Earth, 2011; Bamboozled, 2000; **Chances Are**, 1989; The Company, 2007- (TV miniseries); Experimenter, 2015; **Flight**, 1929; **The Ghost Writer**, 2010; The Good Shepherd, 2006; The Great Gatsby, 2000 (made-for-TV); Head in the Clouds, 2004; **Hawaii**, 1966; Huddle, 1932; I as in Icarus, 1979; Laws of Attraction, 2004; **Lost in Translation**, 2003; Love, Honor and Behave, 1938; **Meet Me in St. Louis**, 1944; Mona Lisa Smile, 2003; **Night and Day**, 1946; **Pigskin Parade**, 1936; **Running on Empty**, 1988; The Skulls, 2000; **Splendor in the Grass**, 1961; The Sport Parade, 1932; Tarzan's Desert Mystery, 1943; Tenure, 2008; The Young Rajah, 1922.

Yakuza (criminal secret society in Japan since the 17th Century): **Across the Pacific**, 1942; **Adrenaline Drive**, 2000; American Yakuza, 1993; Armed Response, 1986; Battles without Honor and Humanity, 2004; Beyond Outrage, 2012; The Bird People in China, 1998; Black Rain, 1989; The Blind Swordsman: Zatoichi, 2004; Blue Tiger, 1994; Boiling Point, 1990; Branded to Kill, 1967; Brother, 2000; The Challenge, 1982; Chocolate, 2009; Cold Fish, 2011; Contract Killer, 1998; Crying Freeman, 1995; Dead or Alive, 2001; **Drunken Angel**, 1959; Everything's Gone Green, 2007; The Fast and the Furious: Tokyo Drift, 2006; Fighter in the Wind, 2004; Fireworks, 1998; The Five, 1998; Fudoh: The New Generation, 1996; Ghost in the Shell, 1995; Ghost in the Shell: Innocence, 2004; Gozu, 2003; Graveyard of Honor, 2003; The Hoodlum Soldier, 1974; Ichi the Killer, 2003; Into the Sun, 2005; Kids Return, 1996; Last Life in the Universe, 2004; Like a Dragon, 2010; My Wife Is a Gangster, 2001; Naked Weapon, 2002; Nameless Gangster: Rules of the Time, 2012; Ninja, 2009; Ninja Assassin, 2009; No Way Back, 1995; Outrage, 2010; Pairan, 2001; Pale Flower, 2005; Pigs and Battleships, 1963; Predators, 2010; The Punisher, 1989; Rain Fall, 2009; Rainy Dog, 1997; Red Sun Rising, 1994; Rising Sun, 1993; RoboCop 3, 1993; Samurai Cop, 1991; Shinjuku Incident, 2010; Showdown in Little Tokyo, 1991; The Slammin' Salmon, 2009; **Sonatine**, 1998; A Stranger of Mine, 2005; The Taste of Tea, 2004; **A Taxing Woman**, 1987; Tokyo Decadence, 1993; **Tokyo Drifter**, 1966; Tokyo Godfathers, 2003; Versus, 2002; War, 2007; Wasabi, 2002; Why Don't You Play in Hell?, 2013; **The Wolverine**, 2013; **The Yakuza**, 1975; Yakuza Apocalypse, 2015; Yakuza Weapon, 2011; Younger and Younger, 1993; Youth of the Beast, 1963; Zatoichi, 1989. For detailed information on Yakuza, see my two-volume work *The Great Pictorial History of World Crime*, Volume II (History, Inc., 2004; illustrated pages 1471-1474).

LINES THAT LIVE FOREVER

Note: The following annotated index, exclusively (and manually) created by the author, offers some of the most memorable lines delivered in theatrically released feature films (chiefly U.S. and British releases, along with notable foreign productions, showing U.S. year of release). All titles shown in boldface represent entries profiled in this work.

Adam's Rib, 1949; Katharine Hepburn, as criminal defense attorney Amanda Bonner, to Judy Holliday, as housewife Doris Attinger, who has recently shot and wounded her philandering husband: "After you shot your husband...how did you feel?" And to which Holliday replies: "Hungry!"...David Wayne, as Kip Laurie, sarcastic suitor of lawyer Hepburn, who is married to lawyer Spencer Tracy: "Lawyers should never marry other lawyers. This is called in-breeding. From this comes idiot children...and other lawyers."

The Adventures of Robin Hood, 1938; Errol Flynn, as Robin Hood, to tyrant Claude Rains, as Prince John, who has usurped the throne of his brother, Richard the Lionheart: "I'll organize revolt, exact a death for a death, and I'll never rest until every Saxon in this shire can stand up free men and strike a blow for Richard and England...I'm only just beginning. From this night forward I'll use every means in my power to fight you!"

The Adventures of Sherlock Holmes, 1939; Basil Rathbone, as the inimitable detective, to eternal companion, Nigel Bruce, playing Dr. John Watson, after solving a complex crime: "Elementary, my dear Watson!"

The African Queen, 1951; Humphrey Bogart as Charlie Allnut, while drunk and enraged at Katharine Hepburn, as prim and proper missionary Rose Sayer: "Well, I ain't sorry for you no more, you crazy psalm-singing, skinny, old maid!"...Bogart, also in his cups, to Hepburn: "What an absurd idea! What an absurd idea! Lady, I may be a born fool, but you got ten absurd ideas to my one, and don't you forget it!"

The Alamo, 1960; John Wayne, as Davy Crockett: "Republic. I like the sound of the word. It means that people can live free, talk free, go or come, buy or sell, be drunk or sober, however they choose. Some words give you a feeling. Republic is one of those words that makes me feel tight in the throat—the same tightness a man gets when his baby takes his first step, or his first baby shaves and makes his first sound as a man. Some words can give you a feeling that makes your heart warm. Republic is one of those words."

All About Eve, 1950; Bette Davis to friends at a party and how she intends to vent her anger: "Fasten your seatbelts. It's going to be a bumpy night."

All the King's Men, 1949; Broderick Crawford as Willie Stark (who becomes the dictatorial governor of a Southern state, not unlike Huey Long of Louisiana), while running for office and addressing a group of rural voters: "Now, shut up! Shut up, all of you! Now listen to me, you hicks! Yeah, you're hicks, too, and they [his political adversaries] fooled you a thousand times like they fooled me. But this time, I'm going to fool somebody. I'm going to stay in this race. I'm on my own and I'm out for blood!"

All the President's Men, 1976; Jason Robards Jr., as Washington *Post* editor Ben Bradlee: "...when is someone going to go on record in this story? You guys are about to write a story that says that the former Attorney General, the highest-ranking law enforcement officer in this country, is a crook! Just be sure you're right."

All Quiet on the Western Front, 1930; Lewis Ayres, as war-embittered veteran Paul Baumer, to a classroom of students after briefly returning from the front: "I shouldn't have come on leave. Up at the front you're either alive or you're dead and that's all. You can't fool anybody about that very long. And up there we know that we're lost and done for whether we're dead or alive. Three years we've had of it, four years! And every day a year, and every night a century! And our bodies are earth, and our thoughts are clay, and we sleep and eat with death! And we're done for because you can't live that way and keep anything inside you! I shouldn't have come on leave. I'll go back tomorrow. I've got four days more, but I can't stand it here! I'll go back tomorrow! I'm sorry."

Amadeus, 1984; Tom Hulce, as Wolfgang Amadeus Mozart, to Jeffrey Jones, as Austrian Emperor Joseph II: "Forgive me, Majesty. I am a vulgar man! But, I assure you, my music is not." And to which Jones replies: "You are passionate, Mozart, but you do not persuade..."

American Graffiti, 1973; Mackenzie Phillips, as Carol: "Your car is uglier than I am!"

An American in Paris, 1951; Gene Kelly as American expatriate artist Jerry Mulligan: "Back home everyone said I didn't have any talent. They might be saying the same thing over here, but it sounds better in French."...Oscar Levant, as Adam Cook: "I'm a concert pianist. That's a pretentious way of saying I'm...unemployed at the moment."...Levant, about his own appearance: "It's not a pretty face, I grant you, but underneath its flabby exterior is an enormous lack of character."

Anatomy of a Murder, 1959; Joseph N. Welch, as Judge Weaver, who is presiding over a sensational murder case; to the court: "One judge is quite like another. The only difference may be in the state of their digestions or their proclivities for sleeping on the bench. For myself, I can digest pig iron. And while I might appear to doze occasionally, you will find that I am easily awakened, particularly if shaken gently by a good lawyer with a nice point of law."

Animal Crackers, 1930; Groucho Marx: "One morning I shot an elephant in my pajamas. How he got in my pajamas I don't know."

Annie Hall, 1977; Woody Allen: "Sun is bad for you. Everything our parents said was good is bad—sun, milk, red meat...college."...Diane Keaton when invariably expressing her frustration: "La-dee-dah, la-dee-dah."...Allen when ruminating about his native city: "Don't you see the rest of the country looks upon New York like we're left-wing, communist, Jewish, homosexual pornographers. I think of us that way sometimes and I live here."

Apocalypse Now, 1979; Robert Duvall, a gung-ho battle-loving U.S. Army commander in Vietnam: "I love the smell of napalm in the morning."

Apollo 13, 1995; Tom Hanks (as astronaut Jim Lovell): "Houston, we have a problem."

Around the World in 80 Days, 1956; Shirley MacLaine, as Princess Aouda, to Cantinflas, as manservant Passepartout, about his enigmatic employer, David Niven, as Phileas Fogg: "Have there been any women in his life?" And to which Cantinflas replies: "I assume he had a mother, but I am not certain."...Niven: "Crisis or no, nothing should interfere with tea!"

As Good as It Gets, 1997; Jack Nicholson to Helen Hunt: "You make me want to be a better man."

Atlantic City, 1980; Susan Sarandon, as Sally, to Burt Lancaster, as

Lou: "Why are you doing this for me?" And to which Lancaster replies: "Hey, it's nothing. Sinatra gives wings to hospitals. We all do what we can."

Auntie Mame, 1958; Rosalind Russell as the flamboyant Mame: "Life is a banquet, and most poor suckers are starving to death."

Avalon, 1990; Lou Jacobi, as Gabriel Krichinsky, offended and enraged, after he arrives late at the family Thanksgiving dinner: "You cut the turkey without me!"

Babe, 1995; James Cromwell to his noisy pet: "That'll do, pig. That'll do."

Back to Bataan, 1945; Ducky Louie, as Maximo Cuenca, a Filipino boy dying in the arms of his American schoolteacher, Beulah Bondi, as Bertha Barnes, after sacrificing himself to save American and Filipino guerrillas from Japanese troops: "Miss Barnes—I'm sorry that I never learned how to spell 'liberty.'" And to which the weeping Bondi replies: "No one ever learned it so well."

Back to the Future, 1985; Lea Thompson, as Lorraine Baines, to Michael J. Fox, as Martin McFly, who will become her son in the future: "Marty, will we ever see you again?" And to which Fox replies: "I guarantee it!"

Bambi, 1942; Will Wright, voiceover for Friend Owl: "Nearly everybody gets twitterpated in the springtime. For example, you're walking along, minding your own business. You're looking neither to the left, nor to the right, when, all of a sudden, you run smack into a pretty face. Woo-woo! You begin to get weak in the knees. Your head's in a whirl. And then you feel light as a feather, and, before you know it, you're walking on air. And then you know what? You're knocked for a loop, and you completely lose your head!"

The Band Wagon, 1953; Fred Astaire, as Tony Hunter: "She was scared...scared as a turkey in November."

The Bank Dick, 1940; W.C. Fields as Egbert Souse, a bumbling bank guard, who becomes alarmed when seeing a child holding a toy gun in the bank and asks the child's mother (Jan Duggan): "Is that gun loaded?" The mother looks him over and replies: "Certainly not! But I think you are!"

Barbary Coast, 1935; Edward G. Robinson, a brutish gambling hall owner, after being snubbed on the street by a leading San Francisco couple: "I'll fix him and that horse-face he calls his wife!"

Batman, 1989; Jack Nicholson as The Joker, to Michael Keaton, as Bruce Wayne/Batman: "Tell me something, my friend. You ever dance with the devil in the pale moonlight?"

Battleground, 1949; Mess sergeant George Chandler, who is thrown into the front lines during the WWII Battle of Bastogne and is given a rifle by GI Herbert Anderson, who begins reciting the manual about the weapon (Chandler to Anderson): "Look, you ain't selling it to me. You're showing me how to fire it."

Beauty and the Beast, 1991; Paige O'Hara, as Belle's voiceover, singing: "I want adventure in the great wide somewhere. / I want it more than I can tell. / And for once it might be grand. / To have someone understand. / I want so much more than what they've got planned..."

Ben-Hur, 1959; Charlton Heston as Judah Ben-Hur, a former galley slave, repeating the words of Jack Hawkins, as Roman admiral Quintus Arias after saving Hawkins' life: "We keep you alive to serve this ship. Row well and live."

The Best Years of Our Lives, 1946; Myrna Loy when responding to her daughter, Teresa Wright, who stated that Loy and her father, Fredric March, never had any trouble in their lives and where Loy addresses March: "We never had any trouble? How many times have I told you I hated you and believed it in my heart? How many times have you said that you were sick and tired of me, that we were all washed up? How many times have we had to fall in love all over again?"

Beyond the Forest, 1949; Bette Davis after entering a house: "What a dump!"

Big, 1988; David Moscow, as young Josh: "I wish I were big."

The Big Broadcast of 1938, 1938; W.C. Fields, as T. Frothingill Bellows, after his wife, Martha Raye, as wife Martha Bellows, has been rescued from the sea: "Throw her back in—let the sharks protect themselves!"

The Big Carnival (aka: Ace in the Hole), 1951; Hard-hearted Jan Sterling after newspaperman Kirk Douglas asks her to attend church to show her concern for her husband, who is trapped in a cave: "I don't go to church. Kneeling bags my nylons."

The Big Chill, 1983; Mary Kay Place, as Meg: "I'm going to wash my hair and puke." And to which Jeff Goldblum, as Michael, replies: "Puke first."

The Big Parade, 1925; Tom O'Brien, as Bull (his dying words on a title card), to John Gilbert, as James Apperson: "I'll meet you in Berlin!"

The Birds, 1963; Doreen Lang, as the mother in a diner, to Tippi Hedren, as Melanie Daniels, who was the first to be attacked by a bird and whom Lang blames for the mass attacks by the feathered creatures: "Why are they doing this? Why are they doing this? They said when you got here, the whole thing started. Who are you? What are you? Where did you come from? I think you are the cause of all of this. I think you are evil! *Evil*!"

Blackboard Jungle, 1955; Anne Francis, as Anne Dadier, to her husband, Glenn Ford, as Richard Dadier: "I was like one of the bad kids in your class. Somebody told me a lie and I believed it. One's as bad as the other."

Blade Runner, 1982; Rutger Hauer, uttering the last words of a fatally wounded outlaw replicant being hunted by police and to Harrison Ford, the detective hunting him: "I've seen things you people wouldn't believe. Attack ships on fire off the shoulder of Orion. I watched C-beams glitter in the dark near the Tannhauser Gate. All those moments will be lost in time...like tears in rain. Time to die."

The Blue Angel, 1931; Marlene Dietrich, as vamp singer Lola Lola, to Emil Jannings, as Professor Immanuel Rath: "I knew you'd be back. They all come back for me."

The Blues Brothers, 1980; Dan Aykroyd, as Elwood: "We're on a mission from God."

Bobby Jones: Stroke of Genius, 2004; Ted Manson, an elderly client complaining to his attorney (who is also the world famous golfer), Jim Caviezel, as Bobby Jones: "But he told me to go to hell!" And to which Caviezel replies: "I checked the law on that, and you don't have to go."

Body and Soul, 1947; John Garfield, as prizefighter Charlie Davis, to Lilli Palmer, as Peg Born (after she calls him "tiger"): "Yeah, that's right.

I got claws. But not for you, Peg, not for you."

Bombshell, 1933; Jean Harlow, as movie star Lola Burns, to her publicity agent, Lee Tracy, as Space Hanlon, who has planted notorious tales about her in the press to boost public interest in her: "How do you think I enjoy reading all that scandal that hasn't an ounce of truth in it?" And to which Tracy replies: "I've told you, sugar. It isn't what *you* like to read. It's what the *public* likes to read."

Boom Town, 1940: Clark Gable, as oilman Big John McMasters, to Claudette Colbert, as Elizabeth Bartlett, the woman he has come to love and will be his wife: "You sure can talk straight to a fella and ball him up at that same time."

Bonnie and Clyde, 1967; Faye Dunaway, as outlaw Bonnie Parker, to a farmer dispossessed by a bank and who has come upon her and Warren Beatty, as Clyde Barrow, while they were target shooting at his vacant home: "We rob banks!"

Born Yesterday, 1950; Judy Holliday, as not-so-dumb blonde mistress Billie, to her sugar daddy, Broderick Crawford, as Harry Brock: "Because when you steal from the government, you're stealing from yourself, you dumb ox!"

The Bourne Identity, 2002; Chris Cooper, as Conklin, to Matt Damon, as Jason Bourne (after Damon asks him "Who am I?"): "You're U.S. Government property. You're a malfunctioning $30 million dollar weapon. You're a total goddamn catastrophe, and, by God, if it kills me, you're going to tell me how this happened."

The Boy in the Striped Pajamas, 2008; David Thewlis, as Father: "You are home, Bruno. Home is where the family is."

Braveheart, 1995; Mel Gibson, as Scottish leader William Wallace when encouraging his men for battle with British forces: "They may take our lives, but they will never take our freedom!"...Gibson: "Every man dies; not every man really lives."

Bride of Frankenstein, 1935; Boris Karloff, as the monster, just before he and others are destroyed: "We belong dead!"

The Bridge on the River Kwai, 1957; Sessue Hayakawa, as Colonel Saito, to Alec Guinness, as Colonel Nicholson (stating what he must do if he fails to complete the bridge): "I will have to kill myself. What would you do if you were me?" And to which Guinness replies: "I suppose if I were you...I would have to kill myself."

Bringing Up Baby, 1938; Cary Grant, as retiring archeologist David Huxley, to Katharine Hepburn, as the free-spirited Susan Vance: "You don't understand—this is *my* car." And to which Hepburn replies: "You mean, this is *your* car, *your* golf ball, *your* car? Is there anything in the world that doesn't belong to you?" And to which Grant answers: "Yes, thank Heaven, *you!*"

Broken Blossoms, 1919; Donald Gisp, as Battling Burrows, to Lillian Gish, his much-abused daughter Lucy Burrows: "Put a smile on yer face, can't yer?" And, in a classic on-screen response, Gish uses two fingers to pathetically push her lips upward into a smile.

Buffalo Bill, 1944; Joel McCrea, as William F. "Buffalo Bill" Cody: "Nobody knows the Indian. I've had to fight them since I was fourteen—Pony Express, stage driver, scout. Indians never do what you'd expect."

The Cabin in the Cotton, 1932; Bette Davis to Richard Barthelmess: "I'd like to kiss you, but I just washed my hair."

Caddyshack, 1980; Bill Murray, a groundskeeper at a golf course, who has absolutely nothing going for him: "So I got that going for me, which is nice."

Call of the Wild, 1935: Clark Gable, as Jack Thornton, after seeing three men escape with his gold, but sink after their canoe strikes a rock and all drown as they are weighted down with the stolen gold: "Well, they wanted gold. Now they got it."

Captain America: The Winter Soldier, 2014; Scarlett Johansson as Natasha Romanoff: "The truth is a matter of circumstances. It's not all things to all people all the time."

Captain Blood, 1935; Basil Rathbone, as French pirate Levasseur while dueling with swords over captive Olivia de Havilland with fellow pirate Errol Flynn, as Captain Peter Blood: "You'll not take her while I live" and to which Flynn replies: "Then I'll take her when you're dead!"... Flynn, after killing Rathbone: "And that, my friend, ends a partnership that should never have begun."

Captain from Castile, 1947; Cesar Romero as Spanish conqueror Hernando Cortez: "Gentlemen, this time last year we were fighting mosquitos in swamps, accepting paltry gifts, and half-starving. But now we stand knocking at the very door of the great Emperor Moctezuma. We shall meet with his Majesty face-to-face, have done with ambassadors and specks of gold. This, gentlemen, is just the beginning!"

Captain Phillips, 2013; Tom Hanks, as Captain Richard Phillips, to kidnapper Barkhad Abdi: "Your problem isn't me talking; your problem is you not listening."

Casablanca, 1942; Humphrey Bogart to Ingrid Bergman (several times) after kissing her: "Here's looking at you, kid."...Ingrid Bergman to Humphrey Bogart when announcing his love for him as gunfire announces the approach of the German army toward Paris in WWII: "Is that cannon fire or is it my heart pounding?"...Bergman to pianist Dooley Wilson when meeting him again in Rick's nightclub: "Play it, Sam, play 'As Time Goes By,"...Bogart (to himself) as he drinks in his closed nightclub after having again met with his one-time lover Bergman: "Of all the gin joints in all the towns in the world, she walks into mine!"...Bogart to Paul Henreid who has told Bogart that he, like all others, has a "destiny either for good or for evil," as Henreid is arrested by Vichy officers: "It seems that destiny has taken a hand."... Claude Rains to Nazi Conrad Veidt who has described Americans as "blundering": "We musn't underestimate the Americans. I was with them when they 'blundered' into Berlin in 1918."...Rains, after Bogart tells him that he is aiming a pistol at his heart: "That is my least vulnerable spot."...Rains to arriving Vichy officers, after he has witnessed Bogart shoot and kill Nazi Conrad Veidt: "Round up the usual suspects."...Bogart to Bergman, reminding her how they loved each other in another town as she is about to go out of his life forever: "We'll always have Paris."

Casino, 1995; Robert De Niro, as Ace Rothstein, operator of a Las Vegas casino: "When you love someone, you've gotta trust them. There's no other way. You've got to give them the key to everything that's yours. Otherwise, what's the point? And, for a while, I believed, that's the kind of love I had."

Champagne for Caesar, 1950; Vincent Price, as wealthy Burnbridge Waters, who sponsors an on-air quiz show and where brilliant contestant Ronald Colman, as Beauregard Bottomley, threatens to win everything, including Price's company: "I now believe that we have a Frankenstein on our hands, and a very well-informed Frankenstein. He must be stopped!"

Changeling, 2008; Angelina Jolie, as Christine Collins, who is battling authorities to find her missing child, Walter: "I used to tell Walter: 'Never start a fight, but always finish it.' I didn't start this fight, but, by God, I'm going to finish it!"

Charge of the Light Brigade, 1936; Errol Flynn, addressing his men before making the charge: "Surat Khan is on the field with the opposing Russian forces, the same Surat Khan who massacred the women and children of Chukoti. Our chance has come! Show no mercy! Let no power on Earth stop you! Prove to the world that no man could kill women and children and live to boast of it! Men of the Twenty-Seventh—our objective is Surat Khan! Forward!"

China Seas, 1935; Wallace Beery, as thief Jamesy MacArdle, to Jean Harlow, as China Doll: "Loving you is the only decent thing I ever did in my entire life. And even that was a mistake."

Chinatown, 1974; John Huston to Jack Nicholson after Nicholson has been brought a plate of fish for lunch: "I believe they should be served with the head."...Hysterical Fae Dunaway to Jack Nicholson when attempting to explain that her child is an incestuous offspring: "She's my daughter! She's my sister! She's my daughter! My sister, my daughter! She's my sister *and* my daughter!"

A Christmas Story, 1983; Melinda Dillon, as Mother Parker, after her young son tells her that he wants a B-B gun for Christmas: "No, you'll shoot your eye out!"

Cimarron, 1931; Irene Dunne, as Sabra Cravat, distraught over the fact that Richard Dix, as Yancey Cravat, her preacher husband, who is also a crusading newspaperman, has shot and killed the ruthless town bully: "Did you have to kill him?" And to which Dix responds: "No, I could have let him kill *me*."

Cinderella Man, 2005; Rene Zellweger, as Mae Braddock, to her husband, Russell Crowe, as prizefighter James J. Braddock, just before he enters the ring to fight for the world's heavyweight championship with Max Baer, and even though she has feared he will be terribly injured in that fight: "Maybe I understand some, about having to fight. So you just remember who you are...You're the Bulldog of Bergen, and the Pride of New Jersey. You're everybody's hope and the kids' hero, and you are the champion of my heart, James J. Braddock!"

Citizen Kane, 1941; Orson Welles to Everett Sloane: "You know, Mr. Bernstein, if I hadn't been very rich, I might have been a really great man."...Welles to financial adviser George Coulouris who has complained about his losing so much money while operating his newspaper: "You're right. I did lose a million dollars last year. I expect to lose a million dollars this year. I expect to lose a million dollars next year. You know, Mr. Thatcher, at the rate of a million dollars a year, I'll have to close this place...in sixty years."...Welles uttering his last cryptic word as he dies: "Rosebud."...Sloane to a newspaper reporter investigating Welles' past: "Old age. It's the only disease, Mr. Thompson, that you don't look forward to being cured of."

City Slickers, 1991; Billy Crystal, as Mitch Robbins, to seasoned cowboy Jack Palance, as Curly, after he holds up one finger to represent "the one thing" that explains the secret of life: "But, what is the one thing?" And to which Palance smiles and replies: "That's what you have to find out."

Close Encounters of the Third Kind, 1977; Richard Dreyfuss as Roy Neary, who has had an encounter with an alien spacecraft and has been acting in an eccentric manner ever since, to his children: "I guess you've noticed something a little strange with Dad. It's okay, though.

I'm still Dad."

Coal Miner's Daughter, 1980; Sissy Spacek, as country singer Loretta Lynn: "I done wrote me a song, Betty Sue. Your mama dadgum songwriter now."

The Color Purple, 1985; Margaret Avery as Shug: "See, Daddy, sinners have souls, too."...Whoopi Goldberg, as Celie: "I'm poor, black, I might even be ugly, but, dear God, I'm here! I'm here!"...Oprah Winfrey, as Sophia: "All my life I had to fight. I had to fight my daddy. I had to fight my uncles. I had to fight my brothers. A girl child ain't safe in a family of men, but I never thought I'd have to fight in my own house!"

Come Back, Little Sheba, 1952; Burt Lancaster, as reformed alcoholic Doc Delaney, after kissing his wife (Shirley Booth) good-bye while on his way to work, and teasingly asked by young Terry Moore, as Marie Buckholder, who boards with them, if he will kiss her, too: "I can't spend my time kissing all the girls."

The Company Men, 2011; Chris Cooper, as Phil Woodward: "You know the worst part?...The world didn't stop. The newspaper still came every morning, the automatic sprinklers went off at six. Jerry next door still washed his car every Sunday...My life ended and nobody noticed."

Cool Hand Luke, 1967; Strother Martin, a vicious chain gang warden, after administering brutal punishment to convicts: "What we've got here is a failure to communicate."

The Count of Monte Cristo, 1934; Robert Donat, as wrongly imprisoned Edmond Dantes, to Sidney Blackmer, as Count Fernand de Mondego, who had conspired to send Donat to prison, and after Donat has bested Blackmer in a duel: "It was not my sword, Mondego, but your past that disarmed you!"

The Crowd, 1928; Title card: "We do not know how big the crowd is, and what opposition it is...until we get out of step with it."

The Curious Case of Benjamin Button, 2008; Brad Pitt, as Benjamin Button: "It's a funny thing about coming home—looks the same, smells the same, feels the same. You'll realize what's changed is you."

The Dark Corner, 1946; Mark Stevens, as private detective Bradford Galt: "I'm clean as a peeled egg...no debts, no angry husbands, no payoffs, nothing."...Also Stevens, feeling his quest to vindicate himself in a murder is hopeless: "There goes my last lead. I feel all dead inside. I'm backed up in a dark corner and I don't know who's hitting me."

The Dark Knight, 2008; Heath Ledger as The Joker: "I believe whatever doesn't kill you, simply makes you...stranger."

The Day of the Locust, 1975; Richard Dysart, as Hollywood filmmaker Claude Estee, about producing films: "Sometimes I wonder what we are doing here, grown men making mud pies to sell to the great unwashed."

The Day the Earth Stood Still, 1951; Patricia Neal as Helen, when meeting powerful robot Gort: "Klaatu barada nicktu!"...Michael Rennie as visiting alien Klaatu, giving a final warning to Earthlings: "...It is no concern of ours how you run your own planet, but if you threaten to extend your violence, this Earth of yours will be reduced to a burned-out cinder. You choice is simple: Join us and live in peace, or pursue your present course and face obliteration. We shall be waiting for your answer. The decision rests with you."

Days of Wine and Roses, 1962; Jack Lemmon, as Joe Clay, who forces his wife, Lee Remick, as Kirsten Clay, to look at themselves in a mirror for the alcoholics they are: "I walked by Union Square bar. I was going to go in. Then I saw myself, my reflection in the window. And I thought, 'I wonder who that bum is?' And then I saw it was me. Look at me! Look at you. You're a bum. Look at you. Look at us. Look at us. C'mon, look at us. See? A couple of bums!"

Dead Poets Society, 1989; Robin Williams as John Keating: "There is a time for daring and there's a time for caution, and a wise man knows which is called for."

Decision before Dawn, 1951; Oskar Werner, as captured German corporal Karl Maurer, who has agreed to spy on his own people during the closing battles of WWII in Germany: "I believe in a life in which one is not afraid, in a life in which people are free and honest with each other. And I know we won't have this in Germany, until we have lost."...O.E. Hasse, as German Colonel von Ecker, who has just condemned a deserter to death and where Werner, as a medic who has just saved Hasse's life from a fatal heart attack, asked that the deserter be spared: "Corporal—your profession is to save lives, even the unworthy. Well, mine is to take it, even the worthy."

The Deer Hunter, 1978; Robert De Niro, as Michael: "The deer has to be taken with one shot. I try to tell people that, but they don't listen."... Chuck Aspegren, as Axel: "Lemme ask you something—how come I never see you eat?" And to which Christopher Walken, as Nick, replies: "I like to starve myself. It keeps the fear up."

The Defiant Ones, 1958; Sidney Poitier, as Noah Cullen, to Tony Curtis, as John "Joker" Jackson, both of whom are chained to each other as runaway convicts from a Southern chain gang: "I ain't *gettin'* mad, Joker. I been mad all my natural life."...Curtis, to a white mob that has captured him and black convict Poitier: "You all can't lynch me! I'm a white man!"

The Departed, 2006; Jack Nicholson as gang boss Frank Costello: "When you decide to be something, you can be it."

Destination Tokyo, 1943; Cary Grant, as Captain Cassidy, commander of a U.S. submarine in WWII, talking to crew members after one of his men has been knifed to death by a Japanese pilot whom the crew member was trying to rescue from the sea, and after explaining that the Japanese airman had been taught to kill in childhood: "There's a lot of Mikes dying right now. And a lot more Mikes will die, until we wipe out a system that puts daggers in the hands of five-year-old children."...John Garfield, as Wolf, a member of the U.S. submarine, who has been selected to go ashore with a few others to hazardly monitor military maneuvers inside of Tokyo Bay, which the submarine has secretly penetrated, and after being asked why he had been chosen to go ashore: "I dunno—strong arm, strong back, weak mind!"

Destry Rides Again, 1939; James Stewart, as Tom Destry Jr., who arrives in a lawless town to tame it as a deputy under the authority of Charles Winninger, as Washington Dimsdale, the town drunk, has mockingly been made sheriff and as Winninger urges Stewart to leave town after learning Stewart is a mild-mannered young man who refuses to wear a gun: "Oh, I think I'll stick around. You know I had a friend once [who] used to collect postage stamps. He always said that the one good thing about a postage stamp [was that] it always sticks to one thing until it gets there...I'm sort of like that, too."...Winninger to Stewart, reluctantly allowing Stewart to stay in town as his deputy: "Here's your badge. Don't let anyone see it."

Detective Story, 1951; Kirk Douglas, as hard-nosed NYPD detective James McLeod, who has struggled to overcome the haunting image of his crooked father: "I built my whole life on hating my father. All the

time, he was inside me, laughing."

Dirty Harry, 1971; Clint Eastwood as SFPD detective "Dirty Harry" Callahan, as he points his revolver at a trapped criminal thinking to fire back: "You've got to ask yourself one question: 'Do I feel lucky?' Well, do you, punk?"

Dr. Strangelove, 1964; Peter Sellers as a milquetoast U.S. President after a struggle takes place in a political inner sanctum: "Gentlemen, you can't fight in here! This is the war room!"

Doctor Zhivago, 1965; Alec Guinness, as Bolshevik General Yevgraf Zhivago (narrating as a parade ensues at the beginning of WWII in Russia): "In bourgeois terms, it was a war between the Allies and Germany. In Bolshevik terms, it was a war between the Allied and German upper classes, and which of them won was of total indifference. My task was to organize defeat [among Russian troops], so as to hasten the onset of revolution. I enlisted under the name of Petrov. The party [Bolshevik Party] looked to the peasant conscript soldiers—many of whom were wearing their first real pair of boots. When their boots had worn out, they'd be ready to listen. When the time came, I was able to take three whole battalions out of the front lines with me, the best day's work I ever did. But for now, there was nothing to be done. There were too many volunteers. Most of it was mere hysteria."

Dodge City, 1939; Errol Flynn, as Wade Hatton (a role model for Western lawman Wyatt Earp), to Olivia de Havilland, as Abbie Irving, the woman he loves: "The only real native of Kansas is the buffalo. He's got a very hard head, a very uncertain temper, and a very lonely future. Apart from that, there's hardly any comparison between you."

Double Indemnity, 1944; Fred MacMurray, as insurance salesman Walter Neff, who has helped murder the husband of Barbara Stanwyck so that he can be with her, but who has been fatally shot by her and where he has killed her, and where he sits bleeding in his office, dictating his lethal tale at the opening: "Yes, I killed him. I killed him for money—and a woman. I didn't get the money and I didn't get the woman. Pretty, isn't it?"...MacMurray to Stanwyck after she implies that he help her murder her husband for a large insurance payment: "Who do you think I was anyway? The guy that walks into a good looking dame's front parlor and says: 'Good afternoon. I sell accident insurance on husbands. ...You got one who's been around too long? One you'd like to turn into a little hard cash?"...Edward G. Robinson, as Barton Keyes, the insurance detective who has been on Stanwyck's trail after the strange death of her husband, to his superior, who refuses to make an insurance payment for that death by stating that the deceased committed suicide by leaping from the end of a moving train (in one of the most dynamically prolonged speeches ever delivered in any film): "Come now, you've never read an actuary table in your life, have you? Why, they have ten volumes on suicide alone—suicide by race, by color, by occupation, by sex, by seasons of the year, by time of day. Suicide, how committed: by poison, by firearms, by drowning, by leaps. Suicide by poison, subdivided by types of poison, such as corrosive, irritant, systemic, gaseous, narcotic, alkaloid, protein, and so forth; suicide by leaps, subdivided by leaps from high places, under the wheels of trains, under the wheels of trucks, under the feet of horses, from steamboats. But, Mr. Norton, of all the cases on record, there's not one single case of suicide by leap from the rear end of a moving train. And do you know how fast that train was moving at the point where the body was found? Fifteen miles an hour. Now, how can anybody jump off a slow-moving train like that with any kind of expectation that he would kill himself? No—no soap, Mr. Norton. We're sunk, and we'll have to pay through the nose and you know it!"

Dracula, 1931; Bela Lugosi, as the eternal vampire Dracula after listening to howling of wolves: "Listen to them—children of the night. What music they make."

E.T.: The Extra-Terrestrial, 1982; Henry Thomas, as Elliott, to E.T.: "You could be happy here. I could take care of you. I wouldn't let anybody hurt you. We could grow up together, E.T."

East of Eden, 1955; Raymond Massey, as Adam Trask, to his son, James Dean, as Cal Trask, who has just offered him money, which Massey has refused: "If you want to give me a present, give me a good life. That's something I can value."...Julie Harris, as Abra, to Massey: "But, you must give him [Dean] some sign, Mr. Trask, some sign that you love him, or he'll never be a man."

Easy Rider, 1969; Peter Fonda, as Captain America: "No, I mean it, you've got a nice place. It's not every man that can live off the land, you know. You do your own thing in your own time. You should be proud."

Elmer Gantry, 1960; Burt Lancaster as Elmer Gantry, a glib and artful preacher (often repeated): "Love is the morning and the evening star."

The Empire Strikes Back (aka: Star Wars: Episode V—The Empire Strikes Back), 1980; Frank Oz, as Yoda voiceover, to Mark Hamill, as Luke Skywalker after Hamill tells him that he will "give it a try": "No. Try not. Do or do not. There is no 'try.'"

The Enforcer, 1951; Jack Lambert, as Philadelphia Tom Zaca, one of the hired killers in Murder, Inc., after naïve new member Zero Mostel asks him who calls boss Ted de Corsia, as Joseph Rico, on the phone: "If you're a good swimmer, you can ask the guy who found out. He's at the bottom of the river."...Everett Sloane, head of Murder, Inc., after killing his first man on a murder-for-hire scheme, and to de Corsia, who becomes his top lieutenant, as both leave the murder scene and where de Corsia is inclined to run: "Don't run. If you run, someone runs after you."

The English Patient, 1996; Ralph Fiennes, as Almasy: "Every night I cut out my heart. But in the morning it was full again."

Exodus, 1960; Lee J. Cobb, as Barak Ben Canaan: "God, don't let my brother die at the end of a British rope!"...David Opatoshu, as Akiva Ben Canaan, to Paul Newman, as his nephew, as Ari Ben Canaan: "In this fatal optimism, you are Haganah. In methodology you are Irgun. But, in your heart, you are Israel."...Eva Marie Saint, to Newman: "Can't you understand that you make me feel like a Presbyterian when you can't, just for a minute or two, forget that you're a Jew."

The Exorcist, 1973; Max von Sydow, as Father Merrin, and Jason Miller, as Father Damien Karras, shouting repeatedly in unison as they coat Linda Blair, as Regan MacNeil, with Holy Water to force a demon into leaving her being: "The Power of Christ compels you!"

The Fallen Idol, 1949; Ralph Richardson, as a very wise house servant, Baines, to youthful Bobby Henrey, as Phillipe, who idolizes him: "There are faults on both sides...We don't have any call to judge. Perhaps she was what she was because I am what I am. We ought to be very careful...because we make one another."

Fargo, 1996; Frances McDormand, as police officer Marge Gunderson, to mindless killer Peter Stormare, as Gaear Grimsrud, whom she has arrested for murder and who sits as a prisoner in the back of her police car, as she drives along a road: "So that was [the body of] Mrs. Lundegaard on the floor in there. And I guess that was [what was left of the body of] your accomplice in the wood chipper. And those three people in Brainerd. And for what—a little bit of money? There's more to life

than a little money, you know? Don't you know that? And here you are, and it's a beautiful day. Well, I just don't understand it."

A Few Good Men, 1992; Jack Nicholson, a martinet Marine commander, to probing investigator Tom Cruise: "You can't handle the truth!"

Field of Dreams, 1989; The voice Kevin Costner hears when thinking about making a baseball field out of his corn crop: "If you build it, he will come."

For Whom the Bell Tolls, 1943; Ingrid Bergman as Maria to Gary Cooper as Robert Jordan: "If you don't love me, I'll love you enough for both of us."...Bergman also to Cooper: "I love you as I loved my father and mother, as I love our unborn children, as I love what I love most in the world, and I love you more. Always remember."

Forrest Gump, 1994; Tom Hanks to a black woman he meets for the first time as they sit on a bench and await the arrival of a bus: "Mama says: 'Stupid is as stupid does.'"

42nd Street, 1933; Theatrical producer Warner Baxter to his protégé Ruby Keeler before sending her onto the stage to appear in the first night of his make-or-break show: "Sawyer, you're going out a youngster, but you've got to come back a star!"

Frankenstein, 1931; Scientist Colin Clive after seeing that his creation, a man made of dead flesh, shows signs of life: "It's alive! It's alive!" (In the original version, Clive cried out: "It's aive! It's alive. In the name of God, now I know what it's like to be God," but these additional words were cut by the censor as being sacrilegious.)

The French Connection, 1971; Gene Hackman, as Jimmy "Popeye" Doyle: "If that's not a drop [drug delivery], I'll open a charge for you at Bloomingdale's!"

From Here to Eternity, 1953; Deborah Kerr, as cheating wife Karen Holmes, to Burt Lancaster, as U.S. Army Sergeant Milton Warden, after he arrives at a public rendezvous: "You certainly chose a lovely spot for our meeting. I've had three chances to be picked up in the last five minutes...If you think this is a mistake, come right out and say so. Well, I guess it's about time for me to be heading home, isn't it? Well, isn't it? And to which Lancaster replies: "What's the matter? What started all this, anyway? You think I'd be here if I thought it was a mistake? Taking a chance on twenty years in Leavenworth for making dates with the company commander's wife? And her acting like...like Lady Astor's horse, and all because I got here on time!"...Montgomery Clift, as Pvt. Robert E. Lee Prewitt: "Nobody ever lies about being lonely."... Clift to Lancaster: "A man don't go his own way, he's nothing." And to which Lancaster replies: "Maybe back in the days of the pioneers a man could go his own way, but today you got to play ball."...Clift to Donna Reed, playing Alma, a dance hall hostess: "Well, what am I? I'm a private no-class dogface. The way most civilians look at that, that's two steps up from nothing."...Reed to Clift, after she insists that she wants to be "proper": "Yes, proper! In another month I'll have enough money saved. Then I'm going to go back to my home town in Oregon, and I'm going to build a house for my mother and myself, and join the country club and take up golf. Then I'll meet the proper man with the proper position, to make a proper wife, and can run a proper home and raise proper children. And I'll be *happy* because when you're *proper* you're *safe!*"

Full Metal Jacket, 1987; Matthew Modine as Marine private J.T. "Joker" Davis while serving in the Vietnam War: "The dead only know one thing. It is better to be alive."

Gandhi, 1982; Ben Kingsley as Mahatma Gandhi: "When I despair, I remember that all through history the way of truth and love has always won. There have been tyrants and murderers, and for a time, they seem invincible, but, in the end, they always fall. Think of it, always."

Gentleman's Agreement, 1947; Gregory Peck, as Phil Green, a journalist for a magazine, who pretends to be Jewish to probe the conduct of anti-Semites, and to Dorothy McGuire, the woman who loves him, and who asks him if he thinks if she is an anti-Semite: "No, I don't. But I've come to see a lot of nice people who hate it [anti-Semitism] and deplore it and protest their innocence, then help it along and wonder why it grows. People who would never beat up a Jew—people who think anti-Semitism is far away in some dark place with low-class morons. That's the biggest discovery I've made—the good people, the nice people."

The Ghost Breakers, 1940; Bob Hope, as Larry Lawrence, a radio broadcaster who concentrates on crime: "Me, I'm mentally retarded. I'm still eleven years old when it comes to the Fourth of July, circuses and haunted castles."…Willie Best, manservant to Bob Hope: "A lot of folks don't like you, boss. I expect some of these mornings when I come to get you out of bed, I'll have to pull the sheet up instead of down."… Richard Carlson, as Geoff Montgomery, as he describes the conduct of zombies in Cuba: "It's worse than horrible because a zombie has no will of his own. You see them sometimes walking around blindly with dead eyes, following orders, not knowing what they do, not caring." To this, Hope replies: "You mean like Democrats?"

Ghostbusters, 1984; Bill Murray: "Dogs and cats living together! Mass hysteria!"

Gigi, 1958; Leslie Caron, as Gigi, after Isabel Jeans, as her Aunt Alicia, has asked her what makes an artist: "Cigars and jewelry."

Gladiator, 2000; Russell Crowe as a Roman general turned gladiator: "My name is Maximus Decimus Meridius, commander of the Armies of the North, general of the Felix Legions, and loyal servant to the true emperor, Marcus Aurelius…Father to a murdered son, husband to a murdered wife, and I will have my vengeance in this life or the next!"

The Godfather, 1972; Marlon Brando to son Al Pacino: "Keep your friends close, but your enemies closer."…Marlon Brando, explaining how he will convince a Hollywood mogul to give a prized movie role to a protégé: "I'm going to make him an offer he can't refuse."

The Godfather, Part II, 1974; Lee Strasberg (in a role loosely based on organized crime boss Meyer Lansky) to Al Pacino: "Michael, we're bigger than U.S. Steel!"…Al Pacino to John Cazale after Pacino has learned that his brother had conspired to have him killed: "I know it was you, Fredo. You broke my heart…you broke my heart!"

Gone with the Wind, 1939: Title card that opens the film: "There was a land of cavaliers and cotton fields known as the Old South. Here, in this pretty world, Gallantry took its last bow. Here was the last ever to be seen of Knights and their Ladies Fair, of Master and Slave…Look for it only in books, for it is no more than a dream remembered, a civilization gone with the wind…"…Clark Gable as Rhett Butler to Vivien Leigh as Scarlett O'Hara: "No, I don't think I will kiss you, although you need kissing badly. That's what's wrong with you. You should be kissed and often, and by someone who knows how."…Leigh, who returns home to her devastated plantation and, starving, finds a turnip and chews on it and then retches, rising with fist raised in hand to vow: "As God is my witness, they're not going to lick me. I'm going to live through all this and when it is over, I'll never be hungry again! No, nor any of my folk. If I have to lie, cheat, steal, or kill. As God is my witness, I'll never be hungry again!"

Goodfellas, 1990; Ray Liotta (narrating): "For as long as I can remember I wanted to be a gangster. To me, that was better than being the President of the United States. To be a gangster was to own the world."

The Graduate, 1967; Dustin Hoffman, a naïve college student, to married woman Anne Bancroft: "Mrs. Robinson, you're trying to seduce me, aren't you?"…Walter Brooke, a businessman friend of the family when giving Hoffman advice on his future: "I just want to say one word to you, one word, 'Plastics.'…There is a great future in plastics."

Grand Hotel, 1932; Greta Garbo as a fading ballerina: "I want to be alone."

The Grapes of Wrath, 1940; Henry Fonda to his mother, Jane Darwell, before he leaves his family as police hunt him, promising her: "I'll be all around in the dark. I'll be everywhere. Wherever you can look, wherever there's a fight, so hungry people can eat, I'll be there. Wherever there's a cop beating up a guy, I'll be there. I'll be in the way guys yell when they're mad. I'll be in the way kids laugh when they're hungry and they know supper's ready, and when the people are eating the stuff they raise and living in the houses they build, I'll be there, too."

Gravity, 2013; George Clooney to Sandra Bullock, realizing that she must save her own life by not attempting to save his as they drift in space: "Ryan, you're going to have to learn to let go."

Gunga Din, 1939; Eduardo Ciannelli, as the Guru leading a small army of Thugs out to conquer India and after his new members have been initiated into his murderous cult that worships the Goddess Kali inside a huge temple: "Rise, our new-made brothers. Rise and kill. Kill, lest you be killed yourselves! Kill for the love of killing! Kill for the love of Kali! Kill! Kill! Kill!"… Cary Grant, as British Sergeant Archibald Cutter, striding all alone into that vast temple packed with murderous Thugs and boldly stating: "Now, you're all under arrest. Her Majesty's very touchy about having her subjects strangled."

Gunfight at the O.K. Corral, 1957; Kirk Douglas, as Doc Holliday, to Burt Lancaster, as Wyatt Earp: "Well spoken. I'll repeat those words at your funeral," after Douglas has warned Lancaster that a small army of cowboys is coming to terrorize the town and even kill him and where Lancaster sternly states to Douglas that he will tolerate no lawbreaking in Dodge City…Lancaster to Dennis Hopper, as Billy Clanton: "All gunfighters are lonely. They die without a dime, a woman, or a friend," after Lancaster has brought Hopper home on a charge of drunkenness and while Hopper contemplates the future of being a gunfighter.

Hail the Conquering Hero, 1944; Eddie Bracken, as Woodrow Lafayette Pershing Truesmith, while addressing a hometown crowd and attempting to refuse their universal nomination that he run for the post of mayor: "I've known all of you all my life. I've mowed your lawns. I've delivered milk for your babies. I even know the dogs and cats."

Halls of Montezuma, 1950; Don Hicks, as Marine Lieutenant Butterfield while under Japanese fire on a Pacific island in WWII, and remarking about Civil War General William T. Sherman's comment about war: "Yeah, he said 'War is Hell.' What did he know? That eight-ball never left the States."

The Harder They Fall, 1956; Rod Steiger, as powerful underworld fight promoter Nick Benko: "The fight game today is like show business. There are no real fighters anymore. They're all actors. The best showman becomes the champ!"

Harry Potter and the Deathly Hollows Part 2, 2011; Michael Gambon, as Professor Albus Dombledore: "Words are, in my not so humble opinion, our most inexhaustible source of magic—capable of both inflicting injury and remedying it."

The Heiress, 1949; Olivia de Havilland, as heiress Catherine Sloper, after having been abandoned by fortune-hunter Montgomery Clift, who is about to return and wrongly thinking he can now marry her and gain her wealth: "He's grown greedier over the years. Before, he only wanted my money. Now, he wants my love as well. Well, he came to the wrong house, and he came twice. I shall see that he does not come a third time."

High Noon, 1952; Katy Jurado, former mistress to Gary Cooper, playing Will Kane, the local lawman who, alone, must face four men coming to kill him, to Grace Kelly, playing Helen, Cooper's wife, who is about to leave him: "What kind of woman are you? How can you leave him like this? Does the sound of guns frighten you that much?" And to which Kelly replies: "I've heard guns. My father and my brother were killed by guns. They were on the right side but that didn't help them any when the shooting started. I watched them die. That's when I became a Quaker. I don't care who's right or who's wrong. There's got to be a better way for people to live."

His Girl Friday, 1940; Rosalind Russell, as newspaper reporter Hildy Johnson, to Cary Grant, as Walter Burns, her conniving editor and sometimes lover: "Walter, you're wonderful, in a loathsome sort of way."

Hotel Rwanda, 2004; Joaquin Phoenix, a documentary filmmaker, who has filmed the atrocity of slaughtered members of the Tutsi tribe: "I think if people see this footage, they'll say 'Oh, my God, that's horrible.' And then they will go on eating their dinners."

How Green Was My Valley, 1941; Irving Pichel, narrating as an adult Huw Morgan: "Men like my father cannot die. They are with me still, real in memory as they were in flesh, loving and beloved forever. How green was my valley then."

The Hucksters, 1947; Clark Gable, as Victor Albee Norman, to Deborah Kerr, as Kay Dorrance: "I don't want anything from you, except you."

Hugo, 2011; Ben Kingsley, as pioneer filmmaker Georges Melies: "My life has taught me one lesson, Hugo, and not the one I thought it would. Happy endings only happen in the movies."

The Hustler, 1961; Paul Newman to George C. Scott: "You tell your boys they better kill me, Bert. They better go all the way with me 'cause if they just bust me up, I'll put all those pieces back together again. Then, so help me, so help me God, Bert, I'm gonna come back here and I'm gonna kill you."

If I Had a Million, 1932; W.C. Fields, as Rollo La Rue, to Alison Skipworth, as his wife Emily, while Fields is doing what he accuses others of doing: "Road hogs—a constant menace to society! They should be wiped out, Emily. Do you hear? Wiped out!"

In Harm's Way, 1965; Burgess Meredith, a U.S. Navy officer before going into a sea battle: "I'm so scared that my bones are clicking like dice on a Reno craps table."...John Wayne, commander of a cruiser, who is also about to go into battle: "All battles are fought by men who'd rather be somewhere else."...Henry Fonda, as Admiral Chester Nimitz: "Well, we all know that the Navy's never wrong, but in this case it was a little weak on being right."

In the Heat of the Night, 1967; Sidney Poitier to Rod Steiger: "They call me Mr. Tibbs!"

Inside Out, 2015; Phyllis Smith as voiceover for Sadness: "Crying

helps me slow down and obsess over the weight of life's problems."

Into the Wild, 2007; Emile Hirsch, as Christopher McCandless while writing into his book: "Happiness is only real when shared."

The Iron Lady, 2011; Meryl Streep, as Margaret Thatcher: "It used to be about trying to do something. Now it's about trying to be someone."

It Happened One Night, 1934; Clark Gable, as newspaper reporter Peter Warne, to Claudette Colbert, as Ellie Andrews, the runaway heiress he has been shepherding home, and while they lie in beds separated by a blanket that serves as a makeshift wall between them as he tells her about the girl of his dreams: "Sure, I've thought about it. Who hasn't? If I could ever meet the right sort of girl. Aww, where you gonna find her? Somebody that's real, somebody that's alive. They don't come that way anymore. Have I ever thought about it? I've even been sucker enough to make plans. You know, I saw an island in the Pacific once. I've never been able to forget it. That's where I'd like to take her. She'd have to be the sort of a girl who'd...well, who'd jump in the surf with me and love it as much as I did. You know, nights when you and the water and the moon all become one. You feel you're part of something big and marvelous. That's the only place to live...where the stars are close over your head you could reach up and stir them around. Certainly, I've been thinking about it. Boy, if I could ever find a girl who was hungry for those things…"

It's a Gift, 1934; W.C. Fields, after someone accuses him of being drunk: "And you're crazy. But I'll be sober tomorrow and you'll be crazy for the rest of your life."

It's a Wonderful Life, 1946; Karolyn Grimes as Zuzu Bailey to her mother Donna Reed and father James Stewart after she hears an ornamental bell ringing on a nearby Christmas tree: "Every time a bell rings, an angel gets his wings."

Jaws, 1975; Roy Scheider to Robert Shaw, after he witnesses the huge shark swimming after Shaw's fishing vessel: "You're gonna need a bigger boat."

The Jazz Singer, 1927; Al Jolson to an applauding audience after finishing a performance: "You ain't heard nothin' yet!"

Jerry McGuire, 1995; Tom Cruise to Rene Zellweger: "You complete me."

Jesse James, 1939; Tyrone Power, as Jesse James, after climbing into the cabin of a moving train, when the engineer asks him what he "aims" to do: "I ain't aimin' to do nothing. I'm doing it. I'm holding up this train!"

Jezebel, 1938; Bette Davis, as self-centered Southern belle Julie, while trying to win Henry Fonda, as Preston Dillard, from another woman: "Can you hear them, the night noises? The mockingbird in the magnolia? See the moss hanging from the moonlight. You can fairly taste the night, can't you? You're part of it...it's part of you, like I am. You can't get away from us...we're both in your blood. This is the country you were born to...the country you know and trust. Your country! Amy [Margaret Lindsay, her competitor for Fonda's heart] wouldn't understand. She'd think there'd be snakes."

Jim Thorpe—All American, 1951; Eula Morgan, as Charlotte Thorpe, the mother of Jim Thorpe, who, as a child, has again run away from school to hunt and fish, to Nestor Paiva, as Hiram Thorpe, his father: "You're his father. You taught him all the things he likes to do. Now teach him what he has to do!"

Judgment at Nuremberg, 1961; Spencer Tracy, as Judge Dan Haywood: "Before the people of the world, let it now be noted in our decision here that this is what we stand for: 'justice, truth, and the value of a single human being,"

Key Largo, 1948; Gangster Edward G. Robinson after he is asked by Humphrey Bogart to explain what Robinson wants in life: "Yeah, that's it, more. That's right! I want more!"

Kind Hearts and Coronets, 1950; Dennis Price as the calculating Louis Mazzini, who busies himself with systematically killing off a number of relatives in order to gain the family inheritance, while romancing two women at the same time, including Joan Greenwood, as Sibella, about whom he artfully states: "I'd say that you were the perfect combination of imperfections. I'd say that your nose was just a little too short, your mouth just a little too wide. But yours was a face that a man could see in his dreams for the whole of his life. I'd say that you were vain, cruel, selfish, deceitful. I'd say that you were adorable."

Kit Carson, 1940; Dana Andrews as frontiersman John C. Fremont and bidding good luck to pioneers before departing with his troops: "Green grass and running water!"

Knute Rockne, All American, 1940; Ronald Reagan, as dying college football player George Gipp to Pat O'Brien, who plays Rockne and who later restates Reagan's remarks to his faltering team: "Sometime when the team is up against it and the breaks are beating the boys, tell them to go out there with all they've got and win just one for the Gipper."

The Lady Eve, 1941; Barbara Stanwyck, as sharper Jean Harrington: "They say a moonlit deck is a woman's business office."

The Last Tycoon, 1976; Robert De Niro as a Hollywood movie mogul (loosely based on MGM executive Irving Thalberg): "I don't think that I have more brains than a writer. I just think that his brains belong to me."

Laura, 1944; Clifton Webb, an arrogant, wealthy newspaper columnist: "I don't use a pen. I write with a goose quill dipped in venom."…Webb to police detective Dana Andrews whom Webb thinks is obsessing about a beautiful woman they both think is dead, but who is very much alive: "You'd better watch out, McPherson, or you'll finish up in a psychiatric ward. I doubt they've ever had a patient who fell in love with a corpse."…Andrews to Gene Tierney, the woman who resurfaces after everyone thinks she has been murdered: "I must say, for a charming, intelligent girl, you certainly surrounded yourself with a remarkable collection of dopes."…Webb, who turns out to be a killer: "Murder is my favorite crime."…Andrews, when asked if he has ever been in love: "A doll in Washington Heights once got a fox fur out of me."

Lawrence of Arabia, 1962; Peter O'Toole, as T.E. Lawrence, to Omar Sharif, as Sherif Ali: "So long the Arabs fight tribe against tribe, so long will they be a little people—greedy, barbarous and cruel, as you are."… Alec Guinness as Prince Feisal: "With Major Lawrence, mercy is a passion. With me, it is merely good manners. You may judge which motive is the more reliable."…Guinness, when replying to O'Toole's expression of love for the desert: "No Arab loves the desert. We love water and green trees. There is nothing in the desert and no man needs nothing."… Jack Hawkins as General Allenby, to O'Toole: "I believe your name will be a household word when you'll have to go to the War Museum to find who Allenby was. You're the most extraordinary man I've ever met!" …O'Toole: "I pray that I may never see the desert again. Hear me, God."

A League of Their Own, 1992; Tom Hanks, as Jimmy Dugan, manager of a female baseball team, to weeping player Bitty Schram, as Evelyn Gardner, after he has criticized her playing: "There's no crying in baseball!"

Leaving Las Vegas, 1995; Elisabeth Shue, as Sera, to Nicolas Cage, as her alcoholic lover Ben Sanderson: "That's nice talk, Ben; keep drinking. Between the 101-proof breath and the occasional bits of drool, some interesting words come out."

The Loved One, 1965; Jonathan Winters, as Henry Glenworthy, a callous director of an expensive cemetery who wants to turn his land into a housing development: "There's got to be a way to get those stiffs off my property!"

The Man from Laramie, 1955; James Stewart, as Will Lockhart, who has been wrongly accused jailed and for killing shiftless Jack Elam (sarcastically): "I came all the way from Laramie to creep up a dark alley to knife the town drunk."

Manhattan Melodrama, 1934; Clark Gable, as Edward J. "Blackie" Gallagher, a condemned man walking to the electric chair as he tells a fellow inmate also awaiting execution: "Die the way you lived, all of a sudden, that's the way to go. Don't drag it out."

Marathon Man, 1976; Laurence Olivier, a wanted Nazi doctor, while torturing Dustin Hoffman by extracting a tooth and repeating a code line about his own security: "Is it safe?"

Marty, 1955; Ernest Borgnine, as Marty, to his closest friend, Joe Mantell, as Angie, after Mantell has told him that the girl who loves Borgnine is not for him: "You don't like her. My mother don't like her. She's a dog, and I'm a fat, ugly man. I'm gonna have a good time tonight. Well, all I know is that I had a good time last night. If we have enough good times together, I'm gonna get down on my knees and ask that girl to marry me. If we make a party on New Year's, I got a date for that party. You don't like her? That's too bad."

Midnight Cowboy, 1969; Dustin Hoffman, a hustler, while walking across a NYC street with friend Jon Voight and indignantly shouting at a driver entering the crosswalk: "I'm walking here! I'm walking here!"

The Misfits, 1961; Clark Gable, as Gay Langland, to Marilyn Monroe, as Roslyn Taber: "Honey, we all got to go sometime, reason or no reason. Dying's as natural as living. The man who is too afraid to die is too afraid to live." (Note: Gable thought this film was the best "I have made," but was extremely frustrated with the erratic behavior and many delays created by his co-star, Monroe, saying about her on the final day's shooting: "I'm glad this picture is finished. She [Monroe] damn near gave me a heart attack." He suffered a heart attack the following day and died in a hospital ten days later on November 16, 1960.)

Mississippi, 1935: W.C. Fields, as Commodore Jackson: "Never mind what I told you! Do as I tell you!"…Fields: "I like women as I like elephants. I like to look at 'em, but I wouldn't own one."

Mr. Smith Goes to Washington, 1939; James Stewart as a novice U.S. senator to his secretary, Jean Arthur: "You see, boys forget what their country means by just reading The Land of the Free in history books. When they get to be men they forget even more. Liberty's too precious a thing to be buried in books, Miss Saunders. Men should hold it up in front of them every single day of their lives and say: 'I'm free to think and to speak. My ancestors couldn't, I can, and my children will. Boys ought to grow up remembering that."

Mommie Dearest, 1981; Faye Dunaway as actress Joan Crawford, who is obsessed by not using anything common, and to her daughter: "No wire hangers, ever!"

Moonstruck, 1987; Cher to Nicolas Cage after he tells her that he loves her: "Snap out of it!"…Cher to her mother, Olympia Dukakis, after she asks Cher if she loves Cage: "Aw, Ma, I love him awful!" (To which Dukakis replies: "Oh, God, that's too bad.")

Murder, Inc., 1960; Peter Falk, as murderous gangster Abe "Kid Twist" Reles: "Take! You see what you can get your hands on, you take! Don't ask questions! Take! What you want, take! What I want, I take! Nothing means nothing unless I got it! What do you got your hands for, huh? Take!"

Mutiny on the Bounty, 1935; Charles Laughton, as the cold-hearted and sadistic Captain William Bligh after asking Eddie Quillan, as seaman Thomas Ellison, his name, and when Ellison complains that he was pressed into service and has a wife and child: "I asked your name, not the history of your misfortunes."…Clark Gable, as Fletcher Christian, leader of the mutiny, to Laughton: "Bligh, you've given your last command on this ship! We'll be men again if we hang for it!"…Laughton, after he and others have been set adrift in a lifeboat, shouting to Gable and other mutineers remaining aboard the *Bounty*: "I'll live to see you—all of you—hanging from the highest yardarm in the British fleet!"… Gable to friend Franchot Tone, as Byam, following a mutiny in which Tone did not participate: "When you're back in England with the fleet again, you'll hear the hue and cry against me. From now on they'll spell mutiny with my name."

My Fair Lady, 1964; Rex Harrison, as Professor Henry Higgins: "There even are places where English completely disappears. In America, they haven't used it for years."…Audrey Hepburn, as Eliza Doolittle: "The difference between a lady and flower girl is not how she behaves, but how she is treated."

My Little Chickadee, 1940; Mae West, as Flower Belle Lee, and while reading from a blackboard: "'I am a good boy. I am a good man. I am a good girl.' What is this—propaganda?"…W.C. Fields, as Cuthbert J. Twillie, after waking up with a tormenting hangover: "I feel as though a midget with muddy feet had been walking over my tongue all night."

Network, 1976; Peter Finch, a mentally disturbed TV anchorman yelling to his viewership to get up and shout: "I'm as mad as hell, and I'm not going to take this anymore!"

Never Give a Sucker an Even Break, 1941; W.C. Fields as The Great Man, to Jody Gilbert, an overweight waitress who seems threatening: "I didn't squawk about the steak, dear. I merely said that I didn't see that old horse that used to be tethered outside here."

No Man of Her Own, 1932; Carole Lombard as Connie Randall: "Oh, I've been busy leading my usual life of sin."

North by Northwest, 1959; Cary Grant, as advertising executive Roger Thornhill, after Eva Marie Saint, playing Eve Kendall, asks him what happened to his first two marriages: "My wives divorced me…They said I led too dull a life."…Grant to intelligence chief Leo G. Carroll, who has asked him to help him save Saint from enemy agents: "Now you listen to me. I'm an advertising man, not a red herring. I've got a job, a secretary, a mother, two ex-wives and several bartenders that depend upon me, and I don't intend to disappoint them all by getting myself 'slightly' killed."…Grant, also to Carroll: "If you fellows can't lick the Vandamms [enemy agent] of this world without asking girls like her [Saint] to bed down with them, and fly away with them and probably never come back, perhaps you ought to start learning how to lose a few cold wars."…Carroll, replying: "I'm afraid we're already doing that."

Objective Burma, 1945; GI George Tobias about leader Errol Flynn to

other dispirited paratroopers trapped behind Japanese lines in WWII: "C'mon. I'd follow him down the barrel of a cannon!"…Errol Flynn to his commander, Warner Anderson, after returning to U.S. lines with only a few of his remaining paratroopers and being congratulated for his mission behind Japanese lines as he hands over the dog tags of his slain men: "Here's what it cost—a handful of Americans."

The Old Fashioned Way, 1934; W.C. Fields as The Great McGonigle: "It ain't a fit night out for man or beast!"

On Golden Pond, 1981; Aging Katharine Hepburn to aging Henry Fonda, her husband, who fears senility is overtaking him: "Listen, mister. You are my knight in shining armor. Don't you forget it! You're going to get back on that horse, and I'm going to be right behind you, holding on tight, and away we're going to go, go, go!"

On the Waterfront, 1954; Marlon Brando to his brother, Rod Steiger, when bemoaning how his gangster brother compelled him to dump a fixed fight when he was a prizefighter: "I could have had class. I could have been a contender. I could have been somebody, instead of a bum, which is what I am, let's face it."

The Oxbow Incident, 1943; Dana Andrews, who, along with two others, is about to be lynched for a crime he and the others did not commit: "Justice? What do you know about justice? You don't even care if you've got the right men or not. All you know is that you've lost something and somebody's got to be punished."

Patton, 1970; George C. Scott, as General George Patton, in his opening address: "Now I want you to remember that no bastard ever won a war by dying for his country. He won it by making the other poor dumb bastard die for his country."… Scott, while traveling along a road filled with marching GIs and after being asked where he is going: "Berlin! I'm going to personally shoot that paper-hanging son-of-a-bitch!" His reference is to German leader Adolf Hitler, who reportedly had once been a paper-hanger, and where Scott receives cheers from his troops.

Persepolis, 2007; Chiara Mastroianni, as Marjane voiceover: "I remember that I led a peaceful, uneventful life as a little girl. I loved fries and ketchup. Bruce Lee was my hero, I wore Adidas sneakers, and had two obsessions: Shaving my legs one day and being the last prophet of the galaxy."

The Philadelphia Story, 1940; Katharine Hepburn, as beautiful, wealthy socialite Tracy Lord: "The time to make up your mind about people is never."…Cary Grant, as C.K. Dexter Haven, to Hepburn: "You'll never be a first class human being or a first class woman until you've learned to have some regard for human frailty."…James Stewart, as jaded write Macaulay Connor: "I would sell my grandmother for a drink, and you know how much I love my grandmother."…Roland Young, as Uncle Willie: "Aww, this is one of those days that the pages of history teach us are best spent lying in bed."…John Howard, as George Kittredge, to Hepburn: "You're like some marvelous, distant, well, queen, I guess. You're so cool and fine, and always so much your own. There's a kind of beautiful purity about you, Tracy, like…like a statue."…Hepburn to Howard: "You're much too good for me, George. You're a hundred times too good. And I'd make you most unhappy, most. That is, I'd do my best to."…Grant to Stewart: "I thought that all writers drank to excess and beat their wives. You know, one time I secretly wanted to be a writer."…Hepburn to Grant: "I'm not interested in myself." And to which Grant replies: "Not interested in yourself, Red? You're fascinated. You're far and away your favorite person in the world."

Pinocchio, 1940; Evelyn Venable, voiceover of the Blue Fairy to puppet

Pinocchio (Dickie Jones voiceover): "A lie keeps growing and growing until it's as plain as the nose on your face."…Venable to Jones: "Prove yourself brave, truthful and unselfish, and someday you *will* be a real boy."…Jiminy Cricket (Cliff Edwards voiceover), deprecating himself for failing in his duties to keep Pinocchio on the straight and narrow: "A fine conscience I turned out to be!"

A Place in the Sun, 1951; Montgomery Clift as George Eastman, to Elizabeth Taylor, as Angela Vickers: "I love you. I've loved you from the first moment I saw you. I guess maybe I've even loved you before I saw you."…Taylor: "Of course. I'm always late—part of my charm."

Planet of the Apes, 1968; Charlton Heston, regaining his voice and star-tling his captors when he shouts: "Take your stinking paws off me, you damn dirty ape!"

The Poseidon Adventure, 1972; Gene Hackman, as the unorthodox minister Reverend Frank Scott: "So what resolution shall we make for the new year? It's to let God know that you have the guts and the will to do it alone. Resolve to fight for yourselves, and for others, for those you love. And that part of God within you will be fighting all the way."

Poltergeist, 1982; Six-year-old Heather O'Rourke, who announces the arrival of otherworld spirits: "They're here!"

The Princess Bride, 1987; Mandy Patinkin to Christopher Guest: "Hello, my name is Inigo Montoya. You killed my father. Prepare to die."…Wallace Shawn, after playing a lethal game of switching poi-soned goblets with Cary Elwes: "Never go in against a Sicilian when death is on the line," and he cackles madly before dropping dead…Billy Crystal as Miracle Max when he is asked to bring Carey Elwes back to life: "It just so happens that your friend here is only *mostly dead*. There's a big difference between *mostly dead* and *all dead*. *Mostly dead* is slightly alive. With *all dead*, well, there is usually only one thing you can do…go through his clothes and look for loose change."

The Private Lives of Elizabeth and Essex, 1939; Bette Davis, as Eliz-abeth I of England: "The necessities of a queen must transcend those of a woman."…Errol Flynn, as Essex, who refuses to share the crown with Davis, accepting the alternative, his death by execution: "And now, may I go? This dying sticks in my mind and makes me poor company."

The Producers, 1967; Kenneth Mars, the crackpot ex-Nazi soldier of WWII, who has written an absurd play praising Adolf Hitler, to Zero Mostel and Gene Wilder, who have agreed to produce that miserable play so it can immediately flop and they can retain investor money: "Hitler was better looking than Churchill! He was a better dresser than Churchill! He had more hair! He told funnier jokes and he could dance the pants off of Churchill!"…Mars to theatergoers in the audience who object to his outlandish behavior: "I am the author. You are the audience. I outrank you!"…Bill Macy, foreman of a jury that has listened to the charges against the outlandish Mostel and Wilder: "We find the defen-dants incredibly guilty!"

Psycho, 1960; Anthony Perkins, who possesses a murderous split per-sonality where he assumes the role of his dead mother to kill women at-tracted to her affectionate son: "A boy's best friend is his mother."

Raiders of the Lost Ark, 1981; Harrison Ford, as archeological adven-turer Indiana Jones, after his mentor, Brody (Denholm Elliott) has warned him about the dangers of the legendary Ark he seeks: "What are you trying to do—scare me? You sound like my mother. We've known each other for a long time. I don't believe in magic, a lot of superstitious hocus-pocus. I'm going after a find of incredible historical significance [and], you're talking about the boogie man."

Rear Window, 1954; Grace Kelly as Lisa: "I wish I were creative." And to which James Stewart, as Jeff, replies: "You are. You're great at creating difficult situations."…Thelma Ritter, as Stella: "Intelligence. Nothing has caused the human race so much trouble as intelligence."… Ritter: "When two people love each other, they come together—wham [!]—like two taxis on Broadway."

Rebel without a Cause, 1955; An anguished James Dean to his arguing parents: "You're tearing me apart!"

Red River, 1948; John Wayne to Montgomery Clift after Clift and other cowboys have taken Wayne's herd of cattle from him and left him wounded on the trail: "Cherry was right. You're soft. You should have let them kill me, 'cause I'm gonna kill you. I'll catch up with you. I don't know when, but I'll catch up. Every time you turn around expect to see me, 'cause one time you'll turn around and I'll be there. I'm gonnna kill you, Matt."

Rocky, 1976; Sylvester Stallone, as Rocky Balboa, to Talia Shire, as Arian, who has just reminded him of a holiday: "Yeah, to you it's Thanksgiving. To me, it's Thursday."…Burgess Meredith, as fight trainer Mickey, to Stallone before they begin training for a heavyweight championship bout: "You're gonna eat lightning, and you're gonna crap thunder!"

San Francisco, 1936; Spencer Tracy as Father Mullin, to Jeanette Mac-Donald, as singer Mary Blake: "You in probably the wickedest, most corrupt city, most Godless city in America. Sometimes it frightens me. I wonder what the end's going to be. But nothing can harm you if you don't allow it to because nothing in the world, no one in the world, is all bad."…Clark Gable, as Blackie Norton, saloon owner on the Barbary Coast, who has just brought a process server to interrupt MacDonald's performance at the opera in order to have her back singing in his saloon: "That process server is the meanest man west of the Rocky Mountains. He'd push his mother off a ferry boat for half a dollar. Yeah, he'd turn the air off in a baby's incubator just to watch the little sucker squirm."

The Sand Pebbles, 1966; Steve McQueen, as U.S. sailor Jake Holman, after being fatally shot at a remote mission in China: "I was home. What happened? What the hell happened?"

Schindler's List, 1993; Liam Neeson, as Oskar Schindler, a German entrepreneurial manufacturer using Jews in his plants, who tells Ralph Fiennes, playing Amon Goeth, murderous commandant of a concentra-tion camp: "Power is when we have justification to kill and we don't." Fiennes nods, pardons a young Jewish worker for his inept service and sends him from his home to the camp, then whimsically shoots and kills the youth from his balcony, as if for sport…Fiennes, addressing his men before ordering the destruction of the Jewish ghetto in Krakow, Poland, as he tries to callously impress them with the warped notion that their genocidal actions are historically significant: "Today is history. Today will be remembered. Years from now the young will ask with wonder about this day. Today is history and you are part of it. Six hundred years ago, when elsewhere they were footing the blame on the Black Death, Casimir the great, so-called, told the Jews they could come to Krakow. They came. They trundled their belongings into the city. They settled. They took hold. They prospered in business, science, education, the arts. They came with nothing. And they flourished. For six centuries there has been a Jewish Krakow. By this evening, those six centuries will be a rumor. They never happened. Today is history."

Shane, 1953; Alan Ladd to fellow gunfighter Jack Palance just before Ladd shoots and kills him: "I hear you're a lowdown Yankee liar."

She Done Him Wrong, 1933; Dance hall hostess Mae West to Cary

Grant: "Why don't you come up some time and see me?"

The Shining, 1980; Berserk Jack Nicholson breaking through a door in an attempt to murder wife Shelley Duvall (and playing on Johnny Carson's introduction on *The Tonight Show*): "Here's Johnny!"

Snow White and the Seven Dwarfs, 1937; Lucile La Verne voiceover as the Wicked Queen: "Magic Mirror on the Wall, who is the fairest of them all?"

Sons of the Desert, 1933: Oliver Hardy to Stan Laurel: "Well, here's another nice mess you've gotten me into."

The Sound of Music, 1965; Julie Andrews, as Maria, a young woman preparing to become a nun in an Austrian convent and who later becomes the governess of seven mischievous children of the Von Trapp family: "You know how Sister Berthe always makes me kiss the floor after we have a disagreement? Well, lately, I've taken to kissing the floor whenever I see her coming just to save time."…Andrews: "When the Lord closes a door, somewhere He opens a window."

Spirited Away, 2003; Daveigh Chase, as Chihiro: "I finally get a bouquet and it's a good-bye present. That's depressing."

Star Wars, 1977; Harrison Ford, as Hans Solo: "May the Force be with you." (This is a play on "May God be with you," where God is replaced by some unseen "Force" by godless persons traveling and battling through space.)

A Streetcar Named Desire, 1951; Vivien Leigh, a Southern belle with a shattered mind to a physician about to take her to a mental institution: "I have always depended upon the kindness of strangers."

Sudden Impact, 1983; Clint Eastwood, as SFPD detective "Dirty Harry" Callahan, while he points his revolver at a criminal thinking to fire back: "Go ahead, make my day!"

Sunset Boulevard, 1950; William Holden staring at an empty, neglected, rat-infested large pool on the estate of a faded film star of the silent era: "And that pool where Vilmy Banky and Rod LaRocque swam ten thousand nights ago."… Gloria Swanson to William Holden: "I *am* big! It's the pictures that got small."…Swanson to Holden: "We didn't need dialogue. We had faces!"…William Holden to aging Gloria Swanson: "There's nothing wrong with being fifty unless you insist on being twenty-five."

Taken, 2008; Liam Neeson to those who have kidnapped his child: "If you let my daughter go now, that'll be the end of it. I will not look for you, I will not pursue you. But, if you don't, I will look for you, I will find you, and I will kill you."

They Died with Their Boots On, 1941; Errol Flynn, as George Armstrong Custer, to Olivia de Havilland, as his wife, Elizabeth Bacon Custer, and before leaving on his last and fatal campaign against the Sioux: "Walking through life with you, ma'am, has been a very gracious thing."…Flynn, just before the Battle of the Little Big Horn and his death: "You can take glory with you when it's your time to go."

The Thing from Another World, 1951; Newspaperman Douglas Spencer, as Ned "Scotty" Scott, after learning about the alien creature who has invaded a remote arctic base: "An intellectual carrot. The mind boggles."…Robert Cornthwaite, as scientist Dr. Arthur Carrington, who insists that the creature not be harmed no matter how lethal it is and that it must, at all costs, be preserved, for the sake of science: "Its development was not handicapped by emotional or sexual factors…We owe to the brain of our species to stand here and die…without destroy-

ing a source of wisdom."…Spencer to Cornthwaite: "Dr. Carrington, you're a man who won the Nobel Prize. You've received every international kudos a scientist can attain. If you were for sale, I could get a million bucks for you from any foreign government. I'm not, therefore, going to stick my neck out to say that you're stuffed absolutely clean full of wild blueberry muffins, but I promise my readers are going to think so."

The Third Man, 1950; Orson Welles, as Harry Lime, a fugitive wanted for peddling lethal drugs, to his onetime close friend Joseph Cotten, as Holly Martins, while furtively meeting on a moving Ferris wheel: "Don't be so gloomy. After all, it's not that awful. Like the fellow says, in Italy for thirty years under the Borgias they had warfare, terror, murder, and bloodshed, but they produced Michelangelo, Da Vinci, and the Renaissance. In Switzerland, they had brotherly love, they had five hundred years of democracy and peace, and what did that produce? The cuckoo clock. So long, Holly."

To Have and Have Not, 1944; Lauren Bacall to Humphrey Bogart: "You know how to whistle, don't you, Steve? You just put your lips together and blow."

To Kill a Mockingbird, 1962; Gregory Peck, as thoughtful lawyer and father Atticus Finch, to Mary Badham, as Scout: "If you just learn a single trick, Scout, you'll get along a lot better with all kinds of folks. You never really understand a person until you consider things from his point of view—until you climb inside of his skin and walk around in it."

Toy Story, 1995; Tom Hanks, as voiceover for Woody: "To infinity and beyond!"

The Treasure of the Sierra Madre, 1948; Veteran prospector Walter Huston to greenhorn gold seekers Humphrey Bogart and Tim Holt when talking about the discovery of gold: "I know what gold does to men's souls…You lose your sense of values and your character changes entirely. Your soul stops being the same as it was before." Huston to Bogart and Holt, after he discovers gold and before he begins a wild jig in his joyful discovery: "You two are so dumb that you don't even see the millions when treading upon them with your own feet!"…Alfonso Bedoya, a Mexican bandit leader, after being asked to show his badge when stating that he is a federal officer: "Badges? We ain't got no badges! We don't need no badges! I don't have to show you any stinking badges!"

12 Angry Men, 1957; Henry Fonda, as Juror No. 8, while sitting with a jury that must decide the guilt or innocence of a boy accused of killing his father, to L. J. Cobb, Juror No. 3: "I feel sorry for you. What it must feel like to want to pull the switch! [To execute the defendant, for which Cobb has been lobbying.] Ever since you walked into this room, you've been acting like a self-appointed public avenger. You want to see this boy die because you personally want it, not because of the facts! You're a sadist!"

12 Years a Slave, 2013; Chiwetel Ejiofor (as Solomon Northup, a free black man who has been abducted and sold into slavery): "I don't want to survive. I want to live."

2001: A Space Odyssey, 1968; Douglas Rain, the voiceover for the devious and disaster-creating computer HAL: "Dave, my mind is going… I can feel it."

The Usual Suspects, 1995; Kevin Spacey, stating: "The greatest trick the Devil ever pulled was convincing the world he didn't exist."

A Walk in the Sun, 1945; Richard Conte, as GI Rivera, after being asked if he thinks he will live long enough to be promoted to the rank of corporal: "Baby, I just want to live long enough to make civilian."... John Ireland, as Windy, a contemplative GI as he examines his fingernails while resting: "A man's hands never seem to get clean, even if he don't touch nothing. They just stay dirty. Some of a special kind of dirty, G.I. dirt. I bet one of those criminologists could take a sample out of a guy's fingernail, put it under a microscope, and say: 'That's G.I. dirt.' The dirt's always the same color, no matter what country you're in."

Wall Street, 1987: Michael Douglas: "Greed, for the lack of a better word, is good."

WALL-E, 2008; Voice in commercial in opening lines: "Too much garbage in your face? There's plenty of space out in space. BnL Starliners leaving each day. We'll clean up the mess while you're away."

West Side Story, 1961; Natalie Wood, as Maria: "All of you! You all killed him! And my brother, and Riff. Not with bullets or guns—with hate! Well, now I can kill, too, because now I have hate!"

The Westerner, 1940; Cowboy Gary Cooper to Walter Brennan, who plays the self-appointed treacherous and corrupt Judge Roy Bean: "When I was a kid, I had a pet rattlesnake. I was fond of it, but I wouldn't turn my back on it."...Brennan to Cooper as they have a drink together in Brennan's saloon: "Don't spill any of that liquor, son. It eats right into the bar."...Brennan after he is asked if he ever met the female idol of his life, singer Lillie Langtry: "No, I never met her. I never met the sun. I never shook hands with the moon, and I've never been introduced to no clouds."

Who Framed Roger Rabbit, 1988; Kathleen Turner (voiceover as the animated Jessica Rabbit), to detective Bob Hoskins: "I'm not bad. I'm just drawn that way."

The Wild Bunch, 1969; William Holden to Bo Hopkins as they are in the course of a robbery and holding customers at gunpoint: "If they move, kill them!"...Hopkins, mortally wounded and remaining behind after the robbery, to lawmen who have shot him: "Well, how'd you like to kiss my sister's black cat's ass?"...Holden to his fellow outlaws, some of whom want to eliminate one of their gang members: "We're not going to get rid of anybody! We're going to stick together just like it used to be! When you side with a man, you stay with him, and if you can't do that, you're like some animal, you're finished! We're finished! All of us!"

The Wizard of Oz, 1939; Judy Garland to her dog as she enters the world of Oz: "Toto, I've a feeling we're not in Kansas anymore."...Margaret Hamilton as the Wicked Witch of the West, to Garland: "Just try and stay out of my way. Just try! I'll get you, my pretty, and your little dog, too!"...Frank Morgan, a bogus wizard manipulating thunderous machines to frighten Garland and her friends, after her dog, Toto, pulls away a curtain to expose Morgan operating those machines: "Pay no attention to that man behind the curtain!"...Morgan to Jack Haley (the Tin Man seeking a heart from the wizard): "A heart is not judged by how much you love, but by how much you are loved by others."

Wuthering Heights, 1939; Laurence Olivier as Heathcliff (mourning with guilt over the loss of the only woman he loved): "Catherine Earnshaw, may you not rest so long as I live on! I killed you! Haunt me then! Haunt your murderer! I know that ghosts have wandered on the Earth. Be with me always. Take any form, drive me mad...only do not leave me in this dark alone where I cannot find you. I cannot live without my life! I cannot die without my soul!"

Yankee Doodle Dandy, 1942: James Cagney, as entertainer-composer George M. Cohan, to an audience when finishing a performance with his family members: "My mother thanks you. My father thanks you. My sister thanks you. And I thank you!"

You Can't Cheat an Honest Man, 1939; W.C. Fields, as Larson E. Whipsnade, to some children annoying him (as all children did): "You kids are disgusting! Staggering around here all day, reeking of popcorn and lollipops!"...Fields: "As my dear old grandfather Litvak said (just before they swung the trap): 'You can't cheat an honest man. Never give a sucker an even break or smarten up a chump.'"...Fields to nemesis Charlie McCarthy, the inimitable wooden dummy so artfully managed by ventriloquist Edgar Bergen: "I shall send over a couple of pet beavers to romp with you."...McCarthy to Fields (who had a bulbous proboscis): "Are you eating a tomato or is that your nose?"

You're Telling Me!, 1934; W.C. Fields, as Sam Bisbee, to Adrienne Ames, as Princess Lescaboura, after Fields mistakenly thinks she is contemplating suicide: "When you wake up in the morning and find yourself dead, you'll regret it."...Fields when cautioning his daughter, Joan Marsh, as Pauline Bisbee, to be careful before deciding to marry: "Pick and choose, dear. Liberty is sweet. Once you're married, it's just like being in jail."

PERSONALITIES QUOTED

Note: The following index cites several hundred film industry personalities, or those historic personalities related to film productions, and who provided quotes about their films and their personal recollections about the film industry that were exclusively acquired by Jay Robert Nash in meetings and interviews with these personalities. Following the names of these personalities are A-Z film titles about which these persons commented, these statements appearing for the first time in this work.

George Abbott (director-writer, 1887-1995): **My Sin**, 1973.

Robert Aldrich (director, 1918-1983): **Attack**, 1956 (see his remarks under *Author's Note* in **Too Late the Hero**); **The Dirty Dozen**, 1967 (see his remarks under *Author's Note* in **Too Late the Hero**); **The Flight of the Phoenix**, 1965; **Hush...Hush, Sweet Charlotte**, 1964; **Kiss Me Deadly**, 1955; **Too Late the Hero**, 1970; **Twilight's Last Gleaming**, 1977; **Ulzana's Raid**, 1972; **Vera Cruz**, 1954; **What Ever Happened to Baby Jane?**, 1962; **World for Ransom**, 1954.

The Amazing Criswell (Jeron Criswell King, psychic, 1907-1982): **Ed Wood**, 1994.

Eric Ambler (author, 1909-1998): **The Mask of Dimitrios**, 1944.

Don Ameche (actor, 1908-1993): **Cocoon**, 1985 (see his remarks under *Author's Note* in **Things Change**); **In Old Chicago**, 1938; **Midnight**, 1939; **Moon over Miami**, 1941; **The Story of Alexander Graham Bell**, 1939; **Swanee River**, 1939; **That Night in Rio**, 1941; **Things Change**, 1988; **Trading Places**, 1983; **Wing and a Prayer**, 1944; **You Can't Have Everything**, 1937.

Dana Andrews (actor, 1909-1992): **The Best Years of Our Lives**, 1946 (see his remarks under *Author's Note* in **Where the Sidewalk Ends**); **Boomerang!**, 1947 (see his remarks under *Author's Note* in **Where the Sidewalk Ends**); **Fallen Angel**, 1945 (see his remarks under *Author's Note* in **Where the Sidewalk Ends**); **Laura**, 1944 (see his remarks under *Author's Note* in **Where the Sidewalk Ends**); **No Minor Vices**, 1948; **The North Star**, 1943; **The Ox-Bow Incident**, 1943; **The Purple Heart**, 1944; **Sealed Cargo**, 1951; **State Fair**, 1946; **Sword in the Desert**, 1949; **Three Hours to Kill**, 1954; **Tobacco Road**, 1941; **A Walk in the Sun**, 1945; **The Westerner**, 1940; **Where the Sidewalk Ends**, 1950; **While the City Sleeps**, 1956; **Wing and a Prayer**, 1944.

Jack Arnold (director, 1916-1992): **The Mouse That Roared**, 1959.

Jean Arthur (actress, 1900-1991): **A Foreign Affair**, 1948; **History Is Made at Night**, 1937; **The More the Merrier**, 1943; **Mr. Deeds Goes to Town**, 1936; **Mr. Smith Goes to Washington**, 1939; **Only Angels Have Wings**, 1939; **The Plainsman**, 1936; **Shane**, 1953; **The Silver Horde**, 1930; **The Talk of the Town**, 1942; **The Whole Town's Talking**, 1935; **You Can't Take It with You**, 1938.

Fred Astaire (actor-dancer-singer, 1899-1987): **The Band Wagon**, 1953 (his remarks about this film are in the *Author's Note* for **Royal Wedding**); **Flying Down to Rio**, 1933; **Follow the Fleet**, 1936; **The Gay Divorcee**, 1934; **Holiday Inn**, 1942; **The Pleasure of His Company**, 1961; **Roberta**, 1935; **Royal Wedding**, 1951; **Shall We Dance**, 1937; **Silk Stockings**, 1957; **The Story of Vernon and Irene Castle**, 1939; **Swing Time**, 1936; **Three Little Words**, 1950; **Top Hat**, 1935; **The Towering Inferno**, 1974; **Yankee Doodle Dandy**, 1942; **Yolanda and the Thief**, 1945; **You Were Never Lovelier**, 1942; **You'll Never Get Rich**, 1941; **The Ziegfeld Follies**, 1945.

Mary Astor (actress, 1906-1987): **The Hurricane**, 1937; **The Maltese Falcon**, 1941; **The Man with Two Faces**, 1934; **Meet Me in St. Louis**, 1944; **Midnight**, 1939; **The Palm Beach Story**, 1942; **The Prisoner of Zenda**, 1937; **Red Dust**, 1932; **Two Arabian Knights**, 1927; **The World Changes**, 1933.

James Henry "Blackie" Audett (1930s bank robber, c. 1902-1979): **Bonnie and Clyde**, 1967.

Lew Ayres (actor, 1908-1996): **Fingers at the Window**, 1942; **Young Dr. Kildare**, 1938.

Anne Bancroft (actress, 1931-2005): **The Miracle Worker**, 1962; **7 Women**, 1966; **The Turning Point**, 1977; **Young Winston**, 1972.

Richard Basehart (actor, 1914-1984): **Fourteen Hours**, 1951; **He Walked by Night**, 1948; **The House on Telegraph Hill**, 1951; **Moby Dick**, 1956; **Reign of Terror**, 1949; **Time Limit**, 1957; **Titanic**, 1953.

Ed Begley (actor, 1901-1970): **Patterns**, 1956; **Sorry, Wrong Number**, 1948; **12 Angry Men**, 1957.

Ralph Bellamy (actor, 1904-1991): **Footsteps in the Dark**, 1941; **The Narrow Corner**, 1933; **Queen of the Mob**, 1940; **Rosemary's Baby**, 1968; **The Secret Six**, 1931; **Spitfire**, 1934; **Stage Door Canteen**, 1943; **Sunrise at Campobello**, 1960; **Trade Winds**, 1938; **Trading Places**, 1983; **The Wedding Night**, 1935.

Saul Bellow (author, 1915-2005): **Specter of the Rose**, 1946.

John Belushi (actor-comedian, 1949-1982): **National Lampoon's Animal House**, 1978.

Paul Benedict (actor, 1938-2008): **The Goodbye Girl**, 1977.

Bruce Bennett (Harold Herman Brix; actor, 1906-2007): **Mildred Pierce**, 1945; **Mystery Street**, 1950; **Sahara**, 1943; **A Stolen Life**, 1946; **Sudden Fear**, 1952; **The Treasure of the Sierra Madre**, 1948.

Joan Bennett (actress, 1910-1990): **Moby Dick**, 1930; **The Reckless Moment**, 1949; **Scarlet Street**, 1945; **Secret beyond the Door**, 1948; **Trade Winds**, 1938; **The Woman in the Window**, 1944; **The Woman on the Beach**, 1947.

Jack Benny (actor-comedian, 1894-1974): **George Washington Slept Here**, 1942; **It's a Mad, Mad, Mad, Mad World**, 1963; **It's in the Bag!**, 1945; **To Be or Not to Be**, 1942.

Ingrid Bergman (actress, 1915-1982): **Arch of Triumph**, 1948 (see her remarks in *Author's Note* under **Saratoga Trunk**); **The Bells of St. Mary's**, 1945 (see her remarks in *Author's Note* under **Saratoga Trunk**); **For Whom the Bell Tolls**, 1943; **Gaslight**, 1944; **The Inn of the Sixth Happiness**, 1958; **Intermezzo: A Love Story**, 1939; **Joan of Arc**, 1948; **The Maltese Falcon**, 1941; **Murder on the Orient Express**, 1974; **Notorious**, 1946; **The Passion of Joan of Arc**, 1929; **Saratoga Trunk**, 1945; **Spellbound**, 1945.

Busby Berkeley (choreographer-director, 1895-1976): **Footlight Parade**, 1933; **42nd Street**, 1933; **Gold Diggers of 1935**, 1935; **Hollywood Hotel**, 1937; **Take Me Out to the Ball Game**, 1949; **They Made Me a Criminal**, 1939.

Richard Boone (actor, 1917-1981): **Hombre**, 1967; **The Shootist**, 1968; **The Tall T**, 1957; **The War Lord**, 1965; **Winter Kills**, 1979.

Ernest Borgnine (actor, 1917-2012): **Bad Day at Black Rock**, 1955 (see his remarks under *Author's Note* in **Pay or Die**); **Marty**, 1955; **Pay or Die**, 1960; **The Poseidon Adventure**, 1972; **Season of Passion**, 1961; **Three Brave Men**, 1956; **Torpedo Run**, 1958; **Vera Cruz**, 1954; **The Vikings**, 1958; **Violent Saturday**, 1955; **The Whistle at Eaton Falls**, 1951; **The Wild Bunch**, 1969.

Charles Boyer (actor, 1899-1978): **The Garden of Allah**, 1936; **Gaslight**, 1944; **History Is Made at Night**, 1937; **Love Affair**, 1939; **Mayerling**, 1937; **Red-Headed Woman**, 1932; **Stavisky**, 1974; **The 13th Letter**, 1951; **Thunder in the East**, 1953; **Together Again**, 1944; **Tovarich**, 1937; **Watch on the Rhine**, 1943.

Peter Boyle (actor, 1935-2006): **The Friends of Eddie Coyle**, 1973.

Eddie Bracken (actor, 1915-2002): **The Miracle at Morgan's Creek**, 1944.

Ray Bradbury (author-screenwriter, 1920-2012): **King Kong**, 1933; **Moby Dick**, 1956.

Marlon Brando (actor, 1924-2004): **East of Eden**, 1955; **The Freshman**, 1990; **The Godfather**, 1972; **Guys and Dolls**, 1955; **Julius Caesar**, 1953; **The Men**, 1950; **The Missouri Breaks**, 1976; **Morituri**, 1965; **Mutiny on the Bounty**, 1962; **On the Waterfront**, 1954; **One-Eyed Jacks**, 1961; **Sayonara**, 1957; **A Streetcar Named Desire**, 1951; **Sudden Fear**, 1952; **Superman**, 1978; **The Teahouse of the August Moon**, 1956; **Viva Zapata!**, 1952; **War and Peace**, 1956; **The Wild One**, 1953; **The Young Lions**, 1958.

Walter Brennan (actor, 1894-1974): **Kentucky**, 1938; **My Darling Clementine**, 1946; **Northwest Passage**, 1940; **Pride of the Yankees**, 1942; **Red River**, 1948; **Scudda-Hoo! Scudda Hay!**, 1948; **Sergeant York**, 1941; **The Showdown**, 1950; **Stand by for Action**, 1942; **Stanley and Livingstone**, 1939; **A Stolen Life**, 1946; **The Story of Irene and Vernon Castle**, 1939; **Support Your Local Sheriff**, 1969; **Swamp Water**, 1941; **Tammy and the Bachelor**, 1957; **Task Force**, 1949; **Three Godfathers**, 1936; **To Have and Have Not**, 1944; **The Westerner**, 1940.

Sandy Bresler (Hollywood agent): **The Graduate**, 1967.

Charles Bronson (actor, 1921-2003): **Hard Times**, 1975; **The Magnificent Seven**, 1960; **Mr. Majestyk**, 1974; **Once upon a Time in the West**, 1969; **The Valachi Papers**, 1972; **Vera Cruz**, 1954; **Villa Rides**, 1968; **The White Buffalo**, 1977.

Louise Brooks (actress, 1906-1985): **Beggars of Life**, 1928; **The Canary Murder Case**, 1929; **Diary of a Lost Girl**, 1929; **Pandora's Box**, 1929; **A Social Celebrity**, 1926; **When You're in Love**, 1937.

Richard Brooks (director-producer-writer, 1912-1992): **Lord Jim**, 1965; **The Professionals**, 1966; **Something of Value**, 1957; **Sweet Bird of Youth**, 1962.

Clarence Brown (director, 1890-1987): **A Free Soul**, 1931; **The Human Comedy**, 1943; **Idiot's Delight**, 1939; **Intruder in the Dust**, 1949; **Night Flight**, 1933; **Of Human Hearts**, 1938; **Plymouth Adventure**, 1952; **The Rains Came**, 1939; **Sadie McKee**, 1934; **They Met in Bombay**, 1941; **The Trail of '98**, 1928; **The White Cliffs of Dover**, 1944; **Wife vs. Secretary**, 1936; **A Woman of Affairs**, 1928; **The Yearling**, 1946.

Lenny Bruce (Leonard Alfred Schneider; comedian, 1925-1966): **Lenny**, 1974.

Charles Bukowski (poet-screenwriter, 1920-1994): **Barfly**, 1987.

Henry Bumstead (art director-production designer, 1915-2006): **Flags of Our Fathers**, 2006; **High Plains Drifter**, 1973.

W. R. Burnett (novelist-screenwriter, 1899-1982): **The Finger Points**, 1931; **Illegal**, 1955; **Little Caesar**, 1931; **San Antonio**, 1949; **Yellow Sky**, 1948.

Richard Burton (actor, 1925-1984): **The Desert Rats**, 1953 (see his remarks under *Author's Note* in **Where Eagles Dare**); **Prince of Players**, 1955; **The Robe**, 1953; **The Spy Who Came in From the Cold**, 1965; **The Taming of the Shrew**, 1957; **Under Milk Wood**, 1973; **The V.I.P.s**, 1963; **Where Eagles Dare**, 1969; **Who's Afraid of Virginia Woolf?**, 1966; **The Wild Geese**, 1978.

James Cagney (actor, 1899-1986): **Angels with Dirty Faces**, 1938 (see his remarks in *Author's Note* in entry for **The Roaring Twenties**); **Boy Meets Girl**, 1938; **The Bride Came C.O.D.**, 1941 (see his remarks under *Author's Note* in **The St. Louis Kid**); **Ceiling Zero**, 1935; **City for Conquest**, 1941; **Come Fill the Cup**, 1951; **Devil Dogs of the Air**, 1935; **Doorway to Hell**, 1930; **Each Dawn I Die**, 1939; **The Fighting 69th**, 1940; **Frisco Kid**, 1935; **The Gallant Hours**, 1960; **G-Men**, 1935; **Here Comes the Navy**, 1934; **High Sierra**, 1941; **The Irish in Us**, 1935; **Jimmy the Gent**, 1934; **Kiss Tomorrow Goodbye**, 1950; **A Lion Is in the Streets**, 1953; **Love Me or Leave Me**, 1955; **Man of a Thousand Faces**, 1957; **The Mayor of Hell**, 1933; **A Midsummer Night's Dream**, 1935; **Mister Roberts**, 1955; **The Millionaire**, 1931; **Never Steal Anything Small**, 1959; **The Oklahoma Kid**, 1939; **One, Two, Three**, 1961; **Picture Snatcher**, 1933; **The Public Enemy**, 1931; **The Roaring Twenties**, 1939; **Run for Cover**, 1955; **The St. Louis Kid**, 1934; **The Seven Little Foys**, 1955; **Shake Hands with the Devil**, 1959; **Sinner's Holiday**, 1930; **Smart Money**, 1931; **Something to Sing About**, 1937; **The Strawberry Blonde**, 1941; **Taxi!**, 1932; **These Wilder Years**, 1956; **13 Rue Madeleine**, 1947; **The Time of Your Life**, 1948; **Torrid Zone**, 1940; **Tribute to a Bad Man**, 1956; **20,000 Years in Sing Sing**, 1932; **The West Point Story**, 1950; **What Price Glory**, 1952; **White Heat**, 1949; **Winner Take All**, 1932; **Yankee Doodle Dandy**, 1942.

Frank Capra (director, 1897-1991): **Dirigible**, 1931; **Flight**, 1929; **A Hole in the Head**, 1959; **It Happened One Night**, 1934; **It's a Wonderful Life**, 1946; **Lady for a Day**, 1933; **Long Pants**, 1927; **Lost Horizon**, 1937; **Meet John Doe**, 1941; **The Miracle Woman**, 1931; **Mr. Deeds Goes to Town**, 1936; **Mr. Smith Goes to Washington**, 1939; **Platinum Blonde**, 1931; **A Pocketful of Miracles**, 1961; **Riding High**, 1950; **Roman Holiday**, 1953; **State of the Union**, 1948; **Submarine**, 1928; **Ten Days That Shook the World**, 1928; **Westward the Women**, 1951; **The Whole Town's Talking**, 1935; **You Can't Take It with You**, 1938.

Richard Carlson (actor, 1912-1977): **King Solomon's Mines**, 1950; **Retreat Hell!**, 1952; **Seminole**, 1953; **The Sound of Fury**, 1950.

Art Carney (actor-comedian, 1918-2003): **Harry and Tonto**, 1974; **The Odd Couple**, 1968.

Johnny Carson (host of *The Tonight Show*, 1925-2005): **Network**, 1976.

Lon Chaney Jr. (actor, 1906-1973): **The Ghost of Frankenstein**, 1942; **The House of Frankenstein**, 1944; **The Indian Fighter**, 1955; **One Million B.C.**, 1940; **Son of Dracula**, 1943; **The Wolf Man**, 1941.

Eduardo Ciannelli (actor, 1889-1964): **Gunga Din**, 1939; **Marked Woman**, 1937.

Dane Clark (actor, 1912-1998): **Pride of the Marines**, 1945; **A Stolen Life**, 1946; **The Very Thought of You**, 1944.

Lee J. Cobb (actor, 1911-1976): **On the Waterfront**, 1954 (see his remarks under *Author's Note* in **Party Girl**); **Party Girl**, 1958; **The Song of Bernadette**, 1943; **12 Angry Men**, 1957.

Claudette Colbert (actress, 1903-1996): **Imitation of Life**, 1934; **It Happened One Night**, 1934; **Midnight**, 1939; **No Time for Love**, 1943; **The Palm Beach Story**, 1942; **Remember the Day**, 1941; **The Secret Heart**, 1946; **She Married Her Boss**, 1935; **The Sign of the Cross**, 1932; **Since You Went Away**, 1944; **The Smiling Lieutenant**, 1931; **So Proudly We Hail**, 1943; **Three Came Home**, 1950; **Three-Cornered Moon**, 1933; **Thunder on the Hill**, 1951; **Tomorrow Is Forever**, 1946; **Tovarich**, 1937; **Under Two Flags**, 1936; **Without Reservations**, 1946.

Marc Connelly (actor-director-playwright-screenwriter, 1890-1980): **The Green Pastures**, 1936.

Elisha Cook Jr. (actor, 1903-1995): **I Wake Up Screaming**, 1941; **The Maltese Falcon**, 1941; **Trial**, 1955.

Gary Cooper (actor, 1901-1961): **A Farewell to Arms**, 1932; **Fighting Caravans**, 1931; **High Noon**, 1952; **Meet John Doe**, 1941; **Morocco**, 1930; **Mr. Deeds Goes to Town**, 1936; **Northwest Mounted Police**, 1940; **Peter Ibbetson**,1935; **The Plainsman**, 1936; **Pride of the Yankees**, 1942; **The Real Glory**, 1939; **Saratoga Trunk**, 1945; **Sergeant York**, 1941; **Souls at Sea**, 1937; **Springfield Rifle**, 1952; **The Story of Dr. Wassell**, 1944; **Task Force**, 1949; **The Texan**, 1930; **They Came to Cordura**, 1959; **Unconquered**, 1947; **Vera Cruz**, 1954; **The Virginian**, 1929; **The Wedding Night**, 1935; **The Westerner**, 1940; **The Winning of Barbara Worth**, 1926; **Wolf Song**, 1929; **The Wreck of the Mary Deare**, 1959; **You're in the Navy Now**, 1951.

Jackie Cooper (actor, 1922-2011): **Treasure Island**, 1934.

Merian C. Cooper (director-producer, 1893-1973): **King Kong**, 1933; **The Last Days of Pompeii**, 1935.

Jeff Corey (actor, 1914-2002): **Little Big Man**, 1970; **True Grit**, 1969.

Joseph Cotten (actor, 1905-1994): **Citizen Kane**, 1941; **Duel in the Sun**, 1943; **The Farmer's Daughter**, 1947; **Hush...Hush, Sweet Charlotte**, 1964; **Journey into Fear**, 1943; **Love Letters**, 1945; **The Magnificent Ambersons**, 1942; **The Man with a Cloak**, 1951; **Portrait of Jennie**, 1949; **September Affair**, 1950; **Shadow of a Doubt**, 1943; **Since You Went Away**, 1944; **The Steel Trap**, 1952; **The Third Man**, 1950; **Tora! Tora! Tora!**, 1970; **Touch of Evil**, 1958; **Twilight's Last Gleaming**, 1977; **Two Flags West**, 1950; **Walk Softly, Stranger**, 1950.

James Craig (actor, 1912-1985): **The Devil and Daniel Webster**, 1941; **Kitty Foyle**, 1940.

Jeanne Crain (actress, 1925-2003): **Margie**, 1946; **State Fair**, 1945; **Winged Victory**, 1944.

Joan Crawford (actress, 1905-1977): **Grand Hotel**, 1932; **Harriet Craig**, 1950; **Humoresque**, 1946; **Love on the Run**, 1936; **Mildred Pierce**, 1945; **Possessed**, 1947; **Rain**, 1932; **Reunion in France**, 1942; **Sadie McKee**, 1934; **The Story of Esther Costello**, 1957; **Strange Cargo**, 1940; **Sudden Fear**, 1952; **Susan and God**, 1940; **They All Kissed the Bride**, 1942; **This Woman Is Dangerous**, 1952; **Torch Song**, 1953; **Tramp, Tramp, Tramp**, 1927; **The Unknown**, 1927;

West Point, 1927; **What Ever Happened to Baby Jane?**, 1962; **When Ladies Meet**, 1941; **A Woman's Face**, 1941; **The Women**, 1939.

[John] Michael Crichton (author-screenwriter, 1942-2008): **Jurassic Park**, 1993; **Them!**, 1954.

Donald Crisp (actor, 1882-1974): **How Green Was My Valley**, 1941; **Lassie Come Home**, 1943; **The Man from Laramie**, 1955 (see his remarks under *Author's Note* in **Saddle in the Wind**); **Mutiny on the Bounty**, 1935; **The Private Lives of Elizabeth and Essex**, 1939; **Saddle in the Wind**, 1958; **The Sea Hawk**, 1940; **Son of Lassie**, 1945; **Svengali**, 1931; **That Certain Woman**, 1937; **The Uninvited**, 1944; **The Valley of Decision**, 1945; **Whispering Smith**, 1948; **The White Angel**, 1936; **Wuthering Heights**, 1939.

John Cromwell (director, 1887-1979): **Of Human Bondage**, 1934; **The Prisoner of Zenda**, 1937; **The Racket**, 1951; **Scandal Sheet**, 1931; **Since You Went Away**, 1944; **So Ends Our Night**, 1941; **Son of Fury: Spitfire**, 1934; **The Story of Benjamin Blake**, 1942; **The Texan**, 1930; **Tom Sawyer**, 1930.

Hume Cronyn (actor, 1911-2003): **Brute Force**, 1947; **Gaily, Gaily**, 1969; **Lifeboat**, 1944; **People Will Talk**, 1951; **The Postman Always Rings Twice**, 1946; **Rope**, 1948; **The Seventh Cross**, 1944; **Shadow of a Doubt**, 1943; **Sunrise at Campobello**, 1960; **There Was a Crooked Man**, 1970.

Bing Crosby (actor-singer, 1903-1977): **Going Hollywood**, 1933; **Going My Way**, 1944; **The Great John L**, 1945; **Holiday Inn**, 1942; **Mississippi**, 1935; **Pennies from Heaven**, 1936; **Riding High**, 1950; **Road to Morocco**, 1942; **Road to Rio**, 1947; **Road to Utopia**, 1946; **Robin and the 7 Hoods**, 1964; **Sing, You Sinners**, 1938; **The Star Maker**, 1939; **Waikiki Wedding**, 1937; **Welcome Stranger**, 1947; **We're Not Dressing**, 1934; **White Christmas**, 1954.

George Cukor (director, 1899-1983): **Gaslight**, 1944; **Gone with the Wind**, 1939; **Holiday**, 1938; **Keeper of the Flame**, 1942; **Les Girls**, 1957; **Little Women**, 1933; **One Hour with You**, 1932; **Our Betters**, 1933; **Pat and Mike**, 1952; **The Philadelphia Story**, 1940; **Romeo and Juliet**, 1936; **The Royal Family of Broadway**, 1930; **A Star Is Born**, 1954; **Susan and God**, 1940; **Sylvia Scarlett**, 1936; **Tarnished Lady**, 1931; **Travels with My Aunt**, 1972; **Two-Faced Woman**, 1941; **What Price Hollywood?**, 1932; **Wild Is the Wind**, 1957; **Winged Victory**, 1944; **The Wizard of Oz**, 1939; **A Woman's Face**, 1941; **The Women**, 1939.

Tony Curtis (actor, 1925-2010): **The Defiant Ones**, 1958 (see his remarks under *Author's Note* in **The Outsider**); **Operation Petticoat**, 1959; **The Outsider**, 1961; **Some Like It Hot**, 1959; **Spartacus**, 1960; **Sweet Smell of Success**, 1957; **Trapeze**, 1956; **The Vikings**, 1958; **Who Was That Lady?**, 1960.

Rodney Dangerfield (actor-comedian, 1921-2004): **Easy Money**, 1983; **The Projectionist**, 1971.

Bette Davis (actress, 1908-1989): **All about Eve**, 1950; **The Bride Came C.O.D.**, 1941; **Fog over Frisco**, 1934; **The Great Lie**, 1941; **The Hard Way**, 1942; **Hollywood Canteen**, 1944 (see her remarks under *Author's Note* in **So Big**); **Hush...Hush, Sweet Charlotte**, 1964; **Jezebel**, 1938; **Jimmy the Gent**, 1934; **Juarez**, 1939; **Kid Galahad**, 1937; **The Letter**, 1940; **The Little Foxes**, 1941; **The Man Who Came to Dinner**, 1942; **Marked Woman**, 1937; **Mr. Skeffington**, 1944; **Now Voyager**, 1940; **Of Human Bondage**, 1934; **The Old Maid**, 1939; **Payment on Demand**, 1951; **The Petrified Forest**, 1936; **Phone Call from a Stranger**, 1952; **A Pocketful of Miracles**, 1961; **The Private**

Lives of Elizabeth and Essex, 1939; Satan Met a Lady, 1936; The Sisters, 1938; So Big, 1932; The Star, 1952; A Stolen Life, 1946; Thank Your Lucky Stars, 1943; That Certain Woman, 1937; Three on a Match, 1932; 20,000 Years in Sing Sing, 1932; The Virgin Queen, 1955; Watch on the Rhine, 1943; Waterloo Bridge, 1931; What Ever Happened to Baby Jane?, 1962.

Laraine Day (actress, 1920-2007): Fingers at the Window, 1942; Foreign Correspondent, 1940; Mr. Lucky, 1943; Sorry, Wrong Number, 1948; Tycoon, 1947.

Frances Dee (actress, 1909-2004): I Walked with a Zombie, 1943; So Ends Our Night, 1941; Souls at Sea, 1937; Wells Fargo, 1937.

William Dieterle (director-actor, 1893-1972): Juarez, 1939; The Life of Emile Zola, 1937; Love Letters, 1945; A Midsummer Night's Dream, 1935; Portrait of Jennie, 1949; Red Mountain, 1951; Rope of Sand, 1949; Salome, 1953; Satan Met a Lady, 1936; The Searching Wind, 1946; September Affair, 1950; The Story of Louis Pasteur, 1936; Tennessee Johnson, 1942; The Turning Point, 1952; Waxworks, 1929; The White Angel, 1936.

Marlene Dietrich (actress, 1901-1992): A Foreign Affair, 1948; The Garden of Allah, 1936; Knight without Armor, 1937; Manpower, 1941; Morocco, 1930; No Highway in the Sky, 1951; Pittsburgh, 1942; Rancho Notorious, 1952; The Scarlet Empress, 1934; Seven Sinners, 1940; Shanghai Express, 1932; The Spoilers, 1942; Stage Fright, 1950; Touch of Evil, 1958; Witness for the Prosecution, 1957.

Joseph Vincent "Little Caesar" Divarco (1911-1986; Chicago mobster and member of the Chicago Outfit): Scarface, 1932.

Edward Dmytryk (director, 1909-1999): Murder, My Sweet, 1944; Raintree County, 1957; Secrets of the Lone Wolf, 1941; The Sniper, 1952; Tender Comrade, 1943; Till the End of Time, 1946; Walk on the Wild Side, 1962; Warlock, 1959; The Young Lions, 1958.

Brian Donlevy (actor, 1901-1972): Impact, 1949; In Old Chicago, 1938; Jesse James, 1939 (see his remarks under Author's Note in The Virginian); The Remarkable Andrew, 1942; Shakedown, 1950; A Southern Yankee, 1948; Stand by for Action, 1942; Two Years before the Mast, 1946; Union Pacific, 1939; The Virginian, 1946; Wake Island, 1942; When the Daltons Rode, 1940; Woman They Almost Lynched, 1953.

Irene Dunne (actress, 1898-1990): A Guy Named Joe, 1943; I Remember Mama, 1948; Love Affair, 1939; The Mudlark, 1950; Penny Serenade, 1941; Roberta, 1935; Show Boat, 1936; Theodora Goes Wild, 1936; Thirteen Women, 1932; Together Again, 1944; The White Cliffs of Dover, 1944.

Julius J. Epstein (screenwriter, 1909-2000): Casablanca, 1942; Four Daughters, 1938; Mr. Skeffington, 1944; No Time for Comedy, 1940; Pete 'n' Tillie, 1972; The Strawberry Blonde, 1941; Yankee Doodle Dandy, 1942.

Douglas Fairbanks Jr. (actor-producer, 1909-2000): Gunga Din, 1939; The Prisoner of Zenda, 1937; Union Depot, 1932; The Young in Heart, 1938.

Peter Falk (actor, 1927-2011): The In-Laws, 1979; Murder by Death, 1976; Murder, Inc., 1960; A Pocketful of Miracles, 1961; The Princess Bride, 1987; Wind across the Everglades, 1958; A Woman under the Influence, 1974.

Alice Faye (actress-singer, 1915-1998): The Great American Broadcast, 1941; In Old Chicago, 1938; On the Avenue, 1937; Poor Little Rich Girl, 1936; Rose of Washington Square, 1939; Sally, Irene and Mary, 1938; Sing, Baby, Sing, 1936; That Night in Rio, 1941; Tin Pan Alley, 1940; Wake Up and Live, 1937; Week-End in Havana, 1941; You Can't Have Everything, 1937.

Tom Fitzpatrick (journalist-newspaper columnist, 1927-2002): Medium Cool, 1969.

Richard Fleischer (director; 1916-2006): The Narrow Margin, 1952; 10 Rillington Place, 1971; Tora! Tora! Tora!, 1970; Trapped, 1949; 20,000 Leagues under the Sea, 1954; The Vikings, 1958; Violent Saturday, 1955.

Henry Fonda (actor, 1905-1982): Drums along the Mohawk, 1939; Fort Apache, 1948; The Fugitive, 1947; The Grapes of Wrath, 1940; Jezebel, 1938; The Lady Eve, 1941; The Long Night, 1947; The Longest Day, 1962; The Mad Miss Manton, 1938; Madigan, 1968; The Male Animal, 1942; Midway, 1976; Mister Roberts, 1955; Murder!, 1930; My Darling Clementine, 1946; Once upon a Time in the West, 1969; The Ox-Bow Incident, 1943; The Return of Frank James, 1940; The Serpent, 1973; Sex and the Single Girl, 1964; Sometimes a Great Notion, 1970; Spawn of the North, 1939; Spencer's Mountain, 1963; The Story of Alexander Graham Bell, 1939; Tales of Manhattan, 1942; That Certain Woman, 1937; There Was a Crooked Man, 1970; The Tin Star, 1957; Too Late the Hero, 1970; Trail of the Lonesome Pine, 1936; 12 Angry Men, 1957; War and Peace, 1956; Warlock, 1959; Wild Geese Calling, 1941; Wings of the Morning, 1937; The Wrong Man, 1956; You Belong to Me, 1941; You Only Live Once, 1937; Young Mr. Lincoln, 1939.

Glenn Ford (actor, 1916-2006): Follow the Sun, 1951; Gilda, 1946; Jubal, 1956; The Man from the Alamo, 1963; Midway, 1976; A Pocketful of Miracles, 1961; Ransom!, 1956; The Rounders, 1965; The Sheepman, 1958; So Ends Our Night, 1941; A Stolen Life, 1946; Texas, 1941; 3:10 to Yuma, 1957; Torpedo Run, 1958; Trial, 1955; The Undercover Man, 1949; The Untouchables, 1987; The Violent Men, 1955; The White Tower, 1950; Young Man with Ideas, 1952.

John Ford (director, 1894-1973): Cheyenne Autumn, 1964; Fort Apache, 1948; Four Sons, 1928; The Fugitive, 1947; The Grapes of Wrath, 1940; The Horse Soldiers, 1959; How Green Was My Valley, 1941; How the West Was Won, 1963; The Hurricane, 1937; The Informer, 1935; The Iron Horse, 1924; The Long Gray Line, 1955; The Long Voyage Home, 1940; The Lost Patrol, 1934; The Man Who Shot Liberty Valance, 1962; Mary of Scotland, 1936; Mighty Joe Young, 1949; Mister Roberts, 1955; Mogambo, 1953; My Darling Clementine, 1946; Pinky, 1949; The Plough and the Stars, 1936; The Prisoner of Shark Island, 1936; The Quiet Man, 1952; The Rising of the Moon, 1957; Rio Grande, 1950; The Searchers, 1956; Sergeant Rutledge, 1960; She Wore a Yellow Ribbon, 1949; Stagecoach, 1939; Steamboat Round the Bend, 1935; Submarine Patrol, 1938; The Sun Shines Bright, 1953; Tabu: A Story of the South Seas, 1931; They Were Expendable, 1945; 3 Godfathers, 1948; Tobacco Road, 1941; Up the River, 1930; Wagonmaster, 1950; Wee Willie Winkie, 1937; What Price Glory, 1952; When Willie Comes Marching Home, 1950; The Whole Town's Talking, 1935; Wild Boys of the Road, 1933; The Wings of Eagles, 1957; The World Moves On, 1934; Young Cassidy, 1965; Young Mr. Lincoln, 1939.

John Frankenheimer (director; 1930-2002): La bete humaine, 1940; The Manchurian Candidate, 1962; Ronin, 1998; Seconds, 1966; Seven Days in May, 1964; The Train, 1965; The Young Savages, 1961.

Everett Freeman (producer-writer, 1911-1991): **The Glass Bottom Boat**, 1966.

Samuel Fuller (director-writer, 1912-1997): **I Shot Jesse James**, 1949; **Park Row**, 1952; **Pickup on South Street**, 1953; **Run of the Arrow**, 1957; **Scandal Sheet**, 1952; **The Steel Helmet**, 1951; **Shock Corridor**, 1963; **Underworld U.S.A.**, 1961; **White Dog**, 1982.

Greta Garbo (actress, 1905-1990): **Anna Christie**, 1930; **As You Desire Me**, 1932; **Camille**, 1937; **Flesh and the Devil**, 1926; **Grand Hotel**, 1932; **I Remember Mama**, 1948; **Mata Hari**, 1931; **The Match King**, 1932; **Ninotchka**, 1939; **The Painted Veil**, 1934; **The Paradine Case**, 1947; **The Princess Comes Across**, 1936; **Queen Christina**, 1933; **Sunset Boulevard**, 1950; **Susan Lenox (Her Fall and Rise)**, 1931; **Tabu: A Story of the South Seas**, 1931; **The Temptress**, 1926; **Torrent**, 1926; **Two-Faced Woman**, 1941; **Wild Orchids**, 1929; **A Woman of Affairs**, 1928.

Ava Gardner (actress, 1922-1990): **The Killers**, 1948; **The Life and Times of Judge Roy Bean**, 1972; **Mogambo**, 1953; **Seven Days in May**, 1964; **Show Boat**, 1951; **Singapore**, 1947; **The Snows of Kilimanjaro**, 1952; **The Sun Also Rises**, 1957; **Whistle Stop**, 1946; **Whistle Stop**, 1946.

Brian Garfield (writer, 1939-): **Death Wish**, 1974.

Lee Garmes (cinematograper-director, 1898-1978): **Morocco**, 1930; **A Social Celebrity**, 1926.

William Taylor "Tay" Garnett (director, 1894-1977): **China Seas**, 1935; **Love Is News**, 1937; **One Minute to Zero**, 1952; **One Way Passage**, 1932; **The Postman Always Rings Twice**, 1946; **Seven Sinners**, 1940; **Soldiers Three**, 1951; **Stand-In**, 1937; **Trade Winds**, 1938; **The Valley of Decision**, 1945; **Wild Harvest**, 1947.

Greer Garson (actress, 1904-1996): **Goodbye, Mr. Chips**, 1939; **Julia Misbehaves**, 1948; **Madame Curie**, 1943; **Mrs. Miniver**, 1942; **Pride and Prejudice**, 1940; **Random Harvest**, 1942; **Sunrise at Campobello**, 1960; **That Forsyte Woman**, 1949; **The Valley of Decision**, 1945; **When Ladies Meet**, 1941.

Jackie Gleason (actor-comedian, 1916-1987): **The Hustler**, 1961 (see Gleason's remarks in *Author's Note* for entry of **Requiem for a Heavyweight**); **Papa's Delicate Condition**, 1963; **Requiem for a Heavyweight**, 1962.

Samuel Goldwyn (producer, 1879-1974): **Dead End**, 1937; **The Hurricane**, 1937; **The Kid from Spain**, 1932; **The Little Foxes**, 1941; **Porgy and Bess**, 1959; **The Princess and the Pirate**, 1944; **Raffles**, 1930; **The Real Glory**, 1939; **Roseanna McCoy**, 1949; **A Song Is Born**, 1948; **Spitfire**, 1943; **Stella Dallas**, 1925; **Stella Dallas**, 1937; **Street Scene**, 1931; **These Three**, 1936; **Up in Arms**, 1944; **We Live Again**, 1934; **The Wedding Night**, 1935; **The Westerner**, 1940; **Whoopee!**, 1930; **The Winning of Barbara Worth**, 1926; **The Wizard of Oz**, 1939; **Wonder Man**, 1945; **Wuthering Heights**, 1939.

Thomas Gomez (actor, 1905-1971): **Force of Evil**, 1948; **Johnny O'Clock**, 1947; **Key Largo**, 1948; **Macao**, 1952; **Pony Soldier**, 1952; **Ride the Pink Horse**, 1947; **Sorrowful Jones**, 1949; **Summer and Smoke**, 1961; **That Midnight Kiss**, 1949; **Trapeze**, 1956; **The Woman on Pier 13**, 1949.

Betty Grable (actress-singer-dancer, 1916-1973): **I Wake Up Screaming**, 1942; **Springtime in the Rockies**, 1942; **Sweet Rosie O'Grady**, 1943; **Three for the Show**, 1955; **Tin Pan Alley**, 1940; **Wabash Avenue**, 1950; **When My Baby Smiles at Me**, 1948; **Whoopee!**, 1930; **A Yank in the R.A.F.**, 1941.

Stewart Granger (actor, 1913-1993): **King Solomon's Mines**, 1950; **The Prisoner of Zenda**, 1952; **Saraband**, 1949; **Scaramouche**, 1952; **Soldiers Three**, 1951; **The Wild North**, 1952; **Young Bess**, 1953.

Cary Grant (actor, 1904-1986): **The Awful Truth**, 1937 (see his remarks under *Author's Note* in **Topper**); **The Eagle and the Hawk**, 1933; **Father Goose**, 1964; **Gunga Din**, 1939; **His Girl Friday**, 1940; **Holiday**, 1938; **Houseboat**, 1958; **I Was a Male War Bride**, 1949; **Monkey Business**, 1952; **Mr. Blandings Builds His Dream House**, 1948; **Mr. Lucky**, 1943; **My Fair Lady**, 1964; **My Favorite Wife**, 1940; **Night and Day**, 1946; **North by Northwest**, 1959; **Notorious**, 1946; **Only Angels Have Wings**, 1939; **Operation Petticoat**, 1959; **Penny Serenade**, 1941; **People Will Talk**, 1951; **The Philadelphia Story**, 1940; **The Pride and the Passion**, 1957; **She Done Him Wrong**, 1933; **A Star Is Born**, 1954; **Suspicion**, 1941; **Suzy**, 1936; **Sylvia Scarlett**, 1936; **The Talk of the Town**, 1942; **That Touch of Mink**, 1962; **This Is the Night**, 1932; **To Catch a Thief**, 1955; **The Toast of New York**, 1937; **Topper**, 1937; **Walk, Don't Run**, 1966; **When You're in Love**, 1937; **Wings in the Dark**, 1935.

Jane Greer (actress, 1924-2001): **Out of the Past**, 1947; **The Prisoner of Zenda**, 1952; **Run for the Sun**, 1956; **Sinbad the Sailor**, 1947; **Station West**, 1948; **They Won't Believe Me**, 1947; **You're in the Navy Now**, 1951.

Andy Griffith (actor, 1926-2012): **A Face in the Crowd**, 1957; **No Time for Sergeants**, 1958.

Alec Guinness (actor, 1914-2000): **Dr. Zhivago**, 1965 (see his remarks in *Author's Note* in **Ryan's Daughter**); **Great Expectations**, 1946; **The Green Man**, 1950; **The Horse's Mouth**, 1958; **Kind Hearts and Coronets**, 1950; **The Ladykillers**, 1956; **The Lavender Hill Mob**, 1951; **Lawrence of Arabia**, 1962; **A Majority of One**, 1961; **Malta Story**, 1954; **The Man in the White Suit**, 1952; **The Mouse That Roared**, 1959; **The Mudlark**, 1950; **Murder by Death**, 1976; **Oliver Twist**, 1951; **Our Man in Havana**, 1960; **Passage to India**, 1984; **The Prisoner**, 1955; **The Promoter**, 1952; **Ryan's Daughter**, 1970; **The Swan**, 1956; **Tunes of Glory**, 1960.

Henry Hathaway (director, 1898-1985): **Fourteen Hours**, 1951; **Garden of Evil**, 1954; **The House on 92nd Street**, 1945; **How the West Was Won**, 1963; **Johnny Apollo**, 1940; **Kiss of Death**, 1947; **The Lives of a Bengal Lancer**, 1935; **North to Alaska**, 1960; **Peter Ibbetson**, 1935; **Rawhide**, 1951; **The Real Glory**, 1939; **Seven Thieves**, 1960; **The Shepherd of the Hills**, 1941; **The Sons of Katie Elder**, 1965; **Souls at Sea**, 1937; **Spawn of the North**, 1938; **13 Rue Madeleine**, 1947; **Trail of the Lonesome Pine**, 1936; **True Grit**, 1969; **23 Paces to Baker Street**, 1956; **The Way of All Flesh**, 1927; **White Witch Doctor**, 1953; **Wing and a Prayer**, 1944; **Wolf Song**, 1929; **You're in the Navy Now**, 1951.

Howard Hawks (director, 1896-1977): **Air Force**, 1943 (see his remarks under *Author's Note* in **Sergeant York**); **Bringing Up Baby**, 1938; **Gentlemen Prefer Blondes**, 1953; **His Girl Friday**, 1940; **I Was a Male War Bride**, 1949; **Monkey Business**, 1952; **Only Angels Have Wings**, 1939; **Paths of Glory**, 1957; **Red River**, 1948; **Rio Bravo**, 1959; **The Road to Glory**, 1936; **Scarface**, 1932; **Sergeant York**, 1941; **A Song Is Born**, 1948; **The Sun Also Rises**, 1957; **The Thing from Another World**, 1951; **Tiger Shark**, 1932; **To Have and Have Not**, 1944; **Twentieth Century**, 1934; **Viva Villa!**, 1934.

Sterling Hayden (actor, 1916-1986): **The Long Goodbye**, 1973; **The**

Naked Alibi, 1954; Prince Valiant, 1954; So Big, 1953; Suddenly, 1954.

Susan Hayward (actress, 1917-1975): The Hairy Ape, 1944; House of Strangers, 1949; I Want to Live!, 1958; I'll Cry Tomorrow, 1955; Jack London, 1943; The Lusty Men, 1952; My Foolish Heart, 1949; The President's Lady, 1953; Rawhide, 1951; Reap the Wild Wind, 1942; Smash Up: The Story of a Woman, 1947; The Snows of Kilimanjaro, 1952; Stolen Hours, 1963; Tap Roots, 1948; They Won't Believe Me, 1947; Top Secret Affair, 1957; Tulsa, 1949; White Witch Doctor, 1953; Young and Willing, 1943.

Rita Hayworth (actress, 1918-1987): Gilda, 1946; The Lady from Shanghai, 1948; Miss Sadie Thompson, 1953; My Gal Sal, 1942; Pal Joey, 1957; Salome, 1953; Separate Tables, 1958; The Story on Page One, 1959; The Strawberry Blonde, 1941; Tales of Manhattan, 1942; They Came to Cordura, 1959; Tonight and Every Night, 1945; You Were Never Lovelier, 1942; You'll Never Get Rich, 1941.

Ben Hecht (journalist-novelist-screenwriter-director-producer, 1894-1964): Barbary Coast, 1935; China Girl, 1942; The Cocoanuts, 1929; Crime without Passion, 1934; Design for Living, 1933; A Farewell to Arms, 1957; The Florentine Dagger, 1935; Frisco Kid, 1935; The Front Page, 1931; Gone with the Wind, 1939; The Great Gabbo, 1929; The Great Profile, 1940; Gunga Din, 1939; Hallelujah, I'm a Bum!, 1933; His Girl Friday, 1940; The Indian Fighter, 1955; It's a Wonderful World, 1939; Kiss of Death, 1947; Let Freedom Ring, 1939; Lifeboat, 1944; Living It Up, 1954; Miracle in the Rain, 1956; Miracle of the Bells, 1948 (additional remarks under Author's Note in Saratoga); Monkey Business, 1931; Nothing Sacred, 1937; Notorious, 1946; O. Henry's Full House, 1952; The Paradine Case, 1947; Peter Ibbetson, 1935; Portrait of Jennie, 1949; Quick Millions, 1931; Rasputin and the Empress, 1932; Rope, 1948; Roseanna McCoy, 1949; Roxie Hart, 1942; Samson and Delilah, 1949; San Francisco, 1936; Saratoga, 1937; Scarface, 1932; The Scoundrel, 1945; The Secret Six, 1931; September Affair, 1950; The Sin of Madelon Claudet, 1931; Specter of the Rose, 1946; Spellbound, 1945; Stagecoach, 1939; A Star Is Born, 1937; Strangers on a Train, 1951; Tales of Manhattan, 1942; Three Comrades, 1938; Topaze, 1933; Twentieth Century, 1934; Underworld, 1927; The Unholy Night, 1929; Viva Villa!, 1934; Walk on the Wild Side, 1962; What Price Hollywood, 1932; Where the Sidewalk Ends, 1950; Wuthering Heights, 1939; A Yank at Oxford, 1938.

Van Heflin (actor, 1910-1971): Act of Violence, 1948 (see his remarks in Author's Note under Week-End with Father); B.F.'s Daughter, 1948 (see his remarks in Author's Note under Week-End with Father); Patterns, 1956; The Prowler, 1951; The Raid, 1954; Shane, 1953; The Strange Love of Martha Ivers, 1946; Tap Roots, 1948; Tennessee Johnson, 1942; They Came to Cordura, 1959; The Three Musketeers, 1948; 3:10 to Yuma, 1957; Tomahawk, 1951; Under Ten Flags, 1960; Week-End with Father, 1951; Woman's World, 1954.

Ernest Hemingway (author, 1899-1961): A Farewell to Arms, 1932; For Whom the Bell Tolls, 1943; The Macomber Affair, 1947; Man's Hope, 1947; The Old Man and the Sea, 1958; Out of Africa, 1985; The Snows of Kilimanjaro, 1952; The Sun Also Rises, 1957; Tender Is the Night, 1962; A Woman of Paris: A Drama of Fate, 1923; The Words, 2012.

Katharine Hepburn (actress, 1907-2003): Gone with the Wind, 1939; Guess Who's Coming to Dinner, 1967; Holiday, 1938; Judgment at Nuremberg, 1962; Keeper of the Flame, 1942; The Lion in Winter, 1968; Little Women, 1933; Long Day's Journey into Night, 1962; Mary of Scotland, 1936; Morning Glory, 1933; On Golden Pond, 1981; Pat and Mike, 1952; The Philadelphia Story, 1940; The Rainmaker, 1957; Rooster Cogburn, 1975; Spitfire, 1934; Stage Door, 1937; Stage Door Canteen, 1943; State of the Union, 1948; Suddenly Last Summer, 1959; Summertime, 1955; Sylvia Scarlett, 1936; Travels with My Aunt, 1972; Undercurrent, 1946; Without Love, 1945; Woman of the Year, 1942.

Charlton Heston (actor, 1923-2008): The Agony and the Ecstasy, 1965 (see his remarks under Author's Note in The Ten Commandments); Ben-Hur, 1959 (see his remarks under Author's Note in The Ten Commandments); Dark City, 1950; El Cid, 1961; The Far Horizons, 1955; 55 Days at Peking, 1963; The Greatest Show on Earth, 1952; The Greatest Story Ever Told, 1965; Khartoum, 1966; Major Dundee, 1965; Midway, 1976; The Naked Jungle, 1954; The Planet of the Apes, 1968; Pony Express, 1953; The President's Lady, 1953; The Ten Commandments, 1956; Touch of Evil, 1958; The War Lord, 1965; Will Penny, 1968; The Wreck of the Mary Deare, 1959.

Alfred Hitchcock (director, 1899-1980): The Birds, 1963; Blackmail, 1929; Dial M for Murder, 1954; Family Plot, 1976; Foreign Correspondent, 1940; Goldfinger, 1964; I Confess, 1953; The Lady Vanishes, 1938; Lifeboat, 1944; The Lodger, 1928; The Man Who Knew Too Much, 1935; The Man Who Knew Too Much, 1956; Marnie, 1964; Monte Carlo, 1930; Mr. and Mrs. Smith, 1941; Murder!, 1930; North by Northwest, 1959; Notorious, 1946; The Paradine Case, 1947; The Private Life of Henry VIII, 1933; Psycho, 1960; Rear Window, 1954; Rebecca, 1940; Rich and Strange, 1932; Rope, 1948; Sabotage, 1937; Saboteur, 1942; The Secret Agent, 1936; Shadow of a Doubt, 1943; Specter of the Rose, 1946; Spellbound, 1945; Stage Fright, 1950; Strangers on a Train, 1951 (see also his further remarks about this film under Author's Note in They Live by Night, 1949); Suspicion, 1941; They Live by Night, 1949; The 39 Steps, 1935; To Catch a Thief, 1955; Topaz, 1969; Torn Curtain, 1966; Touch of Evil, 1958; The Trouble with Harry, 1955; Vertigo, 1958; War of the Worlds, 1953; White Shadows, 1924; Witness for the Prosecution, 1957; The Wreck of the Mary Deare, 1959; The Wrong Man, 1956; Young and Innocent, 1938.

Harry Hoffman (Dustin Hoffman's father, 1907-1992): The Graduate, 1967.

William Holden (actor, 1918-1981): The Devil's Brigade, 1968; Executive Suite, 1954; Golden Boy, 1939; The Horse Soldiers, 1959; I Wanted Wings, 1941; The Key, 1958; Love Is a Many Splendored Thing, 1955; Miss Grant Takes Richmond, 1949; Our Town, 1940; Picnic, 1955; The Rainmaker, 1956; The Remarkable Andrew, 1942; The Roots of Heaven, 1958; Sabrina, 1954; Stalag 17, 1953; Streets of Laredo, 1949; Submarine Command, 1951; Sunset Boulevard, 1950; Texas, 1941; Those Were the Days, 1940; Toward the Unknown, 1956; The Towering Inferno, 1974; The Turning Point, 1952; Union Station, 1950; The Wild Bunch, 1969; Wild Rovers, 1971; Young and Willing, 1943.

Billie Holiday (singer, 1915-1959): Lady Sings the Blues, 1972.

Earl Holliman (actor, 1928-): Forbidden Planet, 1956; Gunfight at the O.K. Corral, 1957; Last Train from Gun Hill, 1959; The Sons of Katie Elder, 1965; Trooper Hook, 1957.

Celeste Holm (actress, 1917-2012): A Letter to Three Wives, 1949; The Private Files of J. Edgar Hoover, 1977; Road House, 1948; The Snake Pit, 1948; Three Little Girls in Blue, 1946.

Bob Hope (actor-comedian-dancer-singer, 1903-2003): The Ghost Breakers, 1940; The Lemon Drop Kid, 1951; My Favorite Blonde,

1942; **Nothing but the Truth**, 1941; **The Paleface**, 1948; **The Princess and the Pirate**, 1944; **Road to Morocco**, 1942; **Road to Rio**, 1947; **Road to Utopia**, 1946; **The Seven Little Foys**, 1955; **Son of Paleface**, 1952; **Sorrowful Jones**, 1949; **They Got Me Covered**, 1943.

Dennis Hopper (actor, 1936-2010): **Apocalypse Now**, 1979; **Easy Rider**, 1969; **Gunfight at the O.K. Corral**, 1957; **Hoosiers**, 1986; **Kid Blue**, 1973; **Rebel without a Cause**, 1955; **Rumble Fish**, 1983; **The Sons of Katie Elder**, 1965; **True Grit**, 1969.

John Houseman (actor-producer-writer, 1902-1988): **Julius Caesar**, 1953; **They Live by Night**, 1949.

Rock Hudson (actor, 1925-1985): **Fighter Squadron**, 1948; **Seminole**, 1953; **Something of Value**, 1957; **The Tarnished Angels**, 1957; **The Undefeated**, 1969; **Written on the Wind**, 1956.

Ruth Hussey (actress, 1911-2005): **H. M. Pulham, Esq.**, 1941; **Tennessee Johnson**, 1942; **The Uninvited**, 1944.

John Huston (actor-director, 1906-1987): **The African Queen**, 1951 (see his remarks in *Author's Note* in entry for **The Red Badge of Courage**); **The Asphalt Jungle**, 1950 (see his remarks in *Author's Note* in entry for **The Red Badge of Courage**); **A Farewell to Arms**, 1957; **High Sierra**, 1941; **A House Divided**, 1931; **Key Largo**, 1948; **The Killers**, 1946; **Law and Order**, 1932; **The Life and Times of Judge Roy Bean**, 1972; **The List of Adrian Messenger**, 1963; **The Maltese Falcon**, 1941; **The Man Who Would Be King**, 1975; **The Misfits**, 1961; **Moby Dick**, 1956; **Moulin Rouge**, 1952; **The Red Badge of Courage**, 1951; **The Roots of Heaven**, 1958; **Sergeant York**, 1941; **The Stranger**, 1946; **Three Strangers**, 1946; **The Treasure of the Sierra Madre**, 1948; **Under the Volcano**, 1984; **The Unforgiven**, 1960; **We Were Strangers**, 1949; **Winter Kills**, 1979; **Wuthering Heights**, 1939.

Betty Hutton (actress, 1921-2007): **The Greatest Show on Earth**, 1952; **Incendiary Blonde**, 1945; **The Miracle of Morgan's Creek**, 1944; **The Perils of Pauline**, 1947; **Red, Hot and Blue**, 1949; **Somebody Loves Me**, 1952; **Star Spangled Rhythm**, 1942; **The Stork Club**, 1945.

William Inge (playwright, 1913-1973): **Picnic**, 1955.

John Ireland (actor, 1914-1992): **Party Girl**, 1958; **Railroaded**, 1947; **Red River**, 1948; **Vengeance Valley**, 1951; **Villa Rides**, 1968; **A Walk in the Sun**, 1945.

Sam Jaffe (actor, 1891-1984): **Gunga Din**, 1939; **Lost Horizon**, 1937; **Rope of Sand**, 1949; **The Scarlet Empress**, 1934; **13 Rue Madeleine**, 1947; **Under the Gun**, 1951.

Nunnally Johnson (director-producer-writer, 1897-1977): **The Gunfighter**, 1950; **Holy Matrimony**, 1943; **Jesse James**, 1939; **The Keys to the Kingdom**, 1944; **The Man in the Gray Flannel Suit**, 1956; **The Moon Is Down**, 1943; **Mr. Peabody and the Mermaid**, 1948; **My Cousin Rachel**, 1952; **Night People**, 1954; **Oh, Men! Oh, Women!**, 1957; **The Prisoner of Shark Island**, 1936; **The Senator Was Indiscreet**, 1947; **The Southerner**, 1945; **Three Came Home**, 1950; **The Three Faces of Eve**, 1957; **Wife, Husband and Friend**, 1939; **The Woman in the Window**, 1944.

Van Johnson (actor, 1916-2008): **The Caine Mutiny**, 1954; **A Guy Named Joe**, 1943; **In the Good Old Summertime**, 1949; **The Last Time I Saw Paris**, 1954; **Scene of the Crime**, 1949; **Thirty Seconds Over Tokyo**, 1944; **23 Paces to Baker Street**, 1956; **Two Girls and a**

Sailor, 1944; **Weekend at the Waldorf**, 1945.

Jennifer, Jones (actress, 1919-2009): **Song of Bernadette**, 1943; **The Towering Inferno**, 1974.

Boris Karloff (actor, 1887-1969): **Frankenstein**, 1931; **The Hunchback of Notre Dame**, 1923; **The Lost Patrol**, 1934; **The Man Who Lived Again**, 1936; **The Mask of Fu Manchu**, 1932; **The Mummy**, 1932; **The Mystery of Mr. Wong**, 1939; **The Old Dark House**, 1932; **The Raven**, 1935; **The Raven**, 1963; **Scarface**, 1932; **The Secret Life of Walter Mitty**, 1947; **Smart Money**, 1931; **Son of Frankenstein**, 1939; **Tower of London**, 1939; **Two Arabian Knights**, 1927; **Unconquered**, 1947; **The Unholy Night**, 1929; **The Walking Dead**, 1936; **You'll Find Out**, 1940.

Danny Kaye (actor-comedian-singer-dancer, 1913-1987): **The Five Pennies**, 1959; **The Kid from Brooklyn**, 1946; **On the Double**, 1961; **On the Riviera**, 1951; **The Secret Life of Walter Mitty**, 1947; **A Song Is Born**, 1948; **Up in Arms**, 1944; **White Christmas**, 1954; **Wonder Man**, 1945.

Elia Kazan (actor-director-producer; 1909-2003): **Man on a Tightrope**, 1953; **On the Waterfront**, 1954; **Panic in the Streets**, 1950; **Pinky**, 1949; **A Streetcar Named Desire**, 1951; **A Tree Grows in Brooklyn**, 1945; **Viva Zapata!**, 1952; **Wanda**, 1971; **Wild River**, 1960.

Buster Keaton (actor-comedian, 1895-1966): **Doughboys**, 1930; **Free and Easy**, 1930; **The General**, 1926; **Go West**, 1925; **In the Good Old Summertime**, 1949; **It's a Mad, Mad, Mad, Mad World**, 1963; **The Navigator**, 1924; **Our Hospitality**, 1923; **San Diego, I Love You**, 1944; **Seven Chances**, 1925; **Sherlock Jr.**, 1924; **A Southern Yankee**, 1948; **Steamboat Bill, Jr.**, 1928; **Three Ages**, 1923; **Too Hot to Handle**, 1938.

William Keighley (director, 1889-1984): **The Fighting 69th**, 1940; **The Man Who Came to Dinner**, 1942; **No Time for Comedy**, 1940; **The Prince and the Pauper**, 1937; **Rocky Mountain**, 1950; **The Street with No Name**, 1948; **Torrid Zone**, 1940.

Brian Keith (actor, 1921-1997): **5 against the House**, 1955; **Run of the Arrow**, 1957; **The Russians Are Coming, The Russians Are Coming!**, 1966; **The Violent Men**, 1955; **The Wind and the Lion**, 1975.

Gene Kelly (actor-singer-dancer-director, 1912-1996): **An American in Paris**, 1951 (see his comments under *Author's Note* in entry for **The Red Shoes**, 1948); **Anchors Aweigh**, 1945 (see his comments under *Author's Note* in **The Three Caballeros**); **For Me and My Gal**, 1942; **Invitation to the Dance**, 1957; **It's Always Fair Weather**, 1955; **Les Girls**, 1957; **Marty**, 1955; **On the Town**, 1949; **The Pirate**, 1948; **The Red Shoes**, 1948; **Singin' in the Rain**, 1952; **Summer Stock**, 1950; **Take Me Out to the Ball Game**, 1949; **Thousands Cheer**, 1943; **The Three Caballeros**, 1944; **The Three Musketeers**, 1948; **Yankee Doodle Dandy**, 1942; **Ziegfeld Follies**, 1945.

Deborah Kerr (actress, 1921-2007): **From Here to Eternity**, 1953; **Heaven Knows, Mr. Allison**, 1957; **The Hucksters**, 1947; **I See a Dark Stranger**, 1947; **The King and I**, 1956; **King Solomon's Mines**, 1950; **The Prisoner of Zenda**, 1952; **Quo Vadis**, 1951; **Separate Tables**, 1958; **The Sundowners**, 1960; **Tea and Sympathy**, 1956; **Thunder in the East**, 1953; **Vacation from Marriage**, 1945; **Young Bess**, 1953.

Henry King (director, 1886-1982): **The Eddy Duchin Story**, 1956; **The Gunfighter**, 1950; **In Old Chicago**, 1938; **Lloyd's of London**, 1936; **Margie**, 1946; **Marie Galante**, 1934; **Prince of Foxes**, 1949; **Remem-**

ber the Day, 1941; **The Snows of Kilimanjaro**, 1952; **Stanley and Livingstone**, 1939; **The Song of Bernadette**, 1943; **State Fair**, 1933; **Stella Dallas**, 1925; **The Sun Also Rises**, 1957; **Tender Is the Night**, 1962; **Tol'able David**, 1921; **Twelve O'Clock High**, 1949; **The White Sister**, 1923; **Wilson**, 1944; **The Winning of Barbara Worth**, 1926; **A Yank in the R.A.F.**, 1941.

Don Knotts (actor-comedian, 1924-2006): **The Incredible Mr. Limpet**, 1964; **The Reluctant Astronaut**, 1967; **The Shakiest Gun in the West**, 1968.

Howard Koch (screenwriter, 1901-1995): **Mission to Moscow**, 1943; **Rhapsody in Blue**, 1945; **Virginia City**, 1940.

Michael Korda (editor, 1933-): **The Four Feathers**, 1939.

Stanley Kramer (director-producer, 1913-2001): **Champion**, 1949; **Eight Iron Men**, 1952; **The Four Poster**, 1952; **Guess Who's Coming to Dinner**, 1967; **High Noon**, 1952; **Home of the Brave**, 1949; **Inherit the Wind**, 1960; **It's a Mad, Mad, Mad, Mad World**, 1963; **Judgment at Nuremberg**, 1962; **The Juggler**, 1953; **The Member of the Wedding**, 1952; **The Men**, 1950; **My Six Convicts**, 1952; **Not as a Stranger**, 1955; **Oklahoma Crude**, 1973; **Pressure Point**, 1962; **The Pride and the Passion**, 1957; **Ship of Fools**, 1965; **The Sniper**, 1952; **The Wild One**, 1953.

Stanley Kubrick (director, 1928-1999): **A.I. Artificial Intelligence**, 2001; **Dr. Strangelove or: How I Learned to Stop Worrying and Love the Bomb**, 1964; **Full Metal Jacket**, 1987; **The Killing**, 1956; **Lolita**, 1962; **Paths of Glory**, 1957; **Rififi**, 1956; **Spartacus**, 1960; **The Shining**, 1980; **2001: A Space Odyssey**, 1968; **Spartacus**, 1960.

Veronica Lake (actress, 1922-1973): **The Blue Dahlia**, 1946 (see her comments in *Author's Note* under **This Gun for Hire**); **The Glass Key**, 1942; **I Married a Witch**, 1942; **I Wanted Wings**, 1941; **Saigon**, 1948; **Slattery's Hurricane**, 1949; **So Proudly We Hail**, 1943; **Sullivan's Travels**, 1941; **This Gun for Hire**, 1942.

Hedy Lamarr (actress, 1913-2000): **H. M. Pulham, Esq.**, 1941; **Samson and Delilah**, 1949; **The Strange Woman**, 1946; **The Three Musketeers**, 1921; **Tortilla Flat**, 1942; **The Trunks of Mr. O.F.**, 1932; **White Cargo**, 1942; **Ziegfeld Girl**, 1941.

Dorothy Lamour (actress, 1914-1996): **The Hurricane**, 1937 (see her remarks under *Author's Note* in **Typhoon**); **The Last Train from Madrid**, 1937; **Road to Rio**, 1947 (see her remarks under *Author's Note* in **Swing High, Swing Low**); **Road to Singapore**, 1940 (see her remarks under *Author's Note* in **Swing High, Swing Low**); **St. Louis Blues**, 1939; **Spawn of the North**, 1939; **Swing High, Swing Low**, 1937; **They Got Me Covered**, 1943; **Typhoon**, 1940; **Wild Harvest**, 1947.

Burt Lancaster (actor-producer, 1913-1994): **Come Back, Little Sheba**, 1952; **Elmer Gantry**, 1960; **From Here to Eternity**, 1953; **Gunfight at the O.K. Corral**, 1957; **His Majesty O'Keefe**, 1954; **I Walk Alone**, 1948; **Jim Thorpe—All American**, 1951; **The Kentuckian**, 1955; **The Killers**, 1946; **Kiss the Blood Off My Hands**, 1948; **The Mark of Zorro**, 1920; **The Professionals**, 1966; **The Rainmaker**, 1956; **Rope of Sand**, 1949; **The Rose Tattoo**, 1955; **Run Silent, Run Deep**, 1958; **The Scalphunters**, 1968; **Separate Tables**, 1958; **Seven Days in May**, 1964; **Sorry, Wrong Number**, 1948; **South Sea Woman**, 1953; **Sweet Smell of Success**, 1957; **Ten Tall Men**, 1951; **Tough Guys**, 1986; **The Train**, 1965; **Trapeze**, 1956; **Twilight's Last Gleaming**, 1977; **Ulzana's Raid**, 1972; **The Unforgiven**, 1960; **Valdez Is Coming**, 1971; **Vengeance Valley**, 1951; **Vera Cruz**, 1954; **The Young Savages**, 1961;

Zulu Dawn, 1979.

Priscilla Lane (actress, 1915-1995): **Four Daughters**, 1938; **The Roaring Twenties**, 1939; **Saboteur**, 1942.

Mark Lawrence (actor, 1910-2005): **The Ox-Bow Incident**, 1943; **San Quentin**, 1937; **This Gun for Hire**, 1942; **Unconquered**, 1947; **The Virginian**, 1946.

Jack Lemmon (actor, 1925-2001): **Good Neighbor Sam**, 1964; **The Great Race**, 1965; **How to Murder Your Wife**, 1965; **Irma La Douce**, 1963; **Missing**, 1982; **Mister Roberts**, 1955; **My Sister Eileen**, 1955; **The Odd Couple**, 1968; **The Out of Towners**, 1970; **Phffft!**, 1954; **The Prisoner of Second Avenue**, 1975; **Save the Tiger**, 1973; **Some Like It Hot**, 1959; **Three for the Show**, 1955; **Tribute**, 1980.

Mervyn LeRoy (producer-director, 1900-1987): **Gold Diggers of 1933**, 1933; **I Am a Fugitive from a Chain Gang**, 1932; **Little Caesar**, 1931; **Madame Curie**, 1943; **Oil for the Lamps of China**, 1935; **Quo Vadis**, 1951; **Random Harvest**, 1942; **Stand Up and Fight**, 1939; **They Won't Forget**, 1937; **Thirty Seconds Over Tokyo**, 1944; **Three Men on a Horse**, 1936; **Three on a Match**, 1932; **Top Speed**, 1930; **Toward the Unknown**, 1956; **Tugboat Annie**, 1933; **Waterloo Bridge**, 1940; **Without Reservations**, 1946; **The Wizard of Oz**, 1939; **The World Changes**, 1933.

Harold Lloyd (actor-comedian-producer-writer, 1893-1971): **The Freshman**, 1925; **Mad Wednesday**, 1950; **Movie Crazy**, 1932; **Safety Last!**, 1924; **Speedy**, 1928.

Peter Lorre (actor-director, 1904-1964): **The Lost One**, 1951; **M**, 1933; **Mad Love**, 1935; **The Maltese Falcon**, 1941; **The Man Who Knew Too Much**, 1935; **The Mask of Dimitrios**, 1944; **Mr. Moto's Gamble**, 1938; **Mr. Moto's Last Warning**, 1939; **Mysterious Mr. Moto**, 1938; **Passage to Marseille**, 1944; **Quicksand**, 1950; **The Raven**, 1963; **Rope of Sand**, 1949; **The Secret Agent**, 1936; **Silk Stockings**, 1957; **Stranger on the Third Floor**, 1940; **Tales of Terror**, 1962; **They Met in Bombay**, 1941; **Think Fast, Mr. Moto**, 1937; **Three Strangers**, 1946; **The Trunks of Mr. O.F.**, 1932; **20,000 Leagues under the Sea**, 1954; **The Verdict**, 1946; **You'll Find Out**, 1940.

Myrna Loy (actress, 1905-1993): **Manhattan Melodrama**, 1934; **The Mask of Fu Manchu**, 1932; **Men in White**, 1934; **Midnight Lace**, 1960; **Mr. Blandings Builds His Dream House**, 1948; **The Rains Came**, 1939; **The Senator Was Indiscreet**, 1947; **Shadow of the Thin Man**, 1941; **Song of the Thin Man**, 1947; **Stamboul Quest**, 1934; **Test Pilot**, 1938; **The Thin Man**, 1934; **The Thin Man Goes Home**, 1945; **Thirteen Women**, 1932; **Too Hot to Handle**, 1938; **Topaze**, 1933; **Transatlantic**, 1931; **When Ladies Meet**, 1933; **Whipsaw**, 1935; **Wife vs. Secretary**, 1936; **Wings in the Dark**, 1935.

Ida Lupino (actress, 1918-1995): **The Hard Way**, 1942; **High Sierra**, 1941; **The Hitch-Hiker**, 1953; **Ladies in Retirement**, 1941; **The Light That Failed**, 1939; **The Lone Wolf Spy Hunt**, 1939; **The Man in the Iron Mask**, 1939; **On Dangerous Ground**, 1951; **Out of the Fog**, 1941; **Road House**, 1947; **The Sea Wolf**, 1941; **Thank Your Lucky Stars**, 1943; **They Drive by Night**, 1940; **Woman in Hiding**, 1950.

Fred MacMurray (actor, 1908-1991): **Double Indemnity**, 1944; **The Egg and I**, 1949; **The Far Horizons**, 1955; **Flight for Freedom**, 1943; **The Gilded Lily**, 1935; **Men with Wings**, 1938; **Miracle of the Bells**, 1948; **Murder, He Says**, 1945; **No Time for Love**, 1943; **Pardon My Past**, 1946; **The Princess Comes Across**, 1936; **Pushover**, 1954; **The Rains of Ranchipur**, 1955; **Remember the Night**, 1940; **Sing, You Sinners**, 1938; **Singapore**, 1947; **Smoky**, 1946; **Standing Room Only**,

1944; **The Street With No Name**, 1948; **Sunset Boulevard**, 1950; **Swing High, Swing Low**, 1937; **The Texas Rangers**, 1936; **There's Always Tomorrow**, 1956; **Trail of the Lonesome Pine**, 1936; **True Confession**, 1937; **Woman's World**, 1954.

Karl Malden (actor, 1912-2009): **On the Waterfront**, 1954 (see his remarks under *Author's Note* in **A Streetcar Named Desire**); **One-Eyed Jacks**, 1961 (see his remarks under *Author's Note* in **A Streetcar Named Desire**); **Patton**, 1970; **A Streetcar Named Desire**, 1951; **Time Limit**, 1957; **Where the Sidewalk Ends**, 1950.

Rouben Mamoulian (director, 1897-1987): **Blood and Sand**, 1941; **City Streets**, 1931; **Golden Boy**, 1939; **Laura**, 1944; **Love Me Tonight**, 1932; **The Mark of Zorro**, 1940; **Mr. Smith Goes to Washington**, 1939; **Porgy and Bess**, 1959; **Queen Christina**, 1933; **Silk Stockings**, 1957; **Summer Holiday**, 1948; **We Live Again**, 1934.

Norman Mailer (author, 1923-2007): **Medium Cool**, 1969; **A Place in the Sun**, 1951.

Joseph Mankiewicz (director-producer, 1909-1993): **Beloved Infidel**, 1959.

Fredric March (actor, 1897-1975): **The Eagle and the Hawk**, 1933; **Hombre**, 1967; **I Married a Witch**, 1942; **Inherit the Wind**, 1960; **Laughter**, 1930; **Les Misérables**, 1935; **Mary of Scotland**, 1936; **My Sin**, 1931; **Nothing Sacred**, 1937; **One Foot in Heaven**, 1941; **The Road to Glory**, 1936; **The Royal Family of Broadway**, 1930; **Seven Days in May**, 1964; **The Sign of the Cross**, 1932; **Smilin' Through**, 1932; **So Ends Our Night**, 1941; **A Star Is Born**, 1937; **Susan and God**, 1940; **There Goes My Heart**, 1938; **Tomorrow the World**, 1944; **Trade Winds**, 1938; **We Live Again**, 1934; **Wild Party**, 1929.

George Marshall (director, 1891-1975): **How the West Was Won**, 1963; **In Old Kentucky**, 1935; **The Sheepman**, 1958; **Show Them No Mercy**, 1935; **Star Spangled Rhythm**, 1942; **Texas**, 1941; **When the Daltons Rode**, 1940; **You Can't Cheat an Honest Man**, 1939.

Herbert Marshall (actor, 1890-1966): **Foreign Correspondent**, 1940 (see his remarks under *Author's Note* in **Trouble in Paradise**); **The Letter**, 1940 (see his remarks under *Author's Note* in **Wicked as They Come**, 1957); **Murder!**, 1930; **The Secret Garden**, 1949; **Till We Meet Again**, 1936; **Trouble in Paradise**, 1932; **The Virgin Queen**, 1955; **When Ladies Meet**, 1941; **Wicked as They Come** (aka: Portrait in Smoke), 1957.

Lee Marvin (actor, 1924-1987): **The Dirty Dozen**, 1967; **Hell in the Pacific**, 1968; **The Killers**, 1964; **Monte Walsh**, 1970; **Paint Your Wagon**, 1969; **Point Blank**, 1967; **The Professionals**, 1966; **The Rack**, 1956; **The Raid**, 1954; **Seminole**, 1953; **Ship of Fools**, 1965; **Violent Saturday**, 1955; **The Wild One**, 1953.

Groucho Marx (actor-comedian, 1890-1977): **Animal Crackers**, 1930; **Duck Soup**, 1933; **Gone with the Wind**, 1939; **Horse Feathers**, 1932; **Monkey Business**, 1931; **A Night at the Opera**, 1935; **A Night in Casablanca**, 1946; **Room Service**, 1938.

James Mason (actor, 1909-1984): **5 Fingers**, 1952; **Hatter's Castle**, 1948; **Hotel Reserve**, 1946; **Lord Jim**, 1965; **Madame Bovary**, 1949; **North by Northwest**, 1959; **Odd Man Out**, 1947; **A Place of One's Own**, 1949; **Prince Valiant**, 1954; **The Prisoner of Zenda**, 1952; **The Reckless Moment**, 1949; **The Seventh Veil**, 1946; **A Star Is Born**, 1954; **Terror House**, 1943; **Thunder Rock**, 1944; **20,000 Leagues Under the Sea**, 1954; **The Verdict**, 1982; **The Wicked Lady**, 1946.

Raymond Massey (actor, 1896-1983): **Dreaming Lips**, 1937; **The Drum**, 1938; **East of Eden**, 1955; **The 49th Parallel**, 1942; **God Is My Co-Pilot**, 1945; **The Hurricane**, 1937; **The Old Dark House**, 1932; **Reap the Wild Wind**, 1942; **Roseanna McCoy**, 1949; **Santa Fe Trail**, 1940; **The Scarlet Pimpernel**, 1935; **Seven Angry Men**, 1955; **Stairway to Heaven**, 1947; **Things to Come**, 1936; **Under the Red Robe**, 1937; **The Woman in the Window**, 1944.

Walter Matthau (actor, 1920-2000): **Hopscotch**, 1980; **Mirage**, 1965; **The Odd Couple**, 1968; **Pete 'n' Tillie**, 1972; **Plaza Suite**, 1971; **The Sunshine Boys**, 1975; **The Taking of Pelham One Two Three**, 1974.

Victor Mature (actor, 1913-1999): **I Wake Up Screaming**, 1942; **Kiss of Death**, 1947; **My Darling Clementine**, 1946; **My Gal Sal**, 1942; **One Million B.C.**, 1940; **Samson and Delilah**, 1949; **The Shanghai Gesture**, 1941; **Violent Saturday**, 1955; **Wabash Avenue**, 1950.

Bill Mauldin (William Henry Mauldin; 1921-2003; illustrator, cartoonist and actor): **The Red Badge of Courage**, 1951; **Up Front**, 1951.

Archie Mayo (director, 1891-1968): **Night After Night**, 1932; **Orchestra Wives**, 1942; **The Petrified Forest**, 1936; **Svengali**, 1931.

Virginia Mayo (actress, 1920-2005): **The Princess and the Pirate**, 1944; **The Secret Life of Walter Mitty**, 1947; **She's Working Her Way through College**, 1952; **The Silver Chalice**, 1954; **A Song Is Born**, 1948; **South Sea Woman**, 1953; **The West Point Story**, 1950; **Westbound**, 1959; **White Heat**, 1949; **Wonder Man**, 1945.

Mike Mazurki (actor, 1907-1990): **Dark City**, 1950; **I Walk Alone**, 1948; **Murder, My Sweet**, 1944; **Night and the City**, 1950; **Nightmare Alley**, 1947; **A Pocketful of Miracles**, 1961; **The Princess and the Pirate**, 1944; **7 Women**, 1966; **The Shanghai Gesture**, 1941; **Some Like It Hot**, 1959; **The Spanish Main**, 1945; **Ten Tall Men**, 1951; **Unconquered**, 1947.

Leo McCarey (director, 1896-1969): **Duck Soup**, 1933; **The Kid from Spain**, 1932; **Love Affair**, 1939; **Make Way for Tomorrow**, 1937; **The Milky Way**, 1936; **My Son John**, 1952; **Ruggles of Red Gap**, 1935; **Six of a Kind**, 1934.

Joel McCrea (actor, 1905-1990): **Foreign Correspondent**, 1940; **Four Faces West**, 1948; **The Lost Squadron**, 1932; **The More the Merrier**, 1943; **The Most Dangerous Game**, 1932; **The Outriders**, 1950 (see his comments under *Author's Note* in **South of St. Louis**); **The Palm Beach Story**, 1942; **The Richest Girl in the World**, 1934; **Ride the High Country**, 1962; **Saddle Tramp**, 1950; **The Silver Horde**, 1930; **South of St. Louis**, 1949; **The Southerner**, 1945; **Stars in My Crown**, 1950; **Stella Dallas**, 1937; **Sullivan's Travels**, 1941; **These Three**, 1936; **Three Blind Mice**, 1938; **Trooper Hook**, 1957; **Union Pacific**, 1939; **The Virginian**, 1946; **The Way of All Flesh**, 1927; **Wells Fargo**, 1937; **Wichita**, 1955; **The Wild Bunch**, 1969.

Charles McGraw (actor, 1914-1980): **The Narrow Margin**, 1952; **One Minute to Zero**, 1952.

Norman Z. McLeod (director, 1898-1964): **It's a Gift**, 1934; **Monkey Business**, 1931; **Road to Rio**, 1947; **The Secret Life of Walter Mitty**, 1947; **There Goes My Heart**, 1938; **Topper**, 1937; **Topper Takes a Trip**, 1939.

Steve McQueen (actor, 1930-1980): **The Cincinnati Kid**, 1965; **The Getaway**, 1972; **The Great Escape**, 1963; **Hell Is for Heroes**, 1962; **Junior Bonner**, 1972; **The Magnificent Seven**, 1960; **Nevada Smith**, 1966; **Never So Few**, 1959; **Papillon**, 1973; **The Sand Pebbles**, 1966;

The Thomas Crown Affair, 1968; **The Towering Inferno**, 1974; **The War Lover**, 1962.

Ralph Meeker (actor, 1920-1988): **Kiss Me Deadly**, 1955; **Paths of Glory**, 1957; **Run of the Arrow**, 1957; **The St. Valentine's Day Massacre**, 1967; **Somebody Loves Me**, 1952; **Winter Kills**, 1979.

Melina Mercouri (actress, 1920-1994): **Gaily, Gaily**, 1969.

Vera Miles (actress, 1929-): **The Man Who Shot Liberty Valance**, 1962; **Psycho**, 1960; **The Searchers**, 1956; **The Wrong Man**, 1956.

Lewis Milestone (director, 1895-1980): **All Quiet on the Western Front**, 1930 (see his remarks under *Author's Note* in **Paths of Glory**); **The General Died at Dawn**, 1936; **Hallelujah, I'm a Bum!**, 1933; **Halls of Montezuma**, 1950; **Mutiny on the Bounty**, 1962; **No Minor Vices**, 1948; **The North Star**, 1943; **Paths of Glory**, 1957; **Pork Chop Hill**, 1959; **PT-109**, 1963; **Rain**, 1932; **The Red Pony**, 1949; **The Strange Love of Martha Ivers**, 1946; **Two Arabian Knights**, 1927; **A Walk in the Sun**, 1945.

Ray Milland (actor, 1905-1986): **The Bad and the Beautiful**, 1952 (see his remarks under *Author's Note* in **The Uninvited**); **It Happens Every Spring**, 1949; **Kitty**, 1946; **The Lost Weekend**, 1945; **The Major and the Minor**, 1942; **Ministry of Fear**, 1944; **Rhubarb**, 1951; **So Evil My Love**, 1948; **Strangers May Kiss**, 1931; **The Thief**, 1952; **Three Brave Men**, 1956; **Till We Meet Again**, 1944; **The Uninvited**, 1944.

Vincent Minnelli (director, 1903-1986): **Father of the Bride**, 1950; **Father's Little Dividend**, 1951; **Meet Me in St. Louis**, 1944; **The Moon and Sixpence**, 1942; **The Pirate**, 1948; **Some Came Running**, 1958; **The Story of Three Loves**, 1953; **Tea and Sympathy**, 1956; **Two Weeks in Another Town**, 1962; **Undercurrent**, 1946; **Ziegfeld Follies**, 1945.

Robert Mitchum (actor, 1917-1997): **The Enemy Below**, 1957; **Farewell, My Lovely**, 1975; **The Friends of Eddie Coyle**, 1973; **Heaven Knows, Mr. Allison**, 1957; **His Kind of Woman**, 1951; **The Last Tycoon**, 1976; **The Longest Day**, 1962; **The Lusty Men**, 1952; **Macao**, 1952; **Midway**, 1976; **Morocco**, 1930; **My Forbidden Past**, 1951; **Night of the Hunter**, 1955; **Not as a Stranger**, 1955; **One Minute to Zero**, 1952; **Out of the Past**, 1947; **Pursued**, 1947; **Rachel and the Stranger**, 1948; **The Racket**, 1951; **The Red Pony**, 1949; **River of No Return**, 1954; **Ryan's Daughter**, 1970; **The Story of G.I. Joe**, 1945; **The Sundowners**, 1960; **Thirty Seconds Over Tokyo**, 1944; **Thunder Road**, 1958; **Till the End of Time**, 1946; **Track of the Cat**, 1954; **Undercurrent**, 1946; **Villa Rides**, 1968; **The Way West**, 1967; **West of the Pecos**, 1945; **When Strangers Marry**, 1944; **Where Danger Lives**, 1950; **White Witch Doctor**, 1953; **The Wonderful Country**, 1960; **The Yakuza**, 1975.

Robert Montgomery (actor-director, 1904-1981): **Lady in the Lake**, 1947; **Mr. and Mrs. Smith**, 1941; **The Mystery of Mr. X**, 1934; **Night Must Fall**, 1937; **Private Lives**, 1931; **Ride the Pink Horse**, 1947; **Riptide**, 1934; **Strangers May Kiss**, 1931; **They Were Expendable**, 1945; **Three Loves Has Nancy**, 1938; **When Ladies Meet**, 1933; **Yellow Jack**, 1938.

Karen Morley (actress, politician and political activist; 1909-2003): **Our Daily Bread**, 1934; **Scarface**, 1932.

Zero Mostel (Samuel Joel Mostel, actor-comedian, 1915-1977): **The Enforcer**, 1951 (see his remarks under *Author's Note* in **Sirocco**); **A Funny Thing Happened on the Way to the Forum**, 1966; **The Producers**, 1968; **Sirocco**, 1951.

Paul Muni (actor, 1895-1967): **Commandos Strike at Dawn**, 1942; **The Good Earth**, 1936; **High Sierra**, 1941; **Hudson's Bay**, 1941; **I Am a Fugitive from a Chain Gang**, 1932; **Inherit the Wind**, 1960; **Juarez**, 1939; **The Life of Emile Zola**, 1937; **Scarface**, 1932; **Seven Faces**, 1929; **A Song to Remember**, 1945; **Stage Door Canteen**, 1943; **The Story of Louis Pasteur**, 1936; **The Valiant**, 1929; **We Are Not Alone**, 1939; **The Woman I Love**, 1937; **The World Changes**, 1933.

Patricia Neal (actress, 1926-2010): **A Face in the Crowd**, 1957; **The Fountainhead**, 1949; **Hud**, 1963 (see her remarks under *Author's Note* in **The Subject Was Roses**); **Operation Pacific**, 1951; **The Subject Was Roses**, 1968; **Week-End with Father**, 1951.

Tom Neal (actor, 1914-1972): **Detour**, 1945; **First Yank Into Tokyo**, 1945; **Flying Tigers**, 1942.

Jean Negulesco (director, 1900-1993): **Humoresque**, 1946; **The Mask of Dimitrios**, 1944; **The Mudlark**, 1950; **Nobody Lives Forever**, 1946; **Phone Call from a Stranger**, 1952; **The Rains of Ranchipur**, 1955; **Road House**, 1948; **Three Came Home**, 1950; **Three Coins in the Fountain**, 1954; **Three Strangers**, 1946; **Titanic**, 1953; **Under My Skin**, 1950; **Woman's World**, 1954.

Paul Newman (actor, 1925-2008): **Butch Cassidy and the Sundance Kid**, 1969 (see his remarks under *Author's Note* in **The Sting**); **The Drowning Pool**, 1975; **Exodus**, 1960; **Harper**, 1966; **Hombre**, 1967; **Hud**, 1963; **The Hustler**, 1961; **The Left-Handed Gun**, 1958; **The Life and Times of Judge Roy Bean**, 1972; **Nobody's Fool**, 1995; **Paris Blues**, 1961; **The Rack**, 1956; **The Silver Chalice**, 1954; **Somebody Up There Likes Me**, 1956; **Sometimes a Great Notion**, 1970; **The Sting**, 1973; **Sweet Bird of Youth**, 1962; **Torn Curtain**, 1966; **The Towering Inferno**, 1974; **The Verdict**, 1982; **Winning**, 1969; **The Young Philadelphians**, 1959.

David Niven (actor, 1910-1983): **55 Days at Peking**, 1963; **Gentleman's Agreement**, 1947; **The Guns of Navarone**, 1961; **La Dolce Vita**, 1961; **Murder by Death**, 1976; **Oh, Men! Oh, Women!**, 1957; **The Pink Panther**, 1964; **Please Don't Eat the Daisies**, 1960; **Raffles**, 1939; **The Real Glory**, 1939; **Separate Tables**, 1958; **Spitfire**, 1943; **Stairway to Heaven**, 1947; **Three Blind Mice**, 1938; **Wuthering Heights**, 1939.

Lloyd Nolan (actor, 1902-1985): **Guadalcanal Diary**, 1943; **A Hatful of Rain**, 1957; **The House Across the Bay**, 1940; **The House on 92nd Street**, 1945; **Johnny Apollo**, 1940; **Lady in the Lake**, 1947; **Manila Calling**, 1942; **The Private Files of J. Edgar Hoover**, 1977; **St. Louis Blues**, 1939; **Sleepers West**, 1941; **Somewhere in the Night**, 1946; **The Street with No Name**, 1948; **The Texas Rangers**, 1936; **Time to Kill**, 1942; **A Tree Grows in Brooklyn**, 1945.

George O'Brien (actor, 1899-1985): **The Iron Horse**, 1924.

Pat O'Brien (actor, 1899-1983): **Boy Meets Girl**, 1938; **Ceiling Zero**, 1935; **The Fighting 69th**, 1940; **Flowing Gold**, 1940; **The Front Page**, 1931; **The Great O'Malley**, 1937; **Having Wonderful Crime**, 1945; **Here Comes the Navy**, 1934; **The Iron Major**, 1943; **Knute Rockne—All American**, 1940; **The Last Hurrah**, 1958; **Oil for the Lamps of China**, 1935; **The People Against O'Hara**, 1951; **Riffraff**, 1947; **San Quentin**, 1937; **Some Like It Hot**, 1959; **'Til We Meet Again**, 1940; **Torrid Zone**, 1940; **Twenty Million Sweethearts**, 1934; **Virtue**, 1932.

Laurence Olivier (actor, 1907-1989): **Fire Over England**, 1937; **The 49th Parallel**, 1942; **Khartoum**, 1966; **Othello**, 1965; **Pride and Prejudice**, 1940; **Rebecca**, 1940; **Richard III**, 1956; **Sleuth**, 1972; **Spar-**

tacus, 1960; **That Hamilton Woman**, 1941; **Wuthering Heights**, 1939.

Jerry Paris (actor-director-producer, 1925-1986): **Good Morning, Miss Dove**, 1955.

Dorothy Parker (short story writer-editor-screenwriter, 1893-1967): **Beloved Infidel**, 1959; **The Man Who Came to Dinner**, 1942; **The Moon's Our Home**, 1936; **Saboteur**, 1942; **The Secret Life of Walter Mitty**, 1947; **A Star Is Born**, 1937; **Suzy**, 1936; **Trade Winds**, 1938.

John Payne (actor, 1912-1989): **The Great American Broadcast**, 1941; **Miracle on 34th Street**, 1944; **99 River Street**, 1953; **The Razor's Edge**, 1946; **Remember the Day**, 1941; **Santa Fe Passage**, 1955; **Sentimental Journey**, 1946; **Springtime in the Rockies**, 1942; **Slightly Scarlet**, 1956; **Star Dust**, 1940; **Sun Valley Serenade**, 1941; **Tennessee's Partner**, 1955; **Tin Pan Alley**, 1940; **To the Shores of Tripoli**, 1942; **Week-End in Havana**, 1941.

Gregory Peck (actor; 1916-2003): **Duel in the Sun**, 1946; **Gentleman's Agreement**, 1947; **The Great Sinner**, 1949; **The Gunfighter**, 1950; **The Guns of Navarone**, 1961; **How the West Was Won**, 1963; **The Keys to the Kingdom**, 1944; **MacArthur**, 1977; **The Macomber Affair**, 1947; **The Man in the Gray Flannel Suit**, 1956; **Man on a Tightrope**, 1953; **Man with a Million**, 1954; **Mirage**, 1965; **Moby Dick**, 1956; **Night People**, 1954; **Old Gringo**, 1989; **The Omen**, 1976; **Only the Valiant**, 1951; **The Paradine Case**, 1947; **Pork Chop Hill**, 1959; **The Purple Plain**, 1954; **Roman Holiday**, 1953; **Ryan's Daughter**, 1970; **The Shootist**, 1976;**The Snows of Kilimanjaro**, 1952; **Spellbound**, 1945; **The Stalking Moon**, 1968; **To Kill a Mockingbird**, 1962; **Twelve O'Clock High**, 1949; **The Valley of Decision**, 1945; **The World in His Arms**, 1952; **The Yearling**, 1946; **Yellow Sky**, 1948.

Arthur Penn (director, 1922-2010): **The Miracle Worker**, 1962; **The Missouri Breaks**, 1976.

Tony Perkins (actor, 1932-1992): **Friendly Persuasion**, 1956; **Is Paris Burning?**, 1966; **Pretty Poison**, 1968; **Psycho**, 1960; **The Tin Star**, 1957; **The Trial**, 1963; **Winter Kills**, 1979.

Christopher Plummer (actor, 1929-): **The Fall of the Roman Empire**, 1964; **The Man Who Would Be King**, 1975; **Murder by Decree**, 1979; **The Return of the Pink Panther**, 1975; **The Sound of Music**, 1965; **Triple Cross**, 1967; **Waterloo**, 1971; **Wind Across the Everglades**, 1958.

William Powell (actor, 1892-1984): **The Great Ziegfeld**, 1936 (see his remarks under *Author's Note* in Ziegfeld Follies); **Life with Father**, 1947; **Mr. Peabody and the Mermaid**, 1948; **My Man Godfrey**, 1936; **One Way Passage**, 1932; **Reckless**, 1935; **Rendezvous**, 1935; **The Senator Was Indiscreet**, 1947; **Shadow of the Thin Man**, 1941; **Song of the Thin Man**, 1947; **Star of Midnight**, 1935; **Take One False Step**, 1949; **The Thin Man**, 1934; **The Thin Man Goes Home**, 1945; **When Knighthood Was in Flower**, 1922; **Ziegfeld Follies**, 1945.

Gary Francis Powers (CIA pilot of downed U-2 spy plane; 1929-1977): **Bridge of Spies**, 2015; **The Serpent**, 1973.

Otto Preminger (actor-director; 1905-1986): **Exodus**, 1960; **Fallen Angel**, 1945; **In Harm's Way**, 1965; **Laura**, 1944; **The Man with the Golden Arm**, 1955; **Porgy and Bess**, 1959; **River of No Return**, 1954; **A Royal Scandal**, 1945; **Stalag 17**, 1953; **They Got Me Covered**, 1943; **The 13th Letter**, 1951; **Where the Sidewalk Ends**, 1950; **Whirlpool**, 1949.

Vincent Price (actor, 1911-1993): **Champagne for Caesar**, 1950; **The Fly**, 1958; **His Kind of Woman**, 1951; **House of Usher**, 1960; **House of Wax**, 1953; **Laura**, 1944; **The Long Night**, 1947; **The Masque of the Red Death**, 1964; **The Pit and the Pendulum**, 1961; **The Private Lives of Elizabeth and Essex**, 1939; **The Raven**, 1963; **Rogue's Regiment**, 1948; **A Royal Scandal**, 1945; **Serenade**, 1956; **The Song of Bernadette**, 1943; **Tales of Terror**, 1962; **The Ten Commandments**, 1956; **Theatre of Blood**, 1973; **Twice Told Tales**, 1963; **The Web**, 1947; **The Whales of August**, 1987; **While the City Sleeps**, 1956; **Wilson**, 1944.

Anthony Quinn (actor-director, 1915-2001): **A Dream of Kings**, 1969; **A High Wind in Jamaica**, 1965; **La Strada**, 1956; **The Last Train from Madrid**, 1937; **Lawrence of Arabia**, 1962; **Lust for Life**, 1956; **The Ox-Bow Incident**, 1943; **The Plainsman**, 1936; **Requiem for a Heavyweight**, 1962; **The Ride Back**, 1957; **Seminole**, 1953; **Seven Cities of Gold**, 1955; **The Shoes of the Fisherman**, 1968; **Sinbad the Sailor**, 1947; **They Died with Their Boots On**, 1941; **Ulysses**, 1955; **Viva Zapata!**, 1952; **Waikiki Wedding**, 1937; **Warlock**, 1959; **A Walk in the Clouds**, 1995; **Wild Is the Wind**, 1957; **The World in His Arms**, 1952; **Zorba the Greek**, 1964.

George Raft (actor, 1901-1980): **The Bowery**, 1933; **Each Dawn I Die**, 1939; **High Sierra**, 1941; **The House Across the Bay**, 1940; **I Stole a Million**, 1939; **Invisible Stripes**, 1940; **Manpower**, 1941; **Night After Night**, 1932; **Nob Hill**, 1945; **Nocturne**, 1946; **Quick Millions**, 1931; **Scarface**, 1932; **Some Like It Hot**, 1959; **Souls at Sea**, 1937; **Spawn of the North**, 1939; **Stage Door Canteen**, 1943; **Taxi!**, 1932; **They Drive by Night**, 1940; **Under-Cover Man**, 1932; **Whistle Stop**, 1946; **You and Me**, 1938.

Claude Rains (actor, 1889-1967): **The Invisible Man**, 1933; **The Man Who Reclaimed His Head**, 1935; **Mr. Skeffington**, 1944; **The Phantom of the Opera**, 1943; **The Prince and the Pauper**, 1937; **Rope of Sand**, 1949; **The Sea Hawk**, 1940; **Sealed Cargo**, 1951; **They Made Me a Criminal**, 1939; **They Won't Forget**, 1937; **The White Tower**, 1950; **The Wolf Man**, 1941.

Basil Rathbone (actor, 1892-1967): **The Adventures of Robin Hood**, 1938 (his remarks about Errol Flynn under *Author's Note* in **The Mark of Zorro**); **Captain Blood**, 1935 (his remarks about Errol Flynn under *Author's Note* in **The Mark of Zorro**); **Dressed to Kill**, 1946; **The Hound of the Baskervilles**, 1939; **The Last Days of Pompeii**, 1935; **Love from a Stranger**, 1937; **The Mark of Zorro**, 1940; **The Pearl of Death**, 1944; **Pursuit to Algiers**, 1945; **Rhythm on the River**, 1940; **Romeo and Juliet**, 1936; **The Scarlet Claw**, 1944; **Sherlock Holmes and the Secret Weapon**, 1942; **Sherlock Holmes Faces Death**, 1943; **Son of Frankenstein**, 1939; **The Spider Woman**, 1944; **A Tale of Two Cities**, 1935; **Tales of Terror**, 1962; **Terror by Night**, 1946; **Tovarich**, 1937; **Tower of London**, 1939; **We're No Angels**, 1955; **The Woman in Green**, 1945.

Nicholas Ray (director, 1911-1979): **55 Days at Peking**, 1963; **Flying Leathernecks**, 1951; **The Greatest Show on Earth**, 1952; **In a Lonely Place**, 1950; **Johnny Guitar**, 1954 (see his remarks under *Author's Note* in Rancho Notorious); **King of Kings**, 1961; **Knock on Any Door**, 1949; **The Lusty Men**, 1952; **Macao**, 1952; **On Dangerous Ground**, 1951; **Party Girl**, 1958; **Rancho Notorious**, 1952; **Rebel Without a Cause**, 1955; **Roseanna McCoy**, 1949; **Run for Cover**, 1955; **A Streetcar Named Desire**, 1951; **They Live By Night**, 1949; **Thieves Like Us**, 1974; **The True Story of Jesse James**, 1957; **Wind Across the Everglades**, 1958.

Erich Maria Remarque (Erich Paul Remark; author of stories and novels; 1898-1970): **All Quiet on the Western Front**, 1930 (see his comments under *Author's Note* in entry for **The Road Back**); **The Road Back**, 1937; **So Ends Our Night**, 1941; **Three Comrades**, 1938.

Michael Rennie (actor, 1909-1971): **5 Fingers**, 1952.

Marjorie Reynolds (actress, 1917-1997): **Holiday Inn**, 1942; **Ministry of Fear**, 1944; **That Midnight Kiss**, 1949; **The Time of Their Lives**, 1946; **Up in Mabel's Room**, 1944.

Jason Robards Jr. (actor, 1922-2000): **Hour of the Gun**, 1967; **Julia**, 1977; **Max Dugan Returns**, 1983; **Pat Garrett and Billy the Kid**, 1973; **The St. Valentine's Day Massacre**, 1967; **Tender Is the Night**, 1962; **A Thousand Clowns**, 1965; **Tora! Tora! Tora!**, 1970.

Edward G. Robinson (actor, 1893-1973): **Dr. Ehrlich's Magic Bullet**, 1940; **Double Indemnity**, 1944; **Five Star Final**, 1931; **The Hatchet Man**, 1932; **Hell on Frisco Bay**, 1956; **A Hole in the Head**, 1959; **House of Strangers**, 1949; **Key Largo**, 1948; **Kid Galahad**, 1937; **Larceny, Inc.**, 1942; **The Last Gangster**, 1937; **Little Caesar**, 1931; **Little Giant**, 1933; **The Man with Two Faces**, 1934; **Manpower**, 1941; **Mr. Winkle Goes to War**, 1944; **Night Has a Thousand Eyes**, 1948; **Our Vines Have Tender Grapes**, 1945; **The Petrified Forest**, 1936; **The Red House**, 1947; **Scarlet Street**, 1945; **The Sea Wolf**, 1941; **Seven Thieves**, 1960; **Silver Dollar**, 1932; **A Slight Case of Murder**, 1938; **Smart Money**, 1931; **Some Like It Hot**, 1959; **The Stranger**, 1946; **Tales of Manhattan**, 1942; **Thunder in the City**, 1937; **Tiger Shark**, 1932; **Tight Spot**, 1955; **Two Weeks in Another Town**, 1962; **The Violent Men**, 1955; **The Whole Town's Talking**, 1935; **The Woman in the Window**, 1944.

Ginger Rogers (actress-dancer-singer, 1911-1995): **Kitty Foyle**, 1940; **Lady in the Dark**, 1944; **The Major and the Minor**, 1942; **Monkey Business**, 1952; **Oh, Men! Oh, Women!**, 1957; **Roberta**, 1935; **Roxie Hart**, 1942; **Shall We Dance**, 1937; **Sitting Pretty**, 1933; **Stage Door**, 1937; **Star of Midnight**, 1935; **Storm Warning**, 1950; **The Story of Vernon and Irene Castle**, 1939; **Swing Time**, 1936; **Tales of Manhattan**, 1942; **Tender Comrade**, 1943; **Tight Spot**, 1955; **To Each His Own**, 1946; **Tom, Dick and Harry**, 1941; **Top Hat**, 1935; **Twenty Million Sweethearts**, 1934; **Weekend at the Waldorf**, 1945; **We're Not Married**, 1952.

Stanley Ralph Ross (actor-composer-producer-screenwriter, 1935-2000): **Chinatown**, 1974; **De-Lovely**, 2004; **The Silver Streak**, 1976; **Tony Rome**, 1967; **Too Late the Hero**, 1970.

Robert Rosson (director-producer-writer, 1906-1966): **The Hustler**, 1961; **Racket Busters**, 1938.

Mike Royko (journalist-newspaper columnist, 1932-1997): **Medium Cool**, 1969.

Gene Ruggiero (film editor, 1910-2002): **Around the World in 80 Days**, 1956; **The Color Purple**, 1985; **Foolish Wives**, 1922; **The Graduate**, 1967; **The Great Caruso**, 1951; **Greed**, 1925; **I Love You Again**, 1940; **Marie Antoinette**, 1938; **Mark of the Vampire**, 1935; **Men of the Fighting Lady**, 1954; **Ninotchka**, 1939; **The Patriot**, 1928; **The People Against O'Hara**, 1951; **Queen Kelly**, 1929; **Rich, Young and Pretty**, 1951; **The Shop Around the Corner**, 1940; **Song of the Thin Man**, 1947; **Spitfire**, 1943; **Stars in My Crown**, 1950; **Tarzan Finds a Son!**, 1939; **Tarzan's Secret Treasure**, 1941; **That Midnight Kiss**, 1949; **The Toast of New Orleans**, 1950; **Torpedo Run**, 1958; **The Wings of Eagles**, 1957.

Jane Russell (actress, 1921-2011): **His Kind of Woman**, 1951; **Macao**, 1952; **The Paleface**, 1948; **Son of Paleface**, 1952; **The Tall Men**, 1956.

Rosalind Russell (actress, 1907-1976): **Flight for Freedom**, 1943; **His Girl Friday**, 1940; **A Majority of One**, 1961; **No Time for Comedy**, 1940; **Rendezvous**, 1935; **Sister Kenny**, 1946; **They Met in Bombay**, 1941; **This Thing Called Love**, 1940; **Under Two Flags**, 1936; **The Velvet Touch**, 1948; **The Women**, 1939.

Ann Rutherford (actress, 1917-2012): **Orchestra Wives**, 1942; **Whistling in Brooklyn**, 1943; **Whistling in Dixie**, 1942; **Whistling in the Dark**, 1941; **Wyoming**, 1940.

Robert Ryan (actor, 1909-1973): **God's Little Acre**, 1958; **House of Bamboo**, 1955; **Inferno**, 1953; **Lonelyhearts**, 1958; **The Naked Spur**, 1953; **Odds Against Tomorrow**, 1969; **On Dangerous Ground**, 1951; **The Professionals**, 1966; **The Proud Ones**, 1956; **The Racket**, 1951; **Return of the Bad Men**, 1948; **The Set-Up**, 1949; **Tender Comrade**, 1943; **Trail Street**, 1947; **The Wild Bunch**, 1969; **The Woman on Pier 13**, 1949; **The Woman on the Beach**, 1947.

Telly Savalas (actor, 1922-1994): **Kelly's Heroes**, 1970; **On Her Majesty's Secret Service**, 1969; **The Scalphunters**, 1968.

George Sanders (actor, 1906-1972): **Confessions of a Nazi Spy**, 1939 (see his comments in *Author's Note* under **The Saint in Palm Springs**); **Foreign Correspondent**, 1940; **Lancer Spy**, 1937; **The Lodger**, 1944; **Love Is News**, 1937; **Man Hunt**, 1941; **The Moon and Sixpence**, 1942; **Mr. Moto's Last Warning**, 1939; **The Picture of Dorian Gray**, 1945; **The Private Affairs of Bel Ami**, 1947; **Rebecca**, 1940; **The Saint in London**, 1939; **The Saint in Palm Springs**, 1941; **The Saint Strikes Back**, 1929; **The Saint's Double Trouble**, 1940; **Samson and Delilah**, 1949; **A Scandal in Paris**, 1946; **The Scarlet Coat**, 1955; **A Shot in the Dark**, 1964; **Son of Fury: The Story of Benjamin Blake**, 1942; **Solomon and Sheba**, 1959; **The Strange Woman**, 1946; **Summer Storm**, 1944; **Tales of Manhattan**, 1942; **They Came to Blow Up America**, 1943; **This Land Is Mine**, 1943; **Village of the Damned**, 1960; **Warning Shot**, 1967; **While the City Sleeps**, 1956; **Witness to Murder**, 1954.

William Saroyan (writer, 1908-1981): **The Human Comedy**, 1943.

Roy Scheider (actor, 1932-2008): **All That Jazz**, 1979 (see his remarks under *Author's Note* in **The Seven Ups**); **Jaws**, 1975; **Marathon Man**, 1976; **The Seven Ups**, 1973; **Sorcerer**, 1977; **2010**, 1984.

Joseph Schildkraut (actor, 1896-1964): **The King of Kings**, 1927; **The Shop Around the Corner**, 1940; **Suez**, 1938.

Budd Schulberg (author-screenwriter, 1914-2009): **A Face in the Crowd**, 1957; **The Harder They Fall**, 1956; **On the Waterfront**, 1954; **A Star Is Born**, 1937; **Wind Across the Everglades**, 1958.

George C. Scott (actor, 1927-1999): **The Flim-Flam Man**, 1967; **The Hospital**, 1971; **The Hustler**, 1961; **Oklahoma Crude**, 1973; **Patton**, 1970; **Taps**, 1981; **They Might Be Giants**, 1971; **White Heat**, 1949.

Randolph Scott (actor, 1898-1987): **Follow the Fleet**, 1936; **The Last of the Mohicans**, 1936; **Pittsburgh**, 1942; **Rage at Dawn**, 1955; **Return of the Bad Men**, 1948; **Ride Lonesome**, 1959; **Ride the High Country**, 1962; **Santa Fe**, 1951; **Seven Men from Now**, 1956; **7th Cavalry**, 1956; **She**, 1935; **The Spoilers**, 1942; **The Tall T**, 1957; **To the Shores of Tripoli**, 1942; **Trail Street**, 1947; **Virginia City**, 1940; **Weary River**, 1929; **Westbound**, 1959; **Western Union**, 1941; **When the Daltons Rode**, 1940.

George Seaton (director, 1911-1979): **Miracle on 34th Street**, 1947; **Teacher's Pet**, 1958; **36 Hours**, 1965.

William A. Seiter (director, 1890-1964): **The Moon's Our Home**, 1936; **This Is My Affair**, 1937; **Three Blind Mice**, 1938; **Why Be Good?**, 1929; **You Were Never Lovelier**, 1942.

Rod Serling (writer of TV and screen scripts, 1924-1975): **Patterns**, 1956; **Requiem for a Heavyweight**, 1962.

Sylvia Sidney (actress, 1910-1999): **An American Tragedy**, 1931 (under *Author's Note* in Sabotage); **City Streets**, 1931; **Dead End**, 1937 (under *Author's Note* in Sabotage); **Fury**, 1936 (under *Author's Note* in Sabotage); **Sabotage**, 1937; **The Searching Wind**, 1946; **Street Scene**, 1931; **Trail of the Lonesome Pine**, 1936; **Violent Saturday**, 1955; **The Wagons Roll at Night**, 1941; **You and Me**, 1938; **You Only Live Once**, 1937.

Don Siegel (director, 1912-1991): **The Invasion of the Body Snatchers**, 1956; **Telefon**, 1977; **Two Mules for Sister Sara**, 1970; **The Verdict**, 1946.

Jean Simmons (actress, 1929-2010): **Guys and Dolls**, 1955; **The Robe**, 1953; **Spartacus**, 1960.

Frank Sinatra (singer-actor-producer, 1915-1998): **5 Against the House**, 1955; **From Here to Eternity**, 1953; **Guys and Dolls**, 1955; **A Hole in the Head**, 1959; **It's Always Fair Weather**, 1955; **The Joker Is Wild**, 1957; **Kings Go Forth**, 1958; **The Man with the Golden Arm**, 1955; **The Manchurian Candidate**, 1962; **Never So Few**, 1959; **Not as a Stranger**, 1955; **Ocean's Eleven**, 1960; **On the Town**, 1949; **Pal Joey**, 1957; **Porgy and Bess**, 1959; **The Pride and the Passion**, 1957; **Robin and the 7 Hoods**, 1964; **Some Came Running**, 1958; **Step Lively**, 1944; **Suddenly**, 1954; **Take Me Out to the Ball Game**, 1949; **The Tender Trap**, 1956; **Tony Rome**, 1967; **The Train**, 1964; **The Verdict**, 1982; **Von Ryan's Express**, 1965; **Winter Kills**, 1979; **Young at Heart**, 1954.

Curt Siodmak (writer, 1902-2000): **I Walked with a Zombie**, 1943; **Son of Dracula**, 1943; **The Wolf Man**, 1941.

Douglas Sirk (director, 1897-1987): **All That Heaven Allows**, 1955 (see his remarks in *Author's Note* under **Week-End with Father**); **Hitler's Madman**, 1943; **Imitation of Life**, 1959; **Lured**, 1947; **Magnificent Obsession**, 1954; **A Scandal in Paris**, 1946. **Shockproof**, 1949; **Summer Storm**, 1944; **The Tarnished Angels**, 1957; **Thunder on the Hill**, 1951; **Week-End with Father**, 1951; **Written on the Wind**, 1956.

Red Skelton (Richard Bernard Skelton, actor-comedian, 1913-1997): **The Fuller Brush Man**, 1948; **A Southern Yankee**, 1948; **Three Little Words**, 1950.

Ann Sothern (actress-singer, 1909-2001): **Folies Bergere**, 1934; **The Whales of August**, 1987; **Whoopee!**, 1930.

Robert Stack (actor; 1919-2003): **Eagle Squadron**, 1942; **The High and the Mighty**, 1954; **House of Bamboo**, 1955; **John Paul Jones**, 1959; **The Mortal Storm**, 1940; **The Scarface Mob**, 1959; **The Tarnished Angels**, 1957; **To Be or Not to Be**, 1942; **Written on the Wind**, 1956; **Written on the Wind**, 1956.

Barbara Stanwyck (actress, 1907-1990): **Double Indemnity**, 1944; **Executive Suite**, 1954; **The File on Thelma Jordan**, 1950; **Golden Boy**, 1939; **The Lady Eve**, 1941; **The Mad Miss Manton**, 1938; **The Man with a Cloak**, 1951; **Meet John Doe**, 1941; **The Miracle Woman**, 1931; **Night Nurse**, 1931; **No Man of Her Own**, 1950; **The Plough and the Stars**, 1936; **Remember the Night**, 1940; **So Big**, 1932; **Sorry, Wrong Number**, 1948; **Stella Dallas**, 1937; **The Strange Love of**

Martha Ivers, 1946; **Sunset Boulevard**, 1950; **These Wilder Years**, 1956; **This Is My Affair**, 1937; **Titanic**, 1953; **Trooper Hook**, 1957; **The Two Mrs. Carrolls**, 1947; **Union Pacific**, 1939; **The Violent Men**, 1955; **Walk on the Wild Side**, 1962; **Witness to Murder**, 1954; **The Woman in Red**, 1935; **You Belong to Me**, 1941.

Rod Steiger (actor, 1925-2002): **Duck, You Sucker!**, 1972; **The Godfather**, 1972 (see his remarks under *Author's Note* in **The Pawnbroker**); **The Harder They Fall**, 1956; **In the Heat of the Night**, 1967; **Last Days of Mussolini**, 1974; **Lion of the Desert**, 1981; **The Loved One**, 1965; **Mars Attacks!**, 1996; **Marty**, 1955; **No Way to Treat a Lady**, 1868; **Oklahoma!**, 1955; **On the Waterfront**, 1954; **Patton**, 1970 (see his remarks under *Author's Note* in **The Pawnbroker**); **The Pawnbroker**, 1965; **Run of the Arrow**, 1957; **Three Into Two Won't Go**, 1969; **W.C. Fields and Me**, 1976; **Waterloo**, 1971.

John Steinbeck (author-screenwriter, 1902-1968): **The Grapes of Wrath**, 1940; **Lifeboat**, 1944; **The Moon is Down**, 1943; **Of Mice and Men**, 1939; **The Pearl**, 1948; **The Red Pony**, 1949; **Strangers on a Train**, 1951; **Tortilla Flat**, 1942; **Viva Zapata!**, 1952.

George Stevens (director, 1904-1975): **Giant**, 1956; **The Greatest Story Ever Told**, 1965; **Gunga Din**, 1939; **I Remember Mama**, 1948; **The More the Merrier**, 1943; **Penny Serenade**, 1941; **A Place in the Sun**, 1951; **Shane**, 1953; **Swing Time**, 1936; **The Talk of the Town**, 1942; **Woman of the Year**, 1942.

James Stewart (actor, 1908-1997): **Anatomy of a Murder**, 1959 (see his remarks under *Author's Note* in **Rope**); **Destry Rides Again**, 1939; **The Far Country**, 1955; **The Flight of the Phoenix**, 1965; **Fool's Parade**, 1971; **The Good Earth**, 1937; **Harvey**, 1950; **How the West Was Won**, 1962; **It's a Wonderful Life**, 1946; **Made for Each Other**, 1939; **Malaya**, 1950; **The Man from Laramie**, 1955; **The Man Who Knew Too Much**, 1956; **The Man Who Shot Liberty Valance**, 1962; **Maytime**, 1937 (see his remarks under *Author's Note* in **Rose Marie**, 1936); **The Mortal Storm**, 1940; **Mr. Hobbs Takes a Vacation**, 1962; **Mr. Smith Goes to Washington**, 1939; **The Murder Man**, 1935; **The Naked Spur**, 1953; **No Highway in the Sky**, 1951; **No Time for Comedy**, 1940; **Of Human Hearts**, 1938; **The Philadelphia Story**, 1940; **Rear Window**, 1954; **Rope**, 1948; **Rose Marie**, 1936; **Shenandoah**, 1965; **The Shootist**, 1976; **The Shop Around the Corner**, 1940; **The Shopworn Angel**, 1948; **The Spirit of St. Louis**, 1957; **Strategic Air Command**, 1955; **The Stratton Story**, 1949; **Thunder Bay**, 1953; **Vertigo**, 1958; **Wife vs. Secretary**, 1936; **Winchester '73**, 1950; **Yellow Jack**, 1938; **You Can't Take It With You**, 1938; **You Gotta Stay Happy**, 1948; **Ziegfeld Girl**, 1941.

Paul Stewart (actor, 1908-1986): **Citizen Kane**, 1941; **The Juggler**, 1953; **Kiss Me Deadly**, 1955; **Prisoner of War**, 1954; **Top Secret Affair**, 1957; **Twelve O'Clock High**, 1949; **The Window**, 1949.

John Sturges (director, 1910-1992): **The Great Escape**, 1963; **Gunfight at the O.K. Corral**, 1957; **The Magnificent Seven**, 1960; **The Magnificent Yankee**, 1950; **Never So Few**, 1959; **The Old Man and the Sea**, 1958; **Right Cross**, 1950; **The Scarlet Coat**, 1955.

Jessica Tandy (actress, 1909-1994): **Driving Mrs. Daisy**, 1989; **The Seventh Cross**, 1944; **A Streetcar Named Desire**, 1951.

Elizabeth Taylor (actress, 1932-2011): **Elephant Walk**, 1954; **Father of the Bride**, 1951; **Giant**, 1956; **Ivanhoe**, 1952; **Lassie Come Home**, 1943; **The Last Time I Saw Paris**, 1954; **Life with Father**, 1947; **The Longest Day**, 1962; **National Velvet**, 1945; **A Place in the Sun**, 1951; **Rhapsody**, 1954; **South Pacific**, 1958; **Suddenly Last Summer**, 1959; **The Taming of the Shrew**, 1967; **The V.I.P.s**, 1963; **Who's Afraid of**

Virginia Woolf?, 1966; **Winter Kills**, 1979.

Robert Taylor (actor, 1911-1969): **Ivanhoe**, 1952; **Johnny Eager**, 1942; **Knights of the Round Table**, 1953; **The Last Hunt**, 1956; **Party Girl**, 1958; **Quentin Durward**, 1955; **Quo Vadis**, 1951; **Saddle in the Wind**, 1958; **Stand by for Action**, 1942; **Stand Up and Fight**, 1939; **The Stratton Story**, 1949; **This Is My Affair**, 1937; **Three Comrades**, 1938; **Undercurrent**, 1946; **Waterloo Bridge**, 1940; **Westward the Women**, 1951; **When Ladies Meet**, 1941; **A Wicked Woman**, 1934; **A Yank at Oxford**, 1938.

Studs Terkel (Louis Terkel, 1912-2008): **Eight Men Out**, 1988.

Richard Thorpe (director, 1896-1991): **Night Must Fall**, 1937; **The Prisoner of Zenda**, 1952; **The Student Prince**, 1954; **The Thin Man Goes Home**, 1945; **Three Little Words**, 1950; **20 Mule Team**, 1940; **Vengeance Valley**, 1951; **White Cargo**, 1942; **Wyoming**, 1940.

Gene Tierney (actress, 1920-1991): **Belle Starr**, 1941 (see her comments under *Author's Note* in **The Return of Frank James**); **Laura**, 1944; **Leave Her to Heaven**, 1945; **The Razor's Edge**, 1946; **The Return of Frank James**, 1940; **The Shanghai Gesture**, 1941; **Son of Fury: The Story of Benjamin Blake**, 1942; **That Wonderful Urge**, 1948; **Thunder Birds**, 1942; **Tobacco Road**, 1941; **Where the Sidewalk Ends**, 1950; **Whirlpool**, 1949.

Franchot Tone (actor, 1905-1968): **Mutiny on the Bounty**, 1935; **Suzy**, 1936; **They Gave Him a Gun**, 1937; **Three Comrades**, 1938; **Three Loves Has Nancy**, 1938; **True to Life**, 1943.

Spencer Tracy (actor; 1900-1967): **Father of the Bride**, 1950; **Inherit the Wind**, 1960; **Judgment at Nuremberg**, 1962; **Keeper of the Flame**, 1942; **The Last Hurrah**, 1958; **The Last Mile**, 1932; **The Murder Man**, 1935; **Northwest Passage**, 1940; **The Old Man and the Sea**, 1958; **Pat and Mike**, 1952; **Plymouth Adventure**, 1952; **The Power and the Glory**, 1933; **Quick Millions**, 1931; **Riffraff**, 1936; **San Francisco**, 1936; **The Seventh Cross**, 1944; **Stanley and Livingstone**, 1939; **State of the Union**, 1948; **Test Pilot**, 1938; **They Gave Him a Gun**, 1937; **Thirty Seconds Over Tokyo**, 1944; **Tortilla Flat**, 1942; **20,000 Years in Sing Sing**, 1932; **Up the River**, 1930; **Whipsaw**, 1935; **Without Love**, 1945; **Woman of the Year**, 1942.

Claire Trevor (actress, 1910-2000): **Dante's Inferno**, 1935; **Dead End**, 1937 (see her remarks under *Author's Note* in **Stagecoach**); **The High and the Mighty**, 1954; **Honky Tonk**, 1941; **How to Murder Your Wife**, 1965; **I Stole a Million**, 1939; **Key Largo**, 1948; **Murder, My Sweet**, 1944; **Raw Deal**, 1947; **Stagecoach**, 1939; **Texas**, 1941; **The Velvet Touch**, 1948; **A Woman of the Town**, 1943.

Dalton Trumbo (author-screenwriter, 1905-1976): **The Gangster**, 1947; **Lonely Are the Brave**, 1962; **The Prowler**, 1951; **The Remarkable Andrew**, 1942; **Roman Holiday**, 1953; **Spartacus**, 1960.

Lana Turner (actress, 1921-1995): **Honky Tonk**, 1941; **Imitation of Life**, 1959; **Johnny Eager**, 1942; **Madame X**, 1966; **The Postman Always Rings Twice**, 1946; **The Rains of Ranchipur**, 1955; **Somewhere I'll Find You**, 1942; **The Three Musketeers**, 1948; **Weekend at the Waldorf**, 1945; **Ziegfeld Girl**, 1941.

King Vidor (director, 1894-1982): **The Fountainhead**, 1948; **H. M. Pulham, Esq.**, 1941; **Hallelujah**, 1929; **The Mask of Fu Manchu**, 1932; **Northwest Passage**, 1940; **Our Daily Bread**, 1934; **Show People**, 1928; **Solomon and Sheba**, 1959; **Stella Dallas**, 1937; **Street Scene**, 1931; **The Texas Rangers**, 1936; **War and Peace**, 1956; **The Wedding Night**, 1935; **The Wizard of Oz**, 1939; **The Yearling**, 1946.

Mike Wallace (journalist-TV commentator, 1918-2012): **Medium Cool**, 1969.

Raoul Walsh (director, 1887-1980): **The Bowery**, 1933; **Captain Blood**, 1935; **Desperate Journey**, 1942; **Fighter Squadron**, 1948; **Gentlemen Jim**, 1942; **In Old Arizona**, 1929; **The Lawless Breed**, 1953; **Manpower**, 1941; **Northern Pursuit**, 1943; **Objective, Burma!**, 1945; **The Roaring Twenties**, 1939; **Rosita**, 1923; **Sadie Thompson**, 1928; **Salty O'Rourke**, 1945; **St. Louis Blues**, 1939; **San Francisco**, 1936; **Saskatchewan**, 1954; **The Sheik**, 1921; **The Strawberry Blonde**, 1941; **They Died with Their Boots On**, 1941; **They Drive by Night**, 1940; **The Thief of Bagdad**, 1924; **Too Much, Too Soon**, 1958; **Uncertain Glory**, 1944; **What Price Glory**, 1926; **White Heat**, 1949; **The World in His Arms**, 1952.

Harry Warren (composer, 1893-1981): **Colleen**, 1936; **Gold Diggers of 1935**, 1935; **Marty**, 1955.

Ruth Warrick (actress, 1915-2005): **Citizen Kane**, 1941; **Mr. Winkle Goes to War**, 1944; **Song of the South**, 1946.

John Wayne (actor-director, 1907-1979): **Circus World**, 1964; **The Dark Command**, 1940; **Donovan's Reef**, 1963; **Duel in the Sun**, 1946; **Easy Rider**, 1969; **El Dorado**, 1967; **Fighting Caravans**, 1931; **The Fighting Seabees**, 1944; **A Fistful of Dollars**, 1964; **Flying Leathernecks**, 1951; **Flying Tigers**, 1942; **Fort Apache**, 1948; **The Green Berets**, 1968; **The Gunfighter**, 1950; **The High and the Mighty**, 1954; **The Horse Soldiers**, 1959; **How the West Was Won**, 1963; **I Cover the War**, 1937; **In Harm's Way**, 1965; **The Long Voyage Home**, 1940; **The Longest Day**, 1962; **The Man Who Shot Liberty Valance**, 1962; **Noah's Ark**, 1928; **North to Alaska**, 1960; **Operation Pacific**, 1951; **Our Hearts Were Young and Gay**, 1944; **Pittsburgh**, 1942; **The Quiet Man**, 1952; **Reap the Wild Wind**, 1942; **Red River**, 1948; **Reunion in France**, 1942; **Rio Bravo**, 1959; **Rio Grande**, 1950; **Rooster Cogburn**, 1975; **Sands of Iwo Jima**, 1949; **The Searchers**, 1956; **Seven Men from Now**, 1956; **Seven Sinners**, 1940; **She Wore a Yellow Ribbon**, 1949; **The Shepherd of the Hills**, 1941; **The Shootist**, 1976; **The Sons of Katie Elder**, 1965; **The Spoilers**, 1942; **Stagecoach**, 1939; **Tall in the Saddle**, 1944; **They Were Expendable**, 1945; **Three Faces West**, 1940; **3 Godfathers**, 1948; **True Grit**, 1969; **Tycoon**, 1947; **The Undefeated**, 1969; **Wake of the Red Witch**, 1949; **The War Wagon**, 1967; **When You're in Love**, 1937; **The Wild Bunch**, 1969; **The Wings of Eagles**, 1957; **Without Reservations**, 1946.

Orson Welles (actor-director, 1915-1985): **Black Magic**, 1949; **Chimes at Midnight**, 1961; **Citizen Kane**, 1941; **Compulsion**, 1959; **Ed Wood**, 1994; **Jane Eyre**, 1944; **Journey into Fear**, 1943; **The Kremlin Letter**, 1970; **The Lady from Shanghai**, 1948; **The Long, Hot Summer**, 1958; **Macbeth**, 1948; **The Magnificent Ambersons**, 1942; **Moby Dick**, 1956; **Monsieur Verdoux**, 1947; **Mr. Arkadin**, 1962; **Othello**, 1955; **Prince of Foxes**, 1949; **The Roots of Heaven**, 1958; **September Affair**, 1950; **Stagecoach**, 1939; **The Stranger**, 1946; **Sweet Smell of Success**, 1957; **The Third Man**, 1950; **Three Cases of Murder**, 1955; **The Three Faces of Eve**, 1957; **Tomorrow Is Forever**, 1946; **Touch of Evil**, 1958; **The Trial**, 1963; **The V.I.P.s**, 1963; **War of the Worlds**, 1953; **Waterloo**, 1971; **When Knighthood Was in Flower**, 1922; **White Heat**, 1949.

William A. Wellman (director, 1896-1975): **Buffalo Bill**, 1944; **Call of the Wild**, 1935; **The Hatchet Man**, 1932; **The High and the Mighty**, 1954; **The Iron Curtain**, 1948; **Island in the Sky**, 1953; **The Light That Failed**, 1939; **The Next Voice You Hear**, 1950; **Night Nurse**, 1931; **Nothing Sacred**, 1937; **The Ox-Bow Incident**, 1943; **The Public Enemy**, 1931; **Roxie Hart**, 1942; **So Big**, 1932; **A Star Is Born**, 1937; **The Story of G.I. Joe**, 1945; **Thunder Birds**, 1942; **Track of the Cat**,

1954; **Westward the Women**, 1951; **Wild Boys of the Road**, 1933; **Yellow Sky**, 1948.

James Whitmore (actor, 1921-2009): **Battleground**, 1949 (see Whitmore's comments in *Author's Note* for **The Red Badge of Courage**); **The Next Voice You Hear**, 1950; **Oklahoma!**, 1955; **The Red Badge of Courage**, 1951; **Them!**, 1954; **Tora! Tora! Tora!**, 1970; **The Undercover Man**, 1949; **Waterhole No. 3**, 1967.

Richard Widmark (actor, 1914-2008): **Kiss of Death**, 1947; **Madigan**, 1968; **Murder on the Orient Express**, 1974; **Night and the City**, 1950; **No Way Out**, 1950; **Panic in the Streets**, 1950; **Pickup on South Street**, 1953; **Red Skies of Montana**, 1952; **Road House**, 1948; **Rollercoaster**, 1977; **Run for the Sun**, 1956; **Slattery's Hurricane**, 1949; **The Street with No Name**, 1948; **Take the High Ground!**, 1953; **Time Limit**, 1957; **Twilight's Last Gleaming**, 1977; **Warlock**, 1959; **The Way West**, 1967; **When the Legends Die**, 1972; **Yellow Sky**, 1948.

Henry Wilcoxon (actor, 1905-1984): **The Crusades**, 1935; **The Greatest Show on Earth**, 1952; **Samson and Delilah**, 1949; **Unconquered**, 1947.

Billy Wilder (director, 1906-2002): **Ball of Fire**, 1941 (see his remarks under *Author's Note* in **A Song Is Born**); **Double Indemnity**, 1944; **Five Graves to Cairo**, 1943; **A Foreign Affair**, 1948; **The Fortune Cookie**, 1966; **The Lost Weekend**, 1945; **Love in the Afternoon**, 1957; **The Major and the Minor**, 1942; **One, Two, Three**, 1961; **Sabrina**, 1954; **The Secret Life of Walter Mitty**, 1947; **The Seven Year Itch**, 1955; **Some Like It Hot**, 1959; **A Song Is Born**, 1948; **The Spirit of St. Louis**, 1957; **Stalag 17**, 1953; **Sunset Boulevard**, 1950; **Witness for the Prosecution**, 1957.

Marie Windsor (actress, 1919-2000): **The Narrow Margin**, 1952; **The Showdown**, 1950; **The Sniper**, 1952.

Jonathan Winters (actor-comedian, 1925-2013): **It's A Mad, Mad, Mad, Mad World**, 1963 (see his remarks under *Author's Note* in **The Russians Are Coming!, The Russians Are Coming!**); **The Russians are Coming, the Russians are Coming**, 1966.

Shelley Winters (actress, 1920-2006): **Larceny**, 1948; **Night of the Hunter**, 1955; **A Place in the Sun**, 1951; **The Poseidon Adventure**, 1972; **Saskatchewan**, 1954; **The Scalphunters**, 1968; **Take One False Step**, 1949; **Winchester '73**, 1950.

Hank Worden (actor, horse wrangler, 1901-1992): **Fort Apache**, 1948; **The Horse Soldiers**, 1959; **The Indian Fighter**, 1955; **Red River**, 1948; **The Searchers**, 1956; **Sergeant Rutledge**, 1960; **3 Godfathers**, 1948; **A Woman of the Town**, 1943.

Fay Wray (actress, 1907-2004): **Doctor X**, 1932 (see her remarks under *Author's Note* in **The Vampire Bat**); **King Kong**, 1933; **The Most Dangerous Game**, 1932; **The Mystery of the Wax Museum**, 1933; **One Sunday Afternoon**, 1933; **The Richest Girl in the World**, 1934; **Tammy and the Bachelor**, 1957; **Thunderbolt**, 1929; **The Vampire Bat**, 1932; **Viva Villa!**, 1934; **The Wedding March**, 1928.

William Wyler (director, 1902-1981): **Counsellor at Law**, 1933; **Dead End**, 1937; **The Desperate Hours**, 1955; **Detective Story**, 1951; **Dodsworth**, 1936; **The Heiress**, 1949; **The Hunchback of Notre Dame**, 1923; **Jezebel**, 1938; **The Letter**, 1940; **The Little Foxes**, 1941; **Mrs. Miniver**, 1942; **Roman Holiday**, 1953; **These Three**, 1936; **Tom Brown of Culver**, 1932; **The Westerner**, 1940; **Wuthering Heights**, 1939.

Jane Wyman (actress, 1917-2007): **The Glass Menagerie**, 1950; **Johnny Belinda**, 1948; **The Lost Weekend**, 1945; **Miracle in the Rain**, 1956; **Princess O'Rourke**, 1943; **So Big**, 1953; **Stage Fright**, 1950; **The Yearling**, 1946.

Frank Garvin Yerby (author, 1916-1991): **The Foxes of Harrow**, 1947.

Loretta Young (actress, 1913-2000): **The Farmer's Daughter**, 1947; **The Hatchet Man**, 1932; **Laugh, Clown, Laugh**, 1928; **Life Begins**, 1932; **Love Is News**, 1937; **The Man from Blankley's**, 1930; **Platinum Blonde**, 1931; **The Story of Alexander Graham Bell**, 1939; **The Stranger**, 1946; **Suez**, 1938; **Three Blind Mice**, 1938; **Wife, Husband and Friend**, 1939; **Zoo in Budapest**, 1933.

Robert Young (actor, 1907-1998): **H. M. Pulham, Esq.**, 1941; **Joe Smith, American**, 1942; **Journey for Margaret**, 1942; **The Mortal Storm**, 1940; **Northwest Passage**, 1940; **Relentless**, 1948; **Remember Last Night?**, 1935; **Spitfire**, 1934; **Sweet Rosie O'Grady**, 1943; **The Searching Wind**, 1946; **The Secret Agent**, 1936; **Sitting Pretty**, 1948; **Stowaway**, 1936; **Strange Interlude**, 1932; **Sweet Rosie O'Grady**, 1943; **They Won't Believe Me**, 1947; **Three Comrades**, 1938; **Tugboat Annie**, 1933; **Western Union**, 1941.

Darryl F. Zanuck (producer-writer, 1902-1979): **The Hound of the Baskervilles**, 1939; **The House of Rothschild**, 1934; **The House on 92nd Street**, 1945; **How Green Was My Valley**, 1941; **Hudson's Bay**, 1941; **I Was an Adventuress**, 1940; **In Old Chicago**, 1938; **Johnny Apollo**, 1940; **The Keys to the Kingdom**, 1944; **Kidnapped**, 1938; **Laura**, 1944; **Leave Her to Heaven**, 1945; **Les Misérables**, 1935; **A Letter to Three Wives**, 1949; **Lifeboat**, 1944; **Little Caesar**, 1931; **The Littlest Rebel**, 1935; **Lloyd's of London**, 1936; **The Longest Day**, 1962; **The Mighty Barnum**, 1934; **Miracle on 34th Street**, 1947; **The Moon Is Down**, 1943; **Mr. Moto's Gamble**, 1938; **My Darling Clementine**, 1946; **Nightmare Alley**, 1947; **No Way Out**, 1950; **On the Avenue**, 1937; **Pickup on South Street**, 1953; **The President's Lady**, 1953; **The Prisoner of Shark Island**, 1936; **The Public Enemy**, 1931; **The Purple Heart**, 1944; **The Razor's Edge**, 1946; **River of No Return**, 1954; **Road House**, 1948; **The Robe**, 1953; **The Roots of Heaven**, 1958; **Rose of Washington Square**, 1939; **Sing, Baby, Sing**, 1936; **The Snake Pit**, 1948; **The Snows of Kilimanjaro**, 1952; **Song of Bernadette**, 1943; **The Sound of Music**, 1965; **Stars and Stripes Forever**, 1952; **The Story of Alexander Graham Bell**, 1939; **The Street With No Name**, 1948; **Suez**, 1938; **The Sun Also Rises**, 1957; **That Night in Rio**, 1941; **A Tree Grows in Brooklyn**, 1945; **Under Two Flags**, 1936; **Unfaithfully Yours**, 1948; **Viva Zapata!**, 1952; **Wee Willie Winkie**, 1937; **Week-End in Havana**, 1941; **Western Union**, 1941; **Wilson**, 1944; **A Yank in the R.A.F.**, 1941; **Yellow Sky**, 1948; **Young Mr. Lincoln**, 1939; **Zorba the Greek**, 1964.

Fred Zinnemann (director, 1907-1997): **From Here to Eternity**, 1953; **A Hatful of Rain**, 1957; **High Noon**, 1952; **Julia**, 1977; **A Man for All Seasons**, 1966; **The Men**, 1950; **My Brother Talks to Horses**, 1947; **Oklahoma!**, 1955; **The Old Man and the Sea**, 1958; **The Search**, 1948; **The Seventh Cross**, 1944; **The Sundowners**, 1960.

PHOTOS: NAME INDEX

1299; Bradna, Olympe, 2218; Brady, Alice, 881, 1402; Branagh, Kenneth, 733, 1623; Brand, Neville, 967; Brandauer, Klaus Maria, 265, 1272, 3549; Brando, Marlon, 51, 648, 1268, 1313, 1334, 1524, 1525, 1526, 1531, 2365, 2366, 2367, 2894, 2895, 2896, 2898, 3069, 3070, 3214, 3216; Braschi, Nicoletta, 1412; Brasselle, Keith, 3559; Brecher, Egon, 121; Bremer, Lucille, 3561; Brennan, Eileen, 1369; Brennan, Walter, 482, 1392, 2652, 2654, 2981, 2983; Brent, Evelyn, 2132, 2818, 2819; Brent, George, 941, 1561, 1575, 1784, 2282; Breslin, Abigail, 1005; Breslin, Spencer, 1973; Brett, Jeremy, 1394; Breuler, Robert, 307; Brewster, Diane, 910; Brian, Mary, 588, 1239, 2889; Brice, Fanny, 3237; Bridges, Beau, 600, 3599; Bridges, Jeff, 493, 932, 2614, 2761, 3038, 3058, 3059; Bridges, Lloyd, 798, 1103, 1783, 2220, 2918, 3039, 3617; Briggs, Matt, 163; Bright, Richard, 1225; Brimley, Wilford, 1423; Britt, May, 3216; Britton, Barbara, 2625, 2910; Britton, Connie, 3297; Broadbent, Jim, 3055, 3277; Broderick, Matthew, 114, 478, 580; Brodie, Steve, 798; Brody, Adam, 3397; Brody, Adrien, 1633; Brolin, Josh, 3362; Bromberg, J. Edward, 1233; Bronson, Charles (Charles Buchinsky), 739, 823, 1529, 2853, 2882, 3019; Brook, Clive, 2089, 2101, 2452, 2773, 2818, 2819; Brook, Faith, 3053; Brooke, Hillary, 908, 1296, 3126; Brooks, Albert, 1139, 2008; Brooks, Howard, 1199; Brooks, Jean, 474, 1075, 2072; Brooks, Louise, 95, 179, 373, 1580; Brooks, Mel, 410, 773; Brophy, Edward, 2120, 2546; Brosnan, Pierce, 324, 2045, 2431, 3494; Brown, James, 20; Brown, Joe E., 636; Brown, Johnny Mack, 2035, 2036; Brown, Stanley, 1206; Brown, Tom, 2666; Brown, Vanessa, 1059; Browne, Coral, 414, 2498; Browning, Emily, 2830, 2831; Bruce, Nigel, 813, 1743, 2102, 2483, 2730, 3497; Bruce, Sally Jane, 1445; Bruce, Virginia, 461, 1371, 1439, 2502, 3097, 3184; Bruhl, Linda, 1582; Bryan, Jane, 1235; Brynner, Yul, 40, 984, 1334, 2181, 2219, 2472, 2473, 2882, 3537; Buchholz, Horst, 2617; Buetel, Jack, 3547; Bujold, Genevieve, 3550; Buka, Donald, 2364; Bull, Joseph, 1454; Bullock, Sandra, 2238; Bunsen Honeydew (animated character), 3482; Buono, Cara, 1432; Burke, Billie, 113, 3213; Burke, James, 341; Burlinson, Tom, 1629; Burnett, Carol, 567; Burns, Bob, 3598; Burns, Edmund, 1186; Burns, Edward, 3297; Burns, George, 2149, 2405; Burr, Raymond, 1809, 3313; Burstyn, Ellen, 1054; Burton, Richard, 1388, 1785, 1889, 2261, 2262, 2448, 2849, 3006, 3008, 3045, 3536; Bush, Beatrice, 1604; Bush, Billy, 313; Bushman, Francis X., 100; Butcher, Adam, 1949; Butler, Gerard, 3373; Buzz Lightyear (animated character), 2715, 2716; Byington, Spring, 2928; Byrne, Gabriel, 1291, 2848;

Caan, James, 648, 649, 1901, 2537, 2538; Cabot, Bruce, 2120, 3581; Caesar, Adolph, 2180; Cage, Nicolas, 1072, 1135, 1332, 1787, 2962, 3057, 3089, 3597; Cagney, James, 43, 187, 366, 428, 501, 539, 601, 644, 1151, 1201, 1315, 1510, 1539, 1638, 1735, 1736, 1737, 1775, 1886, 1887, 1888, 1948, 2080, 2144, 2160, 2359, 2360, 2460, 2510, 2559, 2634, 2745, 2990, 2991, 2992, 3026, 3027, 3028, 3029, 3030, 3031, 3097, 3174, 3175, 3176, 3177, 3649; Cagney, Jeanne, 1754, 3176; Caine, Georgia, 1299; Caine, Michael, 234, 912, 1214, 1322, 1661, 1739, 2680, 3016, 3283, 3482; Calhern, Louis, 54, 422, 964, 1180, 2843, 3569, 3607; Calleia, Joseph, 2708; Calthrop, Donald, 127, 1488; Calvert, Corinne, 2610, 2990, 2991; Cambridge, Godfrey, 2949; Camp, Anna, 3387; Campbell, Glen, 2755; Campbell, John, 2382; Cannavale, Bobby, 3078; Cantor, Eddie, 2119, 2343, 3050; Capponi, Pier Paolo, 505; Cardinale, Claudia, 239, 1529; Cardwell, James, 2382; Carey, Harry, 2218, 2719; Carey, Harry, Jr., 2096, 2592, 2593, 2907; Carey, Macdonald, 2076, 2810; Carey, Philip, 3053; Carl Fredricksen (animated character), 2841, 2842; Carlson, Richard, 1842, 3020, 3612; Carlyle, Richard, 3553; Carmen, Loene, 3178; Carmichael, Hoagy, 3218; Carmichael, Ian, 2006; Carney, Alan, 1351; Carney, Art, 743; Carnovsky, Morris, 343; Carol, Martine, 1118, 3642; Caron, Leslie, 37, 317, 3484; Carr, Jane, 1953; Carra, Raffaella, 2902; Carradine, David, 142, 1745; Carradine, John, 13, 1242; Carradine, Keith, 424, 2227; Carrell, Steve, 3396; Carrere, Tia, 2757; Carrey, Jim, 2759, 3290; Carrez, Florence, 2744; Carrillo, Elpidia, 1452; Carrillo, Leo, 3167; Carroll, John, 532, 533, 2269, 2271; Carroll, Leo G., 2356, 2972; Carroll,

Madeleine, 612, 1115, 1711, 1713, 1714, 2026, 2027, 2565, 2566, 3485; Carroll, Nancy, 1061; Carson, Jack, 57, 924, 1707, 1904, 2359, 2451; Carson, Jean, 1630; Carter, Harper, 2642; Carter, Helena Bonham, 999, 1286, 1908; Carter, Janis, 570; Caruso, Anthony, 60, 916; Casilio, Maria Pia, 2799; Cass, Peggy, 1573; Cassavetes, John, 3137; Cassell, Wally, 3028; Cassidy, Joanna, 2808; Cassini, Nadia, 1739; Cassisi, John, 165; Castelnuovo, Nino, 2801; Castro, Analia, 1505; Cates, Phoebe, 1706; Catlett, Walter, 2437; Caubere, Philippe, 1395; Caulfield, Joan, 345, 1625, 2969; Cavanagh, Paul, 818, 823; Cave, Des, 1573; Caviezel, James, 774; Cazale, John, 648; Chakiris, George, 2977; Chamberlain, Richard, 566, 3558; Champion, Gower, 2118; Champion, Marge, 2118; Chan, Jackie, 1353; Chance, Naomi, 1953; Chandler, Helen, 409; Chandler, Jeff, 157, 937, 3568; Chandler, Kyle, 2406; Chaney, Lon, Jr., 573, 1503, 1536, 3121, 3122; Chaney, Lon, Sr., 840, 1627, 2826, 2827; Channing, Carol, 2577; Channing, Stockard, 2148; Chapin, Billy, 1445; Chaplin, Charles, 246, 656, 657, 689, 976, 1319, 1320, 1324, 2116, 2627; Chaplin, Geraldine, 3033; Chapman, Marguerite, 287; Charisse, Cyd, 75, 1262, 1591, 2129, 2141; Charles, Ray, 134; Charles Darwin (animated character), 3383; Charleson, Ian, 215; Chase, Lewis, 1516; Chastain, Jessica, 2741; Chatterton, Ruth, 396; Chau Thi Kim Xuan, 91; Cheadle, Don, 812; Cheetah (monkey), 3521; Chekhov, Michael, 2241; Cher, 1322, 2411, 3103, 3104; Cherkasov, Nicolai, 929; Cherrill, Virginia, 246; Chevalier, Maurice, 1152, 1154, 1275, 1533, 2162, 3484; Chief Thundercloud, 3593; Chihane, Oxana, 3429; Childers, Ambyr, 3357; Chishu Ryu, 2664; Chiyeko Higashiyama, 2664; Chong, Rae Dawn, 1752; Chow Yun-Fat, 1648; Christensen, Hayden, 2304; Christians, Mady, 3054; Christie, Julie, 473, 733, 755, 2084; Christy, Eileen, 2613; Churchill, Berton, 2270; Ciannelli, Eduardo, 722, 1246, 3102; Cichy, Martin, 504; Claire, Ina, 1457, 1922; Clark, Barney, 1516; Clark, Bobby, 737; Clark, Dane, 1331, 2875; Clarke, Angela, 3670; Clarke, Mae, 1735, 2946; Clayburgh, Jill, 2836; Clift, Montgomery, 585, 586, 1651, 1652, 1653, 1786, 1824, 1825, 1827, 1828, 3215; Clive, Colin, 233; Clive, E. E., 1691; Clooney, George, 275, 1491, 1492, 1618, 2595, 2845, 3315; Clooney, Rosemary, 3021; Close, Glenn, 489, 932, 1847; Cloutier, Suzanne, 1552; Cluzet, Francois, 3332, 3333; Cobb, Lee J., 139, 175, 2767; Coburn, Charles, 875, 1323, 1333, 1569, 2591; Coburn, James, 304, 739; Coco, James, 1543; Coe, Peter, 819; Colbert, Claudette, 138, 253, 419, 442, 563, 632, 920, 921, 2094, 2136, 2137, 2162, 2175, 2176, 2177, 2674, 3107; Coleman, Charles, 3097; Collier, William, Jr., 1104, 2361; Collinge, Patricia, 2074; Collins, Cora Sue, 1178; Collins, Eddie, 1844; Collins, Joan, 634, 2065, 2885, 3684, 3697; Collins, Lynn, 3339; Collins, Ray, 464; Colman, Ronald, 89, 209, 210, 255, 405, 871, 1059, 1094, 1137, 1138, 1711, 1712, 1713, 1714, 1770, 1791, 1792, 2436, 2437, 2441, 2442, 2814, 3485; Combs, Jackie, 2952; Cone, Stephen, 3431; Connelly, Jennifer, 1023; Connery, Sean, 393, 478, 842, 892, 1214, 1236, 1237, 1891, 2458, 2838, 2839, 3084, 3469; Connolly, Billy, 766; Connolly, Walter, 702, 1481, 3603; Connors, Chuck, 108, 1414; Conroy, Frank, 217; Considine, Paddy, 3435; Considine, Tim, 1607; Conte, Richard, 311, 821, 2154, 2559, 2811, 2919, 3012; Converse, Frank, 816; Conway, Tom, 474, 862; Coogan, Jackie, 976, 2669; Coonan, Dorothy, 3061; Cook, Elisha, Jr., 981, 1190; Cook, Peter, 3157; Cook, Tommy, 311; Coolidge, Philip, 863; Cooper, Bradley, 3248, 3249, 3398; Cooper, Charles, 3159; Cooper, Chris, 1253; Cooper, Gary, 32, 195, 249, 295, 319, 383, 484, 485, 498, 542, 559, 605, 611, 612, 734, 775, 870, 1114, 1149, 1261, 1336, 1348, 1349, 1475, 1538, 1621, 1655, 1656, 1697, 1806, 2047, 2048, 2049, 2050, 2051, 2052, 2217, 2218, 2258, 2336, 2459, 2512, 2513, 2804, 2805, 2889, 2981, 2982, 2983, 3092, 3098, 3123, 3153, 3230, 3591, 3604, 3641, 3701; Cooper, Gladys, 2043; Cooper, Jackie, 1844, 2152, 2729, 2730; Coote, Robert, 273, 1161; Cord, Alex, 159; Cording, Harry, 818; Corey, Jeff, 161, 535; Corey, Wendell, 502, 3698; Corrigan, Lloyd, 1053; Corrigan, Ray, 1861; Cort, Bud, 741; Cortez, Ricardo, 2560, 2703; Cosmo, James, 146; Cossart, Ernest, 1006; Costello, Lou, 1537, 1588, 2633, 3041; Costner, Kevin, 36, 321, 496, 1465, 1895, 2133, 2557, 2838, 2839, 3164, 3165, 3166, 3647; Cotillard, Marion, 3392; Cotten, Joseph, 241,

mated character), 2841; Elliott, Bill, 2122; Elliott, Robert, 517; Elliott, Sam, 2673; Ellis, Edward, 3102; Elmo (Muppet character), 12; Elwes, Cary, 1705; Emerson, Faye, 1246, 2802, 2875; Emery, John, 768; Emery, R. Lee, 2124; Eppler, Laramie, 2741; Epps, Mike, 3404; Erickson, Leif, 908, 2446, 3604; Ericson, John, 2810; Ermey, R. Lee, 594; Esmond, Jill, 430, 2568; Esmond, Carl, 3149; Estevez, Emilio, 2277; Etel, Alex, 2944; Evans, Chris, 3473; Evans, Edith, 876; Evans, Gene, 518, 1590, 2318; Evans, Linda, 2578; Evans, Madge, 1613; Everett, Rupert, 869; Ewell, Tom, 2067; Eyer, Richard, 910; Eythe, William, 464, 824, 2202, 3091;

Fabian, 1474; Fabrizio, David, 2407; Fairbanks, Douglas, Jr., 212, 288, 722, 1335, 1712, 2135, 3213; Fairbanks, Douglas, Sr., 609, 1893, 2539, 2541, 2598; Falconetti, Maria, 1595; Falk, Peter, 156, 1369; Fanning, Dakota, 2936; Farhat, Julien, 3430; Farley, Morgan, 964; Farmer, Frances, 2196; Farmiga, Vera, 2845; Farnsworth, Richard, 1423, 2345; Farnum, Dustin, 2263; Farnum, William, 3692; Farrell, Charles, 2070; Farrell, Colin, 2619, 2950; Farrow, Mia, 301, 736, 1741, 1918, 1919, 2078, 3055; Fassbender, Michael, 3169; Faylen, Frank, 1257, 3015; Faye, Alice, 881, 882, 1521, 1916, 2344, 2496, 2915, 2968, 3195; Faye, Julia, 2832; Feist, Harry, 1544; Feldman, Corey, 2283; Feldman, Marty, 11, 3209; Fellini, Federico, 905; Fellows, Edith, 121, 1613; Fenton, Frank, 401; Ferrell, Will, 2352; Ferrer, Jose, 315, 696, 1341, 3013, 3467, 3477, 3686; Ferrer, Mel, 1988, 1990, 2929, 3622; Ferrero, Martin, 966; Fiala, Karel, 1074; Field, Betty, 692, 1503, 2100; Field, Sally, 1469, 1654, 3351; Fields, W.C., 76, 903, 923, 1311, 1401, 1429, 1511, 1677, 2149, 2626, 3193, 3231; Fiennes, Joseph, 448, 2081; Fiennes, Ralph, 455, 459, 2005, 3314, 3399, 3673; Fievel (animated character), 38; Filipi, Carmen, 1612; Finch, Jon, 3623; Finch, Peter, 1427; Finlay, Frank, 566; Finney, Albert, 1291, 1978, 2668, 2784, 2813; Firth, Colin, 999, 1050; Fischer, Sarah, 3412; Fisher, Frances, 2824; Fitzgerald, Barry, 436, 653, 1307, 2793, 2834; Fitzgerald, Geraldine, 1494, 2803, 3077; Fitzgerald, Tara, 752; Fix, Paul, 72; Flaherty, Pat, 3662; Fleming, Rhonda, 2248; Flemying, Robert, 1212; Fletcher, Bramwell, 1363; Flick (dog), 2799; Flicka (horse), 1399; Flippen, Jay C., 891; Flipper (porpoise), 526; Flit (animated character), 1669; Flon, Suzanne, 3686; Florelle, 2603; Fluke, 528; Flynn, Errol, 14, 182, 214, 333, 385, 395, 439, 614, 1249, 1495, 1496, 1720, 1900, 1910, 1960, 2011, 2012, 2013, 2493, 2514, 2515, 2516, 2517, 2518, 2683, 2802, 2887, 3502, 3581; Fonda, Henry, 318, 419, 420, 554, 593, 684, 686, 1025, 1315, 1518, 1570, 1571, 1572, 1843, 1844, 2190, 2721, 2767, 2929, 2930, 2939, 3096, 3158, 3159, 3199, 3219, 3220, 3222, 3611, 3626; Fonda, Jane, 271, 962, 1453, 2526, 2921; Fonda, Peter, 434; Fontaine, Joan, 282, 452, 1082, 1810, 1811, 2044, 2568, 2903, 3141, 3495; Foran, Dick, 1624; Forbes, Bryan, 1069, 3189; Forbes, Ralph, 89; Forbes, Scott, 1546; Ford, Glenn, 297, 488, 570, 1195, 2174, 2506, 2702, 2815, 2883, 3039, 3605; Ford, Harrison, 891, 892, 893, 1688, 1777, 1778, 3109, 3147; Ford, Wallace, 1141, 2076, 2428; Foronjy, Richard, 1702; Forrest, Fredric, 3003; Forrest, Sally, 3010; Forrest, Steve, 1710; Forster, Robert, 1259; Forsyth, Rosemary, 2932; Forsythe, John, 2690, 2751; Fossey, Brigitte, 737; Foster, Barry, 579; Foster, Ben, 3354; Foster, Jodie, 165, 2193; Foster, Norman, 1640; Foster, Preston, 859, 967, 1046, 2028, 3557; Foulger, Byron, 1206; Fowley, Douglas, 1276; Fox, Allan, 2362; Fox, Edward, 335; Fox, James, 2577; Fox, Michael J., 70, 2034; Fox, Sidney, 1378; France Nuyen, 955; Francen, Victor, 281; Franciosa, Anthony, 1125; Francis, Anne, 544; Francis, Kay, 1239, 1540, 2773, 3002, 3018; Francis, Robert, 173; Franciscus, James, 2858; Franco, James, 2244; Francois, Emile, 2042; Franklin, Pamela, 900; Frantz, Chandler, 3365, 3367; Franz, Eduard, 1060, 1171, 3681; Fraser, Brendan, 2008; Fraser, Elizabeth, 2764; Frawley, William, 1537, 1921; Fred Flintstone (animated character), 1191; Freeman, Mona, 2368; Freeman, Morgan, 417, 1489, 2091; Frees, Paul, 2378; Fricker, Brenda, 797; Friend, Rupert, 1361, 3226; Friendlikh, Alice, 1796; Friganza, Trixie, 575; Froling, Ewa, 480; Frost, Nick, 3435; Frye, Dwight, 571; Fuller, Frances, 1538; Funshine Bear (animated character), 189; Futterman, Dan, 1287;

Gaal, Franciska, 162; Gabin, Jean, 683; Gable, Clark, 138, 176, 177, 225, 272, 274, 504, 663, 664, 668, 669, 801, 834, 920, 921, 1153, 1220, 1221, 1305, 1382, 1383, 1384, 1385, 1442, 1460, 1574, 1819, 1820, 1961, 1962, 1964, 1965, 1976, 2035, 2036, 2191, 2346, 2347, 2444, 2463, 2485, 2486, 2524, 2525, 2678, 3037, 3056, 3609, 3610; Gabor, Zsa Zsa, 3686; Gahagan, Helen, 2092, 3470; Galletti, Giovanna, 1544; Gallian, Ketti, 1230; Galloway, Jay, 3416; Gam, Rita, 1446; Gambon, Michael, 744, 1055, 2766; Garber, Victor, 1290; Garbo, Greta, 45, 59, 178, 522, 681, 1250, 1456, 1457, 1575, 1746, 1747, 1748, 1749, 2466, 2467, 2703, 2782, 3071, 3130, 3468, 3636; Garcia, Andy, 769, 2838; Garcia, Rosita, 86; Gardner, Ava, 497, 701, 834, 1087, 1321, 1398, 2058, 2169, 2170, 2171, 2391, 3017, 3600; Garfield, Andrew, 2178; Garfield, John, 199, 476, 546, 560, 615, 750, 1684, 1685, 1696, 2015, 2016, 2017, 2523, 2704, 2809, 2961; Gargan, William, 563; Garland, Judy, 66, 433, 541, 746, 883, 1088, 1110, 1263, 1264, 1647, 2291, 2292, 2293, 2294, 2388, 3114, 3115, 3117, 3118, 3119, 3146; Garner, James, 816, 1379, 1480, 2567, 2607; Garner, Jennifer, 2558; Garner, Peggy Ann, 2740; Garr, Teri, 3208; Garson, Greer, 132, 1359, 1360, 1691, 1791, 1792, 2493, 2857, 3594; Gassman, Vittorio, 1849; Gates, Larry, 3685; Gates, Nancy, 2377; Gaynes, George, 307; Gaynor, Janet, 2070, 2289, 2290, 2395, 3213; Gaynor, Mitzi, 853, 1076, 1387; Gaze, Gwen, 852; Gazara, Ben, 3696; Geer, Will, 3081; Gelfant, Alan, 1432; Gelin, Daniel, 1210; Gemora, Charles, 1378; Genn, Leo, 1762, 2866, 3554; George, Gladys, 1888; Geppetto (animated character), 1645; Geraghty, Brian, 845; Gere, Richard, 290, 1133, 1504, 1690, 2193, 3469; Giacomo, Laura San, 1758; Giamatti, Paul, 237, 3078; Gibson, Gowland, 707, 708; Gibson, Henry, 1124, 1421; Gibson, Mel, 146, 602, 1080, 1170, 1217, 1604, 1793, 2960, 2994, 3179, 3565, 3693; Gielgud, John, 964, 2026, 2027, 3016, 3539, 3556; Gilbert, John, 110, 522, 1746, 2974; Gilbert, Lou, 2896, 2898; Gilford, Jack, 1980; Gillingwater, Claude, 1107, 1676; Gillis, Ann, 14; Gilman, Jared, 3369, 3370; Girard, Joseph W., 2051; Gish, Dorothy, 1549; Gish, Lillian, 117, 754, 1549, 2000, 2821, 2951, 2987, 3082; Gleason, Jackie, 847, 1582; Gleason, James, 768, 1261; Gleeson, Brendan, 146; Gleeson, Domhnall, 3295; Glen, Iain, 1242; Glenn, Scott, 2133, 2134; Glover, Crispin, 70; Glover, Danny, 1080, 1654, 2133; Goddard, Paulette, 200, 624, 788, 1319, 1475, 2175, 2176, 2805; Godfrey, Renee, 2483; Godzilla (animated monster), 3310, 3311, 3312; Golan, Gila, 2858; Golbahari, Marina, 1551; Goldberg, Whoopi, 266; Goldblum, Jeff, 966, 1145; Goldwyn Girls, 1903; Gollum (animated character; Andy Serkis voiceover), 3317; Gomez, Thomas, 546, 973, 1674, 2495; Gong Li, 956; Gonzo the Great (Muppet character), 1366; Gooding, Cuba, Jr., 938, 1271; Goodman, John, 65, 3252, 3418; Goodwin, Bill, 924, 2911; Gordon, C. Henry, 1994, 2282; Gordon, Christine, 862; Gordon, Dexter, 1920; Gordon, Gale, 1557; Gordon, Harold, 2896; Gordon, Ruth, 741, 1918; Gordon-Levitt, Joseph, 42, 3286, 3352, 3353; Gorman, Robert, 1907; Gorney, Karen Lynn, 1979; Gould, Elliott, 181, 1124, 1244; Grable, Betty, 1340, 1387, 2637, 2904, 3172, 3173; Grace, Maggie, 3410; Grace, Topher, 879; Gracy Singh, 1038; Graham, Betty Jane, 1442; Graham, Bill, 3631; Grahame, Gloria, 109, 878; Grandstedt, Greta, 2362; Granger, Farley, 1473, 1911, 2353, 2354, 2356, 2522, 3628, 3684; Granger, Stewart, 995, 1474, 1715, 1988, 1989, 1990, 3068, 3205; Grant, Cary, 16, 64, 67, 155, 213, 360, 429, 722, 782, 790, 825, 833, 864, 880, 894, 1323, 1347, 1351, 1435, 1436, 1468, 1470, 1471, 1472, 1484, 1485, 1541, 1547, 1614, 1631, 1693, 2093, 2414, 2441, 2442, 2497, 2573, 2649, 2650, 2693, 2694, 2695, 3612, 3657; Grant, David, 36; Grant, Hugh, 3275; Grapewin, Charles, 2661; Gray, Coleen, 1002, 1862; Gray, Dulcie, 1295; Grayson, Kathryn, 355, 1001, 2495, 2660, 2852; Greco, Juliette, 1910; Greene, Richard, 814, 971, 2286, 2375, 3183, 3589; Greenstreet, Sydney, 1188, 1245, 2868, 3129; Greenwood, Bruce, 2296, 2557; Greenwood, Charlotte, 3223; Greenwood, Joan, 876, 2620; Greer, Jane, 1562, 1928; Greer, Lucy, 2558; Gregson, John, 2645; Grenfell, Joyce, 2115; Grey, Joel, 2061; Grey, Nan, 2604; Grey, Virginia, 2804; Grier, David Alan, 1846; Griffith, Andy, 472, 1463; Griffith, Melanie, 3147, 3371; Grimes, Gary, 313; Grimes, Karolyn, 927; Grizzard, George, 2940; Grodin,

Charles, 1283; Gryphon, 414; Guardino, Harry, 825; Guest, Christopher, 3587; Guest, Nicholas, 3587; Gugino, Carla, 1865; Guinee, Tim, 1620; Guinness, Alec, 809, 983, 1064, 1556, 1708, 2301, 2763, 3690; Guiry, Thomas, 1041, 1969; Gurie, Sigrid, 2591; Guthrie, Pat, 2392; Guttenberg, Steve, 93, 262; Guzman, Ryan, 3408, 3409; Gwenn, Edmund, 1300, 1301, 1314, 2751; Gwynne, Fred, 1389; Gyllenhaal, Jake, 1727, 3403; Gyllenhaal, Maggie, 2352; Gyasi, David, 3278;

Haade, William, 973, 978; Haas, Lukas, 283, 3109; Hackett, Buddy, 925; Hackman, Gene, 252, 507, 578, 803, 1465, 1683, 2807, 2824; Hadley, Reed, 3604; Hagen, Jean, 2142, 3698; Hagerty, Julie, 1139; Haigh, Louisa, 2109; Hailey, Marian, 1157; Haines, Larry, 2066; Hair, Raymond C., Jr., 2147; Hale, Alan, Sr., 13, 359, 395; Hale, Barbara, 509, 931, 2040, 2975, 3650; Hale, Jonathan, 1952; Haley, Jack, 2915, 3115, 3118; Hall, James, 762; Hall, Jon, 843, 1004; Hall, Juanita, 2225; Hall, Porter, 55, 611, 1299, 2341; Hall, Rebecca, 1665; Hall, Thurston, 2104; Halop, Billy, 3194; Ham (animated character), 2714; Hamilton, George, 2879, 3229; Hamilton, Linda, 324; Hamilton, Margaret, 3116, 3524; Hamilton, Neil, 89, 2986, 3051; Hamlin, Harry, 251; Haney, Carol, 1576; Hanks, Tom, 552, 710, 1070, 1981, 1982, 1983, 2155, 2253, 2480, 3232, 3273, 3630; Hanley, Jimmy, 188; Hannah, Daryl, 2253; Hanson, Lars, 2000; Harbord, Carl, 1945; Hardin, Ty, 1733; Harding, Ann, 471, 1180; Hardwicke, Cedric, 273, 833, 1686, 3039, 3629; Hardy, Oliver, 129, 1558, 1975, 2423, 2953; Hardy, Tom, 3356; Harlow, Jean, 87, 378, 762, 1085, 1659, 1737, 1815, 1819, 1820, 1821, 1863, 1976, 2414, 3056, 3649; Harnois, Elizabeth, 1535; Harper, Jessica, 1397; Harrigan, William, 531; Harris, Barbara, 2580; Harris, Ed, 1672, 2807, 2950; Harris, Julie, 432; Harris, Richard, 2080, 2574, 2822; Harrison, George, 738; Harrison, Rex, 254, 569, 623, 1182, 1394, 1448, 2123, 2820, 3660, 3669; Harron, Robert, 754; Hart, William S., 2762; Hartnett, Josh, 1611; Harvey, Laurence, 1218, 2128, 2921; Hatfield, Hurd, 1637, 3655; Hathaway, Anne, 1765; Hatton, Raymond, 1004, 1186, 1751; Hauer, Rutger, 1037; Haver, June, 1507; Hawke, Ethan, 3025; Hawkins, Jack, 124, 1459, 3242; Hawks, Howard, 2772; Hawn, Goldie, 1716, 2381; Hawthorne, Nigel, 1175; Hayden, Harry, 591; Hayden, Sterling, 60, 394, 981, 1124, 1414, 2173, 2287, 3608; Hayes, Billie, 1102; Hayes, George ("Gabby"), 190, 1845, 2443; Hayes, Helen, 484, 485, 1405, 3633; Hayward, Kara, 3368, 3369; Hayward, Louis, 1199, 1406, 1953, 2349, 2916; Hayward, Susan, 8, 331, 353, 605, 851, 863, 1163, 1687, 1802, 2161, 2172, 2329, 2533, 3040, 3105, 3544, 3574, 3592, 3595, 3638; Hayworth, Rita, 130, 296, 323, 631, 1027, 1400, 1954, 2359, 2360, 2513, 2676, 3200, 3467; Heche, Anne, 2905; Heckart, Eileen, 1297; Hedron, Tippi, 116, 1236, 1237; Heflin, Van, 126, 1171, 1405, 1605, 1729, 1776, 2348, 2449, 2479, 2600, 2605; Heggie, O.P., 2163; Helm, Brigitte, 1278; Helpmann, Robert, 497, 1829; Hemingway, Ernest, 2392; Hemingway, Hadley, 2392; Hemingway, Mariel, 1219; Hemsworth, Chris, 3402; Henderson, Martin, 1866; Henderson, Stephen McKinley, 3353; Hendrix, Wanda, 1307; Henley, Barry Shabaka, 2480; Henn, Carrie, 25; Henreid, Paul, 194, 1486, 1487; Henry Bigg (animated character), 767; Henry, Justin, 1012; Hepburn, Audrey, 223, 1149, 1394, 1891, 1902, 1937, 1938, 2784, 2821, 2909, 2930; Hepburn, Katharine, 9, 19, 113, 155, 233, 357, 716, 790, 1100, 1111, 1123, 1242, 1335, 1518, 1597, 1631, 1783, 1909, 2252, 2265, 2266, 2313, 2314, 2390, 2427, 2816, 3106, 3132, 3133, 3134, 3580, 3583, 3635; Herbert, Holmes, 818; Herbert, Hugh, 763; Herman, Pee-wee, 1612; Hernandez, Jay, 581; Hernandez, Juano, 907, 2189, 3217; Hershey, Barbara, 477, 1738; Hersholt, Jean, 2484; Heston, Charlton, 101, 325, 497, 975, 1183, 1285, 1657, 1687, 2471, 2473, 2708, 2932, 3539, 3643, 3668; Heydt, Louis Jean, 917, 2528; Heyes, Herbert, 1590, 3668; Highmore, Freddie, 2246; Hikari Ishida, 10; Hill, Steven, 3671; Hiller, Wendy, 1182, 1193, 1744, 1947, 2208; Hinds, Samuel S., 2621; Hingle, Pat, 1458; Hirsch, Emile, 3354; Hitchcock, Alfred, 2690, 2691, 2874; Hitchcock, Patricia, 2356; Hobbes, Halliwell, 768, 2928; Hobson, Valerie, 418, 691, 2259, 2260; Hodiak, John, 746, 1092, 1093, 1185; Hoey, Dennis, 818; Hoffman, Dustin, 478, 679, 1012, 1225, 1226, 1282, 1584, 1781, 2684, 2685,

2905, 3671, 3700; Hoffman, Philip Seymour, 3357; Hogan, Paul, 303; Holbrook, Hal, 2288; Holcombe, Harry, 3599; Holden, William, 141, 292, 345, 369, 463, 545, 658, 807, 1150, 1306, 1635, 1636, 1764, 1836, 1938, 2278, 2279, 2280, 2281, 2368, 2373, 2374, 2399, 2400, 2401, 2402, 2403, 2488, 2710, 2712, 2834, 3062, 3063, 3064, 3065; Holiday, Judy, 9, 141, 595; Holland, Tom, 3329, 3331; Holliman, Earl, 1783, 2209, 2210, 2748; Holloway, Stanley, 1596, 2645; Holloway, Sterling, 654; Holm, Celeste, 210, 1879; Holm, Ian, 713, 944; Holmes, Katie, 2489; Holt, Jany, 1799; Holt, Jack, 1961; Holt, Tim, 1177, 2735, 2736, 2738; Homeier, Skip (Skippy), 2675; Homolka, Oscar (Oskar), 436, 3039, 3622; Hope, Bob, 624, 1396, 1578, 1579, 1881, 1883, 1884, 2060, 2295, 3588; Hopkins, Anthony, 445, 1835, 2127, 3152, 3202, 3465, 3534; Hopkins, Miriam, 356, 758, 1512, 2342, 2750, 2887, 3125; Hopper, Dennis, 434, 2755; Hopper, Hedda, 1640; Hopper, William, 2774; Hopton, Russell, 644; Horne, Lena, 2334, 2335; Horton, Edward Everett, 368, 2389; Horton, Louisa, 27; Hoskins, Bob, 1322, 3042, 3043, 3044; Houghton, Katharine, 716; Hounsou, Djimon, 39; Houseman, Arthur, 1558; Houston, Whitney, 3406; Howard, John, 1137; Howard, Leslie, 557, 664, 667, 668, 902, 1501, 1624, 1744, 2284; Howard, Trevor, 858, 1910, 2208, 2901, 2902; Howell, C. Thomas, 1568; Hoyt, John, 161; Huber, Harold, 1004; Hudson, John, 719; Hudson, Rochelle, 1077, 1677, 3061; Hudson, Rock, 1065, 1156, 1179, 2025, 2040, 2189, 2451, 2662, 2806, 3155, 3156, 3598; Hughes, Mary Beth, 1570; Hughes, Wendy, 1122; Hulce, Tom, 33; Hull, Henry, 1093, 1843, 2973; Hunt, Helen, 58, 2994; Hunt, Marsha, 945, 1801; Hunt, Martita, 691; Hunter, Ian, 441; Hunter, Jeffrey, 1947, 2022, 2046; Hunter, Kim, 3001; Huntley, Raymond, 2927; Hurst, Paul, 2036; Hurt, William, 135, 222, 470, 1279; Hussey, Ruth, 1477, 2479, 2828; Huston, Angelica, 1724; Huston, Danny, 1894; Huston, John, 228; Huston, Virginia, 1563; Huston, Walter, 364, 396, 411, 701, 1094, 1502, 2734, 2735, 2737, 3176, 3478, 3547; Hutchinson, Josephine, 2340; Hutton, Betty, 46, 705, 887, 1298, 1299, 2185, 2186, 3569; Hutton, Timothy, 2450; Hyde-White, Wilfred, 660; Hylton, Richard, 518; Hymer, Warren, 2120; Hytten, Olaf, 3126;

Ibsen, Buddy, 1446; Ice Cube (O'Shea Jackson Sr.), 2595; Imrie, Celia, 3262, 3394; Ingram, Rex, 711, 2543; Ireland, John, 29, 859, 1103, 1824; Iron Eyes Cody, 131; Irons, Jeremy, 1847; Isaacs, Jason, 3683; Iturbi, Jose, 2588; Ivan, Rosalind, 2410, 3584; Ives, Burl, 108, 201;

Jackman, Hugh, 3346, 3434; Jackson, Glenda, 804, 2706, 2766; Jackson, Gordon, 17; Jackson, Jonathan, 2760; Jackson, Samuel L., 376; Jackson, Thomas, 2545; Jacobi, Derek, 733; Jacobsson, Ulla, 3242; Jade, Claude, 2690; Jaeckel, Richard, 1099; Jaffe, Sam, 60, 722; Jagger, Dean, 2770, 2771, 2980; James (animated character), 933; James, David, 1032; James, Sidney, 1064; Jannings, Emil, 1044, 1603, 2865, 2952; Janssen, David, 2940; Jarman, Claude, Jr., 907, 1567, 3181; Jarrott, Charles, 3550; Jenkins, Allen, 1948, 2041; Jenkins, Richard, 3341; Jessica Rabbit (animated character; Kathleen Turner voiceover), 3044; Jet Li, 1365; Jethro (animated character), 1700; Jewell, 1859, 1860; Jiminy Cricket (animated character), 1643; Johann, Zita, 3506; Johns, Glynis, 344, 1304, 1582, 2394, 3634; Johnson, Ben, 2095, 2907, 3062; Johnson, Celia, 61; Johnson, Chic, 763; Johnson, Chubby, 174; Johnson, Don, 3285; Johnson, Dwayne, 3307; Johnson, Kay, 427; Johnson, Rita, 440; Johnson, Van, 173, 838, 883, 1056, 2562, 2563, 2778, 2785, 3535; Johnson, Zita, 2618; Jolie, Angelina, 1287, 1955; Jolson, Al, 730, 936, 1916, 2139; Jonathan (animated character), 3323; Jones, Allan, 702, 3603; Jones, Barry, 353, 2059; Jones, Bruce, 1782; Jones, Carolyn, 789; Jones, Christopher, 1933; Jones, Dean, 2702; Jones, Griffith, 3171; Jones, James Earl, 283, 496, 703, 1969; Jones, Jennifer, 192, 423, 1150, 1171, 1681, 2136, 2201, 2202, 2203, 2476, 2961, 3556, 3678; Jones, Sam J., 3414; Jones, Shirley, 1381; Jones, Terry, 3085; Jones, Tommy Lee, 1269, 2795, 3350; Jordan, Dorothy, 2022, 2393; Jordan, Miriam, 2101; Jory, Victor, 220, 500; Jose Carioca (animated character), 2584; Joslin, Samuel, 3329, 3330; Joslyn, Allyn, 1541; Jourdan, Louis, 1082,

O'Connell, Jack, 3422; O'Connor, Carroll, 369; O'Connor, Donald, 2138, 2142, 3619; O'Connor, Frances, 1224; O'Connor, Robert Emmett, 2718; O'Connor, Una, 896, 911, 3110; O'Donnell, Cathy, 2522; O'Donnell, Chris, 1005, 2003, 2601; O'Donnell, Rosie, 1070; O'Donovan, Ross, 1629; Offerman, George, Jr., 2382; O'Gorman, Dean, 3318; O'Hara, Maureen, 125, 476, 569, 1300, 1301, 1755, 1756, 1794, 1869, 2135, 3095; O'Keefe, Dennis, 621, 770, 1075, 2428, 2429, 2844, 2916; Okonedo, Sophie, 812; Oland, Warner, 216, 217, 1409, 2973, 3475, 3487; Oldman, Gary, 3343; Oliver, Edna May, 420; Oliver, Susan, 3229; Oliver, Thelma, 1608; Oliveri, Robert, 800; Olivier, Bernard, 1222; Olivier, Laurence, 84, 192, 764, 765, 975, 1225, 1226, 1691, 1811, 1853, 1854, 2235, 2494, 3160, 3161, 3162, 3163, 3525, 3601; O'Loughlan, Gerald S., 2853; Olsen, Chris, 2451; Olsen, Moroni, 1048, 3609; Olson, Nancy, 3, 2374, 2402, 2834; O'Neal, Ryan, 1155, 1583, 2998; O'Neal, Tatum, 1583; Oreste, 2852; Ormond, Julia, 1005; O'Rourke, Heather, 1673; O'Shea, Michael, 2582; O'Shea, Milo, 1573; Osment, Haley Joel, 2150, 2151; O'Sullivan, Maureen, 2204, 2454, 2455, 2457, 3521; Oswalt, Patton, 3396; O'Toole, Peter, 1066, 1100, 1134, 1380, 1397, 1443, 3583; Otto, Miranda, 259; Oury, Gerard, 3634; Ouspenskaya, Maria, 3121; Overman, Jack, 161; Overmann, Lynn, 2833; Owen, Seena, 1750; Owens, Patricia, 529, 1985;

Pace, Lee, 3699; Pacino, Al, 397, 648, 651, 901, 2003, 2014, 2053, 3407; Page, Gale, 2520; Page, Genevieve, 1718; Page, Geraldine, 2717, 2746; Paget, Debra, 2307; Paiva, Nestor, 1578; Palance, Jack, 248; Palin, Michael, 2628; Pallette, Eugene, 2695; Palmer, Betsy, 2758; Palmer, Lilli, 1461; Palmer, Peter, 1102; Palminteri, Chaz, 158; Paltrow, Gwyneth, 1617, 1727, 2081, 3673; Panchito Pistoles (animated character), 2584; Pangborn, Franklin, 76; Papas, Irene, 2745, 3233, 3550; Paquin, Anna, 2920; Paredes, Marisa, 2597; Parker, Eleanor, 2, 208, 362, 1696, 2875, 2900; Parker, Fess, 332; Parker, Jean, 1111, 3054; Parker, Sarah Jessica, 2311; Parks, Larry, 950, 3616; Parks, Taylor, 728; Parrish, Leslie, 1102; Parsons, Estelle, 2949; Parsons, Louella, 794; Parton, Dolly, 1453; Pastorelli, Robert, 1279; Pate, Michael, 2189; Patel, Dev, 2159, 3260, 3264; Patric, Jason, 619; Patrick (animated character), 2257; Patrick, Lee, 1189; Patrick, Nigel, 149; Patterson, Jay, 756; Pattinson, Robert, 2943; Patton, Will, 1465; Pavan, Marisa, 1198; Pawley, Edward, 644; Paxton, Bill, 2673; Payne, John, 687, 967, 1040, 1300, 1301, 1455, 1803, 2659, 2968; Payton, Barbara, 421, 1542; Pearce, Guy, 2632, 3345; Pearson, Beatrice, 546; Peck, Gregory, 108, 185, 331, 423, 615, 701, 720, 723, 974, 1166, 1198, 1215, 1317, 1318, 1446, 1517, 1542, 1680, 1902, 2169, 2170, 2171, 2172, 2239, 2240, 2241, 2656, 2657, 2769, 2770, 2771, 2857, 3148, 3185, 3186, 3187, 3466, 3574, 3600; Pegg, Simon, 3435; Pena, Elizabeth, 2705; Pendergast, Oaklee, 3329, 3330; Penn, Sean, 267, 342, 1290, 2450, 3309; Pennick, Jack, 2527, 3221; Penry-Jones, Rupert, 1252; Peppard, George, 191, 2662, 2878, 2879; Percy, Esme, 1367; Perez, Vincent, 1519; Perkins, Anthony, 122, 582, 1731, 1732, 2638; Perkins, Elizabeth, 62; Perkins, Osgood, 1992, 1993; Perlman, Ron, 1752; Perreau, Gigi, 647; Perry, Vic, 1634; Persoff, Nehemiah, 21, 740, 1270; Pesci, Joe, 796, 1389, 1390, 1738; Peter, 1789; Peter Pan (animated character), 1622; Peters, Brock, 2657; Peters, Jean, 49, 922, 1433, 1634, 2586, 2895, 3551; Pettersson, Birgitta, 2886; Pfeiffer, Michele, 83, 3034, 3103, 3120; Phelps, Lee, 1736; Phelps, Peter, 1095; Philbin, Mary, 1627; Phillips, Lou Diamond, 1018, 3211; Phoenix, Joaquin, 3358, 3359, 3360, 3361; Phoenix, River, 1931, 2283; Piccoli, Michel, 1594; Pickford, Mary, 1107, 1675, 1774, 1812, 2231, 2322, 2484; Pidgeon, Walter, 272, 326, 544, 1293, 1359, 2903, 2967, 3020, 3659; Pierce, Brock, 508; Pinal, Silvia, 2890; Pinkett, Jada, 1490; Pinocchio (animated character in 1940 production; Dickie Jones voiceover), 1643, 1644, 1645; Pinocchio (animated character in 1996 production; Jonathan Taylor Thomas voiceover), 3488, 3510; Pinter, Harold, 1224; Pinto, Freida, 2159; Pirate Captain (animated character), 3383; Pitt, Brad, 1877, 2068, 2768, 3279, 3308; Pitt, Ingrid, 3007; Pitts, Zasu, 708, 2963; Platt, Louise, 2269, 2270, 2271, 2275; Platt, Oliver, 877, 2601; Pleakley (animated character), 1098; Pleasence, Donald,

3074; Plowright, Joan, 454, 1361, 3055; Plummer, Christopher, 2192, 2222, 2747, 3083, 3517; Po (animated character), 1014; Po, Salvatore, 651; Pocahontas (animated character), 1669; Poitier, Sidney, 351, 716, 884, 1097, 1464, 1678, 1679, 2511; Polk, Oscar, 711; Pollack, Sydney, 2685; Pollard, Michael J., 137; Polo, Teri, 56; Pomeranc, Max, 2024; Portman, Eric, 2958; Portman, Natalie, 2302; Posey, Parker, 1620, 2407; Post, William, Jr., 824; Postlethwaite, Pete, 2848; Powell, Addison, 2590; Powell, Dick, 948, 1373, 1374, 1375, 1521, 2446, 2491, 2658; Powell, Eleanor, 1913; Powell, Jane, 330, 1924, 2588; Powell, William, 89, 322, 461, 704, 712, 854, 1085, 1091, 1221, 1354, 1402, 1540, 1815, 1838, 2041, 2077, 2433, 2545, 2546, 3000, 3507, 3702; Power, Tyrone (Jr.), 1, 124, 125, 130, 172, 184, 438, 866, 881, 882, 939, 994, 1115, 1158, 1228, 1229, 1232, 1233, 1234, 1312, 1451, 1674, 1701, 1802, 1804, 1916, 2196, 2380, 3110, 3111, 3112, 3113, 3172, 3173, 3552, 3579; Powers, Mala, 3477; Pratt, Oliver, 3511; Pratt, Purnell, 517; Prejean, Albert, 2603; Prelle [Presle], Micheline, 2809; Preminger, Otto, 1639, 2280; Presson, Jason, 2331; Preston, Robert, 965, 1168, 1381, 1475, 2911, 2912, 3014; Prevost, Marie, 1767; Price, Connor, 238; Price, Dennis, 674; Price, Vincent, 80, 209, 529, 822, 823, 1062, 1649, 2498, 2711; Probst, Christoph, 3035; Professor Ratigan (animated character), 698; Provost, Jon, 2173; Prud'Homme, Cameron, 1783; Pryor, Richard, 2327, 2328, 2408; Puglia, Frank, 24; Purcell, Noel, 1873; Purdom, Edmund, 2371; Puss and Boots (animated character), 2122; Pyle, Ernie, 2339; Pyrkosz, Witold, 2850;

Quaid, Dennis, 412, 879, 2411, 3166; Quasimodo (animated character in 1996 production of The Hunchback of Notre Dame; Tom Hulce voiceover), 3512; Quasimodo (animated character in 2012 production of Hotel Transylvania; John Lovitz voiceover), 3323; Quayle, Anthony, 2458; Quigley, Rita, 837; Quill, Tim, 732; Quinlan, Kathleen, 148, 2779; Quinn, Aidan, 62, 3514; Quinn, Anthony, 723, 1021, 1022, 1057, 1067, 1840, 1855, 2110, 2896, 2897, 2939, 3239, 3240, 3542, 3571, 3650, 3672;

Radcliffe, Daniel, 744, 3322; Radford, Basil, 188, 1036; Radha Shri Ram, 1875; Radziwilowicz, Jerzy, 1202; Raft, George, 428, 638, 817, 860, 1223, 1466, 1995, 2217, 2218, 2519, 3017, 3191; Rahim, Tahar, 3306; Rai, Aishwarya, 1050; Rain (animated horse), 2251; Rainer, Luise, 670, 704; Raines, Ella, 3625; Rains, Claude, 194, 911, 1358, 1483, 1485, 1628, 2534, 2535, 3005; Raisch, Bill, 1121; Raitt, John, 1576; Ralston, Marcia, 1429; Ralston, Vera, 499; Ramis, Harold, 2369; Rampling, Charlotte, 2305; Randall, Stuart, 2333; Randall, Tony, 3075; Rassam, Julien, 4; Rathbone, Basil, 182, 416, 813, 815, 818, 1046, 1148, 1232, 1743, 2102, 2103, 2104, 2194, 2245, 2483, 2711, 3126, 3497; Ratoff, Gregory, 26; Ray, Aldo, 1449, 2972; Raye, Martha, 1324; Rea, Stephen, 312, 455; Reagan, Ronald, 359, 747, 998, 1053, 1710, 2333, 2900, 3099; Reardon, Mildred, 1186; Redford, Robert, 160, 168, 693, 811, 1877, 2323, 2325, 2589, 2590, 2954, 2955, 3656, 3682, 3700; Redgrave, Michael, 84, 876, 1034, 1035, 1454, 3637; Redgrave, Vanessa, 1328; Redmayne, Eddie, 3347, 3415; Redwing, 2263; Reed, Alyson, 230; Reed, Barbara, 2604; Reed, Donna, 927, 1637, 2529, 2749, 3668; Reed, George, 2416; Reed, Oliver, 314, 566, 1514, 3523; Reed, Philip, 3476; Reeve, Christopher, 2408, 3520; Reeves, Keanu, 2238; Reid, Carl Benton, 2629; Reiner, Carl, 1932; Reinhold, Judge, 106; Reiser, Paul, 377; Remick, Lee, 339, 1125, 1517; Renaldo, Duncan, 2719; Renard, Ken, 2189; Renner, Jeremy, 3267, 3268; Rennie, James, 2440; Rennie, Michael, 337, 1079, 3653, 3672; Renoir, Jean, 2230; Revere, Anne, 2203; Rey, Fernando, 2890; Reymond, Dominque, 2387; Reynolds, Burt, 2424; Reynolds, Corey, 2480; Reynolds, Craig, 1410; Reynolds, Debbie, 1262, 2142, 2837; Reynolds, Gene, 440; Reynolds, Marjorie, 783, 791, 792, 2633, 2844; Rhys Myers, Jonathan, 1252; Ribisi, Giovanni, 1982; Rice, Joan, 784; Richards, Dakota Blue, 659; Richards, Michael, 2743; Richards, Sandra Lee, 3603; Richardson, Miranda, 454; Richardson, Ralph, 149; Rickles, Don, 970; Ridgely, John, 20, 2908; Rigg, Diana, 2498; Riva, Emmanuelle, 3250; Rivera, Chita, 2417; Rizzo the Rat (Muppet character), 1366; Robards, Jason, Jr., 73, 816, 1266, 1447, 2476, 2580, 2697; Robeson, Paul, 2117; Robbins, Tim, 1310, 1664, 2091, 2936; Roberts, Allene, 1822; Roberts, Eric, 1771, 1930; Roberts, Julia, 1690, 2319; Roberts, Rachel, 1816, 1978; Roberts, Theodore, 3533; Roberts, Tony, 47; Robertson, Cliff, 218, 369, 630, 1285, 1733, 2680, 2681; Robin, Dany, 2690; Robinson, Bill "Bojangles," 1106, 1113, 2334, 2335; Robinson, Charles, 1968; Robinson, Edward G., 34, 235, 236, 402, 404, 516, 517, 521, 748, 750, 821, 873, 973, 1048, 1104, 1105, 1223, 1439, 1559, 1822, 2002, 2015, 2016, 2017, 2018, 2065, 2131, 2157, 2160, 2350, 2440, 2618, 3047, 3048, 3127, 3560; Robinson, Julia Anne, 993; Robson, Flora, 3161; Robson, May, 1025; Roby the Robot, 910; Rockwell, Sam, 275; Roger Rabbit (animated character; Charles Fleischer voiceover), 3043; Rogers, Charles "Buddy," 3092, 3093; Rogers, Ginger, 413, 530, 558, 865, 1006, 1029, 1506, 1890, 1921, 2082, 2265, 2332, 2420, 2421, 2688, 2899, 2967; Rogers, Jean, 2928; Rogers, John, 1770; Rogers, Roy, 1403; Rogers, Will Jr., 2343, 3664; Rogers, Will, Sr., 293; Roland, Gilbert, 220, 1057; Rolfe, Erik, 3570; Rollins, Howard, E. Jr., 2179; Roman, Ruth, 406, 2306, 2355, 2356, 3087; Romano, Ray, 2970; Romashin, Anatoly, 1796; Romero, Cesar, 367, 2120, 2966, 3606; Rooney, Mickey, 66, 837, 925, 1088, 1422, 1754, 3146; Roper, Brian, 2029; Rorke, Hayden, 3608; Rosenbloom, Maxie, 34; Ross, Diana, 1033; Ross, Katharine, 2465, 3656; Ross, Thomas W., 1952; Ross, Tyler, 3431, 3432; Roundtree, Richard, 2079; Rourke, Mickey, 78, 377, 1927, 3154, 3180; Roussel, Nathalie, 1395; Rowlands, Gena, 1480, 3137; Roy, Billy, 1593; Rub, Christian, 1108; Rudd, Paul, 3424, 3426, 3427; Ruehl, Mercedes, 1140; Ruffalo, Mark, 3192; Ruggles, Charles, 1462, 1925, 2573; Rule, Janice, 2306; Ruman, Sig, 1437, 2648; Rush, Barbara, 1458; Rush, Gabriel, 3365; Rush, Geoffrey, 999; Russell (animated character), 2842; Russell, Gail, 1555, 2829; Russell, Harold, 104; Russell, Jane, 616, 617, 1165, 1579, 2444; Russell, John, 2393; Russell, Johnnie, 1196; Russell, Keri, 800; Russell, Kurt, 148, 2671, 2672, 2673; Russell, Rosalind, 240, 298, 523, 782, 1404, 1462, 1838, 2145, 2524, 2525, 2814, 2866, 3141, 3142; Russo, Rene, 2576; Ruth, George Herman "Babe," 1697; Rutherford, Gene, 3074; Rutherford, Margaret, 1368, 1372, 1377, 3504; Ryan, Blanchard, 1545; Ryan, Edward, 2382; Ryan, Meg, 294, 2999, 3232; Ryan, Robert, 71, 305, 531, 652, 1500, 1728, 2055, 2722, 3135, 3136; Ryan, Sheila, 621; Ryder, Winona, 1273, 3496;

Saavedra, Catalina, 1181; Sabu, 418, 2542; Sadler, Dudley, 139; Saint, Eva Marie, 1470, 1471, 1472, 1525, 1526, 2567; St. Clair, Lydia, 824; St. John, Jill, 2677; Sakall, S.Z. "Cuddles," 883, 2490, 3175; Salenger, Meredith, 952; Salt, Jennifer, 1848;
Samuel, Xavier, 3287; Sanchez, Jaime, 3063; Sand, Paul, 811; Sandburg, Clinton, 883; Sandars, Clare, 1359; Sande, Walter, 721; Sanders, George, 822, 851, 1115, 1161, 1329, 1952, 2803, 3472, 3518, 3563, 3576, 3590, 3660; Sands, Julian, 1908; Sarandon, Susan, 342, 3103, 3389; Sarrazin, Michael, 2526; Savage, Ann, 363; Savage, John, 350; Savalas, Telly, 3483; Sawyer, Joseph, 785, 981, 1966, 2050; Sayles, John, 444; Scacchi, Greta, 1197, 3033; Scheider, Roy, 935, 2066; Schell, Maria, 734; Schell, Maximilian, 959, 2692, 3214; Schiff, Richard, 1145; Schnabel, Stefan, 379; Schneider, Romy, 2742, 2747; Schoeffling, Michael, 1273, 3067; Schoenaerts, Matthias, 3392, 3393; Scholl, Hans, 3035; Scholl, Sophie, 3035; Schreck, Max, 1478; Schwartzman, Jason, 3369; Schwarzenegger, Arnold, 2757, 3294; Schygulla, Hanna, 1238, 1594; Sciorra, Annabella, 2988; Scofield, Paul, 307, 1192, 1193; Scott, Campbell, 1949; Scott, George C., 525, 810, 1509, 1606, 1607, 3696; Scott, Janette, 2006; Scott, Lizabeth, 325, 343, 1823, 2679; Scott, Martha, 770, 833, 1985, 3612; Scott, Randolph, 136, 190, 226, 287, 289, 401, 500, 591, 1845, 1856, 1858, 2092, 2255, 2659, 2888, 2979, 2980, 3470, 3476; Scott, Zachary, 2224, 2229; Seales, Franklyn, 2227; Sebastian, Dorothy, 2825; Segal, George, 1950, 2706; Sellars, Elizabeth, 77, 497; Selleck, Tom, 1758; Sellers, Peter, 96, 394, 1369, 1641, 3151; Sellon, Charles, 923; Selton, Morton, 2542; Serbedzija, Rade, 969; Serre, Henri, 961; Servillo, Toni, 872; Sessions, Almira, 1299; Sessue

Hayakawa, 2585; Seton, Bruce, 2620; Setsuko Hara, 2664; Severn, Christopher, 1359; Sevigny, Chloe, 1045; Seyfried, Amanda, 3347; Seymour, Anne, 29; Seymour, Dan, 973; Seymour, Jane, 2192; Shah, Naseeruddin, 1325; Shannon, Harry, 244; Sharma, Suraj, 3348; Shaw, Robert, 781, 1193, 2325, 2435; Shearer, Moira, 1829; Shearer, Norma, 386, 576, 1228, 1229, 1719, 2163, 2347, 2372, 3141; Sheen, Charlie, 56, 2601, 2924; Sheen, Martin, 51, 622; Sheffer, Craig, 1877; Shelton, John, 2633; Shepard, Sam, 1864, 2615; Shepherd, Cybill, 1046; Shepherd, Sally, 3126; Sheridan, Ann, 439, 864, 998, 1207, 1208, 2519; Sheridan, Tye, 2741; Sherman, Lowell, 2993; Shields, Arthur, 1615; Shields, Brooke, 1689; Shira (animated saber-toothed lion), 3327; Shirley, Anne, 1374; Shrek (animated character), 2122; Shue, Elisabeth, 1072; Shutta, Ethel, 3050; Sidney, Sylvia, 249, 1934, 2361, 2908, 3191; Signoret, Simone, 17, 2108; Silvera, Frank, 2854; Silverheels, Jay, 1120; Silvers, Phil, 296, 2579; Sim, Alastair, 2268; Simmons, Jean, 449, 2232, 3205; Simms, Ginny, 785, 1435, 3657; Simon, Michel, 2724; Simpson, Russell, 684; Sims, Sylvia, 2876; Sinatra, Frank, 41, 585, 725, 778, 789, 949, 997, 1216, 1218, 1260, 1430, 1479, 1497, 1523, 1577, 1693, 1694, 1892, 2182, 2377, 2378, 2478, 2623, 2677, 2901, 3204, 3676; Sinbad, 508; Sinbad (animated character; Brad Pitt voiceover), 3519; Singer Midgets (Munchkins), 3114; Sinise, Gary, 1310; Sisto, Jeremy, 3388; Sita (animated character), 2146; Sizemore, Tom, 1981, 1982; Sjostrom, Victor, 3072; Skelton, Red, 260, 466, 1276, 2228; Skerritt, Tom, 1244, 2319, 2464; Skinner, Cornelia Otis, 2828; Skipworth, Alison, 2626; Skye, Tone, 1984; Slate, Henry, 568; Slate, Jeremy, 2755; Slater, Christian, 3212; Slater, Helen, 2034; Slinky Dog (animated character), 2714; Sloane, Everett, 241, 1028, 2188; Smart, Jean, 3321; Smestad, Stian, 2109; Smith, Alexis, 282, 1960, 3129; Smith, C. Aubrey, 844, 1114; Smith, Howard, 346; Smith, John, 239; Smith, Kent, 1985, 3658; Smith, Maggie, 1055, 1369, 2728, 3206, 3263; Smith, Will, 1073, 1269, 3362; Snipes, Wesley, 2795; Snow White (animated character), 2167, 2168; Sok, Chanty, 3412; Sokoloff, Vladimir, 2658; Sondergaard, Gale, 2245; Song, Brenda, 2178; Sorel, Jean, 2880; Sorensen, Linda, 951; Sorvino, Paul, 156; Sothern, Ann, 1083; Spacek, Sissy, 1308, 1771, 2345; Spacey, Kevin, 35, 2407; Sparks, Jordin, 3405; Sparky (animated character), 3305; Spence, Bruce, 1885; Spiner, Brent, 2298; Spinetti, Victor, 2310; Spirit (animated horse), 2251; SpongeBob (animated character), 2257; Stack, Robert, 330, 431, 772, 1307, 2451, 2646; Stafford, Frederick, 2690; Stahl, Nick, 2445; Stallone, Sylvester, 338, 1898, 1899, 3294; Stander, Lionel, 1048, 1265, 1348; Stanwyck, Barbara, 119, 402, 403, 502, 658, 1025, 1261, 1302, 1442, 1666, 1837, 2214, 2215, 2216, 2321, 2348, 2510, 2571, 2640, 2642, 2748, 2788, 3557, 3648; Starr, Ringo, 738; Starr, Ron, 1857, 1858; Steele, Barbara, 1649; Steele, Karen, 1856; Stegers, Bernice, 247; Steiger, Rod, 21, 740, 884, 1608, 1929, 2945; Stein, Sammy, 614; Sten, Anna, 2959; Stennett, Frank, 3431; Stepanek, Karel, 2143; Stephens, Harvey, 1517, 3194; Stephens, Robert, 1718; Stephenson, Henry, 3589; Sterling, Jan, 740, 1454; Stern, Daniel, 377, 796; Stevens, Charles, 463, 1893; Stevens, Craig, 3009; Stevens, George, 629, 706, 2899; Stevens, Mark, 322, 1507, 2363; Stevens, Stella, 73; Stewart, Donald Ogden, 2392; Stewart, James, 157, 175, 270, 482, 492, 524, 538, 642, 745, 828, 926, 927, 931, 1173, 1185, 1194, 1210, 1213, 1355, 1356, 1357, 1358, 1417, 1459, 1462, 1502, 1631, 1794, 1808, 1809, 1911, 2099, 2112, 2113, 2114, 2249, 2250, 2357, 2358, 2872, 2873, 2899, 3079, 3080, 3081, 3196, 3197, 3198, 3568, 3613, 3628, 3698; Stewart, Kristen, 3402; Stewart, Patrick, 2297; Stewart, Paul, 750, 2770, 3087, 3088; Stockwell, Dean, 205, 407, 2208; Stone, George E., 558, 589; Stone, Harold J., 2234, 3159; Stone, Lewis, 225, 1748, 2730, 3130; Stone, Milburn, 289; Stone, Sharon, 197; Stowe, Madeleine, 1052; Strasberg, Susan, 1636; Strathairn, David, 2246, 2830; Strauss, Robert, 2278, 2279; Streep, Meryl, 153, 310, 1560, 2130, 2211, 2212, 2213, 3321, 3549; Streisand, Barbra, 596, 761, 1703, 2954, 2955, 2998; Strode, Woody, 2046; Stroheim, Erich von, 59, 128, 514, 537, 1142, 2403, 2963, 2964; Stromboli (animated character), 1644; Studi, Wes, 619; Stuhlberg, Michael, 3362; Sturges, Preston, 2385; Sturgess, Jim, 3276, 3278; Sullavan, Margaret, 2114, 2174; Sullivan, Barry, 206,

621, 1610; Sullivan, Francis L., 3100; Summerville, Slim, 2666; Sumpter, Tina, 3405; Sutherland, Donald, 1244, 1548, 2148; Sutherland, Kiefer, 2601; Swain, Mack, 656; Swanson, Gloria, 1750, 1940, 2399, 2400, 2401, 2403, 2404; Swann, Buddy, 244; Swank, Hilary, 577; Swayze, Patrick, 2445; Sy, Omar, 3332, 3333, 3331; Sydow, Max von, 706, 1759, 2071, 2083, 2609; Sylvester, William, 3182; Szabo, Istvan, 1272; Szigeti, Joseph, 793;

Tai (elephant), 2943; Takahiro Tamura, 2699; Talbot, Lyle, 534, 2777; Taliaferro, Hal, 475; Tamblyn, Russ, 1842, 2977; Tambor, Jeffrey, 389; Tamiroff, Akim, 611, 612, 2707, 3633; Tamlyn Tomita, 955; Tandy, Jessica, 417, 1467; Tati, Jacques, 1407; Tatsuya Nakadai, 1789; Taylor, Don, 1415, 2281; Taylor, Elizabeth, 201, 254, 280, 330, 447, 1056, 1112, 1422, 1651, 1652, 1653, 1786, 1849, 2448, 2849, 3045, 3540; Taylor, Estelle, 3533; Taylor, James, 2787; Taylor, Libby, 868; Taylor, Robert, 2, 81, 178, 280, 316, 370, 779, 930, 947, 1178, 1591, 1762, 1763, 2571, 2587, 2816, 2947, 2948, 2984, 2985, 3171, 3685; Taylor, Rod, 2630, 2631, 3206; Tearle, Godfrey, 2645; Temple, Shirley, 67, 1106, 1109, 1113, 1676, 2136, 2344, 2966, 3223; Terkel, Studs, 444; Terry, Alice, 564; Terry, Nigel, 2426; Terry-Thomas, 2006; Thao, Elvis, 680; Theron, Charlize, 1878, 3401; Thewlis, David, 2068; Thomas, Danny, 867, 3618; Thomas, Jameson, 217; Thomas, Kristin Scott, 459; Thomas, Richard, 3201; Thompson, Emma, 1623, 1698, 1835, 2042, 3101; Thompson, Lea, 70; Thompson, Marshall, 2447; Thornton, Billy Bob, 2158; Thorwarth, Otto, 2038; Thulin, Ingrid, 320; Thurman, Uma, 608, 1169, 3523; Thuy An Luu, 384; Tierney, Gene, 623, 1062, 1071, 1522, 1668, 2090, 2661, 3009, 3012, 3013, 3554, 3611; Tierney, Lawrence, 3577; Tierney, Maura, 2970; Tilly, Meg, 2487; Timberlake, Justin, 3417; Tobias, George, 1593, 2050; Tobin, Genevieve, 1533; Todd, Ann, 1696; Todd, Ann, 149, 1174, 3677; Todd, Richard, 316, 747, 2267, 2268, 2885, 3663; Toland, Gregg, 242; Tomei, Marisa, 1389, 3154; Tomlin, Lily, 1453; Tomlinson, Ricky, 1782; Tone, Franchot, 513, 514, 1114, 1205, 2587; Toomey, Regis, 385; Toothless (animated dragon), 832; Torres, Raquel, 3036; Torvay, Jose, 140; Toshiaki (animated character; James Hiroyuki Liao voiceover), 3304; Toshiro Mifune, 1795, 2608, 3190; Totter, Audrey, 1030, 1031, 2055, 2811; Towers, Constance, 808, 2046; Townsend, Colleen, 3004; Tracy, Spencer, 9, 71, 145, 186, 198, 323, 357, 365, 392, 440, 441, 490, 491, 598, 716, 724, 897, 958, 1048, 1085, 1185, 1230, 1371, 1476, 1477, 1513, 1597, 1615, 1668, 1753, 1863, 1962, 1964, 2069, 2285, 2286, 2313, 2314, 2485, 2486, 2562, 2704, 2777, 2846, 3011, 3106, 3132, 3133, 3134, 3617; Tramp (animated character), 1024; Travers, Bill, 2965; Travers, Henry, 440, 2073, 2286; Travers, Linden, 1036; Travis, Daniel, 1545; Travis, Richard, 1208; Travolta, John, 250, 1279, 1698, 1979, 2847; Treen, Mary, 926; Trevor, Claire, 31, 34, 972, 1375, 2269, 2270, 2273, 2274, 2276, 2488, 3131, 3659; Trikonis, Gus, 2837; Trintignant, Jean-Louis, 3250; Tsai Chin, 955; Tucci, Stanley, 877, 944, 2480; Tulku Jamyang Kunga Tenzin, 1013; Turner, Kathleen, 135, 940, 1723, 1905, 2424, 2933; Turner, Lana, 198, 947, 1060, 1172, 1626, 1684, 1685, 1785, 2191, 2600; Tunie, Tamara, 3300; Turturro, John, 1491, 1492; Tweedledee (animated character; Matt Lucas voiceover), 3522; Tweedledum (animated character; Matt Lucas voiceover), 3522; Twelvetrees, Helen, 2315; Twysden, Duff, 2392; Tyler, Liv, 1667; Tyson, Cathy, 1322; Tzipporah (animated character), 1700;

Udvarnoky, Martin, 1553; Uggie (dog), 3255; Ullmann, Liv, 1619, 2083; Ulrich, Skeet, 1860; Underwood, Edward, 1851; Ure, Mary, 3007; Ustinov, Peter, 1136, 2394, 2972, 3492;

Valentino, Rudolph, 564, 565, 2098, 2199; Valli, Alida, 2556, 2922; Vallone, Raf, 118, 2880; Van Cleef, Lee, 967; Van Dyke, Dick, 1243; Van Fleet, Jo, 3585; Van Houten, Carice, 2855; Van Pallandt, Nina, 1124; Vandervoort, Laura, 3413; Vanel, Charles, 2906; Vang, Bee, 680; Varconi, Victor, 786, 1655; Varden, Norma, 3110; Varela, Nina, 2897; Vartan, Michael, 505; Vaughn, Vince, 1145; Veidt, Conrad, 171, 1211, 1426, 1686, 2259, 2260, 3138; Velez, Lupe, 609, 3123; Velazquez, Nadine,

3300; Venable, Evelyn, 347; Vera-Ellen, 2596, 3022; Verdure, Armand, 3393; Verea, Lisette, 1440; Verne, Kaaren, 2102; Vernon, Howard, 2723; Vernon, John, 2689; Victor Frankenstein (animated character), 3305; Vidor, Florence, 1603; Viharo, Robert, 2882; Vikander, Alicia, 3295, 3391; Villemaire, James, 1254; Viruet, Michael, 3386; Vitale, Millie, 3588; Vitar, Mike, 1969; Vodianova, Natalia, 3503; Vogler, Karl Michael, 133; Voight, Jon, 271, 352, 1281, 1282, 1848, 1930; Voskovec, George, 3083; Vue, Sonny, 680;

Wade, Russell, 626; Wagenheim, Charles, 548; Wagner, Robert, 105, 1000, 1704, 2307, 2641; Wahlberg, Mark, 1618, 3354; Wakefield, Hugh, 1215; Walbrook, Anton, 2877; Walburn, Raymond, 1862, 2094; Walcott, George, 598; Waldis, Otto, 103; Walken, Christopher, 114, 202, 3407; Walker, Helen, 1159, 1370; Walker, Kathryn, 1852; Walker, Polly, 454; Walker, Robert, 2353, 2354, 2355, 2562, 2867; Wall, Robert, 460, 1405; Wallace, Baird, 2462; Wallace, Oscar, 2838; Wallach, Eli, 1099, 2786; Waller, Ariel, 238; Wallis, Quevenzhane, 3257, 3258, 3259; Walters, Jessica, 1663; Walters, Patricia, 1875; Walthall, Henry B., 117; Walton, Douglas, 1373; Warburton, Patrick, 2817; Ward, Simon, 3228; Ward, Sophie, 3225; Ward, Warwick, 2864; Warner, H.B., 991, 3614; Warrick, Ruth, 243, 288; Warwick, Robert, 1312; Washington, Denzel, 3298, 3301, 3632; Washington, Isaiah, 2754; Wasikowska, Mia, 3344; Waters, Ethel, 1642; Waterston, Sam, 982; Watson, Bobby, 786; Watson, Emily, 143; Watson, Emma, 3376, 3379; Watson, Lucile, 1173, 2941, 2942; Watson, Minor, 3662; Watts, Naomi, 1866, 3329, 3331; Wayne, David, 1939, 2478; Wayne, John, 31, 68, 239, 399, 446, 499, 531, 532, 533, 554, 709, 772, 799, 806, 808, 829, 852, 1128, 1129, 1131, 1474, 1650, 1755, 1756, 1757, 1807, 1825, 1826, 1827, 1828, 1867, 1868, 1869, 1870, 1909, 1970, 2020, 2021, 2022, 2023, 2095, 2100, 2111, 2113, 2209, 2210, 2255, 2256, 2269, 2272, 2273, 2275, 2276, 2443, 2528, 2532, 2591, 2592, 2593, 2594, 2749, 2755, 2794, 2806, 2938, 3095, 3107, 3108, 3592, 3674; Wayne, Naunton, 1036; Weaver, Marjorie, 2583; Weaver, Sigourney, 25, 470, 678, 3147, 3179; Weaving, Hugo, 3276; Webb, Clifton, 219, 413, 1062, 1063, 1212, 1346, 2147, 2308, 2640, 2642, 3140, 3679; Webb, Jack, 2561; Weber, Karl, 2917; Weil, Joseph "Yellow Kid," 2326; Weissmuller, Johnny, 2453, 2454, 2455, 2457, 3521; Weisz, Rachel, 3267, 3268; Welch, Joseph, 3696; Welch, Tahnee, 262; Weld, Tuesday, 2537, 3049; Weldon, Ben, 978; Weldon, Joan, 2499, 2500; Weller, Peter, 1896; Welles, Orson, 123, 124, 203, 241, 242, 243, 953, 1027, 1167, 1345, 1552, 1701, 2350, 2351, 2553, 2554, 2555, 2674, 2707, 2708, 2742, 3495, 3501, 3552; Wendy (animated character), 1622; Werner, Oskar, 348, 473, 961, 1118, 2108, 2261, 3642; Wesson, Dick, 2306; West, Dominic, 3338; West, Mae, 868, 1401, 2093; Westcott, Helen, 720; Whalen, Michael, 1676; Whaley, Frank, 580; Wheaton, Will, 2283; Wheeler, Bert, 729; Whishaw, Ben, 3277; Whitaker, Forest, 312; White, Alice, 1638; Whitman, Mae, 3377, 3378; Whitmore, James, 60, 2500, 2698, 2815; Whitney, Helene, 1952; Whitney, Peter, 1370; Whitney, Susan, 3670; Whittaker, Johnnie, 2670; Whitty, Dame May, 521, 1035; Whorf, Richard, 231; Widmark, Richard, 407, 584, 605, 959, 1058, 1581, 1879, 1928, 2364, 2629, 2764, 3003; Wilcoxon, Henry, 253, 309, 1051, 1959; Wilde, Cornel, 207, 705, 1071, 1416, 2206, 2207, 2579, 2732, 2783, 2926, 3140, 3564; Wilder, Gene, 1725, 2310, 2327, 2328, 3208, 3210; Wildman, John, 1386; Wilding, Michael, 2700; Wilhelmi, Erin, 3377, 3378; Wilkinson, Tom, 2426, 3261; William, Warren, 1251, 1343, 1977; Williams, Billy Dee, 1033, 2303; Williams, Charles, 926; Williams, Emlyn, 240; Williams, Esther, 435, 1293, 3620; Williams, Guinn "Big Boy," 395, 2258, 3199; Williams, Rhys, 488; Williams, Robert, 1659; Williams, Robin, 672, 675, 802, 1338, 2988; Williams, Treat, 1702; Williamson, Nicol, 1816, 2061, 2062; Willis, Bruce, 376, 2151, 2768, 2800, 3366; Wilson, Dennis, 2787; Wilson, Elizabeth, 1605; Wilson, Lambert, 1055, 1839; Wilson, Rebel, 3387; Wilson, Teddy, 642; Wilton, Penelope, 3265; Winchell, Walter, 2915; Windsor, Marie, 1103, 1419, 1420, 2121; Winger, Debra, 1504, 2482, 2847; Winninger, Charles, 2604; Winslet, Kate, 503, 1805, 2042, 2643, 2644, 3284; Winstone, Ray, 891; Winters,

PHOTOS: STUDIO INDEX

Note: The following photo credits are shown by production companies, studios and the Jay Robert Nash archives, with page numbers.

ABC Entertainment, 767; ABC Pictures, 2680, 2681; Adriana/Island, 327; Adventure Pictures, 3178; Allied Artists (AA), 21, 97, 497, 582, 909, 1074, 1149, 1573, 1608, 1609, 2547, 3052, 3182, 3515; Almi Pictures, 1505; American International Pictures (AIP), 1248, 3539; American Tobis Company, 1292; Amkino, 85; Analysis Film Releasing Corporation, 1272; Arrival Pictures, 969; Artcraft Pictures Corporation, 1765, 1812, 2322; Artists International, 1068; Astor Pictures, 1020, 2742, 2876; AVCO Embassy Pictures, 304, 1100, 2628, 2706;

BBC Films, 259; British International Pictures, 1367, 1488, 1851; British Screen Productions, 3055;

Cannon Group, 1930; Castle Films, 905; Castle Rock, 410; Cinecom Pictures, 1095, 1197, 1253, 1908; Cinedigm, 3371; Cinema 5 Distributing, 3233; Cinema Guild, 633, 691, 3419, 3420; Cinema Releasing Corporation, 2434, 2526; Cinerama Releasing Corporation, 218, 965, 1157; Cineplex-Odeon, 641; Circle Films, 1425; Claremont Films, 1361; Columbia, 1, 8, 12, 29, 55, 64, 109, 119, 141, 152, 173, 230, 248, 257, 273, 287, 296, 297, 298, 300, 343, 346, 365, 394, 401, 434, 438, 445, 455, 495, 511, 512, 538, 555, 557, 570, 583, 585, 586, 587, 595, 596, 603, 608, 619, 627, 628, 630, 631, 636, 658, 714, 716, 723, 733, 739, 740, 768, 769, 781, 782, 790, 833, 878, 885, 920, 921, 932, 934, 937, 948, 950, 960, 968, 993, 1009, 1012, 1018, 1026, 1027, 1028, 1032, 1047, 1049, 1054, 1066, 1067, 1070, 1099, 1134, 1137, 1138, 1140, 1183, 1191, 1192, 1193, 1194, 1206, 1214, 1265, 1269, 1280, 1302, 1306, 1333, 1338, 1348, 1349, 1355, 1356, 1357, 1358, 1369, 1379, 1404, 1443, 1449, 1454, 1509, 1514, 1515, 1524, 1525, 1526, 1541, 1543, 1556, 1569, 1577, 1587, 1592, 1604, 1613, 1614, 1625, 1635, 1636, 1659, 1703, 1708, 1726, 1816, 1835, 1840, 1856, 1877, 1891, 1943, 1944, 1945, 1954, 1955, 2042, 2084, 2091, 2094, 2107, 2108, 2133, 2134, 2178, 2179, 2180, 2206, 2207, 2243, 2244, 2283, 2327, 2328, 2352, 2369, 2370, 2431, 2441, 2442, 2448, 2464, 2474, 2475, 2488, 2501, 2551, 2579, 2605, 2658, 2663, 2676, 2682, 2684, 2685, 2758, 2772, 2774, 2815, 2853, 2878, 2879, 2883, 2891, 2916, 2917, 2921, 2944, 2949, 2954, 2955, 2961, 3033, 3046, 3047, 3048, 3053, 3069, 3070, 3120, 3157, 3189, 3196, 3197, 3200, 3228, 3234, 3248, 3285, 3293, 3321, 3323, 3362, 3381, 3382, 3383, 3384, 3399, 3400, 3436, 3465, 3467, 3469, 3471, 3496, 3523, 3542, 3564, 3579, 3612, 3616, 3627, 3683, 3696; Compass International Pictures, 731; Continental Distributing Company, 1407, 1978, 2006, 2574, 2617, 2880;

Daiei Studios, 2796; DCA, 2906; Destination Films, 2045; Dimension Films, 1878, 2009, 3322; DisCina International, 1550; Disney/Buena Vista, 3, 42, 92, 122, 263, 332, 375, 437, 508, 672, 698, 800, 933, 952, 955, 1013, 1024, 1098, 1101, 1243, 1310, 1366, 1535, 1669, 1973, 2037, 2038, 2109, 2167, 2168, 2345, 2422, 2425, 2445, 2487, 2578, 2714, 2715, 2716, 2775, 2776, 2817, 2841, 2842, 3025, 3067, 3085, 3269, 3270, 3271, 3272, 3302, 3303, 3304, 3305, 3337, 3338, 3339, 3482, 3499, 3511, 3512, 3516, 3522, 3602, 3634; DNA Films, 3295; DreamWorks, 35, 39, 202, 637, 832, 1073, 1252, 1700, 1866, 1882, 1981, 1982, 1983, 2122, 2251, 2480, 2830, 2831, 2936, 2937, 3349, 3350, 3351, 3352, 3353, 3519, 3534, 3699;

Eagle-Lion, 660, 674, 751, 771, 858, 983, 1304, 1801, 1829, 2428, 2429, 3100, 3561, 3601, 3640, 3662; Ealing, 17, 188, 426, 613, 1064, 1596, 2007, 2620, 2645; Elephant Eye Films, 1181; Elstree/British International, 127, 2054; Embassy, 443, 450, 480, 679, 804, 1123, 1528, 1725, 2792, 3188, 3241, 3242, 3517, 3583; EMI Films, 2477; Empire Pictures, 1019, 1519; Enterprise/Shooting Gallery, 10; Entertainment Networks,

1412; Epoch, 117; Excelsa Films, 1544;

Faces International, 3137; Film Arts Guild, 1478; Film District, 3373; Film Movement, 3306; Films Around the World, 150; Fine Line Features, 505, 1530, 1664, 2311, 3101; First National, 212, 976, 1126, 1699, 2116, 2131, 2456, 2665; Focus Features, 1290, 1325, 1633, 1692, 2639, 3280, 3326, 3365, 3366, 3367, 3368, 3369, 3370, 3396, 3397, 3415, 3435; Fox Searchlight, 1527, 2741, 3078, 3154, 3257, 3258, 3259, 3260, 3261, 3262, 3263, 3264, 3265, 3314, 3394; Fries Entertainment, 2124;

Gamma Film, 3642; Gaumont, 247, 1034, 1035, 1036, 1209, 1686, 1934, 2026, 2027, 2564, 2565, 2566, 3203; GFD, 2958; GK Films, 3226, 3227; Goldwyn Distributing Company, 171, 189; Gramercy, 448, 486, 1045, 1489; Grange, 2851; Grazing Goat Pictures, 3374;

Hemdale, 3016; Hollywood Pictures, 1240, 1350, 2150, 2151, 2671, 2672, 2673, 3038; Horizon/Romulus, 19;

IFC Films, 2387; Image Entertainment, 2492; Independent Artists, 2927; International Film Exchange, 1796; International Spectrafilm, 1017, 1386, 1839; Island Pictures, 1322, 2746, 3514;

Janus Films, 961, 1345, 2071, 2609, 2799, 2886, 3072; Jay Robert Nash Archives, 2326, 2392, 2691, 3035; Jesse L. Lasky Famous Players, 2263;

Kingsley International Pictures, 1069, 2890; Kino International, 2635; Kino Lorber, 3428;

Landau Releasing, 2801; Legende Films, 4442; Lionsgate, 1135, 1545, 2606, 3287, 3324, 3325, 3407, 3575; Lippert, 80, 859, 1103, 2318; London Film Productions, 149, 1007, 1008, 1717, 1853, 1854, 2001, 2059, 2259, 2260, 2390, 2542, 2543, 2552, 2553, 2554, 2555, 2556; Lopert Picture Corporation, 1619, 2083, 2544, 2668, 2763; Lux Film, 118;

Magnolia Pictures, 962, 1452, 2581, 3152, 3391; Majestic Pictures, 2859; Manhattan Films International, 1118; Mayer-Burstyn, 107; Mayflower Pictures, 2123; Max Glass Film, 1799; Medusa, 2462; Metro, 564, 565, 2105; Metropolis Pictures, 661; MGM, 2, 9, 18, 37, 41, 45, 46, 59, 60, 66, 71, 75, 79, 81, 100, 101, 110, 129, 132, 138, 140, 145, 154, 177, 178, 186, 198, 201, 204, 206, 225, 235, 236, 240, 260, 270, 272, 274, 280, 306, 330, 334, 349, 370, 377, 378, 380, 386, 392, 411, 427, 433, 435, 440, 441, 461, 463, 466, 467, 471, 488, 490, 491, 494, 522, 528, 541, 544, 546, 574, 575, 576, 598, 606, 607, 635, 645, 646, 670, 671, 673, 676, 681, 682, 688, 701, 704, 707, 708, 724, 725, 737, 746, 778, 779, 780, 801, 828, 829, 834, 837, 838, 854, 883, 907, 910, 930, 945, 947, 964, 970, 995, 1001, 1030, 1031, 1042, 1043, 1048, 1056, 1060, 1072, 1076, 1085, 1088, 1110, 1112, 1119, 1147, 1151, 1153, 1162, 1171, 1180, 1185, 1200, 1220, 1221, 1228, 1229, 1231, 1250, 1256, 1262, 1263, 1264, 1274, 1275, 1276, 1293, 1294, 1321, 1332, 1359, 1360, 1368, 1371, 1372, 1377, 1382, 1383, 1384, 1385, 1397, 1417, 1422, 1424, 1426, 1427, 1430, 1437, 1438, 1441, 1456, 1457, 1461, 1470, 1471, 1472, 1476, 1477, 1502, 1523, 1551, 1558, 1559, 1567, 1575, 1591, 1597, 1615, 1631, 1637, 1646, 1647, 1649, 1668, 1671, 1673, 1684, 1685, 1691, 1710, 1715, 1719, 1744, 1746, 1747, 1748, 1749, 1758, 1761, 1762, 1763, 1766, 1786, 1791, 1792, 1797, 1798, 1815, 1817, 1818, 1819, 1820, 1821, 1838, 1846, 1849, 1857, 1858, 1863, 1913, 1915, 1923, 1933, 1961, 1962, 1963, 1964, 1965, 1976, 1988, 1989, 1990, 2000, 2003, 2019, 2029, 2035, 2036, 2056, 2057, 2077, 2078, 2079, 2110, 2114, 2118, 2129, 2140, 2141, 2142, 2148, 2163, 2182, 2187, 2188, 2189, 2191, 2198, 2228, 2253, 2282, 2309, 2313, 2314, 2346, 2347, 2357, 2358, 2371, 2372, 2388, 2405, 2409, 2414, 2415, 2423, 2432, 2436, 2437, 2438, 2446, 2447, 2453, 2454, 2455, 2457, 2461, 2466, 2467, 2478, 2479, 2485, 2486, 2493, 2495, 2510, 2524, 2525, 2527, 2528, 2529, 2530, 2531, 2532, 2545, 2546, 2562, 2563, 2567, 2587, 2588, 2592, 2593, 2594, 2596,

2599, 2600, 2623, 2630, 2531, 2660, 2678, 2693, 2694, 2695, 2700, 2702, 2703, 2704, 2719, 2728, 2729, 2730, 2745, 2764, 2782, 2785, 2790, 2816, 2825, 2826, 2827, 2837, 2848, 2849, 2855, 2856, 2857, 2867, 2892, 2893, 2928, 2947, 2948, 2953, 2967, 2974, 2984, 2985, 2986, 3006, 3007, 3008, 3011, 3020, 3023, 3024, 3036, 3037, 3054, 3056, 3068, 3071, 3076, 3082, 3084, 3089, 3095, 3106, 3114, 3115, 3116, 3117, 3118, 3119, 3130, 3132, 3133, 3134, 3138, 3139, 3141, 3142, 3146, 3150, 3153, 3167, 3171, 3179, 3180, 3181, 3184, 3205, 3206, 3207, 3229, 3236, 3237, 3468, 3504, 3507, 3524, 3525, 3535, 3548, 3554, 3556, 3569, 3586, 3594, 3596, 3607, 3609, 3610, 3617, 3620, 3636, 3655, 3666, 3676, 3680, 3685, 3689, 3691, 3698, 3702; Miramax, 63, 221, 234, 237, 238, 258, 275, 312, 454, 459, 503, 675, 752, 766, 869, 956, 1224, 1286, 1328, 1432, 1841, 2158, 2920, 3673; Monogram, 839, 1410, 3001, 3577; MSEG, 283; Mulberry Square, 102; Music Box Films, 872; Mutual, 2627;

National General Pictures, 620, 1086, 1087, 1327, 3545; Nelson Entertainment, 2987, 2999; Nero Films, 1255, 1580; New Front Films, 3073; New Line Cinema, 659, 728, 1005, 1279, 1353, 1480, 2557, 2743, 2905, 3488, 3562; New Market Films, 2950; New World Pictures, 2636; New Yorker, 1238, 2597, 2664; Northern Arts, 1782;

One Pass Media, 2760; Orion, 33, 56, 69, 265, 267, 301, 321, 444, 736, 803, 820, 1222, 1273, 1395, 1465, 1660, 1702, 1741, 1769, 1896, 2127, 2468, 2807, 2808, 3565; Overture Films, 1865; Oxford Films, 3637;

Pabst Film, 373; Paramount, 44, 52, 53, 86, 89, 90, 95, 106, 146, 148, 159, 162, 165, 179, 183, 191, 192, 200, 203, 222, 224, 227, 228, 239, 249, 250, 253, 261, 269, 278, 292, 303, 308, 309, 325, 336, 345, 347, 356, 358, 362, 367, 368, 382, 387, 388, 390, 391, 399, 402, 403, 404, 422, 424, 429, 436, 446, 447, 452, 462, 483, 484, 485, 489, 498, 502, 507, 513, 514, 515, 542, 547, 552, 563, 577, 602, 610, 611, 612, 624, 632, 638, 639, 648, 649, 650, 651, 653, 692, 693, 697, 702, 705, 712, 718, 719, 727, 741, 749, 755, 758, 786, 788, 791, 792, 805, 825, 835, 842, 855, 856, 868, 870, 871, 887, 891, 892, 893, 903, 919, 923, 949, 1010, 1014, 1025, 1029, 1033, 1041; 1044, 1053, 1057, 1061, 1094, 1102, 1109, 1114, 1133, 1143, 1144, 1152, 1154, 1155, 1159, 1164, 1184, 1186, 1210, 1213, 1225, 1226, 1239, 1259, 1277, 1278, 1296, 1298, 1299, 1307, 1309, 1311, 1326, 1336, 1337, 1370, 1376, 1380, 1396, 1405, 1409, 1416, 1421, 1428, 1439, 1460, 1467, 1475, 1494, 1498, 1504, 1511, 1529, 1531, 1533, 1538, 1548, 1555, 1564, 1578, 1579, 1582, 1583, 1586, 1603, 1621, 1630, 1651, 1652, 1653, 1655, 1656, 1662, 1677, 1689, 1722, 1730, 1731, 1732, 1751, 1767, 1774, 1775, 1777, 1778, 1783, 1807, 1808, 1809, 1823, 1831, 1832, 1833, 1836, 1837, 1850, 1862, 1881, 1883, 1884, 1902, 1912, 1917, 1918, 1919, 1922, 1925, 1926, 1937, 1938, 1939, 1946, 1957, 1958, 1959, 1979, 1980, 1987, 1998, 1999, 2024, 2025, 2044, 2053, 2058, 2060, 2085, 2086, 2087, 2088, 2089, 2093, 2098, 2100, 2111, 2112, 2113, 2125, 2126, 2138, 2147, 2149, 2152, 2162, 2175, 2176, 2177, 2185, 2186, 2209, 2210, 2214, 2215, 2216, 2217, 2218, 2237, 2246, 2257, 2261, 2262, 2278, 2279, 2280, 2281, 2295, 2296, 2297, 2298, 2299, 2336, 2342, 2348, 2368, 2373, 2374, 2383, 2384, 2385, 2386, 2399, 2400, 2401, 2402, 2403, 2404, 2406, 2426, 2430, 2439, 2452, 2458, 2463, 2469, 2470, 2471, 2472, 2473, 2481, 2482, 2505, 2506, 2569, 2570, 2573, 2576, 2589, 2590, 2610, 2625, 2626, 2638, 2649, 2650, 2651, 2669, 2686, 2721, 2725, 2726, 2750, 2751, 2753, 2755, 2756, 2759, 2761, 2773, 2786, 2793, 2797, 2804, 2805, 2810, 2818, 2819, 2828, 2829, 2832, 2833, 2834, 2838, 2839, 2840, 2845, 2847, 2852, 2872, 2873, 2874, 2882, 2889, 2910, 2911, 2912, 2913, 2929, 2930, 2931, 2934, 2935, 2940, 2945, 2952, 2960, 2962, 2963, 2964, 2969, 2971, 2972, 2994, 2996, 3000, 3014, 3015, 3021, 3022, 3066, 3092, 3093, 3094, 3109, 3123, 3191, 3192, 3231, 3238, 3298, 3299, 3300, 3301, 3335, 3336, 3363, 3433, 3473, 3487, 3491, 3492, 3508, 3533, 3572, 3576, 3582, 3585, 3588, 3593, 3603, 3619, 3622, 3643, 3644, 3647, 3667, 3668, 3693, 3695; Paramount Vantage, 1287; Pathe Con-

temporary Films, 2744, 2781; Pathé Exchange, 991, 992, 1942, 3614; Pathe International, 3086; Pittsburgh Pictures, 5; Polygram: Gramercy, 342; PRC, 363, 1779; Prominent Films, 2115;

Rank, 61, 3541; Relativity Media, 3244, 3245, 3246, 3247; Republic, 326, 499, 532, 533, 1167, 1331, 1403, 1755, 1756, 1757, 1861, 1869, 1870, 1970, 1971, 1972, 2121, 2393, 2591, 2613, 2914, 3060, 3501, 3608, 3659, 3674; Relativity Media, 3286; Rialto Pictures, 1789; Rizzoli Film, 963; RKO, 31, 32, 50, 67, 68, 99, 103, 104, 111, 113, 131, 136, 155, 195, 226, 233, 241, 242, 243, 244, 245, 305, 364, 421, 474, 476, 481, 487, 509, 523, 530, 531, 535, 536, 553, 554, 593, 626, 722, 729, 732, 783, 841, 857, 862, 880, 895, 896, 915, 918, 926, 927, 943, 953, 985, 986, 987, 988, 1006, 1046, 1075, 1111, 1116, 1141, 1142, 1146, 1163, 1165, 1177, 1205, 1242, 1335, 1339, 1344, 1347, 1351, 1373, 1374, 1375, 1398, 1419, 1420, 1468, 1473, 1483, 1484, 1485, 1501, 1508, 1562, 1563, 1574, 1610, 1622, 1643, 1644, 1645, 1666, 1697, 1764, 1790, 1795, 1845, 1871, 1890, 1929, 1952, 1953, 2030, 2031, 2032, 2033, 2055, 2072, 2082, 2092, 2095, 2096, 2097, 2119, 2132, 2135, 2145, 2197, 2205, 2247, 2248, 2252, 2265, 2266, 2315, 2350, 2351, 2376, 2412, 2420, 2421, 2427, 2443, 2521, 2522, 2533, 2549, 2550, 2560, 2582, 2584, 2624, 2674, 2687, 2688, 2722, 2731, 2791, 2794, 2843, 2866, 2877, 2899, 2907, 2922, 2975, 2993, 3005, 3010, 3039, 3087, 3088, 3102, 3107, 3108, 3125, 3127, 3128, 3135, 3136, 3183, 3470, 3478, 3518, 3547, 3557, 3580, 3591, 3592, 3615, 3629, 3635, 3648, 3663; Roadside Attractions, 3364; Royal Films International, 1956;

Samuel Goldwyn Co., 1122, 1175, 1623, 1678, 1679, 1949, 2200, 2264, 2509, 2705, 2766, 3057, 3143, 3144, 3538; Savoy Pictures, 158; Selznick International, 423, 662, 663, 664, 665, 666, 667, 668, 669, 1173, 1585, 1681, 1682, 1711, 1712, 1713, 1714, 2136, 2137, 2239, 2240, 2241, 2242, 2289, 2290; Shadow Distribution, 2146; Societa Italiana Cines, 1760; Societe Generale des Films, 1595; Solar Productions, 1584; Sony, 4, 91, 451, 874, 1038, 1132, 1516, 1598, 1665, 1672, 1765, 1941, 2424, 2862, 3202, 3250, 3308, 3392, 3393, 3404, 3405, 3406, 3429, 3430; State 6 Films, 3388, 3389, 3390; Studio Canal, 3421; Summit Entertainment, 845, 1084, 3284, 3294, 3329, 3330, 3331, 3375, 3376, 3377, 3378, 3379, 3380, 3408, 3409; Sundance Select, 3340;

Times Film Corp, 2965; Tobis, 2603, 2860, 2861; Toho Company, 2063, 2608, 3190; Touchstone Pictures, 1611, 1690, 1793, 2277, 2709, 2800, 2997, 3042, 3043, 3044, 3479, 3489, 3578, 3671; Trans Lux, 1021, 1022; Triangle Film Corporation, 906; Tribeca, 3297; Trimark Pictures, 1055; TriStar, 22, 58, 62, 164, 478, 580, 618, 622, 756, 802, 938, 1023, 1247, 1342, 1423, 1654, 1706, 2155, 2319, 2411, 2615, 3292, 3567, 3631, 3675; 20th/21st Century Fox, 11, 16, 25, 26, 40, 93, 98, 105, 124, 125, 126, 130, 133, 139, 144, 157, 160, 163, 167, 168, 172, 175, 176, 184, 190, 207, 215, 216, 217, 219, 252, 254, 255, 262, 279, 293, 294, 307, 311, 313, 316, 317, 318, 322, 323, 331, 337, 344, 348, 353, 354, 357, 374, 376, 379, 389, 400, 407, 413, 419, 420, 456, 464, 465, 470, 475, 500, 518, 520, 524, 525, 529, 566, 568, 569, 578, 584, 591, 599, 605, 615, 617, 623, 634, 643, 684, 685, 686, 687, 699, 703, 715, 717, 720, 735, 743, 757, 761, 773, 774, 787, 795, 796, 797, 811, 813, 814, 815, 821, 824, 826, 836, 846, 847, 848, 851, 853, 861, 864, 866, 877, 881, 882, 889, 899, 900, 908, 914, 922, 931, 939, 940, 951, 954, 971, 974, 984, 990, 994, 996, 1002, 1037, 1052, 1058, 1059, 1062, 1063, 1071, 1079, 1083, 1092, 1093, 1106, 1113, 1115, 1117, 1125, 1129, 1130, 1131, 1150, 1158, 1196, 1198, 1203, 1204, 1212, 1227, 1230, 1232, 1233, 1234, 1244, 1271, 1291, 1295, 1300, 1301, 1314, 1323, 1334, 1340, 1346, 1352, 1362, 1387, 1388, 1389, 1390, 1391, 1392, 1399, 1400, 1418, 1433, 1434, 1446, 1448, 1451, 1453, 1458, 1459, 1464, 1466, 1469, 1474, 1493, 1506, 1507, 1517, 1521, 1522, 1553, 1570, 1571, 1572, 1581, 1589, 1606, 1607, 1626, 1629, 1632, 1634, 1639, 1640, 1642, 1657, 1658, 1674, 1676, 1683, 1687, 1695, 1701, 1704, 1705, 1709, 1723, 1724, 1728, 1740, 1752, 1753, 1759, 1776,

PHOTOS: TITLE INDEX

Note: The following photo credits are shown by film title and year with page numbers in parentheses for 1913-2011 entries.

(280); **The Conspirators**, 1944 (281); **The Constant Nymph**, 1943 (282); **Convicts**, 1991 (283); **Coogan's Bluff**, 1968 (284); **Cool Hand Luke**, 1967 (285); **The Corn Is Green**, 1945 (286); **Coroner Creek**, 1948 (287); **The Corsican Brothers**, 1941 (288); **Corvette K-225**, 1943 (289); **The Cotton Club**, 1984 (290); **Counsellor at Law**, 1933 (291); **The Counterfeit Traitor**, 1962 (292); **The County Chairman**, 1935 (293); **Courage Under Fire**, 1996 (294); **The Court-Martial of Billy Mitchell**, 1955 (295); **Cover Girl**, 1944 (296); **Cowboy**, 1958 (297); **Craig's Wife**, 1936 (298); **The Creature from the Black Lagoon**, 1954 (299); **Crime and Punishment**, 1935 (300); **Crimes and Misdemeanors**, 1989 (301); **The Crimson Pirate**, 1952 (302); **"Crocodile" Dundee**, 1986 (303); **Cross of Iron**, 1977 (304); **Crossfire**, 1947 (305); **The Crowd**, 1928 (306); **The Crucible**, 1996 (307); **The Crusades**, 1935 (308, 309); **A Cry in the Dark**, 1988 (310); **Cry of the City**, 1948 (311); **The Crying Game**, 1992 (312); **The Culpepper Cattle Company**, 1972 (313); **Curse of the Werewolf**, 1961 (314); **Cyrano de Bergerac**, 1950 (315);

D-Day: The Sixth of June, 1956 (316); **Daddy Long Legs**, 1955 (317); **Daisy Kenyon**, 1947 (318); **Dallas**, 1950 (319); **The Damned**, 1969 (320); **Dances with Wolves**, 1990 (321); **Dancing in the Dark**, 1949 (322); **Dante's Inferno**, 1935 (323); **Dante's Peak**, 1997 (324); **Dark City**, 1950 (325); **The Dark Command**, 1940 (326); **Dark Eyes**, 1987 (327); **The Dark Mirror**, 1946 (328); **Dark Passage**, 1947 (329); **A Date with Judy**, 1948 (330); **David and Bathsheba**, 1951 (331); **Davy Crockett and the River Pirates**, 1956 (332); **The Dawn Patrol**, 1938 (333); **A Day at the Races**, 1937 (334); **The Day of the Jackal**, 1973 (335); **The Day of the Locust**, 1975 (336); **The Day the Earth Stood Still**, 1951 (337); **Daylight**, 1996 (338); **Days of Wine and Roses**, 1962 (339); **Dead Calm**, 1989 (340); **Dead End**, 1937 (341); **Dead Man Walking**, 1996 (342); **Dead Reckoning**, 1947 (343); **Dear Brigitte**, 1965 (344); **Dear Wife**, 1949 (345); **Death of a Salesman**, 1951 (346); **Death Takes a Holiday**, 1934 (347); **Decision Before Dawn**, 1951 (348); **Deep in My Heart**, 1954 (349); **The Deer Hunter**, 1978 (350); **The Defiant Ones**, 1958 (351); **Deliverance**, 1972 (352); **Demetrius and the Gladiators**, 1954 (353); **The Desert Fox: The Story of Rommel**, 1951 (354); **The Desert Song**, 1953 (355); **Design for Living**, 1933 (356); **Desk Set**, 1957 (357); **The Desperate Hours**, 1955 (358); **Desperate Journey**, 1942 (359); **Destination Tokyo**, 1943 (360); **Destry Rides Again**, 1939 (361); **Detective Story**, 1951 (362); **Detour**, 1945 (363); **The Devil and Daniel Webster**, 1941 (364); **The Devil at Four O'Clock**, 1961 (365); **Devil Dogs of the Air**, 1935 (366); **The Devil Is a Woman**, 1935 (367, 368); **The Devil's Brigade**, 1968 (369); **Devil's Doorway**, 1950 (370); **Dial M for Murder**, 1954 (371); **Diamond Jim**, 1935 (372); **Diary of a Lost Girl**, 1929 (373); **The Diary of Anne Frank**, 1959 (374); **Dick Tracy**, 1990 (375); **Die Hard with a Vengeance**, 1995 (376); **Diner**, 1982 (377); **Dinner at Eight**, 1933 (378); **Diplomatic Courier**, 1952 (379); **The Dirty Dozen**, 1967 (380); **Dirty Harry**, 1971 (381); **Dishonored**, 1931 (382); **Distant Drums**, 1951 (383); **Diva**, 1982 (384); **Dive Bomber**, 1941 (385); **The Divorcee**, 1930 (386); **Dixie**, 1943 (387); **Dr. Cyclops**, 1940 (388); **Dr. Dolittle**, 1998 (389); **Dr. Jekyll and Mr. Hyde**, 1920 (390); **Dr. Jekyll and Mr. Hyde**, 1931 (391); **Dr. Jekyll and Mr. Hyde**, 1941 (392); **Dr. No**, 1962 (393); **Dr. Strangelove or: How I Learned to Stop Worrying and Love the Bomb**, 1964 (394); **Dodge City**, 1939 (395); **Dodsworth**, 1936 (396); **Dog Day Afternoon**, 1975 (397); **Don Juan**, 1926 (398); **Donovan's Reef**, 1963 (399); **Don't Bother to Knock**, 1952 (400); **The Doolins of Oklahoma**, 1949 (401); **Double Indemnity**, 1944 (402, 403, 404); **A Double Life**, 1947 (405); **Down Three Dark Streets**, 1954 (406); **Down to the Sea in Ships**, 1949 (407); **Dracula**, 1931 (408, 409); **Dracula: Dead and Loving It**, 1995 (410); **Dragon Seed**, 1944 (411); **Dragonheart**, 1996 (412); **Dreamboat**, 1952 (413); **Dreamchild**, 1985 (414); **Dreams**, 1990 (415); **Dressed to Kill**, 1946 (416); **Driving Miss Daisy**, 1989 (417); **The Drum**, 1938 (418); **Drums Along the Mohawk**, 1939 (419, 420); **Drums in the**

Deep South, 1951 (421); **Duck Soup**, 1933 (422); **Duel in the Sun**, 1946 (423); **The Duelists**, 1977 (424); **Duma**, 2005 (425); **Dunkirk**, 1958 (426); **Dynamite**, 1929 (427);

Each Dawn I Die, 1939 (428); **The Eagle and the Hawk**, 1933 (429); **Eagle Squadron**, 1942 (430, 431); **East of Eden**, 1955 (432); **Easter Parade**, 1948 (433); **Easy Rider**, 1969 (434); **Easy to Love**, 1953 (435); **Ebb Tide**, 1937 (436); **Ed Wood**, 1994 (437); **The Eddy Duchin Story**, 1956 (438); **Edge of Darkness**, 1943 (439); **Edison, the Man**, 1940 (440); **Edward, My Son**, 1949 (441); **The Egg and I**, 1947 (442); **8½**, 1963 (443); **Eight Men Out**, 1988 (444); **84 Charing Cross Road**, 1987 (445); **El Dorado**, 1967 (446); **Elephant Walk**, 1954 (447); **Elizabeth**, 1998 (448); **Elmer Gantry**, 1960 (449); **The Emerald Forest**, 1985 (450); **The Emperor and the Assassin**, 1999 (451); **The Emperor Waltz**, 1948 (452); **Empire of the Sun**, 1987 (453); **Enchanted April**, 1992 (454); **The End of the Affair**, 1999 (455); **The Enemy Below**, 1957 (456); **The Enforcer**, 1951 (457); **The Enforcer**, 1976 (458); **The English Patient**, 1996 (459); **Enter the Dragon**, 1973 (460); **Escapade**, 1935 (461); **Escape from Alcatraz**, 1979 (462); **Escape from Fort Bravo**, 1953 (463); **The Eve of St. Mark**, 1944 (464); **Everybody Does It**, 1949 (465); **Excuse My Dust**, 1951 (466); **Executive Suite**, 1954 (467); **Exodus**, 1960 (468); **The Exorcist**, 1973 (469); **Eyewitness**, 1981 (470); **Eyes in the Night**, 1942 (471);

A Face in the Crowd, 1957 (472); **Fahrenheit 451**, 1966 (473); **The Falcon and the Coeds**, 1943 (474); **Fallen Angel**, 1945 (475); **The Fallen Sparrow**, 1943 (476); **Falling Down**, 1993 (477); **Family Business**, 1989 (478); **Family Plot**, 1976 (479); **Fanny and Alexander**, 1983 (480); **Fantasia**, 1940 (481); **The Far Country**, 1955 (482); **The Far Horizons**, 1955 (483); **A Farewell to Arms**, 1932 (484, 485); **Fargo**, 1996 (486); **The Farmer's Daughter**, 1947 (487); **The Fastest Gun Alive**, 1956 (488); **Fatal Attraction**, 1987 (489); **Father of the Bride**, 1950 (490); **Father's Little Dividend**, 1951 (491); **The FBI Story**, 1959 (492); **Fearless**, 1993 (493); **The Fearless Vampire Slayers; or Pardon Me but Your Teeth Are in My Neck**, 1967 (494); **A Few Good Men**, 1992 (495); **Field of Dreams**, 1989 (496); **55 Days at Peking**, 1963 (497); **Fighting Caravans**, 1931 (498); **The Fighting Kentuckian**, 1949 (499); **Fighting Man of the Plains**, 1949 (500); **The Fighting 69th**, 1940 (501); **The File on Thelma Jordan**, 1950 (502); **Finding Neverland**, 2004 (503); **The Finger Points**, 1931 (504); **Fiorile**, 1993 (505); **Firefox**, 1982 (506); **The Firm**, 1993 (507); **First Kid**, 1996 (508); **First Yank into Tokyo**, 1945 (509); **A Fistful of Dollars**, 1964 (510); **5 Against the House**, 1955 (511); **Five Easy Pieces**, 1970 (512); **Five Graves to Cairo** (513, 514); **The Five Pennies**, 1959 (515); **Five Star Final**, 1931 (516, 517); **Fixed Bayonets!**, 1951 (518); **The Flame and the Arrow**, 1950 (519); **The Flamingo Kid**, 1984 (520); **Flesh and Fantasy**, 1943 (521); **Flesh and the Devil**, 1926 (522); **Flight for Freedom**, 1943 (523); **The Flight of the Phoenix**, 1965 (524); **The Flim-Flam Man**, 1967 (525); **Flipper**, 1996 (526); **Flower Drum Song**, 1961 (527); **Fluke**, 1995 (528); **The Fly**, 1958 (529); **Flying Down to Rio**, 1933 (530); **Flying Leathernecks**, 1951 (531); **Flying Tigers**, 1942 (532, 533); **Fog Over Frisco**, 1934 (534); **Follow Me Quietly**, 1949 (535); **Follow the Fleet**, 1936 (536); **Foolish Wives**, 1922 (537); **Fool's Parade**, 1971 (538); **Footlight Parade**, 1933 (539); **For a Few More Dollars**, 1967 (540); **For Me and My Gal**, 1942 (541); **For Whom the Bell Tolls**, 1943 (542); **For Your Eyes Only**, 1981 (543); **Forbidden Planet**, 1956 (544); **Force of Arms**, 1951 (545); **Force of Evil**, 1948 (546); **A Foreign Affair**, 1948 (547); **Foreign Correspondent**, 1940 (548, 549, 550, 551); **Forrest Gump**, 1994 (552); **Fort Apache**, 1948 (553, 554); **The Fortune**, 1975 (555); **The Fortune Cookie**, 1966 (556); **49th Parallel**, 1942 (557); **42nd Street**, 1933 (558); **The Fountainhead**, 1949 (559); **Four Daughters**, 1938 (560); **Four Faces West**, 1948 (561); **The Four Feathers**, 1939 (562); **Four Frightened People**, 1934 (563); **The Four Horsemen of the Apocalypse**, 1921 (564, 565); **The Four Musketeers: Milady's Revenge**,

1975 (566); **The Four Seasons**, 1981 (567); **Fourteen Hours**, 1951 (568); **The Foxes of Harrow**, 1947 (569); **Framed**, 1947 (570); **Frankenstein**, 1931 (571, 572); **Frankenstein Meets the Wolf Man**, 1943 (573); **Freaks**, 1932 (574); **Free and Easy**, 1930 (575); **A Free Soul**, 1931 (576); **Freedom Writers**, 2007 (577); **The French Connection**, 1971 (578); **Frenzy**, 1972 (579); **The Freshman**, 1990 (580); **Friday Night Lights**, 2004 (581); **Friendly Persuasion**, 1956 (582); **Fright Night**, 1985 (583); **The Frogmen**, 1951 (584); **From Here to Eternity**, 1953 (585, 586); **The Front**, 1976 (587); **The Front Page**, 1931 (588, 589); **The Front Page**, 1974 (590); **Frontier Marshal**, 1939 (591); **Frost/Nixon**, 2008 (592); **The Fugitive**, 1947 (593); **Full Metal Jacket**, 1987 (594); **Full of Life**, 1956 (595); **Funny Girl**, 1968 (596); **A Funny Thing Happened on the Way to the Forum**, 1966 (597); **Fury**, 1936 (598); **Fury at Furnace Creek**, 1948 (599);

Gaily, Gaily, 1969 (600); **The Gallant Hours**, 1960 (601); **Gallipoli**, 1981 (602); **Gandhi**, 1982 (603); **The Garden of Allah**, 1936 (604); **Garden of Evil**, 1954 (605); **Gaslight**, 1944 (606, 607); **Gattaca**, 1997 (608); **The Gaucho**, 1927 (609); **The Geisha Boy**, 1958 (610); **The General Died at Dawn**, 1936 (611, 612); **The Gentle Gunman**, 1953 (613); **Gentleman Jim**, 1942 (614); **Gentleman's Agreement**, 1947 (615); **Gentlemen Marry Brunettes**, 1955 (616); **Gentlemen Prefer Blondes**, 1953 (617); **Germinal**, 1993 (618); **Geronimo: An American Legend**, 1993 (619); **The Getaway**, 1972 (620); **Getting Gertie's Garter**, 1945 (621); **Gettysburg**, 1993 (622); **The Ghost and Mrs. Muir**, 1947 (623); **The Ghost Breakers**, 1940 (624); **The Ghost of Frankenstein**, 1942 (625); **The Ghost Ship**, 1943 (626); **Ghostbusters**, 1984 (627); **Ghosts of Mississippi**, 1996 (628); **Giant**, 1956 (629); **Gidget**, 1959 (630); **Gilda**, 1946 (631); **The Gilded Lily**, 1935 (632); **Gilles' Wife**, 2004 (633); **The Girl in the Red Velvet Swing**, 1955 (634); **The Girl in White**, 1952 (635); **The Gladiator**, 1938 (636); **Gladiator**, 2000 (637); **The Glass Key**, 1935 (638); **The Glass Key**, 1942 (639); **The Glass Menagerie**, 1950 (640); **The Glass Menagerie**, 1987 (641); **The Glenn Miller Story**, 1954 (642); **The Glory Brigade**, 1953 (643); **G-Men**, 1935 (644); **Go for Broke**, 1951 (645); **Go West**, 1925 (646); **God is My Co-Pilot**, 1945 (647); **The Godfather**, 1972 (648, 649); **The Godfather Part II**, 1974 (650, 651); **God's Little Acre**, 1958 (652); **Going My Way**, 1944 (653); **Gold Diggers of 1933**, 1933 (654); **Gold Diggers of 1935**, 1935 (655); **The Gold Rush**, 1925 (656, 657); **Golden Boy**, 1939 (658); **The Golden Compass**, 2007 (659); **Golden Salamander**, 1951 (660); **The Golem**, 1921 (661); **Gone with the Wind**, 1939 (662, 663, 664, 665, 666, 667, 668, 669); **The Good Earth**, 1937 (670, 671); **Good Morning, Vietnam**, 1987 (672); **Good News**, 1947 (673); **Good-Time Girl**, 1950 (674); **Good Will Hunting**, 1997 (675); **The Goodbye Girl**, 1977 (676); **GoodFellas**, 1990 (677); **Gorillas in the Mist**, 1988 (678); **The Graduate**, 1967 (679); **Gran Torino**, 2008 (680); **Grand Hotel**, 1932 (681, 682); **Grand Illusion**, 1938 (683); **The Grapes of Wrath**, 1940 (684, 685, 686); **The Great American Broadcast**, 1938 (687); **The Great Caruso**, 1951 (688); **The Great Dictator**, 1940 (689); **The Great Escape**, 1963 (690); **Great Expectations**, 1946 (691); **The Great Gatsby**, 1949 (692); **The Great Gatsby**, 1974 (693); **The Great Impersonation**, 1942 (694); **The Great John L.**, 1945 (695); **The Great Man**, 1957 (696); **The Great McGinty**, 1940 (697); **The Great Mouse Detective**, 1986 (698); **The Great Profile**, 1940 (699); **The Great Santini**, 1979 (700); **The Great Sinner**, 1949 (701); **The Great Victor Herbert**, 1939 (702); **The Great White Hope**, 1970 (703); **The Great Ziegfeld**, 1936 (704); **The Greatest Show on Earth**, 1952 (705); **The Greatest Story Ever Told**, 1965 (706); **Greed**, 1925 (707, 708); **The Green Berets**, 1968 (709); **The Green Mile**, 1999 (710); **The Green Pastures**, 1936 (711); **The Greene Murder Case**, 1929 (712); **Greystoke: The Legend of Tarzan, Lord of the Apes**, 1984 (713); **Groundhog Day**, 1993 (714); **Guadalcanal Diary**, 1943 (715); **Guess Who's Coming to Dinner**, 1967 (716); **A Guide for the Married Man**, 1967 (717); **Gunfight at the O.K. Corral**, 1957 (718, 719); **The Gunfighter**, 1950

(720); **Gung Ho!**, 1943 (721); **Gunga Din**, 1939 (722); **The Guns of Navarone**, 1961 (723); **A Guy Named Joe**, 1943 (724); **Guys and Dolls**, 1955 (725); **Gypsy**, 1962 (726);

Hail the Conquering Hero, 1944 (727); **Hairspray**, 2007 (728); **Half Shot at Sunrise**, 1930 (729); **Hallelujah, I'm a Bum!**, 1933 (730); **Halloween**, 1978 (731); **Hamburger Hill**, 1987 (732); **Hamlet**, 1996 (733); **The Hanging Tree**, 1959 (734); **Hangover Square**, 1945 (735); **Hannah and Her Sisters**, 1986 (736); **The Happy Road**, 1957 (737); **A Hard Day's Night**, 1964 (738); **Hard Times**, 1975 (739); **The Harder They Fall**, 1956 (740); **Harold and Maude**, 1971 (741); **Harper**, 1966 (742); **Harry and Tonto**, 1974 (743); **Harry Potter and the Goblet of Fire**, 2005 (744); **Harvey**, 1950 (745); **The Harvey Girls**, 1946 (746); **The Hasty Heart**, 1949 (747); **The Hatchet Man**, 1932 (748); **Hatter's Castle**, 1948 (749); **He Ran All the Way**, 1951 (750); **He Walked by Night**, 1948 (751); **Hear My Song**, 1991 (752); **Heartbreak Ridge**, 1986 (753); **Hearts of the World**, 1918 (754); **Heaven Can Wait**, 1978 (755); **Heaven Help Us**, 1985 (756); **Heaven Knows, Mr. Allison**, 1957 (757); **The Heiress**, 1949 (758); **The Helen Morgan Story**, 1957 (759); **Hell on Frisco Bay**, 1956 (760); **Hello, Dolly!**, 1969 (761); **Hell's Angels**, 1930 (762); **Hellzapoppin'**, 1941 (763); **Henry V**, 1946 (764, 765); **Her Majesty, Mrs. Brown**, 1997 (766); **Here Come the Littles**, 1985 (767); **Here Comes Mr. Jordan**, 1941 (768); **Hero**, 1992 (769); **Hi Diddle Diddle**, 1943 (770); **The Hidden Room**, 1949 (771); **The High and the Mighty**, 1954 (772); **High Anxiety**, 1977 (773); **High Crimes**, 2002 (774); **High Noon**, 1952 (775); **High Plains Drifter**, 1973 (776); **High Sierra**, 1941 (777); **High Society**, 1956 (778); **High Wall**, 1947 (779); **The Hills of Home**, 1948 (780); **The Hireling**, 1973 (781); **His Girl Friday**, 1940 (782); **His Kind of Woman**, 1951 (783); **His Majesty O'Keefe**, 1954 (784); **Hit the Ice**, 1943 (785); **The Hitler Gang**, 1944 (786); **Hoffa**, 1992 (787); **Hold Back the Dawn**, 1941 (788); **A Hole in the Head**, 1959 (789); **Holiday**, 1938 (790); **Holiday Inn**, 1942 (791, 792); **Hollywood Canteen**, 1944 (793); **Hollywood Hotel**, 1937 (794); **Hombre**, 1967 (795); **Home Alone**, 1990 (796); **Home Alone 2: Lost in New York**, 1992 (797); **Home of the Brave**, 1949 (798); **Hondo**, 1953 (799); **Honey, I Blew Up the Kid**, 1992 (800); **Honky Tonk**, 1941 (801); **Hook**, 1991 (802); **Hoosiers**, 1986 (803); **Hopscotch**, 1980 (804); **Horse Feathers**, 1932 (805); **The Horse Soldiers**, 1959 (806, 807, 808); **The Horse's Mouth**, 1958 (809); **The Hospital**, 1971 (810); **The Hot Rock**, 1972 (811); **Hotel Rwanda**, 2004 (812); **The Hound of the Baskervilles**, 1939 (813, 814, 815); **Hour of the Gun**, 1967 (816); **The House Across the Bay**, 1940 (817); **The House of Fear**, 1945 (818); **House of Frankenstein**, 1944 (819); **House of Games**, 1987 (820); **House of Strangers**, 1949 (821); **The House of the Seven Gables**, 1940 (822); **House of Wax**, 1953 (823); **The House on 92nd Street**, 1945 (824); **Houseboat**, 1958 (825); **How Green Was My Valley**, 1941 (826); **How I Won the War**, 1967 (827); **How the West Was Won**, 1963 (828, 829); **How to Murder Your Wife**, 1965 (830); **How to Succeed in Business Without Really Trying**, 1967 (831); **How to Train Your Dragon**, 2010 (832); **The Howards of Virginia**, 1940 (833); **The Hucksters**, 1947 (834); **Hud**, 1963 (835); **Hudson's Bay**, 1941 (836); **The Human Comedy**, 1943 (837, 838); **The Human Monster**, 1940 (839); **The Hunchback of Notre Dame**, 1923 (840); **The Hunchback of Notre Dame**, 1939 (841); **The Hunt for Red October**, 1990 (842); **The Hurricane**, 1937 (843, 844); **The Hurt Locker**, 2009 (845); **Hush...Hush, Sweet Charlotte**, 1964 (846); **The Hustler**, 1961 (847, 848);

I Am a Fugitive from a Chain Gang, 1932 (849, 850); **I Can Get It for You Wholesale**, 1951 (851); **I Cover the War**, 1937 (852); **The I Don't Care Girl**, 1952 (853); **I Love You Again**, 1940 (854); **I Married a Witch**, 1942 (855, 856); **I Remember Mama**, 1948 (857); **I See a Dark Stranger**, 1947 (858); **I Shot Jesse James**, 1949 (859); **I Stole a Million**, 1939 (860); **I Wake Up Screaming**, 1941 (861); **I Walked with a Zombie**, 1943 (862); **I Want to Live!**, 1958 (863); **I Was a Male

War Bride, 1949 (864); I'll Be Seeing You, 1944 (865); I'll Never Forget You, 1951 (866); I'll See You in My Dreams, 1951 (867); I'm No Angel, 1933 (868); An Ideal Husband, 1999 (869); If I Had a Million, 1933 (870); If I Were King, 1938 (871); Il Divo, 2009 (872); Illegal, 1955 (873); The Illusionist, 2010 (874); Impact, 1949 (875); The Importance of Being Earnest, 1952 (876); The Imposters, 1998 (877); In a Lonely Place, 1950 (878); In Good Company, 2004 (879); In Name Only, 1939 (880); In Old Chicago, 1938 (881, 882); In the Good Old Summertime, 1949 (883); In the Heat of the Night, 1967 (884); In the Line of Fire, 1993 (885); In Which We Serve, 1942 (886); Incendiary Blonde, 1945 (887); The Incredible Mr. Limpet, 1967 (888); Independence Day, 1996 (889); The Indian Fighter, 1955 (890); Indiana Jones and the Kingdom of the Crystal Skull, 2008 (891); Indiana Jones and the Last Crusade, 1989 (892); Indiana Jones and the Temple of Doom, 1984 (893); Indiscreet, 1958 (894); The Informer, 1935 (895, 896); Inherit the Wind, 1960 (897, 898); The Inn of the Sixth Happiness, 1958 (899); The Innocents, 1961 (900); Insomnia, 2002 (901); Intermezzo: A Love Story, 1939 (902); International House, 1933 (903); Interview with the Vampire: The Vampire Chronicles, 1994 (904); Intervista, 1992 (905); Intolerance: Love's Struggle Throughout the Ages, 1916 (906); Intruder in the Dust, 1949 (907); Invaders from Mars, 1953 (908); Invasion of the Body Snatchers, 1956 (909); The Invisible Boy, 1957 (910); The Invisible Man, 1933 (911); The Ipcress File, 1965 (912); Irma La Douce, 1963 (913); The Iron Horse, 1924 (914); The Iron Major, 1943 (915); The Iron Mistress, 1952 (916); Island in the Sky, 1953 (917); Isle of the Dead, 1945 (918); It, 1927 (919); It Happened One Night, 1934 (920, 921); It Happens Every Spring, 1949 (922); It's a Gift, 1934 (923); It's a Great Feeling, 1949 (924); It's a Mad, Mad, Mad, Mad World, 1963 (925); It's a Wonderful Life, 1946 (926, 927); It's in the Bag, 1945 (928); Ivan the Terrible, 1947 (929); Ivanhoe, 1952 (930);

The Jackpot, 1950 (931); Jagged Edge, 1985 (932); James and the Giant Peach, 1996 (933); Jason and the Argonauts, 1963 (934); Jaws, 1975 (935); The Jazz Singer, 1927 (936); Jeanne Eagels, 1957 (937); Jerry Maguire, 1996 (938); Jesse James, 1939 (939); The Jewel of the Nile, 1985 (940); Jezebel, 1938 (941); Jim Thorpe—All American, 1951 (942); Joan of Arc, 1948 (943); Joe Gould's Secret, 2000 (944); Joe Smith, American, 1942 (945); Johnny Belinda, 1948 (946); Johnny Eager, 1942 (947); Johnny O'Clock, 1947 (948); The Joker Is Wild, 1957 (949); The Jolson Story, 1946 (950); Jonah Then and Now, 1985 (951); The Journey of Natty Gann, 1985 (952); Journey Into Fear, 1943 (953); Journey to the Center of the Earth, 1959 (954); The Joy Luck Club, 1993 (955); Ju Dou, 1991 (956); Juarez, 1939 (957); Judgment at Nuremberg, 1961 (958, 959); The Juggler, 1953 (960); Jules and Jim, 1962 (961); Julia, 1977 (962); Juliet of the Spirits, 1965 (963); Julius Caesar, 1953 (964); Junior Bonner, 1972 (965); Jurassic Park, 1993 (966);

Kansas City Confidential, 1952 (967); The Karate Kid, 1984 (968); The Keeper: The Legend of Omar Khayyam, 2005 (969); Kelly's Heroes, 1970 (970); Kentucky, 1938 (971); Key Largo, 1948 (972, 973); The Keys to the Kingdom, 1944 (974); Khartoum, 1966 (975); The Kid, 1921 (976); The Kid from Spain, 1932 (977); Kid Galahad, 1937 (978); The Killers, 1946 (979, 980); The Killing, 1956 (981); The Killing Fields, 1984 (982); Kind Hearts and Coronets, 1950 (983); The King and I, 1956 (984); King Kong, 1933 (985, 986, 987, 988); King Kong, 2005 (989); The King of Comedy, 1983 (990); The King of Kings, 1927 (991, 992); The King of Marvin Gardens, 1972 (993); King of the Khyber Rifles, 1953 (994); King Solomon's Mines, 1950 (995); Kingdom of Heaven, 2005 (996); Kings Go Forth, 1958 (997); Kings Row, 1942 (998); The King's Speech, 2010 (999); A Kiss Before Dying, 1956 (1000); Kiss Me Kate, 1953 (1001); Kiss of Death, 1947 (1002); Kiss the Blood Off My Hands, 1948 (1003); Kit

Carson, 1940 (1004); Kit Kittredge: An American Girl, 2008 (1005); Kitty Foyle, 1940 (1006); Knight without Armor, 1937 (1007, 1008); Knock on Any Door, 1949 (1009); Knock on Wood, 1954 (1010); Knute Rockne—All American, 1940 (1011); Kramer vs. Kramer, 1979 (1012); Kundun, 1997 (1013); Kung Fu Panda, 2008 (1014);

L.A. Confidential, 1997 (1015, 1016); La Balance, 1983 (1017); La Bamba, 1987 (1018); La Buche, 2000 (1019); La Dolce Vita, 1961 (1020); La Strada, 1956 (1021, 1022); Labyrinth, 1986 (1023); Lady and the Tramp, 1955 (1024); The Lady Eve, 1941 (1025); Lady for a Day, 1933 (1026); The Lady from Shanghai, 1948 (1027, 1028); Lady in the Dark, 1944 (1029); Lady in the Lake, 1947 (1030, 1031); The Lady Is Willing, 1942 (1032); Lady Sings the Blues, 1972 (1033); The Lady Vanishes, 1938 (1034, 1035, 1036); Ladyhawke, 1985 (1037); Lagaan: Once Upon a Time in India, 2002 (1038); The Land before Time, 1988 (1039); Larceny, 1948 (1040); Lassie, 1994 (1041); Lassie Come Home, 1943 (1042, 1043); The Last Command, 1928 (1044); The Last Days of Disco, 1998 (1045); The Last Days of Pompeii, 1935 (1046); The Last Emperor, 1987 (1047); The Last Gangster, 1937 (1048); The Last Hurrah, 1958 (1049); The Last Legion, 2007 (1050); The Last of the Mohicans, 1936 (1051); The Last of the Mohicans, 1992 (1052); The Last Outpost, 1951 (1053); The Last Picture Show, 1971 (1054); The Last September, 2000 (1055); The Last Time I Saw Paris, 1954 (1056); The Last Train from Madrid, 1937 (1057); The Last Wagon, 1956 (1058); The Late George Apley, 1947 (1059); Latin Lovers, 1953 (1060); Laughter, 1930 (1061); Laura, 1944 (1062, 1063); The Lavender Hill Mob, 1951 (1064); The Lawless Breed, 1953 (1065); Lawrence of Arabia, 1962 (1066, 1067); Le Samourai, 1972 (1068); The League of Gentlemen, 1961 (1069); A League of Their Own, 1992 (1070); Leave Her to Heaven, 1945 (1071); Leaving Las Vegas, 1995 (1072); The Legend of Bagger Vance, 2000 (1073); Lemonade Joe, 1967 (1074); The Leopard Man, 1943 (1075); Les Girls, 1957 (1076); Les Misérables, 1935 (1077, 1078); Les Misérables, 1952 (1079); Lethal Weapon, 1987 (1080); The Letter, 1940 (1081); Letter from an Unknown Woman, 1948 (1082); A Letter to Three Wives, 1949 (1083); Letters to Juliet, 2010 (1084); Libeled Lady, 1936 (1085); The Life and Times of Judge Roy Bean, 1972 (1086, 1087); Life Begins for Andy Hardy, 1941 (1088); The Life of Emile Zola, 1937 (1089); The Life of Riley, 1949 (1090); Life with Father, 1947 (1091); Lifeboat, 1944 (1092, 1093); The Light That Failed, 1939 (1094); The Lighthorsemen, 1988 (1095); Lights of New York, 1928 (1096); Lilies of the Field, 1963 (1097); Lilo & Snitch, 2002 (1098); The Lineup, 1958 (1099); The Lion in Winter, 1968 (1100); The Lion King, 1994 (1101); Li'l Abner, 1959 (1102); Little Big Horn, 1951 (1103); Little Caesar, 1931 (1104, 1105); The Little Colonel, 1935 (1106); Little Lord Fauntleroy, 1921 (1107); Little Man, What Now?, 1934 (1108); Little Miss Marker, 1934 (1109); Little Nellie Kelly, 1940 (1110); Little Women, 1933 (1111); Little Women, 1949 (1112); The Littlest Rebel, 1935 (1113); The Lives of a Bengal Lancer, 1935 (1114); Lloyds of London, 1936 (1115); The Locket, 1946 (1116); The Lodger, 1944 (1117); Lola Montes, 1959 (1118); Lolita, 1962 (1119); The Lone Ranger, 1956 (1120); Lonely Are the Brave, 1962 (1121); Lonely Hearts, 1983 (1122); Long Day's Journey Into Night, 1962 (1123); The Long Goodbye, 1973 (1124); The Long, Hot Summer, 1958 (1125); Long Pants, 1927 (1126); The Long Riders, 1980 (1127); The Long Voyage Home, 1940 (1128); The Longest Day, 1962 (1129, 1130, 1131); Look at Me, 2005 (1132); Looking for Mr. Goodbar, 1977 (1133); Lord Jim, 1965 (1134); Lord of War, 2005 (1135); Lorenzo's Oil, 1992 (1136); Lost Horizon, 1937 (1137, 1138); Lost in America, 1985 (1139); Lost in Yonkers, 1993 (1140); The Lost Patrol, 1934 (1141); The Lost Squadron, 1932 (1142); The Lost Weekend, 1945 (1143, 1144); The Lost World: Jurassic Park, 1997 (1145); Love Affair, 1939 (1146); Love and Death, 1975 (1147); Love from a Stranger, 1937 (1148); Love in the Afternoon, 1957 (1149); Love Is a Many

Splendored Thing, 1955 (1150); **Love Me or Leave Me**, 1955 (1151); **Love Me Tonight**, 1932 (1152); **Love on the Run**, 1936 (1153); **The Love Parade**, 1929 (1154); **Love Story**, 1970 (1155); **Lover Come Back**, 1962 (1156); **Lovers and Other Strangers**, 1970 (1157); **The Luck of the Irish**, 1948 (1158); **Lucky Jordan**, 1942 (1159); **Lullaby of Broadway**, 1951 (1160); **Lured**, 1947 (1161); **Lust for Life**, 1956 (1162); **The Lusty Men**, 1952 (1163);

M, 1933 (1164); **Macao**, 1952 (1165); **MacArthur**, 1977 (1166); **Macbeth**, 1948 (1167); **The Macomber Affair**, 1947 (1168); **Mad Dog and Glory**, 1993 (1169); **Mad Max: Beyond Thunderdome**, 1985 (1170); **Madame Bovary**, 1949 (1171); **Madame X**, 1966 (1172); **Made for Each Other**, 1939 (1173); **Madeleine**, 1950 (1174); **The Madness of King George**, 1994 (1175); **The Magnetic Monster**, 1953 (1176); **The Magnificent Ambersons**, 1942 (1177); **Magnificent Obsession**, 1935 (1178); **Magnificent Obsession**, 1954 (1179); **The Magnificent Yankee**, 1950 (1180); **The Maid**, 2009 (1181); **Major Barbara**, 1941 (1182); **Major Dundee**, 1965 (1183); **Make Way for Tomorrow**, 1937 (1184); **Malaya**, 1950 (1185); **Male and Female**, 1919 (1186); **The Maltese Falcon**, 1941 (1187, 1188, 1189, 1190); **The Man Called Flintstone**, 1966 (1191); **A Man for All Seasons**, 1966 (1192, 1193); **The Man from Laramie**, 1955 (1194); **The Man from the Alamo**, 1953 (1195); **The Man I Married**, 1940 (1196); **A Man in Love**, 1987 (1197); **The Man in the Gray Flannel Suit**, 1956 (1198); **The Man in the Iron Mask**, 1939 (1199); **The Man in the Moon**, 1991 (1200); **Man of a Thousand Faces**, 1957 (1201); **Man of Iron**, 1983 (1202); **Man on a Tightrope**, 1953 (1203, 1204); **The Man on the Eiffel Tower**, 1949 (1205); **The Man They Could Not Hang**, 1939 (1206); **The Man Who Came to Dinner**, 1942 (1207, 1208); **The Man Who Knew Too Much**, 1935 (1209); **The Man Who Knew Too Much**, 1956 (1210); **The Man Who Laughs**, 1928 (1211); **The Man Who Never Was**, 1956 (1212); **The Man Who Shot Liberty Valance**, 1962 (1213); **The Man Who Would Be King**, 1975 (1214); **Man with a Million**, 1954 (1215); **The Man with the Golden Arm**, 1955 (1216); **The Man Without a Face**, 1993 (1217); **The Manchurian Candidate**, 1962 (1218); **Manhattan**, 1979 (1219); **Manhattan Melodrama**, 1934 (1220, 1221); **Manon of the Spring**, 1987 (1222); **Manpower**, 1941 (1223); **Mansfield Park**, 1999 (1224); **Marathon Man**, 1976 (1225, 1226); **Margie**, 1946 (1227); **Marie Antoinette**, 1938 (1228, 1229); **Marie Galante**, 1934 (1230); **Mark of the Vampire**, 1935 (1231); **The Mark of Zorro**, 1940 (1232, 1233, 1234); **Marked Woman**, 1937 (1235); **Marnie**, 1964 (1236, 1237); **The Marriage of Maria Braun**, 1979 (1238); **The Marriage Playground**, 1929 (1239); **The Marrying Man**, 1991 (1240); **Marty**, 1955 (1241); **Mary of Scotland**, 1936 (1242); **Mary Poppins**, 1964 (1243); **M*A*S*H**, 1970 (1244); **The Mask of Dimitrios**, 1944 (1245, 1246); **The Mask of Zorro**, 1998 (1247); **The Masque of the Red Death**, 1964 (1248); **The Master of Ballantrae**, 1953 (1249); **Mata Hari**, 1931 (1250); **The Match King**, 1932 (1251); **Match Point**, 2006 (1252); **Matewan**, 1987 (1253); **Matinee**, 1993 (1254); **Mayerling**, 1937 (1255); **Maytime**, 1937 (1256); **The McConnell Story**, 1955 (1257); **Mean Streets**, 1973 (1258); **Medium Cool**, 1969 (1259); **Meet Danny Wilson**, 1952 (1260); **Meet John Doe**, 1941 (1261); **Meet Me in Las Vegas**, 1956 (1262); **Meet Me in St. Louis**, 1944 (1263, 1264); **Meet Nero Wolfe**, 1936 (1265); **Melvin and Howard**, 1980 (1266); **Memphis Belle**, 1990 (1267); **The Men**, 1950 (1268); **Men in Black**, 1997 (1269); **Men in War**, 1957 (1270); **Men of Honor**, 2000 (1271); **Mephisto**, 1982 (1272); **Mermaids**, 1990 (1273); **The Merry Widow**, 1925 (1274); **The Merry Widow**, 1934 (1275); **Merton of the Movies**, 1947 (1276); **Metropolis**, 1928 (1277, 1278); **Michael**, 1996 (1279); **Mickey One**, 1965 (1280); **Midnight Cowboy**, 1969 (1281, 1282); **Midnight Run**, 1988 (1283); **A Midsummer Night's Dream**, 1935 (1284); **Midway**, 1976 (1285); **Mighty Aphrodite**, 1996 (1286); **A Mighty Heart**, 2007 (1287); **Mildred Pierce**, 1945 (1288, 1289); **Milk**, 2008 (1290); **Miller's Crossing**, 1990 (1291); **The Million**, 1931 (1292); **Million Dollar Mermaid**,

1952 (1293); **Min and Bill**, 1930 (1294); **Mine Own Executioner**, 1949 (1295); **Ministry of Fear**, 1944 (1296); **Miracle in the Rain**, 1956 (1297); **The Miracle of Morgan's Creek**, 1944 (1298, 1299); **Miracle on 34th Street**, 1947 (1300, 1301); **The Miracle Woman**, 1931 (1302); **The Miracle Worker**, 1962 (1303); **Miranda**, 1949 (1304); **The Misfits**, 1961 (1305); **Miss Grant Takes Richmond**, 1949 (1306); **Miss Tatlock's Millions**, 1948 (1307); **Missing**, 1982 (1308); **Mission Impossible II**, 2000 (1309); **Mission to Mars**, 2000 (1310); **Mississippi**, 1935 (1311); **Mississippi Gambler**, 1953 (1312); **The Missouri Breaks**, 1976 (1313); **Mister 880**, 1950 (1314); **Mister Roberts**, 1955 (1315); **Moby Dick**, 1930 (1316); **Moby Dick**, 1956 (1317, 1318); **Modern Times**, 1936 (1319, 1320); **Mogambo**, 1953 (1321); **Mona Lisa**, 1986 (1322); **Monkey Business**, 1952 (1323); **Monsieur Verdoux**, 1947 (1324); **Monsoon Wedding**, 2004 (1325); **The Monster and the Girl**, 1941 (1326); **Monte Walsh**, 1970 (1327); **A Month By the Lake**, 1995 (1328); **The Moon and Sixpence**, 1942 (1329); **Moon Over Parador**, 1988 (1330); **Moonrise**, 1948 (1331); **Moonstruck**, 1987 (1332); **The More the Merrier**, 1943 (1333); **Morituri**, 1965 (1334); **Morning Glory**, 1933 (1335); **Morocco**, 1930 (1336, 1337); **Moscow on the Hudson**, 1984 (1338); **The Most Dangerous Game**, 1932 (1339); **Mother Wore Tights**, 1947 (1340); **Moulin Rouge**, 1952 (1341); **Mountains of the Moon**, 1990 (1342); **The Mouthpiece**, 1932 (1343); **Mr. and Mrs. Smith**, 1941 (1344); **Mr. Arkadin**, 1962 (1345); **Mr. Belvedere Rings the Bell**, 1951 (1346); **Mr. Blandings Builds His Dream House**, 1948 (1347); **Mr. Deeds Goes to Town**, 1936 (1348, 1349); **Mr. Holland's Opus**, 1995 (1350); **Mr. Lucky**, 1943 (1351); **Mr. Moto's Last Warning**, 1939 (1352); **Mr. Nice Guy**, 1998 (1353); **Mr. Peabody and the Mermaid**, 1948 (1354); **Mr. Smith Goes to Washington**, 1939 (1355, 1356, 1357, 1358); **Mrs. Miniver**, 1942 (1359, 1360); **Mrs. Palfrey and the Claremont**, 2005 (1361); **The Mudlark**, 1950 (1362); **The Mummy**, 1932 (1363, 1364); **The Mummy: Tomb of the Dragon Emperor**, 2008 (1365); **The Muppet Christmas Carol**, 1992 (1366); **Murder!**, 1930 (1367); **Murder at the Gallop**, 1963 (1368); **Murder by Death**, 1976 (1369); **Murder, He Says**, 1945 (1370); **The Murder Man**, 1935 (1371); **Murder Most Foul**, 1964 (1372); **Murder, My Sweet**, 1944 (1373, 1374, 1375); **Murder on the Orient Express**, 1974 (1376); **Murder She Said**, 1961 (1377); **Murders in the Rue Morgue**, 1932 (1378); **Murphy's Romance**, 1985 (1379); **Murphy's War**, 1971 (1380); **The Music Man**, 1962 (1381); **Mutiny on the Bounty**, 1935 (1382, 1383, 1384, 1385); **My American Cousin**, 1986 (1386); **My Blue Heaven**, 1950 (1387); **My Cousin Rachel**, 1952 (1388); **My Cousin Vinny**, 1992 (1389, 1390); **My Darling Clementine**, 1946 (1391, 1392); **My Dog Skip**, 2000 (1393); **My Fair Lady**, 1964 (1394); **My Father's Glory**, 1991 (1395); **My Favorite Brunette**, 1947 (1396); **My Favorite Year**, 1982 (1397); **My Forbidden Past**, 1951 (1398); **My Friend Flicka**, 1943 (1399); **My Gal Sal**, 1942 (1400); **My Little Chickadee**, 1940 (1401); **My Man Godfrey**, 1936 (1402); **My Pal Trigger**, 1946 (1403); **My Sister Eileen**, 1942 (1404); **My Son John**, 1952 (1405); **My Son, My Son!**, 1940 (1406); **My Uncle**, 1958 (1407); **My Wild Irish Rose**, 1947 (1408); **The Mysterious Dr. Fu Manchu**, 1929 (1409); **The Mystery of Mr. Wong**, 1939 (1410); **The Mystery of the Wax Museum**, 1933 (1411); **Mystery Train**, 1989 (1412);

Nagana, 1933 (1413); **Naked Alibi**, 1954 (1414); **The Naked City**, 1948 (1415); **The Naked Prey**, 1966 (1416); **The Naked Spur**, 1953 (1417); **The Nanny**, 1965 (1418); **The Narrow Margin**, 1952 (1419, 1420); **Nashville**, 1975 (1421); **National Velvet**, 1945 (1422); **The Natural**, 1984 (1423); **Naughty Marietta**, 1935 (1424); **The Navigator: A Medieval Odyssey**, 1989 (1425); **Nazi Agent**, 1942 (1426); **Network**, 1976 (1427); **Nevada Smith**, 1966 (1428); **Never Give a Sucker an Even Break**, 1941 (1429); **Never So Few**, 1959 (1430); **New York, New York**, 1977 (1431); **Next Stop Wonderland**, 1998 (1432); **Niagara**, 1953 (1433, 1434); **Night and Day**, 1946 (1435, 1436); **A Night at the Opera**, 1935 (1437, 1438); **Night Has a Thousand Eyes**, 1948

(1439); **A Night in Casablanca**, 1946 (1440); **Night Must Fall**, 1937 (1441); **Night Nurse**, 1931 (1442); **Night of the Generals**, 1967 (1443); **The Night of the Hunter**, 1955 (1444, 1445); **Night People**, 1954 (1446); **The Night They Raided Minsky's**, 1968 (1447); **Night Train to Munich**, 1940 (1448); **Nightfall**, 1957 (1449); **Nightmare**, 1942 (1450); **Nightmare Alley**, 1947 (1451); **Nine Lives**, 2005 (1452); **Nine to Five**, 1980 (1453); **1984**, 1956 (1454); **99 River Street**, 1953 (1455); **Ninotchka**, 1939 (1456, 1457); **No Down Payment**, 1957 (1458); **No Highway in the Sky**, 1951 (1459); **No Man of Her Own**, 1932 (1460); **No Minor Vices**, 1948 (1461); **No Time for Comedy**, 1940 (1462); **No Time for Sergeants**, 1958 (1463); **No Way Out**, 1950 (1464); **No Way Out**, 1987 (1465); **Nob Hill**, 1945 (1466); **Nobody's Fool**, 1995 (1467); **None But the Lonely Heart**, 1944 (1468); **Norma Rae**, 1979 (1469); **North by Northwest**, 1959 (1470, 1471, 1472); **The North Star**, 1943 (1473); **North to Alaska**, 1960 (1474); **Northwest Mounted Police**, 1940 (1475); **Northwest Passage**, 1940 (1476, 1477); **Nosferatu**, 1922 (1478); **Not as a Stranger**, 1955 (1479); **The Notebook**, 2004 (1480); **Nothing Sacred**, 1937 (1481, 1482); **Notorious**, 1946 (1483, 1484, 1485); **Now, Voyager**, 1940 (1486, 1487); **Number Seventeen**, 1932 (1488); **Nurse Betty**, 2000 (1489); **The Nutty Professor**, 1996 (1490);

O Brother, Where Art Thou?, 2000 (1490, 1491); **O. Henry's Full House**, 1952 (1493); **O.S.S.**, 1946 (1494); **Objective, Burma!**, 1945 (1495, 1496); **Ocean's Eleven**, 1960 (1497); **The Odd Couple**, 1968 (1498); **Odd Man Out**, 1947 (1499); **Odds Against Tomorrow**, 1959 (1500); **Of Human Bondage**, 1934 (1501); **Of Human Hearts**, 1938 (1502); **Of Mice and Men**, 1939 (1503); **An Officer and a Gentleman**, 1982 (1504); **The Official Story**, 1985 (1505); **Oh Men! Oh Women!**, 1957 (1506); **Oh, You Beautiful Doll**, 1949 (1507); **Oklahoma!**, 1955 (1508); **Oklahoma Crude**, 1973 (1509); **The Oklahoma Kid**, 1939 (1510); **The Old Fashioned Way**, 1934 (1511); **The Old Maid**, 1939 (1512); **The Old Man and the Sea**, 1958 (1513); **Oliver!**, 1968 (1514, 1515); **Oliver Twist**, 2005 (1516); **The Omen**, 1976 (1517); **On Golden Pond**, 1981 (1518); **On Guard**, 2002 (1519); **On Moonlight Bay**, 1951 (1520); **On the Avenue**, 1937 (1521); **On the Riviera**, 1951 (1522); **On the Town**, 1949 (1523); **On the Waterfront**, 1954 (1524, 1525, 1526); **Once**, 2007 (1527); **Once Upon a Time in America**, 1984 (1528); **Once Upon a Time in the West**, 1969 (1529); **Once Were Warriors**, 1995 (1530); **One-Eyed Jacks**, 1961 (1531); **One Flew Over the Cuckoo's Nest**, 1975 (1532); **One Hour with You**, 1932 (1533); **100 Men and a Girl**, 1937 (1534); **One Magic Christmas**, 1985 (1535); **One Million B.C.**, 1940 (1536); **One Night in the Tropics**, 1940 (1537); **One Sunday Afternoon**, 1933 (1538); **One, Two, Three**, 1961 (1539); **One Way Passage**, 1940 (1540); **Only Angels Have Wings**, 1939 (1541); **Only the Valiant**, 1951 (1542); **Only When I Laugh**, 1981 (1543); **Open City**, 1946 (1544); **Open Water**, 2004 (1545); **Operation Pacific**, 1951 (1546); **Operation Petticoat**, 1959 (1547); **Ordinary People**, 1980 (1548); **Orphans of the Storm**, 1921 (1549); **Orpheus**, 1950 (1550); **Osama**, 2004 (1551); **Othello**, 1955 (1552); **The Other**, 1972 (1553); **Our Daily Bread**, 1934 (1554); **Our Hearts Were Young and Gay**, 1944 (1555); **Our Man in Havana**, 1960 (1556); **Our Miss Brooks**, 1956 (1557); **Our Relations**, 1936 (1558); **Our Vines Have Tender Grapes**, 1945 (1559); **Out of Africa**, 1985 (1560); **Out of the Blue**, 1947 (1561); **Out of the Past**, 1947 (1562, 1563); **The Out of Towners**, 1970 (1564); **The Outlaw Josey Wales**, 1976 (1565, 1566); **The Outriders**, 1950 (1567); **The Outsiders**, 1983 (1568); **Over 21**, 1945 (1569); **The Ox-Bow Incident**, 1943 (1570, 1571, 1572);

Paddy, 1970 (1573); **The Painted Desert**, 1931 (1574); **The Painted Veil**, 1934 (1575); **The Pajama Game**, 1957 (1576); **Pal Joey**, 1957 (1577); **The Paleface**, 1948 (1578, 1579); **Pandora's Box**, 1929 (1580); **Panic in the Streets**, 1950 (1581); **Papa's Delicate Condition**, 1963 (1582); **Paper Moon**, 1973 (1583); **Papillon**, 1973 (1584); **The Paradine Case**, 1947 (1585); **The Parallax View**, 1974 (1586); **Para-**

trooper, 1954 (1587); **Pardon My Sarong**, 1942 (1588); **Paris, Texas**, 1984 (1589); **Park Row**, 1952 (1590); **Party Girl**, 1958 (1591); **A Passage to India**, 1984 (1592); **Passage to Marseille**, 1944 (1593); **Passion**, 1982 (1594); **The Passion of Joan of Arc**, 1929 (1595); **Passport to Pimlico**, 1949 (1596); **Pat and Mike**, 1952 (1597); **Pather Panchali**, 1955 (1598); **Paths of Glory**, 1957 (1599, 1600, 1601, 1602); **The Patriot**, 1928 (1603); **The Patriot**, 2000 (1604); **Patterns**, 1956 (1605); **Patton**, 1970 (1606, 1607); **The Pawnbroker**, 1965 (1608); **Pay or Die**, 1960 (1609); **Payment on Demand**, 1951 (1610); **Pearl Harbor**, 2001 (1611); **Pee-Wee's Big Adventure**, 1985 (1612); **Pennies from Heaven**, 1936 (1613); **Penny Serenade**, 1941 (1614); **The People Against O'Hara**, 1951 (1615); **A Perfect Getaway**, 2009 (1616); **A Perfect Murder**, 1998 (1617); **The Perfect Storm**, 2000 (1618); **Persona**, 1967 (1619); **Personal Velocity: Three Portraits**, 2002 (1620); **Peter Ibbetson**, 1935 (1621); **Peter Pan**, 1953 (1622); **Peter's Friends**, 1992 (1623); **The Petrified Forest**, 1936 (1624); **The Petty Girl**, 1950 (1625); **Peyton Place**, 1957 (1626); **The Phantom of the Opera**, 1925 (1627); **The Phantom of the Opera**, 1943 (1628); **Phar Lap**, 1984 (1629); **The Phenix City Story**, 1955 (1630): **The Philadelphia Story**, 1940 (1631); **Phone Call from a Stranger**, 1952 (1632); **The Pianist**, 2002 (1633); **Pickup on South Street**, 1953 (1634); **Picnic**, 1955 (1635, 1636); **The Picture of Dorian Gray**, 1945 (1637); **Picture Snatcher**, 1933 (1638); **The Pied Piper**, 1942 (1639); **Pilgrimage**, 1933 (1640); **The Pink Panther**, 1964 (1641); **Pinky**, 1949 (1642); **Pinocchio**, 1940 (1643, 1644, 1645); **The Pirate**, 1948 (1646, 1647); **Pirates of the Caribbean: At World's End**, 2007 (1648); **The Pit and the Pendulum**, 1961 (1649); **Pittsburgh**, 1942 (1650); **A Place in the Sun**, 1951 (1651, 1652, 1653); **Places in the Heart**, 1984 (1654); **The Plainsman**, 1936 (1655, 1656); **The Planet of the Apes**, 1968 (1657, 1658); **Platinum Blonde**, 1931 (1659); **Platoon**, 1986 (1660); **Play Dirty**, 1969 (1661); **Play It Again, Sam**, 1972 (1662); **Play Misty for Me**, 1971 (1663); **The Player**, 1992 (1664); **Please Give**, 2010 (1665); **The Plough and the Stars**, 1936 (1666); **Plunkett and Macleane**, 1999 (1667); **Plymouth Adventure**, 1952 (1668); **Pocahontas**, 1995 (1669); **Pocketful of Miracles**, 1961 (1670); **Point Blank**, 1967 (1671); **Pollock**, 2000 (1672); **Poltergeist**, 1982 (1673); **Pony Soldier**, 1952 (1674); **The Poor Little Rich Girl**, 1917 (1675); **Poor Little Rich Girl**, 1936 (1676); **Poppy**, 1936 (1677); **Porgy and Bess**, 1959 (1678, 1679); **Pork Chop Hill**, 1959 (1680); **Portrait of Jennie**, 1949 (1681, 1682); **The Poseidon Adventure**, 1972 (1683); **The Postman Always Rings Twice**, 1946 (1684, 1685); **Power**, 1934 (1686); **The President's Lady**, 1953 (1687); **Presumed Innocent**, 1990 (1688); **Pretty Baby**, 1978 (1689); **Pretty Woman**, 1990 (1690); **Pride and Prejudice**, 1940 (1691); **Pride and Prejudice**, 2005 (1692); **The Pride and the Passion**, 1957 (1693, 1694); **The Pride of St. Louis**, 1952 (1695); **Pride of the Marines**, 1945 (1696); **The Pride of the Yankees**, 1942 (1697); **Primary Colors**, 1998 (1698); **The Prince and the Pauper**, 1937 (1699); **The Prince of Egypt**, 1998 (1700); **Prince of Foxes**, 1949 (1701); **Prince of the City**, 1981 (1702); **The Prince of Tides**, 1991 (1703); **Prince Valiant**, 1954 (1704); **The Princess Bride**, 1987 (1705); **Princess Caraboo**, 1994 (1706); **Princess O'Rourke**, 1943 (1707); **The Prisoner**, 1955 (1708); **The Prisoner of Shark Island**, 1936 (1709); **Prisoner of War**, 1954 (1710); **The Prisoner of Zenda**, 1937 (1711, 1712, 1713, 1714); **The Prisoner of Zenda**, 1952 (1715); **Private Benjamin**, 1980 (1716); **The Private Life of Henry VIII**, 1933 (1717); **The Private Life of Sherlock Holmes**, 1970 (1718); **Private Lives**, 1931 (1719); **The Private Lives of Elizabeth and Essex**, 1939 (1720, 1721); **Private Worlds**, 1935 (1722); **Prizzi's Honor**, 1985 (1723, 1724); **The Producers**, 1968 (1725); **The Professionals**, 1966 (1726); **Proof**, 2005 (1727); **The Proud Ones**, 1956 (1728); **The Prowler**, 1951 (1729); **Psycho**, 1960 (1730, 1731, 1732); **PT-109**, 1963 (1733); **Public Enemies**, 2009 (1734); **The Public Enemy**, 1931 (1735, 1736, 1737); **The Public Eye**, 1992 (1738); **Pulp**, 1972 (1739); **The Purple Heart**, 1944 (1740); **The Purple Rose of Cairo**, 1985 (1741); **Pursued**, 1947 (1742); **Pursuit** to Algiers, 1945 (1743); **Pygmalion**, 1938 (1744);

Q, 1982 (1745); **Queen Christina**, 1933 (1746, 1747, 1748, 1749); **Queen Kelly**, 1929 (1750); **Queen of the Mob**, 1940 (1751); **Quest for Fire**, 1982 (1752); **Quick Millions**, 1931 (1753); **Quicksand**, 1950 (1754); **The Quiet Man**, 1952 (1755, 1756, 1757); **Quigley Down Under**, 1990 (1758); **The Quiller Memorandum**, 1966 (1759); **Quo Vadis**, 1913 (1760); **Quo Vadis**, 1951 (1761, 1762, 1763);

Rachel and the Stranger, 1948 (1764); **Rachel Getting Married**, 2008 (1765); **The Rack**, 1956 (1766); **The Racket**, 1928 (1767); **Racket Busters**, 1938 (1768); **Radio Days**, 1987 (1769); **Raffles**, 1930 (1770); **Raggedy Man**, 1981 (1771); **Raging Bull**, 1980 (1772, 1773); **Rags**, 1915 (1774); **Ragtime**, 1981 (1775); **The Raid**, 1954 (1776); **Raiders of the Lost Ark**, 1981 (1777, 1778); **Railroaded**, 1947 (1779); **Rain**, 1932 (1780); **Rain Man**, 1988 (1781); **Raining Stones**, 1994 (1782); **The Rainmaker**, 1956 (1783); **The Rains Came**, 1939 (1784); **The Rains of Ranchipur**, 1955 (1785); **Raintree County**, 1957 (1786); **Raising Arizona**, 1987 (1787); **Ramrod**, 1947 (1788); **Ran**, 1985 (1789); **Rancho Notorious**, 1952 (1790); **Random Harvest**, 1942 (1791, 1792); **Ransom**, 1996 (1793); **The Rare Breed**, 1966 (1794); **Rashomon**, 1951 (1795); **Rasputin**, 1985 (1796); **Rasputin and the Empress**, 1932 (1797, 1798); **Rasputin**, 1939 (1799); **The Raven**, 1935 (1800); **Raw Deal**, 1948 (1801); **Rawhide**, 1951 (1802); **The Razor's Edge**, 1946 (1803, 1804); **The Reader**, 2009 (1805); **The Real Glory**, 1939 (1806); **Reap the Wild Wind**, 1942 (1807); **Rear Window**, 1954 (1808, 1809); **Rebecca**, 1940 (1810, 1811); **Rebecca of Sunnybrook Farm**, 1917 (1812); **Rebel Without a Cause**, 1955 (1813, 1814); **Reckless**, 1935 (1815); **The Reckoning**, 1971 (1816); **The Red Badge of Courage**, 1951 (1817, 1818); **Red Dust**, 1932 (1819, 1820); **Red-Headed Woman**, 1932 (1821); **The Red House**, 1947 (1822); **Red Mountain**, 1951 (1823); **Red River**, 1948 (1824, 1825, 1826, 1827, 1828); **The Red Shoes**, 1948 (1829); **Red Skies of Montana**, 1952 (1830); **Reds**, 1981 (1831, 1832, 1833); **The Reluctant Astronaut**, 1967 (1834); **The Remains of the Day**, 1993 (1835); **The Remarkable Andrew**, 1942 (1836); **Remember the Night**, 1940 (1837); **Rendezvous**, 1935 (1838); **Rendez-vous**, 1987 (1839); **Requiem for a Heavyweight**, 1962 (1840); **Reservoir Dogs**, 1992 (1841); **Retreat, Hell!**, 1952 (1842); **The Return of Frank James**, 1940 (1843, 1844); **Return of the Bad Men**, 1948 (1845); **Return to Me**, 2000 (1846); **Reversal of Fortune**, 1990 (1847); **The Revolutionary**, 1970 (1848); **Rhapsody**, 1954 (1849); **Rhubarb**, 1951 (1850); **Rich and Strange**, 1932 (1851); **Rich Kids**, 1979 (1852); **Richard III**, 1956 (1853, 1854); **The Ride Back**, 1957 (1855); **Ride Lonesome**, 1959 (1856); **Ride the High Country**, 1962 (1857, 1858); **Ride with the Devil**, 1999 (1859, 1860); **The Riders of the Whistling Skull**, 1937 (1861); **Riding High**, 1950 (1862); **Riff-Raff**, 1936 (1863); **The Right Stuff**, 1983 (1864); **Righteous Kill**, 2008 (1865); **The Ring**, 2002 (1866); **Rio Bravo**, 1959 (1867, 1868); **Rio Grande**, 1950 (1869, 1870); **Rio Rita**, 1929 (1871); **The Rise and Fall of Legs Diamond**, 1960 (1872); **The Rising of the Moon**, 1957 (1873); **Risky Business**, 1983 (1874); **The River**, 1951 (1875); **River of No Return**, 1954 (1876); **A River Runs Through It**, 1992 (1877); **The Road**, 2009 (1878); **Road House**, 1948 (1879); **The Road to Glory**, 1936 (1880); **Road to Morocco**, 1942 (1881); **Road to Perdition**, 2002 (1882); **Road to Rio**, 1947, (1883); **Road to Singapore**, 1940 (1884); **The Road Warrior**, 1982 (1885); **The Roaring Twenties**, 1939 (1886, 1887, 1888); **The Robe**, 1953 (1889); **Roberta**, 1935 (1890); **Robin and Marian**, 1976 (1891); **Robin and the 7 Hoods**, 1964 (1892); **Robin Hood**, 1922 (1893); **Robin Hood**, 2010 (1894); **Robin Hood: Prince of Thieves**, 1991 (1895); **RoboCop**, 1987 (1896); **The Rocking Horse Winner**, 1950 (1897); **Rocky**, 1976 (1898, 1899); **Rocky Mountain**, 1950 (1900); **Rollerball**, 1975 (1901); **Roman Holiday**, 1953 (1902); **Roman Scandals**, 1933 (1903); **Romance on the High Seas**, 1948 (1904); **Romancing the Stone**, 1984 (1905); **Romeo + Juliet**, 1996 (1906); **Rookie of the Year**, 1993 (1907);

A Room with a View, 1986 (1908); **Rooster Cogburn**, 1975 (1909); **The Roots of Heaven**, 1958 (1910); **Rope**, 1948 (1911); **Rope of Sand**, 1949 (1912); **Rosalie**, 1937 (1913); **The Rose**, 1979 (1914); **Rose Marie**, 1936 (1915); **Rose of Washington Square**, 1939 (1916); **The Rose Tattoo**, 1955 (1917); **Rosemary's Baby**, 1968 (1918, 1919); **Round Midnight**, 1986 (1920); **Roxie Hart**, 1942 (1921); **The Royal Family of Broadway**, 1930 (1922); **A Royal Scandal**, 1945 (1923); **Royal Wedding**, 1951 (1924); **Ruggles of Red Gap**, 1935 (1925); **Rugrats of Paris**, 2000 (1926); **Rumble Fish**, 1983 (1927); **Run for the Sun**, 1956 (1928); **Run of the Arrow**, 1957 (1929); **Runaway Train**, 1985 (1930); **Running on Empty**, 1988 (1931); **The Russians Are Coming! The Russians Are Coming!** 1966 (1932); **Ryan's Daughter**, 1970 (1933);

Sabotage, 1937 (1934); **Saboteur**, 1942 (1935, 1936); **Sabrina**, 1954 (1937, 1938); **The Sad Sack**, 1957 (1939); **Sadie Thompson**, 1928 (1940); **Safe**, 1995 (1941); **Safety Last!**, 1923 (1942); **Sahara**, 1943 (1943, 1944, 1945); **Saigon**, 1948 (1946); **Sailor of the King**, 1953 (1947); **The St. Louis Kid**, 1934 (1948); **Saint Ralph**, 2005 (1949); **The St. Valentine's Day Massacre**, 1967 (1950, 1951); **The Saint's Double Trouble**, 1940 (1952); **The Saint's Girl Friday**, 1954 (1953); **Salome**, 1953 (1954), **Salt**, 2010 (1955); **Salvatore Giuliano**, 1964 (1956); **Samson and Delilah**, 1949 (1957, 1958, 1959); **San Antonio**, 1945 (1960); **San Francisco**, 1936 (1961, 1962, 1963, 1964, 1965); **San Quentin**, 1937 (1966, 1967); **The Sand Pebbles**, 1966 (1968); **The Sandlot**, 1993 (1969); **Sands of Iwo Jima**, 1949 (1970, 1971, 1972); **The Santa Clause 2**, 2002 (1973); **Santa Fe Trail**, 1940 (1974); **Saps at Sea**, 1940 (1975); **Saratoga**, 1937 (1976); **Satan Met a Lady**, 1936 (1977); **Saturday Night and Sunday Morning**, 1961 (1978); **Saturday Night Fever**, 1977 (1979); **Save the Tiger**, 1973 (1980); **Saving Private Ryan**, 1998 (1981, 1982, 1983); **Say Anything**, 1989 (1984); **Sayonara**, 1957 (1985); **The Scalphunters**, 1968 (1986); **Scandal Sheet**, 1931 (1987); **Scaramouche**, 1952 (1988, 1989, 1990); **Scarface**, 1932 (1991, 1992, 1993, 1994, 1995, 1996, 1997); **The Scarlet Empress**, 1934 (1998, 1999); **The Scarlet Letter**, 1926 (2000); **The Scarlet Pimpernel**, 1935 (2001); **Scarlet Street**, 1945 (2002); **Scent of a Woman**, 1992 (2003); **Schindler's List**, 1993 (2004, 2005); **School for Scoundrels**, 1960 (2006); **Scott of the Antarctic**, 1949 (2007); **The Scout**, 1994 (2008); **Scream**, 1996 (2009); **The Sea Beast**, 1926 (2010); **The Sea Hawk**, 1940 (2011, 2012, 2013); **Sea of Love**, 1989 (2014); **The Sea Wolf**, 1941 (2015, 2016, 2017, 2018); **The Search**, 1948 (2019); **The Searchers**, 1956 (2020, 2021, 2022, 2023); **Searching for Bobby Fischer**, 1993 (2024); **Seconds**, 1966 (2025); **Secret Agent**, 1936 (2026, 2027); **Secret Agent of Japan**, 1942 (2028); **The Secret Garden**, 1949 (2029); **The Secret Life of Walter Mitty**, 1947 (2030, 2031, 2032, 2033); **The Secret of My Success**, 1987 (2034); **The Secret Six**, 1931 (2035, 2036); **Secretariat**, 2010 (2037, 2038); **Selena**, 1997 (2039); **Seminole**, 1953 (2040); **The Senator Was Indiscreet**, 1947 (2041); **Sense and Sensibility**, 1995 (2042); **Separate Tables**, 1958 (2043); **September Affair**, 1950 (2044); **Seraphim Falls**, 2007 (2045); **Sergeant Rutledge**, 1960 (2046); **Sergeant York**, 1941 (2047, 2048, 2049, 2050, 2051, 2052); **Serpico**, 1973 (2053); **The Servant**, 1964 (2054); **The Set-Up**, 1949 (2055); **Seven Brides for Seven Brothers**, 1954 (2056, 2057); **Seven Days in May**, 1964 (2058); **Seven Days to Noon**, 1950 (2059); **The Seven Little Foys**, 1955 (2060); **The Seven-Per-Cent Solution**, 1976 (2061, 2062); **Seven Samurai**, 1956 (2063); **Seven Sinners**, 1964 (2064); **Seven Thieves**, 1960 (2065); **The Seven Ups**, 1973 (2066); **The Seven Year Itch**, 1955 (2067); **Seven Years in Tibet**, 1997 (2068); **The Seventh Cross**, 1944 (2069); **7th Heaven**, 1927 (2070); **The Seventh Seal**, 1958 (2071); **The Seventh Victim**, 1943 (2072); **Shadow of a Doubt**, 1943 (2073, 2074, 2075, 2076); **Shadow of the Thin Man**, 1941 (2077); **Shadows and Fog**, 1992 (2078); **Shaft**, 1971 (2079); **Shake Hands with the Devil**, 1959 (2080); **Shakespeare in Love**, 1998 (2081); **Shall We Dance**, 1937 (2082); **Shame**, 1968 (2083); **Shampoo**, 1975 (2084); **Shane**, 1953 (2085,

2086, 2087); **Shanghai Express**, 1932 (2088, 2089); **The Shanghai Gesture**, 1941 (2090); **The Shawshank Redemption**, 1994 (2091); **She**, 1935 (2092); **She Done Him Wrong**, 1933 (2093); **She Married Her Boss**, 1935 (2094); **She Wore a Yellow Ribbon**, 1949 (2095, 2096, 2097); **The Sheik**, 1921 (2098); **Shenandoah**, 1965 (2099); **The Shepherd of the Hills**, 1941 (2100); **Sherlock Holmes**, 1932 (2101); **Sherlock Holmes and the Secret Weapon**, 1942 (2102); **Sherlock Holmes and the Voice of Terror**, 1942 (2103); **Sherlock Holmes in Washington**, 1943 (2104); **Sherlock Jr.**, 1924 (2105); **The Shining**, 1980 (2106); **Ship of Fools**, 1965 (2107, 2108); **Shipwrecked**, 1991 (2109); **The Shoes of the Fisherman**, 1968 (2110); **The Shootist**, 1976 (2111, 2112, 2113); **The Shop Around the Corner**, 1940 (2114); **The Shop on Main Street**, 1967 (2115); **Shoulder Arms**, 1918 (2116); **Show Boat**, 1936 (2117); **Show Boat**, 1951 (2118); **Show Business**, 1944 (2119); **Show Them No Mercy**, 1935 (2120); **The Showdown**, 1950 (2121); **Shrek 2**, 2004 (2122); **Sidewalks of London**, 1940 (2123); **The Siege of Firebase Gloria**, 1989 (2124); **The Sign of the Cross**, 1932 (2125, 2126); **Silence of the Lambs**, 1991 (2127); **The Silent Enemy**, 1959 (2128); **Silk Stockings**, 1957 (2129); **Silkwood**, 1983 (2130); **Silver Dollar**, 1932 (2131); **The Silver Horde**, 1930 (2132); **Silverado**, 1985 (2133); **Sinbad the Sailor**, 1947 (2135); **Since You Went Away**, 1944 (2136, 2137); **Sing, You Sinners**, 1938 (2138); **The Singing Fool**, 1928 (2139); **Singin' in the Rain**, 1952 (2140, 2141, 2142); **Sink the Bismarck!**, 1960 (2143); **Sinner's Holiday**, 1930 (2144); **Sister Kenny**, 1946 (2145); **Sita Sings the Blues**, 2009 (2146); **Sitting Pretty**, 1948 (2147); **Six Degrees of Separation**, 1993 (2148); **Six of a Kind**, 1934 (2149); **The Sixth Sense**, 1999 (2150, 2151); **Skippy**, 1931 (2152); **Sleeper**, 1973 (2153); **The Sleeping City**, 1950 (2154); **Sleepless in Seattle**, 1993 (2155); **Sleuth**, 1972 (2156); **A Slight Case of Murder**, 1938 (2157); **Sling Blade**, 1996 (2158); **Slumdog Millionaire**, 2008 (2159); **Smart Money**, 1931 (2160); **Smash-Up: The Story of a Woman**, 1947 (2161); **The Smiling Lieutenant**, 1931 (2162); **Smiling Through**, 1932 (2163); **Smoky**, 1946 (2164); **The Snake Pit**, 1948 (2165, 2166); **Snow White and the Seven Dwarfs**, 1937 (2167, 2168); **The Snows of Kilimanjaro**, 1952 (2169, 2170, 2171, 2172); **So Big**, 1953 (2173); **So Ends Our Night**, 1941 (2174); **So Proudly We Hail**, 1943 (2175, 2176, 2177); **The Social Network**, 2010 (2178); **A Soldier's Story**, 1984 (2179, 2180); **Solomon and Sheba**, 1959 (2181); **Some Came Running**, 1958 (2182); **Some Like It Hot**, 1949 (2183, 2184); **Somebody Loves Me**, 1952 (2185, 2186); **Somebody Up There Likes Me**, 1956 (2187, 2188); **Something of Value**, 1957 (2189); **Sometimes a Great Notion**, 1970 (2190); **Somewhere I'll Find You**, 1942 (2191); **Somewhere in Time**, 1980 (2192); **Sommersby**, 1993 (2193); **Son of Frankenstein**, 1939 (2194, 2195); **Son of Fury: The Story of Benjamin Blake**, 1942 (2196); **Son of Kong**, 1933 (2197); **Son of Lassie**, 1946 (2198); **The Son of the Sheik**, 1926 (2199); **A Song Is Born**, 1948 (2200); **The Song of Bernadette**, 1943 (2201, 2202, 2203); **Song O' My Heart**, 1930 (2204); **Song of the South**, 1946 (2205); **A Song to Remember**, 1945 (2206, 2207); **Sons and Lovers**, 1960 (2208); **The Sons of Katie Elder**, 1965 (2209, 2210); **Sophie's Choice**, 1982 (2211, 2212, 2213); **Sorry, Wrong Number**, 1948 (2214, 2215, 2216); **Souls at Sea**, 1937 (2217, 2218); **The Sound and the Fury**, 1959 (2219); **The Sound of Fury**, 1950 (2220); **The Sound of Music**, 1965 (2221, 2222); **Sounder**, 1972 (2223); **South of St. Louis**, 1949 (2224); **South Pacific**, 1958 (2225); **South Sea Woman**, 1952 (2226); **Southern Comfort**, 1981 (2227); **A Southern Yankee**, 1948 (2228); **The Southerner**, 1945 (2229, 2230); **Sparrows**, 1926 (2231); **Spartacus**, 1960 (2232, 2233, 2234, 2235, 2236); **Spawn of the North**, 1938 (2237); **Speed**, 1994 (2238); **Spellbound**, 1945 (2239, 2240, 2241, 2242); **Spider Man**, 2002 (2243); **Spider Man 2**, 2004 (2244); **The Spider Woman**, 1944 (2245); **The Spiderwick Chronicles**, 2008 (2246); **The Spiral Staircase**, 1946 (2247, 2248); **The Spirit of St. Louis**, 1957 (2249, 2250); **Spirit: Stallion of the Cimarron**, 2002 (2251); **Spitfire**, 1934 (2252); **Splash**, 1984 (2253); **Splendor in the Grass**, 1961 (2254); **The Spoilers**, 1942 (2255, 2256); **The SpongeBob**

SquarePants Movie, 2004 (2257); **Springfield Rifle**, 1952 (2258); **The Spy in Black**, 1939 (2259, 2260); **The Spy Who Came in from the Cold**, 1965 (2261, 2262); **The Squaw Man**, 1914 (2263); **The Squid and the Whale**, 2005 (2264); **Stage Door**, 1937 (2265, 2266); **Stage Fright**, 1950 (2267, 2268); **Stagecoach**, 1939 (2269, 2270, 2271, 2272, 2273, 2274, 2275, 2276); **Stakeout**, 1987 (2277); **Stalag 17**, 1953 (2278, 2279, 2280, 2281); **Stamboul Quest**, 1934 (2282); **Stand By Me**, 1986 (2283); **Stand-In**, 1937 (2284); **Stanley and Livingstone**, 1939 (2285, 2286); **The Star**, 1952 (2287); **The Star Chamber**, 1983 (2288); **A Star Is Born**, 1937 (2289, 2290); **A Star Is Born**, 1954 (2291, 2292, 2293, 2294); **Star Spangled Rhythm**, 1942 (2295); **Star Trek**, 2009 (2296); **Star Trek: First Contact**, 1996 (2297); **Star Trek: Nemesis**, 2002 (2298); **Star Trek VI: The Undiscovered Country**, 1991 (2299); **Star Wars: Episode V—The Empire Strikes Back**, 1980 (2300); **Star Wars: Episode IV—A New Hope**, 1977 (2301); **Star Wars: Episode I—The Phantom Menace**, 1999 (2302); **Stars Wars: Episode VI—Return of the Jedi**, 1983 (2303); **Star Wars: Episode II—The Attack of the Clones**, 2002 (2304); **Stardust Memories**, 1980 (2305); **Starlift**, 1951 (2306); **Stars and Stripes Forever**, 1952 (2307, 2308); **Stars in My Crown**, 1950 (2309); **Start the Revolution Without Me**, 1970 (2310); **State and Main**, 2000 (2311); **State Fair**, 1945 (2312); **State of the Union**, 1948 (2313, 2314); **State's Attorney**, 1932 (2315); **Steamboat Bill, Jr.**, 1928 (2316); **Steamboat Round the Bend**, 1935 (2317); **The Steel Helmet**, 1951 (2318); **Steel Magnolias**, 1989 (2319); **The Steel Trap**, 1952 (2320); **Stella Dallas**, 1937 (2321); **Stella Maris**, 1918 (2322); **The Sting**, 1973 (2323, 2324, 2325, 2326); **Stir Crazy**, 1980 (2327, 2328); **Stolen Hours**, 1963 (2329); **A Stolen Life**, 1946 (2330); **The Stone Boy**, 1984 (2331); **Storm Warning**, 1951 (2332, 2333); **Stormy Weather**, 1943 (2334, 2335); **The Story of Dr. Wassel**, 1944 (2336); **The Story of G.I. Joe**, 1945 (2337, 2338, 2339); **The Story of Louis Pasteur**, 1936 (2340, 2341); **The Story of Temple Drake**, 1933 (2342); **The Story of Will Rogers**, 1952 (2343); **Stowaway**, 1936 (2344); **The Straight Story**, 1999 (2345); **Strange Cargo**, 1940 (2346); **Strange Interlude**, 1932 (2347); **The Strange Love of Martha Ivers**, 1946 (2348); **The Strange Woman**, 1946 (2349); **The Stranger**, 1946 (2350, 2351); **Stranger Than Fiction**, 2006 (2352); **Strangers on a Train**, 1951 (2353, 2354, 2355, 2356); **The Stratton Story**, 1949 (2357, 2358); **The Strawberry Blonde**, 1941 (2359, 2360); **Street Scene**, 1931 (2361, 2362); **The Street with No Name**, 1948 (2363, 2364); **A Streetcar Named Desire**, 1951 (2365, 2366, 2367); **The Streets of Laredo**, 1949 (2368); **Stripes**, 1981 (2369); **Stuart Little**, 1999 (2370); **The Student Prince**, 1954 (2371); **The Student Prince in Old Heidelberg**, 1928 (2372); **Submarine Command**, 1951 (2373, 2374); **Submarine Patrol**, 1938 (2375); **Sudden Fear**, 1952 (2376); **Suddenly**, 1954 (2377, 2378); **Suez**, 1938 (2379, 2380); **The Sugarland Express**, 1974 (2381); **The Sullivans**, 1944 (2382); **Sullivan's Travels**, 1941 (2383, 2384, 2385, 2386); **Summer Hours**, 2008 (2387); **Summer Stock**, 1950 (2388); **Summer Storm**, 1944 (2389); **Summertime**, 1955 (2390); **The Sun Also Rises**, 1957 (2391, 2392); **The Sun Shines Bright**, 1953 (2393); **The Sundowners**, 1960 (2394); **Sunrise: A Song of Two Humans**, 1927 (2395, 2396); **Sunrise at Campobello**, 1960 (2397, 2398); **Sunset Boulevard**, 1950 (2399, 2400, 2401, 2402, 2403, 2404); **The Sunshine Boys**, 1975 (2405); **Super 8**, 2011 (2406); **Superman Returns**, 2006 (2407); **Superman III**, 1983 (2408); **Susan and God**, 1940 (2409); **The Suspect**, 1944 (2410); **Suspect**, 1987 (2411); **Suspicion**, 1941 (2412); **Sutter's Gold**, 1936 (2413); **Suzy**, 1936 (2414); **The Swan**, 1956 (2415); **Swanee River**, 1939 (2416); **Sweet Charity**, 1969 (2417); **Sweet Smell of Success**, 1957 (2418, 2419); **Swing Time**, 1936 (2420, 2421); **Swiss Family Robinson**, 1960 (2422); **Swiss Miss**, 1938 (2423); **Switching Channels**, 1988 (2424); **The Sword and the Stone**, 1963 (2425); **Sylvia**, 1985 (2426); **Sylvia Scarlett**, 1935 (2427);

T-Men, 1947 (2428, 2429); **Tabu: A Story of the South Seas**, 1931 (2430); **The Tailor of Panama**, 2001 (2431); **Take Me Out to the Ball**

Game, 1949 (2432); **Take One False Step**, 1949 (2433); **Take the Money and Run**, 1969 (2434); **The Taking of Pelham One Two Three**, 1974 (2435); **A Tale of Two Cities**, 1935 (2436, 2437, 2438); **The Talented Mr. Ripley**, 1999 (2439); **Tales of Manhattan**, 1942 (2440); **The Talk of the Town**, 1942 (2441, 2442); **Tall in the Saddle**, 1944 (2443); **The Tall Men**, 1955 (2444); **Tall Tale: The Unbelievable Adventures of Pecos Bill**, 1995 (2445); **The Tall Target**, 1951 (2446, 2447); **The Taming of the Shrew**, 1967 (2448); **Tap Roots**, 1949 (2449); **Taps**, 1981 (2450); **The Tarnished Angels**, 1958 (2451); **Tarnished Lady**, 1931 (2452); **Tarzan and His Mate**, 1934 (2453); **Tarzan Escapes**, 1936 (2454); **Tarzan Finds a Son!**, 1939 (2455); **Tarzan of the Apes**, 1918 (2456); **Tarzan the Ape Man**, 1932 (2457); **Tarzan's Greatest Adventure**, 1959 (2458); **Task Force**, 1949 (2459); **Taxi!**, 1932 (2460); **Tea and Sympathy**, 1956 (2461); **Tea with Mussolini**, 1999 (2462); **Teacher's Pet**, 1958 (2463); **Tears of the Sun**, 2003 (2464); **Tell Them That Willie Boy Is Here**, 1969 (2465); **The Temptress**, 1926 (2466, 2467); **10**, 1979 (2468); **The Ten Commandments**, 1923 (2469, 2470); **The Ten Commandments**, 1956 (2471, 2472, 2473); **10 Rillington Place**, 1971 (2474); **Ten Tall Men**, 1951 (2475); **Tender Is the Night**, 1962 (2476); **Tender Mercies**, 1977 (2477); **The Tender Trap**, 1956 (2478); **Tennessee Johnson**, 1942 (2479); **The Terminal**, 2004 (2480); **Terms of Endearment**, 1983 (2481, 2482); **Terror by Night**, 1946 (2483); **Tess of the Storm Country**, 1922 (2484); **Test Pilot**, 1938 (2485, 2486); **Tex**, 1982 (2487); **Texas**, 1941 (2488); **Thank You for Smoking**, 2006 (2489); **Thank Your Lucky Stars**, 1943 (2490); **Thanks a Million**, 1935 (2491); **That Evening Sun**, 2009 (2492); **That Forsyte Woman**, 1949 (2493); **That Hamilton Woman**, 1941 (2494); **That Midnight Kiss**, 1949 (2495); **That Night in Rio**, 1941 (2496); **That Touch of Mink**, 1962 (2497); **Theatre of Blood**, 1973 (2498); **Them!**, 1954 (2499, 2500); **Theodora Goes Wild**, 1936 (2501); **There Goes My Heart**, 1938 (2502); **There Was a Crooked Man**, 1970 (2503, 2504); **There Will Be Blood**, 2007 (2505, 2506); **There's No Business Like Show Business**, 1954 (2507); **There's Something About Mary**, 1998 (2508); **These Three**, 1936 (2509); **These Wilder Years**, 1956 (2510); **They Call Me Mr. Tibbs**, 1970 (2511); **They Came to Cordura**, 1959 (2512, 2513); **They Died with Their Boots On**, 1941 (2514, 2515, 2516, 2517, 2518); **They Drive by Night**, 1940 (2519, 2520); **They Knew What They Wanted**, 1940 (2521); **They Live by Night**, 1949 (2522); **They Made Me a Criminal**, 1939 (2523); **They Met in Bombay**, 1941 (2524, 2525); **They Shoot Horses, Don't They?**, 1969 (2526); **They Were Expendable**, 1945 (2527, 2528, 2529, 2530, 2531, 2532); **They Won't Believe Me**, 1947 (2533); **They Won't Forget**, 1937 (2534, 2535); **The Thief**, 1952 (2536); **Thief**, 1981 (2537, 2538); **The Thief of Bagdad**, 1924 (2539, 2540, 2541); **The Thief of Bagdad**, 1940 (2542, 2543); **The Thief of Paris**, 1967 (2544); **The Thin Man**, 1934 (2545); **The Thin Man Goes Home**, 1945 (2546); **The Thin Red Line**, 1964 (2547); **The Thin Red Line**, 1998 (2548); **The Thing from Another World**, 1951 (2549, 2550); **Things Change**, 1988 (2551); **Things to Come**, 1936 (2552); **The Third Man**, 1950 (2553, 2554, 2555, 2556); **Thirteen Days**, 2000 (2557); **13 Going on Thirty**, 2004 (2558); **13 Rue Madeleine**, 1947 (2559); **Thirteen Women**, 1932 (2560); **-30-**, 1959 (2561); **Thirty Seconds Over Tokyo**, 1944 (2562, 2563); **The 39 Steps**, 1935 (2564, 2565, 2566); **36 Hours**, 1965 (2567); **This Above All**, 1942 (2568); **This Gun for Hire**, 1942 (2569, 2570); **This Is My Affair**, 1937 (2571); **This Is the Army**, 1943 (2572); **This Is the Night**, 1932 (2573); **This Sporting Life**, 1963 (2574); **This Woman Is Dangerous**, 1952 (2575); **Thor**, 2011 (2576); **Thoroughly Modern Millie**, 1967 (2577); **Those Callaways**, 1964 (2578); **A Thousand and One Nights**, 1945 (2579); **A Thousand Clowns**, 1965 (2580); **A Thousand Years of Good Prayers**, 2008 (2581); **The Threat**, 1949 (2582); **Three Blind Mice**, 1938 (2583); **The Three Caballeros**, 1944 (2584); **Three Came Home**, 1950 (2585); **Three Coins in the Fountain**, 1954 (2586); **Three Comrades**, 1938 (2587); **Three Daring Daughters**, 1948 (2588); **Three Days of the Condor**, 1975 (2589, 2590); **Three Faces West**,

1940 (2591); **3 Godfathers**, 1948 (2592, 2593, 2594); **Three Kings**, 1999 (2595); **Three Little Words**, 1950 (2596); **Three Lives and Only One Death**, 1997 (2597); **The Three Musketeers**, 1921 (2598); **The Three Musketeers**, 1948 (2599, 2600); **The Three Musketeers**, 1993 (2601); **Three on a Match**, 1932 (2602); **3 Penny Opera**, 1931 (French version; 2603); **Three Smart Girls**, 1936 (2604); **3:10 to Yuma**, 1957 (2605); **3:10 to Yuma**, 2007 (2606); **The Thrill of It All**, 1963 (2607); **Throne of Blood**, 1961 (2608); **Through a Glass Darkly**, 1962 (2609); **Thunder in the East**, 1953 (2610); **Thunder on the Hill**, 1951 (2611); **Thunder Road**, 1958 (2612); **Thunderbirds**, 1952 (2613); **Thunderbolt and Lightfoot**, 1974 (2614); **Thunderheart**, 1992 (2615); **A Ticket to Tomahawk**, 1950 (2616); **Tiger Bay**, 1959 (2617); **Tiger Shark**, 1932 (2618); **Tigerland**, 2000 (2619); **Tight Little Island**, 1949 (2620); **Tight Shoes**, 1941 (2621); **Tightrope**, 1984 (2622); **Till the Clouds Roll By**, 1946 (2623); **Till the End of Time**, 1946 (2624); **Till We Meet Again**, 1944 (2625); **Tillie and Gus**, 1933 (2626); **Tillie's Punctured Romance**, 1914 (2627); **Time Bandits**, 1981 (2628); **Time Limit**, 1957 (2629); **The Time Machine**, 1960 (2630, 2631); **The Time Machine**, 2002 (2632); **The Time of Their Lives**, 1946 (2633); **The Time of Your Life**, 1948 (2634); **Time Regained**, 1999 (2635); **The Tin Drum**, 1980 (2636); **Tin Pan Alley**, 1940 (2637); **The Tin Star**, 1957 (2638); **Tinker Tailor Soldier Spy**, 2011 (2639); **Titanic**, 1953 (2640, 2641, 2642); **Titanic**, 1997 (2643, 2644); **The Titfield Thunderbolt**, 1953 (2645); **To Be or Not to Be**, 1942 (2646, 2647, 2648); **To Catch a Thief**, 1955 (2649, 2650); **To Each His Own**, 1946 (2651); **To Have and Have Not**, 1944 (2652, 2653, 2654); **To Hell and Back**, 1955 (2655); **To Kill a Mockingbird**, 1962 (2656, 2657); **To the Ends of the Earth**, 1948 (2658); **To the Shores of Tripoli**, 1942 (2659); **The Toast of New Orleans**, 1950 (2660); **Tobacco Road**, 1941 (2661); **Tobruk**, 1967 (2662); **Tokyo Joe**, 1949 (2663); **Tokyo Story**, 1972 (2664); **Tol'able David**, 1921 (2665); **Tom Brown of Culver**, 1932 (2666); **Tom Horn**, 1980 (2667); **Tom Jones**, 1963 (2668); **Tom Sawyer**, 1930 (2669); **Tom Sawyer**, 1973 (2670); **Tombstone**, 1993 (2671, 2672, 2673); **Tomorrow Is Forever**, 1946 (2674); **Tomorrow the World**, 1944 (2675); **Tonight and Every Night**, 1945 (2676); **Tony Rome**, 1967 (2677); **Too Hot to Handle**, 1938 (2678); **Too Late for Tears**, 1949 (2679); **Too Late the Hero**, 1970 (2680, 2681); **Too Many Husbands**, 1940 (2682); **Too Much, Too Soon**, 1958 (2683); **Tootsie**, 1982 (2684, 2685); **Top Gun**, 1986 (2686); **Top Hat**, 1935 (2687, 2688); **Topaz**, 1969 (2689, 2690, 2691); **Topkapi**, 1964 (2692); **Topper**, 1937 (2693, 2694, 2695); **Topper Returns**, 1941 (2696); **Tora! Tora! Tora!**, 1970 (2697, 2698, 2699); **Torch Song**, 1953 (2700); **Torn Curtain**, 1966 (2701); **Torpedo Run**, 1958 (2702); **Torrent**, 1926 (2703); **Tortilla Flat**, 1942 (2704); **Tortilla Soup**, 2001 (2705); **A Touch of Class**, 1973 (2706); **Touch of Evil**, 1958 (2707, 2708); **Tough Guys**, 1986 (2709); **Toward the Unknown**, 1956 (2710); **Tower of London**, 1939 (2711); **The Towering Inferno**, 1974 (2712, 2713); **Toy Story**, 1995 (2714); **Toy Story 3**, 2010 (2715); **Toy Story 2**, 1999 (2716); **Toys in the Attic**, 1963 (2717); **Trade Winds**, 1938 (2718); **Trader Horn**, 1931 (2719); **Traffic**, 2000 (2720); **Trail of the Lonesome Pine**, 1936 (2721); **Trail Street**, 1947 (2722); **The Train**, 1965 (2723, 2724); **Train of Life**, 1998 (2725); **Transformers**, 2007 (2726); **Trapeze**, 1956 (2727); **Travels with My Aunt**, 1972 (2728); **Treasure Island**, 1934 (2729, 2730); **Treasure Island**, 1950 (2731); **Treasure of the Golden Condor**, 1953 (2732); **The Treasure of the Sierra Madre**, 1948 (2733, 2734, 2735, 2736, 2737, 2738, 2739); **A Tree Grows in Brooklyn**, 1945 (2740); **The Tree of Life**, 2011 (2741); **The Trial**, 1963 (2742); **Trial and Error**, 1997 (2743); **The Trial of Joan of Arc**, 1965 (2744); **Tribute to a Bad Man**, 1956 (2745); **The Trip to Bountiful**, 1985 (2746); **Triple Cross**, 1967 (2747); **Trooper Hook**, 1957 (2748); **Trouble Along the Way**, 1953 (2749); **Trouble in Paradise**, 1932 (2750); **The Trouble with Harry**, 1955 (2751); **Troy**, 2004 (2752); **True Confessions**, 1937 (2753); **True Crime**, 1999 (2754); **True Grit**, 1969 (2755, 2756); **True Lies**, 1994 (2757); **The True Story of Lynn Stuart**, 1958 (2758); **The Truman Show**, 1998 (2759); **Tuck Everlast-**

ing, 2002 (2760); **Tucker: The Man and His Dream**, 1988 (2761); **Tumbleweeds**, 1925 (2762); **Tunes of Glory**, 1960 (2763); **The Tunnel of Love**, 1958 (2764); **The Turning Point**, 1977 (2765); **Turtle Diary**, 1986 (2766); **12 Angry Men**, 1957 (2767); **12 Monkeys**, 1995 (2768); **Twelve O'Clock High**, 1949 (2769, 2770, 2771); **Twentieth Century**, 1934 (2772); **24 Hours**, 1931 (2773); **20 Million Miles to Earth**, 1957 (2774); **20,000 Leagues Under the Sea**, 1954 (2775, 2776); **20,000 Years in Sing Sing**, 1932 (2777); **23 Paces to Baker Street**, 1956 (2778); **Twilight Zone: The Movie**, 1983 (2779); **Two Arabian Knights**, 1927 (2780); **Two Brothers**, 2004 (2781); **Two-Faced Woman**, 1941 (2782); **Two Flags West**, 1950 (2783); **Two for the Road**, 1967 (2784); **Two Girls and a Sailor**, 1944 (2785); **The Two Jakes**, 1990 (2786); **Two-Lane Blacktop**, 1971 (2787); **The Two Mrs. Carrolls**, 1947 (2788); **Two Mules for Sister Sara**, 1970 (2789); **2001: A Space Odyssey**, 1968 (2790); **Two Tickets to Broadway**, 1951 (2791); **Two Women**, 1961 (2792); **Two Years Before the Mast**, 1946 (2793); **Tycoon**, 1947 (2794);

U.S. Marshals, 1998 (2795); **Ugetsu**, 1954 (2796); **Ulysses**, 1955 (2797); **Ulzana's Raid**, 1972 (2798); **Umberto D**, 1955 (2799); **Unbreakable**, 2000 (2800); **The Umbrellas of Cherbourg**, 1964 (2801); **Uncertain Glory**, 1944 (2802); **Uncle Harry**, 1945 (2803); **Unconquered**, 1947 (2804, 2805); **The Undefeated**, 1969 (2806); **Under Fire**, 1983 (2807, 2808); **Under My Skin**, 1950 (2809); **Under Ten Flags**, 1960 (2810); **Under the Gun**, 1951 (2811); **Under the Volcano**, 1984 (2812, 2813); **Under Two Flags**, 1936 (2814); **The Undercover Man**, 1949 (2815); **Undercurrent**, 1946 (2816); **Underdog**, 2007 (2817); **Underworld**, 1927 (2818, 2819); **Unfaithfully Yours**, 1948 (2820); **The Unforgiven**, 1960 (2821); **Unforgiven**, 1992 (2822, 2823, 2824); **The Unholy Night**, 1929 (2825); **The Unholy Three**, 1925 (2826); **The Unholy Three**, 1930 (2827); **The Uninvited**, 1944 (2828, 2829); **The Uninvited**, 2009 (2830, 2831); **Union Pacific**, 1939 (2832, 2833); **Union Station**, 1950 (2834); **Unknown**, 2011 (2835); **An Unmarried Woman**, 1978 (2836); **The Unsinkable Molly Brown**, 1964 (2837); **The Untouchables**, 1987 (2838, 2839, 2840); **Up**, 2009 (2841, 2842); **Up in Arms**, 1944 (2843); **Up in Mabel's Room**, 1944 (2844); **Up in the Air**, 2009 (2845); **Up the River**, 1930 (2846); **Urban Cowboy**, 1980 (2847); **The Usual Suspects**, 1995 (2848);

The V.I.P.s, 1963 (2849); **Vabank**, 1982 (2850); **Vagabond**, 1985 (2851); **The Vagabond King**, 1956 (2852); **The Valachi Papers**, 1972 (2853); **Valdez Is Coming**, 1971 (2854); **Valkyrie**, 2008 (2855, 2856); **The Valley of Decision**, 1945 (2857); **The Valley of Gwangi**, 1969 (2858); **The Vampire Bat**, 1933 (2859); **Vampyr**, 1932 (2860, 2861); **Van Gogh**, 1991 (2862); **Van Helsing**, 2004 (2863); **Variety**, 1925 (2864, 2865); **The Velvet Touch**, 1948 (2866); **Vengeance Valley**, 1951 (2867); **The Verdict**, 1946 (2868); **The Verdict**, 1982 (2869, 2870, 2871); **Vertigo**, 1958 (2872, 2873, 2874); **The Very Thought of You**, 1944 (2875); **Victim**, 1962 (2876); **Victoria the Great**, 1937 (2877); **The Victors**, 1963 (2878, 2879); **A View from the Bridge**, 1962 (2880); **The Vikings**, 1958 (2881); **Villa Rides**, 1968 (2882); **The Violent Men**, 1955 (2883); **Violent Saturday**, 1955 (2884); **The Virgin Queen**, 1955 (2885); **The Virgin Spring**, 1960 (2886); **Virginia City**, 1940 (2887, 2888); **The Virginian**, 1929 (2889); **Viridiana**, 1962 (2890); **Virtue**, 1932 (2891); **Viva Las Vegas**, 1964 (2892); **Viva Villa!**, 1934 (2893); **Viva Zapata!**, 1952 (2894, 2895, 2896, 2897, 2898); **Vivacious Lady**, 1938 (2899); **The Voice of the Turtle**, 1947 (2900); **Von Ryan's Express**, 1965 (2901, 2902); **Voyage to the Bottom of the Sea**, 1961 (2903);

Wabash Avenue, 1950 (2904); **Wag the Dog**, 1997 (2905); **The Wages of Fear**, 1955 (2906); **Wagon Master**, 1950 (2907); **The Wagons Roll at Night**, 1941 (2908); **Wait Until Dark**, 1967 (2909); **Wake Island**, 1942 (2910, 2911, 2912, 2913); **Wake of the Red Witch**, 1949 (2914); **Wake Up and Live**, 1937 (2915); **Walk a Crooked Mile**, 1948 (2916);

Walk East on Beacon!, 1952 (2917); **A Walk in the Sun**, 1945 (2918, 2919); **A Walk on the Moon**, 1999 (2920); **Walk on the Wild Side**, 1962 (2921); **Walk Softly, Stranger**, 1950 (2922); **The Walking Dead**, 1936 (2923); **Wall Street**, 1987 (2924, 2925); **The Walls of Jericho**, 1948 (2926); **Waltz of the Toreadors**, 1962 (2927); **The War Against Mrs. Hadley**, 1942 (2928); **War and Peace**, 1956 (2929, 2930, 2931); **The War Lord**, 1965 (2932); **The War of the Roses**, 1989 (2933); **The War of the Worlds**, 1953 (2934, 2935); **The War of the Worlds**, 2005 (2936, 2937); **The War Wagon**, 1967 (2938); **Warlock**, 1959 (2939); **Warning Shot**, 1967 (2940); **Watch on the Rhine**, 1943 (2941, 2942); **Water for Elephants**, 2011 (2943); **The Water Horse: Legend of the Deep**, 2007 (2944); **Waterloo**, 1971 (2945); **Waterloo Bridge**, 1931 (2946); **Waterloo Bridge**, 1940 (2947, 2948); **Watermelon Man**, 1970 (2949); **The Way Back**, 2010 (2950); **Way Down East**, 1920 (2951); **The Way of All Flesh**, 1927 (2952); **Way Out West**, 1937 (2953); **The Way We Were**, 1972 (2954, 2955); **The Way West**, 1967 (2956); **We Bought a Zoo**, 2011 (2957); **We Dive at Dawn**, 1943 (2958); **We Live Again**, 1934 (2959); **We Were Soldiers**, 2002 (2960); **We Were Strangers**, 1949 (2961); **The Weather Man**, 2005 (2962); **The Wedding March**, 1928 (2963, 2964); **Wee Geordie**, 1956 (2965); **Wee Willie Winkie**, 1937 (2966); **Week-End at the Waldorf**, 1945 (2967); **Week-End in Havana**, 1941 (2968); **Welcome Stranger**, 1947 (2969); **Welcome to Mooseport**, 2004 (2970); **Wells Fargo**, 1937 (2971); **We're No Angels**, 1955 (2972); **Werewolf of London**, 1935 (2973); **West of Broadway**, 1931 (2974); **West of the Pecos**, 1945 (2975); **West Point Story**, 1950 (2976); **West Side Story**, 1961 (2977, 2978); **Western Union**, 1941 (2979, 2980); **The Westerner**, 1940 (2981, 2982, 2983); **Westward the Women**, 1951 (2984, 2985); **The Wet Parade**, 1932 (2986); **The Whales of August**, 1987 (2987); **What Dreams May Come**, 1998 (2988); **What Price Glory**, 1926 (2989); **What Price Glory**, 1952 (2990, 2991, 2992); **What Price Hollywood**, 1932 (2993); **What Women Want**, 2000 (2994); **Whatever Happened to Baby Jane?**, 1962 (2995); **What's Eating Gilbert Grape**, 1993 (2996); **What's Love Got to Do with It**, 1993 (2997); **What's Up, Doc?**, 1972 (2998); **When Harry Met Sally**, 1989 (2999); **When Knighthood Was in Flower**, 1922 (3000); **When Strangers Marry**, 1944 (3001); **When the Daltons Rode**, 1940 (3002); **When the Legends Die**, 1972 (3003); **When Willie Comes Marching Home**, 1950 (3004); **Where Danger Lives**, 1950 (3005); **Where Eagles Dare**, 1969 (3006, 3007, 3008); **Where the Sidewalk Ends**, 1950 (3009); **While the City Sleeps**, 1956 (3010); **Whipsaw**, 1935 (3011); **Whirlpool**, 1949 (3012, 3013): **Whispering Smith**, 1948 (3014, 3015); **The Whistle Blower**, 1987 (3016); **Whistle Stop**, 1946 (3017); **The White Angel**, 1936 (3018); **The White Buffalo**, 1977 (3019); **White Cargo**, 1942 (3020); **White Christmas**, 1954 (3021, 3022); **The White Cliffs of Dover**, 1944 (3023, 3024); **White Fang**, 1991 (3025); **White Heat**, 1949 (3026, 3027, 3028, 3029, 3030, 3031); **White Hunter Black Heart**, 1990 (3032); **White Mischief**, 1988 (3033); **White Oleander**, 2002 (3034); **The White Rose**, 1983 (3035); **White Shadows of the South Seas**, 1928 (3036); **The White Sister**, 1933 (3037); **White Squall**, 1996 (3038); **The White Tower**, 1950 (3039); **White Witch Doctor**, 1953 (3040); **Who Done It?**, 1942 (3041); **Who Framed Roger Rabbit**, 1988 (3042, 3043, 3044); **Who's Afraid of Virginia Woolf?**, 1966 (3045); **Who Was That Lady?**, 1960 (3046); **The Whole Town's Talking**, 1935 (3047, 3048); **Who'll Stop the Rain**, 1978 (3049); **Whoopee!**, 1930 (3050); **Why Be Good?**, 1929 (3051); **Wichita**, 1955 (3052); **Wicked as They Come**, 1957 (3053); **A Wicked Woman**, 1934 (3054); **Widow's Peak**, 1994 (3055); **Wife vs. Secretary**, 1936 (3056); **Wild at Heart**, 1990 (3057); **Wild Bill**, 1995 (3058, 3059); **The Wild Blue Yonder**, 1951 (3060); **Wild Boys of the Road**, 1933 (3061); **The Wild Bunch**, 1969 (3062, 3063, 3064, 3065); **Wild Harvest**, 1947 (3066); **Wild Hearts Can't Be Broken**, 1991 (3067); **The Wild North**, 1952 (3068); **The Wild One**, 1953 (3069, 3070); **Wild Orchids**, 1929 (3071); **Wild Strawberries**, 1959 (3072); **Wildrose**, 1985 (3073); **Will Penny**, 1968 (3074); **Will Success Spoil Rock Hunter?**, 1957 (3075); **Willow**, 1988 (3076); **Wil-**

son, 1944 (3077); **Win Win**, 2011 (3078); **Winchester '73**, 1950 (3079, 3080, 3081); **The Wind**, 1928 (3082); **Wind Across the Everglades**, 1958 (3083); **The Wind and the Lion**, 1975 (3084); **The Wind in the Willows**, 1997 (3085); **The Wind That Shakes the Barley**, 2007 (3086); **The Window**, 1949 (3087, 3088); **Windtalkers**, 2002 (3089); **Wing and a Prayer**, 1944 (3090, 3091); **Wings**, 1927 (3092, 3093, 3094); **The Wings of Eagles**, 1957 (3095); **Wings of the Morning**, 1937 (3096); **Winner Take All**, 1932 (3097); **The Winning of Barbara Worth**, 1926 (3098); **The Winning Team**, 1952 (3099); **The Winslow Boy**, 1950 (3100); **The Winter Guest**, 1997 (3101); **Winterset**, 1936 (3102); **The Witches of Eastwick**, 1987 (3103, 3104); **With a Song in My Heart**, 1952 (3105); **Without Love**, 1945 (3106); **Without Reservations**, 1946 (3107, 3108); **Witness**, 1985 (3109); **Witness for the Prosecution**, 1957 (3110, 3111, 3112, 3113); **The Wizard of Oz**, 1939 (3114, 3115, 3116, 3117, 3118, 3119); **Wolf**, 1994 (3120); **The Wolf Man**, 1941 (3121, 3122); **Wolf Song**, 1929 (3123); **The Wolfman**, 2010 (3124); **The Woman I Love**, 1937 (3125); **The Woman in Green**, 1945 (3126); **The Woman in the Window**, 1944 (3127, 3128); **The Woman in White**, 1948 (3129); **A Woman of Affairs**, 1928 (3130); **The Woman of the Town**, 1943 (3131); **Woman of the Year**, 1942 (3132, 3133, 3134); **The Woman on Pier 13**, 1949 (3135); **The Woman on the Beach**, 1947 (3136); **A Woman Under the Influence**, 1974 (3137); **A Woman's Face**, 1941 (3138, 3139); **Woman's World**, 1954 (3140); **The Women**, 1939 (3141, 3142); **Wonder Man**, 1945 (3143, 3144); **The Wonderful Country**, 1959 (3145); **Words and Music**, 1948 (3146); **Working Girl**, 1988 (3147); **The World in His Arms**, 1952 (3148, 3149); **The World Is Not Enough**, 1999 (3150); **The World of Henry Orient**, 1964 (3151); **The World's Fastest Indian**, 2005 (3152); **The Wreck of the Mary Deare**, 1959 (3153); **The Wrestler**, 2008 (3154); **Written on the Wind**, 1956 (3155, 3156); **The Wrong Box**, 1966 (3157); **The Wrong Man**, 1956 (3158, 3159); **Wuthering Heights**, 1939 (3160, 3161, 3162, 3163); **Wyatt Earp**, 1994 (3164, 3165, 3166); **Wyoming**, 1940 (3167);

X-Men, 2000 (3168); **X-Men; First Class**, 2011 (3169); **X2: X-Men United**, 2003 (3170);

A Yank at Oxford, 1938 (3171); **A Yank in the R.A.F.**, 1941 (3172, 3173); **Yankee Doodle Dandy**, 1942 (3174, 3175, 3176, 3177); **The Year My Voice Broke**, 1987 (3178); **The Year of Living Dangerously**, 1982 (3179); **The Year of the Dragon**, 1985 (3180); **The Yearling**, 1946 (3181); **The Yellow Balloon**, 1953 (3182); **Yellow Canary**, 1944 (3183); **Yellow Jack**, 1938 (3184); **Yellow Sky**, 1948 (3185, 3186, 3187); **Yesterday, Today and Tomorrow**, 1964 (3188); **Yesterday's Enemy**, 1959 (3189); **Yojimbo**, 1961 (3190); **You and Me**, 1938 (3191); **You Can Count on Me**, 2000 (3192); **You Can't Cheat an Honest Man**, 1939 (3193); **You Can't Get Away with Murder**, 1939 (3194); **You Can't Have Everything**, 1937 (3195); **You Can't Take It With You**, 1938 (3196, 3197); **You Gotta Stay Happy**, 1948 (3198); **You Only Live Once**, 1937 (3199); **You Were Never Lovelier**, 1942 (3200); **You'll Like My Mother**, 1972 (3201); **You Will Meet a Tall Dark Stranger**, 2010 (3202); **Young and Innocent**, 1938 (3203); **Young at Heart**, 1954 (3204); **Young Bess**, 1953 (3205); **Young Cassidy**, 1965 (3206); **Young Dr. Kildare**, 1938 (3207); **Young Frankenstein**, 1974 (3208, 3209, 3210); **Young Guns**, 1988 (3211); **Young Guns II**, 1990 (3212); **The Young in Heart**, 1938 (3213); **The Young Lions**, 1958 (3214, 3215, 3216); **Young Man with a Horn**, 1950 (3217, 3218); **Young Mr. Lincoln**, 1939 (3219, 3220, 3221, 3222); **Young People**, 1940 (3223); **The Young Philadelphians**, 1959 (3224); **Young Sherlock Holmes**, 1985 (3225); **The Young Victoria**, 2009 (3226, 3227); **Young Winston**, 1972 (3228); **Your Cheatin' Heart**, 1964 (3229); **You're in the Navy Now**, 1951 (3230); **You're Telling Me!**, 1934 (3231); **You've Got Mail**, 1998 (3232);

Z, 1969 (3233); **Zathura: A Space Adventure**, 2005 (3234); **Zelig**, 1985 (3235); **Ziegfeld Follies**, 1945 (3236; 3237); **Zodiac**, 2007 (3238); **Zorba the Greek**, 1964 (3239, 3240); **Zulu**, 1964 (3241, 3242);

2012-2015 Films: **Act of Valor**, 2012 (3244, 3245, 3246, 3247); **American Hustle**, 2013 (3248); **American Sniper**, 2015 (3249); **Amour (Love)**, 2012 (3250); **Anna Karenina**, 2012 (3251); **Argo**, 2012 (3252, 3253); **The Artist**, 2012 (3254, 3255, 3256); **Beasts of the Southern Wild**, 2012 (3257, 3258, 3259); **The Best Exotic Marigold Hotel**, 2012 (3260, 3261, 3262, 3263, 3264, 3265); **The Bourne Legacy**, 2012 (3266, 3267, 3268); **Brave**, 2012 (3269, 3270, 3271, 3272); **Cloud Atlas**, 2012 (3273, 3274, 3275, 3276, 3277, 3278); **The Counselor**, 2013 (3279); **Dallas Buyers Club**, 2013 (3280); **The Dark Knight Rises**, 2012 (3281, 3282, 3283); **Divergent**, 2014 (3284); **Django Unchained**, 2012 (3285); **Don Jon**, 2013 (3286); **Drift**, 2013 (3287); **Dr. Seuss' The Lorax**, 2012 (3288, 3289); **Dumb and Dumber To**, 2014 (3290); **Edge of Tomorrow**, 2014 (3291); **Elysium**, 2013 (3292); **The Equalizer**, 2014 (3293); **Escape Plan**, 2013 (3294); **Ex Machina**, 2015 (2395); **Exodus: Gods and Kings**, 2014 (3296); **The Fitzgerald Family Christmas**, 2012 (3297); **Flight**, 2012 (3298, 3299, 3300, 3301); **Frankenweenie**, 2012 (3302, 3303, 3304, 3305); **Free Men**, 2012 (3306); **Furious Seven**, 2015 (3307); **Fury**, 2014 (3308); **Gangster Squad**, 2013 (3309); **Godzilla**, 2014 (3310, 3311, 3312, 3313); **The Grand Budapest Hotel**, 2014 (3314); **Gravity**, 2013 (3315); **The Great Gatsby**, 2013 (3316); **The Hobbit: An Unexpected Journey**, 2012 (3317, 3318, 3319, 3320); **Hope Springs**, 2012 (3321); **Horns**, 2013 (3322); **Hotel Transylvania**, 2012 (3323); **The Hunger Games**, 2012 (3224, 3225); **Hyde Park on the Hudson**, 2012 (3326); **Ice Age: Continental Drift**, 2012 (3327); **The Imitation Game**, 2014 (3328); **The Impossible**, 2012 (3329, 3330, 3331); **The Intouchables**, 2012 (3332, 3333, 3334); **Jack Reacher**, 2012 (3335, 3336); **John Carter**, 2012 (3337, 3338, 3339); **The Kid with a Bike**, 2012 (3340); **Killing Them Softly**, 2012 (3341); **La Rafle**, 2012 (3342); **Lawless**, 2012 (3343, 3344, 3345); **Les Miserables**, 2012 (3346, 3347); **Life of Pi**, 2012 (3348); **Lincoln**, 2012 (3349, 3350, 3351, 3352, 3353); **Lone Survivor**, 2013 (3354); **The Longest Ride**, 2015 (3355); **Mad Max: Fury Road**, 2015 (3356); **The Master**, 2012 (3357, 3358, 3359, 3360, 3361); **Men in Black 3**, 2012 (3362); **Mission Impossible—Rogue Nation**, 2015 (3363); **Mr. Holmes**, 2015 (3364); **Moonrise Kingdom**, 2012 (3365, 3366, 3367, 3368, 3369, 3370); **Night Moves**, 2013 (3371); **Oblivion**, 2013 (3372); **Olympus Has Fallen**, 2013 (3373); **OMG: Oh My God**, 2012 (3374); **The Perks of Being a Wallflower**, 2012 (3375, 3376, 3377, 3378, 3379, 3380); **The Pirates! Band of Misfits**, 2012 (3381, 3382, 3383, 3384); **Pitch Perfect**, 2012 (3385, 3386, 3387); **Robot and Frank**, 2012 (3388, 3389, 3390); **A Royal Affair**, 2012 (3391); **Rust and Bone**, 2012 (3392, 3393); **The Second Best Exotic Marigold Hotel**, 2015 (3394); **The Secret World of Arietty**, 2012 (3395); **Seeking a Friend for the End of the World**, 2012 (3396, 3397); **Silver Linings Playbook**, 2012 (3398); **Skyfall**, 2012 (3399, 3400); **Snow White and the Huntsman**, 2012 (3401, 3402); **Southpaw**, 2015 (3403); **Sparkle**, 2012 (3404, 3405, 3406); **Stand Up Guys**, 2012 (3407); **Step Up Revolution**, 2012 (3408, 3409); **Taken 2**, 2012 (3410, 3411); **Ted**, 2012 (3412, 3413, 3414); **The Theory of Everything**, 2014 (3415); **Trouble with the Curve**, 2012 (3416, 3417, 3418); **The Turin Horse**, 2012 (3419, 3420); **The Two Faces of January**, 2014 (3421); **Unbroken**, 2014 (3422); **Veronica Mars**, 2014 (3423); **Wanderlust**, 2012 (3424, 3425, 3426, 3427); **The Well-Digger's Daughter**, 2012 (3428); **Where Do We Go Now?**, 2012 (3429, 3430); **The Wise Kids**, 2012 (3431, 3432); **The Wolf of Wall Street**, 2013 (3433); **The Wolverine**, 2013 (3434); **The World's End**, 2013 (3435); **Zero Dark Thirty**, 2012 (3436);

Fictional Persons Index: **The Adventures of Baron Munchausen**, 1989 (3471, 3523); **The Adventures of Pinocchio**, 1996 (3488, 3510); **The Adventures of Robin Hood**, 1938 (3502); **The Adventures of Tom Sawyer**, 1938 (3493); **Alice in Wonderland**, 2010 (3522); **Anna**

SUBJECT INDEX

Note: Titles shown in boldface within this anecdotal index represent films reviewed in this work; other entries include theatrically released films, serials, made-for-TV films; TV miniseries and series. No documentaries or made-for-video films are included in this compilation, which, as is the case with all other indices within this work, has been handcrafted by the author.

Acrobats (acrobatic dancing; acrobatics; circus performers): Absolute Beginners, 1986; The Accidental Spy, 2001; **Adam's Rib**, 1949; Adios Sabata, 1970; The Adventures of Prince Achmed, 1926; **An American in Paris**, 1951; American Ninja 5, 1993; Anerican Ninja 3: Blood Hunt, 1989; American Ninja 2: The Confrontation, 1987; **Anchors Aweigh**, 1945; Andrei Rublev, 1983; **Arabian Nights**, 1942; Armour of God, 1986; Around a Small Mountain, 2009; **Around the World in 80 Days**, 1956; Around the World in 80 Days, 1989 (TV miniseries); At the Circus, 1939; **Batman Forever**, 1995; Bear's Kiss, 2002; Beowulf, 1999; Behind the Sun, 2001; The Big Circus, 1959; Big Top Pee-Wee, 1988; Billy Rose's Jumbo, 1962; The Blood of Jesus, 1941; The Blue Bird, 1976; Border Outlaws, 1940; Breaking and Entering, 2006; **Brigadoon**, 1954; Bright Lights, 1935; Call Out the Marines, 1942; Captain America, 1990; Carolina Blues, 1944; Catwoman, 2004; **The Circus**, 1928; **Circus World**, 1964; City Hunter, 1993; **Cleopatra**, 1934; **Closely Watched Trains**, 1967; Cop Out, 2010; **Coraline**, 2009; Cosi, 1986; **The Crimson Pirate**, 1952; **Daddy Long Legs**, 1955; Daredevils of Kung Fu, 1979; Daredevils of the Red Circle, 1939; The Divine Lady, 1929; Dragons Forever, 1988; Epic Movie, 2007; Farewell My Concubine, 1993; Fixer Dugan, 1939; **The Flame and the Arrow**, 1950; The Flame of New Orleans, 1941; **Freaks**, 1932; **A Funny Thing Happened on the Way to the Forum**, 1966; Gals, Incorporated, 1943; Ginger Meggs, 1982; Give a Girl a Break, 1953; Gorilla at Large, 1954; **The Great Profile**, 1940; **The Great Train Robbery**, 1979; The Great Wallendas, 1978 (made-for-TV); **The Greatest Show on Earth**, 1952; Gun Crazy, 1950; Hercules Against the Barbarians, 1964; Here Come the Girls, 1953; Here Comes Cookie, 1935; **The Hindenburg**, 1975; **Hook**, 1991; The Horde, 2012; **The Hunchback of Notre Dame**, 1923; **The Hunchback of Notre Dame**, 1939; **Idiot's Delight**, 1939; **The Illusionist**, 2010; Island of Fire, 1990; **It's Always Fair Weather**, 1955; **Jacquot de Nantes**, 1993; Judex, 1966; **Julia Misbehaves**, 1948; The King and the Clown, 2005; King of the Carnival, 1955; The King's Pirate, 1967; K-20: The Fiend With Twenty Faces, 2008; **La Strada**, 1956; **La Vie en Rose**, 2007; The Last Circus, 2010; The Legend, 1993; The Legend II, 1993; The Legend of Drunken Master, 2000; The Little Adventuress, 1938; Living on Love, 1937; Loose Ankles, 1930; Lost in a Harem, 1944; The Lovers on the Bridge, 1991; Man Is Not a Bird, 1972; **Man on a Tightrope**, 1953; **The Man Who Laughs**, 1928; Maniac, 1980; The Medallion, 2003; Merry Andrew, 1958; Miracles: Mr. Canton and Lady Rose, 1989; Mirrormask, 2005; Mr. Nice Guy, 1997; **Mrs. Wiggs and the Cabbage Patch**, 1934; My Mother's Courage, 1996; Never Weaken, 1921; Nine Days a Queen, 1936; **1900**, 1977; **Ocean's Eleven**, 2001; **On the Town**, 1949; One from the Heart, 1981; One Hundred and One Nights, 1999; **The Pirate**, 1948; Police Academy: Mission to Moscow, 1994; Police Story 3: Supercop, 1992; Polly of the Circus, 1917; Polly of the Circus, 1932; Priest, 2011; Project A, 1983; Project A 2, 1987; The Protector, 1985; Psycho-Circus, 1967; Rain or Shine, 1930; Red Barry, 1938; The Return of Sabata, 1971; Sabata, 1969; **Sally of the Sawdust**, 1925; The Scorpion King: Rise of a Warrior, 2008; **Seven Brides for Seven Brothers**, 1954; Shalimar, 1978; **The Silver Chalice**, 1954; **Singin' in the Rain**, 1952; Slaves in Bondage, 1937; Small Town Girl, 1953; **State Fair**, 1933; **The Story of Three Loves**, 1953; Supercop 2, 1993; **Take Me Out to the Ball Game**, 1949; A Tale of Five Women, 1952; Thank You, Mr. Moto, 1937; **Thirteen Women**, 1932; **The 39 Steps**, 1935; The 39 Steps, 1959;

Thoroughly Modern Millie, 1967; **Thousands Cheer**, 1943; Three Avengers, 1979; **The Three Musketeers**, 1948; To Please a Lady, 1950; **Topkapi**, 1964; The Touch, 2003; **Trapeze**, 1956; Trigger, Jr., 1950; Troopers Three, 1930; Twin Dragons, 1999; Under the Top, 1919; **Vatel**, 2000; **Victor/Victoria**, 1982; **The War of the Roses**, 1989; Wheels on Meals, 1984; When Night Is Falling, 1995; **White Palms**, 2007; You Never Know Women, 1926.

Acrophobia (fear of heights, often wrongly called vertigo; as well as vertigo, which afflicts persons with dizziness who perceive usually a spinning motion due to dysfunction of the vestibular system): The Andromeda Strain, 2008 (TV miniseries); Animal, 1977; **Antz**, 1998; Baby's Day Out, 1994; **The Barefoot Executive**, 1971; The Brave Little Toaster, 1987; The Children of the Century, 1999; **Cliffhanger**, 1993; Continental Divide, 1981; Deewana Mastana, 1997; Dick Francis: Twice Shy, 1989 (made-for-TV); **Divergent**, 2014; Don't Look Down, 1998 (made-for-TV); Driving In, 1990; Empire Falls, 2005 (made-for-TV); Enduring Love, 2004; Evil Under the Sun, 1982; The Face of Fear, 1990 (made-for-TV); Fear of Heights, 1994; **Flame Over India**, 1960; Futureworld, 1976; **Hero**, 1992; **High Anxiety**, 1977; High Lane, 2009; A History of Violence, 2005; Horatio Hornblower: Retribution, 2001 (made-for-TV); The In-Laws, 2003; **Jack the Giant Slayer**, 2013; **Journey to the Center of the Earth**, 1959; Le chanteur de Mexico, 1956; The Legend of Lylah Clare, 1968; A Likely Story, 1947; **The Mad Miss Manton**, 1938; Matador, 1986; The Meteor Man, 1993; The Night the World Exploded, 1957; Open Your Eyes, 1997; OSS 117: Lost in Rio, 2009; The Pagemaster, 1994; Passengers, 2008; Patchwork Family, 2014; Planes, 2013; Police Academy: Mission to Moscow, 1994; **The Reluctant Astronaut**, 1967; Samba, 2014; Steel, 1979; **Stolen Hours**, 1963; **Switching Channels**, 1988; Three Dancing Slaves, 2004; **Thunder Birds**, 1942; **Topkapi**, 1964; Up, Down, Fragile, 1995; **Vanila Sky**, 2001; **Vertigo**, 1958; **White Squall**, 1996; **The Winning Team**, 1952.

Adoption (also see Homeless Children; Orphanages and Orphans, this index): **Abandoned**, 1949; The Abandoned, 2007; Admission, 2013; Adoption, 1975; Adoption, 1979; Anne of Green Gables, 1919; Anne of Green Gables, 1934; Anne of Green Gables, 1952 (TV series); Anne of Green Gables, 1956 (made-for-TV); Anne of Green Gables, 1958 (made-for-TV); Anne of Green Gables, 1972 (TV miniseries); Anne of Green Gables, 1979 (TV series); Anne of Green Gables, 1985 (TV miniseries); **Annie**, 1982; **Annie Get Your Gun**, 1950; **Another Thin Man**, 1939; Arthur 2: On the Rocks, 1988; **Auntie Mame**, 1958; **Ben-Hur: A Tale of the Christ**, 1925; **Ben-Hur**, 1959; Babe, 1995; Baby Boom, 1987; **Bachelor Mother**, 1939; Big Daddy, 1999; The Bigamist, 1953; The Blind Side, 2009; **Blossoms in the Dust**, 1941; **Bombshell**, 1933; Born to Be Bad, 1934; **The Boys from Brazil**, 1978; **Boys Town**, 1938; Bride Flight, 2010; **Bright Eyes**, 1934; Buck Privates Come Home, 1947; Butter, 2011; **Caged**, 1950; **Captain January**, 1936; **Casanova Brown**, 1944; Cass, 2008; **The Cider House Rules**, 1999; Clean Shaven, 1995; **The Corn Is Green**, 1945; **The County Chairman**, 1935; **The Curious Case of Benjamin Button**, 2008; **Daddy Long Legs**, 1919; **Daddy Long Legs**, 1931; **Daddy Long Legs**, 1955; December Boys, 2007; Despicable Me, 2010; **Dimples**, 1936; **Dr. Zhivago**, 1965; Flirting with Disaster, 1996; For Keeps?, 1998; Forbidden, 1932; 40 Pounds of Trouble, 1962; The Glass House, 2001; **The Glenn Miller Story**, 1954; **Georgy Girl**, 1966; Great Expectations, 1917; Great Expectations, 1934; **Great Expectations**, 1946; Great Expectations, 1998; Great Expectations, 2012; Great Expectations, 2013; **The Great Lie**, 1941; Heaven's Prisoners, 1996; **Hook**, 1991; I Could Go on Singing, 1963; **The Inn of the Sixth Happiness**, 1958; **Johnny Belinda**, 1948; **Journey for Margaret**, 1942; Juno, 2007; **The Last Gangster**, 1937; **The Last of the Mohicans**, 1992; Leila, 1999; **Lilo and Stitch**, 2002; **Little Miss Marker**, 1934; Little Miss Marker, 1980; Little Secrets, 2001; **Man of Steel**, 2013; **Manhattan Melodrama**, 1934; Martian Child, 2007; Matilda, 1996; **Men of Boys Town**, 1941; **Mighty Aphrodite**, 1996; Mommie

Dearest, 1981; October Baby, 2011; **The Old Maid**, 1939; **The Omen**, 1976; One Good Cop, 1991; Orphan, 2009; **Penny Serenade**, 1941; **Peter Pan**, 1953; Peter Pan, 2003; **Pollyanna**, 1920; **Pollyanna**, 1960; **The Prince of Egypt**, 1998; Problem Child, 1990; **Raising Arizona**, 1987; Relative Strangers, 2006; **Room for One More**, 1952; **Second Best**, 1994; **The Silver Chalice**, 1954; A Simple Twist of Fate, 1994; Smart People, 2008; **Stella Maris**, 1918; **Stuart Little**, 1999; **Superman**, 1978; **Tarzan**, 1999; **The Ten Commandments**, 1956; **That Certain Woman**, 1937; Then She Found Me, 2008; **There Will Be Blood**, 2007; **Thief**, 1981; 3 Men and a Baby, 1987; **To Each His Own**, 1946; **Tom Jones**, 1963; **Tomorrow the World**, 1944; **The Truman Show**, 1998; **The Tunnel of Love**, 1958; **The Unforgiven**, 1960; Welcome Home, Roxy Carmichael, 1990; **Winning**, 1969; **Woman of the Year**, 1942; **Wuthering Heights**, 1939; Wuthering Heights, 1971; Wuthering Heights, 1992; Wuthering Heights, 2011; **Yours, Mine and Ours**, 1968; Yours, Mine & Ours, 2005.

Advertising Agencies: According to Spencer, 2001; Agency, 1981; Artists and Models, 1937; Beauty for the Asking, 1939; Being Nice, 2014; Bewitched, 1964-1972 (TV series); Bosom Buddies, 1980-1982 (TV series); Bounce, 2000; Branded, 2012; The Circle, 1970; Confessions of a Sociopathic Social Climber, 2005 (made-for-TV); Crazy People, 1990; The Days, 2004- (TV series); Definitely, Maybe, 2008; Derailed, 2005; Distracted, 1970; Doin' the Town, 1941; Elvis Has Left the Building, 2004; The Ex, 2006; **A Face in the Crowd**, 1957; Fancy Dancing, 2002; **Good Neighbor Sam**, 1964; **Good Night, and Good Luck**, 2005; **H.M. Pulham, Esq.**, 1941; Happiness Never Comes Along, 2012; How to Get Ahead in Advertising, 1989; Howl, 2010; **The Hucksters**, 1947; The Human Contact, 2008; I Want to Get Married, 2011; A Job to Kill For, 2006 (made-for-TV); **Kate & Leopold**, 2001; The Last Kiss, 2006; **Laura**, 1944; Live!, 2007; The Long Weekend, 2006; **Lost in America**, 1985; Loulou, 1980; Mad Men, 2007-2015 (made-for-TV); Madison Avenue, 1961; Marjorie Morningstar, 1958; Me and My Girl, 1984-1988 (TV series); **Melancholia**, 2011; Melody Lane, 1941; **A Merry War**, 1998; Million Dollar Murder, 2005 (made-for-TV); **Mr. Blandings Builds His Dream House**, 1948; Ned and Stacey, 1995-1997 (TV series); **No**, 2012; **North by Northwest**, 1959; Oh Happy Day, 2007; Old Dogs, 2009; One Way, 2006; Passkey to Danger, 1946; Perfect Stranger, 2007; Private Road, 1973; Putney Swope, 1969; Sweetheart of the Fleet, 1942; Syrup, 2013; A Taste of Success, 1983; They Want to Marry, 1947; **Three Cases of Murder**, 1955; 388 Arletta Avenue, 2012; Viktor Vogel – Commercial Man, 2001; What to Do in Case of Fire, 2002; Weekend for Three, 1941; **Wicked as They Come**, 1956; **Will Success Spoil Rock Hunter?**, 1957; The Woman in Red, 1984.

Afterlife: **Abbott and Costello Meet Frankenstein**, 1948; **The Adding Machine**, 1969; The Adventures of Mark Twain, 1985; **After Life**, 1998; **Alias Nick Beal**, 1949; **All Dogs Go to Heaven**, 1989; **All Dogs Go to Heaven 2**, 1996; All of Me, 1984; Always, 1989; **Angel on My Shoulder**, 1946; **Angels in the Outfield**, 1951; **Angels in the Outfield**, 1994; **Barabbas**, 1962; **Beetlejuice**, 1988; **Between Two Worlds**, 1944; Beyond Tomorrow, 1940; Blackbeard's Ghost, 1968; **Bram Stoker's Dracula**, 1992; **Cabin in the Sky**, 1943; **The Canterville Ghost**, 1944; **Carousel**, 1956; **Chances Are**, 1989; Charly, 2002; **A Christmas Carol**, 1938; **A Christmas Carol**, 1951; The Cockeyed Miracle, 1946; The Crow, 1990; **Damn Yankees**, 1958; Death Becomes Her, 1992; **Death Takes a Holiday**, 1934; Defending Your Life, 1991; **The Devil and Daniel Webster**, 1941; The Devil Commands, 1941; **Dracula**, 1931; **Dracula: Dead and Loving It**, 1995; **Dracula Has Risen from the Grave**, 1969; **Dracula: Prince of Darkness**, 1966; Dragonfly, 2002; **8½**, 1963; The Egyptian, 1954; Flatliners, 1990; Ghost, 1990; **The Ghost and Mrs. Muir**, 1947; **The Ghost Goes West**, 1936; Ghost Town, 2008; **Ghostbusters**, 1984; **Ghostbusters II**, 1989; **Gladiator**, 2000; **The Greatest Story Ever Told**, 1965; **The Green

Pastures**, 1936; **A Guy Named Joe**, 1943; **Harvey**, 1950; **Heaven Can Wait**, 1943; **Heaven Can Wait**, 1978; Heaven Only Knows, 1947; The Heavenly Kid, 1985; **Hercules**, 1997; **Here Comes Mr. Jordan**, 1941; Hereafter, 2010; **The Horn Blows at Midnight**, 1945; **Horror of Dracula**, 1958; **House of Dracula**, 1945; **House of Frankenstein**, 1944; **I Married a Witch**, 1942; **The Illusionist**, 2006; In Between, 1991; **It's a Wonderful Life**, 1946; **Jesus Christ Superstar**, 1973; Just Like Heaven, 2005; **The King of Kings**, 1927; **King of Kings**, 1961; Kiss Me Goodbye, 1982; Liliom, 1930; **Liliom**, 1935; A Little Bit of Heaven, 2012; Look Both Ways, 2005; Lovelorn, 2011; The Lovely Bones, 2010; Made in Heaven, 1987; Meet Joe Black, 1998; **Michael**, 1996; **Miracle in the Rain**, 1956; **The Miracle of Our Lady of Fatima**, 1952; **The Mummy**, 1932; **The Mummy**, 1999; **The Mummy Returns**, 2001; **The Mummy: Tomb of the Dragon Emperor**, 2008; **The Mummy's Hand**, 1940; My Life, 1993; **Nosferatu**, 1922; **Nosferatu the Vampyre**, 1979; **Oh, God!**, 1977; **The Omen**, 1976; **On Borrowed Time**, 1939; **Outward Bound**, 1930; **Poltergeist**, 1982; **Pirates of the Caribbean: At World's End**, 2007; **Portrait of Jennie**, 1949; Resurrection, 1980; **The Robe**, 1953; The Return of Peter Grimm, 1935; **The Scoundrel**, 1935; **Scrooge**, 1970; **The Seventh Seal**, 1958; **The Sixth Sense**, 1999; Sodom and Gomorrah, 1963; **Somewhere in Time**, 1980; **The Song of Bernadette**, 1943; **Stairway to Heaven**, 1947; **Stir of Echoes**, 1999; **Supernatural**, 1933; **Tales from the Crypt**, 1972; **The Ten Commandments**, 1923; **The Ten Commandments**, 1956; **The Time of Their Lives**, 1946; **Topper**, 1937; **Topper Returns**, 1941; **Topper Takes a Trip**, 1939; **The Uninvited**, 1944; **The Uninvited**, 2009; **Van Helsing**, 2004; **Vanilla Sky**, 2001; **What Dreams May Come**, 1998; **The Witches of Eastwick**, 1987; **You Never Can Tell**, 1951.

Aircraft Carriers: Act of Valor, 2012; **Air Force**, 1943 (WWII); **Apollo 13**, 1995; **The Avengers**, 2012; Battle of the Coral Sea, 1959 (WWII; USS *Lexington*, CV-2; USS *Yorktown*, CV-5); Battleship, 2012; Behind Enemy Lines, 2001(Kosovo Campaign of 1999); **Between Heaven and Hell**, 1956 (WWII); **Bombardier**, 1943 (WWII; USS *Hornet*, CV-8); **The Bridges at Toko-Ri**, 1954 (Korean War; USS *Oriskany*, CV-34); **The Caine Mutiny**, 1954 (WWII; USS *Kearsarge*, CV-33); **Captain Phillips**, 2013; **Crimson Tide**, 1995; **The Deer Hunter**, 1978 (Vietnam War); **Destination Tokyo**, 1943 (WWII; USS *Hornet*, CV-8); **Dive Bomber**, 1941 (pre-WWII; USS *Enterprise*, CV-6); **The Eternal Sea**, 1955 (WWII; USS *Princeton*, CV-37); The Final Countdown, 1980 (WWII; USS *Nimitz*, CVN-68); **Flat Top**, 1952 (Korean War; USS *Princeton*, CV-37); **Flight Command**, 1940 (pre-WWII; USS *Enterprise*, CV-6); The Flight of the Intruder, 1991 (Vietnam War; USS *Independence*, CV-61); The Flyboys, 2008; Freedom Strike, 1998; **The Gallant Hours**, 1960 (WWII); **Godzilla**, 2014; **A Guy Named Joe**, 1943 (WWII; mythical German aircraft carrier); Hell Divers, 1931 (1930s; USS *Saratoga*, CV-3); **Here Come the Waves**, 1944; **Hot Shots!**, 1991; I Am Legend, 2007; **Men of the Fighting Lady**, 1954 (Korean War; USS *Oriskany*, CV-34); Midway (WWII; USS *Enterprise*, CV-6; USS *Hornet*, CV-8; USS *Yorktown*, CV-5); **A Mighty Heart**, 2007; **Olympus Has Fallen**, 2013; **Operation Pacific**, 1951 (WWII); **Our Man Flint**, 1966; **Pacific Rim**, 2013; **Pearl Harbor**, 2001 (WWII; USS *Hornet*, CV-8); **The Purple Heart**, 1944 (WWII; USS *Hornet*, CV-8); **Rescue Dawn**, 2007; **The Right Stuff**, 1983; Rules of Engagement, 2000; **Sink the Bismarck!**, 1960 (WWII; HMS *Ark Royal*, 91); Supercarrier, 1988 (TV series); **Task Force**, 1949 (pre-WWII and WWII; USS *Enterprise*, CV-6; USS *Franklin*, CV-13; USS *Hornet*, CV-8; USS *Langley*, CV-1; USS *Saratoga*, CV-3; USS *Yorktown*, CV-5); **Tears of the Sun**, 2003; **Thirty Seconds Over Tokyo**, 1944 (WWII; USS *Hornet*; CV-8); Top Gun, 1986 (Vietnam War); **Torpedo Run**, 1958 (WWII); **Tora! Tora! Tora!**, 1970 (WWII; Japanese carriers; USS *Hornet*, CV-8); **Transformers**, 2007; **The Wind Rises**, 2014; **Wing and a Prayer**, 1944 (WWII; USS *Yorktown*, CV-10, representing the original *Yorktown*, CV-5); **World War Z**, 2013; **Zero

Dark Thirty, 2012.

Airplanes (bomber; also see Aviators; Pilots; Survival Films, this index): **Above and Beyond**, 1953 (U.S. B-29); **Air Force**, 1943 (U.S. B-17); **Battle of Britain**, 1969 (German Dornier, Heinkel and Junker); Beautiful Dreamer, 2006 (U.S. B-17); **The Best Years of Our Lives**, 1946 (U.S. B-17); Black Book, 2006 (U.S. B-17); **Bombardier**, 1943 (U.S. B-17); Bombers B-52, 1957; **Catch-22**, 1970 (U.S. B-24 Liberator); **Command Decision**, 1948 (U.S. B-17); **Desperate Journey**, 1942 (British Wellington); **Destination Tokyo**, 1943 (U.S. B-25; Japanese seaplane bombers); **Dr. Strangelove**, 1964 (U.S. B-52); Flying Fortress, 1942 (U.S. B-17); Forever Young, 1992 (U.S. B-24); Hiroshima, 1995 (made-for-TV; U.S. B-29); International Lady, 1941 (U.S. B-17); **Johnny in the Clouds** (aka: The Way to the Stars), 1945 (U.S. B-17); **Memphis Belle**, 1990 (U.S. B-17); Missing Jane, 2004 (U.S. B-17); **One of Our Aircraft Is Missing**, 1942 (British Wellington); **Passage to Marseille**, 1944 (German seaplane bombers; French bombers); **Pearl Harbor**, 2001 (U.S. B-25); Red Tails, 2012 (WWII; U.S. B-17); **633 Squadron**, 1964 (British Mosquito); **Strategic Air Command**, 1955 (U.S. B-36; U.S. B-47); **Thirty Seconds Over Tokyo**, 1944 (U.S. B-25); **Tora! Tora! Tora!**, 1970 (U.S. B-17); Torpedo Bombers, 1983 (Soviet bombers); **Twelve O'Clock High**, 1949 (U.S. B-17); **The War Lover**, 1962 (U.S. B-17); We'll Meet Again, 1982 (TV miniseries; U.S. B-17); **The Wild Blue Yonder**, 1951 (U.S. B-29).

Airplanes (charter; also see Aviators; Pilots; Survival Films, this index): **Armored Car Robbery**, 1950; **The Bride Came C.O.D.**, 1941; Bulldog Drummond's Peril, 1938; Catch Me...I'm in Love, 2011; Green Light, 1937; High Explosive, 1943; High Road to China, 1983; **It's a Mad, Mad, Mad, Mad World**, 1963; Johnny Comes Flying Home, 1946; **Six Days Seven Nights**, 1998; Slaughterhouse-Five, 1972; **Tokyo Joe**, 1949.

Airplanes (commercial; passenger; also see Aviators; Pilots; Survival Films, this index): **Absolute Quiet**, 1936; **Alive**, 1993; **Airplane!**, 1980; Airplane II: The Sequel, 1982; Airport, 1970; Airport, 1978 (made-for-TV); Airport, 1996 (TV series); Airport 1975, 1974; Airport '77, 1977; **The Aviator**, 2004; Back from Eternity, 1956; Back to the Beach, 1987; Bridesmaids, 2011; **The Carpetbaggers**, 1964; **Casablanca**, 1942; **Ceiling Zero**, 1936; China Clipper, 1936; Code of the Secret Service, 1939; The Concorde ...Airport '79, 1979; The Crowded Sky, 1960; **Executive Decision**, 1996; Five Came Back, 1939; **Flight**, 2012; Flightplan, 2005; **Flying Tigers**, 1942; **The French Connection**, 1971; Ground Control, 1998; **The High and the Mighty**, 1954; **How to Marry a Millionaire**, 1953; **JFK**, 1991; Judgement in Berlin, 1988; The Langoliers, 1995 (TV miniseries); Left Behind, 2014; **Lost Horizon**, 1937; Lost Horizon, 1973; The Mark, 2012; Mimino, 1977 (helicopter passenger service); **Never Give a Sucker an Even Break**, 1941 (with sleeping berths); Night Plane from Chungking, 1943; **No Highway in the Sky**, 1951; Non-Stop, 2014; **Notorious**, 1946; Operation Thunderbolt, 1978 (raid at Entebbe); Panic Button, 2011; **Phone Call from a Stranger**, 1952; Raid on Entebbe, 1976 (made-for-TV); Red Eye, 2005; Secret Service of the Air, 1939; Sky Liner, 1949; **The Steel Trap**, 1952; Stewardess School, 1986; Stolen Holiday, 1937; 13 Hours by Air, 1936; Tomorrow at Seven, 1933; **Travels With My Aunt**, 1972; Turbulence, 1997; Turbulence 2: Fear of Flying, 1999; **Twilight Zone: The Movie**, 1983; The Very Private Life of Mr. Sim, 2015; View from the Top, 2003; **Wild Tales**, 2014; **Will Success Spoil Rock Hunter?**, 1957 (with sleeping berths); **You Gotta Stay Happy**, 1948; Zero Hour!, 1957.

Airplanes (experimental; also see Aviators; Pilots; Survival Films, this index): The Accidental Hero, 2002 (made-for-TV); **Amelia,** 2009; The Arrow, 1997 (made-for-TV); **The Aviator**, 2004; The Bamboo Saucer, 1968; Batman, 1943 (serial and feature); Beyond the Time Barrier, 1960;

The Blue Max, 1966; **Breaking the Sound Barrier**, 1952; **Ceiling Zero**, 1936; Central Airport, 1933; **Chain Lightning**, 1950; Crimson Romance, 1934; Decision Against Time, 1957; **Dive Bomber**, 1941; Emergency Landing, 1941; Flying Wild, 1941; **Forever Young**, 1992; Green Lantern, 2011; Happy Landing, 1934; House on Haunted Hill, 1959; Jet Job, 1952; King of the Texas Rangers, 1941; Lady Bodyguard, 1943; The Man in the Sky, 1957; **The McConnell Story**, 1955; Men Against the Sky, 1940; Nick Carter, Master Detective, 1939; **Operation Crossbow**, 1965; **The Right Stuff**, 1983; Satellite in the Sky, 1956; Sky Raiders, 1941; The Sound Barrier, 1952; Space, 1985 (TV miniseries); **Space Cowboys**, 2000; Speed Wings, 1934; **Spitfire**, 1942; **Test Pilot**, 1938; **Tobor the Great**, 1954; **Toward the Unknown**, 1956; Wings of the Navy, 1939; X-15, 1961.

Airplanes (fighter; also see Aviators; Pilots; Survival Films, this index): **Ace of Aces**, 1933 (WWI); **Aces High**, 1977 (WWI); **Bataan**, 1943 (WWII); **Battle of Britain**, 1969 (WWII; British Spitfire; British Hurricane); Battleship, 2012 (space); Behind Enemy Lines, 2001 (Bosnia); **The Blue Max**, 1966 (WWI); **The Bridges at Toko-Ri**, 1954 (Korean War; U.S. Navy jet fighters); Dark Blue Yonder, 2001 (WWII; Czechs flying in the R.A.F.; British Spitfire; British Hurricane); **The Dawn Patrol**, 1930 (WWI); **The Dawn Patrol**, 1938 (WWI); Der Stern von Afrika, 1957 (WWII; German fighter planes); **The Eagle and the Hawk**, 1933 (WWI); **Eagle Squadron**, 1942 (WWII; British Spitfire; British Hurricane); The Eternal Zero, 2013 (WWII; Japanese fighter plane); **Fighter Squadron**, 1948 (WWII; U.S. P-47); The Final Countdown, 1980 (WWII; U.S. Navy fighter planes); **Firefox**, 1982 (Cold War; Soviet jet fighter planes); **Flat Top**, 1952 (Korean War; U.S. Navy fighter planes); **Flyboys**, 2008 (WWI); **Flying Tigers**, 1942 (WWII; U.S. P-40); **God Is My Co-Pilot**, 1945 (WWII; U.S. P-40); **The Guns of Navarone**, 1961 (German Luftwaffe fighter planes); **Hell's Angels**, 1930 (WWI); The Hunters, 1958 (Korean War; F-86 Saber Jets); Lafayette Escadrille, 1958 (WWI); L'equipage, 1938 (WWI); **Lilac Time**, 1928 (WWI); Men Must Fight, 1933 (WWI); **Men of the Fighting Lady**, 1954 (Korean War; U.S. Navy jet fighters); **Midway**, 1976 (WWII U.S. Navy fighter planes); **1941**, 1979 (WWII; U.S. P-40); Only Old Men Are Going to Battle, 1974 (WWII; Soviet fighter planes); Pan, 2015 (space); Red Tails, 2012 (WWII; P-40; P-51 Mustang); **Saving Private Ryan**, 1998 (WWII; P-51 Mustang); Sky Fighters, 2005 (French Mirage 2000); **Star Wars: Episode V—The Empire Strikes Back**, 1980 (space); **Star Wars: Episode IV—A New Hope**, 1977 (space); **Star Wars: Episode I—The Phantom Menace**, 1999 (space); **Star Wars: Episode VI—Return of the Jedi**, 1983 (space); **Star Wars: Episode III—Revenge of the Sith**, 2005 (space); **Star Wars: Episode II—The Attack of the Clones**, 2002 (space); **Star Wars: The Clone Wars**, 2008 (space); **Star Wars: The Force Awakens**, 2015 (space); **Task Force**, 1949 (WWII; U.S. Navy fighter planes); The Tuskegee Airmen, 1995 (made-for-TV; WWII; P-40; P-51 Mustang); **Twelve O'Clock High**, 1949 (WWII; German Luftwaffe fighter planes); **Von Richthofen and Brown**, 1971 (WWI); **Wings**, 1927 (WWI); **The Woman I Love**, 1937 (WWI); **A Yank in the R.A.F.**, 1941 (WWII; British Spitfire).

Airplanes (freight, transport; also see Aviators; Pilots; Survival Films, this index); **Air Mail**, 1932; The Big Lift, 1950; **Captains of the Clouds**, 1942; Cast Away, 2000; Flight from Glory, 1937; **Flight of the Phoenix**, 1965; Flight of the Phoenix, 2004; **Force 10 from Navarone**, 1978; **Island in the Sky**, 1953; Johnny Comes Flying Home, 1946; **Night Flight**, 1933; **Only Angels Have Wings**, 1939; **The Spirit of St. Louis**, 1957 (U.S. Air Mail); **The Thing from Another World**, 1951; Tokyo Joe, 1949.

Airplanes (private; also see Aviators; Pilots; Survival Films, this index): **Air Force One**, 1997; **Here Comes Mr. Jordan**, 1941; **It's a Mad, Mad, Mad, Mad World**, 1963.

Alcoholics and Alcoholism: Aberdeen, 2001; **Across the Pacific**, 1942; **The African Queen**, 1951; **Ah, Wilderness!**, 1935; Airport 1975, 1974; **All Fall Down**, 1962; All or Nothing, 2002; All Over the Guy, 2001; **American Heart**, 1993; **Anatomy of a Murder**, 1959; Angela's Ashes, 1999; **Anna Christie**, 1931; **Arthur**, 1981; **The Bad and the Beautiful**, 1952; **The Bad News Bears**, 1976; **Barfly**, 1987; **The Beachcomber**, 1938; **Beloved Infidel**, 1959; **The Best Years of Our Lives**, 1946; Beyond the Limit, 1983; **The Big Carnival**, 1951; **The Big Knife**, 1955; **Black Angel**, 1946; The Bottom of the Bottle, 1956; **The Boxer**, 1997; Brideshead Revisited, 2008; **Broken Blossoms**, 1919; **Bullets Over Broadway**, 1994; **Bulworth**, 1998; **Cat on a Hot Tin Roof**, 1958; **Catherine the Great**, 1934; **City Lights**, 1931; Clean and Sober, 1988; **The Clown**, 1953; **Come Back, Little Sheba**, 1952; **Come Fill the Cup**, 1951; The Comic, 1969; **Coney Island**, 1943; **Corrina, Corrina**, 1994; **Corsair**, 1931; **The Country Girl**, 1954; **Crazy Heart**, 2009; **The Crowd Roars**, 1932; **The Crowd Roars**, 1938; Cutter's Way, 1981; **Days of Wine and Roses**, 1962; **Easy Rider**, 1969; **El Dorado**, 1967; **Elephant Walk**, 1954; **The Entertainer**, 1960; **The Fallen Sparrow**, 1943; Flight, 2012; The Forbidden Street, 1949; **48 Hours**, 1982; **The Foxes of Harrow**, 1947; **The Fugitive Kind**, 1960; The Goddess, 1958; **The Great Ziegfeld**, 1936; Green Light, 1937; **Harvey**, 1950; **Heaven Can Wait**, 1943; **The Helen Morgan Story**, 1957; **Hoosiers**, 1986; **Hud**, 1963; **I Walked with a Zombie**, 1943; **I'll Cry Tomorrow**, 1955; Ironweed, 1987; Jack Slade, 1953; Jealousy, 1945; **Jim Thorpe—All American**, 1951; **The Joker Is Wild**, 1957; **Kongo**, 1932; **Leaving Las Vegas**, 1995; **The Legend of Bagger Vance**, 2000; **Long Day's Journey into Night**, 1962; **The Lost Weekend**, 1945; A Love Song for Bobby Long, 2004; **Lullaby of Broadway**, 1951; **The Man Who Fell to Earth**, 1976; **My Dream Is Yours**, 1949; **My Favorite Year**, 1982; A New Kind of Love, 1963; **The Night of the Hunter**, 1955; The Night of the Iguana, 1964; **Nightmare Alley**, 1947; **Nixon**, 1995; **No Down Payment**, 1957; **One True Thing**, 1998; **A Patch of Blue**, 1965; **The People Against O'Hara**, 1951; **Pollock**, 2000; The Principal, 1987; The Racketeer, 1929; **The Rains Came**, 1939; **The Rains of Ranchipur**, 1955; **Reckless**, 1935; Repeat Performance, 1947; **Rio Bravo**, 1959; **The Road to Glory**, 1936; **The Roaring Twenties**, 1939; **Rooster Cogburn**, 1975; **The Roots of Heaven**, 1958; **The Rose**, 1979; **'Round Midnight**, 1986; The Rum Diary, 2011; The Russia House, 1990; **The Servant**, 1964; **Shadows**, 1959; Slap Shot, 1977; **Smash-Up: The Story of a Woman**, 1947; **Some Came Running**, 1958; **The Sound and the Fury**, 1959; **Stagecoach**, 1939; **A Star Is Born**, 1937; **A Star Is Born**, 1954; A Star Is Born, 1976; **State's Attorney**, 1932; **Sling Blade**, 1996; **The Struggle**, 1931; **Summer Holiday**, 1948; **The Sun Also Rises**, 1957; **Tales of Terror**, 1962; **Tender Is the Night**, 1962; **Tender Mercies**, 1983; **Them!**, 1954; **There Will Be Blood**, 2007; **Time Without Pity**, 1957; **Too Much, Too Soon**, 1958; **A Tree Grows in Brooklyn**, 1945; **The Two Jakes**, 1990; **Two Weeks in Another Town**, 1962; **Under Capricorn**, 1949; **Under the Volcano**, 1984; **The Verdict**, 1982; **W.C. Fields and Me**, 1976; **Wabash Avenue**, 1950; **A Wedding**, 1978; **West of Broadway**, 1931; **The Wet Parade**, 1932; Where Love Has Gone, 1964; White Shadows in the South Seas, 1928; **Who's Afraid of Virginia Woolf?**, 1966; **The Wild One**, 1953; **Wind Across the Everglades**, 1958; The Winning Season, 2009; **Written on the Wind**, 1956; **Wuthering Heights**, 1939; **Young Man with a Horn**, 1950; **The Young Philadelphians**, 1959.

Aliens (invading or visiting Earth): **The Abyss**, 1989; **The Arrival**, 1996; Battlefield Earth, 2000; Buck Rogers, 1939 (serial); **Close Encounters of the Third Kind**, 1977; **The Day the Earth Stood Still**, 1951; **The Day the Earth Stood Still**, 2008; The Earth Dies Screaming, 1964; Earth vs. the Flying Saucers, 1956; End of the World, 1977; Frankenstein Meets the Space Monster, 1965; Gog, 1954; I Married a Monster from Outer Space, 1958; **Invaders from Mars**, 1953; The Invasion, 2007; **Invasion of the Body Snatchers**, 1956; **Invasion of the Body Snatchers**, 1978; Invasion of the Saucer Men, 1957; Invasion of the Star Creatures, 1962; It Came from Outer Space, 1953; Kronos, 1957; The Magnetic Monster, 1953; The Man from Planet X, 1951; **Mars Attacks!**, 1998; The Mysterians, 1957; Robot Monster, 1953; The Space Children, 1958; Target Earth, 1954; **The Thing**, 1982; The Thing from Another World, 1951; **This Island Earth**, 1955; **20 Million Miles to Earth**, 1957; The 27th Day, 1957; **War of the Worlds**, 1953; **War of the Worlds**, 2005;

Amnesia (loss of memory): The Accidental Hero, 2002 (made-for-TV); **The Addams Family**, 1991; **The Adventures of Baron Munchausen**, 1989; Agatha, 1979; Agatha Christie: A Life in Pictures, 2004 (made-for-TV); **Agnes of God**, 1985; Akira, 1988; All Around the Town, 2002 (made-for-TV); Aloha Oe, 1915; Amateur, 1995; American Dreamer, 1984; American Ninja, 1985; Amnesia, 1994; Amnesia, 1997; Amnesia, 2002; Amnesia, 2004 (made-for-TV); **Anastasia**, 1956; Anastasia, 1967 (made-for-TV); Anastasia, 1997; Anastasia: The Mystery of Anna, 1986 (made-for-TV); Angel Eyes, 2001; Angel Heart, 1987; Another Woman, 1994 (made-for-TV); Apart, 2011; Apocrypha, 2011; Archangel, 1991; **As You Desire Me**, 1932; Autumn, 1916; Ave Maria, 1918; The Awakening of Candra, 1983 (made-for-TV); **Away from Her**, 2007; The Back Trail, 1924; **Beautiful Creatures**, 2013; Beautiful Dreamer, 2006; Beautiful Memories, 2003; Bed and Breakfast, 1992; **Before I Go to Sleep**, 2014; Before I Hang, 1940; Beneath Western Skies, 1944; Beware My Lovely, 1952; The Bird People in China, 1998; **Black Angel**, 1946; The Black Box, 2005; Black Crown, 1951; Blackout, 1996 (made-for-TV); Blackout, 2008; **Blind Alley**, 1939; Blind Horizon, 2004; **The Blue Dahlia**, 1946; Body and Soul, 1915; The Bourne Identity, 1988 (made-for-TV); **The Bourne Identity**, 2002; The Bourne Supremacy, 2004; Boys, 1996; A Bride's Silence, 1917; The Brighton Strangler, 1945; Buck Rogers, 1977; The Buffalo Son, 2009; The Bumblebee Flies Anyway, 2000; Buried, 2010; By Berwin Banks, 1920; Called Back, 1933; Calling Dr. Gillespie, 1942; Captain Midnight, 1942; **Caravan**, 1946; The Catman of Paris, 1946; Chain of Evidence, 1957; **Charlie Chan at the Opera**, 1936; Chrysalis, 2008; **The Chase**, 1946; The City of Lost Children, 1995; Clean Slate, 1994; Code Name: The Cleaner, 2007; **Conspiracy Theory**, 1997; **The Constant Husband**, 1955; **Courage of Lassie**, 1946; Crime Doctor, 1943; Crime Doctor's Manhunt, 1946; The Crooked Way, 1949; **Crossroads**, 1942; Cure, 2001; Cypher, 2002; Dangerous Intrigue, 1936; Dangerous Moonlight, 1942; Dangerously They Live, 1941; Dark City, 1998; **The Dark Past**, 1948; The Dark Room, 1999 (made-for-TV); The Dark Room, 2006; Dazzle, 1999; Dead Again, 1991; Deadline at Dawn, 1946; Deadly Messages, 1985 (made-for-TV); The Dead Pit, 1989; Death by Hanging, 1971; Delirious, 1991; Desire and Hell at Sunset Motel, 1991; Desperate Escape, 2010 (made-for-TV); Desperately Seeking Susan, 1985; Diaboliquement votre, 1967; Dr. Gillespie's New Assistant, 1942; **A Double Life**, 1947; Driftwood, 1997; Eden Log, 2007; The Element of Crime, 1984; **The English Patient**, 1996; Experiment, 2008; Eyes of Texas, 1948; Facing Windows, 2003; Fall In, 1942; Fallen, 2004 (made-for-TV); Falling for You, 1995 (made-for-TV); False Identity, 1990; The Far Frontier, 1948; The Fifth Patient, 2007; 50 First Dates, 2004; The Fighting Sheriff, 1925; Final Approach, 1991; The Flag Lieutenant, 1919; Footlights and Shadows, 1920; For the Term of His Natural Life, 1929; The Forger of London, 1961; The Forgotten, 2004; The Fourth Man, 2007; Frankenstein's Daughter, 1958; Fugue State, 2008; A Gamble with Hearts, 1923; Gangbusters Kung-Fu, 1983; Garden of Lies, 1915; Garrison's Finish, 1923; The Gathering, 2003; A Gentleman of Quality, 1919; Ginger, 1935; The Girl and the Millionaire, 1965; Girl from Nowhere, 1919; The Goat, 1985; God of Gamblers, 1989; Good Bye Lenin!, 2003; The Gorgon, 1965; **The Great Dictator**, 1940; The Great White Trail, 1917; The Groundstar Conspiracy, 1972; Gypsy Angels, 1980; **Hallelujah, I'm a Bum!**, 1933; Hana and Alice, 2004; The Hangover, 2009; Hardwired, 2009; Hellhole, 1985; Here Come the Coeds, 1945; **High Wall**, 1947; Hornblower: Mutiny, 2001 (made-for-TV);

Hot Sauce, 1997; How to Make a Monster, 1958; **The Howling**, 1981; I Am the Cheese, 1983; I Know Who You Are, 2001; **I Love You Again**, 1940; Identity Unknown, 1945; The Imp, 1919; **Impact**, 1949; In the Shadow of Evil, 1995 (made-for-TV); Inferno, 2000; Into the Arms of Strangers, 2007; The Invisible Man's Revenge, 1944; The Island of Surprise, 1916; Istanbul, 1957; Jab Tak Hai Jaan, 2012; The Jacket, 2005; Jackie Chan's Who Am I?, 1998; Jane Doe, 1983 (made-for-TV); Jericho Mansions, 2004; Jigsaw, 1968; John Forrest Finds Himself, 1920; Johnny Mnemonic, 1995; Journal of a Crime, 1934; Judy Forgot, 1915; The Key to Yesterday, 1914; Killers 2: The Beast, 2002; Kisses for Breakfast, 1941; Kitty, 1929; The Kovak Box, 2006; The Lady Forgets, 1989 (made-for-TV); Laid to Rest, 2009; Landslide, 1992; Lapse of Memory, 1992; L'assassino... e al telefono, 1972; Last Rites, 1999 (made-for-TV); **Libel**, 1959; Lightning in a Bottle, 1998; **A Little Princess**, 1995; The Long Kiss Goodnight, 1996; **The Long Wait**, 1954; Looking for Miguel, 2007; Lost Honeymoon, 1947; **Love Letters**, 1945; Love Without Question, 1920; Luminous Motion, 1998; **Madonna of the Seven Moons**, 1946; A Maid of Belgium, 1917; The Majestic, 2001; The Man Called Noon, 1973; The Man from Left Field, 1993 (made-for-TV); Man in the Dark, 1953; The Man in the Road, 1957; The Man Who Forgot, 1919; The Man Who Lost Himself, 2005; The Man Who Won, 1919; The Man Without a Past, 2002; Man Without Memory, 1984; **Marnie**, 1964; Married to a Stranger, 1997 (made-for-TV); The Matrimonial Bed, 1930; The Mayor of Filbert, 1919; Mean Creek, 2004; **Meet Me After the Show**, 1951; Memories of a Murder, 1990 (made-for-TV); Memories of Midnight, 1991 (made-for-TV); The Memory, 2006; **Men in Black**, 1997; **Men in Black II**, 2002; Mindstorm, 2001; **Mirage**, 1965; Mist in the Valley, 1923; **Mr. Arkadin**, 1962; Mister Buddwing, 1966; A Modern Cain, 1921; Monster on Campus, 1958; Moondram Pirai, 1982; The Morning After, 1986; MugShot, 1996; **Muholland Dr.**, 2001; Mummy's Boys, 1936; The Mummy's Curse, 1944; **The Muppets Take Manhattan**, 1984; **Murder!**, 1930; Murder by Night, 1989; **Murder on Monday**, 1953; My Amnesia Girl, 2010; The Net, 1923; Never Forget, 2008; New York November, 2011; The Next One, 1984; The Night Before, 1988; **Nightmare**, 1956; Nightmare Street, 1998 (made-for-TV); **Nosferatu: The Vampire**, 1979; One Exciting Weekend, 1946; One Man Justice, 1937; One True Love, 2008; The Other Woman, 1921; The Other Side of Midnight, 1977; Out, 1982; Out for Blood, 1993; Out of Nowhere, 1997 (made-for-TV); Overboard, 1987; P.J., 2008; **Paris, Texas**, 1984; Patsy, 2008; The Pawn, 2010; Paycheck, 2003; Pig, 2011; **Possessed**, 1947; The Price of Power, 1916; Primal Fear, 1996; Project X, 1968; A Pure Formality, 1995; Pure Luck, 1991; Red Lob, 1990; Regarding Henry, 1991; Remember?, 1939; Return of the Lash, 1947; The Road to Hong Kong, 1962; **Random Harvest**, 1942; Rascals, 1938; The Red Squirrel, 1993; Resident Evil, 2002; Resurrected, 1989; The Return of the Soldier, 1985; The Right of Way, 1931; The Road to Broadway, 1926; **RoboCop**, 1987; Roma, Citta Liberia, 1946; Rose Red, 2002 (TV miniseries); Run a Crooked Mile, 1969 (made-for-TV); Sadma, 1983; Sailaab, 1990; Santa Who?, 2000 (made-for-TV); Satanic, 2006; The Satin Girl, 1923; The Scarf, 1951; The Sea, 2003; Second Nature, 2003 (made-for-TV); Second Skin, 2000; The Secret Adversary, 1983 (made-for-TV); See Jane Run, 1995 (made-for-TV); The Sender, 1982; Sessions of the Mind, 2008; The 7th Commandment, 1961; **Shadow on the Wall**, 1950; Shadowplay, 2007; Shadows of the Past, 1991; Shattered, 1991; Shock, 1934; Shock, 1946; The Sign of the Poppy, 1916; The Sin That Was His, 1920; The Skywayman, 1920; A Sleeping Memory, 1917; Sleepwalker, 1998; Slightly Dangerous, 1943; **The Snake Pit**, 1948; Snow 2: Brain Freeze, 2008; So This Is Washington, 1943; Sod Sisters, 1969; **Somewhere in the Night**, 1946; Sound of My Voice, 2011; Southland Tales, 2007; **Spellbound**, 1945; Spider-Man 3, 2007; **Star Trek: The Search for Spock**, 1984; State of Mind, 2003 (made-for-TV); Stragglers, 2004; The Straight Way, 1916; The Strange Awakening, 1960; Strange Experiment, 1937; The Stranger, 1987; The Stranger Came Home, 1954; Stranger in My Bed, 1987 (made-for-TV); Stranger in the Family, 1991 (made-for-

TV); A Stranger to Love, 1996 (made-for-TV); Street of Chance, 1942; Street of Memories, 1940; **Suddenly, Last Summer**, 1959; **Sullivan's Travels**, 1941; Sunday, 2008; **Sundays and Cybele**, 1962; The Sundown Trail, 1919; Surf, 1949; The Survivor, 1981; Suture, 1993; Sweet Dreams, 1996 (made-for-TV); A Tale of Five Cities, 1952; A Tale of Two Sisters, 2003; **Tenebre**, 1987; Terminal City Ricochet, 1990; There Goes the Groom, 1937; **The Thief of Bagdad**, 1940; **36 Hours**, 1965; Three Live Ghosts, 1936; The Three Lives of Karen, 1997 (made-for-TV); Through Stormy Waters, 1920; Ticket to Paradise, 1936; Time Burst: The Final Alliance, 1989; Timebomb, 1991; Tomie, 1999; **Total Recall**, 1990; Total Recall, 2012; Trance, 2013; Trauma, 1962; Tropical Love, 1921; Trumpet Island, 1920; The Truth About Layla, 2009; Two in the Dark, 1936; Two O'Clock Courage, 1945; The UFO Incident, 1975 (made-for-TV); **Ulysses**, 1955; Unico in the Island of Magic, 1983; Universal Soldier: Regeneration, 2009; Unknown, 2006; **Unknown**, 2011; **The Unsuspected**, 1947; An Unusual Love, 2000; Up in the World, 1956; Upside Down, 2012; The Usurper, 1919; The Vampire, 1957; Vanilla Sky, 2001; Vengeance, 2010; Versus, 2002; A Very Brady Sequel, 1996; Violence, 1947; Vital, 205; Vive la France!, 1918; Voice in the Wind, 1944; **The Walking Dead**, 1926; War of the Worlds, 1988 (TV series); Welcome to Blood City, 1977; What Shall I Do?, 1924; The Wheel of Destiny, 1927; When the Lights Go On Again, 1944; Where I Live, 1947; While You Were Sleeping, 1995; The White Cat, 1950; With a Vengeance, 1992 (made-for-TV); **Without Love**, 1945; Wolves of the Range, 1943; **The Woman in Green**, 1945; Woman to Woman, 1934; The Woman with No Name, 1951; A Woman's Devotion, 1956; Women and Gold, 1925; Women in the Mirror, 2002; Wrecked, 2010; **X-Men**, 2000; **X2**, 2003; **X-Men Origins: Wolverine**, 2009; Yellow Fin, 1951; Yesterday's Target, 1996.

Anti-Communism: Assignment: Paris, 1952; Arctic Flight, 1952; Avalanche Express, 1979; Big Jim McLain, 1952; Billion Dollar Brain, 1967; A Bullet for Joey, 1955; Captain Scarface, 1953; Counterspy Meets Scotland Yard, 1950; **The Deadly Affair**, 1967; **Die Another Day**, 2002; **Diplomatic Courier**, 1952; **Dr. Strangelove**, 1964; The Double, 2011; The Double Man, 1968; The Fearmakers, 1958; The Falcon and the Snowman, 1985; Family of Spies, 1990 (made-for-TV); 5 Steps to Danger, 1957; Foreign Intrigue, 1956; The Fourth Protocol, 1987; **From Russia with Love**, 1964; **Funeral in Berlin**, 1966; The Girl in the Kremlin, 1957; Hell and High Water, 1954; High Treason, 1952; The Hunter, 1952 (TV series); **I Was a Communist for the F.B.I.**, 1951; Invasion U.S.A., 1952; Invasion U.S.A., 1985; **The Ipcress File**, 1965; **The Iron Curtain**, 1948; Jet Attack, 1958; The Jigsaw Man, 1984; The Journey, 1959; **The Kremlin Letter**, 1970; License to Kill, 1989; The Looking Glass War, 1970; The Mackintosh Man, 1973; **Man on a Tightrope**, 1953; **The Manchurian Candidate**, 1962; The Manchurian Candidate, 2004; **My Son John**, 1952; **Night People**, 1954; **Pickup on South Street**, 1952; Rambo: First Blood Part II, 1985; Rambo III, 1988; Red Dawn, 1984; Red Dawn, 2012; The Red Menace, 1949; Red Scorpion, 1989; **Salt**, 2010; Satan Never Sleeps, 1962; Security Risk, 1954; Shack Out on 101, 1955; Spies Like Us, 1985; **The Spy Who Came in from the Cold**, 1965; **The Spy Who Loved Me**, 1977; The Russia House, 1990; **The Thief**, 1952; Topaz, 1969; **Torn Curtain**, 1966; Trial, 1955; **Walk a Crooked Mile**, 1948; **Walk East on Beacon!**, 1952; The Whip Hand, 1951; **The Whistle Blower**, 1987; **The Woman on Pier 13**, 1949.

Anti-Semitism (hatred or prejudice against Jews or the Hebrew religion): Adventureland, 2009; Aimee & Jaguar, 1999; American History X, 1998; **An American Tail**, 1986; Anne Frank: The Whole Story, 2001 (TV miniseries); **Annie Hall**, 1977; Apt Pupil, 1998; Au revoir les infants, 1987; **Auntie Mame**, 1958; **Barton Fink**, 1991; **The Battleship Potemkin**, 1925; The Believer, 2001; **Ben Hur: A Tale of the Christ**, 1925; **Ben-Hur**, 1959; Betrayed, 1988; **Biloxi Blues**, 1988; The Black Dahlia, 2006; The Book of Esther, 2013; **The Boy in the Striped Pa-**

jamas, 2008; **Bugsy**, 1991; The Bunker, 1981 (made-for-TV); **Cabaret**, 1972; **The Cardinal**, 1963; The Chamber, 1996; Chaplin, 1992; **Chariots of Fire**, 1981; **Cimarron**, 1931; **Commandos Strike at Dawn**, 1942; Conspiracy, 2001 (made-for-TV); **The Counterfeit Traitor**, 1962; **The Counterfeiters**, 2008; The Courageous Heart of Irena Sendler, 2009 (made-for-TV); Crossfire, 1947; **The Damned**, 1969; Dancing on the Edge, 2013 (TV miniseries); Defiance, 2008; The Delta Force, 1986; Delta of Venus, 1995; The Devil's Arithmetic, 1999 (made-for-TV); **Diary of a Chambermaid**, 1946; **Diary of a Chambermaid**, 1964; Diary of a Chambermaid, 2015; **The Diary of Anne Frank**, 1959; The Dictator, 2012; **Downfall**, 2004; **Driving Miss Daisy**, 1989; **An Education**, 2009; Eichmann, 2007; **Europa Europa**, 1991; Everything Is Illuminated, 2005; Evil, 2003; **Exodus**, 1960; **Exodus: Gods and Kings**, 2014; **Fateless**, 2005; Fatherland, 1994 (made-for-TV); **Fiddler on the Roof**, 1971; Focus, 2001; From Hell, 2001; **Gentleman's Agreement**, 1947; **The Girl with the Dragon Tattoo**, 2011; **The Golem**, 1937; **The Golem: How He Came Into the World**, 1921; Good, 2008; **Gran Torino**, 2008; **Grand Illusion**, 1938; **The Great Dictator**, 1940; **Hangmen Also Die**, 1943; Higher Learning, 1995; **The Hitler Gang**, 1944; Hitler: The Rise of Evil, 2003 (TV miniseries); **Hitler's Madman**, 1943; Holocaust, 1978 (TV miniseries); Homicide, 1991; I Love You, I Love You Not, 1996; **Ida**, 2013; The Infidel, 2010; Inglourious Basterds, 2009; Invincible, 2001; **Is Paris Burning?**, 1966; It Runs in the Family, 2003; **Ivanhoe**, 1952; Ivanhoe, 1982 (made-for-TV); Ivanhoe, 1997 (TV miniseries); Jack the Ripper, 1988 (TV series); **The Juggler**, 1953; **Junebug**, 2005; The Kennedys, 2011 (TV miniseries); The Last Supper, 1995; The Last Train, 2006; Liberty Heights, 1999; **The Life of Emile Zola**, 1937; **Love and Death**, 1975; **The Loved One**, 1965; Mad Men, 2007-2015 (TV series); **The Man in the Glass Booth**, 1975; The Man Who Cried, 2000; Max, 2002; The Meaning of Life, 1983; **The Merchant of Venice**, 2004; **A Mighty Heart**, 2007; **Mississippi Burning**, 1988; **Morituri**, 1965; **The Mortal Storm**, 1940; Mother Night, 1996; Mrs. Henderson Presents, 2005; **Murder by Decree**, 1979; Music Box, 1989; Naked Among Wolves, 2015 (made-for-TV); The Notebook, 2013; One Night with the King, 2006; Paris 36, 2008; The Passion of Christ, 2004; **The People vs. Fritz Bauer**, 2015; **The Pianist**, 2002; Porky's, 1981; Postal, 2007; Pretty Persuasion, 2005; **Quiz Show**, 1994; The Real Blonde, 1997; **The Remains of the Day**, 1993; RKO 281, 1999 (made-for-TV); **Saving Private Ryan**, 1998; **Schindler's List**, 1993; School Ties, 1992; **Shadows and Fog**, 1992; **Ship of Fools**, 1965; A Single Man, 2009; **Sophie Scholl: The Final Days**, 2006; **The Stranger**, 1946; Suite Francaise, 2014; **Sunshine**, 2000; Swing Kids, 1993; **Swing Vote**, 2008; **Sword in the Desert**, 1949; Tart, 2001; **Ted**, 2012; **The Ten Commandments**, 1923; **The Ten Commandments**, 1956; Therese, 2012; **36 Hours**, 1965; **Twilight Zone: The Movie**, 1983; **The Two Jakes**, 1990; Voyage of the Damned, 1976; Where the Truth Lies, 2005; **The White Countess**, 2005; **White Hunter Black Heart**, 1990; The Winds of War, 1983 (TV miniseries); **The Young Lions**, 1958; **Z**, 1969.

Archeologists: Adventures of Captain Marvel, 1941 (serial); The Awakening, 1980; The Beautiful Somewhere, 2006; **Boy on a Dolphin**, 1957; **Charlie Chan in Egypt**, 1935; Charlie Chan's Murder Cruise, 1940; The Curse of King Tut's Tomb, 2006 (made-for-TV); Dig, 2015; Drums of Fu Manchu, 1940; The Feathered Serpent, 1948; The Fifth Element, 1997; **Five Graves to Cairo**, 1943; The Flying Serpent, 1946; The Gathering, 2003; Ghosts of Mars, 2001; The Golden Mask, 1953; **Golden Salamander**, 1950; Heavy Metal, 1981; The Hound of the Baskervilles, 1988 (made-for-TV); **I Live My Life**, 1935; **Indiana Jones and the Kingdom of the Crystal Skull**, 2008; **Indiana Jones and the Last Crusade**, 1989; **Indiana Jones and the Temple of Doom**, 1984; Lara Croft; Tomb Raider, 2001; Lara Croft Tomb Raider: The Cradle of Life, 2003; The Long Shadow, 1992; Lost City of the Jungle, 1946; The Lovers, 1958; The Man from Earth, 2007; Mr. Moto Takes a Vacation, 1939; **The Mummy**, 1932; Mummy's Boys, 1936; **The Mummy's Hand**, 1940; The Mummy's Shroud, 1967; The Mummy's Tomb, 1942; **One Million B.C.**, 1940; **Pardon My Sarong**, 1942; Pandora and the Flying Dutchman, 1951; Paradise Lost, 1999; Pascali's Island, 1988; Phantom of Chinatown, 1940; Pharaoh's Curse, 1957; Prisoners of the Sun, 2013; **Pursuit to Algiers**, 1945; The Pyramid, 2014; **Raiders of the Lost Ark**, 1981; **The Riders of the Whistling Skull**, 1937; The Royal Tenenbaums, 2001; Secret of the Incas, 1954; Suicide Squad, 2016; Tarzan and the Amazons, 1945; **Tea with Mussolini**, 1999; Terry and the Pirates, 1940 (serial); That Man from Rio, 1964; Time Walker, 1982; The White Orchid, 1954.

Armored Cars: The Adventures of the Masked Phantom, 1939; Akira, 1988; Alex Rider: Operation Stormbreaker, 2006; Alien Outpost, 2014; The Alpha Caper, 1973 (made-for-TV); **The Amazing Spider-Man 2**, 2014; American Ninja, 1985; **American Sniper**, 2014; Analyze That, 2002; Armed and Dangerous, 1986; Armored, 2009; Armored Car, 1937; **Armored Car Robbery**, 1950; The Aura, 2005; Babylon A.D., 2008; Batman, 1943; **Batman Begins**, 2005; **Batman Forever**, 1995; Behind the Headlines, 1937; Bethune: The Making of a Hero, 1990; Beverly Hills Cop II, 1987; The Big Chase, 1954; Blueprint for Robbery, 1961; **Bonnie and Clyde**, 1967; The Book of Eli, 2010; Born Reckless, 1937; **Brazil**, 1985; Brick Mansions, 2014; **The Brink's Job**, 1978; Burnt Money, 2000; **Captain America: The Winter Soldier**, 2014; **Cars 2**, 2011; **Cast a Giant Shadow**, 1966; The Cats, 1968; City Park, 1934; Clear and Present Danger, 1994; The Code, 2002; Colombiana, 2011; Cowboy Bebop: The Movie, 2001; Cradle 2 the Grave, 2003; The Crimson Ghost, 1946; **Criss Cross**, 1949; Danger Ahead, 1940; **The Dark Knight**, 2008; **The Dark Knight Rises**, 2012; Death Race, 2008; Desperado, 1995; Dick Tracy Returns, 1938; **Die Another Day**, 2002; **Die Hard**, 1988; Dillinger, 1945; The Dion Brothers, 1974; **Divergent**, 2014; Eagle Eye, 2008; **Edge of Tomorrow**, 2014; Elysium, 2013; Empire State, 2013; The Enemy General, 1960; Equilibrium, 2002; **The Expendables 3**, 2014; The Expendables 2, 2012; Fast Five, 2011; The Fat Man, 1951; Forfeit, 2007; 44 Minutes: The North Hollywood Shoot-Out, 2003 (made-for-TV); Free Zone, 2005; Getaway, 2013; Getting Any?, 1994; G.I. Joe: Retaliation, 2013; G.I. Joe: The Rise of Cobra, 2009; **G-Men**, 1935; A Good Day to Die Hard, 2013; The Green Hornet, 2011; Guns, Girls, and Gangsters, 1959; Harley Davidson and the Marlboro Man, 1991; Heat, 1995; Heist, 2009; Highway 301, 1950; Highway West, 1941; The Hoodlum, 1951; Im Schatten der Macht, 1987; **In the Name of the Father**, 1993; **The In-Laws**, 1979; **The Interview**, 2014; Into the Storm, 2014; The Invisible Monster, 1950; **Invisible Stripes**, 1939; The Island, 2005; The Italian Job, 1969; Jack Ryan: Shadow Recruit, 2014; **Kansas City Confidential**, 1952; The Kidnapping of the President, 1980; The Killer Elite, 1975; **The Ladykillers**, 1956; **The Lavender Hill Mob**, 1951; **Lawrence of Arabia**, 1962; Lethal Weapon 3, 1992; The Lone Wolf Meets a Lady, 1940; The Lookout, 2007; Machete Kills, 2013; Million Dollar Haul, 1935; Mr. Moto Taks a Vacation, 1939; Money Movers, 1979; Monsters of the Dark Continent, 2014; Navy Seals, 1990; The Nest, 2002; The One, 2001; **Operation Daybreak**, 1975; Operation Rogue, 2014; Outside the Wall, 1950; Oyster Farmer, 2004; **Patton**, 1970; Play It Loud!, 2003; Police Academy 6: City Under Siege, 1989; Psycho-Circus, 1967; **Public Enemies**, 2009; The Purge Anarchy, 2014; **Olympus Has Fallen**, 2013; The Rebel Set, 1959; Redemption, 2013; Resident Evil: Retribution, 2012; Riders, 2002; RoboCop, 2014; Sabotage, 2014; **Scanners**, 1981; **'71**, 2014; Sniper Legacy, 2014; **Some Mother's Son**, 1996; Speed Racer, 2008; **Spider Man**, 2002; Spider Man 3, 2007; The Spider Returns, 1941; **The Story of G.I. Joe**, 1945; **Stripes**, 1981; **Take the Money and Run**, 1969; Takers, 2010; Tango and Cash, 1989; They Came to Rob Las Vegas, 1968; **They Met in Bombay**, 1941; Three Brothers, 1982; Tomorrow Never Dies, 1997; The Town, 2010; Transforers: Age of Extinction, 2014; Transit, 2012; Trollhunter, 2010; The Underneath, 1995; **A Walk in the Sun**, 1945; **What Doesn't Kill You**, 2008; Where the Money Is, 2000; **X-Men: First Class**, 2011.

Armored Cars (military): **American Sniper**, 2014; The Battle of the Bulge, 1965; **A Bridge Too Far**, 1977; **Captain America: The Winter Soldier**, 2014; **Cast a Giant Shadow**, 1966; **Edge of Tomorrow**, 2014; The Enemy General, 1960; The Expendables 3, 2014; The Expendables 2, 2012; G.I. Joe: Retaliation, 2019; G.I. Joe: The Rise of Cobra, 2009; **Lawrence of Arabia**, 1962; Navy Seals, 1990; **Operation Daybreak**, 1975; '71, 2014; **Stripes**, 1981; **A Walk in the Sun**, 1945.

Armored Cars (police): **Bonnie and Clyde**, 1967; **Gabriel over the White House**, 1933; RoboCop, 2014; Sabotage, 2014.

Armored Cars (security): **The Amazing Spiderman 2**, 2014; American Ultra, 2015; Analyze That, 2002; The Alpha Caper, 1973 (made-for-TV); Armored, 2009; Armored Car, 1937; **Armored Car Robbery**, 1950; The Aura, 2005; **Avengers: Age of Ultron**, 2015; The Bastard, 1968; **Batman Begins**, 2005; **Batman Forever**, 1995; Behind the Head-lines, 1937; The Big Chase, 1954; Black, 2009; Blueprint for Robbery, 1961; Born Reckless, 1937; **Brazil**, 1985; **The Brink's Job**, 1978; Chappie, 2015; City Park, 1934; The Code, 2004; **Criss Cross**, 1949; Danger Ahead, 1940; **The Dark Knight**, 2008; **The Dark Knight Rises**, 2012; Dead Presidents, 1995; Dick Tracy Returns, 1938 (serial); **Die Another Day**, 2002; **Die Hard**, 1988; Dillinger, 1945; **Divergent**, 2014; **Elysium**, 2013; Empire State, 2013; Equilibrium, 2002; Escobar: Paradise Lost, 2014; Fast Five, 2011; The Fat Man, 1951; **Furious 7**, 2015; **G-Men**, 1935; A Good Day to Die Hard, 2013; Guns, Girls, and Gangsters, 1958; Harley Davidson and the Marlboro Man, 1991; Heat, 1995; Heist, 2009; Highway 301, 1950; Highway West, 1941; The Hoodlum, 1951; **The Hunger Games: Mockingjay—Part 2**, 2015; In Time, 2011; **The In-Laws**, 1979; Insurgent, 2015; **The Interview**, 2014; **Invisible Stripes**, 1939; The Island, 2005; The Italian Job, 1969; Jack Ryan: Shadow Recruit, 2014; **Kansas City Confidential**, 1952; L.A. Takedown, 1989 (made-for-TV); **The Ladykillers**, 1956; Las Vegas Beat, 1961 (made-for-TV); The Last Ride, 2004 (made-for-TV); **The Lavender Hill Mob**, 1951; Le convoyeur, 2005; Le deuxieme souffle, 1966; The Lone Wolf Meets a Lady, 1940; Machete Kills, 2013; **Mad Max: Fury Road**, 2015; Million Dollar Haul, 1935; Mr. Moto Takes a Vacation, 1939; Momentum, 2003; Money Movers, 1978; **Olympus Has Fallen**, 2013; Outside the Wall, 1950; Police Academy 6: City Under Siege, 1989; Psycho-Circus, 1966; The Purge: Anarchy, 2014; Real Time, 2002; The Rebel Set, 1959; The Spider Returns, 1941 (ser-ial); **Spectre**, 2015; **Spider-Man**, 2002; Spider-Man 3, 2007; Steal, 2002; **Take the Money and Run**, 1969; Takers, 2010; Teenage Mutant Ninja Turtles, 2014; They Came to Rob Las Vegas, 1968; The Town, 2010; Transformers: Age of Extinction, 2014; Transit, 2012; **X-Men: First Class**, 2011.

Astronauts (also see Aviators; Explorers; Martians; Pilots; Space, this index): Abbott and Costello Go to Mars, 1953; The Aftermath, 1982; **Alien**, 1979; Alien Apocalypse, 2005 (made-for-TV); **Aliens**, 1986; Al-ternative 3, 1977 (made-for-TV); The Angry Red Planet, 1959; Apollo 18, 2011; **Apollo 13**, 1995; Armageddon, 1998; The Astronaut Farmer, 2006; Astronaut: The Last Push, 2012; The Astronaut Wives Club, 2015 (TV series); Astronauts, 1981-1982 (TV series); Astronauts, 2002 (made-for-TV); The Astronaut's Wife, 1999; Aurora, 1998; Back to the Planet of the Apes, 1981 (made-for-TV); Barbarella, 1968; Battle for Terra, 2007; Battle of the Stars, 1978; **Beneath the Planet of the Apes**, 1970; Beyond the Stars, 1989; **The Black Hole**, 1979; Blackstar, 1981-1982 (TV series); Buck Rogers, 1939 (serial); Buck Rogers in the 25th Century, 1979-1981 (TV series); **Capricorn One**, 1978; Cat-Women of the Moon, 1953; Challenger, 1990 (made-for-TV); **Close Encounters of the Third Kind**, 1977; Conquest of Space, 1955; Contamination, 1980; Cosmonaut, 2009; The Cosmonaut, 2013; Countdown, 1967; The Crawling Hand, 1963; Dark Breed, 1996; **The Day the Earth Stood Still**, 1951; **The Day the Earth Stood Still**, 2008; The Day the Sky Ex-ploded, 1958; **Deep Impact**, 1998; Defying Gravity, 2009- (TV series);

Destination Moon, 1950; The Earth Dies Screaming, 1964; Earthstorm, 2006 (made-for-TV); Escape from Mars, 1999 (made-for-TV); **Escape from the Planet of the Apes**, 1971; Europa Report, 2013; Extant, 2014- (TV series); Fantastic Four, 2005; The Far Side of the Moon, 2003; Final Days of Planet Earth, 2006 (made-for-TV); First Man Into Space, 1959; First Men in the Moon, 1964; First Spaceship on Venus, 1960; Five Mil-lion Years to Earth, 1968; Flash Gordon's Flight to Mars, 1938; Flight to Mars, 1951; 400 Days, 2015; Frankenstein Meets the Spacemonster, 1965; From the Earth to the Moon, 1998 (TV miniseries); Galaxy of Terror, 1981; **Gattaca**, 1997; Ghosts of Mars, 2011; Gorath, 1962; **Gravity**, 2013; Green Lantern, 2011; Houston, We've Got a Problem, 1974 (made-for-TV); Hyper Space, 1989; I Dream of Jeannie, 1965-1970 (TV series); Impact, 2009 (TV miniseries); The Incredible Melting Man, 1977; The Infinite Worlds of H.G. Wells, 2001 (TV miniseries); Inside Planet Earth, 2009 (made-for-TV); **Interstellar**, 2014; Iron Sky, 2012; Invasion of Astro-Monster, 1965; It's About Time, 1966-1967 (TV series); Journey to Saturn, 2008; **Journey to the Far Side of the Sun**, 1969; Journey to the Seventh Planet, 1962; Land of the Lost, 2009; The Last Days on Mars, 2013; Le orme, 1975; Los astronautas, 1964; Love, 2011; Making Mr. Right, 1987; **Marooned**, 1969; Mars Attacks the World, 1938; **The Martian**, 2015; Max Q, 1998 (made-for-TV); Men Into Space, 1959-1960 (TV series); Meteor, 1979; Mission Star-dust, 1967; **Mission to Mars**, 2000; **Moon**, 2009; Moon Shot, 1994 (made-for-TV); Moon Zero Two, 1969; **Moonraker**, 1979; Moonshot, 2009 (made-for-TV); Moontrap, 1989; Northstar, 1986 (made-for-TV); **Oblivion**, 2013; Odyssey 5, 2002-2004 (TV series); On the Silver Globe, 1988; Outlander, 2009; Planet 51, 2009; Planet of Dinosaurs, 1977; **Planet of the Apes**, 1968; Planet of the Apes, 1974- (TV series); **Planet of the Apes**, 2001; Planet of the Vampires, 1965; Planeta bur, 1962; Planetes, 2003-2004 (TV series); **Prometheus**, 2012; Red Planet, 2000; **The Reluctant Astronaut**, 1967; Return to Earth, 1976 (made-for-TV); Return to the Planet of the Apes, 1975-1976 (TV series); Riders to the Stars, 1958; **The Right Stuff**, 1983; Robinson Crusoe on Mars, 1964; RocketMan, 1997; Rocket's Red Glare, 2000 (made-for-TV); **Rocketship X-M**, 1950; Sergeant Dead Head, 1965; Silent Running, 1972; Solar Crisis, 1990; Space, 1985 (TV miniseries); The Space Chil-dren, 1958; Space Chimps, 2008; **Space Cowboys**, 2000; Space: 1999, 1975-1977 (TV series); SpaceCamp, 1986; Species II, 1998; Star Trek, 1966-1969 (TV Series); Star Trek, 2009; **Star Trek: First Contact**, 1996; **Star Trek: Generations**, 1994; **Star Trek: Insurrection**, 1998; **Star Trek: Into Darkness**, 2013; **Star Trek: Nemesis**, 2002; **Star Trek: The Motion Picture**, 1979; **Star Trek II: The Wrath of Khan**, 1982; **Star Trek III: The Search for Spock**, 1984; **Star Trek IV: The Voyage Home**, 1986; **Star Trek V: The Final Frontier**, 1989; **Star Trek VI: The Undiscovered Country**, 1991; **Star Wars: Episode V— The Empire Strikes Back**, 1980; **Star Wars: Episode IV—A New Hope**, 1977; **Star Wars: Episode I—The Phantom Menace**, 1999; **Star Wars: Episode VI—Return of the Jedi**, 1983; **Star Wars: Episode III—Revenge of the Sith**, 2005; **Star Wars: Episode II— The Attack of the Clones** , 2002; **Star Wars: The Clone Wars**, 2008; **Star Wars: The Force Awakens**, 2015; Stowaway to the Moon, 1975 (made-for-TV); Stranded, 2001; Strange New World, 1975 (made-for-TV); Sunshine, 2007; **Superman II**, 1981; Superman IV: The Quest for Peace, 1987; Tales of Tomorrow, 1951-1953 (TV series; "Test Flight," 1951 episode; "Appointment on Mars," 1952 episode; "Plague from Space," 1952 episode); **Terms of Endearment**, 1983; Thunderbirds, 2004; A Ticket to Space, 2006; Time Warp, 1981 (made-for-TV); **To-morrowland**, 2015; **Transformers**, 2007; Transformers: Dark of the Moon, 2011; Trapped in Space, 1995 (made-for-TV); A Trip to Mars, 1918; 12 to the Moon, 1960; **20 Million Miles to Earth**, 1957; **2001: A Space Odyssey**, 1968; **2010**, 1984; Unidentified Flying Oddball, 1979; Virus, 1999; Voyage to the End of the Universe, 1963; Voyage to the Prehistoric Planet, 1965; War of the Planets, 1977; Watchmen, 2009; Way...Way Out, 1966; The Wild Blue Yonder, 2005; World Without End, 1956; X-15, 1961; Yongary, Monster from the Deep, 1967; **You**

Only Live Twice, 1967; **Zathura: A Space Adventure**, 2005.

Atomic Bomb: **Above and Beyond**, 1953; Atomic War Bride, 1960; The Beast from 20,000 Fathoms, 1953; Black Rain, 1989; A Boy and His Dog, 1975; **Cloak and Dagger**, 1946; Come See the Paradise, 1990; Day One, 1989 (made-for-TV); The Day the Sky Exploded, 1958; The Devil, Probably, 1977; **Dr. Strangelove**, 1964; **Emperor**, 2012; **Empire of the Sun**, 1987; The Enola Gay: The Men, the Mission, the Atomic Bomb, 1980 (made-for-TV); **Fail Safe**, 1964; Fail Safe, 2000 (made-for-TV); **Fat Man and Little Boy**, 1989; Five, 1951; The Fourth Protocol, 1987; Ghosts of Mars, 2001; Golden Rendezvous, 1977; **Goldfinger**, 1964; The Good German, 2006; Ground Zero, 1987; The Highest Honor, 1982; Hiroshima, 1995 (made-for-TV); **Hiroshima; Mon Amour**, 1960; Hiroshima: Out of the Ashes, 1990 (made-for-TV); **The House on 92nd Street**, 1945; Imposter, 2001; Island of Lost Women, 1959; Jack Reacher: Never Go Back, 2016; Japan's Longest Day, 1967; **Kiss Me Deadly**, 1955; **Kundun**, 1997; The Little House, 2014; **Lorenzo's Oil**, 1992; **MacArthur**, 1977; The Man from U.N.C.L.E., 2015; The Man Who Saw Tomorrow, 1981; The Man Who Stole the Sun, 1979; The Manhattan Project, 1986; The Mirror, 1975; Mona Lisa Smile, 2003; Octopussy, 1983; On the Beach, 1959; Oppenheimer, 1980 (TV miniseries); Outbreak, 1995; Panic in Year Zero!, 1962; **Pickup on South Street**, 1953; Rhapsody in August, 1991; The Salton Sea, 2002; Satellite in the Sky, 1956; The Second Front, 2005; **Seven Days to Noon**, 1950; Striking Range, 2006; The Sum of All Fears, 2002; **Them!**, 1954; **The Thief**, 1952; Threads, 1984 (made-for-TV); **Thunderball**, 1965; **The War of the Worlds**, 1953; **The Wolverine**, 2013; Women in the Night, 1948; Young Einstein, 1988.

Attorneys: **Abe Lincoln in Illinois**, 1940; **Abused Confidence**, 1938; **Accused**, 1936; **The Accused**, 1949; The Accused, 1988; **Accused— Stand Up**, 1930; **The Accusing Finger**, 1936; **Achilles' Love**, 2000; An Act of Murder, 1948; **Adam's Rib**, 1949; **The Addams Family**, 1991; **The Adventures of Huckleberry Finn**, 1960; Affare Dreyfus, 1968 (TV miniseries); **Along the Great Divide**, 1951; **The Amazing Dr. Clitterhouse**, 1938; **An American Tragedy**, 1931; **Amistad**, 1999; **Anatomy of a Murder**, 1959; Anatomy of a Psycho, 1961; ...And Justice for All, 1979; And the Sea Will Tell, 1991 (made-for-TV); **Angel Face**, 1952; **The Asphalt Jungle**, 1950; **The Bachelor and the Bobby-Soxer**, 1947; The Ballad of Josie, 1967; **Barefoot in the Park**, 1967; **Becoming Jane**, 2007; Before I Hang, 1940; Before the Deluge, 1954; Bernie, 2011; Best Wishes for Tomorrow, 2007; **Bewitched**, 1945; Beyond a Reasonable Doubt, 1956; Black and White, 2002; **Black Legion**, 1937; Blind Faith, 1990 (made-for-TV); Blondes at Work, 1938; Blood & Orchids, 1986 (TV miniseries); Bluebeard, 1963; **Blume in Love**, 1973; Body of Evidence, 1993; **Body Heat**, 1981; Body of My Enemy, 1976; **Boomergang**, 1947; **Bordertown**, 1935; **Breaker Morant**, 1980; The Brief, 2004-2005 (TV series); Buchanan Rides Alone, 1958; Buried Alive, 1939; **The Caine Mutiny**, 1954; **Canyon Passage**, 1946; **Cape Fear**, 1962; **Cape Fear**, 1991; **The Case of the Black Cat**, 1936; The Case of the Stuttering Bishop, 1937; **Cass Timberlane**, 1947; **The Castle**, 1997; **Castle on the Hudson**, 1940; **Character**, 1997; Charlie Chan at the Wax Museum, 1940; The Charmer, 1987 (TV miniseries); The Chatterley Affair, 2006 (made-for-TV); The Cheat, 1931; **Chicago**, 2002; **Citizen Kane**, 1941; **City Streets**, 1931; **City That Never Sleeps**, 1953; **A Civil Action**, 1998; **The Clairvoyant**, 1935; **Class Action**, 1991; **The Client**, 1994; **Clueless**, 1995; **Compulsion**, 1959; Conduct Unbecoming, 1975; **The Conspirator**, 2011; **The Constant Husband**, 1955; **Counselor at Law**, 1933; Counter Investigation, 2007; **The County Chairman**, 1935; **Court Martial**, 1954; **The Court-Martial of Billy Mitchell**, 1955; **The Cousins**, 1959; **Crack in the Mirror**, 1960; Crazy in Alabama, 1999; **Crime Without Passion**, 1934; **Criminal Court**, 1946; **Crossroads**, 1942; Damini—Lightning, 1993; Darrow, 1991 (made-for-TV); Deadlocked, 2000 (made-for-TV); Destry Rides Again, 1932; **Destry Rides Again**, 1939; **The Devil and Daniel**

Webster, 1941 (aka: All That Money Can Buy); Dishonored Lady, 1947; Dorothea Angermann, 1959; **Double Jeopardy**, 1999; The Drake Case, 1929; Dress Gray, 1986 (made-for-TV); The Dreyfus Case, 1930; **The Dreyfus Case**, 1931; 88 Minutes, 2007; **Emma**, 1932; **Erin Brockovich**, 2000; Evelyn Prentice, 1934; **A Few Good Men**, 1992; **Find Me Guilty**, 2006; **The Firm**, 1993; For the Defense, 1954 (made-for-TV); Fracture, 2007; **Fury**, 1936; The Girl Who Kicked the Hornets' Nest, 2009; The Glass Shield, 1994; Good Day for a Hanging, 1959; Gupt: The Hidden Truth, 1997; **Hang 'Em High**, 1968; **High Crimes**, 2002; **Hour of the Gun**, 1967; **The Hour of Thirteen**, 1952; The Hourglass Sanatorium, 1973; **Huckleberry Finn**, 1939; I Accuse!, 1958; **I Want to Live!**, 1958; **Illegal**, 1955; **Impact**, 1949; The Incident, 1990 (made-for-TV); Incident in a Small Town, 1994 (made-for-TV); **Inherit the Wind**, 1960; Inherit the Wind, 1988 (made-for-TV); The Iron Sheriff, 1957; **J. Edgar**, 2011; **Jagged Edge**, 1985; Jasper, Texas, 2003 (made-for-TV); **JFK**, 1991; **Jimmy the Gent**, 1934; **Joan of Arc**, 1948; **Johnny Belinda**, 1948; **The Judge**, 2014; **Judgment at Nuremberg**, 1961; Judicial Consent, 1994; Kavanagh QC, 1995-2001 (TV series); L.A. Law, 1986-1994 (TV series); La Chienne, 1931; **La Chienne**, 1975; **The Lady from Shanghai**, 1948; L'affaire Dreyfus, 1995 (made-for-TV); L'affare Dreyfus, 1968 (made-for-TV); The Laramie Project, 2002 (made-for-TV); The Last Innocent Man, 1987 (made-for-TV); The Lawyer, 1970; **Leave Her to Heaven**, 1945; The Learning Tree, 1969; The Legend of Lizzie Borden, 1975 (made-for-TV); **Let Us Live**, 1939; **Libel**, 1959; **Libeled Lady**, 1936; **The Life of Emile Zola**, 1937; **The Lincoln Lawyer**, 2011; **A Lion Is in the Streets**, 1953; Lizzie Borden Took an Ax, **2014** (made-for-TV); **M**, 1933; **M**, 1951; **Madeleine**, 1950; **A Man for All Seasons**, 1966; Man Made Monster, 1941; **The Man They Could Not Hang**, 1939; **Manhattan Melodrama**, 1934; Marshal of Gunsmoke, 1944; Mary, 1931; **The Messenger: The Story of Joan of Arc**, 1999; Midnight in the Garden of Good and Evil, 1997; The Missing Juror, 1944; **Mississippi Burning**, 1988; **The Missouri Breaks**, 1976; **The Monster and the Girl**, 1941; **The Mouthpiece**, 1932; **Murder!**, 1930; The Murder of Mary Phagan, 1988 (TV miniseries); **Mutiny on the Bounty**, 1935; **Mutiny on the Bounty**, 1962; **My Cousin Vinny**, 1992; The Naked Edge, 1961; The Night of January 16th, 1941; Night Without Justice, 2004; No One Killed Jessica, 2011; **Oscar Wilde**, 1960; Oscar Wilde, 1972 (made-for-TV); The Outrage, 1964; **Pandora's Box**, 1929; **The Paradine Case**, 1947; **Party Girl**, 1958; **The Passion of Joan of Arc**, 1928; Penguin Pool Murder, 1932; **The People Against O'Hara**, 1951; The People v. Leo Frank, 2009; The People vs. Jean Harris, 1981 (made-for-TV); The People vs. Larry Flynt, 1996; Perfect Stranger, 2007; **Peyton Place**, 1957; Philadelphia, 1993; Physical Evidence, 1989; Piccadilly, 1929; **A Place in the Sun**, 1951; Primal Fear, 1996; Prisoner of Honor, 1991 (made-for-TV); **Providence**, 1977; Question of Love, 1978; **The Rack**, 1956; **The Return of Frank James**, 1940; **Reversal of Fortune**, 1990; Roses Are for the Rich, 1987 (made-for-TV); **Roxie Hart**, 1942; **Runaway Jury**, 2003; Salome's Last Dance, 1988; **Scarlet Street**, 1945; **The Secret Six**, 1931; Separated by Murder, 1994 (made-for-TV); Shark, 2006-2008 (TV series); **The Shawshank Redemption**, 1994; Side Effects, 2013; **Silkwood**, 1983; Sleep Murder, 2004 (made-for-TV); Sleepers, 1996; **A Soldier's Story**, 1984; Sorry Ain't Enough, 2006; **The Sound of Fury**, 1950; **The Star Chamber**, 1983; **State's Attorney**, 1932; Storeyville, 1992; The Story on Page One, 1959; The Strange Case of Dr. Rx, 1942; **Stranger on the Third Floor**, 1940; Suing the Devil, 2011; **Summer Storm**, 1944; **Suspect**, 1987; Sway, 2007; **Taxi!**, 1932; **They Won't Believe Me**, 1947; **They Won't Forget**, 1937; **This Land Is Mine**, 1943; **Three Strangers**, 1946; **Time Limit**, 1957; **To Kill a Mockingbird**, 1962; Tom und Hacke, 2012; **Tombstone**, 1993; **Trial**, 1955; **The Trial**, 1963; The Trial, 2010; Trial and Error, 1962; **Trial and Error**, 1997; **The Trial of Joan of Arc**, 1965; The Trial of Madeleine Smith, 1949; **The Trial of Mary Dugan**, 1929; The Trials of Oscar Wilde, 1960; **True Grit**, 1969; **True Grit**, 2010; The Truth, 1960; **12 Angry Men**, 1957; Twilight of Honor, 1963; Two Men in Town, 1976; Two

Seconds, 1932; **The Undercover Man**, 1949; **The Unholy Three**, 1925; **The Unholy Three**, 1930; **The Untouchables**, 1987; **The Valiant**, 1929; **Valiant Is the Word for Carrie**, 1936; **Valley of the Heart's Delight**, 2009; **The Verdict**, 1982; The Weight of Water, 2000; West of Memphis, 2012; **White Mischief**, 1988; **Whose Life Is It Anyway?**, 1981; A Wife Confesses, 1961; Wilde, 1997; **Witness**, 1985; **Witness for the Prosecution**, 1957; **A Woman's Face**, 1941; **Wyatt Earp**, 1994; You Are There, 1953-1957 (TV series); Young Adam, 2003; The Young Land, 1959; **The Young Savages**, 1961.

Avalanches: The Abominable Snowman, 1957; **Agent Cody Banks**, 2003; **Alive**, 1993; Alaska Seas, 1954; Aspen Extreme, 1993; The Avalanche, 1946; Avalanche, 1969; Avalanche, 1978; Avalanche, 1994 (made-for-TV); Avalache, 1999; Avalanche Alley, 2001 (made-for-TV); Avalanche Express, 1979; Avalanche Sharks, 2014 (made-for-TV); Back to God's Country, 1953; **Balto**, 1995; Bear Island, 1979; Belle & Sebastian, 2013; Blood Tracks, 1985; Blue Mountain Skies, 1939; Bridal Suite, 1939; The Bulldog Breed, 1960; Canadian Mounties vs. Atomic Invaders, 1953 (serial); Careful, 1992; Carson City, 1952; The Challenge, 1938; Challenge to White Fang, 1974; The Claim, 2000; Conan the Barbarian, 2011; The Crawling Eye, 1958; The Crimson Rivers, 2000; Dance Program, 1938; Dangerous Mission, 1954; The Day the Earth Moved, 1974 (made-for-TV); Devil's Pass, 2013; Doktor Faustus, 1982; Dusty Ermine, 1937; The Eiger Sanction, 1975; Everest, 2007 (TV miniseries); **Everest**, 2015; Extreme Ops, 2002; Faces of Death, 1981; **The Far Country**, 1955; The Fight Before Christmas, 2008; Final Ascent, 2000 (made-for-TV); The Flight Before Christmas, 2008; Flight from Ashiya, 1965; Flight to Mars, 1951; **Force Majeure**, 2014; G.I. Joe: Retaliation, 2013; George!, 1972; Ghost of Zorro, 1949; Godzilla Raids Again, 1955; Green Fire, 1954; Happy Feet, 2006; Heroes of the Flames, 1931 (serial); High Ice, 1980 (made-for-TV); **Ice Age**, 2002; **Ice Age: Continental Drift**, 2012; Ice Quake, 2010 (made-for-TV); Idiocracy, 2006; In Search of the Castaways, 1962; Inception, 2010; The Invisible Monster, 1950; Invitation, 1952; The James Brothers of Missouri, 1949; Jungle Raiders, 1945; King of the Texas Rangers, 1949 (serial); **Kit Carson**, 1940; K2, 1991; **The Lady Vanishes**, 1938; Last Holiday, 2006; Latitude Zero, 1969; **The Lord of the Rings: The Fellowship of the Ring**, 2001; **Lost Horizon**, 1937; Lost Horizon, 1973; Man Beast, 1956; **The Man Who Would Be King**, 1975; Men of Action, 1935; Men of the North, 1930; Meteor, 1979; Milarepa, 2006; The Mole People, 1956; The Monster and the Ape, 1945; **Mulan**, 1998; **The Mummy: Tomb of the Dragon Emperor**, 2008; **Murder on the Orient Express**, 1974; New Year's Day, 2000; North Face, 2008; **Northern Pursuit**, 1943; **On Her Majesty's Secret Service**, 1969; **One Million B.C.**, 1940; The Oregon Trail, 1939; **Our Man Flint**, 1966; Pack Train, 1953; The Painted Stallion, 1937; Panther Girl of the Kongo, 1955; The Passage, 1979; Pathfinder, 1987; Pathfinder, 2007; The Perfect Sense, 2011; Perils of Nyoka, 1942 (serial); The Phantom, 1943 (serial); **The Professionals**, 1966; Quintet, 1979; Raiders of Ghost City, 1944 (serial); Rancho Grande, 1940; The Rawhide Terror, 1934; Red Planet Mars, 1952; **The Revenant**, 2015; Riddick, 2013; Riders of Death Valley, 1941; **The Riders of the Whistling Skull**, 1937; **Road to Utopia**, 1946; Robinson Crusoe on Mars, 1964; **Seven Brides for Seven Brothers**, 1954; **Seven Chances**, 1925; **Seven Years in Tibet**, 1997; **She**, 1935; Sherpa, 2015; Shopworn, 1932; Silver Canyon, 1951; **The Simpsons Movie**, 2007; Snow Beast, 2011; Snow Trail, 1947; **Snowpiercer**, 2014; Something New, 1920; Son of Zorro, 1947 (serial); **Spawn of the North**, 1938; Storm Over Mont Blanc, 1930; **Superman**, 1978; Thunder Mountain, 1935; To the Last Man, 1933; **The Trail of '98**, 1928; The Treasure of Pancho Villa, 1955; The Truth Below, 2011; 2012, 2009; Up to His Ears, 1965; Valley of the Eagles, 1951; Vertical Limit, 2000; Water Rustlers, 1939; The White Desert, 1925; The White Hell of Pitz Palu, 1953; **The Wild North**, 1952; The Wildest Dream, 2000; **The World Is Not Enough**, 1999; Youth in Revolt, 1938; Zorro's Fighting Legion, 1939 (serial). For more information on avalanches through-

out history, see my book *Darkest Hours: A Narrative Encyclopedia of Worldwide Disasters from Ancient Times to the Present* (Nelson-Hall, 1976).

Aviators (WWI, 1914-1918; also see Airplanes; Astronauts; Pilots; Survival Films, this index): **Ace of Aces**, 1933; **Aces High**, 1977; The Adventures of Young Indiana Jones: Attack of the Hawkman, 1995 (made-for-TV); **The Blue Max**, 1966; Body and Soul, 1931; **Captain Eddie**, 1945; **The Court-Martial of Billy Mitchell**, 1955; Crimson Romance, 1934; Darling Lili, 1970; **The Dawn Patrol**, 1930; **The Dawn Patrol**, 1938; **The Eagle and the Hawk**, 1933; Flight Into Darkness, 1938; **Flyboys**, 2006; **The Great Dictator**, 1940; **The Great Waldo Pepper**, 1975; Hell in the Heavens, 1934; **Hell's Angels**, 1930; Lafayette Escadrille, 1958; The Last Flight, 1931; The Legion of the Condemned, 1928; L'equipage, 1938 (aka: Flight into Darkness; remade as **The Woman I Love**, 1937); **Lilac Time**, 1928; **The Lost Squadron**, 1932; **Mata Hari**, 1931; Men Must Fight, 1933; **The Red Baron**, 2010; Revenge of the Red Baron, 1994; Richthofen, 1929; A Romance of the Air, 1918; The Sky Hawk, 1929; **The Story of Vernon and Irene Castle**, 1939; **Suzy**, 1936; **The Tarnished Angels**, 1958; **To Each His Own**, 1946; Today We Live, 1933; **Von Richthofen and Brown**, 1971; War Nurse, 1930; **War of the Worlds: Goliath**, 2012; **Wings**, 1927; **The Woman I Love**, 1937; Young Eagles, 1930; **Zeppelin**, 1971.

Aviators (WWII, 1939-1945; European and North African Theaters; also see Airplanes; Astronauts; Pilots; Survival Films, this index; Bomber Planes, Fighter Planes in Objects and Structures Index): **The Adventures of Tartu** (aka: Sabotage Agent; 1943; R.A.F.; German Luftwaffe); Angels One Five, 1954 (R.A.F.); **Battle of Britain**, 1969 (R.A.F.; German Luftwaffe); Battle Squadron Lutzow, 1941 (German Luftwaffe); **Battleground**, 1949 (U.S. Air Force); **The Best Years of Our Lives**, 1946 (U.S. Air Force); **A Bridge Too Far**, 1977 (U.S. Air Force; R.A.F.); **Captains of the Clouds**, 1942 (R.A.F.; German Luftwaffe); **Catch-22**, 1970 (U.S.); **Command Decision**, 1948 (U.S. Air Force); The Crew of the Dora, 1943 (German Luftwaffe; Soviet Air Force); Dark Blue World, 2001 (Czech pilots in the R.A.F.); **The Desert Fox: The Story of Rommel**, 1951; **Desperate Journey**, 1942 (R.A.F.; German Luftwaffe); The Devil's General, 1957 (German Luftwaffe); **Eagle Squadron**, 1942 (R.A.F.); Eagles Over London, 1973 (R.A.F.); **The English Patient**, 1996; **Fighter Squadron**, 1948 (U.S. Air Force); Flying Fortress, 1942 (U.S. Air Force); **Force 10 from Navarone**, 1978; Forever Young, 1992; **The Great Escape**, 1963 (U.S. Air Force; R.A.F.; German Luftwaffe); **The Guns of Navarone**, 1961; **The Heroes of Telemark**, 1965 (R.A.F.); **Hope and Glory**, 1987 (German Luftwaffe; R.A.F.); International Lady, 1941; **Into the White**, 2012 (R.A.F.; German Luftwaffe); **Johnny in the Clouds** (aka: The Way to the Stars; R.A.F.), 1945; **The Longest Day**, 1962 (R.A.F.; German Luftwaffe); **The McKenzie Break**, 1970 (German Luftwaffe; R.A.F.); **Memphis Belle**, 1990 (U.S. Air Force; German Luftwaffe); Missing Jane, 2004; **One of Our Aircraft Is Missing**, 1942 (R.A.F.); **The One That Got Away**, 1958 (German Luftwaffe); Only Old Men Are Going to Battle, 1974 (Soviet Air Force; German Luftwaffe); **Patton**, 1970; Red Tails, 2012 (Tuskegee pilots in Italy; U.S. Air Force); **Sahara**, 1943 (German Luftwaffe); **Saving Private Ryan**, 1998; Secret Flight, 1952 (German Luftwaffe; R.A.F.); **633 Squadron**, 1964 (R.A.F.); **Spitfire**, 1943 (R.A.F.); **Stairway to Heaven** (aka: A Matter of Life and Death), 1947; The Star of Africa, 1957 (German Luftwaffe; R.A.F.); Stukas, 1941 (German Luftwaffe); **13 Rue Madeleine**, 1947 (U.S. Air Force); **To Be or Not to Be**, 1942 (Polish pilots in the R.A.F.); Torpedo Bombers, 1983 (Soviet Air Force); The Tuskegee Airmen, 1995 (made-for-TV; U.S. Air Force); **Twelve O'Clock High**, 1949 (U.S. Air Force); **Valkyrie**, 2008; **Von Ryan's Express**, 1965 (German Luftwaffe); **A Walk in the Sun** (aka: Salerno Beachhead; German Luftwaffe; U.S. Air Force), 1945; **The War Lover**, 1962 (U.S. Air Force); We'll Meet

Again, 1982 (TV miniseries); The Winds of War, 1983 (TV miniseries); **A Yank in the R.A.F.**, 1941.

Aviators (WWII, 1939-1945; Pacific Theater; also see Airplanes; Astronauts; Pilots; Survival Films, this index; Bomber Planes, Fighter Planes in Objects and Structures Index): **Above and Beyond**, 1953; Aerial Gunner, 1943; **Air Force**, 1943; The Bamboo Blonde, 1946; **Bataan**, 1943; Battle of the Coral Sea, 1959; **Bombardier**, 1943; Bombs Over Burma, 1943; **China Girl**, 1942; **China Sky**, 1945; **Destination Tokyo**, 1943; **Empire of the Sun**, 1987; The Final Countdown, 1980; **Flight for Freedom**, 1943; **Flying Leathernecks**, 1951; **Flying Tigers**, 1942; **God Is My Co-Pilot**, 1945; **The Great Raid**, 2005; **A Guy Named Joe**, 1943; High Barbaree, 1947; **Midway**, 1976; **1941**, 1979; Night Plane from Chungking, 1943; **1941**, 1979; **Pearl Harbor**, 2001; Pilot No. 5, 1943; **The Purple Heart**, 1944; **The Purple Plain**, 1954; Storm Over the Pacific, 1960; **Task Force**, 1949; **Thirty Seconds Over Tokyo**, 1944; **Tora! Tora! Tora!**, 1970; **We've Never Been Licked**, 1943; **The Wild Blue Yonder**, 1951; **Wing and a Prayer**, 1944.

Aviators (Korean War, 1950-1953; also see Airplanes; Astronauts; Pilots; Survival Films, this index; Bomber Planes, Fighter Planes in Objects and Structures Index): **The Bridges at Toko-Ri**, 1954; The Hunters, 1958; **Men of the Fighting Lady**, 1954.

Aviation Pioneers (also see Airplanes; Astronauts; Pilots; Survival Films, this index; Bomber Planes, Fighter Planes in Objects and Structures Index): **Air Mail**, 1932; **Amelia**, 2009 (Amelia Earhart); **Around the World in 80 Days**, 1956; **The Aviator**, 2004 (Howard Hughes); Bieder der Flieger, 1941; Blaze of Noon, 1947; **Breaking the Sound Barrier**, 1952; **Captain Eddie**, 1945 (Eddie Rickenbacker); **Captains of the Clouds**, 1942; **Ceiling Zero**, 1936; **Chain Lightning**, 1950; China Clipper, 1936; **Christopher Strong**, 1933; The Conquest of the Air, 1940; **The Court-Martial of Billy Mitchell**, 1955; **The Crack-Up**, 1937; **Dirigible**, 1931; **Flight**, 1929; **Flight for Freedom**, 1943 (role model for Amelia Earhart); The Flying Irishman, 1939 (Douglas "Wrong Way" Corrigan); Gallant Journey, 1946; **The Great Waldo Pepper**, 1975; **The Hindenburg**, 1975; **The Lost Squadron**, 1932; Men Against the Sky, 1940; **Night Flight**, 1933; **Only Angels Have Wings**, 1939; **The Right Stuff**, 1983; **The Spirit of St. Louis**, 1957 (Charles A. Lindbergh); **Spitfire**, 1943 (R.J. Mitchell; Geoffrey Crisp); **The Tarnished Angels**, 1958; **Task Force**, 1949; **Test Pilot**, 1938; **Those Magnificent Men in Their Flying Machines; or, How I Flew from London to Paris in 25 Hours 11 Minutes**, 1965; **Wings in the Dark**, 1935.

Babysitters: Adventures in Babysitting, 1987; Alone in the Dark, 1982; The Amateurs, 2005; The Amityville Horror, 1979; Among the Living, 2014; Angela, 1995; Anne of Green Gables, 1985 (TV miniseries); Anything for Her, 2008; Are We There Yet?, 2005; Ask Me Anything, 2014; The Baby, 1973; The Babysitter, 1969; The Babysitter, 1980 (made-for-TV); The Babysitter, 1995; Babysitter, 2015; Babysitter Wanted, 2009; The Babysitters, 2007; Babysitters Beware, 2009; The Babysitters Club, 1990- (TV series); The Babysitters Club, 1995; The Babysitter's Seduction, 1996 (made-for-TV); Babysitting, 2014; **Before Midnight**, 2013; The Biederbecke Connection, 1988 (TV miniseries); Biutiful, 2010; Blended, 2014; Blondie for Victory, 1942; Bob the Butler, 2005; The Canal, 2014; Child's Play, 1988; Chinese Puzzle, 2013; **The Company You Keep**, 2013; The Crazy Stranger, 1997; Crazy, Stupid, Love, 2011; The Crazysitter, 1994; **Daddy Day Care**, 2003; Daddy or Mommy, 2015; Date Night, 2010; **Diary of a Mad Housewife**, 1970; Dirty Work, 1998; The Divorce, 2003; **Don't Bother to Knock**, 1952; Don't Tell Mom the Babysitter's Dead, 1991; **The Door in the Floor**, 2004; Dummy, 2002; East Side of Heaven, 1939; **Erin Brockovich**, 2000; Eyes Wide Shut, 1999; The Five Senses, 1999; **Flight of the Red Balloon**, 2008; **Fort Bliss**, 2014; **Forty Shades of Blue**, 2005; French

Women, 2014; G.I. Blues, 1960; The Gate, 1987; Georgia Rule, 2007; Good Kids, 2016; **GoodFellas**, 1990; The Guardian, 1990; Hall Pass, 2011; **Halloween**, 1978; The Hand That Rocks the Cradle, 1992; Happy Christmas, 2014; Hard Candy, 2005; Home Alone 3, 1997; Horsemen, 2009; The Hours, 2002; I Saw What You Did, 1965; In Her Skin, 2009; **The Incredibles**, 2004; **Jerry Maguire**, 1996; **Kramer vs. Kramer**, 1979; **Labyrinth**, 1986; The Last Mimzy, 2007; **The Last Wave**, 1978; Life as We Know It, 2010; A Little Help, 2010; A Map of the World, 1999; **Maps to the Stars**, 2014; The Meddler, 2015; Mrs. Doubtfire, 1993; Mostly Martha, 2001; My Babysitter's a Vampire, 2010 (made-for-TV); Mystic Pizza, 1988; **The Nanny**, 1965; No Reservations, 2007; The New Daughter, 2009; Obsessed, 2009; **Odds against Tomorrow**, 1959; **Only Two Can Play**, 1962; Orphans, 1998; The Pacifier, 2005; The Page Turner, 2006; Palo Alto, 2013; **Pierrot Le Fou**, 1968; Playing It Cool, 2014; **Please Don't Eat the Daisies**, 1960; **Poltergeist**, 1982; **Raising Arizona**, 1987; Rally 'Round the Flag, Boys!, 1958; The Rebound, 2009; **The Ring**, 2002; The Safety of Objects, 2001; The Shipping News, 2001; The Sitter, 2011; **Sitting Pretty**, 1948; The Spy Next Door, 2010; **Stir of Echoes**, 1999; Summer Girl, 1983 (made-for-TV); Sunshine Cleaning, 2008; The Swimmer, 1968; That Brennan Girl, 1946; Trick or Treats, 1982; The Truth About Emanuel, 2013; Uncle Buck, 1989; Up the Sandbox, 1972; Weekend with the Babysitter, 1970; When a Stranger Calls, 1979; When a Stranger Calls, 2006; When a Stranger Calls Back, 1993 (made-for-TV); Woman Doctor, 1939; Year of the Dog, 2007.

Bank Robbers and Bank Robberies (U.S. Old West): The Adventures of Frank and Jesse James, 1948; Along the Rio Grande, 1941; American Outlaws, 2001; **The Apple Dumpling Gang**, 1975; Arizona Express, 1924; Arizona Legion, 1939; **The Assassination of Jesse James by the Coward Robert Ford**, 2007; Bad Man's River, 1971; **Bad Man's Territory**, 1946; **Bad Men of Missouri**, 1941; Badlands of Dakota, 1941; Badlands of Montana, 1957; The Bandit Trail, 1941; Bandolero!, 1968; Beau Bandit, 1930; Beyond the Purple Hills, 1950; Beyond the Rio Grande, 1930; Beyond the Sacramento, 1940; Black Jack, 1968; The Blazing Sun, 1950; Border Wolves, 1938; Borderline Caballero, 1936; Brothers of the West, 1937; Bullet for a Badman, 1964; **Butch Cassidy and the Sundance Kid**, 1969; Butch and Sundance: The Early Days, 1979; Cahill, U.S. Marshal, 1973; Call of the Prairie, 1936; Carson City Cyclone, 1943; Cattle Raiders, 1938; Cherokee Strip, 1940; **A Chump at Oxford**, 1940; Come On, Rangers, 1938; The Daltons' Women, 1950; Dangerous Nan McGrew, 1930; Days of Jesse James, 1939; The Deadline, 1931; The Deadly Trackers, 1973; Death Rides a Horse, 1967; Death Valley Manhunt, 1943; The Desert Trail, 1935; The Desperados, 1943; **The Doolins of Oklahoma**, 1949; Dude Ranch, 1931; The Fabulous Texan, 1947; **The Fastest Gun Alive**, 1956; The Fighting Lawman, 1953; Fighting Mad, 1939; Five Guns to Tombstone, 1960; Forlorn River, 1937; Fort Dodge Stampede, 1951; Frank & Jesse, 1995; The Frisco Kid, 1979; Frontier Outlaws, 1944; Fury at Gunsight Pass, 1956; Galloping On, 1925; Gauchos of El Dorado, 1941; Ghost-Town Gold, 1936; God's Gun, 1977; Goin' South, 1978; Good Day for a Hanging, 1959; The Great Jesse James Raid, 1953; **The Great Missouri Raid**, 1951; **The Great Northfield, Minnesota Raid**, 1972; Gun the Man Down, 1956; Gunbelt, 1953; Gunsight Ridge, 1957; Harmony Trail, 1944; Harry Tracy: The Last of the Wild Bunch, 1982; He Who Shoots First, 1966; Hell Canyon Outlaws, 1957; Hells Heels, 1930; Hell's Heroes, 1929; Hidden Gold, 1832; Haunted Trails, 1949; **I Shot Jesse James**, 1949; The James Brothers of Missouri, 1949; Jesse James, 1927; **Jesse James**, 1939; Jesse James as the Outlaw, 1921; Jesse James Rides Again, 1947; **Johnny Guitar**, 1954; Kansas Raiders, 1950; The Kid Rides Again, 1943; Land of Haunted Men, 1943; The Laramie Kid, 1935; The Last Days of Frank and Jesse James, 1986 (made-for-TV); The Last Outlaw, 1936; Lawless Breed, 1946; The Lawless Frontier, 1934; Lawless Riders, 1935; **The Lone Ranger**, 2013; The Lone Rider Crosses the Rio, 1941; **The Long Riders**, 1980; The Lucky Texan,

1934; The Magnificent Seven Ride!, 1972; The Man from Death Valley, 1931; The Man from Hell, 1934; The Man from Utah, 1934; The Man from Tumbleweeds, 1940; Marked Men, 1919; Marshal of Cedar Rock, 1953; Marshal of Heldorado, 1950; Marshal of Laredo, 1945; Masked Raiders, 1949; The Maverick Queen, 1956; Men of America, 1932; The Mexicali Kid, 1938; The Moonlighter, 1953; The Nevadan, 1950; The Oklahoma Cyclone, 1930; **One-Eyed Jacks**, 1961; Outlaw Women, 1952; Outlaws of the Rockies, 1945; Outlaws of Santa Fe, 1944; The Phantom Rider, 1946; **Rage at Dawn**, 1955; Rancho Notorious, 1952; Rawhide Rangers, 1941; The Renegade, 1943; The Return of Jesse James, 1950; **Return of the Bad Men**, 1948; Ride a Crooked Trail, 1958; Ride, Cowboy, Ride, 1939; Ride, Vaquero!, 1953; The Rider of the Law, 1935; Riders of the Rio Grande, 1943; Ridin' on a Rainbow, 1941; Road Agent, 1941; Rocky Mountain Rangers, 1940; **Run for Cover**, 1955; Rustler's Valley, 1937; The Sagebrush Family Trails West, 1940; Salt Lake Raiders, 1950; Shooting High, 1940; Silver Canyon, 1951; Six Shootin' Sheriff, 1938; Six-Gun Law, 1948; Son of Billy the Kid, 1949; Son of the Border, 1933; Sonora Stagecoach, 1944; South of Heaven, West of Hell, 2000; Southwest Passage, 1954; The Spikes Gang, 1974; **The Spoilers**, 1942; Stampede, 1949; Stormy Trails, 1936; Sunset Pass, 1946; The Texas Bad Man, 1932; Texas Dynamo, 1950; Three Desperate Men, 1951; Three Godfathers, 1916; **Three Godfathers**, 1936; **3 Godfathers**, 1948; The Three Outlaws, 1956; Trail of the Yukon, 1949; Trail Riders, 1941; Trouble in Sundown, 1939; **The True Story of Jesse James**, 1957; Under Colorado Skies, 1947; Untamed Justice, 1929; **When the Daltons Rode**, 1940; The Whirlwind, 1933; Whirlwind, 1951; Whirlwind Raiders, 1948; Wild and Woolly, 1937; **The Wild Bunch**, 1969; Wild Horse Phantom, 1944; Wild Mustang, 1935; **Wild Rovers**, 1971; **Winchester '73**, 1950; Winning of the West, 1953; Wolves of the Range, 1943; Wyoming Renegades, 1954; **Yellow Sky**, 1948; **The Younger Brothers**, 1949. Note: For detailed information on the most notorious bank robbers of the Old West, see my books *Bloodletters and Badmen* (M. Evans, 1973); *Encyclopedia of World Crime*; 8 volumes (CrimeBooks, Inc., 1990); *The Great Pictorial History of World Crime*; 2 volumes (History, Inc., 2004).

Barbary Coast (San Francisco, c. 1860-1911; red light district): **Barbary Coast**, 1935; Barbary Coast, 1975-1976 (TV series); Barbary Coast Gent, 1944; The Desperadoes, 1943; The Fastest Guitar Alive, 1967; Flame of Barbary Coast, 1945; Frisco Jenny, 1932; **Frisco Kid**, 1935; Frisco Sal, 1945; **Gentleman Jim**, 1942; Inside Straight, 1951; Law of the Barbary Coast, 1949; **Nob Hill**, 1945; Old San Francisco, 1927; The Penalty, 1920; **San Francisco**, 1936; San Francisco Docks, 1940; The San Francisco Story, 1952; The Sea Flower, 1918; The Vagabond Prince, 1916; Wharf Angel, 1934.

Bare Knuckle Fighters: American Brawler, 2013; Among Dead Men, 2008; Any Gun Can Play, 1967; **Any Way Which You Can**, 1980; Bare Knuckles, 2013; Bear Island, 1979; Bruc, the Manhunt, 2010; Crossing the Line, 1990; Damage, 2009; **Django Unchained**, 2012; Dog Bite Dog, 2006; **Every Which Way But Loose**, 1978; The Expendables 3, 2014; Fighting, 2009; Fist of Honor, 1993; 47 Ronin, 2013; **Gentleman Jim**, 1942 (James J. Corbett; John L. Sullivan); Gladiator Cop, 1995; **The Great John L**, 1945 (John L. Sullivan); **Hard Times**, 1975; Knockaround Guys, 2001; Last Man Standing, 1987; The Last of the Knucklemen, 1979; The Learning Tree, 1969; The Legend of Hercules, 2014; Life, 1999; Like It Is, 1998; Lionheart, 1990; Locked Down, 2010; Machete, 2010; Mandingo, 1975; McLintock!, 1963; Night of the Warrior, 1991; **Out of the Furnace**, 2013; **Pompeii**, 2014; **The Quiet Man**, 1952; Raiders of the South, 1947; Rigged, 2008; Robot Overlords, 2014; Rust and Bone, 2012; **The Scalphunters**, 1968; Schizo, 2004; **Sherlock Holmes**, 2009; **Snatch**, 2000; Street Warrior, 2008 (made-for-TV); Sunday Too Far Away, 1975; **Texas**, 1941; The Two Faces of Dr. Jekyll, 1960; Vegasland, 2008; Without Mercy, 1995; **Wyatt Earp**, 1994; **Young Guns**, 1988.

Baseball: The Adventures of Frank Merriwell, 1936 (serial); Alibi Ike, 1935 (Chicago Cubs); Amos, 1985 (made-for-TV); **Angels in the Outfield**, 1951 (Pittsburgh Pirates); **Angels in the Outfield**, 1994 (California Angels); **The Babe**, 1992 (George Herman "Babe" Ruth; New York Yankees); Babe Ruth, 1991 (made-for-TV; New York Yankees); **The Babe Ruth Story**, 1948 (New York Yankees); Back in the Game, 2013- (TV series); **The Bad News Bears**, 1976; **Bang the Drum Slowly**, 1973; The Battery, 2012; Battlefield Baseball, 2003; The Benchwarmers, 2006; The Big Picture, 1989 (George Herman "Babe" Ruth); **The Bingo Long Traveling All Stars & Motor Kings**, 1976; The Blonde, 2001 (TV miniseries; based on Marilyn Monroe and her relationship with New York Yankees player Joe DiMaggio); Boys, 1996; **Brewster's Millions**, 1985; The Bronx Is Burning, 2007 (TV series; New York Yankees); **Bull Durham**, 1988; **Cannery Row**, 1982; Casey at the Bat, 1916; Casey at the Bat, 1927; Cobb, 1994 (Ty Cobb; Detroit Tigers); **Damn Yankees**, 1958 (New York Yankees); Deadball, 2011; Deadline at Dawn, 1946; Dempsey, 1983 (made-for-TV; George Herman "Babe" Ruth; New York Yankees); Don't Look Back: The Story of Leroy "Satchel" Paige, 1981 (made-for-TV; Negro Leagues); Eastbound & Down, 2009-2013 (TV series); **Eight Men Out**, 1988 (1919 Chicago White Sox); **Elmer the Great**, 1933 (Chicago Cubs); Everybody Loves Raymond, 1996-2005 (TV series); The Fan, 1996 (San Francisco Giants); **Fear Strikes Out**, 1957 (Jimmy Piersall; Boston Red Sox); **Field of Dreams**, 1989 (1919 Chicago White Sox); For Love of the Game, 1999 (Detroit Tigers); **42**, 2013 (Jackie Robinson; Brooklyn Dodgers); The Goddess, 1958 (based on Marilyn Monroe and her relationship with New York Yankees player Joe DiMaggio); Henry & Me, 2014 (George Herman "Babe" Ruth; Lefty Gomez; Thurman Munson; Reggie Jackson; Michael Kay; Joe Girardi; Mickey Mantle; New York Yankees); Hit and Run, 1924; Holes, 2003; Hot Curves, 1930; House on Haunted Hill, 1999; How Do You Know, 2010; I'm With Lucy, 2002; Insignificance, 1985 (based on Marilyn Monroe and her relationship with New York Yankees player Joe DiMaggio); Ironweed, 1987; It Happened in Flatbush, 1942; **It Happens Every Spring**, 1949 (fictitious St. Louis team); **The Jackie Robinson Story**, 1950 (Brooklyn Dodgers); **Jim Thorpe—All American**, 1951 (New York Giants); The Kid from Cleveland, 1949 (Cleveland Indians); The Kid from Left Field, 1979 (made-for-TV); Kill the Umpire, 1950 (Texas League); Ladies' Day, 1943; **A League of Their Own**, 1992; **Little Big League**, 1994 (Minnesota Twins); Love Affair: The Eleanor and Lou Gehrig Story, 1978 (made-for-TV; Lou Gehrig; George Herman "Babe" Ruth; New York Yankees); Love Finds You in Sugarcreek, 2014 (made-for-TV); Major League, 1989 (Cleveland Indians); **Make Mine Music**, 1946 (animated sequence of Casey at the Bat); Manhattan Merry-Go-Round, 1942; Marilyn: The Untold Story, 1980 (made-for-TV; based on Marilyn Monroe and her relationship with New York Yankees player Joe DiMaggio); **Meet John Doe**, 1941; The Men's Club, 1986; A Mile in His Shoes, 2011 (made-for-TV); Mr. Baseball, 1992; Mr. Dynamite, 1941; Moneyball, 2011 (Oakland Athletics); Moonlight in Havana, 1942; **The Natural**, 1984 (based on Edward Stephen Waitkus, who played for the Chicago Cubs, Philadelphia Phillies and Baltimore Orioles and who was shot and critically wounded on June 14, 1949, at Chicago's Edgewater Beach Hotel by deranged fan and stalker Ruth Ann Steinhagen, 1929-2012); Never Been Kissed, 1999; Norma Jean & Marilyn, 1996 (made-for-TV; based on Marilyn Monroe and her relationship with New York Yankees player Joe DiMaggio); **The Odd Couple**, 1968; One Hit from Home, 2012; Outrage, 2003; Outside Ozona, 1998; **The Pride of St. Louis**, 1952 (Jerome "Dizzy" Dean; St. Louis Cardinals; Chicago Cubs); **The Pride of the Yankees**, 1942 (Lou Gehrig; New York Yankees); Rocket Gibraltar, 1988; The Rookie, 2002 (Jim Morris; Tampa Bay Devil Rays); **Rookie of the Year**, 1993 (Chicago Cubs); Safe at Home!, 1962 (Roger Maris; Mickey Mantle; New York Yankees); **The Sandlot**, 1993; **The Scout**, 1994 (New York Yankees); Seven Minutes in Heaven, 1985; **Ship of Fools**, 1965; Shuffleton's Barbershop, 2013 (made-for-TV); Signs, 2002; Simple Men, 1992; 61*, 2001 (made-for-

TV; Roger Maris; Mickey Mantle; New York Yankees); Soul of the Game, 1996 (made-for-cable-TV; Negro Leagues; Leroy "Satchel" Paige; Josh Gibson; Jackie Robinson); **Space Jam**, 1996 (Michael Jordan; Birmingham Barons, minor league team of Chicago White Sox); **Strategic Air Command**, 1955 (St. Louis Cardinals); **The Stratton Story**, 1949 (Monty Stratton; Chicago White Sox); Summer Catch, 2001; Summer Wars, 2009; Swellhead, 1935; **Take Me Out to the Ball Game**, 1949; Tall Tales & Legends, 1985-1987 (TV series; "Casey at the Bat," 1986 episode); **That Touch of Mink**, 1962 (Roger Maris; Mickey Mantle; Yogi Berra; New York Yankees); **Trouble with the Curve**, 2012; 20,000 Men a Year, 1939; Two's Company, 1973 (made-for-TV); **The Upside of Anger**, 2005; **The Winning Team**, 1952 (Grover Cleveland Alexander; Philadelphia Phillies; Chicago Cubs; St. Louis Cardinals); **Woman of the Year**, 1942; Wrecking Crew, 1942.

Basketball: Above the Rim, 1994; **The Absent-Minded Professor**, 1961; Across the Universe, 2007; After the Sunset, 2004; **Air Bud**, 1997; **Airplane!**, 1980; Alien: Resurrection, 1997; Along Came Polly, 2004; The Amazing Spider-Man, 2012; **American Beauty**, 1999; American History X, 1988; **Angels with Dirty Faces**, 1938; Another Earth, 2011; Are We There Yet?, 2005; The Astronaut Farmer, 2006; August Rush, 2007; **The Bachelor and the Bobby-Soxer**, 1947; Bad Boys, 1995; BASEketball, 1998; Basketball, 2013- (TV series); The Basketball Diaries, 1995; Battle Royale, 2001; Bedazzled, 2000; **Believe in Me**, 2007; **Big**, 1988; **Big Fish**, 2003; Billy Madison, 1995; **Black Hawk Down**, 2001; Blended, 2014; Blue Chips, 1994; The Breakfast Club, 1989; Brotherly Love, 2015; Buffy the Vampire Slayer, 1992; The Butterfly Effect, 2004; The Cable Guy, 1996; Charlie Bartlett, 2007; **Children of a Lesser God**, 1986; City of Angels, 1998; Coach Carter, 2005; **Coming to America**, 1988; Conviction, 2010; Cosmopolis, 2012; **Dawn of the Dead**, 1979; **The Deep End of the Ocean**, 1999; **The Deer Hunter**, 1978; **Delivery Man**, 2013; Doctor Strange, 2016; **Don Jon**, 2013; **The Door in the Floor**, 2004; Doubt, 2008; Dreamcatcher, 2003; Drive Me Crazy, 1999; Easy A, 2010; Elizabethtown, 2005; Enough, 2002; Escape from L.A., 1996; **Escape Plan**, 2013; The Expendables, 2010; The Experiment, 2001; The Experiment, 2010; Fallen, 1998; Finding Forrester, 2000; The Flintstones, 1994; Flubber, 1997; **Forget Paris**, 1995; Fresh, 1994; Good Burger, 1997; Grand Canyon, 1991; **Grease**, 1978; **The Great Santini**, 1979; The Green Hornet, 2011; **Hair**, 1979; Half Nelson, 2006; Halls of Anger, 1970; Hancock, 2008; Hang Time, 1995-2000 (TV series); Happy Days, 1974-1984 (TV series); The Harlem Globetrotters, 1951; **Harry Brown**, 2009; He Got Game, 1998; Hitch, 2005; **Hoosiers**, 1986; How to Lose a Guy in 10 Days, 2003; **Husbands and Wives**, 1992; **In Good Company**, 2004; In Her Shoes, 2005; Infinitely Polar Bear, 2014; Into the Storm, 2014; It's Kind of a Funny Story, 2010; **The Italian Job**, 2003; **The Interview**, 2014; Jack, 1996; Juice, 1992; Just Wright, 2010; The Kids Are All Right, 2010; The Kingdom, 2007; **The Last Picture Show**, 1971; **Like Mike**, 2002; Like Stars on Earth, 2007; Love & Basketball, 2000; The Luck of the Irish, 2001 (made-for-TV); Made of Honor, 2008; Martian Child, 2007; Mean Creek, 2004; Meatballs, 1979; **Meet Me in St. Louis**, 1944; **Mr. & Mrs. Smith**, 2005; Mr. Nobody, 2009; Monster House, 2006; **My Bodyguard**, 1980; **My Dog Skip**, 2000; My Girl, 1991; My Stepmother Is an Alien, 1988; Nancy Drew, 2007; Napoleon Dynamite, 2004; New Jack City, 1991; New York, I Love You, 2008; Now and Then, 1995; One Crazy Summer, 1986; **One Flew Over the Cuckoo's Nest**, 1975; Orphan, 2009; Out of Sight, 1998; Pain & Gain, 2013; Panic Room, 2002; Paycheck, 2003; **Picnic**, 1955; **Planet of the Apes**, 2001; Pleasantville, 1998; **Please Give**, 2010; Porky's, 1981; Prefontaine, 1997; Prime, 2005; Primer, 2003; The Princess Diaries, 2001; **Prometheus**, 2012; Push, 2009; Radio, 2003; Raising Helen, 2004; Rebound, 2005; Revenge of the Nerds, 1984; Romeo Must Die, 2000; **Runaway Jury**, 2003; Running Scared, 1986; Rushmore, 1998; The Sacrament, 2013; Self/less, 2015; 17 Again, 2009; Shaft, 2000; Short Cuts, 1993; Sleepers, 1996; The Smurfs, 2011; **Solitary Man**, 2009;

Space Jam, 1996; Spider-Man 3, 2007; **Splendor in the Grass**, 1961; Step Up, 2006; **Stripes**, 1981; Teen Wolf, 1985; Think Like a Man, 2012; The Three Stooges, 2012; **To Live and Die in L.A.**, 1985; Trainwreck, 2015; **Transformers**, 2007; 25th Hour, 2002; 21 Grams, 2003; Two for the Money, 2005; **Up in the Air**, 2009; A Walk to Remember, 2002; We Need to Talk About Kevin, 2011; **West Side Story**, 1961; What Happens in Vegas, 2008; While You Were Sleeping, 1995; White Men Can't Jump, 1992; The Winning Season, 2009; Without Limits, 1998.

Battleships (warships): **Above Us the Waves**, 1956 (*Tirpitz*); The Adventures of Smilin' Jack, 1943 (serial); **Air Force**, 1943; **Anchors Aweigh**, 1945; Atragon, 1963; **The Avengers**, 2012; The Baby and the Battleship, 1957; Battleship, 2012; **The Battleship Potemkin**, 1925; Beach Red, 1967; Corregidor, 1943; **The Court-Martial of Billy Mitchell**, 1955; **D-Day; The Sixth of June**, 1956; December 7th: The Movie, 1943; **Destination Tokyo**, 1943; Don Winslow of the Coast Guard, 1943 (serial); **Father Goose**, 1964; Final Yamato, 1983; **Flat Top**, 1952; **The Fleet's In**, 1942; **Follow the Fleet**, 1936; For the Love of Mary, 1948; **The Frogmen**, 1951; **Gabriel Over the White House**, 1933; **The Gallant Hours**, 1960; Girls at Sea, 1958; Give Me a Sailor, 1938; **Godzilla**, 2014; Gorgo, 1961; **Guadalcanal Diary**, 1943; **The Guns of Navarone**, 1961; **Hell Below**, 1933; Hell Raiders of the Deep, 1954; **Here Comes the Navy**, 1934; **In Harm's Way**, 1965; In the Navy, 1941; **In Which We Serve**, 1942; Lady Be Careful, 1936; The Last Ship, 2014- (TV series); Let's Go Navy!, 1951; The Little Hut, 1957; **The Longest Day**, 1962; **Malta Story**, 1954; Miditerraneo, 1992; **Midway**, 1976; Midshipman Jack, 1933; Moonzund, 1987; Off Limits, 1952; Okinawa, 1952; On the Beach, 1959; Operation Bikini, 1963; **Pearl Harbor**, 2001; The Philadelphia Experiment, 1984; Prisoner of Japan, 1942; Pursuit of the Graf Spee, 1956 (*Admiral Graf Spee*); Remember Pearl Harbor, 1942; Rules of Engagement, 2000; **Sands of Iwo Jima**, 1949; The Sea Chase, 1955; Shout at the Devil, 1976; **Sink the Bismarck!**, 1960; Son of a Sailor, 1933; Space Battleship Yamato, 1977; Space Battleship Yamato, 2010; Spare a Copper, 1941; **Stand By for Action**, 1942; **Submarine D-1**, 1937; **Task Force**, 1949; **Tell It to the Marines**, 1926; Three Cockeyed Sailors, 1941; Today We Live, 1933; **Tora! Tora! Tora!**, 1970; Torpedoed, 1937; Under Siege, 1992; The Valiant, 1962; War and Remembrance, 1988- (TV miniseries); **X-Men: First Class**, 2011; Yamato, 2005.

Beggars (also see Hoboes, this index): **A nous la liberté**, 1931; Accattone, 1961; Adventures in Manhattan, 1936; **Ali Baba and the Forty Thieves**, 1944; Amazing Grace, 2006; America America, 1963; Angela's Ashes, 1999; Arabian Adventure, 1979; **Arabian Nights**, 1942; Arabian Nights, 1974; Around the World in 80 Days, 2004; Babes in Bagdad, 1952; Bagdad, 1949; **The Battle of Algiers**, 1967; Beggars in Ermine, 1934; **Beggars of Life**, 1928; **The Beggars Opera**, 1953; **Ben-Hur**, 1959; **Bicycle Thieves**, 1949; **Black Narcissus**, 1947; Blake of Scotland Yard, 1937; Brother Sun, Sister Moon, 1972; The Brothers Grimm, 2005; The Burning Hell, 1974; **Carrie**, 1952; Charlie Chan in Paris, 1935; The Cherry Orchard, 2002; **Cinderella Man**, 2005; **A Clockwork Orange**, 1971; **Code Unknown: Incomplete Tales of Several Journeys**, 2000; **Colonel Blimp**, 1945; The Comedians, 1967; **A Connecticut Yankee in King Arthur's Court**, 1949; Cousin Bette, 1998; The Counterfeit Coin, 1960; Cradle Will Rock, 1999; Cromwell, 1970; **The Curse of the Werewolf**, 1961; Daughter of the Tong, 1939; Days of Being Wild, 1991; The Desert Hawk, 1944; Diana and Me, 1997; Drag Me to Hell, 2009; The Driller Killer, 1979; The Evil of Frankenstein, 1964; Eye of the Beholder, 1999; Farewell, Home Sweet Home, 1999; Fearless, 2006; **Fellini Satyricon**, 1969; **Fiddler on the Roof**, 1971; A Fool and His Money, 1989; Four Flies on Grey Velvet, 1971; Free Men, 2011; Gervaise, 1957; Girls in the Night, 1953; **The Good Earth**, 1937; Half Baked, 1998; Hellbenders, 1967; Holy Motors, 2012; **The Hunchback of Notre Dame**, 1923; **The Hunchback of**

Notre Dame, 1939; The Hunchback of Notre Dame, 1956; **The Hunch-back of Notre Dame**, 1995; Hunger, 1968; I Am Cuba, 1964; I Come with the Rain, 2009; In the Middle of the World, 2004; The Invention of Lying, 2009; K-PAX, 2001; **The Illusionist**, 2006; In This World, 2002; **Into the West**, 1993; Jack the Ripper, 1988- (TV series); Johns, 1996; Kandahar, 2001; Katie Tippel, 1976; **Kim**, 1950; King of Beggars, 1993; Kismet, 1930; **Kismet**, 1944; Kismet, 1955; Knockabout, 1979; **La Chienne**, 1975; Lady Caroline Lamb, 1972; **Lady Jane**, 1986; Lady Oscar, 1979; Lady Snowblood, 1973; **Last Holiday**, 1950; The Last Minute, 2001; Le Grand Voyage, 2005; L'enfant, 2005; **Les Misérables**, 1935; **Les Misérables**, 1952; **Les Misérables**, 1995; **Les Misérables**, 1998; Let Joy Reign Supreme, 1977; Life Is Hot in Cracktown, 2009; Life of Brian, 1979; Lost City of the Jungle, 1946 (serial); Love in Bloom, 1935; The Lovers on the Bridge, 1991; **M**, 1931; **Macao**, 1952; **Madame Bovary**, 1949; Madame Bovary, 1991; Midnight's Children, 2012; Mondo, 1997; **Monsieur Vincent**, 1948; **The Mudlark**, 1950; **My Man Godfrey**, 1936; Nazarin, 1968; **Nicholas Nickleby**, 2002; **Night and the City**, 1950; A Night in Old Mexico, 2013; **The Night of the Hunter**, 1955; Night Sun, 1990; Oblomov, 1980; **Odd Man Out**, 1947; **Orphans of the Storm**, 1921; **Osama**, 2004; Painted Fire, 2002; **The Painted Veil**, 1934; **The Painted Veil**, 2006; Paris 36, 2008; **Pepe Le Moko**, 1941; **Persepolis**, 2007; Philanthropy, 2002; Poetic Justice, 1993; The Prince and the Pauper, 1915; The Prince and the Pauper, 1920; **The Prince and the Pauper**, 1937; The Prince and the Pauper, 1977; The Prince and the Pauper, 1990; The Prince and the Pauper, 2007; **Princess Caraboo**, 1994; The Prodigal, 1955; The Rainbow Thief, 1990; Ran, 1985; **The Razor's Edge**, 1946; The Razor's Edge, 1984; Rent, 2005; **Salaam Bombay!**, 1988; Seize the Day, 1986; The Seventh Sin, 1957; Slacker, 1991; Sneakers, 1982; The Sorcerer's Apprentice, 1978; The Street of Forgotten Men, 1925; Sudan, 1945; **Suddenly, Last Summer**, 1959; **Sullivan's Travels**, 1941; Sweeney Todd: The Demon Barber of Fleet Street, 2007; Tambourine, 2008; **The Thief of Bagdad**, 1924; **The Thief of Bagdad**, 1940; **A Thousand and One Nights**, 1945; **Trading Places**, 1983; Traffic Signal, 2007; **The Treasure of the Sierra Madre**, 1948; **Umberto D**, 1955; **Variety Lights**, 1965; **Viridiana**, 1962; **The Wages of Fear**, 1955; Water, 2005; Where Angels Fear to Tread, 1991; **Wild Boys of the Road**, 1933; The Young and the Damned, 1952.

Bellboys and Bellhops at Hotels: **Arise My Love**, 1940; The Bell Boy, 1918; The Bellboy, 1960; **Blonde Crazy**, 1931; Born to Kill, 1947; Century Hotel, 2001; Crazy in Alabama, 1999; Cuban Fireball, 1951; Daredevil Drivers, 1938; A Date with the Falcon, 1942; Daughter of the Tong, 1939; **Don't Bother to Knock**, 1952; Father Was a Fullback, 1949; Fired Wife, 1943; Four Rooms, 1995; **Fourteen Hours**, 1951; The French Key, 1936; Garden State, 2004; The Gay Deception, 1935; Gildersleeve on Broadway, 1943; Go Into Your Dance, 1935; **The Grand Budapest Hotel**, 2014; Her Highness and the Bellboy, 1945; Here We Go Again, 1942; **High Sierra**, 1941; **Hollywood Hotel**, 1937; Honeymoon Hotel, 1934; **The Horn Blows at Midnight**, 1945; **Hotel**, 1967; **Hotel Berlin**, 1945; **Hotel Reserve**, 1946; **Hotel Rwanda**, 2004; Irish Luck, 1939; Joe Palooka in the Counterpunch, 1949; Kentucky Moonshine, 1938; **Kid Galahad**, 1937; The Killer That Stalked New York, 1950; A King in New York, 1957; Ladies' Man, 1947; The Lady and the Monster, 1944; Lady Tubbs, 1935; Ma and Pa Kettle Go to Town, 1950; Ma and Pa Kettle on Vacation, 1953; Maisie Gets Her Man, 1942; Maisie Goes to Reno, 1944; Mr. Moto Takes a Vacation, 1939; **The Monster and the Girl**, 1941; Moonlight in Havana, 1942; Motel Confidential, 1969; Mountain Music, 1937; Murder in the Air, 1940; Nancy Drew...Reporter, 1939; Night Club Girl, 1945; **A Night in Casablanca**, 1946; **No Way Out**, 1987; Page Miss Glory, 1935; **Pee-wee's Big Adventure**, 1985; Public Enemies, 1941; Red Light, 1949; **Remember the Day**, 1941; **The Second Best Exotic Marigold Hotel**, 2015; She's for Me, 1943; A Shot in the Dark, 1935; Showgirls, 1995; Smart Woman, 1948; **Some Like It Hot**, 1959; Something for the Birds,

1952; **A Southern Yankee**, 1948; **Spellbound**, 1945; The Strange Love of Molly Louvain, 1932; Strictly in the Groove, 1942; Swingin' on a Rainbow, 1945; Texas, Brooklyn and Heaven, 1948; Three of a Kind, 1936; Times Square Lady, 1935; Times Square Playboy, 1936; **Topper**, 1937; Twenty Plus Two, 1961; The Walls Came Tumbling Down, 1946; Wanted: Jane Turner, 1936; We Were Dancing, 1942; **Week-End at the Waldorf**, 1945; **Week-End in Havana**, 1941; You're Out of Luck, 1941.

Bigamists and Bigamy: The Abandoned, 1945; Almost Married, 1932; **Bathing Beauty**, 1944; Big Trouble in Little China, 1986; The Bigamist, 1916; The Bigamist, 1921; The Bigamist, 1953; The Bigamist, 1956; A Bride of the Seventh Heaven, 2004; **Bureau of Missing Persons**, 1933; **The Captain's Paradise**, 1953; **Carrie**, 1952; The Case of the Curious Bride, 1935; Charlie Chan at Monte Carlo, 1937; **Cleopatra**, 1934; **Cleopatra**, 1963; Coffee, Tea or Me?, 1973 (made-for-TV); **The Constant Husband**, 1955; Curse of the Fly, 1965; D.O.A., 1988; Dangerous Number, 1937; Deceived, 1991; Double Standard, 1988 (made-for-TV); The Duo, 1997; Enemies: A Love Story, 1989; Every Woman's Dream, 1996 (made-for-TV); **The Falcon in Mexico**, 1944; First Lady, 1937; Fletch, 1985; Frequent Flyer, 1996 (made-for-TV); **Girl Shy**, 1924; **The Good Earth**, 1937; The Great Vazquez, 2010; Handle with Care, 1977; Hangman's House, 1928; Hearts in Exile, 1915; Hell's Highway, 1932; Honeymoon Deferred, 1950; **Into the Wild**, 2007; Jenny Jenny, 1966; **Jimmy the Gent**, 1934; Kisses for Breakfast, 1941; Krull, 1983; Lady Audley's Secret, 1949 (made-for-TV); Lady Behave!, 1937; A Lady in Love, 1920; Lady Liberty, 1972; Leonie, 2010; **Libeled Lady**, 1936; Lilly Turner, 1933; Linda, 1929; Living Dangerously, 1936; Love at Large, 1990; Love's Wilderness, 1924; Lucky Them, 2013; Madame Butterfly, 1995; Madame Butterfly, 2010; The Man Who Wouldn't Die, 1942; The Man with Three Wives, 1993 (made-for-TV); The Matrimonial Bed, 1930; **Meet Me after the Show**, 1951; Micki + Maude, 1984; **The Miracle of Morgan's Creek**, 1944; Miss Lulu Bett, 1921; A Modern Musketeer, 1917; Move Over, Darling, 1963; **My Favorite Wife**, 1940; My One and Only, 2009; Northfork, 2003; Out of Control, 2003; Parole Girl, 1933; The Parole Officer, 2001; Peach-O-Reno, 1931; The Price She Paid, 1917; The Remarkable Mr. Pennnypacker, 1959; Run for Your Wife, 2012; Service, 2008; **Sex and the Single Girl**, 1964; Shadows, 1919; She Led Two Lives, 1994 (made-for-TV); Skeletons, 2010; The Substitute Wife, 1994 (made-for-TV); Sunflower, 1970; Surrender, 1950; Swing Your Lady, 1938; A Table for One, 1999; A Tale of Two Wives, 2003 (made-for-TV); The Tattooed Stranger, 1950; Thirteen Conversations About One Thing, 2001; Three Sons o' Guns, 1941; The Toll of the Sea, 1922; **Tony Rome**, 1967; Three's a Crowd, 1969 (made-for-TV); Trapped by the Mormons, 1922; **Ugetsu**, 1954; Valentino, 1977; The Viking Who Became a Bigamist, 1969; The Wax Model, 1917; Whirlpool, 1934; **Witness for the Prosecution**, 1957.

Black Market: **Abandoned**, 1949; ...And the Fifth Horseman Is Fear, 1968; Angelina, 1948; Anything for Her, 2008; Army of Shadows, 1969; Atlantic Wall, 1970; Au revoir les enfants, 1987; The Barefoot Battalion, 1954; The Beasts of Marseilles, 1959; Below the Deadline, 1946; The Berliner, 1952; A Better Life, 2011; Biutiful, 2010; Black Market Rustlers, 1943; Blood Diamond, 2006; The Boss of Big Town, 1942; The Brave One, 2007; Buffalo Soldiers, 2001; **Casablanca**, 1942; **City of Torment**, 1950; Coma, 1978; The Cyclist, 1987; The Darkest Corner of Paradise, 2010; Delicatessen, 1991; Dilemma of Two Angels, 1948; Down with Misery, 1945; **Empire of the Sun**, 1987; Escape by Night, 1960; Faraway, So Close!, 1993; **Fateless**, 2005; **First Yank Into Tokyo**, 1945; **A Foreign Affair**, 1948; Foreign Land, 1997; Four Bags Full, 1957; Frantic, 1988; French Leave, 1948; Germany Year Zero, 1949; The Good German, 2006; Government Agents vs. Phantom Legion, 1951; **The Great Raid**, 2005; Home Alone 3, 1997; **House of Bamboo**, 1955; **I Was a Male War Bride**, 1949; In Praise of Older

Women, 1997; **Julia**, 2008; Khadak, 2007; **Kiss the Blood Off My Hands**, 1948; **The Last Metro**, 1981; The Last Ride, 1944; Le chemin des ecoliers, 1960; L'enfant, 2005; Leningrad, 2011; Life of Brian, 1979; Machuca, 2005; Madame Brouette, 2003; **The Man Between**, 1953; The Market: A Tale of Trade, 2009; **Mr. Arkadin**, 1962; Monsieur Batignole, 2003; No Place for a Lady, 1943; Nora inu, 1963; **Open City**, 1946; **Operation Mad Ball**, 1957; **Pacific Rim**, 2013; The Paris Express, 1953; Peddlin' in Society, 1950; **Persepolis**, 2007; Pigs and Battleships, 1963; The Printing, 1990; **The Public Eye**, 1992; Pu-239, 2007; The Racket Man, 1944; Repo Men, 2010; **Reunion in France**, 1942; Rush Hour 2, 2001; **Saigon**, 1948; **The Shawshank Redemption**, 1994; **The Ship That Died of Shame**, 1956; **Shoeshine**, 1947; The Silk Noose, 1948; **Sirocco**, 1951; Sister, 2012; The Slingshot, 1994; Sun Alley, 2000; Sympathy for Mr. Vengeance, 2002; **Taking Sides**, 2003; Tangier Incident, 1953; The Tattooed Swordsman, 1971; Temptress Moon, 1997; They Made Me a Fugitive, 1948; Tiara Tahiti, 1963; **The Third Man**, 1950; **This Land Is Mine**, 1943; The Tiger and the Widow, 1981; **To End All Wars**, 2001; **Tokyo Joe**, 1949; Tom und Hacke, 2012; Tomorrow We Live, 1942; **Up Front**, 1951; Vera Drake, 2004; Videodrome, 1983; Violette, 2013; The War Boys, 2009; Yami no kodomotachi, 2008; You Can't Escape Forever, 1942.

Blacksmiths: **Alexander Nevsky**, 1939; Amy Foster, 1997; Andrei Rublev, 1966; **Antonia's Line**, 1995; Apache Drums, 1951; **Arabian Nights**, 1942; Army of Darkness, 1992; Bells of San Fernando, 1947; A Big Hand for the Little Lady, 1966; **Back to the Future Part III**, 1990; The Black Knight, 1954; Bright Leaf, 1950; A Canterbury Tale, 1944; Captain Kidd, 1945; The Children Are Watching Us, 1944; **Chisum**, 1970; The Christmas Kid, 1967; Conan the Barbarian, 2011; **A Connecticut Yankee in King Arthur's Court**, 1949; The Cowboy Counsellor, 1932; **The Crusades**, 1935; Daredevils of the West, 1943 (serial); Deadwood Dick, 1940; Death Hunt, 1981; The Desert Hawk, 1950; Down Texas Way, 1942; The Farmer Takes a Wife, 1935; **Fighting Caravans**, 1931; **The Flame and the Arrow**, 1950; For Love and Gold, 1966; **Four Sons**, 1928; Gervaise, 1956; The Girl of the Golden West, 1938; Ghost of Zorro, 1949 (serial); God's Country and the Man, 1937; The Great Adventures of Wild Bill Hickok, 1938 (serial); Great Expectations, 1934; **Great Expectations**, 1946; Gunslingers, 1950; **Hang 'Em High**, 1968; **The Harvey Girls**, 1946; Hellboy II: The Golden Army, 2008; **The Hobbit: An Unexpected Journey**, 2012; **How to Train Your Dragon**, 2010; The Hunted, 1995; **In Old Arizona**, 1929; The Iron Age, 1982 (TV miniseries); **The Iron Mistress**, 1952; Jade Warrior, 2006; Jesse James Rides Again, 1947; Joe Palooka Meets Humphrey, 1950; Judge Priest, 1934; The Kaiser, the Beast of Berlin, 1918; **Kingdom of Heaven**, 2005; A Knight's Tale, 2001; **The Last Days of Pompeii**, 1935; The Little Convict, 1979; Lone Texas Ranger, 1945; The Lonely Man, 1957; The Lucky Texan, 1934; The Man from Hell, 1934; **Moby Dick**, 1930; **Moby Dick**, 1956; **My Life So Far**, 1999; My Outlaw Brother, 1951; **The Navigator: A Medieval Odyssey**, 1988; **Ned Kelly**, 1970; No Name on the Bullet, 1959; **The Paleface**, 1948; The Phantom Stage, 1939; The Pirates of Blood River, 1962; **Pirates of the Caribbean: The Curse of the Black Pearl**, 2003; The Proposition, 2005; **Queen Christina**, 1933; **Quentin Durward**, 1955; Range Law, 1944; The Return of the Durango Kid, 1945; Rogue of the Range, 1936; Romulus, My Father, 2008; Rose of the Rancho, 1936; **Rosewood**, 1997; Sam Whiskey, 1969; Santa Claus, 1959; Savage Islands, 1983; Secret Service in Darkest Africa, 1943 (serial); **The Seventh Seal**, 1958; **Shane**, 1953; **She Wore a Yellow Ribbon**, 1949; The Singing Blacksmith, 1938; Son of the Morning Star, 1991 (TV miniseries); **The Sons of Katie Elder**, 1965; The Spanish Sword, 1962; Stagecoach Buckeroo, 1942; **The Stalking Moon**, 1968; Stormy Trails, 1936; Swing Your Lady, 1938; **The Tall T**, 1957; They Made Me a Killer, 1946; A Tornado in the Saddle, 1942; **The Two Faces of January**, 2014; **Unconquered**, 1947; Underworld: Rise of the Lycans, 2009; The Village Blacksmith, 1922; **Virginia City**, 1940; Vulcan: Son of

Giove, 1962; **Wake Island**, 1942; Western Trails, 1938; Wheels of Destiny, 1934; **The Woman on the Beach**, 1947; The Young and the Damned, 1952.

Bordellos: Assassins, 2010; Bad Girls, 1994; **The Ballad of Cable Hogue**, 1970; **Belle de jour**, 1968; **Belle Toujours**, 2006; **The Bicycle Thieves**, 1949; Big Trouble in Little China, 1986; Bordello, 1981; Bordello, 1985; Bordello of Blood, 1996; Brothel, 2008; Bright Leaf, 1950; **Butch Cassidy and the Sundance Kid**, 1969; **The Cheyenne Social Club**, 1970; **Closely Watched Trains**, 1967; The Counterfeiters of Paris, 1961; Cowards Bend the Knee or the Blue Hands, 2004; **The Curious Case of Benjamin Button**, 2008; Dirty Dingus Magee, 1970; Flap, 1970; **A Funny Thing Happened on the Way to the Forum**, 1966; **Gaily, Gaily**, 1969; Gangs of New York, 2002; **The Godfather: Part II**, 1974; **The Great Northfield, Minnesota Raid**, 1972; **The Great Train Robbery**, 1979; **Hang 'Em High**, 1968; House of Pleasure for Women, 1976; **The Long Riders**, 1980; **McCabe & Mrs. Miller**, 1971; A Night in Old Mexico, 2013; **North to Alaska**, 1960; **Open City**, 1946; Outrageous Fortune, 1987; Place Without Limits, 1978; **Public Enemies**, 2009; Quick, Let's Get Married, 1964; Rancho Deluxe, 1975; Rouge, 1987; **Seabiscuit**, 2003; Spartan, 2004; **Stagecoach**, 1939; Stand-Up Guys, 2012; **Susan Lenox; Her Fall and Rise**, 1931; Taxi Driver, 1976; **There Was a Crooked Man**, 1970; **True Confessions**, 1981; **Unforgiven**, 1992; **Walk on the Wild Side**, 1962; **Welcome to Hard Times**, 1967; West Beirut, 1999; What Did You Do in the War, Daddy?, 1966; **The White Buffalo**, 1977; **Wild Bill**, 1995; **Wyatt Earp**, 1994; **Yesterday, Today and Tomorrow**, 1964.

Bounty Hunters (historic and Old West): Ace High, 1969; Acquasanta Joe, 1971; The Adventures of Brisco County Jr., 1993-1994 (TV series); **The Adventures of Huckleberry Finn**, 1960; Alias Smith and Jones, 1971-1973 (TV series; several episodes depicting bounty hunters); And Now...Make Your Peace with God, 1968; Any Gun Can Play, 1968; Apache Warrior, 1957; Avenging Angel, 2007 (made-for-TV); Black Spurs, 1965; The Big Gundown, 1968; Bordertown, 1989-1991 (TV series; several episodes depicting bounty hunters); The Bounty Man, 1972 (made-for-TV); The Bounty Hunter, 1954; Bounty Hunter in Trinity, 1972; The Bounty Killer, 1965; The Capture of Grizzly Adams, 1982 (made-for-TV); Catlow, 1971; **Chisum**, 1970; Cimarron City, 1958-1960 (TV series; several episodes depicting bounty hunters); Cimarron Strip, 1967-1968 (TV series; several episodes depicting bounty hunters); Cowboy G-Men, 1952-1953 (TV series; several episodes depicting bounty hunters); The Dangerous Days of Kiowa Jones, 1966 (made-for-TV); Dawn Rider, 2012; Dead Bones, 2008; Dead Men Don't Count, 1968; The Deputy, 1959-1961 (TV series; several episodes depicting bounty hunters); Desolation Canyon, 2006 (made-for-TV); Django, A Bullet for You, 1969; Dust, 2003; Execution, 1968; An Eye for an Eye, 1966; The Firebrand, 1962; **For a Few Dollars More**, 1967; **Geronimo: An American Legend**, 1993; God Made Them...I Kill Them, 1968; **The Good, the Bad and the Ugly**, 1967; The Grand Duel, 1974; The Great Silence, 1968; Grim Prairie Trails: Hit the Trail...to Terror, 1990; Gunsmoke, 1955-1975 (TV series; several episodes depicting bounty hunters); Hannah's Law, 2012 (made-for-TV); Hannie Caulder, 1972; Hard Bounty, 1995; He Who Shoots First, 1966; High Bounty, 1995; High Plains Invaders, 2009 (made-for-TV); Inn of the Damned, 1975; Into the Badlands, 1991 (made-for-TV); Joe Kidd, 1972; Johnny Ringo, 1959-1960 (TV series; several episodes depicting bounty hunters); Last of the Dogmen, 1995; Lawman, 1958-1962 (TV series; several episodes depicting bounty hunters); Life Is Tough Enough, Eh Providence?, 1972; Lonesome Dove: The Outlaw Years, 1995-1996 (TV series); Luke and the Tenderfoot, 1955 (TV series; several episodes depicting bounty hunters); Maverick, 1957-1962 (TV series; several episodes depicting bounty hunters); Meaner Than Hell, 2009; **The Missouri Breaks**, 1976; **The Naked Spur**, 1953; The Night Before Christmas, 1994; **The Outlaw Josey Wales**, 1976; Overland Trail, 1960 (TV series; several episodes depicting bounty hunters); **Pat Garrett and Billy the Kid**, 1973; Per il gusto di uccidere, 1966; **The Professionals**, 1966; Quintana: Dead or Alive, 1969; Renegade, 2004; Renegade Riders, 1968; The Retrieval, 2013; The Return of Sabata, 1972; Return of Shanghai Joe, 1975; The Reward, 1965; **Ride Lonesome**, 1959; The Rifleman, 1958-1963 (TV series; several episodes depicting bounty hunters); Rio Diablo, 1993 (made-for-TV); Sabata, 1969; Saddle Tramp Women, 1972; Santee, 1973; **Seraphim Falls**, 2007; **The Shooting**, 1966; Shotgun, 1955; Sidekicks, 1974 (made-for-TV); Six Gun, 2008; Stagecoach West, 1960-1961 (TV series; several episodes depicting bounty hunters); Strange Empire, 2014- (TV series; several episodes depicting bounty hunters); 10,000 Dollars for a Massacre, 1967; **3:10 to Yuma**, 1957; **3:10 to Yuma**, 2007; Take a Hard Ride, 1975; Tales of Wells Fargo, 1957-1972 (TV series; several episodes depicting bounty hunters); The Texan, 1958-1960 (TV series; several episodes depicting bounty hunters); The Texican, 1966; Three Crosses Not to Die, 1968; **The Tin Star**, 1957; Trackdown, 1957-1959 (TV series; several episodes depicting bounty hunters); The Tracker, 1988 (made-for-TV); **True Grit**, 1969; **True Grit**, 2010; The Ugly Ones, 1968; Un par de asesinos, 1970; Una lunga fila di croci, 1969; **Unforgiven**, 1992; Unforgiven, 2014; Vengeance Is Mine, 1968; Wanted: Dead or Alive, 1958-1961 (TV series); **The Wild Bunch**, 1969; Wild Times, 1980 (TV miniseries); **Young Guns**, 1988; **Young Guns II**, 1990.

Boxcars: As Far as My Feet Will Carry Me, 2001; **Beggars of Life**, 1928; Big Bad Love, 2001; Blue Ridge Fall, 1999; Blues in the Night, 1941; **Boom Town**, 1940; Boxcar Bertha, 1972; The Brain, 1969; **Champion**, 1949; The Dream Catcher, 1999; **Emperor of the North Pole**, 1973; The Fighting Peacemaker, 1926; Fortress of War, 2010; **The General**, 1926; The Girl in Lovers Lane, 1960; Girls of the Road, 1940; Gun Crazy, 1950; Hell-Fire Austin, 1932; I'm Not There, 2007; Kid Courageous, 1935; **Meet John Doe**, 1941; Perils of the Wilderness, 1956 (serial); **Picnic**, 1955; **The Professionals**, 1966; **Schindler's List**, 1993; Slaughterhouse-Five, 1972; **Sullivan's Travels**, 1941; **They Shoot Horses, Don't They?**, 1969; **To End All Wars**, 2001; Twenty Four Seven, 1997; **Von Ryan's Express**, 1965; The Water Diviner, 2014; **Wild Boys of the Road**, 1933; **You Only Live Once**, 1937.

Boxers and Boxing (prizefighters and amateur fighters): **The Abysmal Brute**, 1923; Action Jackson, 1988; **Adventures of a Young Man**, 1962; After Dark, My Sweet, 1990; Against the Ropes, 2004; Ali, 2001 (Muhammad Ali); Ali: An American Hero, 2000 (made-for-TV; Muhammad Ali); **The Animal Kingdom**, 1932; **Annapolis**, 2006; **Any Which Way You Can**, 1980 (Bare Knuckle); **April Showers**, 1923; Aryan: Unbreakable, 2006; Back Roads, 1981; Backfire, 1950; Bad Boy, 1949; The Bad Man of Brimstone, 1937; The Bad Penny, 2010; Behind the Rising Sun, 1943; Bell-Bottom George, 1944; Below the Deadline, 1936; The Big Chance, 1933; The Big Game, 1936; **The Big Knife**, 1955; The Big Man, 1991 (Bare Knuckle); Black Cloud, 2004; The Black Dahlia, 2006; The Blonde Bomber, 1936 (Joe Palooka); Blood and Bone, 2009; Bluebeard's Eighth Wife, 1938; **Body and Soul**, 1947; Body and Soul, 2000; The Boxer, 1963; **The Boxer**, 1997; **Broken Blossoms**, 1919; Broken Journey, 1948; The Brute, 1920; **Buck Privates**, 1941; Busted Up, 1987; Cain and Mabel, 1936; The Calcium Kid, 2005; Calling All Kids, 1937 (Joe Palooka); The Card, 1922; Carman: The Champion, 2001; **Carmen Jones**, 1954; Carnera: The Walking Mountain, 2008 (Primo Carnera); Casablanca Driver, 2004; **The Champ**, 1931; **The Champ**, 1979; **Champion**, 1949; The Choke's on You, 1936 (Joe Palooka); **Cinderella Man**, 2005 (James J. Braddock, Max Baer); **City for Conquest**, 1940; City Heat, 1984; **City Lights**, 1931; Corinthian Jack, 1921; The Crime Patrol, 1936; The Crooked Circle, 1957; **The Crowd Roars**, 1938; Dempsey, 1983 (made-for-TV; Jack Dempsey); **Designing Woman**, 1957; Detective, 1985; Diggstown, 1992; Doin' Time, 1985; Duke of Chicago, 1949; Emergency Call, 1952; **Every Which Way But Loose**, 1978 (Bare Knuckle); **Fat City**,

1972; Fight and Win, 1924 (Jack Dempsey as a prizefighter); The Fighter, 1952; The Fighter, 1983 (made-for-TV); **The Fighter**, 2010; The Fighting Gentleman, 1932; Fighting Tommy Riley, 2004; **First Kid**, 1996; Fists of Steel, 1991 (Bare Knuckle); Flying Fists, 1937; Footlight Serenade, 1942; For the Love of Pete, 1936 (Joe Palooka); **From Here to Eternity**, 1953; From Mexico with Love, 2009; Fugitive from the Sky, 1936; Gangster Squad, 2013; **Gentleman Jim**, 1942 (James J. Corbett, John L. Sullivan); Gentleman Joe Palooka, 1946; Girlfight, 2000; Gladiator, 1992; Glory Alley, 1952; The Goddess, 1958; **Golden Boy**, 1939; Goldie and the Boxer, 1979 (made-for-TV); **The Great John L.**, 1945 (John L. Sullivan); **The Great White Hope**, 1970 (Jack Johnson); The Great White Hype, 1996; The Greatest, 1977 (Muhammad Ali); Grudge Match, 2013; **Halls of Montezuma**, 1950; Hammer, 1972; The Hammer, 2007; **Hard Times**, 1975 (Bare Knuckle); **The Harder They Fall**, 1956 (role model for Primo Carnera); Harvest Melody, 1943; Heart of a Champion: The Ray Mancini Story, 1985 (made-for-TV; Ray "Boom Boom" Mancini); Hell's Cargo, 1935; **Here Comes Mr. Jordan**, 1941; Here's How, 1936 (Joe Palooka); Homeboy, 1988; **The Homecoming**, 1973; Hot News, 1953; House of Cards, 1968; **How Green Was My Valley**, 1941; **The Hurricane**, 1999 (Rubin "Hurricane" Carter); I Spy, 2002; In This Corner, 1948; Invitation to Happiness, 1939; **The Irish in Us**, 1935; Iron Man, 1951; **It's Always Fair Weather**, 1955; Jim Bougne, Boxeur, 1923; Joe and Max, 2002 (made-for-TV; Joe Louis, Max Schmeling); **The Joe Louis Story**, 1953; Joe Palooka, Champ, 1946; Joe Palooka in Fighting Mad, 1948; Joe Palooka in Humphrey Takes a Chance, 1950; Joe Palooka in the Big Fight, 1949; Joe Palooka in the Counterpunch, 1949; Joe Palooka in the Knockout, 1947; Joe Palooka in the Square Circle, 1950; Joe Palooka in Triple Cross, 1951; Joe Palooka in Winner Take All, 1948; Joe Palooka Meets Humphrey, 1950; The Joe Palooka Story, 1954-1955 (TV series); The Keeper, 2009; Kelly the Second, 1936; Kick Me Again, 1937 (Joe Palooka); The Kid: Chamaco, 2010; **The Kid from Brooklyn**, 1946; **Kid Galahad**, 1937; Kid Galahad, 1962; Kid Monk Baroni, 1952; Killer McCoy, 1947; **The Killers**, 1946; Killer's Kiss, 1955; King of Chinatown, 1939; Knockout, 2000; **L.A. Confidential**, 1997; Ladies and the Champ, 2001 (made-for-TV); Lady and the Gent, 1932; Lady Caroline Lamb, 1973; Last of the Breed, 1996; Laughing Irish Eyes, 1936; **Les Misérables**, 1995; Like It Is, 1998; Lionheart, 1990 (Bare Knuckle); The Main Event, 1979; Matilda, 1978 (boxing kangaroo); Max Schmeling, 2010; **Medium Cool**, 1969; **Mighty Joe Young**, 1949; The Mighty McGurk, 1947; **The Milky Way**, 1936; **Million Dollar Baby**, 2004; **Million Dollar Mermaid**, 1952 (boxing kangaroo); The Miracle Kid, 1941; Mr. Celebrity, 1941; Mr. Moto's Gamble, 1938; Mo, 2006; My Baby's Daddy, 2004; Nancy Drew…Reporter, 1939; Native Son, 1951; Navy Bound, 1951; News Hounds, 1947; Never Back Down, 2008 (Bare Knuckle); Never Back Down 2: The Beatdown, 2011 (Bare Knuckle); **Night and the City**, 1992; Night of the Warrior, 1991; **99 River Street**, 1953; Nothing to Lose, 1994; Off Limits, 1953; **On the Waterfront**, 1954; Once to Every Man, 1918; One for the Money, 2012; The Opponent, 2000; Over the Wall, 1938; Pacquiao: The Movie, 2006; **Palooka**, 1934 (Joe Palooka); Paradise, 2004; **Pat and Mike**, 1952; Percy & Thunder, 1993; Performance, 1970; The Personality Kid, 1934; Phantom Punch, 2008 (Sonny Liston); **Pittsburgh**, 1942; Play It to the Bone, 1999; Poor Boy's Game, 2007; Prison Shadows, 1936; The Prizefighter, 1979; The Prizefighter and the Lady, 1933 (Max Baer, Primo Carnera); Pulp Fiction, 1994; Punch and Beauty, 1936 (Joe Palooka); The Quest, 1996 (kickboxing); **The Quiet Man**, 1952; **Raging Bull**, 1980 (Jake La Motta); **Random Harvest**, 1942; Reflections in a Golden Eye, 1967; **Requiem for a Heavyweight**, 1962; Resurrecting the Champ, 2007; Revolution, 2006; **Right Cross**, 1950; **The Ring**, 1927; Ringside Maisie, 1941; **Rocky**, 1976; **Rocky II**, 1979; Rocky III, 1982; Rocky IV, 1985; Rocky Balboa, 2006; The Rough Lover, 1918; **The Set-Up**, 1949; Snake Eyes, 1998; Snatch, 2000; Some Blondes Are Dangerous, 1937; **Somebody Up There Likes Me**, 1956 (Rocky Graziano, Tony Zale); Southland Tales, 2006; **Southpaw**, 2015; Southside, 2003; Split

Decisions, 1988; The Square Ring, 1955; Stars Over Broadway, 1935; Straight Right, 2000; **The Street With No Name**, 1948; Strength and Honor, 2007; Sworn Enemy, 1936; Taking the Count, 1937 (Joe Palooka); **Tension**, 1949; Terrible Joe Moran, 1984 (made-for-TV); **Thank Your Lucky Stars**, 1943; **They Made Me a Criminal**, 1939; They Never Come Back, 1932; Thirst Aid, 1937 (Joe Palooka); Three Sons O' Guns, 1941; **Tin Pan Alley**, 1940; The Tip-Off, 1931; Tough Enough, 1983; **Triumph of the Spirit**, 1989; Unchained, 1955; Undisputed, 2002; Undisputed: Last Man Standing, 2006; Valentino, 1977; Walkover, 1969; When's Your Birthday?, 1937; Where God Left His Shoes, 2007; Wildcat Saunders, 1936; **Winner Take All**, 1932; Woman-Wise, 1937; The Wonder Man, 1920; **World in My Corner**, 1956; **Wyatt Earp**, 1994; The Young Americans, 1993; **Ziegfeld Girl**, 1941.

Brainwashing: Aamir, 2008 (terrorist cult indoctrination); American Ultra, 2015; Angel Dust, 1994 (cult indoctrination); The Anomaly, 2014; **Around the World in 80 Days**, 1956 (Thuggee cult indoctrination); Around the World in 80 Days, 1989 (made-for-TV; Thuggee cult indoctrination); The Assassin, 1965; Assignment: Paris, 1952 (Soviet indoctrination); Balkan Spy, 1984 (government indoctrination); Blood Diamond, 2006; **The Bourne Legacy**, 2012; The Brain from Planet Arous, 1957 (alien indoctrination); Brainwashed, 1961 (Nazi indoctrination); **Brazil**, 1985 (futuristic Big Brother indoctrination); **Captain America: The Winter Soldier**, 2014; Captive, 1986 (male chauvinism indoctrination); Chained, 2012; Children of Sorrow, 2012 (cult indoctrination); Citizen Tania, 1989 (Patty Hearst; indoctrination by revolutionaries); **A Clockwork Orange**, 1971 (experimental indoctrination to rehab criminals); Closet Land, 1991; The Collection, 2012; **Commandos Strike at Dawn**, 1942 (Nazi indoctrination); Cypher, 2002 (corporate indoctrination); The Defector, 1966 (government indoctrination); Demon Seed, 1977; Disturbing Behavior, 1998; Dirty Hearts, 2011 (Japanese nationalism indoctrination); Drunk History, 2013- (TV series; "San Francisco," 2013 episode; Patty Hearst; indoctrination by revolutionaries); Equilibrium, 2002 (futuristic Big Brother indoctrination); Faults, 2014 (cult indoctrination); The Fearmakers, 1958 (Korean War POW indoctrination); The 5th Wave, 2016; **The 49th Parallel** (aka: The Invaders), 1942 (Nazi indoctrination); **Full Metal Jacket**, 1987 (military indoctrination); The Great Water, 2004 (Soviet indoctrination); **Gunga Din**, 1939 (Thuggee cult indoctrination); Hitler's Children, 1943 (Nazi indoctrination); Hot Fuzz, 2007; Human Experiments, 1979 (medical indoctrination); **The Hunger Games: Mockingjay—Part 1**, 2014; **The Hunger Games: Mockingjay—Part 2**, 2015; Idiocracy, 2006; Igor, 2008 (indoctrination by scientific community); In Like Flint, 1967 (indoctrination of an all-female community); **Indiana Jones and the Temple of Doom**, 1984 (Thuggee cult indoctrination); The Interrogation of Michael Crowe, 2002 (made-for-TV; indoctrination by police); Invader, 1992 (alien indoctrination); **Invaders from Mars**, 1953 (alien indoctrination); **The Ipcress File**, 1965 (government indoctrination of scientists); The Island, 1980; Johnny English Reborn, 2011; Kept Woman, 2015 (made-for-TV); Killers from Space, 1951; **Kingsman: The Secret Service**, 2014; The Kiss, 1988; Land of the Blind, 2006; The Last of the Manson Girls, 2015 (made-for-TV; killer cult indoctrination); Legend, 1985; **The Long Goodbye**, 1973 (cult indoctrination); Madame Sin, 1972; Magnetic, 2015 (alien indoctrination); **The Manchurian Candidate**, 1962 (Korean War POW indoctrination); The Manchurian Candidate, 2004 (First Gulf War); **The Mind Benders**, 1963 (scientific indoctrination); **Miss Sadie Thompson**, 1953 (religious indoctrination); Mysterious Two, 1982 (made-for-TV; alien indoctrination); **1984**, 1956; **The Naked Gun: From the Files of Police Squad**, 1988; **1984**, 1956 (futuristic Big Brother indoctrination); **Nineteen Eighty Four**, 1984 (futuristic Big Brother indoctrination); Octane, 2003 (cult indoctrination); Omkara, 2006; **On Her Majesty's Secret Service**, 1969; Oranges Are Not the Only Fruit, 1989 (TV miniseries); The Ordeal of Patty Hearst, 1979 (made-for-TV; indoctrination by revolutionaries); **Our Man Flint**, 1966; Pafnucio Santo, 1977 (Patty Hearst;

indoctrination by revolutionaries); **The Parallax View**, 1974 (corporate indoctrination); Patty Hearst, 1988 (indoctrination by revolutionaries); The Poughkeepsie Tapes, 2007; Priest, 1994; **The Prisoner**, 1955 (Soviet indoctrination); **Prisoner of War**, 1954 (Korean War POW indoctrination); **The Rack**, 1956 (Korean War POW indoctrination); **Rain**, 1932 (religious indoctrination); Remote Control, 1988 (alien indoctrination); Resident Evil: Extinction, 2007; Return from Witch Mountain, 1978; Revenge of the Stepford Wives, 1980 (made-for-TV; female chauvinism indoctrination); The Sacrament, 2013; **Sadie Thompson**, 1928 (religious indoctrination); Sgt. Pepper's Lonely Hearts Club Band, 1978; **The Shadow**, 1994; Shallow Hal, 2001; Shivers, 1981 (Soviet indoctrination); Shock Treatment, 1981; Simon, 1980 (scientist cabal indoctrination); Sinbad of the Seven Seas, 1989; **Sleeper**, 1973 (futuristic Big Brother indoctrination); **Split Image**, 1982 (religious cult indoctrination); **Star Trek II: The Wrath of Khan**, 1982; Steel Toes, 2007; The Stepford Children, 1987 (made-for-TV); The Stepford Husbands, 1996 (made-for-TV; female chauvinism indoctrination); **The Stepford Wives**, 1975 (male chauvinism indoctrination); The Stepford Wives, 2004 (male chauvinism indoctrination); The Stone Killer, 1973; Street Fighter, 1994; **Telefon**, 1977 (indoctrinated Soviet assassins in the U.S.); They Live, 1988 (alien indoctrination); Thirst, 1979 (killer cult indoctrination); **36 Hours**, 1965 (WWII POW indoctrination); This Is England, 2006 (Skinhead indoctrination); **This Land Is Mine**, 1943 (Nazi indoctrination); **Ticket to Heaven**, 1981 (religious indoctrination); Timebomb, 1991; **Total Recall**, 1990; Torture Room, 2007 (CIA indoctrination); Undersea Kingdom, 1936 (serial); Upstream Color, 2013; V for Vendetta, 2005 (futuristic Big Brother indoctrination); V: The Final Battle, 1984 (TV miniseries); Videodrome, 1983 (media indoctrination); Volunteers, 1985; War of the Satellites, 1958 (alien indoctrination); **Whirlpool**, 1949 (indoctrination of a rich woman through hypnosis); Worlds Apart, 2008; Zoolander, 2001 (indoctrination to commit an assassination).

Bridges: **Alvarez Kelly**, 1966 (Confederate cattle rustlers blow up a bridge to prevent pursuit); **Arch of Triumph**, 1948 (man saves woman from jumping into the Seine River in Paris and they become star-crossed lovers); **Across the Bridge**, 1957 (fugitive attempting to flee into and back from Mexico over a bridge); **Bataan**, 1943 (guarding a bridge on Luzon during the Philippine Defense of 1942 in WWII); **The Bowery**, 1933 (NYC's Brooklyn Bridge spanning the East River and from which Steve Brodie, played by George Raft, leaps and survives on July 23, 1886); The Bridge, 2011- (TV series); The Bridge, 2013- (TV series); The Bridge, 2015 (made-for-TV); **The Bridge at Remagen**, 1969; The Bridge of San Luis Rey, 1929 (five people plunge to their deaths when a rope bridge gives way in the Peruvian Alps); The Bridge of San Luis Rey, 1944 (five people plunge to their deaths when a rope bridge gives way in the Peruvian Alps); The Bridge of San Luis Rey, 2004 (five people plunge to their deaths when a rope bridge gives way in the Peruvian Alps); **Bridge of Spies**, 2015 (Glienicke Bridge connecting Potsdam and Berlin); **A Bridge Too Far**, 1977 (1944 Allied Market Garden Operation in the Netherlands depicting the Son, Grave, Nijmegen and Arnhem bridges); **The Bridge on the River Kwai**, 1957; **The Bridges at Toko-Ri**, 1954 (military objective in the Korean War); **The Bridges of Madison County**, 1995; Cop Land, 1997 (distressed young cop leaps from the NYC's George Washington Bridge spanning the Hudson River and linking Manhattan, New York to Fort Lee, New Jersey); **The Core**, 2003 (radiation from Earth's disturbed core cuts the Golden Gate Bridge in San Francisco in half); **Duck, You Sucker!**, 1972 (guarding a bridge in Mexico during the 1910-1920 Revolution); **For Whom the Bell Tolls**, 1943 (blowing up a bridge in Segovia, Spain in May 1937); **Force 10 from Navarone**, 1978 (Allied commandos assigned to destroy a strategic bridge in Yugoslavia during WWII); **The General**, 1926 (giant trestle bridge spectacularly collapses from fire during a Civil War battle, sending a running train into a gorge); The Ghost and the Darkness, 1996 (bridge builders in 1896 East Africa are attacked by two lions to seek out humans for food, based on an actual case where as many as thirty-five victims were claimed by the beasts before they were killed); **Godzilla**, 2014 (gigantic monster destroys Golden Gate Bridge in San Francisco, California); **Gone with the Wind**, 1939 (heroine Scarlett O'Hara hides with family members beneath a bridge during a rainstorm as Union troops ride across the span); **The Great Raid**, 2005 (Filipino guerrillas damage a bridge and prevent Japanese troops from crossing it while U.S. rangers liberate more than 500 Allied prisoners from nearby Cabanatuan Prison Camp on Luzon, Philippines on January 30, 1945, during WWII); **The Green Berets**, 1968 (U.S. commandos kidnap a North Vietnamese general and blow up a bridge to prevent pursuit); **Gunga Din**, 1939 (shaky rope bridge in India over which a gold-seeker crosses to discover a den of killer-cult Thugs worshipping the goddess Kali, and from which a number of pursuing Thugs fall to their deaths); **In the Heat of the Night**, 1967 (Southern sheriff pursues a murder suspect across a bridge); **The Horse Soldiers**, 1959 (Union raiders in the Deep South blow up a bridge to prevent Confederates from pursuing them); **It Came from Beneath the Sea**, 1955 (mammoth octopus destroys the Golden Gate Bridge in San Francisco); **It's a Wonderful Life**, 1946 (despondent businessman leaps from a bridge but his life is saved by his guardian angel); **Kelly's Heroes**, 1970 (GIs use a pontoon bridge to span a river after a bridge is destroyed); **King Kong**, 1933 (mammoth ape destroys a log bridge over a gorge to which escaping men cling); **King Kong**, 2005 (mammoth ape destroys a log bridge over a gorge to which escaping men cling); **Knight Without Armor**, 1937 (bombing assassination attempt is made on a member of royalty on a bridge in St. Petersburg during the Russian Revolution); **The Last Bridge**, 1954; **The Longest Day**, 1962 (British commandos seizing and holding the Pegasus Bridge spanning the Caen Canal between Ouistreham and Caen, in Normandy, France, on June 6, 1944, in WWII); Megashark vs. Giant Octopus, 2009 (giant shark bites the Golden Gate Bridge in San Francisco in half); Meteor Storm, 2010 (made-for-TV; meteor shower destroys The Golden Gate Bridge in San Francisco); **The Naked City**, 1948 (NYC's Williamsburg Bridge spanning the East River and across which a murderer flees); **Pacific Rim**, 2013 (futuristic monsters destroy the Golden Gate Bridge in San Francisco); **Paper Moon**, 1973 (Rulo Bridge spanning the Missouri River); **The Raid**, 1954 (Confederates raiding and robbing the banks of St. Albans, Vermont, on October 19, 1864, escape by burning a bridge to prevent pursuit by Union cavalry); **Saving Private Ryan**, 1998 (GIs hold an important bridge against overwhelming German forces during the 1944 Normandy invasion of WWII); Six Bridges to Cross, 1955 (Bridges leading in and out of Boston, Massachusetts over which thieves might escape following a heist patterned after the 1950 Brink's Robbery); **The Snows of Kilimanjaro**, 1952 (lovers meeting on a bridge spanning the Seine River in Paris); **The Sons of Katie Elder**, 1965 (four brothers under arrest are pinned down beneath a low bridge while assassins-for-hire attempt to kill them); **Sorcerer**, 1977 (trucks carrying life-threatening nitro must cross a rickety rope bridge while traversing a South American jungle); **They Were Expendable**, 1945 (U.S. troops blow up a bridge on Mindanao, Philippines, to prevent pursuit by Japanese forces in WWII); **The 39 Steps**, 1935 (innocent man accused of murder escapes detectives on a stopped train by hiding in the girders of the Forth Bridge spanning the Firth of Forth River in Scotland); **Touch of Evil**, 1958 (confession of a crooked cop is secretly recorded while he stands on a bridge in a small town bordering Mexico); **The Untouchables**, 1987 (Costner and Connery meet at Chicago's North Michigan Avenue Bridge; Costner and his agents intercept a shipment of Canadian liquor at Hardy Creek Bridge at Great Falls, Montana); A View from the Bridge, 1962 (NYC's Brooklyn Bridge spanning the East River); **The Wages of Fear**, 1955 (trucks carrying life-threatening nitro must cross a rickety rope bridge while traversing a South American jungle; remade as **Sorcerer**, 1977); **Waterloo Bridge**, 1931 (bridge in London where star-crossed lovers meet); **Waterloo Bridge**, 1940 (bridge in London where star-crossed lovers meet); **The Wild Bunch**, 1969 (destruction of a bridge sends U.S. Cav-

alry troopers plunging into a river); **X-Men: The Last Stand**, 2006 (Magneto and his mutants rip away the foundation of the Golden Gate Bridge and use the structure as a span to link San Francisco to the island of Alcatraz).

Brink's Robbery (robbery of security firm, collector of currency in all city banks in Boston, Massachusetts, by eight burlgars on the night of January 17, 1950; all the thieves were captured and imprisoned, but only $58,000 of the $2.7 million stolen was recovered): **The Brink's Job**, 1978; Brinks: The Great Robbery, 1976 (made-for-TV); Blueprint for Robbery, 1961; Six Bridges to Cross, 1955.

British Raj (British control of colonial India): **Around the World in 80 Days**, 1956; The Bandit of Zhobe, 1959; **Before the Rains**, 2008; Bengal Brigade, 1954; The Bengali Night, 1988; Bhowani Junction, 1956; **Black Narcissus**, 1947; **The Black Watch**, 1929; **Bonnie Scotland**, 1935; The Brigand of Kandahar, 1965; Carry On...Up the Khyber, 1968; **The Charge of the Light Brigade**, 1936; The Chess Players, 1978; **Clive of India**, 1935; The Crucifer of Blood, 1991 (made-for-TV); **The Drum**, 1938; **Flame Over India**, 1960; Frontier, 1968 (TV series); Ganadevata, 1979; **Gandhi**, 1982; The Green Goddess, 1923; **Gunga Din**, 1939; **Indiana Jones and the Temple of Doom**, 1984; The Jewel in the Crown, 1984 (TV miniseries); Jinnah, 1998; **Jungle Book**, 1942; Junoon, 1979; **Kim**, 1950; Kim, 1984 (made-for-TV); **King of the Khyber Rifles**, 1953; Khyber Patrol, 1954; The Legend of Bhagat Singh, 2002; **The Lives of a Bengal Lancer**, 1935; The Long Duel, 1967; **The Man Who Would Be King**, 1975; Mard, 1985; Miss Beatty's Children, 1992; The Moonstone, 1997 (made-for-TV); Neel Akasher Neechey, 1959; 1942: A Love Story, 1994; Palay Khan, 1986; **Passage to India**, 1984; **The Rains Came**, 1939; **The Rains of Ranchipur**, 1955; Rang De Basanti, 2006; The Rising: The Ballad of Mangal Pandey, 2005; **The River**, 1951; Rudyard Kipling's The Jungle Book, 1994; Shadows of Time, 2005; Sharpe's Challenge, 2006 (made-for-TV); Sharpe's Peril, 2010 (made-for-TV); **Soldiers Three**, 1951; Staying On, 1980 (made-for-TV); Storm Over Bengal, 1938; The Stranglers of Bombay, 1960; Those Daring Young Men in Their Jaunty Jalopies, 1969; **Thunder in the East**, 1953; 22 June 1897, 1979; Veta, 2014; Water, 2006; **Wee Willie Winkie**, 1937.

Broadway Productions and Shows (also see Stage Performers; Vaudeville and Vaudeville Performers, this index): **All About Eve**, 1950; **All That Jazz**, 1979; At the Stage Door, 1921; Author! Author!, 1982; **Babes on Broadway**, 1941; **The Band Wagon**, 1953; **The Barkleys of Broadway**, 1949; **Bedtime Story**, 1941; The Big Street, 1942; **Birdman or (The Unexpected Virtue of Ignorance)**, 2014; **Black Widow**, 1954; **Bloodhounds of Broadway**, 1952; Blossoms on Broadway, 1937; Bowery to Broadway, 1944; **The Boy Friend**, 1971; Bring Your Smile Along, 1955; Broadway, 1929; **Broadway**, 1942; The Broadway Boob, 1926; Broadway Broke, 1923; Broadway Daddies, 1928; **The Broadway Melody**, 1929; **Broadway Melody of 1936**, 1935; **Broadway Melody of 1938**, 1937; **Broadway Melody of 1940**, 1940; Broadway Scandals, 1929; Chasing Rainbows, 1930; Chicken a la King, 1928; Chip Off the Old Block, 1944; Cinderella Swings It, 1943; **City for Conquest**, 1940; **The Country Girl**, 1954; Cowboy in Manhattan, 1943; David Harum, 1934; **Deep in My Heart**, 1954; Delightfully Dangerous, 1945; **De-Lovely**, 2004; **Diamond Jim**, 1936; **A Double Life**, 1947; **Down to Earth**, 1947; The Eddie Cantor Story, 1953; Ellis Island, 1984 (TV miniseries); Follow the Band, 1943; **Footlight Parade**, 1933; Footlight Serenade, 1942; Forty Naughty Girls, 1937; **42nd Street**, 1933; **Funny Girl**, 1968; **Funny Lady**, 1975; The Gentleman from Louisiana, 1936; George White's Scandals, 1934; Gildersleeve on Broadway, 1943; The Girl He Didn't Buy, 1928; **Gold Diggers of 1933**, 1933; **Gold Diggers of 1935**, 1935; **Gold Diggers of 1937**, 1936; Good Morning, Judge, 1943; The Great Flirtation, 1934; **The Great Victor Herbert**, 1939; **The Great Ziegfeld**, 1936; Grief Street, 1931; Haywire,

1980 (made-for-TV); **The Helen Morgan Story**, 1957; **I'll See You in My Dreams**, 1951; It Could Be Worse, 2013 (TV miniseries); **The Jazz Singer**, 1927; The Jazz Singer, 1952; The Jazz Singer, 1980; **Jeanne Eagels**, 1957; **Jolson Sings Again**, 1949; **The Jolson Story**, 1946; Lillian Russell, 1940; Lillie, 1978 (TV miniseries); Lily in Love, 1985; Look for the Silver Lining, 1949; Love Happy, 1949; **Love Me or Leave Me**, 1955; Lovestruck: The Musical, 2013 (made-for-TV); Lucky Me, 1954; **Lullaby of Broadway**, 1951; Make a Wish, 1937; The Matinee Idol, 1928; **Meet Me After the Show**, 1951; Mr. Big, 1943; My Best Gal, 1944; **My Gal Sal**, 1942; **My Wild Irish Rose**, 1947; **New York, New York**, 1977; **Night and Day**, 1946; On Broadway, 2007; Polly of the Follies, 1922; **Prince of Players**, 1955; **The Producers**, 1967; The Producers, 2005; Rainbow Over Broadway, 1933; Regal Cavalcade, 1935; Repeat Performance, 1947; Scattergood Meets Broadway, 1941; **The Seven Little Foys**, 1955; Smash, 2012-2013 (TV series); **Somebody Loves Me**, 1952; **Stage Door**, 1937; Stage Door, 1948 (made-for-TV); **Star!**, 1968; Staying Alive, 1983; **The Story of Vernon and Irene Castle**, 1939; **The Story of Will Rogers**, 1952; Submissions Only, 2010- (TV series); **Tea for Two**, 1950; **This Is the Army**, 1943; **Three for the Show**, 1955; Thrill of a Lifetime, 1937; **Till the Clouds Roll By**, 1946; **Tonight We Sing**, 1953; Two Blondes and a Redhead, 1947; **The Velvet Touch**, 1948; **W.C. Fields and Me**, 1976; Walking Down Broadway, 1938; Wives and Lovers, 1963; **Words and Music**, 1948; **Yankee Doodle Dandy**, 1942; You're the One, 1941; **Ziegfeld Follies**, 1945; **Ziegfeld Girl**, 1941; Ziegfeld: The Man and His Women, 1978 (made-for-TV).

Bronco Riding and Breakin Broncos (horses; also see: Rodeos and Rodeo Performers, this index): All the Pretty Horses, 2000; **American Sniper**, 2014; Arena, 1953; **The Big Country**, 1958; **Boom Town**, 1940; **Bus Stop**, 1956; Dirty Dingus Magee, 1970; **Giant**, 1956; The Hi-Lo Country, 1998; **Hondo**, 1953; **J. W. Coop**, 1971; **Junior Bonner**, 1972; A Lady Takes a Chance, 1943; **The Lusty Men**, 1952; The Man from Utah, 1934; **The Misfits**, 1961; **Monte Walsh**, 1970; Pardners, 1956; Pocket Money, 1972; **Ride 'Em Cowboy**, 1942; Rodeo, 1952; Rodeo Girl, 1980 (made-for-TV); Somewhere in Sonora, 1933; **These Thousand Hills**, 1959; Tickle Me, 1965; **Western Union**, 1941.

Brothers: **Abilene**, 1999; **Across to Singapore**, 1928; **Adam Had Four Sons**, 1941; **The Adventure of Sherlock Holmes' Smarter Brother**, 1975; **All the Brothers Were Valiant**, 1953; **American Flyers**, 1985; Among the Living, 1941; **The Assassination of Jesse James by the Coward Robert Ford**, 2007 (James and Ford brothers); **Bad Man's Territory**, 1946 (James brothers); **Bad Men of Missouri**, 1941 (Younger and James brothers); **Beau Geste**, 1926; **Beau Geste**, 1939; Beau Geste, 1966; **The Beautiful Country**, 2005; Bloody Mama, 1970 (Barker brothers); **Broken Lance**, 1954; Brothers, 2005; **Brothers**, 2009; The Brothers Grimm, 2005; **The Brothers Karamazov**, 1958; **Cat Ballou**, 1965; **Chances**, 1931; **The Charge of the Light Brigade**, 1936; **City Slickers**, 1991; **City Slickers II: The Legend of Curly's Gold**, 1994; **Come Blow Your Horn**, 1963; **The Corsican Brothers**, 1941; **The Cotton Club**, 1984; **Dallas**, 1950; **Duel in the Sun**, 1946; **East of Eden**, 1955; **Escape from Alcatraz**, 1979; The Fabulous Baker Boys, 1989; The Fabulous Dorseys, 1947; Face of a Fugitive, 1959; **The Falcon's Brother**, 1942; **The Fighting 69th**, 1940; Five Little Peppers and How They Grew, 1939; **Four Sons**, 1928; **Gentleman Jim**, 1942; **The Godfather**, 1972; **Godfather II**, 1974; **Gone with the Wind**, 1939 (Tarleton twins); **The Great Missouri Raid**, 1951 (James and Younger brothers); **The Great Northfield, Minnesota Raid**, 1972 (James and Younger Brothers); Gun for a Coward, 1957; **Gunfight at the O. K. Corral**, 1957 (Earp, Clanton and McLowery brothers); Gunfighters of Abilene, 1960; **Gung Ho!**, 1943; Gunman's Walk, 1958; **Hearts of the World**, 1918; **Hour of the Gun**, 1967 (Earp, Clanton and McLowery brothers); **House of Numbers**, 1957; **How Green Was My Valley**, 1941; **In Old Chicago**, 1938 (O'Leary brothers); **Jesse James**, 1939

(James brothers); **The Kennel Murder Case**, 1933; **La Bamba**, 1987; **Law and Order**, 1932 (Earp brothers as role models); **The Long Riders**, 1980 (James, Younger, Miller and Ford brothers); **Moonstruck**, 1987; **The Mortal Storm**, 1940; **Murder, He Says**, 1945; **My Darling Clementine**, 1946 (Earp and Clanton brothers); My Dear Brother, 1973; My Outlaw Brother, 1951; **Nazi Agent**, 1942; The Newton Boys, 1998; **The Public Enemy**, 1931; **Rage at Dawn**, 1955 (Reno brothers); **Rain Man**, 1988; **The Return of Frank James**, 1940 (Ford brothers); **Richard III**, 1956 (Edward and Richard, heirs to the British throne); **Sands of Iwo Jima**, 1949; **Santa Fe**, 1951; **Saving Private Ryan**, 1998; **The Sea Wolf**, 1941; **The Seven Little Foys**, 1955; **Sing, You Sinners**, 1938; **The Spiral Staircase**, 1946; **The Straight Story**, 1999; **The Sullivans**, 1944; **The Tall Men**, 1956; **Tombstone**, 1993 (Earp, Clanton and McLowery brothers); **Tombstone: The Town Too Tough to Die**, 1942 (Earp brothers); **Tower of London**, 1939 (Edward and Richard, heirs to the British throne); Tower of London, 1962 (Edward and Richard, heirs to the British throne); **The True Story of Jesse James**, 1957 (James and Younger brothers); **Underground**, 1941; **Viva Zapata!**, 1952; **Western Union**, 1941; **When the Daltons Rode**, 1940; **Winchester '73**, 1950; **Wyatt Earp**, 1994 (Earp, Clanton and McLowery brothers); **The Younger Brothers**, 1949.

Buffalo: **Across the Great Divide**, 1976; Animals United, 2010; **Around the World in 80 Days**, 1956; The Bad Man of Brimstone, 1937; **The Big Trail**, 1930; **Bless the Beasts and Children**, 1971; **Buffalo Bill**, 1944; The Buffalo Boy, 2004; Buffalo Dreams, 2005 (made-for-TV); Buffalo Rider, 1978; Bury My Heart at Wounded Knee, 2007 (made-for-TV); The Calgary Stampede, 1925; **Cheyenne Autumn**, 1964; **The Covered Wagon**, 1923; **"Crocodile" Dundee**, 1986; Crossfire Trail, 2001 (made-for-TV); **Dances with Wolves**, 1990; **Davy Crockett: King of the Wild Frontier**, 1955; Dead Man's Walk, 1996 (TV miniseries); **Dodge City**, 1939; Dynamite Warrior, 2007; **Ephraim's Rescue**, 2013; **Fighting Caravans**, 1931; Flaming Frontiers, 1938; Fort Worth, 1951; The Gun That Won the West, 1955; Heroes of the West, 1932 (serial); **Home on the Range**, 2004; **How the West Was Won**, 1962; Indian Paint, 1965; **The Iron Horse**, 1924; The Last Frontier, 1926; **The Last Hunt**, 1956; The Legend of the Lone Ranger, 1952; Maisie, 1939; **The Outlaws Is Coming**, 1965; Pawnee, 1957; **The Plainsman**, 1936; **Pony Express**, 1953; Red Fork Range, 1931; **The Ruling Class**, 1972; **The Searchers**, 1956; **She Wore a Yellow Ribbon**, 1949; Son of the Morning Star, 1991 (made-for-TV); **Spirit: Stallion of the Cimarron**, 2002; The Thundering Herd, 1933; Treachery Rides the Range, 1936; **Union Pacific**, 1939; Walking Thunder, 1997; **The Way West**, 1967; **West of Thunder**, 2012; Where the Buffalo Roam, 1938; **The White Buffalo**, 1977; Winnetou: The Last Shot, 1968; With Buffalo Bill on the U.P. Trail, 1926; **Wyatt Earp**, 1994.

Bullfighting: Americano, 2005; **Around the World in 80 Days**, 1956; Baton Rouge, 1988; Belmonte, 1995; **Blood and Sand**, 1922; **Blood and Sand**, 1941; The Bobo, 1967; Bolero, 1984; **The Brave Bulls**, 1951; The Bridge of San Luis Rey, 2004; Bullfighter and the Lady, 1951; The Bullfighters, 1945; Carmen, 1915; Carmen, 1921; Carmen on Ice, 1990 (made-for-TV); **Cowboy**, 1958; **Death in Grenada**, 1996; Friends, 1971; It Started with a Kiss, 1959; The Kid from Amarillo, 1951; **The Kid from Spain**, 1932; The Loves of Carmen, 1948; The Magnificent Matador, 1955; Matador, 1986; The Matador, 2005; A Matador's Mistress (aka: Manolete), 2010; Mexican Hayride, 1948; More Wild, Wild West, 1980 (made-for-TV); **On Her Majesty's Service**, 1969; Once Upon a Time in Mexico, 2003; Pandora and the Flying Dutchman, 1951; The Pleasure Seekers, 1964; Return of the Seven, 1866; The Siren of Seville, 1924; **The Snows of Kilimanjaro**, 1952; **Strangers May Kiss**, 1931; **The Sun Also Rises**, 1957; **Surviving Picasso**, 1996; Talk of Angels, 1998; **A Touch of Class**, 1973; **Zelig**, 1983.

Cameo Appearances by Film stars (either as themselves, or as bit characters, and their studios or production companies): **Around the World in 80 Days**, 1956 (United Artists); The Brady Bunch Movie, 1995 (Paramount); **Callaway Went Thataway**, 1951 (MGM); Crocodile Dundee in Los Angeles, 2001 (Paramount); Don't Worry, We'll Think of a Title, 1966 (United Artists); **Duffy's Tavern**, 1945 (Paramount); 8 Seconds, 1994 (New Line Cinema); **Follow the Boys**, 1944 (Universal); **The Great Muppet Caper**, 1981 (Universal); **The Greatest Story Ever Told**, 1965 (United Artists); Hollywood, 1923 (Paramount); **Hollywood Canteen**, 1944 (Warner Brothers); **Hollywood Cavalcade**, 1939 (Twentieth Century Fox); **Hollywood Hotel**, 1937 (Warner Brothers); **Hollywoodland**, 2006 (Focus Features); **It's a Great Feeling**, 1949 (Warner Brothers); **It's a Mad, Mad, Mad, Mad World**, 1963 (United Artists); **It's in the Bag**, 1945 (United Artists); Last Action Hero, 1993 (Columbia); Meet Wally Sparks, 1997 (Trimark Pictures); **Midway**, 1976 (Universal); Mr. Music, 1950 (Paramount); The Muse, 1999 (October Films); **Ocean's Eleven**, 1960 (Warner Brothers); **Ocean's Eleven**, 2001 (Warner Brothers); Ocean's Twelve, 2004 (Warner Brothers); Paramount on Parade, 1930; Pink Cadillac, 1989 (Warner Brothers); **The Player**, 1992 (Fine Line Features); Private Buckeroo, 1942 (Universal); **Say Anything**, 1989 (Twentieth Century Fox); Show Girl in Hollywood, 1930 (Warner Brothers); **Silent Movie**, 1976 (Twentieth Century Fox); **Souls for Sale**, 1923 (Goldwyn Pictures); **Stage Door Canteen**, 1943 (United Artists); **Star Spangle Rhythm**, 1942 (Paramount); **Starlift**, 1951 (Warner Brothers); **Thank Your Lucky Stars**, 1943 (Warner Brothers); **This Is the Army**, 1943 (Warner Brothers); **Thousands Cheer**, 1943 (MGM); **Too Late the Hero**, 1970 (Cinerama Releasing Corporation); The Yanks Are Coming, 1942 (PRC).

Catholic Nuns: **Agnes of God**, 1985; **Airplane!**, 1980; **Amen**, 2002; **Appointment with Danger**, 1951; Au revoir les enfants, 1987; Bad Lieutenant, 1992; **The Bells of St. Mary's**, 1945; **Black Narcissus**, 1947; **The Blues Brothers**, 1980; Change of Habit, 1970; Child of Darkness, Child of Light, 1991 (made-for-TV); **Come to the Stable**, 1949; The Dangerous Lives of Altar Boys, 2002; The Da Vinci Code, 2006; **Dead Man Walking**, 1995; **The Enforcer**, 1976; The Flying Nun, 1967-1970 (TV series); **Foreign Correspondent**, 1940; **Going My Way**, 1944; **The Grand Budapest Hotel**, 2014; **Heaven Knows, Mr. Allison**, 1957; **The Hunchback of Notre Dame**, 1923; **The Hunchback of Notre Dame**, 1939; **The Hunchback of Notre Dame**, 1996; **Ida**, 2013 **The Keys of the Kingdom**, 1944; **The Lady Vanishes**, 1938; **Les Misérables**, 1935; **Les Misérables**, 1955; **Les Misérables**, 1995; **Les Misérables**, 1998; **Lilies of the Field**, 1963; **The Longest Day**, 1962; Luther, 2003; **The Nun**, 1971; The Nun, 2013; **The Nun's Story**, 1959; The Order, 2003; Papillon, 1973; Paradise Road, 1997; **Portrait of Jennie**, 1949; **Robin and Marian**, 1976; The Singing Nun, 1966; Sister Act, 1992; Sister Act 2: Back in the Habit, 1993; **The Song of Bernadette**, 1943; **The Sound of Music**, 1965; **Tea with Mussolini**, 1999; The Trouble with Angels, 1966; **Two Mules for Sister Sara**, 1970; The White Sister, 1915; **The White Sister**, 1923; **The White Sister**, 1933; The White Sister, 1973; Wide Awake, 1998.

Cavalry Charges (U.S. Cavalry during the Indian Wars): Arrow in the Dust, 1954; **Arrowhead**, 1953; Battles of Chief Pontiac, 1952; Breakheart Pass, 1975; Bugles in the Afternoon, 1952; **Buffalo Bill**, 1944 (charge of the U.S. 5th Cavalry at War Bonnet Creek on the Cheyenne River, South Dakota, July 17, 1876); Buffalo Bill, 1965; Column South, 1953; Comanche, 1956; The Command, 1954; Custer of the West, 1967 (Custer Massacre); **Davy Crocket, Indian Scout**, 1950; A Distant Trumpet, 1964; Duel at Diablo, 1966; **Fort Apache**, 1948 (recreation of Custer Massacre); Fort Yuma, 1955; **Geronimo**, 1939 (footage from **The Plainsman**, 1936); **Geronimo: An American Legend**, 1993; The Great Sioux Massacre, 1965 (Custer Massacre); The Great Sioux Uprising, 1953; Into the West, 2005 (TV miniseries); **Kit Carson**, 1940; **The Last Outpost**, 1951; **Little Big Horn**, 1951; **Little Big Man**, 1970

(Custer Massacre); **Only the Valiant**, 1951; **The Plainsman**, 1936 (Custer Massacre); **Rio Grande**, 1950; **The Searchers**, 1956; **She Wore a Yellow Ribbon**, 1949; Sitting Bull, 1954 (Custer Massacre); Son of the Morning Star, 1991 (made-for-TV; Custer Massacre); **Stagecoach**, 1939; **They Died with Their Boots On**, 1941 (U.S. Civil War and Indian Wars, including Custer Massacre); They Rode West, 1954; **Two Flags West**, 1950; **Ulzana's Raid**, 1972; War Arrow, 1953.

Cavalry Charges (Other than U.S. Cavalry during the Indian Wars): **Abraham Lincoln**, 1930 (Union cavalry during the Civil War); Alexander, 2004 (Greek cavalry charge against Persian forces in Asia Minor, 333 B.C.); **Alexander the Great**, 1956 (Grecian War in Asia Minor, 333 B.C.); Alexander the Great, 2006 (animated Grecian War in Asia Minor, 333 B.C.); **The Alamo**, 1960 (Mexican cavalry against the Alamo in 1836); **The Alamo**, 2004 (Mexican and Texas volunteer cavalry at the Alamo and Jan Jacinto in 1836); Amigo, 2010 (Philippine-American War, 1899-1902); The Avenger, 1964 (Trojan War, 1194-1184 B.C.); Bengal Brigade, 1954 (British-Indian cavalry in 1857 India); The Blue and the Gray, 1982 (TV miniseries; American Civil War); **Braveheart**, 1995 (English and Scottish cavalry at the battles of Stirling Bridge in 1297 and Falkirk in 1298); Cavalry Command, 1958 (1902, during the Philippine-American War, 1899-1902); **The Charge of the Light Brigade**, 1936 (British cavalry in 19th-Century India and the charge at the Battle of Balaclava, 1854, in the Crimean War); **The Charge of the Light Brigade**, 1968 (remake of the 1936 film); **The Chronicles of Narnia: Prince Caspian**, 2008; The Conqueror, 1956 (Genghis Khan; 12th-Century Mongolia); **Dark Command**, 1940 (Quantrill's guerrillas during American Civil War); **Dr. Zhivago**, 1965 (Cossack cavalry in Russian Revolution and Civil War, 1917-1922); **The Fall of the Roman Empire**, 1964 (Roman cavalry in 3rd Century A.D.); **The Fighting Kentuckian**, 1949 (expatriated French cavalry in Louisiana in 1815); The First Texan, 1956 (Texas volunteer cavalry at San Jacinto, 1836); George Washington, 1984 (TV miniseries; American Revolution); **Gladiator**, 2000 (Roman cavalry in 3rd-Century A.D.); **Glory**, 1989 (U.S. Civil War); Gone to Texas, 1986 (made-for-TV; Texas volunteer cavalry at San Jacinto in 1836); **Gunga Din**, 1939 (British cavalry charge against Thug forces in 19th-Century India); **The Horse Soldiers**, 1959 (Union cavalry during the American Civil War emulating Grierson's Raid to Baton Rouge on April 17-May 2, 1863); Ironclad, 2011 (1215, in the English civil war against King John); **Juarez**, 1939 (French cavalry charge against the forces of Juarez during the ill-fated brief reign of Maximilian I of Mexico, 1864-1867); Kansas Raiders, 1950 (Quantrill's guerrillas during the American Civil War); **The Last Command**, 1955 (Mexican cavalry in the attack against the Alamo in 1836); **The Last Samurai**, 2003 (1870s Japan); **The Lighthorsemen**, 1987 (Australian cavalry charge at the Battle of Beersheba on October 31, 1917, in WWI); **The Lives of a Bengal Lancer**, 1935 (British cavalry in 19th-Century India); **The Lion in Winter**, 1968 (12th Century France); The Lord of the Rings, 1978; Love Me Tender, 1956 (U.S. Civil War); **Major Dundee**, 1965 (Mexico, 1865; French lancers and U.S. Cavalry); The Man Behind the Gun, 1953 (American Civil War); **Man of Conquest**, 1939 (Texas volunteer cavalry at San Jacinto, 1836); **The Mummy**, 1999 (French Foreign Legion in North Africa); **The Patriot**, 2000 (American Revolution); The Postman, 1997; The Proud and the Damned, 1972 (American Civil War); **The Red Badge of Courage**, 1951 (U.S. and Confederate cavalry during the Civil War); **Ride with the Devil**, 1999 (Quantrill's guerrillas during the American Civil War, the charges in the raid against Lawrence, Kansas, on August 21, 1863); **Rob Roy**, 1995 (18th-Century Scotland); **Rob Roy: The Highland Rogue**, 1954 (18th Century Scotland); **Rocky Mountain**, 1950 (Confederate cavalry against Indians during the Civil War); Rough Riders, 1997 (made-for-TV; Spanish-American War of 1898); **Santa Fe Trail**, 1940 (U.S. troops at Harpers Ferry during the John Brown insurrection in 1859); The Shadow Riders, 1982 (made-for-TV; American Civil War); Sharpe's Challenge, 2006 (made-for-TV; 19th-Century

India); **Spirit: Stallion of the Cimarron**, 2002; Taras Bulba, 1962 (16th-Century Ukraine); **They Came to Cordura**, 1959 (U.S. cavalry in its campaign in Mexico in 1916-1917 against Pancho Villa); Timbuktu, 1959 (French cavalry in North Africa); Two for Texas, 1998 (made-for-TV; Texas volunteer cavalry at San Jacinto, 1836); **The Undefeated**, 1969 (Mexico, 1865); **Virginia City**, 1940 (American Civil War); **Viva Villa!**, 1934 (Mexican Revolution, 1910-1920); **Viva Zapata!**, 1952 (Mexican Revolution, 1910-1920); **War Horse**, 2011 (British cavalry charge in 1914 during WWI); **Waterloo**, 1970 (French cavalry at the Battle of Waterloo, 1815).

Central Park (New York, New York): **All Through the Night**, 1942; The Anderson Tapes, 1971; **Antz**, 1998; Arbitrage, 2012; **The Band Wagon**, 1953; **Barefoot in the Park**, 1967; **Beau James**, 1957; Big City Blues, 1932; Born to Dance, 1936; **Cat People**, 1942; Central Park, 1932; **The Clock**, 1945; Everyone Says I Love You, 1996; The Extra Man, 2010; Factory Girl, 2006; Fantasy 2000, 1999; **Ghost Town**, 2008; **Hallelujah; I'm a Bum!**, 1933; Holiday Affair, 1949; Ice-Capades, 1941; **King Kong**, 2005; Last Embrace, 1979; **Lights of New York**, 1928; Maid in Manhattan, 2002; The Man Who Played God, 1932; Maniac, 1980; Melinda and Melinda, 2004; Murder on a Bridle Path, 1936; **The Out of Towners**, 1970; Pardon Our Nerve, 1939; **Pillow Talk**, 1959; Sentimental Journey, 1984 (made-for-TV); Sleepwalkers, 2015; A Troll in Central Park, 1994; **Wall Street**, 1987.

Chases (on foot as human prey): **Drums Along the Mohawk**, 1939 (Henry Fonda is chased by Mohawk braves for many miles); **The Most Dangerous Game**, 1932 (Joel McCrea and Fay Wray are hunted on a jungle island by a deranged aristocrat); The Mountain Men, 1980 (Charlton Heston must evade Blackfoot Indians stalking him in the Far West in 1838); **The Naked Prey**, 1966 (Cornel Wilde is pursued by African warriors); **Run for the Sun**, 1956 (Richard Widmark and Jane Greer must outrun Nazi pursuers in the South American wilds); **Run of the Arrow**, 1957 (where Rod Steiger must outrun Sioux Braves to survive); Surviving the Game, 1994 (man takes a well-paying job as a servant in a hunting party in the Rocky Mountains, only to discover that he has become the hunters' prey).

Chases (pursuing outlaws and renegade Indians in the Old West; also see Posses, this index): Adventures in Silverado, 1948; Adventures of Frank and Jesse James, 1948 (serial); The Adventures of Red Ryder, 1940 (serial); Al Jennings of Oklahoma, 1951; Albuquerque, 1948; **Along Came Jones**, 1945; Along the Navajo Trail, 1945; Ambush at Dark Canyon, 2012; The Animals, 1970; Bad Company, 1972; Bad Girls, 1994; **Bad Man's Territory**, 1946; **Bad Men of Missouri**, 1941; Bad Men of Tombstone, 1949; The Badge of Marshal Brennan, 1957; Badlands of Montana, 1957; The Bandit Trail, 1941; Bandolero!, 1968; Barbary Coast Gent, 1944; Belle Starr's Daughter, 1948; Big Jake, 1971; Billy the Kid, 1930; **Billy the Kid**, 1941; Billy the Kid, 1989 (made-for-TV); Billy the Kid Returns, 1938; Billy the Kid's Gun Justice, 1940; Black Aces, 1937; Black Bandit, 1938; Black Bart, 1948; Blackthorn, 2011; Blazing Sixes, 1937; Bone Tomahawk, 2015; Border Roundup, 1942; Borderland, 1937; The Bravados, 1958; Brimstone, 1949; Bullet Code, 1940; Bullet for a Badman, 1964; Butch and Sundance: The Early Days, 1979; **Butch Cassidy and the Sundance Kid**, 1969; Call the Mesquiteers, 1938; The Carson City Kid, 1940; Carson City Raiders, 1948; Cattle Stampede, 1943; Cave of Outlaws, 1951; Chato's Land, 1972; Check Your Guns, 1948; **Chisum**, 1970; The Cimarron Kid, 1952; Clash of the Wolves, 1925; Colorado, 1940; **Colorado Territory**, 1949; Colt .45, 1950; The Conquerors, 1932; The Cowboy and the Bandit, 1935; The Cowboy and the Indians, 1949; Crooked River, 1950; Curtin Call at Cactus Creek, 1950; **Dallas**, 1950; The Deadly Companions, 1971; Deadwood Dick, 1940 (serial); Death Hunt, 1981; Devil Riders, 1943; **The Doolins of Oklahoma**, 1949; The Dude Bandit, 1933; Dude Cowboy, 1941; The Duel at Silver Creek, 1952; El Paso Stampede,

1953; **Face to Face**, 1976; The Far Side of Jericho, 2006; **The Fastest Gun Alive**, 1956; The Fighting Redhead, 1949; Forlorn River, 1926; Forlorn River, 1937; Fort Dobbs, 1958; Four Guns to the Border, 1954; **Fury at Furnace Creek**, 1948; Gangster's Den, 1945; The Gay Ranchero, 1948; Ghost of Zorro, 1949 (serial); Git along Little Dogies, 1937; Goin' South, 1978; The Good Bad Man, 1916; Good Day for a Hanging, 1959; Gordon of Ghost City, 1933; **The Great Missouri Raid**, 1951; **The Great Northfield, Minnesota Raid**, 1972; Gun Brothers, 1956; Gun Glory, 1957; Gun Law, 1938; Gun Street, 1961; Gunfight, 1961; Gunfighters, 1947; The Gunfighters, 1987 (made-for-TV); Gunfire at Indian Gap, 1957; Gunman's Walk, 1958; Gunpoint, 1966; The Halliday Brand, 1957; **Hang 'Em High**, 1968; **The Hanging Tree**, 1959; Harmony Trail, 1944; Heart of the Golden West, 1942; Hidden Gold, 1940; Hills of Old Wyoming, 1937; Hittin' the Trail, 1937; Hollywood Cowboy, 1937; Home on the Prairie, 1939; Homesteaders of Paradise Valley, 1947; **Hour of the Gun**, 1967; The Hunting Party, 1971; The James Brothers of Missouri, 1949; **Jesse James**, 1939; Jesse James Rides Again, 1947 (serial); **Johnny Guitar**, 1954; **Jubal**, 1956; The Kid from Texas, 1950; The King and Four Queens, 1956; The Last Days of Frank and Jesse James, 1986 (made-for-TV); The Last Frontier, 1932; The Last Hard Men, 1976; The Last Outlaw, 1993 (made-for-TV); The Last Posse, 1953; The Last Stagecoach West, 1957; Law of the Canyon, 1947; Lawless Breed, 1946; **The Lawless Breed**, 1953; The Lawless Range, 1935; Lawless Valley, 1938; **The Left-Handed Gun**, 1958; The Legend of the Lone Ranger, 1952; The Light of Western Stars, 1940; Lightning Raiders, 1945; Lightning Range, 1933; Loaded Pistols, 1948; The Local Bad Man, 1932; The Lone Ranger Rides Again, 1939 (serial); The Lone Star Ranger, 1930; **The Long Riders**, 1980; The Man from Colorado, 1948; The Man Who Loved Cat Dancing, 1973; The Marshal's Daughter, 1953; The Michigan Kid, 1947; Mrs. Sundance, 1974 (made-for-TV); Mule Train, 1950; The Mysterious Rider, 1938; 'Neath Arizona Skies, 1934; Nevada, 1944; The Nevada Buckeroo, 1931; Nevada City, 1941; The Nevadan, 1950; New Frontier, 1939; Oh, Susanna!, 1936; The Oklahoma Cyclone, 1930; **One-Eyed Jacks**, 1961; The Outlaw, 1943; **The Outlaw Josey Wales**, 1976; Outlaw Trail, 1944; Overland Stage Riders, 1938; **The Ox-Bow Incident**, 1943; Paradise Canyon, 1935; **Pat Garrett and Billy the Kid**, 1973; The Phantom of the West, 1931; The Phantom Rider, 1936 (serial); The Phantom Rider, 1946 (serial); Posse, 1975; Posse, 1993; Posse from Hell, 1961; Prairie Moon, 1938; Pride of the West, 1938; **Rancho Notorious**, 1952; Randy Rides Alone, 1934; Range War, 1939; **Rango**, 2011; The Red Rider, 1934; Red River Range, 1938; **Relentless**, 1948; Renegade Trail, 1939; Renegades, 1946; **Return of the Bad Men**, 1948; Return of the Seven, 1966; The Reward, 1965; Ride Him, Cowboy, 1932; Ride in the Whirlwind, 1966; Riders of the Range, 1950; The Riders of the Whistling Skull, 1937; Rim of the Canyon, 1949; **Robin Hood of El Dorado**, 1936; Rogue of the Rio Grande, 1930; Rollin' Plains, 1938; Rootin' Tootin' Rhythm, 1937; **Run for Cover**, 1955; Running Target, 1956; Rustler's Valley, 1937; Sagebrush Trail, 1933; **Santa Fe**, 1951; Santa Fe Stampede, 1938; Scarlet River, 1933; **The Searchers**, 1956; The Secret of Convict Lake, 1951; **Seraphim Falls**, 2007; The Shadow Riders, 1982 (made-for-TV); Shanghai Noon, 2000; Sheriff of Sage Valley, 1942; Shooting High, 1940; Sierra, 1950; Silver Canyon, 1951; Silver Lode, 1954; The Silver Whip, 1953; **Silverado**, 1985; Son of God's Country, 1948; Son of the Border, 1933; Son of Zorro, 1947; **The Sons of Katie Elder**, 1965; South of Heaven, West of Hell, 2000; Southwest Passage, 1954; Stormy Trails, 1936; Sunset Range, 1935; Sunset Pass, 1946; **Tension at Table Rock**, 1956; The Test, 1935; Texas Masquerade, 1944; Three Desperate Men, 1951; **The Three Godfathers**, 1916; **Three Godfathers**, 1936; **3 Godfathers**, 1948; Three on the Trail, 1936; **3:10 to Yuma**, 2007; Three Young Texans, 1954; Timber Stampede, 1939; Toll of the Desert, 1935; **Tombstone**, 1993; The Tracker, 1988 (made-for-TV); Trail of Kit Carson, 1945; Triple Justice, 1940; Trouble in Sundown, 1939; Trouble in Texas, 1937; **True Grit**, 1969; **True Grit**, 2010; **The True Story of Jesse James**, 1957; Under

Texas Skies, 1940; Under Western Stars, 1938; Undercover Man, 1942; The Unholy Four, 1970; The Virginian, 1914; **The Virginian**, 1929; **The Virginian**, 1946; **Wagon Master**, 1950; Wagon Trail, 1935; West of the Divide, 1934; **Western Union**, 1941; **When the Daltons Rode**, 1940; Where the Buffalo Roam, 1938; **Whispering Smith**, 1948; **The Wild Bunch**, 1969; Wild Horse Mesa, 1932; **Wild Rovers**, 1971; **Wyatt Earp**, 1994; Wyoming Outlaw, 1939; Wyoming Renegades, 1954; **Yellow Sky**, 1948; **Young Guns**, 1988; **Young Guns II**, 1990; Young Guns of Texas, 1962; **Young Jesse James**, 1960; The Younger Brothers, 1949.

Chefs and Cooks: **The Adventures of Robin Hood**, 1938; **All Quiet on the Western Front**, 1930; Angels Fall, 2007 (made-for-TV); Anything Can Happen, 1952; **Back to Bataan**, 1945; **Bataan**, 1943; **Battleground**, 1949; A Better Life, 2012; Big Night, 1996; **The Blues Brothers**, 1980; **Buck Privates**, 1941; Burning Man, 2011; Burnt, 2015; **Carnival of Sinners**, 1947; The Case of the Curious Bride, 1935; Chef!, 1993-1996 (TV series); The Chef, 2005; **Chef**, 2014; Chef's Special, 2009; Chowder, 2007-2010 (TV series); **Cover Girl**, 1944; **Cowboy**, 1958; **Christmas in Connecticut**, 1945; **The Culpepper Cattle Company**, 1972; **The Dark Knight Rises**, 2012; **Destination Tokyo**, 1943; **The Devil Wears Prada**, 2006; **Dinner Rush**, 2000; Dishdogz, 2006; The Duchess of Duke Street, 1976-1977 (TV series); East Side Story, 2006; Eat Drink Man Woman, 1994; Everybody Sing, 1938; Felicia's Journey, 1999; The Fighting Chefs, 2013; Follow the Leader, 1930; Fools for Scandal, 1938; Freddie, 2005-2006 (TV series); **The Freshman**, 1990; The Glass Slipper, 1955; **The Godfather**, 1972; The Golden Palace, 1992-1993 (TV series); **The Great Race**, 1965; **Guadalcanal Diary**, 1943; Haute Cuisine, 2013; He Stayed for Breakfast, 1940; **Here Comes Cookie**, 1935; **History Is Made at Night**, 1937; Hit Parade of 1947, 1947; **The Hundred-Foot Journey**, 2014; I Am Love, 2010; **If You Could Only Cook**, 1936; **Julie & Julia**, 2009; Kitchen Confidential, 2005- (TV series); **The Killers**, 1946; Lady Bodyguard, 1943; Le Chef, 2012; Le Grand Chef, 2007; Le Grand Chef 2: Kimchi Battle, 2010; **Let's Dance**, 1950; **The Longest Day**, 1962; Love's Kitchen, 2011; Majestic Hotel Cellars, 1945; A Matter of Minutes, 1959; **Mr. Nice Guy**, 1998; **Monte Walsh**, 1970; Monte Walsh, 2003 (made-for-TV); Mostly Martha, 2001; **Murder by Death**, 1976; My Big Love, 2008; **My Darling Clementine**, 1946; A Night at the Ritz, 1935; **A Night in Casablanca**, 1946; No Reservations, 2007; Obliging Young Lady, 1942; **Pack Up Your Troubles**, 1932; Panman, 2011; **Patton**, 1970; Perfect Sense, 2011; **PT 109**, 1963; Queen for a Day, 1951; The Ramen Girl, 2008; The Ranger, the Cook and a Hole in the Sky, 1995 (made-for-TV); **Ratatouille**, 2007; **Red River**, 1948; Recipe for Disaster, 2003 (made-for-TV); Simply Irresistible, 1999; The Slammin' Salmon, 2009; Soul Kitchen, 2010; Spanglish, 2004; **The Swan**, 1956; **They Were Expendable**, 1945; Three's Company, 1977-1984 (TV series); **Till We Meet Again**, 1936; **To Catch a Thief**, 1955; Toast, 2011; Today's Special, 2009; **Tortilla Soup**, 2001; Vatel, 2000; **Wake Island**, 1942; **Who Is Killing the Great Chefs of Europe?**, 1978; You Really Got Me, 2001.

Chinatown: **After the Thin Man**, 1936 (San Francisco); Alice, 1990 (New York); **The Beautiful Country**, 2005 (New York); Big Trouble in Little China, 1986 (San Francisco); Bizarre, Bizarre, 1939 (London); **Blade Runner**, 1982 (Los Angeles); **Broken Blossoms**, 1919 (London); **The Cameraman**, 1928 (New York); The Cat's-Paw, 1934; China Town, 1962 (Calcutta, India); China Town, 2006; **Chinatown**, 1974 (Los Angeles); Chinatown, 2009 (New York); Chinatown After Dark, 1931; Chinatown Nights, 1929; Chinese Puzzle, 2013; Confessions of an Opium Eater, 1962 (San Francisco); The Corruptor, 1999 (New York); **The Cuban Love Song**, 1931; Customs Agent, 1950 (Shanghai); The Cyclone, 1920; Daughter of the Tong, 1939; **The Dead Pool**, 1988 (San Francisco); Detective Lloyd, 1932 (London); Doomed to Die, 1940; Drums of Fu Manchu, 1940 (serial); **Eyewitness**, 1981 (New

York); Falling in Love, 1984; **Flower Drum Song**, 1961 (San Francisco); **Godzilla**, 2014; The Golden Child, 1986; The Golden Eye, 1948; Gremlins, 1984; Hair-Trigger Casey, 1936; **Hammett**, 1982 (San Francisco); **The Hatchet Man**, 1932 (San Francisco); The Illegal Immigrant, 1985; The Imp, 1919; Jade, 1995; The Jitters, 1989; The Killer Elite, 1975; The Killing of a Chinese Bookie, 1976; King of Chinatown, 1939; King of New York, 1990; **The Lady from Shanghai**, 1948 (San Francisco); The Law of the Tong, 1931; Married Before Breakfast, 1937; Mask of the Dragon, 1951 (Los Angeles); Mr. Moto Takes a Vacation, 1939 (San Francisco); **Mr. Nice Guy**, 1998; Murder in the First, 1995; My Life, 1993; **The Mysterious Mr. Wong**, 1935; The Mystery of the Leaping Fish, 1916 (New York); Nancy Drew, 2007 (Los Angeles); Outside the Law, 1920 (San Francisco); Ransom, 1928; Red, 2010; Red Barry, 1938 (serial); The Replacement Killers, 1998; Repo Men, 2010; Revenge of the Green Dragons, 2014 (New York); Rush Hour, 1998 (Los Angeles); **San Andreas**, 2015 (Los Angeles); Shadow of Chinatown, 1936 (serial); Shadows Over Chinatown, 1946 (San Francisco); Shanghai Joe, 1973; The Son-Daughter, 1932 (San Francisco); Sons of the Gods, 1930 (San Francisco); Starsky & Hutch, 2004 (San Francisco); Survivor, 2015 (New York); The Sweetest Thing, 2002; Swim Little Fish Swim, 2012 (New York); **Thoroughly Modern Millie**, 1967 (New York); Ticker, 2001 (San Francisco); The Tong Man, 1919 (San Francisco); Torchy Blane in Chinatown, 1939 (New York); **A Touch of Class**, 1973; Tracers, 2015 (New York); True Believer, 1989; **True Lies**, 1994; Twinkletoes, 1926; Wharf Angel, 1934 (San Francisco); What a Girl Wants, 2003 (London); **What's Up, Doc?**, 1972; The War of the Tongs, 1917; The Weapons of Death, 1981 (San Francisco).

Circling the Wagons (defense technique to use covered wagons as an enclosure against Indian attacks in U.S. Old West): **The Big Trail**, 1930; **Brigham Young: Frontiersman**, 1940; **The Covered Wagon**, 1923; **Fighting Caravans**, 1931; **Hondo**, 1953; **Kit Carson**, 1940; Ranger Courage, 1937; **Red River**, 1948; Saddlemates, 1941; The Thundering Herd, 1933; **Virginia City**, 1940; **Wagon Master**, 1950; **Westward Ho the Wagons**, 1956; **Westward the Women**, 1951.

Circus, Carnival and Arcade Performers (also see Acrobats, this index): Across the Universe, 2007; Adam Resurrected, 2008; Adventureland, 2009; **Air Bud: Golden Receiver**, 1998; The Ape, 1940; Arizona Mahoney, 1936; **Around the World in 80 Days**, 1956; At the Circus, 1939; Au Hazard Balthazar, 1970; Barnum!, 1986 (made-for-TV); Bells of Rosarita, 1945; Bengal Tiger, 1936; Berserk, 1967; Beyond the Blue Horizon, 1942; The Big Cage, 1933; The Big Circus, 1959; **Big Fish**, 2003; The Big Show, 1961; Big Top, 1950-1957 (TV series); Big Top Pee-Wee, 1988; Bill and Coo, 1948; Billy Rose's Jumbo, 1862; Bimbo the Great, 1961; **Bingo**, 1991; **Black Magic**, 1949; Blind Justice, 1916; The Boy Who Stole the Elephant, 1970 (made-for-TV); Bozo's Circus, 1961-1980 (TV series); **Bringing Up Baby**, 1938; **Bronco Billy**, 1980; A Bug's Life, 1998; **Buffalo Bill**, 1944; Bye Bye Blackbird, 2005; **The Cabinet of Dr. Caligari**, 1921; Caged Fury, 1948; **Capricious Summer**, 1968; Captive Wild Women, 1943; Carnival, 1935; Carnivale, 2003-2005 (TV series); **Carny**, 1980; **Chad Hanna**, 1940; Charlie Chan at the Circus, 1936; **The Circus**, 1928; The Circus, 1951; Circus, 1988 (made-for-TV); Circus, 1989 (TV series); Circus, 2010 (TV series); Circus Angel, 1965; Circus Boy, 1947; Circus Boy, 1956-1958 (TV series); Circus Cavalcade, 1945; The Circus Clown, 1934; Circus Girl, 1937; The Circus Kid, 1926; The Circus Kid, 1928; Circus of Horrors, 1960; Circus of the Dead, 2014; The Circus Queen Murder, 1933; **Circus World**, 1964; The City of Lost Children, 1995; Clowning Around, 1992; Dangerous Curves, 1929; **Dante's Inferno**, 1935; The Dark Tower, 1943; Darkest Africa, 1936; The Devil's Circus, 1926; Dhoom: 3, 2013; **Dumbo**, 1941; 8½, 1963; Elephant, 2011; The Enigma of Kasper Hauser, 1975; Escape to Grizzly Mountain, 2000; Far from the Madding Crowd, 1967; The Fat Man, 1951; **Finding Neverland**, 2004; Fixer Dugan, 1939; **Flesh and Fantasy**, 1943; The Flying Devils,

1985; 4 Devils, 1928; **Freaks**, 1932; Frontier Circus, 1961-1962 (TV series); Fun and Fancy Free, 1947; Funny Bones, 1995; The Girl on the Bridge, 1999; Gorilla at Large, 1954; The Great Wallendas, 1978 (made-for-TV); **The Greatest Show on Earth**, 1952; **The Hairy Ape**, 1944; **He Who Gets Slapped**, 1924; The Holy Mountain, 1973; **I Am David**, 2004; I'll Give a Million, 1935; **I'm No Angel**, 1933; Inland Empire, 2006; Inside Daisy Clover, 1965; **Invitation to the Dance**, 1956; It's a Small World, 1950; Jealousy, 1925; **Juliet of the Spirits**, 1965; King of the Arena, 1933; King of the Circus, 1925; King of Thieves, 2004; **La Strada**, 1956; **La Vie en Rose**, 2007; **Lady in the Dark**, 1944; Larger Than Life, 1996; The Last Circus, 2010; **Laugh, Clown, Laugh**, 1928; Legend of the Werewolf, 1975; Let's Fall in Love, 1933; Life Is a Circus, 1960; **Lili**, 1953; Little Big Top, 2006; The Little Unicorn, 2002; **Lola Montes**, 1959; **Mad Max: Beyond Thunderdome**, 1985; Madeline, 1998; **Man on a Tightrope**, 1953; **The Man Who Laughs**, 1928; Mary, 1931; The Men in Her Life, 1941; Merry Andrew, 1958; **The Mighty Barnum**, 1934; **The Miracle Woman**, 1931; A Modern Hero, 1934; The Monkey Talks, 1927; **Moscow on the Hudson**, 1984; Mother Machree, 1928; **Murder!**, 1930; **Murders in the Rue Morgue**, 1932; Ned Kelly, 2003; **Nightmare Alley**, 1947; Octopussy, 1983; Once in a Blue Moon, 1935; Only One Night, 1939; Open Season 3, 2011; **Our Vines Have Tender Grapes**, 1945; Outrage, 1993; P.T. Barnum, 1999; **Papa's Delicate Condition**, 1963; Parade, 1974 (made-for-TV); Peck's Bad Boy, 1921; Peck's Bad Boy with the Circus, 1938; **Pennies from Heaven**, 1936; Polly of the Circus, 1917; Polly of the Circus, 1932; Rain or Shine, 1930; Red Stallion in the Rockies, 1949; Red Wagon, 1936; Ring Circus, 1954; Ring of Fear, 1954; **Saboteur**, 1942; **Sally of the Sawdust**, 1925; Santa Sangre, 1990; Sawdust and Tinsel, 1956; Sawdust Tales, 1997; **7 Faces of Dr. Lao**, 1964; The Shadow, 1937; She Made Her Bed, 1934; The Side Show, 1931; Sideshow, 1928; **Sinner's Holiday**, 1930; Something Wicked This Way Comes, 1983; **Souls for Sale**, 1923; **Stage Door**, 1937; **The Story of Three Loves**, 1953; Street Angel, 1928; **The Stunt Man**, 1980; Sunny, 1930; **Susan Lenox; Her Fall and Rise**, 1931; Swing High, 1930; Things Are Looking Up, 1935; **Thirteen Women**, 1932; **Thousands Cheer**, 1943; Three-Ring Marriage, 1928; A Tiger Walks, 1964; Tillie's Punctured Romance, 1928; **The Tin Drum**, 1980; **Toby Tyler, or Ten Weeks with a Circus**, 1960; Tough Luck, 2003; Trapeze, 1931; **Trapeze**, 1956; Tricks of Life, 1935; True to the Army, 1942; **Two Brothers**, 2004; Two Flaming Youths, 1927; Under the Big Top, 1938; Under the Top, 1919; **The Unholy Three**, 1925; **The Unholy Three**, 1930; **The Unknown**, 1927; The Valley of the Gwangi, 1969; Variétés, 1935; Varsity Blues, 1999; **The Wagons Roll at Night**, 1941; **Water for Elephants**, 2011; Whispering Moon, 2006; **Wings of Desire**, 1988; **The Winning Team**, 1952; The Woman for Joe, 1955; The Woman from Hell, 1929; **You Can't Cheat an Honest Man**, 1939; You Never Know Women, 1926; **Zouzou**, 1989.

Clairvoyants (mediums, soothsayers, palm-readers, fortune-tellers, and psychics ostensibly gifted with ESP [extrasensory perception] or telepathy to see the future and/or the hidden past as well as the ability to contact the dead through séances; also see Fortune-Tellers; Séances, this index): A l'aventure, 2009; The Abominable Snowman, 1957; **Alexander the Great**, 1956; Along the Navajo Trail, 1945; The Amazing Mr. X, 1948; Angel Heart, 1987; **The Assassination of Jesse James by the Coward Robert Ford**, 2007; Baffled!, 1973 (made-for-TV); **Beetle Juice**, 1988; Before Dawn, 1933; The Big Moment, 1934; The Black Camel, 1931; The Black Cat, 1981; **The Black Cauldron**, 1985; The Black Dahlia Haunting, 2012; **The Black Hole**, 1979; Black Magic; 1944; **Black Magic**, 1949; The Black Rainbow, 1989; **Black Rainbow**, 1991; **Blithe Spirit**, 1945; Blur, 2007; **The Boston Strangler**, 1978 (Peter Hurkos); **Broadway Danny Rose**, 1984; **The Cabinet of Dr. Caligari**, 1921; Carrie, 1976; Carrie, 2002 (made-for-TV); The Champions, 1968-1969 (TV series); **The Changeling**, 1980; Charlie Chan at Treasure Island, 1939; Children of the Damned, 1964; **The Circus**,

1928; **The Clairvoyant**, 1935; The Clairvoyant, 1982; **Claudia and David**, 1946; **Cleopatra**, 1934; **Cleopatra**, 1963; **Close Your Eyes**, 2003; The Clown at Midnight, 1999; **Confessions of a Dangerous Mind**, 2002; Constantine, 2005; The Crawling Eye, 1958; Crime Ring, 1938; Crossfire, 2000; The Crystal Ball, 1943; The Cuckoos, 1930; **Dante's Inferno**, 1935; The Dark Mirror, 1920; **Dead of Night**, 1945; The Dead Zone, 1983; Deathtrap, 1982; Deep Red, 1976; The Demon, 1981; The Devil's Rain, 1975; The Diary of Ellen Rimbauer, 2003 (made-for-TV); Dr. Terror's House of Horrors, 1965; Don't Look Now, 1973; **The Doorway to Hell**, 1930; Drag Me to Hell, 2009; Dreamscape, 1984; Elvira Madigan, 1967; Escape to Witch Mountain, 1975; Eyes of Laura Mars, 1978; **Fanfan the Tulip**, 1953; **The Falcon and the Coeds**, 1943; **Fallen Angel**, 1945; **Family Plot**, 1976; Fear, 1990; Fear in the Night, 1947; Final Destination, 2000; Firestarter, 1984; **Flesh and Fantasy**, 1943; **For Whom the Bell Tolls**, 1943; The Fortune Teller, 1920; From Hell, 2001; The Frozen Ghost, 1945; The Fury, 1978; Games, 1967; Ghost, 1990; The Gift, 2001; The Gifted One, 1989 (made-for-TV); God of Gamblers III: Back to Shanghai, 1991; Golden Earrings, 1947; **The Green Mile**, 1999; Hard Boiled Mahoney, 1947; **The Haunting**, 1963; Hearts in Atlantis, 2001; Hell's Highway, 1932; Hereafter, 2010; **High Anxiety**, 1977; **The Hindenburg**, 1975; Honeymoon in Bali, 1939; **Houdini**, 1953; The House of the Spirits, 1994; Horror, 2003; I Love a Mystery, 1945; **I'm No Angel**, 1933; The Innkeepers, 2011; **It Happened Tomorrow**, 1944; Jack Be Nimble, 1993; Jennifer, 1978; **Julius Caesar**, 1953; Just Like Heaven, 2005; Key to the City, 1950; **A Kid for Two Farthings**, 1956; Kiss Daddy Goodbye, 1981; **Kung Fu Panda**, 2011; **Labyrinth**, 1986; **The Landlord**, 1970; **The Last Days of Pompeii**, 1935; The Legend of Hell House, 1973; **The Leopard Man**, 1943; Live and Let Die, 1973; **The Long Night**, 1947; **Love Is a Many Splendored Thing**, 1955; The Man in Grey, 1943; Manhattan Baby, 1982; Matador, 1988; Mean Business, 1979; The Medium, 1921; **The Medium**, 1951; Medium, 2007; The Medusa Touch, 1978; Melody Trail, 1935; **Min and Bill**, 1930; The Mind Reader, 1933; **Ministry of Fear**, 1944; **Miracles for Sale**, 1939; **Murder by Decree**, 1979; **The Navigator: A Medieval Odyssey**, 1988; Next, 2007; **Network**, 1976; **Night Has a Thousand Eyes**, 1948; **The Night My Number Came Up**, 1955; **Nightmare**, 1942; **Nightmare Alley**, 1947; The Omega Factor, 1979 (TV series); On a Clear Day You Can See Forever, 1970; Once Upon a Time, 1976; 100 Days, 1991; One Night in Rome, 1924; **Palmy Days**, 1931; **Panic**, 1946; Party Crasher: My Bloody Birthday, 2000; Patrick, 1978; **Pee-wee's Big Adventure**, 1985; **Pepe Le Moko**, 1937; The Pit, 1981; Powder, 1995; The Power, 1968; The Premonition, 1976; **The Psychic**, 1979; Psychic Killer, 1975; The Psychotronic Man, 1979; Push, 2009; **Rashomon**, 1951; **Red Lights**, 2012; **Ring**, 1998; Ring 2, 1999; **The Ring**, 2002; **Road to Utopia**, 1946; Rocket Gibraltar, 1988; Rose Red, 2002 (TV miniseries); **Scanners**, 1981; The Sender, 1982; **7 Faces of Dr. Lao**, 1964; **The Shadow**, 1994; **The Shining**, 1980; The Shout, 1978; **Sisters**, 1973; The Sixth Sense, 1972; **The Sixth Sense**, 1999; The Sky Is Falling, 2001; Slacker, 1991; Something Weird, 1967; South of Caliente, 1951; **Stalker**, 1982; Starstruck, 1982; **State Fair**, 1933; **State Fair**, 1946; State Fair, 1962; **Stir of Echoes**, 1999; Suez, 1938; Suspect Zero, 2004; Taken, 2002 (TV miniseries); 10 Promises to My Dog, 2008; That's So Raven, 2003-2007 (TV series); The Thirteenth Chair, 1919; The Thirteenth Chair, 1930; **The Thirteenth Chair**, 1937; The 39 Steps, 1959; The Tommyknockers, 1993; **Touch of Evil**, 1958; **Unbreakable**, 2000; **The Unholy Night**, 1929; **The Uninvited**, 1944; Upcoming Scenery, 1996; **Village of the Damned**, 1960; Village of the Damned, 1995; The Watcher in the Woods, 1980; Wendigo, 2001; **What Women Want**, 2000; White Noise, 2005; White Palace, 1990; **The Wizard of Oz**, 1939; **The Wolf Man**, 1941; The X-Files, 1993-2002 (TV series); **X-Men**, 2000.

Classic Fathers (Benevolent): *Brian Aherne*: **My Son, My Son!**, 1940; *Warner Baxter*: **Adam Had Four Sons**, 1941; *Donald Crisp*: **Lassie**,

Come Home, 1943; National Velvet, 1945; *Alan Hale Sr.*: Gentleman Jim, 1942; The Strawberry Blonde, 1941; *Walter Huston*: Dragon Seed, 1944; Of Human Hearts, 1938; Yankee Doodle Dandy, 1942; *Raymond Massey*: Abe Lincoln in Illinois, 1940; East of Eden, 1955; *John Mills*: Swiss Family Robinson, 1960; *Thomas Mitchell*: The Sullivans, 1941; *Gregory Peck*: Gentleman's Agreement, 1947; The Yearling, 1946; *William Powell*: Life with Father, 1947; *Russell Simpson*: The Grapes of Wrath, 1940; *James Stewart*: Dear Brigitte, 1965; Mr. Hobbs Takes a Vacation, 1962; Shenandoah, 1965; *Clifton Webb*: Cheaper by the Dozen, 1950; Titanic, 1953.

Classic Fathers (Malevolent): *Walter Brennan*: My Darling Clementine, 1946; *Lee J. Cobb*: The Brothers Karamazov, 1958; Man of the West, 1958; *Donald Crisp*: Broken Blossoms, 1919; *Victor Kilian*: Huckleberry Finn, 1939; *Donald Pleasence*: Will Penny, 1968.

Classic Fistfights (also see Bare Knuckle Fighters, this index): Angel and the Badman, 1947 (between John Wayne and others in a saloon); The Big Country, 1958 (between Gregory Peck and Charlton Heston on an open plain); Canyon Passage, 1946 (between Dana Andrews and Ward Bond in a saloon); Champion, 1949 (between prizefighter Kirk Douglas and gangsters inside a deserted boxing arena); Destry Rides Again, 1939 (between Marlene Dietrich and Una Merkel inside a saloon); Dodge City, 1939 (scores of cowboys, Union and Confederate veterans of the Civil War, battle inside of a saloon in a calamitous brawl that utterly wrecks the place); Donovan's Reef, 1963 (between John Wayne and Lee Marvin and others in a bar); 48 Hours, 1982 (between Nick Nolte and Eddie Murphy); From Here to Eternity, 1953 (between Montgomery Clift and John Dennis outside a military barracks); Giant, 1956 (between Rock Hudson and Mickey Simpson in a diner); The Gunfight at Dodge City, 1959 (between Joel McCrea and Don Haggerty); Gunga Din, 1939 (between Cary Grant and several other British soldiers; between three British soldiers—Cary Grant, Douglas Fairbanks Jr. and Victor McLaglen—and many Indian natives who are secret Thugs in a remote mountain village); High Noon, 1952 (between Gary Cooper and Lloyd Bridges inside a livery stable); It's a Mad, Mad, Mad, Mad World, 1963 (hilarious bumbling fight between comedians Milton Berle and Terry-Thomas); Johnny Apollo, 1940 (between Tyrone Power and Lloyd Nolan inside a prison library); The Most Dangerous Game, 1932 (between Joel McCrea and Leslie Banks inside a castle chamber); The Narrow Margin, 1952 (between Charles McGraw and David Clarke inside the compartment of a moving train); On the Waterfront, 1954 (between Marlon Brando and Lee J. Cobb outside a waterfront shack); The Quiet Man, 1952 (between John Wayne and Victor McLaglen through an Irish countryside); Red River, 1948 (between John Wayne and Montgomery Clift); Ride the High Country, 1962 (between Joel McCrea and Randolph Scott); The Scalphunters, 1968 (between frontiersman Burt Lancaster and slave Ossie Davis); Shane, 1953 (between Alan Ladd and Ben Johnson, who is knocked rolling along a bar; between Ladd and Van Heflin and many other cowboys; between Ladd and Heflin); She Wore a Yellow Ribbon, 1949 (between Victor McLaglen and four cavalry troopers in a commissary); The Spoilers, 1942 (between John Wayne and Randolph Scott, through the second floor of a saloon to the first floor and into the street in a four-minute battle); The Treasure of the Sierra Madre, 1948 (between Humphrey Bogart, Tim Holt and Barton MacLane, who is knocked rolling along a bar); White Heat, 1949 (between convict James Cagney and several prison guards inside a prison mess hall); Wild Bill, 1995 (Jeff Bridges, as lawman James Butler Hickok, battling four cavalrymen in a saloon); The Young Lions, 1958 (between GI Montgomery Clift and several members of his platoon in training camp).

Classic Mothers (Benevolent; also see Domineering Mothers, this index): *Mary Astor*: Meet Me in St. Louis, 1944; *Fay Bainter*: The Human Comedy, 1943; *Beulah Bondi*: It's a Wonderful Life, 1946; Mr. Smith Goes to Washington, 1939; Of Human Hearts, 1938; Our Town, 1940; Track of the Cat, 1954; *Alice Brady*: In Old Chicago, 1937 (as Mrs. Molly O'Leary); My Man Godfrey, 1936; Young Mr. Lincoln, 1939; *Jane Darwell*: All Through the Night, 1941; Brigham Young: Frontiersman, 1940; The Devil and Daniel Webster, 1941; The Grapes of Wrath, 1940 (as Ma Joad); Jesse James, 1939 (mother of Frank and Jesse James); It Happened in Flatbush; *Rosemary DeCamp*: By the Light of the Silvery Moon, 1953; On Moonlight Bay, 1951; *Irene Dunne*: Anna and the King of Siam, 1946; I Remember Mama, 1948; Life with Father, 1947; My Favorite Wife, 1940; The White Cliffs of Dover, 1944; *Jessie Royce Landis*: It Happens Every Spring, 1949; North by Northwest, 1959; To Catch a Thief, 1955; *Dorothy McGuire*: Friendly Persuasion, 1956; The Greatest Story Ever Told, 1965 (as the Virgin Mary); Old Yeller, 1957; Swiss Family Robinson, 1960; A Tree Grows in Brooklyn, 1949; *Beryl Mercer*: All Quiet on the Western Front, 1930; Outward Bound, 1930; The Public Enemy, 1931; *Ann Revere*: Body and Soul, 1947; Gentleman's Agreement, 1947; The Great Missouri Raid, 1951 (mother of Frank and Jesse James); National Velvet, 1945; A Place in the Sun, 1951; Scudda Hoo! Scudda Hay!, 1949; The Song of Bernadette, 1943 (mother of Saint Bernadette); *Selena Royle*: Come Fill the Cup, 1951; Courage of Lassie, 1946; A Date with Judy, 1948; Gallant Journey, 1946; The Green Years, 1946; Joan of Arc, 1948 (Joan's mother); Night and Day, 1946; The Romance of Rosy Ridge, 1947; The Sullivans (aka: The Fighting Sullivans), 1944 (mother of the five Sullivan brothers, all killed in WWII when their ship, the light cruiser USS *Juneau*, CL-52 was destroyed in the naval battle off Guadalcanal on November 13, 1942); Summer Holiday, 1948; Thirty Seconds Over Tokyo, 1944; Till the End of Time, 1946; *Margaret Wycherly*: Sergeant York, 1941; *Jane Wyman*: So Big, 1953; The Yearling, 1946.

Classic Mothers (Malevolent; also see Domineering Mothers, this index): *Angela Lansbury*: The Manchurian Candidate, 1962; *Shelley Winters*: Bloody Mama, 1970 (as Ma Barker); *Margaret Wycherly*: White Heat, 1949; *Blanche Yurka*: Queen of the Mob, 1940 (in role modeled on Ma Barker).

Classic Swordfights: Adventures of Don Juan, 1948 (between Errol Flynn and Robert Douglas); The Adventures of Robin Hood, 1938 (between Errol Flynn and Basil Rathbone); The Black Pirate, 1926 (between Douglas Fairbanks Sr. and Anders Randolf); The Black Swan, 1942 (between Tyrone Power and George Sanders); Captain Blood, 1935 (between Errol Flynn and Basil Rathbone); The Corsican Brothers, 1941 (between Douglas Fairbanks Jr. and Akim Tamiroff); The Mark of Zorro, 1940 (between Tyrone Power and Basil Rathbone); Prince of Foxes, 1949 (Tyrone Power and several opponents); The Prisoner of Zenda, 1937 (between Ronald Colman and Douglas Fairbanks Jr.); The Prisoner of Zenda, 1952 (between Stewart Granger and James Mason); Scaramouche, 1952 (between Stewart Granger and Mel Ferrer); The Sea Hawk, 1940 (between Errol Flynn and Henry Daniell); The Three Musketeers, 1948 (between Gene Kelly and Sol Gorss).

Coal Miners and Mines (also see Miners and Mining Towns, this index): Act of Vengeance, 1986 (made-for-TV); Ariel, 1989; As Far as My Feet Will Carry Me, 2001; A Bachelor's Life Abroad, 1992; Benek, 2007; Big Bad John, 1990; Billy Elliott, 2000; Black Beauty, 1987 (made-for-TV); Black Diamonds, 1932; Black Fury, 1935; Blind Shaft, 2003; Brassed Off, 1997; The Brave Don't Cry, 1952; The Citadel, 1938; Coal Miner's Daughter, 1980; Comradeship, 1932; Confidential Agent, 1945; The Corn Is Green, 1945; Dear Wendy, 2005; Devaki, 2005; The Devil's Messenger, 1961; Dynamite, 1930; The Eyes of Van Gogh, 2005; Factory Girl, 2006; Fury Below, 1936; Germinal, 1993; Harlan County War, 2000 (made-for-TV); How Green Was My Valley, 1941; The Invisible Man Returns, 1940; Ip Man, 2010; Iron Man, 1951; Jack London, 1943; Kentucky Woman, 1983 (made-for-TV);

Larks on a String, 1991; **Lassie**, 2006; **Leatherheads**, 2008; Little Accidents, 2014; Little Miss Optimist, 1917; **The Littlest Horse Thieves**, 1977; **Lust for Life**, 1956; Margaret's Museum, 1996; **Matewan**, 1987; Mine Games, 2012; **The Miracle of the Bells**, 1948; **Mission to Moscow**, 1943; **The Molly Maguires**, 1970; My Bloody Valentine, 2009; **My Son, My Son!**, 1940; **October Sky**, 1999; One Missed Call 2, 2005; Pit Pony, 1997 (made-for-TV); **Pittsburgh**, 1942; Railroad Man, 1999; The Rainbow, 1989; **Random Harvest**, 1942; **The Razor's Edge**, 1946; Roses Are for the Rich, 1987 (made-for-TV); Silent Hill, 2006; Solino, 2003; Solomon & Gaener, 2000; **Songcatcher**, 2000; **Sons and Lovers**, 1960; Speakerman: The Boo, 2004; Spring Night, Summer Night, 1967; **The Stars Look Down**, 1941; Sub terra, 2003; **Superman III**, 1983; **This Sporting Life**, 1963; A Touch of Sin, 2013; Victory, 1996; **The Way Back**, 2010; Who's Cheating?, 1924; **Women in Love**, 1970; Zoolander, 2001.

Columnists (newspapers and magazines; also see Reporters, this index; also see Paul Gallico, Sheilah Graham, Hedda Hopper, William Barclay "Bat" Masterson, Louella Parsons, Damon Runyon, Walter Winchell in Historical Persons Index): **Advice to the Lovelorn**, 1933; Agatha, 1979; **All About Eve**, 1950; The Appointment, 1991; Attraction, 2001; **Beau James**, 1957 (Walter Winchell narrating); The Bellboy, 1960 (Walter Winchell narrating); **Beloved Infidel**, 1959 (Sheilah Graham); The Big Game, 1936; The Big Story, 1949-1958 (TV series; Walter Winchell); Big Trouble, 2002; The Birds, the Bees and the Italians, 1967; **Black Angel**, 1946; **Blessed Event**, 1932 (role modeled on Walter Winchell); Blonde for a Day, 1946; A Bloody Canvas, 2008 (made-for-TV; Paul Gallico); **The Blue Gardenia**, 1953; Bogie, 1980 (made-for-TV; Louella Parsons); Breakfast in Hollywood, 1946 (Hedda Hopper); **The Bride Came C.O.D.**, 1941; The Bride Vanishes, 1939; The Bride Wore Crutches, 1940; Bright Young Things, 2003; **Broadway Melody of 1936**, 1935; Broadway Thru a Key-Hole, 1933 (Walter Winchell and other columnists); Café Society, 1995; **The Cat's Meow**, 2001 (Louella Parsons); **Chicago**, 2002; **Christmas in Connecticut**, 1945; Citizen Cohn, 1992 (made-for-TV; Walter Winchell); **Citizen Kane**, 1941; Climax!, 1954-1958 (TV series; "The Louella Parsons Story," 1956 episode); College Confidential, 1960 (Walter Winchell, Sheilah Graham); Confessions of a Shopaholic, 2009; Continental Divide, 1981; The Corpse Came C.O.D., 1947 (Louella Parsons, Hedda Hopper); **Crime of Passion**, 1957; **Daisy Kenyon**, 1947 (Walter Winchell, Damon Runyon); Damon Runyon's Pueblo, 1981 (made-for-TV); Dan in Real Life, 2007; Dash and Lilly, 1999 (made-for-TV; Walter Winchell); Dempsey, 1983 (made-for-TV; Damon Runyon); Divorcing Jack, 1998; Dondi, 1961 (Walter Winchell); The Drag-Net, 1936; F. Scott Fitzgerald in Hollywood, 1976 (made-for-TV; Sheilah Graham); **A Face in the Crowd**, 1957 (Walter Winchell); Finnegan Begin Again, 1985 (made-for-TV); Fitzgerald, 2002 (made-for-TV; Sheilah Graham); **Five Star Final**, 1931; **The Fountainhead**, 1949; **The Front Page**, 1931; **The Front Page**, 1974; The Girl Hunters, 1963; The Gossip Columnist, 1980 (made-for-TV); The Great Jewel Robber, 1950 (Sheilah Graham); The Hearst and Davies Affair, 1985 (made-for-TV; Louella Parsons); Heartburn, 1986; Her Highness and the Bellboy, 1945; Hi, Nellie!, 1934; High Tide, 1947; **Hollywood Hotel**, 1937 (Louella Parsons); The Honor of the Press, 1932; Hot News, 1953; The House Across the Street, 1949; House of Horrors, 1946; How to Handle Women, 1928; How to Lose a Guy in 10 Days, 2003; Human Cargo, 1936; **I Wake Up Screaming**, 1942; **Impact**, 1949 (Sheilah Graham); Impact Point, 2008; **Incendiary Blonde**, 1945 (Louella Parsons); International Crime, 1938; Is It Just Me?, 2010; The Josephine Baker Story, 1991 (made-for-TV; Walter Winchell); The Jury's Secret, 1938; Kraft Music Hall, 1967-1971 (TV series; "Stagedoor Johnny," 1967 episode; Walter Winchell); Laughter on the 23rd Floor, 2003 (made-for-TV; Walter Winchell); **Laura**, 1944; Lepke, 1975 (Walter Winchell); **Lonelyhearts**, 1958; Love and Hisses, 1937 (Walter Winchell); **Love is News**, 1937; The Lucy Show, 1962-1968 (TV series; "Lucy the Gun Moll,"

1966 episode; Walter Winchell); Lux Video Theater, 1950-1959 (TV series; Sheilah Graham in two episodes); Ma! He's Making Eyes at Me, 1940; Madison Sq. Garden, 1932 (Damon Runyon playing himself; Paul Gallico playing himself); Malice in Wonderland, 1985 (made-for-TV; Louella Parsons, Hedda Hopper); The Man Who Dared, 1946; Marilyn and Me, 1991 (made-for-TV; Walter Winchell, Louella Parsons); Marilyn: The Untold Story, 1980 (made-for-TV; Louella Parsons); Marlene, 2000 (Louella Parsons); **Meet John Doe**, 1941; **Mr. Deeds Goes to Town**, 1936; Mr. Soft Touch, 1949; **The Murder Man**, 1935; A New Kind of Love, 1963; **The Odd Couple**, 1968; One Mile from Heaven, 1937; **Over 21**, 1945; The Paper, 1994; The Patsy, 1964 (Hedda Hopper); The Payoff, 1935; **Pepe**, 1960 (Hedda Hopper); The Phantom of 42nd Street, 1945; **The Private Files of J. Edgar Hoover**, 1977 (Walter Winchell, Damon Runyon); **Red, Hot and Blue**, 1949; The Rat Pack, 1998 (made-for-TV; Walter Winchell); **The Reluctant Dragon**, 1941 (Walter Winchell); The Right Approach, 1961 (Hedda Hopper); Ring of Passion, 1978 (made-for-TV; Damon Runyon, Paul Gallico); RKO 281, 1999 (made-for-TV; Louella Parsons, Hedda Hopper); **Roxie Hart**, 1942; Runaway Bride, 1999; Saving Sarah Caine, 2007; **Scandal Sheet**, 1931; **Scandal Sheet**, 1952; The Scarlett O'Hara War, 1980 (made-for-TV; Walter Winchell, Louella Parsons); Sex and the City, 1998-2004 (TV series); Shinbone Alley, 1970; Shirley Temple Story, 1976 (Louella Parsons); Single Room Furnished, 1966 (Walter Winchell); Smart Woman, 1948; Social Register, 1934; The Soloist, 2009; **Something to Sing About**, 1937; **Sorrowful Jones**, 1949 (Walter Winchell narrating); Spy Ship, 1942; **Starlift**, 1951 (Louella Parsons); **State of the Union**, 1948; **The Stork Club**, 1945 (Louella Parsons); **Sunset Boulevard**, 1950 (Hedda Hopper); **Sweet Smell of Success**, 1957 (role modeled on Walter Winchell); Taking a Chance on Love, 2009 (made-for-TV); **Teacher's Pet**, 1958; Telephone Time, 1956-1958 (TV series; "I Get Along Without You Very Well," 1957 episode; Walter Winchell); That's Right—You're Wrong, 1939 (Sheilah Graham); **There's No Business Like Show Business**, 1954 (Walter Winchell narrating); They Asked for It, 1939; **-30-**, 1959; To Please a Lady, 1950; Trocadero, 1944; The Untouchables, 1959-1963 (TV series; Walter Winchell narrating); Vicki, 1953 (remake of I Wake Up Screaming); Wake Up and Live, 1937 (Walter Winchell); The Walls Came Tumbling Down, 1946; The Walter Winchell File, 1957-1958 (TV series); The Walter Winchell Show, 1956 (TV series); Where Are You, Sophia?, 2009; **While the City Sleeps**, 1956; Wild Harvest, 1962 (Walter Winchell narrating); Wild in the Streets, 1968 (Walter Winchell); Winchell, 1998 (made-for-TV; Walter Winchell); **Without Reservations**, 1946 (Louella Parsons); **Woman of the Town**, 1943 (Bat Masterson, Louella Parsons); **Woman of the Year**, 1942; Woman-Wise, 1937; **The Women**, 1939 (Hedda Hopper); X Marks the Spot, 1931; You Can't Escape Forever, 1942; **Young Man of Manhattan**, 1930.

Comatose State: **An American Werewolf in London**, 1981; **Awakenings**, 1990; **Bean**, 1997; **Belle de Jour**, 1968; **Birdy**, 1984; **The Client**, 1994; **Crimes of the Heart**, 1986; **The Cross of Lorraine**, 1943; **Demetrius and the Gladiators**, 1954; **Fingers at the Window**, 1942; **Forever Young**, 1992; **Gabriel Over the Whitehouse**, 1933; **He Walked by Night**, 1948; **I Walked with a Zombie**, 1943; **Insidious**, 2010; **The Mind of Mr. Soames**, 1970; **Muriel's Wedding**, 1994; **Open Range**, 2003; **Reversal of Fortune**, 1990; **Rocky II**, 1979; **They Call It Sin**, 1932; **Three Women**, 1977; **The Verdict**, 1982; **White Zombie**, 1932.

Communist Spies (and the political witch-hunting they spawned in the U.S. during the late 1940s and early 1950s): **The Aviator**, 2004; Chaplin, 1992; The 49th Man, 1953; **The Front**, 1976; **Good Night and Good Luck**, 2005; **I Was a Communist for the FBI**, 1951; **The Iron Curtain**, 1948; A King in New York, 1957; **Marathon Man**, 1976; Mona Lisa Smile, 2003; **My Son John**, 1952; **One of the Hollywood Ten**, 2000; **Pickup on South Street**, 1953; The Red Menace, 1949; Security Risk, 1954; **The Thief**, 1952; **Three Brave Men**, 1956; **Trial**, 1955; **The Way We Were**, 1973; **The Woman on Pier 13**, 1949.

Con Artists and Confidence Games: **The Addams Family**, 1991; Always a Bride, 1954 (marriage scam); American Hustle, 2013; The Barefoot Mailman, 1951 (real estate scams); **Beat the Devil**, 1953 (land scam involving uranium); **Bedknobs and Broomsticks**, 1971 (bogus magic spells); Beg, Borrow or Steal, 1937 (art scams); The Big Bluff, 1955 (fortune hustlers); A Big Hand for the Little Lady, 1966 (cards); The Big Lebowski, 1998; The Big Shakedown, 1934 (bogus goods); **Black Magic**, 1949 (fake magic and healing); **Blonde Crazy**, 1931 (short cons); **Body and Soul**, 1947 (rigged prizefighting); The Brothers Grimm, 2005 (exorcisms); Came a Hot Friday, 1985 (betting scams); The Case of the Lucky Legs, 1935 (phony beauty contests); **Catch Me If You Can**, 2002 (forgeries); **Champion**, 1949 (rigged prizefighting); **The Clairvoyant**, 1935 (mind reading); **The Color of Money**, 1986 (pool sharks); The Con Artist, 2011; Confidence, 2003 (accounting scams); The Crystal Ball, 1943 (bogus fortune-tellers); Darkened Rooms, 1929 (spiritual mediums); Diggstown, 1992 (rigged prizefighting); Dirty Rotten Scoundrels, 1988 (Big Con); The Distinguished Gentleman, 1992 (political scams); Don't Tell the Wife, 1937 (phony gold mine stocks); **Elmer Gantry**, 1960 (fake healing); **Fallen Angel**, 1945 (spiritual mediums); The Flame of New Orleans, 1941 (impersonations); **The Flim-Flam Man**, 1967 (short and street cons); Flying Lariats, 1931 (gold brick scam); **Fog Over Frisco**, 1934 (stocks and bonds); **The Fortune**, 1975 (fortune hustlers); **Foul Play**, 1978; **The Freshman**, 1990 (fake gourmet cuisine); **Get Shorty**, 1995 (film swindles); The Gift (clairvoyance); Golden Earrings, 1947 (bogus fortune-tellers); **The Great McGinty**, 1940 (political scams); **The Grifters**, 1990 (short cons); **The Harder They Fall**, 1956 (rigged prizefighting); **Hold Your Man**, 1933 (short cons); **The Honeymoon Killers**, 1969 (Martha Beck, Raymond Fernandez; murderous marital scams); **Honkey Tonk**, 1941 (impersonations); Hooray for Love, 1935 (fake show productions); **Hot Millions**, 1968 (insurance claim fraud); **House of Games**, 1987 (gambling scams); **Houdini**, 1953 (spiritual mediums); **How to Steal a Million**, 1966 (art forgeries); **Huckleberry Finn**, 1931 (short cons); **Huckleberry Finn**, 1939 (short cons); **The Hustler**, 1961 (pool sharks); **I Love You Again**, 1940 (oil and real estate scams); **I Was an Adventuress**, 1940 (fortune hustlers); **Jimmy the Gent**, 1934 (fortune hustlers); **Kind Lady**, 1951 (fortune hustlers); **The Lady Eve**, 1941 (cards); Lonely Hearts, 1991 (money schemes); Lonely Hearts, 2006 (Martha Beck, Raymond Fernandez; murderous marital scams); **The Long Night**, 1947 (bogus magic); **Matchstick Men**, 2003 (phony contests); Maverick, 1994 (cards); **Mean Streets**, 1973; **Midnight Cowboy**, 1969; **The Medium**, 1951 (spiritual mediums); **The Mighty Barnum**, 1940 (fake exhibits); The Mind Reader, 1933 (phony clairvoyant); **Ministry of Fear**, 1944 (spiritual mediums); **The Miracle Woman**, 1931 (fake healing); **Mr. Lucky**, 1943 (charity scams); **The Music Man**, 1962 (musical instruments scam); The Naughty Nineties, 1945 (cards); **Night and the City**, 1950 (rigged wrestling); **Night and the City**, 1992 (rigged prizefighting); **Nightmare Alley**, 1947 (spiritual mediums); **Nobody Lives Forever**, 1946 (fortune hustlers); Nothing But the Best, 1964 (bank scams); On the Level, 1930 (real estate scams); Oz the Great and Powerful, 2013 (fake magic); **Palmy Days**, 1931 (phony psychic); **Paper Moon**, 1973 (short cons); **Papillon**, 1973 (stocks and bonds); **Paradise Alley**, 1978 (rigged wrestling); Public Wedding, 1937 (marriage scams); **The Rainmaker**, 1956 (weather conjuror); **Red Lights**, 2012 (paranormal scams); Rings on Her Fingers, 1942 (impersonations; fortune hustlers); **Road to Singapore**, 1940 (short cons); **Road to Zanzibar**, 1941 (short cons); The Scam, 2012; Search for Beauty, 1934 (phony publications); **The Set-Up**, 1949 (rigged prizefighting); Seven Times Lucky, 2004 (Big Con); Shade, 2003 (cards); Skin Game, 1971 (faked bounty hunting for runaway slaves); **Stavisky**, 1974 (stocks and bonds); **The Sting**, 1973 (card games; fake betting parlor as a Big Store game); **Support Your Local Gunfighter**, 1971 (impersonations); Sus-

picion, 1941 (money schemes); Tarnished Angel, 1938 (fake healing); **The Toast of New York**, 1937 (Jim Fisk; stocks and bonds); Tommy Boy, 1995; **Trading Places**, 1983; **The Treasure of the Sierra Madre**, 1948 (employment scams); **The Twelve Chairs**, 1970 (short cons); **The Two Faces of January**, 2014 (tourist scams); **Wall Street**, 1987 (stocks and bonds; insider trading); **Yolanda and the Thief**, 1945 (fortune hustlers); **The Young in Heart**, 1938 (fortune hustlers). Note: For detailed information on the most notorious confidence artists and confidence games, see my books *Hustlers and Con Men: An Anecdotal History of the Confidence Man and His Games* (M. Evans, 1976); *Encyclopedia of World Crime*; 8 volumes (CrimeBooks, Inc., 1990); *The Great Pictorial History of World Crime*; 2 volumes (History, Inc., 2004).

Concentration and POW Camps (German): **Above Suspicion**, 1943; Adam Resurrected, 2008; **Amen**, 2002; **Arch of Triumph**, 1948; Arch of Triumph, 1985 (made-for-TV); The Aryan Couple, 2004; Bent, 1997; **The Big Red One**, 1980; **The Boy in the Striped Pajamas**, 2008; **The Captive Heart**, 1948; **Carve Her Name with Pride**, 1958; **Cast a Giant Shadow**, 1966; Charlie Grant's War, 1984 (made-for-TV); Christabel, 1988 (made-for-TV); **The Colditz Story**, 1957; Colette, 2013; Concentration Camp, 1938; **The Counterfeiters**, 2008; Death in Love, 2009; Defiance, 2009; Desire Me, 1947; Eichmann, 2009; Enemies: A Love Story, 1989; Enemy of Women, 1944; **Escape**, 1940; Escape from Sobibor, 1987 (made-for-TV); Esther's Diary, 2010; **Europa Europa**, 1991; The Execution, 1985 (made-for-TV); For My Baby, 1999; God on Trial, 2008 (made-for-TV); Good, 2008; The Good German, 2006; **The Great Escape**, 1963; **The Grey Zone**, 2002; **Hart's War**, 2002; Haven, 2001 (made-for-TV); The Hiding Place, 1975; Hitler: Beast of Berlin, 1939; Hitler's SS: Portrait in Evil, 1985 (made-for-TV); **The House on Telegraph Hill**, 1951; **It Happened Here**, 1966; **Judgment at Nuremberg**, 1961; **The Juggler**, 1953; Kapo, 1964; **Life Is Beautiful**, 1999; Lili Marleen, 1981; Lore, 2012; Mendel, 1998; Milena, 1991; Mother Night, 1996; **Morituri**, 1965; **The Mortal Storm**, 1940; My Mother's Courage, 1996; Naked Among Wolves, 2015 (made-for-TV; Buchenwald); **Night Train to Munich**, 1940; **The Odessa File**, 1976; **Odette**, 1951; Olga, 2004; Once Upon a Honeymoon, 1942; Out of the Ashes, 2003 (made-for-TV); **The Pawnbroker**, 1965; **Pimpernel Smith**, 1941; **The Reader**, 2009; The Relief of Belsen, 2007 (made-for-TV); **Schindler's List**, 1993; **The Search**, 1948; **The Seventh Cross**, 1944; **Sophie's Choice**, 1982; **Stalag 17**, 1953; **The Stranger**, 1946 (shown in newsreel footage); **Sunshine**, 2000; **Taking Sides**, 2003; **Three Faces West**, 1940; **Triumph of the Spirit**, 1989; **Underground**, 1941; **The Wooden Horse**, 1951; **The Young Lions**, 1958.

Confederates operating in the Far West during the American Civil War: **Arizona**, 1940; Arizona Raiders, 1965 (Quantrill's guerrillas); **Escape from Fort Bravo**, 1953; **The Good, the Bad and the Ugly**, 1966; Kansas Raiders, 1950 (Quantrill's guerrillas); Last Stand at Saber River, 1997 (made-for-TV); **The Outriders**, 1950; **Ride with the Devil**, 1999 (Quantrill's guerrillas); **Rocky Mountain**, 1950; Siege at Red River, 1952; **Springfield Rifle**, 1952; A Time for Killing, 1967; **Two Flags West**, 1950; **Virginia City**, 1940.

Congressional Medal of Honor: **Buffalo Bill**, 1944; **Courage Under Fire**, 1996; **Dead Reckoning**, 1947; Decoration Day, 1990 (made-for-TV); **Heartbreak Ridge**, 1986; The Last Castle, 2001; **The Manchurian Candidate**, 1962; The Pacific, 2010 (TV miniseries); The Rock, 1996; **Sergeant York**, 1941; **To Hell and Back**, 1955.

Conscientious Objectors: Age of Innocence, 1977; Ali, 2001; Bartleby, 2001; **Birdy**, 1984; Carrington, 1995; **Castle Keep**, 1969; Children of the Revolution, 1997; The Conscientious Objector, 2004; Conscientious Objector Adolf, 1937; Cowards, 1970; **Death Wish**, 1974; The Deep Six, 1958; **The Four Feathers**, 1939; The Four Feathers, 2002; Ginger and Rosa, 2012; **Gosford Park**, 2001; The Greatest, 1977; Hedd Wyn, 1996; The Human Condition I: No Greater Love, 1959; The Human Condition II: Road to Eternity, 1961; Nothing to Report, 1973; Punishment Park, 1971; **Sergeant York**, 1941; Siege at Red River, 1954; **The Steel Helmet**, 1951; **This Above All**, 1942; The Volunteer, 1917; The Year That Trembled, 2002.

Contests: Carry on Girls, 1973 (beauty); The Case of the Lucky Legs, 1935 (beauty); Central Park, 1932 (beauty); Chasing Papi, 2003 (beauty); Cool Breeze, 1972; **Christmas in July**, 1940 (slogans); **The Crowd**, 1928; Dead Ringers, 1988 (beauty); Ella Cinders, 1926 (beauty); **The Entertainer**, 1960 (beauty); The Everlasting Secret Family, 1988 (beauty); Fast and Furious, 1939 (beauty); Faustina, 1957 (beauty); **The Firemen's Ball**, 1968 (beauty); Flawless, 1999; Goodbye, Norma Jean, 1976 (beauty); **Girl Crazy**, 1943 (beauty); Girls in the Night, 1953 (beauty); The Great Masquerade, 1974 (beauty); Hear Me Good, 1957 (beauty); **Hear My Song**, 1991 (beauty); **The Helen Morgan Story**, 1957 (beauty); Holiday Camp, 1948 (beauty); I Am Cuba, 1964 (beauty); I Know What You Did Last Summer, 1997 (beauty); I Married a Woman, 1958 (beauty); **Iron Man 3**, 2013 (beauty); **Jeanne Eagels**, 1957 (beauty); The Lady Without Camelias, 1953 (beauty); **Little Miss Sunshine**, 2006 (beauty); Miss Congeniality, 2000 (beauty); **Miss Firecracker**, 1989 (beauty); Pick a Star, 1937 (beauty); Playing Around, 1930 (beauty); Sing As We Go!, 1934 (beauty); **Smile**, 1975 (beauty); The Thing Called Love, 1993 (beauty); **We're Not Married!**, 1952 (beauty).

Counterfeiters and Counterfeiting: The Amazing Mr. Nordill, 1947; The Argyle Case, 1917; Arizona Territory, 1950; Bad Men of the Border, 1945; Bank Alarm, 1937; The Big Swindle, 2004; Blondie's Secret, 1948; Boys' School, 1938; Brannigan, 1975; Buckeroo from Powder River, 1947; Call to Danger, 1968 (made-for-TV); The Christmas Star, 1986; Come on Cowboys, 1937; Company Business, 1991; The Counterfeiters, 1948; **The Counterfeiters**, 2007; The Crimson Gardenia, 1919; The Crooked Circle, 1932; Cruel Deception, 2003 (made-for-TV); Dangerous Money, 1946; **Dressed to Kill**, 1946; East Side Kids, 1940; The Fighting Coward, 1935; Fighting Trouble, 1956; Firebrand Jordan, 1930; The Flaming Clue, 1920; Foreign Intrigue, 1951-1955 (TV series; "International Counterfeiters," 1951 episode); The Gray Horizon, 1919; Hideout in the Alps, 1937; The House of Fear, 1915; House of Secrets, 1957; I Escaped from the Gestapo, 1943; **In the Line of Fire**, 1993; King of the Carnival, 1955; **Lethal Weapon 4**, 1998; The Mandarin Mystery, 1936; Midnight Taxi, 1937; **Mister 880**, 1950; Murder on the Yukon, 1940; Northern Frontier, 1935; 9 Souls, 2004; Nine Queens, 2001; Outlaws of the Rio Grande, 1941; Paradise Canyon, 1935; Perilous Holiday, 1946; Poor Little Peppina, 1916; Project Ninja Daredevils, 1986; Renfrew of the Royal Mounted, 1937; Riding High, 1943; Rush Hour 2, 2001; Secret Service of the Air, 1939; **She Done Him Wrong**, 1933; Sins of Paris, 1953; Sweet and Lowdown, 1999; **T-Men**, 1947; **The Testament of Dr. Mabuse**, 1952; Three Supermen in Santo Domingo, 1986; Too Many Winners, 1947; Torchy Gets Her Man, 1938; Treasury Men in Action, 1950-1955 (TV series); Trick, 2010; **Two Merry Adventurers**, 1937; Under Mexicali Stars, 1950; Under Suspicion, 1916; Undercover Agent, 1939; **Union Depot**, 1932. Note: For detailed information on the most notorious counterfeiters, see my books *Bloodletters and Badmen* (M. Evans, 1973); *Encyclopedia of World Crime*; 8 volumes (CrimeBooks, Inc., 1990); *The Great Pictorial History of World Crime*; 2 volumes (History, Inc., 2004).

Courtrooms and Trials (individuals cross-referenced in Historical Persons Index; also see Attorneys; Military Tribunals, this index): **Abused Confidence**, 1938; **Across the Pacific**, 1942 (military tribunal); **Accused**, 1936; **The Accused**, 1949; The Accused, 1988; Accused—Stand Up, 1930; **The Adventures of Huckleberry Finn**, 1960; Affare Dreyfus, 1968 (TV miniseries; Alfred Dreyfus); **An Act of Murder**,

1948; **Adam's Rib**, 1949; **Along the Great Divide**, 1951; **The Amazing Dr. Clitterhouse**, 1938; **An American Tragedy**, 1931 (based on the 1908 Chester Gillette murder case); **Amistad**, 1999 (based upon the 1839 mutiny case by slaves on board the ship *La Amistad*); **Anatomy of a Murder**, 1959 (murder defense based upon "irresistible impulse" and loosely based on the 1932 Massie murder trial in Hawaii where Clarence Darrow acted as defense attorney); Anatomy of a Psycho, 1961; ...And Justice for All, 1979; And the Sea Will Tell, 1991 (made-for-TV); **Angel Face**, 1952; **The Bachelor and the Bobby-Soxer**, 1947; The Ballad of Josie, 1967; Before I Hang, 1940; Before the Deluge, 1954; Bernie, 2011 (based on the murder of millionaire Marjorie Nugent in Carthage, Texas); Best Wishes for Tomorrow, 2007 (trial of WWII Japanese war criminals); **Bewitched**, 1945; Beyond a Reasonable Doubt, 1956; Black and White, 2002; **Black Legion**, 1937 (based on the Detroit, Michigan, terrorist organization, 1933-1936, led by Harvey Davis); Blind Faith, 1990 (made-for-TV); Blondes at Work, 1938; Blood & Orchids, 1986 (TV miniseries; loosely based on the 1932 Massie murder trial in Hawaii where Clarence Darrow acted as defense attorney); Bluebeard, 1963 (based on French serial killer Henri Landru, who was found guilty of murdering at least eleven women and was beheaded by the guillotine in 1922); Body of Evidence, 1993; Body of My Enemy, 1976; **Boomerang**, 1947 (based on the 1924 murder of Father Hubert Dahme in Bridgeport, Connecticut, and the resultant trial of Harold Israel, who was saved from conviction by prosecutor Homer Cummings, and who later became the U.S. Attorney General); **Bordertown**, 1935 (murder case where wife kills her husband and falsely implicates a man she loves because he rejects her, which was loosely remade as **They Drive by Night**, 1940, and Blowing Wild, 1953); **Breaker Morant**, 1980 (based upon the 1902 court-martial of British officers Harry "Breaker" Morant, Peter Handcock and four others on charges of murder during the Boer War and for which the two principals were executed); The Brief, 2004-2005 (TV series); **Broken Lance**, 1954 (trial against a rancher and his sons for invading a copper mine); Buchanan Rides Alone, 1958; Buried Alive, 1939; **The Caine Mutiny**, 1954 (U.S. military tribunal); **Canyon Passage**, 1946; **The Case of the Black Cat**, 1936; The Case of the Stuttering Bishop, 1937; **Character**, 1997; Charlie Chan at the Wax Museum, 1940; The Charmer, 1987 (TV miniseries); The Chatterley Affair, 2006 (made-for-TV); The Cheat, 1931; **Chicago**, 2002 (based on the 1924 murder committed by married Beulah Annan, who shot her lover in the back and was nevertheless acquitted by a Chicago jury); **A Civil Action**, 1998; **The Clairvoyant**, 1935; **Class Action**, 1991; **The Client**, 1994; **Compulsion**, 1959 (based on the 1924 Loeb and Leopold murder case and criminal defense attorney Clarence Darrow who is played by Orson Welles); **Conduct Unbecoming**, 1975 (man accused of molesting a woman); **The Confession**, 1970 (kangaroo trial by Soviets in Czechoslovakia); **The Conspirator**, 2011; **The Constant Husband**, 1955 (trial for bigamy); **Convicted**, 1950 (wrongly accused of murder); **Counselor at Law**, 1933 (based on the courtroom exploits of criminal defense attorney William Fallon); Counter Investigation, 2007; **The Count of Monte Cristo**, 1934; **The Count of Monte Cristo** 2002; **Court Martial**, 1954 (military tribunal); **The Court-Martial of Billy Mitchell**, 1955 (U.S. military tribunal); Crazy in Alabama, 1999; **Criminal Court**, 1946 (criminal attorney defends his sweetheart and himself in a murder case); **Crossroads**, 1938; **Crossroads**, 1942; **The Crucible**, 1996 (Salem witch trials in 1692-1693); Damini—Lightning, 1993; Darrow, 1991 (made-for-TV; life of attorney Clarence Darrow); Deadlocked, 2000 (made-for-TV); Destry Rides Again, 1932; **Destry Rides Again**, 1939; **The Devil and Daniel Webster**, 1941 (aka: All That Money Can Buy; Webster defends a mortal who has made a pact with the Devil); Dishonored Lady, 1947; Dorothea Angermann, 1959; **Double Jeopardy**, 1999; The Drake Case, 1929; Dress Gray, 1986 (made-for-TV); The Dreyfus Case, 1930; **The Dreyfus Case**, 1931 (Alfred Dreyfus); 88 Minutes, 2007; **Emma**, 1932; **Erin Brockovich**, 2000; Evelyn Prentice, 1934; The Exorcism of Emily Rose, 2005; **A Few Good Men**, 1992 (U.S. military trial); **Find Me**

Guilty, 2006 (based upon the 1985 case against members of organized crime in New Jersey, reputedly aligned with the New York Thomas Lucchese crime family headquartered in NYC); **The Firm**, 1993; For the Defense, 1954 (made-for-TV); Fracture, 2007; **Fury**, 1936 (based upon the 1933 kidnapping-murder of department store heir Brooke Hart and the lynching of his killers, Thomas Harold Thurmond and Maurice Holmes by a mob in San Jose, California); **Gandhi**, 1982; The Girl Who Kicked the Hornets' Nest, 2009; The Glass Shield, 1994; Good Day for a Hanging, 1959; The Great Sioux Massacre, 1965 (U.S. military tribunal following the Custer massacre of 1876); Gupt: The Hidden Truth, 1997; **Hang 'Em High**, 1968; **High Crimes**, 2002; **Hour of the Gun**, 1967 (trials in Tombstone, Arizona in 1881 involving the Earp-Clanton factions); **The Hour of Thirteen**, 1952; The Hourglass Sanatorium, 1973 (Alfred Dreyfus); **Huckleberry Finn**, 1939; I Accuse!, 1958 (Alfred Dreyfus); **I Want to Live!**, 1958 (based on the 1955 murder trial of Barbara Graham); **Illegal**, 1955 (based on the courtroom exploits of criminal defense attorney William Fallon); **Impact**, 1949; The Incident, 1990 (made-for-TV); Incident in a Small Town, 1994 (made-for-TV); In Cold Blood, 1967 (based on mass murderers Perry Smith and Richard Hickock); **Inherit the Wind**, 1960 (based on the 1925 John T. Scopes "Monkey Trial"); Inherit the Wind, 1988 (made-for-TV; 1925 Scopes trial); The Iron Sheriff, 1957; **J. Edgar**, 2011 (trials resulting from the investigations of the FBI as led by J. Edgar Hoover); **Jagged Edge**, 1985; Jasper, Texas, 2003 (made-for-TV; based upon the 1998 murder of black man James Byrd Jr., by three white racists); **JFK**, 1991 (trials resulting from the investigations launched by New Orleans district attorney Jim Garrison into the assassination of President John F. Kennedy); **Jimmy the Gent**, 1934; **Joan of Arc**, 1948; **Joan the Woman**, 1916 (Joan of Arc); **Johnny Belinda**, 1948; **The Judge**, 2014; **Judgment at Nuremberg**, 1961 (post-WWII Nazi trial); Judicial Consent, 1994; Kavanagh QC, 1995-2001 (TV series); **King & Country**, 1964 (British military tribunal); L.A. Law, 1986-1994 (TV series); La Chienne, 1931; **La Chienne**, 1975; **The Lady from Shanghai**, 1948; L'affaire Dreyfus, 1995 (made-for-TV; Alfred Dreyfus); L'affare Dreyfus, 1968 (made-for-TV; Alfred Dreyfus); The Laramie Project, 2002 (made-for-TV; based on the 1988 murder of Matthew Shepard); The Last Innocent Man, 1987 (made-for-TV); The Lawyer, 1970; **Leave Her to Heaven**, 1945; The Learning Tree, 1969; The Legend of Lizzie Borden, 1975 (made-for-TV; based on the 1892 ax murders of Borden's father and stepmother in Fall River, Massachusetts; she was acquitted); **Let Us Live**, 1939; **The Letter**, 1940 (trial of wife who has killed her lover); **Libel**, 1959; **Libeled Lady**, 1936; **The Life of Emile Zola**, 1937 (Alfred Dreyfus); **The Lincoln Lawyer**, 2011; **A Lion Is in the Streets**, 1953 (based on Louisiana demagogue Huey Long); Lizzie Borden Took an Ax, 2014 (made-for-TV; based on the 1892 ax murders of Borden's father and stepmother in Fall River, Massachusetts; she was acquitted); **M**, 1933 (trial held by criminals judging a child molester and killer); **M**, 1951 (trial held by criminals judging a child molester and killer); **Madeleine**, 1950 (based on the 1857 murder case of Madeleine Smith, accused of killing her lover in Glasgow, Scotland); **A Man for All Seasons**, 1966 (based on the 1535 trial for treason by Sir Thomas More); Man Made Monster, 1941; **The Man They Could Not Hang**, 1939; The Man Who Sued God, 2001; **Manhattan Melodrama**, 1934 (loosely based on the 1928 NYC murder of gambler and crime boss Arnold Rothstein); Marshal of Gunsmoke, 1944; Mary, 1931; Melvilisom, 2011 (Indian military trial); **The Messenger: The Story of Joan of Arc**, 1999; Midnight in the Garden of Good and Evil, 1997; **Miracle on 34th Street**, 1947 (sanity hearing); The Missing Juror, 1944; **Mississippi Burning**, 1988 (based on the 1964 murders of three Civil Rights activists and the resultant trial of KKK members); **The Missouri Breaks**, 1976; **Mr. Deeds Goes to Town**, 1936 (sanity hearing); **Mister 880**, 1950 (trial of an elderly counterfeiter); **The Monster and the Girl**, 1941; **The Mouthpiece**, 1932 (based on the courtroom exploits of criminal defense attorney William Fallon); **Murder!**, 1930; The Murder of Mary Phagan, 1988 (TV miniseries; based upon the 1913 wrongful conviction of Leo Frank for the murder of Mary Phagan, a young girl in Atlanta, Georgia, and Frank's lynching by the KKK in 1915); **Mutiny on the Bounty**, 1935 (military tribunal); **Mutiny on the Bounty**, 1962 (British military tribunal); **My Cousin Vinny**, 1992; The Naked Edge, 1961; The Night of January 16th, 1941; Night Without Justice, 2004 (based upon the 1933 kidnapping-murder of department store heir Brooke Hart and the lynching of his killers, Thomas Harold Thurmond and Maurice Holmes by a mob in San Jose, California); No One Killed Jessica, 2011; **Oscar Wilde**, 1960; Oscar Wilde, 1972 (made-for-TV); The Outrage, 1964; **The Ox-Bow Incident**, 1943 (trial by lynch mob); **Pandora's Box**, 1929; **The Paradine Case**, 1947; **Party Girl**, 1958 (trials of a criminal attorney in 1920s Chicago); **The Passion of Joan of Arc**, 1928; The Passion of the Christ, 2004; **Paths of Glory**, 1957 (French military tribunal in WWI); Penguin Pool Murder, 1932; **The People Against O'Hara**, 1951; The People v. Leo Frank, 2009 (based upon the 1913 wrongful conviction of Leo Frank for the murder of Mary Phagan, a young girl in Atlanta, Georgia, and Frank's lynching by the KKK in 1915); The People vs. Jean Harris, 1981 (made-for-TV); The People vs. Larry Flynt, 1996; Perfect Stranger, 2007; **Peyton Place**, 1957; Philadelphia, 1993; Physical Evidence, 1989; Piccadilly, 1929; **A Place in the Sun**, 1951 (based on the 1908 Chester Gillette murder case); Primal Fear, 1996; Prisoner of Honor, 1991 (made-for-TV; Alfred Dreyfus); **Providence**, 1977; Question of Love, 1978; **The Rack**, 1956 (U.S. court-martial of a U.S. officer accused of treason in Korean War); **The Return of Frank James**, 1940; **Reversal of Fortune**, 1990 (based upon the 1982 Claus von Bulow murder trial); Roses Are for the Rich, 1987 (made-for-TV); **Roxie Hart**, 1942 (based on the 1924 murder committed by married Beulah Annan, who shot her lover in the back and was nevertheless acquitted by a Chicago jury); Rules of Engagement, 2000 (U.S. military trial); **Runaway Jury**, 2003; Salome's Last Dance, 1988 (Oscar Wilde); **Scarlet Street**, 1945; **The Secret Six**, 1931; Separated by Murder, 1994 (made-for-TV); **Sergeant Rutledge**, 1960 (U.S. military tribunal); Shark, 2006-2008 (TV series); Shaurya, 2008 (Indian military trial); **The Shawshank Redemption**, 1994; Side Effects, 2013; **Silkwood**, 1983; Sleep Murder, 2004 (made-for-TV); Sleepers, 1996; **A Soldier's Story**, 1984 (U.S. military tribunal); **Solomon and Sheba**, 1959; **Somebody Up There Likes Me**, 1956 (U.S. court-martial of prizefighter Rocky Graziano); Sorry Ain't Enough, 2006; **The Sound of Fury**, 1950 (based upon the 1933 kidnapping-murder of department store heir Brooke Hart and the lynching of his killers, Thomas Harold Thurmond and Maurice Holmes by a mob in San Jose, California); **Stairway to Heaven**, 1947 (trial held in Heaven); **The Star Chamber**, 1983; **State's Attorney**, 1932 (loosely based on the career of criminal defense attorney William Fallon); Storeyville, 1992; The Story on Page One, 1959; The Strange Case of Dr. Rx, 1942; **Stranger on the Third Floor**, 1940; Suing the Devil, 2011; **Summer Storm**, 1944; Suspect, 1987; Sway, 2007; **Taxi!**, 1932; **They Won't Believe Me**, 1947; **They Won't Forget**, 1937 (based upon the 1913 wrongful conviction of Leo Frank for the murder of Mary Phagan, a young girl in Atlanta, Georgia, and Frank's lynching by the KKK in 1915); **This Land Is Mine**, 1943; **Three Strangers**, 1946; **Time Limit**, 1957 (U.S. court-martial of a U.S. officer accused of treason in Korean War); A Time to Kill, 1996; **To Kill a Mockingbird**, 1962; Tom und Hacke, 2012; **Tombstone**, 1993 (trials in Tombstone, Arizona, in 1881 involving the Earp-Clanton factions); **Town Without Pity**, 1961; **Trial**, 1955; **The Trial**, 1963; The Trial, 2010; Trial and Error, 1962; **Trial and Error**, 1997; **The Trial of Joan of Arc**, 1965; The Trial of Madeleine Smith, 1949 (made-for-TV; based on the 1857 muder case of Madeleine Smith, accused of murdering her lover in Glasgow, Scotland); **The Trial of Joan of Arc**, 1965; **The Trial of Mary Dugan**, 1929; The Trials of Oscar Wilde, 1960; **True Grit**, 1969; **True Grit**, 2010; The Truth, 1960; **12 Angry Men**, 1957 (chiefly takes place inside of a jury room); Twilight of Honor, 1963; Two Men in Town, 1976; Two Seconds, 1932; **The Undercover Man**, 1949 (based on the 1931 tax evasion case of Chicago crime boss Al Capone); **The Unholy Three**, 1925; **The Unholy**

Three, 1930; **The Untouchables**, 1987 (based on the 1931 tax evasion case of Chicago crime boss Al Capone); **The Valiant**, 1929; **Valiant Is the Word for Carrie**, 1936; **Valley of the Heart's Delight**, 2009 (based upon the 1933 kidnapping-murder of department store heir Brooke Hart and the lynching of his killers, Thomas Harold Thurmond and Maurice Holmes by a mob in San Jose, California); **The Verdict**, 1982 (medical malpractice case); **Virginia City**, 1940 (U.S. military tribunal); The Weight of Water, 2000; West of Memphis, 2012; **White Mischief**, 1988 (based on the 1941 murder trial in Kenya of Sir Henry "Jock" Delves Broughton, accused of killing Josslyn Hay, Earl of Erroll, over the affections of Broughton's much younger wife); **Whose Life Is It Anyway?**, 1981 (euthanasia case); A Wife Confesses, 1961; Wilde, 1997 (Oscar Wilde); **Witness**, 1985; **Witness for the Prosecution**, 1957; **A Woman's Face**, 1941; **The Wreck of the Mary Deare**, 1959; **Wyatt Earp**, 1994 (trials in Tombstone, Arizona, in 1881 involving the Earp-Clanton factions); You Are There, 1953-1957 (TV series; "The Dreyfus Case," 1953 episode); Young Adam, 2003; The Young Land, 1959; **Young Mr. Lincoln**, 1939; **The Young Savages**, 1961. Note: For detailed information on the most important criminal trials, see my books *Bloodletters and Badmen* (M. Evans, 1973); *Encyclopedia of World Crime*; 8 volumes (CrimeBooks, Inc., 1990); *The Great Pictorial History of World Crime*; 2 volumes (History, Inc., 2004); *"I Am Innocent": A Comprehensive Encyclopedic History of the World's Wrongly Convicted Persons* (Da Capo Press, 2008).

Covered Wagons (also see Circling the Wagons, this index): Across the Plains, 1939; Adventures of Frank and Jesse James, 1948; **Arizona**, 1940; Arrow in the Dust, 1954; Bad Men, 1926; **Bend of the River**, 1952; Beyond the Last Frontier, 1943; Beyond the Law, 1975; The Big Stampede, 1932; **The Big Trail**, 1930; The Big Trees, 1952; The Blocked Trail, 1943; **Brigham Young: Frontiersman**, 1940; **Broken Lance**, 1954; Bullwhip, 1958; Can't Help Singing, 1944; **Canyon Passage**, 1946; Cavalry, 1936; The Cherokee Strip, 1937; **Chisum**, 1970; **Cimarron**, 1931; Cimarron, 1960; **City Slickers**, 1991; Cole Younger, Gunfighter, 1958; **The Command**, 1954; Conagher, 1991 (made-for-TV); **The Covered Wagon**, 1923; Covered Wagon Days, 1940; Covered Wagon Raid, 1950; Covered Wagon Trails, 1930; Covered Wagon Trails, 1940; Crooked River, 1950; **The Culpepper Cattle Company**, 1972; Daniel Boone: Frontier Trail Rider, 1966; **Dark Command**, 1940; **Davy Crockett: Indian Scout**, 1950; Desperados of the West, 1950; The Desperate Mission, 1969 (made-for-TV); **Dodge City**, 1939; **Drums Along the Mohawk**, 1939; El Condor, 1970; End of the Trail, 1932; **Fighting Caravans**, 1931; Fighting Pioneers, 1935; Finger on the Trigger, 1965; Flame of Barbary Coast, 1945; **For a Few More Dollars**, 1967; Fort Worth, 1951; Fort Yuma, 1955; 4 Dollars of Revenge, 1966; **The General**, 1926; Ghost of Zorro, 1949; The Great Sioux Massacre, 1965; Heroes of the West, 1930; Home on the Range, 1946; Home on the Range, 2004; **Hondo**, 1953; **How the West Was Won**, 1962; In Old California, 1942; **In Old Chicago**, 1938; Into the West, 2005 (TV miniseries); **Kit Carson**, 1940; Land Raiders, 1970; **The Lawless Breed**, 1953; The Lone Ranger, 1938; The Lone Ranger Rides Again, 1939; Man in the Saddle, 1951; Man with the Steel Whip, 1954; Massacre Canyon, 1954; **Mogambo**, 1953; Monte Walsh, 2003 (made-for-TV); **North to Alaska**, 1960; The Oklahoman, 1957; **Once Upon a Time in the West**, 1969; **Open Range**, 2003; The Oregon Trail, 1939; **The Outriders**, 1950; **The Painted Desert**, 1931; **The Paleface**, 1948; Pioneers of the West, 1940; Prairie Schooners, 1940; **The Proud Ones**, 1956; Puss in Boots, 2011; **Rango**, 2011; Red Fork Range, 1931; **Red River**, 1948; **Ride with the Devil**, 1999; Riders of the Deadline, 1943; Riding West, 1944; **Rio Grande**, 1950; Rolling Down the Great Divide, 1942; The Sacketts, 1979 (made-for-TV); Saddlemates, 1941; Sam Whiskey, 1969; **The Scalphunters**, 1968; Scarlet River, 1933; September Dawn, 2007; **Shane**, 1953; **She Wore a Yellow Ribbon**, 1949; **Seven Men from Now**, 1956; **7th Cavalry**, 1956; **The Shakiest Gun in the West**, 1968; Shoot, Gringo...Shoot!, 1968; The Silver Treasure,

1926; **Silverado**, 1985; The Singing Cowboy, 1936; Sitting Bull, 1954; Soldier Blue, 1970; Son of Oklahoma, 1932; Song of the Buckeroo, 1938; The Stranger Wore a Gun, 1953; Take a Hard Ride, 1975; Tall Man Riding, 1955; **The Tall Men**, 1956; The Tall Stranger, 1957; The Tall Texan, 1953; **The Texan**, 1930; **Texas**, 1941; **They Died with Their Boots On**, 1941; **3 Godfathers**, 1948; The Thundering Herd, 1933; Thundering Thomas, 1929; To the Last Man, 1933; The Topeka Terror, 1945; **The Undefeated**, 1969; Untamed, 1955; Valley of Vengeance, 1944; Vengeance, 1977; **Vera Cruz**, 1954; **Virginia City**, 1940; **Wagon Master**, 1950; Wagon Wheels, 1934; Wagon Train, 1957-1965 (TV series); Wagons East, 1954; Wagons West, 1952; West of the Rockies, 1931; **The Westerner**, 1940; **Westward Ho the Wagons**, 1956; **Westward the Women**, 1951; Wheels of Destiny, 1934; **Wyoming**, 1947.

Cowardice in Battle: **All Quiet on the Western Front**, 1930 (WWII; Western Front in France); **Attack**, 1956 (WWII; European Theater); The Battle of the Bulge, 1965 (WWII; European Theater); **Battleground**, 1949 (WWII; European Theater); **The Bridge at Remagen**, 1969 (WWII; European Theater); **The Caine Mutiny**, 1954 (WWII; Pacific Theater; emotional breakdown); **Cross of Iron**, 1977 (WWII; European Theater; Russian Front); **A Farewell to Arms**, 1932 (WWI; Italian Front); **A Farewell to Arms**, 1957 (WWI; Italian Front); **Flying Leathernecks**, 1951 (WWII; Pacific Theater); **For Whom the Bell Tolls**, 1943 (Spanish Civil War, 1936-1939); **Fury**, 2014 (WWII; European Theater); **Is Paris Burning?**, 1966 (WWII; recapturing of Paris from German forces in 1944); **The Longest Day**, 1962 (WWII; European Theater; Normandy Invasion); **Patton**, 1970 (WWII, European Theater; emotional breakdown); **The Patriot**, 2000 (American Revolutionary War); **Platoon**, 1986 (Vietnam War); **Pork Chop Hill**, 1959 (Korean War); **The Red Badge of Courage**, 1951 (American Civil War); **Sands of Iwo Jima**, 1949 (WWII; Pacific Theater); **Saving Private Ryan**, 1998 (WWII; Normandy Invasion in France); **Twelve O'-Clock High**, 1949 (WWII; European Theater); **A Walk in the Sun**, 1945 (WWII; European Theater, Salerno Invasion of Italy; emotional breakdown).

Cowboys: **Abilene Town**, 1946; **Ace of the Saddle**, 1919; **Adventures of Gallant Bess**, 1948; All the Pretty Horses, 2000; **Along Came Jones**, 1945; **Alvarez Kelly**, 1966; American Outlaws, 2001; **American Sniper**, 2014; **An American Tail: Fievel Goes West**, 1991; **Annie Get Your Gun**; 1950; **Annie Oakley**, 1935; **Appaloosa**, 2008; **Bend of the River**, 1952; **The Big Country**, 1958; **Billy the Kid**, 1941; **Bite the Bullet**, 1975; **Blazing Saddles**, 1974; **Branding Broadway**, 1918; Brokeback Mountain, 2005; **Bus Stop**, 1956; **Callaway Went Thataway**, 1951; **The Cariboo Trail**, 1950; **Cat Ballou**, 1965; **Cattle Drive**, 1951; **The Cheyenne Social Club**, 1970; **Chisum**, 1970; **City Slickers**, 1991; **City Slickers II: The Legend of Curly's Gold**, 1994; **Cowboy**, 1958; **The Cowboys**, 1972; Cowboys & Aliens, 2011; **The Culpepper Cattle Company**, 1972; **Dallas Buyers Club**, 2013; **Dodge City**, 1939; **El Dorado**, 1967; **The Far Country**, 1955; **A Fistful of Dollars**, 1964; **For a Few More Dollars**, 1967; **The Good; the Bad and the Ugly**, 1967; **Gunfight at the O.K. Corral**, 1957; **The Gunfighter**, 1950; Gunsmoke: Return to Dodge, 1987 (made-for-TV); **Hang 'Em High**, 1968; Heaven's Gate, 1980; **Hidalgo**, 2004; **High Noon**, 1952; **High Plains Drifter**, 1973; **Hombre**, 1967; **How the West Was Won**, 1962; Jonah Hex, 2011; **The Last Picture Show**, 1971; **The Left-Handed Gun**, 1958; **The Lego Movie**, 2014; **The Lone Ranger**, 2013; **Lonely Are the Brave**, 1962; **The Magnificent Seven**, 1960; **The Man Who Shot Liberty Valance**, 1962; Maverick, 1994; McLintock!, 1963; **Midnight Cowboy**, 1969; **A Million Ways to Die in the West**, 2014; **The Misfits**, 1961; **The Missouri Breaks**, 1976; **Monte Walsh**, 1970; **My Darling Clementine**, 1946; **Night at the Museum**, 2006; **Night at the Museum: Battle of the Smithsonian**, 2009; **Oklahoma!**, 1955; **Once Upon a Time in the West**, 1969; **Open Range**, 2003; **The Outlaw**

Josey Wales, 1976; **The Ox-Bow Incident**, 1943; **Pale Rider**, 1985; **Pat Garrett and Billy the Kid**, 1973; **The Plainsman**, 1936; The Quick and the Dead, 1987 (made-for-TV); The Quick and the Dead, 1995; **Quigley Down Under**, 1990; **Rango**, 2011; Rawhide, 1959-1965 (TV series); **Red River**, 1948; The Rifleman, 1958-1963 (TV series); **Rio Bravo**, 1959; Rio Lobo, 1970; The Salvation, 2014; **The Searchers**, 1956; **Shane**, 1953; Shanghai Noon, 2000; **Silverado**, 1985; **Stagecoach**, 1939; Temple Grandin, 2010 (made-for-TV); **These Thousand Hills**, 1959; **3:10 to Yuma**, 1957; **3:10 to Yuma**, 2007; **Tombstone**, 1993; **Tombstone, the Town Too Tough to Die**, 1942; **Toy Story**, 1995; **Toy Story 3**, 2010; **Toy Story 2**, 1999; **True Grit**, 1969; **True Grit**, 2010; **Unforgiven**, 1992; **Urban Cowboy**, 1980; **Vengeance Valley**, 1951; **The Virginian**, 1929; **The Virginian**, 1946; The Virginian, 2000 (made-for-TV); Walker, Texas Ranger, 1993-2001 (TV series); **The Westerner**, 1940; **Wild Bill**, 1995; **Wild Bill Hickok**, 1923; **Wild Bunch**, 1969; **Wild Rovers**, 1971; Wild Wild West, 1999; **Will Penny**, 1968; **The Winning of Barbara Worth**, 1926; **Earp**, 1994; **Young Guns**, 1988; **Young Guns II**, 1990.

Crooked Cops and Law Enforcement Officials: Ambushed, 1998; American Gangster, 2007; Armed and Dangerous, 1986; **The Asphalt Jungle**, 1950; Assault on Precinct 13, 1976; Assault on Precinct 13, 2005; The Bag Man, 2014; **The Beast of the City**, 1932; **The Big Heat**, 1953; Black Mama, White Mama, 1973; Blind Fury, 1990; Bones, 2001; Brain Drain, 1998; Brewster McCloud, 1970; Brokedown Place, 1999; Catchfire, 1990; Challenge of the Ninja, 1989; Chasing Ghosts, 2005; Cleopatra Jones, 1973; **The Cooler**, 2003; Crime Story, 1996; Crossfire Trail, 2001 (made-for-TV); Dead Badge, 1994; Dead Cert, 1974; Desperation, 2006 (made-for-TV); Down 'n' Dirty, 2001; The Dream Team, 1989; An Eye for an Eye, 1981; Four Brothers, 2005; The Gauntlet, 1977; **The Godfather**, 1972; Going the Distance, 2004; **Gunfight at the O.K. Corral**, 1957; The Happy Hooker, 1975; Hard Boiled, 1993; Hard Ca$h, 2002; Hard to Kill, 1990; Herbie Goes to Monte Carlo, 1977; **Hombre**, 1967; **I Wake Up Screaming**, 1941; I'm Gonna Git You, Sucka, 1988; Ironheart, 1992; Justice, 2000 (made-for-TV); Kaminey: The Scoundrels, 2009; **Kansas City Confidential**, 1952; **The Killing**, 1956; Knockaround Guys, 2002; **L.A. Confidential**, 1997; Leon: The Professional, 1994; Lord of Darkness, 2013; **Madigan**, 1968; Man of the House, 2005; Manhattan Chase, 2000; The Marine, 2006; The Mod Squad, 1999; Money Talks, 1997; Monster from Bikini Beach, 2008; Murphy's Law, 1986; The Negotiator, 1998; New Jersey Drive, 1995; No Way Out, 2008; On the Edge, 2002; Out of Bounds, 1986; Paap, 2003; Palmetto, 1998; A Piece of the Action, 1977; Pier 5, Havana, 1959; Pray for Death, 1985; Prison Break, 2005-2009 (TV series); **The Racket**, 1951; Rapid Fire, 1992; **The Saint Strikes Back**, 1939; She's on Duty, 2005; Renegades, 1989; **Rio Lobo**, 1970; Romeo Is Bleeding, 1994; Saw II, 2005; Scared Silent, 2002; Secuesto Express, 2005; **Serpico**, 1973; Shaft, 2000; **Sharkey's Machine**, 1981; Six Ways to Sunday, 1998; 16 Blocks, 2006; **The Street with No Name**, 1948; **Sunset**, 1988; Sunset Heat, 1992; **Sweet Smell of Success**, 1957; Sworn to Justice, 1997; **There Was a Crooked Man**, 1970; Third World Cop, 2000; Tickle Me, 1965; **Tight Spot**, 1955; **Tombstone**, 1993; **Touch of Evil**, 1958; Traffic in Crime, 1946; **Underworld U.S.A.**, 1961; The Untouchables, 1959-1963 (TV series); **The Untouchables**, 1987; Wild Thing, 1987; With Murder in Mind, 1992 (made-for-TV); **Witness**, 1985; **Wyatt Earp**, 1994. Note: For detailed information on corrupt police officials and policemen, see my books *Bloodletters and Badmen* (M. Evans, 1973); *Encyclopedia of World Crime*; 8 volumes (CrimeBooks, Inc., 1990); *The Great Pictorial History of World Crime*; 2 volumes (History, Inc., 2004); *"I Am Innocent": A Comprehensive Encyclopedic History of the World's Wrongly Convicted Persons* (Da Capo Press, 2008).

Cruisers (warships): **The Bridge on the River Kwai**, 1957 (USS *Houston* referenced); **Cruiser Emden**, 1932; **The Gallant Hours**, 1960;

Guadalcanal Diary, 1943; **In Harm's Way**, 1965; **Midway**, 1976; Pursuit of the Graf Spee, 1956 (*Admiral Graf Spee*); **Sands of Iwo Jima**, 1949; The Sea Chase, 1955; **Sink the Bismarck!**, 1960; **The Story of Dr. Wassell**, 1944 (USS *Marblehead*); **The Sullivans**, 1944 (USS *Juneau*); **Task Force**, 1949; Under Ten Flags, 1960.

Dance Marathons: Blind Date, 1934; Hard to Handle, 1933; The Hoodlum Saint, 1946; The Lottery Bride, 1930; **They Shoot Horses, Don't They?**, 1969.

Dentists: **Babel**, 2006; Baby Doll, 1956; The Baxter, 2005; **Bells Are Ringing**, 1960; Blue Denim, 1959; **Blue Jasmine**, 2013; **Bordertown**, 1935; Butley, 1974; **Cactus Flower**, 1969; **Changeling**, 2008; Charlie and the Chocolate Factory, 2005; **Cinderella Liberty**, 1973; Coffee and Cigarettes, 2004; Confessions of a Dangerous Mind, 2002; Criss Cross, 2010; **Dark Command**, 1940; The Dentist, 1996; Dentist on the Job, 1963; The Dentist 2, 1998; **Diamonds Are Forever**, 1971; **The Diary of Anne Frank**, 1959; Dillinger, 1945; Django Unchained, 2012; **"Doc,"** 1971; **Down Memory Lane**, 1949 (with W.C. Field's classic dentist short); A Dry White Season, 1989; **Equus**, 1977; The Farmer Takes a Wife, 1935; The Fat Man, 1951; **Finding Nemo**, 2003; Flaming Bullets, 1945; **Footsteps in the Dark**, 1941; **Ghost Town**, 2008; **The Girl in the Red Velvet Swing**, 1955; **The Great Moment**, 1944; **Gunfight at the O.K. Corral**, 1957; The Hangover, 2009; The Hawk of Wild River, 1952; The Heart of New York, 1932; **His Majesty O'Keefe**, 1954; **Hell Below**, 1933; Here Comes the Band, 1935; **Hollow Triumph**, 1948; **Hour of the Gun**, 1967; Husbands, 1970; **The In-Laws**, 1979; **It's A Mad, Mad, Mad, Mad World**, 1963; **A Kid for Two Farthings**, 1956; Kiss Me, Stupid, 1964; **Lethal Weapon 4**, 1998; Like It Is, 1998; **The Little Shop of Horrors**, 1960; Little Shop of Horrors, 1986; Love Serenade, 1997; Man About Town, 2006; **The Man Who Knew Too Much**, 1935; **Marathon Man**, 1976; **Marie Galante**, 1934; **M*A*S*H***, 1970; The Mind Reader, 1933; The Moonshine War, 1970; Novocaine, 2001; **Off the Map**, 2003; The Old Man Who Read Love Stories, 2001; **One Sunday Afternoon**, 1933; Outlaws of Stampede Pass, 1943; **The Paleface**, 1948; **Pardon Us**, 1931; **Pearl Harbor**, 2001; **Reds**, 1981; Ride, Vaquero!, 1953; Rio Lobo, 1970; **Running on Empty**, 1988; The Secret Lives of Dentists, 2003; Serial Mom, 1994; A Serious Man, 2009; **The Shakiest Gun in the West**, 1968; Sidewalks of New York, 2001; Silly Billies, 1936; **Splash**, 1984; Son of a Badman, 1949; **A Southern Yankee**, 1948; **Stamboul Quest**, 1934; The Story of Us, 1999; **The Strawberry Blonde**, 1941; Studs Lonigan, 1960; **Texas**, 1941; The Thing You Do!, 1996; **Tombstone**, 1993; **Tombstone, the Town Too Tough to Die**, 1942; **Topsy-Turvy**, 1999; Trail of Terror, 1943; Two Men Went to War, 2004; Waiting for Guffman, 1996; Welcome Home, 1935; The Whole Nine Yards, 2000; The Whole Ten Yards, 2004; Wild Bill Hickok Rides, 1942; Wives and Lovers, 1963; **Wyatt Earp**, 1994.

Destroyers (and corvettes; warships): **Action in the North Atlantic**, 1943; **Air Force**, 1942; Away All Boats, 1956; **The Bedford Incident**, 1965; **The Caine Mutiny**, 1954; **Corvette K-225**, 1943; **The Cruel Sea**, 1953; **Das Boot**, 1982; The Deep Six, 1958; **Destination Tokyo**, 1943; **Destroyer**, 1943; **The Enemy Below**, 1957; **The Guns of Navarone**, 1961; **In Harm's Way**, 1965; **In Which We Serve**, 1942; **Morituri**, 1965; The Navy Comes Through, 1942; Okinawa, 1952; Prisoner of Japan, 1942; **PT-109**, 1963; **Run Silent, Run Deep**, 1958; The Sea Chase, 1955; **Sink the Bismarck!**, 1960; **Stand By for Action**, 1942; **Tora! Tora! Tora!**, 1970; **Torpedo Run**, 1958; U-Boat Prisoner, 1944; **U-571**, 2000; **Up Periscope**, 1959.

Diamond Miners and Mines (also see Miners and Mining Towns): Adventure in Diamonds, 1940; African Treasure, 1952; The Ambassador, 2011; Bat Men of Africa, 1966 (made-for-TV); Blonde Savage, 1947; The Claw Monsters, 1996 (made-for-TV); Darkest Africa, 1936 (serial);

Diamonds, 2009 (made-for-TV); Flatfoot in Africa, 1978; Fortune in Diamonds, 1941; **Gentlemen Prefer Blondes**, 1953; The Invisible Man's Revenge, 1944; **King Solomon's Mines**, 1937; **King Solomon's Mines**, 1950; Koyla, 1997; Lost Money, 1919; Master of the Game, 1984 (TV miniseries); Miraculous Journey, 1948; Mr. Natwarlal, 1979; Mountains of the Moon, 2014; The Nature Girl, 1919; Panther Girl of the Kongo, 1955; Picture Brides, 1934; Pink Gods, 1922; The Pink Jungle, 1968; Piranha, 1972; Prince of Diamonds, 1930; **Road to Zanzibar**, 1941; **Rope of Sand**, 1949; The Sins of Rosanne, 1920; **Snow White and the Seven Dwarfs**, 1937; Soldiers of Fortune, 1955-1957 (TV series; "Doubled in Diamonds," 1956 episode); South of Suez, 1940; Thou Art the Man, 1920; The Whispering Skull, 1944; White Fire, 1985; White Man, 1924; Wings Over Africa, 1936.

Dirigibles (lighter-than-air craft): The Airship, 1994; Around the World in 80 Days, 1989 (TV miniseries); The Assassination Bureau, 1969; Batman: The Animated Series, 1992-1995 (TV series); British Intelligence, 1940; Buck Rogers, 1939 (serial); Buck Rogers, 1977 (edited version of 1939 serial); Charlie Chan at the Olympics, 1937; **The Court-Martial of Billy Mitchell**, 1955; Darling Lili, 1970; **The Desert Fox: The Story of Rommel**, 1951; **Devil Dogs of the Air**, 1935; **Dirigible**, 1931; Equilibrium, 2002; The Fabulous World of Jules Verne, 1961; The Fighting Devil Dogs, 1938 (serial); Fly Away Baby, 1937; **Flyboys**, 2008; The Go Getter, 1937; **The Golden Compass**, 2007; The Great Love, 1918; Hell Divers, 1931; **Hell's Angels**, 1930; **Here Comes the Navy**, 1934; **The Hindenburg**, 1975; Hindenburg, 2007 (made-for-TV); Hindenburg: The Last Flight, 2011 (made-for-TV); **Hope and Glory**, 1987; **Indiana Jones and the Last Crusade**, 1989; The Island at the Top of the World, 1974; Joe and Max, 2002 (made-for-TV); **Kiki's Delivery Service**, 1989; King of the Texas Rangers, 1941 (serial); The League of Extraordinary Gentlemen, 2003; The Lost Jungle, 1934; The Lost Zeppelin, 1929; The Lottery Bride, 1930; Madam Satan, 1930; Master of the World, 1961; Murder in the Air, 1940; **The Red Tent**, 1971; Riverworld, 2010 (made-for-TV); Robinson Crusoe of Clipper Island, 1936 (serial); Shanghai Knights, 2003; Sky Bandits, 1986; Sky Captain and the World of Tomorrow, 2004; The Sky Hawk, 1929; Snow White, 2012; Southland Tales, 2006; Steamboy, 2004; The Sum of All Fears, 2002; Synecdoche, New York, 2008; Tailspin Tommy in the Great Air Mystery, 1935 (serial); **Thunder in the City**, 1937; Two Years' Vacation, 1967; **Up**, 2009; A Very Long Engagement, 2005; A View to Kill, 1985; **Waterloo Bridge**, 1931; **Wings**, 1927; **Zeppelin**, 1971; Zeppelin, 1981.

Divers (underwater divers searching for treasure, salvage or making repairs on ships below the waterline or in scientific or military service): **The Abyss**, 1989; **Act of Valor**, 2012; The Adventures of TinTin, 2011; Bear Island, 1979; **Bedknobs and Broomsticks**, 1971; Beneath the 12-Mile Reef, 1953; **Boy on a Dolphin**, 1957; The Bulldog Breed, 1960; City in the Sea, 1965; **Cocoon**, 1985; **Creature from the Black Lagoon**, 1954; The Deep, 1977; DeepStar Six, 1989; **The Diving Bell and the Butterfly**, 2007; Doc Savage: The Man of Bronze, 1975; The Dragon Murder Case, 1934; The Embalmer, 1965; The Fabulous World of Jules Verne, 1961; **Fanny**, 1961; Ffolkes, 1980; The Flesh Eaters, 1964; Fool's Gold, 2008; **The Frogmen**, 1951; Ghost in the Shell, 1996; Isle of Fury, 1936; **It Came from Beneath the Sea**, 1955; **King of California**, 2007; Leviathan, 1989; Loch Ness, 1996; The Mechanic, 1972; **Men of Honor**, 2000; **Mud**, 2013; **Mysterious Island**, 1961; Parker, 2013; The Perils of Pauline, 1914; **The Perils of Pauline**, 1947; The Phantom Submarine, 1940; Pineapple Express, 2008; **Reap the Wild Wind**, 1942; Red Barry, 1938; Revenge of the Creature, 1955; The Sea Hound, 1947 (serial); Sh! The Octopus, 1937; **Sink the Bismarck!**, 1960; Sphere, 1998; That Burning Feeling, 2013; **They Were Expendable**, 1945; **Tillie and Gus**, 1933; **Titanic**, 1997; **20,000 Leagues Under the Sea**, 1954; Undersea Girl, 1957; Underwater!, 1955; **Voyage to the Bottom of the Sea**, 1961; **Wake of the Red

Witch, 1949; When Eight Bells Toll, 1971.

Domineering Mothers (also see Classic Mothers, this index): **Adventures of a Young Man**, 1962; **Almost Famous**, 2000; The Anniversary, 1968; Arthur, 2011; Black Swan, 2010; Bloody Mama, 1970; Brave, 2012; Butterflies Are Free, 1972; Carrie, 1976; The Crime Doctor's Warning, 1945; Crooklyn, 1994; Dead Alive, 1992; Deranged, 1987; Die, Mommie, Die!, 2003; Dirty Laundry, 2006; Don't Go in the House, 1980; Ed Gein, 2000; Eleanor and Franklin, 1976 (made-for-TV); Enter Laughing, 1967; Envy, 1999; Felicia's Journey, 1999; **The Fighter**, 2010; **Fourteen Hours**, 1951; Frances, 1982; **The Glass Menagerie**, 1950; **The Glass Menagerie**, 1987; **Gold Diggers of 1935**, 1935; The Gruesome Twosome, 1967; **Gypsy**, 1962; Happiness Ahead, 1934; Heavy, 1995; His Greatest Gamble, 1934; Hush, 1998; **I'll Cry Tomorrow**, 1955; **It's a Gift**, 1934; **It's a Mad, Mad, Mad, Mad World**, 1963; Life of Brian, 1979; **The Lion in Winter**, 1968; Little Voice, 1998; Love at First Kill, 2008; **The Loved One**, 1965; Ma and Pa Kettle Back on the Farm, 1951; **The Manchurian Candidate**, 1962; **The Messenger: The Story of Joan of Arc**, 1999; Mommie Dearest, 1981; Mother's Day, 2010; My Reputation, 1946; New York Stories, 1989; Only the Lonely, 1991; The Patsy, 1928; Persecution, 1975; **Phone Call from a Stranger**, 1952; **The Pride of the Yankees**, 1942; **Psycho**, 1960; Psycho, 1998; Psycho III, 1986; **Queen of the Mob**, 1940; **Rachel, Rachel**, 1968; Red White & Blue, 2010; Requiem, 2006; **Robin Hood**, 2010; Sailor Beware, 1957; **Separate Tables**, 1958; Serial Mom, 1994; Shopworn, 1932; **Splendor in the Grass**, 1961; **The Story on Page One**, 1959; A Stranger in My Arms, 1959; The Strangler, 1964; **A Summer Place**, 1959; **Sunrise at Campobello**, 1960; Teddy Bear, 2012; **Terms of Endearment**, 1983; Throw Momma from the Train, 1987; Too Much Sleep, 2001; **Too Much, Too Soon**, 1958; **What's Love Got to Do with It**, 1993; Where Love Has Gone, 1964; **White Heat**, 1949; **White Oleander**, 2002; **Wild at Heart**, 1990; Will There Really Be a Morning, 1983 (made-for-TV); Willard, 1971; Willard, 2003; **The Yearling**, 1946.

Doughboys (U.S. soldiers in WWI): **Alexander's Ragtime Band**, 1938; Anybody Here Seen Kelly?, 1928; Beyond Victory, 1931; **The Big Parade**, 1925; **Blockheads**, 1938; **By the Light of the Silvery Moon**, 1953; Company K, 2004; **Doughboys**, 1930; F. Scott Fitzgerald and the Last of the Belles, 1974 (made-for-TV); **The Fighting 69th**, 1940; **For Me and My Gal**, 1942; **Four Sons**, 1928; **Gold Diggers of 1933**, 1933; **The Great Gatsby**, 1926; **The Great Gatsby**, 1949; **The Great Gatsby**, 1974; The Great Gatsby, 2000 (made-for-TV); **H. M. Pulham, Esq.**, 1941; **Half Shot at Sunrise**, 1930; **Hell's Angels**, 1930; Heroes for Sale, 1933; **I Am a Fugitive from a Chain Gang**, 1932; **The Iron Major**, 1943; Johnny Got His Gun, 1971; Legends of the Fall, 1994; Look for the Silver Lining, 1949; The Lost Battalion, 1919; The Lost Battalion, 2001 (made-for-TV); The Man Who Broke 1,000 Chains, 1987 (made-for-TV); Marianne, 1929; My Buddy, 1944; **Noah's Ark**, 1928; **On Moonlight Bay**, 1951; Only Yesterday, 1933; **Pack Up Your Troubles**, 1932; **The Public Enemy**, 1931; **The Razor's Edge**, 1946; **Rendezvous**, 1935; **The Roaring Twenties**, 1939; **Sergeant York**, 1941; The Shopworn Angel, 1928; **The Shopworn Angel**, 1938; **Shoulder Arms**, 1918; Sons o' Guns, 1936; **They Gave Him a Gun**, 1937; **This Is the Army**, 1943; Three Live Ghosts, 1936; **Tin Pan Alley**, 1940; **To Each His Own**, 1946; **Two Arabian Knights**, 1927; **What Price Glory**, 1926; **What Price Glory**, 1952; **Wilson**, 1944; **Wings**, 1927; **Yankee Doodle Dandy**, 1942.

Drilling, Storing and Wildcatting for Oil: The Arizona Cowboy, 1950; Armageddon, 1998; **Armored Car Robbery**, 1950; Beyond the Pecos, 1945; Black Gold, 1928; Black Gold, 1936; Black Gold, 1947; Blackmail, 1939; Blondie Plays Cupid, 1940; Blood and Oil, 2010 (mad-for-TV); Blowing Wild, 1953; **Boom Town**, 1940; **Breaking the Waves**, 1996; Buffalo Bill Rides Again, 1947; Burning Gold, 1936; Campbell's

Kingdom, 1960; The City of Lost Children, 1995; Clambake, 1967; Clipped Wings, 1937; Colt Comrades, 1943; Conquest of Cheyenne, 1946; Country Gentlemen, 1936; Cyclone Kid, 1931; **The Day the Earth Stood Still**, 2008; **Death of a Scoundrel**, 1956; Death Valley Manhunt, 1943; Desperadoes of the West, 1950; The Devil's Pipeline, 1940; **Diamonds Are Forever**, 1971; **The FBI Story**, 1959; Fear Is the Key, 1973; Ffolkes, 1980; **The Fighting Seabees**, 1944; Flaming Gold, 1932; **The Flight of the Phoenix**, 1965; The Flight of the Phoenix, 2004; **Flowing Gold**, 1940; **Giant**, 1956; Git Along Little Dogies, 1937; Goin' to Town, 1935; The Good, the Bad, the Weird, 2008; Gotta Run!, 1982; Gran Casino, 1947; The Green Hornet Strikes Again!, 1940 (serial); **Harper**, 1966; Hellfighters, 1968; High Explosive, 1943; **How to Marry a Millionaire**, 1953; **Hud**, 1963; In Old Oklahoma, 1943; India, 1993; The Jailbird, 1920; **Jarhead**, 2005; Jeep Herders, 1949; Jesse James Rides Again, 1947; Joe Dirt, 2001; Ladies' Man, 1947; **The Last Time I Saw Paris**, 1954; The Last Winter, 2007; Lay That Rifle Down, 1955; Legendary, 2010; **The Life and Times of Judge Roy Bean**, 1972; The Lone Hand Texan, 1947; Louisiana Story, 1948; Lucky Me, 1954; Man from Oklahoma, 1945; **Man of Steel**, 2013; Mexicali Rose, 1939; Million Dollar Racket, 1937; Mr. Reckless, 1948; Murder in Texas, 1981 (made-for-TV); Near Dark, 1987; Neglected Women, 1924; **Nightfall**, 1956; **Oil for the Lamps of China**, 1935; The Oil Raider, 1934; Oiltown, U.S.A., 1953; **Oklahoma Crude**, 1973; On Deadly Ground, 1994; Outlaws of the Orient, 1937; Pueblo Terror, 1931; Red Dirt, 2000; Red Rock West, 1993; The Return of Mr. Moto, 1965; The Rig, 2010; **The Secret Life of Words**, 2005; **Shockproof**, 1949; Siberiade, 1979; Sin Town, 1942; Smilla's Feeling for Snow, 1997; **Sorcerer**, 1977; Spoilers of the Plains, 1951; The Stars Fell on Henrietta, 1995; Superman and the Mole-Men, 1951; Texas Masquerade, 1944; **There Will Be Blood**, 2007; Thunderbirds, 2004; The Tiger Woman, 1944; Tongues of Flame, 1924; **Touch of Evil**, 1958; **The Treasure of the Sierra Madre**, 1948; Treat 'Em Rough, 1942; **Tulsa**, 1949; **The Two Jakes**, 1990; Ulzhan, 2007; A View to Kill, 1985; **The Wages of Fear**, 1955; The Wheeler-Dealers, 1963; Where the Truth Lies, 2005; The Wild Angels, 1966; Wildcat, 1942.

Drug Smugglers: **Act of Valor**, 2012; American Gangster, 2007; Ararat, 2002; Bad Boys II, 2003; The Bank Job, 2008; **Batman Begins**, 2005; Behind the Mask, 1932; **Beverly Hills Cop**, 1984; Black Dynamite, 2009; Blow, 2001; Borderline, 1950; Brokedown Palace, 1999; The Business, 2005; Crashing Courage, 1923; Crossing the Bridge, 1992; Desperado, 1995; **The Discreet Charm of the Bourgeoisie**, 1972; The Falcon and the Snowman, 1985; Fast & Furious, 2009; Forbidden Cargo, 1954; **The French Connection**, 1971; **French Connection II**, 1975; **The Guard**, 2011; Harsh Times, 2006; Indochine, 1992; An Innocent Man, 1989; Inspector Morse, 1987-2000 (TV series); The Italian Connection, 1973; **Kill the Messenger**, 2014; **The Lineup**, 1978; Live and Let Die, 1973; Looking for Trouble, 1926; Maria Full of Grace, 2004; The Mechanic, 1972; **Midnight Express**, 1978; Mr. Nice, 2011; **Non-Stop**, 2014; Open Gate, 2011; Outland, 1991; Outrage, 2010; Police Story 3: Supercop, 1996; **Ray**, 2004; Rapid Fire, 1992; Revenge of the Ninja, 1983; **The Rose Tattoo**, 1955; Scarface, 1983; The Sicilian Girl, 2010; Snitch, 2013; 10th & Wolf, 2006; **The Three Burials of Melquiades Estrada**, 2006; Through Thick and Thin, 1927; **To the Ends of the Earth**, 1948; **Traffic**, 2000; Trans-Europ-Express, 1968; **Transsiberian**, 2008; Traffik, 1989 (TV miniseries); **Underworld U.S.A.**, 1961; Unseen Enemies, 1925; The Warning, 1927; We're the Millers, 2013; **Who'll Stop the Rain**, 1978; **Year of the Dragon**, 1985. Note: For detailed information on drug smuggling, see my books *Bloodletters and Badmen* (M. Evans, 1973); *Encyclopedia of World Crime*; 8 volumes (CrimeBooks, Inc., 1990); *The Great Pictorial History of World Crime*; 2 volumes (History, Inc., 2004).

Dual Roles (also see Twins, this index): Adaptation, 2002; Alien 3, 1992; Around the World in 80 Days, 2004; **Baahubali: The Beginning**, 2015;

Back to the Future Part III, 1990; Bad Company, 2002; Before Night Falls, 2000; Bicentennial Man, 1999; **Bram Stoker's Dracula**, 1992; Captain America, 1944 (serial); Captain America, 1990; **Cat Ballou**, 1965; **Casualties of War**, 1989; Chaplin, 1992; Coffee and Cigarettes, 2003; **Colonel Blimp**, 1945; **Come and Get It**, 1936; **Confessions of a Rogue**, 1948; Constantine, 2005; **The Corsican Brothers**, 1941; **Cover Girl**, 1944; **Crack in the Mirror**, 1960; The Dark Half, 1993; **The Dark Mirror**, 1946; Dave, 1993; Dead Again, 1991; Dead Ringer, 1964; Dead Ringers, 1988; **Django Unchained**, 2012; Don, 2006; Double Impact, 1991; Duplicate, 1998; **Fahrenheit 451**, 1966; Fan, 2016; Female Trouble, 1974; **The Great Dictator**, 1940; **The Great Race**, 1965; History of the World: Part I, 1981; **It Came from Outer Space**, 1953; **A Kiss Before Dying**, 1956; The Last Starfighter, 1984; Leaves of Grass, 2009; **Liquid Sky**, 1982; **The Love Bug**, 1968; **The Man in the Iron Mask**, 1939; The Man in the Iron Mask, 1998; Marked for Death, 1990; **Mary Poppins**, 1964; Mary Reilly, 1996; Maximum Risk, 1996; Mother Night, 1996; Obsession, 1976; The One, 2001; **The Parent Trap**, 1961; **The Parent Trap**, 1998; **Peter Pan**, 1953; **Pocahontas**, 1995; **The Prisoner of Zenda**, 1922; **The Prisoner of Zenda**, 1937; **The Prisoner of Zenda**, 1952; **The Purple Rose of Cairo**, 1985; Replicant, 2001; Roy, 2015; The 6th Day, 2000; So I Married an Axe Murderer, 1993; **The Social Network**, 2010; Special Effects, 1984; **The Spiderwick Chronicles**, 2008; **A Stolen Life**, 1946; Superman, 1948 (serial); **Superman**, 1978; **Superman Returns**, 2006; **Superman II**, 1981; **Superman III**, 1983; Tango & Cash, 1989; **Tanu Weds Manu Returns**, 2015; Teenage Mutant Ninja Turtles, 1990; **The Time Machine**, 1960; **To Each His Own**, 1946; The Tomb of Ligeia, 1964; Twin Dragons, 1992; **Vertigo**, 1958; **Windwalker**, 1980; **The Woman in White**, 1948.

Earthquakes: Adventures of Captain Marvel, 1941; **Advice to the Lovelorn**, 1933; Aftershock, 2012 (Chile); **The Apple Dumpling Gang**, 1975 (California); Arachnophobia, 1990 (South America); Around the World under the Sea, 1966; Atlantis, the Lost Continent, 1961; Attack of the Crab Monsters, 1957; The Black Dahlia, 2006 (Los Angeles, California); The Black Scorpion, 1957 (Mexico); The Book of Life, 1998; The Border, 1982 (Texas); Border Treasure, 1950; The Bridge of San Luis Rey, 2004; Bug, 1975; A Canterbury Tale, 1949; Captain Corelli's Mandolin, 2001; **The China Syndrome**, 1979 (California); City Beneath the Sea, 1953 (Jamaica); The Clan of the Cave Bear, 1986; **The Core**, 2003 (California); Crack in the World, 1965; Creatures the World Forgot, 1971; **Dante's Peak**, 1997 (Pacific Northwest); **The Day of the Locust**, 1975 (Long Beach, California, March 10-11, 1933); Deluge, 1933; **The Devil at Four O'Clock**, 1961 (Pacific island); Earthquake, 1974 (Los Angeles, California); Encino Man, 1992; Escape from L.A., 1996; Evita, 1996; **Fantasia**, 1940; **Fellini Satyricon**, 1969 (Italy); 50 Ways to Leave Your Lover, 2004 (Los Angeles, California); Flame of the Barbary Coast, 1945 (the Great San Francisco Earthquake, 1906); Flash Gordon, 1980; Freaky Friday, 2003; Frisco Jenny, 1932 (the Great San Francisco Earthquake, 1906); Gallant Journey, 1946 (California); Ghost Diver, 1957; Grand Canyon, 1991 (California); **Green Dolphin Street**, 1947 (New Zealand); Hell Morgan's Girl, 1917 (the Great San Francisco Earthquake, 1906); Her Jungle Love, 1938; The House of the Spirits, 1993 (Chile); **Ice Age**, 2002; Impulse, 1984; In Search of the Castaways, 1962; **Indiana Jones and the Last Crusade**, 1989; **Journey to the Center of the Earth**, 1959; **Journey to the Center of the Earth**, 2008; Journey to the Seventh Planet, 1962; A Kid in King Arthur's Court, 1995; **The King of Kings**, 1927 (Golgotha during the crucifixion of Jesus); King of the Rocket Men, 1949; L. A. Story, 1991 (Los Angeles, California); **The Land Before Time**, 1988; Land of the Lost, 2009; Lara Croft Tomb Raider: The Cradle of Life, 2003; **The Last Days of Pompeii**, 1935 (volcanic eruption of Vesuvius and earthquake in Italy, 79 A.D.); The Last Patrol, 2000; **The Last Tycoon**, 1976 (Los Angeles, California); Life or Something Like It, 2002; Looking for Trouble, 1934 (Long

Beach, California, 1933); Lust for Gold, 1949 (Arizona); Mackenna's Gold, 1969 (Colorado); Mamma Mia!, 2008; The Man Who Loved Women, 1983; The Mist, 2007; The Mole People, 1956 (Middle East); The Monster That Challenged the World, 1957 (California); **The Mummy**, 1999; Namus, 1925; The Neptune Factor, 1973; The Night the World Exploded, 1957 (California); Ocean's Thirteen, 2007; Old San Francisco, 1927 (the Great San Francisco Earthquake, 1906); **One Million B.C.**, 1940; One Million Years, B.C., 1966; Passage to Zarahemla, 2007; **Penny Serenade**, 1941 (the Great Kanto Earthquake, Japan, 1923); Phenomenon, 1996; Pirates, 1998; Playing Mona Lisa, 2000 (San Francisco, California); **The Poseidon Adventure**, 1972 (earthquake producing a Seismic Sea Wave); Proud Flesh, 1925; **The Rains Came**, 1939 (India); **The Rains of Ranchipur**, 1955 (India); **San Francisco**, 1936 (the Great San Francisco Earthquake, 1906); **The Secret Garden**, 1993; The Seventh Sign, 1988; **The Shock**, 1923 (the Great San Francisco Earthquake, 1906); **The Sisters**, 1938 (the Great San Francisco Earthquake, 1906); **Somebody Loves Me**, 1952 (the Great San Francisco Earthquake, 1906); **The Son of Kong**, 1933; The Space Between Us, 1999 (San Francisco, California); **Superman Returns**, 2006; **The Thief of Bagdad**, 1940; **The Two Jakes**, 1990 (Southern California); Undersea Kingdom, 1936; A View to Kill, 1985; A Virtuous Vamp, 1919 (the Great San Francisco Earthquake, 1906); Volcano, 1997 (Los Angeles, California); **War of the Worlds**, 2005; **When Worlds Collide**, 1951. Note: For more information on earthquakes throughout history, see my book *Darkest Hours: A Narrative Encyclopedia of Worldwide Disasters from Ancient Times to the Present* (Nelson-Hall, 1976).

Elephants: **Airplane!**, 1980; **Around the World in 80 Days**, 1956; **Babar: The Movie**, 1989; Blood Diamond, 2006; **Cabiria**, 1914; **The Care Bears Movie**, 1985; **Chad Hanna**, 1940; **The Circus**, 1928; **Circus World**, 1964; **Clive of India**, 1935; Despicable Me, 2010; **Dumbo**, 1941; **Elephant Boy**, 1937; **Elephant Walk**, 1954; **Eternal Sunshine of the Spotless Mind**, 2004; Gangs of New York, 2002; **Gladiator**, 2000; **The Greatest Show on Earth**, 1952; **Gunga Din**, 1939; **Inside Out**, 2015; **Life of Pi**, 2012; **The Lives of a Bengal Lancer**, 1935; The Lord of the Rings: The Return of the King, 2003; **The Lord of the Rings: The Two Towers**, 2002; **Night at the Museum**, 2006; **1941**, 1979; **Our Vines Have Tender Grapes**, 1945; Polly of the Circus, 1917; Polly of the Circus, 1932; **The Roots of Heaven**, 1958; **Sally of the Sawdust**, 1925; Shirley of the Circus, 1922; **The Snows of Kilimanjaro**, 1952; Stardust, 2007; **Tarzan**, 1999; **Tarzan and His Mate**, 1934; **Tarzan Escapes**, 1936; **Tarzan Finds a Son!**, 1939; **Tarzan of the Apes**, 1918; **Tarzan the Ape Man**, 1932; **Tarzan's Greatest Adventure**, 1959; **Tarzan's Secret Treasure**, 1941; **Tarzan's Three Challenges**, 1963; **The Thief of Bagdad**, 1940; **300**, 2006; 300: Rise of an Empire, 2014; **Trader Horn**, 1931; Transformers: Dark of the Moon, 2011; **12 Monkeys**, 1995; **20 Million Miles to Earth**, 1957; **Water for Elephants**, 2011.

Elevator Operators: All Good Things, 2010; **The Apartment**, 1960; Attack of the Puppet People, 1958; Behind That Curtain, 1929; Bermuda Mystery, 1944; Biff Baker, U.S.A., 1952-1954 (TV series; "Grey Market," 1952 episode); Blossoms on Broadway, 1937; The Bride Comes Home, 1935; **Carefree**, 1938; Case of the Missing Man, 1935; Cigarette Girl, 1947; City Girl, 1938; **Confessions of Boston Blackie**, 1941; **Counselor at Law**, 1933; **Cover Girl**, 1944; **Cry of the City**, 1948; Deadline for Murder, 1946; Dr. Gillespie's New Assistant, 1942; **Don't Bother to Knock**, 1952; **Double Indemnity**, 1944; **Dressed to Kill**, 1941; Easy to Love, 1934; Elevator Girls in Bondage, 1972; Emergency Squad, 1940; **Employee's Entrance**, 1933; Expensive Husbands, 1937; **A Face in the Crowd**, 1957; Fairy Tales, 1978; Federal Agent, 1936; Fifteen Maiden Lane, 1936; Footlight Fever, 1941; **Force of Evil**, 1948; Gildersleeve on Broadway, 1943; Girl Trouble, 1942; Good Sport, 1931; **The Grand Budapest Hotel**, 2014; Here

Comes Trouble, 1948; Honeymoon in Bali, 1939; Honolulu Lou, 1941; **The Horn Blows at Midnight**, 1945; How's About It, 1943; The Hudsucker Proxy, 1994; I Married a Woman, 1958; I Want a Divorce, 1940; It's in the Air, 1935; **It's in the Bag**, 1945; **The Jackpot**, 1950; Kettle of Fish, 2006; **King of Burlesque**, 1936; **King of the Hill**, 1993; Lightnin' in the Forest, 1948; Little Manhattan, 2005; Living Out Loud, 1998; **Love Crazy**, 1941; **The Major and the Minor**, 1942; **The Man in the Gray Flannel Suit**, 1956; The Mysterious Miss X, 1939; Navy Secrets, 1939; **North by Northwest**, 1959; One Hour Late, 1934; Pacific Rendezvous, 1942; The Party's Over, 1934; The Patient in Room 18, 1938; Perry Mason, 1957-1966 (TV series; "The Case of the Daring Decoy," 1958 episode; "The Case of the Terrified Typist," 1958 episode); The Piano Lesson, 1995 (made-for-TV); The Pilgrim Lady, 1947; **Pillow Talk**, 1959; Please Believe Me, 1950; **Pretty Woman**, 1990; The Royal Tenenbaums, 2001; Senorita from the West, 1945; Shadow of the Law, 1930; The Silken Affair, 1957; Skyscraper Souls, 1932; **The Sleeping City**, 1950; Slightly Honorable, 1939; Something to Live For, 1952; Special Agent K-7, 1936; Suddenly It's Spring, 1947; Swing It, Soldier, 1941; That Man's Here Again, 1937; They Made Her a Spy, 1939; **They Won't Forget**, 1937; The Toe Tactic, 2008; Top of the Town, 1937; **Topper**, 1937; **The Towering Inferno**, 1974; Twin Falls Idaho, 1999; Under the Rainbow, 1981; Up in the Air, 1940; A Very Honorable Guy, 1934; The Witness Chair, 1936; Who Killed Gail Preston?, 1938; You're Out of Luck, 1941.

Emperors (Austria-Hungary; historical; also see entries for individuals in Historical Persons Index): **Amadeus**, 1984 (Joseph II); **Mayerling**, 1937 (Franz Joseph); Mayerling, 1969 (Franz Joseph).

Emperors (China; historical; also see entries for individuals in Historical Persons Index): **The Adventures of Marco Polo**, 1938 (Kublai Khan of China); The Adventures of Marco Polo, 1956 (made-for-TV; Kuglai Khan of China); The Conqueror, 1956 (Genghis Khan); Genghis Khan, 1965 (Genghis Khan); **The Last Emperor**, 1987 (Henry Pu Yi); Marco Polo, 1962 (Kublai Khan); Marco Polo, 1982 (TV miniseries; Kublai Khan); Marco Polo, 2007 (made-for-TV; Kublai Khan); Marco Polo, 2014- (TV series; Kublai Khan); **Marco the Magnificent**, 1966 (Kublai Khan).

Emperors (France; historical; also see entries for individuals in Historical Persons Index): **The Count of Monte Cristo**, 1934 (Napoleon I); **The Count of Monte Cristo**, 2002 (Napoleon I); **Desirée**, 1954 (Napoleon I); **Juarez**, 1939 (Napoleon III); **Napoleon**, 1927 (Napoleon I); **Reign of Terror**, 1949 (Napoleon I); **Scaramouche**, 1952 (Napoleon I); **The Song of Bernadette**, 1943 (Napoleon III); **Suez**, 1938 (Napoleon III); **War and Peace**, 1956 (Napoleon I); **War and Peace**, 1968 (Napoleon I); **Waterloo**, 1971 (Napoleon I).

Emperors (Roman Empire; historical; also see entries for individuals in Historical Persons Index): **Ben Hur: A Tale of the Christ**, 1925 (Tiberius); **Ben-Hur**, 1959 (Tiberius); Caligula, 1980 (Caligula); Cleopatra, 1912 (Augustus/Octavius); Cleopatra, 1917 (Augustus/Octavius); **Cleopatra**, 1963 (Augustus/Octavius); **Demetrius and the Gladiators**, 1954 (Caligula, Claudius); **The Fall of the Roman Empire**, 1964 (Marcus Aurelius, Commodus); **Gladiator**, 2000 (Marcus Aurelius, Commodus); Imperium: Augustus, 2003 (made-for-TV; Augustus/Octavius); **Night at the Museum**, 2006 (Augustus/Octavius); **Night at the Museum: Battle of the Smithsonian**, 2009 (Augustus/Octavius); **Quo Vadis**, 1913 (Nero); **Quo Vadis**, 1951 (Nero); **The Robe**, 1953 (Tiberius, Caligula); **The Sign of the Cross**, 1932 (Nero); **The Silver Chalice**, 1954 (Nero).

Emperors (Russia; historical; also see entries for individuals in Historical Persons Index): **Catherine the Great**, 1934 (Paul I); **Ivan the Terrible**, 1947 (Ivan IV); **Nicholas and Alexandra**, 1971 (Nicholas II);

Peter the Great, 1986 (TV miniseries; Peter I); **The Scarlet Empress**, 1934 (Paul I).

Empire State Building (New York, New York): **An Affair to Remember**, 1957; **Counselor at Law**, 1933; **Dodsworth**, 1936; Fly Away Baby, 1937; Happiness Ahead, 1934; **King Kong**, 1933; **On the Town**, 1949; **Sleepless in Seattle**, 1993; **The Thief**, 1952.

Empresses (Russia; historical; also see entries for individuals in Historical Persons Index): **Catherine the Great**, 1934 (Catherine II); **John Paul Jones**, 1959 (Catherine the Great/Catherine II); **Nicholas and Alexandra**, 1971; **The Scarlet Empress**, 1934 (Catherine the Great/Catherine II).

Espionage (American Civil War): **Abraham Lincoln**, 1930 (Lincoln assassination; Secret Service); **The Great Locomotive Chase**, 1956; **The Horse Soldiers**, 1959 (Union and Confederate espionage during the American Civil War); The Lincoln Conspiracy, 1977 (Secret Service); Operator 13, 1934; **Prince of Players**, 1955 (Abraham Lincoln assassination; Secret Service); **The Prisoner of Shark Island**, 1936 (Abraham Lincoln assassination; Secret Service); The Rose and the Jackal, 1990 (made-for-TV; Confederate and Union spies); **A Southern Yankee**, 1948 (Confederate and Union spies); **The Tall Target**, 1951 (Abraham Lincoln; pre-American Civil War); **Virginia City**, 1940 (Confederate and Union spies). Note: For more information on espionage during the American Civil War, see my book *Spies: A Narrative Encyclopedia of Dirty Deeds and Double Dealing from Biblical Times to Today* (M. Evans, 1997).

Espionage (Cold War and thereafter): Agent 8¾ (aka: Hot Enough for June, 1965 (MI6; KGB); Alex Rider: Operation Stormbreaker, 2006 (MI6); Assignment K, 1968 (MI6; East German Stasi); Assignment: Paris, 1952; Arctic Flight, 1952; Avalanche Express, 1979; Bang! Bang! You're Dead! (aka: Our Man in Marrakesh), 1966; Battle beneath the Earth, 1968 (Chinese Intelligence); **Berlin Express**, 1948 (neo-Nazism); Billion Dollar Brain, 1967 (MI5); The Black Windmill, 1974 (MI6; IRA); Blue Ice, 1992 (MI6); **The Bourne Identity**, 2002 (CIA); **The Bourne Ultimatum**, 2007 (CIA); **Breach**, 2007 (FBI turncoat Robert Hanssen; CIA; KGB); **Bridge of Spies**, 2015 (Francis Gary Powers; Rudolf Abel; CIA; KGB); Bullet to Beijing, 1997 (made-for-TV; MI5; KGB); Callan, 1974 (SIS; KGB); Caravan to Vaccares, 1974 (KGB); Carry On Spying, 1965; The Case of the Red Monkey (aka: Little Red Monkey), 1955 (Scotland Yard's Special Branch; CIA; KGB); **Casino Royale**, 2006 (MI6; CIA); **The Chairman**, 1969 (CIA); Charlie Muffin, 1983 (made-for-TV; MI6; KGB); **Charlie Wilson's War**, 2007 (CIA); Che!, 1969 (KGB); Company Business, 1991 (CIA; KGB); Company Man, 2001 (CIA); **Confessions of a Dangerous Mind**, 2002 (CIA); **Conspirator**, 1949 (MI5; KGB); **Cornered**, 1945 (neo-Nazism); Counterspy Meets Scotland Yard, 1950; Criminal, 2016 (CIA); A Dandy in Aspic, 1968 (MI6; KGB); Danger Route, 1968 (MI6); **The Deadly Affair**, 1967 (MI5; KGB); Death Has a Bad Reputation, 1990 (made-for-TV; MI6; Carlos the Jackal); Death Train, 1993 (made-for-TV; MI6); The Devil Makes Three, 1952 (U.S. Army intelligence; neo-Nazism); The Devil's Agent, 1962 (KGB; Stasi); Dick Barton at Bay, 1950 (MI5); Dick Barton Strikes Back, 1949 (MI5); Dick Barton, Special Agent, 1948 (MI6); **Die Another Day**, 2002; **Diplomatic Courier**, 1952 (KGB; U.S. Army intelligence); **Dr. Strangelove**, 1964; The Double, 2011; The Double Man, 1968 (CIA; KGB); The Executioner, 1970 (MI5; KGB); The Executioner (aka: Permission to Kill), 1975; The Falcon and the Snowman, 1985 (KGB; FBI); Family of Spies, 1990 (made-for-TV; the Walker family); Fathom, 1967 (NATO); Foreign Exchange, 1970 (made-for-TV; KGB; MI6); Foreign Intrigue, 1956; The Fourth Protocol, 1987 (KGB); **From Russia with Love**, 1964; **Funeral in Berlin**, 1966 (MI5; KGB); Hammerhead, 1968 (MI6; NATO); Hell and High Water, 1954; High Treason, 1952 (Scotland Yard's Special Branch;

KGB); Highly Dangerous, 1951 (MI6; KGB); The Holcroft Covenant, 1985 (neo-Nazism); The Human Factor, 1979 (MI6; KGB); The Hunter, 1952 (TV series); **I Was a Communist for the F.B.I.**, 1951 (FBI; KGB); The Innocent, 1995 (MI6; CIA; KGB; Berlin Tunnel); Innocent Bystanders, 1973 (MI6; KGB; CIA); The Intelligence Men, 1965 (MI5; KGB); The Internecine Project, 1974 (MI6); **The Ipcress File**, 1965 (MI5); **The Iron Curtain**, 1948 (MGB/MVD; RCMP); Jet Attack, 1958 (KGB); The Jigsaw Man, 1984 (KGB; MI6; Kim Philby); Johnny English, 2003 (MI6; KGB); Johnny English Reborn (aka: Johnny English Returns), 2011 (MI6; KGB); Keep Your Fingers Crossed (aka: Catch Me a Spy), 1971 (KGB; MI6); **Kingsman: The Secret Service**, 2014; **The Kremlin Letter**, 1970 (KGB); License to Kill, 1989; The Liquidator, 1966 (MI6); The Looking Glass War, 1970 (MI6; KGB); The Mackintosh Man, 1973 (MI6); Madame Sin, 1972 (CIA); **The Man Between**, 1953 (MI6; KGB); The Man in the Glass Booth, 1975 (role model for Adolf Eichmann; Mossad); Man on a String, 1960 (CIA; KGB); **The Man Who Knew Too Much**, 1956 (MI5; KGB); **The Manchurian Candidate**, 1962; The Manchurian Candidate, 2004; **Marathon Man**, 1976; Master Spy, 1964 (MI5; KGB); Midnight in Saint Petersburg, 1996 (MI6; KGB); MI-5 (aka: Spooks: The Greater Good), 2015 (MI5); **My Son John**, 1952 (MGB/MVD; FBI); The Naked Runner, 1967 (MI6; KGB); **Night People**, 1954 (KGB; U.S. G-2); Night Train to Paris, 1964 (French intelligence; KGB); Nightwatch, 1995 (made-for-TV; UN agents); No. 1 of the Secret Service, 1970 (MI6); **North by Northwest**, 1959 (CIA; KGB); **Notorious**, 1946 (neo-Nazism; FBI); Notorious, 1992 (made-for-TV); The Numbers Station, 2013 (CIA); **The Odessa File**, 1974 (neo-Nazism); Otley, 1969; Operation Eichmann, 1961 (neo-Nazism; Mossad); Operation Manhunt, 1954 (KGB; Canadian intelligence; RCMP); **Our Man in Havana**, 1959 (MI6); Page Eight, 2011 (MI5); **Pickup on South Street**, 1952 (NKVD; KGB; FBI); **The Quiller Memorandum**, 1966 (neo-Nazism); Ring of Treason (aka: Ring of Spies), 1964 (MI5; KGB; Portland Spy Ring); **Salt**, 2010; Salting the Battlefield, 2014 (made-for-TV; MI5; CIA); The 2nd Best Secret Agent in the Whole Wide World (aka: Licensed to Kill), 1965 (MI6); Security Risk, 1954; The Sell-Out, 1977 (CIA; KGB; Mossad); **Shadow Dancer**, 2012 (MI5; IRA); Shoot First (aka: Rough Shoot), 1953 (MI5; KGB); Some Girls Do, 1971; Some May Live, 1967 (U.S. Army intelligence); Spies Like Us, 1985; Spooks, 2002-2011 (TV series; MI5); The Spy Killer, 1969 (made-for-TV; MI6; KGB); Spy Story, 1976 (MI6; KGB); **The Spy Who Came in from the Cold**, 1965 (KGB; MI6; MI5); **The Spy Who Loved Me**, 1977; The Russia House, 1990 (MI6; KGB); **The Stranger**, 1946 (neo-Nazism); Subterfuge, 1969 (MI6); Survivor, 2015 (MI6); They Can't Hang Me, 1955 (Scotland Yard's Special Branch; KGB); **The Thief**, 1952 (KGB; FBI); **The Third Man**, 1950 (MI6; KGB); **Three Days of the Condor**, 1975 (CIA); Tinker Tailor Soldier Spy, 1979 (TV miniseries); **Tinker Tailor Soldier Spy**, 2011 (MI5; KGB); **Topaz**, 1969 (CIA; KGB); **Torn Curtain**, 1966 (CIA; KGB); Turks and Caicos, 2014 (made-for-TV; MI5; CIA); **Walk a Crooked Mile**, 1948 (FBI; Scotland Yard's Special Branch; KGB); **Walk East on Beacon!**, 1952 (FBI; KGB); Where the Bullets Fly, 1967; Where the Spies Are, 1966; **The Whistle Blower**, 1987 (MI6); **The Woman on Pier 13**, 1949 (KGB; FBI). Note: For more information on espionage during the Cold War, see my book *Spies: A Narrative Encyclopedia of Dirty Deeds and Double Dealing from Biblical Times to Today* (M. Evans, 1997).

Espionage (Historical): **Abraham Lincoln**, 1930 (Lincoln assassination; Secret Service); Adventures of Casanova, 1948 (18th-Century France); Cardinal Richelieu, 1935 (17th-Century France); The Dreyfus Case, 1931 (Alfred Dreyfus; Deuxieme Bureau; Abteilung IIIb); The Dreyfus Case, 1940 (Alfred Dreyfus; Deuxieme Bureau; Abteilung IIIb); **Fire Over England**, 1937 (Elizabethan espionage); **The Four Feathers**, 1939 (SIS during the Mahdist War of 1881-1899); **The Horse Soldiers**, 1959 (Union and Confederate espionage during the American Civil War); **I Accuse!**, 1958 (Alfred Dreyfus; Deuxieme Bureau;

Abteilung IIIb); **Jack London**, 1943 (Russo-Japanese War; Kempeitai); **Kim**, 1950 (SIS; 19th-Century India); The King's Thief, 1955; **The Life of Emile Zola**, 1937 (Alfred Dreyfus; Deuxieme Bureau; Abteilung IIIb); The Lincoln Conspiracy, 1977 (Secret Service); Madame Du Barry, 1934; **Mary of Scotland**, 1936 (Elizabethan espionage); Mary Queen of Scots, 1971 (Elizabethan espionage); Mary Queen of Scots, 2013 (Elizabethan espionage); **The Mask of Dimitrios**, 1944 (Industrial espionage; Turkish intelligence; pre-WWII); **The Molly Maguires**, 1970 (U.S. Sinn Fein in 19th Century; Pinkerton agents); Operator 13, 1934 (Union and Confederate intellicence agents in the American Civil War); **Prince of Players**, 1955 (Abraham Lincoln assassination; Secret Service); **The Prisoner of Shark Island**, 1936 (Abraham Lincoln assassination; Secret Service); **Reign of Terror**, 1949 (French Revolution); The Riddle of the Sands, 1984 (1901; SIS; Abwehr); Spy of Napoleon, 1936 (Deuxieme Bureau; Franco-Prussian War of 1870); **The Scarlet Coat**, 1955 (American Revolution); **The Tall Target**, 1951 (Abraham Lincoln; pre-American Civil War); **The Three Musketeers**, 1921 (17th-Century France); **The Three Musketeers**, 1948 (17th-Century France); **The Three Musketeers**, 1974 (17th Century France); **The Three Musketeers**, 1993 (17th-Century France); **Young Bess**, 1953 (Elizabethan era). Note: For more information on historical espionage see my book *Spies: A Narrative Encyclopedia of Dirty Deeds and Double Dealing from Biblical Times to Today* (M. Evans, 1997).

Espionage (Post-WWII neo-Nazism): **Berlin Express**, 1948; **Captain Carey, U.S.A.**, 1950; **Cornered**, 1945; The Holcroft Covenant, 1985; **Notorious**, 1946; **The Odessa File**, 1974; **The Quiller Memorandum**, 1966; **The Stranger**, 1946. Note: For more information on espionage during the neo-Nazi era, see my book *Spies: A Narrative Encyclopedia of Dirty Deeds and Double Dealing from Biblical Times to Today* (M. Evans, 1997).

Espionage (Pre-WWII): **Above Suspicion**, 1943; **Arch of Triumph**, 1948; Arch of Triumph, 1984 (made-for-TV); **Blood on the Sun**, 1945; **Confessions of a Nazi Spy**, 1939; **Escape**, 1940; **Flight for Freedom**, 1943; **The General Died at Dawn**, 1936; Head in the Clouds, 2004; **The Hindenburg**, 1975; **The Lady Vanishes**, 1938; The Lady Vanishes, 1979; **Love on the Run**, 1936; **Marie Galante**, 1934; **Man Hunt**, 1941; **The Man Who Knew Too Much**, 1935; **The Mask of Dimitrios**, 1944 (industrial espionage; Turkish intelligence; pre-WWII); **Night Train to Munich**, 1940; **Sabotage**, 1937; Second Bureau, 1937; **The Seventh Cross**, 1944; **The 39 Steps**, 1935. Note: For more information on espionage prior to WWII, see my book *Spies: A Narrative Encyclopedia of Dirty Deeds and Double Dealing from Biblical Times to Today* (M. Evans, 1997).

Espionage (Spanish Civil War): **Confidential Agent**, 1945; Espionage Agent, 1939; **The Fallen Sparrow**, 1943. Note: For more information on espionage during the Spanish Civil War, see my book *Spies: A Narrative Encyclopedia of Dirty Deeds and Double Dealing from Biblical Times to Today* (M. Evans, 1997).

Espionage (World War I): **Arms and the Woman**, 1916; **The Battle Cry of Peace**, 1915; Britannic, 2000 (made-for-cable TV); British Agent, 1934; British Intelligence, 1940; Darling Lili, 1970 (Abteilung IIIb); **Dark Journey**, 1937 (Abteilung IIIb); Dawn, 1928 (Edith Cavell; SIS; Abteilung IIIb); **Dishonored**, 1931 (Abteilung IIIb); Espionage, 1937; Fraulein Doktor, 1969 (Abteilung IIIb); Guilty Melody, 1936; **Hearts of the World**, 1918 (Abteilung IIIb); **I Was a Spy**, 1934 (Abteilung IIIb; SIS); Jack Tar, 1915; **Knight without Armor**, 1937 (SIS); **Lancer Spy**, 1937, Abteilung IIIb); **Lawrence of Arabia**, 1962 (SIS); Madame Spy, 1934; Mademoiselle Docteur, [1937] 1948 (Abteilung IIIb); Mademoiselle from Armentieres, 1928 (SIS; Abteilung IIIb); The Man Who Stayed at Home, 1915 (MI5; Abteilung IIIb); Mare Nostrum, 1926; **Mata Hari**, 1931 (Abteilung IIIb; French intelligence);

Mata Hari, Agent H21, 1964 (French i; Abteilung IIIb); Mata Hari, 1985 (French intelligence; Abteilung IIIb); **Nurse Edith Cavell**, 1939 (SIS; Abteilung IIIb); **Rendezvous**, 1935; **Secret Agent**, 1936; The Secret Agent, 1996; **Spies**, 1929; **The Spy in Black**, 1939; Spy 77 (aka: On Secret Service), 1936 (Austrian and Italian Intelligence services); **Stamboul Quest**, 1934 (Abteilung IIIb); **Suzy**, 1936; The Thirty - Steps, 1980; This Mad World, 1930; Under Secret Orders, 1943; The W Plan, 1931 (SIS); Would You Believe It!, 1930 (SIS; Abteilung IIIb); Young Eagles, 1930. Note: For more information on espionage during WWI see my book, *Spies: A Narrative Encyclopedia of Dirty Deeds and Double Dealing from Biblical Times to Today* (M. Evans, 1997).

Espionage (prior to and during World War II): **Above Suspicion**, 1943 (MI6; Abwehr; Gestapo); **Across the Pacific**, 1942 (U.S. Army G-2; Kempeitai); Action in Arabia, 1944 (MI6; O.S.S.); Address Unknown, 1944 (Gestapo); **Adventures of Tartu**, 1943 (Gestapo; MI6); Adventures of the Flying Cadets, 1943 (Gestapo); **Against the Wind**, 1949 (SOE); Aimee & Jaguar, 1999 (German underground; Gestapo); All My Loved Ones, 2000 (Czech underground; Gestapo); **All through the Night**, 1942 (Abwehr); **Amen**, 2002 (Gestapo); **An American Guerrilla in the Philippines**, 1950 (U.S. Naval Intelligence; Filipino Underground; Japanese Intelligence; Kempeitai); The Angels of Death Island, 2003 (O.S.S.); Angry Harvest, 1986 (Gestapo); Anne Frank: The Whole Story, 2001 (TV miniseries; Gestapo); **Arch of Triumph**, 1948 (Gestapo; Abwehr; pre-WWII); Arch of Triumph, 1984 (made-for-TV; Gestapo; Abwehr; pre-WWII); The Army of Shadows, 2006 (French underground; Gestapo); The Aryan Couple, 2004 (Gestapo); The Assassination of Trotsky, 1972 (KGB); **The Assissi Underground**, 1985 (Italian underground; Gestapo); At Dawn We Die (aka: Tomorrow We Live), 1943 (French Underground; Gestapo); Au revoir les enfants: Goodbye Children, 1987 (Gestapo); Back-Room Boy, 1942 (Abwehr); **Back to Bataan**, 1945 (Filipino underground; Japanese intelligence; Kempeitai); **Background to Danger**, 1943 (O.S.S.; Abwehr); Balkan Express 2, 1989 (Gestapo); Battle for the Railway, 1978 (Gestapo); **Beachhead**, 1954 (U.S. military intelligence); Beast of Berlin, 1939 (Gestapo); The Beasts of Marseilles, 1957 (Gestapo); Before the Fall, 2005 (Gestapo); Behind the Rising Sun, 1943 (Japanese intelligence; Kempeitai); **Berlin Correspondent**, 1942 (Abwehr; Gestapo); Betrayal from the East, 1945 (Japanese intelligence; Kempeitai); Betrayed, 1954 (MI6; Dutch underground; Abwehr; Gestapo); Bijo gomon, 1967 (Kempeitai); Black Book, 2007 (Gestapo); Black Dragons, 1942 (Kempeitai); **Blood on the Sun**, 1945 (Japanese intelligence; Kempeitai); Bombay Clipper, 1942 (Japanese intelligence; Kempeitai); Bonhoeffer: Agent of Grace, 2000 (German underground; Gestapo); Breakthrough, 1981 (German underground; Gestapo); Bulldog Sees It Through, 1940 (MI6; Abwehr); **Canaris**, 1955 (Abwehr; MI6; SIS); **Carve Her Name with Pride**, 1958 (SOE; Abwehr); **Casablanca**, 1942 (Gestapo); **China Girl**, 1942 (Japanese spies in China; Kempei Tai); Circle of Deception, 1961 (MI6; SOE; Abwehr; Gestapo); **Cloak and Dagger**, 1946 (O.S.S.; Abwehr; Gestapo); Clouds over Europe (aka: Foreign Sabotage; Q Planes), 1939 (MI5; Abwehr); **Commandos Strike at Dawn**, 1942 (Norwegian underground; Abwehr; Gestapo); **Confessions of a Nazi Spy**, 1939 (Abwehr; FBI; Gestapo; pre-WWII); Contraband (aka: Blackout), 1940 (Abwehr); Cottage to Let (aka: Bombsight Stolen), 1943 (Abwehr); Count Five and Die, 1958 (O.S.S.; MI6; Abwehr); Counter-Espionage, 1942 (MI5; Abwehr); **The Counterfeit Traitor**, 1962; **The Counterfeiters**, 2008 (Operation Bernhard; Gestapo); **Cross of Iron**, 1977 (Gestapo); **The Cross of Lorraine**, 1943 (French Underground; Gestapo); **The Damned**, 1969 (Gestapo); The Day and the Hour, 1964 (French underground; Gestapo); **Decision before Dawn**, 1951 (U.S. Army intelligence; O.S.S.; Abwehr; Gestapo); **The Desert Fox: The Story of Rommel**, 1951 (Abwehr; Gestapo; plot to overthrow Hitler); **Desperate Journey**, 1942 (Abwehr; Gestapo); **Destination Tokyo**, 1943 (U.S. Navy intelligence); **The Diary of Anne Frank**, 1959 (Gestapo); **Divided We Fall**, 2000 (Czech underground; Gestapo); Dr.

Petiot, 1990 (Gestapo); **The Eagle Has Landed**, 1977 (Abwehr); **Edge of Darkness**, 1943 (Norwegian underground; Gestapo); Enemy Agent, 1940 (Abwehr; FBI; German agents after plans for the B-17 bomber and its bomb-sight); Enemy of Women, 1944 (Joseph Goebbels; Abwehr; Gestapo); **Enigma**, 2001 (British code breakers at Bletchley Park); Escape from Hong Kong, 1942 (Kempeitai); **Eye of the Needle**, 1981 (Abwehr); **Eyes in the Night**, 1942 (Abwehr); **The Falcon's Brother**, 1942 (Abwehr); **Father Goose**, 1964 (Allied Intelligence Bureau; ASIO; coastwatchers); Fatherland, 1994 (made-for-TV; Gestapo); Female Agents, 2008 (French Underground; SOE; Gestapo); The Final Solution: The Wannsee Conference, 1987 (made-for-TV; Gestapo); **First Yank into Tokyo**, 1945 (O.S.S.; Japanese i; Kempeitai); **5 Fingers**, 1952 (MI6; Abwehr; Gestapo); Flame and Citron, 2008 (Danish Resistance; Gestapo); **Flight for Freedom**, 1943 (U.S. Army intelligence; Kempeitai; pre-WWII); **Foreign Correspondent**, 1940 (Abwehr; Scotland Yard's Special Branch); **The 49th Parallel** (aka: The Invaders), 1942 (Abwehr; RCMP); The Four Horsemen of the Apocalypse, 1962 (French underground; Gestapo); Free Men, 2012 (French underground; Gestapo); **The General Died at Dawn**, 1936 (Chinese intelligence; pre-WWII); **Generale Della Rovere**, 1961 (Italian underground; Gestapo); Good, 2008 (Gestapo); The Good Shepherd, 2007 (O.S.S.); **The Great Escape**, 1963 (French underground; Gestapo); **The Great Raid**, 2005 (Kempeitai); **Hangmen Also Die**, 1943 (Gestapo); Haven, 2001 (made-for-TV; Gestapo); Head in the Clouds, 2004 (Gestapo; pre-WWII); **The Heroes of Telemark**, 1965 (Norwegian underground; Abwehr); Hidden Enemy, 1940 (Abwehr); The Highest Honor, 1982 (Kempeitai); **The Hindenburg**, 1975 (Gestapo; pre-WWII); **The Hitler Gang**, 1944 (Abwehr; Gestapo); Hitler's Children, 1943 (Gestapo); **Hitler's Madman**, 1943 (Gestapo); Hitler's S.S.: Portrait in Evil, 1985 (made-for-TV; Gestapo); Holocaust, 1978 (TV miniseries; Gestapo); **Hotel Berlin**, 1945 (Gestapo); **Hotel Reserve**, 1946 (French intelligence; MI6; Abwehr, pre-WWII); **The House on 92nd Street**, 1945 (Abwehr; FBI); I Escaped from the Gestapo, 1943 (FBI); **I See a Dark Stranger**, 1947 (Abwehr; MI5); I Was an American Spy, 1951 (Filipino underground; Japanese intelligence; Kempeitai); **In Harm's Way**, 1965 (Allied Intelligence Bureau; ASIO; coastwatchers); **Indiana Jones and the Last Crusade**, 1989 (Gestapo); Jacob the Liar, 1977 (Gestapo); Jacob the Liar, 1999 (Gestapo); Jenny's War, 1985 (made-for-TV; Gestapo); **Joan of Paris**, 1942 (French underground; Gestapo); Joe and Max, 2002 (made-for-TV; Gestapo); **Journey into Fear**, 1943 (Turkish intelligence; Abwehr); Lacombe, Lucien, 1974 (French Underground; Gestapo); **The Lady Vanishes**, 1938 (MI6; Abwehr; pre-WWII); The Lady Vanishes, 1979 (MI6; Abwehr; pre-WWII); Landscape Aafter Battle, 1978 (Gestapo); **The Last Emperor**, 1987 (Kempeitai); **The Last Metro**, 1981 (French Underground; Gestapo); Law and Disorder, 1940 (MI5; Scotland Yard's Special Branch; Abwehr); Let George Do It! (aka: To Hell with Hitler), 1940 (MI6; Abwehr); **Letters from Iwo Jima**, 2006 (Kempeitai); Lightning Conductor, 1938 (MI5; Abwehr); Lili Marleen, 1981 (Gestapo); The Lone Wolf Spy Hunt, 1939; **The Lost One** (aka: Der Verlorene), 1984 (Gestapo); Lucie Aubrac, 1999 (French underground; Gestapo); A Man Escaped, 1957 (Gestapo); The Man from Morocco, 1946 (MI6; Abwehr); **Man Hunt**, 1941 (Abwehr; Gestapo; pre-WWII); **The Man Who Knew Too Much**, 1935 (Scotland Yard's Special Branch; Abwehr; pre-WWII); **The Man Who Never Was**, 1956 (NID; Abwehr); **Manila Calling**, 1942 (Filipino underground; Japanese intelligence; Kempeitai); Max Manus: Man of War, 2009 (Gestapo); **Meet Boston Blackie**, 1941; **Ministry of Fear**, 1944 (Abwehr; Scotland Yard's Special Branch); Mr. Klein, 1977 (Gestapo); Monsieur Batignole, 2003 (French underground; Gestapo); **Morituri**, 1965 (MI6; Gestapo); My Favorite Spy, 1942 (U.S Army intelligence); Naked among Wolves, 1967 (Gestapo); **Nazi Agent**, 1942 (Abwehr; Gestapo); **Never So Few**, 1959 (MI; O.S.S.); Night Boat to Dublin, 1946 (MI5; Abwehr); Night of the Fox, 1990 (made-for-TV; MI6; SOE; Abwehr); **The Night of the Generals**, 1967 (Abwehr, Gestapo); **Night Train to Munich**, 1940

(MI6; Abwehr; Gestapo; pre-WWII); **Northern Pursuit**, 1943 (Canadian intelligence); **Notorious**, 1946 (FBI); **Odette**, 1951 (SOE; Abwehr); Once upon a Honeymoon, 1942 (Gestapo); **Open City** (aka: Rome: Open City), 1946 (Gestapo); **Operation Daybreak**, 1975 (Czech underground; Gestapo); **Operation Crossbow**, 1965 (O.S.S.; MI6; Abwehr); **Operation Secret**, 1952 (O.S.S.; Abwehr; Gestapo); **O.S.S.**, 1946 (Abwehr; Gestapo); Papy fait de la resistance, 1983 (French underground; Gestapo); Paris Calling, 1942 (French underground; Gestapo); Paris underground, 1945 (French underground; Gestapo); **The Pianist**, 2002 (Gestapo); **Pimpernel Smith**, 1942 (MI6; Abwehr; Gestapo); Prisoner of Japan, 1942 (Kempeitai); **The Purple Heart**, 1944 (Kempeitai); The Red Nights of the Gestapo, 1977 (MI6; plot to overthrow Hitler); Remember Pearl Harbor, 1942 (Abwehr; Kempeitai); **Reunion in France**, 1942 (French Underground; Gesapo); Rogue Male, 1977 (made-for-TV; Abwehr; Gestapo); Rotation, 1950 (Gestapo); **Rogue's Regiment**, 1948 (O.S.S.); **Sabotage**, 1937 (Abwehr; pre-WWII); **Saboteur**, 1942 (FBI; Abwehr); The Savior, 1971 (French Unudground; Gestapo); Sebastian, 1968 (MI5; KGB); Second Bureau, 1937 (French intelligence; pre-WWII); **Secret Agent of Japan**, 1942 (Kempeitai); Secret People, 1952; Seven Minutes, 1989 (Gestapo); **The Seventh Cross**, 1944 (German underground; Gestapo; pre-WWII); The Seventh Survivor, 1942 (MI6; Abwehr); **Sherlock Holmes and the Secret Weapon**, 1942 (MI5; MI6; Scotland Yard's Special Branch; Abwehr; Gestapo); **Sherlock Holmes in Washington**, 1943 (Abwehr; FBI); Seven Miles from Alcatraz, 1942; Shining Through, 1992 (O.S.S.; Abwehr); **Sink the Bismarck!**, 1960 (NID); **633 Squadron**, 1964 (Gestapo); Snowbound, 1949 (MI6; Abwehr); **Soldier of Orange**, 1979 (Dutch Underground; Gestapo); Sons of the Sea, 1939 (NID; Abwehr); **Sophie Scholl: The Final Days**, 2006 (German underground; White Rose; Gestapo); Spies of the Air, 1940 (Scotland Yard's Special Branch; Abwehr); Spy for a Day, 1940 (MI6; MI5; Abwehr); Spy Ship, 1942 (Abwehr); Squadron Leader X, 1943 (Abwehr; MI5); **Stalag 17**, 1953 (Abwehr; Gestapo); **Sunshine**, 2000 (Gestapo); **Tea with Mussolini**, 1999 (Gestapo); **They Came to Blow Up America**, 1943 (Abwehr); **They Met in the Dark**, 1945 (NID; Abwehr); **13 Rue Madeleine**, 1947 (O.S.S.; Abwehr; Gestapo); **36 Hours**, 1965 (Abwehr); **This Gun for Hire**, 1942 (fifth columnists working for Japan); This Was Paris, 1942 (MI6; French underground; Abwehr); A Time to Love and a Time to Die, 1958 (Gestapo); **To Be or Not to Be**, 1942 (Polish underground; MI6; Abwehr; Gestapo); **To Have and Have Not**, 1944 (Gestapo); The Torso Murder Mystery (aka: Traitor Spy), 1940 (MI6; Abwehr); Tower of Terror, 1942 (MI6; Abwehr); **The Train**, 1965 (French underground; Gestapo); **Triple Cross**, 1966 (MI5; MI6; Abwehr); **The Two-Headed Spy**, 1959 (MI6; Abwehr; Gestapo); **U-47**, 1958 (Gestapo); **Unbroken**, 2014 (Kempeitai); **Uncertain Glory**, 1944 (French underground; Gestapo); **Underground**, 1941 (Gestapo); Underground, 1997 (Gestapo); Unseen Enemy, 1942 (Abwehr; Kempeitai); **Valkyrie**, 2008 (German underground; Gestapo; plot to overthrow Hitler); **Von Ryan's Express**, 1965 (Gestapo); Walter Defends Sarajevo, 1972 (Gestapo); Waterfront, 1944 (Abwehr); **We've Never Been Licked**, 1943 (Kempeitai); **When Willie Comes Marching Home**, 1950 (French underground; Gestapo); **Where Eagles Dare**, 1968 (MI6; U.S. Army Intelligence; O.S.S.; NID; SOE; Gestapo; Abwehr); The Whip Hand, 1951 (Abwehr); **The White Rose**, 1983 (German underground; Gestapo); Women in Bondage, 1943 (German underground; Gestapo); **The Wooden Horse**, 1951 (Gestapo); **Yellow Canary**, 1944 (Abwehr; NID); Zamach, 1959 (Polish underground; Gestapo); **Zelary**, 2004 (Czech underground; Gestapo). Note: For more information on espionage prior to and during WWII, see my book *Spies: A Narrative Encyclopedia of Dirty Deeds and Double Dealing from Biblical Times to Today* (M. Evans, 1997).

Euthanasia (mercy killing): Ace of Hearts, 2008; **An Act of Murder**, 1948; Alexander, 2004; Amazon, 1990; **Amen**, 2002; America, 2010; **Amour**, 2012; As the Earth Turns, 1934; **The Barbarian Invasions**,

2003; Before Night Falls, 2000; Behind the Red Door, 2003; Betty Blue, 1986; Before the Devil Knows You're Dead, 2007; Bicentennial Man, 1999; Blue Denim, 1959; Bringing Out the Dead, 1999; **Captain from Castile**, 1947; Criticial Care, 1997; Cut Loose, 2009; The Descent, 2005; Dormant Beauty, 2012; Dream with the Fishes, 1997; **The English Patient**, 1996; The Event, 2003; The Exterminator, 1980; The Farewell Party, 2014; The Fifth Cord, 1971; Firelight, 1997; **For Whom the Bell Tolls**, 1943; The Fountain, 2006; **The Giver**, 2014; Glorious 39, 2009; Gods and Monsters, 1998; Good, 2008; **The Greatest Show on Earth**, 1952; Guzaarish, 2010; Hold-Up, 2000; Honey, 2013; The Hotel New Hampshire, 1984; House, 1986; House of D, 2004; I Accuse, 1941; Igby Goes Down, 2002; The Illustrated Man, 1969; Imaginary Heroes, 2004; **It Happened Here**, 1966; I've Loved You So Long, 2008; Johnny Got His Gun, 1971; Kings & Queen, 2004; Last Cab to Darwin, 2015; **Lawrence of Arabia**, 1962; The Legacy, 2010; Magnus, 2007; Menschen, 2013; **Million Dollar Baby**, 2004; **Ministry of Fear**, 1944; **Moon**, 2009; **Old Gringo**, 1989; **Of Mice and Men**, 1939; **Of Mice and Men**, 1992; **One Flew Over the Cuckoo's Nest**, 1975; **One True Thing**, 1998; **Pan's Labyrinth**, 2007; Pinapple Express, 2008; The Reckoning, 2002; Right to Die, 1987 (made-for-TV); R-Point, 2004; The Sacred Flame, 1929; The Safety of Objects, 2001; The Sea Inside, 2004; Sex Drive, 2008; Short Night of Glass Dolls, 1971; Simon, 2004; Solace, 2016; The Sunchaser, 1996; Tapas, 2005; **They Shoot Horse, Don't They?**, 1969: A Thousand Kisses, 2006; **The Three Lives of Thomasina**, 1963; Tour de Force, 2014; 12 and Holding, 2005; The Unbearable Lightness of Being, 1988; Walking and Talking, 1996; **Whose Life Is It Anyway?**, 1981; **The Wild Bunch**, 1969; The Witnesses, 2007; Year of the Dog, 2007; You Don't Know Jack, 2010 (made-for-TV).

Exploration and Explorers: **The Adventures of Marco Polo**, 1938 (China); **Aguirre, The Wrath of God**, 1977 (South America); **Alien**, 1979 (Space); **Animal Crackers**, 1930 (African explorer); **Atlantis: The Lost Empire**, 2001 (legendary undersea city); Beyond the Rocks, 1922 (Swiss Alps); **The Big Sky**, 1952 (American Far West); Black Gold, 1936 (oil); The Blonde Captive, 1931 (Australian outback); **Boom Town**, 1940 (oil); Bridger, 1976 (made-for-TV; American Far West); Bye Bye Columbus, 1991 (made-for-TV; North America); Call Me Bwana, 1963 (Africa); Carl Peters, 1941 (Tanzania and Tanganyika); Carry on Columbus, 1992 (North America); Castaway, 2000 (island); The Call of the Soul, 1919 (North Pole); Christophe Columb, 1916 (North America); Christophe Columb, 1975 (made-for-TV; North America); **Christopher Columbus**, 1949 (North America); Christopher Columbus, 1985 (TV miniseries; North America); Christopher Columbus: The Discovery, 1992 (North America); Columbus, 1923 (North America); Conquest of Space, 1955; Cristobal Colon, 1943 (North America); Cristobal Colon, 1982 (North America); **Crusoe**, 1988 (island); Darkest Africa, 1936; Dawn of America, 1951 (North America); **Destination Moon**, 1950 (Space); Explorers, 1985 (Space); **The Far Horizons**, 1955 (Lewis and Clark expedition to the American Far West in 1804-1806); **Flowing Gold**, 1940 (oil); Fools in the Dark, 1924 (Orient); The Forbidden Quest, 1994 (Antarctica); 1492: Conquest of Paradise, 1992 (North America); Glory & Honor, 1998 (made-for-TV; Peary's 1909 expedition to the North Pole); Green Hell, 1940 (South American jungles); **Greystoke: The Legend of Tarzan; Lord of the Apes**, 1984 (Africa); **God's Little Acre**, 1958 (hidden treasure); Hawk of the Wilderness, 1938 (island); Hell's Headquarters, 1932 (ivory hunting in Africa); Isabel, 2011- (TV series; North America); **Journey to the Center of the Earth**, 1959; **Journey to the Center of the Earth**, 2008; **Journey to the Far Side of the Sun**, 1969 (space); Journey to the Seventh Planet, 1962 (space); Juana la loca...de vez en cuando, 1983 (North America); Jungle Moon Men, 1955 (Africa); **King Kong**, 1933 (island); **King Kong**, 2005 (island); **King Solomon's Mines**, 1937 (African treasure); **King Solomon's Mines**, 1950 (missing person); **Kit Carson**, 1940 (American Far West); **The Land That**

Time Forgot, 1975 (island); **The Lost World**, 1925 (Amazon jungle); The Lost World, 1999-2002 (TV series; island); The Lost World, 2002 (made-for-TV; Amazon Jungle); Lust for Gold, 1949 (search for the Lost Dutchman Mine in Arizona); The Magic Voyage, 1992 (North America); Marco Polo, 1962 (China); **Marooned**, 1969 (space); Meet the Baron, 1933 (Africa); **Mission to Mars**, 2000 (space); The Mountain Men, 1980 (American Far West); **Mountains of the Moon**, 1990 (Nile River); Mutiny in the Arctic, 1941; **Mysterious Island**, 1961; The New World, 2005 (Virginia); **Northwest Passage**, 1940 (American Far West); **On the Avenue**, 1937 (Arctic explorer); Perils of the Jungle, 1927 (Africa); **Planet of the Apes**, 1968 (space); **Planet of the Apes**, 2001 (space); **Pony Express**, 1953 (American Far West); **Prometheus**, 2012 (space); **The Right Stuff**, 1983 (space); **Rio 2**, 2014 (Amazon Jungle); Robinson Crusoe, 1954 (island); Robinson Crusoe, 1970 (island); Robinson Crusoe, 1973 (island); Robinson Crusoe, 1997 (island); **Rocketship X-M**, 1950 (space); Safari, 1940 (West Africa); Sahara, 2009 (West Africa); The Savage Woman, 1918 (Abyssinia); **Scott of the Antarctic**, 1949; Secret of the Incas, 1954 (hidden treasure in Peruvian jungles); **Son of Kong**, 1933 (island); Star Trek, 1966-1969 (TV series; space); **Star Trek**, 2009 (space); **Star Trek: First Contact**, 1996 (space); **Star Trek: Generations**, 1994 (space); **Star Trek: Insurrection**, 1998 (space); **Star Trek: Nemesis**, 2002 (space); **Star Trek: The Motion Picture**, 1979 (space); **Star Trek II: The Wrath of Khan**, 1982 (space); **Star Trek III: The Search for Spock**, 1984 (space); **Star Trek IV: The Voyage Home**, 1986 (space); **Star Trek V: The Final Frontier**, 1989 (space); **Star Trek VI: The Undiscovered Country**, 1991 (space); **Tarzan, the Ape Man**, 1932 (ivory in Africa); **Tarzan**, 1999 (Africa); **There Will Be Blood**, 2000 (oil); Tiger Fangs, 1943 (Malaya); **The Treasure of the Sierra Madre**, 1948 (gold in Mexico); **Swiss Family Robinson**, 1960 (island); **The Time Machine**, 1960 (Time Travel); **The Time Machine**, 2002 (Time Travel); **2001: A Space Odyssey**, 1968; **2010**, 1984 (Space); **Up**, 2009 (South America); The Viking, 1928 (North America); Voyage to the Bottom of the Sea, 1964-1968 (TV series); **We of the Never Never**, 1983 (Australian outback).

Factory Workers: **A Nous La Liberte**, 1931; **Adalen 31**, 1969; **Adventures of Tartu**, 1943 (Czech defense workers for Germany); **An American Tragedy**, 1931; **As Young as You Feel**, 1951; **Brute Force**, 1947 (prison workers); **Carmen Jones**, 1954 (parachute factory in WWII); **The Company Men**, 2011; **Each Dawn I Die**, 1939 (prison workers); 8 Mile, 2002; Gangway for Tomorrow, 1943 (U.S. defense workers in WWII); George Lopez, 2002-2007 (TV series); **Gung Ho!**, 1943 (U.S. defense workers in WWII); In Time, 2011; **Kid Blue**, 1973; **Kiss of Death**, 1947 (prison workers); **Modern Times**, 1936; Monster, 2003; **Norma Rae**, 1979; **An Officer and a Gentleman**, 1982; **Schindler's List**, 1993 (forced Jewish defense workers for Germany); **Sleepy Lagoon**, 1943 (U.S. defense workers in WWII); **A Streetcar Named Desire**, 1951; **Tender Comrade**, 1943 (U.S. defense workers in WWII); **There Was a Crooked Man**, 1970 (prison workers); Total Recall, 2012; The Voices, 2014; **The Whistle at Eaton Falls**, 1951; **White Heat**, 1949 (prison workers).

Famous Female Singers: Adriana, 2004 (Maria Callas, portrayed by Antonio Moco); After the Ball, 1957 (Vesta Tilley; portrayed by Margaret Sawyer as a child; Pat Kirkwood as an adult Tilley); Bessie, 2015 (made-for-cable TV; Bessie Smith, portrayed by Queen Latifah); Bowery to Broadway, 1944 (Lillian Russell, portrayed by Louise Allbritton); Callas e Onassis, 2005 (made-for-TV; Maria Callas, portrayed by Luisa Ranieri); **Callas Forever**, 2002 (Maria Callas, portrayed by Fanny Ardant); **The Cotton Club**, 1984 (Fanny Brice, portrayed by Rosalind Harris); Daphne, 2007 (Gertrude Lawrence, portrayed by Janet McTeer); David Harum, 1934 (Lillian Russell, portrayed by Ruth Gillette); **Diamond Jim**, 1936 (Lillian Russell, portrayed by Binnie Barnes); Downton Abbey, 2010- (TV series; Nellie Melba, portrayed by Kiri Te Kanawa); Edith and Marcel, 1984 (Edith Piaf, portrayed by Evelyne Bouix); Edith es Marlene, 1992 (made-for-TV; Edith Piaf, portrayed by Erzsebet Kutvolgyi); Edith Piaf: Une breve rencontre, 1993 (made-for-TV; Sophie Artur); **Funny Girl**, 1968 (Fanny Brice, portrayed by Barbra Streisand); **Funny Lady**, 1975 (Fanny Brice, portrayed by Barbra Streisand); The Gentleman from Louisiana, 1936 (Lillian Russell, portrayed by Ruth Gillette); Grace of Monaco, 2014 (Maria Callas, portrayed by Paz Vega); **The Great Ziegfeld**, 1936 (Lillian Russell, portrayed by Ruth Gillette; Marilyn Miller, portrayed by Rosina Lawrence); **The Helen Morgan Story**, 1957 (portrayed by Ann Blyth); Ike: The War Years, 1979 (TV series; Gertrude Lawrence, portrayed by Patricia Michael); **I'll Cry Tomorrow**, 1955 (Lillian Roth, portrayed by Susan Hayward); **Interrupted Melody**, 1955 (Marjorie Lawrence, portrayed by Eleanor Parker; singing vocals by Eileen Farrell); ITV Sunday Night Drama, 1959-1980 (TV series; "Remember Jack Buchanan," 1980 episode; Gertrude Lawrence, portrayed by Cheryl Kennedy); Jackie Bouvier Kennedy Onassis, 2000 (made-for-TV; Maria Callas, portrayed by Leslie Cottle); **La Vie en Rose**, 2007 (Edith Piaf, portrayed by Marion Cotillard); **Lady Sings the Blues**, 1972 (Billie Holiday, portrayed by Diana Ross); Lillie, 1978 (TV miniseries; Lillian Russell, portrayed by Christina Greateaux); Lillian Russell, 1940 (portrayed by Alice Faye); Look for the Silver Lining, 1949 (Marilyn Miller, portrayed by June Haver); Lost Empires, 1986 (TV miniseries; Vesta Tilley, portrayed by Julia Parrott); **Love Me or Leave Me**, 1955 (Ruth Etting, portrayed by Doris Day); The Man Who Lived at the Ritz, 1989 (made-for-TV; Edith Piaf, portrayed by Nathalie Cerda); Melba, 1953 (Nellie Melba, portrayed by Patrice Munsel); Melba, 1988 (TV series; Nellie Melba, portrayed by Linda Cropper, singing vocals by Yvonne Kenny); Mitzi…Roaring the 1920s, 1976 (TV special; Bessie Smith, portrayed by Linda Hopkins); **My Wild Irish Rose**, 1947 (Lillian Russell, portrayed by Andrea King); Onassis: The Richest Man in the World, 1988 (made-for-TV; Maria Callas, portrayed by Jane Seymour); Parade of Stars, 1983 (made-for-TV; Fanny Brice, portrayed by Dorothy Loudon; Helen Morgan, portrayed by Dinah Shore); Playhouse 90, 1956-1961 (TV series; "The Helen Morgan Story," 1957 episode; portrayed by Polly Bergen); Sinatra, 1992 (made-for-TV; Jo Stafford, portrayed by Maggie Egan; Billie Holiday, portrayed by Leata Galloway); **So This Is Love**, 1953 (Grace Moore, portrayed by Kathryn Grayson); **Somebody Loves Me**, 1952 (Blossom Seeley, portrayed by Betty Hutton); **Stage Door Canteen**, 1943 (Gertrude Lawrence, portrayed by herself); **Star!**, 1968 (Gertrude Lawrence, portrayed by Julie Andrews); Stars in Their Eyes, 1990- (TV series; Billie Holiday, portrayed by Deborah Christopher; Maria Callas, portrayed by Nicola Kirsch; Edith Piaf, portrayed in two separate episodes by Marie Lloyd and Esther Rantzen); **Till the Clouds Roll By**, 1946 (Marilyn Miller, portrayed by Judy Garland); Touched by an Angel, 1995-2003 (TV series; "God Bless the Child," 2000 episode; Billie Holiday, portrayed by Paula Jai Parker); **What's Love Got to Do with It**, 1993 (Tina Turner, portrayed by herself); **With a Song in My Heart**, 1952 (Jane Froman, portrayed by Susan Hayward); **Yankee Doodle Dandy**, 1942 (Fay Templeton, portrayed by Irene Manning); Ziegfeld: The Man and His Women, 1978 (made-for-TV; Fanny Brice, portrayed by Catherine Jacoby; Marilyn Miller, portrayed by Pamela Peadon).

Fathers and Daughters (emotional relationships cited): **The Barretts of Wimpole Street**, 1934 (domineering father; stressful); **The Barretts of Wimpole Street**, 1957 (domineering father; stressful); **Chinatown**, 1974 (stressful; incest-related); **Father of the Bride**, 1950 (amiable); **Four Daughters**, 1938 (stressful; amiable); **The Heiress**, 1949 (domineering father; stressful); **I Remember Mama**, 1948 (amiable); **The Littlest Rebel**, 1935 (amiable; daughter successfully pleads for her father's life); **Max Dugan Returns**, 1983 (stressful; amiable); **Meet Me in St. Louis**, 1944 (stressful; amiable); **My Fair Lady**, 1964 (amiable); **The Philadelphia Story**, 1940 (amiable); **Pygmalion**, 1938 (amiable);

Them!, 1954 (fellow scientists; amiable); **Too Much, Too Soon**, 1958 (stressful relationship between actor John Barrymore and daughter Diana).

Fathers and Sons (emotional relationships cited): **Adam Had Four Sons**, 1941 (amiable); **All My Sons**, 1948 (stressful); **The Bicycle Thieves**, 1949 (role model/stressful); **The Big Country**, 1958 (stressful); **Broken Lance**, 1954 (domineering father; stressful with three sons; amiable with one son); **Character**, 1997 (stressful); **Dear Brigitte**, 1965 (role model; amiable); **Duel in the Sun**, 1946 (stressful with oldest son; overly protective father with younger son); **Exodus: Gods and Kings**, 2014 (amiable; stressful; amiable); **Fort Apache**, 1948 (role model; amiable); Geronimo, 1939 (domineering father; stressful); Gunman's Walk, 1958 (stressful; overly protective father); **How Green Was My Valley**, 1941 (amiable; stressful); **Hud**, 1963 (stressful with older son; amiable with younger son); **I Never Sang for My Father**, 1970 (stressful); **In Harm's Way**, 1965 (stressful; amiable); **House of Strangers**, 1949 (domineering father; stressful with three sons; amiable with one son); **Ivanhoe**, 1952 (stressful; amiable); **The Kentuckian**, 1955 (role model; amiable); **The Last Days of Pompeii**, 1935 (overly protective father; amiable); **Last Train from Gun Hill**, 1959 (stressful; overly protective father); **The Lives of a Bengal Lancer**, 1935 (domineering father; stressful); **The Long, Hot Summer**, 1958 (domineering father and weak-willed son); **The Man from Laramie**, 1955 (stressful; overly protective father); **Man of the West**, 1958 (domineering, villainous father with slavishly obedient and equally lethal sons); **The Man Who Knew Too Much**, 1956 (role model; amiable); **Mr. Hobbs Takes a Vacation**, 1962 (role model; amiable); **My Darling Clementine**, 1946 (domineering, villainous father with slavishly obedient and equally lethal sons); **My Son, My Son!**, 1940 (amiable; overly protective father); **The Oklahoma Kid**, 1939 (stressful); **Rebel Without a Cause**, 1955 (stressful; weak-willed father); **Red River**, 1948 (role model; stressful; competitive father figure); **Rio Grande**, 1950 (domineering father; stressful; amiable); **Rosewood**, 1997 (white bigoted father with resentful son); **Shenandoah**, 1965 (amiable); **Sometimes a Great Notion**, 1970 (amiable); **Sons and Lovers**, 1960 (stressful; uneducated father, educated son); **Sounder**, 1972 (role model; amiable); **The Sullivans** (aka: The Fighting Sullivans), 1944 (role model; amiable); **Titanic**, 1953 (stressful; amiable); **Vengeance Valley**, 1951, (stressful; overly protective father); **Wagon Master**, 1950 (domineering, villainous father with slavishly obedient and equally lethal sons); **Will Penny**, 1968 (domineering, villainous father with slavishly obedient and equally lethal sons); **Wyatt Earp**, 1994 (amiable); **The Yearling**, 1946 (role model; amiable).

Feminists and Suffragettes: Abbott and Costello Meet Dr. Jekyll and Mr. Hyde, 1953; An American Girl Holiday, 2004 (made-for-TV); **Belles on Their Toes**, 1952; The Bostonians, 1984; **Colonel Blimp** (aka: The Life and Death of Colonel Blimp), 1945; The Deputy, 1959-1961 (TV series; "Lady with a Mission," 1960 episode); Die Suffragette, 1914; Fame Is the Spur, 1949; Iron-Jawed Angels, 2004 (made-for-TV); **Kind Hearts and Coronets**, 1950; Lillian Russell, 1940; Made in Dagenham, 2010; **Mary Poppins**, 1964; **Miss Potter**, 2006; Mrs. Santa Claus, 1996 (made-for-TV); Parade's End, 2012 (TV miniseries); Party Over Here, 2016- (TV series; "Suffragettes," 2016 episode); Possession, 2002; The Rainbow, 1989; The Restless Gun, 1957-1959 (TV series; "The Suffragette," 1958 episode); Savage Messiah, 1972; Sherlock Holmes, 1954-1955 (TV series; "The Case of the Careless Suffragette," 1955 episode); **Sleepy Lagoon**, 1943; **The Strawberry Blonde**, 1941; The Suffragette, 1951 (made-for-TV); Suffragette, 2015; **Sweet Land**, 2005; The Tall Man, 1960-1962 (TV series; "Petticoat Crusade," 1961 episode); **Thunder Rock**, 1944; Upstairs, Downstairs, 1971-1975 (TV series; "A Special Mischief," 1972 episode); **Van Gogh**, 1991; **The Winslow Boy**, 1950; **The Winslow Boy**, 1999.

Feuds (Appalachian feuds in Kentucky, Tennessee and West Virginia): The Apostle of Vengeance, 1916; Feudin' Fools, 1952; Hatfields and McCoys, 2012 (TV miniseries); Hatfields and McCoys: Bad Blood, 2012; **The Brotherhood**, 1968; The Hatfields and the McCoys, 1975 (made-for-TV); **Kentucky**, 1938; Kentucky Kernels, 1934; Kentucky Moonshine, 1938; Mountain Justice, 1930; **Our Hospitality**, 1923; **Roseanna McCoy**, 1949; **Sergeant York**, 1941; The Stronger Love, 1916; To the Last Man, 1933; **Tol'able David**, 1921; The Trail of the Lonesome Pine, 1914; The Trail of the Lonesome Pine, 1916; The Trail of the Lonesome Pine, 1923; **The Trail of the Lonesome Pine**, 1936.

Film Clips (integrating newsreels of real-life persons or dramatic scenes to enhance a dramatic film or films being watched in theaters, churches, prisons or on TV): **Across the Pacific**, 1942 (watching a Japanese film in a theater in Panama); American Playhouse, 1981- (TV series; "Overdrawn at the Memory Bank," 1985 episode; watching **Casablanca**, 1942); **The Bad and the Beautiful**, 1952 (film executives watch film auditions); **Blazing Saddles**, 1974 (Gene Wilder and others watch **Blazing Saddles** in a theater at the end of the film); **Bonnie and Clyde**, 1967 (watching **Gold Diggers of 1933**, 1933, in a theater); **Citizen Kane**, 1941 (posing with world leaders); **Crossfire**,1947 (watching a film while hiding in a theater); Dead Men Don't Wear Plaid, 1982 (interrelating with characters in clips from other film noir productions); **Each Dawn I Die**, 1939 (convicts watching a film in prison); **Halloween**, 1978 (watching **The Thing from Another World**, 1951 on TV); **Hugo**, 2011 (watching the early works of Georges Melies, including scenes from Melies' thirteen-minute short, A Trip to the Moon, 1902); **I Wake Up Screaming**, 1941 (watching a film while hiding in a theater); Last Action Hero, 1993 (magic ticket transports viewers in and out of films such as **The Seventh Seal**, 1958); A Life More Ordinary, 2002 (enriching a dull life by living within film scenes); **The Man in the Gray Flannel Suit**, 1956 (Gregory Peck's children watching **Yellow Sky**, 1948, on TV, a film in which Peck also starred); A Nightmare on Elm Street, 1984 (watching The Evil Dead, 1981, on TV); **O Brother, Where Art Thou**, 2000 (convicts watching Myrt and Marge, 1933, in a theater); **Prometheus**, 2012 (android watches **Lawrence of Arabia**, 1962); Sex and the City 2, 2010 (watching **It Happened One Night**, 1934, on TV); **The Shawshank Redemption**, 1994 (convicts watching **Gilda**, 1946); **Somebody Up There Likes Me**, 1956 (watching a romantic film in a theater); **Sullivan's Travels**, 1941 (chain gang convicts watching a cartoon in a church); Twister, 1996 (watching **The Shining**, 1980, in a drive-in theater); **12 Monkeys**, 1995 (watching Alfred Hitchcock's **Vertigo**, 1958); **What Price Hollywood?**, 1932 (film executives watch film auditions); **White Heat**, 1949 (watching **Task Force**, 1949, in a drive-in theater); **Zelig**, 1983 (posing with international celebrities).

Filmmakers and Filmmaking (movies about making movies and movie personalities): Adaptation, 2002; **After the Fox**, 1966; **All That Jazz**, 1979; Analyze That, 2002; **Anchors Aweigh**, 1945; **Annie Hall**, 1977; **The Anniversary Party**, 2001; Ararat, 2002; **The Aviator**, 2004; **The Bad and the Beautiful**, 1952; **The Bank Dick**, 1940; **The Barefoot Contessa**, 1954; **Barton Fink**, 1991; **Beloved Infidel**, 1959; Beyond the Sea, 2004; **The Big Knife**, 1955; The Black Camel, 1931; **Blazing Saddles**, 1974; **Bluebeard's Seven Wives**, 1926; **Bolt**, 2008; **Bombshell**, 1933; **Boy Meets Girl**, 1938; **Bugsy**, 1991; The Buster Keaton Story, 1957; **Callaway Went Thataway**, 1951; **Camera Buff**, 1983; **The Cameraman**, 1928; **The Carpetbaggers**, 1964; **The Cat's Meow**, 2001; **Caught in the Draft**, 1941; Celebrity, 1998; Chaplin, 1992; **Cinema Paradiso**, 1988; Color Me Kubrick, 2006; **The Cotton Club**, 1984; **The Country Girl**, 1954; **Crimes and Misdemeanors**, 1989; **Dancing in the Dark**, 1949; **Day for Night**, 1973; **The Day of the Locust**, 1975; **De-Lovely**, 2004; **Ed Wood**, 1994; **8½**, 1963; The Extra Girl, 1923; **Follow the Boys**, 1944; **Footlight Parade**, 1933; Frances, 1982; **Free and Easy**, 1930; The French Lieutenant's Woman, 1981; Gable and Lombard, 1976; **Get Shorty**, 1995; **The Godfather**, 1972;

Going Hollywood, 1933; **Good Morning, Babylon**, 1987; **The Great Waldo Pepper**, 1975; Harlow, 1965 (with Carroll Baker); Harlow, 1965 (with Carole Lynley); **Hearts of the West**, 1975; **The Helen Morgan Story**, 1957; **Henry Aldrich Gets Glamour**, 1942; **Hitchcock**, 2012; **Hold Back the Dawn**, 1941; **Holiday Inn**, 1942; Hollywood Boulevard, 1976; **Hollywood Canteen**, 1944; **Hollywood Cavalcade**, 1939; Hollywood Hotel, 1937; Hollywood Shuffle, 1987; Hollywood Story, 1951; **Hollywoodland**, 2006; **Hugo**, 2011; **I Wake Up Screaming**, 1941; **In a Lonely Place**, 1950; **Incendiary Blonde**, 1945; It Happened in Hollywood, 1937; **It's a Great Feeling**, 1949; **Jeanne Eagels**, 1957; **Jolson Sings Again**, 1949; **The Jolson Story**, 1946; **King Kong**, 1933; **L.A. Confidential**, 1997; **La Dolce Vita**, 1961; **Lady Killer**, 1933; **The Last Command**, 1928; The Last Movie, 1971; **The Last Tycoon**, 1976; **Leaving Las Vegas**, 1995; The Legend of Lylah Clare, 1968; **Lost in Translation**, 2003; **The Lost Squadron**, 1932; **Love Me or Leave Me**, 1955; **The Loved One**, 1965; **Mad About Music**, 1938; **The Magic Box**, 1952; **Man of a Thousand Faces**, 1957; Man on the Moon, 1999; **Merton of the Movies**, 1947; **Midnight in Paris**, 2011; **The Miracle of the Bells**, 1948; **Miss Tatlock's Millions**, 1948; Mrs. Parker and the Vicious Circle, 1994; Mommie Dearest, 1981; **Moon Over Parador**, 1988; **Movie Crazy**, 1932; **My Favorite Year**, 1982; **Mulholland Dr.**, 2011; **My Week with Marilyn**, 2011; Nickelodeon, 1976; Nine, 2009; **One of the Hollywood Ten**, 2000; The Oscar, 1966; **Paramount on Parade**, 1930; **The Perils of Pauline**, 1947; **The Player**, 1992; **Postcards from the Edge**, 1990; **The Purple Rose of Cairo**, 1985; **Ragtime**, 1981; Second Fiddle, 1939; **Shadow of the Vampire**, 2000; **Show People**, 1928; **Silent Movie**, 1976; **Singin' in the Rain**, 1952; **Sitting Pretty**, 1933; **Something to Sing About**, 1937; **Souls for Sale**, 1923; Special Effects, 1984; **Stand-In**, 1937; **A Star Is Born**, 1937; **A Star Is Born**, 1954; **Star Spangled Rhythm**, 1942; **Stardust Memories**, 1980; **Starlift**, 1951; **The Stuntman**, 1980; **Sullivan's Travels**, 1941; **Sunset**, 1988; **Sunset Boulevard**, 1950; **Thank Your Lucky Stars**, 1943; **Two Weeks in Another Town**, 1962; Valentino, 1951; Valentino, 1977; **W.C. Fields and Me**, 1976; **Wag the Dog**, 1997; **The Way We Were**, 1973; **What Price Hollywood?**, 1932; **Whatever Happened to Baby Jane?**, 1962; **White Hunter, Black Heart**, 1990; **Who Framed Roger Rabbit**, 1988; Won Ton Ton: The Dog Who Saved Hollywood, 1976; The World's Greatest Lover, 1977.

Films with Live Action and Animation: Absolutely Anything, 2015; The Adventures of Rocky and Bullwinkle, 2000; Alice, 1988; Alice in Wonderland, 1949 (French version); **Anchors Aweigh**, 1945; **Annie Hall**, 1977; Arthur and the Invisibles, 2007; Arthur 3: The War of the Two Worlds, 2010; Arthur 2: The Revenge of the Maltazards, 2009; Babes in Toyland, 1961; **Bedknobs and Broomsticks**, 1971; Belle's Tales of Friendship, 1999; Best Player, 2011 (made-for-TV); Brasil Animado, 2011; Captain EQ, 1986; Casper: A Spirited Beginning, 1997; **Charlotte's Web**, 2006; A Christmas Carol, 2009; Christmas Carol: The Movie, 2001; The Congress, 2014; Conspirators of Pleasure, 1997; Cool World, 1992; Coonskin, 1975; Creepshow, 1982; Creepshow 2, 1987; Dangerous When Wet, 1953; The Daydreamer, 1966; Dibu 3, 2002; **Dinosaur**, 2000; Dot and the Kangaroo, 1977; **Elf**, 2003; **Enchanted**, 2007; Evil Toons, 1992; The Extraordinary Adventures of Adele Blanc-Sec, 2010; A Fairly Odd Christmas, 2012 (made-for-TV); A Fairly Odd Movie: Grow Up, Timmy Turner!, 2011 (made-for-TV); A Fairly Odd Summer, 2014 (made-for-TV); Fantasia 2000, 1999; Fat Albert, 2004; Faust, 1995; (500) Days of Summer, 2009; The Flying Machine, 2011; Fun and Fancy Free, 1947; Garm Wars: The Last Druid, 2014; The Great Rock 'n' Roll Swindle, 1990; Greedy Guts, 2001; Gulliver's Travels, 1981; The Hairy Tooth Fairy, 2007; Happy Feet, 2006; Happy Feet 2, 2011; Hollywood Party, 1934; **Honey, I Blew Up the Kid**, 1992; **Honey, I Shrunk the Kids**, 1989; Hop, 2011; How to Eat Fried Worms, 2006; Howl, 2010; Immortal (Ad Vitam), 2004; **The Incredible Mr. Limpet**, 1964; The Invincible Piglet, 2015; **James and the Giant Peach**, 1996; Journey Back to Oz, 1974; Judy Moody and the Not Bummer Summer, 2011; King of Jazz, 1930; The Lego Movie, 2014; The Lizzie McGuire Movie, 2003; Lunacy, 2006; Main Krishna Hoon, 2013; The Many Adventures of Winnie the Pooh, 1977; Maria, Mirabella, 1981; **Mary Poppins**, 1964; McDull, the Alumni, 2006; **Melody Time**, 1948; Metamorphoses, 1978; Monkeybone, 2001; **Monty Python and the Holy Grail**, 1975; Monty Python's Life of Brian, 1979; Moonwalker, 1988; Movie 43, 2013; Mrs. Doubtfire, 1993; **My Dream Is Yours**, 1949; My Friend Ganesha, 2007; My Friend Ganesha 3, 2010; My Friend Ganesha 2, 2009; Natural Born Killers, 1994; Neon Genesis Evangelion: The End of Evangelion, 2002; The New Gulliver, 1935; **9 to 5**, 1980; O'Faby, 1993; Osmosis Jones, 2001; Out of an Old Man's Head, 1969; The Outrageous Baron Munchausen, 1964; The Pagemaster, 1994; **Pete's Dragon**, 1977; **The Phantom Tollbooth**, 1970; Pink Floyd; The Wall, 1982; **The Pink Panther**, 1964; The Pink Panther, 2006; The Pink Panther 2, 2009; **The Pink Panther Strikes Again**, 1976; Pooh's Heffalump Halloween Movie, 2005; Problem Child 2, 1991; Ra One, 2011; **Raggedy Ann and Andy**, 1977; Re-Animated, 2006 (made-for-TV); **The Reluctant Dragon**, 1941; **The Return of the Pink Panther**, 1975; **Revenge of the Pink Panther**, 1978; Robosapien: Rebooted, 2013; Rock-A-Doodle, 1992; Run Lola Run, 1999; The Secret of the Magic Gourd, 2007; **A Shot in the Dark**, 1964; The Smurfs, 2011; The Smurfs 2, 2013; Son of the Pink Panther, 1993; **Song of the South**, 1946; **Space Jam**, 1996; The SpongeBob Movie: Sponge Out of Water, 2015; **The SpongeBob SquarePants Movie**, 2004; Stay Tuned, 1992; The Stolen Airship, 1967; Super, 2011; Surviving Life, 2010; Tank Girl, 1995; Taxandria, 1994; Thomas and the Magic Railroad, 2000; **The Three Caballeros**, 1944; Trail of the Pink Panther, 1982; The Trigger Movie, 2000; Tron, 1982; Troop Beverly Hills, 1989; Twice upon a Time, 1983; A Very Harold & Kumar 3D Christmas, 2011; Volere Volare, 1993; Walking with Dinosaurs 3D, 2013; **Wall-E**, 2008; The Water Babies, 1978; **Who Framed Roger Rabbit**, 1988; **Winnie the Pooh**, 2011; Winnie the Pooh: A Valentine for You, 1999; Winnie the Pooh: A Very Merry Pooh Year, 2002; Xanadu, 1980; Yogi Bear, 2010.

Firefighters and Firefighting: Ablaze, 2002; The Accidental Husband, 2008; Alarm Code 112, 1996 (TV series); Always, 1989; Arson Gang Busters, 1938; Arson Squad, 1945; The Arson Squad, 1961 (made-for-TV); Backdraft, 1991; Backfire!, 1995; Bad Day on the Block, 1997; **Battle of Britain**, 1969; The Bells Go Down, 1943; Blackmail, 1939; **Boom Town**, 1940; **The Bowery**, 1933; Burning Flame, 2009 (TV series); Blue Smoke, 2007; Chicago Fire, 2012- (TV series); City on Fire, 1979; City on Fire, 1987; Code Red, 1981-1982 (TV series); Collateral Damage, 2002; Emergency!, 1972-1979 (TV series); Damrell's Fire, 2006 (made-for-TV); A Dangerous Summer, 1982; **The Egg and I**, 1947; The False Alarm, 1926; **Fahrenheit, 451**, 1966; 15 Minutes, 2001; Fire!, 1977 (made-for-TV); Fire, 1995-1996 (TV series); The Fire Brigade, 1926; Fire on Kelly Mountain, 1973 (made-for-TV); Fire Serpent, 2007 (made-for-TV); Fire: Trapped on the 37th Floor, 1991 (made-for-TV); The Fire Raisers, 1934; Firefight, 2003; Firefighter, 1986 (made-for-TV); The Firefighters, 1975; Firehouse, 1987; Firehouse, 1997 (made-for-TV); Firehouse Dog, 2007; **Fireman: Save My Child**, 1932; **Fireman: Save My Child**, 1954; **The Fireman's Ball**, 1968; Fireproof, 2008; Fires Were Started, 1943; Firestorm, 1998; Firestorm: The Last Stand at Yellowstone, 2006 (made-for-TV); Flames, 1932; **Flat Top**, 1952; The Forest Rangers, 1942; 49 Days, 2006; The Fourth Alarm, 1930; Frequency, 2000; The Guys, 2002; Heart of Fire, 1997 (made-for-TV); Heaven's Fire, 1999 (made-for-TV); Hellfighters, 1968; Heroes of the Flames, 1931; Holy Joe, 1999 (made-for-TV); Hook and Ladder, 1924; Hook and Ladder No. 9, 1927; I Do (but I Don't), 2004 (made-for-TV); **I Married a Witch**, 1942; **In Old Chicago**, 1938; Inferno, 1998; Inferno, 2001 (made-for-TV); The January Man, 1989; Kindergarten Cop, 1990; **Ladder 49**, 2004; The Last Alarm, 1940; Lifeline, 1997; The Little Rascals, 1994; London's Burning: The Movie, 1986 (made-for-TV); London's Burning, 1988-2002 (TV series); **The**

North Star, 1943; On Fire, 1987 (made-for-TV); On Fire, 1996; One True Love, 2000 (made-for-TV); **Our Vines Have Tender Grapes**, 1945; Pine Canyon Is Burning, 1977 (made-for-TV); Planes: Fire & Rescue, 2014; Point of Origin, 2002 (made-for-TV); Quarantine, 2008; The Quinns, 1977 (made-for-TV); **Red Skies of Montana**, 1952; Rescue Me, 20004-2011 (TV series); Rescue Heroes, 2000- (TV series); Romance of the Redwoods, 1939; Roxanne, 1987; **San Francisco**, 1936; Scorched, 2008 (made-for-TV); Smoke Jumpers, 1996 (made-for-TV); Superfire, 2002 (made-for-TV); **Task Force**, 1949; **The Testament of Dr. Mabuse**, 1952; Third Watch, 1999-2005 (TV series); **This Above All**, 1942; **Tora! Tora! Tora!**, 1970; **The Towering Inferno**, 1974; Trespass, 1992; Trial by Fire, 2008 (made-for-TV); The Triangle Factory Fire Scandal, 1979 (made-for-TV); **Tulsa**, 1949; Turk 182!, 1985; Uncommon Valor, 1983 (made-for-TV); Volcano, 1997; Where's That Fire?, 1940; Wildcat, 1942.

Flappers (modern girls of the 1920s): The Adventurous Sex, 1925; The American Venus, 1926; **The Artist**, 2012; Beautiful But Dumb, 1928; Bernice Bobs Her Hair, 1976 (made-for-TV); The Big Fight, 1930; The Big Party, 1930; Black Oxen, 1924; Bobbed Hair, 1925; Border Romance, 1929; **Bright Young Things**, 2003; Broadway Billy, 1926; Broadway Daddies, 1928; **The Broadway Melody**, 1929; **Bugsy Malone**, 1976; **Bullets Over Broadway**, 1984; Call Her Savage, 1932; **The Canary Murder Case**, 1929; Capone, 1975; The Cat's Meow, 2002; **Chicago**, 2002; Children of Divorce, 1927; The City Gone Wild, 1927; Classified, 1925; Coquette, 1929; **The Cotton Club**, 1984; Dancing Days, 1926; Dancing Mothers, 1926; The Daring Years, 1923; **Diary of a Lost Girl**, 1929; Empty Hearts, 1924; Enchantment, 1921; Enemies of Women, 1923; Flaming Youth, 1923; French Dressing, 1927; Get Your Man, 1927; **Girl Shy**, 1924; **Good News**, 1947; Her Splendid Folly, 1933; Her Wild Oat, 1927; Hula, 1927; **The Immigrant**, 2014; In Borrowed Plumes, 1926; It, 1927; Just Another Blonde, 1926; Kid Boots, 1926; Joanna, 1925; Ladies at Play, 1926; Ladies of Leisure, 1930; The Last Man on Earth, 1924; **Leatherheads**, 2008; **Long Pants**, 1927; Love 'Em and Leave 'Em, 1926; **Love Me or Leave Me**, 1955; The Mad Whirl, 1925; Man Bait, 1927; The Masked Angel, 1928; Maxie, 1985; **Midnight in Paris**, 2011; Mobsters, 1991; Mother Knows Best, 1928; Mrs. Parker and the Vicious Circle, 1994; The Nest, 1927; **Night Nurse**, 1931; Not on the Lips, 2004; Our Dancing Daughters, 1928; The Painted Flapper, 1924; **Pandora's Box**, 1929; Paradise for Two, 1927; The Patsy, 1928; The Perfect Flapper, 1924; **Pete Kelly's Blues**, 1955; The Phantom of the House, 1929; The Plastic Age, 1925; Powder My Back, 1928; The Price of a Party, 1924; Prodigal Daughters, 1923; The Rich Are Always with Us, 1932; Red Hair, 1928; **The Ring**, 1927; The Road to Ruin, 1928; **The Roaring Twenties**, 1939; Rolled Stockings, 1927; **Roxie Hart**, 1942; Sally's Shoulders, 1928; The Saturday Night Kid, 1929; **Singin' in the Rain**, 1952; Sinners in Silk, 1924; **A Social Celebrity**, 1926; Soiled, 1925; **Some Like It Hot**, 1959; **Splendor in the Grass**, 1961; The Street of Forgotten Men, 1925; Subway Sadie, 1926; Tanned Legs, 1929; **Thoroughly Modern Millie**, 1967; Une jeune fille a la fenetre, 2001; We Moderns, 1925; What Fools Men, 1925; **Why Be Good?**, 1929; **The Wild Party**, 1929; Womanhandled, 1925.

Florida Everglades: Adaptation, 2002; All about the Benjamins, 2002; Band of the Hand, 1986; Blackwater, 2007; **Distant Drums**, 1951; Drums of Destiny, 1937; Empire of the Ants, 1977; Four Sheets to the Wind, 2007; Gentle Ben, 1967-1969 (TV series); Gloria's Romance, 1916; Invasion U.S.A., 1985; Just Cause, 1995; Naked in the Sun, 1957; The Nest of the Cuckoo Birds, 1965; Pick-Up, 1975; Project X, 1987; R.I.T., 2009; Ramshackle House, 1924; Red, 2010; **Seminole**, 1953; Seminole Uprising, 1955; Shark River, 1953; Stanley, 1972; Sting of Death, 1966; The Substitute, 1996; Sun Don't Shine, 2012; Thunder and Lightning, 1977; War Arrow, 1953; **Wind Across the Everglades**, 1958; Yellowneck, 1955.

Flying Carpets: **Aladdin**, 1992; The Big Lebowski, 1998; Destiny, 1924; The Flying Carpet, 1960; Once Upon a Time in Wonderland, 2013- (TV series): **The Thief of Bagdad**, 1924; **The Thief of Bagdad**, 1940; The Wizard of Bagdad, 1960.

Flying Cars: **The Absent-Minded Professor**, 1961; Aladdin, 1986; Astro Boy, 2009; **Back to the Future**, 1985; **Back to the Future III**, 1990; **Back to the Future II**, 1988; **Blade Runner**, 1982; **Cars 2**, 2011; **Chitty Chitty Bang Bang**, 1968; The Covenant, 2006; Dragonball: Evolution, 2009; The Fifth Element, 1997; Flubber, 1997; Galaxy Quest, 1999; **Grease**, 1978; **Harry Potter and the Chamber of Secrets**, 2002; Heavy Metal, 1981; **Herbie Fully Loaded**, 2005; Herbie Goes Bananas, 1980; Herbie Goes to Monte Carlo, 1977; **Herbie Rides Again**, 1974; **I Married a Witch**, 1940; Invasion of the Neptune Men, 1961; Judge Dredd, 1995; The Last Starfighter, 1984; Looney Tunes: Back in Action, 2003; **The Love Bug**, 1968; The Man with the Golden Gun, 1974; **Men in Black II**, 2002; Munchie, 1982; **Pippi on the Run**, 1977; Repo Man, 1984; The Sandman and the Lost Sand of Dreams, 2010; **Son of Flubber**, 1963; **Star Trek: Into Darkness**, 2013; Team America: World Police, 2004; Terminal Velocity, 1994; Thunderbirds, 2004; Total Recall, 2012.

Flying Horses: The Adventures of Prince Ahmed, 1926; **Clash of the Titans**, 1981 (Pegasus); **Clash of the Titans**, 2010 (Pegasus); **Harry Potter and the Goblet of Fire**, 2005; Little Prince and the Eight-Headed Dragon, 1964; The Magic Pony, 1977; Star Fairies, 1985 (made-for-TV); **The Thief of Bagdad**, 1924; **The Thief of Bagdad**, 1940; **Winter's Tale**, 2014.

Football (American football): **About a Boy**, 2002; **Air Bud: Golden Receiver**, 1998 (high school); **All the King's Men**, 1949 (college); All the Right Moves, 1983 (high school); Any Given Sunday, 1999 (professional); Arli$$, 1996-2002 (TV series; professional); Ashby, 2015 (high school); Badlands, 1973; **Beautiful People**, 1999; Bella and the Bulldogs, 2015- (TV series; high school); **Bend It Like Beckham**, 2002; **Big Fish**, 2003; The Big Short, 2015; **Black Sunday**, 1977 (professional; terrorist threat during Super Bowl X); The Blob, 1988; Blue Mountain State, 2010-2011 (TV series; college); **Boyhood**, 2014 (college); Boyz n the Hood, 1991; Brian's Song, 1971 (made-for-TV; professional; Brian Piccolo; Gale Sayers; Chicago Bears); **Brother Rat**, 1938 (college); **Brown of Harvard**, 1926 (college); **Cat on a Hot Tin Roof**, 1958; Chronicle, 2012; Coach, 1989-1997 (TV series; college); College Coach, 1933; The Comebacks, 2007 (college); Concussion, 2015 (professional); **Corsair**, 1931; Crush, 2013 (high school); **Daddy Day Care**, 2003; **The Dark Knight Rises**, 2012; **Dawn of the Dead**, 1979; Dazed and Confused, 1993 (high school); **The Deer Hunter**, 1978; **Draft Day**, 2014 (professional; Cleveland Browns); The Emperor's Club, 2002 (high school); Facing the Giants, 2006 (high school); The 5th Quarter, 2010 (college); Fired Up!, 2009 (high school); The Firm, 2009; **Flight**, 2012; **The Freshman**, 1925 (college); **Friday Night Lights**, 2004 (high school); Friday Night Lights, 2006-2011 (TV series; high school); **Forrest Gump**, 1994; **The Fortune Cookie**, 1966 (professional); The Game, 2006-2015 (professional); The Girl from Manhattan, 1948 (professional); **Good News**, 1947 (college); Gridiron Gang, 2006 (juvenile detention center team); Hancock, 2008; **Heaven Can Wait**, 1978 (professional; Los Angeles Rams); The Ice Storm, 1997; **Invincible**, 2006 (professional; Philadelphia Eagles); **The Iron Major**, 1943 (Frank Cavanaugh; college; Fordham); **Jerry Maguire**, 1996; **Jim Thorpe—All American**, 1951 (college; Carlisle; professional; Chicago Bulldogs); Johnny Be Good, 1988 (college); **Knute Rockne—All American**, 1940 (college; Notre Dame); The Last Boy Scout, 1991 (professional); The League, 2009-2015 (TV series); **Leatherheads**, 2008 (professional); Lock Up, 1989 (prison football); **The Long Gray Line**, 1955 (college; West Point); **The Longest Yard**, 1974 (prison football); The Longest Yard, 2005 (prison football); **Lucas**, 1986 (high

school); **The Male Animal**, 1942 (college); **Muriel's Wedding**, 1995; **Mustang**, 2015; **My All-American**, 2015 (college; University of Texas); Necessary Roughness, 1991 (college; Texas State); **North Dallas Forty**, 1979 (professional; role model for Dallas Cowboys); Notes on a Scandal, 2006; One-Hour Photo, 2002; **The Perks of Being a Wallflower**, 2012 (high school); **Picnic**, 1955; Pigskin Parade, 1936 (college); The Pink Panther, 2006; Point Break, 1991; Primer, 2004; **Remember the Titans**, 2000 (high school); Ride Along, 2014; **Robin Hood**, 1973; **Rudy**, 1993 (college; Notre Dame); **Saturday's Hero**, 1951 (college); **The Secret in Their Eyes**, 2009; Semi-Tough, 1977 (professional); **Son of Flubber**, 1963 (high school); **Speed**, 1994; Start Cheering, 1938 (college); **Ted**, 2012; **Three Kings**, 1999; Transformers: Age of Extinction, 2014; Two for the Money, 2005 (college); The Waterboy, 1998 (college); We Are Marshall, 2006; Wildcats, 1986 (high school).

Fortune-Hunters: Affair in Reno, 1957; **Anastasia**, 1956; Anything for a Thrill, 1937; **Atlantis: The Lost Empire**, 2001; Beauty for the Asking, 1939; The Big Cube, 1969; The Body Disappears, 1941; **Bonnie Scotland**, 1935; Bridal Suite, 1939; -But the Flesh Is Weak, 1932; The Butterfly Man, 1920; Calm Yourself, 1935; The Car of Chance, 1917; **The Case of the Black Cat**, 1936; **Cast a Dark Shadow**, 1958; Castles for Two, 1917; **Charley's Aunt**, 1941; **The Clairvoyant**, 1935; Clarence, 1937; The Clean Gun, 1917; Come Through, 1917; The Comic, 1969; **Convention City**, 1933; **Counselor at Law**, 1933; Cupid the Cowpuncher, 1920; Desperate Remedies, 1994; The Devil to Pay!, 1930; **Dial M for Murder**, 1954; Diamonds and Pearls, 1917; Diplomacy, 1916; Doughnuts and Society, 1936; The Europeans, 1979; **Fallen Angel**, 1945; Fiesta, 1941; Fifteen Wives, 1934; Fight for Your Lady, 1937; Footlights and Shadows, 1920; 45 Minutes from Broadway, 1920; Four Girls in White, 1939; Free and Easy, 1941; The French Line, 1954; The Gay Lord Quex, 1919; **Gentleman Prefer Blondes**, 1953; **Gentlemen Marry Brunettes**, 1955; Gold Diggers in Paris, 1938; Gold Diggers of Broadway, 1929; **Gold Diggers of 1933**, 1933; **Gold Diggers of 1935**, 1935; **Gold Diggers of 1937**, 1936; The Golden Arrow, 1936; **Hands Across the Table**, 1935; Hard to Handle, 1933; **The Hardys Ride High**, 1939; **The Heiress**, 1949; Help Wanted—Male, 1920; Her First Elopement, 1920; **Here Comes Cookie**, 1935; Here Comes Happiness, 1941; High Play, 1917; Higher and Higher, 1943; His Temporary Wife, 1920; The Honorable Algy, 1916; **The House on Telegraph Hill**, 1951; **How the West Was Won**, 1962; **How to Marry a Millionaire**, 1953; Human Driftwood, 1916; **I'll Cry Tomorrow**, 1955; **In Name Only**, 1939; In Search of Arcady, 1919; It Happened in Honolulu, 1916; It's All Yours, 1937; Johnny-on-the-Spot, 1919; Ladies' Man, 1947; The Lady Refuses, 1931; Latin Lovers, 1953; **Libeled Lady**, 1936; The Life of the Party, 1937; Life's Twist, 1920; The Little Intruder, 1919; Live Sparks, 1920; **Love from a Stranger**, 1937; Madame Bo-Peep, 1917; Maisie Was a Lady, 1941; The Man in Possession, 1931; The Man Who Took a Chance, 1917; The Marriage of Kitty, 1915; Marry the Girl, 1937; The Master Hand, 1915; Mayblossom, 1917; Men, 1918; The Men She Married, 1916; Mile a Minute Love, 1937; Million Dollar Racket, 1937; Millionaire Playboy, 1940; Millipilleri, 1966; Miss Deception, 1917; **Mr. Arkadin**, 1962; Molly Go Get 'Em, 1918; **Monsieur Verdoux**, 1947; **Moon Over Miami**, 1941; The Morals of Marcus, 1915; The Moth, 1917; **The Mummy**, 1999; Music in My Heart, 1940; The Mysterious Pilot, 1937; New Adventures of Get Rich Quick Wallingford, 1931; A New Leaf, 1971; Next Time I Marry, 1938; No Other Woman, 1928; Nobody Home, 1919; **Nobody Lives Forever**, 1946; One Frightened Night, 1935; Outcast, 1917; Paradise for Three, 1938; Period of Adjustment, 1962; Please Believe Me, 1950; The Plow Girl, 1916; Prison's Playground, 1920; Red Lights Ahead, 1936; The Reward of Patience, 1916; **Road to Rio**, 1947; **Robin Hood of El Dorado**, 1936; The Romance Promoters, 1920; Rouge and Riches, 1920; Ruby Gentry, 1952; Senorita from the West, 1945; Set Free, 1927; The Shuttle, 1918; The Silent Partner, 1917; The Singing Vagabond, 1935;

A Song of Sixpence, 1917; South Pacific Trail, 1952; **The Strange Woman**, 1947; **Sudden Fear**, 1952; Supernatural, 1933; **Suspicion**, 1941; **The Taming of the Shrew**, 1967; There Goes the Groom, 1937; These Glamour Girls, 1939; The Thousand Dollar Husband, 1916; A Thousand to One, 1920; Three of a Kind, 1936; Through the Wrong Door, 1919; **Tom, Dick and Harry**, 1941; **Topper Takes a Trip**, 1939; Turning the Tables, 1919; Unashamed, 1932; Under the Greenwood Tree, 1918; Unto Those Who Sin, 1916; The Veiled Marriage, 1920; The Vortex, 1918; **Walking on Air**, 1936; The Week-End, 1920; **We're Not Dressing**, 1934; **The Wings of the Dove**, 1997; **Witness for the Prosecution**, 1957; Woman Chases Man, 1937; Wooden Shoes, 1917; **The Young in Heart**, 1938.

Fortune-Tellers (also see Clairvoyants; Séances, this index): Along the Navajo Trail, 1945; Are You With It?, 1948; Batman, 1943; A Bay of Blood, 1971; Bear's Kiss, 2002; **Before Sunrise**, 1995; **The Bicycle Thief**, 1946; Black Magic, 1944; **Black Magic**, 1949; The Black Widow, 1947; **Broadway Danny Rose**, 1984; Broadway Rhythm, 1944; Brotherhood of the Wolf, 2001; Bunco Squad, 1950; Bunker Bean, 1936; Burnt Money, 2001; California Frontier, 1938; Carny, 2009 (made-for-TV); The Case of the Black Parrot, 1941; Celebrity, 1998; Chinese Odyssey 2002, 2003; **The Circus**, 1928; The Countess of Baton Rouge, 1997; Crime Doctor's Man Hunt, 1946; Crime Ring, 1938; The Crystal Ball, 1943; Cuban Fireball, 1951; **The Cuckoos**, 1930; Danger! Women at Work, 1943; Dangerous Davies: The Last Detective, 1981 (made-for-TV); **Dante's Inferno**, 1935; Dead Man's Folly, 1986 (made-for-TV); The Devil's Messenger, 1961; Dirty Gertie from Harlem, U.S.A., 1946; **Doctor Mabuse**, 2013; **The Doorway to Hell**, 1930; Du Barry Was a Lady, 1943; Edmond, 2005; Eye's Bayou, 1997; Feast of Love, 2007; **Fellini Satyricon**, 1969; Feudin' Rhythm, 1949; Fight for Your Lady, 1937; First Snow, 2006; Five Angles on Murder, 1952; **Flesh and Fantasy**, 1943; For Your Consideration, 2006; **For Whom the Bell Tolls**, 1943; Forever, Lulu, 1987; The Fortune Teller, 1920; The Fortune Teller, 1946; Frankie and Johnny, 1966; Freshman Love, 1936; Games, 2007; The Gift, 2000; Golden Earrings, 1947; The Great Jasper, 1933; Greenwich Village, 1944; Hard Boiled Mahoney, 1947; Head in the Clouds, 2004; Heaven on Earth, 1931; Hell's Highway, 1932; Holes, 2003; Honeymoon in Bali, 1939; The Hottest State, 2006; **I'm No Angel**, 1933; Inside Daisy Clover, 1965; It Can't Last Forever, 1937; I've Been Waiting for You, 1998 (made-for-TV); I've Got Your Number, 1934; Journey to the Sun, 2001; **A Kid for Two Farthings**, 1956; **La Vie en Rose**, 2007; **Labyrinth**, 1986; **The Landlord**, 1970; The Last Days of Man on Earth, 1974; Le grand jeu, 1934; The Legend of Suram Fortress, 1987; **The Leopard Man**, 1943; Let Joy Reign Supreme, 1977; Live and Let Die, 1973; Long Life, Happiness & Prosperity, 2003; Lord of Illusions, 1995; Love, Honor and Goodbye, 1945; **Love Is A Many Splendored Thing**, 1955; Lucky Me, 1954; The Man from Monterey, 1933; Man from Music Mountain, 1938; **The Man in Grey**, 1946; **The Medium**, 1951; Melody Trail, 1935; **Men in Black III**, 2012; **Mildred Pierce**, 1945; **Min and Bill**, 1930; The Mind Reader, 1933; **Ministry of Fear**, 1944; **Miracle in Milan**, 1951; A Modern Hero, 1934; Murder-Rock: Dancing Death, 1984; **The Murderers Among Us**, 1946; My Lucky Star, 1938; My Mom's a Werewolf, 1989; The Mysterious Mrs. Musslewhite, 1917; **Network**, 1976; Night of Terror, 1933; **Nightmare Alley**, 1947; Noi the Albino, 2003; Old Mother Riley's Circus, 1941; Once Upon a Time, 1973; One Night in Rome, 1924; **Onegin**, 1999; **Only You**, 1994; **Ossessione**, [1942] 1959; **The Painted Veil**, 1934; **Palmy Days**, 1931; **Panic**, 1947; Papa, Mama, My Wife and Me, 1955; **Pee-wee's Big Adventure**, 1985; **Pepe Le Moko**, 1937; The Perils of Pauline, 1914; **The Perils of Pauline**, 1947; Playmates, 1941; The Puppetmaster, 1993; The Rainbow Thief, 1990; **The River**, 1951; The River, 1997; The Rogue's Tavern, 1936; Rough Riders' Round Up, 1939; Roustabout, 1964; The Royal Mounted Rides Again, 1945; The Saddest Music in the World, 2004; **Santa Fe Trail**, 1940; Saving Face, 2004; **7 Faces of Dr. Lao**, 1964; A Shadow You Soon Will Be, 1994;

Sherlock Holmes: A Game of Shadows, 2011; **Shoeshine**, 1947; Sing as We Go, 1934; Sinister Hands, 1932; Sinners in Paradise, 1938; Six-Gun Trail, 1938; Slacker, 1991; **Son of Dracula**, 1943; South of Caliente, 1951; South of the Border, 1939; Starstruck, 1982; **State Fair**, 1945; Sudden Manhattan, 1996; **Suez**, 1938; Swashbuckler, 1971; **Tales from the Crypt**, 1972; Theatre of Death, 1967; The 13th Warrior, 1999; The 39 Steps, 1959; Tokyo Decadence, 1993; Torture Garden, 1968; **Touch of Evil**, 1958; Villa des Roses, 2002; **The Wagons Roll at Night**, 1941; **A Walk on the Moon**, 1999; When's Your Birthday?, 1937; **The Wizard of Oz**, 1939; **The Wolf Man**, 1941; Wolves of the Range, 1943; Yankee, 1966; You Can't Escape Forever, 1942.

French Guiana (penal colony and Devil's Island): **The Devil Doll**, 1936; Devil's Island, 1926; **Devil's Island**, 1939; Escape from Devil's Island, 1935; Hell on Devil's Island, 1957; I Escaped from Devil's Island, 1973; L'affaire Seznec, 1993 (made-for-TV); **The Life of Emile Zola**, 1937 (which depicts Alfred Dreyfus' incarceration at Devil's Island); **Pappillon**, 1973; **Passage to Marseille**, 1944; **Strange Cargo**, 1940; Terror of the Bloodhunters, 1962; **We're No Angels**, 1955; Women of Devil's Island, 1962.

French Resistance (during the German occupation of France in WWII, 1940-1944): **The Accompanist**, 1993; **Against the Wind**, 1949; The Annuity, 1972; The Army of Shadows, 2006; At Dawn We Die, 1943; Atlantic Wall, 1970; Au revoir les enfants, 1987; The Battle of the Rails, 1949; Belle and Sebastian, 2014; Black Thursday, 1974; A Captain's Honor, 1982; **Carve Her Name with Pride**, 1958; Charlotte Gray, 2001; Churchill's Leopards, 1970; A Circle of Deception, 1961; **Cornered**, 1945; **The Cross of Loraine**, 1943; The Day and the Hour, 1964; Dawn Devils, 1946; **Diplomacy**, 2014; Fall from Grace, 1994 (made-for-TV); Female Agents, 2008; The Four Horsemen of the Apocalypse, 1962; Fortunate, 1960; Gates of the Night, 1950; Head in the Clouds, 2004; The Inglorious Bastards, 1981; **Is Paris Burning?**, 1966; Jean Moulin, 2003 (made-for-TV); **Joan of Paris**, 1942; Lacombe, Lucien, 1974; L'affiche rouge, 1977; **The Last Metro**, 1981; The Last Train, 1973; Le neige et le feu, 1991; Line of Demarcation, 1966; **The Longest Day**, 1962; Make Mine a Double, 1961; A Man Escaped, 1957; Manon, 1950; Miss V from Moscow, 1942; Mr. Klein, 1977; Mr. Orchid, 1948; **O.S.S.**, 1946; **Odette**, 1951; The Old Gun, 1976; **Operation Secret**, 1952; Papy fait de la resistance, 1983; Paris After Dark, 1943; Paris Underground, 1945; Pétain, 1994; Resistance, 2003; **Reunion in France**, 1942; **Safe Conduct**, 2002; A Self-Made Hero, 1997; Shock Troops, 1968; Silence of the Sea, 2004 (made-for-TV); Strange Game, 1968; Strange Gardens, 2007; The Tenth Man, 1988 (made-for-TV); **13 Rue Madeleine**, 1947; Tomorrow Is My Turn, 1962; **Topaz**, 1969; **Touchez pas au Grisbi**, 1960; **The Train**, 1965; **Triple Cross**, 1967; **Uncertain Glory**, 1944; **When Willie Comes Marching Home**, 1950. Note: For more information on the French Resistance during WWII, see my book *Spies: A Narrative Encyclopedia of Dirty Deeds and Double Dealing from Biblical Times to Today* (M. Evans, 1997).

Genies: Abrakadabra, 1994; Aladdin, 1987; **Aladdin**, 1992; Aladdin, 1994-1995 (TV series); Aladdin and His Lamp, 1952; Aladdin and His Magic Lamp, 1968; Aladdin and the Wonderful Lamp, 1917; Aladdin on Ice, 1995 (made-for-TV); Aladin, 2009; Alf's Button, 1920; Arabian Adventure, 1979; Arabian Nights, 2000 (made-for-TV); Bedazzled, 2000; The Bottle Imp, 1917; The Brass Bottle, 1923; The Brass Bottle, 1964; Djinn, 2008; Djinn, 2013; Bernard and the Genie, 1991 (made-for-TV): The Boy and the Pirates, 1960; Chris and His Wonderful Lamp, 1917; **Clash of the Titans**, 2010; Ducktales the Movie: Treasure of the Lost Lamp, 1990; The Flying Carpet, 1960; The Genie, 1953; I Dream of Jeannie, 1965-1970 (TV series); I Dream of Jeannie...Fifteen Years Later, 1985 (made-for-TV): I Still Dream of Jeannie, 1992 (made-for-TV); The Incredible Genie, 1999; **Invitation to the Dance**, 1956; Jinn, 2014; Kazaam, 1996; The Lamp, 2011 (made-for-TV); Les 1001 nuits,

1990; Life Is a Circus, 1962; Little Miss Devil, 1951; Long Time Dead, 2002; Magic Mansion, 1965-1967 (TV series); Mio in the Land of Faraway, 1988; Once Upon a Time in Wonderland, 2013- (TV series); **1001 Arabian Nights**, 1959; The Outing, 1987; The Pee-Wee Herman Show, 1981 (made-for-TV); Red Sands, 2009; Sabu and the Magic Ring, 1957; Scooby-Doo in Arabian Nights, 1994 (made-for-TV): **The 7th Voyage of Sinbad**, 1958; The Singing Princess, 1967; Skin Deep, 1989; The Tale of Despereaux, 2008; **The Thief of Bagdad**, 1940; The Thief of Bagdad, 1978 (made-for-TV); **A Thousand and One Nights**, 1945; **Turnabout**, 1940; Weird Science, 1985; Wishmaster, 1997; The Wizard of Bagdad, 1960; The Wonders of Aladdin, 1961.

Gladiators: Androcles and the Lion, 1953; Atlantis, the Lost Continent, 1961; Atlas, 1961; **Barabbas**, 1962; **Ben-Hur**, 1959; Challenge of the Gladiator, 1965; **Clash of the Titans**, 1981; **Clash of the Titans**, 2010; Conan the Barbarian, 1982; **Demetrius and the Gladiators**, 1954; **The Eagle**, 2011; Fabiola, 1951; **Gladiator**, 2000; **The Hunger Games**, 2012; **Hunger Games: Catching Fire**, 2013; **Hunger Games: Mockingjay—Part 1**, 2014; **The Hunger Games: Mockingjay – Part 2**, 2015; **The Last Days of Pompeii**, 1935; **Mad Max: Beyond Thunderdome**, 1985; Pompeii, 2014; **Quo Vadis**, 1913; **Quo Vadis**, 1951; S.P.Q.R.: 2000 and a Half Years Ago, 1994; **The Sign of the Cross**, 1932; Sins of Rome, 1954; Spartacus, 1913; **Spartacus**, 1960; Spartacus, 1976 (made-for-TV); Spartacus, 2004 (made-for-TV); Spartacus, 2008 (made-for-TV); Spartacus and the Ten Gladiators, 1964; Spartacus: Gods of the Arena, 2011- (TV miniseries); Spartacus: War of the Damned, 2010-2013; Tron, 1982; The Two Gladiators, 1964; Up Pompeii!, 1969- (TV series).

Global Warming: **A.I. Artificial Intelligence**, 2001; Alternative 3, 1977 (made-for-TV); **The Arrival**, 1996; **Beasts of the Southern Wild**, 2012; **Before Sunset**, 2004; Category 7: The End of the World, 2005 (made-for-TV); Changing Climates, Changing Times, 2008 (made-for-TV); The Colony, 2013; **The Day after Tomorrow**, 2004; Earth 2100, 2009 (made-for-TV); Empty, 2011; The Extra Man, 2010; The Fire Next Time, 1993 (made-for-TV); Flood, 2007; The Future, 2011; Future Weather, 2011; A Glaring Emission, 2010; **The Golden Compass**, 2007; Half Life, 2008; Happy Accidents, 2000; **Ice Age**, 2002; Ice Age: The Meltdown, 2006; The Lake House, 2006; Loch Ness, 1996; Lost City Raiders, 2008 (made-for-TV); NYC: Tornado Terror, 2008 (made-for-TV); **Our Man Flint**, 1966; Pete Winning and the Pirates, 2013- (TV series); Pete Winning and the Pirates: The Motion Picture, 2015; Quantum of Solace, 2008; Split Second, 1992; Solar Attack, 2006 (made-for-TV); The Steam Experiment, 2009; Stonados, 2013 (made-for-TV); Sunshine State, 2002; 10 Promises to My Dog, 2008; The Thaw, 2009; Waterworld, 1995; **Voyage to the Bottom of the Sea**, 1961; X-Mas, Inc., 2008.

Gold Fields, Gold Miners and Gold Mines (also see Miners and Mining Towns): Aces Wild, 1936; Across the Pacific, 1914; **The Adventures of Bullwhip Griffin**, 1967; Adventures of Frank and Jesse James, 1948; **The Adventures of Mark Twain**, 1944; The Adventures of the Masked Phantom, 1939; Angelique, 2013; Apache Rifles, 1964; **The Apple Dumpling Gang**, 1975; **At Play in the Fields of the Lord**, 1991; Back to God's Country, 1953; Bad Men of Tombstone, 1949; **The Badlanders**, 1958; Badlands of Dakota, 1941; Bait, 1954; Bandits of Dark Canyon, 1947; **Barbary Coast**, 1935; Barbary Coast Gent, 1944; Battling with Buffalo Bill, 1931 (serial); Beaten, 1924; The Beautiful Blonde from Bashful Bend, 1949; Behind Southern Lines, 1952; Beings, 1998; Belle of the Yukon, 1944; **Bend of the River**, 1952; Beyond the Sierras, 1928; Black Arrow, 1944; Black Bart, 1948; Blind Warrior, 1987; The Blocked Trail, 1943; Border Feud, 1987; Border Roundup, 1942; Border Vengeance, 1925; Born to Gamble, 1935; Born to the West, 1926; **The Bride Came C.O.D.**, 1941; The Broken Law, 1924; The Bronze Buckeroo, 1939; Bulldog Courage, 1935; Burning Daylight,

1928; Bury Me Not on the Lone Prairie, 1941; California, 1947; California Firebrand, 1948; Call of the Coyote: A Legend of the Golden West, 1934; Call of the Desert, 1930; **The Call of the Wild**, 1935; The Call of the Wild, 1972; **The Cariboo Trail**, 1950; Carmen of the Klondike, 1918; Carson City, 1952; Carson City Raiders, 1948; The Chechahcos, 1924; The Cheyenne Kid, 1933; Choco, 2012; The Cisco Kid and the Lady, 1939; **City Slickers II: The Legend of Curly's Gold**, 1994; The Claim, 2000; Clancy of the Mounted, 1933; The Comeback, 1917; Country Gentlemen, 1936; The Courageous Avenger, 1935; Cowboy and the Senorita, 1944; **The Cowboys**, 1972; Crimes at the Dark House, 1940; The Crooked Trail, 1936; Cross Fire, 1933; Curse of the Forty-Niner, 2002; Danger Valley, 1937; Dark Mountain, 2013; Dead Man's Gold, 1948; Deadwood, 2004-2006 (TV series); Death Valley Rangers, 1943; Desert Gold, 1936; Desert Phantom, 1936; Desire Under the Elms, 1958; Doughnuts and Society, 1936; Draegerman Courage, 1937; **The Dude Goes West**, 1948; Edge of Eternity, 1959; Eight Legged Freaks, 2002; El Cortez, 2006; Eureka, 1984; Fandango, 1970; **The Far Country**, 1955; **Fighting Caravans**, 1931; Fighting Frontier, 1943; The Firebrand, 1962; The Flame of the Yukon, 1926; Flaming Frontiers, 1938; **For a Few More Dollars**, 1966; **Framed**, 1947; The Frozen Limits, 1939; **Garden of Evil**, 1954; The Gay Defender, 1927; Gay Purr-ee, 1962; Ghost Valley, 1932; The Girl from Outside, 1919; Girl Rush, 1944; Goin' South, 1978; Gold, 2013; Gold Fever, 1952; Gold Fever in Lapland, 1999; Gold Is Where You Find It, 1938; **The Gold Rush**, 1925; The Golden Eye, 1948; The Golden Stallion, 1927; The Golden Trail, 1940; Goldrush: A Real Alaskan Adventure, 1998 (made-for-TV); Goldtown Ghost Riders, 1953; Gordon of Ghost City, 1933; Grand Larceny, 1991 (made-for-TV); The Great Divide, 1929; The Great Jesse James Raid, 1953; **Greed**, 1924; Gun Fever, 1958; Gun Gospel, 1927; Gunmen of Abilene, 1950; Guns of Hate, 1948; Hands Up!, 1926; **The Hanging Tree**, 1959; Haunted Gold, 1932; The Haunted Mine, 1946; Heading West, 1946; Heathens and Thieves, 2012; Heir to Trouble, 1935; Hell on Devil's Island, 1957; Hellhounds of the West, 1922; Hidden Gold, 1940; Holes, 2003; Home on the Range, 1935; **How the West Was Won**, 1962; If One Is Born a Swine, 1967; In Old Sacramento, 1946; The Indians Are Coming, 1930; **Jack London**, 1943; Jack McCall, Desperado, 1953; Junction City, 1952; Jungle Drums of Africa, 1953; Kid Courageous, 1935; King of the Wild, 1931 (serial); Klondike Fever, 1980; Klondike Kate, 1943; Lady in a Jam, 1942; The Law Rides, 1936; The Lawless Frontier, 1934; Le ruffian, 1983; The Legend of White Fang, 1992-1994 (TV series); Lightning Raiders, 1945; Lightning Range, 1934; The Lightning Warrior, 1931 (serial); The Lone Defender, 1934; The Lone Rider and the Bandit, 1942; The Lone Rider Fights Back, 1941; Lonesome Trail, 1945; The Lost Special, 1932 (serial); The Luck of the Roaring Camp, 1937; Lure of the Yukon, 1924; Lust for Gold, 1949; Mad Dog Morgan, 1976; The Man from Colorado, 1949; Man from Music Mountain, 1938; A Man from Nowhere, 1920; Man from the Black Hills, 1952; The Man Who Played Square, 1924; Mandie and the Cherokee Treasure, 2010; **The Mask of Zorro**, 1998; Men in the Raw, 1923; The Mints of Hell, 1919; Montana Territory, 1952; Mourning Becomes Electra, 1947; The Mysterious Rider, 1942; **The New Land**, 1973; **Nikki, Wild Dog of the North**, 1961; No Man's Gold, 1926; North of Arizona, 1935; The North Star, 1996; **North to Alaska**, 1960; North to the Klondike, 1942; Oblomov, 1980; On Our Merry Way, 1948; One More Train to Rob, 1971; Orphans of the North, 1940; The Overland Express, 1938; Overland Trails, 1948; **Paint Your Wagon**, 1969; The Pal from Texas, 1939; **Pale Rider**, 1985; Pals in Paradise, 1926; Panther Girl of the Kongo, 1955; The Pecos Kid, 1935; A Perilous Journey, 1953; Perils of the Royal Mounted, 1942; Phantom Gold, 1938; The Phantom Rider, 1936 (serial); Pirates on Horseback, 1941; The Plunderer, 1915; The Prime Gig, 2001; Quick Millions, 1939; The Raiders, 1952; Range Riders, 1934; **Relentless**, 1948; Renegade, 2004; Revenue Agent, 1950; **Ride the High Country**, 1962; Rider from Tucson, 1950; The Rider of Death Valley, 1932; A River of Skulls, 2011; **Road to Utopia**, 1946; **Robin Hood of El Dorado**, 1936; Rockin' in the Rockies, 1945; A Romance of the Redwoods, 1917; Rough Riders' Round-up, 1939; The Royal Mounted Rides Again, 1945 (serial); Rugged Gold, 1994 (made-for-TV); The Ruthless Four, 1960; Sagebrush Troubadour, 1935; Salt of the Earth, 1917; The San Francisco Story, 1952; Santa Fe Stampede, 1938; Scared Stiff, 1953; The Secret Menace, 1931; Secrets of the Wasteland, 1941; Senorita from the West, 1934; Senorita from the West, 1945; Set Free, 1927; Sheriff of Tombstone, 1941; Seven Guns for Timothy, 1966; The Silent Code, 1935; The Silent Hero, 1927; Silly Billies, 1936; The Singing Cowboy, 1936; A Sky Full of Stars for a Roof, 1968; The Sombrero Kid, 1942; Something New, 1920; Son of a Gun, 2014; Son of the Morning Star, 1991 (made-for-TV); Son of Zorro, 1947; South of Death Valley, 1949; Special Investigator, 1936; The Spoilers, 1914; The Spoilers, 1923; **The Spoilers**, 1930; **The Spoilers**, 1942; The Spoilers, 1955; Spook Ranch, 1925; Stage to Chino, 1940; Stagecoach Express, 1942; The Strangeness, 1987; A Stone's Throw, 2006; Sudden Bill Dorn, 1937; **Support Your Local Sheriff**, 1991; **Sutter's Gold**, 1936; Sweet Georgia, 1972; The Texas Rambler, 1935; Texas Terrors, 1940; Thanks for Listening, 1937; There Goes the Groom, 1937; The 33 of San Jose, 2010; Those Redheads from Seattle, 1953; Thunder Mountain, 1935; Thunder Over Arizona, 1956; A Tornado in the Saddle, 1942; Trail of Kit Carson, 1945; Trails of Adventure, 1933; Trapped, 2010; **The Treasure of the Sierra Madre**, 1948; Two Brothers in Trinity, 1972; Tyrant of Red Gulch, 1928; Unconquered Bandit, 1935; Under the Fiesta Stars, 1941; The Valiant Hombre, 1948; The Valley of Bravery, 1926; Valley of the Lawless, 1936; Valley of Vanishing Men, 1924; The Valley of Vanishing Men, 1942 (serial); Wanda Nevada, 1979; **Way Out West**, 1937; **Welcome to Hard Times**, 1967; **Wells Fargo**, 1937; We're Going to Be Rich, 1938; West of Carson City, 1940; Westbound Mail, 1937; Western Vengeance, 1924; Whispering Smith Rides, 1927; **White Fang**, 1991; White Fang 2: Myth of the White Wolf, 1994; **Wild Geese Calling**, 1941; Wings of the Hawk, 1953; Women and Gold, 1925; The Yellow Bullet, 1917; Yellow Dust, 1936; **Yellow Sky**, 1948; Young Buffalo Bill, 1940.

Golden Gate Bridge (San Francisco Bay, California; location): **The Abyss**, 1989; **The Age of Adaline**, 2015; **Air Force**, 1943; **Alone on the Pacific**, 1964; **Ant-Man**, 2015; Bee Season, 2005; **Big Hero 6**, 2014; Big Trouble in Little China, 1986; **Blue Jasmine**, 2013; Blue State, 2007; **Bolt**, 2008; The Book of Eli, 2010; Born to Kill, 1947; Boys and Girls, 2000; **The Caine Mutiny**, 1954; **The Cheap Detective**, 1978; Coach Carter, 2005; The Core, 2003; Crazy in Alabama, 1999; Dark Passage, 1947; **Dawn of the Planet of the Apes**, 2014; **Destination Tokyo**, 1943; **Dirty Harry**, 1971; Dogfight, 1991; **Double Jeopardy**, 1999; Dream for an Insomniac, 1996; Drive, 1997; Electric Dreams, 1984; **Escape from Alcatraz**, 1979; Escape in the Fog, 1945; Eye of the Beholder, 1999; Fanboys, 2009; Final Analysis, 1992; 5 Star Day, 2010; Flight of the Navigator, 1986; **Flower Drum Song**, 1961; 40 Days and 40 Nights, 2002; **Foul Play**, 1978; **Godzilla**, 2014; The Golden Gate Murders, 1979 (made-for-TV); **Good Neighbor Sam**, 1964; **Herbie Rides Again**, 1974; **The High and the Mighty**, 1954; House of Sand and Fog, 2003; **How the West Was Won**, 1962; Hulk, 2003; If I Had My Way, 1940; **Impact**, 1949; In Love and War, 1958; Innerspace, 1987; **Interview with the Vampire: The Vampire Chronicles**, 1994; **It Came from Beneath the Sea**, 1955; Jack the Bear, 1993; Just Like Heaven, 2005; The Killer Elite, 1975; **The Lady from Shanghai**, 1948; Land of the Lost, 2009; **The Lincoln Lawyer**, 2011; **The Lineup**, 1958; **The Love Bug**, 1968; **Magnum Force**, 1973; Memoirs of an Invisible Man, 1992; Mr. Wong, Detective, 1938; Monsters vs. Aliens, 2009; Need for Speed, 2014; **Nim's Island**, 2008; On the Beach, 1959; **Pacific Rim**, 2013; The Princess Diaries, 2001; The Presidio, 1988; Race Street, 1948; The Rock, 1996; **San Andreas**, 2015; The Sessions, 2012; **Shadow of a Doubt**, 1943; **Shadow of the Thin Man**, 1941; **Star Trek**, 2009; **Star Trek IV: The Voyage Home**, 1986; **Star Trek: Into Darkness**, 2013; **Star Trek: The Motion Picture**, 1979;

Sudden Fear, 1952; **Sudden Impact**, 1983; **Superman**, 1978; Superman IV: The Quest for Peace, 1987; Terminator Genisys, 2015; **Terminator Salvation**, 2009; **This Gun for Hire**, 1942; Thunderbirds, 2004; Ticker, 2001; **Ticket to Heaven**, 1981; **Time After Time**, 1979; **The Time of Your Life**, 1948; **The Towering Inferno**, 1974; Under Siege, 1992; **Vertigo**, 1958; A View to Kill, 1985; **Wake Island**, 1942; Wildcat Bus, 1940; **X-Men: The Last Stand**, 2006; **Zodiac**, 2007.

Golf, Golfers and Golfing: Animal House, 1978; Another Dawn, 1937; The Big Broadcast of 1938, 1938; Birdie and Bogey, 2004; **Bobby Jones: Stroke of Genius**, 2004; The Bride Goes Wild, 1948; **Bringing Up Baby**, 1938; The Browning Version, 1994; The Caddy, 1953; **Caddyshack**, 1980; Caddyshack II, 1988; Call Me Bwana, 1963; **Colonel Blimp**, 1945; **Dead of Night**, 1945; **Enter the Dragon**, 1973; **Falling Down**, 1993; **Follow the Sun**, 1951; Robert Adams, D. Scotty Chisholm, John Close, Al Demaret, Jimmy Demaret, Mortie Dutra, Bob Evans, Ralph Guldahl, Ben Hogan, Cary Middlecoff, Eric Monti, Frank Peters, Joe Rocca, Sam Snead, Jimmy Thompson); **Frost/Nixon**, 2008; A Gentleman's Game, 2002; **Going My Way**, 1944; Golf Punks, 1998; Golfballs!, 1999; **Guarding Tess**, 1994; **A Guide for the Married Man**, 1967; **The Great Gatsby**, 1974; **The Greatest Game Ever Played**, 2005 (Francis DeSales Ouimet; Henry William "Harry" Vardon; Edward Rivers J. "Ted" Ray; Edward Edgar "Eddie" Lowery); Happy Gilmore, 1996; Hole in One, 2010; **I Love You Again**, 1940; The Idle Class, 1921; Leap Year, 1924; **The Legend of Bagger Vance**, 2000 (Bobby Jones; Walter Hagen); Let's Be Happy, 1957; **Men of Boys Town**, 1941; Merrily We Live, 1938; Miracle on the 17th Green, 1999 (made-for-TV); Mr. Music, 1950; **Murder She Said**, 1961; My Fellow Americans, 1996; My Past, 1931; The Naughty Flirt, 1931; **Ordinary People**, 1980; **The Parent Trap**, 1961; **Pat and Mike**, 1952; The Rag Man, 1925; **Rhubarb**, 1951; Ruby Gentry, 1952; **The Short Game**, 2013; **Since You Went Away**, 1944; **Space Jam**, 1996; Spring Fever, 1927; **The Sting**, 1973; Stopover Tokyo, 1957; Street of Women, 1932; **Tea and Sympathy**, 1956; **Thoroughly Modern Millie**, 1967; The Tiger Woods Story, 1998 (made-for-TV); **Tin Cup**, 1996; **A Touch of Class**, 1973; **Trouble in Paradise**, 1932; **True Confessions**, 1981; **The Truman Show**, 1998; **The Two Jakes**, 1990; **Welcome to Mooseport**, 2004; **When Ladies Meet**, 1933; **Wilson**, 1944; Who's Your Caddy?, 2007.

Grasshoppers (locusts): All the Little Animals, 1998; **The Ballad of Cable Hogue**, 1970; Beginning of the End, 1957; **Brigham Young: Frontiersman**, 1940; **A Bug's Life**, 1998; Days of Heaven, 1978; Everything Is Illuminated, 2005; **Exodus: Gods and Kings**, 2014; **Dracula: Dead and Loving It**, 1995; **The Good Earth**, 1937; **Hidalgo**, 2004; **James and the Giant Peach**, 1996; Mondays in the Sun, 2002; **My Mother's Castle**, 1991; **Nowhere in Africa**, 2001; Rancho Deluxe, 1975; **The Ruling Class**, 1972; Short Circuit, 1986; **The Ten Commandments**, 1923; **The Ten Commandments**, 1956; Treeless Mountain, 2008; **Walkabout**, 1971; Young Pioneers, 1976 (made-for-TV).

Guerrillas: **An American Guerrilla in the Philippines**, 1950 (WWII); **Back to Bataan**, 1945 (Philippines, WWII); Battle at Bloody Beach, 1961 (Philippines, WWII); **Best of the Badmen**, 1951 (southern guerrillas, American Civil War); **China**, 1943 (Chinese in WWII); **China Sky**, 1945 (Chinese in WWII); **Dark Command**, 1940 (southern guerrillas, American Civil War); **Fighting Man of the Plains**, 1949 (southern guerrillas, American Civil War); Kansas Raiders, 1950 (southern guerrillas, American Civil War); **Manila Calling**, 1942 (Philippines, WWII); **The Outlaw Josey Wales**, 1976 (northern and southern guerrillas, American Civil War); **The Outriders**, 1950 (southern guerrillas, American Civil War); **Quantrill's Raiders**, 1958 (southern guerrillas, American Civil War); **The Real Glory**, 1939 (Philippines; Moro Rebellion); **Red Mountain**, 1951 (southern guerrillas, American Civil War); **Ride with the Devil**, 1999 (southern guerrillas, American Civil

War); **Rocky Mountain**, 1950 (southern guerrillas, American Civil War); **Woman They Almost Lynched**, 1953 (southern guerrillas, American Civil War); and **Young Jesse James**, 1960 (southern guerrillas, American Civil War).

Gunfighters (U.S. Old West): **Across the Sierras**, 1941; Alias Jesse James, 1959; **Along Came Jones**, 1945; **Angel and the Badman**, 1947; **Appaloosa**, 2008; **Badman's Territory**, 1946 (Frank and Jesse James; Dalton Brothers; Belle Starr); **Bad Men of Missouri**, 1941 (Jesse James; Younger Brothers); **Belle Starr**, 1941 (Sam Starr); **Best of the Badmen**, 1951 (Frank and Jesse James; Younger Brothers); **Blazing Saddles**, 1974; Billy the Kid, 1930; **Billy the Kid**, 1941; **Butch Cassidy and the Sundance Kid**, 1969; **Calamity Jane**, 1953 (Wild Bill Hickok); **Cat Ballou**, 1965; **Chisum**, 1970 (Billy the Kid); **Cimarron**, 1931; Cole Younger, Gunfighter, 1958; **The Culpepper Cattle Company**, 1972; **Dallas**, 1950 (Wild Bill Hickok); The Daltons Ride Again, 1945; **Dawn at Socorro**, 1954 (Doc Holliday; Earp Brothers); Death of a Gunfighter, 1969; **Destiny Rides Again**, 1939; **Doc**, 1971 (Doc Holliday); **Dodge City**, 1939 (role modeled on Wyatt Earp); **The Doolins of Oklahoma**, 1949 (Bill Doolin, George "Bittercreek" Newcomb; Bill "Tulsa Jack" Blake; William "Little Bill" Raidler); **The Fastest Gun Alive**, 1956; **Fighting Man of the Plains**, 1949 (Jesse James; Cole Younger); **A Fistful of Dollars**, 1967; **For a Few Dollars More**, 1967; **Frontier Marshal**, 1939 (Doc Holliday; Wyatt Earp); **The Good, the Bad and the Ugly**, 1967; **The Great Missouri Raid**, 1951 (Frank and Jesse James; Younger Brothers); **The Great Northfield, Minnesota Raid**, 1972 (Frank and Jesse James; Younger Brothers); **A Gunfight**, 1971; **Gunfight at the O.K. Corral**, 1957 (Doc Holliday; Earp Brothers); **The Gunfighter**, 1950; Gunslingers, 1950; **Hang 'Em High**, 1968; Heaven with a Gun, 1969; **Hell's Hinges**, 1916; **High Noon**, 1952; **High Plains Drifter**, 1973; **Hour of the Gun**, 1967 (Doc Holliday; Earp Brothers; Curly Bill Brocious); Jack Slade, 1953; The James Brothers of Missouri, 1949; **Jesse James**, 1939 (Frank and Jesse James); Joe Kidd, 1972; **Johnny Guitar**, 1954; **Last Train from Gun Hill**, 1959; **Law and Order**, 1932 (Doc Holliday; Earp Brothers); **The Lawless Breed**, 1953 (John Wesley Hardin); **A Lawless Street**, 1955; **Lawman**, 1975; **The Life and Times of Judge Roy Bean**, 1972; **Little Big Man**, 1970 (Wild Bill Hickok); **The Long Riders**, 1980 (Jesse and Frank James; Younger Brothers); **The Magnificent Seven**, 1960; **Man from Del Rio**, 1956; **McCabe and Mrs. Miller**, 1971; Montana Belle, 1952 (Belle Starr); **My Darling Clementine**, 1946 (Doc Holliday; Earp Brothers); **Nevada Smith**, 1966; **The Oklahoma Kid**, 1939; **One-Eyed Jacks**, 1961; **Open Range**, 2003; **The Outlaw Josey Wales**, 1976; **Pale Rider**, 1975; **Pat Garrett & Billy the Kid**, 1973; **The Plainsman**, 1936 (Wild Bill Hickok); The Quick and the Dead, 1995; **Rancho Notorious**, 1952; **Red River**, 1948; **The Return of Frank James**, 1940; The Return of Jack Slade, 1955; **Return of the Bad Men**, 1948 (Younger Brothers; Dalton Brothers; Sundance Kid; Billy the Kid; Bill Doolin); Return of the Gunfighter, 1967; **Ride the High Country**, 1962; **Rio Bravo**, 1959; **Rooster Cogburn**, 1975; **Saddle the Wind**, 1958; **Shane**, 1953; **The Shootist**, 1976; **Silverado**, 1985; **The Sons of Katie Elder**, 1965; **Stagecoach**, 1939; **Stars in My Crown**, 1950; **Support Your Local Gunfighter**, 1971; Three Amigos, 1986; **3:10 to Yuma**, 1957; **3:10 to Yuma**, 2007; **The Tin Star**, 1957; **Tombstone**, 1993 (Doc Holliday; Earp Brothers; Johnny Ringo; Curly Bill Brocious); **Tombstone: The Town Too Tough to Die**, 1942 (Doc Holliday; Earp Brothers); Trail Street, 1947 (Bat Masterson); **True Grit**, 1969; **True Grit**, 2010; **The True Story of Jesse James**, 1957; **Tumbleweeds**, 1925; **Unforgiven**, 1992; **The Virginian**, 1929; **The Virginian**, 1946; **Warlock**, 1959 (Doc Holliday; Wyatt Earp); **The Westerner**, 1940; **When the Daltons Rode**, 1940; **Whispering Smith**, 1948; **The White Buffalo**, 1977 (Wild Bill Hickok); **Wichita**, 1955 (Wyatt Earp); **Wild Bill**, 1995 (Wild Bill Hickok); **Wild Bill Hickok**, 1923; Wild Bill Hickok Rides, 1942; **The Wild Bunch**, 1969; **Wyatt Earp**, 1994 (Doc Holliday; Johnny Ringo; Curly Bill Brocious); **Young Guns**, 1988 (Billy the Kid);

Young Guns II, 1990 (Billy the Kid); Young Jesse James, 1960 (Frank and Jesse James; Younger Brothers; Belle Starr); **The Younger Brothers**, 1949. Note: For more information of gunfighters in the U.S. Old West, see my book *Encyclopedia of Western Lawmen and Outlaws* (Paragon House, 1992).

Gunsmiths: The American, 2010; **Carbine Williams**, 1952; **The Day of the Jackal**, 1973 (blacksmith); Forty Guns, 1957; **The Grey Fox**, 1983; Hannie Caulder, 1971; Legends of Anika, 1956; The Lone Rider Crosses the Rio, 1941; Masters of the Universe, 1987; The Mexican, 2001; **Nevada Smith**, 1966; Night Riders of Montana, 1951; Rocky Mountain Rangers, 1940; **Son of Fury: The Story of Benjamin Blake**, 1942; Trail of Kit Carson, 1945; Trail to Gunsight, 1944; Wanted, 2008; The Wild Frontier, 1947.

Hangmen and Hangings (official executioners and executions): Apprentice, 2016 (Wan Hanafi Su; Firdaus Rahman, prison executioners); Bandolero!, 1968 (James Stewart, who impersonates an Old West hangman in order to rescue his imprisoned brother); Battle of the Brave, 2004 (Maxime Allard as the official hangman); **Blazing Saddles**, 1974; The Bravados, 1958 (Joe DeRita, who impersonates an Old West hangman in an effort to release four condemned prisoners); Burke and Hare, 2010; Captain of the Guard, 1930 (Stanley Field as the hangman); **Changeling**, 2008 (graphic 1930 hanging of serial killer Gordon Stewart Northcott [confessed to murdering five boys], played by Jason Butler Harner); The Chant of Jimmie Blacksmith, 1980; **The Crucible**, 1996; Crypt of the Vampire, 1984; Django: Prepare a Coffin, 1968; **Drum Beat**, 1954 (Old West hanging of Indian outlaw Captain Jack, played by Charles Bronson); Feast of July, 1995 (Tim Perrin as the hangman); **Geronimo: An American Legend**, 1993 (Old West graphic hangings of three Apache Indians convicted of murder); The Grand Duel, 1972 (Furio Meniconi as the hangman); **Hang 'Em High**, 1968 (Bert Freed, an official executioner, who, in one sequence, hangs six convicted men of the Old West at once at a public execution); **The Hunchback of Notre Dame**, 1939; In Cold Blood, 1967 (graphic hanging of convicted mass murderers Perry Smith and Richard Hickock); Janosik: A True Story, 2009; **Kind Hearts and Coronets**, 1950 (executioner Miles Malleson, who is to hang Dennis Price, convicted of murdering his relatives in order to gain the family inheritance in a black comedy); The Lady and the Bandit, 1951 (Frank Hagney as Dick Turpin's (Louis Hayward) hangman); **Ned Kelly**, 1970 (hanging of Australian outlaw played by Mick Jagger); **Night of the Hunter**, 1955 (Paul Bryar as the official hangman); Noose for a Gunman, 1960; Perfume: The Story of a Murderer, 2006 (Enric Arquimbau); **Pierrepoint: The Last Hangman**, 2007 (Timothy Spall as Britain's last official executioner); **Robin Hood: Men in Tights**, 1993 (Robert Ridgely as a hangman); Safe in Hell, 1931; **The Scarlet Coat**, 1955 (the 1780 hanging of British spymaster Major John Andre, played by Michael Wilding, during the American Revolution); **The Scarlet Empress**, 1934; Taking Sides, 2001; **Tom Horn**, 1980 (graphic hanging of Old West scout-turned-killer Tom Horn, played by Steve McQueen). Note: For more information on hangmen or official executioners, see my eight-volume work *Encyclopedia of World Crime* (CrimeBooks, Inc., 1990).

Harmonica Players and Harmonica Playing: **Alice in Wonderland**, 1951; All Mine to Give, 1957; **All Quiet on the Western Front**, 1930; Always in My Heart, 1942; At the Circus, 1939; Atonement, 2007; August Rush, 2007; **Australia**, 2008; Baby Doll, 1956; The Ballad of the Sad Café, 1991; Battle Beyond the Stars, 1980; The Big Bounce, 2004; **Blood Work**, 2002; Blue Hawaii, 1961; **The Blues Brothers**, 1980; Boxcar Bertha, 1972; The Brothers Bloom, 2008; **The Cardinal**, 1963; **The Cat's Meow**, 2001; **Charley Varrick**, 1973; Chatahoochee, 1989; **City Slickers**, 1991; The Cranes Are Flying, 1960; Creation, 2009; **Cross of Iron**, 1977; Crossroads, 1986; Dark City, 1998; Day of Anger, 1967; The Deadly Companions, 1961; December Boys, 2007; **Drums** in the Deep South, 1951; **Empire of the Sun**, 1987; Escape to Witch Mountain, 1975; Factory Girl, 2006; Fateless, 2005; The Favor, 1994; Frankie and Johnny, 1966; **Free Willy**, 1993; **Grand Illusion**, 1938; **The Great Northfield, Minnesota Raid**, 1972; **Guns at Batasi**, 1964; **Hair**, 1979; Harmonica, 1974; **Hidalgo**, 2004; **The High and the Mighty**, 1954; **Home from the Hill**, 1960; **Hope and Glory**, 1987; **Houseboat**, 1958; I Spit on Your Grave, 1978; I'm Not There, 2007; **Into the West**, 1993; It Always Rains on Sunday, 1949; Jack Frost, 1998; **Jean de Florette**, 1987; Joe and Max, 2002 (made-for-TV); **Johnny in the Clouds** (AKA: Way to the Stars), 1945; **Joyeux Noel**, 2005; The Kettles in the Ozarks, 1956; The Killer, 1989; Knightriders, 1983; **La Terra Trema**, 1947; Lackawanna Blues, 2005 (made-for-TV); The Lair of the White Worm, 1988; Lamb, 1985; Last Tango in Paris, 1972; **Letter from an Unknown Woman**, 1948; **The Lighthorsemen**, 1988; Like Water for Chocolate, 1992; **The Little Colonel**, 1935; Love Me Tender, 1956; **Major Dundee**, 1965; **Manhattan**, 1979; **Manon of the Spring**, 1987; **Meet John Doe**, 1941; **Memphis Belle**, 1990; **Midnight Express**, 1978; Monte Walsh, 2003 (made-for-TV); Moonlighting, 1985-1989 (TV series); **The Muppet Movie**, 1979; My Bloody Valentine, 1981; My Boy Jack, 2007 (made-for-TV); **Mysterious Island**, 1961; **The Naked City**, 1948; Nobody's Fool, 1986; **The Notebook**, 2004; Nowhere Boy, 2009; **Once Upon a Time in the West**, 1969; One False Move, 1992; **One Magic Christmas**, 1985; **Ossessione**, 1959; **The Other**, 1972; Paper Heart, 2009; **Pepe Le Moko**, 1937; **The Perks of Being a Wallflower**, 2012; **Pigskin Parade**, 1936; The Pinchcliffe Grand Prix, 1975; Pot o' Gold, 1941; The Princess Diaries, 2001; The Recruit, 2003; **Rio Bravo**, 1959; **Room Service**, 1938; **Run of the Arrow**, 1957; Savannah Smiles, 1982; Scarecrows, 1988; **Seeking a Friend for the End of the World**, 2012; **Shane**, 1953; **The Shawshank Redemption**, 1994; Sholay, 1975; **Singin' in the Rain**, 1952; Slipstream, 2007; Something Wicked This Way Comes, 1983; Songs, 2004; **Star Spangled Rhythm**, 1942; **State Fair**, 1945; Staying Together, 1989; Stone Cold, 1991; Stoned, 2005; The Stranger Wore a Gun, 1953; Summer Storm, 2004; **Sweet Land**, 2005; The Telegraph Trail, 1933; They Live, 1988; **They Were Expendable**, 1945; Time of the Gypsies, 1988; **The Tin Drum**, 1980; **Tin Pan Alley**, 1940; **The Treasure of the Sierra Madre**, 1948; The Truce, 1997; **20,000 Years in Sing Sing**, 1932; The Unbelievable Truth, 1989; **The Undefeated**, 1969; **Vagabond**, 1985; **Vera Cruz**, 1954; **The Wages of Fear**, 1955; **We're No Angels**, 1956; When the Cat's Away, 1996; **Whispering Smith**, 1948; **Windtalkers**, 2002; Without a Paddle, 2004; Wolf Creek 2, 2013; **The Woman on the Beach**, 1947; **The Yearling**, 1946; **You Can't Take It With You**, 1938; **The Young Savages**, 1961.

Headless Horsemen: **Adventures of Ichabod and Mr. Toad**, 1949; **The Curse of the Cat People**, 1944; Curse of the Headless Horseman, 1972; **Gladiator**, 2000; The Headless Horseman, 1922; Headless Horseman, 2007; The Legend of Sleepy Hollow, 1980 (made-for-TV); The Legend of Sleepy Hollow, 1999 (made-for-TV); The New Misadventures of Ichabod Crane, 1979 (made-for-TV); Sleepy Hollow, 1999; Sleepy Hollow, 2013- (TV series); Sleepy Hollow High, 2000.

Heavenly Visitors: **All Dogs Go to Heaven**, 1989; **All Dogs Go to Heaven 2**, 1996; An Angel Comes to Brooklyn, 1945; The Angel Levine, 1970; **Angels in the Outfield**, 1951; **Angels in the Outfield**, 1994; Barbarella, 1968; **The Bishop's Wife**, 1947; Brother John, 1971; **Cabin in the Sky**, 1943; **Carousel**, 1956; Charley and the Angel, 1973; City of Angels, 1998; **A Christmas Carol**, 1938; **A Christmas Carol**, 1951; A Christmas Carol, 2009; For Heaven's Sake, 1950; Forever, Darling, 1956; **The Green Pastures**, 1936; **A Guy Named Joe**, 1943; **Heaven Can Wait**, 1978; Heaven Only Knows, 1947; **Here Comes Mr. Jordan**, 1941; **The Horn Blows at Midnight**, 1945; I Married an Angel, 1942; **It's a Wonderful Life**, 1947; **Liliom**, 1935; Made in Heaven, 1987; **Michael**, 1996; **The Milagro Beanfield War**, 1988; **The Next Voice You Hear**, 1950; **One Magic Christmas**, 1985; The

Preacher's Wife, 1996; **Scrooge**, 1970; The Sentinel, 1977; **Stairway to Heaven**, 1947; **Strange Cargo**, 1940.

High Wire Artists (Tight-Rope Walkers): Berserk, 1967; Billy Rose's Jumbo, 1962; Boot Hill, 1969; Butch and Sundance: The Early Days, 1979; **Capricious Summer**, 1968; **The Circus**, 1928; Circus Girl, 1937; **Circus World**, 1964; The Dark Tower, 1943; Delightfully Dangerous, 1945; Elvira Madigan, 1967; Fixer Dugan, 1939; The Flame of New Orleans, 1941; **Flesh and Fantasy**, 1943; The Great Wallendas, 1978 (made-for-TV); **The Greatest Show on Earth**, 1952; Here Come the Girls, 1953; Homicide for Three, 1948; **Invitation to the Dance**, 1956; King of the Carnival, 1955; **La Strada**, 1956; The Little Adventuress, 1938; Little Big Top, 2006; Looking for Cheyenne, 2005; Madagascar 3: Europe's Most Wanted, 2012; The Monster, 1925; My Friend Joe, 1996; New York Stories, 1989; Obsession, 1997; One from the Heart, 1981; **Pippi on the Run**, 1977; **The Pirate**, 1948; Ring of Fear, 1954; **Road to Rio**, 1947; Roseanna's Grave, 1997; Save the Green Planet, 2003; Starstruck, 1982; Still Life, 2006; **The Story of Three Loves**, 1953; Swashbuckler, 1976; Tarzan's Desert Mystery, 1943; The Twelve Tasks of Asterix, 1976; **Van Helsing**, 2004; **The Walk**, 2015.

Hitmen: Abduction, 2011; Above the Law, 1998; **Absolute Power**, 1997; Action Jackson, 1988; **Al Capone**, 1959; Alex Cross, 2012; Alien Nation, 1988; The American, 2010; American Ultra, 2015; **Analyze This**, 1999; **Any Which Way You Can**, 1980; Ashby, 2015; Assassination, 2015; **Assassination Games**, 2011; Assassins, 1995; The Asian Connection, 2016; The Avengers, 1998; **The Bag Man**, 2014; Bangkok Dangerous, 2008; **Batman: Mask of the Phantasm**, 1993; Batman: The Killing Joke, 2016; Be Cool, 2005; **Beverly Hills Cop**, 1984; **The Big Heat**, 1953; The Big Hit, 1998; Big Trouble, 2002; A Bittersweet Life, 2005; Black Dynamite, 2009; **Black Hand**, 1950; Black Mass, 2015; Black Rain, 1989; **Blood Work**, 2002; The Boondock Saints, 1999; **Border Incident**, 1949; **The Bourne Legacy**, 2012; **Bring Me the Head of Alfredo Garcia**, 1974; Broken City, 2013; **The Brotherhood**, 1968; Bullets, 2012; **Bullitt**, 1968; Bully, 2001; **Bulworth**, 1998; **Cape Fear**, 1991; **Casino**, 1995; **Charley Varrick**, 1973; **Chinatown**, 1974; **Cloak and Dagger**, 1984; **The Client**, 1994; **Cloud Atlas**, 2012; Cocaine Cowboys, 2006; Code of Silence, 1985; Collateral, 2004; Coma, 1978; Commando, 1985; **Confessions of a Dangerous Mind**, 2002; **The Conformist**, 1971; The Contract, 2006; Crank, 2006; **Crimes and Misdemeanors**, 1989; The Crow: City of Angels, 1996; Crying Freeman, 1995; Daredevil, 2003; Darkman, 1990; **The Day of the Jackal**, 1973; **The Dead Pool**, 1988; Death to Smoochy, 2002; Death Warrant, 1990; **The Departed**, 2006; Despardo, 1995; **Diamonds Are Forever**, 1971; **Dr. No**, 1962; Donnie Brasco, 1997; Double Impact, 1991; Drive, 2011; Drive Angry, 2011; **The Drop**, 2014; Eastern Promises, 2007; The Eiger Sanction, 1975; Enough, 2000; **The Equalizer**, 2014; Erased, 2012; **Eraser**, 1996; An Eye for an Eye, 1981; Eye for an Eye, 1996; Fallen Angels, 1995; **The Family**, 2013; **Family Plot**, 1976; **Fargo**, 1996; Fargo, 2014- (TV series); **The Firm**, 1993; Flame and Citron, 2008; **For Your Eyes Only**, 1981; **Foul Play**, 1978; Foxy Brown, 1974; **The French Connection**, 1971; Fresh, 1994; From Dusk Till Dawn, 1996; From Paris with Love, 2010; **The Frozen Ground**, 2013; F/X, 1986; Game of Death, 1978; **Gangster Squad**, 2013; The Gauntlet, 1977; **Get Carter**, 1971; Get Carter, 2000; **Get Shorty**, 1995; **The Getaway**, 1972; **The Getaway**, 1993; **Gloria**, 1980; Gloria, 1999; **The Godfather**, 1972; The Godfather: Part III, 1990; **The Godfather: Part II**, 1974; Gomorrah, 2009; **The Good, the Bad and the Ugly**, 1967; **GoodFellas**, 1990; Grosse Pointe Blank, 1997; The Gunman, 2015; Harley Davidson and the Marlboro Man, 1991; Hard to Kill, 1990; **High Plains Drifter**, 1973; The Hitman, 1991; Hitman: Agent 47, 2015; Hitmen, 2011; **Hoffa**, 1992; Homefront, 2013; Hoodlum, 1997; I Am Wrath, 2016; **I Was a Communist for the F.B.I.**, 1951; The Iceman, 2012; Ichi the Killer, 2001; **Il Divo**, 2008; **In Bruges**, 2008; Intolerable Cruelty, 2003; **Jack Reacher**, 2012; The Jackal, 1997; **JFK**,

1991; **John Wick**, 2014; The Juror, 1996; Kangaroo Jack, 2003; Kill List, 2011; Kill Me Three Times, 2014; Kill the Irishman, 2011; The Killer, 1989; The Killer Elite, 1975; Killer Elite, 2011; Killer Joe, 2011; **The Killers**, 1946; **The Killers**, 1964; **The Killing**, 1956; **Killing Them Softly**, 2012; Killshot, 2008; King of New York, 1990; The Last Boy Scout, 1991; Layer Cake, 2004; **Le Samourai**, 1972; Leon: The Professional, 1994; **Lethal Weapon 2**, 1989; **License to Kill**, 1989; The Limey, 1991; Live and Let Die, 1973; Lone Wolf McQuade, 1983; Looper, 2012; Lucky Number Seven, 2006; Machete, 2010; Machete Kills, 2013; Mafia!, 1998; **Magnum Force**, 1973; The Man Who Knew Too Little, 1997; The Man with the Golden Gun, 1974; **Marathon Man**, 1976; **Married to the Mob**, 1988; Marked for Death, 1990; Masterminds, 2016; The Matador, 2005; **McCabe & Mrs. Miller**, 1971; The Mechanic, 1972; The Mechanic, 2011; Men at Work, 1990; The Merry Gentleman, 2008; The Mexican, 2001; **Michael Clayton**, 2007; **Midnight Run**, 1988; Mobsters, 1991; Munich, 2005; Mr. Nobody, 2009; Mr. Right, 2015; Money Talks, 1997; **Moonraker**, 1979; **Mulholland Dr.**, 2001; **The Muppet Movie**, 1979; **The Narrow Margin**, 1952; Narrow Margin, 1990; The Net, 1995; New Jack City, 1991; Next of Kin, 1989; Ninja, 2009; **No Country for Old Men**, 2007; The Numbers Station, 2013; Once Upon a Time in Mexico, 2003; **Once Upon a Time in the West**, 1969; Oscar, 1991; Out for Justice, 1991; Paranoia, 2013; Parker, 2013; **Patriot Games**, 1992; **Pay or Die**, 1960; **Payback**, 1999; **Pierrot Le Fou**, 1968; **The Pelican Brief**, 1993; **The Pink Panther Strikes Again**, 1976; **Point Blank**, 1967; Point Blank, 2011; Point of No Return, 1993; Precious Cargo, 2016; Predators, 2010; **Prizzi's Honor**, 1985; Pulp Fiction, 1994; The Punisher, 2004; Quarry, 2016- (TV series); **Quigley Down Under**, 1990; **Radio Days**, 1987; Rage, 2014; Rapid Fire, 1992; The Replacement Killers, 1998; Repo Men, 2010; Revolver, 2005; Ripley's Game, 2002; **Road to Perdition**, 2002; **Robin Hood: Men in Tights**, 1993; The Rookie, 1990; Rumble in the Bronx, 1995; **Run All Night**, 2015; Rush Hour, 1998; Safe, 2012; **Salt**, 2010; Savages, 2012; **Scanners**, 1981; **Scarface**, 1932; Scarface, 1983; See Spot Run, 2001; **Shaft**, 1971; **Shane**, 1953; **The Shootist**, 1976; **Sicario**, 2015; Sin City, 2005; Sister Act, 1992; The 6th Day, 2000; Skin Trade, 2014; Slacker, 1991; Sleepers, 1992; **Snatch**, 2000; **The Sons of Katie Elder**, 1965; The Sopranos, 1999-2007 (TV series); The Specialist, 1994; **The Spy Who Loved Me**, 1977; Standoff, 2016; Starsky & Hutch, 2004; Stone Cold, 1991; **Sudden Impact**, 1983; The Sum of All Fears, 2002; Survivor, 2015; Tango & Cash, 1989; **Thief**, 1981; Things to Do in Denver When You're Dead, 1995; **Three Days of the Condor**, 1975; **The Three Musketeers**, 1993; Thursday, 1998; Timecop, 1994; To Die For, 1995; The Tourist, 2010; The Tournament, 2009; Tracers, 2015; **Traffic**, 2000; Trespass, 1992; True Romance, 1993; **U.S. Marshals**, 1998; **The Untouchables**, 1987; **The Usual Suspects**, 1995; Vampire in Brooklyn, 1995; **Veronica Guerin**, 2003; A View to Kill, 1985; War, 2007; Wasabi, 2001; **The Way of the Dragon**, 1972; Weekend at Bernie's, 1989; The Whole Nine Yards, 2000; The Whole Ten Yards, 2004; **Wild at Heart**, 1990; **Wild Bill**, 1995; **The Wild Geese**, 1978; Wild Target, 2010; **The Wolverine**, 2013; **Year of the Dragon**, 1985; **You Only Live Twice**, 1967; Zero Effect, 1998.

Hoboes (also see Beggars, this index): **A nous la liberte**, 1931; The Abandonment, 1916; **Across the Bridge**, 1957; **Adventures of a Young Man**, 1962; The Adventures of Rex and Rinty, 1935 (serial); Almost a Gentleman, 1939; Always a Bridesmaid, 1943; American Psycho, 2000; The Arkansas Traveler, 1938; The Assistant, 1997; **The Ballad of Cable Hogue**, 1970; Bank Alarm, 1937; **Barefoot in the Park**, 1967; **The Beachcomber**, 1938; **Beggars of Life**, 1928; **Beloved Infidel**, 1959; The Big Show-Off, 1945; Bindlestiffs, 2012; A Bird in the Bush, 2008; The Black Dahlia, 2006; Black Eagle, 1948; **Boom Town**, 1940; **Border Incident**, 1949; Born to Fight, 1936; Boulder Dam, 1936; **Bound for Glory**, 1976; Bowery at Midnight, 1942; Boxcar Bertha, 1972; Breakfast with Scot, 2008; Bruce Almighty, 2003; Bud Abbott and Lou Costello in Hollywood, 1945; **Burn Em 'Up Barnes**, 1921; Calling All

Husbands, 1940; Central Park, 1932; Chronically Unfeasible, 2000; C.H.U.D., 1984; **Cinderella Man**, 2005; **City Lights**, 1931; **Come Live With Me**, 1941;Come the Morning, 1993; **Conflict**, 1945; The Cosmic Monster, 1958; Cosmopolis, 2012; Crimson Gold, 2003; The Crossing Guard, 1995; Danger Lights, 1930; Date with Death, 1959; Drillbit Taylor, 2008; **Easy Living**, 1937; **Elmer Gantry**, 1960; **Emperor of the North Pole**, 1973; End of Days, 1999; **Escape in the Desert**, 1945; **A Face in the Crowd**, 1957; The Falcon Strikes Back, 1943; The Fighting Peacemaker, 1926; Flying Fists, 1937; The Footloose Heiress, 1937; Gangway for Tomorrow, 1943; The Gay Falcon, 1941; Girls on the Road, 1940; **The Gold Rush**, 1925; **The Grapes of Wrath**, 1940; **The Great Debaters**, 2007; Grind, 2003; Happenstance, 2001; Heaven with a Barbed Wire Fence, 1939; Henry and Dizzy, 1942; Heroes for Sale, 1933; Hidden Places, 2006 (made-for-TV); Hobo with a Shotgun, 2011; A Hobo's Christmas, 1987 (made-for-TV); **I Am a Fugitive from a Chain Gang**, 1932; The Illustrated Man, 1969; I'll Give a Million, 1937; I'm Not There, 2007; **Into the Wild**, 2007; Iron Sky, 2012; It Happened on Fifth Avenue, 1947; **It Happened One Night**, 1934; **Joe Gould's Secret**, 2000; Joe the King, 1999; **The Journey of Natty Gann**, 1985; Junior Army, 1942; **The Kid**, 1921; Killer: A Journal of Murder, 1995; King of the Underworld, 1939; Kisses for Breakfast, 1941; **Kit Kittredge: An American Girl**, 2008; La Chienne, 1931; **Lady Killer**, 1933; The Landloper, 1918; **Little Caesar**, 1931; The Little Red Schoolhouse, 1936; The Littlest Hobo, 1979-1985 (TV series); The Live Wire, 1925; Long Live the Hobos, 1995; **The Lost Squadron**, 1932; Love on a Bet, 1936; The Lovers on the Bridge, 1991; Maisie, 1939; The Man Who Found Himself, 1937; The Man Without a Past, 2002; The Manipulator, 1971; Masked and Anonymous, 2003; **Meet John Doe**, 1941; **Melvin and Howard**, 1980; Merrily We Live, 1938; Midnight Court, 1937; **Miracle in Milan**, 1951; Miss Nobody, 1926; Mr. Nobody, 2011; Mokey, 1942; The Moonlighter, 1953; Mountain Rhythm, 1939; My Man, 1997; **My Man Godfrey**, 1936; My Summer Vacation, 1996; New York, I Love You, 2009; **Nightmare Alley**, 1947; Oliver & Company, 1988; On the Road, 2012; On Our Merry Way, 1948; **Our Hospitality**, 1923; The Outfit, 1993; The Penalty, 1941; **The Petrified Forest**, 1936; Pippi, 2006; The Plot Thickens, 1936; The Polar Express, 2004; Prince of Darkness, 1987; The Rainmakers, 1935; Resurrecting the Champ, 2007; **Riffraff**, 1936; Samuel Fuller's Street of No Return, 1991; **Scarecrow**, 1973; **Seabiscuit**, 2003; **Starlight Hotel**, 1988; **The Stratton Story**, 1949; **Sullivan's Travels**, 1941; Superman and the Mole-Men, 1951; Syncopation, 1942; **Thank You for Smoking**, 2006; That I May Live, 1937; **Them!**, 1954; There Goes My Girl, 1937; They Wanted to Marry, 1937; Things That Hang from Trees, 2006; **The Time of Your Life**, 1948; Tombstone Terror, 1935; **The Treasure of the Sierra Madre**, 1948; **The Trouble with Harry**, 1955; **12 Monkeys**, 1995; 24 Hour Party People, 2002; The Ultimate Life, 2013; **Union Depot**, 1932; **Vagabond**, 1985; **Wanda**, 1971; **The Way of All Flesh**, 1927; The Way of All Flesh, 1941; Wendy and Lucy, 2008; **Wild Boys of the Road**, 1933; **Wyatt Earp**, 1994; Young Fugitives, 1938.

Hollywood Blacklist (those Hollywood personalities and other personnel in the industry, including television in NYC, as well as academics, who were blacklisted during the witch-hunting actions of U.S. Senator Joseph McCarthy and the U.S. House Un-American Activities Committee during the late 1940s and early 1950s): Chaplin, 1992; Dash and Lilly, 1999 (made-for-TV; based on the lives of Lillian Hellman and Dashiell Hammett, the latter having been imprisoned and blacklisted for previous Communist activities); Fear on Trial, 1975 (made-for-TV; based on blacklisted TV/radio personality John Henry Faulk); **The Front**, 1976; **Good Night, and Good Luck**, 2005; Guilty by Suspicion, 1991; The Majestic, 2001; **Marathon Man**, 1976; **One of the Hollywood Ten**, 2000; **Trumbo**, 2015; **The Way We Were**, 1973.

Home Front (WWII): **Adventure for Two**, 1945 (U.K.); Air Raid Wardens, 1943 (U.S.); Allotment Wives, 1945 (U.S.); Blondie for Victory,

1942 (U.S.); Bridge to the Sun, 1961 (Japan); **Follow the Boys**, 1944 (U.S.); **Hail the Conquering Hero**, 1944 (U.S.); **The Human Comedy**, 1943 (U.S.); The Impatient Years, 1944 (U.S.); **Mrs. Miniver**, 1942 (U.K.); Music for Millions, 1944 (U.S.); **Our Vines Have Tender Grapes**, 1945 (U.S.); **Radio Days**, 1987 (U.S.); Rationing, 1944 (U.S.); Rosie the Riveter, 1944 (U.S.); **Since You Went Away**, 1944 (U.S.); Song of the Open Road, 1944 (U.S.); **Tender Comrade**, 1944 (U.S.); **This Above All**, 1942 (U.K.); **The Very Thought of You**, 1944 (U.S.); Victory Song, 1945 (Japan); **The War Against Mrs. Hadley**, 1942 (U.S.); **When Willie Comes Marching Home**, 1950 (U.S.); Youth Runs Wild, 1944 (U.S.).

Home Invasions: Act of Valor, 2012; The Aggression Scale, 2012; The Air I Breathe, 2007; Angst, 1983; Assassins, 1995; Bad Boys, 1995; **Batman**, 1989; **Batman Forever**, 1995; **Beverly Hills Cop**, 1989; The Big Lebowski, 1998; Black Christmas, 1974; Black Christmas, 2006; **Blind Alley**, 1939; Boxcar Bertha, 1972; Boys Don't Cry, 1999; The Cable Guy, 1996; **Cape Fear**, 1962; **Cape Fear**, 1991; Cassandra's Dream, 2007; Cheery Tree Lane, 2010; **A Christmas Story**, 1983; The Chronicles of Reddick, 2004; **A Clockwork Orange**, 1971; **Close Encounters of the Third Kind**, 1977; Cobra, 1986; Coffy, 1973; The Collector, 2009; Contagion, 2011; Contraband, 2012; Copycat, 1995; Crime Wave, 1954; **Cul-de-sac**, 1966; Curfew, 1989; The Dark Hours, 2005; **The Dark Knight Rises**, 2012; **The Dark Past**, 1948; Daybreakers, 2009; Death Weekend, 1976; **Death Wish**, 1974; Desperado, 1995; **The Desperate Hours**, 1955; The Desperate Hours, 1990; Devil in a Blue Dress, 1995; The Devil's Own, 1997; **Dial M for Murder**, 1954; **Escape in the Desert**, 1945; Fast Five, 2011; **Fatal Attraction**, 1987; Fear, 1996; The Fear Inside, 1992; Felon, 2008; Fight for Your Life, 1977; Firewall, 2006; Flesh and Bone, 1993; Foxy Brown, 1974; Frequency, 2000; **The Fugitive**, 1993; Funny Games, 1997; Funny Games, 2008; **A Funny Thing Happened on the Way to the Forum**, 1966; Gangster Squad, 2013; The Girl Next Door, 2004; **G-Men**, 1935; **The Great Train Robbery**, 1979; Grosse Point Blank, 1997; The Hand That Rocks the Cradle, 1992; **He Ran All the Way**, 1951; Henry: Portrait of a Serial Killer, 1990; Hesher, 2010; Hider in the House, 1991; High Tension, 2005; **Home Alone**, 1990; Home Invasion, 2012; Hostage, 2005; The House on the Edge of the Park, 1985; **The Hurt Locker**, 2009; If I Die Before I Wake, 1998; In Cold Blood, 1967; **In the Line of Fire**, 1993; In Their Skin, 2012; Inside, 2007; **The Ipcress File**, 1965; **Invaders from Mars**, 1953; Invaders from Mars, 1986; The Jackal, 1997; **Key Largo**, 1948; **Kidnapped**, 1938; **Kidnapped**, 1960; **Kidnapped**, 1971; Kill the Irishman, 2011; **Lady in a Cage**, 1964; Lakeview Terrace, 2008; Last Action Hero, 1993; Last House on Dead End Street, 1977; The Last House on the Left, 1972; The Last House on the Left, 2009; Law Abiding Citizen, 2009; **Lethal Weapon 2**, 1989; Limitless, 2011; **The Lincoln Lawyer**, 2011; **Live Free or Die Hard**, 2007; The Long Kiss Goodnight, 1996; The Lost Boys, 1987; The Lovely Bones, 2009; Machete, 2010; **Manhunter**, 1986; **Marathon Man**, 1976; Martin, 1976; Martyrs, 2008; **Nevada Smith**, 1966; The Omega Man, 1971; **The Outlaw Josey Wales**, 1976; Pacific Heights, 1990; Pain & Gain, 2013; Panic Room, 2002; **Patriot Games**, 1993; The Penthouse, 1967; The People Under the Stairs, 1991; **A Perfect Murder**, 1998; **The Petrified Forest**, 1936; **Point Blank**, 1967; Posse from Hell, 1961; A Prayer for the Dying, 1987; Prisoners, 2013; The Proposition, 2006; **The Prowler**, 1951; The Purge, 2013; The Ref, 1994; Rolling Thunder, 1977; Savages, 2012; **Scream**, 1996; **The Seven Ups**, 1973; Shoot Out, 1971; Silent House, 2011; Single White Female, 1992; Skyfall, 2012; **Something of Value**, 1957; The Sorcerer's Apprentice, 2010; **Sorry, Wrong Number**, 1948; The Strangers, 2008; Straw Dogs, 1971; Straw Dogs, 2011; **Suddenly**, 1954; Supremacy, 2014; Them, 2006; **Thief**, 1981; Tiger House, 2014; Trespass, 2011; **Unbreakable**, 2000; **The Unforgiven**, 1960; Underworld: Awakening, 2012; **Unknown**, 2011; Unlawful Entry, 1992; Unleashed, 2005; Visiting Hours, 1982; **Wait Until Dark**, 1967; When a Stranger Calls, 1979; When a Stranger Calls, 2006;

When a Stranger Calls Back, 1993; White Sands, 1992; **The Whole Town's Talking**, 1935; **The Wild Geese**, 1978; **Will Penny**, 1968; **Year of the Dragon**, 1985; You're Next, 2011.

Homeless Children (also see Adoption; Ophans, this index): **American Heart**, 1993; **Annie**, 1982; Annie, 1999 (made-for-TV); Annie, 2014; The Betty Hutton Show, 1959-1960 (TV series; "Jenny," 1959 episode); Beyond the Blackboard, 2011 (made-for-TV); Border Street, 1950; **China Sky**, 1945; Chiquititas, 2013-2015 (TV series); Curly Sue, 1991; **Convicts**, 1991; Dr. Who, 2005 (TV series; 'The Empty Child," 2005 episode); **The Eddy Duchin Story**, 1956; The Giants, 2012; God Bless the Child, 1988 (made-for-TV); **The Grapes of Wrath**, 1940; Highway to Heaven, 1984-1989 (TV series; "Alone," 1986 episode); Johnny, 1999; **The Kid with a Bike**, 2012; Lucky Trouble, 2011; **Manhattan Melodrama**, 1934; **The Night of the Hunter**, 1955; No Place Like Home, 1989 (made-for-TV); **Oliver!**, 1968; **Olivier, Oliver Twist**, 1922; **Oliver Twist**, 1951; **Oliver Twist**, 2005; **Olivier**, 1992; Pixote, 1981; Podranka, 1977; Solo Dio mi fermera, 1957; Song of Arizona, 1946; **Sparrows**, 1926; **The Story of G.I. Joe**, 1945; The Story of Me, 2009; Stray Dogs, 2004; **These Wilder Years**, 1956; **The Three Godfathers**, 1916; **Three Godfathers**, 1936; **3 Godfathers**, 1948; **To Hell and Back**, 1955; **Wild Boys of the Road**, 1933; **Woman of the Year**, 1942; **The Young Lions**, 1958.

Horse Races, Horse Racing and Horses: Angel, 1937; **Anna Karenina**, 1935; Atta Boy's Last Chance, 1916; Bandits of the West, 1953; Beautiful Joe, 2000; **The Belles of St. Trinian's**, 1954; Big Boy, 1930; The Big Race, 1934; The Big Street, 1942; **Bite the Bullet**, 1975; Black Beauty, 1933; Black Beauty, 1971; **Black Beauty**, 1994; Black Gold, 1947; **The Black Stallion**, 1979; The Black Stallion Returns, 1983; Blondie's Holiday, 1947; **Blue Skies**, 1946; The Bold Frontiersman, 1948; **Boots Malone**, 1952; Born to the Saddle, 1953; The Boy from Indiana, 1950; Boy Woodburn, 1922; **Brewster's Millions**, 1945; **Brewster's Millions**, 1985; Broadway Bill, 1934; **Broadway Melody of 1938**, 1937; Calamity Jane and Sam Bass, 1949; **Casey's Shadow**, 1978; Catch the Dream, 2013; **The Champ**, 1931; **The Champ**, 1979; Champions, 1984; **Charlie Chan at the Racetrack**, 1936; The Christmas Stallion, 1992 (made-for-TV); **Closely Watched Trains**, 1967; Come On George!, 1939; **Conspiracy Theory**, 1997; Counterfeit Love, 1923; Country Fair, 1937; Courage of Black Beauty, 1957; Coyote Trails, 1935; Crazy Over Horses, 1951; **The Crowd Roars**, 1938; **A Day at the Races**, 1937; A Dead Certainty, 1920; Dead Heat, 2002; **Dear Brigitte**, 1965; Death Force, 1989; The Derby Stallion, 2005; Don't Bet on Blondes, 1935; **Down Argentine Way**, 1940; The Fabulous Suzanne, 1946; Fast Companions, 1932; 50 Million Frenchmen, 1931; The Fighting Chance, 1955; The Flame of Araby, 1951; **The Flamingo Kid**, 1984; The Flying Fifty-Five, 1924; 40 Pounds of Trouble, 1962; Free and Easy, 1941; The Gay Deception, 1935; Gentleman from Dixie, 1941; A Girl in Every Port, 1952; Going Places, 1938; Goin' to Town, 1935; The Golden Stallion, 1927; The Golden Stallion, 1949; **The Great Dan Patch**, 1949; The Great Mike, 1944; Green Grass of Wyoming, 1948; **The Grifters**, 1990; **Guys and Dolls**, 1955; Harmony Trail, 1944; Harrigan's Kid, 1943; He Married His Wife, 1940; Heart of Virginia, 1948; **Hidalgo**, 2004; Hit the Saddle, 1937; **Home in Indiana**, 1944; Horse Crazy, 2001; **The Horse Whisperer**, 1998; In Old Cheyenne, 1931; It Ain't Hay, 1943; Just Tony, 1922; **Kentucky**, 1938; Kentucky Blue Streak, 1935; **The Killing**, 1956; King of the Wild Horses, 1933; King of the Wild Stallions, 1959; Kissing Cup's Race, 1920; Konga, the Wild Stallion, 1939; The Lady's from Kentucky, 1939; **The Last Time I Saw Paris**, 1954; **The Lawless Breed**, 1953; **The Lemon Drop Kid**, 1951; Let It Ride, 1989; **Little Miss Marker**, 1934; Little Miss Marker, 1980; Little Miss Thoroughbred, 1938; The Lone Ranger, 1938; **The Lone Ranger**, 1956; **The Lone Ranger**, 2013; Long Odds, 1922; Long Shot, 1939; Lost Stallions: The Journey Home, 2008; The Man from Button Willow, 1965; **The Man from Snowy River**,

1983; Michael Shayne, Private Detective, 1940; Midnight Stallion, 2013; **The Misfits**, 1961; Mr. Celebrity, 1941; **Moon Over Miami**, 1941; Mustang!, 1959; Mustang Country, 1976; **My Brother Talks to Horses**, 1947; **My Fair Lady** 1964; **My Friend Flicka**, 1943; **My Lucky Star**, 2012; A Nag in the Bag, 1938; **National Velvet**, 1945; On the Nose, 2001; On the Right Track, 1981; The Painted Stallion, 1937; The Payoff, 1935; **Phar Lap**, 1984; Play-Girl, 1932; The Pope of Greenwich Village, 1984; Powder River Rustlers, 1949; Pride of the Blue Grass, 1939; Queen of Broadway, 1942; Queen of the Turf, 1921; **The Quiet Man**, 1952; Racing Lady, 1937; Racing Luck, 1935; Racing Luck, 1948; Racing Stripes, 2005; The Rainbow Jacket, 1954; Rare Breed, 1984; Ready to Run, 2000 (made-for-TV); Red Fork Range, 1931; The Red Stallion, 1947; The Reivers, 1969; Riders of the Black Hills, 1938; **Riding High**, 1950; Ridin' Thru, 1934; **The Rocking Horse Winner**, 1950; Run for the Roses, 1977; **Saratoga**, 1937; **Seabiscuit**, 2003; **Secretariat**, 2010; Sergeant Murphy, 1938; Shergar, 1999; Silks and Saddles, 1936; **Sing, You Sinners**, 1938; Snowfire, 1958; A Song of Kentucky, 1929; **Sorrowful Jones**, 1949; South of Caliente, 1951; The Speed Maniac, 1919; Speed to Burn, 1938; **Spirit: Stallion of the Cimarron**, 2002; Sport of Kings, 1947; The Sport Parade, 1932; **Sporting Blood**, 1931; Sporting Blood, 1940; Sporting Chance, 1931; A Sporting Double, 1922; Sporting Love, 1936; Stable Companions, 1922; **Stablemates**, 1938; The Stallion, 1972 (made-for-TV); Starlight, the Untamed, 1925; **The Sting**, 1973; **The Story of Seabiscuit**, 1949; Straight Place and Show, 1938; **The Sundowners**, 1960; The Texan, 1932; That Gang of Mine, 1940; That's My Man, 1947; The Thoroughbred, 1925; Thoroughbred, 1935; Thoroughbreds Don't Cry, 1937; Thunder, 1977-1978 (TV series); **The Time of Your Life**, 1948; **Three Men on a Horse**, 1936; **Thunderhead—Son of Flicka**, 1945; Torchy Gets Her Man, 1938; Trail to San Antone, 1947; Trainer and Temptress, 1925; The True Story of Seabiscuit, 2003 (made-for-TV); The Turf Conspiracy, 1918; Two in Revolt, 1936; Two Thoroughbreds, 1939; The Unknown Ranger, 1936; Wall Street Cowboy, 1939; **War Horse**, 2011; What Price Loving Cup?, 1923; **White Mischief**, 1988; Wild Horse Mesa, 1947; The Wild Stallion, 2009; Win, Place or Steal, 1975; Wine, Women and Horses, 1937; **Wings of the Morning**, 1937; The Winner's Circle, 1948; You Can't Buy Luck, 1937; The Young Black Stallion, 2003.

Housing Shortages: The Big Lift, 1950 (during post-WWII Berlin, Germany); **A Foreign Affair**, 1948 (during post-WWII in Berlin, Germany); Government Girl, 1943 (during WWII in Washington, D.C.); Johnny Doesn't Live Here Anymore, 1944 (during WWII in New York, N.Y.); Meet the People, 1944 (during WWII in New York, N.Y.); **The More the Merrier**, 1943 (during WWII in Washington, D.C.); **Since You Went Away**, 1944 (during WWII, U.S.); So This Is Washington, 1943 (during WWII in Washington, D.C.); **Standing Room Only**, 1944 (during WWII in Washington, D.C.); **Walk, Don't Run**, 1966 (during the Summer Olympic Games of 1964 in Tokyo, Japan); **Without Love**, 1945 (during WWII in Washington, D.C.).

Human Guinea Pigs (in medical operations, eugenics and scientific experiments): After the Truth, 1999 (Joseph Mengele); And the Violins Stopped Playing, 1981 (Joseph Mengele); The Andromeda Strain, 1971; The Andromeda Strain, 2008 (TV miniseries); **The Boys from Brazil**, 1978 (Joseph Mengele); Brain Twisters, 1991; Bug, 2006; The Caller, 1987; **The Chairman**, 1969; Commando Mengele, 1987 (Joseph Mengele); Control, 2004; Cube Zero, 2005; Danger 5, 2011- (TV series; "Lizard Soldiers of the Third Reich," 2012 episode; "Revenge of the Lizardmen," 2015 episode; Joseph Mengele in both episodes); Devil's Plot, 1948; **Dr. Ehrlich's Magic Bullet**, 1940; **Dr. Jekyll and Mr. Hyde**, 1920; **Dr. Jekyll and Mr. Hyde**, 1931; **Dr. Jekyll and Mr. Hyde**, 1941; The Experiment, 2002; **Fantastic Voyage**, 1966; Flesh for Frankenstein, 1974; Frozen Scream, 1975; The German Doctor, 2014 (Joseph Mengele); Green Light, 1937; **The Grey Zone**, 2002 (Joseph

Mengele); Heroes of the North, 2010-2011 (TV series; Joseph Mengele); Human Experiments, 1979; The Hydric Zone, 2015- (TV series; "Rise of the Mutant Wetlands," 2015 episode; Joseph Mengele); I.Q., 1994; Ilsa: She Wolf of the SS, 1975; **The Invisible Man**, 1933; **The Invisible Man Returns**, 1940; Kessler, 1981 (TV miniseries; Joseph Mengele); The Mad Doctor of Market Street, 1942; The Mad Monster, 1942; The Man with Nine Lives, 1940; The Manster, 1959; **Marathon Man**, 1976 (role modeled on Joseph Mengele); Maruta 2: Laboratory of the Devil, 1992 (Japanese eugenics on captives in Manchuria during WWII); Men Behind the Sun, 1989 (Japanese eugenics on captives in Manchuria during WWII); Out of the Ashes, 2003 (made-for-TV; Joseph Mengele); The Passing, 1985; Playing for Time, 1980 (made-for-TV; Joseph Mengele); Push, 2009; Saru, 2003; **Schindler's List**, 1993 (Joseph Mengele); **The Story of Louis Pasteur**, 1936; Subject Two, 2006; Surf Nazis Must Die, 1987 (Joseph Mengele); Terminal Choice, 1985; **Tobor the Great**, 1954; The Unborn, 2009 (Joseph Mengele); Walking the Dead, 2000- (TV series; "Yahrzeit: Part 1," "Yahrzeit: Part 2," 2007 episodes; Joseph Mengele); Whiffs, 1975; Wit, 2001 (made-for-TV); Women's Camp 119, 1977; Wyrmwood: Road of the Dead, 2014; **Yellow Jack**, 1938.

Hurricanes (also see Typhoons, this index): **Abandon Ship!**, 1957; Adventure Girl, 1934; **The Adventures of Baron Munchausen**, 1989; **Band of Angels**, 1957; **Beasts of the Southern Wild**, 2012; Beyond the Poseidon Adventure, 1979; **The Black Stallion**, 1979; **The Bounty**, 1984; **Clash of the Titans**, 1981; **The Count of Monte Cristo**, 1934; Crash Landing, 2005; **The Curious Case of Benjamin Button**, 2008; Earthstorm, 2006 (made-for-TV); **Flipper**, 1996; Flood, 2007; Forces of Nature, 1999; 40 Days and Nights, 2012; Four Mothers, 1941; 14 Hours, 2005 (made-for-TV; tropical storm Allison of 2001); Haunted Harbor, 1944; **A High Wind in Jamaica**, 1965; Hours, 2013 (Hurricane Katrina of 2005); **The Hurricane**, 1937; Hurricane, 1974 (made-for-TV); Hurricane, 1979; Hurricane Island, 1951; **In the Heart of the Sea**, 2015; Invasion, 2005-2006 (TV series); Journey 2: The Mysterious Island, 2012; **Key Largo**, 1948; The Lost Continent, 1968; **Mysterious Island**, 1961; The New Adventures of Tarzan, 1935 (serial); Nights in Rodanthe, 2008; **Nim's Island**, 2008; Orphans, 1998; **Our Man Flint**, 1966; **The Perfect Storm**, 2000; Phantom Ship, 1935; Port Sinister, 1953; **Portrait of Jennie**, 1949; **The Poseidon Adventure**, 1972; **The Prisoner of Shark Island**, 1936; Return to Boggy Creek, 1977; A Rising Tide, 2015 (Hurricane Sandy of 2012); Salty, 1973; Sea Devils, 1937; She Gods of Shark Reef, 1958; Sheltered, 2010; Shutter Island, 2010; **Six Days Seven Nights**, 1998; **Slattery's Hurricane**, 1949; **Souls at Sea**, 1937; **Souls for Sale**, 1923; The Stars Fell on Henrietta, 1995; **Steamboat Bill Jr.**, 1928; Trader Tom of the China Seas, 1954 (serial); When Tomorrow Comes, 1939; Yellowneck, 1955. Note: For more information on hurricanes throughout history, see my book, *Darkest Hours: A Narrative Encyclopedia of Worldwide Disasters from Ancient Times to the Present* (Nelson-Hall, 1976).

Hypnosis, Hypnotism and Hypnotists: **Abbott and Costello Meet Frankenstein**, 1948; Abbott and Costello Meet the Killer, Boris Karloff, 1949; The Adventures of Rocky and Bullwinkle, 2000; The Affairs of Anatol, 1921; Alice, 1990; Amy George, 2011; Archangel, 1991; Atlantis, the Lost Continent, 1961; Audrey Rose, 1977; Battle Beneath the Earth, 1968; The Bells, 1918; **Beautiful People**, 1999; **Bewitched**, 1945; The Black Cat, 1984; The Black Doll, 1938; **Black Magic**, 1949; Black Shadows, 1920; **Blithe Spirit**, 1945; **Blind Alley**, 1939; The Blood Beast Terror, 1969; Blood of Dracula, 1957; The Bride and the Beast, 1958; Bride of the Monster, 1956; The Brides of Fu Manchu, 1966; **Broadway Danny Rose**, 1984; **The Cabinet of Dr. Caligari**, 1921; Calling Dr. Death, 1943; Captain America, 1944; Captain Kronos—Vampire Hunter, 1974; **Carefree**, 1938; Carnival Magic, 1981; Carry on Spying, 1964; The Case of Becky, 1921; Chandu the Magician, 1932; Charlie Chan at Treasure Island, 1939; **Close Your Eyes,**

2002; Communion, 1989; Conan the Barbarian, 1982; Contamination, 1982; Count Yorga, Vampire, 1970; **The Court Jester**, 1956; Cowboy from Brooklyn, 1938; The Crawling Eye, 1958; Cure, 2001; The Curse of the Alpha Stone, 1985; **Curse of the Demon**, 1958; The Curse of the Jade Scorpion, 2001; **The Dark Past**, 1948; The Dark Tower, 1943; Dead Again, 1991; Dead on Sight, 1994; The Dead Pit, 1989; Devil Doll, 1964; The Devil Rides Out, 1968; The Devil's Mask, 1946; The Devonsville Terror, 1983; Disturbing Behavior, 1998; **Divorce American Style**, 1967; Doctor Dracula, 1978; Dr. Morelle: The Case of the Missing Heiress, 1949; Cat-Women of the Moon, 1953; **Dracula**, 1931; **Dracula**, 1979; **Dracula**, 1992; **Dracula: Dead and Loving It**, 1995; **Dracula Has Risen from His Grave**, 1969; Dracula—Prince of Darkness, 1966; **Dracula's Daughter**, 1936; Elvira's Haunted Hills, 2002; Evil Deeds, 2012; The Evil of Frankenstein, 1964; Exorcist II: The Heretic, 1977; Faces in the Crowd, 2011; Fear in the Night, 1947; The Fighting Gringo, 1917; **Flash Gordon**, 1936; Four Rooms, 1995; The Frozen Ghost, 1945; Future Shock, 1994; Girl Crazy, 1932; Ghost Chasers, 1951; Glitch!, 1988; **The Great Buck Howard**, 2009; Happiness Runs, 2010; Her Jungle Love, 1938; Hold That Hypnotist, 1957; Horrors of the Black Museum, 1959; **The Hot Rock**, 1972; **House of Dracula**, 1945; How to Be Very, Very Popular, 1955; How to Make a Monster, 1958; Hypnosis, 1963; The Hypnotist, 2001; Hypnotized, 1932; I Was a Teenage Werewolf, 1957; **The Illusionist**, 2006; I'm from the City, 1938; Invasion of the Star Creatures, 1962; The Invisible Avenger, 1958; Island Empire, 2006; J. D.'s Revenge, 1976; Judgment, 1992; **The Jungle Book**, 1942; **The Jungle Book**, 1967; The Keeper, 1976; **Kim**, 1950; King of the Zombies, 1941; The Killer Eye, 1999; Kiss the Girls, 1997; Kisses for Breakfast, 1941; Konga, 1961; **Let's Kill Uncle Before Uncle Kills Us**, 1966; Lizzie, 1957; London After Midnight, 1927; Lord Love a Duck, 1966; Lost in a Harem, 1944; Love at First Bite, 1979; The Love Captive, 1934; The Magician, 1926; The Man in the Moonlight, 1919; **The Man Who Knew Too Much**, 1934; The Man Who Saw Tomorrow, 1922; **The Man with Two Faces**, 1934; **The Manchurian Candidate**, 1962; **Mark of the Vampire**, 1935; The Mask of Diijon, 1946; The Matrimonial Bed, 1930; Mausoleum, 1983; Mesmerized, 1986; Messengers, 2004; **Mirage**, 1965; Mr. Hex, 1946; Mountain Rhythm, 1939; **Mountains of the Moon**, 1990; **Nicholas and Alexandra**, 1971; No Dessert, Dad, Till You Mow the Lawn, 1994; Nothing But the Night, 1975; On a Clear Day You Can See Forever, 1970; **On Her Majesty's Secret Service**, 1969; One Hour Before Dawn, 1920; Operation Kid Brother, 1967; **Palmy Days**, 1931; Paranormal Xperience 3D, 2011; **The Pirate**, 1948; The Pit and the Pendulum, 2009; The Plague of the Zombies, 1966; Possession, 2008; Psycho Beach Party, 2000; Raising Cain, 1992; **Rasputin**, 1985; **Rasputin and the Empress**, 1932; **Rasputin the Mad Monk**, 1966; Rawhead Rex, 1987; **The Razor's Edge**, 1946; Reckless, 1995; Revenge of the Ninji, 1983; **Road to Rio**, 1947; **Running Wild**, 1927; The Search for Bridey Murphy, 1956; **The Secret Life of Walter Mitty**, 1947; **The Seven-Per-Cent Solution**, 1976; **The Seventh Veil**, 1946; **The Shadow**, 1994; Shadow of Chinatown, 1936; The She Creature, 1956; She's Got Everything, 1937; Sin You Sinners, 1963; Sing Your Worries Away, 1942; **Sisters**, 1973; **Stir of Echoes**, 1999; Sum of Existence, 2005; **Svengali**, 1931; **Tales of Terror**, 1962; A Taste of Blood, 1967; The Terror, 1963; Terror, 1979; Theater of Death, 1967; **The Thief of Bagdad**, 1940; **Thirteen Women**, 1932; **The Three Faces of Eve**, 1957; The Tomb of Ligeia, 1965; Tomie, 1999; Trilby, 1923; Twilight of the Ice Nymphs, 1997; The Two-Soul Woman, 1918; The Undead, 1957; Under the Top, 1919; Undersea Kingdom, 1936; The Unholy Night, 1929; Unmasked, 1929; The Untameable, 1923; Vampire at Midnight, 1988; Violent Love, 1967; Voodoo Man, 1944; What Happened Then?, 1934; **Whirlpool**, 1949; White Goddess, 1953; Wild Wild West, 1999; The Witch, 1916; **The Woman in Green**, 1945; **The Year My Voice Broke**, 1987; **Zelig**, 1983.

Hypochondriacs: All Mine to Give, 1957; **Amelie**, 2001; **The Aviator**,

2004; **The Band Wagon**, 1953; Bandits, 2001; Born Romantic, 2000; Burn Notice, 2007-2013 (TV series); Carry On Matron, 1972; Checking Out, 1989; **The Citadel**, 1938; Crimes at the Dark House, 1943; **A Day at the Races**, 1937; Day of the Wacko, 2002; **Dr. Bull**, 1933; Dr. Socrates, 1935; Dogville, 2004; Down to Earth, 1917; **The Egg and I**, 1947; Emma, 1972 (TV miniseries); Emma, 1996 (made-for-TV); Ethan Frome, 1993; Ferris Bueller's Day Off, 1986; **The Gangster**, 1947; **Gold Diggers of 1937**, 1936; The Great Madcap, 1977; A Guy and a Gal, 1975; **Hannah and Her Sisters**, 1986; Hav Plenty, 1997; Home, 2009; How I Was Systematically Destroyed by an Idiot, 1983; Hypochondriac, 1979; I Take This Woman, 1940; In the Land of Women, 2007; An Indecent Obsession, 1985; Innerspace, 1987; Le Corbeau: The Raven, 1948; **The Little Shop of Horrors**, 1960; Lovely Loneliness, 2009; Madagascar, 2005; Meet the Girls, 1938; A Night of Terror, 1937; **Not as a Stranger**, 1955; **The Odd Couple**, 1968; **Piku**, 2015; Pinching Penny, 2011; **Play It Again, Sam**, 1972; Poison Ivy, 1992; **Pollyanna**, 1960; **Red Desert**, 1965; The Saddest Music in the World, 2003; Saddle Pals, 1947; **Send Me No Flowers**, 1964; **Sorry, Wrong Number**, 1948; Sorry, Wrong Number, 1989 (made-for-TV); **The Street with No Name**, 1948; **The Strawberry Blonde**, 1941; **Swing High, Swing Low**, 1937; Uptown Girls, 2003; Ship Ahoy, 1942; Supercondriaque, 2014; The Switch, 2010; Trilogy: Two, 2002; 2 Days in Paris, 2007; **Up in Arms**, 1944; Wake Up Love, 1997; **Whoopee!**, 1930; **Why Worry?**, 1923; Wild and Wonderful, 1964; Wonderful Summer, 2010; You Really Got Me, 2001.

Illegal Immigrants: A.C.A.B., 2012 (Italy); Across the Line, 2000 (Mexicans in U.S.); Across the Universe, 2007 (England); **Arch of Triumph**, 1948 (France); **Babel**, 2006 (Mexicans in U.S.); Bad Lieutenant: Port of Call New Orleans, 2009 (Senegalese in U.S.); Beautiful People, 2000 (Yugoslavians in England); Best Seller, 1987 (U.S.); A Better Life, 2011 (Mexicans in U.S.); The Big Lift, 1950 (Germany); Biutiful, 2010 (Spain); Black Gold, 1947 (Chinese in U.S.); **Black Hand**, 1950 (Italians in U.S.); Bolivia, 2003 (Bolivian in Argentina); The Border, 1982 (Mexicans in U.S.); Border Cop, 1980 (Mexicans in U.S.); **Border Incident**, 1949 (Mexicans in U.S.); Border Lost, 2008 (Mexicans in U.S.); Borderline, 1980 (Mexicans in U.S.); Born in East L.A., 1987 (U.S. citizen and Mexicans in Mexico and U.S.); **Bread and Roses**, 2002 (Mexicans in U.S.); Brothers in Trouble, 1997 (Pakistanis in England); **Casablanca**, 1942 (French Morocco); **Changeling**, 2008 (Canadians in U.S.); **The Class**, 2008 (France); **Code Unknown: Incomplete Tales of Several Journeys**, 2000 (France); Cordon, 2014- (TV series; Antwerp, Belgium); The Corruptor, 1999 (Chinese in U.S.); **The Counterfeit Traitor**, 1962 (Jew hiding aboard ship from Denmark to Sweden during WWII); The Craic, 1999 (Irish in Australia); **Crash**, 2005 (U.S.); Crossing Over, 2009 (Australians, Bangladesh, Koreans, Mexicans, Nigerians in U.S.); Daughter of the Tong, 1939 (Chinese in U.S.); **The Diary of Anne Frank**, 1959 (Jews hiding in Amsterdam, Netherlands, during WWII); The Diary of Anne Frank, 2009 (Jews hiding in Amsterdam, Netherlands, during WWII); Dirty Pretty Things, 2003 (Nigerians in U.S.); Distant Lights, 2003 (Ukrainians in Germany); Dolan's Cadillac, 2009 (Mexicans in U.S.); Eden Is West, 2009 (France); The Edge of Heaven, 2008 (Turks in Germany); El Norte, 1984 (Guatemalans in U.S.); **Elysium**, 2013 (Earth and exclusive space station); Eternity and a Day, 1998 (Albanian in Greece); Exiles, 2004 (French in Algeria); **Exodus**, 1960 (Jews on board a ship in British-controlled Cyprus); The Fairy, 2012 (France); Fast Food Nation, 2006 (Mexicans in U.S.); 15 Minutes, 2001 (Eastern Europeans in U.S.); **A Foreign Affair**, 1948 (Germany); Freeloaders, 2012 (U.S.); From Mexico with Love, 2009 (Mexicans in U.S.); Frontera, 2014 (Mexicans in U.S.); **Frozen River**, 2008 (Canadians in U.S.); The Garden Murder Case, 1936 (U.S.); **The Glass Wall**, 1953 (U.S.); The Guru, 2003 (India natives in U.S.); **Haemoo**, 2014 (Chinese in Korea); Happenstance, 2001 (France); Harsh Times, 2006 (Mexicans in U.S.); **Hold Back the Dawn**, 1941 (Europeans in Mexico); The Home Song Stories, 2008

(Chinese in Australia); I Witness, 2003 (Mexicans in U.S.); Illegal, 2011 (Russians in Belgium); Then Illegal Immigrant, 1985 (Chinese in U.S.); Immigrants, 2008 (U.S.); **In America**, 2003 (Irish in U.S.); Innocent, 2005 (Canada); Journey of Hope, 1991 (Turks in Switzerland); Judith, 1966 (German Nazi hiding in Israel in 1948); **The Juggler**, 1953 (Jews in Israel in 1949); **King of California**, 2007 (Chinese boat people in U.S.); King of Thieves, 2004 (Germany); La nostra vita, 2010 (Italy); La vida precoz y breve de Sabina Rivas, 2012 (Hondurans, Mexicans in U.S.); Ladron que roba a ladron, 2007 (Mexicans in U.S.); Last Rites, 1988 (U.S.); Le Havre, 2011 (France); Le petit lieutenant, 2006 (Russian in France); **Lethal Weapon 4**, 1998 (Chinese in U.S.); **Lone Star**, 1996 (Mexicans in U.S.); The Long Run, 2001 (Namibian in South Africa); Lost Souls, 1980 (Chinese in Hong Kong); Lovers, 1999 (Yugoslavian in France); Machete, 2010 (Mexicans in U.S.); Mala Noche, 1986 (Mexicans in U.S.); Man in the Shadow, 1958 (Mexicans in U.S.); Maria Full of Grace, 2004 (Columbian girl and Mexicans in U.S.); The Master, 1989 (Chinese in U.S.); **Men in Black**, 1997 (Other World creatures on Earth); **Men in Black II**, 2002 (Other World creatures on Earth); **Morituri**, 1965 (Jew on board a German freighter during WWII); **A Most Wanted Man**, 2014 (Germany); My Father's Guests, 2010 (France); My Fellow Americans, 1996 (Mexicans in U.S.); Never Forever, 2007 (Koreans in U.S.); Northless, 2009 (Mexicans in U.S.); On the Border, 1998 (made-for-TV; Mexicans in U.S.); **Panic in the Streets**, 1950 (U.S.); Paraiso Travel, 2008 (Colombians in U.S.); Path of Hope, 1952 (Italians in France); **Pay or Die**, 1960 (Italians in U.S.); Prime Suspect 6: The Last Witness, 2003 (TV miniseries; Yugoslavians in U.S.); Princesas, 2006 (Spain); The Puffy Chair, 2005 (U.S.); Quicksand, 2003 (Monaco); Riding Speed, 1934 (Mexicans in U.S.); Room to Rent, 2001 (Egyptian in England); Row Your Boat, 1999 (Chinese in U.S.); Ruby & Quentin, 2003 (France); Samba, 2014 (France); **The Search**, 1948 (Germany); Secret Service of the Air, 1936 (U.S.); Shelter Me, 2007 (Italy); Shinjuku Incident, 2009 (Chinese in Japan); Sin Nombre, 2009 (Hondurans, Mexicans in U.S.) Spanglish, 2004 (Mexicans in U.S.); Spare Parts, 2003 (Croatians in Italy); **Sugar**, 2008 (Dominican in U.S.); Swallowtail Butterfly, 1996 (Japan); Sweet Fifteen, 1990 (made-for-TV; Mexicans in U.S.); **Swing Vote**, 2008 (Mexicans in U.S.); **Sword in the Desert**, 1949 (Jews in British-controlled Palestine); Tequilas Sunrise, 1988 (Mexicans in U.S.); **The Terminal**, 2004 (U.S.); Terraferma, 2011 (Sicily); That Girl in Yellow Boots, 2011 (India); **The Three Burials of Melquiades Estrada**, 2006 (Mexicans in U.S.); Three Worlds, 2013 (France); **To Have and Have Not**, 1944 (French Martinque); The Tong Man, 1919 (Chinese in U.S.); **Under the Same Moon**, 2008 (Mexicans in the U.S.); Undocumented, 2010 (Mexicans in U.S.); **Unknown**, 2011 (Germany); Up and Down, 2004 (Czech Republic); Vampires, 2011 (Belgium); **A View from the Bridge**, 1962 (Italians in U.S.); The Visitor, 2008 (Senegalese, Syrians in U.S.); The War Boys, 2009 (Mexicans in U.S.); The Wedding Banquet, 1993 (Chinese in U.S.); Welcome, 2009 (France); The Wendell Baker Story, 2005 (Mexicans in U.S.); Wetbacks, 1956 (Mexicans in U.S.); While My Pretty One Sleeps, 1997 (Canada); Without a Paddle, 2004 (Mexicans and Costa Ricans in U.S.); The Yellow Sea, 2011 (North Korea).

Incognito: The Adorable Deceiver, 1926 (Balkan king and princess daughter disguise themselves when fleeing to America from revolutionaries with the crown jewels); Bachelor in Paradise, 1961 (famous author goes undercover); Back Trail, 1948 (former outlaw serves as respectable town banker); The Beasts of Marseilles, 1959; Betty, 1997 (famous actress disguises her identity); The Big Mouth, 1967; Big Town Girl, 1937 (department store clerk hides her identity as a famous radio singing star); Business Under Distress, 1938 (efficiency expert goes undercover to solve financial problems at a nightclub); Death Duel, 1977; **The Desert Song**, 1943 (sheik poses as a lowly positioned Arab); **The Desert Song**, 1953 (sheik poses as a lowly positioned Arab); **The Devil and Miss Jones**, 1941 (tycoon takes a job as a clerk in his own department store); Elvis Meets Nixon, 1997 (made-for-TV); Emperor Chien Lung, 1976;

Expensive Husbands, 1937 (prince disguises himself as a waiter at an upscale European hotel); Go-Get-'Em Haines, 1936 (reporter goes undercover to nab criminals); The Goose Girl, 1915 (German nobleman disguises his identity); **The Green Man**, 1957; Gun Smoke, 1945; **The Gunfighter**, 1950 (former outlaw serves as town's marshal); Headline Crasher, 1937 (senator's son goes undercover to aid his father's reelection); Hey Hey It's Esther Blueburger, 2008; Highways by Night, 1942; **Hollow Triumph**, 1948 (fatal irony takes place after a man disguises himself with plastic surgery); Hollywood Road Trip, 2015; **Holy Matrimony**, 1943 (famous painter works under a pseudonym to ruin greedy art dealers); Honeymoon, 2014; **I Married a Witch**, 1942 (infamous Salem witch pretends to be a victim in a modern-day fire); Incognito, 1998 (art expert disguises herself to expose creator of faked famous paintings); Incognito, 1999 (bodyguard disguises himself to protect rape victim); Incognito, 2005 (TV series); Incognito, 2009 (ambitious singer disguises himself to advance his career); Incognito, 2012- (TV series); Intent to Kill, 1959 (South American president disguises himself to evade assassins); **It Happened One Night**, 1934 (heiress disguises herself on flight from tycoon father); Jesse James Rides Again, 1947 (infamous outlaw goes undercover to aid ranchers); **Knight Without Armor**, 1937 (countess disguises herself as a peasant to escape Bolshevik killers during the Russian Revolution); The Lady Hermit, 1971 (Kung Fu master goes undercover); Lafayette, 1963; The Man with 100 Faces, 1938 (society lion goes undercover as a modern-day Robin Hood); Man with the Steel Whip, 1954; Mary Jane's Pa, 1935 (long-absent father returns to aid daughter by pretending to be her housekeeper); **Melvin and Howard**, 1980 (billionaire Howard Hughes disguises himself as a hobo); Mississippi Gambler, 1942 (criminal disguises himself with plastic surgery); Orlando, 1993 (British nobleman remains young forever under many aliases); The Panther's Claw, 1942 (famous person becomes a secret blackmailer); Park Avenue Logger, 1937 (rich man's son disguises his identity); The Rogue's Tavern, 1936; Set Free, 1927 (stuntman works as clerk to rescue female storeowner); **Sitting Pretty**, 1948 (famous author goes undercover as a babysitter to write a scandalous book about neighbors); Sudan, 1945 (Egyptian queen pretends to be a commoner); **Sullivan's Travels**, 1941 (famous film director pretends to be a hobo); A Taste for Women, 1964 (cannibals pretend to operate a gourmet restaurant while looking for the ideal woman to serve at their next full-moon sacrifice); **They All Kissed the Bride**, 1942; **The Thief of Bagdad**, 1924 (sultan pretends to be a commoner); **The Thief of Bagdad**, 1940 (sultan pretends to be a commoner); Time Out for Romance, 1937 (society lady hides her identity when escaping an unhappy marriage); The Tourist, 2010; Twilight on the Prairie, 1944 (musicians pretend to be cowboys to aid rancher); Two Gun Lady, 1955 (woman becomes a sharpshooter and goes undercover to hunt down her parents' killers); Undercover, 2015- (TV series); **The Vagabond King**, 1930; **The Vagabond King**, 1956; Western Justice, 1934 (three men uses aliases in an effort to bring water to a drought-ridden town); With Pleasure, Madame, 1937 (British diplomat disguises himself for reasons of State); **Without Reservations**, 1946 (famous author pretends to be a non-entity); Woman in Distress, 1937 (reporter goes undercover to expose art fraud).

Indianapolis 500 (also see Race Cars and Racar Drivers, this index): The Big Wheel, 1949; **The Crowd Roars**, 1932; Indianapolis Speedway, 1939; Road Demon, 1938; Speedway, 1929; Ten Laps to Go, 1936; Turbo, 2013; **Winning**, 1969.

Infantry (in WWII): Ambush Bay, 1966 (Philippines, 1944; U.S., Japanese troops); **American Guerrilla in the Philippines**, 1950 (Philippine defense, 1942; Leyte, 1944; U.S., Filipino, Japanese troops); The Americanization of Emily, 1964 (Normandy, France, June 6, 1944; U.S., German troops); Anzio, 1962 (Operation Shingle, amphibious landing at Anzio, Italy, January 22, 1944; U.S., German troops); **Attack**, 1956 (France, 1944; U.S., German troops); Back Door to Hell, 1964 (Philippines, Leyte, 1944; U.S., Japanese troops); **Back to Bataan**, 1945 (Bataan, Philippines, 1942; Leyte, Philippines, 1944; U.S., Filipino, Japanese troops); Band of Brothers, 2001 (TV miniseries; Normandy, France, June 6, 1944, and thereafter; U.S., German troops); **Bataan**, 1943 (Bataan, Philippines, 1942; U.S., Filipino, Japanese troops); Battle at Bloody Beach, 1961 (Philippine Resistance, 1943; Filipino and Japanese troops); **Battle Cry**, 1955 (Guadalcanal, 1942; Tarawa, 1943; U.S., Japanese troops); **Battle of the Bulge**, 1965 (Belgium, France and Luxembourg; Bastogne, December 16, 1944-January 25, 1945); **Battleground**, 1949 (Battle of the Bulge, Belgium, France, and Luxembourg; Bastogne, December 16, 1944-January 25, 1945; U.S., German troops); Beach Red, 1967 (Bougainville, 1943-1944, U.S., Japanese troops); **Beachhead**, 1954 (Choiseul Island in Bougainville Campaign, 1943-1945; U.S., Japanese troops); **Between Heaven and Hell**, 1956 (Philippines, 1944; U.S., Japanese troops); **The Big Red One**, 1980 (North Africa, 1943; Italy, 1943; France, 1944; U.S., German troops); The Blockhouse, 1974 (Normandy, France, June 6, 1944; U.S., German troops); Blood Oath, 1990 (Laha Massacre, 1942); **Breakthrough**, 1950 (France, 1944; U.S., German troops); **The Bridge at Remagen**, 1969 (Ludendorff Bridge spanning the Rhine River, March 1945; U.S. and German troops); **The Bridge on the River Kwai**, 1957 (Burma, 1942-1943; British, Japanese troops); **A Bridge Too Far**, 1977 (Operation Market Garden, Holland, September 17-25, 1944; U.S., British, German troops); **Cast a Giant Shadow**, 1966 (France, 1944; Germany, 1945; U.S., German troops); **China Sky**, 1945 (Sino-Japanese War, 1937-1945; Chinese, Japanese troops); Combat!, 1962-1967 (TV series; France, 1944; U.S., German troops); **Commandos Strike at Dawn**, 1942 (Norway, 1940; British, German troops); Corregidor, 1943 (Philippine Defense, 1941-1942; U.S., Japanese troops); **Counter Attack**, 1945 (Eastern Front; Russian, German troops); **Cross of Iron**, 1977 (Russian front, German, Russian troops); **Cry Havoc**, 1943 (Bataan, Philippines, 1941-1942; U.S., Filipino, Japanese troops); Cry of Battle, 1963 (Philippine Defense, 1941-1942; U.S., Filipino, Japanese troops); **Days of Glory**, 2006 (France, 1940; French, German troops); D-Day 6.6.1944, 2004 (made-for-TV; Normandy, France, June 6, 1944; U.S., German troops); **D-Day: The Sixth of June**, 1956 (Normandy, France, June 6, 1944; U.S., British and German troops); **The Desert Fox: The Story of Rommel**, 1951 (North Africa, 1941-1943; France, 1944; German, British, U.S. troops); **The Desert Rats**, 1953 (Battle for Tobruk, Libya, 1942; British, German troops); **The Devil's Brigade**, 1968 (Italy, 1943; U.S., German troops); **The Dirty Dozen**, 1967 (France; U.S., German troops); **Dragon Seed**, 1944 (Sino-Japanese War, 1942; Chinese, Japanese troops); **Eight Iron Men**, 1952 (Italy, 1943; U.S., German troops); **Enemy at the Gates**, 2001 (Battle of Stalingrad, August 23, 1942-February 2, 1943; German, Russian troops); **The Fighting Seabees**, 1944 (Pacific, 1943; U.S., Japanese troops); **First to Fight**, 1967 (Guadalcanal, 1942; U.S., Japanese troops); **Five Graves to Cairo**, 1943 (Libyan desert, 1942; British, German troops); **Flags of Our Fathers**, 2006 (Iwo Jima, 1945; U.S., Japanese troops); **The Flying Leathernecks**, 1951 (Guadalcanal, 1942; U.S., Japanese troops); **Force of Arms**, 1951 (Battle of San Pietro Infine, Italy, December 8-17, 1943; U.S., German troops); **Go for Broke!**, 1951 (Italy, France; U.S. [Japanese-American], German troops); **The Great Raid**, 2005 (spectacular raid against Japanese prison camp at Cabanatuan, Luzon, Philippines, where more than 500 prisoners were rescued on April 30, 1945; U.S., Japanese troops); **Guadalcanal Diary**, 1943 (Guadalcanal, 1942; U.S., Japanese troops); **Gung Ho!**, 1943 (Makin Island Raid, August 17-18, 1942; U.S., Japanese troops); **Halls of Montezuma**, 1951 (Okinawa, 1945; U.S., Japanese troops); **Hell Is for Heroes**, 1962 (Siegfried Line, Germany, August 1944-early 1945; U.S., German troops); **Home of the Brave**, 1949 (Pacific, 1944; U.S., Japanese troops); I Was an American Spy, 1951 (Philippine Defense, 1941-1944; U.S.-Filipino resistance fighters, Japanese troops; based on the exploits of Claire Phillips, 1908-1960); **Immortal Sergeant**, 1943 (North Africa, 1942; Canadian, German troops); **Kelly's Heroes**, 1970 (France, 1944; U.S., German

troops); **Letters from Iwo Jima**, 2006 (Iwo Jima, 1945; Japanese, U.S. troops); **The Longest Day**, 1962 (Normandy, France, June 6, 1944; U.S., British, French, German troops); **MacArthur**, 1977 (Philippine defense, 1941-1942, Pacific islands to Leyte, Philippines, 1943-1944; U.S., Japanese troops); **Manila Calling**, 1942 (Philippine defense, 1942; U.S., Japanese troops); **Marine Raiders**, 1944 (Guadalcanal, 1942; Solomon Islands, 1943; U.S., Japanese troops); Memorial Day, 2011 (France, 1944; U.S., German troops); **Merrill's Marauders**, 1962 (Burma, 1944); Miracle at St. Anna, 2008 (Italy, 1943; U.S., German troops); **Mr. Winkle Goes to War**, 1944 (Pacific island; U.S., Japanese troops); The Mountain Road, 1960 (China, 1944; Chinese, Japanese troops); The Naked and the Dead, 1958 (Pacific island, U.S., Japanese troops); **Never So Few**, 1959 (Burma, 1943; U.S.-led Burmese, Japanese troops); **No Man Is an Island**, 1962 (Guam, 1941-1944; U.S., Japanese troops); None but the Brave, 1965 (Pacific island; U.S., Japanese troops); **Objective, Burma!**, 1945 (based on the 1944 raids by Merrill's Marauders in 1944; U.S., Japanese troops); **The Outsider**, 1961 (portraying the exploits of Marine and Native American Ira Hayes, one of those who raised the American flag at Mount Suribachi during the battle of Iwo Jima, and who is enacted by Tony Curtis; U.S., Japanese troops); The Pacific, 2010 (cable-TV miniseries; Guadalcanal, 1942; Peleliu, 1944; Iwo Jima, 1945; U.S., Japanese troops); Paradise Road, 1997 (Sumatra, 1941-1945; British, Japanese troops); **Patton**, 1970 (North Africa, Sicily, France; U.S., German troops); **Play Dirty, 1969** (raid on Rommel's fuel depot in Libya, 1943; British, German troops); **Pride of the Marines**, 1945 (Guadalcanal, 1942; U.S., Japanese troops); Prisoner of Japan, 1942 (Pacific island; U.S., Japanese troops); Raid on Rommel, 1971 (Libya, 1943; British, German troops); Rommel, 2012 (made-for-TV; North Africa, 1941-1943; France, 1944; U.S., British, German troops); **Sahara**, 1943 (Libyan desert, 1943; U.S., British, German troops); Salute to the Marines, 1943 (Philippine defense, 1941-1942); **Sands of Iwo Jima**, 1949 (Tarawa, 1943; Iwo Jima, 1945; U.S., Japanese troops); **Saving Private Ryan**, 1998 (Normandy, France, June 6, 1944, and thereafter; U.S., German troops); Sea of Sand (aka: Desert Patrol), 1961 (North Africa, 1943; British, German troops); **So Proudly We Hail!**, 1943 (Philippine Defense, Bataan and Corregidor, 1941-1942; U.S., Japanese troops); **Somewhere I'll Find You**, 1942 (Manila, Philippine Defense, 1941-1942; U.S., Japanese troops); **South Sea Woman**, 1953 (Guadalcanal, 1942; U.S., Japanese troops); Storming Juno, 2010 (made-for-TV; Normandy, France, June 6, 1944; British, German troops); **The Story of Dr. Wassell**, 1944 (Java, 1942; Dutch, Japanese troops); **The Story of G.I. Joe**, 1945 (North Africa, Italy, 1943; U.S., German troops); **Tarawa Beachhead**, 1958 (Guadalcanal, 1942; Tarawa, 1943; U.S., Japanese troops); **They Met in Bombay**, 1941 (China, 1941; British, Japanese troops); **The Thin Red Line**, 1964 (Guadalcanal, 1942; U.S., Japanese troops); **The Thin Red Line**, 1998 (Guadalcanal, 1942; U.S., Japanese troops); **Three Came Home**, 1950 (Battle of Borneo, 1941-1942; British, Japanese troops); **Thunderbirds**, 1952 (Sicily, Italy, 1943; France, 1944; U.S., German troops); **To Hell and Back**, 1955 (Sicily, Italy, 1943; Southern France, 1944; U.S., German troops); **Tobruk**, 1967 (Tobruk, Libya, 1942; British, German troops); **Too Late the Hero**, 1970 (New Hebrides; British, Japanese troops); The Unknown Soldier, 1955 (Finland, 1941; Finnish, Russian troops); **Up Front**, 1951 (Italy, 1943; U.S., German troops); **Valkyrie**, 2008 (North Africa, 1942; German troops); **Wake Island**, 1942 (Wake Island defense, 1942; U.S., Japanese troops); **A Walk in the Sun**, 1945 (Italy, 1943; U.S., Italian, German troops); **The Winter War**, 1989 (Finland, 1939; Finnish, Russian troops); **A Yank on the Burma Road**, 1942 (Burma, 1942; U.S., Chinese, Japanese troops); **The Young Lions**, 1958 (France, 1940; North Africa, 1941-1943; France, 1944; Germany, 1945; German, French, British, U.S. troops).

Investigative Reporters: **Abandoned**, 1949 (reporter probes illegal baby adoption racket in Los Angeles); **Absence of Malice**, 1981 (investigative reporter probing a Florida crime family wrongly accuses a family member); The Adventures of Nellie Bly, 1981 (made-for-TV; pioneer female investigative reporter of the late 1880s); **All the King's Men**, 1949 (exposing political corruption in the Deep South, based on Louisiana's political demagogue Huey Long); **All the President's Men**, 1976 (the uncovering of President Richard Nixon's involvement in Watergate); Bordertown, 2006 (investigating a series of murders along the border between Juarez, Mexico, and El Paso, Texas); **Call Northside 777**, 1948 (uncovering evidence to prove the innocence of a wrongly-convicted man in Chicago; based on the Joseph Majczek case); **Capricorn One**, 1978 (exposing fraud in the U.S. space program); **Chicago Deadline**, 1949 (dogged reporter tracks down the killer of a dead girl); **The China Syndrome**, 1979 (TV anchorwoman investigates a cover-up at a nuclear plant in California); The Clearstream Affair, 2014 (probing European financing); **The Company You Keep**, 2013 (tracking down a wanted Weather Underground activist); Cover Up, 1991 (probing corrupt politicians); Cronicas, 2004 (Miami reporter goes to Ecuador in search of a serial killer); Dance, Fool, Dance, 1931 (female cub reporter investigates bootleggers); Deadline, 2012 (probing the twenty-year-old murder of a black youth in Alabama); **Deadline U.S.A.**, 1952 (several newspaper reporters risk their lives in exposing the murderous operations of a crime boss); **Dr. X**, 1932 (reporter investigates the experiments of a mad scientist); Edison, 2005; Exclusive, 1992 (made-for-TV; television reporter probes the murders of six persons at a swanky lounge); **Five Star Final**, 1931 (scandal sheet investigative reporter exposes a couple's background that leads to suicide); **Foreign Correspondent**, 1940 (investigating the disappearance of a Dutch diplomat); The Fourth Angel, 2001 (investigation following the murder of a man's wife and child); The Good Shepherd, 2004 (investigating a priest accused of murder); Guilty of Treason, 1950 (probe into the persecution of Catholic Cardinal Mindzhenty); **The Harder They Fall**, 1956 (reporter turned fight promoter decides to expose corrupt prizefighting); **The Insider**, 1999 (probing of tobacco companies by "60 Minutes" researcher); **Keeper of the Flame**, 1942 (unearthing evidence that a recently deceased American icon was a traitor); **Kill the Messenger**, 2014 (probe into the CIA's cocaine trafficking); **The Last Hurrah**, 1958 (investigating political corruption in Boston); Lois & Clark: The New Adventures of Superman, 1993-1997 (TV series); The Mad Ghoul, 1943 (reporter investigates the experiments of a mad scientist); **Man of Steel**, 2013; Messenger of Death, 1988 (probing the mass murder of a Mormon family); **The Murder Man**, 1935; The Murder of Mary Phagan, 1988 (TV miniseries; probe into the murder of a fifteen-year-old factory worker in Atlanta, Georgia, and for which Leo Max Frank was wrongly convicted, imprisoned and later lynched, 1913-1915); **The Odessa File**, 1974 (tracking down Nazi war criminals after WWII); **The Parallax View**, 1974 (uncovering a corporate conspiracy behind the death of a U.S. senator); **The Pelican Brief**, 1993 (uncovering a dangerous conspiracy); Perfect Stranger, 2007 (reporter goes undercover to identify a killer); Pilot Error, 2014 (reporter probes an airplane crash that took the lives of 212 passengers); Primeval, 2007; Quid Pro Quo, 2008 (investigating a disturbing subculture); **The Return of Dr. X**, 1939 (reporter investigates the experiments of a mad scientist); **Ring**, 1998 (tracking down a mysterious videotape that has brought death to several viewers); **The Ring**, 2002; Rise: Blood Hunter, 2007; Savage, 1973 (made-for-TV; probe into the background of a U.S. Supreme Court nominee); **The Secret Six**, 1931 (investigative reporters compete to expose a crime boss); Seeking Justice, 2011; Shattered Glass, 2003 (exposing an investigative reporter who has faked his reports); Silver City, 2004 (a discovered corpse prompts investigation into the campaign of a Colorado's governor); **Spotlight**, 2015 (exposing the widespread child molestation among Catholic priests in Boston and elsewhere); State of Play, 2003 (TV miniseries; probing the activities of Washington politicians following the murder of a congressional aide); State of Play, 2009; Tab Lloyd: Investigative Reporter, 1985 (made-for-TV); Tank Malling, 1989; **10 Days in a Madhouse**, 2015 (investigative reporter Nellie Bly goes undercover to expose malpractice in an insane asylum in 1887); They

Won't Forget, 1937 (reporter probes the murder of a girl in a factory, and its manager is wrongly convicted and lynched; based on the Leo Max Frank case of 1913-1915); Ulterior Motives, 1993 (probing aerospace leaders selling secrets); **Woman in Gold**, 2015 (investigating Austrian officials who may have stolen invaluable artworks from a Jewish refugee).

Invisibility: **Abbott and Costello Meet Frankenstein**, 1948; Abbott and Costello Meet the Invisible Man, 1951; Abraham Lincoln, Vampire Hunter, 2012; The Adventures of Baron Munchausen, 1943; **The Adventures of Baron Munchausen**, 1989; Alice, 1990; **Alice in Wonderland**, 1951; **Alice in Wonderland**, 2010; Alien Trespass, 2009; Alone in the Dark, 2005; Alter Egos, 2012; **The Amazing Spider-Man 2**, 2014; The Amazing Transparent Man, 1960; American Ninja, 1985; Arthur and the Invisibles, 2006; **Australia**, 2008; **The Avengers**, 2012; Barbarella, 1968; Batman and Robin, 1949; Blackbeard's Ghost, 1968; **Brigadoon**, 1954; **The Canterville Ghost**, 1944; Captain Video: Master of the Stratosphere, 1951 (serial); Chandu on the Magic Island, 1935; The Chronicles of Narnia: The Voyage of the Dawn Treader, 2010; **Clash of the Titans**, 1981; The Cosmic Man, 1959; The Covenant, 2006; The Darkest Hour, 2011; The Devil and Max Devlin, 1981; Dr. Orloff's Invisible Monster, 1970; Don Juan, My Dear Ghost, 1990; The Dunwich Horror, 1970; The Entity, 1982; Equinox, 1970; Fantastic Four, 1967- (TV series); The Fantastic Four, 1994; Fantastic Four, 2005; Fantastic Four, 2015; Fiend Without a Face, 1958; Final Fantasy: The Spirits Within, 2001; Flash Gordon, 1936 (serial); **Forbidden Planet**, 1956; G.I. Joe: The Rise of Cobra, 2009; Gawain and the Green Knight, 1973; Ghost, 1990; **The Ghost and Mrs. Muir**, 1947; **The Ghost Breakers**, 1940; Ghost Dad, 1990; **The Ghost Goes West**, 1936; Ghost in the Shell, 1995; The Ghosts of Hanley House, 1968; Gildersleeve's Ghost, 1944; **The Golden Voyage of Sinbad**, 1974; Griff the Invisible, 2010; **Harry Potter and the Chamber of Secrets**, 2002; **Harry Potter and the Goblet of Fire**, 2005; **Harry Potter and the Half-Blood Prince**, 2009; **Harry Potter and the Prisoner of Azkaban**, 2004; **Harry Potter and the Sorcerer's Stone**, 2001; The Heavenly Kid, 1985; Henry's Night In, 1969; Heroes, 2006-2010 (TV series); The Hobbit, 1977 (made-for-TV); **The Hobbit: An Unexpected Journey**, 2012; **The Hobbit: The Battle of the Five Armies**, 2014; **The Hobbit: The Desolation of Smaug**, 2013; Hollow Man, 2000; **The Incredibles**, 2004; The Invisible, 2007; **Invisible Agent**, 1942; The Invisible Avenger, 1958; **The Invisible Boy**, 1957; The Invisible Boy, 2014; Invisible Eyes, 2009; Invisible Invaders, 1959; The Invisible Kid, 1988; **The Invisible Man**, 1933; The Invisible Man, 2000-2002 (TV series); Invisible Man Appears, 1949; **The Invisible Man Returns**, 1940; The Invisible Man's Revenge, 1944; The Invisible Monster, 1950; Invisible Sister, 2015 (made-for-TV); Invisible Temptation, 1996; The Invisible Terror, 1963; The Invisible Woman, 1940; The Invisible Woman, 2009; It All Came True, 1998; It Follows, 2014; The Jade Box, 1930 (serial); Jupiter Ascending, 2015; The Last Unicorn, 1982; The League of Extraordinary Gentlemen, 2003; Let There Be Light, 1998; The Life and Adventures of Santa Clause, 1985 (made-for-TV); Long Live Ghosts!, 1977; **The Lord of the Rings: The Fellowship of the Ring**, 2001; The Lord of the Rings: The Return of the King, 2003; Magic Boy, 1959; The Magical Land of the Leprechauns, 1999 (made-for-TV); Man in Outer Space, 1962; The Man Who Wasn't There, 1983; Manhunt in Space, 1956 (made-for-TV); Matchless, 1967; Memoirs of an Invisible Man, 1992; Mr. Horatio Knibbles, 1971; Mr. India, 1987; Mr. Superinvisible, 1970; **Monsters, Inc.**, 2001; Mother of Tears, 2008; My Favorite Martian, 1963-1966 (TV series); My Favorite Martian, 1999; Mystery Men, 1999; The Mystery of the Third Planet, 1981; Now You See Him, Now You Don't, 1972; Paranormal Activity 3, 2011; Paul, 2011; **Pete's Dragon**, 1977; The Phantom Creeps, 1939 (serial); Predator, 1987; Predator 2, 1990; Predators, 2010; Private Snuffy Smith, 1942; The Prodigy, 2005; The Purple Monster Strikes, 1945 (serial); Renaissance, 2006; The Return of Chandu, 1934; The Return of the King, 1980 (made-for-TV); Rise of the Silver Surfer, 2007; R-Point, 2004; School Spirit, 1985; **The Shadow**, 1994; Sound of Horror, 1966; Space Ghost, 1966-1968 (TV series); Special, 2006; **Star Trek V: The Final Frontier**, 1989; **Star Trek IV: The Voyage Home**, 1986; **Star Trek: Generations**, 1994; **Star Trek: Insurrection**, 1998; **Star Trek: Nemesis**, 2002; **Star Trek III: The Search for Spock**, 1984; Stardust, 2007; Supergirl, 1984; Superhero Movie, 2008; There Once Was a King..., 1955; **Thor: The Dark World**, 2013; **The Time of Their Lives**, 1946; Tom's Midnight Garden, 1999; Tooth Fairy, 2010; **Topper**, 1937; **Topper Returns**, 1941; **Topper Takes a Trip**, 1938; Vampire in Brooklyn, 1995; The Vanishing Shadow, 1934 (serial); Voices, 2007; The Wonderful World of the Brothers Grimm, 1982; The Worst Witch, 1986 (made-for-TV); Yoga Class, 2009; Zoom, 2006.

Jazz Players, Jazz Bands and Jazz Music: **All Dogs Go to Heaven**, 1989; All Night Long, 1963; American Blue Note, 1989; An American in Rome, 1954; American Pop, 1981; **Anatomy of a Murder**, 1959; And All That Jazz, 1983; At the Circus, 1939; **The Benny Goodman Story**, 1956; Belle of the Nineties, 1934; The Big Bang, 2010; Bird, 1988; Birth of the Blues, 1941; The Black Glove, 1954; **Blackboard Jungle**, 1955; **The Blues Brothers**, 1980; Blues in the Night, 1941; Bombay Velvet, 2015; Bullet to the Head, 2012; **The Cabin in the Cotton**, 1932; Chico & Rita, 2010; **Compulsion**, 1959; **The Cotton Club**, 1984; The Crimson Canary, 1945; Dancing on the Edge, 2013 (TV miniseries); Dementia, 1955; Dr. Rhythm, 1937; The Drag-Net, 1936; Drillinge an Bord, 1959; Every Other Weekend, 1991; The Fabulous Dorseys, 1947; False Face, 1977; **The Five Pennies**, 1959; **Follow the Boys**, 1944; **Follow the Fleet**, 1936; The Gene Krupa Story, 1959; Glory Alley, 1952; **Groundhog Day**, 1993; Hard Boiled, 1993; Havoc, 1972; **High Society**, 1956; **Houseboat**, 1958; **The Hustler**, 1961; Imaginary Heroes, 2004; Innocent Sorcerers [1960], 2014; Jam Session, 1944; **The Jazz Singer**, 1927; The Jazzband Five, 1932; Just Friends, 1993; Just Wright, 2010; Kansas City, 1996; Kettle of Fish, 2006; **King of California**, 2007; King of Jazz, 1930; The Kovak Box, 2006; Kung Fu Hustle, 2004; The Lady Says No, 1951; **Lady Sings the Blues**, 1972; Make Believe Ballroom, 1949; A Man Called Adam, 1966; **Miles Ahead**, 2015; Mo' Better Blues, 1990; **My Man Godfrey**, 1936; New Orleans, 1947; **New York, New York**, 1977; Night Owl, 1993 (made-for-TV); **Nightmare**, 1956; **Paris Blues**, 1961; The Party's Over, 1966; **Pete Kelly's Blues**, 1955; **Play Misty for Me**, 1971; **Rachel Getting Married**, 2008; **Rififi**, 1956; **Roberta**, 1935; 'Round Midnight', 1986; **St. Louis Blues**, 1939; St. Louis Blues, 1958; Second Chorus, 1940; Shadows, 1959; **The Snows of Kilimanjaro**, 1952; **A Song Is Born**, 1948; Space Is the Place, 1974; **Stormy Monday**, 1988; **Stormy Weather**, 1943; The Strip, 1951; **The Sun Also Rises**, 1957; Sweet and Low-Down, 1944; Sweet and Low-down, 1999; **Sweet Smell of Success**, 1957; Swing, 1999; Swing Kids, 1993; The Ten, 2007; Thank You Satan, 1989; **Three on a Match**, 1932; Thrill of a Romance, 1945; The Tic Code, 2000; **Tightrope**, 1984; Tony Takitani, 2005; Too Late Blues, 1962; Treme, 2010-2013 (TV series); 28 Days, 2000; Up at the Villa, 2000; **Vabank**, 1982; Where the Boys Are, 1960; **Whiplash**, 2014; You, the Living, 2007; **Young and Innocent**, 1938; **Young Man with a Horn**, 1950.

Jewel Thieves: **Absolute Power**, 1997; Adriane's Castle, 2011; Adventure in Diamonds, 1940; The Adventures of Kitty O'Day, 1945; **The Adventures of Sherlock Holmes**, 1939; After Midnight with Boston Blackie, 1943; Alex in Wonderland, 1940; **Algiers**, 1938; Amateur Crook, 1937; **The Amazing Dr. Clitterhouse**, 1938; Amazon, 2000; And Now...Ladies and Gentlemen...,2003; Arsene Lupin Returns, 1938; **The Asphalt Jungle**, 1950; Atlantic Adventure, 1935; **The Bat Whispers**,1930; **Beau Geste**, 1926; **Beau Geste**, 1939; Below the Border, 1942; Below the Deadline, 1936; **Big Deal on Madonna Street**, 1960; Big Brown Eyes, 1936; The Black Tulip, 1964; The Blackbird, 1926; Blood Nasty, 1989; Blue Streak, 1999; The Border Patrolman, 1936; Boston Blackie Goes Hollywood, 1942; Boston Blackie's Little

Pal, 1918; Bullets for O'Hara, 1941; Cairo, 1963; The Cartier Affair, 1984 (made-for-TV); **Casbah**, 1948; Case of the Missing Man, 1935; Castle in the Sky, 1989; **Castle on the Hudson**, 1940; Charlie Chan in Rio, 1941; China Passage, 1937; Chinatown after Dark, 1931; Cleaverville, 2007 (made-for-TV); C-Man, 1949; Confessions, 1925; The Connection, 1973 (made-for-TV); Cool Breeze, 1972; Counterfeit Lady, 1936; Crown Jewels, 1918; The Curse of the Jade Scorpion, 2001; Danger: Diabolik, 1968; Danger Zone, 1951; A Date with the Falcon, 1942; Deadfall, 1968; The Deputy Drummer, 1935; **Desire**, 1936; The Devil Has Seven Faces, 1971; Diamonds on Wheels, 1974 (made-for-TV); Double Danger, 1938; Double Trouble, 1967; Double Trouble, 1992; Dragnet, 1947; Entrapment, 1999; Eye in the Sky, 2007; The Fiendish Plot of Dr. Fu Manchu, 1980; A Fine Pair, 1968; **The Finger Man**, 1964; The Flyin' Cowboy, 1928; Foolish Monte Carlo, 1920; Fric-Frac, 1939; The Gay Falcon, 1941; The Goose and the Gander, 1935; **Grand Hotel**, 1932; The Gray Ghost, 1917; The Great Diamond Robbery, 1954; **The Great Jewel Robber**, 1950; **The Great Muppet Caper**, 1981; Hearts or Diamonds?, 1918; Heist, 2001; High Flyers, 1937; High Jinks in Society, 1949; High Society, 1995; His Father's Son, 1917; Hot Ice, 1978; **The Hot Rock**, 1972; **The Hour of Thirteen**, 1952; I Am a Thief, 1934; In His Grip, 1921; Ireland's Border Line, 1939; Irma Vep, 1997; Itchy Fingers, 1979; Jack of Diamonds, 1967; Jack of Diamonds, 2011 (made-for-TV); Java Heat, 2013; Jay and the Silent Bob Strike Back, 2001; **The Jewel of the Nile**, 1985; Jewel Thief, 1967; Jiggs and Maggie in Society, 1947; Junk, 2000; **The Killers**, 1946; Kuro tokage, 1969; Lady Ice, 1973; Lassiter, 1984; The Last of Mrs. Cheyney, 1937; Le Doulos, 1962; The Lincoln Highwayman, 1919; The Lone Wolf in London, 1947; The Lone Wolf Returns, 1926; The Lone Wolf Returns, 1935; Loot, 1919; Lord Jeff, 1938; Love Happy, 1949; Love in High Gear, 1932; Love Letters: A Romantic Trilogy, 2001; The Magic of David Copperfield II, 1979 (TV special); The Man Who Came to Dinner, 1967; Married Before Breakfast, 1937; Mary Ryan, Detective, 1949; Meet the Girls, 1938; Men of the Night, 1934; Metro, 1997; Midnight Limited, 1940; Mr. Dane's Danger, 1916; The Moonstone, 1934; The Moth, 1934; **Murder, My Sweet**, 1944; Murph the Surf, 1975; Music for Madame, 1937; My Lady's Garter, 1920; The Mysterious Mr. Tiller, 1917; **The Mystery of Mr. X**, 1934; Mystery in Dracula's Castle, 1973 (made-for-TV); Night Class, 2001; Ninja in Action, 1987; Now or Never, 1935; **Number Seventeen**, 1932; Oh, What a Night, 1944; Once Upon a Time, 2008; Our Lips Are Sealed, 2000; Out of Sight, 1998; Outside the Law, 1920; Palace Guard, 1991- (TV series); **Pepe Le Moko**, 1937; The Phantom, 1916; **The Pink Panther**, 1964; **The Return of the Pink Panther**, 1975; **Raffles**, 1930; **Raffles**, 1939; Remote Control, 1930; The Return of Raffles, 1932; **Rififi**, 1956; Rififi in Amsterdam, 1962; Rififi in Tokyo, 1963; **Robot and Frank**, 2012; Rough Cut, 1980; Rubber Heels, 1927; School for Girls, 1934; **The Score**, 2001; A Scream in the Night, 1943; Secret Agent X-9, 1937; The Servant Question, 1920; Seven Footprints to Satan, 1929; Shalimar, 1978; Sleeping Dogs, 1998; The Solitaire Man, 1933; Sophie Lang Goes West, 1937; The Squeeker, 1931; Stateline Motel, 1975; Stop That Cab, 1951; Sunshine Dad, 1916; **Superman**, 1978; Tarzan the Tiger, 1929; Terror by Night, 1946; **They Met in Bombay**, 1941; **Thief**, 1981; **The Thief of Paris**, 1967; The Thief Who Came to Dinner, 1973; Thirteen Hours by Air, 1936; Time Locks and Diamonds, 1917; Time Out for Romance, 1937; **To Catch a Thief**, 1955; **Topkapi**, 1964; The Trans-Atlantic Mystery, 1932; Trapped by Boston Blackie, 1948; The Trembling Hour, 1919; **Trouble in Paradise**, 1932; Under Suspicion, 1916; Under Suspicion, 1918; **The Unholy Three**, 1925; **The Unholy Three**, 1930; The Wager, 1916; Why Me?, 1990; Yaadon Ki Baaraat, 1973; Yesterday Once More, 2004; Young Detectives on Wheels, 1987; You're Never Too Young, 1955. Note: For detailed information on the most notorious jewel thieves, see my books *Bloodletters and Badmen* (M. Evans, 1973); *Encyclopedia of World Crime*; 8 volumes (CrimeBooks, Inc., 1990); *The Great Pictorial History of World Crime*; 2 volumes (History, Inc., 2004).

Jockeys (horse riding; horseraces): All Hat, 2007; The Amateur Gentleman, 1926; The Big Race, 1934; **Bite the Bullet**, 1975; Black Beauty, 1933; **Black Beauty**, 1994; **The Black Stallion**, 1979; **Boots Malone**, 1952; Bred in Old Kentucky, 1926; Broadway Bill, 1934; Bush Christmas, 1983; Calamity Jane and Sam Bass, 1949; **Casey's Shadow**, 1978; Charlie Chan at the Race Track, 1836; Country Fair, 1937; Crazy Over Horses, 1951; **A Day at the Races**, 1937; Dead Cert, 1974; Dead Heat, 2002; The Derby Stallion, 2005; Dick Francis: Twice Shy, 1989 (made-for-TV); Down the Stretch, 1936; The Ex-Mrs. Bradford, 1936; The Fabulous Suzanne, 1946; Fast Companions, 1932; The Fighting Chance, 1955; The Garden Murder Case, 1936; The Gentleman from Arizona, 1939; Going Places, 1938; A Great Coup, 1919; **The Great Dan Patch**, 1949; Heart of Virginia, 1948; **Hidalgo**, 2004; Hillbilly Blitzkrieg, 1942; **Home in Indiana**, 1944; The Horsemen, 1951; Horsing Around, 2005; Hot Heels, 1927; Impossible Dream, 1973; It's in the Air, 1935; Jiggs and Maggie in Jackpot Jitters, 1949; **Kentucky**, 1938; Kentucky Blue Streak, 1935; The Kentucky Derby, 1922; **The Lawless Breed**, 1953; Lena Rivers, 1932; The Life of the Party, 1930; The Little Adventuress, 1938; Little Johnnie Jones, 1929; Little Miss Thoroughbred, 1938; Little Vic, 1977 (TV miniseries); Ma and Pa Kettle at the Fair, 1952; Mr. Celebrity, 1941; Money from Home, 1953; Monte Carlo Nights, 1934; **My Brother Talks to Horses**, 1947; **National Velvet**, 1945; One Man Law, 1932; The Payoff, 1935; **Phar Lap**, 1984; Pride of the Blue Grass, 1939; Queen of Broadway, 1942; **The Quiet Man**, 1952; Racetrack, 1933; Racing Blood, 1936; Racing Lady, 1937; Racing Luck, 1935; Racing Luck, 1948; The Rank Outsider, 1920; **Ride the High Country**, 1962; Riders in the Sky, 1968; **Riding High**, 1950; **The Rocking Horse Winner**, 1950; **Saratoga**, 1937; **Seabiscuit**, 2003; **Secretariat**, 2010; The Shamrock Handicap, 1926; **Shadow of the Thin Man**, 1941; Shergar, 1999; Silks and Saddles, 1936; **Sing, You Sinners**, 1938; Speed to Burn, 1938; **Sporting Blood**, 1931; Sporting Blood, 1940; Sporting Chance, 1931; The Sporting Lover, 1926; **Stablemates**, 1938; **The Story of Seabiscuit**, 1949; Straight Place and Show, 1938; **The Sundowners**, 1960; Sweepstakes Winner, 1939; That Gang of Mine, 1940; That's My Man, 1947; Thoroughbreds Don't Cry, 1937; Three Girls from Home, 1953; **Thunderhead—Son of Flicka**, 1945; Too Many Winners, 1947; Trail to San Antone, 1947; Two Dollar Bettor, 1951; Two in Revolt, 1936; **Under My Skin**, 1950; Under the Pampas Moon, 1935; Unwelcome Stranger, 1935; Wall of Noise, 1963; Wedding Night in the Rain, 1967; Wildfire, 2005-2008 (TV series); Wine, Women and Horses, 1937; The Winner's Circle, 1948; **Yankee Doodle Dandy**, 1942.

Jousting and Jousts (medieval knights): The Adventures of Sir Lancelot, 1956-1957 (TV series); The Black Shield of Falworth, 1954; **Braveheart**, 1995 (with stones); **Camelot**, 1967; **The Canterville Ghost**, 1944; Colossus and the Amazon Queen, 1960; **A Connecticut Yankee**, 1931; **A Connecticut Yankee in King Arthur's Court**, 1949; **The Court Jester**, 1956; The Crown of Fire, 1990; The Curse of Marialva, 1991; The Dark Avenger, 1955; Diane, 1956; Elizabeth I, 2005- (TV miniseries); **Excalibur**, 1981; Game of Thrones, 2011- (TV series); Gawain and the Green Knight, 1973; **Ivanhoe**, 1952; Ivanhoe, 1982 (made-for-TV); Ivanhoe, 1986 (made-for-TV; animated); Jabberwocky, 1977; A Kid in King Arthur's Court, 1995; **King Richard and the Crusaders**, 1954; **Knights of the Round Table**, 1953; A Knight's Tale, 2001; Lancelot of the Lake, 1974; **The Lion in Winter**, 1968; Merlin, 2008-2012 (TV series); Perceval, 1978; **Prince Valiant**, 1954; Richard the Lionheart, 1962- (TV series); **Robin Hood**, 1922; Rogues of Sherwood Forest, 1950; **Shrek the Third**, 2007; Sword of Lancelot, 1963; **Tower of London**, 1939; Tristan + Isolde, 2006; The Tudors, 2007-2010 (TV series); Warriors, 2008- (TV series).

Kleptomania and Kleptomaniacs: The Adventures of Tintin, 2011; Bee Season, 2005; Blood Money, 1933; The Breakfast Club, 1985; **The Brink's Job**, 1978; Borstal Boy, 2001; Call the Midwife, 2012- (TV series); **The Children's Hour**, 1961; Cockeyed Cavaliers, 1934; Combat High, 1986 (made-for-TV); Death of a Salesman, 1985 (made-for-TV); **Detective Story**, 1951; **The Family**, 2013; Female Perversions, 1996; Girl in the Cadillac, 1995; The Glass Slipper, 1955; Gran Casino, 1947; Hardly a Butterfly, 1998; Hawaii, Oslo, 2005; Haxan: Witchcraft Through the Ages, 1922; High Flyers, 1937; Hold That Blonde!, 1945; Hold That Kiss, 1938; Home in San Antone, 1949; **House of Games**, 1987; **I Was an Adventuress**, 1940; If It's Tuesday, This Must Be Belgium, 1969; I'm a Cyborg, But That's OK, 2007; **In the Name of the Father**, 1993; Jack of Diamonds, 1967; The Kid from Kokomo, 1939; Kleptomania, 1995; The Little Thief, 1989; **The Locket**, 1946; The Loft, 2015- (TV series); The Longest Night, 1936; **Love Crazy**, 1941; MacShayne: The Final Roll of the Dice, 1994; **Maid in Manhattan**, 2002; **Marnie**, 1964; **Mr. Moto's Gamble**, 1938; Mom, Dad and Her, 2008 (made-for-TV); Nothing to Lose, 1997; On the Count of Zero, 2007; **The Onion Field**, 1979; Outrageous Fortune, 2005- (TV series); Paste, 1916; Penelope, 1966; The Phantom of the Range, 1936; The Princess and the Cobbler, 1993; Raw Nerve, 1999; Rocket Science, 2007; Rocky Times, 2000 (made-for-TV); Schism, 2008; Seventh Heaven, 1998; Since You've Been Gone, 1998 (made-for-TV); Sing Me a Love Song, 1936; **Slightly Scarlet**, 1956; **Spellbound**, 1945; Spider, 2002; Steal Me, 2005; Sweet and Lowdown, 1999; The Thank You Girls, 2009; Thieves, 2007; Three Live Ghosts, 1936; 3000 Miles to Graceland, 2001; What Have I Done to Deserve This?, 1985; **Whirlpool**, 1949; Wild Target, 2010.

Knife-Throwers and Knife-Throwing: **Accused**, 1936; **Accused—Stand Up**, 1930; Adam Resurrected, 2008; **Addams Family Values**, 1993; The Adventures of the Masked Phantom, 1939; **Alice in Wonderland**, 2010; Alien: Resurrection, 1997; **Avatar**, 2009; Berserk, 1967; The Big Gundown, 1966; Big Jake, 1971; Big Trouble in Little China, 1986; The Bodyguard, 1992; Breed of the Border, 1924; **Brave**, 2012; **Bronco Billy**, 1980; Commando, 1985; **City Slickers**, 1991; **The Count of Monte Cristo**, 2002; The Crow, 1994; Daughter of Don Q, 1947; **Dawn of the Dead**, 1979; **Die Hard with a Vengeance**, 1995; **Divergent**, 2014; Dracula Untold, 2014; **Dumb and Dumber To**, 2014; **El Dorado**, 1967; Excape from New York, 1981; The Expendables, 2010; The Expendables 2, 2012; **A Fistful of Dollars**, 1967; Four Guns to the Border, 1954; **Freaks**, 1932; Gangs of New York, 2002; **Gangster Squad**, 2013; The Girl on the Bridge, 1999; **The Great Beauty**, 2013; **The Green Berets**, 1968; **Gunfight at the O.K. Corral**, 1957; **Hanna**, 2011; Head Over Heels, 2001; The Heat, 2013; Hercules, 2014; **Hidalgo**, 2004; **The Hobbit: The Desolation of Smaug**, 2013; **The Hunger Games**, 2012; **The Iron Mistress**, 1952; Jack Armstrong, 1947 (serial); **The Jewel of the Nile**, 1985; Just Off Broadway, 1942; Knight and Day, 2010; Kung Fu Hustle, 2004; Lariats and Six-Shooters, 1931; **The Last Samurai**, 2003; The League of Extraordinary Gentlemen, 2003; The Lottery Lover, 1935; **Mad Love**, 1935; **The Magnificent Seven**, 1960; The Magnificent Seven, 2016; Mahler, 1974; Maisie Gets Her Man, 1942; The Matrix, 1999; The Mechanic, 1972; **Mr. & Mrs. Smith**, 2005; **Moonraker**, 1979; **The Most Dangerous Game**, 1932; **The Mummy: Tomb of the Dragon Emperor**, 2008; Murder on the Waterfront, 1943; **North by Northwest**, 1959; **Now You See Me**, 2013; Octopussy, 1983; **The Pajama Game**, 1957; Phantom of the Rue Morgue, 1954; Pompeii, 2014; Predator, 1987; **The Princess Bride**, 1987; **Pursuit to Algiers**, 1945; Raiders of the Desert, 1941; Riddick, 2013; Riding Romance, 1925; **Robin Hood: Men in Tights**, 1993; **Robin Hood: Prince of Thieves**, 1991; Santa Sangre, 1989; The Scorpion King, 2002; **Se7en**, 1995; Seventh Son, 2014; The Shanghai Drama, 1938; **Sherlock Holmes: A Game of Shadows**, 2011; **Show Business**, 1944; The Sideshow, 1928; **Skyfall**, 2012; Spy, 2015; Starship Troopers, 1997; **This Is the End**, 2013; This Means War, 2012; Traffic in Souls, 1937; Trigger Fingers, 1924; **True Lies**, 1994; Twilight on the Rio Grande, 1947; Under Siege, 1992; Underworld: Awakening, 2012; The Unknown, 1927; Upstage, 1926; Upstream, 1927; V for Vendetta, 2005; **Victor Frankenstein**, 2015; Viva Maria!, 1965; **Wait**

Until Dark, 1967; Wanted, 2008; Warm Bodies, 2013; **The Warriors**, 1979; **X-Men: First Class**, 2011; White House Down, 2013; **Yojimbo**, 1961.

Lion Tamers and Lions: **The Adventures of Huckleberry Finn**, 1960; Big Top Pee-Wee, 1988; Billy Rose's Jumbo, 1962; Captive Wild Woman, 1943; **Chad Hanna**, 1940; Circus Girl, 1937; The Circus Kid, 1928; **Clarence, the Cross-Eyed Lion**, 1965; Congo Bill, 1938; Fixer Dugan, 1939; Frontier Circus, 1961-1962 (TV series; "Depths of Fear," 1961 episode); **The Greatest Show on Earth**, 1953; **I'm No Angel**, 1933; Kristina Talking Pictures, 1976; La tendre ennemie, 1936; La venenosa, 1928; Las doce sillas, 1962; The Lost Jungle, 1934; **Man on a Tightrope**, 1953; The Mighty Gorga, 1969; The Miracle, 1991; Only One Night, 1939; The Postman Always Rings Twice, 1981; Psycho-Circus, 1966; Rain or Shine, 1930; Red Barry, 1938; Red Wagon, 1933; Ring of Fear, 1954; Roselyne and the Lions, 1989; She Made Her Bed, 1934; Side Show, 1981 (made-for-TV); **The Wagons Roll at Night**, 1941; Zirkus Palestina, 1998.

Los Angeles River (and its storm drains): **Blue Thunder**, 1983; **Chinatown**, 1974; Cleopatra Jones, 1973; **The Core**, 2003; Drive, 2011; Gone in 60 Seconds, 2000; **Grease**, 1978; The Gumball Rally, 1976; **He Walked by Night**, 1948; In Time, 2011; **The Italian Job**, 2003; It's Alive, 1974; Last Action Hero, 1993; **Point Blank**, 1976; Point Break, 1991; Repo Man, 1984; **Road Block**, 1951; Terminator 2: Judgment Day, 1991; **Them!**, 1954; **-30-**, 1959; **To Live and Die in L.A.**, 1985; **Transformers**, 2007.

Lumbering and Lumberjacks: The Adventures of Frank Merriwell, 1936 (12-episode serial); All Mine to Give, 1958; As Cool as I Am, 2013; Big Timber, 1950; The Big Trees, 1952; The Blazing Forest, 1952; **Blue Skies**, 1946; Carnival Boat, 1932; Carolina Moon, 1940; **Come and Get It**, 1936; Conflict, 1936; The Fighting Trooper, 1934; Flying Fists, 1937; The Forest King, 1922; Freckles, 1960; Girl in the Woods, 1958; The Girl of Lost Lake, 1916; God's Country, 1946; God's Country and the Woman, 1937; The Great Alaskan Mystery, 1944; Guns of the Timberland, 1960; The Ice Flood, 1926; John Petticoats, 1919; **The Journey of Natty Gann**, 1985; The Kettles on Old MacDonald's Farm, 1957; King of the Lumberjacks, 1940; Law of the Timber, 1941; Lumberjack, 1944; The Lumberjack of All Trades, 2006; Men of the Timberland, 1941; The Mysterious Pilot, 1937 (15-episode serial); **North to Alaska**, 1960; Park Avenue Logger, 1937; Raw Timber, 1937; Roaring Timber, 1937; Romance of the Redwoods, 1939; Rough Romance, 1930; Secret Patrol, 1936; **Seven Brides for Seven Brothers**, 1954; **Sometimes a Great Notion**, 1970; Spoilers of the Forest, 1957; **The Strange Woman**, 1946; **Tall Tale: The Unbelievable Adventures of Pecos Bill**, 1995; Tall Timbers, 1940; Then Came the Woman, 1926; Thunder in the Pines, 1948; Timber!, 1942; Timber Fury, 1950; The Timber Queen, 1922; Timber Stampede, 1939; Timber Terrors, 1935; Timber Tramps, 1975; Timberjack, 1955; The Tougher They Come, 1950; Trouble in High Timber Country, 1980 (made-for-TV); Twilight, 1919; Valley of the Giants, 1938; **Wild Geese Calling**, 1941.

Lynch Mobs and Lynching (also see Ku Klux Klan): Across the Deadline, 1925; Across the Plains, 1928; **Across the Sierras**, 1941; Adios Gringo, 1968; Adventures in Silverado, 1948; The Adventures of Huck Finn, 1993; **Agneepath**, 2012; **Along the Great Divide**, 1951; Among the Living, 1941; The Animal, 2001; Arizona Bound, 1941; The Arizona Raiders, 1936; Attack on Terror: The FBI vs. the Ku Klux Klan, 1975 (made-for-TV); The Avenger, 1931; **Back to Bataan**, 1945; **Back to the Future Part III**, 1990; Bad Company, 1972; **Bad Day at Black Rock**, 1955; Bad Man from Red Butte, 1940; The Badge of Marshal Brennan, 1957; **The Baron of Arizona**, 1950; Bandits of the West, 1953; Beyond the Purple Hills, 1950; Big Calibre, 1935; Billy the Kid's Fighting Pals, 1941; **The Birth of a Nation**, 1915; The Black Klansman,

1966; **The Black Legion**, 1937; **Blazing Saddles**, 1974; The Blue Moon, 1920; **Boomerang**, 1947; Born to the Saddle, 1953; Branded a Bandit, 1924; **The Bride of Frankenstein**, 1935; **Brigham Young: Frontiersman**, 1940; **Broken Arrow**, 1950; The Broken Gate, 1920; Buchanan Rides Alone, 1958; Bucking the Truth, 1926; Buffalo Soldiers, 1997 (made-for-TV); **The Cabin in the Cotton**, 1932; Cadillac Records, 2008; California Mail, 1936; California Passage, 1950; Cameo Kirby, 1914; Candyman, 1992; Canoa, 1976; Captain Corelli's Mandolin, 2001; Cattle Raiders, 1938; The Chase, 1966; Chronicles, 2005; The Claim, 2000; Colorado Ranger, 1950; Condemned to Live, 1935; Covered Wagon Days, 1940; The Cowboy and the Bandit, 1935; The Crimson Trail, 1935; Cross Fire, 1933; Crossed Trails, 1948; Dangerously Close, 1986; Dark Night of the Scarecrow, 1981 (made-for-TV); **The Day of the Locust**, 1975; Defiance, 2008; **The Defiant Ones**, 1958; The Devil Commands, 1941; The Devil's Saddle Legion, 1937; Diggstown, 1992; **Dodge City**, 1939; Down Texas Way, 1942; Down the Wyoming Trail, 1939; Duel at Silver Creek, 1952; Emma Smith: My Story, 2008; The Fighting Legion, 1930; **Fighting Man of the Plains**, 1949; Firebrands of Arizona, 1944; Firecreek, 1968; 5 Card Stud, 1968; Five Guns to Tombstone, 1960; **Frankenstein**, 1931; Frankenstein, 1994; **Frankenstein Created Woman**, 1965; **Frisco Kid**, 1935; Frontier Law, 1943; Frontier Vengeance, 1940; **Fury**, 1936; **Fury at Furnace Creek**, 1948; The Furies, 1950; Fuzzy Settles Down, 1944; The Gambling Terror, 1937; Gangs of New York, 2002; Gangs of Sonora, 1941; Gentlemen with Guns, 1946; **Gone with the Wind**, 1939; **The Great Debaters**, 2007; **The Great Missouri Raid**, 1951; **Gunfight at the O.K. Corral**, 1957; Gunfighters, 1947; Gunfighters of Abilene, 1960; Guns of the Magnificent Seven, 1969; Guns of the Pecos, 1937; The Halliday Brand, 1957; **Hang 'Em High**, 1968; Hangman's Knot, 1952; **The Hanging Tree**, 1959; Hansel & Gretel: Witch Hunters, 2013; Heaven Only Knows, 1947; Henry Goes Arizona, 1939; Her Inspiration, 1918; Hidden Valley Outlaws, 1944; Hopalong Cassidy, 1935; Hopalong Cassidy Returns, 1936; **Hotel Rwanda**, 2004; **Huckleberry Finn**, 1939; **The Hunchback of Notre Dame**, 1939; Hurry Sundown, 1967; **I Confess**, 1953; I Spit on Your Grave, 1959; I'm Not There, 2007; In Old California, 1942; In Old Montana, 1939; **The Intruder**, 1962; **Intruder in the Dust**, 1949; Iron Mountain Trail, 1953; Jamaica Inn, 1939; The James Brothers of Missouri, 1949; Jesse James vs. the Daltons, 1954; **Johnny Guitar**, 1954; Joseph Smith: Prophet of the Restoration, 2005; The Journey of August King, 1995; **Journey to Shiloh**, 1968; Juke Girl, 1942; Kill the Umpire, 1950; Laughing at Trouble, 1936; Laughter in Hell, 1933; Law and Order, 1953; The Law of the Wild, 1934; A Law Unto Himself, 1916; **The Lawless**, 1950; Lincz, 2010; Little Miss Roughneck, 1938; The Lone Defender, 1934; The Lone Hand, 1920; The Lone Ranger Rides Again, 1939; The Lone Rider in Texas Justice, 1942; The Long Hot Summer, 1985 (made-for-TV); The Long Rope, 1961; **M**, 1931; **M**, 1951; **A Man Alone**, 1955; The Man from Colorado, 1948; The Man from Death Valley, 1931; **The Man from the Alamo**, 1953; Marshal of Laredo, 1945; **Masterson of Kansas**, 1954; Meanwhile, Back at the Ranch, 1976; The Midnight Stage, 1919; **Mississippi Burning**, 1988; **The Missouri Breaks**, 1976; The Missourians, 1950; Mixed Company, 1974; The Moonlighter, 1953; Mountain Justice, 1937; The Murder of Mary Phagan, 1988 (TV miniseries); My Fighting Gentleman, 1917; **My Little Chickadee**, 1940; The Mysterious Rider, 1938; The Mystery Squadron, 1933; **Napoleon**, 1927; Nation Aflame, 1937; **No Name on the Bullet**, 1959; **The Night of the Hunter**, 1955; **1900**, 1977; **O Brother, Where Art Thou**, 2000; The Oakdale Affair, 1919; **The Oklahoma Kid**, 1939; Oklahoma Raiders, 1944; **The Oxbow Incident**, 1943; **Panic**, 1947; Paradise Express, 1937; Paradise Valley, 1934; Paying His Debt, 1918; **The Phantom of the Opera**, 1962; **Places in the Heart**, 1984; Prairie Schooners, 1940; Prescott Kid, 1934; Prince of the Plains, 1949; The Proposition, 2006; The Quiet Gun, 1957; **Rage at Dawn**, 1955; Rain of Light, 2001; Range Law, 1944; Range War, 1939; **Rango**, 2011; Raw Edge, 1956; Red Foam, 1920; Red Fork Range, 1931; Return of the Outlaws, 2009; The

Return of Wild Bill, 1940; Riders of Death Valley, 1941; Riding Shotgun, 1954; **Robin Hood of El Dorado**, 1936; Rock River Renegades, 1942; A Romance of the Redwoods, 1917; Roots, 1977 (TV miniseries); Rose of the Rancho, 1936; **Rosewood**, 1997; Rough Night in Jericho, 1967; Santa Fe Bound, 1936; Santa Fe Stampede, 1938; Scars of Jealousy, 1923; Shep Comes Home, 1948; Sierra Stranger, 1957; The Silver Bullet, 1935; Silver Canyon, 1951; Silver Load, 1954; Silver Trails, 1948; The Silver Whip, 1953; Sinful Davy, 1969; Sing, Cowboy, Sing, 1937; The Skeleton Key, 2005; Sophie and the Moonhanger, 1996 (made-for-TV); Song of the Saddle, 1936; **The Sound of Fury**, 1950; South of Arizona, 1938; Stagecoach Buckeroo, 1942; Stand Up and Fight, 1939; **Stars in My Crown**, 1950; **Storm Warning**, 1951; Strange Case of Dr. Meade, 1938; **The Sun Shines Bright**, 1953; Superman and the Mole-Men, 1951; Swifty, 1935; **The Talk of the Town**, 1942; A Tenderfoot Goes West, 1936; Texas Masquerade, 1944; **They Won't Forget**, 1937; **Three Hours to Kill**, 1954; Thunder Over the Plains, 1953; The Terror of Tiny Town, 1938; That Wild West, 1924; …tick…tick… tick, 1970; **The Tin Star**, 1957; **To Kill a Mockingbird**, 1962; The Topeka Terror, 1945; The Traitor, 1936; The Traitor Within, 1942; Transient Lady, 1935; **Trial**, 1955; **Tribute to a Bad Man**, 1956; Trigger Law, 1944; Trouble in Sundown, 1939; **The True Story of Jesse James**, 1957; Tumbleweed, 1953; Two-Fisted Sheriff, 1937; **Unforgiven**, 1992; The Unpainted Woman, 1919; Valley of Terror, 1937; **Valley of the Heart's Delight**, 2006; Vendetta, 1999 (made-for-TV); Vigilante Terror, 1953; The Violent Ones, 1967; **The Virginian**, 1929; Wagon Tracks West, 1943; **Warlock**, 1959; Wayward Son, 1999; Weekend of Shadows, 1978; The Western Code, 1932; The Whispering Skull, 1944; Whispering Smith Rides, 1927; White Eagle, 1932; White Lie, 1991 (made-for-TV); The Wildcat, 1917; The Wildcat of Tucson, 1940; Winner Takes All, 1918; **The Winning of Barbara Worth**, 1926; Within Our Gates, 1920; A Woman of Redemption, 1918; **Woman They Almost Lynched**, 1953; The Work and the Glory II: American Zion, 2005; **Wyatt Earp**, 1994; Yodelin' Kid from Pine Ridge, 1937; **Young Guns II**, 1990; **Young Mr. Lincoln**, 1939; **The Young One**, 1961. Note: For detailed information on lynch mobs and lynching, see my books *Bloodletters and Badmen* (M. Evans, 1973); *Encyclopedia of World Crime*; 8 volumes (CrimeBooks, Inc., 1990); *The Great Pictorial History of World Crime*; 2 volumes (History, Inc., 2004).

Magic and Magicians (illusionists; also see Witchcraft; Wizards, this index): **The Accompanist**, 1993; Adam Resurrected, 2008; The Adventures of Sir Galahad, 1949 (serial; Merlin); A-Haunting We Will Go, 1942; The Alchemist, 1983; Ali Baba Goes to Town, 1937 The Amazing Mr. X, 1948; Are These Our Parents?, 1944; Around the Bend, 2004; Arrested Development, 2003- (TV series); Barry Lyndon, 1975; **Bedknobs and Broomsticks**, 1971; **The Black Cauldron**, 1985; Black Magic, 1944; **Black Magic**, 1949 (Cagliostro); Blake's Magic, 1983- (TV series); Blackstar, 1981-1982 (TV series); Blondie Has Servant Trouble, 1940; **The Blue Angel**, 1931; Bogus, 1996; **Bombardier**, 1943; Boston Blackie and the Law, 1946; Breakfast on Pluto, 2005; **Broadway Danny Rose**, 1984; Bunco Squad, 1950; Buster's World, 1984; Captain Sinbad, 1963; The Care Bears Movie, 1985; The Care Bears Adventure in Wonderland, 1987; Careful, He Might Hear You, 1983; Carnival Magic, 1981; **The Cat's Paw**, 1934; Catweazle, 1970-1971 (TV series); Celine and Julie Go Boating, 1974; Chac, 1975; Chandu on the Magic Island, 1935; Chandu the Magician, 1932; Charlie Chan at Treasure Island, 1939; The Children Are Watching Us, 1947; The Church, 1990; **The Circus**, 1928; The Color of Magic, 2008- (TV miniseries); Conan the Adventurer, 1992-1993 (TV series); Conan the Barbarian, 1982; Conan the Destroyer, 1984; **A Connecticut Yankee**, 1931 (Merlin); **A Connecticut Yankee in King Arthur's Court**, 1949 (Merlin); A Connecticut Yankee in King Arthur's Court, 1989 (made-for-TV: Merlin); Cousin Bette, 1998; Cowboy Canteen, 1944; **Curse of the Demon**, 1958; Daniel the Wizard, 2004; Deep Red, 1975; Desperate Acts of Magic, 2013; Destiny, 1921; The Devil's Rain, 1975; Doctor

Death: Seeker of Souls, 1973; Dr. Kildare's Wedding Day, 1941; Doctor Strange, 2016; **Dressed to Kill**, 1941; **8½**, 1963; El Mago, 1949; Even Money, 2006; The Everlasting Secret Family, 1988; **Excalibur**, 1981 (Merlin); Face in the Sky, 1933; **Fallen Angel**, 1945; **Fantasia**, 1940; Fantasia 2000, 1999; The Fantasticks, 1995; Fear, 1946; 50 Million Frenchmen, 1931; **Follow the Boys**, 1944; Fugitive Valley, 1941; The Funhouse, 1981; **The Geisha Boy**, 1958; Geisha Girl, 1952; **The Golden Voyage of Sinbad**, 1974; **The Great Buck Howard**, 2009; The Great Houdini, 1976 (made-for-TV); Guinevere Jones, 2002 (TV series; Merlin); Guzaarish, 2010; **Harry Potter and the Chamber of Secrets**, 2002; **Harry Potter and the Deathly Hallows Part 1**, 2010; **Harry Potter and the Deathly Hollows Part 2**, 2011; **Harry Potter and the Goblet of Fire**, 2005; **Harry Potter and the Half-Blood Prince**, 2009; Harry Potter and the Order of the Phoenix, 2007; **Harry Potter and the Prisoner of Azkaban**, 2004; **Harry Potter and the Sorcerer's Stone**, 2001; **Having Wonderful Crime**, 1945; The Hobbit, 1977 (made-for-TV); **The Hobbit: An Unexpected Journey**, 2012; **The Hobbit: The Battle of the Five Armies**, 2014; **The Hobbit: The Desolation of Smaug**, 2013; The Holy Mountain, 1973; Honolulu Lu, 1941; The Horde, 2012; **Houdini**, 1953; Houdini, 2014 (TV miniseries); **Hugo**, 2011; **Hugo the Hippo**, 1976; The Illusionist, 1983; **The Illusionist**, 2006; **The Illusionist**, 2010; The Imaginarium of Doctor Parnassus, 2009; **The Immigrant**, 2014; In the Name of Sherlock Holmes, 2011; The Incredible Burt Wonderstone, 2013; Intervista, 1992; Invincible, 2001; It All Came True, 1940; Journey Back to Oz, 1974; **Journey into Fear**, 1943; Judex, 1963; **King Arthur**, 2004 (Merlin); King Arthur and the Knights of Justice, 1992-1993 (TV series; Merlin); Knightriders, 1981; Ladies in Love, 1936; **The Lady Vanishes**, 1938; The Last Magic Show, 2007; The Last Unicorn, 1982; Legends of Oz: Dorothy's Return, 2014; Lilly Turner, 1933; The Limping Man, 1953; Lloyd, 2001; **The Long Night**, 1947; Lord of Illusions, 1995; The Lord of the Rings, 1978; **The Lord of the Rings: The Fellowship of the Ring**, 2001; The Lord of the Rings: The Return of the King, 2003; **The Lord of the Rings: The Two Towers**, 2002; The Lord Protector, 1996; Lost in a Harem, 1944; Love on the Ground, 1984; Love 'Em and Leave 'Em, 1926; Lucinda's Spell, 2000; Magic Boy, 1961; **Magic in the Moonlight**, 2014; The Magic Show, 1983; **The Magic Sword**, 1962 (Merlin); The Magician, 1926; **The Magician**, 1959; The Magician, 1972-1974 (TV series); The Magician of Lublin, 1979; Magicians, 1982 (made-for-TV); Magicians, 2000; Magicians, 2007; The Magicians, 2015 (TV series); Magos y gigantes, 2004; The Magus, 1968; The Man Who Wagged His Tail, 1961; The Man Who Wouldn't Die, 1942; Mary Jane's Pa, 1935; The Mask of Diijon, 1946; The Master and Margaret, 1972; Merlin, 1993; Merlin, 1998 (TV miniseries); Merlin, 2008-2012 (TV series); Merlin and the Sword, 1985 (made-for-TV); Merlin: The Return, 2000; Merlin's Apprentice, 2006 (TV miniseries); Mexican Spitfire's Elephant, 1942; Mickey's 60th Birthday, 1988 (made-for-TV); Milarepa, 1974; Milarepa, 2006; Miracles for Sale, 1939; Mr. Merlin, 1981-1982 (TV series); Modesty Blaise, 1966; **Movie Crazy**, 1932; **The Mummy's Hand**, 1940; The Mummy's Tomb, 1942; The Muppets' Wizard of Oz, 2005 (made-for-TV); The Murderer Lives at Number 21, 1947; The Mystery of the Yellow Room, 2003; Needful Things, 1993; New Faces of 1937, 1937; The New Wizard of Oz, 1914; Next, 2007; **Nightmare Alley**, 1947; **Nights of Cabiria**, 1957; No Surrender, 1986; Now You See It, 2005 (made-for-TV); **Now You See Me**, 2013; Now You See Me 2, 2016; **The Official Story**, 1985; On Our Merry Way, 1948; One Hundred and One Nights, 1995; **Oz the Great and Powerful**, 2014; Paganini, 1923; Parade, 1974 (made-for-TV); **Pardon My Sarong**, 1942; **Passport to Pimlico**, 1949; The Patchwork Girl of Oz, 1914; The Phantom of Paris, 1931; Port Said, 1948; Postcards from the Zoo, 2012; The Prestige, 2006; The Prince and the Evening Star, 1979; **The Princess Bride**, 1987; The Princess and the Pauper, 1997 (made-for-TV); Quest for Camelot, 1998 (Merlin); Quicker Than the Eye, 1988; **The Raven**, 1963; The Return of Chandu, 1934; The Return of the King, 1980 (made-for-TV); Return to Oz, 1964 (made-for-TV); Return to Oz, 1985;

Road to Zanzibar, 1941; Roar, 1997- (TV series); Roaring Fire, 1982; Rough Magic, 1995; The Ruby Princess Runs Away, 2001; Rasputin, 2010; Rise and Shine, 1941; Ruslan and Ludmila, 2006; Santa Claus, 1959; **The Secret of NIMH**, 1982; The Sentinel, 1977; **7 Faces of Dr. Lao**, 1964; **Seven Sinners**, 1940; **The 7th Voyage of Sinbad**, 1958; **Shadows and Fog**, 1992; She's Got Everything, 1937; Shine on Harvest Moon, 1944; **Shrek**, 2001; **Shrek Forever After**, 2010; **Shrek the Third**, 2007; **Shrek 2**, 2004; The Sideshow, 1928; The Sign of Death, 1939; **The Silver Chalice**, 1954; **Sinbad and the Eye of the Tiger**, 1977; **Sinbad: Legend of the Seven Seas**, 2003; Sinbad of the Seven Seas, 1989; Sinbad: The Battle of the Dark Knights, 1998; **Sinbad the Sailor**, 1947; Sing Your Worries Away, 1942; The Singing Princess, 1967; Siren of Bagdad, 1953; The Slayers, 1995 (TV series); Sleeping Beauty, 2014; Snow Queen, 2002 (made-for-TV); Something Wicked This Way Comes, 1983; Songs from the Second Floor, 2000; The Sorcerer's Apprentice, 2010; Spellbound, 2011; Spooks Run Wild, 1941; Sprung! The Magic Roundabout, 2005; Star Fairies, 1985 (made-for-TV); Stardust on the Stage, 1942; Still Life, 2006; **Stolen Kisses**, 1969; The Strange Mr. Gregory, 1945; The Stripper, 1963; Stunt Rock, 1980; Sued for Libel, 1939; **Swing Time**, 1936; Swinging Hostess, 1944; **The Sword in the Stone**, 1963 (Merlin); **The Tales of Hoffmann**, 1951; Terry and the Pirates, 1940; Their Big Moment, 1934; These Foolish Things, 2005; Thief of Damascus, 1952; **This Gun for Hire**, 1942; **The Three Caballeros**, 1944; Three Girls About Town, 1941; **Three Little Words**, 1950; **The 3 Worlds of Gulliver**, 1960; Toofan, 1989; Top Banana, 1954; Tricked, 2013- (TV series); Troll, 1986; Two on a Guillotine, 1965; Unico in the Island of Magic, 1983; Up in the World, 1956; **Variety Lights**, 1965; The Vault of Horror, 1973; War Witch, 2012; Welcome Home, 1935; West of Zanzibar, 1928; When the Cat Comes, 1963; When's Your Birthday?, 1937; **Willow**, 1988; Witchville, 2010 (made-for-TV); The Wiz, 1978; The Wizard, 1989; The Wizard, 2015; The Wizard of Baghdad, 1960; The Wizard of Gore, 1970; The Wizard of Gore, 2007; The Wizard of Mars, 1965; The Wizard of Oz, 1925; **The Wizard of Oz**, 1939; The Wizard of Oz, 1982; The Wizard of Oz, 1990-1991 (TV series); The Wizard of Oz on Ice, 1996 (made-for-TV); The Wizard of Stone Mountain, 2011; Wizards, 1977; Wizards of the Demon Sword, 1991; The Wizards of the Lost Kingdom, 1985; Wizards of the Lost Kingdom II, 1989; Wizards of Waverly Place: The Movie, 2009 (made-for-TV); Wizards of Waverly Place, 2007-2012 (TV series); The Woman in Black, 2012; The Worst Witch, 1986 (made-for-TV); You Never Know Women, 1926; **Young and Innocent**, 1938; Your Highness, 2011; Zu: Warriors from the Magic Mountain, 1983.

Mars and Martians: Aelita: Queen of Mars, 1929; Alfred Hitchcock Presents, 1955-1962 (TV series; "Human Interest Story," 1959 episode); The Angry Red Planet, 1959; Attack from Mars, 1988; Batman: The Brave and the Bold, 2008-2011 (TV series); Ben X, 2007; Bill & Ted's Bogus Journey, 1991; Contamination, 1980; The Day Mars Invaded Earth, 1963; D-Day on Mars, 1966 (made-for-TV); Devil Girl from Mars, 1954; Doom, 2005; Duck Dodgers, 2003- (TV series); Five Million Years to Earth, 1968; Flash Gordon's Flight to Mars, 1938; Flight to Mars, 1951; Flying Disc Man from Mars, 1950; Flying Saucer Rock 'N' Roll, 2006; Frankenstein Meets the Space Monster, 1965; Ghosts of Mars, 2011; The Great Martian War, 1913-1917, 2013 (made-for-TV); The Infinite Worlds of H.G. Wells, 2001 (TV miniseries); **Invaders from Mars**, 1953; It! The Terror from Beyond Space, 1958; John Carter, 2012; Justice League, 2001-2006 (TV series; "Secret Origins," 2001 episode; "Secret Origins: Part II," 2001 episode; "Injustice for All," 2002 episode; "The Cat and the Canary," 2005 episode); Looney Tunes: Back in Action, 2003; Los astronautas, 1964; **Mars Attacks!**, 1996; Mars Attacks the World, 1938; Mars Needs Moms, 2011; Mars Needs Women, 1967 (made-for-TV); A Martian Christmas, 2008; The Martian Chronicles, 1980 (TV miniseries); Martians Go Home, 1989; Mercano the Martian, 2002; Missile Monsters, 1958; **Mission to Mars**, 2000; Murdoch Mysteries, 2008- (TV series; "The Annoying Red Planet,"

2008 episode); My Favorite Martian, 1963-1966 (TV series); My Favorite Martian, 1999; Pajama Party, 1964; The Purple Monster Strikes, 1945; Quartermass and the Pit, 1958 (TV miniseries); Radio-Mania, 1922; **Rocketship X-M**, 1950; Santa Claus Conquers the Martians, 1964; Santo vs. la invasion de los marcianos, 1967; Satan's Satellites, 1958 (feature version of serial Zombies of the Stratosphere); Tales of Tomorrow, 1951-1953 (TV series; "Test Flight," 1951 episode; "Appointment on Mars," 1952 episode; "Plague from Space," 1952 episode); Tracker, 2001-2002 (TV series); A Trip to Mars, 1918; Twilight Zone, 1961-1964 (TV series; "People Are Alike All Over," 1960 episode; "Mr. Dingle, the Strong," 1961 episode); **The War of the Worlds**, 1953; The War of the Worlds, 1988 (TV series); **The War of the Worlds**, 2005; The War of the Worlds: Next Century, 1981; Warlords of the Deep, 1978; Wehan Ke Log, 1967; The Wizard of Mars, 1965; Zombies of the Stratosphere, 1952 (serial).

Medical Malpractice: Awake, 2007; The Babymaker: The Dr. Cecil Jacobson Story, 1994 (made-for-TV); Bedside, 1934; Betrayal of Trust, 1994 (made-for-TV); Cimarron City, 1958-1960 (TV series; "Medicine Man," 1958 episode); **The Citadel**, 1938; The Critical List, 1978 (made-for-TV); Dead Sleep, 1992; **Detective Story**, 1951; The Good Doctor, 2011; Green Light, 1937; The Hand That Rocks the Cradle, 1992; Heaven, 1999; **The Horse Soldiers**, 1959 (John Wayne talks about the malpracticing doctors who brought about his wife's death); **The Hospital**, 1971; In the Matter of Karen Ann Quinlan, 1977 (made-for-TV); Infection, 2004; Inspector Morse, 1987-2000 (TV series; "Deadly Slumber," 1993 episode); Isolation, 2011; Jeans, 1998; Kingdom Hospital, 2004 (TV series; "Goodbye Kiss," 2004 episode); **Kings Row**, 1942; A Little Help, 2010; M*A*S*H*, 1972-1983 (TV series; "The Novocaine Mutiny," 1976 episode; "Preventative Medicine," 1979 episode); Malpractice, 2001; **Miracle on 34th Street**, 1947; Miracle on 34th Street, 1973 (made-for-TV); Negotiator, 2003 (made-for-TV); **Not as a Stranger**, 1955; Open Heart, 2004 (made-for-TV); The Penalty, 1920; Saving Hope, 2012- (TV series; "Defense," 2013 episode); Speaking of Sex, 2001; Terminal Choice, 1985; True Crimes: The First 72 Hours, 2003 (TV series; "Good Doctor," 2006 episode); **The Verdict**, 1982; Waking the Dead, 2000- (TV series; "Double Bind," 2007 episode); **Where Does It Hurt?**, 1972.

Mental Illnesses: **Anatomy of a Murder**, 1959 (irresistible impulse to commit violence); **An Angel at My Table**, 1990; **Arsenic and Old Lace**, 1944 (grandiose delusions); **Away from Her**, 2007; **A Beautiful Mind**, 2001 (paranoia); **Bedlam**, 1946 (many types); **The Best of Youth**, 2003; **Birdy**, 1984; Black Swan, 2011 (animal metamorphosis); **A Bill of Divorcement**, 1932 (shellshock); **The Cabinet of Dr. Caligari**, 1921 (controlled somnambulism); **The Caine Mutiny**, 1954 (paranoia); **Catherine the Great**, 1934 (delusions); Chattahoochee, 1990; **A Clockwork Orange**, 1971 (obsessive compulsion to commit violence); The Crime Doctor's Gamble, 1947; **The Dark Mirror**, 1946 (split personality); **The Exorcist**, 1973 (demonic possession); A Fine Madness, 1966; Frances, 1982 (manic depressive psychosis); Frankie and Alice, 2010; **Good Will Hunting**, 1997; **Harvey**, 1950 (schizophrenia; delusionary visions); **Home of the Brave**, 1949; Instinct, 1999; Irresistible, 2006; The Keeper of the Bees, 1935; **The Madness of King George**, 1994 (paranoia stemming from porphyria, or blood contamination); **Marnie**, 1964 (paranoia; guilt complex); **Mine Own Executioner**, 1947; **Mirage**, 1965 (amnesia); Nuts, 1987; On the Edge, 2001; **One Flew Over the Cuckoo's Nest**, 1975 (many types); **Play Misty for Me**, 1971 (possessive jealousy); **Private Worlds**, 1935; Psycho, 1960; **Random Harvest**, 1942 (amnesia); Samuel Bleak, 2011; **The Shining**, 1980 (schizophrenia); **The Silence of the Lambs**, 1991 (psychopathic serial killer and cannibal); **The Sixth Sense**, 1999; **The Snake Pit**, 1948 (schizophrenia); **The Sniper**, 1952 (woman hater; compulsive killer); **Spellbound**, 1945 (guilt complex); **Spiderman**, 2002 (superiority complex); Sybil, 1976 (made-for-TV; split personality); **The Three Faces** of Eve, 1957 (split personality); **12 Monkeys**, 1995; **White Heat**, 1949 (superiority complex); Woman Who Came Back, 1945.

Mermaids: Aquamarine, 2007; **The Chronicles of Narnia: The Lion, the Witch, and the Wardrobe**, 2005; **The Glass Bottom Boat**, 1966; **Harry Potter and the Goblet of Fire**, 2005; **Hook**, 1991; **Hugo**, 2011; **The Little Mermaid**, 1989; **Local Hero**, 1983; Mako Mermaids, 2013- (TV series); **Miranda**, 1949; **Mr. Peabody and the Mermaid**, 1948; **Peter Pan**, 1953; **Pirates of the Caribbean: On Stranger Tides**, 2011; **Shrek 2**, 2004; **Splash**, 1984; **Whirlpool**, 1949.

Merry-Go-Rounds: An American Crime, 2007; **An American in Paris**, 1951; Americana, 1981; At Close Range, 1986; Betrayed, 1988; Bitter Moon, 1992; Black Eye, 1974; Boy A, 2007; Bye Bye Braverman, 1968; Cain and Mabel, 1936; Carnival Story, 1954; **Carousel**, 1956; Chaos Theory, 2008; **Charade**, 1963; **Cloak and Dagger**, 1946; Comedy of Innocence, 2000; **The Crowd**, 1928; The Crush, 1993; The Destructors, 1974; The Devil to Pay!, 1930; The Divine Lady, 1929; Down the Shore, 2011; Eagle Eye, 2008; **The Egg and I**, 1947; The Eighth Day, 1996; Elizabethtown, 2005; Fading Gigolo, 2013; Gorilla at Large, 1954; Gun Crazy, 1950; Fear and Loathing in Las Vegas, 1998; Firecracker, 2005; **Flight of the Red Balloon**, 2008; Focus, 2001; **Frozen River**, 2008; The Glass Cage, 1964; **The Grand Budapest Hotel**, 2014; **Greed**, 1924; **Hanna**, 2011; He Got Game, 1998; He Knows You're Alone, 1980; The Heart Is a Lonely Hunter, 1968; **Hell Below**, 1933; How to Save a Marriage and Ruin Your Life, 1968; **Hugo**, 2011; **Hustle**, 1975; I Love You, I Love You Not, 1996; I'm Going Home, 2001; **Jeanne Eagels**, 1957; Kindergarten Cop, 1990; **La Ronde**, 1954; Little Athens, 2005; **M**, 1951; Magnifico, 2003; Malice in Wonderland, 2009; A Man Betrayed, 1941; Man with a Movie Camera, 1929; Minority Report, 2002; Mr. Right, 2009; **The Murder Man**, 1935; My Brother Is an Only Child, 2007; The Neighbor No. Thirteen, 2006; Night Tide, 1961; **Now You See Me**, 2013; **Oh! What a Lovely War**, 1969; The Omen, 2006; **One Sunday Afternoon**, 1933; The Parent Trap II, 1986 (made-for-TV); **Philomena**, 2013; **Poppy**, 1936; The Red Ibis, 1975; The Return, 2006; **Ride the Pink Horse**, 1947; Road Show, 1941; Rock My World, 2002; **Ronin**, 1998; Savannah Smiles, 1982; **Saving Mr. Banks**, 2013; Serial (Bad) Weddings, 2014; Shaan, 1980; **Shadow of the Thin Man**, 1941; Shoot 'Em Up, 2007; A Soldier's Plaything, 1930; Something Wicked This Way Comes, 1983; **State Fair**, 1945; **The Sting**, 1973; Stoker, 2013; **Strangers on a Train**, 1951; The Student Body, 1976; **Sudden Impact**, 1983; **These Three**, 1936; The Thief Lord, 2006; 3 Days to Kill, 2014; Trans, 1998; **Thunder in the City**, 1937; The Tree of Wooden Clogs, 1980; 24 Hours to Die, 2008; The Trip, 1967; The Unbearable Lightness of Being, 1988; The Warrior's Way, 2010; Wassup Rockers, 2005; **Whistle Stop**, 1946; Woman Obsessed, 1959; The Woodsman, 2004; Wretched Lives, 2001; You Can't Write a Letter, 2013.

Military Hospitals: **All Quiet on the Western Front**, 1930 (WWI); Battle Circus, 1953 (Korean War); **Battle Cry**, 1955 (WWII); **Battleground**, 1949 (WWII); **The Birth of a Nation**, 1915 (American Civil War); **The Blue Max**, 1966 (WWI); **The Bridge on the River Kwai**, 1957 (WWII); **Bright Victory**, 1951 (WWII); **Coming Home**, 1978 (Vietnam War); Cry Havoc, 1943 (WWII); **D-Day: The Sixth of June**, 1956 (WWII); **M*A*S*H***, 1970 (Korean War); **Mata Hari**, 1931 (WWI); **The Men**, 1950 (WWII); **Patton**, 1970 (WWII); **Pride of the Marines**, 1945 (WWII); **So Proudly We Hail!**, 1943 (WWII); **They Were Expendable**, 1945 (WWII); **The Victors**, 1963 (WWII); **The Young Lions**, 1958 (WWII).

Military Schools: About Face, 1952; Annapolis, 2006; Annapolis Salute, 1937; Arizona, 1931 (West Point); **Best Foot Forward**, 1943; Blondie Goes to College, 1942; **Brother Rat**, 1938 (Virginia Military Institute); Brother Rat and a Baby, 1940 (Virginia Military Institute); **Chip Off**

the Old Block, 1944; The Contender, 1944; Damien: Omen II, 1978; Dinky, 1935; Divorce in the Family, 1932; Dress Gray, 1986 (made-for-TV); The Duke of West Point, 1938; **Flesh and the Devil**, 1926; **Flirtation Walk**, 1934 (West Point); Francis Goes to West Point, 1952; Hitler's Children, 1943; Hold 'Em, Navy, 1937 (Annapolis); **The Horse Soldiers**, 1959; Junior Army, 1942; **The Long Gray Line**, 1955 (West Point); The Lords of Discipline, 1983; The Lottery Lover, 1935; **MacArthur**, 1977 (West Point); **The Major and the Minor**, 1942; Mardi Gras, 1958; Military Academy, 1940; Military Academy with That Tenth Avenue Gang, 1950; **Napoleon**, 1927; On Dress Parade, 1939; Prep and Pep, 1928; The Private War of Major Benson, 1955; **Rosalie**, 1937 (West Point); **Santa Fe Trail**, 1940 (West Point); Sky Giant, 1938; Square Shoulders, 1929; **The Strange One**, 1957; Sweet and Low-Down, 1944; **Taps**, 1981; **Task Force**, 1949 (Annapolis); **They Died with Their Boots On**, 1941 (West Point); **Tom Brown of Culver**, 1932; Too Many Parents, 1936; **West Point**, 1927; West Point of the Air, 1935; **The West Point Story**, 1950; Women at West Point, 1979 (made-for-TV).

Mimes: Alegria, 1999; An Angel Comes to Brooklyn, 1945; **Batman**, 1989; **The Best of Youth**, 2003; Bitter Victory, 1957; Blow-Up, 1966; **Children of Paradise**, 1946; **City That Never Sleeps**, 1953; **The Conversation**, 1974; **The Day of the Locust**, 1975; El Topo, 1970; EuroTrip, 2004; **Fellini Satyricon**, 1969; 500 Days of Summer, 2009; Glory Daze, 1995; Half Baked, 1998; **I'll Never Forget You**, 1951; Japanese Story, 2003; Julia, 2011; **La Strada**, 1956; The Last Butterfly, 1991; Mademoiselle, 2001; **Man of a Thousand Faces**, 1957; Man of the House, 1995; Manglehorn, 2014; **Mr. Hulot's Holiday**, 1954; Modesty Blaise, 1966; **My Uncle**, 1958; The Nanny Diaries, 2007; Open Your Eyes, 1997; **Ran**, 1985; The Reckoning, 2002; **Robin Hood: Men in Tights**, 1993; Shake It, 2001; Shakes the Clown, 1991; Shanks, 1974; **Silent Movie**, 1976; Singles, 1992; Starsky & Hutch, 2004; Strange Days, 1995; Suburban Commando, 1991; **Superman III**, 1983; Team America: World Police, 2004; This Is Spinal Tap, 1984; Transformers: The Revenge of the Fallen, 2009; **The Walk**, 2015; **The White Countess**, 2005.

Miners and Mining Towns (also see Gold Fields, this index): Across the Pacific, 1914 (gold); **The Adventures of Bullwhip Griffin**, 1967 (gold); An American Romance, 1944 (iron); Ariel, 1989 (coal); **The Ballad of Little Jo**, 1993; **Barabbas**, 1962 (sulfur); **Barbary Coast**, 1935 (gold); The Beautiful Blonde from Bashful Bend, 1949 (gold); **Billy Elliott**, 2000 (coal); Black Bart, 1948 (gold); Black Diamonds, 1932 (coal); **Black Fury**, 1935 (coal); Blind Shaft, 2003 (coal); Born to the West, 1926 (gold); **Brassed Off**, 1997 (coal); **Broken Lance**, 1954 (copper); The Chechahcos, 1924 (gold); **The Citadel**, 1938 (coal); The Claim, 2000 (gold); Clancy of the Mounted, 1933 (gold); **Coal Miner's Daughter**, 1980; **Confidential Agent**, 1945 (coal); The Crooked Trail, 1936 (gold); **Dr. Cyclops**, 1940 (radium); **The Dude Goes West**, 1948 (gold); **Dynamite**, 1930 (coal); The Eyes of Van Gogh, 2005 (coal); Fandango, 1970 (gold); **The Far Country**, 1955 (gold); The Flame of the Yukon, 1917 (gold); Fury Below, 1936 (coal); **Germinal**, 1993 (coal); Goin' South, 1978 (gold); Gold Fever, 1952; Gold Is Where You Find It, 1938; **The Gold Rush**, 1925; **Greed**, 1924 (gold); Harlan County War, 2000 (made-for-TV; coal); Heading West, 1946 (gold); Holes, 2003 (gold); **How Green Was My Valley**, 1941 (coal); In Old Sacramento, 1946 (gold); The Indians Are Coming, 1930 (gold); **The Invisible Man Returns**, 1940 (coal); Iron Man, 1951 (coal); **Jack London**, 1943 (gold); Kentucky Woman, 1983 (made-for-TV; coal); Klondike Kate, 1943 (gold); **Leatherheads**, 2008 (coal); The Little Horse Thieves, 1977 (coal); The Lone Defender, 1934 (gold); The Lone Rider and the Bandit, 1942 (gold); The Luck of Roaring Camp, 1937 (gold); Lust for Gold, 1949; **Lust for Life**, 1956 (coal); Mad Dog Morgan, 1976 (gold); The Man from Colorado, 1949 (gold); Margaret's Museum, 1996 (coal); **Matewan**, 1987 (coal); **The Miracle of the Bells**,

1948 (coal); **The Molly Maguires**, 1970 (coal); Montana Territory, 1952 (gold); **My Son, My Son!**, 1940 (coal); North Country, 2005 (iron ore); **North to Alaska**, 1960; **October Sky**, 1999 (coal); **Paint Your Wagon**, 1969 (gold); **Pale Rider**, 1985 (gold); **Pittsburgh**, 1942 (coal); The Rainbow, 1989 (coal); **Random Harvest**, 1942 (coal); **The Razor's Edge**, 1946 (coal); **Ride the High Country**, 1962 (gold); Rockin' in the Rockies, 1945 (gold); The San Francisco Story, 1952 (gold); Senorita from the West, 1934 (gold); The Silent Hero, 1927 (gold); Silver City, 1951; Silver River, 1948; Solino, 2003 (coal); Son of the Morning Star, 1991 (made-for-TV; gold); **Sons and Lovers**, 1960 (coal); **Spartacus**, 1960; The Spoilers, 1914 (gold); **The Spoilers**, 1930 (gold); **The Spoilers**, 1942 (gold); The Spoilers, 1955 (gold); Spring Night, Summer Night, 1967 (coal); Stage to Chino, 1940 (gold); Stagecoach Express, 1942 (gold); **The Stars Look Down**, 1941 (coal); **Sutter's Gold**, 1936; **This Sporting Life**, 1963 (coal); Thunder Mountain, 1935 (gold); **The Treasure of the Sierra Madre**, 1948 (gold); The Valiant Hombre, 1948 (gold); **Welcome to Hard Times**, 1967 (gold); **White Fang**, 1991 (gold); **Wild Geese Calling**, 1941 (gold); Wings of the Hawk, 1953 (gold); **Women in Love**, 1970 (coal); **Yellow Sky**, 1948; Zoolander, 2001 (coal).

Missionaries (Africa): **The African Queen**, 1951 (German East Africa); Bill Wallace of China, 1967; Black and White in Color, 1977 (French Senegal in WWI); Captive Girl, 1950; Cardinal Messias, 1939 (Ethiopia; Guglielmo Massaia, 1809-1889; Catholic cardinal and capuchin friar); Darkest Africa, 1936; Dominion: Prequel to the Exorcist, 2005 (East Africa); **The Exorcist**, 1973 (East Africa); The Exorcist: The Beginning, 2004 (East Africa); **Gandhi**, 1982 (South Africa); Gold Coast, 2015; **King Solomon's Mines**, 1937; **King Solomon's Mines**, 1950; King Solomon's Mines, 1985; King Solomon's Mines, 2004; **Kongo**, 1932; **Mogambo**, 1953 (Kenya); Monster from Green Hell, 1957; **Mountains of the Moon**, 1990; **The Nun's Story**, 1959 (Congo); **Of Gods and Men**, 2011 (Algeria); The Roses of the Desert, 2006 (Libya); **Stanley and Livingstone**, 1939 (East Africa; Tanganyika); The Temple of Dusk, 1918; **Trader Horn**, 1931; Untamed, 1955 (South Africa); West of Zanzibar, 1928 (East Africa); **White Cargo**, 1942 (Congo); **White Witch Doctor**, 1953 (Belgian Congo); Wild Zone, 1989; **Zulu**, 1964 (Natal Province, South Africa, 1879).

Missionaries (Asia): Barricade, 1939 (China); Bethune: The Making of a Hero, 1993 (China; Norman Bethune, Canadian missionary physician, 1890-1939); Breed of the Sea, 1926 (China); **The Bitter Tea of General Yen**, 1933 (China); Black Kiss, 2004 (Japan); **Black Narcissus**, 1947 (Tibet); **The Cat's-Paw**, 1934 (China); Charlie Chan in Shanghai, 1935 (China); **China Sky**, 1945 (China); **Flying Tigers**, 1942 (China); **God Is My Co-Pilot**, 1945 (China); Hudson Taylor, 1981 (China; British Protestant missionary, 1832-1905); **The Inn of the Sixth Happiness**, 1958 (1936-1938 China; Gladys Aylward); Journey of Honor, 1991 (17th-Century Japan); **The Keys of the Kingdom**, 1944 (China; Tibet); **The Left Hand of God**, 1955 (China); Lorenzo Ruiz, 1988 (Japan; Filipino Catholic saint, 1600-1637); **Lost Horizon**, 1937 (China); Lost Horizon, 1973 (China); Night Plane from Chunking, 1943 (China); Painted Fire, 2002 (19th-Century Korea); Pavilion of Women, 2001 (China); Rambo, 2008 (Burma); The Right to Love, 1930 (China); **Rogue's Regiment**, 1948 (Indochina); **The Sand Pebbles**, 1966 (China, 1926); Satan Never Sleeps, 1962 (China); **7 Women**, 1966 (China); **Shanghai Express**, 1932 (China); Shanghai Surprise, 1986 (China); The Sickle or the Cross, 1949 (China); Shogun, 1980 (TV miniseries; Japan); Silence, 1971 (17th-Century Japan); **Singapore**, 1947; State Department: File 649, 1949 (China); The Temple of Dusk, 1918 (Japan); Transsiberian, 2008 (China); West of Shanghai, 1937 (China).

Missionaries (Australia and New Zealand): **Australia**, 2008; **Green Dolphin Street**, 1947 (New Zealand); Shadow of the Boomerang, 1960 (Australia).

Missionaries (Caribbean Islands): **I Walked with a Zombie**, 1943; **White Zombie**, 1932 (Haiti).

Missionaries (Europe): Au revoir les enfants, 1987 (France); The Awakening, 1956 (Italy); Beowulf & Grendel, 2005 (Denmark); The Best Two Years, 2004 (Netherlands); **The Bicycle Thieves**, 1949; A Canterbury Tale, 1949 (England); **Chariots of Fire**, 1981; Daens, 1992 (Belgium; Adolf Daens, Catholic priest, 1839-1907); The Errand of Angels, 2008 (Austria); **Major Barbara**, 1941 (Salvation Army; England); Mendel, 1998 (Norway); **Monsieur Vincent**, 1948 (Catholic priest St.Vincent de Paul, 1581-1660; Black Plague of the 17th Century); St. Paul, 2000 (Rome, Italy; 1st Century); The Saratov Approach, 2013 (Russia); Shining Victory, 1941 (Scotland); The Singing Nun, 1966 (Belgium).

Missionaries (India): Beyond the Next Mountain, 1987; The Darjeeling Limited, 2007; Flammen im Paradies, 1997; **Gandhi**, 1982; **The Rains Came**, 1939; **The Rains of Ranchipur**, 1955; **The Razor's Edge**, 1946; **Thunder in the East**, 1953.

Missionaries (Latin America): Cabeza de Vaca, 1992 (Mexico); **Captain from Castile**, 1947 (Hernan Cortes; 16th-Century Mexico); El Mago, 1949 (Mexico); Mission to Glory: A True Story, 1977 (Mexico; Father Eusebio Francisco Kino, 17th-18th Centuries); The Mosquito Coast, 1986.

Missionaries (Middle East): Auction of Souls, 1919 (Turkey); **The Crusades**, 1935 (12th-Century Jerusalem; Third Crusade; Richard the Lionheart, Saladin); **King Richard and the Crusaders**, 1954 (12th-Century Jerusalem; Third Crusade; Richard the Lionheart, Saladin); **Kingdom of Heaven**, 2005 (12th-Century Jerusalem; Saladin); Ministry of Vengeance, 1989 (Lebanon).

Missionaries (North America): Apache Rifles, 1964 (Arizona); **The Apostle**, 1997; **Black Robe**, 1991 (Canada); **The Color Purple**, 1985; The First Legion, 1951; God's Army, 2000 (Los Angeles); **Guys and Dolls**, 1955 (Salvation Army; NYC); Hate Crime, 2005; Holyman Undercover, 2010 (Hollywood); Land of Plenty, 2004 (Los Angeles); Mission to Glory: A True Story, 1977 (Arizona; California; Father Eusebio Francisco Kino, 17th-18th Centuries); **A Place in the Sun**, 1951 (Chicago); The Power of God, 1942; The Reaping, 2007 (Louisiana); **Seraphin Falls**, 2007; **Seven Cities of Gold**, 1955 (18th-Century California; Father Junipero Serra); **She Done Him Wrong**, 1933 (NYC; The Bowery; Salvation Army type organization); Soul of the Slums, 1931 (NYC); States of Grace, 2005 (Mormon missionary in Santa Monica, California); **Tales of Manhattan**, 1942 (NYC); **There Will Be Blood**, 2007 (Southwest; California); Wesley, 2009 (John Wesley; 1732 Georgia).

Missionaries (Pacific Ocean): **The Beachcomber**, 1938 (Dutch East Indies); Black Paradise, 1926; Breed of the Sea, 1926; Down Among the Sheltering Palms, 1953; First Fruits, 1982 (West Indies); The Flaming Signal, 1933; Godless Men, 1920; **Hawaii**, 1966; I'll Give My Life, 1960 (New Guinea); In a Savage Land, 1999 (New Guinea); Isle of Destiny, 1940; Mission Batangas, 1968 (Philippines); Molokai, 1999 (Hawaii); The Other Side of Heaven, 2001 (Tongan Islands); Paradise Road, 1997 (Sumatra); Peace Child, 1972; Pearl of the South Pacific, 1955; **Rain**, 1932 (Pago Pago); Return to Paradise, 1953 (Polynesian island); **Sadie Thompson**, 1928 (Pago Pago); Savage Islands, 1983; The Sleeping Dictionary, 2003 (Borneo); Wilson's Reward, 1980 (made-for-TV; West Indies); A Woman There Was, 1919.

Missionaries (South America): **At Play in the Fields of the Lord**, 1991 (Argentina; Brazil); **Fitzcarraldo**, 1982 (Brazil); The Mission, 1986; Last Flight Out, 2004 (Colombia); Jerico, 1992 (16th-Century

Venezuela); **Murphy's War**, 1971 (Orinoco River, Venezuela); Valley of Mystery, 1967 (made-for-TV; Venezuela).

Mississippi River: The Adventures of Huck Finn, 1993; **The Adventures of Huckleberry Finn**, 1960; The Adventures of Huckleberry Finn, 1984 (animated; made-for-TV); **The Adventures of Mark Twain**, 1944; **The Adventures of Tom Sawyer**, 1938; The Adventures of Tom Sawyer, 1986; **Band of Angels**, 1957; **Banjo on My Knee**, 1936; Bed of Roses, 1933; Belle Le Grand, 1951; Cameo Kirby, 1914; **The Cincinnati Kid**, 1965; Davy Crockett on the Mississippi, 1976 (made-for-TV); Delirium, 1979; Dixie Jamboree, 1944; Duel on the Mississippi, 1955; **Fighting Caravans**, 1931; The Flame of New Orleans, 1941; Frankie and Johnny, 1966; Frontier Woman, 1956; The Gambler from Natchez, 1954; Heaven on Earth, 1931; Hitchin' Posts, 1920; **Huckleberry Finn**, 1931; **Huckleberry Finn**, 1939; Huckleberry Finn, 1975 (made-for-TV); I Dream of Jeanie, 1952; **In the Heat of the Night**, 1967; **The Iron Mistress**, 1952; The Jack-Knife World, 1920; Jesse James Rides Again, 1947 (serial); Lady for a Night, 1942; Land of Liberty, 1939; Land of Sky Blue Water, 2011; The Louisiana Hussy, 1959; Mark Twain: Beneath the Laughter, 1979 (made-for-TV); **Mississippi**, 1935; **The Mississippi Gambler**, 1953; Mississippi Rhythm, 1949; Mysterious Crossing, 1936; The Mystery Man, 1935; Mystery of the Riverboat, 1944 (serial); The Naughty Nineties, 1945; Obsession, 1976; Old Louisiana, 1937; The Painted Stallion, 1937; River Lady, 1948; Riverboat Rhythm, 1946; The Runaway Barge, 1975 (made-for-TV); **The Secret Life of Walter Mitty**, 1947; Showboat, 1929; **Showboat**, 1936; Showboat, 1951; **Steamboat Round the Bend**, 1935; **The Straight Story**, 1999; Swamp Fire, 1946; Syncopation, 1942; To Survive, 2014; Tom Sawyer, 1917; **Tom Sawyer**, 1930; **Tom Sawyer**, 1973; Tom Sawyer, 1973 (made-for-TV); Tom Sawyer, 2011; Tom Sawyer & Huckleberry Finn, 2014; Uncle Tom's Cabin, 1918; **Uncle Tom's Cabin**, 1927; The Way of All Men, 1930; **Wild River**, 1960; Yes Sir, Mr. Bones, 1951.

Moonshiners and Moonshining: Amigo, 2011; Bad Georgia Road, 1977; **The Belles of St. Trinian's**, 1954; Big Bad Mama, 1974; Bootleggers, 1974; The Burning Hills, 1956; **Carbine Williams**, 1952; **The Cat's Meow**, 2001; Cherokee Uprising, 1953; **Coal Miner's Daughter**, 1980; Dixie Dynamite, 1976; **The Egg and I**, 1947; **The Flim-Flam Man**, 1967; Foxfire Light, 1982; Frozen Heart, 1993; Harlan County War, 2000 (made-for-TV); Hooch, 1977; Hot Lead and Cold Feet, 1978; The Howling Miller, 1982; It's Up to Us, 1973; The Jerk, 1979; Judith of the Cumberlands, 1916; Juha, 2003; Kentucky Moonshine, 1938; King of the Pack, 1926; Kissin' Cousins, 1964; The Last American Hero, 1973; The Last of the High Kings, 1988; **Lawless**, 2012; Lucky Lady, 1975; **Make Mine Music**, 1946; A Man Without a Wife, 1983; Mongoland, 2000; Monsieur Gangster, 1963; Moonrunners, 1975; Moonshine, 2006; Moonshine County Express, 1977; Moonshine Highway, 1996 (made-for-TV); Moonshine Mountain, 1964; The Moonshine War, 1970; **My Dog Skip**, 2000; The Nest of the Cuckoo Bird, 1965; The Night Watch, 1926; **Nightmare Alley**, 1947; Our Mr. Sun, 1956 (made-for-TV); **Paper Moon**, 1973; The Quiet Village, 1997; The Road Hustlers, 1968; Rocco and His Brothers, 1962; Ruby Gentry, 1953; The Rutherford County Line, 1987; The Scarlet Drop, 1918; Sheffey, 1977; The Shepherd of the Hills, 1919; **The Shepherd of the Hills**, 1941; The Silent Avenger, 1926; Soggy Bottom U.S.A., 1981; Song of Warsaw, 1953; Swamp County, 1966; The Tender Warrior, 1971; **They Live by Night**, 1949; **Thunder Road**, 1958; **Walking Tall**, 1973; **White Lightning**, 1973; **A Wicked Woman**, 1934; **The Wind Journeys**, 2010. Note: For detailed information on moonshiners and moonshining, see my books *Bloodletters and Badmen* (M. Evans, 1973); *Encyclopedia of World Crime*; 8 volumes (CrimeBooks, Inc., 1990); *The Great Pictorial History of World Crime*; 2 volumes (History, Inc., 2004).

Mountain Climbing, Mountain Climbers and Mountaineers: The Abom-inable Snowman, 1957 (Yeti); The Ascent, 1994; **Aguirre: The Wrath of God**, 1972; **Alive**, 1993 (Andes Mountains); **Auntie Mame**, 1958 (Matterhorn); Bergwind, 1963; Beyond the Edge, 2014 (Everest; Edmund Hillary and Tenzing Norgay); Beyond the Rocks, 1922; **Blind Husbands**, 1919 (Dolomites); The Blue Light, 1934; Bridal Suite, 1939; The Bulldog Breed, 1960; Canoa, 1976; Cast Away, 2000; The Challenge, 1939 (ill-fated 1865 climb on Matterhorn); **Cliffhanger**, 1993; The Climb, 1986; The Climb, 2002; Courage Mountain, 1990; Death Hunt, 1981; Demon of the Himalayas, 1935; **The Devil's Brigade**, 1968; Devil's Pass, 2013; **Drums in the Deep South**, 1951; The Eiger Sanction, 1975; The Endless Knot, 2007; Everest, 2007 (TV miniseries); **Everest**, 2015; **A Farewell to Arms**, 1932; **A Farewell to Arms**, 1957; Final Ascent, 2000 (made-for-TV); Five Days One Summer, 1982 (Swiss Alps); The Giant of the Dolomites, 1927; The Girl from the Chartreuse, 2005; **The Gold Rush**, 1925 (Alaska); **Goodbye, Mr. Chips**, 1939; Goodbye, Mr. Chips, 2002; Gran Paradiso, 2000; The Great Leap, 1927; **The Guns of Navarone**, 1961; High Ice, 1980 (made-for-TV); Himalaya, 2016; The Holy Mountain, 1927; The Holy Mountain, 1973; Into Thin Air: Death on Everest, 1997 (made-for-TV); Kleine Scheidegg, 1937 (Swiss Alps); K2, 1992; **Letter from an Unknown Woman**, 1948; **The Longest Day**, 1962 (climbing Pointe du Hoc, a 100-foot cliff, during the 1944 Normandy invasion); Lost Continent, 1951; **Lost Horizon**, 1937 (Himalayas); Love and Bullets, 1979 (Matterhorn); Lowlands, 1981; Magic Boy, 1961; Man Beast, 1956 (Yeti); Midnight Eagle, 2007; Mount Hakkoda, 2014 (ill-fated Japanese military exercise in 1902); The Mountain, 1956; The Mountain Calls, 1938 (ill-fated 1865 climb on Matterhorn); Mountain Crystal, 1949; The Mountaineers, 1925; Mountains on Fire, 1931 (shot in the Dolomites); Nanga Parbat, 2010 (ill-fated 1970 climb); Never Again as Before, 2005; **Nim's Island**, 2008; North Face, 2008 (Eiger in the Bernese Alps); 127 Hours, 2011; Operation Edelweiss, 1954; The Passage, 1979 (Pyrenees); **Pathfinder**, 1988; The Peak Scaler, 1937; The Place of the Dead, 1997; Premier de Cordee, 1999 (made-for-TV); **Private Lives**, 1931; The Rebel, 1933 (Austrian Alps); **Road to Utopia**, 1946; S.O.S. Iceberg, 1934 (Bernina Alps); Sacred Waters, 1932; Sacred Waters, 1962; Scream of Stone, 1991 (Cerro Torre); **Secret Agent**, 1936; **Seven Years in Tibet**, 1997; **She**, 1935; Shoot to Kill, 1988; The Silent Barrier, 1920; Snowbound, 1949; The Son of the White Mountain, 1933; **The Squaw Man**, 1914; Stars at Noon, 1959; Storm and Sorrow, 1990 (made-for-TV); Storm Over Mont Blanc, 1932; Struggle for the Matterhorn, 1929; Survival Quest, 1988; **Third Man on the Mountain**, 1959; **The Treasure of the Sierra Madre**, 1948; Vertical Limit, 2000; The Vulture Wally, 1921; **The Werewolf of London**, 1935 (Tibetan Mountains); What Lies Above, 2004; **Where Eagles Dare**, 1969; **White Fang**, 1991 (Alaskan Gold Rush); The White Hell of Pitz Palu, 1930; The White Hell of Pitz Palu, 1953; **The White Tower**, 1950 (role model for Matterhorn); Wide Country, 1962-1963 (TV series; "A Cry from the Mountain," 1963 episode); A Wife Confesses, 1961; With a Friend Like Harry, 2001 (Matterhorn); Yevade Subramanyam, 2015 (Everest).

Movie Moguls: **The Aviator**, 2004; **The Bad and the Beautiful**, 1952; **The Carpetbaggers**, 1964; **The Day of the Locust**, 1975; **It's a Great Feeling**, 1949; **The Last Tycoon**, 1976; **The Miracle of the Bells**, 1948; **Silent Movie**, 1976; **Singin' in the Rain**, 1952; **A Star Is Born**, 1937; **A Star Is Born**, 1954; A Star Is Born, 1976; **Sullivan's Travels**, 1941; **Sunset Boulevard**, 1950; **What Price Hollywood?**, 1932.

Movie Stars: **The Aviator**, 2004; **The Bad and the Beautiful**, 1952; **Best Foot Forward**, 1943; **Bombshell**, 1933; **The Carpetbaggers**, 1964; **The Cotton Club**, 1984; **Hollywood Canteen**, 1944; **Hollywood Cavalcade**, 1939; **It's a Great Feeling**, 1949; **J. Edgar**, 2011; **The Purple Rose of Cairo**, 1985; **Souls for Sale**, 1923; **The Star**, 1952; **A Star Is Born**, 1937; **A Star Is Born**, 1954; **Thank Your Lucky Stars**, 1943; **What Price Hollywood?**, 1932; **Will Success Spoil Rock Hunter?**, 1957.

Movie Theaters: **Across the Pacific**, 1942; Another 48 Hours, 1990; **The Artist**, 2012; **The Aviator**, 2004; **Annie Hall**, 1977; **Beautiful Creatures**, 2013; **Blazing Saddles**, 1974; The Blob, 1957; The Blob, 1988; Blow Out, 1981; The Bodyguard, 1992; **Bonnie and Clyde**, 1967; **Breathless**, 1961; **Brief Encounter**, 1945; Broken City, 2013; Bulletproof Monk, 2003; The Butterfly Effect, 2004; **Cape Fear**, 1991; **Captain America: The First Avenger**, 2011; **Catch Me If You Can**, 2002; **The Cider House Rules**, 1999; **Cinema Paradiso**, 1988; **Clash by Night**, 1952; **A Clockwork Orange**, 1971; Come See the Paradise, 1990; **Coogan's Bluff**, 1968; **Crimes and Misdemeanors**, 1989; **Crossfire**, 1947; Dancer in the Dark, 2000; **The Day of the Locust**, 1975; **Desperately Seeking Susan**, 1985; Dillinger, 1945; Dillinger, 1973; **Diner**, 1982; **Don Jon**, 2013; The Doors, 1991; Earthquake, 1974; **Ed Wood**, 1994; **84 Charing Cross Road**, 1987; Far from Heaven, 2002; 500 Days of Summer, 2009; **The 400 Blows**, 1959; **Get Shorty**, 1995; Ghost World, 2001; **The Godfather**, 1972; Greetings, 1968; The Good German, 2006; **Groundhog Day**, 1993; **Hangmen Also Die**, 1943; The Hard Way, 1991; Hitchcock, 2012; Home of the Brave, 2006; **Hud**, 1963; **Hustle**, 1975; **I Wake Up Screaming**, 1941; **In America**, 2003; **J. Edgar**, 2011; **Jarhead**, 2005; **The Killers**, 1946; **The Last Emperor**, 1987; **The Last Picture Show**, 1971; **A Little Romance**, 1979; Lovelace, 2013; Married Life, 2007; **Matinee**, 1993; **My Dog Skip**, 2000; **The Muppet Movie**, 1979; **The Muppets Take Manhattan**, 1984; **1941**, 1979; The Omega Man, 1971; **Once Upon a Time in America**, 1984; **The Pelican Brief**, 1993; **The Perks of Being a Wallflower**, 2012; **Play It Again, Sam**, 1972; **Public Enemies**, 2009; **The Purple Rose of Cairo**, 1985; Racing with the Moon, 1984; **Ragtime**, 1981; **The Rainmaker**, 1997; **Reds**, 1981; Regarding Henry, 1991; **Sabotage**, 1937; **Saboteur**, 1942; **Saving Mr. Banks**, 2013; **Seabiscuit**, 2003; **The Seven Year Itch**, 1955; **Shadow of a Doubt**, 1943; **Silent Movie**, 1976; **Singin' in the Rain**, 1952; Sky Captain and the World of Tomorrow, 2004; **Somebody Up There Likes Me**, 1956; **The SpongeBob SquarePants Movie**, 2004; **Stir of Echoes**, 1999; The Tingler, 1959; True Romance, 1993; **12 Monkeys**, 1995; Valentino, 1977; **The War of the Worlds**, 1953; White House Down, 2013; **You've Got Mail**, 1998; **Zodiac**, 2007.

Multiple Personalities (Dissociative Identity Disorder; Multiple Personality Disorder): All Around the Town, 2002 (made-for-TV); Angel's Dance, 1999; The Befallen, 2003 (TV miniseries); **Bewitched**, 1945; Color of Night, 1994; Dark Corners, 2006; Dear Diary, 1989; **Dr. Jekyll and Mr. Hyde**, 1920; **Dr. Jekyll and Mr. Hyde**, 1931; **Dr. Jekyll and Mr. Hyde**, 1941; Dorothy Mills, 2008; Eden Log, 2007; Femme Fatale, 1991; The Five of Me, 1981 (made-for-TV); Flirting with Danger, 2006 (made-for-TV); Frankie & Alice, 2010; H, 2002; **Hangover Square**, 1945; Hangover Square, 2009; Her Deadly Rival, 1995 (made-for-TV); Heroes, 2006-2010 (TV series); A History of Violence, 2005; House of Dust, 2013; I'm Not There, 2007; Identity, 2003; Keep My Grave Open, 1976; Keiho, 1999; Lizzie, 1957; Loose Cannons, 1990; Mad Detective, 2008; **Madonna of the Seven Moons**, 1945; Me Myself and I, 1992; Me, Myself & Irene, 2000; **Mirage**, 1965; Mirage, 1995; Never Talk to Strangers, 1995; 9, 2009; The Nines, 2007; Norma Jean & Marilyn, 1996 (made-for-TV); On the Count of Zero, 2007; One Life to Live, 1968-2013 (TV series); Passion of the Mind, 2000; Primal Fear, 1996; **Psycho**, 1960; Psycho, 1998; Psycho Beach Party, 2000; Raising Cain, 1992; Rampage: The Hillside Strangler Murders, 2006; A Reflection of Fear, 1992; The Scribbler, 2014; Secret Window, 2004; Session 9, 2001; Shattered Image, 1998; 6 Souls, 2010; Ski Patrol, 1990; Sybil, 1976 (TV miniseries); The Terror Inside, 1996 (made-for-TV); Thr3e, 2007; **The Three Faces of Eve**, 1957; Three Lives and Only One Death, 1997; Twin Peaks, 1990-1991 (TV series); Twin Peaks: Fire Walk with Me, 1992; United States of Tara, 2009-2011 (TV series); Voice, 2005; Voices Within: The Lives of Truddi Chase, 1990 (made-for-TV); Wicked Wicked Games, 2006- (TV series); **Zelig**, 1983.

Nazi Germany (prior to WWII): **Above Suspicion**, 1943 (Honeymooners act as British spies in Nazi Germany prior to WWII); Address Unknown, 1944 (art dealer returns to his native Germany to embrace Nazi beliefs); Bonhoeffer: Agent of Grace, 2000 (life of German clergyman Dietrich Bonhoeffer, who opposed Hitler's regime); **The Book Thief**, 2013 (Germans opposed to the Nazi regime who hide Jews prior to WWII); **Confessions of a Nazi Spy**, 1939 (espionage agents in Germany and the U.S. prior to WWII); **The Damned**, 1969 (the rise of Hitler's SA Storm Troopers and SS); Enemy of Women, 1944 (rise of Nazi propaganda minister Paul Joseph Goebbels); **Escape**, 1940 (American attempts to get his mother released from a Nazi concentration camp in 1938); Good, 2008 (the rise of National Socialism); **The Hindenburg**, 1975 (the sabotaging of the Nazi dirigible LZ 129 in 1937); Hitler: Beast of Berlin, 1939 (anti-Nazi activists in Germany prior to WWII); **The Hitler Gang**, 1944 (the rise of Adolf Hitler in Germany); Hitler's SS: Portrait in Evil, 1985 (made-for-TV); Joe and Max, 2002 (made-for-TV; story of German prizefighter Max Schmeling, who fought U.S. boxer Joe Louis); **Julia**, 1977 (American playwright Lillian Hellman smuggles money into Nazi Germany to aid her closest friend and other members of the underground); **The Man I Married**, 1940 (American woman marries a German, who becomes a Nazi); **The Mortal Storm**, 1940 (rise of Hitler's SA Storm Troopers); **None Shall Escape**, 1944 (the rise to power of a Nazi officer); Pastor Hall, 1940 (profile of German clergyman Martin Neimuller, who opposed the Nazis); Seven Journeys, 1951 (profiles seven owners of a car during the years of Nazi Germany); **Spitfire**, 1943 (scenes showing how Germany is building a massive air force before WWII); **Taking Sides**, 2003 (the life of Berlin orchestra leader Wilhelm Furtzwanger); **13 Minutes**, 2015 (profiling Georg Elser, who attempted the assassination of Adolf Hitler in 1939); **The Tin Drum**, 1980 (the Nazi takeover of Danzig).

Nazi Indoctrination of Children (and Hitler Youth): Before the Fall, 2005; Border Street, 1950; **The Boys from Brazil**, 1978; **The Bridge at Remagen**, 1969; **Cabaret**, 1972; **Commandos Strike at Dawn**, 1942; **Confessions of a Nazi Spy**, 1939; David, 1982; **Decision Before Dawn**, 1951; Der Unhold, 1996; **Downfall**, 2004; Enemy of Women, 1944 (profile of Nazi propaganda chief Joseph Goebbels); **Europa Europa**, 1991; **49th Parallel**, 1942; Hande hoch, 1942 (Nazi propaganda drama); Himmelhunde, 1942 (Nazi propaganda drama); **The Hitler Gang**, 1944; Hitler's Children, 1943; Jakko, 1941 (Nazi propaganda drama); Jurgens, 1941 (Nazi propaganda drama); Kopf hoch, Johannes!, 1941 (Nazi propaganda drama); **Mission to Moscow**, 1943; **The Mortal Storm**, 1940; Our Flags Lead Us Forward, 1933 (Nazi propaganda drama); Rotation, 1950; S.A.-Mann Brand, 1934 (Nazi propaganda drama); Silent Night, 2002 (made-for-TV); **Stalag 17**, 1953; **This Land Is Mine**, 1943; **The Tin Drum**, 1980; **Tomorrow the World**, 1944.

Nazi Resurgence (post-WWII): **Berlin Express**, 1948; **The Blues Brothers**, 1980; **The Boys from Brazil**, 1978; **Captain Carey, U.S.A.**, 1950; **Cornered**, 1945; **The House on Carroll Street**, 1988; **The Man in the Glass Booth**, 1975; **Marathon Man**, 1976; **Notorious**, 1946; **The Odessa File**, 1974; **Rogue's Regiment**, 1948; **The Stranger**, 1946; **Talk Radio**, 1989.

Nazi Spies (also see Espionage, this index): **Above Suspicion**, 1943; The Adventures of Smilin' Jack, 1943; **Adventures of Tartu**, 1943; Arizona Gang Busters, 1940; Bell-Bottom George, 1944; **Berlin Express**, 1948; Blue, White and Perfect, 1942; **Captain Carey, U.S.A.**, 1950; **Confessions of a Nazi Spy**, 1939; **Cornered**, 1945; Cottage to Let, 1943; The Dawn Express, 1942; **The Eagle Has Landed**, 1976; **Eye of the Needle**, 1965; **Escape**, 1940; **Escape in the Desert**, 1945; **The Falcon's Brother**, 1942; **Foreign Correspondent**, 1940; **The 49th Parallel**, 1942; **The House on Carroll Street**, 1988; **The House on 92nd Street**, 1945; Junior Army, 1942; **Man Hunt**, 1941; **The Man Who Never Was**, 1956; **Marathon Man**, 1976; Mountain Rhythm, 1944;

Murder in the Air, 1940; **Nazi Agent**, 1942; The Next of Kin, 1943; Night Plane from Chungking, 1943; **Night Train to Munich**, 1940; **Northern Pursuit**, 1943; **Notorious**, 1946; **The Odessa File**, 1976; Odette, 1951; **Passage to Marseille**, 1944; Remember Pearl Harbor, 1942; **Rogue's Regiment**, 1948; **Schindler's List**, 1993; The Sea Wolves, 1981; The Secret Code, 1942; **The Seventh Cross**, 1944; **Stalag 17**, 1953; Step by Step, 1946; **The Stranger**, 1946; The Sultan's Daughter, 1944; Texas Man Hunt, 1942; **They Came to Blow Up America**, 1943; **Tobruk**, 1967; Traitor Spy, 1940; U-Boat Prisoner, 1944; **Where Eagles Dare**, 1969; Where the Trail Ends, 1942. Note: For more information on Nazi spies, see my book *Spies: A Narrative Encyclopedia of Dirty Deeds and Double Dealing from Biblical Times to Today* (M. Evans, 1997).

Nazis: **Above Suspicion**, 1943; The Adventures of Smilin' Jack, 1943; **Adventures of Tartu**, 1943; **Amen**, 2002; Arizona Gang Busters, 1940; Beasts of Berlin, 1939; Bell-Bottom George, 1944; **Berlin Express**, 1948; Blood Creek, 2009; Blue, White and Perfect, 1942; **The Boys from Brazil**, 1978; **Cabaret**, 1972; **Casablanca**, 1942; **Confessions of a Nazi Spy**, 1939; **Cornered**, 1945; Cottage to Let, 1943; **Escape**, 1940; **Escape in the Desert**, 1945; **The Falcon's Brother**, 1942; **Foreign Correspondent**, 1940; **The 49th Parallel**, 1942; Four Sons, 1940; **The House on Carroll Street**, 1988; **The House on 92nd Street**, 1945; Junior Army, 1942; **Man Hunt**, 1941; **The Man I Married**, 1940; **The Man in the Glass Booth**, 1975; **The Man Who Never Was**, 1956; **Marathon Man**, 1976; **The Mortal Storm**, 1940; Mountain Rhythm, 1944; Murder in the Air, 1940; **Nazi Agent**, 1942; The Next of Kin, 1943; Night Plane from Chungking, 1943; **Night Train to Munich**, 1940; **Northern Pursuit**, 1943; **Notorious**, 1946; **The Odessa File**, 1976; Odette, 1951; **Passage to Marseille**, 1944; Remember Pearl Harbor, 1942; **Rogue's Regiment**, 1948; **Schindler's List**, 1993; The Sea Wolves, 1981; The Secret Code, 1942; **The Seventh Cross**, 1944; **Stalag 17**, 1953; Step by Step, 1946; **The Stranger**, 1946; The Sultan's Daughter, 1944; Texas Man Hunt, 1942; **They Came to Blow Up America**, 1943; **Tobruk**, 1967; Traitor Spy, 1940; U-Boat Prisoner, 1944; **Where Eagles Dare**, 1969; Where the Trail Ends, 1942.

Newlyweds: **Addams Family Values**, 1993; After Tomorrow, 1932; Amy Foster, 1997; The Big Year, 2011; Cheri, 2009; **Claudia**, 1943; Cry Hollow, 1952; Curse of the Fly, 1965; Dark Country, 2009; Dead Men Tell, 1941; Dr. Gillespie's New Assistant, 1942; **Earth vs. the Flying Saucers**, 1956; **The English Patient**, 1996; **Eye of the Needle**, 1965; Faster, 2010; **Father Goose**, 1964; **Father of the Bride**, 1950; Fire, 1997; Fools Rush In, 1997; French Dressing, 1927; **Hard Eight**, 1997; Helena from the Wedding, 2010; **The High and the Mighty**, 1954; **His Kind of Woman**, 1951; Honeymoon, 2013; The Honeymoon's Over, 1939; **The Hurricane**, 1937; I Bury the Living, 1958; **Idiot's Delight**, 1939; In a Savage Land, 1999; In the Meantime, Darling, 1944; **It Happened One Night**, 1934; Kaos, 1984; Kamikaze, 2014; The Kettles on Old MacDonald's Farm, 1957; The Kiss of the Vampire, 1963; **Knock on Any Door**, 1949; Love and Kisses, 1965; Machete, 1958; **The More the Merrier**, 1943; **The Naked Jungle**, 1954; Neglected by His Wife, 1947; Newlyweds, 1993-1994 (TV series); Newlyweds, 2011; **Niagara**, 1953; **Not as a Stranger**, 1955; One Week, 1920; **A Perfect Getaway**, 2009; The Piano Room, 2013; **Picnic**, 1955; The Rocky Horror Picture Show, 1975; **Rocky II**, 1979; Ruby Gentry, 1952; **Sands of Iwo Jima**, 1949; **Saturday's Children**, 1940; Seventh Moon, 2008; **The Tall T**, 1957; To Rome with Love, 2012; True as a Turtle, 1957; Turned Out Nice Again, 1941; Ulysses and the Stars, 1976; Walk the Proud Land, 1956; Wedding in White, 1973; The White Sheik, 1956; **Woman of the Year**, 1942.

Newsreel Cameramen: Above the Clouds, 1933; **Action in the North Atlantic**, 1943; Alan and Naomi, 1992; **All the King's Men**, 1949; All Things Fair, 1995; The Americanization of Emily, 1964; The Annuity,

1972; Anything for a Thrill, 1937; Atlantic Flight, 1937; **The Black Stallion**, 1979; **Buck Privates**, 1941; **Bullets or Ballots**, 1936; Burn 'Em Up Barnes, 1934; Call It Luck, 1934; **The Cameraman**, 1928; **Captain America: The First Avenger**, 2011; **China Girl**, 1942; **Citizen Kane**, 1941; The Deadly Invention, 1961; 5 Days of War, 2011; Five of a Kind, 1938; **Fury**, 1936; Gable and Lombard, 1976; The Girl from Jones Beach, 1949; Headline Shooter, 1933; **The Hindenburg**, 1975; **Hope and Glory**, 1987; Hot News, 1928; **I Cover the War**, 1937; I.Q., 2004; Ice-Capades, 1941; **Irene**, 1940; **J. Edgar**, 2011; Jericho, 1937; **King Kong**, 1933; Ladies Crave Excitement, 1935; The Lady Banker, 1980; **Lady on a Train**, 1945; The Last Winter, 1984; The Lion Has Wings, 1940; The Lone Wolf Takes a Chance, 1941; Lucky Devils, 1941; The Majestic, 2001; Men of the Hour, 1935; **Mission to Moscow**, 1943; **Mr. Moto's Last Warning**, 1939; Mr. Wise Guy, 1942; Murder in the First, 1995; **Newsfront**, 1979; Okinawa, 1952; The Other Side of Midnight, 1977; **Passport to Pimlico**, 1949; **Pierrepoint: The Last Hangman**, 2007; Pierrot le fou, 1969; **Public Enemies**, 2009; Ray of Sunshine, 1933; Red Light, 1949; **Riffraff**, 1936; **The Senator Was Indiscreet**, 1947; Shanghai 1937, 1997 (made-for-TV); Sharpshooters, 1938; **Since You Went Away**, 1944; Smith of Minnesota, 1942; **Sons of the Desert**, 1933; The Spirit of Stanford, 1942; **Star Dust**, 1940; **State of the Union**, 1948; **Sunset Boulevard**, 1950; **Too Hot to Handle**, 1938; **Top Secret Affair**, 1957; **Tramp, Tramp, Tramp**, 1926; **The Undercover Man**, 1949; Watch the Birdie, 1950; The Winning Ticket, 1935; **Who Framed Roger Rabbit**, 1988; **Zelig**, 1983.

Ocean Liners: **Abandon Ship!**, 1957; **An Affair to Remember**, 1957; Amarcord, 1973; America America, 1963; **Amelia**, 2009; Appointment with Death, 1988; **April in Paris**, 1952; Arsene Lupin Returns, 1938; Assault on a Queen, 1966; Atlantic Adventure, 1935; Baby Face, 1933; **Beau James**, 1957; Beauty for Sale, 1933; **Between Two Worlds**, 1944; The Big Broadcast of 1938, 1938; Biography of a Bachelor Girl, 1935; The Birds and the Bees, 1956; Black Sheep, 1935; **The Black Stallion**, 1979; Blondie Goes Latin, 1941; Blue, White and Perfect, 1942; **Bluebeard's Seven Wives**, 1926; **A Blueprint for Murder**, 1953; Boat Trip, 2002; The Branded Woman, 1920; Buttons, 1927; **The Captain Hates the Sea**, 1934; **Captains Courageous**, 1937; **Cavalcade**, 1933; The Chambermaid on the Titanic, 1997; **Charlie Chan at the Racetrack**, 1936; Charlie Chan on Broadway, 1937; Charlie Chan's Murder Cruise, 1940; Cocktail Hour, 1933; **Colleen**, 1936; **Confessions of a Nazi Spy**, 1939; Consolation Marriage, 1931; A Countess from Hong Kong, 1967; Cracked Nuts, 1931; Dangerous Money, 1946; Deadly Honeymoon, 2010 (made-for-TV); Death Cruise, 1974 (made-for-TV); Dick Tracy vs. Cueball, 1946; Diplomaniacs, 1933; Dr. Monica, 1934; The Doctor Takes a Wife, 1940; **Dodsworth**, 1936; East of Shanhai, 1931; **Flesh and Fantasy**, 1943; Flesh and the Woman, 1954; **Foreign Correspondent**, 1940; The French Line, 1953; **Funny Girl**, 1968; The Gay Deception, 1935; **Gentlemen Prefer Blondes**, 1953; **The Ghost Breakers**, 1940; Ghost Ship, 2002; **The Girl from Missouri**, 1934; Girl in the Street, 1937; The Girl on the Bridge, 1999; Going Highbrow, 1935; Gold Diggers in Paris, 1938; The Great Lover, 1949; High Pressure, 1932; **History Is Made at Night**, 1937; **The House on 92nd Street**, 1945; How Sweet It Is!, 1968; **I Love You Again**, 1940; I Was an Adventuress, 1940; **The Imposters**, 1998; **In Name Only**, 1939; Indiscreet, 1931; Isadora, 1968; It's a Date, 1940; Jack of Diamonds, 1967; **Juggernaut**, 1974; Kid Millions, 1934; **King of Burlesque**, 1936; **The Lady Eve**, 1941; Lady with a Past, 1932; **The Last Voyage**, 1960; Le voleur d'enfants, 1991; The Legend of 1900, 1998; **Libeled Lady**, 1936; **Lifeboat**, 1944; The Little American, 1917; The Lone Wolf Strikes, 1940; **Love Affair**, 1939; Love Before Breakfast, 1936; The Love Boat, 1976 (made-for-TV); The Mad Doctor of Market Street, 1942; Made on Broadway, 1933; Mama Steps Out, 1937; The Man Who Cried, 2000; **Marnie**, 1964; Mary Stevens, M.D., 1933; Melody Cruise, 1933; **Melody Time**, 1948; Men of Chance, 1931; Mr. & Mrs. Bridge, 1990; Mr. Moto Takes a Vaction, 1939; **Monkey Business**, 1931; **The Mouse**

That Roared, 1959; Mystery Liner, 1934; **The Navigator**, 1924; **A Night at the Opera**, 1935 (classic crowded cabin scene); **A Night to Remember**, 1958 (*Titanic*); **One Way Passage**, 1932; **Outward Bound**, 1930; Paris Holiday, 1958; **A Passage to India**, 1984; **The Pearl of Death**, 1944; **Pepe Le Moko** [1937], 1941; Please Believe Me, 1950; **Pocketful of Miracles**, 1961; Poseidon, 2006; **The Poseidon Adventure**, 1972; **The Princess Comes Across**, 1936; **The Promoter**, 1952; **Pursuit to Algiers**, 1945; Reaching for the Moon, 1930; Red Barry, 1938; **The Richest Girl in the World**, 1934; **Road to Morocco**, 1942; **Road to Rio**, 1947; **Road to Utopia**, 1946; **Romance on the High Seas**, 1948; **Sabrina**, 1954; The Saint in Palm Springs, 1941; **The Saint Takes Over**, 1940; Saving the Titanic, 2012 (made-for-TV); Search for Beauty, 1934; The Secret of Madame Blanche, 1933; **Shall We Dance**, 1937; **Ship of Fools**, 1965; Sin Takes a Holiday, 1930; S.O.S. Titanic, 1979 (made-for-TV); **So This Is Love**, 1953; **The Story of Three Loves**, 1953; **Stowaway**, 1936; Student Tour, 1934; Sunny, 1930; Susan Slade, 1961; Terror Aboard, 1933; **Three Smart Girls**, 1936; Through the Breakers, 1928; Till the Clouds Roll By, 1946; Times Square Lady, 1935; **Titanic** [1943], 1950; **Titanic**, 1953; **Titanic**, 1997; Titanic, 2012 (TV miniseries); Torchy Blane in Panama, 1938; **Trade Winds**, 1938; Transatlantic Merry-Go-Round, 1934; **The Triplets of Belleville**, 2003; **The Unsinkable Molly Brown**, 1964 (*Titanic*); Way for a Sailor, 1930; **Week-End in Havana**, 1941; Westward Passage, 1932; Woman Chases Man, 1937; **Words and Music**, 1948; **The Young in Heart**, 1938; Zombies on Broadway, 1945.

Orphanages and Orphans (also see Adoption; Homeless Children, this index): **Abandoned**, 1949; **About Schmidt**, 2002; **Across the Great Divide**, 1976; **After the Wedding**, 2006; Albatross, 2011; **All Dogs Go to Heaven**, 1989; **All Dogs Go to Heaven 2**, 1996; The Amazing Spider-Man, 2012; **The Amazing Spider-Man 2**, 2014; **An American Tail**, 1986; **An American Tail: Fievel Goes West**, 1991; **Anchors Aweigh**, 1945; **Angels in the Outfield**, 1951; **Angels in the Outfield**, 1994; Anne of Green Gables, 1919; Anne of Green Gables, 1934; Anne of Green Gables, 1952 (TV series); Anne of Green Gables, 1956 (made-for-TV); Anne of Green Gables, 1958 (made-for-TV); Anne of Green Gables, 1972 (TV miniseries); Anne of Green Gables, 1979 (TV series); Anne of Green Gables, 1985 (TV miniseries); Anne of Green Gables: The Continuing Story, 2000 (made-for-TV); Anne of Avonlea, 1987 (TV miniseries); **Annie**, 1982; Annie, 1999 (made-for-TV); Annie, 2014; **Annie Get Your Gun**, 1950; **Anthony Adverse**, 1936; **Antwone Fisher**, 2002; **The Apple Dumpling Gang**, 1975; Astro Boy, 2009; August Rush, 2007; **Auntie Mame**, 1958; **Australia**, 2008; **Avengers: Age of Ultron**, 2015; **Babe**, 1995; **Babe: Pig in the City**, 1998; **Batman**, 1989; **Batman and Robin**, 1997; **Batman Begins**, 2005; **Batman Forever**, 1995; **Batman: Mask of the Phantasm**, 1993; **Batman Returns**, 1992; **Beautiful Creatures**, 2013; **Bedknobs and Broomsticks**, 1971; **Before Midnight**, 2013; Belle & Sebastian, 2013; **The Bells of St. Mary's**, 1945; Big Daddy, 1999; **Bright Eyes**, 1934; **Big Eyes**, 2014; Biutiful, 2010; **Blossoms in the Dust**, 1941; **Boys Town**, 1938; **Brother Bear**, 2003; **Captain January**, 1936; **The Care Bears Movie**, 1985; Castle in the Sky, 1986; Child 44, 2014; The Chorus, 2004; Christmas Oranges, 2012; **The Cider House Rules**, 1999; **Cinderella**, 1950; City of Ember, 2008; The City of Lost Children, 1995; **Coco Before Chanel**, 2009; **Contact**, 1997; **Coraline**, 2009; Crossing Over, 2009; Curly Sue, 1991; **The Da Vinci Code**, 2006; **The Dark Knight Rises**, 2012; Dark Places, 2015; **David Copperfield**, 1935; David Copperfield, 1999 (TV miniseries); December Boys, 2007; Despicable Me, 2010; The Devil's Backbone, 2001; The Devil's Own, 1997; **Dick Tracy**, 1990; **Doctor Zhivago**, 1965; Dorian Gray, 2009; Double Impact, 1991; The Duchess, 2008; **The Eagle**, 2011; Eastern Promises, 2007; **Elf**, 2003; **Elysium**, 2013; Enter the Void, 2011; Escape to Witch Mountain, 1975; Evelyn, 2002; Fantastic Four, 2015; **Far from the Madding Crowd**, 2015; Farewell, My Queen, 2012; A Few Best Men, 2011; **Finding Neverland**, 2004; Flowers in the Attic, 1987; **The Flowers of War**, 2011; Fly

Away Solo, 2015; The Forbidden Kingdom, 2008; 47 Ronin, 2013; **The Fox and the Hound**, 1981; Fred Clause, 2007; **Frozen**, 2013; Gangs of New York, 2002; The Girl Next Door, 2007; **The Godfather**, 1972; **The Godfather: Part II**, 1974; **The Golden Compass**, 2007; **Good Will Hunting**, 1997; **Gosford Park**, 2001; Gotham, 2014 (TV series); **The Grand Budapest Hotel**, 2014; Grave of the Fireflies, 1988; **Great Expectations**, 1946; Great Expectations, 2012; **The Green Berets**, 1968; **Greystoke: The Legend of Tarzan, Lord of the Apes**, 1984; **Guardians of the Galaxy**, 2014; Hansel & Gretel: Witch Hunters, 2013; **Harry Potter and the Goblet of Fire**, 2005; Harry Potter and the Order of the Phoenix, 2007; **Harry Potter and the Sorcerer's Stone**, 2001; Haven, 2010- (TV series); Hearts in Atlantis, 2001; **Heidi**, 1937; Heidi, 1993 (made-for-TV); Hercules, 2014; **Hero**, 2002; A History of Violence, 2005; Hitman: Agent 47, 2015; Holes, 2003; **Hombre**, 1967; **Hook**, 1991; **Hotel Rwanda**, 2004; The House at the End of the Street, 2012; **Hugo**, 2011; Hustle, 2004-2012 (TV series); I Am Number Four, 2011; I Stand Alone, 1998; Ice Age: The Meltdown, 2006; **Ida**, 2013; **Identity Thief**, 2013; **Interview with the Vampire: The Vampire Chronicles**, 1994; It Takes Two, 1995; **James and the Giant Peach**, 1996; **Jane Eyre**, 1944; Jayne Eyre, 1996; **Jane Eyre**, 2011; Jumanji, 1995; **Jungle Book**, 1942; **The Jungle Book**, 1967; The Jungle Book, 1994; The Jungle Book 2, 2003; **The Kid**, 1921; Killers, 2010; **Kiss of Death**, 1947; **The Kite Runner**, 2007; **The Last Days of Pompeii**, 1935; The Last Kingdom, 2015- (TV series); **The Last of the Mohicans**, 1920; **The Last of the Mohicans**, 1936; **The Last of the Mohicans**, 1992; The Legend of 1900, 1998; **Les Misérables**, 1935; **Les Misérables**, 1952; **Les Misérables**, 1995; **Les Misérables**, 1998; **Les Misérables**, 2012; Life as We Know It, 2010; **Life of Pi**, 2012; **Lilo & Stitch**, 2002; **Little Big Man**, 1970; **A Little Princess**, 1995; **The Little Shop of Horrors**, 1960; Little Shop of Horrors, 1986; Lost in the Sun, 2015; **The Lunchbox**, 2013; **Mad Max**, 1980; **Mad Max: Beyond Thunderdome**, 1985; **Madeline**, 1998; **The Man from Snowy River**, 1983; **Man of Steel**, 2013; Mary and Max, 2009; Mary Shelley's Frankenstein, 1994; Meet the Robinsons, 2007; Mercury Rising, 1998; MI-5, 2015; **Modern Times**, 1936; **Moonrise Kingdom**, 2012; The Musketeer, 2001; **Mustang**, 2015; **Nevada Smith**, 1966; Neverland, 2011 (TV miniseries); Newsies, 1992; **Nicholas Nickelby**, 2002; **The Night of the Hunter**, 1955; No Reservations, 2007; **Noah**, 2014; **The November Man**, 2014; **Oliver!**, 1968; **Oliver Twist**, 1922; **Oliver Twist**, 1951; **Oliver Twist**, 2005; Oliver Twist, 2007 (TV miniseries); **Olivier, Olivier**, 1992; **The Omen**, 1976; The Omen, 2006; The Order, 2003; Original Sin, 2001; Orphan, 2001; Orphan, 2009; The Orphanage, 2008; Orphans, 1987; Orphans, 2000; Orphans, 2007; **Orphans of the Storm**, 1921; Our Little Sister, 2015; **The Outsiders**, 1983; **Oz the Great and Powerful**, 2014; **The Painted Veil**, 1934; **The Painted Veil**, 2007; **Paper Moon**, 1973; Pan, 2015; Party of Five, 1994-2000 (TV series); **Penny Serenade**, 1941; Perfume: The Story of a Murderer, 2006; **Peter Pan**, 1953; **Pete's Dragon**, 1977; **The Picture of Dorian Gray**, 1945; Playing It Cool, 2014; **Pompeii**, 2014; Practical Magic, 1998; **Predestination**, 2014; The Pretender, 1996-2000 (TV series); Prince of Persia: The Sands of Time, 2010; The Princess Diaries 2: Royal Engagement, 2004; A Princess for Christmas, 2011 (made-for-TV); Raising Helen, 2004; **Red River**, 1948; **The Red Violin**, 1999; Reign of Fire, 2002; **The Rescuers**, 1977; **Road to Perdition**, 2002; The Room, 2003; The Saint, 1997; **Salt**, 2010; **The Searchers**, 1956; **The Secret Garden**, 1949; **The Secret Garden**, 1993; **Seven Samurai**, 1956; **'71**, 2014; Shanghai Knights, 2003; **Skyfall**, 2012; **The Silence of the Lambs**, 1991; **Slumdog Millionaire**, 2008; **Southpaw**, 2015; Spectre, 2015; **Spider-Man**, 2002; **Spider-Man 2**, 2004; Stay, 2005; **Star Wars: The Force Awakens**, 2015; Stuart Little, 1999; **Superman**, 1978; **Superman Returns**, 2006; **Superman III**, 1983; **Superman II**, 1981; Superstar, 1991; Survivor, 2015; A Tale of Two Sisters, 2003; Teenage Mutant Ninja Turtles, 2014; Terminator Genisys, 2015; Theeb, 2014; **Them!**, 1954; **There Will Be Blood**, 2007; **These Wilder Years**, 1956; **The Three Godfathers**, 1916; **Three Godfathers**, 1936; **3 Godfathers**,

1948; 300: Rise of an Empire, 2014; Tideland, 2005; Tracers, 2015; Tristan + Isolde, 2006; **Tron: Legacy**, 2010; **Up**, 2009; Upside Down, 2012; Vanity Fair, 2000; The Vampire Diaries, 2009- (TV series); A Very Long Engagement, 2004; **A Walk Among the Tombstones**, 2014; **A Walk in the Clouds**, 1995; Walking with Dinosaurs 3D, 2013; **Water for Elephants**, 2011; **The Way Back**, 2010; Weekend, 2011; When Marnie Was There, 2014; **Wild Hearts Can't Be Broken**, 1991; **The Witches**, 1990; **The Wolverine**, 2013; **Woman of the Year**, 1942; **Wuthering Heights**, 1939; Wuthering Heights, 2011; **You Can Count on Me**, 2000; **Young Guns**, 1988; Young Guns II, 1990.

Painters and Paintings: **Adventures of Don Juan**, 1948; The Adventures of Picasso, 1978; **The Agony and the Ecstasy**, 1965 (Michelangelo; Raphael); **An American in Paris**, 1951; **Animal Crackers**, 1930; **April Showers**, 1923; **Beggar on Horseback**, 1925; **The Big Clock**, 1948; **Body and Soul**, 1947; **Captain Carey, U.S.A.**, 1950; **Come to the Stable**, 1949; Dali, 1991; Dead Man's Eyes, 1944; El Greco, 1967 (Domenico Teotocopulo); El Greco, 2009 (Domenico Teotocopulo); Goya's Ghost, 2007 (Francisco Jose de Goya); **The Horse's Mouth**, 1958; **Hugo**, 2011 (Salvador Dali); Lautrec, 1999 (Henri de Toulouse-Lautrec); **The Light That Failed**, 1939; Little Ashes, 2009 (Salvador Dali); Lives and Deaths of the Poets, 2011; **Lust for Life**, 1956 (Vincent van Gogh); Max, 2002 (Adolf Hitler); **Midnight in Paris**, 2011 (Salvador Dali); **The Moon and Sixpence**, 1942 (role model for Paul Gauguin); **Moulin Rouge**, 1952 (Henri de Toulouse-Lautrec); The Naked Maja, 1958 (Francisco Jose de Goya); **O. Henry's Full House**, 1952; **Odd Man Out**, 1947; **Patton**, 1970; **The Picture of Dorian Gray**, 1945; **Portrait of Jennie**, 1949; **Rembrandt**, 1936; **Scarlet Street**, 1945; **Strangers on a Train**, 1951; **Surviving Picasso**, 1996; **The Trouble with Harry**, 1955; **The Two Mrs. Carrolls**, 1947; **Van Gogh**, 1992; **Vincent and Theo**, 1990 (Vincent van Gogh).

Parachuting and Parachutists: **Act of Valor**, 2012 (U.S. Navy SEALS battling terrorists); **Against the Wind**, 1949 (WWII; espionage); **Air Force**, 1943 (WWII; Wake Island; Philippine Defense, 1942); Air Hawks, 1935; Army of Shadows, 2006 (WWII; Resistance and espionage in France); **The Avengers**, 2012; Balibo, 2009; Bastards, 2006 (WWII); **Battle of Britain**, 1969 (WWII; Battle of Britain in the skies over England, 1940); The Battle of Sutjeska, 1973 (WWII; Yugoslavia); Beach Blanket Bingo, 1955; The Big Hop, 1928; **Bombardier**, 1943 (WWII); **A Bridge Too Far**, 1977 (WWII; Battle of Arnhem, September 17-26, 1944); **The Bridges at Toko-Ri**, 1954 (Korean War); The Burma Conspiracy, 2011; **Captain America: The First Avenger**, 2011; **Captain America: The Winter Soldier**, 2014; Captain Corelli's Mandolin, 2001 (WWII; Greece, 1941-1943); **Carve Her Name with Pride**, 1958 (WWII; SOE; espionage; Violette Szabo); Central Airport, 1933; Danny Deckchair, 2003; Dark Blue World, 2001 (WWII; RAF); **Decision Before Dawn**, 1951 (WWII; espionage in Germany); Delta Force 2: The Colombian Connection, 1990; The Day of the Wolves, 1971; Decision Against Time, 1857 (test pilots); Dirty Dozen: The Deadly Mission, 1987 (made-for-TV); The Dirty Dozen: The Fatal Mission, 1988 (made-for-TV); Don't Look Now…We're Being Shot At!. 1969 (WWII; German-occupied France); **The Expendables 3**, 2014; Farewell to the King, 1989 (WWII; Borneo); Flying Devils, 1933 (Air shows; barnstorming pilots); **Flying Leathernecks**, 1951 (WWII; Guadalcanal, 1942); **The Flying Tigers**, 1942 (WWII; China); **Force 10 from Navarone**, 1978 (WWII; sabotage in Yugoslavia); The Giant Claw, 1957 (UFOs); **Godzilla**, 2014; Gorilla's Waltz, 1959; Greaser's Palace, 1972; **The Incredibles**, 2004; **Invisible Agent**, 1942 (WWII espionage in Germany); Iron Man, 2008; Jacquot de Nantes, 1993; Keep 'Em Flying, 1941; Kingsman: The Secret Service, 2013; **The Longest Day**, 1962 (WWII; Normandy invasion, June 6, 1944); Management, 2008; **Mission to Moscow**, 1943 (WWII); The Monster That Challenged the World, 1957; Most Wanted, 1997; The Next of Kin, 1943 (WWII; Nazi espionage in England); **O.S.S.**, 1946 (WWII; espionage in France); **Objective,**

Burma!, 1945 (WWII); **Odette**, 1951 (WWII; SOE; espionage; Odette Sanson); **Operation Daybreak**, 1975 (WWII; Czechoslovakia; assassination of Nazi leader Reinhard Heydrich, on June 4, 1942); Operation Delta Force, 1997 (made-for-TV); Operation Leopard, 1980 (Africa; Congo); **Paisan**, 1948 (Allied invasion of Sicily and Italy, 1943-1944); Parachute Battalion, 1941; Parachute Jumper, 1933; Parachute Nurse, 1942; **Paratrooper**, 1954 (WWII); Riders, 2002; **Red Skies of Montana**, 1952 (firefighters); Reign of Fire, 2002; Rule No. 1, 2003; **Safe Conduct**, 2002 (WWII; Resistance in German-occupied France); **Saints and Soldiers**, 2005 (WWII; Battle of Bastogne, December 1944; Malmedy Massacre, December 17, 1944); Salute to the Marines, 1943 (WWII; Philippine Defense, 1942); Scarecrows, 1988; The Second Front, 2005; Son of the Pink Panther, 1993; The Spider Returns, 1941; **Star Trek**, 2009; Stealth, 2005; Stretch, 2014; **The Tarnished Angels**, 1958 (air Show in New Orleans in early 1930s; barnstorming pilots); The Ten, 2007; **13 Rue Madeleine**, 1947 (WWII; espionage in France); The 317th Platoon, 1965 (Vietnam War); **To Be or Not to Be**, 1942 (WWII; Resistance in Poland); **Top Gun**, 1986; Torchy Blane in Panama, 1938; Toto the Hero, 1991; Trinity: Gambling for High Stakes, 1978; The Twelve Days of Christmas Eve, 2004 (made-for-TV); Valiant, 2005; What War May Bring, 2010 (WWII; Resistance in German-occupied France); **What's New, Pussycat?**, 1965; **Where Eagles Dare**, 1969 (WWII; espionage in Bavaria); Where the Boys Are, 1960; Where the Boys Are, 1984; **The Wild Geese**, 1978 (mercenaries in Africa); The Wild Thornberrys Movie, 2002; Wrong Side Up, 2005.

Parrots: Action in Arabia, 1944; Admissions, 2004; **The Adventures of Robinson Crusoe**, 1954; **Aladdin**, 1992; Alexander, 2004; **Aloma of the South Seas**, 1941; The Animal, 2001; **Argo**, 2012; The Arizona Cyclone, 1928; Around the World, 1943; Auggie Rose, 2000; Because of Winn-Dixie, 2005; **Bell Book and Candle**, 1958; **The Big Steal**, 1949; **Black Narcissus**, 1947; **Blithe Spirit**, 1945; The Blue Butterfly, 2004; The Blue Lagoon, 1949; Boots and Saddles, 1937; Borderline, 1950; Breakfast for Two, 1937; **The Buccaneer**, 1938; Buddy, 1997; The Burmese Harp, 1956; **Casablanca**, 1942; The Case of the Black Parrot, 1941; Casino Royale, 1967; **Champagne for Caesar**, 1950; City Without Men, 1943; Daddy Day Care, 2003; Dead Men Tell, 1941; **The Death of Tarzan**, 1968; Deep Blue Sea, 1999; Delusions of Grandeur, 1971; **Doctor Dolittle**, 1967; Doctor, You've Got to Be Kidding!, 1967; Dragonfly, 2002; Duplex, 2003; **Dynamite**, 1929; The Emperor's New Groove, 2000; Eureka, 1983; **The Fallen Idol**, 1949; Fatal Instinct, 1993; Fifty Million Frenchmen, 1931; Fighting Love, 1927; Fire on the Amazon, 1993; **The Fuller Brush Girl**, 1950; The Girl Next Door, 2004; Georgia Rule, 2007; The Ghost Comes Home, 1940; Ghost of Dragstrip Hollow, 1959; The Great Lover, 1931; The Heavenly Body, 1944; **Hello, Frisco, Hello**, 1943; Hitting a New High, 1937; Home Alone 3, 1997; **I Married a Witch**, 1942; The Invisible Man's Revenge, 1944; Iron Man 2, 2010; The January Man, 1989; Johnny Dangerously, 1984; **The Keys of the Kingdom**, 1944; **A Kid for Two Farthings**, 1956; **The Killing**, 1956; Kiss Me, Stupid, 1964; Ladies They Talk About, 1933; **The Lady from Shanghai**, 1948; **The Ladykillers**, 1956; Lillian Russell, 1940; A Little Help, 2010; **The Little Princess**, 1939; **Little Women**, 1933; **Love Crazy**, 1941; Love Happens, 2009; Love in the Time of Cholera, 2007; Man on Fire, 2004; Maniac, 1963; Man's Best Friend, 1993; Marie Antoinette, 2006; **Melody Time**, 1948; Merrily We Live, 1938; Mr. Robinson Crusoe, 1932; The Mosquito Coast, 1986; Mozart and the Whale, 2005; Murder on a Bridle Path, 1936; **My Dog Skip**, 2000; **My Father's Glory**, 1991; Naked Lunch, 1991; Ned Kelly, 2003; The Next Best Thing, 2000; **Nicholas Nickleby**, 2002; A Night in Old Mexico, 2013; Once a Thief, 1990; Once in a Lifetime, 2014; 102 Dalmatians, 2000; Over Her Dead Body, 2008; Panama Lady, 1939; The Party, 1968; Peter Pan, 2003; **Pierrot le fou**, 1968; **The Pink Panther Strikes Again**, 1976; **Pippi in the South Seas**, 1974; **Pirates of the Caribbean: At World's End**, 2007; **Pirates of the Caribbean: The Curse of the Black Pearl**, 2003; **Platinum Blonde**, 1931; **Pride** and Prejudice, 1940; The Rainbow Thief, 1990; Range Defenders, 1937; **Reap the Wild Wind**, 1942; Red Road, 2006; **The Return of the Pink Panther**, 1975; **Revenge of the Pink Panther**, 1978; **Riffraff**, 1947; **Rio**, 2011; **Rio Rita**, 1942; **Rio 2**, 2014; **The River**, 1951; Robinson Crusoe, 2003 (made-for-TV); Rough Riders, 1997 (TV series); **San Antonio**, 1945; Scalawag, 1973; **Sense and Sensibility**, 1995; **Serpico**, 1973; **The 7th Voyage of Sinbad**, 1958; A Simple Heart, 2008; The Slave, 1962; Sleepless, 2001; **South Sea Woman**, 1953; A Special Day, 1977; **Spirits of the Dead**, 1969; Stowaway in the Sky, 1960; Swing It, Sailor!, 1938; Switch, 1991; **There Was a Crooked Man**, 1970; 3 Bad Men, 1926; **The Three Caballeros**, 1944; The Third Eye, 1966; **The Third Man**, 1950; Torchy Gets Her Man, 1938; Torso, 1973; **Treasure Island**, 1934; **Treasure Island**, 1950; Treasure Island, 1972; The Trouble with Spies, 1987; The Two Faces of Fear, 1972; **The Two Jakes**, 1990; Undersea Kingdom, 1936 (serial); **The Unholy Three**, 1925; **The Unholy Three**, 1930; Vanity Fair, 2004; **Vatel**, 2000; Volcano, 1997; **Walkabout**, 1971; **Whistling in Dixie**, 1942; White Slave Ship, 1961; Wide Sargasso Sea, 1993; The Wild Life, 2016; Wild Orchid, 1989; Wild Target, 2010; The Wizard of Baghdad, 1960; The Woman in Black, 2012; **The Year My Voice Broke**, 1987; **Yolanda and the Thief**, 1945; Zazie, 1961; **Zorba the Greek**, 1964.

Pearl Divers and Pearl Diving: Adventure's End, 1937; Amphibian Man, 2006; Anokha Moti, 2000; Badjao: The Sea Gypsies, 1962; Beyond the Reef, 1981; The Blue Lagoon, 1980; Brides of Sulu, 1937; Cruel Sea, 1972; The Flaming Signal, 1933; Hitokui ama, 1958; In a Savage Land, 1999; Isle of Fury, 1936; My Mother the Mermaid, 2004; The Millionaire Pirate, 1919; Paradise Island, 1930; Port of Hate, 1939; Return to the Blue Lagoon, 1991; Soldiers of Fortune, 1955-1957 (TV series; "Pearls Off Dondra Head," 1955 episode); **Tabu: A Story of the South Seas**, 1931; Tarzan and the Mermaids, 1948; A Thief in Paradise, 1925; Vengeance of the Deep, 1938; **Wake of the Red Witch**, 1948; Wallaby Jim of the Islands, 1937; **White Shadows in the South Seas**, 1928; A Woman There Was, 1919; Zetsurin ama: Shimari-gai, 1985.

Pet Stores: Because of Winn-Dixie, 2005; **Beethoven**, 1992; **The Birds**, 1963; The Black Dahlia, 2006; **Cars 2**, 2011; Downloading Nancy, 2008; **The Drop**, 2014; Five Corners, 1987; G-Force, 2009; The Go-Getter, 2007; **Greed**, 1924; Grumpy Cat's Worst Christmas Ever, 2014 (made-for-TV); Hellraiser, 1987; Hotel for Dogs, 2009; In Her Shoes, 2005; Johnny Dangerously, 1984; **Lady and the Tramp**, 1955; The Man of the Year, 2003; Me and You, 2012; **Mother**, 1996; The Nine Lives of Christmas, 2014 (made-for-TV); Outbreak, 1995; **Pee-wee's Big Adventure**, 1985; **Rocky**, 1976; **Rumble Fish**, 1983; See Spot Run, 2001; Tracers, 2015.

Pilots (air mail): **Air Mail**, 1932; The Aviator, 1985; **The Spirit of St. Louis**, 1957.

Pilots (auto-gyros): **International House**, 1933; **It Happened One Night**, 1934.

Pilots (auxiliary planes in military actions): **Cast a Giant Shadow**, 1966; **Villa Rides**, 1968.

Pilots (barnstormers; pilots at airshows or delivering air mail): Ace Eli and Rodger of the Skies, 1973; Air Eagles, 1931; **Air Mail**, 1932; **Amelia**, 2009; **Captains of the Clouds**, 1942; **Flight for Freedom**, 1943; **Flight from Glory**, 1937; **The Flight of the Phoenix**, 1965; Flying Devils, 1933; The Flying Fool, 1929; The Flying Irishman, 1939; **The Flying Tigers**, 1942; **The Great Waldo Pepper**, 1975; Gypsy Angels, 1980; The Gypsy Moths, 1969; I'm Still Alive, 1940; **The Lost Squadron**, 1932; **Night Flight**, 1933; **Only Angels Have Wings**, 1939; Planes, 2013; **The Spirit of St. Louis**, 1957; Spitfire, 1943; **The Tarnished Angels**, 1957; **Test Pilot**, 1938; **Those Magnificent Men in**

Their Flying Machines, 1965.

Pilots (cargo planes): Alaska, 1996; The Big Lift, 1948 (Berlin airlift); **Calcutta**, 1947; **Flight from Glory**, 1937; **The Flight of the Phoenix**, 1965; The Flight of the Phoenix, 2004; **Island in the Sky**, 1953; The Last Flight of Noah's Ark, 1980; **Night Flight**, 1933; **Only Angels Have Wings**, 1939; **Slattery's Hurricane**, 1949; **Tokyo Joe**, 1949; **You Gotta Stay Happy**, 1948.

Pilots (charter): **The Bride Came C.O.D.**, 1941; **Captains of the Clouds**, 1942; High Road to China, 1983; **It's a Mad, Mad, Mad, Mad World**, 1963; **Six Days Seven Nights**, 1998.

Pilots (Cold War): By Dawn's Early Light, 1990 (made-for-TV); **Bridge of Spies**, 2015 (Francis Gary Powers); **Dr. Strangelove**, 1964; **Fail Safe**, 1964; A Gathering of Eagles, 1963; Jet Pilot, 1957; **Top Gun**, 1986; **Strategic Air Command**, 1955.

Pilots (Crashes): **Alive**, 1993; The Aviator, 1985; **Back from Eternity**, 1956; **Catch-22**, 1970; Five Came Back, 1939; **Flight**, 2012; **Here Comes Mr. Jordan**, 1941; **Hero**, 1992; **Lost Horizon**, 1937; Lt. Robin Crusoe, U.S.N., 1966; Passengers, 2008; **Phone Call from a Stranger**, 1952; **Run for the Sun**, 1956; **Six Days Seven Nights**, 1998; The Snow Walker, 2003.

Pilots (crimes committed involving aircraft): **Air Force One**, 1997; Airborne, 2012 (made-for-TV); Black Sunday, 1977 (Goodyear Blimp at Super Bowl); Breakout, 1975 (helicopter used to free inmate from Mexican prison); The Delta Force, 1986; **Executive Decision**, 1996; Flight 93, 2006 (made-for-TV); Flightplan, 2005; **Magnum Force**, 1973; Murder on Flight 502, 1975 (made-for-TV); Red Eye, 2005; Snakes on a Plane, 2006; Turbulence, 1997; Turbulence 2: Fear of Flying, 1999; **Twelve O'Clock High**, 1949; **U.S. Marshals**, 1998.

Pilots (crop dusting): **Independence Day**, 1996; It Happened at the World's Fair, 1963; **North by Northwest**, 1959.

Pilots (dirigibles): **Dirigible**, 1931; **Flyboys**, 2008; **Hell's Angels**, 1930; **The Hindenburg**, 1975; **Zeppelin**, 1971.

Pilots (fantasy): **A Guy Named Joe**, 1943; **Here Comes Mr. Jordan**, 1941; The Little Prince, 1974; **Stairway to Heaven**, 1947.

Pilots (firefighting): Always, 1989; Hellfighters, 1968 (helicopter); **Red Skies of Montana**, 1952.

Pilots (herding Mustangs): **The Misfits**, 1961.

Pilots (hobby): **Here Comes Mr. Jordan**, 1941; **Thoroughly Modern Millie**, 1967.

Pilots (Korean War): Bombers B-52, 1957; **The Bridges at Toko-Ri**, 1954; **Flat Top**, 1952; The Hook, 1963; The Hunters, 1958; **Men of the Fighting Lady**, 1954; **Starlift**, 1951.

Pilots (Passenger Craft): **Air Force One**, 1997 (U.S. President); Airborne, 2012 (made-for-TV); **Airplane!**, 1980; Airplane II: The Sequel, 1982; Airport, 1970; Airport, 1978 (made-for-TV); Airport, 1996 (TV series); Airport 1975, 1974; Airport '77, 1977; **The Aviator**, 2004; **Back from Eternity**, 1956; **The Carpetbaggers**, 1964 (loosely based on Howard Hughes); **Ceiling Zero**, 1936; China Clipper, 1936; The Concorde ...Airport '79, 1979; Five Came Back, 1939; **Flight**, 2012; **Flying Tigers**, 1942; **The French Connection**, 1971; Ground Control, 1998; **The High and the Mighty**, 1954; **How to Marry a Millionaire**, 1953; **JFK**, 1991; The Langoliers, 1995 (TV miniseries); **Lost Horizon**, 1937;

Lost Horizon, 1973; Mimino, 1977 (helicopter passenger service); **Never Give a Sucker an Even Break**, 1941 (with sleeping berths); **No Highway in the Sky**, 1951; Non-Stop, 2014; **Notorious**, 1946; Panic Button, 2011; **Phone Call from a Stranger**, 1952; **The Steel Trap**, 1952; Turbulence, 1997; Turbulence 2: Fear of Flying, 1999; View from the Top, 2003; **Will Success Spoil Rock Hunter?**, 1957 (with sleeping berths); **You Gotta Stay Happy**, 1948; Zero Hour!, 1957.

Pilots (police Craft): **Blue Thunder**, 1983.

Pilots (racing): **Spitfire**, 1943; **The Tarnished Angels**, 1958; **Test Pilot**, 1938.

Pilots (reconnaissance): Battle of the Bulge, 1965; **Bridge of Spies**, 2015 (Francis Gary Powers); **Flight for Freedom**, 1943; **Objective, Burma!**, 1945.

Pilots (record-setting): **Amelia**, 2009 (Amelia Earhart); **The Aviator**, 2004 (Howard Hughes); **Flight for Freedom**, 1943 (based on Amelia Earhart); **The Spirit of St. Louis**, 1957 (Charles A. Lindbergh's solo flight to Paris in 1927).

Pilots (rescue missions): **The Day after Tomorrow**, 2004; **Island in the Sky**, 1953.

Pilots (Space): **Alien**, 1979; **Aliens**, 1986; **Apollo 13**, 1995; The Astronaut Farmer, 2006; The Astronaut's Wife, 1999; **The Black Hole**, 1979; **Capricorn One**, 1978; **Destination Moon**, 1950; **Elysium**, 2013; **Gravity**, 2013; **Guardians of the Galaxy**, 2014; **Independence Day**, 1996; **Interstellar**, 2014; Moon Pilot, 1962; **Planet of the Apes**, 1968; **Planet of the Apes**, 2001; **Prometheus**, 2012; **Rocketship X-M**, 1950; Space, 1985 (TV miniseries); Sphere, 1998; **Star Trek**, 2009; **Star Trek: First Contact**, 1996; **Star Trek: Generations**, 1994; **Star Trek: Insurrection**, 1998; **Star Trek: Into Darkness**, 2013; **Star Trek: Nemesis**, 2002; **Star Trek: The Motion Picture**, 1979; **Star Trek II: The Wrath of Khan**, 1982; **Star Trek III: The Search for Spock**, 1984; **Star Trek IV: The Voyage Home**, 1986; **Star Trek V: The Final Frontier**, 1989; **Star Trek VI: The Undiscovered Country**, 1991; **Star Wars: Episode V—The Empire Strikes Back**, 1980; **Star Wars: Episode IV—A New Hope**, 1977; **Star Wars: Episode I—The Phantom Menace**, 1999; **Star Wars: Episode VI—Return of the Jedi**, 1983; **Star Wars: Episode III—Revenge of the Sith**, 2005; **Star Wars: Episode II—The Attack of the Clones**, 2002; **Star Wars: The Clone Wars**, 2008; **Star Wars: The Force Awakens**, 2015; **20 Million Miles to Earth**, 1957; **2001: A Space Odyssey**, 1968; **2010**, 1984.

Pilots (stunt): **Ceiling Zero**, 1936; **Devil Dogs of the Air**, 1935; **The Great Waldo Pepper**, 1975; **The Lost Squadron**, 1932.

Pilots (test): The Accidental Hero, 2002 (made-for-TV); **Amelia**, 2009; The Arrow, 1997 (made-for-TV); **The Aviator**, 2004; The Bamboo Saucer, 1968; Batman, 1943 (serial and feature); Beyond the Time Barrier, 1960; **The Blue Max**, 1966; **Breaking the Sound Barrier**, 1952; **Ceiling Zero**, 1936; Central Airport, 1933; **Chain Lightning**, 1950; **The Crack-Up**, 1937; Crimson Romance, 1934; Decision against Time, 1957; Devil's Squadron, 1936; **Dive Bomber**, 1941; Emergency Landing, 1941; Flight Lieutenant, 1942; Flying Wild, 1941; **Forever Young**, 1992; Green Lantern, 2011; Happy Landing, 1934; House on Haunted Hill, 1959; Jet Job, 1952; King of the Texas Rangers, 1941 (serial); Lady Bodyguard, 1943; Macross Plus, 1994 (TV miniseries); The Man in the Sky, 1957; **The McConnell Story**, 1955; Men against the Sky, 1940; Nick Carter, Master Detective, 1939; **Operation Crossbow**, 1965; **The Right Stuff**, 1983; Satellite in the Sky, 1956; Sky Raiders, 1941 (serial); The Sound Barrier, 1952; Space, 1985 (TV miniseries); **Space Cowboys**, 2000; Speed Wings, 1934; **Spitfire**, 1942; **Test Pilot**, 1938; Tobor

the Great, 1954; **Toward the Unknown**, 1956; Wings of the Navy, 1939; X-15, 1961.

Pilots (U.S. military operations): **Black Hawk Down**, 2001 (assault helicopters in Battle of Mogadishu, Somolia, October 3-4, 1993); Coast Guard, 1939; **Devil Dogs of the Air**, 1935; **Dr. Strangelove**, 1964; **Fail Safe**, 1964; **Flight**, 1929; **Flight Command**, 1940; Into the Sun, 1992; **King Kong**, 1933; Project X, 1987; Stealth, 2005; **The Thing**, 1982; **The Thing from Another World**, 1951.

Pilots (Vietnam War): Air America, 1990 (CIA operation); Bat*21, 1988; **The Green Berets**, 1968 (assault helicopters); Flight of the Intruder, 1991; **Rescue Dawn**, 2007; **We Were Soldiers**, 2002 (assault helicopters; jet fighter planes).

Pilots (WWI): **Ace of Aces**, 1933; **Aces High**, 1977; **The Blue Max**, 1966; **Captain Eddie**, 1945 (Edward Rickenbacker); **The Dawn Patrol**, 1930; **The Dawn Patrol**, 1938; **The Eagle and the Hawk**, 1933; **Flyboys**, 2008; **The Great Dictator**, 1940; **Hell's Angels**, 1930; Lafayette Escadrille, 1958; L'equipage, 1938; **Lilac Time**, 1928; Men Must Fight, 1933; **The Red Baron**, 2010 (Manfred von Richthofen); **To Each His Own**, 1946; **Von Richthofen and Brown**, 1971 (Manfred von Richthofen); **Wings**, 1927; **The Woman I Love**, 1937.

Pilots (WWII): **Above and Beyond**; 1953; **Air Force**, 1943; **Bataan**, 1943; **Battle of Britain**, 1969; Battle of the Bulge, 1965; **Battleground**, 1949; Beautiful Dreamer, 2006; **The Best Years of Our Lives**, 1946; **The Blue Dahlia**, 1946; **Bombardier**, 1943; **A Bridge Too Far**, 1977; **Catch-22**, 1970; Charlotte Gray, 2001; **China Sky**, 1945; **Command Decision**, 1948; **The Dam Busters**, 1955; **Desperate Journey**, 1942; **Destination Gobi**, 1953; **Destination Tokyo**, 1943; **Eagle Squadron**, 1942; **Empire of the Sun**, 1987; **The English Patient**, 1996; Every Time We Say Goodbye, 1986; Fighter Attack, 1953; **Fighter Squadron**, 1948; **The Fighting Seabees**, 1944; **Flying Leathernecks**, 1951; **Flying Tigers**, 1942; **Foreign Correspondent**, 1940; **God Is My Co-Pilot**, 1945; **The Great Raid**, 2005; **A Guy Named Joe**, 1943; **Halls of Montezuma**, 1950; Hanover Street, 1979; **Hell in the Pacific**, 1968; **The Heroes of Telemark**, 1965; Kiss Them for Me, 1957; **The Left Hand of God**, 1955; **The Longest Day**, 1962; **Memphis Belle**, 1990; **Midway**, 1976; **Mrs. Miniver**, 1942; **Murphy's War**, 1971; **Objective, Burma!**, 1945; **Passage to Marseille**, 1944; **Patton**, 1970; **Pearl Harbor**, 2001; **The Purple Plain**, 1954; **Reach for the Sky**, 1956; **Sahara**, 1943; **Saving Private Ryan**, 1998; **The Secret Life of Walter Mitty**, 1947; **633 Squadron**, 1964; **Spitfire**, 1943; **Stairway to Heaven**, 1947; **Task Force**, 1949; **13 Rue Madeleine**, 1947; **Thirty Seconds over Tokyo**, 1944; **To Be or Not to Be**, 1942; **To Each His Own**, 1946; **Tora! Tora! Tora!**, 1970; Torpedo Bombers, 1983; **Twelve O'Clock High**, 1949; **Wake Island**, 1942; **The War Lover**, 1962; **We've Never Been Licked**, 1943; **Where Eagles Dare**, 1969; **The Wild Blue Yonder**, 1951; **Wing and a Prayer**, 1944; **The Wings of Eagles**, 1957; **A Yank in the R.A.F.**, 1941.

Pirates: Abbott and Costello Meet Captain Kidd, 1952; **The Adventures of Baron Munchausen**, 1989; The Adventures of Long John Silver, 1955-1957 (TV series); The Adventures of Tintin, 2011; Against All Flags, 1952; Animal Treasure Island, 1971; Anne of the Indies, 1951; Avenger of the Seven Seas, 1962; Barbary Pirate, 1949; Batman: The Brave and the Bold, 2008-2011 (TV series); Batman: The Movie, 1966; **Ben-Hur**, 1959; **The Black Pirate**, 1926; The Black Pirate, 1944; The Black Pirates, 1954; Black Sails, 2014- (TV series); **The Black Swan**, 1942; Blackbeard, 2006 (made-for-TV); Blackbeard: Terror at Sea, 2006 (made-for-TV); Blackbeard, the Pirate, 1952; Blackbeard's Ghost, 1968; Blackie the Pirate, 1971; The Boy and the Pirates, 1960; **The Buccaneer**, 1938; The Buccaneer, 1958; Buccaneer's Girl, 1950; The Buccaneers, 1956-1957 (TV series); **Cabiria**, 1914; Candleshoe, 1977;

Captain America: The Winter Soldier, 2014; Captain Blood, 1924; Captain Blood, 1935; Captain Calamity, 1936; Captain Caution, 1940; Captain Horatio Hornblower, 1951; Captain Kidd, 1945; Captain Kidd and the Slave Girl, 1954; Captain Phillips, 2013; Captain Pirate, 1952; Captain Sabertooth, 2004; Caribbean, 1952; Castle in the Sky, 1987; China Seas, 1935; Chocolat, 2000; Clothes Make the Pirate, 1925; The Count of Monte Cristo, 1934; The Count of Monte Cristo, 2002; The Crimson Pirate, 1952; Cutthroat Island, 1995; Dancing Pirate, 1936; Davy Crockett and the River Pirates, 1956; The Devil Ship-Ship Pirates, 1964; Double Crossbones, 1951; The Expendables 3, 2014; Fair Wind to Java, 1953; Fairy Tale: A True Story, 1997; The Fall, 2006; Ferry to Hong Kong, 1961; Finding Neverland, 2004; For Love and Gold, 1966; Frenchman's Creek, 1944; Frenchman's Creek, 1998 (made-for-TV); Fury at Smuggler's Bay, 1963; Ghost in the Noonday Sun, 1984; The Golden Hawk, 1952; The Goonies, 1985; Guardians of the Galaxy, 2014; Hamlet, 1948; Hamlet, 1990; Hamlet, 1996; A High Wind in Jamaica, 1965; A Hijacking, 2013; Hook, 1991; How the West Was Won, 1962; Ice Age: Continental Drift, 2012; The Ice Pirates, 1984; The Island, 1980; Jamaica Inn, 1939; Jamaica Inn, 1983 (made-for-TV); The Jewel of the Nile, 1985; Jolly Roger, 2001; Kidnapped, 1938; Kidnapped, 1960; Kidnapped, 1971; The King's Pirate, 1967; Last of the Buccaneers, 1950; The Lego Movie, 2014; The Life Aquatic with Steve Zissou, 2004; The Light at the Edge of the World, 1971; The Little Mermaid, 1989; Long John Silver, 1954; The Lord of the Rings: The Return of the King, 2003; The Lost Continent, 1968; The Lost World of Sinbad, 1965; The Masked Pirate, 1949; The Master of Ballantrae, 1953; Monsieur Vincent, 1949; Moonfleet, 2013 (TV miniseries); Morgan, the Pirate, 1960; Muppet Treasure Island, 1996; Mysterious Island, 1951; Mysterious Island, 1961; The Mysterious Island, 1973; The Mysterious Island, 1975 (made-for-TV); Mysterious Island, 2005 (made-for-TV); Mysterious Island, 2012; Naughty Marietta, 1935; Neverland, 2011 (TV miniseries); New Moon, 1940; Nim's Island, 2008; Pearl of the South Pacific, 1955; The Perils of Pauline, 1914; Peter Pan, 1924; Peter Pan, 1953; Peter Pan, 1955 (made-for-TV); Peter Pan, 1960 (made-for-TV); Peter Pan, 2000 (made-for-TV); Peter Pan, 2003; Pippi in the South Seas, 1974; The Pirate, 1948; The Pirate and the Slave Girl, 1959; The Pirate Fairy, 2014; The Pirate Movie, 1982; Pirates, 1986; Pirates, 1998; The Pirates! Band of Misfits, 2012; Pirates: Blood Brothers, 1999 (TV miniseries); The Pirates of Blood River, 1962; The Pirates of Dark Water, 1991-1992 (TV series); The Pirates of Penzance, 1983; Pirates of the Caribbean: At World's End, 2007; Pirates of the Caribbean: The Curse of the Black Pearl, 2003; Pirates of the Caribbean: Dead Man's Chest, 2006; Pirates of the Caribbean: On Stranger Tides, 2011; Pirates of the Coast, 1960; Pirates of the Plain, 1999; Pirates of Tortuga, 1961; Pirates of Treasure Island, 2006; Pirates of Tripoli, 1955; Port Sinister, 1953; Prince of Pirates, 1953; The Princess and the Pirate, 1944; The Princess Bride, 1987; The Princess and the Pirate, 1944; Project A, 1983; Project A 2, 1987; The Queen of the Pirates, 1961; Queen of the Seas, 1963; Rage of the Buccaneers, 1963; Raiders of the Seven Seas, 1953; Reap the Wild Wind, 1942; Return to Never Land, 2002; Return to Treasure Island, 1988; Revenge of the Pink Panther, 1978; The River Pirates, 1988; Robinson Crusoe, 1970; Rosencrantz & Guildenstern Are Dead, 1991; Satyricon, 1970; Savage Islands, 1983; The Sea Hawk, 1924; The Sea Hawk, 1940; The Secret of Treasure Island, 1938; Shipwrecked, 1991; Shrek the Third, 2007; Sinbad: Legend of the Seven Seas, 2003; Sinbad the Sailor, 1947; Six Days Seven Nights, 1998; The Son of Captain Blood, 1972; The Spanish Main, 1945; Spartacus, 1960; Spawn of the North, 1938; The SpongeBob SquarePants Movie, 2004; Star Wars: The Clone Wars, 2008; Stardust, 2007; Stranded, 2002 (made-for-TV); Swashbuckler, 1976; Swiss Family Robinson, 1960; Terry and the Pirates, 1940 (serial); The Three Musketeers, 1993; Treasure Island, 1917; Treasure Island, 1920; Treasure Island, 1934; Treasure Island, 1950; Treasure Island, 1987 (made-for-TV); Treasure Island, 1990 (made-for-TV);

Treasure Island, 1999; Treasure Island, 2007; Treasure Planet, 2002; Tripoli, 1950; True Caribbean Pirates, 2006 (made-for-TV); Twelfth Night or What You Will, 1996; The Vikings, 1958; Wallaby Jim of the Islands, 1937; When a Man Loves, 1927; When Eight Bells Toll, 1971; Wild Sargasso Sea, 1993; The Wind and the Lion, 1975; Women of Devil's Island, 1962; Yellowbeard, 1983; Yankee Buccaneer, 1952; Yankee Pasha, 1954; Young Bess, 1953. Note: For detailed information on pirates, see my books *Encyclopedia of World Crime*; 8 volumes (Crime-Books, Inc., 1990); *The Great Pictorial History of World Crime*; 2 volumes (History, Inc., 2004).

Plastic Surgery: The Air I Breathe, 2007; All about My Mother, 1999; American Mary, 2012; Anna Nicole, 2007; Another Face, 1935; Another Pretty Face, 2002 (made-for-TV); Anthony Zimmer, 2006; Arsenic and Old Lace, 1944; Arsenic and Old Lace, 1969 (made-for-TV); Arthur 3: The War of the Two Worlds, 2010; Ash Wednesday, 1973; Bad Teacher, 2011; Behind the Candelabra, 2013 (made-for-TV); Below the Deadline, 1936; Bernard and Doris, 2007; Beyond Recognition, 2003; Black Dragons, 1942; Blackout, 1985 (made-for-TV); Borderline Murder, 2011 (made-for-TV); The Brain That Wouldn't Die, 1962; Brazil, 1985; Brief Crossing, 2002; Burn After Reading, 2008; Calendar Girl, 1993; Campus Confidential, 2005 (made-for-TV); Cape of Good Hope, 2004; Captain America, 1990; Carnage, 2002; Cassandra's Dream, 2007; Celebrity, 1998; Charlie Chan at the Wax Museum, 1940; A Chorus Line, 1985; Chrysalis, 2008; Circus of Horrors, 1960; City Girl, 1938; Confetti, 2006; Corruption, 1968; Cronos, 1994; Dan in Real Life, 2007; The Dancer Upstairs, 2002; Dark Passage, 1947; Dead End, 1937; Death Becomes Her, 1992; The Devil's Double, 2011; The Diabolical Dr. Z, 1967; Diamonds Are Forever, 1971; Doc Hollywood, 1991; Dr. Renault's Secret, 1942; Doctors Don't Tell, 1941; The Dolly Sisters, 1945; Escape from L.A., 1996; Eyes Without a Face, 1962; Face/Off, 1997; The Face Behind the Mask, 1941; A Face to Die For, 1996 (made-for-TV); Faceless, 1987; False Face, 1977; False Faces, 1932; Fedora, 1978; First Yank Into Tokyo, 1945; For Your Consideration, 2006; Foxy Brown, 1974; Get Smart, 2008; The Ghost Walks, 1934; The Girl in the Kremlin, 1957; The Girl Most Likely to…, 1973; G-Men Never Forget, 1948; Good Luck Chuck, 2007; Goodbye, Columbus, 1969; Goodnight Mommy, 2014; The Great Beauty, 2013; The Guest, 2014; He Who Dares: Downing Street Siege, 2014; Head Over Heels, 2001; Hello Again, 1987; Hired Killer, 1966; His Kind of Woman, 1951; Hollow Triumph, 1948; I Could Never Be Your Woman, 2007; The Illegal Immigrant, 1985; Ira & Abby, 2006; It's Complicated, 2009; Jail Bait, 1954; The Jigsaw Man, 1984; Johnny Handsome, 1989; Just Before Dawn, 1946; Just Go With It, 2011; Kid Monk Baroni, 1952; Killer Babes, 2007; A King in New York, 1957; L.A. Confidential, 1997; Logan's Run, 1976; Looker, 1981; Lovely & Amazing, 2001; Made in Italy, 2008; Man in the Mirror: The Michael Jackson Story, 2004 (made-for-TV); The Man Who Lived Twice, 1936; Mask of Death, 1996; Me, Myself & Irene, 2000; Melvin Goes to Dinner, 2003; The Menace, 1932; The Merry Widow, 2007; Mirror, Mirror, 1979 (made-for-TV); Mississippi Gambler, 1942; Mouth to Mouth, 1997; Movie 43, 2013; Murder in Texas, 1981 (made-for-TV); My Only Love, 1982; Mystery of the 13th Guest, 1943; The Naked Kiss, 1964; Nighthawks, 1981; Nights in Rodanthe, 2008; Nip/Tuck, 2003-2010 (TV series); Norma Jean & Marilyn, 1996 (made-for-TV); Once upon a Time in Mexico, 2003; Open Windows, 2014; Open Your Eyes, 1999; Operation Kid Brother, 1967; The Osterman Weekend, 1983; Partners in Crime, 2012; Passenger 57, 1992; Peep World, 2010; Perfect People, 1988 (made-for-TV); Petunia, 2012; Plastic Man, 1999 (made-for-TV); The Point Men, 2001; Predestination, 2014; Priceless, 2008; The Promise, 1979; Providence, 1999-2002 (TV series); Public Enemies, 2009; Public Hero No. 1, 1935; Quicksilver Highway, 1997 (made-for-TV); The Raven, 1935; Remo Williams: The Adventure Begins, 1985; Repo! The Genetic Opera, 2008; Revenge, 2000; Richard, 1972; The Right to Romance, 1933; Romy and Michele's High School Reunion,

1997; Roxanne, 1987; The Second Face, 1950; Second Nature, 2003 (made-for-TV); **Seconds**, 1966; Seducing Doctor Lewis, 2003; Sgt. Pepper's Lonely Hearts Club Band, 1978; A Serious Man, 2009; The Shape of Things, 2003; Shattered, 1991; **Sherlock Holmes; A Game of Shadows**, 2011; Sherman Oaks, 1995-1997 (TV series); Shiri, 2002; Short Night of Glass Dolls, 1971; Sin City: A Dame to Kill For, 2014; Singles, 1992; The Skin I Live In, 2011; Smile, 2005; Smokin' Aces, 2006; Southland Tales, 2006; Speed Racer, 2008; Spin the Bottle, 2000; **Stolen Face**, 1952; Thirteen, 2003; The Three Trials, 2006; **Thunderball**, 1965; Time, 2006; The Tourist, 2010; **Traffic**, 2000; 12 and Holding, 2006; 2012, 2009; **Vanilla Sky**, 2001; White Fire, 1985; **Winner Take All**, 1932; A Woman's Face, 1939; **A Woman's Face**, 1941; Why Me?, 1984 (made-for-TV); You Are a Widow, Sir, 2012.

Politicians: **Abe Lincoln in Illinois**, 1940; **Abraham Lincoln**, 1930; **Absolute Quiet**, 1936; **The Accusing Finger**, 1936; **Advise and Consent**, 1962; **The Agony and the Ecstasy**, 1965; **Alias Nick Beal**, 1949; **All the King's Men**, 1949; **Amistad**, 1997; **Anna Karenina**, 1935; **Anna Karenina**, 1948; **The Battle Cry of Peace**, 1915; **The Beast of the City**, 1932; **Beau James**, 1957; **Beneath the Planet of the Apes**, 1970; **The Best Man**, 1964; **The Birth of a Nation**, 1915; **Blue Skies**, 1946; **Born Yesterday**, 1951; **The Buccaneer**, 1938; **Buffalo Bill**, 1944; **Bullitt**, 1968; **Bulworth**, 1998; **Call Me Madam**, 1953; **Camera Buff**, 1983; **Captain Fury**, 1939; **The Candidate**, 1972; **The Cat's Paw**, 1934; **The Changeling**, 1980; **Charlie Wilson's War**, 2007; **Christopher Strong**, 1933; **Citizen Kane**, 1941; **Cleopatra**, 1934; **Cleopatra**, 1963; **Counselor at Law**, 1933; **The County Chairman**, 1935; **Doc**, 1971; **Death in Granada**, 1996; **Duck Soup**, 1933; **The Enforcer**, 1976; **Escape from the Planet of the Apes**, 1971; **A Face in the Crowd**, 1957; **The Far Horizons**, 1955; **Flamingo Road**, 1949; **A Foreign Affair**, 1948; **Frenzy**, 1972; **Frost/Nixon**, 2008; **Fury**, 1936; **Gabriel over the White House**, 1933; **The Gangster**, 1947; **The Getaway**, 1972; **The Getaway**, 1993; **Gettysburg**, 1993; **The Glass Key**, 1935; **The Glass Key**, 1942; **G-Men**, 1935; **Good Night; and Good Luck**, 2005; **The Great McGinty**, 1940; **Guarding Tess**, 1994; **Hail the Conquering Hero**, 1944; **Her Majesty; Mrs. Brown**, 1997; **The Hitler Gang**, 1944; **Hoffa**, 1992; **Hoover**, 2000; **Hour of the Gun**, 1967; **The House on Carroll Street**, 1988; **I'm Nobody's Sweetheart Now**, 1940; **In Old Chicago**, 1938; **Independence Day**, 1996; **Inherit the Wind**, 1960; **It Happened Here**, 1966; **J. Edgar**, 2011; **JFK**, 1991; **Julius Caesar**, 1953; **Julius Caesar**, 1970; **Khartoum**, 1966; **The Last Days of Pompeii**, 1935; **The Last Hurrah**, 1958; **Lawrence of Arabia**, 1962; **A Lion Is in the Streets**, 1953; **The Loneliness of the Long Distance Runner**, 1962; **The Luck of the Irish**, 1948; **MacArthur**, 1977; **Man of Conquest**, 1939; **The Man Who Shot Liberty Valance**, 1962; **The Manchurian Candidate**, 1962; **Mars Attacks!**, 1996; **The Mayor of Hell**, 1933; **Michael Collins**, 1996; **Milk**, 2008; **Miller's Crossing**, 1990; **The Miracle of Morgan's Creek**, 1944; **The Mudlark**, 1950; **Muriel's Wedding**, 1994; **My Wild Irish Rose**, 1947; **News Is Made at Night**, 1939; **Nixon**, 1995; **The Omen**, 1976; **Our Daily Bread**, 1934; **Our Man Flint**, 1966; **Pearl Harbor**, 2001; **The Pelican Brief**, 1993; **The President's Lady**, 1953; **Primary Colors**, 1998; **The Prisoner of Shark Island**, 1936; **The Private Files of J. Edgar Hoover**, 1977; **The Racket**, 1928; **The Racket**, 1951; **Random Harvest**, 1942; **The Remains of the Day**, 1993; **The Remarkable Andrew**, 1942; **Remember the Day**, 1941; **The Ruling Class**, 1972; **Salvatore Giuliano**, 1966; **San Francisco**, 1936; **The Seduction of Joe Tynan**, 1979; **The Sicilian**, 1987; **Silver Dollar**, 1932; **Sleepy Lagoon**, 1943; **So Well Remembered**, 1947; **Spartacus**, 1960; **Stand by for Action**, 1942; **Stand Up and Cheer!**, 1934; **State of the Union**, 1948; **Storm in a Teacup**, 1938; **The Sun Shines Bright**, 1953; **Sunrise at Campobello**, 1960; **Sunshine**, 1999; **Susan Lenox: Her Fall and Rise**, 1931; **They Died with Their Boots On**, 1941; **They Won't Forget**, 1937; **The 39 Steps**, 1935; **This Is My Affair**, 1937; **Tora! Tora! Tora!**, 1970; **Tucker: The Man and His Dream**, 1988; **Virginia City**, 1940; **Viva Villa!**, 1934;

Viva Zapata!, 1952; **Wag the Dog**, 1997; **The Walls of Jericho**, 1948; **The Way We Were**, 1973; **Wilson**, 1944; **The Wind and the Lion**, 1975; **Yankee Doodle Dandy**, 1942; **Young Dr. Kildare**, 1938; **Z**, 1969.

Posses (also see Chases, pursuing outlaws and renegade Indians in the Old West, this index): Adventures in Silverado, 1948; Adventures of Frank and Jesse James, 1948 (serial); The Adventures of Red Ryder, 1940 (serial); Al Jennings of Oklahoma, 1951; Albuquerque, 1948; **Along Came Jones**, 1945; Along the Navajo Trail, 1945; Ambush at Dark Canyon, 2012; The Animals, 1970; The Ape, 1940; Bad Company, 1972; Bad Girls, 1994; **Bad Man's Territory**, 1946; **Bad Men of Missouri**, 1941; Bad Men of Tombstone, 1949; The Badge of Marshal Brennan, 1957; Badlands of Montana, 1957; The Bandit Trail, 1941; Bandolero!, 1968; Barbary Coast Gent, 1944; Belle Starr's Daughter, 1948; Big Jake, 1971; Billy the Kid, 1930; **Billy the Kid**, 1941; Billy the Kid, 1989 (made-for-TV); Billy the Kid Returns, 1938; Billy the Kid's Gun Justice, 1940; Black Aces, 1937; Black Bandit, 1938; Black Bart, 1948; Blackthorn, 2011; Blazing Sixes, 1937; Bone Tomahawk, 2015; Border G-Man, 1938; Border Roundup, 1942; Borderland, 1937; The Bravados, 1958; Breaker! Breaker!, 1977; Brimstone, 1949; Bullet Code, 1940; Bullet for a Badman, 1964; Butch and Sundance: The Early Days, 1979; **Butch Cassidy and the Sundance Kid**, 1969; Cabin Fever, 2002; **The Cabin in the Cotton**, 1932; Call the Mesquiteers, 1938; **The Capture**, 1950; The Carson City Kid, 1940; Carson City Raiders, 1948; Cattle Stampede, 1943; Cave of Outlaws, 1951; Chato's Land, 1972; Check Your Guns, 1948; The Cimarron Kid, 1952; **Chisum**, 1970; Clash of the Wolves, 1925; Colorado, 1940; **Colorado Territory**, 1949; Colt .45, 1950; The Conquerors, 1932; The Cowboy and the Bandit, 1935; The Cowboy and the Indians, 1949; Cowboys and Aliens, 2011; Crooked River, 1950; The Cursed, 2010; Curtin Call at Cactus Creek, 1950; **Dallas**, 1950; Deadwood Dick, 1940 (serial); The Deadly Companions, 1971; Death Hunt, 1981; **The Defiant Ones**, 1958; The Devil and Leroy Bassett, 1973; Devil Riders, 1943; The Devil's Rejects, 2005; **The Doolins of Oklahoma**, 1949; The Dude Bandit, 1933; Dude Cowboy, 1941; The Duel at Silver Creek, 1952; El Paso Stampede, 1953; Face to Face, 1976; The Far Side of Jericho, 2006; **The Fastest Gun Alive**, 1956; The Fighting Redhead, 1949; A Florida Enchantment, 1914; Forlorn River, 1926; Forlorn River, 1937; Fort Dobbs, 1958; Four Guns to the Border, 1954; **Fury at Furnace Creek**, 1948; Gangster's Den, 1945; The Gay Ranchero, 1948; Ghost of Zorro, 1949 (serial); Git Along Little Dogies, 1937; Goin' South, 1978; The Good Bad Man, 1916; Good Day for a Hanging, 1959; Gordon of Ghost City, 1933; **The Great Missouri Raid**, 1951; **The Great Northfield, Minnesota Raid**, 1972; **Greed**, 1924; Gun Brothers, 1956; Gun Crazy, 1950; Gun Glory, 1957; Gun Law, 1938; Gun Street, 1961; Gunfight, 1961; Gunfighters, 1947; The Gunfighters, 1987 (made-for-TV); Gunfire at Indian Gap, 1957; Gunman's Walk, 1958; Gunpoint, 1966; The Halliday Brand, 1957; **Hang 'Em High**, 1968; **The Hanging Tree**, 1959; Harmony Trail, 1944; Heart of the Golden West, 1942; Hidden Gold, 1940; Hills of Old Wyoming, 1937; Hittin' the Trail, 1937; Hollywood Cowboy, 1937; Home on the Prairie, 1939; Homesteaders of Paradise Valley, 1947; Hooded Angels, 2002; **Hour of the Gun**, 1967; The Hunting Party, 1971; I Spit on Your Grave, 1959; The James Brothers of Missouri, 1949; **Jesse James**, 1939; Jesse James Rides Again, 1947 (serial); **Johnny Guitar**, 1954; **Jubal**, 1956; The Kid from Texas, 1950; The King and Four Queens, 1956; The Last Days of Frank and Jesse James, 1986 (made-for-TV); The Last Frontier, 1932; The Last Hard Men, 1976; The Last Outlaw, 1993 (made-for-TV); The Last Posse, 1953; The Last Stagecoach West, 1957; The Last Witch Hunter, 2015; Law of the Canyon, 1947; Lawless Breed, 1946; **The Lawless Breed**, 1953; The Lawless Range, 1935; Lawless Valley, 1938; **The Left-Handed Gun**, 1958; The Legend of the Lone Ranger, 1952; The Light of Western Stars, 1940; Lightning Raiders, 1945; Lightning Range, 1933; Loaded Pistols, 1948; The Local Bad Man, 1932; The Lone Ranger Rides Again,

1939 (serial); The Lone Star Ranger, 1930; **The Long Riders**, 1980; Man and Boy, 1971; The Man from Colorado, 1948; Man Hunt, 1936; The Man Who Loved Cat Dancing, 1973; The Marshal's Daughter, 1953; Merlin, 1993; The Michigan Kid, 1947; Milarepa, 2006; Mrs. Sundance, 1974 (made-for-TV); Mule Train, 1950; **My Little Chickadee**, 1940; The Mysterious Rider, 1938; 'Neath Arizona Skies, 1934; Nevada, 1944; The Nevada Buckeroo, 1931; Nevada City, 1941; The Nevadan, 1950; New Frontier, 1939; **O Brother, Where Art Thou**, 2000; Oh, Susanna!, 1936; The Oklahoma Cyclone, 1930; **On Dangerous Ground**, 1951; Once Upon a Time in the North, 2012; **One-Eyed Jacks**, 1961; The Outlaw, 1943; **The Outlaw Josey Wales**, 1976; Outlaw Trail, 1944; Overland Stage Riders, 1938; **The Ox-Bow Incident**, 1943; Paradise Canyon, 1935; **Pat Garrett and Billy the Kid**, 1973; The Phantom of the West, 1931; The Phantom Rider, 1936 (serial); The Phantom Rider, 1946 (serial); Posse, 1975; Posse, 1993; Posse from Hell, 1961; Prairie Moon, 1938; Pride of the West, 1938; Prince of the Himalayas, 2006; **Rancho Notorious**, 1952; Randy Rides Alone, 1934; Range War, 1939; **Rango**, 2011; Red Hill, 2010; The Red Rider, 1934; Red River Range, 1938; **Relentless**, 1948; Renegade Trail, 1939; Renegades, 1946; **Return of the Bad Men**, 1948; Return of the Seven, 1966; The Reward, 1965; Ride Him, Cowboy, 1932; Ride in the Whirlwind, 1966; Riders of the Range, 1950; The Riders of the Whistling Skull, 1937; Rim of the Canyon, 1949; **Robin Hood of El Dorado**, 1936; Rogue of the Rio Grande, 1930; Rollin' Plains, 1938; Rootin' Tootin' Rhythm, 1937; Rough Riders, 1997 (made-for-TV); **Run for Cover**, 1955; Running Target, 1956; Rustler's Valley, 1937; Sagebrush Trail, 1933; **Santa Fe**, 1951; Santa Fe Stampede, 1938; Scarlet River, 1933; **The Searchers**, 1956; The Secret of Convict Lake, 1951; **Seraphim Falls**, 2007; The Shadow Riders, 1982 (made-for-TV); Shanghai Noon, 2000; Sheriff of Sage Valley, 1942; Shooting High, 1940; Sierra, 1950; Silver Canyon, 1951; Silver Lode, 1954; The Silver Whip, 1953; **Silverado**, 1985; Skull and Crown, 1935; Slither, 2006; Son of God's Country, 1948; Son of the Border, 1933; Son of Zorro, 1947; **The Sons of Katie Elder**, 1965; South of Heaven, West of Hell, 2000; Southwest Passage, 1954; Special Agent, 1949; Stormy Trails, 1936; Stranger on the Run, 1967 (made-for-TV); Sunset Range, 1935; Sunset Pass, 1946; **Tell Them Willie Boy Is Here**, 1969; **Tension at Table Rock**, 1956; The Test, 1935; Texas Masquerade, 1944; Three Desperate Men, 1951; **The Three Godfathers**, 1916; **Three Godfathers**, 1936; **3 Godfathers**, 1948; Three on the Trail, 1936; **3:10 to Yuma**, 2007; Three Young Texans, 1954; Thunder, 1983; Timber Stampede, 1939; Toll of the Desert, 1935; **Tombstone**, 1993; The Tracker, 1988 (made-for-TV); The Tracker, 2002; Trail of Kit Carson, 1945; Triple Justice, 1940; Trouble in Sundown, 1939; Trouble in Texas, 1937; **True Grit**, 1969; **True Grit**, 2010; **The True Story of Jesse James**, 1957; Under Texas Skies, 1940; Under Western Stars, 1938; Undercover Man, 1942; The Unholy Four, 1970; The Virginian, 1914; **The Virginian**, 1929; **The Virginian**, 1946; **Wagon Master**, 1950; Wagon Trail, 1935; West of the Divide, 1934; **Western Union**, 1941; **When the Daltons Rode**, 1940; Where the Buffalo Roam, 1938; **Whispering Smith**, 1948; White Sun of the Desert, 1973; **The Wild Bunch**, 1969; Wild Horse Mesa, 1932; **Wild Rovers**, 1971; Wisconsin Death Trip, 1999; **Wyatt Earp**, 1994; Wyoming Outlaw, 1939; Wyoming Renegades, 1954; **Yellow Sky**; 1948; **Young Guns**, 1988; **Young Guns II**, 1990; Young Guns of Texas, 1962; **Young Jesse James**, 1960; The Younger Brothers, 1949. Note: For more information of posses of the Old West, see my book *Encylcopedia of Western Lawmen and Outlaws* (Paragon House, 1992).

POWs (prisoners-of-war in WWII): Albert, R.N. (aka: Break to Freedom), 1955 (British POWs in a German camp); Another Time, Another Place, 1984 (three Italian POWs are put to work on a farm in Scotland in 1943); As Far as My Feet Will Carry Me, 2001 (German POW escapes from a Soviet camp in Siberia); **Back to Bataan**, 1945 (begins with the spectacular raid against Japanese POW camp at Cabanatuan, Luzon, Philippines, where more than 500 prisoners were rescued on April 30, 1945); Battle of the Coral Sea, 1959 (based on the USS *Perch*, a submarine that was depth-charged by Japanese ships and captured in 1942, its crew held in a Japanese prison camp, along with Australian POWs, and where some escape); The Beasts of Marseilles (aka: Seven Thunders), 1959 (British POWs escape to be hidden by Resistance fighters in Nazi-occupied France); **The Bridge on the River Kwai**, 1957 (British troops in a Japanese POW camp in Burma, 1942-1943); **Brothers**, 2009 (held by terrorists in Afghanistan); Brylcreem Boys, 1999 (Allied and Axis servicemen interned in neutral Ireland); The Camp on Blood Island, 1958 (Japanese POW camp holding British captives in Malaya); **The Captive Heart**, 1948 (Czech officer escapes Dachau concentration camp to join British POWs, and then escapes from a German POW camp); City of War: The Story of John Rabe, 2009; **The Colditz Story**, 1955 (Allied officers escaping from a so-called escape-proof castle in Germany); **Cornered**, 1945 (Nazi concentration camp); **The Cow and I**, 1961 (French POW working on a German farm escapes back to France); **The Cross of Lorraine**, 1943 (French POWs escape a German prison camp); Danger Within (aka: Breakout), 1960 (British POWs held in Italian prison camp in 1943); **Decision before Dawn**, 1951 (German POWs held in a U.S. Army prison); The Doctor of Stalingrad, 1958 (German POWs held by the Soviets); The Elusive Corporal, 1963 (French POWs in a German prison camp); **Empire of the Sun**, 1987 (Allied prisoners in Shanghai, 1939-1945); Eroica (aka: Heroism), 1966 (Polish POWs in a German prison camp); **Escape**, 1940 (from a German concentration camp); **Escape in the Desert**, 1945 (German POWs escaping a prison camp in the U.S.); Escape to Athena, 1979 (Allied POWs escape from a German prison camp on a Greek island); Escape to Victory (aka: Victory), 1981 (Allied POWs flee a German prison camp); 5th Day of Peace, 1970 (German POWs in a Canadian Army prison camp in Amsterdam); **Force 10 from Navarone**, 1978 (Allied POWs escape from a Nazi camp in Yugoslavia); **The Great Escape**, 1963 (mass escape of Allied prisoners from a German POW camp; uses many of the escape techniques shown in The Password Is Courage, 1962); The Great Escape II: The Untold Story, 1988 (made-for-TV; mass escape of Allied prisoners from a German POW camp); **The Great Raid**, 2005 (details the spectacular raid against a Japanese POW camp at Cabanatuan, Luzon, Philippines, where more than 500 prisoners were rescued on April 30, 1945); Hannibal Brooks, 1969 (British POW in charge of Munich Zoo escapes with an elephant to Switzerland); **Hart's War**, 2002 (Allied POWs held in a German camp escape); The Highest Honor, 1984 (British POWs in Singapore in 1943); The Human Condition, 1959; In Transit, 2009 (German POWS interned in a Soviet prison camp); **Katyn**, 2008 (Polish POWS in a Soviet prison camp who were executed in the March 1940 Katyn Massacre by Soviets); King Rat, 1965 (Allied POWs in Malaysia); The Longest Hundred Miles, 1967 (Allied prisoners in the Philippines); **The McKenzie Break**, 1970 (German POWs escape from a British prison camp in Scotland); **Merry Christmas, Mr. Lawrence**, 1983 (British soldiers in a Japanese POW camp); **Northern Pursuit**, 1943 (German POWs escape from a Canadian prison camp); **The One That Got Away**, 1958 (biopic of Luftwaffe pilot Franz von Werra, 1914-1941, who was captured by the British, but later escaped when shipped to Canada); Paradise Road, 1997 (Allied female POWs held in a Japanese prison camp); The Password Is Courage, 1962 (British POWs in a German prison camp escape by using a fire engine; uses the technique to destroy a passing German ammunition train employed in **Stalag 17**, 1953, but escape techniques used in this film were later employed in **The Great Escape**, 1963); **The Purple Heart**, 1944 (Doolittle Raid against Japan, April 18, 1942; U.S. airmen tried for the attack held in a Japanese prison); **The Railway Man**, 2014 (British captives in Japanese POW camp, who are used as laborers to build the Thai-Burma Railway); Reach for the Sky, 1957 (biopic of RAF pilot Douglas Bader, 1910-1982, who was captured by the Germans in WWII, escaped several times, but was recaptured); Return from the River Kwai, 1989 (British POWs in Burma); **Sailor of the King**, 1953 (British sailor escapes from German custody); The Secret of Blood Island, 1965 (British soldiers in a Japanese POW camp aid a female agent to escape); The Secret War of Harry Frigg, 1968 (U.S. generals held captive at an Italian castle and later escape from a German prison camp); 7 Women from Hell, 1961 (Allied women captives in a Japanese POW camp); **Stalag 17**, 1953 (American POWs escape from a German prison camp); Summer of My German Soldier, 1978 (German POWs in a prison camp in the U.S.); **Three Came Home**, 1950 (British male and female captives in Japanese POW camps); **To End All Wars**, 2001 (British troops in a POW camp in Burma); 2000 Women, 1951 (British female POWs held in prison camps in Nazi-occupied France); **Unbroken**, 2014 (biopic of Louis Zamperini, 1917-2014, who survived several Japanese prison camps); **Von Ryan's Express**, 1965 (mass escape by Allied POWs from an Italian prison camp); **Where Eagles Dare**, 1968 (American POW posing as a U.S. general rescued from a German fortress in the Alps); Women of Valor, 1986 (made-for-TV; U.S. Army nurses captured on Bataan and Corregidor, who are held as POWs in a Japanese prison camp); **The Wooden Horse**, 1951 (British POWs escape from a German prison camp in WWII).

Prehistoric Beasts and Man: Adventures in Dinosaur City, 1991; Age of Dinosaurs, 2013; Anonymous Rex, 2004 (made-for-TV); Barney's Great Adventure, 1998; The Beast from 20,000 Fathoms, 1953; The Beast of Hollow Mountain, 1956; Beast Wars: 1996-1999 (TV series); Bog, 1984; **Brother Bear**, 2003; Carnosaur, 1993; Carnosaur 2, 1995; Carnosaur 3: Primal Species, 1996; Caveman, 1981; The Crater Lake Monster, 1977; The Croods, 2013; The Day Time Ended, 1980; The Deadly Mantis, 1957; Denver: The Last Dinosaur, 1988-1990 (TV series); Destroy All Monsters, 1969; Dino Time, 2012; **Dinosaur**, 2000; Dinosaur Island, 1994; The Dinosaur Project, 2012; Dinosaur Train, 2009 (TV series); Dinosaurs, 1991-1994 (TV series); Dinosaurus!, 1960; Eegah, 1962; **Fantasia**, 1940; The Flintstones, 1994; The Flintstones: On the Rocks, 2001 (made-for-TV); The Flying Serpent, 1946; Galaxy of the Dinosaurs, 1992; Gamera vs. Guillon, 1969; Gertie the Dinosaur, 1914 (12-minute short); The Giant Behemoth, 1959; Giant of the 20th Century, 1978; Godzilla (1954), 2004; **Godzilla: King of the Monsters**, 1956; Godzilla, Mothra and King Ghidorah: Giant Monsters All Out Attack, 2003; Godzilla vs. Gigan, 1977; Godzilla vs. Mechagodzilla, 1977; Gumby Adventures, 1988-2002 (TV series); Harry and His Bucketful of Dinosaurs, 2005 (TV series); Horror Express, 1973; **Ice Age**, 2002; **Ice Age: Continental Drift**, 2012; **Ice Age: Dawn of the Dinosaurs**, 2009; Iceman, 1984; Island of the Lost, 1967; The Jetsons Meet the Flintstones, 1987 (made-for-TV); **Journey to the Center of the Earth**, 1959; **Journey to the Center of the Earth**, 2008; Journey to the Center of Time, 1967; **Jurassic Park**, 1993; Jurassic Park III, 2001; King Dinosaur, 1955; **King Kong**, 1933; **King Kong**, 2005; **The Land Before Time**, 1988; **The Land Before Time II: The Great Valley Adventure**, 1994; Land of the Lost, 1974-1977 (TV series); Land of the Lost, 1991-1992 (TV series); Land of the Lost, 2009; **The Land That Time Forgot**, 1975; The Land Unknown, 1957; The Last Dinosaur, 1977; The Legend of the Dinosaurs, 1977; Loch Ness, 1996; Lost Continent, 1951; **The Lost World**, 1925; The Lost World, 1998 (made-for-TV); The Lost World, 1999-2002 (TV series); The Lost World, 2002 (made-for-TV); **The Lost World: Jurassic Park**, 1997; The Man Called Flintstone, 1966; **Night at the Museum**, 2006; **Night at the Museum: Battle of the Smithsonian**, 2009; **One Million B.C.**, 1940; One Million Years, B.C., 1967; The People That Time Forgot, 1977; The Pit, 1981; Planet of Dinosaurs, 1981; Planet Raptor, 2009; Predator X, 2009 (made-for-TV); Prehistoric Women, 1950; Prehistoric Women, 1967; Prehysteria!, 1993; Primeval, 2007 (TV series); **Q**, 1982; Reptilicus, 1963; Rise of the Dinosaurs, 2013; RRRrrrr!!!, 2004; The Sea Serpent, 1984; Sliders, 1995-2000 (TV series); **Son of Kong**, 1933; A Sound of Thunder, 2005; Stanley's Dinosaur Round-Up, 2006; Tammy and the T-Rex, 1994; Teenage Caveman, 1958; **Three Ages**, 1923; Transformers, 1984 (TV series); T-Rex: Back to the Cretaceous, 1998 (45-minute short); The Tribe, 1974; Trog, 1970; **20 Million Miles to Earth**, 1957; Two Lost

Worlds, 1951; Unknown Island, 1948; Untamed Women, 1952; Valley of the Dragons, 1961; Voyage to the Planet of Prehistoric Women, 1968; Voyage to the Prehistoric Planet, 1965; Vulcan, 1999; We're Back!: A Dinosaur's Story, 1993; When Dinosaurs Ruled the Earth, 1971; When Women Lost Their Tails, 1972; Where Time Began, 1978; Women of the Prehistoric Planet, 1966; Yor, the Hunter from the Future, 1983.

Prison Escapes and Escape Attempts: **A nous la liberte**, 1931; Aces: Iron Eagle III, 1992; **Adventures of Don Juan**, 1948; After the Dance, 1935; **After the Fox**, 1966; Alias Boston Blackie, 1942; Albert, R.N. (aka: Break to Freedom), 1955 (British POWs in a German camp in WWII); Alien Thunder, 1974; Animal Factory, 2000; Ariel, 1990; **Arise My Love**, 1940; Around the Bend, 2004; As Far as My Feet Will Carry Me, 2001 (German POW escapes from a Soviet camp in Siberia in WWII); Asylum, 2003; The A-Team, 2010; **Back to Bataan**, 1945 (escape of more than 500 American POWs held at the Japanese concentration camp in Cabanatuan, Philippines, in January 1945 in a daring WWII raid by U.S. Army Rangers); Bandits, 1997; Bandits, 2001; Battle of the Coral Sea, 1959 (based on the USS *Perch*, a submarine that was depth-charged by Japanese ships and captured in 1942 in WWII, its crew held in a Japanese prison camp, along with Australian POWs, and some escape); The Beasts of Marseilles (aka: Seven Thunders), 1959 (British POWs escape to be hidden by Resistance fighters in Nazi-occupied France in WWII); **The Beggars Opera**, 1953; Between Midnight and Dawn, 1950; Beyond Re-Animator, 2003; **The Big House**, 1930; Billy the Kid, 1930 (the Kid's escape from the Lincoln County Jail, New Mexico); **Billy the Kid**, 1941 (the Kid's escape from the Lincoln County Jail, New Mexico); **Birdman of Alcatraz**, 1962; **Bite the Bullet**, 1975 (from a chain gang); Black Mama, White Mama, 1973 (women's prison); Black Tuesday, 1954; Blackmail, 1939 (from a chain gang); Bon Voyage, 2003; Born American, 1986; Borstal Boy, 2000; Breakout, 1975 (the helicopter escape shown in this film inspired the real life helicopter escape of swindler Dale Otto Remling from the Southern Michigan State Prison in Jackson, Michigan, in 1975); The Bridge of San Luis Rey, 1944; **The Bridge on the River Kwai**, 1957 (from a Japanese POW camp in WWII); The Broken Land, 1962; **Brute Force**, 1947; **Caged**, 1950 (women's prison); Caged Fury, 1990 (women's prison); Caged Heat, 1974 (women's prison); Canon City, 1948 (from Colorado State Penitentiary); **Captain from Castile**, 1947; **The Captive Heart**, 1948 (Czech officer escapes Dachau concentration camp to join British POWs, and then escapes from a German POW camp in WWII); Carlito's Way, 1993; Casanova's Big Night, 1954; **Castle on the Hudson**, 1940 (from Sing Sing state prison at Ossining, N.Y.); The Ceremony, 1963; **The Chairman**, 1969; Chattahoochee, 1990; A Circle of Deception, 1961; City of Fear, 1959 (from San Quentin State Prison, California); **The Colditz Story**, 1955 (Allied officers escaping from a so-called escape-proof castle in Germany in WWII); **The Concrete Jungle**, 1962; **The Conspirators**, 1944; **Cool Hand Luke**, 1967 (from a chain gang); **The Count of Monte Cristo**, 1934 (from the Chateau d'If); **The Count of Monte Cristo**, 2002 (from the Chateau d'If); Crashout, 1955; The Crimson Blade, 1964; **The Cross of Lorraine**, 1943 (French POWs escape a German prison camp in WWII); Danger Within (aka: Breakout), 1960 (British POWs escape from an Italian prison camp in 1943 in WWII); **The Dark Knight**, 2008; **Dark Passage**, 1947 (from San Quentin State Prison, California); Daughter of the Tong, 1939; **The Defiant Ones**, 1958 (from a chain gang); Desperate Measures, 1998; **The Devil Doll**, 1936; **Devil's Island**, 1939 (from French Guiana); The Devil's Saddle Legion, 1937; Dillinger, 1945 (his escape from the jail at Crown Point, Indiana, with a wooden gun); Dillinger, 1973 (his escape from the jail at Crown Point, Indiana, with a wooden gun); Don't Turn 'Em Loose, 1936; Down by Law, 1986; **Each Dawn I Die**, 1939; Eddie Macon's Run, 1983; El Condor, 1970; **Escape**, 1940 (from a German concentration camp); **Escape from Alcatraz**, 1979; Escape from Devil's Island, 1935 (from French Guiana); Escape from DS-3, 1981; **Escape from Fort Bravo**, 1953 (from a

Union prison in the U.S. Civil War); Escape from New York, 1981; **Escape from the Planet of the Apes**, 1971; **Escape in the Desert**, 1945; Escape Plan, 2013; Escape to Athena, 1979 (Allied POWs escape from a German prison camp on a Greek island in WWII); Escape to Victory (aka: Victory), 1981 (Allied POWs flee a German prison camp in WWII); The Escapist, 2006; The Escapist, 2008; **Exodus**, 1960; Fiesta, 1995; The Fighting Marshal, 1931; The Fighting Prince of Donegal, 1966; Firestorm, 1998; Five Guns to Tombstone, 1960; Flesh and the Spur, 1956; **The Flim-Flam Man**, 1967; For the Term of His Natural Life, 1927; **Force 10 from Navarone**, 1978 (escape from a Nazi camp in Yugoslavia in WWII); Forgotten Girls, 1940 (women's prison); Fortress, 1992; Fortunes of Captain Blood, 1950; **The Four Feathers**, 1939; **Frenzy**, 1972; **The Fugitive**, 1947; The Fugitive, 1963; **The Fugitive**, 1993; Fugitive at Large, 1939; Fugitive Lovers, 1934; Fugitives, 1929; G.I. Joe: Retaliation, 2013; A Gentleman After Dark, 1942; **Get the Gringo**, 2012; The Getaway, 1941; Girls of the Big House, 1945 (women's prison); Girls on Probation, 1938 (women's prison); **Grand Illusion**, 1938 (from a German POW camp in WWI); The Grave, 1996; **The Great Escape**, 1963 (mass escape of Allied prisoners from a German POW camp in WWII); The Great Escape II: The Untold Story, 1988 (made-for-TV; mass escape of Allied prisoners from a German POW camp in WWII); **Great Expectations**, 1946; Great Expectations, 1998; **The Great Raid**, 2005 (escape of more than 500 American POWs held at the Japanese concentration camp in Cabanatuan, Philippines, in January 1945 in a daring WWII raid by U.S. Army Rangers); The Green-Eyed Blonde, 1957; Gunman from Laredo, 1959; Guns, Girls and Gangsters, 1959; Hangfire, 1991; The Hangover Part III, 2013; Hannibal Brooks, 1969 (British POW in charge of Munich Zoo escapes with an elephant to Switzerland in WWII); The Hard Word, 2003; **Harry Potter and the Prisoner of Azkaban**, 2004; Harry Tracy: The Last of the Wild Bunch, 1983; **Hart's War**, 2002 (Allied POWs held in a German camp escape in WWII); Hearts in Exile, 1915; Heaven, 2002; Hell on Devil's Island, 1957 (from French Guiana); Hell's Highway, 1932 (from a chain gang); Hero and the Terror, 1988; **His Girl Friday**, 1940; His Majesty, the American, 1919; Hollow Point, 1996; **The Hot Rock**, 1972; **House of Frankenstein**, 1944; **House of Numbers**, 1957 (from San Quentin State Prison, California); House of Whipcord, 1975 (women's prison); The Human Shield, 1991; **The Hurricane**, 1937; **I Am a Fugitive from a Chain Gang**, 1932; I Escaped from Devil's Island, 1973 (from French Guiana); I Love You Phillip Morris, 2009; I Was Framed, 1942; Innocent Prey, 1991; Inside Out, 1976; **Inside the Walls of Folsom Prison**, 1951 (from the state prison in California); Instinct, 1999; Instinct to Kill, 2001; **The Invisible Man Returns**, 1940; Iron Man 2, 2010; Island in the Sky, 1938; Jacktown, 1962; Johnny Firecloud, 1975; The Killer Is Loose, 1956; **Kung Fu Panda**, 2008; Ladies They Talk About, 1933; **Ladyhawke**, 1985; L'affaire Seznec, 1993 (made-for-TV; from French Guiana); **Larceny, Inc.**, 1942; Lazy River, 1934; **The Left-Handed Gun**, 1958 (Billy the Kid's escape from the Lincoln County Jail); Les Miserables, 1917; Les Miserables, 1927; Les Miserables, 1934; **Les Miserables**, 1935; Les Miserables, 1952; **Les Miserables**, 1953; Les Miserables, 1958; Les Miserables, 1967 (TV series); Les Miserables, 1978 (made-for-TV); Les Miserables, 1982; **Les Miserables**, 1995; **Les Miserables**, 1998; Les Miserables, 2000 (TV series); Les Miserables, 2007; **Les Miserables**, 2012; Les Miserables in Concert: The 25th Anniversary, 2010; Little Miss Broadway, 1947; Lock Up, 1989; **The Loneliness of the Long Distance Runner**, 1962; Los Miserables, 1944; The Man from Dakota, 1940; Man Hunt, 1936; **The Man in the Iron Mask**, 1939; **The Man in the Iron Mask**, 1998; The Man in the Moonlight, 1919; The Man of Shame, 1915; Man on a Ledge, 2012; Maniac, 1963; The Man Who Came Back, 2008; The Mask, 1994; **The McKenzie Break**, 1970 (German POWs escape from a British prison camp in Scotland in WWII); **Men in Black 3**, 2012; **Midnight Express**, 1978; **Mission Impossible: Ghost Protocol**, 2011; Morgan's Ferry, 2001; **Mr. Majestyk**, 1974; Mrs. Soffel, 1984; Murder on the Blackboard, 1934; Murphy's Law, 1986; The Musketeer, 2001;

Mysterious Island, 1961 (from a Confederate prison in the American Civil War); **Nevada Smith**, 1966 (from a chain gang); Nobody's Baby, 2001; **Northern Pursuit**, 1943 (German POWs escape from a Canadian prison camp in WWII); O Brother, Where Art Thou, 2000 (from a chain gang); **One-Eyed Jacks**, 1961; **The One That Got Away**, 1958 (biopic of Luftwaffe pilot Franz von Werra, 1914-1941, who was captured by the British, but later escaped when shipped to Canda); Out of Sight, 1998; **The Outriders**, 1950 (from a Union prison camp in the American Civil War); Over the Wall, 1938 (from Sing Sing Prison, N.Y.); Overkill, 1996; **Pappillon**, 1973 (Devil's Island; from French Guiana); **Pardon Us**, 1931; **Passage to Marseille**, 1944 (patriotic French prisoners escape from French Guiana in order to fight for France in WWII); The Password Is Courage, 1962 (British POWs in a German prison camp escape by using a fire engine in WWII); **Pat Garrett and Billy the Kid**, 1973 (the Kid's escape from the Lincoln County Jail, New Mexico); Payback, 2007; A Perfect World, 1993; The Phantom of Paris, 1931; Phantom of the Paradise, 1974; **Planet of the Apes**, 1968; Prison-A-Go-Go!, 2003; Prison Break, 2005-2009 (TV series); Prison Heat, 1993; **The Prisoner of Shark Island**, 1936 (from the Union prison in the Dry Tortugas in the American Civil War); **Public Enemies**, 2009 (from State Prison, Michigan City, Indiana; Dillinger's escape from the jail at Crown Point, Indiana); **Public Hero No. 1**, 1935; **Raising Arizona**, 1987; **Raw Deal**, 1948; Reach for the Sky, 1957 (biopic of RAF pilot Douglas Bader, 1910-1982, who was captured by the Germans in WWII, escaped several times, but was recaptured); Red Heat, 1988; Redemption of the Ghost, 2002; Renegades of the West, 1932; Return to Warbow, 1958; **Riffraff**, 1936; **Rob Roy: The Highland Rogue**, 1954; **Robbery**, 1967; Robin Hood: Ghosts of Sherwood 3-D, 2012; **Robin Hood: Prince of Thieves**, 1991; Roger Toughy, Gangster, 1944 (from the state prison in Joliet, Illinois); Rogue of the Range, 1936; Romeo Must Die, 2000; **Runaway Train**, 1985; Running Target, 1956; Sagebrush Trail, 1933; **Sailor of the King**, 1953 (British sailor escapes from German custody in WWII); **The Saint's Double Trouble**, 1940; **San Quentin**, 1937 (from the state prison in California); Savannah Smiles, 1982; The Scar of Shame, 1927; **The Sea Hawk**, 1940 (galley slaves from a Spanish galleon); The Secret of Blood Island, 1965 (British soldiers in a Japanese POW camp aid a female agent to escape in WWII); Secret Service of the Air, 1939; The Secret Invasion, 1964; The Secret War of Harry Frigg, 1968 (U.S. generals held captive at an Italian castle and later escape from a German prison camp in WWII); Seven Miles from Alcatraz, 1942; **The Seventh Cross**, 1944 (from a German concentration camp); **The Shawshank Redemption**, 1994; She Mob, 1968 (women's prison); Sitting Target, 1972; Sleeper, 2012; Smashing the Money Ring, 1939; Snow White and the Three Stooges, 1961; **The Son of Monte Cristo**, 1940; **Stalag 17**, 1953 (American POWs escape from a German prison camp in WWII); Spy Game, 2001; **Star Trek III: The Search for Spock**, 1984; 6,000 Enemies, 1939; **Stir Crazy**, 1980; Strange Alibi, 1941; **Strange Cargo**, 1940 (from French Guiana); Street Fighter, 1994; **The Sugarland Express**, 1974; **Superman II**, 1981; Superman IV: The Quest for Peace, 1987; **20,000 Years in Sing Sing**, 1933 (from the state prison at Ossining, N.Y.); **The Sword and the Rose**, 1953; **Take the Money and Run**, 1969; Taking Care of Business, 1990; Terror of the Bloodhunters, 1962; **There Was a Crooked Man**, 1970; **The Three Musketeers**, 1948; Three Who Loved, 1931; **Tom Horn**, 1980 (from the jail in Cheyenne, Wyoming); Torchy Blane...Playing with Dynamite, 1939; Toronto Stories, 2008; **Toy Story 3**, 2010; Tracy the Outlaw, 1928 (Harry Tracy); **Twilight's Last Gleaming**, 1977; **U.S. Marshals**, 1998; **Uncertain Glory**, 1944; **Up the River**, 1930; Violent Women, 1960 (women's prison); **Virginia City**, 1940 (from a Confederate prison in the American Civil War); **Von Ryan's Express**, 1965 (mass escape by Allied POWs from an Italian prison camp in WWII); **The Way Back**, 2010; Wedding Daze, 2006; Welcome to Collinwood, 2002; **We're No Angels**, 1955 (from French Guiana); The Wheels of Justice, 1915; **Where Eagles Dare**, 1968 (American POW posing as a U.S. general rescued from a German fortress in the Alps in WWII);

Where the West Begins, 1938; **White Heat**, 1949 (from the state prison in Joliet, Illinois); White Lightning, 1973; Wild Horse Phantom, 1944; **The Whole Town's Talking**, 1935; Wild Geese II, 1985; Women in Cages, 1971 (women's prison); Women of Devil's Island, 1962 (from French Guiana; women's prison); Women Without Men, 1956 (women's prison); **The Wooden Horse**, 1951 (British POWs escape from a German prison camp in WWII); X-Men: The Last Stand, 2006; **You Can't Get Away with Murder**, 1939; **You Only Live Once**, 1937; **Young Guns**, 1988 (Billy the Kid's escape from the Lincoln County Jail, New Mexico); **Young Guns II**, 1990. Note: For detailed information on prison escapes by criminals, see my books *Bloodletters and Badmen* (M. Evans, 1973); *Encyclopedia of World Crime*; 8 volumes (Crime-Books, Inc., 1990); *The Great Pictorial History of World Crime*; 2 volumes (History, Inc., 2004).

Projectionists, Projection Rooms and Film Projectors: **Adam's Rib**, 1949; The Adventures of George the Projectionist, 2006; Apartment Zero, 1988; Attack from Mars, 1988; **The Aviator**, 2004; **The Bad and the Beautiful**, 1952; **The Barefoot Executive**, 1971; **Blazing Saddles**, 1974; The Blind Owl, 1987; The Blob, 1958; Blow Out, 1981; **A Bridge Too Far**, 1977; Bulletproof Monk, 2003; Bye Bye Brasil, 1980; **The Cameraman**, 1928; Chillerama, 2011; **Cinema Paradiso**, 1988; **Citizen Kane**, 1941; **Clash by Night**, 1952; Coming Soon, 2008; **Desperately Seeking Susan**, 1985; **Each Dawn I Die**, 1939; **Edison; The Man**, 1940; Electric Shadows, 2004; The Ex-Mrs. Bradford, 1936; Fight Club, 1999; Fortress of War, 2011; **Fury**, 1936; Ginger Meggs, 1988; The Good Life, 2007; Graziella, 2015; **Hellzapoppin**, 1941; How to Make a Monster, 1958; Inglourious Basterds, 2009; The Inner Circle, 1991; Joni's Promise, 2005; Kings of the Road, 1976; **L. A. Confidential**, 1997; Last Action Hero, 1993; **The Last Picture Show**, 1971; Le film de les nuls, 1994; **MacArthur**, 1977; **The Magic Box**, 1952; The Magic Box, 2002; Mr. Love, 1985; **Mister Roberts**, 1955; The Nice Guys, 2016; Perhaps Love, 2005; Popcorn, 2007; The Preview Murder Mystery, 1936; The Projectionist, 1971; Projectionist, 2008; **The Purple Rose of Cairo**, 1985; **Quadrophenia**, 1979; **Silent Movie**, 1976; **Singin' in the Rain**, 1952; Sioux City Sue, 1946; Snafu, 1945; Splendor, 1989; **The Stranger**, 1946; **Sullivan's Travels**, 1941; The Talk of Hollywood, 1929; Targets, 1968; Things to Do in Denver When You're Dead, 1995; Vanishing on 7th Street, 2010; Watch the Birdie, 1950; **What Price Hollywood?**, 1932; Wish You Were Here, 1987.

Psychiatrists, Psychiatry, Psychologists and Psychology (also see Asylums; Multiple Personalities, this index): Abandon, 2002; Abduction, 2011; The Adored, 2012; **Agnes of God**, 1985; **Airplane!**, 1980; Airplane II: The Sequel, 1982; All about My Mother, 1999; All around the Town, 2002 (made-for-TV); All Good Things, 2010; All over the Guy, 2001; **The Amazing Dr. Clitterhouse**, 1938; **American Sniper**, 2014; Amos & Andrew, 1993; Analyze That, 2002; **Analyze This**, 1999; **Anatomy of a Murder**, 1959; **An Angel at My Table**, 1990; **Angel on My Shoulder**, 1946; Angel's Dance, 1999; **Another Woman**, 1988; **Antwone Fisher**, 2002; **Antz**, 1998; Anything Else, 2003; **Arsenic and Old Lace**, 1944; **As Good as It Gets**, 1997; As Time Goes By, 1992-2005 (TV series); Assassin of the Tsar, 1991; Assassin's Bullet, 2012; Assault on Precinct 13, 2005; **The Astonished Heart**, 1950; Asylum, 2005; Audrey Rose, 1977; Autumn Leaves, 1956; **The Bachelor and the Bobby-Soxer**, 1947; Bad Dreams, 1988; Bad Timing, 1980; Basic Instinct, 1992; Basic Instinct 2, 2006; Battle Los Angeles, 2011; **Batman Begins**, 2005; **Batman Forever**, 1995; The Beast from 20,000 Fathoms, 1953; **A Beautiful Mind**, 2001; **Bedlam**, 1946; The Befallen, 2003 (TV miniseries); **Before I Go to Sleep**, 2014; **Before Sunrise**, 1995; Behind Locked Doors, 1948; Benny & Joon, 1993; Berserk, 1967; **Bewitched**, 1945; **The Best of Youth**, 2003; Birds of Prey, 2002-2003 (TV series); **Birdy**, 1984; **Black Sunday**, 1977; **Blind Alley**, 1939; Blind Dating, 2006; Blood and Black Lace, 1964; The Blue Elephant, 2014; **Blume in Love**, 1973; Bones, 2005- (TV series); **Boomerang**,

1947; Borderline, 2002 (made-for-TV); Brainstorm, 2001; Brave, 1994; **A Bridge Too Far**, 1977; **Bringing Up Baby**, 1938; Broken Flowers, 2005; The Butcher's Wife, 1991; **Butterfield 8**, 1960; The Butterfly Effect, 2004; **The Cabinet of Dr. Caligari**, 1921; The Cabinet of Dr. Caligari, 1962; **The Caine Mutiny**, 1954; Call Me Bwana, 1963; Candyman, 1992; The Canyons, 2013; Captain Newman, M.D., 1963; Captive Wild Women, 1943; **Carefree**, 1938; **Carnival of Souls**, 1962; Cast Away, 2000; **Cat People**, 1942; Caught, 1949; Cecilie, 2007; The Cell, 2000; **Chances Are**, 1989; Charlie and the Chocolate Factory, 2005; Charlie Bartlett, 2007; **Cheaper by the Dozen**, 1950; Cheers, 1982-1993 (TV series); Christmas Eve, 1947; The Chorus, 2004; Citizen X, 1995 (made-for-TV); **A Clockwork Orange**, 1971; Clue, 1985; Color of Night, 1994; Coma, 1978; **Conflict**, 1945; **The Constant Husband**, 1955; The Couch Trip, 1988; **C.R.A.Z.Y.**, 2005; Crazy as Hell, 2002; Crazy in Alabama, 1999; Crazy Moon, 1987; Crazy People, 1990; Crazylove, 2005; The Cure, 1997; Dark City, 1998; Dark Corners, 2006; The Dark Hours, 2005; **The Dark Past**, 1948; Dark Shadows, 2012; Dead Again, 1991; Dead Heat on a Merry-Go-Round, 1966; Dead Men Tell, 1941; **Dead of Night**, 1945; Dead of Winter, 1987; The Dead Zone, 1983; Dear Diary, 1989; **Deconstructing Harry**, 1997; Defying Gravity, 2009- (TV series); **The Departed**, 2006; **Desire**, 1936; Desire Me, 1947; **Diary of a Mad Housewife**, 1970; Dishonored Lady, 1947; Don Juan DeMarco, 1994; Donnie Darko, 2001; Don't Be Afraid of the Dark, 2010; Don't Say a Word, 2001; Dorothy Mills, 2008; **Dr. Cyclops**, 1940; Dr. Katz, Professional Therapist, 1995-2002 (TV series); Dr. T and the Women, 2000; **Dracula's Daughter**, 1936; The Dream Team, 1989; Dreamcatcher, 2003; **Dressed to Kill**, 1980; Ed, 2000-2004 (TV series); Eden Log, 2007; Edward Scissorhands, 1990; 88 Minutes, 2007; End of Days, 1999; The Entity, 1982; **Equus**, 1977; **Escape from the Planet of the Apes**, 1971; The Evening Star, 1996; Everything You Always Wanted to Know About Sex * But Were Afraid to Ask, 1972; Evil Eye, 1963; Exit in Red, 1996; **The Exorcist**, 1973; **Experiment Perilous**, 1944; Expresso Bongo, 1959; Eye See You, 2002; Eyes Wide Shut, 1999; **Face to Face**, 1976; **Faces**, 1968; Far from Heaven, 2002; Fear of Fear, 1975 (made-for-TV); **Fear Strikes Out**, 1957; **Fearless**, 1993; Femme Fatale, 1991; A Few Days in September, 2006; 15 Minutes, 2001; 5th Avenue Girl, 1939; Filth, 2013; Final Analysis, 1992; A Fine Madness, 1966; Firestarter, 1984; The Fisher King, 1991; The Five of Me, 1981 (made-for-TV); Flash of Genius, 2008; Flirting with Danger, 2006 (made-for-TV); The Forbidden Room, 2015; The Forgotten, 1973; The Forgotten, 2004; **Fourteen Hours**, 1951; The Fourth Kind, 2009; Frances, 1982; Frankie & Alice, 2010; Franklyn, 2008; Frasier, 1993-2004 (TV series); Freud, 1962; From Beyond, 1986; **The Front Page**, 1931; **The Front Page**, 1974; **The Fugitive**, 1993; Garden State, 2004; Ghost World, 2001; The Girl Who Kicked the Hornets' Nest, 2009; The Girl Who Played with Fire, 2009; Glen or Glenda, 1953; **The Gnome-Mobile**, 1967; **Good Will Hunting**, 1997; **Greenberg**, 2010; Grosse Pointe Blank, 1997; The Guardian, 1990; Gun Shy, 2000; Hairspray, 1988; **Halloween**, 1978; Hands of the Ripper, 1971; Hannibal, 2001; Hannibal, 2013-2015 (TV series); **Harvey**, 1950; Harvey (1972 (made-for-TV); Harvey, 1996 (made-for-TV); **The Haunting**, 1963; The Haunting, 2009; A Haunting at Silver Falls, 2013; He Was a Quiet Man, 2007; Head-On, 2004; Heat and Dust, 1983; Hector and the Search for Happiness, 2014; Hemlock Grove, 2013-2015 (TV series); Her Deadly Rival, 1995 (made-for-TV); Heroes, 2006-2010 (TV series); **The Hidden Room**, 1949; **High Anxiety**, 1977; **High Wall**, 1947; **His Girl Friday**, 1940; A History of Violence, 2005; **Hollow Triumph**, 1948; Hollywood Ending, 2002; **Home of the Brave**, 1949; The Hourglass Sanatorium, 1973; House of Dust, 2013; **House of Games**, 1987; The House on Haunted Hill, 1959; How to Get Ahead in Advertising, 1989; **The Howling**, 1981; The Hudsucker Proxy, 1994; Huff, 2004-2006 (TV series); The Human Stain, 2003; **The Hurt Locker**, 2009; I Dream of Jeannie, 1965-1970 (TV series); **I Never Promised You a Rose Garden**, 1977; I, the Jury, 1953; I, the Jury, 1982; Identity, 2003; Igby Goes Down, 2002; I'm Not There, 2007; Imaginary Friend, 2012 (made-for-

TV); **The Impossible Years**, 1968; The In Crowd, 2000; In the Mouth of Madness, 1994; The Incredible Hulk, 2008; **The Incredible Shrinking Man**, 1957; **The Informant!**, 2009; Inspector Morse, 1987-2000 (TV series); Instinct, 1999; The Invasion, 2007; **Invasion of the Body Snatchers**, 1956; **Invasion of the Body Snatchers**, 1978; Invisible Ghost, 1941; Irresistible, 2006; It's Kind of a Funny Story, 2010; **Joe Gould's Secret**, 2000; Johnny English Reborn, 2011; Just Like Heaven, 2005; **Kate & Leopold**, 2001; Keep My Grave Open, 1976; Keiho, 1999; Killer, 1994; Killer: A Journal of Murder, 1992; **The King of Marvin Gardens**, 1972; The Kingdom, 1994 (TV miniseries); Kings & Queen, 2004; **Kings Row**, 1942; Klute, 1971; K-PAX, 2001; **Lady in the Dark**, 1944; Lantana, 2001; The Last Kiss, 2001; Laurel Canyon, 2002; The Lazarus Project, 2008; **Le Week-End**, 2014; Let's Live a Little, 1948; Little Children, 2006; Lizzie, 1957; **The Locket**, 1946; The Loft, 2014; London, 2005; Loose Cannons, 1990; Lost Angels, 1989; Love at First Bite, 1979; **Love Crazy**, 1941; **Lover Come Back**, 1962; Lovesick, 1983; Ludwig, 1972; Lunacy, 2005; **M**, 1951; Mad Detective, 2008; Mad House, 2004; **Madonna of the Seven Moons**, 1945; Man on a Swing, 1974; The Man Who Loved Women, 1983; **The Manchurian Candidate**, 1962; The Manchurian Candidate, 2004; **Manhunter**, 1986; **The Mark**, 1961; Mary and Max, 2009; The Mask, 1994; **The Master**, 2012; Matador, 1986; Me Myself and I, 1992; Me, Myself & Irene, 2000; The Medusa Touch, 1978; The Memory of a Killer, 2003; **Midnight Lace**, 1960; **Mine Own Executioner**, 1949; **Ministry of Fear**, 1944; **Mirage**, 1965; Mirage, 1995; Mirrors, 2008; Mistresses, 2013- (TV series); Molly, 1999; Monster-in-Law, 2005; **Montenegro**, 1981; Moonlight Mile, 2002; Mostly Martha, 2001; Move Over, Darling, 1963; **Mr. & Mr. Bridge**, 1990; **Mr. Deeds Goes to Town**, 1936; Mr. Frost, 1990; Mr. Jones, 1993; Mrs. Harris, 2005 (made-for-TV); Mumford, 1999; **Murder, My Sweet**, 1944; **My Favorite Wife**, 1940; My Soul to Take, 2010; My World Dies Screaming, 1958; The Naked Face, 1984; The Net, 1995; Never Talk to Strangers, 1995; The New York Ripper, 1982; New York Stories, 1989; The Night Caller, 1975; **Night Has a Thousand Eyes**, 1948; Nightbreed, 1990; **Nightmare Alley**, 1947; 9, 2009; Nine Months, 1995; The Nines, 2007; Nobody Else but You, 2011; Norma Jean & Marilyn, 1996 (made-for-TV); Nothing without You, 2012; **Now, Voyager**, 1942; The Number 23, 2007; **Nuts**, 1987; Obsessed, 1992 (made-for-TV); Off the Map, 2003; **The Omen**, 1976; The Omen, 2006; On a Clear Day You Can See Forever, 1970; On the Count of Zero, 2007; On the Edge, 2001; **One Flew Over the Cuckoo's Nest**, 1975; One Life to Live, 1968-2013 (TV series); One Night at McCool's, 2001; **The 1,000 Eyes of Dr. Mabuse**, 1960; Open Your Eyes, 1997; **Ordinary People**, 1980; Orphan, 2009; Oz, 1997-2003 (TV series); Panic, 2000; Passion of the Mind, 2000; **The Peanuts Movie**, 2015; Peeping Tom, 1960; Phobia, 1980; **Possessed**, 1947; The Possession, 2012; Premonition, 2007; **The President's Analyst**, 1967; **Pressure Point**, 1962; Prick of Your Ears, 1987; Primal Fear, 1996; Prime Suspect: The Scent of Darkness, 1995 (made-for-TV); **The Prince of Tides**, 1991; **The Prisoner of Second Avenue**, 1975; The Private Lives of Pippa Lee, 2009; Private Practice, 2007-2013 (TV series); Prozac Nation, 2001; **Psycho**, 1960; Psycho, 1998; Psycho Beach Party, 2000; Psycho II, 1983; **The Pumpkin Eater**, 1964; Queen Bee, 1955; Rage in Heaven, 1941; Raising Cain, 1992; Rampage: The Hillside Strangler Murders, 2006; **Random Harvest**, 1942; **Rebel Without a Cause**, 1955; Red Dragon, 2002; The Red Robin, 2013; A Reflection of Fear, 1992; Reflections in a Golden Eye, 1967; Reform School Girl, 1957; Requiem for a Dream, 2000; **Revenge of the Pink Panther**, 1978; Ring of Fear, 1954; Romance, 1999; Romantics Anonymous, 2010; Ruby & Quentin, 2003; **The Ruling Class**, 1972; **Safe**, 1995; **The Santa Clause**, 1994; Schizo, 1976; Screaming Mimi, 1958; The Scribbler, 2014; Secret Window, 2004; The Serpent and the Rainbow, 1988; Session 9, 2001; **The Seven-Per-Cent Solution**, 1976; **The Seven Year Itch**, 1955; **Shadow on the Wall**, 1950; **Shakespeare in Love**, 1998; Shattered Image, 1998; Shattered Mind, 1996 (made-for-TV); She Wouldn't Say Yes, 1945; Sherlock Holmes and the Case of

the Silk Stocking, 2004 (made-for-TV); She's So Lovely, 1999; Shock, 1946; **Shock Corridor**, 1963; **Shockproof**, 1949; Shrink, 2009; Shutter Island, 2010; Side Effects, 2013; **The Silence of the Lambs**, 1991; Silent Fall, 1994; **Silver Linings Playbook**, 2012; The Singing Detective, 2003; Six Feet Under, 2001-2005 (TV series); 6 Souls, 2010; **The Sixth Sense**, 1999; Ski Patrol, 1990; Slaughterhouse-Five, 1972; The Sleeping Tiger, 1954; **Smile**, 1975; **The Snake Pit**, 1948; **The Sniper**, 1952; The Snowtown Murders, 2011; Society, 1989; Solaris, 2002; **The Song of Bernadette**, 1943; The Sopranos, 1999-2007 (TV series); The Soul Keeper, 2002; Soul Man, 1986; **Space Jam**, 1996; Space Station 76, 2014; Speaking of Sex, 2001; **Spellbound**, 1945; **Splendor in the Grass**, 1961; **The Squid and the Whale**, 2005; Stay, 2005; The Stepfather, 1987; **The Stepford Wives**, 1975; Stereo, 1969; Still of Night, 1982; Stonehearst Asylum, 2014; Strange Illusion, 1945; The Stranger, 1987; **Stranger Than Fiction**, 2006; The Strangler, 1964; **Suddenly, Last Summer**, 1959; Suicide Room, 2011; Summer Things, 2002; Surviving Christmas, 2004; Surviving the Game, 1994; Sybil, 1976 (TV miniseries); Take Shelter, 2011; **Take the Money and Run**, 1969; Taking Chance, 2009 (made-for-TV); Talk to Her, 2002; Talaash, 2012; **Tender Is the Night**, 1962; **Terminator 3: Rise of the Machines**, 2003; The Terror Inside, 1996 (made-for-TV); **That Touch of Mink**, 1962; That's My Boy, 1951; **Them!**, 1954; There Goes the Neighborhood, 1992; They, 2002; **They Might Be Giants**, 1971; **The Third Secret**, 1964; Thirst, 1961; **36 Hours**, 1965; **The Thomas Crown Affair**, 1968; The Thomas Crown Affair, 1999; Thr3e, 2007; **Three Cases of Murder**, 1955; **The Three Faces of Eve**, 1957; **Three Lives and Only One Death**, 1997; Three on a Couch, 1966; **The Time of Their Lives**, 1946; Transamerica, 2005; Trust the Man, 2005; **12 Monkeys**, 1995; 22 Jump Street, 2014; Twin Peaks, 1990-1991 (TV series); Twin Peaks: Fire Walk with Me, 1992; The Uncanny, 1977; Under the Sand, 2000; United States of Tara, 2009-2011 (TV series); The Unsaid, 2001; Used People, 1992; Vampire's Kiss, 1988; Vera Drake, 2004; Veronika Decides to Die, 2009; A Very Long Engagement, 2004; A Very Special Favor, 1965; The Very Thought of You, 1998; The Virgin Suicides, 1999; Voice, 2005; The Voices, 2014; Voices Within: The Lives of Truddi Chase, 1990 (made-for-TV); **Voyage to the Bottom of the Sea**, 1961; The Wackness, 2008; The Ward, 2010; Watch Out, We're Mad, 1974; The Watcher, 2000; What a Way to Go!, 1964; What Have I Done to Deserve This?, 1984; **What Lies Beneath**, 2000; **What Women Want**, 2000; Whatever Works, 2009; **What's New Pussycat?**, 1965; **Whirlpool**, 1949; Whispers in the Dark, 1992; **White Bird in a Blizzard**, 2014; White Frog, 2012; **White Heat**, 1949; Who's Been Sleeping in My Bed?, 1963; Wicked Wicked Games, 2006- (TV series); Wire in the Blood, 2002- (TV series); Wish You Were Here, 1987; **Without Warning**, 1952; **Witness to Murder**, 1954; **A Woman Under the Influence**, 1974; **The World of Henry Orient**, 1964; **The Wrong Man**, 1956; **Zelig**, 1983; Zotz!, 1962.

Publicity Agents: As Luck Would Have It, 2011; **The Barefoot Contessa**, 1955; **Bluebeard's Seven Wives**, 1926; **Bombshell**, 1933; **Bridget Jones's Diary**, 2001; **Callaway Went Thataway**, 1951; Career, 1959; The Drifter, 1944; The Fuzzy Pink Nightgown, 1957; **The Harder They Fall**, 1956; His Family Tree, 1935; His Lordship, 1932; Ice-Capades, 1941; It's Tough to Be Famous, 1933; Mary Lou, 1948; Musical Airwaves, 1936; Petticoat Larceny, 1943; Shooting High, 1940; Sing Boy Sing, 1958; **A Star Is Born**, 1937; **A Star Is Born**, 1954; Sweet Music, 1935; **Sweet Smell of Success**, 1957; Swamp Woman, 1941; Welcome Mr. Marshall!, 1953; Young and Beautiful, 1934.

Race Cars and Racecar Drivers (also see Indianapolis 500): **Across the Continent**, 1922; **Adventures of Ichabod and Mr. Toad**, 1949; **American Graffiti**, 1973 (drag racing); Army of One, 1993; **At Any Price**, 2012; The Best of Youth, 2003; Better Off Dead..., 1985 (drag racing); Bikini Beach, 1964 (drag racing); Blonde Comet, 1941; Bobby Deerfield, 1977; Born Reckless, 1937; Born to Speed, 1947 (midget car racing); Børning, 2014; Buck Privates Come Home, 1947; The Bucket List, 2007; Burn 'Em Up Barnes, 1921; The Cannonball Run, 1981; **Cars**, 2006; **Cars 2**, 2011; **Casino Royale**, 1967; Catch Me If You Can, 1989 (drag racing); Charlie's Angels, 2000; The Circuit, 2008 (made-for-TV); Clambake, 1967; Collision Course, 1989 (drag racing); Crack o' Dawn, 1925; Crazy Beautiful You, 2015; The Crossing, 1990 (drag racing); **The Crowd Roars**, 1932; Daddy-O, 1958 (drag racing); Dance with a Stranger, 1985; Daredevil Drivers, 1938; Days of Thunder, 1990; Deadhead Miles, 1973 (drag racing); Death Race 2000, 1975; Deuce Coupe, 1992 (drag racing); Double Exposure, 1983; Dragstrip Girl, 1957 (drag racing); Drive, 2011; Driven, 2001; The Dukes of Hazard, 2005; The Fast and the Furious, 1955 (drag racing); The Fast and the Furious, 2001 (drag racing); Fast & Furious, 2009; Fast Company, 1979 (drag racing); Fast Five, 2011; The Fifth Cord, 1975; The Final Destination, 2009 (stockcar racing); Fireball Run: The Movie, 2010; The Flaw, 1955; Footloose, 2011 (drag racing); **Furious Seven**, 2015; Ghost of Dragstrip Hollow, 1959 (drag racing); Girls Town, 1959 (drag racing); Gloria's Romance, 1916; Gone in Sixty Seconds, 2000 (drag racing); Grand Prix, 1966; **Grease**, 1978 (drag racing); **The Great Race**, 1965 (vintage autos); Grind, 1997 (drag racing); Heart Like a Wheel, 1983 (drag racing); The Heavenly Kid, 1985 (drag racing); Heroes, 1977; High School Caesar, 1960 (drag racing); High School High, 1996 (drag racing); High Speed, 1932; Hi-Riders, 1978 (drag racing); Hot Rod, 1979 (made-for-TV; drag racing); Hot Rods to Hell, 1967 (drag racing); In Spite of Danger, 1935; Initial D, 2005; Isadora, 1968; Jump, 1971 (stock car racing); **The Killers**, 1964; The Last American Hero, 1973 (NASCAR); The Last Chase, 1981; **The Last Stand**, 2013; **Le Mans**, 1971; The Lively Set, 1964 (drag racing); **The Love Bug**, 1968 (stock car racing); Mad Drivers, 1978; Malibu Express, 1985; Metal Skin, 1994; Michel Vaillant, 2003 (Le Mans); Midnight Spares, 1983; More American Griffiti, 1979 (drag racing); Need for Speed, 2014; Nitro, 2007; Octane, 2008; Pandora and the Flying Dutchman, 1951; The Pinchcliffe Grand Prix, 1981; The Pom Pom Girls, 1976 (drag racing); The Presidio, 1988; The Prince and Me, 2004; The Race, 1916; Race, 2008; Race for Life, 1954; **The Racers**, 1955; Racin' for a Livin', 2006 (TV series; stock car racing); Racing Hearts, 1923; The Radio Detective, 1926; **Rebel Without a Cause**, 1955 (drag racing); Redline, 2009; Return to Macon County, 1975 (drag racing); The Roaring Road, 1919; Roaring Roads, 1935; **Rush**, 2013; **Seabiscuit**, 2003; Separate Ways, 1981; Soiled, 1925; Speed Demon, 2003; The Speed Classic, 1928; The Speed Lovers, 1968; Speed Racer, 2008; Speedway, 1929 (Indianapolis 500); Speedway Junky, 1999; Spinout, 1966; Stoker Ace, 1983 (NASCAR); Super Speed, 1925; **Swing Vote**, 2008; Tail Lights Fade, 1999 (drag racing); Taming the Apex, 2013 (Le Mans); Teenage Rebel, 1956 (drag racing); Ten Laps to Go, 1936; Those Daring Young Men in Their Jaunty Jalopies, 1969; Thunder Run, 1986 (drag racing); Thunderbolt, 1995 (street racing); **Time Without Pity**, 1957; To Please a Lady, 1950 (midget car racing); Tomboy, 1985; Too Much Speed, 1921; **Toy Story 2**, 1999; Trinity: Gambling for High Stakes, 1978 (stock car racing); **Tucker: The Man and His Dream**, 1988; Tulips, 2004; Turbo, 2013 (Indianapolis 500); **Two-Lane Blacktop**, 1971 (drag racing); Van Nuys Blvd., 1979 (drag racing); **Viva Las Vegas**, 1964; **White Lightning**, 1973; The Wild McCullochs, 1975 (drag racing); The Wind in the Willows, 1987 (made-for-TV); **Wings**, 1927; **Winning**, 1969 (Indianapolis 500); The Wraith, 1986 (drag racing); Wreck-It Ralph, 2012; The Young Racers, 1963 (Grand Prix).

Radio (Announcers, Commentators and Hosts): **The Arrival**, 1996 (signals from space); **Beloved Infidel**, 1959; **Blue Skies**, 1946; **Bound for Glory**, 1976 (recording sessions); **The Buddy Holly Story**, 1978 (recording sessions); **Choose Me**, 1984; **Coal Miner's Daughter**, 1980 (recording sessions); **High Sierra**, 1941; **1941**, 1979 (at a dance competition); **O Brother, Where Art Thou**, 2000 (recording sessions); **Radio Days**, 1987; **Singin' in the Rain**, 1952 (at a Hollywood premiere); **A Star Is Born**, 1937 (at a Hollywood premiere); **A Star Is Born**, 1954 (at a Hollywood premiere); **They Shoot Horses, Don't They?**, 1969 (at a marathon dance); **The War of the Worlds**, 1953.

Ranchers and Ranches: **Absolute Quiet**, 1936; **Ace of the Saddle**, 1919; **The Big Country**, 1958 (cattle); **Blood on the Moon**, 1948 (cattle); **Border Incident**, 1949; **Broken Lance**, 1954 (cattle); **Brother Orchid**, 1940; **Cat Ballou**, 1965; **Cattle Drive**, 1951; Cattle Empire, 1958; **Changeling**, 2008; **Chisum**, 1970; **Courage of Lassie**, 1946; **The Culpepper Cattle Company**, 1972; **Giant**, 1956 (cattle); **Gunfight at the O.K. Corral**, 1957 (cattle); Gunman's Walk, 1958 (cattle); Heaven's Gate, 1980 (cattle); **Last Train from Gun Hill**, 1959 (cattle); **The Missouri Breaks**, 1976 (horses); **Monte Walsh**, 1970 (cattle); **My Friend Flicka**, 1943 (horses); **Oklahoma!**, 1955 (cattle); **Open Range**, 2003 (cattle); **Quigley Down Under**, 1990 (cattle); **Ramrod**, 1947 (cattle); **Red River**, 1948 (cattle); **Rio Bravo**, 1959 (cattle); **Shane**, 1953 (cattle); **South of St. Louis**, 1949 (cattle); **Thunderhead—Son of Flicka**, 1945 (horses); **Tribute to a Bad Man**, 1956 (cattle); **The Virginian**, 1929 (cattle); **The Virginian**, 1946 (cattle); **The Westerner**, 1940 (cattle); **Will Penny**, 1968 (cattle).

Reincarnation (also see Fictional Persons Index, Dracula): **The Adding Machine**, 1969; All of Me, 1988; Always, 1989; The Amityville Horror, 1979; **Angel on My Shoulder**, 1946; The Antichrist, 1974; Audrey Rose, 1977; Avalon High, 2010 (made-for-TV); The Aztec Mummy Against the Humanoid Robot, 1958; Battlestar Gallactica, 2004-2009 (TV series); **Before Sunrise**, 1995; **Before Sunset**, 2004; **Before the Rains**, 2008; Being Human, 1994; Belladonna, 2008; Beloved, 1998; Birth, 2004; Bizarre, 1970; Black Death, 2010; Blacula, 1972; Bloodstained Shadow, 1978; Bloom, 2003; Bram Stoker's Dracula, 1974 (made-for-TV); The Bride and the Beast, 1958; Buffy the Vampire Slayer, 1992; Bunker Bean, 1936; Burned at the Stake, 1981; **The Cave of the Yellow Dog**, 2006; **Chances Are**, 1989; Chaotic Ana, 2007; Chemical Wedding, 2008; Children of the Revolution, 1997; Circulation, 2008; **Cloud Atlas**, 2012; Corridor of Mirrors, 1948; The Creeping Flesh, 1973; Crowhaven Farm, 1970 (made-for-TV); Curse of the Faceless Man, 1958; Daughters of Satan, 1972; Dead Again, 1991; The Dead Are Alive, 1972; Defending Your Life, 1991; Déjà Vu, 1985; The Devonsville Terror, 1983; Divine Lovers, 1997; Dr. Who, 1963-1989 (TV series); Dr. Who, 2005- (TV series); Don't Die Without Telling Me Where You're Going, 1995; The Double Life of Veronique, 1991; Down to Earth, 2001; Dragon Wars: D-War, 2007; **Dracula**, 1931; **Dracula**, 1979; **Dracula**, 1992; Dracula, 2013-2014 (TV series); **Dracula: Dead and Loving It**, 1995; **Dracula Has Risen from His Grave**, 1969; **Dracula—Prince of Darkness**, 1966; **Dracula Untold**, 2014; **Dracula's Daughter**, 1936; Eega, 2012; Embrace the Vampire, 1995; Enter the Void, 2010; Eternity, 1990; Eve and the Fire Horse, 2006; **Fluke**, 1995; **The Flying Deuces**, 1939; Fright, 1956; Garfield Has 9 Lives, 1988 (made-for-TV); **Ghostbusters II**, 1989; Goodbye Charlie, 1964; Goya in Bordeaux, 2000; Haunted, 1977; The Haunted Mansion, 2003; Hearts and Souls, 1993; **Heaven Can Wait**, 1978; **Here Comes Mr. Jordan**, 1941; His Majesty Minor, 2007; Hollywood Party, 1934; House of Dark Shadows, 1970; **The House of Dracula**, 1945; **The House of Frankenstein**, 1944; The Hudsucker Proxy, 1994; Hush Little Baby, 2007 (made-for-TV); **I Married a Witch**, 1942; I Origins, 2014; Ice Angel, 2000 (made-for-TV); I'm with Lucy, 2002; India, 1993; **Interview with the Vampire: The Vampire Chronicles**, 1994; I've Lived Before, 1956; J.D.'s Revenge, 1976; Jack Brown Genius, 1996; Jack Frost, 1998; Jade Warrior, 2006; Jupiter Ascending, 2015; **Justice in Mind**, 2013; Karz, 1980; The Kingdom, 1994 (TV miniseries); **Kundun**, 1997; The Lair of the White Worm, 1988; The Legacy, 1978; Legend of Eight Samurai, 1983; Legend of the Mummy, 1998; Little Buddha, 1993; The Living Idol, 1957; Logan's Run, 1976; **Lord Jim**, 1965; Lost Souls, 2000; Love at First Bite, 1979; The Lovers, 2015; Lovers of the Arctic Circle, 1999; Made in Heaven, 1987; Madhumati, 1958; Mammoth, 2009; The Man Beyond, 1922; **The Man Who Would**

Be King, 1975; The Man with Two Lives, 1942; The Manitou, 1978; Mannequin: On the Move, 1991; Mary Shelley's Frankenstein, 1994; The Matrix, 1999; Mean Spirit, 2003; Medusa, 1973; Merlin, 1993; Midnight Bayou, 2009 (made-for-TV); Mummies Alive!, 1997-1998 (TV series); **The Mummy**, 1932; **The Mummy**, 1999; **The Mummy Returns**, 2001; **The Mummy: Tomb of the Dragon Emperor**, 2008; The Mummy's Curse, 1944; **The Mummy's Hand**, 1940; The Mummy's Ghost, 1944; The Mummy's Revenge, 1973; My Blood Runs Cold, 1965; My Mother the Car, 1965-1966 (TV series); My Talks with Dean Spanley, 2009; The Myth, 2005; Naked Weapon, 2002; Night of Dark Shadows, 1971; **The Notebook**, 2004; Oh Heavenly Dog, 1980; **The Omen**, 1976; On a Clear Day You Can See Forever, 1970; One Hell of a Guy, 2000; Out on a Limb, 1987 (TV miniseries); Over My Dead Body, 1995; P.S., 2004; Past Life, 2010- (TV series); Past Tense, 2006 (made-for-TV); **Patton**, 1970; The Phantom of the Opera, 1989; The Possessed, 1977 (made-for-TV); Professor Beware, 1938; Rahtree Reborn, 2009; The Reincarnation of Isabel, 1973; The Reincarnation of Peter Proud, 1975; The Return, 2006; The Return of Chandu, 1934; Revelation, 2002; Rinne, 2006; Riverworld, 2010 (made-for-TV); The Road to Yesterday, 1925; Rockula, 1990; Room to Rent, 2000; Running on Karma, 2003; Salome's Last Dance, 1988; Samurai Reincarnation, 1981;The Search for Bridey Murphy, 1956; **She**, 1935; She, 1965; She, 2001; The She-Creature, 1956; Shinbone Alley, 1970; **The Shining**, 1980; Sidhartha, 1973; **Son of Dracula**, 1943; **Star Trek III: The Search for Spock**, 1984; **The Story of Three Loves**, 1953; Strange Paradise, 1969-1970 (TV series); The Stranger Within, 1974 (made-for-TV); The Supernaturals, 1986; Susie Q, 1986 (made-for-TV); Switch, 1991; **Tales of Terror**, 1962; Tank Girl, 1995; **The Three Lives of Thomasina**, 1963; Tomie, 1999; The Trotsky, 2009; The Truce, 1997; The Undead, 1957; Underwater Love, 2011; Valley of Flowers, 2006; What Time Is It There?, 2001; **The Wicker Man**, 1975; The Wraith, 1986; Xena: Warrior Princess, 1995-2001 (TV series); **What Dreams May Come**, 1998; While I Live, 1947; **Windwalker**, 1980; Wonderful World, 2009; Yesterday's Children, 2000 (made-for-TV); **You Never Can Tell**, 1951; Zarafa, 2012.

Reporters (newspapers): **Abandoned**, 1949; **Absence of Malice**, 1981 (investigative reporter); **Absolute Quiet**, 1936; **The Adventures of Mark Twain**, 1944 (Old West reporters); **Al Capone**, 1959; **All the King's Men**, 1949; **All the President's Men**, 1976 (investigative reporters Bob Woodward and Carl Bernstein); **Almost Famous**, 2000; Angels and Demons, 2009; **Angels in the Outfield**, 1951; Anzio, 1968 (war correspondent); **Arise My Love**, 1940; **Batman**, 1989; **The Big Carnival**, 1951; **Big Eyes**, 2014; Black Mass, 2015; **Call Northside 777**, 1948; **Chicago**, 2002; **Chicago Deadline**, 1949; **Christmas Holiday**, 1944; **Cimarron**, 1931; Cimarron, 1960; **Cinderella Man**, 2005; **Circle of Deceit**, 1982; **Citizen Kane**, 1941; **A Clockwork Orange**, 1971; **Cloud Atlas**, 2012; **Compulsion**, 1959; **Comrade X**, 1940; **"Crocodile" Dundee**, 1986; **The Dark Knight**, 2008; **Detective Story**, 1951 (police reporter); **Dodge City**, 1939 (Old West reporters); **Everest**, 2015; **Fairy Tale: A True Story**, 1997; **Five Star Final**, 1931; **Foreign Correspondent**, 1940; **The Front Page**, 1931; **The Front Page**, 1974; **Gaily, Gaily**, 1969; **Gone Girl**, 2014; **The Green Berets**, 1968 (war correspondent); **Guadalcanal Diary**, 1943 (war correspondent in WWII); **The Harder They Fall**, 1956 (sports; boxing); **Harry Potter and the Goblet of Fire**, 2005; Hemingway & Gellhorn, 2012 (made-for-TV; war correspondents covering the Spanish Civil War); **High Sierra**, 1941; **His Girl Friday**, 1940; **Houdini**, 1953; **It Happened One Night**, 1934; **Jack London**, 1943 (war correspondent in the Russo-Japanese War); **L. A. Confidential**, 1997 (police reporters); **The Last Hurrah**, 1958; **Lonelyhearts**, 1958; **Love Is News**, 1937; **Man of Steel**, 2013; **The Man Who Shot Liberty Valance**, 1962 (Old West reporter); **Meet John Doe**, 1941; **Mr. Deeds Goes to Town**, 1936; **Mr. Smith Goes to Washington**, 1939 (political reporters in Washington, D.C.); Mr. Soft Touch, 1949; **The Murder Man**, 1935; **Nothing Sa-**cred, 1937; **Objective, Burma!**, 1945 (war correspondent); **Once upon a Time in America**, 1984; **Passage to Marseille**, 1944; **Patton**, 1970 (war correspondents in WWII); **Picture Snatcher**, 1933; **The Purple Heart**, 1944 (war correspondents); **Ratatouille**, 2007; **Ring**, 1998; **The Ring**, 2002; **San Andreas**, 2015; **Scandal Sheet**, 1931; **Scandal Sheet**, 1952; **Scarface**, 1932; **The Secret Six**, 1931 (police reporters); Spider-Man 3, 2007; **Spotlight**, 2015 (investigative reporters); **The Story of G.I. Joe**, 1945 (Ernie Pyle, war correspondent in WWII); **Superman**, 1978; **Superman Returns**, 2006; **Superman III**, 1983; **Superman II**, 1981; **The Tarnished Angels**, 1958; **Teacher's Pet**, 1958; **They Won't Forget**, 1937 (police reporter); **That Wonderful Urge**, 1948; **-30-**, 1959; **Tombstone**, 1993 (Old West reporter); **We Were Soldiers**, 2002 (war correspondent); **While the City Sleeps**, 1956; **The Wolf of Wall Street**, 2013; **Zodiac**, 2007.

Riverboats and Steamboats (also see Mississippi River, this index): **Abe Lincoln in Illinois**, 1940; **The Adventures of Huckleberry Finn**, 1960; **The Adventures of Mark Twain**, 1944; **The African Queen**, 1951; **Anna and the King of Siam**, 1946; **Annie Get Your Gun**, 1950; **Around the World in 80 Days**, 1956; **Band of Angels**, 1957; **Banjo on My Knee**, 1936; **Barbary Coast**, 1935; **Bend of the River**, 1952; Dakota, 1945; **Death on the Nile**, 1978; **The Four Feathers**, 1939; **The Foxes of Harrow**, 1947; **Glory**, 1989; **Gone with the Wind**, 1939; How the West Was Won, 1962; **Huckleberry Finn**, 1931; **Huckleberry Finn**, 1939; **The Iron Mistress**, 1952; **Jezebel**, 1938; **The Kentuckian**, 1955; **Khartoum**, 1966; **The King and I**, 1956; **Mississippi**, 1935; **The Mississippi Gambler**, 1953; **The Plainsman**, 1936; **The Secret Life of Walter Mitty**, 1947; **Showboat**, 1936; **Showboat**, 1951; **Steamboat Bill Jr.**, 1928; **Steamboat Round the Bend**, 1935.

Rodeos and Rodeo Performers: **Adventures of Gallant Bess**, 1948; The Adventures of Spin and Marty, 1955 (TV series); All My LovedOnes, 1999; **American Sniper**, 2014; Arena, 1953; The Arizona Cowboy, 1950; Bells of Capistrano, 1942; A Better Life, 2011; **Boom Town**, 1940; Born Reckless, 1938; Branded a Coward, 1935; Bronco Buster, 1952; The Bull-Dogger, 1921; **Bus Stop**, 1956; The Busters, 1978 (made-for-TV); The Calgary Stampede, 1925; Call the Mesquiteers, 1938; Carolina Moon, 1940; Charlie & Boots, 2010; The Cheyenne Kid, 1933; Christmas Eve, 1947; Convict Cowboy, 1995 (made-for-TV); Cotter, 1973; The Cowboy and the Ballerina, 1984 (made-for-TV); The Cowboy and the Blonde, 1941; The Cowboy and the Lady, 1938; Cowboy Blues, 1946; Cowboy from Brooklyn, 1938; Cowboy Up, 2002; Cowboys and Indians, 2013; Cowboys Don't Cry, 1988; The Crimson Skull, 1922; **Dallas Buyers Club**, 2013; The Denver Dude, 1927; The Desert Trail, 1935; Did You Hear about the Morgans?, 2009; Down Laredo Way, 1953; Drift Fence, 1936; Dudes, 1987; Eddie Macon's Run, 1983; Everything That Rises, 1998 (made-for-TV); F.T.W., 1994; Feud of the West, 1936; Flap, 1970; **Flicka**, 2006; The Flyin' Cowboy, 1928; Frontier Town, 1938; The Gentleman from Arizona, 1939; Getting Married in Buffalo Jump, 1990 (made-for-TV); **Girl Crazy**, 1943; Girl's Night, 1998; Great Guns, 1941; Gun Crazy, 1950; Hard Time Romance, 1991; Harley Davidson and the Marlboro Man, 1991; Heroes of the Saddle, 1940; The Hi-Lo Country, 1998; The Honkers, 1972; Honor of the West, 1939; **Hud**, 1963; Hurrican Smith, 1941; In Cold Blood, 1967; **J. W. Coop**, 1971; **Junior Bonner**, 1972; The Kid from Gower Gulch, 1950; **King of the Cowboys**, 1943; A Lady Takes a Chance, 1943; **The Last Picture Show**, 1971; Law of the Pampas, 1939; Lights of Old Santa Fe, 1944; Lone Cowboy, 1933; Lone Wolf McQuade, 1983; Lure of Gold, 1922; **The Lusty Men**, 1952; Maisie, 1939; Man from Rainbow Valley, 1946; The Man from Snowy River: Arena Spectacular, 2003 (made-for-TV); The Man from Utah, 1934; The Manhunt, 1984; Melody Trail, 1935; Mesquite Buckeroo, 1939; **The Misfits**, 1961; The Money Corral, 1919; Moonlight on the Prairie, 1935; Mustang!, 1959; Mustang, 1975; Never a Dull Moment, 1950; North Beach and Rawhide, 1985 (made-for-TV); Northwest Stampede, 1948; Open Gate, 2011; Pardners,

1956; Painted Hero, 1997; **Pee-wee's Big Adventure**, 1985; Pink Lemonade, 2006; Pure Country, 1992; Range Land, 1949; **The Rare Breed**, 1966; The Red Rider, 1934; Rhythm of the Saddle, 1938; **Rhythm on the Range**, 1936; Rhythm Round-Up, 1945; The Ride, 1997; **Ride 'Em, Cowboy**, 1942; Ride 'em, Cowgirl, 1939; Ride 'em High, 1927; Ride Him, Cowboy, 1932; Riders of Pasco Basin, 1940; Rodeo, 1952; Rodeo Girl, 1980 (made-for-TV); Rodeo Girls, 2013-2014 (TV series); Rodeo King and the Senorita, 1951; Rolling Home, 1946; **The Rounders**, 1965; Rovin' Tumbleweeds, 1939; Ruby Jean and Joe, 1996 (made-for-TV); Run, Appaloosa, Run, 1966; The Saddle Buster, 1932; The Sagebrush Family Trails West, 1940; Sagebrush Heroes, 1945; Satins and Spurs, 1954 (made-for-TV); Second Chances, 1998; Seconds, 1994; The Secret Menace, 1931; Shadows of the Past, 2009; The Singing Outlaw, 1937; Skipped Parts, 2000; SLC Punk!, 1999; Smoky River Serenade, 1947; Somewhere in Sonora, 1933; Song of Texas, 1943; Song of the Trail, 1936; The Spirit of the West, 1932; Stay Away, Joe, 1968; Still Holding On: The Legend of Cadillac Jack, 1998 (made-for-TV); **Stir Crazy**, 1980; Stoney Burke, 1962-1963 (TV series); Swing in the Saddle, 1944; Swing the Western Way, 1947; Take It Big, 1944; Temple Grandin, 2010 (made-for-TV); Texas to Bataan, 1942; Throw a Saddle on a Star, 1946; **Thunder Birds**, 1942; Tickle Me, 1965; A Time for Revenge, 1997; The Tonto Kid, 1934; Trigger, Jr., 1950; Trouble in Texas, 1937; Tucson, 1949; The Twinkle in God's Eye, 1955; Under Western Skies, 1926; **An Unfinished Life**, 2005; The Utah Kid, 1944; **The Valley of Gwangi**, 1969; Waking Life, 2001; The Walking Hills, 1949; The Westerner, 1934; **When the Legends Die**, 1972; The Whirlwind Rider, 1934; White Sands, 1992; Wide Country, 1962-1963 (TV series); The Wild West Show, 1928; Wolves of the Range, 1921; Yodelin' Kid from Pine Ridge, 1937.

Samurai Warriors: Assassins, 2011; Battle with Top-Class Samuri, 1980; **Brazil**, 1985; **Chushingura**, 1963; Duel to Death, 1983; Forgotten Warrior, 1986; 47 Ronin, 2013; 47 Samurai, 1963; Ghost Dog: The Way of the Samurai, 2000; **The Hidden Fortress**, 1959; Highlander: The Final Dimension, 1995; Kanketsu Sasaki Kojiro: Ganryo-jima ketto, 1951; **The Last Samurai**, 2003; Lone Wolf and Cub: Baby Cart at the River Styx, 1997; Lone Wolf and Cub: Baby Cart in Peril, 1997; Lone Wolf and Cub: Baby Cart in the Land of Demons, 1997; Lone Wolf and Cub: Baby Cart to Hades, 1973; Lone Wolf and Cub: Sword of Vengeance, 1973; Lone Wolf and Cub: White Heaven in Hell, 1997; **Rashomon**, 1951; Rurouni Kenshin: Wandering Samurai, 1996-1998 (TV series); Samurai, 2009 (made-for-TV); Samurai Avenger: The Blind Wolf, 2009; Samurai Commando Mission 1549, 2005; Samurai Jack, 2001-2004 (TV series); Samurai I: Musashi Miyamoto, 1955; Samurai Reincarnation, 1981; Samurai III: Duel at Ganryu Island, 1967; Samurai Two: Duel at Ichijoji Temple, 1967; Samurai X: Reflection, 2001- (TV series); **Sanjuro**, 1963; Sengoku jieitai, 1981; **Seven Samurai**, 1956; Shadow Hunters 2: Echo of Destiny, 1972; Shinsengumi: Assassins of Honor, 1970; The Shogun's Samurai, 1984; Sleepy Eyes of Death: Sword of Fire, 1965; The Sword of Doom, 1966; **Throne of Blood**, 1961; **Ugetsu**, 1954; Village of Eight Gravestones, 1978; **Yojimbo**, 1961; Yoroiden Samurai Troopers, 1988-1995 (TV series).

Scandal Sheets (including tabloid newspapers; also see Newspaper Reporters and newspapers, this index): Buried Alive, 1939; Cain and Mabel, 1936l; Dirt, 2007-2008 (TV series); **Five Star Final**, 1931; **The Front Page**, 1931; **The Front Page**, 1974; Go to Hell, 1999; **His Girl Friday**, 1940; **It Happened One Night**, 1934; **L.A. Confidential**, 1997; **Lonelyhearts**, 1958; **Love Is News**, 1937; **Mr. Deeds Goes to Town**, 1936; **The Murder Man**, 1935; The Naked Truth, 1995-1998 (TV series); **Picture Snatcher**, 1933; **Platinum Blonde**, 1931; Scandal Sheet, 1931; Scandal Sheet, 1939; Scandal Sheet, 1952; Scandal Sheet, 1985 (made-for-TV); **Sex and the Single Girl**, 1964; **The Story on Page One**, 1959; **While the City Sleeps**, 1956; Winchell, 1998 (made-for-TV).

Schizophrenia: After Darkness, 1985; **The Amazing Dr. Clitterhouse**, 1938; **An Angel at My Table**, 1990; Angel Baby, 1997; Autumn Leaves, 1956; Barefoot, 2014; **A Beautiful Mind**, 2001; Benny & Joon, 1993; **Bewitched**, 1945; The Brighton Strangler, 1945; Buddy Boy, 2000; **Bunny Lake I Missing**, 1965; The Butcher Boy, 1998; Camille Claudel, 1989; Canvas, 2006; The Cell, 2000; Clean, Shaven, 1999; **Compulsion**, 1959; **Conspiracy Theory**, 1997; Crimes of Passion, 1984; **The Dark Knight**, 2008; **David and Lisa**, 1962; Dead Ringers, 1998; Donnie Darko, 2001; **A Double Life**, 1947; eXistenZ, 1999; The Exorcism of Emily Rose, 2005; Family Life, 1972; Fight Club, 1999; **Fingers at the Window**, 1942; From Beyond, 1986; **Fury**, 1936; Girl, Interrupted, 1999; **Good News**, 1947; Hide and Seek, 2005; **I Never Promised You a Rose Garden**, 1977; Identity, 2003; Igby Goes Down, 2002; Images, 1972; **The Innocents**, 1961; Ironweed, 1987; It's Kind of a Funny Story, 2010; Julien Donkey-Boy, 1999; Keane, 2004; **King's Row**, 1942; K-PAX, 2001; Lilith, 1964; **The Lord of the Rings: The Two Towers**, 2002; The Mad Ghoul, 1943; **Magic**, 1978; Me, Myself & Irene, 2000; Mirrors, 2008; Mr. Brooks, 2007; Music Within, 2007; Neverwas, 2005; Ordet, 1943; **One Flew Over the Cuckoo's Nest**, 1975; The Passion of Darkly Noon, 1995; **Possessed**, 1947; **Proof**, 2005; **Repulsion**, 1965; Revolver, 2007; The Saint of Fort Washington, 1993; **Scarecrow**, 1973; Schizoid, 1980; Schizopolis, 1997; The Science of Sleep, 2006; Secret Window, 2004; **Shine**, 1996; Shutter Island, 2010; **The Snake Pit**, 1948; The Soloist, 2009; **Spellbound**, 1945; Spider, 2002; **Stranger Than Fiction**, 2006; Summer of Sam, 1999; Take Shelter, 2011; **The Third Secret**, 1964; **The Three Faces of Eve**, 1957; Twin Peaks: Fire Walk with Me, 1992; **The Uninvited**, 2009.

Séances: The Amazing Mr. X, 1948; **Anna Karenina**, 1935; **Anna Karenina**, 1948; The Awakening, 2011; **Beetlejuice**, 1988; The Bishop of the Ozarks, 1923; Black Magic, 1944; **Blithe Spirit**, 1945; Blood Brides, 1974; Blood Nasty, 1989; Bunco Squad, 1950; **The Changeling**, 1980; **Charlie Chan's Secret**, 1936; City of Pirates, 1989; City of the Living Dead, 1983; **Curse of the Demon**, 1958; Dangerous Corner, 1934; Danton, 1983; Dark and Stormy Night, 2009; Darkened Rooms, 1929; Daughter of the Mind, 1969 (made-for-TV); The Devil Commands, 1941; **Dr. Mabuse: The Gambler**, 1922; Drag Me to Hell, 2009; Dulcimer Street, 1948; **Family Plot**, 1976; Fantomas vs. Scotland Yard, 1967; Fog Island, 1945; Frenzy, 1946 (aka: Latin Quarter); The Ghost, 1965; Ghost, 1990; Ghost Chasers, 1951; The Ghost Goes Wild, 1947; Good Morning, Night, 2004; **The Half-Way House**, 1945; Hands of the Ripper, 1972; The Haunting of Julia, 1981; **Houdini**, 1953; **The Hound of the Baskervilles**, 1939; Inland Empire, 2006; Innocent Husbands, 1925; Invincible, 2001; I've Got Your Number, 1934; **Juliet of the Spirits**, 1965; **La Dolce Vita**, 1961; The Legend of Hell House, 1973; Let's Scare Jessica to Death, 1971; **Magic in the Moonlight**, 2014; The Medium, 1951; The Medium, 1960 (made-for-TV); **Ministry of Fear**, 1944; **Miracles for Sale**, 1939; Night of Terror, 1933; Night of the Demons, 1988; **Nightmare Alley**, 1947; Now and Then, 1995; **The 1,000 Eyes of Dr. Mabuse**, 1960; **The Others**, 2001; The Perfume of the Lady in Black, 1974; The Phantom Thief, 1946; Phenomena, 1985; Photographing Fairies, 1997; Pillow of Death, 1945; The Prestige, 2006; A Quiet Place in the Country, 1970; Religious Racketeers, 1938; The Return of Peter Grimm, 1935; Séance, 2000 (made-for-TV); Séance, 2009; **Séance on a Wet Afternoon**, 1964; Sinister Hands, 1932; The Spider, 1931; Strutter, 2012; Sucker Money, 1933; Summerland, 2010; Supernatural, 1933; Talaash, 2012; Telstar: The Joe Meek Story, 2009; Ten, 2014; Their Big Moment, 1934; 13 Ghosts, 1960; The Thirteenth Chair, 1929; **The Thirteenth Chair**, 1937; **The Time of Their Lives**, 1946; Trauma, 1994; **The Unholy Night**, 1929; **The Uninvited**, 1944; Uninvited, 2003; **Walking with the Ferryman**, 2014; The Watcher in the Woods, 1980; **What Lies Beneath**, 2000; **You'll Find Out**, 1940; **You Will Meet a Tall Dark Stranger**, 2010.

Sending Combatants into Harm's Way dDuring Revolutions and Wars (motivations and emotional responses): **Aces High**, 1977 (WWI; out of a perverse sense of authority); **Admiral Yamamoto**, 1968 (WWII; Isoroku Yamamoto; a sense of duty and to achieve personal victory); **Air Force**, 1943 (WWII; out of a sense of duty and guilt); **All Quiet on the Western Front**, 1930 (WWI; out of a perverse sense of patriotism and authority); Anzio, 1968 (WWII; out of neglect and apprehension); **Apocalypse Now**, 1979 (Vietnam War; out of a perverse love of battle and sense of authority); **Attack**, 1956 (WWII; out of irresponsibility, neglect and revenge); **Battle Cry**, 1955 (WWII; out of sense of duty and guilt); **Battle of Britain**, 1969 (WWII; out of a sense of duty and guilt by British commanders; out of a sense of achieving victory at all costs by German commanders, and, on the part of Hermann Goering, a sense of personal achievement); Battle of the Bulge, 1965 (WWII; out of a sense of duty and guilt on the part of U.S. commanders; out of a sense of achieving victory at all costs on the part of German commanders); **The Blue Max**, 1966 (WWI; out of a sense of duty and guilt); **The Bridges at Toko-Ri**, 1954 (Korean War; out of a sense of duty and guilt); **The Caine Mutiny**, 1954 (WWII; out of mental instability, fear and possible cowardice); **Casualties of War**, 1989 (Vietnam War; out of a perverse and sadistic sense of authority); **Command Decision**, 1948 (WWII; out of sense of duty and guilt); **Cross of Iron**, 1977 (WWII; out of a perverse sense of authority); **The Dawn Patrol**, 1930 (WWI; out of sense of duty and guilt); **The Dawn Patrol**, 1938 (WWI; out of a sense of duty and guilt); **The Desert Fox: The Story of Rommel**, 1951 (WWII; Erwin Rommel; out of a sense of duty and to achieve personal victory); **Doctor Zhivago**, 1965 (WWI; Russian Revolution of 1917; Russian Civil War, 1918-1922; character Pasha in WWI; out of a sense of patriotism, but later as a revolutionary leader out of a perverse sense of sadistic authority); **The Eagle and the Hawk**, 1933 (WWI; out of a sense of duty and guilt); **The Fighting 69th**, 1940 (WWI; out of a sense of duty and guilt); **Fixed Bayonets!**, 1951 (Korean War; out of a sense of duty and guilt and on the unwillingness to take command on the part of a corporal); **Full Metal Jacket**, 1987 (out of a perverse sense of dedication to duty); **The Gallant Hours**, 1960 (WWII; Admiral William Halsey Jr.; out of a sense of duty and guilt); **The Glory Brigade**, 1953 (Korean War; out of a sense of duty and guilt); **The Green Berets**, 1968 (Vietnam War; out of a sense of duty and guilt); **Halls of Montezuma**, 1950 (WWII; out of a sense of duty and guilt); **Hamburger Hill**, 1987 (Vietnam War; out of a sense of duty and guilt); **Heartbreak Ridge**, 1986 (U.S. invasion of Grenada in 1983; out of duty and guilt); **Hell Is for Heroes**, 1962 (WWII; out of a perverse sense of authority and love of battle); **In Harm's Way**, 1965 (out of a sense of duty and guilt on the part of one admiral; out of a sense of perverse authority on the part of another admiral); Inchon, 1982 (Korean War; Douglas MacArthur; out of a sense of duty and to achieve personal victory); **Journey's End**, 1930 (WWI; out of a sense of duty and guilt); **Juarez**, 1939 (Mexican Revolution of 1866-1867; out of a sense of duty and guilt on the part of Benito Juarez; out of a sense of maintaining authority on the part of Maximilian von Hapsburg); **The Last of the Mohicans**, 1936 (French and Indian War, 1754-1763 or Seven Years' War; out of a sense of duty by British commanders, but no sense of guilt; out of a sense of duty and guilt by French General Louis-Joseph de Montcalm); The Last of the Mohicans, 1971 (TV miniseries; French and Indian War, 1754-1763 or Seven Years' War; out of a sense of duty by British commanders, but no sense of guilt; out of a sense of duty and guilt by French General Louis-Joseph de Montcalm); **The Last of the Mohicans**, 1992 (French and Indian War, 1754-1763 or Seven Years' War; out of a sense of duty by British commanders, but no sense of guilt; out of a sense of duty and guilt by French General Louis-Joseph de Montcalm); **Lawrence of Arabia**, 1962 (WWI; T.E. Lawrence; out of a sense of duty, but later out of a sense of sadistic authority); **Letters from Iwo Jima**, 2006 (WWII; out of a perverse sense of authority and suicidal dedication to duty); **MacArthur**, 1977 (WWII; Korean War; out of a sense of duty and to achieve personal victory); MacArthur, 1976 (made-for-TV; WWII; Korean War; out of a sense of duty and to achieve per-

sonal victory); **Major Dundee**, 1965 (Mexican Revolution of 1866-1867; out of a sense of duty and guilt); **Men in War**, 1957 (Korean War; out of a sense of duty and guilt); **Men of the Fighting Lady**, 1954 (Korean War; out of a sense of duty and guilt); **Midway**, 1976 (WWII; Admiral Chester Nimitz; out of a sense of duty and guilt and to achieve a personal victory); The Naked and the Dead, 1958 (WWII; out of a perverse sense of authority on the part of a general and a perverse love of battle on the part of a sergeant); **Northwest Passage**, 1940 (French and Indian War, 1754-1763 or Seven Years' War; Robert Rogers of Rogers Rangers; out of a sense of duty and revenge); **Old Gringo**, 1989 (Mexican Revolution of 1910-1920; out of a sense of duty and a perverse sense of authority); **Paths of Glory**, 1957 (WWI; out of perverse pride of authority on the part of generals and out of cowardice by a lieutenant); **Patton**, 1970 (WWII; out of a sense of duty and to achieve personal victory); **Platoon**, 1986 (Vietnam War; out of a sense of duty by one sergeant; out of a perverse and sadistic sense of authority by another sergeant); **Pearl Harbor**, 2001 (WWII; Colonel James H. Doolittle; out of a sense of duty and guilt); **Pork Chop Hill**, 1959 (Korean War; out of sense of willingness to spend lives on the part of U.S. commanders and a sense of duty and guilt on the part of a company commander); **The Purple Heart**, 1944 (WWII; Doolittle Raid; out of a sense of duty and guilt); **The Real Glory**, 1939 (Philippine-American War, 1899-1902; out of a sense of duty and guilt); **Retreat, Hell!**, 1952 (Korean War; out of a sense of duty); **Rogue's Regiment**, 1948 (French Indo-China War, 1946-1954; out of a sense of duty); **Sergeant York**, 1941 (WWI; Alvin C. York; out of a sense of duty); **The Siege of Firebase Gloria**, 1989 (Vietnam War; out of a sense of duty and guilt); **The Steel Helmet**, 1951 (Korean War; out of a sense of duty and guilt); **The Story of G.I. Joe**, 1945 (WWII; out of a sense of duty and guilt); **Submarine Command**, 1951 (WWII; Korean War; out of a sense to seek vindication); **Task Force**, 1949 (WWII; out of a sense of duty and guilt); **They Came to Cordura**, 1959 (Pershing's 1916 expedition into Mexico; cavalry charge ordered out of a perverse pride in achieving victory for political purposes); **They Were Expendable**, 1945 (out of a sense of duty and guilt); **The Thin Red Line**, 1998 (WWII: out of a perverse pride in achieving a personal victory on the part of a colonel); **Thirty Seconds over Tokyo**, 1944 (WWII; James H. Doolittle; out of a sense of duty and guilt); **Tora! Tora! Tora!**, 1970 (WWII; Isoroku Yamamoto; out of a sense of duty and to achieve personal victory); **Twelve O'Clock High**, 1949 (WWII; out of a sense of duty and guilt); **Unconquered**, 1947 (French and Indian War, 1754-1763 or Seven Years' War; out of a sense of duty by British commanders, where one callously uses the bodies of his own dead troops to hoodwink the enemy); **The Undefeated**, 1969 (Mexican Revolution of 1866-1867; out of a sense of maintaining independence on the part of a former Confederate officer); **Villa Rides**, 1968 (Mexican Revolution of 1910-1920; Pancho Villa; out of a sense of duty and a perverse sense of authority); **Viva Villa!**, 1934 (Mexican Revolution of 1910-1920; Pancho Villa; out of a sense of duty and a perverse sense of authority); **Viva Zapata!**, 1952 (Mexican Revolution of 1910-1920; Emiliano Zapata; out of a sense of duty and guilt); **The War Lover**, 1962 (WWII; out of perverse love of battle); **What Price Glory**, 1926 (WWI; out of a sense of duty and guilt); **What Price Glory**, 1952 (WWI; out of a sense of duty and guilt); **Wing and a Prayer**, 1944 (WWII; out of a sense of duty and guilt); **The Woman I Love**, 1937 (WWI; out of being an alleged jinx); **Wooden Crosses**, 1932 (WWI; out of a perverse sense of authority); **The Young Lions**, 1958 (WWII; German segments: out of a perverse sense of authority).

Serial Killers (also see Historical Persons Index): **Arsenic and Old Lace**, 1944; Bluebeard, 1963 (Henri Desire Landru); **The Bird with the Crystal Plumage**, 1970; Bluebeard's Ten Honeymoons, 1960 (Henri Desire Landru); **The Boston Strangler**, 1968 (Albert DeSalvo); Bridge Across Time, 1985 (Jack the Ripper); **Cast a Dark Shadow**, 1958; **Changeling**, 2008 (Gordon Stewart Northcott); Charlie Chan at the Wax Museum, 1940 (wax exhibit of Henri Desire Landru); **Children** of Paradise, 1946 (Pierre Lecenaire); Citizen X, 1995 (made-for-TV; Andrei Chikatilo); **Close Your Eyes**, 2003; Desire Landru, 2005 (made-for-TV; Henri Desire Landru); Edge of Sanity, 1989 (Jack the Ripper); From Hell, 2001 (Jack the Ripper); Hands of the Ripper, 1972 (Jack the Ripper); Jack the Ripper, 1960; Jack the Ripper, 1973 (TV miniseries); Jack the Ripper, 1979; Jack the Ripper, 1988 (TV series); Killer: A Journal of Murder, 1995 (Carl Panzram); Landru: The Bluebeard of Paris, 1923 (Henri Desire Landru); **The Lodger**, 1928 (Jack the Ripper); **The Lodger**, 1944 (Jack the Ripper); Lulu, 1980 (Jack the Ripper); **Man in the Attic**, 1953 (Jack the Ripper); Men Think Only of That, 1954 (Henri Desire Landru); **Monsieur Verdoux**, 1947 (Henri Desire Landru); Monster, 2003 (Aileen Carol Wuornos); **Murder by Decree**, 1979 (Jack the Ripper); **Pandora's Box**, 1929 (Jack the Ripper); The Phantom Fiend, 1935 (Jack the Ripper); The Ripper, 1997 (Jack the Ripper); Room to Let, 1950 (Jack the Ripper); **The Ruling Class**, 1972 (Jack the Ripper); Seven Murders for Scotland Yard, 1971 (Jack the Ripper); Sinister, 2012; **A Study in Terror**, 1966 (Jack the Ripper); **10 Rillington Place**, 1971 (John Reginald Halliday Christie); **Time After Time**, 1979 (Jack the Ripper); Waxwork, 1988 (Jack the Ripper); Waxwork II: Lost in Time, 1992 (Jack the Ripper); **Waxworks**, 1929 (Jack the Ripper).

Sharecroppers and Tenant Farmers: **All the King's Men**, 1949; **Between Heaven and Hell**, 1956; **The Cabin in the Cotton**, 1932; **The Cincinnati Kid**, 1965; Claudelle English, 1961; **Come Next Spring**, 1956; Desire in the Dust, 1960; Down in the Delta, 1998; **Dragonwyck**, 1946; **The Grapes of Wrath**, 1940; **The Great Debaters**, 2007; **Hallelujah**, 1929; His Brother's Ghost, 1945; **Home from the Hill**, 1960; In Old Missouri, 1940; The Jerk, 1979; Life Goes On, 1938; **A Lion Is in the Streets**, 1953; **The Long Hot Summer**, 1958; Native Land, 1942; **Our Daily Bread**, 1934; **Pardon Us**, 1931; **Ray**, 2004; Roots: The Next Generation, 1979 (TV miniseries); **Sergeant York**, 1941; The Skin Game, 1931; **Song of the South**, 1946; **Sounder**, 1972; Sounder Part 2, 1976; **The Southerner**, 1945; **Tales of Manhattan**, 1942; **Tobacco Road**, 1941; **Tol'able David**, 1921; Under the North Star, 2009; White Bondage, 1937; **Within Our Gates**, 1920.

Sharks: Aatank, 1996; Ace Ventura: Pet Detective, 1994; The Adventures of Sharkboy and Lavagirl, 3-D, 2008; The Adventures of Tintin, 2011; **All Is Lost**, 2013; Around the World Under the Sea, 1966; Avalanche Sharks, 2013; Bad Lieutenant: Port of Call New Orleans, 2009; Bait, 2012; Battle at Bloody Beach, 1961; The Beach, 2000; The Beast from 20,000 Fathoms, 1953; Beneath the 12-Mile Reef, 1953; The Bermuda Triangle, 1978; **Bird of Paradise**, 1932; **The Black Bird**, 1975; Blood in the Water, 2009 (made-for-TV); The Blue Lagoon, 1980; Beyond the Reef, 1980; Cave of the Sharks, 1978; Creature, 1998 (made-for-TV); Cruel Jaws, 1995 (made-for-TV); Cyclone, 1978; Dark Tide, 2012; The Deep, 1977; Deep Blood, 1990; Deep Blue Sea, 1999; DeepStar Six, 1989; Devil Fish, 1986; Dinoshark, 2010; Escape from L.A., 1996; The Fighting Devil Dogs, 1938; **Finding Nemo**, 2003; **Flipper**, 1996; **The Flying Deuces**, 1939; **For Your Eyes Only**, 1981; Ghost Shark, 2013; Ghost Shark 2: Urban Jaws, 2014; Gone Fishing, 2012; Harbor of Missing Men, 1950; **Hawaii**, 1966; Hello Down There, 1969; **Hook**, 1991; Hugo the Hippo, 1975; **The Hurricane**, 1937; Hurricane Smith, 1952; I Escaped from Devil's Island, 1973; **Ice Age: Continental Drift**, 2012; **The Incredible Mr. Limpet**, 1964; Into the Blue, 2005; Into the Deep, 1994; Island of Lost Women, 1959; Islands of the Stream, 1977; **Jaws**, 1975; Jaws in Japan, 2009; **Jaws 2**, 1978; Jaws: The Revenge, 1987; Jaws 3-D, 1983; Jersey Shore Shark Attack, 2012 (made-for-TV); Journey 2: The Mysterious Island, 2012; Jungle Man, 1941; Jurassic Shark, 2012; **Kon-Tiki**, 2013; Lara Croft Tomb Raider: The Cradle of Life, 2003; The Last Flight of Noah's Ark, 1980; The Last Shark, 1982; The Legend of the Titanic, 1999; **Lethal Weapon 4**, 1998; **Let's Kill Uncle Before He Kills Us**, 1966; Leviathan, 1989; **Life of Pi**, 2012; **License to Kill**, 1989; Live and Let Die, 1973; Loch Ness, 1996; The Lost Continent, 1968; The Lost Tribe, 1949; Madagascar:

Escape 2 Africa, 2008; Mako: The Jaws of Death, 1976; Malibu Beach, 1978; Malibu Shark Attack, 2009 (made-for-TV); The Man from Acapulco, 1973; Manfish, 1956; Mara Maru, 1952; Mega Shark vs. Mecha Shark, 2014; Megalodon, 2002; The Middle Passage, 2000; Miss Castaway and the Island Girls, 2004; Monster from the Ocean Floor, 1954; Monster Shark, 1984; **The Most Dangerous Game**, 1932; Never Say Never Again, 1983; **Nim's Island**, 2008; **The Old Man and the Sea**, 1958; On a Clear Day, 2005; **Open Water**, 2004; Orca, 1977; The Pagan, 1929; **Pardon My Sarong**, 1942; Penguin Pool Murder, 1932; **The Perfect Storm**, 2000; Phantom Ship, 1935; **Pippi in the South Seas**, 1970; **The Prisoner of Shark Island**, 1936; Proteus, 1995; Red Water, 2003 (made-for-TV); The Reef, 2011; Revenge of the Creature, 1955; Return to the Blue Lagoon, 1991; The Sailor Who Fell from Grace from the Sea, 1976; Sand Sharks, 2011 (made-for-TV); The Sea, 2002; The Sea Chase, 1955; **The Sea Wolf**, 1941; Shark!, 1969; Shark, 2010; Shark Attack, 1999 (made-for-TV); Shark Bait, 2006; The Shark Hunter, 1979; Shark Hunter, 2001; The Sharkfighters, 1956; Shark in Venice, 2008; Shark Kill, 1976 (made-for-TV); Shark Night 3D, 2011; Shark Swarm, 2008 (made-for-TV); Shark Tale, 2004; Shark Tank, 2009- (TV series); Shark Week, 2012; Sharkman, 2005 (made-for-TV); Sharknado, 2013 (made-for-TV); Sharknado 2: The Second One, 2014; (made-for-TV); Shark's Paradise, 1986 (made-for-TV); Shark's Treasure, 1975; Sharktopus, 2010 (made-for-TV); Sharktopus vs. Pteracuda, 2014 (made-for-TV); She Gods of Shark Reef, 1958; The Ship from Shanghai, 1930; **Shrek 2**, 2004; Spring Break Shark Attack, 2005 (made-for-TV); **The Spy Who Loved Me**, 1977; **Soul Surfer**, 2011; The Steel Claw, 1961; Storm Bound, 2007; **Strange Cargo**, 1940; Subterfuge, 1996; Super Shark, 2011; Swamp Shark, 2011 (made-for-TV); **Swiss Family Robinson**, 1960; **Tabu: A Story of the South Seas**, 1931; **Thunderball**, 1965; Tideland, 2006; **Tiger Shark**, 1932; Tiko and the Shark, 1962; Tintorera: Killer Shark, 1978; **Treasure Island**, 1934; **Treasure Island**, 1950; 12 Days of Terror, 2005 (made-for-TV); 20,000 Leagues Under the Sea, 1916; **20,000 Leagues Under the Sea**, 1954; Twilight for the Gods, 1958; 2-Headed Shark Attack, 2012; Underwater!, 1955; **Voyage to the Bottom of the Sea**, 1961; **Wake of the Red Witch**, 1948; White Shadows in the South Seas, 1928; Yankee Buccaneer, 1952.

Sharps Rifle (designed by Christian Sharps in 1848, a long-range, large-bore, single-shot rifle widely known for its pinpoint accuracy, effective to a range of 1200 yards): **Billy Two Hats**, 1974; **Geronimo: An American Legend**, 1993; **Quigley Down Under**, 1990; **Rancho Deluxe**, 1975; **Silverado**, 1985; **True Grit**, 1969; **True Grit**, 2010; **Unforgiven**, 1992; **Up**, 2009; **Valdez Is Coming**, 1971.

Ship Hijackings (attempted seizures and seizures of ships): **All the Brothers Were Valiant**, 1953; **Amistad**, 1997; **The Bounty**, 1984; **The Caine Mutiny**, 1954; **Captain Blood**, 1935; **Captain Horatio Hornblower**, 1951; **Captain Phillips**, 2013; **China Seas**, 1935; City Hunter, 1993; Final Voyage, 1999; The French Atlantic Affair, 1979 (TV miniseries); **The Ghost Ship**, 1943; Golden Rendezvous, 1978; **A Hijacking**, 2013; **King of Alcatraz**, 1938; **The Land That Time Forgot**, 1975; The Lightship, 1986; **Morituri**, 1965; **Mutiny on the Bounty**, 1935; **Mutiny on the Bounty**, 1962; **Passage to Marseille**, 1944; **The Sea Hawk**, 1940; **The Sea Wolf**, 1941; Speed 2: Cruise Control, 1997; **Two Years before the Mast**, 1946; Under Siege, 1992; Voyage of Terror: The Achille Lauro Affair, 1990 (made-for-TV).

Shooting Galleries: Absolute Hundred, 2001; American Gun, 2005; American Violet, 2008; **Annie Get Your Gun**, 1950; **Annie Oakley**, 1935; **Back to the Future Part III**, 1990; Beach Patrol, 1959 (made-for-TV); Beverly Hills Cop II, 1987; Blood Diamond, 2006; Boccaccio '70, 1962; **Buffalo Bill**, 1944 (Joel McCrea, playing the legendary Buffalo Bill, is reduced by poverty into appearing as an attraction at a lowlife shooting gallery); **The Cincinnati Kid**, 1965; Coldblooded,

1995; Crime Doctor's Manhunt, 1946; The Crystal Ball, 1943; Cutter's Way, 1981; Dear Wendy, 2004; Divine Intervention, 2002; **East of Eden**, 1955; Female, 1933; The Five People You Meet in Heaven, 2004 (made-for-TV); Ghoulies II, 1988; Gun Crazy, 1950; Heldorado, 1946; Hot Fuzz, 2007; It Takes a Thief, 1960; The Last Flight, 1931; Love and Anarchy, 1973; Maisie, 1939; **Midnight Cowboy**, 1969; **A Million Ways to Die in the West**, 2014; **Mr. & Mrs. Smith**, 2005; Narc, 2002; **The Murder Man**, 1935; **On the Avenue**, 1937; The Party's Over, 1934; **Pat and Mike**, 1952; **Pilgrimage**, 1933; The Rear Gunner, 1943; **Ride the High Country**, 1962; San Fernando Valley, 1944; Shooting Gallery, 1995 (TV series); Shooting Gallery, 2011 (TV series); A Soldier's Plaything, 1930; **The Sniper**, 1952; **The Spider Woman**, 1944 (targets are the faces of Japan's Emperor Hirohito, Italy's dictator Benito Mussolini, and Germany's dictator Adolf Hitler); Spy Hard, 1996; **Stage Fright**, 1950; Taxi Driver, 1976; Strike Me Pink, 1936; Sudden Death, 1977; Suicide Fleet, 1931; **This Gun for Hire**, 1942 (Robert Preston, a police detective, unerringly wins every trophy at a shooting gallery until he fails to miss his shot when lover Veronica Lake appears, edifying gallery owner Mikhail Rasumny no end); **Thunder in the City**, 1937; The Tuxedo, 2002; The Underdog, 1943; **A Walk in the Sun**, 1945 (Richard Conte, a machine gunner fighting in Italy during WWII, 1939-1945, talks about how he could never hit any targets at a shooting gallery when he was a civilian); **Whistle Stop**, 1946; **The Wolf Man**, 1941(Lon Chaney Jr. cannot bring himself to shoot the target of a wolf, suspecting that he is possessed of lycanthropy and just such a fellow beast in human form); Youth Runs Wild, 1944; Zachariah, 1971.

Slaves (slave traders; slavery): **Abe Lincoln in Illinois**, 1940; **Abraham Lincoln**, 1930; **Adanggman**, 2000; **The Adventures of Robinson Crusoe**, 1954; Aferim!, 2015; Alex Haley's Queen, 1993 (TV miniseries); Amazing Grace, 2007; American Playhouse, 1981-1992 (TV series; "Solomon Northup's Odyssey," 1984 episode); **Amistad**, 1997; **Anna and the King of Siam**, 1946; Anna and the King, 1999; **Anthony Adverse**, 1936; **Band of Angels**, 1957; **Barabbas**, 1962; **Battle for the Planet of the Apes**, 1973; **Belle**, 2014; **Belle Starr**, 1941; Beloved, 1998; **Ben Hur: A Tale of the Christ**, 1925; **Ben-Hur**, 1959; **The Birth of a Nation**, 1915; **Blade Runner**, 1982; Boy Slaves, 1939; Brother Future, 1991 (made-for-TV); Burn!, 1969; **Cabiria**, 1914; Cameo Kirby, 1914; **Captain Blood**, 1935; Caribbean, 1952; Ceddo, 1978; The Chronicles of Narnia: The Voyage of the Dawn Treader, 2010; Cobra Verde, 1987; **Cold Mountain**, 2003; **The Color Purple**, 1985; **Conquest of the Planet of the Apes**, 1972; **Crusoe**, 1988; **Dark Command**, 1940; **The Dark Crystal**, 1982; **Demetrius and the Gladiators**, 1954; **Django Unchained**, 2012; **Dragon Seed**, 1944; **Dragonheart**, 1996; Drum, 1976; The Egyptian, 1954; El Cimarron, 2006; **The Emperor Jones**, 1933; Enslavement; The True Story of Fanny Kemble, 2000 (made-for-TV); Fiddlers Three, 1946; **The Four Feathers**, 1939; The Four Feathers, 2002; **Freedom**, 2014; **Friendly Persuasion**, 1956; **The Foxes of Harrow**, 1947; **Freedom** (aka: Something Whispered), 2014; **A Funny Thing Happened on the Way to the Forum**, 1966; Ganga Zumba, 1972; Genghis Khan, 1965; **Gettysburg**, 1993; **Gladiator**, 2000; **Glory**, 1989; **Gods and Generals**, 2003; **Gone with the Wind**, 1939; The Gorgeous Hussy, 1936; Hearts Divided, 1936; Her Purchase Price, 1919; **The Horse Soldiers**, 1959; **Huckleberry Finn**, 1931; **Huckleberry Finn** (aka: The Adventures of Huckleberry Finn), 1939; I Am Slave, 2011; **Indiana Jones and the Temple of Doom**, 1984; Indochine, 1992; The Island of Dr. Moreau, 1977; The Island of Dr. Moreau, 1996; Island of Doomed Men, 1940; **Island of Lost Souls**, 1932; Jefferson in Paris, 1995; **Jezebel**, 1938; **John Paul Jones**, 1959; Joseph, 1995 (made-for-TV); Joseph and the Amazing Technicolor Dreamcoat, 2000; The Journey of August King, 1995; **Journey to Shiloh**, 1968; The Keeping Room, 2014; **Khartoum**, 1966; **The King and I**, 1956; The King and I, 1999; Land of the Pharaohs, 1955; **The Last Days of Pompeii**, 1935; The Last Supper, 1978; The Legend of Nigger Charley, 1972; **Lincoln**, 2012; Little Senegal, 2002; **The Littlest**

Rebel, 1936; Manderlay, 2005; Mandingo, 1975; **Mansfield Park**, 1999; The Matrix, 1999; **Metropolis**, 1927; The Middle Passage, 2001; The Mission, 1986; **The Naked Prey**, 1965; New Moon, 1940; North and South, 1985 (TV miniseries); **Northwest Passage**, 1940; **The Patriot**, 2000; **Pirates of the Caribbean: Dead Man's Chest**, 2006; **Planet of the Apes**, 1968; **Planet of the Apes**, 2001; **The Prince of Egypt**, 1998; **The Prisoner of Shark Island**, 1936; The Prodigal, 1955; Quilombo, 1986; **Quo Vadis**, 1913; **Quo Vadis**, 1951; Returner, 2003; **Ride with the Devil**, 1999; **The Robe**, 1953; Roots, 1977 (TV miniseries); Roots: The Gift, 1988 (made-for-TV); **Samson and Delilah**, 1949; **Sanders of the River**, 1935; Sankofa, 1993; **Santa Fe Trail**, 1940 (John Brown); Savannah, 2013; **The Scalphunters**, 1968; **The Sea Hawk**, 1940; **Seven Angry Men**, 1955 (John Brown); Shaft in Africa, 1973; Skin Game, 1971; The Slave, 1962; The Slave Hunters, 2010 (TV miniseries); Slavers, 1980; Slaves, 1969; Solomon Northup's Odyssey (aka: Half Slave, Half Free), 1984 (made-for-TV); **Song of Freedom**, 1936; **Souls at Sea**, 1937; **Spartacus**, 1960; Spartacus, 2004 (made-for-TV); **Stanley and Livingstone**, 1939; **Star Wars: Episode I—The Phantom Menace**, 1999; **Star Wars: Episode VI—Return of the Jedi**, 1983; Tamango, 1959; Tarzan of the Apes, 1918; **300**, 2006; **The Ten Commandments**, 1923; **The Ten Commandments**, 1956; **Tennessee Johnson**, 1942; **They Died with Their Boots On**, 1941; Topsy and Eva, 1927; Tula: The Revolt, 2014; **12 Years a Slave**, 2013; **20,000 Leagues under the Sea**, 1954; Uncle Tom's Cabin, 1914; Uncle Tom's Cabin, 1918; **Uncle Tom's Cabin**, 1927; Uncle Tom's Cabin, 1969; **The Vikings**, 1958; Way Down South, 1939.

Sleepwalkers and Sleepwalking (Somnambulism): **Abbott and Costello Meet Frankenstein**, 1948; The Affairs of Cellini, 1934; **The Cabinet of Dr. Caligari**, 1921; The Chinese Room, 1968; City of Pirates, 1985; Class Trip, 1998; **The Conjuring**, 2013; Count Dracula, 1977 (made-for-TV); Dark Corners, 2006; Dark Water, 2002; Dead Awake, 2001; The Doll, 1919; Donnie Darko, 2001; Don't Look Down, 2008; Don't Look Now...We're Being Shot At!, 1969; **Dracula**, 1931; **Dracula**, 1979; **Dracula**, 1992; **Dracula: Dead and Loving It**, 1995; **Dracula Has Risen from His Grave**, 1969; Dracula in Istanbul, 1953; **Dracula—Prince of Darkness**, 1966; **Dracula's Daughter**, 1936; Experience Preferred...but Not Essential, 1983; Eye of the Devil, 1966; The Eyes of Annie Jones, 1964; **Fort Bliss**, 2014; Gone Fishin', 1997; Half Angel, 1951; Haxan: Witchcraft Through the Ages, 1922; He Married His Wife, 1940; He Said, She Said, 1991; **The Horn Blows at Midnight**, 1945; Hot Water, 1924; Jericho Mansions, 2003; Killer Joe, 2011; La sonnambula, 1954; The Legend of Hell House, 1973; Leif, 1987; **The Lieutenant Wore Skirts**, 1956; Loch Ness, 1996; **Macbeth**, 1948; **Macbeth**, 1971; **Macbeth**, 2015; **Mark of the Vampire**, 1935; Neel Kamal, 1968; The New Daughter, 2009; A Nightmare on Elm Street 2: Freddy's Revenge, 1985; **Nosferatu**, 1922; **Nosferatu: The Vampire**, 1979; **Paranormal Activity**, 2009; The Parasomniac, 2010; The Private Lives of Pippa Lee, 2009; Reign Over Me, 2007; **Run & Jump**, 2013; The Science of Sleep, 2006; **Secondhand Lions**, 2003; Side Effects, 2013; Silent Hill, 2006; Sinister, 2012; The Skull, 1965; Sleep Murder, 2004 (made-for-TV); Sleepwalk With Me, 2012; The Sleepwalker Killing, 1997 (made-for-TV); Sleepwalkers, 1992; Stepbrothers, 2008; The Towrope, 2012; Turtles Can Fly, 2004; Vampire Over London, 1952; **Viridiana**, 1962; **When Father Was Away on Business**, 1985; **Without Love**, 1945; **The Woman in Green**, 1945; Wreckers, 2011.

Snipers (crime and law enforcement): **Absolute Power**, 1997; Across 110th Street, 1972; **The Adventure of Sherlock Holmes' Smarter Brother**, 1975; **The Amazing Spider-Man 2**, 2014; The American, 2010; Assault on Precinct 13, 2005; Big Jake, 1971; Billion Dollar Brain, 1967; Billy Jack, 1971; Blood Simple, 1985; **Bloody Sunday**, 2002; Charming Billy, 1999; **Colorado Territory**, 1949; Dark Alibi, 1946; **The Dark Knight**, 2008; The Dark Knight Rises, 2012; **The Day of the Jackal**, 1973; Dick Tracy Returns, 1938; **Die Hard**, 1988; **Die**

Hard: With a Vengeance, 1995; **Dirty Harry**, 1971; **Dr. No**, 1962; **Dog Day Afternoon**, 1975; **The Falcon's Brother**, 1942; Flashpoint, 1984; **The French Connection**, 1971; The Gauntlet, 1977; **G-Men**, 1935; Grosse Pointe Blank, 1997; Hard Target, 1993; Heat, 1995; **High Sierra**, 1941; Hitman, 2007; Hostage, 2005; **The Hunted**, 2003; The Hunting Party, 1971; **In the Line of Fire**, 1993; **The In-Laws**, 1979; The Jackal, 1997; Joe Kidd, 1972; Kill the Irishman, 2011; The Killer Elite, 1975; The Last Boy Scout, 1991; Leon: The Professional, 1994; **Lethal Weapon**, 1987; **The Life and Times of Judge Roy Bean**, 1972; Little Murders, 1971; **The Long Good Friday**, 1982; **The Magnificent Seven**, 1960; **The Man from Laramie**, 1955; **The Man Who Knew Too Much**, 1956; **The Manchurian Candidate**, 1962; The Manchurian Candidate, 2004; The Mechanic, 1972; **North West Mounted Police**, 1940; **Papillon**, 1973; **Pat Garrett and Billy the Kid**, 1973; A Perfect World, 1993; **Point Blank**, 1967; Point Blank, 1998; **Ronin**, 1998; Scarface, 1983; **Sherlock Holmes: A Game of Shadows**, 2011; Shooter, 2007; **Silver Streak**, 1976; **The Sniper**, 1952; Snitch, 2013; **The Sons of Katie Elder**, 1965; Stander, 2003; **Suddenly**, 1954; **The Sugarland Express**, 1974; Swamp Women, 1956; **The Taking of Pelham One Two Three**, 1974; **The Taking of Pelham 1 2 3**, 2009; **Thief**, 1981; **3:10 to Yuma**, 2007; **To Live and Die in L.A.**, 1985; **The Turning Point**, 1952; **U.S. Marshals**, 1998; **The Usual Suspects**, 1995; **Valdez Is Coming**, 1971; Vantage Point, 2008; **Warlock**, 1959; Winter Kills, 1979; **The Woman in Green**, 1945. Note: For detailed information on criminal snipers, see my books *Bloodletters and Badmen* (M. Evans, 1973); *Encyclopedia of World Crime*; 8 volumes (CrimeBooks, Inc., 1990); *The Great Pictorial History of World Crime*; 2 volumes (History, Inc., 2004).

Snipers (intelligence and military): Aerial Gunner, 1943; **Air Force**, 1943; **All Quiet on the Western Front**, 1930; **American Sniper**, 2014; **Back to Bataan**, 1945; **Bataan**, 1943; Beach Red, 1967; **Beachhead**, 1954; Behind Enemy Lines, 2001; **Between Heaven and Hell**, 1956; **The Big Red One**, 1980; **Black Hawk Down**, 2001; **The Bourne Identity**, 2002; The Bourne Supremacy, 2004; **The Bridge at Remagen**, 1969; **The Bridges at Toko-Ri**, 1954; **A Bridge Too Far**, 1977; **Casualties of War**, 1989; Clear and Present Danger, 1994; **Cold Mountain**, 2003; **Courage Under Fire**, 1996; **Cross of Iron**, 1977; **Cry Havoc**, 1943; Days of Glory, 1944; **Enemy at the Gates**, 2001; Executive Action, 1973; **The Fighting Seabees**, 1944; **Flags of Our Fathers**, 2006; **For Your Eyes Only**, 1981; **For Whom the Bell Tolls**, 1943; The Four Feathers, 2009; **From Russia with Love**, 1963; **Full Metal Jacket**, 1987; **Gettysburg**, 1993; **Goldfinger**, 1964; **The Great Raid**, 2005; **The Green Berets**, 1968; **Green Zone**, 2011; **Guadalcanal Diary**, 1943; **Gunga Din**, 1939; **The Guns of Navarone**, 1961; **The Hurt Locker**, 2009; I Was an American Spy, 1951; **Joyeux Noel**, 2005; **Kelly's Heroes**, 1970; **Letters from Iwo Jima**, 2006; **The Lives of a Bengal Lancer**, 1935; The Living Daylights, 1987; **The Lost Patrol**, 1934; The Mark of Cain, 2008; **Men in War**, 1957; Miracle at St. Anna, 2008; **Platoon**, 1986; Rambo, 2008; **Sands of Iwo Jima**, 1949; **Saving Private Ryan**, 1998; Shock, 1934; Ski Patrol, 1940; Sniper, 1993; Soldiers, 2010; **The Steel Helmet**, 1951; **Tears of the Sun**, 2003; **The Thin Red Line**, 1964; **The Thin Red Line**, 1998; **Three Kings**, 1999; **Thunderbirds**, 1952; **Twilight's Last Gleaming**, 1977; The Wild Geese, 1978; **X-Men Origins: Wolverine**, 2009; **Zulu**, 1964.

Soda Jerks: Assassin of Youth, 1937; **The Bank Dick**, 1940 (Shemp Howard); **The Best Years of Our Lives**, 1946 (Dana Andrews); Blast from the Past, 1999; Blue Denim, 1959; Calling All Marines, 1939; College, 1927 (Buster Keaton); The Constant Woman, 1933; **Dames**, 1934; **The Gangster**, 1947 (Harry Morgan); **Good News**, 1947 (Peter Lawford); The Great Rupert, 1950; Happiness C.O.D., 1935; **Has Anybody Seen My Gal?**, 1952; The Headleys at Home, 1938; **It's a Wonderful Life**, 1946; Larceny, Inc., 1942; **My Sister Eileen**, 1942; **My Sister Eileen**, 1955; **99 River Street**, 1953; One Hour Late, 1934; Playing

Around, 1930; **Pleasantville**, 1998 (Jeff Daniels); Reefer Madness, 1936; Slightly Dangerous, 1943; **The Sniper**, 1952; **Speedy**, 1928 (Harold Lloyd); Start Cheering, 1938; **Stranger on the Third Floor**, 1940; **Tension**, 1949; **They Won't Forget**, 1937 (Elisha Cook Jr.); **Thousands Cheer**, 1944; 20,000 Men a Year, 1939; **Who Done It?**, 1942 (Bud Abbott and Lou Costello); **Wide Open Faces**, 1938 (Joe E. Brown); Zis Boom Bah, 1941.

Soviet Defectors in the Cold War (1922-1989): Avalanche Express, 1979; The Beast of Yucca Flats, 1961; Condorman, 1981; Danger Route, 1968; The Fourth Protocol, 1987; **The Hunt for Red October**, 1990; Judgment in Berlin, 1988; The Looking Glass War, 1970; **Man on a Tightrope**, 1953; **Moscow on the Hudson**, 1984; **Ninotchka**, 1939; Red Heat, 1985; **Salt**, 2010; **The Serpent**, 1973; Singing the Blues in Red, 1988; **The Spy Who Came in from the Cold**, 1965; **Topaz**, 1969; White Nights, 1985.

Space (also see Astronauts; Explorers; Martians, this Index): **The Abyss**, 1989; **Alien**, 1979; **Aliens**, 1986; The Angry Red Planet, 1959; **Apollo 13**, 1995; **The Arrival**, 1996; Attack from Mars, 1988; Battlefield Earth, 2000; Ben X, 2007; Bill & Ted's Bogus Journey, 1991; **The Black Hole**, 1979; Buck Rogers, 1939 (serial); **Capricorn One**, 1978; **Close Encounters of the Third Kind**, 1977; Conquest of Space, 1955; **Contact**, 1997; Contamination, 1980; Countdown, 1968; The Day Mars Invaded Earth, 1963; **The Day the Earth Stood Still**, 1951; **The Day the Earth Stood Still**, 2008; D-Day on Mars, 1966 (made-for-TV); **Destination Moon**, 1950; Devil Girl from Mars, 1954; Doom, 2005 (on Mars); Duck Dodgers, 2003- (TV series); The Earth Dies Screaming, 1964; Earth vs. the Flying Saucers, 1956; **Elysium**, 2013; End of the World, 1977; Explorers, 1985; Five Million Years to Earth, 1968; Flash Gordon's Flight to Mars, 1938; Flight to Mars, 1951; Flying Disc Man from Mars, 1950; Flying Saucer Rock 'N' Roll, 2006; Frankenstein Meets the Space Monster, 1965; Ghosts of Mars, 2011; Gog, 1954; **Gravity**, 2013; The Great Martian War, 1913-1917, 2013 (made-for-TV); I Married a Monster from Outer Space, 1958; The Infinite Worlds of H.G. Wells, 2001 (TV miniseries); **Invaders from Mars**, 1953; The Invasion, 2007; **Invasion of the Body Snatchers**, 1956; **Invasion of the Body Snatchers**, 1978; Invasion of the Saucer Men, 1957; Invasion of the Star Creatures, 1962; It Came from Outer Space, 1953; It! The Terror from Beyond Space, 1958; John Carter, 2012; **Journey to the Far Side of the Sun**, 1969; Journey to the Seventh Planet, 1962; Justice League, 2001-2006 (TV series; "Secret Origins," 2001 episode; "Secret Origins: Part II," 2001 episode; "Injustice for All," 2002 episode; "The Cat and the Canary," 2005 episode); Kronos, 1957; Looney Tunes: Back in Action, 2003; Los astronautas, 1964; The Magnetic Monster, 1953; The Man from Planet X, 1951; **Marooned**, 1969; **Mars Attacks!**, 1998; Mars Attacks the World, 1938; Mars Needs Moms, 2011; Mars Needs Women, 1967 (made-for-TV); A Martian Christmas, 2008; The Martian Chronicles, 1980 (TV miniseries); Martians Go Home, 1989; Mercano the Martian, 2002; Missile Monsters, 1958; **Mission to Mars**, 2000; Murdoch Mysteries, 2008- (TV series: "The Annoying Red Planet," 2008 episode); My Favorite Martian, 1963-1966 (TV series); My Favorite Martian, 1999; The Mysterians, 1957; Pajama Party, 1964; Pitch Black, 2000; **Planet of the Apes**, 1968; **Planet of the Apes**, 2001; **Prometheus**, 2012; The Purple Monster Strikes, 1945; Quartermass and the Pit, 1958 (TV miniseries); Queen of Outer Space, 1958; Radio-Mania, 1922; **The Right Stuff**, 1983; Robot Monster, 1953; **Rocketship X-M**, 1950; Santa Claus Conquers the Martians, 1964; Santo vs. la invasion de los marcianos, 1967; Satan's Satellites, 1958 (feature version of serial Zombies of the Stratosphere); Space, 1985 (TV miniseries); The Space Children, 1958; **Space Cowboys**, 2000; Space Station 76, 2014; Star Trek, 1966-1969 (TV series); **Star Trek**, 2009; **Star Trek: First Contact**, 1996; **Star Trek: Generations**, 1994; **Star Trek: Insurrection**, 1998; **Star Trek: Into Darkness**, 2013; **Star Trek: Nemesis**, 2002; **Star Trek: The Motion Picture**, 1979; **Star Trek II: The Wrath of Khan**, 1982;

Star Trek III: The Search for Spock, 1984; Star Trek IV: The Voyage Home, 1986; Star Trek V: The Final Frontier, 1989; Star Trek VI: The Undiscovered Country, 1991; Star Wars: Episode V—The Empire Strikes Back, 1980; Star Wars: Episode IV—A New Hope, 1977; Star Wars: Episode I—The Phantom Menace, 1999; Star Wars: Episode VI—Return of the Jedi, 1983; Star Wars: Episode III—Revenge of the Sith, 2005; Star Wars: Episode II—The Attack of the Clones , 2002; Star Wars: The Clone Wars, 2008; Star Wars: The Force Awakens, 2015; Tales of Tomorrow, 1951-1953 (TV series; "Test Flight," 1951 episode; "Appointment on Mars," 1952 episode; "Plague from Space," 1952 episode); Target Earth, 1954; The Thing, 1982; The Thing from Another World, 1951; This Island Earth, 1955; Tracker, 2001-2002 (TV series); A Trip to Mars, 1918; 20 Million Miles to Earth, 1957; The 27th Day, 1957; Twilight Zone, 1961-1964 (TV series; "People Are Alike All Over," 1960 episode; "Mr. Dingle, the Strong," 1961 episode); 2001: A Space Odyssey, 1968; 2010, 1984; War of the Worlds, 1953; The War of the Worlds, 1988 (TV series); War of the Worlds, 2005; Warlords of the Deep, 1978; Wehan Ke Log, 1967; The Wizard of Mars, 1965; The World of the Worlds: Next Century, 1981; Zombies of the Stratosphere, 1952 (serial).

Spiritualism and Spiritualists: Astral City: A Spiritual Journey, 2010; Black Magic, 1944; Black Magic, 1949; Blithe Spirit, 1945; Déjà vu, 1985; Family Plot, 1976; The Girl with the Dragon's Tattoo, 2011; Grandma's Boy, 2006; The Grim Reaper, 1976; A-Haunting We Will Go, 1942; The Haunting, 1963; Houdini, 1953; The Illusionist, 2006; Innocent Husbands, 1925; The Manitou, 1978; Ministry of Fear, 1944; Nightmare Alley, 1947; OMG: Oh My God!, 2021; Paranormal Activity, 2009; Parasaito Ivu, 1997; Pa-siyam, 2004; The Phantom Thief, 1946; Photographing Fairies, 1997; Poltergeist, 1982; Poltergeist: The Legacy, 1996; Poltergeist III, 1988; Poltergeist II: The Other Side, 1986; Possession, 2002; The Rites of May, 1977; Sucker Money, 1933; Supernatural, 1933; The Thirteenth Chair, 1937; The Uninvited, 1944; Walking with the Ferryman, 2014; You Will Meet a Tall Dark Stranger, 2010; You'll Find Out, 1940; The Zero Hour, 1918.

Spirits: The Adding Machine, 1969; Adventures of Ichabod and Mr. Toad, 1949; The Adventures of Prince Achmed, 1926; The Adventures of Sir Galahad, 1949; After Life, 1998; An American Carol, 2008; The Amityville Horror, 1979; The Amityville Horror, 2005; Amityville 3-D, 1983; An American Werewolf in London, 1981; An American Werewolf in Paris, 1997; Andrea: The Revenge of the Spirit, 2005; Angel on My Shoulder, 1946; Apartment 1303, 2007; Apartment 1303 3D, 2012; Art of the Devil, 2005; The Asphyx, 1973; Banshee!!!, 2008; Bedazzled, 2000; Beetlejuice, 1988; Begotten, 1991; Behind the Wall, 2008; Belladonna of Sadness, 1973; Beloved, 1998; Beyond the Door, 1975; Beyond the Door II, 1977; Beyond the Door III, 1989; Beyond Tomorrow, 1940; Bhooter Bhabishyat, 2012; Bhoothnath, 2008; The Bible: In the Beginning, 1966; Big Trouble in Little China, 1986; Black Butler, 2014; Black Robe, 1991; Blackbeard's Ghost, 1968; The Blair Witch Project, 1999; Blithe Spirit, 1945; Blondie Has Servant Trouble, 1940; Body of Water, 2011; Book of Blood, 2009; The Book of Life, 2014; The Boy Who Wanted to Be a Bear, 2003; Brave, 2012; Brother Bear, 2003; Bunshinsaba, 2012; Burned at the Stake, 1981; The Canterville Ghost, 1944; The Canterville Ghost, 1975 (made-for-TV); The Canterville Ghost, 1985 (made-for-TV); The Canterville Ghost, 1986 (made-for-TV); The Canterville Ghost, 1996 (made-for-TV); The Canterville Ghost, 1997 (made-for-TV); The Canterville Ghost, 2001 (made-for-TV); The Canterville Ghost, 2005 (made-for-TV); Casper, 1995; Carnival of Souls, 1962; Carousel, 1956; The Cat and the Canary, 1927; The Cat and the Canary, 1939; The Cat and the Canary, 1978; Cello, 2005; Chamatkar, 1992; The Changeling, 1980; A Chinese Ghost Story, 1988; A Chinese Ghost Story, 1997; Christ Stopped at Eboli, 1979; A Christmas Carol, 1938; A Christmas Carol, 1951; Christmas Carol, 1978 (made-for-TV); Christmas Carol, 1984 (made-

for-TV); Christmas Carol, 1986 (made-for-TV); A Christmas Carol, 1999 (made-for-TV); A Christmas Carol, 2000 (made-for-TV); Christmas Carol: The Movie, 2012; Christmas Ride, 2013; Cinco, 2010; City That Never Sleeps, 1953; Clash of the Titans, 2010; Concentration Camp, 1938; Conjurer, 2008; The Conjuring, 2013; Coraline, 2009; Corpse Bride, 2005; The Curse of the Crying Woman, 1969; The Dangerous Lives of Altar Boys, 2002; Darby O'Gill and the Little People, 1959; The Dark, 2006; Dark Circles, 2013; Dark Water, 2002; Dark Water, 2005; Daughter of the Mind, 1969 (made-for-TV); Dead Friend, 2004; Dead of Night, 1945; Dead Silence, 2007; Dead Weekend, 2014; Deadly Visitor, 1973 (made-for-TV); Death at Love House, 1976 (made-for-TV); Death of a Ghost Hunter, 2007; Dementia, 2014; The Demoniacs, 1977; Demonic Beauty, 2002; The Devil and Daniel Webster, 1941; The Devil's Backbone, 2011; Distant Lights, 1987; Don't Be Afraid of the Dark, 1973 (made-for-TV); Don't Be Afraid of the Dark, 2011; Don't Click, 2012; Don't Go to Sleep, 1982 (made-for-TV); Don't Panic, 1978; Dorm, 2006; Drag Me to Hell, 2009; Dragonheart, 1996; The Dreaming, 1988; Dreamkeeper, 2003 (made-for-TV); The Echo, 2008; Eliza's Horoscope, 1975; The Enemy, 1974; Enter the Void, 2010; The Entity, 1983; Esprit d'amour, 1983; Evil Angel, 2009; The Exorcism of Emily Rose, 2005; Extended Play, 2006; The Eye, 2002; The Eye, 2008; The Eye 10, 2005; The Eye 2, 2004; The Fall of the House of Usher, 1928; Feardotcom, 2002; Fear No Evil, 1969 (made-for-TV); Feng Sui, 2004; Feng Sui, 2014; Field of Dreams, 1989; Final Fantasy: The Spirits Within, 2001; The Fog, 1980; The Fog, 2005; 1408, 2007; Fragile, 2005; Fridge, 2012; The Frighteners, 1996; Ghastly, 2011; The Ghost, 1963; Ghost, 1990; The Ghost, 2001; Ghost, 2010; Ghost, 2012; The Ghost and Mrs. Muir, 1947; The Ghost and Mr. Chicken, 1966; Ghost Banana Tree, 2005; The Ghost Breakers, 1940; The Ghost Catchers, 1944; Ghost Dad, 1990; The Ghost Goes West, 1936; Ghost in the Machine, 1993; The Ghost of Rashmon Hall, 1953; Ghost Rider, 2007; Ghost Ship, 2002; Ghost Story, 1981; The Ghost Talks, 1929; Ghost Town, 2008; The Ghost Walks, 1934; The Ghost That Walks Alone, 1944; Ghostbusters, 1984; Ghostbusters II, 1989; The Ghostmaker, 2012; Ghostwatch, 1992; The Ghosts of Berkeley Square, 1947; The Ghosts of Edendale, 2003; Ghosts of Girlfriends Past, 2009; The Ghosts of Hanley House, 1968; Ghosts of Mars, 2001; Ghosts That Still Walk, 1977; The Gift, 2000; Golden Door, 2006; Golden Earrings, 2010; Golpo Holeo Shotti, 2014; Gothika, 2003; Grave Encounters, 2011; Grave Secrets: The Legacy of Hilltop Drive, 1992 (made-for-TV); The Gravedancers, 2006; The Grudge, 2004; The Grudge 3, 2009; The Grudge 2, 2006; Gugure! Kokkuri-san, 2014 (TV series); A Guy Named Joe, 1943; The Halloween Tree, 1993 (made-for-TV); Hamlet, 1948; Hamlet, 1964; Hamlet, 1969; Hamlet, 1990; Hamlet, 1996; Hamlet, 2000; Hamlet, 2010 (made-for-TV); Hamlet, 2014; Harry Potter and the Chamber of Secrets, 2002; Harry Potter and the Deathly Hallows Part 1, 2010; Harry Potter and the Deathly Hollows Part 2, 2011; Harry Potter and the Goblet of Fire, 2005; Harry Potter and the Half-Blood Prince, 2009; Harry Potter and the Order of the Phoenix, 2007; Harry Potter and the Prisoner of Azkaban, 2004; Harry Potter and the Sorcerer's Stone, 2001; The Haunted, 1991 (made-for-TV); Haunted, 1995; The Haunted Mansion, 2003; The Haunting, 1963; The Haunting, 1999; The Haunting in Connecticut, 2009; The Haunting in Connecticut 2: The Ghosts of Georgia, 2013; The Haunting of Helena, 2013; The Haunting of Julia, 1981; The Healing, 2012; Heart and Souls, 1993; Heaven Can Wait, 1943; Heaven Can Wait, 1978; Here Comes Mr. Jordan, 1941; Hidalgo, 2004; High Plains Drifter, 1973; High Spirits, 1988; Hold That Ghost, 1941; The Horn Blows at Midnight, 1945; Horror, 2003; House, 1977; House, 1986; House of Evil, 1978; House on Haunted Hill, 1959; House on Haunted Hill, 1999; The House That Never Dies, 2014; House II: The Second Story, 1987; The House Where Evil Dwells, 1982; How Awful about Allan, 1970 (made-for-TV); How to Drown Dr. Mracek, the Lawyer, 1975; Hum Kaun Hai?, 2004; I Am ZoZo, 2012; I Married a Witch, 1942; Idle Hands, 1999; The Innocents, 1961; Insidious, 2011;

The Invasion of Carol Enders, 1973 (made-for-TV); Invisible Adversaries, 1977; Invisible Ghost, 1941; The Invited, 2010; Isabel, 1968; Jack Frost, 1998; Jekhane Bhooter Bhoy, 2012; Jessabelle, 2014; Jessica: A Ghost Story, 1992; The Journals of Knud Rasmussen, 2006; Jungle Boy, 1998; Ju-on: The Grudge, 2003; Just Like Heaven, 2005; Kairo, 2001; The Keeper of the Bees, 1935; Kilometer 31, 2006; The Kingdom, 1994 (TV miniseries); Krasue Valentine, 2006; **Kwaidan**, 1965; La Liorona, 1960; Lady in White, 1988; Lake Mungo, 2008; The Last Airbender, 2010; The Legend of Hell House, 1973; **Liliom**, 1935; The Living and the Dead, 2006; Long Time Dead, 2002; The Lord of the Rings: The Return of the King, 2003; The Lovely Bones, 2009; The Magic Snowman, 1987; The Magical Legend of the Leprechauns, 1999; The Maid, 2006; Man with the Steel Whip, 1954; Marchlands, 2011 (TV miniseries); The Marsh, 2006; The Matrimony, 2007; Maxie, 1985; **Maytime**, 1937; **The Messenger: The Story of Joan of Arc**, 1999; The Messengers, 2007; A Midsummer Night's Sex Comedy, 1982; **Miracle in the Rain**, 1955; Mostly Ghostly, 2008; Mother of Tears, 2008; **My Neighbor Totoro**, 1993; My Own Love Song, 2010; Night Angel, 1990; The Night Child, 1976; Nightmare, 2007 (made-for-TV); The Nightmare Before Christmas, 1993; A Nightmare on Elm Street, 1984; Nightwing, 1979; Nomads, 1986; Now and Forever, 2002; Nutcracker, 2001; Oculus, 2014; **On Borrowed Time**, 1939; 100 Feet, 2008; One Missed Call, 2005; One Missed Call 2, 2006; The Oracle, 1985; The Orphanage, 2008; **The Other**, 1972; The Other Side of the Tracks, 2008; **The Others**, 2001; Ouija, 2014; Over Her Dead Body, 2008; Painted Fire, 2002; The Painted Stallion, 1937; **Pan's Labyrinth**, 2007; **Papillon**, 1973; Paranormal Activity, 2007; Paranormal Activity 3, 2013; Paranormal Activity 2, 2010; ParaNorman, 2012; Phantasmagoria, 2014; Phantom Brother, 1988; The Phantom Rider, 1946; Photographing Fairies, 1997; The Piano Lesson, 1996 (made-for-TV); Pizza, 2012; Pizza 2: Villa, 2013; Playing Beatie Bow, 1986; **Poltergeist**, 1982; Poltergeist III, 1988; Poltergeist II, 1986; **Portrait of Jennie**, 1949; Practical Magic, 1988; Presence of Mind, 1999; **Princess Mononoke**, 1999; Pulse, 1988; Pulse, 2001; Pulse, 2006; Purgatory, 1999 (made-for-TV); R.I.P.D., 2013; Ravenous, 1999; The Red Shoes, 2005; **The Remarkable Andrew**, 1942; The Return of Peter Grimm, 1935; Resurrection Mary, 2008; Riding the Bullet, 2004; **Ring**, 1998; **The Ring**, 2002; Ring 2, 1999; Rinne, 2006; The Rising Light, 2013; The Rite, 2011; **Road to Morocco**, 1942; Route 666, 2001; The Ruins, 2008; Saint Ange, 2005; Sandcastles, 1972 (made-for-TV); Satan's Blade, 1984; Saving Hope, 2012- (TV series); Scary Movie 2, 2001; Schalken the Painter, 1979 (made-for-TV); Scooby-Doo, 2002; Scooby-Doo 2: Monsters Unleashed, 2004; The Screaming Skull, 1958; **Scrooge**, 1970; Scrooged, 1988; Segundo Mano, 2011; The She-Creature, 1956; Shadows of a Stranger, 2014; **The Shining**, 1980; Shock, 2004; **Short Peace**, 2014; Shutter, 2004; Shutter, 2008; Shutterbug, 2009; Silent Tongue, 1993; Silk, 2007; Simeon, 1992; The Sixth Man, 1997; **The Sixth Sense**, 1999; Sleepy Hollow, 1999; Sleepy Hollow, 2013 (TV series); Spectres, 2012; Spirit Warriors: The Shortcut, 2003; **Spirited Away**, 2003; **Star Wars: Episode IV—A New Hope**, 1977; Stay Alive, 2006; **Stir of Echoes**, 1999; Stir of Echoes 2: The Homecoming, 2007; Stormhouse, 2012; **The Sullivans**, 1944; Supernatural, 2005- (TV series); Susie Q, 1996 (made-for-TV); The Sweet House of Horrors, 1989; **Tales of Terror**, 1962; Tears of Ka li, 2004; The Tempest, 1960 (made-for-TV); The Tempest, 1979; The Tempest, 2010; The Terror, 1963; That's My Boy, 1932; 13 Ghosts, 1960; This England, 1941; This House Possessed, 1981 (made-for-TV); **Throne of Blood**, 1961; Till Death, 1978; **The Time of Their Lives**, 1946; **Topper**, 1937; **Topper Returns**, 1941; **Topper Takes a Trip**, 1939; Tormented, 1960; Tormented, 2009; Torture Garden, 1967; Tower of Terror, 1997; The Triangle, 2001 (made-for-TV); Trick or Treat, 1986; Truly Madly Deeply, 1991; The Turn of the Screw, 1959 (made-for-TV); The Turn of the Screw, 1974 (made-for-TV); The Turn of the Screw, 1982 (made-for-TV); The Turn of the Screw, 1992; The Turn of the Screw, 1994 (made-for-TV); The Turn of the Screw, 2000 (made-for-TV); The Turn of the Screw, 2003; The Turn

of the Screw, 2009 (made-for-TV); Two Thousand Maniacs, 1964; 2001 Maniacs, 2005; **Ugetsu**, 1954; Universal Grove, 2007; Universal Signs, 2008; **The Uninvited**, 1944; The Uninvited, 1996 (made-for-TV); The Uninvited, 2001; The Unseeable, 2006; Venus in Furs, 1970; The Victim, 2006; Visitor, 2004; Voices, 2007; The Watcher in the Woods, 1980; Wendigo, 2001; What Lies Beneath, 2000; When a Man Sees Red, 1934; When the Lights Went Out, 2012; Where Got Ghost?, 2009; White Lady, 2006; White Noise, 2005; White Noise 2, 2007; Wild Flowers, 2000; Windstruck, 2004; Witchboard, 1986; Witchboard III: The Possession, 1995; Witchboard 2, 1993; The Woman in Black, 1989 (made-for-TV); The Woman in Black, 2012; The Woods, 2006; The Wraith, 1986; **Wuthering Heights**, 1939; **You'll Find Out**, 1940; Zorro Rides Again, 1937.

Spoofs (Westerns): **Along Came Jones**, 1945; The Beautiful Blonde from Bashful Bend, 1949; Big Money Rustlas, 2010; **Blazing Saddles**, 1974; Carry On Cowboy, 1965; **Cat Ballou**, 1965; Crazy Westerners, 1973; Dirty Dingus Magee, 1970; For a Few Dollars Less, 1966; Go West, 1940; **Lemonade Joe**, 1966; **The Lone Ranger**, 2013; **A Million Ways to Die in the West**, 2014; **The Outlaws Is Coming**, 1965; Petticoat Planet, 1996; **Ride 'Em Cowboy**, 1942; Rustlers' Rhapsody, 1985; **The Secret Life of Walter Mitty**, 1947 (western daydream sequence); Shanghai Express, 1986; **Support Your Local Gunfighter**, 1971; **Support Your Local Sheriff**, 1969; Texas across the River, 1966; **Waterhole No. 3**, 1967; **Way Out West**, 1937; Zachariah, 1971.

Stage Performers (also see Broadway Productions and Shows; Vaudeville and Vaudeville Performers, this index): **Accent on Youth**, 1935; **The Actress**, 1928; **Alexander's Ragtime Band**, 1938; **All about Eve**, 1950; **All That Jazz**, 1979; **Almost Famous**, 2000; American Hot Wax, 1978; Always Leave Them Laughing, 1949; And the Angels Sing, 1944; **Annie Get Your Gun**, 1950 (Annie Oakley); **Annie Oakley**, 1935; Anything Goes, 1956; Applause, 1929; **April in Paris**, 1952; **The Assassination of Jesse James by the Coward Robert Ford**, 2007; **Babes in Arms**, 1939; **The Band Wagon**, 1953; **The Barkleys of Broadway**, 1949; **The Benny Goodman Story**, 1956; Billy Rose's Jumbo, 1962; Black Swan, 2010; Black Tights, 1962; **Blonde Venus**, 1932; **Bloodhounds of Broadway**, 1952; **The Blue Angel**, 1931; **Blue Skies**, 1946; Bolero, 1934; **Boy Meets Girl**, 1938; **Broadway**, 1942; **Broadway Danny Rose**, 1984; **The Broadway Melody**, 1929; **Broadway Melody of 1936**, 1935; **Broadway Melody of 1938**, 1937; **Broadway Melody of 1940**, 1940; **The Buddy Holly Story**, 1978; **Bullets Over Broadway**, 1994; Burlesque, 2010; **Cabaret**, 1972; **Call Me Mister**, 1951; Can-Can, 1960; Career, 1959; Champagne Charlie, 1948; Charlie Chan at the Opera, 1937; **A Chorus Line**, 1985; **Circus World**, 1964; **Citizen Kane**, 1941; The Climax, 1944; **Coney Island**, 1943; **Dames**, 1934; **The Dolly Sisters**, 1945; **A Double Life**, 1947; **The Entertainer**, 1960; The Fabulous Dorseys, 1947 (Jimmy and Tommy Dorsey); **Finding Neverland**, 2004 (J.M. Barrie); **Flying Down to Rio**, 1933; **Footlight Parade**, 1933; Footlight Serenade, 1942; **For Me and My Gal**, 1942; **42nd Street**, 1933; **Freaks**, 1932; **The Gang's All Here**, 1943; The Gene Krupa Story, 1959; **Gentlemen Marry Brunettes**, 1955; **Gentlemen Prefer Blondes**, 1953; George White's 1935 Scandals, 1935; George White's Scandals, 1934; **The Girl in the Red Velvet Swing**, 1955 (Evelyn Nesbit, Stanford White, Harry K. Thaw); **The Glenn Miller Story**, 1954; **Gold Diggers of 1933**, 1933; **Gold Diggers of 1935**, 1935; **Gold Diggers of 1937**, 1936; **The Great American Broadcast**, 1938; **The Great Caruso**, 1951; **The Great Ziegfeld**, 1936 (Anna Held, Billie Burke); **The Greatest Show on Earth**, 1952; **Gypsy**, 1962; **Hearts of the West**, 1975; **The Helen Morgan Story**, 1957; **Hello, Frisco, Hello**, 1943; **Holiday Inn**, 1942; **Hollywood Canteen**, 1944; **Hollywood Cavalcade**, 1939; **Hollywood Hotel**, 1937; **The I Don't Care Girl**, 1953 (Eva Tanguay); **I'll Cry Tomorrow**, 1955 (Lillian Roth); **I'll See You in My Dreams**, 1951 (Gus Kahn, Walter Donaldson); **The Illusionist**, 2006; **In Old Chicago**, 1938; **Incendiary Blonde**,

1945 (Texas Guinan); **It's Always Fair Weather**, 1955; **Jeanne Eagels**, 1957; **The Joker Is Wild**, 1957 (Joe E. Lewis); **King Creole**, 1958; **King of Burlesque**, 1936; **La Bamba**, 1987 (Ritchie Valens, Buddy Holley, The Big Bopper); Last Summer in the Hamptons, 1995; **Les Girls**, 1957; **Let's Dance**, 1950; Lillian Russell, 1940; **Limelight**, 1952; Little Miss Broadway, 1938; **Love Me or Leave Me**, 1955 (Ruth Etting); Lucky Me, 1954; **Lullaby of Broadway**, 1951; **Man of a Thousand Faces**, 1957 (Lon Chaney Sr.); **Meet Me after the Show**, 1951; **Meet Me in Las Vegas**, 1956; **Merton of the Movies**, 1947; **Mother Wore Tights**, 1947; **Moulin Rouge**, 1952 (Henri de Toulouse-Lautrec); Moulin Rouge!, 2001; **Movie Crazy**, 1932; Music Is Magic, 1935; **My Blue Heaven**, 1950; **My Dream Is Yours**, 1949; **My Gal Sal**, 1942 (Paul Dresser); **My Wild Irish Rose**, 1947 (Chauncey Olcott); **New York, New York**, 1977; **A Night at the Opera**, 1935; **Nightmare Alley**, 1947; Nijinsky, 1980; **No Time for Comedy**, 1940; **On the Avenue**, 1937; **Orchestra Wives**, 1942; **Pal Joey**, 1957; **Party Girl**, 1958; **The Perils of Pauline**, 1947 (Pearl White); **The Phantom of the Opera**, 1925; **The Phantom of the Opera**, 1943; **The Phantom of the Opera**, 1962; **The Phantom of the Opera**, 2004; **Prince of Players**, 1955 (Edwin Booth, John Wilkes Booth, Junius Brutus Booth); **The Producers**, 1967; **Red, Hot and Blue**, 1949; **Romance on the High Seas**, 1948; **Rose of Washington Square**, 1939 (Fanny Brice); **The Royal Family of Broadway**, 1930; **Sally of the Sawdust**, 1925; **Scaramouche**, 1923; **Scaramouche**, 1952; **The Seven Little Foys**, 1955 (Eddie Foy Sr.); **Shakespeare in Love**, 1998; **Shall We Dance**, 1937; Shine on Harvest Moon, 1944 (Nora Bayes, Jack Norworth); **Show Boat**, 1936; **Show Boat**, 1951; **Show Business**, 1944; **Show People**, 1928; **Sing, Baby, Sing**, 1936; **Singin' in the Rain**, 1952; **Somebody Loves Me**, 1952 (Blossom Seeley); **Song O' My Heart**, 1930; **Souls for Sale**, 1923; **The Specter of the Rose**, 1946; **Springtime in the Rockies**, 1942; **Stage Beauty**, 2004; **Stage Door**, 1937; **Stage Door Canteen**, 1943; **Stage Fright**, 1950; **Stand-In**, 1937; **Star!**, 1968; **A Star Is Born**, 1954; **Star Spangled Rhythm**, 1942; **Starlift**, 1951; **The Story of Vernon and Irene Castle**, 1939; **The Stunt Man**, 1980; **Sunset**, 1988 (Tom Mix, Wyatt Earp); **Sweet Dreams**, 1985; **Sweet Rosie O'Grady**, 1943; **Swing Time**, 1936; **The Tales of Hoffman**, 1951; **Tea for Two**, 1950; **Thank Your Lucky Stars**, 1943; **There's No Business Like Show Business**, 1954; **Three for the Show**, 1955; **Three Little Words**, 1950 (Bert Kalmar, Harry Ruby); 365 Nights in Hollywood, 1934; **Till the Clouds Roll By**, 1947 (Jerome Kern); **Tin Pan Alley**, 1940; **Too Many Husbands**, 1940; **Top Hat**, 1935; **Trapeze**, 1956; **The Unfinished Dance**, 1947; **The Velvet Touch**, 1948; **Viva Las Vegas**, 1954; **Wabash Avenue**, 1950; **The West Point Story**, 1950; **What Price Hollywood?**, 1932; **When My Baby Smiles at Me**, 1948; **Words and Music**, 1948 (Richard Rodgers, Lorenz Hart); **Yankee Doodle Dandy**, 1942 (George M. Cohan); **You'll Never Get Rich**, 1941; You're My Sweetheart, 1937; **Ziegfeld Follies**, 1945; **Ziegfeld Girl**, 1941.

Stagecoaches: Across the Rio Grande, 1949; **Across the Sierras**, 1941; Adventures in Silverado, 1948; Adventures of Frank and Jesse James, 1948 (serial); Al Jennings of Oklahoma, 1951; Albuquerque, 1948; Alias John Law, 1935; **The Apple Dumpling Gang**, 1975; **Arizona**, 1940; Arizona Bound, 1927; Arizona Bound, 1941; Arizona Stagecoach, 1942; The Arizona Wildcat, 1939; Bad Man of Deadwood, 1941; **The Ballad of Cable Hogue**, 1970; Below the Border, 1942; Billy the Kid Trapped, 1942; Bitter Creek, 1954; Black Bart, 1948; Black Hills, 1947; Blazing the Western Trail, 1945; Born to the Saddle, 1953; Brand of the Outlaws, 1936; Brimstone, 1949; **Broken Arrow**, 1950; **Calamity Jane**, 1953; The Carson City Kid, 1940; Cave of Outlaws, 1951; Code of the West, 1947; Convict Stage, 1965; Cow Country, 1953; The Cowboy Millionaire, 1935; Crooked River, 1950; Crossed Trails, 1948; The Dalton Girls, 1957; Daredevils of the West, 1943 (serial); Dead Man's Trail, 1952; Deadwood Dick, 1940 (serial); Desert Gold, 1936; Desperadoes of the West, 1950 (serial); Devil Riders, 1943; The El Paso Kid, 1946; Fast on the Draw, 1950; Five Guns to Tombstone, 1960; Five Guns West, 1955;

For the Service, 1936; **Fort Apache**, 1948; Frontier Outlaws, 1944; Frontier Vengeance, 1940; Fugitive of the Plains, 1943; The Gentleman from Texas, 1946; Ghost of Zorro, 1949; The Grand Duel, 1974; The Great Adventures of Wild Bill Hickok, 1938 (serial); Great Stagecoach Robbery, 1945; Gun Fury, 1953; Gun Town, 1946; **Gunfight at the O.K. Corral**, 1957; Gunsight Ridge, 1957; The Hawk of Powder River, 1948; Heart of Arizona, 1938; Hidden Guns, 1952; **Hombre**, 1967; **In Old Arizona**, 1929; In Old Sacramento, 1946; Iron Mountain Trail, 1953; The James Brothers of Missouri, 1949; Jesse James Rides Again, 1947; **Johnny Guitar**, 1954; The Kid Ranger, 1936; Last of the Pony Riders, 1953; Law of the Lash, 1947; Lawless Riders, 1935; Lightning Bryce, 1919; The Llano Kid, 1939; The Lone Star Ranger, 1930; Lone Texas Ranger, 1945; Lonesome Trail, 1945; **The Long Riders**, 1980; The Lost Trail, 1945; The Man from Hell's Edges, 1932; The Man from Tumbleweeds, 1940; The Man from Utah, 1934; **The Man Who Shot Liberty Valance**, 1962; Man with the Steel Whip, 1954 (serial); Marked Trails, 1944; The Marksman, 1953; The Michigan Kid, 1947; Montana Territory, 1952; **My Darling Clementine**, 1946; The Nevada Buckeroo, 1931; Nevada City, 1941; New Mexico, 1951; Night Stage to Galveston, 1952; Noose for a Gunman, 1960; Oklahoma Terror, 1939; The Old Texas Trail, 1944; The Old West, 1952; The Oregon Trail, 1939; Oregon Trail, 1945; Outlaw Trail, 1944; Outlaws of Texas, 1950; Overland Mail, 1942; **The Ox-Bow Incident**, 1943; Partners on the Trail, 1944; The Phantom Cowboy, 1935; The Phantom Cowboy, 1941; The Phantom Rider, 1936 (serial); The Phantom Rider, 1946 (serial); **Pony Express**, 1953; Pony Express Days, 1940; Powder River, 1953; Powder River Rustlers, 1949; Raiders of Ghost City, 1944 (serial); Range beyond the Blue, 1947; Range Defenders, 1937; Range Land, 1949; Range War, 1939; Renegades, 1946; The Return of the Durango Kid, 1945; Return of the Lash, 1947; Rider from Tucson, 1950; Riders of Death Valley, 1941; Riders of the Dawn, 1937; Riders of the Frontier, 1939; Rim of the Canyon, 1949; Rock Island Trail, 1950; **Rocky Mountain**, 1950; Rogue of the Range, 1936; Rogue of the Rio Grande, 1930; Romance of the Rio Grande, 1941; Rose of the Rancho, 1936; Roughshod, 1949; The Sabre and the Arrow, 1953; Salome Where She Danced, 1945; Salt Lake Raiders, 1950; San Antone Ambush, 1949; **San Antonio**, 1945; The Second Greatest Sex, 1955; Seven Guns to Mesa, 1958; Sheriff of Sage Valley, 1942; The Silver Whip, 1953; Son of Oklahoma, 1932; Son of Zorro, 1947; Song of the Saddle, 1936; Sonora Stagecoach, 1944; Stage to Mesa City, 1947; **Stagecoach**, 1939; Stagecoach, 1966; Stagecoach, 1986 (made-for-TV); Stagecoach Driver, 1951; Stagecoach Express, 1942; Stagecoach War, 1940; Stagecoach West, 1960 (TV series); Storm Over Wyoming, 1950; Sunset Trail, 1939; Surrender, 1950; Target, 1952; Tex Granger: Midnight Rider of the Plains, 1948 (serial); Texans Never Cry, 1951; **Texas**, 1941; The Texas Kid, 1943; Texas Lawman, 1951; Texas Masquerade, 1944; Three on the Trail, 1936; **3:10 to Yuma**, 1957; Thunder Mountain, 1947; The Thundering Trail, 1951; **A Ticket to Tomahawk**, 1950; **Tombstone, the Town Too Tough to Die**, 1942; Tonto Basin Outlaws, 1941; Topeka, 1953; Topeka Terror, 1945; Trailing Danger, 1947; Trailin' West, 1936; Trigger Law, 1944; Trigger Trail, 1944; Triple Justice, 1940; **Trooper Hook**, 1957; Tucson Raiders, 1944; Two Gun Sheriff, 1941; **Ulzana's Raid**, 1972; Under Montana Skies, 1930; The Utah Kid, 1944; The Valiant Hombre, 1948; The Valley of Vanishing Men, 1942 (serial); The Vanishing Outpost, 1951; The Vanishing Westerner, 1950; Vengeance of Rannah, 1936; The Vigilante: Fighting Hero of the West, 1947 (serial); Vigilante Terror, 1953; Wagon Trail, 1935; **Warlock**, 1959; **Wells Fargo**, 1937; Wells Fargo Days, 1944; West of Tombstone, 1942; Western Cyclone, 1943; Western Heritage, 1948; **Western Union**, 1941; Western Trails, 1938; The Westward Trail, 1948; Where the Buffalo Roam, 1938; Whirlwind, 1951; White Eagle, 1941; Wild Beauty, 1946; Wild Girl, 1932; **Winchester '73**, 1950; **Woman They Almost Lynched**, 1953; Wyoming Wildcat, 1941.

Stampedes (buffalo): Ao: The Last Hunter, 2010; **Bless the Beasts and**

Children, 1971; **How the West Was Won**, 1962; The Last Frontier, 1932; **The Last Hunt**, 1956; The Thundering Herd, 1933.

Stampedes (cattle): **Abilene Town**, 1946; Across the Plains, 1928; **Alvarez Kelly**, 1966; **Arizona**; 1940; **Australia**, 2008; Back in the Saddle, 1941; Bar 20 Rides Again, 1935; The Big Land, 1957; **Billy the Kid**, 1941; Border Wolves, 1938; Bullets and Saddles, 1943; **The Cariboo Trail**, 1950; Cast a Long Shadow, 1959; Cattle Stampede, 1943; **Cowboy**, 1958; Deadwood Dick, 1940 (serial); **Dodge City**, 1939; Drift Fence, 1936; Fargo, 1952; The Field, 1990; Fort Worth, 1951; Galloping Thunder, 1946; Guilty Trails, 1938; Gun for a Coward, 1957; The Halliday Brand, 1957; He Rides Tall, 1964; Man in the Saddle, 1951; The Old Corral, 1936; The Old Chisholm Trail, 1942; The Outcast, 1954; The Outsider, 2002 (made-for-TV); Overland Mail, 1942; **Ramrod**, 1947; **Red River**, 1948; Roll Along, Cowboy, 1937; **The Showdown**, 1950; Sioux City Sue, 1946; Six Gun Mesa, 1950; Stampede, 1936; Stampede, 1949; Streets of Ghost Town, 1950; **3:10 to Yuma**, 2007; **The Tall Men**, 1956; Tamara Drewe, 2010; Ten Wanted Men, 1955.

Steelworkers: Acciaio, 1933; All the Right Moves, 1983; Bootmen, 2000; **The Deer Hunter**, 1978; The Fighter, 1983 (made-for-TV); Flashdance, 1983; Flesh and Blood, 1968 (made-for-TV); The Full Monty, 1997; Heart of Steel, 1983 (made-for-TV); Her Husband's Secretary, 1937; Homefront, 1991-1993 (TV series); Hot Steel, 1940; Kept Husbands, 1931; The Light at Dusk, 1916; **Man of Marble**, 1981; Man of Iron, 1935; No Other Woman, 1933; **Rudy**, 1993; Stranded, 1935; Tomato, 1990; Two Seconds, 1932; Udaan, 2011; 24 City, 2008; **The Valley of Decision**, 1945.

Stevedores (dockworkers; longshoremen): Alfred Hitchcock Presents, 1955-1962 (TV series; "Shopping for Death," 1956 episode); **Cinderella Man**, 2005; **Edge of the City**, 1957; French Leave, 1948; Gakra, 1931; Harbor Command, 1957-1958 (TV series; "Final Score," 1957 episode); Justice, 1954-1956 (TV series; "Flight from Fear," 1955 episode); Kavanagh QC, 1995-2001 (TV series; "True Commitment," 1996 episode); The Keegans, 1976 (made-for-TV); Kill the Irishman, 2011; Money for Nothing, 1993; The Moon in the Gutter, 1983; **On the Waterfront**, 1954; **Ossessione**, 1959; Passion Flower, 1930; San Francisco Docks, 1940; The Silver Treasure, 1926; Slaughter on Tenth Avenue, 1957; Special Agent 7, 1958-1959 (TV series; "The Inside Man," 1959 episode; 'The Longshoreman," 1959 episode); Starsky and Hutch, 1975-1979 (TV series; "Terror on the Docks," 1975 episode); **Triumph of the Spirit**, 1989; **A View from the Bridge**, 1962; **War of the Worlds**, 2005; Waterfront, 1939.

Stockbrokers (and Investment Bankers): The Abandonment, 1916; All My Loved Ones, 1999; All of It, 1998; American Psycho, 2000; Any Woman, 1925; The April Fools, 1969; Bernie, 2011; The Bet, 2006; Blood Will Tell, 1917; The Bonfire of the Vanities, 1990; The Boss' Wife, 1986; **Brewster's Millions**, 1945; **Brewster's Millions**, 1985; Bruiser, 2000; Bucking Broadway, 1917; Bull, 2000- (TV series); Bull's Market, 1970; The Cheat, 1915; City Limits, 1934; **The Crowd Roars**, 1938; Dealers, 1989; Derailed, 2005; **A Dispatch from Reuters**, 1940; Don't Tell the Wife, 1937; Each Pearl a Tear, 1916; East of Ludgate Hill, 1937; Fast and Loose, 1939; The First 9½ Weeks, 1998; The Flash of Fate, 1918; Forbidden Fruit, 1915; From Headquarters, 1915; Gone, but Not Forgotten, 2003; Good Advice, 2001; A Good Year, 2006; Hiding Out, 1987; Hitch, 2005; I Melt with You, 2011; In Between, 1994; In Your Wildest Dreams, 1991; **Johnny Apollo**, 1940; Joshua, 2007; Jungle 2 Jungle, 1997; Kiss the Bride, 2002; The Log of the Black Pearl, 1975 (made-for-TV); Lucky Losers, 1950; The Marriage of a Young Stockbroker, 1971; **The Match King**, 1932 (based on the life of Swedish stock swindler Ivar Kreuger); Maurice, 1997; Memoirs of an Invisible Man, 1992; Million Dollar Weekend, 1948; Modern Husbands, 1919; Net Worth, 2001; New Faces of 1937, 1937; **Nicholas Nickleby**,

2002; **Night at the Museum**, 2006; The Ninth Guest, 1934; Overnight, 2007; Paris Interlude, 1934; The Path of Darkness, 1916; The Patient in Room 18, 1938; Penguin Pool Murder, 1932; The Plunger, 1920; The Pursuit of Happiness, 2006; Quicksilver, 1986; Reaching for the Moon, 1930; The Rich Are Always with Us, 1932; Rumpole of the Bailey, 1978-1992 (TV series); **Runaway Jury**, 2003; The Scarlet Road, 1918; Second Chance, 1972 (made-for-TV); The Secretary, 1995 (made-for-TV); Seize the Day, 1986; Soldiers of Fortune, 2012; A Soul for Sale, 1918; **Stavisky**, 1974 (French stock swindler Serge Stavisky); Steambath, 1973 (made-for-TV); The Strong Way, 1917; Surviving the Game, 1994; Swingtown, 2008; These Glamour Girls, 1939; They're Off, 1918; Times Square Playboy, 1936; To Honor and Obey, 1917; **The Toast of New York**, 1937 (profiles stock manipulator James "Big Jim" Fisk Jr.); **12 Angry Men**, 1957; 25th Hour, 2002; Two for the Money, 2005; Universal Grove, 2007; Urbania, 2000; **Van Gogh**, 1991; **Wall Street**, 1987; The Wall Street Mystery, 1931; A Wall Street Tragedy, 1916; **Washington Square**, 1997; The Way of a Man with a Maid, 1918; The White Raven, 1917; The Wife He Bought, 1918; Wildness of Youth, 1922; **The Wolf of Wall Street**, 2013; Wolves of Wall Street, 2002; You Can't Fool Your Wife, 1923.

Storms at Sea: **Abandon Ship!**, 1957; **The Adventures of Baron Munchausen**, 1989; **The Adventures of Robinson Crusoe**, 1954; The Adventures of Swiss Family Robinson, 1998 (TV series); **All the Brothers Were Valiant**, 1953; **Aloma of the South Seas**, 1926; **Alone on the Pacific**, 1964; **An American Tail**, 1986; The Bermuda Depths, 1978 (made-for-TV); Beyond the Poseidon Adventure, 1979; Bitter Moon, 1994; **The Black Stallion**, 1979; **The Bounty**, 1984; **The Caine Mutiny**, 1954; Cast Away, 2000; **China Seas**, 1935; The Chronicles of Narnia: The Voyage of the Dawn Treader, 2010; **Cloud Atlas**, 2012; Crusoe, 1988; **Dead Calm**, 1989; Deep Waters, 1948; **Doctor Dolittle**, 1967; **Down to the Sea in Ships**, 1949; Eight Bells, 1935; **Far from Home: The Adventures of Yellow Dog**, 1995; Ffolkes, 1980; **The Finest Hours**, 2015; Flood, 2007; **Foreign Correspondent**, 1940; **Frozen**, 2013; The Giants of Thessaly, 1963; Golden Door, 2006; Golden Rendezvous, 1978; **The Golden Voyage of Sinbad**, 1974; Goliath Against the Giants, 1963; Gorgo, 1961; The Guardian, 2006; **The Guns of Navarone**, 1961; **Hawaii**, 1966; Hawks of the Wilderness, 1938; Hercules in the Haunted World, 1964; Hornblower: Duty, 2003 (made-for-TV); Hornblower: Mutiny, 2001 (made-for-TV); **The Hurricane**, 1937; **Ice Age: Continental Drift**, 2012; The Immortal Voyage of Captain Drake, 2009 (made-for-TV); **Indiana Jones and the Last Crusade**, 1989; Jamaica Inn, 1939; **Journey to the Center of the Earth**, 1959; **Journey to the Center of the Earth**, 2008; Journey 2: The Mysterious Island, 2012; Kidnapped, 1948; **King Kong**, 2005; **Kon-Tiki**, 2013; **The Last Voyage**, 1960; **Life of Pi**, 2012; **Lifeboat**, 1944; Mantango, 1963; Mara Maru, 1952; **Master and Commander: The Far Side of the World**, 2003; **Mysterious Island**, 1961; **Napoleon**, 1927; New Moon, 1940; **Nim's Island**, 2008; **No Way Out**, 1987; North of Nome, 1936; **Ordinary People**, 1980; **Pacific Rim**, 2013; **The Perfect Storm**, 2000; **Pirates of the Caribbean: The Curse of the Black Pearl**, 2003; Plymouth Adventure, 1952; Port Sinister, 1953; **The Poseidon Adventure**, 1972; **Reap the Wild Wind**, 1942; Robinson Crusoe, 1997; Safe Harbor, 2009 (made-for-TV); The Sea Beast, 2008 (made-for-TV); Sea Wife, 1957; The Sea Wolf, 2008 (made-for-TV); **Ship of Fools**, 1965; **Sinbad: Legend of the Seven Seas**, 2003; **Six Days Seven Nights**, 1998; **Souls at Sea**, 1937; Swiss Family Robinson, 1940; **Swiss Family Robinson**, 1960; **Tarzan**, 1999; Tarzan and the Green Goddess, 1938; 300: Rise of the Empire, 2014; **The Thief of Bagdad**, 1940; **Thunder Bay**, 1953; **Thunder Rock**, 1944; **The Truman Show**, 1998; **Two Years Before the Mast**, 1946; Una noche, 2012; Virus, 1999; **Wake of the Red Witch**, 1948; **White Squall**, 1996; **The Wolf of Wall Street**, 2013; **The Wreck of the Mary Deare**, 1959; Yankee Buccaneer, 1952. Note: For more information on destructive storms at sea throughout history, see my book *Darkest Hours: A Nar-*

rative Encyclopedia of Worldwide Disasters from Ancient Times to the Present (Nelson-Hall, 1976).

Street Gangs: Aberdeen, 2000; Adventures in Babysitting, 1987; **American Graffiti**, 1973; American Me, 1992; **An American Tail**, 1986; Angel, 1999-2004 (TV series); Angel Town, 1990; The Angels Wash Their Faces, 1939; **Angels with Dirty Faces**, 1938; Assault on Precinct 13, 1976; Attack the Block, 2011; Attack the Gas Station!, 1999; Band of the Hand, 1986; **Batman Forever**, 1995; **Batman: The Dark Knight Returns, Part 1**, 2012; Batman; The Movie, 1999 (made-for-TV); *batteries not included, 1987; The Baytown Outlaws, 2013; **Being There**, 1979; A Better Life, 2011; The Big Boss, 1981; Big Trouble in Little China, 1986; Billy Jack Goes to Washington, 1971; **Blackboard Jungle**, 1955; Boyz n the Hood, 1991; A Brighter Summer Day, 2011; Brighton Rock, 1947; Brighton Rock, 2011; Bruce Almighty, 2003; Bulletproof Monk, 2003; **City of God**, 2000; City of Joy, 1992; City of Men, 2002-2005 (TV series); Clockers, 1995; **A Clockwork Orange**, 1971; **Colors**, 1988; The Cool World, 1963; The Corruptor, 1999; Crank, 2006; **Crash**, 2005; Crime in the Streets, 1956; Crime Spree, 2003; **Dead End**, 1937; **Death Wish**, 1974; Death Wish 3, 1985; Death Wish II, 1982; **The Departed**, 2006; Deuces Wilde, 2002; Downtown, 1990; 8 Mile, 2002; End of Watch, 2012; **The Enforcer**, 1976; Escape from New York, 1981; A Family Thing, 1996; Gangs of New York, 2002; Germany Year Zero, 1949; **Gran Torino**, 2008; **Grease**, 1978; Harsh Times, 2006; Hazard, 2005; Heartless, 2009; Hey Good Lookin'!, 1982; **The Hoodlum Priest**, 1961; Hue and Cry, 1951; **In the Heat of the Night**, 1967; Josh, 2000; Kids Return, 1996; Kill the Irishman, 2011; **King Creole**, 1958; King of New York, 1990; Knights of the City, 1986; **Knock on Any Door**, 1949; Kung Fu Hustle, 2005; Life Is Hot in Crackdown, 2009; Lionheart, 1991; **Los Olvidados**, 1950; **Mean Streets**, 1973; **Medium Cool**, 1969; The New Centurions, 1972; The New Kids, 1985; 1990: The Bronx Warriors, 1982; **No Way Out**, 1950; **On the Waterfront**, 1954; **The Onion Field**, 1979; Only the Strong, 1993; **The Outsiders**, 1983; Painted Fire, 2002; The Perfect Weapon, 1991; Police Academy 2: Their First Assignment, 1985; **The Public Enemy**, 1931; **The Purple Gang**, 1960; The Quest, 1996; Ratcatcher, 1999; Red Heat, 1988; Ring of Fire, 1991; River Gang, 1945; **Romeo + Juliet**, 1996; **Rumble Fish**, 1983; Rumble in the Bronx, 1996; **Salaam Bombay!**, 1988; The Sandpit Generals, 1972; Seven Hours to Judgment, 1988; Sinners and Saints, 2010; Six Bridges to Cross, 1965; **Somebody Up There Likes Me**, 1956; Sons of Anarchy, 2004-2008 (TV series); Straw Dogs, 1971; Teenage Mutant Ninja Turtles, 1990; Teenage Mutant Ninja Turtles II: The Secret of the Ooze, 1991; Tell No One, 2006; **They Call Me Mr. Tibbs!**, 1970; 3:15, 1986; **The Tin Drum**, 1980; **To Live and Die in L.A.**, 1985; Tokyo Tribe, 2014; Touch and Go, 1986; **Trading Places**, 1983; Training Day, 2001; **The Warriors**, 1979; **West Side Story**, 1961; **Wild at Heart**, 1990; **Wild Boys of the Road**, 1933; **Who's That Knocking at My Door**, 1967; **The Young Savages**, 1961.

Submarines: **Above Us the Waves**, 1956 (Atlantic; WWII); **The Abyss**, 1989; **Action in the North Atlantic,** 1943 (WWII); **Arise, My Love**, 1940 (Atlantic; WWII); Around the World Under the Sea, 1966; **Atlantis: The Lost Empire**, 2001; The Atomic Submarine, 1959 (Cold War); **Back to Bataan**, 1945 (Pacific; Leyte, Philippines invasion of 1944); Battle of the Coral Sea, 1959 (Pacific; WWII); **The Bedford Incident**, 1965 (Arctic; Cold War); Below, 2002 (Atlantic; WWII); **Captain America: The First Avenger**, 2011; **Corvette K-225** (Atlantic; WWII); **Crash Dive**, 1943; **Crimson Tide**, 1995; **The Cruel Sea**, 1953 (Atlantic; WWII); Dangerously They Live, 1941; **Dark Journey**, 1937 (Atlantic; WWI); Darling Lili, 1970; **Das Boot**, 1981 (Atlantic, Mediterranean, WWII); **The Desert Fox: The Story of Rommel**, 1951 (Mediterranean; WWII); **Destination Tokyo**, 1943 (Pacific; WWII); Destroyer, 1943 (Atlantic; WWII); Devil and the Deep, 1932; **Diamonds Are Forever**, 1971; Down Periscope, 1996; **The Enemy Below**, 1957 (Atlantic; WWII); **Eye of the Needle**, 1981 (Irish Sea; WWII);

Fantastic Voyage, 1966; **Firefox**, 1982; **For Your Eyes Only**, 1981; **49th Parallel**, 1941 (Hudson's Bay; WWII); Full Fathom Five, 1990; **Generale Della Rovere**, 1961; Gray Lady Down, 1978; **The Great Race**, 1965; **Gung Ho!**, 1943 (Pacific; Makin Island Raid; WWII); Hell and High Water, 1964 (Pacific; Cold War); **Hell Below**, 1933; Hellcats of the Navy, 1957 (Pacific; WWII); **The Hunt for Red October**, 1990; I Was an American Spy, 1951 (Pacific; WWII); Ice Station Zebra, 1968 (Arctic; Cold War); In Enemy Hands, 2004 (Atlantic; WWII); **In Which We Serve**, 1943 (Atlantic; Mediterranean; WWII); **The Incredible Mr. Limpet**, 1964 (Pacific; WWII); **It Came from Beneath the Sea**, 1955; K-19: The Widowmaker, 2002; **The Land That Time Forgot**, 1975 (South Atlantic; WWI); **Lifeboat**, 1944 (Atlantic; WWII); **License to Kill**, 1989; **The Man Who Never Was**, 1956 (Atlantic; WWII); **The McKenzie Break**, 1970 (Atlantic; WWII); **Men of Honor**, 2000; **Morituri**, 1965 (Atlantic; WWII); **Murphy's War**, 1971 (South Atlantic; WWII); **Mysterious Island**, 1961 (Pacific); Mystery Submarine, 1950 (South Atlantic; WWII); **Nazi Agent**, 1942 (Atlantic; WWII); Never Say Never Again, 1983; **1941**, 1979 (Pacific; WWII); **Northern Pursuit**, 1943; Okinawa, 1952 (Pacific; WWII); On the Beach, 1959; Operation Disaster, 1950; **Operation Pacific**, 1951 (WWII); **Operation Petticoat**, 1959 (Pacific; WWII); **Our Man Flint**, 1966; **Pearl Harbor**, 2001 (Pacific; WWII); Phantom, 2013; Prisoner of Japan, 1942 (Pacific; WWII); **Raiders of the Lost Ark**, 1981; **Run Silent, Run Deep**, 1958 (Pacific; WWII); **The Russians Are Coming! The Russians Are Coming!** 1966; Sea Wife, 1957 (Pacific; WWII); **Sealed Cargo**, 1951; **The Silver Fleet**, 1945; **The Spy in Black**, 1939 (Atlantic; WWI); **Spy Kids**, 2001; **The Spy Who Loved Me**, 1977; **Submarine**, 1928; **Submarine Command**, 1951 (Pacific; WWII; Korean War); Submarine Seahawk, 1958 (Pacific; WWII); **Submarine Patrol**, 1938; **Submarine X-1**, 1969 (Atlantic; WWII); **Task Force**, 1949 (Pacific; WWII); **They Came to Blow Up America**, 1943 (Atlantic; WWII); **They Were Expendable**, 1945 (Pacific; WWII); Titanic, 1997 (Atlantic; finding and exploring the ship's wreck); **Tora! Tora! Tora!**, 1970 (Pacific; attack on Pearl Harbor; WWII); **Torpedo Alley**, 1953 (Pacific; Korean War); **Torpedo Run**, 1958 (Pacific; WWII); **20,000 Leagues Under the Sea**, 1954 (Pacific); **U-571**, 2000 (Atlantic; WWII); U-47, 1958 (Atlantic; WWII); **Up Periscope**, 1959 (Pacific; WWII); **Voyage to the Bottom of the Sea**, 1961; **We Dive at Dawn**, 1943 (Atlantic; WWII); **Yellow Submarine**, 1958; **You Only Live Twice**, 1967.

Surfers and Surfing: Back to the Beach, 1987; The Big Bounce, 2004; Big Wednesday, 1978; Blue Crush, 2002; Blue Juice, 1995; Chairman of the Board, 1998; Chasing Mavericks, 2012; The Cove, 2009; Don't Make Waves, 1967; **Drift**, 2013; The Drifter, 2009; First Love, 2010; Isolated, 2013; **Jaws**, 1975; **Jaws 2**, 1978; John from Cincinnati, 2007- (TV series); Laguna Beach: The Real Orange County, 2002-2006 (TV series); **Lilo & Stitch**, 2002; Local Boys, 2002; Loch Ness, 1996; Muscle Beach Party, 1964; North Shore, 1987; Off the Lip, 2004; **Open Water**, 2004; Open Water 2, 2006; Point Break, 1991; The Prince and the Surfer, 1999; Psycho Beach Party, 2000; Ride the Wild Surf, 1964; A Scene at the Sea, 1991; Shout for Joy, 1983; **Soul Surfer**, 2011; Surf Ninjas, 1993; Surf School, 2006; **Surf's Up**, 2007; Teen Beach Movie, 2013 (made-for-TV); There Goes My Baby, 1994; Without a Paddle, 2004.

Surveillance: **The Adventures of Sherlock Holmes**, 1939; **The Amazing Spider-Man 2**, 2014; **American Hustle**, 2013; American Ultra, 2015; The Anderson Tapes, 1971; **Ant-Man**, 2015; **The Asphalt Jungle**, 1950; **The Aviator**, 2004; **Batman Begins**, 2005; **Batman Forever**, 1995; **The Bourne Identity**, 2002; **The Bourne Ultimatum**, 2007; **Bridge of Spies**, 2015; The Cabin in the Woods, 2012; **Captain America: The First Avenger**, 2011; **Captain America: The Winter Soldier**, 2014; **Casino**, 1995; **Casino Royale**, 2006; **Catch Me If You Can**, 2002; Chappie, 2015; Children of Men, 2006; **The Conversation**, 1974; **The Dark Knight**, 2008; **The Dark Knight Rises**, 2012; **The De-**

parted, 2006; **Divergent**, 2014; **Elysium**, 2013; **The Equalizer**, 2014; Equilibrium, 2002; **Fahrenheit 451**, 1966; **Furious 7**, 2015; G.I. Joe: Retaliation, 2013; **Gone Girl**, 2014; **Guardians of the Galaxy**, 2014; Heat, 1995; **The Hot Rock**, 1972; **The House on Carroll Street**, 1988; **The House on 92nd Street**, 1945; **The Hunger Games: Catching Fire**, 2013; **The Hunger Games: Mockingjay—Part 2**, 2015; In Time, 2011; **The Incredibles**, 2004; Inferno, 2016; Insurgent, 2015; **Iron Man 3**, 2013; **Jack Reacher**, 2012; Jack Reacher: Never Go Back, 2016; **Jurassic Park**, 1993; **Jurassic World**, 2015; **Kingsman: The Secret Service**, 2014; **L. A. Confidential**, 1997; **The Lives of Others**, 2006; Logan's Run, 1976; London Has Fallen, 2016; **The Martian**, 2015; The Mechanic, 2011; MI-5, 2015; **Mission Impossible: Ghost Protocol**, 2011; **Mission Impossible – Rogue Nation**, 2015; Need for Speed, 2014; **Now You See Me**, 2013; **Oblivion**, 2013; Oldboy, 2003; **Olympus Has Fallen**, 2013; Person of Interest, 2011-2016 (TV series); Pineapple Express, 2008; **Point Break**, 2015; **Public Enemies**, 2009; The Purge, 2013; Quantum of Solace, 2008; Red, 2010; **The Secret in Their Eyes**, 2009; **Serpico**, 1973; **Skyfall**, 2012; The Sopranos, 1999-2007 (TV series); **Spectre**, 2015; **Splash**, 1984; Surveillance, 2000; **Stakeout**, 1987; **Star Trek: Into Darkness**, 2013; Surveillance, 2006; Surveillance, 2008; Surveillance, 2013 (made-for-TV); **T-Men**, 1947; **Taken**, 2008; This Means War, 2012; **Thor**, 2011; **Tinker Tailor Soldier Spy**, 2011; **Tomorrowland**, 2015; **Topkapi**, 1964; Transformers: Age of Extinction, 2014; **Tron: Legacy**, 2010; Underworld: Awakening, 2012; **Vertigo**, 1958; **Walk East on Beacon!**, 1952; White Collar, 2009-2014 (TV series); **World War Z**, 2013; **X-Men Origins: Wolverine**, 2009; **Zero Dark Thirty**, 2012.

Survival Films (airplane and helicopter crashes): **Ace of Aces**, 1933 (WWI France); **Aces High**, 1977 (WWI France); **Air Force**, 1943 (WWII; U.S. B-17 bomber crash-landing at Luzon, Philippines); **Alive**, 1993 (passenger plane in the Andes); **The Aviator**, 2004 (experimental plane); Back from Eternity, 1956 (passenger plane in the Amazon rainforest); **Black Hawk Down**, 2001 (U.S. Air Force helicopters crash-landing in Mogadishu, Somalia, in 1993); **The Blue Max**, 1966 (WWI France); **A Bridge Too Far**, 1977 (WWII Netherlands; glider crashes); **Captain Eddie**, 1945 (WWII Pacific); Cast Away, 2000 (Fed Ex plane crashes on deserted island); **Command Decision**, 1948 (WWII; U.S. B-17 bomber crash-landing at airbase in England); The Crowded Sky, 1960 (collison of two planes); **The Dawn Patrol**, 1930 (WWI France); **The Dawn Patrol**, 1938 (WWI France); **Desperate Journey**, 1942 (WWII Germany; British Lancaster bomber); **The Eagle and the Hawk**, 1933 (WWI France); **The Flight of the Phoenix**, 1965 (transport plane crash-lands in the Sahara Desert); Flight of the Phoenix, 2004 (transport plane crashlands in the Sahara Desert); Five Came Back, 1939 (passenger plane in the Amazon rainforest); **Flyboys**, 2008 (WWI France); **Flying Tigers**, 1942 (WWII China; crash landings by passenger and fighter planes); **The Green Berets**, 1968 (U.S. Air Force helicopter crashlanding in Vietnam); **A Guy Named Joe**, 1943 (WWII in Europe and the Pacific); **Hell's Angels**, 1930 (WWI France); **Here Comes Mr. Jordan**, 1941 (private plane); High Flight, 1957; **Island in the Sky**, 1953 (forced landing of transport plane in the wastelands of Labrador); **Into the White**, 2014 (WWII Norway); **The Longest Day**, 1962 (WWII France; glider crashes); **Lost Horizon**, 1937 (passenger plane in the Himalayas); Lost Horizon, 1973 (passenger plane in the Himalayas); **No Highway in the Sky**, 1951 (forced landing because of suspected faulty passenger plane construction); **Objective, Burma!**, 1945 (WWII Burma; glider crashes); **Pearl Harbor**, 2001 (WWII; U.S. B-25 bomber crash-landing in China); **Phone Call from a Stranger**, 1952 (commercial plane crash); Planes, 2013; Planes: Fire & Rescue, 2014; **The Red Baron**, 2010 (WWI France); **The Right Stuff**, 1983; **Saving Private Ryan**, 1998 (WWII France; glider crash); **Test Pilot**, 1938 (monoplane forced landing; bomber crash); **Thirty Seconds over Tokyo**, 1944 (WWII; U.S. B-25 bomber crash-landing in China); **Toward the Unknown**, 1956; **Twelve O'Clock High**, 1949 (WWII; U.S.

B-17 bomber crash-landing at airbase in England); **Unbroken**, 2014 (WWII Pacific); **Von Richthofen and Brown**, 1971 (WWI France); **We Were Soldiers**, 2002 (U.S. Air Force helicopters crash-landing in Vietnam); **Wings**, 1927 (WWI France). Note: For more information on airplane and helicopter crashes throughout history, see my book *Darkest Hours: A Narrative Encyclopedia of Worldwide Disasters from Ancient Times to the Present* (Nelson-Hall, 1976).

Survival Films (behind enemy lines): **Above Suspicion**, 1943 (pre-WWII; espionage in Germany); **The Adventures of Tartu**, 1943 (WWII; espionage in Romania); **Against the Wind**, 1948 (WWII; SOE espionage in France); Age of Heroes, 2011 (WWII; Nazi-occupied Norway); **The Alamo**, 1960 (Texas-Mexican War of 1836); **The Alamo**, 2004 (Texas-Mexican War of 1836); **All Quiet on the Western Front**, 1930 (WWII; France); All the Young Men, 1960 (Korean War); Anzio, 1968 (WWII; Italy); **Arrowhead**, 1953 (U.S. Cavalry vs. Apaches); Attack Force Z, 1982 (WWII; Pacific); **Back to Bataan**, 1945 (WWII; Filipino resistance in Japanese-occupied Philippines); Band of Brothers, 2001 (TV miniseries; WWII; France); Battle of the Bulge, 1965 (WWII; Belgium); **Beachhead**, 1954 (WWII; jungle on island); **Beau Geste**, 1926 (French Foreign Legion); **Beau Geste**, 1939 (French Foreign Legion); Beau Geste, 1966 (French Foreign Legion); Behind Enemy Lines, 1986 (Vietnam War); Behind Enemy Lines, 1985 (made-for-TV; WWII; Nazi-occupied Norway); Behind Enemy Lines, 1987 (Vietnam War); Behind Enemy Lines, 1997 (Vietnam War); Behind Enemy Lines, 2001 (Bosnian Crisis); **Bombardier**, 1943 (WWII; Pacific); **A Bridge Too Far**, 1977 (WWII; Holland); **The Bridge on the River Kwai**, 1957 (WWII; from a Japanese prison camp in Burma); **The Bridges at Toko-Ri**, 1954 (Korean War); **Carve Her Name with Pride**, 1958 (WWII; Violette Szabo; espionage in France); **Cast a Giant Shadow**, 1966 (Israeli war of Independence); Centurion, 2010 (Britain 117 A.D.); **The Charge of the Light Brigade**, 1936 (19th-Century India; Crimean War); **The Charge of the Light Brigade**, 1968 (Crimean War); Charlotte Gray, 2001 (WWII; espionage-sabotage in Nazi-occupied France); Clear and Present Danger, 1994 (Colombia); **Cloak and Dagger**, 1946 (WWII; espionage in Italy); **The Cockleshell Heroes**, 1955 (WWII; British navy commandoes); **Commandoes Strike at Dawn**, 1942 (WWII; British commando raid in Nazi-occupied Norway); **Courage Under Fire**, 1996 (Desert Storm in the Gulf War of 1990-1991); Dark of the Sun, 1968 (Congo); Days of Glory, 1944 (WWII; Russia); **Decision Before Dawn**, 1951 (WWII; espionage in Nazi-controlled Germany); The Deep Six, 1958 (WWII; Pacific); **The Desert Fox: The Story of Rommel**, 1951 (WWII; raid on Rommel's headquarters in North Africa); **The Desert Rats**, 1953 (WWII; North Africa); **Desperate Journey**, 1942 (WWII; Germany); **The Devil's Brigade**, 1968 (WWII; Italy); **The Dirty Dozen**, 1967 (WWII; to attack a German headquarters); The Dogs of War, 1980 (Africa); **The Drum**, 1938 (19th-Century India); **Escape**, 1940 (pre-WWII; from a German concentration camp); **Escape from Fort Bravo**, 1953 (U.S. Cavalry vs. Indians); 5 Days of War, 2011 (journalists caught up in the Russo-Georgian War of 2008); **Five Graves to Cairo**, 1943 (WWII; espionage in the Libyan desert); **Fixed Bayonets!**, 1951 (Korean War); **For Whom the Bell Tolls**, 1943 (sabotage in the Spanish Civil War, 1936-1939); **Force 10 from Navrone**, 1978 (WWII; sabotage in Yugoslavia); **The Four Feathers**, 1939 (British troops in Sudan); The Four Feathers, 2002 (British troops in Sudan); **Go for Broke**, 1951 (WWII; Italy and France); Gone to Texas, 1986 (made-for-TV; Texas-Mexican War of 1836); **Grand Illusion**, 1938 (WWI; from a German POW camp); **The Great Escape**, 1963 (WWII; from a German prison camp); The Great Escape II: The Untold Story, 1988 (WWII; from a German prison camp); **The Great Raid**, 2005 (WWII; U.S. commando attack against the Japanese POW camp at Cabanatuan, Luzon, Philippines, in January 1945); **Gung Ho!**, 1943 (WWII; Makin Island raid in the Pacific); **Gunga Din**, 1939 (19th-Century India); **The Guns of Navrone**, 1961 (WWII; sabotage on a Nazi-held Greek island); **Halls of Montezuma**, 1950 (WWII; Pacific island); **Heaven Knows, Mr. Allison**, 1957 (WWII; Japanese-held island in the Pacific); Hell to Eternity, 1960 (WWII; Guy Gabaldon on Saipan); **Hell's Angels**, 1930 (WWI; pilots crashing behind enemy lines); **The Heroes of Telemark**, 1965 (WWII; sabotage in Nazi-occupied Norway); **The Horse Soldiers**, 1959 (Union cavalry raid into the Deep South during the American Civil War); The Hunters, 1958 (Korean War); **Joan of Paris**, 1942 (WWII; allied airmen in France); **Kelly's Heroes**, 1970 (WWII; France); **King of the Khyber Rifles**, 1953 (19th-Century India); **Kings Go Forth**, 1958 (WWII; France); **The Last Command**, 1955 (Texas-Mexican War of 1836; The Alamo); Legionnaire, 1998 (French Foreign Legion); Lions for Lambs, 2007 (Afghan War); **The Lives of a Bengal Lancer**, 1935 (19th-Century India); **Lone Survivor**, 2013 (Afghan war); **The Longest Day**, 1962 (WWII; France); **Major Dundee**, 1965 (U.S. Cavalry battling Apaches and French troops in Mexico); **Marine Raiders**, 1944 (WWII; Pacific); **Mata Hari**, 1931 (WWI; espionage in France); Mata Hari, 1965 (WWI; espionage in France); **A Midnight Clear**, 1992 (WWII; France); Miracle at St. Anna, 2008 (WWII; Italy); **No Man Is an Island**, 1962 (WWII; George R. Tweed on the Island of Guam); **Northwest Passage**, 1940 (French-Indian War); **O.S.S.**, 1946 (WWII; espionage in France); **Objective Burma!**, 1945 (WWII; commando raid behind Japanese lines in Burma); **Odette**, 1951 (WWII; Odette Sanson; espionage in France); Only the Brave, 2006 (WWII; Italy and France); **Operation Crossbow**, 1965 (WWII; espionage-sabotage in Germany); **Operation Secret**, 1952 (WWII; espionage in Nazi-occupied France); Operator 13, 1934 (espionage in American Civil War); **Pearl Harbor**, 2001 (WWII; pilots crashing behind Japanese lines); **The Pianist**, 2002 (WWII; escaping the Holocaust); **The Purple Plain**, 1954 (WWII; crashlanding in Japanese-occupied Burma); **The Raid**, 1954 (American Civil War; St. Albans, Vermont, raid of 1864); Raid on Rommel, 1971 (WWII; Libyan desert); **Rescue Dawn**, 2007 (Vietnam War); **Retreat, Hell!**, 1952 (Korean War); **Rio Grande**, 1950 (U.S. Cavalry fighting Apaches in Mexico); **Saints and Soldiers**, 2005 (WWII; surviving the Malmedy Massacre in France); Seal Team Eight: Behind Enemy Lines, 2014 (African Congo); **Sergeant York**, 1941 (WWI; Battle of the Argonne); **7th Cavalry**, 1956 (U.S. Cavalry vs. Sioux); **The Seventh Cross**, 1944 (preWWII; from a German concentration camp); **Shenandoah**, 1965 (American Civil War); **Shoulder Arms**, 1918 (WWII; Western Front); A Southern Yankee, 1948 (espionage in American Civil War); **Stagecoach**, 1939 (white passengers vs. Apaches); **Star Wars: The Clone Wars**, 2008 (futuristic wars); The Steel Claw, 1951 (WWII; Filipino resistance in Japanese-controlled Philippines); **The Steel Helmet**, 1951 (Korean War); **Tears of the Sun**, 2003 (Nigerian jungles); **Ten Tall Men**, 1951 (French Foreign Legion); **They Came to Cordura**, 1959 (U.S. Cavalry during the 1916 U.S. incursion into Mexico); They Raid by Night, 1942 (WWII; espionage in Nazi-occupied Norway); **13 Rue Madeleine**, 1947 (WWII; espionage in France); **The Three Musketeers**, 1921 (France during the 100 Years' War); **The Three Musketeers**, 1948 (France during the 100 Years' War); **The Three Musketeers**, 1974 (France during the 100 Years' War); **The Three Musketeers**, 1993 (France during the 100 Years' War); Tobruk, 1967 (WWII; Libyan desert); **Too Late the Hero**, 1970 (WWII; Japanese-held island); **Von Ryan's Express**, 1965 (WWII; escape from a POW camp in Italy); **Where Eagles Dare**, 1969 (WWII; raid on German alpine headquarters); **Windtalkers**, 2002 (WWII; Pacific); **Wings**, 1927 (WWI; pilots crashing behind enemy lines); **The Young Lions**, 1958 (WWII; Germany).

Survival Films (in lifeboats, rafts or sinking vessels): **Abandon Ship!**, 1957 (lifeboat); **Action in the North Atlantic**, 1943 (raft); **The Adventures of Robinson Crusoe**, 1954; The Adventures of Tintin, 2011; **The African Queen**, 1951; **All Is Lost**, 2013 (sailboat at sea); **Arise My Love**, 1940 (lifeboats); Atlantic Adventure, 1935 (lifeboat); Atlantis, 1914; **Beat the Devil**, 1953; **Ben-Hur**, 1959 (raft); Black Island, 1979; The Blue Lagoon, 1949; The Blue Lagoon, 1980; **The Bounty**, 1984

(lifeboat); Britannic, 2000 (made-for-TV); By the Bluest of Seas, 1936 (fishing boat); **Captain Eddie**, 1945 (lifeboat); **Captain Phillips**, 2013; The Chambermaid on the Titanic, 1998 (lifeboats); **Crash Dive**, 1943; **Crusoe**, 1988; Crusoe, 2008-2009 (TV series); Cyclone, 1979 (tour boat); **Dead Calm**, 1989 (yacht); Death Ship, 1980 (floating wreckage); The Devil Pays Off, 1941 (lifeboat); The Disappeared, 2013 (lifeboat); Eight Bells, 1935 (lifeboat); Go-Get-'Em Haines, 1936; **The Heroes of Telemark**, 1965; **The Hurricane**, 1937 (lifeboats; sailboat); **I Love You Again**, 1940 (lifeboat); **In Which We Serve**, 1942 (lifeboat); The Intruder, 1933 (lifeboat); Island Captives, 1937 (lifeboat); The Island of Dr. Moreau, 1977; **Island of Lost Souls**, 1932; **Jaws**, 1975 (fishing boat); **Jaws 2**, 1978 (sailboats); **Juggernaut**, 1974 (lifeboat); Jungle Bride, 1933; King Kong, 1976; **The Land That Time Forgot**, 1988; The Last Survivors, 1975 (made-for-TV); **The Last Voyage**, 1960; The Legend of the Titanic, 1999; **Life of Pi**, 2012 (lifeboat); **Lifeboat**, 1944 (lifeboat); Lt. Robin Crusoe, U.S.N., 1966; Little Robinson Crusoe, 1924; **Lord Jim**, 1965 (lifeboats); The Lost Continent, 1968; Madame Spy, 1942 (lifeboat); Miss Robin Crusoe, 1954; **The Most Dangerous Game**, 1932; **Mutiny on the Bounty**, 1935 (lifeboat); **Mutiny on the Bounty**, 1962 (lifeboat); **A Night to Remember**, 1958 (*Titanic*; lifeboats); **Nim's Island**, 2008; No Greater Love, 1995 (made-for-TV; *Titanic*; lifeboats); Once upon a Honeymoon, 1942 (lifeboat); **Open Water**, 2004; Out to Sea, 1997; **The Poseidon Adventure**, 1972; The Poseidon Adventure, 2005; **Prometheus**, 2012; Regeneration, 1923 (lifeboat); **Road to Rio**, 1947 (raft); Robinson Crusoe, 1927; Robinson Crusoe, 1997; S.O.S. Titanic, 1979 (made-for-TV; lifeboats); Scarlet Seas, 1928; Sea Wife, 1957 (liferaft); The Sea Wolf, 1920 (always at sea); **The Sea Wolf**, 1941 (always at sea); The Sea Wolf, 1971 (TV miniseries; always at sea); The Sea Wolf, 2008 (made-for-TV; always at sea); Seas Beneath, 1931 (lifeboat); Seven Were Saved, 1947 (liferaft); Shout at the Devil, 1976; **Souls at Sea**, 1937 (lifeboat); **The Spy in Black**, 1939 (lifeboats); **Stand by for Action**, 1942; Stranded, 2002 (made-for-TV); Strange Holiday, 1970 (made-for-TV); Swiss Family Robinson, 1940; **Swiss Family Robinson**, 1960; A Talking Picture, 2003; **Titanic**, 1943 (lifeboats); **Titanic**, 1953 (lifeboats); **Titanic**, 1997 (lifeboats); Titanic, 2012 (TV miniseries); Titanic: The Legend Goes On, 2000; **Topper Returns**, 1941; Two Came Back, 1997 (made-for-TV; liferaft); **U-571**, 2000; **Unbroken**, 2014 (liferafts); Under False Colors, 1917 (lifeboat); **The Unsinkable Molly Brown**, 1964 (*Titanic*; lifeboats); Waterworld, 1995; When a Man Loves, 1927; Whom the Gods Destroy, 1934 (lifeboat). Note: For more information on ship sinkings throughout history, see my book *Darkest Hours: A Narrative Encyclopedia of Worldwide Disasters from Ancient Times to the Present* (Nelson-Hall, 1976).

Survival Films (marooned or shipwrecked on an island): The Admirable Crichton, 1918; The Admirable Crichton, 1957; The Admirable Crichton, 1968 (made-for-TV); **The Adventures of Robinson Crusoe**, 1954; The Adventures of Robinson Crusoe, 1964 (TV miniseries); **The Black Pirate**, 1926; **The Black Stallion**, 1979: The Blue Lagoon, 1949; The Blue Lagoon, 1980; Capt. Grant's Family, 1938; Cast Away, 2000; Castaway, 1974 (TV series); Castaway, 1986; Castaway, 2010 (TV series); The Castaways, 2003 (made-for-TV); The Castaways on Gilligan's Island, 1979 (made-for-TV); The Cat Creeps, 1946; **Crusoe**, 1988; **Davy Crockett and the River Pirates**, 1965; Dear Claudia, 1999; **Heaven Knows, Mr. Allison**, 1957 (WWII; Japanese-held island in the Pacific); Everywhere but Here, 2008; For the Term of His Natural Life, 1927; Forbidden Island, 1999 (TV series); Gilligan's Island, 1964-1967 (TV series); Gumnaam, 1965; **Hell in the Pacific**, 1968; In Search of the Castaways, 1962; Island of Desire, 1952; The Island of Dr. Moreau, 1977; The Island of Dr. Moreau, 1996; **Island of Lost Souls**, 1934; Island of Lost Women, 1959; The Isle of Love, 1916; **The Land That Time Forgot**, 1988; The Last Flight of Noah's Ark, 1980; L'enfant d'eau, 1995; Lost, 2004-2010 (TV series); Lost Flight, 1970 (made-for-TV); The Lost Tribe, 2009; Love Wrecked, 2005; Lt. Robin Crusoe,

U.S.N., 1966; Madagascar, 2005; Marooned, 1933; Mercy Island, 1941 (on a Florida key); Miss Castaway and the Island Girls, 2004; Miss Robin Crusoe, 1954; Mr. Robinson Crusoe, 1932; **The Most Dangerous Game**, 1932; **Mutiny on the Bounty**, 1935 (at sea in a lifeboat; island); **Mutiny on the Bounty**, 1962 (at sea in a lifeboat; island); **My Favorite Wife**, 1940; **Mysterious Island**, 1961; Mysterious Island, 2005 (made-for-TV); The New People, 1969-1970 (TV series; island); None but the Brave, 1965; Pirates, 1998; **Pirates of the Caribbean: Curse of the Black Pearl**, 2003; **Pirates of the Caribbean: Dead Man's Chest**, 2006; Rainbow Island, 1944; Rescue from Gilligan's Island, 1978 (made-for-TV); The Return of Chandu, 1934; Return to the Blue Lagoon, 1991; Robinson Crusoe, 1927; Run, Rebecca, Run!, 1981; The Savage Is Loose, 1974; Screamers, 1981; The Sea Lion, 1921; Sea Wife, 1957; Selvaggi, 1995; She Demons, 1958; Shore Acres, 1920; The Show Down, 1917; **Six Days Seven Nights**, 1998; **Son of Kong**, 1933; **Swiss Family Robinson**, 1960; The Tale of Tsar Saltan, 1967; Temptation Island, 1980; Temptation Island, 2011; Treasure Island, 1918; **Treasure Island**, 1934; **Treasure Island**, 1950; Treasure Island, 1972; Treasure Island II, 1999; Welcome to the Jungle, 2013; **We're Not Dressing**, 1934; Wild Women, 1918. Note: For more information on ship sinkings and shipwrecks throughout history, see my book *Darkest Hours: A Narrative Encyclopedia of Worldwide Disasters from Ancient Times to the Present* (Nelson-Hall, 1976).

Survival Films (mountains): **Alive**, 1993 (Andes mountains); **Back from Eternity**, 1956; Five Came Back, 1939; Frozen, 2010; Into Thin Air: Death on Everest, 1997 (made-for-TV; 1997 Mount Everest climbing disaster); **Rocky Mountain**, 1950; Survival Quest, 1989; **The Wall**, 2012.

Survival Films (post-apocalyptic disasters): The Book of Eli, 2010; The Dark Hour, 2007 (ruins after war); The Divide, 2012; I Am Legend, 2007 (virus); On the Beach, 1959 (worldwide nuclear holocaust); The Omega Man, 1971 (worldwide biological warfare); Pandorum, 2009; Panic in the Year Zero!, 1962; **Planet of the Apes**, 1968; **Planets of the Apes**, 2001; Soylent Green, 1973; The Ultimate Warrior, 1976; The World, the Flesh and the Devil, 1959; Z.P.G., 1972.

Survival Films (prehistoric eras): **One Million B.C.**, 1940; One Million Years, B.C., 1966; **Quest for Fire**, 1982; When Dinosaurs Ruled the Earth, 1970; When Women Lost Their Tales, 1972.

Survival Films (space): **Apollo 13**, 1995; **The Black Hole**, 1979; Countdown, 1968; **Destination Moon**, 1950; Doom, 2005 (on Mars); **Gravity**, 2013; **Interstellar**, 2014; **Marooned**, 1969; **Mission to Mars**, 2000; Pitch Black, 2000; Queen of Outer Space, 1958; **Star Trek**, 2009; **Star Trek II: The Wrath of Khan**, 1982; **2001: A Space Odyssey**, 1968; **2010**, 1984; **When Worlds Collide**, 1951.

Survival Films (tsunamis or tidal waves caused by undersea earthquakes): **The Abyss**, 1989; Aftershock, 2012; Akira, 1988; **Atlantis: The Lost Empire**, 2001; Bait, 2012; Bruce Almighty, 2003; **The Day After Tomorrow**, 2004; Deathwave, 2009; End Day, 2005 (made-for-TV); Escape from L.A., 1996; **Godzilla**, 2014; Gorath, 1962; Hereafter, 2010; Himizu, 2014 (based on the 2011 Tohoku earthquake and tsunami); Homeland, 2014 (based on the 2011 Tohoku earthquake and tsunami); Immortals, 2011; **The Impossible**, 2012 (based on the 2004 Indian Ocean tsunami); **Interstellar**, 2014 (tidal waves on a distant planet); Isle of Forgotten Sins, 1943; Japan Sinks, 2006; **Krakatoa, East of Java**, 1969; Land of Hope, 2012 (based on the 2011 Tohoku earthquake and tsunami); **The Last Wave**, 1978; Lost City Raiders, 2008 (made-for-TV); Malibu Shark Attack, 2009 (made-for-TV); Mind Games, 2004; The Omen, 2006; Orange County, 2002; Pirates, 1998; **Pompeii**, 2014; **Ponyo**, 2008; **The Poseidon Adventure**, 1972; Rescue from Gilligan's Island, 1978 (made-for-TV); Reunion, 2013 (based on

the 2011 Tohoku earthquake and tsunami); **San Adreas**, 2015; The Sorcerer and the White Snake, 2013; The Ten Avatars, 2008; Tidal Wave, 1973; Tidal Wave, 2009; Tokyo Fiancée, 2014; **Tomorrowland**, 2015; Tsunami, 2005 (made-for-TV); Tsunami: The Aftermath, 2006 (made-for-cable; based on the 2004 Indian Ocean tsunami); A View to Kill, 1985; Vinyan, 2008; When Dinosaurs Ruled the Earth, 1970; Wonderful Town, 2007. Note: For more information on tsunamis and tidal waves throughout history, see my book *Darkest Hours: A Narrative Encyclopedia of Worldwide Disasters from Ancient Times to the Present* (Nelson-Hall, 1976).

Survival Films (underground): **The Big Carnival** (aka: Ace in the Hole), 1951; Buried, 2010 (buried alive in a coffin); Daylight, 1996 (tunnel); The Incredible Petrified World, 1957; **Journey to the Center of the Earth**, 1959 (underground city of Atlantis); **Journey to the Center of the Earth**, 2008; Sanctum, 2011; **She**, 1935 (world beneath the earth); Warlords of the Deep, 1978 (beneath the bottom of the sea).

Survival Films (wilderness): As Far as My Feet Will Carry Me, 2001 (Siberian wastelands); Castaway on the Moon, 2010; Coast Guard, 1939 (arctic region); Death Hunt, 1981 (Yukon in Canada); **Deliverance**, 1972; Dersu Uzala: The Hunter, 1975; The Edge, 1997; **Far From Home: The Adventures of Yellow Dog**, 1995 (in British Columbia); The Grey, 2011 (Alaska); The Hunted, 2003 (Pacific Northwest); **Into the White**, 2014 (WWII Norway); **Into the Wild**, 2007 (Alaska); **The Naked Jungle**, 1954 (African jungle); **Rabbit-Proof Fence**, 2003 (Australian outback); **The Revenant**, 2015; Sands of the Kalahari, 1965 (Africa); Scenic Route, 2013 (California desert); **Scott of the Antarctic**, 1949 (Antarctic region); Tarzan the Mighty, 1928 (African jungle); **The Way Back**, 2010.

Tanks (in WWII; 1939-1945): **American Guerrilla in the Philippines**, 1950; **Back to Bataan**, 1945; Band of Brothers, 2001 (TV miniseries); Battle of the Bulge, 1965; **The Big Red One**, 1980; **Breakthrough**, 1950; **The Bridge at Remagen**, 1969; **A Bridge Too Far**, 1977; **Burnt By the Sun**, 1994; **Comrade X**, 1940; **Days of Glory**, 2006; The Days of Rage, 2001; **The Desert Fox: The Story of Rommel**, 1951; **The Desert Rats**, 1953; **The Devil's Brigade**, 1968; The Fighting Rats of Tobruk, 1951; **The Fighting Seabees**, 1944; **Five Graves to Cairo**, 1943; **Force of Arms**, 1951; **Fury**, 2014; **The Great Raid**, 2005; **Guadalcanal Diary**, 1943; **Halls of Montezuma**, 1950; **The Hurt Locker**, 2009; Kelly's Heroes, 1970; **The North Star**, 1943; **Patton**, 1970; **Play Dirty**, 1969; Raid on Rommel, 1971; **Sahara**, 1943; Sahara, 1995 (made-for-TV); **Sands of Iwo Jima**, 1949; **Saving Private Ryan**, 1998; Sea of Sand (aka: Desert Patrol), 1961; **The Story of G.I. Joe**, 1945; The Tanks Are Coming, 1951; **To Hell and Back**, 1955; **Tobruk**, 1967; **A Walk in the Sun**, 1945; **Windtalkers**, 2002.

Telegraphers: **Bad Day at Black Rock**, 1955; **Cloak and Dagger**, 1946; **Destination Tokyo**, 1943; **Edison: The Man**, 1940; **Fort Apache**, 1948; **The Great Locomotive Chase**, 1956; **Gunga Din**, 1939; Gunslingers, 1950; **High Noon**, 1952; Last of the Pony Riders, 1953; Love Me Tender, 1956; **A Night to Remember**, 1958 (*Titanic*); **O.S.S.**, 1946; Postal Union, 1937; Renegades of the Sage, 1949; **The Return of Frank James**, 1940; **Return of the Bad Men**, 1948; Rolling Caravans, 1938; **Stagecoach**, 1939; The Telegraph Trail, 1933; **Them!**, 1954; **13 Rue Madeleine**, 1947; Three Desperate Men, 1951; Through the Fog, 1948; The Timber Trail, 1948; **Titanic**, 1943; **Titanic**, 1953; **Titanic**, 1997; **Trail Street**, 1947; **Wake Island**, 1942; **Western Union**, 1941; **Wing and a Prayer**, 1944; **Young Tom Edison**, 1940.

Time Travel: **Back to the Future**, 1985 (past); **Back to the Future Part III**, 1990 (past); **Back to the Future Part II**, 1989 (past); **Berkeley Square**, 1933 (past); **Big**, 1988; **A Christmas Carol**, 1938 (past; future); **The Chronicles of Narnia: Prince Caspian**, 2008; **The Chron-**

icles of Narnia: The Lion, the Witch and the Wardrobe, 2005; **A Connecticut Yankee**, 1931 (past); **A Connecticut Yankee in King Arthur's Court**, 1949 (past); **The Final Countdown**, 1980 (past); **I'll Never Forget You**, 1951 (past); **It's a Wonderful Life**, 1946 (past); **Men in Black III**, 2012 (past); **The Time Machine**, 1960 (future); **The Time Machine**, 2002 (future); **12 Monkeys**, 1995 (past); **Twilight Zone: The Movie**, 1983 (past).

Train Attacks: Al Jennings of Oklahoma, 1951 (robbery in Old West); **The Assassination of Jesse James by the Coward Robert Ford**, 2007 (robbery in Old West); **Butch Cassidy and the Sundance Kid**, 1969 (robbery in Old West); **Dodge City**, 1939 (outlaws attempting to retrieve a captured gang member in Old West); Frank and Jesse, 1995 (robbery in Old West); **Flying Tigers**, 1942 (train attacked from the air during WWII); **The General**, 1926 (military espionage in American Civil War); **The General Died at Dawn**, 1936 (warlord attacks in 1930s China); **The Great Locomotive Chase**, 1956 (military espionage in American Civil War); **The Great Missouri Raid**, 1951 (robbery in Old West); **Jesse James**, 1939 (robbery in Old West); **The Lady Vanishes**, 1938 (espionage, attempt to kidnap an elderly female British spy); **Lawrence of Arabia**, 1962 (military action in WWI); **The Lone Ranger**, 2013 (Indian attack in Old West); **The Long Riders**, 1980 (robbery in Old West); Night Passage, 1957 (robbery in Old West); **Old Gringo**, 1989 (Mexican Revolution); **The Professionals**, 1966 (Mexican Revolution); **Silver Streak**, 1976 (attack against spies who have taken over a passenger train); **The Taking of Pelham One Two Three**, 1974 (taking over a NYC subway train to hold hostages for ransom); **The Taking of Pelham 1 2 3**, 2009 (taking over a NYC subway train to hold hostages for ransom); **Tough Guys**, 1986 (modern-day robbery); The Train Robbers, 1973 (robbery in Old West); **The Train**, 1965 (train bound for Germany with stolen art treasures attacked by French saboteurs); **The Treasure of the Sierra Madre**, 1948 (robbery in Mexico); **Union Pacific**, 1939 (Indian attack in Old West); **Villa Rides**, 1968 (train attacked from the air during Mexican Revolution); **Viva Villa!**, 1934 (Mexican Revolution); **Viva Zapata!**, 1952 (Mexican Revolution); **Von Ryan's Express**, 1965 (train attacked from the air during WWII); **The Wild Bunch**, 1969 (robbery of weapons from U.S. Army).

Train Crashes and Wrecks: Abraham Lincoln: Vampire Hunter, 2012; Amy, 1981; **Arsenal**, 1929 (accident); Atomic Train, 1999 (made-for-TV); Back in Circulation, 1937; **Back to the Future Part III**, 1990; **Batman Begins**, 2005; Battle for the Railway, 1978 (sabotage in WWII); **Beggars of Life**, 1928 (accident); Between Two Women, 1937 (accident); The Big Trees, 1952; The Black Scorpion, 1957; Breakheart Pass, 1975; **The Bridge on the River Kwai**, 1957 (sabotage in WWII; train exploded off trestle); Carnival Boat, 1932; **Carrie**, 1952; The Cassandra Crossing, 1976; Castle in the Sky, 1986; **The Clairvoyant**, 1935 (ability to accurately predict accidents); **Cloak and Dagger**, 1946 (sabotage in WWII); Collision Earth, 2011 (made-for-TV); Crack in the World, 1965; **Crack-Up**, 1946; **The Crime of Monsieur Lange**, 1936; **Crossroads**, 1942; Dangers of the Canadian Mounted, 1948; The Day of the Roses, 1998 (made-for-TV; dramatic inquiry into the Granville train disaster in Sidney, Australia, January 18, 1977. where eighty-three persons were killed and 210 injured); Dick Tracy Returns, 1938 (serial); Dragon Head, 2003 (accident); **Duel in the Sun**, 1946 (sabotage; train exploded off tracks); The Earth Dies Screaming, 1964; Faust, 2000; Fireball, 2009 (made-for-TV); **For Whom the Bell Tolls**, 1943 (sabotage; train exploded off tracks); Four Girls in White, 1939; From Inside, 2008; **The General**, 1926 (collapsing on burning trestle in American Civil War); The Giant Gila Monster, 1959; **Godzilla: King of the Monsters**, 1956; **GoldenEye**, 1995; **The Greatest Show on Earth**, 1952 (sabotage; car blocking tracks causing train to telescope into another); Hancock, 2008; The Hands of Orlac, 1924 (accident); Horror Express, 1972; **How the West Was Won**, 1962; **Hugo**, 2011; The Hurricane Express, 1932 (serial; sabotage); I Want to Forget, 1918; Ice Twisters, 2009

(made-for-TV); **The Invisible Man**, 1933 (sabotage); **The Iron Horse**, 1924 (accident); **Jimmy the Gent**, 1934 (accident); **King Kong**, 1933 (elevated train in NYC destroyed by giant ape); King of the Lumberjacks, 1940; **Kings Row**, 1942 (accident); Lady from Chungking, 1942 (sabotage in WWII); **The Last Command**, 1928; Law of the Timber, 1941; **Lawrence of Arabia**, 1962 (sabotage in WWI; train exploded off tracks); The Local Bad Man, 1932; **The Longest Day**, 1962 (sabotage in WWII; French Resistance fighters exploding train off tracks); **The Lone Ranger**, 2013 (collapsing on destroyed trestle); Look Both Ways, 2005; **Mad Love**, 1935 (accident); The Man Who Found Himself, 1937 (accident); Mrs. Winterbourne, 1996; Murder in the Air, 1940; Murder in the Private Car, 1934; My Parents Are Divorced, 1959; The Mysterious Pilot, 1937 (serial); Naina, 2005 (ability to predict disasters); **No Man of Her Own**, 1950 (accident); North of the Rio Grande, 1937; **Number Seventeen**, 1932; 100 Rifles, 1969; Other Men's Women, 1931 (accident); Pancho Villa, 1972; **Pan's Labyrinth**, 2007; Paradise Express, 1937; Peacock, 2010 (accident); The Phantom's Secret, 1917; The Polar Express, 2004; Priest, 2011; The Promise, 1917; Red Tails, 2008; **Ring of Fire**, 1961; The Rugrats Movie, 1998; Ruler of the Road, 1918 (negligence; engineer falls asleep at the throttle); The Ruling Voice, 1931; The Runaway Express, 1926; **Saratoga Trunk**, 1945; Scotty of the Scouts, 1926; **Secret Agent**, 1936 (accident); **The Senator Was Indiscreet**, 1947; **Sherlock Holmes and the Voice of Terror**, 1942 (sabotage); **Silver Streak**, 1976 (runaway train crashing into Chicago's Union Station); **Skyfall**, 2012; A Slave of Fashion, 1925; **Sleepers West**, 1941 (sabotage); The Sleeping Car, 1990; **Snowpiercer**, 2014; Stormy, 1935; Steele of the Royal Mounted, 1925; Strange Illusion, 1945; The Straight Way, 1916; The Swarm, 1978; **This Land Is Mine**, 1943 (sabotage in WWII); A Thousand to One, 1920; Three Sinners, 1928; Tideland, 2005; The Tornado, 1924; Trader Tom of the China Seas, 1954 (serial); **The Train**, 1965 (sabotage in WWII; runaway train at railroad station in France); Transcontinental Limited, 1926; Troubles of a Bride, 1924; The Turmoil, 1924; Two Women, 1919; Un soir, un train, 1968; **Unbreakable**, 2000 (accident); **Union Pacific**, 1939 (Indian attack wrecks train); Viadukt, 1983 (based on mass murderer and psychopath Sylvestre Matuschka [b. 1892], who blew up several trains in Hungary for sexual gratification, most notably destroying the Orient Express [Vienna Express] on September 13, 1931, killing twenty-two persons and injuring another 120 people; he was sentenced to death, but his sentence was commuted; he escaped from prison in 1944 in WWII and was never again seen); **Viva Zapata!**, 1952 (sabotage; train exploded off tracks in Mexican Revolution of 1910-1920); Wanted, 2008; When the Wind Blows, 1986; The Whip, 1917; Whispering Smith, 1916 (accident and sabotage); Whispering Smith, 1926 (accident and sabotage); **Whispering Smith**, 1948 (accident and sabotage); **The Young in Heart**, 1938 (accident); Zombies of the Stratosphere, 1952. Note: For more information on train crashes throughout history, see my book *Darkest Hours: A Narrative Encyclopedia of Worldwide Disasters from Ancient Times to the Present* (Nelson-Hall, 1976).

Train Stations: **An Affair to Remember**, 1957 (New York's Penn Station); Amateur, 1994 (New York's Grand Central Station); **Anna Karenina**, 1935; **Anna Karenina**, 1948; **Anna Karenina**, 2012; Arthur, 2011 (New York's Grand Central Station); Bad Company, 2002; Bhowani Junction, 1956; **Blade Runner**, 1982 (Los Angeles' Union Station); **Brief Encounter**, 1945; Broken City, 2013 (New York's Grand Central Station); **Bugsy**, 1991 (Los Angeles' Union Station); Carlito's Way, 1993 (New York's Grand Central Station); **Catch Me If You Can**, 2002; **Central Station**, 1998 (Rio de Janeiro); Chain Reaction, 1996 (Chicago's Union Station); **The Clock**, 1945 (New York's Penn Station); The Code, 2009 (New York's Grand Central Station); **The Cotton Club**, 1984 (New York's Grand Central Station); Dead Men Don't Wear Plaid, 1982 (Los Angeles' Union Station); Dear Heart, 1964 (New York's Penn Station); Drag Me to Hell, 2009 (Los Angeles' Union Station); Duplicity, 2009 (New York's Grand Central Station); **Eternal**

Sunshine of the Spotless Mind, 2004 (New York's Grand Central Station); Extreme Measures, 1996 (New York's Grand Central Station); Falling in Love, 1984 (New York's Grand Central Station); The Fisher King, 1991 (New York's Grand Central Station); **Flags of Our Fathers**, 2006 (Chicago's Union Station); **The Freshman**, 1990 (New York's Grand Central Station); **Friends with Benefits**, 2011 (New York's Grand Central Station); Gable and Lombard, 1976 (Los Angeles' Union Station); **Gaily, Gaily**, 1969 (Chicago's LaSalle Street Station); **Gandhi**, 1982; **Grand Central Murder**, 1942 (New York's Grand Central Station); Hackers, 1995 (New York's Grand Central Station); **The House on Carroll Street**, 1988 (New York's Grand Central Station); In the Mood, 1987 (Los Angeles' Union Station); Just My Luck, 2006 (New York's Grand Central Station); The Killer That Stalked New York, 1950 (New York's Penn Station); Killer's Kiss, 1955 (New York's Penn Station); **Knight without Armor**, 1937 (remote station in Russia); **Man of Steel**, 2013 (Chicago's Union Station); **Men in Black II**, 2002 (New York's Grand Central Station); **Midnight Run**, 1988 (New York's Grand Central Station); **Mr. Holmes**, 2015; **Murder on the Orient Express**, 1974 (Istanbul); My Best Friend's Wedding, 1997 (Chicago's Union Station); **North by Northwest**, 1959 (New York's Grand Central Station to Chicago's LaSalle Street Station); Old Dogs, 2009 (New York's Grand Central Station); **The Out of Towners**, 1970 (New York's Grand Central Station); **The Palm Beach Story**, 1942 (New York's Penn Station); **Pearl Harbor**, 2001 (Los Angeles' Union Station); **Pride of the Marines**, 1945; **The Prince of Tides**, 1991 (New York's Grand Central Station); **Public Enemies**, 2009 (Chicago's Union Staton); Reign Over Me, 2007 (New York's Grand Central Station); Revolutionary Road, 2008 (New York's Grand Central Station); **The Seven Year Itch**, 1955 (New York's Penn Station); A Shock to the System, 1990 (New York's Grand Central Station); **The Silver Streak**, 1976 (Los Angeles' Union Station; later crashes into Chicago's Union Station); **Spellbound**, 1945 (New York's Penn Station); State of Grace, 1990 (New York's Grand Central Station); **Strangers on a Train**, 1951 (New York's Penn Station); **Superman**, 1978 (New York's Grand Central Station); **Sweet Charity**, 1969 (New York's Grand Central Station); The Switch, 2010 (New York's Grand Central Station); Tadpole, 2000 (New York's Grand Central Station); **The Taking of Pelham 1 2 3**, 2009 (New York's Grand Central Station); **The Thin Man Goes Home**, 1945 (New York's Grand Central Station); **To Live and Die in L.A.**, 1985 (Los Angeles' Union Station); **The Train**, 1965 (Paris, France and many other stations); Under the Rainbow, 1981 (Los Angeles' Union Station); Unfaithful, 2002; **Union Depot**, 1932; **Union Station**, 1950 (Los Angeles); **The Untouchables**, 1987 (shootout in Chicago's Union Station); **The Way We Were**, 1973 (Los Angeles' Union Station); Winter's Tale, 2014; **You're a Big Boy Now**, 1966 (New York's Penn Station).

Trapeze Artists: Alegria, 1999; **Annie Get Your Gun**, 1950; **The Aristocats**, 1970; The Big Cage, 1933; Big Top Pee-Wee, 1988; The Biggest Robbery Never Told, 2002; Charlie Chan at the Circus, 1936; **The Circus**, 1928; Circus Girl, 1937; Circus of Horrors, 1960; **Circus World**, 1964; Comrade Kim Goes Flying, 2012; **Dante's Inferno**, 1935; The Dark Tower, 1943; Das Schlangenei, 1978; Fire-Eater, 1998; 4 Devils, 1928; **Freaks**, 1932; The Girl of Your Dreams, 1988; Gorilla at Large, 1954; **The Greatest Show on Earth**, 1952; Homicide for Three, 1948; **I'm No Angel**, 1933; It's Easier for a Camel…, 2004; Las Vegas Lady, 1975; Madagascar 3: Europe's Most Wanted, 2012; The Master Touch, 1974; O'Shaughnessy's Boy, 1935; **Pandora's Box**, 1929; Phantom of the Rue Morgue, 1954; Polly of the Circus, 1932; Seven Murders for Scotland Yard, 1971; **The Story of Three Loves**, 1953; Strike Me Pink, 1936; **Thirteen Women**, 1932; Trapeze, 1932; **Trapeze**, 1956; Trigger, Jr., 1950; Tsirk, 1936; **Two Tickets to Broadway**, 1951; Undiscovered, 2005; **Van Helsing**, 2004; **Variety**, 1925; **Water for Elephants**, 2011; When Night Is Falling, 1995; **Wings of Desire**, 1988.

Trapped Human Beings (in caves, in ruined, bombed-out or locked base-ment buildings, aboard sinking ships): **Action in the North Atlantic**, 1943 (inside a cabin with a buckled door on a sinking ship); **The Big Carnival**, 1951 (cave); **Blockade**, 1938 (bombed-out building); **Counter-Attack**, 1945 (bombed-out building); **Foreign Correspondent**, 1940 (inside a shot-down airplane sinking at sea); **It's a Mad, Mad, Mad, Mad World**, 1963 (locked store basement); **Journey to the Center of the Earth**, 1959 (underground chambers); **Journey to the Center of the Earth**, 2008 (underground chambers); **King Solomon's Mines**, 1950 (treasure cave); **The Last Voyage**, 1960 (wedged by wreckage on a sinking ship); **The Tin Star**, 1957 (cave); **Titanic**, 1997 (handcuffed to a pipe on sinking ship); **True Grit**, 1969 (inside a snakepit).

Trench Warfare (WWI): **All Quiet on the Western Front**, 1930; All Quiet on the Western Front, 1979 (made-for-TV); Behind the Lines, 1997; The Better 'Ole, 1926 (Western Front); **The Big Parade**, 1925 (Western Front); **Blockheads**, 1938 (Western Front); **The Blue Max**, 1966 (Western Front); Company K, 2004 (Western Front); **Doctor Zhivago**, 1965 (Eastern Front); **A Farewell to Arms**, 1932 (Italian Front); **A Farewell to Arms**, 1957 (Italian Front); The Fear, 2015 (Western Front); **The Fighting 69th**, 1940 (Western Front); Fraulein Doktor, 1969 (Western Front); **Gallipoli**, 1981 (Turkish Front); Heroes for Sale, 1933 (Western Front); **Joan the Woman**, 1916 (Western Front); **Journey's End**, 1930 (Western Front); **Joyeux Noel**, 2005 (Western Front); **The Lighthorsemen**, 1988 (Turkish Front); The Lost Batallion, 2001 (made-for-TV; Western Front); Many Years Ago, 1970 (Western Front); **My Son, My Son!**, 1940 (Western Front); **Noah's Ark**, 1928 (Western Front); **Passchendaele**, 2008 (Western Front); **Paths of Glory**, 1957 (Western Front); The Patriots, 1933 (Eastern Front); **Random Harvest**, 1942 (Western Front); **The Road to Glory**, 1936 (Western Front); **Sergeant York**, 1941 (Western Front); Shock Troop, 1934 (Western Front); **Shoulder Arms**, 1918 (Western Front); The Trench, 1999; **12 Monkeys**, 1995 (Western Front); 21 Brothers, 2011 (Western Front); **Two Arabian Knights**, 1927 (Western Front); A Very Long Engagement, 2004; **War Horse**, 2011 (Western Front); **Westfront 1918**, 1931; **What Price Glory**, 1926 (Western Front); **What Price Glory**, 1952 (Western Front); **Wings**, 1927 (Western Front); **Wooden Crosses**, 1932 (Western Front).

Truck Drivers and Trucks: **All Quiet on the Western Front**, 1930; **Back to Bataan**, 1945; **Beverly Hills Cop**, 1984; **Bicycle Thieves**, 1949; **The Big Parade**, 1925; Big Trouble in Little China, 1986; **Black Hawk Down**, 2001; The Blind Side, 2009; **Brazil**, 1985; **Breakdown**, 1997; Breaker! Breaker!, 1977; **The Castle**, 1997; **Catch-22**, 1970; Charlie and the Chocolate Factory, 2005; **The Dark Knight Rises**, 2012; **Dark Passage**, 1947; **The Desert Rats**, 1953; **Downfall**, 2004; Duel, 1971 (made-for-TV); **Empire of the Sun**, 1987; **The English Patient**, 1996; Equilibrium, 2002; The Fast and the Furious, 2001; **The Grapes of Wrath**, 1940; **The Great Debaters**, 2007; **The Great Escape**, 1963; **Home Alone**, 1990; **Hotel Rwanda**, 2004; **I Am a Fugitive from a Chain Gang**, 1932; **The Impossible**, 2012; Inside Man, 2006; **Insomnia**, 1997; **Interstellar**, 2014; **Into the Wild**, 2007; **It's a Mad, Mad, Mad, Mad World**, 1963; **Jarhead**, 2005; Joy Ride, 2001; **Lawrence of Arabia**, 1962; **License to Kill**, 1989; **Lonely Are the Brave**, 1962; **Mad Max**, 1980; **Mad Max: Fury Road**, 2015; **Man of Steel**, 2013; The Matrix, 1999; **Midnight Express**, 1978; **Midnight Run**, 1988; The Motorcycle Diaries, 2004; **Night of the Living Dead**, 1968; **One Hundred and One Dalmatians**, 1961; **Open City**, 1946; **The Perks of Being a Wallflower**, 2012; **Play Dirty**, 1969; Red Ball Express, 1952; **The Road**, 2009; **The Roaring Twenties**, 1939; **Rust and Bone**, 2012; **Saboteur**, 1942; **The St. Valentine's Day Massacre**, 1967; Smoky and the Bandit, 1977; Smoky and the Bandit II, 1980; **Sorcerer**, 1977; **The Southerner**, 1945; Spider-Man 3, 2007; **Tea with Mussolini**, 1999; **They Drive by Night**, 1940; **Thieves' Highway**, 1949; **Tobruk**, 1967; **Transformers**, 2007; The Unbearable Lightness of Being, 1988; **The Wages of Fear**, 1955; **The Wagons Roll at Night**,

1941; War Dogs, 2016; **The War of the Worlds**, 1953; **War of the Worlds**, 2005; You Can't Escape Forever, 1942.

Tuberculosis: **Alfie**, 1966; All Mine to Give, 1957; America America, 1963; ...And the Earth Did Not Swallow Him, 1995; Ask the Dust, 2006; **At Play in the Fields of the Lord**, 1991; **Australia**, 2008; Bel Ami, 2012; **The Bells of St. Mary's**, 1945; Bethune: The Making of a Hero, 1990; **Bram Stoker's Dracula**, 1992; A Brief Vacation, 1973; Bright Star, 2009; Broken Promise, 2009; Butley, 1974; **Camille**, 1937; **Chicago Deadline**, 1949; Chief Crazy Horse, 1955; **Chocolat**, 2000; **The Citadel**, 1938; The Cloud-Capped Star, 1960; **Confessions of Boston Blackie**, 1941; **The Constant Gardener**, 2005; **The Counterfeiters**, 2008; **Dawn at Socorro**, 1954; **Days of Heaven**, 1978; **DeLovely**, 2004; **Detour**, 1945; The Devil's Backbone, 2001; **Diary of a Chambermaid**, 1964; Diary of a Chambermaid, 2015; **Diary of a Country Priest**, 1964; **Dr. Ehrlich's Magic Bullet**, 1940; The Doctor's Dilemma, 1958; **Drunken Angel**, 1948; **The End of the Affair**, 1999; Fight Club, 1999; **Fires on the Plain**, 1962; **Frontier Marshal**, 1939; Good, 2008; **Gunfight at the O.K. Corral**, 1957; Gunfire, 1950; **Heavenly Creatures**, 1994; **Hold Back the Dawn**, 1941; Honkytonk Man, 1982; Hot Blood, 1956; **Hour of the Gun**, 1967; **The Immigrant**, 2014; Infinity, 1996; Kafka, 1991; La Boheme, 1926; **Les Misérables**, 1935; **Les Misérables**, 1952; **Les Misérables**, 1992; **Les Misérables**, 1998; **Les Misérables**, 2012; **Long Day's Journey into Night**, 1962; Levity, 2003; Lisa, 2001; Long Live Death, 1971; **Lost Horizon**, 1937; **A Man Called Peter**, 1955; The Man Who Knew Infinity, 2015; The Man Who Played God, 1932; **Map of the Human Heart**, 1993; **Midnight Cowboy**, 1969; **The Miracle of the Bells**, 1948; **Moliere**, 2007; **Moulin Rouge**, 1952; Moulin Rouge, 2001; **The Murderers among Us**, 1948; **My Darling Clementine**, 1946; My Neighbor Totoro, 1988; The Necessities of Life, 2008; **The Nun's Story**, 1959; **Of Human Bondage**, 1934; **Only the Valiant**, 1951; Other Men's Women, 1931; Outside the Law, 2010; The Phantom Carriage, 1921; The Phantom Wagon, 1939; Priest of Love, 1981; The Puppetmaster, 1993; Ravenous, 1999; **Rififi**, 1956; Same Old Song, 1997; Scandal, 1950; School for Love, 1955; The Sicilian, 1987; The Sins of the Children, 1930; The Snow Walker, 2003; **The Song of Bernadette**, 1943; Street of Shame, 1956; **Sunshine**, 2000; **There Will Be Blood**, 2007; **This Property Is Condemned**, 1966; **Three Comrades**, 1938; **Three Godfathers**, 1936; 3 Seasons in Hell, 2009; **Tombstone**, 1993; **Trio**, 1950; **Two English Girls**, 1972; **The Wind Rises**, 2014; Winter's Tale, 2014; **Wyatt Earp**, 1994.

Twins (and lookalikes; also see Dual Roles, this index): The Ace of Scotland Yard, 1929; **Adam and Evil**, 1927; Adaptation, 2002; Adolf Armstarke, 1937; Adventures of Texas Jack, 1934; Ali Baba Goes to Town, 1937; **Alice in Wonderland**, 1933; **Alice in Wonderland**, 1951; **Alice in Wonderland**, 2010; Alien 3, 1992; Among the Living, 1941; Angels and Insects, 1996; Anna the Adventuress, 1920; The Arizona Cyclone, 1928; Around the World in 80 Days, 2004; Atom Man vs. Superman, 1950; **Back to the Future Part III**, 1990; Bad Company, 2002; Bad Man from Red Butte, 1940; Bad Man of Deadwood, 1941; The Baron's African War, 1966 (made-for-TV; repackaging of Republic's 1943 serial "Secret Service in Darkest Africa"); Barry McKenzie Holds His Own, 1974; **The Beast of the City**, 1932; Before Night Falls, 2000; **Berkeley Square**, 1933; Bicentennial Man, 1999; Big Calibre, 1935; The Big Show, 1936; Bikini Beach, 1964; Billy the Kid Returns, 1938; Black Bandit, 1938; Black Is White, 1920; **Black Magic**, 1949; The Black Room, 1935; Black Waters, 1929; Blake of Scotland Yard, 1937; Blazing Across the Pecos, 1948; Blazing the Western Trail, 1945; A Blind Bargain, 1922; Blueprint, 2003; Bonanza Town, 1951; Born to Gamble, 1935; Both Barrels Blazing, 1945; Brazil, 1944; Breed of the Sea, 1926; Brenda Starr, Reporter, 1945; Brothers, 1930; Bruce Gentry, 1949; **Bullitt**, 1968; Buried Treasure, 1921; **Callaway Went Thataway**, 1951; Canadian Mounties vs. Atomic Invaders, 1953; Captain America, 1944;

Captain America, 1979 (made-for-TV); Captain America, 1990; Carolina Blues, 1944; **Casualties of War**, 1989; **Cat Ballou**, 1965; Chaplin, 1992; Chatterbox, 1943; The Cheerful Fraud, 1926; The Chinese Cat, 1944; **A Chump at Oxford**, 1940; The Circus Clown, 1934; **City Slickers II: The Legend of Curly's Gold**, 1994; A Close Call for Boston Blackie, 1946; Cobra Woman, 1944; The Cobra Strikes, 1948; Coffee and Cigarettes, 2004; Conceiving Ada, 1997; Confessions of a Vice Baron, 1943; The Conquerors, 1932; Constantine, 2005; Copacabana, 1947; Corpus Christi Bandits, 1945; **The Corsican Brothers**, 1941; **Cover Girl**, 1944; Covered Wagon Days, 1940; Crime Doctor's Man Hunt, 1946; Crime Over London, 1936; Crimes at the Dark House, 1940; Cuban Fireball, 1951; Custer's Last Stand, 1936; Daredevils of the Red Circle, 1939; The Daring Young Man, 1942; The Dark Half, 1993; The Dark Mirror, 1920; **The Dark Mirror**, 1946; Dark Streets, 1929; A Date with the Falcon, 1942; Dave, 1993; Dead Again, 1991; Dead Men Walk, 1943; Dead Ringer, 1964; Dead Ringers, 1988; Deadwood Dick, 1940; Deceptions, 1985 (made-for-TV); The Desert Hawk, 1944; The Desert Horseman, 1946; **Django Unchained**, 2012; **Don Q: Son of Zorro**, 1925; Don Ricardo Returns, 1946; Don't Get Personal, 1942; Double, Double, Toil and Trouble, 1993 (made-for-TV); Double Impact, 1991; **Dracula**, 1992; The Drifter, 1944; The Driftin' Kid, 1941; Duplicate, 1998; Eadie Was a Lady, 1945; Echo, 1997 (made-for-TV); **Enemy**, 2014; England Made Me, 1973; Equinox, 1992; The Errand Boy, 1961; **Fahrenheit 451**, 1966; False Face, 1977; The Far Side of the Moon, 2005; The Fighting Frontiersman, 1946; The Fighting Renegade, 1939; **Folies Bergere**, 1935; The Forbidden City, 1918; The Forbidden Street, 1949; Four Mothers, 1941; Freddie Steps Out, 1946; Frontier Gunlaw, 1946; Fugitive at Large, 1939; Fugitive from Sonora, 1943; Galloping Thunder, 1946; The Gay Deceiver, 1926; The Gay Vagabond, 1941; Genealogies of a Crime, 1998; Get That Man, 1935; Ghost of Zorro, 1949; The Ghosts of Yesterday, 1918; The Girl Without a Soul, 1917; G-Men Never Forget, 1948; God's Gun, 1976; Gold Dust Gertie, 1931; **The Great Dictator**, 1940; **The Great Race**, 1965; The Green Archer, 1940; Gunfire, 1950; Gunning for Vengeance, 1946; The Hawk of Wild River, 1952; Heading West, 1946; The Hell of Frankenstein, 1960; Her Splendid Folly, 1933; **Here Come the Waves**, 1944; His Brother's Ghost, 1945; History of the World: Part I, 1981; Hit and Run, 1957; **House of Numbers**, 1957; House of Terror, 1973; **I'll Never Forget You**, 1951; In His Brother's Place, 1919; The Indians Are Coming, 1930; Irish Luck, 1925; **It Came from Outer Space**, 1953; Jesse James at Bay, 1941; Joe Palooka Meets Humphrey, 1950; Joy of Living, 1938; Junction City, 1952; Just Suppose, 1926; Kaminey: The Scoundrels, 2009; The Kid from Amarillo, 1951; King of the Bullwhip, 1950; A Kiss Before Dying, 1993; Kissin' Cousins, 1964; **The Krays**, 1990; La Conga Nights, 1940; Lady of the Night, 1925; Landrush, 1946; The Last Days of Boot Hill, 1947; The Last Starfighter, 1984; Law and Order, 1942; Lawless Breed, 1946; **The Lawless Breed**, 1953; Lawless Empire, 1945; The Lawless Rider, 1954; Leaves of Grass, 2009; **Les Misérables**, 1935; **Les Misérables**, 1952; **Les Misérables**, 1995; **Les Misérables**, 1998; Les Misérables, 2000 (TV miniseries); Lightning Guns, 1950; Lights of Old Broadway, 1925; **Liquid Sky**, 1982; **Little Lord Fauntleroy**, 1921; Little Miss Broadway, 1938; The Lizzie McGuire Movie, 2003; The Lone Hand Texan, 1947; The Lone Ranger Rides Again, 1939; Lonely Wives, 1931; The Long Shadow, 1992; Lord of the Flies, 1963; **The Love Bug**, 1968; Make Mine a Double, 1961; **The Man in the Iron Mask**, 1939; **The Man in the Iron Mask**, 1998; **The Man Who Loved Redheads**, 1955; Manhattan Moon, 1935; Man's Country, 1938; Marked for Death, 1990; Marriage in Transit, 1925; **Mary Poppins**, 1964; Mary Reilly, 1996; Mask of Death, 1996; The Masked Pirate, 1949; Maximum Risk, 1996; Mexican Spitfire's Elephant, 1942; The Million Dollar Dollies, 1918; Miss V from Moscow, 1942; **Mistaken**, 2013; Mr. Lemon of Orange, 1931; Mr. Murder, 1998 (made-for-TV); Model Behavior, 2000 (made-for-TV); Modesty Blaise, 1966; The Mosquito Coast, 1986; Mother Night, 1996; Murder by Television, 1935; **Murder He Says**, 1945; **Nazi Agent**, 1942; Now or

Never, 1935; Obsession, 1976; Om Shanti Om, 2007; **On the Riviera**, 1951; The One, 2001; One Touch of Venus, 1948; The Other Me, 2000 (made-for-TV); Outlaw Treasure, 1955; Outlaws of Santa Fe, 1944; Outlaws of the Rockies, 1945; **The Parent Trap**, 1961; **The Parent Trap**, 1998; Partners in Crime, 1928; The Persuader, 1957; **Peter Pan**, 1953; The Phantom, 1943; The Phantom Cowboy, 1935; Phantom Patrol, 1936; The Phantom Rider, 1946; Phantom Valley, 1948; Pioneers of the West, 1940; **Pocahontas**, 1995; Port Said, 1948; Prairie Raiders, 1947; Prairie Rustlers, 1945; **Prem Ratan Dhan Payo**, 2015; **The Prince and the Pauper**, 1937; **The Prince of Tides**, 1991; **The Prisoner of Zenda**, 1922; **The Prisoner of Zenda**, 1937; **The Prisoner of Zenda**, 1952; **The Purple Rose of Cairo**, 1985; Redline, 1997; Renegades of the Sage, 1948; Replicant, 2001; The Return of Daniel Boone, 1941; The Return of the Durango Kid, 1945; Riders of the Lone Star, 1947; Rim of the Canyon, 1949; The River Pirates, 1988; Riverboat Rhythm, 1946; River's End, 1940; Road to Paradise, 1930; Romance of the Rio Grande, 1941; **The Saint's Double Trouble**, 1940; Schizopolis, 1997; Scouts to the Rescue, 1939; A Scream in the Night, 1935; Sealed Lips, 1942; Secret Agent X-9, 1937; The Secret Code, 1942; The Secret of Treasure Island, 1938; Secret Service in Darkest Africa, 1943 (serial); Secrets of Scotland Yard, 1944; Separated by Murder, 1994 (made-for-TV); The Shadow Returns, 1946; She Gets Her Man, 1945; Shooting High, 1940; The Sickle or the Cross, 1949; The 6th Day, 2000; Sky Raiders, 1941; Slap Shot, 1977; Slightly Scandalous, 1946; Smart Politics, 1948; So I Married an Axe Murderer, 1993; So You Won't Talk, 1940; **The Social Network**, 2010; Son of a Badman, 1949; The Son of Dr. Jekyll, 1951; **The Son of the Sheik**, 1926; Son of Zorro, 1947; Special Effects, 1984; Speed to Spare, 1937; The Sphinx, 1933; The Spider Returns, 1941; The Spider's Web, 1938; **The Spiderwick Chronicles**, 2008; Spy Smasher, 1942; Stars Over Texas, 1946; **Start the Revolution Without Me**, 1970; **Stella Maris**, 1918; **A Stolen Life**, 1946; The Strange Death of Adolf Hitler, 1943; Sunset in El Dorado, 1945; The Sunset Legion, 1928; Superman, 1948; Swing Out, Sister, 1945; Swing It, Soldier, 1941; The Tabasco Kid, 1932; **A Tale of Two Cities**, 1935; **A Tale of Two Cities**, 1958; A Tale of Two Cities, 1980 (made-for-TV); Tango & Cash, 1989; **Tanu Weds Manu Returns**, 2015; Teenage Mutant Ninja Turtles, 1990; Texas Dynamo, 1950; **Thank Your Lucky Stars**, 1943; A Thousand Elephants, 2008; **The Time Machine**, 1960; The Tioga Kid, 1948; Tom and Thomas, 2002; The Tomb of Ligeia, 1964; Tombstone Terror, 1935; Trail of Terror, 1943; **Trail Street**, 1947; Trail to Laredo, 1948; Trapped in Tia Juana, 1932; **The Truman Show**, 1998; Tumbledown Ranch in Arizona, 1941; Twice Blessed, 1945; Twin Dragons, 1992; **Two-Faced Woman**, 1941; Two-Fisted Stranger, 1946; Two Gun Sheriff, 1941; Two Sisters, 1929; Under California Stars, 1948; **Vertigo**, 1958; The Vigilante: Fighting Hero of the West, 1947; Watch the Birdie, 1950; West of Sonora, 1948; Westwind, 2011; Wheel of Chance, 1928; While the Patient Slept, 1935; Whirlwind Raiders, 1948; **Whistling in Dixie**, 1942; White Comanche, 1968; **The White Shadow**, 1924; **The Whole Town's Talking**, 1935; The Wife of General Ling, 1938; Wild Horse Rustlers, 1943; **Windwalker**, 1980; **The Woman in White**, 1948; **Wonder Man**, 1945; The Wonderful Adventure, 1915; **Wyoming**, 1947; Zorro Rides Again, 1937.

Typhoons (cyclones; also see Hurricanes, this index): **The Adventures of Robinson Crusoe**, 1954; **The Caine Mutiny**, 1954; Captain China, 1950; China Clipper, 1936; **China Seas**, 1935; **Crusoe**, 1989; **The Day After Tomorrow**, 2004; Dearest, 2012; Deluge, 1933; Devil Ship, 1947; Eight Bells, 1935; Ferry to Hong Kong, 1959; Hell-Ship Morgan, 1936; Her Jungle Love, 1938; Iisa, 2015; Island Wives, 1922; None But the Grave, 1965; Perils of Pauline, 1933 (serial); **Reap the Wild Wind**, 1942; Robinson Crusoe, 1997; Sea Horses, 1926; The Sea Is Watching, 2002; Still the Water, 2014; Trap, 2015; **Typhoon**, 1940; Typhoon Club, 1985; **White Shadows in the South Seas**, 1928; A Woman There Was, 1919. Note: For more information on typhoons throughout history, see my book *Darkest Hours: A Narrative Encyclopedia of Worldwide Disasters from Ancient Times to the Present* (Nelson-Hall, 1976).

U.S. Presidents: **Abe Lincoln in Illinois**, 1940; **Abraham Lincoln**, 1930; **Absolute Power**, 1997; **Advise and Consent**, 1962; **Air Force One**, 1997; **All the President's Men**, 1976 (Richard Nixon); **The American President**, 1995; **Amistad**, 1997 (John Quincy Adams; Martin Van Buren); **Being There**, 1979; **The Best Man**, 1964; **The Buccaneer**, 1938 (Andrew Jackson); **Buffalo Bill**, 1944 (Theodore Roosevelt); **Drumbeat**, 1954 (U.S. Grant); **Escape from the Planet of the Apes**, 1971; **Fail Safe**, 1964; **The Far Horizons**, 1955 (Thomas Jefferson); **Forrest Gump**, 1994; **Frost/Nixon**, 2008 (Richard Nixon); **Gabriel over the White House**, 1933; **Guarding Tess**, 1994; **Hoover**, 2000; **In the Line of Fire**, 1993; **Independence Day**, 1996; **J. Edgar**, 2011 (Franklin D. Roosevelt; Dwight D. Eisenhower; Richard Nixon); **JFK**, 1991 (John F. Kennedy); **Lincoln**, 2012; **MacArthur**, 1977 (Franklin D. Roosevelt; Harry Truman); **Man of Conquest**, 1939 (Andrew Jackson); **Mars Attacks!**, 1996; **Nixon**, 1995 (Richard Nixon); **The Omen**, 1976; **Our Man Flint**, 1966; **Pearl Harbor**, 2001 (Franklin D. Roosevelt); **The Pelican Brief**, 1993; **The President's Lady**, 1953 (Andrew Jackson); **The Prisoner of Shark Island**, 1936 (Abraham Lincoln); **The Private Files of J. Edgar Hoover**, 1977 (Franklin D. Roosevelt; John F. Kennedy; Lyndon B. Johnson); **The Remarkable Andrew**, 1942 (Andrew Jackson); **The Right Stuff**, 1983; **Silver Dollar**, 1932 (Chester A. Arthur); **Sunrise at Campobello**, 1960 (Franklin D. Roosevelt); **Tennessee Johnson**, 1942 (Andrew Johnson); **They Died with Their Boots On**, 1941 (U.S. Grant); **This Is My Affair**, 1937 (William McKinley; Theodore Roosevelt); **Virginia City**, 1940 (Abraham Lincoln); **Wag the Dog**, 1997; **Wilson**, 1944 (Woodrow Wilson); **The Wind and the Lion**, 1975 (Theodore Roosevelt); **Yankee Doodle Dandy**, 1942 (Franklin D. Roosevelt); **Young Mr. Lincoln**, 1939 (Abraham Lincoln).

Undercover Agents (law enforcement; also see Incognito): Airheads, 1994; American Ganster, 2007 (police mole inside drug cartel operated by black criminal mastermind); **Appointment with Danger**, 1951 (U.S. postal inspector goes undercover to trap thieves); Arizona Raiders, 1965 (former Quantrill riders join Arizona rangers to trap fellow guerrillas); **Batman Begins**, 2005; **The Beast of the City**, 1932 (police detective joins gang to expose its operations); **Beverly Hills Cop**, 1984 (Detroit cop penetrates L.A. drug ring); Beverly Hills Cop III, 1994; Beverly Hills Cop II, 1987; Blood In, Blood Out, 1993; **Border Incident**, 1949 (federal agent goes undercover to expose illegal immigrant smugglers); Brick Mansions, 2014; Brooklyn's Finest, 2009; Bulletproof, 1996; Cop Out, 2010; **The Departed**, 2006 (police detective and mole in police department try to locate each other while participating in criminal operations in South Boston); Desert Patrol, 1938 (ranger goes undercover to arrest criminals); District B13, 2006; The Eagle's Brood, 1935 (Hopalong Cassidy goes undercover to find killer); Eastern Promises, 2007; The Fast and the Furious, 2001 (cop goes undercover to solve truck robberies); Fast & Furious, 2009 (cop goes undercover to smash drug smugglers); Fighting Frontier, 1943 (undercover lawman); **The French Connection**, 1971; Frontier Feud, 1945 (U.S. marshals go undercover to solve murders); Gangland Undercover, 2015 (TV miniseries; drug dealer becomes undercover agent to capture drug offenders); **Gangster Squad**, 2013 (LAPD officers infiltrate gang run by Mickey Cohen in 1949); Gone in Sixty Seconds, 2000; **House of Bamboo**, 1955 (U.S. Army agent goes undercover by joining criminal gang in Tokyo, Japan, to solve murders); Incognito, 1958 (FBI agent acts as consul in France while tracking counterfeiters of U.S. dollars); Infernal Affairs, 2002; Jump Street, 2012 (cops infiltrate high school); Kindergarten Cop, 1990 (cop becomes kindergarten teacher to expose drug ring); Last Days of Boot Hill, 1947 (Treasury agents go undercover to find stolen money); The Last Stagecoach West, 1957 (special agent goes undercover to capture outlaws); Lawless Empire, 1945; **Lethal Weapon**, 1987; **Lethal Weapon 4**, 1998; **Lethal Weapon 3**, 1992; **Lethal Weapon 2**, 1989;

Let's Be Cops, 2014 (two men faking cops pursue criminals); The Lone Hand Texan, 1947 (man goes undercover to aid wildcatter); The Lost Trail, 1945 (U.S. marshal goes undercover to solve robberies); Man of Evil, 1948; Marked for Murder, 1945 (Texas Rangers go undercover to stop range war); Memento, 2001 (ex-insurance investigator goes after his wife's killers); Miami Vice, 1984-1990 (TV series); **The Mob**, 1951 (police detective disguises himself as longshoreman to expose waterfront crime); The Mod Squad, 1968-1973 (TV series); Mountain Justice, 1930 (man goes undercover to find his father's killer); New Jack City, 1991; Point Break, 1991 (cop goes undercover to capture bank robbers); Police Academy, 1984; Police Academy 5; Assignment: Miami Beach, 1988; Police Academy 4: Citizens on Patrol, 1987; Police Academy 3: Back in Training, 1986; Police Academy 2: Their First Assignment, 1985; Powder River Rustlers, 1949 (railroad agent goes undercover to locate abducted man); Prairie Raiders, 1947 (man goes undercover to expose land-grabbing scheme); **The Private Life of Sherlock Holmes**, 1970; The Raid: Redemption, 2011; The Raid 2, 2014; Red River Renegades, 1946 (postal inspectors go undercover to solve robberies); **Reservoir Dogs**, 1992 (cop infiltrates a ring of jewel thieves); The Return of Jack Slade, 1955 (son of famous lawman, goes undercover to trap outlaws); Riders of the Lone Star, 1947 (man goes undercover to find a long-missing outlaw); RoboCop, 2014; Running Scared, 2006; Rush Hour, 1998; Rush Hour 2, 2001; A Scanner Darkly, 2006; Scarface, 1983 (police mole in drug cartel operations); **Serpico**, 1973 (NYPD cop investigates corrupt cops); **The Seven Ups**, 1973 (NYPD detectives investigate murder of fellow cop who disguised himself as chauffeur for gang bosses); She's Dangerous!, 1937 (female detective goes undercover to track down bond thieves); Sin City, 2005; So Undercover, 2012 (private detective becomes FBI agent to infiltrate college sorority); Stranger from Santa Fe, 1945 (U.S. marshals go undercover to locate rustlers); **The Street with No Name**, 1948 (FBI agent goes undercover to trap criminal gang); Sundown in Santa Fe, 1948 (lawman goes undercover to track down killers); **T-Men**, 1947 (Secret Service agents go undercover to find counterfeiters); Thick as Thieves, 2009; Total Recall, 2012; 21 Jump Street, 1987-1991 (TV series); 22 Jump Street, 2014 (cops go undercover at a college); UC: Undercover, 2001-2002 (TV series; federal agents combat crime); **U.S. Marshals**, 1998 (agent operating undercover becomes murder suspect); Under Cover, 1987 (police detective attends South Carolina high school to bust drug ring); Undercover Agent, 1939 (postal clerk tracks down sweepstakes counterfeiters); Undercover Brother, 2002; The Vigilantes Return, 1947 (undercover lawman); We Own the Night, 2007 (undercover police detective exposes Russian Mafia); **White Heat**, 1949 (federal agent goes undercover to trap notorious criminal); The Whole Nine Yards, 2000. Note: For detailed information on law enforcement undercover agents, see my books *Bloodletters and Badmen* (M. Evans, 1973); *Encyclopedia of World Crime*; 8 volumes (CrimeBooks, Inc., 1990); *The Great Pictorial History of World Crime*; 2 volumes (History, Inc., 2004).

Valets: The Admirable Crichton, 1957; The Admirable Crichton, 1968; **Around the World in Eighty Days**, 1956; Around the World in 80 Days, 1989; Around the World in 80 Days, 2004; **Arthur**, 1981; Bad Little Angel, 1939; **Batman**, 1989 (his valet appears in other films in the series and/or sequels); Because of Him, 1946; The Benson Murder Case, 1930; **Bulldog Drummond Strikes Back**, 1934 (his valet appears in all other films of the series); Cats Don't Dance, 1997; **A Chump at Oxford**, 1940; **Cornered**, 1945; Counter-Espionage, 1942; A Date with the Falcon, 1942; Desire, 1937; **The Diary of a Chambermaid**, 1946; The Dresser, 1983; **5 Fingers**, 1952; Give Out Sisters, 1942; **The Ghost Breakers**, 1940; **Gosford Park**, 2001; **The Great Ziegfeld**, 1936; Hard to Get, 1938; **Holy Matrimony**, 1943; **The Hound of the Baskervilles, 1939**; **How to Murder Your Wife**, 1965; **The Hucksters**, 1947; **The Innocents**, 1961; **The Lady Eve**, 1941; **The Last Emperor**, 1987; The Limey, 1999; The Lone Wolf in Mexico, 1947; The Lottery Lover, 1935;

Madame Bovary, 1991; **Mr. Deeds Goes to Town**, 1936; **Murder on the Orient Express**, 1974; Murder on the Orient Express, 2001; **My Man Godfrey**, 1936; **A Night at the Opera**, 1935; **A Night in Casablanca**, 1946; One Dangerous Night, 1943; **The Paradine Case**, 1947; People Will Talk, 1935; **People Will Talk**, 1951; **Platinum Blonde**, 1931; **The Remains of the Day**, 1993; **The Return of the Pink Panther**, 1975; **Ruggles of Red Gap**, 1935; Seven Years Bad Luck, 1921; The Smart Set, 1928; Smartest Girl in Town, 1936; A Successful Calamity, 1932; **Sullivan's Travels**, 1941; **The Talk of the Town**, 1942; **Three Smart Girls**, 1936; **Top Hat**, 1935; **Topsy-Turvy**, 1999; **Walking on Air**, 1936; You'd Be Surprised, 1926.

Vampires: **Abbott and Costello Meet Frankenstein**, 1948; The ABC Saturday Night Superstar Movie, 1972-1974 (TV series; "The Mad, Mad, Mad Monsters," animated 1972 episode); About Adam, 2000; Abraham Lincoln: Vampire Hunter, 2012; The Addiction, 1995; Against the Dark, 2009; Ahkea Khots, 1961; Alraune, 1918; Andy Warhol's Dracula, 1974 (aka: Blood for Dracula); Awake, 2007; Batman Dracula, 1964; Batman Fights Dracula, 1967; Billy the Kid vs. Dracula, 1966; Black Sabbath, 1964; Black Sunday, 1960; Black Vampire, 1988; Blacula, 1972; The Black Water Vampire, 2014; Blade, 1998; Blade: Trinity, 2004; Blade II, 2002; Blood, 1974; Blood and Donuts, 1995; Blood and Roses, 1960; Blood Bath, 1966; Blood Beast Terror (aka: The Vampire Beast Craves Blood), 1969; The Blood Drinkers (aka: The Vampire People), 1966; Blood for Dracula, 1974; Blood of Dracula's Castle, 1969; Blood of the Vampire, 1958; Blood: The Last Vampire, 2000; Blood: The Last Vampire, 2009; Blood Ties, 1991 (made-for-TV); BloodRayne, 2006; Bonnie & Clyde vs. Dracula, 2008; Bordello of Blood, 1996; Bram Stoker's Dracula, 1974; **Bram Stoker's Dracula** (aka: Dracula), 1992; The Breed, 2001; The Brides of Dracula, 1960; Buffy the Vampire Slayer, 1992; Buffy the Vampire Slayer, 1997-2003 (TV series); Byzantium, 2013; Captain Kronos—Vampire Hunter, 1974; The Caretaker, 2012; Carry on Christmas, 1969 (made-for-TV); Chica Vampiro, 2013 (TV series); Cirque du Freak: The Vampire's Assistant, 2009; Count Dracula, 1973; Count Dracula's Great Love, 1974; Count Yorga, Vampire, 1970; Countess Dracula, 1971; Cowboys and Vampires, 2010; The Creeps, 1997; Cronos, 1994; The Curse of Dracula, 1979 (TV series); Curse of the Undead, 1959; **Curse of the Vampires**, 1970; Crypt of the Vampire, 1964; **The Dark Crystal**, 1982; Dark Prince: The True Story of Dracula, 2000; Dark Shadows, 2012; Daughters of Darkness, 1971; Day Watch (aka: Night Watch II), 2006; Daybreakers, 2009; Desire, the Vampire, 1982 (made-for-TV); The Devil's Commandment (aka: Vampires), 1957; Die Hard Dracula, 1998; Doctor Dracula, 1978; Dr. Terror's Gallery of Horrors, 1967; **Dracula**, 1931; Dracula, 1931 (Mexican version); Dracula, 1972 (made-for-TV); Dracula, 1973 (made-for-TV); **Dracula**, 1979; Dracula, 1980 (animated made-for-TV); Dracula, 2002 (made-for-TV;); Dracula, 2007 (made-for-TV); Dracula, 2013- (TV series); Dracula A.D. 1972, 1972; Dracula and Son, 1979; Dracula contra Frankenstein, 1972; **Dracula: Dead and Loving It**, 1995; Dracula in Istanbul, 1953; Dracula in Pakistan, 1967; **Dracula Has Risen from the Grave**, 1969; Dracula: Pages from a Virgin's Diary, 2003; **Dracula: Prince of Darkness**, 1966; Dracula Reborn, 2012; Dracula Rising, 1993; The Dracula Saga, 1973; Dracula: The Dark Prince, 2013; Dracula (The Dirty Old Man), 1969; Dracula: The Series, 1990-1991 (TV series); Dracula 3D, 2013; Dracula 3000: Infinite Darkness, 2004 (made-for-TV); Dracula II: Ascension, 2003; Dracula 2000, 2000; Dracula 2012, 2013; Dracula Untold, 2014; Dracula vs. Frankenstein (aka: Blood of Frankenstein), 1971; **Dracula's Daughter**, 1936; Dracula's Death, 1921; Dracula's Dog (aka: Zoltan: Hound of Dracula), 1978; Dracula's Family Visit, 2006; Dracula's Guest, 2008; Drakula halala, 1921; El Vampiro, 1957; Embrace of the Vampire, 1995; The Empire of Dracula, 1967; The Era of Vampires, 2003; Eulogy for a Vampire, 2009; **The Fearless Vampire Killers**, 1967; Fist of the Vampire, 2007; The Forsaken, 2001; Frankenstein and Me, 1997; Frankenstein's Aunt, 1987; Freckled Max and Spook, 1987;

Fright Night, 1985; Fright Night, 2011; Fright Night Part II, 1989; Fright Night 2, 2013; From Dusk Till Dawn, 1996; Frostbite (aka: Frostbitten), 2006; Ganja & Hess, 1973; Genuine, 1920; Ghost in the Water, 1982 (made-for-TV); God of Vampires, 2010; Grave of the Vampire, 1972; The Great Bear Scare, 1983 (animated feature made-for-TV); Guess What Happened to Count Dracula?, 1970; Habit, 1997; The Hamiltons, 2006; Haunted, 1993; The Hilarious House of Frankenstein, 1971 (TV series); Hope, 2001 (made-for-TV); **Horror of Dracula** (AKA: Dracula), 1958; Horror of the Blood Monsters (aka: Vampire Men of the Lost Planet), 1970; Hotel Transylvania, 2012 (animated feature); House of Dark Shadows, 1970; **House of Dracula**, 1945; **House of Frankenstein**, 1944; House of the Wolf Man, 2009; The Hunger, 1983; Hysterical, 1983; I Am Legend, 2007; I Kissed a Vampire, 2012; I Sell the Dead, 2008; Immortality, 2000; Innocent Blood, 1992; **Interview with the Vampire: The Vampire Chronicles**, 1994; Jonathan (aka: Jonathan: Vampire Sterben Nicht), 1970; Joe Vampire, 2012; Jugular Wine: A Vampire Odyssey, 1994; The Keep, 1983; The Ketchup Vampires, 1992; Killer Barbys vs. Dracula, 2005; Kiss of the Damned, 2013; The Kiss of the Vampire, 1963; La fille de Dracula (aka: Dracula's Daughter), 1972; Ladies Night, 1983; Lady Dracula, 1977; The Lair of the White Worm, 1988; Lake of Dracula, 1973; The Last Man on Earth, 1924; The Last Man on Earth, 1964; Le viol du vampire (aka: The Rape of the Vampire), 1968; The League of Extraordinary Gentlemen, 2003; The Legend of the 7 Golden Vampires, 1979; Lemora: A Child's Tale of the Supernatural, 1975; Leptirica, 1973 (made-for-TV); Let Me In, 2010; Let the Right One In, 2008; Let's Scare Jessica to Death, 1971; Lifeforce, 1985; Lilith and Ly, 1919; The Little Vampire, 1986 (TV series); The Little Vampire, 2000; Little Vampire, 2004 (TV series); London after Midnight (aka: The Hypnotist), 1927; The Lost Boys, 1987; Lost Boys: The Thirst, 2010; Lost Boys: The Tribe, 2008; Lost Empires, 1986 (TV miniseries); Love at First Bite, 1979; Love Bites, 1993; Lust for a Vampire, 1971; Lust of the Vampire, 1963; Mad Monster Party?, 1967 (animated feature); **Mark of the Vampire**, 1935; Martin, 1978; Matinee Theater, 1955-1958 (TV series; "Dracula," two 1956 episodes); Midnight Son, 2011; Mr. Vampire, 1916; Modern Vampires, 1998 (made-for-TV); Mona the Vampire, 1999-2003 (TV series); Monkeybone, 2001; The Monster Club, 1981; Monster Mash: The Movie, 1995; Monster Squad, 1976 (TV series); The Monster Squad, 1987; Moon Child, 2004; The Moth Diaries, 2012; My Babysitter's a Vampire, 2010 (made-for-TV); My Babysitter's a Vampire, 2011-2012 (TV series); My Best Friend Is a Vampire (aka: I Was a Teenage Vampire), 1988; My Son the Vampire (aka: Vampire over London), 1963; My Stepbrother Is a Vampire !?!, 2013; Mystery and Imagination, 1966-1970 (TV series; "Dracula," 1968 episode); Nadja, 1995; Near Dark, 1987; Never on a Sunday, 2006; New Blood Rising, 2014; A Night of Horror, 1916; Night of the Vampire Hunter, 2000; Night of the Vampires, 1966; Night People, 2006; Night Watch, 2004; Ninjas vs. Vampires, 2010; Nocturna: Granddaughter of Dracula, 1979; **Nosferatu**, 1922; **Nosferatu the Vampyre**, 1979; Not Like Others (aka: Vampyrer), 2008; Not of This Earth, 1957; Not of This Earth, 1988; Not of This Earth, 1995; The Nude Vampire, 1970; Old Dracula (aka: Old Drac; Vampira), 1975; The Omega Man, 1971; Once Bitten, 1985; One More Time, 1970; Only Lovers Left Alive, 2013; Perfect Creature, 2007; Planet of the Vampires, 1965; Priest, 2011; Queen of the Damned, 2002; Rabid, 1977; The Rape of the Vampire, 1968; Red Blooded American Girl, 1990; Renfield the Undead, 2011; Requiem for a Vampire, 1973; **The Return of Dr. X**, 1939; The Return of Dracula, 1958; **The Return of the Vampire**, 1944; A Return to Salem's Lot, 1987; Rise: Blood Hunter, 2007; Robo Vampire, 1988; Rockula, 1990; Rosario + Vampire, 2008 (TV series); Saint Dracula 3D, 2012; Samurai Vampire Bikers from Hell, 1992; The Satanic Rites of Dracula, 1978; Scars of Dracula, 1970; **Shadow of the Vampire**, 2000; The Shiver of the Vampires, 1978; Sifu vs. Vampire, 2014; Slayer, 2006 (made-for-TV); Sleepwalkers, 1992; Son of Darkness: To Die For II, 1991; **Son of Dracula**, 1943; Son of Dracula, 1974; Stake Land, 2010; Strange Things Happen at

Sundown, 2003; Sun Shadows: Faithful Kiss, 2011; Sundown: The Vampire in Retreat, 1989; Tales of a Vampire, 1993; Taste the Blood of Dracula, 1970; Teenage Space Vampires, 1999; Terror of Dracula, 2012; Thirst, 1979; The Thirst, 2006; Thirst, 2009; Thirty Days of Night, 2007; Thirty Days of Night: Dark Days, 2010; To Die For, 1989; Trouble Every Day, 2001; Twilight, 2008; The Twilight Saga: Eclipse, 2010; The Twilight Saga: New Moon, 2009; The Twins Effect, 2003; Two Orphan Vampires, 1997; Ultraviolet, 2006; Underworld, 2003; Underworld: Awakening, 2012; Underworld: Evolution, 2006; Underworld: Rise of the Lycans, 2009; Valerie and Her Week of Wonders, 1971; Vamp, 1986; Vampira, 1956 (TV series); Vampira, 1971 (made-for-TV); Vampira, 1994; The Vampire (aka: El Vampiro), 1957; The Vampire, 1968; The Vampire, 2007; Vampire, 2010; Vampire, 2011; The Vampire, 2013; Vampire Academy, 2014; The Vampire and the Ballerina, 1962; **The Vampire Bat**, 1933; Vampire Bats, 2005; Vampire Blvd., 2004; Vampire Boys, 2011; Vampire Boys II: The New Brood, 2013; Vampire Camp, 2012; Vampire Child, 1999; Vampire Circus, 1972; Vampire City, 2009; Vampire Clan, 2002; Vampire Cop, 1990; Vampire Cop Ricky, 2006; The Vampire Diaries, 2009 (TV series); Vampire Diary, 2007; Vampire Dog, 2012; Vampire Effect, 2003; Vampire High, 2001 (TV series); The Vampire Hookers (aka; Sensuous Vampires; Cemetery Girls), 1979; Vampire Hunter D, 1993; Vampire Hunter D: Bloodlust, 2001; Vampire Idol, 2011-2012 (TV series); Vampire in Brooklyn, 1995; Vampire in Vegas, 2009; Vampire in Venice (aka: Nosferatu in Venice), 1988; Vampire Killers, 2009; The Vampire Lovers, 1970; Vampire Night, 2000; Vampire Noir, 2007; Vampire Over London, 1952; Vampire Prosecutor, 2011 (TV series); The Vampire Secrets, 2011 (TV series); Vampire Sunrise, 2014; Vampire Vixens from Venus, 1995; The Vampires (aka: Las Vampiras; The Vampire Girls), 1969; Vampires, 1986; Vampires (aka: John Carpenter's Vampires), 1998; Vampires, 2011; Vampires, 2012 (TV series); Vampires Anonymous, 2003; Vampire's Embrace, 1991; The Vampire's Ghost, 1945; Vampires in Venice, 2013; Vampire's Kiss, 1989; Vampires: Los Muertos, 2002; The Vampire's Night Orgy, 1974; The Vampires of Bloody Island, 2009; Vampires of Warsaw, 1925; Vampires: Rise of the Fallen, 2012; The Vampire's Seduction, 1998; Vampires Suck, 2010; A Vampire's Tale, 2009; Vampires: The Turning, 2005; The Vampire's Tomb, 2013; Vampiresas, 1996 (made-for-TV); Vampiresas 1930, 1962; Vampiro, 2009; Vamps, 2012; **Vampyr**, 1932; Vampyres, 1975; **Van Helsing**, 2004; Vegas Vampires, 2007; Vlad (aka: The True Life of Dracula), 1982; Vlad, 2003; Vlad Tepes, 1979; Waxwork, 1988; Way of the Vampire, 2005; We Are the Night, 2010; The Worst Crime of Them All! (aka: Mondo Keyhole), 1966.

Vaudeville and Vaudeville Performers (also see Broadway Productions and Shows; Stage Performers, this index): All I Desire, 1953; Always Leave Them Laughing, 1949; Applause, 1929; Atlantic City, 1944; **Babes in Arms**, 1939; Beautiful But Broke, 1944; Behind the Eight Ball, 1942; **The Blue Angel**, 1931; **Blue Skies**, 1946; Brain Donors, 1992; Bright Lights, 1935; **Broadway**, 1942; **The Broadway Melody**, 1929; Broadway to Hollywood, 1933; Burlesque, 2010; **Cavalcade**, 1933; Celine and Julie Go Boating, 1974; Chaplin, 1992; **Chicago**, 2002; **Children of Paradise**, 1946; **City for Conquest**, 1940; The Comic, 1969; **Coney Island**, 1943; Copacabana, 1947; **The Crowd**, 1928; **Curly Top**, 1935; Curtain Call at Cactus Creek, 1950; **The Day of the Locust**, 1975; **Daybreak**, 1940; Comet Over Broadway, 1938; Crazy House, 1943; The Daughter of Rosie O'Grady, 1950; Dizzy Dames, 1935; **Dr. Jekyll and Mr. Hyde**, 1941; **The Dolly Sisters**, 1945; **Easter Parade**, 1948; Elstree Calling, 1930; **The Entertainer**, 1960; Flirting with Fate, 1938; The Florodora Girl, 1930; Follies Girl, 1943; **For Me and My Gal**, 1942; **Funny Girl**, 1968; George White's 1935 Scandals, 1935; George White's Scandals, 1934; George White's Scandals, 1945; Give My Regards to Broadway, 1948; Glorifying the American Girl, 1929; **Grand Illusion**, 1938; **The Great Flamarion**, 1945; **The Great Ziegfeld**, 1936; **Gypsy**, 1962; **The Hard Way**, 1943; He

Found a Star, 1941; **Hello, Frisco, Hello**, 1943; **Here Comes Cookie**, 1935; **Houdini**, 1953; **How the West Was Won**, 1962; **Idiot's Delight**, 1939; It All Came True, 1940; **The Jolson Story**, 1946; **King Kong**, 2005; Lady of Burlesque, 1943; **Limelight**, 1952; Little Miss Broadway, 1938; London Town, 1953; Lord Byron of Broadway, 1930; Lucky Me, 1954; Make Mine Laughs, 1949; **Man of a Thousand Faces**, 1957; The Merry Monahans, 1944; Million Dollar Baby, 1934; Mrs. Henderson Presents, 2005; **Mrs. Wiggs of the Cabbage Patch**, 1934; Moon Over Harlem, 1938; **Morning Glory**, 1933; **Mother Wore Tights**, 1947; **My Favorite Blonde**, 1942; **My Wild Irish Rose**, 1947; **Night Has a Thousand Eyes**, 1948; **Nightmare Alley**, 1947; On Your Toes, 1939; Painted Faces, 1929; **The Picture of Dorian Gray**, 1945; **Poor Little Rich Girl**, 1936; **The Princess and the Pirate**, 1944; The Prizefighter and the Lady, 1933; **Public Hero No. 1**, 1935; Puttin' on the Ritz, 1930; Radio City Revels, 1938; **River of No Return**, 1954; **Road to Bali**, 1952; **Road to Utopia**, 1946; **Rose of Washington Square**, 1939; **Sadie McKee**, 1934; **San Francisco**, 1936; Sarah and Son, 1930; Say One for Me, 1959; The Serpent's Egg, 1978; **The Seven Little Foys**, 1955; Shine on Harvest Moon, 1944; **Show Business**, 1944; Show Folks, 1929; **Singin' in the Rain**, 1952; **Somebody Loves Me**, 1952; Stage Mother, 1933; **Star!**, 1968; The Stooge, 1952; **The Sunshine Boys**, 1975; **Sweet Rosie O'Grady**, 1943; Swing Hostess, 1944; Syncopation, 1929; **Take Me Out to the Ball Game**, 1949; Tarnished Angel, 1938; **That's Right—You're Wrong**, 1939; **There's No Business Like Show Business**, 1954; They Learned about Women, 1930; **The 39 Steps**, 1935; The 39 Steps, 1960; **Thoroughly Modern Millie**, 1967; Three of a Kind, 1944; **Tin Pan Alley**, 1940; Upstream, 1927; Valentino, 1977; Vaudeville, 1986; **Wabash Avenue**, 1950; Wake Up and Dream, 1934; **Weary River**, 1929; **When My Baby Smiles at Me**, 1948; **Yankee Doodle Dandy**, 1942; You Never Know Women, 1926; **Young People**, 1940; **Ziegfeld Follies**, 1945; **Ziegfeld Girl**, 1941.

Ventriloquists (and their dummies): Alfred Hitchcock Presents, 1955-1965 (TV series; "And So Died Riabouchinska," 1956 episode; "Final Performance," 1965 episode); All's Faire in Love, 2009; **Annie**, 1982; Arizona Stage Coach, 1942; Avargal, 1977; Best in Show, 2000; **Big Fish**, 2003; The Big Show, 1936; Bright Lights, 1935; **Broadway Danny Rose**, 1984; The Bronze Buckeroo, 1939; **Bugsy Malone**, 1976; Bullets and Saddles, 1943; Call the Mesquiteers, 1938; Charlie McCarthy, Detective, 1939 (Edgar Bergen and Charlie McCarthy); Charlie's Haunt, 1950 (Edgar Bergen and Charlie McCarthy); **Chicago**, 2002; **Coming Home**, 1978; Cowboy Canteen, 1944; Cradle Will Rock, 1999; Crash Canyon, 2011- (TV series); Crime Ring, 1938; The Danny Kaye Show, 1963-1967 (TV series; several episodes); **Dead of Night**, 1945; Dead Silence, 2007; Death Defying Acts, 2008; Der Mann mitt dem Glasauge, 1969; **Devil Doll**, 1964; Dinner for Schmucks, 2010; Don't Make Waves, 1967; Dummy, 2002; El as negro, 1943; Ellery Queen's Penthouse Mystery, 1941; Fight for Your Lady, 1937; Find the Blackmailer, 1943; For Your Consideration, 2006; Fugitive Valley, 1941; Fun and Fancy Free, 1947 (Edgar Bergen and Charlie McCarthy); Getting Any?, 1994; Getting Home, 2007; Go Chase Yourself, 1938; Go for It, 1983; Gold Diggers in Paris, 1938; The Goldwyn Follies, 1938 (Edgar Bergen and Charlie McCarthy); **The Great Gabbo**, 1929; Gunsmoke Ranch, 1937; Harmony Trail, 1944; Here We Go Again, 1942 (Edgar Bergen and Charlie McCarthy); Hidden Danger, 1948; Hit the Saddle, 1937; I Love Hitler, 1984; **The Illusionist**, 2010; The Immortals, 1995; **The In-Laws**, 1979; The Jack Benny Program, 1950-1965 (TV series; "Christmas Show," 1960 episode); Jeff Dunham: Birth of a Dummy, 2011; **Knock on Wood**, 1954; Knots, 1975; La 7eme cible, 1984; Land of Hunted Men, 1943; The Last of Sheila, 1973; The Last Request, 2006; Letter of Introduction, 1938 (Edgar Bergen and Charlie McCarthy); Look Who's Laughing, 1941 (Edgar Bergen and Charlie McCarthy); **Magic**, 1978; Magic Mansion, 1965-1967 (TV series); Manhattan Merry-Go-Round, 1937; The Men's Club, 1986; **The Miracle Woman**, 1931; **Mr. Moto's Last Warning**, 1939; **The Muppet**

Movie, 1979; The Night Is Young, 1987; **1941**, 1979; Overland Stage Raiders, 1938; The Paper Man, 1963; Pecker, 1998; Pin, 1989; **Poppy**, 1936; The Purple Vigilantes, 1938; Range Defenders, 1937; **Reap the Wild Wind**, 1942; Red River Range, 1938; **The Riders of the Whistling Skull**, 1937; Roaring Fire, 1982; Rock River Renegades, 1942; **Rosalie**, 1937; Santa Fe Stampede, 1938; Seed of Chucky, 2004; The Shadow of the Eagle, 1932; The Sheriff of Medicine Bow, 1948; Sheriff of Sundown, 1944; Soap, 1977-1981 (TV series); Song of the Open Road, 1944 (Edgar Bergen and Charlie McCarthy); **Stage Door Canteen**, 1943 (Edgar Bergen and Charlie McCarthy); Stop! Look! And Laugh!, 1960; Swing, Cowboy, Swing, 1946; Swing Out the Blues, 1943; The Ten, 2007; Terror Firmer, 1999; The 39 Steps, 2008 (made-for-TV); The Three Mesquiteers, 1936; Tonto Basin Outlaws, 1941; Trigger Trail, 1944; Tumbledown Ranch in Arizona, 1941; 20 Years After, 2008; Twilight Zone, 1959-1964 (TV series; "Caesar and Me," 1964 episode); Two Fisted Justice, 1943; Unashamed, 1938; Underground Rustlers, 1941; **The Unholy Three**, 1925; **The Unholy Three**, 1930; **Variety Lights**, 1965; A Very Long Engagement, 2004; West of Pinto Basin, 1940; **What's Up, Tiger Lily?**, 1966; When a Stranger Calls Back, 1993 (made-for-TV); **You Can't Cheat an Honest Man**, 1939 (Edgar Bergen and Charlie McCarthy); Zapatlela, 1993.

Vikings: Erik the Conqueror, 1963; Erik the Viking, 1989; **Exodus: Gods and Kings**, 2014; The Long Ships, 1964; The Norseman, 1980; **Northmen: A Viking Saga**, 2014; Tales of the Vikings, 1959 (TV series); The 13th Warrior, 1999; The Viking, 1928; The Viking Sagas, 1997; Viking Quest, 2014 (made-for-TV); Vikingdom, 2013; **The Vikings**, 1958; Vikings!, 1980 (TV series); Vikings, 2013- (TV series).

Volcanic Eruptions: **Aloma of the South Seas**, 1941; Alvin and the Chipmunks: Chipwrecked, 2011; Apocalypse Pompeii, 2014; Atlantis, The Lost Continent, 1961; **Atlantis: The Lost Empire**, 2001; Behemoth, 2011 (made-for-TV); Black Paradise, 1926; The Black Scorpion, 1957 (Mexico); Colossus and the Headhunters, 1963; Congo, 1995; **The Croods**, 2013; **Dante's Peak**, 1997 (Pacific Northwest); The Deep, 2012; Deep Core, 2000; **The Devil at Four O'Clock**, 1961; Devil Goddess, 1955; Doomsday Prophecy, 2011 (made-for-TV); **Fantasia**, 1940; Her Jungle Love, 1938; Hercules the Avenger, 1965; In Search of the Castaways, 1962; **Journey to the Center of the Earth**, 1959; **Journey to the Center of the Earth**, 2008; Journey 2: The Mysterious Island, 2012; King of the Rocket Men, 1949; **King Solomon's Mines**, 1937; King Solomon's Mines, 1985; **Krakatoa: East of Java**, 1969 (May-August 1883); Krakatoa, 2008 (made-for-TV; May-August 1883); **The Land That Time Forgot**, 1975; The Last Days of Pompeii, 1913 (Vesuvius, 79 A.D.); **The Last Days of Pompeii**, 1935 (Vesuvius, 79 A.D.); Last Days of the Dinosaurs, 2010 (made-for-TV); Leopardi, 2014; The Lord of the Rings: The Return of the King, 2003; Lost Continent, 1951; Magma: Volcanic Disaster, 2006 (made-for-TV); Melody in Love, 1978; **Mysterious Island**, 1961; Mysterious Island, 2005 (made-for-TV); **The Naked Kiss**, 1964; **Night at the Museum: Secret of the Tomb**, 2014; The Night the World Exploded, 1957; 100 Degrees below Zero, 2013; **Our Man Flint**, 1966; Phantom of the Jungle, 1955; **Pompeii**, 2014 (Vesuvius, 79 A.D.); Raptor Island, 2004 (made-for-TV); Robinson Crusoe of Clipper Island, 1936; Robot Monster, 1953; Rodan, 1956; St. Helens, 1981; Scorcher, 2002; The Secret Life of Walter Mitty, 2013; The Secret of Treasure Island, 1938; 79 A.D., 1962 (Vesuvius); She Demons, 1958; **Son of Kong**, 1933; **Star Trek: Into Darkness**, 2013; Stromboli, 1950; Supergirl, 1984; Superman IV: The Quest for Peace, 1987; **Switching Channels**, 1988; **The Time Machine**, 1960; 2012, 2009; Two Lost Worlds, 1951; Untamed Women, 1952; Volcano, 1997 (Los Angeles, California); When Time Ran Out, 1980; **The White Sister**, 1923; The Wild, 2006; Wrath of the Titans, 2012; Yog: Monster from Space, 1970. Note: For more information on volcanic eruptions throughout history, see my book *Darkest Hours: A Narrative Encyclopedia of Worldwide Disasters from Ancient Times to* *the Present* (Nelson-Hall, 1976).

War Correspondents (and photo journalists, newsreel reporters): The Angel Wore Red, 1960 (Spanish Civil War, 1936-1939); Another Time, Another Place, 1958 (WWII; Europe); Attack on Leningrad, 2011 (WWII, 1939-1945; Europe); The Biggest Battle, 1978 (WWII; Europe); **Blood on the Sun**, 1945 (Second Sino-Japanese War, 1931-1945; Tanaka Plan); **Circle of Deceit**, 1982 (Lebanese Civil War, 1975-1990); **Command Decision**, 1948 (WWII; Europe); Cry Freedom, 1987 (South Africa); **Das Boot**, 1982 (WWII; Atlantic, Mediterranean); Down among the Sheltering Palms, 1953 (WWII; Pacific); **The Fighting Seabees**, 1944 (WWII; Pacific Theater); 5 Days of War, 2011 (Russo-Georgian War, 2008); **Foreign Correspondent**, 1940 (WWII; Europe); **Full Metal Jacket**, 1987 (Vietnam War); Generation Kill, 2008 (TV miniseries; Iraq War, 2003-2011); **The Green Berets**, 1968 (Vietnam War); **Guadalcanal Diary**, 1943 (WWII; Pacific Theater); Guest Wife, 1945 (WWII; Home Front); Hemingway & Gellhorn, 2012 (made-for TV; Spanish civil war, 1936-1939); Immortal Sergeant, 1943 (WWII; North Africa); **Jack London**, 1943 (Russo-Japanese War, 1904-1905); Kandahar, 2001 (Civil War in Afghanistan, 1989-1992); **The Killing Fields**, 1984 (Cambodia); **Lawrence of Arabia**, 1962 (WWI; Middle East); Live from Bagdad, 2002 (made-for-TV; Gulf War, 1990-1991); **My Son, My Son!**, 1940 (WWI, 1914-1918; Western Front); **Mysterious Island**, 1961 (American Civil War, 1861-1865); No Man's Land, 2001 (Bosnia and Herzegovina, 1993); **Objective Burma!**, 1945 (WWII); **The Purple Heart**, 1944 (WWII; Doolittle Raid against Tokyo, 1942); Rough Riders, 1997 (made-for-TV; Spanish-American War, 1898); Salome Where She Danced, 1945 (Austro-Prussian War, 1866); Salvador, 1986 (El Salvador, 1980); Secret Service in Darkest Africa, 1943 (WWII; Africa); **Somewhere I'll Find You**, 1942 (WWII; Pacific); **The Story of G.I. Joe**, 1945 (WWII; North Africa, Sicily, Italy); Suicide Squadron, 1942 (WWII; Europe); Tokyo Rose, 1946 (WWII; Pacific); **Too Hot to Handle**, 1938 (Second Sino-Japanese War, 1931-1945); Triage, 2009 (Iraq-Kurdistan); **Under Fire**, 1983 (Nicaragua, 1979); War Correspondent, 1932 (Second Sino-Japanese War, 1931-1945); **We Were Soldiers**, 2002 (Vietnam War); Witness in the War Zone, 1987 (Lebanese Civil War, 1975-1990); **The Year of Living Dangerously**, 1982 (Indonesia); **Yesterday's Enemy**, 1959 (WWII; Burma).

Werewolves: **Abbott and Costello Meet Frankenstein**, 1948; **An American Werewolf in London**, 1981; An American Werewolf in Paris, 1997; The Beast Must Die, 1974; Being Human, 2008-2014 (TV series); **Big Fish**, 2003; Big Wolf on Campus, 1999-2002 (TV series); Bitten, 2014- (TV series); Blood of Dracula's Castle, 1969; The Boy Who Cried Werewolf, 1973; The Boy Who Cried Werewolf, 2010 (made-for-TV); Brotherhood of the Wolf, 2001; The Brothers Grimm, 2005; Buffy the Vampire Slayer, 1997-2003; The Cabin in the Woods, 2012; The Company of Wolves, 1984; Cry of the Banshee, 1970; Cry of the Werewolf, 1944; **The Curse of the Werewolf**, 1961; Dark Shadows, 2012; Death Valley, 2011- (TV series); Despicable Me, 2010; Dr. Terror's House of Horrors, 1965; Dog Soldiers, 2002; **Dracula**, 1931; **Dracula**, 1979; **Dracula**, 1992; **Dracula Has Risen from His Grave**, 1969; **Dracula—Prince of Darkness**, 1966; Dracula 2000, 2000; **Frankenstein Meets the Wolf Man**, 1943; **Fright Night**, 1985; The Gates, 2010- (TV series); Ginger Snaps, 2000; Grimm, 2011- (TV series); Grindhouse, 2007; **Harry Potter and the Deathly Hallows Part 1**, 2010; **Harry Potter and the Deathly Hollows Part 2**, 2011; **Harry Potter and the Half-Blood Prince**, 2009; **Harry Potter and the Prisoner of Azkaban**, 2004; Hemlock Grove, 2013 (made-for-TV); Holloweentown, 1998 (made-for-TV); **Hotel Transylvania**, 2012; **The House of Dracula**, 1945; **The House of Frankenstein**, 1944; Howl, 2015; **The Howling**, 1981; **I Was a Teenage Werewolf**, 1957; Kaos, 1984; Legend of the Werewolf, 1975; The Machinest, 2004; Mad at the Moon, 1992; The Mad Monster, 1942; Mad Monster Party, 1967; The

Midnight Hour, 1985 (made-for-TV); The Monster Club, 1981; The Monster Squad, 1987; The Munsters, 1964-1966 (TV series); My Mom's a Werewolf, 1989; Never Cry Werewolf, 2008 (made-for-TV); The Neverending Story, 1984; Night of the Werewolf, 1981; **The Nightmare Before Christmas**, 1993; **Nosferatu**, 1922; **Nosferatu: The Vampire**, 1979; Penny Dreadful, 2014- (TV series); **Providence**, 1977; Red: Werewolf Hunter, 2010; **The Return of the Vampire**, 1944; Sanctuary, 2008- (TV series); Scream of the Wolf, 1974 (made-for-TV); She-Wolf of London, 1990-1991 (TV series); Silver Bullet, 1985; Spring, 2014; Supernatural, 2005- (TV series); Tales of Halloween, 2015; Teen Wolf, 1985; Teen Wolf, 2011- (TV series); The 10th Kingdom, 2000 (TV miniseries); Transylvania 6-5000, 1985; True Blood, 2008-2014 (TV series); Underworld, 2003; Underworld: Evolution, 2006; Underworld: Rise of the Lycans, 2009; The Undying Monster, 1942; The Vampire Diaries, 2009- (TV series); **Van Helsing**, 2004; Waxwork, 1988; What We Do in the Shadows, 2014; The Werewolf, 1956; Werewolf, 1987-1988 (TV series); Werewolf, 2012; **Werewolf of London**, 1935; The Werewolf of Washington, 1973; Werewolf Women, 1977; **When Animals Dream**, 2014; **Wolf**, 1994; Wolf Children, 2012; Wolf Girl, 2001 (made-for-TV); **The Wolf Man**, 1941; Wolfblood, 2012- (TV series); **Wolfen**, 1981; Wolfman, 1979; **The Wolfman**, 2010; Wolves, 2014; Wolf's Rain, 2003- (TV series).

Witchcraft (witches and trials; also see Wizards, this index; also see separate indices: Events: Salem Witch Trials; Fictional Characters: Merlin; Historical Characters: Elizabeth Bathory, Joan of Arc, Cagliostro/Joseph Balsamo, Tomas Torquemada; Organizations: Spanish Inquisition): The Adventures of Baron Munchausen, 1943 (Cagliostro); The Adventures of Sir Galahad, 1949 (serial; Merlin); The Adventures of Sir Lancelot, 1956-1957 (TV series; Merlin); The Affair of the Necklace, 2001 (Cagliostro); An Age of Kings, 1960 (TV series Joan of Arc); Agora, 2010; Amy Foster, 1998; Andrei Rublev, 1973; Angelique, 1964; The Antichrist, 1974; Antichrist, 2009; Arthur the King, 1985 (made-for-TV; Merlin); Arthur's Quest, 1999 (made-for-TV; Merlin); Barbarina: The King's Dancer, 1932 (Cagliostro); Baron Blood, 1972 (Elizabeth Bathory); Bathory, 2011 (Elizabeth Bathory); Bathory: Countess of Blood, 2008 (Elizabeth Bathory); The Bathory Legend, 2010 (TV series; Elizabeth Bathory); Battle of the Brave, 2004; The Beastmaster, 1982; **Bedknobs and Broomsticks**, 1971; **Bell Book and Candle**, 1958; Bewitched, 1964-1972 (TV series); Bewitched, 2005; Bill & Ted's Excellent Adventure, 1989 (Joan of Arc); **The Black Cauldron**, 1985; **Black Magic**, 1949 (Cagliostro); Black Noon, 1971 (made-for-TV); Black Sunday, 1961; The Blair Witch Project, 1999; Bless Me, Ultima, 2013; Blood Cousins, 2012; The Blood on Satan's Claw, 1971; Bloodbath, 1999 (Elizabeth Bathory); The Brotherhood of Satan, 1971; Brotherhood of the Wolf, 2001; Burn, Witch, Burn, 1962; Burned at the Stake, 1981 (New England of the Pilgrims; Salem witch trials); Bye Bye Columbus, 1991 (Torquemada; Spanish Inquisition); Cabeza de Vaca, 1992; Cagliostro, 1929; Cagliostro, 1977; **Camelot**, 1967 (Merlin); Camelot, 1982 (made-for-TV; Merlin); Camelot, 2011 (TV miniseries; Merlin); Captain Alatriste: The Spanish Musketeer, 2007 (Spanish Inquisition); **Captain from Castile**, 1947 (Spanish Inquisition); Carry on Laughing!, 1975 (TV series; Merlin); Carry on Columbus, 1992 (Torquemada; Spanish Inquisition); **Casanova**, 2005; The Case of Becky, 1921 (Cagliostro); The Castle of Cagliostro, 1991; Celestial Clockwork, 1996; Charmed, 1998-2006 (TV series); Chastity Bites, 2013 (Elizabeth Bathory); Child's Play, 1988; The Circle, 2015; **Christopher Columbus**, 1949 (Spanish Inquisition); Christopher Columbus: The Discovery, 1992 (Torquemada; Spanish Inquisition); **The Chronicles of Narnia: Prince Caspian**, 2008; **The Chronicles of Narnia: The Lion, the Witch and the Wardrobe**, 2005; The Church, 1989; The City of the Dead, 1961; **Clash of the Titans**, 1981 (Stygian Witches); **Cloud Atlas**, 2012; The Collingswood Story, 2002; Conan the Barbarian, 1982; Conan the Destroyer, 1984; The Conjuring, 2013; **A Connecitcut Yankee**, 1931 (Merlin); A Connecticut Yankee,

1955 (made-for-TV; Merlin); A Connecticut Yankee in King Arthur's Court, 1921 (Merlin); **A Connecticut Yankee in King Arthur's Court**, 1949 (Merlin); A Connecticut Yankee in King Arthur's Court, 1989 (made-for-TV: Merlin); **The Conqueror Worm**, 1968; Conquest of Paradise, 1992 (Spanish Inquisition); The Countess, 2009 (Elizabeth Bathory);); Countess Dracula, 1972 (Elizabeth Bathory); The Coven, 2015; The Covenant, 2006; The Craft, 1996; Cristobal Colon, de oficio…descubridor, 1982 (Torquemada; Spanish Inquisition); Cronos, 1994 (Spanish Inquisition); Crowhaven Farm, 1970 (made-for-TV; New England of the Pilgrims); The Crucible, 1958 (New England of the Pilgrims; Salem Witch Trials); **The Crucible**, 1996 (New England of the Pilgrims; Salem Witch Trials); The Crucible, 2014 (New England of the Pilgrims; Salem Witch Trials); The Crusaders #357: Experiment in Evil!, 2008 (Elizabeth Bathory); Cry of the Banshee, 1970; Crypt of the Vampire, 1964; Crystal Cave, 1996 (made-for-TV; Merlin); Curse of the Crimson Altar, 1968; **Curse of the Demon**, 1958; Curse of the Devil, 1977 (Elizabeth Bathory); Da Vinci's Demons, 2013 (TV series; Torquemada; Spanish Inquisition); Dangerous Beauty, 1998; Dark Shadows, 1991- (TV series); Daughters of Darkness, 1971 (Elizabeth Bathory); Daughters of Destiny, 1954 (Joan of Arc); Daughters of Satan, 1972; **Day of Wrath**, 1948 (17th-Century Denmark witch hunts); Day Watch, 2007; Deadly Women, 2005-2010 (TV series; Elizabeth Bathory); Death Becomes Her, 1992; Deep in the Woods, 2010; Der Fall Jeanne d'Arc, 1966 (made-for-TV; Joan of Arc); The Devil's Daughter, 1939; District 9, 2009; The Doors, 1991; Double, Double Toil and Trouble, 1993 (made-for-TV); Dracula A.D. 1972, 1972; Dracula's Curse, 2006 (Elizabeth Bathory); Drag Me to Hell, 2009; El Greco, 1966 (Spanish Inquisition); El Greco, 2009 (Spanish Inquisition); Elizabeth Bathory, 2014; **Elizabeth: The Golden Age**, 2007 (Spanish Inquisition); Elvira: Mistress of the Dark, 1988; The Erotic Rites of Frankenstein, 1973 (Cagliostro); Eternal, 2005 (Elizabeth Bathory); Eve's Bayou, 1997; Eye of the Devil, 1967; **Excalibur**, 1981 (Merlin); **The Exorcist**, 1973; **Fantasia**, 1940; Faust, 1926; **Fire Over England**, 1937 (Spanish Inquisition); Firewalker, 1986; Flame in the Wind, 1971 (Spanish Inquisition); Forbidden Empire, 2014; 47 Ronin, 2013; Formula of Love, 1984 (Cagliostro); The Fountain, 2006 (Spanish Inquisition); Four Rooms, 1995; Francis the First, 1947 (Cagliostro); Frankenstein's Aunt, 1987 (TV series; Elizabeth Bathory); Freckled Max and Spooks, 1987 (Elizabeth Bathory); From Within, 2008; Game of Swords, 2006 (Spanish Inquisition); Game of Thrones, 2011- (TV series); Giovanna d'Arco al rogo, 1954 (Joan of Arc); The Good Witch, 2008 (made-for-TV); The Gospel according to God, 2004 (Torquemada; Spanish Inquisition); Goya in Bordeaux, 2000 (Spanish Inquisition); Goya's Ghost, 2007 (Spanish Inquisition); Guinevere, 1994 (made-for-TV; Merlin); Halloweentown, 1998 (made-for-TV); Halloweentown High, 2004 (made-for-TV); Halloweentown II: Kalabar's Revenge, 2001 (made-for-TV); Hansel and Gretel, 1987; Hansel & Gretel: Warriors of Witchcraft, 2013; **Harry Potter and the Chamber of Secrets**, 2002; **Harry Potter and the Deathly Hallows Part 1**, 2010; **Harry Potter and the Deathly Hollows Part 2**, 2011; **Harry Potter and the Goblet of Fire**, 2005; **Harry Potter and the Half-Blood Prince**, 2009; Harry Potter and the Order of the Phoenix, 2007; **Harry Potter and the Prisoner of Azkaban**, 2004; **Harry Potter and the Sorcerer's Stone**, 2001; A Haunting in Salem, 2011; Haxan: Witchcraft Through the Ages, 1929; Heinrich VI.—Der Krieg der Rosen 1. Teil, 1969 (made-for-TV; Joan of Arc); Hellboy Animated: Blood and Iron, 2007 (made-for-TV; Elizabeth Bathory); Henry VIII and His Six Wives, 1972; History of the World, Part I, 1981 (Torquemada; Spanish Inquisition); Hocus Pocus, 1993 (New England of the Pilgrims to modern times; Salem witch trials); The Holy Inquisition, 1975 (Spanish Inquisition); The House of the Devil, 2009; The House That Dripped Blood, 1971; The House That Would Not Die, 1970 (made-for-TV); Howl's Moving Castle, 2005; **The Hunchback of Notre Dame**, 1923; **The Hunchback of Notre Dame**, 1939; The Hunchback of Notre Dame, 1982 (made-for-TV); **The Hunchback of Notre Dame**, 1996; **I Married a Witch**, 1942 (New

England of the Pilgrims to modern times; Salem witch trials); If Paris Were Told to Us, 1956 (Joan of Arc); Inferno, 1980; The Inheritance, 2011; The Initiation of Sarah, 2006 (made-for-TV); **Into the Woods**, 2014; Inquisition, 1976 (Spanish Inquisition); Isabel, 2011-2014 (TV series; Torquemada; Spanish Inquisition); Jane B. for Agnes V., 1988 (Joan of Arc); Jeanne au bucher, 1966 (made-for-TV; Joan of Arc); Jeanne d'Arc au bucher, 1993 (made-for-TV; Joan of Arc); Jeanne d'Arc au bucher, 2007 (Joan of Arc); Jeanne d'Arc au bucher, 2012 (made-for-TV; Joan of Arc); Jeanne d'Arc auf dem Scheiterhaufen, 1960 (made-for-TV; Joan of Arc); Jeanne d'Arc, le pouvoir de l'innocence, 1989 (made-for-TV; Joan of Arc); Jeanne la Pucelle I—Les batailles, 1994 (Joan of Arc); Jeanne la Pucelle II—Les prisons, 1994 (Joan of Arc); Jeanne oder Die Lerche, 1956 (made-for-TV; Joan of Arc); Jeanne oder Die Lerche, 1966 (made-for-TV; Joan of Arc); Joan of Arc, 1914; Joan of Arc, 1935; **Joan of Arc**, 1948; Joan of Arc, 1952 (made-for-TV); Joan of Arc, 1999 (TV series); Joan of Arc, 2003 (made-for-TV); Joan the Woman, 1916 (Joan of Arc); Joseph Balsamo, 1973 (TV series; Cagliostro); Juana la loca…de vez en cuando, 1983 (Torquemada; Spanish Inquisition); Kaliostro, 1918 (Cagliostro); A Kid in King Arthur's Court, 1995 (Merlin); **Kiki's Delivery Service**, 1989; **King Arthur**, 2004 (Merlin); **King Solomon's Mines**, 1937; **King Solomon's Mines**, 1950; King Solomon's Mines, 1976; A Knight in Camelot, 1998 (made-for-TV; Merlin); **Knights of the Round Table**, 1953 (Merlin); **Kwaidan**, 1965; La comtesse de Charny (Cagliostro); La mort mystererieuse de Nina Chereau, 1988 (made-for-TV; Elizabeth Bathory); Lancelot of the Lake, 1970 (made-for-TV; Merlin); L'araignee, 1981 (Cagliostro); The Lark, 1957 (made-for-TV; Joan of Arc); The Lark, 1958 (made-for-TV; Joan of Arc); **The Last Legion**, 2007 (Merlin); The Last Valley, 1971; Le chevalier d'Eon, 2006- (TV series; Cagliostro); Left Bank, 2008; The Legend of Blood Castle, 1974 (Elizabeth Bathory); The Legend of King Arthur, 1979 (TV series; Merlin); The Legend of Prince Valiant, 1991-1994 (TV series; Merlin); Legend of the Seeker, 2008-2010 (TV series); Les chats bottes, 1971 (Joan of Arc); Les gloutonnes, 1975 (Cagliostro); Let Joy Reign Supreme, 1977 (Spanish Inquisition); Lisa and the Devil, 1973; **The Little Mermaid**, 1989; Little Witches, 1996; The Lord of the Rings, 1978; **The Lord of the Rings: The Fellowship of the Ring**, 2001; **The Lord of the Rings: The Two Towers**, 2002; The Lords of Salem, 2002 (New England of the Pilgrims; Salem witch trials); Lucinda's Spell, 2000; **Macbeth**, 1948; **Macbeth**, 1971; **Macbeth**, 2015; The Maid of Orleans, 1993 (made-for-TV; Joan of Arc); Maid of Salem, 1937 (New England of the Pilgrims; Salem witch trials); **Maleficent**, 2014; Maleficarum, 2011 (Spanish Inquisition); Mama Dracula, 1980 (Elizabeth Bathory); Man of La Mancha, 1972 (Spanish Inquisition); Mark of the Devil, 1972; Mark of the Devil, Part II, 1974; Metamorphosis, 2010 (Elizabeth Bathory); Merlin, 1998 (TV miniseries); Merlin, 2008-2012 (TV series); Merlin: The Return, 2000; **The Messenger: The Story of Joan of Arc**, 1999; The Midnight Game, 2013; Midnight Offerings, 1981 (made-for-TV); Midnight's Child, 1992 (made-for-TV); Miracoloni, 1981 (Joan of Arc); Mirror Mirror, 2012; The Missing 2003; The Mists of Avalon, 2001 (made-for-TV; Merlin); Mondo Weirdo, 1990 (Elizabeth Bathory); Monster Man, 2003; More Than a Miracle, 1967; The Mother of Tears, 2008; The Mystic Tales of Nikolas Winter, 2012 (Cagliostro); Nachalo, 1970 (Joan of Arc); The Name of the Rose, 1986; Necromancy, 1972; Necropolis, 1970 (Elizabeth Bathory); Night Fangs, 2005 (Elizabeth Bathory); Night Gallery, 1969-1973 (TV series); Night of the Werewolf, 1985 (Elizabeth Bathory); The Night of the Witches, 1973; Night Watch, 2006; The Ninth Gate, 2000; The Oblong Box, 1969; Once Upon a Classic, 1976-1979 (TV series; Merlin); **Oz the Great and Powerful**, 2014; The Pagan Queen, 2009; **Paranormal Activity**, 2009; Paranormal Activity 3, 2011; Paranormal Activity 2: Tokyo Night, 2010; **The Passion of Joan of Arc**, 1929; Passions, 1999-2008 (TV series); **The Pit and the Pendulum**, 1961 (Spanish Inquisition); The Pit and the Pendulum, 1991 (Torquemada; Spanish Inquisition); Poison for the Fairies, 1984; Practical Magic, 1998; Puffball: The Devil's Eyeball, 2007; Pumpkinhead, 1988; Puritan Passions, 1923 (New England of the Pilgrims; Salem witch trials); Queen's Necklace, 1947 (Cagliostro); Quest for Camelot, 1998 (Merlin); The Return of the King, 1980 (made-for-TV); Return of the Moonwalker, 2013 (Cagliostro); Return to Halloweentown, 2006 (made-for-TV); **Rosemary's Baby**, 1968; Rosemary's Baby, 2014 (TV miniseries); Royal Affairs in Versailles, 1957 (Cagliostro); Sabrina, the Animated Series, 1999-2001 (TV series); Sabrina, the Teenage Witch, 1996 (made-for-TV); Sabrina, the Teenage Witch, 1996-2003 (TV series); The Sacrifice, 1986; Saint Joan, 1957 (Joan of Arc); Saint Joan, 1958 (made-for-TV; Joan of Arc); Saint Joan, 1967 (made-for-TV; Joan of Arc); Saint Joan the Maid, 1929 (Joan of Arc); Sainte Jeanne, 1969 (made-for-TV; Joan of Arc); Salem witch trials, 2002 (New England of the Pilgrims); Satan's School for Girls, 1973 (made-for-TV); Satan's School for Girls, 2000; The Scarecrow, 1972 (made-for-TV; New England of the Pilgrims); Season of the Witch, 1972; Season of the Witch, 2011; The Secret Circle, 2011-2012 (TV series); **The Secret of Kells**, 2009; Secret Passage, 2004 (Spanish Inquisition); The Secret Village, 2013 (New England of the Pilgrims; Salem witch trials); **7 Faces of Dr. Lao**, 1964 (Merlin); **The Seventh Seal**, 1958; Seventh Son, 2014; The Shades, 2015; Shine, Shine, My Star, 1970 (Joan of Arc); Shock House, 2011 (Elizabeth Bathory); **Shrek**, 2001; **Shrek Forever After**, 2010; **Shrek the Third**, 2007; **Shrek 2**, 2004; Siege of the Saxons, 1963 (Merlin); The Silence of Joan, 2011 (Joan of Arc); Silent Night, Deadly Night 4, 1990; Simon: King of the Witches, 1971; A Simple Wish, 1997; **Sinbad and the Eye of the Tiger**, 1977; The Skeleton Key, 2005; The Skull, 1965; **Sleeping Beauty**, 1959; Sleepy Hollow, 1999; The Snow Queen, 1995; Snow White: A Tale of Terror, 1997; **Snow White and the Huntsman**, 2012; **Snow White and the Seven Dwarfs**, 1937; Snow White: The Fairest of Them All, 2001 (made-for-TV); Solomon Kane, 2009; **Something of Value**, 1957 (witchcraft in Kenya); Something Wicked This Way Comes, 1983; The Sorcerer's Apprentice, 2010; Sorceress, 1995; Spellbinder, 1988; **Spitfire**, 1934; Stardust, 2007; Stay Alive, 2006 (Elizabeth Bathory); The Story of Mankind, 1957 (Joan of Arc); Stranger in Our House, 1978 (made-for-TV); Studio One in Hollywood, 1948-1958 (TV series; Merlin); Subversion, 1979 (Cagliostro); Supergirl, 1984; Superstition, 1985; Suspiria, 1977; **The Sword in the Stone**, 1963 (Merlin); Sword of Lancelot, 1963 (Merlin); Tabitha, 1976-1978 (TV series); Tamara, 2005; Teen Witch, 1989; Terror, 1979; **The Three Lives of Thomasina**, 1963; The Three Musketeers, 2011 (Cagliostro); Thriller, 1960-1962 (TV series; "The Prisoner in the Mirror," 1961 episode; Cagliostro); The Time Tunnel, 1966-1967 (TV series; Merlin); Tin Man, 2007 (TV miniseries); Tomb of the Werewolf, 2004 (Elizabeth Bathory); Torquemada, 1989 (Spanish Inquisition); The Touch of Satan, 1971; **The Trial of Joan of Arc**, 1965; Troll, 1986; Troll 2, 1990; **Ulysses**, 1955 (Circe); Un amour de sorciere, 1997; Unidentified Flying Oddball, 1979 (Merlin); Vagen till Klockrike, 1953 (Cagliostro); Vampire Secrets, 2006 (made-for-TV; Elizabeth Bathory); **The Virgin Spring**, 1960; The Vertical Smile, 1973 (Joan of Arc); **The Wandering Jew**, 1935 (Spanish Inquisition); **The Wandering Jew**, 1949 (Spanish Inquisition); **The Wandering Jew: The Life of Theodore Herzl**, 1923 (Spanish Inquisition); Warlock, 1989; Warlock Moon, 1973; Warlock: The Armageddon, 1993; **Weekend**, 1968; Weird Woman, 1944; The Werewolf vs. the Vampire Woman, 1972 (Elizabeth Bathory); The White Queen, 2013 (TV miniseries); Wicked Stepmother, 1989; **The Wicker Man**, 1975; Witchboard, 1987; Witchboard 2: The Devil's Doorway, 1993; Witchcraft, 1964; Witchcraft, 1988; Witchcraft III: The Kiss of Death, 1991; Witchcraft II: The Temptress, 1990; Witchery, 1988; The Witches, 1967; The Witches, 1969; **The Witches**, 1990; Witches' Brew, 1980; **The Witches of Eastwick**, 1987; The Witches of Eastwick, 1992 (made-for-TV); Witches of the Caribbean, 2005; Witches' Brew, 1980; Witching and Bitching, 2013; The Witch's Curse, 1963; Witch's Night Out, 1978 (made-for-TV); Witchville, 2010 (made-for-TV); **The Wizard of Oz**, 1939; **Woman Who Came Back**, 1945 (New England of the Pilgrims; Salem witch trials); The Woods, 2006; The Worst Witch, 1986 (made-for-TV);

The Worst Witch, 1998-2001 (TV series); A Young Connecticut Yankee in King Arthur's Court, 1996 (Merlin). Note: For detailed information on witchcraft trials, see my books *Encyclopedia of World Crime*; 8 volumes (CrimeBooks, Inc., 1990); *The Great Pictorial History of World Crime*; 2 volumes (History, Inc., 2004).

Witch Doctors: Altered States, 1980; Arizona Dream, 1992; Art of the Devil, 2004; **Australia**, 2008; Belizaire the Cajun, 1986; Booloo, 1938; Cabeza de Vaca, 1991; Captive Girl, 1950; Carry on up the Jungle, 1970; Child's Play, 1988; The Comedians, 1967; Congo Bill, 1948; Dance with the Devil, 1997; Danger Island, 1931; Darkest Africa, 1936; Daughter of the Jungle, 1949; The Dead, 2010; Demon Hunter, 1983; **The Diving Bell and the Butterfly**, 2007; Down Among the Sheltering Palms, 1953; East of Sudan, 1964; Exorcist II: The Heretic, 1977; Father and Sons, 2003; The Four Skulls of Jonathan Drake, 1959; Hawk of the Wilderness, 1948; How to Stuff a Wild Bikini, 1965; Jungle Drums of Africa, 1953; Jungle Gents, 1954; Jungle Girl, 1941; Jungle Gold, 1966 (made-for-TV); Jungle Jim, 1948; Jungle Mystery, 1932; Jungle Raiders, 1945; Killers of Kilimanjaro, 1959; **King Kong**, 1933; King of the Islands, 1936; **King Solomon's Mines**, 1937; **King Solomon's Mines**, 1950; King Solomon's Mines, 1976; The Kingdom, 1994 (TV miniseries); Land of Fury, 1954; The Last King of Scotland, 2006; Law of the Jungle, 1942; The League of Extraordinary Gentlemen, 2003; Madagascar: Escape 2 Africa, 2008; Manhunt in the Jungle, 1958; Manhunters of the Caribbean, 1936; The Men's Club, 1986; The Mighty Gorga, 1969; Mirrors, 1978; The New World, 2005; The Oblong Box, 1969; **Operation Petticoat**, 1959; Outbreak, 1995; The Perfect Snob, 1941; **The Princess and the Frog**, 2009; The Punisher, 2004; Robinson Crusoe of Clipper Island, 1936; The Rum Diary, 2011; Sacrifice!, 1972; **The Snows of Kilimanjaro**, 1952; **Something of Value**, 1957; **Son of Kong**, 1933; Souls, 2010; The Stick, 1988; Tarzan and the She-Devil, 1953; Tarzan's Fight for Life, 1958; Tarzan's Savage Fury, 1952; **Too Hot to Handle**, 1938; Uncivilized, 1937; U-238 and the Witch Doctor, 1966 (made-for-TV); Vengeance, 1930; Voodoo Woman, 1957; Walk into Hell, 1956; White Goddess, 1953; **White Witch Doctor**, 1953; **White Zombie**, 1932; Yesterday, 2004.

Wizards (also see Magicians; Witchcraft, this index): After the Wizard, 2010; Adventure Time, 2010- (TV series); Arabela, 1979 (TV series); Arabian Knights, 1968 (TV series); Arthur's Quest, 1999 (made-for-TV; Merlin); **Bedknobs and Broomsticks**, 1971; **The Black Cauldron**, 1985; Blackstar, 1981-1982 (TV series); Captain Sinbad, 1962; The Care Bears Adventure in Wonderland, 1987; **The Care Bears Movie**, 1985; Chac, 1975; The Church, 1990; The Color of Magic, 2008- (TV miniseries); Conan the Adventurer, 1992-1993 (TV series); Conan the Barbarian, 1982; Conan the Destroyer, 1984; **A Connecticut Yankee**, 1931 (Merlin); **A Connecticut Yankee in King Arthur's Court**, 1949 (Merlin); A Connecticut Yankee in King Arthur's Court, 1989 (made-for-TV: Merlin); Daniel the Wizard, 2004; Deathstalkers, 1983; The Desert Hawk, 1944; Dr. Strange, 1978 (made-for-TV); Dragons: Fire and Ice, 2004 (made-for-TV); Dragonworld: The Legend Continues, 1999; The Dresden Files, 2007- (TV series); **Dragonslayer**, 1981; **Excalibur**, 1981 (Merlin); Fairy Tail, 2009- (TV series); **Fantasia**, 1940; **Fellini Satyricon**, 1969; Fire and Ice, 1983; The Flight of Dragons, 1982; Guinevere Jones, 2002 (TV series; Merlin); **Harry Potter and the Chamber of Secrets**, 2002; **Harry Potter and the Deathly Hallows Part 1**, 2010; **Harry Potter and the Deathly Hollows Part 2**, 2011; **Harry Potter and the Goblet of Fire**, 2005; **Harry Potter and the Half-Blood Prince**, 2009; Harry Potter and the Order of the Phoenix, 2007; **Harry Potter and the Prisoner of Azkaban**, 2004; **Harry Potter and the Sorcerer's Stone**, 2001; The Hobbit, 1977 (made-for-TV); **The Hobbit: An Unexpected Journey**, 2012; **The Hobbit: The Battle of the Five Armies**, 2014; **The Hobbit: The Desolation of Smaug**, 2013; **Hugo**, 2011; Ice from the Sun, 1999; Into the Labyrinth, 1981-1982 (TV series); **Jack the Giant Killer**, 1962; Journey Back to Oz, 1974; King Arthur and the Knights of Justice, 1992-1993 (TV series; Merlin); Knightriders, 1981; Legends of Oz: Dorothy's Return, 2014; Legend of the Seeker, 2008-2010 (TV series); **The Lego Movie**, 2014; The Lord of the Rings, 1978; **The Lord of the Rings: The Fellowship of the Ring**, 2001; The Lord of the Rings: The Return of the King, 2003; **The Lord of the Rings: The Two Towers**, 2002; The Lord Protector, 1996; Lucinda's Spell, 2000; Magic Boy, 1961; **The Magic Sword**, 1962 (Merlin); Magos y gigantes, 2004; Merlin, 1993; Merlin, 1998 (TV miniseries); Merlin and the Sword, 1985 (made-for-TV); Merlin: The Return, 2000; Merlin's Apprentice, 2006 (TV miniseries); Mr. Merlin, 1981-1982 (TV series); **Monty Python and the Holy Grail**, 1975; The Muppets' Wizard of Oz, 2005 (made-for-TV); The New Wizard of Oz, 1914; **Oz the Great and Powerful**, 2014; Paganini, 1923; The Prestige, 2006; The Prince and the Evening Star, 1979; **The Princess Bride**, 1987; The Princess and the Pauper, 1997 (made-for-TV); Quest for Camelot, 1998 (Merlin); The Return of the King, 1980 (made-for-TV); Return to Oz, 1964 (made-for-TV); Return to Oz, 1985; Roar, 1997- (TV series); The Ruby Princess Runs Away, 2001; Ruslan and Ludmila, 2006; Santa Claus, 1959; **The Secret of NIMH**, 1982; **Shrek**, 2001; **Shrek Forever After**, 2010; **Shrek the Third**, 2007; **Shrek 2**, 2004; The Sign of Death, 1939; Sinbad of the Seven Seas, 1989; Sinbad: The Battle of the Dark Knights, 1998; The Singing Princess, 1967; The Slayers, 1995 (TV series); Sleeping Beauty, 2014; The Sorcerer's Apprentice, 2010; Sprung! The Magic Roundabout, 2005; Star Fairies, 1985 (made-for-TV); Stunt Rock, 1980; **The Sword in the Stone**, 1963 (Merlin); Troll, 1986; **Willow**, 1988; The Wiz, 1978; The Wizard, 1989; The Wizard, 2015; The Wizard of Baghdad, 1960; The Wizard of Gore, 1970; The Wizard of Gore, 2007; The Wizard of Mars, 1965; The Wizard of Oz, 1925; **The Wizard of Oz**, 1939; The Wizard of Oz, 1982; The Wizard of Oz, 1990-1991 (TV series); The Wizard of Oz on Ice, 1996 (made-for-TV); The Wizard of Stone Mountain, 2011; Wizards, 1977; Wizards of the Demon Sword, 1991; The Wizards of the Lost Kingdom, 1985; Wizards of the Lost Kingdom II, 1989; Wizards of Waverly Place, 2007-2012 (TV series); The Woman in Black, 2012; The Worst Witch, 1986 (made-for-TV); Your Highness, 2011.

Women Bathing; Arabesque, 1966 (Sophia Loren in shower); **Blonde Crazy**, 1931 (Joan Blondell bathing in a bathtub); **Cabin in the Sky**, 1943 (Lena Horne taking a bubble bath; scene cut in most versions); **Cleopatra**, 1963 (Elizabeth Taylor in bathing pool sailing miniature boats); **David and Bathsheba**, 1951 (Susan Hayward as Bathsheba in a bath while Gregory Peck, as David, sees her bathing from a distant balcony); **Duel in the Sun**, 1946 (Jennifer Jones bathing in a pond); **Fatal Attraction**, 1987 (Glenn Close in bathtub); **The Fighting Kentuckian**, 1949 (Vera Rhuba Ralston in a tall metallic tub); Jet Pilot, 1957 (Janet Leigh in a shower); **Kit Carson**, 1940 (Lynn Bari in crude running water trough); **Knight Without Armor**, 1937 (Marlene Dietrich bathing in a tub full of soap bubbles while the Russian Civil War rages nearby); National Lampoon's Vacation, 1983 (Beverly D'Angelo in shower); A Nightmare on Elm Street, 1984 (Heather Langenkamp in bathtub); **The Notorious Landlady**, 1962 (Kim Novak taking a bubble bath); **Pony Express**, 1953 (Rhonda Fleming and Jan Sterling, both in individual bathtubs separated by a curtain); **Pretty Woman**, 1990 (Julia Roberts in bathtub); **Psycho**, 1960 (Janet Leigh in shower); **Red Dust**, 1932 (Jean Harlow in a water tank); **The Seven Year Itch**, 1955 (Marilyn Monroe in bathtub); Short Circuit, 1986 (Ally Sheedy in bathtub); **Sign of the Cross**, 1932 (Claudette Colbert in milk bath); **Splash**, 1984 (Daryl Hannah in bathtub as a mermaid); **The Tall Men**, 1956 (Jane Russell bathing in a river); **Unconquered**, 1947 (Paulette Goddard in a water barrel); **Will Success Spoil Rock Hunter?**, 1957 (Jayne Mansfield taking a bubble bath); Weird Science, 1985 (Kelly LeBrock in shower); Wildcats, 1986 (Goldie Hawn in bathtub); **The Women**, 1939 (Joan Crawford taking a bubble bath); **Yolanda and the Thief**, 1945 (Lucille Bremer taking a bubble bath).

Wrestlers and Wrestling (including Judo and Jiu-Jitsu): Abbott and Costello in the Foreign Legion, 1950; **Abe Lincoln in Illinois**, 1940; **Across the Pacific**, 1942; Alias Betty, 2001; Alias the Champ, 1949; **American Graffiti**, 1973; Baby It's You, 1983; **Bad Day at Black Rock**, 1955; Behind the Rising Sun, 1943; The Big Show-Off, 1945; Billy Madison, 1995; The Blue Umbrella, 2005; Blue Valentine, 2010; **Blood on the Sun**, 1945; The Body Snatcher, 1957; Bodyhold, 1949; The Breakfast Club, 1985; The Calamari Wrestler, 2005; The Chinese Connection, 1972; The Crammer, 1958; Diary of a Wimpy Kid, 2010; **Ed Wood**, 1994; Fancypants, 2011; **Fellini Satyricon**, 1969; Fighting Coast Guard, 1951; **The Fighting Kentuckian**, 1949; Fighting Through, 1934; **Force 10 from Navarone**, 1978; Foxcatcher, 2014; A Girl, a Guy, and a Gob, 1941; The Girl from Mexico, 1939; Goliath and the Rebel Slave, 1963; Goliath and the Sins of Babylon, 1963; Hadley's Rebellion, 1987; Hercules Unchained, 1959; Highlander, 1986; **Holly-woodland**, 2006; Idiocracy, 2006; Kid Courageous, 1935; Kid Nightingale, 1939; **The Killing**, 1956; Legendary, 2010; The Magic of Lassie, 1978; Magnificent Brute, 1936; **Man on the Flying Trapeze**, 1935; Man on the Moon, 1999; **The Manchurian Candidate**, 1962; Micki & Maude, 1984; **Mighty Joe Young**, 1949; Mr. Moto in Danger Island, 1939; **Morgan!**, 1966; **The Mummy Returns**, 2001; Munich, 2005; **The Naked City**, 1948; **Night and the City**, 1950; No Place to Go, 1939; **Paper Moon**, 1973; Park Avenue Logger, 1937; The Payoff, 1935; People Will Talk, 1935; Pulp Fiction, 1994; **Quo Vadis**, 1951; **Requiem for a Heavyweight**, 1962; **Risky Business**, 1983; Rocky III, 1982; **Samson and Delilah**, 1949; Santa Sangre, 1990; Secret Venture, 1955; **The Sign of the Cross**, 1932; Spartacus and the Ten Gladiators, 1964; **Spider-Man**, 2002; Sudan, 1945; Swing Fever, 1943; Swing Your Lady, 1938; **The Sword and the Rose**, 1953; Take Down, 1979; Tarzan and the Leopard Woman, 1946; True Legend, 2011; Uptown New York, 1932; The Vampires, 1969; Vision Quest, 1985; **Walking Tall**, 1973; Walking Tall Part II, 1975; The Waterboy, 1998; We're in the Money, 1935; **The World according to Garp**, 1982; The Wrestler, 1974; **The Wrestler**, 2008; The Wrestler and the Clown, 1958.

Yellow Fever (aka: Bronze John; Yellow Jack; Yellow Plague; an acute viral disease spread by and contracted from the bite of a female mosquito): Blood and Honor, 2000; **Captain Horatio Hornblower**, 1951; The Courage to Love, 2000 (made-for-TV; New Orleans); **Jezebel**, 1938 (New Orleans); **The Liberator**, 2014; Magnificent Doll, 1946; **A Man Alone**, 1955; The Navy Lark, 1959; The Ordeal of Dr. Mudd, 1980 (made-for-TV; Dr. Samuel Alexander Mudd; Dry Tortugas); The Planter, 1917; **The Prisoner of Shark Island**, 1936 (Dr. Samuel Alexander Mudd; Dry Tortugas); The Rifleman, 1958-1963 (TV series; "Panic," 1959 episode); Telephone Time, 1956-1958 (TV series; "The Quality of Mercy," 1958 episode: Dr. Samuel Alexander Mudd; Dry Tortugas); **Washington Square**, 1997; Westinghouse Desilu Playhouse, 1958-1960 (TV series; "The Case for Dr. Mudd," 1958 episode: Dr. Samuel Alexander Mudd; Dry Tortugas); White Legion, 1936 (Panama Canal); Women of Valor, 1977 (made-for-TV); **Yellow Jack**, 1938 (Cuba).

Ziegfeld Follies: **Beau James**, 1957; **Deep in My Heart**, 1954; The Eddie Cantor Story, 1953; **Funny Girl**, 1968; Glorifying the American Girl, 1929; **The Great Ziegfeld**, 1936; **I'll See You in My Dreams**, 1951; **The Jolson Story**, 1946; Look for the Silver Lining, 1949; Polly of the Follies, 1922; **Singin' in the Rain**, 1952; **The Story of Will Rogers**, 1952; **W.C. Fields and Me**, 1976; **Ziegfeld Follies**, 1945; **Ziegfeld Girl**, 1941; Ziegfeld: The Man and His Women, 1978 (made-for-TV).

Zionism: **Cast a Giant Shadow**, 1966; **The Chosen**, 1982; Eden, 2001; The Earth Cries Out, 1949; Escaping Tel Aviv, 2009; **Exodus**, 1960; **The Fixer**, 1968; Focus, 2001; Four Blood Moons, 2015; Holocaust, 1978 (TV miniseries); Judith, 1966; **The Juggler**, 1953; Killer Kid,

1994; **The Lighthorsemen**, 1988; **Rosewater**, 2014; **Sword in the Desert**, 1949; **The Syrian Bride**, 2004; A Woman Called Golda, 1982 (made-for-TV).

Zombies: **Dawn of the Dead**, 1979; **The Ghost Breakers**, 1940; **I Walked with a Zombie**, 1943; iZombie, 2015- (TV series); King of the Zombies, 1941; **Phantasm**, 1979; The Plague of the Zombies, 1966; Pride and Prejudice and Zombies, 2016; Satan's Satellites, 1958 (feature version of serial Zombies of the Stratosphere); The Serpent and the Rainbow, 1988; **White Zombie**, 1932; Zombie, 1980; Zombie and the Ghost Train, 1991; Zombie Diaries 2, 2011; Zombie Hunter, 2013; The Zombie King, 2013; Zombieland, 2009; Zombieland, 2013 (made-for-TV); Zombies of the Stratosphere, 1952 (serial).

Zoos: **An American Werewolf in London**, 1981; Anchorman: The Legend of Ron Burgundy, 2004; Creature Comforts, 1996; Elephant Fury, 1956; Fierce Creatures, 1997; **Harry Potter and the Sorcerer's Stone**, 2001; **Hero**, 1992; **Rise of the Planet of the Apes**, 2011; **We Bought a Zoo**, 2011; Withnail & I, 1987; **Zoo in Budapest**, 1933; Zookeeper, 2011.